BY APPOINTMENT TO
HER MAJESTY THE QUEEN
PHILATELISTS
STANLEY GIBBONS LTD
LONDON

Stanley Gibbons
Stamp Catalogue

Commonwealth and British Empire Stamps 1840 – 1970

121st edition 2019

Stanley Gibbons Ltd • London and Ringwood

By Appointment to
Her Majesty The Queen
Philatelists
Stanley Gibbons Ltd
London

Published by Stanley Gibbons Ltd
Editorial and Publications:
7 Parkside, Christchurch Road, Ringwood,
Hants BH24 3SH

British Library Cataloguing in
Publication Data.
A catalogue record for this book is available
from the British Library.

ISBN-13: 978-1-911304-28-9

Item No. R 2813-19

Printed and bound in Italy
by Lego SpA

Contents

Orange Free State 1882-86 £5 green postal fiscal, showing the remarkable plate variety 'VRY-STAAT' (with hyphen), which is believed to occur only once on the two-pane sheet of 120. The only recorded unused example.

Preface to the 2019 Edition

FOR the first 30 years of its existence the Stanley Gibbons Stamp Catalogue was published in a single volume, giving the Company's selling prices for the stamps of the whole world. Then, in 1895 it was split into two volumes, 'Part 1' covering the stamps of the British Empire only.

That handy, pocket-sized volume grew and grew as the years passed and the new stamp issues increased in the 1970s, and '80s, until, by the 2002 edition it had become two substantial A4 volumes, each the size of the book you are currently reading.

Since then the number of issues has continued to grow year-on-year, as postal administrations and their agencies attempt to sell as much material as they can to an ever-declining number of new issue purchasers; so I suspect that by now the two volumes of 2002 would be, at least four, had we continued to publish 'Part 1' in the old way.

I fear such a product would be totally impractical, today, so full listings of Commonwealth stamps will be found in the 'yellow' series of one-country or regional catalogues, each volume appearing every three to four years, or so. These list all the stamps of their respective territories from the very earliest to the latest new issues, all in the same detail as provided in this volume, thus catering for the general Commonwealth collector up to 1970 as well as the complete one-country collector.

One might assume from this that unless the Commonwealth stamp market is in 'boom mode', this edition would be little different to last year's; but nothing could be further from the truth.

The fact is that, as more and more collectors begin to delve more deeply into the earlier issues of their chosen country, further information comes to light, much of which is being published in the pages of specialist society journals, or is reported directly to us for incorporation into the next edition.

Some of the more significant additions and improvements to this catalogue are noted below, but, as last year, I invite anyone who has a suggestion for the next one to email me at *hjefferies@stanleygibbons.com*, preferably with scans of any items for potential listing.

PRICES

We might not always be happy to admit to it, but as a user of this catalogue for 60 years, myself, I know that the prime area of interest for many collectors is the price changes.

This is only as it should be since, for the first half of 2018, the members of Stanley Gibbons Commonwealth Specialist Department have been carefully reviewing every price in the light of auction realisations, sales, stock levels and the advice and comments received from collectors and other members of the philatelic trade.

The resulting prices are therefore as accurate as they can possibly be and, while we are all aware that some stamps are available at lower prices elsewhere, I must stress, once again, that the prices shown in this catalogue are for stamps in fine condition 'free of damage and in the case of used stamps with genuine cancellations, struck during the period the stamps were current. Furthermore, they are all covered by Stanley Gibbons' lifetime guarantee of genuineness. So, when you are buying elsewhere it is always advisable to check every purchase: is it as described? Is it free of damage and in fine condition? Can you confirm that the postmark is correct? If you can answer positively to these questions, then you are buying a stamp of 'catalogue quality'; if not, the best advice is to leave it, or, if you really must have it, secure the best price possible, and certainly a significant discount off 'full catalogue'.

Happily, for users of this catalogue, the Commonwealth stamp market remains very healthy. Ten years of low inflation and low interest rates, not to mention the possible impact of Brexit, seem not to have worried collectors in the slightest, while the current lack of 'speculation' in the home market at least, means that prices are being driven entirely by collectors seeking to add to their collections. This is healthy for the hobby and gives confidence for the future. In a way, steep price increases across the board, may sound good, but we know from past experience that they are unlikely to be sustained for long and will usually be 'corrected' in due course. On the other hand, gradual and selected increases, with a few areas of faster growth, as determined by the market, are much more sustainable.

This is the position we are in today, with widespread, but selective and generally fairly modest price growth in most areas and periods up to about 1960. While some 'blue chip' items are certainly affected (the Western Australia 4d. 'Inverted frame' rises from £140,000 to £180,000!), much of the action is centred on stamps with prices of less than £50 – just the sort of thing being targeted by the 'ordinary collector', as opposed to the 'investor'. The West Indies, Africa, Asia and the Pacific territories are all seeing similar growth, although there are also a few reductions here and there, as the results of previous speculative activity are rectified in countries such as Hong Kong, Pitcairn Islands and Singapore.

The Dominions; **Australia, Canada and New Zealand** show similar patterns, as does **Great Britain** up to 1952, although some significant price reductions are recorded among the commemorative issues of the 1960s, bringing the catalogue back into line with the market.

Much more dramatic increases are recorded in the **Australian States**, following major international auctions, with mint 'Sydney Views', Queensland postal fiscals, South Australia 'Long' types, Tasmania 'Couriers' and the Victoria 'Stamp Statute' and 'Stamp Duty' series standing out in particular.

Prices are up again for **India** also, notably for mint 19th-century issues, George VI watermark varieties and telegraphs, and while increases in **Indian States** may not be as widespread as in the past few years, mint Gwalior stands out in the Convention States and Bussahir, Duttia, Morvi and Poonch in the Feudatory States.

Elsewhere, the Middle East territories are strong, with **Aden and States**, **Bahrain**, **Bushire** and **Iraq** standing out and every stamp in the **Baghdad** listing marked up again, while, in **Malaya**, **Indian** stamps used in Malacca and Thailand used in Perlis are also all marked up, some substantially so.

Varieties of watermark and printing remain popular, while many Telegraph stamps see further increases, notably in **Bechuanaland**, **Ceylon** and **Rhodesia**.

Among other pricing developments more prices are now given for fiscally used high values (Malaya) and in **India** for Edward VII and George V high values with telegraphic cancels. Further effort has been put into giving prices for hitherto unpriced plate and watermark varieties, although, I must say that it is important that we at least see scans of items for pricing as quite a few put forward recently have forged or 'philatelically contrived' cancels. We have had a good response in the past year to my request for scans of items which would allow us to fill some of those 'pricing gaps' and I am grateful to all those who have been in touch. If you have further items to add, please use the email address above.

REVISIONS OF THIS EDITION

Probably the most significant addition to the 2018 edition was the listing of Indian Stamps used at the two main post offices in **Aden**. It was felt at the time that there was insufficient information to prepare similar listings for the lesser offices, such as Perim and Khormaksar, but as new reports have come in, we have prepared an abbreviated listing of those values we have seen so far. Additions to this list would be welcome in the hope that we may be able to upgrade the sub-offices to a fully priced listing in a future edition.

In **Australia**, following advice from Glen Stevens, new notes are provided to help distinguish the three single Crown over A watermarks found on the Kangaroo and Map definitives.

There are a number of new notes in **India and States**, notably a description of the settings of the first 'Service' overprints of India and, in Gwalior, a new 9mm spacing variety on the King Edward VII official stamps (which occurred in the 15th horizontal row of the 8mm setting stamps (O39/O46 and O49/O50) is now listed and priced.

Indian stamps used in **Kuwait**, both in the period before 1929, when Kuwait first issued its own stamps, and in the period between 1941 and 1945, when administration of the post office reverted to India, are now fully listed and priced, with high values cancelled telegraphically separately priced. We are grateful to Thomas Johansen and Khaled Abdulmughni for their assistance in compiling this listing.

Further progress has been made in transferring the last few black and white images into colour, in **Mauritius** we now have a fine illustration of a 'Post Paid', thanks to our friends at David Feldman in Geneva, while Paul Wreglesworth and members of the New Zealand Society of Great Britain have replaced the old illustrations of the different dies on the 1882-1900 'Second Sidefaces'. Also in **New Zealand**, the papermakers' names found on the 'no watermark' Chalon head stamps of 1855 (SG 4/6) are now given.

Another new colour illustration appears in **Tobago**, where a long-listed variety which has never been illustrated, the 'Slash flaw repaired' variety, is now shown.

There are a number of new plate flaws and watermark varieties in this edition and I would like to thank the many correspondents who have assisted in this process. Among those who I would particularly like to mention are Markand Dave, Bryan Short, Neil Grover and Ron Winter.

Finally, once again, there has been a complete review of the 'General Philatelic Information and Guidelines' at the front of the catalogue. As usual, I urge all catalogue users to re-read this section each year.

This catalogue could not exist without the help of my colleagues in the Commonwealth Stamps Specialist Department of Stanley Gibbons in the Strand, or those members of the Catalogue Department and Studio in Ringwood, all of whom play a vital part in bringing the job to fruition. Thank you all.

Hugh Jefferies
Catalogue Editor
August 2018

The Stanley Gibbons Group Plc

Stanley Gibbons Limited,
Stanley Gibbons Auctions
399 Strand, London WC2R 0LX
Tel: +44 (0)207 836 8444
Fax: +44 (0)207 836 7342
E-mail: help@stanleygibbons.com
Website: www.stanleygibbons.com
for all departments, Auction and Specialist Stamp Departments.

Open Monday–Friday 9.30 a.m. to 5 p.m.
Shop. Open Monday–Friday 9 a.m. to 5.30 p.m.
and Saturday 9.30 a.m. to 5.30 p.m.

Stanley Gibbons Publications,
Gibbons Stamp Monthly
and *Philatelic Exporter*
7 Parkside, Christchurch Road, Ringwood,
Hampshire BH24 3SH.
Tel: +44 (0)1425 472363
Fax: +44 (0)1425 470247
E-mail: support@stanleygibbons.com
Publications Mail Order.
Tel: +44 (0)1425 472363

Monday–Friday 8.30 a.m. to 5 p.m.

Stanley Gibbons Publications Overseas Representation
Stanley Gibbons Publications are represented overseas by the following

Australia
Renniks Publications Pty Ltd
Unit 3 37-39 Green Street,
Banksmeadow, NSW 2019, Australia
Tel: +612 9695 7055
Website: www.renniks.com

Canada
Unitrade Associates
99 Floral Parkway, Toronto,
Ontario M6L 2C4, Canada
Tel: +1 416 242 5900
Website: www.unitradeassoc.com

Germany
Schaubek Verlag Leipzig
Am Glaeschen 23, D-04420
Markranstaedt, Germany
Tel: +49 34 205 67823
Website: www.schaubek.de

Italy
Ernesto Marini S.R.L.
V. Struppa, 300, Genova, 16165, Italy
Tel: +3901 0247-3530
Website: www.ernestomarini.it

Japan
Japan Philatelic
PO Box 2, Suginami-Minami,
Tokyo 168-8081, Japan
Tel: +81 3330 41641
Website: www.yushu.co.jp

Netherlands (also covers Belgium Denmark, Finland & France)
Uitgeverij Davo BV
PO Box 411, Ak Deventer, 7400
Netherlands
Tel: +315 7050 2700
Website: www.davo.nl

New Zealand
House of Stamps
PO Box 12, Paraparaumu,
New Zealand
Tel: +61 6364 8270
Website: www.houseofstamps.co.nz

Philatelic Distributors
PO Box 863
15 Mount Edgecumbe Street
New Plymouth 4615, New Zealand
Tel: +6 46 758 65 68
Website: www.stampcollecta.com

Norway
SKANFIL A/S
SPANAV. 52 / BOKS 2030
N-5504 HAUGESUND, Norway
Tel: +47-52703940
E-mail: magne@skanfil.no

Singapore
C S Philatelic Agency
Peninsula Shopping Centre #04-29
3 Coleman Street, 179804, Singapore
Tel: +65 6337-1859
Website: www.cs.com.sg

South Africa
Peter Bale Philatelics
PO Box 3719, Honeydew,
2040, South Africa
Tel: +27 11 462 2463
Tel: +27 82 330 3925
E-mail: balep@iafrica.com

Sweden
Chr Winther Sorensen AB
Box 43, S-310 20 Knaered, Sweden
Tel: +46 43050743
Website: www.collectia.se

Stamps Added

Great Britain	87c, 95, 198b, 218a, 218aw, 221a, 227a, 243, 267a, 267aw,290a, 400wk, 619a, 632b, 632c, 637a, 637pa, 681a, 681b, 681pa, 681pb, 690a, 690pa, 712b, 712pb, 713c, 713pc, 716h, 716ph, 815g
Used Abroad	
Colombia	Z109a
Peru	Z101a
Mail Boat Cancellations	Z172a
Aden	
Hadhramaut	11a
Australia	122a, D97w, SB5ab, SB10c, SB14a, SB19a
New South Wales	SB1c, SB3a
Queensland	266a
S. Australia	O27c, SB4a
Papua	154a
Bahamas	107b
Brunei	39a, 39x
Burma	35w
Cameroon	74aa
Ceylon	168x, SB3b
Cyprus	65w
Dominica	53asa
Ghana	D13ca, D18ca, D23ca
Gibraltar	Z57a, Z83a, 27a, 244a
Gold Coast	6y, 13e, 72ac, D8ca
Grenada	D2a, D9a, D13a
Hong Kong	188a, 188ba
India	31b, 221b, 223a, 233bw
Chamba	37a, 53ba
Gwalior	O39b, O41a/O46a, O49a, O50a
Jaipur	O34a/b
Ireland	141a, 143ab
Kenya Uganda and Tanganyika	135c
Kuwait	32b, 34a
Leeward Islands	80c
Malaya	
Straits Settlements	44w, 58a, 92w, 155aw, 193bx, 197y, 198ay, 199x, 202by
Federated Malay States	38ay
Johore	13a
Kedah	Z211, Z240
Kelantan	Z39b
Malacca	67b
Sungei Ujong	50a
Pahang	89d
Perak	43a, 87w
Perlis	46a
Selangor	136a, 137a, 142c
Trengganu	106b
Japanese Occupation	J246b
Malta	48c, 51c/55c, 61c/63c, 102sa, 252b
Morocco Agencies	26d
Muscat	Z1a
New Zealand	782ba, O128aw
Niue	24f
Nigeria	7y
Lagos	21w
North Borneo	67sa
Labuan	43d, 54c
Japanese Occupation	JD3, JD5
St Christopher	13c, 18x
St Vincent	131x
Samoa	116a
South Africa	64ba, O14a, O26a, O28a, O40, O40a
Natal	22y, 54by, 60y, 61w, 93w, 147ay, 147y
Orange Free State	F11a, F11b
Transvaal	246w
South West Africa	D1c
Trinidad and Tobago	D9ab, D17ab, D25ab
Uganda	T6c
Zanzibar	4p, 4pj

Catalogue Numbers Altered

The table below is a cross-reference of those catalogue numbers which have been altered in this edition.

	Old	New
Aden	82a	82b
Australia		
New South Wales	O32da	deleted
	O32db	deleted
Ceylon	SB3a	SB3b
Egypt	85a	deleted
	89a	deleted
Gibraltar	Z83a	Z83b
Hong Kong	102ay	102y
	188a	188b
India	O125/O149b	O121/O150
Jaipur	O34a	O34c
Jamaica	71f	deleted
Kenya, Uganda and Tanganyika	135c	135d
Malaya		
Straits Settlements	155a/as	155b/bs
Johore	7	deleted
Kelantan	Z396	Z397
North Borneo		
Labuan	8a	deleted
	19a	deleted
	32a	deleted
	JD3	JD4
South West Africa	A203a	deleted
Tanganyika	M44a	deleted
Zanzibar	5l	deleted

The Importance of Condition

The prices in the Stanley Gibbons Catalogue are for stamps in 'fine condition' – but what exactly does 'fine' mean, and what effect might a slight defect have upon the price? We visit Stanley Gibbons Specialist Stamp Department to find out

To quote in full the relevant paragraph in the introduction to the current Stanley Gibbons Commonwealth and British Empire Stamps Catalogue; 'The prices quoted in this catalogue are the estimated selling prices of Stanley Gibbons Ltd at the time of publication. They are, unless it is specifically stated otherwise, for examples in fine condition for the issue concerned. Superb examples are worth more, those of a lower quality, considerably less.' This single paragraph is probably the most significant piece of information in the entire catalogue – but one that is frequently ignored or forgotten. The big question, of course, is just how much more is 'more' and how much less is 'less'?

Not surprisingly, the ability to answer that question depends on experience. A knowledgeable philatelist will be able to assess fairly quickly what the price of a particular stamp should be in relation to that quoted in the catalogue. Many sellers, however, both professional and collector, find it simpler to price items for sale by a standard percentage of 'catalogue'; probably only marking down those that are actually damaged. This can mean that stamps in better than 'fine' condition are underpriced, while poorer ones are too expensive; something which buyers need to bear in mind.

Talking to the experts, it quickly becomes obvious that every single feature of a stamp needs to be considered separately before a judgement on its overall condition can be passed. So this article will look at each of those features individually, before drawing them all together and attempting to assess how much more than catalogue price a superb example might be worth and, conversely, how low a price should be put on one of lower quality.

Gum

This would seem to be a relatively easy one – after all, it says in the catalogue; 'The prices for unused stamps of Queen Victoria to King George V are for lightly hinged examples. Unused prices for King Edward VIII to Queen Elizabeth issues are for unmounted mint.' Well, at least the definition of unmounted is pretty clear, while lightly hinged means, in theory, a single hinge mark, although, apparently, two or three might be acceptable if the hinges have been lightly applied and carefully removed. The stamps printed by De La Rue for the majority of Colonial postal administrations during the first three decades of the twentieth century have stood up reasonably well to stamp hinges, so finding lightly mounted examples of such stamps should not be too difficult. However, Canadian stamps, for example, which were printed on softer paper and had thicker gum, are more difficult to find in fine mounted condition and should be valued accordingly.

Heavier hinging is acceptable for stamps issued before around 1890 but the majority of the gum should be clear and 'unblemished'. If the stamp has been mounted on a number of occasions or if there is a heavy hinge still attached, the price would drop to about half catalogue and from there on would decline fairly rapidly.

For a twentieth century stamp without gum a price of about one tenth of catalogue would be more or less the order of the day (unless it was normally issued that way, of course!). However, many early issues are extremely rare with gum and in these cases anything up to full catalogue price would be appropriate. Prices for early Western **Australia** and Sarawak are, for example, without gum, gummed stamps being worth a premium. The first perforated issues of British Guiana are also rarely found with gum, so ungummed examples would be worth a higher proportion of catalogue price than usual – about one third, or more – while Turks Islands provisionals and early **New Zealand** Chalon heads without gum might rate half catalogue or above.

As for the premium that should be put on earlier stamps in unmounted condition, that will vary from issue to issue and from country to country. Clearly, the older the stamp the less likely it is that it will be easy to find by those seeking 'unmounted' perfection. The *Great Britain Concise* catalogue gives both mounted and unmounted prices for all stamps issued between 1887 and 1935 and the premium ranges from zero up to 100 per cent, or even more, depending on the relative scarcity of the stamp in unmounted condition.

Some stamps are more acceptable than others without gum

The discounts for mounted issues of the Third Reich period can be dramatic

As for post-1935 stamps in lightly mounted condition, the story is just as complicated. As it says in the catalogue; 'Some stamps from the King George VI period are often difficult to find in unmounted mint condition. In such instances we would expect that collectors would need to pay a high proportion of the price quoted to obtain mounted mint examples. Generally speaking, lightly mounted mint stamps from this reign, issued before 1945, are in considerable demand.' This may hold good for Commonwealth stamps, but on the continent the demand for unmounted has severely affected the market for even lightly mounted specimens. The current *Part 7, Germany, Catalogue* provides some clear examples of this. This catalogue gives unmounted and mounted mint prices for all Third Reich issues, from 1933 to 1945, with unmounted prices only for later issues. The differences are quite dramatic, with the 1936 Local Government Congress set (SG 614/7) rated at £23.00 unmounted, but only £5.25 lightly hinged, and the 1942 Hamburg Derby stamp (SG 804) is priced at £28.00 and £7.50, respectively. Thus, for most mounted mint post-war European stamps, one should probably be thinking in terms of deducting 75 or 85 per cent from the catalogue price.

Even for King George VI stamps the discount for mounted mint can vary

As suggested earlier, Commonwealth collectors are fortunate in that the price differential is not nearly so dramatic. On average, mounted mint prices for post-war King George VI sets are approximately 'half catalogue'. Again, there are exceptions. To take three examples; the first King George VI 3d. of Ascension, the black and ultramarine stamp (42), would only rate around 25 per cent of catalogue in mounted condition, on the other hand, the 1938 set of Perak (103/21) would be more like two thirds, while for some of the Indian Convention States high values the proportion would be even higher, providing the gum is white and not toned. For the first issues of the present reign the proportion drops to around a third, but after about 1965 there is really very little demand for mounted examples of anything other than the more expensive sets, even in fine lightly hinged condition.

Some gum toning can be acceptable on certain King George VI issues

Whether or not a hinge has been attached to it is not the only gum feature that can affect the value of a stamp. Discoloration or toning can also be significant. Stamps which have spent time in the tropics frequently suffer from gum browning and, in extreme cases, cracking and 'crazing', sometimes affecting the face of the stamp as well as the back. The value of such specimens should be marked down accordingly. For stamps of King George VI one would normally aim for no gum toning at all, but the first 10s. definitive of Grenada only exists toned, so that would be considered 'fine for the issue concerned'; later stamps in the series should have cream or white gum, depending on the original issue. Again, the vast majority of the first Hong Kong definitives have at least some gum toning, so here the discount for lightly toned examples would be smaller than usual.

The demand for unmounted mint, as well as very real concerns that the gum applied to nineteenth

6 Reasons

1 CHOICE: 20,000+/- different lots in each auction

You'll experience an extraordinary Worldwide range of stamps, collections, covers, classic to modern, ranging from £5 to £100,000 offered from 508 different Countries/ categories/subjects, strong in British, British Empire, Europe naturally, but also including Asia, Americas and thematic. If you collect it, chances are we've got it in one of our massive philatelic auctions… ***Request/View Catalogue on-line now***

2 VALYOU: No Buyer's Premium (NO B P)

If you abhor buyer's premiums as much as we do, especially when you may be paying up to 25% more for that same Dealer/Auction's own stock, this is a major reason why you'll find winning lots at UPA so refreshingly different, because there's NO B.P. to pay, and NO added extras either… ***Request/View Catalogue on-line now***

3 Guarantee: Total NO quibble refund policy

You can be confident in our peace of mind No Quibble total refund guarantee. Why is it that so few auctions fail to understand that Happy Bidders make repeat buyers? We've offered our Total 'Peace of Mind' guarantee for the past 18 years. Rather than lose business it has won respect and garnered more business, which is why you can bid with complete confidence… ***Request/View Catalogue on-line now***

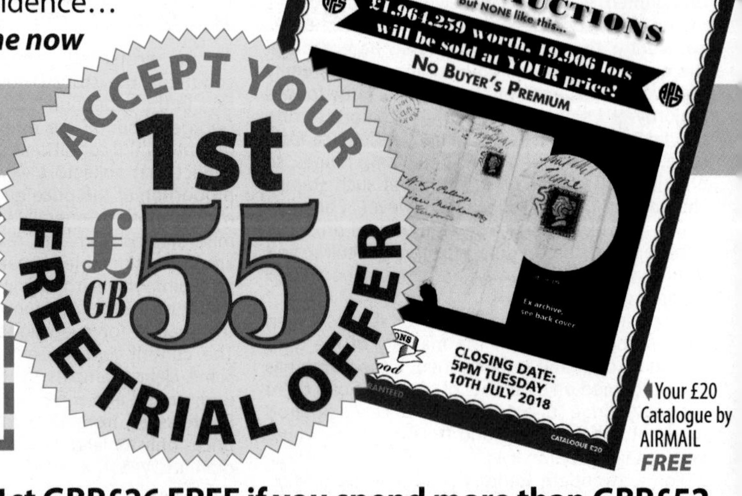

Order/View Your FREE Catalogue on-line NOW and I'll give You your 1st **£55** Auction winnings **FREE** so You can test my auction

Your £20 Catalogue by AIRMAIL ***FREE***

Returning client after 12 months: Your 1st GBP£26 FREE if you spend more than GBP£52

century issues was, in itself, potentially damaging, has inevitably led to a certain amount of regumming. Stanley Gibbons' policy is not to sell stamps which have been regummed, especially since the new layer of gum may disguise damage or attempts at repair. It is important, therefore, that the edges of early mint stamps be checked very carefully to make sure that there are no suspicious signs of gum on the surface. (There is one set of stamps, China SG 457/9, which was gummed after printing and perforating, while stamps printed on top of the gum are clearly not a problem – but these are very much the exceptions.)

Margins

Another feature which has long been a part of the 'Stamp Improver's' repertoire has been the adding of margins to stamps which have been deficient in them. Once again, this 'service' has developed because of the premium placed by collectors on 'fine four-margin' examples of stamps like the Penny Black. For some years now the *Part 1* and *GB Concise* catalogues have provided guidance on this matter; illustrating 'good', 'fine', 'very fine' and 'superb' examples of the first postage stamp. As stated, the standard adopted in the catalogue is for stamps described as 'fine', which, in terms of margins, means that the area outside the printed design should be 'approximately one half of the distance between two adjoining unsevered stamps'–on all four sides, of course! Anything more than this will take the stamp into the 'very fine' or 'superb' categories, with the stamp's price rising accordingly. Ultimately, one arrives at a point where the stamp has 'stolen' the margins from all of its neighbours, in which case exaggerated expressions such as 'gargantuan' or 'jumbo' margins are frequently resorted to. Such examples are, indeed, rare and would expect to be valued accordingly; at least double catalogue price and probably more, if other aspects of its condition are 'up to scratch'.

Beware of stamps to which margins have been added

Stamps with abnormally large margins are worth a substantial premium

One factor which needs to be borne in mind is that the distance between two adjoining unsevered stamps varied quite a lot in the early days. So what would be considered only 'fair', or even 'narrow', for the Indian lithographs or the first issue of Norway would be 'enormous' on the early issues of several British colonies whose stamp printing plates were laid down by Perkins Bacon. Ceylon, Queensland and Tasmania are typical examples of countries whose stamps, suffer from this problem – and where narrow margins do not necessarily prevent a stamp being described as 'fine'.

Mention of the **India**n lithographs raises the issue of octagonal stamps which have been cut to shape – often to fit into the spaces provided for them by the manufacturers of early stamp albums! Again, the catalogue provides helpful guidance with a note explaining that 'catalogue prices for Four Annas stamps are for cut-square specimens with clear margins and in good condition. Cut-to-shape copies are worth from 3% to 20% of these prices according to condition.'

For more conventionally-shaped imperforate issues, a stamp which has lost one of its margins might be priced as high as half catalogue if it is fine in all other respects, but the price declines rapidly if more than one side is affected. Of course, there are exceptions; the Penny Black, because of its unique desirability, can merit a higher proportion of catalogue price, even with no margins at all, than just about any other stamp – certainly more than its much scarcer partner, the Two Pence Blue!

What might be described as 'narrow margins' for one stamp could be wide for another

Perforations

When we look at the influence which perforations have on value, the situation is no less complicated. Here there are two factors to consider, the condition of the perforations themselves and centring of the stamp image within them.

It makes sense to seek out stamps that are perfectly centred

Centring is easy to understand; in a perfect stamp the space between the edge of the design and the perforations should be equal on all sides. For most modern stamps, perforated on comb machines, good centring is normal and perfect centring would not merit a premium. Even 100 years ago the quality controls at De La Rue, where most British and colonial stamps were produced, were such that poorly centred stamps, particularly the keyplate types, are seldom encountered, so once again, it is hardly an issue. The attractive engraved pictorials, popular with post offices in the mid-twentieth century and popular with collectors to this day, were more variable – irrespective of which firm printed and perforated them. A stamp slightly off-centre could still merit the description 'fine', but if it is visibly off-centre in more than one direction or the design touches the perforations, then a discount from catalogue price could be expected – the clearer the displacement, the bigger the discount. If, of course, the perforations pass right through the middle of the stamp, it becomes an error – and that's a completely different story!

Early stamps are seldom found perfectly centred, especially those printed from plates laid down before perforating was introduced

The moral is that it certainly makes sense to try and seek out stamps that are perfectly centred, although in the case of the above issues it would be unlikely that you would be charged extra for them.

When discussing the problem of finding imperf stamps with good margins, it was noted that the designs were sometimes placed so close together on the plate that it required considerable care on the part of the post office clerk to separate stamps from the sheet without cutting into them. This became even more of a problem when stamps printed from those same plates were required to be perforated. It is not surprising that, in view of the materials they had to work with and the experimental nature of perforating machinery at the time, early stamps are seldom found perfectly centred. For this reason it would be unrealistic to suggest that a slightly off-centre perforated Penny Red was less than 'fine', although to command full catalogue price, the perforations should not touch the design.

Centring is also an important issue among more modern line-perforated stamps, notably those of the USA and Canada – right up to quite recent times. Here, poorly centred stamps were the norm and even a slightly off-centre example could merit the description 'fine'. Because of the inaccuracy of the perforating machines, the stamps can also vary in size quite a bit, and oversized, well-centred stamps, because of their relative scarcity, can be the subject of fierce competition when they come up at auction and can fetch prices vastly in excess of catalogue. In the case of cheaper stamps five or ten times catalogue price is not unknown.

Nibbled, Short or Pulled?

Perforations are easily damaged, especially if the gauge is coarse and the paper soft. On a De La Rue keyplate issue, with a standard perforation of 14, one would expect a 'fine' stamp to have all its perforation 'teeth' intact. One 'nibbled' or 'nibbed' perf tooth (slightly short) would call for a slight discount, but the more teeth affected or the shorter the tooth the greater the reduction in price. Incidentally, a 'short perf' would still show a vestigial 'tooth', a 'missing perf' shows no tooth at all and a 'pulled perf' signifies that there is a 'hole' in the stamp where the perforation tooth was pulled away). Even worse than a short perf on one of the sides is a short corner. Here again, the more of the corner missing the lower the price – but if the damage has resulted in part of the stamp design being torn away then the stamp would be unlikely to be worth more than a tenth of catalogue and possibly much less.

Canadian coil stamps with full perfs are far from common

Whereas on a perf 14 stamp a damaged perforation tooth would be considered a defect which would force a reduction in the price, on a perf 8 stamp, such as some of the Canadian coil stamps of the 1920s and 30s, stamps with full perfs are far from common. Here, one or two shortish perfs would probably be acceptable, providing they were not too short. Such a stamp with all its perforations could command a premium over full catalogue price, especially if it was also well centred. As the gauge increases, however, the impact of short perfs increases, so that a King George V 'Seahorse' with one or two short perfs would probably carry a 20 per cent discount, any more than that and the price would drop to half catalogue.

Check the perfs on King George V Seahorses

Today, only a small premium is paid for plate number examples of most colonial stamps

Great Britain control numbers are widely available

Booklet stamps

Damaged perforations are not only caused by careless separation. Until very recently, most stamp booklets were made up from reels of stamps, bound into covers by stapling, stitching or gluing and then guillotined to produce the finished books. Inevitably, this cutting was seldom totally accurate, resulting in the majority of booklet panes being trimmed on at least one side. Prices for stamp booklets in the Stanley Gibbons catalogues are for examples with 'average' perforations – that is, slightly trimmed; the prices for booklet panes are for examples with full perforations. If a pane of six has good perforations at the top and side, but is trimmed along the foot, then its value should be based on the three stamps in the top row, the three stamps at the bottom being virtually discounted.

A single stamp which only occurs in booklet panes, such as most of the definitive watermark varieties of Queen Elizabeth **Great Britain**, should also have full perforations. Trimmed perfs bring the price down significantly and if they are missing completely than even a scarce variety would only merit a tenth of catalogue.

One should expect to pay a t premium for a modern plate block

Catalogue prices for booklet panes are for examples with full perforations

Wing margins

Another perforation issue is 'wing margins'. When De La Rue began producing the surface-printed stamps of Great Britain, their printing plates were made up of separate sections which printed as 'panes'. In the case of the 1861 3d., for example, the printed sheet of 240 stamps was made up of 12 panes of 20 stamps. Between each pane there was a 'gutter' and where the panes were side-by-side the gutter was perforated down the centre, giving the stamps at the side of the pane a wide (5mm) margin – the 'wing margin'. Wing margins were frowned upon by early collectors, who liked their stamps to fit exactly into the stamp-size rectangles printed for them by album manufacturers. As a result, stamps with wing margins generally commanded a lower price than stamps from the centre of the pane which had 'normal' perforations and many stamps had their wing margins cut off or had fake perforations added to provide collectors with stamps of the required shape.

Fashions change, and wing margins are now no longer despised, indeed, because of their slightly larger size, they frequently compare well with a 'normal' and they certainly show a postmark to better advantage. Thus, there is no longer a discount for a wing margined stamp, although we have not yet reached a situation where one has to pay a premium for their relative scarcity!

Sadly, however, those stamps which were 'doctored' in order to appeal to earlier fashions are now considered to be considerably devalued, except in the case of a good basic stamp such as the 2s. brown, or perhaps where the stamp has some other redeeming feature such as an attractive cancellation. For more run-of-the-mill stamps a price of one tenth of catalogue would usually be appropriate. With this in mind, of course, it pays to be aware of the corner letters of British surface-printed stamps which should have wing margins, in order to spot ones which have had fake perforations added. This information is given in both *'Part 1'* and the GB Specialised Catalogue.

De La Rue printed stamps by the same technique for many British colonies; stamps which do not have corner letters to allow today's collectors to identify those with 'dodgy perfs'. The early stamps of Hong Kong are an obvious example and, bearing in mind the prices which these can fetch in fine condition, it behoves us all to be aware of stamps which may have had wing margins removed and to check them carefully before purchase.

Wing margins were frowned upon by early collectors but not any longer!

Marginal premium

For modern stamps, an intact sheet margin should not add to the value, although one should now expect to pay a significant premium for a plate block or imprint block over the price for a plain block of four. For most earlier twentieth century stamps, also, a plain margin will do little for a stamp's value, but if that piece of margin includes a control number, plate number or printer's imprint then the difference can be very significant indeed! Great Britain control numbers were widely collected at the time they were current and are widely available to this day. Reference to volume 2 of the *Great Britain Specialised Catalogue* demonstrates that, in spite of the fact that there was only one control single in a sheet of 240 stamps, apart from a few rare examples, they generally only merit a premium of between 50 and 100 per cent over the price of a normal mounted mint example. Plate number singles of colonial stamps occurred once or twice a sheet but, judging from the infrequency with which one encounters them, they were not sought after at the time of issue and are still undervalued today – again a small premium over the price of a fine mint basic stamp is all one should expect.

However, perhaps the Australian market indicates that this may not always be the case. In Australia huge premiums are now being paid for imprint strips and singles at auction. At a sale in Australia a 5s. Kangaroo, third watermark, mounted mint 'CA' monogram single, catalogue price for a single stamp £250, sold for A$21,000 – getting on for £9000 after tax and premium were added!

Even a partial marginal inscription can make a great difference to the price of a Penny Red

The first stamps of Great Britain bore an inscription in the sheet margins, advising the public as to the price of the stamps, where they should be placed on the letter and warning against the removal of 'the cement'. The early surface-printed stamps also bore inscriptions in the sheet margins. The latter are not currently considered to impact significantly on the value of the stamp to which they are attached, but a partial marginal inscription can make a great difference to the price of a Penny Black or Penny Red, and a complete corner, with plate number attached, will be very desirable indeed.

What's the damage?

We have looked at some aspects of damage in this article, notably in relation to perforations, so let us conclude by reviewing other aspects of damage.

All young collectors are advised from the outset to avoid torn stamps, and the advice obviously holds good throughout one's philatelic life. However, that is not to say that all torn stamps are worthless, because even a torn example of a desirable stamp is still collectable and can therefore command a price. In a GB context, a fine used £5 orange or 2s. brown with a 3mm tear, but otherwise superb, would probably rate about one third of catalogue price. A more common stamp, such as a 2s.6d. or 5s. value, would be worth much less and, naturally, the larger or more obvious the tear, the greater its impact on the price.

A 'bend' will generally not be evident on the face of a stamp, only on the back, and will result in a 10 or 15 per cent reduction in price; a gum crease is the natural result of gum ageing and its effect on value will depend upon the damage caused to the face of the stamp. A crease is clearly evident on the surface of the stamp and will result in a more common stamp being worth between one fifth and one tenth of catalogue, depending on the harshness of the crease and where it is – a crease across a corner will be less significant than one right across the middle, for example. A 'wrinkle' gives the appearance of a series of light creases, whose effect on value will depend on its extent and clarity. Once again, a crease or wrinkle on a valuable stamp will be less significant in percentage terms than one on a more common one – all other factors being equal.

The impact a thin will have will similarly depend upon its extent and the effect it may have on the surface of the stamp; a surface abrasion having a greater impact than a hinge thin. Some of the chalk-surfaced key types of the early twentieth century are particularly prone to 'rubbing' and, again, this will always reduce the price of a stamp, the size of the reduction depending upon the degree of the damage and the scarcity of the stamp itself.

Perfins

Stamps bearing perforated initials were at one time treated as little better than rubbish and many were destroyed. The fact that there is now a specialist society devoted to perfins should indicate that the situation has changed; but it is fair to say that the majority of collectors avoid them like the plague. Many official perfins are now listed, in the catalogue and some of them carry a price higher than they would as normals. Some, indeed, are very desirable, notably the China 'Large Dragons' perforated 'NCH' by the *North China Herald*. Demand from specialist perfin collectors has pushed up the price for 'proving covers' that is, covers which show which organisation used a particular set of initials, while some commercial perfins are sought after and command a premium over the price of an unperfined stamp. Nevertheless, a set of perforated initials would still usually result in an otherwise fine stamp being worth only about one tenth of catalogue.

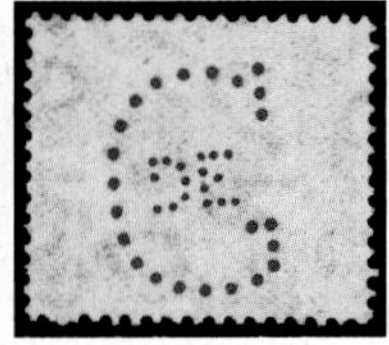

Perfins can enhance the value of a stamp

Fading

One of the reasons why the firm of De La Rue held such an important position in stamp production in the British Empire at the turn of the last century was the security offered by their fugitive inks. The green ink they used, in particular, dissolved into a pale yellow-green upon immersion in water. A footnote in the catalogue under the 1883 definitives of Great Britain comments; 'The above prices are for stamps in the true dull green colour. Stamps which have been soaked, causing the colour to run, are virtually worthless.' This seems rather harsh, particularly in the case of the difficult 9d., but fairly reflects the current market position. The comment is just as relevant to many other stamps, both from Britain and the colonies. The same inks were used in the production of many colonial middle and high values, such as the Federated Malay States 'elephants'. Such stamps, when water affected, would be worth from one fifth to one tenth of catalogue, depending on the degree of discolouration.

Water damage is not only a problem for the typographed issues of De La Rue. Although it is generally recognised that recess-printing inks are more stable, there are examples of such stamps which are susceptible to 'washing' – some of the Rhodesian 'double heads', for example, can be de-valued in this way.

Colour change is not, of course, brought about only through immersion in water; sunlight can sometimes have a very significant effect and seriously faded stamps should be viewed in the same way as 'washed' ones – more common items being 'virtually worthless', rarer ones rating up to one fifth of catalogue, providing that the fading is not too serious.

Tone spots – the brownish spots encountered on many stamps which have been stored in damp conditions – especially in the tropics – will also reduce the value of a stamp or cover; the degree of reduction once again depending upon the extent of the toning and the value of the stamp in fine condition. A few toned perforation tips should, say the experts, be viewed in the same way as if they were 'short'. A small brown spot in the centre of a stamp, providing it cannot be seen on the front, would reduce an otherwise fine King George VI stamp to around half catalogue, or quarter catalogue if it were mounted as well. Earlier stamps would require similar discounting but toned examples of more modern issues should be considered almost valueless. Similarly, any stamp with extensive or more disfiguring brown marks should be avoided, especially as the fault can 'migrate' to other stamps.

Fugitive inks were used for many colonial middle and high values

Cancellation quality

When describing the postmarks of the nineteenth century, the word 'obliteration' is synonymous with 'cancellation' – because, of course, that was what they were designed to do – to 'obliterate' the stamp in such a way as to prevent any opportunity for reuse. The Maltese cross is an attractive cancellation, especially when applied in red or one of the 'fancy' colours, but many early Great Britain line-engraved adhesives are heavily cancelled by over-inked black crosses, which detract considerably from the beauty of the stamps. A 'fine' cancellation should be lightly applied, if possible leaving a substantial part of the design – ideally including the Queen's profile – clear of the cancellation. Also desirable are well centred examples displaying all, or nearly all of the cancellation on the stamp. This is particularly true where the cancellation is more significant than the stamp, such as a Wotton-under-Edge Maltese cross. Here, you would want to have as full a cancellation as possible, although it would still be preferable to have it lightly applied.

The Maltese cross is an attractive cancellation, especially when applied in red

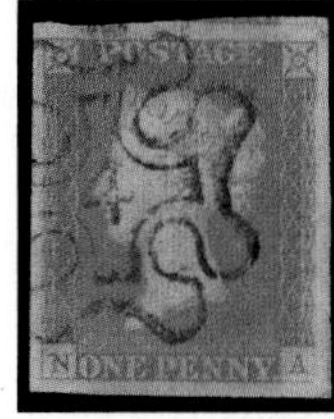

Where the cancellation is more important than the stamp it should be clear, upright and lightly applied

This rule remains valid after the arrival of the '1844' numeral cancellation. The duplex postmark, incorporating a circular datestamp alongside the numeral obliterator, was not introduced in London until early 1853, so for nine years nearly every stamp continued to be 'obliterated' by a barred numeral. On the odd occasion where another form of cancellation was used, such as the circular 'Town' marks or 'Penny Post' handstamps, the postmark has become more desirable than the stamp anyway. For stamps used during those nine years, therefore, lightly applied postmarks which leave a significant part of the design clear continue to be desirable and stamps which fall short of this will not be categorised as 'fine'.

Other countries followed the practices established by the British Post Office, using 'anonymous' cancels which can only be identified by individual peculiarities, or numeral postmarks of one form or another.

Numeral postmarks which leave a significant part of the design clear are desirable

Line-engraved stamps cancelled only by the datestamp would be rated 'superb'

Again, stamps with lightly applied cancellations should be sought out for preference, although it is necessary to bear in mind the current postal practices in the country or at the individual post office concerned. In spite of the fact that pen cancellations are not generally popular among collectors, where this was a normal method of cancellation, as on the first issue of St Helena, for example, they would be acceptable, although in practice most such examples have since been cleaned in an attempt to make them appear unused. Indeed, early GB stamps with manuscript cancels, such as the hand-drawn 'Maltese cross' of Dunnet, often fetch high prices at auction if their provenance is sound.

Circular datestamps

With the arrival of the Duplex cancellation, the possibility that a stamp might receive the circular dated portion of the handstamp increases, although this was not supposed to happen. Here, we should perhaps return to the statement in the front of the Stanley Gibbons catalogue, that: 'The prices are ... for examples in fine condition for the issue concerned. Superb examples are worth more, those of a lower quality, considerably less'. Thus, a postally used stamp cancelled by a lightly applied numeral portion of the postmark would generally be considered 'fine', while one which showed only the dater portion would be rated as 'superb', especially where that datestamp is upright, well-centred and lightly but clearly applied. A stamp in this condition could rate two or three times the price of a fine example, all other factors being equal.

Squared circles are collectable in their own right

As Duplex postmarks were replaced by new forms of cancellation such as squared circle handstamps and various forms of machine cancellation, new criteria come into play, but essentially the aim is the same, to find stamps which have been attractively cancelled. Squared circles were designed to combine the date and place of posting (in the central circle) and the obliteration (in the form of the corner bars) in one small and convenient handstamp. Their adoption by many postal administrations around the world would seem to indicate what a good idea they were felt to be at the time. In the case of squared circles it is necessary to make your own judgement: heavily inked bars obscuring the main feature of a stamp's design would not be 'fine', but a light but legible postmark which allows the design to show through would be. Of course, once again, squared circles are very collectable in their own right, so a clear complete (or almost complete) cancellation would almost certainly outweigh the 'marking down' which might normally be applied because the stamp itself was almost obscured.

'Socked on the nose' cancellations have become more popular, especially if they show something significant like the misspelling 'MAURITUS'

Just as in the case of wing margins and perfins, discussed above, fashions are changing in relation to cancellations. In the past, the aim was to find stamps on which the cancellation fell across just one corner of the design, leaving the major part of it clear. Today, interest in exactly where and when the stamp was cancelled, not to mention the possibility that such partial cancellations may have been forged, have made clear, centrally applied or 'socked-on-the-nose' cancellations much more desirable – although, again, they do need to be lightly applied.

Towards the end of the nineteenth century, rubber packet, newspaper and parcel cancellers began to appear. These, inevitably, obliterated more of the stamp's design than a steel datestamp and any stamp cancelled in this way would fall well short of 'fine'. The rectangular parcel cancellations which replaced the old parcel labels in the twentieth century are also shunned by all, other than postal historians seeking particular markings

Manuscript cancellations

We have briefly touched upon this issue already, but it is worth pursuing in greater depth. The reason why many collectors eschew stamps cancelled by pen marks is that they very often suggest fiscal, rather than postal, use. Fiscally used stamps are normally much cheaper than postally used examples, even with the significant increase in interest in revenue stamps which has taken place in the last decade. However, individual post offices in a number of countries have resorted to this form of cancellation from time to time and examples are sometimes even more desirable than the same stamp with a clear dated postmark. On the other hand, Australian postage due stamps are often found correctly cancelled in manuscript, rather than by a dated postmark. Although these are perfectly collectable, they are certainly nowhere near as desirable as similar examples with a 'proper' postmark and would probably rate no more than 20 per cent of catalogue, if that.

Individual post offices have resorted to manuscript cancellations from time to time: the Gold Coast stamp was used in Dodowah

Returning to fiscal cancellations, these take a number of forms and, since the stamps concerned are often of high face value, some are more desirable than others. The early 'Arms' high values of Rhodesia are relatively common fiscally used, cancelled by rubber handstamps in a variety of colours and often perfined as well. Such examples would rate barely 5 per cent of the catalogue price of postally used examples. The New Zealand 'long' Queen Victoria and 'Arms' high values were designed for both postal and fiscal use and the prices given for them in the catalogue are for examples with clear postal cancellations. However, some revenue cancels are similar in form to postal ones, so it is important that sufficient of the cancel falls on the stamp to guarantee postal use. Again, fiscally used examples would generally rate only 5 per cent or so of the price of postally used ones, while, among stamps which have seen revenue use, clear black 'Stamp Office' and other similar types are much more desirable than purple rubber handstamps, embossed cancels, manuscript markings and stamps which have been perforated through.

Early 'Arms' high values of Rhodesia are relatively common fiscally used

It is important that sufficient of the cancel falls on the stamp to guarantee postal use

Telegraphic postmarks

Generally speaking, just as stamp collectors prefer stamps which have not been fiscally used, they are also not keen on those which have identifiable telegraphic cancellations. Often, the same canceller was used for both purposes, in which case a stamp, once removed from a telegraph form would be indistinguishable from a postally used example and would therefore be equally acceptable. However, Indian high values that have been used telegraphically can often be identified by their cancellations which have three concentric arcs in the segments of the postmark immediately above and below the band across the centre of the cancellation which contains the date of sending. It is noted in the catalogue, for example, that India SG 147, the Edward VII 25r., can be supplied at one third of the price quoted in the catalogue (currently £1500), with a telegraphic cancellation. Other values should be similarly discounted.

1s. greens from plates 5 and 6 are not worth a premium

In light of this, it may seem strange that Great Britain Queen Victoria high values which were almost exclusively used for telegraphic or accounting purposes should be more highly priced than any which were used postally, simply because the quality of cancellation was vastly superior and, here, the prices quoted in the catalogue would be for telegraphically used examples, since this would be the only way of obtaining 'fine used'. Probably, the vast majority of fine used middle values, from 4d. to 2s. were also once attached to telegraph forms and many are relatively common in this form; notably the ls. green from plates 5 and 6, which would not be worth a premium over catalogue in this condition, while others, notably the 2½d. rosy mauve or any 9d. value would merit the premiums, sometimes substantial premiums, quoted in the catalogue for 'well centred, lightly used'.

It has sometimes been remarked upon that some GB surface-printed issues are more highly priced in the main GB listing than they are in some of the 'used abroad' sections. An 1873-80 2½d. rosy mauve (SG 141), for example, is priced at £80 in the GB listing, but £28 used in Suez, £24 used in Constantinople, £21 used in Gibraltar and just £17 used in Malta. This is not because there is less interest in GB used abroad, but because the prices are for 'fine condition for the issue concerned'. GB stamps used in Malta are generally fairly heavily cancelled by the 'A25' obliterator and the price quoted would be for an example in this form, whereas the price in the GB listing would be for a considerably better stamp. The two conclusions which can be drawn from this are that, firstly, a British stamp with a light Malta c.d.s. should be priced according to the GB listing, where that price is higher, and, secondly, that one should expect to pay very considerably less than the price in the GB section of the catalogue for a stamp with an 'average' numeral cancellation, which would only rate between 10 and 20 percent of catalogue, depending on the scarcity of the stamp and the extent to which it is obliterated by the postmark.

A British stamp with light Malta c.d.s. should be priced according to the GB listing

Wartime Malay States stamps should have identifiable pre-occupation datestamps (left), not post-war cancellations, such as that on the 6c. (right)

It is worth mentioning at this point that, to be worth full catalogue price, a stamp also needs to be used 'in period'. There are notes in the catalogue (such as that below Perak No. 121 or Muscat No. O10) indicating that the price shown is for a stamp with clearly identifiable contemporary cancellation. Stamps used later, in the case of Malayan States after the Japanese occupation had ended, are worth much less than catalogue price, even though they were still valid for postage in the early post-war period.

Collectors should be wary of any stamp with a non-contemporary ('posthumous') cancellation, however fine it may appear in all other respects, and expect to pay proportionately less for it. It must be remembered, of course, that some stamps were in normal use over prolonged periods, so it pays to be aware of the 'correct' postmark types for all stamps.

Be wary of stamps with non-contemporary cancellations, however attractive they may seem

Forged cancellations

The problem of forged cancellations has gained much greater prominence in the last few years. This is at least partly due to the increased demand for fine quality insofar as mint stamps are concerned. Heavily mounted or toned stamps are, as commented earlier, worth only a small fraction of catalogue price, so there is clearly an opportunity for the unscrupulous to turn them into 'fine used', in order to enhance their value. Fiscally used stamps may also have had their cancellations removed and any remains of them covered up by forged postmarks, while a great many stamps simply command a higher price used than they do mint, having been little used at the time they were current.

The upshot is that we all need to be aware of stamps which, at first sight, appear to be used, but bear cancellations which cannot be identified, A nice clean ring across the corner of a stamp, an apparently smeared c.d.s. on which neither the place of posting nor the date can be seen, or a general black smudge, reminiscent of many modern British Post Office operational postmarks, should all be avoided, unless they are known to be typical of the place and period concerned.

Fiscally used stamps may have their cancellations removed and covered up

'Madame Joseph' cancellations are becoming very collectable

Such stamps are really of 'spacefiller' status only and would usually not merit a price of more than one tenth of catalogue, if that.

More sophisticated forged cancellations also exist, of course and it is fair to say that the extent of this problem has only recently been recognised. Some of them are becoming collectable in their own right. However, these have now become of such interest that a stamp catalogued at less than about £10 is often of greater value with a clear Madame Joseph cancellation than it would be genuinely used. Higher value stamps would be discounted, though, but would still rate around one third of the price of a genuine example, taking the cheaper of the used or unused prices. Thus, a 1933 Falkland Islands Centenary £1 with the famous Port Stanley, '6 JA 33' forged postmark sells for about £750. Other forged cancellations are of less interest, especially more modern ones and those which have been drawn on by hand!

Another new development is 'postmarks' applied by ink-jet printer. In such cases close magnification will show the cancellation to be made up of a series of dots rather than the clearly inked lines of a genuine marking.

Look out for forged cancellations which have been drawn by hand or applied by ink-jet printer!

'Chops' and manuscript endorsements bring down the value of a used stamp

While on the subject of 'drawn in by hand', collectors in the past – including some very eminent ones – were in the habit of 'enhancing' slightly unclear postal markings by drawing over them in Indian ink. Less expensive stamps are seriously devalued in this condition, especially if the postmark is a heavy or disfiguring one. Major rarities would be less devalued in percentage terms, however, and could still rate up to about one third the price of an 'unenhanced' stamp with the same cancellation.

Many businesses in Asian countries, especially forwarding agents, were in the habit of cancelling their stamps with 'chops', while individuals frequently wrote across them in manuscript in order to discourage theft. Catalogue prices are for stamps without such endorsements, with a neat handstamped 'chop' reducing the price by at least one third and a handwritten one by around two thirds.

Cancelled to order

Prices in the catalogue are, generally, for fine postally used, but for many modern issues they relate to cancelled to order examples. This does not refer to the selling of cancelled stamps for less than face value for the making up of stamp packets, as was the practice in many Eastern European countries between the 1950s and 1990s, and in North Borneo up to 1912 or Ghana in the 1950s. These latter examples are noted in the catalogue, with separate prices for the North Borneo stamps, while it is noted that catalogue prices for Ghana refer to cancelled to order, properly postally used stamps being worth a little more.

As the volume of worldwide stamp issues has escalated in the last 30 years and the cost of having postally used stamps removed from envelopes, soaked, dried and sorted has risen, it is no longer practicable for the stamp trade to supply fine postally used examples of most modern issues. They are therefore supplied cancelled by the postal administration concerned at the same price as mint examples, although as new issues they may be slightly more expensive, owing to the extra handling costs involved. Catalogue price is therefore for stamps 'cancelled to order' or 'cancelled by favour', although fine postally used examples would merit the same price. Unfortunately, as collectors in Britain and the USA are aware, 'fine' and 'postally used' are two expressions which are rarely used together when discussing modern issues, since our respective postal administrations have deliberately returned to the philosophy of their Victorian predecessors and 'obliterated', rather than 'cancelled', any stamp being used to prepay postage. In the circumstances, therefore, catalogue price for used twentieth or twenty-first century GB refers to stamps cancelled by a light circular or oval datestamp. Rubber packet or parcel handstamps, ink-jet cancellations slogan postmarks or wavy lines are worthy only of a small proportion of catalogue, the size of that proportion depending, once again, on the appearance of the stamp and its relative scarcity.

Modern GB prices are for c.d.s. used, wavy lines are worth only a small proportion of catalogue

That, indeed, encapsulates the relationship between condition and price. In this article we have reviewed the various aspects of 'condition' and how they can vary from country to country and from issue to issue. The catalogue price is for 'fine for the issue concerned', meaning fine in every respect, although a better than fine cancellation might outweigh a slight deficiency in centring, to allow a stamp to still be classified as 'fine'.

The end result is that, when buying, it is vitally important to carefully consider the condition of the item as well as its price and whether or not you want it and, when satisfied on all three counts, make your purchase – before anyone else gets in first!

This is an updated version of a series of articles published in Gibbons Stamp Monthly *in 2003 under the title of* 'Defining "Fine"'.

General Philatelic Information and Guidelines to the Scope of Stanley Gibbons Commonwealth catalogues

These notes reflect current practice in compiling the Stanley Gibbons Commonwealth Catalogues.

The Stanley Gibbons Stamp Catalogue has a very long history and the vast quantity of information it contains has been carefully built up by successive generations through the work of countless individuals. Philately is never static and the Catalogue has evolved and developed over the years. These notes relate to the current criteria upon which a stamp may be listed or priced. These criteria have developed over time and may have differed somewhat in the early years of this catalogue. These notes are not intended to suggest that we plan to make wholesale changes to the listing of classic issues in order to bring them into line with today's listing policy, they are designed to inform catalogue users as to the policies currently in operation.

PRICES

The prices quoted in this Catalogue are the estimated selling prices of Stanley Gibbons Ltd at the time of publication. They are, unless it is specifically stated otherwise, for examples in fine condition for the issue concerned. Superb examples are worth more; those of a lower quality considerably less.

All prices are subject to change without prior notice and Stanley Gibbons Ltd may from time to time offer stamps below catalogue price. Individual low value stamps sold at 399 Strand are liable to an additional handling charge. Purchasers of new issues should note the prices charged for them contain an element for the service rendered and so may exceed the prices shown when the stamps are subsequently catalogued. Postage and handling charges are extra.

No guarantee is given to supply all stamps priced, since it is not possible to keep every catalogued item in stock. Commemorative issues may, at times, only be available in complete sets and not as individual values.

Quotation of prices. The prices in the left-hand column are for unused stamps and those in the right-hand column are for used.

A dagger (†) denotes that the item listed does not exist in that condition and a blank, or dash, that it exists, or may exist, but we are unable to quote a price.

We welcome information concerning items which are currently unpriced. Such assistance may lead to them being priced in future editions.

Prices are expressed in pounds and pence sterling. One pound comprises 100 pence (£1 = 100p).

The method of notation is as follows: pence in numerals (e.g. 10 denotes ten pence); pounds and pence, up to £100, in numerals (e.g. 4.25 denotes four pounds and twenty-five pence); prices above £100 are expressed in whole pounds with the '£' sign shown.

Unused stamps. Great Britain and Commonwealth: the prices for unused stamps of Queen Victoria to King George V are for lightly hinged examples. Unused prices for King Edward VIII, King George VI and Queen Elizabeth issues are for unmounted mint or 'mint never hinged' (MNH).

Some stamps from the King George VI period are often difficult to find in unmounted mint condition. In such instances we would expect that collectors would need to pay a high proportion of the price quoted to obtain mounted mint examples. Generally speaking lightly mounted mint stamps from this reign, issued before 1945, are in considerable demand.

Used stamps. The used prices are normally for stamps fine postally used, which for the vast majority of those issued since 1900 refers to cancellation with a clear circular or oval dated postmark. It may also include stamps cancelled to order, where this practice exists, or with commemorative or 'first day' postmarks.

A pen-cancellation on early issues can sometimes correctly denote postal use. Instances are individually noted in the Catalogue in explanation of the used price given.

Prices quoted for bisects on cover or large piece are for those dated during the period officially authorised.

Stamps not sold unused to the public (e.g. some official stamps) are priced used only.

The use of 'unified' designs, that is stamps inscribed for both postal and fiscal purposes, results in a number of stamps of very high face value. In some instances these may not have been primarily intended for postal purposes, but if they are so inscribed we include them. The used prices shown refer to stamps postally used, although fiscally used examples are sometimes priced in brackets. Collectors should be careful to avoid stamps with fiscal cancellations that have had their cancellations removed and fraudulent postmarks applied.

Cover prices. To assist collectors, cover prices are quoted for issues up to 1945 at the beginning of each country.

The system gives a general guide in the form of a factor by which the corresponding used price of the basic loose stamp should be multiplied when found in fine average condition on cover.

Care is needed in applying the factors and they relate to a cover which bears a single of the denomination listed; if more than one denomination is present the most highly priced attracts the multiplier and the remainder are priced at the simple figure for used singles in arriving at a total.

The cover should be of non-philatelic origin; bearing the correct postal rate for the period and distance involved and cancelled with the markings normal to the offices concerned. Purely philatelic items have a cover value only slightly greater than the catalogue value for the corresponding used stamps. This applies generally to those high-value stamps used philatelically rather than in the normal course of commerce. Low-value stamps, e.g. ¼d. and ½d., are desirable when used as a single rate on cover and merit an increase in 'multiplier' value.

First day covers in the period up to 1945 are not within the scope of the system and the multiplier should not be used. As a special category of philatelic usage, with wide variations in valuation according to scarcity, they require separate treatment.

Oversized covers, difficult to accommodate on an album page, should be reckoned as worth little more than the corresponding value of the used stamps. The condition of a cover also affects its value. Except for 'wreck covers', serious damage or soiling reduce the value where the postal markings and stamps are ordinary ones. Conversely, visual appeal adds to the value and this can include freshness of appearance, important addresses, old-fashioned but legible hand-writing, historic town-names, etc.

The multipliers are a base on which further value would be added to take account of the cover's postal historical importance in demonstrating such things as unusual, scarce or emergency cancels, interesting routes, significant postal markings, combination usage, the development of postal rates, and so on.

Minimum price. The minimum catalogue price quoted is 10p. For individual stamps prices between 10p. and 95p. are provided as a guide for catalogue users. The lowest price charged for individual stamps or sets purchased from Stanley Gibbons Ltd is £1

Set prices. Set prices are generally for one of each value, excluding shades and varieties, but including major colour changes. Where there are alternative shades, etc., the cheapest is usually included. The number of stamps in the set is always stated for clarity. The prices for sets containing *se-tenant* pieces are based on the prices quoted for such combinations, and not on those for the individual stamps.

Varieties. Where plate or cylinder varieties are priced in used condition the price quoted is for a fine used example with the cancellation well clear of the listed flaw.

Specimen stamps. The pricing of these items is explained under that heading.

Stamp booklets. Prices are for complete assembled booklets in fine condition with those issued before 1945 showing normal wear and tear. Incomplete booklets and those which have been 'exploded' will, in general, be worth less than the figure quoted.

Repricing. Collectors will be aware that the market factors of supply and demand directly influence the prices quoted in this Catalogue. Whatever the scarcity of a particular stamp, if there is no one in the market who wishes to buy it cannot be expected to achieve a high price. Conversely, the same item actively sought by numerous potential buyers may cause the price to rise.

All the prices in this Catalogue are examined during the preparation of each new edition by the expert staff of Stanley Gibbons and repriced as necessary. They take many factors into account, including supply and demand, and are in close touch with the international stamp market and the auction world.

Commonwealth cover prices and advice on postal history material originally provided by Edward B Proud.

GUARANTEE

All stamps are guaranteed originals in the following terms:

If not as described, and returned by the purchaser, we undertake to refund the price paid to us in the original transaction. If any stamp is certified as genuine by the Expert Committee of the Royal Philatelic Society, London, or by BPA Expertising Ltd, the purchaser shall not be entitled to make any claim against us for any error, omission or mistake in such certificate.

Consumers' statutory rights are not affected by the above guarantee.

The recognised Expert Committees in this country are those of the Royal Philatelic Society, 41 Devonshire Place, London W1G, 6JY, and BPA Expertising Ltd, PO Box 1141, Guildford, Surrey GU5 0WR. They do not undertake valuations under any circumstances and fees are payable for their services.

CONDITION GUIDE

To assist collectors in assessing the true value of items they are considering buying or in reviewing stamps already in their collections, we now offer a more detailed guide to the condition of stamps on which this catalogue's prices are based.

For a stamp to be described as 'Fine', it should be sound in all respects, without creases, bends, wrinkles, pin holes, thins or tears. If perforated, all perforation 'teeth' should be intact, it should not suffer from fading, rubbing or toning and it should be of clean, fresh appearance.

Margins on imperforate stamps: These should be even on all sides and should be at least as wide as half the distance between that stamp and the next. To have one or more margins of less than this width, would normally preclude a stamp from being described as 'Fine'. Some early stamps were positioned very close together on the printing plate and in such cases 'Fine' margins would necessarily be narrow. On the other hand, some plates were laid down to give a substantial gap between individual stamps and in such cases margins would be expected to be much wider.

An 'average' four-margin example would have a narrower margin on one or more sides and should be priced accordingly, while a stamp with wider, yet even, margins than 'Fine' would merit the description 'Very Fine' or 'Superb' and, if available, would command a price in excess of that quoted in the catalogue.

Gum: Since the prices for stamps of King Edward VIII, King George VI and Queen Elizabeth are for 'unmounted' or 'never hinged' mint, even stamps from these reigns which have been very lightly mounted should be available at a discount from catalogue price, the more obvious the hinge marks, the greater the discount.

Catalogue prices for stamps issued prior to King Edward VIII's reign are for mounted mint, so unmounted examples would be worth a premium. Hinge marks on 20th century stamps should not be too obtrusive, and should be at least in the lightly mounted category. For 19th century stamps more obvious hinging would be acceptable, but stamps should still carry a large part of their original gum—'Large part o.g.'—in order to be described as 'Fine'.

Centring: Ideally, the stamp's image should appear in the exact centre of the perforated area, giving equal margins on all sides. 'Fine' centring would be close to this ideal with any deviation having an effect on the value of the stamp. As in the case of the margins on imperforate stamps, it should be borne in mind that the space between some early stamps was very narrow, so it was very difficult to achieve accurate perforation, especially when the technology was in its infancy. Thus, poor centring would have a less damaging effect on the value of a 19th century stamp than on a 20th century example, but the premium put on a perfectly centred specimen would be greater.

Cancellations: Early cancellation devices were designed to 'obliterate' the stamp in order to prevent it being reused and this is still an important objective for today's postal administrations. Stamp collectors, on the other hand, prefer postmarks to be lightly applied, clear, and to leave as much as possible of the design visible. Dated, circular cancellations have long been 'the postmark of choice', but the definition of a 'Fine' cancellation will depend upon the types of cancellation in use at the time a stamp was current—it is clearly illogical to seek a circular datestamp on a Penny Black.

'Fine', by definition, will be superior to 'Average', so, in terms of cancellation quality, if one begins by identifying what 'Average' looks like, then one will be half way to identifying 'Fine'. The illustrations will give some guidance on mid-19th century and mid-20th century cancellations of **Great Britain**, but types of cancellation in general use in each country and in each period will determine the appearance of 'Fine'.

As for the factors discussed above, anything less than 'Fine' will result in a downgrading of the stamp concerned, while a very fine or superb cancellation will be worth a premium.

Combining the factors: To merit the description 'Fine', a stamp should be fine in every respect, but a small deficiency in one area might be made up for in another by a factor meriting an 'Extremely Fine' description.

Some early issues are so seldom found in what would normally be considered to be 'Fine' condition, the catalogue prices are for a slightly lower grade, with 'Fine' examples being worth a premium. In such cases a note to this effect is given in the catalogue, while elsewhere premiums are given for well-centred, lightly cancelled examples.

Stamps graded at less than fine remain collectable and, in the case of more highly priced stamps, will continue to hold a value. Nevertheless, buyers should always bear condition in mind.

Contents. The Catalogue is confined to adhesive postage stamps, including miniature sheets. For particular categories the rules are:

(a) Revenue (fiscal) stamps are listed only where they have been expressly authorised for postal duty.

(b) Stamps issued only precancelled are included, but normally issued stamps available additionally with precancel have no separate precancel listing unless the face value is changed.

(c) Stamps prepared for use but not issued, hitherto accorded full listing, are nowadays foot-noted with a price (where possible).

(d) Bisects (trisects, etc.) are only listed where such usage was officially authorised.

(e) Stamps issued only on first day covers or in presentation packs and not available separately are not listed but may be priced in a footnote.

(f) New printings are only included in this Catalogue where they show a major philatelic variety, such as a change in shade, watermark or paper. Stamps which exist with or without imprint dates are listed separately; changes in

MARGINS ON IMPERFORATE STAMPS

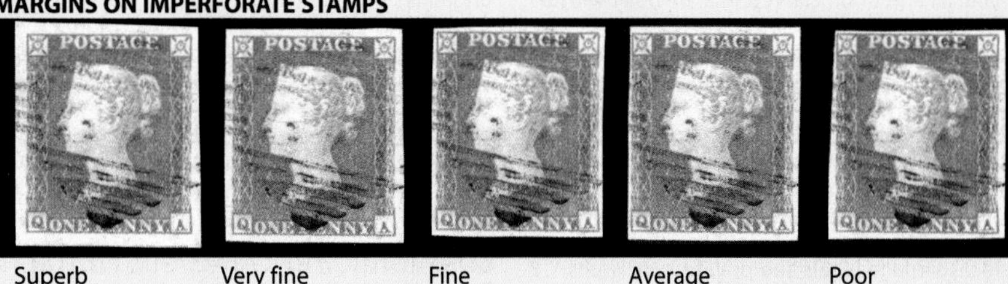

Superb | Very fine | Fine | Average | Poor

GUM

Unmounted | Very lightly mounted | Lightly mounted | Mounted/large part original gum (o.g.). | Heavily mounted small part o.g

CENTRING

Superb | Very fine | Fine | Average | Poor

CANCELLATIONS

Superb | Very fine | Fine | Average | Poor

Superb | Very fine

Fine | Average | Poor

imprint dates are mentioned in footnotes.
(g) Official and unofficial reprints are dealt with by footnote.
(h) Stamps from imperforate printings of modern issues which occur perforated are covered by footnotes, but are listed where widely available for postal use.

Exclusions. The following are excluded:
(a) non-postal revenue or fiscal stamps;
(b) postage stamps used fiscally (although prices are now given for some fiscally used high values);
(c) local carriage labels and private local issues;
(d) bogus or phantom stamps;
(e) railway or airline letter fee stamps, bus or road transport company labels or the stamps of private postal companies operating under licence from the national authority;
(f) cut-outs;
(g) all types of non-postal labels and souvenirs;
(h) documentary labels for the postal service, e.g. registration, recorded delivery, air-mail etiquettes, etc.;
(i) privately applied embellishments to official issues and privately commissioned items generally;
(j) stamps for training postal officers.

Full listing. 'Full listing' confers our recognition and implies allotting a catalogue number and (wherever possible) a price quotation.

In judging status for inclusion in the catalogue broad considerations are applied to stamps. They must be issued by a legitimate postal authority, recognised by the government concerned, and must be adhesives valid for proper postal use in the class of service for which they are inscribed. Stamps, with the exception of such categories as postage dues and officials, must be available to the general public, at face value, in reasonable quantities without any artificial restrictions being imposed on their distribution.

For errors and varieties the criterion is legitimate (albeit inadvertent) sale through a postal administration in the normal course of business. Details of provenance are always important; printers' waste and deliberately manufactured material are excluded.

Certificates. In assessing unlisted items due weight is given to Certificates from recognised Expert Committees and, where appropriate, we will usually ask to see them.

Date of issue. Where local issue dates differ from dates of release by agencies, 'date of issue' is the local date. Fortuitous stray usage before the officially intended date is disregarded in listing.

Catalogue numbers. Stamps of each country are catalogued chronologically by date of issue. Subsidiary classes are placed at the end of the country, as separate lists, with a distinguishing letter prefix to the catalogue number, e.g. D for postage due, O for official and E for express delivery stamps.

The catalogue number appears in the extreme left-column. The boldface Type numbers in the next column are merely cross-references to illustrations.

A catalogue number with a suffix will normally relate to the main number, so 137a will be a variant of No. 137, unless the suffix appears as part of the number in the left-hand column such as **Great Britain** No. 20*a*, in which case that should be treated as the main number. A number with multiple suffixes will relate to the first letter or letters of that suffix, so 137ab will be a variant of 137a and 137aba a variant of 137ab. The exception is an "aa" suffix, which will precede an "a" and always refers to the main number, so 137aa relates to 137, not 137a.

Once published in the Catalogue, numbers are changed as little as possible; really serious renumbering is reserved for the occasions when a complete country or an entire issue is being rewritten. The edition first affected includes cross-reference tables of old and new numbers.

Our catalogue numbers are universally recognised in specifying stamps and as a hallmark of status.

Illustrations. Stamps are illustrated at three-quarters linear size. Stamps not illustrated are the same size and format as the value shown, unless otherwise indicated. Stamps issued only as miniature sheets have the stamp alone illustrated but sheet size is also quoted. Overprints, surcharges, watermarks and postmarks are normally actual size. Illustrations of varieties are often enlarged to show the detail. Stamp booklet covers are illustrated half-size, unless otherwise indicated.

The colour illustrations of stamps are intended as a guide only, they may differ in shade from the originals

Designers. Designers' names are quoted where known, though space precludes naming every individual concerned in the production of a set. In particular, photographers supplying material are usually named only where they also make an active contribution in the design stage; posed photographs of reigning monarchs are, however, an exception to this rule.

CONTACTING THE CATALOGUE EDITOR

The editor is always interested in hearing from people who have new information which will improve or correct the Catalogue. As a general rule he must see and examine the actual stamps before they can be considered for listing; photographs or photocopies are insufficient evidence.

Submissions should be made in writing to the Catalogue Editor, Stanley Gibbons Publications at the Ringwood office. The cost of return postage for items submitted is appreciated, and this should include the registration fee if required.

Where information is solicited purely for the benefit of the enquirer, the editor cannot undertake to reply if the answer is already contained in these published notes or if return postage is omitted. Written communications are greatly preferred to enquiries by telephone or e-mail and the editor regrets that he or his staff cannot see personal callers without a prior appointment being made. Correspondence may be subject to delay during the production period of each new edition.

The editor welcomes close contact with study circles and is interested, too, in finding reliable local correspondents who will verify and supplement official information in countries where this is deficient.

We regret we do not give opinions as to the genuineness of stamps, nor do we identify stamps or number them by our Catalogue.

TECHNICAL MATTERS

The meanings of the technical terms used in the catalogue will be found in our *Philatelic Terms Illustrated.*

References below to (more specialised) listings are to be taken to indicate, as appropriate, the Stanley Gibbons *Great Britain Specialised Catalogue* in five volumes or the *Great Britain Concise Catalogue*.

1. Printing

Printing errors. Errors in printing are of major interest to the Catalogue. Authenticated items meriting consideration would include: background, centre or frame inverted or omitted; centre or subject transposed; error of colour; error or omission of value; double prints and impressions; printed both sides; and so on. Apparent "double prints" including overprints, on stamps printed by offset litho arising from movement of the rubber "blanket" involved in this process are however, outside the scope of this catalogue, although they may be included in more specialised listings. Designs *tête-bêche*, whether intentionally or by accident, are listable. *Se-tenant* arrangements of stamps are recognised in the listings or footnotes. Gutter pairs (a pair of stamps separated by blank margin) are not included in this volume. Colours only partially omitted are not listed. Stamps with embossing omitted are reserved for our more specialised listings.

Printing varieties. Listing is accorded to major changes in the printing base which lead to completely new types. In recess-printing this could be a design re-engraved; in photogravure or photolithography a screen altered in whole or in part. It can also encompass flat-bed and rotary printing if the results are readily distinguishable.

To be considered at all, varieties must be constant.

Early stamps, produced by primitive methods, were prone to numerous imperfections; the lists reflect this, recognising re-entries, retouches, broken frames, misshapen letters, and so on. Printing technology has, however, radically improved over the years, during which time photogravure and lithography have become predominant. Varieties nowadays are more in the nature of flaws and these, being too specialised for this general catalogue, are almost always outside the scope.

In no catalogue, however, do we list such items as: dry prints, kiss prints, doctor-blade flaws, colour shifts or registration flaws (unless they lead to the complete omission of a colour from an individual stamp), lithographic ring flaws, and so on. Neither do we recognise fortuitous happenings like paper creases or confetti flaws.

"Varieties of varieties". We no longer provide individual listings for combinations of two or more varieties; thus a plate variety or overprinting error will not be listed for various watermark orientations.

Overprints (and surcharges). Overprints of different types qualify for separate listing. These include overprints in different colours; overprints from different printing processes such as litho and typo; overprints in totally different typefaces, etc. Major errors in machine-printed overprints are important and listable. They include: overprint inverted or omitted; overprint double (treble, etc.); overprint diagonal; overprint double, one inverted; pairs with one overprint omitted, e.g. from a radical shift to an adjoining stamp; error of colour; error of type fount; letters inverted or omitted, etc. If the overprint is handstamped, few of these would qualify and a distinction is drawn. We continue, however, to list pairs of stamps where one has a handstamped overprint and the other has not.

Albino prints or double prints, one of them being albino (i.e. showing an uninked impression of the printing plate) are listable unless they are particularly common in this form (see the note below Travancore No. 32fa, for example). We do not, however, normally list reversed albino overprints, caused by the accidental or deliberate folding of sheets prior to overprinting (British Levant Nos. 51/8).

Varieties occurring in overprints will often take the form of broken letters, slight differences in spacing, rising spaces, etc. Only the most important would be considered for listing or footnote mention.

Sheet positions. If space permits we quote sheet positions of listed varieties and authenticated data is solicited for this purpose.

De La Rue plates. The Catalogue classifies the general plates used by De La Rue for printing British Colonial stamps as follows:

VICTORIAN KEY TYPE

Die I

1. The ball of decoration on the second point of the crown appears as a dark mass of lines.
2. Dark vertical shading separates the front hair from the bun.
3. The vertical line of colour outlining the front of the throat stops at the sixth line of shading on the neck.
4. The white space in the coil of the hair above the curl is roughly the shape of a pin's head.

Die II

1. There are very few lines of colour in the ball and it appears almost white.
2. A white vertical strand of hair appears in place of the dark shading.
3. The line stops at the eighth line of shading.
4. The white space is oblong, with a line of colour partially dividing it at the left end.

Plates numbered 1 and 2 are both Die I. Plates 3 and 4 are Die II.

GEORGIAN KEY TYPE

Die I

A. The second (thick) line below the name of the country is cut slanting, conforming roughly to the shape of the crown on each side.

B. The labels of solid colour bearing the words "POSTAGE" and "& REVENUE" are square at the inner top corners.

C. There is a projecting "bud" on the outer spiral of the ornament in each of the lower corners.

Die II

A. The second line is cut vertically on each side of the crown.

B. The labels curve inwards at the top.

C. There is no "bud" in this position.

Unless otherwise stated in the lists, all stamps with watermark Multiple Crown CA (w **8**) are Die I while those with watermark Multiple Crown Script CA (w **9**) are Die II. The Georgian Die II was introduced in April 1921 and was used for Plates 10 to 22 and 26 to 28. Plates 23 to 25 were made from Die I by mistake.

2. Paper

All stamps listed are deemed to be on (ordinary) paper of the wove type and white in colour; only departures from this are normally mentioned.

Types. Where classification so requires we distinguish such other types of paper as, for example, vertically and horizontally laid; wove and laid bâtonné; card(board); carton; cartridge; glazed; granite; native; pelure; porous; quadrillé; ribbed; rice; and silk thread.

Wove paper Laid paper

Granite paper Quadrillé paper

Burelé band

The various makeshifts for normal paper are listed as appropriate. The varieties of double paper and joined paper are recognised. The security device of a printed burelé band on the back of a stamp, as in early Queensland, qualifies for listing.

Descriptive terms. The fact that a paper is handmade (and thus probably of uneven thickness) is mentioned where necessary. Such descriptive terms as "hard" and "soft"; "smooth" and "rough"; "thick", "medium" and "thin" are applied where there is philatelic merit in classifying papers.

Coloured, very white and toned papers. A coloured paper is one that is coloured right through (front and back of the stamp). In the Catalogue the colour of the paper is given in italics, thus:
black/*rose* = black design on rose paper.

Papers have been made specially white in recent years by, for example, a very heavy coating of chalk. We do not classify shades of whiteness of paper as distinct varieties. There does exist, however, a type of paper from early days called toned. This is off-white, often brownish or buffish, but it cannot be assigned any definite colour. A toning effect brought on by climate, incorrect storage or gum staining is disregarded here, as this was not the state of the paper when issued.

"Ordinary" and "Chalk-surfaced" papers. The availability of many postage stamps for revenue purposes made necessary some safeguard against the illegitimate re-use of stamps with removable cancellations. This was at first secured by using fugitive inks and later by printing on paper surfaced by coatings containing either chalk or china clay, both of which made it difficult to remove any form of obliteration without damaging the stamp design.

This catalogue lists these chalk-surfaced paper varieties from their introduction in 1905. Where no indication is given, the paper is "ordinary".

The "traditional" method of indentifying chalk-surfaced papers has been that, when touched with a silver wire, a black mark is left on the paper, and the listings in this catalogue are based on that test. However, the test itself is now largely discredited, for, although the mark can be removed by a soft rubber, some damage to the stamp will result from its use.

The difference between chalk-surfaced and pre-war ordinary papers is fairly clear: chalk-surfaced papers being smoother to the touch and showing a characteristic sheen when light is reflected off their surface. Under good magnification tiny bubbles or pock marks can be seen on the surface of the stamp and at the tips of the perforations the surfacing appears "broken". Traces of paper fibres are evident on the surface of ordinary paper and the ink shows a degree of absorption into it.

Initial chalk-surfaced paper printings by De La Rue had a thinner coating than subsequently became the norm. The characteristics described above are less pronounced in these printings.

During and after the Second World War, substitute papers replaced the chalk-surfaced papers, these do not react to the silver test and are therefore classed as "ordinary", although differentiating them without recourse to it is more difficult, for, although the characteristics of the chalk-surfaced paper remained the same, some of the ordinary papers appear much smoother than earlier papers and many do not show the watermark clearly. Experience is the only solution to identifying these, and comparison with stamps whose paper type is without question will be of great help.

Another type of paper, known as "thin striated" was used only for the Bahamas 1s. and 5s. (Nos. 155a, 156a, 171 and 174) and for several stamps of the **Malaya**n states. Hitherto these have been described as "chalk-surfaced" since they gave some reaction to the silver test, but they are much thinner than usual chalk-surfaced papers, with the watermark showing clearly. Stamps on this paper show a slightly 'ribbed' effect when the stamp is held up to the light. Again, comparison with a known striated paper stamp, such as the 1941 Straits Settlements Die II 2c. orange (No. 294) will prove invaluable in separating these papers.

Glazed paper. In 1969 the Crown Agents introduced a new general-purpose paper for use in conjunction with all current printing processes. It generally has a marked glossy surface but the degree varies according to the process used, being more marked in recess-printing stamps. As it does not respond to the silver test this presents a further test where previous printings were on chalky paper. A change of paper to the glazed variety merits separate listing.

Green and yellow papers. Issues of the First World War and immediate postwar period occur on green and yellow papers and these are given separate Catalogue listing. The original coloured papers (coloured throughout) gave way to surface-coloured papers, the stamps having "white backs"; other stamps show one colour on the front and a different one at the back. Because of the numerous variations a grouping of colours is adopted as follows:

Yellow papers

(1) The original *yellow* paper (throughout), usually bright in colour. The gum is often sparse, of harsh consistency and dull-looking. Used 1912–1920.

(2) The *white-backs*. Used 1913–1914.

(3) A bright lemon paper. The colour must have a pronounced greenish tinge, different from the "yellow" in (1). As a rule, the gum on stamps using this lemon paper is plentiful, smooth and shiny, and the watermark shows distinctly. Care is needed with stamps printed in green on yellow paper (1) as it may appear that the paper is this lemon. Used 1914–1916.

(4) An experimental *orange-buff* paper. The colour must have a distinct brownish tinge. It is not to be confused with a muddy yellow (1) nor the misleading appearance (on the surface) of stamps printed in red on yellow paper where an engraved plate has been insufficiently wiped. Used 1918–1921.

(5) An experimental *buff* paper. This lacks the brownish tinge of (4) and the brightness of the yellow shades. The gum is shiny when compared with the matt type used on (4). Used 1919–1920.

(6) A *pale yellow* paper that has a creamy tone to the yellow. Used from 1920 onwards.

Green papers

(7) The original "green" paper, varying considerably through shades of blue-green and yellow-green, the front and back sometimes differing. Used 1912–1916.

(8) The *white backs*. Used 1913–1914.

(9) A paper blue-green on the surface with *pale olive* back. The back must be markedly paler than the front and this and the pronounced olive tinge to the back distinguish it from (7). Used 1916–1920.

(10) Paper with a vivid green surface, commonly called *emerald-green*; it has the olive back of (9). Used 1920.

(11) Paper with *emerald-green* both back and front. Used from 1920 onwards.

3. Perforation and Rouletting

Perforation gauge. The gauge of a perforation is the number of holes in a length of 2 cm. For correct classification the size of the holes (large or small) may need to be distinguished; in a few cases the actual number of holes on each edge of the stamp needs to be quoted.

Measurement. The Gibbons *Instanta* gauge is the standard for measuring perforations. The stamp is viewed against a dark background with the transparent gauge put on top of it. Though the gauge measures to decimal accuracy, perforations read from it are generally quoted in the Catalogue to the nearest half. For example:

Just over perf 12¾ to just under 13¼ = perf 13
Perf 13¼ exactly, rounded up = perf 13½
Just over perf 13¼ to just under 13¾ = perf 13½
Perf 13¾ exactly, rounded up = perf 14

However, where classification depends on it, actual quarter-perforations are quoted.

Notation. Where no perforation is quoted for an issue it is imperforate. Perforations are usually abbreviated (and spoken) as follows, though sometimes they may be spelled out for clarity. This notation for rectangular stamps (the majority) applies to diamond shapes if "top" is read as the edge to the top right.

P 14: perforated alike on all sides (read: "perf 14").

P 14×15: the first figure refers to top and bottom, the second to left and right sides (read: "perf 14 by 15"). This is a compound perforation. For an upright triangular stamp the first figure refers to the two sloping sides and second to the base. In inverted triangulars the base is first and the second figure to the sloping sides.

P 14–15: perforation measuring anything between 14 and 15: the holes are irregularly spaced, thus the gauge may vary along a single line or even along a single edge of the stamp (read: "perf 14 to 15").

P 14 *irregular*: perforated 14 from a worn perforator, giving badly aligned holes irregularly spaced (read: "irregular perf 14").

P *comp(ound)* 14×15: two gauges in use but not necessarily on opposite sides of the stamp. It could be one side in one gauge and three in the other; or two adjacent sides with the same gauge. (Read: "perf compound of 14 and 15".) For three gauges or more, abbreviated as "P 12, 14½, 15 *or compound*" for example.

P 14, 14½: perforated approximately 14¼ (read: "perf 14 or 14½"). It does *not* mean two stamps, one perf 14 and the other perf 14½. This obsolescent notation is gradually being replaced in the Catalogue.

Imperf: imperforate (not perforated)

Imperf×P 14: imperforate at top ad bottom and perf 14 at sides.

P 14×*imperf*: perf 14 at top and bottom and imperforate at sides.

Such headings as "P 13×14 (*vert*) and P 14×13 (*horiz*)" indicate which perforations apply to which stamp format—vertical or horizontal.

Some stamps are additionally perforated so that a label or tab is detachable; others have been perforated for use as two halves. Listings are normally for whole stamps, unless stated otherwise.

Imperf×perf

Other terms. Perforation almost always gives circular holes; where other shapes have been used they are specified, e.g. square holes; lozenge perf. Interrupted perfs are brought about by the omission of pins at regular intervals. Perforations merely simulated by being printed as part of the design are of course ignored. With few exceptions, privately applied perforations are not listed.

In the 19th century perforations are often described as clean cut (clean, sharply incised holes), intermediate or rough (rough holes, imperfectly cut, often the result of blunt pins).

Perforation errors and varieties. Authenticated errors, where a stamp normally perforated is accidentally issued imperforate, are listed provided no traces of perforation (blind holes or indentations) remain. They must be provided as pairs, both stamps wholly imperforate, and are only priced in that form.

Note that several postal administrations and their agencies are now deliberately releasing imperforate versions of issued stamps in restricted quantities and at premium prices. These are not listable, but, where possible, their existance will be noted

Stamps imperforate between stamp and sheet margin are not listed in this catalogue, but such errors on **Great Britain** stamps will be found in the *Great Britain Specialised Catalogue*.

Pairs described as "imperforate between" have the line of perforations between the two stamps omitted.

Imperf between (horiz pair): a horizontal pair of stamps with perfs all around the edges but none between the stamps.

Imperf between (vert pair): a vertical pair of stamps with perfs all around the edges but none between the stamps.

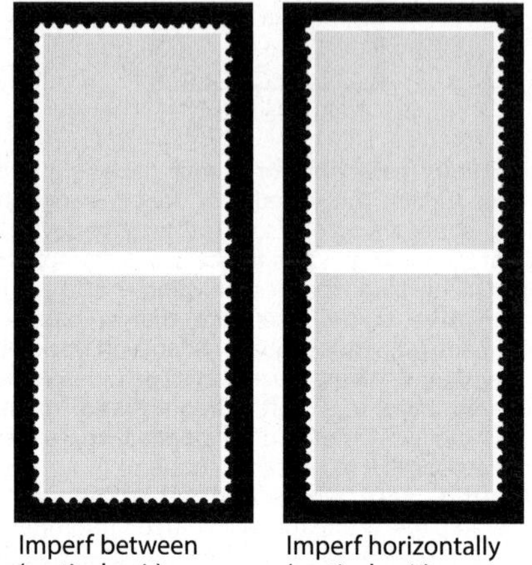

Imperf between (vertical pair) — Imperf horizontally (vertical pair)

Where several of the rows have escaped perforation the resulting varieties are listable. Thus:

Imperf vert (horiz pair): a horizontal pair of stamps perforated top and bottom; all three vertical directions are imperf—the two outer edges and between the stamps.

Imperf horiz (vert pair): a vertical pair perforated at left and right edges; all three horizontal directions are imperf—the top, bottom and between the stamps.

Straight edges. Large sheets cut up before issue to post offices can cause stamps with straight edges, i.e. imperf on one side or on two sides at right angles. They are not usually listable in this condition and are worth less than corresponding stamps properly perforated all round. This does not, however, apply to certain stamps, mainly from coils and booklets, where straight edges on various sides are the manufacturing norm affecting every stamp. The listings and notes make clear which sides are correctly imperf.

Malfunction. Varieties of double, misplaced or partial perforation caused by error or machine malfunction are not listable, neither are freaks, such as perforations placed diagonally from paper folds, nor missing holes caused by broken pins.

Types of perforating. Where necessary for classification, perforation types are distinguished. These include:

Line perforation from one line of pins punching single rows of holes at a time.

Comb perforation from pins disposed across the sheet in comb formation, punching out holes at three sides of the stamp a row at a time.

Harrow perforation applied to a whole pane or sheet at one stroke.

Rotary perforation from toothed wheels operating across a sheet, then crosswise.

Sewing machine perforation. The resultant condition, clean-cut or rough, is distinguished where required.

Pin-perforation is the commonly applied term for pin-roulette in which, instead of being punched out, round holes are pricked by sharp-pointed pins and no paper is removed.

Mixed perforation occurs when stamps with defective perforations are re-perforated in a different gauge.

Punctured stamps. Perforation holes can be punched into the face of the stamp. Patterns of small holes, often in the shape of initial letters, are privately applied devices against pilferage. These (perfins) are outside the scope except for Australia, Canada, Cape of Good Hope, Papua and Sudan where they were used as official stamps by the national administration. Identification devices, when officially inspired, are listed or noted; they can be shapes, or letters or words formed from holes, sometimes converting one class of stamp into another.

Rouletting. In rouletting the paper is cut, for ease of separation, but none is removed. The gauge is measured, when needed, as for perforations. Traditional French terms descriptive of the type of cut are often used and types include:

Arc roulette (percé en arc). Cuts are minute, spaced arcs, each roughly a semicircle.

Cross roulette (percé en croix). Cuts are tiny diagonal crosses.

Line roulette (percé en ligne or *en ligne droite)*. Short straight cuts parallel to the frame of the stamp. The commonest basic roulette. Where not further described, "roulette" means this type.

Rouletted in colour or coloured roulette (percé en lignes colorées or *en lignes de coleur)*. Cuts with coloured edges, arising from notched rule inked simultaneously with the printing plate.

Saw-tooth roulette (percé en scie). Cuts applied zigzag fashion to resemble the teeth of a saw.

Serpentine roulette (percé en serpentin). Cuts as sharply wavy lines.

Zigzag roulette (percé en zigzags). Short straight cuts at angles in alternate directions, producing sharp points on separation. US usage favours "serrate(d) roulette" for this type.

Pin-roulette (originally *percé en points* and now *perforés trous d'epingle*) is commonly called pin-perforation in English.

4. Gum

All stamps listed are assumed to have gum of some kind; if they were issued without gum this is stated. Original gum (o.g.) means that which was present on the stamp as issued to the public. Deleterious climates and the presence of certain chemicals can cause gum to crack and, with early stamps, even make the paper deteriorate. Unscrupulous fakers are adept in removing it and regumming the stamp to meet the unreasoning demand often made for "full o.g." in cases where such a thing is virtually impossible.

The gum normally used on stamps has been gum arabic until the late 1960s when synthetic adhesives were introduced. Harrison and Sons Ltd for instance used polyvinyl alcohol known to philatelists as PVA. This is almost invisible except for a slight yellowish tinge which was incorporated to make it possible to see that the stamps had been gummed. It has advantages in hot countries, as stamps do not curl and sheets are less likely to stick together. Gum arabic and PVA are not distinguished in the lists except that where a stamp exists in both forms this is indicated in the footnotes. Our more specialised catalogues provide separate listing of gums for **Great Britain**

5. Watermarks

Stamps are on unwatermarked paper except where the heading to the set says otherwise.

Detection. Watermarks are detected for Catalogue description by one of four methods: (1) holding stamps to the light; (2) laying stamps face down on a dark background; (3) adding a few drops of petroleum ether 40/60 to the stamp laid face down in a watermark tray; (4) by use of the Stanley Gibbons Detectamark, or other equipment, which work by revealing the thinning of the paper at the watermark. (Note that petroleum ether is highly inflammable in use and can damage photogravure stamps.)

Listable types. Stamps occurring on both watermarked and unwatermarked papers are different types and both receive full listing.

Single watermarks (devices occurring once on every stamp) can be modified in size and shape as between different issues; the types are noted but not usually separately listed. Fortuitous absence of watermark from a single stamp or its gross displacement would not be listable.

To overcome registration difficulties the device may be repeated at close intervals *(a multiple watermark)*, single stamps thus showing parts of several devices. Similarly, a *large sheet watermark* (or *all-over watermark*) covering numerous stamps can be used. We give informative notes and illustrations for them. The designs may be such that numbers of stamps in the sheet automatically lack watermark: this is not a listable variety. Multiple and all-over watermarks sometimes undergo modifications, but if the various types are difficult to distinguish from single stamps notes are given but not separate listings.

Papermakers' watermarks are noted where known but not listed separately, since most stamps in the sheet will lack them. Sheet watermarks which are nothing more than officially adopted papermakers' watermarks are, however, given normal listing.

Marginal watermarks, falling outside the pane of stamps, are ignored except where misplacement has caused the adjoining row to be affected, in which case they may be footnoted.

They usually consist of straight or angled lines and double-lined capital letters, they are particularly prevalent on some Crown CC and Crown CA watermark stamps.

Watermark errors and varieties. Watermark errors are recognised as of major importance. They comprise stamps intended to be on unwatermarked paper but issued watermarked by mistake, or stamps printed on paper with the wrong watermark. Varieties showing letters omitted from the watermark are also included, but broken or deformed bits on the dandy roll are not listed unless they represent repairs.

Watermark positions. The diagram shows how watermark position is described in the Catalogue. Paper has a side intended for printing and watermarks are usually impressed so that they read normally when looked through from that printed side. However, since philatelists customarily detect watermarks by looking at the back of the stamp the watermark diagram also makes clear what is actually seen.

Illustrations in the Catalogue are of watermarks in normal positions (from the front of the stamps) and are actual size where possible.

Differences in watermark position are collectable varieties. This Catalogue now lists inverted, sideways inverted and reversed watermark varieties on Commonwealth stamps from the 1860s onwards except where the watermark position is completely haphazard or, due to the method of printing, appear in equal quantities, upright and inverted (e.g. Papua Nos. 47/83). In such cases it should be assumed that the price is the same, either way.

Where a watermark comes indiscriminately in various positions our policy is to cover this by a general note: we do not give separate listings because the watermark position in these circumstances has no particular philatelic importance.

AS DESCRIBED (Read through front of stamp)		AS SEEN DURING WATERMARK DETECTION (Stamp face down and back examined)
GvR	Normal	GvR
GvR	Inverted	GvR
GvR	Reversed	GvR
GvR	Inverted and Reversed	GvR
GvR	Sideways	GvR
GvR	Sideways Inverted	GvR

As shown in the diagram, a watermark described as 'sideways' will normally show the top of the watermark (as shown in its illustration), pointing to the left of the stamp, as seen from the front and to the right as seen from the back.

For clarification, or in cases where the 'normal' watermark is 'sideways inverted' a note is generally provided at the foot of the relevant listing, particularly where sideways and sideways inverted varieties exist.

Standard types of watermark. Some watermarks have been used generally for various British possessions rather than exclusively for a single colony. To avoid repetition the Catalogue classifies 11 general types, as under, with references in the headings throughout the listings being given either in words or in the form ("W w **9**") (meaning "watermark type w **9**"). In those cases where watermark illustrations appear in the listings themselves, the respective reference reads, for example, W **153**, thus indicating that the watermark will be found in the normal sequence of illustrations as (type) **153**.

The general types are as follows, with an example of each quoted.

W	*Description*	*Example*
w **1**	Large Star	St. Helena No. 1
w **2**	Small Star	Turks Is. No. 4
w **3**	Broad (pointed) Star	Grenada No. 24
w **4**	Crown (over) CC, small stamp	Antigua No. 13
w **5**	Crown (over) CC, large stamp	Antigua No. 31
w **6**	Crown (over) CA, small stamp	Antigua No. 21
w **7**	Crown CA (CA over Crown), large stamp	Sierra Leone No. 54
w **8**	Multiple Crown CA	Antigua No. 41
w **9**	Multiple Script CA	Seychelles No. 158
w **9*a***	do. Error	Seychelles No. 158a
w **9*b***	do. Error	Seychelles No. 158b
w **10**	V over Crown	N.S.W. No. 327
w **11**	Crown over A	N.S.W. No. 347

CC in these watermarks is an abbreviation for "Crown Colonies" and CA for "Crown Agents". Watermarks w **1**, w **2** and w **3** are on stamps printed by Perkins, Bacon; w **4** onwards on stamps from De La Rue and other printers.

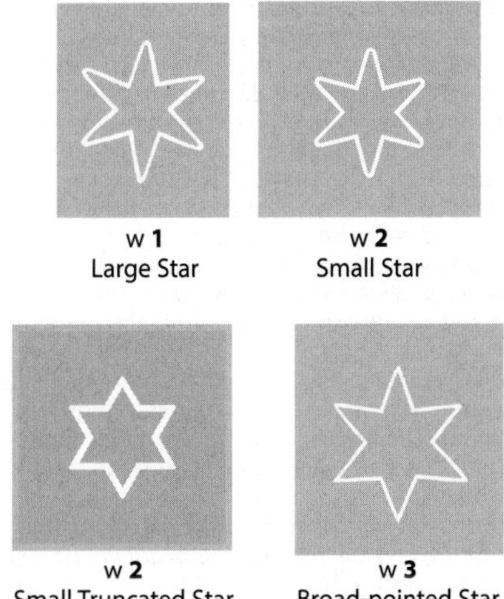

w **1** Large Star

w **2** Small Star

w **2** Small Truncated Star

w **3** Broad-pointed Star

Watermark w **1**, *Large Star*, measures 15 to 16 mm across the star from point to point and about 27 mm from centre to centre vertically between stars in the sheet. It was made for long stamps like Ceylon 1857 and St. Helena 1856.

Watermark w **2**, *Small Star* is of similar design but measures 12 to 13½mm from point to point and 24 mm from centre to centre vertically. It was for use with ordinary-size stamps such as Grenada 1863–71.

When the Large Star watermark was used with the smaller stamps it only occasionally comes in the centre of the paper. It is frequently so misplaced as to show portions of two stars above and below and this eccentricity will very often help in determining the watermark.

Watermark w **2*a***, *Small Truncated Star,* only used for Queensland stamps of 1868-74.

Watermark w **3**, *Broad-pointed Star*, resembles w **1** but the points are broader.

w **4**
Crown (over) CC

w **5**
Crown (over) CC

Two *Crown (over) CC* watermarks were used: w **4** was for stamps of ordinary size and w **5** for those of larger size.

w **6**
Crown (over) CA

w **7**
CA over Crown

Two watermarks of *Crown CA* type were used, w **6** being for stamps of ordinary size. The other, w **7**, is properly described as *CA over Crown*. It was specially made for paper on which it was intended to print long fiscal stamps: that some were used postally accounts for the appearance of w **7** in the Catalogue. The watermark occupies twice the space of the ordinary Crown CA watermark, w **6**. Stamps of normal size printed on paper with w **7** watermark show it *sideways*; it takes a horizontal pair of stamps to show the entire watermark.

w **8**
Multiple Crown CA

w **9**
Multiple Script CA

Multiple watermarks began in 1904 with w **8**, *Multiple Crown CA,* changed from 1921 to w **9**, *Multiple Script CA*. On stamps of ordinary size portions of two or three watermarks appear and on the large-sized stamps a greater number can be observed. The change to letters in script character with w **9** was accompanied by a Crown of distinctly different shape.

It seems likely that there were at least two dandy rolls for each Crown Agents watermark in use at any one time with a reserve roll being employed when the normal one was withdrawn for maintenance or repair.

Both the Mult Crown CA and the Mult Script CA types exist with one or other of the letters omitted from individual impressions. It is possible that most of these occur from the reserve rolls as they have only been found on certain issues. The MCA watermark experienced such problems during the early 1920s and the Script over a longer period from the early 1940s until 1951.

During the 1920s damage must also have occurred on one of the Crowns as a substituted Crown has been found on certain issues. This is smaller than the normal and consists of an oval base joined to two upright ovals with a circle positioned between their upper ends. The upper line of the Crown's base is omitted, as are the left and right-hand circles at the top and also the cross over the centre circle.

Substituted Crown

The *Multiple Script CA* watermark, w **9**, is known with two errors, recurring among the 1950–52 printings of several territories. In the first a crown has fallen away from the dandy-roll that impresses the watermark into the paper pulp. It gives w **9a**, *Crown missing*, but this omission has been found in both "Crown only" (*illustrated*) and "Crown CA" rows. The resulting faulty paper was used for Bahamas, Johore, Seychelles and the postage due stamps of nine colonies

w **9a**: Error, Crown missing

w **9b**: Error, St. Edward's Crown

When the omission was noticed a second mishap occurred, which was to insert a wrong crown in the space, giving w **9b**, St. Edward's Crown. This produced varieties in Bahamas, Perlis, St. Kitts-Nevis and Singapore and the incorrect crown likewise occurs in (Crown only) and (Crown CA) rows.

w **10**
V over Crown

w **11**
Crown over A

Resuming the general types, two watermarks found in issues of several Australian States are: w **10**, *V over Crown*, and w **11**, *Crown over A*.

w **12**
Multiple St. Edward's Crown Block CA

w **13**
Multiple PTM

The *Multiple St. Edward's Crown Block CA* watermark, w **12**, was introduced in 1957 and besides the change in the Crown (from that used in Multiple Crown Script CA, w **9**) the letters reverted to block capitals. The new watermark began to appear sideways in 1966 and these stamps are generally listed as separate sets.

The watermark w **13**, *Multiple PTM*, was introduced for new Malaysian issues in November 1961.

6. Colours

Stamps in two or three colours have these named in order of appearance, from the centre moving outwards. Four colours or more are usually listed as multicoloured.

In compound colour names the second is the predominant one, thus:

orange-red = a red tending towards orange;
red-orange = an orange containing more red than usual.

Standard colours used. The 200 colours most used for stamp identification are given in the Stanley Gibbons Stamp Colour Key. The Catalogue has used the Stamp Colour Key as standard for describing new issues for some years. The names are also introduced as lists are rewritten, though exceptions are made for those early issues where traditional names have become universally established.

Determining colours. When comparing actual stamps with colour samples in the Stamp Colour Key, view in a good north daylight (or its best substitute; fluorescent "colour matching" light). Sunshine is not recommended. Choose a solid portion of the stamp design; if available, marginal markings such as solid bars of colour or colour check dots are helpful. Shading lines in the design can be misleading as they appear lighter than solid colour. Postmarked portions of a stamp appear darker than normal. If more than one colour is present, mask off the extraneous ones as the eye tends to mix them.

Errors of colour. Major colour errors in stamps or overprints which qualify for listing are: wrong colours; one colour inverted in relation to the rest; albinos (colourless impressions), where these have Expert Committee certificates; colours completely omitted, but only on unused stamps (if found on used stamps the information is footnoted) and with good credentials, missing colours being frequently faked.

Colours only partially omitted are not recognised, Colour shifts, however spectacular, are not listed.

Shades. Shades in philately refer to variations in the intensity of a colour or the presence of differing amounts of other colours. They are particularly significant when they can be linked to specific printings. In general, shades need to be quite marked to fall within the scope of this Catalogue. Furthermore, the listings refer to colours as issued; they may deteriorate into something different through the passage of time. Collectors are warned against according any significance to colours which may have been altered by immersion in water or exposure to sunlight, but time, alone will sometimes cause colours to change, notably some of the letterpress De la Rue stamps of the late 19th and early 20th centuries.

Modern colour printing by lithography is prone to marked differences of shade, even within a single run, and variations can occur within the same sheet. Such shades are not listed.

Aniline colours. An aniline colour meant originally one derived from coal-tar; it now refers more widely to colour of a particular brightness suffused on the surface of a stamp and showing through clearly on the back.

Colours of overprints and surcharges. All overprints and surcharges are in black unless stated otherwise in the heading or after the description of the stamp.

7. Specimen Stamps

Originally, stamps overprinted SPECIMEN were circulated to postmasters or kept in official records, but after the establishment of the Universal Postal Union supplies were sent to Berne for distribution to the postal administrations of member countries.

During the period 1884 to 1928 most of the stamps of British Crown Colonies required for this purpose were overprinted SPECIMEN in various shapes and sizes by their printers from typeset formes. Some locally produced provisionals were handstamped locally, as were sets prepared for presentation. From 1928 stamps were punched with holes forming the word SPECIMEN, each firm of printers using a different machine or machines. From 1948 the stamps supplied for UPU distribution were no longer punctured, although receiving authorities sometimes applied SPECIMEN markings of their own.

Stamps of some other Commonwealth territories were overprinted or handstamped locally, while stamps of **Great Britain** and those overprinted for use in overseas postal agencies (mostly of the higher denominations) bore SPECIMEN overprints and handstamps applied by the Inland Revenue or the Post Office.

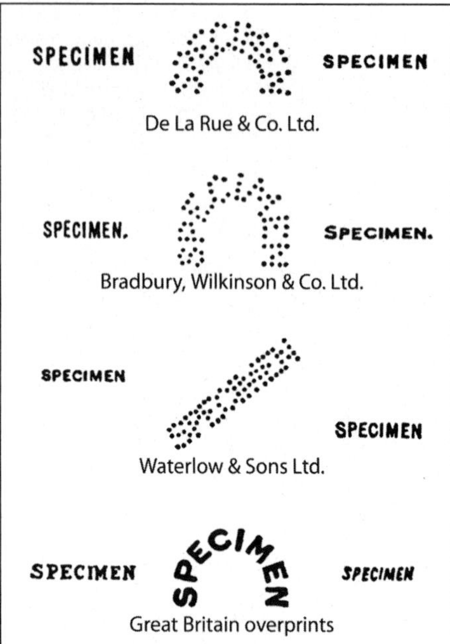

Some of the commoner types of overprints or punctures are illustrated here. Collectors are warned that dangerous forgeries of the punctured type exist.

The *Stanley Gibbons Commonwealth Catalogues* record those Specimen overprints or perforations intended for distribution by the UPU to member countries and we are grateful to James Bendon, author and publisher of *UPU Specimen Stamps, 1878 – 1961,* a much expanded edition of which was published in 2015, for his assistance with these listings. The Specimen overprints of Australia and its dependent territories, which were sold to collectors by the Post Office, are also included.

Various Perkins Bacon issues exist obliterated with a "CANCELLED" within an oval of bars handstamp.

Perkins Bacon "CANCELLED" Handstamp

This was applied to six examples of those issues available in 1861 which were then given to members of Sir Rowland Hill's family. 75 different stamps (including four from Chile) are recorded with this handstamp although others may possibly exist. The unauthorised gift of these "CANCELLED" stamps to the Hill family was a major factor in the loss of the Agent General for the Crown Colonies (the forerunner of the Crown Agents) contracts by Perkins Bacon in the following year. Where examples of these scarce items are known to be in private hands the catalogue provides a price.

For full details of these stamps see *CANCELLED by Perkins Bacon* by Peter Jaffé (published by Spink in 1998).

All other Specimens are outside the scope of this volume.

In specifying type of specimen for individual high-value stamps, "H/S" means handstamped, "Optd" is overprinted and "Perf" is punctured. Some sets occur mixed, e.g. "Optd/Perf". If unspecified, the type is apparent from the date or it is the same as for the lower values quoted as a set.

Prices. Prices for stamps up to £1 are quoted in sets;

higher values are priced singly. Where specimens exist in more than one type the price quoted is for the cheapest. Specimen stamps have rarely survived even as pairs; these and strips of three, four or five are worth considerably more than singles.

8. Luminescence

Machines which sort mail electronically have been introduced in recent years. In consequence some countries have issued stamps on flourescent or phosphorescent papers, while others have marked their stamps with phosphor bands.

The various papers can only be distinguished by ultraviolet lamps emitting particular wavelengths. They are separately listed only when the stamps have some other means of distinguishing them, visible without the use of these lamps. Where this is not so, the papers are recorded in footnotes or headings.

For this catalogue we do not consider it appropriate that collectors be compelled to have the use of an ultraviolet lamp before being able to identify stamps by our listings. Some experience will also be found necessary in interpreting the results given by ultraviolet. Collectors using the lamps, nevertheless, should exercise great care in their use as exposure to their light is potentially dangerous to the eyes.

Phosphor bands are listable, since they are visible to the naked eye (by holding stamps at an angle to the light and looking along them, the bands appear dark). Stamps existing with or without phosphor bands or with differing numbers of bands are given separate listings. Varieties such as double bands, bands omitted, misplaced or printed on the back are not listed.

Detailed descriptions appear at appropriate places in the listings in explanation of luminescent papers; see, for example, Australia above No.363, Canada above Nos. 472 and 611, Cook Is. above 249, etc.

For **Great Britain**, where since 1959 phosphors have played a prominent and intricate part in stamp issues, the main notes above Nos. 599 and 723 should be studied, as well as the footnotes to individual listings where appropriate. In general the classification is as follows.

Stamps with phosphor bands are those where a separate cylinder applies the phosphor after the stamps are printed. Issues with "all-over" phosphor have the "band" covering the entire stamp. Parts of the stamp covered by phosphor bands, or the entire surface for "all-over" phosphor versions, appear matt. Stamps on phosphorised paper have the phosphor added to the paper coating before the stamps are printed. Issues on this paper have a completely shiny surface.

Further particularisation of phosphor – their methods of printing and the colours they exhibit under ultraviolet – is outside the scope of this catalogue. The more specialised listings should be consulted for this information.

9. Coil Stamps

Stamps issued only in coil form are given full listing. If stamps are issued in both sheets and coils the coil stamps are listed separately only where there is some feature (e.g. perforation or watermark sideways) by which singles can be distinguished. Coil stamps containing different stamps *se-tenant* are also listed.

Coil join pairs are too random and too easily faked to permit listing; similarly ignored are coil stamps which have accidentally suffered an extra row of perforations from the claw mechanism in a malfunctioning vending machine.

10. Stamp Booklets

Stamp booklets are now listed in this catalogue.

Single stamps from booklets are listed if they are distinguishable in some way (such as watermark or perforation) from similar sheet stamps.

Booklet panes are listed where they contain stamps of different denominations *se-tenant*, where stamp-size labels are included, or where such panes are otherwise identifiable. Booklet panes are placed in the listing under the lowest denomination present.

Particular perforations (straight edges) are covered by appropriate notes.

The majority of stamps booklets were made up from normal sheets and panes may be bound upright or inverted and booklets may be stapled or stitched at either the left or right-hand side. Unless specifically mentioned in the listings, such variations do not command a price premium.

11. Miniature Sheets and Sheetlets

We distinguish between "miniature sheets" and "sheetlets" and this affects the catalogue numbering. An item in sheet form that is postally valid, containing a single stamp, pair, block or set of stamps, with wide, inscribed and/or decorative margins, is a miniature sheet if it is sold at post offices as an indivisable entity. As such the Catalogue allots a single MS number and describes what stamps make it up. The sheetlet or small sheet differs in that the individual stamps are intended to be purchased separately for postal purposes. For sheetlets, all the component postage stamps are numbered individually and the composition explained in a footnote. Note that the definitions refer to post office sale—not how items may be subsequently offered by stamp dealers.

12. Forgeries and Fakes

Forgeries. Where space permits, notes are considered if they can give a concise description that will permit unequivocal detection of a forgery. Generalised warnings, lacking detail, are not nowadays inserted, since their value to the collector is problematic.

Forged cancellations have also been applied to genuine stamps. This catalogue includes notes regarding those manufactured by "Madame Joseph", together with the cancellation dates known to exist. It should be remembered that these dates also exist as genuine cancellations.

For full details of these see *Madame Joseph Forged Postmarks* by Derek Worboys (published by the Royal Philatelic Society London and the British Philatelic Trust in 1994) or *Madame Joseph Revisited* by Brian Cartwright (published by the Royal Philatelic Society London in 2005).

Fakes. Unwitting fakes are numerous, particularly "new shades" which are colour changelings brought about by exposure to sunlight, soaking in water contaminated with dyes from adherent paper, contact with oil and dirt from a pocketbook, and so on. Fraudulent operators, in addition, can offer to arrange: removal of hinge marks; repairs of thins on white or coloured papers; replacement of missing margins or perforations; reperforating in true or false gauges; removal of fiscal cancellations; rejoining of severed pairs, strips and blocks; and (a major hazard) regumming. Collectors can only be urged to purchase from reputable sources and to insist upon Expert Committee certification where there is any kind of doubt.

The Catalogue can consider footnotes about fakes where these are specific enough to assist in detection.

Abbreviations

Printers

A.B.N. Co.	American Bank Note Co, New York.
B.A.B.N.	British American Bank Note Co. Ottawa
B.W.	Bradbury Wilkinson & Co, Ltd.
C.B.N.	Canadian Bank Note Co, Ottawa.
Continental B.N. Co.	Continental Bank Note Co.
Courvoisier	Imprimerie Courvoisier S.A., La-Chaux-de-Fonds, Switzerland.
D.L.R.	De La Rue & Co, Ltd, London.
Enschedé	Joh. Enschedé en Zonen, Haarlem, Netherlands.
Harrison	Harrison & Sons, Ltd. London
P.B.	Perkins Bacon Ltd, London.
Waterlow	Waterlow & Sons, Ltd, London.

General Abbreviations

Alph	Alphabet
Anniv	Anniversary
Comp	Compound (perforation)
Des	Designer; designed
Diag	Diagonal; diagonally
Eng	Engraver; engraved
F.C. or f.c.	Fiscal Cancellation
H/S	Handstamped
Horiz	Horizontal; horizontally
Imp, Imperf	Imperforate
Inscr	Inscribed
L	Left
Litho	Lithographed
mm	Millimetres
MS	Miniature sheet
N.Y.	New York
Opt(d)	Overprint(ed)
P or P-c	Pen-cancelled
P, Pf or Perf	Perforated
Photo	Photogravure
Pl	Plate
Pr	Pair
Ptd	Printed
Ptg	Printing
R	Right
R.	Row
Recess	Recess-printed
Roto	Rotogravure
Roul	Rouletted
S	Specimen (overprint)
Surch	Surcharge(d)
T.C.	Telegraph Cancellation
T	Type
Typo	Typographed
Un	Unused
Us	Used
Vert	Vertical; vertically
W or wmk	Watermark
Wmk s	Watermark sideways

(†) = Does not exist

(–) (or blank price column) = Exists, or may exist, but no market price is known.

/ between colours means "on" and the colour following is that of the paper on which the stamp is printed.

Colours of Stamps

Bl (blue); blk (black); brn (brown); car, carm (carmine); choc (chocolate); clar (claret); emer (emerald); grn (green); ind (indigo); mag (magenta); mar (maroon); mult (multicoloured); mve (mauve); ol (olive); orge (orange); pk (pink); pur (purple); scar (scarlet); sep (sepia); turq (turquoise); ultram (ultramarine); verm (vermilion); vio (violet); yell (yellow).

Colour of Overprints and Surcharges

(B.) = blue, (Blk.) = black, (Br.) = brown, (C.) = carmine, (G.) = green, (Mag.) = magenta, (Mve.) = mauve, (Ol.) = olive, (O.) = orange, (P.) = purple, (Pk.) = pink, (R.) = red, (Sil.) = silver, (V.) = violet, (Vm.) or (Verm.) = vermilion, (W.) = white, (Y.) = yellow.

Arabic Numerals

As in the case of European figures, the details of the Arabic numerals vary in different stamp designs, but they should be readily recognised with the aid of this illustration.

International Philatelic Glossary

English	French	German	Spanish	Italian
Agate	Agate	Achat	Agata	Agata
Air stamp	Timbre de la poste aérienne	Flugpostmarke	Sello de correo aéreo	Francobollo per posta aerea
Apple Green	Vert-pomme	Apfelgrün	Verde manzana	Verde mela
Barred	Annulé par barres	Balkenentwertung	Anulado con barras	Sbarrato
Bisected	Timbre coupé	Halbiert	Partido en dos	Frazionato
Bistre	Bistre	Bister	Bistre	Bistro
Bistre-brown	Brun-bistre	Bisterbraun	Castaño bistre	Bruno-bistro
Black	Noir	Schwarz	Negro	Nero
Blackish Brown	Brun-noir	Schwärzlichbraun	Castaño negruzco	Bruno nerastro
Blackish Green	Vert foncé	Schwärzlichgrün	Verde negruzco	Verde nerastro
Blackish Olive	Olive foncé	Schwärzlicholiv	Oliva negruzco	Oliva nerastro
Block of four	Bloc de quatre	Viererblock	Bloque de cuatro	Bloco di quattro
Blue	Bleu	Blau	Azul	Azzurro
Blue-green	Vert-bleu	Blaugrün	Verde azul	Verde azzuro
Bluish Violet	Violet bleuâtre	Bläulichviolett	Violeta azulado	Violtto azzurrastro
Booklet	Carnet	Heft	Cuadernillo	Libretto
Bright Blue	Bleu vif	Lebhaftblau	Azul vivo	Azzurro vivo
Bright Green	Vert vif	Lebhaftgrün	Verde vivo	Verde vivo
Bright Purple	Mauve vif	Lebhaftpurpur	Púrpura vivo	Porpora vivo
Bronze Green	Vert-bronze	Bronzegrün	Verde bronce	Verde bronzo
Brown	Brun	Braun	Castaño	Bruno
Brown-lake	Carmin-brun	Braunlack	Laca castaño	Lacca bruno
Brown-purple	Pourpre-brun	Braunpurpur	Púrpura castaño	Porpora bruno
Brown-red	Rouge-brun	Braunrot	Rojo castaño	Rosso bruno
Buff	Chamois	Sämisch	Anteado	Camoscio
Cancellation	Oblitération	Entwertung	Cancelación	Annullamento
Cancelled	Annulé	Gestempelt	Cancelado	Annullato
Carmine	Carmin	Karmin	Carmín	Carminio
Carmine-red	Rouge-carmin	Karminrot	Rojo carmín	Rosso carminio
Centred	Centré	Zentriert	Centrado	Centrato
Cerise	Rouge-cerise	Kirschrot	Color de ceresa	Color Ciliegia
Chalk-surfaced paper	Papier couché	Kreidepapier	Papel estucado	Carta gessata
Chalky Blue	Bleu terne	Kreideblau	Azul turbio	Azzurro smorto
Charity stamp	Timbre de bienfaisance	Wohltätigkeitsmarke	Sello de beneficenza	Francobollo di beneficenza
Chestnut	Marron	Kastanienbraun	Castaño rojo	Marrone
Chocolate	Chocolat	Schokolade	Chocolate	Cioccolato
Cinnamon	Cannelle	Zimtbraun	Canela	Cannella
Claret	Grenat	Weinrot	Rojo vinoso	Vinaccia
Cobalt	Cobalt	Kobalt	Cobalto	Cobalto
Colour	Couleur	Farbe	Color	Colore
Comb-perforation	Dentelure en peigne	Kammzähnung, Reihenzähnung	Dentado de peine	Dentellatura e pettine
Commemorative stamp	Timbre commémoratif	Gedenkmarke	Sello conmemorativo	Francobollo commemorativo
Crimson	Cramoisi	Karmesin	Carmesí	Cremisi
Deep Blue	Blue foncé	Dunkelblau	Azul oscuro	Azzurro scuro
Deep bluish Green	Vert-bleu foncé	Dunkelbläulichgrün	Verde azulado oscuro	Verde azzurro scuro
Design	Dessin	Markenbild	Diseño	Disegno
Die	Matrice	Urstempel. Type, Platte	Cuño	Conio, Matrice
Double	Double	Doppelt	Doble	Doppio
Drab	Olive terne	Trüboliv	Oliva turbio	Oliva smorto
Dull Green	Vert terne	Trübgrün	Verde turbio	Verde smorto
Dull purple	Mauve terne	Trübpurpur	Púrpura turbio	Porpora smorto
Embossing	Impression en relief	Prägedruck	Impresión en relieve	Impressione a relievo
Emerald	Vert-eméraude	Smaragdgrün	Esmeralda	Smeraldo
Engraved	Gravé	Graviert	Grabado	Inciso
Error	Erreur	Fehler, Fehldruck	Error	Errore
Essay	Essai	Probedruck	Ensayo	Saggio
Express letter stamp	Timbre pour lettres par exprès	Eilmarke	Sello de urgencia	Francobollo per espresso
Fiscal stamp	Timbre fiscal	Stempelmarke	Sello fiscal	Francobollo fiscale
Flesh	Chair	Fleischfarben	Carne	Carnicino
Forgery	Faux, Falsification	Fälschung	Falsificación	Falso, Falsificazione
Frame	Cadre	Rahmen	Marco	Cornice

English	French	German	Spanish	Italian
Granite paper	Papier avec fragments de fils de soie	Faserpapier	Papel con filamentos	Carto con fili di seta
Green	Vert	Grün	Verde	Verde
Greenish Blue	Bleu verdâtre	Grünlichblau	Azul verdoso	Azzurro verdastro
Greenish Yellow	Jaune-vert	Grünlichgelb	Amarillo verdoso	Giallo verdastro
Grey	Gris	Grau	Gris	Grigio
Grey-blue	Bleu-gris	Graublau	Azul gris	Azzurro grigio
Grey-green	Vert gris	Graugrün	Verde gris	Verde grigio
Gum	Gomme	Gummi	Goma	Gomma
Gutter	Interpanneau	Zwischensteg	Espacio blanco entre dos grupos	Ponte
Imperforate	Non-dentelé	Geschnitten	Sin dentar	Non dentellato
Indigo	Indigo	Indigo	Azul indigo	Indaco
Inscription	Inscription	Inschrift	Inscripción	Dicitura
Inverted	Renversé	Kopfstehend	Invertido	Capovolto
Issue	Émission	Ausgabe	Emisión	Emissione
Laid	Vergé	Gestreift	Listado	Vergato
Lake	Lie de vin	Lackfarbe	Laca	Lacca
Lake-brown	Brun-carmin	Lackbraun	Castaño laca	Bruno lacca
Lavender	Bleu-lavande	Lavendel	Color de alhucema	Lavanda
Lemon	Jaune-citron	Zitrongelb	Limón	Limone
Light Blue	Bleu clair	Hellblau	Azul claro	Azzurro chiaro
Lilac	Lilas	Lila	Lila	Lilla
Line perforation	Dentelure en lignes	Linienzähnung	Dentado en linea	Dentellatura lineare
Lithography	Lithographie	Steindruck	Litografía	Litografia
Local	Timbre de poste locale	Lokalpostmarke	Emisión local	Emissione locale
Lozenge roulette	Percé en losanges	Rautenförmiger Durchstich	Picadura en rombos	Perforazione a losanghe
Magenta	Magenta	Magentarot	Magenta	Magenta
Margin	Marge	Rand	Borde	Margine
Maroon	Marron pourpré	Dunkelrotpurpur	Púrpura rojo oscuro	Marrone rossastro
Mauve	Mauve	Malvenfarbe	Malva	Malva
Multicoloured	Polychrome	Mehrfarbig	Multicolores	Policromo
Myrtle Green	Vert myrte	Myrtengrün	Verde mirto	Verde mirto
New Blue	Bleu ciel vif	Neublau	Azul nuevo	Azzurro nuovo
Newspaper stamp	Timbre pour journaux	Zeitungsmarke	Sello para periódicos	Francobollo per giornali
Obliteration	Oblitération	Abstempelung	Matasello	Annullamento
Obsolete	Hors (de) cours	Ausser Kurs	Fuera de curso	Fuori corso
Ochre	Ocre	Ocker	Ocre	Ocra
Official stamp	Timbre de service	Dienstmarke	Sello de servicio	Francobollo di
Olive-brown	Brun-olive	Olivbraun	Castaño oliva	Bruno oliva
Olive-green	Vert-olive	Olivgrün	Verde oliva	Verde oliva
Olive-grey	Gris-olive	Olivgrau	Gris oliva	Grigio oliva
Olive-yellow	Jaune-olive	Olivgelb	Amarillo oliva	Giallo oliva
Orange	Orange	Orange	Naranja	Arancio
Orange-brown	Brun-orange	Orangebraun	Castaño naranja	Bruno arancio
Orange-red	Rouge-orange	Orangerot	Rojo naranja	Rosso arancio
Orange-yellow	Jaune-orange	Orangegelb	Amarillo naranja	Giallo arancio
Overprint	Surcharge	Aufdruck	Sobrecarga	Soprastampa
Pair	Paire	Paar	Pareja	Coppia
Pale	Pâle	Blass	Pálido	Pallido
Pane	Panneau	Gruppe	Grupo	Gruppo
Paper	Papier	Papier	Papel	Carta
Parcel post stamp	Timbre pour colis postaux	Paketmarke	Sello para paquete postal	Francobollo per pacchi postali
Pen-cancelled	Oblitéré à plume	Federzugentwertung	Cancelado a pluma	Annullato a penna
Percé en arc	Percé en arc	Bogenförmiger Durchstich	Picadura en forma de arco	Perforazione ad arco
Percé en scie	Percé en scie	Bogenförmiger Durchstich	Picado en sierra	Foratura a sega
Perforated	Dentelé	Gezähnt	Dentado	Dentellato
Perforation	Dentelure	Zähnung	Dentar	Dentellatura
Photogravure	Photogravure, Heliogravure	Rastertiefdruck	Fotograbado	Rotocalco
Pin perforation	Percé en points	In Punkten durchstochen	Horadado con alfileres	Perforato a punti
Plate	Planche	Platte	Plancha	Lastra, Tavola
Plum	Prune	Pflaumenfarbe	Color de ciruela	Prugna
Postage Due stamp	Timbre-taxe	Portomarke	Sello de tasa	Segnatasse
Postage stamp	Timbre-poste	Briefmarke, Freimarke, Postmarke	Sello de correos	Francobollo postale
Postal fiscal stamp	Timbre fiscal-postal	Stempelmarke als Postmarke verwendet	Sello fiscal-postal	Fiscale postale
Postmark	Oblitération postale	Poststempel	Matasello	Bollo
Printing	Impression, Tirage	Druck	Impresión	Stampa, Tiratura
Proof	Épreuve	Druckprobe	Prueba de impresión	Prova

English	French	German	Spanish	Italian
Provisionals	Timbres provisoires	Provisorische Marken. Provisorien	Provisionales	Provvisori
Prussian Blue	Bleu de Prusse	Preussischblau	Azul de Prusia	Azzurro di Prussia
Purple	Pourpre	Purpur	Púrpura	Porpora
Purple-brown	Brun-pourpre	Purpurbraun	Castaño púrpura	Bruno porpora
Recess-printing	Impression en taille douce	Tiefdruck	Grabado	Incisione
Red	Rouge	Rot	Rojo	Rosso
Red-brown	Brun-rouge	Rotbraun	Castaño rojizo	Bruno rosso
Reddish Lilac	Lilas rougeâtre	Rötlichlila	Lila rojizo	Lilla rossastro
Reddish Purple	Poupre-rouge	Rötlichpurpur	Púrpura rojizo	Porpora rossastro
Reddish Violet	Violet rougeâtre	Rötlichviolett	Violeta rojizo	Violetto rossastro
Red-orange	Orange rougeâtre	Rotorange	Naranja rojizo	Arancio rosso
Registration stamp	Timbre pour lettre chargée (recommandée)	Einschreibemarke	Sello de certificado lettere	Francobollo per raccomandate
Reprint	Réimpression	Neudruck	Reimpresión	Ristampa
Reversed	Retourné	Umgekehrt	Invertido	Rovesciato
Rose	Rose	Rosa	Rosa	Rosa
Rose-red	Rouge rosé	Rosarot	Rojo rosado	Rosso rosa
Rosine	Rose vif	Lebhaftrosa	Rosa vivo	Rosa vivo
Roulette	Percage	Durchstich	Picadura	Foratura
Rouletted	Percé	Durchstochen	Picado	Forato
Royal Blue	Bleu-roi	Königblau	Azul real	Azzurro reale
Sage green	Vert-sauge	Salbeigrün	Verde salvia	Verde salvia
Salmon	Saumon	Lachs	Salmón	Salmone
Scarlet	Écarlate	Scharlach	Escarlata	Scarlatto
Sepia	Sépia	Sepia	Sepia	Seppia
Serpentine roulette	Percé en serpentin	Schlangenliniger Durchstich	Picado a serpentina	Perforazione a serpentina
Shade	Nuance	Tönung	Tono	Gradazione de colore
Sheet	Feuille	Bogen	Hoja	Foglio
Slate	Ardoise	Schiefer	Pizarra	Ardesia
Slate-blue	Bleu-ardoise	Schieferblau	Azul pizarra	Azzurro ardesia
Slate-green	Vert-ardoise	Schiefergrün	Verde pizarra	Verde ardesia
Slate-lilac	Lilas-gris	Schierferlila	Lila pizarra	Lilla ardesia
Slate-purple	Mauve-gris	Schieferpurpur	Púrpura pizarra	Porpora ardesia
Slate-violet	Violet-gris	Schieferviolett	Violeta pizarra	Violetto ardesia
Special delivery stamp	Timbre pour exprès	Eilmarke	Sello de urgencia	Francobollo per espressi
Specimen	Spécimen	Muster	Muestra	Saggio
Steel Blue	Bleu acier	Stahlblau	Azul acero	Azzurro acciaio
Strip	Bande	Streifen	Tira	Striscia
Surcharge	Surcharge	Aufdruck	Sobrecarga	Soprastampa
Tête-bêche	Tête-bêche	Kehrdruck	Tête-bêche	Tête-bêche
Tinted paper	Papier teinté	Getöntes Papier	Papel coloreado	Carta tinta
Too-late stamp	Timbre pour lettres en retard	Verspätungsmarke	Sello para cartas retardadas	Francobollo per le lettere in ritardo
Turquoise-blue	Bleu-turquoise	Türkisblau	Azul turquesa	Azzurro turchese
Turquoise-green	Vert-turquoise	Türkisgrün	Verde turquesa	Verde turchese
Typography	Typographie	Buchdruck	Tipografia	Tipografia
Ultramarine	Outremer	Ultramarin	Ultramar	Oltremare
Unused	Neuf	Ungebraucht	Nuevo	Nuovo
Used	Oblitéré, Usé	Gebraucht	Usado	Usato
Venetian Red	Rouge-brun terne	Venezianischrot	Rojo veneciano	Rosso veneziano
Vermilion	Vermillon	Zinnober	Cinabrio	Vermiglione
Violet	Violet	Violett	Violeta	Violetto
Violet-blue	Bleu-violet	Violettblau	Azul violeta	Azzurro violetto
Watermark	Filigrane	Wasserzeichen	Filigrana	Filigrana
Watermark sideways	Filigrane couché liegend	Wasserzeichen	Filigrana acostado	Filigrana coricata
Wove paper	Papier ordinaire, Papier uni	Einfaches Papier	Papel avitelado	Carta unita
Yellow	Jaune	Gelb	Amarillo	Giallo
Yellow-brown	Brun-jaune	Gelbbraun	Castaño amarillo	Bruno giallo
Yellow-green	Vert-jaune	Gelbgrün	Verde amarillo	Verde giallo
Yellow-olive	Olive-jaunâtre	Gelboliv	Oliva amarillo	Oliva giallastro
Yellow-orange	Orange jaunâtre	Gelborange	Naranja amarillo	Arancio giallastro
Zig-zag roulette	Percé en zigzag	Sägezahnartiger Durchstich	Picado en zigzag	Perforazione a zigzag

Specialist Philatelic Societies

Requests for inclusion on this page should be sent to the Catalogue Editor.

Great Britain Philatelic Society
Membership Secretary – Victoria Lajer,
Stanley Gibbons Ltd., 399 Strand,
London WC2R 0LX

Great Britain Collectors Club
Secretary - Mr S. McGill
10309 Brookhollow Circle,
Highlands Ranch, CO 80129, USA

Channel Islands Specialists Society
Membership Secretary – Sheila Marshall
1 Grove Farm Drive, Leeds, West Yorkshire
LS16 6DD

GB Overprints Society
Membership Secretary – Mr A. Haymes,
20 Sheldon Drive, Wells, Somerset BA5 2HB.

Aden & Somaliland Study Group
UK Representative – Mr M. Lacey
108 Dalestorth Road, Sutton-in-Ashfield
Notts NG17 3AA

Ascension Study Circle
Secretary – Dr. R.C.F. Baker
Greys, Tower Road, Whitstable,
Kent CT5 3ER

Australian States Study Circle
Royal Sydney Philatelic Club
Membership Secretary – Mr P. Brigden
c/o R.S.P.C., GPO Box 1751,
Sydney, NSW 2001,
Australia

British Society of Australian Philately
Secretary – Dr P.G.E. Reid
12 Holly Spring Lane, Bracknell,
Berks RG12 2JL

Society of Australasian Specialists/Oceania
Secretary – Mr S. Leven
P.O. Box 24764, San Jose, CA 95154-4764 U.S.A.

Bechuanalands and Botswana Society
Membership Secretary – Mr O. Peetoom,
Roos, East Yorkshire
HU12 0LD

Bermuda Collectors Society
President – Mr J. Pare
405 Perimeter St, Mt. Horeb,
Wisconsin 52572, USA

British Caribbean Philatelic Study Group
International Director – Mr D.N. Druett
Pennymead Auctions, 1 Brewerton Street,
Knaresborough, North Yorkshire HG5 8AZ

British West Indies Study Circle
Membership Secretary – Mr S. Jarvis
5 Redbridge Drive, Andover,
Hampshire SP10 2LF

Burma (Myanmar) Philatelic Study Circle
Secretary – Mr M. Whittaker,
1 Ecton Leys, Rugby, Warwickshire,
CV22 5SL, UK

Canadian Philatelic Society of Great Britain
Secretary – Mr J. Watson,
Lyngarth, 106 Huddersfield Road, Penistone
South Yorkshire S36 7BX

Cape and Natal Study Circle
Acting Secretary – Mr J. Dickson,
Lismore House, Great Lane, Shepton Beauchamp,
Somerset TA19 0LJ

Ceylon Study Circle
Secretary – Mr R.W.P. Frost
42 Lonsdale Road, Cannington, Bridgewater,
Somerset TA5 2JS

Cyprus Study Circle
Secretary – Mr R. Wheeler
47 Drayton Avenue, Ealing, London
W13 0LE

East Africa Study Circle
Secretary – Mr M.D. Vesey-Fitzgerald,
Gambles Cottage, 18 Clarence Road,
Lyndhurst, Hants SO43 7AL

Egypt Study Circle
Secretary – Mr M. Murphy,
11 Waterbank Road, Bellingham London SE6 3DJ

Falklands Islands Study Group
Membership Secretary – Morva White
42 Colton Road, Shrivenham,
Swindon Wilts SN6 5JX

Gibraltar Study Circle
Membership Secretary – Mr E. D. Holmes,
29 Highgate Road, Woodley, Reading RG5 3ND

Hong Kong Study Circle
Membership Secretary -- Mr N Halewood
Midoricho 1-9-204, Ashiya-shi
Japan 659-0042

Indian Ocean Study Circle
Secretary – Mrs S. Hopson
Field Acre, Hoe Benham, Newbury,
Berkshire RG20 8PD

India Study Circle
Secretary – Mr B Gilham
11 Victoria Crescent, Town Moor,
Doncaster DN2 5BW

Irish Philatelic Circle
Acting Secretary – Mr B. Warren
PO Box 12624, Rathfarnham,
Dublin 16, Ireland

King George V Silver Jubilee Study Circle
President – Mr N. Donen
31-4525 Wilkinson Road, Victoria, BC,
V8Z 5C3, Canada

King George VI Collectors Society
Membership Secretary – Mr M. Axe
Barbizon Cottage, Marringdean Road,
Billingshurst RH14 9HQ

Malaya Study Group
Membership Secretary - Mr M Roper
25 King Edward Avenue
Aylesbury HP21 7JD

Malta Study Circle
Membership Secretary – Mr C. Searle
4 Sunderland Place, Wellesbourne,
Warwick CV35 9LE

New Zealand Society of Great Britain
Membership Secretary - Mrs E. Diamond
9 Ashley Drive, Walton on Thames,
Surrey KT12 1JL

Orange Free State Study Circle
Secrertary – Mr J.R. Stroud
28 Oxford Street, Burnham-on-Sea,
Somerset TA8 1LQ

Pacific Islands Study Circle
Honorary Secretary – Mr J.D. Ray
24 Woodvale Avenue, London SE25 4AE

Pakistan Study Circle
Membership Secretary – Mr M. Robinson
35 Ethelburt Avenue, Bassett Green,
Southampton SO16 3DG

Papuan Philatelic Society
Chairman – Mr M. Robinson
P.O. Box 3275, Birkdale,
Queensland 4159, Australia

Pitcairn Islands Study Group (U.K.)
Honorary Secretary – Mr D. Sleep
6 Palace Gardens, 100 Court Road, Eltham,
London SE9 5NS

Rhodesian Study Circle
Membership Secretary - Mr A. Plumbe
25 Oakwood Drive, Bingley,
West Yorkshire BD16 4SJ

Royal Philatelic Society of New Zealand
Secretary – Mr G. Wilson
P.O. Box 1269, Wellington, New Zealand

St. Helena, Ascension and Tristan da Cunha Philatelic Society
Secretary – Mr. Klaus D. Hahn
P.O. Box 14, 71145 Bondorf,
Germany

Samoa Specialists, Fellowship of
Secretary – Mr S.G. Zirinsky
P.O. Box 230049, Ansonia Station
New York, NY10023, USA

Sarawak Specialists Society
(also Brunei, North Borneo and Labuan)
Secretary – Dr. R.G. Johnson
9 Chipstead Park Close, Sevenoaks, Kent TN13 2ST

South African Collectors' Society
General Secretary – Mr C. Oliver
Telephone 020 8940 9833

Philatelic Society of Sri Lanka
Secretary – Mr H. Goonawardena, J.P.
44A Hena Road, Mt. Lavinia 10370, Sri Lanka

Sudan Study Group
Secretary – Mr P. Grigg
19 Howmead, Berkeley, Glos GL13 9AR

Transvaal Study Circle
Honorary Treasurer – Mr J. Woolgar
c/o 9 Meadow Road, Gravesend,
Kent DA11 7LR

West Africa Study Circle
Membership Secretary – Mr J. Hossack
28 Saxon's Close, Leighton Buzzard
LU7 3LT

Western Australia Study Circle
Secretary – Mr B. Pope
P.O Box 423, Claremount
Western Australia 6910

Select Bibliography

The literature on British Commonwealth stamps is vast, but works are often difficult to obtain once they are out of print. The selection of books below has been made on the basis of authority together with availability to the general reader, either as new or secondhand. Very specialised studies, and those covering aspects of postal history to which there are no references in the catalogue, have been excluded.

The following abbreviations are used to denote publishers:

CRL Christie's Robson Lowe;
HH Harry Hayes;
PB Proud Bailey Co. Ltd. and Postal History Publications Co.;
PC Philip Cockrill;
RPSL Royal Philatelic Society, London;
SG Stanley Gibbons Ltd.

Where no publisher is quoted, the book is published by its author.

GENERAL

Encylopaedia of British Empire Postage Stamps. Vols 1-6. Edited Robson Lowe. (CRL, 1951–1991)

Specimen Stamps of the Crown Colonies 1857-1948. Marcus Samuel. (RPSL, 1976 and 1984 Supplement)

Cancelled by Perkins Bacon. P. Jaffé. (Spink & Son Ltd., 1998)

U.P.U. Specimen Stamps 1878-1961. J. Bendon. (2015)

King George V Key Plates of the Imperium Postage and Revenue Design. P. Fernbank. (Second edition, British West Indies Study Circle, 2013)

Silver Jubilee of King George V Stamps Handbook. A.J. Ainscough. (Ainweel Developments, 1985)

The Commemorative Stamps of the British Commonwealth. H.D.S. Haverbeck. (Faber, 1955)

The Printings of King George VI Colonial Stamps. W.J.W. Potter & Lt-Col R.C.M. Shelton. (1952 and later facsimile edition)

King George VI Large Key Type Stamps of Bermuda, Leeward Islands, Nyasaland. R.W. Dickgiesser and E.P. Yendall. (Triad Publications, 1985)

The King George VI Large Key Type Revenue and Postage High Value Stamps 1937–1952. E. Yendall (RPSL, 2008)

War Tax Stamps of the British Empire, First World War – The West Indies. J.G.M. Davis (RPSL, 2009)

Madame Joseph Forged Postmarks. D. Worboys. (RPSL, 1994)

Madame Joseph Revisited. B.M. Cartwright. (RPSL, 2005)

G.B. Used Abroad: Cancellations and Postal Markings. J. Parmenter. (The Postal History Society, 1993)

GREAT BRITAIN

For extensive bibliographies see G.B. Specialised Catalogues. Vols 1-5. (Stanley Gibbons)

Stamps and Postal History of the Channel Islands. W. Newport. (Heineman, 1972)

ADEN

The Postal History of British Aden 1839-1967. Major R.W. Pratt. (PB, 1985)

The Postal History of Aden and Somaliland Protectorate. E. B. Proud. (PB, 2004)

ANTIGUA

Antigua, the Stamps and Postal History. C Freeland and J.M. Jordan (B.W.I. Study Circle, 2016)

ASCENSION

Ascension. The Stamps and Postal History. J.H. Attwood. (CRL, 1981)

AUSTRALIA

The Postal History of New South Wales 1788-1901. Edited J.S. White. (Philatelic Association of New South Wales, 1988)

South Australia. The Long Stamps 1902-12. J.R.W. Purves. (Royal Philatelic Society of Victoria, 1978)

The Departmental Stamps of South Australia. A.R. Butler. (RPSL, 1978)

A Priced Listing of the Departmental Stamps of South Australia. A.D. Presgrave. (2nd edition, 1999)

Stamps and Postal History of Tasmania. W.E. Tinsley. (RPSL, 1986)

The Pictorial Stamps of Tasmania 1899-1912. K.E. Lancaster. (Royal Philatelic Society of Victoria, 1986)

The Stamps of Victoria. G. Kellow. (B. & K. Philatelic Publishing, 1990)

Western Australia. The Stamps and Postal History. Edited M. Hamilton and B. Pope. (W. Australian Study Group, 1979)

Postage Stamps and Postal History of Western Australia. Vols 1-3. M. Juhl. (1981-83)

The Chapman Collection of Australian Commonwealth Stamps. R. Chapman. (Royal Philatelic Society of Victoria, 1999)

Nauru 1915--1923. K. Buckingham. (The British Philatelic Association Expertising Educational Charity, 2004)

The Postal History of British New Guinea and Papua 1885-1942. R. Lee. (CRL, 1983)

Collector's Guide to the Stamps of British New Guinea and the Territory of Papua, 1884-1942. M. L. Parr and M. Robinson (PnR Publications, 2013)

The Stamps of the Territory of New Guinea, 1952–1932 Huts Issues. R. Heward, R. Garratt and D. Heward (2008)

Norfolk Island. A Postal and Philatelic History, 1788-1969. P. Collas & R. Breckon. (B. & K. Philatelic Publishing, 1997)

BAHAMAS

The Postage Stamps and Postal History of the Bahamas. H.G.D. Gisburn, (SG, 1950 and later facsimile edition)

Bahamas Stamps and Postal Stationery to 1970. Ed. P. Fernbank (B.W.I. Study Circle, 2017)

BARBADOS

The Stamps of Barbados. E.A. Bayley. (1989)

Advanced Barbados Philately. H.F. Deakin. (B.W.I. Study Circle, 1997)

Barbados, The Britannia Issues. M.F. Roett. (B.W.I. Study Circle, 2013)

BASUTOLAND

The Cancellations and Postal Markings of Basutoland/ Lesotho Post Offices. A. H. Scott. (Collectors Mail Auctions (Pty) Ltd., 1980)

BATUM

British Occupation of Batum. P.T. Ashford. (1989)

BECHUANALAND

The Postage Stamps, Postal Stationery and Postmarks of the Bechuanalands. H.R. Holmes. (RPSL, 1971)

BERMUDA

The Postal History and Stamps of Bermuda. M.H. Ludington. (Quarterman Publications Inc., 1978)

The King George V High-value Stamps of Bermuda, 1917-1938. M. Glazer. (Calaby Publishers, 1994)

The Postal History of Bermuda. E.B. Proud. (PB, 2003)

BRITISH GUIANA

The Postage Stamps and Postal History of British Guiana. W.A. Townsend & F.G. Howe. (RPSL, 1970)

British Guiana: The provisionals of 1882. R. Maisel (B.W.I. Study Circle, 2013)

BRITISH HONDURAS

The Postal History of British Honduras. E.B. Proud. (PB, 1999)

BRITISH INDIAN OCEAN

The Postal History of B.I.O.T., Maldive Islands and Seychelles. E. B. Proud (PB, 2006)

BRITISH OCCUPATION OF GERMAN COLONIES

G.R.I. R.M. Gibbs. (CRL, 1989)

BRITISH PACIFIC OCEAN

The Postal History of the British Solomon Islands and Tonga. E.B. Proud (PB, 2006)

The Postal History of the Gilbert and Ellice Islands and New Hebrides. E.B. Proud. (PB, 2006)

BRITISH POSTAL AGENCIES IN EASTERN ARABIA

The Postal Agencies in Eastern Arabia and the Gulf. N. Donaldson. (HH, 1975) and Supplement (Bridger & Kay Guernsey Ltd., 1994)

BRITISH SOLOMON ISLANDS

British Solomon Islands Protectorate. Its Postage Stamps and Postal History. H.G.D. Gisburn. (T. Sanders (Philatelist) Ltd., 1956)

BRITISH WEST AFRICA

The Postal History and Handstamps of British West Africa. C. McCaig. (CRL, 1978)

BRITISH WEST INDIES

The Postal History of the Cayman Islands and Turks & Caicos Islands. E.B. Proud (PB, 2006)

The Postal History of St. Lucia and St. Vincent. E.B. Proud and J. C. Aleong (PB, 2006)

BURMA

Burma Postal History. G. Davis and D Martin. (CRL, 1971 and 1987 Supplement).

The Postal History of Burma. E.B. Proud. (PB, 2002)

CAMEROONS

The Postal Arrangements of the Anglo-French Cameroons Expeditionary Force 1914-1916. R.J. Maddocks. (1996)

CANADA

The Postage Stamps and Postal History of Newfoundland. W.S. Boggs. (Quarterman Publications Inc., 1975)

Stamps of British North America. F. Jarrett. (Quarterman Publications Inc., 1975)

The Postage Stamps and Postal History of Canada. W.S. Boggs. (Quarterman Publications Inc., 1974)

The First Decimal Issue of Canada 1859-68. G. Whitworth. (RPSL, 1966)

The Five Cents Beaver Stamp of Canada. G. Whitworth. (RPSL, 1985)

The Small Queens of Canada. J. Hillson. (CRL, 1989)

Canada Small Queens Re-Appraised. J. Hillson. (Canadian Philatelic Society of Great Britain, 1999)

Canada's Postage Stamps of the Small Queen Era, 1870-1897. J. Hillson and J.E. Nixon (Vincent Graves Greene Philatelic Research Foundation, 2008)

The Edward VII Issue of Canada, G.C. Marler, (National Postal Museum, Canada, 1975)

The Admiral Issue of Canada. G.C. Marler. (American Philatelic Society, 1982)

CEYLON

The Postal History of Ceylon. E. B. Proud (PB, 2006)

CYPRUS

Cyprus 1353-1986. W. Castle. (CRL 3rd edition, 1987)

DOMINICA

Dominica Postal History, Stamps and Postal Stationery to 1935. E.V. Toeg. (B.W.I. Study Circle, 1994)

EGYPT

Egypt Stamps & Postal History. P.A.S. Smith. (James Bendon, 1999)

The Nile Post. J. H. Chalhoub. (2003)

FALKLAND ISLANDS

The Postage Stamps of the Falkland Islands and Dependencies. B.S.H. Grant. (SG, 1952 and later facsimile edition)

The Falkland Islands Philatelic Digest. Nos. 1 & 2. M. Barton and R Spafford. (HH, 1975 and 1979)

The De La Rue Definitives of the Falkland Islands 1901-1929. J.P. Bunt. (1986 and 1996 Supplement)

The Falkland Islands. The 1891 Provisionals. M. Barton. (BPA Expertising Educational Trust, 2002)

The War Stamp Overprints of the Falkland Islands 1918-1920. J.P. Bunt. (1981)

The Falkland Islands. Printings of the Pictorial Issue of 1938-49. C.E. Glass. (CRL, 1979)

The Postal History of the Falkland Islands and Dependencies. E.B. Proud (PB, 2006)

FIJI

Fiji's Times Express Stamps. D.E. Gillis (Pacific Islands Study Circle, 2011)

Fiji Philatelics. D.E.F. Alford. (Pacific Islands Study Circle, 1994)

Fiji Queen Victoria One Shilling and Five Shillings Postage Stamps 1881-1902. R.F. Duberal. (Pacific Islands Study Circle, 2003)

The Postal History of Fiji 1911-1952. J.G. Rodger. (Pacific Islands Study Circle, 1991)

GAMBIA

The Stamps and Postal History of the Gambia. Edited J.O. Andrew. (CRL, 1985)

The Postal History of the Gambia. E.B. Proud. (PB, 1994)

GIBRALTAR

Posted in Gibraltar. W. Hine-Haycock. (CRL, 1978 and 1983 Supplement)

Gibraltar. The Postal History and Postage Stamps. Vol 1 to 1885. G. Osborn. (Gibraltar Study Circle, 1995)

The Postal History of Gibraltar. R.J.M. Garcia & E.B. Proud. (PB, 1998)

Gibraltar, Collecting King George VI. E. Chambers. (The Gibraltar Study Circle, 2003)

GOLD COAST

The Postal History of the Gold Coast. E.B. Proud. (PB, 1995)

The Postal Services of the Gold Coast, 1901-1957. Edited M. Ensor. (West Africa Study Circle, 1998)

The Postal Services of the Gold Coast to 1901. Edited J. Sacher. (RPSL, 2003)

HONG KONG

The Philatelic History of Hong Kong. Vol 1. (Hong Kong Study Circle, 1984)

Hong Kong Postage Stamps of the Queen Victoria Period. R.N. Gurevitch. (1993)

Hong Kong. The 1898 10c. on 30c. Provisional Issue. A.M. Chu. (1998)

The Postal History History of Hong Kong. E.B. Proud (PB, 2004)

British Post Offices in the Far East. E.B. Proud. (PB, 1991)

Cancellations of the Treaty Ports of Hong Kong. H. Schoenfield. (1988)

The Crown Colony of Wei Hai Wei. M.Goldsmith and C.W. Goodwyn. (RPSL, 1985)

INDIA

India 1935 Silver Jubilee Stamps. N. Levinge and R. Prasad. (King George V Silver Jubilee Study Circle, 2018)

C.E.F. The China Expeditionary force 1900-1923. D.S. Virk, J.C. Hume, G. Sattin. (Philatelic Congress of India, 1992)

India Used Abroad. V.S. Dastur. (Mysore Philatelics, 1982)

The Indian Postal Agencies in the Persian Gulf Area. A. Parsons. (Sahara Publications Ltd., 2001)

A Handbook on Gwalior Postal History and Stamps. V.K. Gupta. (1980)

The Stamps of Jammu & Kashmir. F. Staal. (The Collectors Club, 1983)

Sorath Stamps and Postal History. R.A. Malaviya. (Ravi Prakashan, 1999)

IRAQ

The Postal History of Iraq. P.C. Pearson and E.B. Proud. (PB, 1996)

Baghdad in British Occupation: The Story of the 1917 Provisional Stamps. F. Khalastchy (RPSL, 2017)

IRELAND

Irish Stamp Booklets 1931-1991. C.J. Dulin. (1998)

British Stamps Overprinted for use in Ireland during the Transitional Period. Barry Cousins (Irish Philatelic Circle, 2008)

JAMAICA

Encyclopaedia of Jamaican Philately. Vol 1. D.Sutcliffe & S. Jarvis. (1997); *Vol 6.* S. Jarvis. (2001) (B.W.I. Study Circle)

Jamaica, the Definitive and Commemorative Stamps and Postal Stationery of the Reign of King George VI. H.A.H. James. (The King George VI Collectors Society, 1999)

KENYA

British East Africa. The Stamps and Postal Stationery. J. Minns. (RPSL, 1982 and 1990 Supplement) (New edition, revised and updated, George T. Krieger, 2006)

The Postal History of Kenya. E.B. Proud. (PB, 1992)

LEEWARD ISLANDS

The Leeward Islands – Notes for Philatelists. M.N. Oliver. (B.W.I. Study Circle, second edition, 2011)

MALAYA

The Postal History of British Malaya. Vols 1-3. E.B. Proud. (PB, 2nd edition, 2000)

The Postage Stamps of Federated Malay States. W.A. Reeves. (Malaya Study Group, 1978)

Kedah and Perlis. D.R.M. Holley. (Malaya Study Group, 1995)

Kelantan. Its Stamps and Postal History. W.A. Reeves and B.E. Dexter. (Malaya Study Group, 1992)

The Postal History of the Occupation of Malaya and British Borneo 1941-1945. E.B. Proud and M.D. Rowell. (PB, 1992)

Pahang 1888 to 1903, The Chersonese Collection (BPA Expertising Educational Charity, 2009)

MALTA

Malta. The Postal History and Postage Stamps. Edited R.E. Martin. (CRL, 1980 and 1985 Supplement)

MAURITIUS

The Postal History and Stamps of Mauritius. P. Ibbotson. (RPSL, 1991); Revisions and additions Supplement (Indian Ocean Study Circle, 1995)

The Postal History of Mauritius. E.B. Proud. (PB, 2001)

MONTSERRAT

Montserrat to 1965. L.E. Britnor. (B.W.I. Study Circle. 3rd edition, 2010)

MOROCCO AGENCIES

British Post Offices and Agencies in Morocco 1857-1907 and Local Posts 1891-1914. R.K. Clough. (Gibraltar Study Circle, 1984)

The Stamps of the Morocco Agencies. Ed. D.A. Stotter (GB Overprints Society, 2011)

NEW ZEALAND

The Postage Stamps of New Zealand. Vols I-VII. (Royal Philatelic Society of New Zealand. 1939—98)

The Early Cook Islands Post Office. A.R. Burge (Hawthorn Pres, 1978)

The Postal History and Postage Stamps of the Tokelau/Union Islands. A.H. Burgess. (Pacific Islands Study Circle, 2nd edition, 1998)

A Postal History of the Samoan Islands (Parts I and II). Edited R. Burge. (Royal Philatelic Society of New Zealand, 1987-89)

The Stamps and Postal History of Nineteenth Century Samoa. R.P. Odenweller. (RPSL and The Royal Philatelic Society of New Zealand, 2004)

The 1893 New Zealand Advertisement Stamps. J.A. Robb (Christchurch (N.Z.) Philatelic Society, 2006)

New Zealand Stamps Overprinted "O.P.S.O". C. Capill (New Zealand Society of Great Britain and Royal Philatelic Society of New Zealand, 2010)

The Postage Stamps of New Zealand 1855-1873: The Chalon Head Issues and *Chalon Sorting Guide* R.P. Odenweller (RPSL, 2009 and 2014)

The 1898 Pictorial Issue of New Zealand its Design, Printing and Use. D. Diamond (New Zealand Society of Great Britian, 2014)

NIGERIA

The Postal Services of the British Nigeria Region. J. Ince and J. Sacher. (RPSL, 1992)

The Postal History of Nigeria. E.B. Proud (PB, 1995)

The Oil Rivers and Niger Coast Surcharged Provisionals and Bisected Stamps. J. Sacher (RPSL, 2009)

NORTH BORNEO

A Concise Guide to the Queen Issues of Labuan. R. Price. (Sarawak Specialists Society, 1991)

The Stamps and Postal History of North Borneo. Parts 1-3. L.H. Shipman and P.K. Cassells. (Sarawak Specialists Society, 1976-88)

The Postal History of British Borneo. E.B. Proud. (PB, 2003)

NORTHERN RHODESIA

Northern Rhodesia – The Mkushi Postage Dues and the renamed Old Mkushi Post Office Otto Peetoom (2005)

The King George VI Postage and Revenue Stamps of Northern Rhodesia Alan Drysdall, Ian Lane and Jean Cheston (Rhodesia Study Circle, 2006)

NYASALAND

The Postal History of Nyasaland. E.B. Proud. (PB, 1997)

PALESTINE

The Stamps & Postal Stationery of Palestine Mandate 1918-1948. D. Dorfman. (Edward G. Rosen, 2001)

The Postal History of Palestine and Transjordan. E.B. Proud. (PB, 2006)

PITCAIRN ISLANDS

Pitcairn Islands Philately. D.E. Hume. (3rd edition, 2006)

RHODESIA

Mashonaland. A Postal History 1890—96. Dr. A.R. Drysdall and D. Collis. (CRL, 1990)

Rhodesia. A Postal History. R.C. Smith. (1967 and 1970 Supplement)

The Rhodesia Philatelist. (Ormskirk Stamps)

ST. HELENA

St. Helena, Postal History and Stamps. E. Hibbert. (CRL, 1979)

The George V Badge Issues of St Helena and Ascension. R. Stanton and W. Thorpe (West Africa Study Circle, 2012)

The Postal History of Ascension, St. Helena & Tristan da Cunha. E.B. Proud. (PB, 2005)

ST. KITTS-NEVIS

A Study of the King George VI Stamps of St. Kitts-Nevis. P.L. Baldwin. (Murray Payne Ltd., 2nd edition, 1997)

The Philately of Nevis. F. Borromeo. (British West Indies Study Circle, 2001)

Nevis-The Stamps and Postal History (1661-1890). F. Borromeo and C. Freeland (British West Indies Study Circle, 2015)

ST VINCENT

St Vincent 1899-1965. C. Freeland, R. Bond and R. Boylan (B.W.I, Study Circle 2017).

SARAWAK

The Stamps and Postal History of Sarawak. W.A. Forrester-Wood. (Sarawak Specialists Society, 1959 and 1970 Supplement)

Sarawak: The Issues of 1871 and 1875. W. Batty-Smith and W.E.Watterson. (1990)

SEYCHELLES

Seychelles Postal History and Postage Stamps to 1976. S. Hopson & B.M. McCloy. (Indian Ocean Study Circle, 2002)

The Postal History of B.I.O.T., Maldive Islands and Seychelles. E.B Proud (PB 2006)

SIERRA LEONE

The Postal Service of Sierra Leone. P.O. Beale. (RPSL, 1988)

The Postal History of Sierra Leone. E.B. Proud. (PB, 1994)

Sierra Leone King George VI Definitive Stamps. F. Walton. (West Africa Study Circle, 2001)

SOUTH AFRICA

Postmarks of the Cape of Good Hope. R. Goldblatt. (Reijger Publishers (Pty) Ltd., 1984)

Stamps of the Orange Free State. Parts 1-3. G.D. Buckley & W.B. Marriott. (O.F.S. Study Circle, 1967--80)

The Postal History of the Orange Free State. R Allison. (BPA Expertising, 2016)

Transvaal Philately. Edited I.B. Mathews. (Reijer Publishers (Pty) Ltd., 1986)

Transvaal. The Provisional Issues of the First British Occupation. Dr. A.R. Drysdall. (James Bendon, 1994)

Die Pietersburg-seëls ran die Anglo-Boereoorlog. C. Breedt and J. Groenewald (Philatelic Federation of South Africa, 2007)

The Wherewithal of Wolmaransstad. H. Birkhead and J. Groenewald. (Philatelic Foundation of Southern Africa, 1999)

Die Vryburg-sëëls van die Anglo-Boereoorlog. J Groenewald. (Philatelic Federation of South Africa, 2010)

The Transvaal 'Spread Wings' 6d. Stamps, 1870-1878. I. Jorgensen. (Transvaal Study Circle, 2017)

SOUTH WEST AFRICA

The Overprinted Stamps of South West Africa to 1930. N. Becker. (Philatelic Holdings (Pty) Ltd., 1990)

SUDAN

Sudan. The Stamps and Postal Stationery of 1867 to 1970. E.C.W. Stagg. (HH, 1977)

The Camel Postman 1898-1998. R. Stock. (Sudan Study Group, 2001)

The Postal History of Sudan. E. B Proud (PB, 2006)

SWAZILAND

Swaziland Philately to 1968. Ed. P. van der Molen (RPSL, 2013)

TANGANYIKA

The Postal History of Tanganyika. 1915-1961. E.B. Proud. (PB, 1989)

TOGO

Togo-The Postal History of the Anglo-French Occupation 1914-22. J. Martin and F. Walton. (West Africa S.C., 1995)

Togo Overprints on Stamps of the Gold Coast 1915–1920. P. Duggan. (West Africa S.C. 2005)

TRANSJORDAN

The Stamps of Jordan 1920—1965. A.H. Najjar. (Sahara Publications Ltd., 1998)

TRINIDAD AND TOBAGO

The Postal History of Trinidad and Tobago. J.C. Aleong and E.B. Proud. (PB, 1997)

Trinidad, a Philatelic History to 1913. Sir J. Marriott, KCVO, RDP, M. Medlicott and R.A. Ramkissoon (British West Indies Study Circle and British Caribbean Philatelic Study Group, 2010)

Tobago, the Philatelic Story of a Small Island. P.C. Ford, C. Freeland and E. Barrow (British West Indies Study Circle, 2014)

TRISTAN DA CUNHA

The History and Postal History of Tristan da Cunha. G. Crabb. (1980)

TURKS AND CAICOS ISLANDS

Turks Islands and Caicos Islands to 1950. J.J. Challis. (Roses Caribbean Philatelic Society, 1983)

UGANDA

The Postal History of Uganda and Zanzibar. E.B. Proud. (PB, 1993)

ZANZIBAR

Zanzibar 1895 – 1904. T.W. Hall. (Reprint, East Africa Study Circle, 2002)

The Postage Dues of Zanzibar 1875 – 1964, The Stamps, the Covers and their Story. J. Griffith-Jones (B.P.A. Expertising, 2014)

Great Britain

UNITED KINGDOM OF GREAT BRITAIN AND IRELAND

QUEEN VICTORIA
20 June 1837–22 January 1901

PARLIAMENTARY ENVELOPES. When the Uniform Penny Postage was introduced on 10 January 1840 the free franking privileges of Members of Parliament were abolished. During the same month, special envelopes were introduced for mail posted from the Houses of Parliament and these remained in use until the introduction of stamps and the Mulready stationery in May 1840. Envelopes are priced in used condition only.

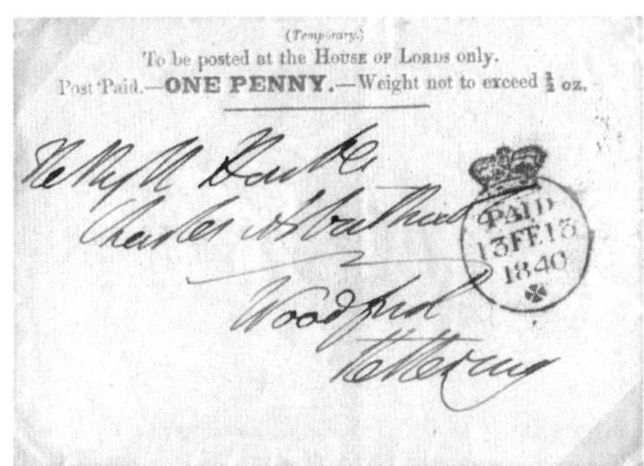

Inscribed 'Houses of Parliament' in black (16 Jan 1840)

PE2	1d. envelope	from	£18000
PE3	2d. envelope	from	£45000
PE4	4d. envelope	from	

Inscribed 'House of Lords' in vermilion (Jan 1840)

PE5	1d. envelope	from	£25000
PE8	2d. envelope		

Inscribed 'House of Commons' in black (Jan 1840)

PE9	1d. envelope	from	£6000

MULREADY ENVELOPES AND LETTER SHEETS, so called from the name of the designer, William Mulready, were issued concurrently with the first British adhesive stamps.

A large number of letter sheets and much smaller quantity of envelopes were sold by businesses, advertising to promote their services.

Letter sheets

ME1	1d.black	£350	£550
	a.With advertisements printed inside	£750	£850
ME3	2d.blue	£425	£2400
	a.With advertisements printed inside ... From		£3200

Envelopes

ME2	1d. black	£350	£550
	a.With advertisements printed inside	£2500	£4000
ME4	2d.blue	£450	£2500
	a.With advertisements printed inside ... From		£3500

LINE-ENGRAVED ISSUES

GENERAL NOTES

Brief notes on some aspects of the line-engraved stamps follow, but for further information and a full specialist treatment of these issues collectors are recommended to consult Volume 1 of the Stanley Gibbons *Great Britain Specialised Catalogue*.

Alphabet I

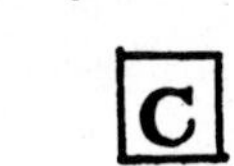

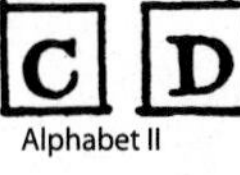

Alphabet II

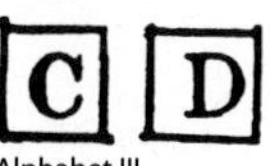

Alphabet III

Alphabet IV

Typical Corner Letters of the four Alphabets

Alphabets. Four different styles were used for the corner letters on stamps prior to the issue with letters in all four corners, these being known to collectors as:

Alphabet I. Used for all plates made from 1840 to the end of 1851. Letters small.

Alphabet II. Plates from 1852 to mid-1855. Letters larger, heavier and broader.

Alphabet III. Plates from mid-1855 to end of period. Letters tall and more slender.

Alphabet IV. 1861. 1d. Die II, Plates 50 and 51 only. Letters were hand-engraved instead of being punched on the plate. They are therefore inconsistent in shape and size but generally larger and outstanding.

While the general descriptions and the illustrations of typical letters given above may be of some assistance, only long experience and published aids can enable every stamp to be allocated to its particular Alphabet without hesitation, as certain letters in each are similar to those in one of the others.

Blued Paper. The blueing of the paper of the earlier issues is believed to be due to the presence of prussiate of potash in the printing ink, or in the paper, which, under certain conditions, tended to colour the paper when the sheets were damped for printing. An alternative term is *bleuté* paper.

Corner Letters. The corner letters on the early British stamps were intended as a safeguard against forgery, each stamp in the sheet having a different combination of letters. Taking the first 1d. stamp, printed in 20 horizontal rows of 12, as an example, the lettering is as follows:

Row 1.	A A, A B, A C, etc. to A L.
Row 2.	B A, B B, B C, etc. to B L.
	and so on to
Row 20	T A, T B, T C, etc. to T L.

On the stamps with four corner letters, those in the upper corners are in the reverse positions to those in the lower corners.
Thus in a sheet of 240 (12×20) the sequence is:

	AA	BA	CA		LA
Row 1.				etc. to	
	AA	AB	AC		AL
	AB	BB	CB		LB
Row 2.				etc. to	
	BA	BB	BC		BL
	and so on to				
	AT	BT	CT		LT
Row 20.				etc. to	
	TA	TB	TC		TL

Placing letters in all four corners was not only an added precaution against forgery but was meant to deter unmarked parts of used stamps being pieced together and passed off as an unused whole.

Dies. The first die of the 1d. was used for making the original die of the 2d., both the No Lines and White Lines issues. In 1855 the 1d. Die I was amended by retouching the head and deepening the lines on a transferred impression of the original. This later version, known to collectors as Die II, was used for making the dies for the 1d. and 2d. with letters in all four corners and also for the 1½d.

The two dies are illustrated above No. 17 in the catalogue.

Double letter

Guide line in corner

Guide line through value

Double Corner Letters. These are due to the workman placing his letter-punch in the wrong position at the first attempt, when lettering the plate, and then correcting the mistake; or to a slight shifting of the punch when struck. If a wrong letter was struck in the first instance, traces of a wrong letter may appear in a corner in addition to the correct one. A typical example is illustrated.

Guide Lines and Dots. When laying down the impressions of the design on the early plates, fine vertical and horizontal guide lines were marked on the plates to assist the operative. These were usually removed from the gutter margins, but could not be removed from the stamp impression without damage to the plate, so that in such cases they appear on the printed stamps, sometimes in the corners, sometimes through 'POSTAGE' or the value. Typical examples are illustrated.

Guide dots or cuts were similarly made to indicate the spacing of the guide lines. These too sometimes appear on the stamps.

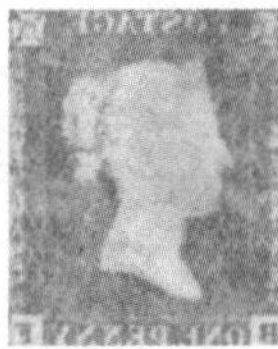

Ivory Head

'Ivory Head'. The so-called 'ivory head' variety is one in which the Queen's Head shows white on the back of the stamp. It arises from the comparative absence of ink in the head portion of the design, with consequent absence of blueing. (See 'Blued Paper', on page 1).

Line-engraving. In this context 'line-engraved' is synonymous with recess-printing, in which the engraver cuts recesses in a plate and printing (the coloured areas) is from these recesses. 'Line-engraved' is the traditional philatelic description for these stamps; other equivalent terms found are 'engraving in *taille-douce*' (French) or 'in *intaglio*' (Italian).

Plates. Until the introduction of the stamps with letters in all four corners, the number of the plate was not indicated in the design of the stamp, but was printed on the sheet margin. By long study of identifiable blocks and the minor variation in the design, coupled with the position of the corner letters, philatelists are now able to allot many of these stamps to their respective plates. Specialist collectors often endeavour to obtain examples of a given stamp printed from its different plates and our catalogue accordingly reflects this depth of detail.

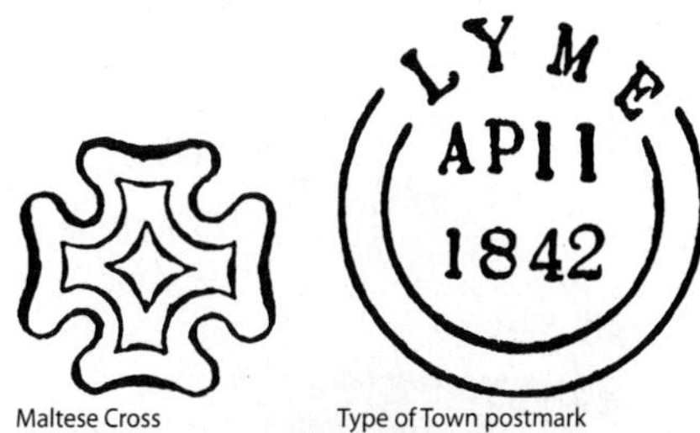

Maltese Cross — Type of Town postmark

Type of Penny Post cancellation

Example of 1844 type postmark

Postmarks. The so-called 'Maltese Cross' design was the first employed for obliterating British postage stamps and was in use from 1840 to 1844. Being hand-cut, the obliterating stamps varied greatly in detail and some distinctive types can be allotted to particular towns or offices. Local types, such as those used at Manchester, Norwich, Leeds, etc., are keenly sought. A red ink was first employed, but was superseded by black, after some earlier experiments, in February 1841. Maltese Cross obliterations in other colours are rare.

Obliterations of this type, numbered 1 to 12 in the centre, were used at the London Chief Office in 1843 and 1844.

Some straight-line cancellations were in use in 1840 at the Penny Post receiving offices, normally applied on the envelope, the adhesives then being obliterated at the Head Office. They are nevertheless known, with or without Maltese Cross, on the early postage stamps.

In 1842 some offices in south west England used dated postmarks in place of the Maltese Cross, usually on the back of the letter since they were not originally intended as obliterators. These town postmarks have likewise been found on adhesives.

In 1844 the Maltese Cross design was superseded by numbered obliterators of varied type, one of which is illustrated. They are naturally comparatively scarce on the first 1d. and 2d. stamps.

Like the Maltese Cross they are found in various colours, some of which are rare.

Re-entry

'Union Jack' re-entry

Re-entries. Re-entries on the plate show as a doubling of part of the design of the stamp generally at top or bottom. Many re-entries are very slight while others are most marked. A typical one is illustrated.

The *'Union Jack'* re-entry, so-called owing to the effect of the re-entry on the appearance of the corner stars (see illustration) occurs on stamp L K of Plate 75 of the 1d. red, Die I.

T A (T L)

M A (M L)

Varieties of Large Crown Watermark

I — II

Two states of Large Crown Watermark

Watermarks. Two watermark varieties, as illustrated, consisting of crowns of entirely different shape, are found in sheets of the Large Crown paper and fall on stamps lettered M A and T A (or M L and T L when the paper is printed on the wrong side). Both varieties are found on the 1d. rose-red of 1857, while the M A (M L) variety comes also on some plates of the 1d. of 1864 (Nos. 43, 44) up to about Plate 96. On the 2d. the T A (T L) variety is known on plates 8 and 9, and the

M A (M L) on later prints of plate 9. These varieties may exist inverted, or inverted reversed on stamps lettered A A and A L and H A and H L, and some are known.

In 1861 a minor alteration was made in the Large Crown watermark by the removal of the two vertical strokes, representing *fleurs-de-lis*, which projected upwards from the uppermost of the three horizontal curves at the base of the Crown. Hence two states are distinguishable, as illustrated.

CONDITION—IMPERFORATE LINE-ENGRAVED ISSUES

The prices quoted for the 1840 and 1841 imperforate Line engraved issues are for 'fine' examples. As condition is most important in assessing the value of a stamp, the following definitions will assist collectors in the evaluation of individual examples.

Four main factors are relevant when considering quality.

(a) Impression. This should be clean and the surface free of any rubbing or unnatural blurring which would detract from the appearance.

(b) Margins. This is perhaps the most difficult factor to evaluate. Stamps described as 'fine', the standard adopted in this catalogue for pricing purposes, should have margins of the recognised width, defined as approximately one half of the distance between two adjoining unsevered stamps. Stamps described as 'very fine' or 'superb' should have margins which are proportionately larger than those of a 'fine' stamp. Examples with close margins should not, generally, be classified as 'fine'.

(c) Cancellation. On a 'fine' stamp this should be reasonably clear and not noticeably smudged. A stamp described as 'superb' should have a neat cancellation, preferably centrally placed or to the right.

(d) Appearance. Stamps, at the prices quoted, should always be without any tears, creases, bends or thins and should not be toned on either the front or back. Stamps with such defects are worth only a proportion of the catalogue price.

Poor

Average

Fine

Very Fine

Superb

The actual size illustrations of 1840 1d. blacks show the various grades of quality. When comparing these illustrations it should be assumed that they are all from the same plate and that they are free of any hidden defects.

PRINTERS. Nos. 1/53*a* were recess-printed by Perkins, Bacon & Petch, known from 1852 as Perkins Bacon & Co.

STAMPS ON COVER. Prices are quoted, for those Victorian and Edwardian issues usually found used on cover. In general these prices refer to single examples of the cheapest versions of each basic stamp, with other shades, plates or varieties, together with unusual frankings and postmarks, being worth more. However multiples of some stamps may be more common than single usages and in this case the covers might be worth considerably less than the price quoted.

1

1a

2 Small Crown

(Eng Charles and Frederick Heath)

1840 (6 May). Letters in lower corners. Wmk Small Crown, W **2**. Imperf.

			Unused	Used	Used on cover
1	**1**	1d. intense black	£17500	£525	
2		1d. black	£12500	£375	£750
		Wi. Watermark inverted	£50000	£2500	
3		1d. grey-black (worn plate)	£16500	£500	
4	**1a**	2d. deep full blue	£45000	£1200	
5		2d. blue	£38000	£950	£2500
		Wi. Watermark inverted	£90000	£6250	
6		2d. pale blue	£48000	£1000	

The 1d. stamp in black was printed from Plates 1 to 11. Plate 1 exists in two states (known to collectors as 1a and 1b), the latter being the result of extensive repairs.

Repairs were also made to plates 2, 5, 6, 8, 9, 10 and 11, and certain impressions exist in two or more states.

The so-called 'Royal reprint' of the 1d. black was made in 1864, from Plate 66, Die II, on paper with Large Crown watermark, inverted. A printing was also made in carmine, on paper with the same watermark, upright.

For 1d. black with 'VR' in upper corners see No. V1 under Official Stamps.

The 2d. stamps were printed from Plates 1 and 2.

Plates of 1d. black

	Unused	Used
1*a*	£18500	£375
1*b*	£12500	£375
2	£12500	£375
3	£20000	£500
4	£13000	£400
5	£12500	£375
6	£13500	£375
7	£13500	£400
8	£16500	£525
9	£21000	£625
10	£26500	£950
11	£23000	£4600

Varieties of 1d. black

		Unused	Used
a.	On *bleuté* paper (Plates 1 to 8) *from*		£775
b.	Double letter in corner *from*	£13000	£400
bb.	Re-entry *from*	£13500	£450
bc.	'PB' re-entry (Plate 5, 3rd state)	—	£10500
c.	Guide line in corner	£13000	£400
cc.	Large letters in each corner (E J, I L, J C and P A) (Plate 1b) *from*	£13500	£550
d.	Guide line through value	£13000	£450
g.	Obliterated by Maltese Cross		
	In red	—	£425
	In black	—	£375
	In blue	—	£12000
	In magenta	—	£3000
	In yellow	—	—
	In violet		£12000
h.	Obliterated by Maltese Cross with number in centre *from*	—	£20000
	No. 1	—	£20000
	No. 2	—	£20000
	No. 3	—	£20000
	No. 4	—	£20000
	No. 5	—	£20000
	No. 6	—	£20000
	No. 7	—	£20000
	No. 8	—	£20000
	No. 9	—	£20000
	No. 10	—	£20000
	No. 11	—	£20000
	No. 12	—	£20000
i.	Obliterated 'Penny Post' in black (without Maltese Cross) *from*	—	£5500
j.	Obliterated by town postmark (without Maltese Cross)		
	In black *from*	—	£17500
	In yellow *from*	—	£60000
	In red *from*	—	£18500
k.	Obliterated by 1844 type postmark in black *from*	—	£1800

Plates of 2d. blue

Plate		Unused	Used
1	*Shades from*	£38000	£950
2	*Shades from*	£48000	£1100

Varieties of 2d. blue

		Unused	Used
a.	Double letter in corner	—	£1000
aa.	Re-entry	—	£1100
b.	Guide line in corner	—	£975
c.	Guide line through value	—	£975
e.	Obliterated by Maltese Cross		
	In red	—	£1200
	In black	—	£950
	In blue	—	£15000
	In magenta	—	£12000
f.	Obliterated by Maltese Cross with number in centre *from*	—	£18000
	No. 1	—	£18000
	No. 2	—	£18000
	No. 3	—	£18000
	No. 4	—	£18000
	No. 5	—	£18000
	No. 6	—	£18000
	No. 7	—	£18000
	No. 8	—	£18000
	No. 9	—	£18000
	No. 10	—	£18000
	No. 11	—	£18000
	No. 12	—	£18000
g.	Obliterated 'Penny Post' in black (without Maltese Cross) *from*	—	£16000
h.	Obliterated by town postmark (without Maltese Cross) in black *from*	—	£10000
i.	Obliterated by 1844 type postmark		
	In black *from*	—	£2500
	In blue *from*	—	£18000

1841 (10 Feb). Printed from 'black' plates. Wmk W **2**. Paper more or less blued. Imperf.

			Unused	Used	Used on cover
7	**1**	1d. red-brown (*shades*)	£2700	£130	£240
		a. 'PB' re-entry (Plate 5, 3rd state)	—	£2600	
		Wi. Watermark inverted (Plates 1b, 8 and 10) *from*	—	£3250	

The first printings of the 1d. in red-brown were made from Plates 1b, 2, 5 and 8 to 11 used for the 1d. black.

1d. red-brown from 'black' plates

Plate	*Unused*	*Used*
1*b*	£23000	£375
2	£25000	£325
5	£12000	£200
8	£13000	£190
9	£6500	£190
10	£2800	£190
11	£11500	£130

1841 (late Feb). Plate 12 onwards. Wmk W **2**. Paper more or less blued. Imperf.

			Unused	Used	Used on cover
8	**1**	1d. red-brown	£600	35·00	45·00
		Wi. Watermark inverted	£5000	£400	
8*a*		1d. red-brown on very blue paper	£700	35·00	
9		1d. pale red-brown (worn plates)	£675	45·00	
10		1d. deep red-brown	£900	50·00	
11		1d. lake-red	£5250	£850	
12		1d. orange-brown	£2000	£275	

Error. No letter 'A' in right lower corner (Stamp B (A), Plate 77)

			Unused	Used
12*a*	**1**	1d. red-brown	—	£26000

The error 'No letter A in right corner' was due to the omission to insert this letter on stamp B A of Plate 77. The error was discovered some months after the plate was registered and was then corrected.

There are innumerable variations in the colour shade of the 1d. 'red' and those given in the above list represent colour groups each covering a wide range.

Varieties of 1d. red-brown, etc.

		Un	Used
b.	Major re-entry from	—	90·00
c.	Double letter in corner from	—	40·00
d.	Double Star (Plate 75) 'Union Jack' re-entry	£34000	£3000
e.	Guide line in corner	—	35·00
f.	Guide line through value	—	40·00
g.	Thick outer frame to stamp	—	38·00
h.	Ivory head	£600	38·00
j.	Left corner letter 'S' inverted (Plates 78, 105, 107) *from*	—	£160
k.	P converted to R (Plates 30/1, 33, 83, 86) *from*	—	80·00
l.	Obliterated by Maltese Cross		
	In red	—	£4800
	In black	—	65·00
	In blue	—	£675
m.	Obliterated by Maltese Cross with number in centre		
	No. 1	—	£180
	No. 2	—	£180
	No. 3	—	£225
	No. 4	—	£600
	No. 5	—	£180
	No. 6	—	£160
	No. 7	—	£160
	No. 8	—	£160
	No. 9	—	£180
	No. 10	—	£320
	No. 11	—	£350
	No. 12	—	£350
n.	Obliterated 'Penny Post' in black (without Maltese Cross)	—	£1100
o.	Obliterated by town postmark (without Maltese Cross)		
	In black *from*	—	£825
	In blue *from*	—	£2700
	In green *from*	—	£5500
	In yellow *from*	—	—
	In red *from*	—	£15000
p.	Obliterated by 1844 type postmark		
	In blue *from*	—	£250
	In red *from*	—	£9750
	In green *from*	—	£3250
	In violet *from*	—	£4000
	In black *from*	—	35·00

Stamps with thick outer frame to the design are from plates on which the frame-lines have been straightened or recut, particularly Plates 76 and 90.

For 'Union Jack' re-entry see General Notes to Line-engraved Issues.

In 'P converted to R' the corner letter 'R' is formed from the 'P', the distinctive long tail having been hand-cut.

KEY TO LINE-ENGRAVED ISSUES

SG Nos.	*Description*	*Date*	*Wmk*	*Perf*	*Die*	*Alphabet*
		THE IMPERFORATE ISSUES				
1/3	1d. black	6.5.40	SC	Imp	I	I
4/6	2d. no lines	8.5.40	SC	Imp	I	I
		PAPER MORE OR LESS BLUED				
7	1d. red-brown	Feb 1841	SC	Imp	I	I
8/12	1d. red-brown	Feb 1841	SC	Imp	I	I
8/12	1d. red-brown	6.2.52	SC	Imp	I	II
13/15	2d. white lines	13.3.41	SC	Imp	I	I
		THE PERFORATED ISSUES				
		ONE PENNY VALUE				
16*a*	1d. red-brown	1848	SC	Roul	I	I
16*b*	1d. red-brown	1850	SC	16	I	I

SG Nos.	Description	Date	Wmk	Perf	Die	Alphabet
16c	1d. red-brown	1853	SC	16	I	II
17/18	1d. red-brown	Feb 1854	SC	16	I	II
22	1d. red-brown	Jan 1855	SC	14	I	II
24/5	1d. red-brown	28.2.55	SC	14	II	II
21	1d. red-brown	1.3.55	SC	16	II	II
26	1d. red-brown	15.5.55	LC	16	II	II
29/33	1d. red-brown	Aug 1855	LC	14	II	III
	NEW COLOURS ON WHITE PAPER					
37/41	1d. rose-red	Nov 1856	LC	14	II	III
36	1d. rose-red	26.12.57	LC	16	II	III
42	1d. rose-red	1861	LC	14	II	IV
	TWO PENCE VALUE					
19, 20	2d. blue	1.3.54	SC	16	I	I
23	2d. blue	22.2.55	SC	14	I	I
23a	2d. blue	5.7.55	SC	14	I	II
20a	2d. blue	18.8.55	SC	16	I	II
27	2d. blue	20.7.55	LC	16	I	II
34	2d. blue	20.7.55	LC	14	I	II
35	2d. blue	2.7.57	LC	14	I	III
36a	2d. blue	1.2.58	LC	16	I	III
	LETTERS IN ALL FOUR CORNERS					
48/9	½d. rose-red	1.10.70	W 9	14	—	
43/4	1d. rose-red	1.4.64	LC	14	II	
53a	1½d. rosy mauve	1860	LC	14	II	
51/3	1½d. rose-red	1.10.70	LC	14	II	
45	2d. blue	July 1858	LC	14	II	
46/7	2d. thinner lines	7.7.69	LC	14	II	

Watermarks: SC = Small Crown, T **2**. LC = Large Crown, T **4**.
Dies: See notes above No. 17 in the catalogue.
Alphabets: See General Notes to this section.

3 White lines added

1841 (13 Mar)–**51**. White lines added. Wmk W **2**. Paper more or less blued. Imperf.

			Unused	Used	Used on cover
13	**3**	2d. pale blue	£9500	£110	
14		2d. blue	£6250	90·00	£350
		Wi. Watermark inverted	£24000	£875	
15		2d. deep full blue	£8500	£110	
15aa		2d. violet-blue (1851)	£28000	£1800	

The 2d. stamp with white lines was printed from Plates 3 and 4.

No. 15*aa* came from Plate 4 and the quoted price is for examples on thicker, lavender tinted paper.

Plates of 2d. blue

Plate	Unused	Used
3 shades.....*from*	£6250	£100
4 shades.....*from*	£6250	90·00

Varieties of 2d. blue

		Unused	Used
a.	Guide line in corner	—	£110
b.	Guide line through value	£6750	£110
bb.	Double letter in corner	—	£120
be	Re-entry	£8250	£200
c.	Ivory head	£6250	£100
e.	Obliterated by Maltese Cross		
	In red	—	—
	In black	—	£275
	In blue	—	£5000
f.	Obliterated by Maltese Cross with number in centre		
	No. 1	—	£700
	No. 2	—	£700
	No. 3	—	£700
	No. 4	—	£700
	No. 5	—	£850
	No. 6	—	£700
	No. 7	—	£1200
	No. 8	—	£1000
	No. 9	—	£1200
	No. 10	—	£1500
	No. 11	—	£850
	No. 12	—	£550
g.	Obliterated by town postmark (without Maltese Cross)		
	In black.....*from*	—	£3500
	In blue.....*from*	—	£4500
h.	Obliterated by 1844 type postmark		
	In black.....*from*	—	90·00
	In blue.....*from*	—	£1000
	In red.....*from*	—	£28000
	In green.....*from*	—	£9000

1841 (Apr). Trial printing (unissued) on Dickinson silk-thread paper. No wmk. Imperf.

16 **1** 1d. red-brown (Plate 11)............ £7750

Eight sheets were printed on this paper, six being gummed, two ungummed, but we have only seen examples without gum.

1848. Wmk W **2**. Rouletted approx 11½ by Henry Archer.

16a **1** 1d. red-brown (Plates 70, 71)............ £25000

1850. Wmk W **2**. P 16 by Henry Archer.

			Unused	Used	Used on cover
16b	**1**	1d. red-brown (Alphabet 1) (from Plates 90–101, 105, 107, 108, 116) *from*	£3500	£625	£2000
		*b*Wi. Watermark inverted	—	£3750	

1853. *Wmk* W **2**. Government Trial Perforation.

			Un	Used
16c	**1**	1d. red-brown (P 16) (Alphabet II) (*on cover*)		†

SEPARATION TRIALS. Although the various trials of machines for rouletting and perforating were unofficial, Archer had the consent of the authorities in making his experiments, and sheets so experimented upon were afterwards used by the Post Office.

As Archer ended his experiments in 1850 and plates with corner letters of Alphabet II did not come into issue until 1852, perforated stamps with corner letters of Alphabet I may safely be assumed to be Archer productions, if genuine.

The Government trial perforation is believed to have been done on Archer's machines after they had been purchased in 1853. As Alphabet II was by that time in use, the trials can be distinguished from the perforated stamps listed below by being dated prior to 24 February 1854, the date when the perforated stamps were officially issued.

Die I, Alphabet I, stamps from plates 74 and 113 perforated 14 have been recorded for many years, but it is now generally recognised that the type of comb machine used, producing one extension hole in the side margins, cannot be contemporary with other trials of this period.

Die I

Die II

4 Large Crown

Die I: The features of the portrait are lightly shaded and consequently lack emphasis.

Die II: (Die I retouched): The lines of the features have been deepened and appear stronger. The eye is deeply shaded and made more lifelike. The nostril and lips are more clearly defined, the latter appearing much thicker. A strong downward stroke of colour marks the corner of the mouth. There is a deep indentation of colour between lower lip and chin. The band running from the back of the ear to the chignon has a bolder horizontal line below it than in Die I.

1854–57. Paper more or less blued.

(a) Wmk Small Crown, W **2**. *P 16.*

			Unused	Used	Used on cover
17	**1**	1d. red-brown (Die I) (24.2.54)	£375	35·00	60·00
		a. Imperf three sides (horiz pair)	†	£7500	
		Wi. Watermark inverted	—	£200	
18		1d. yellow-brown (Die I)	£450	50·00	
19	**3**	2d. deep blue (Plate 4) (12.3.54)	£4700	£100	£200
		a. Imperf three sides (horiz pair)	†	—	
		Wi. Watermark inverted	—	£325	
20		2d. pale blue (Plate 4)	£5500	£110	
20a		2d. blue (Plate 5) (18.8.55)	£10000	£350	£550
		*a*Wi. Watermark inverted	—	£900	
21	**1**	1d. red-brown (Die II) (22.2.55)	£550	65·00	£110
		a. Imperf (Plates 2, 14)			
		Wi. Watermark inverted	£1750	£260	
		(b) Wmk Small Crown, W **2**. P 14.			
22	**1**	1d. red-brown (Die I) (1.55)	£1000	90·00	£160
		Wi. Watermark inverted	—	£300	
23	**3**	2d. blue (Plate 4) (22.2.55)	£13000	£225	£375
		Wi. Watermark inverted	£18500	£650	
23a		2d. blue (Plate 5) (4.7.55)	£14000	£350	£525
		*a*Wi. Watermark inverted	—	£750	
		b. Imperf (Plate 5)			
24	**1**	1d. red-brown (Die II) (27.2.55)	£700	70·00	£110
		Wi. Watermark inverted	£2400	£350	
24a		1d. deep red-brown (very blue paper) (Die II)	£850	£110	
25		1d. orange-brown (Die II)	£1900	£170	
		(c) Wmk Large Crown, W **4**. *P 16.*			
26	**1**	1d. red-brown (Die II) (15.5.55)	£2500	£130	£240
		a. Imperf (Plate 7)			
		Wi. Watermark inverted	—	£450	
27	**3**	2d. blue (Plate 5) (20.7.55)	£18500	£450	£575
		a. Imperf	—	£12000	
		Wi. Watermark inverted	—	£1000	
		(d) Wmk Large Crown, W **4**. *P 14.*			
29	**1**	1d. red-brown (Die II) (6.55)	£240	22·00	40·00
		a. Imperf (*shades*) (Plates 22, 24, 25, 32, 43)	£4000	£3500	
		Wi. Watermark inverted	£1000	£150	
30		1d. brick-red (Die II)	£375	45·00	
31		1d. plum (Die II) (2.56)	£3800	£900	
32		1d. brown-rose (Die II)	£375	55·00	
33		1d. orange-brown (Die II) (3.57)	£725	60·00	
34	**3**	2d. blue (Plate 5) (20.7.55)	£2850	70·00	£200
		Wi. Watermark inverted	—	£325	
35		2d. blue (Plate 6) (2.7.57)	£3400	70·00	£200
		a. Imperf	—	£12000	
		b. Imperf horiz (vert pair)	†	—	
		Wi. Watermark inverted	—	£325	

* 17/35a **For well-centred, lightly used +125%**

1856–58. Wmk Large Crown, W **4**. Paper no longer blued.

			Unused	Used	Used on cover
		(a) P 16.			
36	**1**	1d. rose-red (Die II) (26.12.57)	£2750	80·00	£160
		Wi. Watermark inverted	—	£475	
36a	**3**	2d. blue (Plate 6) (1.2.58)	£14500	£375	£550
		*a*Wi. Watermark inverted	—	£1000	
		(b) Die II. P 14.			
37	**1**	1d. red-brown (11.56)	£2400	£375	£1100
38		1d. pale red (9.4.57)	£100	35·00	
		a. Imperf	£4800	£3600	
		s. Optd 'SPECIMEN' (6, 7, 10)	£200		
39		1d. pale rose (3.57)	£110	35·00	
40		1d. rose-red (9.57)	50·00	12·00	23·00
		a. Imperf	£5000	£3800	
		b. Imperf vert (horiz pair)	†	—	
		Wi. Watermark inverted	£180	85·00	
41		1d. deep rose-red (7.57)	£160	20·00	

1861. Letters engraved on plate instead of punched (Alphabet IV).

			Unused	Used	Used on cover
42	**1**	1d. rose-red (Die II) (Plates 50 and 51)	£250	40·00	70·00
		a. Imperf	—	£5750	
		Wi. Watermark inverted	£750	£200	

*36/42a **For well-centred, lightly used +125%**

One Penny. The numbering of the 1d. plates recommenced at 1 on the introduction of Die II. Plates 1 to 21 were Alphabet II from which a scarce plum shade exists. Corner letters of Alphabet III appear on Plate 22 and onwards. As an experiment, the corner letters were engraved by hand on Plates 50 and 51 in 1856, instead of being punched (Alphabet IV), but punching was again resorted to from Plate 52 onwards. Plates 50 and 51 were not put into use until 1861.

Two Pence. Unlike the 1d. the old sequence of plate numbers continued. Plates 3 and 4 of the 2d. had corner letters of Alphabet I, Plate 5 Alphabet II and Plate 6 Alphabet III. In Plate 6 the white lines are thinner than before.

In both values, varieties may be found as described in the preceding issues – ivory heads, inverted watermarks, re-entries, and double letters in corners.

The change of perforation from 16 to 14 was decided upon late in 1854 since the closer holes of the former gauge tended to cause the sheets of stamps to break up when handled, but for a time both gauges were in concurrent use. Owing to faulty alignment of the impressions on the plates and to shrinkage of the paper when dampened, badly perforated stamps are plentiful in the line-engraved issues.

5

6

Showing position of the plate number on the 1d. and 2d. values. (Plate 170 shown)

1864–79. 'Letters in all four corners.' Wmk Large Crown, W **4**. Die II. P **14**.

			Unused	Used*	Used on cover
43	**5**	1d. rose-red (1.4.64)	27·00	2·75	8·00
		s. Optd 'SPECIMEN' (pl. 146)			
44		1d. lake-red	27·00	2·75	
		a. Imperf.....*from*	£8500	£4500	
		Wi. Watermark inverted..*from*	£110	35·00	

* 43/4a **For well-centred, lightly used +125%**

The following plate numbers are known imperf (No. 44a); 72, 79, 80, 81, 82, 83, 84, 85, 86, 87, 88, 90, 91, 92, 93, 96, 97, 98, 100, 101, 102, 103, 104, 105, 107, 108, 109, 112, 113, 114, 116, 117, 120, 121, 122, 136, 137, 142, 146, 148, 158, 162, 164, 166, 171, 174, 191 and 202.

The numbering of this series of 1d. red plates follows after that of the previous 1d. stamp, last printed from Plate 68.

Plates 69, 70, 75, 126 and 128 were prepared for this issue but rejected owing to defects, and stamps from these plates do not exist, so that specimens which appear to be from these plates (like many of those which optimistic collectors believe to be from Plate 77) bear other plate numbers. Owing to faulty engraving or printing it is not always easy to identify the plate number. Plate 77 was also rejected but some stamps printed from it were used. One specimen is in the Tapling Collection and six or seven others are known. Plates 226 to 228 were made but not used.

Specimens from most of the plates are known with inverted watermark. The variety of watermark described in the General Notes to this section occurs on stamp M A (or M L) on plates up to about 96 (*Prices from £120 used*).

Re-entries in this issue are few, the best being on stamps M K and T K of Plate 71 and on S L and T L, Plate 83.

Plate	Un	Used	Plate	Un	Used
71	55·00	4·00	103	70·00	4·50
72	60·00	5·00	104	£100	6·00
73	60·00	4·00	105	£130	9·00
74	60·00	2·75	106	75·00	2·75
76	55·00	2·75	107	80·00	9·00
77	—	£600000	108	£110	3·00
78	£130	2·75	109	£120	4·50
79	48·00	2·75	110	80·00	11·00
80	65·00	2·75	111	70·00	3·00
81	65·00	3·00	112	90·00	3·00
82	£130	5·00	113	70·00	15·00
83	£155	9·00	114	£325	15·00
84	80·00	3·00	115	£130	3·00
85	60·00	4·00	116	£100	11·00
86	70·00	5·00	117	65·00	2·75
87	48·00	2·75	118	70·00	2·75
88	£190	9·50	119	65·00	2·75
89	60·00	2·75	120	27·00	2·75
90	60·00	2·75	121	60·00	11·00
91	75·00	7·00	122	27·00	2·75
92	55·00	2·75	123	60·00	2·75
93	70·00	2·75	124	42·00	2·75
94	65·00	6·00	125	60·00	2·75
95	60·00	2·75	127	75·00	3·00
96	65·00	2·75	129	60·00	10·00
97	60·00	4·50	130	75·00	3·00
98	70·00	7·00	131	85·00	20·00
99	75·00	6·00	132	£190	27·00
100	80·00	3·00	133	£160	11·00
101	80·00	11·00	134	27·00	2·75
102	65·00	2·75	135	£130	30·00

Plate	Un	Used	Plate	Un	Used
136	£130	24·00	181	65·00	2·75
137	42·00	3·00	182	£130	6·50
138	32·00	2·75	183	75·00	4·00
139	80·00	20·00	184	48·00	3·00
140	32·00	2·75	185	70·00	4·00
141	£160	11·00	186	90·00	3·00
142	95·00	30·00	187	70·00	2·75
143	80·00	17·00	188	95·00	12·00
144	£130	25·00	189	95·00	8·50
145	48·00	3·00	190	70·00	7·00
146	60·00	7·00	191	48·00	9·00
147	70·00	4·00	192	70·00	2·75
148	60·00	4·00	193	48·00	2·75
149	60·00	7·00	194	70·00	10·00
150	27·00	2·75	195	70·00	10·00
151	80·00	11·00	196	70·00	6·50
152	80·00	7·50	197	75·00	11·00
153	£140	11·00	198	60·00	7·00
154	70·00	2·75	199	75·00	7·00
155	70·00	3·00	200	80·00	2·75
156	65·00	2·75	201	48·00	6·00
157	70·00	2·75	202	80·00	10·00
158	48·00	2·75	203	48·00	20·00
159	48·00	2·75	204	75·00	3·00
160	48·00	2·75	205	75·00	4·00
161	80·00	9·00	206	75·00	11·00
162	70·00	9·00	207	80·00	11·00
163	70·00	4·00	208	75·00	18·00
164	70·00	4·00	209	65·00	10·00
165	65·00	2·75	210	90·00	15·00
166	65·00	7·00	211	95·00	25·00
167	65·00	2·75	212	80·00	13·00
168	70·00	10·00	213	80·00	13·00
169	80·00	9·00	214	90·00	23·00
170	55·00	2·75	215	90·00	23·00
171	27·00	2·75	216	95·00	23·00
172	48·00	2·75	217	95·00	9·00
173	95·00	11·00	218	90·00	10·00
174	50·00	2·75	219	£130	85·00
175	80·00	4·50	220	60·00	9·00
176	80·00	3·00	221	95·00	20·00
177	60·00	2·75	222	£110	50·00
178	80·00	4·50	223	£130	75·00
179	70·00	3·00	224	£165	65·00
180	80·00	6·50	225	£3200	£800

1858-76 Wmk Large Crown. Die II. *P.* 14

			Un	*Used**	*Used on cover*
45	**6**	2d. blue (thick lines) (7.58)	£350	15·00	50·00
		a. Imperf (Plate 9)		£13000	
		Wi. Watermark inverted	£1700	£240	
		Plate			
		7	£2000	65·00	
		8	£1850	45·00	
		9	£350	15·00	
		12	£3000	£140	
46		2d. blue (thin lines) (1.7.69)	£375	27·00	75·00
		s. Optd 'SPECIMEN' (pl. 15)	£250		
		Wi. Watermark inverted	£2250	£300	
47		2d. deep blue (thin lines)	£375	30·00	
		a. Imperf (Plate 13)	£12000		
		Plate			
		13	£375	30·00	
		14	£500	38·00	
		15	£525	38·00	

* 45/7 **For well-centred, lightly used +125%**

Plates 10 and 11 of the 2d. were prepared but rejected. Plates 13 to 15 were laid down from a new roller impression on which the white lines were thinner.

There are some marked re-entries and repairs, particularly on Plates 7, 8, 9 and 12.

Stamps with inverted watermark may be found and also the T A (T L) and M A (M L) watermark varieties (see General Notes to this section).

Though the paper is normally white, some printings showed blueing and stamps showing the 'ivory head' may therefore be found.

7

Showing the plate number (9)

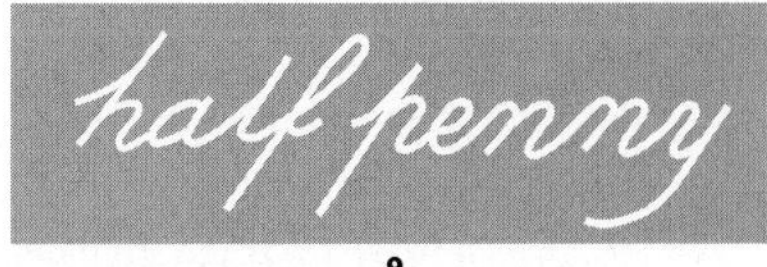

9

1870 (1 Oct)-79. Wmk W **9**, extending over three stamps. P 14.

			Unused	*Used**	*Used on cover*
48	**7**	½d. rose-red	£110	30·00	70·00
49		½d. rose	£110	30·00	
		a. Imperf (Plates 1, 4, 5, 6, 8, 14) *from*	£4500	£3200	
		s. Optd 'SPECIMEN' (pl. 10)	£225		
		Wi. Watermark inverted	£450	£150	
		Wj. Watermark reversed	£450	£150	
		Wk. Watermark inverted and reversed	£300	£100	
		Plate			
		1	£325	£100	
		3	£240	55·00	
		4	£150	50·00	
		5	£110	30·00	
		6	£120	30·00	
		8	£600	£120	
		9	£6000	£850	
		10	£130	30·00	
		11	£120	30·00	
		12	£120	30·00	
		13	£120	30·00	
		14	£120	30·00	
		15	£175	50·00	
		19	£300	65·00	
		20	£350	85·00	

* 48/9a **For well-centred, lightly used +200%**

The ½d. was printed in sheets of 480 (24×20) so that the check letters run from

AA AX
to
TA TX

Plates 2, 7, 16, 17 and 18 were not completed while Plates 21 and 22, though made, were not used.

Owing to the method of perforating, the outer side of stamps in either the A or X row (ie the left or right side of the sheet) is imperf.

Stamps may be found with watermark inverted or reversed, or without watermark, the latter due to misplacement of the paper when printing.

8

Position of plate number

1870 (1 Oct)-74. *Wmk* W **4**. P 14.

			Unused	*Used**	*Used on cover*
51	**8**	1½d. rose-red	£500	75·00	£275
		sa. Optd 'SPECIMEN' (pl. 3)	£300		
52		1½d. lake-red	£600	75·00	
		a. Imperf (Plates 1 and 3) *from*	£10000	†	
		Wi. Watermark inverted	£3000	£500	
		Plate			
		(1)	£725	£110	
		3	£500	75·00	
		Error of lettering. OP–PC for CP–PC (Plate 1)			
53	**8**	1½d. rose-red	£30000	£2000	£7500
		Prepared for use in 1860, but not issued; blued paper.			
53a	**8**	1½d. rosy mauve (Plate 1)	£8500	—	
		b. Error of lettering, OP–PC for CP–PC	—	†	

* 51/3 **For well-centred, lightly used +125%**

Owing to a proposed change in the postal rates, 1½d. stamps were first printed in 1860, in rosy mauve, No. 53a, but the change was not approved and the greater part of the stock was destroyed, although three or four postally used examples have been recorded.

In 1870 a 1½d. stamp was required and was issued in rose-red. Plate 1 did not have the plate number in the design of the stamps, but on stamps from Plate 3 the number will be found in the frame as shown above. Plate 2 was defective and was not used.

The error of lettering OP–PC on Plate 1 was apparently not noticed by the printer, and therefore not corrected.

EMBOSSED ISSUES

Volume 1 of the Stanley Gibbons *Great Britain Specialised Catalogue* gives further detailed information on the embossed issues.

PRICES. The prices quoted are for cut-square stamps with average to fine embossing. Stamps with exceptionally clear embossing are worth more.

10

11

12

13

Position of die number

(Primary die engraved at the Royal Mint by William Wyon. Stamps printed at Somerset House)

1847–54. Imperf (For paper and watermark see footnote).

			Unused	*Used*	*Used on cover*
54	**10**	1s. pale green (11.9.47)	£24000	£1000	£1900
55		1s. green	£24000	£1000	
56		1s. deep green	£28500	£1200	
		Die 1 (1847)	£24000	£1000	
		Die 2 (1854)	£26500	£1100	
57	**11**	10d. brown (6.11.48)	£11500	£1500	£3200
		Die 1 (1848)	£12000	£1500	
		Die 2 (1850)	£11500	£1500	
		Die 3 (1853)	£11500	£1500	
		Die 4 (1854)	£13000	£1750	
58	**12**	6d. mauve (watermark reversed) (1.3.54)	£19500	£1000	
59		6d. dull lilac	£19500	£1000	£1900
60		6d. purple (watermark upright)	£19500	£1000	
		Wi. Watermark inverted	£19500	£1000	
		Wk. Watermark inverted and reversed	£19500	£1000	
61		6d. violet	£32000	£4000	

The 1s. and 10d. are on 'Dickinson' paper with 'silk' threads. The 6d. is on paper watermarked V R in single-lined letters, W **13**, which may be found in four ways–upright, inverted, upright reversed, and inverted reversed. In this listing the reversed watermark is taken to be 'normal'. **Collectors are reminded that Types 10/12 were also used to print postal stationery. 6d. stamps without watermark and 10d. and 1s. stamps without 'silk' threads come from this source and should not be confused with the adhesives, Nos. 54/61.**

The die numbers are indicated on the base of the bust. Only Die 1 (1 *W* W) of the 6d. was used for the adhesive stamps. The 10d. is from Die 1 (W.W.1 on stamps), and Dies 2 to 4 (2W.W., 3W.W. and 4W.W.) but the number and letters on stamps from Die 1 are seldom clear and many specimens are known without any trace of them. Because of this the stamp we previously listed as 'No die number' has been deleted. That they are from Die 1 is proved by the existence of blocks showing stamps with and without the die number. The 1s. is from Dies 1 and 2 (W.W.1, W.W.2).

The normal arrangement of the 'silk' threads in the paper was in pairs running down each vertical row of the sheets, the space between the threads of each pair being approximately 5 mm and between pairs of threads 20 mm. Varieties due to misplacement of the paper in printing show a single thread on the first stamp from the sheet margin and two threads 20 mm apart on the other stamps of the row. Faulty manufacture is the cause of stamps with a single thread in the middle.

Through bad spacing of the impressions, which were handstruck, all values may be found with two impressions more or less overlapping. Owing to the small margin allowed for variation of spacing, specimens with good margins on all sides are not common.

Double impressions are known of all values.

Later printings of the 6d. had the gum tinted green to enable the printer to distinguish the gummed side of the paper.

SURFACE-PRINTED ISSUES

GENERAL NOTES

Volume 1 of the Stanley Gibbons *Great Britain Specialised Catalogue* gives further detailed information on the surface-printed issues.

'Abnormals'. The majority of the great rarities in the surface printed group of issues are the so-called 'abnormals', whose existence is due to the practice of printing six sheets from every plate as soon as made, one of which was kept for record purposes at Somerset House, while the others were perforated and usually issued. If such plates were not used for general production or if, before they came into full use, a change of watermark or colour took place, the six sheets originally printed would differ from the main issue in plate, colour or watermark and, if issued would be extremely rare.

The abnormal stamps of this class listed in this Catalogue and distinguished, where not priced, by an asterisk (*) are:

No.	
78	3d. Plate 3 (with white dots)
152	4d. vermilion, Plate 16
153	4d. sage-green, Plate 17
109	6d. mauve, Plate 10
124/124*a*	6d. pale chestnut and 6d. chestnut, Plate 12
145	6d. pale buff, Plate 13
88	9d. Plate 3 (hair lines)
98	9d. Plate 5 (see footnote to No. 98)
113	10d. Plate 2
91	1s. Plate 3 ('Plate 2')
148/150	1s. green, Plate 14
120	2s. blue, Plate 3

Those which may have been issued, but of which no specimens are known, are 2½d. wmk Anchor, Plates 4 and 5; 3d. wmk Emblems, Plate 5; 3d. wmk Spray, Plate 21, 6d. grey, wmk Spray, Plate 18; 8d. orange, Plate 2; 1s. wmk Emblems, Plate 5; 5s. wmk Maltese Cross, Plate 4.

The 10d. Plate 1, wmk Emblems (No. 99), is sometimes reckoned among the abnormals, but was an error, due to the use of the wrong paper.

Corner Letters. With the exception of the 4d., 6d. and 1s. of 1855–1857, the ½d., 1½d., 2d. and 5d. of 1880, the 1d. lilac of 1881 and the £5 (which had letters in lower corners only, and in the reverse order to the normal), all the surface-printed stamps issued prior to 1887 had letters in all four corners, as in the later line-engraved stamps. The arrangement is the same, the letters running in sequence right across and down the sheets, whether these were divided into panes or not. The corner letters existing naturally depend on the number of stamps in the sheet and their arrangement.

Imprimaturs and Imperforate Stamps. The Post Office retained in their records (now in the National Postal Museum) one imperforate sheet from each plate, known as the Imprimatur (or officially approved) sheet. Some stamps were removed from time to time for presentation purposes and have come on to the market, but these imperforates are not listed as they were not issued. Full details can be found in Volume 1 of the *Great Britain Specialised Catalogue*.

However, other imperforate stamps are known to have been issued and these are listed where it has been possible to prove that they do not come from the Imprimatur sheets. It is therefore advisable to purchase these only when accompanied by an Expert Committee certificate of genuineness.

Plate Numbers. All stamps from No. 75 to No. 163 bear in their designs either the plate number or, in one or two earlier instances, some other indication by which one plate can be distinguished from another. With the aid of these and of the corner letters it is thus possible to 'reconstruct' a sheet of stamps from any plate of any issue or denomination.

Surface-printing. In this context the traditional designation 'surface-

printing' is synonymous with letterpress—the printers' term—as meaning printing from (the surface of) raised type while philatelists often use the expression 'Typo(graphy)', although this is beginning to fall out of favour. It is also called relief printing, as the image is in relief (in French, *en épargne*), unwanted parts of the design having been cut away. Duplicate impressions can be electrotyped or stereotyped from an original die, the resulting clichés being locked together to form the printing plate.

Wing Margins. As the vertical gutters (spaces) between the panes, into which sheets of stamps of most values were divided until the introduction of the Imperial Crown watermark, were perforated through the centre with a single row of holes, instead of each vertical row of stamps on the inner side of the panes having its own line of perforation as is now usual, a proportion of the stamps in each sheet have what is called a 'wing margin' about 5 mm wide on one or other side.

The stamps with 'wing margins' are the watermark Emblems and Spray of Rose series (3d., 6d., 9d., 10d., 1s. and 2s.) with letters D, E, H or I in the south-east corner, and the watermark Garter series (4d. and 8d.) with letters F or G in the south-east corner. Knowledge of this lettering will enable collectors to guard against stamps with wing margin cut down and re-perforated, but note that wing margin stamps of Nos. 62 to 73 are also to be found re-perforated.

'USED' PRICES. In the case of high value surface-printed issues, used prices refer to stamps bearing telegraphic cancellations.

PRINTERS. The issues of Queen Victoria, Nos. 62/214, were typo by Thomas De La Rue & Co.

PERFORATIONS. All the surface-printed issues of Queen Victoria are perf 14, with the exception of Nos. 126/9.

KEY TO SURFACE-PRINTED ISSUES 1855-1883

SG Nos.	*Description*	*Watermark*	*Date of Issue*
	NO CORNER LETTERS		
62	4d. carmine	Small Garter	31.7.55
63/65	4d. carmine	Medium Garter	25.2.56
66/66a	4d. carmine	Large Garter	Jan 1857
69/70	6d. lilac	Emblems	21.10.56
71/73	1s. green	Emblems	1.11.56
	SMALL WHITE CORNER LETTERS		
75/77	3d. carmine	Emblems	1.5.62
78	3d. carmine (dots)	Emblems	Aug 1862
79/82	4d. red	Large Garter	15.1.62
83/85	6d. lilac	Emblems	1.12.62
86/88	9d. bistre	Emblems	15.1.62
89/91	1s. green	Emblems	1.12.62
	LARGE WHITE CORNER LETTERS		
92	3d. rose	Emblems	1.3.65
102/103	3d. rose	Spray	July 1867
93/94	4d. vermilion	Large Garter	4.7.65
96/97	6d. lilac	Emblems	7.3.65
104/107	6d. lilac	Spray	21.6.67
108/109	6d. lilac	Spray	8.3.69
122/124	6d. chestnut	Spray	12.4.72
125	6d. grey	Spray	24.4.73
98	9d. straw	Emblems	30.10.65
110/111	9d. straw	Spray	3.10.67
99	10d. brown	Emblems	11.11.67
112/114	10d. brown	Spray	1.7.67
101	1s. green	Emblems	19.1.65
115/117	1s. green	Spray	13.7.67
118/120b	2s. blue	Spray	1.7.67
121	2s. brown	Spray	27.2.80
126/7	5s. rose	Cross	1.7.67
128	10s. grey	Cross	26.9.78
129	£1 brown-lilac	Cross	26.9.78
130, 134	5s. rose	Anchor	25.11.82
131, 135	10s. grey-green	Anchor	Feb 1883
132, 136	£1 brown-lilac	Anchor	Dec 1882
133, 137	£5 orange	Anchor	21.3.82
	LARGE COLOURED CORNER LETTERS		
138/139	2½d. rosy mauve	Anchor	1.7.75
141	2½d. rosy mauve	Orb	1.5.76
142	2½d. blue	Orb	5·2.80
157	2½d. blue	Crown	23.3.81
143/144	3d. rose	Spray	5.7.73
158	3d. rose	Crown	Jan 1881
159	3d. on 3d. lilac	Crown	1.1.83
152	4d. vermilion	Large Garter	1.3.76
153	4d. sage-green	Large Garter	12.3.77
154	4d. brown	Large Garter	15.8.80
160	4d. brown	Crown	9.12.80
145	6d. buff	Spray	15.3.73
146/147	6d. grey	Spray	20.3.74
161	6d. grey	Crown	1.1.81
162	6d. on 6d. lilac	Crown	1.1.83
156a	8d. purple-brown	Large Garter	July 1876
156	8d. orange	Large Garter	11.9.76
148/150	1s. green	Spray	1.9.73
151	1s. brown	Spray	14.10.80
163	1s. brown	Crown	24.5.81

Watermarks:		
	Anchor	W **40, 47**
	Cross	W **39**
	Crown	W **49**
	Emblems	W **20**
	Large Garter	W **17**
	Medium Garter	W **16**
	Orb	W **48**
	Small Garter	W **15**
	Spray	W **33**

Please note that all watermark illustrations are *as ssen from the front of thestamp.*

14

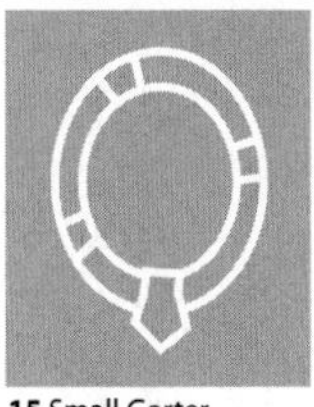
15 Small Garter

16 Medium Garter

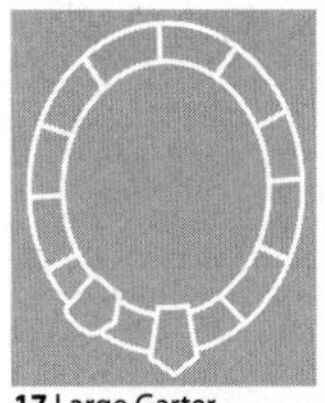
17 Large Garter

1855–57. No corner letters.

(a) Wmk Small Garter, W **15**. *Highly glazed, deeply blued paper (31 July 1855)*

			Unused	*Used**	*Used on cover*
62	**14**	4d. carmine (*shades*)	£8500	£450	£780
		a. Paper slightly blued	£9000	£450	
		b. White paper	£20000	£1100	
		Wi. Watermark inverted	£11000	£1200	

(b) Wmk Medium Garter, W **16**.

(i) Thick, blued highly glazed paper 25 February 1856.

63	**14**	4d. carmine (*shades*)	£14000	£575	£1100
		a. White paper	£12000		
		Wi. Watermark inverted	—	£1250	

(ii) Ordinary thin white paper – September 1856

64	**14**	4d. pale carmine	£13000	£500	£1000
		a. Stamp printed double	†	—	
		Wi. Watermark inverted	£17000	£1200	

(iii) Ordinary white paper, specially prepared ink – 1 November 1856

65	**14**	4d. rose or deep rose	£13000	£525	£1000
		Wi Watermark inverted	†	—	

(c) Wmk Large Garter, W **17**. *Ordinary white paper – January 1857.*

66	**14**	4d. rose-carmine	£2100	£150	£225
		a. Rose	£1750	£150	
		*a*Wi. Watermark inverted	£4800	£400	
		*a*Wj. Watermark inverted and reversed			
		b. Thick glazed paper	£6500	£375	
		*b*Wi. Watermark inverted			

* 62/6b **For well-centred, lightly used** +125%

18

19

20 Emblems wmk (normal)

20a Watermark error, three roses and shamrock

20b Watermark error, three roses and thistle

(d) Wmk Emblems, W **20**.

			Unused	*Used**	*Used on cover*
68	**18**	6d. lilac	£1350	£110	£240
69	**18**	6d. deep lilac (21.10.56)	£1800	£175	
70		6d. pale lilac	£1350	£125	£240
		a. Azure paper	£9000	£950	
		b. Thick paper	£4000	£425	
		c. Error. Watermark W **20a**			
		Wi. Watermark inverted	£3000	£400	
		Wj. Watermark reversed		£475	
		Wk. Watermark inverted and reversed			
71	**19**	1s. deep green (1.11.56)	£5750	£550	
72		1s. green	£3250	£350	£425
73		1s. pale green	£3250	£350	
		a. Azure paper	—	£2000	
		b. Thick paper	—	£400	
		c. Imperf		†	—
		Wi. Watermark inverted	—	£700	
		Wj. Watermark reversed	—	£1400	
		Wk. Watermark inverted and reversed			

* 69/73b **For well-centred, lightly used** +125%

21

22

23

24

25 Plate 2

A.White dots added

B. Hair lines

1862–64. A small uncoloured letter in each corner, the 4d. wmk Large Garter, W **17**, the others Emblems, W **20**.

			Unused	*Used**	*Used on cover*
75	**21**	3d. deep carmine-rose (Plate 2) (1.5.62)	£4800	£575	
76		3d. bright carmine-rose	£2700	£350	£600
		a. Error. Watermark W **20b** (stamp TF)		£9000	
		Wi .Watermark inverted	—	£1200	
77		3d. pale carmine-rose	£2700	£350	
		b. Thick paper	£4000	£475	
		Wj. Watermark reversed			
78		3d. rose (with white dots, Type A, Plate 3) (8.62)	£45000	£17000	
		a. Imperf (Plate 3)	£6750		
79	**22**	4d. bright red (Plate 3) (15.1.62)	£2200	£170	
80		4d. pale red	£2000	£140	£300
		Wi. Watermark inverted	—	£375	
81		4d. bright red (Hair lines, Type B, Plate 4) (16.10.63)	£2300	£185	
82		4d. pale red (Hair lines, Type B, Plate 4)	£2100	£150	£300
		a. Imperf (Plate 4)	£2750		
		Wi. Watermark inverted	£6700	£375	
83	**23**	6d. deep lilac (Plate 3) (1.12.62)	£2800	£160	
84		6d. lilac	£2250	£140	£225
		a. Azure paper	—	£1400	
		b. Thick paper	—	£375	
		c. Error. Shamrock missing from wmk (stamp TF)		£4000	
		d. Error. Watermark W **20b** (stamp TF)	—	£8000	
		e. Hyphen omitted (KA)*		£7750	
		Wi. Watermark inverted	£8250	£450	
		Wj. Watermark reversed		£550	
		Wk. Watermark inverted and reversed	£12000		
85		6d. lilac (Hair lines, Plate 4) (20.4.64)	£3000	£250	£350
		a. Imperf (watermark inverted)	£3250		
		Eb. Imperf and watermark upright	£3500		
		c. Thick paper	£4000	£280	
		d. Error. Watermark W **20b** (stamp TF)			
		Wi. Watermark inverted	£8250	£475	
		Wj. Watermark reversed			
		Wk. Watermark inverted and reversed			
86	**24**	9d. bistre (Plate 2) (15.1.62)	£5800	£575	£1200
		Wi. Watermark inverted	£10000	£700	
		Wj. Watermark reversed	—	£850	
		Wk. Watermark inverted and reversed			
87		9d. straw	£4000	£475	£1000
		a. On azure paper			
		b. Thick paper	£6000	£550	
		c. Error. Shamrock missing from wmk (stamp TF)	†	—	
		d. Error. Watermark W **20b** (stamp TF)	†	—	
		Wi. Watermark inverted	£6800	£650	
88		9d. bistre (Hair lines, Plate 3) (5.62)	£32000	£13500	
89	**25**	1s. deep green (Plate No. 1 = Plate 2) (1.12.62)	£4800	£500	
90		1s. green (Plate No. 1 = Plate 2)	£3200	£300	£450
		a. 'K' in lower left corner in white circle (stamp KD)	£20000	£2750	
		awi. Watermark inverted	—	£4250	
		ab. 'K' normal (stamp KD)	—	£2200	
		b. On azure paper			
		c.Error. Watermark W 20b (stamp TF)			
		d. Thick paper	—	£375	
		da. Thick paper, 'K' in circle as No. 90a	—	£3750	
		Wi. Watermark inverted	—	£450	
		Wj. Watermark reversed			
		Wk. Watermark inverted and reversed	—	£475	
91		1s. deep green (Plate No. 2 = Plate 3)	£35000		
		a. Imperf	£7250		
		*a*Wi. Watermark inverted	£7250		

* 75/91 **For well-centred, lightly used** +125%

The 3d. as T **21**, but with network background in the spandrels, was never issued. Optd 'SPECIMEN' *price* £800.

The plates of this issue may be distinguished as follows:

3d.	Plate 2	No white dots.
	Plate 3	White dots as illustration A.
4d.	Plate 3	No hair lines. Roman I next to lower corner letters.
	Plate 4	Hair lines in corners. (Illustration B.). Roman II.
6d.	Plate 3	No hair lines.
	Plate 4	Hair lines in corners.
9d.	Plate 2	No hair lines.
	Plate 3	Hair lines in corners. Beware of faked lines.
1s.	Plate 2	Numbered 1 on stamps.
	Plate 3	Numbered 2 on stamps and with hair lines.

* One used example on piece has been recorded, cancelled by a Glasgow Duplex postmark dated 06.1.1863.

The 9d. on azure paper (No. 87a) is very rare, only one confirmed example being known.

The variety 'K' in circle, No. 90a, is believed to be due to a damaged letter having been cut out and replaced. It is probable that the punch was driven in too deeply, causing the flange to penetrate the surface, producing an indentation showing as an uncoloured circle.

The watermark variety 'three roses and a shamrock' illustrated in W **20a** was evidently due to the substitution of an extra rose for the thistle in a faulty watermark bit. It is found on stamp TA of Plate 4 of the 3d., Plates 1 (No. 70c), 3, 5 and 6 of the 6d., Plate 4 of the 9d. and Plate 4 of the 1s.

Similar problems occurred on stamp TF of the 6d. and 9d. Here the shamrock emblem became detached and used examples are known showing it omitted. It was replaced by a third rose (W **20b**) and this variety exists on the 6d. (Nos. 84/5 and 97) and 9d. (Nos. 87 and 98).

26

27

28 (with hyphen)

28a (without hyphen)

29

30

31

1865–67. Large uncoloured corner letters. Wmk Large Garter (4d.); others Emblems.

			Unused	Used*	Used on cover
92	26	3d. rose (Plate 4) (1.3.65)	£2500	£250	£500
		a. Error. Watermark W 20a	£6500	£1250	
		b. Thick paper	£3500	£325	
		Wi. Watermark inverted	—	£600	
		Wj. Watermark reversed			
		Wk. Watermark inverted and reversed			
93	27	4d. dull vermilion (4.7.65)	£650	90·00	
94		4d. vermilion	£575	75·00	£140
		a. Imperf (Plates 11, 12)	£8500		
		Wi. Watermark inverted	£575	75·00	
95		4d. deep vermilion	£650	90·00	
		Plate			
		7 (1865)	£650	£130	
		8 (1866)	£600	90·00	
		9 (1867)	£600	90·00	
		10 (1868)	£825	£150	
		11 (1869)	£625	90·00	
		12 (1870)	£575	75·00	
		13 (1872)	£650	75·00	
		14 (1873)	£775	£110	
96	28	6d. dp lilac (with hyphen) (7.3.65)	£1900	£200	
97		6d. lilac (with hyphen)	£1200	£140	£225
		a. Thick paper	£1600	£175	
		b. Stamp doubly printed (Plate 6)	—	£15000	
		c. Error. Watermark W 20a (Pl 5, 6) *from*	—	£2400	
		d. Error. Watermark W 20b (Plate 5)			
		e. Imperf (Plate 5)			
		Wi. Watermark inverted	—	£250	
		Wj. Watermark reversed			
		Wk. Watermark inverted and reversed	†	—	
		Plate			
		5 (1865)	£1150	£140	
		6 (1867)	£3800	£250	
98	29	9d. straw (Plate 4) (25.10.65)	£4800	£600	£1400
		a. Thick paper	£5800	£850	
		b. Error. Watermark W 20a	—	£2500	
		c. Error. Watermark W 20b (stamp TF)	£13000		
		Wi. Watermark inverted	—	£1650	
99	30	10d. red-brown (Plate 1) (11.11.67)	*	£55000	
101	31	1s. green (Plate 4) (19.1.65)	£2850	£275	£450
		a. Error. Watermark W 20a	—	£1700	
		ab. Error. Watermark W 20b			
		b. Thick paper	£3500	£380	
		c. Imperf between (vertical pair)	—	£16000	
		Wi. Watermark inverted	—	£650	
		Wia. Imperf watermark inverted			
		Wk. Watermark inverted and reversed	—	£650	

* 92/101c **For well-centred, lightly used** +**100%**

From mid-1866 to about the end of 1871 4d. stamps of this issue appeared generally with watermark inverted.

Unused examples of No. 98 from Plate 5 exist, but this was never put to press and all evidence points to such stamps originating from a portion of the Imprimatur sheet which was perforated by De La Rue in 1887 for insertion in albums to be presented to members of the Stamp Committee (*Price* £20000 *unused*).

The 10d. stamps, No. 99, were printed in error on paper watermarked 'Emblems' instead of on 'Spray of Rose'.

32

33 Spray of Rose

34

1867–80 *Wmk* Spray of Rose. W **33**.

			Unused	Used*	Used on cover
102	26	3d. deep rose (12.7.67)	£800	£100	
103		3d. rose	£525	60·00	£110
		a. Imperf (Plates 5, 6) *from*	£11000		
		Wi. Watermark inverted	£2250	£300	
		Plate			
		4 (1867)	£1850	£300	
		5 (1868)	£525	70·00	
		6 (1870)	£550	70·00	
		7 (1871)	£650	70·00	
		8 (1872)	£625	60·00	
		9 (1872)	£625	70·00	
		10 (1873)	£875	£150	
104	28	6d. lilac (with hyphen) (Plate 6) (21.6.67)	£1900	£175	£250
		a. Imperf		£6000	
		Wi. Watermark inverted	—	£350	
105		6d. deep lilac (with hyphen) (Plate 6)	£1900	£175	
106		6d. purple (with hyphen) (Plate 6)	£1900	£200	
107		6d. bright violet (with hyphen) (Plate 6) (22.7.68)	£1800	£200	
108	28a	6d. dull violet (without hyphen) (Plate 8) (8.3.69)	£1250	£190	
		Wi. Watermark inverted	—	£275	
109		6d. mauve (without hyphen)	£700	90·00	£140
		a. Imperf (Plate Nos. 8 and 9)	£12000	£5000	
		Wi. Watermark inverted	—	£250	
		Plate			
		8 (1869, mauve)	£800	£140	
		9 (1870, mauve)	£700	90·00	
		10 (1869, mauve)	*	£37500	
110	29	9d. straw (Plate No. 4) (3.10.67)	£2500	£325	£525
		Wi. Watermark inverted	—	£650	
111		9d. pale straw (Plate No. 4)	£2400	£300	
		a. Imperf (Plate 4)	£22000		
112	30	10d. red-brown (1.7.67)	£3600	£400	£850
		Wi. Watermark inverted	—	£1000	
113		10d. pale red-brown	£3600	£400	
114		10d. deep red-brown	£5000	£600	
		a. Imperf (Plate 1)	£17000		
		Plate			
		1 (1867)	£3600	£400	
		2 (1867)	£55000	£17000	
115	31	1s. deep green (13.7.67)	£1300	70·00	
117		1s. green	£800	45·00	90·00
		a. Imperf between (horiz pair) (Pl 7)			
		b. Imperf (Plate 4)	£10000	£6500	
		Wi. Watermark inverted	£2400	£180	
		Plate			
		4 (1867)	£975	65·00	
		5 (1871)	£800	45·00	
		6 (1871)	£1200	45·00	
		7 (1873)	£1400	90·00	
118	32	2s. dull blue (1.7.67)	£4200	£225	£825
		s. Optd 'SPECIMEN'	£600		
		Wi. Watermark inverted	—	£950	
119		2s. deep blue	£5000	£240	
		a. Imperf (Plate 1)	£23000		
120		2s. pale blue	£5000	£275	
		aa. Imperf (Plate 1)	£22000		
120*a*		2s. cobalt	£25000	£3000	
120*b*		2s. milky blue	£24000	£2000	
		Plate			
		1 (1867)	£4200	£225	
		3 (1868)	*	£16500	
121		2s. brown (Plate No. 1) (27.2.80)	£30000	£4250	
		a. Imperf	£30000		
		b. No watermark	†	—	
		s. Optd 'SPECIMEN' (9)	£3800		
		Wi. Watermark inverted	—	£6000	

* 102/21 **For well-centred, lightly used** +**75%**

Examples of the 1s. from Plates 5 and 6 without watermark are postal forgeries used at the Stock Exchange Post Office in the early 1870s. (*Prices from* £850)

1872–73. Uncoloured letters in corners. Wmk Spray, W **33**.

			Unused	Used*	Used on cover
122	34	6d. deep chestnut (Plate 11) (12.4.72)	£1300	£125	
122*a*		6d. chestnut (Plate 11) (22.5.72)	£800	65·00	£150
		Wi. Watermark inverted	—	£325	
122*b*		6d. pale chestnut (Plate 11) (1872)	£700	65·00	
123		6d. pale buff (18.10.72)	£1100	£125	£250
		Wi. Watermark inverted	—	£375	
		Plate			
		11 (1872, pale buff)	£1100	£125	
		12 (1872, pale buff)	£3400	£350	
124		6d. chestnut (Plate 12) (1872)	*	£3800	
124*a*		6d. pale chestnut (Plate 12) (1872)	*	£3500	
125		6d. grey (Plate No. 12) (24.4.73)	£1900	£300	£375
		a. Imperf	£15000		
		Wi. Watermark inverted	£6250	—	

* 122/5 **For well-centred, lightly used** +**50%**

35

36

37

38

39 Maltese Cross

40 Large Anchor

1867–83. Uncoloured letters in corners.

(a) Wmk Maltese Cross, W **39**. *P* 15½×15.

			Unused	Used*
126	35	5s. rose (1.7.67)	£11000	£675
127		5s. pale rose	£11000	£675
		a. Imperf (Plate 1)	£18000	
		s. Optd 'SPECIMEN' (pl. 2)	£1750	
		Plate		
		1 (1867)	£11000	£675
		2 (1874)	£18000	£1500
128	36	10s. greenish grey (Plate 1) (26.9.78)	£60000	£3200
		s. Optd 'SPECIMEN'	£4250	
129	37	£1 brown-lilac (Plate 1) (26.9.78)	£90000	£4500
		s. Optd 'SPECIMEN'	£6250	
		(b) Wmk Large Anchor, W **40**. *P* 14.		
		(i) Blued paper.		
130	35	5s. rose (Plate 4) (25.11.82)	£42000	£4800
		Wi. Watermark inverted	—	£18000
131	36	10s. grey-green (Plate 1) (2.83)	£135000	£5200
132	37	£1 brown-lilac (Plate 1) (12.82)	£175000	£10000
133	38	£5 orange (Plate 1) (21.3.82)	£70000	£15000
		s. Optd 'SPECIMEN' (9, 11)	£3500	
		(ii) White paper.		
134	35	5s. rose (Plate 4)	£35000	£4200
135	36	10s. greenish grey (Plate 1)	£160000	£4500
136	37	£1 brown-lilac (Plate 1)	£200000	£9000
137	38	£5 orange (Plate 1)	£14500	£4750

* 126/37 **For well-centred, lightly used** +**75%**

41 **42** **43**

44 **45** **46**

47 Small Anchor

48 Orb

1873–80. Large coloured letters in the corners.

(a) Wmk Small Anchor, W **47**.

No.	Type	Description	Unused	Used*	Used on cover
138	**41**	2½d. rosy mauve (*blued paper*) (1.7.75)	£875	£190	
		a. Imperf			
		Wi. Watermark inverted	£3000	£350	
		Plate			
		1 (*blued paper*) (1875)	£875	£190	
		2 (*blued paper*) (1875)	£8000	£1650	
		3 (*blued paper*) (1875)	—	£5750	
139		2½d. rosy mauve (*white paper*)	£675	£120	£180
		Wi. Watermark inverted	£2750	£250	
		Plate			
		1 (*white paper*) (1875)	£675	£120	
		2 (*white paper*) (1875)	£675	£120	
		3 (*white paper*) (1875)	£1000	£175	
		Error of Lettering L H—F L *for* L H—H L (*Plate* 2).			
140	**41**	2½d. rosy mauve	£34000	£2750	

(b) Wmk Orb, W **48**.

No.	Type	Description	Unused	Used*	Used on cover
141	**41**	2½d. rosy mauve (1.5.76)	£525	85·00	£125
		sb. Optd 'SPECIMEN' (pl. 6)	£220		
		Wi. Watermark inverted	£1900	£225	
		Plate			
		3 (1876)	£1350	£150	
		4 (1876)	£525	85·00	
		5 (1876)	£525	85·00	
		6 (1876)	£525	85·00	
		7 (1877)	£525	85·00	
		8 (1877)	£525	85·00	
		9 (1877)	£525	85·00	
		10 (1878)	£550	85·00	
		11 (1878)	£525	85·00	
		12 (1878)	£525	85·00	
		13 (1878)	£525	85·00	
		14 (1879)	£525	85·00	
		15 (1879)	£525	85·00	
		16 (1879)	£525	85·00	
		17 (1880)	£1700	£300	
142	**41**	2½d. blue (5.2.80)	£575	55·00	90·00
		s. Optd 'SPECIMEN' (pl. 17) (9)	£160		
		Wi. Watermark inverted	£2100	£275	
		Plate			
		17 (1880)	£575	75·00	
		18 (1880)	£575	55·00	
		19 (1880)	£575	55·00	
		20 (1880)	£575	55·00	

(c) Wmk Spray, W **33**.

No.	Type	Description	Unused	Used*	Used on cover
143	**42**	3d. rose (5.7.73)	£450	80·00	£120
		sb. Optd 'SPECIMEN' (pl. 18)	£250		
		Wi. Watermark inverted	£1650	£350	
144		3d. pale rose	£450	80·00	
		Plate			
		11 (1873)	£450	80·00	
		12 (1873)	£525	80·00	
		14 (1874)	£525	80·00	
		15 (1874)	£450	80·00	
		16 (1875)	£450	80·00	
		17 (1875)	£525	80·00	
		18 (1875)	£525	80·00	
		19 (1876)	£450	80·00	
		20 (1879)	£850	£140	
145	**43**	6d. pale buff (Plate 13) (15.3.73)	*	£25000	
146		6d. deep grey (20.3.74)	£600	£120	£150
		sa. Optd 'SPECIMEN' (pl. 15)	£300		
147		6d. grey	£500	90·00	
		Wi. Watermark inverted	£1800	£350	
		13 (1874)	£500	90·00	
		14 (1875)	£500	90·00	
		15 (1876)	£500	90·00	
		16 (1878)	£500	90·00	
		17 (1880)	£950	£180	
148	**44**	1s. deep green (1.9.73)	£1100	£225	
150		1s. green	£650	£160	£240
		sa. Optd 'SPECIMEN' (pl. 12)	£350		
		Wi. Watermark inverted	£2400	£400	
		Plate			
		8 (1873)	£825	£175	
		9 (1874)	£825	£175	
		10 (1874)	£775	£200	
		11 (1875)	£775	£175	
		12 (1876)	£650	£160	
		13 (1876)	£650	£160	
		14 (—)*	*	£40000	
151		1s. orange-brown (Plate 13) (14.10.80)	£4750	£700	£1800
		s. Optd 'SPECIMEN'	£550		
		Wi. Watermark inverted	£11000	£1800	

(d) Wmk Large Garter, W **17**.

No.	Type	Description	Unused	Used*	Used on cover
152	**45**	4d. vermilion (1.3.76)	£3200	£525	£1100
		Wi. Watermark inverted	—	£1000	
		Plate			
		15 (1876)	£3200	£525	
		16 (1877)	*	£35000	
153		4d. sage-green (12.3.77)	£1400	£300	£600
		s. Optd 'SPECIMEN' (pl. 15)	£350		
		Wi. Watermark inverted	£3000	£625	
		Plate			
		15 (1877)	£1600	£325	
		16 (1877)	£1400	£300	
		17 (1877)	*	£20000	
154		4d. grey-brown (Plate 17) (15.8.80)	£2800	£550	£1700
		a. Imperf	£22000		
		s. Optd 'SPECIMEN'	£350		
		Wi. Watermark inverted	—	£1200	
156	**46**	8d. orange (Plate 1) (11.9.76)	£1850	£350	£625
		s. Optd 'SPECIMEN'	£350		
		Wi. Watermark inverted	—	£900	

*138/56 **For well-centred, lightly used +100%**

1876 (July). *Prepared for use but not issued.*

No.	Type	Description	Unused
156*a*	**46**	8d. purple-brown (Plate 1)	£9750

49 Imperial Crown

3d

(50)

1880–83. *Wmk Imperial Crown, W* **49**.

No.	Type	Description	Unused	Used*	Used on cover
157	**41**	2½d. blue (23.3.81)	£450	35·00	55·00
		Wi. Watermark inverted	—	£550	
		Plate			
		21 (1881)	£500	45·00	
		22 (1881)	£450	45·00	
		23 (1881)	£450	35·00	
158	**42**	3d. rose (3.81)	£500	£100	£175
		Wi. Watermark inverted	—	£580	
		Plate			
		20 (1881)	£900	£150	
		21 (1881)	£500	£100	
159	**50**	3d. on 3d lilac (C.) (Plate 21) (1.1.83)	£650	£160	£450
		s. Optd 'SPECIMEN'	£300		
		Wi. Watermark inverted			
160	**45**	4d. grey-brown (8.12.80)	£450	75·00	£190
		Wi. Watermark inverted	—	£650	
		Plate			
		17 (1880)	£475	80·00	
		18 (1882)	£450	75·00	
161	**43**	6d. grey (1.1.81)	£400	80·00	£120
		Wi. Watermark inverted	—	£650	
		Plate			
		17 (1881)	£425	80·00	
		18 (1882)	£400	80·00	
162	**50**	6d. on 6d. lilac (C.) (Plate 18) (1.1.83)	£675	£150	£425
		a. Slanting dots (various) *from*	£1800	£450	
		b. Optd double	—	£12500	
		s. Optd 'SPECIMEN' (9)	£300		
		Wi. Watermark inverted	£3500	£850	
163	**44**	1s. orange-brown (24.5.81)	£750	£170	£550
		Wi. Watermark inverted	£3250	£950	
		Plate			
		13 (1881)	£875	£170	
		14 (1881)	£750	£170	

* 157/63 **For well-centred, lightly used +75%**

The 1s. plate 14 (line perf 14) exists in purple but was not issued in this shade (*Price* £15000 *unused*). Examples were included in a few of the Souvenir Albums prepared for members of the 'Stamp Committee of 1884'.

KEY TO SURFACE-PRINTED ISSUES
1880–1900

SG Nos.	*Description*	*Date of Issue*
164/165	½d. green	14.10.80
187	½d. slate-blue	1.4.84
197/*e*	½d. vermilion	1.1.87
213	½d. blue-green	17.4.1900
166	1d. Venetian red	1.1.80
170/171	1d. lilac, Die I	12.7.81
172/174	1d. lilac, Die II	12.12.81
167	1½d. Venetian red	14.10.80
188	1½d. lilac	1.4.84
198	1½d. purple and green	1.1.87
168/*a*	2d. rose	8.12.80
189	2d. lilac	1.4.84
199/200	2d. green and red	1.1.87
190	2½d. lilac	1.4.84
201	2½d. purple on blue paper	1.1.87
191	3d. lilac	1.4.84
202/204	3d. purple on yellow paper	1.1.87
192	4d. dull green	1.4.84
205/*a*	4d. green and brown	1.1.87
206	4½d. green and carmine	15.9.92
169	5d. indigo	15.3.81
193	5d. dull green	1.4.84
207	5d. purple and blue, Die I	1.1.87
207*a*	5d. purple and blue, Die II	1888
194	6d. dull green	1.4.84
208/*a*	6d. purple on rose-red paper	1.1.87
195	9d. dull green	1.8.83
209	9d. purple and blue	1.1.87
210/*b*	10d. purple and carmine	24.2.90
196	1s. dull green	1.4.84
211	1s. green	1.1.87
214	1s. green and carmine	11.7.1900
175	2s.6d. lilac on blued paper	2.7.83
178/9	2s.6d. lilac	1884
176	5s. rose on blued paper	1.4.84
180/181	5s. rose	1884
177/*a*	10s. ultramarine on blued paper	1.4.84
182/183*a*	10s. ultramarine	1884
185	£1 brown-lilac, wmk Crowns	1.4.84
186	£1 brown-lilac, wmk Orbs	6.1.88
212	£1 green	28.1.91

Note that the £5 value used with the above series is listed as Nos. 133 and 137.

52 **53** **54** **55**

56

1880–81. Wmk Imperial Crown, W **49**.

No.	Type	Description	Unused	Used*	Used on cover
164	**52**	½d. deep green (14.10.80)	55·00	22·00	30·00
		a. Imperf	£5000		
		b. No watermark	£10000		
		s. Optd 'SPECIMEN'	60·00		
		Wi. Watermark inverted	£2400	£575	
165		½d. pale green	55·00	22·00	
166	**53**	1d. Venetian red (1.1.80)	35·00	15·00	30·00
		a. Imperf	£5800		
		b. Error. *Wmk* **48**	†	£27000	
		s. Optd 'SPECIMEN'	£100		
		Wi. Watermark inverted	—	£350	
167	**54**	1½d. Venetian red (14.10.80)	£250	60·00	£160
		s. Optd 'SPECIMEN'	80·00		
		Wi. Watermark inverted	†	—	
168	**55**	2d. pale rose (8.12.80)	£340	£120	£300
		s. Optd 'SPECIMEN'	£110		
		Wi. Watermark inverted	£3000	£850	
168*a*		2d. deep rose	£360	£120	
169	**56**	5d. indigo (15.3.81)	£725	£175	£325
		a. Imperf	£6750	£4500	
		s. Optd 'SPECIMEN'	£160		
		Wi. Watermark inverted	—	£4800	
Set of 5			£1275	£350	

* 164/9 **For well-centred, lightly used +75%**

Two used examples of the 1d. value have been reported on the Orb (fiscal) watermark.

57

Die I

Die II

1881. Wmk Imperial Crown, W **49**.

(a) 14 dots in each corner, Die I (12 July)

No.	Type	Description	Unused	Used*	Used on cover
170	**57**	1d. lilac	£225	45·00	60·00
		s. Optd 'SPECIMEN'	70·00		
		Wi. Watermark inverted	—	£600	
171		1d. pale lilac	£225	45·00	

(b) 16 dots in each corner, Die II (13 December).

No.	Type	Description	Unused	Used*	Used on cover
172	**57**	1d. lilac	2·75	2·20	4·00
		s. Optd 'SPECIMEN' (9, 12)	60·00		
		Wi. Watermark inverted	60·00	35·00	
172*a*		1d. bluish lilac	£475	£150	
173		1d. deep purple	2·75	2·20	
		a. Printed both sides	£900	†	
		b. Frame broken at bottom	£975	£350	
		c. Printed on gummed side	£900	†	
		d. Imperf three sides (pair)	£8250	†	
		e. Printed both sides but impression on back inverted	£1000	†	
		f. No watermark	£8000	†	
		g. Blued paper	—		
174		1d. mauve	2·75	1·70	
		a. Imperf (pair)	£7500		

* 170/4 **For well-centred, lightly used +50%**

1d. stamps with the words 'PEARS SOAP' printed on the back in orange, blue or mauve *price from £550, unused.*

The variety 'frame broken at bottom' (No. 173b) shows a white space just inside the bottom frame-line from between the 'N' and 'E' of 'ONE' to below the first 'N' of 'PENNY', breaking the pearls and cutting into the lower part of the oval below 'PEN'.

58

59

60

1883–84. Coloured letters in the corners. Wmk Large Anchor, W **40**.

(a) Blued paper.

No.	Type	Description	*Unused*	*Used**
175	**58**	2s.6d. lilac (2.7.83)	£6750	£1500
		s. Optd 'SPECIMEN'	£625	
176	**59**	5s. rose (1.4.84)	£18000	£4000
177	**60**	10s. ultramarine (1.4.84)	£40000	£8250
177*a*		10s. cobalt (5.84)	£62000	£13500

(b) White paper.

No.	Type	Description	*Unused*	*Used**
178	**58**	2s.6d. lilac	£600	£160
		s. Optd 'SPECIMEN'	£425	
179		2s.6d. deep lilac	£825	£225
		a. On blued paper	£9000	£3600
		Wi. Watermark inverted	—	£11500
180	**59**	5s. rose	£1100	£250
		Wi. Watermark inverted	†	£12500
181		5s. crimson	£975	£250
		s. Optd 'SPECIMEN'	£450	
182	**60**	10s. cobalt	£42000	£8250
183		10s. ultramarine	£2250	£525
		s. Optd 'SPECIMEN'	£550	
183*a*		10s. pale ultramarine	£2500	£550

* 175/83a **For well-centred, lightly used +50%**

For No. 180 perf 12 see second note below No. 196.

61

Broken frames, Plate 2

1884 (1 Apr). Wmk Three Imperial Crowns, W **49**.

No.	Type	Description	*Unused*	*Used**
185	**61**	£1 brown-lilac	£32000	£3000
		a. Frame broken	£60000	£5000
		Wi. Watermark inverted	—	£38000

1888 (Feb). Wmk Three Orbs, W **48**.

No.	Type	Description	*Unused*	*Used**
186	**61**	£1 brown-lilac	£72000	£4500
		a. Frame broken	£150000	£9000

* 185/6a **For well-centred, lightly used +50%**

The broken-frame varieties, Nos. 185a and 186a, are on Plate 2 stamps JC and TA, as illustrated. See also No. 212a.

62 63 64

65 66

1883 (1 Aug). (9d.) or 1884 (1 Apr) (others). Wmk Imperial Crown, W **49** (sideways on horiz designs).

No.	Type	Description	*Unused*	*Used**	*Used on cover*
187	**52**	½d. slate-blue	35·00	10·00	20·00
		a. Imperf	£3750		
		s. Optd 'SPECIMEN'	50·00		
		Wi. Watermark inverted	£3000	£350	
188	**62**	1½d. lilac	£125	45·00	£120
		a. Imperf	£3750		
		s. Optd 'SPECIMEN'	85·00		
		Wi. Watermark inverted	£3000	£280	
189	**63**	2d. lilac	£230	80·00	£150
		a. Imperf	£4800		
		s. Optd 'SPECIMEN'	85·00		
		Wi. Watermark sideways inverted			
190	**64**	2½d. lilac	95·00	20·00	30·00
		a. Imperf	£4800		
		s. Optd 'SPECIMEN'	85·00		
		Wi. Watermark sideways inverted	£600		
191	**65**	3d. lilac	£280	£100	£180
		a. Imperf	£4800		
		s. Optd 'SPECIMEN'	85·00		
		Wi. Watermark inverted	†	£1200	
192	**66**	4d. dull green	£580	£210	£350
		a. Imperf	£4800		
		s. Optd 'SPECIMEN'	£190		
193	**62**	5d. dull green	£580	£210	£350
		a. Imperf	£5500		
		s. Optd 'SPECIMEN'	£190		
194	**63**	6d. dull green	£625	£240	£380
		a. Imperf	£5750		
		s. Optd 'SPECIMEN'	£220		
		Wi. Watermark sideways inverted	£1400		
195	**64**	9d. dull green (1.8.83)	£1250	£480	£4750
		s. Optd 'SPECIMEN'	£425		
		Wi. Watermark sideways inverted	£2000	£775	
196	**65**	1s. dull green	£1600	£325	£625
		a. Imperf	£8750		
		s. Optd 'SPECIMEN'	£375		
		Wi. Watermark-inverted			
Set of 10			£5000	£1600	

* 187/96 **For well-centred, lightly used +100%**

The normal sideways watermark shows the top of the crown pointing to the right *as seen from the back of the stamp.*

The above prices are for stamps in the true dull green colour. Stamps which have been soaked, causing the colour to run, are virtually worthless.

Stamps of the above set and No. 180 are also found perf 12; these are official perforations, but were never issued. A second variety of the 5d. is known with a line instead of a stop under the 'd' in the value; this was never issued and is therefore only known unused (*Price* £38,000).

71 72 73 74 75 76 77 78 79 80 81 82

Die I Die II

Die I: Square dots to right of 'd'.
Die II: Thin vertical lines to right of 'd'.

1½d. Deformed leaf (Duty plate 4, R. 19/1)

1887 (1 Jan)–**92**. 'Jubilee' issue. New types. The bicoloured stamps have the value tablets, or the frames including the value tablets, in the second colour. Wmk Imperial Crown, W **49** (Three Crowns on £1).

No.	Type	Description	*Mint*	*Used**	*Used on cover*
197	**71**	½d. vermilion	1·75	1·20	7·00
		a. Printed on gummed side	£3500		
		b. Printed both sides			
		c. Doubly printed	£32000		
		d. Imperf (showing bottom margins)	£5000		
		s. Optd 'SPECIMEN' (9, 10, 12)	35·00		
		Wi. Watermark inverted	60·00	60·00	
197*e*		½d. orange-vermilion	1·75	1·20	
198	**72**	1½d. dull purple and pale green	18·00	8·00	25·00
		a. Purple part of design double	—	£9000	
		b. Deformed leaf	£800	£450	
		s. Optd 'SPECIMEN' (12)	55·00		
		Wi. Watermark inverted	£1200	£500	
199	**73**	2d. green and scarlet	£425	£260	
200		2d. grey-green and carmine	35·00	15·00	28·00
		s. Optd 'SPECIMEN'	60·00		
		Wi. Watermark inverted	£1200	£525	
201	**74**	2½d. purple/*blue*	25·00	5·00	8·00
		a. Printed on gummed side	£15000		
		b. Imperf three sides	£9500		
		c. Imperf	£12000		
		Ed. Missing 'd' in value	†	£9500	
		s. Optd 'SPECIMEN'	75·00		
		Wi. Watermark inverted	£3500	£1400	
202	**75**	3d. purple/*yellow*	25·00	5·00	38·00
		a. Imperf (wmk inverted)	£11000		
		s. Optd 'SPECIMEN'	60·00		
		Wi. Watermark inverted	—	£725	
203		3d. deep purple/*yellow*	30·00	5·00	
204		3d. purple/*orange* (1890)	£800		
205	**76**	4d. green and purple-brown	40·00	18·00	42·00
		aa. Imperf	£12000		
		s. Optd 'SPECIMEN'	60·00		
		Wi. Watermark inverted	£1200	£650	
205*a*		4d. green and deep brown	40·00	18·00	
206	**77**	4½d. green and carmine (15.9.92)	11·00	45·00	£100
		Wi. Watermark inverted			
206*a*		4½d. green and deep bright carmine	£750	£650	
207	**78**	5d. dull purple and blue (Die I)	£800	£120	£275
		s. Optd 'SPECIMEN'	£110		
207*a*		5d. dull purple and blue (Die II) (1888)	42·00	15·00	50·00
		Wi. Watermark inverted	£17000	£1250	
208	**79**	6d. purple/*rose-red*	40·00	15·00	95·00
		s. Optd 'SPECIMEN'	65·00		
		Wi. Watermark inverted	£7500	£2000	
208*a*		6d. deep purple/*rose-red*	40·00	15·00	
209	**80**	9d. dull purple and blue	75·00	48·00	£275
		s. Optd 'SPECIMEN'	70·00		
		Wi. Watermark inverted	£8000	£2800	
210	**81**	10d. dull purple and carmine (*shades*) (24.2.90)	60·00	45·00	£300
		aa. Imperf	£17500		
		s. Optd 'SPECIMEN'	£110		
		Wi. Watermark inverted	£9500	£3000	
210*a*		10d. dull purple and deep dull carmine	£625	£250	
210*b*		10d. dull purple and scarlet	95·00	65·00	
211	**82**	1s. dull green	£275	80·00	£190
		s. Optd 'SPECIMEN'	75·00		
		Wi. Watermark inverted	£1700	£975	
212	**61**	£1 green (28.1.91)	£4000	£800	
		a. Frame broken	£8500	£2000	
		s. Optd 'SPECIMEN'	£1100		
		Wi. Watermark inverted	£110000	£13000	

* 197/212a **For well-centred, lightly used +50%**

The broken-frame varieties, No. 212a, are on Plate 2 stamps JC or TA, as illustrated above No. 185.

½d. stamps with 'PEARS SOAP' printed on the back in orange, blue or mauve, *price from £525 each.*

No used price is quoted for No. 204 as it is not possible to authenticate the paper colour on stamps in used condition.

1900. Colours changed. Wmk Imperial Crown, W **49**.

No.	Type	Description	*Mint*	*Used**	*Used on cover*
213	**71**	½d. blue-green (17.4)	2·00	2·25	6·50
		a. Printed on gummed side	—	†	
		b. Imperf	£7500		
		Wi. Watermark inverted	75·00	95·00	
214	**82**	1s. green and carmine (11.7)	65·00	£140	£1000
		Wi. Watermark inverted	£1900	£1100	
Set of 14			£650	£380	

* 213/14 **For well-centred, lightly used +50%**

The ½d. No. 213, in bright blue, is a colour changeling caused by a constituent of the ink used for some months in 1900.

PRICES. Please note that, with the exception of Government Parcels stamps, the price columns in this section are for mounted mint, used and used on cover examples. For Government Parcels they are for mint and used only.

KING EDWARD VII

22 January 1901 – 6 May 1910

PRINTINGS. Distinguishing De La Rue printings from the provisional printings of the same values made by Harrison & Sons Ltd. or at Somerset House may prove difficult in some cases. For very full guidance Volume 2 of the Stanley Gibbons *Great Britain Specialised Catalogue* should prove helpful.

Note that stamps perforated 15×14 must be Harrison; the 2½d., 3d. and 4d. in this perforation are useful reference material, their shades and appearance in most cases matching the Harrison perf 14 printings.

Except for the 6d. value, all stamps on chalk-surfaced paper were printed by De La Rue.

Of the stamps on ordinary paper, the De La Rue impressions are usually clearer and of a higher finish than those of the other printers. The shades are markedly different except in some printings of the 4d., 6d. and 7d. and in the 5s., 10s. and £1.

Used stamps in good, clean, unrubbed condition and with dated postmarks can form the basis of a useful reference collection, the dates often assisting in the assignment to the printers.

USED STAMPS. For well-centred, lightly used examples of King Edward VII stamps, add the following percentages to the used prices quoted below:

De La Rue printings (Nos. 215/266)—3d. values + 35%, 4d. orange + 100%, 6d. + 75%, 7d. and 1s. + 25%, all other values + 50%. *Harrison printings* (Nos. 267/286)—all values and perforations + 75%. *Somerset House printings* (Nos. 287/320)—1s. values + 25%, all other values + 50%.

83 84 85 86 87 88 89 90 91 92 93

94 95 96

97

Deformed tablet (Pl. D4, R. 5/9)

(Des E. Fuchs)

1902 (1 Jan)–**10**. Printed by De La Rue & Co. Wmk Imperial Crown W **49** (½d. to 1s. Three Crowns on £1); Large Anchor, W **40** (2s.6d. to 10s.). Ordinary paper. P 14.

			Mtd mint	*Used*	*Used on cover*
215	**83**	½d. dull blue-green (1.1.02)	2·00	1·50	2·50
		Wi. Watermark inverted	£2750	£2000	
216		½d. blue-green	2·00	1·50	
217		½d. pale yellowish green (26.11.04)	2·00	1·50	2·50
218		½d. yellowish green	2·00	1·50	
		a. Pair. No. 218 plus St Andrew's Cross label	£175	£200	
		aw. Pair. No. 218 Wi plus St Andrew's Cross label	£175	£200	
		b. Booklet pane. No. 218×5 plus St Andrew's Cross label	£700	£550	
		bw. Booklet pane. No. 218×5 plus St Andrew's Cross label. Wmk inverted	£700	£550	
		d. Doubly printed (bottom row on one pane) (Control H9)	£27500		
		Wi. Watermark inverted	12·00	9·00	
219		1d. scarlet (1.1.02)	2·00	1·50	2·50
220		1d. bright scarlet	2·00	1·50	
		a. Imperf (pair)	£35000		
		Wi. Watermark inverted	4·00	4·00	
221	**84**	1½d. dull purple and green (21.3.02)	50·00	24·00	
		a. Deformed leaf	£825	£425	
222		1½d. slate-purple and green	50·00	24·00	50·00
		Wi. Watermark inverted	—	£900	
223		1½d. pale dull purple and green (chalk-surfaced paper) (7.05)	45·00	24·00	
224		1½d. slate-purple and bluish green (chalk-surfaced paper)	45·00	22·00	
225	**85**	2d. yellowish green and carmine-red (25.3.02)	70·00	25·00	50·00
		Wi. Watermark inverted			
226		2d. grey-green and carmine-red (1904)	85·00	35·00	
227		2d. pale grey-green and carmine-red (chalk-surfaced paper) (4.06)	45·00	32·00	
		a. Deformed tablet	£1000	£750	
		Wi. Watermark inverted	£20000		
228		2d. pale grey-green and scarlet (chalk-surfaced paper) (1909)	45·00	32·00	
229		2d. dull blue-green and carmine (chalk-surfaced paper) (1907)	90·00	50·00	
230	**86**	2½d. ultramarine (1.1.02)	20·00	15·00	25·00
231		2½d. pale ultramarine	20·00	15·00	
		Wi. Watermark inverted	—	£4200	
232	**87**	3d. dull purple/orange-yellow (20.3.02)	50·00	18·00	35·00
		Wi. Watermark inverted			
		a. Chalk-surfaced paper (3.06)	£250	£100	
232*b*		3d. deep purple/orange-yellow	45·00	18·00	
232*c*		3d. pale reddish purple/orange-yellow (chalk-surfaced paper) (3.06)	£225	85·00	
233		3d. dull reddish purple/yellow (lemon back) (chalk-surfaced paper)	£225	85·00	
233*b*		3d. pale purple/lemon (chalk-surfaced paper)	45·00	20·00	
234		3d. purple/lemon (chalk-surfaced paper)	45·00	20·00	
235	**88**	4d. green and grey-brown (27.3.02)	70·00	35·00	
		Wi. Watermark inverted			
236		4d. green and chocolate-brown	70·00	35·00	
		a. Chalk-surfaced paper (1.06)	40·00	20·00	45·00
		Wi. watermark inverted		£9500	
238		4d. deep green and chocolate-brown (chalk-surfaced paper) (1.06)	40·00	20·00	
239		4d. brown-orange (1.11.09)	£180	£140	
240		4d. pale orange (12.09)	20·00	18·00	40·00
241		4d. orange-red (12.09)	25·00	20·00	
242	**89**	5d. dull purple and ultramarine (14.5.02)	65·00	22·00	50·00
		a. Chalk-surfaced paper (5.06)	60·00	22·00	
243		5d. slate-purple and ultramarine (14.5.02)	55·00	22·00	
		a. slate-purple and ultramarine (chalk-surfaced paper) (5.06)	55·00	22·00	
		as. Optd 'SPECIMEN' (17)	£700		
		Wi. Watermark inverted	£5500		
245	**83**	6d. pale dull purple (1.1.02)	45·00	22·00	60·00
		a. Chalk-surfaced paper (1.06)	45·00	22·00	
246		6d. slate-purple	45·00	22·00	
248		6d. dull purple (chalk-surfaced paper) (1.06)	45·00	22·00	
		Wi. Watermark inverted	—	£3500	
249	**90**	7d. grey-black (4.5.10)	15·00	22·00	£200
249*a*		7d. deep grey-black	£115	£100	
250	**91**	9d. dull purple and ultramarine (7.4.02)	£140	75·00	£250
		a. Chalk-surfaced paper (6.05)	£140	75·00	
		aWi. Watermark inverted	—	£3500	
251		9d. slate-purple and ultramarine	£140	75·00	
		a. Chalk-surfaced paper (6.05)	£120	75·00	
		as. Optd 'SPECIMEN' (17)	£725		
254	**92**	10d. dull purple and carmine (3.7.02)	£150	75·00	£225
		a. No cross on crown	£425	£300	
		b. Chalk-surfaced paper (9.06)	£140	75·00	
255		10d. slate-purple and carmine (chalk-surfaced paper) (9.06)	£140	75·00	
		a. No cross on crown	£450	£275	
256		10d. dull purple and scarlet (chalk-surfaced paper) (9.10)	£140	75·00	
		a. No cross on crown	£425	£250	
257	**93**	1s. dull green and carmine (24.3.02)	£100	40·00	£175
		a. Chalk-surfaced paper (9.05)	£100	40·00	
259		1s. dull green and scarlet (chalk-surfaced paper) (9.10)	£100	55·00	
260	**94**	2s.6d. lilac (5.4.02)	£280	£150	£1250
		s. Optd 'SPECIMEN' (15, 16)	£400		
		Wi. Watermark inverted	£5000	£3500	
261		2s.6d. pale dull purple (chalk-surfaced paper) (7.10.05)	£350	£180	
		Wi. Watermark inverted	£7500	£4250	
262		2s.6d. dull purple (chalk-surfaced paper)	£350	£180	
263	**95**	5s. bright carmine (5.4.02)	£450	£220	£1850
		s. Optd 'SPECIMEN'	£400		
		Wi. Watermark inverted	£65000	£5750	
264		5s. deep bright carmine	£450	£220	
265	**96**	10s. ultramarine (5.4.02)	£1000	£500	
		s. Optd 'SPECIMEN'	£500		
		Wi. Watermark inverted	£85000	£40000	
266	**97**	£1 dull blue-green (16.6.02)	£2000	£825	
		s. Optd 'SPECIMEN'	£1400		
		Wi. Watermark inverted	£110000	£24000	

97a

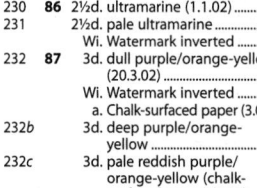

1910 (May). Prepared for use, by De La Rue but not issued. Wmk Imperial Crown, W **49**. P 14.

266*a*	**97a**	2d. Tyrian plum	£115000

One example of this stamp is known used, but it was never issued to the public.

1911. Printed by Harrison & Sons. Ordinary paper. Wmk Imperial Crown W **49**.

(a) P 14.

267	**83**	½d. dull yellow-green (3.5.11)	2·75	4·00	6·00
		a. Pair. No. 267 plus St Andrew's Cross label	£300	£300	
		aw. Pair. No. 267Wi plus St Andrew's Cross label	£300	£300	
		Wi. Watermark inverted	60·00	60·00	
268		½d. dull green	3·00	4·00	
269		½d. deep dull green	11·00	10·00	
270		½d. pale bluish green	40·00	40·00	
		a. Booklet pane. Five stamps plus St Andrew's Cross label	£800	£650	
		aw. Booklet pane. Five stamps plus St Andrew's Cross label. Wmk inverted	£800	£650	
		c. Watermark sideways	†	£35000	
		d. Imperf (pair)	£40000	†	
271		½d. bright green (fine impression) (6.11)	£275	£170	
272		1d. rose-red (3.5.11)	8·00	15·00	18·00
		a. No watermark (brick-red)	50·00	—	
		Wi. Watermark inverted	50·00	50·00	
273		1d. deep rose-red	8·00	15·00	
274		1d. rose-carmine	55·00	50·00	
275		1d. aniline pink (5.11)	£750	£400	
275*a*		1d. aniline rose	£180	£140	
276	**86**	2½d. bright blue (10.7.11)	65·00	38·00	55·00
		Wi. Watermark inverted	£1250		
277	**87**	3d. purple/*lemon* (12.9.11)	£150	£250	£550
277*a*		3d. grey/*lemon*	£4500		
278	**88**	4d. bright orange (12.7.11)	£120	55·00	£175
Set of 5			£290	£290	

(b) P 15×14.

279	**83**	½d. dull green (30.10.11)	40·00	45·00	£100
		Wi. Watermark inverted	†	£3500	
279*a*		½d. deep dull green	45·00	45·00	
280		1d. rose-red (4.10.11)	45·00	25·00	
281		1d. rose-carmine	15·00	15·00	30·00
		Wi. Watermark inverted	†	—	
282		1d. pale rose-carmine	22·00	15·00	
283	**86**	2½d. bright blue (14.10.11).	22·00	15·00	35·00
284		2½d. dull blue	22·00	15·00	
		Wi. Watermark inverted	—	£3000	
285	**87**	3d. purple/*lemon* (22.9.11)	45·00	15·00	40·00
285*a*		3d. grey/*lemon*	£3250		
286	**88**	4d. bright orange (11.11.11)	30·00	15·00	65·00
Set of 5			£130	90·00	

No. 272a was probably a trial printing.

1911–13. Printed at Somerset House. Ordinary paper. Wmk as 1902–1910. P 14.

287	**84**	1½d. reddish purple and bright green (13.7.11).	45·00	38·00	
288		1½d. dull purple and green	30·00	30·00	60·00
289		1½d. slate-purple and green (1.12)	30·00	30·00	
290	**85**	2d. deep dull green and red (8.8.11)	28·00	22·00	55·00
		a. Deformed tablet	£925	£550	
291		2d. deep dull green and carmine	30·00	25·00	
292		2d. grey-green and bright carmine (carmine shows clearly on back) (11.3.12)	28·00	28·00	
293	**89**	5d. dull reddish purple and bright blue (7.8.11)	30·00	22·00	65·00
294		5d. deep dull reddish purple and bright blue	30·00	22·00	
295	**83**	6d. royal purple (31.10.11)	50·00	90·00	
296		6d. bright magenta (chalk-surfaced paper) (31.10.11)	£12500		
297		6d. dull purple	30·00	22·00	90·00
298		6d. reddish purple (11.11)	30·00	28·00	
		a. No cross on crown (*various shades*)	£1200		
299		6d. very deep reddish purple (11.11)	55·00	45·00	
300		6d. dark purple (3.12)	35·00	28·00	
301		6d. dull purple 'Dickinson' coated paper* (3.13)	£250	£190	
303		6d. deep plum (chalk-surfaced paper) (7.13)	30·00	75·00	
		a. No cross on crown	£1250		
305	**90**	7d. slate-grey (1.8.12)	15·00	22·00	£200
306	**91**	9d. reddish purple and light blue (24.7.11)	95·00	75·00	
306*a*		9d. deep dull reddish purple and deep brt blue (9.11)	95·00	75·00	
307		9d. dull reddish purple and blue (10.11)	60·00	60·00	£190

No.	Type	Description	Unused	Used	Cover
307a		9d. deep plum and blue (7.13)	60·00	60·00	
308		9d. slate-purple and cobalt-blue (3.12)	£160	£110	
309	92	10d. dull purple and scarlet (9.10.11)	95·00	75·00	
310		10d. dull reddish purple and aniline pink	£275	£225	
311		10d. dull reddish purple and carmine (5.12)	80·00	60·00	£225
		a. No cross on crown	£1800		
312	93	1s. dark green and scarlet (13.7.11)	£120	60·00	
313		1s. deep green and scarlet (9.10.11)	80·00	40·00	
		Wi. Watermark inverted	£150	†	
314		1s. green and carmine (15.4.12)	60·00	35·00	£200
315	94	2s.6d. dull greyish purple (15.9.11)	£950	£450	
316		2s.6d. dull reddish purple	£300	£180	£1700
		Wi. Watermark inverted	†	—	
317		2s.6d. dark purple	£325	£190	
318	95	5s. carmine (29.2.12)	£425	£200	£1750
319	96	10s. blue (14.1.12)	£1100	£600	
320	97	£1 deep green (3.9.11)	£2000	£750	

* No. 301 was on an experimental coated paper which does not respond to the silver test.

King George V
6 May 1910 – 20 January 1936

Further detailed information on the issues of King George V will be found in Volume 2 of the Stanley Gibbons *Great Britain Specialised Catalogue*.

PRINTERS. Types 98 to 102 were letterpress printed by Harrison & Sons Ltd, with the exception of certain preliminary printings made at Somerset House and distinguishable by the controls 'A.11', 'B.11' or 'B.12' (the Harrison printings do not have a full stop after the letter). The booklet stamps, Nos. 334/7, and 344/5 were printed by Harrison only.

WATERMARK VARIETIES. Many British stamps to 1967 exist without watermark owing to misplacement of the paper, and with either inverted, reversed, or inverted and reversed watermarks. A proportion of the low-value stamps issued in booklets have the watermark inverted in the normal course of printing.

Low values with *watermark sideways* are normally from stamp rolls used on machines with sideways delivery or, from June 1940, certain booklets.

STAMPS WITHOUT WATERMARK. Stamps found without watermark, due to misplacement of the sheet in relation to the dandy roll, are not listed here but will be found in the *Great Britain Specialised Catalogue*.

The 1½d. and 5d. 1912–22, and ½d., 2d. and 2½d., 1924–26, listed here, are from whole sheets completely without watermark.

98

99

100 Simple Cypher

For type difference with T **101/2** see notes below the latter.

Die A

Die B

Dies of Halfpenny

Die A. The three upper scales on the body of the right hand dolphin form a triangle; the centre jewel of the cross inside the crown is suggested by a comma.

Die B. The three upper scales are incomplete; the centre jewel is suggested by a crescent.

Die A

Die B

Dies of One Penny

Die A. The second line of shading on the ribbon to the right of the crown extends right across the wreath; the line nearest to the crown on the right hand ribbon shows as a short line at the bottom of the ribbon.

Die B. The second line of shading is broken in the middle; the first line is little more than a dot.

(Des Bertram Mackennal and G. W. Eve. Head from photograph by W. and D. Downey. Die eng J. A. C. Harrison)

1911–12. Wmk Imperial Crown, W **49**. Perf 15×14.

No.	Type	Description	Unused	Used
321	98	½d. pale green (Die A) (22.6.11)	5·00	4·00
322		½d. green (Die A) (22.6.11)	4·00	4·00
		a. Error. Perf 14 (8.11)	£20000	£1000
		Wi. Watermark inverted	—	£2000
323		½d. bluish green (Die A)	£300	£180
324		½d. yellow-green (Die B)	12·00	1·50
325		½d. bright green (Die B)	8·00	1·50
		a. Watermark sideways	—	£5500
		Wi. Watermark inverted	20·00	7·50
326		½d. bluish green (Die B)	£160	£100
327	99	1d. carmine-red (Die A) (22.6.11)	4·50	2·50
		c. Watermark sideways	†	£17000
		Wi. Watermark inverted	£1500	£1250
328		1d. pale carmine (Die A) (22.6.11)	14·00	3·00
		a. No cross on crown	£850	£500
329		1d. carmine (Die B)	10·00	3·00
		Wi. Watermark inverted	20·00	7·50
330		1d. pale carmine (Die B)	10·00	4·00
		a. No cross on crown	£800	£500
331		1d. rose-pink (Die B)	£125	45·00
332		1d. scarlet (Die B) (6.12)	45·00	18·00
		Wi. Watermark inverted	45·00	18·00
333		1d. aniline scarlet (Die B)	£240	£110
		Wi. Watermark inverted	£240	£110

For note on the aniline scarlet No. 333 see below No. 343.

1912 (28 Sept). Booklet stamps. Wmk Royal Cypher ('Simple'), W **100**. Perf 15×14.

No.	Type	Description	Unused	Used
334	98	½d. pale green (Die B)	45·00	40·00
335		½d. green (Die B)	45·00	40·00
		Wi. Watermark inverted	45·00	40·00
		Wj. Watermark reversed	£1100	£800
		Wk. Watermark inverted and reversed	£1100	£800
336	99	1d. scarlet (Die B)	30·00	30·00
		Wi. Watermark inverted	30·00	30·00
		Wj. Watermark reversed	£1100	£800
		Wk. Watermark inverted and reversed	—	£850
337		1d. bright scarlet (Die B)	30·00	30·00

101

102

103 Multiple Cypher

Type differences

½d. In T **98** the ornament above 'P' of 'HALFPENNY' has two thin lines of colour and the beard is undefined. In T **101** the ornament has one thick line and the beard is well defined.

1d. In T **99** the body of the lion is unshaded and in T **102** it is shaded.

1912 (1 Jan). Wmk Imperial Crown, W **49**. Perf 15×14.

No.	Type	Description	Unused	Used
338	101	½d. deep green	15·00	8·00
339		½d. green	8·00	4·00
340		½d. yellow-green	8·00	4·00
		a. No cross on crown	£100	55·00
		Wi. Watermark inverted	£1100	£650
341	102	1d. bright scarlet	5·00	2·00
		a. No cross on crown	£110	55·00
		b. Printed double, one albino	£275	
		Wi. Watermark inverted	£425	£400
342		1d. scarlet	5·00	2·00
343		1d. aniline scarlet*	£175	£100
		a. No cross on crown	£1400	

* Our prices for the aniline scarlet 1d. stamps, Nos. 333 and 343, are for the specimens in which the colour is suffused on the surface of the stamp and shows through clearly on the back. Specimens without these characteristics but which show 'aniline' reactions under the quartz lamp are relatively common.

1912 (Aug). Wmk Royal Cypher (Simple), W **100**. Perf 15×14.

No.	Type	Description	Unused	Used
344	101	½d. green	7·00	3·00
		a. No cross on crown	£225	£175
		Wi. Watermark inverted	£375	£275
		Wj. Watermark reversed	£375	£275
		Wk. Watermark inverted and reversed	12·00	20·00
345	102	1d. scarlet	8·00	4·50
		a. No cross on crown	£100	50·00
		Wi. Watermark inverted	18·00	25·00
		Wj. Watermark reversed	£125	£125
		Wk. Watermark inverted and reversed	12·00	20·00

1912 (Sept). Wmk Royal Cypher ('Multiple'), W **103**. Perf 15×14.

No.	Type	Description	Unused	Used
346	101	½d. green (Oct)	12·00	8·00
		a. No cross on crown	£200	£150
		b. Imperf	£175	
		c. Watermark sideways	†	£4000
		d. Printed on gummed side	—	†
		Wi. Watermark inverted	12·00	20·00
		Wj. Watermark reversed	15·00	20·00
		Wk. Watermark inverted and reversed	£100	£110
347		½d. yellow-green	15·00	8·00
348		½d. pale green	15·00	8·00
349	102	1d. bright scarlet	18·00	10·00
350		1d. scarlet	18·00	10·00
		a. No cross on crown	£150	60·00
		b. Imperf	£150	
		c. Watermark sideways	£190	£220
		d. Watermark sideways. No cross on crown	£750	
		Wi. Watermark inverted	30·00	35·00
		Wj. Watermark reversed	30·00	35·00
		Wk. Watermark inverted and reversed	£1000	£650

104

105

106

107

108

No. 357a

No. 357ab

No. 357ac

Die I

Die II

Two Dies of the 2d.

Die I.— Inner frame-line at top and sides close to solid of background. *Four* complete lines of shading between top of head and oval frame-line. These four lines do *not* extend to the oval itself. White line round 'TWOPENCE' thin.

Die II.— Inner frame-line farther from solid of background. *Three* lines between top of head and extending to the oval. White line round 'TWOPENCE' thicker.

(Des Bertram Mackennal (heads) and G. W. Eve (frames). Coinage head (½, 1½, 2, 3 and 4d.); large medal head (1d., 2½d.); intermediate medal head (5d. to 1s.); small medal head used for fiscal stamps. Dies eng J. A. C. Harrison) (Letterpress by Harrison & Sons Ltd., except the 6d. printed by the Stamping Department of the Board of Inland Revenue, Somerset House. The latter also made printings of the following which can only be distinguished by the controls: ½d. B.13; 1½d. A.12; 2d. C.13; 2½d. A.12; 3d. A12, B.13, C.13; 4d. B.13; 5d. B.13; 7d. C.13; 8d. C.13; 9d. agate B.13; 10d. C.13; 1s. C.13)

1912–24. Wmk Royal Cypher ('Simple'), W **100**. Chalk-surfaced paper (6d.). Perf 15×14.

No.	Type	Description	Unused	Used
351	105	½d. green (16.1.13)	1·00	1·00
		a. Partial double print (half of bottom row) (Control G15)	£25000	
		b. Gummed both sides	—	—
		Wi. Watermark inverted	3·00	1·50
		Wj. Watermark reversed	55·00	60·00
		Wk. Watermark inverted and reversed	4·00	3·50
352		½d. bright green	1·00	1·00
353		½d. deep green	5·00	2·00
354		½d. yellow-green	6·00	3·00
355		½d. very yellow (Cyprus) green (1914)	£9000	†
356		½d. blue-green	40·00	25·00
357	104	1d. bright scarlet (8.10.12)	1·00	1·00
		a. 'Q' for 'O' (R. 1/4) (Control E14)	£175	£175
		ab. 'Q' for 'O' (R. 4/11) (Control T22)	£350	£190
		ac. Reversed 'Q' for 'O' (R. 15/9) (Control T22)	£300	£240
		ad. Inverted 'Q' for 'O' (R. 20/3)	£375	£240
		b. *Tête-bêche* (pair)	£80000	†
		Wi. Watermark inverted	2·00	1·00
		Wj. Watermark reversed	95·00	£110
		Wk. Watermark inverted and reversed	3·00	3·00
358		1d. vermilion	5·00	2·50
359		1d. pale rose-red	20·00	5·00
360		1d. carmine-red	11·00	5·00
361		1d. scarlet-vermilion	£125	50·00
		a. Printed on back	£300	†
362	105	1½d. red-brown (15.10.12)	6·00	1·50
		a. 'PENCF' (R. 15/12)	£300	£250
		b. Booklet pane. Four stamps plus two printed labels (2.24)	£600	£500
		bw. Booklet pane. Four stamps plus two printed labels, watermark inverted	£600	£500
		Wi. Watermark inverted	5·00	2·00
		Wj. Watermark reversed	50·00	50·00
		Wk. Watermark inverted and reversed	8·00	8·00
363		1½d. chocolate-brown	11·00	2·00
		a. No watermark	£240	£240
364		1½d. chestnut	3·00	1·00

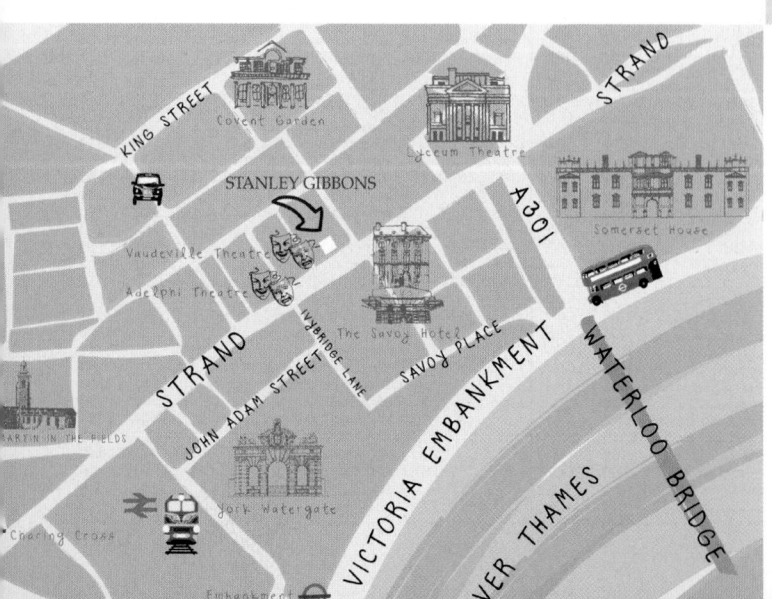

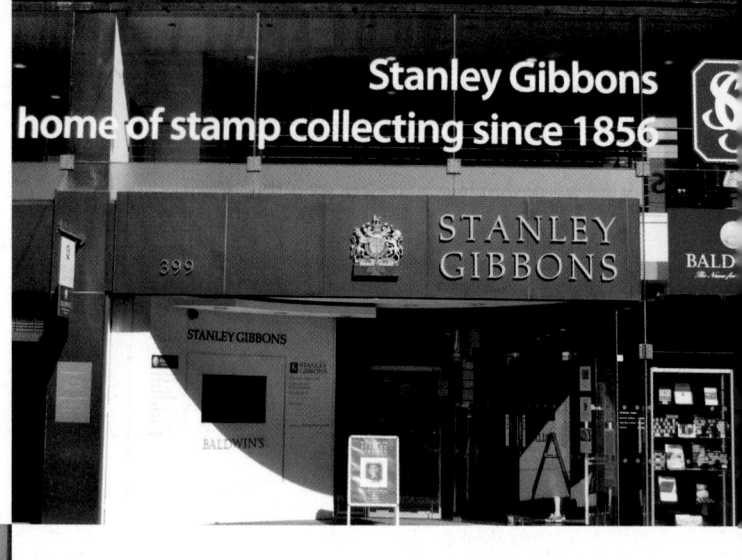

No.	Type	Description	Unused	Used
		a. 'PENCF' (R. 15/12)	£125	£110
365		1½d. yellow-brown	20·00	16·00
366	106	2d. orange-yellow (Die I) (20.8.12)	8·00	3·00
367		2d. reddish orange (Die I) (11.13)	6·00	3·00
368		2d. orange (Die I)	4·00	3·00
		Wi. Watermark inverted	12·00	12·00
		Wj. Watermark reversed	15·00	15·00
		Wk. Watermark inverted and reversed	10·00	10·00
369		2d. brt orange (Die I)	5·00	3·00
370		2d. orange (Die II) (9.21)	5·00	3·50
		Wi. Watermark inverted	40·00	40·00
		Wk. Watermark inverted and reversed	£140	£130
371	104	2½d. cobalt-blue (18.10.12)	12·00	4·00
371*a*		2½d. bright blue (1914)	12·00	4·00
372		2½d. blue	12·00	4·00
		Wi. Watermark inverted	85·00	85·00
		Wj. Watermark reversed	65·00	65·00
		Wk. Watermark inverted and reversed	28·00	28·00
373		2½d. indigo-blue* (1920)	£3500	£2500
373*a*		2½d. dull Prussian blue* (12.20)	£1500	£850
374	106	3d. dull reddish violet (9.10.12)	12·00	3·00
375		3d. violet	8·00	3·00
		Wi. Watermark inverted	95·00	£110
		Wj. Watermark reversed	£500	£500
		Wk. Watermark inverted and reversed	30·00	30·00
376		3d. bluish violet (11.13)	9·00	3·00
377		3d. pale violet	10·00	3·00
378		4d. deep grey-green (15.1.13)	45·00	25·00
379		4d. grey-green	15·00	2·00
		Wi. Watermark inverted	30·00	30·00
		Wj. Watermark reversed	£350	£350
		Wk. Watermark inverted and reversed	90·00	£100
380		4d. pale grey-green	25·00	5·00
381	107	5d. brown (30.6.13)	15·00	5·00
		Wi. Watermark inverted	£1200	£1100
		Wj. Watermark reversed	†	—
		Wk. Watermark inverted and reversed	£400	£400
382		5d. yellow-brown	15·00	5·00
		a. No watermark	£1200	
383		5d. bistre-brown	£185	75·00
384		6d. dull purple (1.8.13)	25·00	10·00
385		6d. reddish purple (8.13)	15·00	7·00
		a. Perf 14 (9.20)	90·00	£110
		Wi. Watermark inverted	50·00	60·00
		Wj. Watermark reversed	£4500	
		Wk. Watermark inverted and reversed	£100	£100
386		6d. deep reddish purple	50·00	5·00
387		7d. olive (1.8.13)	20·00	10·00
		Wi. Watermark inverted	50·00	60·00
		Wj. Watermark reversed	†	—
		Wk. Watermark inverted and reversed	£5000	
388		7d. bronze-green (1915)	70·00	25·00
389		7d. sage-green (1917)	70·00	18·00
390		8d. black/*yellow* (1.8.13)	32·00	11·00
		Wi. Watermark inverted	£150	£150
		Wj. Watermark reversed	£250	£250
		Wk. Watermark inverted and reversed	£5500	
391		8d. black/*yellow-buff* (granite) (5.17)	40·00	15·00
392	108	9d. agate (30.6.13)	15·00	6·00
		a. Printed double, one albino		
		Wi. Watermark inverted	£175	£175
		Wk. Watermark inverted and reversed	£175	£175
393		9d. deep agate	25·00	6·00
393*a*		9d. olive-green (9.22)	£110	30·00
		*a*Wi. Watermark inverted	£900	£825
		*a*Wk. Watermark inverted and reversed	£1100	£1000
393*b*		9d. pale olive-green	£120	40·00
394		10d. turquoise-blue (1.8.13)	22·00	20·00
		Wi. Watermark inverted	£3000	£2500
		Wk. Watermark inverted and reversed	£325	£300
394*a*		10d. deep turquoise-blue	90·00	30·00
395		1s. bistre (1.8.13)	20·00	4·00
		s. Optd 'SPECIMEN'	£375	
		Wi. Watermark inverted	£250	£225
		Wk. Watermark inverted and reversed	70·00	70·00
396		1s. bistre-brown	35·00	12·00
Set of 15			£250	95·00

Imperf stamps of this issue exist but may be war-time colour trials.

† The impression of No. 361a is set sideways and is very pale. Nos. 362a and 364a occur on Plates 12 and 29 and are known from Controls L18, M18, M19, O19 and Q21. The flaws were corrected by 1921.

* No. 373 comes from Control O20 and also exists on toned paper. No. 373*a* comes from Control R21 and also exists on toned paper, but both are unlike the rare Prussian blue shade of the 1935 2½d. Jubilee issue.

Examples of the 2d., T **106** which were in the hands of philatelists, are known bisected in Guernsey from 27 December 1940 to February 1941.

See also Nos. 418/29.

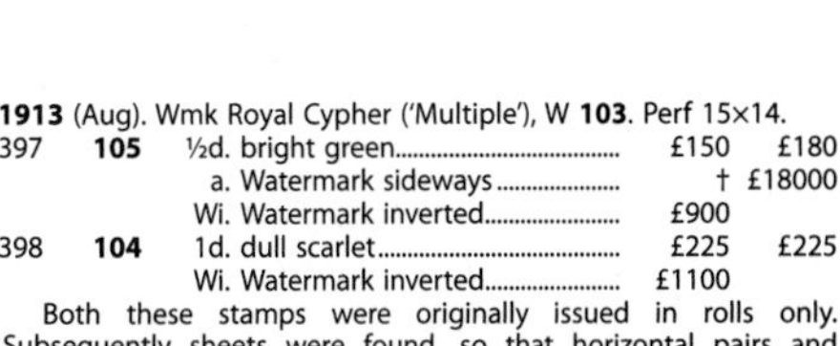

1913 (Aug). Wmk Royal Cypher ('Multiple'), W **103**. Perf 15×14.

No.	Type	Description	Unused	Used
397	105	½d. bright green	£150	£180
		a. Watermark sideways	†	£18000
		Wi. Watermark inverted	£900	
398	104	1d. dull scarlet	£225	£225
		Wi. Watermark inverted	£1100	

Both these stamps were originally issued in rolls only. Subsequently sheets were found, so that horizontal pairs and blocks are known but are of considerable rarity.

109

A

110 Single Cypher

Major Re-entries on 2s.6d.

Nos. 400a and 406/7a

No. 415b.

(Des Bertram Mackennal. Dies eng J. A. C. Harrison. Recess)

High values, so-called 'Sea Horses' design: T **109**. *Background around portrait consists of horizontal lines, Type A. Wmk Single Cypher, W* **110**. *P* 11×12.

1913 (30 June). Printed by Waterlow Bros & Layton.

No.	Type	Description	Unused	Used
399	109	2s.6d. deep sepia-brown	£400	£200
		s. Optd 'SPECIMEN' (23, 26)	£650	
400		2s.6d. sepia-brown	£300	£150
		a. Re-entry (Plate 3, R. 2/1)	£1800	£800
		Wk. Watermark inverted and reversed	†	—
401		5s. rose-carmine	£625	£325
		s. Optd 'SPECIMEN' (26)	£950	
402		10s. indigo-blue (1 Aug)	£1200	£475
		s. Optd 'SPECIMEN' (23, 26, 29)	£1200	
403		£1 green (1 Aug)	£3500	£1400
		s. Optd 'SPECIMEN' (23, 26)	£3250	
404		£1 dull blue-green (1 Aug)	£3500	£1600

* 399/404 **For well-centred, lightly used+35%**

1915 (Sept–Dec). Printed by De la Rue & Co.

No.	Type	Description	Unused	Used
405	109	2s.6d. deep yellow-brown (Oct)	£375	£250
		Wi. Watermark inverted	£1500	
406		2s.6d. yellow-brown (inc. worn plates)	£325	£225
		a. Re-entry (Plate 3, R. 2/1)	£2000	£950
		Wi. Watermark inverted	£1250	£875
		Wj. Watermark reversed	£1250	£1000
		Wk. Watermark inverted and reversed	£4000	
407		2s.6d. grey-brown (inc. worn plates)	£400	£300
		a. Re-entry (Plate 3, R. 2/1)	£2000	£950
		Wi. Watermark inverted	£1250	£1000
		Wj. Watermark reversed	£1250	£1000
408		2s.6d. sepia (seal-brown)	£325	£250
		Wi. Watermark inverted	£1250	£1000
		Wj. Watermark reversed	£1250	£1000
409		5s. bright carmine	£650	£400
		Wi. Watermark inverted	£4750	
		Wj. Watermark reversed	£4500	
		Wk. Watermark inverted and reversed	£18000	†
410		5s. pale carmine (worn plate)	£800	£500
411		10s. deep blue (Dec)	£3750	£1000
412		10s. blue	£3250	£875
		Wk. Watermark inverted and reversed	—	†
413		10s. pale blue	£3500	£875

* 405/13 **For well-centred, lightly used +45%**

No. 406/7 were produced from the original Waterlow plates as were all De La Rue 5s. and 10s. printings. Examples of No. 406/7, 410 and 411 occur showing degrees of plate wear. 412wi. one damaged mint example is recorded.

1918 (Dec)–**19**. Printed by Bradbury, Wilkinson & Co, Ltd.

No.	Type	Description	Unused	Used
413*a*	109	2s.6d. olive-brown	£190	£100
414		2s.6d. chocolate-brown	£160	75·00
415		2s.6d. reddish brown	£160	75·00
415*a*		2s.6d. pale brown	£175	85·00
		b. Major re-entry (Plate 3/5L, R. 1/2)	£1000	£500
416		5s. rose-red (1.19)	£325	£135
417		10s. dull grey-blue (1.19)	£475	£175
Set of 4 (inc. no. 403)			£4000	£1500

* 413*a*/17 **For well-centred, lightly used +35%**

DISTINGUISHING PRINTINGS. Note that the £1 value was only printed by Waterlow.

Waterlow and De La Rue stamps measure exactly 22.1 mm vertically. In the De La Rue printings the gum is usually patchy and yellowish, and the colour of the stamp, particularly in the 5s., tends to show through the back. The holes of the perforation are smaller than those of the other two printers, but there is a thick perforation tooth at the top of each vertical side.

In the Bradbury Wilkinson printings the height of the stamp is 22.6 – 23.1 mm due to the use of curved plates. On most of the 22.6 mm high stamps a minute coloured guide dot appears in the margin just above the middle of the upper frame-line.

For (1934) re-engraved Waterlow printings see Nos. 450/2.

UNITED KINGDOM OF GREAT BRITAIN AND NORTHERN IRELAND

111 Block Cypher

111a

The watermark T **111a**, as compared with T **111**, differs as follows: Closer spacing of horizontal rows (12½ mm instead of 14½ mm). Letters shorter and rounder. Watermark thicker. The dandy roll to produce watermark T **111a** was provided by Somerset House in connection with experiments in paper composition undertaken during 1924–1925. These resulted in a change from rag only paper to that made from a mixture including esparto and sulphite.

(Letterpress by Waterlow & Sons, Ltd (all values except 6d.) and later, 1934–1935, by Harrison & Sons, Ltd (all values). Until 1934 the 6d. was printed at Somerset House where a printing of the 1½d. was also made in 1926 (identifiable only by control E.26). Printings by Harrisons in 1934–1935 can be identified, when in mint condition, by the fact that the gum shows a streaky appearance vertically, the Waterlow gum being uniformly applied, but Harrisons also used up the balance of the Waterlow 'smooth gum' paper)

1924 (Feb)–**26**. Wmk Block Cypher, W **111**. Perf 15×14.

No.	Type	Description	Unused	Used
418	105	½d. green	1·00	1·00
		a. Watermark sideways (5.24)	9·00	3·25
		aWi. Watermark sideways inverted	£450	
		b. Doubly printed	£12000	†
		c. No watermark	—	—
		Wi. Watermark inverted	3·50	1·00
419	104	1d. scarlet	1·00	1·00
		a. Watermark sideways	20·00	15·00
		b. Experimental paper, W **111a** (10.24)	22·00	
		c. Partial double print, one inverted	—	
		d. Inverted 'Q' for 'O' (R. 20/3)	£500	
		Wi. Watermark inverted	4·00	1·50
420	105	1½d. red-brown	1·00	1·00
		a. *Tête-bêche* (pair)	£500	£800
		b. Watermark sideways (8.24)	10·00	3·50
		bWi. Watermark sideways inverted	£900	
		c. Printed on the gummed side	£750	
		d. Booklet pane. Four stamps plus two printed labels (3.24)	£225	£190
		dw. Booklet pane. Four stamps plus two printed labels, watermark inverted	£225	£190
		f. Booklet pane. Four stamps plus two printed labels, watermark sideways		
		g. Experimental paper, W **111a** (10.24)	£120	£120
		h. Double impression	—	†
		Wi. Watermark inverted	2·00	1·00
421	106	2d. orange (Die II) (7.24)	2·50	2·50
		a. No watermark	£1800	
		b. Watermark sideways (7.26)	£100	£100
		c. Partial double print	£35000	†
		Wi. Watermark inverted	55·00	55·00
422	104	2½d. blue (10.10.24)	5·00	3·00
		a. No watermark	£2800	
		b. Watermark sideways	†	£18000
		Wi. Watermark inverted	90·00	90·00
423	106	3d. violet (10.10.24)	10·00	2·50
		Wi. Watermark inverted	90·00	90·00
424		4d. grey-green (10.10.24)	12·00	2·50
		a. Printed on the gummed side	£4250	†
		Wi. Watermark inverted	£150	£150
425	107	5d. brown (17.10.24)	20·00	3·00
		Wi. Watermark inverted	£150	£150
426		6d. reddish purple (chalk-surfaced paper) (9.24)	12·00	2·50
		Wi. Watermark inverted	60·00	60·00
		Wk. Watermark inverted and reversed	£450	£400
426*a*		6d. purple (6.26)	4·00	1·50
		aWi. Watermark inverted	90·00	90·00
427	108	9d. olive-green (11.11.24)	12·00	3·50
		Wi. Watermark inverted	£120	£120
428		10d. turquoise-blue (28.11.24)	40·00	40·00
		Wi. Watermark inverted	£2750	£2400
429		1s. bistre-brown (10.24)	22·00	3·00
		Wi. Watermark inverted	£375	£375
418/429 *Set of* 12			£110	60·00

The normal sideways watermark shows the top of the Crown pointing to the right, *as seen from the back of the stamp.*

There are numerous shades in this issue.

The 6d. on chalk-surfaced and ordinary papers was printed by both Somerset House and Harrisons. The Harrison printings have streaky gum, differ slightly in shade, and that on chalk-surfaced paper is printed in a highly fugitive ink. The prices quoted are for the commonest (Harrison) printing in each case.

The dandy roll to produce watermark T **111a** was provided by Somerset House in connection with experiments in paper composition undertaken during 1924–1925. These resulted in a change from rag only paper to that made from a mixture including esparto and sulphite.

112

(Des H. Nelson. Eng J. A. C. Harrison. Recess Waterlow)

1924–25. 'British Empire Exhibition.' W **111**. Perf 14.

*(a) Dated '**1924**' (23.4.24).*

430	**112**	1d. scarlet	10·00	11·00
431		1½d. brown	15·00	15·00

*(b) Dated '**1925**' (9.5.25).*

432	**112**	1d. scarlet	15·00	30·00
433		1½d. brown	40·00	70·00

113

114

115

116 St George and the Dragon

117

Des J. Farleigh (T **113** and **115**), E. Linzell (T **114**) and H. Nelson (T **116**). Eng C. G. Lewis (T **113**), T. E. Storey (T **115**), both at the Royal Mint; J. A. C. Harrison, of Waterlow (T **114** and **116**). Letterpress by Waterlow from plates made at the Royal Mint, except T **116**, recess by Bradbury, Wilkinson from die and plate of their own manufacture

1929 (10 May). 'Ninth UPU Congress, London'.

*(a) W **111**. P 15×14.*

434	**113**	½d. green	2·25	2·25
		a. Watermark sideways	55·00	50·00
		Wi. Watermark inverted	15·00	12·00
435	**114**	1d. scarlet	2·25	2·25
		a. Watermark sideways	95·00	90·00
		Wi. Watermark inverted	15·00	12·00
436		1½d. purple-brown	2·25	1·75
		a. Watermark sideways	60·00	55·00
		b. Booklet pane. Four stamps plus two printed labels	£375	£325
		bw Booklet pane. Four stamps plus two printed labels, watermark inverted	£375	£325
		Wi. Watermark inverted	5·00	6·00
437	**115**	2½d. blue	10·00	10·00
		Wi. Watermark inverted	£2750	£1100

*(b) W **117**. P 12.*

438	**116**	£1 black	£750	£550
		s. Optd 'SPECIMEN' (32, red opt)	£3000	
Set of 4 (to 2½d.)			15·00	14·50

PRINTERS. All subsequent issues were printed in photogravure by Harrison & Sons Ltd *except where otherwise stated.*

118

119

120

121

122

1934–36. W **111**. Perf 15×14.

439	**118**	½d. green (17.11.34)	50	50
		a. Watermark sideways	10·00	5·00
		aWi. Watermark sideways inverted	£450	£150
		b. Imperf three sides	£5250	
		Wi. Watermark inverted	11·00	1·50
440	**119**	1d. scarlet (24.9.34)	50	50
		a. Imperf (pair)	£5000	
		b. Printed on gummed side	£750	
		c. Watermark sideways (30.4.35)	20·00	12·00
		cWi. Watermark sideways inverted	£125	—
		d. Double impression	†	£24000
		e. Imperf between (pair)	£8500	
		f. Imperf (three sides) (pair)	£7000	
		Wi. Watermark inverted	9·00	3·00
441	**118**	1½d. red-brown (20.8.34)	50	50
		a. Imperf (pair)	£1250	
		b. Imperf (three sides) (lower stamp in vert pair)	£4800	
		c. Imperf between (horiz pair)		
		d. Watermark sideways	10·00	5·00
		dWi. Watermark sideways inverted		
		e. Booklet pane. Four stamps plus two printed labels (1.35)	£200	£170
		ew. Booklet pane. Four stamps plus two printed labels, watermark inverted	£200	£170
		Wi. Watermark inverted	4·00	1·00
442	**120**	2d. orange (19.1.35)	75	75
		a. Imperf (pair)	£5750	
		b. Watermark sideways (30.4.35)	£125	90·00
443	**119**	2½d. bright blue (18.3.35)	1·50	1·25
444	**120**	3d. reddish violet (18.3.35)	1·50	1·25
		Wi. Watermark inverted	—	£9000
445		4d. deep grey-green (2.12.35)	2·00	1·25
		Wi. Watermark inverted	†	£9000
446	**121**	5d. yellow-brown (17.2.36)	6·50	2·75
447	**122**	9d. deep olive-green (2.12.35)	12·00	2·25
448		10d. turquoise-blue (24.2.36)	15·00	10·00
449		1s. bistre-brown (24.2.36)	15·00	1·25
		a. Double impression	—	†
		s. Optd 'SPECIMEN'	£125	
Set of 11			50·00	20·00

Owing to the need for wider space for the perforations the size of the designs of the ½d. and 2d. were once, and the 1d. and 1½d. twice reduced from that of the first printings.

The format description, size in millimetres and SG catalogue number are given but further details will be found in the *Great Britain Specialised Catalogue*, Volume 2.

The normal sideways watermark shows the top of the Crown pointing to the right, *as seen from the back of the stamp.*

The ½d. imperf three sides, No. 439b, is known in a block of four, from a sheet, to which the bottom pair is imperf at top and sides.

Description	*Size*	*SG Nos.*	*Date of Issue*
½d. intermediate format	18.4×22.2	—	19.11.34
½d. small format	17.9×21.7	439	14.2.35
1d. large format	18.7×22.5	—	24.9.34
1d. intermediate format	18.4×22.2	—	1934
1d. small format	17.9×21.7	440	8.2.35
1½d. large format	18.7×22.5	—	20.8.34
1½d. intermediate format	18.4×22.2	—	1934
1½d. small format	17.9×21.7	441	7.2.35
2d. intermediate format	18.4×22.2	—	21.1.35
2d. small format	18.15×21.7	442	1935

There are also numerous minor variations, due to the photographic element in the process.

Examples of 2d., T **120**, which were in the hands of philatelists are known bisected in Guernsey from 27 December 1940 to February 1941.

B

123

(Eng. J.A.C. Harrison. Recess Waterlow)

1934 (16 Oct). T **109** (re-engraved). Background around portrait consists of horizontal and diagonal lines, Type B. W **110**. Perf 11×12.

450	**109**	2s.6d. chocolate-brown	80·00	40·00
451		5s. bright rose-red	£175	85·00
452		10s. indigo	£350	80·00
Set of 3			£575	£190

There are numerous other minor differences in the design of this issue.

(Des B. Freedman)

1935 (7 May). 'Silver Jubilee.' W **111**. Perf 15×14.

453	**123**	½d. green	1·00	1·00
		Wi. Watermark inverted	8·00	3·00
454		1d. scarlet	1·50	2·00
		Wi. Watermark inverted	8·00	4·00
455		1½d. red-brown	1·00	1·00
		Wi. Watermark inverted	3·00	1·50
456		2½d. blue	5·00	6·50
456*a*		2½d. Prussian blue	£13750	£15000
453/456 *Set of* 4			7·50	9·50

The 1d., 1½d. and 2½d. values differ from T **123** in the emblem in the panel at right.

Four sheets of No. 456*a*, printed in the wrong shade, were issued in error by the Post Office Stores Department on 25 June 1935. It is known that three of the sheets were sold from the sub-office at 134 Fore Street, Upper Edmonton, London, between that date and 4 July.

King Edward VIII
20 January – 10 December 1936

Further detailed information on the stamps of King Edward VIII will be found in Volume 2 of the Stanley Gibbons *Great Britain Specialised Catalogue.*

PRICES. From S.G. 457 prices quoted in the first column are for stamps in unmounted mint condition.

124

125

(Des H. Brown, adapted Harrison using a photo by Hugh Cecil)

1936. W **125**. Perf 15×14.

457	**124**	½d. green (1.9.36)	30	30
		a. Double impression		
		Wi. Watermark inverted	10·00	5·00
458		1d. scarlet (14.9.36)	60	50
		Wi. Watermark inverted	9·00	5·00
459		1½d. red-brown (1.9.36)	30	30
		a. Booklet pane. Four stamps plus two printed labels (10.36)	£100	
		aw. Booklet pane. Four stamps plus two printed labels, watermark inverted	£100	
		d Imperf (pair)	£40000	
		Wi. Watermark inverted	1·00	1·00
460		2½d. bright blue (1.9.36)	30	85
Set of 4			1·25	1·75

KING GEORGE VI
11 December 1936 – 6 February 1952

Further detailed information on the stamps of King George VI will be found in Volume 2 of the Stanley Gibbons *Great Britain Specialised Catalogue.*

126 King George VI and Queen Elizabeth

127

Colon flaw (Cyl. 7 No dot, R. 10/1, later corrected)

(Des E. Dulac)

1937 (13 May). 'Coronation.' W **127**. Perf 15×14.

461	**126**	1½d. maroon	30	30
		a. Colon flaw	70·00	

128

129

130

King George VI and National Emblems

(Des Types **128/9**, E. Dulac (head) and E. Gill (frames). T **130**, E. Dulac (whole stamp))

1937–47. W **127**. Perf 15×14.

462	**128**	½d. green (10.5.37)	30	25
		a. Watermark sideways (1.38)	75	60
		ab. Booklet pane of 4 (6.40)	£110	
		Wi. Watermark inverted	10·00	60
463		1d. scarlet (10.5.37)	30	25
		a. Watermark sideways (2.38)	20·00	9·00
		ab. Booklet pane of 4 (6.40)	£175	

		Wi. Watermark inverted	40·00	3·00
464		1½d. red-brown (30.7.37)	30	25
		a. Watermark sideways (2.38)	1·25	1·25
		b. Booklet pane. Four stamps plus two printed labels (8.37)	£140	
		bw. Booklet pane. Four stamps plus two printed labels. Watermark inverted	£140	
		e. Imperf three sides (pair)	£6500	
		Wi. Watermark inverted	15·00	1·25
465		2d. orange (31.1.38)	1·20	50
		a. Watermark sideways (2.38)	75·00	40·00
		b. Bisected (*on cover*)	†	50·00
		Wi. Watermark inverted	60·00	22·00
466		2½d. ultramarine (10.5.37)	40	25
		a. Watermark sideways (6.40)	75·00	35·00
		b. *Tête-bêche* (horiz pair)	£22000	
		Wi. Watermark inverted	55·00	22·00
467		3d. violet (31.1.38)	5·00	1·00
468	**129**	4d. grey-green (21.11.38)	60	75
		a. Imperf (pair)	£9000	
		b. Imperf three sides (horiz pair)	£9500	
469		5d. brown (21.11.38)	3·50	85
		a. Imperf (pair)	£8500	
		b. Imperf three sides (horiz pair)	£9000	
470		6d. purple (30.1.39)	1·50	60
471	**130**	7d. emerald-green (27.2.39)	5·00	60
		a. Imperf three sides (horiz pair)	£9000	
472		8d. bright carmine (27.2.39)	7·50	80
473		9d. deep olive-green (1.5.39)	6·50	80
474		10d. turquoise-blue (1.5.39)	7·00	80
		aa. Imperf (pair)		
474*a*		11d. plum (29.12.47)	3·00	2·75
475		1s. bistre-brown (1.5.39)	9·00	75
		s. Optd 'SPECIMEN'	£160	
Set of 15			45·00	10·00

For later printings of the lower values in apparently lighter shades and different colours, see Nos. 485/490 and 503/508.

No. 465b was authorised for use in Guernsey from 27 December 1940 until February 1941.

Nos. 468b and 469b are perforated at foot only and each occurs in the same sheet as Nos. 468a and 469a.

No. 471a is also perforated at foot only, but occurs on the top row of a sheet.

131

132

133

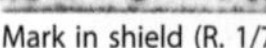
Mark in shield (R. 1/7)

Gashed diadem (R. 2/7)

Gashed crown (R. 5/5)

Broken stem (R. 1/4)

Blot on scroll (R. 2/5)

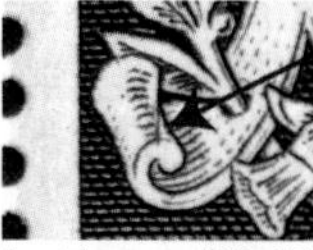
Scratch on scroll (R. 4/6)

(Des E. Dulac (T **131**) and Hon. G. R. Bellew (T **132**). Eng J. A. C. Harrison. Recess Waterlow)

1939–48. W **133**. Perf 14.

476	**131**	2s.6d. brown (4.9.39)	£100	8·00
		aa. Mark in shield	£190	85·00
		ab. Gashed diadem	£190	85·00
		ac. Gashed crown	£190	85·00
		as. Optd 'SPECIMEN' (23)	£300	
476*b*		2s.6d. yellow-green (9.3.42)	15·00	1·50
		bs. Optd 'SPECIMEN' (23)	£300	
477		5s. red (21.8.39)	20·00	2·00
		s. Optd 'SPECIMEN' (23)	£300	
478	**132**	10s. dark blue (30.10.39)	£260	22·00
		aa. Broken stem	£275	80·00
		ab. Blot on scroll	£275	80·00
		ac. Scratch on scroll	£350	£100
		as. Optd 'SPECIMEN' (23)	£500	
478*b*		10s. ultramarine (30.11.42)	45·00	5·00
		bs. Optd 'SPECIMEN' (30)	£425	
478*c*		£1 brown (1.10.48)	25·00	26·00
		cs. Optd 'SPECIMEN' (30)	—	
Set of 6			£425	60·00

134 Queen Victoria and King George VI

(Des H. L. Palmer)

1940 (6 May). Centenary of First Adhesive Postage Stamps. W **127**. P 14½×14.

479	**134**	½d. green	30	75
480		1d. scarlet	1·00	75
481		1½d. red-brown	50	1·50
482		2d. orange	1·00	75
		a. Bisected (*on cover*)	†	40·00
483		2½d. ultramarine	2·25	50
484		3d. violet	3·00	3·50
479/84 *Set of* 6			8·75	5·25

No. 482a was authorised for use in Guernsey. See notes on War Occupation Issues.

1941–42. Head as Nos. 462/7, but with lighter background to provide a more economic use of the printing ink. W **127**. Perf 15×14.

485	**128**	½d. pale green (1.9.41)	30	30
		a. *Tête-bêche* (horiz pair)	£18000	
		b. Imperf (pair)	£8500	
		Wi. Watermark inverted	4·00	50
486		1d. pale scarlet (11.8.41)	30	30
		a. Watermark sideways (10.42)	5·00	4·50
		b. Imperf (pair)	£8000	
		c. Imperf three sides (horiz pair)	£8500	
487		1½d. pale red-brown (28.9.42)	60	80
488		2d. pale orange (6.10.41)	50	50
		a. Watermark sideways (6.42)	28·00	19·00
		b. *Tête-bêche* (horiz pair)	£18000	
		c. Imperf (pair)	£7500	
		d. Imperf pane*	£20000	
		Wi. Watermark inverted	4·00	1·00
489		2½d. light ultramarine (21.7.41)	30	30
		a. Watermark sideways (8.42)	15·00	12·00
		b. *Tête-bêche* (horiz pair)	£18000	
		c. Imperf (pair)	£4800	
		d. Imperf pane*	£15000	
		e. Imperf three sides (horiz pair)	£7500	
		Wi. Watermark inverted	1·50	1·00
490		3d. pale violet (3.11.41)	2·50	1·00
Set of 6			3·50	2·75

135

136

Extra porthole aft (Cyl. 11 No dot, R. 16/1)

Extra porthole fore (Cyl. 8 Dot, R. 5/6)

Seven berries (Cyl. 4 No dot, R. 12/5)

(Des H. L. Palmer (T **135**) and R. Stone (T **136**))

1946 (11 June). 'Peace.' W **127**. Perf 15×14.

491	**135**	2½d. ultramarine	20	20
		a. Extra porthole aft	95·00	
		b. Extra porthole fore	£120	
492	**136**	3d. violet	20	50
		a. Seven berries	35·00	

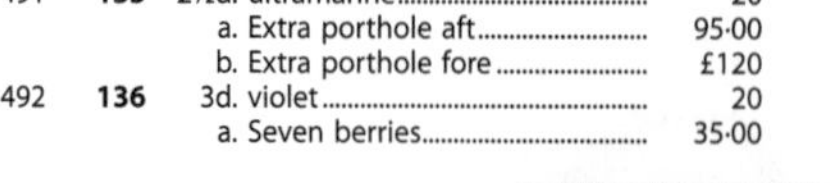

137

138 King George VI and Queen Elizabeth

(Des G. Knipe and Joan Hassall from photographs by Dorothy Wilding)

1948 (26 Apr). 'Royal Silver Wedding.' W **127**. Perf 15×14 (2½d.) or 14×15 (£1).

493	**137**	2½d. ultramarine	35	20
494	**138**	£1 blue	40·00	40·00

1948 (10 May). Stamps of 1d. and 2½d. showing seaweed-gathering were on sale at eight Head Post Offices in Great Britain, but were primarily for use in the Channel Islands and are listed there (see after Great Britain Postal Fiscals).

139 Globe and Laurel Wreath

140 'Speed'

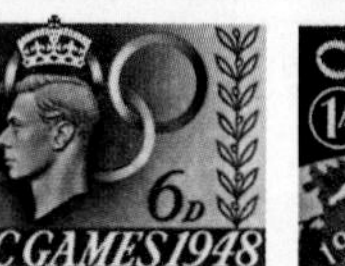

141 Olympic Symbol

142 Winged Victory

Crown flaw (Cyl. 1 No dot, R. 20/2, later retouched)

(Des P. Metcalfe (T **139**), A. Games (T **140**), S. D. Scott (T **141**) and E. Dulac (T **142**))

1948 (29 July). 'Olympic Games.' W **127**. Perf 15×14.

495	**139**	2½d. ultramarine	50	10
496	**140**	3d. violet	50	50
		a. Crown flaw	75·00	
497	**141**	6d. bright purple	3·25	75
498	**142**	1s. brown	4·50	2·00
495/475 *Set of* 4			8·00	3·00

143 Two Hemispheres

144 UPU Monument, Berne

145 Goddess Concordia, Globe and Points of Compass

146 Posthorn and Globe

Lake in Asia (Cyl. 3 Dot, R. 14/1)

Lake in India (Cyl. 2 No dot, R. 8/2)

(Des Mary Adshead (T **143**), P. Metcalfe (T **144**), H. Fleury (T **145**) and Hon. G. R. Bellew (T **146**))

1949 (10 Oct). '75th Anniversary of Universal Postal Union.' W **127**. Perf 15×14.

499	**143**	2½d. ultramarine	25	10
		a. Lake in Asia	£145	
		b. Lake in India	£100	
500	**144**	3d. violet	25	50
501	**145**	6d. bright purple	50	75
502	**146**	1s. brown	1·00	1·25
499/502 *Set of* 4			1·50	2·50

1950–52. 4d. as No. 468 and others as Nos. 485/9, but colours changed. W **127**. Perf 15×14.

503	**128**	½d. pale orange (3.5.51)	30	30
		a. Imperf (pair)	£7000	
		b. *Tête-bêche* (horiz pair)	£20000	
		c. Imperf pane*	£18000	
		Wi. Watermark inverted	50	50
504		1d. light ultramarine (3.5.51)	30	30
		a. Watermark sideways (5.51)	1·10	1·25
		b. Imperf (pair)	£4800	
		c. Imperf three sides (horiz pair)	£6500	
		d. Booklet pane. Three stamps plus three printed labels (3.52)	18·00	
		dw. Booklet pane. Three stamps plus three printed labels. Watermark inverted	18·00	
		e. Booklet pane. Three stamps plus three printed labels. Watermark inverted. Partial *tête-bêche* pane	£8500	
		Wi. Watermark inverted	4·50	2·50
505		1½d. pale green (3.5.51)	65	60
		a. Watermark sideways (9.51)	3·25	5·00
		Wi. Watermark inverted	6·00	1·00
506		2d. pale red-brown (3.5.51)	75	40
		a. Watermark sideways (5.51)	1·75	2·00
		b. *Tête-bêche* (horiz pair)	£18000	
		c. Imperf three sides (horiz pair)	£8000	
		Wi. Watermark inverted	6·00	6·50
507		2½d. pale scarlet (3.5.51)	60	40
		a. Watermark sideways (5.51)	1·75	1·75
		b. *Tête-bêche* (horiz pair)		
		Wi. Watermark inverted	2·00	1·25
508	**129**	4d. light ultramarine (2.10.50)	2·00	1·75
		a. Double impression	†	£7000
Set of 6			4·00	3·25

* BOOKLET ERRORS. Those listed as 'imperf panes' show one row of perforations either at the top or at the bottom of the pane of 6.

No. 504c is perforated at foot only and occurs in the same sheet as No. 504b.

No. 506c is also perforated at foot only.

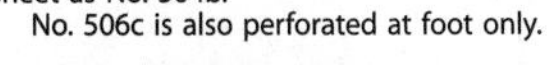

147 HMS *Victory*

148 White Cliffs of Dover

149 St George and the Dragon

150 Royal Coat of Arms

(Des Mary Adshead (T **147/8**), P. Metcalfe (T **149/50**). Recess Waterlow)

1951 (3 May). W **133**. P 11×12.

509	**147**	2s.6d. yellow-green	7·50	1·00
510	**148**	5s. red	35·00	1·00
511	**149**	10s. ultramarine	15·00	7·50
512	**150**	£1 brown	45·00	18·00
Set of 4			£100	25·00

151 'Commerce and Prosperity'

152 Festival Symbol

(Des E. Dulac (T **151**), A. Games (T **152**))

1951 (3 May). 'Festival of Britain.' W **127**. P 15×14.

513	**151**	2½d. scarlet	20	15
514	**152**	4d. ultramarine	30	35

USED PRICES. For Nos. 515 onwards the used prices quoted are for examples with circular dated postmarks.

Queen Elizabeth II
6 February 1952

Further detailed information on the stamps of Queen Elizabeth II will be found in Volumes 3, 4 and 5 of the Stanley Gibbons *Great Britain Specialised Catalogue*.

153 Tudor Crown

154

155

156

157

158

159

160

Queen Elizabeth II and National Emblems

I II

Two types of the 2½d.

Type I:— In the frontal cross of the diadem, the top line is only half the width of the cross.

Type II:— The top line extends to the full width of the cross and there are signs of strengthening in other parts of the diadem.

(Des Enid Marx (T **154**), M. Farrar-Bell (Types **155/156**), G. Knipe (T **157**), Mary Adshead (T **158**), E. Dulac (Types **159/160**). Portrait by Dorothy Wilding)

1952–54. W **153**. Perf 15×14.

515	**154**	½d. orange-red (31.8.53)	25	15
		Wi. Watermark inverted (3.54)	2·00	2·00
516		1d. ultramarine (31.8.53)	30	20
		a. Booklet pane. Three stamps plus three printed labels	40·00	
		aw. Booklet pane. Three stamps plus three printed labels. watermark inverted	35·00	
		Wi. Watermark inverted (3.54)	6·00	3·00
517		1½d. green (5.12.52)	25	20
		a. Watermark sideways (15.10.54)	1·20	1·20
		b. Imperf pane*		
		Wi. Watermark inverted (5.53)	1·30	1·30
518		2d. red-brown (31.8.53)	30	20
		a. Watermark sideways (8.10.54)	2·00	2·00
		Wi. Watermark inverted (3.54)	30·00	22·00
519	**155**	2½d. carmine-red (Type I) (5.12.52)	30	15
		a. Watermark sideways (15.11.54)	12·00	12·00
		b. Type II (booklets) (5.53)	1·30	1·30
		bWi. Watermark inverted (5.53)	1·00	1·00
520		3d. deep lilac (18.1.54)	1·50	90
521	**156**	4d. ultramarine (2.11.53)	3·25	1·30
522	**157**	5d. brown (6.7.53)	1·00	3·50
523		6d. reddish purple (18.1.54)	4·00	1·00
		a. Imperf three sides (pair)	£3750	
524		7d. bright green (18.1.54)	9·50	5·50
525	**158**	8d. magenta (6.7.53)	1·25	85
526		9d. bronze-green (8.2.54)	23·00	4·75
527		10d. Prussian blue (8.2.54)	18·00	4·75
528		11d. brown-purple (8.2.54)	35·00	15·00
529	**159**	1s. bistre-brown (6.7.53)	80	50
530	**160**	1s.3d. green (2.11.53)	4·50	3·25
531		1s.6d. grey-blue (2.11.53)	14·00	3·75
515/531 *Set of 17*			£100	40·00

* BOOKLET ERRORS. This pane of 6 stamps is completely imperf (see No. 540a, etc).

Stamps with *sideways watermark* come from left-side delivery coils and stamps with *inverted watermark* are from booklets.

See also Nos. 540/56, 561/6, 570/94 and 599/618a.

161

162

163

164

(Des E. Fuller (2½d.), M. Goaman (4d.), E. Dulac (1s.3d.), M. Farrar-Bell (1s.6d.). Portrait (except 1s.3d.) by Dorothy Wilding)

1953 (3 June). Coronation. W **153**. Perf 15×14.

532	**161**	2½d. carmine-red	20	20
533	**162**	4d. ultramarine	80	40
534	**163**	1s.3d. deep yellow-green	3·00	1·00
535	**164**	1s.6d. deep grey-blue	6·50	2.00
532/535 *Set of 4*			10·00	3·50

165 St Edward's Crown

166 Carrickfergus Castle

167 Caernarvon Castle

168 Edinburgh Castle

169 Windsor Castle

(Des L. Lamb. Portrait by Dorothy Wilding. Recess Waterlow (until 31.12.57) and De La Rue (subsequently))

1955–58. W **165**. Perf 11×12.

536	**166**	2s.6d. black-brown (23.9.55)	15·00	2·00
		a. De La Rue printing (17.7.58)	30·00	2·50
		Wi. Watermark inverted	†	£3000
537	**167**	5s. rose-carmine (23.9.55)	40·00	4·00
		a. De La Rue printing. *Scarlet-vermilion* (30.4.58)	65·00	10·00
538	**168**	10s. ultramarine (1.9.55)	90·00	14·00
		a. De La Rue printing. *Dull ultramarine* (25.4.58)	£225	22·00
539	**169**	£1 black (1.9.55)	£140	35·00
		a. De La Rue printing (28.4.58)	£350	65·00
Set of 4 (Nos. 536/9)			£250	50·00
Set of 4 (Nos. 536a/9a)			£600	90·00

See also Nos. 595/8a & 759/62.

On 1 January 1958, the contract for printing the high values, Types **166** to **169**, was transferred to De La Rue & Co, Ltd. The work of the two printers is very similar, but the following notes will be helpful to those attempting to identify Waterlow and De La Rue stamps of the W **165** issue.

The De La Rue sheets are printed in pairs and have a -| or |-shaped guide-mark at the centre of one side-margin, opposite the middle row of perforations, indicating left and right-hand sheets respectively.

The Waterlow sheets have a small circle (sometimes crossed) instead of a '|-' and this is present in both side-margins opposite the 6th row of stamps, though one is sometimes trimmed off. Short dashes are also present in the perforation gutter between the marginal stamps marking the middle of the four sides and a cross is at the centre of the sheet. The four corners of the sheet have two lines forming a right-angle as trimming marks, but some are usually trimmed off. All these gutter marks and sheet trimming marks are absent in the De La Rue printings. De La Rue used the Waterlow die and no alterations were made to it, so that no difference exists in the design or its size, but the making of new plates at first resulted in slight but measurable variations in the width of the gutters between stamps, particularly the horizontal, as follows:

	Waterlow	De La Rue
Horiz gutters, mm	3.8 to 4.0	3.4 to 3.8

Later D.L.R. plates were however less distinguishable in this respect.

For a short time in 1959 the D.L.R. 2s.6d. appeared with one dot in the bottom margin below the first stamp.

It is possible to sort singles with reasonable certainty by general characteristics. The individual lines of the D.L.R. impression are cleaner and devoid of the whiskers of colour of Waterlow's, and the whole impression lighter and softer.

Owing to the closer setting of the horizontal rows the strokes of the perforating comb are closer; this results in the topmost tooth on each side of De La Rue stamps being narrower than the corresponding teeth in Waterlow's which were more than normally broad.

Shades also help. The 2s.6d. D.L.R. is a warmer, more chocolate shade than the blackish brown of Waterlow; the 5s. a lighter red with less carmine than Waterlow's; the 10s. more blue and less ultramarine; the £1 less intense black.

The paper of D.L.R. printings is uniformly white, identical with that of Waterlow printings from February 1957 onwards, but earlier Waterlow printings are on paper which is creamy by comparison.

In this and later issues of Types **166/9** the dates of issue given for changes of watermark or paper are those on which supplies were first sent by the Supplies Department to Postmasters.

A used example of No. 538a has been reported with watermark inverted.

1955–58. W **165**. Perf 15×14.

540	**154**	½d. orange-red (booklets 8.55, sheets 12.12.55)	20	15
		a. Part perf pane*	£5250	
		Wi. Watermark inverted (9.55)	45	40
541		1d. ultramarine (19.9.55)	30	15
		a. Booklet pane. Three stamps plus three printed labels	18·00	
		aw. Booklet pane. Three stamps plus three printed labels. watermark inverted	18·00	
		b. *Tête-bêche* (horiz pair)		
		Wi. Watermark inverted (9.55)	65	60
542		1½d. green (booklet 8.55, sheets 11.10.55)	25	30
		a. Watermark sideways (7.3.56)	35	70
		b. *Tête-bêche* (horiz pair)	—	
		Wi. Watermark inverted (8.55)	75	70
543		2d. red-brown (6.9.55)	25	35
		aa. Imperf between (vert pair)	£4750	
		a. Watermark sideways (31.7.56)	55	70
		ab. Imperf between (horiz pair)	£4750	
		Wi. Watermark inverted (9.55)	11·00	9·00
543*b*		2d. light red-brown (17.10.56)	30	20
		ba. *Tête-bêche* (horiz pair)	—	
		bb. Imperf pane*	£6000	
		bc. Part perf pane*	£6000	
		bWi. Watermark inverted (1.57)	9·00	7·00
		d. Watermark sideways (5.3.57)	8·00	7·00
544	**155**	2½d. carmine-red (Type I) (28.9.55)	30	25
		a. Watermark sideways (Type I) (23.3.56)	1·50	1·80
		b. Type II (booklets 9.55, sheets 1957)	45	45
		ba. *Tête-bêche* (horiz pair)	—	
		bb. Imperf pane*	—	
		bc. Part perf pane*	£5250	
		bWi. Watermark inverted (9.55)	55	70
545		3d. deep lilac (17.7.56)	40	25
		aa. *Tête-bêche* (horiz pair)	£3000	
		a. Imperf three sides (pair)	£2750	
		b. Watermark sideways (22.11.57)	18·00	17·00
		Wi. Watermark inverted (1.10.57)	1·25	1·25
546	**156**	4d. ultramarine (14.11.55)	1·30	45
547	**157**	5d. brown (21.9.55)	6·00	6·00
548		6d. reddish purple (20.12.55)	4·50	1·20
		aa. Imperf three sides (pair)	£5250	
		a. Deep claret (8.5.58)	4·50	1·40
		ab. Imperf three sides (pair)	£5250	
549		7d. bright green (23.4.56)	50·00	10·00
550	**158**	8d. magenta (21.12.55)	7·00	1·30
551		9d. bronze-green (15.12.55)	20·00	2·75
552		10d. Prussian blue (22.9.55)	20·00	2·75
553		11d. brown-purple (28.10.55)	1·00	1·10
554	**159**	1s. bistre-brown (3.11.55)	22·00	65
555		1s.3d. green (27.3.56)	30·00	1·60
556	**160**	1s.6d. grey-blue (27.3.56)	23·00	1·60
540/556 *Set of 18*			£160	27·00

The dates given for Nos. 540/556 are those on which they were first issued by the Supplies Dept to postmasters.

In December 1956 a completely imperforate sheet of No. 543*b* was noticed by clerks in a Kent post office, one of whom purchased it against P.O. regulations. In view of this irregularity we do not consider it properly issued.

Types of 2½d. In this issue, in 1957, Type II formerly only found in stamps from booklets, began to replace Type I on sheet stamps.

* BOOKLET ERRORS. Those listed as 'imperf panes' show one row of perforations either at top or bottom of the booklet pane; those as 'part perf panes' have one row of 3 stamps imperf on three sides.

170 Scout Badge and 'Rolling Hitch'

171 'Scouts coming to Britain'

172 Globe within a Compass

(Des Mary Adshead (2½d.), P. Keely (4d.), W. H. Brown (1s.3d.))

1957 (1 Aug). 'World Scout Jubilee Jamboree.' W **165**. Perf 15×14.

557	**170**	2½d. carmine-red	20	20
558	**171**	4d. ultramarine	50	50
559	**172**	1s.3d. green	3·00	2·00
557/559 *Set of 3*			3·50	2·50

173

½d. to 1½d., 2½d., 3d.

2d.

Graphite line arrangements (Stamps viewed from back)

(Adapted F. Langfield)

1957 (12 Sept). 46th Inter-Parliamentary Union Conference. W **165**. Perf 15×14.

560	**173**	4d. ultramarine	40	40

GRAPHITE-LINED ISSUES. These were used in connection with automatic sorting machinery, first introduced experimentally at Southampton in December 1957.

The graphite lines were printed in black on the back, beneath the gum; two lines per stamp, except for the 2d.

In November 1959 phosphor bands were introduced (see notes after No. 598).

1957 (19 Nov). Graphite-lined issue. Two graphite lines on the back, except 2d. value, which has one line. W **165**. Perf 15×14.

561	**154**	½d. orange-red	50	40
562		1d. ultramarine	70	60
563		1½d. green	2·00	1·75
		a. Both lines at left	£1600	£600
564		2d. light red-brown	2·40	2·40
		a. Line at left	£700	£250
565	**155**	2½d. carmine-red (Type II)	8·50	7·00
566		3d. deep lilac	1·40	1·20
561/566 *Set of 6*			14·00	12·00

No. 564a results from a misplacement of the line and horizontal pairs exist showing one stamp without line. No. 563a results from a similar misplacement.

See also Nos. 587/94.

176 Welsh Dragon

177 Flag and Games Emblem

178 Welsh Dragon

(Des R. Stone (3d.), W. H. Brown (6d.), P. Keely (1s.3d.))

1958 (18 July). Sixth British Empire and Commonwealth Games, Cardiff. W **165**. Perf 15×14.

567	**176**	3d. deep lilac	10	10
568	**177**	6d. reddish purple	30	30
569	**178**	1s.3d. green	1.00	1.00
Set of 3			1.20	1.20

179 Multiple Crowns

1958–65. W **179**. Perf 15×14.

570	**154**	½d. orange-red (25.11.58)	10	10
		a. Watermark sideways (26.5.61)	75	75
		c. Part perf pane*	£4500	
		Wi. Watermark inverted (11.58)	1·50	1·50
		k. Chalk-surfaced paper (15.7.63)	2·50	2·75
		kWi. Watermark inverted	2·75	3·00
		l. Booklet pane. No. 570a×4	7·50	
		m. Booklet pane. No. 570k×3 *se-tenant* with 574k	9·00	
		n. Booklet pane. No. 570a×2 *se-tenant* with 574l×2 (1.7.64)	2·25	
571		1d. ultramarine (booklets 11.58, sheets 24.3.59)	10	10
		aa. Imperf (vert pair from coil)		
		a. Watermark sideways (26.5.61)	1·50	1·50
		b. Part perf pane*	£5000	
		c. Imperf pane	£6500	
		d. *Tête-bêche* (horiz pair)		
		Wi. Watermark inverted (11.58)	50	50
		l. Booklet pane. No. 571a×4	12·00	
		m. Booklet pane. No. 571a×2 *se-tenant* with 575a×2 (1d. values at left) (16.8.65)	12·00	
		ma. Ditto. 1d. values at right	13·00	
572		1½d. green (booklets 12.58, sheets 30.8.60)	10	15
		a. Imperf three sides (horiz strip of 3)	£8500	
		b. Watermark sideways (26.5.61)	9·00	9·00
		c. *Tête-bêche* (horiz pair)		
		Wi. Watermark inverted (12.58)	1·50	1·25
		l. Booklet pane. No. 572b×4	40·00	
573		2d. light red-brown (4.12.58)	10	10
		a. Watermark sideways (3.4.59)	1·00	1·00
		Wi. Watermark inverted (10.4.61)	£140	70·00
574	**155**	2½d. carmine-red (Type II) (booklets 11.58, sheets 15.9.59)	10	20
		a. Imperf strip of 3		
		b. *Tête-bêche* (horiz pair)	—	
		c. Imperf pane*	—	
		ca. Part perf pane	£3750	
		Wi. Watermark inverted (Type II) (11.58)	4·50	3·00
		e. Watermark sideways (Type I) (10.11.60)	40	60
		ea. Imperf strip of 6		
		f. Type I (wmk upright) (4.10.61)	70	70
		k. Chalk-surfaced paper (Type II) (15.7.63)	50	80
		kWi. Do. Watermark inverted (15.7.63)	75	1·30
		l. Watermark sideways (Type II) (1.7.64)	70	1·30
575		3d. deep lilac (booklets 11.58, sheets 8.12.58)	20	15
		a. Watermark sideways (24.10.58)	50	55
		b. Imperf pane*	£4250	
		c. Part perf pane*	£4000	
		d. Phantom 'R' (Cyl 41 no dot)	£375	
		Eda. Do. First retouch	30·00	
		Edb. Do. Second retouch	30·00	
		e. Phantom 'R' (Cyl 37 no dot)	55·00	
		Eea. Do. Retouch	20·00	
		Wi. Watermark inverted (11.58)	50	55
		l. Booklet pane. No. 575a×4 (26.5.61)	3·25	
576	**156**	4d. ultramarine (29.10.58)	45	35
		a. Deep ultramarine†† (28.4.65)	15	15
		ab. Watermark sideways (31.5.65)	70	55
		ac. Imperf pane*	£5500	
		ad. Part perf pane*	£4500	
		ae. Double impression	—	
		al. Booklet pane. No. 576ab×4 (16.8.65)	3·25	
		aWi. Watermark inverted (21.6.65)	60	75
577		4½d. chestnut (9.2.59)	10	25
578	**157**	5d. brown (10.11.58)	30	40
579		6d. deep claret (23.12.58)	30	25
		a. Imperf three sides (pair)	£4000	
		b. Imperf (pair)	£4500	
580		7d. brt green (26.11.58)	50	45
581	**158**	8d. magenta (24.2.60)	60	40
582		9d. bronze-green (24.3.59)	60	40
583		10d. Prussian blue (18.11.58)	1·00	50
584	**159**	1s. bistre-brown (30.10.58)	75	30
585		1s.3d. green (17.6.59)	75	30
586	**160**	1s.6d. grey-blue (16.12.58)	5·00	40
570/586 *Set of 17 (one of each value)*			9·00	4·25

* BOOKLET ERROR. See note after No. 556.

†† This 'shade' was brought about by making more deeply etched cylinders, resulting in apparent depth of colour in parts of the design. There is no difference in the colour of the ink.

Sideways watermark. The 2d., 2½d., 3d. and 4d. come from coils and the ½d., 1d., 1½d., 2½d., 3d. and 4d. come from booklets. In coil stamps the sideways watermark shows the top of the watermark to the left *as seen from the front of the stamp*. In the *booklet* stamps it comes equally to the left or right.

Nos. 570k and 574k only come from 2s. 'Holiday Resort' experimental undated booklets issued in 1963, in which one page contained 1 × 2½d. *se-tenant* with 3×½d. (See No. 570m).

No. 574l comes from coils, and the 'Holiday Resort' experimental booklets dated '1964' comprising four panes each containing two of these 2½d. stamps *se-tenant* vertically with two ½d. No. 570a. (See No. 570n).

2½d. imperf. No. 574a comes from a booklet with watermark upright. No. 574da is from a coil with sideways watermark.

No. 574ca is partially perforated at top. Only one example has been recorded, from which the top right stamp has been removed.

No. 574e comes from sheets bearing cylinder number 42 and is also known on vertical delivery coils.

In 1964 No. 575 was printed from cylinder number 70 no dot and dot on an experimental paper which is distinguishable by an additional watermark letter 'T' lying on its side, which occurs about four times in the sheet, usually in the side margins, 48,000 sheets were issued.

No. 575 is known imperforate and *tête-bêche*. These came from booklet sheets which were not issued *(price £70 per pair)*.

Phantom 'R' varieties

179a Nos. 575d and 615a (Cyl 41 no dot)

179b No. 575Eda

179c No. 575e (Cyl 37 no dot)

3d. An incomplete marginal rule revealed an 'R' on cyls 37 and 41 no dot below R. 20/12. It is more noticeable on cyl 41 because of the wider marginal rule. The 'R' on cyl 41 was twice retouched, the first being as illustrated here (No. 575Eda) and traces of the 'R' can still be seen in the second retouch.

No. 575d is best collected in a block of 4 or 6 with full margins in order to be sure that it is not 615a with phosphor lines removed.

The retouch on cyl 37 is not easily identified: there is no trace of the 'R' but the general appearance of that part of the marginal rule is uneven.

DOLLIS HILL TRIAL STAMPS. From 1957 to 1972 trials were carried out at the Post Office Research Station, Dollis Hill, London, to determine the most efficient method of applying phosphor to stamps in connection with automatic letter sorting. Stamps were frequently applied to 'live' mail to test sorting machinery.

The 2d. light red-brown and 3d. deep lilac stamps from these trials exist on unwatermarked paper, *prices from* £300 (2d.), £350 (3d.), *mint or used*.

WHITER PAPER. On 18 May 1962 the Post Office announced that a whiter paper was being used for the current issue (including Nos. 595/8). This is beyond the scope of this catalogue, but the whiter papers are listed in Vol. 3 of the Stanley Gibbons *Great Britain Specialised Catalogue*.

1958 (24 Nov)–**61**. Graphite-lined issue. Two graphite lines on the back, except 2d. value, which has one line. W **179**. Perf 15×14.

587	**154**	½d. orange-red (15.6.59)	9·00	9·00
		Wi. Watermark inverted (4.8.59)	3·25	4·00
588		1d. ultramarine (18.12.58)	2·00	1·50
		a. Misplaced graphite lines (7.61)*	80	1·20
		b. Three graphite lines	65·00	60·00
		Wi. Watermark inverted (4.8.59)	1·50	2·00
589		1½d. green (4.8.59)	90·00	80·00
		Wi. Watermark inverted (4.8.59)	75·00	60·00
590		2d. light red-brown (24.11.58)	10·00	3·50
		a. One line at exteme left as seen from back	£975	
591	**155**	2½d. carmine-red (Type II) (9.6.59)	12·00	10·00
		Wi. Watermark inverted (21.8.59)	65·00	50·00
592		3d. deep lilac (24.11.58)	90	65
		a. Misplaced graphite lines (5.61)*	£550	£425
		b. One graphite line	£2500	—
		c. Three graphite lines	£150	£120
		Wi. Watermark inverted (4.8.59)	1·00	1·25
593	**156**	4d. ultramarine (29.4.59)	5·50	5·00
		a. Misplaced graphite lines (1961)*	£2400	
594		4½d. chestnut (3.6.59)	6·50	5·00
Set of 8 (cheapest)			£110	70·00

Nos. 587/9 were only issued in booklets or coils (587/8).

* No. 588a (in coils), and Nos. 592a/c and 593a (all in sheets) result from the use of a residual stock of graphite-lined paper. As the use of graphite lines had ceased, the register of the lines in relation to the stamps was of no importance and numerous misplacements occurred - two lines close together, one line only, etc. No. 588a refers to two lines at left or right; No. 592a refers to stamps with two lines only at left and both clear of the perforations No. 592b refers to stamps with a single line and Nos. 588b, 592c and 593a to stamps with two lines at left (with left line down perforations) and traces of a third line down the opposite perforations.

No. 592 Wi was included in 4s.6d. booklets, L15 and L16, dated April and June 1959. These represent production dates not issue dates.

(Recess D.L.R. (until 31.12.62), then B.W.)

1959–68. W **179**. Perf 11×12.

595	**166**	2s.6d. black-brown (22.7.59)	10·00	75
		Wi. Watermark inverted	—	£3250
		a. B.W. printing (1.7.63)	35	40
		aWi. Watermark inverted	£3250	£280
		k. Chalk-surfaced paper (30.5.68)	50	1·50
596	**167**	5s. scarlet-vermilion (15.6.59)	45·00	2·00
		Wi. Watermark inverted	£9000	£600
		a. B.W. ptg. *Red (shades)* (3.9.63)	1·20	50
		ab. Printed on the gummed side	£1600	
		aWi. Watermark inverted	£400	£300
597	**168**	10s. blue (21.7.59)	55·00	5·00
		a. B.W. ptg. *Bright ultramarine* (16.10.63)	4·50	4·50
		aWi. Watermark inverted	—	£3250
598	**169**	£1 black (23.6.59)	£120	12·00

No.	Type	Description	Unused	Used
		Wi. Watermark inverted	—	£2500
		a. B.W. printing (14.11.63)	13·00	8·00
		aWi. Watermark inverted	£15000	£3750
		k. Chalk-surfaced paper	£5250	
Set of 4 (Nos. 595/8)			£195	17·00
Set of 4 (Nos. 595a/8a)			15·00	11·00

The B.W. printings have a marginal Plate Number. They are generally more deeply engraved than the DLR showing more of the Diadem detail and heavier lines on Her Majesty's face. The vertical perf is 11.9 to 12 against DLR 11.8.

See also Nos. 759/62.

PHOSPHOR BAND ISSUES. These are printed on the front and are wider than graphite lines. They are not easy to see but show as broad vertical bands at certain angles to the light.

Values representing the rate for printed papers (and when this was abolished in 1968 for second issue class mail) have one band and others two, three or four bands as stated, according to the size and format.

In the small size stamps the bands are on each side with the single band at left (*except where otherwise stated*). In the large size commemorative stamps the single band may be at left, centre or right, varying in different designs. The bands are vertical on both horizontal and vertical designs *except where otherwise stated*.

The phosphor was originally applied by letterpress but later usually by photogravure and sometimes using flexography, a relief printing process using rubber cylinders.

Three different types of phosphor have been used, distinguishable by the colour emitted under an ultra-violet lamp, the first being green, then blue and now violet. Different sized bands are also known. All these are fully listed in Vol. 3 of the Stanley Gibbons *Great Britain Specialised Catalogue*.

Varieties. Misplaced and missing phosphor bands are known but such varieties are beyond the scope of this Catalogue.

1959 (18 Nov). Phosphor-Graphite issue. Two phosphor bands on front and two graphite lines on back, except 2d. value, which has one band on front and one line on back. (a) W **165**. Perf 15×14.

No.	Type	Description	Unused	Used
599	**154**	½d. orange-red	4·25	4·25
600		1d. ultramarine	11·00	11·00
601		1½d. green	4·50	4·50
		(b) W **179**.		
605	**154**	2d. light red-brown (1 band)	6·00	4·25
		a. Error. *W* **165**	£200	£175
606	**155**	2½d. carmine-red (Type II)	22·00	18·00
607		3d. deep lilac	12·00	8·00
608	**156**	4d. ultramarine	20·00	16·00
609		4½d. chestnut	30·00	20·00
599/609 *Set of 8*			£100	80·00

Examples of the 2½d., No. 606, exist showing watermark W **165** in error. It is believed that phosphor-graphite stamps of this value with this watermark were not used by the public for postal purposes.

1960 (22 June)–**67**. Phosphor issue. Two phosphor bands on front, except where otherwise stated. W **179**. Perf 15×14.

No.	Type	Description	Unused	Used
610	**154**	½d. orange-red	10	15
		a. Watermark sideways (14.7.61)	15·00	15·00
		Wi. Watermark inverted (14.8.60)	1·50	1·50
		l. Booklet pane. No. 610a×4	45·00	
611		1d. ultramarine	10	10
		a. Watermark sideways (14.7.61)	1·10	1·10
		l. Booklet pane. No. 611a×4	10·00	
		m. Booklet pane. No. 611a×2 *se-tenant* with 615d×2† (16.8.65)	18·00	
		ma. Booklet pane. No. 611a×2 *se-tenant* with 615dEa×2 (16.8.65)	18·00	
		n. Booklet pane. No. 611a×2 *se-tenant* with 615b×2†† (11.67)	10·00	
		Wi. Watermark inverted (14.8.60)	65	65
612		1½d. green	15	15
		a. Watermark sideways (14.7.61)	18·00	18·00
		l. Booklet pane. No. 612a×4	50·00	
		Wi. Watermark inverted (14.8.60)	25·00	22·00
613		2d. light red-brown (1 band)	22·00	22·00
613*a*		2d. light red-brown (2 bands) (4.10.61)	10	15
		aa. Imperf three sides*** (pair)	—	
		ab. Watermark sideways (6.4.67)	1·00	1·00
614	**155**	2½d. carmine-red (Type II) (2 bands)*	40	30
		Wi. Watermark inverted (14.8.60)	£170	£140
614*a*		2½d. carmine-red (Type II) (1 band) (4.10.61)	60	75
		aWi. Watermark inverted (3.62)	50·00	42·00
614*b*		2½d. carmine-red (Type I) (1 band) (4.10.61)	45·00	40·00
615		3d. deep lilac (2 bands)	60	55
		aa. Phantom 'R' (Cyl 41 no dot)	55·00	
		a. Imperf three sides (horiz pair)	£2000	
		b. Watermark sideways (14.7.61)	1·80	1·80
		l. Booklet pane. No. 615b×4	25·00	
		Wi. Watermark inverted (14.8.60)	50	90
615*c*		3d. deep lilac (1 band at right) (29.4.65)	60	55
		cEa. Band at left	60	70
		cWi. Watermark inverted (band at right) (2.67)	8·00	7·00
		cWia. Watermark inverted (band at left) (2.67)	80·00	80·00
		d. Watermark sideways (band at right) (16.8.65)	5·50	5·00
		dEa. Watermark sideways (band at left)	5·50	5·00
		e. One centre band (8.12.66)	40	45
		ea. Wmk sideways (19.6.67)	1·00	1·00
		eWi. Watermark inverted (8.67)	4·00	4·00
616	**156**	4d. ultramarine	3·50	3·50
		a. Deep ultramarine (28.4.65)	25	25
		aa. Part perf pane	£5500	
		ab. Wmk sideways	1·10	1·10
		al. Booklet pane. No. 616ab×4	2·50	
		aWi. Watermark inverted (21.6.65)	75	75
616*b*		4½d. chestnut (13.9.61)	55	30
616*c*	**157**	5d. brown (9.6.67)	55	35
617		6d. purple	55	30
617*a*		7d. bright green (15.2.67)	70	50
617*b*	**158**	8d. magenta (28.6.67)	70	55
617*c*		9d. bronze-green (29.12.66)	70	65
617*d*		10d. Prussian blue (30.12.66)	1·00	1·00
617*e*	**159**	1s. bistre-brown (28.6.67)	1·00	35
618		1s.3d. green	1·90	2·50
618*a*	**160**	1s.6d. grey-blue (12.12.66)	2·00	2·00
610/618*a Set of 17*			10·50	8·00

The automatic facing equipment was brought into use on 6 July 1960 but the phosphor stamps may have been released a few days earlier.

The stamps with watermark sideways are from booklets except Nos. 613ab and 615ea which are from coils. No. 616ab comes from both booklets and coils.

No. 615a. See footnote after No. 586.

* No. 614 with two bands on the creamy paper was originally from cylinder 50 dot and no dot. When the change in postal rates took place in 1965 it was reissued from cylinder 57 dot and no dot on the whiter paper. Some of these latter were also released in error in districts of S.E. London in September 1964. The shade of the reissue is slightly more carmine.

***This comes from the bottom row of a sheet which is imperf at bottom and both sides.

† Booklet pane No. 611m shows the 1d. stamps at left and No. 611ma the 1d. stamps at right.

†† Booklet pane No. 611n comes from 2s. booklets of January and March 1968. The two bands on the 3d. stamp were intentional because of the technical difficulties in producing one band and two band stamps *se-tenant*.

The Phosphor-Graphite stamps had the phosphor applied by letterpress but the Phosphor issue can be divided into those with the phosphor applied letterpress and others where it was applied by photogravure. Moreover the photogravure form can be further divided into those which phosphoresce green and others which phosphoresce blue under ultraviolet light. From 1965 violet phosphorescence was introduced in place of the blue. All these are fully listed in Vol. 3 of the Stanley Gibbons *Great Britain Specialised Catalogue*.

Unlike previous one-banded phosphor stamps, No. 615c has a broad band extending over two stamps so that alternate stamps have the band at left or right (same prices either way). No. 615cWi comes from the 10s phosphor booklet of February 1967 and No. 615eWi comes from the 10s. phosphor booklets of August 1967 and February 1968.

No. 615a (Phantom 'R'), see illustration following No. 586.

180 Postboy of 1660

181 Posthorn of 1660

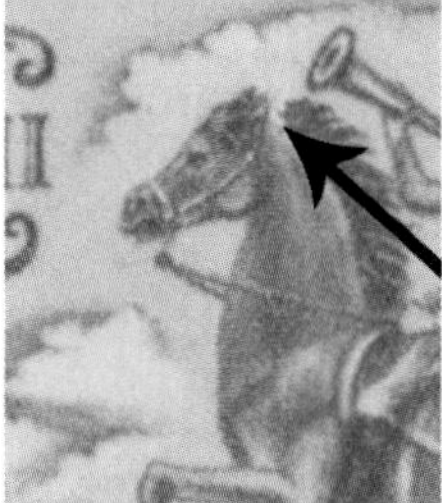

Broken mane (Cyl. 1 No dot, R. 17/2)

(Des R. Stone (3d.), Faith Jaques (1s.3d.))

1960 (7 July). Tercentenary of Establishment of General Letter Office. W **179** (sideways on 1s.3d.). Perf 15×14 (3d.) or 14×15 (1s.3d.).

No.	Type	Description	Unused	Used
619	**180**	3d. deep lilac	20	20
		a. Broken mane	70·00	
620	**181**	1s.3d. green	1.60	1.80

182 Conference Emblem

(Des R. Stone (emblem, P. Rahikainen))

1960 (19 Sept). First Anniversary of European Postal and Telecommunications Conference. Chalk-surfaced paper. W **179**. Perf 15×14.

No.	Type	Description	Unused	Used
621	**182**	6d. bronze-green and purple	1·00	20
622		1s.6d. brown and blue	5·50	2·25

SCREENS. Up to this point all photogravure stamps were printed in a 200 screen (200 dots per linear inch), but all later commemorative stamps are a finer 250 screen. Exceptionally No. 622 has a 200 screen for the portrait and a 250 screen for the background.

184 'Growth of Savings'

183 Thrift Plant

185 Thrift Plant

(Des P. Gauld (2½d.), M. Goaman (others))

1961 (28 Aug). Centenary of Post Office Savings Bank. Chalk-surfaced paper. W **179** (sideways on 2½d.) Perf 14×15 (2½d.) or 15×14 (others).

No.	Type	Description	Unused	Used
		A. 'Timson' Machine		
623A	**183**	2½d. black and red	10	10
		a. Black omitted	—	
624A	**184**	3d. orange-brown and violet	10	10
		a. Orange-brown omitted	£600	
625A	**185**	1s.6d. red and blue	1·00	1·20
Set of 3			1·00	1.20
		B. 'Thrissell' Machine		
623B	**183**	2½d. black and red	1·50	1·50
624B	**184**	3d. orange-brown and violet	30	30
		a. Orange-brown omitted	£1750	

2½d. TIMSON. Cyls 1E-1F. Deeply shaded portrait (brownish black).

2½d. THRISSELL. Cyls 1D-1B or 1D (dot)-1B (dot). Lighter portrait (grey-black).

3d. TIMSON. Cyls 3D-3E. Clear, well-defined portrait with deep shadows and bright highlights.

3d. THRISSELL. Cyls 3C-3B or 3C (dot)-3B (dot). Dull portrait, lacking in contrast.

Sheet marginal examples *without* single extension perf hole on the short side of the stamp are always 'Timson', as are those with large punch-hole *not* coincident with printed three-sided box guide mark.

The 3d. 'Timson' perforated completely through the right hand side margin comes from a relatively small part of the printing perforated on a sheet-fed machine.

Normally the 'Timsons' were perforated in the reel, with three large punch-holes in both long margins and the perforations completely through both short margins. Only one punch-hole coincides with the guide-mark.

The 'Thrissells' have one large punch-hole in one long margin, coinciding with guide-mark and one short margin imperf (except sometimes for encroachments).

186 C.E.P.T. Emblem

187 Doves and Emblem

188 Doves and Emblem

(Des M. Goaman (doves T. Kurpershoek))

1961 (18 Sept). European Postal and Telecommunications (C.E.P.T.) Conference, Torquay. Chalk-surfaced paper. W **179**. Perf 15×14.

No.	Type	Description	Unused	Used
626	**186**	2d. orange, pink and brown	10	10
		a. Orange omitted	£15000	
		b. Pink omitted		
627	**187**	4d. buff, mauve and ultramarine	10	10
628	**188**	10d. turquoise, pale green and Prussian blue	20	20
		a. Pale green omitted	£24000	
		b. Turquoise omitted	7250	
Set of 3			30	30

189 Hammer Beam Roof, Westminster Hall

190 Palace of Westminster

(Des Faith Jaques)

1961 (25 Sept). Seventh Commonwealth Parliamentary Conference. Chalk-surfaced paper. W **179** (sideways on 1s.3d.) Perf 15×14 (6d.) or 14×15 (1s.3d.).

No.	Type	Description	Unused	Used
629	**189**	6d. purple and gold	10	10
		a. Gold omitted	£2200	
630	**190**	1s.3d. green and blue	1·20	1·20
		a. Blue (Queen's head) omitted	£40000	
		b. Green omitted		

191 'Units of Productivity'

192 'National Productivity'

193 'Unified Productivity'

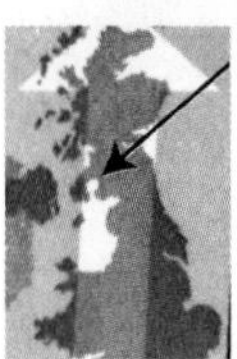

3d. Lake in Scotland (Cyls. 2A-2B Dot, R. 1/3)

3d. Kent omitted (Cyls. 2C-2B No. Dot, R. 18/2)

(Des D. Gentleman)

1962 (14 Nov). 'National Productivity Year. Chalk-surfaced paper. W **179** (inverted on 2½d. and 3d.). Perf 15×14.

631	**191**	2½d. myrtle-green and carmine-red (*shades*)	10	10
		Ea. Blackish olive and carmine-red	25	15
		p. One phosphor band. *Blackish olive and carmine-red*	60	50
632	**192**	3d. light blue and violet (*shades*)	25	25
		a. Light blue (Queen's head) omitted	£5750	
		b. Lake in Scotland	65·00	
		c. Kent omitted	70·00	
		p. Three phosphor bands	1·50	80
633	**193**	1s.3d. carmine, light blue and deep green	80	80
		a. Light blue (Queen's head) omitted	£15000	
		p. Three phosphor bands	35·00	22·00
Set of 3 (Ordinary)			1·00	1·00
Set of 3 (Phosphor)			35·00	22·00

194 Campaign Emblem and Family

195 Children of Three Races

(Des M. Goaman)

1963 (21 Mar). Freedom from Hunger. Chalk-surfaced paper. W **179** (inverted). Perf 15×14.

634	**194**	2½d. crimson and pink	10	10
		p. One phosphor band	3·00	1·20
635	**195**	1s.3d. bistre-brown and yellow	1·00	1·00
		p. Three phosphor bands	30·00	23·00

196 'Paris Conference'

(Des R. Stone)

1963 (7 May). Paris Postal Conference Centenary. Chalk-surfaced paper. W **179** (inverted). Perf 15×14.

636	**196**	6d. green and mauve	20	20
		a. Green omitted	£5500	
		p. Three phosphor bands	3·00	2.75

197 Posy of Flowers

198 Woodland Life

'Caterpillar' flaw (Cyl. 3B Dot, R. 3/2)

(Des S. Scott (3d.), M. Goaman (4½d.))

1963 (16 May). National Nature Week. Chalk-surfaced paper. W **179**. Perf 15×14.

637	**197**	3d. yellow, green, brown and black	10	10
		a. 'Caterpillar' flaw	75·00	
		p. Three phosphor bands	30	30
		pa. 'Caterpillar' flaw	75·00	
638	**198**	4½d. black, blue, yellow, magenta and brown-red	15	15
		p. Three phosphor bands	1·40	1·40

199 Rescue at Sea

200 19th-century Lifeboat

201 Lifeboatmen

(Des D. Gentleman)

1963 (31 May). Ninth International Lifeboat Conference, Edinburgh. Chalk-surfaced paper. W **179**. Perf 15×14.

639	**199**	2½d. blue, black and red	10	10
		p. One phosphor band	50	60
640	**200**	4d. red, yellow, brown, black and blue	20	20
		p. Three phosphor bands	50	60
641	**201**	1s.6d. sepia, yellow and grey-blue	1·50	1·50
		p. Three phosphor bands	48·00	28·00
Set of 3 (Ordinary)			1·50	1·50
Set of 3 (Phosphor)			48·00	28·00

202 Red Cross

203

204

(Des H. Bartram)

1963 (15 Aug). Red Cross Centenary Congress. Chalk-surfaced paper. W **179**. Perf 15×14.

642	**202**	3d. red and deep lilac	25	25
		a. Red omitted	£16000	
		p. Three phosphor bands	1·10	1·00
		pa. Red omitted	—	
643	**203**	1s.3d. red, blue and grey	1·25	1·25
		p. Three phosphor bands	35·00	30·00
644	**204**	1s.6d. red, blue and bistre	1·25	1·25
		p. Three phosphor bands	35·00	27·00
Set of 3 (Ordinary)			2·50	2·50
Set of 3 (Phosphor)			65·00	55·00

205 Commonwealth Cable

(Des P. Gauld)

1963 (3 Dec). Opening of COMPAC (Trans-Pacific Telephone Cable). Chalk-surfaced paper. W **179**. Perf 15×14.

645	**205**	1s.6d. blue and black	1·25	1.25
		a. Black omitted	£7000	
		p. Three phosphor bands	7.25	7.00

206 Puck and Bottom (*A Midsummer Night's Dream*)

207 Feste (*Twelfth Night*)

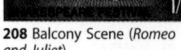

208 Balcony Scene (*Romeo and Juliet*)

209 Eve of Agincourt (*Henry V*)

210 Hamlet contemplating Yorick's Skull *Hamlet* and Queen Elizabeth II

(Des D. Gentleman. Photo Harrison & Sons (3d., 6d., 1s.3d., 1s.6d.). Des C. and R. Ironside. Recess B.W. (2s.6d.))

1964 (23 Apr). Shakespeare Festival. Chalk-surfaced paper. W **179**. Perf 11×12 (2s.6d.) or 15×14 (others).

646	**206**	3d. yellow-bistre, black and deep violet-blue (*shades*)	10	10
		p. Three phosphor bands	25	25
647	**207**	6d. yellow, orange, black and yellow-olive (*shades*)	20	20
		p. Three phosphor bands	75	75
648	**208**	1s.3d. cerise, blue-green, black and sepia (*shades*)	40	40
		Wi. Watermark inverted	£950	
		p. Three phosphor bands	2·00	2·00
		pWi. Watermark inverted	£400	
649	**209**	1s.6d. violet, turquoise, black and blue (*shades*)	60	60
		Wi. Watermark inverted		£1300
		p. Three phosphor bands	2.50	2.50
650	**210**	2s.6d. deep slate-purple (*shades*)	1·20	1·20
		Wi. Watermark inverted	£1000	
Set of 5 (Ordinary)			2.00	2.00
Set of 4 (Phosphor)			5·00	5·00

211 Flats near Richmond Park *Urban Development*

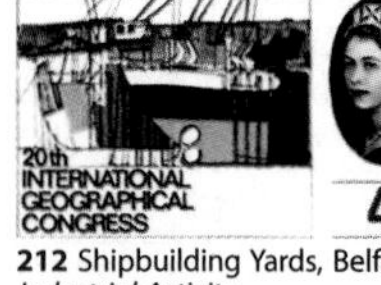
212 Shipbuilding Yards, Belfast *Industrial Activity*

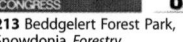

213 Beddgelert Forest Park, Snowdonia *Forestry*

214 Nuclear Reactor, Dounreay *Technological Development*

(Des D. Bailey)

1964 (1 July). '20th International Geographical Congress', London. Chalk-surfaced paper. W **179**. Perf 15×14.

651	**211**	2½d. black, olive-yellow, olive-grey and turquoise-blue	10	10
		p. One phosphor band	40	50
652	**212**	4d. orange-brown, red-brown, rose, black and violet	30	30
		a. Violet (face value) omitted	275	
		c. Violet and red-brown (dock walls) omitted	500	
		d. Red brown (dock walls) omitted		
		Wi. Watermark inverted	£850	
		p. Three phosphor bands	1·20	1·20
653	**213**	8d. yellow-brown, emerald, green and black	80	80
		a. Green (lawn) omitted	£24000	
		Wi. Watermark inverted	£2200	
		p. Three phosphor bands	2·50	3·50
654	**214**	1s.6d. yellow-brown, pale pink, black and brown	1.40	1.40
		Wi. Watermark inverted	55·00	
		p. Three phosphor bands	28·00	22·00
Set of 4 (Ordinary)			2.00	2.00
Set of 4 (Phosphor)			30·00	25·00

A used example of the 4d. is known with the red-brown omitted.

215 Spring Gentian

216 Dog Rose

217 Honeysuckle

218 Fringed Water Lily

(Des M. and Sylvia Goaman)

1964 (5 Aug). Tenth International Botanical Congress', Edinburgh. Chalk-surfaced paper. W **179**. Perf 15×14.

655	**215**	3d. violet, blue and sage-green	25	25
		a. Blue omitted	£20000	
		b. Sage-green omitted	£24000	
		p. Three phosphor bands	40	40
656	**216**	6d. apple-green, rose, scarlet and green	30	30
		p. Three phosphor bands	2·50	2·75
657	**217**	9d. lemon, green, lake and rose-red	80	80
		a. Green (leaves) omitted	£22000	
		Wi. Watermark inverted	75·00	
		p. Three phosphor bands	4·50	4·50
658	**218**	1s.3d. yellow, emerald, reddish violet and grey-green	1·20	1·20
		a. Yellow (flowers) omitted	£45000	
		Wi. Watermark inverted	£2500	
		p. Three phosphor bands	25·00	20·00
Set of 4 (Ordinary)			2.00	2.00
Set of 4 (Phosphor)			30·00	25·00

Unissued Goaman designs of the 3d and 9d values on perforated and gummed paper are known.

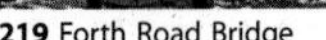

219 Forth Road Bridge

220 Forth Road and Railway Bridges

(Des A. Restall)

1964 (4 Sept). Opening of Forth Road Bridge. Chalk-surfaced paper. W **179**. Perf 15×14.

659	**219**	3d. black, blue and reddish violet..	10	10
		p. Three phosphor bands	50	50
660	**220**	6d. blackish lilac, light blue and carmine-red	20	20
		a. Light blue omitted	£6500	
		Wi. Watermark inverted	5·00	
		p. Three phosphor bands	2.25	2.25
		pWi. Watermark inverted	£800	

221 Sir Winston Churchill

(Des D. Gentleman and Rosalind Dease, from photograph by Karsh)

1965 (8 July). 'Churchill Commemoration'. Chalk-surfaced paper. W **179**. Perf 15×14.

I. 'REMBRANDT' Machine

661	**221**	4d. black and olive-brown	15	15
		Wi. Watermark inverted	3·00	
		p. Three phosphor bands	20	20

II. 'TIMSON' Machine

661*a*	**221**	4d. black and olive-brown	50	50

III. 'L. & M. 4' Machine

662	–	1s.3d. black and grey	45	45
		Wi. Watermark inverted	£140	
		p. Three phosphor bands	1.00	1·00

The 1s.3d. shows a closer view of Churchill's head.

4d. REMBRANDT, Cyls 1A-1B dot and no dot. Lack of shading detail on Churchill's portrait. Queen's portrait appears dull and coarse. This is a rotary machine which is sheet-fed.

4d. TIMSON. Cyls 5A-6B no dot. More detail on Churchill's portrait –furrow on forehead, his left eyebrow fully drawn and more shading on cheek. Queen's portrait lighter and sharper. This is a reel-fed two-colour 12-in. wide rotary machine and the differences in impressions are due to the greater pressure applied by this machine.

1s.3d. Cyls 1A-1B no dot. The 'Linotype and Machinery No. 4' machine is an ordinary sheet-fed rotary press machine. Besides being used for printing the 1s.3d. stamps it was also employed for overprinting the phosphor bands on both values.

Two examples of the 4d. value exist with the Queen's head omitted, one due to something adhering to the cylinder and the other due to a paper fold. The stamp also exists with Churchill's head omitted, also due to a paper fold.

222 Simon de Montfort's Seal

223 Parliament Buildings (after engraving by Hollar, 1647)

(Des S. Black (6d.), R. Guyatt (2s.6d.))

1965 (19 July). 700th Anniversary of Simon de Montfort's Parliament. Chalk-surfaced paper. W **179**. Perf 15×14.

663	**222**	6d. olive-green	10	10
		p. Three phosphor bands	50	50
664	**223**	2s.6d. black, grey and pale drab	40	40
		Wi. Watermark inverted	60·00	

224 Bandsmen and Banner

225 Three Salvationists

(Des M. Farrar-Bell (3d.), G. Trenaman (1s.6d.))

1965 (9 Aug). Salvation Army Centenary. Chalk-surfaced paper. W **179**. Perf 15×14.

665	**224**	3d. indigo, grey-blue, cerise, yellow and brown	10	10
		p. One phosphor band	20	20
666	**225**	1s.6d. red, blue, yellow and brown	60	60
		p. Three phosphor bands	90	90

226 Lister's Carbolic Spray

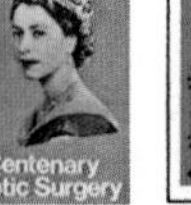

227 Lister and Chemical Symbols

(Des P. Gauld (4d.), F. Ariss (1s.))

1965 (1 Sept). Centenary of Joseph Lister's Discovery of Antiseptic Surgery. Chalk-surfaced paper. W **179**. Perf 15×14.

667	**226**	4d. indigo, brown-red and grey-black	10	10
		a. Brown-red (tube) omitted	600	
		b. Indigo omitted	£7000	
		p. Three phosphor bands	25	25
		pa. Brown-red (tube) omitted	£6750	
668	**227**	1s. black, purple and new blue	40	40
		Wi. Watermark inverted	£675	
		p. Three phosphor bands	1·00	1·00
		pWi. Watermark inverted	£550	

228 Trinidad Carnival Dancers

229 Canadian Folk-dancers

(Des D. Gentleman and Rosalind Dease)

1965 (1 Sept). Commonwealth Arts Festival. Chalk-surfaced paper. W **179**. Perf 15×14.

669	**228**	6d. black and orange	10	10
		p. Three phosphor bands	40	40
670	**229**	1s.6d. black and light reddish violet	40	40
		p. Three phosphor bands	1·20	1·20

230 Flight of Supermarine Spitfires

231 Pilot in Hawker Hurricane Mk I

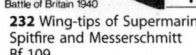

232 Wing-tips of Supermarine Spitfire and Messerschmitt Bf 109

233 Supermarine Spitfires attacking Heinkel He-111H Bomber

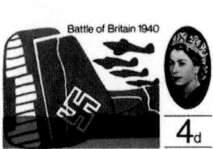

234 Supermarine Spitfire attacking Junkers Ju 87B 'Stuka' Dive-bomber

235 Hawker Hurricanes Mk I over Wreck of Dornier Do-17Z Bomber

236 Anti-aircraft Artillery in Action

237 Air-battle over St Paul's Cathedral

(Des D. Gentleman and Rosalind Dease (4d.×6 and 1s.3d.), A. Restall (9d.))

1965 (13 Sept). 25th Anniv of Battle of Britain. Chalk-surfaced paper. W **179**. Perf 15×14.

671	**230**	4d. yellow-olive and black	25	25
		a. Block of 6. Nos. 671/6	2·50	2·50
		p. Three phosphor bands	40	40
		pa. Block of 6. Nos. 671p/6p	3·75	3·75
672	**231**	4d. yellow-olive, olive-grey and black	25	25
		p. Three phosphor bands	40	40
673	**232**	4d. red, new blue, yellow-olive, olive-grey and black	25	25
		p. Three phosphor bands	40	40
674	**233**	4d. olive-grey, yellow-olive and black	25	25
		p. Three phosphor bands	40	40
675	**234**	4d. olive-grey, yellow-olive and black	25	25
		p. Three phosphor bands	40	40
676	**235**	4d. olive-grey, yellow-olive, new blue and black	25	25
		a. New blue omitted	†	£6500
		p. Three phosphor bands	40	40
677	**236**	9d. bluish violet, orange and slate purple	1·70	1·70
		Wi. Watermark inverted	£100	
		p. Three phosphor bands	2.00	2·00
678	**237**	1s.3d. Lt grey, dp grey, black, Lt blue and bright blue	1·70	1·70
		a. Face value omitted*	£1500	
		Wi. Watermark inverted	£190	
		p. Three phosphor bands	2.00	2·00
		pWi. Watermark inverted	5·00	
		Set of 8 (Ordinary)	5·50	5·50
		Set of 8 (Phosphor)	7·00	7·00

Nos. 671/6 were issued together *se-tenant* in blocks of 6 (3×2) within the sheet. No. 676a is only known commercially used on cover from Truro.

* No. 678a is caused by a 12 mm downward shift of black which resulted in the value being omitted from the top row of one sheet.

238 Tower and Georgian Buildings

239 Tower and 'Nash' Terrace, Regent's Park

(Des C. Abbott)

1965 (8 Oct). Opening of Post Office Tower. Chalk-surfaced paper. W **179** (sideways on 3d.). Perf 14×15 (3d.) or 15×14 (1s.3d.).

679	**238**	3d. olive-yellow, new blue and bronze-green	10	10
		a. Olive-yellow (Tower) omitted	£6000	£2250
		p. One phosphor band at right	15	15
		pEa. Band at left	15	15
		pEb. Horiz pair. Nos. 679p/pEa	30	50
680	**239**	1s.3d. bronze-green, yellow-green and blue	20	20
		Wi. Watermark inverted	£175	
		p. Three phosphor bands	30	30
		pWi. Watermark inverted	£200	

The one phosphor band on No. 679p was produced by printing broad phosphor bands across alternate vertical perforations. Individual stamps show the band at right or left.

240 U.N. Emblem

241 I.C.Y. Emblem

Broken circle (Cyl. 1A Dot, R. 11/4)

Lake in Russia (Cyl. 1A Dot, R. 19/3)

(Des J. Matthews)

1965 (25 Oct). 20th Anniv of U.N.O. and International Co-operation Year. Chalk-surfaced paper. W **179**. Perf 15×14.

681	**240**	3d. black, yellow-orange and light blue	10	10
		a. Broken circle	65·00	
		b. Lake in Russia	65·00	
		p. One phosphor band	25	25
		pa. Broken circle	65·00	
		pb. Lake in Russia	65·00	
682	**241**	1s.6d. black, brt purple and light blue	35	35
		Wi. Watermark inverted		£2200
		p. Three phosphor bands	1.00	1·00

242 Telecommunications Network

243 Radio Waves and Switchboard

1s.6d. Red pin with arm (Cyl. 1D, R. 1/4)

(Des A. Restall)

1965 (15 Nov). International Telecommunications Union Centenary. Chalk-surfaced paper. W **179**. Perf 15×14.

683	**242**	9d. red, ultramarine, deep slate, violet, black and pink	20	20
		Wi. Watermark inverted	30·00	
		p. Three phosphor bands	75	75
		pWi. Watermark inverted	£110	

684 **243** 1s.6d. red, greenish blue, indigo, black and light pink 40 40
a. Light pink omitted £4000 £2500
b. Red pin with arm .... —
Wi. Watermark inverted £300
p. Three phosphor bands 2.00 2.00
pb. Red pin with arm .... 35·00

Originally scheduled for issue on 17 May 1965, supplies from the Philatelic Bureau were sent in error to reach a dealer on that date and another dealer received his supply on 27 May.

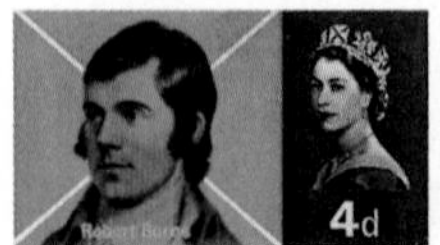

244 Robert Burns (after Skirving chalk drawing)

245 Robert Burns (after Nasmyth portrait)

(Des G. Huntly)

1966 (25 Jan). 'Burns Commemoration.' Chalk-surfaced paper. W **179**. Perf 15×14.

685 **244** 4d. black, dp violet-blue and new blue 10 10
p. Three phosphor bands 20 20

686 **245** 1s.3d. black, slate-blue and yellow-orange 20 20
p. Three phosphor bands 90 90

246 Westminster Abbey

247 Fan Vaulting, Henry VII Chapel

(Des Sheila Robinson. Photo Harrison (3d.). Des and eng Bradbury, Wilkinson. Recess (2s.6d.))

1966 (28 Feb). 900th Anniversary of Westminster Abbey. Chalk-surfaced paper (3d.). W **179**. Perf 15×14 (3d.) or 11×12 (2s.6d.).

687 **246** 3d. black, red-brown and new blue 10 10
p. One phosphor band 10 10

688 **247** 2s.6d. black 30 30

248 View near Hassocks, Sussex

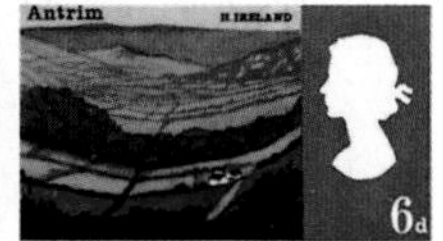

249 Antrim, Northern Ireland

250 Harlech Castle, Wales

251 Cairngorm Mountains Scotland

6d. 'AN' for 'AND' (Cyl. 1A No dot, R. 10/3)

(Des L. Rosoman. Queen's portrait, adapted by D. Gentleman from coinage)

1966 (2 May). Landscapes. Chalk-surfaced paper. W **179**. Perf 15×14.

689 **248** 4d. black, yellow-green and new blue 10 10
p. Three phosphor bands 10 10

690 **249** 6d. black, emerald and new blue 10 10
a. 'AN' for 'AND' .... 65·00
Wi. Watermark inverted .... 6·00
p. Three phosphor bands 10 10
pa. 'AN' for 'AND' .... 65·00
pWi. Watermark inverted £170

691 **250** 1s.3d. black, greenish yellow and greenish blue 15 15
p. Three phosphor bands 15 15

692 **251** 1s.6d. black, orange and Prussian blue 15 15
Wi. Watermark inverted .... 22·00
p. Three phosphor bands 15 15

Set of 4 (Ordinary) 40 40
Set of 4 (Phosphor) 40 40

Blocks of four of Nos. 689 and 690 are known with the Queen's head and face value omitted on one stamp and a partial omission on the second, due to a paper fold (*Price per block*. £10000)

252 Players with Ball

253 Goalmouth Mêlée

254 Goalkeeper saving Goal

(Des D. Gentleman (4d.), W. Kempster (6d.), D. Caplan (1s.3d.). Queen's portrait adapted by D. Gentleman from coinage)

1966 (1 June). World Cup Football Championship. Chalk-surfaced paper. W **179** (sideways on 4d.). Perf 14×15 (4d.) or 15×14 (others).

693 **252** 4d. red, reddish purple, bright blue, flesh and black 10 10
p. Two phosphor bands 10 10

694 **253** 6d. black, sepia, red, apple-green and blue 10 10
a. Black omitted £200
b. Apple-green omitted £6000
c. Red omitted £10000
Wi. Watermark inverted .... 5·00
p. Three phosphor bands 10 10
pa. Black omitted £2800

695 **254** 1s.3d. black, blue, yellow, red and light yellow-olive 15 15
a. Blue omitted £350
Wi. Watermark inverted £150
p. Three phosphor bands 15 15
pWi. Watermark inverted .... 2·00

Set of 3 (Ordinary) 30 30
Set of 3 (Phosphor) 30 30

255 Black-headed Gull

256 Blue Tit

257 European Robin

258 Blackbird

(Des J. Norris Wood)

1966 (8 Aug). British Birds. Chalk-surfaced paper. W **179**. Perf 15×14.

696 **255** 4d. grey, black, red, emerald-green, brt blue, greenish yellow and bistre 10 10
Wi. Watermark inverted .... 4·00
a. Block of 4. Nos. 696/9 .... 40 40
ab. Black (value), etc. omitted* (*block of four*) £20000
c. Black only omitted* .... —
aWi. Watermark inverted (*block of four*) .... 18·00
p. Three phosphor bands 10 10
pWi. Watermark inverted .... 20·00
pa. Block of 4. Nos. 696p/9p 40 40
paWi. Watermark inverted (*block of four*) .... 85·00

697 **256** 4d. black, greenish yellow, grey, emerald-green, brt blue and bistre 10 10
b. Black '4d' only omitted £2000
Wi. Watermark inverted .... 4·00
p. Three phosphor bands 10 10
pWi. Watermark inverted .... 20·00

698 **257** 4d. red, greenish yellow, black, grey, bistre, reddish brown and emerald-green 10 10
a. Black only omitted ....
Wi. Watermark inverted .... 4·00
p. Three phosphor bands 10 10
pWi. Watermark inverted .... 20·00

699 **258** 4d. black, reddish brown, greenish yellow, grey and bistre** 10 10
b. Black '4d' only omitted*** £2000
Wi. Watermark inverted .... 4·00
p. Three phosphor bands 10 10
pWi. Watermark inverted .... 20·00

Set of 4 (Ordinary) 40 40
Set of 4 (Phosphor) 40 40

Nos. 696/9 were issued together *se-tenant* in blocks of four within the sheet.

Nos. 697b and 699b are the result of a partial impression of the black, rendering the '4d' only omitted.

* In No. 696ab the blue, bistre and reddish brown are also omitted but in No. - 696c + 698c only the black is omitted.

** In No. 699 the black was printed over the bistre.

*** A partial omission caused by a dry print affecting only the face value on the last column of the sheet.

Other colours omitted, and the stamps affected:

d. Greenish yellow (Nos. 696/9) £950
pd. Greenish yellow (Nos. 696p/9p) £2000
e. Red (Nos. 696 and 698) £1100
f. Emerald-green (Nos. 696/8) £200
pf. Emerald-green (Nos. 696p/8p) £200
g. Bright blue (Nos. 696/7) £700
pg. Bright blue (Nos. 696p and 697p) £5000
h. Bistre (Nos. 696/9) £200
ph. Bistre (Nos. 696p/9p) £2000
j. Reddish brown (Nos. 698/9) £125
pj. Reddish brown (Nos. 698p and 699p) £175

The prices quoted are for each stamp.

259 Cup Winners

1966 (18 Aug). England's World Cup Football Victory. Chalk-surfaced paper. W **179** (sideways). Perf 14×15.

700 **259** 4d. red, reddish purple, bright blue, flesh and black 10 10

These stamps were only put on sale at post offices in England, the Channel Islands and the Isle of Man, and at the Philatelic Bureau in London and also, on 22 August, in Edinburgh on the occasion of the opening of the Edinburgh Festival as well as at Army post offices at home and abroad.

260 Jodrell Bank Radio Telescope

261 British Motor-cars

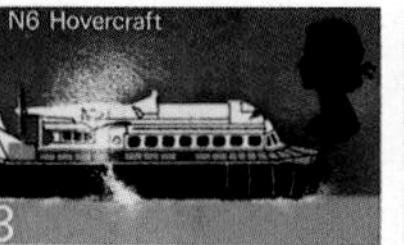

262 'SRN 6' Hovercraft

263 Windscale Reactor

(Des D. and A. Gillespie (4d., 6d.), A. Restall (others))

1966 (19 Sept). British Technology. Chalk-surfaced paper. W **179**. Perf 15×14.

701 **260** 4d. black and lemon 10 10
p. Three phosphor bands 10 10

702 **261** 6d. red, dp blue and orange 10 10
a. Red (Mini-cars) omitted .... £20000 —
b. Deep blue (Jaguar & inscr) omitted £17000
p. Three phosphor bands 10 10

703 **262** 1s.3d. black, orange-red, slate and light greenish blue 15 15
p. Three phosphor bands 20 20

704 **263** 1s.6d. black, yellow-green, bronze-green, lilac and deep blue 15 15
p. Three phosphor bands 20 20

Set of 4 (Ordinary) 40 40
Set of 4 (Phosphor) 50 50

264 **265**

266 **267**

268 **269**

270 Norman Ship

271 Norman Horsemen attacking Harold's Troops

Club flaw (Cyl. 1A No dot, R. 7/2)

(All the above are scenes from the Bayeux Tapestry)

(Des D. Gentleman. Photo. Queen's head die-stamped (6d., 1s.3d.))

1966 (14 Oct). 900th Anniversary of Battle of Hastings. Chalk-surfaced paper. W **179** (sideways on 1s.3d.). Perf 15×14.

No.	Type	Description	Unused	Used
705	**264**	4d. black, olive-green, bistre, deep blue, orange, magenta, green, blue and grey	10	10
		a. Strip of 6. Nos. 705/10	60	60
		ab. Imperforate strip of six	£3500	
		aWi. Strip of 6. Watermark inverted	45·00	
		Wi. Watermark inverted	7·00	
		p. Three phosphor bands	10	10
		pa. Strip of 6. Nos. 705p/10p	60	60
		pWi. Watermark inverted	3·00	
		paWi. Strip of 6. Watermark inverted	20·00	
706	**265**	4d. black, olive-green, bistre, deep blue, orange, magenta, green, blue and grey	10	10
		Wi. Watermark inverted	7·00	
		p. Three phosphor bands	10	10
		pWi. Watermark inverted	2·00	
707	**266**	4d. black, olive-green, bistre, deep blue, orange, magenta, green, blue and grey	10	10
		Wi. Watermark inverted	7·00	
		p. Three phosphor bands	10	10
		pWi. Watermark inverted	3·00	
708	**267**	4d. black, olive-green, bistre, deep blue, magenta, green, blue and grey	10	10
		Wi. Watermark inverted	7·00	
		p. Three phosphor bands	10	10
		pWi. Watermark inverted	3·00	
709	**268**	4d. black, olive-green, bistre, deep blue, orange, magenta, green, blue and grey	10	10
		Wi. Watermark inverted	7·00	
		p. Three phosphor bands	10	10
		pWi. Watermark inverted	3·00	
710	**269**	4d. black, olive-green, bistre, deep blue, orange, magenta, green, blue and grey	10	10
		Wi. Watermark inverted	7·00	
		p. Three phosphor bands	10	10
		pWi. Watermark inverted	3·00	
711	**270**	6d. black, olive-green, violet, blue, green and gold	10	10
		Wi. Watermark inverted	42·00	
		p. Three phosphor bands	10	10
		pWi. Watermark inverted	75·00	
712	**271**	1s.3d. black, lilac, bronze-green, rosine, bistre-brown and gold	20	30
		a. Lilac omitted	£5250	
		b. Club flaw	28·00	
		Wi. Watermark sideways inverted (top of crown pointing to right)*	50·00	
		p. Four phosphor bands	20	40
		pa. Lilac omitted	£1250	
		pb. Club flaw	28·00	
		pWi. Watermark sideways inverted (top of crown pointing to right)*	50·00	
Set of 8 (Ordinary)			85	1·00
Set of 8 (Phosphor)			85	1·00

Nos. 705/10 show battle scenes and they were issued together *se-tenant* in horizontal strips of six within the sheet.

* The normal sideways watermark shows the tops of the Crowns pointing to the left, as seen from the *back of the stamp*.

Other colours omitted in the 4d. values and the stamps affected:

b. Olive-green (Nos. 705/10)	50·00
pb. Olive-green (Nos. 705p/10p)	50·00
c. Bistre (Nos. 705/10)	50·00
pc. Bistre (Nos. 705p/10p)	50·00
d. Deep blue (Nos. 705/10)	60·00
pd. Deep blue (Nos. 705p/10p)	60·00
e. Orange (Nos. 705/7 and 709/10)	50·00
pe. Orange (Nos. 705p/7p and 709p/10p)	50·00
f. Magenta (Nos. 705/10)	50·00
pf. Magenta (Nos. 705p/10p)	50·00
g. Green (Nos. 705/10)	45·00
pg. Green (Nos. 705p/10p)	45·00
h. Blue (Nos. 705/10)	35·00
ph. Blue (Nos. 705p/10p)	50·00
j. Grey (Nos. 705/10)	35·00
pj. Grey (Nos. 705p/10p)	40·00
pk. Magenta and green (Nos. 705p/10p)	—

The prices quoted are for each stamp.

Nos. 705 and 709, with grey and blue omitted, have been seen commercially used, posted from Middleton-in-Teesdale.

The 6d. phosphor is known in a yellowish gold as well as the reddish gold as used in the 1s.3d.

Three examples of No. 712 in a right-hand top corner block of 10 (2×5) are known with the Queen's head omitted as a result of a double paper fold prior to die-stamping. The perforation is normal. Of the other seven stamps, four have the Queen's head misplaced and three are normal.

MISSING GOLD HEADS. The 6d. and 1s.3d. were also issued with the die-stamped gold head omitted but as these can also be removed by chemical means we are not prepared to list them unless a way is found of distinguishing the genuine stamps from the fakes which will satisfy the Expert Committees.

The same remarks apply to Nos. 713/14.

272 King of the Orient

273 Snowman

Missing 'T' (Cyl. 1E No dot, R. 6/2)

(Des Tasveer Shemza (3d.), J. Berry (1s.6d.) (winners of children's design competition). Photo, Queen's head die-stamped)

1966 (1 Dec). Christmas, Children's Paintings. Chalk-surfaced paper. W **179** (sideways on 3d.). Perf 14×15.

No.	Type	Description	Unused	Used
713	**272**	3d. black, blue, green, yellow, red and gold	10	10
		a. Queen's head double*	—	†
		ab. Queen's head double, one albino	£500	
		b. Green omitted		£4250
		c. Missing 'T'	25·00	
		p. One phosphor band at right	10	10
		pEa. Band at left	10	10
		pEb. Horiz pair. Nos. 713p/pEa	20	20
		pc. Missing 'T'	45·00	
714	**273**	1s.6d. blue, red, pink, black and gold	10	10
		a. Pink (hat) omitted	£3800	
		Wi. Watermark inverted	30.00	
		p. Two phosphor bands	10	10
		pWi. Watermark inverted	90·00	

No. 713a refers to stamps showing two impressions, one directly below the other, both with embossing. Examples showing two partial strikes on opposite sides of the stamp, caused by a colour shift are common.

The single phosphor band on No. 713p was produced by printing broad phosphor bands across alternate perforations. Individual* show the band at right or left.

274 Sea Freight

275 Air Freight

Broken undercarriage leg (Cyl. 2, No dot, R. 13/6)

(Des C. Abbott)

1967 (20 Feb). European Free Trade Association (EFTA). Chalk-surfaced paper. W **179**. Perf 15×14.

No.	Type	Description	Unused	Used
715	**274**	9d. deep blue, red, lilac, green, brown, new blue, yellow and black	10	10
		a. Black (Queen's head, etc.), brown, new blue and yellow omitted	£1300	
		b. Lilac omitted	£140	
		c. Green omitted	£140	
		d. Brown (rail trucks) omitted	95·00	
		e. New blue omitted	£140	
		f. Yellow omitted	£140	
		p. Three phosphor bands	10	10
		pb. Lilac omitted	£225	
		pc. Green omitted	£140	
		pd. Brown omitted	95·00	
		pe. New blue omitted	£140	
		pf. Yellow omitted	£180	
		pWi. Watermark inverted	95·00	
716	**275**	1s.6d. violet, red, deep blue, brown, green, blue-grey, new blue, yellow and black	10	10
		a. Red omitted		
		b. Deep blue omitted	£550	
		c. Brown omitted	£140	
		d. Blue-grey omitted	£140	
		e. New blue omitted	£140	
		f. Yellow omitted	£140	
		g. Green omitted	£3750	
		h. Broken undercarriage leg	40·00	
		Wi. Watermark inverted	30·00	
		p. Three phosphor bands	10	10
		pa. Red omitted		
		pb. Deep blue omitted	£140	£140
		pc. Brown omitted	95·00	
		pd. Blue-grey omitted	£140	
		pf. New blue omitted	£140	
		ph. Broken undercarriage leg	40·00	
		pWi. Watermark inverted	30·00	

276 Hawthorn and Bramble

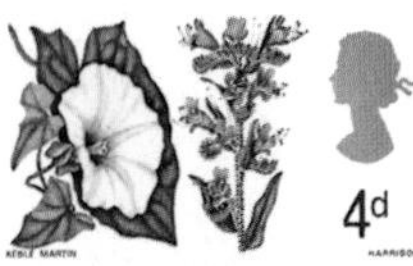

277 Larger Bindweed and Viper's Bugloss

278 Ox-eye Daisy, Coltsfoot and Buttercup

279 Bluebell, Red Campion and Wood Anemone

280 Dog Violet

281 Primroses

(Des Rev. W. Keble Martin (T **276/9**), Mary Grierson (others))

1967 (24 Apr). British Wild Flowers. Chalk-surfaced paper. W **179**. Perf 15×14.

No.	Type	Description	Unused	Used
717	**276**	4d. grey, lemon, myrtle-green, red, agate and slate-purple	10	10
		a. Block of 4. Nos. 717/20	40	40
		aWi. Block of 4. Watermark inverted	9·00	
		b. Grey double*		
		c. Red omitted	£4000	
		f. Slate-purple omitted	£5500	
		Wi. Watermark inverted	2·00	
		p. Three phosphor bands	10	10
		pa. Block of 4. Nos. 717p/20p	40	40
		paWi. Block of 4. Watermark inverted	9·00	
		pd. Agate omitted	£3500	
		pf. Slate-purple omitted	£500	
		pWi. Watermark inverted	2·00	
718	**277**	4d. grey, lemon, myrtle-green, red, agate and violet	10	10
		b. Grey double*		
		Wi. Watermark inverted	2·00	
		p. Three phosphor bands	10	10
		pd. Agate omitted	£3500	
		pe. Violet omitted		
		pWi. Watermark inverted	2·00	
719	**278**	4d. grey, lemon, myrtle-green, red and agate	10	10
		b. Grey double*		
		Wi. Watermark inverted	2·00	
		p. Three phosphor bands	10	10
		pd. Agate omitted	£3500	
		pWi. Watermark inverted	2·00	
720	**279**	4d. grey, lemon, myrtle-green, reddish purple, agate and violet	10	10
		b. Grey double*		
		c. Reddish purple omitted	£2000	
		d. Value omitted†	£9500	
		Wi. Watermark inverted	2·00	
		p. Three phosphor bands	10	10
		pd. Agate omitted	£3500	
		pe. Violet omitted		
		pWi. Watermark inverted	2·00	
721	**280**	9d. lavender-grey, green, reddish violet and orange-yellow	15	15
		Wi. Watermark inverted	1·30	
		p. Three phosphor bands	15	15
722	**281**	1s.9d. lavender-grey, green, greenish yellow and orange	15	15
		p. Three phosphor bands	15	15
Set of 6 (Ordinary)			50	50
Set of 6 (Phosphor)			50	50

Nos. 717/20 were issued together *se-tenant* in blocks of four within the sheet.

* The double impression of the grey printing affects the Queen's head, value and inscription.

† No. 720d was caused by something obscuring the face value on R14/6 during the printing of one sheet.

PHOSPHOR BANDS. Issues from No. 723 are normally with phosphor bands only, except for the high values but most stamps have appeared with the phosphor bands omitted in error. Such varieties are listed under 'Ey' numbers and are priced unused only.

PHOSPHORISED PAPER. Following the adoption of phosphor bands the Post Office started a series of experiments involving the addition of the phosphor to the paper coating before the stamps were printed. No. 743c was the first of these experiments to be issued for normal postal use.

PVA GUM. Polyvinyl alcohol was introduced by Harrisons in place of gum arabic in 1968. As it is almost invisible a small amount of pale yellowish colouring was introduced to make it possible to check that the stamps had been gummed. Although this can be distinguished from gum arabic in unused stamps there is, of course, no means of detecting it in used examples. Where the two forms of gum exist on the same stamps, the PVA type are listed under 'Ev' numbers, except in the case of the 1d. and 4d. (vermilion), both one centre band, which later appeared with gum arabic and these have 'Eg' numbers. 'Ev' and 'Eg' numbers are priced unused only. All stamps printed from No. 763 onwards were issued with PVA gum only *except where otherwise stated.*

It should be further noted that gum arabic is shiny in appearance, and that, normally, PVA gum has a matt appearance. However, depending upon the qualities of the paper ingredients and the resultant absorption of the gum, occasionally, PVA gum has a shiny appearance. In such cases, especially in stamps from booklets, it is sometimes impossible to be absolutely sure which gum has been used except by testing the stamps chemically which destroys them. Therefore, whilst all gum arabic is shiny it does not follow that all shiny gum is gum arabic.

282 **282a**

I II

Two types of the 2d.

I. Value spaced away from left side of stamp (cylinders 1 no dot and dot).

II. Value close to left side from new multipositive used for cylinders 5 no dot and dot onwards. The portrait appears in the centre, thus conforming to the other values.

Three types of the Machin head, known as Head A, B or C, are distinguished by specialists. These are illustrated in Vol. 3 of the *Great Britain Specialised Catalogue*.

(Des after plaster cast by Arnold Machin)

1967 (5 June)–**70**. Chalk-surfaced paper. Two phosphor bands except where otherwise stated. PVA gum except Nos. 725m, 728, 729, 731, 731Ea, 740, 742/Ea, 743/a and 744/Ea. No wmk. Perf 15×14.

No.	Type	Description	Unused	Used
723	**282**	½d. orange-brown (5.2.68)	10	10
		Ey. Phosphor omitted	30·00	
724		1d. light olive (*shades*) (2 bands) (5.2.68)	10	10
		a. Imperf (coil strip)†	£3500	
		b. Part perf pane*	£5000	
		c. Imperf pane*	£5750	
		d. Uncoated paper (1970)**	£150	
		Ey. Phosphor omitted	4·00	
		l. Booklet pane. No. 724×2 *se-tenant* with 730×2 (6.4.68)	3·00	
		lEy. Booklet pane. Phosphor omitted	90·00	
		m. Booklet pane. No. 724×4 *se-tenant* with 734×2 (6.1.69)	90	
		mEy. Booklet pane. Phosphor omitted	£225	
		n. Booklet pane. No. 724×6, 734×3, 734Eb×3 & 735×3 *se-tenant* (1.12.69)	8·50	
		na. Booklet pane. Uncoated paper**	£925	
		nEy. Booklet pane. Phosphor omitted	£225	
725		1d. yellowish olive (1 centre band) (16.9.68)	45	45
		Eg. Gum arabic (27.8.69)	1.00	
		l. Booklet pane. No. 725×4 *se-tenant* with 732×2	4·00	
		lEy. Booklet pane. Phosphor omitted	35·00	
		m. Coil strip. No. 728×2 *se-tenant* with 729, 725Eg & 733Eg (27.8.69)	1·90	
726		2d. lake-brown (Type I) (2 bands) (5.2.68)	10	10
		Ey. Phosphor omitted	40·00	
727		2d. lake-brown (Type II) (2 bands) (1969)	10	10
		Ey. Phosphor omitted	2·00	
728		2d. lake-brown (Type II) (1 centre band) (27.8.69)	35	40
729		3d. violet (*shades*) (1 centre band) (8.8.67)	10	10
		a. Imperf (vert pair)	£950	
		Ey. Phosphor omitted	4·00	
		Ev. PVA gum (*shades*) (12.3.68)	1.00	
		Evy. Phosphor omitted	4·00	
730		3d. violet (2 bands) (6.4.68)	10	15
		a. Uncoated paper**	£6000	
731		4d. deep sepia (*shades*) (2 bands)	10	10
		Ey. Phosphor omitted	4·00	
		Ea. Deep olive-brown	1·00	1·00
		Eay. Phosphor omitted	6·00	
		b. Part perf pane*	£4000	
		Ev. PVA gum (*shades*) (22.1.68)	1·00	
		Evy. Phosphor omitted	4·00	
732		4d. deep olive-brown (*shades*) (1 centre band) (16.9.68)	10	10
		a. Part perf pane*	£4250	
		l. Booklet pane. Two stamps plus two printed labels	1·00	
		lEy. Booklet pane. Phosphor omitted	45·00	
733		4d. bright vermilion (1 centre band) (6.1.69)	10	10
		a. *Tête-bêche* (horiz pair)	£5000	
		b. Uncoated paper**	20·00	
		Ey. Phosphor omitted	4·00	
		l. Booklet pane. Two stamps plus two printed labels (3.3.69)	1·00	
		lEy. Booklet pane. Phosphor omitted	75·00	
		Eg. Gum arabic (27.8.69)	1·00	
		Egy. Phosphor omitted	£1650	
734		4d. bright vermilion (1 band at left) (6.1.69)	65	75
		a. Uncoated paper**	£475	
		Eb. One band at right (1.12.69)	1·00	1·00
		Eba. Ditto. Uncoated paper**	£425	
735		5d. royal blue (*shades*) (1.7.68)	10	10
		a. Imperf pane*	£3500	
		b. Part perf pane*	£2500	
		c. Imperf (pair)††	£275	
		d. Uncoated paper**	40·00	
		Ey. Phosphor omitted	6·50	
		Ee. Deep blue	1·00	1·00
		Eey. Phosphor omitted	6·00	
736		6d. brt reddish purple (shades) (5.2.68)	10	10
		Ey. Phosphor omitted	35·00	
		Ea. Bright magenta	9·00	9·00
		Eb. Claret	1·25	1·25
		Eby. Phosphor omitted	45·00	
737	**282a**	7d. bright emerald (1.7.68)	25	25
		Ey. Phosphor omitted	£100	
738		8d. bright vermilion (1.7.68)	10	15
		Ey. Phosphor omitted	£450	
739		8d. light turquoise-blue (6.1.69)	25	25
		Ey. Phosphor omitted	80·00	
740		9d. myrtle-green (8.8.67)	1·00	1·50
		Ey. Phosphor omitted	60·00	
		Ev. PVA gum (29.11.68)	1·00	
		Evy. Phosphor omitted	85·00	
741	**282**	10d. drab (1.7.68)	25	25
		a. Uncoated paper**	85.00	
		Ey. Phosphor omitted	70·00	
742		1s. light bluish violet (*shades*)	20	20
		Ey. Phosphor omitted	85·00	
		Ea. Pale bluish violet	1·00	1·00
		Ev. Ditto. PVA gum (26.4.68)	1·00	
		Evy. Phosphor omitted	12·00	
743		1s.6d. greenish blue and deep blue (*shades*) (8.8.67)	25	25
		a. Greenish blue omitted	£160	
		Ey. Phosphor omitted	15·00	
		Ev. PVA gum (28.8.68)	1.00	
		Eva. Greenish blue omitted	£100	
		Evy. Phosphor omitted	22·00	
		Evb. Prussian blue and indigo	7.00	7.00
		Evby. Phosphor omitted	18·00	
		c. Phosphorised paper (*Prussian blue and indigo*) (10.12.69)	30	35
		ca. Prussian blue omitted	£450	
744		1s.9d. dull orange and black (*shades*)	25	25
		Ey. Phosphor omitted	65·00	
		Ea. Bright orange and black	1·00	1·00
		Ev. PVA gum (*bright orange and black*) (16.11.70)	2·50	
Set of 16 (one of each value and colour)			2·00	2·25

* BOOKLET ERRORS. See note after No. 556.

** Uncoated paper. This does not respond to the chalky test, and may be further distinguished from the normal chalk-surfaced paper by the fibres which clearly show on the surface, resulting in the printing impression being rougher, and by the screening dots which are not so evident. The 1d., 4d. and 5d. come from the £1 'Stamps for Cooks' Booklet (1969); the 3d. and 10d. from sheets (1969). The 20p. and 50p. high values (Nos. 830/1) exist with similar errors.

† No. 724a occurs in a vertical strip of four, top stamp perforated on three sides, bottom stamp imperf three sides and the two middle stamps completely imperf.

†† No. 735c comes from the original state of cylinder 15 which is identifiable by the screening dots which extend through the gutters of the stamps and into the margins of the sheet. This must not be confused with imperforate stamps from cylinder 10, a large quantity of which was stolen from the printers early in 1970.

The 1d. with centre band and PVA gum (725) only came in the September 1968 10s. booklet (No. XP6). The 1d., 2d. and 4d. with centre band and gum arabic (725Eg, 728 and 733Eg respectively) only came in the coil strip (725m). The 3d. (No. 730) appeared in booklets on 6.4.68, from coils during Dec 68 and from sheets in Jan 1969. The 4d. with one side band at left (734) came from 10s. (band at left) and £1 (band at left or right) booklet *se-tenant* panes, and the 4d. with one side band at right (734Eb) came from the £1 booklet *se-tenant* panes only.

The 4d. (731) in shades of washed-out grey are colour changelings which we understand are caused by the concentrated solvents used in modern dry cleaning methods.

283 'Master Lambton' (Sir Thomas Lawrence)

284 'Mares and Foals in a Landscape' (George Stubbs)

285 'Children Coming Out of School' (L. S. Lowry)

(Des S. Rose)

1967 (10 July). 'British Paintings' (1st series). Chalk-surfaced paper. Two phosphor bands. No wmk. Perf 14×15 (4d.) or 15×14 (others).

No.	Type	Description	Unused	Used
748	**283**	4d. rose-red, lemon, brown, black, new blue and gold	10	10
		a. Gold (value and Queen's head) omitted	£275	
		b. New blue omitted	£15000	
		Ey. Phosphor omitted	7·00	
749	**284**	9d. Venetian red, ochre, grey-black, new-blue, greenish yellow and black	10	10
		a. Black (Queen's head and value) omitted	£1000	
		ab. Black (Queen's head only) omitted	£2100	
		Ey. Phosphor omitted	£500	
750	**285**	1s.6d. greenish yellow, grey, rose, new blue, grey-black and gold.	10	10
		a. Gold (Queen's head) omitted		
		b. New blue omitted	£275	
		c. Grey (clouds and shading) omitted	£150	
		Ey. Phosphor omitted	£300	
Set of 3			30	30

286 *Gipsy Moth IV*

(Des M. and Sylvia Goaman)

1967 (24 July). 'Sir Francis Chichester's World Voyage'. Chalk-surfaced paper. Three phosphor bands. No wmk. Perf 15×14.

No.	Type	Description	Unused	Used
751	**286**	1s.9d. black, brown-red, light emerald and blue	10	10

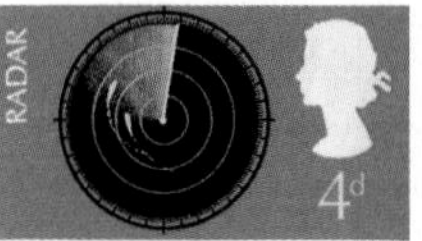

287 Radar Screen

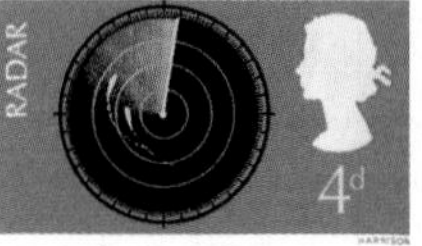

288 *Penicillium notatum*

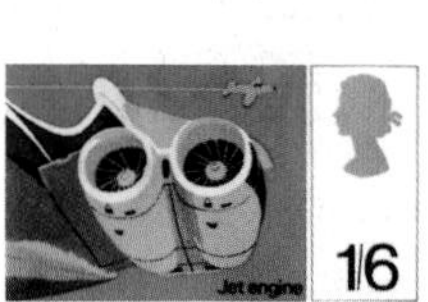

289 Vickers VC-10 Jet Engines

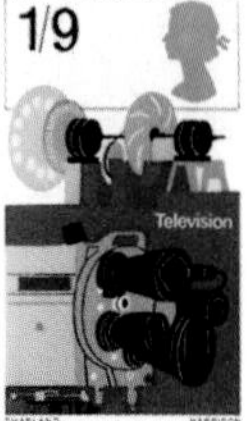

290 Television Equipment

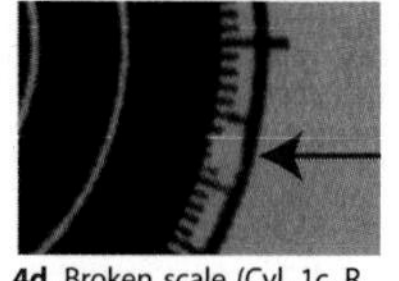

4d. Broken scale (Cyl. 1c, R. 10/2)

(Des C. Abbott (4d., 1s.), Negus-Sharland team (others))

1967 (19 Sept). British Discovery and Invention. Chalk-surfaced paper. Three phosphor bands (4d.) or two phosphor bands (others). W **179** (sideways on 1s.9d.). Perf 14×15 (1s.9d.) or 15×14 (others).

No.	Type	Description	Unused	Used
752	**287**	4d. greenish yellow, black and vermilion	10	10
		a. Broken scale	45·00	
		Ey. Phosphor omitted	5·00	
753	**288**	1s. blue-green, lt greenish blue, slate-purple and bluish violet	10	10
		Wi. Watermark inverted	20·00	
		Ey. Phosphor omitted	10·00	
754	**289**	1s.6d. black, grey, royal blue, ochre and turquoise-blue	10	10
		Wi. Watermark inverted	£240	
		Ey. Phosphor omitted	£525	
755	**290**	1s.9d. black, grey-blue, pale olive-grey, violet and orange	10	10
		a. Pale olive-grey omitted		£4500
		b. Orange (Queen's head) omitted	£30000	
		Ey. Phosphor omitted	£525	
Set of 4			40	40

WATERMARK. All issues from this date are on unwatermarked paper unless otherwise stated

291 'The Adoration of the Shepherds' (School of Seville)

292 'Madonna and Child' (Murillo)

293 'The Adoration of the Shepherds' (Louis le Nain)

(Des S. Rose)

1967 Christmas, Paintings. Chalk-surfaced paper. One phosphor band (3d.) or two phosphor bands (others). Perf 15×14 (1s.6d.) or 14×15 (others).

756	**291**	3d. olive-yellow, rose, blue, black and gold (27.11)	10	15
		a. Gold (value and Queen's head) omitted	£110	
		ab. Gold (Queen's head only) omitted	£2750	
		b. Printed on the gummed side	£625	
		c. Rose omitted	£3250	
		Ey. Phosphor omitted	1·00	
757	**292**	4d. bright purple, greenish yellow, new blue, grey-black and gold (18.10)	10	15
		a. Gold (value and Queen's head) omitted	80·00	
		ab. Gold (Queen's head only) omitted	£4500	
		b. Gold ('4D' only) omitted	£2500	
		c. Greenish yellow (Child, robe and Madonna's face) omitted	£7500	
		d. Greenish yellow and gold omitted	£15000	
		Ey. Phosphor omitted	£125	
758	**293**	1s.6d. bright purple, bistre, lemon, black, orange-red, ultramarine and gold (27.11)	15	15
		a. Gold (value and Queen's head) omitted	£15000	
		ab. Gold (value only) omitted	£3000	
		b. Ultramarine omitted	£750	
		c. Lemon omitted	£20000	
		Ey. Phosphor omitted	12·00	
Set of 3			30	30

Distinct shades exist of the 3d. and 4d. values but are not listable as there are intermediate shades. For the 4d., stamps from one machine show a darker background and give the appearance of the yellow colour being omitted, but this is not so and these should not be confused with the true missing yellow No. 757c.

No. 757b comes from stamps in the first vertical row of a sheet.

The 3d. and 4d. values are known imperforate. They are of proof status.

(Recess Bradbury, Wilkinson)

1967–68. No wmk. White paper. Perf 11×12.

759	**166**	2s.6d. black-brown (1.7.68)	10	20
760	**167**	5s. red (10.4.68)	50	50
761	**168**	10s. bright ultramarine (10.4.68)	4.50	2·00
762	**169**	£1 black (4.12.67)	6·50	2·00
Set of 4			10·00	4·25

PVA GUM. All the following issues from this date have PVA gum *except where footnotes state otherwise.*

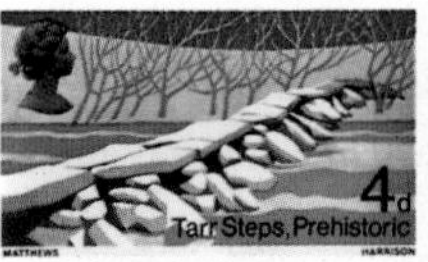

294 Tarr Steps, Exmoor

295 Aberfeldy Bridge

296 Menai Bridge

297 M4 Viaduct

(Des A. Restall (9d.), L. Rosoman (1s.6d.), J. Matthews (others))

1968 (29 Apr). British Bridges. Chalk-surfaced paper. Two phosphor bands. Perf 15×14.

763	**294**	4d. black, bluish violet, turquoise-blue and gold	10	10
		a. Printed on gummed side	35·00	
		Ey. Phosphor omitted	10.00	
764	**295**	9d. red-brown, myrtle-green, ultramarine, olive-brown, black and gold	10	15
		a. Gold (Queen's head) omitted	£225	
		b. Ultramarine omitted	†	£7000
		Ey. Phosphor omitted	15·00	
765	**296**	1s.6d. olive-brown, red-orange, brt green, turquoise-green and gold	15	20
		a. Gold (Queen's head) omitted	£375	
		b. Red-orange (rooftops) omitted	£375	
		Ey. Phosphor omitted	50·00	
766	**297**	1s.9d. olive-brown, greenish yellow, dull green, dp ultramarine and gold	15	25
		a. Gold (Queen's head) omitted	£325	
		Ey. Phosphor omitted	10·00	
		Eya. Gold (Queen's head) & Phosphor omitted	£3500	—
Set of 4			45	65

Used examples of the 1s.6d. and 1s.9d. are known with both the gold and the phosphor omitted.

298 'TUC' and Trades Unionists

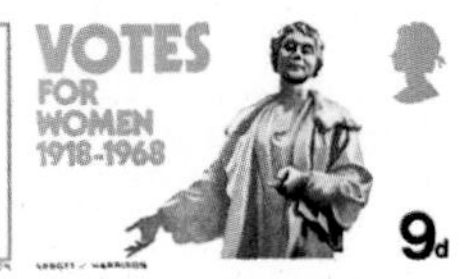
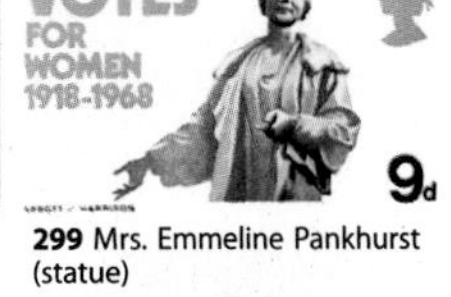

299 Mrs. Emmeline Pankhurst (statue)

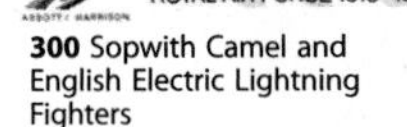
300 Sopwith Camel and English Electric Lightning Fighters

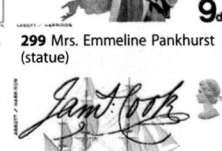

301 Captain Cook's *Endeavour* and Signature

(Des D. Gentleman (4d.), C. Abbott (others))

1968 (29 May). Anniversaries (1st series). Events described on stamps. Chalk surfaced paper. Two phosphor bands. Perf 15×14.

767	**298**	4d. emerald, olive, blue and black	10	10
		Ey. Phosphor omitted	12·00	
768	**299**	9d. reddish violet, bluish grey and black	10	10
		Ey. Phosphor omitted	7·00	
769	**300**	1s. olive-brown, blue, red, slate-blue and black	15	20
		Ey. Phosphor omitted	10·00	
770	**301**	1s.9d. yellow-ochre and blackish brown	20	25
		Ey. Phosphor omitted	£190	
Set of 4			50	60

302 'Queen Elizabeth I' (unknown artist)

303 'Pinkie' (Sir Thomas Lawrence)

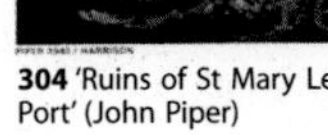
304 'Ruins of St Mary Le Port' (John Piper)

305 'The Hay Wain' (John Constable)

(Des S. Rose)

1968 (12 Aug). British Paintings (2nd series). Queen's head embossed. Chalk-surfaced paper. Two phosphor bands. Perf 15×14 (1s.9d.) or 14×15 (others).

771	**302**	4d. black, vermilion, greenish yellow, grey and gold	10	10
		a. Gold (value and Queen's head) omitted	£300	
		b. Vermilion omitted*	£700	
		Ec. Embossing omitted	90·00	
		Ey. Phosphor omitted	1·50	
		Eya. Gold (value and Queen's head) and phosphor omitted	£4000	
772	**303**	1s. mauve, new blue, greenish yellow, black, magenta and gold	10	15
		a. Gold (value and Queen's head) omitted	£7500	
		Eb. Gold (value and Queen's head), embossing and phosphor omitted	£650	
		Ec. Embossing omitted		
		Ey. Phosphor omitted	7·00	
773	**304**	1s.6d. slate, orange, black, mauve, greenish yellow, ultramarine and gold	15	20
		a. Gold (value and Queen's head) omitted	£300	
		Eb. Embossing omitted	£300	
		Ey. Phosphor omitted	10·00	
774	**305**	1s.9d. greenish yellow, black, new blue, red and gold	15	20
		a. Gold (value and Queen's head) and embossing omitted	£900	
		b. Red omitted	£10000	
		Ec. Embossing omitted	£140	
		Ey. Phosphor omitted	20·00	
Set of 4			45	60

No. 774a is only known with the phosphor also omitted.

* The effect of this is to leave the face and hands white and there is more yellow and olive in the costume.

The 4d. also exists with the value only omitted resulting from a colour shift.

306 Boy and Girl with Rocking Horse

307 Girl with Doll'sHouse

308 Boy with TrainSet

(Des Rosalind Dease. Head printed in gold and then embossed)

1968 (25 Nov). Christmas, Children's Toys. Chalk-surfaced paper. One centre phosphor band (4d.) or two phosphor bands (others). Perf 15×14 (4d.) or 14×15 (others).

775	**306**	4d. black, orange, vermilion, ultramarine, bistre and gold	10	10
		a. Gold omitted	£6000	
		b. Vermilion omitted*	£525	
		c. Ultramarine omitted	£500	
		d. Bistre omitted		
		e. Orange omitted	†	—
		Ef. Embossing omitted	6·00	
		Ey. Phosphor omitted	5·00	
		Eya. Embossing and phosphor omitted		
776	**307**	9d. yellow-olive, black, brown, yellow, magenta, orange, turquoise-green and gold	15	15
		a. Yellow omitted	£175	
		b. Turquoise-green (dress) omitted	£22000	
		Ec. Embossing omitted	6·00	
		Ey. Phosphor omitted	10·00	
		Eya. Embossing and phosphor omitted	10·00	
777	**308**	1s.6d. ultramarine, yellow-orange, bright purple, blue-green, black and gold	15	20
		Ea. Embossing omitted		
		Ey. Phosphor omitted	15·00	
Set of 3			35	40

* The effect of the missing vermilion is shown on the rocking horse, saddle and faces which appear orange instead of red.

A single used example of the 4d. exists with the bistre omitted.

No. 775c is only known with phosphor also omitted.

Two machines were used for printing for the 4d. value:

Stamps from cylinders 1A-1B-2C-1D-1E in combination with 1F, 2F or 3F (gold) were printed entirely on the Rembrandt sheet-fed machine. They invariably have the Queen's head level with the top of the boy's head and the sheets are perforated through the left side margin.

Stamps from cylinders 2A-2B-3C-2D-2E in combination with 1F, 2F, 3F or 4F (gold) were printed on the reel-fed Thrissell machine in five colours (its maximum colour capacity) and subsequently sheet-fed on the Rembrandt machine for the Queen's head and the embossing. The position of the Queen's head is generally lower than on the stamps printed at one operation but it varies in different parts of the sheet and is not, therefore, a sure indication for identifying single stamps. Another small difference is that the boy's grey pullover is noticeably 'moth-eaten' in the Thrissell printings and is normal on the Rembrandt. The Thrissell printings are perforated through the top margin.

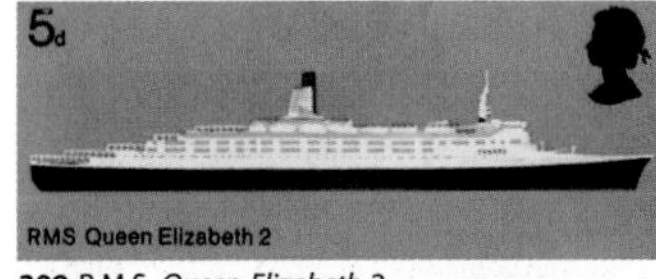

309 R.M.S. *Queen Elizabeth 2*

310 Elizabethan Galleon

311 East Indiaman

312 *Cutty Sark*

313 S.S. *Great Britain*

314 R.M.S. *Mauretania*

(Des D. Gentleman)

1969 (15 Jan). British Ships. Chalk-surfaced paper. Two vertical phosphor bands at right (1s.), one horizontal phosphor band (5d.) or two phosphor bands (9d.). Perf 15×14.

No.	Type	Description	Unused	Used
778	**309**	5d. black, grey, red and turquoise..	10	10
		a. Black (Queen's head, value, hull and inscr) omitted	£3500	
		b. Grey (decks, etc.) omitted	£225	
		c. Red (inscription) omitted	£225	
		Ey. Phosphor omitted	5·00	
		Eya. Red and phosphor omitted	£190	
779	**310**	9d. red, blue, ochre, brown, black and grey	10	10
		a. Strip of 3. Nos. 779/81	40	50
		ab. Red and blue omitted	£3250	
		ac. Blue omitted	£3250	
		Ey. Phosphor omitted	12·00	
		Eya. Strip of 3. Nos. 779/81. Phosphor omitted	40·00	
780	**311**	9d. ochre, brown, black and grey...	10	10
		Ey. Phosphor omitted	12·00	
781	**312**	9d. ochre, brown, black and grey...	10	10
		Ey. Phosphor omitted	12·00	
782	**313**	1s. brown, black, grey, green and greenish yellow	15	15
		a. Pair. Nos. 782/3	50	60
		ab. Greenish yellow omitted	£4500	
		Ey. Phosphor omitted	28·00	
		Eya. Pair. Nos. 782/3. Phosphor omitted	65·00	
783	**314**	1s. red, black, brown, carmine and grey	15	15
		a. Carmine (hull overlay) omitted	£40000	
		b. Red (funnels) omitted	£30000	
		c. Carmine and red omitted	£30000	
		Ey. Phosphor omitted	30·00	
Set of 6			80	1·00

The 9d. and 1s. values were arranged in horizontal strips of three and pairs respectively throughout the sheet. No. 779ab is known only with the phosphor also omitted.

315 Concorde in Flight

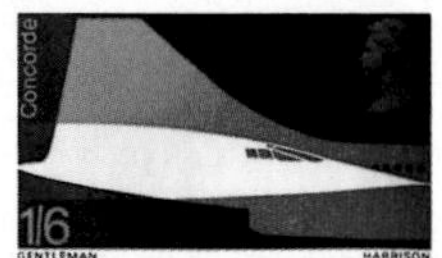

316 Plan and Elevation Views

317 Concorde's Nose and Tail

(Des M. and Sylvia Goaman (4d.), D. Gentleman (9d., 1s.6d.))

1969 (3 Mar). First Flight of Concorde. Chalk-surfaced paper. Two phosphor bands. Perf 15×14.

No.	Type	Description	Unused	Used
784	**315**	4d. yellow-orange, violet, greenish blue, blue-green and pale green	10	10
		a. Violet (value etc.) omitted	£750	
		b. Yellow-orange omitted	£750	
		Ey. Phosphor omitted	1·00	
		Eya. Yellow-orange and phosphor omitted	£750	
785	**316**	9d. ultramarine, emerald, red and grey-blue	15	15
		a. Face value and inscr omitted	—	
		Ey. Phosphor omitted	£100	
786	**317**	1s.6d. deep blue, silver-grey and light blue	15	15
		a. Silver-grey omitted	£750	
		Ey. Phosphor omitted	9·00	
Set of 3			35	35

No. 785a is caused by a colour shift of the grey-blue. On the only known example the top of the Queen's head appears across the perforations at foot. No. 786a affects the Queen's head which appears in the light blue colour.

318 Queen Elizabeth II
(See also Type **357**)

(Des after plaster cast by Arnold Machin. Recess Bradbury, Wilkinson)

1969 (5 Mar). Perf 12.

No.	Type	Description	Unused	Used
787	**318**	2s.6d. brown	20	20
788		5s. crimson-lake	85	25
789		10s. deep ultramarine	3·00	3·75
790		£1 bluish black	1·75	75
Set of 4			5·00	4·50

For decimal issue, see Nos. 829/31*b* and notes after No. 831*b*.

319 Page from *Daily Mail*, and Vickers FB-27 Vimy Aircraft

320 Europa and CEPT Emblems

321 ILO Emblem

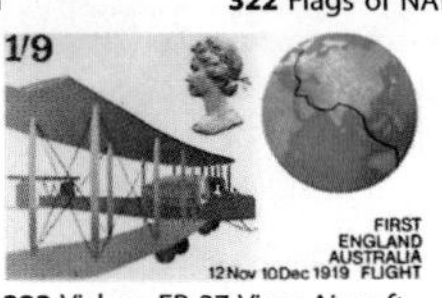

322 Flags of NATO Countries

323 Vickers FB-27 Vimy Aircraft and Globe showing Flight

(Des P. Sharland (5d., 1s., 1s.6d.), M. and Sylvia Goaman (9d., 1s.9d.))

1969 (2 Apr). 'Anniversaries' (2nd series). Events described on stamps. Chalk-surfaced paper. Two phosphor bands. Perf 15×14.

No.	Type	Description	Unused	Used
791	**319**	5d. black, pale sage-green, chestnut and new blue	10	10
		Ey. Phosphor omitted		
792	**320**	9d. pale turquoise, dp blue, lt emerald-green and black	10	15
		aEy. Phosphor omitted		
		a. Uncoated paper*	£1800	
		Ey. Phosphor omitted	18·00	
793	**321**	1s. brt purple, dp blue and lilac	15	20
		Eya. Phosphor omitted	10·00	
794	**322**	1s.6d. red, royal blue, yellow-green, black, lemon and new blue	15	20
		e. Black omitted	£125	
		f. Yellow-green (from flags) omitted	85·00	
		g. Lemon (from flags) omitted	†	£4500
		Ey. Phosphor omitted	9·00	
		Eya. Yellow-green and phosphor omitted	85·00	
795	**323**	1s.9d. yellow-olive, greenish yellow and pale turquoise-green	25	30
		a. Uncoated paper*	£275	
		Ey. Phosphor omitted	6·00	
Set of 5			65	80

*Uncoated paper. The second note after No. 744 also applies here.

No. 794g is only known used on First Day Cover from Liverpool.

A trial of the 9d value in green and red is known.

324 Durham Cathedral **325** York Minster

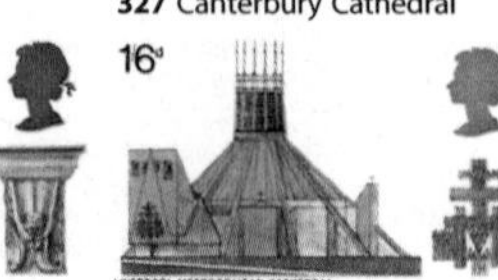

326 St Giles, Edinburgh **327** Canterbury Cathedral

9d 16d

328 St Paul's Cathedral **329** Liverpool Metropolitan Cathedral

(Des P. Gauld)

1969 (28 May). British Architecture (1st series). Cathedrals. Chalk-surfaced paper. Two phosphor bands. Perf 15×14.

No.	Type	Description	Unused	Used
796	**324**	5d. grey-black, orange, pale bluish violet and black	10	10
		a. Block of 4. Nos. 796/9	40	50
		ab. Block of 4. Uncoated paper†	£1000	
		b. Pale bluish violet omitted	£12500	
797	**325**	5d. grey-black, pale bluish violet, new blue and black	10	10
		b. Pale bluish violet omitted	£12500	
798	**326**	5d. grey-black, purple, green and black	10	10
		c. Green omitted*	£100	
799	**327**	5d. grey-black, green, new blue and black	10	10
800	**328**	9d. grey-black, ochre, pale drab, violet and black	15	20
		a. Black (value) omitted	£250	
		Ey. Phosphor omitted	45·00	
		Eya. Black and phosphor omitted	£325	
801	**329**	1s.6d. grey-black, pale turquoise, pale reddish violet, pale yellow-olive and black	20	25
		a. Black (value) omitted	£2750	
		b. Black (value) double	£500	
		Ey. Phosphor omitted	20·00	
Set of 6			70	85

Nos. 796/9 were issued together *se-tenant* in blocks of four throughout the sheet.

* The missing green on the roof top is known on R. 2/5, R. 8/5 and R. 10/5 but all are from different sheets and it only occurred in part of the printing, being 'probably caused by a batter on the impression cylinder'. Examples are also known with the green partly omitted.

† Uncoated paper. The second note after No. 744 also applies here.

330 The King's Gate, Caernarvon Castle

331 The Eagle Tower, Caernarvon Castle

332 Queen Eleanor's Gate, Caernarvon Castle

333 Celtic Cross, Margam Abbey

334 H.R.H. The Prince of Wales (after photograph by G. Argent)

(Des D. Gentleman)

1969 (1 July). 'Investiture of H.R.H. The Prince of Wales.' Chalk-surfaced paper. Two phosphor bands. Perf 14×15.

No.	Type	Description	Unused	Used
802	**330**	5d. dp olive-grey, lt olive-grey, dp grey, light grey, red, pale turquoise-green, black and silver	10	10
		a. Strip of 3. Nos. 802/4	30	50
		b. Black (value and inscr) omitted	£700	
		c. Red omitted*	£1250	
		d. Deep grey omitted**	£500	
		e. Pale turquoise-green omitted	£1250	
		f. Light grey omitted	£9500	
		Ey. Phosphor omitted	5·00	
		Eya. Strip of 3. Nos. 802/4. Phosphor omitted	15·00	
803	**331**	5d. dp olive-grey, lt olive-grey, dp grey, light grey, red, pale turquoise-green, black and silver	10	10
		b. Black (value and inscr) omitted	£700	
		c. Red omitted*	£1250	
		d. Deep grey omitted**	£500	
		e. Pale turquoise-green omitted	£1250	
		f. Light grey (marks on walls, window frames, etc) omitted	£9500	—
		Ey. Phosphor omitted	5·00	
804	**332**	5d. dp olive-grey, lt olive-grey, dp grey, lt grey, red, pale turquoise-green, black and silver	10	10
		b. Black (value and inscr) omitted	£700	
		c. Red omitted*	£1250	
		d. Deep grey omitted**	£500	
		e. Pale turquoise-green omitted	£1250	
		f. Light grey omitted	£9500	
		Ey. Phosphor omitted	5·00	
805	**333**	9d. dp grey, lt grey, black and gold	15	20
		Ey. Phosphor omitted	25·00	
806	**334**	1s. blackish yellow-olive and gold	15	20
		Ey. Phosphor omitted	18·00	
Set of 5			55	80

Nos. 802/4 were issued together *se-tenant* in strips of three throughout the sheet.

* The 5d. value is also known with the red misplaced downwards and where this occurs the red printing does not take very well on the silver background and in some cases is so faint it could be mistaken for a missing red. However, the red can be seen under a magnifying glass and caution should therefore be exercised when purchasing copies of Nos. 802/4c.

** The deep grey affects the dark portions of the windows and doors.

No. 803f is only known commercially used on cover.

335 Mahatma Gandhi

(Des B. Mullick)

1969 (13 Aug). 'Gandhi Centenary Year.' Chalk-surfaced paper. Two phosphor bands. Perf 15×14.

807 **335** 1s.6d. black, green, red-orange and grey 25 30
b. Printed on the gummed side £1750
Ey. Phosphor omitted .... 4·00

336 National Giro 'G' Symbol

337 Telecommunications–International Subscriber Dialling

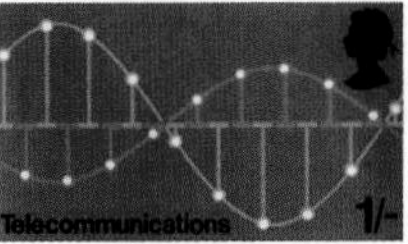

338 Telecommunications–Pulse Code Modulation

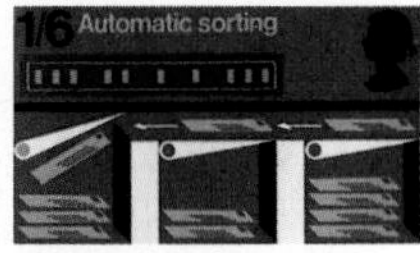

339 Postal Mechanisation–Automatic Sorting

(Des D. Gentleman. Litho De La Rue)

1969 (1 Oct). Post Office Technology Commemoration. Chalk-surfaced paper. Two phosphor bands. Perf 13½×14.

808 **336** 5d. new blue, greenish blue, lavender and black 10 10
Ey. Phosphor omitted .... 5·00
809 **337** 9d. emerald, violet-blue and black 10 10
810 **338** 1s. emerald, lavender and black 15 15
Ey. Phosphor omitted £325
811 **339** 1s.6d. bright purple, light blue, grey-blue and black 20 20
Set of 4 .... 50 50

340 Herald Angel

341 The Three Shepherds

342 The Three Kings

(Des F. Wegner. Queen's head (and stars 4d., 5d. and scrollwork 1s.6d.) printed in gold and then embossed)

1969 (26 Nov). Christmas, Traditional Religious Themes. Chalk-surfaced paper. Two phosphor bands (5d., 1s.6d.) or one centre band (4d.). Perf 15×14.

812 **340** 4d. vermilion, new blue, orange, brt purple, light green, bluish violet, blackish brown and gold 10 10
a. Gold (Queen's head etc.) omitted £12000
Eb. Centre band 3½ mm 30 20
813 **341** 5d. magenta, light blue, royal blue, olive-brown, green, greenish yellow, red and gold 10 10
a. Lt blue (sheep, etc.) omitted £110
b. Red omitted* £2200
c. Gold (Queen's head) omitted £1200
d. Green omitted £375
e. Olive-brown, red and gold omitted £15000
Ef. Embossing omitted .... 25·00
Ey. Phosphor omitted .... 5·00
814 **342** 1s.6d. greenish yellow, brt purple, bluish violet, dp slate, orange, green, new blue and gold 15 15
a. Gold (Queen's head etc.) omitted £150
b. Deep slate (value) omitted £525
c. Greenish yellow omitted £475
e. New blue omitted £140
Ef. Embossing omitted .... 12·00
Ey. Phosphor omitted .... 6·00
Eya. Embossing and phosphor omitted .... 12·00
Set of 3 .... 30 30

* The effect of the missing red is shown on the hat, leggings and purse which appear as dull orange.

No. 812 has one centre band 8 mm. wide but this was of no practical use in the automatic facing machines and after about three-quarters of the stamps had been printed the remainder were printed with a 3½mm. band (No. 812Eb).

No. 813e was caused by a paper fold and also shows the phosphor omitted.

Used copies of the 5d. have been seen with the olive-brown or greenish yellow (tunic at left) omitted.

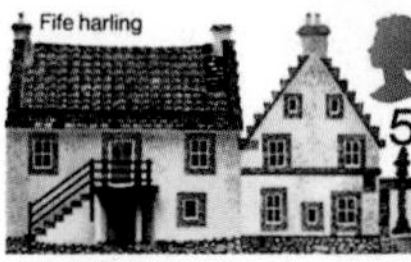

343 Fife Harling

344 Cotswold Limestone

345 Welsh Stucco

346 Ulster Thatch

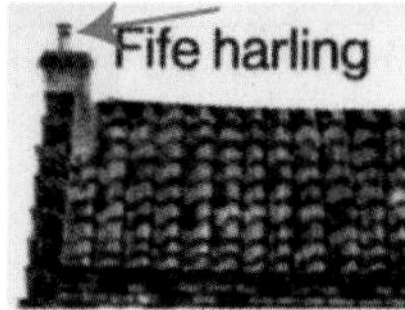

5d. Lemon omitted from left chimney (Cyl. 1H, R. 12/2)

(Des D. Gentleman (5d., 9d.), Sheila Robinson (1s., 1s.6d.))

1970 (11 Feb). British Rural Architecture. Chalk-surfaced paper. Two phosphor bands. Perf 15×14.

815 **343** 5d. grey, grey-black, black, lemon, greenish blue, orange-brown, ultramarine and green 10 10
a. Lemon omitted £160
b. Grey (Queen's head and cottage shading) omitted .... —
c. Greenish blue (door) omitted .... † £4800
d. Grey black (inscription & face value) omitted £20000
e. Grey black (face value only) omitted £17000
f. Green omitted (cobblestones).
g. Lemon omitted from left chimney .... 35·00
Ey. Phosphor omitted .... 2·00
816 **344** 9d. orange-brown, olive-yellow, bright green, black, grey-black and grey 15 15
Ey. Phosphor omitted .... 10·00
817 **345** 1s. deep blue, reddish lilac, drab and new blue 15 15
a. New blue omitted £125
Ey. Phosphor omitted .... 15·00
818 **346** 1s.6d. greenish yellow, black, turquoise-blue and lilac 20 25
a. Turquoise-blue omitted £17500
Ey. Phosphor omitted .... 5·00
Set of 4 .... 55 60

Used examples of the 5d. exist, one of which is on piece, with the greenish blue colour omitted.

347 Signing the Declaration of Arbroath

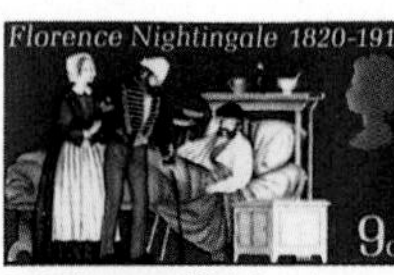

348 Florence Nightingale attending Patients

349 Signing of International Co-operative Alliance

350 Pilgrims and *Mayflower*

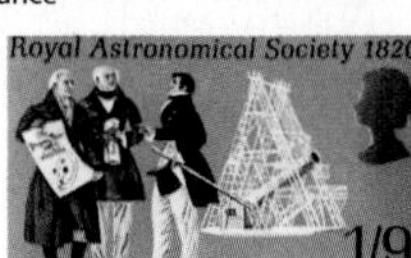

351 Sir William Herschel, Francis Baily, Sir John Herschel and Telescope

(Des F. Wegner (5d., 9d. and 1s.6d.), Marjorie Saynor (1s., 1s.9d.). Queen's head printed in gold and then embossed)

1970 (1 Apr). Anniversaries (3rd series). Events described on stamps. Chalk-surfaced paper. Two phosphor bands. Perf 15×14.

819 **347** 5d. black, yellow-olive, blue, emerald, greenish yellow, rose-red, gold and orange-red 10 10
a. Gold (Queen's head) omitted £3500
b. Emerald omitted £475
Ey. Phosphor omitted £375
820 **348** 9d. ochre, deep blue, carmine, black, blue-green, yellow-olive, gold and blue 10 10
a. Ochre omitted £475
Eb. Embossing omitted .... 15·00
Ey. Phosphor omitted .... 5·00
821 **349** 1s. green, greenish yellow, brown, black, cerise, gold and lt blue 15 15
a. Gold (Queen's head) omitted .... 90·00
Eb. Green and embossing omitted £150
c. Green omitted £150
d. Brown omitted £300
Ee. Embossing omitted .... 12·00
Ey. Phosphor omitted .... 5·00
Eya. Brown and phosphor omitted £300
Eyb. Embossing and phosphor omitted .... 22·00
822 **350** 1s.6d. greenish yellow, carmine, deep yellow-olive, emerald, black, blue, gold and sage-green 20 20
a. Gold (Queen's head) omitted £300
b. Emerald omitted £150
Ec. Embossing omitted .... 6·00
Ey. Phosphor omitted .... 5·00
823 **351** 1s.9d. black, slate, lemon, gold and bright purple 20 20
a. Lemon (trousers and document) omitted £10000 £6000
Eb. Embossing omitted .... 75·00
Ey. Phosphor omitted .... 5·00
Set of 5 .... 70 70

No. 823a is known mint, or used on First Day Cover postmarked London WC.

352 'Mr. Pickwick and Sam Weller' (*Pickwick Papers*)

353 'Mr. and Mrs. Micawber' (*David Copperfield*)

354 'David Copperfield and Betsy Trotwood' (*David Copperfield*)

355 'Oliver asking for more' (*Oliver Twist*)

356 'Grasmere' (from engraving by J. Farrington, R.A.)

(Des Rosalind Dease. Queen's head printed in gold and then embossed)

1970 (3 June). Literary Anniversaries (1st series). Death Centenary of Charles Dickens (novelist) (5d.×4) and Birth Bicentenary of William Wordsworth (poet) (1s.6d.). Chalk-surfaced paper. Two phosphor bands. Perf 14×15.

824 **352** 5d. black, orange, silver, gold and magenta 10 10
a. Block of 4. Nos. 824/7 .... 40 60
ab. Imperf (block of four) £2250
ac. Silver (inscr) omitted (block of four) .... —
825 **353** 5d. black, magenta, silver, gold and orange 10 10
826 **354** 5d. black, light greenish blue, silver, gold and yellow-bistre 10 10
b. Yellow-bistre (value) omitted £8500
827 **355** 5d. black, yellow-bistre, silver, gold and light greenish blue 10 10
b. Yellow-bistre (background) omitted £22000
c. Lt greenish blue (value) omitted* £775
d. Lt greenish blue and silver (inscr at foot) omitted £32000
828 **356** 1s.6d. yellow-olive, black, silver, gold and bright blue 15 20
a. Gold (Queen's head) omitted £10000
b. Silver ('Grasmere') omitted £250
c. Bright blue (face value) omitted £20000
d. Bright blue and silver omitted £25000
Ee. Embossing omitted .... 6·00
Ey. Phosphor omitted .... 5·00
Eya. Embossing and phosphor omitted .... 22·00
Set of 5 .... 50 70

Nos. 824/7 were issued together *se-tenant* in blocks of four throughout the sheet.

* No. 827c (unlike No. 826b) comes from a sheet on which the colour was only partially omitted so that, although No. 827 was completely without the light greenish blue colour, it was still partially present on No. 826.

Essays exist of Nos. 824/7 showing the Queen's head in silver and with different inscriptions. (*Price £13000 per block of 4*).

357 (Value redrawn)

(Des after plaster cast by Arnold Machin. Recess B.W.)

1970 (17 June)–**72**. Decimal Currency. Chalk-surfaced paper or phosphorised paper (10p.). P 12.

No.	Type	Description	Unused	Used
829		10p. cerise	50	50
830		20p. olive-green	60	20
831		50p. deep ultramarine	1·25	25
831*b*	**357**	£1 bluish black (6.12.72)	2·25	40
829/831*b* *Set of 4*			3·25	1·20

The 20p. and 50p. exist on thinner, uncoated paper and are listed in the *Great Britain Concise Catalogue*.

A whiter paper was introduced in 1973. The £1 appeared on 27 Sept. 1973, the 20p. on 30 Nov. 1973 and the 50p. on 20 Feb. 1974.

The 50p. was issued on 1 Feb. 1973 on phosphorised paper. This cannot be distinguished from No. 831 with the naked eye.

The £1, T **318**, was also issued, on 17 June 1970, in sheets of 100 (10×10) instead of panes of 40 (8×5) but it is not easy to distinguish from No. 790 in singles. It can be readily differentiated when in large strips or marginal pieces showing sheet markings or plate numbers.

358 Runners

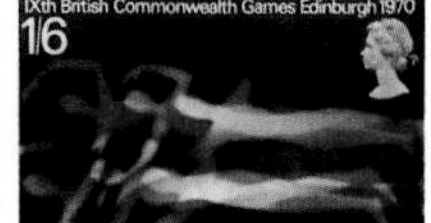

359 Swimmers

360 Cyclists

(Des A. Restall. Litho D.L.R.)

1970 (15 July). Ninth British Commonwealth Games. Chalk-surfaced paper. Two phosphor bands. Perf 13½×14.

No.	Type	Description	Unused	Used
832	**358**	5d. pink, emerald, greenish yellow and deep yellow-green	10	10
		a. Greenish yellow omitted	—	
		Ey. Phosphor omitted	£200	
833	**359**	1s.6d. light greenish blue, lilac, bistre-brown and Prussian blue	15	15
		Ey. Phosphor omitted	60·00	
834	**360**	1s.9d. yellow-orange, lilac, salmon and deep red-brown	15	15
832/834 *Set of 3*			45	45

1840 first engraved issue

361 1d. Black (1840)

1847 first embossed issue

362 1s. Green (1847)

1855 first surface printed issue

363 4d. Carmine (1855)

(Des D. Gentleman)

1970 (18 Sept). Philympia 70 Stamp Exhibition. Chalk-surfaced paper. Two phosphor bands. Perf 14×14½.

No.	Type	Description	Unused	Used
835	**361**	5d. grey-black, brownish bistre, black and dull purple	10	10
		a. Dull purple (Queen's head) omitted	—	
		Ey. Phosphor omitted	5·00	
836	**362**	9d. light drab, bluish green, stone, black and dull purple	15	15
		Ey. Phosphor omitted	12·00	
837	**363**	1s.6d. carmine, light drab, black and dull purple	20	20
		Ey. Phosphor omitted	4·00	
835/837 *Set of 3*			40	40

364 Shepherds and Apparition of the Angel

365 Mary, Joseph and Christ in the Manger

366 The Wise Men bearing gifts

(Des Sally Stiff after De Lisle Psalter. Queen's head printed in gold and then embossed)

1970 (25 Nov). Christmas, Robert De Lisle Psalter. Chalk-surfaced paper. One centre phosphor band (4d.) or two phosphor bands (others). Perf 14×15.

No.	Type	Description	Unused	Used
838	**364**	4d. brown-red, turquoise-green, pale chestnut, brown, grey-black, gold and vermilion	10	10
		Ea. Embossing omitted	50·00	
		Ey. Phosphor omitted	60·00	
839	**365**	5d. emerald, gold, blue, brown-red, ochre, grey-black and violet	10	10
		a. Gold (Queen's head) omitted	†	£3500
		b. Emerald omitted	£140	
		c. Imperf (pair)	£400	
		d. Ochre omitted	£5500	†
		Ed. Embossing omitted	15·00	
		Ey. Phosphor omitted	5·00	
840	**366**	1s.6d. gold, grey-black, pale turquoise-green, salmon, ultramarine, ochre and yellow-green	15	15
		a. Salmon omitted	£220	
		b. Ochre omitted	£140	
		Ec. Embossing omitted	35·00	
		Ey. Phosphor omitted	5·00	
		Eya. Embossing and phosphor omitted		
838//840 *Set of 3*			30	30

COUNTRY ISSUES

For country issues of Guernsey and Jersey, *see* after Great Britain Postal Fiscals

Printers (£ s. d. stamps of all regions);—Photo Harrison & Sons. Portrait by Dorothy Wilding Ltd.

DATES OF ISSUE. Conflicting dates of issue have been announced for some of the country issues, partly explained by the stamps being released on different dates by the Philatelic Bureau in Edinburgh or the Philatelic Counter in London and in the countries. We have adopoted the practice of giving the earliest known dates, since once released the stamps could have been used anywhere in the UK.

I. ISLE OF MAN

1

2

(Des J. Nicholson. Portrait by Dorothy Wilding Ltd. Photo Harrison)

1958 (18 Aug)–**68**. W **179**. P 15×14.

No.	Type	Description	Unused	Used
1	**1**	2½d. carmine-red (8.6.64)	70	70
2	**2**	3d. deep lilac	50	50
		a. Chalk-surfaced paper (17.5.63).	6·50	6·50
		p. One centre phosphor band (27.6.68)	20	20
3		4d. ultramarine (7.2.66)	1·00	1·00
		p. Two phosphor bands (5.7.67)	30	30
1/3p *Set of 3*			1·00	1·00

No. 2a was released in London sometime after 17 May 1963, this being the date of issue in Douglas.

1968–69. No wmk. Chalk-surfaced paper. PVA gum. One centre phosphor band (Nos. 5/6) or two phosphor bands (others). P 15×14.

No.	Type	Description	Unused	Used
4	**2**	4d. blue (24.6.68)	25	30
5		4d. olive-sepia (4.9.68)	30	30
		Ey. Phosphor omitted	25·00	
6		4d. bright vermilion (26.2.69)	45	45
7		5d. royal blue (4.9.68)	45	45
		Ey. Phosphor omitted	£175	
4/7 *Set of 4*			1·25	1·25

II. NORTHERN IRELAND

N 1

N 2

N 3

(Des W. Hollywood (3d., 4d., 5d.), L. Pilton (6d., 9d.), T. Collins (1s.3d., 1s.6d.))

1958–67. W **179**. P 15×14.

No.	Type	Description	Unused	Used
NI1	**N 1**	3d. deep lilac (18.8.58)	15	15
		p. One centre phosphor band (9.6.67)	25	25
NI2		4d. ultramarine (7.2.66)	15	15
		p. Two phosphor bands (10.67)	15	15
NI3	**N 2**	6d. deep claret (29.9.58)	50	50
NI4		9d. bronze-green (2 phosphor bands) (1.3.67)	40	40
NI5	**N 3**	1s.3d. green (29.9.58)	50	50
NI6		1s.6d. grey-blue (2 phosphor bands) (1 .3.67)	40	40
		Ey. Phosphor omitted	£225	
NI1/NI6 *Set of 6*			1·90	1·90

1968–69. No wmk. Chalk-surfaced paper. One centre phosphor band (Nos. NI8/9) or two phosphor bands (others). P 15×14.

No.	Type	Description	Unused	Used
NI7	**N 1**	4d. deep bright blue (27.6.68)	25	25
		Ev. PVA gum (23.10.68)	30·00	
NI8		4d. olive-sepia (4.9.68)	25	25
		Ey. Phosphor omitted		
NI9		4d. bright vermilion (26.2.69)	30	30
		Ey. Phosphor omitted	4·50	
NI10		5d. royal blue (4.9.68)	40	40
		Ey. Phosphor omitted	25·00	
NI11	**N 3**	1s.6d. grey-blue (20.5.69)	1·50	1·50
		Ey. Phosphor omitted	£500	
NI7/NI11 *Set of 5*			2·00	2·00

No. N17 was only issued in Northern Ireland with gum arabic. After it had been withdrawn from Northern Ireland but whilst still on sale at the philatelic counters elsewhere, about 50 sheets with PVA gum were sold over the London Philatelic counter on 23 October 1968, and some were also on sale at the British Philatelic Exhibition Post Office in October, without any prior announcement. The other values exist with PVA gum only.

III. SCOTLAND

S 1

S 2

S 3

(Des G. Huntly (3d., 4d., 5d), J. Fleming (6d., 9d.), A. Imrie (1s.3d., 1s.6d.))

1958–67. W **179**. P 15×14.

No.	Type	Description	Unused	Used
S1	**S 1**	3d. deep lilac (18.8.58)	15	15
		p. Two phosphor bands (29.1.63).	7·50	6·00
		pa. One phosphor band at right (30.4.65)	25	25
		pb. Band at left	25	25
		pc. Horizontal pair. Nos. S1pa/S1pb.	60	75
		pd. One centre phosphor band (9.11.67)	15	25
S2		4d. ultramarine (7.2.66)	20	20
		p. Two phosphor bands	20	20
S3	**S 2**	6d. deep claret (29.9.58)	25	25
		p. Two phosphor bands (29.1.63).	25	25
S4		9d. bronze-green (2 phosphor bands) (1.3.67)	40	40
S5	**S 3**	1s.3d. green (29.9.58)	40	40
		p. Two phosphor bands (29.1.63).	50	50
S6		1s.6d. grey-blue (2 phosphor bands) (1.3.67)	60	60
S1/S6 *Set of 6*			1·80	1·80

The one phosphor band on No. S1pa was produced by printing broad phosphor bands across alternate vertical perforations. Individual stamps show the band at right or left (same prices either way).

1967–70. No wmk. Chalk-surfaced paper. One centre phosphor band (S7, S9/10) or two phosphor bands (others). P 15×14.

No.	Type	Description	Unused	Used
S7	**S 1**	3d. deep lilac (16.5.68)	15	15
		Ey. Phosphor omitted	7·00	
		Ev. PVA gum	10	
S8		4d. deep bright blue (28.11.67)	30	30
		Ey. Phosphor omitted	10·00	
		Ev. PVA gum	10	
S9		4d. olive-sepia (4.9.68)	15	15
		Ey. Phosphor omitted	3·00	
S10		4d. bright vermilion (26.2.69)	15	15
		Ey. Phosphor omitted	2·50	
S11		5d. royal blue (4.9.68)	25	25
		Ey. Phosphor omitted	55·00	
S12	**S 2**	9d. bronze-green (28.9.70)	4·00	4·00
		Ey. Phosphor omitted	£275	
S13	**S 3**	1s.6d. grey-blue (12.12.68)	1·25	1·25
		Ey. Phosphor omitted	£125	
S7/S13 *Set of 7*			5·75	5·75

Nos. S7/8 exist with both gum arabic and PVA gum; others with PVA gum only.

IV. WALES

From the inception of the Country stamps, the Welsh versions were tendered to members of the public at all Post Offices within the former County of Monmouthshire but the national alternatives were available on request. By August 1961 the policy of 'dual stocking' of definitive stamps was only maintained at Abergavenny, Chepstow. Newport and Pontypool. Offices with a Monmouthshire postal address but situated outside the County, namely Beachley, Brockweir. Redbrook. Sedbury, Tutshill, Welsh Newton and Woodcroft, were not supplied with the Welsh stamps.

W 1

W 2

W 3

(Des R. Stone)

1958–67. W **179**. P 15×14.

No.	Type	Description	Unused	Used
W1	**W 1**	3d. deep lilac (18.8.58)	15	15
		p. One centre phosphor band (16.5.67)	20	15
W2		4d. ultramarine (7.2.66)	20	20
		p. Two phosphor bands (10.67)	20	20
W3	**W 2**	6d. deep claret (29.9.58)	35	35
W4		9d. bronze-green (2 phosphor bands) (1.3.67)	35	35

		Ey. Phosphor omitted	£375	
W5	W 3	1s.3d. green (29.9.58)	40	40
W6		1s.6d. grey-blue (2 phosphor bands) (1.3.67)	40	40
		Ey. Phosphor omitted	50·00	
W1/W6 *Set of 6*			1·75	1·75

1967–69. No wmk. Chalk-surfaced paper. One centre phosphor band (W 7, W 9/W 10) or two phosphor bands (others). P 15×14.

W7	W 1	3d. deep lilac (6.12.67)	15	15
		Ey. Phosphor omitted	70·00	
W8		4d. ultramarine (21.6.68)	15	15
W9		4d. olive-sepia (4.9.68)	15	15
W10		4d. bright vermilion (26.2.69)	15	15
		Ey. Phosphor omitted	2·00	
W11		5d. royal blue (4.9.68)	15	15
		Ey. Phosphor omitted	3·00	
W12	W 3	1s.6d. grey-blue (1.8.69)	2·00	2·00
W7/W12 *Set of 6*			2·50	2·50

The 3d. exists with gum arabic only; the remainder with PVA gum only.

STAMP BOOKLETS

For a full listing of Great Britain stamp booklets see the *Great Britain Concise Catalogue* published each Spring.

POSTAGE DUE STAMPS

PERFORATIONS. All postage due stamps to No. D89 are perf 14×15.

WATERMARKS. The normal sideways watermark shows the tops of the crowns pointing to the right, *as seen from the back of the stamp*.

D 1

D 2

(Des G. Eve. Typo Somerset House (early trial printings of ½d., 1d., 2d. and 5d.; all printings of 1s.) or Harrison (later printings of all values except 1s.)).

1914 (20 Apr)–**22.** W **100** (Simple Cypher) sideways.

D1	D 1	½d. emerald	50	25
		Wi. Wmk sideways-inverted	2·00	2·00
		Wj. Wmk sideways-reversed	18·00	20·00
		Wk. Wmk sideways-inverted and reversed	—	20·00
D2		1d. carmine	50	25
		a. Pale carmine	75	50
		Wi. Wmk sideways-inverted	2·00	2·00
		Wj. Wmk sideways-reversed	—	20·00
		Wk. Wmk sideways-inverted and reversed	18·00	20·00
D3		1½d. chestnut (1922)	48·00	20·00
		Wi. Wmk sideways-inverted	70·00	24·00
D4		2d. agate	50	25
		Wi. Wmk sideways-inverted	3·75	3·75
		Wk. Wmk sideways-inverted and reversed	18·00	18·00
D5		3d. violet (1918)	9·00	75
		a. Bluish violet	10·00	2·75
		Wi. Wmk sideways-inverted	40·00	40·00
		Wk. Wmk sideways-inverted and reversed	—	—
D6		4d. dull grey-green (12.20)	£150	50·00
		Wi. Wmk sideways-inverted	40·00	5·00
D7		5d. brownish cinnamon	7·00	3·50
		Wi. Wmk sideways-inverted	20·00	20·00
D8		1s. bright blue (1915)	40·00	5·00
		a. Deep bright blue	40·00	5·00
		Wi. Wmk sideways-inverted	40·00	40·00
		Wk. Wmk sideways-inverted and reversed	—	—
		s. Optd 'SPECIMEN'	45·00	
D1/D8 *Set of 8*			£130	32·00

Stamps from the above issue are known bisected and used for half their face value at the following sorting offices:

1d. Barrhead (1922), Bristol (1918), Cowes (1923), Elgin (1921), Kidlington (1922, 1923), Kilburn, London NW (1923), Malvern (1915), Palmers Green, London N (1922), Plaistow, London E (1916), River, Dover (1922), Rock Ferry, Birkenhead (1915, 1918), St Ouens, Jersey (1924), Salford, Manchester (1914), South Tottenham, London N (1921), Warminster (1922), Wavertree, Liverpool (1921), Whitchurch (1922), Winton, Bournemouth (1921), Wood Green, London N (1921)

2d. Anerley, London SE (1921), Bethnal Green, London E (1918), Christchurch (1921), Didcot (1919), Ealing, London W (1921), Hythe, Southampton (1923), Kirkwall (1922), Ledbury (1922), Malvern (1921, 1923), Sheffield (1921), Shipley (1922), Streatham, London SW (1921), Victoria Docks & North Woolwich (1921), West Kensington, London W (1921, 1922)

3d. Malvern (trisected and used for 1d.) (1921), Warminster (1922)

(Typo Waterlow)

1924. As 1914–1922, but on thick chalk-surfaced paper.

D9	D 1	1d. carmine	6·00	6·00
		Wi. Wmk sideways-inverted		

(Typo Waterlow and (from 1934) Harrison)

1924–31. W **111** (Block Cypher) sideways.

D10	D 1	½d. emerald (6.25)	1·25	75
		Wi. Wmk sideways-inverted	5·00	2·50
D11		1d. carmine (4.25)	60	25
		Wi. Wmk sideways-inverted	—	30·00
D12		1½d. chestnut (10.24)	48·00	22·00
		Wi. Wmk sideways-inverted	—	75·00
D13		2d. agate (7.24)	1·00	25
		Wi. Wmk sideways-inverted	—	30·00
D14		3d. dull violet (10.24)	1·50	25
		a. Printed on gummed side	£125	†
		Wi. Wmk sideways-inverted	—	40·00
		b. Experimental paper W **111a**	95·00	95·00
D15		4d. dull grey-green (10.24)	15·00	4·25
		Wi. Wmk sideways-inverted	40·00	40·00
D16		5d. brownish cinnamon (1.31)	65·00	45·00
D17		1s. deep blue (9.24)	8·50	50
		Wi. Wmk sideways-inverted	55·00	—
D18	D 2	2s.6d. purple/*yellow* (5.24)	85·00	1·75
		Wi. Wmk sideways-inverted	—	90
		s. Optd 'SPECIMEN'	55·00	
D10/D18 *Set of 9*			£200	70·00

Stamps from the above issue are known bisected and used for half their face value at the following sorting offices:

1d. Ashton under Lyne (1932), Hastings (1930), Penryn, Cornwall (1928), Shenfield (1926), Wimbledon, London SW (1925)

2d. Perranwell Station (1932)

1936–37. W **125** (E 8 R) sideways.

D19	D 1	½d. emerald (6.37)	15·00	11·00
D20		1d. carmine (5.37)	2·00	1·75
D21		2d. agate (5.37)	15·00	12·00
D22		3d. dull violet (3.37)	2·00	2·00
D23		4d. dull grey-green (12.36)	65·00	35·00
D24		5d. brownish cinnamon (11.36)	90·00	30·00
		a. Yellow-brown (1937)	40·00	28·00
D25		1s. deep blue (12.36)	25·00	8·50
D26	D 2	2s.6d. purple/*yellow* (5.37)	£325	12·00
D19/D26 *Set of 8 (cheapest)*			£450	£100

The 1d. of the above issue is known bisected and used for half its face value at the following sorting office:

1d. Solihull (1937)

1937–38. W **127** (G VI R) sideways.

D27	D 1	½d. emerald (5.38)	13·00	3·75
D28		1d. carmine (5.38)	3·00	50
		Wi. Wmk sideways-inverted	2·75	—
D29		2d. agate (5.38)	11·00	30
		Wi. Wmk sideways-inverted	£150	—
D30		3d. violet (12.37)	11·10	30
		Wi. Wmk sideways-inverted	£150	—
D31		4d. dull grey-green (9.37)	£110	10·00
		Wi. Wmk sideways-inverted	£300	—
D32		5d. yellow-brown (11.38)	17·00	75
		Wi. Wmk sideways-inverted	£150	—
D33		1s. deep blue (10.37)	80·00	75
		Wi. Wmk sideways-inverted	£150	—
D34	D 2	2s.6d. purple/*yellow* (9.38)	85·00	1·25
D27/D34 *Set of 8*			£300	16·00

The 2d. from the above issue is known bisected and used for half its face value at the following sorting offices:

2d. Boreham Wood (1951), Camberley (1951), Harpenden (1951, 1954), St Albans (1951)

DATES OF ISSUE. The dates for Nos. D35/D39 are those on which stamps were first issued by the Supplies Department to postmasters.

1951–52. Colours changed and new value (1½d.). W **127** (G VI R) sideways.

D35	D 1	½d. yellow-orange (18.9.51)	3·50	3·50
		a. Bright orange	55·00	
D36		1d. violet-blue (6.6.51)	1·50	75
		Wi. Wmk sideways-inverted	—	
D37		1½d. green (11.2.52)	2·00	2·00
		Wi. Wmk sideways-inverted	£140	£140
D38		4d. blue (14.8.51)	50·00	22·00
		Wi. Wmk sideways-inverted	†	£1000
D39		1s. ochre (6.12.51)	28·00	5·25
		Wi. Wmk sideways-inverted	£2800	—
D35/9 *Set of 5*			75·00	30·00

The 1d. of the above issue is known bisected and used for half its face value at the following sorting offices:

1d. Camberley (1954), Capel, Dorking (1952)

1954–55. W **153** (Mult Tudor Crown and E 2 R) sideways.

D40	D 1	½d. orange (8.6.55)	7·00	5·25
		Wi. Wmk sideways-inverted	£150	£150
D41		2d. agate (28.7.55)	26·00	23·00
		Wi. Wmk sideways-inverted	—	—
D42		3d. violet (4.5.55)	75·00	60·00
D43		4d. blue (14.7.55)	26·00	32·00
		a. Imperf (pair)	£250	
D44		5d. yellow-brown (19.5.55)	20·00	20·00
D45	D 2	2s.6d. purple/*yellow* (11.54)	£150	5·75
		Wi. Wmk sideways-inverted	—	—
D40/5 *Set of 6*			£250	£130

1955–57. W **165** (Mult St Edward's Crown and E 2 R) sideways.

D46	D 1	½d. orange (16.7.56)	2·75	3·25
		Wi. Wmk sideways-inverted	85·00	—
D47		1d. violet-blue (7.6.56)	5·00	1·50
D48		1½d. green (13.2.56)	8·50	7·00
		Wi. Wmk sideways-inverted	85·00	—
D49		2d. agate (22.5.56)	45·00	3·50
D50		3d. violet (5.3.56)	6·00	1·50
		Wi. Wmk sideways-inverted	£100	—
D51		4d. blue (24.4.56)	25·00	6·00
		Wi. Wmk sideways-inverted	£175	—
D52		5d. brown-ochre (23.3.56)	26·00	20·00
D53		1s. ochre (22.11.55)	65·00	2·25
		Wi. Wmk sideways-inverted	—	—
D54	D 2	2s.6d. purple/*yellow* (28.6.57)	£200	8·50
		Wi. Wmk sideways-inverted	—	—
D55		5s. scarlet/*yellow* (25.1 1.55)	£150	32·00
		Wi. Wmk sideways-inverted	—	£375
D46/55 *Set of 10*			£475	75·00

Stamps from the above issue are known bisected and used for half their face value at the following sorting offices:

1d. Beswick, Manchester (1958), Huddersfield (1956), London SE (1957)

2d. Eynsham, Oxford (1956), Garelochhead, Helensburgh (1956), Harpenden (1956), Hull (1956), Kingston on Thames (1956), Leicester Square, London WC (1956), London WC (1956)

3d. London SE (1957) 4d. Poplar, London E (1958)

1959–63. W **179** (Mult St Edward's Crown) sideways.

D56	D 1	½d. orange (18.10.61)	15	1·25
		Wi. Wmk sideways-inverted	2·50	2·50
D57		1d. violet-blue (9.5.60)	15	50
		Wi. Wmk sideways-inverted	£125	—
D58		1½d. green (5.10.60)	2·50	2·50
D59		2d. agate (14.9.59)	1·10	50
		Wi. Wmk sideways-inverted	£200	—
D60		3d. violet (24.3.59)	30	30
		Wi. Wmk sideways-inverted	85·00	85·00
D61		4d. blue (17.12.59)	30	30
		Wi. Wmk sideways-inverted	£300	—
D62		5d. yellow-brown (6.11.61)	45	60
		Wi. Wmk sideways-inverted	5·00	6·00
D63		6d. purple (29.3.62)	50	30
		Wi. Wmk sideways-inverted	£400	£400
D64		1s. ochre (11 .4.60)	90	30
		Wi. Wmk sideways-inverted	75·00	75·00
D65	D 2	2s.6d. purple/*yellow* (11.5.61)	3·00	50
		Wi. Wmk sideways-inverted	15·00	15·00
D66		5s. scarlet/*yellow* (8.5.61)	8·50	1·00
		Wi. Wmk sideways-inverted	25·00	25·00
D67		10s. blue/*yellow* (2.9.63)	11·50	5·75
		Wi. Wmk sideways-inverted	40·00	25·00
D68		£1 black/*yellow* (2.9.63)	45·00	8·00
D56/D68 *Set of 13*			65·00	20·00

Whiter paper. The note after No. 586 also applies to Postage Due stamps.

Stamps from the above issue are known bisected and used for half their face value at the following sorting offices:

1d. Chieveley, Newbury (1962, 1963), Henlan, Llandyssil (1961), Mayfield (1962), St Albans (1964)

2d. Doncaster (?)

The 1d. is known bisected at various offices between November 1961 and July 1964. The 2d. is known bisected at Doncaster.

1968–69. Typo. No wmk. Chalk-surfaced paper.

D69	D 1	2d. agate (11.4.68)	75	1·00
		Ev. PVA gum	75	
D70		3d. violet (9.9.68)	1·00	1·00
D71		4d. blue (6.5.68)	1·00	1·00
		Ev. PVA gum	£2250	
D72		5d. orange-brown (3.1.69)	8·00	11·00
D73		6d. purple (9.9.68)	2·25	1·75
D74		1s. ochre (19.11.68)	4·00	2·50
D69/D74 *Set of 6*			15·00	16·00

The 2d. and 4d. exist with gum arabic and PVA gum; the remainder with PVA gum only.

Stamps from the above issue are known bisected and used for half their face value at the following sorting offices:

4d. Northampton (1970)

6d. Kilburn, London NW (1968)

1968–69. Photo. No wmk. Chalk-surfaced paper. PVA gum.

D75	D 1	4d. blue (12.6.69)	7·00	6·75
D76		8d. red (3.10.68)	50	1·00

Nos. D75/D76 are smaller, 21½×17½ mm.

The 4d. is known bisected in April 1970 (Northampton).

D 3

D 4

(Des J. Matthews. Photo Harrison)

1970 (17 June)–**75.** Decimal Currency. Chalk-surfaced paper.

D77	D 3	½p. turquoise-blue (15.2.71)	15	2·50
D78		1p. deep reddish purple (15.2.71)	15	15
D79		2p. myrtle-green (15.2.71)	20	15
D80		3p. ultramarine (15.2.71)	20	15
D81		4p. yellow-brown (15.2.71)	25	15
D82		5p. violet (15.2.71)	25	15
D83		7p. red-brown (21.8.74)	35	1·00
D84	D 4	10p. carmine	30	30
D85		11p. slate-green (18.6.75)	50	1·00
D86		20p. olive-brown	60	25
D87		50p. ultramarine	2·00	1·25
D88		£1 black	4·00	1·00
D89		£5 orange-yellow and black (2.4.73)	25·00	1·50
D77/D89 *Set of 13*			30·00	7·75

The 2p. was bisected at Exeter on 25 October 1977.

DEPARTMENTAL OFFICIALS

The following Official stamps were exclusively for the use of certain government departments. Until 1882 official mail used ordinary postage stamps purchased at post offices, the cash being refunded once a quarter. Later the government departments obtained Official stamps by requisition.

Official stamps may have been on sale to the public for a short time at Somerset House but they were not sold from post offices. The system of only supplying the Government departments with stamps was open to abuse so that all official stamps were withdrawn on 13 May 1904.

PRICES. Please note that, with the exception of Government Parcels Stamps, the price columns in this section are for mounted mint, used and used on cover examples. For Government Parcels Stamps they are for mint and used only.

OVERPRINTS, PERFORATIONS, WATERMARKS. All official stamps were overprinted by Thomas De La Rue & Co. and are perf 14. Except for the 5s., and 10s. on Anchor, they are on Crown watermarked paper unless otherwise stated.

OFFICIAL STAMP

In 1840 the 1d. black (Type **1**), with 'V R' in the upper corners, was prepared for official use, but was never issued for postal purposes. Obliterated specimens are those which were used for experimental trials of obliterating inks, or those that passed through the post by oversight.

V 1

1840. Prepared for use but not issued; 'V' 'R' in upper corners. Imperf.

V1	V 1	1d. black	£32000	£35000

INLAND REVENUE

These stamps were used by revenue officials in the provinces, mail to and from Head Office passing without a stamp. The London Office used these stamps only for foreign mail.

I.R. OFFICIAL (O 1) I. R. OFFICIAL (O 2)

Optd with Types O **1** (½d. to 1s.) or O **2** (others).

1882–1901. Stamps of Queen Victoria.

(a) Issues of 1880–1881

		Unused	**Used*	*Used on cover*
O1	½d. deep green (1.11.82)	£135	60·00	£120
O2	½d. pale green	90·00	40·00	
O3	1d. lilac (Die II) (1.10.82)	8·00	6·00	30·00
	a. Optd in blue-black	£300	£125	
	b. 'OFFICIAL' omitted	—	£12500	
	c. Imperf	£4500		
	ca. Imperf, optd in blue-black	£4500		
	Wi. Watermark inverted	—	£2200	
O4	6d. grey (Plate 18) (3.11.82)	£575	£140	

No. O3 with the lines of the overprint transposed is an essay.

(b) Issues of 1884–1888

O5	½d. slate-blue (8.5.85)	85·00	35·00	£135
O6	2½d. lilac (12.3.85)	£525	£180	£1400
O7	1s. dull green (12.3.85)	£6000	£1900	
O8	5s. rose (blued paper) (Wmk Anchor) (12.3.85)	£17500	£6500	
	a. Raised stop after 'R'	£18500	£7250	
O9	5s. rose (Wmk Anchor) (3.90)	£12000	£2500	
	a. Raised stop after 'R'	£14000	£3200	
	b. Optd in blue-black	£14000	£3200	
O9*c*	10s. cobalt (blued paper) (Wmk Anchor) (12.3.85)	£38000	£9500	
	ca. Raised stop after 'R'			
	cb. cobalt (white paper) (Wmk Anchor)	£22000	£7750	
O9*d*	10s. ultramarine (blued paper) (Wmk Anchor) (12.3.85)	£25000	£7500	
	da Raised stop after 'R'	£27000	£8500	
O10	10s. ultramarine (Wmk Anchor) (3.90)	£11500	£3750	
	a. Raised stop after 'R'	£12500	£4500	
	b. Optd in blue-black	£12500	£4500	
O11	£1 brown-lilac (Wmk Crowns) (12.3.85)	£75000	£30000	
	a. Frame broken	£100000	—	
O12	£1 brown-lilac (Wmk Orbs) (3.90)	£100000	£40000	
	a. Frame broken	£150000		
	b. Optd in blue-black	£160000		

(c) Issues of 1887–1892.

O13	½d. vermilion (15.5.88)	15·00	7·00	£110
	a. Without 'I.R.'	£7000		
	b. Imperf	£7000		
	c. Optd double (imperf)	£8000		
	s. Optd 'SPECIMEN' (9, 15)	£120		
O14	2½d. purple/*blue* (2.92)	£175	30·00	£450
	s. Optd 'SPECIMEN' (9, 13, 15)	£120		
O15	1s. dull green (9.89)	£1000	£375	£3750
	a. Optd in blue-black	£2250		
	s. Optd 'SPECIMEN' (9, 15)	£260		
O16	£1 green (6.92)	£12500	£2500	
	a. No stop after 'R'	—	£4000	
	b. Frame broken	£20000	£5250	
	s. Optd 'SPECIMEN' (9, 10, 15)	£2250		

(d) Issues of 1887 and 1900.

O17	½d. blue-green (4.01)	20·00	15·00	£350
	s. Optd 'SPECIMEN' (15)	£160		
O18	6d. purple/*rose-red* (1.7.01)	£500	£150	
	s. Optd 'SPECIMEN' (15, 16)	£250		
O19	1s. green and carmine (12.01)	£4250	£1800	
	s. Optd 'SPECIMEN' (15)	£1100		

* O1/19 **For well-centred, lightly used +35%**

Nos. O3, O13, O15 and O16 may be found showing worn impressions of the overprints with thicker letters.

1902–04. Stamps of King Edward VII. Ordinary paper.

O20	½d. blue-green (4.2.02)	32·00	4·50	£150
O21	1d. scarlet (4.2.02)	22·00	3·00	95·00
O22	2½d. ultramarine (19.2.02)	£1000	£280	
O23	6d. pale dull purple (14.3.04)	£475000	£300000	
O24	1s. dull green and carmine (29.4.02)	£3750	£900	
O25	5s. bright carmine (29.4.02)	£45000	£11000	
	a. Raised stop after 'R'	£50000	£13000	
O26	10s. ultramarine (29.4.02)	£100000	£48000	
	a. Raised stop after 'R'	£125000	£48000	
O27	£1 dull blue-green (29.4.02)	£62500	£25000	

Although an issue date of 4 February has long been recorded, the 1d. is not currently known used before 24 February and the ½d. before early March 1902.

OFFICE OF WORKS

These were issued to Head and Branch (local) offices in London and to Branch (local) offices at Birmingham, Bristol, Edinburgh, Glasgow, Leeds, Liverpool, Manchester and Southampton. The overprints on stamps of value 2d. and upwards were created later in 1902, the 2d. for registration fees and the rest for overseas mail.

O.W. OFFICIAL (O 3)

Optd with Type O **3**

1896 (24 Mar)–**02.** Stamps of Queen Victoria.

		Unused	**Used*	*Used on Cover*
O31	½d. vermilion	£350	£150	£800
O32	½d. blue-green (2.02)	£475	£225	
O33	1d. lilac (Die II)	£500	£150	£1000
O34	5d. dull purple and blue (II) (29.4.02)	£4000	£1400	
O35	10d. dull purple and carmine (28.5.02)	£7250	£2250	

1902 (11 Feb)–**03.** Stamps of King Edward VII. Ordinary paper.

O36	½d. blue-green (2.02)	£575	£180	£2000
O37	1d. scarlet	£575	£180	£425
O38	2d. yellowish green and carmine-red (27.4.02)	£2000	£450	£3250
O39	2½d. ultramarine (29.4.02)	£3400	£675	£4250
O40	10d. dull purple & carmine (28.5.03)	£47500	£7000	

* O31/O40 **For well-centred, lightly used +25%.**

ARMY

Letters to and from the War Office in London passed without postage. The overprinted stamps were distributed to District and Station Paymasters nationwide, including Cox and Co., the Army Agents, who were paymasters to the Household Division.

ARMY OFFICIAL (O 4) ARMY OFFICIAL (O 5)

1896 (1 Sept)–**01.** Stamps of Queen Victoria optd with Type O 4 (½d., 1d.) or O 5 (2½d., 6d.).

		Unused	**Used*	*Used on cover*
O41	½d. vermilion	8·00	3·00	65·00
	a. 'OFFICIAI' (R.13/7)	£300	£130	
	b. Lines of optd transposed	£4700		
	Wi. Watermark inverted	£800	£375	
O42	½d. blue-green (6.00)	10·00	15·00	
	Wi. Watermark inverted	£1000	£650	
O43	1d. lilac (Die II)	8·00	7·00	£110
	a. 'OFFICIAI' (R.13/7)	£240	£150	
O44	2½d. purple/*blue*	50·00	35·00	£775
O45	6d. purple/*rose-red* (20.9.01)	£110	60·00	£1700

Nos. O41a and O43a occur in sheets overprinted by Forme 1.

ARMY OFFICIAL (O 6)

1902–03. Stamps of King Edward VII optd with Type O **4** (Nos. O48/50) or Type O **6** (No. O52). Ordinary paper.

O48	½d. blue-green (11.2.02)	5·50	2·25	£100
O49	1d. scarlet (11.2.02)	5·50	2·25	£100
	a. 'ARMY' omitted	†	—	
O50	6d. pale dull purple (23.8.02)	£175	80·00	
O52	6d. pale dull purple (12.03)	£3000	£1600	

GOVERNMENT PARCELS

These stamps were issued to all departments, including Head Office, for use on parcels weighing over 3 lb. Below this weight government parcels were sent by letter post to avoid the 55% of the postage paid from accruing to the railway companies, as laid down by parcel-post regulations. Most government parcels stamps suffered heavy postmarks in use.

GOVT PARCELS (O 7)

Optd as Type O **7**

1883 (1 Aug)–**86.** Stamps of Queen Victoria.

O61	1½d. lilac (1.5.86)	£400	£100
	a. No dot under 'T'	£775	£175
	b. Dot to left of 'T'	£775	£175
O62	6d. dull green (1.5.86)	£3500	£1400
O63	9d. dull green	£2750	£1200
O64	1s. orange-brown (watermark Crown, Pl 13)	£1750	£300
	a. No dot under 'T'	£2750	£500
	b. Dot to left of 'T'	£2750	£500
O64*c*	1s. orange-brown (Pl 14)	£3500	£600
	ca. No dot under 'T'	£4500	£850
	cb. Dot to left of 'T'		

1887–90. Stamps of Queen Victoria.

O65	1½d. dull purple and pale green (29.10.87)	£160	28·00
	a. No dot under 'T'	£260	75·00
	b. Dot to right of 'T'	£260	75·00
	c. Dot to left of 'T'	£260	75·00
	s. Optd 'SPECIMEN'	£300	
O66	6d. purple/*rose-red* (19.12.87)	£275	75·00
	a. No dot under 'T'	£375	£120
	b. Dot to right of 'T'	£375	£120
	c. Dot to left of 'T'	£375	£120
	s. Optd 'SPECIMEN'	£250	
O67	9d. dull purple and blue (21.8.88)	£425	£120
	a. Optd in blue-black		
	s. Optd 'SPECIMEN'	£300	
	Wi. Watermark inverted		
O68	1s. dull green (25.3.90)	£700	£275
	a. No dot under 'T'	£1000	£500
	b. Dot to right of 'T'	£1000	£500
	c. Dot to left of 'T'	£1000	£500
	d. Optd in blue-black		
	s. Optd 'SPECIMEN'	£300	

1891–1900. Stamps of Queen Victoria.

O69	1d. lilac (Die II) (18.6.97)	£100	30·00
	a. No dot under 'T'	£160	75·00
	b. Dot to left of 'T'	£160	75·00
	c. Optd inverted	£7500	£3500
	d. Optd inverted. Dot to left of 'T'	£8500	£4500
	Wi. Watermark inverted	—	£500
O70	2d. grey-green and carmine (24.10.91)	£250	50·00
	a. No dot under 'T'	£400	£125
	b. Dot to left of 'T'	£400	£125
	s. Optd 'SPECIMEN' (9, 11, 13, 15)	£300	
O71	4½d. green and carmine (29.9.92)	£400	£275
	b. Dot to right of 'T'		
	Wi. Watermark inverted	—	£9000
O72	1s. green and carmine (11.00)	£650	£275
	a. Optd inverted	†	£17500

*O61/72 **For well-centred lightly used +100%**

The 'no dot under T' variety occurred on R.12/3 and 20/2. The 'dot to left of T' comes four times in the sheet on R.2/7, 6/7, 7/9 and 12/9. The best example of the 'dot to right of T' is on R.20/1. All three varieties were corrected around 1897.

1902. Stamps of King Edward VII. Ordinary paper.

O74	1d. scarlet (30.10.02)	75·00	22·00
O75	2d. yellowish green and carmine-red (29.4.02)	£225	60·00
O76	6d. pale dull purple (19.2.02)	£275	60·00
	a. Opt double, one albino	£35000	
O77	9d. dull purple and ultramarine (28.8.02)	£650	£175
O78	1s. dull green and carmine (17.12.02)	£1350	£300

BOARD OF EDUCATION

BOARD OF EDUCATION (O 8)

Optd with Type O **8**

1902 (19 Feb). Stamps of Queen Victoria.

O81	5d. dull purple and blue (II)	£5750	£1500
O82	1s. green and carmine	£12000	£6000

1902 (19 Feb)–**04.** Stamps of King Edward VII. Ordinary paper.

O83	½d. blue-green	£180	40·00	£550
O84	1d. scarlet	£180	40·00	£550
O85	2½d. ultramarine	£4850	£450	
O86	5d. dull purple and ultram (6.2.04)	£35000	£10000	
O87	1s. dull green and carmine (23.12.02)	£200000		

ROYAL HOUSEHOLD

R.H. OFFICIAL (O 9)

1902. Stamps of King Edward VII optd with Type O **9**. Ordinary paper.

O91	½d. blue-green (29.4.02)	£375	£200	£1100
O92	1d. scarlet (19.2.02)	£325	£175	£1000

ADMIRALTY

ADMIRALTY OFFICIAL (O 10) ADMIRALTY OFFICIAL (O 11) (with different 'M')

1903 (1 Apr). Stamps of King Edward VII optd with Type O **10**. Ordinary paper.

O101	½d. blue-green	30·00	15·00	
O102	1d. scarlet	20·00	8·00	£300
O103	1½d. dull purple and green	£325	£150	
O104	2d. yellowish green and carmine-red	£350	£160	
O105	2½d. ultramarine	£475	£150	
O106	3d. purple/*yellow*	£425	£160	

1903–04. Stamps of King Edward VII optd with Type O **11**. Ordinary paper.

O107	½d. blue-green (9.03)	60·00	25·00	£500
O108	1d. scarlet (12.03)	60·00	25·00	£160
O109	1½d. dull purple and green (2.04)	£1200	£650	
O110	2d. yellowish green and carmine red (3.04)	£2700	£900	
O111	2½d. ultramarine (3.04)	£2900	£950	
O112	3d. dull purple/*orange-yellow* (12.03)	£2600	£400	

Stamps of various issues perforated with a Crown and initials ('H.M.O.W.', 'O.W.', 'B.T.' or 'S.O.') or with initials only ('H.M.S.O.' or 'D.S.I.R.') have also been used for official purposes, but these are outside the scope of the catalogue.

POSTAL FISCAL STAMPS

PRICES. Prices in the used column are for stamps with genuine postal cancellations dated from the time when they were authorised for use as postage stamps. Beware of stamps with fiscal cancellations removed and fraudulent postmarks applied.

VALIDITY. The 1d. Surface-printed stamps were authorised for postal use from 1 June 1881 and at the same time the 1d. postage issue, No. 166, was declared valid for fiscal purposes. The 3d. and 6d. values, together with the Embossed issues were declared valid for postal purposes by another Act effective from 1 January 1883

SURFACE-PRINTED ISSUES

(Typo Thomas De La Rue & Co)

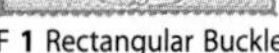

F **1** Rectangular Buckle

F **2**

F **3** Octagonal Buckle

F **4**

F **5** Double-lined Anchor

F **6** Single-lined Anchor

1853–57. P 15½x15.

*(a) Wmk F **5** (inverted) (1853–55)*

			Un	*Used*	*Used on cover*
F1	F **1**	1d. light blue (10.10.53)	50·00	65·00	£225
		Wi. Wmk upright	£180	—	
		Wj. Emk reversed*	£180	—	
F2	F **2**	1d. ochre (10.53)	£130	£160	£600
		a. *Tête-bêche* (in block of four)	£22000		
		Wi. Wmk upright	—	—	
F3	F **3**	1d. pale turquoise-blue (12.53)	45·00	60·00	£350
F4		1d. light blue/*blue* (12.53)	90·00	95·00	£550
		Wi. Wmk upright	£160	£225	
F5	F **4**	1d. reddish lilac/*blue glazed paper* (25.3.55)	£130	£160	£450
		Wi. Wmk upright	£200	£300	

* Watermark reversed: with the stamp upright and *viewed from the front*, the cable finishes to the right of the base of the anchor shaft.

Only one example is known of No. F2a outside the National Postal Museum and the Royal Collection.

*(b) Wmk F **6** (1856–57)*

F6	F **4**	1d. reddish lilac (*shades*)	12·00	9·50	£180
		Wi. Wmk inversed	£160	—	
		Wj. Wmk reversed	£180	—	
F7		1d. reddish lilac/*bluish* (*shades*) (1857)	12·00	9·50	£180
		Wj. Wmk reversed	£180	—	

(F **7**)

1860 (3 Apr). No. F7 optd with Type F 7, in red

F8	F **4**	1d. dull reddish lilac/*blue*	£950	£725	£1500
		Wj. Wmk reversed	—	—	

BLUE PAPER. In the following issues we no longer distinguish between bluish and white paper. There is a range of papers from white or greyish to bluish.

F **8**

F **9**

F **10**

1860–67. Bluish to white Paper. P 15½x15.

		*(a) Wmk F **6** (1860)*			
F 9	F **8**	1d. reddish lilac (5.60)	14·00	18·00	£180
		Wi. Wmk inverted	£130	—	
F10	F **9**	3d. reddish lilac (6.60)	£550	£340	£550
F11	F **10**	6d. reddish lilac (10.60)	£220	£220	£450
		Wi. Wmk inverted	£275	£220	
		Wj. Wmk reversed	£275	£220	
		*(b) W **40**. (Anchor 16 mm high) (1864)*			
F12	F **8**	1d. pale reddish lilac (Nov)	12·00	14·00	£180
		Wi. Wmk inverted	—	—	
F13	F **9**	3d. pale reddish lilac	£275	£210	£550
F14	F **10**	6d. pale reddish lilac	£240	£210	£550
		Wi. Wmk inverted	£360	—	
		*(c) W **40** (Anchor 18 mm high) (1867)*			
F15	F **8**	1d. reddish lilac	25·00	27·00	£275
F16	F **9**	3d. reddish lilac	£120	£120	£450
F17	F **10**	6d. reddish lilac	£110	95·00	£300

For stamps perf 14, see Nos. F24/7.

F **11**

F **12**

Four Dies of Type F 12

Nos. F19/F21 show 'O' of 'ONE' circular. No. F22 (Die 4) shows a horizontal oval

Four Dies of T F 12

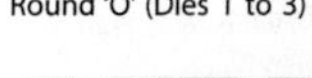

Round 'O' (Dies 1 to 3)

Oval 'O' (Die 4)

Small corner ornaments (Dies 1 and 2)

Medium corner ornaments (Die 3)

Large corner ornaments (Die 4)

Four lines of shading In left-hand ribbon (Die 1)

Two lines of shading in left-hand ribbon (Die 2)

Three lines of shading In left-hand ribbon (Die 3)

Heavy shading in both ribbons (Die 4)

Band of crown shaded (Dies 1 and 2)

Band of crown unshaded (Die 3)

Band of crown unshaded at front only (Die 4)

Die 1: Round 'O' in 'ONE'
Small corner ornaments
Four lines of shading in left-hand ribbon
Band of crown shaded

Die 2: Round 'O' in 'ONE'
Small corner ornaments
Two lines of shading in left-hand ribbon
Band of crown shaded

Die 3: Round 'O' in 'ONE'
Medium corner ornaments
Three lines of shading in left-hand ribbon
Band of crown unshaded

Die 3: Oval 'O' in 'ONE'
Large corner ornaments
Heavy shading in both ribbons
Band of crown unshaded at front only

1867–81. White to bluish paper. P 14.

		*(a) W **47** (Small Anchor)*			
F18	F **11**	1d. purple (1.9.67)	22·00	24·00	£140
		Wi. Wmk inverted	£130	—	
F19	F **12**	1d. purple (Die 1) (6.68)	7·50	9·00	£140
		Wi. Wmk inverted	90·00	—	
F20		1d. purple (Die 2) (6.76)	27·00	22·00	£300
F21		1d. purple (Die 3) (3.77)	14·00	18·00	£220
F22		1d. purple (Die 4) (7.78)	8·50	10·00	£120
		*(b) W **48** (Orb)*			
F23	F **12**	1d. purple (Die 4) (1.81)	8·50	5·00	£110
		Wi. Wmk inverted	£130	—	

1881. White to bluish paper. P 14.

		*(a) W **40** (Anchor 18 mm high) (Jan)*			
F24	F **9**	3d. reddish lilac	£850	£525	£1000
F25	F **10**	6d. reddish lilac	£400	£225	£450
		*(b) W **40** (Anchor 20 mm high) (May)*			
F26	F **9**	3d. reddish lilac	£625	£425	£700
F27	F **10**	6d. reddish lilac	£360	£210	£450

ISSUES EMBOSSED IN COLOUR

(Made at Somerset House)

The embossed stamps were struck from dies not appropriated to any special purpose on paper which had the words 'INLAND REVENUE' previously printed, and thus became available for payment of any duties for which no special stamps had been provided.

The die letters are included in the embossed designs and holes were drilled for the insertion of plugs showing figures indicating dates of striking.

F **13**

F **14**

(F **15**)

INLAND
REVENUE

(F **16**)

1860 (3 Apr)**–71.** Types F 13/F 14 and similar types embossed on bluish paper. No wmk. Imperf.

		Un	*Used*
F28	2d. pink (Die A) (1.1.71)	£775	
F29	3d. pink (Die C)	£210	
	a. *Tête-bêche* (vert pair)	£1700	
F30	3d. pink (Die D)	£775	
F31	6d. pink (Die T)		
F32	6d. pink (Die U)	£400	
	a. *Tête-bêche* (vert pair)		
F33	9d. pink (Die C) (1.1.71)	£1000	
F34	1s. pink (Die E) (28.6.61)	£775	
	a. *Tête-bêche* (vert pair)		
F35	1s. pink (Die F) (28.6.61)	£300	
	a. *Tête-bêche* (vert pair)	£1200	
F36	2s. pink (Die K) (6.8.61)	£775	
F37	2s.6d. pink (Die N) (28.6.61)		
F38	2s.6d. pink (Die O) (28.6.61)	£400	

1871 (Aug). As last but perf 12½.

F39	2d. pink (Die A)	£500	
	a. *Tête-bêche* (vert pair)		
F42	9d. pink (Die C)	£1200	
F43	1s. pink (Die E)	£775	
F44	1s. pink (Die F)	£700	
F45	2s.6d. pink (Die O)	£400	

1874 (Nov). T F **15** embossed on white paper. Underprint T F 16, in green. W **47** (Small Anchor). P 12½.

F48	1s. pink (Die F)	£775	

It is possible that the 2d., 9d. and 2s.6d. may not exist with the thin underprint, Type F **16**, in this shade

1875 (Nov)**–80.** Types F 13/F15 and similar but colour changed and underprint as F 15. On white or bluish paper.

F50	2d. vermilion (Die A) (1880)	£600	
F51	9d. vermilion (Die C) (1876)	£775	
F52	1s. vermilion (Die E)	£500	
F53	1s. vermilion (Die F)	£1200	
F54	2s.6d. vermilion (Die O) (1878)	£500	

1882 (Oct). As last but W **48** (Orbs).

F55	2d. vermilion (Die A)	†	
F56	9d. vermilion (Die C)	†	
F57	1s. vermilion (Die E)	†	
F58	2s.6d. vermilion (Die O)	£1000	£775

Although specimen overprints of Nos. F55/7 are known there is some doubt if these values were issued.

The sale of Inland Revenue stamps up to the 2s. value ceased from 30 December 1882 and stocks were called in and destroyed. The 2s.6d. value remained on sale until 2 July 1883 when it was replaced by the 2s.6d. 'Postage & Revenue' stamp. Inland Revenue stamps still in the hands of the public continued to be accepted for revenue and postal purposes.

TELEGRAPH STAMPS. A priced listing of the Post Office telegraph stamps appears in Volume 1 of the Stanley Gibbons *Great Britain Specialised Catalogue* and in the *Great Britian Concise Catalogue*. The last listing for the private telegraph companies in the Part 1 Catalogue was in the 1940 edition. For military telegraph stamps, see under Bechuanaland, Egypt and British Field Offices in South Africa.

CHANNEL ISLANDS

GENERAL ISSUE

C **1** Gathering Vraic

C **2** Islanders gathering Vraic

Broken Wheel (R. 20/5)

(Des J. R. R. Stobie (1d.) or from drawing by E. Blampied (2½d.). Photo Harrison)

1948 (10 May). Third Anniversary of Liberation. W **127** of Great Britain. P 15×14.

C1	C **1**	1d. scarlet	25	55
C2	C **2**	2½d. ultramarine	25	60
		a. Broken Wheel	75·00	

Supplies of these stamps were also available from eight head post offices on the mainland of Great Britain.

GUERNSEY

WAR OCCUPATION ISSUES

Stamps issued under the authority of the Guernsey States during the German Occupation

BISECTS. On 24 December 1940 authority was given, by Post Office notice, that prepayment of penny postage could be effected by using half a British 2d. stamp, diagonally bisected. Such stamps were first used on 27 December 1940.

The 2d. stamps generally available were those of the Postal Centenary issue, 1940 (S.G. 482) and the first colour of the King George VI issue (S.G. 465). These are listed under Nos. 482a and 465b. A number of the 2d. King George V, 1912–1922, and of the King George V photogravure stamp (S.G. 442) which were in the hands of philatelists, were also bisected and used.

1

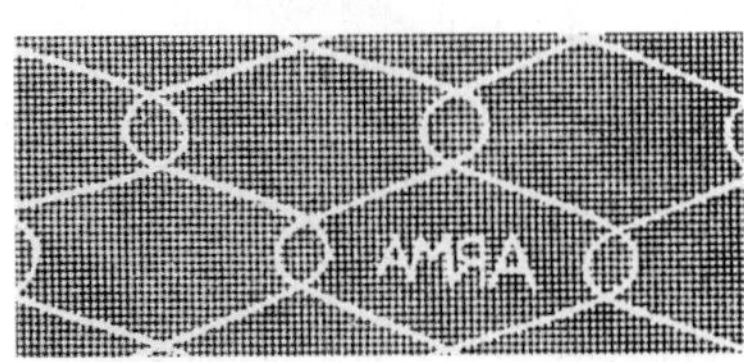

1a Loops (half actual size)

(Des E. W. Vaudin. Typo Guernsey Press Co Ltd)

1941–44. Rouletted.

		(a) White paper. No wmk		
1	**1**	½d. light green (7.4.41)	6·00	3·50
		a. Emerald-green (6.41)	6·50	3·50
		b. Bluish green (11.41)	35·00	15·00
		c. Bright green (2.42)	25·00	12·00
		d. Dull green (9.42)	5·00	3·50
		e. Olive-green (2.43)	45·00	25·00
		f. Pale yellowish green (7.43 and later) (*shades*)	5·00	3·50
		g. Imperf (pair)	£250	
		h. Imperf between (horiz pair)	£800	
		i. Imperf between (vert pair)	£950	
2		1d. scarlet (18.2.41)	3·25	2·00
		a. Pale vermilion (7.43) (etc.)	5·00	2·00
		b. Carmine (1943)	3·50	2·00
		c. Imperf (pair)	£200	90·00
		d. Imperf between (horiz pair)	£800	
		da. Imperf vert (centre stamp of horiz strip of 3)		
		e. Imperf between (vert pair)	£950	
		f. Printed double (scarlet shade)	£150	
3		2½d. ultramarine (12.4.44)	18·00	15·00
		a. Pale ultramarine (7.44)	15·00	10·00
		b. Imperf (pair)	£550	
		c. Imperf between (horiz pair)	£1250	
		*(b) Bluish French bank-note paper. W **1a** (sideways)*		
4	**1**	½d. bright green (11.3.42)	32·00	25·00
5		1d. scarlet (9.4.42)	18·00	25·00

The dates given for the shades of Nos. 1/3 are the months in which they were printed as indicated on the printer's imprints. Others are issue dates.

REGIONAL ISSUES

DATES OF ISSUE. Conflicting dates of issue have been announced for some of the regional issues, partly explained by the stamps being released on different dates by the Philatelic Bureau in Edinburgh or the Philatelic Counter in London and in the regions. We have adopted the practice of giving the earliest known dates, since once released the stamps could have been used anywhere in the U.K

2

3

(Des E. A. Piprell. Portrait by Dorothy Wilding Ltd. Photo Harrison & Sons)

1958 (18 Aug)**–67.** W **179** of Great Britain. P 15×14.

6	**2**	2½d. rose-red (8.6.64)	40	50
7	**3**	3d. deep lilac	30	40
		p. One centre phosphor band (24.5.67)	20	30
8		4d. ultramarine (7.2.66)	40	50
		p. Two phosphor bands (24.10.67)	15	25
6/8p *Set of 3*			70	1·25

1968–69. No wmk. Chalk-surfaced paper. PVA gum*. One centre phosphor band (Nos. 10/11) or two phosphor bands (others). P 15×14.

9	**3**	4d. pale ultramarine (16.4.68)	10	20
10		4d. olive-sepia (4.9.68)	10	15
11		4d. bright vermilion (26.2.69)	20	25
12		5d. royal blue (4.9.68)	30	40
9/12 *Set of 4*			50	1·00

No. 9 was not issued in Guernsey until 22 April.

* PVA Gum. See note after No. 722 of Great Britain.

INDEPENDENT POSTAL ADMINISTRATION

4 Castle Cornet and Edward the Confessor

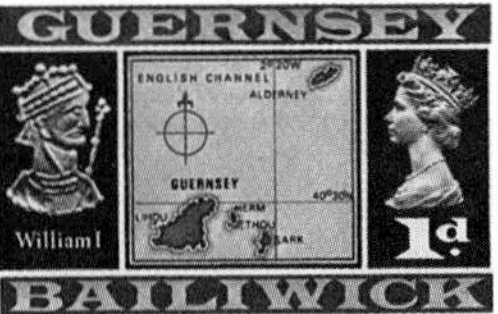

5 View of Sark Two Types of 1d. and 1s.6d.

6 Martello Tower and Henry II

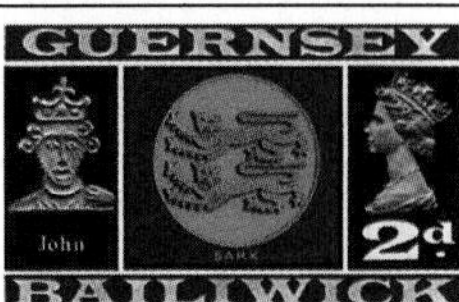

7 Arms of Sark and King John

8 Arms of Alderney and Edward III

9 Guernsey Lily and Henry V

10 Arms of Guernsey and Elizabeth I

11 Arms of Alderney and Charles II

12 Arms of Sark and George III

13 Arms of Guernsey and Queen Victoria

14 Guernsey Lily and Elizabeth I

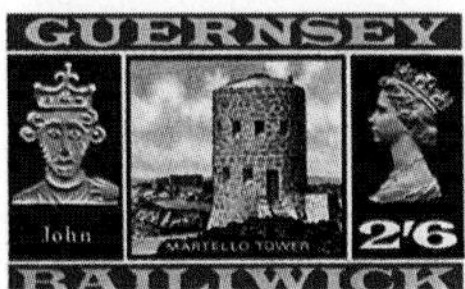

15 Martello Tower and King John

16 View of Sark

17 View of Alderney

18 View of Guernsey

(Des R. Granger Barrett. Photo Harrison (½d. to 2s.6d.), Delrieu (others))

1969 (1 Oct)–**70**. Perf 14 (½d. to 2s.6d.) or 12½ (others), all comb.

13	**4**	½d. deep magenta and black (a)	10	10
		a. Thin paper	60	60
14	**5**	1d. bright blue and black (I) (a)	10	10
		a. Thin paper (b)	50	50
14*b*		1d. bright blue and black (thin paper) (II) (eg)	30	30
		c. Booklet stamp with margins (thick paper) (C)	40	40
15	**6**	1½d. yellow-brown and black (a)	10	10
16	**7**	2d. gold, bright red, deep blue and black (a)	10	10
		a. Thin paper (g)	40	40
17	**8**	3d. gold, pale greenish yellow, orange-red and black (a)	15	15
		a. Error. Wmk Block CA	£1400	
		ai. Wmk inverted	£1250	
		b. Thin paper (g)	50	50
18	**9**	4d. multicoloured (a)	20	10
		a. Booklet stamp with margins (C)	40	45
		ab. Yellow omitted	£775	
		ac. Emerald (stem) omitted	£775	
19	**10**	5d. gold, bright vermilion, bluish violet and black (a)	20	10
		a. Booklet stamp with margins (C)	50	50
		b. *gold* (inscription etc.) omitted (booklets)	£1400	
20	**11**	6d. gold, pale greenish yellow, light bronze-green and black (a)	20	30
		a. Thin paper (g)	45	45
21	**12**	9d. gold, bright red, crimson and black (a)	30	30
		a. Thin paper (g)	3·00	1·70
22	**13**	1s. gold, bright vermilion, bistre and black (a)	30	30
		a. Thin paper (g)	1·00	75
23	**5**	1s.6d. turquoise-green and black (I) (a)	25	30
		a. Thin paper (d)	1·70	3·25
23*b*		1s.6d. turquoise-green and black (thin paper) (II) (eg)	2·00	1·70
24	**14**	1s.9d. multicoloured (a)	1·00	1·00
		a. Emerald (stem) omitted	£875	
		b. Thin paper (g)	1·50	1·90
25	**15**	2s.6d. brt reddish violet and black (a)	3·00	2·50
		a. Thin paper (g)	4·50	4·00
26	**16**	5s. multicoloured (a)	2·50	2·75
27	**17**	10s. multicoloured (a)	12·00	14·00
		a. Perf 13½×13 (f)	26·00	32·00
28	**18**	£1 multicoloured (a)	2·20	2·20
		a. Perf 13½×13 (fh)	2·20	2·20
13/28a *Set of* 16			20·00	23·00

The booklet panes consist of single perforated stamps with wide margins all round intended to fit automatic machines designed for the Great Britain 2s. booklets. They are therefore found with three margins when detached from booklets or four margins when complete.

There was no postal need for the ½d. and 1½d. values as the ½d. coin had been withdrawn prior to their issue in anticipation of decimalisation. These values were only on sale at the Philatelic Bureau and the Crown Agents as well as in the USA

Nos. 14*b* and 23*b* are known only on thin paper and Nos. 13, 14, 16, 17, 20, 21, 22, 23, 24 and 25 also exist on thin paper.

19 Isaac Brock as Colonel

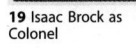

23 HMS *L103* (landing craft) entering St Peter's Harbour

(Litho Format)

1969 (1 Dec). Birth Bicentenary of Sir Isaac Brock. T **19** and similar multicoloured designs. P 13½×14 (2s.6d.) or 14×13½ (others).

29	4d. Type **19**	20	20
30	5d. Sir Isaac Brock as Major-General	20	20
31	1s.9d. Isaac Brock as Ensign	50	50
32	2s.6d. Arms and flags (*horiz*)	50	50
29/32 *Set of* 4		1·25	1·25

(Des and photo Courvoisier)

1970 (9 May). 25th Anniversary of Liberation. T **23** and similar designs. Granite paper. P 11½.

33	4d. blue and pale blue	20	20
34	5d. brown-lake and pale grey	30	20
35	1s.6d. bistre-brown and buff	85	85
33/35 *Set of* 3		1·10	1·10

Designs: Horiz—5d. HMS *Bulldog* and HMS *Beagle* (destroyers) entering St Peter's Port. Vert—1s.6d. Brigadier Snow reading Proclamation.

26 Guernsey 'Toms'

32 St Peter Church, Sark

(Des and photo Courvoisier)

1970 (12 Aug). Agriculture and Horticulture. T **26** and similar horiz designs. Multicoloured. Granite paper. P 11½.

36	4d. Type **26**	55	20
37	5d. Guernsey Cow	60	20
38	9d. Guernsey Bull	1·25	75
39	1s.6d. Freesias	1·50	2·00
36/39 *Set of* 4		3·50	2·75

(Des and photo Courvoisier)

1970 (11 Nov). Christmas. Guernsey Churches (1st series). T **32** and similar multicoloured designs. Granite paper. P 11½.

40	4d. St Anne's Church, Alderney (*horiz*)	20	10
41	5d. St Peter's Church (*horiz*)	20	10
42	9d. Type **32**	60	50
43	1s.6d. St Tugual Chapel, Herm	70	70
40/43 *Set of* 4		1·50	1·20

Further stamps in this series appear after 1970.

STAMP BOOKLETS

For a full listing of Guernsey stamp booklets see *Collect Channel Islands and Isle of Man Stamps.*

POSTAGE DUE STAMPS

D **1** Castle Cornet

(Des R. Granger Barrett. Photo Delrieu)

1969 (1 Oct). Value in black; background colour given. No wmk. P 12½×12.

D1	D **1**	1d. plum	1·50	1·20
D2		2d. bright green	1·50	1·20
D3		3d. vermilion	2·25	3·00
D4		4d. ultramarine	2·50	3·50
D5		5d. yellow-ochre	4·50	3·50
D6		6d. turquoise-blue	4·50	3·50
D7		1s. lake-brown	7·50	6·50
D1/D7 *Set of* 7			22·00	20·00

JERSEY

WAR OCCUPATION ISSUES

Stamps issued under the authority of the Jersey States during the German Occupation

5

(Des Major N. V. L. Rybot. Typo *Jersey Evening Post*, St Helier)

1941–43. White paper (thin to thick). No wmk. P 11.

1	**5**	½d. bright green (29.1.42)	8·00	6·00
		a. Imperf between (vert pair)	£900	
		b. Imperf between (horiz pair)	£800	
		c. Imperf (pair)	£300	
		d. On greyish paper (1.43)	12·00	12·00
2		1d. scarlet (1.4.41)	8·00	5·00
		a. Imperf between (vert pair)	£900	
		b. Imperf between (horiz pair)	£800	
		c. Imperf (pair)	£325	
		d. On chalk-surfaced paper	55·00	48·00
		e. On greyish paper (1.43)	14·00	14·00

6 Old Jersey Farm

7 Portelet Bay

8 Corbière Lighthouse

9 Elizabeth Castle

10 Mont Orgueil Castle

11 Gathering Vraic (seaweed)

(Des E. Blampied. Eng H. Cortot. Typo French Govt Works, Paris)

1943–44. No wmk. P 13½.

3	**6**	½d. green (1.6.43)	12·00	12·00
		a. Rough, grey paper (6.10.43)	15·00	14·00
4	**7**	1d. scarlet (1.6.43)	3·00	50
		a. On newsprint (28.2.44)	3·50	75
5	**8**	1½d. brown (8.6.43)	8·00	5·75
6	**5**	2d. orange-yellow (8.6.43)	7·50	2·00
7	**9**	2½d. blue (29.6.43)	3·00	1·00
		a. On newsprint (25.2.44)	1·00	1·75
		ba. Thin paper*	£225	
8	**11**	3d. violet (29.6.43)	3·00	2·75
3/8 *Set of 6*			30·00	21·00

* On No. 7ba the design shows clearly through the back of the stamp.

REGIONAL ISSUES

DATES OF ISSUE. The note at the beginning of the Guernsey Regional Issues also applies here

INVALIDATION. The regional issues for Jersey were invalidated for use in Jersey and Guernsey on 1 November 1969 but remained valid for use in the rest of the United Kingdom. Nos. 15/41 (except No. 29) and Nos. D1/D6 were invalidated on 14 February 1972

12

13

(Des E. Blampied (T **12**), W Gardner (T **13**) Portrait by Dorothy Wilding Ltd. Photo Harrison & Sons)

1958 (18 Aug)**–67.** W **179** of Great Britain. P 15×14.

9	**12**	2½d. carmine-red (8.6.64)	75	1·00
		a. Imperf three sides (pair)	£3250	
10	**13**	3d. deep lilac	30	40
		p. One centre phosphor band (9.6.67)	15	25
11		4d. ultramarine (7.2.66)	25	30
		p. Two phosphor bands (5.9.67)	15	25
9/11p *Set of 3*			80	1·25

1968–69. No wmk. Chalk-surfaced paper. PVA gum*. One centre phosphor band (4d. values) or two phosphor bands (5d.). P 15×14.

12	**13**	4d. olive-sepia (4.9.68)	15	25
13		4d. bright vermilion (26.2.69)	15	25
14		5d. royal blue (4.9.68)	15	50
12/14 *Set of 3*			40	90

* PVA Gum. See note after No. 722 of Great Britain.

INDEPENDENT POSTAL ADMINISTRATION

14 Elizabeth Castle

23 Queen Elizabeth II (after Cecil Beaton)

27 Queen Elizabeth II (after Cecil Beaton)

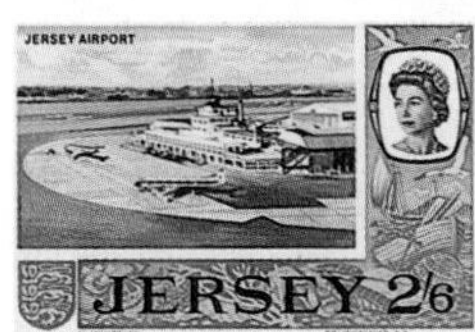

24 Jersey Airport

(Des V. Whiteley. Photo Harrison (½d. to 1s.9d.); Courvoisier (others))

1969 (1 Oct). Types 14/27 and similar horiz designs as T **14** (½d. to 1s.6d.) or T **24** (5s., 10s., £1). Multicoloured. Granite paper. P 14 (½d. to 1s.9d.) or 12 (others).

15	½d. Type **14**	10	60
16	1d. La Hougue Bie (prehistoric tomb) (*shades*)	10	10
	a. Booklet stamp with blank margins	75	
17	2d. Portelet Bay	10	10
18	3d. La Corbière Lighthouse	10	10
	b. Orange omitted	£425	
19	4d. Mont Orgueil Castle by night	10	10
	a. Booklet stamp with blank margins	50	
	c. Gold omitted		
20	5d. Arms and Royal Mace	10	10
21	6d. Jersey Cow	10	10
22	9d. Chart of English Channel	10	20
23	1s. Mont Orgueil Castle by day	25	25
24	1s.6d. As 9d.	80	80
25	1s.9d. Type **23**	1·00	1·00
26	2s.6d. Type **24**	1·60	1·60
27	5s. Legislative Chamber	4·50	4·50
28	10s. The Royal Court	9·00	9·00
	a. Error. Green border*	£5500	
29	£1 Type **27** (*shades*)	1·90	1·90
15/29 *Set of 15*		17·00	17·00

* During the final printing of the 10s. a sheet was printed in the colours of the 50p., No. 56, i.e. green border instead of slate.

The 3d. is known with the orange omitted.

There was no postal need for the ½d. value as the ½d. coin had been withdrawn prior to its issue in anticipation of decimalisation.

Nos. 16a and 19a come from 2s. booklets for the automatic machines formerly used for the Great Britain 2s. booklets (see also note after Guernsey No. 28).

Various papers were used by Harrisons. The ½d. and 1d. exist on much thicker paper from 2s. booklets and the 2d. to 1s.9d. exist on thinner paper having white instead of creamy gum.

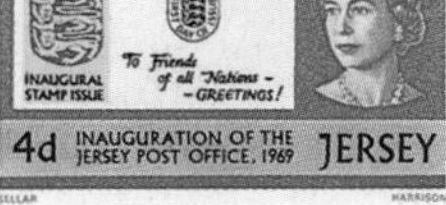

28 First Day Cover

29 Lord Coutanche, former Bailiff of Jersey

(Des R. Sellar. Photo Harrison)

1969 (1 Oct). Inauguration of Post Office. P 14.

30	**28**	4d. multicoloured	10	10
31		5d. multicoloured	10	10
32		1s.6d. multicoloured	30	40
33		1s.9d. multicoloured	60	80
30/33 *Set of 4*			1·00	1·25

(Des Rosalind Dease. Photo Courvoisier)

1970 (9 May). 25th Anniversary of Liberation. T **29** and similar multicoloured designs. Granite paper. P 11½.

34	4d. Type **29**	20	20
35	5d. Sir Winston Churchill	20	20
36	1s.6d. *Liberation* (Edmund Blampied) (*horiz*)	60	60
37	1s.9d. SS *Vega* (*horiz*)	80	80
34/37 *Set of 4*		1·40	1·40

33 'A Tribute to Enid Blyton'

(Des Jennifer Toombs. Photo Courvoisier)

1970 (28 July). 'Battle of Flowers' Parade. T **33** and similar horiz designs. Multicoloured. Granite paper. P 11½.

38	4d. Type **29**	20	10
39	5d. 'Rags to Riches' (Cinderella and pumpkin)	20	20
40	1s.6d. 'Gourmet's Delight' (lobster and cornucopia)	2·00	1·75
41	1s.9d. 'We're the Greatest' (ostriches)	2·00	1·75
38/41 *Set of 4*		4·00	3·50

37 Martello Tower, Archirondel

(Des V. Whiteley. Photo Harrison (½ to 9p.), Courvoisier (others))

1970 (1 Oct)**–74.** Decimal Currency. Designs as Nos. 15/28, but with values inscr in decimal currency as in T **37**, and new horiz design as T **14** (6p.). Chalk-surfaced paper (4½, 5, 8p.), granite paper (10, 20, 50p.). P 14 (½p. to 9p.) or 12 (others).

42	½p. Type **14** (15.2.71)	10	10
	a. Booklet stamp with blank margins	20	
43	1p. La Corbière Lighthouse (*shades*) (15.2.71)	10	10
	a. Orange omitted	£500	
44	1½p. Jersey Cow (15.2.71)	10	10
45	2p. Mont Orgueil Castle by night (15.2.71)	10	10
	a. Booklet stamp with blank margins	60	
46	2½p. Arms and Royal Mace (15.2.71)	10	10
	a. Booklet stamp with blank margins	60	
	ab. Gold (Mace) omitted	£775	
	ac. Gold (Mace) printed double	£575	
47	3p. La Hougue Bie (prehistoric tomb) (15.2.71)	10	10
	a. Booklet stamp with blank margins (1.12.72)	60	
48	3½p. Portelet Bay (15.2.71)	10	10
	a. Booklet stamp with blank margins (1.7.74)	25	
49	4p. Chart of English Channel (15.2.71)	10	10
49*a*	4½p. Arms and Royal Mace (1.11.74)	75	75
	ab. Uncoated paper	£400	
50	5p. Mont Orgueil Castle by day (15.2.71)	10	10
50*a*	5½p. Jersey Cow (1.11.74)	75	75
51	6p. Type **37** (15.2.71)	20	10
52	7½p. Chart of English Channel (15.2.71)	50	50
52*a*	8p. Mont Orgueil Castle by night (1.11.74)	75	75
53	9p. Type **23** (15.2.71)	70	70
54	10p. Jersey Airport	40	30
55	20p. Legislative Chamber	90	80
56	50p. The Royal Court	1·00	1·00
42/56 *Set of 18*		4·00	4·00

Original printings of the ½p. to 4p., 5p. and 6p. to 9p. were with PVA gum; printings from 1974 (including original printings of the 4½p. and 5½p.) have dextrin added (see notes after 1971 Great Britain Decimal Machin issue). The 10p. to 50p. have gum arabic.

The border of No. 56 has been changed from turquoise-blue to dull green.

STAMP BOOKLETS

For a full listing of Jersey stamp booklets see Collect *Channel Islands and Isle of Man Stamps*.

POSTAGE DUE STAMPS

D **1**

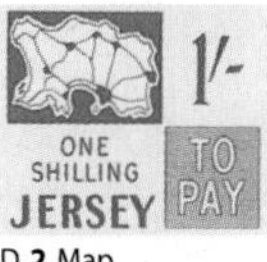

D **2** Map

(Des F. Gudnier. Litho Bradbury, Wilkinson)

1969 (1 Oct). P 14×13½.

D1	D **1**	1d. bluish violet	65	1·10
D2		2d. sepia	90	1·10
D3		3d. magenta	1·00	1·10
D4	D **2**	1s. bright emerald	5·50	5·00
D5		2s.6d. olive-grey	10·00	12·00
D6		5s. vermilion	13·00	15·00
D1/D6 *Set of 6*			28·00	32·00

Specialists in British Commonwealth Stamps

IMPERIUM STAMPS LTD

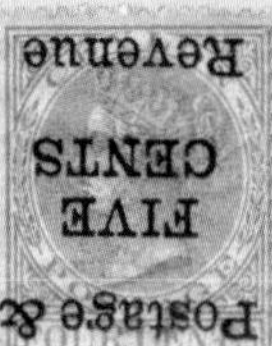

www.imperiumstamps.co.uk

For all your commonwealth requirements from 1840 to 1970

PO BOX 6051 TAMWORTH STAFFS B78 3JB ENGLAND TEL 01827 67579
Website: www.imperiumstamps.co.uk | Email: sales@imperiumstamps.co.uk

British Post Offices Abroad

The origins of the network of Post Offices, Postal Agencies and Packet Agents can be recognised from the 18th-century, but the system did not become established until the expansion of trade, following the end of the Napoleonic Wars in 1815.

Many offices were provided in newly acquired dependent territories, and were then, eventually, transferred from the control of the British Post Office to the evolving local administrations.

Those in foreign countries, nearly always based on existing British Consular appointments, were mostly connected to the network of British Packet lines which had been re-established in 1814. They tended to survive until the country in which they were situated established its own efficient postal service or joined the UPU The term 'Post Office Agent' was employed by the British GPO and 'Packet Agent' by the shipping lines to describe similar functions.

Listed in this section are the Crowned-circle handstamps and GB stamps used in the Post Offices and Agencies situated in foreign countries. Those for the territories within the scope of this catalogue will be found under the following headings:

Prices. Catalogue prices quoted in this section, and throughout the volume, covering stamps of Great Britain used abroad are for used examples with the cancellation or handstamp clearly legible. Poor impressions of the cancellations and handstamps are worth much less than the prices quoted.

They also take into account the fact that many identifiable cancellations of the post offices abroad render the stamps they obliterate in less than 'fine' condition. As a result, some stamps listed in this section are priced at less than the same items used in Great Britain, where the prices are for fine examples. Lightly cancelled stamps used in offices abroad would be worth a premium over the prices quoted.

CROWNED-CIRCLE HANDSTAMPS

Following the introduction, in 1840, of adhesive stamps in Great Britain there was considerable pressure from a number of the dependent territories for the British Post Office to provide something similar for their use.

Such suggestions were resisted, however, because of supposed operational problems, but the decision was taken, in connection with an expansion of the Packet Service, to issue a uniform series of handstamps and date stamps to the offices abroad, both in the dependent territories and in foreign countries.

Under the regulations circulated in December 1841, letters and packets forwarded through these offices to the United Kingdom or any of its territories were to be sent unpaid, the postage being collected on delivery. Where this was not possible, for example from a British colony to a foreign colony or between two foreign ports, then a *crowned-circle handstamp* was to be applied with the postage, paid in advance, noted alongside in manuscript.

Examples of these handstamps were supplied over 20 years from 1842, but many continued to fulfil other functions long after the introduction of adhesive stamps in the colony concerned.

Our listings cover the use of these handstamps for their initial purpose and the prices quoted are for examples used on cover during the pre-adhesive period.

In most instances the dates quoted are those on which the handstamp appears in the GPO Record Books, but it seems to have been normal for the handstamps to be sent to the office concerned immediately following this registration. The only known examples of certain hanstamps are those in The Record Books; these include St Michaels (Azores), Cobija (Bolivia), St Vincent (Cape Verde Islands), Cartagena (CC1) and Chagres (Colombia), Cap Haitien (Haiti), Greytown (Nicaragua), Corunna (Spain), and Charleston, Mobile, New Orleans and Savannah (United States of America).

Many of the handstamps were individually cut by hand, so that each has its own characteristics, but for the purposes of the listing they have been grouped into nine Types as shown in the adjacent column. No attempt has been made to identify them by anything but the most major differences, so that minor differences in size and in the type of the crown have been ignored.

DOUBLE CIRCLE

CC 1 CC 1a

Curved 'PAID'

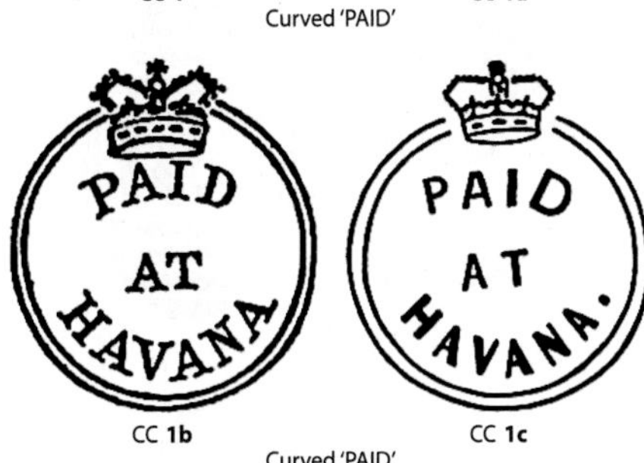

CC 1b CC 1c

Curved 'PAID'

CC 2

Straight 'PAID'

SINGLE CIRCLE

CC 3 CC 4

Straight 'PAID'

CC 5

Curved 'PAID'

CC 6 Straight 'PAID' CC 7 Curved 'PAID'

GREAT BRITAIN STAMPS USED ABROAD

Prices quoted are for single stamps not on cover unless otherwise stated. Stamps on cover are worth considerably more in most cases.

In many instances obliterators allocated to post offices abroad were, at a later date re-allocated to offices at home. Postmarks on issues later than those included in our lists can therefore safely be regarded as *not* having been 'used abroad'.

INDEX

TYPES OF OBLITERATOR FOR GREAT BRITAIN STAMPS USED ABROAD

HORIZONTAL OVAL

(1) (2)

(3)

(4)

(5)

(6)

(7)

VERTICAL OVAL

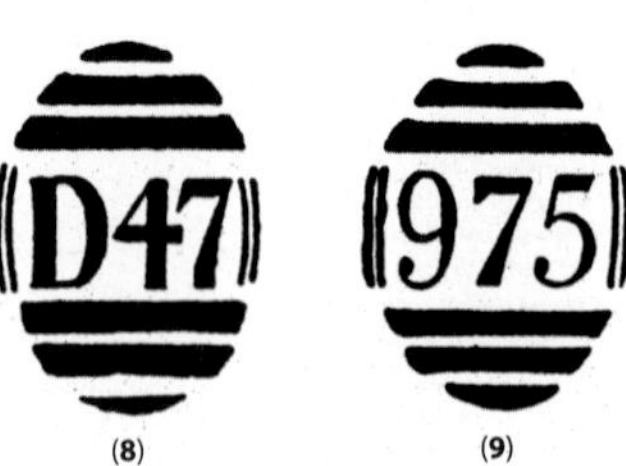

(8) (9)

(10)

(11)

(11A)

(12)

(13)

(14)

(14A)

(14B)

(15)

CIRCULAR DATE STAMPS

(16)

(16A)

(17)

(17A)

(17B)

(18)

(19)

(20)

(21)

Late fee

(22)

ARGENTINE REPUBLIC

BUENOS AYRES

The first regular monthly British mail packet service was introduced in 1824, replacing a private arrangement which had previously existed for some years.

Great Britain stamps were used from 1860 until the office closed at the end of June 1873. Until 1878 the British Consul continued to sell stamps which were used in combination with an Argentine value prepaying the internal rate. The British stamps on such covers were cancelled on arrival in England.

CROWNED-CIRCLE HANDSTAMPS

CC1 CC **7** BUENOS AYRES (Black or B.) (5.1.1851) .... *Price on cover* £850

Stamps of GREAT BRITAIN cancelled 'B32' as Types **2**, **12** or **13** in black or blue.

1860–73.

Z1	1d. rose-red (1857)	45·00
Z2	1d. rose-red (1864) .... *From*	40·00
	Plate Nos. 71, 72, 73, 74, 76, 78, 79, 80, 81, 82, 85, 87, 89, 90, 91, 92, 93, 94, 95, 96, 97, 99, 101, 103, 104, 107, 108, 110, 112, 113, 114, 117, 118, 119, 120, 121, 123, 125, 127, 129, 130, 131, 135, 136, 138, 139, 140, 142, 143, 145, 147, 149, 150, 151, 155, 159, 163, 164, 166, 169, 172.	
Z3	2d. blue (1858–69) .... *From*	50·00
	Plate Nos. 8, 9, 12, 13, 14.	
Z4	3d. carmine-rose (1862)	£270
Z5	3d. rose (1865) (Plate No. 4)	£120
Z6	3d. rose (1867–1873) .... *From*	60·00
	Plate Nos. 4, 5, 6, 7, 8, 9, 10.	
Z7	4d. rose (1857)	£120
Z8	4d. red (1862) (Plate Nos. 3, 4)	£110
Z9	4d. vermilion (1865–1873) .... *From*	50·00
	Plate Nos. 7, 8, 9, 10, 11, 12, 13.	
Z10	6d. lilac (1856)	£100
Z11	6d. lilac (1862) (Plate Nos. 3, 4)	
Z12	6d. lilac (1865–1867) (Plate Nos. 5, 6) .... *From*	80·00
Z13	6d. lilac (1867) (Plate No. 6)	90·00
Z14	6d. violet (1867–1870) (Plate Nos. 6, 8, 9)... *From*	70·00
Z15	6d. buff (1872) (Plate No. 11)	85·00
Z16	6d. chestnut (1872) (Plate No. 11)	50·00
Z17	9d. bistre (1862)	£325
Z18	9d. straw (1862)	£300
Z19	9d. straw (1865)	£475
Z20	9d. straw (1867)	£300
Z21	10d. red-brown (1867)	£325
Z22	1s. green (1856)	£275
Z23	1s. green (1862)	£170
Z24	1s. green (1865) (Plate No. 4)	£160
Z25	1s. green (1867–1873) (Plate Nos. 4, 5, 6, 7) *From*	45·00
Z26	1s. green (1873–1877) (Plate No. 8)	
Z27	2s. blue (1867)	£175
Z28	5s. rose (1867) (Plate No. 1)	£500

A 'B32' obliteration was later used by Mauritius on its own stamps.

AZORES

ST MICHAELS (SAN MIGUEL)

A British Postal Agency existed at Ponta Delgada, the chief port of the island, to operate with the services of the Royal Mail Steam Packet Company.

CROWNED-CIRCLE HANDSTAMPS

CC1 CC **1b** ST. MICHAELS (27.5.1842)

Although recorded in the GPO Proof Books, no example of No. CC1 is known on cover.

BOLIVIA

COBIJA

It is believed that the British Postal Agency opened in 1862. The stamps of Great Britain were used between 1865 and 1878. They can be found used in combination with Bolivia adhesive stamps paying the local postage. The Agency closed in 1881, the town having been occupied by Chile in 1879

CROWNED-CIRCLE HANDSTAMPS

CC1	CC **4** COBIJA (29.3.1862)	

Although recorded in the GPO Proof Books, no example of No. CC1 is known on cover.

Stamps of GREAT BRITAIN cancelled 'C39' as Types **4**, **8** or **12**.

1865–78.

Z1	1d. rose-red (Plate Nos. 85, 93, 95, 156)	
Z2	2d. blue (1858–1869) (Plate No. 14)	
Z3	3d. rose (1867–1873) (Plate No. 6)	
Z4	3d. rose (1873–1876) (Plate Nos. 16, 19)	
Z5	4d. sage-green (1877) (Plate No. 15)	£1000
Z6	6d. violet (1867–1870) (Plate No. 9)	£1000
Z7	6d. buff (1872) (Plate No. 11)	
Z8	6d. grey (1874–1876) (Plate Nos. 13, 14, 15, 16)	£800
Z9	1s. green (1867–1873) (Plate Nos. 4, 5)	£850
Z10	1s. green (1873–1877) (Plate Nos. 10, 11, 12, 13)	£850
Z11	2s. blue (1867)	£1300
Z12	5s. rose (1867–1874) (Plate No. 2)	£2400

BRAZIL

The first packets ran to Brazil in 1808 when the Portuguese royal family went into exile at Rio de Janeiro. The Agencies at Bahia and Pernambuco did not open until 1851. All three agencies used the stamps of Great Britain from 1866 and these can be found used in combination with Brazil adhesive stamps paying the local postage. The agencies closed on 30 June 1874

BAHIA

CROWNED-CIRCLE HANDSTAMPS

CC1	CC **7** BAHIA (Black *or* B.) (6.1.1851) *Price on cover From*	£3750

Stamps of GREAT BRITAIN cancelled 'C81' as T **12**.

1866–74.

Z1	1d. rose-red (1864–1879) *From* Plate Nos. 90, 93, 96, 108, 113, 117, 135, 140, 147, 155.	50·00
Z2	1½d. lake-red (1870–1874) (Plate No. 3)	£110
Z3	2d. blue (1858–59) (Plate Nos. 9, 12, 13, 14)	65·00
Z4	3d. rose (1865) (Plate No. 4)	£140
Z5	3d. rose (1867–1873) (Plate Nos. 4, 6, 8, 9, 10)	80·00
Z6	3d. rose (1873–1879) (Plate No. 11)	
Z7	4d. vermilion (1865–1873) *From* Plate Nos. 8, 9, 10, 11, 12, 13.	50·00
Z8	6d. lilac (1865–1867) (Plate No. 5)	
Z9	6d. lilac (1867) (Plate No. 6)	£100
Z10	6d. violet (1867–1870) (Plate Nos. 6, 8, 9) *From*	£95
Z11	6d. buff (1872–1873) (Plate Nos. 11, 12) *From*	£100
Z12	6d. chestnut (1872) (Plate No. 11)	£100
Z13	6d. grey (1873) (Plate No. 12)	£225
Z14	6d. grey (1874–76) (Plate No. 13)	
Z15	9d. straw (1865)	£425
Z16	9d. straw (1867)	£250
Z17	1s. green (1865) (Plate No. 4)	£170
Z18	1s. green (1867–1873) (Plate Nos. 4, 5, 6, 7) *From*	60·00
Z19	1s. green (1873–1877) (Plate Nos. 8, 9)	£100
Z20	2s. blue (1867)	£275
Z21	5s. rose (1867) (Plate No. 1)	£500

PERNAMBUCO

CROWNED-CIRCLE HANDSTAMPS

CC2	CC **7** PERNAMBUCO (Black *or* R.) (6.1.1851) *Price on cover From*	£3750

Stamps of GREAT BRITAIN cancelled 'C82' as Type 12 or with circular date stamp as Type 16 in black or blue.

1866–74.

Z22	1d. rose-red (1864–1879) *From* Plate Nos. 85, 108, 111, 130, 131, 132, 149, 157, 159, 160, 187.	50·00
Z23	2d. blue (1858–1869) *From* Plate Nos. 9, 12, 13, 14.	60·00
Z23*a*	3d. rose (1865) (Plate No. 4)	£120
Z24	3d. rose (1867–1873) (Plate Nos. 4, 5, 6, 7, 10)	75·00
Z25	3d. rose (1873–1877) (Plate No. 11)	
Z26	4d. vermilion (1865–1873) *From* Plate Nos. 9, 10, 11, 12, 13, 14.	50·00
Z27	6d. lilac (1865–1867) (Plate Nos. 5, 6)	
Z28	6d. lilac (1867) (Plate No. 6)	85·00
Z29	6d. violet (1867–1870) (Plate Nos. 8, 9) *From*	75·00
Z30	6d. buff (1872–1873) (Plate Nos. 11, 12) *From*	90·00
Z31	6d. chestnut (1872) (Plate No. 11)	75·00
Z32	6d. grey (1873) (Plate No. 12)	
Z33	9d. straw (1865)	£425
Z34	9d. straw (1867)	£225
Z35	10d. red-brown (1867)	£325
Z36	1s. green (1865) (Plate No. 4)	£170
Z37	1s. green (1867–1873) (Plate Nos. 4, 5, 6, 7) *From*	75·00
Z38	2s. blue (1867)	£250
Z39	5s. rose (1867–1874) (Plate Nos. 1, 2) *From*	£500

RIO DE JANEIRO

CROWNED-CIRCLE HANDSTAMPS

CC3	CC **7** RIO DE JANEIRO (Black, B. *or* G.) (6.1.1851) *Price on cover From*	£850

Stamps of GREAT BRITAIN cancelled 'C83' as T **12**.

1866–74.

Z40	1d. rose-red (1857)	45·00
Z41	1d. rose-red (1864–1879) *From* Plate Nos. 71, 76, 80, 82, 86, 94, 97, 103, 113, 117, 119, 123, 130, 132, 134, 135, 146, 148, 159, 161, 166, 185, 200, 204.	40·00
Z42	2d. blue (1858–1869) *From* Plate Nos. 9, 12, 13, 14.	45·00
Z43	3d. rose (1867–1873) *From* Plate Nos. 4, 5, 6, 7, 8, 9.	60·00
Z44	3d. rose (1873–1877) (Plate No. 11)	
Z45	4d. vermilion (1865–1873) *From* Plate Nos. 8, 9, 10, 11, 12, 13, 14.	50·00
Z46	6d. lilac (1865–1867) (Plate No. 5)	£100
Z47	6d. lilac (1867) (Plate No. 6)	75·00
Z48	6d. violet (1867–1870) (Plate Nos. 6, 8, 9) *From*	70·00
Z49	6d. buff (1872) (Plate No. 11)	75·00
Z50	6d. chestnut (1872) (Plate No. 11)	55·00
Z51	6d. grey (1873) (Plate No. 12)	£225
Z52	9d. straw (1865)	£400
Z53	9d. straw (1867)	£200
Z54	10d. red-brown (1867)	£300
Z55	1s. green (1865) (Plate No. 4)	£140
Z56	1s. green (1867–1873) (Plate Nos. 4, 5, 6, 7) *From*	50·00
Z57	1s. green (1873–1877) (Plate Nos. 8, 9)	80·00
Z58	2s. blue (1867)	£160
Z59	5s. rose (1867–1874) (Plate Nos. 1, 2) *From*	£450

CAPE VERDE ISLANDS

The British Packet Agency at St Vincent opened in 1851 as part of the revised service to South America. The agency was closed by 1860.

CROWNED-CIRCLE HANDSTAMPS

CC1	CC **6** ST. VINCENT C.DE.V. (6.1.1851)	

Although recorded in the GPO Proof Books, no example of No. CC1 is known on cover.

CHILE

The British Postal Agency at Valparaiso opened on 7 May 1846, to be followed by further offices at Caldera (1858) and Coquimbo (1863). The stamps of Great Britain were introduced in 1865 and can be found used in combination with Chile adhesives paying the local postage. All three offices closed on 31 March 1881 when Chile joined the UPU

CALDERA

Stamps of GREAT BRITAIN cancelled 'C37' as in Type 4 in black and blue.

1865–81.

Z1	1d. rose-red (1864–1879) *From* Plate Nos. 71, 72, 88, 90, 95, 160, 195.	70·00
Z2	1½d. lake-red (1870–1874) (Plate No. 3)	
Z3	2d. blue (1858–1869) (Plate Nos. 9, 13)	80·00
Z4	3d. rose (1865) (Plate No. 4)	£110
Z5	3d. rose (1867–1873) (Plate Nos. 5, 7)	90·00
Z6	3d. rose (1873–1876) *From* Plate Nos. 11, 12, 16, 17, 18, 19.	80·00
Z7	4d. red (1862) (Plate No. 4)	
Z8	4d. vermilion (1865–1873) *From* Plate Nos. 8, 11, 12, 13, 14.	80·00
Z9	4d. sage-green (1877) (Plate No. 16)	
Z10	6d. lilac (1862) (Plate No. 4)	£100
Z11	6d. lilac (1865–1867) (Plate Nos. 5, 6) *From*	£130
Z12	6d. violet (1867–180) (Plate Nos. 6, 8, 9) *From*	£100
Z13	6d. buff (1872) (Plate No. 11)	
Z14	6d. chestnut (1872) (Plate No. 11)	
Z15	6d. grey (1873) (Plate No. 12)	
Z16	6d. grey (1874–1880) *From* Plate Nos. 13, 14, 15, 16, 17.	80·00
Z17	8d. orange (1876)	£350
Z18	9d. straw (1867)	£300
Z19	10d. red-brown (1867)	£375
Z20	1s. green (1865) (Plate No. 4)	
Z21	1s. green 1867–1873 (Plate Nos. 4, 5, 6) *From*	75·00
Z22	1s. green (1873–1877) *From* Plate Nos. 8, 10, 11, 12, 13.	£100
Z23	2s. blue (1867)	£250
Z23*a*	2s. cobalt (1867)	
Z24	2s. brown (1880)	£2250
Z25	5s. rose (1867–1874) (Plate No. 2)	£750

COQUIMBO

Stamps of GREAT BRITAIN cancelled 'C40' as in T **4** or with circular date stamp as T **16**.

1865–81.

Z26	½d. rose-red (1870–1879) (Plate No. 14)	
Z27	1d. rose-red (1857)	
Z28	1d. rose-red (1864–1879) (Plate Nos. 85, 204)	
Z29	2d. blue (1858–69) (Plate Nos. 9, 14)	
Z30	3d. rose (1865)	
Z31	3d. rose (1872) (Plate No. 8)	
Z32	3d. rose (1873–1876) (Plate Nos. 18, 19) *From*	80·00
Z33	4d. red (1863) (Plate No. 4) (*Hair lines*)	
Z34	4d. vermilion (1865–1873) (Plate Nos. 12, 14)	80·00
Z35	4d. sage-green (1877) (Plate Nos. 15, 16) *From*	£250
Z36	6d. lilac (1862) (Plate Nos. 3, 4) *From*	£110
Z37	6d. lilac (1865–1867) (Plate No. 5)	
Z38	6d. lilac (1867) (Plate No. 6)	£100
Z39	6d. violet (1867–1870) (Plate Nos. 6, 8, 9) *From*	£100
Z40	6d. buff (1872–1873) (Plate Nos. 11, 12) *From*	£100
Z41	6d. chestnut (1872) (Plate No. 11)	
Z42	6d. grey (1873) (Plate No. 12)	£225
Z43	6d. grey (1874–1876) *From* Plate Nos. 13, 14, 15, 16.	80·00
Z44	8d. orange (1876)	
Z45	9d. straw (1862)	£350
Z46	9d. straw (1867)	£275
Z47	10d. red-brown (1867)	£325
Z48	1s. green (1865) (Plate No. 4)	£170
Z49	1s. green (1867–1873) (Plate Nos. 4, 5, 6)	80·00
Z50	1s. green (1873–1877) *From* Plate Nos. 8, 10, 11, 12, 13.	£100
Z51	2s. blue (1867)	£250
Z51*a*	2s. cobalt (1867)	
Z52	2s. brown (1880)	£2250
Z53	5s. rose (1867–1874) (Plate Nos. 1, 2) *From*	£700

VALPARAISO

CROWNED-CIRCLE HANDSTAMPS

CC1	CC **1** VALPARAISO (R.) (*without stop*) (13.1.1846) *Price on cover*	£450
CC2	VALPARAISO. (R.) (*with stop*) (16.7.1846) *Price on cover*	£500

Stamps of GREAT BRITAIN cancelled 'C30', as in Types **12**, **14** and 14A (without 'PAID' before 1870) or with circular date stamp as Type 16 in black blue or red.

1865–81.

Z54	½d. rose-red (1870–1879) *From* Plate Nos. 6,11, 12, 13, 14.	65·00
Z55	1d. rose-red (1864–1879) *From* Plate Nos. 80, 84, 85, 89, 91, 101, 106, 113, 116, 122, 123, 138, 140, 141, 146, 148, 149, 152, 157, 158, 162, 166, 167, 175, 178, 181, 185, 186, 187, 189, 190, 195, 197, 198, 199, 200, 201, 207, 208, 209, 210, 211, 212, 213, 214, 215, 217.	40·00
Z56	1½d. lake-red (1870–1874) (Plate Nos, 1, 3) *From*	65·00
Z57	2d. blue (1858–1869) (Plate Nos. 9, 13, 14, 15)	45·00
Z58	2½d. rosy mauve (1875), white paper Plate No. 2.	£200
Z59	2½d. rosy mauve (1876) (Plate Nos. 4, 8)	£180
Z60	3d. carmine-rose (1862)	
Z61	3d. rose (1865) (Plate No. 4)	
Z62	3d. rose (1867–1873) *From* Plate Nos. 5, 6, 7, 8, 9, 10.	50·00
Z63	3d. rose (1873–1876) *From* Plate Nos. 11, 12, 14, 16, 17, 18, 19.	45·00
Z63*a*	4d. red (1862) (Plate Nos. 3, 4)	
Z64	4d. vermilion (1865–1873) *From* Plate Nos. 9, 10, 11, 12, 13, 14.	50·00
Z65	4d. vermilion (1876) (Plate No. 15)	£300
Z66	4d. sage-green (1877) (Plate Nos. 15, 16) *From*	£200
Z67	4d. grey-brown (1880) wmk Large Garter Plate No. 17.	
Z68	6d. lilac (1862) (Plate Nos. 3, 4) *From*	£100
Z69	6d. lilac (1865) (Plate Nos. 5, 6)	
Z70	6d. lilac (1867) (Plate No. 6)	
Z71	6d. violet (1867–1870) (Plate Nos. 6, 8, 9) *From*	70·00
Z72	6d. buff (1872–1873) (Plate Nos. 11, 12) *From*	80·00
Z73	6d. chestnut (1872) (Plate No. 11)	45·00
Z74	6d. grey (1873) (Plate No. 12)	£210
Z75	6d. grey (1874–1880) *From* Plate Nos. 13, 14, 15, 16, 17.	45·00
Z76	6d. grey (1881) (Plate No. 17)	
Z77	8d. orange (1876)	£300
Z78	9d. straw (1862)	
Z79	9d. straw (1865)	
Z80	9d. straw (1867)	£200
Z81	10d. red-brown (1867)	£275
Z82	1s. green (1865) (Plate No. 4)	
Z83	1s. green (1867–73) *From* Plate Nos. 4, 5, 6, 7.	45·00
Z84	1s. green (1873–77) *From* Plate Nos. 8, 9, 10, 11, 12, 13.	65·00
Z85	1s. orange-brown (1880) (Plate No. 13)	£375
Z86	2s. blue (1867)	£120
Z86*a*	2s. cobalt (1867)	£1500
Z87	2s. brown (1880)	£1900
Z88	5s. rose (1867–74) (Plate Nos. 1, 2) *From*	£400
Z89	10s. grey-green (1878) (wmk Cross)	£4000
Z90	£1 brown-lilac (1878) (wmk Cross)	£5000

1880.

Z91	1d. Venetian red	£100
Z92	1½d. Venetian red	£150

COLOMBIA

The system of British Postal Agencies in the area was inaugurated by the opening of the Carthagena office in 1825. In 1842 agencies at Chagres, Panama and Santa Martha were added to the system. A further office opened at Colon in 1852, this port also being known as Aspinwall. During 1872 the system was further enlarged by an office at Savanilla, although this agency was later, 1878, transferred to Barranquilla.

Stamps of Great Britain were supplied to Carthagena, Panama and Santa Martha in 1865, Colon in 1870 and Savanilla in 1872. Combination covers with Colombia stamps paying the local postage are known from Santa Martha and Savanilla as are similar covers from Panama showing Costa Rica and El Salvador stamps.

All offices, except Chagres which had ceased to operate in 1855, closed for public business on 30 June 1881. Colon and Panama continued to exist as transit offices to deal with the mail across the isthmus. Both finally closed on 31 March 1921.

CARTHAGENA

CROWNED-CIRCLE HANDSTAMPS

CC1	CC **1b** CARTHAGENA (15.1.1841)	
CC2	CC **1** CARTHAGENA (Black or R.) (1.7.1846) *Price on cover From*	£1000

Although recorded in the GPO Proof Books, no example of No. CC1 is known on cover.

Stamps of GREAT BRITAIN cancelled 'C56' as in T **4**.

1865–81.

Z1	½d. rose-red (1870–79) (Plate No. 10)	
Z2	1d. rose-red (1864–1879) *From* Plate Nos. 78, 87, 100, 111, 113, 117, 119, 125, 172, 189, 217.	55·00
Z3	2d. blue (1858–1869) (Plate Nos. 9, 14) *From*	55·00
Z4	3d. rose (1865) (Plate No. 4)	
Z5	3d. rose (1865–1868) (Plate Nos. 4, 5)	
Z6	3d. rose (1873–1879) (Plate Nos. 12, 17, 18) *From*	60·00
Z7	4d. vermilion (1865–1873) *From* Plate Nos. 7, 8, 9, 10, 11, 12, 13, 14.	55·00
Z8	4d. vermilion (1876) (Plate No. 15)	£300
Z9	4d. sage-green (1877) (Plate Nos. 15, 16) *From*	£200
Z10	6d. lilac (1865–1867) (Plate Nos. 5, 6)	
Z11	6d. violet (1867–1870) (Plate Nos. 6, 8) *From*	85·00
Z12	6d. grey (1873) (Plate No. 12)	£210
Z13	6d. grey (1874–1876) *From* Plate Nos. 13, 14, 15, 16.	70·00
Z14	8d. orange (1876)	£350
Z15	9d. straw (1865)	
Z16	1s. green (1865)	
Z17	1s. green (1867–1873) (Plate Nos. 4, 5, 7) *From*	70·00

Z18	1s. green (1873–1877) *From* Plate Nos. 8, 9, 10, 11, 12, 13.	80·00
Z19	1s. orange-brown (1880)	
Z20	2s. blue (1867)	£300
Z21	5s. rose (1867) (Plate No. 1)	£550

Cancelled 'C65' (incorrect handstamp, supplied in error) as Type 12.

1866–81.

Z22	½d. rose-red (1870–1879) (Plate No. 10)	
Z23	1d. rose-red (1864–1879) *From* Plate Nos. 100, 106, 111, 123.	80·00
Z23*a*	1½d. lake-red (1870) (Plate No. 3)	
Z24	2d. blue (1858–1869) (Plate No. 9, 14)	80·00
Z25	2d. rose (1880)	
Z26	2½d. blue (1880) (Plate No. 19)	
Z27	3d. rose (1867–1873) (Plate No. 9)	
Z28	3d. rose (1873–1879) (Plate Nos. 14, 17, 19, 20) ...	
Z29	4d. vermilion (1865–1873) *From* Plate Nos. 7, 8, 9, 11, 12, 13 14.	60·00
Z30	4d. vermilion (1876) (Plate No. 15)	£300
Z31	4d. sage-green (1877) (Plate Nos. 15, 16) *From*	£200
Z32	6d. violet (1867–1870) (Plate Nos. 6, 8)	£100
Z33	6d. pale buff (1872) (Plate No. 11)	
Z34	6d. grey (1873) (Plate No. 12)	£225
Z35	6d. grey (1874–1880) *From* Plate Nos. 13, 14, 15, 16, 17.	75·00
Z36	8d. orange (1876)	£400
Z37	9d. straw (1865)	£450
Z38	1s. green (1865) (Plate No. 4)	£130
Z39	1s. green (1867) (Plate Nos. 4, 5, 6, 7) *From*	75·00
Z40	1s. green (1873–1877) *From* Plate Nos. 8, 11, 12, 13.	90·00
Z41	1s. orange-brown (1880)	
Z42	2s. blue (1867)	£650
Z43	2s. brown (1880)	£2750
Z44	5s. rose (1867) (Plate Nos. 1, 2) *From*	£650

CHAGRES

CROWNED-CIRCLE HANDSTAMPS

CC3	CC **1** CHAGRES (16.9.1846)	

Although recorded in the GPO Proof Books, no example of No. CC3 is known on cover.

COLON

CROWNED-CIRCLE HANDSTAMPS

CC4	CC **5** COLON (R.) (21.6.1854) *Price on cover*	£4750

Stamps of GREAT BRITAIN cancelled 'E88' as in Type 12 or circular date stamp as Type 16, 16A and 17A.

1870–81.

Z45	1d. rose-red (1864–1879) *From* Plate Nos. 107, 121, 122, 123, 125, 127, 130, 131, 133, 136, 138, 142, 150, 151, 152, 153, 155, 156, 157, 158, 160, 169, 170, 171, 174, 176, 178, 179, 184, 187, 188, 194, 195, 201, 209, 213, 214, 217.	50·00
Z46	1d. Venetian red (1880)	£120
Z47	1½d. lake-red (1870–1874) (Plate No. 3)	£100
Z48	2d. blue (1858–1869) (Plate Nos. 14, 15)	50·00
Z49	2d. pale rose (1880)	£150
Z50	3d. rose (1867–1873) (Plate Nos. 6, 9)	
Z51	3d. rose (1873–1876) *From* Plate Nos. 11, 12, 16, 18, 19, 20.	60·00
Z52	4d. vermilion (1865–1873) *From* Plate Nos. 10, 11, 12, 13 14.	60·00
Z53	4d. vermilion (1876) (Plate No. 15)	£300
Z54	4d. sage-green (1877) (Plate Nos. 15, 16) *From*	£225
Z55	4d. grey-brown (1880) wmk Large Garter Plate No. 17.	£350
Z56	4d. grey-brown (1880) wmk Crown Plate No. 17.	75·00
Z57	6d. violet (1867–1870) (Plate Nos. 6, 8, 9)	
Z58	6d. buff (1872) (Plate No. 11)	
Z59	6d. chestnut (1872) (Plate No. 11)	70·00
Z60	6d. grey (1873) (Plate No. 12)	
Z61	6d. grey (1874–1880) *From* Plate Nos. 13, 14, 15, 16, 17.	60·00
Z62	8d. orange (1876)	£375
Z63	9d. straw (1867)	£275
Z63*a*	10d. red-brown (1867)	
Z64	1s. green (1867–1873) *From* Plate Nos. 4, 5, 6, 7.	55·00
Z65	1s. green (1873–1877) *From* Plate Nos. 8, 9, 10, 11, 12, 13.	70·00
Z66	1s. orange-brown (1880) (Plate 13)	£375
Z67	1s. orange-brown (1881) (Plate 13)	£140
Z68	2s. blue (1867)	£225
Z69	2s. brown (1880)	£2250
Z70	5s. rose (1867) (Plate Nos. 1, 2) *From*	£700

PANAMA

CROWNED-CIRCLE HANDSTAMPS

CC5	CC **1** PANAMA (R.) (24.8.1846) *Price on cover*	£1900

Stamps of GREAT BRITAIN cancelled 'C35' as in Types **4**, **11A**, **14B** or as **21**.

1865–81.

Z71	½d. rose-red (1870–1879) *From* Plate Nos. 10, 11, 12, 13, 14, 15, 19.	50·00
Z72	1d. rose-red (1864–1879) *From* Plate Nos. 71, 72, 76, 81, 85, 87, 88, 89, 93, 95, 96, 101, 104, 114, 122, 124, 130, 138, 139, 142, 159, 168, 171, 172, 174, 177, 179, 180, 182, 184, 185, 187, 189, 191, 192, 193, 196, 197, 200, 203, 204, 205, 207, 208, 209, 210, 211, 213, 214, 215, 218, 224.	40·00
Z73	1½d. lake-red (1870–1874) (Plate No. 3)	75·00
Z74	2d. blue (1858–1869) *From* Plate Nos. 9, 12, 13, 14, 15.	45·00
Z75	2½d. rosy mauve (1875) (Plate No. 1)	£250
Z76	2½d. rosy mauve (1876–1880) (Plate Nos. 4, 12, 16)	£200
Z77	2½d. blue (1880) (Plate No. 19)	
Z78	2½d. blue (1881) (Plate Nos. 22, 23)	
Z79	3d. carmine-rose (1862)	£300
Z80	3d. rose (1865) (Plate No. 4)	
Z81	3d. rose (1867–1873) *From* Plate Nos. 4, 5, 6, 7, 8, 9.	50·00
Z82	3d. rose (1873–1876) *From* Plate Nos. 12, 14, 15, 16, 17, 18, 19, 20.	40·00
Z83	3d. rose (1881) (Plate Nos. 20, 21)	
Z84	4d. red (1863) (Plate No. 4) (*Hair lines*)	£110
Z85	4d. vermilion (1865–1873) *From* Plate Nos. 7, 8, 9, 10, 11, 12, 13, 14.	50·00
Z86	4d. vermilion (1876) (Plate No. 15)	£300
Z87	4d. sage-green (1877) (Plate Nos. 15, 16) *From*	£200
Z88	4d. grey-brown (1880) wmk Crown *From* Plate Nos. 17 18.	55·00
Z89	6d. lilac (1862) (Plate Nos. 3, 4) *From*	95·00
Z90	6d. lilac (1865–1867) (Plate Nos. 5, 6) *From*	75·00
Z91	6d. lilac (1867) (Plate No. 6)	
Z92	6d. violet (1867–1870) (Plate Nos. 6, 8, 9)	70·00
Z93	6d. buff (1872–1873) (Plate Nos. 11, 12) *From*	75·00
Z94	6d. chestnut (Plate No. 11)	50·00
Z95	6d. grey (1873) (Plate No. 12)	£210
Z96	6d. grey (1874–1880) *From* Plate Nos. 13, 14, 15, 16, 17.	50·00
Z97	6d. grey (1881) (Plate No. 17)	70·00
Z98	8d. orange (1876)	£300
Z99	9d. straw (1862)	£350
Z100	9d. straw (1867)	£250
Z101	10d. red-brown (1867)	£300
Z102	1s. green (1865) (Plate No. 4)	£140
Z103	1s. green (1867–1873) *From* Plate Nos. 4, 5, 6, 7.	45·00
Z104	1s. green (1873–1877) *From* Plate Nos. 8, 9, 10, 11, 12, 13.	60·00
Z105	1s. orange-brown (1880) (Plate No. 13)	£400
Z106	1s. orange-brown (1881) (Plate No. 13)	£110
Z107	2s. blue (1867)	£140
Z108	2s. brown (1880)	£1900
Z109	5s. rose (1867–1874) (Plate Nos. 1, 2) *From*	£450
Z109a	10s. greenish grey (1878)	

1880.

Z110	1d. Venetian red	55·00
Z111	2d. rose	£120
Z112	5d. indigo	£190

Later stamps cancelled 'C35' are believed to originate from sailors' letters or other forms of maritime mail.

SANTA MARTHA

CROWNED-CIRCLE HANDSTAMPS

CC6	CC **1b** SANTA MARTHA (R.) (15.12.1841) *Price on cover*	£1900

Stamps of GREAT BRITAIN cancelled 'C62' as in T **4**.

1865–81.

Z113	½d. rose-red (1870–1879) (Plate No. 6)	90·00
Z114	1d. rose-red (1864–1879) (Plate No. 106)	75·00
Z115	2d. blue (1858–1869) (Plate Nos. 9, 13)	90·00
Z116	4d. vermilion (1865–1873) *From* Plate Nos. 7, 8, 9, 11, 12, 13, 14.	60·00
Z117	4d. sage-green (1877) (Plate No. 15)	£250
Z118	4d. grey-brown (1880) wmk Large Garter Plate No. 17.	£375
Z119	4d. grey-brown (1880) wmk Crown Plate No. 17.	£100
Z120	6d. lilac (1865–1867) (Plate No. 5)	£100
Z121	6d. grey (1873) (Plate No. 12)	
Z122	6d. grey (1874–1876) (Plate No. 14)	
Z123	8d. orange (1876)	£375
Z123*a*	9d. bistre (1862)	
Z124	1s. green (1865) (Plate No. 4)	£160
Z125	1s. green (1867–1873) (Plate Nos. 5, 7) *From*	85·00
Z126	1s. green (1873–1877) (Plate No. 8)	
Z127	2s. blue (1867)	£325
Z128	5s. rose (1867) (Plate No. 2)	£650

SAVANILLA (BARRANQUILLA)

Stamps of GREAT BRITAIN cancelled 'F69' as in T **12**.

1872–81.

Z129	½d. rose-red (1870–1879) (Plate No. 6)	90·00
Z130	1d. rose-red (1864–1879) (Plate Nos. 122, 171)	75·00
Z131	1½d. lake-red (1870–1874) Plate No. 3)	£110
Z131*a*	2d.. blue (1858–1869) (Plate No. 15)	
Z132	3d. rose (1867–1873) (Plate No. 7)	
Z133	3d. rose (1873–1876) (Plate No. 20)	£120
Z134	3d. rose (1881) (Plate No. 20)	£120
Z135	4d. verm (1865–1873) *From* Plate Nos. 12, 13, 14.	65·00
Z136	4d. vermilion (1876) (Plate No. 15)	£325
Z137	4d. sage-green (1877) (Plate Nos. 15, 16) *From*	£225
Z138	4d. grey-brown (1880) wmk Large Garter Plate No. 17.	£375
Z139	4d. grey-brown (1880) wmk Crown Plate No. 17.	75·00
Z140	6d. buff (1872) (Plate No. 11)	
Z141	6d. grey (1878) (Plate Nos. 16, 17) *From*	85·00
Z142	8d. orange (1876)	£375
Z143	1s. green (1867–1873) (Plate Nos. 5,7)	85·00
Z144	1s. green (1873–1877) (Plate Nos. 8, 11, 12, 13) ..	90·00
Z145	1s. orange-brown (1880)	£450
Z146	2s. blue (1867)	£300
Z147	5s. rose (1867–1874) (Plate No. 2)	£650

CUBA

The British Postal Agency at Havana opened in 1762, the island then being part of the Spanish Empire. A further office, at St Jago de Cuba, was added in 1841.

Great Britain stamps were supplied to Havana in 1865 and to St Jago de Cuba in 1866. They continued in use until the offices closed on 30 May 1877.

HAVANA

CROWNED-CIRCLE HANDSTAMPS

1890.

CC1	CC **1b** HAVANA (13.11.1841) *Price on cover*	£1200
CC2	CC **1c** HAVANA (1848) *Price on cover*	£1200
CC3	CC **2** HAVANA (14.7.1848) *Price on cover*	£1000

Stamps of GREAT BRITAIN cancelled 'C58' as in Types **4**, or as Types **14**, **14B**.

1865–77.

Z1	½d. rose-red (1870) (Plate Nos. 6, 12)	75·00
Z2	1d. rose-red (1864–1879) Plate Nos. 86, 90, 93, 115, 120, 123, 144, 146, 171, 174, 208.	65·00
Z3	2d. blue (1858–1869) (Plate Nos. 9, 14, 15)	75·00
Z4	3d. rose (1867–1873) (Plate No. 4)	£140
Z5	3d. rose (1873–1876) (Plate Nos. 18, 19)	
Z6	4d. vermilion (1865–1873) *From* Plate Nos. 7, 8, 10, 11, 12, 13, 14.	65·00
Z7	4d. vermilion (1876) (Plate No. 15)	£300
Z8	6d. lilac (1865) (with hyphen) (Plate No. 5)	
Z9	6d. grey (1874–1876) (Plate No. 15)	
Z10	8d. orange (1876)	£375
Z11	9d. straw (1867)	£300
Z12	10d. red-brown (1867)	£325
Z13	1s. green (1865) (Plate No. 4)	£160
Z14	1s. green (1867–1873) (Plate Nos. 4, 5, 7) *From*	75·00
Z15	1s. green (1873–1877) (Plate Nos. 10, 12, 13) *From*	£110
Z16	2s. blue (1867)	£275
Z17	5s. rose (1867–1874) (Plate Nos. 1, 2) *From*	£650

ST. JAGO DE CUBA

CROWNED-CIRCLE HANDSTAMPS

CC4	CC **1b** ST JAGO-DE-CUBA (R.) (15.12.1841) *Price on cover*	£6000

Stamps of GREAT BRITAIN cancelled 'C88' as T **12**.

1866–77.

Z18	½d. rose-red (1870–1879) (Plate Nos. 4, 6, 14)	
Z19	1d. rose-red (1864–1879) *From* Plate Nos. 100, 105, 106, 109, 111, 120, 123, 138, 144, 146, 147, 148, 171, 208.	£225
Z20	1½d. lake-red (1870–1874) (Plate No. 3)	
Z21	2d. blue (1858–1869) (Plate Nos. 9, 12, 13, 14)	£325
Z22	3d. rose (1867) (Plate No. 5)	
Z23	4d. vermilion (1865–1873) *From* Plate Nos. 9, 10, 11, 12, 13, 14.	£350
Z24	4d. vermilion (1876) (Plate No. 15)	£850
Z25	6d. violet (1867–1870) (Plate Nos. 6, 8, 9) *From*	£700
Z26	6d. buff (Plate No. 11)	
Z27	9d. straw (1865)	
Z27*a*	9d. straw (1867)	£900
Z28	10d. red-brown (1867)	£900
Z29	1s. green (1867–1873) (Plate Nos. 4, 5, 6) *From*	£700
Z30	1s. green (1873–1877) (Plate Nos. 9, 10, 12, 13) ..	
Z31	2s. blue (1867)	
Z32	5s. rose (1867) (Plate 1)	

DANISH WEST INDIES

ST. THOMAS

The British Postal Agency at St Thomas opened in January 1809 and by 1825 was the office around which many of the packet routes were organised.

Great Britain stamps were introduced on 3 July 1865 and can be found used in combination with Danish West Indies adhesives paying the local postage.

Following a hurricane in October 1867 the main British packet office was moved to Colon in Colombia.

The British Post Office at St Thomas closed to the public on I September 1877, but continued to operate as a transit office for a further two years

CROWNED-CIRCLE HANDSTAMPS

CC1	CC **1** ST. THOMAS (R.) (20.2.49) *Price on cover*	£500
CC2	CC **6** ST. THOMAS (R.) (1.5.1855) *Price on cover*	£1800

Stamps of GREAT BRITAIN cancelled 'C51' as in Types **4**, **12** or **14**.

1865–79.

Z1	½d. rose-red (1870–1879) Plate Nos. 5, 6, 8, 10, 11, 12.	40·00
Z2	1d. rose-red (1857)	
Z3	1d. rose-red (1864–1879) *From* Plate Nos. 71, 72, 79, 81, 84, 85, 86, 87, 88, 89, 90, 93, 94, 95, 96, 97, 98, 99, 100, 101, 102, 105, 106, 107, 108, 109, 110, 111, 112, 113, 114, 116, 117, 118, 119, 120, 121, 122, 123, 124, 125, 127, 129, 130, 131, 133, 134, 136, 137, 138, 139, 140, 141, 142, 144, 145, 146, 147, 148, 149, 150, 151, 152, 154, 155, 156, 157, 158, 159, 160, 161, 162, 163, 164, 165, 166, 167, 169, 170, 171, 172, 173, 174, 175, 176, 177, 178, 179, 180, 181, 182, 184, 185, 186, 187, 189, 190, 197.	30·00
Z4	1½d. lake-red (1870–1874) (Plate Nos. 1, 3)	65·00
Z5	2d. blue (1858–1869) *From* Plate Nos. 9, 12, 13, 14, 15.	35·00
Z6	3d. rose (1865) (Plate No. 4)	90·00
Z7	3d. rose (1867–1873) *From* Plate Nos. 4, 5, 6, 7, 8, 9, 10.	45·00
Z8	3d. rose (1873–1876) *From* Plate Nos. 11, 12, 14, 15, 16, 17, 18, 19.	35·00
Z9	4d. red (1862) (Plate Nos. 3, 4)	75·00
Z10	4d. vermilion (1865–1873) *From* Plate Nos. 7, 8, 9, 10, 11, 12, 13, 14.	50·00
Z11	4d. vermilion (1876) (Plate No. 15)	£300
Z12	4d. sage-green (1877) (Plate Nos. 15, 16) *From*	£200
Z14	6d. lilac (1864) (Plate No. 4)	£150
Z15	6d. lilac (1865–1867) (Plate Nos. 5, 6) *From*	75·00
Z16	6d. lilac (1867) (Plate No. 6)	75·00
Z17	6d. violet (1867–1870) (Plate Nos. 6, 8, 9) *From*	70·00
Z18	6d. buff (1872–1873) (Plate Nos. 11, 12) *From*	75·00

Z19 6d. chestnut (1872) (Plate No. 11) 45·00
Z20 6d. grey (1873) (Plate No. 12) £210
Z21 6d. grey (1874–1876) *From* 45·00
Plate Nos. 13, 14, 15, 16.
Z22 8d. orange (1876) £275
Z23 9d. straw (1862) £275
Z24 9d. bistre (1862) £300
Z25 9d. straw (1865) £375
Z26 9d. straw (1867) £200
Z27 10d. red-brown (1867) £275
Z28 1s. green (1865) (Plate No. 4) £140
Z29 1s. green (1867–1873) (Plate Nos. 4, 5, 6, 7) *From* 35·00
Z30 1s. green (1873–1877) *From* 60·00
Plate Nos, 8, 9, 10, 11, 12, 13.
Z31 2s. blue (1867) £130
Z32 5s. rose (1867–1874) (Plate Nos. 1, 2) *From* £450

DOMINICAN REPUBLIC

British Postal Agencies may have existed in the area before 1867, but it is only from that year that details can be found concerning offices at Porto Plata and St Domingo. Both were closed in 1871, but re-opened in 1876.

Although postmarks were supplied in 1866 it seems likely that Great Britain stamps were not sent until the offices re-opened in 1876.

Covers exist showing Great Britain stamps used in combination with those of Dominican Republic with the latter paying the local postage. Both agencies finally closed in 1881.

PORTO PLATA

Stamps of GREAT BRITAIN cancelled 'C86' or circular date stamp as in Types **8** or **17**.

1876–81.

Z1 ½d. rose-red (1870–1879) *From* 90·00
Plate Nos. 10, 12, 14.
Z2 1d. rose-red (1864–1879) *From* 80·00
Plate Nos. 123, 130, 136, 146, 151, 178, 199, 200, 205, 217.
Z3 1½d. lake-red (1870–1874) (Plate No. 3) £110
Z4 2d. blue (1858–1869) (Plate Nos. 14, 15) £120
Z5 2½d. rosy mauve (1876–1879) *From* £250
Plate Nos. 13, 14.
Z6 3d. rose (1873–1876) (Plate No. 18) £120
Z7 4d. vermilion (1873) (Plate No. 14) £120
Z8 4d. vermilion (1876) (Plate No. 15) £325
Z9 4d. sage-green (1877) (Plate No. 15) £275
Z10 6d. violet (1867–1870) (Plate No. 8)
Z11 6d. grey (1874–1876) (Plate No. 15) £110
Z12 8d. orange (1876) £425
Z13 1s. green (1867–1873) (Plate Nos. 4, 7) *From* £110
Z14 1s. green (1873–1877) *From* £110
Plate Nos. 11, 12, 13.
Z15 2s. blue (1867) £300
Z15*a* 5s. rose (1867–1883) (Plate No. 2)

ST. DOMINGO

Stamps of GREAT BRITAIN cancelled 'C87' or circular date stamp as in Types **12** or **16**.

1876–81.

Z16 ½d. rose-red (1870–1879) *From* £120
Plate Nos. 5, 6, 8, 10, 11, 13.
Z17 1d. rose-red (1864–1879) *From* £100
Plate Nos. 146, 154, 171, 173, 174, 176, 178, 133, 136, 190, 197, 220.
Z18 1½d. lake-red (1870–1874) (Plate No. 3) £150
Z19 2d. blue (1858–1869) (Plate Nos. 13, 14) £150
Z20 3d. rose (1873–1876) (Plate No. 18)
Z21 4d. vermilion (1865–1873) *From* £150
Plate Nos. 11, 12, 14.
Z22 4d. vermilion (1876) (Plate No. 15) £500
Z23 4d. sage-green (1877) (Plate No. 15) £350
Z24 6d. grey (1874–1876) (Plate No. 15) £150
Z25 9d. straw (1867)
Z26 1s. green (1867) (Plate No. 4)
Z27 1s. green (1873–1877) *From* £150
Plate Nos. 10, 11, 12, 13.
Z28 2s. blue (1867)

ECUADOR

GUAYAQUIL

The first British Postal Agent in Guayaquil was appointed in 1848.

Great Britain stamps were supplied in 1865 and continued to be used until the agency closed on 30 June 1880. They can be found used in combination with stamps of Ecuador with the latter paying the local postage.

Stamps of GREAT BRITAIN cancelled 'C41' as T **4**.

1865–80.

Z1 ½d. rose-red (1870–1879) (Plate Nos. 5, 6) 60·00
Z2 1d. rose-red (1857)
Z3 1d. rose-red (1864–1879) 50·00
Plate Nos. 74, 78, 85, 92, 94, 105, 110, 115, 133, 140, 145, 166, 174, 180, 186, 216.
Z4 1½d. lake-red (1870–1874) (Plate No. 3) 90·00
Z5 2d. blue (1858–1869) (Plate Nos. 9, 12, 13, 14) *From* 50·00
Z6 3d. carmine-rose (1862) £275
Z7 3d. rose (1865) (Plate No. 4) £120
Z8 3d. rose (1867–1873) (Plate Nos. 5, 6, 7, 9, 10) *From* 55·00
Z9 3d. rose (1873–1876) *From* 55·00
Plate Nos. 11, 12, 15, 16, 17, 18, 19, 20.
Z10 4d. red (1862) (Plate Nos. 3, 4) £140
Z11 4d. vermilion (1865–1873) *From* 60·00
Plate Nos. 7, 8, 9, 10, 11, 12, 13, 14.
Z12 4d. vermilion (1876) (Plate No. 15) £300
Z13 4d. sage-green (1877) (Plate Nos. 15, 16) *From* £200
Z14 6d. lilac (1864) (Plate No. 4) £150
Z15 6d. lilac (1865–1867) (Plate Nos. 5, 6) *From* 75·00
Z16 6d. lilac (1867) (Plate No. 6)
Z17 6d. violet (1867–1870) (Plate Nos. 6, 8, 9) *From* 70·00
Z18 6d. buff (1872–1873) (Plate Nos. 11,12) *From* 80·00
Z19 6d. chestnut (1872) (Plate No. 11)
Z20 6d. grey (1873) (Plate No. 12)
Z21 6d. grey (1874–1876) *From* 55·00
Plate Nos. 13, 14, 15, 16.
Z22 8d. orange (1876) £350
Z23 9d. straw (1862) £300
Z24 9d. straw (1867) £225
Z25 10d. red-brown (1867) £325
Z26 1s. green (1865) (Plate No. 4) £160
Z27 1s. green (1867–1873) (Plate Nos. 4, 5, 6, 7) *From* 50·00
Z28 1s. green (1873–1877) *From* 85·00
Plate Nos. 8, 9, 10, 11, 12, 13.
Z29 2s. blue (1867) £175
Z30 2s. brown (1880) £2500
Z31 5s. rose (1867–1874) (Plate Nos. 1, 2) *From* £525

FERNANDO PO

The British government leased naval facilities on this Spanish island from 1827 until 1834. A British Consul was appointed in 1849 and a postal agency was opened on 1 April 1858.

The use of Great Britain stainps was authorised in 1858, but a cancellation was not supplied until 1874. The office remained open until 1877.

CROWNED-CIRCLE HANDSTAMPS

CC1 CC **4** FERNANDO-PO (R.) (19.2.1859) *Price on cover* £7000

Stamps of GREAT BRITAIN cancelled '247' as T **9**.

1874–77.

Z1 4d. vermilion (1865–1872) (Plate Nos. 13, 14) £2250
Z2 4d. vermilion (1876) (Plate No. 15) £2000
Z3 6d. grey (1874–1876) (Plate Nos. 13, 14, 15, 16) £2000

GUADELOUPE

A British Packet Agency was established on Guadeloupe on 1 October 1848 and continued to function until 1874.

No. CC1 is often found used in conjunction with French Colonies (General Issues) adhesive stamps.

A similar packet agency existed on Martinique from 1 October 1848 until 1879, but no crowned-circle handstamp was issued for it.

CROWNED-CIRCLE HANDSTAMPS

CC1 CC **1** GUADALOUPE (R., B. or Black) (9.3.1849) *Price on cover* £2250

HAITI

The original British Postal Agencies in Haiti date from 1830 when it is known a Packet Agency was established at Jacmel. An office at Port-au-Prince followed in 1842, both these agencies remaining in operation until 30 June 1881.

During this period short-lived agencies also operated in the following Haitian towns: Aux Cayes (1848 to 1863, Cap Haitien (1842 to 1863), Gonaives (1849 to 1857) and St Marc (1854 to 1861). A further agency may have operated at Le Mole around the year 1841.

Great Britain stamps were supplied to Jacmel in 1865 and to Port-au-Prince in 1869.

CAP HAITIEN

CROWNED-CIRCLE HANDSTAMPS

CC1 CC **1b** CAPE-HAITIEN (R.) (31.12.1841)

Although recorded in the GPO Proof Books, no example of No. CC1 is known on cover.

JACMEL

CROWNED-CIRCLE HANDSTAMPS

CC2 CC **1b** JACMEL (R.) (29.6.1843) *Price on cover* £950

Stamps of GREAT BRITAIN cancelled 'C59' as Type 4 or with circular date stamp as Type 16A.

1865–81.

Z1 ½d. rose-red (1870–1879) *From* 70·00
Plate Nos. 4, 5, 6, 10, 11, 12, 14, 15.
Z2 1d. rose-red (1864–1879) *From* 50·00
Plate Nos. 74, 81, 84, 87, 95, 106, 107, 109, 122, 136, 137, 139, 146, 148, 150, 151, 152, 156, 157, 159, 160, 162, 164, 166, 167, 170, 171, 179, 181, 183, 184, 186, 187, 189, 192, 194, 198, 200, 204, 206, 215, 219.
Z3 1½d. lake-red (1870–1874) (Plate No. 3) 75·00
Z4 2d. blue (1858–1869) (Plate Nos. 9, 13, 14, 15) 50·00
Z5 2½d. rosy mauve (1876) (Plate No. 4)
Z6 3d. rose (1867–1873) *From* 50·00
Plate Nos. 5, 6, 7, 8, 9, 10.
Z7 3d. rose (1873–1876) 50·00
Plate Nos. 11, 12, 14, 16, 17, 18, 19.
Z8 4d. red (1863) (Plate No. 4) (*Hair lines*) £120
Z9 4d. vermilion (1865–1873) *From* 50·00
Plate Nos. 7, 8, 9, 10, 11, 12, 13, 14.
Z10 4d. vermilion (1876) (Plate No. 15) £300
Z11 4d. sage-green (1877) (Plate Nos. 15, 16) *From* £200
Z12 4d. grey-brown (1880) wmk Large Garter £325
Plate No. 17.
Z13 4d. grey-brown (1880) wmk Crown 55·00
Plate No. 17.
Z14 6d. lilac (1867) (Plate Nos. 5, 6) 80·00
Z15 6d. violet (1867–1870) (Plate Nos. 8, 9) 75·00
Z16 6d. buff (1872–1873) (Plate Nos. 11, 12) *From* 80·00
Z17 6d. chestnut (1872) (Plate No. 11)
Z18 6d. grey (1873) (Plate No. 12)
Z19 6d. grey (1874–1876) *From* 55·00
Plate Nos. 13, 14, 15, 16, 17.
Z20 8d. orange (1876) £325
Z21 9d. straw (1862) £275
Z22 9d. straw (1867) £200
Z23 10d. red-brown (1867) £300
Z24 1s. green (1865) (Plate No. 4) £140
Z25 1s. green (1867–1873) (Plate Nos. 4, 5, 6, 7) *From* 50·00
Z26 1s. green (1873–1877) *From* 65·00
Plate Nos. 8, 9, 10, 11, 12, 13.
Z27 1s. orange-brown (1880) (Plate No. 13) £375
Z28 2s. blue (1867) £150
Z29 2s. brown (1880) £2500
Z30 5s. rose (1867–1874) (Plate Nos. 1, 2) *From* £500

1880.

Z31 ½d. green (1880) 80·00
Z32 1d. Venetian red 80·00
Z33 1½d. Venetian red £110
Z34 2d. rose £150

PORT-AU-PRINCE

CROWNED-CIRCLE HANDSTAMPS

CC3 CC **1b** PORT-AU-PRINCE (R.) (29.6.1843) *Price on cover* £2500

Stamps of GREAT BRITAIN cancelled 'E53' as in Types **8**, **12** or **16**.

1869–81.

Z35 ½d. rose-red (1870–1879) *From* 60·00
Plate Nos. 5, 6, 10, 11, 12, 13, 14.
Z36 1d. rose-red (1864–1879) *From* 55·00
Plate Nos. 87, 134, 154,146, 159, 167, 171, 173, 174, 177, 181, 183, 187, 189, 193, 199, 200, 201, 202, 206, 209, 210, 218, 219.
Z37 1½d. lake-red (1870–1874) (Plate No. 3) 85·00
Z38 2d. blue (1858–1869) (Plate Nos. 9, 14, 15) 55·00
Z40 2½d. rosy mauve (1876–1879) (Plate Nos. 3, 9) *From* £175
Z41 3d. rose (1867–1873) (Plate Nos. 6, 7)
Z42 3d. rose (1873–1879) (Plate Nos. 17, 18, 20) *From* 55·00
Z43 4d. vermilion (1865–1873) *From* 55·00
Plate Nos. 11, 12, 13, 14.
Z44 4d. vermilion (1876) (Plate No. 15) £300
Z45 4d. sage-green (1877) (Plate Nos. 15, 16) *From* £200
Z46 4d. grey-brown (1880) wmk £325
Large Garter Plate No. 17.
Z47 4d. grey-brown (1880) wmk Crown 55·00
Plate No. 17.
Z48 6d. grey (1874–1876) (Plate Nos. 15, 16)
Z49 8d. orange (1876) £350
Z50 1s. green (1867–1873) (Plate Nos. 4, 5, 6, 7) *From* 55·00
Z51 1s. green (1873–1877) *From* 70·00
Plate Nos. 8, 9, 10, 11, 12, 13.
Z52 1s. orange-brown (1880) (Plate No. 13) £375
Z53 1s. orange-brown (1880) (Plate No. 13) £120
Z54 2s. blue (1867) £175
Z55 2s. brown (1880) £2750
Z56 5s. rose (1867–1874) (Plate Nos. 1, 2) *From* £550
Z57 10s. greenish grey (1878) £4500

1880.

Z58 ½d. green 80·00
Z59 1d. Venetian red 80·00
Z60 1½d. Venetian red £110
Z61 2d. rose £150

MACAO

A British Consular Post Office opened in 1841. It had been preceded by the Macao Boat Office, possibly a private venture, which operated in the 1830s. The office closed when the consulate closed on 30 September 1845, but was back in operation by 1854.

The Agency continued to function, in conjunction with the Hong Kong Post Office, until 28 February 1884 when Portugal joined the UPU

CROWNED-CIRCLE HANDSTAMPS

Z **2**

CC1 – PAID AT MACAO (crowned-oval 20 *mm* wide) (R.) (1844) *Price on cover* £32500
CC2 Z **2** Crown and Macao (1881)

No. CC2 with the Crown removed was used by the Portuguese post office in Macao as a cancellation until 1890.

A locally-cut mark, as T CC **2**, inscribed 'PAGO EM MACAO' is known on covers between 1870 and 1877. It was probably used by the Portuguese postmaster to send letters via the British Post Office (*Price* £10000).

MADEIRA

The British Packet Agency on this Portuguese island was opened in 1767 and was of increased importance from 1808 following the exile of the Portuguese royal family to Brazil. The South American packets ceased to call in 1858. It appears to have closed sometime around 1860.

CROWN-CIRCLE HANDSTAMPS

CC1 CC **1b** MADEIRA (R.) (28.2.1842) *Price on cover* £17500

MEXICO

The British Postal Agency at Vera Cruz opened in 1825, following the introduction of the Mexican Packet service. No handstamps were supplied, however, until 1842, when a similar agency at Tampico was set up.

Great Britain stamps were used at Tampico from 1867, but, apparently, were never sent to the Vera Cruz office. Combination covers exist showing the local postage paid by Mexican adhesives. The Agency at Vera Cruz closed in 1874 and that at Tampico in 1876.

TAMPICO

CROWNED-CIRCLE HANDSTAMPS

CC1 CC **1b** TAMPICO (R.) (13.11.1841) *Price on cover* £1800

No. CC1 may be found on cover, used in conjunction with Mexico adhesive stamps.

Stamps of GREAT BRITAIN cancelled 'C63' as T **4**.

1867–76.

Z1 1d. rose-red (1864–1879) *From* £150
Plate Nos. 81, 85, 89, 96, 103, 117, 139, 147.
Z2 2d. blue (1858–1869) (Plate Nos. 9, 14) £200
Z3 4d. vermilion (1865–1873) *From* £150
Plate Nos. 7, 8, 10, 11, 12, 13, 14.
Z4 1s. green (1867–1873) (Plate Nos. 4, 5, 7, 8) £225
Z5 2s. blue (1867) £600

VERA CRUZ

CROWNED-CIRCLE HANDSTAMPS

CC2 CC **1b** VERA CRUZ (R.) (13.11.1841) *Price on cover* £2250
CC3 VERA CRUZ (Black) (*circa* 1845). *Price on cover* £1000

NICARAGUA

GREYTOWN

British involvement on the Mosquito Coast of Nicaragua dates from 1655 when contacts were first made with the indigenous Misquito Indians. A formal alliance was signed in 1740 and the area was considered as a British dependency until the Spanish authorities negotiated a withdrawal in 1786.

The Misquitos remained under British protection, however, and, following the revolutionary period in the Spanish dominions, this eventually led to the appropriation, by the Misquitos with British backing, of the town of San Juan del Norte, later renamed Greytown.

The port was included in the Royal West Indian Mail Steam Packet Company's mail network from January 1842, forming part of the Jamaica District. This arrangement only lasted until September of that year, however, although packets were once again calling at Greytown by November 1844. Following the discovery of gold in California the office increased in importance, owing to the overland traffic, although the first distinctive postmark is not recorded in use until February 1856.

A subsidiary agency, without its own postmark, operated at Bluefields from 1857 to 1863.

The British Protectorate over the Misquitos ended in 1860, but the British Post Office at Greytown continued to operate, being supplied with Great Britain stamps in 1865. These are occasionally found used in combination with Nicaragua issues, which had only internal validity.

The British Post Office at Greytown closed on 1 May 1882 when the Republic of Nicaragua joined the UPU

CROWNED-CIRCLE HANDSTAMPS

CC1 C **4** GREYTOWN (R.) (14.4.1859)

Although recorded in the GPO Proof Books, no example of No. CC1 is known on cover.

Stamps of GREAT BRITAIN cancelled 'C57' as in T **4** (issued 1865), T **14A** (issued 1875), or with circular postmark as T **16** (issued 1864).

1865–82.

Z1 ½d. rose-red (1870–1879) (Plate Nos. 5, 10, 11) 80·00
Z2 1d. rose-red (1864–1879) 60·00
Plate Nos. 180, 197, 210.
Z3 1½d. lake-red (1870) (Plate No. 3) 85·00
Z4 2d. blue (1858–1869) (Plate Nos. 9, 14, 15)
Z5 3d. rose (1873–1876) (Plate Nos. 17, 18, 19, 20) 60·00
Z6 3d. rose (1881) (Plate No. 20)
Z7 4d. vermilion (1865–1873) *From* 60·00
Plate Nos. 8, 10, 11, 12, 13, 14.
Z8 4d. vermilion (1876) (Plate No. 15) £300
Z9 4d. sage-green (1877) (Plate Nos. 15, 16) *From* £200
Z10 4d. grey-brown (1880) wmk Large Garter £325
Plate No. 17.
Z11 4d. grey-brown (1880) wmk Crown 90·00
Plate No. 17.
Z12 6d. grey (1874–1876) (Plate Nos. 14, 15, 16, 17) 95·00
Z13 8d. orange (1876) £325
Z14 1s. green (1865) (Plate No. 4)
Z15 1s. green (1867–1873) (Plate Nos. 6, 7)
Z16 1s. green (1873–1877) *From* 65·00
Plate Nos. 8, 10, 12, 13.
Z17 1s. orange-brown (1880) (Plate No. 13) £375
Z18 1s. orange-brown (1881) (Plate No. 13) £110
Z19 2s. blue (1867) £225
Z20 2s. brown (1880) £2750
Z21 5s. rose (1867–1874) (Plate Nos. 1, 2) *From* £550
Z22 5s. rose (1882) (Plate No. 4), *blue paper* £3000
Z23 10s. greenish grey (1878) £4500

1880.

Z24 1d. Venetian red 80·00
Z25 1½d. Venetian red 80·00

PERU

British Agencies in Peru date from 1846 when offices were established at Arica and Callao. The network was later expanded to include agencies at Paita (1848), Pisco (1868) and Iquique and Islay (both 1869). This last office was transferred to Mollendo in 1877.

It is believed that a further agency existed at Pisagua, but no details exist.

Great Britain stamps were supplied from 1865 and are often found in combination with Peru adhesives which paid the local postal tax.

The Postal Agency at Pisco closed in 1870 and the remainder in 1879, the towns of Arica, Iquique and Pisagua passing to Chile by treaty in 1883.

ARICA

CROWNED-CIRCLE HANDSTAMPS

CC1 CC **1** ARICA (Black) (5.11.1850) *Price on cover* £4750

Stamps of Great Britain cancelled 'C36' as Types **4**, **12**, **14B** and **16A** in black, blue or red.

1865–79.

Z1 ½d. rose-red (1870–1879) *From* 75·00
Plate Nos. 5, 6, 10, 11, 13.
Z2 1d. rose-red (1864–1879) *From* 65·00
Plate Nos. 102, 139, 140, 163, 167.
Z3 1½d. lake-red (1870–1874) (Plate No. 3)
Z4 2d. blue (1858–1869) (Plate Nos. 13, 14) 75·00
Z5 3d. rose (1867–1873) (Plate Nos. 5, 9) 90·00
Z6 3d. rose (1873–1876) *From* 70·00
Plate Nos. 11, 12, 17, 18, 19.
Z7 4d. vermilion (1865–1873) *From* 70·00
Plate Nos. 10, 11, 12, 13, 14.
Z8 4d. vermilion (1876) (Plate No. 15)
Z9 4d. sage-green (1877) (Plate Nos. 15, 16) £225
Z10 6d. lilac (1862) (Plate Nos. 3, 4)
Z11 6d. lilac (1865–1867) (Plate No. 5)
Z12 6d. violet (1867–1870) (Plate Nos. 6, 8, 9) *From* 80·00
Z13 6d. buff (1872) (Plate No. 11) £100
Z14 6d. chestnut (1872) (Plate No. 11) £100
Z15 6d. grey (1873) (Plate No. 12) £225
Z16 6d. grey (1874–1876) *From* 60·00
Plate Nos. 13, 14, 15, 16.
Z17 8d. orange (1876)
Z18 9d. straw (1862)
Z19 9d. straw (1865)
Z20 9d. straw (1867) £250
Z21 10d. red-brown (1867)
Z22 1s. green (1862)
Z23 1s. green (1865)
Z24 1s. green (1867–1873) (Plate Nos. 4, 5, 6, 7) *From* 65·00
Z25 1s. green (1873–1877) *From* 75·00
Plate Nos. 8, 9, 10, 11, 12, 13.
Z26 2s. blue (1867) £250
Z27 5s. rose (1867–1874) (Plate Nos. 1, 2) *From* £600

CALLAO

CROWNED-CIRCLE HANDSTAMPS

CC2 CC **1** CALLAO (R.) (13.1.1846) *Price on cover* £800

A second version of No. CC 2, showing 'PAID' more curved, was supplied in July 1847.

No. CC2 can be found used on covers from 1865 showing the local postage paid by a Peru adhesive.

Stamps of GREAT BRITAIN cancelled 'C38' as in Types **4**, **12** and **14B**, with circular date stamp as T **16A** or with boxed handstamp T **22**.

1865–79.

Z28 ½d. rose-red (1870–1879) *From* 45·00
Plate Nos. 5, 6, 10, 11, 12, 13, 14.
Z29 1d. rose-red (1864–1879) *From* 40·00
Plate Nos. 74, 88, 89, 93, 94, 97, 108, 120, 121, 123, 127, 128, 130, 134, 137, 139, 140, 141, 143, 144, 145, 146, 148, 149, 156, 157, 160, 163, 167, 171, 172, 173, 175, 176, 180, 181, 182, 183, 185, 187, 190, 193, 195, 198, 199, 200, 201, 204, 206, 209, 210, 212, 213, 215.
Z30 1½d. lake-red (1870–1874) (Plate No. 3)
Z31 2d. blue (1858–1869) *From* 40·00
Plate Nos. 9, 12, 13, 14, 15.
Z32 3d. carmine-rose (1862)
Z33 3d. rose (1865) (Plate No. 4) £100
Z34 3d. rose (1867–1873) *From* 50·00
Plate Nos. 5, 6, 7, 8, 9, 10.
Z35 3d. rose (1873–1876) *From* 50·00
Plate Nos. 11, 12, 14, 15, 16, 17, 18, 19.
Z36 4d. red (1862) (Plate Nos. 3, 4)
Z37 4d. vermilion (1865–1873) *From* 40·00
Plate Nos. 8, 10, 11, 12, 13, 14.
Z38 4d. vermilion (1876) (Plate No. 15) £300
Z39 4d. sage-green (1877) (Plate Nos. 15, 16) £200
Z40 6d. lilac (1862) (Plate Nos. 3, 4)
Z40*a* 6d. lilac (1865) (Plate No. 5)
Z41 6d. lilac (1867)
Z42 6d. violet (1867–1870) *From* 70·00
Plate Nos. 6, 8, 9.
Z43 6d. buff (1872–1873) (Plate Nos. 11, 12) *From* 70·00
Z44 6d. chestnut (1872) (Plate No. 11) 50·00
Z45 6d. grey (1873) (Plate No. 12) £210
Z46 6d. grey (1874–1880) *From* 50·00
Plate Nos. 13, 14, 15, 16.
Z47 8d. orange (1876) £275
Z48 9d. straw (1862)
Z49 9d. straw (1865) £400
Z50 9d. straw (1867) £200
Z51 10d. red-brown (1867) £275
Z52 1s. green (1865)
Z53 1s. green (1867–1873) *From* 45·00
Plate Nos. 4, 5, 6, 7.
Z54 1s. green (1873–1877) *From* 60·00
Plate Nos. 8, 9, 10, 11, 12, 13.
Z55 2s. blue (1867) £120
Z56 5s. rose (1867–1874) (Plate Nos. 1, 2) *From* £450

IQUIQUE

Stamps of GREAT BRITAIN cancelled 'D87' as T **12** in black or blue.

1865–79.

Z57 ½d. rose-red (1870–1879) (Plate Nos. 5, 6, 13, 14) 75·00
Z58 1d. rose-red (1864–1879) 60·00
Plate Nos. 76, 179, 185, 205.
Z59 2d. blue (1858–1869) (Plate Nos. 9, 12, 13, 14) 60·00
Z60 3d. rose (1867–1873) (Plate Nos. 5, 6, 7, 8, 9) *From* 65·00
Z61 3d. rose (1873–1876) (Plate Nos. 12, 18, 19) 75·00
Z62 4d. vermilion (1865–1873) *From* 70·00
Plate Nos. 12, 13, 14.
Z63 4d. vermilion (1876) (Plate No. 15) £300
Z64 4d. sage-green (1877) (Plate Nos. 15, 16) *From* £200
Z65 6d. mauve (1869) (Plate Nos. 8, 9)
Z66 6d. buff (1872–1873) (Plate Nos. 11, 12) *From* £110
Z67 6d. chestnut (1872) (Plate No. 11)
Z68 6d. grey (1873) (Plate No. 12) £225
Z69 6d. grey (1874–1876) (Plate Nos. 13, 14, 15, 16) 80·00
Z70 8d. orange (1876) £350
Z71 9d. straw (1867) £200
Z72 10d. red-brown (1867)
Z73 1s. green (1867–1873) (Plate Nos. 4, 6, 7) *From* 60·00
Z74 1s. green (1873–1877) *From* 80·00
Plate Nos. 8, 9, 10, 11, 12, 13.
Z75 2s. blue (1867) £250
Z75*a* 5s. rose (1857) (Plate No. 2)

ISLAY (*later* MOLLENDO)

CROWNED-CIRCLE HANDSTAMPS

CC4 CC **1** ISLAY (Black) (23.10.1850) *Price on cover* £5000

Stamps of GREAT BRITAIN cancelled 'C42' as T **4** or with circular date stamp as T **16**.

1865–79.

Z76 1d. rose-red (1864–1879) *From* 60·00
Plate Nos. 78, 84, 87, 88, 93, 96, 97, 103, 125, 134.
Z77 1½d. lake-red (1870–1874) (Plate No. 3)
Z78 2d. blue (1858–1869) (Plate Nos. 9, 13, 15) 60·00
Z79 3d. carmine-rose (1862)
Z80 3d. rose (1865) £120
Z81 3d. rose (1867–1873) (Plate Nos. 4, 5, 6, 10). *From* 80·00
Z82 4d. red (1862) (Plate Nos. 3, 4) £130
Z83 4d. vermilion (1867–1873) *From* 80·00
Plate Nos. 9, 10, 11, 12, 13.
Z84 4d. vermilion (1876) (Plate No. 15)
Z85 4d. sage-green (1877) (Plate Nos. 15, 16) *From* £200
Z86 6d. lilac (1862) (Plate Nos, 3, 4) *From* 90·00
Z87 6d. lilac (1865) (Plate No. 5) 80·00
Z88 6d. violet (1867–1870) (Plate Nos. 6, 8, 9) *From* 80·00
Z88*a* 6d. chestnut (1872) (Plate No. 11)
Z89 6d. buff (1873) (Plate No. 12)
Z90 6d. grey (1873) (Plate No. 12)
Z91 6d. grey (1874–1876) *From* 65·00
Plate Nos. 13, 14, 15, 16.
Z92 9d. straw (1865) £375
Z93 9d. straw (1867) £225
Z94 10d. red-brown (1867) £300
Z95 1s. green (1865) (Plate No. 4)
Z96 1s. green (1867–1873) (Plate Nos. 4, 5, 6, 7) *From* 60·00
Z97 1s. green (1873–1877) *From* 80·00
Plate Nos. 8, 10, 12, 13.
Z98 2s. blue (1867)
Z99 5s. rose (1867) (Plate No. 1)

PAITA

CROWNED-CIRCLE HANDSTAMPS

CC5 CC **1** PAITA (Black) (5.11.1850) *Price on cover* £6500

Stamps of GREAT BRITAIN cancelled 'C43' as T **4** or with circular date stamp as T **16A** in black or blue.

1865–79.

Z99*a* ½d. rose-red (Plate No. 6)
Z100 1d. rose-red (1864–1879) (Plate Nos. 127, 147) £120
Z101 2d. blue (1858–1869) (Plate Nos. 9, 14) £120
Z101*a* 3d. Carmine-rose (1862)
Z102 3d. rose (1867–1873) (Plate Nos. 5, 6) £120
Z103 3d. rose (1876) (Plate Nos. 17, 18, 19) £120
Z104 4d. vermilion (1865–1873) *From* £120
Plate Nos. 9, 10, 11, 12, 13, 14.
Z104*a* 4d. vermilion (1876) (Plate No. 15) £425
Z105 4d. sage-green (1877) (Plate No. 15)
Z106 6d. lilac (1862) (Plate No. 3) £175
Z107 6d. lilac (1865–1867) (Plate Nos. 5, 6) *From* £150
Z108 6d. violet (1867–1870) (Plate Nos. 6, 8, 9) *From* £150
Z109 6d. buff (1872–1873) (Plate Nos. 11, 12) *From* £150
Z110 6d. chestnut (Plate No. 11) £120
Z111 6d. grey (1873) (Plate No. 12) £400
Z112 6d. grey (1874–1876) (Plate Nos. 13, 14, 15)
Z113 9d. straw (1862)
Z114 10d. red-brown (1867) £450
Z115 1s. green (1865) (Plate No. 4)
Z116 1s. green (1867–1873) (Plate No. 4) £140
Z117 1s. green (1873–1877) (Plate Nos. 8, 9, 10, 13) £160
Z118 2s. blue (1867) £425
Z119 5s. rose (1867) (Plate No. 1) £850

PISAGUA(?)

Stamps of GREAT BRITAIN cancelled 'D65' as T **12**.

Z119*a* 1d. rose-red (1864–1879)
Z119*b* 2d. blue (1858–1869)
Z120 2s. blue (1867)

There is no record of an office opening at Pisagua. The few known examples of 'D65' in red are on loose stamps. The 2s. blue listing, based on a single cover cancelled 'D65' in black, is without any datestamp confirming its origin.

We continue to list this office pending further research.

PISCO AND CHINCHA ISLANDS

Stamps of GREAT BRITAIN cancelled 'D74' as T **12**.

1865–70.

Z121 2d. blue (1858–1869) (Plate No. 9)
Z122 4d. vermilion (1865–1873) (Plate Nos. 10, 12) £1400
Z123 6d. violet (1868) (Plate No. 6) £1800
Z124 1s. green (1867) (Plate No. 4)
Z125 2s. blue (1867) £2400

PORTO RICO

A British Postal Agency operated at San Juan from 1844. On 24 October 1872 further offices were opened at Aguadilla, Arroyo, Mayaguez and Ponce, with Naguabo added three years later.

Great Britain stamps were used from 1865 to 1877, but few letters appear to have used the San Juan postal agency between 1866 and 1873 due to various natural disasters and the hostile attitude of the local authorities. All the British Agencies closed on 1 May 1877.

AGUADILLA

Stamps of GREAT BRITAIN cancelled 'F84' as T **8**.

1873–77.

Z1 ½d. rose-red (1870) (Plate No. 6) £150
Z2 1d. rose-red (1864–1879) £140
Plate Nos. 119, 122, 139, 149, 156, 160.
Z3 2d. blue (1858–1869) (Plate No. 14)
Z4 3d. rose (1867–1873) (Plate Nos. 7, 8, 9)
Z5 3d. rose (1873–1876) (Plate No. 12)
Z6 4d. vermilion (1865–1873) *From* £100
Plate Nos. 12, 13, 14.
Z7 4d. vermilion (1876) (Plate No. 15) £325
Z7*a* 6d. pale buff (1872–1873) (Plate No. 11)
Z8 6d. grey (1874–1876) (Plate Nos. 13, 14)
Z9 9d. straw (1867) £400
Z10 10d. red-brown (1867) £475
Z11 1s. green (1867–1873) (Plate Nos. 4, 5, 6, 7) *From* £125
Z12 1s. green (1873–1877) *From* £125
Plate Nos. 8, 9, 10, 11, 12.
Z13 2s. blue (1867) £350

ARROYO

Stamps of GREAT BRITAIN cancelled 'F83' as T **8** (black or red) or with circular date stamps as Types **17** and **17B**.

1873–77.

Z14 ½d. rose-red 1870) (Plate No. 5) £120
Z15 1d. rose-red (1864–1879) £100
Plate Nos. 149, 150, 151, 156, 164, 174, 175.
Z16 1½d. lake-red (1870) (Plate Nos. 1, 3)
Z17 2d. blue (1858–1869) (Plate No. 14)
Z18 3d. rose (1867–1873) (Plate Nos. 5, 7, 10) *From* £100
Z19 3d. rose 1873–76 *From* £100
Plate Nos. 11, 12, 14, 16, 18.
Z20 4d. verm (1865–1873) (Plate Nos. 12, 13, 14) *From* 90·00
Z21 4d. vermilion (1876) (Plate No. 15) £350
Z22 6d. chestnut (1872) (Plate No. 11) £120
Z23 6d. pale buff (1872) (Plate No. 11) £120
Z23*a* 6d. grey (1873) (Plate No. 12)
Z24 6d. grey (1874–1876) (Plate Nos. 13, 14, 15) £100
Z25 9d. straw (1867) £350
Z26 10d. red-brown (1867) £400
Z27 1s. green (1865) (Plate No. 4)
Z28 1s. green (1867–1873) (Plate Nos. 4, 5, 6, 7) *From* 90·00
Z29 1s. green (1873–1877) *From* £100
Plate Nos. 8, 9, 10, 11, 12, 13.
Z30 2s. blue (1867) £325
Z31 5s. rose (1867–1874) (Plate No. 2)

MAYAGUEZ

Stamps of GREAT BRITAIN cancelled 'F85' as T **8** in black or blue.

1873–77.

Z32 ½d. rose-red (1870) *From* 60·00
Plate Nos. 4, 5, 6, 8, 10, 11.
Z33 1d. rose-red (1864–1879) *From* 50·00
Plate Nos. 76, 120, 121, 122, 124, 134, 137, 140, 146, 148, 149, 150, 151, 154, 155, 156, 157, 160, 167, 170, 171, 174, 175, 176, 178, 180, 182, 185, 186, 189.
Z34 1½d. lake-red (1870–1874) (Plate Nos. 1, 3) 50·00
Z35 2d. blue (1858–1869) (Plate Nos. 13, 14, 15) 50·00
Z36 3d. rose (1867–1873) (Plate Nos. 7, 8, 9, 10) *From* 65·00
Z37 3d. rose (1873–1876) *From* 60·00
Plate Nos. 11, 12, 14, 15, 16, 17, 18, 19.
Z38 4d. vermilion (1865–1873) *From* 50·00
Plate Nos. 11, 12, 13, 14.
Z39 4d. vermilion (1876) (Plate No. 15) £300
Z40 4d. sage-green (1877) (Plate No. 15)
Z41 6d. mauve (1870) (Plate No. 9) £120
Z42 6d. buff (1872) (Plate No. 11) 80·00
Z43 6d. chestnut (1872) (Plate No. 11) 70·00
Z44 6d. grey (1873) (Plate No. 12) £200
Z45 6d. grey (1874–1880) *From* 60·00
Plate Nos. 13, 14, 15, 16.
Z46 8d. orange (1876) £325
Z47 9d. straw (1867) £275
Z48 10d. red-brown (1867) £350
Z49 1s. green (1867–1873) (Plate Nos. 4, 5, 6, 7) *From* 50·00
Z50 1s. green (1873–1877) *From* 60·00
Plate Nos. 8, 9, 10, 11, 12.
Z51 2s. blue (1867) £200
Z52 5s. rose (1867–1874) (Plate Nos. 1, 2) £600

NAGUABO

Stamps of GREAT BRITAIN cancelled '582' as T **9**.

1875–77.

Z53 ½d. rose-red (1870–1879) (Plate Nos. 5. 12, 14)
Z54 1d. rose-red (1864–1879) (Plate Nos. 150, 159, 165) £800
Z55 3d. rose (1873–1876) (Plate Nos. 17, 18) £1100
Z56 4d. vermilion (1872–1873) (Plate Nos. 13, 14) *From* £1100
Z57 4d. vermilion (1876) (Plate No. 15) £1500
Z58 6d. grey (1874–1876) (Plate Nos. 14, 15)
Z59 9d. straw (1867)
Z60 10d. red-brown (1867) £1700
Z61 1s. green (1873–1877) (Plate Nos. 11, 12) £1100
Z62 2s. dull blue (1867) (Plate No. 1) £1900

PONCE

Stamps of GREAT BRITAIN cancelled 'F88' as T **8**.

1873–77.

Z63 ½d. rose-red (1870) (Plate Nos. 5, 10, 12) 70·00
Z64 1d. rose-red (1864–1879) *From* 60·00
Plate Nos. 120, 121, 122, 123, 124, 146, 148, 154, 156, 157, 158, 160, 167, 171, 174, 175, 179, 186, 187.
Z65 1½d. lake-red (1870–1874) (Plate No. 3) £110
Z66 2d. blue (1858–1869) (Plate Nos. 13, 14) 60·00
Z67 3d. rose (1867–1873) (Plate Nos. 7, 8, 9)
Z68 3d. rose (1873–1876) 70·00
Plate Nos. 12, 16, 17, 18, 19.
Z69 4d. vermilion (1865–1873) *From* 60·00
Plate Nos. 8, 9, 12, 13, 14.
Z70 4d. vermilion (1876) (Plate No. 15) £300
Z71 4d. sage-green (1877) (Plate Nos. 15, 16) *From* £200
Z72 6d. buff (1872–1873) (Plate Nos. 11, 12) *From* 75·00
Z73 6d. chestnut (1872) (Plate No. 11) 75·00
Z74 6d. grey (1873) (Plate No. 12)
Z75 6d. grey (1874–1876) (Plate Nos. 13, 14, 15) *From* 65·00
Z76 9d. straw (1867) £275
Z77 10d. red-brown (1867) £325
Z78 1s. green (1867–1873) (Plate Nos. 4, 6, 7) 60·00
Z79 1s. green (1873–1877) *From* 65·00
Plate Nos. 8, 9. 10, 11, 12, 13.
Z80 2s. blue (1867)
Z81 5s. rose (1867–1874) (Plate Nos. 1, 2) *From* £650

SAN JUAN

CROWNED-CIRCLE HANDSTAMPS

CC1 CC **1** SAN JUAN PORTO RICO (R. *or* Black) (25.5.1844) *Price on cover* £650

No. CC1 may be found on cover, used in conjunction with Spanish colonial adhesive stamps paying the local postage.

Stamps of GREAT BRITAIN cancelled 'C61' as in Types **4**, **8**, **12**, **14A** or **16**.

1865–77.

Z82 ½d. rose-red (1870) (Plate Nos. 5, 10, 15) *From* 55·00
Z83 1d. rose-red (1857)
Z84 1d. rose-red (1864–1879) *From* 45·00
Plate Nos. 72, 73, 74, 81, 84, 90, 94, 100, 101, 102, 107, 117, 122, 124, 125, 127, 130, 137, 138, 139, 140, 145, 146, 149, 153, 156, 159, 160, 162, 163, 169, 171, 172, 173, 174, 175, 179, 180, 182, 186.
Z85 1½d. lake-red (1870–1874) (Plate Nos. 1, 3) *From* 70·00
Z86 2d. blue (1858–1869) (Plate Nos. 9, 13, 14) *From* 50·00
Z87 3d. rose (1865) (Plate No. 4) 90·00
Z88 3d. rose (1867–1873) *From* 55·00
Plate Nos. 5, 6, 7, 8, 9, 10.
Z89 3d. rose (1873–1876) *From* 55·00
Plate Nos. 11, 12, 14, 15, 16, 17, 18.
Z90 4d. vermilion (1865–1873) *From* 50·00
Plate Nos. 7, 8, 9, 10, 11, 12, 13, 14.
Z91 4d. vermilion (1876) (Plate No. 15) £300
Z92 6d. lilac (1865–1867) (Plate Nos. 5, 6) *From* 75·00
Z93 6d. lilac (1867) (Plate No. 6) 75·00
Z94 6d. violet (1867–1870) (Plate Nos. 6, 8, 9) *From* 70·00
Z95 6d. buff (1872–1873) (Plate Nos. 11, 12) *From* 75·00
Z96 6d. chestnut (1872) (Plate No. 11) 50·00
Z97 6d. grey (1873) (Plate No. 12)
Z98 6d. grey (1874–1876) (Plate Nos. 13, 14, 15) *From* 50·00
Z99 9d. straw (1862) £300
Z100 9d. straw (1865) £375
Z101 9d. straw (1867) £200
Z102 10d. red-brown (1867) £275
Z103 1s. green (1865) (Plate No. 4) £140
Z104 1s. green (1867–1873) (Plate Nos. 4, 5, 6, 7) *From* 50·00
Z105 1s. green (1873–1877) *From* 65·00
Plate Nos. 8, 9, 10, 11, 12, 13.
Z106 2s. blue (1867) £140
Z107 5s. rose (1867) (Plate Nos. 1, 2) *From* £450

RUSSIA

ARMY FIELD OFFICES IN THE CRIMEA, THE BLACK SEA AND CONSTANTINOPLE

1854–56.

Crown between Stars

Z1 1d. red-brown (1841), imperf £875
Z2 1d. red-brown (1854), Die I, wmk Small Crown, perf 16
Z3 1d. red-brown (1855), Die II, wmk Small Crown, perf 16 £275
Z4 1d. red-brown, Die I, wmk Small Crown, perf 14
Z5 1d. red-brown (1855), Die II, Small Crown, perf 14
Z6 2d. blue (1841) imperf £1800
Z7 2d. blue, Small Crown (1854), perf 16 (Plate No. 4)
Z8 1s. green (1847), embossed £3000

Star between Cyphers

Z9 1d. red-brown (1841), imperf
Z10 1d. red-brown (1854), Die I, wmk Small Crown, perf 16 90·00
Z11 1d. red-brown (1855), Die II, wmk Small Crown, perf 16 £110
Z12 1d. red-brown (1855), Die I, wmk Small Crown, perf 14 £120
Z13 1d. red-brown (1855), Die II, wmk Small Crown, perf 14 £110
Z14 1d. red-brown (1855), Die II, wmk Large Crown, perf 16 £150
Z15 1d. red-brown (1855), Die II, wmk Large Crown, perf 14 50·00
Z16 2d. blue (1841), imperf £2000
Z17 2d. blue (1854), wmk Small Crown, perf 16 *From* £160
Plate Nos. 4, 5.
Z18 2d. blue (1855), wmk Small Crown, perf 14 £275
Plate No. 4.
Z19 2d. blue (1855), wmk Large Crown, perf 16 £325
Plate No. 5.
Z20 2d. blue (1855), wmk Large Crown, perf 14 £190
Plate No. 5.
Z22 6d. violet (1854), embossed £2250
Z23 1s. green (1847), embossed £2250

On 12 March 1854 Britain, France and Turkey signed an alliance against Russia. A British force arrived in Constantinople in April 1854 and the Anglo-French Black Sea Fleet based itself at Varna, Bulgaria, the following month. 'Crown between Stars' obliterators were supplied for use at Army Field Post Offices at Constantinople and Varna from July 1854 and in the Crimea, following the arrival of Allied Forces, on 14 September 1854. The 'Star between Cyphers' obliterator was in use from March 1855 in the Crimea and at the British barracks at Scutari, near Constantinople.

SPAIN

Little is known about the operation of British Packet Agencies in Spain, other than the dates recorded for the various postal markings in the GPO Proof Books. The Agency at Corunna is said to date from the late 17th-century when the Spanish packets for South America were based there. No. CC1 was probably issued in connection with the inauguration of the P & O service to Spain in 1843. The Spanish port of call was changed to Vigo in 1846 and the office at Corunna was then closed. Teneriffe became a port-of-call for the South American packets in 1817 and this arrangement continued until 1858.

CORUNNA

CROWNED-CIRCLE HANDSTAMPS

CC1 CC **1b** CORUNNA (28.2.1842)

Although recorded in the GPO Proof Books no example of No. CC1 on cover is known.

TENERIFFE (CANARY ISLANDS)

CROWNED-CIRCLE HANDSTAMPS

CC2 CC **7** TENERIFFE (6.1.1851) *Price on cover* £3750
CC3 CC **4** TENERIFFE (23.10.1857) *Price on cover* £3750

No. CC2/3 can be found used on covers from Spain to South America with the rate from Spain to Teneriffe paid in Spanish adhesive stamps.

UNITED STATES OF AMERICA

The network of British Packet Agencies, to operate the trans-Atlantic Packet system, was re-established in 1814 after the War of 1812.

The New York Agency opened in that year to be followed by further offices at Boston, Charleston (South Carolina), New Orleans, Savannah (Georgia) (all in 1842), Mobile (Alabama) (1848) and San Francisco (1860). Of these agencies Charleston and Savannah closed the same year (1842) as did New Orleans, although the latter was re-activated from 1848 to 1850. Mobile closed 1850, Boston in 1865, New York in 1882 and San Francisco, for which no postal markings have been recorded, in 1883.

Although recorded in the GPO Proof Books no actual examples of the Crowned-circle handstamps for Charleston, Mobile, New Orleans and Savannah are known on cover.

The GPO Proof Books record, in error, a Crowned-circle handstamp for St Michaels, Maryland. This handstamp was intended for the agency on San Miguel in the Azores.

CHARLESTON

CROWNED-CIRCLE HANDSTAMPS

CC1 CC **1b** CHARLESTON (15.12.1841)

MOBILE

CROWNED-CIRCLE HANDSTAMPS

CC2 CC **1b** MOBILE (15.12.1841)

NEW ORLEANS

CROWNED-CIRCLE HANDSTAMPS

CC3 CC **1b** NEW ORLEANS (15.12.1841)
CC4 CC **1** NEW ORLEANS (27.4.1848)

NEW YORK

CROWNED-CIRCLE HANDSTAMPS

CC5 CC **1b** NEW YORK (R.) (15.12.1841) *Price on cover* £35000

SAVANNAH

CROWNED-CIRCLE HANDSTAMPS

CC6 CC **1b** SAVANNAH (15.12.1841)

Although recorded in the GPO Proof Books, no examples of Nos. CC1/CC4 or CC6 are known on cover.

URUGUAY

MONTEVIDEO

British packets commenced calling at Montevideo in 1824 on passage to and from Buenos Aires.

Great Britain stamps were in use from 1864. Combination covers exist with the local postage paid by Uruguay adhesive stamps. The agency was closed on 31 July 1873.

CROWNED-CIRCLE HANDSTAMPS

CC1 CC **5** MONTEVIDEO (Black) (6.1.1851) *Price on cover* £1400

Stamps of GREAT BRITAIN cancelled 'C28' as T **4**.

1864–73.

Z1 1d. rose-red (1864) 75·00
Plate Nos. 73, 92, 93, 94, 119, 148, 154, 157, 171.
Z2 2d. blue (1858–1869) (Plate Nos. 9, 13) 75·00
Z3 3d. rose (1865) (Plate No. 4)
Z4 3d. rose (1867–1871) (Plate Nos. 4, 5, 7) *From* 85·00
Z6 4d. rose (1857)
Z7 4d. red (1862) (Plate No. 4)
Z8 4d. vermilion (1865–1870) *From* 85·00
Plate Nos. 7, 8, 9, 10, 11, 12.
Z9 6d. lilac (1856)
Z10 6d. lilac (1862) (Plate No. 4) £175
Z11 6d. lilac (1865–1867) (Plate Nos. 5, 6) *From* £100
Z12 6d. lilac (1867) (Plate No. 6)
Z13 6d. violet (1867–1870) (Plate Nos. 8, 9) *From* 90·00
Z14 6d. buff (1872)
Z15 6d. chestnut (1872)
Z16 9d. straw (1862)
Z17 9d. straw (1865)
Z18 9d. straw (1867) £325
Z19 10d. red-brown (1867) £375
Z20 1s. green (1862) £190
Z21 1s. green (1865) (Plate No. 4) £170
Z22 1s. green (1867–1873) (Plate Nos. 4, 5) *From* 85·00
Z23 2s. blue (1867) £275
Z24 5s. rose (1867) (Plate No. 1) £675

VENEZUELA

British Postal Agencies were initially opened at La Guayra and Porto Cabello on 1 January 1842. Further offices were added at Maracaibo in 1842 and Ciudad Bolivar during January 1868. Porto Cabello closed in 1858 and Maracaibo was also short-lived. The remaining offices closed at the end of 1879 when Venezuela joined the UPU.

Great Britain stamps were used at La Guayra from 1865 and at Ciudad Bolivar from its establishment in 1868. They can be found used in combination with Venezuela adhesives paying the local postage.

CIUDAD BOLIVAR

Stamps of GREAT BRITAIN cancelled 'D22' as T **12**, or circular date stamps as Types **16** (black) or **17** (red).

1868–79.

Z1 1d. rose-red (1864–1879) (Plate No. 133) £300
Z2 2d. blue (1858–1869) (Plate No. 13)
Z3 3d. rose (1867–1873) (Plate No. 5)
Z4 3d. rose (1873–1879) (Plate No. 11) £425
Z5 4d. vermilion (1865–1873) *From* £425
Plate Nos. 9, 11, 12, 14.
Z6 4d. sage-green (1877) (Plate Nos. 15, 16) *From* £450
Z7 4d. grey-brown (1880) wmk Crown (Plate No. 17). £1100
Z8 9d. straw (1867) £550
Z9 10d. red-brown (1867)
Z10 1s. green (1867–1873) (Plate Nos. 4, 5, 7) *From* £400
Z11 1s. green (1873–1877) (Plate Nos. 10, 12, 13) *From* £575
Z12 2s. blue (1867) £1200
Z13 5s. rose (1867–1874) (Plate Nos. 1, 2) *From* £2200

LA GUAYRA

CROWNED-CIRCLE HANDSTAMPS

CC1 CC **1b** LA GUAYRA (Black) (15.12.1841)
Price on cover £3250

Stamps of GREAT BRITAIN cancelled 'C60' as T **4**, circular date stamp as Types **16** and **17** or with No. CC1.

1865–80.

Z14 ½d. rose-red (1870) Plate No. 6)
Z15 1d. rose-red (1864–1879) *From* 70·00
Plate Nos. 81, 92, 96, 98, 111, 113, 115, 131, 138, 144, 145, 154, 177, 178, 180, 196.
Z16 1½d. lake-red (1870–1874) (Plate No. 3)
Z17 2d. blue (1858–1869) (Plate Nos. 13, 14) 70·00
Z18 3d. rose (1873–1876) *From* 80·00
Plate Nos. 14, 15, 17, 18, 19.
Z19 4d. vermilion (1865–1873) *From* 70·00
Plate Nos. 7, 9, 11, 12, 13, 14.
Z20 4d. vermilion (1876) (Plate No. 15) £300
Z21 4d. sage-green (1877) (Plate Nos. 15, 16) *From* £225
Z22 6d. lilac (1865) (Plate No. 5)
Z23 6d. violet (1867–1870) (Plate Nos. 6, 8)
Z24 6d. buff (1872–1873) (Plate Nos. 11, 12) *From* £100
Z25 6d. grey (1873) (Plate No. 12) £225
Z26 6d. grey (1874–1876) (Plate Nos. 13, 14, 15, 16) 70·00
Z27 8d. orange (1876) £300
Z28 9d. straw (1862)
Z29 9d. straw (1867)
Z30 10d. red-brown (1867)
Z31 1s. green (1865) (Plate No. 4) £160
Z32 1s. green (1867–1873) (Plate Nos. 4, 7)
Z33 1s. green (1873–1877) *From* 85·00
Plate Nos. 8, 9, 10, 11, 12, 13.
Z34 2s. blue (1867) £275
Z35 5s. rose (1867–1874) (Plate No. 1, 2) *From* £600

MARACAIBO

CROWNED-CIRCLE HANDSTAMPS

CC2 CC **1b** MARACAIBO (31.12.1841)
No examples of No. CC2 on cover have been recorded.

PORTO CABELLO

CROWNED-CIRCLE HANDSTAMPS

CC3 CC **1b** PORTO-CABELLO (R.) (15.12.1841)
Price on cover £3500

MAIL BOAT OBLITERATIONS

The following cancellations were supplied to GPO sorters operating on ships holding mail contracts from the British Post Office. They were for use on mail posted on board, but most examples occur on letters from soldiers and sailors serving overseas which were forwarded to the mailboats without postmarks.

P. & O. MEDITERRANEAN AND FAR EAST MAILBOATS

The first such cancellation, 'A17' as T **2**, was issued to the Southampton–Alexandria packet in April 1858, but no examples have been recorded.

The GPO Proof Book also records 'B16', in T **2**, as being issued for marine sorting in November 1859, but this postmark was subsequently used by the Plymouth and Bristol Sorting Carriage.

Sorting on board P. & O. packets ceased in June 1870 and many of the cancellation numbers were subsequently reallocated using Types **9**, **11** or **12**.

Stamps of GREAT BRITAIN cancelled 'A80' as T **2**.

1859 (Mar)–**70.**

Z1 1d. rose-red (1857). Die II, wmk Large Crown, perf 14 50·00
Z2 6d. lilac (1856) £160

Stamps of GREAT BRITAIN cancelled 'A81' as T **2**.

1859 (Mar)–**70.**

Z3 1d. rose-red (1857), Die II, wmk Large Crown, *perf* 14 50·00
Z4 1d. rose-red (1864–1879) *From* 45·00
Plate Nos, 84, 85, 86, 91, 97.
Z5 2d. blue (1858–1869) (Plate No. 9) 60·00
Z6 4d. red (1862) (Plate No. 4) £120
Z7 4d. vermilion (1865–1873) (Plate No. 8) 60·00
Z8 6d. lilac (1856) £160
Z9 6d. lilac (1862) (Plate No. 3) £120
Z10 6d. lilac (1865–1867) (Plate Nos. 5, 6) *From* £100
Z11 6d. lilac (1867) (Plate No. 6) £100
Z12 6d. violet (1867–1870) (Plate Nos. 6, 8) *From* 75·00
Z13 10d. red-brown (1867) £500
Z14 1s. green (1856) £300

Stamps of GREAT BRITAIN cancelled 'A82' as T **2**.

1859 (Mar)–**70.**

Z15 1d. rose-red (1857), Die II, wmk Large Crown, perf 14 60·00
Z16 2d. blue (1858) (Plate No. 7) 65·00
Z17 4d. rose (1856) £225
Z18 6d. lilac 1856) £200
Z19 6d. lilac (1865–1867) (Plate Nos. 5. 6) *From* £130
Z20 6d. lilac (1867) (Plate No. 6) £110

Stamps of GREAT BRITAIN cancelled 'A83' as T **2**.

1859 (Apr)–**70.**

Z21 1d. rose-red (1857), Die II, wmk Large Crown, perf 14 50·00
Z22 1d. rose-red (1864–1879) *From* 45·00
Plate Nos. 73, 74, 84, 91, 92, 109.
Z23 3d. carmine-rose (1862) £275
Z24 4d. rose (1857) £200
Z25 4d. red (1862) £110
Z26 4d. vermilion (1865–1873) (Plate Nos. 9, 10) .. *From* 60·00
Z27 6d. lilac (1856) £160
Z28 6d. lilac (1862) £125
Z29 6d. lilac (1865–1867) (Plate Nos. 5, 6) *From* £100
Z30 6d. violet (1867–1870) (Plate Nos. 6, 8) *From* 75·00
Z31 10d. red-brown (1867) £500
Z32 1s. green (1862) £300

Stamps of GREAT BRITAIN cancelled 'A84' as T **2**.

1859 (Apr)–**70.**

Z33 1d. rose-red (1857), Die II, wmk Large Crown, perf 14 £110

Stamps of GREAT BRITAIN cancelled 'A85' as T **2**.

1859 (Apr)–**70.**

Z34 1d. rose-red (1857), Die II, wmk Large Crown, perf 14 50·00
Z35 1d. rose-red (1864–1879) *From* 45·00
Plate Nos. 79, 97, 103.
Z36 3d. carmine-rose (1862) £275
Z37 4d. red (1862) £110
Z38 6d. lilac (1856) £160
Z39 6d. lilac (1862) (Plate Nos. 3, 4) *From* £120
Z40 6d. lilac (1865–1867) (Plate No. 5) £100
Z41 6d. lilac (1867) (Plate No. 6) 90·00
Z42 1s. green (1862) £325

Stamps of GREAT BRITAIN cancelled 'A86' as T **2**.

1859 (Apr)–**70.**

Z43 1d. rose-red (1857), Die II, wmk Large Crown, perf 14 50·00
Z44 1d. rose-red (1864–1879) *From* 45·00
Plate Nos. 73, 84, 94, 97, 114, 118.
Z45 3d. rose (1865) £250
Z46 3d. rose (1867–1873) (Plate Nos. 4, 5) *From* 75·00
Z47 4d. rose (1857) £200
Z48 4d. red (1862) (Plate No. 4) £110
Z49 4d. vermilion (1865–1873) (Plate No. 10) 80·00
Z50 6d. lilac (1856) £160
Z51 6d. lilac (1862) (Plate Nos. 3, 4) *From* £120
Z52 6d. lilac (1865–1867) (Plate Nos. 5, 6) *From* £100
Z53 6d. lilac (1867) (Plate Nos. 6, 8) *From* 75·00
Z54 10d. red-brown (1867) £450
Z55 1s. green (1862) £300

Stamps of GREAT BRITAIN cancelled 'A87' as T **2**.

1859 (Apr)–**70.**

Z56 1d. rose-red (1857), Die II, wmk Large Crown, perf 14 65·00
Z57 4d. rose (1856) £250
Z58 6d. lilac (1867) (Plate No. 6) £120

Stamps of GREAT BRITAIN cancelled 'A88' as T **2**.

1859 (Apr)–**70.**

Z59 1d. rose-red (1857), Die II, wmk Large Crown, perf 14 50·00
Z60 1d. rose-red (1864–1879) *From* 45·00
Plate Nos. 74, 80, 85.
Z61 4d. rose (1857) £225
Z62 4d. red (1862) £120
Z63 4d. vermilion (1865–1873) (Plate No. 8) 60·00
Z64 6d. lilac (1856)
Z65 6d. lilac (1862) (Plate No. 4) £160
Z66 6d. lilac (1865–1867) (Plate No. 5) £120
Z67 6d. lilac (1867) (Plate No. 6) £100
Z68 6d. violet (1867–1870) (Plate No. 8) 75·00
Z69 10d. red-brown (1867) £525
Z70 1s. green (1856) £325

Stamps of GREAT BRITAIN cancelled 'A89' as T **2**.

1859 (Apr)–**70.**

Z71 1d. rose-red (1857), Die II, wmk Large Crown, perf 14 £110
Z72 6d. lilac (1856) £300

Stamps of GREAT BRITAIN cancelled 'A90' as T **2**.

1859 (June)–**70.**

Z73 1d. rose-red (1857), Die II, wmk Large Crown, perf 14 75·00
Z74 4d. rose (1856)
Z75 6d. lilac (1856) £250
Z76 6d. lilac (1865–1867) (Plate Nos. 5, 6) *From* £160
Z77 9d. straw (1867)

Stamps of GREAT BRITAIN cancelled 'A99' as T **2**.

1859 (June)–**70.**

Z78 1d. rose-red (1857), Die II, wmk Large Crown, perf 14 50·00
Z79 1d. rose-red (1864–1879) *From* 45·00
Plate Nos. 93, 97, 99, 118.
Z80 4d. rose (1857) £200
Z81 4d. red (1862) £110
Z82 4d. vermilion (1865–1873) (Plate No. 11) 60·00
Z83 6d. lilac (1856)
Z84 6d. lilac (1862) £160
Z85 6d. lilac (1865–1867) (Plate Nos. 5, 6) *From* £120
Z86 10d. red-brown (1867) £500

Stamps of GREAT BRITAIN cancelled 'B03' as T **2**.

1859 (Aug)–**70.**

Z87 1d. rose-red (1857), Die II, wmk Large Crown, perf 14 65·00
Z88 1d. rose-red (1864–1879) (Plate Nos. 109, 116) .. *From* 50·00
Z89 3d. rose (1865) (Plate No. 4) £100
Z90 6d. lilac (1856) £170
Z91 6d. lilac (1867) (Plate No. 6) £140
Z92 6d. violet (1867–1870) (Plate Nos. 6, 8) *From* £100
Z93 10d. red-brown (1867) £550

Stamps of GREAT BRITAIN cancelled 'B12' as T **2**.

1859 (Oct)–**70.**

Z94 1d. rose-red (1857), Die II, wmk Large Crown, perf 14 65·00
Z95 1d. rose-red (1864–1879) (Plate No. 94) 50·00
Z96 3d. rose (1865) (Plate No. 4) £100
Z97 4d. red (1862) £120
Z98 4d. vermilion (1865–1873) (Plate No. 8) 75·00
Z99 6d. lilac (1856)
Z100 6d. lilac (1862) £170
Z101 6d. lilac (1865–1867) (Plate Nos. 5, 6) *From* £140
Z102 6d. violet (1867–1870) (Plate No. 8) 95·00

Stamps of GREAT BRITAIN cancelled 'B56' as T **2**.

1861 (July)–**70.**

Z103 1d. rose-red (1864–1870) (Plate Nos. 84, 97) 50·00
Z104 2d. blue (1858–1869) (Plate No. 9) 60·00
Z105 4d. red (1862) (Plate No. 4) £120
Z106 4d. vermilion (1865–1873) (Plate Nos. 7, 8) 70·00
Z107 6d. lilac (1862) (Plate Nos. 3, 4) *From* £140
Z108 6d. lilac (1865–1867) (Plate Nos. 5, 6) *From* £120
Z109 6d. violet (1867–1871) (Plate Nos. 6, 8) *From* £100

Stamps of GREAT BRITAIN cancelled 'B57' as T **2**.

1861 (July)–**70.**

Z110 1d. rose-red (1857), Die II, wmk Large Crown, perf 14 60·00
Z111 1d. rose-red (1864–1879) (Plate No. 81) 50·00
Z112 2d. blue (1858–1869) (Plate No. 9) 70·00
Z113 4d. red (1862) £120
Z114 4d. vermilion (1865–1873) (Plate Nos. 7, 8) 70·00
Z115 6d. lilac (1865–1867) (Plate Nos. 5, 6) *From* £120

Stamps of GREAT BRITAIN cancelled 'C79' as T **12**.

1866 (June)–**70.**

Z116 6d. violet (1867–1870) (Plate Nos. 6, 8) *From* £100
Z117 10d. red-brown (1867) £475

CUNARD LINE ATLANTIC MAILBOATS

These were all issued in June 1859. No examples arc known used after August 1868. 'B61' is recorded as being issued in March 1862, but no examples are known. Cancellation numbers were subsequently reallocated to offices in Great Britain or, in the case of 'A91', the British Virgin Islands.

Stamps of GREAT BRITAIN cancelled 'A91' as T **2**.

1859 (June)–**68.**

Z130 1d. rose-red (1857), Die II, wmk Large Crown, perf 14 70·00
Z131 1d. rose-red (1864–1879) (Plate No. 121) 60·00
Z132 2d. blue (1855), wmk Small Crown, perf 14
Z133 2d. blue (1858–1869) (Plate Nos. 8, 9) 95·00
Z134 4d. rose (1857) £250
Z135 4d. red (1862) £130
Z136 6d. lilac (1856) £175
Z137 6d. lilac (1862) £160
Z138 6d. lilac (1865–1867) £120
Z139 9d. straw (1862)
Z140 1s. green (1856) £350

Stamps of GREAT BRITAIN cancelled 'A92' as T **2**

1859 (June)–**68**.

Z141	1d. rose-red (1857), Die II, wmk Large Crown, perf 14	70·00
Z142	1d. rose-red (1864–1879) (Plate Nos. 93, 97) *From*	60·00
Z143	6d. lilac (1856)	£175
Z144	6d. lilac (1862) (Plate No. 3)	£160
Z145	6d. lilac (1865–1867) (Plate Nos. 5, 6) *From*	£120

Stamps of GREAT BRITAIN cancelled 'A93' as T **2**.

1859 (June)–**63**.

Z146	1d. rose-red (1857), Die II, wmk Large Crown, perf 14	70·00
Z147	1d. rose-red (1864–1879) (Plate No. 85)	60·00
Z148	6d. lilac (1856)	£175
Z149	6d. lilac (1865–1867) (Plate No. 6)	£160
Z150	10d. red-brown (1867)	£525

Stamps of GREAT BRITAIN cancelled 'A94' as T **2**.

1859 (June)–**68**.

Z151	1d. rose-red (1857), Die II, wmk Large Crown, perf 14	95·00
Z152	1d. rose-red (1864–1879) (Plate Nos. 74, 97)	70·00
Z153	4d. vermilion (1865–1873) (Plate No. 7)	£100
Z154	6d. lilac (1856)	£200
Z155	6d. lilac (1862)	£160
Z156	6d. lilac (1865–1867) (Plate Nos. 5, 6) *From*	£140

Stamps of GREAT BRITAIN cancelled 'A95' as T **2**.

1859 (June)–**68**.

Z157	1d. rose-red (1857), Die II, wmk Large Crown, perf 14	65·00
Z158	1d. rose-red (1864–1879) *From* Plate Nos. 72, 89, 97.	55·00
Z159	3d. rose (1867–1873) (Plate No. 5)	95·00
Z160	4d. red (1862)	£130
Z161	4d. vermilion (1865–1873) (Plate No. 8)	80·00
Z162	6d. lilac (1862)	£190
Z163	6d. lilac (1865–1867) (Plate No. 5)	£160
Z164	6d. lilac (1867) (Plate No. 6)	£130
Z165	1s. green (1856)	£300

Stamps of GREAT BRITAIN cancelled 'A96' as T **2**.

1859 (June)–**68**.

Z166	1d. rose-red (1857), Die II, wmk Large Crown, perf 14	70·00
Z167	4d. vermilion (1865–1873) (Plate No. 7)	£100
Z168	6d. lilac (1856)	£180
Z169	1s. green (1856)	£350

Stamps of GREAT BRITAIN cancelled 'A97' as T **2**.

1859 (June)–**68**.

Z170	1d. rose-red (1857), Die II, wmk Large Crown, perf 14	70·00
Z171	1d. rose-red (1864–1879) (Plate No. 71)	60·00
Z172	4d. Red (1862) (Plate No. 3)	£140
Z172*a*	6d. lilac (1862)	£180

Stamps of GREAT BRITAIN cancelled 'A98' as T **2**.

1859 (June)–**68**.

Z173	1d. rose-red (1857), Die II, wmk Large Crown, perf 14	70·00
Z174	4d. red (1862)	£140
Z175	6d. lilac (1856)	£200
Z176	6d. lilac (1862) (Plate No. 4)	£160
Z177	6d. lilac (1865–1867) (Plate Nos. 5, 6) *From*	£120

ALLAN LINE ATLANTIC MAILBOATS

British GPO sorters worked on these Canadian ships between November 1859 and April 1860. Cancellations as Type **2** numbered 'B17', 'B18', 'B27', 'B28', 'B29' and 'B30' were issued to them, but have not been reported used on Great Britain stamps during this period. All were subsequently reallocated to British post offices.

SPANISH WEST INDIES MAILBOATS

'D26' was supplied for use by British mail clerks employed on ships of the Herrara Line operating between St Thomas (Danish West Indies), Cuba, Dominican Republic and Porto Rico.

Stamps of GREAT BRITAIN cancelled 'D26' as T **12**.

1868–71.

Z190	1d. rose-red (1864–1879) (Plate Nos. 98, 125)	
Z191	4d. vermilion (1865–1873) (Plate Nos. 9, 10, 11)	£1500
Z192	6d. violet (1867–1870) (Plate No. 8)	
Z193	1s. green (1867) (Plate No. 4)	£1500

Abu Dhabi

1964. 100 Naye Paise = 1 Rupee 1966. 1000 Fils = 1 Dinar

Abu Dhabi is the largest of the former Trucial States on the Persian Gulf, which are now combined to form the United Arab Emirates. The others, which all issued stamps, are Ajman (with Manama), Dubai, Fujeira, Ras al Khaima, Sharjah and Umm al Qiwain. They were known as the Trucial States because in May 1853 they all signed the Perpetual Maritime Truce Agreement with the United Kingdom, under which they undertook to give up piracy and the slave trade.

Sheikh Shakhbut bin Sultan
1928–6 August 1966

BRITISH POSTAL ADMINISTRATION

The postal service was established on 30 March 1963 and the stamps of the British Postal Agencies in Eastern Arabia (see *British Postal Agencies in Eastern Arabia* in this catalogue) were used until 29 March 1964.

1 Sheikh Shakhbut bin Sultan

2 Mountain Gazelle

3 Ruler's Palace

4 Oil Rig and Camels

(Des M. C. Farrar-Bell. Photo Harrison (T **1/2**). Des C. T. Kavanagh (T **3**), Miss P. M. Goth (T **4**). Recess Bradbury Wilkinson)

1964 (30 Mar). P 14½ (T **1/2**) or 13×13½ (T **3/4**).

1	**1**	5n.p. green	6·50	6·00
2		15n.p. red-brown	4·75	3·75
3		20n.p. ultramarine	4·75	2·25
		a. Perf 13×13½	£750	
4		30n.p. red-orange	4·75	2·25
5	**2**	40n.p. reddish violet	8·50	1·50
6		50n.p. bistre	8·50	3·50
7		75n.p. black	11·00	8·50
8	**3**	1r. emerald	6·50	3·25
9		2r. black	11·00	6·00
10	**4**	5r. carmine-red	25·00	15·00
11		10r. deep ultramarine	29·00	17·00
1/11 *Set of* 11			£110	60·00

5

6

7

Saker Falcon on Gloved Hand

(Des V. Whiteley. Photo Harrison)

1965 (30 Mar). Falconry. P 14½.

12	**5**	20n.p. light brown and grey-blue	15·00	3·25
13	**6**	40n.p. light brown and blue	18·00	3·25
14	**7**	2r. sepia and turquoise-green	32·00	16·00
12/14 *Set of* 3			60·00	20·00

Sheikh Zaid bin Sultan al Nahyan
6 August 1966

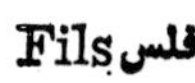

(**8**)

(Surch by Arabian Ptg & Publishing House, Bahrain)

1966 (1 Oct). New Currency. Nos. 1/11 surch as T **8**, with bars obliterating portrait of deposed Sheikh. P 13×13½ (20f.), others as before.

15	**1**	5f. on 5n.p. green	15·00	7·00
16		15f. on 15n.p. red-brown	22·00	13·00
17		20f. on 20n.p. ultramarine	22·00	9·00
		b. Perf 14½	£350	£325
		ba. Surch inverted	£800	£1400
18		30f. on 30n.p. red-orange	20·00	26·00
		a. Arabic '2' for '3' in surch (R. 7/8)	£9000	
		b. Surch double, one albino	£400	
19	**2**	40f. on 40n.p. reddish violet	18·00	1·50
20		50f. on 50n.p. bistre	60·00	60·00
21		75f. on 75n.p. black	60·00	60·00
		a. Surch double, one albino	£400	
22	**3**	100f. on 1r. emerald	18·00	5·00
23		200f. on 2r. black	18·00	15·00
24	**4**	500f. on 5r. carmine-red	30·00	38·00
25		1d. on 10r. deep ultramarine	55·00	70·00
		a. Short extra bar below portrait (R. 7/3)	£475	
15/25 *Set of* 11			£300	£275

The 40f., 50f. and 75f. are surcharged 'Fils' only, as in Type **8**. The remainder have the new value expressed in figures also. On the 1d. the old value is obliterated by bars.

No. 18a was quickly corrected. Only five sheets with the error are believed to have been sold.

The Abu Dhabi Post Department took over the postal services on 1 January 1967. Later stamp isssues will be found in Stanley Gibbons *Arabia Catalogue*.

Aden

The first post office in Aden opened during January 1839, situated in what became known as the Crater district. No stamps were initially available, but, after the office was placed under the Bombay Postal Circle, stocks of the 1854 ½a. and 1a. stamps were placed on sale in Aden from 10 October 1854. Supplies of the 2a. and 4a. values did not arrive until December. Most Indian issues from the 1854 lithographs up to 1935 Silver Jubilee set can be found with Aden postmarks.

During January 1858 a further office, Aden Steamer Point, was opened in the harbour area and much of the business was transferred to it by 1869. The original Aden post office, in Crater, was renamed Aden Cantonment, later to be changed again to Aden Camp.

The first cancellation used with the Indian stamps was a plain diamond of dots. This type was also used elsewhere so that attribution to Aden is only possible when on cover. Aden was assigned '124' in the Indian postal number system, with the sub-office at Aden Steamer Point being '132'. After a short period '124' was used at both offices, cancellations being identifiable by the spacing and shape of the numerals. It is possible that '132' was also used at an office in India.

1858 '124' Cancellation

1870 Aden Duplex

1872 Aden Steamer Point Duplex

Both post offices used '124' until 1871 when Aden Cantonment was assigned '125', only to have this swiftly amended to '124A' in the same year.

1871 Aden Cantonment '125' Cancellation

1871 Aden Cantonment '124A' Cancellation

Cancellations inscribed 'Aden Steamer Point' disappear after 1874 and this office was then known simply as Aden. Following this change the office was given number 'B-22' under the revised Indian PO scheme and this number appears as a major part of the cancellations from 1875 to 1886, either on its own or as part of a duplex. Aden Camp, the alternative name for the Cantonment office, became 'B-22/1'.

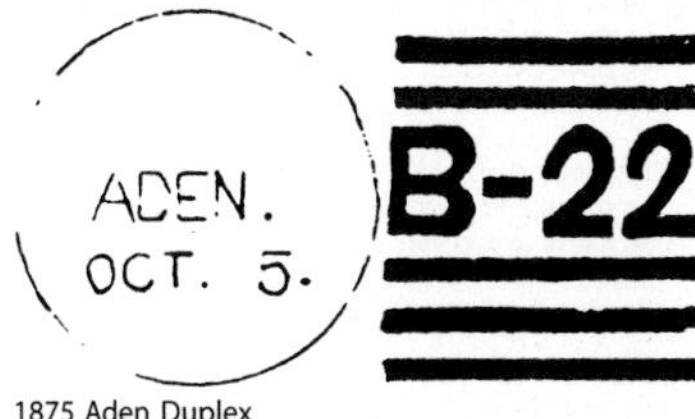

1875 Aden Duplex

Squared-circle types for Aden and Aden Cantonment were introduced in 1884 and 1888 to be in turn replaced by standard Indian double and single circle from 1895 onwards. A rectangular 'Support the Jubilee Fund' slogan handstamp was in use in April and May 1935.

INDIA USED IN ADEN

Aden – Steamer Point/GPO or Aden Camp

1854-55 (Nos. 2/31)

Z1	½a. blue Die I	£100
Z2	½a. blue Die II	£250
Z3	½a. blue Die III	£200
Z4	1a. red Die I	£150
Z5	1a. red Die II	£150
Z6	1a. red Die III	£750
Z7	2a. green	£100
Z8	4a. blue and red (Head Die I)	£2000
Z9	4a. blue and red (Head Die II)	£1500
Z10	4a. blue and red (Head Die III)	£1100

1855 Blue glazed paper (Nos. 35/6)
Z14 4a. black 50·00
Z15 8a. carmine 75·00

1856-64 No wmk (Nos. 37/49)
Z16 ½a. blue 35·00
Z17 1a. brown 20·00
Z18 2a. dull pink 80·00
Z19 2a. yellow-buff 75·00
Z20 2a. yellow 85·00
Z21 2a. orange 85·00
Z22 4a. black 20·00
Z23 4a. green £120
Z24 8a. carmine 75·00

1860 (Nos. 51/3)
Z25 8p. purple/*bluish*
Z26 8p. purple/*white* 50·00

1865 Watermark T **13** (Nos. 51/65)
Z27 ½a. blue 30·00
Z28 8p. purple 50·00
Z29 1a. brown 10·00
Z30 2a. orange 15·00
Z31 4a. green 85·00
Z32 8a. carmine (Die I) £200

1866 Opt on 6a. fiscal (Nos. 66/8)
Z34 6a. purple (T **15**) £550
Z35 6a. purple (T **16**) £850

1866-78 (Nos. 69/76)
Z36 ½a. blue Die II 6·00
Z37 4a. green Die I 18·00
Z38 4a. green Die II 15·00
Z39 6a.8p. slate 90·00
Z40 8a. rose Die II 20·00

1874-76 Additional values (Nos. 77/82)
Z41 9p. mauve 60·00
Z42 6a. pale brown 15·00
Z43 12a. Venetian red 90·00
Z44 1r. slate £100

1882-90 (Nos. 84/101)
Z45 ½a. blue-green 2·00
Z46 9p. rose 15·00
Z47 1a. brown-purple 2·00
Z48 1a.6p. sepia 8·00
Z49 2a. blue 3·00
Z50 3a. orange 18·00
Z51 3a. brown-orange 5·00
Z52 4a. olive-green 6·00
Z53 4a.6p. yellow-green 12·00
Z54 8a. magenta 10·00
Z55 12a. purple/*red* 25·00
Z56 1r. slate 18·00

1891 Surcharge (No. 102)
ZX58 2½a. on 4a.6p. yellow-green 10·00

1892-97 (Nos. 103/109)
Z59 2a.6p. yellow-green 4·00
Z60 1r. green and carmine 15·00
Z61 2r. carmine and yellow-brown 50·00
Z62 3r. brown and green 55·00
Z63 5r. ultramarine and violet 85·00

1898 Surcharge (No. 110)
Z64 ¼. on ½a. blue-green 12·00

1899-1902 Changed colours (Nos. 111/118)
Z65 3p. aniline carmine 3·00
Z66 3p. grey £250*
Z67 ½a. yellow-green 4·00
Z68 1a. carmine 3·00
Z69 2a. pale violet 10·00
Z70 2a.6p. ultramarine 12·00

*The 3p. grey was never placed on sale in Aden, but was of course valid for postage there. Most purported examples with Aden cancels are forgeries.

1902 King Edward VII (Nos. 119/141)
Z71 3p. grey 3·00
Z72 ½a. green 1·50
Z73 1a. carmine 1·50
Z74 2a. mauve 2·50
Z75 2a.6p. ultramarine 2·00
Z76 3a. orange-brown 3·00
Z77 4a. olive 4·00
Z78 6a. maize 7·00
Z79 8a. purple 6·00
Z80 12a. purple/*red* 15·00
Z81 1r. green and carmine 9·00
Z82 2r. carmine and yellow-brown 35·00
Z83 3r. brown and green 65·00
Z84 5r. ultramarine and violet £110

1905 (No. 148)
Z88 ¼ on ½a. green 9·00

1906 Inscr 'POSTAGE AND REVENUE' (Nos. 149/150)
Z89 ½a. green 1·50
Z90 1a. carmine 1·50

1911-22 King George V Wmk Single Star (Nos. 151/191)
Z91 3p. grey 3·00
Z92 ½a. green 1·25
Z93 1a. carmine 1·25
Z94 1½a. chocolate (Type A) 7·00
Z95 1½a. chocolate (Type B) 18·00
Z96 2a. purple 2·00
Z97 2a.6p. ultramarine (No. 170) 14·00
Z98 2a.6p. ultramarine (No. 171) 1·50
Z99 3a. orange 1·75
Z100 4a. olive-green 2·25
Z101 6a. brown-ochre 3·50
Z102 8a. deep mauve 3·50
Z103 12a. carmine-lake 6·00
Z104 1r. brown and green 7·00
Z105 2r. carmine and brown 12·00
Z106 5r. ultramarine and violet 25·00

1921-22 Surcharges (Nos. 192/196)
Z110 ¼ on ½a. green 10·00
Z111 9p. on 1a. carmine 12·00

1922-26 Wmk Single Star (Nos. 197/200)
Z112 1a. chocolate 2·00
Z113 1½a. rose-carmine 5·00
Z114 2a.6p. orange 8·00
Z115 3a. ultramarine 4·00

1926-33 Wmk Multiple Star (Nos. 201/219)
Z116 3p. slate 1·50
Z117 ½a. green 1·25
Z118 1a. chocolate 1·00
Z119 1½a. rose-carmine 4·00
Z120 2a. bright purple (No. 205) 40·00
Z121 2a. purple (No. 206) 1·25
Z122 2a.6p. orange 2·00
Z123 3a. ultramarine 2·50
Z124 4a. sage-green (No. 210) 2·50
Z125 4a. sage-green (No. 211) 2·00
Z126 8a. reddish purple 3·00
Z127 12a. claret 3·50
Z128 1r. chocolate and green 3·00
Z129 2r. carmine and orange 4·00
Z130 5r. ultramarine and purple 25·00
Z131 10r. green and scarlet 40·00
Z132 15r. blue and olive

1931 Inauguration of New Delhi (Nos. 226/231)
Z140 ¼a. olive-green and orange-brown 15·00
Z141 ½a. violet and green 1·75
Z142 1a. mauve and chocolate 1·75
Z143 2a. green and blue 3·00
Z144 3a. chocolate and carmine 6·00
Z145 1r. violet and green 75·00

1932-36 (Nos. 232/239)
Z146 ½a. green 2·00
Z147 9p. deep green 3·00
Z148 1a. chocolate 1·50
Z149 1a.3p. mauve 3·50
Z150 2a. vermilion (No. 236) 15·00
Z151 +2a. vermilion (No. 236*b*) 3·00
Z152 2a. vermilion (No. 236*c*) 5·00
Z153 3a. carmine 3·00
Z154 3a.6p. ultramarine 5·00

1935 Silver Jubilee (Nos. 240/246)
Z156 ½a. black and yellow-green 3·00
Z157 9p. black and grey-green 3·50
Z158 1a. black and brown 2·50
Z159 1¼a. black and bright violet 3·00
Z160 2½a. black and orange 7·00
Z161 3½a. black and dull ultramarine 22·00
Z162 8a. black and purple 12·00

OFFICIAL STAMPS

1866 No Watermark (Nos. O1/O5)
Z201 ½a. blue
Z202 1a. brown
Z203 8a. carmine £225

1866-72 Wmk T **13** (Nos. O6/O14)
Z204 ½a. blue £180
Z205 8p. purple
Z206 1a. brown £180
Z207 2a. yellow £375
Z208 4a. green (T **11**) £450
Z209 4a. green (T **17**)

1867-73 (Nos. O20/O30a)
Z211 ½a. blue (Die I) 30·00
Z212 ½a. blue (Die II)
Z213 1a. brown 30·00
Z214 2a. yellow 30·00
Z215 4a. green 25·00
Z216 8a. rose 35·00

1874-82 (Nos. O31/O35)
Z217 ½a. blue 15·00
Z218 1a. brown 15·00
Z219 2a. orange 30·00
Z220 4a. green 25·00
Z221 8a. rose 40·00

1883-99 (Nos. O37*a*/O48)
Z224 3p. aniline carmine 15·00
Z225 ½a. deep blue-green 10·00
Z226 1a. brown-purple 10·00
Z227 2a. blue 15·00
Z228 4a. olive-green 20·00
Z229 8a. magenta 28·00
Z230 1r. green and carmine 50·00

1900 (Nos. O49/O52)
Z231 ½a. yellow-green 15·00
Z232 1a. carmine 12·00
Z233 2a. mauve 20·00

1902-09 King Edward VII (Nos. O54/O65)
Z234 3p. grey 15·00
Z235 ½a. green 8·00
Z236 1a. carmine 7·00
Z237 2a. mauve 12·00
Z238 4a. olive 15·00
Z239 6a. olive-bistre 20·00
Z240 8a. claret 18·00
Z241 1r. green and carmine 35·00

1906 New Types (Nos. O66/O67)
Z242 ½a. green 8·00
Z243 1a. carmine 8·00

1909 (Nos. O68/O69)
Z244 2r. carmine and yellow-brown 45·00
Z245 5r. ultramarine and violet 55·00

1912-13 King George V (wmk Single Star) (Nos. O73/O92)
Z249 3p. grey 6·00
Z250 ½a. light green 3·00
Z251 1a. carmine 3·00
Z252 2a. purple 5·00
Z253 4a. olive-green 10·00
Z254 6a. yellow-bistre 15·00
Z255 8a. deep mauve 15·00
Z256 1r. brown and green 18·00
Z257 2r. rose-carmine and brown 30·00

1922 (No. O98)
Z263 1a. chocolate 5·00

1926-31 (Wmk Multiple Star) (Nos. O109/O117)
Z272 3p. slate 5·00
Z273 ½a. green 4·00
Z274 1a. chocolate 4·00
Z275 2a. purple 5·00
Z276 4a. sage-green 7·00
Z277 8a. reddish purple 10·00
Z278 12a. claret 20·00
Z279 1r. chocolate and green 20·00

ADEN SUB-OFFICES

The following Indian stamps have been reported used in the Aden sub-post offices. We would welcome details of potential additions to these lists, so that comprehensive, priced listings may be included in future editions of this catalogue.

DTHALI (opened 1903, initially using 'EXPERIMENTAL P.O. B-84' postmark; closed 1907)
1899–1902 Queen Victoria (Nos. 111/118) 3p., (No. 111) ½a, 1a.
1902 King Edward VII (Nos. 119/147) ½a., 1a.
Official stamps Queen Victoria (Nos. O49/O52) ½a.

KAMARAN (opened *c.* 1915, but no civilian postmarks known before 1925)
1911–22 King George V (Nos. 151/191) 1a., 3a., 4a.
1922–26 King George V (Nos. 197/200) 1a., 3a.
1926–33 King George V (Nos. 201/219) 3p.
1931 New Delhi (Nos. 226/231) ¼a.
1932–36 King George V (Nos. 232/239) ½a.
1935 Silver Jubilee (Nos. 240/246) ½a., 1a., 1¼a.
Official stamps 1912–13 King George V (Nos. O73/O96) 1a., 4a., 1r.
1922 King George V (No. O98) 1a.

KHORMAKSAR (opened 1892; closed 1915; reopened 1925)
1911–22 King George V (Nos. 151/191) 1a.
1931 New Delhi (Nos. 226/231) ¼a., ½a., 1a., 2a., 3a., 1r
Official Stamps 1912–13 King George V (Nos. O73/O96) 1a.
1922 King George V (No. O98) 1a.

MAALA (opened 1923; closed 1931)
Official stamps 1922 King George V (No. O98) 1a.

NOBAT DAKIM (opened 1904, initially using 'EXPERIMENTAL P.O. B-84' postmark; closed 1905)
1900 Queen Victoria (Nos. 111/118) 1a.

PERIM (opened 1915; closed 1936)
1905 King Edward VII (Nos. 149/150) 1a.
1912–22 King George V (Nos. 151/191) ½a., 1a., 3a., 8a.
1926–33 King George V (Nos. 201/219) 3p., ½a., 1a., 2a. (No. 20b), 2a.6p.
1935 Silver Jubilee (Nos. 240/246) ½a., 8a.
Official stamps 1912–13 King George V (Nos. O73/O96) ½a.

SHEIKH OTHMAN (opened 1891; closed 1915; reopened 1922; closed 1937)
1911–22 King George V (Nos. 151/191) ½a., 1a., 1½a. (No. 163) 2a.
1926–33 King George V (Nos. 201/219) 1a., 1½a.
1932–36 King George V (Nos. 232/239) 1a.
1931 New Delhi (Nos. 226/231) ½a.
Official stamps 1883–99 Queen Victoria (Nos. O37a/O48) 3p (No. O37a).

PRICES FOR STAMPS ON COVER TO 1945	
Nos. 1/15	*from* × 6
Nos. 16/27	*from* × 3

(Currency. 12 pies = 1 anna; 16 annas = 1 rupee)

1 Dhow

(Recess D.L.R.)

1937 (1 Apr). Wmk Mult Script CA sideways. P 13×12.

1	**1**	½a. yellow-green	4·50	3·00
2		9p. deep green	5·00	3·75
3		1a. sepia	3·75	2·00
4		2a. scarlet	6·00	3·25
5		2½a. bright blue	8·50	2·50
6		3a. carmine	11·00	8·50
7		3½a. grey-blue	9·50	6·00
8		8a. pale purple	27·00	13·00
9		1r. brown	60·00	13·00
10		2r. yellow	£120	42·00
11		5r. deep purple	£300	£140
		a. Bright aniline purple	£450	£180
12		10r. olive-green	£750	£650
1/12 *Set of* 12			£1200	£800
1s/12s Perf 'SPECIMEN' *Set of* 12			£800	

1937 (12 May). Coronation. As Nos. 95/97 of Antigua, but ptd by D.L.R. P 14.

13	1a. sepia	65	1·40
14	2½a. light blue	75	1·40
	w. Wmk inverted	£2000	£3250
15	3½a. grey-blue	1·00	3·25
13/15 *Set of* 3		2·25	5·50
13s/15s Perf 'SPECIMEN' *Set of* 3		£160	

3 Aidrus Mosque, Crater

4 Adenese Camel Corps

5 The Harbour

6 Adenese Dhow

7 Mukalla

8 *Capture of Aden, 1839* (Captain Rundle)

(Recess Waterlow)

1939 (19 Jan)–**48**. Wmk Mult Script CA. P 12½.

16	**3**	½a. yellowish green	2·25	60
		a. Bluish green (13.9.48)	5·50	4·00
17	**4**	¾a. red-brown	3·00	1·25
18	**5**	1a. pale blue	1·75	40
19	**6**	1½a. scarlet	3·00	60
20	**3**	2a. sepia	2·00	25
21	**7**	2½a. deep ultramarine	2·00	30
22	**8**	3a. sepia and carmine	2·00	25
23	**7**	8a. red-orange	2·50	40
23*a*	**8**	14a. sepia and light blue (15.1.45)	4·75	1·00
24	**6**	1r. emerald-green	5·50	2·75
25	**5**	2r. deep blue and magenta	13·00	3·25
26	**4**	5r. red-brown and olive-green	40·00	17·00
27	**8**	10r. sepia and violet	50·00	18·00
16/27 *Set of* 13			£120	40·00
16s/27s Perf 'SPECIMEN' *Set of* 13			£375	

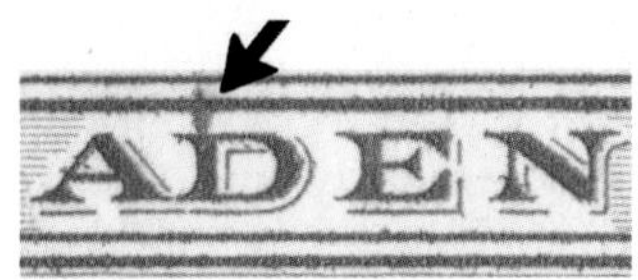

1½a. Accent over 'D' (R. 7/1)

1946 (15 Oct). Victory. As Nos. 110/111 of Antigua.

28	1½a. carmine	40	1·75
	a. Accent over 'D'	60·00	75·00
29	2½a. blue	1·00	1·00
	w. Wmk inverted	£2000	
28s/29s Perf 'SPECIMEN' *Set of* 2		£140	

Examples of the 'Accent over 'D" are known officially corrected by scratching out the mark with a sharp point.

1949 (17 Jan). Royal Silver Wedding. As Nos. 112/113 of Antigua.

30	1½a. scarlet (P 14×15)	75	2·25
31	10r. mauve (P 11½×11)	40·00	55·00

1949 (10 Oct). 75th Anniversary of UPU. As Nos. 114/117 of Antigua, surch with new values by Waterlow.

32	2½a. on 20c. ultramarine	60	1·50
33	3a. on 30c. carmine-red	2·00	1·50
34	8a. on 50c. orange	2·00	2·00
	a. 'C' of 'CA' omitted from watermark	£1600	
35	1r. on 1s. blue	1·60	6·00
32/35 *Set of* 4		5·50	10·00

(New Currency. 100 cents = 1 shilling)

5
CENTS
(**12**)

1951 (1 Oct). Nos. 18 and 20/27 surch with new values, in cents or shillings, as T **12**, or in one line between bars (30c.) by Waterlow.

36	5c. on 1a. pale blue	35	40
37	10c. on 2a. sepia	25	45
38	15c. on 2½a. deep ultramarine	55	1·25
	a. Surch double	£1600	
39	20c. on 3a. sepia and carmine	50	40
40	30c. on 8a. red-orange (R.)	1·00	65
41	50c. on 8a. red-orange	1·75	35
	a. Surch double, one albino	£3500	
42	70c. on 14a. sepia and light blue	2·50	1·50
43	1s. on 1r. emerald-green	3·25	30
44	2s. on 2r. deep blue and magenta	16·00	3·75
	a. Surch albino	£1500	
45	5s. on 5r. red-brown and olive-green	30·00	17·00
46	10s. on 10r. sepia and violet	42·00	17·00
36/46 *Set of* 11		85·00	38·00

1953 (2 June). Coronation. As No. 120 of Antigua.

47	15c. black and green	1·75	1·50

14 Minaret

15 Camel transport

16 Crater

17 Mosque

18 Dhow

19 Map

20 Salt works

21 Dhow building

21a Colony's badge

22 Aden Protectorate levy

23 Crater Pass

24 Tribesman

25 *Aden in 1572* (F. Hogenberg)

25c. Crack in wall (R. 1/5)

(Recess Waterlow, D.L.R. from 5 Dec 1961)

1953 (15 June)–**63**. T **14/25**. Wmk Mult Script CA. P 13½×13 (No. 72), 12×13½ (Nos. 57, 64, 66, 68) or 12 (others).

48	**14**	5c. yellowish green	20	10
49		5c. bluish green (1.6.55)	3·00	3·50
		a. Perf 12×13½ (12.4.56)	35	1·25
50	**15**	10c. orange	40	10
51		10c. vermilion (1.2.55)	1·75	30
52	**16**	15c. blue-green	1·50	60
53		15c. greenish grey (26.4.59)	10·00	6·50
		a. Deep greenish grey (16.1.62)	23·00	24·00
		b. Greenish slate (13.11.62)	30·00	20·00
54	**17**	25c. carmine-red	1·00	55
		a. Crack in wall	65·00	35·00
55		25c. deep rose-red (15.3.56)	7·50	2·00
		a. Rose-red (13.3.62)	24·00	8·50
56	**18**	35c. deep ultramarine	2·50	1·00
57		35c. deep blue (15.10.58)	8·00	6·00
		a. Violet-blue (17.2.59)	15·00	4·50
58	**19**	50c. dull blue	50	10
59		50c. deep blue (1.7.55)	4·50	2·50
		a. Perf 12×13½ (12.4.56)	1·25	20
		aw. Wmk inverted	†	£900
60	**20**	70c. brown-grey	70	10
61		70c. black (20.9.54)	2·00	1·50
		a. Perf 12×13½ (12.4.56)	2·00	20
62	**21**	1s. sepia and reddish violet	70	10
63		1s. black and violet (1.7.55)	2·00	10
64	**21a**	1s.25 blue and black (16.7.56)	16·00	60
		a. Dull blue and black (16.1.62)	24·00	1·25
65	**22**	2s. sepia and rose-carmine	1·75	50
66		2s. black and carmine-red (1.3.56)	16·00	50
		aw. Wmk inverted	†	£1500
		b. Black and carmine-rose (22.1.63)	48·00	18·00
67	**23**	5s. sepia and dull blue	3·25	1·00
68		5s. black and deep dull blue (11.4.56)	17·00	1·50
		a. Black and blue (11.12.62)	45·00	18·00
69	**24**	10s. sepia and olive	3·50	8·00
70		10s. black and bronze-green (20.9.54)	17·00	1·75
71	**25**	20s. chocolate and reddish lilac	8·50	10·00
72		20s. black and deep lilac (7.1.57)	65·00	22·00
		a. Deep black and deep lilac (14.5.58)	85·00	27·00
48/72 *Set of* 25			£160	55·00

On No. 70 the tribesman's skirt is shaded with cross-hatching instead of with mainly diagonal lines as in No. 69.

1954 (27 Apr). Royal Visit. As No. 62 but inscr 'ROYAL VISIT 1954' at top.

73	1s. sepia and reddish violet	1·00	1·00

تعديل
الدستور
١٩٥٩
(**26**)

REVISED
CONSTITUTION
1959
(**27**)

1959 (26 Jan). Revised Constitution. No. 53 optd with T **26**, and No. 64 optd with T **27**, in red, by Waterlow.

74	15c. slate-green	60	2·50
75	1s.25 blue and black	1·00	1·50

1963 (4 June). Freedom from Hunger. As No. 146 of Antigua.

76	1s.25 bluish green (Protein foods)	1·25	2·25

1964 (5 Feb)–**65**. As Nos. 48, etc. but wmk w **12**. P 12 (10c., 15c., 25c., 1s.) or 12×13½ (others).

77	**14**	5c. green (16.2.65)	4·75	12·00
78	**15**	10c. bright orange	2·50	1·25
79	**16**	15c. greenish grey	1·00	6·50
		w. Wmk inverted	£130	
80	**17**	25c. carmine-red	3·50	50
81	**18**	35c. indigo-violet	8·00	6·00
82	**19**	50c. indigo-blue	1·75	1·75
		aw. Wmk inverted	†	£1200
		b. Pale indigo-blue (16.2.65)	2·75	2·75
83	**20**	70c. black	3·50	5·50
		a. Brownish grey (16.2.65)	6·50	13·00
84	**21**	1s. black and violet (10.3.64)	12·00	3·50
85	**21a**	1s.25 ultramarine and black (10.3.64)	18·00	2·25
86	**22**	2s. black and carmine-rose (16.2.65)	7·50	38·00
77/86 *Set of* 10			55·00	65·00

The Stamps of Aden were withdrawn on 31 March 1965 and superseded by those of the South Arabian Federation.

ADEN PROTECTORATE STATES

KATHIRI STATE OF SEIYUN

The stamps of ADEN were used in Kathiri State of Seiyun from 22 May 1937 until 1942. A further office was opened at Tarim on 11 December 1940.

PRICES FOR STAMPS ON COVER TO 1945
Nos. 1/11 *from* × 10

1 Sultan of Seiyun

2 Seiyun

3 Tarim

4 Mosque, Seiyun

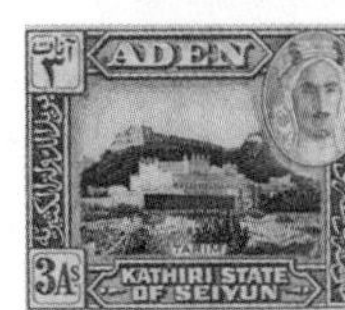

5 Fortress, Tarim

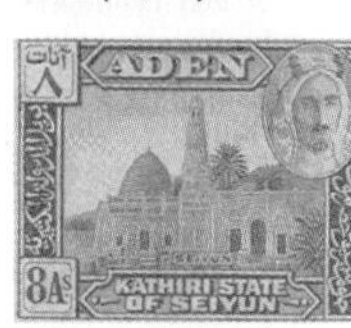

6 Mosque, Seiyun

7 South Gate, Tarim

8 Kathiri House

9 Mosque Entrance, Tarim

VICTORY
ISSUE
8TH JUNE 1946
(**10**)

(Recess D.L.R.)

1942 (July–Oct). T **1/9** Wmk Mult Script CA. T **1**, P 14; others P 12×13 (vert) or 13×12 (horiz).

1	**1**	½a. blue-green	20	2·00
2		¾a. brown	60	4·50
3		1a. blue	70	2·25
4	**2**	1½a. carmine	70	2·75
5	**3**	2a. sepia	50	2·75
6	**4**	2½a. blue	1·25	2·75
7	**5**	3a. sepia and carmine	1·75	4·50
8	**6**	8a. red	3·25	1·50
9	**7**	1r. green	7·50	5·00
10	**8**	2r. blue and purple	16·00	27·00
11	**9**	5r. brown and green	38·00	35·00
1/11 *Set of* 11			60·00	80·00
1s/11s Perf 'SPECIMEN' *Set of* 11			£325	

1946 (15 Oct). Victory. No. 4 optd with T **10**, and No. 6 optd similarly but in four lines, by De La Rue.

12		1½a. carmine	20	65
13		2½a. blue (R.)	20	35
		a. Opt inverted	£1300	
		b. Opt double	£1800	
12s/13s Perf 'SPECIMEN' *Set of* 2			£120	

A flaw occurred on the plate to the right of the top of the fort on R. 10/6 (not known on No. 4), all examples of which were officially scratched out with a sharp point.

1949 (17 Jan). Royal Silver Wedding. As Nos. 112/113 of Antigua.

14		1½a. scarlet	30	4·50
15		5r. green	18·00	17·00

1949 (10 Oct). 75th Anniversary of UPU. As Nos. 114/117 of Antigua, surch with new values by Waterlow.

16		2½a. on 20c. ultramarine	15	2·00
17		3a. on 30c. carmine-red	1·25	3·50
18		8a. on 50c. orange	25	6·50
19		1r. on 1s. blue	30	2·50
16/19 *Set of* 4			1·75	13·00

5 CTS (**11**) **50 CENTS** (**12**) **5/-** (**13**)

1951 (1 Oct). Currency changed. Nos. 3 and 5/11 surch as T **11** (5c.), **12** (10c. ('CTS'), 15c. ('CTS'), 20c. and 50c.) or **13** (1s. to 5s.), by Waterlow.

20		5c. on 1a. blue (R.)	15	2·75
21		10c. on 2a. sepia	30	2·25
22		15c. on 2½a. blue	20	3·00
23		20c. on 3a. sepia and carmine	25	3·00
24		50c. on 8a. red	1·25	2·25
25		1s. on 1r. green	3·25	4·75
26		2s. on 2r. blue and purple	14·00	42·00
27		5s. on 5r. brown and green	38·00	65·00
20/27 *Set of* 8			50·00	£110

1953 (2 June). Coronation. As No. 120 of Antigua.

28		15c. black and deep green (Queen Elizabeth II)	60	2·00

14 Sultan Hussein

15 Tarim

(Des Freya Stark and H. Ingram. Recess D.L.R.)

1954 (15 Jan). As Nos. 1/11 (but with portrait of Sultan Hussein as in T **14/15**). Wmk Mult Script CA. T **14**, P 12½; others P 12×13 (vert) or 13×12 (horiz).

29	**14**	5c. sepia	10	25
30		10c. deep blue	15	25
31	**2**	15c. deep bluish green	20	25
32	**15**	25c. carmine-red	20	25
33	**4**	35c. deep blue	20	25
34	**5**	50c. deep brown and carmine-red	20	20
35	**6**	1s. brown-orange	20	20
36	**7**	2s. deep yellow-green	5·00	3·50
37	**8**	5s. deep blue and violet	11·00	15·00
38	**9**	10s. yellow-brown and violet	13·00	15·00
29/38 *Set of* 10			27·00	32·00

16 Qarn Adh Dhabi

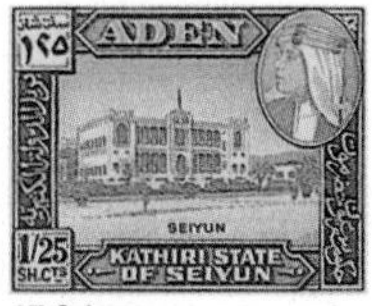
17 Seiyun

18 Gheil Omer

(Recess D.L.R.)

1964 (1 July). T **16/18**. W w **12**. P 12×13 (70c.) or 13×12 (others).

39	**16**	70c. black	4·25	2·50
40	**17**	1s.25 blue-green	4·50	11·00
41	**18**	1s.50 deep reddish violet	4·50	11·00
39/41 *Set of* 3			12·00	22·00

Stamps after this date can be found listed under South Arabia.

QU'AITI STATE IN HADHRAMAUT

The stamps of ADEN were used in Qu'aiti State in Hadhramaut from 22 April 1937 until 1942. The main post office was at Mukalla. Other offices existed at Du'an (*opened* 1940), Gheil Ba Wazir (*opened* 1942), Haura (*opened* 1940), Shibam (*opened* 1940) and Shihr (*opened* 1939).

PRICES FOR STAMPS ON COVER TO 1945
Nos. 1/11 *from* × 15

I. ISSUES INSCR 'SHIHR AND MUKALLA'.

1 Sultan of Shihr and Mukalla

2 Mukalla Harbour

3 Gateway of Shifir

4 Shibam

5 Outpost of Mukalla

6 'Einat

7 Du'an

8 Mosque in Hureidha

9 Meshhed

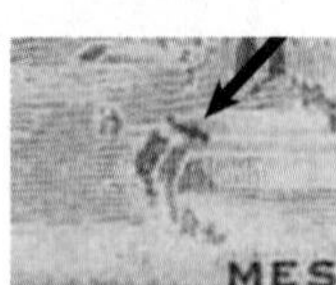
5r. Extra wall in earthworks (R.10/2)

(Recess D.L.R.)

1942 (July)–**46**. T **1/9**. Wmk Mult Script CA. P 14 (½ to 1a.), 12×13 (1½, 2, 3a. and 1r.) or 13×12 (others).

1	**1**	½a. blue-green	1·75	50
		a. Olive-green (12.46)	30·00	42·00
2		¾a. brown	2·50	30
3		1a. blue	1·00	1·00
4	**2**	1½a. carmine	2·00	50
5	**3**	2a. sepia	2·00	1·75
6	**4**	2½a. blue	50	30
7	**5**	3a. sepia and carmine	1·50	1·00
8	**6**	8a. red	1·25	40
9	**7**	1r. green	7·50	4·75
		a. 'A' of 'CA' missing from wmk	£1300	£1200
10	**8**	2r. blue and purple	20·00	18·00
11	**9**	5r. brown and green	40·00	24·00
		a. 'Extra wall'	£325	
1/11 *Set of* 11			70·00	45·00
1s/11s Perf 'SPECIMEN' *Set of* 11			£325	

VICTORY
ISSUE
8TH JUNE
1946
(**10**)

1946 (15 Oct). Victory. No. 4 optd. with T **10** and No. 6 optd similarly, but in three lines, by De La Rue.

12		1½a. carmine	15	1·25
13		2½a. blue (R.)	15	50
12s/13s Perf 'SPECIMEN' *Set of* 2			£120	

1949 (17 Jan). Royal Silver Wedding. As Nos. 112/113 of Antigua.

14		1½a. scarlet	50	4·50
15		5r. green	17·00	18·00

1949 (10 Oct). 75th Anniversary of UPU. As Nos. 114/117 of Antigua, surch with new values by Waterlow.

16		2½a. on 20c. ultramarine	15	1·00
17		3a. on 30c. carmine-red	1·40	4·00
18		8a. on 50c. orange	25	4·00
19		1r. on 1s. blue	30	50
		a. Surch omitted	£4000	
16/19 *Set of* 4			1·90	8·50

1951 (1 Oct). Currency changed. Surch with new values in cents or shillings as T **11** (5c.), **12** (10c. ('CTS'), 15c., 20c. and 50c.) or **13** (1s. to 5s.) of Seiyun, by Waterlow.

20		5c. on 1a. blue (R.)	15	30
21		10c. on 2a. sepia	15	30
22		15c. on 2½a. blue	15	30
23		20c. on 3a. sepia and carmine	30	1·00
		a. Surch double, one albino	£600	
24		50c. on 8a. red	50	3·00
25		1s. on 1r. green	2·25	55
26		2s. on 2r. blue and purple	8·50	32·00
27		5s. on 5r. brown and green	24·00	45·00
20/27 *Set of* 8			32·00	75·00

1953 (2 June). Coronation. As No. 120 of Antigua.

28		15c. black and deep blue (Queen Elizabeth II)	1·00	65

II. ISSUES INSCR 'HADHRAMAUT'

11 Metal Work

12 Mat-making

13 Weaving

14 Pottery

15 Building

16 Date cultivation

17 Agriculture

18 Fisheries

19 Lime burning

20 Dhow building

21 Agriculture

22 Lime burning

(Des Mme M. de Sturler Raemaekers. Recess D.L.R.)

1955 (1 Sept)–**63**. T **11/22**. Wmk Mult Script CA. P 11½×13-13½ (vert) or 14 (horiz).

29	5c. greenish blue	1·00	10
30	10c. grey-black	1·25	10
31	15c. deep green	1·00	10
	a. Bronze-green (9.3.63)	1·50	40
32	25c. carmine-red	50	10
33	35c. blue	1·00	10
34	50c. orange-red	1·50	10
	a. Red-orange (9.3.63)	1·25	30
35	90c. sepia	70	15
36	1s. black and deep lilac	1·00	10
37	1s.25 black and red-orange	75	55
38	2s. black and indigo	4·00	60
39	5s. black and bluish green	5·00	3·00
40	10s. black and lake	19·00	8·00
29/40 *Set of* 12		32·00	11·50

22a Metal Work

1963 (20 Oct). As Nos. 29/40 but with inset portrait of Sultan Awadh bin Saleh el-Qu'aiti as in T **22a** and wmk w **12**.

41	5c. greenish blue	10	1·75
42	10c. grey-black	10	1·50
43	15c. bronze-green	10	1·75
44	25c. carmine-red	15	75
45	35c. blue	15	2·00
46	50c. red-orange	15	1·00
47	70c. deep brown (as 90c.)	20	75
48	1s. black and deep lilac	25	30
49	1s.25 black and red-orange	60	6·50
50	2s. black and indigo-blue	3·25	3·75
51	5s. black and bluish green	17·00	32·00
52	10s. black and lake	32·00	32·00
41/52 *Set of* 12		48·00	75·00

Stamps after this date can be found listed under South Arabia.

Aitutaki see Cook Islands

Anguilla

Following the grant of Associated Statehood to St Christopher, Nevis and Anguilla, on 27 February 1967, the Island Council of Anguilla declared the island independent and the St Kitts-Nevis authorities left the island on 30 May 1967. Mail communications, which had all been via St Kitts, were severed for four weeks and when they were resumed, via St Thomas in the US Virgin Islands, prepayment was denoted by a rectangular handstamp in violet with the postage rate incorporated within it. Nos. 1/16 were subsequently issued by the Island Council and were accepted for international mail. On 7 July 1969 the Anguilla post office was officially recognised by the Government of St Christopher, Nevis and Anguilla and normal postal communications via St Christopher were resumed. By the Anguilla Act of 21 July 1971, Anguilla was restored to direct British control.

A degree of internal self-government with an Executive Council was introduced on 10 February 1976 and the links with St Kitts-Nevis were officially severed on 18 December 1980.

(Currency. 100 cents = 1 Eastern Caribbean dollar)

Independent Anguilla

(**1**)

2 Mahogany Tree, The Quarter

1967 (4 Sept). Nos. 129/144 of St Kitts-Nevis optd as T **1**, by Island Press Inc, St. Thomas, US Virgin Islands.

1	½c. New lighthouse, Sombrero	70·00	26·00
2	1c. Loading sugar cane, St. Kitts	80·00	11·00
3	2c. Pall Mall Square, Basseterre	75·00	3·00
4	3c. Gateway, Brimstone Hill Fort, St. Kitts	80·00	8·50
	w. Wmk inverted	—	50·00
5	4c. Nelson's Spring, Nevis	80·00	6·50
6	5c. Grammar School, St. Kitts	£400	50·00
7	6c. Crater, Mt. Misery, St. Kitts	£130	20·00
8	10c. Hibiscus	75·00	11·00
9	15c. Sea Island cotton, Nevis	£150	17·00
10	20c. Boat building, Anguilla	£400	26·00
11	25c. White-crowned Pigeon	£425	50·00
	w. Wmk inverted	£275	80·00
12	50c. St. George's Church Tower, Basseterre	£6000	£900
13	60c. Alexander Hamilton	£9000	£2250
14	$1 Map of St. Kitts-Nevis	£4250	£750
15	$2.50 Map of Anguilla	£3250	£475
16	$5 Arms of St. Christopher, Nevis and Anguilla	£3500	£500
1/16 *Set of* 16		£25000	£4250

Owing to the limited stocks available for overprinting, the sale of the above stamps was personally controlled by the Postmaster and no orders from the trade were accepted.

(Des John Lister Ltd. Litho A. & M.)

1967 (27 Nov)–**68**. T **2** and similar horiz designs. P 12½×13.

17	1c. dull green, bistre-brown and pale orange	10	1·00
18	2c. bluish green and black (21.3.68)	10	3·00
19	3c. black and light emerald (10.2.68)	10	10
20	4c. cobalt-blue and black (10.2.68)	10	10
21	5c. multicoloured	10	10
22	6c. light vermilion and black (21.3.68)	10	10
23	10c. multicoloured	15	10
24	15c. multicoloured (10.2.68)	3·50	20
25	20c. multicoloured	1·25	2·75
26	25c. multicoloured	60	20
27	40c. apple green, light greenish blue and black	1·00	25
28	60c. multicoloured (10.2.68)	5·00	6·50
29	$1 multicoloured (10.2.68)	1·75	3·25
30	$2.50 multicoloured (21.3.68)	2·00	7·50
31	$5 multicoloured (10.2.68)	3·00	4·25
17/31 *Set of* 15		16·00	25·00

Designs:—1c. T **2**; 2c. Sombrero Lighthouse; 3c. St Mary's Church; 4c. Valley Police Station; 5c. Old Plantation House, Mt. Fortune; 6c. Valley Post Office; 10c. Methodist Church, West End; 15c. Wall-Blake Airport; 20c. Beech A90 King Air aircraft over Sandy Ground; 25c. Island Harbour; 40c. Map of Anguilla; 60c. Hermit Crab and Starfish; $1 Hibiscus; $2.50, Local scene; $5, Spiny Lobster.

17 Yachts in Lagoon

18 Purple-throated Carib

(Des John Lister Ltd. Litho A. & M.)

1968 (11 May). Anguillan Ships. T **17** and similar horiz designs. Multicoloured. P 14.

32	10c. Type **17**	35	10
33	15c. Boat on beach	40	10
34	25c. *Warspite* (schooner)	55	15
35	40c. *Atlantic Star* (schooner)	65	20
32/35 *Set of* 4		1·75	50

(Des John Lister Ltd. Litho A. & M.)

1968 (8 July). Anguillan Birds. T **18** and similar multicoloured designs. P 14.

36	10c. Type **18**	65	20
37	15c. Bananaquit	80	25
38	25c. Black-necked Stilt (*horiz*)	85	25
39	40c. Royal Tern (*horiz*)	90	40
36/39 *Set of* 4		3·00	1·00

19 Guides' Badge and Anniversary Years

(Des John Lister Ltd. Litho A. & M.)

1968 (14 Oct). 35th Anniversary of Anguillan Girl Guides. T **19** and similar multicoloured designs. P 13×13½ (10, 25c.) or 13½×13 (others).

40	10c. Type **19**	10	25
41	15c. Badge and silhouettes of Guides (*vert*)	15	25
42	25c. Guides' badge and Headquarters	20	35
43	40c. Association and Proficiency badges (*vert*)	25	50
40/43 *Set of* 4		65	1·25

20 The Three Kings

(Des John Lister Ltd. Litho A. & M.)

1968 (18 Nov). Christmas. T **20** and similar designs. P 13.

44	1c. black and cerise	10	10
45	10c. black and light greenish blue	10	10
46	15c. black and chestnut	15	10
47	40c. black and blue	15	10
48	50c. black and dull green	20	15
44/48 *Set of* 5		60	50

Designs: Vert—10c. The Wise Men; 15c. Holy Family and manger. Horiz—1c. T **20**; 40c. The Shepherds; 50c. Holy Family and donkey.

21 Bagging Salt

INDEPENDENCE JANUARY, 1969

(**21a**)

(Des John Lister Ltd. Litho A. & M.)

1969 (4 Jan). Anguillan Salt Industry. T **21** and similar horiz designs. Multicoloured. P 13.

49	10c. Type **21**	25	35
50	15c. Packing salt	30	40
51	40c. Salt pond	35	45
52	50c. Loading salt	35	75
49/52 *Set of* 4		1·10	1·75

1969 (17 Jan*). Expiration of Interim Agreement on Status of Anguilla. Nos. 17/24 and 26/27 optd with T **21a**.

52*a*	1c. dull green, bistre-brown and pale orange	10	40
52*b*	2c. bluish green and black	10	40
52*c*	3c. black and light emerald	10	40
52*d*	4c. cobalt-blue and black	10	40
52*e*	5c. multicoloured	10	20
52*f*	6c. light vermilion and black	10	20
52*g*	10c. multicoloured	10	30
52*h*	15c. multicoloured	90	30
52*i*	25c. multicoloured	80	30
52*j*	40c. apple green, light greenish blue and black	1·75	40
52*a/j* *Set of* 10		3·50	3·00

*Earliest known postmark date. The remaining values of the 1967–68 series, Nos. 17/31, also come with this overprint. The complete set exists on large first day covers postmarked 9 January 1969. The values listed above have been reported used on commercial mail from Anguilla.

22 *The Crucifixion* (Studio of Massys)

(Des John Lister Ltd. Litho Format)

1969 (31 Mar). Easter Commemoration. T **22** and similar vert design. P 13½.

53	25c. multicoloured	25	15
54	40c. multicoloured	35	15

Design:—25c. T **22**; 40c. *The Last Supper* (ascribed to Roberti).

23 Amaryllis

(Des John Lister Ltd. Litho Format)

1969 (10 June). Flowers of the Caribbean. T **23** and similar horiz designs. Multicoloured. P 14.

55	10c. Type **23**	15	20
56	15c. Bougainvillea	15	25
57	40c. Hibiscus	20	50
58	50c. Cattleya Orchid	70	1·60
55/58 *Set of 4*		1·10	2·25

24 Superb Gaza, Channelled Turban, Chestnut Turban and Carved Star Shell

(Des John Lister Ltd. Litho A. & M.)

1969 (22 Sept). Sea Shells. T **24** and similar horiz designs. Multicoloured. P 14.

59	10c. Type **24**	30	25
60	15c. American Thorny Oyster	30	25
61	40c. Scotch, Royal and Smooth Scotch Bonnets	45	30
62	50c. Atlantic Trumpet Triton	50	30
59/62 *Set of 4*		1·40	1·00

(25)

(26)

(27)

(28)

(29)

1969 (1 Oct). Christmas. Nos. 17, 25/28 optd with T **25/29**.

63	1c. dull green, bistre-brown and light orange	10	10
64	20c. multicoloured	20	10
65	25c. multicoloured	20	10
66	40c. apple-green, light greenish blue and black	25	15
67	60c. multicoloured	40	20
63/67 *Set of 5*		1·00	55

30 Spotted Goatfish

31 *Morning Glory*

(Des John Lister Ltd. Litho A. & M.)

1969 (1 Dec). Fish. T **30** and similar horiz designs. Multicoloured. P 14.

68	10c. Type **30**	45	15
69	15c. Blue-striped Grunt	60	15
70	40c. Nassau Grouper	75	20
71	50c. Banded Butterflyfish	80	20
68/71 *Set of 4*		2·40	65

(Des John Lister Ltd. Litho A. & M.)

1970 (23 Feb). Flowers. T **31** and similar vert designs. Multicoloured. P 14.

72	10c. Type **31**	20	10
73	15c. Blue Petrea	20	10
74	40c. Hibiscus	35	20
75	50c. Flame Tree	35	25
72/75 *Set of 4*		1·00	55

32 *The Crucifixion* (Masaccio)

33 Scout Badge and Map

(Des John Lister Ltd. Litho Format)

1970 (26 Mar). Easter. T **32** and similar multicoloured designs. P 13½.

76	10c. *The Ascent to Calvary* (Tiepolo) (*horiz*)	15	10
77	20c. Type **32**	20	10
78	40c. *Deposition* (Rosso Fiorentino)	25	15
79	60c. *The Ascent to Calvary* (Murillo) (*horiz*)	25	15
76/79 *Set of 4*		75	45

(Des John Lister Ltd. Litho A. & M.)

1970 (10 Aug). 40th Anniversary of Scouting in Anguilla. T **33** and similar horiz designs. Multicoloured. P 13.

80	10c. Type **33**	15	30
81	15c. Scout camp and cubs practising first-aid	20	30
82	40c. Monkey Bridge	25	40
83	50c. Scout HQ Building and Lord Baden-Powell	35	55
80/83 *Set of 4*		85	1·40

34 Boatbuilding

(Des John Lister Ltd. Litho Format)

1970 (23 Nov). Various horiz designs as T **34**. Multicoloured. P 14.

84	1c. Type **34**	30	40
85	2c. Road Construction	30	40
86	3c. Quay, Blowing Point	30	20
87	4c. Broadcaster, Radio Anguilla	30	50
88	5c. Cottage Hospital Extension	40	50
89	6c. Valley Secondary School	30	50
90	10c. Hotel Extension	30	30
91	15c. Sandy Ground	30	30
92	20c. Supermarket and Cinema	70	30
93	25c. Bananas and Mangoes	35	1·00
94	40c. Wall Blake Airport	4·00	3·25
95	60c. Sandy Ground Jetty	65	3·50
96	$1 Administration Buildings	1·25	1·40
97	$2.50 Livestock	1·50	4·00
98	$5 Sandy Hill Bay	3·25	3·75
84/98 *Set of 15*		13·00	18·00

35 *The Adoration of the Shepherds* (Reni)

(Des John Lister Ltd. Litho Questa)

1970 (11 Dec). Christmas. T **35** and similar vert designs. Multicoloured. P 13½.

99	1c. Type **35**	10	20
100	20c. *The Virgin and Child* (Gozzoli)	30	25
101	25c. *Mystic Nativity* (detail, Botticelli)	30	30
102	40c. *The Santa Margherita Madonna* (detail, Mazzola)	40	30
103	50c. *The Adoration of the Magi* (detail, Tiepolo)	40	30
99/103 *Set of 5*		1·25	1·25

Antigua

It is believed that the first postmaster for Antigua was appointed under Edward Dummer's scheme in 1706. After the failure of his service, control of the overseas mails passed to the British GPO Mail services before 1850 were somewhat haphazard, until St. John's was made a branch office of the British GPO in 1850. A second office, at English Harbour, opened in 1857.

The stamps of Great Britain were used between May 1858 and the end of April 1860, when the island postal service became the responsibility of the local colonial authorities. In the interim period, between the take-over and the appearance of Antiguan stamps, the crowned-circle handstamps were again utilised and No. CC1 can be found used as late as 1869.

For illustrations of the handstamp and postmark types see BRITISH POST OFFICES ABROAD notes, following GREAT BRITAIN.

CC 1

CC 3

ST JOHN'S

CROWNED-CIRCLE HANDSTAMPS

CC1 CC **1** ANTIGUA (St John's) (9.3.1850) (R.) *Price on cover* £650

Stamps of GREAT BRITAIN cancelled 'A02' as Type **2**.

1858–60.

Z1	1d. rose-red (1857), P 14	£750
Z2	2d. blue (1855), P 14 (Plate No. 6)	£1800
Z3	2d. blue (1858) (Plate Nos. 7, 8, 9)	£1000
Z4	4d. rose (1857)	£600
Z5	6d. lilac (1856)	£180
Z6	1s. green (1856)	£3250

ENGLISH HARBOUR

CROWNED-CIRCLE HANDSTAMPS

CC2 CC **3** 'ENGLISH HARBOR' (10.12.1857) *Price on cover* £9000

Stamps of GREAT BRITAIN cancelled 'A18' as Type **2**.

1858–60.

Z6a	1d. rose red (1857)	£3250
Z7	2d. blue (1858) (Plate No. 7)	£6000
Z8	4d. rose (1857)	£6000
Z9	6d. lilac	£2000
Z10	1s. green (1856)	

PRICES FOR STAMPS ON COVER TO 1945

No. 1	*from* × 10
Nos. 2/4	†
Nos. 5/10	*from* × 20
Nos. 13/14	*from* × 30
No. 15	*from* × 60
Nos. 16/18	*from* × 50
Nos. 19/23	*from* × 12
No. 24	*from* × 50
Nos. 25/30	*from* × 10
Nos. 31/51	*from* × 4
Nos. 52/54	*from* × 10
Nos. 55/61	*from* × 4
Nos. 62/80	*from* × 3
Nos. 81/90	*from* × 4
Nos. 91/94	*from* × 5
Nos. 95/97	*from* × 4
Nos. 98/109	*from* × 3

CROWN COLONY

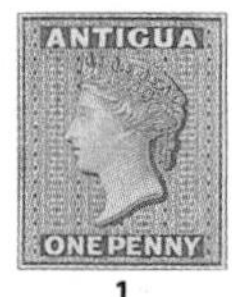

1

3

(Eng C. Jeens after drawing by Edward Corbould. Recess P.B.)

1862 (Aug). No wmk.

(a) Rough perf 14 to 16

1	**1**	6d. blue-green	£800	£550

(b) P 11 to 12½

2	**1**	6d. blue-green	£7500	

(c) P 14 to 16×11 to 12½

3	**1**	6d. blue-green	£3250	

(d) P 14 to 16 compound with 11 to 12½

4	**1**	6d. blue-green	£3250	

Nos. 2/4 may be trial perforations. They are not known used.

1863 (Jan)–**67**. Wmk Small Star. W w **2** (sideways on 6d.). Rough perf 14 to 16.

5	**1**	1d. rosy mauve	£130	80·00
6		1d. dull rose (1864)	£120	55·00
		a. Imperf between (vert pair)	£32000	

7 1d. vermilion (1867) £250 30·00
a. Imperf between (horiz pair) £32000
b. Wmk sideways £250 42·00
8 6d. green (*shades*) £700 26·00
a. Wmk upright — £200
9 6d. dark green £750 26·00
10 6d. yellow-green £4250 £100

Caution is needed in buying No. 10 as some of the shades of No. 8 verge on yellow-green.

The 1d. rosy mauve exists showing trial perforations of 11 to 12½ and 14 to 16 (*Price, £8500 unused*).

(Recess D.L.R. from P.B. plates)

1872. Wmk Crown CC. P 12½.
13 **1** 1d. lake £200 17·00
w. Wmk inverted £275 80·00
x. Wmk reversed £180 17·00
y. Wmk inverted and reversed
14 1d. scarlet £200 24·00
w. Wmk inverted £200 65·00
x. Wmk reversed — 32·00
15 6d. blue-green £550 11·00
w. Wmk inverted — £120
x. Wmk reversed £500 14·00
y. Wmk inverted and reversed — £140

1876. Wmk Crown CC. P 14.
16 **1** 1d. lake £225 11·00
a. Bisected (½d.) (1883) (*on cover*) † £8000
x. Wmk reversed — 38·00
17 1d. lake-rose £225 11·00
w. Wmk inverted £400 £100
x. Wmk reversed — 35·00
y. Wmk inverted and reversed
18 6d. blue-green £425 21·00
w. Wmk inverted † £140
x. Wmk reversed £350 22·00
y. Wmk inverted and reversed £500 85·00

(Recess (T **1**); typo (T **3**) De La Rue & Co).

1879. Wmk Crown CC. P 14.
19 **3** 2½d. red-brown £600 £170
a. Large '2' in '2½' with slanting foot £11000 £2750
20 4d. blue £250 13·00

Top left triangle detached
(Pl 2 R. 3/3 of right pane)

1882. Wmk Crown CA. P 14.
21 **3** ½d. dull green 5·00 20·00
a. Top left triangle detached £350 £550
22 2½d. red-brown £190 55·00
a. Top left triangle detached
b. Large '2' in '2½' with slanting foot £3500 £1300
23 4d. blue £275 13·00
a. Top left triangle detached — £750

1884. Wmk Crown CA. P 12.
24 **1** 1d. carmine-red 60·00 20·00
w. Wmk inverted
y. Wmk inverted and reversed

The 1d. scarlet is a colour changeling.

1884–87. Wmk Crown CA. P 14.
25 **1** 1d. carmine-red 2·25 3·75
w. Wmk inverted — £110
x. Wmk reversed 75·00 35·00
y. Wmk inverted and reversed
26 1d. rose 60·00 12·00
27 **3** 2½d. ultramarine (1887) 7·00 14·00
a. Large '2' in '2½' with slanting foot £160 £250
b. Top left triangle detached £400 £475
28 4d. chestnut (1887) 2·25 3·00
a. Top left triangle detached £350 £375
29 **1** 6d. deep green 60·00 £120
30 **3** 1s. mauve (1886) £160 £140
a. Top left triangle detached £2000 £2000
25/30 *Set of 5* £200 £250
27s, 28s, 30s Optd 'SPECIMEN' *Set of 3* £150

Nos. 25 and 26 postmarked 'A12' in place of 'A02' were used in St Christopher between January and March 1890.

2½ 2½ 2½
A B C

The variety 'Large '2' in '2½' with slanting foot' occurs on R. 7/1 of the duty plate on all printings. At this position the 'NN' of 'PENNY' also sustained damage in about 1886, leaving three vertical strokes shortened. A and B (above) represent two states of the flaw at R. 7/1. Head plate 2, first used for Antigua in 1886, was a double-pane plate of 120, but the same 60-set duty plate remained in use, the variety thus occurring on R. 7/1 of each pane. A very similar flaw (C above) appeared at R. 3/1 of the duty plate (on which the 'NN' was undamaged) early in the life of No. 27 and thus occurs on both panes of that stamp.

From 31 October 1890 until July 1903 Leeward Islands general issues were used. Subsequently both general issues and the following separate issues were in concurrent use until July 1956, when the general Leeward Islands stamps were withdrawn.

4

5

(Typo D.L.R.)

1903 (July)–**07**. Wmk Crown CC. Ordinary paper. P 14.
31 **4** ½d. grey-black and grey-green 3·75 6·50
32 1d. grey-black and rose-red 15·00 1·25
w. Wmk inverted † £400
33 2d. dull purple and brown 7·50 25·00
34 2½d. grey-black and blue 19·00 24·00
a. Chalk-surfaced paper (1907) 50·00 70·00
35 3d. grey-green and orange-brown 11·00 20·00
36 6d. purple and drab 32·00 55·00
w. Wmk inverted £190 £250
37 1s. blue and dull purple 55·00 65·00
a. Chalk-surfaced paper (1907) 75·00 £140
38 2s. grey-green and pale violet 90·00 £130
39 2s.6d. grey-black and purple 27·00 75·00
40 **5** 5s. grey-green and violet £110 £180
a. Chalk-surfaced paper (1907) £190 £250
31/40 *Set of 10* £325 £500
31s/40s Optd 'SPECIMEN' *Set of 10* £200

1908–17. Wmk Mult Crown CA. Chalk-surfaced paper (2d., 3d. to 2s.). P 14.
41 **4** ½d. green 4·75 4·75
w. Wmk inverted † £425
42 ½d. blue-green (1917) 8·00 7·50
43 1d. red (1909) 12·00 2·25
44 1d. scarlet (5.8.15) 9·50 3·25
w. Wmk inverted £425
45 2d. dull purple and brown (1912) 4·75 32·00
46 2½d. ultramarine 23·00 18·00
a. Blue 38·00 25·00
47 3d. grey-green and orange-brown (1912) 6·50 19·00
48 6d. purple and drab (1911) 7·50 40·00
49 1s. blue and dull purple 27·00 70·00
50 2s. grey-green and violet (1912) £110 £130
41/50 *Set of 8* £170 £275
41s, 43s, 46s Optd 'SPECIMEN' *Set of 3* 90·00

1913. As T **5**, but portrait of George V. Wmk Mult Crown CA. Chalk-surfaced paper. P 14.
51 5s. grey-green and violet 95·00 £150
s. Optd 'SPECIMEN' 90·00

WAR STAMP
(7)

8

1916 (Sept)–**17**. No. 41 optd with T **7** by D.L.R.
52 **4** ½d. green (Bk.) 4·75 3·75
53 ½d. green (R.) (1.10.17) 1·50 3·50
w. Wmk inverted † —

1918 (July). Optd with T **7**. Wmk Mult Crown CA. P 14.
54 **4** 1½d. orange 2·00 2·00
52s/4s Optd 'SPECIMEN' *Set of 3* £120

(Typo D.L.R.)

1921 (1 July)–**29**. P 14.

(a) Wmk Mult Crown CA. Chalk-surfaced paper
55 **8** 3d. purple/*pale yellow* 4·75 15·00
56 4d. grey-black and red/*pale yellow* (1922) 2·25 5·50
57 1s. black/*emerald* 4·25 9·00
y. Wmk inverted and reversed £400
58 2s. purple and blue/*blue* 13·00 38·00
59 2s.6d. black and red/*blue* 19·00 65·00
60 5s. green and red/*pale yellow* (1922) 8·50 50·00
61 £1 purple and black/*red* (1922) £275 £400
55/61 *Set of 7* £300 £500
55s/61s Optd 'SPECIMEN' *Set of 7* £200

(b) Wmk Mult Script CA. Chalk-surfaced paper (3d. to 4s.)
62 **8** ½d. dull green 3·00 50
63 1d. carmine-red 4·25 50
64 1d. bright violet (1923) 8·50 1·50
a. Mauve (1926?) 20·00 7·00
65 1d. bright scarlet (1929) 42·00 4·25
67 1½d. dull orange (1922) 6·00 5·00
68 1½d. carmine-red (1926) 9·00 1·75
69 1½d. pale red-brown (1929) 3·00 60
70 2d. grey 4·50 75
a. Wmk sideways † £3500
71 2½d. bright blue 9·50 17·00
72 2½d. orange-yellow (1923) 2·50 17·00
73 2½d. ultramarine (1927) 18·00 3·25
74 3d. purple/*pale yellow* (1925) 15·00 6·50
75 6d. dull and bright purple 8·50 4·25
76 1s. black/*emerald* (1929) 6·00 3·25
77 2s. purple and blue/*blue* (1927) 11·00 65·00
78 2s.6d. black and red/*blue* (1927) 50·00 50·00
79 3s. green and violet (1922) 50·00 £100
80 4s. grey-black and red (1922) 50·00 75·00
62/80 *Set of 18* £200 £300
62s/80s Optd or Perf (Nos. 65, 69, 76) 'SPECIMEN' *Set of 18* £450

9 Old Dockyard, English Harbour

10 Government House, St John's

11 Nelson's *Victory*

12 Sir Thomas Warner's *Concepcion*

(Des Mrs. W. M. N. Goodwin (5s.), Waterlow (others). Recess Waterlow)

1932 (27 Jan). Tercentenary. Wmk Mult Script CA. P 12½.
81 **9** ½d. green 4·50 7·50
82 1d. scarlet 6·00 9·00
83 1½d. brown 4·75 4·75
84 **10** 2d. grey 8·50 27·00
85 2½d. deep blue 8·50 8·50
86 3d. orange 8·50 12·00
87 **11** 6d. violet 15·00 12·00
88 1s. olive-green 20·00 32·00
89 2s.6d. claret 55·00 80·00
90 **12** 5s. black and chocolate £120 £160
81/90 *Set of 10* £225 £325
81s/90s Perf 'SPECIMEN' *Set of 10* £250

Examples of all values are known showing a forged St. John's postmark dated 'MY 18 1932'.

13 Windsor Castle

(Des H. Fleury. Recess D.L.R.)

1935 (6 May). Silver Jubilee. Wmk Mult Script CA. P 13½×14.
91 **13** 1d. deep blue and carmine 3·00 4·25
f. Diagonal line by turret £100 £140
92 1½d. ultramarine and grey 2·75 1·75
93 2½d. brown and deep blue 7·00 1·75
g. Dot to left of chapel £225 £250
94 1s. slate and purple 8·50 18·00
a. Frame printed double, one albino £2000
h. Dot by flagstaff £375 £550
91/94 *Set of 4* 19·00 23·00
91s/4s Perf 'SPECIMEN' *Set of 4* £110

For illustrations of plate varieties see Ominbus section following Zanzibar.

14 King George VI and Queen Elizabeth

(Des D.L.R. Recess B.W.)

1937 (12 May). Coronation. Wmk Mult Script CA. P 11×11½.
95 **14** 1d. carmine **1·00** 3·50
96 1½d. yellow-brown **1·00** 3·00
97 2½d. blue **2·25** 3·50
95/7 *Set of 3* **3·75** 9·00
95s/97s Perf 'SPECIMEN' *Set of 3* £100

15 English Harbour

16 Nelson's Dockyard

16a Fort James

16b St John's Harbour

(Des A. W. Morley. Recess Waterlow)

1938 (15 Nov)–**51**. Wmk Mult Script CA. P 12½.
98 **15** ½d. green 40 1·25
99 **16** 1d. scarlet 3·50 2·50
a. Red (8.42) 5·50 3·00

100		1½d. chocolate-brown	10·00	2·50
		a. Dull reddish brown (12.43)	3·00	4·25
		b. Lake-brown (7.49)	32·00	14·00
101	15	2d. grey	1·50	1·50
		a. Slate-grey (6.51)	9·50	10·00
102	16	2½d. deep ultramarine	1·75	80
103	16a	3d. orange	1·50	1·00
104	16b	6d. violet	5·50	1·25
105		1s. black and brown	8·00	2·25
		a. Black and red-brown (7.49)	32·00	11·00
		ab. Frame ptd double, one albino	£6000	
		b. 'A' of 'CA' missing from wmk	£1100	
106	16a	2s.6d. brown-purple	55·00	22·00
		a. Maroon (8.42)	38·00	22·00
107	16b	5s. olive-green	18·00	15·00
108	16	10s. magenta (1.4.48)	22·00	38·00
109	16a	£1 slate-green (1.4.48)	45·00	70·00
98/109 *Set of* 12			£130	£140
98s/109s Perf 'SPECIMEN' *Set of* 12			£300	

17 Houses of Parliament, London

(Des and recess D.L.R.)

1946 (1 Nov). Victory. Wmk Mult Script CA. P 13½×14.

110	17	1½d. brown	30	10
111		3d. red-orange	30	50
110s/11s Perf 'SPECIMEN' *Set of* 2			90·00	

18 King George VI and Queen Elizabeth    **19**

(Des and photo Waterlow (T **18**). Design recess; name typo B.W. (T **19**))

1949 (3 Jan). Royal Silver Wedding. Wmk Mult Script CA.

112	18	2½d. ultramarine (P 14×15)	1·00	2·75
113	19	5s. grey-olive (P 11½×11)	15·00	16·00

20 Hermes, Globe and Forms of Transport    **21** Hemispheres, Jet-powered Vickers Viking Airliner and Steamer

22 Hermes and Globe   **23** UPU Monument

(Recess Waterlow (T **20, 23**). Designs recess, name typo B.W. (T **21/2**))

1949 (10 Oct). 75th Anniversary of Universal Postal Union. Wmk Mult Script CA.

114	20	2½d. ultramarine (P 13½–14)	55	1·50
115	21	3d. orange (P 11×11½)	2·25	4·25
116	22	6d. purple (P 11×11½)	55	4·00
117	23	1s. red-brown (P 13½–14)	55	1·50
114/17 *Set of* 4			3·50	10·00

(New Currency. 100 cents = 1 West Indian, later Eastern Caribbean, dollar)

24 Arms of University   **25** Princess Alice

(Recess Waterlow)

1951 (16 Feb). Inauguration of BWI University College. Wmk Mult Script CA. P 14×14½.

118	24	3c. black and brown	1·00	2·25
119	25	12c. black and violet	1·00	2·25

26 Queen Elizabeth II   **27** Martello Tower

(Des and eng B.W. Recess D.L.R.)

1953. (2 June). Coronation. Wmk Mult Script CA. P 13½×13.

120	26	2c. black and deep yellow-green	30	75

(Recess Waterlow until 1961, then D.L.R.)

1953 (2 Nov)–**62**. Designs previously used for King George VI issue, but with portrait of Queen Elizabeth II as in T **27**. Wmk Mult Script CA. P 13×13½ (horiz) or 13½×13 (vert).

120*a*	16a	½c. brown (3.7.56)	40	40
121	15	1c. slate-grey	30	2·50
		a. Slate (7.11.61)	4·00	6·00
122	16	2c. green	30	10
123		3c. black and orange-yellow	40	20
		a. Black and yellow-orange (5.12.61)	3·50	3·75
124	15	4c. scarlet	1·25	10
		a. Brown-red (11.12.62)	1·25	50
125	16	5c. black and slate-lilac	2·50	40
126	16a	6c. yellow-ochre	3·00	10
		a. Dull yellow-ochre (5.12.61)	13·00	3·50
127	27	8c. deep blue	2·50	10
128	16b	12c. violet	2·50	10
129		24c. black and chocolate	6·00	15
130	27	48c. purple and deep blue	14·00	4·25
131	16a	60c. maroon	13·00	2·50
132	16b	$1.20 olive-green	4·75	70
		a. Yellowish olive (10.8.55)	4·25	1·00
133	16	$2.40 bright reddish purple	20·00	12·00
134	16a	$4.80 slate-blue	28·00	38·00
120*a*/134 *Set of* 15			85·00	55·00

See also Nos. 149/158.

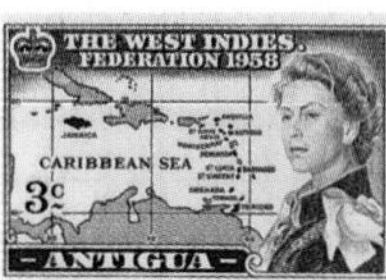

28 Federation Map

COMMEMORATION ANTIGUA CONSTITUTION 1960

(29)

(Recess B.W.)

1958 (22 Apr). Inauguration of British Caribbean Federation. W w **12**. P 11½×11.

135	28	3c. deep green	1·60	40
136		6c. blue	1·60	3·25
137		12c. scarlet	1·75	75
135/137 *Set of* 3			4·50	4·00

MINISTERIAL GOVERNMENT

1960 (1 Jan). New Constitution. Nos. 123 and 128 optd with T **29**.

138		3c. black and orange-yellow (R)	20	45
139		12c. violet	20	30

30 Nelson's Dockyard and Admiral Nelson    **31** Stamp of 1862 and RMSP *Solent I* at English Harbour

(Recess B.W.)

1961 (14 Nov). Restoration of Nelson's Dockyard. W w **12**. P 11½×11.

140	30	20c. purple and brown	2·00	1·60
141		30c. green and blue	2·00	3·75

(Des A. W. Morley. Recess B.W.)

1962 (1 Aug). Stamp Centenary. W w **12**. P 13½.

142	31	3c. purple and deep green	90	10
143		10c. blue and deep green	1·00	10
144		12c. deep sepia and deep green	1·10	10
145		50c. orange-brown and deep green	1·50	3·25
142/145 *Set of* 4			4·00	3·25

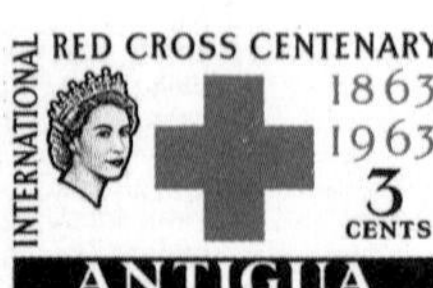

32 Protein Foods   **33** Red Cross Emblem

(Des M. Goaman. Photo Harrison)

1963 (4 June). Freedom from Hunger. W w **12**. P 14×14½.

146	32	12c. bluish green	20	15

(Des V. Whiteley. Litho B.W.)

1963 (2 Sept). Red Cross Centenary. W w **12**. P 13½.

147	33	3c. red and black	30	1·00
148		12c. red and blue	45	1·25

(Recess D.L.R.)

1963 (16 Sept)–**65**. As 1953–1961 but wmk w **12**.

149	16a	½c. brown (13.4.65)	2·75	2·00
150	15	1c. slate (13.4.65)	1·50	1·00
151	16	2c. green	70	30
152		3c. black and yellow-orange	45	20
153	15	4c. brown-red	30	3·75
154	16	5c. black and slate-lilac	20	20
		a. Black and reddish violet (15.1.65)	20	20
155	16a	6c. yellow-ochre	75	30
156	27	8c. deep blue	40	20
157	16b	12c. violet	3·25	20
158		24c. black and deep chocolate	9·00	1·00
		a. Black and chocolate-brown (28.4.65)	13·00	3·75
149/158 *Set of* 10			17·00	8·00

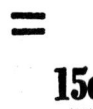

34 Shakespeare and Memorial Theatre, Stratford-upon-Avon

15c.

(35)

(Des R. Granger Barrett. Photo Harrison)

1964 (23 Apr). 400th Birth Anniversary of William Shakespeare. W w **12**. P 14×14½.

164	34	12c. orange-brown	30	10
		w. Wmk inverted	80·00	

1965 (1 Apr). No. 157 surch with T **35**.

165		15c. on 12c. violet	40	10

36 ITU Emblem

(Des M. Goaman. Litho Enschedé)

1965. I.T.U. Centenary. W w **12**. P 11×11½.

166	36	2c. light blue and light red	25	15
167		50c. orange-yellow and ultramarine	75	1·25

37 ICY Emblem

(Des V. Whiteley. Litho Harrison)

1965 (25 Oct). International Co-operation Year. W w **12**. P 14½.

168	37	4c. reddish purple and turquoise-green	25	60
169		15c. deep bluish green and lavender	40	40

38 Sir Winston Churchill, and St Paul's Cathedral in Wartime

(Des Jennifer Toombs. Photo Harrison)

1966 (24 Jan). Churchill Commemoration. Printed in black, cerise and gold and with background in colours stated. W w **12**. P 14.

170	38	½c. new blue	10	2·50
		a. Value omitted	£850	
171		4c. deep green	65	10
172		25c. brown	1·50	45
173		35c. bluish violet	1·50	55
170/3 *Set of* 4			3·25	3·25

No. 170a was caused by misplacement of the gold and also shows 'ANTIGUA' moved to the right.

39 Queen Elizabeth II and Duke of Edinburgh

(Des H. Baxter. Litho B.W.)

1966 (4 Feb). Royal Visit. W w **12**. P 11×12.

174	39	6c. black and ultramarine	1·50	1·40
175		15c. black and magenta	1·50	1·40

40 Footballer's Legs, Ball and Jules Rimet Cup

(Des V. Whiteley. Litho Harrison)

1966 (1 July). World Cup Football Championship. W w **12** (sideways). P 14.

176	**40**	6c. violet, yellow-green, lake and yellow-brown	20	75
177		35c. chocolate, blue-green, lake and yellow-brown	60	25

41 WHO Building

(Des M. Goaman. Litho Harrison)

1966 (20 Sept). Inauguration of WHO Headquarters, Geneva. W w **12** (sideways). P 14.

178	**41**	2c. black, yellow-green and light blue	20	25
179		15c. black, light purple and yellow-brown	1·25	25

42 Nelson's Dockyard

43 Old Post Office, St John's

44 Health Centre

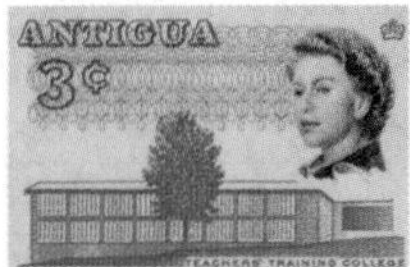

45 Teachers' Training College

46 Martello Tower, Barbuda

47 Ruins of Officers' Quarters, Shirley Heights

48 Government House, Barbuda

49 Princess Margaret School

50 Air Terminal Building

51 General Post Office

52 Clarence House

53 Government House, St John's

53a Administration Building

53b Courthouse, St John's

53c Magistrates' Court

53d St John's Cathedral

(Des, eng and recess B.W.)

1966 (1 Nov)–**70**. W w **12**. Ordinary paper. P 11½×11.

180	**42**	½c. green and turquoise-blue	10	1·50
		a. Perf 13½ (24.6.69)	10	2·50
181	**43**	1c. purple and cerise	10	30
		a. Perf 13½ (24.6.69)	10	1·50
		ab. Glazed paper (30.9.69)	75	20
182	**44**	2c. slate-blue and yellow-orange	10	20
		a. Perf 13½ (24.6.69)	10	75
		ab. Glazed paper (30.9.69)	1·25	10
183	**45**	3c. rose-red and black	30	30
		a. Perf 13½ (24.6.69)	15	15
184	**46**	4c. slate-violet and brown	2·50	10
		a. Perf 13½ (24.6.69)	15	30
		ab. Glazed paper (6.4.70)	16·00	1·75
185	**47**	5c. ultramarine and yellow-olive	1·75	10
		a. Perf 13½ (24.6.69)	15	10
		ab. Glazed paper (30.9.69)	40	10
186	**48**	6c. salmon and purple	2·50	30
		a. Perf 13½ (24.6.69)	15	1·00
187	**49**	10c. emerald and rose-red	15	10
		a. Perf 13½ (24.6.69)	15	15
		ab. Glazed paper (30.9.69)	4·00	10
188	**50**	15c. brown and new blue	2·75	10
		a. Perf 13½ (*glazed paper*) (30.9.69)	70	10
189	**51**	25c. slate-blue and sepia	35	20
		a. Perf 13½ (*glazed paper*) (30.9.69)	45	10
190	**52**	35c. cerise and blackish brown	1·50	55
		a. Perf 13½ (*glazed paper*) (30.9.69)	60	1·00
191	**53**	50c. dull green and black	6·00	2·50
		a. Perf 13½ (*glazed paper*) (30.9.69)	1·00	2·25
192	**53a**	75c. greenish blue and ultramarine	8·00	5·00
193	**53b**	$1 cerise and yellow-olive	15·00	2·50
		aa. Carmine and yellow-olive (14.5.68)	55·00	17·00
		a. Perf 13½ (*glazed paper*) (30.9.69)	1·25	5·00
194	**53c**	$2.50 black and cerise	15·00	10·00
		a. Perf 13½ (*glazed paper*) (30.9.69)	1·50	8·00
195	**53d**	$5 olive-green and slate-violet	16·00	6·50
		a. Perf 13½ (*glazed paper*) (30.9.69)	14·00	24·00
180/195 *Set of* 16			55·00	25·00
180a/195a *Set of* 15			18·00	40·00

54 'Education'

55 'Science'

56 'Culture'

(Des Jennifer Toombs. Litho Harrison)

1966 (1 Dec). 20th Anniversary of UNESCO W w **12** (sideways). P 14.

196	**54**	4c. slate-violet, red, yellow and orange	20	10
197	**55**	25c. orange-yellow, violet and deep olive	45	10
198	**56**	$1 black, bright purple and orange	90	2·25
196/198 *Set of* 3			1·40	2·25

ASSOCIATED STATEHOOD

57 State Flag and Maps

(Des W. D. Cribbs. Photo Harrison)

1967 (27 Feb). Statehood. T **57** and similar horiz designs. Multicoloured. W w **12** (sideways*). P 14.

199	4c. Type **57**	10	10
200	15c. State Flag	10	20
	w. Wmk Crown to right of CA	1·25	
201	25c. Premier's Office and State Flag	10	25
202	35c. As 15c.	15	25
199/202 *Set of* 4		40	70

*The normal sideways watermark shows Crown to left of CA, as seen from the back of the stamp.

60 Gilbert Memorial Church

4c. Line projecting from near corner of building stretching two thirds way up roof (R. 1/2)

(Des G. Drummond (from sketches by W. D. Cribbs). Photo Harrison)

1967 (18 May). Attainment of Autonomy by the Methodist Church. T **60** and similar horiz designs. W w **12**. P 14½×13½.

203	4c. black and orange-red	10	10
	a. Roof flaw	8·00	
204	25c. black and bright green	15	15
205	35c. black and bright blue	15	15
203/205 *Set of* 3		35	35

Designs:—4c. T **60**; 25c. Nathaniel Gilbert's House; 35c. Caribbean and Central American map.

63 Coat of Arms

64 *Susan Constant* (settlers' ship)

65 Van Risen's map of 1665

(Des V. Whiteley (from sketches by W. D. Cribbs). Photo Harrison)

1967 (21 July). 300th Anniversary of Treaty of Breda and Grant of New Arms. W w **12** (sideways*). P 14½×14.

206	**63**	15c. multicoloured	20	10
		w. Wmk Crown to right of CA	10·00	10·00
207		35c. multicoloured	20	10

*The normal sideways watermark shows Crown to left of CA, *as seen from the back of the stamp.*

(Des (from sketches by W. D. Cribbs) and recess B.W.)

1967 (14 Dec). 300th Anniversary of Barbuda Settlement. T **64/5**. W w **12**. P 11½×11.

208	**64**	4c. deep ultramarine	45	10
209	**65**	6c. purple	45	1·50
210	**64**	25c. emerald	50	20
211	**65**	35c. black	55	25
208/11 *Set of* 4			1·75	1·75

66 Tracking Station

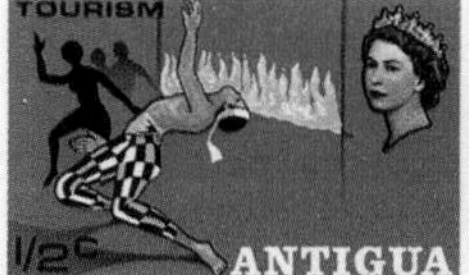

70 Limbo-dancing

(Des G. Vasarhelyi (from sketches by W. D. Cribbs). Photo Harrison)

1968 (29 Mar). NASA Apollo Project. Inauguration of Dow Hill Tracking Station. T **66** and similar vert designs in deep blue, orange yellow and black. W w **12** (sideways). P 14½×14.

212	4c. Type **66**	10	10
213	15c. Antenna and spacecraft taking off	20	10
214	25c. Spacecraft approaching Moon	20	10
215	50c. Re-entry of space capsule	30	40
212/215 *Set of* 4		70	60

(Des (½c. and 50c. from sketches by W. D. Cribbs) and photo Harrison)

1968 (1 July). Tourism. T **70** and similar horiz designs. Multicoloured. W w **12**. P 14½×14.

216		½c. Type **70**	10	50
217		15c. Water-skiing and bathers	30	10
218		25c. Yachts and beach	30	10
219		35c. Underwater swimming	30	10
220		50c. Type **70**	35	1·25
216/220 *Set of 5*			1·25	1·75

74 Old Harbour in 1768

(Des R. Granger Barrett (from sketches by W.D. Cribbs). Recess B.W.)

1968 (31 Oct). Opening of St. John's Deep Water Harbour. T **74** and similar horiz designs. W w **12**. P 13.

221		2c. light blue and carmine	10	40
222		15c. light yellow-green and sepia	35	10
223		25c. olive-yellow and blue	40	10
224		35c. salmon and emerald	50	10
225		$1 black	90	2·25
221/225 *Set of 5*			2·00	2·50

Designs:—2c., $1 T **74**; 15c. Old Harbour in 1829; 25c. Freighter and chart of New Harbour; 35c. New Harbour, 1968.

78 Parliament Buildings

(Des R. Granger Barrett (from sketches by W.D. Cribbs). Photo Harrison)

1969 (3 Feb). Tercentenary of Parliament. T **78** and similar square designs. Multicoloured. W w **12** (sideways). P 12½.

226		4c. Type **78**	10	10
227		15c. Antigua Mace and bearer	20	10
228		25c. House of Representatives' Room	20	10
229		50c. Coat of Arms and Seal of Antigua	30	1·60
226/229 *Set of 4*			70	1·75

82 Freight Transport

(Des Jennifer Toombs. Litho D.L.R.)

1969 (14 Apr). First Anniversary of CARIFTA (Caribbean Free Trade Area). T **82** and similar design. W w **12** (sideways on 4c., 15c). P 13.

230		4c. black and reddish purple	10	10
231		15c. black and turquoise-blue	20	30
232		25c. chocolate, black and yellow-ochre	25	30
233		35c. chocolate, black and yellow-brown	25	30
230/233 *Set of 4*			70	90

Designs: Horiz—4, 15c. Type **82**. Vert—25, 35c. Crate of cargo.

Nos. 234 to 248 are redundant.

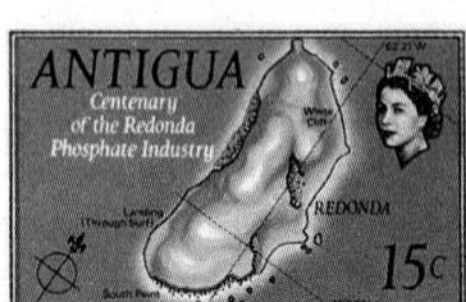

84 Island of Redonda (Chart)

(Des R. Granger Barrett. Photo Enschedé)

1969 (1 Aug). Centenary of Redonda Phosphate Industry. T **84** and similar horiz design. W w **12** (sideways). P 13×13½.

249		15c. Type **84**	20	10
250		25c. Redonda from the sea	20	10
251		50c. Type **84**	45	75
249/251 *Set of 3*			75	85

86 *The Adoration of the Magi* (Marcillat)

(**88**)

(Des adapted by V. Whiteley. Litho Enschedé)

1969 (15 Oct). Christmas. Stained-glass Windows. T **86** and similar vert design. Multicoloured. W w **12** (sideways*). P 13×14.

252		6c. Type **86**	10	10
253		10c. *The Nativity* (unknown German artist, 15th-century)	10	10
254		35c. Type **86**	25	10
255		50c. As 10c.	50	40
		w. Wmk Crown to right of CA	23·00	
252/255 *Set of 4*			85	60

*The normal sideways watermark shows Crown to left of CA, *as seen from the back of the stamp.*

1970 (2 Jan). No. 189 surch with T **88**.

256		20c. on 25c. slate-blue and sepia	20	10

89 Coat of Arms

90 Sikorsky S-38 Flying Boat

(Des and photo Harrison)

1970 (30 Jan)–**73**. Coil Stamps. W w **12**. P 14½×14.

A. Chalk-surfaced paper. Wmk upright (30.1.70)

257A	**89**	5c. blue	10	40
258A		10c. emerald	10	35
259A		25c. crimson	20	35
257A/259A *Set of 3*			35	1·00

B. Glazed paper. Wmk sideways (5.3.73)

257B	**89**	5c. blue	1·25	2·75
258B		10c. emerald	1·25	2·75
259B		25c. crimson	1·75	2·25
257B/9B *Set of 3*			3·75	7·00

These stamps were issued on Multiple Crown CA Diagonal paper in 1975.

(Des R. Granger Barrett. Litho J.W.)

1970 (16 Feb). 40th Anniversary of Antiguan Air Services. T **90** and similar designs. Multicoloured. W w **12** (sideways). P 14½.

260		5c. Type **90**	50	10
261		20c. Dornier Do-X flying boat	80	10
262		35c. Hawker Siddeley H.S. 748	1·00	10
263		50c. Douglas C-124C Globemaster II	1·00	1·75
264		75c. Vickers Super VC-10	1·25	3·00
260/264 *Set of 5*			4·00	4·50

91 Dickens and Scene from *Nicholas Nickleby*

(Des Jennifer Toombs (from sketches by W.D. Cribbs). Litho Walsall)

1970 (19 May). Death Centenary of Charles Dickens. T **91** and similar horiz designs. W w **12** (sideways). P 14.

265		5c. bistre, sepia and black	10	10
266		20c. light turquoise-blue, sepia and black	20	10
267		35c. violet-blue, sepia and black	30	10
268		$1 rosine, sepia and black	75	80
265/268 *Set of 4*			1·25	1·00

Designs:—5c. T **91**; 20c. Dickens and Scene from *Pickwick Papers*; 35c. Dickens and Scene from *Oliver Twist*; $1 Dickens and Scene from *David Copperfield*.

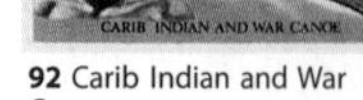
92 Carib Indian and War Canoe

93 *The Small Passion* (detail) (Dürer)

(Des J.W. Litho Questa)

1970 (19 Aug)–**75**. Horiz designs as T **92**. Multicoloured. Toned paper. W w **12** (sideways*). P 14.

269		½c. Type **92**	10	1·50
270		1c. Columbus and *Nina*	30	1·50
271		2c. Sir Thomas Warner's emblem and *Concepcion*	40	3·25
		a. Whiter paper (20.10.75)	1·50	3·25
272		3c. Viscount Hood and HMS *Barfleur*	40	2·00
		w. Wmk Crown to right of CA	4·00	4·00
273		4c. Sir George Rodney and HMS *Formidable*	40	3·00
274		5c. Nelson and HMS *Boreas*	50	40
275		6c. William IV and HMS *Pegasus*	1·75	5·00
276		10c. 'Blackbeard' and pirate ketch	80	20
277		15c. Captain Collingwood and HMS *Pelican*	14·00	1·00
278		20c. Nelson and HMS *Victory*	1·25	40
279		25c. *Solent I* (paddle-steamer)	1·00	40
280		35c. George V (when Prince George) and HMS *Canada* (screw corvette)	3·50	80
281		50c. HMS *Renown* (battle cruiser)	3·00	6·00
282		75c. *Federal Maple* (freighter)	3·00	6·00
283		$1 *Sol Quest* (yacht) and class emblem	3·00	1·50
284		$2.50 HMS *London* (destroyer)	9·50	7·50
285		$5 *Pathfinder* (tug)	2·00	6·00
269/285 *Set of 17*			38·00	40·00

*The normal sideways watermark shows Crown to left of CA *as seen from the back of the stamp.*

Stamps in these designs were issued with upright watermark between 1972 and 1974 and the $5 value was issued with a change of watermark in 1975.

(Des G. Drummond. Recess and litho D.L.R.)

1970 (28 Oct). Christmas. T **93** and similar vert design. W w **12**. P 13½×14.

286	**93**	3c. black and turquoise-blue	10	10
287	–	10c. dull purple and pink	10	10
288	**93**	35c. black and rose-red	30	10
289	–	50c. black and lilac	45	50
286/289 *Set of 4*			85	70

Design:—10c., 50c. *Adoration of the Magi* (detail) (Dürer).

94 4th King's Own Regt, 1759

(Des P. W. Kingsland. Litho Questa)

1970 (14 Dec). Military Uniforms (1st series). T **94** and similar vert designs. Multicoloured. W w **12**. P 14×13½.

290		½c. Type **94**	10	10
291		10c. 4th West India Regiment, 1804	65	10
292		20c. 60th Regiment, The Royal American, 1809	1·00	10
293		35c. 93rd Regiment, Sutherland Highlanders, 1826–34	1·25	10
294		75c. 3rd West India Regiment, 1851	1·75	2·00
290/294 *Set of 5*			4·25	2·10
MS295 128×146 mm. Nos. 290/4			5·50	11·00

STAMP BOOKLET

1968 (2 Oct). Blue cover. Stitched.

SB1	$1.20 booklet containing 5c., 10c. and 15c. (Nos. 185, 187, 188) in blocks of 4	8·50

BARBUDA

DEPENDENCY OF ANTIGUA

PRICES FOR STAMPS ON COVER TO 1945
Nos. 1/11 *from* × 5

BARBUDA
(**1**)

1922 (13 July). Stamps of Leeward Islands optd with T **1**. All Die II. Chalk-surfaced paper (3d. to 5s.).

(a) Wmk Mult Script CA

1	**11**	½d. deep green	1·50	13·00
2		1d. bright scarlet	1·50	13·00
		x. Wmk reversed	£900	£900
3	**10**	2d. slate-grey	1·50	7·00
		x. Wmk reversed	£100	
4	**11**	2½d. bright blue	1·50	7·50
		w. Wmk inverted	38·00	£120
5		6d. dull and bright purple	2·00	18·00
6	**10**	2s. purple and blue/*blue*	15·00	55·00
7		3s. bright green and violet	35·00	80·00
8		4s. black and red (R.)	45·00	80·00

(b) Wmk Mult Crown CA

9	**10**	3d. purple/*pale yellow*	1·75	16·00
10	**12**	1s. black/*emerald* (R.)	1·50	8·00
11		5s. green and red/*pale yellow*	65·00	£130
1/11 *Set of 11*			£150	£375
1s/11s Optd 'SPECIMEN' *Set of 11*			£225	

Examples of all values are known showing a forged Barbuda postmark of 'JU 1 23'.

Stocks of the overprinted stamps were exhausted by October 1925 and issues of Antigua or Leeward Islands were then used in Barbuda until 1968.

The following issues for Barbuda were also valid for use in Antigua.

(**New Currency. 100 cents = 1 Eastern Caribbean dollar**)

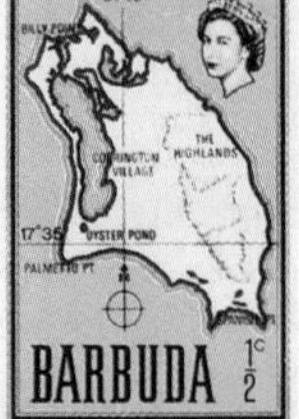

2 Map of Barbuda

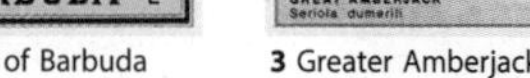

3 Greater Amberjack

(Des R. Granger Barrett. Litho Format)

1968 (19 Nov)–**70**. Designs as T **2**/**3**. P 14.

12		½c. brown, black and pink	65	3·75
13		1c. orange, black and flesh	1·75	35
14		2c. blackish brown, rose-red and rose	2·25	1·75

15		3c. blackish brown, orange-yellow and lemon	2·00	55
16		4c. black, bright green and apple-green	3·00	3·75
17		5c. blue-green, black and pale blue-green	2·25	20
18		6c. black, bright purple and pale lilac	1·50	3·25
19		10c. black, ultramarine and cobalt	2·00	1·75
20		15c. black, blue-green and turquoise-green	2·25	4·00
20*a*		20c. multicoloured (22.7.70)	2·00	2·00
21		25c. multicoloured (6.2.69)	1·50	25
22		35c. multicoloured (5.2.69)	3·00	25
23		50c. multicoloured (5.2.69)	1·00	2·25
24		75c. multicoloured (5.2.69)	1·00	80
25		$1 multicoloured (6.3.69)	50	1·50
26		$2.50 multicoloured (6.3.69)	55	2·00
27		$5 multicoloured (6.3.69)	65	2·25
12/27 *Set of* 17			24·00	27·00

Designs: ½ to 15c. Type **2**. Horiz as T **3**—20c. Great Barracuda; 35c. French Angelfish; 50c. Porkfish; 75c. Princess Parrotfish; $1, Long-spined Squirrelfish; $2.50, Bigeye; $5, Blue Chromis.

10 Sprinting and Aztec Sun-stone

14 *The Ascension* (Orcagna)

(Des R. Granger Barrett. Litho Format)

1968 (20 Dec). Olympic Games, Mexico. T **10** and similar horiz designs. Multicoloured. P 14.

28		25c. Type **10**	40	50
29		35c. High-jumping and Aztec statue	45	50
30		75c. Dinghy-racing and Aztec lion mask	50	1·75
28/30 *Set of* 3			1·25	2·50
MS31		85×76 mm. $1 Football and engraved plate	2·00	3·25

(Des R. Granger Barrett. Litho Format)

1969 (24 Mar). Easter Commemoration. P 14.

32	**14**	25c. black and light blue	15	45
33		35c. black and deep carmine	15	50
34		75c. black and bluish lilac	15	55
32/34 *Set of* 3			40	1·40

15 Scout Enrolment Ceremony

18 *Sistine Madonna* (Raphael)

(Des R. Granger Barrett. Litho Format)

1969 (7 Aug). Third Caribbean Scout Jamboree. T **15** and similar horiz designs. Multicoloured. P 14.

35		25c. Type **15**	35	55
36		35c. Scouts around camp fire	45	65
37		75c. Sea Scouts rowing boat	55	1·40
35/37 *Set of* 3			1·25	2·40

(Des. R. Granger Barrett. Litho Format)

1969 (20 Oct). Christmas. P 14.

38	**18**	½c. multicoloured	10	30
39		25c. multicoloured	10	15
40		35c. multicoloured	10	20
41		75c. multicoloured	20	35
38/41 *Set of* 4			30	90

19 William I (1066–87)

(**20**)

(Des R. Granger Barrett. Litho Format (Nos. 42/49) or Questa (others))

1970–71. English Monarchs. T **19** and similar vert designs. Multicoloured. P 14½×14.

42		35c. Type **19** (16.2.70)	30	15
43		35c. William II (2.3.70)	10	15
44		35c. Henry I (16.3.70)	10	15
45		35c. Stephen (1.4.70)	10	15
46		35c. Henry II (15.4.70)	10	15
47		35c. Richard I (1.5.70)	10	15
48		35c. John (15.5.70)	10	15
49		35c. Henry III (1.6.70)	10	15
50		35c. Edward I (15.6.70)	10	15
51		35c. Edward II (1.7.70)	10	15
52		35c. Edward III (15.7.70)	10	15
53		35c. Richard II (1.8.70)	10	15
54		35c. Henry IV (15.8.70)	10	15
55		35c. Henry V (1.9.70)	10	15
56		35c. Henry VI (15.9.70)	10	15
57		36c. Edward IV (1.10.70)	10	15
58		35c. Edward V (15.10.70)	10	15
59		35c. Richard III (2.11.70)	10	15
60		35c. Henry VII (16.11.70)	35	15
61		35c. Henry VIII (1.12.70)	35	15
62		35c. Edward VI (15.12.70)	35	15
63		35c. Lady Jane Grey (2.1.71)	35	15
64		35c. Mary I (15.1.71)	35	15
65		35c. Elizabeth I (1.2.71)	35	15
66		35c. James I (15.2.71)	35	15
67		35c. Charles I (1.3.71)	35	15
68		35c. Charles II (15.3.71)	35	15
69		35c. James II (1.4.71)	35	15
70		35c. William III (15.4.71)	35	15
71		35c. Mary II (1.5.71)	35	15
72		35c. Anne (15.5.71)	35	15
73		35c. George I (1.6.71)	35	15
74		35c. George II (15.6.71)	35	15
75		35c. George III (1.7.71)	35	15
76		35c. George IV (15.7.71)	35	15
77		35c. William IV (2.8.71)	35	60
78		35c. Victoria (16.8.71)	35	60
42/78 *Set of* 37			7·50	6·00

Further values in this series were issued in 1984.

1970 (26 Feb). No. 12 surch with T **20**.

79	**2**	20c. on ½c. brown, black and pink	20	20
		a. Surch inverted	60·00	
		b. Surch double	55·00	

21 *The Way to Calvary* (Ugolino)

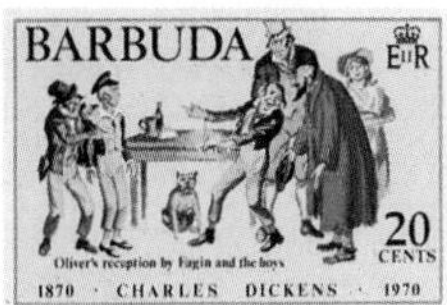

22 Oliver is introduced to Fagin (*Oliver Twist*)

(Des R. Granger Barrett. Litho Questa)

1970 (16 Mar). Easter Paintings. T **21** and similar vert designs. Multicoloured. P 14.

80		25c. Type **21**	15	45
		a. Horiz strip of 3. Nos. 80/82	40	1·25
81		35c. *The Deposition from the Cross* (Ugolino)	15	45
82		75c. *Crucifix* (The Master of St. Francis)	15	45
80/82 *Set of* 3			40	1·25

Nos. 80/82 were printed together, *se-tenant*, in horizontal strips of three throughout the sheet.

(Des R. Granger Barrett. Litho Questa)

1970 (10 July). Death Centenary of Charles Dickens. T **22** and similar horiz design. Multicoloured. P 14.

83		20c. Type **22**	45	40
84		75c. Dickens and Scene from *The Old Curiosity Shop*	80	1·40

23 *Madonna of the Meadow* (Bellini)

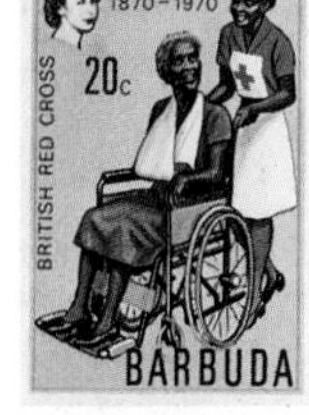

24 Nurse with Patient in Wheelchair

(Des R. Granger Barrett. Litho Questa)

1970 (15 Oct). Christmas. T **23** and similar horiz designs. Multicoloured. P 14.

85		20c. Type **23**	10	25
86		50c. *Madonna, Child and Angels* (from Wilton diptych)	15	35
87		75c. *The Nativity* (della Francesca)	15	50
85/7 *Set of* 3			30	1·00

(Des R. Granger Barrett. Litho Questa)

1970 (21 Dec). Centenary of British Red Cross. T **24** and similar multicoloured designs. P 14.

88		20c. Type **24**	15	40
89		35c. Nurse giving patient magazines (*horiz*)	20	45
90		75c. Nurse and mother weighing baby (*horiz*)	25	85
88/90 *Set of* 3			55	1·50

Ascension

DEPENDENCY OF ST. HELENA

Ascension, first occupied in 1815, was retained as a Royal Navy establishment from 1816 until 20 October 1922 when it became a dependency of St. Helena by Letters Patent.

Under Post Office regulations of 1850 (ratings) and 1854 (officers) mail from men of the Royal Navy serving abroad had the postage prepaid in Great Britain stamps, supplies of which were issued to each ship. Great Britain stamps used on Ascension before 1860 may have been provided by the naval officer in charge of the postal service.

The British GPO assumed responsibility for such matters in 1860, but failed to send any stamps to the island until January 1867.

Until about 1880 naval mail, which made up most early correspondence, did not have the stamps cancelled until arrival in England. The prices quoted for Nos. Z1/Z3 and Z6 are for examples on cover showing the Great Britain stamps cancelled on arrival and an Ascension postmark struck elsewhere on the front of the envelope.

The use of British stamps ceased in December 1922.

The following postmarks were used on Great Britain stamps from Ascension:

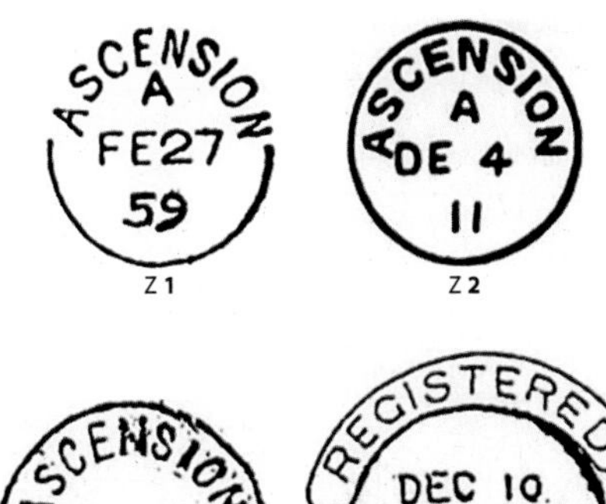

Z 1 Z 2 Z 3 Z 4

Z 5

Postmark Type	*Approx Period of Use*	*Diameter*	*Index Letter*
Z **1**	1862	20 mm	A
Z **2**	1864–1872	20 mm	A
	1872–1878	21½ mm	A
	1879–1889	19½ mm	A
	1891–1894	21½ mm	C
	1894–1902	22 mm	A
	1903–1907	20½ mm	A
	1908–1920	21 mm	A or none
	1909–1920	23 mm	C sideways (1909), none (1910–11), B (1911–20)
Z **3**	1920–1922	24 mm	none
Z **4**	1897–1903 Reg'd	23 mm	none
Z **5**	1900–1902 Reg'd	28 mm	C
	1903–1904 Reg'd	29 mm	A

Postmark Type Z **1** appears in the GPO proof book for 1858, but the first recorded use is 3 November 1862.

Forged postmarks exist. Those found most frequently are genuine postmarks of the post-1922 period with earlier date slugs fraudulently inserted, namely a 20 mm postmark as Type Z **2** (because of the shape of the 'O' in 'ASCENSION' this is often known as the 'Square O' postmark) and a 24 mm postmark as Type Z **3** but with the index letter A.

Stamps of GREAT BRITAIN cancelled with Types Z **2/5**. *Prices quoted for Nos. Z1/Z6 are for complete covers.*

Line-engraved issues.

Z1	1d. red-brown (1855)	£9000
Z2	1d. rose-red (1864–79) *From*	£3250
	Plate Nos. 71, 74, 76, 78, 83, 85, 96, 100, 102, 103, 104, 122, 134, 138, 154, 155, 157, 160, 168, 178	

Surface-printed issues (1856–1883)

Z2*a*	6d. lilac (1856)	
Z3	6d. lilac (1865) (Plate No. 5)	£9000
Z4	1s. green (1865) (Plate No. 4)	
Z5	1s. green (1867) (Plate No. 7)	
Z6	6d. grey (1874) (Plate Nos. 15, 16)	£7500
Z6*a*	6d. on 6d. lilac (1883)	
Z7	1d. lilac (1881) (16 dots)	90·00

1887–92.

Z8	½d. vermilion	£130
Z9	1½d. purple and green	£850
Z10	2d. green and carmine	£350
Z11	2½d. purple/*blue*	£170
Z12	3d. purple/*yellow*	£700
Z13	4d. green and brown	£450
Z14	4½d. green and carmine	£1300
Z15	5d. dull purple and blue	£500

Z16	6d. purple/*rose-red*	£400
Z17	9d. purple and blue	£1100
Z17*a*	10d. dull purple and carmine	£1300
Z18	1s. green	£1300

1900.

Z19	½d. blue-green	£160
Z20	1s. green and carmine	£1400

1902–11. King Edward VII issues.

Z21	½d. green	£100
Z22	1d. red	32·00
Z23	1½d. purple and green	£400
Z24	2d. green and carmine	£200
Z25	2½d. blue	£225
Z26	3d. purple/*yellow*	£400
Z27	4d. green and brown	£1000
Z28	4d. orange (1909)	£400
Z29	5d. purple and ultramarine	£400
Z30	6d. purple	£350
Z31	7d. grey-black (1910)	£475
Z32	9d. purple and ultramarine (1910)	£600
Z32*a*	10d. dull purple and scarlet	£800
Z33	1s. green and carmine	£200
Z33*a*	2s.6d. dull reddish purple (1911)	£1800
Z34	5s. carmine	£2500
Z35	10s. ultramarine	£3750
Z35*a*	£1 green	£8500

1911–12. T **98/9** of Great Britain.

Z36	½d. green (Die A)	£225
Z37	½d. yellow-green (Die B)	£100
Z38	1d. scarlet (Die B)	£100

1912. T **101/2** of Great Britain.

Z38*a*	½d. green	£100
Z38*b*	1d. scarlet	95·00

1912–22.

Z39	½d. green (1913)	85·00
Z40	1d. scarlet	38·00
Z41	1½d. red-brown	£100
Z42	2d. orange (Die I)	95·00
Z42*a*	2d. orange (Die II) (1921)	£900
Z43	2½d. blue	£130
Z44	3d. violet	£180
Z45	4d. grey-green (1913)	£225
Z46	5d. brown (1913)	£325
Z47	6d. purple (1913)	£180
Z47*a*	7d. green (1913)	£750
Z47*b*	8d. black/*yellow* (1913)	£800
Z48	9d. agate (1913)	£700
Z49	9d. olive-green (1922)	£1900
Z50	10d. turquoise-blue (1913)	£750
Z51	1s. bistre (1913)	£225
Z52	2s.6d. brown (1918)	£2250
Z53	5s. rose-red (1919)	£3750

Supplies of some values do not appear to have been sent to the island and known examples originate from maritime or, in the case of high values, philatelic mail.

PRICES FOR STAMPS ON COVER

Nos. 1/34	*from* × 5
Nos. 35/37	*from* × 10
Nos. 38/47	*from* × 6

ASCENSION
(1)

2d. Line through 'P' of 'POSTAGE' (R. 3/6)

2d. Blot on scroll (R. 3/10)

1922 (2 Nov). Stamps of St. Helena, showing Government House or the Wharf, optd with T **1** by D.L.R.

(a) Wmk Mult Script CA

1	½d. black and green	7·50	29·00
	x. Wmk reversed	£1500	
2	1d. green	8·50	28·00
3	1½d. rose-scarlet	17·00	48·00
4	2d. black and grey	17·00	13·00
	a. Line through 'P' of 'POSTAGE'	£500	£650
	b. Blot on scroll	£500	£650
5	3d. bright blue	13·00	30·00
6	8d. black and dull purple	27·00	55·00
7	2s. black and blue/*blue*	£110	£130
8	3s. black and violet	£140	£160

(b) Wmk Mult Crown CA

9	1s. black/*green* (R.)	28·00	48·00
1/9 *Set of* 9		£325	£475
1s/9s Optd 'SPECIMEN' *Set of* 9		£800	

Nos. 1, 4 and 6/8 are on special printings which were not issued without overprint.

Examples of all values are known showing a forged Ascension postmark dated 'MY 24 23'.

PLATE FLAWS ON THE 1924–1933 ISSUE. Many constant plate varieties exist on both the vignette and duty plates of this issue.

The major varieties are illustrated and listed below.

This issue utilised the same vignette plate as the St. Helena 1922–1937 set so that these flaws occur there also.

2 Badge of St. Helena

Broken mainmast. Occurs on R. 2/1 of all values.

Torn flag. Occurs on R. 4/6 of all values except the 5d. Retouched on sheets of ½d., 1d. and 2d. printed after 1927.

Cleft rock. Occurs on R. 5/1 of all values.

Broken scroll. (R. 1/4)

1½d. line through 'C' (R. 1/6)

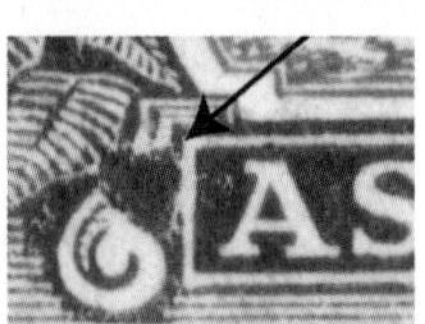

8d. 'Shamrock' flaw (R. 4/1)

(Typo D.L.R.)

1924 (20 Aug)–**33.** Wmk Mult Script CA. Chalk-surfaced paper. P 14.

10	**2**	½d. grey-black and black	6·50	20·00
		a. Broken mainmast	£130	£300
		b. Torn flag	£200	£375
		c. Cleft rock	£110	£275
11		1d. grey-black and deep blue-green	6·00	18·00
		a. Broken mainmast	£140	£300
		b. Torn flag	£150	£300
		c. Cleft rock	£130	£300
11*d*		1d. grey-black and bright blue-green (1933)	£110	£500
		da. Broken mainmast	£1000	
		dc. Cleft rock	£1000	
12		1½d. rose-red	10·00	48·00
		a. Broken mainmast	£150	£400
		b. Torn flag	£160	£400
		c. Cleft rock	£150	£400
		d. Broken scroll	£180	£450
		e. line through 'C'	£180	£450
13		2d. grey-black and grey	24·00	13·00
		a. Broken mainmast	£275	£300
		b. Torn flag	£350	£400
		c. Cleft rock	£250	£300
14		3d. blue	8·00	18·00
		a. Broken mainmast	£160	£300
		b. Torn flag	£160	£300
		c. Cleft rock	£150	£300
15		4d. grey-black and black/*yellow*	50·00	95·00
		a. Broken mainmast	£500	£850
		b. Torn flag	£500	£850
		c. Cleft rock	£475	£850
15*d*		5d. purple and olive-green (8.27)	23·00	26·00
		da. Broken mainmast	£375	£475
		dc. Cleft rock	£350	£475
16		6d. grey-black and bright purple	60·00	£120
		a. Broken mainmast	£650	£1000
		b. Torn flag	£650	£1000
		c. Cleft rock	£650	£1000
17		8d. grey-black and bright violet	20·00	48·00
		a. Broken mainmast	£325	£600
		b. Torn flag	£325	£600
		c. Cleft rock	£300	£600
		d. 'Shamrock' flaw	£375	£650
18		1s. grey-black and brown	21·00	55·00
		a. Broken mainmast	£400	£650
		b. Torn flag	£400	£650
		c. Cleft rock	£375	£650
19		2s. grey-black and blue/*blue*	75·00	£120
		a. Broken mainmast	£750	£1100
		b. Torn flag	£750	£1100
		c. Cleft rock	£700	£1100
20		3s. grey-black and black/*blue*	£100	£100
		a. Broken mainmast	£900	£1000
		b. Torn flag	£900	£1000
		c. Cleft rock	£850	£1000
10/20 *Set of* 12			£350	£600
10s/20s Optd 'SPECIMEN' *Set of* 12			£1000	

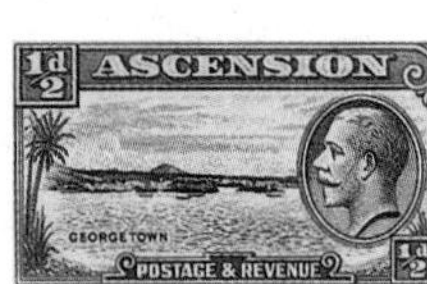

3 Georgetown

4 Ascension Island

5 The Pier

6 Long Beach

7 Three Sisters

8 Sooty Tern and Wideawake Fair

9 Green Mountain

'Teardrops' flaw (R. 4/5)

(Des and recess D.L.R.)

1934 (2 July). T **3/9** and similar designs. Wmk Mult Script CA. P 14.

21	**3**	½d. black and violet	90	80
22	**4**	1d. black and emerald	1·75	1·50
		a. Teardrops flaw	£150	£180
23	**5**	1½d. black and scarlet	1·75	2·25
24	**4**	2d. black and orange	1·75	2·50
		a. Teardrops flaw	£300	£375
25	**6**	3d. black and ultramarine	2·50	1·50
26	**7**	5d. black and blue	2·25	3·25
27	**4**	8d. black and sepia	4·25	6·50
		a. Teardrops flaw	£500	£700
28	**8**	1s. black and carmine	18·00	12·00
29	**4**	2s.6d. black and bright purple	45·00	48·00
		a. Teardrops flaw	£1700	£1900
30	**9**	5s. black and brown	55·00	60·00
21/30 *Set of* 10			£120	£120
21s/30s Perf 'SPECIMEN' *Set of* 10			£500	

1935 (6 May). Silver Jubilee. As Nos. 91/94 of Antigua, but ptd by Waterlow. P 11×12.

31	1½d. deep blue and scarlet	3·50	15·00
	l. Kite and horizontal log	£475	£650
32	2d. ultramarine and grey	11·00	38·00
	l. Kite and horizontal log	£1000	
33	5d. green and indigo	23·00	32·00
	k. Kite and vertical log	£400	£550
	l. Kite and horizontal log	£1000	£1100
34	1s. slate and purple	23·00	42·00
	l. Kite and horizontal log	£950	£1200
31/4 *Set of* 4		55·00	£110
31s/4s Perf 'SPECIMEN' *Set of* 4		£425	

For illustrations of plate varieties see Omnibus section following Zanzibar.

1937 (19 May). Coronation. As Nos. 95/97 of Antigua, but printed by D.L.R. P 14.

35		1d. green	50	1·40
36		2d. orange	1·00	60
37		3d. bright blue	1·00	50
35/37 *Set of 3*			2·25	2·25
35s/7s Perf 'SPECIMEN' *Set of 3*			£450	

10 Georgetown

11 Green Mountain

12 Three Sisters

13 The Pier

14 Long Beach

½d. Long centre bar to 'E' in 'GEORGETOWN' (R. 2/3)

'Mountaineer' flaw (R. 4/4) (1d., 2d., and 4d. ptgs from 1945)

'Davit' flaw (R. 5/1) (all ptgs of 1½d. and 2s.6d.)

'Cut mast and railings' (R. 3/1) (1½d. and 2s.6d. ptgs from 1946)

'Boulder' flaw (R. 5/4) (6d. and 10s. part of 1938 ptg and all subsequent)

(Recess D.L.R.)

1938 (12 May)–**53**. T **10/14**. Wmk Mult Script CA. P 13½.

38	**10**	½d. black and violet	8·00	4·00
		a. Long centre bar to E	£325	£275
		b. Perf 13. Black and bluish violet (17.5.44)	1·40	4·00
		ba. Long centre bar to E	90·00	£170
39	**11**	1d. black and green	45·00	13·00
39*a*		1d. black and yellow-orange (8.7.40)	14·00	9·00
		b. Perf 13 (5.42)	45	60
		ba. Mountaineer flaw	£350	£450
		c. Perf 14 (17.2.49)	70	16·00
		ca. Mountaineer flaw	£225	£750
39*d*	**12**	1d. black and green, P 13 (1.6.49)	60	1·50
40	**13**	1½d. black and vermilion	9·50	1·40
		a. Davit flaw	£400	£225
		b. Perf 13 (17.5.44)	1·00	80
		ba. Davit flaw	£200	£170
		bb. Cut mast and railings	£275	£300
		c. Perf 14 (17.2.49)	3·75	13·00
		ca. Davit flaw	£350	£550
		cb. Cut mast and railings	£400	£550
40*d*		1½d. black and rose-carmine, P 14 (1.6.49)	2·50	1·00
		da. Davit flaw	£130	£190
		db. Cut mast and railings	£130	£190
		e. Black and carmine	12·00	5·00
		ea. Davit flaw	£450	£425
		eb. Cut mast and railings	£450	£425
		f. Perf 13 (25.2.53)	45	6·50
		fa. Davit flaw	£140	
		fb. Cut mast and railings	£140	£400
41	**11**	2d. black and red-orange	10·00	1·00
		a. Perf 13 (17.5.44)	80	40
		aa. Mountaineer flaw	£450	£350
		b. Perf 14 (17.2.49)	3·50	35·00
		ba. Mountaineer flaw	£350	£900
41*c*		2d. black and scarlet, P 14 (1.6.49)	1·75	1·75
		ca. Mountaineer flaw	£275	£400
42	**14**	3d. black and ultramarine	£100	26·00
42*a*		3d. black and grey (8.7.40)	20·00	4·25
		b. Perf 13 (17.5.44)	70	1·00
42*c*	**11**	4d. black and ultramarine (8.7.40)	17·00	3·75
		d. Perf 13 (17.5.44)	5·00	2·50
		da. Mountaineer flaw	£1000	£700
43	**12**	6d. black and blue	14·00	2·25
		a. Boulder flaw	£225	£160
		b. Perf 13 (17.5.44)	12·00	7·00
		ba. Boulder flaw	£225	£200
44	**10**	1s. black and sepia	22·00	3·00
		a. Perf 13 (17.5.44)	4·75	2·00
45	**13**	2s.6d. black and deep carmine	45·00	12·00
		a. Frame printed double, one albino	£5000	£5000
		b. Davit flaw	£1600	£850
		c. Perf 13 (17.5.44)	27·00	38·00
		ca. Davit flaw	£1400	£1800
		cb. Cut mast and railings	£2500	£3000
46	**14**	5s. black and yellow-brown	95·00	12·00
		a. Perf 13 (17.5.44)	40·00	45·00
47	**12**	10s. black and bright purple	£110	48·00
		a. Boulder flaw	£900	£500
		b. Perf 13 (17.5.44)	48·00	60·00
		ba. Boulder flaw	£600	£600
38b/47b *Set of 16*			£250	£110
38s/47s Perf 'SPECIMEN' *Set of 13*			£1000	

1946 (21 Oct). Victory. As Nos. 110/111 of Antigua.

48	2d. red-orange	40	1·00
49	4d. blue	40	1·00
48s/9s Perf 'SPECIMEN' *Set of 2*		£450	

1948 (20 Oct). Royal Silver Wedding. As Nos. 112/113 of Antigua.

50	3d. black	50	30
51	10s. bright purple	50·00	50·00

1949 (10 Oct). 75th Anniversary of Universal Postal Union. As Nos. 114/117 of Antigua.

52	3d. carmine	1·00	2·00
53	4d. deep blue	4·00	1·50
54	6d. olive	2·00	3·50
55	1s. blue-black	2·00	1·50
	a. 'A' of 'CA' missing from Wmk	—	£1500
52/55 *Set of 4*		8·00	7·75

1953 (2 June). Coronation. As No. 120 of Antigua.

56	3d. black and grey-black	1·00	2·75

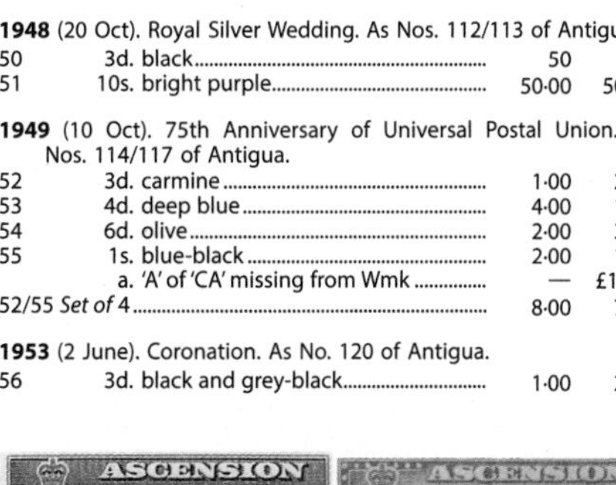

15 Water Catchment

16 Map of Ascension

17 View of Georgetown

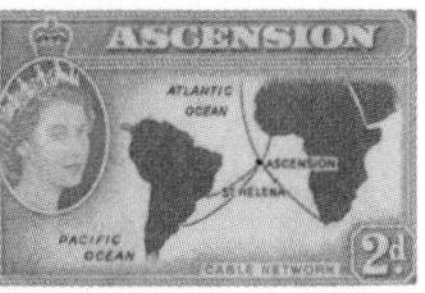
18 Map showing cable network

19 Mountain road

20 White-tailed Tropicbird ('Boatswain Bird')

21 Yellow-finned Tuna

22 Rollers on the seashore

23 Young turtles

24 Land Crab

25 Sooty Tern ('Wideawake')

26 Perfect Crater

27 View of Ascension from North-west

(Recess B.W.)

1956 (19 Nov). T **19/27**. Wmk Mult Script CA. P 13.

57	**15**	½d. black and brown	10	50
58	**16**	1d. black and magenta	4·50	2·75
59	**17**	1½d. black and orange	1·50	1·25
60	**18**	2d. black and carmine-red	6·00	3·50
61	**19**	2½d. black and orange-brown	2·25	3·50
62	**20**	3d. black and blue	6·00	1·25
63	**21**	4d. black and deep turquoise-green	1·25	2·00
64	**22**	6d. black and indigo	1·75	2·75
65	**23**	7d. black and deep olive	4·25	2·00
66	**24**	1s. black and vermilion	1·50	1·75
67	**25**	2s.6d. black and deep dull purple	30·00	9·00
68	**26**	5s. black and blue-green	42·00	19·00
69	**27**	10s. black and purple	55·00	40·00
57/69 *Set of 13*			£140	80·00

28 Brown Booby

(Des after photos by N. P. Ashmole. Photo Harrison)

1963 (23 May). T **28** and similar horiz designs. W w **12**. P 14×14½.

70	1d. black, lemon and new blue	1·50	30
71	1½d. black, cobalt and ochre	2·00	1·00
	a. Cobalt omitted	£150	
72	2d. black, grey and bright blue	1·25	30
73	3d. black, magenta and turquoise-blue	1·75	30
74	4½d. black, bistre-brown and new blue	1·75	30
	w. Wmk inverted	£550	
75	6d. bistre, black and yellow-green	1·25	30
76	7d. black, brown and reddish violet	1·25	30
77	10d. black, greenish yellow and blue-green	1·25	50
78	1s. multicoloured	1·25	30
79	1s.6d. multicoloured	4·50	1·75
80	2s.6d. multicoloured	8·50	12·00
81	5s. multicoloured	10·00	13·00
82	10s. multicoloured	13·00	15·00
83	£1 multicoloured	21·00	17·00
70/83 *Set of 14*		60·00	55·00

Designs:—1d. T **28**; 1½d. White-capped Noddy; 2d. White Tern; 3d. Red Billed Tropicbird; 4½d. Common Noddy; 6d. Sooty Tern; 7d. Ascension Frigatebird; 10d. Blue-faced Booby; 1s. White-tailed Tropicbird; 1s.6d. Red-billed Tropicbird; 2s.6d. Madeiran Storm Petrel; 5s. Red-footed Booby (brown phase); 10s. Ascension Frigatebirds; £1 Red-footed Booby (white phase).

1963 (4 June). Freedom from Hunger. As Nos. 146 of Antigua.

84	1s.6d. carmine	75	40

1963 (2 Sept). Red Cross Centenary. As Nos. 147/148 of Antigua.

85	3d. red and black	1·00	1·25
86	1s.6d. red and blue	1·50	2·25

1965 (17 May). ITU Centenary. As Nos. 166/167 of Antigua.

87	3d. magenta and bluish violet	50	65
88	6d. turquoise-blue and light chestnut	75	65

1965 (25 Oct). International Co-operation Year. As Nos. 168/169 of Antigua.

89	1d. reddish purple and turquoise-green	40	60
90	6d. deep bluish green and lavender	60	90

1966 (24 Jan). Churchill Commemoration. As Nos. 170/173 of Antigua.

91	1d. new blue	40	75
92	3d. deep green	1·25	1·00
93	6d. brown	1·40	1·25
94	1s.6d. bluish violet	1·60	1·50
91/94 *Set of 4*		4·25	4·00

1966 (1 July). World Cup Football Championship. As Nos. 176/177 of Antigua.

95	3d. violet, yellow-green, lake and yellow-brown	75	1·00
96	6d. chocolate, blue-green, lake and yellow-brown	75	1·25

1966 (20 Sept). Inauguration of WHO Headquarters, Geneva. As Nos. 178/179 of Antigua.

97	3d. black, yellow-green and light blue	1·75	1·00
98	1s.6d. black, light purple and yellow-brown	4·75	2·00

36 Satellite Station

37 BBC Emblem

(Des V. Whiteley. Photo Harrison)

1966 (7 Nov). Opening of Apollo Communications Satellite Earth Station. W w **12**. (sideways). P 14×14½.

99	**36**	4d. black and reddish violet	10	10
100		8d. black and deep bluish green	15	15
101		1s.3d. black and olive-brown	15	20
102		2s.6d. black and turquoise-blue	15	20
99/102 *Set of 4*			50	60

(Des BBC staff. Photo, Queen's head and emblem die-stamped, Harrison)

1966 (1 Dec). Opening of BBC Relay Station. W w **12**. P 14½.

103	**37**	1d. gold and ultramarine	10	10
104		3d. gold and myrtle-green	15	15
		w. Wmk inverted	50	1·00
105		6d. gold and reddish violet	15	15
106		1s.6d. gold and red	15	15
103/106 *Set of 4*			50	50

1967 (1 Jan). 20th Anniv of UNESCO As Nos. 196/198 of Antigua.

107	3d. slate-violet, red, yellow and orange	1·75	1·50
108	6d. orange-yellow, violet and deep olive	2·25	2·00
109	1s.6d. black, bright purple and orange	3·25	2·50
107/109 *Set of 3*		6·50	5·50

44 Human Rights Emblem and Chain Links

(Des and litho Harrison)

1968 (8 July). Human Rights Year. W w **12** (sideways*). P 14½×14.

110	**44**	6d. light orange, red and black	30	15
111		1s.6d. light grey-blue, red and black	40	25
112		2s.6d. light green, red and black	40	30
		w. Wmk Crown to right of CA	£800	
110/112 *Set of 3*			1·00	65

*The normal sideways watermark shows Crown to left of CA, *as seen from the back of the stamp.*

45 Black Durgon ('Ascension Black-Fish')

46 HMS *Rattlesnake*

(Des M. Farrar Bell. Litho D.L.R.)

1968 (23 Oct). Fish (1st series). T **45** and similar horiz designs. W w **12** (sideways*). P 13.

113	4d. black, slate and turquoise-blue	30	35
114	8d. multicoloured	35	60
	w. Wmk Crown to right of CA	£475	
115	1s.9d. multicoloured	40	65
116	2s.3d. multicoloured	40	65
113/116 *Set of 4*		1·25	2·00

Designs:—4d. T **45**; 8d. Scribbled Filefish ('Leather-jacket'); 1s.9d. Yellow-finned Tuna; 2s.3d. Short-finned Mako.

*The normal sideways watermark shows Crown to left of CA, *as seen from the back of the stamp.*

See also Nos. 117/120 and 126/129.

(Des M. Farrar Bell. Litho D.L.R.)

1969 (3 Mar). Fish (2nd series). Horiz designs as T **45**. Multicoloured. W w **12** (sideways). P 13½×13.

117	4d. Sailfish	55	80
118	6d. White Seabream ('Old Wife')	70	1·00
119	1s.6d. Yellowtail	90	2·00
120	2s.11d. Rock Hind ('Jack')	1·10	2·25
117/120 *Set of 4*		3·00	5·50

(Des L. Curtis. Photo Harrison)

1969 (1 Oct). Royal Naval Crests (1st series). T **46** and similar vert designs. W w **12** (sideways*). P 14×14½.

121	4d. multicoloured	50	30
122	9d. multicoloured	60	35
123	1s.9d. deep blue, pale blue and gold	80	45
124	2s.3d. multicoloured	90	55
121/124 *Set of 4*		2·50	1·50
MS125 165×105 mm. Nos. 121/124. P 14½		6·50	13·00
	w. Wmk Crown to right of CA	£1300	

Designs:—4d. T **46**; 9d. HMS *Weston*; 1s.9d. HMS *Undaunted*; 2s.3d. HMS *Eagle*.

*The normal sideways watermark shows Crown to left of CA, *as seen from the back of the stamp.*

See also Nos. 130/**MS**134.

(Des M. Farrar Bell. Litho D.L.R.)

1970 (6 Apr). Fish (3rd series). Horiz designs as T **45**. Multicoloured. W w **12** (sideways*). P 14.

126	4d. Wahoo	3·00	2·75
	w. Wmk Crown to right of CA	£500	
127	9d. Ascension Jack ('Coalfish')	3·50	2·75
	w. Wmk Crown to right of CA	1·25	1·25
128	1s.9d. Pompano Dolphin	4·00	3·50
129	2s.3d. Squirrelfish ('Soldier')	4·00	3·50
	w. Wmk Crown to right of CA	1·25	1·50
126/129w *Set of 4*		8·50	8·00

*The normal sideways watermark shows Crown to left of CA, *as seen from the back of the stamp.*

(Des L. Curtis. Photo D.L.R.)

1970 (7 Sept). Royal Naval Crests (2nd series). Designs as T **46**. Multicoloured. W w **12**. P 12½.

130	4d. HMS *Penelope*	1·00	1·00
131	9d. HMS *Carlisle*	1·25	1·25
132	1s.6d. HMS *Amphion*	1·50	1·50
133	2s.6d. HMS *Magpie*	1·50	1·50
130/133 *Set of 4*		4·75	4·75
MS134 153×96 mm. Nos. 130/133		7·50	14·00

STAMP BOOKLET

1963 (23 May). Buff cover. Stitched.

SB1	10s.6d. booklet containing 1d., 1½d., 2d., 3d., 6d. and 1s.6d. (Nos. 70/3, 75, 79), each in block of 4	70·00

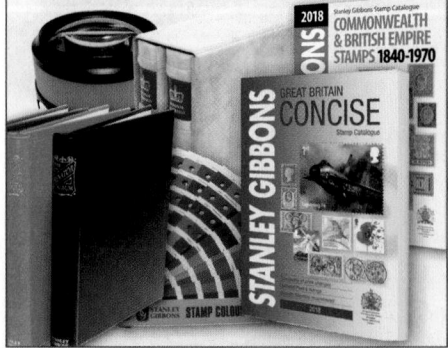

Australia

The Australian colonies of New South Wales, Queensland, South Australia, Tasmania, Victoria and Western Australia produced their own issues before federation in 1901. Stamps inscribed for the individual states continued in use after federation until the end of December 1912.

WATERMARK VARIETIES. Some stamp printers in the Australian colonies paid little attention to the position of the watermark in the sheets they produced so that some entire printings had the watermark inverted, some 50% upright and 50% inverted while on others the inverted watermarks were restricted to odd sheets. Reversed, inverted and reversed, and on stamps with sideways watermarks, sideways inverted and sideways inverted and reversed watermarks, are frequently encountered, especially on the stamps of New South Wales and the later issues of Tasmania, Victoria and Western Australia. In such circumstances it is impossible to provide accurate prices for such items, so, generally, only those watermark varieties occurring on stamps printed in Great Britain are included in the following listings.

DOUBLE PRINTS. Numerous examples of 'double prints,' also 'printed double, one albino' varieties are found on the locally printed line-engraved stamps of the Australian colonies. These are particularly prevalent in the stamps of South Australia and Tasmania. We no longer list such varieties.

NEW SOUTH WALES

PRICES FOR STAMPS ON COVER

Nos. 1/83	from × 2
Nos. 84/87	from × 3
No. 88	—
Nos. 89/96	from × 2
Nos. 97/98	—
Nos. 99/101	from × 2
Nos. 102/113	from × 3
No. 114	from × 10
Nos. 115/117	from × 2
Nos. 118/127	from × 3
Nos. 131/153	from × 2
Nos. 154/170	from × 3
Nos. 171/181	—
Nos. 186/202	from × 2
Nos. 203/206	from × 10
Nos. 207/221	from × 5
Nos. 222/237	from × 6
Nos. 238/242	—
Nos. 243/244	from × 6
Nos. 253/264	from × 10
Nos. 265/268	from × 15
Nos. 269/270	from × 2
Nos. 271/273	from × 10
Nos. 280/281	from × 2
Nos. 288/297	from × 10
Nos. 298/312	from × 12
Nos. 313/331	from × 10
No. 332	—
Nos. 333/349	from × 12
No. 350	—
Nos. 351/363	from × 12
No. O1	—
Nos. O2/O12	from × 4
Nos. O13/O18	—
Nos. O19/O34	from × 20
Nos. O35/O38	—
Nos. O39/O47	from × 40
Nos. O48/O53	—
Nos. O54/O58	from × 20
No. O59	—
Nos. D1/D7	from × 50
Nos. D8/D10	—
Nos. D11/D15	from × 50

EMBOSSED LETTER SHEETS AND ENVELOPES. From 1 November 1838 the Sydney GPO supplied letter sheets pre-stamped with an albino embossing, as illustrated, at 1½d. each or 1s.3d. per dozen. From January 1841 the price was reduced to 1s. per dozen. The public were also able to present their own stationery for embossing. The circular design measures approximately 29 mm in diameter, and examples are known on laid or wove paper of varying colours. Embossing continued until 1 May 1852 after which the Post Office refused to carry mail which was not franked with postage stamps. The die was used for reprints in 1870 and 1898 before it was destroyed later the same year.

A 1

PRINTERS. The early issues of New South Wales were printed on a press supervised by the Inspector of Stamps, Charles Kay. On 1 January 1857 this responsibility passed to the Government printer who produced all subsequent issues, *unless otherwise stated*.

SPECIMEN OVERPRINTS. Those listed are from UPU distributions between 1892 and 1903. Further 'Specimen' overprints exist, but these were used for other purposes. From 1891 examples of some of these Specimens, together with cancelled stamps, were sold to collectors by the NSW Post Office.

NEW SOUTH WALES USED IN NEW CALEDONIA. From October 1859 mail for Europe from New Caledonia was routed via Sydney and franked with New South Wales stamps in combination with local issues. Such NSW stamps were cancelled on arrival in Sydney.

1

2

(Eng Robert Clayton, Sydney)

1850 (1 Jan). T **1**. Plate I. No clouds.

(a) Soft yellowish paper

1	1d. crimson-lake	£16000	£550
2	1d. carmine	£16000	£500
3	1d. reddish rose	£15000	£475
4	1d. brownish red	£16000	£500

(b) Hard bluish paper

5	1d. pale red	£15000	£475
6	1d. dull lake	£16000	£500

1850 (Aug). T **2**. Plate I re-engraved by Henry C. Jervis, commonly termed Plate II. With clouds.

(a) Hard toned white to yellowish paper

7	1d. vermilion	£13000	£375
8	1d. dull carmine	£13000	£375
	a. No trees on hill (R. 2/2)	£17000	£750
	b. Hill unshaded (R. 2/3)	£17000	£750
	c. Without clouds (R. 3/5)	£17000	£750

(b) Hard greyish or bluish paper

9	1d. crimson-lake	£13000	£375
10	1d. gooseberry-red	£16000	£550
11	1d. dull carmine	£13000	£375
12	1d. brownish red	£13000	£350
	a. No trees on hill (R. 2/2)	£17000	£750
	b. Hill unshaded (R. 2/3)	£17000	£750
	c. Without clouds (R. 3/5)	£17000	£750

(c) Laid paper

13	1d. carmine	£18000	£700
14	1d. vermilion	£19000	£650
	a. No trees on hill (R. 2/2)	—	£1200
	b. Hill unshaded (R. 2/3)	—	£1200
	c. Without clouds (R. 3/5)	—	£1200

Each image was individually engraved on the plate.

The varieties quoted with the letters 'a', 'b', 'c' of course exist in each shade; the prices quoted are for the commonest shade, and the same applies to the following portions of this list.

Nos. 1/14 were printed in sheets of 25 (5×5).

Note that in genuine examples of Nos 1/14 the star is directly below the 'T' of 'POSTAGE'. Otherwise convincing forgeries exist where the star is between the 'T' and the 'A'.

LAID PAPER. Nos. 13/14, 34/35, 38 and 43*d*/43*e* can be found showing parts of the papermaker's watermark (T. H. SAUNDERS 1847 in double-lined capitals and the figure of Britannia seated in an oval beneath a crown).

3

4

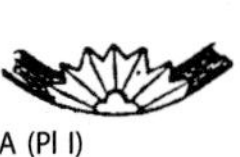
A (Pl I)

Illustrations A, B, C and D are sketches of the lower part of the inner circular frame, showing the characteristic variations of each plate.

(Eng John Carmichael)

1850 (1 Jan). Plate I. Vertical-lined background. T **3**.

(a) Early impressions, full details of clouds, etc

15	2d. greyish blue	£21000	£550
16	2d. deep blue	—	£650
	a. Double lines on bale (R. 2/7)	—	£1100

(b) Intermediate impressions

16*b*	2d. greyish blue	£12000	£325
16*c*	2d. deep blue	£13000	£400

(c) Later impressions, clouds, etc., mostly gone, T **4**

17	2d. greyish blue	£10000	£190
18	2d. dull blue	£10000	£180

(d) Stamps in the lower row partially retouched (end Jan)

19	2d. greyish blue	£12000	£300
20	2d. dull blue	£13000	£350

5

Pick and shovel omitted (R. 1/10)

B (Pl II)

C (Pl III)

(Plate entirely re-engraved by Henry C. Jervis)

1850 (Apr–July). T **5**. Plate II. Horizontal-lined background. Bale on left side supporting the seated figure, dated. Dot in centre of the star In each corner.

(a) Early impressions

21	2d. indigo	£16000	£350
22	2d. lilac-blue	—	£1300
23	2d. grey-blue	£16000	£300
24	2d. bright blue	£16000	£300
	a. Fan as in Pl III, but with shading outside (R. 1/1)	—	£550
	b. Fan as in Pl III, but without shading, and inner circle intersects the fan (R. 1/2)	—	£600
	c. Fan as B, but inner circle intersects fan (R. 1/3)	—	£600
	d. No whip and inner circle intersects fan (R. 1/4)	—	£600
	e. No whip (R. 1/8, 2/8)	—	£475
	f. Pick and shovel omitted (R. 1/10)	£20000	£600
	g. 'CREVIT' omitted (R. 2/1)	—	£950

(b) Worn impressions

25	2d. dull blue	£10000	£170
26	2d. Prussian blue	£10000	£200
	a. Fan as in Pl III, but with shading outside (R. 1/1)	£14000	£425
	b. Fan as in Pl III, but without shading, and inner circle intersects the fan (R. 1/2)	—	£425
	c. Fan as B, but inner circle intersects fan (R. 1/3)	—	£425
	d. No whip and inner circle intersects fan (R. 1/4)	—	£425
	e. No whip (R. 1/8, 2/8)	£14000	£350
	f. Pick and shovel omitted (R. 1/10)	—	£425
	g. 'CREVIT' omitted (R. 2/1)	£16000	£650

(c) Bottom row retouched with dots and dashes in lower spandrels (from July)

27	2d. Prussian blue	£11000	£325
28	2d. dull blue	£11000	£225
	e. No whip (R. 2/8)	—	£375
	g. 'CREVIT' omitted (R. 2/1)	—	£550

(Plate re-engraved a second time by Henry C. Jervis)

1850 (Sept). Plate III. Bale not dated and single-lined, except on No. 30c which is doubled-lined. No dots in stars.

29	2d. ultramarine	£11000	£225
30	2d. deep blue	£11000	£225
	a. No whip (R. 2/3, 2/7)	—	£375
	b. Fan with 6 segments (R. 2/8)	—	£500
	c. Double lines on bale (R. 1/7, 1/10, 1/12)	—	£350

(Plate re-engraved a third time by Henry C. Jervis)

1851 (Jan). Plate IV. Double-lined bale, and circle in centre of each star.

(a) Hard bluish grey wove paper

31	2d. ultramarine	£11000	£200
32	2d. Prussian blue	£11000	£170
33	2d. bright blue	£11000	£190
	a. Hill not shaded (R. 1/12)	—	£325
	b. Fan with 6 segments (R. 2/8)	—	£325
	c. No clouds (R. 2/10)	—	£325
	d. Retouch (R. 2/1)	—	£400
	e. No waves (R. 1/9, 2/5)	—	£275

(b) Stout yellowish vertically laid paper

34	2d. ultramarine	£12000	£250
35	2d. Prussian blue	£13000	£275
	a. Hill not shaded (R. 1/12)	—	£425
	b. Fan with 6 segments (R. 2/8)	—	£425
	c. No clouds (R. 2/10)	£16000	£425
	d. Retouch (R. 2/1)	£16000	£500
	e. No waves (R. 1/9, 2/5)	—	£375
	f. 'PENOE' (R. 1/10, 2/12)	—	£450

The retouch, Nos. 33d and 35d., occurs outside the left margin line on R. 2/1.

6

D (Pl V)

7

(Plate re-engraved a fourth time by Henry C. Jervis)

1851 (Apr.). T **6**. Plate V. Pearl in fan.

(a) Hard greyish wove paper

36	2d. ultramarine	£11000	£180
37	2d. dull blue	£11000	£180
	a. Pick and shovel omitted (R. 2/5)	—	£375
	b. Fan with 6 segments (R. 2/8)	—	£375

(b) Stout yellowish vertically laid paper

38	2d. dull ultramarine	£15000	£425
	a. Pick and shovel omitted (R. 2/5)	—	£650
	b. Fan with 6 segments (R. 2/8)	—	£650

Nos. 15/38 were printed in sheets of 24 (12×2), although the existence of an inter-panneau *tête-bêche* pair from Plate II indicates that the printer applied two impressions of the plate to each sheet of paper. The two panes were normally separated before issue. The original Plate I was re-cut four times to form Plates II to V. An interesting variety occurs on R. 1/9-11 and 2/7 in all five plates. It consists of ten loops of the engine-turning on each side of the design instead of the normal nine loops.

(Eng Henry C. Jervis)

1850 (1 Jan)–**51**. T **7**.

(a) Soft yellowish wove paper

39	3d. yellow-green	£12000	£325
40	3d. myrtle green	£22000	£1400
41	3d. emerald-green	£14000	£350
	a. No whip (R. 4/3–4)	—	£500
	b. 'SIGIIIUM' for 'SIGILLUM' (R. 5/3)	—	£700

(b) Bluish to grey wove paper (July 1850)

42 3d. yellow-green £12000 £275
43 3d. emerald-green £13000 £275
b. No whip (R. 4/3–4) — £400
c. 'SIGIIIUM' for 'SIGILLUM' (R. 5/3) — £600

(c) Yellowish to bluish laid paper (Jan 1851)

43*d* 3d. bright green £18000 £600
43*e* 3d. yellowish green £16000 £500
f. No whip (R. 4/3–4) — £850
g. 'SIGIIIUM' for 'SIGILLUM' (R. 5/3) — £1200

Nos. 39/43*e* were printed in sheets of 25 (5×5).

8

9

(Des A. W. Manning from sketch by W. T. Levinge; eng on steel by John Carmichael, Sydney)

1851 (18 Dec)–**52**. Imperf.

(a) Thick yellowish paper

44 **8** 1d. carmine £4500 £300
a. No leaves right of 'SOUTH' (R. 1/7, 3/1) — £500
b. Two leaves right of 'SOUTH' (R. 2/5) — £750
c. 'WALE' (R. 1/9) — £750

(b) Bluish medium wove paper (1852)

45 **8** 1d. carmine £2250 £160
46 1d. scarlet £2250 £160
47 1d. vermilion £2250 £140
48 1d. brick-red £2250 £140
a. No leaves right of 'SOUTH' (R. 1/7, 3/1) £4000 £350
b. Two leaves right of 'SOUTH' (R. 2/5) — £450
c. 'WALE' (R. 1/9) — £450

(c) Thick vertically laid bluish paper (1852?)

49 **8** 1d. orange-brown £7500 £450
50 1d. claret £7500 £475
a. No leaves right of 'SOUTH' (R. 1/7, 3/1) — £850
b. Two leaves right of 'SOUTH' (R. 2/5) — £1100
c. 'WALE' (R. 1/9) — £1200

Nos. 44/50 were printed in sheets of 50 (10×5).

(Eng John Carmichael (Nos. 51/59), Henry C. Jervis (Nos. 60/64))

1851 (24 July)–**55**. Imperf.

(a) Plate I

(i) Thick yellowish wove paper

51 **8** 2d. ultramarine £2250 £120

(ii) Fine impressions, blue to greyish medium paper

52 **8** 2d. ultramarine £1800 35·00
53 2d. chalky blue £1700 35·00
54 2d. dark blue £1700 35·00
55 2d. greyish blue £1700 35·00

(iii) Worn plate, blue to greyish medium paper

56 **8** 2d. ultramarine £1200 35·00
57 2d. Prussian blue £1200 35·00

(iv) Worn plate, blue wove medium paper

58 **8** 2d. ultramarine £1100 35·00
59 2d. Prussian blue £1100 35·00

(b) Plate II. Stars in corners (Oct 1853)

(i) Bluish medium to thick wove paper

60 **9** 2d. deep ultramarine £2500 £130
61 2d. indigo £2500 £100
a. 'WAEES' (R. 3/3) — £475

(ii) Worn plate, hard blue wove paper

62 **9** 2d. deep Prussian blue £2500 £120
a. 'WAEES' (R. 3/3) — £475

*(c) Plate III, being Plate I (T **8**) re-engraved by H. C. Jervis. Background of crossed lines (Sept 1855)*

(i) Medium bluish wove paper

63 – 2d. Prussian blue £1400 75·00
a. 'WALES' partly covered with wavy lines (R. 1/3) £5000 £275

(ii) Stout white wove paper

64 – 2d. Prussian blue £1400 75·00
a. 'WALES' partly covered with wavy lines (R. 1/3) £5000 £275

Nos. 51/64 were printed in sheets of 50 (10×5).

(Eng John Carmichael)

1852 (3 Dec). Imperf.

(a) Medium greyish blue wove paper

65 **8** 3d. deep green £6000 £225
66 3d. green £5000 £160
67 3d. dull yellow-green £4250 £110
a. 'WAEES' with centre bar of first 'E' missing (R. 4/7) — £450

(b) Thick blue wove paper

69 **8** 3d. emerald-green £6000 £250
71 3d. blue-green £6000 £275
a. 'WAEES' with centre bar of first 'E' missing (R. 4/7) — £750

Nos. 65/71 were printed in sheets of 50 (10×5).

1852 (Apr)–**53**. Imperf.

(a) Plate I

(i) Medium white wove paper

72 **8** 6d. Vandyke-brown — £1100
a. 'WALLS' (R. 2/3) — £2500

(ii) Medium bluish grey wove paper

73 **8** 6d. Vandyke-brown £5500 £250
74 6d. yellow-brown £6000 £275
75 6d. chocolate-brown £5500 £250
76 6d. grey-brown £5500 £250
a. 'WALLS' (R. 2/3) — £1000

(b) Plate I re-engraved by H. C. Jervis. Coarse background (June 1853)

77 – 6d. brown £6000 £300
78 – 6d. grey-brown £5500 £300

Reprints from the original plates of the 6d. and 8d. were produced in a variety of colours, including those in which the stamps had been issued. Unused examples of Nos. 72/81 should only be purchased from a reliable source.

Nos. 72/76 and 77/78 were printed in sheets of 25 (5×5).

(Eng Henry C. Jervis)

1853 (May). Imperf. Medium bluish paper.

79 8d. dull yellow £20000 £600
80 8d. orange-yellow £20000 £600
81 8d. orange £21000 £650
a. No bow at back of head (R. 1/9) — £2000
b. No leaves right of 'SOUTH' (R. 3/1) — £2000
c. No lines in spandrel (R. 2/2, 3/2, 4/2) — £1100

Nos. 79/81 were issued in sheets of 50 (10×5).

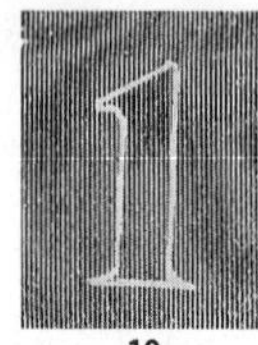
10

NOTE. All watermarked stamps from No. 82 to No. 172 have double-lined figures, as T 10.

1854 (Jan–Mar). Yellowish wove paper. Wmk double-lined '**1**', '**2**', or '**3**' as T **10**, to match face value. Imperf.

82 **8** 1d. red-orange (2.54) £550 38·00
83 1d. orange-vermilion £550 38·00
a. No leaves right of 'SOUTH' (R. 1/7, 3/1) £1000 £110
b. Two leaves right of 'SOUTH' (R. 2/5) £1400 £170
c. 'WALE' (R. 1/9) £1400 £170
84 – 2d. ultramarine (Pl III) (1.54) £450 15·00
85 – 2d. Prussian blue (Pl III) £450 15·00
86 – 2d. chalky blue (Pl III) £450 12·00
a. 'WALES' partly covered by wavy lines (R. 1/3) £1200 65·00
87 **8** 3d. yellow-green (3.54) £800 50·00
a. 'WAEES' with centre bar of first 'E' missing (R. 4/7) £200 £200
b. Error. Wmk '**2**' £7500 £1600

Nos. 82/87 were printed in sheets of 50 (10×5).

11 12

13 14

(6d. and 1s. des E. H. Corbould after sketches by W. T. Levinge. Printed by New South Wales Govt Ptg Dept from Perkins Bacon plates)

1854 (1 Feb)–**59**. Wmk double-lined '**5**', '**6**', '**8**' or '**12**' to match face value. Imperf.

88 **11** 5d. dull green (1.12.55) £1400 £650
89 **12** 6d. deep slate £2250 35·00
a. Wmk sideways † £1200
90 6d. greenish grey £1900 35·00
91 6d. slate-green £1900 35·00
92 6d. bluish grey £1900 55·00
93 6d. fawn £2000 95·00
a. Wmk '**8**' (15.8.59) £4250 £110
94 6d. grey £1900 55·00
95 6d. olive-grey £1900 35·00
96 6d. greyish brown £1900 35·00
a. Wmk '**8**' (15.8.59) £4250 £110
ab. Wmk sideways — £500
97 **13** 8d. golden yellow (1.12.55) £25000 £1600
98 8d. dull yellow-orange £24000 £1500
99 **14** 1s. rosy vermilion (2.54) £5500 75·00
a. Wmk '**8**' (20.6.57) £10000 £180
100 1s. pale red £5000 70·00
101 1s. brownish red £5500 80·00

Nos. 93a, 96a and 99a come from printings made when supplies of the correct numeral watermarks were unavailable.

Plate proofs of the 6d. in red-brown and of the 1s. in deep blue on unwatermarked paper exist handstamped 'CANCELLED' in oval of bars (see note on Perkins Bacon 'CANCELLED' in Catalogue introduction) (*Price £15000 each*).

A single used example of No. 91 exists printed on both sides. It is in the Royal Philatelic Collection.

For further examples of Types **11**/**14** on different watermarks see Nos. 141/153, 160/170, 215, 218, 231/233, 236 and 329.

15

16

(Eng John Carmichael)

1856 (1 Jan)–**59**. For Registered Letters. No wmk. Imperf.

(a) Soft medium yellowish paper

102 **15** (6d.) vermilion and Prussian blue £2000 £180
a. Frame printed on back £12000 £5000
103 (6d.) salmon and indigo £1900 £200
104 (6d.) orange and Prussian blue £1900 £250
105 (6d.) orange and indigo £1900 £225

(b) Hard medium bluish wove paper, with manufacturer's wmk in sans-serif, double-lined capitals across sheet and only showing portions of letters on a few stamps in a sheet

106 **15** (6d.) orange and Prussian blue (4.59) £2500 £275

For further examples of Type **15** on different watermarks see Nos. 119/127.

2d. Major retouch (Plate I, R. 2/12)

2d. Major retouch (Plate I, R. 9/8)

(Printed by New South Wales Govt Ptg Dept from plates engraved by Perkins Bacon & Co)

1856 (7 Jan)–**60**. Wmk double-lined '**1**', '**2**' or '**3**' to match face value. Imperf.

(a) Recess

107 **16** 1d. orange-vermilion (6.4.56) £400 24·00
a. Error. Wmk '**2**' † £8500
108 1d. carmine-vermilion £400 24·00
109 1d. orange-red £425 24·00
a. Printed on both sides £3750 £2500
110 2d. deep turquoise-blue (Pl I) £375 14·00
111 2d. ultramarine (Pl I) £350 14·00
112 2d. blue (Pl I) £350 14·00
a. Major retouch (1858) £2250 £450
b. Error. Wmk '**1**' † £8500
c. Wmk '**5**' (3.57) £950 70·00
113 2d. pale blue (Pl I) £350 14·00
114 2d. blue (Pl II) (1.60) £950 65·00
115 3d. yellow-green (10.10.56) £1800 £110
116 3d. bluish green £1900 £120
117 3d. dull green £1900 £120
a. Error, Wmk '**2**' — £4000

(b) Lithographic transfer of Plate I

118 **16** 2d. pale blue (3.8.59) — £800
a. Retouched — £2500

For further examples of Type **16** on different watermarks see Nos. 131/140, 154/158, 171/172, 211/212, 226/228 and 327/328.

Two plates were used for the 2d. The 2d. Plate I was retouched, on a total of ten positions, Nos. 112a and 133a refer to the third retouch of R. 2/12 and R. 9/8. Earlier retouches of these exist. Stamps from Plate II are wider apart and are more regularly spaced. There is also a white patch between 'A' of 'WALES' and the back of the Queen's head on later printings from Plate II, but this is not obvious on the early printings.

On the 3d. the value is in block letters on a white background. No. 112c comes from a printing made when supplies of the '2' paper were unavailable. There are only two known of No. 112b one of which is in the Royal Collection. Two used examples are known with '8' watermark, both of which are in museum collections.

The 1d. exists privately rouletted 10, a used pair of which is known postmarked 15 May 1861.

No. 114 was mainly used at post offices in Queensland.

The lithographic retouches (No. 118a) occur on the three stamps at the left of the bottom row of the sheet and consist of strong horizontal lines below 'TWO PENCE'.

STAMPS WITH STRAIGHT EDGES. Stamps between Nos. 119 and 244 and also Nos. 327/329 can be found with one or two sides imperforate. These come from the outside rows which were not perforated between the stamps and the sheet margins. Being from the edge of the sheet such stamps are often found without watermark or showing portions of the double-lined 'NEW SOUTH WALES' marginal watermark.

1860 (Feb)–**63**. For Registered Letters.

(a) P 12

(i) Hard medium bluish wove paper with manufacturer's wmk in sans-serif, double-lined capitals across sheet, showing portions of letters on a few stamps

119 **15** (6d.) orange and Prussian blue £1100 80·00
120 (6d.) orange and indigo £1100 85·00

(ii) Coarse, yellowish wove paper with manufacturer's wmk in Roman capitals (Feb 1860)

121	**15**	(6d.) rose-red and Prussian blue	£700	55·00
122		(6d.) rose-red and indigo	£800	£100
123		(6d.) salmon and indigo		

(b) P 13

(i) Coarse, yellowish wove paper with manufacturer's wmk in Roman capitals (1862)

124	**15**	(6d.) rose-red and Prussian blue	£800	70·00

(ii) Yellowish wove paper. Wmk double-lined '6' (May 1863)

125	**15**	(6d.) rose-red and Prussian blue	£350	24·00
126		(6d.) rose-red and indigo	£450	32·00
127		(6d.) rose-red and pale blue	£350	22·00

2d. Major retouch around neck and above 'TWO PENCE' (Plate II, R. 5/9)

1860 (14 Feb)–**72**. Wmk double-lined figure of value.

(a) P 12

131	**16**	1d. orange-red	£375	25·00
132		1d. scarlet	£300	25·00
133		2d. pale blue (Pl I)	£750	£140
		a. Retouched	—	£1400
134		2d. greenish blue (Pl II)	£275	13·00
136		2d. Prussian blue (Pl II)	£275	13·00
		a. Error. Wmk '1'	—	£3500
		b. Retouched (*shades*)	—	£425
137		2d. Prussian blue (Pl I) (3.61)	£300	14·00
138		2d. dull blue (Pl I)	£275	13·00
139		3d. yellow-green (1860)	£1900	60·00
140		3d. blue-green	£1000	48·00
141	**11**	5d. dull green (1863)	£475	£120
142		5d. yellowish green (1863)	£475	£120
143	**12**	6d. grey-brown	£850	65·00
144		6d. olive-brown	£850	75·00
145		6d. greenish grey	£950	60·00
146		6d. fawn	£900	85·00
147		6d. mauve	£850	38·00
148		6d. violet	£750	19·00
149	**13**	8d. lemon-yellow	—	£2000
150		8d. orange	£7500	£1300
151		8d. red-orange	£7500	£1300
152	**14**	1s. brownish red	£1700	75·00
153		1s. rose-carmine	£1700	75·00

(b) P 13

154	**16**	1d. scarlet (1862)	£170	25·00
155		1d. dull red	£170	25·00
156		3d. blue-green (12.62)	£110	13·00
157		3d. yellow-green	£120	9·50
		a. Wmk '6' (7.72)	£250	15·00
158		3d. dull green	£120	9·00
		a. Wmk '6' (7.72)	£275	18·00
160	**11**	5d. bluish green (12.63)	£150	38·00
161		5d. bright yellow-green (8.65)	£300	80·00
162		5d. sea-green (1866)	£170	40·00
162*a*		5d. dark bluish green (11.70)	£110	25·00
163	**12**	6d. reddish purple (Pl I) (7.62)	£250	6·50
164		6d. mauve	£250	6·50
165		6d. purple (Pl II) (1864)	£180	4·75
		a. Wmk '5' (7.66)	£800	28·00
		ab. Wmk '5' sideways	†	£1200
		b. Wmk '12' (12.66 and 1868)	£750	23·00
166		6d. violet	£190	6·50
		a. Wmk '5' (7.66)	—	38·00
167		6d. aniline mauve	£1300	£140
167*a*	**13**	8d. red-orange (1862)	£550	55·00
167*b*		8d. yellow-orange	£600	45·00
		ba. Wmk sideways	†	£1200
167*c*		8d. bright yellow	£550	45·00
168	**14**	1s. rose-carmine (1862)	£375	8·50
169		1s. carmine	£350	9·50
170		1s. crimson-lake	£350	9·50

(c) Perf compound 12×13

171	**16**	1d. scarlet (1862)	—	£2250
172		2d. dull blue (1.62)	£2750	£400

No. 133 was made by perforating a small remaining stock of No. 113. Nos. 137/138 were printed from the original plate after its return from London, where it had been repaired.

No. 136b refers to the second retouch on R. 5/9. Other retouches to plate II exist.

Nos. 157a, 158a and 165a/165b come from printings made when supplies of paper with the correct face value were unavailable.

The Royal Philatelic Collection contains examples of Nos. 131 and 168 in imperf between pairs.

For later printings in these types, with different watermarks and perforations, see Nos. 195, 211/212, 215, 218, 226/228, 231/233, 236, 269/270 and 327/329.

24

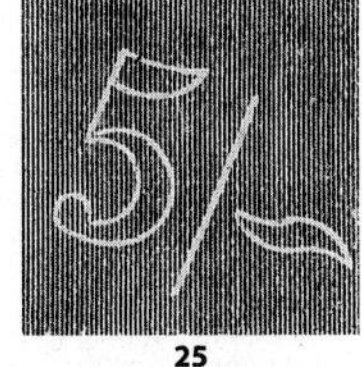

25

(Des E. H. Corbould, R.I.)

1861–88. W **25**. Various perfs.

174	**24**	5s. dull violet, P 12 (1861)	£2250	£325
		a. Perf 13 (1861)	£350	35·00
175		5s. royal purple, P 13 (1872)	£850	70·00
176		5s. deep rose-lilac, P 13 (1875)	£250	35·00
177		5s. deep purple, P 13 (1880)	£300	50·00
		a. Perf 10 (1882)	£325	75·00
178		5s. rose-lilac, P 10 (1883)	£300	55·00
179		5s. purple, P 12 (1885)	—	70·00
		a. Perf 10×12 (1885)	—	£180
180		5s. reddish purple, P 10 (1886)	£300	60·00
		a. Perf 12×10 (1887)	£450	65·00
		b. Mixed perfs 10 and 12	—	†
181		5s. rose-lilac, P 11 (1888)	£350	£140

This value was replaced by Nos. 261, etc. in 1888 but reissued in 1897, *see* Nos. 297*c*/297*e*.

26

27

28

(Printed by De La Rue & Co, Ltd, London and perf at Somerset House, London)

1862–65. Surfaced paper. P 14.

(i) W **27**

186	**26**	1d. dull red (Pl I) (1.4.64)	£250	90·00

(ii) No wmk

187	**26**	1d. dull red (Pl II) (1.65)	£250	80·00
188	**28**	2d. pale blue (25.3.62)	£250	95·00

(Printed from the De La Rue plates in the Colony)

1862 (12 Apr). Wmk double-lined '**2**' (No. 189) or '**5**' (No. 190). P 13.

189	**28**	2d. blue	£120	38·00
		a. Perf 12	£225	50·00
		b. Perf 12×13	£600	£200
190		2d. dull blue (9.62)	£120	40·00

29

1863–69. W **29**. P 13.

191	**26**	1d. pale red (3.69)	£275	38·00
192	**28**	2d. pale blue (4.63)	60·00	3·00
		a. Perf 12		
193		2d. cobalt-blue	60·00	3·00
194		2d. Prussian blue	65·00	3·75

1864–65. W **27**. P 13.

195	**16**	1d. pale red (6.64)	£130	60·00
196	**26**	1d. dark red-brown (Pl I)	£325	48·00
197		1d. brownish red (Pl II)	85·00	10·00
		a. Imperf between (horiz pair)	†	£2500
198		1d. brick-red (Pl II)	85·00	10·00
		a. Highly surfaced paper (1865)	£325	£180
199	**28**	2d. pale blue	£250	6·00

Plates I and II were made from the same die; they can only be distinguished by the colour or by the marginal inscription.

1865–66. Thin to very thin wove paper. No wmk. P 13.

200	**26**	1d. brick-red	£225	48·00
201		1d. brownish red	£225	48·00
202	**28**	2d. pale blue (11.65)	£140	6·00

32

34

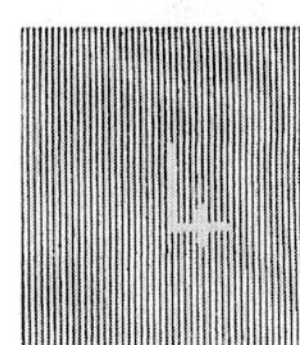

33

35

1867 (Sept)–**93**. W **33** and **35**.

203	**32**	4d. red-brown, P 13	£130	8·50
204		4d. pale red-brown, P 13	£130	8·50
205	**34**	10d. lilac, P 13	55·00	8·50
		a. Imperf between (horiz pair)	£3000	
		s. Optd 'Specimen'	30·00	
206		10d. lilac, P 11 (1893)	18·00	10·00
		a. Perf 10	19·00	12·00
		b. Perf 10×11 or 11×10	27·00	12·00
		c. Perf 12×11	£160	16·00

See also Nos. 269/270.

36

37

38

NINEPENCE

(39)

From 1871 to 1903 the 9d. is formed from the 10d. by a black surch. (T **39**), 15 mm long on Nos. 219 to 220g, and 13½ mm long on subsequent issues.

1871–1902. W **36**.

207	**26**	1d. dull red, P 13 (8.71)	42·00	3·50
		a. Imperf vert (horiz pair)	†	£2750
		b. Imperf between (horiz pair)	†	£2750
208		1d. salmon, P 13 (1878)	42·00	3·75
		a. Perf 10 (6.80)	£250	40·00
		b. Perf 10×13 (6.80)	70·00	8·50
		ba. Perf 13×10	35·00	2·75
		c. *Scarlet*. Perf 10 (4.82)	—	£180
209	**28**	2d. Prussian-blue, P 13 (11.71)	55·00	1·75
		a. Perf 11×12, comb (11.84)	£250	40·00
		c. Imperf between (horiz pair)	†	£3250
210		2d. pale blue, P 13 (1876)	50·00	1·75
		a. Perf 10 (6.80)	£250	23·00
		b. Perf 10×13 (6.80)	£100	16·00
		ba. Perf 13×10	35·00	1·25
		c. Surfaced paper. Perf 13	—	£200
211	**16**	3d. yellow-green, P 13 (3.74)	75·00	5·00
		a. Perf 10 (6.80)	90·00	12·00
		b. Perf 11 (1902)	£160	£100
		c. Perf 12 (5.85)	—	£150
		d. Perf 10×12 or 12×10 (5.85)	£150	40·00
		e. Perf 11×12 (1902)	£130	40·00
212		3d. bright green, P 10 (6.80)	£120	20·00
		a. Perf 13×10 (6.80)	£110	24·00
		b. Perf 13		
213	**32**	4d. pale red-brown, P 13 (8.77)	£120	22·00
214		4d. red-brown, P 13	£120	17·00
		a. Perf 10 (6.80)	£225	60·00
		b. Perf 10×13 (6.80)	£150	24·00
		ba. Perf 13×10	£130	7·00
215	**11**	5d. bluish green, P 10 (8.84)	42·00	48·00
		a. Perf 12 (5.85)	£250	£100
		b. Perf 10×13 or 13×10		
		c. Perf 10×12 (5.85)	£120	65·00
		ca. Perf 12×10	60·00	48·00
216	**37**	6d. bright mauve, P 13 (1.1.72)	£100	2·25
		a. Imperf between (horiz pair)	†	£3000
217		6d. pale lilac, P 13 (1878)	£100	2·25
		a. Perf 10 (6.80)	£200	12·00
		b. Perf 10×13 (6.80)	£140	16·00
		ba. Perf 13×10	£120	2·50
		c. Imperf between (horiz pair). (Perf 13×10)	†	£3000
218	**13**	8d. yellow, P 13 (3.77)	£225	17·00
		a. Wmk sideways	†	—
		b. Perf 10 (6.80)	£350	26·00
		c. Perf 13×10 (6.80)	£250	24·00
219	**34**	9d. on 10d. pale red-brown, P 13 (8.71)	75·00	6·00
220		9d. on 10d. red-brown, P 13 (1878)	75·00	14·00
		a. Perf 10 (6.80)	17·00	12·00
		b. Perf 12 (5.85)	24·00	22·00
		c. Perf 11 (12.85)	60·00	12·00
		d. Perf 12×10 (5.85)	£275	£180
		e. Perf 10×11 or 11×10 (12.85)	70·00	22·00
		g. Perf 12×11, comb (1.84)	18·00	6·50
		ga. Perf 11×12		
		gs. Optd 'Specimen'	28·00	
221	**38**	1s. black, P 13 (1.4.76)	£170	14·00
		aa. Imperf horiz (vert pair)	†	£3000
		a. Perf 10 (6.80)	£225	26·00
		b. Perf 10×13 (6.80)	£250	48·00
		ba. Perf 13×10	£180	16·00
		c. Perf 11		
		e. Imperf (pair)	†	£2750

Stamps from this series without watermark are from the edge of the sheet.

A used horizontal pair of the 2d. Prussian-blue imperf vertically, is in the Royal Philatelic Collection.

Nos. 211b and 211e were printed in 1902 on wmk **36** paper, left over when it was superseded by wmk **40**.

Collectors should note that for issues prior to 1888 (other than those specifically described as 'Perf 11×12, comb' our classification of perforations follows the long-standing convention whereby 'Perf 12' denotes a perforation of 11½, 12 and 'Perf 13' denotes one of 12½, 13.

BISECTS. Between 1887 and 1913 various 1d. and 2d. stamps can be found vertically or diagonally bisected. This was unauthorised.

40

1882 (Apr)–**97**. W **40**.

222	**26**	1d. salmon, P 10	45·00	3·00
		a. Perf 13		
		b. Perf 10×13	†	£200
		ba. Perf 13×10	65·00	3·00
223		1d. orange *to* scarlet, P 13	£850	£450
		a. Perf 10	25·00	2·50
		ab. Imperf between (horiz pair)	†	£3750

		b. Perf 10×13	£120	9·50
		c. Perf 10×12 or 12×10 (4.85)	£275	65·00
		d. Perf 11×10 (12.85)	£475	£120
		e. Perf 12×11 (12.85)	—	£120
		f. Perf 11×12, comb (1.84)	11·00	1·50
		h. Perf 11 (12.85)	—	£140
224	28	2d. pale blue, P 13	£450	90·00
		a. Perf 10	50·00	1·25
		b. Perf 10×13	£150	7·50
		ba. Perf 13×10	70·00	3·25
225		2d. Prussian blue, P 10	60·00	1·00
		b. Perf 12 (4.85)	—	£225
		c. Perf 11 (12.85)	—	£100
		d. Perf 12×11 (12.85)	£400	£100
		e. Perf 10×12 (4.85)	£225	65·00
		ca. Perf 12×10	£400	£100
		f. Perf 10×11 or 11×10 (12.85)	£450	£150
		g. Perf 11×12, comb (1.84)	13·00	1·00
		ga. Printed double	†	£700
		gb. Imperf three sides (left stamp of horizontal pair)	£2250	
226	16	3d. yellow-green, P 10 (1886)	35·00	2·25
		b. Wmk sideways		
		bs. Optd 'Specimen'	27·00	
		c. Perf 10×12	£180	42·00
		ca. Perf 12×10	£140	18·00
		d. Perf 11	10·00	1·00
		da. Imperf vert (horiz pair)	£700	
		e. Perf 11×12 or 12×11	6·00	1·00
		f. Perf 12	15·00	2·50
		g. Imperf (pair)	£500	
227		3d. bluish green, P 10	38·00	2·25
		a. Wmk sideways	60·00	11·00
		b. Perf 11	27·00	2·50
		ba. Imperf between (horiz pair)		
		c. Perf 10×11	38·00	3·25
		ca. Perf 11×10	£100	35·00
		d. Perf 11×12 or 12×11	11·00	2·75
		e. Perf 10×12 or 12×10	50·00	4·25
228		3d. emerald-green, P 10 (1893)	65·00	10·00
		a. Wmk sideways	—	22·00
		b. Perf 10×11	65·00	6·50
		ba. Perf 11×10	£120	42·00
		c. Perf 10×12	60·00	6·50
		ca. Perf 12×10	80·00	9·00
		d. Perf 12×11	—	15·00
229	32	4d. red-brown, P 10	£120	5·50
		a. Perf 10×12 (4.85)	—	£160
		b. Perf 11×12, comb (1.84)	£120	3·00
230		4d. dark brown, P 10	£120	4·75
		a. Perf 12 (4.85)	£325	£200
		b. Perf 10×12 (4.85)	£225	60·00
		ba. Perf 12×10	£325	£150
		c. Perf 11×12, comb (1.84)	85·00	3·00
231	11	5d. dull green, P 10 (1890)	50·00	3·25
		as. Optd. 'Specimen'	27·00	
		b. Perf 11×10	70·00	
		c. Perf 12×10 (4.85)	£100	8·00
232		5d. bright green, P 10	75·00	16·00
		b. Perf 10×11 (12.85)	80·00	11·00
		ba. Perf 11×10	80·00	14·00
		c. Perf 10×12 (4.85)	£160	45·00
		ca. Perf 12×10	£110	75·00
233		5d. blue-green, P 10	26·00	1·75
		a. Perf 12 (4.85)	27·00	1·75
		ab. Wmk sideways	80·00	
		aba. Mixed perfs 12 and 13		
		b. Perf 11 (12.85)	11·00	1·25
		c. Perf 10×11 (12.85)	50·00	3·25
		d. Perf 11×12 or 12×11 (12.85)	11·00	1·25
		da. Wmk sideways (P 11×12)	80·00	25·00
		e. Imperf (pair)	£475	
234	37	6d. pale lilac, P 10	£100	1·50
		a. Perf 10×13 or 13×10	—	£300
		b. Perf 10×12 or 12×10 (4.85)	£110	1·75
235		6d. mauve, P 10	£100	1·50
		a. Perf 12 (4.85)	£130	10·00
		b. Perf 11 (12.85)	£130	8·00
		c. Perf 10×12 (4.85)	£110	8·50
		ca. Perf 12×10	£110	2·50
		cb. Imperf between (horiz pair)	†	£2750
		d. Perf 11×12 (12.85)	£130	14·00
		da. Perf 12×11	£110	2·00
		e. Perf 11×10 or 10×11(12.85)	£120	2·75
236	13	8d. yellow, P 10 (1883)	£250	20·00
		a. Perf 12 (4.85)	£350	30·00
		b. Perf 11 (12.85)	£250	25·00
		c. Perf 10×12 (4.85)	£300	60·00
		ca. Perf 12×10	£275	55·00
236*d*	34	9d. on 10d. red-brown, P 11×12 (28.2.97)	20·00	23·00
		das. Optd 'Specimen'	28·00	
		db. Perf 12	13·00	23·00
		dc. Perf 11	12·00	23·00
		dca. Surch double	£325	£425
236*e*		10d. violet, P 11×12 (1897)	35·00	27·00
		eas. Optd 'Specimen'	32·00	
		eb. Perf 12×11½	12·00	23·00
		ec. Perf 12	23·00	30·00
		ed. Perf 11	27·00	32·00
237	38	1s. black, P 10	£160	7·50
		a. Perf 11 (12.85)	£275	20·00
		b. Perf 10×12	—	£250
		c. Perf 10×13		
		ca. Perf 13×10	£275	28·00
		d. Perf 11×12, comb (1.84)	£150	7·50

41 42

1885–86. W **41** (sideways).

(i) Optd 'POSTAGE', in black

238	42	5s. lilac and green, P 13 (15.10.85).		
		a. Perf 10		
		b. Perf 12×10	£800	£140
239		10s. lilac and claret, P 13 (17.5.86)		
		a. Perf 12	£1700	£225
		ab. Opt double	—	†
240		£1 lilac and claret, P 13 (17.5.86)	—	£8000
		a. Perf 12	£11000	£5000

(ii) Overprinted in blue

241	42	10s. mauve and claret, P 10	£1900	£225
		as. Optd 'Specimen'	80·00	
		b. Perf 12	£300	70·00
		c. Perf 12×11		
242		£1 rose-lilac and claret, P 12×10	£10000	£5000

1886–87. W **41**.

243	26	1d. scarlet, P 10 (12.86)	60·00	17·00
		a. Perf 11×12, comb	20·00	9·50
244	28	2d. deep blue, P 10 (12.87)	£100	23·00
		a. Perf 11×12, comb	42·00	7·50
		b. Imperf (pair)	†	£3000

45 View of Sydney

46 Emu

47 Captain Cook

48 Queen Victoria and Arms of Colony

49 Superb Lyrebird

50 Eastern Grey Kangaroo

51 Map of Australia

52 Capt. Arthur Phillip, first Governor and Lord Carrington, Governor in 1888

(Des M. Tannenberg (1d., 6d.), Miss Catherine Devine (2d., 8d.), H. A. Barraclough (4d.), Govt Ptg Office (1s.), C. Turner (5s.), Mrs Mary Stoddard (20s.). Eng W. Bell).

1888 (1 May)–**89**. Centenary of New South Wales.

(a) W **40**. *P 11×12*

253	45	1d. lilac (9.7.88)	15·00	1·00
		a. Perf 12×11½	24·00	1·25
		b. Perf 12	16·00	50
		c. Imperf (pair)	£2250	
		d. Mauve	14·00	50
		da. Imperf between (pair)		
		db. Perf 12×11½	17·00	70
		dc. Perf 12	17·00	70
254	46	2d. Prussian blue (1.9.88)	22·00	50
		a. Imperf (pair)	£375	£550
		b. Imperf three sides (right stamp of horiz pair)	£1700	
		c. Perf 12×11½	22·00	40
		d. Perf 12	22·00	40
		e. Chalky blue	17·00	40
		ea. Perf 12×11½		
		eb. Perf 12	22·00	60
255	47	4d. purple-brown (8.10.88)	29·00	5·50
		a. Perf 12×11½	50·00	8·50
		b. Perf 12	50·00	5·00
		c. Perf 11	£300	95·00
		d. Red-brown	17·00	5·00
		da. Perf 12×11½	20·00	4·50
		db. Perf 12	20·00	4·50
		e. Orange-brown, P 12×11½	42·00	5·00
		f. Yellow-brown, P 12×11½	24·00	5·00
256	48	6d. carmine (26.11.88)	35·00	4·50
		a. Perf 12×11½	50·00	5·00
		b. Perf 12	35·00	11·00
257	49	8d. lilac-rose (17.1.89)	25·00	9·00
		a. Perf 12×11½	60·00	16·00
		b. Perf 12	25·00	9·50
		c. Magenta	85·00	16·00
		ca. Perf 12×11½	42·00	9·50
		cb. Perf 12	48·00	9·50
258	50	1s. maroon (21.2.89)	55·00	2·50
		a. Perf 12×11½	55·00	3·00
		b. Perf 12	60·00	2·50
		c. Violet-brown	55·00	3·00
		ca. Imperf (pair)	£1400	
		cb. Perf 12×11½	80·00	4·75
		cc. Perf 12	80·00	2·75
253s/8s Optd 'Specimen' *Set of 6*			£200	

(b) W **41**. *P 11×12*

259	45	1d. lilac (1888)	70·00	
		a. Mauve	50·00	7·50
260	46	2d. Prussian blue (1888)	£110	7·00

(c) W **25** *(sideways on 20s.) P 10*

261	51	5s. deep purple (13.3.89)	£425	55·00
		a. Deep violet	£425	60·00
262	52	20s. cobalt-blue (27.4.88)	£750	£160

Nos. 255c and 261/262 are line perforated, the remainder are comb.

A lithographed postal forgery exists of the 2d. on unwatermarked paper and perforated 11 (*Price £450, used*). These were in use in Sydney between March and May 1895, a similar forgery of the 2s. 6d. is also known.

53

54

1890. W **53** (5s.) or **54** (20s.). P 10.

263	51	5s. lilac	£275	32·00
		a. Perf 11	£375	50·00
		ab. Imperf between (horiz pair)		
		b. Perf 12	£450	55·00
		c. Perf 10×11 or 11×10	£375	32·00
		d. Mauve	£375	32·00
		da. Perf 11	£375	50·00
264	52	20s. cobalt-blue	£500	£160
		a. Perf 11	£500	90·00
		b. Perf 10×11		
		c. Ultramarine, P 11	£425	90·00
		ca. Perf 12	£450	£150
		cb. Perf 11×12 or 12×11	£375	90·00
263s/4s Optd 'SPECIMEN' (5s.) or 'Specimen' *Set of 2*			£225	

55 Allegorical figure of Australia

Halfpenny

(56)

SEVEN-PENCE HALFPENNY

(57)

(Des Miss Catherine Devine)

1890 (22 Dec). W **40**.

265	55	2½d. ultramarine, P 11×12 comb	18·00	60
		as. Optd 'Specimen'	30·00	
		b. Perf 12×11½, comb	50·00	50·00
		c. Perf 12, comb	23·00	1·00

WATERMARK VARIETIES: The attention of collectors is drawn to the note on inverted and reversed watermarks on the stamps of the Australian States at the top of the Australia listings.

1891 (5 Jan). Surch as T **56** and **57**. W **40**.

266	26	½d. on 1d. grey, P 11×12 comb	4·50	6·00
		b. Surch double	£800	
267	37	7½d. on 6d. brown, P 10	5·50	10·00
		a. Perf 11	5·00	3·75
		b. Perf 12	14·00	4·50
		c. Perf 11×12 or 12×11	6·50	3·50
		d. Perf 10×12	7·00	5·00
268	38	12½d. on 1s. red, P 10	19·00	35·00
		b. Perf 11	14·00	27·00
		c. Perf 11×12, comb	14·00	19·00
		d. Perf 12×11½, comb	15·00	26·00
		e. Perf 12, comb	32·00	20·00
266/268s Optd 'SPECIMEN' *Set of 3*			85·00	

An unused example of No. 268 exists with the lower line of the T **57** surcharge omitted.

1891 (1 July). Wmk '10' as W **35**. P 10.

269	16	3d. green	16·00	80·00
270		3d. dark green	6·50	19·00

58

Type I. Narrow 'H' in 'HALF'

1892 (21 Mar)–**99**. Type I. W **40**.

271	58	½d. grey, P 10	65·00	2·50
		a. Perf 11	95·00	8·50
		b. Perf 10×12 or 12×10	90·00	12·00
		c. Perf 11×12	5·50	40
		cs. Optd 'SPECIMEN'	22·00	
		d. Perf 12	5·50	1·00
		e. Imperf (pair)		
272		½d. slate, P 11×12 (1897)	4·75	40
		a. Perf 12×11½	4·75	55
		b. Perf 12	4·75	40
		c. Imperf three sides (left stamp of horiz pair). Perf 12×11½	£1900	
273		½d. bluish green, P 11×12 (1.99)	8·00	40
		a. Perf 12×11½	2·00	1·00
		b. Perf 12	8·50	1·75

The perforations 11×12, 12×11½, 12, are from comb machines.

The die for T **58** was constructed from an electro taken from the die of the De La Rue 1d., T **26**, with 'ONE' replaced by 'HALF' and two '½' plugs added to the bottom corners. These alterations proved to be less hard-wearing than the remainder of the die and defects were visible by the 1905 plate of No. 333. It seems likely that repairs were undertaken before printing from the next plate in late 1907 which produced stamps as Type II.

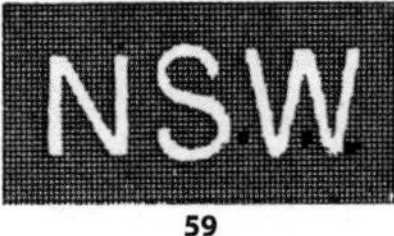

59

1894–1904. Optd 'POSTAGE' in blue. W **59** (sideways).
274 **42** 10s. mauve and claret, P 10 ..... £600 £160
275 10s. violet and claret, P 12 ..... £325 50·00
a. Perf 11 ..... £500 90·00
b. Perf 12×11 ..... £350 60·00
276 10s. violet and aniline crimson, P 12×11 ..... £325 55·00
a. Chalk-surfaced paper (1903) ..... £375 60·00
b. Perf 12 ..... £425 85·00
277 10s. violet and rosine (*chalk-surfaced paper*), P 12 (1904) ..... £375 85·00
a. Perf 11 ..... £425 90·00
b. Perf 12×11 ..... £375 55·00
278 10s. violet and claret (*chalk-surfaced paper*), P 12×11 (1904) ..... £475 95·00
279 £1 violet and claret, P 12×11 .....

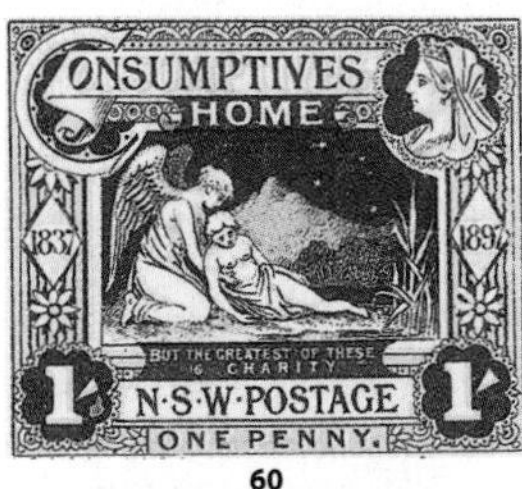

60

61

(Des C. Turner. Litho Govt Printing Office, Sydney)

1897 (22–28 June). Diamond Jubilee and Hospital Charity. T **60/1**. W **40**. P 12×11 (1d.) or 11 (2½d.).
280 **60** 1d. (1s.) green and brown (22.6) ..... 50·00 50·00
281 **61** 2½d. (2s.6d.) gold, carmine and blue (28.6) £250 £225
280s/1s Optd 'Specimen' *Set of 2* £300

These stamps, sold at 1s. and 2s.6d. respectively, paid postage of 1d. and 2½d. only, the difference being given to a Consumptives' Home.

62

63

64

Dies of the 1d.

Die I

Die II

1d. Die I. The first pearl on the crown on the left side is merged into the arch, the shading under the fleur-de-lis is indistinct, the 'S' of 'WALES' is open.

Die II. The first pearl is circular, the vertical shading under the fleur-de-lis clear, the 'S' of 'WALES' not so open.

Dies of the 2½d.

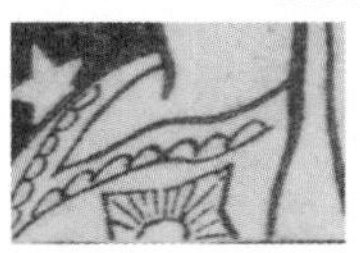
Die I

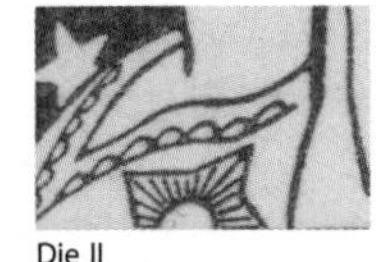
Die II

2½d. Die I. There are 12 radiating lines in the star on the Queen's breast.

Die II. There are 16 radiating lines in the star and the eye is nearly full of colour.

(Des D. Souter (2d., 2½d.). Eng W. Amor)

1897 (22 June)–**99**. W **40** (sideways on 2½d.). P 12×11 (2½d.) or 11×12 (others).
288 **62** 1d. carmine (Die I) ..... 5·00 1·00
a. Perf 12×11½ ..... 5·00 1·00
s. Optd 'Specimen' ..... 24·00
289 1d. scarlet (Die I) ..... 10·00 1·25
a. Perf 12×11½ ..... 10·00 1·50
b. Perf 12 ..... 10·00 1·75
ba. Imperf horiz (vert pair) £850
290 1d. rose-carmine (Die II) (10.97) ..... 5·00 50
a. Perf 12×11½ ..... 4·00 50
b. Perf 12 ..... 7·00 50
c. Imperf (pair) ..... £750 †
d. Imperf between (pair) £1200
291 1d. salmon-red (Die II) (P 12×11½) ..... 7·50 1·25
a. Perf 12 ..... 10·00 1·75
292 **63** 2d. deep dull blue ..... 17·00 1·50
a. Perf 12×11½ ..... 8·50 1·50
b. Perf 12 ..... 17·00 1·50
s. Optd 'Specimen' ..... 24·00
293 2d. cobalt-blue ..... 18·00 1·00
a. Perf 12×11½ ..... 7·00 1·00
b. Perf 12 ..... 15·00 1·00
294 2d. ultramarine (1.12.97) ..... 15·00 50
a. Perf 12×11½ ..... 4·25 50
b. Perf 12 ..... 4·25 50
s. Optd 'Specimen' ..... 25·00
295 **64** 2½d. purple (Die I) ..... 29·00 2·50
a. Perf 11½×12 ..... 30·00 2·50
b. Perf 11 ..... 30·00 3·75
s. Optd 'Specimen' ..... 25·00
296 2½d. deep violet (Die II) (11.97) ..... 40·00 2·25
a. Perf 11½×12 ..... 30·00 2·25
b. Perf 12 ..... 32·00 2·25
297 2½d. Prussian blue (17.1.99) ..... 26·00 3·25
a. Perf 11½×12 ..... 7·00 3·50
b. Perf 12 ..... 7·00 4·50

The perforations 11×12, 12×11½ and 12 are from comb machines, the perforation 11 is from a single-line machine.

Nos. 288/296 were originally issued in celebration of Queen Victoria's Diamond Jubilee.

1897–99. Reissue of T **24**. W **25**. P 11.
297*c* 5s. reddish purple (*shades*) ..... 48·00 13·00
ca. Imperf between (horiz pair) £9500
d. Perf 12 ..... 70·00 42·00
e. Perf 11×12 or 12×11 ..... 50·00 19·00

1898–99. W **40**. P 11×12.
297*f* **48** 6d. emerald-green ..... 32·00 32·00
fa. Perf 12×11½ ..... 38·00 20·00
fb. Perf 12 ..... 28·00 20·00
fs. Optd 'Specimen' ..... 27·00
297*g* 6d. orange-yellow (1899) ..... 35·00 12·00
ga. Perf 12×11½ ..... 17·00 11·00
gb. Perf 12 ..... 35·00 11·00
gc. Yellow, P 12×11½ ..... 17·00 6·00

1899 (Oct). Chalk-surfaced paper. W **40** (sideways on 2½d.). P 12×11½ or 11½×12 (2½d.), comb.
298 **58** ½d. blue-green (Type I) ..... 3·75 1·50
a. Imperf (pair) £250 £350
299 **62** 1d. carmine (Die II) ..... 6·00 1·00
a. Imperf horiz (vert pair) £1000
300 1d. scarlet (Die II) ..... 6·00 1·00
a. Imperf three sides (block of four) £1200
b. Perf 11 ..... † £1200
c. Mixed perfs 12×11½ and 11 .....
301 1d. salmon-red (Die II) ..... 23·00 1·75
a. Imperf (pair) £275 £350
b. Mixed perfs 12×11½ and 11 .....
302 **63** 2d. cobalt-blue ..... 5·50 1·00
a. Imperf (pair) £300
b. Imperf horiz (vert pair) £1800
303 **64** 2½d. Prussian blue (Die II) ..... 9·00 1·00
a. Imperf (pair) £350
303*b* **47** 4d. red-brown ..... 35·00 16·00
c. Imperf (pair) £600
304 4d. orange-brown ..... 18·00 7·50
305 **48** 6d. deep orange ..... 50·00 4·75
a. Imperf (pair) £600
306 6d. orange-yellow ..... 16·00 9·00
307 6d. emerald-green ..... 90·00 25·00
a. Imperf (pair) £600
308 **49** 8d. magenta ..... 45·00 5·50
309 **34** 9d. on 10d. dull brown ..... 11·00 22·00
a. Surcharge double £275 £600
b. Albino surcharge £275
310 10d. violet ..... 25·00 28·00
311 **50** 1s. maroon ..... 27·00 3·50
312 1s. purple-brown ..... 27·00 4·25
a. Imperf (pair) £700

65 The spacing between the Crown and 'NSW' is 1 mm in T **65** as against 2 mm in T **40**

66 Superb Lyrebird

67

1902–03. Chalk-surfaced paper. W **65** (sideways on 2½d.). P 12×11½ or 11½×12 (2½d.), comb.
313 **58** ½d. blue-green (Type I) ..... 4·75 40
a. Perf 12×11 ..... 4·75 40
b. Mixed perfs 12×11½ and 11 ..... £650
314 **62** 1d. carmine (Die II) ..... 2·75 20
a. Perf 11 ..... † £1100
315 **63** 2d. cobalt-blue ..... 7·50 1·50
a. Imperf (pair) £400
b. Perf 11 ..... — —
c. Mixed perfs 12×11½ and 11 .....
316 **64** 2½d. dark blue (Die II) ..... 14·00 1·00
317 **47** 4d. orange-brown ..... 55·00 14·00
318 **48** 6d. yellow-orange ..... 22·00 9·00
319 6d. orange ..... 30·00 3·25
320 6d. orange-buff ..... 50·00 3·75
321 **49** 8d. magenta ..... 22·00 8·50
322 **34** 9d. on 10d. brownish orange ..... 10·00 5·00
323 10d. violet ..... 25·00 27·00
324 **50** 1s. maroon ..... 75·00 2·75
325 1s. purple-brown ..... 75·00 2·75
326 **66** 2s.6d. green (1903) ..... 45·00 23·00
s. Optd 'SPECIMEN' ..... 80·00

1903–08. W **65**.
327 **16** 3d. yellow-green, P 11 ..... 14·00 1·75
b. Perf 12 ..... 14·00 1·75
ba. Imperf between (horiz pair) .....
c. Perf 11×12 or 12×11 ..... 10·00 1·00
328 3d. dull green, P 12 ..... 50·00 5·00
a. Perf 11×12 or 12×11 ..... 25·00 3·75
b. Perf 11 ..... 25·00 3·75
329 **11** 5d. dark blue-green, P 11×12 or 12×11 ..... 10·00 1·50
a. Wmk sideways ..... 35·00 7·00
b. Perf 11 ..... 28·00 1·50
ba. Wmk sideways ..... — 65·00
c. Perf 12 ..... 50·00 6·50
ca. Wmk sideways ..... £120 65·00
d. Imperf (pair) £450

Stamps from this series without watermark are from the edge of the sheet.

(Typo Victoria Govt Printer, Melbourne)

1903 (18 July). Wmk double-lined V over Crown. W w **10**.
330 **67** 9d. brown and ultramarine, P 12¼×12½, comb ..... 18·00 3·25
s. Optd 'SPECIMEN.' ..... 48·00
331 9d. brown and deep blue, P 12¼×12½, *comb* ..... 18·00 3·25
332 9d. brown and blue, P 11 ..... £4500 £1600

Type II. Broad 'H' in 'HALF'

68

1905 (1 Oct)–**10**. Chalk-surfaced paper. W **68** (sideways on 2½d.). P 12×11½ or 11½×12 (2½d.) comb, unless otherwise stated.
333 **58** ½d. blue-green (Type I) ..... 4·50 1·00
a. Perf 11½×11 ..... 17·00 2·50
b. Type II (1908) ..... 2·75 1·25
ba. Type I (substituted cliché) in pair with Die II ..... 95·00 85·00
bb. Perf 11½×11 ..... 3·25 1·25
bc. Mixed perfs 12×11½ and 11 .....
334 **62** 1d. rose-carmine (Die II) ..... 2·75 10
a. Double impression £550 £650
b. Perf 11½×11 ..... 10·00 75
335 **63** 2d. deep ultramarine ..... 2·25 40
b. Perf 11½×11 ..... 2·75 40
c. Perf 11 .....
336 2d. milky blue (1910) ..... 4·75 20
a. Perf 11 ..... 60·00 80·00
b. Perf 11½×11 ..... 4·75 30
337 **64** 2½d. Prussian blue (Die II) ..... 4·00 2·75
338 **47** 4d. orange-brown ..... 10·00 4·25
339 4d. red-brown ..... 13·00 5·50
340 **48** 6d. dull yellow ..... 19·00 4·50
a. Perf 11½×11 ..... 23·00 6·50
341 6d. orange-yellow ..... 19·00 2·50
a. Perf 11½×11 ..... 28·00 7·50
342 6d. deep orange ..... 16·00 2·50
a. Perf 11 ..... £350
343 6d. orange-buff ..... 23·00 2·75
a. Perf 11½×11 ..... 32·00 6·00
344 **49** 8d. magenta ..... 27·00 8·00
345 8d. lilac-rose ..... 55·00 8·00
346 **34** 10d. violet ..... 19·00 9·00
a. Perf 11½×11 ..... 13·00 6·00
b. Perf 11 ..... 13·00 7·00
347 **50** 1s. maroon ..... 27·00 1·75
348 1s. purple-brown (1908) ..... 42·00 2·75
349 **66** 2s.6d. blue-green ..... 90·00 45·00
a. Perf 11½×11 ..... 80·00 19·00
b. Perf 11 ..... 45·00 24·00

No. 333ba occurred when a block of four units from the Type II plate (R. 3/5-4/6) were replaced by new clichés, one of which (right pane, R. 4/6) was Type I.

69

1905 (Dec). W **69**. Chalk-surfaced paper. P 11.
350 **52** 20s. cobalt-blue ..... £375 80·00
a. Perf 12 ..... £400 85·00
b. Perf 11×12 or 12×11 ..... £375 70·00

(Typo Victoria Govt Printer, Melbourne)

1905 (Dec). Wmk double-lined 'A' and Crown, W w **11**. P 12×12½ comb.
351 **67** 9d. brown and ultramarine ..... 27·00 1·75
a. Perf 11 ..... £120 70·00
b. Mixed perfs 12×12½ and 11 ..... £1600
352 9d. yellow-brown and ultramarine ..... 18·00 1·75
a. Perf 11 ..... £130 75·00

1907 (July–Dec). W w **11** (sideways on 2½d.). P 12×11½ or 11½×12 (2½d.), comb, unless otherwise stated.
353 **58** ½d. blue-green (Type I) ..... 4·75 7·00
354 **62** 1d. dull rose (Die II) ..... 27·00 5·00

355	63	2d. cobalt-blue	7·50	5·00
		a. Wmk sideways	—	£325
356	64	2½d. Prussian blue (Die II)	70·00	£130
357	47	4d. orange-brown	32·00	32·00
358	48	6d. orange-buff	50·00	50·00
359		6d. dull yellow	50·00	50·00
360	49	8d. magenta	32·00	50·00
361	34	10d. violet, P 11 (12.07)	35·00	60·00
362	50	1s. purple-brown	75·00	12·00
		a. Perf 11	†	£1700
363	66	2s.6d. blue-green	£120	£120

Stamps from this series without watermark are from the edge of the sheet.

STAMP BOOKLETS

There are very few surviving examples of Nos. SB1/SB4. Listings are provided for those believed to have been issued with prices quoted for those known to still exist.

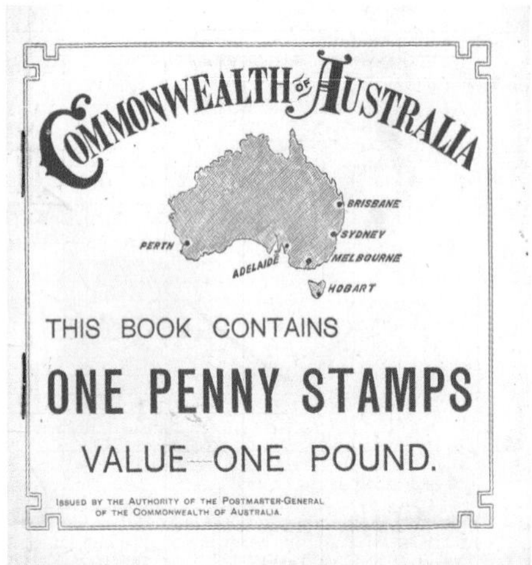

B **1** *(Illustration reduced. Actual size* 150×175 *mm)*

1904 (May)–**09**. Black on red cover as Type B **1** and picture of one of six different State GPO's on back. Stapled.

SB1	£1 booklet containing 240×1d. in four blocks of 30 and two blocks of 60	
	a. Red-brown on pink cover (1909)	
	b. Blue on pink cover	
	c. Purple-brown on pink cover	

1904 (May). Black on grey cover as No. SB1. Stapled.

SB2	£1 booklet containing 120×2d. in four blocks of 30	

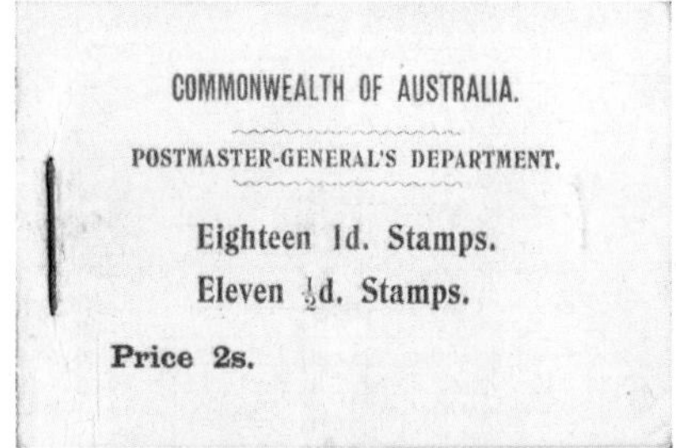

B **2** *(Illustration reduced. Actual size* 85×57 *mm)*

1910 (May). Black on cream. cover 80-85×55-57 mm, as Type B **2**.

SB3	2s. booklet containing 11×½d. (No. 333), either in block of 6 plus block of 5 or block of 11, and 18×1d. (No. 334), either in three blocks of 6 or block of 6 plus block of 12	£7000
	a. Red-brown on pink cover	

Unsold stocks of Nos. SB3/SB3a were uprated with one additional ½d. in May 1911.

1911 (Aug). Red on pink cover as No. SB3. Stapled.

SB4	2s. booklet containing 12×½d. (No. 333), either in two blocks of 6 or block of 12, and 18×1d. (No. 334) either in three blocks of 6 or one block of 6 plus block of 12	£6000

OFFICIAL STAMPS

O S (O 1) O S (O 2) O S (O 3)

The space between the letters is normally 7 mm as illustrated, except on the 5d. and 8d. (11–11½ *mm*), 5s. (12 *mm*) and 20s. (14 *mm*). Later printings of the 3d., W **40**, are 5½ mm, and these are listed. A wide (8.5 *mm*) variety exists at R. 4/4 on all values other than the 3d., 5d., 8d., 5s., 10s. and 20s.

Varieties of Type O **1** exist with 'O' sideways.

Nos. O1/O35 overprinted with Type O **1**

1879. Wmk double-lined '**6**'. P 13.

O1	16	3d. dull green	—	£600

1879 (Oct)–**85**. W **36**. P 13.

O2	26	1d. salmon	55·00	2·75
		a. Perf 10 (5.81)	£190	38·00
		b. Perf 13×10 (1881)	65·00	4·50
O3	28	2d. blue	55·00	2·50
		a. Perf 10 (7.81)	£225	35·00
		b. Perf 10×13 (1881)	80·00	25·00
		ba. Perf 13×10	65·00	3·50
		d. Perf 11×12 (11.84?)	—	£225
O4	16	3d. dull green (R.) (12.79)	£1000	£375
O5		3d. dull green (3.80)	£325	75·00
		a. Perf 10 (1881)	£190	65·00
		b. Yellow-green. Perf 10 (10.81)	£180	30·00
		ba. Perf 13×10 (1881)	£170	30·00
		bb. Perf 12 (4.85)	£225	55·00
		be. Perf 10×12 or 12×10 (4.85)	£225	55·00
O6	32	4d. red-brown	£325	9·50
		a. Perf 10 (1881)	—	£225
		b. Perf 10×13 (1881)	£350	90·00
		ba. Perf 13×10	£275	14·00
O7	11	5d. green, P 10 (8.84)	27·00	35·00
O8	37	6d. pale lilac	£300	7·00
		a. Perf 10 (1881)	£425	42·00
		b. Perf 13×10 (1881)	£275	42·00
O9	13	8d. yellow (R.) (12.79)	—	£600
O10		8d. yellow (1880)	—	50·00
		a. Perf 10 (1881)	£500	90·00
O11	34	9d. on 10d. brown, P 10 (30.5.80)	£1100	£1000
		s. Optd 'Specimen'	65·00	
O12	38	1s. black (R.)	£500	24·00
		a. Perf 10 (1881)	—	40·00
		b. Perf 10×13 (1881)	—	50·00
		ba. Perf 13×10	—	12·00

Other stamps are known with red overprint but their status is in doubt.

1880–88. W **25**.

		(a) P 13		
O13	24	5s. deep purple (15.2.80)	£850	£100
		a. Royal purple	—	£300
		b. Deep rose-lilac	£850	£100
		(b) P 10		
O14	24	5s. deep purple (9.82)	£850	£170
		a. Opt double	£4250	£1700
		b. Rose-lilac (1883)	£600	£120
		ba. Opt double, one albino		
		(c) P 10×12		
O15	24	5s. purple (10.86)		
		(d) P 12×10		
O16	24	5s. reddish purple (1886)	£750	£120
		(e) P 12		
O17	24	5s. purple	†	£650
		(f) P 11		
O18	24	5s. rose-lilac (1888)	£475	95·00

1880 (31 May). W **35**. P 13.

O18*a*	34	10d. lilac	£425	£120
		ab. Perf 10 and 11, compound	£425	£200
		ac. Perf 10	£425	
		aca. Opt double, one albino	£475	
		as. Optd 'Specimen'	70·00	

1882–85. W **40**. P 10.

O19	26	1d. salmon	80·00	4·75
		a. Perf 13×10	—	£130
O20		1d. orange *to* scarlet	28·00	2·00
		a. Perf 10×13	—	£130
		b. Perf 11×12, comb (1.84)	14·00	1·40
		c. Perf 10×12 or 12×10 (4.85)	—	£110
		d. Perf 12×11 (12.85)		
O21	28	2d. blue	42·00	1·00
		a. Perf 10×13 or 13×10	£200	75·00
		c. Perf 11×12, comb (1.84)	9·50	1·00
		ca. Opt double	£950	£400
		e. Perf 12×11 (12.85)		
O22	16	3d. yellow-green (7 *mm*)	15·00	5·00
		aa. Opt double, one albino	£160	
		a. Wmk sideways	£225	£110
		b. Perf 12 (4.85)	£120	80·00
		ba. Opt double, one albino	£250	
		c. Perf 12×10 (4.85)	—	7·50
		ca. Opt double	†	£650
		d. Perf 12×11		
O23		3d. bluish green (7 *mm*)	32·00	8·50
		a. Perf 12 (4.85)	£120	80·00
		b. Perf 12×10 (4.85)		
		c. Perf 10×11 (12.85)		
O24		3d. yellow-green (5½ *mm*)	16·00	5·50
		a. Wmk sideways	40·00	38·00
		as. Optd 'Specimen'	38·00	
		b. Perf 10×12 or 12×10 (4.85)	28·00	5·50
		c. Perf 10×11 or 11×10 (12.85)	—	7·00
O25		3d. bluish green (5½ *mm*)	12·00	11·00
		a. Wmk sideways		
		b. Perf 10×12 or 12×10 (4.85)	17·00	12·00
		c. Perf 10×11 or 11×10 (12.85)	5·00	4·25
O26	32	4d. red-brown	75·00	5·50
		a. Perf 11×12, comb (1.84)	19·00	4·00
		b. Perf 10×12 (4.85)	—	70·00
O27		4d. dark brown	42·00	4·00
		a. Perf 11×12, comb (1.84)	20·00	4·00
		b. Perf 12 (4.85)	£250	£150
		c. Perf 10×12 (4.85)	£250	90·00
O28	11	5d. dull green	25·00	27·00
		a. Perf 12×10 (4.85)		
O29		5d. blue-green	26·00	35·00
		a. Perf 12 (4.85)	£100	£120
		as. Optd 'Specimen'	38·00	
		b. Perf 10×11	15·00	20·00
		c. Perf 11	†	£150
O30	37	6d. pale lilac	22·00	5·50
		a. Perf 11 (12.85)	55·00	8·00
O31		6d. mauve	22·00	7·00
		a. Perf 12 (4.85)	—	45·00
		b. Perf 10×12 or 12×10 (4.85)	22·00	6·50
		d. Perf 11×10 (12.85)	22·00	7·00
		e. Perf 11×12		
		ea. Perf 12×11 (12.85)	85·00	19·00
O32	13	8d. yellow	26·00	11·00
		aa. Opt double	†	£1300
		a. Perf 12 (4.85)	£150	45·00
		b. Perf 10×12 or 12×10 (4.85)	26·00	11·00
		ba. Opt double	£1300	
		d. Perf 11 (12.85)	26·00	28·00
O33	38	1s. black (R.)	55·00	15·00
		a. Perf 10×13	—	60·00
		b. Perf 11×12, comb (1.84)	29·00	8·00
		ba. Opt double	—	£500

1886–87. W **41**. P 10.

O34	26	1d. scarlet	£100	8·00
O35	28	2d. deep blue	†	£600
		a. Perf 11×12, comb	†	£600

1887–90. Nos. 241/2 optd in black.

		(a) With Type O 1		
O36	42	10s. mauve and claret, P 12 (1890)	—	£3750
		(b) With Type O 2 (30 April 1889)		
O37	42	10s. mauve and claret P 12	£6000	£1400
		as. Optd 'Specimen'	£110	
		b. Perf 10	£7500	£3000
		(c) With Type O 3 (7 Jan 1887)		
O38	42	£1 mauve and claret, P 12×10	£40000	£19000

Only nine examples of No. O38 are recorded, three of which are mint. One of the used stamps, in the Royal Collection, shows overprint Type O **3** double.

1888 (17 July)–**90**. Optd as Type O **1**.

		(a) W 40. P 11×12		
O39	45	1d. lilac	6·00	1·00
		a. Perf 12	3·75	1·00
		b. Mauve	3·50	1·00
		ba. Perf 12	3·75	1·00
O40	46	2d. Prussian blue (15.10.88)	4·50	60
		aa. Opt double, one albino		
		ab. Opt double	—	†
		a. Perf 12	9·00	2·50
O41	47	4d. purple-brown (10.10.89)	11·00	4·25
		a. Perf 12	18·00	6·00
		b. Perf 11		
		c. Red-brown	13·00	3·75
		ca. Opt double	†	£650
		cb. Perf 12	22·00	6·00
O42	48	6d. carmine (16.1.89)	9·00	10·00
		a. Perf 12	20·00	10·00
		ab. Opt double	—	†
O43	49	8d. lilac-rose (1890)	26·00	12·00
		a. Perf 12	55·00	17·00
O44	50	1s. maroon (9.1.90)	45·00	4·00
		a. Perf 12	45·00	4·50
		b. Purple-brown	42·00	4·75
		ba. Opt double		
		bb. Perf 12	45·00	7·00
O39s/O44s Optd 'Specimen' *Set of* 6			£250	
		(b) W 41. P 11×12 (1889)		
O45	45	1d. mauve		
O46	46	2d. blue		
		(c) W 25. P 10		
O47	51	5s. deep purple (R.) (9.1.90)	£2000	£800
O48	52	20s. cobalt-blue (10.3.90)	£20000	£1100

1890 (15 Feb)–**91**. Optd as Type O **1**. W **53** (5s.) or **54** (20s.). P 10.

O49	51	5s. lilac	£650	£170
		a. Mauve	£400	£100
		b. Dull lilac, P 12	£800	£170
O50	52	20s. cobalt-blue (3.91)	£21000	£1100
O49s/O50s Optd 'SPECIMEN' *Set of* 2			£250	

The used prices quoted for Nos. O48 and O50 are for cancelled-to-order examples.

1891 (Jan). Optd as Type O **1**. W **40**.

		(a) On No. 265. P 11×12		
O54	55	2½d. ultramarine	14·00	11·00
		(b) On Nos. 266/268		
O55	26	½d. on 1d. grey, P 11×12	70·00	80·00
		a. Opt double	£1500	†
O56	37	7½d. on 6d. brown, P 10	50·00	70·00
O57	38	12½d. on 1s. red, P 11×12	70·00	£110
O54s/O57s Optd 'Specimen' *Set of* 4			£150	

1892 (May). No. 271 optd as Type O **1**. P 10.

O58	58	½d. grey	14·00	20·00
		a. Perf 11×12	5·50	17·00
		as. Optd 'SPECIMEN'	32·00	
		b. Perf 12	12·00	12·00
		c. Perf 12×11½	35·00	18·00

Official stamps were withdrawn from the government departments on 31 December 1894.

POSTAGE DUE STAMPS

D **1**

(Dies eng by A. Collingridge. Typo Govt Printing Office, Sydney)

1891 (1 Jan)–**97**. W **40**. P 10.

D1	D 1	½d. green (21.1.92)	12·00	7·00
D2		1d. green	35·00	4·00
		a. Imperf vert (horiz pair)	†	£6000
		b. Perf 11 (1896)	23·00	3·50
		c. Perf 12	80·00	40·00
		d. Perf 12×10 (1892)	80·00	40·00
		e. Perf 10×11 (1894)	38·00	8·00
		f. Perf 11×12 or 12×11	25·00	3·50
D3		2d. green	24·00	4·00
		a. Perf 11	24·00	3·50
		b. Perf 12 (1897)	80·00	40·00
		c. Perf 12×10 (1894)	80·00	40·00
		d. Perf 10×11 (1894)	32·00	11·00
		e. Perf 11×12 or 12×11	24·00	4·00
		f. Wmk sideways	70·00	20·00
D4		3d. green	65·00	14·00
		a. Perf 10×11 (1893)	65·00	14·00
D5		4d. green	60·00	3·75
		a. Perf 11		
		b. Perf 10×11 (1893)	50·00	3·75
		c. Perf 10×12	†	£1000
D6		6d. green	60·00	15·00
D7		8d. green	£120	27·00
D8		5s. green	£275	50·00
		a. Perf 11	£750	£180
		b. Perf 11×12	—	£325

D9		10s. green	£750	70·00
		a. Perf 12×10	£550	
D10		20s. green	£850	£100
		a. Perf 12	£1500	
		b. Perf 12×10	£650	
D1s/D10s Optd 'SPECIMEN' *Set of* 10 (incl D3fs)			£225	

Used prices for 10s. and 20s. are for cancelled-to-order stamps. Postally used examples are very rare.

1900. Chalk-surfaced paper. W **40**. P 11.

D12	D **1**	1d. emerald-green	27·00	4·75
		a. Perf 12	50·00	13·00
		b. Perf 11×12 or 12×11	29·00	4·25
D13		2d. emerald-green	35·00	6·50
		a. Perf 12	—	£100
		b. Perf 11×12 or 12×11	26·00	6·50
D14		3d. emerald-green, P 11×12 or 12×11	90·00	27·00
D15		4d. emerald-green (7.00)	60·00	13·00

TELEGRAPH STAMPS

T **1**

(Des of vignette H. T. Glover. Vignette litho, frame typo Govt Printer)

1871 (1 Feb). W **41** (sideways). Bluish paper. P 13.

T1	1d. black and brownish red	£180
T2	2d. black and blue	£275
T3	6d. black and Indian red	£275
T4	1s. black and bright blue	£400
T5	2s. black and brown	£750
T6	4s. black and mauve	£950
T7	6s. black and carmine	£1400
T8	8s. black and lilac	£1700
	a. Perf 10	£1500

New South Wales became part of the Commonwealth of Australia on 1 January 1901

QUEENSLAND

The area which later became Queensland was previously part of New South Wales known as the Moreton Bay District. The first post office, at Brisbane, was opened in 1834 and the use of New South Wales stamps from the District became compulsory from 1 May 1854.

Queensland was proclaimed a separate colony on 10 December 1859, but continued to use New South Wales issues until 1 November 1860.

Post Offices opened in the Moreton Bay District before 10 December 1859, and using New South Wales stamps, were

Office	*Opened*	*Numeral Cancellation*
Brisbane	1834	95
Burnett's Inn/Goode's Inn/Nanango	1850	108
Callandoon	1850	74
Condamine	1856	151
Dalby	1854	133
Drayton	1846	85
Gayndah	1850	86
Gladstone	1854	131
Goode's Inn	1858	108
Ipswich	1846	87
Maryborough	1849	96
Rockhampton	1858	201
Surat	1852	110
Taroom	1856	152
Toowoomba	1858	214
Warwick	1848	81

PRICES FOR STAMPS ON COVER

Nos. 1/3	*from* × 2
Nos. 4/56	*from* × 3
Nos. 57/58	—
Nos. 59/73	*from* × 4
Nos. 74/82	*from* × 2
Nos. 83/109	*from* × 3
Nos. 110/113	*from* × 2
Nos. 116/117	*from* × 3
Nos. 118/127	—
Nos. 128/150	*from* × 4
Nos. 151/165	—
Nos. 166/178	*from* × 10
Nos. 179/183	*from* × 4
Nos. 184/206	*from* × 15
No. 207	—
Nos. 208/228	*from* × 15
No. 229	*from* × 100
No. 230	—
Nos. 231/254	*from* × 15
Nos. 256/262*c*	*from* × 10
Nos. 264*a*/264*b*	*from* × 2
Nos. 265/266	*from* × 20
Nos. 270/274	—
Nos. 281/285	*from* × 10
Nos. 286/308	*from* × 12
Nos. 309/313	—
Nos. F1/F37	—

PERKINS BACON 'CANCELLED'. For notes on these handstamps, showing 'CANCELLED' between horizontal bars forming an oval, see Catalogue Introduction.

1

2 Large Star

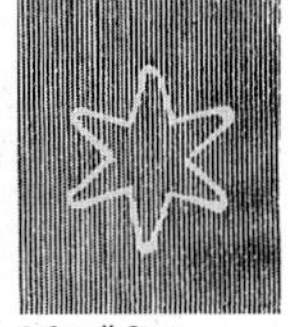
3 Small Star

(Dies eng W. Humphrys. Recess P.B.)

1860. W **2**.

(a) Imperf

1	**1**	1d. carmine-rose	£6500	£800
2		2d. blue	£18000	£2000
3		6d. green	£11000	£850
		(b) Clean-cut perf 14–16		
4	**1**	1d. carmine-rose	£3000	£300
5		2d. blue	£1500	£110
		a. Imperf between (horiz pair)	†	—
6		6d. green (15.11)	£1500	70·00

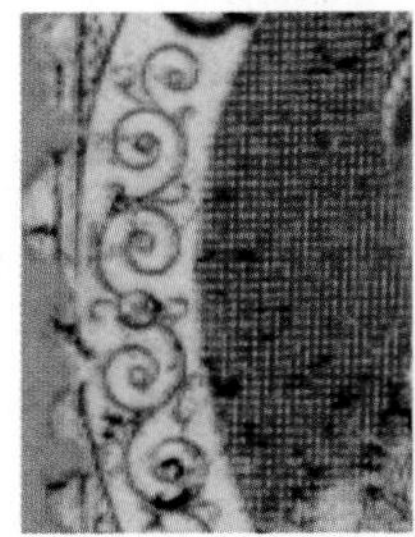
3d. re-entry

3d. retouch (R.2/8)

The 3d. re-entry which occurs on one stamp in the second row, shows doubling of the left-hand arabesque and the retouch has redrawn spandrel dots under 'EN' of 'PENCE', a single dot in the centre of the circle under 'E' and the bottom outer frame line closer to the spandrel's frame line.

1860–61. W **3**.

		(a) Clean-cut perf 14–16		
7	**1**	2d. blue	£1100	£110
		a. Imperf between (horiz pair)	†	£11000
8		3d. brown (15.4.61)	£850	75·00
		a. Re-entry	—	£275
		b. Retouch	—	£275
9		6d. green	£1500	75·00
10		1s. violet (15.11.60) (H/S 'CANCELLED' in oval £10000)	£1600	£110
11		'REGISTERED' (6d.) olive-yellow (1.61) (H/S 'CANCELLED' in oval £10000)	£1100	£100
		a. Imperf between (pair)	£13000	
		(b) Clean-cut perf 14 at Somerset House (7.61)		
12	**1**	1d. carmine-rose (H/S 'CANCELLED' in oval £9500)	£425	60·00
13		2d. blue (H/S 'CANCELLED' in oval £9500)	£950	65·00
		(c) Rough perf 14–16 (9.61)		
14	**1**	1d. carmine-rose	£110	50·00
15		2d. blue	£325	28·00
		a. Imperf between (horiz pair)	£10000	
16		3d. brown (H/S 'CANCELLED' in oval £11000)	85·00	32·00
		a. Imperf vert (horiz pair)	£10000	
		b. Re-entry	£400	£140
		c. Retouch (R. 2/8)	—	£140
17		6d. deep green (H/S 'CANCELLED' in oval £10000)	£600	30·00
18		6d. yellow-green	£700	30·00
19		1s. violet	£1200	90·00
20		'REGISTERED' (6d.) orange-yellow	£120	40·00

The perforation of No. 8 is that known as 'intermediate between clean-cut and rough', No. 20 can also be found with a similar perforation.

Line through design

(Printed and perforated by Thomas Ham, Brisbane)

1862–67. Thick toned paper. No wmk.

		(a) P 13 rough perforations (1862–1863)		
21	**1**	1d. Indian red (16.12.62)	£500	75·00
22		1d. orange-vermilion (2.63)	£110	17·00
		a. Imperf (pair)	—	£2750
23		2d. pale blue (16.12.62)	£140	27·00
24		2d. blue	85·00	9·00
		a. Imperf (pair)	—	£2500
		b. Imperf between (horiz pair)	†	£15000
		c. Imperf between (vert pair)	£5500	
25		3d. brown	£120	45·00
		a. Re-entry	—	£140
		b. Retouch (R. 2/8)	—	£140
26		6d. apple green (17.4.63)	£180	15·00
		a. Line through design at right	—	£130
		b. Line through design at left	—	£130
27		6d. yellow-green	£170	12·00
		a. Imperf between (horiz pair)	†	£16000
		b. Line through design at right	—	£110
		c. Line through design at left	—	£110
28		6d. pale bluish green	£275	45·00
		a. Imperf (pair)	—	£2750
		b. Line through design at right	—	£225
		c. Line through design at left	—	£225
29		1s. grey (14.7.63)	£375	24·00
		a. Imperf between (horiz pair)	†	£17000
		b. Imperf between (vert pair)	†	—
		s. Handstamped 'SPECIMEN'	55·00	

The top or bottom row of perforations was sometimes omitted from the sheet, resulting in stamps perforated on three sides only.

Prior to the plates being printed from in Brisbane, damage occurred to the 6d. plate in the form of a scratch across two adjoining stamps. The position of the pair in the plate is not yet recorded. One joined pair is known.

This flaw was not corrected until around 1869 when, after plate cleaning, only faint traces remain. These are hard to see.

The Royal Philatelic Collection contains an example of No. 22 imperf between (horizontal pair), used.

		(b) P 12½×13 rough (1863–1867)		
30	**1**	1d. orange-vermilion	£120	32·00
31		2d. blue	£110	20·00
32		3d. brown	£130	27·00
		a. Re-entry	—	£130
		b. Retouch (R. 2/8)	—	£130
33		6d. apple green	£225	50·00
		a. Line through design at right	—	£300
		b. Line through design at left	—	£300
34		6d. yellow-green	£225	50·00
		a. Line through design at right	—	£300
		b. Line through design at left	—	£300
35		6d. pale bluish green		
		a. Line through design at right		
		b. Line through design at left		
36		1s. grey	£600	45·00
		a. Imperf between (horiz pair)		

This paper was used again for a very limited printing in 1867 which can be properly regarded as the First Government Printing. The perforations were now clean-cut. The designs and the background to the head are very well defined, the plates having been cleaned when transferred to the Government Printing Office.

	(c) P 13 Clean-cut (1867)		
37	1d. orange-vermilion	£120	28·00
38	2d. blue	90·00	11·00
40	6d. apple green	£225	19·00
41	6d. yellow-green	£225	23·00
42	6d. deep green		

Previously listed and then removed, the significance of this issue has been reassessed and it is now re-listed under this paper.

Copies of the 3d. and 1s. have been identified with these characteristics but there are no records of them being printed at this time.

1864–65. W **3**.

		(a) P 13		
44	**1**	1d. orange-vermilion (1.65)	£120	60·00
		a. Imperf between (horiz pair)	£6000	
45		2d. pale blue (1.65)	£120	17·00
46		2d. deep blue	£120	17·00
		a. Imperf between (vert pair)	£9000	
		b. Imperf between (horiz pair)	†	£16000
		c. Bisected (1d.) (*on cover*)	†	£4000
47		6d. yellow-green (1.65)	£225	22·00
		a. Line through design at right	—	£160
		b. Line through design at left	—	£160
48		6d. deep green	£275	22·00
		a. Line through design at right	—	£160
		b. Line through design at left	—	£160
49		'REGISTERED' (6d.) orange-yellow (21.6.64)	£180	35·00
		b. Imperf		
		(b) P 12½×13		
50	**1**	1d. orange-vermilion	£160	80·00
50*a*		2d. deep blue	£275	80·00

The 'REGISTERED' stamp was reprinted in 1895. See note below No. 82.

1866 (24 Jan). Wmk 'QUEENSLAND/POSTAGE — POSTAGE/STAMPS — STAMPS' in three lines in script capitals with double wavy lines above and below the wmk and single wavy lines with projecting sprays between each line of words. There are ornaments ('fleurons') between 'POSTAGE' 'POSTAGE' and between 'STAMPS' 'STAMPS'. Single stamps only show a portion of one or two letters of this wmk.

		(a) P 13		
51	**1**	1d. orange-vermilion	£200	45·00
52		2d. blue	£100	17·00
		(b) P 12½×13		
52*a*	**1**	1d. orange-vermilion	£275	75·00
52*b*		2d. blue	£275	75·00

First transfer

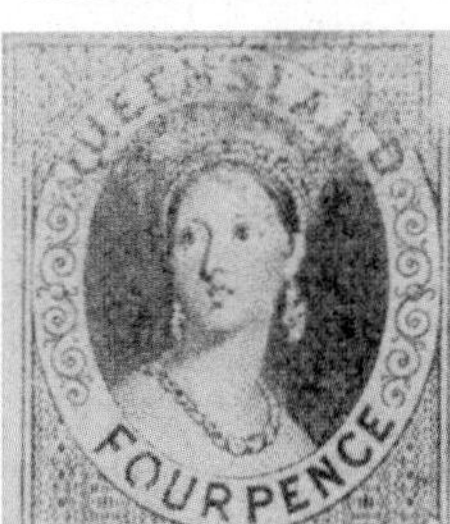

Double transfer

1866–67. Lithographed on thick paper. No wmk. P 13.

	(a) First Transfer (Sept 1866) 'FOUR' in taller thin letters		
53	4d. reddish lilac (*shades*)	£475	32·00
	a. Re-entry	—	£130
	b. Double transfer	£5500	£2500

54		4d. grey-lilac (*shades*)	£475	32·00
		a. Re-entry	—	£130
		b. Double transfer	—	£2500

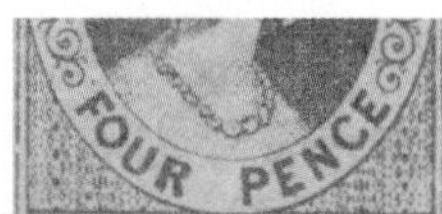

Second transfer

(b) Second Transfer (Feb 1867) 'FOUR' in shorter letters

55		4d. lilac (*shades*)	£475	22·00
		a. Retouch (R. 2/8)	—	£120
		b. 'FOUR' missing	—	£550
56		4d. grey-lilac (*shades*)	£475	22·00
		a. Retouch (R. 2/8)	—	£120
		b. 'FOUR' missing	—	£600
		s. Handstamped 'SPECIMEN'	60·00	
57		5s. bright rose	£1400	£180
58		5s. pale rose	£1300	£140
		a. Imperf between (vert pair)	†	£9000
		s. Handstamped 'SPECIMEN'	75·00	

The 4d. was lithographed from two separate transfers from the 3d. plate and the 5s. was taken from the 1s. plate.

The alterations in values were made by hand on the stones and there are minor varieties in the shape and position of the letters.

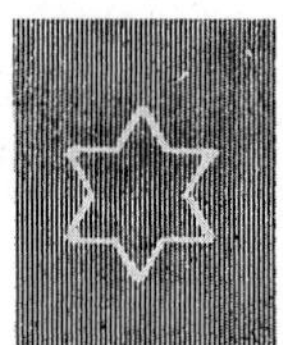

4. Small Truncated Star

2d. Pl II. Dot by 'U'

2d. Pl II. Dots near arabesque

1868–74. Wmk small truncated Star, W **4** on each stamp, and the word 'QUEENSLAND' in single-lined Roman capitals four times in each sheet. P 13.

59	**1**	1d. orange-vermilion (18.1.71)	95·00	7·50
60		2d. pale blue (3.4.68) (Pl I)	80·00	5·00
61		2d. blue (18.1.71) (Pl I)	75·00	3·50
62		2d. bright blue (Pl I)	85·00	2·75
63		2d. greenish blue (Pl I)	£150	2·75
64		2d. dark blue (Pl I)	85·00	2·75
65		3d. olive-green (27.2.71)	£200	7·00
		a. Re-entry	—	65·00
		b. Retouch (R. 2/8)	—	65·00
66		3d. greenish grey	£225	6·50
		a. Re-entry	—	60·00
		b. Retouch (R. 2/8)	—	60·00
67		3d. brown	£120	5·50
		a. Re-entry	—	55·00
		b. Retouch (R. 2/8)	—	55·00
68		6d. yellow-green (10.11.71)	£250	7·50
69		6d. green	£225	10·00
70		6d. deep green	£300	17·00
71		1s. greenish grey (13.11.72)	£850	50·00
72		1s. brownish grey	£850	50·00
73		1s. mauve (19.2.74)	£400	23·00
59s/73s H/S 'SPECIMEN' *Set of 5*			£275	

(b) P 12 (about Feb 1874)

74	**1**	1d. orange-vermilion	£500	30·00
75		2d. blue (Pl II)	£950	75·00
76		3d. greenish grey	—	£225
		a. Re-entry		
		b. Retouch (R. 2/8)		
77		3d. brown	£750	£225
		a. Re-entry		
		b. Retouch (R. 2/8)		
78		6d. green	£1800	50·00
79		1s. mauve	£850	55·00

(c) P 13×12

80	**1**	1d. orange-vermilion	—	£200
81		2d. blue (Pl II)	£1600	45·00
82		3d. greenish grey	—	£350

A second plate of the 2d. denomination was sent by Perkins Bacon to the Colony in 1872 and it was first printed from in August of that year. The new plate is helpful in separating many of the 2d. printings up to 1879.

Plate II of the 2d. may be identified by a smudged dot to the left of 'U' in 'QUEEN' and tiny dots near the lower curl of the right arabesque.

Reprints were made in 1895 of all five values on Wmk W **4**, and perforated 13; the colours are:—1d. orange and brownish orange, 2d. deep dull blue (Pl II), 3d. brown, 6d green, 1s. red-violet and dull violet. The 'Registered' was also reprinted with these on the same paper, but perforated 12. One sheet of the 2d. reprint is known to have had the perforations missing between the fourth and fifth vertical rows.

5

6

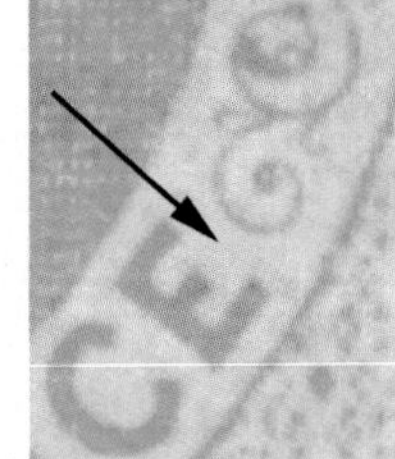

4d. First transfer

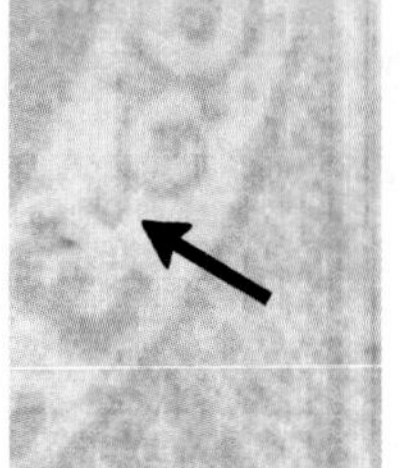

4d. Second transfer

The first transfer of the 4d. was taken from the 3d. plate, identified by the lack of the curl at the foot of the arabesque, the second was from Plate II of the 2d. On the first transfer the 'P' of 'POSTAGE' is to the right of the centre of the Queen's necklace, on the second transfer it is to the left of it.

(4d., litho. Other values recess)

1868–78. Wmk Crown and Q. W **5**.

(a) P 13 (1868–1875)

83	**1**	1d. orange-vermilion (10.11.68)	£110	6·00
		a. Imperf (pair)	£800	
84		1d. pale rose-red (4.11.74)	90·00	16·00
85		1d. deep rose-red	£160	16·00
86		2d. pale blue (20.11.68) (Pl I)	85·00	2·00
87		2d. deep blue (4.11.74) (Pl II)	80·00	4·50
88		3d. brown (11.6.75)	£130	15·00
		a. Re-entry	—	85·00
		b. Retouch (R. 2/8)	—	85·00
89		4d. yellow (*shades*) (1st transfer) (1.1.75)	£2500	£110
		s. Handstamped 'SPECIMEN'	£110	
90		6d. deep green (9.4.69)	£200	9·00
91		6d. yellow-green	£190	6·50
92		6d. pale apple-green (1.1.75)	£225	9·00
		a. Imperf (pair)	£700	
93		1s. mauve	£400	65·00

(b) P 12 (1876–78)

94	**1**	1d. deep orange-vermilion	75·00	6·00
95		1d. pale orange-vermilion	85·00	6·00
96		1d. rose-red	85·00	11·00
97		1d. flesh	£120	13·00
98		2d. pale blue (Pl II)	£130	15·00
99		2d. bright blue (Pl II)	70·00	1·75
100		2d. deep blue (Pl II)	70·00	2·00
101		3d. brown	£120	9·50
		a. Re-entry	—	70·00
		b. Retouch (R. 2/8)	—	70·00
102		4d. yellow (*shades*) (1st transfer)	£1700	50·00
103		4d. buff-yellow (*shades*) (2nd transfer)	£1700	50·00
104		6d. deep green	£250	10·00
105		6d. green	£225	4·25
106		6d. yellow-green	£250	4·50
107		6d. apple-green	£275	7·00
108		1s. mauve	£100	9·00
109		1s. purple	£250	5·00
		a. Imperf between (vert pair)	†	—

(c) P 13×12 or 12×13

110	**1**	1d. orange-vermilion	—	£150
110*a*		1d. rose-red	—	£180
111		2d. deep blue (Pl II)	£1400	£250
112		4d. yellow	—	£650
113		6d. deep green	—	£550

(d) P 12½×13 (1868)

114	**1**	1d. orange-vermilion	—	£600
115		2d. deep blue (Pl I)	—	£600
115*a*		3d. brown	†	—
115*b*		6d. yellow-green	†	£1400

(e) P 12½ (1868)

115*c*	**1**	2d. deep blue (Pl I)	†	£1000
115*d*	**1**	2d. deep blue (Pl II)	†	£750

Reprints of the above were made in 1895 on thicker paper, Wmk. W **6**, perf 12. The colours are:—1d. vermilion-red, 2d. deep dull blue and pale ultramarine, 3d. brown, 6d. dull yellow-green and 1s. lilac-grey.

The Royal Philatelic Collection contains an example of No. 95 imperf between (vert pair), used.

1879. No wmk. P 12.

116	**1**	6d. pale emerald-green	£400	27·00
117		1s. mauve (*fiscal cancel* £5)	£225	£100

No. 117 has a very indistinct lilac *burelé* band at back.

Nos. 116/117 can be found showing portions of a papermaker's watermark, either T. H. Saunders & Co or A. Pirie & Sons.

1880. Lithographed from transfers from the 1s. die. Wmk Crown and Q. W **6**. P 12.

118	**1**	2s. pale blue	£160	60·00
119		2s. blue (*fiscal cancel* £4)	£160	60·00
		a. Imperf vert (horiz pair)	£9000	
120		2s. deep blue (*fiscal cancel* £4)	£190	60·00
121		2s.6d. dull scarlet	£350	80·00
122		2s.6d. bright scarlet (*fiscal cancel* £4)	£350	80·00
123		5s. pale yellow-ochre	£550	£120
124		5s. yellow-ochre (*fiscal cancel* £5)	£550	£120
125		10s. reddish brown	£950	£200
126		10s. bistre-brown	£950	£200
127		20s. rose (*fiscal cancel* £7)	£2250	£275

Of the 2s. and 20s. stamps there are five types of each, and of the other values ten types of each.

Beware of fiscally used copies that have been cleaned and provided with forged postmarks.

7

Die I

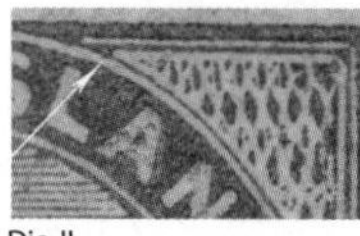

Die II

Dies I and II often occur in the same sheet.

Die I. The white horizontal inner line of the triangle in the upper right-hand corner merges into the outer white line of the oval above the 'L'.

Die II. The same line is short and does not touch the inner oval.

1879–81. Typo. P 12.

(a) Wmk Crown and Q. W **5**

128	**7**	1d. reddish brown (Die I) (15.5.79)	£150	50·00
		a. Die II	£225	50·00
		ab. Imperf between (horiz pair)	†	£2250
		ac. 'QOEENSLAND'	£1800	£275
129		1d. orange-brown (Die I)	£200	50·00
130		2d. blue (Die I) (10.4.79)	£140	13·00
		a. 'PENGE' (R. 12/6)	£1000	£130
		b. 'QUEENSbAND' (R. 5/6)	—	£130
		c. 'QU' joined	—	£130
131		4d. orange-yellow (6.6.79)	£1400	£100

(b) No wmk, with lilac burelé band on back

132	**7**	1d. reddish brown (Die I) (21.10.79)	£800	£120
		a. Die II	£900	£140
		ab. 'QOEENSLAND'	—	£1900
133		2d. blue (Die I) (21.10.79)	£800	60·00
		a. 'PENGE' (R. 12/6)	£4000	£700
		b. 'QUEENSbAND' (R. 5/6)		

(c) Wmk Crown and Q. W **6**

134	**7**	1d. reddish brown (Die I) (31.10.79)	85·00	9·50
		b. Die II	£120	9·50
		ba. 'QOEENSLAND'	£600	60·00
135		1d. dull orange (Die I)	65·00	12·00
		a. Die II	70·00	13·00
		ab. 'QOEENSLAND'	£325	60·00
		ac. Imperf between (horiz pair)	†	—
136		1d. scarlet (Die I) (7.3.81)	60·00	11·00
		aa. Imperf vert (horiz pair)	†	£2250
		a. Die II	65·00	11·00
		ab. 'QOEENSLAND'	£325	38·00
137		2d. blue (Die I) (10.4.79)	85·00	4·00
		a. 'PENGE'	£400	50·00
		b. 'QUEENSbAND'	£400	50·00
		c. Die II	£100	6·50
138		2d. grey-blue (Die I)	85·00	3·25
		a. 'PENGE'	£400	50·00
		b. 'QUEENSbAND'	£400	50·00
		c. Die II	£100	6·50
139		2d. bright blue (Die I)	90·00	3·00
		a. 'PENGE'	£400	50·00
		b. 'QUEENSbAND'	£400	50·00
		c. Imperf between (horiz pair)	£2500	£2500
		d. Die II	£100	6·50
140		2d. deep blue (Die I)	90·00	3·25
		a. 'PENGE'	£400	50·00
		b. 'QUEENSbAND'	£400	50·00
		c. Die II	90·00	8·50
141		4d. orange-yellow	£450	22·00
		a. Imperf vert (horiz pair)	£12000	
142		6d. deep green	£180	7·50
143		6d. yellow-green	£190	7·00
		a. Imperf vertically (horiz pair)		
144		1s. deep violet (3.80)	£190	11·00
145		1s. pale lilac	£180	17·00

The variety 'QO' is No. 48 in the first arrangement, and No. 44 in a later arrangement on the sheets.

All these values have been seen imperf and unused, but we have no evidence that any of them were used in this condition.

The above were printed in sheets of 120, from plates made up of 30 groups of four electrotypes. There are four different types in each group, and two such groups of four are known of the 1d. and 2d., thus giving eight varieties of these two values. There was some resetting of the first plate of the 1d., and there are several plates of the 2d.; the value in the first plate of the latter value is in thinner letters, and in the last plate three types in each group of four have the 'TW' of 'TWO' joined, the letters of 'PENCE' are larger and therefore much closer together, and in one type the 'O' of 'TWO' is oval, that letter being circular in the other types.

(8)

9

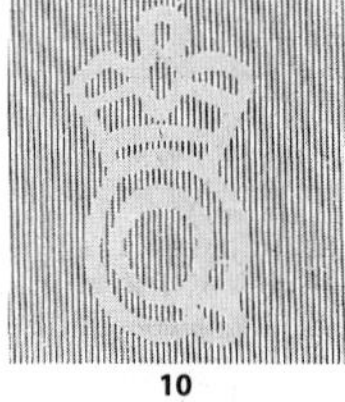

10

1880 (21 Feb). Surch with T **8**.

151	**7**	½d. on 1d. (No. 134) (Die I)	£375	£225
		a. Die II	£850	£475
		ab. 'QOEENSLAND'	£2250	£1300

Examples with 'Half-penny' reading downwards are forged surcharges.

£1 Re-entry (R. 1/2)

£1 Retouch (R. 6/4)

(Eng H. Bourne. Recess Govt Printing Office, Brisbane, from plates made by B.W.)

1882 (13 Apr)–**95**. P 12.

(a) W **5** *(twice sideways). Thin paper*

No.	Type	Description	Unused	Used
152	**9**	2s. bright blue (14.4.82)	£300	65·00
153		2s.6d. vermilion (12.7.82)	£130	27·00
154		5s. rose	£130	28·00
155		10s. brown (12.7.82)	£250	50·00
156		£1 deep green (30.5.83)	£550	£140
		a. Re-entry (R. 1/2)	—	£325
		b. Retouch (R. 6/4)	—	£325
152s/156s (ex 2s. 6d.) H/S 'SPECIMEN' *Set of 4*			£300	

(b) W **10**. *Thick paper (10.11.86)*

No.	Type	Description	Unused	Used
157	**9**	2s. bright blue	£325	65·00
158		2s.6d. vermilion	55·00	27·00
159		5s. rose	55·00	42·00
160	**9**	10s. brown	£130	50·00
161		£1 deep green	£325	85·00
		a. Re-entry (R. 1/2)	£850	£200
		b. Retouch (R. 6/4)	£850	£200

(c) W **6** *(twice sideways). Thin paper (1895)*

No.	Type	Description	Unused	Used
162	**9**	2s.6d. vermilion	90·00	45·00
163		5s. rose	95·00	26·00
164		10s. brown	£475	£110
165		£1 deep green	£375	£100
		a. Re-entry (R. 1/2)	£900	£250
		b. Retouch (R. 6/4)	£900	£250

The re-entry on the £1 shows as a double bottom frame line and the retouch occurs alongside the bottom right numeral.

See also Nos. 270/271, 272/274 and 309/312.

11

12

In T **12** the shading lines do not extend entirely across, as in T **11**, thus leaving a white line down the front of the throat and point of the bust.

4d. 'PENGE' for 'PENCE' (R. 9/1)

4d. 'EN' joined in 'PENCE' (R. 4/6)

1882 (1 Aug)–**91**. W **6**.

(a) P 12

No.	Type	Description	Unused	Used
166	**11**	1d. pale vermilion-red (23.11.82)	12·00	1·00
		a. Double impression		
167		1d. deep vermilion-red	12·00	1·00
168		2d. blue	24·00	1·00
		a. Imperf between (horiz pair)	†	£3000
169		4d. pale yellow (18.4.83)	50·00	3·25
		a. 'PENGE' for 'PENCE'	£325	50·00
		b. 'EN' joined in 'PENCE'	£275	40·00
		c. Imperf (11.91)	†	£500
170		6d. green (6.11.82)	35·00	2·00
171		1s. violet (6.2.83)	55·00	13·00
172		1s. lilac	28·00	8·00
173		1s. deep mauve	25·00	8·00
174		1s. pale mauve	13·00	8·00
		a. Imperf	†	—

(b) P 9½×12 (1884)

No.	Type	Description	Unused	Used
176	**11**	1d. pale red	£160	65·00
177		2d. blue	£550	85·00
178		1s. mauve	£275	80·00

The above were printed from plates made up of groups of four electrotypes as previously. In the 1d. the words of value are followed by a full stop. There are four types of the 4d., 6d. and 1s., eight types of the 1d., and 12 types of the 2d.

No. 169c is from a sheet used at Roma post office and comes cancelled with the '46' numeral postmark.

1887 (5 May)–**89**. W **6**.

(a) P 12

No.	Type	Description	Unused	Used
179	**12**	1d. vermilion-red	18·00	1·00
180		2d. blue	18·00	1·00
		a. Oval white flaw on Queen's head behind diadem (R. 12/5)	75·00	9·00
181		2s. deep brown (12.3.89)	80·00	85·00
182		2s. pale brown	70·00	75·00

(b) P 9½×12

No.	Type	Description	Unused	Used
183	**12**	2d. blue	£425	80·00

These are from new plates; four types of each value grouped as before. The 1d. is without stop. In all values No. 2 in each group of four has the 'L' and 'A' of 'QUEENSLAND' joined at the foot, and No. 3 of the 2d. has 'P' of word 'PENCE' with a long downstroke.

The 2d. is known bisected and used as a 1d. value.

13

14

1890. W **6** (sideways on ½d.). P 12½, 13 (comb machine).

No.	Type	Description	Unused	Used
184	**13**	½d. pale green	20·00	2·25
185		½d. deep green	15·00	2·25
186		½d. deep blue-green	7·50	2·25
187	**12**	1d. vermilion-red	8·50	50
		a. Imperf (pair)	£300	£325
		b. Oval broken by tip of bust (R. 10/3)	50·00	5·00
		c. Double impression	†	£650
188		2d. blue (old plate)	9·50	50
189		2d. pale blue (old plate)	9·50	50
190		2d. pale blue (retouched plate)	11·00	1·00
		a. 'FWO' for 'TWO' (R. 8/7)	—	30·00
191	**14**	2½d. carmine	17·00	2·50
192	**12**	3d. brown	9·00	4·00
193	**11**	4d. yellow	18·00	4·00
		a. 'PENGE' for 'PENCE'	£110	35·00
		b. 'EN' joined in 'PENCE'	90·00	30·00
194		4d. orange	27·00	4·00
		a. 'PENGE' for 'PENCE'	£160	35·00
		b. 'EN' joined in 'PENCE'	£130	30·00
195		4d. lemon	29·00	8·00
		a. 'PENGE' for 'PENCE'	£170	50·00
		b. 'EN' joined in 'PENCE'	£140	45·00
196		6d. green	11·00	2·00
197	**12**	2s. red-brown	45·00	55·00
198		2s. pale brown	55·00	60·00

This issue is perforated by a new vertical comb machine, gauging about 12¾×12¾. The 3d. is from a plate similar to those of the last issue, No. 2 in each group of four types having 'L' and 'A' joined at the foot. The ½d. and 2½d. are likewise in groups of four types, but the differences are very minute. In the retouched plate of the 2d. the letters 'L' and 'A' no longer touch in No. 2 of each group and the 'P' in No. 3 is normal.

1895. W **10**.

A. Thick paper

(a) P 12½, 13

No.	Type	Description	Unused	Used
202	**12**	1d. vermilion-red (16.1.95)	4·75	60
		a. Oval broken by tip of bust (R. 10/3)	45·00	6·50
203		1d. red-orange	4·75	60
		a. Oval broken by tip of bust (R. 10/3)	45·00	6·50
204		2d. blue (retouched plate) (16.1.95)	6·50	60
		a. 'FWO' for 'TWO' (R. 8/7)	90·00	24·00

(b) P 12

No.	Type	Description	Unused	Used
205	**11**	1s. mauve (8.95)	45·00	29·00

B. Unwmkd paper; with blue burelé band at back. P 12½, 13

No.	Type	Description	Unused	Used
206	**12**	1d. vermilion-red (19.2.95)	2·50	2·75
		a. Oval broken by tip of bust (R. 10/3)	22·00	24·00
		b. 'PE' of 'PENNY' omitted (R. 1/2)	£375	£400
206*c*		1d. red-orange	2·50	2·75

C. Thin paper. Crown and Q faintly impressed. P 12½, 13

No.	Type	Description	Unused	Used
207	**12**	2d. blue (retouched plate) (6.95)	13·00	£160
		a. 'FWO' for 'TWO' (R. 8/7)	£150	

15 16 17 18

1895–96.

A. W **6** *(sideways on ½d.)*

(a) P 12½, 13

No.	Type	Description	Unused	Used
208	**15**	½d. green (11.5.95)	3·25	2·00
		a. Double impression	£2000	£2000
209		½d. deep green	3·25	2·00
		a. Printed both sides	£275	
210	**16**	1d. orange-red (28.2.95)	3·75	50
211		1d. pale red	8·50	75
212		2d. blue (19.6.95)	35·00	50
213	**17**	2½d. carmine (8.95)	24·00	5·50
214		2½d. rose	24·00	5·50
215	**18**	5d. purple-brown (10.95)	27·00	5·00

(b) P 12

No.	Type	Description	Unused	Used
217	**16**	1d. red (8.95)	90·00	50·00
218		2d. blue (8.95)	80·00	30·00

B. Thick paper. W **10** *(sideways) (part only on each stamp)*

(a) P 12½, 13

No.	Type	Description	Unused	Used
219	**15**	½d. green (6.8.95)	2·75	7·00
220		½d. deep green	2·75	7·00

(b) P 12

No.	Type	Description	Unused	Used
221	**15**	½d. green	45·00	
222		½d. deep green	45·00	

C. No wmk; with blue burelé band at back

(a) P 12½, 13

No.	Type	Description	Unused	Used
223	**15**	½d. green (1.8.95)	10·00	8·50
		a. Without *burelé* band	75·00	
224		½d. deep green	10·00	

(b) P 12

No.	Type	Description	Unused	Used
225	**15**	½d. green	22·00	
		a. Without *burelé* band	£140	

Nos. 223a and 225a are from the margins of the sheet.

D. Thin paper, with Crown and Q faintly impressed. P 12½, 13.

No.	Type	Description	Unused	Used
227	**15**	½d. green	2·00	7·00
228	**16**	1d. orange-red	3·25	2·50

19

1896–1902. W **6**. P 12½, 13.

No.	Type	Description	Unused	Used
229	**19**	1d. vermilion	20·00	70
230		6d. green (1902)	†	£16000

Only used examples of No. 230 are known, mostly with readable postmarks from 1902. It is suggested that electrotypes of this unissued design were inadvertently entered in a plate of No. 249.

20 21 22

23 24 25

'Cracked plate'

Die I Die II

Two Dies of 4d.:

Die I. Serif of horizontal bar on lower right 4d. is clear of vertical frame line.

Die II. Serif joins vertical frame line.

1897–1908. Figures in all corners. W **6** (sideways on ½d.). P 12½, 13 (comb).

No.	Type	Description	Unused	Used
231	**20**	½d. deep green	5·00	8·50
		a. Perf 12	—	£150
232	**21**	1d. orange-vermilion	2·50	40
233		1d. vermilion	2·50	40
		a. Perf 12 (1899)	8·00	3·50
234		2d. blue	8·50	40
		a. Cracked plate	£200	40·00
		b. Perf 12 (1905)	£700	7·00
		ba. Cracked plate	£2750	£250
235		2d. deep blue	7·50	40
		a. Cracked plate	£180	40·00
236	**22**	2½d. rose (10.98)	17·00	29·00
237		2½d. purple/*blue* (20.1.99)	9·50	3·25
238		2½d. brown-purple/*blue*	9·50	3·25
239		2½d. slate/*blue* (5.08)	9·00	9·00
240	**21**	3d. brown (10.98)	10·00	3·00
241		3d. deep brown	8·00	3·00
242		3d. reddish brown (1906)	13·00	5·00
243		3d. grey-brown (1907)	26·00	5·50
244		4d. yellow (Die I) (10.98)	13·00	3·25
		a. Die II	32·00	11·00
245		4d. yellow-buff (Die I)	11·00	3·25
		a. Die II	26·00	11·00
246	**23**	5d. purple-brown	9·00	3·00
247		5d. dull brown (1906)	9·50	11·00
248		5d. black-brown (1907)	16·00	7·00
249	**21**	6d. green (1.4.98)	8·50	2·75
250		6d. yellow-green	7·00	3·50
251	**24**	1s. pale mauve (1.7.99)	14·00	3·75
252		1s. dull mauve	14·00	3·75
253		1s. bright mauve	20·00	5·00
254	**25**	2s. turquoise-green	35·00	50·00

Stamps of this issue also exist with the irregular line perforation 12½, 13.

The 1d. perf 12×9½ exists used and unused but their status has not yet been established (*price* £120 *unused*).

The cracked plate variety on the 2d. developed during 1901 and shows as a white break on the Queen's head and neck. The electro was later replaced.

1897–98. W **6**.

(a) Zigzag roulette in black
(ab) Zigzag roulette in green
(b) The same but plain
(c) Roulette (a) and also (b)
(d) Roulette (b) and perf 12½, 13
(e) Roulette (a) and perf 12½, 13
(f) Compound of (a), (b), and perf 12½, 13

No.	Type	Description	Unused	Used
256	**21**	1d. vermilion (*a*)	18·00	14·00
		a. Zigzag roulette in green (*ab*)	£250	
257		1d. vermilion (*b*)	19·00	7·50

258 1d. vermilion (*c*) 20·00 27·00
259 1d. vermilion (*d*) 9·50 6·50
260 1d. vermilion (*e*) 75·00 95·00
261 1d. vermilion (*f*) 95·00 £100

26

(Des M. Kellar)

1899 (Sept.)–**1906**. W **6**. P 12½, 13 (comb).
262 **26** ½d. deep green 3·25 2·50
a. Grey-green 2·50 2·50
b. Green (P 12) (1905) £110 65·00
c. Pale green (1906) 12·00 4·50

Stamps of T **26** without wmk, are proofs.
Stamps of this issue also exist with the irregular line perforation 12½, 13.

27 27a

(Des F. Elliott)

1900 (19 June). Anglo-Boer War Patriotic Fund. W **6**. P 12.
263 **27** 1d. (6d.) claret £140 £120
264 **27a** 2d. (1s.) violet £350 £275

These stamps, sold at 6d. and 1s. respectively, paid postage of 1d. and 2d. only, the difference being contributed to The Anglo-Boer War Patriotic Fund.

28

QUEENSLAND QUEENSLAND
A B

TWO TYPES OF 'QUEENSLAND'. Three different pairs of plates were produced for Type **28**, each plate being of 120 impressions (12×10). In Type A the letters of 'QUEENSLAND' are 1mm tall and in Type B they are 1.5mm.

Plate 1: All Type A
Plate 2: Initially, all Type A, but in 1905 Type B clichés were substituted at R. 1/6, 2/6 and 3/6
Plate 3: All Type B
Plate 4: All Type B
Plate 5: All Type A
Plate 6: All Type A

(Typo Victoria Govt Printer, Melbourne)

1903 (4 July)–**05**. W w **10**. P 12½.
265 **28** 9d. brown and ultramarine (A) 55·00 8·00
266 9d. brown and ultramarine (B) (1905) 40·00 8·00
a. Pair, types A and B *se-tenant* £250

The first two printings, No. 265, were all from plates 1 and 2, prior to the substitutions on plate 2. The third printing in May 1905 involved both plates 1 and 2 (after substitutions), together with 3 and 4 (both Type B). For the final printing on W w **10** paper, plates 3 and 4 were again used.

1903 (Oct). As Nos. 162 and 165. W **6** (twice sideways). P 12½, 13 (irregular line).
270 **9** 2s.6d. vermilion £225 60·00
271 £1 deep green £2000 £700
a. Re-entry (R. 1/2) £4000 £1400
b. Retouch (R. 6/4) £4000 £1400

(Litho Govt Ptg Office, Brisbane, from transfers of the recess plates)

1905 (Nov)–**06**. W **6** (twice sideways).

(a) P 12½, 13 (irregular line)
272 **9** £1 deep green £1100 £170
a. Re-entry (R. 1/2) £2250 £400
b. Retouch (R. 6/4) £2250 £400

(b) P 12
273 **9** 5s. rose (7.06) £170 £100
274 £1 deep green (7.06) £550 £130
a. Re-entry (R. 1/2) £1000 £300
b. Retouch (R. 6/4) £1000 £300

30 32

Redrawn types of T **21**

T **30**. The head is redrawn, the top of the crown is higher and touches the frame, as do also the back of the chignon and the point of the bust. The forehead is filled in with lines of shading, and the figures in the corners appear to have been redrawn also.

T **32**. The forehead is plain (white instead of shaded), and though the top of the crown is made higher, it does not touch the frame; but the point of the bust and the chignon still touch. The figure in the right lower corner does not touch the line below, and has not the battered appearance of that in the first redrawn type. The stamps are very clearly printed, the lines of shading being distinct.

1906 (Sept). W **6**. P 12½, 13 (comb).
281 **30** 2d. dull blue (*shades*) 11·00 6·00

(Typo Victoria Govt Printer, Melbourne)

1906 (Sept)–**10**. Wmk Crown and double-lined A, W w **11**.

(a) P 12×12½
282 **28** 9d. brown and ultramarine (A) (1909) 75·00 7·50
283 9d. brown and ultramarine (B) 23·00 4·50
283*a* 9d. pale brown and blue (A) (1909) 70·00 7·50
284 9d. pale brown and blue (B) 14·00 4·50

(b) P 11 (1910)
285 **28** 9d. brown and blue (B) £5000 £800

(c) Compound perf 12×12½ and 11
285*a* 9d. brown and ultramarine (B) † £1600

For the first three printings on W w **11** paper, plates 3 and 4 (Type B) were used. For the fourth printing in January 1909 plates 5 and 6 (Type A) were introduced and used in conjunction with 3 and 4. The final two printings in September 1911 and January 1912 were probably all from plates 3 and 4.

33

1907–11. W **33**.

(a) P 12½, 13 (comb)
286 **26** ½d. deep green 2·00 4·50
287 ½d. deep blue-green 2·00 4·50
288 **21** 1d. vermilion 3·00 30
a. Imperf (pair) £400
289 **30** 2d. dull blue 38·00 3·75
289*a* 2d. bright blue (3.08) 29·00 22·00
290 **32** 2d. bright blue (4.08) 5·00 30
291 **21** 3d. pale brown (8.08) 24·00 2·75
292 3d. bistre-brown 12·00 3·75
293 4d. yellow (Die I) 12·00 4·50
a. Die II 42·00 14·00
294 4d. grey-black (Die I) (4.09) 25·00 7·00
a. Die II 50·00 16·00
295 **23** 5d. dull brown 38·00 22·00
295*a* 5d. sepia (12.09) 22·00 26·00
296 **21** 6d. yellow-green 22·00 4·25
297 6d. bright green 19·00 8·00
298 **24** 1s. violet (1908) 22·00 4·00
299 1s. bright mauve 20·00 4·00
300 **25** 2s. turquoise-green (8.08) 38·00 50·00

Stamps of this issue also exist with the irregular line perforation 12½, 13. This was used when the comb perforation was under repair.

(b) P 13×11 to 12½ (May 1911)
301 **26** ½d. deep green 7·00 13·00
302 **21** 1d. vermilion 7·50 7·00
303 **32** 2d. blue 10·00 9·00
304 **21** 3d. bistre-brown 18·00 27·00
305 4d. grey-black 70·00 90·00
a. Die II £140 £160
306 **23** 5d. dull brown 26·00 70·00
307 **21** 6d. yellow-green 38·00 55·00
308 **23** 1s. violet 60·00 85·00

The perforation (*b*) is from a machine introduced to help cope with the demands caused by the introduction of penny postage. The three rows at top (or bottom) of the sheet show varieties gauging 13×11½, 13×11, and 13×12, respectively, these are obtainable in strips of three showing the three variations.

(Litho Govt Ptg Office, Brisbane)

1907 (Oct)–**11**. W **33** (twice sideways). P 12½, 13 (irregular line).
309 **9** 2s.6d. vermilion 42·00 50·00
a. Dull orange (1910) 80·00 90·00
b. Reddish orange (1911) £180 £225
310 5s. rose (12.07) 80·00 65·00
a. Deep rose (1910) £100 90·00
b. Carmine-red (1911) £250 £275
311 10s. blackish brown £150 75·00
a. Sepia (1911) £425 £300
312 £1 bluish green £400 £130
a. Re-entry (R. 1/2) £800 £300
b. Retouch (R. 6/4) £800 £300
c. Deep bluish green (1910) £550 £350
ca. Re-entry (R. 1/2) £1200 £700
cb. Retouch (R. 6/4) £1200 £700
d. Deep yellowish green (1911) £1800 £1400
da. Re-entry (R. 1/2) £4250 £2750
db. Retouch (R. 6/4) £4250 £2750

The 1911 printings are on thinner, whiter paper.
The lithographic stones used for Nos. 272/274 and 309/312 took the full sheet of 30 so the varieties on the £1 recess-printed version also appear on the stamps printed by lithography.

1911. W **33**. Perf irregular compound, 10½ to 12½.
313 **21** 1d. vermilion £1500 £700

This was from another converted machine, formerly used for perforating Railway stamps. The perforation was very unsatisfactory.

STAMP BOOKLETS

There are very few surviving examples of Nos. SB1/SB4. Listings are provided for those believed to have been issued with prices quoted for those known to still exist.

1904 (1 Jan)–**09**. Black on a red cover as Type B **1** of New South Wales. Stapled.
SB1 £1 booklet containing 240×1d. in four blocks of 30 and two blocks of 60
a. Red on pink cover (1909)
b. Blue on pink cover £15000

1904 (1 Jan). Black on grey cover as No. SB1. Stapled.
SB2 £1 booklet containing 120×2d. in four blocks of 30

1910 (May). Black on cream cover as Type B **2** of New South Wales. Stapled.
SB3 2s. booklet containing 11×½d. (No. 301), either in block of 6 plus block of 5 or block of 11 and 18×1d. (No 302), either in three blocks of 6 or block of 6 plus block of 12

Unsold stock of No. SB3 was uprated with one additional ½d. in May 1911.

1911 (Aug). Red on pink cover as No. SB3. Stapled.
SB4 2s. booklet containing 12×½d. (No. 301), either in two blocks of 6 or block of 12, and 18×1d. (No. 302), either in three blocks of 6 or block of 6 plus block of 12 £6000
a. Red on white cover £5500

POSTAL FISCALS

Authorised for use from 1 January 1880 until 1 July 1892

CANCELLATIONS. Beware of stamps which have had pen-cancellations cleaned off and then had faked postmarks applied. Used prices quoted are for postally used examples between the above dates.

F 1 F 2

1866–68. Litho, Govt Ptg Office.

A. No wmk. P 13
F1 **F 1** 1d. blue £140 30·00
F2 6d. deep violet £250 £130
F3 1s. blue-green £225 90·00
F4 2s. brown £400 £225
F5 2s.6d. dull red £500 £180
F6 5s. yellow £1300 £450
F6*a* 6s. light brown £2000
F7 10s. green £1600 £600
F8 20s. rose £2750 £1200

B. Wmk F 2. P 13
F9 **F 1** 1d. blue 80·00 70·00
F10 6d. deep violet £250 £160
F11 6d. blue £750 £475
F12 1s. blue-green £225 95·00
F13 2s. brown £400 £180
F13*a* 5s. yellow £1300 £400
F14 10s. green £1600 £600
F15 20s. rose £2750 £1300

F 3 F 3a

1871–72. Litho, Govt Ptg Office. P 12 or 13.

A. Wmk Large Crown and Q, Wmk F **3a**
F16 **F 3** 1d. mauve 65·00 26·00
F17 6d. red-brown £120 55·00
a. Imperf vert (horiz pair)
F18 1s. green £150 55·00
F19 2s. blue £225 80·00
F20 2s.6d. brick-red £400 £170
F21 5s. orange-brown £500 £250
F22 10s. brown £1100 £500
F23 20s. rose £2500 £750

B. No wmk. Blue burelé band at back
F24 **F 3** 1d. mauve 75·00 26·00
F25 6d. red-brown £120 55·00
F26 6d. mauve £550 £170
F27 1s. green £180 55·00
F28 2s. blue £300 £180
F29 2s.6d. vermilion £500 £200
F30 5s. yellow-brown £700 £250
F31 10s. brown £1200 £500
F32 20s. rose £2500 £750

No. F19 is known imperforate horizontally (vert pair), with fiscal cancellation.

F 4

F 5

1878–79. Typo.

A. No wmk. Lilac burelé band at back. P 12

F33 F **4** 1d. violet £225 £110

*B. Wmk Crown and Q, W **5**. P 12*

F34 F **4** 1d. violet .... £140 80·00
d. Imperf between (horiz pair).......

Stamps as Type F **5** may not have been issued until after 1 July 1892 when the proper use of duty stamps for postal service was terminated but there are several examples which appear to have genuinely passed through the post during the 1890's. Unless they are dated during 1892 their postal use was certainly unauthorised although they may have been accepted.

Queensland became part of the Commonwealth of Australia on 1 January 1901.

SOUTH AUSTRALIA

PRICES FOR STAMPS ON COVER

Nos. 1/3	*from* × 3
No. 4	†
Nos. 5/12	*from* × 2
Nos. 13/18	*from* × 3
Nos. 19/43	*from* × 4
Nos. 44/49*b*	—
Nos. 50/110	*from* × 3
No. 111	—
Nos. 112/134	*from* × 6
Nos. 135/145	*from* × 3
Nos. 146/166	*from* × 5
Nos. 167/170*a*	*from* × 10
Nos. 171/172*a*	—
Nos. 173/194*a*	*from* × 12
Nos. 195/208	—
Nos. 229/231	*from* × 12
No. 232	—
Nos. 233/242	*from* × 12
Nos. 268/275	*from* × 30
Nos. 276/279	—
Nos. 280/288	*from* × 30
Nos. 289/292	—
Nos. 293/304	*from* × 15
No. 305	—
Nos. O1/O13	—
Nos. O14/O36	*from* × 20
Nos. O37/O42	*from* × 5
Nos. O43/O44	*from* × 50
Nos. O45/O47	—
Nos. O48/O52	*from* × 30
No. O53	—
Nos. O54/O85	*from* × 50
Nos. O86/O87	—

SPECIMEN OVERPRINTS. Those listed are from UPU distributions between 1889 and 1895. Further 'Specimen' overprints exist, but these were used for other purposes.

PERKINS BACON 'CANCELLED'. For notes on these handstamps, showing 'CANCELLED' between horizontal bars forming an oval, see Catalogue Introduction.

1

2 Large Star

(Eng Wm Humphrys. Recess P.B.)

1855 (1 Jan–Oct). Printed in London. W **2**. Imperf.

1 **1** 1d. dark green (10.55) (H/S 'CANCELLED' in oval £13000) £12000 £500
2 2d. rose-carmine (*shades*) (H/S 'CANCELLED' in oval £13000) .... £800 85·00
3 6d. deep blue (10.55) (H/S 'CANCELLED' in oval £11000) £5500 £170

Prepared and sent to the Colony, but not issued

4 **1** 1s. violet (H/S 'CANCELLED' in oval £25000) £40000

A printing of 500,000 of these 1s. stamps was delivered, but, as the colour was liable to be confused with that of the 6d. stamp, this stock was destroyed on 5 June 1857. It is believed that surviving examples of No. 4 come from Perkins Bacon remainders which came on to the market in the late 1890s.

Proofs of the 1d. and 6d. without wmk exist, and these are found with forged star watermarks added, and are sometimes offered as originals.

For reprints of the above and later issues, see note after No. 194.

1856–58. Printed by Printer of Stamps, Adelaide, from Perkins Bacon plates. W **2**. Imperf.

5 **1** 1d. deep yellow-green (15.6.58) £9500 £550
6 1d. yellow-green (11.10.58) £8500 £650
7 2d. orange-red (4.58) .... £2250 80·00
8 2d. blood-red (14.11.56) .... £3000 60·00
a. Printed on both sides .... † £1300
9 2d. red (*shades*) (23.4.56) .... £750 40·00
a. Printed on both sides .... † £850
10 6d. slate-blue (7.57) £4750 £200
11 1s. red-orange (8.7.57) .... — £750
12 1s. orange (11.6.58) £13000 £475

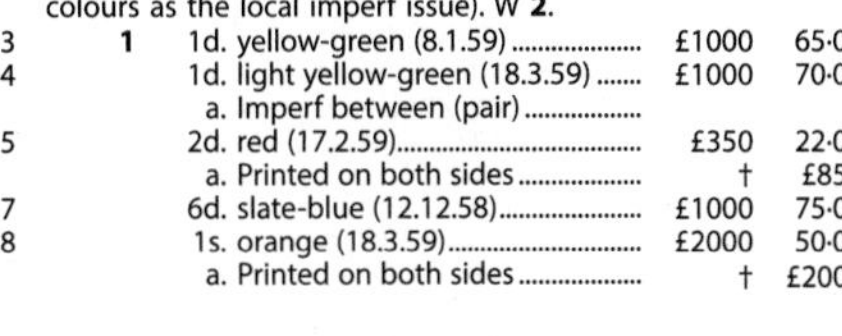

1858–59. Rouletted. (This first rouletted issue has the same colours as the local imperf issue). W **2**.

13 **1** 1d. yellow-green (8.1.59) .... £1000 65·00
14 1d. light yellow-green (18.3.59) .... £1000 70·00
a. Imperf between (pair) ....
15 2d. red (17.2.59) .... £350 22·00
a. Printed on both sides .... † £850
17 6d. slate-blue (12.12.58) .... £1000 75·00
18 1s. orange (18.3.59) .... £2000 50·00
a. Printed on both sides .... † £2000

3

4

(5)

The 'TEN PENCE' surcharge (T **5**) was produced from a setting of six (3×2). There are noticable differences between the six types.

1860–69. Second rouletted issue, printed (with the exception of No. 24) in colours only found rouletted or perforated. Surch with T **5** (Nos. 35/7). W **2**.

19 **1** 1d. bright yellow-green (22.4.61) .... £150 50·00
20 1d. dull blue-green (17.12.63) .... £160 50·00
21 1d. sage-green .... £170 50·00
a. Imperf between (horiz pair) ....
22 1d. pale sage-green (27.5.65) £150
23 1d. deep green (1864) .... £600 85·00
24 1d. deep yellow-green (1869) £325
24*a* 2d. pale red .... £275 4·00
b. Printed on both sides .... † £550
25 2d. pale vermilion (3.2.63) .... £160 4·75
26 2d. bright vermilion (19.8.64) .... £160 3·75
a. Imperf between (horiz pair) £3750 £800
27 **3** 4d. dull violet (24.1.67) .... £180 50·00
28 **1** 6d. violet-blue (19.3.60) .... £500 8·00
29 6d. greenish blue (11.2.63) .... £325 4·75
30 6d. dull ultramarine (25.4.64) .... £275 4·75
a. Imperf between (horiz pair) .... † £2500
31 6d. violet-ultramarine (11.4.68) .... £475 7·00
32 6d. dull blue (26.8.65) .... £400 7·50
a. Imperf between (pair) .... † £3000
33 6d. Prussian blue (7.9.69) .... £1500 50·00
33*a* 6d. indigo .... — 70·00
34 **4** 9d. grey-lilac (24.12.60) .... £160 9·00
a. Imperf between (horiz pair) .... † £4500
35 10d. on 9d. orange-red (B.) (20.7.66) .... £600 50·00
36 10d. on 9d. yellow (B.) (29.7.67) .... £800 30·00
37 10d. on 9d. yellow (Blk.) (14.8.69) .... £4000 80·00
a. Surch inverted at the top .... † £7000
c. Roul×perf 10 .... † —
38 **1** 1s. yellow (25.10.61) .... £1500 32·00
a. Imperf horiz (vert pair) .... † £6000
39 1s. grey-brown (10.4.63) .... £450 32·00
40 1s. dark grey-brown (26.5.63) .... £425 32·00
41 1s. chestnut (25.8.63) .... £375 11·00
42 1s. lake-brown (27.3.65) .... £250 12·00
a. Imperf between (horiz pair) .... † £2500
43 **3** 2s. rose-carmine (24.1.67) .... £550 32·00
a. Imperf between (vert pair) .... † £2750

1868–71. Remainders of old stock subsequently perforated by the 11½–12½ machine.

(a) Imperf stamps. P 11½–12½

44 **1** 2d. pale vermilion (2.68) .... — £1300
45 2d. vermilion (18.3.68) .... — £1400

(b) Rouletted stamps. P 11½–12½

46 **1** 1d. bright green (9.11.69) .... — £750
47 2d. pale vermilion (15.8.68) £2500 £650
48 6d. Prussian blue (8.11.69) .... — £400
aa. Horiz pair perf all round, roul between ....
48*a* 6d. indigo .... — £500
49 **4** 9d. grey-lilac (29.3.71) £2750 £250
a. Perf×roulette .... — £275
49*b* **1** 1s. lake-brown (23.5.70) ....

1867–70. W **2**. P 11½–12½×roulette.

50 **1** 1d. pale bright green (2.11.67) .... £450 29·00
51 1d. bright green (1868) .... £425 24·00
52 1d. grey-green (26.1.70) .... £475 29·00
a. Imperf between (horiz pair) ....
53 1d. blue-green (29.11.67) .... £600 65·00
54 **3** 4d. dull violet (7.68) £3250 £160
55 4d. dull purple (1869) .... — £130
56 **1** 6d. bright pale blue (29.5.67) .... £1100 19·00
57 6d. Prussian blue (30.7.67) .... £1000 19·00
a. Printed on both sides ....
58 6d. indigo (1.8.69) .... £1200 26·00
59 **4** 10d. on 9d. yellow (B.) (2.2.69) .... £1800 35·00
a. Printed on both sides .... — £1300
60 **1** 1s. chestnut (4.68) .... £550 20·00
61 1s. lake-brown (3.3.69) .... £550 20·00

NOTE. The stamps perf 11½, 12½, or compound of the two, are here combined in one list, as both perforations are on the one machine, and all the varieties may be found in each sheet of stamps. This method of classifying the perforations by the machines is by far the most simple and convenient.

3-PENCE
(6)

7 (=Victoria W **19**)

1868–79. Surch with T **6** (Nos. 66/8). W **2**. P 11½–12½.

62 **1** 1d. pale bright green (8.2.68) .... £375 70·00
63 1d. grey-green (18.2.68) .... £325 70·00
64 1d. dark green (20.3.68) .... £190 22·00
a. Printed on both sides .... † £1100
65 1d. deep yellow-green (28.6.72) .... £180 22·00
a. Imperf between (horiz pair) .... † £3250
66 **3** 3d. on 4d. Prussian blue (Blk.) (7.2.71) .... — £850
67 3d. on 4d. sky-blue (Blk.) (12.8.70) .... £650 20·00
a. Imperf ....
b. Rouletted .... — £1400
68 3d. on 4d. deep ultramarine (Blk.) (9.72) .... £180 9·00
a. Surch double .... † £3750
b. Additional surch on back .... — £3000
c. Surch omitted £40000 £20000
70 4d. dull purple (1.2.68) .... £120 15·00
71 4d. dull violet (1868) .... £110 8·00
72 **1** 6d. bright pale blue (23.2.68) .... £700 11·00
73 6d. Prussian blue (29.9.69) .... £375 7·00
a. Perf 11½×imperf (horiz pair) .... † £2250
74 6d. indigo (1869) .... £375 17·00
75 **4** 9d. claret (7.72) .... £200 8·00
76 9d. bright mauve (1.11.72) .... £200 8·00
a. Printed on both sides .... † £900
77 9d. red-purple (15.1.74) .... £120 8·00
78 10d. on 9d. yellow (B.) (15.8.68) .... £2250 50·00
a. Wmk Crown and S A (W **10**) (1868) .... — £1700
79 10d. on 9d. yellow (Blk.) (13.9.69) .... £475 65·00
80 **1** 1s. lake-brown (9.68) .... £225 18·00
81 1s. chestnut (8.10.72) .... £200 20·00
82 1s. dark red-brown .... £170 12·00
83 1s. red-brown (6.1.69) .... £180 12·00
84 **3** 2s. pale rose-pink (10.10.69) £2250 £180
85 2s. deep rose-pink (8.69) .... — £120
86 2s. crimson-carmine (16.10.69) .... £190 21·00
87 2s. carmine (1869) .... £180 13·00
a. Printed on both sides .... † £750

No. 68c comes from two sheets on which, it is believed, some stamps showed the surcharge omitted and others the surcharge double. One of the used examples of No. 68c is known postmarked in 1875 and many of the others in 1879.

No. 78a was a trial printing made to test the perforating machine on the new D.L.R. paper.

A used example of No. 70 in imperf between horiz pair is in the Royal Philatelic Collection.

1870–71. W **2**. P 10.

88 **1** 1d. grey-green (6.70) .... £375 25·00
89 1d. pale bright green (9.8.70) .... £375 22·00
90 1d. bright green (1871) .... £325 22·00
91 **3** 3d. on 4d dull ultramarine (R.) (6.8.70) £1600 £120
92 3d. on 4d pale ultramarine (Blk.) (14.2.71) .... £600 35·00
93 3d. on 4d ultramarine (Blk.) (14.8.71) .... £375 40·00
93*a* 3d. on 4d. Prussian blue (Blk.) (16.12.71) .... — £1000
94 4d. dull lilac (1870) .... £225 11·00
95 4d. dull purple (1871) .... £200 11·00
96 **1** 6d. bright blue (19.6.70) .... £400 17·00
97 6d. indigo (11.10.71) .... £600 16·00
98 1s. chestnut (4.1.71) .... £375 42·00

NOTE. Stamps perf 10 all round were produced by a new rotary machine, introduced early in 1870. This machine was not large enough to perforate entire sheets, and perforation therefore had to be completed with the perf 11½–12½ line machine, giving rise to the compound perforations listed as Nos. 99/110.

1870–73. W **2**. P 10×11½–12½, 11½–12½×10, or compound.

99 **1** 1d. pale bright green (11.10.70) .... £375 24·00
a. Printed on both sides ....
100 1d. grey-green .... £350 18·00
101 1d. deep green (19.6.71) .... £225 11·00
102 **3** 3d. on 4d. pale ultramarine (Blk.) (9.11.70) .... £600 80·00
103 4d. dull lilac (11.5.72) .... — 20·00
104 4d. slate-lilac (5.3.73) .... £225 20·00
105 **1** 6d. Prussian blue (2.3.70) .... £325 8·00
106 6d. bright Prussian blue (26.10.70) .... £350 10·00
107 **4** 10d. on 9d. yellow (Blk.) (1.70) .... £350 65·00
108 **1** 1s. chestnut (17.6.71) .... £425 80·00
109 **3** 2s. rose-pink (24.4.71) .... — £225
110 2s. carmine (2.3.72) .... £375 65·00

1871 (17 July). W **7**. P 10.

111 **3** 4d. dull lilac £5500 £325
a. Printed on both sides .... † £4500

8 Broad Star

8 PENCE
(9)

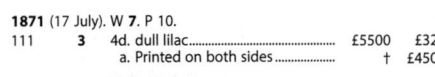

1876–1900. Surch with T **9** (Nos. 118/21). W **8**.

(a) P 11½–12½

112 **3** 3d. on 4d. ultramarine (1.6.79) .... £180 35·00
a. Surch double .... † £1900

113 4d. violet-slate (15.3.79) £170 16·00
114 4d. plum (16.4.80) 95·00 7·50
115 4d. deep mauve (8.6.82) 95·00 6·00
116 1 6d. indigo (2.12.76) £225 5·00
a. Imperf between (horiz pair) † —
117 6d. Prussian blue (7.78) £170 4·50
118 4 8d. on 9d. brown-orange (7.76) £250 10·00
119 8d. on 9d. burnt umber (1880) £250 12·00
a. Surch double † —
120 8d. on 9d. brown (9.3.80) £250 12·00
a. Imperf between (vert pair) £5000
121 8d. on 9d. grey-brown (10.5.81) £200 7·00
a. Surch double — £2750
122 9d. purple (9.3.80) £110 12·00
a. Printed on both sides — £650
123 9d. rose-lilac (21.8.80) 30·00 4·50
a. Printed on both sides † £600
124 9d. rose-lilac (*large holes*) (26.5.00) 20·00 4·50
125 1 1s. red-brown (3.11.77) 95·00 2·75
a. Imperf between (horiz pair) † £2500
126 1s. reddish lake-brown (1880) 95·00 3·75
127 1s. lake-brown (9.1.83) £100 3·00
128 1s. Vandyke brown (1891) £110 8·50
129 1s. dull brown (1891) 95·00 3·25
130 1s. chocolate (*large holes*) (6.5.97) 27·00 3·50
a. Imperf vert (horiz pair) £450
131 1s. sepia (*large holes*) (22.5.00) 27·00 6·50
a. Imperf between (vert pair) £650
132 3 2s. carmine (15.2.77) 55·00 7·50
a. Imperf between (horiz pair) † £3250
133 2s. rose-carmine (1885) 65·00 8·00
134 2s. rose-carmine (*large holes*) (6.12.98) 40·00 8·00

The perforation with larger, clean-cut holes resulted from the fitting of new pins to the machine.

No. 123a is known with the impression on the back either sideways or inverted. The Royal Philatelic Collection contains an unused marginal pair of the former.

(b) P 10

135 1 6d. Prussian blue (11.11.79) £225 26·00
136 6d. bright blue (1879) £250 21·00
136*a* 1s. reddish lake-brown £550

(c) P 10×11½–12½, 11½–12½×10, or compound

137 3 4d. violet-slate (21.5.79) £200 24·00
138 4d. dull purple (4.10.79) 90·00 2·75
139 1 6d. Prussian blue (29.12.77) £150 2·75
140 6d. bright blue £180 6·00
141 6d. bright ultramarine £130 2·75
142 1s. reddish lake-brown (9.2.85) £150 11·00
143 1s. dull brown (29.6.86) £190 14·00
144 3 2s. carmine (27.12.77) £110 6·50
145 2s. rose-carmine (1887) £100 6·00
a. Imperf between (horiz pair) † £3000

10

11

12

1901–02. Wmk Crown SA (wide). W **10**. P 11½–12½ (large holes).

146 4 9d. claret (1.2.02) 20·00 26·00
147 1 1s. dark brown (12.6.01) 22·00 16·00
148 1s. dark reddish brown (1902) 25·00 19·00
a. Imperf horiz (vert pair) £3000 £3000
149 1s. red-brown (aniline) (18.7.02) 25·00 38·00
150 3 2s. crimson (29.8.01) 45·00 16·00
151 2s. carmine 27·00 12·00

(Plates and electrotypes by D.L.R. Printed in Adelaide)

1868–76. W **10**.

(a) Rouletted

152 12 2d. deep brick-red (8.68) £170 7·00
153 2d. pale orange-red (5.10.68) £160 2·75
a. Printed on both sides † £750
b. Imperf between (horiz pair) † £1600
c. Imperf horiz (vert pair) † £3000

(b) P 11½–12½

154 11 1d. blue-green (10.1.75) £180 48·00
155 12 2d. pale orange-red (5.5.69) £1400 £250

(c) P 11½–12½×roulette

156 12 2d. pale orange-red (20.8.69) — £170

(d) P 10×roulette

157 12 2d. pale orange-red (7.5.70) £550 45·00

(e) P 10

158 11 1d. blue-green (4.75) £110 8·50
159 12 2d. brick-red (4.70) 65·00 4·00
160 2d. orange-red (1.7.70) 25·00 1·00
a. Printed on both sides † £425

(f) P 10×11½–12½, 11½–12½×10, or compound

161 11 1d. blue-green (27.8.75) £200 48·00
a. Imperf between (horiz pair) † £1500
162 12 2d. brick-red (19.1.71) £750 40·00
163 2d. orange-red (3.2.71) £225 40·00
a. Imperf (8.76) £1200 £1100

1869. Wmk Large Star W **2**.

(a) Rouletted

164 12 2d. orange-red (13.3.69) £190 26·00

(b) P 11½–12½×roulette

165 12 2d. orange-red (1.8.69) £2000 £120

(c) P 11½–12½

165*a* 12 2d. orange-red (7.69) — £1200

1871 (15 July). Wmk V and Crown, W **7**. P 10.

166 12 2d. brick-red £200 50·00

13

HALF-
PENNY
(14)

1876–1904. Wmk Crown SA (close). W **13**.

(a) P 10 (1876–1885)

167 11 1d. blue-green (9.2.76) 42·00 1·50
a. Yellowish green (11.78) 55·00 1·75
b. Deep green (11.79) 29·00 30
bb. Printed double † —
168 12 2d. orange-red (8.76) 55·00 50
a. Dull brick-red (21.5.77) 60·00 1·00
b. Blood-red (31.10.79) £300 4·75
c. Pale red (4.85) 19·00 40

(b) P 10×11½–12½, 11½–12½×10 or compound (1877–1880)

169 11 1d. deep green (11.2.80) 85·00 15·00
a. Blue-green (2.3.80) 40·00 7·50
170 12 2d. orange-red (4.9.77) £190 15·00
a. Dull brick-red (6.80) £190 15·00

(c) P 11½–12½ (1877–1884)

171 11 1d. blue-green (2.84) — £160
172 12 2d. orange-red (14.9.77) — £160
a. Blood-red (1.4.80) — £160

(d) P 15 (1893)

173 11 1d. green (8.5.93) 50·00 1·00
174 12 2d. pale orange (9.2.93) 29·00 1·00
a. Orange-red 28·00 1·00
b. Imperf between (vert pair) £950

(e) P 13 (1895–1903)

175 11 1d. pale green (11.1.95) 12·00 1·00
a. Green 12·00 20
b. Imperf between (vert pair) £1800
176 1d. rosine (8.8.99) 12·00 75
a. Scarlet (23.12.03) 8·00 1·25
b. Deep red 9·50 1·50
177 12 2d. pale orange (19.1.95) 16·00 20
a. *Orange-red* (9.5.95) 23·00 20
178 2d. bright violet (10.10.99) 7·00 20

(f) P 12×11½ (comb) (1904)

179 11 1d. rosine (2.2.04) 14·00 1·75
a. Scarlet (25.7.04) 8·50 1·00
180 12 2d. bright violet (11.10.04) 14·00 1·00

Examples of the 1d. pale green with thicker lettering come from a worn plate.

1882 (1 Jan). No. 167 surch with T **14**.

181 11 ½d. on 1d. blue-green 14·00 14·00

15

16

17

18

1883–99. W **13** (sideways on ½d.).

(a) P 10 (1883–1895)

182 15 ½d. chocolate (1.3.83) 19·00 2·25
a. Imperf between (horiz pair) † £1500
b. Red-brown (4.4.89) 10·00 2·25
c. Brown (1895) 5·50 4·75
183 16 3d. sage-green (12.86) 40·00 2·75
a. Olive-green (6.6.90) 26·00 6·00
b. Deep green (12.4.93) 23·00 6·00
s. Optd 'SPECIMEN' 40·00
184 17 4d. pale violet (3.90) 60·00 3·00
a. Aniline violet (3.1.93) 55·00 8·00
s. Optd 'SPECIMEN' 40·00
185 18 6d. pale blue (4.87) 75·00 3·75
a. Blue (5.5.87) 60·00 1·25
s. Optd 'SPECIMEN' 40·00

(b) P 10×11½–12½, 11½–12½×10 or compound (1891)

186 15 ½d. red-brown (25.9.91) 35·00 13·00
a. Imperf between (horiz pair) £1000

(c) P 11½–12½ (1890)

187 15 ½d. red-brown (12.10.90) 45·00 10·00

(d) P 15 (1893–1894)

188 15 ½d. pale brown (1.93) 12·00 1·50
aa. Imperf between (horiz pair)
a. Deep brown 12·00 1·50
b. Imperf between (horiz pair) £425
c. Perf 12½ between (pair) £350 90·00
189 17 4d. purple (1.1.94) 50·00 4·25
a. Slate-violet 50·00 4·50
190 18 6d. blue (20.11.93) 75·00 4·25

(e) P 13 (1895–1899)

191 15 ½d. pale brown (9.95) 5·50 60
a. Imperf between (horiz pair)
b. Deep brown (19.3.97) 6·00 45
192 16 3d. pale olive-green (26.7.97) 15·00 3·50
a. Deep olive-green (27.11.99) 6·00 3·50
193 17 4d. violet (21.1.96) 6·00 1·00
194 18 6d. pale blue (3.96) 12·00 1·50
a. Blue 11·00 1·50

REPRINTS. In 1884, and in later years, reprints on paper wmkd Crown SA, W **10**, were made of Nos. 1, 2, 3, 4, 12, 13, 14, 15, 19, 24, 27, 28, 32, 33, 34, 35, 36, 37, 38, 40, 43, 44, 49a, 53, 65, 67, 67 with surcharge in red, 70, 71, 72, 73, 78, 79, 81, 83, 86, 90, 118, 119, 120, 121, 122, 155, 158, 159, 164, 181, 182. They are overprinted 'REPRINT'.

In 1889 examples of the reprints for Nos. 1/3, 12, 15, 19, 27, 32/38, 44, 67, 67 surcharged in red, 70/71, 73, 83, 86, 118, 121/122, 158/159, 164 and 181/182, together with No. 141 overprinted 'SPECIMEN', were supplied to the UPU for distribution.

19

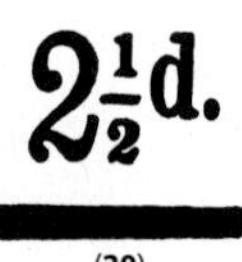
(20)

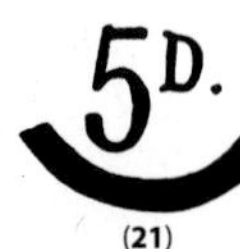
(21)

(Plates and electrotypes by D.L.R. Printed in Adelaide)

1886 (20 Dec)–**96.** T **19** (inscr 'POSTAGE & REVENUE'). W **13**. Parts of two or more wmks, on each stamp, sometimes sideways. P 10.

195 2s.6d. mauve £140 17·00
a. Perf 11½–12½. *Dull violet* £100 9·00
bb. Bright aniline violet £110 9·00
196 5s. rose-pink £160 19·00
a. Perf 11½–12½ £120 19·00
ab. Rose-carmine £120 22·00
197 10s. green £325 75·00
a. Perf 11½–12½ £250 70·00
198 15s. brownish yellow £850 £375
a. Perf 11½–12½ £900 £250
199 £1 blue £600 £180
a. Perf 11½–12½ £500 £170
200 £2 Venetian red £4750 £550
a. Perf 11½–12½ £4500 £500
201 50s. dull pink £5500 £800
a. Perf 11½–12½ £5000 £700
202 £3 sage green £6500 £800
a. Perf 11½–12½ £6000 £750
203 £4 lemon £12000
a. Perf 11½–12½ £10000 £1400
204 £5 grey £10000
a. Perf 11½–12½ £10000
205 £5 brown (P 11½–12½) (1896) £6000 £1100
206 £10 bronze £11000 £2000
a. Perf 11½–12½ £9500 £1400
207 £15 silver £38000
a. Perf 11½–12½ £35000 £2500
208 £20 claret £45000
a. Perf 11½–12½ £42000 £2750
195s/208s Optd 'SPECIMEN' *Set of 14** £1400

Variations exist in the length of the words and shape of the letters of the value inscription.

The 2s.6d. dull violet, 5s. rose-pink, 10s., £1 and £5 brown exist perf 11½–12½ with either large or small holes; the 2s.6d. aniline, 5s. rose-carmine, 15s., £2 and 50s. with large holes only and the remainder only with small holes.

Stamps perforated 11½–12½ small holes, are, generally speaking, rather rarer than those with the 1895 (large holes) gauge.

Stamps perf 10 were issued on 20 Dec 1886. Stamps perf 11½–12½ (small holes) are known with earliest dates covering the period from June 1890 to Feb 1896. Earliest dates of stamps with large holes range from July 1896 to May 1902.

*The listing of the 'SPECIMEN' set distributed by the UPU comprises stamps with W **13**, perf 10, with an overprint 12¼ mm long, except No. 205 which is perf 11½–12½, with an overprint 15¼ mm long. These should not be confused with the same values with other 'SPECIMEN' overprints, usually on stamps perf 11½–12½, and often with W **10**, which were prepared for presentation purposes and for inclusion in sets for sale to collectors.

1891 (1 Jan)–**93.** T **17/18** surch with T **20/1**. W **13**.

(a) P 10

229 17 2½d. on 4d. pale green (Br.) 8·00 2·50
a. Fraction bar omitted £110 80·00
b. Deep green 8·00 1·75
ba. Fraction bar omitted £110 75·00
bb. '2' and '½' closer together 26·00 16·00
bc. Imperf between (horiz pair)
bd. Imperf between (vert pair) † £3750
s. Optd 'SPECIMEN' 35·00
230 18 5d. on 6d. pale brown (C.) 19·00 8·00
a. Deep brown 19·00 7·50
b. No stop after '5D' £170
s. Optd 'SPECIMEN' 35·00

(b) P 10×11½–12½ or 11½–12½×10

231 17 2½d. on 4d. pale green (Br.) 65·00 6·50
a. Deep green 65·00 6·50

(c) P 11½–12½

232 17 2½d. on 4d. deep green 85·00 90·00

(d) P 15

233 17 2½d. on 4d. green (14.10.93) 60·00 2·75
a. Fraction bar omitted
b. '2' and '½d.' closer £130 20·00

On Nos. 229bb and 233b the base of the '1' of '½' and the back of the large '2' are 0.5 mm apart. On normal stamps the spacing is 1 mm.

22 Red Kangaroo

23

24 GPO, Adelaide

(Des M. Tannenberg, plates by D.L.R.)

1894 (1 Mar)–**1906.** W **13**.

(a) P 15

234 22 2½d. violet-blue 50·00 8·50
235 23 5d. brown-purple 45·00 4·25
234s/5s Optd 'SPECIMEN' *Set of 2* 70·00

(b) P 13

236 22 2½d. violet-blue (11.2.95) 35·00 1·75
237 2½d. indigo (25.3.98) 10·00 2·00
238 23 5d. Brown-purple (1.96) 11·00 1·75
a. Purple 11·00 1·75

(c) P 12×11½ (comb)

239 **22** 2½d. indigo (4.7.06) 16·00 6·00
240 **23** 5d. dull purple (1.05) 21·00 2·50

(Typo D.L.R.)

1899 (27 Dec)–**1905**. W **13**.

(a) P 13

241 **24** ½d. yellow-green 7·50 1·50

(b) P 12×11½ (comb)

242 **24** ½d. yellow-green (7.05) 8·00 2·75

25

The measurements given indicate the length of the value inscription in the bottom label. The dates are those of the earliest known postmarks.

1902–04. As T **19**, but top tablet as T **25** (thin 'POSTAGE'). W **13**.

(a) P 11½–12½

268 3d. olive-green (18½ *mm*) (1.8.02) 19·00 3·00
a. Wmk sideways † £1700
269 4d. red-orange (17 *mm*) (29.11.02) 38·00 4·75
270 6d. blue-green (16–16½ *mm*) (29.11.02) 14·00 3·50
271 8d. ultramarine (19 *mm*) (25.4.02) 8·50 19·00
272 8d. ultramarine (16½ *mm*) (22.3.04) 12·00 19·00
a. 'EIGNT' (R.2/9) £2500 £3000
273 9d. rosy lake (19.9.02) 17·00 13·00
a. Imperf between (vert pair) £2750
274 10d. dull yellow (29.11.02) 18·00 20·00
275 1s. brown (18.8.02) 27·00 8·00
a. Imperf between (horiz pair)
b. Imperf between (vert pair) £2750
c. 'POSTAGE' and value in red-brown £1400 £1100
276 2s.6d. pale violet (19.9.02) 80·00 50·00
a. Bright violet (2.2.03) 42·00 15·00
277 5s. rose (17.10.02) £120 75·00
278 10s. green (1.11.02) £200 90·00
279 £1 blue (1.11.02) £500 £250

(b) P 12

280 3d. olive-green (20 *mm*) (15.4.04) 32·00 3·50
a. 'POSTAGE' omitted; value below 'AUSTRALIA' £4500
281 4d. orange-red (17½–18 *mm*) (18.2.03) 25·00 3·00
282 6d. blue-green (15 *mm*) (14.11.03) 26·00 18·00
283 9d. rosy lake (2.12.03) £130 35·00

No. 280a comes from the bottom row of the sheet. Other stamps show the value below 'AUSTRALIA' with 'POSTAGE' over the bottom frame (*Price £950, unused*).

A used example of No. 273 in imperf between horiz pair is in the Royal Philatelic Collection.

PRINTER. Stamp printing in Adelaide ceased in 1909 when the Printer of Stamps, J. B. Cooke, was appointed head of the Commonwealth Stamp Printing Branch in Melbourne. From 9 March 1909 further printings of current South Australia stamps were made in Melbourne.

26

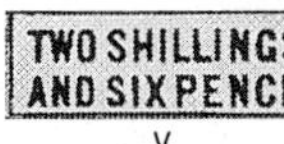

V

TWO SHILLINGS
AND SIXPENCE

X

In Type X the letters in the bottom line are slightly larger than in Type V, especially the 'A', 'S' and 'P'.

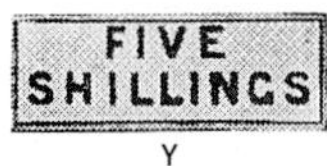

Y

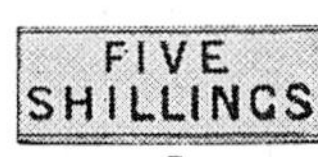

Z

In Type Z the letters 'S' and 'G' are more open than in Type Y.

Nos. 196/196a and 277 are similar to Type Y with all letters thick and regular and the last 'S' has the top curve rounded instead of being slightly flattened.

1904–11. As T **19**, but top tablet as T **26** (thick 'POSTAGE'). W **13**. P 12.

284 6d. blue-green (27.4.04) 42·00 3·00
a. Imperf between (vert pair) £5000
285 8d. bright ultramarine (4.7.05) 19·00 8·50
a. Value closer (15¼ *mm*) 70·00 28·00
b. Dull ultramarine (2.4.08) 27·00 6·50
ba. Ditto. Value closer (15¼ *mm*) £110 20·00
286 9d. rosy lake (17–17¼ *mm*) (18.7.04) 25·00 6·50
a. Value 16½–16¾ mm (2.06) 65·00 8·50
b. Brown-lake. Perf 12½ small holes (11.3.11) 17·00 27·00
287 10d. dull yellow (8.07) 18·00 26·00
a. Imperf between (horiz pair) £3250 £3500
b. Imperf between (vert pair) £4250
288 1s. brown (12.4.04) 32·00 4·00
a. Imperf between (vert pair) £2750
b. Imperf between (horiz pair) £3250
289 2s.6d. bright violet (V.) (14.7.05) 75·00 45·00
a. Dull violet (X) (8.06) 75·00 27·00
290 5s. rose-scarlet (Y) (13.7.04) 80·00 48·00
a. Scarlet (Z) (8.06) 80·00 48·00
b. Pale rose. Perf 12½ (*small holes*) (Z) (6.10) £130 70·00
291 10s. green (26.8.08) £200 £150
292 £1 blue (29.12.04) £325 £170
a. Perf 12½ (*small holes*) (6.10) £250 £160

The 'value closer' variety on the 8d. occurs six times in the sheet of 60. The value normally measures 16½ mm but in the variety it is 15¼ mm.

The 9d., 5s. and £1, perf 12½ (small holes), are late printings made in 1910–11 to use up the Crown SA paper.

No. 286*b* has the value as Type C of the 9d. on Crown over A paper.

27

1905–12. W **27**. P 12×11½ (new comb machine).

293 **24** ½d. pale green (4.07) 18·00 1·25
a. Yellow-green 8·50 1·25
b. Thin ready gummed paper (1912) 6·00 8·00
ba. Mixed perf 12×11½ and 12½ £850
294 **11** 1d. rosine (2.12.05) 7·50 20
a. Scarlet (4.11) 4·00 1·25
295 **12** 2d. bright violet (2.2.06) 27·00 30
aa. Imperf three sides (horiz pair) £3000
a. Mauve (4.08) 7·50 30
296 **22** 2½d. indigo-blue (14.9.10) 9·00 15·00
297 **23** 5d. brown-purple (11.3.08) 30·00 6·50

No. 295aa is perforated at foot.

Three types of the 9d., perf 12½, distinguishable by the distance between 'NINE' and 'PENCE'.

A. Distance 1¾ mm. B. Distance 2¼ mm. C. Distance 2½ mm.

1906–12. T **19** ('POSTAGE' thick as T **26**). W **27**. P 12 or 12½ (small holes).

298 3d. sage-green (19 *mm*) (26.6.06) 16·00 5·50
a. Imperf between (horiz pair) † £5500
b. Perf 12½. *Sage-green (17 mm)* (9.12.09) 17·00 12·00
c. Perf 12½. *Deep olive* (20 *mm*) (7.10) 75·00 11·00
d. Perf 12½. *Yellow-olive* (19 *mm*) (16.12.11) 80·00 60·00
da. Perf 12½. *Bright olive-green* (19–19¾ *mm*) Thin ready gummed paper (8.9.11) 12·00 26·00
e. Perf 11 (17 *mm*) (1910) £1000 £700
299 4d. orange-red (10.9.06) 12·00 3·00
a. Orange 12·00 3·00
b. Perf 12½. *Orange* 25·00 8·50
c. Thin ready gummed paper (19.8.12) 25·00 35·00
300 6d. blue-green (1.9.06) 17·00 3·00
a. Perf 12½ (21.4.10) 8·00 10·00
ab. Perf 12½. Imperf between (vert pair) £2500 £2750
b. Thin ready gummed paper (3.12) 10·00 20·00
301 8d. bright ultramarine (P 12½) (8.09) 10·00 23·00
a. Value closer (8.09) 45·00 85·00
302 9d. brown-lake (3.2.06) 23·00 5·50
aa. Imperf between (horiz strip of three) £5000
a. Imperf between (vert pair) £2250
b. Deep lake (9.5.08) 50·00 9·00
c. Perf 12½. *Lake* (A) (5.9.09) 11·00 11·00
d. Perf 12½. *Lake* (B) (7.09) 48·00 12·00
e. Perf 12½. *Brown-lake* 48·00 12·00
ea. Perf 12½. *Deep lake*. Thin paper (C) 38·00 12·00
f. Perf 11 (1909) † £1500
303 1s. brown (30.5.06) 12·00 5·00
aa. Imperf between (vert pair) £3500
a. Imperf between (horiz pair) £3750
b. Perf 12½ (10.3.10) 10·00 8·00
c. Thin ready gummed paper (4.8.11) 14·00 16·00
304 2s.6d. bright violet (X) (10.6.09) 75·00 32·00
a. Perf 12½. *Pale violet* (X) (6.10) 75·00 35·00
ab. Perf 12½. *Deep purple* (X) Thin ready gummed paper (15.11.12) £120 £130
305 5s. bright rose (P 12½) (Z) Thin ready gummed paper (24.4.11) £140 £150

The 'value closer' variety of the 8d. occurred 11 times in the sheet of 60 in the later printing only. On No. 301 the value measures 16½ mm while on No. 301a it is 15¼ mm.

The 1s. brown, perf compound of 11½ and 12½, formerly listed is now omitted, as it must have been perforated by the 12 machine, which in places varied from 11½ to 13. The 4d. has also been reported with a similar perforation.

STAMP BOOKLETS

There are very few surviving examples of Nos. SB1/SB4. Listings are provided for those believed to have been issued with prices quoted for those known still to exist.

1904 (1 Jan)–**09**. Black on red cover as Type B **1** of New South Wales. Stapled.

SB1 £1 booklet containing 240×1d. in four blocks of 30 and two blocks of 60
a. Red on pink cover (1909)
b. Blue on pink cover £15000

1904 (1 Jan). Black on grey cover as No. SB1. Stapled.

SB2 £1 booklet containing 120×2d. in four blocks of 30

1910 (May). Black on cream cover as Type B **2** of New South Wales. Stapled.

SB3 2s. booklet containing 11×½d. (No. 241), either in block of 6 plus block of 5 or block of 11, and 18×1d. (No. 176*a*), either in three blocks of 6 or block of 6 plus block of 12

Unsold stock of No. SB3 was uprated with one additional ½d. in May 1911.

1911 (Aug). Red on pink cover as No. SB3. Stapled.

SB4 2s. booklet containing 12×½d. (No. 241), either in two blocks of 6 or block of 12, and 18×1d. (No. 176*a*), either in three blocks of 6 or block of 6 plus block of 12 £7000
a. Red on green cover

On some examples of No. SB4 11 of the ½d. stamps were in blocks, with the 12th added separately.

OFFICIAL STAMPS

A. Departmentals

Following suspected abuses involving stamps supplied for official use it was decided by the South Australian authorities that such supplies were to be overprinted with a letter, or letters, indicating the department of the administration to which the stamps had been invoiced.

The system was introduced on 1 April 1868 using overprints struck in red. Later in the same year the colour of the overprints was amended blue, and, during the latter months of 1869, to black.

In 1874 the Postmaster-General recommended that this some-what cumbersome system be replaced by a general series of 'O.S.' overprints with the result that the separate accounting for the Departmentals ceased on 30 June of that year. Existing stocks continued to be used, however, and it is believed that much of the residue was passed to the Government Printer to pay postage on copies of the *Government Gazette*.

We are now able to provide a check list of these most interesting issues based on the definitive work. *The Departmental Stamps of South Australia* by A. R. Butler, FRPSL, RDP, published by the Royal Philatelic Society, London in 1978.

No attempt has been made to assign the various overprints to the catalogue numbers of the basic stamps, but each is clearly identified by both watermark and perforation. the colours are similar to those of the contemporary postage stamps, but there can be shade variations. Errors of overprint are recorded in footnotes, but not errors occurring on the basic stamps used.

Most departmental overprints are considered to be scarce to rare in used condition, with unused examples, used multiples and covers being regarded as considerable rarities.

Forgeries of a few items do exist, but most can be readily identified by comparison with genuine examples. A number of forged overprints on stamps not used for the genuine issues also occur.

A. (Architect)

Optd in red with stop. W **2**. 2d. (Roul), 4d. (P 11½–12½), 6d. (Roul), 1s. (Roul)

Optd in red without stop W **2**. Roul. 1d., 2d., 6d., 1s.

Optd in black. *(a)* W **2**. 4d. (P 10×11½–12½), 6d. (P 11½–12½), 2s. (Roul)

(b) W **10**. 2d. D.L.R. (Roul), 2d. D.L.R. (P 10)

A.G. (Attorney-General)

Optd in red. W **2**. Roul. 1d., 2d., 6d., 1s.

Optd in blue. *(a)* W **2**. Roul. 6d.

(b) W **10**. Roul. 2d. D.L.R.

Optd in black. *(a)* W **2**. 1d (P 11½–12½×Roul), 4d. (P 11½–12½), 4d. (P 10), 6d. (P 11½–12½×Roul), 6d. (P 11½–12½), 1s. (P 11½–12½×Roul), 1s. (P 11½–12½) 1s. (P 10)

(b) W **10**. 2d. D.L.R. (Roul), 2d. D.L.R. (P 10)

A.O. (Audit Office)

Optd in red. W **2**. 2d. (Roul), 4d. (P 11½–12½), 6d. (Roul)

Optd in blue. *(a)* W **2**. P 11½–12½. 1d., 6d.

(b) W **10**. Roul. 2d. D.L.R.

Optd in black. *(a)* W **2**. 1d. (P 11½–12½), 1d. (P 10), 2d. D.L.R. (Roul), 4d. (P 11½–12½) 4d. (P 10), 4d. (P 10×11½–12½), 6d. (Roul), 6d. (P 11½–12½), 1s. (P 11½–12½), 1s. (P 11½–12½×Roul)

(b) W **7**. P 10. 4d.

(c) W **10**. 2d. D.L.R. (Roul), 2d. D.L.R. (P 10)

B.D. (Barracks Department)

Optd in red. W **2**. Roul. 2d., 6d., 1s.

B.G. (Botanic Garden)

Optd in black. *(a)* W **2**. 1d. (P 11½–12½×Roul), 1d. (P 11½–12½), 1d. (P 10×11½–12½), 2d. D.L.R. (Roul), 6d. (Roul), 6d. (P 11½–12½×Roul), 6d. (P 11½–12½), 1s. (P 11½–12½×Roul), 1s. (P 11½–12½), 1s. (P 10), 1s. (P 10×11½–12½)

(b) W **7**. P 10, 2d. D.L.R.

(c) W **10**. 2d. D.L.R. (Roul), 2d. D.L.R. (P 10)

The 6d. (W **2**. Roul) is known without stop after 'B'.

B.M. (Bench of Magistrates)

Optd in red. W **2**. Roul. 2d.

Optd in black. W **10**. Roul. 2d. D.L.R.

C. (Customs)

Optd in red. W **2**. 1d. (Roul), 2d. (Roul), 4d. (P 11½–12½), 6d. (Roul), 1s. (Roul)

Optd in blue *(a)* W **2**. Roul. 1d., 4d., 6d., 1s., 2s.

(b) W **10**. Roul. 2d. D.L.R.

Optd in black. *(a)* W **2**. 1d. (Roul), 1d. (P 10), 1d. (P 10×11½–12½), 4d. (P 11½–12½), 4d. (P 10), 4d. (P 10×11½–12½), 6d. (Roul), 6d. (P 11½–12½), 6d. (P 10), 1s. (P 11½–12½×Roul), 1s. (P 11½–12½), 2s. (Roul)

(b) W **7**. P 10. 2d. D.L.R.

(c) W **10**. 2d. D.L.R. (Roul), 2d. D.L.R. (P 10×Roul), 2d. D.L.R. (P 10), 2d. D.L.R. (P 10×11½–12½)

The 2d. (W **10**. Roul) with black overprint is known showing the error 'G' for 'C'.

C.D. (Convict Department)

Optd in red. W **2**. 2d. (Roul), 4d. (P 11½–12½), 6d. (Roul), 1s. (Roul)

Optd in black. *(a)* W **2**. 1d. (P 11½–12½×Roul), 2d. D.L.R. (Roul), 4d. (P 11½–12½), 6d. (Roul), 6d. (P 11½–12½×Roul, 1s. (P 11½–12½×Roul)

(b) W **10**. 2d. D.L.R. (Roul), 2d. D.L.R. (P 11½–12½), 2d. D.L.R. (P 11½–12½×Roul)

C.L. (Crown Lands)

Optd in red. W **2**. 2d. (Roul), 4d. (P 11½–12½), 6d. (Roul), 1s. (Roul)

Optd in blue. *(a)* W **2**. Roul. 4d., 6d.

(b) W **10**. Roul. 2d. D.L.R.

Optd in black. *(a)* W **2**. 2d. D.L.R. (Roul), 4d. (P 11½–12½), 4d. (P 10), 4d. (P 10×11½–12½), 6d. (Roul), 6d. (P 11½–12½), 1s. (P 11½–12½×Roul), 2s. (Roul), 2s. (P 11½–12½)

(b) W **7**. P 10. 2d. D.L.R., 4d.

(c) W **10**. 2d. D.L.R. (Roul), 2d. D.L.R. (P 10), 2d. D.L.R. (P 10×11½–12½)

The 2s. (W **2**. P 11½–12½) with black overprint is known showing the stop omitted after 'L'.

C.O. (Commissariat Office)

Optd in red. W **2**. (Roul), 4d. (P 11½–12½) 6d. (Roul), 1s. (Roul)
Optd in black. (*a*) W **2**. 4d. (P 10), 4d. (P 10×11½–12½), 6d. (P 11½–12½), 1s. (P 11½–12½), 2s. (Roul), 2s. (P 11½–12½)
(*b*) W **10**. 2d. D.L.R. (Roul), 2d. D.L.R. (P 10)

The 6d. (W **2**. Roul) with red overprint is known showing the error 'O' for 'C', and the 2s. (W **2**. P 11½–12½) with black overprint with the stop omitted after 'O'.

C.P. (Commissioner of Police)

Optd in red. W **2**. 2d. (Roul). 4d. (P 11½–12½), 6d. (Roul)

C.S. (Chief Secretary)

Optd in red. W **2**. 2d. (Roul), 4d. (P 11½–12½), 6d. (Roul), 1s. (Roul)
Optd in blue. (*a*) W **2**. Roul. 4d., 6d.
(*b*) W **10**. Roul. 2d. D.L.R.
Optd in black. (*a*) W **2**. 2d. D.L.R. (Roul), 4d. (Roul), 4d. (P 11½–12½×Roul), 4d. (P 11½–12½), 4d. (P 10), 4d. (P 10×11½–12½), 6d. (P 11½–12½×Roul), 6d. (P 11½–12½), 6d. (P 10), 6d. (P 10×11½–12½), 1s. (P 11½–12½×Roul), 1s. (P 11½–12½), 1s. (P 10), 1s. (P 10×11½–12½), 2s. (P 10×11½–12½)
(*b*) W **7**. P 10. 2d.
(*c*) W **10**. 2d. D.L.R. (Roul), 2d. D.L.R. (P 10)

The 6d. and 1s. (W **2**. Roul) with red overprint are known showing the error 'G' for 'C'.

C.Sgn. (Colonial Surgeon)

Optd in red. W **2**. 2d. (Roul), 4d. (P 11½–12½), 6d. (Roul)
Optd in black. (*a*) W **2**. 2d. D.L.R. (Roul), 4d. (P 10), 4d. (P 10×11½–12½), 6d. (Roul), 6d. (P 11½–12½×Roul) 6d. (P 11½–12½)
(*b*) W **10**. 2d. D.L.R. (Roul), 2d. D.L.R. (P 11½–12½×Roul), 2d. (P 10×Roul), 2d. D.L.R. (P 10)

Two types of overprint exist on the 2d. D.L.R., the second type having block capitals instead of the serifed type used for the other values.

D.B. (Destitute Board)

Optd in red. W **2**. 1d. (Roul), 2d. (Roul), 4d. (P 11½–12½), 6d. (Roul), 1s. (Roul)
Optd in blue. (*a*) W **2**. 2d. D.L.R. (Roul), 4d. (P 11½–12½), 6d. (Roul)
(*b*) W **10**. Roul. 2d. D.L.R.
Optd in black. (*a*) W **2**. 1d. (P 11½–12½), 4d. (P 11½–12½), 4d. (P 10), 6d. (P 10×11½–12½) 1s (P 10)
(*b*) W **10**. 2d. D.L.R. (Roul), 2d. D.L.R. (P 11½–12½), 2d. D.L.R. (P 10), 2d. D.L.R. (P 10×11½–12½)

The 2d. D.L.R. (W **10**. P 10) with black overprint is known showing the stop omitted after 'D'.

D.R. (Deeds Registration)

Optd in red. W **2**. Roul, 2d., 6d.

E. (Engineer)

Optd in red. W **2**. 2d. (Roul), 4d. (P 11½–12½), 6d. (Roul), 1s. (Roul)
Optd in blue. (*a*) W **2**. Roul. 1s.
(*b*) W **10**. Roul. 2d. D.L.R.
Optd in black. (*a*) W **2**. 4d. (P 11½–12½), 4d. (P 10), 4d. (P 10×11½–12½), 6d. (P 11½–12½), 1s. (P 11½–12½×Roul), 1s. (P 11½–12½), 1s. (P 10×11½–12½)
(*b*) W **7**. P 10. 4d.
(*c*) W **10**. P 10. 2d. D.L.R.

E.B. (Education Board)

Optd in red. W **2**. 2d. (Roul), 4d. (P 11½–12½), 6d. (Roul)
Optd in blue. (*a*) W **2**. Roul. 4d., 6d.
(*b*) W **10**. Roul. 2d. D.L.R.
Optd in black. (*a*) W **2**. 2d. D.L.R. (Roul), 4d (Roul), 4d. (P 11½–12½), 4d. (P 10), 6d. (P 11½–12½×Roul), 6d. (P 11½×12½)
(*b*) W **7**. P 10. 2d. D.L.R.
(*c*) W **10**. 2d. D.L.R. (Roul), 2d. D.L.R. (P 10), 2d. D.L.R. (P 10×11½–12½)

G.F. (Gold Fields)

Optd in black. (*a*) W **2**. Roul. 6d.
(*b*) W **10**. 2d. D.L.R. (P 10×Roul), 2d. D.L.R. (P 10)

G.P. (Government Printer)

Optd in red. W **2**. Roul. 1d., 2d., 6d., 1s.
Optd in blue. (*a*) W **2**. Roul. 1d., 6d., 1s., 2s.
(*b*) W **10**. Roul. 2d. D.L.R.
Optd in black. (*a*) W **2**. 1d. (Roul), 1d. (P 11½–12½×Roul), 1d. (P 11½–12½) 1d. (P 10) 1d. (P 10×11½–12½), 6d. (P 11½–12½×Roul), 1s. (P 10×11½–12½), 2s. (Roul), 2s. (P 11½–12½) 2s. (P 10×11½–12½)
(*b*) W **10**. 2d. D.L.R. (Roul), 2d. D.L.R. (P 10)

The 1d. and 1s. (W **2**. Roul) with red overprint are known showing 'C.P.' instead of 'G.P.'.

G.S. (Government Storekeeper)

Optd in red. W **2**. Roul. 2d.

G.T. (Goolwa Tramway)

Optd in red. W **2**. 1d. (Roul), 2d. (Roul), 4d. (P 11½–12½), 6d. (Roul), 1s. (Roul)
Optd in black. (*a*) W **2**. 2d. D.L.R. (Roul), 4d. (P 11½–12½)
(*b*) W **10**. Roul. 2d. D.L.R.

The 2d. and 6d. (both W **2**. Roul) with red overprint are known showing the stop omitted after 'T'. The 6d, and 1s. (W **2**. Roul) with red overprint are known showing 'C.T.', instead of 'G.T.'.

H. (Hospitals)

Optd in black. (*a*) W **2**. P 10×11½–12½. 4d.
(*b*) W **7**. P 10. 2d. D.L.R.
(*c*) W **10**. 2d. D.L.R. (P 10), 2d. D.L.R. (P 10×11½–12½)

H.A. (House of Assembly)

Optd in red. W **2**. 1d. (Roul), 2d. (Roul), 4d. (P 11½–12½), 6d. (Roul), 1s. (Roul)
Optd in black. (*a*) W **2**. 1d. (P 11½–12½), 1d. (P 10) 1d. (P 10×11½–12½), 4d. (P 11½–12½), 4d. (P 10) 6d. (Roul), 6d. (P 11½–12½) 1s. (P 11½–12½×Roul), 1s. (P 11½–12½)
(*b*) W **10**. 2d. D.L.R. (Roul), 2d. D.L.R. (P 10)

I.A. (Immigration Agent)

Optd in red. W **2**. 1d. (Roul), 2d. (Roul), 4d. (P 11½–12½), 6d. (Roul)

I.E. (Intestate Estates)

Optd in black. W **10**. P 10. 2d. D.L.R.

I.S. (Inspector of Sheep)

Optd in red. W **2**. Roul. 2d., 6d.
Optd in blue. W **2**. P 11½–12½. 6d.
Optd in black. (*a*) W **2**. 2d. D.L.R. (Roul), 6d. (P 11½–12½×Roul)
(*b*) W **10**. 2d. D.L.R. (Roul). 2d. D.L.R. (P 10)

L.A. (Lunatic Asylum)

Optd in red. W **2**. 1d. (Roul), 2d. (Roul), 4d. (P 11½–12½), 6d. (Roul), 1s. (Roul)
Optd in black. (*a*) W **2**. 4d. (P 11½–12½), 4d. (P 10), 4d. (P 10×11½–12½), 6d. (P 11½–12½), 1s. (P 11½–12½), 2s. (Roul)
(*b*) W **10**. 2d. D.L.R. (Roul), 2d. D.L.R. (P 10)

L.C. (Legislative Council)

Optd in red. W **2**. Roul. 2d., 6d.
Optd in black. (*a*) W **2**. Roul. 6d.
(*b*) W **10**. 2d. D.L.R. (Roul), 2d. D.L.R. (P 10×Roul)

The 2d. and 6d. (both W **2**. Roul) with red overprint are known showing the stop omitted after 'C'.

L.L. (Legislative Librarian)

Optd in red. W **2**. 2d. (Roul), 4d. (P 11½–12½), 6d. (Roul)
Optd in black. (*a*) W **2**. P 11½–12½. 6d.
(*b*) W **10**. P 10. 2d. D.L.R.

The 2d. and 6d. (both W **2**. Roul) with red overprint are known showing the stop omitted from between the two letters.

L.T. (Land Titles)

Optd in red. W **2**. 2d. (Roul), 4d. (P 11½–12½), 6d. (Roul), 1s. (Roul)
Optd in blue. W **10**. Roul. 2d. D.L.R.
Optd in black. (*a*) W **2**. 4d. (P 11½–12½), 4d. (P 10), 4d. (P 10×11½–12½), 6d. (P 11½–12½×Roul), 6d. (P 11½–12½), 6d. (P 10), 6d. (P 10×11½–12½)
(*b*) W **7**. P 10. 2d. D.L.R.
(*c*) W **10**. 2d. D.L.R. (Roul), 2d. D.L.R. (P 10)

The 2d. and 6d. (both W **2**. Roul) with red overprint are known showing the stop omitted after 'T'.

M. (Military)

Optd in red. W **2**. Roul. 2d., 6d., 1s.
Optd in black. W **2**. 6d. (P 11½–12½×Roul), 1s. (P 11½–12½×Roul), 2s. (Roul)

M.B. (Marine Board)

Optd in red. W **2**. 1d. (Roul), 2d. (Roul), 4d. (Roul), 4d. (P 11½–12½), 6d. (Roul), 1s. (Roul)
Optd in black. (*a*) W **2**. 1d. (Roul), 1d. (P 11½–12½), 2d. D.L.R. (Roul), 4d. (P 11½–12½×Roul), 4d. (P 11½–12½), 4d. (P 10), 4d. (P 10×11½–12½), 6d. (Roul), 6d. (P 11½–12½), 6d. (P 10), 6d. (P 10×11½–12½), 1s. (P 11½–12½×Roul), 1s. (P 11½–12½) 1s. (P 10), 1s. (P 10×11½–12½)
(*b*) W **7**. P 10. 4d.
(*c*) W **10**. Roul. 2d. D.L.R.

M.R. (Manager of Railways)

Optd in red. W **2**. Roul. 2d., 6d.
Optd in black. (*a*) W **2**. 1d. (P 11½–12½), 1d. (P 10), 2d. D.L.R. (Roul), 4d. (Roul), 4d. (P 11½–12½), 6d. (P 11½–12½×Roul), 1s. (P 11½–12½×Roul), 2s. (P 11½–12½ 1, 2s. (P 10×11½–12½)
(*b*) W **10**. 2d. D.L.R. (Roul), 2d. D.L.R. (P 10), 2d. D.L.R. (P 10×11½–12½)

M.R.G. (Main Roads Gambierton)

Optd in red without stops. W **2**. Roul. 2d., 6d.
Optd in blue without stops. W **10**. Roul. 2d. D.L.R.
Optd in black without stops. W **10**. 2d. D.L.R. (Roul), 2d. D.L.R. (Roul 10)
Optd in black with stops. W **10**. 2d. D.L.R. (Roul), 2d. D.L.R. (Roul 10)

The 2d. D.L.R. (W **10**. P 10) with black overprint is known showing the stops omitted after 'M' and 'R'.

N.T. (Northern Territory)

Optd in black (*a*) W **2**. P 11½–12½. 1d., 3d. on 4d., 6d., 1s.
(*b*) W **10**. 2d. D.L.R. (Roul), 2d. D.L.R. (P 10)

O.A. (Official Assignee)

Optd in red. W **2**. 2d. (Roul), 4d. (P 11½–12½)
Optd in blue. W **10**. Roul. 2d. D.L.R.
Optd in black. (*a*) W **2**. P 10. 4d.
(*b*) W **7**. P 10. 2d. D.L.R.
(*c*) W **10**. 2d. D.L.R. (Roul), 2d. D.L.R. (P 10×roul), 2d. D.L.R. (P 10)

P. (Police)

Optd in blue. (*a*) W **2**. Roul. 6d.
(*b*) W **10**. Roul. 2d. D.L.R.
Optd in black. (*a*) W **2**. 6d. (P 11½–12½×Roul), 6d. (P 11½–12½), 6d. (P 10)
(*b*) W **7**. P 10. 2d. D.L.R.
(*c*) W **10**. 2d. D.L.R. (Roul), 2d. D.L.R. (P 11½–12½), 2d. D.L.R. (P 11½–12½×Roul), 2d. D.L.R. (P 10×Roul), 2d. D.L.R. (P 10), 2d. D.L.R. (P 10×11½–12½)

P.A. (Protector of Aborigines)

Optd in red. W **2**. Roul. 2d., 6d.
Optd in black. (*a*) W **2**. P. 2d. D.L.R., 6d.
(*b*) W **10**. 2d. D.L.R. (Roul), 2d. D.L.R. (P 10)

P.O. (Post Office)

Optd in red. W **2**. Roul. 1d., 2d., 6d., 1s.
Optd in blue. (*a*) W **2**. Roul. 2d.
(*b*) W **10**. Roul. 2d. D.L.R.
Optd in black. (*a*) W **2**. 1d. (P 10×11½–12½), 2d. D.L.R. (Roul), 2d. D.L.R. (P 11½–12½×Roul), 4d. (P 11½–12½), 6d. (Roul), 6d. (P 11½×12½), 1s. (P 11½–12½×Roul), 1s. (P 11½×12½) 1s. (P 11½–12½), 1s. (P 10) 1s. (P 10×11½–12½)
(*b*) W **10**. 2d. D.L.R. (Roul), 2d. (P 11½–12½×Roul), 2d. D.L.R. (P 10×Roul), 2d. D.L.R. (P 10)

The 4d. (W **2**. P 11½–12½) with black overprint is known showing the stop omitted after 'O'.

P.S. (Private Secretary)

Optd in red. W **2**. 1d. (Roul), 2d. (Roul), 4d. (P 11½–12½), 6d. (Roul), 1s. (Roul)
Optd in black. (*a*) W **2**. 1d. (P 11½–12½×Roul), 1d. (P 11½–12½), 1d. (P 10), 2d. (Roul), 3d. (in black) on 4d. (P 11½–12½), 3d. (in red) on 4d. (P 10), 3d. (in black) on 4d. (P 10), 4d. (P 11½–12½), 4d. (P 10), 4d. (P 10×11½–12½) 6d. (Roul), 6d. (P 11½–12½×Roul), 6d. (P 11½–12½), 6d. (P 10), 9d. (Roul), 9d. (P 11½–12½) 10d. on 9d. (P 10), 10d. on 9d. (P 10×11½–12½), 1s. (P 11½–12½×Roul)
(*b*) W **7**. P 10. 2d. D.L.R.
(*c*) W **10**. 2d. D.L.R. (Roul), 2d. D.L.R. (P 10)

P.W. (Public Works)

Optd in red without stop after 'W'. W **2**. Roul. 2d., 6d., 1s.
Optd in black. (*a*) W **2**. 2d. D.L.R. (Roul), 4d. (P 10), 6d. (Roul), 6d. (P 11½–12½), 1s. (P 11½–12½×Roul)
(*b*) W **10**. 2d. D.L.R. (Roul), 2d. D.L.R. (P 10)

R.B. (Road Board)

Optd in red. W **2**. 1d. (Roul), 2d. (Roul), 4d. (P 11½–12½), 6d. (Roul), 1s. (Roul)
Optd in blue without stops. W **10**. Roul. 2d D.L.R
Optd in black. (*a*) W **2**. 1d. (P 11½–12½×Roul), 1d. (P 10), 4d. (Roul), 4d. (P 10), 6d. (P 10), 2s. (Roul)
(*b*) W **7**. P 10. 2d. D.L.R.
(*c*) W **10**. 2d. D.L.R. (Roul), 2d. D.L.R. (P 10×Roul), 2d. D.L.R. (P 10)

The 6d. (W **2**. Roul) with red overprint is known showing the stop omitted after 'B'.

R.G. (Registrar-General)

Optd in red. W **2**. Roul. 2d., 6d., 1s.
Optd in blue. (*a*) W **2**. P 11½–12½×Roul. 6d.
(*b*) W **10**. 2d. D.L.R. (Roul), 2d. D.L.R. (P 11½–12½×Roul)
Optd in black. (*a*) W **2**. 2d. D.L.R. (Roul), 6d. (P 10), 6d. (P 10×11½–12½), 1s. (P 11½–12½×Roul), 1s. (P 10)
(*b*) W **7**. P 10. 2d. D.L.R.
(*c*) W **10**. 2d. D.L.R. (Roul), 2d. D.L.R. (P 10×Roul), 2d. D.L.R. (P 10), 2d. D.L.R. (P 10×11½–12½)

The 2d. (W **2**. Roul) with red overprint is known showing 'C' for 'G'.

S. (Sheriff)

Optd in red. W **2**. Roul. 2d., 6d.
Optd in blue. W **10**. Roul. 2d. D.L.R.
Optd in black. (*a*) W **2**. 6d. (Roul), 6d. (P 11½–12½×Roul), 6d. (P 11½–12½), 6d. (P 10)
(*b*) W **10**. 2d. D.L.R. (Roul), 2d. D.L.R. (P 10×Roul), 2d. D.L.R. (P 10)

S.C. (Supreme Court)

Optd in red. W **2**. Roul. 2d. 6d.
Optd in black. W **10**. P 10. 2d. D.L.R.

S.G. (Surveyor-General)

Optd in red. W **2**. 2d. (Roul), 4d. (P 11½–12½), 6d. (Roul)
Optd in blue. (*a*) W **2**. Roul. 4d.
(*b*) W **10**. Roul. 2d. D.L.R.
Optd in black. (*a*) W **2**. 2d. D.L.R. (Roul), 4d. (P 11½–12½), 4d. (P 10) 4d. (P 10×11½–12½), 6d. (P 11½–12½×Roul), 6d. (P 11½–12½), 6d. (P 10), 6d. (P 10×11½–12½)
(*b*) W **7**. P 10. 2d. D.L.R.
(*c*) W **10**. 2d. D.L.R. (Roul), 2d. D.L.R. (P 11½–12½), 2d. D.L.R. (P 10×Roul), 2d. D.L R (P 10)

The 2d. (W **7** and W **10**. P 10) with black overprint are known showing 'C' for 'G'.

S.M. (Stipendiary Magistrate)

Optd in red. W **2**. Roul. 1d., 2d., 4d., 6d., 1s.
Optd in blue. (*a*) W **2**. Roul. 2d., 4d., 6d.
(*b*) W **10**. Roul. 2d. D.L.R.
Optd in black. (*a*) W **2**. 1d. (P 11½–12½), 1d. (P 10), 2d. D.L.R. (Roul), 4d. (Roul), 4d. (P 11½–12½×Roul), 4d. (P 11½–12½), 4d. (P 10), 4d. (P 10×11½–12½), 6d. (P 11½–12½×Roul), 6d. (P 11½–12½), 6d. (P 10), 6d. (P 10×11½–12½), 1s. (P 11½–12½×Roul)
(*b*) W **7**. P 10. 2d. D.L.R.
(*c*) W **10**. 2d. D.L.R. (Roul), 2d. D.L.R. (P 11½–12½), 2d. D.L.R. (P 10×Roul) 2d. D.L.R. (P 10), 2d D.L.R. (P 10×11½–12½)

The 2d. and 4d. (both W **2**. Roul) with red overprint are known showing the stop omitted after 'M'.

S.T. (Superintendent of Telegraphs)

Optd in red. W **2**. Roul. 2d., 6d.
Optd in blue. W **10**. Roul. 2d. D.L.R.

Optd in black. (*a*) W **2**. Roul. 2d. D.L.R., 6d.
(*b*) W **7**. P 10. 2d. D.L.R.
(*c*) W **10**. 2d. D.L.R. (Roul), 2d. D.L.R. (P 10×Roul), 2d. D.L.R. (P 10)

The 2d. and 6d. (both W **2**. Roul) with red overprint are known showing the stop omitted after 'T'.

T. (Treasury)

Optd in red. W **2**. 1d. (Roul), 2d. (Roul), 4d. (P 11½–12½×Roul), 6d. (Roul), 1s. (Roul)
Optd in blue. (*a*) W **2**. Roul. 1d., 4d., 6d.
(*b*) W **10**. Roul. 2d. D.L.R.
Optd in black. (*a*) W **2**. 1d. (P 10), 2d. D.L.R. (Roul), 4d. (Roul), 4d. (P 11½–12½), 4d. (P 10), 6d. (Roul), 6d. (P 11½–12½), 1s. (P 11½–12½×Roul), 1s. (P 10×11½–12½), 2s. (Roul), 2s. (P 11½–12½), 2s. (P 10×11½–12½)
(*b*) W **7**. P 10. 2d. D.L.R.
(*c*) W **10**. 2d. D.L.R. (Roul), 2d. D.L.R. (P 10)

T.R. (Titles Registration)

Optd in black. (*a*) W **2**. 4d. (P 11½–12½), 4d. (P 10×11½–12½), 6d. (P 11½–12½), 1s. (P 11½–12½)
(*b*) W **10**. P 10. 2d. D.L.R.

V. (Volunteers)

Optd in black. (*a*) W **2**. 4d. (P 10×11½–12½), 6d. (P 11½–12½), 1s. (P 11½–12½)
(*b*) W **10**. P 10. 2d. D.L.R.
(*c*) W **10**. 2d. D.L.R. (Roul), 2d. D.L.R. (P 10×Roul), 2d. D.L.R. (P 10)

The 2d. (W **10**. P 10×Roul) overprinted in black is only known showing the stop omitted after 'V'.

VA. (Valuator of Runs)

Optd in black without stop after 'V'. (*a*) W **2**. Roul. 4d.
(*b*) W **10**. P 10. 2d. D.L.R.

VN. (Vaccination)

Optd in black without stop after 'V'. W **2**. 4d. (P 10), 4d. (P 10×11½–12½)

W. (Waterworks)

Optd in red. W **2**. Roul. 2d.
Optd in black. W **10**. 2d. D.L.R. (Roul), 2d. D.L.R. (P 10)

The 2d. (W **2**. Roul) with red overprint is known showing the stop omitted after 'W'.

B. General

O.S. (O **1**) **O.S.** (O **2**)

1874–77. Optd with Type O **1**. W **2**.

(a) P 10

O1 **3** 4d. dull purple (18.2.74) £3000 £550

(b) P 11½–12½×10

O2 **1** 1d. green (2.1.74) — £475
O3 **3** 4d. dull violet (12.2.75) £140 7·00
O4 **1** 6d. Prussian blue (20.10.75) £200 12·00
O4*a* **3** 2s. rose-pink
O5 2s. carmine (3.12.76) £900 £150

(c) P 11½–12½

O6 **1** 1d. deep yellow-green (30.1.74) £3750 £400
a. Printed on both sides — £1300
O7 **3** 3d. on 4d. ultramarine (26.6.77) £9000 £3500
a. No stop after 'S' — £4500
O8 4d. dull violet (13.7.74) 95·00 9·50
a. No stop after 'S' — 75·00
O9 **1** 6d. bright blue (31.8.75) £300 22·00
a. 'O.S.' double — £375
O10 6d. Prussian blue (27.3.74) £275 9·50
a. No stop after 'S' — £100
O11 **4** 9d. red-purple (22.3.76) £4500 £1900
a. No stop after 'S' £5000 £2500
O12 **1** 1s. red-brown (5.8.74) £120 6·50
a. 'O.S.' double — £350
b. No stop after 'S' £400 85·00
O13 **3** 2s. crimson-carmine (13.7.75) £375 32·00
a. No stop after 'S' — £150
b. No stops — £200
c. Stops at top of letters

1876–85. Optd with Type O **1**. W **8**.

(a) P 10

O14 **1** 6d. bright blue (1879) £200 20·00

(b) P 10×11½–12½, 11½–12½×10, or compound

O15 **3** 4d. violet-slate (24.1.78) £130 8·50
O16 4d. plum (29.11.81) 75·00 2·75
O17 4d. deep mauve 75·00 2·50
a. No stop after 'S' £250 50·00
b. No stop after 'O'
c. 'O.S.' double
d. 'O.S.' inverted — £325
e. Imperf between (horiz pair)
O18 **1** 6d. bright blue (1877) £160 5·50
a. 'O.S.' inverted
b. No stop after 'O'
c. Mixed perfs 10 and 11½–12½ — †
O19 6d. bright ultramarine (27.3.85) £160 5·50
a. 'O.S.' inverted
b. 'O.S.' double
c. 'O.S.' double, one inverted — £600
d. No stop after 'S' £650 80·00
e. No stops after 'O' and 'S'
O20 1s. red-brown (27.3.83) £100 7·00
a. 'O.S.' inverted
b. No stop after 'O'
c. No stop after 'S' — 85·00
O21 **3** 2s. carmine (16.3.81) £325 9·00
a. 'O.S.' inverted — £550
b. No stop after 'S' — £120

(c) P 11½–12½

O22 **3** 3d. on 4d. ultramarine £8500
O23 4d. violet-slate (14.3.76) £225 28·00
O24 4d. deep mauve (19.8.79) 95·00 14·00
a. 'O.S.' inverted † £850
b. 'O.S.' double, one inverted
c. No stop after 'S' — 90·00
O25 **1** 6d. Prussian blue (6.77) £150 7·50
a. 'O.S.' double — £190
b. 'O.S.' inverted
O26 **4** 8d. on 9d. brown (9.11.76) £6500 £3250
a. 'O.S.' double £7500
b. 'O' only — £3500
O26*c* 9d. purple £9000
O27 **1** 1s. red-brown (12.2.78) 60·00 8·50
a. 'O.S.' inverted £750 £275
b. No stop after 'S' £375 90·00
c. 'O.S.' double † £500
O28 1s. lake-brown (8.11.83) 75·00 4·25
O29 **3** 2s. rose-carmine (12.8.85) £275 8·50
a. 'O.S.' double — £325
b. 'O.S.' inverted — £375
c. No stop after 'S' — 95·00

1891–1902. Optd with Type O **2**.

(a) W **8**. *P 11½–12½*

O30 **1** 1s. lake-brown (18.4.91) 90·00 11·00
O31 1s. Vandyke brown £100 8·50
O32 1s. dull brown (2.7.96) 80·00 5·50
a. No stop after 'S' — £100
O33 1s. sepia (*large holes*) (4.1.02) 75·00 5·50
a. 'O.S.' double — £500
b. No stop after 'S'
O34 **3** 2s. carmine (26.6.00) £160 15·00
a. No stop after 'S'

(b) W **8**. *P 10×11½–12½*

O35 **3** 2s. rose-carmine (9.11.95) £160 10·00
a. No stop after 'S' £500
b. 'O.S.' double

(c) W 10. P 11½–12½

O36 **1** 1s. dull brown (1902) £110 50·00

1874–76. Optd with Type O **1**. W **10**.

(a) P 10

O37 **11** 1d. blue-green (30.9.75) £250 45·00
a. 'O.S.' inverted
b. No stop after 'S'
O38 **12** 2d. orange-red (18.2.74) 65·00 8·00
a. No stop after 'S' — 60·00
b. 'O.S.' double

(b) P 10×11½–12½, 11½–12½×10, or compound

O39 **11** 1d. blue-green (16.9.75)
a. No stop after 'S'
O40 **12** 2d. orange-red (27.9.76) — 32·00

(c) P 11½–12½

O41 **11** 1d. blue-green (13.8.75) — 65·00
a. 'O.S.' inverted
b. No stop after 'S'
O42 **12** 2d. orange-red (20.5.74) — £160

1876–80. Optd with Type O **1**. W **13**.

(a) P 10

O43 **11** 1d. blue-green (2.10.76) 35·00 1·75
a. 'O.S.' inverted — £130
b. 'O.S.' double £275 £130
c. 'O.S.' double, one inverted
d. No stops — 70·00
e. No stop after 'O'
f. No stop after 'S' — 25·00
g. Deep green 55·00 1·00
ga. 'O.S.' double — £180
O44 **12** 2d. orange-red (21.9.77) 17·00 1·00
a. 'O.S.' inverted — 75·00
b. 'O.S.' double £275 £140
c. 'O.S.' double, one inverted
d. 'O.S.' double, both inverted — £400
e. No stops — £130
f. No stop after 'O' — 32·00
g. No stop after 'S'
h. Dull brick-red 75·00 1·00

(b) P 10×11½–12½, 11½–12½×10 or compound

O45 **11** 1d. deep green (14.8.80) — 65·00
a. 'O.S.' double
O46 **12** 2d. orange-red (6.4.78) £110 32·00
a. 'O.S.' inverted — £350
b. No stop after 'S' — £150

(c) P 11½–12½

O47 **12** 2d. orange-red (15.7.80) — £100

1882 (20 Feb). No. 181 optd with Type O **1**.

O48 **11** ½d. on 1d. blue-green £130 25·00
a. 'O.S.' inverted

1888 (15 Nov)–**91**. Nos. 184 and 185*a* optd with Type O **1**. P 10.

O49 **17** 4d. pale violet (24.1.91) £140 12·00
O50 **18** 6d. blue 60·00 1·50
a. 'O.S.' double
b. No stop after 'S'

1891. Nos. 229*b* and 231*a*/232 optd with Type O **1**.

(a) P 10

O51 **17** 2½d. on 4d. deep green (Br.) (1.8) £130 14·00
a. '2' and '½' closer together — 50·00
b. 'O.S.' inverted
c. 'O.S.' double
d. 'OS.' omitted (in vert pair with normal) † £4500
e. No stop after 'S'

(b) P 10×11½–12½ or 11½–12½×10.

O52 **17** 2½d. on 4d. deep green (Br.) (1.10) £150 30·00

(c) P 11½–12½

O53 **17** 2½d. on 4d. deep green (Br.) (1.6) £275 90·00

1891–96. Optd with Type O **2**. W **13**.

(a) P 10

O54 **11** 1d. deep green (22.4.91) 75·00 2·00
a. 'OS.' double £250 £100
b. 'O.S.' double, one inverted
c. No stop after 'S' £120 13·00
d. Blackish blue opt £250 4·50
O55 **12** 2d. orange-red (22.4.91) 65·00 3·50
a. 'O.S.' double
b. 'O.S.' double, both inverted
c. No stop after 'S' — 28·00

(b) P 15

O56 **11** 1d. green (8.9.94) 30·00 1·25
a. 'O.S.' double
b. No stop after 'S'
c. 'O.S.' inverted
O57 **12** 2d. orange-red (16.6.94) 28·00 60
a. 'O.S.' double — £100
b. 'O.S.' inverted — 70·00

(c) P 13

O58 **11** 1d. green (20.5.95) 42·00 1·50
a. No stop after 'S' £180 15·00
O59 **12** 2d. orange-red (11.2.96) 50·00 50
a. 'O.S.' double £400
b. No stop after 'S' £160 10·00
c. 'O.S.' inverted

1891–99. Optd with Type O **2**. W **13** (sideways on ½d.).

(a) P 10

O60 **15** ½d. brown (2.5.94) 55·00 13·00
a. 'O.S.' inverted £275
b. No stop after 'S' £160 55·00
O61 **17** 4d. pale violet (13.2.91) 75·00 5·00
a. 'O.S.' double
b. 'S.' omitted — £180
c. No stop after 'S'
d. Aniline violet (31.8.93) 75·00 12·00
da. 'O.S.' double
dc. No stop after 'S'
O62 **18** 6d. blue (4.4.93) 45·00 2·50
a. No stop after 'S'
b. Blackish blue opt

(b) P 10×11½–12½

O63 **15** ½d. brown (26.3.95) 55·00 8·00

(c) P 11½–12½

O64 **15** ½d. red-brown (13.6.91) 85·00 15·00

(d) P 15

O65 **15** ½d. pale brown (8.6.95) 80·00 22·00
O66 **17** 4d. slate-violet (4.4.95) £100 6·50
a. 'O.S.' double £500 £160
O67 **18** 6d. blue (20.9.93) 65·00 4·25

(e) P 13

O68 **15** ½d. deep brown (17.5.98) 65·00 6·00
a. Opt triple, twice sideways £500
b. 'O.S.' inverted
O69 **17** 4d. violet (12.96) £130 3·00
a. 'O.S.' double £750 £150
b. No stop after 'S' £375 60·00
O70 **18** 6d. blue (13.9.99) 70·00 3·25
a. No stop after 'S' £275 85·00

1891–95. Nos. 229*b*, 230*a* and 231*a* optd with Type O **2**.

(a) P 10

O71 **17** 2½d. on 4d. deep green (Br.) (18.8.94) 50·00 30·00
a. Fraction bar omitted
b. '2' and '½' closer together £120 55·00
c. 'O.S.' inverted £600
d. No stop after 'S' — 90·00
O72 **18** 5d. on 6d. deep brown (C.) (2.12.91) 55·00 18·00
a. No stop after '5D' £250
b. No stop after 'S' £200 75·00

(b) P 10×11½–12½

O73 **17** 2½d. on 4d. deep green (Br.) (17.9.95) — 90·00
a. 'O.S.' double

1897–1901. Nos. 235/6 and 238*a* optd with Type O **2**.

(a) P 15

O74 **23** 5d. brown-purple (29.3.01) £130 24·00

(b) P 13

O75 **22** 2½d. violet-blue (12.5.97) £120 8·50
a. No stop after 'S' — 75·00
O76 **23** 5d. purple (29.9.01) £130 29·00
a. No stop after 'S'

O. S. (O **3**)

1899–1901. Optd with Type O **3**. W **13**. P 13.

O80 **24** ½d. yellow-green (12.2.00) 24·00 9·00
a. 'O.S.' inverted £200
b. No stop after 'S' 95·00
O81 **11** 1d. rosine (22.9.99) 29·00 1·60
a. 'O.S.' inverted £200 £120
b. 'O.S.' double † £650
c. No stop after 'S' £120 22·00
O82 **12** 2d. bright violet (1.6.00) 35·00 80
a. 'O.S.' inverted £200 85·00
b. 'O.S.' double
c. No stop after 'S' £110 20·00
O83 **22** 2½d. indigo (2.10.01) 85·00 19·00
a. 'O.S.' inverted £600 £225
b. No stop after 'S' £325
O84 **17** 4d. violet (18.11.00) 85·00 5·50
a. 'O.S.' inverted £650
b. No stop after 'S' £275
O85 **18** 6d. blue (8.10.00) 45·00 5·50
a. No stop after 'S' £150

1891 (May). Optd as Type O **3** but wider. W **13**. P 10.

O86 **19** 2s.6d. pale violet £8500 £6500
O87 5s. pale rose £9000 £7500

Only one sheet (60) of each of these stamps was printed.

The use of stamps overprinted 'O S' was made invalid by the Posts and Telegraph Act of 1 November 1902.

South Australia became part of the Commonwealth of Australia on 1 January 1901.

TASMANIA

PRICES FOR STAMPS ON COVER

Nos. 1/4	*from* × 6
Nos. 5/12	*from* × 5
Nos. 14/24	*from* × 3
Nos. 25/56	*from* × 5
Nos. 57/77	*from* × 6
Nos. 78/79	—
Nos. 80/90	*from* × 3
No. 91	—
Nos. 92/109	*from* × 3
No. 110	—
Nos. 111/123	*from* × 3
Nos. 124/126	—
Nos. 127/134	*from* × 5
Nos. 135/155	*from* × 4
Nos. 156/158	*from* × 20
Nos. 159/166	*from* × 10
Nos. 167/169	*from* × 15
Nos. 170/174	*from* × 6
Nos. 216/222	*from* × 15
Nos. 223/225	—
Nos. 226/227	*from* × 15
Nos. 229/236	*from* × 20
Nos. 237/257	*from* × 10
No. 258	—
Nos. 259/262	*from* × 10
Nos. F1/F25	—
Nos. F26/F29	*from* × 15
Nos. F30/F39	—

SPECIMEN OVERPRINTS. Those listed are from UPU distributions between 1892 and 1904. Further 'Specimen' overprints exist, but these were used for other purposes.

1

2

3

(Eng C.W. Coard. Recess H. and C. Best at the *Courier* newspaper, Hobart)

1853 (1 Nov). 24 varieties in four rows of six each. No wmk. Imperf.

(a) Medium soft yellowish paper with all lines clear and distinct

1	1	1d. pale blue	£13000	£1500
2		1d. blue	£13000	£1500

(b) Thin hard white paper with lines of the engraving blurred and worn

3	1	1d. pale blue	£12000	£1300
4		1d. blue	£12000	£1300

1853 (1 Nov). No wmk. Imperf. In each plate there are 24 varieties in four rows of six each.

(a) Plate I. Finely engraved. All lines in network and background thin, clear, and well defined

(i) First state of the plate, brilliant colours

5	2	4d. bright red-orange	£10000	£1000
6		4d. bright brownish orange	—	£1300

(ii) Second state of plate, with blurred lines and worn condition of the central background

7	2	4d. red-orange	£7500	£475
8		4d. orange	£7000	£450
9		4d. pale orange	—	£450

(b) Plate II. Coarse engraving, lines in network and background thicker and blurred

10	2	4d. orange	£7000	£425
11		4d. dull orange	£7000	£375
12		4d. yellowish orange	£7000	£375

In the 4d. Plate I, the outer frame-line is thin all round. In Plate II it is, by comparison with other parts, thicker in the lower left angle.

The 4d. is known on vertically laid paper from proof sheets. Examples from Plate I have the lines close together and those from Plate II wide apart (*Price* £11,000 *unused*).

In 1879 reprints were made of the 1d. in blue and the 4d., Plate I, in brownish yellow, on thin, tough, white wove paper, and perforated 11½. In 1887, a reprint from the other plate of the 4d. was made in reddish brown and black on thick white paper, imperforate, and in 1889 of the 1d. in blue and in black, and of the 4d. (both plates) in yellow and in black on white card, imperforate. As these three reprints were defaced after the stamps had been superseded, all these reprints show two, or three thick strokes across the Queen's head.

All three plates were destroyed in July 1950.

PERKINS BACON 'CANCELLED'. For notes on these handstamps, showing 'CANCELLED' between horizontal bars forming an oval, see Catalogue Introduction.

(Eng W. Humphrys, after water-colour sketch by E. Corbould. Recess P.B.)

1855 (17 Aug–16 Sept). Wmk Large Star. W w **1**. Imperf.

14	3	1d. carmine (16.9) (H/S 'CANCELLED' in oval £12000)	£1100	£900
15		2d. deep green (16.9)	£6000	£550
16		2d. green (16.9) (H/S "CANCELLED" in oval £13000)	£6000	£450
17		4d. deep blue	£6000	£130
18		4d. blue (H/S "CANCELLED" in oval £12000)	£6000	£130

Proofs of the 1d. and 4d. on thick paper, *without watermark*, are sometimes offered as the issued stamps. The 6d. dull lilac on this watermark was prepared, but not issued. Examples exist from a creased proof sheet (*Price £750 unused*).

(Recess H. and C. Best, Hobart, from P.B. plates)

1856 (Apr)–**57**. No wmk. Imperf.

(a) Thin white paper

19	3	1d. pale brick-red (4.56)	£13000	£650
20		2d. dull emerald-green (1.57)	£16000	£950
21		4d. deep blue (5.57)	£3250	£140
22		4d. blue (5.57)	£3250	£140
23		4d. pale blue (5.57)	—	£180

(b) Pelure paper

24	3	1d. deep red-brown (11.56)	£9500	£750

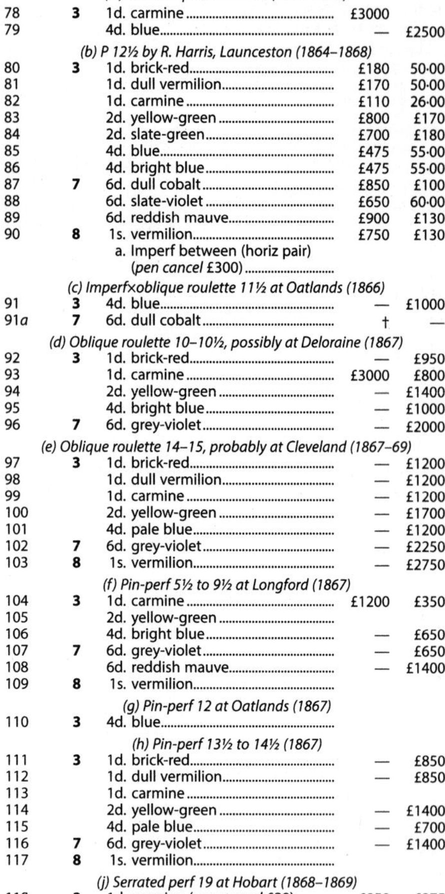
4 7 8

(Recess H. Best (August 1857–May 1859), J. Davies (August 1859–March 1862), J. Birchall (March 1863), M. Hood (October 1863–April 1864), Govt Printer (from July 1864), all from P.B. plates)

1857 (Aug)–**67**. Wmk double-lined numerals '1', '2' or '4' as W **4** on appropriate value. Imperf.

25	3	1d. deep red-brown	£1000	50·00
26		1d. pale red-brown	£650	40·00
27		1d. brick-red (1863)	£475	40·00
28		1d. dull vermilion (1865)	£400	35·00
29		1d. carmine (1867)	£375	30·00
30		2d. dull emerald-green	—	£140
31		2d. green	—	65·00
32		2d. yellow-green	£1000	£120
33		2d. deep green (1858)	£950	75·00
34		2d. slate-green (1860)	£425	85·00
35		4d. deep blue	—	85·00
36		4d. pale blue	£475	26·00
37		4d. blue	£475	28·00
38		4d. bright blue	£475	28·00
		a. Printed on both sides	†	—
39		4d. cobalt-blue	—	90·00

Printings before July 1864 were all carried out at the *Courier* printing works which changed hands several times during this period.

CANCELLATIONS. Beware of early Tasmanian stamps with pen-cancellations cleaned off and faked postmarks applied.

(Recess P.B.)

1858. Wmk double-lined numerals '6' or '12' as W **4**. Imperf.

40	7	6d. dull lilac (H/S 'CANCELLED' in oval £13000)	£1500	90·00
41	8	1s. vermilion (*shades*) (H/S 'CANCELLED' in oval £12000)	£800	80·00

(Recess J. Davies (March 1860), J. Birchall (April 1863), Govt Printer (from February 1865), all from P.B. plates)

1860 (Mar)–**67**. Wmk double-lined '6' as W **4**. Imperf.

44	7	6d. dull slate-grey	£950	85·00
45		6d. grey	—	90·00
46		6d. grey-violet (4.63)	£850	85·00
47		6d. dull cobalt (2.65)	£1400	£140
48		6d. slate-violet (2.65)	£950	75·00
49		6d. reddish mauve (4.67)	£1300	£180

In 1871 reprints were made of the 6d. (in mauve) and the 1s. on white wove paper, and perforated 11½. They are found with or without 'REPRINT'. In 1889 they were again reprinted on white card, imperforate. These later impressions are also found overprinted 'REPRINT' and perforated 11½.

PERFORATED ISSUES. From 1 October 1857 the Tasmania Post Office only supplied purchasers requiring five or more complete sheets of stamps. The public obtained their requirements, at face value, from licensed stamp vendors, who obtained their stocks at a discount from the Post Office.

From 1863 onwards a number of the stamp vendors applied their own roulettes or perforations. The Hobart firm of J. Walch & Sons achieved this so successfully that they were given an official contract in July 1869 to perforate sheets for the Post Office. The Government did not obtain a perforating machine until late in 1871.

1863–71. Double-lined numeral watermarks. Various unofficial roulettes and perforations.

(a) By J. Walch & Sons, Hobart

(i) Roulette about 8, often imperf×roul (1863–1868)

50	3	1d. brick-red	—	£475
51		1d. carmine	£900	£300
52		2d. yellow-green	—	£1200
53		2d. slate green		
54		4d. pale blue	—	£450
55	7	6d. dull lilac	—	£500
56	8	1s. vermilion	—	£1300

(ii) P 10 (1864–1869)

57	3	1d. brick-red	£200	60·00
58		1d. dull vermilion	£200	50·00
59		1d. carmine	£150	50·00
60		2d. yellow-green	£850	£160
61		2d. slate-green	£800	£200
62		4d. pale blue	£425	20·00
63		4d. blue	£425	20·00
64	7	6d. grey-violet	£650	25·00
65		6d. dull cobalt	£850	£100
66		6d. slate-violet	—	50·00
67		6d. reddish mauve	£900	£100
68	8	1s. vermilion	£700	60·00
		a. Imperf vert (horiz pair)		

(iii) P 12 (1865–1871—from July 1869 under contract to the Post Office)

69	3	1d. dull vermilion	£170	
70		1d. carmine	£130	23·00
		a. Error. Wmkd '2' (*pen cancel* £300)	—	£2750
71		2d. yellow-green	£650	£100
72		4d. deep blue	£375	21·00
73		4d. blue	£375	23·00
74		4d. cobalt-blue	—	60·00
75	7	6d. slate-violet	£475	29·00
		a. Imperf between (vert pair)		
76		6d. reddish mauve	£190	42·00
		a. Imperf between (vert or horiz pair) (*pen cancel* £225)		
77	8	1s. vermilion	£475	75·00
		b. Imperf between (horiz pair) (*pen cancel* £300)	—	£3500

(iv) Perf compound 10×12 (1865–1869)

78	3	1d. carmine	£3000	
79		4d. blue	—	£2500

(b) P 12½ by R. Harris, Launceston (1864–1868)

80	3	1d. brick-red	£180	50·00
81		1d. dull vermilion	£170	50·00
82		1d. carmine	£110	26·00
83		2d. yellow-green	£800	£170
84		2d. slate-green	£700	£180
85		4d. blue	£475	55·00
86		4d. bright blue	£475	55·00
87	7	6d. dull cobalt	£850	£100
88		6d. slate-violet	£650	60·00
89		6d. reddish mauve	£900	£130
90	8	1s. vermilion	£750	£130
		a. Imperf between (horiz pair) (*pen cancel* £300)		

(c) Imperf×oblique roulette 11½ at Oatlands (1866)

91	3	4d. blue	—	£1000
91*a*	7	6d. dull cobalt	†	—

(d) Oblique roulette 10–10½, possibly at Deloraine (1867)

92	3	1d. brick-red	—	£950
93		1d. carmine	£3000	£800
94		2d. yellow-green	—	£1400
95		4d. bright blue	—	£1000
96	7	6d. grey-violet	—	£2000

(e) Oblique roulette 14–15, probably at Cleveland (1867–69)

97	3	1d. brick-red	—	£1200
98		1d. dull vermilion	—	£1200
99		1d. carmine	—	£1200
100		2d. yellow-green	—	£1700
101		4d. pale blue	—	£1200
102	7	6d. grey-violet	—	£2250
103	8	1s. vermilion	—	£2750

(f) Pin-perf 5½ to 9½ at Longford (1867)

104	3	1d. carmine	£1200	£350
105		2d. yellow-green		
106		4d. bright blue	—	£650
107	7	6d. grey-violet	—	£650
108		6d. reddish mauve	—	£1400
109	8	1s. vermilion		

(g) Pin-perf 12 at Oatlands (1867)

110	3	4d. blue		

(h) Pin-perf 13½ to 14½ (1867)

111	3	1d. brick-red	—	£850
112		1d. dull vermilion	—	£850
113		1d. carmine		
114		2d. yellow-green	—	£1400
115		4d. pale blue	—	£700
116	7	6d. grey-violet	—	£1400
117	8	1s. vermilion		

(j) Serrated perf 19 at Hobart (1868–1869)

118	3	1d. carmine (*pen-cancel* £20)	£950	£275
119		2d. yellow-green	—	£950
120		4d. deep blue	£2000	£275
121		4d. cobalt-blue	—	£275
122	7	6d. slate-violet	—	£1200
123	8	1s. vermilion		

(k) Roul 4½, possibly at Macquarie River (1868)

124	3	4d. blue		
125	7	6d. reddish mauve		
126	8	1s. vermilion		

An example of the 1d. carmine is known perforated 10 on three sides and serrated 19 on the fourth.

These local separations (Nos. 91/126) were sometimes applied only between the horizontal rows or vertical columns of sheets, so that pairs can be found 'imperforate vertically' or 'imperforate horizontally'.

For stamps perforated 11½ or 12 by the Post Office see Nos. 134*a*/43.

11

12

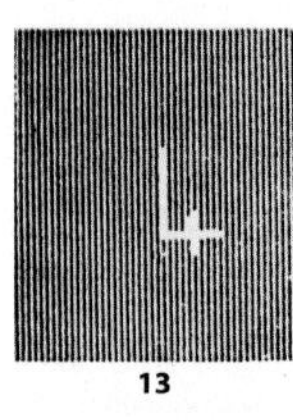
13

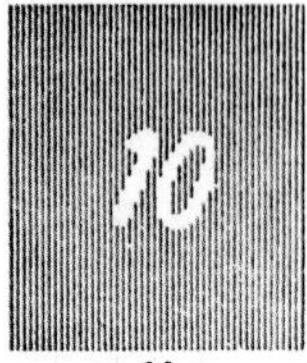
14

(Typo Govt Printer, Hobart, from plates made by D.L.R.)

1870 (1 Nov)–**71**. Wmk single-lined numerals W **12** (2d.), **13** (1d., 4d.) or **14** (1d., 10d.).

(a) P 12 by J. Walch & Sons

127	11	1d. rose-red (wmk '10')	£120	22·00
		b. Deep rose-red	£130	17·00
128		1d. rose-red (wmk '4') (3.71)	£140	65·00
		a. Imperf (pair)	—	—
129		2d. yellow-green	£180	12·00
		b. Blue-green	£190	12·00
		ba. Double print		
130		4d. blue	£1200	£475
131		10d. black	24·00	50·00
		a. Imperf (pair)	£700	

(b) P 11½ by the Post Office (1871)

132	11	1d. rose-red (wmk '10')	£1100	
133		2d. yellow-green	£300	18·00
		a. Blue-green	£180	9·50
		ab. Double print	£5000	£1800
134		10d. black	50·00	50·00
		aa. Imperf vert (horiz pair)		

The above were printed on paper obtained from New South Wales.

See also Nos. 144/155, 156/158, 159/166, 170/174, 226/227, 242 and 255/256.

(Recess P.B.)

1871. Wmk double-lined numeral '**12**'. P 11½ by the Post Office.

134*a*	**8**	1s. vermilion		

(Recess Govt Printer, Hobart)

1871–91. Double-lined numeral watermarks as W **4**. Perforated by the Post Office.

(a) P 11½

135	**7**	6d. dull lilac	£275	22·00
136		6d. lilac	£250	22·00
		a. Imperf between (vert pair)	—	£1700
		b. Imperf between (horiz pair)		
137		6d. deep slate-lilac (3.75)	£250	22·00
		a. Imperf (pair)	—	£1300
138		6d. bright violet (5.78)	£275	35·00
		b. Imperf between (horiz pair)	£4500	
139		6d. dull reddish lilac (10.79)	£200	40·00
140	**8**	1s. brown-red (1.73)	£350	65·00
		a. Imperf between (horiz pair)		
141		1s. orange-red (3.75)	£350	65·00
141*a*		1s. orange (5.78)		

(b) P 12

142	**7**	6d. reddish purple (1884)	£170	20·00
		a. Imperf between (horiz pair)	£2750	
143		6d. dull claret (7.91)	50·00	14·00

The perforation machine used on Nos. 142/3 was previously owned by J. Walch and Sons and passed to the ownership of the Government in 1884. It may have been used to perforate leftover sheets of previous printings.

15

16

'Wedge' flaw (Right pane R. 10/6)

Line through 'THREE PE' (Left pane R. 10/1)

(Typo Govt Printer, Hobart, from plates made by D.L.R.)

1871 (25 Mar)–**78**. W **15**.

(a) P 11½

144	**11**	1d. rose (5.71)	17·00	2·50
		a. Imperf (pair) (*pen cancel* £150)	—	£1300
		b. Bright rose	16·00	2·50
		c. Carmine	23·00	3·25
		d. Pink	23·00	3·50
		e. Vermilion (4.75)	£275	75·00
		f. Wedge flaw	£350	55·00
145		2d. deep green (11.72)	75·00	2·50
		a. Blue-green	50·00	2·50
		b. Yellow-green (12.75)	£250	4·50
146		3d. pale red-brown	70·00	4·25
		a. Imperf (pair)	£600	£1000
		b. Imperf horiz (vert pair)	£3750	
		c. Deep red-brown	75·00	4·50
		d. Purple-brown (1.78)	75·00	4·25
		da. Line through 'THREE PE'	£550	80·00
		e. Brownish purple	65·00	4·25
147		4d. pale yellow (8.8.76)	£160	50·00
		a. Ochre (7.78)	95·00	9·00
		b. Buff	80·00	12·00
148		9d. blue (2.10.71)	30·00	8·00
		a. Imperf (pair)	£550	
		b. Double print	†	£3250
149		5s. purple (*pen cancel* £3.75)	£350	80·00
		b. Mauve	£325	80·00

(b) P 12

150	**11**	1d. rose	£140	32·00
		a. Carmine	£150	35·00
		b. Wedge flaw	—	£180
151		2d. green	£650	£140
152		3d. red-brown	£130	22·00
		a. Deep red-brown	£130	22·00
153		4d. buff	£350	25·00
154		9d. pale blue	55·00	
		a. Imperf between (horiz pair)	£4000	
155		5s. purple	£550	
		a. Mauve	£450	

(Typo D.L.R.)

1878 (28 Oct). W **16**. P 14.

156	**11**	1d. carmine	12·00	1·00
		a. Rose-carmine	6·50	1·00
		b. Scarlet	21·00	1·25
157		2d. pale green	12·00	1·00
		a. Green	11·00	1·00
158		8d. dull purple-brown	14·00	10·00

(Typo Govt Printer, Hobart (some printings of 1d. in 1891 by *Mercury Press*) from plates made by Victoria Govt Printer, Melbourne (½d.) or D.L.R. (others))

1880 (Apr)–**91**. W **16**.

(a) P 11½

159	**11**	½d. orange (8.3.89)	3·25	3·25
		a. Deep orange	3·25	3·25
160		1d. dull red (14.2.89)	16·00	3·50
		a. Vermilion-red	12·00	2·50
		b. Wedge flaw	£150	45·00
161		3d. red-brown	23·00	5·00
		a. Imperf (pair)	£450	
		b. Line through 'THREE PE'	£275	80·00
162		4d. deep yellow (1.83)	85·00	18·00
		a. Chrome-yellow	85·00	20·00
		b. Olive-yellow	£150	27·00
		c. Buff	40·00	9·50

(b) P 12

163	**11**	½d. orange	6·00	7·00
		a. Deep orange	6·00	7·00
		ab. Wmk sideways		
164		1d. pink (1891)	42·00	18·00
		a. Imperf (pair)	£400	£425
		b. Rosine	40·00	13·00
		c. Dull rosine	40·00	14·00
		ca. Imperf (pair)	£375	
		d. Wedge flaw	£275	85·00
165		3d. red-brown	8·00	8·50
		a. Imperf between (horiz pair)	£2250	
		b. Line through 'THREE PE'	£110	95·00
166		4d. deep yellow	£150	32·00
		a. Chrome-yellow	£170	27·00
		ab. Printed both sides	£1500	

SPECIMEN AND PRESENTATION REPRINTS OF TYPE 11. In 1871 the 1d., 2d., 3d., 4d. blue, 9d., 10d. and 5s. were reprinted on soft white wove paper to be followed, in 1879, by the 4d. yellow and 8d. on rough white wove. Both these reprintings were perforated 11½. In 1886 it was decided to overprint remaining stocks with the word 'REPRINT'.

In 1889 Tasmania commenced sending sample stamps to the UPU in Berne and a further printing of the 4d. blue was made, imperforate, on white card. This, together with the 5s. in mauve on white card, both perforated 11½ and overprinted 'REPRINT', were included in presentation sets supplied to members of the states' legislatures in 1901.

Halfpenny
(**17**)

d.
2½
(**18**) (2¼ *mm* between 'd', and '2')

d.
2½
(**19**) (3½ *mm* between 'd' and '2')

1889 (1 Jan). No. 156*b* surch locally with T **17**.

167	**11**	½d. on 1d. scarlet	10·00	25·00
		a. 'al' in 'Half' printed sideways (R. 1/2)	£2250	£2000

No. 167a occurred in a second printing and was later corrected.

A reprint on white card, perforated 11½ or imperforate, overprinted 'REPRINT' was produced in 1901.

1891 (1 Jan–June). Surch locally by lithography. W **16**.

(a) With T **18**. *P 11½*

168	**11**	2½d. on 9d. pale blue	22·00	4·25
		a. Surch double, one inverted	£700	£800
		b. Deep blue (5.91)	13·00	8·00

(b) With T **19**. *P 12*

169	**11**	2½d. on 9d. pale blue (5.91)	5·00	3·75
		a. Blue surch.		

A reprint, using a third setting, perforated 11½ and overprinted 'REPRINT' was produced in 1901.

(Typo Govt Printer, Hobart)

1891 (Apr–Aug). W **15**.

(a) P 11½

170	**11**	½d. orange	75·00	55·00
		a. Brown-orange	55·00	50·00
171		1d. rosine	23·00	10·00
		a. Wedge flaw	£225	90·00

(b) P 12

172	**11**	½d. orange	65·00	50·00
		a. Imperf (pair)	£300	
173		1d. dull rosine	45·00	45·00
		a. Rosine	55·00	45·00
		b. Wedge flaw	£375	£275
174		4d. bistre (8.91)	24·00	38·00

20

21

21a

(Typo D.L.R.)

1892 (12 Feb)–**99**. W **16**. P 14.

216	**20**	½d. orange and mauve (11.92)	2·75	1·25
217	**21**	2½d. purple	2·75	1·75
218	**20**	5d. pale blue and brown	7·50	3·75
219		6d. violet and black (11.92)	16·00	4·75
220	**21a**	10d. purple-lake and deep green (30.1.99)	11·00	14·00
221	**20**	1s. rose and green (11.92)	12·00	3·00
222		2s.6d. brown and blue (11.92)	32·00	38·00
223		5s. lilac and red (3.2.97)	90·00	28·00
224		10s. mauve and brown (11.92)	£190	£120
225		£1 green and yellow (2.97)	£500	£500
216/225 *Set of* 10			£750	£650
216s/225s Optd 'SPECIMEN' *Set of* 10			£650	

See also Nos. 243 and 257/258.

(Typo Govt Printer, Hobart)

1896. W **16**. P 12.

226	**11**	4d. pale bistre	15·00	7·00
227		9d. pale blue	9·50	3·00
		a. Blue	9·50	3·75

22 Lake Marion

23 Mount Wellington

24 Hobart

25 Tasman's Arch

26 Spring River, Port Davey

27 Russell Falls

28 Mount Gould, Lake St. Clair

29 Dilston Falls

30

(Eng L. Phillips. Recess D.L.R.)

1899 (Dec)–**1900**. W **30** (sideways on vert designs). P 14.

229	**22**	½d. deep green (31.3.00)	8·50	6·50
230	**23**	1d. bright lake (13.12.99)*	5·50	1·75
231	**24**	2d. deep violet (15.12.99)*	24·00	1·75
232	**25**	2½d. indigo (1900)	22·00	3·75
233	**26**	3d. sepia (1900)	20·00	6·00
234	**27**	4d. deep orange-buff (1900)	24·00	9·00
235	**28**	5d. bright blue (31.3.00)	38·00	11·00
236	**29**	6d. lake (31.3.00)	32·00	40·00
229/236 *Set of* 8			£150	70·00
229s/236s Optd 'Specimen' *Set of* 8			£550	

*Earliest known postmark dates.

See also Nos. 237/239, 240/241, 245/248, 249/254, 259, 260 and 261/262.

DIFFERENCES BETWEEN LITHOGRAPHED AND TYPOGRAPHED PRINTINGS OF TYPES 22/9

LITHOGRAPHED	TYPOGRAPHED
General appearance fine.	*Comparatively crude and coarse appearance.*
½d. All 'V over Crown' wmk.	All 'Crown over A' wmk.
1d. The shading on the path on the right bank of the river consists of very fine dots. In printings from worn stones the dots hardly show.	The shading on the path is coarser, consisting of large dots and small patches of colour.
The shading on the white mountain is fine (or almost absent in many stamps).	The shading on the mountain is coarse, and clearly defined.
2d. Three rows of windows in large building on shore, at extreme left, against inner frame.	Two rows of windows.
3d. Clouds very white.	Clouds dark.
Stars in corner ornaments have long points.	Stars have short points.
Shading of corner ornaments is defined by a coloured outer line.	Shading of ornaments terminates against white background.
4d. Lithographed only.	—
6d. No coloured dots at base of waterfall.	Coloured dots at base of waterfall.
Outer frame of value tablets is formed by outer line of design.	Thick line of colour between value tablets and outer line.
	Small break in inner frame below second 'A' of 'TASMANIA'.

(Litho, using transfers from D.L.R. plates, Victoria Government Printing Office, Melbourne)

1902 (Jan)–**05**. Wmk V over Crown, W w **10** (sideways on ½d., 2d.). P 12½.

237 **22** ½d. green (2.03) ... 5·50 1·50
a. Wmk upright ... 28·00 27·00
b. Perf 11 (1904) ... 6·50 15·00
c. Perf comp of 12½ and 11 ... £200 £140
d. Perf comp of 12½ and 12 ... £600
s. Optd 'SPECIMEN' ... £120
238 **23** 1d. carmine-red ... 20·00 1·75
239 **24** 2d. deep reddish violet ... 14·00 70
a. Perf 11 ... 14·00 9·00
b. Perf comp of 12½ and 11 ... £180 90·00
c. Wmk upright (2.04) ... 90·00 17·00
d. Deep rose-lilac (4.05) ... 20·00 2·00
da. Perf 11 ... 12·00 2·50
db. Perf comp of 12½ and 11 ... £225 £100
s. Optd 'SPECIMEN' ... £130

As the V and Crown paper was originally prepared for stamps of smaller size, portions of two or more watermarks appear on each stamp.

We only list the main groups of shades in this and the following issues. There are variations of shade in all values, particularly in the 2d. where there is a wide range, also in the 1d. in some issues.

(Typo, using electrotyped plates, Victoria Govt Ptg Office, Melbourne)

1902 (Oct)–**04**. Wmk V over Crown, W w **10**. P 12½.

240 **23** 1d. pale red (wmk sideways) ... 18·00 4·50
a. Perf 11 ... 50·00 13·00
b. Perf comp of 12½ and 11 ... £500 £100
c. Wmk upright (1.03) ... 27·00 13·00
ca. Perf 11 ... 65·00 16·00
d. Rose-red (wmk upright) (4.03) ... 15·00 4·25
da. Perf 11 ... 27·00 4·25
db. Perf comp of 12½ and 11 ... £475 £100
ds. Optd 'SPECIMEN' ... £120
241 1d. scarlet (wmk upright) (9.03) ... 20·00 3·75
a. Perf 11 ... 25·00 4·00
b. Perf comp of 12½ and 11 ... — 60·00
c. Rose-scarlet (1904) ... 20·00 3·75
ca. Perf 11 ... 9·00 4·25
cb. Perf comp of 12½ and 11 ... £180 60·00

The 1d. scarlet of September 1903 was from new electrotyped plates which show less intense shading.

(Typo Victoria Govt Ptg Office, Melbourne)

1903 (Apr–Dec). Wmk V over Crown, W w **10**. P 12½.

242 **11** 9d. blue (4.03) ... 23·00 3·75
a. Perf 11 ... 8·50 18·00
b. Perf comp of 12½ and 11 ... £950 £950
c. Wmk sideways ... £350 £160
d. Pale blue ... 22·00 10·00
e. Bright blue ... 23·00 12·00
f. Ultramarine ... £425
g. Indigo ... £225
243 **20** 1s. rose and green (12.03) ... 50·00 9·00
a. Perf 11 ... 90·00 80·00
242s/243s Optd 'SPECIMEN' *Set of 2* ... £225

1½d. (31) ONE PENNY (32)

1904 (29 Dec). No. 218 surch with T **31**.

244 **20** 1½d. on 5d. pale blue and brown ... 1·50 1·75
s. Optd 'SPECIMEN' ... 70·00

Stamps with inverted surcharge or without surcharge *se-tenant* with stamps with normal surcharge were obtained irregularly and were not issued for postal use.

PRINTER. The Victoria Govt Ptg Office became the Commonwealth Stamp Printing Branch in March 1909.

(Litho, using transfers from D.L.R. plates, Victoria Govt Ptg Office, Melbourne)

1905 (Sep)–**12**. Wmk Crown over A, W w **11** (sideways on horiz stamps). P 12½.

245 **24** 2d. deep purple ... 19·00 1·50
a. Perf 11 ... 50·00 3·00
b. Perf comp of 12½ and 11 ... 30·00 9·00
c. Perf comp of 12½ and 12 ... £200 £120
d. Perf comp of 11 and 12 ... £375 £200
e. Slate-lilac (1906) ... 25·00 1·75
ea. Perf 11 ... 60·00 3·25
eb. Perf comp of 12½ and 11 ...
ed. Perf comp of 11 and 12 ... £350 £200
ee. Perf comp of 12½ and 12 ...
f. Reddish lilac (1907) ... 45·00 4·00
fa. Perf 11 ... 50·00 7·50
fb. Perf comp of 12½ and 11 ... £160
246 **26** 3d. brown (1906) ... 14·00 5·00
a. Perf 11 (9.05) ... 32·00 42·00
b. Perf comp of 12½ and 11 ... £275 £275
247 **27** 4d. pale yellow-brown (3.07) ... 22·00 4·75
a. Perf 11 ... 65·00 21·00
b. Orange-buff (5.09) ... 65·00 5·50
ba. Perf 11 ... 65·00 30·00
bb. Perf comp of 12½ and 11 ... £500 £475
c. Brown-ochre (wmk sideways). Perf 11 (6.11) ... 30·00 55·00
ca. Perf comp of 12½ and 11 ... — £750
d. Orange-yellow (3.12) ... 16·00 40·00
da. Perf 11 ... 48·00 65·00
db. Perf comp of 12½ and 11 ... £500 £500
248 **29** 6d. lake (7.08) ... 80·00 9·00
a. Perf 11 ... 95·00 9·00
b. Perf comp of 12½ and 11 ... £500 £500

Stamps with perf compound of 12½ and 12 or 11 and 12 are found on sheets which were sent from Melbourne incompletely perforated along the outside edge of the pane or sheet. The missing perforations were applied in Hobart using a line machine measuring 12 (11.8 is the exact gauge). This perforation can only occur on one side of a stamp.

(Typo, using electrotyped plates, Victoria Govt Ptg Office, Melbourne).

1905 (Aug)–**11**. Wmk Crown over A, W w **11** (sideways on horiz designs). P 12½.

249 **22** ½d. yellow-green (10.12.08) ... 3·00 1·00
a. Perf 11 ... 3·00 75
b. Perf comp of 12½ and 11 ... £130 32·00
c. Perf comp of 11 and 12 ... £325
d. Wmk upright (1909) ... 25·00 8·50
da. Perf 11 ... £110
250 **23** 1d. rose-red ... 8·00 40
a. Perf 11 ... 7·50 30
b. Perf comp of 12½ and 11 ... 5·50 7·00
c. Perf comp of 12½ and 12 ... £180 65·00
d. Perf comp of 11 and 12 ... £200 65·00
e. Wmk sideways (1907) ... 25·00 3·00
ea. Perf 11 ... 26·00 4·00
eb. Perf comp of 12½ and 11 ... 95·00 23·00
f. Imperf (pair) ... £700 £750
250*g* 1d. carmine-red (3.10) ... 15·00 3·50
ga. Perf 11 ... 15·00 3·50
gb. Perf comp of 12½ and 11 ... 21·00 9·50
gc. Perf comp of 12½ and 12 ... £170 60·00
gd. Perf comp of 11 and 12 ... £200 63·00
gf. Wmk sideways ... 15·00 3·25
gg. Perf 11 ... 16·00 3·25
gh. Perf comp of 12½ and 11 ... 19·00 9·00
h. Carmine-vermilion (1911) ... 19·00 13·00
ha. Perf 11 ... 22·00 12·00
hb. Perf comp of 12½ and 11 ... 65·00 15·00
hc. Perf comp of 12½ and 12 ...
hd. Perf comp of 11 and 12 ...
251 **24** 2d. plum (8.07) ... 38·00 1·00
a. Wmk upright ... 50·00 5·50
b. Perf 11 ... 6·50 30
ba. Wmk upright (12.07) ... 50·00 5·50
c. Perf comp of 12½ and 11 ... 42·00 18·00
d. Perf comp of 12½ and 12 ... £450 £140
e. Perf comp of 11 and 12 ... £275 £110
f. Bright reddish violet (1910) ... 14·00 4·50
fa. Perf 11 ... 13·00 2·25
fb. Perf comp of 12½ and 11 ... 55·00 22·00
fc. Perf comp of 12½ and 12 ... £450 £130
253 **26** 3d. brown (3.09) ... 23·00 12·00
a. Wmk upright ...
b. Perf 11 ... 30·00 15·00
c. Perf comp of 12½ and 11 ... £425 £450
254 **29** 6d. carmine-lake (12.10) ... 24·00 45·00
a. Perf 11 ... 24·00 55·00
b. Perf comp of 12½ and 11 ... £450
c. Dull carmine-red (3.11) ... 25·00 55·00
ca. Wmk upright ... 60·00 65·00
cb. Perf 11 ... 27·00 65·00
cc. Perf comp of 12½ and 11 ... £475 £500

The note after No. 248 re perfs compound with perf 12 also applies here.

Nos. 250/250f were printed from the same plates as Nos. 241/241cb. Nos. 250*g*/250ghd are from a further pair of new plates and the images are sharper.

(Typo Victoria Govt Printing Office, Melbourne).

1906–09. Wmk Crown over A, W w **11**. P 12½.

255 **11** 8d. purple-brown (1907) ... 27·00 25·00
a. Perf 11 ... 19·00 8·50
256 9d. blue (1907) ... 7·50 6·50
a. Perf 11 ... 7·50 10·00
b. Perf comp of 12½ and 11 (1909) ... £110
c. Perf comp of 12½ and 12 (1909) ... £425
d. Perf comp of 11 and 12 ... £550
257 **20** 1s. rose and green (1907) ... 13·00 9·50
a. Perf 11 (1907) ... 29·00 50·00
b. Perf comp of 12½ and 11 ... 23·00 55·00
c. Perf comp of 12½ and 12 ... £275
258 10s. mauve and brown (1906) ... £275 £275
a. Perf 11 ... £475 £475
b. Perf comp of 12½ and 12 ... £850

The note after No. 248 re perfs compound with perf 12, also applies here.

(Typo, using stereotyped plates, Commonwealth Stamp Ptg Branch, Melbourne)

1911 (Jan). Wmk Crown over A, W w **11** (sideways). P 12½.

259 **24** 2d. bright violet ... 21·00 7·00
a. Wmk upright ... 50·00 14·00
b. Perf 11 ... 9·50 5·50
ba. Wmk upright ... 42·00 12·00
c. Perf comp of 12½ and 11 ... £130 38·00
d. Perf comp of 12½ and 12 ... £500

Stamps from this stereotyped plate differ from No. 251 in the width of the design (33 to 33¾ *mm*, against just over 32 *mm*), in the taller, bolder letters of 'TASMANIA', in the slope of the mountain in the left background, which is clearly outlined in white, and in the outer vertical frame-line at left, which appears 'wavy'. Compare Nos. 260, etc, which are always from this plate.

1912 (Oct). No. 259 surch with T **32**. P 12½.

260 **24** 1d. on 2d. bright violet (R.) ... 1·00 1·00
a. Perf 11 ... 1·50 3·50
b. Perf comp of 12½ and 11 ... £275 £300

(Typo, using electrotyped plates, Commonwealth Stamp Ptg Branch, Melbourne).

1912 (Dec). Thin ready gummed paper, white gum (as Victoria, 1912)*. W w **11** (sideways on 3d.). P 12½.

261 **23** 1d. carmine-vermilion ... 26·00 18·00
a. Perf 11 ... 21·00 18·00
b. Perf comp of 12½ and 11 ... † £600
262 **26** 3d. brown ... 70·00 £100

*See note below Victoria No. 455.

STAMP BOOKLETS

There are very few surviving examples of Nos. SB1/SB4. Listings are provided for those believed to have been issued with prices quoted for those known to still exist.

1904 (1 Jan)–**09**. Black on red cover as Type B **1** of New South Wales. Stapled.

SB1 £1 booklet containing 240×1d. in 12 blocks of 20 (5×4) ...
a. Red on pink cover (1909) ...
b. Blue on pink cover ...

1904 (1 Jan). Black on grey cover as No. SB1. Stapled.

SB2 £1 booklet containing 120×2d. in four blocks of 30 ...

1910 (1 May). Black on white cover as Type B **2** of New South Wales. Stapled.

SB3 2s. booklet containing 11×½d. (No. 249), either in block of 6 plus block of 5 or block of 11, and 18×1d. (No. 250), either in three blocks of 6 or block of 6 plus block of 12 ... £7500

Unsold stock No. SB3 was uprated with one additional ½d. in May 1911.

1911 (Aug). Red on pink cover as No. SB3. Stapled.

SB4 2s. booklet containing 12×½d. (No. 249), either in two blocks of 6 or block of 12, and 18×1d. (No. 250), either in three blocks of 6 or block of 6 plus block of 12 ... £6500

POSTAL FISCAL STAMPS

VALIDITY. Nos. F1/F29 were authorised for postal purposes on 1 November 1882.

CLEANED STAMPS. Beware of postal fiscal stamps with pen-cancellations removed.

F 1 F 2 F 3 F 4

(Recess Alfred Bock, Hobart)

1863–80. Wmk double-lined '1'. W **4**.

(a) Imperf

F1 **F 1** 3d. green (1.65) ... £750 £275
F2 **F 2** 2s.6d. carmine (11.63) ... £750 £275
F3 2s.6d. lake (5.80) ...
F4 **F 3** 5s. brown (1.64) ... £1500 £800
F5 5s. sage-green (1880) ... £1000 £400
F6 **F 4** 10s. orange (1.64) ... £1800 £800
F7 10s. salmon (5.80) ... £1500 £800

(b) P 10

F8 **F 1** 3d. green ... £500 £180
F9 **F 2** 2s.6d. carmine ... £450
F10 **F 3** 5s. brown ... £650
F11 **F 4** 10s. orange ... £600

(c) P 12

F12 **F 1** 3d. green ... £450 £190
F13 **F 2** 2s.6d. carmine ... £350 £180
F14 **F 3** 5s. brown ... £650
F15 5s. sage-green ... £450 £190
F16 **F 4** 10s. orange ... £550 £275
F17 10s. salmon ... £500 £225

(d) P 12½

F18 **F 1** 3d. green ... £650
F19 **F 2** 2s.6d. carmine ... £600
F20 **F 3** 5s. brown ... £900
F21 **F 4** 10s. orange-brown ... £700

(e) P 11½

F22 **F 1** 3d. green ... £800
F23 **F 2** 2s.6d. lake ... £350 £190
F24 **F 3** 5s. sage-green ... £450 £180
F25 **F 4** 10s. salmon ... £600 £350

See also No. F30.

In 1879, the 3d., 2s.6d., 5s. (brown), and 10s. (orange) were reprinted on thin, tough, white paper, and are found with or without 'REPRINT'. In 1889 another reprint was made on white card, imperforate and perforated 12. These are also found with or without 'REPRINT'.

F **5** Duck-billed Platypus

REVENUE
(F **6**)

(Typo D.L.R.)

1880 (19 Apr). W **16** (sideways). P 14.

F26 **F 5** 1d. slate ... 48·00 10·00
F27 3d. chestnut ... 27·00 5·00
F28 6d. mauve ... £100 2·50
F29 1s. rose-pink ... £160 30·00
a. Perf comp of 14 and 11 ...

All values are known imperf, but not used.

Reprints are known of the 1d. in deep blue and the 6d. in lilac. The former is on yellowish white, the latter on white card. Both values also exist on wove paper, perf 12, with the word 'REPRINT'.

1888. W **16**. P 12.

F30 **F 2** 2s.6d. lake ... £150 90·00
a. Imperf between (horiz pair) ... £2500

1900 (15 Nov). Optd with Type F **6**.

(a) On Types F 2 and F 4

F32 **F 2** 2s.6d. lake (No. F30) ... £500 £500
a. 'REVFNUE' ... £800
b. Opt inverted ... £1700
c. Imperf (pair) ... £1400

F33 **F 4** 10s. salmon (No. F17) £800 £750
a. 'REVFNUE'

(b) On Nos. F27 and F29

F34 **F 5** 3d. chestnut 42·00 35·00
a. Double opt, one vertical £225 £250
F35 1s. rose-pink

(c) On stamps as Nos. F26/F29, but typo locally. W **16**. *P 12*

F36 **F 5** 1d. blue 25·00 30·00
b. Imperf vert (horiz pair) £550
c. 'REVENUE' inverted £200
d. 'REVENUE' double £325 £325
e. Pale blue 25·00
F37 6d. mauve £120
a. Double print £800
F38 1s. pink £375 £350

(d) On No. 225

F39 **20** £1 green and yellow £275 £225
a. Opt double, one vertical £475 £450

It was not intended that stamps overprinted with Type F **6** should be used for postal purposes, but an ambiguity in regulations permitted such usage until all postal fiscal stamps were invalidated for postal purposes on 30 November 1900.

F38 is known with 'REVENUE' inverted, fiscally used.

Printings of some of the above with different watermarks, together with a 2d. as Nos. F36/F38, did not appear until after the stamps had become invalid for postal purposes.

Tasmania became part of the Commonwealth of Australia on 1 January 1901.

VICTORIA

PRICES FOR STAMPS ON COVER

Nos. 1/17	*from* × 2
Nos. 18/22	*from* × 4
Nos. 23/24	*from* × 2
No. 25	*from* × 3
Nos. 26/32	*from* × 2
No. 33	*from* × 6
No. 34	*from* × 8
Nos. 35/39	*from* × 4
No. 40	*from* × 3
Nos. 41/53	*from* × 2
No. 54	*from* × 3
No. 55	—
No. 56	*from* × 4
Nos. 57/72	*from* × 2
No. 73	*from* × 3
Nos. 74/80	*from* × 2
No. 81	*from* × 3
Nos. 82/87	*from* × 4
Nos. 88/200	*from* × 3
Nos. 201/206	*from* × 5
Nos. 207/208	*from* × 10
Nos. 209/214	*from* × 5
Nos. 215/219	—
Nos. 220/226	*from* × 20
Nos. 227/233	—
Nos. 234/237	*from* × 20
Nos. 238/252	—
Nos. 253/256	*from* × 20
No. 257	*from* × 10
No. 258	*from* × 20
No. 259	*from* × 10
Nos. 260/264	—
Nos. 265/266	*from* × 20
Nos. 267/273	*from* × 10
Nos. 274/291	—
Nos. 292/304	*from* × 10
Nos. 305/309	*from* × 5
Nos. 310/323	*from* × 10
Nos. 324/328	—
No. 329	*from* × 12
Nos. 330/350	*from* × 8
Nos. 351/352	—
Nos. 353/354	*from* × 4
No. 355	*from* × 10
Nos. 356/373	*from* × 15
Nos. 374/375	*from* × 3
Nos. 376/398	*from* × 10
Nos. 399/400	—
Nos. 401/406	*from* × 10
Nos. 407/415	—
Nos. 416/430	*from* × 10
Nos. 431/432	—
Nos. 433/443	*from* × 4
Nos. 444/453	—
Nos. 454/455	*from* × 10
Nos. 456/463	*from* × 6
No. 464	—
Nos. D1/D8	*from* × 30
Nos. D9/D10	—
Nos. D11/D37	*from* × 30

During the expansion of the Australian settlements in the fourth decade of the 19-century the growing population of the Port Phillip District in the south of New South Wales led to a movement for its creation as a separate colony. This aspiration received the approval of the British Government in 1849, but the colony of Victoria, as it was to be called, was not to be created until 1 July 1851.

In the meantime the New South Wales Legislative Council voted for the introduction of postal reforms, including the use of postage stamps, from 1 January 1850, and this act was also to apply to the Port Phillip District where stamps inscribed 'VICTORIA' would predate the creation of that colony by 18 months.

Until the end of 1859 the stamps of Victoria, with the exception of Nos. 40 and 73, were produced by local contractors working under the supervision of the colonial administration.

SPECIMEN OVERPRINTS. Those listed are from UPU distributions in 1892 and 1897. Further 'Specimen' overprints exist, but these were used for other purposes.

HAM PRINTINGS. The first contractor was Thomas Ham of Melbourne. He was responsible for the initial printings of the 'Half-Length' 1d., 2d. and 3d., together with the replacement 'Queen-on-Throne' 2d. The first printings were produced from small sheets of 30 (5×6) laid down directly from the engraved die which showed a single example of each value. Subsequent printings, of which No. 4*a* was the first, were in sheets of 120 (two panes of 60) laid down using intermediate stones of various sizes. Impressions from the first printings were fine and clear, but the quality deteriorated when intermediate stones were used.

1 Queen Victoria ('Half Length')

(Lithographed by Thomas Ham, Melbourne)

1850 (3 Jan)–**53**. Imperf.

1d. Thin line at top

2d. Fine border and background

3d. White area to left of orb

(a) Original state of dies: 1d. (tops of letters of 'VICTORIA' reach to top of stamp); 2d. (fine border and background); 3d. (thicker white outline around left of orb, central band of orb does not protrude at left). No frame-lines on dies

1 **1** 1d. orange-vermilion £35000 £10000
a. Orange-brown † £2250
b. Dull chocolate-brown £22000 £2500
2 2d. lilac-mauve (*shades*) (Stone A) £16000 £1000
3 2d. brown-lilac (*shades*) (Stone B) £14000 £500
a. Grey-lilac — £550
4 3d. bright blue (*shades*) £8500 £600
a. Blue (shades) £7500 £450
ab. Retouched (between Queen's head and right border) (No. 11 in transfer group) (8 varieties) — £600
ac. Retouched (under 'V') (No. 10 in transfer group) £14000 £1000

With the exception of No. 4*a* the above were printed from small stones of 30 (5×6) laid down directly from the engraved die which showed a single example of each value. There were two stones of the 2d. and one for each of the other values. No. 4*a* is the second printing of the 3d. for which the sheet size was increased to 120, the printing stone being constructed from an intermediate stone of 15 (5×3).

1d. Thick line at top

2d. Coarse background

3d. White area small and band protruding to left of orb

(b) Second state of dies: 1d. (more colour over top of letters of 'VICTORIA'); 2d. (fine border as (a) but with coarse background); 3d. (thinner white outline around left of orb, central band of orb protrudes at left)

5 **1** 1d. red-brown (*shades*) (2.50) £10000 £450
a. Pale dull red-brown £8500 £450
6 2d. grey-lilac (*shades*) (1.50) £7500 £200
a. Dull grey £14000 £225
7 3d. blue (*shades*) (6.51) £5000 £190
a. Retouched (22 varieties).... *from* £6000 £350

Printed in sheets of 120 (10×12) with the printing stones constructed from intermediate stones of 30 (5×6) for the 1d. and 2d. or 10 (5×2) for the 3d. It is believed that the use of the smaller intermediate stone for the latter resulted in the many retouches.

Frame-lines added

(c) Third state of dies: As in (b) but with frame-lines added, very close up, on all four sides

8 **1** 1d. dull orange-vermilion (11.50) £6000 £650
a. Dull red (shades) £5000 £200
9 1d. deep red-brown (5.51) £13000 £1200
a. Brownish red (shades) £4750 £180
b. Dull rose (shades) £4750 £180
10 2d. grey (*shades*) (8.50) £8500 £200
a. Olive-grey (shades) £9000 £200
11 3d. blue (*shades*) (12.52) £3000 90·00
a. Deep blue (shades) £3500 90·00
b. Pale greenish blue (shades) £4250 £170

Printed in sheets of 120 (12×10) produced from intermediate stones of 30 (6×5) for No. 8 and 12 (6×2) for the others.

White veil

(d) As (c) but altered to give, for the 1d. and 3d., the so-called 'white veils', and for the 2d., the effect of vertical drapes to the veil

12 **1** 1d. reddish brown (6.51) £7500 £170
a. Bright pinky red (shades) £2500 £170
13 2d. drab (1.51) £8500 £190
a. Grey-drab £8500 £180
b. Lilac-drab £8500 £180
c. Red-lilac — £1300
d. Void lower left corner † £22000
14 3d. blue (*shades*) (1.53) £1300 80·00
a. Deep blue (shades) £1400 80·00
b. Greenish blue (shades) £1700 85·00
c. Retouched (9 varieties) £2750 £180

Printed in sheets of 120 (12×10) produced from intermediate stones of 12 (6×2) on which the details of the veil were amended as described above.

The 'void corner' error occurred on the printing stone. It is believed that only four examples still exist.

2d. Coarse border and background

(e) Fourth state of 2d. die only: Coarse border and background. Veil details as in original die

15 **1** 2d. red-lilac (*shades*) (5.50) £8000 £325
a. Lilac £8000 £350
b. Grey £10000 £425
c. Dull brownish lilac £8000 £180
d. Retouched lower label—value omitted *from* † £15000
e. Other retouches (17 varieties) *from* £9500 £350

Printed in sheets of 120 (12×10) produced from an intermediate stone of 30 (6×5).

(f) 2d. as (e), but with veils altered to give effect of vertical drapes

16 **1** 2d. lilac-grey (1.51) £6000 £170
a. Deep grey £7000 £170
b. Brown-lilac (shades) £5500 £110
17 2d. cinnamon (*shades*) (2.51) £3750 £170
a. Drab (shades) £4000 95·00
b. Pale dull brown (shades) £3750 £120
c. Greenish grey £3750 £110
d. Olive-drab (shades) £4000 £190
e. Buff £12000 £250

Printed in sheets of 120 (12×10) produced from two successive intermediate stones of 30 (6×5) on which the details of the veil were amended as described above.

This was the final printing of the 2d. 'Half Length' as the die for this value had been damaged. A replacement 2d. design was ordered from Thomas Ham.

For the later printings of the 1d. and 3d. in this design see Nos. 23/24, 26/31, 48/49 and 78/79.

2 Queen-on-Throne

3

(Recess-printed by Thomas Ham)

1852 (27 Dec). Imperf.

18 **2** 2d. reddish brown £800 30·00
a. Chestnut — £140
b. Purple-brown £900 30·00

Printed in sheets of 50 (10×5) from a hand-engraved plate of the same size. Each stamp in the sheet had individual corner letters made-up of various combinations, none of which contained the letter 'J'.

Reprints were made in 1891 using the original plate, on paper wmk V over Crown, both imperf and perf 12½.

For later printings of this design see Nos. 19/22 and 36/39.

CAMPBELL & CO PRINTINGS. In May 1853 the Victoria postal authorities placed an order for 1d. and 6d. stamps in the 'Queen-on-Throne' design with Perkins Bacon in London. These would not arrive for some time, however, and supplies of Ham's printings were rapidly becoming exhausted. Local tenders were, therefore, solicited for further supplies of the 1d. and 3d. 'Half Lengths' and the 2d. 'Queen-on-Throne'. That received from J. S. Campbell & Co was accepted. The stamps were produced by lithography, using transfers from either the 'Half Length' engraved die or the 2d. 'Queen-on-Throne' engraved plate of 50. Stamps from the Campbell & Co printings can be distinguished from later printings in lithography by the good quality paper used.

(Lithographed by J. S. Campbell & Co, Melbourne, using transfers taken from Ham's engraved plate)

1854 (Jan–July). Good quality white or toned paper. Imperf.

(a) Clear impressions with details around back of throne generally complete

19	2	2d. brownish purple	£800	40·00
		a. Grey-brown	£1000	40·00
		b. Purple-black	—	40·00
		c. Dull lilac-brown (toned paper only)	£1000	50·00

(b) Poor impressions with details around back of throne not fully defined

20	2	2d. violet-black (2.54)	£950	48·00
		a. Grey-black	£1000	48·00
		b. Grey-lilac	£950	48·00
		c. Dull brown (on toned)	£950	48·00
		ca. Substituted transfer (in pair)	—	£3000

(c) Weak impressions with background generally white without details. Toned paper only

21	2	2d. grey-purple (7.54)	£650	35·00
		a. Purple-black	£650	35·00

(d) Printings using an intermediate stone. Impression flat and blurred. Background details usually complete. Toned paper only

22	2	2d. grey-drab (*shades*) (5.54)	£900	40·00
		a. Black	—	£140

Nos. 19/21 were produced using transfers taken directly from the original Ham engraved plate. It is believed that the different strengths of the impressions were caused by the amount of pressure exerted when the transfers were taken. The stamps were printed in sheets of 100 (2 panes 10×5). On one stone a block of four at bottom left, lettered 'FL GM' over 'QV RW', was damaged and the stone was repaired by using a block of four substituted transfers. These were lettered 'VZ WA' over 'FL GM'. No. 20ca covers any one of these substituted transfers in pair with normal. As horizontal pairs these are lettered 'WA HN' or 'GM SX' and as vertical 'VZ' over 'VZ' or 'WA' over 'WA'.

For No. 22 an intermediate stone was used to produce a printing stone of 300 (6 panes 10×5). The insertion of a further stage into the process caused the blurred appearance of stamps from this printing. No. 22*a* is believed to come from proof sheets issued to post offices for normal use. Examples are usually cancelled with Barred Oval 108 and Barred Numerals 1 and 2.

(Lithographed by J.S. Campbell & Co, Melbourne)

1854 (Feb–June). Good quality wove paper. Imperf.

23	1	1d. orange-red (*shades*)	£3500	£140
		a. Rose	£6500	£750
24		3d. blue (*shades*) (6.54)	£1500	50·00
		a. Retouched under 'C' of 'VICTORIA'	—	£150

The 1d. was produced in sheets of 192 (two panes of 96 (12×8)) and the 3d. in sheets of 320 (two panes of 160 (18×9)). Both printing stones were constructed from transfers taken from intermediate stones of 24 (6×4). The spacing between stamps is far wider than on the Ham printings. The 3d. panes of 160 were constructed using six complete transfers of 24 and three of six with the final impression in the bottom two rows removed.

The 1d. Campbell printings have the frame lines almost completely absent due to lack of pressure when taking transfers.

The 3d. retouch, No. 24a, occurs on R. 3/5 of the intermediate stone.

CAMPBELL & FERGUSSON PRINTINGS. Increased postal rates in early 1854 led to a requirement for a 1s. value and in April a contract for this stamp was awarded to Campbell & Fergusson (the new corporate style of J. S. Campbell & Co). Further contracts to print the 1d. and 3d. 'Half Lengths' and the 2d. 'Queen-on-Throne' followed. All were produced by lithography with the two 'Half Lengths' using transfers from the original engraved die and the 2d. 'Queen-on-Throne' transfers from Ham's original engraved plate.

All Campbell & Fergusson printings were on paper of a poorer quality than that used for the earlier contract.

(Lithographed by Campbell & Fergusson)

1854 (6 July). Poorer quality paper. Imperf.

25	3	1s. blue (*shades*)	£1200	45·00
		a. Greenish blue	£1400	45·00
		b. Indigo-blue	—	£200

No. 25 was produced in sheets of 100 (8×12 with an additional stamp appearing at the end of rows 6 to 9). The printing stones used each contained four such sheets. They were constructed from an intermediate stone of 40 (8×5) taken from a single engraved die. Each pane of 100 showed two complete transfers of 40, one of 20, and one of a vertical strip of four.

For this stamp rouletted or perforated see Nos. 54 and 81.

(Lithographed by Campbell & Fergusson)

1854 (July)–**57**. Poorer quality paper. Imperf.

26	1	1d. brown (*shades*)	£3250	£130
		a. Brick-red (shades)	£3500	£110
		b. Dull red (shades)	£3750	£110
27		1d. Orange-brown (*shades*) (8.55)	£3500	£140
		a. Dull rose-red (shades)	£4000	80·00
		b. Bright rose-pink	£6500	£160
		c. Retouched (6 varieties)	£6000	£450
28		1d. pink (*shades*) (2.55)	£1500	48·00
		a. Rose (shades)	£1500	48·00
		b. Lilac-rose (shades)	£1600	48·00
		c. Dull brown-red (shades)	£1800	£140
		d. Retouched (8 varieties)	£2500	£325
29		3d. bright blue (*shades*) (7.57)	£2500	70·00
		a. Greenish blue (shades)	£2100	55·00
		b. Retouch under 'C' of 'VICTORIA'	£3250	£130
30		3d. Prussian blue (*shades*) (11.56)	£3250	95·00
		a. Milky blue	£4000	£150
		b. Retouch under 'C' of 'VICTORIA'	—	£275
31		3d. steel-blue (*shades*) (heavier impression) (5.55)	—	65·00
		a. Greenish blue (shades)	£2100	48·00
		b. Blue (shades)	£2100	48·00
		c. Deep blue (shades)	£1800	48·00
		d. Indigo (shades)	—	55·00

The 1d. was produced in sheets of 400 (2 panes 20×10) constructed from transfers originating from the J. S. Campbell & Co intermediate stone. Each pane contained six complete transfers of 24, three of 12, two of eight and one of four.

The 3d. was produced in sheets of 320 (2 panes of 160) (No. 29), 200 (No. 30) or 400 (2 panes of 200) (No. 31.) The stone for No. 29 was constructed from transfers taken from the J. S. Campbell intermediate stone with the retouch on R. 3/5 still present. The panes of 160 contained six transfers of 24 and three of six with the last impression in both rows 8 and 9 removed. Quality of impression is generally poor. The stone for No. 30, once again taken from the Campbell intermediate stone, was laid down in the same combination of transfers as the 1d. value. Impressions from it were, however, so poor that transfers from a new intermediate stone were used for No. 31. Impressions from this stone, on which the panes of 200 were in a similar layout to the 1d. were much further apart than those on the stones used to produce Nos. 29/30.

The Campbell & Fergusson printings of the 'Half Lengths' are listed in the order in which they were printed.

CALVERT PRINTINGS. Contracts for the provision of other values required by the postal rate changes in 1853 were placed with Samuel Calvert of Melbourne who used typography as the printing process. Calvert continued to print, and later roulette, stamps for the Victoria Post Office until March 1858 when it was discovered that he had placed some of the stock in pawn.

4

5

6

(Typographed from woodblocks by Samuel Calvert)

1854 (1 Sept)–**55**. Imperf.

32	4	6d. reddish brown (13.9.54)	£1200	75·00
		a. Dull orange	£650	19·00
		b. Orange-yellow	£650	19·00
33	5	6d. ('TOO LATE') lilac and green (1.1.55)	£3500	£250
34	6	1s. ('REGISTERED') rose-pink and blue (1.12.54)	£4250	£200
35	4	2s. dull bluish green/*pale yellow*	£6000	£200

No. 33 was provided to pay the additional fee on letters posted after the normal closure of the mails. This service was only available in the larger towns; examples are usually postmarked Castlemaine, Geelong or Melbourne. The service was withdrawn on 30 June 1857 and remaining stocks of the 'TOO LATE' stamps were used for normal postal purposes.

No. 34 was issued to pay the registration fee and was so used until 5 January 1858 after which remaining stocks were used for normal postage.

These four values were produced from individually-engraved boxwood woodblocks. The 6d. was in sheets of 100 printed by two impressions from two plates of 25. The 2s. was in sheets of 50 from a single plate of 25. The bicoloured 'TOO LATE' and 'REGISTERED' stamps are unusual in that Calvert used a common woodblock 'key' plate of 25 for both values combined with 'duty' plates made up from metal stereos. Both values were originally in sheets of 50, but the 'REGISTERED' later appeared in sheets of 100 for which a second 'key' plate of 25 was utilised.

For these stamps rouletted or perforated see Nos. 53, 55/58, 60/61 and 82.

(Lithographed by Campbell & Fergusson)

1855 (Mar)–**56**. Poorer quality paper. Imperf.

(a) Printings from stones which were not over-used; background around top of throne generally full and detail good

36	2	2d. lilac (*shades*) (7.55)	£600	35·00
		a. Purple (shades)	£600	35·00
		b. 'TVO' for 'TWO'	£9500	£1400

(b) Early printings from stones which were over-used. Similar characteristics to those above, though detail is not quite so full. Distinctive shades

37	2	2d. brown	—	80·00
		a. Brown-purple	£650	27·00
		b. Warm purple	—	27·00
		c. Rose-lilac	—	27·00
		d. Substituted transfer (pair)	—	£750

(c) Later printings from the same stones used for No. 37 when in a worn condition. Impressions heavy, coarse and overcoloured; details blurred; generally white background around top of throne

38	2	2d. dull lilac-mauve (1856)	£650	50·00
		a. Dull mauve	£650	50·00
		b. Grey-violet	—	50·00
		c. Red-lilac	—	50·00
		d. Substituted transfer (pair)	—	£750

(d) Printings from a stone giving blotchy and unpleasing results, with poor definition. Mainly shows in extra colour patches found on most stamps

39	2	2d. dull purple (7.55)	—	70·00
		a. Dull grey-lilac	£650	70·00
		b. On thick card paper	—	£650

The Campbell & Fergusson 2d. 'Queen-on-Throne' printings were in sheets of 200 (4 panes 10×5) constructed from transfers taken from the original Ham engraved plate.

Four separate stones were used. On Stone A a creased transfer running through R. 4/8, 4/9 and 5/8 caused the 'TVO' variety on the stamp from the bottom row of one pane. On Stone C the impression in the first vertical row of one pane were found to be so faulty that they were replaced by substituted transfers taken from elsewhere on the sheet causing abnormal horizontal pairs lettered 'UY BF', 'TX MQ', 'DI WA', 'SW GM' and 'CH RW'. The vertical pairs from the substituted transfers are lettered 'UY' over 'TX' and 'DI' over 'SW'.

PERKINS BACON 'CANCELLED'. For notes on this handstamp, showing 'CANCELLED' between horizontal bars forming an oval, see Catalogue Introduction.

7 Queen-on-Throne

8 'Emblems'

(Recess Perkins Bacon & Co, London)

1856 (23 Oct). Wmk Large Star. Imperf.

40	7	1d. yellow-green (H/S 'CANCELLED' in oval £12000)	£300	45·00

Supplies of this stamp, and the accompanying 6d. which was only issued rouletted (see No. 73), arrived in the colony at the end of 1854, but the 1d. was not placed on sale until almost two years later.

No. 40 was reprinted from the original plate in 1891. Examples, in either dull yellow-green or bright blue-green, are imperforate and on V over Crown watermarked paper.

(Typographed from electrotypes by Calvert)

1857 (26 Jan–6 Sept). Imperf.

(a) Wmk Large Star, W w **1**

41	8	1d. yellow-green (18.2)	£275	29·00
		a. Deep green	£375	40·00
		b. Printed on both sides	†	£2750
42		4d. vermilion	£600	11·00
		a. Brown-vermilion	£550	9·50
		b. Printed on both sides	†	£2750
43		4d. dull red (20.7)	£450	8·50
44		4d. dull rose (6.9)	£550	8·50

(b) No wmk. Good quality medium wove paper

45	8	2d. pale lilac (25.5)	£700	12·00
		a. Grey-lilac	£700	12·00

Nos. 41/45 were produced in sheets of 120, arranged as four panes of 30 (6×5) (1d. and 4d.) or 12 panes of 10 (2×5) (2d.), using electrotypes taken from a single engraved die of each value.

The setting of the 4d. was rearranged before the printing of Nos. 43/44.

Only two examples of No. 41b and No. 42b have been recorded.

For this printing rouletted or perforated see Nos. 46/47, 50/52, 59, 74 and 77.

ROULETTES AND PERFORATIONS. In August 1857 a rouletting machine was provided at the GPO, Melbourne, to enable the counter clerks to separate stamp stocks before sale to the public. This machine produced roulettes of 7½–9 in one direction across six rows at a time. There was also a single wheel device which gauged 7–7½. Both were in use between the earliest known date of 12 August and the end of 1857.

Calvert was granted a separate contract in October 1857 to roulette the stamps he printed, but only Nos. 57/61 had been produced when it was found, in April 1858, that he had pawned a quantity of the sheets. His contracts were terminated and his successor, F. W. Robinson, used a roulette machine of a different gauge before switching to a gauge 12 perforating machine in January 1859.

1857 (12 Aug–Sept). Rouletted 7–9 by counter clerks at GPO, Melbourne.

46	8	1d. yellow-green (No. 41)	£650	£110
47		2d. pale lilac (No. 45)	—	50·00
		a. Grey-lilac	—	50·00
48	1	3d. blue (*shades*) (No. 24)	£3500	£250
		a. Retouch under 'C' of 'VICTORIA'	†	£475
49		3d. bright blue (*shades*) (No. 29)	—	£250
		a. Greenish blue (shades)	£3500	£225
		b. Retouch under 'C' of 'VICTORIA'	†	£600
50	8	4d. vermilion (No. 42)	—	£100
51		4d. dull red (No. 43)	—	42·00
52		4d. dull rose (No. 44) (9.57)	—	28·00
53	4	6d. reddish brown (No. 32)	—	£100
		a. Dull orange	—	60·00
		b. Orange-yellow	—	70·00
54	3	1s. blue (*shades*) (No. 25)	—	£110
		a. Greenish blue	—	£110
55	6	1s. ('REGISTERED') rose-pink and blue (No. 34)	£11000	£400
56	4	2s. dull bluish green/*pale yellow* (No. 35)	£9500	£650

With the exception of the 1s., Nos. 54/54*a*, these stamps are normally found rouletted on one or two sides only.

1857 (Oct). Rouletted by Calvert.

(a) Rouletted 7–9 on all four sides and with finer points than No. 53b

57	4	6d. orange-yellow (No. 32*b*)	—	£100

(b) Serpentine roulette 10–10½

58	4	6d. orange-yellow (No. 32*b*)	£3500	£180

(c) Serrated 18–19

59	8	2d. grey-lilac (No. 45*a*)	£1600	£600
60	4	6d. orange-yellow (No. 32*b*)	£4750	£160

(d) Compound of serrated 18–19 and serpentine 10–10½

61	4	6d. orange-yellow (No. 32*b*)	—	£600

No. 59 was not covered by the contract given to Calvert, but it is believed to be a test run for the rouletting machine. No. 61 always shows serrated 18–19 on three sides and the serpentine roulette at the top or bottom of the stamp.

(Typo from electrotypes by Calvert)

1858 (14 Jan–Apr). Good quality white wove paper. No wmk.

(a) Rouletted 7–9 on all four sides

62	8	1d. pale emerald	£550	32·00
		a. Emerald-green	£550	32·00
63		4d. rose-pink (18.1)	£425	7·50
		a. Bright rose	£425	7·50
		b. Reddish pink	—	11·00
		c. Imperf horiz (vert pair)	†	£650

(b) Imperf (Apr)

64	8	1d. pale emerald	£425	23·00
		a. Emerald-green	—	26·00
65		4d. rose-pink	£500	23·00
		a. Bright rose	—	23·00
		b. Reddish pink	—	30·00

Nos. 62/65 were produced in sheets of 120, arranged as four panes of 30 (6×5).

The Royal Collection contains a used horizontal pair of the 4d. showing the vertical roulettes omitted.

The majority of Nos. 64/65 were issued in April after Calvert's contracts had been terminated, although there is some evidence that imperforate sheets of the 4d., at least, were issued earlier.

For the 1d. of this issue perforated see No. 75.

ROBINSON PRINTINGS. Calvert's contracts were cancelled in April 1858 and the work was then placed with F. W. Robinson, who had unsuccessfully tendered in 1856. The same electrotypes were used, but a perforating machine was introduced from January 1859. Robinson continued to print and perforate stamps under contract until the end of 1859 when the Victoria Post Office purchased his equipment to set up a Stamp Printing Branch and appointed him Printer of Postage Stamps.

(Typo from electrotypes by Robinson)

1858 (May–Dec).

(a) Imperf

(i) Coarse quality wove paper

No.	Type	Description	Unused	Used
66	8	4d. dull rose (*oily ink*)	—	80·00

(ii) Smooth vertically-laid paper

No.	Type	Description	Unused	Used
67	8	4d. dull rose (*oily ink*)	—	55·00
		a. Dull rose-red	—	55·00
68		4d. dull rose-red (*normal ink*) (20.5)	£650	35·00

(b) Rouletted 5½–6½

(i) Smooth-laid paper

No.	Type	Description	Unused	Used
69	8	2d. brown-lilac (*shades*) (*horiz laid*) (6.58)	£300	12·00
		a. Vert laid paper (21.9)	£450	15·00
70		2d. violet (*horiz laid*) (27.11)	£375	6·50
		a. Dull violet	£425	18·00
71		4d. pale dull rose (*vert laid*) (1.6)	£325	4·00
		a. Horiz laid paper	†	£900
		b. Dull rose-red	£275	4·00
		c. Rose-red	£275	4·00
		ca. Serrated 19	†	£550

(ii) Good quality wove paper

No.	Type	Description	Unused	Used
72	8	1d. yellow-green (24.12)	£475	45·00

Nos. 66/72 were produced in sheets of 120, arranged as four panes of 30 (6×5).

For stamps of this issue perforated see Nos. 76 and 80.

(Recess Perkins Bacon & Co, London)

1858 (1 Nov). Wmk Large Star, W w **1**. Rouletted 5½–6½.

No.	Type	Description	Unused	Used
73	7	6d. bright blue	£550	18·00
		a. Light blue	£600	28·00

No. 73 was received from London at the same time as the 1d., No. 40, but was kept in store until November 1858 when the stock was rouletted by Robinson. When issued the gum was in a poor state.

Imperforate examples exist from Perkins Bacon remainders. Examples are known handstamped 'CANCELLED' in oval of bars. *Price* £11000.

Imperforate reprints, in shades of indigo, were made from the original plate in 1891 on V over Crown watermarked paper.

1859 (Jan–May). P 12 by Robinson.

No.	Type	Description	Unused	Used
74	8	1d. yellow-green (No. 41)	—	£500
75		1d. emerald-green (No. 64*a*)	—	£500
		a. Imperf between (horiz pair)		
76		1d. yellow-green (as No. 72) (11.1)	£425	20·00
		a. Imperf horiz (vert pair)	—	£450
		b. Thin, glazed ('Bordeaux') paper	†	£160
77		2d. pale lilac (No. 45)	—	£450
		a. Grey-lilac	—	£550
78	1	3d. blue (*shades*) (No. 24) (2.2)	£2500	£140
		a. Retouch under 'C' of 'VICTORIA'	—	£400
79		3d. greenish blue (*shades*) (No. 29*a*)	†	£425
		a. Retouch under 'C' of 'VICTORIA'	†	£1200
80	8	4d. dull rose-red (No. 68)	—	£325
81	3	1s. blue (*shades*) (No. 25) (4.2)	£400	16·00
		a. Greenish blue	£425	13·00
		b. Indigo-blue	—	45·00
		c. Retouched (shading omitted at left)		
82	4	2s. dull bluish green/*pale yellow* (No. 35) (5.59)	£650	55·00

The 1s. was reprinted in 1891 using transfers taken from the original die. These reprints were on V over Crown watermarked paper and perforated 12½.

For perforated 6d. black and 2s. blue both as Type **4** see Nos. 102 and 129/130.

(Typo from electrotypes by Robinson)

1859 (17 May–23 Dec). P 12.

(a) Good quality wove paper

No.	Type	Description	Unused	Used
83	8	4d. dull rose	£350	7·00
		a. Roul 5½–6½	†	£850

(b) Poorer quality wove paper

No.	Type	Description	Unused	Used
84	8	1d. dull green (7.59)	£300	30·00
		a. Green (11.11)	£300	30·00
85		4d. rose-carmine (16.7)	£350	7·50
		a. *Rose-pink* (*thick paper*) (30.11)	—	15·00

A used vertical pair as No. 85 is known rouletted between, apparently to correct an imperforate between error.t

(c) Horizontally laid paper with the lines wide apart

No.	Type	Description	Unused	Used
86	8	1d. dull green (18.7)	£425	
		a. Laid lines close together	—	50·00
		b. Green (*shades*) (10.59)	£325	30·00
87		4d. rose-pink (*shades*) (23.12)	£300	7·50
		a. Laid lines close together	—	10·00

STAMP PRINTING BRANCH. On 1 January 1860 F. W. Robinson was appointed Printer of Postage Stamps and his equipment purchased by the Post Office to establish the Stamp Printing Branch. All later Victoria issues were printed by the Branch which became part of the Victoria Government Printing Office in December 1885. In 1909 the Commonwealth Stamp Printing Office under J. B. Cooke was established in Melbourne and produced stamps for both the states and Commonwealth until 1918.

9

10

11

(Des and eng F. Grosse. Typo from electrotypes)

1860 (31 Jan)–**66**. P 12.

(a) No wmk

No.	Type	Description	Unused	Used
88	9	3d. deep blue (*horiz laid paper*)	£650	75·00
		a. Light blue		
89		4d. rose-pink (*thin glazed Bordeaux paper*) (21.4.60)	—	42·00
		a. Rose	£600	42·00
		ab. Thicker coarser paper (7.60)	£600	42·00

(b) On paper made by T. H. Saunders of London wmkd with the appropriate value in words as W **10**

No.	Type	Description	Unused	Used
90	9	3d. pale blue (1.61)	£325	7·00
		a. Bright blue (10.61)	£325	8·50
		b. Blue (4.63)	£325	6·00
		c. Deep blue (4.64)	£325	6·00
		d. 'TRREE' for 'THREE' in wmk	—	£700
91		3d. maroon (13.2.66)	£400	30·00
		a. Perf 13	£400	32·00
92		4d. rose-pink (1.8.60)	—	9·50
		a. Rose-red	£200	4·75
		b. Rose-carmine	—	9·50
		c. Dull rose	£200	4·75
		d. Printed on 'FIVE SHILLINGS' diagonal wmk paper (11.9.62)	£3500	23·00
93		6d. orange (25.10.60)	£8000	£450
94		6d. black (20.8.61)	£450	9·00
		a. Grey-black	£450	9·00

(c) On paper made by De La Rue wmkd with the appropriate value as a single-lined numeral as W **11**

No.	Type	Description	Unused	Used
95	9	4d. dull rose-pink (9.10.62)	£200	6·00
		a. Dull rose	£200	6·50
		b. Rose-red	—	6·00
		c. Roul 8 (28.7.63)	£2250	£250
		d. Imperf (14.7.63)	—	75·00
		e. Perf 12½×12		
		f. Perf 12½		

All three values were produced in sheets of 120, initially as four panes of 30 (6×5). Printings of the 3d. from 1864 were in a changed format of six panes of 20 (4×5).

The 'TRREE' watermark error comes from early printings of No. 90 on R. 10/7.

Two examples of the 4d. on Saunders paper are known bisected in 1863, but such use was unauthorised.

Nos. 95c/95d were issued during July and August 1863 when the normal perforating machine had broken down. They are best collected used on piece and cancelled within the period (July-September 1863).

Nos. 95e/95f were perforated or part-perforated with a machine gauging 12¼-12½, borrowed from the Government Printer in 1863, while the perf 12 machine was being repaired.

Reprints, from new plates, were made of the 3d. and 4d. in 1891 on 'V over Crown' paper and perforated 12½.

1860 (Apr)–**63**. P 12.

(a) No wmk

No.	Type	Description	Unused	Used
96	8	1d. bright green (*horiz laid paper*)		
97		1d. bright green (*thin, glazed Bordeaux paper*) (25.5.60)	—	75·00

(b) On paper made by T. H. Saunders of London wmkd with the appropriate value in words as W **10**

No.	Type	Description	Unused	Used
98	8	1d. pale yellowish green (8.7.60)	£140	9·00
		a. Yellow-green	£160	9·00
		b. Error. Wmkd 'FOUR PENCE'	†	£10000
99		2d. brown-lilac (7.7.61)	—	60·00
100		2d. bluish slate (8.61)	£225	6·00
		a. Greyish lilac (9.61)	£250	6·50
		b. Slate-grey (1.62)	—	6·00
		c. Printed on 'THREE PENCE' wmkd paper. *Pale slate* (27.12.62)	£250	30·00
		ca. Bluish grey (2.63)	£275	30·00

(c) On paper made by De La Rue wmkd single-lined '2', W **11**

No.	Type	Description	Unused	Used
101	8	2d. dull reddish lilac (24.4.63)	£350	17·00
		a. Grey-lilac (10.63)	£350	35·00
		ab. Error. Wmkd '6'	†	£6500
		b. Grey-violet (11.63)	£275	32·00
		c. Slate (12.63)	£350	45·00

Only two examples of No. 98b have been recorded, one of which is in the Royal Collection.

1861 (22 June). On paper made by T. H. Saunders of London wmkd 'SIX PENCE' as W **10**. P 12.

No.	Type	Description	Unused	Used
102	4	6d. black	£475	80·00

No. 102 was produced as an emergency measure after the decision had been taken to change the colour of the current 6d. from orange (No. 93) to black (No. 94). During the changeover the old Calvert 'woodblock' plates were pressed into service to provide two months' supply.

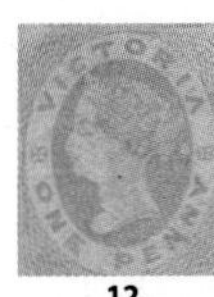

12

13

(Des, eng and electrotyped De Gruchy & Leigh, Melbourne. Typo)

1861 (1 Oct)–**64**. P 12.

(a) On paper made by T. H. Saunders of London. Wmk 'ONE PENNY' as W **10**

No.	Type	Description	Unused	Used
103	12	1d. pale green	£190	25·00
		a. Olive-green	—	26·00

(b) On paper made by De La Rue. Wmk single-lined '1' as W **11**

No.	Type	Description	Unused	Used
104	12	1d. olive-green (1.2.63)	£150	28·00
		a. Pale green (9.63)	£150	20·00
		b. Apple-green (4.64)	£150	19·00

(c) On paper supplied to Tasmania by Perkins Bacon. Wmk double-lined '1', W **4** *of Tasmania*

No.	Type	Description	Unused	Used
105	12	1d. yellow-green (10.12.63)	£275	26·00
		a. Dull green	—	26·00
		b. Imperf between (pair)	†	—

All printings were in sheets of 120 containing four panes of 30 (6×5).

Reprints from new plates were made in 1891 on paper watermarked 'V over Crown' and perforated 12½.

(Frame die eng F. Grosse. Typo from electrotypes)

1862 (26 Apr)–**64**. Centre vignette cut from T **9** with a new frame as T **13**.

(a) On paper made by T. H. Saunders of London. Wmk 'SIX PENCE' as W **10**. *P 12*

No.	Type	Description	Unused	Used
106	13	6d. grey	£250	21·00
		a. Grey-black	£250	23·00
		b. Jet-black	£275	25·00

(b) On paper made by De La Rue. Wmk single-lined '6' as W **11**

No.	Type	Description	Unused	Used
107	13	6d. grey (P 12) (18.6.63)	£200	7·00
		a. Jet-black	—	9·00
		b. Grey-black	£200	7·50
		c. Perf 13. *Jet-black*	£225	9·00
		ca. Grey-black	£225	9·00

Printings before August 1863 were in sheets of 120 containing four panes of 30 (6×5). For subsequent printings of No. 107 the format was changed to six panes of 20 (4×5).

Reprints from new plates were made in 1891 on paper watermarked 'V over Crown' and perforated 12½.

SINGLE-LINED NUMERAL WATERMARK PAPERS. The first consignment of this paper, showing watermarks as W **11**, arrived in Victoria during October 1862. Five further consignments followed, all but the last supplied by De La Rue.

The complexity of the scheme for different watermarks for each value, together with the time required to obtain further supplies from Great Britain, resulted in the emergency use of paper obtained from Tasmania and of the wrong numeral watermark on certain printings.

The final order for this paper was placed, in error with the firm of T. H. Saunders of London. Although the actual watermarks are the same (the dandy rolls were the property of the Victoria Government and supplied to each firm in turn) there are considerable differences between the two types of paper. That manufactured by Saunders is of a more even quality and is smoother, thicker, less brittle and less white than the De La Rue type.

De La Rue supplied white paper watermarked '1', '2', '4', '6' and '8', blue paper watermarked '1' and green paper watermarked '2'. The Saunders consignment of October 1865 contained white paper watermarked '1', '4' and '6', blue paper watermarked '1', green paper watermarked '2' and pink paper watermarked '10'.

It is helpful for comparison purposes to note that all white paper watermarked '2' or '8' can only be De La Rue and all pink paper watermarked '10' can only be Saunders.

14 15 16 17 18

(Des and eng F. Grosse. Typo from electrotypes)

1863–73. 'Laureated' series.

(a) On paper made by De La Rue wmkd with the appropriate value in single-lined numerals as W **11**

No.	Type	Description	Unused	Used
108	14	1d. pale green (P 12) (9.9.64)	£130	16·00
		a. Perf 12½×12 (9.64)		
		b. Perf 13 (10.10.64)	£120	8·50
		c. Bluish green (P 13)	£100	6·50
		ca. Printed double	†	£1500
		d. Green (P 12) (7.65)	£120	6·50
		da. Perf 13	£100	7·00
		e. Deep green (P 12) (12.65)	£150	7·00
		ea. Perf 13	—	7·00
		eb. Perf 12×13	—	13·00
		f. Bright yellow-green (P 13)	—	24·00
109		2d. violet (P 12) (1.4.64)	£160	14·00
		a. Dull violet (P 12) (10.64)	£170	14·00
		ab. Perf 12½×12	£750	
		ac. Perf 12½		
		ad. Perf 13	£160	9·50
		b. Dull lilac (P 13) (4.65)	£140	9·50
		ba. Perf 12 (7.66)	—	19·00
		bb. Perf 12×13 (7.66)	—	20·00
		c. Reddish mauve (P 13) (11.65)	£150	20·00
		d. Rose-lilac (P 13) (1.66)	£140	12·00
		da. Perf 12×13 or 13×12	£130	12·00
		e. Grey (P 12) (7.66)	£190	15·00
		ea. Perf 13	£130	6·00
110		4d. deep rose (P 12) (11.9.63)	£275	5·50
		a. Printed double	†	£1500
		b. Rose-pink (P 12) (9.63)	£200	3·00
		c. Pink (P 12) (7.5.64)	£200	3·00
		ca. Error. Wmkd single-lined '8'	†	£8000
		cb. Perf 12½×12 (9.64)		
		d. Dull rose (P 13) (10.64)	£180	3·00
		e. Dull rose-red (P 13)	£180	3·00
		ea. Perf 12 (8.65)	£275	75·00
111	16	6d. blue (P 12) (13.2.66)	£140	11·00
		a. Perf 13	£140	4·75
		b. Perf 12×13	£130	11·00
112	14	8d. orange (P 13) (22.2.65)	£850	£120
113	17	1s. blue/*blue* (P 13) (10.4.65)	£300	6·00
		a. Perf 12×13 (4.66)	£300	6·00
		ab. Imperf between (vert pair)	†	£7000
		b. Bright blue/blue (P 13) (6.67)	£250	6·50
		c. Indigo-blue/blue (P 13) (3.68)	—	4·00
		d. Dull blue/blue (P 12) (6.74)	—	3·75

(b) Emergency printings on Perkins Bacon paper borrowed from Tasmania. Wmk double-lined '4' as W **4** *of Tasmania*

No.	Type	Description	Unused	Used
114	14	4d. deep rose (P 12) (7.1.64)	£275	12·00
		a. Pale rose (P 12)	—	12·00
		b. Dull reddish rose (P 13) (11.8.65)	£275	12·00
		ba. Perf 12	—	12·00
		bb. Perf 12×13	—	23·00
		c. Red (P 13) (4.12.65)	£275	12·00

(c) Emergency printings on De La Rue paper as W **11**, *but showing incorrect single-lined numeral. P 13*

115 **14** 1d. bright yellow-green (wmkd '8') (27.12.66) £325 29·00
116 1d. bright yellow-green (wmkd '6') (6.67) — 70·00
117 2d. grey (wmkd '8') (18.1.67) £300 7·00
118 **15** 3d. lilac (wmkd '8') (29.9.66) £275 50·00
119 **16** 10d. grey (wmkd '8') (21.10.65) £1100 £150
a. Grey-black £1100 £160

(d) On paper made by T. H. Saunders wmkd with the appropriate value in single-lined numerals as W **11**

120 **14** 1d. deep yellow-green (P 12×13) (1.66) £225 30·00
a. Perf 13 (3.66) £130 15·00
b. Perf 12 (7.66) — 30·00
121 4d. rose-red (P 13) (12.12.65) £160 4·75
aa. Wmk sideways † —
a. Perf 12×13 or 13×12 (2.66) £250 9·50
b. Perf 12 (4.66) — 9·50
122 **16** 6d. blue (P 13) (28.5.66) £140 3·75
a. Perf 12 £140 7·00
b. Perf 12×13 £140 4·75
123 10d. dull purple/*pink* (P 13) (22.3.66) £325 7·00
a. Perf 12×13 £375 8·00
b. Blackish brown/pink (P 13) (12.69) £325 7·00
c. Purple-brown/pink (P 13) (11.70)
124 **17** 1s. bright blue/*blue* (P 13) (5.12.70) £180 4·75
a. Pale dull blue/blue (P 12) (1.73) £275 9·50
ab. Perf 13 — 20·00
b. Indigo-blue/blue (P 12) (9.73) — 15·00
ba. Perf 13 £180 7·00

(e) Emergency printings on Saunders paper as W **11**, *but showing incorrect single-lined numeral. P 13*

125 **14** 1d. bright yellow-green (wmkd '4') (6.3.67) £225 55·00
126 1d. bright yellow-green (wmkd '6') (6.67) £325 70·00
127 2d. grey (wmkd '4') (21.2.67) £250 9·50
128 2d. grey (wmkd '6') (13.5.67) £375 10·00

The 1d., 2d., 4d. and 8d. were originally produced in sheets of 120 containing eight panes of 15 (3×5). The 3d. and 6d. were in sheets of 120 (12×10) and the 1d. (from February 1866), 2d. (from July 1866) and 4d. (from April 1866) subsequently changed to this format. The 10d. was in sheets of 120 containing 20 panes of 6 (2×3). The 1s. was originally in sheets of 60 containing three panes of 20 (4×5), but this changed to 120 (12×10) in April 1866.

Nos. 108a, 109ab/109ac and 110cb were perforated or part-perforated with a machine gauging 12½, borrowed from the Government Printer in September 1864, while the perf 12 machine was being repaired.

Only single examples are thought to exist of Nos. 110a, 110ca and 113ab and two of No. 108ca.

For later emergency printings on these papers see Nos. 153/166.

(Typo from composite woodblock and electrotype plate)

1864–80. Wmk single-lined '2' as W **11**.

(a) On De La Rue paper.

129 **4** 2s. light blue/*green* (P 13) (22.11.64) £475 13·00
a. Dark blue/green (P 12) (9.65) £500 21·00
ab. Perf 13 (6.66) £475 9·50
b. Blue/green (P 13) (6.68) £425 7·00
c. Greenish blue/green (P 13) (7.73) £425 9·50
ca. Perf 12 £450 11·00
d. Deep greenish blue/green (P 12½) (7.80) £425 9·50

(b) On Saunders paper.

130 **4** 2s. dark blue/*green* (P 13) (23.11.67) £475 8·50
a. Blue/green (P 13) (10.71) £475 8·50
ab. Perf 12 (8.74) £500 9·00
c. Deep greenish blue/green (P 12½) (5.80) £450 7·00

Nos. 129/130 were produced in sheets of 30 containing two panes of 15 (3×5). The plate contained 18 of the original woodblock impressions and twelve electrotypes taken from them.

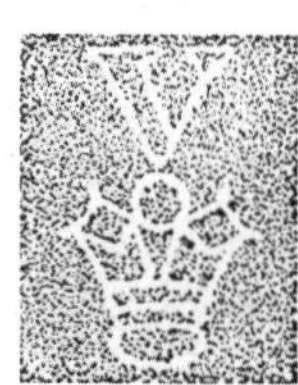
19

20

V OVER CROWN WATERMARKS. The changeover from the numeral watermarks to a general type to be used for all values was first suggested at the end of 1865, but the first supplies did not reach Melbourne until April 1867. Five different versions were used before the V over Crown watermark was superseded by the Commonwealth type in 1905. The five versions are listed as follows:

Type **19** De La Rue paper supplied 1867 to 1882. Shows four points at the top of the crown with the left and right ornaments diamond-shaped
Type **33** De La Rue paper supplied 1882 to 1895. No points at the top of the crown with the left and right ornaments oval-shaped
Type **82** Waterlow paper supplied 1896 to 1899. Wide base to crown
Type **85** Waterlow paper used for postal issues 1899 to 1905. Wide top to crown
Type **104** James Spicer and Sons paper used for postal issues August and September 1912. Narrow crown

(Typo from electrotypes)

1867–81. Wmk. V over Crown. W **19**.

(a) P 13

131 **14** 1d. bright yellow-green (10.8.67) £120 4·25
a. Bright olive-green (1.69) £180 24·00
b. Yellow-green (4.69) £130 4·25
c. Dull green (3.70) £130 4·00
d. Pale green (10.70) £120 4·00
e. Grass-green (1871) £120 4·25
f. Bluish green (shades) (7.72) £120 4·75
fa. Wmk sideways † —
g. Green (shades) (9.72) £120 3·75
ga. Wmk sideways † —
132 2d. slate-grey *(shades)* (26.8.67) £140 4·00
a. Grey-lilac (29.1.68) £140 6·00
b. Lilac (26.8.68) £110 3·75
ba. Wmk sideways † —
c. Dull mauve (shades) (10.68) £110 4·00
d. Lilac-grey (1.69) — 4·25
e. Lilac-rose (2.69) £120 3·75
f. Mauve (4.69) £140 4·00
g. Red-lilac (5.69) £120 3·50
h. Dull lilac (6.69) £120 3·00
i. Silver-grey (9.69) £225 11·00
133 **15** 3d. lilac (28.8.67) £475 55·00
a. Grey-lilac (6.68) £500 60·00
134 3d. yellow-orange (12.6.69) 90·00 17·00
aa. Wmk sideways † —
a. Dull orange (6.70) 75·00 10·00
ab. Wmk sideways † —
b. Orange (3.73) — 10·00
c. Bright orange (3.73) 90·00 10·00
d. Orange-brown (glazed paper) (10.78) 65·00 29·00
135 **14** 4d. dull rose (28.11.67) £140 8·00
a. Wmk sideways † 70·00
b. Aniline red (shades) (21.4.69) — 11·00
c. Rose-pink (11.69) — 7·50
d. Rose (shades) (8.71) £140 3·75
e. Dull rose (glazed paper) (5.3.79) £140 6·50
f. Dull rose-red (glazed paper) (11.79) — 10·00
g. Bright lilac-rose (aniline) (glazed paper) (2.80) £150 6·00
h. Rosine (aniline) (glazed paper) (9.80) £375 9·50
136 **16** 6d. deep blue (15.1.68) — 8·00
a. Blue (21.12.68) 95·00 6·00
ab. Wmk sideways † —
b. Indigo-blue (10.69) 95·00 6·00
c. Prussian blue (9.72) 95·00 7·00
d. Indigo (4.73) 95·00 7·00
e. Dull blue (worn plate) (3.74) — 7·50
f. Dull ultramarine (2.12.75) £110 7·50
g. Light Prussian blue (12.75) £150 7·50
h. Dull violet-blue (7.77) — 17·00
i. Blue (glazed paper) (6.78) £120 7·50
j. Dull milky-blue (glazed paper) (9.79) £120 8·00
k. Prussian blue (glazed paper) (4.80) — 8·00
l. Light blue (glazed paper) (4.81) £120 8·50
m. Deep blue (glazed paper) (10.81) £120 8·00
137 **14** 8d. lilac-brown/*pink* (24.1.77) £250 5·50
a. Purple-brown/pink (2.78) £250 5·50
b. Chocolate/pink (8.78) £275 10·00
ba. Compound perf 13×12 † £325
c. Red-brown/pink (12.78) £110 5·00
d. Wmk sideways † £400
138 **17** 1s. light blue/*blue* (11.5.75) £275 23·00
139 **18** 5s. blue/*yellow* (26.12.67) £4000 £450
a. Wmk reversed — £500
140 5s. indigo-blue and carmine (I) (8.10.68) £800 55·00
a. Blue and carmine (4.69) £750 24·00
b. Pale bright blue and carmine (glazed paper) (24.7.77) £900 55·00
c. Grey-blue and carmine (glazed paper) (4.78) £750 28·00
d. Wmk sideways. *Deep lavender-blue and carmine* (4.6.80) £750 50·00
141 5s. bright blue and red (II) *(glazed paper)* (12.5.81) £700 28·00
a. Indigo-blue and red (glazed paper) — 55·00

(b) P 12

142 **14** 1d. pale green (10.71) £140 10·00
a. Grass-green (1871) £120 10·00
b. Bluish green (shades) (7.72) — 15·00
c. Green (shades) (9.72) £120 8·00
143 **15** 3d. dull orange (5.72) 80·00 8·00
a. Orange (3.73) — 3·25
b. Bright orange (3.73) — 3·25
c. Dull orange-yellow (glazed paper) (12.80)
144 **14** 4d. rose *(shades)* (8.71) £140 3·00
a. Compound perf 12×13 — £400
b. Dull rose (glazed paper) (3.79) — 3·25
c. Dull rose-red (glazed paper) (11.79) — 6·50
d. Bright lilac-rose (aniline) (glazed paper) (2.80) £275 18·00
e. Rosine (aniline) (glazed paper) (9.80) £160 15·00
145 **16** 6d. deep blue (2.2.72)
a. Prussian blue (9.72) £100 9·50
b. Indigo (4.73) £110 10·00
c. Dull blue (worn plate)
d. Blue (glazed paper) (6.78) — 9·50
e. Dull milky-blue (glazed paper) — 9·50
f. Light blue (glazed paper) (4.81) — 10·00
146 **14** 8d. red-brown/*pink (glazed paper)* (11.80) £250 24·00
147 **17** 1s. light blue/*blue* (5.75) — 13·00
148 **18** 5s. bright blue and red (II) *(glazed paper)* (5.81) £700 15·00
a. Indigo-blue and red £800 19·00

(c) P 12½

149 **15** 3d. dull orange-yellow *(glazed paper)* (12.80) £120 17·00
150 **14** 4d. rosine *(aniline) (glazed paper)* (9.80)
151 **16** 6d. Prussian blue *(glazed paper)* (4.80)
a. Light blue (glazed paper) (4.81)
b. Deep blue (glazed paper) (10.81) £110 10·00
152 **14** 8d. lilac-brown/*pink* (8.77) £250 24·00
a. Red-brown/pink (glazed paper) (11.80) † £500

The same electrotypes as the previous issues were used for this series with the exception of the 5s. which was a new value. The 1d., 2d., 3d., 4d., 6d. and 1s. plates were arranged to print sheets of 120 (12×10) and the 8d. conformed to this when reintroduced in 1877. New plates for the 1d. (1868), 2d. (1869) and 6d. (1875) were constructed by Robinson's successor, J. P. Atkinson, using the improved facilities then available.

Atkinson was also responsible for the printing of the 5s. value. The original printings in blue on yellow paper were produced in sheets of 25, or possibly 50, using a vertical strip of five electrotypes. Due to its size the 5s. did not exactly fit the watermarked paper and, to avoid a preprinted sheet number, a proportion of the printing was made on the back of the paper creating the reversed watermark variety, No. 139a. These varieties occur in the first printing only as Atkinson created a plate of 25 for the second printing in March 1868.

Two Types of the 5s.: Printings of the 5s. bicoloured to April 1880 were made from electrotypes taken from the monocoloured plate. These showed a blue line beneath the crown (Type I). In early 1881 this plate was found to be too worn for further use and a new die was made from which a plate of 100 was constructed. Stamps from this plate are without the blue line beneath the crown (Type II).

PERFORATIONS 1859-1883. Collectors should note that our descriptions of perforations follow a longstanding convention.

'Perf 12' (1859 to mid–1866 and mid–1871 to 1883)–line perf machines perforating between 11½ and 12.

'Perf 13' (1864 to 1881)–line perf machines generally gauging between 12½ and 12¾, two of which were converted to comb perforation in 1871. It should be noted that, following a repair in 1879, one of these machines produced an irregular gauge varying between 12¼ and13½.

'Perf 12½' (1863 and 1864)–a line perforating machine borrowed from the Government Printer while the perf 12 machine was being repaired. Stamps perforated (or part-perforated) on this machine were Nos. 95e/95f, 108a, 109ab/109ac and 110cb. All are rare.

'Perf 12½' (late 1879 onwards)–line or comb machines gauging exactly 12½.

'Mixed perforations'–this description covers stamps where both gauges are present on the same side or sides of the stamp, as a result of reperforation.

(Typo from electrotypes)

1867–70. Emergency printings on various papers due to shortages of V over Crown paper. P 13.

(a) Perkins Bacon paper borrowed from Tasmania. Wmkd double-lined numerals as W **4** *of Tasmania*

153 **14** 1d. pale yellowish green (wmkd '1') (24.9.67) £150 14·00
a. Deep yellow-green (10.67) £150 14·00
154 1d. pale yellow-green (wmkd '4') (27.5.68) £2750 £130
155 2d. grey-lilac (wmkd '4') (3.2.68) £300 5·00
a. Slate (4.68) £300 3·50
b. Mauve (7.68) — 4·50
c. Imperf (pair) † £5500
156 2d. mauve (wmkd '1') (30.6.68) £300 5·50
157 **15** 3d. grey-lilac (wmkd '1') (8.68) £400 80·00
158 **14** 4d. dull rose-red (wmkd '4') (5.68) £300 5·00
159 **16** 6d. blue (wmkd '4') (20.6.68) £375 45·00
a. Indigo-blue — 48·00
160 6d. blue (wmkd '1') (28.7.68) £200 14·00
161 6d. dull blue (wmkd '2') (1870) † £4750

(b) Saunders paper. Wmkd in words as W **10**

162 **14** 1d. pale yellow-green (wmkd 'SIX PENCE') (23.3.68) £950 75·00
a. Wmk sideways † —
164 **16** 6d. blue (wmkd 'SIX PENCE') (20.5.68) £750 60·00
a. Indigo-blue — 60·00
165 6d. dull blue (wmkd 'THREE PENCE') (6.12.69) £500 35·00
a. Deep blue — 40·00
166 6d. dull blue (wmkd 'FOUR PENCE') (21.5.70) £750 50·00
a. Deep blue — 55·00

(c) V over Crown, W **19**, *coloured paper*

167 **14** 2d. mauve/*lilac* (7.68) £200 6·50
a. *Lilac/lilac* £200 6·50

(d) Saunders single-lined numeral '4' as W **11**

168 **16** 6d. dull blue (21.5.70) † £3250

The supply of paper was so short during 1868 that many odds and ends were utilised. Nos. 161 (five known) and 168 (ten known) are the rarest of these emergency printings.

The 2d. slate-grey is known watermarked 'SIX PENCE'. The single example is in the Royal Philatelic Collection,

(Printed in Melbourne from a double electrotyped plate of 240 supplied by D.L.R.)

1870 (28 Jan)–**73.** Wmk V over Crown. W **19**

169 **20** 2d. brown-lilac (P 13) £130 3·00
a. Dull lilac-mauve (9.70) £120 1·25
b. Mauve (worn plate) (3.73) £120 1·25
170 2d. dull lilac-mauve (P 12) (28.7.71) £120 2·50
a. Mauve (worn plate) (3.73) £120 2·25

9 9

NINEPENCE

(21)

1871 (22 Apr). No. 123c surch with T **21** in blue.

171 **16** 9d. on 10d. purple-brown/*pink* £900 13·00
a. Blackish brown/pink £950 15·00
b. Surch double † £3250
c. Wmk sideways † —

22

23

24

25

26

27

(Des and eng W. Bell. Typo from electrotyped plates)

1873 (25 Mar)–**74**. Saunders paper. Wmk single-lined '10' as W **11**.

172	**25**	9d. pale brown/*pink* (P 13)	£225	45·00
		a. Red-brown/pink (7.74)	£200	42·00
173		9d. pale brown/*pink* (P 12)	£250	45·00

½ ½

HALF

(**28**)

1873 (25 June). No. 131*g* surch with T **28** in red.

174	**14**	½d. on 1d. green (P 13)	95·00	20·00
		a. Grass-green	£100	20·00
		b. Short '1' at right (R. 1/3)	—	£100
		c. Mixed perf 13 and 12	†	—
175		½d. on 1d. green (P 12)	£120	20·00
		a. Grass-green	£120	20·00
		b. Short '1' at right (R. 1/3)	—	£100

Die I

Die II

Two Dies of 2d.:
Die I. Single-lined outer oval
Die II. Double-lined outer oval

(Des and eng W. Bell. Typo from electrotyped plates)

1873–87. Wmk V over Crown, W **19** (sideways on ½d.).

(a) P 13

176	**22**	½d. rose-red (10.2.74)	38·00	3·25
		a. Lilac-rose (1874)	38·00	3·50
		b. Rosine (shades) (glazed paper)	35·00	3·25
		c. Pale red (glazed paper) (1882)	38·00	3·25
		d. Mixed perf 13 and 12	†	£400
		e. Perf 12×13		
177	**23**	1d. *dull bluish green* (14.12.75)	75·00	2·50
		a. Green (shades) (1877)	75·00	2·50
		b. Yellow-green (glazed paper)	85·00	2·25
		c. Mixed perf 13 and 12		
178	**24**	2d. deep lilac-mauve (I) (1.10.73)	£100	1·00
		a. Dull violet-mauve	£100	1·00
		b. Dull mauve	£100	1·00
		c. Pale mauve (worn plate) (glazed paper) (1.79)	£100	1·25
		d. Mixed perf 13 and 12	£600	£375
179		2d. lilac-mauve (II) *(glazed paper)* (17.12.78)	95·00	1·25
		a. Grey-mauve (1.80)	—	2·75
		b. Pale mauve (6.80)	£130	2·75
		c. Vert pair, lower stamp imperf horiz	†	£3250
180	**26**	1s. indigo-blue/*blue* (16.8.76)	£160	4·75
		a. Wmk sideways	†	£750
		b. Deep blue/blue (7.77)	£170	4·00
		c. Pale blue/blue (3.80)	£170	4·75
		ca. Wmk sideways	†	£750
		d. Bright blue/blue (9.80)	£190	7·50
		e. Bright blue/blue (glazed paper) (21.11.83)	£190	5·50
		f. Pale blue/blue (glazed paper)		
		g. Mixed perf 13 and 12	†	—

(b) P 12

181	**22**	½d. rose-red (1874)	38·00	7·00
		a. Lilac-rose (1874)	38·00	7·00
		b. Rosine (shades) (glazed paper)	38·00	7·00
		c. Pale red (glazed paper) (1882)	38·00	7·00
182	**23**	1d. dull bluish green (1875)	85·00	10·00
		a. Green (shades) (1877)	80·00	13·00
		b. Yellow-green (glazed paper)	—	12·00
183	**24**	2d. deep lilac-mauve (I) (1873)	—	15·00
		a. Dull violet-mauve	—	15·00
		b. Dull mauve	£130	6·00
		c. Pale mauve (worn plate) (glazed paper) (1879)	£140	7·00
184		2d. lilac-mauve (II) *(glazed paper)* (1878)	£140	6·00
		a. Grey-mauve (glazed paper) (1880)	—	7·00
		b. Pale mauve (glazed paper) (1880)	—	8·50
185	**25**	9d. lilac-brown/*pink* (1.12.75)	£300	18·00
186	**26**	1s. deep blue/*blue* (1880)	—	7·50
		a. Bright blue/blue (1880)	—	7·50

(c) P 12½

187	**22**	½d. rosine *(shades) (glazed paper)* (1880)		
		a. Pale red (glazed paper) (1882)		
188	**23**	1d. yellow-green *(glazed paper)* (1880)		
189	**24**	2d. grey-mauve (II) *(glazed paper)* (1880)		
		a. Pale mauve (1880)		
190	**27**	2s. deep blue/*green* (glazed paper) (8.7.81)	£300	24·00
		a. Light blue/green (glazed paper) (4.83)		
		ab. Wmk sideways	£300	24·00
		b. Ultramarine/green (glazed paper) (6.84)	—	28·00
		ba. Wmk sideways	—	60·00

8d 8d

EIGHTPENCE

(**29**)

1876 (1 July). No. 185 surch with T **29** in blue.

191	**25**	8d. on 9d. lilac-brown/*pink*	£650	35·00
		a. 'F.IGHTPENCE'	—	£600

No. 191a was caused by a broken 'E' and it occurred once in each sheet of 120.

1877–79. Saunders paper. Wmk '10' as W **11**.

192	**14**	8d. lilac-brown/*pink* (P 13)	—	£500
		a. Purple-brown/pink (2.78)	£275	20·00
		b. Chocolate/pink (8.78)	†	£600
		c. Red-brown/pink (8.79)	£225	8·50
193		8d. red-brown/*pink* (P 12) (8.79)	£400	28·00
194		8d. red-brown/*pink* (P 12½) (8.79)	—	60·00

Nos. 192/194 occur amongst the V over Crown printings, the two types of pink paper having become mixed.

1878 (21 Feb–5 Apr). Emergency printings on coloured papers. Wmk V over Crown, W **19** (sideways on ½d.). P 13.

195	**22**	½d. rose-red/*pink* (1.3.78)	95·00	50·00
196	**23**	1d. yellow-green/*yellow* (5.3.78)	£160	40·00
197		1d. yellow-green/*drab* (5.4.78)	£275	75·00
198	**24**	2d. dull violet-mauve/*lilac* (21.2.78)	—	£1500
199		2d. dull violet-mauve/*green* (23.2.78)	£375	50·00
		a. Mixed perfs 12 and 13		
200		2d. dull violet-mauve/*brown* (21.3.78)	£350	50·00

There was a shortage of white V over Crown, W **19**, watermarked paper in the early months of 1878 and various coloured papers were used for printings of the ½d., 1d. and 2d. values until fresh stocks of white paper were received.

No. 198 is often misidentified. It can be confused with discoloured examples of Nos. 178/178*b*, and has often been faked.

30

31

32

(Des and eng C. Naish. Typo from electrotyped plates)

1880 (3 Nov)–**84**. Wmk V over Crown. W **19**.

201	**30**	1d. green (P 12½) (2.84)	£190	27·00
202	**31**	2d. sepia (P 12½)	80·00	3·50
		a. Sepia-brown (2.81)	80·00	3·50
		b. Brown (aniline) (5.81)	80·00	3·50
		c. Dull black-brown (10.81)	—	3·50
		d. Dull grey-brown (3.82)	75·00	3·50
203		2d. sepia (P 13)		
		a. Mixed perf 13 and 12	†	£650
204		2d. sepia (P 12)	—	£150
		a. Sepia-brown (2.81)	—	£150
		b. Brown (aniline) (5.81)	—	£150
205		2d. mauve *(worn plate)* (P 12½) (2.84)	£400	17·00
206	**32**	4d. rose-carmine (P 12½) (10.81)	£120	9·00
		aa. Wmk sideways	†	—
		a. Rosine (7.82)	£120	8·50

Nos. 201 and 205 are subsequent printings of stamps first produced on watermark W **33**.

33

1882–84. Wmk V over Crown W **33** (sideways on ½d.). P 12½.

207	**22**	½d. rosine (3.83)	65·00	22·00
		a. Perf 12	—	45·00
208	**23**	1d. yellow-green (9.82)	85·00	7·50
		a. Perf 12		
209	**30**	1d. yellow-green (29.10.83)	85·00	5·50
		a. Green (1.84)	80·00	5·50
		b. Pale green (5.84)	80·00	3·25
210	**31**	2d. dull grey-brown (15.8.82)	65·00	2·25
		a. Chocolate (3.83)	65·00	2·25
		ab. Perf 12	†	£425
211		2d. mauve (20.12.83)	80·00	5·50
		a. Worn plate (2.84)	80·00	5·50
		b. Perf 12	†	£750
		c. Mixed perf 12 and 12½	†	£750
212	**15**	3d. yellow-orange (13.4.83)	£120	30·00
		a. Dull brownish orange	£120	40·00
213	**32**	4d. rose-red (3.83)	£120	18·00
214	**16**	6d. dull violet-blue (10.11.82)	£100	7·00
		a. Indigo-blue (11.83)	£100	7·00
		b. Light ultramarine (8.84)	£100	9·00

Reprints were made in 1891 of the 'Laureated' 1d., 2d., 3d. (in yellow), 4d., 6d., 8d. (in orange-yellow), 10d. (in greenish slate) and 5s. (in blue and red), of the Bell ½d., 1d., 2d. (Die II), 9d. and 1s. and of the Naish 2d. (in brown), 4d. (in pale red) and 2s. With the exception of the Bell 9d., which was watermarked W **19**, all were watermarked W **33** and perforated 12½. Some were from new plates.

THE POST OFFICE ACT OF 1883. Following official concern as to the number of different series of adhesive stamps, both fiscal and postal, used in Victoria it was decided that the system should be unified to the extent that the postage stamps, Stamp Statute fiscals and Stamp Duty fiscals should be replaced by a single series valid for all three purposes. As the Stamp Duty series contained the largest number of values it was adopted as the basis of the new range.

The regulations for the changeover were detailed in the Post Office Act of 1883 which came into force on 1 January 1884. From that date all existing Stamp Statute (first produced in 1871) and Stamp Duty (first produced in 1879) issues became valid for postal purposes, and the previous postage stamps could be used for fiscal fees.

Until matters could be organised printings of some of the existing postage values continued and these will be found included in the listings above.

Printing of the Stamp Statute series was discontinued in early 1884.

The existing Stamp Duty range was initially supplemented by postage stamps overprinted 'STAMP DUTY' for those values where the available fiscal design was considered to be too large to be easily used on mail. These overprints were replaced by smaller designs inscribed 'STAMP DUTY'.

Stamp Statute and Stamp Duty values which became valid for postal purposes on 1 January 1884 have previously been listed in this catalogue as Postal Fiscals. Under the circumstances this distinction appears somewhat arbitrary and all such stamps are now shown in the main listing. Used prices quoted are for examples with postal cancellations. In some instances prices are also provided for fiscally used and these are marked 'F.C.'.

Nos. 215/292 were extensively used for fiscal purposes. Collectors are warned against the many examples of these stamps which have been cleaned and provided with fake gum or forged cancels.

In practice, many of these stamps are not known to exist in genuine unused or postally used condition and only fiscally cancelled examples are available. This applies especially to stamps of high face value such as Nos. 249/252.

34

35

36

37

Designs (all vert ex £5): 1d. head of Queen Victoria, facing right, in circular medallion, 3d. T **34**, 4d. obverse and reverse of 4d. coin showing Queen Victoria and Britannia, respectively, 6d. head of Queen Victoria surrounded by oval garter, 1s. Queen Victoria within octagonal frame, 2s. T **35**, 2s.6d. T **36**, 5s., 10s. and £1 Head of Queen Victoria within oval frames, £5 T **37**. A 12s.6d. value showing the royal Coat of Arms was also printed, but not issued.

(Des and dies eng J. Turner (3d., 2s.6d.), W. Bell (others). Typo from electrotypes)

1884 (1 Jan*). Stamp Statute series. Vert designs as T **34/6**, and others showing Queen Victoria within various frames, and T **37**. P 13.

*(a) Wmk single-lined numerals according to face value, as W **11**, (sideways). Paper manufactured by T. H. Saunders unless otherwise stated*

215		1s. blue/*blue*	£275	50·00
		a. Perf 12	£300	55·00
216		2s. blue/*green (D.L.R. paper)*	£350	£110
		a. Perf 12	£350	£110
217		2s. deep blue/*green*	£325	
		a. Perf 12	—	£110
		b. Wmk upright		
218		10s. brown-olive/*pink*		
219		10s. red-brown/*pink*	£3000	£450
		a. Wmk upright Perf 12		

*(b) Wmk V over Crown W **19** (sideways). P 13*

220		1d. pale green	£150	70·00
		a. Green (wmk upright) (P 12½)	£200	£110
221		3d. mauve	£2000	£600
222		4d. rose	£1500	£550
		a. Wmk upright	£1600	
223		6d. blue	£250	50·00
		a. Ultramarine	£225	40·00
		ab. Perf 12	£250	42·00
224		1s. blue/*blue*	£225	50·00
		a. Perf 12	£250	55·00
		b. Ultramarine/blue (P 12½)	—	85·00
		ba. Perf 12	—	70·00
		c. Deep blue/blue (P 12½)	£250	50·00
		ca. Perf 12	£250	50·00
225		2s. blue/*green*	£425	£110
		a. Perf 12	£425	
		b. Deep blue/blue-green (glazed paper)	£425	£120
		ba. Perf 12	£425	£130
226		2s.6d. orange	—	£325
		a. Perf 12		
		b. Yellow (glazed paper)	£1600	
		ba. Perf 12	£1600	£350
		c. Orange-yellow (glazed paper) (P 12½)	—	£350
		ca. Perf 12		
227		5s. blue/*yellow*	£800	£130
		a. Perf 12	£800	
		b. Wmk upright		
		ba. Perf 12		
		c. Ultramarine/lemon (glazed paper) (P 12½)	£850	£150
		ca. Wmk upright		
228		10s. brown/*pink*	£3250	£450
		a. Purple-brown/pink	£3250	£450
		ab. Perf 12	£3250	

229 £1 slate-violet/*yellow* £4000 £475
a. Wmk upright..........
b. *Mauve/yellow*..........
ba. Perf 12.......... £4000 £450
bb. Perf 12½.......... £4000 £450
230 £5 black and yellow-green.......... £22000
a. Perf 12..........
b. Wmk upright. Perf 12½ (F.C. £450)... £22000

(c) Wmk V over Crown (sideways) W **33**

231 1d. yellowish green (P 12½).......... £150 £120
232 2s.6d. pale orange-yellow (P 12).......... £1800 £350
233 £5 black and yellow-green (wmk upright) (P 12) (F.C. £375).......... —

½d

HALF

(**38**)

1884 (1 Jan*). No. 220 surch with T **38** in red.
234 ½d. on 1d. pale green.......... £130 £120

*The dates quoted are those on which the stamps became valid for postal purposes. The ½d., 1d., 4d., 6d., 1s., 5s. and £1 were issued for fiscal purposes on 26 April 1871. The 10s. was added to the series in June 1871, the £5 in September 1871, the 2s.6d. in July 1876 and the 3d. in October 1879.

All values of the Stamp Statute series were reprinted in 1891 on paper watermarked W **19** (5s., 10s., £1) or W **33** (others). The £5 was pulled from the original plate, but the others were produced from new electrotypes taken from the original dies.

39

40

41

42

43

44

45

46

47

48

49

50

51

52

53

54

55

56 57

58

59

60

61

(Des H. Samson and F. Oxenbould (T **39**), C. Jackson and L. Lang (all others except T **40**). Dies eng C. Jackson, J. Turner, J. Whipple, A. Williams and other employees of Sands & MacDougall. T **40** die eng C. Naish)

1884 (1 Jan*)–**96**. Existing Stamp Duty series.

(a) Litho. Wmk V over Crown. W **19** *(sideways). P 13*

235 **39** 1d. blue-green.......... £170 60·00
a. Perf 12.......... £170 60·00
b. Perf 12½..........
236 **43** 1s.6d. rosine.......... £400 65·00
a. Perf 12.......... — 75·00
b. Perf 12½.......... £400
237 **45** 3s. purple/*blue*.......... £1000 £100
a. Perf 12.......... £1000 £100
b. Perf 12½..........
238 **46** 4s. orange-red.......... £180 22·00
a. Perf 12.......... £180 22·00
b. Perf 12½..........
239 **48** 6s. apple-green.......... £550 75·00
a. Perf 12½.......... £550
240 **49** 10s. brown/*rose* (*glazed paper*).......... £2750 £130
a. Perf 12..........
b. Perf 12½..........
c. Wmk upright..........
cb. Perf 12½..........
241 **50** 15s. mauve.......... £10000 £650
242 **51** £1 red-orange.......... £1200 £120
a. Perf 12½.......... £1200 £120
243 **52** £1.5s. dull rose (wmk upright).......... £6500 £600
244 **53** £1.10s. deep grey-olive.......... £8000 £400
a. Wmk upright.......... — £425
245 – 35s. grey-violet (wmk upright) (F.C. £375).......... £17000
246 **54** £2 blue.......... — £250
247 **55** 45s. dull brown-lilac.......... £12000 £550
248 **56** £5 rose-red (wmk upright) (F.C. £150).......... £17000 £1800
249 **57** £6 blue/*pink* (wmk upright) (*glazed paper*) (F.C. £200).......... —
250 **58** £7 violet/*blue* (wmk upright) (F.C. £200).......... —
251 **59** £8 brownish red/*yellow* (wmk upright) (*glazed paper*) (F.C. £200).......... —
252 **60** £9 yellow-green/*green* (wmk upright) (*glazed paper*) (F.C. £200).......... —

(b) Typo from electrotypes

(i) Wmk V over Crown. W **19** *(sideways). P 13*

253 **39** 1d. yellowish green.......... £140 60·00
a. Perf 12.......... £140 60·00
b. Perf 12½.......... £140

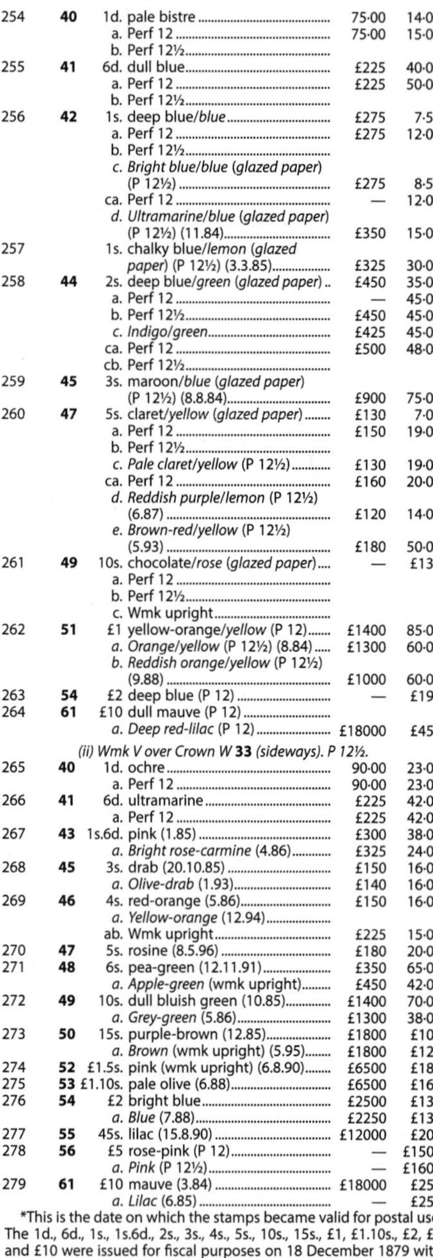

254 **40** 1d. pale bistre.......... 75·00 14·00
a. Perf 12.......... 75·00 15·00
b. Perf 12½..........
255 **41** 6d. dull blue.......... £225 40·00
a. Perf 12.......... £225 50·00
b. Perf 12½..........
256 **42** 1s. deep blue/*blue*.......... £275 7·50
a. Perf 12.......... £275 12·00
b. Perf 12½..........
c. *Bright blue/blue (glazed paper)* (P 12½).......... £275 8·50
ca. Perf 12.......... — 12·00
d. *Ultramarine/blue (glazed paper)* (P 12½) (11.84).......... £350 15·00
257 1s. chalky blue/*lemon* (*glazed paper*) (P 12½) (3.3.85).......... £325 30·00
258 **44** 2s. deep blue/*green* (*glazed paper*).. £450 35·00
a. Perf 12.......... — 45·00
b. Perf 12½.......... £450 45·00
c. *Indigo/green*.......... £425 45·00
ca. Perf 12.......... £500 48·00
cb. Perf 12½..........
259 **45** 3s. maroon/*blue* (*glazed paper*) (P 12½) (8.8.84).......... £900 75·00
260 **47** 5s. claret/*yellow* (*glazed paper*).......... £130 7·00
a. Perf 12.......... £150 19·00
b. Perf 12½..........
c. *Pale claret/yellow* (P 12½).......... £130 19·00
ca. Perf 12.......... £160 20·00
d. *Reddish purple/lemon* (P 12½) (6.87).......... £120 14·00
e. *Brown-red/yellow* (P 12½) (5.93).......... £180 50·00
261 **49** 10s. chocolate/*rose* (*glazed paper*).... — £130
a. Perf 12..........
b. Perf 12½..........
c. Wmk upright..........
262 **51** £1 yellow-orange/*yellow* (P 12).......... £1400 85·00
a. *Orange/yellow* (P 12½) (8.84).......... £1300 60·00
b. *Reddish orange/yellow* (P 12½) (9.88).......... £1000 60·00
263 **54** £2 deep blue (P 12).......... — £190
264 **61** £10 dull mauve (P 12)..........
a. *Deep red-lilac* (P 12).......... £18000 £450

(ii) Wmk V over Crown W **33** *(sideways). P 12½.*

265 **40** 1d. ochre.......... 90·00 23·00
a. Perf 12.......... 90·00 23·00
266 **41** 6d. ultramarine.......... £225 42·00
a. Perf 12.......... £225 42·00
267 **43** 1s.6d. pink (1.85).......... £300 38·00
a. *Bright rose-carmine* (4.86).......... £325 24·00
268 **45** 3s. drab (20.10.85).......... £150 16·00
a. *Olive-drab* (1.93).......... £140 16·00
269 **46** 4s. red-orange (5.86).......... £150 16·00
a. *Yellow-orange* (12.94)..........
ab. Wmk upright.......... £225 15·00
270 **47** 5s. rosine (8.5.96).......... £180 20·00
271 **48** 6s. pea-green (12.11.91).......... £350 65·00
a. *Apple-green* (wmk upright).......... £450 42·00
272 **49** 10s. dull bluish green (10.85).......... £1400 70·00
a. *Grey-green* (5.86).......... £1300 38·00
273 **50** 15s. purple-brown (12.85).......... £1800 £100
a. *Brown* (wmk upright) (5.95).......... £1800 £120
274 **52** £1.5s. pink (wmk upright) (6.8.90).......... £6500 £180
275 **53** £1.10s. pale olive (6.88).......... £6500 £160
276 **54** £2 bright blue.......... £2500 £130
a. *Blue* (7.88).......... £2250 £130
277 **55** 45s. lilac (15.8.90).......... £12000 £200
278 **56** £5 rose-pink (P 12).......... — £1500
a. *Pink* (P 12½).......... — £1600
279 **61** £10 mauve (3.84).......... £18000 £250
a. *Lilac* (6.85).......... — £250

*This is the date on which the stamps became valid for postal use. The 1d., 6d., 1s., 1s.6d., 2s., 3s., 4s., 5s., 10s., 15s., £1, £1.10s., £2, £5 and £10 were issued for fiscal purposes on 18 December 1879 with the £1.5s., 35s., 45s., £6 and £9 added to the range later the same month and the 6s., £7 and £8 in January 1880.

Used prices for the £1.5s., £1.10s., £2 (No. 276*a*), 45s. and £10 watermarked W **33** are for examples from the cancelled-to-order sets sold to collectors by the Victoria postal authorities between September 1900 and 30 June 1902.

Similar Stamp Duty designs were prepared for 7s., 8s., 9s., 11s., 12s., 13s., 14s., 16s., 17s., 18s., and 19s., but were never issued.

The two different 1d. designs were reprinted in 1891 on W **33** paper.

For these designs with later watermarks see Nos. 345/50 and 369/71.

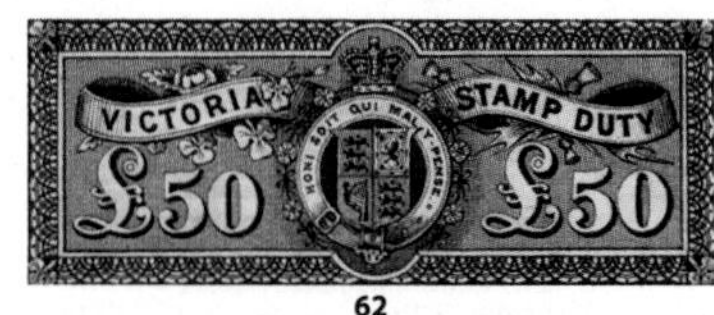

62

(Des C. Jackson and L. Lang. Dies eng C. Jackson)

1884 (1 Jan*)–**00**. High value Stamp Duty series.

(a) Recess-printed direct from the die

(i) Wmk V over Crown W **19** *(sideways). P 12½*

280 **62** £25 yellow-green (F.C. £150)..........
a. Wmk upright..........
b. Perf 13..........
c. *Deep green* (F.C. £150)..........
ca. Wmk upright..........
281 £50 bright mauve (F.C. £225)..........
a. Wmk upright..........
b. Perf 13..........
282 £100 crimson-lake (F.C. £325)..........
a. Wmk upright..........
b. Perf 13..........

(ii) Wmk V over Crown W **33** *(sideways). P 12½*

283 **62** £25 yellow-green..........
a. Perf 12..........
b. *Deep green* (1.85) (F.C. £150).......... £60000 £1400
c. *Bright blue-green* (10.90) (F.C. £150)..........
ca. Wmk upright..........

No.	Type	Description	Unused	Used
284		£50 dull lilac-mauve (wmk upright) (F.C. £190)		
		a. Black-violet (10.90) (F.C. £170)	£70000	£1400
		ab. Wmk upright		
285		£100 crimson (F.C. £325)		
		a. Wmk upright		
		b. Perf 12 (F.C. £325)		
		c. Aniline crimson (wmk upright) (2.85) (F.C. £325)	£80000	£1800
		d. Scarlet-red (5.95)	—	£1800
		da. Wmk upright	—	£1700
		(b) Litho. Wmk V over Crown W **33** *(sideways). P 12½*		
286	**62**	£25 dull yellowish green (1.86) (F.C. £100)		
		a. Wmk upright (11.87)		
		b. Dull blue-green (9.88) (F.C. £100)		
		ba. Wmk upright		
287		£50 dull purple (1.86) (F.C. £120)		
		a. Wmk upright		
		b. Bright violet (11.89) (F.C. £120)		
		ba. Wmk upright		
288		£100 rosine (1.86) (F.C. £200)		
		a. Wmk upright		
		(c) Typo from electrotyped plates. Wmk V over Crown. W **33**. *P 12½*		
289	**62**	£25 dull blue-green (12.97)	—	£500
290		£50 bright mauve (10.97)	—	£650
291		£100 pink-red (10.1900)	—	£1100

*This is the date on which the stamps became valid for postal use. All three values were issued for fiscal purposes on 18 December 1879.

Used prices for Nos. 283*b*, 284*a*, 285*c*/285*d* and 289/291 are for examples from the cancelled-to-order sets described beneath No. 279*a*. 'F.C.' indicates that the price quoted is for a stamp with a fiscal cancellation.

For the £25 and £50 with watermark W **82** see Nos. 351/352.

63

(Des and die eng C. Naish. Typo from electrotyped plates)

1884 (23 Apr)–**92**. New design inscr 'STAMP DUTY'. Wmk V over Crown, W **33** (sideways). P 12½.

No.	Type	Description	Unused	Used
292	**63**	2s.6d. brown-orange	£225	35·00
		a. Yellow (8.85)	£160	15·00
		b. Lemon-yellow (2.92)	£160	34·00

For this design on later watermarks see Nos. 344 and 370.

64 65 66 67 68

(Des and dies eng C. Naish. Typo from electrotyped plates)

1885 (1 Jan)–**95**. New designs inscr 'STAMP DUTY'. P 12½.

No.	Type	Description	Unused	Used
		(a) W **19**		
293	**68**	8d. rose/*pink*	55·00	12·00
		a. Rose-red/pink (2.88)	55·00	12·00
294	**66**	1s. deep dull blue/*lemon* (11.85)	£180	19·00
		a. Dull blue/yellow (6.86)	£180	20·00
295	**68**	2s. olive/*bluish green* (12.85)	£150	6·50
		(b) W **33**		
296	**64**	½d. pale rosine	35·00	3·00
		a. Deep rosine (7.85)	40·00	3·75
		b. Salmon (9.85)	40·00	3·75
297	**65**	1d. yellowish green (1.85)	32·00	3·75
		a. Dull pea-green (2.85)	32·00	3·75
298	**66**	2d. lilac	55·00	3·00
		a. Mauve (1886)	55·00	3·00
		b. Rosy-mauve (1886)	65·00	3·00
299	**65**	3d. yellowish brown	60·00	4·25
		a. Pale ochre (9.86)	12·00	2·25
		b. Bistre-yellow (9.92)	12·00	2·25
300	**67**	4d. magenta	£120	7·50
		a. Bright mauve-rose (12.86)	£120	8·50
		b. Error. *Lilac* (12.86)	£12000	£1700
301	**65**	6d. chalky blue (1.85)	£180	12·00
		a. Bright blue (3.85)	£140	10·00
		b. Cobalt (7.85)	£140	4·75
302	**68**	8d. bright scarlet/*pink* (3.95)	32·00	16·00
303		2s. olive-green/*pale green* (1.90)	55·00	7·00
304		2s. apple-green (12.8.95)	32·00	90·00
		a. Blue-green (29.10.95)	22·00	32·00

The plates for the 1d., 6d., 1s. and 2s. were derived from the dies of the 2d. (1s.), 3d. (1d. and 6d.) and 8d. (2s.). In each instance lead moulds of six impressions were taken from the original die and the face values altered by hand creating six slightly different versions.

Two states of the 2d. die exist with the second showing a break in the top frame line near the right-hand corner. This damaged die was used for seven impressions on Plate 1 and all 120 on Plate 2.

No. 300b occurred during the December 1886 printing of the 4d. when about fifty sheets were printed in the colour of the 2d. by mistake. The sheets were issued to Melbourne post offices and used examples are known postmarked between 21 December 1886 and 4 March 1887. Nine unused are also believed to exist.

Reprints of the ½d., 1d., 2d., 4d., 6d. and 1s. values were made in 1891 from the existing plates. The 1s. was watermarked W **19** and the remainder W **33**.

For some of these values used with later watermarks see Nos. 336, 343, 361 and 369.

(69)

1885 (Feb–Nov). Optd with T **69**. P 12½.

No.	Type	Description	Unused	Used
		(a) W **19**		
305	**15**	3d. dull orange-yellow (*glazed paper*) (B.) (11.85)	—	£850
306	**26**	1s. pale blue/*blue* (*glazed paper*) (P 13)	£130	55·00
		a. Deep blue/*blue*	—	60·00
		b. Blue opt (F.C. £350)	£5500	£2250
307	**27**	2s. ultramarine/*green* (*glazed paper*) (3.85)	£180	19·00
		a. Wmk sideways	£200	26·00
		(b) W **33**		
308	**15**	3d. yellow-orange (B.) (11.85)	70·00	55·00
		a. Dull brownish orange (B.)	75·00	55·00
309	**32**	4d. rose-red (B.) (11.85)	60·00	80·00

Unauthorised reprints of the 4d. and 1s., both with blue overprints and watermarked W **33**, were made during 1895–96. The 4d. reprint, which is in pale red, also exists without the overprint.

70 71 72 73 74 75 76 77 78

79

80

(Des S. Reading (1d.) (No. 313), M. Tannenberg (2½d., 5d.), C. Naish (1s.6d.), P. Astley (others). Dies eng C. Naish (2d., 4d. (both existing dies with lines added behind Queen's head) and 1s.6d.), S. Reading (originally as an employee of Fergusson & Mitchell) (others). Typo from electrotyped plates)

1886 (26 July)–**96**. Wmk V over Crown. W **33** (sideways on ½d., 1s., £5, £7 to £9). P 12½.

No.	Type	Description	Unused	Used
310	**70**	½d. lilac-grey (28.8.86)	45·00	13·00
		a. Grey-black	—	48·00
311		½d. pink (15.2.87)	45·00	2·50
		a. Rosine (aniline) (1889)	19·00	1·50
		b. Rose-red (1891)	15·00	1·25
		c. Vermilion (1896)	19·00	3·75
312	**71**	1d. green	22·00	3·75
		a. Yellow-green (1887)	22·00	3·75
313	**72**	1d. dull chestnut (1.1.90)	32·00	2·75
		a. Deep red-brown (1890)	32·00	2·75
		b. Orange-brown (1890)	32·00	75
		c. Brown-red (1890)	32·00	75
		d. Yellow-brown (1891)	32·00	50
		e. Bright yellow-orange	£120	32·00
		f. Brownish orange (1894)	14·00	40
314	**73**	2d. pale lilac (17.12.86)	40·00	70
		a. Pale mauve (1887)	45·00	30
		b. Deep lilac (1888, 1892)	19·00	30
		c. Purple (1894)	13·00	40
		d. Violet (1895)	13·00	40
		e. Imperf	—	£1000
315	**74**	2½d. red-brown/*lemon* (1.1.91)	40·00	4·00
		a. Brown-red/yellow (1892)	28·00	1·00
		b. Red/yellow (1893)	23·00	70
316	**75**	4d. rose-red (1.4.87)	55·00	1·50
		a. Red (1893)	26·00	1·50
317	**76**	5d. purple-brown (1.1.91)	38·00	3·75
		a. Pale reddish brown (1893)	14·00	3·50
318	**77**	6d. bright ultramarine (27.8.86)	60·00	5·00
		a. Pale ultramarine (1887)	48·00	60
		b. Dull blue (1891)	42·00	75
319	**25**	9d. apple-green (18.10.92)	30·00	16·00
320		9d. carmine-rose (15.10.95)	70·00	28·00
		a. Rosine (aniline) (1896)	70·00	26·00
321	**78**	1s. dull purple-brown (14.3.87)	£120	5·50
		a. Lake (1890)	95·00	6·50
		b. Carmine-lake (1892)	55·00	3·75
		c. Brownish red (1896)	55·00	8·00
322	**79**	1s.6d. pale blue (9.88)	£180	80·00
323		1s.6d. orange (19.9.89)	40·00	25·00
		a. Red-orange (1893)	40·00	13·00
324	**80**	£5 pale blue and maroon (7.2.88)†	£14000	£180
325		£6 yellow and pale blue (1.10.87)†	£15000	£200
326		£7 rosine and black (17.10.89)†	£16000	£250
327		£8 mauve and brown-orange (2.8.90)†	£16000	£275
328		£9 apple-green and rosine (21.8.88)†	£17000	£300

†The used prices provided for these stamps are for cancelled-to-order examples.

Unauthorised reprints of the ½d. lilac-grey and 1s.6d. pale blue were made in 1894–1895 on W **33** paper and perforated 12½. These differ in shade from the originals and have rougher perforations. It should be noted that the original printing of No. 322 does not occur with inverted watermark, but the reprint does.

A single example of No. 314e is known postmarked '737' (Foster). A second, postmarked '249' (Mortlake), was reported in 1892. It is known that an imperforate sheet was sold at Mortlake PO in 1890. Other examples are believed to be clandestine.

Later printings of the £5 to £9 values, as No. 324/328 but on W **85** paper perforated 12½ or 11, were not valid for postal use (*Unused prices, £325 for £5 value, from £500 for £6 to £9 values*).

A £10 value as Type **80** was prepared, but not issued.

1891 (17 June). Wmk V over Crown. W **19**. P 12½.

No.	Type	Description	Unused	Used
329	**72**	1d. orange-brown/*pink*	18·00	5·00

No. 329 was an emergency printing during a shortage of white W **33** paper.

81

82

(Die eng A. Williams (1½d.). Typo from electrotyped plates).

1896 (11 June)–**99**. Wmk V over Crown. W **82** (sideways on ½d., 1½d., 1s., 2s.6d. to 15s.). P 12½.

No.	Type	Description	Unused	Used
330	**70**	½d. light scarlet (1.7.96)	11·00	6·50
		a. Carmine-rose (1897)	11·00	3·50
		b. Deep carmine-red (coarse impression) (1899)	—	7·50
		c. Wmk upright	£110	65·00
331		½d. emerald (1.8.99)	38·00	10·00
		a. Wmk upright	†	£100
332	**72**	1d. brown-red (13.6.96)	15·00	1·00
		a. Brownish orange (1897)	11·00	10
		b. Wmk sideways	†	—
333	**81**	1½d. apple-green (7.10.97)	3·00	8·50
334	**73**	2d. violet	30·00	60
		a. Wmk sideways	†	90·00
335	**74**	2½d. blue (1.8.99)	27·00	32·00
336	**65**	3d. ochre (11.96)	24·00	2·75
		a. Buff (1898)	13·00	2·75
		b. Wmk sideways	†	—
337	**75**	4d. red (6.97)	55·00	13·00
338	**76**	5d. red-brown (7.97)	40·00	2·25
339	**77**	6d. dull blue (9.96)	38·00	1·25
340	**25**	9d. rosine (8.96)	70·00	7·50
		a. Rose-carmine (1898)	—	7·50
		b. Dull rose (1898)	45·00	7·50
		c. Wmk sideways		
341	**78**	1s. brownish red (3.97)	38·00	4·75
		a. Wmk upright	—	—
342	**79**	1s.6d. brown-orange (8.98)	£100	65·00
343	**68**	2s. blue-green (4.97)	£100	16·00
344	**63**	2s.6d. yellow (9.96)	£200	23·00
		a. Wmk upright (1898)	£225	23·00
345	**45**	3s. olive-drab (12.96)	£130	38·00
		a. Wmk upright (1898)	£130	38·00
346	**46**	4s. orange (9.97)	£170	50·00
347	**47**	5s. rosine (2.97)	£180	25·00
		a. Rose-carmine (1897)	£180	25·00
		b. Wmk upright. *Rosine* (1899)	£180	28·00
348	**48**	6s. pale yellow-green (4.99)†	£225	42·00
349	**49**	10s. grey-green (4.97)	£1300	50·00
		a. Blue-green (1898)	£1300	27·00
350	**50**	15s. brown (4.97)†	£1100	85·00
351	**62**	£25 dull bluish green (1897)†	—	£375
352		£50 dull purple (1897)†	—	£550

†The used prices provided for these stamps are for cancelled-to-order examples.

83

84

(Des M. Tannenberg. Dies eng A. Mitchelhill. Typo from electrotyped plates)

1897 (22 Oct). Diamond Jubilee and Hospital Charity Fund. Wmk V over Crown. W **82** (sideways). P 12½.

No.	Type	Description	Unused	Used
353	**83**	1d. (1s.) blue	20·00	23·00
354	**84**	2½d. (2s.6d) red-brown	£130	80·00
353s/354s		Optd 'Specimen' *Set of 2*	£200	

These stamps were sold at 1s. and 2s.6d., but only had postal validity for 1d. and 2½d. with the difference going to the Fund.

1899 (1 Aug). Wmk V over Crown. W **33** (sideways). P 12½.

No.	Type	Description	Unused	Used
355	**81**	1½d. brown-red/*yellow*	4·75	7·50

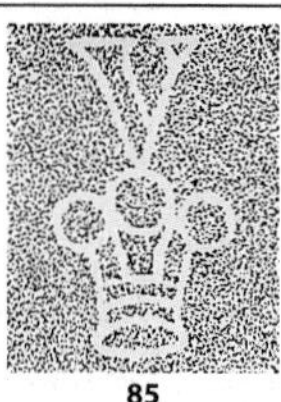

85

1899 (1 Aug)–**1901**. Wmk V over Crown. W **85** (sideways on ½d., 1s. and 2s.6d. to 10s.). P 12½.

No.	Type	Description	Unused	Used
356	**70**	½d. emerald	5·00	4·00
		a. *Deep blue-green*	6·50	2·50
		b. Wmk upright	—	13·00
357	**72**	1d. rose-red	17·00	1·00
		a. *Rosine* (1900)	7·50	10
		b. Wmk sideways	—	—
358		1d. olive (6.6.01)	13·00	4·00
359	**73**	2d. violet	45·00	1·75
		a. Wmk sideways	†	—
360	**74**	2½d. blue (10.99)	50·00	3·25
361	**65**	3d. bistre-yellow (9.99)	7·50	10·00
		a. Wmk sideways	†	—
362		3d. slate-green (20.6.01)	40·00	22·00
363	**75**	4d. rose-red (12.99)	29·00	12·00
364	**76**	5d. red-brown (10.99)	50·00	12·00
365	**77**	6d. dull ultramarine (1.00)	42·00	11·00
366	**25**	9d. rose-red (9.99)	24·00	4·00
		a. Wmk sideways		
367	**78**	1s. brown-red (5.00)	42·00	12·00
368	**79**	1s.6d. orange (2.00)	40·00	70·00
369	**68**	2s. blue-green (6.00)	55·00	50·00
370	**63**	2s.6d. yellow (1.00)	£650	40·00
371	**45**	3s. pale olive (4.00)†	£250	50·00
372	**47**	5s. rose-red (4.00)	£200	50·00
373	**49**	10s. green (3.00)†	£1000	50·00

†The used prices provided for these stamps are for cancelled-to-order examples.

From 1 July 1901 stamps inscribed 'STAMP DUTY' could only be used for fiscal purposes.

86 Victoria Cross

87 Australian Troops in South Africa

(Des Sands and MacDougall (1d.), J. Sutherland (2d.). Dies eng S. Reading. Typo from electrotyped plates)

1900 (22 May). Anglo-Boer War Patriotic Fund. Wmk V over Crown. W **85** (sideways). P 12½.

No.	Type	Description	Unused	Used
374	**86**	1d. (1s.) olive-brown	£160	£100
375	**87**	2d. (2s.) emerald-green	£300	£250

These stamps were sold at 1s. and 2s., but only had postal validity for 1d. and 2d. with the difference going to the Fund.

FEDERATION. The six Australian colonies were federated as the Commonwealth of Australia on 1 January 1901. Under the terms of the Post and Telegraph Act their postal services were amalgamated on 1 March 1901, but other clauses to safeguard the financial position of the individual States provided them with a large degree of independence until 13 October 1910 when issues of each state could be used throughout Australia. Postage stamps for the Commonwealth of Australia did not appear until January 1913.

It was agreed in 1901 that stamp printing should be centralised at Melbourne under J. B. Cooke of South Australia who was appointed Commonwealth Stamp Printer. By 1909 the Commonwealth Stamp Printing Branch in Melbourne was producing stamps for Papua, South Australia, Tasmania and Western Australia in addition to those of Victoria.

On federation it was decided to separate postal and fiscal stamp issues so Victoria needed urgent replacements for the current Stamp Duty series which reverted to fiscal use only on 30 June 1901.

1901 (29 Jan). Re-use of previous designs without 'POSTAGE' inscr. Wmk V over Crown. W **82** (2s.) or W **85** (others) (sideways on ½d.). P 12×12½.

No.	Type	Description	Unused	Used
376	**22**	½d. bluish green	2·75	4·00
		a. 'VICTCRIA' (R. 7/19)	42·00	65·00
377	**31**	2d. reddish violet	17·00	5·50
378	**15**	3d. dull orange	15·00	5·50
379	**32**	4d. bistre-yellow	25·00	32·00
380	**16**	6d. emerald	13·00	18·00
381	**26**	1s. yellow	80·00	48·00
382	**27**	2s. blue/*pink*	42·00	75·00
383	**18**	5s. pale red and deep blue	55·00	80·00

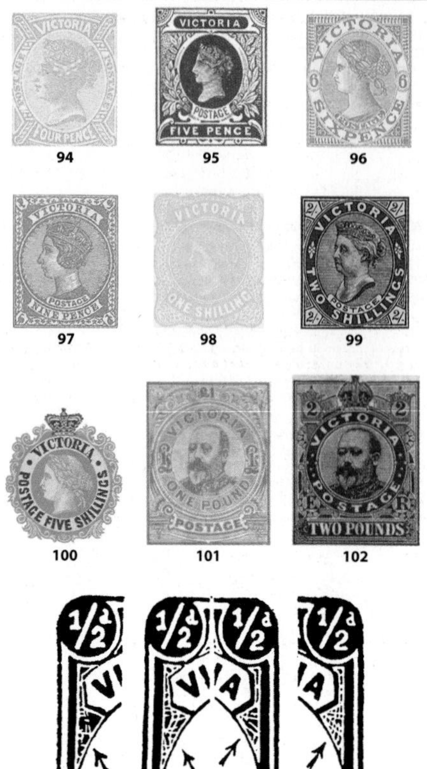

Three die states of ½d.:

I. Outer vertical line of colour to left of 'V' continuous except for a break opposite the top of 'V'. Triangles either end of 'VICTORIA' are more or less solid colour.

II. Die re-engraved. Three breaks in outer line of colour left of 'V'. White lines added to left triangle.

III. Die re-engraved. As II, but equivalent triangle at right also contains white lines.

I

II

III

I and II

III

Three die states of 1d.:

I. Thick lines fill top of oval above Queen's head.

II. Die re-engraved. Lines thinner, showing white space between.

III. Die re-engraved. As II, but with bottom left value tablet recut to show full point separated from both '1' and the circular frame.

Two die states of 2d.:

I. Frame line complete at top right corner. Bottom right corner comes to a point.

II. Break in right frame line just below the top corner. Bottom right corner is blunted.

Two types of 1s.:

A. 'POSTAGE' 6 mm long (produced by a hand punch applied twice to each impression on the previous 1s. electrotyped plate. Slight variations in position occur).

B. 'POSTAGE' 7 mm long (produced from new electrotyped plates incorporating the 'POSTAGE' inscriptions).

(Eng S. Reading after photo by W. Stuart (£1, £2))

1901 (29 Jan)–**10**. Previous issues with 'POSTAGE' added and new designs (£1, £2). Wmk V over Crown. W **85** (sideways on ½d., 1½d., £1, £2).

No.	Type	Description	Unused	Used
		(a) P 12×12½ (½d. to 2s.) or 12½ (½d., 5s. to £2)		
384	**88**	½d. blue-green (I) (26.6.01)	7·50	1·00
		a. Wmk upright (1903)	3·25	3·25
		b. Die state II (6.04)	14·00	2·25
		ba. Wmk upright	14·00	1·75
		c. Die state III (6.05)	24·00	3·25
385	**89**	1d. rose (I)	21·00	1·75
		a. *Dull red* (12.02)	21·00	1·75
		ab. Wmk sideways	£200	75·00
		b. Die state II (4.01)	7·00	15
		ba. *Dull red* (12.02)	8·00	15
		bb. Wmk sideways	£200	75·00
		c. Die state III. *Pale rose-red*	6·00	3·00
		ca. Wmk sideways	60·00	60·00
386	**90**	1½d. maroon/*yellow* (9.7.01)	12·00	10·00
		a. Wmk upright. *Brown-red/yellow* (9.01)	5·00	55
		b. *Dull red-brown/yellow* (1906)	3·50	1·00
		ba. *On yellow-buff back* (1908)	4·00	1·50
387	**91**	2d. lilac (I) (26.6.01)	26·00	2·00
		a. Die state II	50·00	4·50
		b. *Reddish violet* (1902)	30·00	1·00
		ba. Die state II	55·00	3·25
		c. *Bright purple* (II) (1905)	10·00	1·50
		d. *Rosy mauve* (II) (1905)		
		e. Wmk sideways	42·00	
388	**92**	2½d. dull blue	16·00	40
		a. *Deep blue* (1902)	14·00	40
		b. Wmk sideways	†	£950
389	**93**	3d. dull orange-brown (5.7.01)	17·00	2·75
		a. *Chestnut* (1901)	19·00	1·00
		b. *Yellowish brown* (1903)	20·00	1·00
		ba. Wmk sideways	21·00	40·00
390	**94**	4d. bistre-yellow (26.6.01)	9·50	1·00
		a. *Brownish bistre* (1905)	13·00	2·25
391	**95**	5d. reddish brown	23·00	1·00
		a. *Purple-brown* (1903)	14·00	1·75
392	**96**	6d. emerald (5.7.01)	13·00	1·00
		a. *Dull green* (1904)	16·00	2·50
393	**97**	9d. dull rose-red (5.7.01)	30·00	4·50
		a. Wmk sideways (1901)	50·00	35·00
		b. *Pale red* (1901)	20·00	2·00
		c. *Dull brownish red* (1905)	42·00	8·00
394	**98**	1s. yellow-orange (A) (5.7.01)	35·00	3·75
		a. *Yellow* (1902)	25·00	3·25
		b. Type B (4.03)	24·00	3·50
		ba. *Orange* (1904)	22·00	3·00
		bb. Wmk sideways (1905)	75·00	35·00
395	**99**	2s. blue/*rose* (5.7.01)	30·00	2·00
		a. Wmk sideways	£1200	£1000
398	**100**	5s. rose-red and pale blue (5.7.01).	60·00	27·00
		a. *Scarlet and deep blue*	70·00	27·00
		b. *Rosine and blue* (12.04)	70·00	27·00
399	**101**	£1 carmine-rose (18.11.01)	£350	£130
400	**102**	£2 deep blue (2.6.02)	£750	£300
		(b) P 11		
401	**88**	½d. blue-green (I) (9.02)	22·00	9·50
		a. Wmk upright (1903)	3·25	5·50
		b. Die state II (6.04)	21·00	6·00
		ba. Wmk upright	21·00	8·00
		c. Die state III (6.05)	22·00	7·00
402	**89**	1d. dull red (I) (12.02)	90·00	50·00
		a. Die state II	28·00	11·00
		ab. *Pale red* (*aniline*) (3.03)	26·00	4·50
		ac. *Pale rose* (*aniline*) (1904)	48·00	9·00
		b. Die state III. *Pale rose-red* (7.05)	90·00	50·00
403	**90**	1½d. dull red-brown/*yellow* (1910)	£160	£100
404	**91**	2d. bright purple (II) (1905)	£750	£300
		a. *Rosy mauve* (II) (1905)	†	£250
405	**93**	3d. yellowish brown (1903)	6·50	18·00
		a. Wmk sideways	27·00	65·00
406	**96**	6d. emerald (2.03)	12·00	26·00
		a. *Dull green* (1905)	£1000	£550
407	**101**	£1 rose (5.05)	£375	£170
408	**102**	£2 deep blue (1905)	£2000	£1400
		(c) Compound or mixed perfs of 12×12½ or 12½ and 11		
409	**88**	½d. blue-green (I) (1901)	60·00	21·00
		a. Wmk upright (1903)	60·00	24·00
		b. Die state II (1904)	60·00	45·00
		ba. Wmk upright	65·00	50·00
410	**89**	1d. dull red (I) (1902)	—	£450
		a. Die state II	£900	£225
411	**90**	1½d. maroon/*yellow* (1903)	£1400	£800
412	**91**	2d. reddish violet (I) (1903)	†	£1300
413	**93**	3d. dull orange-brown (1902)	—	£1600
414	**96**	6d. emerald (1903)	†	£1600
415	**100**	5s. rosine and blue (12.04)	£3750	

Examples of the 1d. Die state II perforated 12×12½ exist with two black lines printed across the face of the stamp. These were prepared in connection with stamp-vending machine trials.

WATERMARK VARIETIES: The attention of collectors is drawn to the note on inverted and reversed watermarks on the stamps of the Australian States at the top of the Australia listings.

1905–13. Wmk Crown over A, W w **11** (sideways on ½d., £1, £2).

No.	Type	Description	Unused	Used
		(a) P 12×12½ (½d. to 1s.) or 12½ (½d., 1d., 2½d., 6d., 5s. to £2)		
416	**88**	½d. blue-green (*shades*) (III) (21.10.05)	4·50	1·75
		a. Wmk upright	15·00	8·00
		b. Thin, ready gummed paper (6.12)	5·00	13·00
		ba. Wmk upright	5·00	14·00
417	**89**	1d. rose-red (III) (16.7.05)	5·00	25
		a. *Pale rose* (1907)	2·00	10
		b. *Rose-carmine* (1911)	11·00	3·50
		c. Wmk sideways	14·00	10·00
		d. Thin, ready gummed paper (10.12)	4·50	5·50
418	**91**	2d. dull mauve (II) (13.9.05)	6·00	1·75
		a. *Lilac* (1906)	12·00	2·00
		b. *Reddish violet* (1907)	11·00	25
		c. *Bright mauve* (1910)	6·00	1·50
		ca. Thin, ready gummed paper (8.12)	42·00	8·00
419	**92**	2½d. deep dull blue (10.08)	5·00	1·75
		a. *Dull blue* (11.09)	3·00	40
		b. *Indigo* (7.09)	28·00	5·00

No.	Type	Description	Unused	Used
420	**93**	3d. orange-brown (11.11.05)	22·00	1·25
		a. Yellow-orange (1908)	19·00	4·00
		b. Dull orange-buff (1909)	8·50	1·25
		c. Ochre (1912)	8·00	14·00
421	**94**	4d. yellow-bistre (15.1.06)	9·00	65
		a. Olive-bistre (1908)	8·50	65
		b. Yellow-olive (1912)	7·00	3·75
422	**95**	5d. chocolate (14.8.06)	8·50	9·50
		a. Dull reddish brown (1908)	7·50	8·00
		b. Wmk sideways	†	£850
		c. Thin, ready gummed paper (19.10.12)	13·00	26·00
423	**96**	6d. dull green (25.10.05)	27·00	80
		a. Dull yellow-green (1907)	17·00	80
		b. Emerald (1909)	17·00	1·10
		c. Yellowish green (1911)	20·00	6·00
		d. Emerald. Thin, ready gummed paper (11.12)	38·00	50·00
424	**97**	9d. brown-red (11.12.05)	42·00	11·00
		a. Orange-brown (1906)	38·00	11·00
		b. Red-brown (1908)	50·00	12·00
		c. Pale dull rose (1909)	21·00	12·00
		d. Rose-carmine (1910)	14·00	3·25
		e. Wmk sideways	£350	£100
425	**98**	1s. orange (B) (13.2.06)	13·00	2·00
		a. Yellow-orange (1906)	11·00	2·00
		b. Yellow (1908)	17·00	2·00
		ba. Thin, ready gummed paper (11.12)	30·00	25·00
		c. Pale orange. Thin, ready gummed paper (1913)	30·00	50·00
430	**100**	5s. rose-red and ultramarine (12.07)	80·00	28·00
		a. Rose-red and blue (1911)	90·00	50·00
		ab. Wmk sideways	£120	55·00
431	**101**	£1 salmon (12.2.07)	£350	£140
		a. Dull rose (1910)	£350	£140
		ab. Wmk upright (1911)	£375	£160
432	**102**	£2 dull blue (18.7.06)	£750	£425
		(b) P 11		
433	**88**	½d. blue-green (*shades*) (III) (1905) .	1·60	30
		a. Wmk upright. Thin, ready gummed paper (1912)	23·00	32·00
434	**89**	1d. rose-red (III) (1905)	8·50	3·00
		a. Pale rose (1907)	4·00	2·75
		b. Rose-carmine (1911)	7·00	8·50
		ba. Wmk sideways	35·00	32·00
		c. Thin, ready gummed paper (10.12)	16·00	5·50
435	**91**	2d. lilac (II) (1906)	†	£375
		a. Reddish violet (1907)	85·00	27·00
		b. Bright mauve (1910)	35·00	27·00
436	**92**	2½d. blue (1908)	60·00	38·00
		a. Indigo (1909)	20·00	27·00
437	**93**	3d. orange-brown (1905)	10·00	19·00
		a. Yellow-orange (1908)	†	£200
		b. Dull orange-buff (1909)	15·00	27·00
		c. Ochre (1912)	9·00	19·00
		d. Wmk sideways	†	£300
438	**94**	4d. yellow-bistre (1906)	15·00	29·00
		a. Olive-bistre (1909)		
		b. Yellow-olive (1912)	8·50	29·00
439	**95**	5d. chocolate (1906)	†	£1500
		a. Dull reddish brown (1908)	†	£1500
440	**96**	6d. emerald (1909)	10·00	26·00
		a. Yellowish green (1911)	21·00	38·00
441	**97**	9d. rose-carmine (1910)	†	£1300
442	**98**	1s. yellow-orange (B) (1906)	†	£375
		a. Orange (1910)	£1400	
443	**100**	5s. rose-red and ultramarine (12.07)	85·00	11·00
444	**101**	£1 salmon (12.2.07)	£475	£170
445	**102**	£2 dull blue (1.07)	£1300	£600
		(c) Compound or mixed perfs of 12×12½ or 12½ and 11		
446	**88**	½d. blue-green (*shades*) (III) (1905) .	28·00	18·00
		a. Wmk upright. Thin, ready gummed paper (1912)	£200	£160
447	**89**	1d. rose-red (III) (1905)	95·00	80·00
		a. Pale rose (1907)	—	80·00
		b. Rose-carmine (1911)	—	80·00
448	**91**	2d. reddish violet (II) (1907)	£650	£375
449	**93**	3d. orange-brown (1905)	†	£1200
		a. Ochre (1912)	£650	
450	**94**	4d. bistre (1908)	†	£1600
451	**96**	6d. emerald (1909)	—	£1600
		a. Yellowish green (1911)	†	£900
452	**97**	9d. orange-brown (1906)	†	£1800
		a. Red-brown (1908)	†	£1800
453	**98**	1s. yellow-orange (1906)	£2000	
453*a*		£1 dull rose	†	£12000
		(d) Rotary comb perf 11½×12¼		
454		1d. scarlet-red	4·50	2·00
		a. Thin, ready gummed paper *Rose-carmine*	2·75	5·00
		ab. Rose-red	2·75	5·00
		ac. Wmk sideways	35·00	30·00
455	**91**	2d. lilac (II) (1910)	45·00	2·75

The original Crown over A watermark paper used by Victoria was of medium thickness and had toned gum applied after printing. Stocks of this paper lasted until 1912 when further supplies were ordered from a new papermakers, probably W. Joynson and Son. This paper was much thinner and was supplied with white gum already applied. The first delivery arrived in June 1912 and a second in September of the same year.

The rotary comb perforating machine gauging 11½×12¼ was transferred from South Australia in 1909 when J. B. Cooke moved to Melbourne.

Examples of the 1d. perforated 12½ or 11 exist with two black lines across the face of the stamp. These were prepared in connection with stamp-vending machine trials.

ONE PENNY
(103)

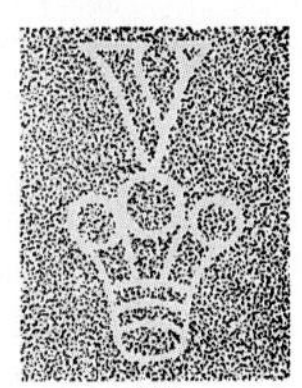
104

1912 (29 June). No. 455 surch with T **103** in red.

No.	Type	Description	Unused	Used
456	**91**	1d. on 2d. lilac (II)	1·00	60

1912 (1 Aug–Sept). Wmk V over Crown. W **104**.

No.	Type	Description	Unused	Used
		(a) P 12½ (½d.) or 12×12½		
457	**88**	½d. bluish green (III)	3·00	10·00
458	**89**	1d. rose-carmine (III)	6·00	6·50
		a. Wmk sideways	50·00	50·00
459	**91**	2d. reddish violet (II) (9.12)	3·00	9·00
		a. Lilac	6·50	15·00
460	**97**	9d. rose-carmine	32·00	50·00
		(b) P 11		
461	**88**	½d. bluish green (III)	20·00	45·00
462	**89**	1d. rose-carmine (III)	50·00	30·00
		a. Wmk sideways	£120	£120
463	**97**	9d. rose-carmine	50·00	75·00
		(c) Compound perfs of 12×12½ or 12½ and 11		
464	**97**	9d. rose-carmine	†	£1800

Nos. 457/464 were emergency printings caused by the non-arrival of stocks of the thin, ready gummed Crown over A watermarked paper. Paper watermarked W **104** had been introduced in 1911 and was normally used for Victoria fiscal stamps. This watermark can be easily distinguished from the previous W **85** by its narrow crown.

STAMP BOOKLETS

There are very few surviving examples of Nos. SB1/SB4. Listings are provided for those believed to have been issued with prices quoted for those known to still exist.

1904 (Mar)–**09**. Black on red cover as Type B **1** of New South Wales. Stapled.

No.	Description	Price
SB1	£1 booklet containing 240×1d. in four blocks of 30 and two blocks of 60	
	a. Red on pink cover (1909)	£22000
	b. Blue on pink cover	£20000

1904 (Mar). Black on grey cover as No. SB1. Stapled.

No.	Description	Price
SB2	£1 booklet containing 120×2d. in four blocks of 30	

1910 (May). Black on white cover as Type B **2** of New South Wales. Stapled.

No.	Description	Price
SB3	2s. booklet containing 11×½d. (No. 426), either in block of 6 plus block of 5 or block of 11, and 18×1d. (No. 427), either in three blocks of 6 or block of 6 plus block of 12	£5500
	a. Black on pale green cover	£6000

Unsold stock of No. SB3 was uprated with one additional ½d. in May 1911.

1911 (1 Aug). Red on pink cover as No. SB3. Stapled.

No.	Description	Price
SB4	2s. Booklet containing 12×½d. (No. 426), either in two blocks of 6 or block of 12, and 18×1d. (No. 427), either in three blocks of 6 or block of 6 plus block of 12	£6000

POSTAGE DUE STAMPS

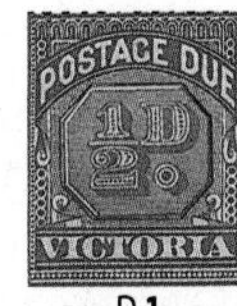

D 1

(Dies eng A. Williams (values) and J. McWilliams (frame). Typo)

1890 (1 Nov)–**94**. Wmk V over Crown, W **33**. P 12×12½.

No.	Type	Description	Unused	Used
D1	D **1**	½d. dull blue and brown-lake (24.12.90)	8·50	8·50
		a. Dull blue and deep claret	6·50	7·00
D2		1d. dull blue and brown-lake	7·00	2·25
		a. Dull blue and brownish red (1.93)	16·00	2·50
D3		2d. dull blue and brown-lake	14·00	2·25
		a. Dull blue and brownish red (3.93)	27·00	2·50
D4		4d. dull blue and brown-lake	32·00	6·00
		a. Dull blue and pale claret (5.94)	35·00	11·00
D5		5d. dull blue and brown-lake	29·00	4·75
D6		6d. dull blue and brown-lake	25·00	10·00
D7		10d. dull blue and brown-lake	75·00	55·00
D8		1s. dull blue and brown-lake	50·00	11·00
D9		2s. dull blue and brown-lake	£140	70·00
D10		5s. dull blue and brown-lake	£190	£110
D1/D10 *Set of* 10			£500	£250
D1as/D10s H/S *'Specimen.' Set of* 10			£475	

A used example of the 6d. showing compound perforation of 12×12½ and 11 exists in the Royal Collection.

1895 (17 Jan)–**96**. Colours changed. Wmk V over Crown. W **33**. P 12×12½.

No.	Type	Description	Unused	Used
D11	D **1**	½d. rosine and bluish green	10·00	2·50
		a. Pale scarlet and yellow-green (3.96)	5·50	4·00
D12		1d. rosine and bluish green	15·00	2·00
		a. Pale scarlet and yellow-green (3.96)	6·00	2·75
D13		2d. rosine and bluish green	28·00	3·00
		a. Pale scarlet and yellow-green (3.96)	25·00	1·50
D14		4d. rosine and bluish green	12·00	1·50
		a. Pale scarlet and yellow-green (3.96)	10·00	2·75
D15		5d. rosine and bluish green	38·00	38·00
		a. Pale scarlet and yellow-green (3.96)	19·00	25·00
D16		6d. rosine and bluish green	25·00	25·00
D17		10d. rosine and bluish green	48·00	10·00
D18		1s. rosine and bluish green	24·00	3·50
D19		2s. pale red and yellowish green (28.3.95)	90·00	26·00
D20		5s. pale red and yellowish green (28.3.95)	£140	40·00
D11/D20 *Set of* 10			£350	£120

1897 (1 July)–**99**. Wmk V over Crown. W **82**. P 12×12½.

No.	Type	Description	Unused	Used
D21	D **1**	1d. pale scarlet and yellow-green	22·00	2·00
		a. Dull red and bluish green (8.99)	20·00	2·75
D22		2d. pale scarlet and yellow-green	38·00	2·00
		a. Dull red and bluish green (6.99)	38·00	2·25
D23		4d. pale scarlet and yellow-green	60·00	2·75
		a. Dull red and bluish green (8.99)	60·00	2·75
D24		5d. pale scarlet and yellow-green	55·00	8·00
D25		6d. pale scarlet and yellow-green	15·00	7·50
D21/D25 *Set of* 5			£170	20·00

1900 (1 June)–**04**. Wmk V over Crown. W **85**. P 12×12½.

No.	Type	Description	Unused	Used
D26	D **1**	½d. rose-red and pale green	26·00	6·00
		a. Pale red and deep green (8.01)	7·00	5·00
		b. Scarlet and deep green (1.03)	—	30·00
		c. Aniline rosine and green (6.04)	18·00	10·00
D27		1d. rose-red and pale green	24·00	1·75
		a. Pale red and deep green (9.01)	26·00	1·50
		b. Scarlet and deep green (2.02)	26·00	1·00
		c. Aniline rosine and green (9.03)	26·00	1·25
D28		2d. rose-red and pale green (7.00)	17·00	2·25
		a. Pale red and deep green (9.01)	26·00	3·50
		b. Scarlet and deep green (2.02)	26·00	1·25
		c. Aniline rosine and green (9.03)	26·00	2·00
D29		4d. rose-red and pale green (5.01)	50·00	15·00
		a. Pale red and deep green (9.01)	50·00	2·75
		b. Scarlet and deep green (6.03)	50·00	4·75
		c. Aniline rosine and green (6.04)	50·00	4·75
D30		5d. scarlet and deep green (1.03)	24·00	13·00
D31		1s. scarlet and deep green (3.02)	26·00	16·00
D32		2s. scarlet and deep green (1.03)	£180	95·00
D33		5s. scarlet and deep green (1.03)	£225	£100
D26/D33 *Set of* 8			£500	£200

1905 (Dec)–**09**. Wmk Crown over A, W w **11**. P 12×12½.

No.	Type	Description	Unused	Used
D34	D **1**	½d. aniline rosine and pale green (1.06)	28·00	22·00
		a. Scarlet and pale yellow-green (7.07)	5·50	13·00
		b. Dull scarlet and pea-green (3.09)	6·50	14·00
		ba. Compound perf 12×12½ and 11.	£1600	£1600
D35		1d. aniline rosine and pale green	70·00	9·50
		a. Scarlet and pale yellow-green (5.06)	6·50	2·75
		b. Dull scarlet and pea-green (1.07)	10·00	2·75
D36		2d. aniline scarlet and deep yellow-green (5.06)	48·00	6·00
		a. Dull scarlet and pea-green (11.07)	14·00	3·00
D37		4d. dull scarlet and pea-green (1908)	22·00	27·00
D34*a*/D37 *Set of* 4			42·00	42·00
		Prepared for use but not issued		
D38	D **1**	5d. dull scarlet and pea-green	£3000	£1700

The 5d. value on this paper was prepared in 1907–1908 but not put into use. A few examples were subsequently included in presentation sets, either mint or cancelled-to-order.

WESTERN AUSTRALIA

PRICES FOR STAMPS ON COVER

Nos. 1/6	*from* × 6
Nos. 15/32	*from* × 4
Nos. 33/46	*from* × 5
Nos. 49/51	*from* × 6
Nos. 52/62	*from* × 10
Nos. 63/63*a*	*from* × 8
No. 67	—
Nos. 68/92*a*	*from* × 10
Nos. 94/102	*from* × 40
Nos. 103/105	*from* × 8
Nos. 107/110*a*	*from* × 12
Nos. 111*a*/111*b*	—
Nos. 112/116	*from* × 25
Nos. 117/125	*from* × 10
Nos. 126/128	—
Nos. 129/134	*from* × 8
Nos. 135/136	—
Nos. 138/148	*from* × 12
Nos. 151/163	*from* × 5
Nos. 168/169	*from* × 20
Nos. 170/171	*from* × 4
Nos. 172/173	*from* × 40
Nos. F11/F22	*from* × 10
Nos. T1/T2	—

SPECIMEN OVERPRINTS. Those listed are from UPU distributions between 1889 and 1892. Further 'Specimen' overprints exist, but those were used for other purposes.

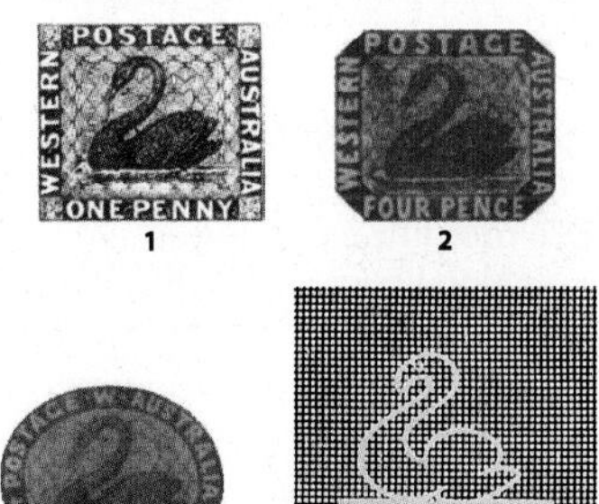

1 2 3 4

GUM. The 1854 and 1857–1859 issues are hardly ever seen with gum, so the unused prices quoted are for examples without gum.

(Eng W. Humphrys. Recess P.B.)

1854 (1 Aug). W **4** (sideways).

No.	Type	Description	Unused	Used
		(a) Imperf		
1	**1**	1d. black	£1500	£300
		(b) Rouletted 7½ to 14 and compound		
2	**1**	1d. black	£4500	£750

ANDREW PROMOTING PHILATELY ON THE ALAN TITCHMARSH SHOW ITV

Selling Your Stamps?

Summary Tip #18:
When it comes to Selling – all collections are Not created Equal

by Andrew McGavin

Dear Colleague,

I will return to the surprisingly large subject of 'certificates' in another article – but this article is prompted by developments we have observed over the past few years when purchasing private stamp collections.

Traditionally there are 5 different ways to sell your stamps:

1. The Stamp Dealer or Stamp Auction buying on their own account.
2. Dealers 'runners'.
3. Private Treaty – the idea of Private Treaty is that collectors 'place' their collection with a dealer or auction that charges a small commission (or the buyer a commission) to purchase the collection outright. Historically 'Private Treaty' has acquired notoriety as an excuse for the company handling the transaction to 'buy-in' the collection for themselves. Fortunately things are more transparent now.
4. Selling through auction on your own account – the auction house charges you a commission and handling costs.
5. Finally – the internet now permits you to sell your stamps on-line upon your own account via internet giants such as 'eBay'.

In selling your stamps there are two principles to understand. Collectors want to buy stamps that are missing in their collections: this is why Dealers exist. Dealers buy collections to 'break-down' into usually smaller units that collectors need for their collections: generally speaking breaking down for sale into small/smaller units adds 'value' and profit for the dealer.

Some collectors are 'hoarders' and will buy general lots – other collectors will buy intermediate sized collections in order to 'extract' the stamps they want ... and then 'turn' the balance back for resale to dealer or auction. The idea that collectors will buy large complete intact collections at retail prices is quaint and outmoded. In almost 40 years of dealing I have seen few intact collections purchased by collectors and continued by new collectors. Collectors enjoy creating their own collections. Few collectors have the budget to purchase a substantial intact collection and develop it still further.

Know your 'strengths' – (know the strength of your collection).

Choosing who is best to approach to sell your stamps or handle them depends upon your knowing the 'strength' and merits of your collection. For example ... on a basic level – if your collection consists of all different modern British sets that you have bought from the Post Office at 'face value' ... the last thing you want to do is send this collection to auction. All you will be doing is paying an auction's commissions – up to 35% for them to sell your stamps, most probably, to a dealer below 'face value' – who will use a fair percentage of them upon commercial correspondence.

A few phone calls to dealers will elicit the percentage of 'face value' that the trade is paying for stamps that there are too many of – because the Post Office has recently printed and sold them.

Just don't forget to ask if there is anything 'better' in the period that you are selling – that may command a higher price.

In our next article we'll focus on the merits of the 5 different ways to sell your stamps ... and which may be best for you.

Happy collecting from us all,

PS. If you find this 'tip' interesting please forward it to a philatelic friend.

Andrew McGavin
Managing Director: Universal Philatelic Auctions, Omniphil & Avon Approvals, Avon Mixtures, Universal Philatelic (Ebay)

To read the rest of this series 'SELLING YOUR STAMPS?' see the relevant pages listed below:

Summary Tip 18 – page 42 (Australia)
Summary Tip 19 – page 206 (Egypt)
Summary Tip 20 – page 266 (India)

To read the final instalment, Summary Tips 21 and 22 – 'Selling via Online Auction' simply e-mail and request to: *info@upastampauctions.co.uk*

Also, at the back of this catalogue to see how UPA can pay you upto 36% more for your collection

In addition to the supplies received from London a further printing, using the original plate and watermarked paper from Perkins, Bacon, was made in the colony before the date of issue.

The 1d. is also known pin-perforated.

(Litho H. Samson (later A. Hillman), Government Lithographer)

1854 (1 Aug)–**55**. W **4** (sideways).

(a) Imperf

3 2 4d. pale blue £375 £200
a. Blue £450 £250
b. Deep dull blue £2750 £850
c. Slate-blue (1855) £4000 £1300
d. 'T' of 'POSTAGE' shaved off to a point at foot (R. 7/5, 7/10, 7/15, 7/20) £2250 £1000
e. Top of letters of 'AUSTRALIA' cut off so that they are barely 1 mm high .... † £32000
f. 'PEICE' instead of 'PENCE' .... † £40000
g. 'CE' of 'Pence' close together .... † £32000
h. Frame inverted (R. 8/1, 8/6, 8/11, 8/16) .... † £180000
i. Tilted border (R. 7/4, 7/9, 7/14, 7/19) £3250 £1600
j. 'WEST' in squeezed-down letters and 'F' of 'FOUR' with pointed foot (R. 2/17) £4000 £1700
k. 'ESTERN' in squeezed-down letters and 'U' of 'FOUR' squeezed up (R. 3/17) £5500 £2750
l. Small 'S' in 'POSTAGE' (R. 4/17) £4000 £1700
m. 'EN' of 'PENCE' shorter (R. 6/4) £3250 £1400
n. 'N' of 'PENCE' tilted to right with thin first downstroke (R. 6/16) £3250 £1400
o. Swan and water above 'ENCE' damaged (R. 6/20) £4250 £1700
p. 'F' of 'FOUR' slanting to left (R. 7/17) £3750 £1600
q. 'WESTERN' in squeezed-down letters only 1½ mm high (R. 8/17) £4250 £1800
r. 'P' of 'PENCE' with small head (R. 9/15) £3750 £1500
s. 'RALIA' in squeezed-down letters only 1½ mm high (R. 9/16) £4000 £1600
t. 'PE' of 'PENCE' close together (R. 10/15) £3750 £1500
u. 'N' of 'PENCE' narrow (R. 10/16) £3750 £1500
v. Part of right cross-stroke and downstroke of 'T' of 'POSTAGE' cut off (R. 11/15) £3250 £1400
w. 'A' in 'POSTAGE' with thin right limb (R. 11/16) £3750 £1500
x. Coloured line above 'AGE' of 'POSTAGE' (R. 8/6) £3750 £1600
y. No outer line above 'GE' of 'POSTAGE' and coloured line under 'FOU' of 'FOUR' (R. 8/11) £3750 £1800

4 3 1s. salmon £25000 £4750
a. Deep red-brown £2000 £1100
b. Grey-brown (1.55) £700 £400
c. Pale brown (10.55) £500 £325

(b) Rouletted 7½ to 14 and compound

5 2 4d. pale blue £4000 £700
a. Blue .... — £700
b. Slate-blue (1855) .... — £2750
6 3 1s. grey-brown (1.55) £8000 £1200
a. Pale brown (10.55) £7500 £1100

Both values are also known pin-perforated.

The 4d. value was prepared by Horace Samson from the Perkins Bacon 1d. plate. A block of 60 (5×12, cols 16-20) was taken as a 'plate to stone' transfer and each frame was then erased. A new lithographic frame, drawn on stone, was transferred 60 times to make up the intermediate stone.

There were a number of transfer varieties, one of the most prominent being the 'T' of 'POSTAGE' shaved at foot (No. 3d).

Four transfers were taken from the intermediate stone to make printing stone No. I with 240 impressions. Samson printed the initial supply of 100 sheets in deep dull blue (No. 3*b*) in July 1854.

Printing stone No. 1 had three scarce creased transfers whose positions in the sheet have yet to be established (Nos. 3e/3g).

Further supplies were printed in January 1855 by Alfred Hillman, Samson's successor. A severe interruption to printing, almost certainly a broken stone, occurred when the fourth sheet was being pulled. On examining the intermediate stone preparatory to making a new printing stone it was found that the frame of R. 8/1 had been damaged and needed replacing.

This was done, but in so doing, Hillman accidentally produced the transfer error 'Inverted Frame' (No. 3h). Printing Stone No. 2 was made as before and bore a range of transfer varieties (Nos. 3j/3w) along with four 'Inverted Frames'. This printing was in blue (No. 3*a*). Some time after completion of the required 97 sheets, the 'Inverted Frame' was corrected on each of the four positions to make printing stone No. 2A. All four corrections are identifiable and on two of them, traces of the inverted frame remain visible (Nos. 3x/3y).

Printing stone No. 2A was used for the third printing undertaken in October 1855, producing 175 sheets of slate-blue (No. 3*c*.) stamps and for the fourth and final printing, totalling 1500 sheets in pale blue (No. 3), undertaken in December 1855.

The 1s. value was produced in much the same way, based on a transfer of cols. 10-14 from the Perkins Bacon 1d. plate.

5

(Litho A. Hillman, Government Lithographer)

1857 (7 Aug)–**59**. W **4** (sideways).

(a) Imperf

15 5 2d. brown-black/*red* (26.2.58) £9000 £550
a. Printed both sides £11000 £800
16 2d. brown-black/*Indian red* (26.2.58) £9000 £850
a. Printed both sides £11000 £900
17 6d. golden bronze £22000 £2500
18 6d. black-bronze £10000 £650
19 6d. grey-black (1859) £10000 £550

(b) Rouletted 7½ to 14 and compound

20 5 2d. brown-black/*red* £15000 £1900
a. Printed both sides .... — £2250
21 2d. brown-black/*Indian red* .... — £1900
22 6d. black-bronze £15000 £1300
23 6d. grey-black .... — £1300

The 2d. and 6d. are known pin-perforated.

Prices quoted for Nos. 15/23 are for 'cut-square' examples. Collectors are warned against 'cut-round' copies with corners added.

(Recess in the colony from P.B. plates)

1860 (11 Aug)–**64**. W **4** (sideways on 2d. and 6d.).

(a) Imperf

24 1 2d. pale orange .... £130 80·00
25 2d. orange-vermilion .... £150 80·00
a. Wmk upright ....
25*b* 2d. deep vermilion £1900 £800
26 4d. blue (Wmk upright) (21.6.64) £350 £2500
a. Wmk sideways £800
27 4d. deep blue (Wmk upright) £350 £2500
28 6d. sage-green (27.7.61) £3250 £400
28*a* 6d. deep sage-green .... — £550

(b) Rouletted 7½ to 14

29 1 2d. pale orange £850 £275
30 2d. orange-vermilion £900 £275
31 4d. deep blue (Wmk upright) £6000
32 6d. sage-green £6000 £750

WATERMARK VARIETIES: On several stamps, Nos. 1 to 46, watermark W **4** exists with the Swan's head to the left or right and reversed in either direction. We do not list these varieties.

PERKINS BACON 'CANCELLED'. For notes on these handstamps, showing 'CANCELLED' between horizontal bars forming an oval, see Catalogue Introduction.

(Recess P.B.)

1861. W **4** (sideways).

(a) Intermediate perf 14–16

33 1 1d. rose £750 £140
34 2d. blue .... £250 40·00
35 4d. vermilion £1900 £2000
36 6d. purple-brown £1100 £110
37 1s. yellow-green £2000 £250

(b) P 14 at Somerset House

38 1 1d. rose .... £375 65·00
39 2d. blue .... £160 45·00
40 4d. vermilion £475 £180

(c) Perf clean-cut 14–16

41 1 2d. blue .... £110 24·00
a. Imperf between (pair) .... † —
42 6d. purple-brown .... £550 50·00
43 1s. yellow-green .... £1000 80·00
a. Wmk upright £1400 £150

(d) P 14–16 very rough (July)

44 1 1d. rose-carmine (H/S 'CANCELLED' in oval £18000) .... £350 50·00
45 6d. purple/*blued* (H/S 'CANCELLED' in oval £12000) £4250 £500
46 1s. deep green (H/S 'CANCELLED' in oval £11000) £4750 £375

Perkins Bacon experienced considerable problems with their perforating machine during the production of these stamps.

The initial printing showed intermediate perforation 14–16. Further supplies were then sent, in late December 1860, to Somerset House to be perforated on their comb 14 machine. The Inland Revenue Board were only able to process the three lower values, although the 6d. purple-brown and 1s. yellow-green are known from this perforation overprinted 'SPECIMEN'.

The Perkins Bacon machine was repaired the following month and the 6d., 1s. and a further supply of the 2d. were perforated on it to give a clean-cut 14-16 gauge.

A final printing was produced in July 1861, but by this time the machine had deteriorated so that it produced a very rough 14–16.

(Recess D.L.R. from P.B. plates)

1863 (16 Dec)–**64**. No wmk. P 13.

49 1 1d. carmine-rose .... 80·00 4·75
50 1d. lake .... 80·00 4·75
51 6d. deep lilac (15.4.64) .... £350 50·00
51*a* 6d. dull violet (15.4.64) .... £400 55·00

Both values exist on thin and on thick papers, the former being the scarcer.

Both grades of paper show a marginal sheet watermark, 'T H SAUNDERS 1860' in double-lined large and small capitals, but parts of this watermark rarely occur on the stamps.

(Recess D.L.R. from P.B. plates)

1864 (27 Dec)–**79**. Wmk Crown CC (sideways* on 1d.). P 12½.

52 1 1d. bistre .... 90·00 9·50
w. Wmk Crown to right of CC .... 90·00 9·50
x. Wmk sideways reversed .... 90·00 9·50
y. Wmk Crown to right of CC and reversed .... 95·00 11·00
53 1d. yellow-ochre (16.10.74) .... £120 15·00
w. Wmk Crown to right of CC .... £120 15·00
54 2d. chrome-yellow (18.1.65) .... £100 7·00
x. Wmk reversed .... £120 8·00
55 2d. yellow .... £110 8·00
a. Wmk sideways (5.79) .... £275 24·00
aw. Wmk Crown to right of CC .... £275 24·00
b. Error. Mauve (1879) £22000 £15000
w. Wmk inverted .... £300 45·00
x. Wmk reversed .... £110 8·00
y. Wmk inverted and reversed .... £300 45·00
56 4d. carmine (18.1.65) .... £150 7·00
a. Doubly printed £30000
w. Wmk inverted .... £475 45·00
x. Wmk reversed .... £160 8·50
y. Wmk inverted and reversed .... — 65·00
57 6d. violet (18.1.65) .... £180 6·00
a. Doubly printed .... † £22000
b. Wmk sideways £850 £325
bw. Wmk Crown to right of CC ....
w. Wmk inverted .... — 65·00
x. Wmk reversed .... £180 6·00
58 6d. indigo-violet .... £475 35·00
w. Wmk inverted ....
x. Wmk reversed .... £475 35·00
59 6d. lilac (1872) .... £300 6·00
y. Wmk inverted and reversed £425
60 6d. mauve (12.5.75) .... £275 6·00
x. Wmk reversed .... £275 6·00
y. Wmk inverted and reversed £425
61 1s. bright green (18.1.65) .... £275 20·00
s. Handstamped 'SPECIMEN.' £225
w. Wmk inverted ....
y. Wmk inverted and reversed £300
62 1s. sage-green (10.68) .... £475 35·00

*The normal sideways watermark shows Crown to left of CC, *as seen from the back of the stamp.*

Beware of fakes of No. 55b made by altering the value tablet of No. 60.

7

ONE PENNY

(8)

(Typo D.L.R.)

1871 (29 Oct)–**73**. Wmk Crown CC (sideways). P 14.

63 7 3d. pale brown .... 60·00 6·00
a. Cinnamon (1873) .... 60·00 4·75
s. Handstamped 'SPECIMEN.' £150

1874 (10 Dec). No. 55 surch with T **8** by Govt Printer.

67 1 1d. on 2d. yellow (G.) .... £750 55·00
b. Surch triple .... † £7500
x. Wmk reversed .... £750 60·00
y. Wmk inverted and reversed .... — £200

Forged surcharges of T **8** are known on stamps wmk Crown CC perf 14, and on Crown CA, perf 12 and 14.

(Recess D.L.R. from P.B. plates)

1876–81. Wmk Crown CC (sideways*). P 14.

68 1 1d. ochre .... 95·00 3·75
w. Wmk Crown to right of CC .... 95·00 3·75
69 1d. bistre (1878) .... £170 5·50
w. Wmk Crown to right of CC .... — 6·50
x. Wmk sideways reversed .... £275 20·00
y. Wmk Crown to right of CC and reversed .... £275 20·00
70 1d. yellow-ochre (1879) .... £110 2·75
71 2d. chrome-yellow .... £120 1·75
a. Wmk upright (1877) .... £140 3·00
aw. Wmk inverted .... £350 55·00
ax. Wmk reversed .... £275 25·00
ay. Wmk inverted and reversed ....
bw. Wmk Crown to right of CC .... £120 2·00
by. Wmk Crown to right of CC and reversed .... £250 22·00
74 4d. carmine (1881) £650 £120
a. Wmk upright .... † —
y. Wmk Crown to right of CC and reversed £650 £150
75 6d. lilac (1877) .... £225 4·00
a. Wmk upright (1879) .... £750 15·00
bw. Wmk Crown to right of CC .... £225 4·00
75*c* 6d. reddish lilac (1879) .... £275 6·00

*The normal sideways watermark shows Crown to left of CC, *as seen from the back of the stamp.*

(Recess D.L.R. from P.B. plates)

1882 (Mar)–**85**. Wmk Crown CA (sideways*).

(a) P 14

76 1 1d. yellow-ochre .... 30·00 2·00
w. Wmk Crown to right of CA .... 30·00 2·00
x. Wmk sideways reversed ....
y. Wmk Crown to right of CA and reversed .... — 20·00
77 2d. chrome-yellow .... 42·00 2·00
a. Wmk upright .... † —
w. Wmk Crown to right of CA .... 48·00 2·50
x. Wmk sideways reversed .... — 20·00
y. Wmk Crown to right of CA and reversed .... — 20·00
78 4d. carmine (8.82) .... £190 15·00
a. Wmk upright (1885) .... — £110
aw. Wmk inverted .... — £200
ax. Wmk reversed .... — £200
w. Wmk Crown to right of CA .... £190 15·00
x. Wmk sideways reversed .... — 42·00
79 6d. reddish lilac (1882) .... £140 3·00
80 6d. lilac (1884) .... £140 4·00
s. Handstamped 'SPECIMEN.' £150
w. Wmk Crown to right of CA .... £150 5·00
x. Wmk sideways reversed .... — 35·00
y. Wmk Crown to right of CA and reversed .... £225 35·00

(b) P 12×14

81 1 1d. yellow-ochre (2.83) £2750 £170

(c) P 12

82 1 1d. yellow-ochre (2.83) .... £100 5·50
w. Wmk Crown to right of CA .... £120 7·00
83 2d. chrome-yellow (6.83) .... £170 5·00
w. Wmk Crown to right of CA .... £170 6·00
y. Wmk Crown to right of CA and reversed .... — 20·00
84 4d. carmine (5.83) .... £300 60·00
w. Wmk Crown to right of CA .... £300 60·00
85 6d. lilac (6.83) .... £550 55·00
w. Wmk Crown to right of CA .... £550 55·00
y. Wmk Crown to right of CA and reversed .... — 85·00

*The normal sideways watermark shows Crown to left of CA, *as seen from the back of the stamp.*

(Typo D.L.R.)

1882 (July)–**95**. Wmk Crown CA (sideways). P 14.

86 7 3d. pale brown .... 17·00 4·00
87 3d. red-brown (12.95) .... 10·00 4·00

The 3d. stamps in other colours, watermark Crown CA and perforated 12, are colour trials dating from 1883.

½ 1d. 1d.
(9) (10) (11)

1884 (19 Feb). Surch with T **9**, in red, by Govt Printer.

89	**1**	½d. on 1d. yellow-ochre (No. 76)	30·00	45·00
		a. Thin bar	£110	£160
		w. Wmk Crown to right of CA	30·00	45·00
90		½d. on 1d. yellow-ochre (No. 82)	17·00	30·00
		w. Wmk Crown to right of CA	17·00	30·00

Inverted or double surcharges are forgeries made in London about 1886.

The 'Thin bar' varieties occur on R. 12/3, R. 12/8, R. 12/13 and R. 12/18, and show the bar only 0.2 mm thick.

1885 (May). Nos. 63/63*a* surch, in green, by Govt Printer.

(a) Thick '1' with slanting top, T **10** *(Horizontal Rows 1/5)*

91		1d. on 3d. pale brown	90·00	35·00
		a. Cinnamon	85·00	35·00
		b. Vert pair. Nos. 91/92	£375	

(b) Thin '1' with straight top, T **11** *(Horizontal Row 6)*

92		1d. on 3d. pale brown	£200	75·00
		a. Cinnamon	£180	75·00

12

13

14

15

(Typo D.L.R.)

1885 (May)–**93**. Wmk Crown CA (sideways). P 14.

94	**12**	½d. yellow-green	7·00	1·00
		a. Green	4·50	1·00
		w. Wmk Crown to right of CA	—	£110
95	**13**	1d. carmine (2.90)	48·00	1·00
		w. Wmk Crown to right of CA	—	70·00
96	**14**	2d. bluish grey (6.90)	32·00	4·25
		a. Grey	30·00	4·25
		w. Wmk Crown to right of CA	—	£110
97	**15**	2½d. deep blue (1.5.92)	26·00	2·25
		a. Blue	26·00	2·25
		w. Wmk Crown to right of CA	—	£120
98		4d. chestnut (7.90)	15·00	2·50
99		5d. bistre (1.5.92)	19·00	4·25
100		6d. bright violet (1.93)	21·00	2·00
		w. Wmk Crown to right of CA	—	£160
101		1s. pale olive-green (4.90)	45·00	5·50
102		1s. olive-green	40·00	5·00
94s/101s (ex 1d., 6d.) Handstamped 'SPECIMEN.' (Nos. 96, 98, 101) or optd 'SPECIMEN' *Set of 6*			£550	

The normal sideways watermark shows Crown to left of CA, *as seen from the back of the stamp.*

(Recess D.L.R. from P.B. plates)

1888 (Mar–Apr). Wmk Crown CA (sideways). P 14.

103	**1**	1d. carmine-pink	32·00	3·50
104		2d. grey	85·00	1·25
		w. Wmk Crown to right of CA	£120	
		y. Wmk Crown to right of CA and reversed	£180	
105		4d. red-brown (4.88)	80·00	32·00
		x. Wmk sideways reversed	£120	
103s/105s H/S 'SPECIMEN.' *Set of 3*			£275	

The watermark shows Crown to right of CA on No. 103 and to the left of CA on 104/5, *as seen from the back of the stamp.*

ONE PENNY (16) Half-penny (17)

1893 (Feb). Surch with T **16**, in green, by Govt Printer.

107	**7**	1d. on 3d. pale brown (No. 63)	15·00	10·00
108		1d. on 3d. cinnamon (No. 63*a*)	15·00	10·00
		a. Double surcharge	£2000	
109		1d. on 3d. pale brown (No. 86)	85·00	16·00

1895 (21 Nov). Surch with T **17** by Govt Printer.

(a) In green

110	**7**	½d. on 3d. pale brown (No. 63)	10·00	42·00
110*a*		½d. on 3d. cinnamon (No. 63*a*)	10·00	42·00
		b. Surcharge double	£1600	

(b) In red and in green

111*a*	**7**	½d. on 3d. cinnamon (No. 63*a*)	£110	£300
111*b*		½d. on 3d. red-brown (No. 87)	85·00	£180

Green was the adopted surcharge colour but a trial had earlier been made in red on stamps watermarked Crown CC. As they proved unsatisfactory they were given another surcharge in green. The trial stamps were inadvertently issued and, to prevent speculation, a further printing of the duplicated surcharge was made, but on both papers, Crown CC (No. 111*a*) and Crown CA (No. 111*b*).

18

19

20

21

(Typo D.L.R.)

1898 (Dec)–**1907**. Wmk W Crown A, W **18**. P 14.

112	**13**	1d. carmine	10·00	30
		w. Wmk inverted	—	£140
113	**14**	2d. bright yellow (1.99)	35·00	3·00
		w. Wmk inverted	—	£150
114	**19**	2½d. blue (1.01)	18·00	1·25
		w. Wmk inverted	£375	
115	**20**	6d. bright violet (10.06)	48·00	4·75
		w. Wmk inverted	—	£300
116	**21**	1s. olive-green (4.07)	55·00	7·00
		w. Wmk inverted	—	£200

22

23

24

25

26

27

28

29

30

31

32

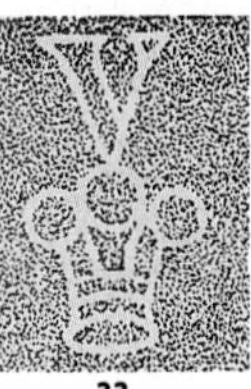
33

(Des M. Tannenberg (2s.6d., 5s.) Typo Victoria Govt Printer, Melbourne, Commonwealth Stamp Ptg Branch from March 1909)

1902 (Oct)–**11**. Wmk V over Crown, W **33** (sideways on horiz designs).

(a) P 12½ or 12½×12 (horiz), 12×12½ (vert)

117	**22**	1d. carmine-rose (1.03)	29·00	1·00
		a. Wmk upright (10.02)	25·00	3·25
118	**23**	2d. yellow (4.1.03)	28·00	4·75
		a. Wmk upright (1903)	65·00	8·00
119	**24**	4d. chestnut (4.03)	45·00	4·25
		a. Wmk upright	£600	£600
120	**15**	5d. bistre (4.9.05)	£150	90·00
121	**25**	8d. apple-green (3.03)	21·00	4·75
122	**26**	9d. yellow-orange (5.03)	55·00	38·00
		a. Wmk upright (11.03)	£120	30·00
123	**27**	10d. red (3.03)	32·00	11·00
124	**28**	2s. bright red/*yellow*	85·00	45·00
		a. Wmk sideways	£250	26·00
		b. Orange/yellow (7.06)	55·00	12·00
		c. Brown-red/yellow (5.11)	45·00	28·00
125	**29**	2s.6d. deep blue/*rose*	55·00	22·00
126	**30**	5s. emerald-green	85·00	50·00
127	**31**	10s. deep mauve	£180	£100
		a. Bright purple (1910)	£950	£450
128	**32**	£1 orange-brown (1.11.02)	£425	£190
		a. Orange (10.7.09)	£750	£350

(b) P 11

129	**22**	1d. carmine-rose	£400	50·00
		a. Wmk upright (1905)	†	£500
130	**23**	2d. yellow	£425	60·00
		a. Wmk upright	†	£500
131	**24**	4d. chestnut	£1400	£425
132	**15**	5d. bistre	50·00	75·00
133	**26**	9d. yellow-orange	£180	£180
134	**28**	2s. bright red/*yellow*	£300	£180
		a. Orange/yellow	£425	£225

(c) Perf compound of 12½ or 12½×12 and 11

135	**22**	1d. carmine-rose	£1300	£650
		a. Wmk upright	†	£650
136	**23**	2d. yellow	£1900	£1100
137	**24**	4d. chestnut		

Type **22** is similar to Type **13** but larger.

WATERMARK VARIETIES: The attention of collectors is drawn to the note on inverted and reversed watermarks on the stamps of the Australian States at the top of the Australia listings.

34

35

1905–12. Wmk Crown over double-lined A W **34** (sideways).

(a) P 12½ or 12½×12 (horiz), 12×12½ (vert)

138	**12**	½d. green (6.10)	4·50	8·50
139	**22**	1d. rose-pink (10.05)	23·00	3·75
		a. Wmk upright (1.06)	11·00	1·25
		b. Carmine (1909)	13·00	1·25
		c. Carmine-red (1912)	13·00	12·00
140	**23**	2d. yellow (15.11.05)	8·50	2·00
		a. Wmk upright (4.10)	†	£350
141	**7**	3d. brown (2.06)	65·00	5·50
142	**24**	4d. bistre-brown (12.06)	60·00	19·00
		a. Pale chestnut (1908)	48·00	18·00
		b. Bright brown-red (14.10.10)	25·00	6·50
143	**15**	5d. pale olive-bistre (8.05)	38·00	30·00
		a. Olive-green (1.09)	38·00	30·00
		b. Pale greenish yellow (2.12)	60·00	£110
144	**25**	8d. apple-green (20.4.12)	23·00	80·00
		a. Wmk upright	†	—
145	**26**	9d. orange (11.5.06)	35·00	6·00
		a. Red-orange (6.10)	60·00	6·00
		b. Wmk upright (7.12)	70·00	32·00
146	**27**	10d. rose-orange (16.2.10)	24·00	29·00
148	**30**	5s. emerald-green (wmk upright) (9.07)	£190	£140

(b) P 11

150	**12**	½d. green	£3000	
151	**22**	1d. rose-pink (1908)	50·00	35·00
		a. Carmine-red	60·00	32·00
		b. Wmk upright (2.06)	90·00	32·00
152	**23**	2d. yellow	50·00	48·00
153	**7**	3d. brown	24·00	17·00
154	**24**	4d. yellow-brown	£1200	£275
		a. Pale chestnut	£1500	£400
155	**15**	5d. pale olive-bistre	60·00	11·00
		a. Olive-green	27·00	20·00
157	**26**	9d. orange	£200	£200
		a. Red-orange	—	£200
		b. Wmk upright (1912)	—	£900

(c) Perf compound of 12½ or 12½×12 and 11

161	**22**	1d. rose-pink (wmk upright)	£1200	£500
		a. Wmk sideways	£1500	£800
162	**23**	2d. yellow	£1200	£550
163	**7**	3d. brown	£1500	£1500
163*a*		5d. olive-green	†	£1800
164	**26**	9d. red-orange		

The prices provided for Nos. 154/154*a* are for examples perforated 'OS'.

1912 (25 Mar–9 Apr). Wmk Crown over single-lined A W **35** (sideways). P 11½×12.

168	**20**	6d. bright violet (9.4.12)	18·00	30·00
169	**21**	1s. sage-green	32·00	48·00
		a. Perf 12½ (single line)	—	£2500

1912 (7 Aug). Thin, ready gummed paper with white gum (as Victoria*). Wmk Crown over double-lined A W **34** (sideways).

170	**7**	3d. brown (P 12½)	75·00	75·00
		a. Wmk upright	£200	£190
171		3d. brown (P 11)		
		a. Wmk upright		

*See note below Victoria No. 455.

ONE PENNY
(36)

1912 (6 Nov). Nos. 140 and 162 surch with T **36** in Melbourne.

(a) P 12½ ×12

172	**23**	1d. on 2d. yellow	3·25	3·50
		a. Wmk upright	8·50	17·00

(b) Perf compound of 12½×12 and 11

173	**23**	1d. on 2d. yellow	£750	£450
		a. Wmk upright	£750	

STAMP BOOKLETS

There are very few surviving examples of Nos. SB1/SB4. Listings are provided for those believed to have been issued with prices quoted for those known to still exist.

1904 (1 Jan)–**09**. Black on red cover as Type B **1** of New South Wales. Stapled.

SB1	£1 booklet containing 240×1d. in four blocks of 30 and two blocks of 60	
	a. Red on pink cover (1909)	£20000
	b. blue on pink cover	

1904 (1 Jan). Black on grey cover as No. SB1. Stapled.

SB2	£1 Booklet containing 120×2d. in four blocks of 30	

1910 (May). Black on cream cover as Type B **2** of New South Wales. Stapled.

SB3	2s. booklet containing 11×½d. (No. 138), either in block of 6 plus block of 5 or block of 11, and 18×1d. (No. 139) either in three blocks of 6 or block of 6 plus block of 12	£7500

Unsold stock of No. SB3 was uprated with one additional ½d. in May 1911.

1911 (1 Aug). Red on pink cover as No. SB3. Stapled.

SB4	2s. Booklet containing 12×½d. (No. 138), either in two blocks of 6 or block of 12, and 18×1d. (No. 139), either in three blocks of 6 or block of 6 plus block of 12	£7500

POSTAL FISCAL STAMPS

By the Post and Telegraph Act of 5 September 1893 the current issue of fiscal stamps up to and including the 1s. value, Nos. F11/F15, was authorised for postal use.

These stamps had been initially supplied, for fiscal purposes, in February 1882 and had been preceded by a series of 'I R' surcharges and overprints on postage stamps which were in use for a period of about six months. Examples of these 1881–1882 provisionals can be found postally used under the terms of the 1893 Act but, as they had not been current for fiscal purposes for over eleven years, we no longer list them.

F 3

(Typo D.L.R.)

1893 (5 Sept). Definitive fiscal stamps of Feb 1882. Wmk CA over Crown. P 14.

F11	F 3	1d. dull purple	35·00	7·00
F12		2d. dull purple	£325	80·00
F13		3d. dull purple	£120	10·00
F14		6d. dull purple	£180	17·00
F15		1s. dull purple	£300	32·00

The 1s. value is as Type F **3** but with rectangular outer frame and circular frame surrounding swan.

Higher values in this series were not validated by the Act for postal use.

Two varieties of watermark exist on these stamps. Initial supplies showed an indistinct watermark with the base of the 'A' 4 mm wide. From 1896 the paper used showed a clearer watermark on which the base of the 'A' was 5 mm wide.

1897. Wmk W Crown A, W **18**. P 14.

F19	F 3	1d. dull purple	40·00	7·00
F20		3d. dull purple	£120	10·00
F21		6d. dull purple	£170	12·00
F22		1s. dull purple	£300	42·00

The above were invalidated for postal purposes from 1 January 1901.

TELEGRAPH STAMPS

T 1

1879 (9 Apr). Wmk Crown CC. P 14.

T1	T 1	1d. bistre	£110	23·00
		a. Perf 12½	£110	23·00
T2		6d. lilac	£550	£225

The 1d. Telegraph Stamps were authorised for postal purposes from 25 October 1886.

OFFICIAL STAMPS

From 1 August 1862 stamps of various issues were punched with a circular hole, the earlier size being about 3 mm. in diameter and the latter 4 mm. These were used on official correspondence by the Commissariat and Convict Department, branches of the Imperial administration separate from the colonial government. This system of punching ceased in March 1886. Subsequently many stamps between Nos. 94 and 148 may be found punctured, 'PWD', 'WA' or 'OS'.

Western Australia became part of the Commonwealth of Australia on 1 January 1901.

COMMONWEALTH OF AUSTRALIA

On 1 March 1901 control of the postal service passed to the federal administration although it was not until 13 October 1910 that the issues of the various states became valid for use throughout Australia. Postal rates were standardised on 1 May 1911.

The first national postage due stamps appeared in July 1902, but it was not until January 1913 that postage stamps inscribed 'AUSTRALIA' were issued.

PRICES FOR STAMPS ON COVER TO 1945

Nos. 1/3	*from* × 10
No. 4	*from* × 4
Nos. 5/12	*from* × 10
Nos. 13/16	—
Nos. 17/19	*from* × 10
Nos. 20/23	*from* × 10
No. 24	*from* × 8
No. 25	*from* × 2
Nos. 26/27	*from* × 8
Nos. 28/30	—
Nos. 35/37	*from* × 5
Nos. 38/39	*from* × 8
Nos. 40/41	*from* × 20
Nos. 42/45	—
No. 47	*from* × 5
Nos. 48/51	*from* × 8
Nos. 52/53	*from* × 5
Nos. 56/57	*from* × 10
Nos. 58/61	*from* × 8
No. 62	*from* × 5
No. 63	*from* × 2
No. 64	*from* × 15
No. 65	*from* × 5
No. 66	—
No. 73	*from* × 20
Nos. 74/75	*from* × 5
Nos. 76/77	*from* × 4
Nos. 78/81	*from* × 8
Nos. 82/84	*from* × 6
Nos. 85/104	*from* × 4
No. 105	*from* × 15
Nos. 106/110	*from* × 6
Nos. 111/114	—
No. 115	*from* × 3
Nos. 116/118	*from* × 5
Nos. 119/120	*from* × 8
Nos. 121/129	*from* × 5
Nos. 130/131	*from* × 25
No. 132	*from* × 3
Nos. 133/135	*from* × 10
Nos. 136/138	*from* × 4
Nos. 139/139*a*	*from* × 3
No. 140	*from* × 8
Nos. 141/142	*from* × 4
No. 143	*from* × 6
No. 146	*from* × 20
Nos. 147/148	*from* × 3
No. 149	*from* × 6
Nos. 150/152	*from* × 3
Nos. 153/153*a*	*from* × 12
No. 154	*from* × 15
No. 155	*from* × 4
No. 156	*from* × 15
Nos. 157/158	*from* × 3
Nos. 159/160	*from* × 6
No. 161	*from* × 10
Nos. 162/163	*from* × 4
Nos. 164/211	*from* × 2
Nos. D1/D118	*from* × 8
Nos. O1/O3	*from* × 10
Nos. O4/O6	*from* × 4
Nos. O7/O8	*from* × 10
Nos. O9/O15	—
Nos. O16/O18	*from* × 10
No. O19	*from* × 3
No. O20	*from* × 15
No. O21	*from* × 3
Nos. O22/O23	*from* × 10
No. O24/O30	—
Nos. O31/O34	*from* × 10
Nos. O35/O37	—
Nos. O38/O42	*from* × 15
Nos. O43/O47	*from* × 10
No. O48	*from* × 30
Nos. O49/O53	—
No. O54	*from* × 6
No. O60	*from* × 4
No. O61	*from* × 30
No. O62	—
No. O63	*from* × 5
Nos. O64/O65	*from* × 15
Nos. O66/O67	*from* × 8
No. O68	*from* × 20
No. O69	*from* × 10
Nos. O70/O74	*from* × 15
No. O75	—
Nos. O76/O77	*from* × 15
No. O78	—
Nos. O79/O84	*from* × 8
No. O85	*from* × 6
Nos. O86/O87	*from* × 3
No. O88	—
No. O89	*from* × 15
Nos. O90/O96	*from* × 6
No. O97	*from* × 20
Nos. O98/O110	*from* × 6
Nos. O111	*from* × 10
Nos. O112/O117	*from* × 20
Nos. O118/O118*b*	—
Nos. O119/O122	*from* × 20
Nos. O126	*from* × 100
Nos. O127	*from* × 5
Nos. O128	*from* × 200
Nos. O129/O131	*from* × 50
Nos. O132/O133	*from* × 10
Nos. O134/O136	*from* × 40

PRINTERS. Except where otherwise stated, all Commonwealth stamps to No. 581 were printed under Government authority at Melbourne. Until 1918 there were two establishments (both of the Treasury Dept)—the Note Printing Branch and the Stamp Printing Branch. The former printed T **3** and **4**.

In 1918 the Stamp Printing Branch was closed and all stamps were printed by the Note Printing Branch. In 1926 control was transferred from the Treasury to the Commonwealth Bank of Australia, and on 14 January 1960 the branch was attached to the newly established Reserve Bank of Australia.

Until 1942 stamps bore in the sheet margin the initials or names of successive managers and from 1942 to March 1952 the imprint 'Printed by the Authority of the Government of the Commonwealth of Australia'. After November 1952 (or Nos. D129/D131 for Postage Dues) imprints were discontinued.

SPECIMEN OVERPRINTS. These come from Specimen sets, first made available to the public on 15 December 1913. In these sets the lower values were cancelled-to-order, but stamps with a face value of over 5s. or later 50c. were overprinted 'SPECIMEN' in different types. These overprints are listed as they could be purchased from the Australian Post Office.

It is, however, believed that examples of No. 112 overprinted 'SPECIMEN' were distributed by the UPU in 1929. Supplies of the 1902 and 1902–04 postage due stamps overprinted 'SPECIMEN' were supplied to the UPU by some of the states.

KANGAROO AND MAP, CROWN OVER A WATERMARKS. Three different Single Crown over A watermarked papers were used to print the Kangaroo and Map stamps of Australia (T **1**).

T **2**, generally known as the 'First' or 'Wide Crown' watermark was used only for the set issued in 1913-1914. The Crown is distinctive and is usually quite well centred on the stamp, while the paper has a clear *horizontal* mesh.

T **5**, the 'Second' or 'Pointed Crown' watermark, as used for the first King's Head stamps of 1913-1914, is as wide as T **2**, but the 'points' on either side of the cross are usually clear. The paper mesh is *vertical*. It was used provisionally for printings of values between 2d. and 5s., but because it was designed for stamps of slightly larger size, it is frequently poorly centred on the stamp.

T **6**, the 'Third' or 'Narrow Crown' watermark has a noticeably narrower Crown than T **2** or **5**. It is generally well centred on the stamp and the paper has a *vertical* mesh.

1

2

Die I

Die II

Dies of Type 1 (mono-coloured values only):—

Die I. Break in inner frame line at lower left level with top of words of value.

Die II. Die repaired showing no break.

Die I was only used for the ½d., 1d., 2d. and 3d. Several plates were produced for each except the 3d. When the second plate of the 3d. was being prepared the damage became aggravated after making 105 out of the 120 units when the die was returned for repair. This gave rise to the *se-tenant* pairs showing the two states of the die.

Die II was used until 1945 and deteriorated progressively with damage to the frame lines and rounding of the corners.

Specialists recognise seven states of this die, but we only list the two most major of the later versions.

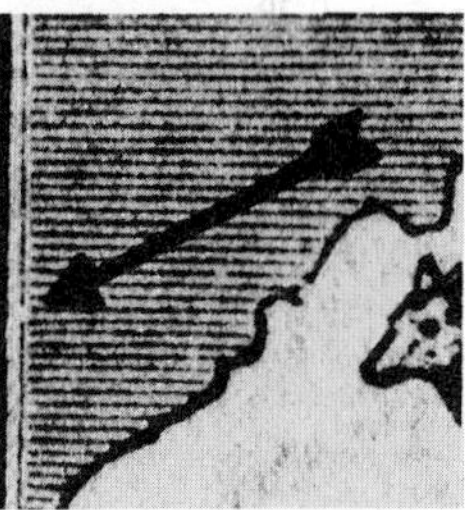

Die IIA. This state is as Die II, but, in addition, shows a break in the inner left-hand frame line, 9 mm from the top of the design (occurs on 1d., 2d. and 6d.).

Die IIB. As Die IIA, but now also showing break in outer frame line above 'ST', and (not illustrated) an incomplete corner to the inner frame line at top right (occurs on 3d., 6d., 9d., 1s. and £1 (No. 75)).

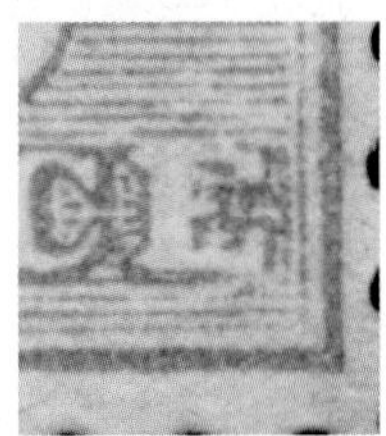

No. 9a shows a badly distorted second 'E' in 'PENCE', which is unmistakable. It occurs on the upper plate right pane R. 10/6 and was replaced by a substitute cliché in Die IIA (No. 9b) in the November 1913 printing.

(Des B. Young. Eng S. Reading. Typo J. B. Cooke)

1913 (2 Jan)–**14**. W **2**. P 12.

1	1	½d. green (Die I) (14.1.13)	10·00	6·50
		bw. Wmk inverted	85·00	32·00
		c. Wmk sideways	†	£35000
		cw. Wmk sideways inverted	†	£28000
2		1d. red (Die I)	20·00	1·75
		a. Wmk sideways	£1600	£275
		aw. Wmk sideways inverted	£1800	£300
		b. Carmine	19·00	1·75
		cw. Wmk inverted	85·00	22·00
		d. Die II *Red* (16.1.13)	16·00	1·00
		da. Wmk sideways	£1600	£325
		daw. Wmk sideways inverted	£1800	£350
		db. Carmine	17·00	1·75
		dw. Wmk inverted	90·00	30·00
		e. Die IIA. *Red* (4.14)	32·00	1·25
		eb. Carmine	32·00	1·75
		ew. Wmk inverted	£170	32·00
3		2d. grey (Die I) (15.1.13)	55·00	6·50
		w. Wmk inverted	£130	35·00
4		2½d. indigo (Die II) (27.1.13)	50·00	23·00

No.	Type	Description	Mint	Used
5		3d. olive (Die I) (28.1.13)	80·00	11·00
		a. Imperf three sides (horiz pair)	£75000	
		aa. Imperf three sides (lower stamp of vert pair)	£45000	
		b. in pair with Die II	£1400	£750
		c. Yellow-olive	85·00	11·00
		ca. In pair with Die II	£1400	£750
		dw. Wmk inverted	£200	80·00
		e. Die II *Olive*	£475	£100
		ea. Yellow-olive	£475	95·00
		ew. Wmk inverted	£950	£375
6		4d. orange (Die II) (19.2.13)	£100	26·00
		a. Orange-yellow	£500	85·00
8		5d. chestnut (Die II) (18.1.13)	90·00	48·00
9		6d. ultramarine (Die II) (18.1.13)	80·00	20·00
		a. Retouched 'E'	£2500	£950
		b. Die IIA (substituted cliché) (11.13)	£6500	£2250
		w. Wmk inverted	£1100	£400
10		9d. violet (Die II) (1.2.13)	80·00	27·00
11		1s. emerald (Die II) (25.1.13)	90·00	27·00
		a. Blue-green	£150	29·00
		w. Wmk inverted	£1500	80·00
12		2s. brown (Die II) (28.1.13)	£275	85·00
13		5s. grey and yellow (Die II) (20.3.13)	£450	£200
14		10s. grey and pink (Die II) (20.3.13)	£900	£700
15		£1 brown and ultramarine (Die II) (20.3.13)	£3000	£2500
16		£2 black and rose (Die II) (8.4.13)	£6500	£4000
1/16 *Set of 15*			£10000	£7000
14s/16s Handstamped *'Specimen' Set of 3*			£1400	

The watermark on Nos. 1c, 2a and 2da shows the Crown pointing to the left and on Nos. 1cw, 2aw and 2daw pointing to the right, *as seen from the back of the stamp.* One example of 1c and two examples of 1cw are known, all used.

The 3d. was printed from two plates, of which the upper plate contained 105 stamps as Die I and 15 as Die II (at left pane R. 7/1-2, 8/1-5, 9/1-3, 10/1-5). The lower plate contained Die I stamps only.

No. 5a is from the top row of a sheet, with perforations at foot only. No. 5aa is from the bottom two rows of a different sheet.

See also Nos. 24/30 (W **5**), 35/45*b* (W **6**), 73/75 (W **6**, new colours), 107/114 (W **7**), 132/138 (W **15**), 212 (2s. re-engraved).

3

4 Laughing Kookaburra

(Des R. A. Harrison. Eng and recess T. S. Harrison)

1913 (9 Dec)–**14**. No wmk. P 11.

No.	Type	Description	Mint	Used
17	**3**	1d. red	4·25	6·50
		a. Imperf between (horiz pair)	£5500	
		b. Imperf between (vert pair)	£2750	
		c. Pale rose-red	10·00	16·00
		ca. Imperf between (vert pair)	£3250	
		cb. Imperf between (horiz pair)	£5500	
19	**4**	6d. claret (26.8.14)	75·00	55·00

All printings from Plate 1 of the 1d. were in the shade of No. 17*c*. This plate shows many retouches.

5

5a

Thin '1' in fraction at right (Plate 5 right pane R. 8/1)

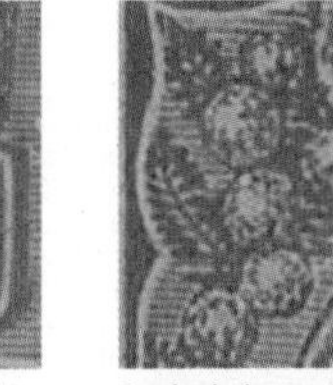

Cracked electro (Plate 5 left pane R. 8/4)

1d. Die II

Dot before '1' (Plate 3 right pane R. 4/3)

'Secret mark' (Plate 4 left pane R. 1/1)

Flaw under neck (Plate 4 left pane R. 7/1)

'RA' joined (Plate 4 left pane R. 10/6)

4d. Line through 'FOUR PENCE' (Pl. 2 right pane R. 2/6)

1d. Die II. The flaw distinguishing the so-called Die II, a white upward spur to the right of the base of the '1' in the left value tablet, is now known to be due to a defective roller-die. It occurred on all stamps in the second and third vertical rows of upper left plate, right pane. Each of the 20 defective impressions differs slightly; a typical example is illustrated above.

(Dies eng P.B. Typo J. B. Cooke until May 1918, then T. S. Harrison)

1914 (17 July)–**20**. W **5**. P 14¼×14 (comb).

No.	Type	Description	Mint	Used
20	**5a**	½d. bright green (22.2.15)	4·00	1·00
		a. Perf 14¼ (line) (12.15)	£12000	£600
		b. Green (1916)	4·00	1·00
		c. Yellow-green (1916)	32·00	13·00
		d. Thin '1' in fraction at right	£23000	£8000
		e. Cracked electro	£8500	£4000
		w. Wmk inverted	23·00	9·50
21		1d. carmine-red (*shades*) (Die I) (P 14¼ (line))	48·00	7·50
		a. Die II	£18000	£3250
		bw. Wmk inverted	†	£14000
		c. Perf 14¼×14 (comb)	13·00	1·00
		ca. Rusted cliché (Pl 2 right pane R. 6/4 and 5) (9.16)	£18000	£450
		cb. Substituted cliché (Pl 2 right pane R. 6/5) (2.18)	£2000	60·00
		cc. Pale carmine (shades) (1917)	14·00	1·00
		cd. Rose-red (1917)	17·00	2·50
		ce. Carmine-pink (1918)	£170	11·00
		cf. Carmine (aniline) (1920)	22·00	3·25
		cg. Dot before '1'	£110	12·00
		ch. 'Secret mark'	£110	12·00
		ci. Flaw under neck	£110	12·00
		cj. 'RA' joined	£110	12·00
		cw. Wmk inverted	27·00	3·00
		cz. Wmk sideways	†	£50000
		d. Die II *Carmine-red (shades)*	£425	6·50
		db. Substituted cliché (Pl 2 right pane R. 6/4) (2.18)	£2000	60·00
		dc. Pale carmine (shades)	£475	8·00
		dw. Wmk inverted	£1300	£120
22		4d. orange (6.1.15)	42·00	2·50
		a. Yellow-orange (1915)	42·00	3·25
		b. Lemon-yellow (3.16)	85·00	14·00
		c. Pale orange-yellow (1.17)	£110	12·00
		d. Dull orange (1920)	55·00	3·25
		e. Line through 'FOUR PENCE' (*all shades*) *From*	£350	£110
		w. Wmk inverted	45·00	12·00
23		5d. brown (*P* 14¼ (line)) (22.2.15)	50·00	7·50
		aw. Wmk inverted	£1400	£950
		b. Perf 14¼×14 (comb)	28·00	2·00
		ba. Yellow-brown (1920)	30·00	2·75
		bw. Wmk inverted	£800	£650

The variety No. 20d was caused by the engraving of a new fraction in a defective electro in 1918.

No. 21ca was caused by rusting on two positions of the steel Plate 2 and shows as white patches on the back of the King's neck and on, and beside, the top of the right frame (right pane R. 6/4) and on the left frame, wattles, head and ears of kangaroo (right pane R. 6/5). These were noticed in December 1916 when the damaged impressions were removed and replaced by a pair of copper electros (Die II for R. 6/4 and Die I for R. 6/5), showing rounded corners and some frame damage, the former also showing a white spot under tail of emu. In time the tops of the crown quickly wore away.

One example of No. 21cz has been recorded. It shows wmk crown to right *(as seen from the back of the stamp).*

Most of Nos. 20/23 were perforated 14 by a comb machine (exact gauge 14.25×14), but printings of the ½d. in December 1915, of the 1d. in July and August 1914 and of the 5d. until June 1917 were perforated by a line machine measuring 14.2.

See also Nos. 47/47k (W **5**, rough paper), 48/52 (W **6a**), 53/53*a* (1d. Die III), 56/66*b* and 76/81 (W **5**, new colours), 82 (W **6a**), 83/84 (no wmk), 85/104 (W **7**), 124/131 (W **15**).

(Typo J. B. Cooke)

1915 (15 Jan–July). W **5**. P 12.

No.	Type	Description	Mint	Used
24	**1**	2d. grey (Die I)	£100	12·00
		w. Wmk inverted	†	£18000
25		2½d. indigo (Die II) (7.15)	90·00	32·00
26		6d. ultramarine (Die II) (4.15)	£200	22·00
		a. Bright blue	£425	70·00
		b. Die IIA. *Ultramarine* (substituted cliché) (Upper plate right pane R. 10/6)	£8500	£3000
		ba. Bright blue	£10000	£4000
		w. Wmk inverted	†	£40000
27		9d. violet (Die II) (9.7)	£200	48·00
		w. Wmk inverted	£4250	£1800
28		1s. blue-green (Die II) (4.15)	£180	35·00
29		2s. brown (Die II) (3.15)	£700	£120
30		5s. grey and yellow (Die II) (12.2)	£1000	£350
		a. Yellow portion doubly printed	£15000	£4000
		w. Wmk inverted	£1300	£500
24/30 *Set of 7*			£2250	£550

6

6a

2d. No. 35a (Upper plate left pane R. 10/1)

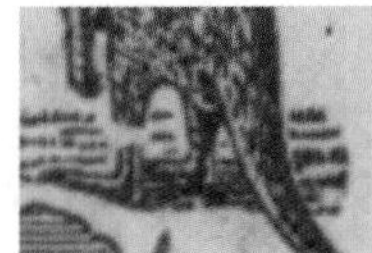

6d. Nos. 38da and 73a (Upper plate left pane R. 1/6)

(Typo J. B. Cooke (to May 1918), T. S. Harrison (to February 1926), A. J. Mullett (to June 1927) and thereafter J. Ash).

1915 (8 Oct)–**27**. W **6** (narrow Crown). P 12.

No.	Type	Description	Mint	Used
35	**1**	2d. grey (Die I) (11.15)	50·00	9·50
		a. Die IIA substituted cliché (upper plate left pane R. 10/1)*	£11000	£1900
		bw. Wmk inverted	75·00	32·00
		c. Silver-grey (shiny paper)	50·00	22·00
		d. Die IIA. *Silver-grey (shiny paper)* (3.18)	70·00	25·00
		daw. Wmk inverted	†	£10000
		dba. Grey (1920)	75·00	32·00
36		2½d. deep blue (Die II) (7.17)	28·00	10·00
		aw. Wmk inverted	£140	90·00
		b. Deep indigo (1919)	50·00	9·00
		ba. '1' of fraction omitted (Lower plate left pane R. 6/3)	£55000	£35000
37		3d. yellow-olive (Die I)	40·00	4·75
		a. In pair with Die II	£550	£425
		b. Olive-green (1917)	42·00	4·50
		ba. In pair with Die II	£600	£425
		cw. Wmk inverted	£100	48·00
		d. Die II *Yellow-olive*	£225	55·00
		da. Olive-green	£250	55·00
		dw. Wmk inverted	£600	£350
		e. Die IIB. *Light olive* (12.22)	60·00	13·00
38		6d. ultramarine (Die II) (15.12.15)	80·00	7·50
		a. Die IIA (substituted cliché) (Upper plate rt pane R. 10/6)	£7500	£1800
		b. Dull blue (6.18)	90·00	11·00
		ba. Die IIA (substituted cliché)	£7500	£1900
		cw. Wmk inverted	£450	£100
		d. Die IIB. *Bright ultramarine* (23.7.21)	90·00	23·00
		da. Leg of kangaroo broken	£2250	£700
		dw. Wmk inverted	£650	£250
39		9d. violet (Die II) (3.7.16)	65·00	11·00
		aw. Wmk inverted	£500	£110
		b. Die IIB. (16.4.19)	75·00	19·00
		bw. Wmk inverted	£300	£100
		c. Die II (substituted cliché) in pair with Die IIB	£750	£600
40		1s. blue-green (Die II) (6.16)	60·00	8·00
		aw. Wmk inverted	£275	£120
		b. Die IIB (11.20)	75·00	9·00
		ba. Wmk sideways (13.12.27)	60·00	£400
		bw. Wmk inverted	£275	£120
41		2s. brown (Die II) (6.16)	£275	14·00
		a. Imperf three sides (horiz pair)	£110000	
		b. Red-brown (aniline)	£3250	£500
		w. Wmk inverted	£3750	£425
42		5s. grey and yellow (Die II) (4.18)	£275	£110
		a. Grey and orange (1920)	£450	£170
		b. Grey and deep yellow	£325	£130
		ba. Wmk sideways	†	£85000
		c. Grey and pale yellow	£275	£110
		w. Wmk inverted	£1300	£1100
43		10s. grey and pink (Die II) (5.2.17)	£550	£350
		a. Grey and bright aniline pink (10.18)	£500	£325
		ab. Wmk sideways	£42000	£19000
		aw. Wmk inverted	£2750	£1600
		b. Grey and pale aniline pink (1922)	£600	£350
44		£1 chocolate and dull blue (Die II) (7.16)	£3000	£1600
		a. Chestnut and bright blue (6.17)	£3250	£1800
		ab. Wmk sideways	†	£50000
		aw. Wmk inverted	£4500	£3500
		b. Bistre-brown and bright blue (7.19)	£3250	£1800
		ba. Frame printed double, one albino	£8500	
45		£2 black and rose (Die II) (12.19)	£5000	£3250
		a. Grey and crimson (1921)	£4750	£3250
		b. Purple-black and pale rose (6.24)	£4500	£2750
35/45*b Set of 11*			£8000	£4250
43s/45s Optd *'SPECIMEN' Set of 3*			£850	

*The Die IIA of No. 35a is a substituted cliché introduced to repair a crack which occurred on R. 10/1 of the upper plate left pane. Its Die IIA characteristics are more pronounced than on the sheet stamps from this die, with the break at left extending to the outer, in addition to the inner, frame line.

One plate of the 3d. contained mixed Die I and Die II stamps as described.

No. 39c comes from eight substituted clichés taken from plate 2 (Die II) and inserted in plate 3 (Die IIB) at position left pane R. 3/6 and in plate 4 (Die IIB) at positions left pane R. 1/3-4, 2/3-4 and 8/6 and right pane R. 2/1 and R. 9/1. This substitution took place in August 1927 towards the end of the printings on W **6**. The variety can also be found on stamps with W **7** and W **15**, see Nos. 108a and 133a.

All values were printed by both Cooke and Harrison, and the 9d., 1s. and 5s. were also printed by Mullett and Ash.

The watermark on No. 40ba shows the Crown printing to the right, that on Nos. 42ba and 43ab shows the Crown pointing to the left *as seen from the back of the stamp.*

1916 (Nov)–**18**. Rough, unsurfaced paper, locally gummed. W **5**. P 14.

47 **5a** 1d. scarlet (Die I) 30·00 3·00
a. Deep red (1917) 30·00 2·50
b. Rose-red (1918) 35·00 2·75
ba. Substituted cliché (Pl 2 right pane R. 6/5) £2000 75·00
c. Rosine (1918) £400 28·00
ca. Substituted cliché (Pl 2 right pane R. 6/5) £3750 £425
d. Dot before '1' £150 20·00
e. Secret mark £150 20·00
f. Flaw under neck £150 20·00
g. 'RA' joined £150 20·00
hw. Wmk inverted 60·00 12·00
i. Die II *Rose-red* (1918) £500 23·00
ia. Substituted cliché (Pl 2 right pane R. 6/4) £2000 75·00
iw. Wmk inverted £1200 £160
j. Die II *Rosine* (1918) £1500 £180
ja. Substituted cliché (Pl 2 right pane R. 6/4) £3750 £425
k. No wmk £6500 £5000

All examples of the 5d. on this paper were perforated 'OS' and will be found listed as No. O60.

No. 47k is the result of misplacement of the sheet during printing. To qualify, there should be no trace of the Crown over A or a line watermark.

(Typo J. B. Cooke to May 1918 thereafter T. S. Harrison)

1918 (4 Jan)–**20**. W **6a** (Mult). P 14.

48 **5a** ½d. green (*shades*) 8·50 2·00
a. Thin 1 in fraction at right £100 £140
b. Wmk sideways † £30000
bw. Wmk sideways inverted † £30000
c. Cracked electro £350 £375
w. Wmk inverted 29·00 16·00
49 1d. carmine-pink (Die I) (23.1.18) £250 £140
aw. Wmk inverted † £27000
b. Deep red (1918) £5500 £3000
bw. Wmk inverted † £40000
c. Dot before '1' £1200 £475
d. Secret mark £1200 £475
e. Flaw under neck £1200 £475
f. 'RA' joined £1200 £475
50 1d. carmine (10.12.19) 30·00 17·00
aw. Wmk inverted £1400 £3000
b. Deep red (aniline) (1920) £850 £325
c. Dot before '1' £300 £100
d. Secret mark £300 £100
e. Flaw under neck £300 £100
f. 'RA' joined £300 £100
51 1½d. black-brown (30.1.19) 6·50 4·00
a. Very thin paper (2.19) 22·00 17·00
w. Wmk inverted 45·00 35·00
52 1½d. red-brown (4.19) 14·00 2·25
a. Chocolate (1920) 14·00 2·25
w. Wmk inverted £120 70·00

No. 48 was printed by Cooke and Harrison, Nos. 49/49*b* by Cooke only and Nos. 50/52*a* by Harrison only. Nos. 49/49*b* have rather yellowish gum, that of No. 50 being pure white.

The watermark on No. 48b shows the Crown pointing to the left and on No. 48bw pointing to the right, *as seen from the back of the stamp*. Two examples of No. 48b and two of No. 48bw are known.

1d. Die III

1d. Die III. In 1917 a printing (in sheets of 120) was made on paper originally prepared for printing War Savings Stamps, with watermark T **5**. A special plate was made for this printing, differing in detail from those previously used. The shading round the head is even; the solid background of the words 'ONE PENNY' is bounded at each end by a white vertical line; and there is a horizontal white line cutting the vertical shading lines at left on the King's neck.

(Typo J. B. Cooke)

1918 (15 July). Printed from a new Die III plate on white unsurfaced paper, locally gummed. W **5**. P 14.

53 **5a** 1d. rose-red 75·00 38·00
a. Rose-carmine 75·00 38·00
w. Wmk inverted £160 £100

(Typo T. S. Harrison or A. J. Mullett (1s.4d. from March 1926))

1918 (9 Nov)–**23**. W **5**. P 14.

56 **5a** ½d. orange (8.11.23) 5·50 2·00
w. Wmk inverted 8·50 11·00
57 1d. violet (*shades*) (12.2.22) 8·50 1·50
a. Imperf three sides (horiz pair) £50000
b. Red-violet 10·00 2·25
c. Dot before '1' 70·00 17·00
d. Secret mark 70·00 17·00
e. Flaw under neck 70·00 17·00
f. 'RA' joined 70·00 17·00
58 1½d. black-brown 8·50 1·50
w. Wmk inverted 60·00 22·00
59 1½d. deep red-brown (4.19) 16·00 1·00
a. Chocolate (1920) 11·00 60
w. Wmk inverted 65·00 35·00
60 1½d. bright red-brown (20.1.22) 40·00 4·00
61 1½d. green (7.3.23) 6·00 1·00
a. Coarse unsurfaced paper (1923) £475 £180
w. Wmk inverted † £18000
62 2d. brown-orange (9.20) 14·00 1·00
a. Dull orange (1921) 16·00 1·00
w. Wmk inverted † £5500
63 2d. bright rose-scarlet (19.1.22) 19·00 1·50
a. Dull rose-scarlet 19·00 1·50
w. Wmk inverted £19000
64 4d. violet (21.6.21) 18·00 15·00
a. Line through 'FOUR PENCE' (Pl 2 right pane R. 2/6) £34000 £9000
b. 'FOUR PENCE' in thinner letters (Pl 2 right pane R. 2/6) £475 £300
65 4d. ultramarine (*shades*) (23.3.22) 50·00 7·50
a. 'FOUR PENCE' in thinner letters (Pl 2 right pane R. 2/6) £475 £170
b. Pale milky blue 90·00 14·00
w. Wmk inverted 90·00 £275
66 1s.4d. pale blue (2.12.20) 90·00 35·00
a. Dull greenish blue 95·00 28·00
b. Deep turquoise (1922) £3500 £2750
56/66 *Set of 11* £225 55·00

In addition to a number of mint pairs of No. 57a from two sheets purchased at Gumeracha, South Australia, with the bottom row imperforate on three sides, a single used example of No. 57 imperforate on three sides is known.

No. 61a was printed on a batch of coarse unsurfaced paper during 1923. Examples may be indentified by a clear vertical mesh in the paper, with mint stamps having a yellowish gum.

The 4d. ultramarine was originally printed from the Cooke plates but the plates were worn in mid-1923 and Harrison prepared a new pair of plates. Stamps from these plates can only be distinguished by the minor flaws which are peculiar to them.

The variety of Nos. 64 and 65 with 'FOUR PENCE' thinner, was caused by the correction of the line through 'FOUR PENCE' flaw early in the printing of No. 64.

(Typo T. S. Harrison (to February 1926), A. J. Mullett (to June 1927), thereafter J. Ash)

1923 (6 Dec)–**24**. W **6**. P 12.

73 **1** 6d. chestnut (Die IIB) 28·00 1·75
a. Leg of kangaroo broken (Upper plate left pane R. 1/6) 75·00 £120
w. Wmk inverted † £23000
74 2s. maroon (Die II) (1.5.24) 80·00 32·00
w. Wmk inverted £2250 £1700
75 £1 grey (Die IIB) (1.5.24) £650 £350
s. Optd 'SPECIMEN' £120

The 6d. and 2s. were printed by all three printers, but the £1 only by Harrison.

No. 73a was corrected during the Ash printing.

(Typo T. S. Harrison (to February 1926), thereafter A. J. Mullett)

1924 (1 May–18 Aug). P 14.

(a) W **5**

76 **5a** 1d. sage-green 6·00 1·50
a. Dot before '1' 55·00 13·00
b. Secret mark 55·00 13·00
c. Flaw under neck 55·00 13·00
d. 'RA' joined 55·00 13·00
w. Wmk inverted 24·00 10·00
77 1½d. scarlet (*shades*) 3·00 40
a. Very thin paper £110 50·00
b. 'HALEPENCE' (Pl 22 left pane R. 4/4) 30·00 38·00
c. 'RAL' of AUSTRALIA' thin (Pl 22 left pane R. 5/4) 32·00 38·00
d. Curved '1' and thin fraction at left (Pl 24 right pane R. 7/5) 32·00 38·00
w. Wmk inverted 50·00 24·00
78 2d. red-brown 17·00 7·00
a. Bright red-brown 22·00 8·00
w. Wmk inverted † £24000
79 3d. dull ultramarine 26·00 2·00
a. Imperf three sides (horiz pair) £13000
80 4d. olive-yellow 35·00 5·50
a. Olive-green 32·00 6·00
w. Wmk inverted † £17000
81 4½d. violet 24·00 3·50

(b) W **6a**

82 **5a** 1d. sage-green (20.5) 15·00 11·00
a. Dot before '1' 90·00 75·00
b. Secret mark 90·00 75·00
c. Flaw under neck 90·00 75·00
d. 'RA' joined 90·00 75·00
w. Wmk inverted † £18000

(c) No wmk

83 **5a** 1d. sage-green (18.8) 7·50 11·00
a. Dot before '1' 60·00 75·00
b. Secret mark 60·00 75·00
c. Flaw under neck 60·00 75·00
d. 'RA' joined 60·00 75·00
84 1½d. scarlet (14.8) 25·00 9·50
76/84 *Set of 9* £140 45·00

Nos. 78/78*a* and 82/84 were printed by Harrison only but the remainder were printed by both Harrison and Mullett.

In the semi-transparent paper of Nos. 51a and 77a the watermark is almost indistinguishable.

Nos. 77b, 77c and 77d are typical examples of retouching of which there are many others in these issues. In No. 77c the letters 'RAL' differ markedly from the normal. There is a white stroke cutting the oval frame-line above the 'L', and the right-hand outer line of the Crown does not cut the white frame-line above the 'A'.

It is believed that No. 79a occurs on the bottom row of at least four sheets purchased from post offices in Victoria during 1926.

7

I

II

New Dies

1d. For differences see note above No. 20.

1½d. From new steel plates made from a new die. Nos. 87*a* and 96*a* are the Ash printings, the ink of which is shiny.

2d. Die I. Height of frame 25.6 mm. Left-hand frame-line thick and uneven behind Kangaroo. Pearls in Crown vary in size.
Die II. Height of frame 25.6 mm. Left-hand frame-line thin and even. Pearls in Crown are all the same size.
Die III. Height 25.1 mm; lettering and figures of value bolder than Die I.

3d. Die II has bolder letters and figures than Die I, as illustrated above.

5d. Die II has a bolder figure '5' with flat top compared with Die I of the earlier issues.

(Typo A. J. Mullett or J. Ash (from June 1927))

1926–30. W **7**.

(a) P 14

85 **5a** ½d. orange (10.3.27) 6·50 7·50
w. Wmk inverted £120 £100
86 1d. sage-green (23.10.26) 6·00 1·00
a. Dot before '1' 70·00 20·00
b. Secret mark 70·00 20·00
c. Flaw under neck 95·00 30·00
d. 'RA' joined 95·00 30·00
w. Wmk inverted 26·00 12·00
87 1½d. scarlet (5.11.26) 14·00 2·50
a. Golden scarlet (1927) 23·00 2·50
w. Wmk inverted 30·00 10·00
89 2d. red-brown (Die I) (17.8.27) 40·00 48·00
90 3d. dull ultramarine (12.26) 30·00 5·00
w. Wmk inverted † £12000
91 4d. yellow-olive (17.1.28) 55·00 40·00
92 4½d. violet (26.10.27) 23·00 3·75
93 1s.4d. pale greenish blue (6.9.27) £130 80·00
w. Wmk inverted † £23000
85/93 *Set of 8* £275 £170

(b) P 13½×12½

94 **5a** ½d. orange (21.11.28) 2·50 1·00
95 1d. sage-green (Die I) (23.12.26) 5·50 70
aa. Dot before '1' £120 42·00
ab. Secret mark £150 65·00
ac. Flaw under neck £150 60·00
ad. 'RA' joined £150 60·00
aw. Wmk inverted 32·00 25·00
b. Die II (6.28) 50·00 80·00
bw. Wmk inverted £1900 £1800
96 1½d. scarlet (14.1.27) 3·25 1·00
a. Golden scarlet (1927) 5·50 1·00
w. Wmk inverted 16·00 2·50
97 1½d. red-brown (16.9.30) 7·00 7·50
98 2d. red-brown (Die II) (28.4.28) 19·00 9·50
99 2d. golden scarlet (Die II) (2.8.30) 24·00 2·75
a. Die III (9.9.30) 8·00 1·00
ab. No wmk £1300 £2750
ac. Tête-bêche (pair) £200000
aw. Wmk inverted (*from booklets*) 9·50 1·60
100 3d. dull ultramarine (Die I) (28.2.28) 38·00 6·50
aw. Wmk inverted £190 £3000
b. Die II *Deep ultramarine* (28.9.29) 20·00 1·40
bw. Wmk inverted † £13000
102 4d. yellow-olive (19.4.29) 35·00 3·25
w. Wmk inverted † £12000
103 4½d. violet Die I* (11.28) 75·00 35·00
103*a* 5d. orange-brown Die II (27.8.30) 45·00 7·00
104 1s.4d. turquoise (30.9.28) £120 26·00
w. Wmk inverted † £21000
94/104 *Set of 11* £300 80·00

Owing to defective manufacture, part of the sheet of the 2d. (Die III), discovered in July 1931, escaped unwatermarked; while the watermark in other parts of the same sheet was faint or normal.

Only one example of No. 99*ac* is known.

*For the 4½d Die II see No. 120a.

8 Parliament House, Canberra

(Des R. A. Harrison. Die eng J. A. C. Harrison (Waterlow, London). Plates and printing by A. J. Mullett)

1927 (9 May). Opening of Parliament House, Canberra. No wmk. P 11.

105 **8** 1½d. brownish lake 50 50
a. Imperf between (vert pair) £5500
b. Imperf between (horiz pair) £13000 £13000

(Eng H. W. Bell. Recess J. Ash)

1928 (29 Oct–2 Nov). Fourth National Stamp Exhibition, Melbourne. As T **4**. No wmk. P 11.
106 3d. blue (2.11) 4·50 6·50
MS106*a* 65×70 mm. No. 106×4 £120 £200
ab. Imperf (pane of four) £150000

No. **MS**106*a* comes from special sheets of 60 stamps divided into 15 blocks of 4 (5×3) and separated by wide gutters perforated down the middle, printed and sold at the Exhibition.

(Typo J. Ash)

1929 (Feb)–**30**. W **7**. P 12.
107 **1** 6d. chestnut (Die IIB) (25.9.29) 38·00 4·50
108 9d. violet (Die IIB) 45·00 29·00
a. Die II (substituted cliché) in pair with Die IIB £450 £500
109 1s. blue-green (Die IIB) (12.6.29) 55·00 11·00
w. Wmk inverted † £23000
110 2s. maroon (Die II) (3.29) 90·00 17·00
111 5s. grey and yellow (Die II) (30.11.29) £250 £110
112 10s. grey and pink (Die II) £475 £500
114 £2 black and rose (Die II) (11.30) £4500 £750
107/114 *Set of 7* £5000 £1300
112s/114s Optd 'SPECIMEN' *Set of 2* £450

For No. 108a see note below No. 45*b*.

9 DH66 Biplane and Pastoral Scene

'Long wing' flaw (R. 2/1 of booklet pane)

(Des R. A. Harrison and H. Herbert. Eng A. Taylor. Recess J. Ash)

1929 (20 May). Air. No wmk. P 11.
115 **9** 3d. green (*shades*) 9·00 4·25
a. Booklet stamp 32·00 22·00
b. 'Long wing' flaw £300 £180

No. 115 was originally issued in preparation for the inauguration of the Perth to Adelaide air service on 2 June 1929.

Variations of up to ¾ mm in the design size of No. 115 are due to paper shrinkage on the printings produced by the 'wet' process. The last printing, in 1935, was printed by the 'dry' method.

Booklet stamps may be identified by a dot in the centre of the horizontal margin between each stamp. The dot may appear above or below the design and is sometimes removed by perforation.

10 Black Swan

11 *Capt. Charles Sturt* (J. H. Crossland)

Re-entry ('T' of 'AUSTRALIA' clearly double) (Pl 2 R. 7/4)

(Des G. Pitt Morrison. Eng F. D. Manley. Recess J. Ash)

1929 (28 Sept). Centenary of Western Australia. No wmk. P 11.
116 **10** 1½d. dull scarlet 2·25 2·00
a. Re-entry 60·00 80·00

(Des R. A. Harrison. Eng F. D. Manley. Recess J. Ash)

1930 (2 June). Centenary of Exploration of River Murray by Capt. Sturt. No wmk. P 11.
117 **11** 1½d. scarlet 1·25 1·00
118 3d. blue 9·50 9·50

No. 117 with manuscript surcharge of '2d. paid P M L H I' was issued by the Postmaster of Lord Howe Island during a shortage of 2d. stamps between 23 August and 17 October 1930 (*Price* £750 *un. or used*). A few copies of the 1½d. value No. 96*a* were also endorsed (*Price* £1700 *un. or used*). These provisionals are not recognised by the Australian postal authorities.

TWO

(**12**)

13 Fokker F. VIIa/3m *Southern Cross* above Hemispheres

4½d. Original die

4½d. Redrawn die

1930 (28 July–2 Aug). T **5a** surch as T **12**. W **7**. P 13½×12½.
119 2d. on 1½d. golden scarlet 3·00 1·00
120 5d. on 4½d. violet (2.8) 15·00 17·00
a. Without surcharge £7500 45·00

No. 120 is from a redrawn die in which the words 'FOURPENCE HALFPENNY' are noticeably thicker than in the original die and the figure '4' has square instead of tapering serifs. The redrawn die also shows thin white lines to the left and right of the tablet carrying 'FOURPENCE HALFPENNY'.

Stamps from the redrawn die without the surcharge were not intended to be issued. Some stamps, *cancelled to order*, were included in sets supplied by the post office. A few mint copies, which escaped the cancellation were found and some may have been used postally.

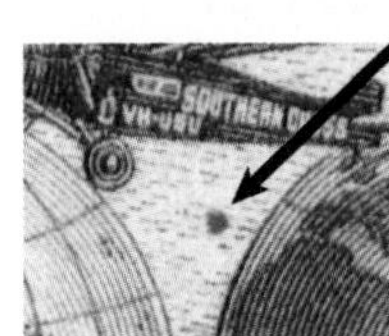

3d. 'Falling mailbag' (Pl 3. R. 3/1)

6d. Re-entry ('FO' and 'LD' double) (Pl 1 R. 5/5)

(Des and eng F. D. Manley. Recess John Ash)

1931 (19 Mar). Kingsford Smith's Flights. No wmk. P 11.

(a) Postage
121 **13** 2d. rose-red 2·25 1·00
122 3d. blue 8·50 7·00
a. 'Falling mailbag' £120 £100

(b) Air. Inscr 'AIR MAIL SERVICE' at sides
123 **13** 6d. violet 6·50 17·00
a. Re-entry 50·00 £110
121/123 *Set of 3* 15·00 22·00

15

17 Superb Lyrebird

(Typo John Ash).

1931–36. W **15**.

(a) P 13½×12½
124 **5a** ½d. orange (2.33) 11·00 5·00
125 1d. green (Die I) (10.31) 4·00 20
w. Wmk inverted 45·00 10·00
x. Wmk reversed £2000 £1300
126 1½d. red-brown (10.36) 9·50 15·00
127 2d. golden scarlet (Die III) (18.12.31) 2·75 10
w. Wmk inverted (*from booklets*) 6·00 50
128 3d. ultramarine (Die II) (30.9.32) 23·00 1·00
w. Wmk inverted £13000 £13000
129 4d. yellow-olive (2.33) 23·00 1·00
w. Wmk inverted † £10000
130 5d. orange-brown (Die II) (25.2.32) 23·00 20
w. Wmk inverted † £7000
131 1s.4d. turquoise (18.8.32) 50·00 2·50
w. Wmk inverted † £15000
124/131 *Set of 8* £130 22·00

(b) P 12
132 **1** 6d. chestnut (Die IIB) (20.4.32) 40·00 40·00
133 9d. violet (Die IIB) (20.4.32) 45·00 2·25
a. Die II (substituted cliché) in pair with Die IIB £350 £275
134 2s. maroon (Die II) (6.8.35) 12·00 1·00
135 5s. grey and yellow (Die II) (12.32) £170 20·00
136 10s. grey and pink (Die II) (31.7.32) £425 £150
137 £1 grey (Die IIB) (11.35) £650 £275
138 £2 black and rose (Die II) (6.34) £4250 £600
132/138 *Set of 7* £5000 £900
136s/138s Optd 'SPECIMEN' *Set of 3* 90·00

Stamps as No. 127, but without watermark and perforated 11, are forgeries made in 1932 to defraud the PO (*Price* £400, *unused*).

For re-engraved type of No. 134, see No. 212.

For No. 133a see note below No. 45*b*.

(Des and eng F. D. Manley. Recess John Ash)

1931 (4 Nov). Air Stamp. As T **13** but inscr 'AIR MAIL SERVICE' in bottom tablet. No wmk. P 11.
139 6d. sepia 22·00 17·00

1931 (17 Nov). Air. No. 139 optd with Type O **4**.
139*a* 6d. sepia 32·00 60·00

This stamp was not restricted to official use but was on general sale to the public.

(Des and eng F. D. Manley. Recess John Ash)

1932 (15 Feb). No wmk. P 11.
140 **17** 1s. green 45·00 2·75
a. Yellow-green 55·00 5·00

18 Sydney Harbour Bridge

19 Laughing Kookaburra

(Des R. A. Harrison. Eng F. D. Manley. Printed John Ash)

1932 (14 Mar). Opening of Sydney Harbour Bridge.

(a) Recess. No wmk. P 11
141 **18** 2d. scarlet 7·00 4·25
142 3d. blue 10·00 11·00
143 5s. blue-green £425 £200

(b) Typo. W **15**. *P 10½*
144 **18** 2d. scarlet 7·00 2·00
141/144 *Set of 4* £425 £200

Stamps as No. 144 without wmk and perf 11 are forgeries made in 1932 to defraud the PO (*Price* £1000, *unused*).

The used price for No. 143 is for a cancelled to order example. Postally used examples are worth more.

(Des and eng F. D. Manley. Recess John Ash)

1932 (1 June). W **15**. P 13½×12½.
146 **19** 6d. red-brown 18·00 55
w. Wmk inverted † £7000

20 Melbourne and R. Yarra

21 Merino Ram

(Des and eng F. D. Manley. Recess John Ash)

1934 (2 July–Aug). Centenary of Victoria. W **15**. P 10½.
147 **20** 2d. orange-vermilion 4·75 1·75
a. Perf 11½ (8.34) 14·00 1·75
148 3d. blue 4·75 5·50
a. Perf 11½ (8.34) 7·50 8·00
149 1s. black 55·00 22·00
a. Perf 11½ (8.34) 65·00 24·00
147/149 *Set of 3* 55·00 26·00
147a/149a *Set of 3* 75·00 30·00

Stamps were originally issued perforated 10½, but the gauge was subsequently changed to 11½ in August 1934 due to difficulties in separating stamps in the first perforation.

(Des and eng F. D. Manley. Recess John Ash)

1934 (1–26 Nov). Death Centenary of Captain John Macarthur (founder of Australian sheep farming). W **15**. P 11½.
150 **21** 2d. carmine-red (A) 8·00 1·75
150*a* 2d. carmine-red (B) (26.11) 26·00 3·25
151 3d. blue 17·00 18·00
152 9d. bright purple 38·00 50·00
150/152 *Set of 3* (excluding No. 150*a*) 55·00 60·00

Type A of the 2d. shows shading on the hill in the background varying from light to dark (as illustrated). Type B has the shading almost uniformly dark.

22 Hermes

23 Cenotaph, Whitehall

(Des F. D. Manley. Eng E. Broad and F. D. Manley. Recess John Ash until April 1940; W. C. G. McCracken thereafter)

1934 (1 Dec)–**48**.

(a) No wmk. P 11
153 **22** 1s.6d. dull purple 45·00 2·00

(b) W **15**. *Chalk-surfaced paper. P 13½×14*
153*a* **22** 1s.6d. dull purple (22.10.37) 11·00 45
b. Thin rough ordinary paper (12.2.48) 2·75 1·40

(Des B Cottier; adapted and eng F. D. Manley. Recess John Ash)

1935 (18 Mar). 20th Anniversary of Gallipoli Landing. W **15**. P 13½×12½ or 11 (1s.).
154 **23** 2d. scarlet 3·25 30
155 1s. black (chalk-surfaced) 45·00 45·00

The 1s. perforated 13½×12½ is a plate proof (*Price* £1600, *unused*).

24 King George V on *Anzac*

3d. Apostrophe after second 'E' of 'GEORGE' (Sheet C, lower pane R. 4/2)

25 Amphitrite and Telephone Cable

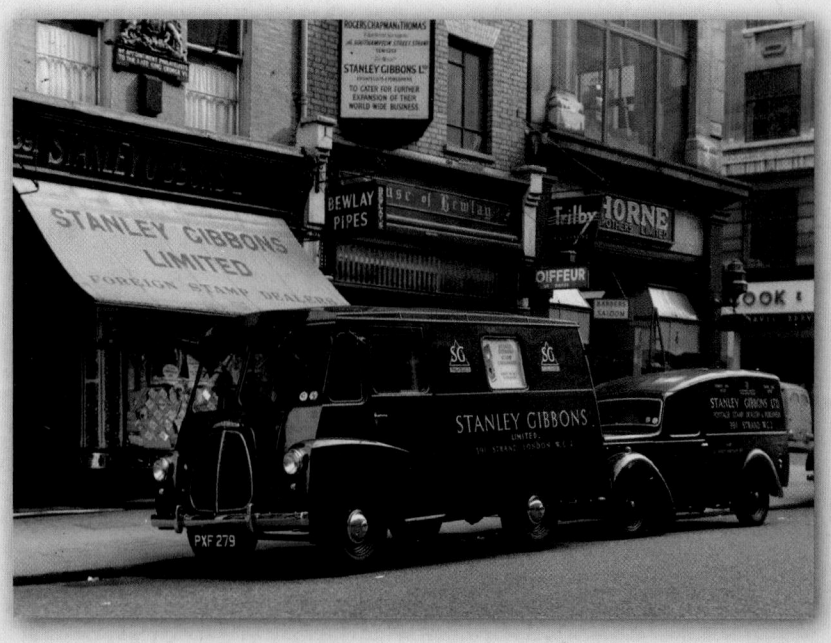

(Des and eng F. D. Manley. Recess John Ash)

1935 (2 May). Silver Jubilee. Chalk-surfaced paper. W **15** (sideways). P 11½.

156	**24**	2d. scarlet	3·25	30
		a. Printed double, one albino	£300	£150
157		3d. blue	10·00	11·00
		a. Apostrophe flaw	£120	£120
158		2s. bright violet	35·00	48·00
156/158 *Set of* 3			42·00	55·00

(Des and eng F. D. Manley. Recess John Ash)

1936 (1 Apr). Opening of Submarine Telephone Link to Tasmania. W **15**. P 11½.

159	**25**	2d. scarlet	2·75	50
160		3d. blue	4·50	2·75

26 Site of Adelaide, 1836; Old Gum Tree, Glenelg; King William St, Adelaide

(Des and eng F. D. Manley. Recess John Ash)

1936 (3 Aug). Centenary of South Australia. W **15**. P 11½.

161	**26**	2d. carmine	4·25	40
162		3d. blue	12·00	3·50
163		1s. green	22·00	14·00
161/163 *Set of* 3			35·00	16·00

27 Wallaroo

28 Queen Elizabeth

28a Queen Elizabeth

29

30 King George VI

30a

31 King George VI

32 Koala

33 Merino Ram

34 Laughing Kookaburra

35 Platypus

36 Superb Lyrebird

38 Queen Elizabeth

39 King George VI

40 King George VI and Queen Elizabeth

Dies of 3d.:

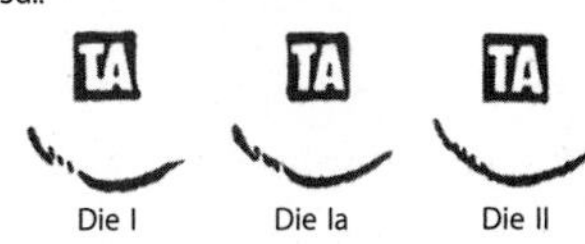

Die I　Die Ia　Die II

Die I. The letters 'TA' of 'POSTAGE' at right are joined by a white flaw; the outline of the chin consists of separate strokes.

No. 168a is a preliminary printing made with unsuitable ink and may be detected by the absence of finer details; the King's face appears whitish and the wattles are blank. The greater part of this printing was distributed to the Press with advance notices of the issue.

Die Ia. As Die I, but 'T' and 'A' have been clearly separated by individual retouches made on the plates.

Die II A completely new die. 'T' and 'A' are separate and a continuous line has been added to the chin. The outline of the cheek extends to about 1 mm above the lobe of the King's right ear.

Die III. Differs from Dies I and II in the King's left eyebrow which is shaded downwards from left to right instead of from right to left. This die also shows more of the epaulette at the right of the stamp, similar to the 1s.4d. value.

½d. Line to Kangaroo's ear (Right pane R. 6/8)

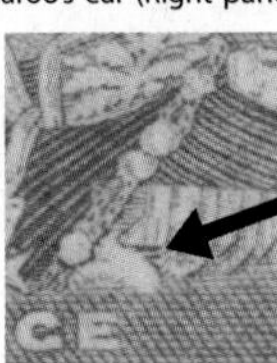

2d. Medal flaw (Right pane R. 2/5)

6d. 'Top hat' flaw (Lower plate, right pane R. 3/3)

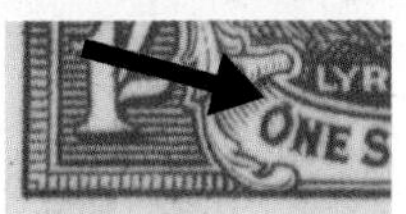

1s. Roller flaw over 'o' of 'one' (Upper plate, right pane R. 1-6/6)

(Des R. A. Harrison (T **28/30**), F. D. Manley (T **27**, **31/36**), H. Barr (T **38/39**), H. Barr and F. D. Manley (T **40**). Eng F. D. Manley and T. C. Duffell (T **34**), T. C. Duffell (revised lettering for T **28a**, **30a**), F. D. Manley and E. Broad (T **38/40**), F. D. Manley (others). All recess with John Ash, W. C. G. McCracken or 'By Authority ...' imprints)

1937–49. Chalk-surfaced paper (3d. (No. 168/168c), 5s., 10s., £1). W **15** (sideways on 5d., 9d., 5s. and 10s.).

(a) P 13½×14 (vert designs) or 14×13½ (horiz)

164	**27**	½d. orange (3.10.38)	2·50	50
165	**28**	1d. emerald-green (10.5.37)	1·25	50
166	**29**	1½d. maroon (20.4.38)	9·00	5·50
167	**30**	2d. scarlet (10.5.37)	1·25	50
168	**31**	3d. blue (Die I) (2.8.37)	65·00	25·00
		a. 'White wattles' (from 1st ptg)	£170	85·00
		b. Die Ia (2.8.37)	£160	8·50
		c. Die II (3.38)	65·00	7·00
		ca. Bright blue (ordinary thin paper) (20.12.38)	60·00	4·00
170	**32**	4d. green (1.2.38)	7·00	2·25
171	**33**	5d. purple (1.12.38)	2·50	60
172	**34**	6d. purple-brown (2.8.37)	20·00	1·50
173	**35**	9d. chocolate (1.9.38)	9·00	2·50
174	**36**	1s. grey-green (2.8.37)	50·00	2·75
175	**31**	1s. 4d. pale magenta (3.10.38)	3·50	2·50
		a. Deep magenta (1943)	5·50	2·50

(b) P 13½

176	**38**	5s. claret (1.4.38)	28·00	2·00
		a. Thin rough ordinary paper (*shades*) (4.2.48)	5·50	4·25
177	**39**	10s. dull purple (1.4.38)	50·00	17·00
		a. Thin rough ordinary paper (11.48)	50·00	35·00
		s. Optd 'SPECIMEN'	35·00	
178	**40**	£1 bluish slate (1.11.38)	70·00	35·00
		a. Thin rough ordinary paper (4.4.49)	70·00	75·00
		s. Optd 'SPECIMEN'	£800	
164/178 *Set of* 14			£250	65·00

(c) P 15×14 (vert designs) or 14×15 (horiz) (1d. and 2d. redrawn with background evenly shaded and lettering strengthened)

179	**27**	½d. orange (28.1.42)	55	70
		a. Line to kangaroo's ear	45·00	35·00
		b. Coil pair (1942)	23·00	40·00
		ba. Coil block of four (1943)	£1000	
180	**28a**	1d. emerald-green (1.8.38)	10·00	60
181		1d. maroon (10.12.41)	3·50	1·00
		a. Coil pair (1942)	14·00	28·00
182	**29**	1½d. maroon (21.11.41)	8·00	17·00
183		1½d. emerald-green (10.12.41)	2·50	2·50
184	**30a**	2d. scarlet (11.7.38)	10·00	20
		a. Coil pair (10.41)	£350	£450
		b. Medal flaw	£350	£130
		w. Wmk inverted (*from booklets*)	16·00	75
185		2d. bright purple (10.12.41)	75	2·00
		a. Coil pair (1942)	50·00	75·00
		b. Medal flaw	85·00	£100
		w. Wmk inverted (*from coils*)	£170	£130
186	**31**	3d. bright blue (Die III) (11.40)	45·00	4·00
187		3d. purple-brown (Die III) (10.12.41)	1·25	10
188	**32**	4d. green (10.42)	1·00	10
		w. Wmk inverted	—	£10000
189	**33**	5d. purple (17.12.45)	65	2·25
190	**34**	6d. red-brown (6.42)	3·50	10
		a. Purple-brown (1944)	1·75	10
		ab. 'Top hat' flaw	£1500	£1700
191	**35**	9d. chocolate (12.9.43)	1·00	30
192	**36**	1s. grey-green (29.3.41)	2·75	10
		a. Roller flaw	85·00	38·00
		w. Wmk inverted	£6000	£6000
179/192 *Set of* 14			75·00	27·00

The watermark on No. 191 shows Crown to the left of C of A, on Nos. 171, 173 and 189 it is to the right, *as seen from the back of the stamp*.

For unwmkd issue, see Nos. 228/230*d*.

Thin paper. Nos. 176a, 177a, 178a. In these varieties the watermark is more clearly visible on the back and the design is much less sharp. On early printings of No. 176a the paper appears tinted.

SPECIAL COIL PERFORATION. This special perforation of large and small holes on the narrow sides of the stamps was introduced after 1939 for stamps issued in coils and was intended to facilitate separation. Where they exist they are listed as 'Coil pairs'.

The following with 'special coil' perforation were placed on sale in *sheets*: Nos. 179, 205, 222*a* (1952), 228, 230, 237, 262 (1953), 309, 311, and 314. These are listed as 'Coil blocks of four'.

Coils with 'normal' perforations also exist for Nos. 180 and 184.

41 *Governor Phillip at Sydney Cove* (J. Alcott)

2d. 'Man with tail' flaw (Left pane R. 7/1. Later retouched)

(Des and eng E. Broad and F. D. Manley. Recess J. Ash)

1937 (1 Oct). 150th Anniversary of Foundation of New South Wales. W **15**. P 13½×14.

193	**41**	2d. scarlet	3·75	30
		a. 'Man with tail' flaw	£750	£140
194		3d. bright blue	9·50	2·25
195		9d. purple	30·00	14·00
193/195 *Set of* 3			38·00	15·00

42 AIF and Nurse

(Des and eng F. D. Manley from drawing by Virgil Reilly. Recess W. C. G. McCracken)

1940 (15 July). Australian Imperial Forces. W **15** (sideways). P 14×13½.

196	**42**	1d. green	2·50	2·75
197		2d. scarlet	2·00	1·50
198		3d. blue	18·00	11·00
199		6d. brown-purple	35·00	30·00
196/199 *Set of* 4			50·00	40·00

(43)　**(44)**　**(45)**

(Opts designed by F. D. Manley)

1941 (10 Dec). Nos. 184, 186 and 171 surch with T **43/5**.

200	**30a**	2½d. on 2d. scarlet (V.)	1·00	70
		a. Pair, one without surcharge	£20000	
		b. Medal flaw	£450	£250
201	**31**	3½d. on 3d. bright blue (Y. on Black)	2·50	2·50
202	**33**	5½d. on 5d. purple (V.)	4·25	7·00
200/202 *Set of* 3			7·00	9·00

Nos. 200/202 were prepared in connection with the imposition of a ½d. 'war tax' increase on most postage rates.

One sheet of the 2½d. on 2d. was discovered showing the surcharge omitted on R. 1/4 and R. 1/5.

46 Queen Elizabeth

46a Queen Elizabeth

47 King George VI

48 King George VI

49 King George VI

50 Emu

(Des F. D. Maley. Eng F. D. Manley and T. C. Duffell (T **46/46a**) or F. D. Manley (others))

1942–50. Recess. W **15**. P 15×14.

203	**46**	1d. brown-purple (2.1.43)	3·25	10
		a. Coil pair (1944)	22·00	42·00
204	**46a**	1½d. green (1.12.42)	3·00	10
		w. Wmk inverted	†	£10000
205	**47**	2d. bright purple (4.12.44)	1·75	2·00
		b. Coil pair (1.49)	90·00	£120
		ba. Coil block of four (5.50)	£2750	
206	**48**	2½d. scarlet (7.1.42)	60	10
		a. Imperf (pair)*	£6500	
		w. Wmk inverted (*from booklets*)	7·50	2·25
207	**49**	3½d. bright blue (3.42)	3·75	60
		a. Deep blue	2·50	60
208	**50**	5½d. slate-blue (12.2.42)	1·25	20
203/208 *Set of* 6			11·00	2·50

*No. 206a comes in horizontal pair with the right-hand stamp completely imperforate and the left-hand stamp imperforate at right only.

Coils with normal perforations exist for 1d.

For stamps as Nos. 204/205 but without watermark see Nos. 229/230.

The following items are understood to have been the subject of unauthorised leakages from the Commonwealth Note and Stamp Printing Branch and are therefore not listed by us.

It is certain that none of this material was distributed to post offices for issue to the public.

Imperforate all round. 1d. Princess Elizabeth; 1½d. Queen; 2½d. King; 4d. Koala; 6d. Kookaburra; 9d. Platypus; 1s. Lyrebird (small) (also imperf three sides); 1s.6d. Air Mail (T **22**); 2½d. Mitchell; 2½d. Newcastle (also imperf three sides or imperf vertically).

Also 2½d. Peace, unwatermarked; 2½d. King, *tête-bêche*; 3½d. Newcastle, in dull ultramarine; 2½d. King on 'toned' paper.

52 Duke and Duchess of Gloucester

(Des F. D. Manley. Eng F. D. Manley and T. C. Duffell. Recess)

1945 (19 Feb). Arrival of Duke and Duchess of Gloucester in Australia. W **15**. P 14½.

209	**52**	2½d. lake	20	10
210		3½d. ultramarine	40	1·25
211		5½d. indigo	50	1·25
209/211 *Set of 3*			1·00	2·25

A

B

1945 (24 Dec). Kangaroo type, as No. 134, but re-engraved as B. W **15**. P 12.

212	**1**	2s. maroon	4·50	7·50
		w. Wmk inverted	†	£24000

No. 134 has two background lines between the value circle and 'TWO SHILLINGS'; No. 212 has only one line in this position. There are also differences in the shape of the letters.

53 Star and Wreath

54 Flag and dove

55 Angel and Queensland

56 Sir Thomas Mitchell

(Des F. D. Manley (2½d.), F. D. Manley and G. Lissenden (3½d.), G. Lissenden (5½d.). Eng F. D. Manley. Recess)

1946 (18 Feb). Victory Commemoration. W **15** (sideways on 5½d.). P 14½.

213	**53**	2½d. scarlet	20	10
214	**54**	3½d. blue	75	1·75
215	**55**	5½d. green	75	1·00
213/215 *Set of 3*			1·50	2·50

These designs were re-issued in 1995 with face values in decimal currency.

(Des F. D. Manley. Eng F. D. Manley and T. C. Duffell. Recess)

1946 (14 Oct). Centenary of Mitchell's Exploration of Central Queensland. W **15**. P 14½.

216	**56**	2½d. scarlet	25	10
217		3½d. blue	75	2·00
218		1s. grey-olive	75	75
216/218 *Set of 3*			1·60	2·50

57 Lt. John Shortland RN

58 Steel Foundry

59 Coal Carrier/Cranes

(Des and eng G. Lissenden (5½d.), F. D. Manley (others). Recess)

1947 (8 Sept). 150th Anniversary of City of Newcastle, New South Wales. W **15** (sideways on 3½d.). P 14½ or 15×14 (2½d.).

219	**57**	2½d. lake	20	10
220	**58**	3½d. blue	60	1·50
221	**59**	5½d. green	60	75
219/221 *Set of 3*			1·25	2·00

60 Queen Elizabeth II when Princess

(Des R. A. Harrison. Eng. F. D. Manley. Recess)

1947 (20 Nov)–**52**. Marriage of Princess Elizabeth. P 14×15.

*(a) W **15** (sideways)*

222	**60**	1d. purple	15	1·00

(b) No wmk

222*a*	**60**	1d. purple (8.48)	10	10
		b. Coil pair (1.50)	2·25	5·50
		c. Coil block of four (9.52)	5·50	

No. 222 was originally prepared to mark the 21st birthday of Princess Elizabeth, but production delays resulted in it being issued on her wedding day instead.

61 Hereford Bull

61a Hermes and Globe

62 Aboriginal Art

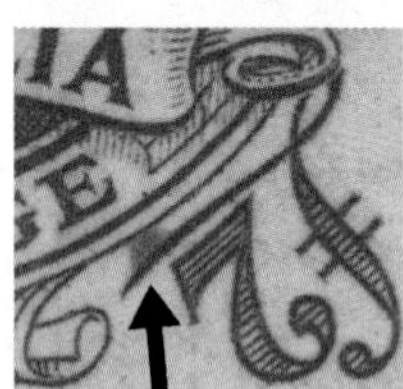

62a Commonwealth Coat of Arms

Roller flaw below 'E' of 'POSTAGE' (R. 4/1 and 5/1). Later retouched.

(Des G. Sellheim (T **62**), F. D. Manley (others). Eng G. Lissenden (T **62**), F. D. Manley (1s.3d., 1s.6d., 5s.), F. D. Manley and R. J. Becker (10s., £1, £2). Recess)

1948 (16 Feb)–**56**. W **15**.

(a) Wmk sideways. P 14½

223	**61**	1s.3d. brown-purple	2·50	2·00
223*a*	**61a**	1s.6d. blackish brown (1.9.49)	1·00	10
224	**62**	2s. chocolate	1·50	10

(b) Wmk upright. P 14½×13½

224*a*	**62a**	5s. claret (11.4.49)	4·00	20
		ab. Thin paper (1951)	£110	75·00
224*b*		10s. purple (3.10.49)	20·00	85
		bws. Wmk inverted, optd 'SPECIMEN'.	£5000	
224*c*		£1 blue (28.11.49)	42·00	4·25
224*d*		£2 green (16.1.50)	85·00	16·00
		da. Roller flaw	£160	£110
223/224*d* *Set of 7*			£140	21·00
224*bs*/224*ds* *Optd 'SPECIMEN' Set of 3*			£160	

(c) No wmk. P 14½

224*e*	**61a**	1s.6d. blackish brown (2.12.56)	12·00	1·50
224*f*	**62**	2s. chocolate (27.6.56)	8·50	1·50

The frames of Nos. 224*b* and 224*c*/224*d* differ slightly from Type **62a**. No. 224*aab* is an emergency printing on white Harrison paper instead of the toned paper used for No. 224*a*.

63 William J. Farrer

64 F. von Mueller

65 Boy Scout

(Des and eng F. D. Manley. Recess)

1948 (12 July). William J. Farrer (wheat research) Commemoration. W **15**. P 15×14.

225	**63**	2½d. scarlet	40	10

(Des and eng F. D. Manley. Recess)

1948 (13 Sept). Sir Ferdinand von Mueller (botanist) Commemoration. W **15**. P 15×14.

226	**64**	2½d. lake	30	10

(Des and eng F. D. Manley. Recess)

1948 (15 Nov). Pan-Pacific Scout Jamboree, Wonga Park. W **15** (sideways). P 14×15.

227	**65**	2½d. lake	30	10

See also No. 254.

½d. Sky retouch (normally unshaded near hill) (right pane R. 6/8) (No. 228*a* retouched in 1951)

1s. 'Green mist' retouch. A large area to the left of the bird's feathers is recut (Upper plate left pane R. 9/3)

1948–56. No wmk. P 15×14 or 14×15 (9d.).

228	**27**	½d. orange (15.9.49)	20	10
		a. Line to kangaroo's ear	38·00	40·00
		b. Sky retouch	60·00	65·00
		c. Coil pair (1950)	1·00	3·25
		ca. Line to kangaroo's ear	95·00	
		cb. Sky retouch (in pair)	£350	
		d. Coil block of four (1953)	2·75	
229	**46a**	1½d. green (17.8.49)	2·00	2·75
230	**47**	2d. bright purple (20.12.48)	1·75	3·25
		aa. Coil pair	3·50	14·00
230*a*	**32**	4d. green (18.8.56)	2·00	2·25
230*b*	**34**	6d. purple-brown (18.8.56)	9·00	1·00
230*c*	**35**	9d. chocolate (13.12.56)	18·00	4·50
230*d*	**36**	1s. grey-green (13.12.56)	5·00	1·25
		da. 'Green mist' retouch	£4500	£3250
		db. Roller flaw	42·00	30·00
228/230*d* *Set of 7*			35·00	13·50

66 *Henry Lawson* (Sir Lionel Lindsay)

67 Mounted Postman and Convair CV 240 Aircraft

(Des F. D. Manley. Eng. E. R. M. Jones. Recess)

1949 (17 June). Henry Lawson (poet) Commemoration. P 15×14.

231	**66**	2½d. maroon	40	10

(Des Sir Daryl Lindsay and F. D. Manley. Eng F. D. Manley. Recess)

1949 (10 Oct). 75th Anniversary of Founding of UPU. P 15×14.

232	**67**	3½d. ultramarine	60	1·00

68 John, Lord Forrest of Bunbury

69 Queen Elizabeth

70 King George VI

(Des and eng F. D. Manley. Recess)

1949 (28 Nov). John, Lord Forrest of Bunbury (explorer and politician) Commemoration. W **15**. P 15×14.

233	**68**	2½d. lake	60	10

(Des and eng F. D. Manley. Recess)

1950 (12 Apr)–**52**.

*(a) W **15**. P 15×14*

234	**70**	2½d. scarlet (12.4.50)	10	10
235		3d. scarlet (28.2.51)	15	25
		aa. Coil pair (4.51)	17·00	50·00

(b) No wmk

236	**69**	1½d. green (19.6.50)	1·25	40
237		2d. yellow-green (28.3.51)	15	10
		a. Coil pair	6·50	10·00
		b. Coil block of four (11.52)	13·00	
237*c*	**70**	2½d. purple-brown (23.5.51)	15	80
237*d*		3d. grey-green (14.11.51)	15	10
		da. Coil pair (12.51)	24·00	55·00
234/237*d* *Set of 6*			1·75	1·50

On 14 October 1951 No. 235 was placed on sale in sheets of 144 originally intended for use in stamp booklets. These sheets contain three panes of 48 (16×3) with horizontal gutter margin between.

71 Aborigine

72 Reproduction of First Stamps of New South Wales

73 Reproduction of First Stamps of Victoria

(Des and eng F. D. Manley. Recess)

1950 (14 Aug). W **15**. P 15×14.

238	**71**	8½d. brown	1·00	1·00

For T **71** in a larger size, see Nos. 253/253*b*.

(Des and eng G. Lissenden (T **72**), E. R. M. Jones (T **73**). Recess)

1950 (27 Sept). Centenary of First Adhesive Postage Stamps in Australia. P 15×14.

239	**72**	2½d. maroon	50	10
		a. Horiz pair. Nos. 239/240	1·00	1·50
240	**73**	2½d. maroon	50	10

Nos. 239/240 were printed alternately in vertical columns throughout the sheet.

74 Sir Edmund Barton **75** Sir Henry Parkes

76 *Opening First Federal Parliament* (T. Roberts) **77** Federal Parliament House, Canberra

(Des and eng F. D. Manley. Recess)

1951 (1 May). 50th Anniversary of Commonwealth of Australia. P 15×14.

241 **74** 3d. lake ... 1·50 10
a. Horiz pair. Nos. 241/242 ... 3·00 3·00
242 **75** 3d. lake ... 1·50 10
243 **76** 5½d. blue ... 65 2·25
244 **77** 1s.6d. purple-brown ... 1·25 50
241/244 *Set of 4* ... 4·50 2·75

Nos. 241/242 were printed alternately in vertical columns throughout the sheet.

78 E. H. Hargraves **79** C. J. Latrobe

(Des and eng F. D. Manley. Recess)

1951 (2 July). Centenaries of Discovery of Gold in Australia and of Responsible Government in Victoria. P 15×14.

245 **78** 3d. maroon ... 1·10 10
a. Horiz pair. Nos. 245/246 ... 2·25 3·75
246 **79** 3d. maroon ... 1·10 10

Nos. 245/246 were printed alternately in vertical columns throughout the sheet.

80 **81** King George VI **82**

(Des E. R. M. Jones (7½d.), F. D. Manley (others) Eng. F. D. Manley. Recess)

1951–52. W **15** (sideways on 1s.0½d.). P 14½ (1s.0½d.) or 15×14 (others).

247 **80** 3½d. brown-purple (28.11.51) ... 10 10
a. Imperf between (horiz pair) ... £18000
248 4½d. scarlet (20.2.52) ... 15 1·25
249 6½d. brown (20.2.52) ... 20 2·00
250 6½d. emerald-green (9.4.52) ... 30 55
251 **81** 7½d. blue (31.10.51) ... 15 1·50
a. Imperf three sides (vert pair) ... £25000
252 **82** 1s.0½d. indigo (19.3.52) ... 1·50 1·00
247/252 *Set of 6* ... 2·10 5·75

No. 251a occurs on the left-hand vertical row of one sheet.

(Des F. D. Manley. Eng E. R. M. Jones. Recess)

1952 (19 Mar)–**65.** P 14½.

*(a) W **15** (sideways*)*

253 2s.6d. deep brown ... 2·25 1·00
aw. Wmk Crown to left of C of A ... £5000 £1500

(b) No wmk

253*b* 2s.6d. deep brown (30.1.57) ... 3·50 75
ba. Sepia (10.65) ... 12·00 14·00

Design:—2s.6d. As T **71** but larger (21×25½ *mm*).

*The normal sideways watermark on No. 253 shows Crown to right of C of A, *as seen from the back of the stamp.*

No. 253*bba* was an emergency printing and can easily be distinguished from No. 253*b* as it is on white Harrison paper, No. 253*b* being on toned paper.

(Des and eng F. D. Manley. Recess)

1952 (19 Nov). Pan-Pacific Scout Jamboree, Greystanes. As T **65**, but inscr '1952-53'. W **15** (sideways). P 14×15.

254 3½d. brown-lake ... 20 10

83 Butter **84** Wheat **85** Beef

(Des PO artists; adapted G. Lissenden. Typo)

1953 (11 Feb). Food Production. P 14½.

255 **83** 3d. emerald ... 30 10
a. Strip of 3. Nos. 255/257 ... 1·60 2·75
256 **84** 3d. emerald ... 30 10
257 **85** 3d. emerald ... 30 10
258 **83** 3½d. scarlet ... 30 10
a. Strip of 3. Nos. 258/260 ... 1·60 2·75
259 **84** 3½d. scarlet ... 30 10
260 **85** 3½d. scarlet ... 30 10
255/260 *Set of 6* ... 3·00 55

The three designs in each denomination appear in rotation, both horizontally and vertically, throughout the sheet.

86 Queen Elizabeth II **87** Queen Elizabeth II

(Des F. D. Manley from photograph by Dorothy Wilding Ltd. Eng D. Cameron. Recess)

1953–56. P 15×14.

(a) No wmk

261 **86** 1d. purple (19.8.53) ... 15 15
261*a* 2½d. blue (23.6.54) ... 20 15
262 3d. deep green (17.6.53) ... 20 10
aa. Coil pair ... 5·00 8·00
ab. Coil block of four (9.53) ... 15·00
262*a* 3½d. brown-red (2.7.56) ... 1·00 30
262*b* 6½d. orange (9.56) ... 1·75 2·75

*(b) W **15***

263 **86** 3½d. brown-red (21.4.53) ... 20 10
263*a* 6½d. orange (23.6.54) ... 3·00 50
261/263*a Set of 7* ... 6·00 3·50

(Des and eng F. D. Manley. Recess)

1953 (25 May). Coronation. P 15×14.

264 **87** 3½d. scarlet ... 40 10
265 7½d. violet ... 75 1·40
266 2s. dull bluish green ... 2·50 2·50
264/266 *Set of 3* ... 3·25 3·50

88 Young Farmers and Calf

(Des PO artist; adapted P. E. Morriss. Eng E. R. M. Jones. Recess)

1953 (3 Sept). 25th Anniversary of Australian Young Farmers' Clubs. P 14½.

267 **88** 3½d. red-brown and deep green ... 10 10

89 Lt.-Gov. D. Collins **90** Lt.-Gov. W. Paterson

91 Sullivan Cove, Hobart, 1804

(Des E. R. M. Jones, eng D. Cameron (T **89/90**); des and eng G. Lissenden (T **91**). Recess)

1953 (23 Sept). 150th Anniversary of Settlement in Tasmania. P 15×14.

268 **89** 3½d. brown-purple ... 50 10
a. Horiz pair. Nos. 268/269 ... 1·00 1·75
269 **90** 3½d. brown-purple ... 50 10
270 **91** 2s. green ... 1·25 3·25
268/270 *Set of 3* ... 2·00 3·25

Nos. 268/269 were printed alternately in vertical columns throughout the sheet.

92 Stamp of 1853

(Des R. L. Beck; eng G. Lissenden. Recess)

1953 (11 Nov). Tasmanian Postage Stamp Centenary. P 14½.

271 **92** 3d. rose-red ... 20 40

93 Queen Elizabeth II and Duke of Edinburgh

94 Queen Elizabeth II

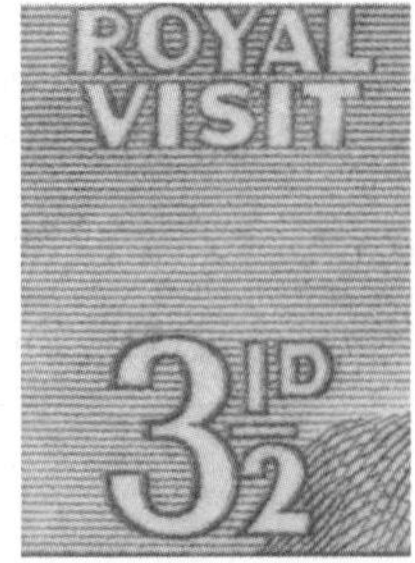

Re-entry. Vertical lines doubled in 'ROYAL VISIT' and '3½D'. (Lower plate left pane R. 8/2)

(Des and eng F. D. Manley; border and lettering on 7½d. des by R. M. Warner. Recess)

1954 (2 Feb). Royal Visit. P 14.

272 **93** 3½d. scarlet ... 20 10
a. Re-entry ... 45·00 21·00
273 **94** 7½d. purple ... 30 1·25
274 **93** 2s. dull bluish green ... 60 65
272/274 *Set of 3* ... 1·00 1·75

95 'Telegraphic Communications' **96** Red Cross and Globe

(Des R. M. Warner. Eng P. E. Morriss. Recess)

1954 (7 Apr). Australian Telegraph System Centenary. P 14.

275 **95** 3½d. brown-red ... 20 10

(Des B. Stewart. Eng P. E. Morriss. Design recess: cross typo)

1954 (9 June). 40th Anniversary of Australian Red Cross Society. P 14½.

276 **96** 3½d. ultramarine and scarlet ... 20 10

97 Mute Swan **98** Locomotives of 1854 and 1954

(Des R. L. Beck. Eng G. Lissenden. Recess)

1954 (2 Aug). Western Australian Postage Stamp Centenary. P 14½.

277 **97** 3½d. black ... 20 10

(Des R. M. Warner. Eng G. Lissenden. Recess)

1954 (13 Sept). Australian Railways Centenary. P 14.

278 **98** 3½d. purple-brown ... 30 10

99 Territory Badge **100** Olympic Games Symbol **101** Rotary Symbol, Globe and Flags

(Des F. D. Manley. Eng G. Lissenden. Recess)

1954 (17 Nov). Australian Antarctic Research. P 14½×13½.

279 **99** 3½d. grey-black ... 20 10

(Des R. L. Beck. Eng P. E. Morriss. Recess)

1954 (1 Dec)–**55.** Olympic Games Propaganda. P 14.

280 **100** 2s. deep bright blue ... 1·00 1·00
280*a* 2s. deep bluish green (30.11.55) ... 2·00 2·50

(Des and eng D. Cameron. Recess)

1955 (23 Feb). 50th Anniversary of Rotary International. P 14×14½.

281 **101** 3½d. carmine ... 10 10

101a Queen Elizabeth II **101b** Queen Elizabeth II **102** Queen Elizabeth II

(Des F. D. Manley from bas-relief by W. L. Bowles. Eng D. Cameron (7½d.), G. Lissenden (others). Recess)

1955 (9 Mar)–**57.** P 15×14 (T **101a/101b**) or 14½ (T **102**).

*(a) W **15** (sideways)*

282 **102** 1s.0½d. deep blue ... 1·00 1·25

(b) No wmk

282*a*	**101a**	4d. lake (13.3.57)	55	10
		ab. Booklet pane of 6	7·50	
282*b*	**101b**	7½d. violet (13.11.57)	1·25	1·50
		ba. Double print	£5500	
282*c*	**101a**	10d. deep grey-blue (6.3.57)	60	1·00
282*d*	**102**	1s.7d. red-brown (13.3.57)	1·25	45
282/282*d* *Set of 5*			4·25	3·75

No. 282*a*ab from booklet SB33 has the outer edges of the pane imperforate, producing single stamps with one or two adjacent sides imperforate.

The doubling on No. 282*b*ba affects the lower part of the design only.

103 American Memorial, Canberra

104 Cobb & Co. Coach (from etching by Sir Lionel Lindsay)

(Des R. L. Beck (head by F. D. Manley). Eng F. D. Manley. Recess)

1955 (4 May). Australian–American Friendship. P 14×14½.

283	**103**	3½d. violet-blue	10	10

(Design adapted and eng by F. D. Manley. Recess)

1955 (6 July). Mail-coach Pioneers Commemoration. P 14½×14.

284	**104**	3½d. blackish brown	25	10
285		2s. reddish brown	1·00	1·75

105 YMCA Emblem and Map of the World

106 Florence Nightingale and Young Nurse

Broken triangle flaw (R. 8/5)

(Des E. Thake. Eng P. E. Morriss. Design recess; emblem typo)

1955 (10 Aug). World Centenary of YMCA P 14½×14.

286	**105**	3½d. deep bluish green and red	20	10
		a. Red (emblem) omitted	£28000	
		b. Broken triangle	15·00	

Only one unused example of No. 286a has been reported. A further defective example exists used on cover.

(Des and eng F. D. Manley. Recess)

1955 (21 Sept). Nursing Profession Commemoration. P 14×14½.

287	**106**	3½d. reddish violet	10	10

107 Queen Victoria

108 Badges of New South Wales, Victoria and Tasmania

(Des and eng D. Cameron. Recess)

1955 (17 Oct). Centenary of First South Australian Postage Stamps. P 14½.

288	**107**	3½d. green	10	10

Imperf pairs of No. 288 are known. They come from die proof blocks of four.

(Des and eng F. D. Manley. Recess)

1956 (26 Sept). Centenary of Responsible Government in New South Wales, Victoria and Tasmania. P 14½×14.

289	**108**	3½d. brown-lake	10	10

109 Arms of Melbourne

110 Olympic Torch and Symbol

111 Collins Street, Melbourne

112 Melbourne across R. Yarra

(Des P. E. Morriss; eng F. D. Manley (4d.). Des and eng F. D. Manley (7½d.) Recess. Des and photo Harrison from photographs by M. Murphy and sketches by L. Coles (1s.). Des and photo Courvoisier from photographs by M. Murphy (2s.))

1956 (31 Oct). Olympic Games, Melbourne. P 14½ (4d.), 14×14½ (7½d., 1s.) or 11½ (2s.).

290	**109**	4d. carmine-red	30	10
291	**110**	7½d. deep bright blue	55	1·40
292	**111**	1s. multicoloured	70	30
293	**112**	2s. multicoloured	1·40	2·75
290/293 *Set of 4*			2·75	4·00

A 3½d. value, as T **109**, was prepared, but not issued following a postage rate increase. Archive examples of the stamps and a 3s.6d. booklet containing two panes of six were released into the market in the 1980s.

115 South Australia Coat of Arms

116 Map of Australia and Caduceus

(Des and eng P. E. Morriss. Recess)

1957 (17 Apr). Centenary of Responsible Government in South Australia. P 14½.

296	**115**	4d. red-brown	10	10

(Des J. E. Lyle; adapted B. Stewart. Eng D. Cameron. Recess)

1957 (21 Aug). Flying Doctor Service. P 14½×14.

297	**116**	7d. ultramarine	15	10

117 'The Spirit of Christmas'

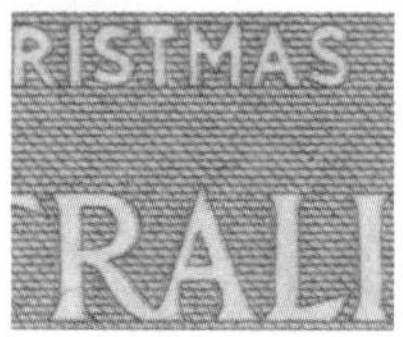

Re-entry. 'ISTMAS' and 'TRALI' double. (Upper plate left pane R. 10/1)

(Des and eng D. Cameron from a painting by Sir Joshua Reynolds. Recess)

1957 (6 Nov). Christmas. P 14½×14.

298	**117**	3½d. scarlet	10	20
		a. Re-entry	9·50	14·00
299		4d. purple	10	10

118 Lockheed L.1049 Super Constellation Airliner

Re-entry on final 'A' of 'AUSTRALIA' (Upper plate right pane R. 7/6)

(Des and eng P. E. Morriss. Recess)

1958 (6 Jan). Inauguration of Australian 'Round the World' Air Service. P 14½×14.

301	**118**	2s. deep blue	1·00	1·00
		a. Re-entry	55·00	55·00

119 Hall of Memory, Sailor and Airman

120 Sir Charles Kingsford Smith and Fokker F.VIIa/3m *Southern Cross*

(Des and eng G. Lissenden. Recess)

1958 (10 Feb). T **119** and similar horiz design. P 14½×14.

302		5½d. brown-red	50	30
		a. Horiz pair. Nos. 302/303	1·25	4·75
303		5½d. brown-red	50	30

No. 303 shows a soldier and service-woman respectively in place of the sailor and airman. Nos. 302/303 are printed alternately in vertical columns throughout the sheet.

(Des J. E. Lyle. Eng F. D. Manley. Recess)

1958 (27 Aug). 30th Anniversary of First Air Crossing of the Tasman Sea. P 14×14½.

304	**120**	8d. deep ultramarine	60	1·00

121 Silver Mine, Broken Hill

122 The Nativity

(Des R. H. Evans; adapted and eng F. D. Manley. Recess)

1958 (10 Sept). 75th Anniversary of Founding of Broken Hill. P 14½×14.

305	**121**	4d. chocolate	30	10

(Des D. Cameron. Eng P. E. Morriss. Recess)

1958 (5 Nov). Christmas. P 14½×15.

306	**122**	3½d. deep scarlet	20	30
307		4d. deep violet	20	10

123

124

126

127

128 Queen Elizabeth II

129

Type I Short break in outer line to bottom right of '4'

Type II Line unbroken

Type A Four short lines inside '5'

Type B Five short lines inside '5'

1d. Re-entry. Line running through base of 'RALIA' (Lower right plate, right pane R. 1/8).

3½d. Re-entry to 'E' and left frame (Upper left plate, left pane R. 1/10)

(Des G. Lissenden from photographs by Baron Studios. Eng F. D. Manley (2d.), D. Cameron (3d.). P. E. Morriss (others). Recess)

1959–63. P 14×15 (horiz) or 15×14 (vert).

308	**123**	1d. deep slate-purple (2.2.59)	10	10
		a. Deep slate-lilac (1961)	2·00	30
		b. Re-entry	24·00	20·00
309	**124**	2d. brown (21.3.62)	60	20
		a. Coil pair (1962)	4·50	7·00
		b. Coil block of four (1963)	14·00	
311	**126**	3d. blue-green (20.5.59)	15	10
		a. Coil pair (8.59)	4·00	6·50
		b. Coil block of four	14·00	
312	**127**	3½d. deep green (18.3.59)	15	15
		a. Re-entry	25·00	25·00
313	**128**	4d. carmine-lake (Type I) (2.2.59)	3·00	10
		a. Carmine-red	3·00	10
		ab. Booklet pane of 6 (18.3.59)	20·00	
		b. Type II	3·00	10
		ba. Carmine-red	3·00	10

314	**129**	5d. deep blue (Type A or B) (1.10.59)	1·50	10
		a. Vert *se-tenant* pair (A and B)	3·50	6·50
		b. Coil pair (18.7.60)	10·00	15·00
		c. Coil block of four (7.61)	55·00	
		d. Booklet pane of 6 (23.3.60)	11·00	
		da. Imperf between (horiz pair)	£11000	
308/314 *Set of 6*			4·75	65

No. 313. Produced in printer's sheets, of 640 split into sheets of 160 for issue. Type I occurs on the two upper sheets from the printers' sheet and on ten positions from the left pane of the lower right sheet. Type II occurs on all stamps from the lower sheets except for ten positions from the left pane of lower right sheet.

No. 314. Both types occur in alternate horizontal rows in the sheet (Type A in Row 1, Type B in Row 2, and so on), and their value is identical. Booklet pane No. 314d from SB35/SB36a contains two Type A and four Type B.

Nos. 309a/309b, 311a/311b and 314b/314c have horizontal coil perforations as described after No. 191.

Nos. 313ab from booklets SB34/SB34a and 314d from booklets SB35/SB36a have the outer edges of the panes imperforate, producing stamps with one or two adjacent sides imperforate.

A single example (imperforate at base) of No.314da is known, apparently from a miscut booklet pane.

Printings of the 2d. (from March 1965) and of the 3d. (from April 1965), both including coils, were on Helecon paper.

131 Numbat

132 Tiger Cat

133 Eastern Grey Kangaroos

134 Common Rabbit-Bandicoot

135 Platypus

136 Thylacine

137 Christmas Bells

138 Flannel Flower

139 Wattle

140 Banksia

141 Waratah

142 Aboriginal Stockman

Normal

2s. 'T' retouch (Right plate R. 6/8)

(Des Eileen Mayo (6d., 8d., 9d., 11d., 1s., 1s.2d.), B. Stewart (5s.), Margaret Stones (others). Eng P. Morriss (11d.) F. D. Manley (1s.), B. Stewart (others). Recess)

1959–64. T **131/142**. W **15** (5s.), no wmk (others). P 14×15 (1s.2d.), 15×14 (6d. to 1s.), 14½×14 (5s.) or 14½ (others).

316	**131**	6d. brown (30.9.60)	1·75	10
317	**132**	8d. red-brown (11.5.60)	1·00	10
		a. Pale red-brown (9.61)	1·50	10
318	**133**	9d. deep sepia (21.10.59)	2·25	55
319	**134**	11d. deep blue (3.5.61)	1·00	15
320	**135**	1s. deep green (9.9.59)	3·00	40
321	**136**	1s.2d. deep purple (21.3.62)	1·00	15
322	**137**	1s.6d. crimson/*yellow* (3.2.60)	2·50	1·40
323	**138**	2s. grey-blue (8.4.59)	70	10
		a. 'T' retouch	60·00	48·00
324	**139**	2s.3d. green/*maize* (9.9.59)	1·00	10
324*a*		2s.3d. yellow-green (28.10.64)	2·50	75
325	**140**	2s.5d. brown/*yellow* (16.3.60)	4·50	1·00
326	**141**	3s. scarlet (15.7.59)	1·75	20
327	**142**	5s. red-brown (26.7.61)	14·00	3·00
		a. White paper. *Brown-red* (17.6.64)	90·00	7·50
316/327 *Set of 13*			32·00	6·50

No. 327 is on toned paper. No. 327*a* was a late printing on the white paper referred to in the note below No. 360.

An experimental printing of the 11d. was made on Helecon paper in December 1963. See note below No. 362.

All printings of the 8d., 11d., 1s.2d. and 2s.3d. (No. 324*a*) were on Helecon paper from April 1965.

143 Postmaster Isaac Nichols boarding the brig *Experiment*

144 Parliament House, Brisbane, and Arms of Queensland

(Des R. Shackel; adapted and eng F. D. Manley. Recess)

1959 (22 Apr). 150th Anniversary of the Australian Post Office. P 14½×14.

331	**143**	4d. slate	15	10

(Des and eng G. Lissenden. Recess and typo)

1959 (5 June). Centenary of Self-Government in Queensland. P 14×14½.

332	**144**	4d. lilac and green	10	10

145 The Approach of the Magi

146 Girl Guide and Lord Baden-Powell

(Des and eng F. D. Manley. Recess)

1959 (4 Nov). Christmas. P 15×14.

333	**145**	5d. deep reddish violet	10	10

(Des and eng B. Stewart. Recess)

1960 (18 Aug). 50th Anniversary of Girl Guide Movement. P 14½×14.

334	**146**	5d. deep ultramarine	30	15

147 *The Overlanders* (Sir Daryl Lindsay)

148 Archer and Melbourne Cup

Two types:

I. Mane rough

II. Mane smooth

Major re-entry below rider's right arm (Lower left plate R. 4/4). This occurs only on Type I.

Type II occurs on Pane A, Row 2 Nos. 8 and 9, Row 4 Nos. 1 to 12, Row 5 Nos. 10 to 12, and on Pane C, Row 4 Nos. 5 to 12, Row 5 Nos. 1 to 9, and Rows 6 to 10 inclusive; the stamps in Row 4 Nos. 5 to 12 and Row 5 Nos. 1 to 9 are considered to be of an intermediate type with the mane as in Type II but the ear and rein being as in Type I. All the rest are Type I.

(Adapted and eng P. E. Morriss. Recess)

1960 (21 Sept). Centenary of Northern Territory Exploration. P 15×14½.

335	**147**	5d. magenta (I)	50	15
		a. Major re-entry	65·00	42·00
		b. Type II	3·50	2·00

(Des F. D. Manley. Eng G. Lissenden. Recess)

1960 (12 Oct). 100th Melbourne Cup Race Commemoration. P 14½.

336	**148**	5d. sepia	20	10

149 Queen Victoria

150 Open Bible and Candle

(Des F. D. Manley. Eng B. Stewart. Recess)

1960 (2 Nov). Centenary of First Queensland Postage Stamp. P 14½×15.

337	**149**	5d. deep myrtle-green	25	10

Re-entry. '19' of '1960' partially double (Lower left plate R. 5/2). On upper left plate R. 10/10 there is a similar partial doubling of '19' but to right of '1' and inside '9'. Same price for either variety.

(Des K. McKay. Adapted and eng B. Stewart. Recess)

1960 (9 Nov). Christmas. P 15×14½.

338	**150**	5d. carmine-red	10	10
		a. Re-entry	24·00	20·00

151 Colombo Plan Bureau Emblem

152 Melba (after bust by Sir Bertram Mackennal)

(Des and eng G. Lissenden. Recess)

1961 (30 June). Colombo Plan. P 14×14½.

339	**151**	1s. red-brown	30	10

No. 339 was issued on Helecon paper in April 1965. See note after No. 362.

(Des and eng B. Stewart. Recess)

1961 (20 Sept). Birth Centenary of Dame Nellie Melba (singer). P 14½×15.

340	**152**	5d. blue	30	15

153 Open Prayer Book and Text

(Des G. Lissenden. Eng P. E. Morriss. Recess)

1961 (8 Nov). Christmas. P 14½×14.

341	**153**	5d. brown	10	10

154 J. M. Stuart

155 Flynn's Grave and Nursing Sister

(Des W. Jardine. Eng P. E. Morriss. Recess)

1962 (25 July). Centenary of Stuart's Crossing of Australia from South to North. P 14½×15.

342	**154**	5d. brown-red	40	10

(Des F. D. Manley. Photo)

1962 (5 Sept). 50th Anniversary of Australian Inland Mission. P 13½.

343	**155**	5d. multicoloured	45	15

Used examples apparently showing the red colour omitted are now considered to be faked.

156 'Woman'

157 Madonna and Child

(Des D. Dundas. Eng G. Lissenden. Recess)

1962 (26 Sept). 'Associated Country Women of the World' Conference, Melbourne. P 14×14½.

344	**156**	5d. deep green	10	10

(Des and eng G. Lissenden. Recess)

1962 (17 Oct). Christmas. P 14½.

345	**157**	5d. violet	15	10

158 Perth and Kangaroo Paw (plant)

159 Arms of Perth and Running Track

(Des R. M. Warner (5d.), G. Hamori (2s.3d.) Photo Harrison)

1962 (1 Nov). Seventh British Empire and Commonwealth Games, Perth. P 14 (5d.) or 14½×14 (2s.3d.).

346	**158**	5d. multicoloured	50	10
		a. Red omitted	£7000	
347	**159**	2s.3d. black, red, blue and green	2·00	2·75

160 Queen Elizabeth II

161 Queen Elizabeth II and Duke of Edinburgh

(Des and eng after portraits by Anthony Buckley, P. E. Morriss (5d.), B. Stewart (2s.3d.). Recess)

1963 (18 Feb). Royal Visit. P 14½.

348	**160**	5d. deep green	35	10
349	**161**	2s.3d. brown-lake	1·50	3·25

162 Arms of Canberra and W. B. Griffin (architect)

163 Centenary Emblem

(Des and eng B. Stewart. Recess)

1963 (8 Mar). 50th Anniversary of Canberra. P 14½×14.

350	**162**	5d. deep green	15	10

(Des G. Hamori. Photo)

1963 (8 May). Red Cross Centenary. P 13½×13.

351	**163**	5d. red, grey-brown and blue	60	10

164 Blaxland, Lawson and Wentworth on Mt. York

(Des T. Alban. Eng P. E. Morriss. Recess)

1963 (28 May). 150th Anniversary of First Crossing of Blue Mountains. P 14½×14.

352	**164**	5d. ultramarine	15	10

165 'Export'

166 Queen Elizabeth II

(Des and eng B. Stewart. Recess)

1963 (28 Aug). Export Campaign. P 14½×14.

353	**165**	5d. red	10	10

(Des and eng P. E. Morriss from photograph by Anthony Buckley. Recess)

1963 (9 Oct)–**65**. P 15×14.

354	**166**	5d. deep green	1·00	10
		a. Booklet pane of 6	22·00	
		b. Imperf between (horiz pair) (31.7.64)	1·50	2·50
354*c*		5d. red (30.6.65)	55	10
		ca. Coil pair	19·00	38·00
		cb. Booklet pane of 6	22·00	

The 5d. deep green exists from both sheets and booklets on Helecon paper produced in error.

The 5d. red was issued with or without Helecon added to the ink. All coil and booklet printings included Helecon in the ink, except for a small printing produced in error. Examples of the sheet and booklet printings with Helecon ink have been found on Helecon *paper*.

Nos. 354a and 354ccb have the outer edges of the panes imperforate producing single stamps with one or two adjacent sides imperforate. They come from booklets SB37/SB38a.

No. 354b comes from sheets of uncut booklet panes containing 288 stamps (16×18) with wide margins intersecting the sheet horizontally below each third row, alternate rows of stamps imperforate between vertically and the outer left, right and bottom margins imperforate. This means that in each sheet there are 126 pairs of stamps imperf between vertically, plus a number with wide imperforate margins attached, as shown in the illustration.

A 5d. in a similar design, printed in blue and brown with vertical edges imperforate, was prepared, but not issued.

167 Tasman and *Heemskerk*

168 Dampier and *Roebuck*

169 Captain Cook (after painting by Nathaniel Dance)

170 Flinders and *Investigator*

171 Bass and *Tom Thumb* (whaleboat)

172 Admiral King and *Mermaid* (survey cutter)

£2 Roller flaw, right-hand frame line at top (R. 1/3).

(Des W. Jardine. Eng B. Stewart (4s.), P. E. Morriss (5s., 7s., 6d., £1), M. Jones (10s). Recess)

1963–65. T **167/172**. No wmk (4s.) or W **15** (others), (sideways on 5s., £1). P 14 or 14½ (5s., £1, £2).

355	**167**	4s. ultramarine (9.10.63)	3·00	55
356	**168**	5s. red-brown (25.11.64)	5·00	1·25
357	**169**	7s.6d. olive (26.8.64)	19·00	21·00
358	**170**	10s. brown-purple (26.2.64)	25·00	5·00
		a. White paper. *Deep brown-purple* (14.1.65)	25·00	8·00
359	**171**	£1 deep reddish violet (26.2.64)	38·00	16·00
		a. White paper. *Deep bluish violet* (16.11.64)	48·00	30·00
360	**172**	£2 sepia (26.8.64)	55·00	75·00
		a. Roller flaw	£225	
355/360 *Set of 6*			£120	£110
357s/360s Optd 'SPECIMEN' *Set of 4*			£475	

Nos. 358 and 359 were printed on a toned paper but all the other values are on white paper, the unwatermarked paper of the 4s. being rather thicker.

173 'Peace on Earth ...'

174 'Commonwealth Cable'

(Des R. M. Warner. Eng B. Stewart. Recess)

1963 (25 Oct). Christmas. P 14½.

361	**173**	5d. greenish blue	10	10

(Des P. E. Morriss. Photo)

1963 (3 Dec). Opening of COMPAC (Trans-Pacific Telephone Cable). Chalk-surfaced paper. P 13½.

362	**174**	2s.3d. red, blue, black and pale blue	1·50	3·00

HELECON (PHOSPHOR) STAMPS. 'Helecon', a chemical substance of the zinc sulphide group, has been incorporated in stamps in two different ways, either in the ink with which the stamps are printed, or included in the surface coating of the stamp paper.

Owing to the difficulty of identification without the use of a UV lamp we do not list the Helecon stamps separately but when in stock can supply them after testing under the lamp.

The first stamp to be issued on Helecon was the 11d. Bandicoot (No. 319) from an experimental printing of four million released to the public in December 1963. The next printing, on ordinary paper, was released in September 1964. The experimental printing was coarse, showing a lot of white dots and the colour is slate-blue, differing from both the ordinary and the later Helecon paper.

Further Helecon printings followed from March 1965. Almost all issues from No. 378 onwards were on Helecon paper or paper coated with Derby Luminescence.

175 Yellow-tailed Thornbill

176 Black-backed Magpie

177 Galah

178 Golden Whistler

179 Blue Wren

180 Scarlet Robin

181 Straw-necked Ibis

(Des Betty Temple-Watts. Photo)

1964 (11 Mar)–**65**. Birds. T **175/181** and similar designs. Chalk-surfaced paper. P 13½.

363	**175**	6d. brown, yellow, black and bluish green (19.8.64)	1·50	50
		a. Brown, yellow, black and *emerald-green*	3·00	2·75
364	**176**	9d. black, grey and pale green	1·00	2·75
365	**177**	1s.6d. pink, grey, dull purple and black	75	1·40
366	**178**	2s. yellow, black and pink (21.4.65)	1·40	50
367	**179**	2s.5d. deep royal blue, light violet-blue, yellow-orange, grey and black	1·75	3·50
		a. Ordinary paper. *Deep blue, light blue, orange-brown, blue-grey and black* (7.65)	5·00	7·50
368	**180**	2s.6d. black, red, grey and green (21.4.65)	2·50	4·50
		a. Red omitted (white breast)	£20000	£20000
369	**181**	3s. black, red, buff and yellow-green (21.4.65)	2·50	2·25
363/369 *Set of 7*			10·00	14·00

No. 367*a* was from a printing, made in 1962, on unsurfaced Wiggins Teape paper, the rest of the set being on chalk-surfaced Harrison paper. Apart from the differences in shade, the inscriptions, particularly 'BLUE WREN', stand out very much more clearly on No. 367*a*. Although two colours are apparent in both stamps, the grey and black were printed from one cylinder.

The 6d. (No. 363) and 2s.5d. were only issued on ordinary paper. The 9d. and 1s.6d. exist on ordinary or Helecon paper. The 6d. (No. 363*a*), 1s., 2s.6d. and 3s. were issued on Helecon paper only.

182 Bleriot XI Aircraft (type flown by M. Guillaux, 1914)

5d. Re-entry to second 'A' of 'AUSTRALIA' (Upper right plate, R. 4/4 subsequently retouched)

(Des K. McKay. Adapted and eng P. E. Morriss. Recess)

1964 (1 July). 50th Anniversary of First Australian Airmail Flight. P 14½×14.

No.	Type	Description	Unused	Used
370	**182**	5d. olive-green	30	10
		a. Re-entry	£275	£200
371		2s.3d. scarlet	1·75	2·75

183 Child looking at Nativity Scene

184 Simpson and his Donkey

(Des P. E. Morriss and J. Mason. Photo)

1964 (21 Oct). Christmas. Chalk-surfaced paper. P 13½.

No.	Type	Description	Unused	Used
372	**183**	5d. red, blue, buff and black	10	10
		a. Red omitted	£5000	£3250
		b. Black omitted	£3250	

The red ink is soluble and can be removed by bleaching and it is therefore advisable to obtain a certificate from a recognised expert committee before purchasing No. 372a. The used price quoted is for an example on cover.

(Des C. Andrew (after statue, Shrine of Remembrance, Melbourne). Eng E. R. M. Jones. Recess)

1965 (14 Apr). 50th Anniversary of Gallipoli Landing. P 14×14½.

No.	Type	Description	Unused	Used
373	**184**	5d. drab	50	10
374		8d. blue	75	2·50
375		2s.3d. reddish purple	1·50	2·50
373/375 *Set of 3*			2·50	4·50

185 'Telecommunications'

186 Sir Winston Churchill

(Des J. McMahon and G. Hamori. Photo)

1965 (10 May). ITU Centenary. Chalk-surfaced paper. P 13½.

No.	Type	Description	Unused	Used
376	**185**	5d. black, brown, orange-brown and blue	70	10
		a. Black (value and pylon) omitted	£5000	

(Des P. E. Morriss from photo by Karsh. Photo)

1965 (24 May). Churchill Commemoration. Chalk-surfaced paper. P 13½.

No.	Type	Description	Unused	Used
377	**186**	5d. black, pale grey, grey and light blue	30	10
		a. Pale grey (facial shading) omitted	£6000	
		b. Grey ('AUSTRALIA') omitted	†	£7000

No. 377a occurred on stamps from the bottom row of one sheet.

No. 377 exists on ordinary or Helecon paper in approximately equal quantities.

HELECON PAPER. All stamps from No. 378 were on Helecon paper, *unless otherwise stated.*

187 General Monash

188 Hargrave and 'Multiplane' Seaplane (1902)

(Des O. Foulkes and W. Walters. Photo)

1965 (23 June). Birth Centenary of General Sir John Monash (engineer and soldier). P 13½.

No.	Type	Description	Unused	Used
378	**187**	5d. multicoloured	15	10

(Des G. Hamori. Photo)

1965 (4 Aug). 50th Death Anniversary of Lawrence Hargrave (aviation pioneer). P 13½.

No.	Type	Description	Unused	Used
379	**188**	5d. purple-brown, black, yellow-ochre and purple	25	10
		a. Purple (value) omitted	£500	£500

189 ICY Emblem

190 Nativity Scene

(Des H. Fallu from UN theme. Photo)

1965 (1 Sept). International Co-operation Year. P 13½.

No.	Type	Description	Unused	Used
380	**189**	2s.3d. emerald and light blue	1·00	1·50

(Des J. Mason. Photo)

1965 (20 Oct). Christmas. P 13½.

No.	Type	Description	Unused	Used
381	**190**	5d. multicoloured	15	10
		a. Gold omitted	£5500	
		b. Blue omitted	£1000	
		c. Brown omitted	£5000	

No. 381a comes from the bottom row of a sheet in which the gold is completely omitted, the background appearing as black with 'CHRISTMAS 1965' and 'AUSTRALIA' omitted. The row above had the gold missing from the lower two-fifths of the stamp. As the gold ink can be chemically removed, No. 381a should only be purchased from a reputable source. It is not known used.

Pre-decimal stamps, including 'states' issues, remained valid for postage until 14 February 1968.

(New Currency. 100 cents = 1 dollar)

191 Queen Elizabeth II

192 Blue-faced Honeyeater

193 White-tailed Dascyllus ('Humbug Fish')

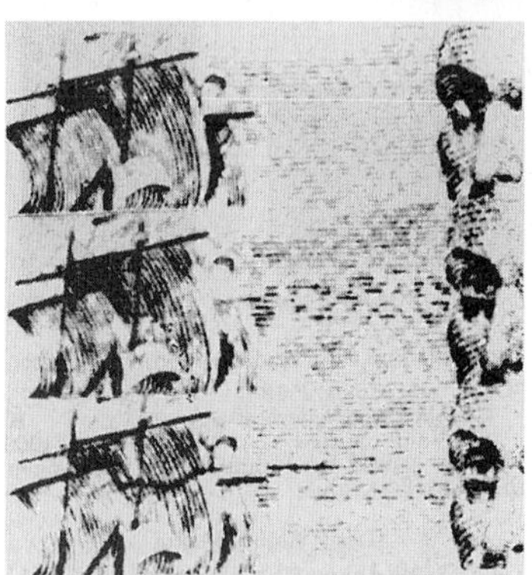

Nos. 401 (top), 401a (centre) and 401b (bottom). No. 401b shows the final form of the variety with a plate crack visible in sky and across sail (Lower sheet left pane. R. 10/1)

(Des Betty Temple-Watts (6c. (No. 387), 13c., 24c.), Eileen Mayo (7c. (No. 388) to 10c.). Recess (T **191**, 40c. to $4). Photo (others))

1966 (14 Feb)–**73**. Decimal currency. T **191/3** and similar designs, some reused from previous issues. P 15×14 (T **191**), 14 (40c., 75c., $1), 14½ (50c., $2, $4) or 13½ (others).

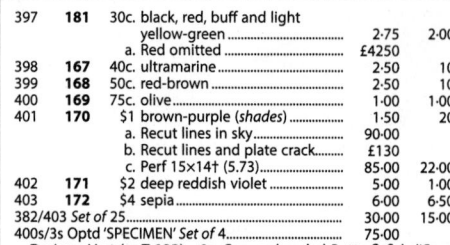

No.	Type	Description	Unused	Used
382	**191**	1c. deep red-brown	25	10
383		2c. olive-green	70	10
384		3c. slate-green	70	10
385		4c. red	20	10
		a. Booklet pane. Five stamps plus one printed label	16·00	
386	**175**	5c. brown, yellow, black and emerald-green	25	10
		a. Brown (plumage) omitted	£4750	
		b. Brown, yellow, black and blue-green (1.67)	25	20
386*c*	**191**	5c. deep blue (29.9.67)	70	10
		ca. Booklet pane. Five stamps plus one printed label	8·00	
		cb. Imperf in horiz strip of 3*	£3000	
387	**192**	6c. olive-yellow, black, blue and pale grey	1·00	1·50
		aa. Blue (eye markings) omitted	£3250	
387*a*	**191**	6c. orange (28.9.70)	1·00	10
388	**193**	7c. black, grey, salmon and brown	60	10
388*a*	**191**	7c. purple (1.10.71)	1·00	10
389	–	8c. red, yellow, blue-green and blackish green	60	1·00
390	–	9c. brown-red, purple-brown, black and light yellow-olive	60	20
391	–	10c. orange, blackish brown, pale turquoise blue and olive-brown	60	10
		a. Orange omitted	£5500	
392	–	13c. red black, grey and light turquoise-green	1·00	25
		a. Red omitted	£4500	
		b. Grey (plumage and legs) omitted	£4250	
393	**177**	15c. rose-carmine, black, grey and light bluish green	1·00	2·25
		a. Rose-carmine omitted	£7500	
		b. Grey omitted	£4000	
394	**178**	20c. yellow, black and pink	1·00	15
		a. Yellow (plumage) omitted	£5000	
395	–	24c. ultramarine, yellow, black and light brown	65	1·25
396	**180**	25c. black, red, grey and green	1·00	30
		a. Red omitted	£20000	
397	**181**	30c. black, red, buff and light yellow-green	2·75	2·00
		a. Red omitted	£4250	
398	**167**	40c. ultramarine	2·50	10
399	**168**	50c. red-brown	2·50	10
400	**169**	75c. olive	1·00	1·00
401	**170**	$1 brown-purple (*shades*)	1·50	20
		a. Recut lines in sky	90·00	
		b. Recut lines and plate crack	£130	
		c. Perf 15×14† (5.73)	85·00	22·00
402	**171**	$2 deep reddish violet	5·00	1·00
403	**172**	$4 sepia	6·00	6·50
382/403 *Set of 25*			30·00	15·00
400s/3s Optd 'SPECIMEN' *Set of 4*			75·00	

Designs: Vert (as T **193**)—8c. Copper-banded Butterflyfish ('Coral Fish'); 9c. Hermit Crab; 10c. Orange Clownfish ('Anemone Fish'). (As T **192**)—13c. Red-necked Avocet; 15c. Galah; 20c. Golden Whistler; 30c. Straw-necked Ibis. Horiz (as T **192**)—24c. Azure Kingfisher; 25c. Scarlet Robin. As T **167**—75c. Captain Cook; $1 Flinders and *Investigator*. As T **168**—$2 Bass and whaleboat; $4 Admiral King and *Mermaid* (survey cutter).

*This shows two stamps imperforate all round and one imperforate at left only.

†The exact gauge of No. 401c is 14.8×14.1. No. 401 is 14.25×13.95.

Nos. 385a (from booklets SB39/SB39a) and 386ca (from booklets SB42/SB43a) have the outer edges of the pane imperforate producing single stamps with one or two adjacent sides imperforate.

No. 385 was normally printed in Helecon ink. Early in 1967 experimental printings on different kinds of paper coated with Helecon or Derby Luminescents phosphor were put on sale. These cannot be distinguished by the naked eye.

199 Queen Elizabeth II

200 'Saving Life'

1966 (14 Feb)–**67**. Coil stamps. Photo. P 15×imperf.

No.	Type	Description	Unused	Used
404	**199**	3c. black, light brown and green	45	1·40
405		4c. black, light brown and light vermilion	35	1·40
405*a*		5c. black, light brown and new blue (29.9.67)	40	10
404/405*a* *Set of 3*			1·10	2·50

(Des L. Mason. Photo)

1966 (6 July). 75th Anniversary of Royal Life Saving Society. P 13½.

No.	Type	Description	Unused	Used
406	**200**	4c. black, bright blue and blue	15	10

201 Adoration of the Shepherds

(Des L. Stirling, after medieval engraving. Photo)

1966 (19 Oct). Christmas. P 13½.

No.	Type	Description	Unused	Used
407	**201**	4c. black and yellow-olive	10	10
		a. Value omitted	£3750	

No. 407a was caused by a partial omission of the yellow-olive so that there was no colour surrounding the white face value.

202 *Eendracht*

203 Open Bible

(Des F. Eidlitz. Photo)

1966 (24 Oct). 350th Anniversary of Dirk Hartog's Landing in Australia. P 13½.

No.	Type	Description	Unused	Used
408	**202**	4c. multicoloured	10	10
		a. Red (sphere) omitted	£5000	
		b. Gold omitted	£2750	

(Des L. Stirling. Photo)

1967 (7 Mar). 150th Anniversary of British and Foreign Bible Society in Australia. P 13½.

No.	Type	Description	Unused	Used
409	**203**	4c. multicoloured	10	10

204 Ancient Keys and Modern Lock

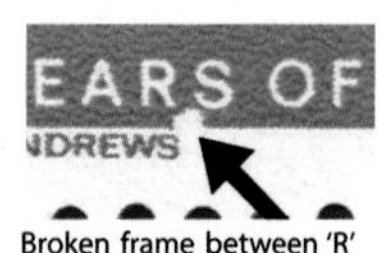

Broken frame between 'R' and 'S' of 'YEARS' (Left-hand pane, R. 8/1)

(Des G. Andrews. Photo)

1967 (5 Apr). 150th Anniversary of Australian Banking. P 13½.

No.	Type	Description	Unused	Used
410	**204**	4c. black, light blue and emerald	10	10
		a. Broken frame	3·50	

205 Lions Badge and 50 Stars **206** YWCA Emblem

(Des M. Ripper. Photo)

1967 (7 June). 50th Anniversary of Lions International. P 13½.
411 **205** 4c. black, gold and blue 10 10

(Des H. Williamson. Photo)

1967 (21 Aug). World YWCA Council Meeting, Monash University, Melbourne. P 13½.
412 **206** 4c. deep blue, ultramarine, light purple and light blue 10 10

207 Anatomical Figures

5c
(208)

(Des R. Ingpen. Photo)

1967 (20 Sept). Fifth World Gynaecology and Obstetrics Congress, Sydney. P 13½.
413 **207** 4c. black, blue and light reddish violet 10 10

1967 (29 Sept). No. 385 surch with T **208**.
414 **191** 5c. on 4c. red 25 10
a. Booklet pane. Five stamps plus one printed label .... 1·00

No. 414 was only issued in 50c. or $1 booklets, Nos. SB40/SB41ab, with the outer edges of the pane imperforate so all stamps have one or two adjacent sides imperforate. It only exists printed in Helecon ink.

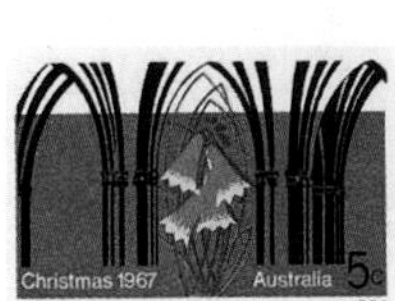

209 Christmas Bells and Gothic Arches **210** Religious Symbols

(Des M. Ripper (5c.), Erica McGilchrist (25c.). Photo)

1967. (18 Oct-27 Nov) Christmas. P 13½.
415 **209** 5c. multicoloured (18.10.67) 20 10
a. Imperf three sides (vert pair) £13000
416 **210** 25c. multicoloured (27.11.67) .... 80 1·60

No. 415a show the stamps perforated at left only.

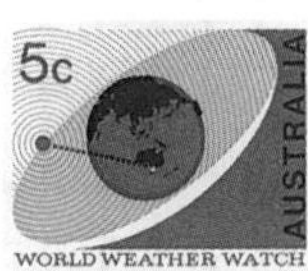

211 Satellite in Orbit **212** World Weather Map

(Des J. Mason. Photo)

1968 (20 Mar). World Weather Watch. P 13½.
417 **211** 5c. orange-brown, pale blue, black and ochre 30 10
418 **212** 20c. orange-brown, blue and black . 1·10 3·00
a. White (radio waves) omitted £1500
b. Orange-brown (triangle) omitted £4250

213 Radar Antenna **214** Kangaroo Paw (Western Australia)

(Des R. Ingpen. Photo)

1968 (20 Mar). World Telecommunications via *Intelsat II*. P 13½.
419 **213** 25c. greenish blue, black and light blue-green .... 1·00 2·00

Type I. Type II.

The 30c. was reprinted in 1971 from new cylinders so that Type II shows greater areas of white in the pink tones of the petals.

(Des Nell Wilson (6c., 30c.); R. and P. Warner (13c., 25c.); Dorothy Thornhill (15c., 20c.). Photo)

1968 (10 July)–**71**. State Floral Emblems. T **214** and similar vert designs. Multicoloured. P 13½.
420 6c. Type **214** .... 45 1·25
421 13c. Pink Heath (Victoria) 50 70
422 15c. Tasmanian Blue Gum (Tasmania) 50 40
423 20c. Sturt's Desert Pea (South Australia). 1·00 75
424 25c. Cooktown Orchid (Queensland) .... 1·10 75
425 30c. Waratah (New South Wales) (Type I) 50 10
a. Green (leaves) omitted £3750
b. Type II (29.6.71) .... 4·75 2·00
420/425 *Set of 6* .... 3·50 3·50

220 Soil Sample Analysis

(Des R. Ingpen. Photo)

1968 (6 Aug). International Soil Science Congress and World Medical Association Assembly. T **220** and similar horiz design. P 13½.
426 **220** 5c. orange-brown, stone, greenish blue and black 10 10
a. Nos. 426/427 *se-tenant* with gutter margin between .... 6·00 14·00
427 – 5c. greenish blue, dull olive-yellow, rose and black 10 10

Design:—No. 427, Rubber-gloved hands, syringe and head of Hippocrates.

The above were printed in sheets of 100 containing a pane of 50 of each design.

The major shades formerly listed have been deleted as there is a range of intermediate shades.

222 Athlete carrying Torch, and Sunstone Symbol **223** Sunstone Symbol and Mexican Flag

(Des H. Williamson. Photo)

1968 (2 Oct). Olympic Games, Mexico City. P 13½.
428 **222** 5c. multicoloured 30 10
429 **223** 25c. multicoloured .... 40 1·50
a. Green (left-hand panel) omitted £3500

224 Houses and Dollar Signs **225** Church Window and View of Bethlehem

(Des Erica McGilchrist. Photo)

1968 (16 Oct). Building and Savings Societies Congress. P 13½.
430 **224** 5c. multicoloured 10 60

(Des G. Hamori. Photo)

1968 (23 Oct). Christmas. P 13½.
431 **225** 5c. multicoloured 10 10
a. Green window (gold omitted) .. £850
b. Red (inscr) omitted £2500

226 Edgeworth David (geologist)

(Des Note Ptg Branch (Nos. 432, 434) A. Cook (others). Recess, background litho)

1968 (6 Nov). Famous Australians (1st series). T **226** and similar vert portraits. P 15×14.
432 5c. myrtle-green/*pale green* 25 20
a. Booklet pane. Five stamps plus one printed label .... 1·00
433 5c. black/*pale blue* 25 20
a. Booklet pane. Five stamps plus one printed label .... 1·00
434 5c. blackish brown/*pale buff* 25 20
a. Booklet pane. Five stamps plus one printed label .... 1·00
435 5c. deep violet/*pale lilac* 25 20
a. Booklet pane. Five stamps plus one printed label .... 1·00
432/435 *Set of 4* 90 70

Designs:—No. 432, Type **226**; No. 433, A. B. Paterson (poet); No. 434, Albert Namatjira (artist); No. 435, Caroline Chisholm (social worker).

Nos. 432/435 were only issued in $1 booklets, Nos. SB44/SB44a, with the outer edges of the pane imperforate so all stamps have one or two adjacent sides imperforate.

See also Nos. 446/449, 479/482.

230 Macquarie Lighthouse **231** Pioneers and Modern Building, Darwin

(Des and eng Note Ptg Branch. Recess; background litho)

1968 (27 Nov). 150th Anniversary of Macquarie Lighthouse. P 14½×13½.
436 **230** 5c. black and pale yellow .... 50 1·00

Used examples are known with the pale yellow background colour omitted.

(Des Marietta Lyon. Photo)

1969 (5 Feb). Centenary of Northern Territory Settlement. P 13½.
437 **231** 5c. blackish brown, yellow-olive and yellow-ochre 10 10

232 Melbourne Harbour **233** Concentric Circles (symbolising Management, Labour and Government)

(Des J. Mason. Photo)

1969 (26 Feb). Sixth Biennial Conference of International Association of Ports and Harbours, Melbourne. P 13½.
438 **232** 5c. multicoloured 20 10

(Des G. Hamori. Photo)

1969 (4 June). 50th Anniversary of International Labour Organisation. P 13½.
439 **233** 5c. multicoloured 15 10
a. Gold (middle circle) omitted...... £3750

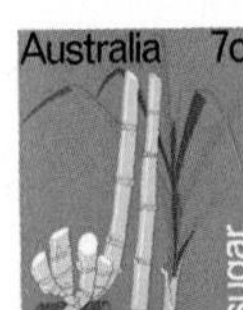

234 Sugar Cane

(Des R. Ingpen. Photo)

1969 (17 Sept). Primary Industries. T **234** and similar vert designs. Multicoloured. P 13½.
440 7c. Type **234** .... 50 1·50
441 15c. Timber .... 75 2·00
a. Black ('Australia' and value) omitted £1700
442 20c. Wheat 30 50
443 25c. Wool .... 50 1·50
440/443 *Set of 4* .... 1·90 5·00

238 The Nativity (stained-glass window) **240** Edmund Barton

(Des G. Hamori (5c.), J. Coburn (25c.). Photo)

1969 (15 Oct). Christmas. T **238** and similar multicoloured designs. P 13½.
444 5c. Type **238** 20 10
a. Magenta (robe) omitted £1800
b. Yellow omitted £1800
445 25c. 'Tree of Life', Christ in Crib and Christmas Star (abstract) .... 1·00 2·00

(Des from drawings by J. Santry. Recess, background litho)

1969 (22 Oct). Famous Australians (2nd series). Prime Ministers. T **240** and similar vert designs each black on pale green. P 15×14.

446 5c. Type **240** ... 30 20
a. Booklet pane. Five stamps plus one printed label ... 1·10
447 5c. Alfred Deakin ... 30 20
a. Booklet pane. Five stamps plus one printed label ... 1·10
448 5c. J. C. Watson ... 30 20
a. Booklet pane. Five stamps plus one printed label ... 1·10
449 5c. G. H. Reid ... 30 20
a. Booklet pane. Five stamps plus one printed label ... 1·10
446/449 *Set of 4* ... 1·10 70

Nos. 446/449 were only issued in $1 booklets, Nos. SB45/SB45a, with the outer edges of the pane imperforate so all stamps have one or two adjacent sides imperforate.

244 Capt. Ross Smith's Vickers Vimy, 1919

247 Symbolic Track and Diesel Locomotive

(Des E. Thake. Photo)

1969 (12 Nov). 50th Anniversary of First England–Australia Flight. T **244** and similar horiz designs. P 13½.

450 5c. olive-green, pale blue, black and red ... 15 15
a. Strip of 3. Nos. 450/452 ... 1·50 2·25
451 5c. black, red and olive-green ... 15 15
452 5c. olive-green, black, pale blue and red ... 15 15
450/452 *Set of 3* ... 1·50 40

Designs:—No. 450, Type **244**; No. 451, Lt. H. Fysh and Lt. P. McGinness on 1919 survey with Ford Model T runabout; No. 452, Capt. Wrigley and Sgt. Murphy in Royal Aircraft Factory B.E.2E taking off to meet the Smiths.

The three designs appear *se-tenant*, both horizontally and vertically, throughout the sheet.

(Des B. Sadgrove. Photo)

1970 (11 Feb). Sydney–Perth Standard Gauge Railway Link. P 13½.

453 **247** 5c. multicoloured ... 15 10

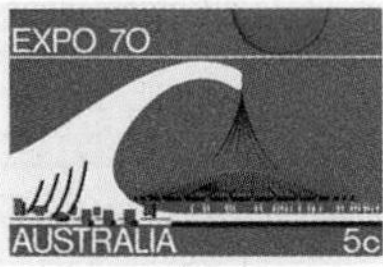

248 Australian Pavilion, Osaka **251** Australian Flag

(Des J. Copeland (5c.), A. Leydin (20c.). Photo)

1970 (16 Mar). World Fair, Osaka. T **248** and similar horiz design. P 13½.

454 5c. multicoloured ... 15 10
455 20c. orange-red and black ... 35 65

Design:—5c. T **248**; 20c. 'Southern Cross' and 'from the Country of the South with warm feelings' (message).

(Des PO Artists (5c.), J. Mason (30c.). Photo)

1970 (31 Mar). Royal Visit. T **251** and similar horiz design. P 13½.

456 5c. black and deep ochre ... 25 15
457 30c. multicoloured ... 85 2·50

Design:—5c. Queen Elizabeth II and Prince Philip; 30c. T **251**.

252 Lucerne Plant, Bull and Sun **253** Captain Cook and HMS *Endeavour*

5c. (No. 459). Red mark on sail at left (Top pane, R. 5/1)

(Des R. Ingpen. Photo)

1970 (13 Apr). 11th International Grasslands Congress, Queensland. P 13½.

458 **252** 5c. multicoloured ... 10 80

(Des R. Ingpen and 'Team' (T. Keneally, A. Leydin, J. R. Smith). Photo)

1970 (20 Apr). Bicentenary of Captain Cook's Discovery of Australia's East Coast. T **253** and similar multicoloured designs. P 13½.

459 5c. Type **253** ... 30 10
a. Strip of 5. Nos. 459/463 ... 1·40 1·50
aa. Black omitted ... £16000
b. Red mark on sail ... 3·00
460 5c. Sextant and HMS *Endeavour* ... 30 10
461 5c. Landing at Botany Bay ... 30 10
462 5c. Charting and exploring ... 30 10
463 5c. Claiming possession ... 30 10
464 30c. Captain Cook, HMS *Endeavour*, sextant, aborigines and kangaroo (*63×30 mm*) ... 1·00 2·50
459/464 *Set of 6* ... 2·25 2·75
MS465 157×129 mm. Nos. 459/64. Imperf ... 4·50 4·50

The 5c. stamps were issued horizontally *se-tenant* within the sheet, to form a composite design in the order listed.

Several used single 5c. stamps are also known with the black omitted.

50,000 miniature sheets were made available by the Post Office to the organisers of the Australian National Philatelic Exhibition which overprinted them in the white margin at each side of the 30c. stamp with 'Souvenir Sheet AUSTRALIAN NATIONAL PHILATELIC EXHIBITION' at left and 'ANPEX 1970 SYDNEY 27 APRIL–1 MAY' at right in light red-brown and they were also serially numbered. These were put on sale at the exhibition on the basis of one sheet to each visitor paying 30c. for admission. Although still valid for postage, since the stamps themselves had not been defaced, these sheets were not sold at post offices.

Subsequently further supplies were purchased and similarly overprinted and numbered by a private firm without the authority of the Post Office and ANPEX took successful legal action to stop their further sale to the public. This firm also had the unoverprinted sheets rouletted in colour between the stamps whilst further supplies of the normal sheets were overprinted with reproductions of old coins and others with an inscription commemorating the opening of Melbourne Airport on 1st July 1970, but all these are private productions. Further private productions have been reported.

259 Sturt's Desert Rose

AUSTRALIA I. **AUSTRALIA** II.

Two types of 2c.

I. 'AUSTRALIA' thin: '2c' thin; flower name lightly printed.

II. Redrawn. 'AUSTRALIA' thicker; '2c' much more heavily printed; flower name thicker and bolder.

(Des Note Ptg Branch. Photo)

1970–75. Coil Stamps. Vert designs as T **259**. Multicoloured. White fluorescent paper (10c.). Perf 15×imperf.

465*a* 2c. Type **259** (I) (1.10.71) ... 40 30
ab. White fluorescent paper ... 40
b. Type II (white fluorescent paper) ... 1·50 1·25
ba. Yellow omitted ... £2000
bb. Grey omitted ... £2250
466 4c. Type **259** (27.4.70) ... 85 2·25
467 5c. Golden Wattle (27.4.70) ... 20 10
aa. Yellow omitted ... £2250
a. White fluorescent paper ... 20
468 6c. Type **259** (28.9.70) ... 1·25 1·00
a. Green (leaves) omitted ... £3000
468*b* 7c. Sturt's Desert Pea (1.10.71) ... 40 70
ba. Black (berries, '7c.' and inscr) omitted ... £2000
bb. Buff (shadows on flowers) omitted ... £225
bc. Buff and green (leaves) omitted ... 80·00
bd. White fluorescent paper (10.73) ... 40
468*d* 10c. As 7c. (15.1.75) ... 60 2·00
465*a*/468*d* *Set of 6* ... 3·25 5·50

Nos. 465*a*/468*d* have horizontal coil perforations described after No. 191.

One used example of No. 468 is known with the magenta omitted.

Examples of No. 468*b*bb also show the green colour displaced downwards.

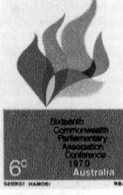

264 Snowy Mountains Scheme **265** Rising Flames

7c. Broken pylon leg (Left pane, R. 7/4).

(Des L. Mason (7c.), R. Ingpen (8c., 9c.), B. Sadgrove (10c.). Photo)

1970 (31 Aug). National Development (1st series). T **264** and similar horiz designs. Multicoloured. P 13½.

469 7c. Type **264** ... 20 2·00
a. Broken pylon leg ... 8·00
470 8c. Ord River Scheme ... 10 20
a. Red omitted ... £4250
471 9c. Bauxite to aluminium ... 15 20
472 10c. Oil and Natural Gas ... 30 10
469/472 *Set of 4* ... 65 2·25

(Des G. Hamori, Photo)

1970 (2 Oct). 16th Commonwealth Parliamentary Association Conference, Canberra. P 13½.

473 **265** 6c. multicoloured ... 10 10

266 Milk Analysis and Dairy Herd **267** The Nativity

(Des R. Honisett. Photo)

1970 (7 Oct). 18th International Dairy Congress, Sydney. P 13½.

474 **266** 6c. multicoloured ... 10 10

(Des W. Beasley. Photo)

1970 (14 Oct). Christmas. P 13½.

475 **267** 6c. multicoloured ... 10 10
a. Yellow omitted ... £2250

268 UN 'Plant' and Dove of Peace **269** Boeing 707 and Avro 504

(Des Monad Design and Visual Graphics. Photo)

1970 (19 Oct). 25th Anniversary of United Nations. P 13½.

476 **268** 6c. multicoloured ... 15 10

(Des G. Hamori. Photo)

1970 (2 Nov). 50th Anniversary of QANTAS Airline. T **269** and similar horiz design. Multicoloured. P 13½.

477 6c. Type **269** ... 30 10
478 30c. Avro 504 and Boeing 707 ... 70 2·25

270 The Duigan Brothers (Pioneer Aviators)

(Des A. Cook (No. 480), T. Adams (No. 482), Note Ptg Branch (others). Recess (background litho))

1970 (16 Nov). Famous Australians (3rd series). T **270** and similar vert designs. P 15×14.

479 6c. blue ... 35 20
a. Booklet pane. Five stamps plus one printed label ... 1·60
480 6c. black/*cinnamon* ... 35 20
a. Booklet pane. Five stamps plus one printed label ... 1·60
481 6c. purple/*pale pink* ... 35 20
a. Booklet pane. Five stamps plus one printed label ... 1·60
482 6c. brown-lake/*flesh* ... 35 20
a. Booklet pane. Five stamps plus one printed label ... 1·60
479/482 *Set of 4* ... 1·25 75

Designs:—No. 479 Type **270**; No. 480 Lachlan Macquarie (Governor of N.S.W.); No. 481 Adam Lindsay Gordon (poet); No. 482 E.J. Eyre (explorer).

Nos. 479/482 were only issued in 60c. or $1.20 booklets, Nos. SB46/SB48a, with the outer edges of the pane imperforate so all stamps have one or two adjacent sides imperforate.

STAMP BOOKLETS

Illustrations of booklet covers are reduced to ½ size, *unless otherwise stated.*

All booklets from 1913 to 1949 were stapled.

Note that the cover colours in these listings refer only to the outside covers. Inside colours may differ from those given.

1913 (17 Jan). Red on pink cover, 75×60 mm as New South Wales Type B **2** (SB1) or blue on pink cover as New South Wales Type B **1** and picture of State GPO on back, 150×175 mm (SB2).

SB1 2s. booklet containing 12×½d. and 18×1d. (Nos. 1/2) in blocks of 6 ... £2250
SB2 £1 booklet containing 240×1d. (No. 2) in blocks of 30 ... £18000

B **1** *(Illustration reduced. Actual size 80×60 mm)*

1914 (6 Oct)–**18**. Red on pink cover, 75×60 mm as Type B **1** (Nos. SB2*a*/SB3), black on red cover, 80×60 mm (No. SB4) or blue on pink cover as New South Wales Type B **1** and picture of State GPO on back, 150×175 mm (No. SB5).

SB2*a* 2s. booklet containing 12×½d. and 18×1d. (Nos. 1, 21c) in blocks of 6 £4000
SB3 2s. booklet containing 12×½d. and 18×1d. (Nos. 20, 21c) in blocks of 6 (1915) £3500
SB4 2s. booklet containing 24×1d. (No. 21c) in blocks of 6 (10.5.17) £3500
a. Black on green cover £4000
b. Red on green cover £3750
SB5 £1 booklet containing 240×1d. (No. 21c) in blocks of 30 £17000
a. Back cover without GPO picture (1918) £19000
ab. Purple-brown on pink cover

Records show that a £1 booklet containing 120×2d. stamps was issued in very limited quantities during 1914. No examples are known to have survived.

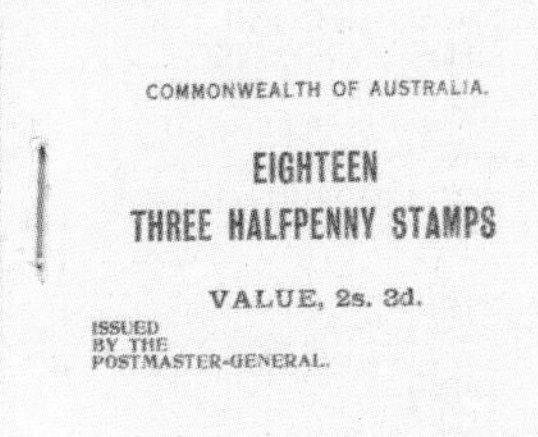

B **1a** *(Illustration reduced. Actual size 80×60 mm)*

COMMONWEALTH OF AUSTRALIA.
—160—
THREE-HALFPENNY STAMPS.
VALUE, ONE POUND.
ISSUED BY THE POSTMASTER-GENERAL.

B **1b** *(Illustration reduced. Actual size 165×120 mm)*

1919 (Jan–Apr). Black on pink, 80×60 mm, as Type B **1a** (Nos. SB6/SB7), black on green, 80×60 mm (Nos. SB8/SB9b) or black on green, 165×120 mm as Type B **1b** (Nos. SB9*c*/SB9*d*) covers.

SB6 2s.3d. booklet containing 18×1½d. (No. 58) in blocks of 6 £3000
a. Black on green cover £3000
SB7 2s.3d. booklet containing 18×1½d. (No. 51) in blocks of 6 £3000
a. Black on green cover £3000
SB8 2s.3d. booklet containing 18×1½d. (No. 59) in blocks of 6 (4.19) £3000
a. Black on pink cover £3000
SB9 2s.3d. booklet containing 18×1½d. (No. 52) in blocks of 6 (4.19) £3000
a. Black on pink cover
b. Black on blue cover £3000
SB9*c* £1 booklet containing 160×1½d. (No. 51) in blocks of 20 £19000
SB9*d* £1 booklet containing 160×1½d. (No. 52) in blocks of 20 (4.19) £17000

COMMONWEALTH OF AUSTRALIA
120
TWOPENNY STAMPS
VALUE ONE POUND
ISSUED BY THE POSTMASTER-GENERAL
SPECIAL NOTE.—The rate on letters to America is 3d. per half ounce or fraction of half ounce

B **1c** *(Illustration reduced. Actual size 157×90 mm)*

1920 (Dec)–**22**. Black on blue, (Nos. SB10, SB12), black on white (SB11) or black on brown (SB14) covers. 80×60mm as T B **1a** (SB10/SB11) or 157×90mm as T B **1c** (SB12/SB14).

SB10 2s. booklet containing 12×2d. (No. 62) in blocks of 6 £3500
a. Black on pink cover £3500
b. Black on orange cover (3.22) £4000
c. Black on green cover
SB11 2s. booklet containing 12×2d. (No. 63) in blocks of 6 (3.22) £4250
a. Black on orange cover (7.22) £3750
b. Black on pink cover £3500
c. Brown on buff cover £3750
d. Brown on pink cover £3750
SB12 £1 booklet containing 120×2d. (No. 62) in blocks of 15 (1.21) £18000
a. Black on pink cover
SB13 £1 booklet containing 90×2d. and 15×4d. (Nos. 63, 65) in blocks of 15 (3.22)
SB14 £1 booklet containing 120×2d. (No. 63) in blocks of 15 (8.22) £17000

a. Black on orange cover

COMMONWEALTH OF AUSTRALIA
160
THREE HALFPENNY STAMPS
VALUE, ONE POUND
ISSUED BY THE POSTMASTER-GENERAL
SPECIAL NOTE.—THE RATE ON LETTERS TO AMERICA IS 3D. FOR THE FIRST OUNCE AND 1½D. FOR EACH ADDITIONAL OUNCE

B **1d** *(Illustration reduced. Actual size 155×90 mm)*

1923 (Oct)–**24**. Black on rose, 80×60 mm (No. SB15), or green on pale green, 80×60 mm (No. SB16) or green on pale green, 155×90 mm, as Type B **1d** (Nos. SB17/SB18) covers.

SB15 2s.3d. booklet containing 18×1½d. (No. 61) in blocks of 6 £3000
a. Black on pale green cover £3000
b. Green on pale green cover £2500
SB16 2s.3d. booklet containing 18×1½d. (No. 77) in blocks of 6 (5.24) £2250
SB17 £1 booklet containing 160×1½d. (No. 61) in blocks of 20 (3.24) £15000
SB18 £1 booklet containing 160×1½d. (No. 77) in blocks of 20 (5.24) £15000

1927 (Jan–June). Green on pale green covers, 82×57 mm (Nos. SB19/SB20) or 150×100 mm (No. SB21). Inscr 'COMMONWEALTH OF AUSTRALIA' at top.

SB19 2s.3d. booklet containing 18×1½d. (No. 87) in blocks of 6 £1400
a. 'COMMONWEALTH OF AUSTRALIA' omitted
SB20 2s.3d. booklet containing 18×1½d. (No. 96) in blocks of 6 £1400
SB21 £1 booklet containing 160×1½d. (No. 96) in blocks of 20 (6.27) £13000

COMMONWEALTH OF AUSTRALIA
BOOKLET OF
CANBERRA COMMEMORATIVE STAMPS
ISSUED 9TH MAY, 1927.
SIXTEEN 1½d STAMPS
PRICE
2/-

B **1e** *(Illustration reduced. Actual size 115×75 mm)*

1927 (9 May). Opening of Parliament House, Canberra. Green on pale green cover 115×75 mm, as Type B **1e** with picture of HMS *Renown* on back (2s.).

SB22 2s. booklet containing 16×1½d. (No. 105) in blocks of 8 90·00

Examples of a 10s. booklet containing 80×1½d. (No. 105) are known without a front cover and with the back cover blank. There is no record that this was an official issue.

1928 (Nov). Green on pale green cover, 83×58 mm.

SB23 2s.3d. booklet containing 18×1½d. (No. 96*a* or 96w) in blocks of 6 £450

COMMONWEALTH OF AUSTRALIA
Twelve Air Mail Stamps and Labels — Price, 3/-
AIR MAIL
SAVES TIME
Information covering conditions and fees applicable to air mail is shown on inside and back of covers.

B **1f** *(Illustration reduced. Actual size 85×60 mm)*

COMMONWEALTH OF AUSTRALIA
12 AIR MAIL STAMPS & LABELS
PRICE—THREE SHILLINGS
USE THE AIR MAIL
The Australia - Singapore - England service is now in operation.

B **1g** *(Illustration reduced. Actual size 85×60 mm)*

1930 (July)–**35**. Air. Black on blue cover, 85×60 mm, as Type B **1f** (No. SB24) or B **1g** (No. SB24a).

SB24 3s. booklet containing 12×3d. (No. 115a) in blocks of 4 plus two panes of air mail labels £850
a. Black on pale green cover (5.35) £1700

1930 (9 Sept)–**33**. Green on pale green covers inscr 'USE THE AIR MAIL' on the back (2s), 83×58 mm (Nos. SB25/SB*a*ab), 160×115 mm (Nos. 26/*a*).

SB25 2s. booklet containing 12×2d. (No. 99a or 99aw) in blocks of 6 £425
SB25*a* 2s. booklet containing 12×2d. (No. 127 or 127w) in blocks of 6 (1.32) £425
ab. Cover with parcel rates on back (1933) £550
SB26 £1 booklet containing 120×2d. (No. 99) in blocks of 20 £11000
SB26*a* £1 booklet containing 120×2d. (No. 99a) in blocks of 20 £11000

1934 (June). Black on cream cover inscr 'Address your mail fully...' on front, 81×55 mm.

SB26*b* 2s. booklet containing 12×2d. (No. 127 or 127w) in blocks of 6 £650

1935–38. Black on green cover with Commonwealth Savings Bank advertisement on front inscr 'WHEREVER THERE IS A MONEY ORDER POST OFFICE' 78×55 mm.

SB26*c* 2s. booklet containing 12×2d. (No. 127 or 127w) in blocks of 6 £475
ca. Front cover inscr 'IN MOST MONEY ORDER OFFICES' (1936) £450
cb. Ditto with waxed interleaves (1938) £550

1938 (Dec). Black on green cover as No. SB26*c* but 70×46 mm. Postal rates on interleaves.

SB27 2s. booklet containing 12×2d. (No. 184 or 184w) in blocks of 6 £500
a. With waxed interleaves. Postal rates on back cover £850
b. Black on buff cover £700

1942 (Aug). Black on buff cover, size 73×47½ mm. Postal rates on interleaves.

SB28 2s.6d. booklet containing 12×2½d. (No. 206 or 206w) in blocks of 6, upright within the booklet £110
a. With waxed interleaves. Postal rates on back cover £250

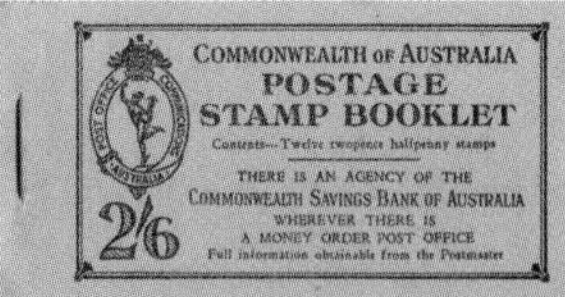

B **1h**

1949 (Sept). Black on buff cover, size 79½×42½ mm as Type B **1h**.

SB29 2s.6d. booklet containing 12×2½d. (No. 206) in blocks of 6, sideways within the booklet 80·00

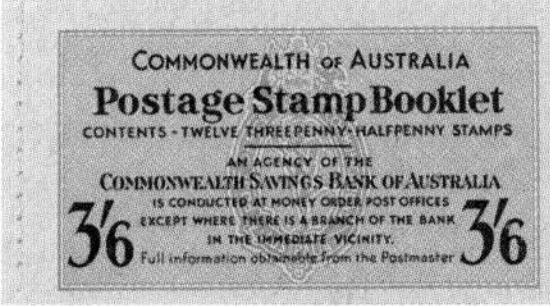

B **1i**

1952 (24 June). Vermilion and deep blue on green cover as Type B **1i**.

SB30 3s.6d. booklet containing 12×3½d. (No. 247) in blocks of 6 19·00
a. With waxed interleaves 90·00

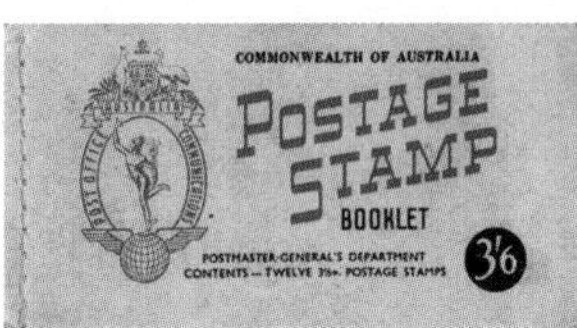

B **1j**

1953 (8 July)–**56**. Vermilion and deep blue on green cover, 80×41 mm, as Type B **1j**.

SB31 3s.6d. booklet containing 12×3½d. (No. 263) in blocks of 6 11·00
a. With waxed interleaves 30·00
SB32 3s.6d. booklet containing 12×3½d. (No. 262*a*) in blocks of 6 (7.56) 23·00
a. With waxed interleaves 85·00

For a 3s.6d. booklet containing 12×3½d. Olympics stamps, see note below No. 293.

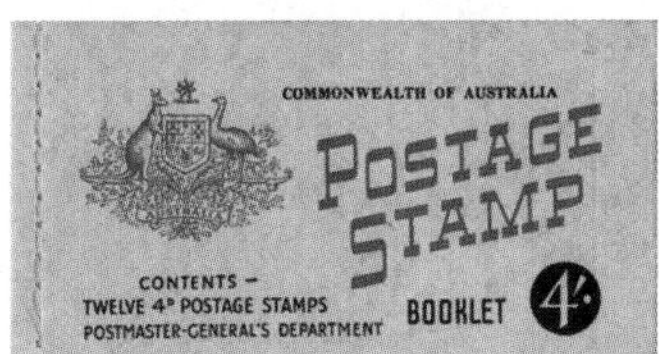

B **2**

1957 (13 Mar)–**59**. Vermilion and deep blue on green cover, 80×41 mm, as Type B **2**.

SB33 4s. booklet containing two panes of 6×4d. (No. 282*a*ab) 14·00
a. With waxed interleaves 55·00
SB34 4s. booklet containing two panes of 6×4d. (No. 313ab) (18.3.59) 38·00
a. With waxed interleaves 90·00

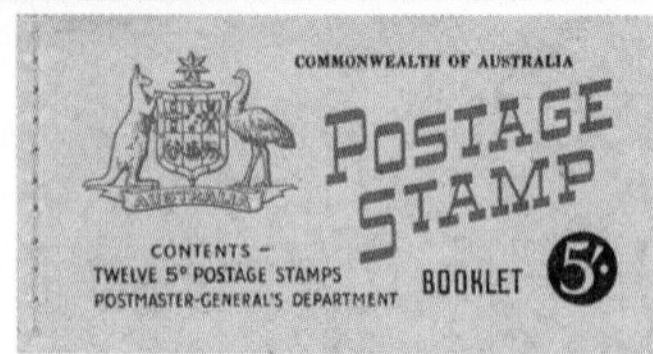

B 3

1960 (23 Mar). Vermilion and deep blue on green cover, 80×41 mm, as Type B **3**.

SB35	5s. booklet containing two panes of 6×5d. (No. 314d)	22·00
	a. With waxed interleaves	50·00

B 4

1962 (1 July)–**65**. Rose and emerald on green cover, 80×41 mm, as Type B **4**.

SB36	5s. booklet containing two panes of 6×5d. (No. 314d)	50·00
	a. With waxed interleaves (1963)	£130
SB37	5s. booklet containing two panes of 6×5d. (No. 354a) (17.6.64)	50·00
	a. With waxed interleaves	£120
SB38	5s. booklet containing two panes of 6×5d. (No. 354ccb) (13.7.65)	60·00
	a. With waxed interleaves	£150

B 5

1966 (14 Feb). Greenish blue and black on yellow-olive cover, 80×41 mm, as Type B **5**.

SB39	60c. booklet containing three panes of 5×4c. and 1 label (No. 385a)	45·00
	a. With waxed interleaves	£130

1967 (29 Sept). Greenish blue and black on yellow-olive covers, 80×41 mm, as Type B **5**.

(a) Surcharged covers

SB40	50c. booklet containing two panes of 5×5c. on 4c. and 1 label (No. 414a)	12·00
SB41	$1 booklet containing four panes of 5×5c. on 4c. and 1 label (No. 414a)	4·50
	a. Normal cover as Type B **5**	5·00
	ab. With waxed interleaves	65·00

(b) Normal covers

SB42	50c. booklet containing two panes of 5×5c. and 1 label (No. 386cca)	17·00
SB43	$1 booklet containing four panes of 5×5c. and 1 label (No. 386cca)	23·00
	a. With waxed interleaves	75·00

Booklets SB40/SB41ab were intended as provisional issues until supplies of the new 5c. became available in booklet form, but in the event these were put on sale on the same date.

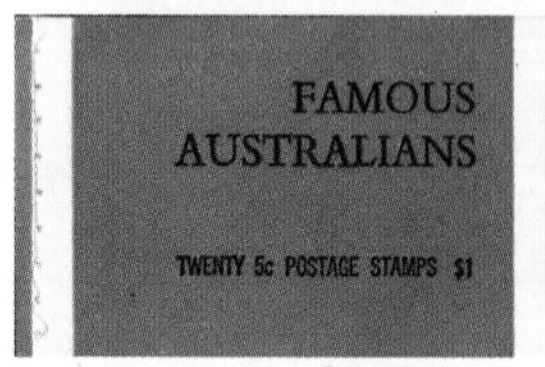

B 6

1968 (6 Nov). Famous Australians (1st series). Black, red, white and blue cover, 80×41 mm, as Type B **6**.

SB44	$1 booklet containing four panes of 5×5c. and 1 label (Nos. 432a, 433a, 434a, 435a)	3·50
	a. With waxed interleaves	55·00

B 7

1969 (22 Oct). Famous Australians (2nd series). Olive-green, gold and black cover, 80×41 mm, as Type B **7**.

SB45	$1 booklet containing four panes of 5×5c. and 1 label (Nos. 446a, 447a, 448a, 449a)	4·00
	a. With waxed interleaves	65·00

B 8

(Des B. Young. Eng S. Reading. Typo J. B. Cooke)

1970 (16 Nov). Famous Australians (3rd series). Multicoloured on white covers, 41×80 mm, as Type B **8**.

SB46	60c. booklet containing two panes of 5×6c. and 1 label (Nos. 479a, 480a)	14·00
SB47	60c. booklet containing two panes of 5×6c. and 1 label (Nos. 481a, 482a)	14·00
SB48	$1.20 booklet containing four panes of 5×6c. and 1 label (Nos. 479a, 480a, 481a, 482a)	7·50
	a. With waxed interleaves	65·00

Military Post Booklets

Issued for the use of Australian Forces in Vietnam

MB 1

1967 (30 May–Sept). Yellow-green and black on white cover as Type MB **1**. Pane attached by selvedge.

MB1	50c. booklet containing 5c. (No. 386) in block of 10	80·00
	a. Containing No. 386*b* (9.67)	80·00

1968 (1 Mar). Yellow-green and black on white cover as Type MB **1**. Pane attached by selvedge.

MB2	50c. booklet containing 5c. (No. 386*c*) in block of 10	50·00

POSTAGE DUE STAMPS

POSTAGE DUE PRINTERS. Nos. D1/D62 were typographed at the New South Wales Government Printing Office, Sydney. They were not used in Victoria.

D 1

D 2

D 3

Type D **1** adapted from plates of New South Wales Type D **1**. No letters at foot.

1902 (1 July). Chalk-surfaced paper. Wmk Type D **2** (inverted on 1d., 3d. and 4d.).

(a) P 11½, 12

D1	D **1**	½d. emerald-green or dull green	3·50	7·50
D2		1d. emerald-green	26·00	13·00
		w. Wmk upright	45·00	26·00
D3		2d. emerald-green	65·00	16·00
		w. Wmk inverted	£130	
D4		3d. emerald-green	50·00	32·00
		w. Wmk upright	55·00	38·00
D5		4d. emerald-green	50·00	15·00
		w. Wmk upright	65·00	25·00
D6		6d. emerald-green	60·00	12·00
		w. Wmk inverted	55·00	12·00
D7		8d. emerald-green or dull green	£100	85·00
D8		5s. emerald-green or dull green	£200	75·00
D1/D8 *Set of* 8			£475	£200
D1s/D7s Opt 'SPECIMEN' *Set of* 7			£350	

(b) P 11½, 12, compound with 11

D9	D **1**	1d. emerald-green	£350	£160
		w. Wmk upright	£375	£150
D10		2d. emerald-green	£500	£180
		w. Wmk inverted	£600	£225

(c) P 11

D12	D **1**	1d. emerald-green (*wmk upright*)	£2500	£900

Stamps may be found showing portions of the marginal watermark 'NEW SOUTH WALES POSTAGE'.

1902 (July)–**04**. Type D **3** (with space at foot filled in). Chalk-surfaced paper. Wmk Type D **2** (inverted on 3d., 4d., 6d., 8d. and 5s.).

(a) P 11½, 12

D13	D **3**	1d. emerald-green (10.02)	£300	£140
D14		2d. emerald-green (3.03)	—	£170
D15		3d. emerald-green (3.03)	£375	£110
D17		5d. emerald-green	70·00	20·00
D18		10d. emerald-green *or* dull green	95·00	24·00
D19		1s. emerald-green	80·00	20·00
D20		2s. emerald-green	£140	18·00

(b) P 11½, 12, compound with 11

D22	D **3**	½d. emerald-green *or* dull green (3.04)	22·00	18·00
		w. Wmk inverted	24·00	20·00
D23		1d. emerald-green *or* dull green (10.02)	21·00	4·50
		w. Wmk inverted	21·00	4·50
D24		2d. emerald-green *or* dull green (3.03)	50·00	3·00
		w. Wmk inverted	50·00	3·00
D25		3d. emerald-green *or* dull green (3.03)	90·00	17·00
		w. Wmk upright	£120	32·00
D26		4d. emerald-green *or* dull green (5.03)	75·00	23·00
		w. Wmk upright	75·00	25·00
D27		5d. emerald-green	65·00	23·00
D28		6d. emerald-green (3.04)	75·00	11·00
D29		8d. emerald-green (3.04)	£140	60·00
D30		10d. emerald-green *or* dull green	£120	19·00
D31		1s. emerald-green	£110	29·00
D32		2s. emerald-green	£190	27·00
D33		5s. emerald-green *or* dull green (5.03)	£450	24·00

(c) P 11

D34	D **3**	½d. emerald-green *or* dull green (wmk inverted) (3.04)	£600	£325
D35		1d. emerald-green *or* dull green (10.02)	£170	32·00
		w. Wmk inverted	£200	42·00
D36		2d. emerald-green (3.03)	£250	30·00
		w. Wmk inverted	£250	30·00
D37		3d. emerald-green *or* dull green (3.03)	£150	60·00
		w. Wmk upright	£160	60·00
D38		4d. emerald-green *or* dull green (5.03)	£275	70·00
		w. Wmk upright	£275	70·00
D39		5d. emerald-green	£400	55·00
D40		6d. emerald-green (3.04)	£110	16·00
D41		1s. emerald-green	£500	38·00
D42		5s. emerald-green (5.03)	£1700	£300
D43		10s. dull green (10.03)	£2000	£1800
D44		20s. dull green (10.03)	£4250	£2250
D13/D44 *Set of* 14			£6500	£4000
D13s/D44s Opt 'SPECIMEN' *Set of* 14			£1100	

The 10s. and 20s. values were only issued in New South Wales.

The used prices quoted for Nos. D43/D44 are for cancelled to order examples.

D 4

D 6

1906 (Jan)–**08**. Chalk-surfaced paper. Wmk Crown over single-lined A Type D **4**.

(a) P 11½, 12, compound with 11

D45	D **3**	½d. green (1.07)	16·00	18·00
		w. Wmk inverted	16·00	18·00
D46		1d. green	28·00	5·50
		w. Wmk inverted	28·00	6·50
D47		2d. green	75·00	9·00
		w. Wmk inverted	75·00	9·00
D48		3d. green (7.08)	£700	£325
D49		4d. green (4.07)	70·00	23·00
		w. Wmk inverted	70·00	23·00
D50		6d. green (3.08)	£300	25·00
		w. Wmk inverted	£300	25·00
D45/D50 *Set of* 6			£1000	£350

(b) P 11

D51	D **3**	1d. dull green	£3000	£1100
		aw. Wmk inverted	£3000	£1100
D51*b*		2d. green	†	£4750
D52		4d. dull green (4.07)	£5500	£3250

No. D51*b* is only known pen-cancelled.

Shades exist.

1907 (July–Sept). Chalk-surfaced paper. Wmk Crown over double-lined A Type w **11** (inverted on ½d.). P 11½×11.

D53	D **3**	½d. dull green	35·00	75·00
		w. Wmk upright	55·00	£100
D54		1d. dull green (8.07)	£140	75·00
		w. Wmk inverted	£140	75·00
D55		2d. dull green (9.07)	£275	£160
		w. Wmk inverted	£300	£180
D56		4d. dull green (9.07)	£275	£150
		w. Wmk inverted	£275	£160
		y. Wmk inverted and reversed	£700	
D57		6d. dull green (9.07)	£325	£225
		w. Wmk inverted	—	£375
D53/D57 *Set of* 5			£900	£600

1908 (Sept)–**09**. Stroke after figure of value. Chalk-surfaced paper. Wmk Crown over single-lined A Type D **4** (inverted on 10s.).

(a) P 11½×11

D58	D **6**	1s. dull green (1909)	£140	18·00
D59		5s. dull green	£275	48·00

(b) P 11

D60	D **6**	2s. dull green (1909)	£1000	£17000
D61		10s. dull green (1909)	£2500	£26000
D62		20s. dull green (1909)	£7500	£40000

Nos. D61/D62 were only issued in New South Wales. The used prices quoted for Nos. D60/D62 are for examples with verified postal cancellations from the period of issue.

D 7

Die I Die II

1d.

Die I Die II

2d.

(Typo J. B. Cooke, Melbourne)

1909 (1 July)–**10**. Wmk Crown over double-lined A, Type w **11**.

*(a) P 12×12½ (comb)**

D63 **D 7** ½d. rosine and yellow-green (8.09) 16·00 32·00
D64 1d. rosine and yellow-green (I) 14·00 4·00
b. Die II (7.10) 38·00 2·00
D65 2d. rosine and yellow-green (I) 38·00 6·00
a. Die II (8.10) 50·00 2·00
aw. Wmk inverted † £5500
D66 3d. rosine and yellow-green (9.09) 42·00 20·00
D67 4d. rosine and yellow-green (8.09) 42·00 5·00
D68 6d. rosine and yellow-green (8.09) 27·00 2·75
D69 1s. rosine and yellow-green (8.09) 30·00 3·25
D70 2s. rosine and yellow-green (8.09) 70·00 10·00
D71 5s. rosine and yellow-green (10.09) 90·00 12·00
D72 10s. rosine and yellow-green (11.09) £250 £150
D73 £1 rosine and yellow-green (11.09) £500 £300
D63/D73 *Set of* 11 £950 £475

(b) P 11 (line)

D74 **D 7** 1d. rose and yellow-green (II) £3750 £1400
D74*a* 2d. rose and yellow-green (II) £24000 £15000
D75 6d. rose and yellow-green £35000 £24000

*Nos. D64/D64b and D65a are also known perf 12½ (line).

Only one unused example, without gum, and another pen-cancelled are known of No. D74*a*.

The 1d. of this printing (No. D74) is distinguishable from No. D78 by the colours, the green being very yellow and the rose having less of a carmine tone. The paper is thicker and slightly toned, that of No D78 being pure white; the gum is thick and yellowish, No. D78 having thin white gum.

All later issues of the 1d. and 2d. are Die II.

(Typo J.B. Cooke (later ptgs by T. S. Harrison))

1913 (July)–**23**. Thin paper. White gum. Wmk Crown over double-lined A W w **11**.

(a) P 12½ (line)

D76 **D 7** ½d. scarlet and pale yellow-green (7.13) 32·00 27·00
w. Wmk inverted £110 £110

(b) P 11

D77 **D 7** ½d. rosine and bright apple-green (10.14) 20·00 20·00
a. Wmk sideways 6·50 14·00
D78 1d. rosine and bright apple-green (8.14) 23·00 4·00
a. Wmk sideways 29·00 2·50
w. Wmk inverted £100 75·00

(c) P 14

D79 **D 7** ½d. rosine and bright apple-green (11.14) £225 £275
a. Carmine and apple-green (Harrison) (1919) 9·00 18·00
D80 1d. rosine and bright apple-green (9.14) £170 17·00
a. Scarlet and pale yellow-green (2.18) 20·00 16·00
aw. Wmk inverted † £1400
b. Carmine and apple-green (Harrison) (1919) 18·00 3·75
D81 2d. scarlet and pale yellow-green (11.17) 17·00 12·00
a. Carmine and apple-green (Harrison) (11.18) 30·00 6·50
D82 3d. rosine and apple-green (5.16) 85·00 32·00
a. Wmk sideways £7500 £4500
D83 4d. carmine and apple-green (Harrison) (4.21) £110 55·00
b. Carmine and pale yellow-green £110 50·00
ba. Wmk sideways £1000 £475
D85 1s. scarlet and pale yellow-green (6.23) 25·00 15·00
D86 10s. scarlet and pale yellow-green (5.21) £1500
D87 £1 scarlet and pale yellow-green (5.21) £950 £2750
D79*a*/D87 *Set of* 8 £2500

(d) Perf 14 compound with 11

D88 **D 7** 1d. carmine and apple-green £12000

(Typo T. S. Harrison (to Feb 1926), A. J. Mullett (to June 1927) and J. Ash (thereafter))

1922 (Feb)–**30**. Wmk Crown over A W **6**.

(a) P 14

D91 **D 7** ½d. carmine and yellow-green (17.5.23) 3·50 8·50
D92 1d. carmine and yellow-green 4·00 1·00
w. Wmk inverted £6000
D93 1½d. carmine and yellow-green (3.25) 1·50 9·00
w. Wmk inverted † £6000
D94 2d. carmine and yellow-green 3·50 2·25
D95 3d. carmine and yellow-green 9·50 5·50
D96 4d. carmine and yellow-green 35·00 23·00
D97 6d. carmine and yellow-green (8.22) 26·00 16·00
w. Wmk inverted

(b) P 11

D98 **D 7** 4d. carmine and yellow-green (22.9.30) 17·00 8·00
D91/D98 *Set of* 8 90·00 65·00

All values perforated 14 were printed by Harrison and all but the 1d. by Mullett and Ash. The 4d. perforated 11 was produced by J. Ash. There is a wide variation of shades in this issue.

(Typo J. Ash)

1931 (Oct)–**36**. Wmk Multiple Crown and C of A W **15**.

(a) P 14

D100 **D 7** 1d. carmine and yellow-green (10.31) 7·00 11·00
a. Imperf between (horiz pair) † £20000
D102 2d. carmine and yellow-green (19.10.31) 7·00 11·00

(b) P 11

D105 **D 7** ½d. carmine and yellow-green (4.34) 12·00 20·00
D106 1d. carmine and yellow-green (21.11.32) 7·50 3·25
D107 2d. carmine and yellow-green (1933) 17·00 2·00
D108 3d. carmine and yellow-green (5.36) 75·00 70·00
D109 4d. carmine and yellow-green (23.5.34) 19·00 5·00
D110 6d. carmine and yellow-green (4.36) £375 £325
D111 1s. carmine and yellow-green (8.34) 55·00 35·00
D105/D111 *Set of* 7 £475 £400

D 8

D 9

A.

B.

C.

Type A. Solid rectangle inside 'D' (ptgs of ½d., 1d., 2d., 4d. and 6d. from 1909 to 1945)
Type B. Shaded area inside 'D' (ptgs of 3d. from 1909 to 1945)
Type C. Solid segment of circle inside 'D' (ptgs of all values below 1s. from 1946)

D.

E.

Type D. Six lines of shading above numeral and four below (ptgs of 1s. from 1909 to 1945)
Type E. Larger '1' with only three background lines above; hyphen more upright (ptgs of 1s. from 1946 to 1953)

(Frame recess. Value typo J. Ash (to 1940, then W. C. G. McCracken))

1938 (July–Sept). W **15**. P 14½×14.

D112 **D 8** ½d. carmine and green (A) (9.38) 3·00 6·00
D113 1d. carmine and green (A) 18·00 2·00
D114 2d. carmine and green (A) 26·00 3·25
D115 3d. carmine and green (B) (8.38) 65·00 26·00
D116 4d. carmine and green (A) (8.38) 8·00 1·00
D117 6d. carmine and green (A) (8.38) 75·00 48·00
D118 1s. carmine and green (D) (8.38) 40·00 12·00
D112/D118 *Set of* 7 £200 85·00

Shades exist.

1946–57. Redrawn as Type C and E (1s). W **15**. P 14½×14.

D119 **D 9** ½d. carmine and green (9.56) 1·50 4·50
D120 1d. carmine and green (17.6.46) 1·25 80
w. Wmk inverted £6500
D121 2d. carmine and green (9.46) 6·00 1·25
w. Wmk inverted † £7000
D122 3d. carmine and green (6.8.46) 6·50 1·25
D123 4d. carmine and green (30.7.52) 8·50 2·50
D124 5d. carmine and green (16.12.48) 21·00 13·00
D125 6d. carmine and green (19.8.47) 13·00 2·25
D126 7d. carmine and green (26.8.53) 2·75 1·50
D127 8d. carmine and green (24.4.57) 4·50 15·00
D128 1s. carmine and green (9.47) 17·00 1·75
D119/D128 *Set of* 10 70·00 40·00

There are many shades in this issue.

D 10

1953 (26 Aug)–**59**. W **15**. P 14½×14.

D129 1s. carmine and yellow-green (17.2.54) 8·50 1·25
a. Carmine and deep green 12·00 5·50
D130 2s. carmine and yellow-green 14·00 5·00
a. Carmine and deep green £400 £130
D131 5s. carmine and green 14·00 1·50
a. Carmine and deep green (6.59) 12·00 1·00
D129/D131 *Set of* 3 32·00 7·00
D129*a*/D131*a* *Set of* 3 £400 £130

A new die was introduced for No. D131*a*. This differs from the original in having a distinct gap between the two arms of the '5'. On No. D131 these two features are joined.

Two Dies of ½d.:
Die I. Six dots in base of '2'
Die II. Seven dots in base of '2'

I.

II.

Two Dies of 1d. to 10d.:
Die I. Numeral, 'D' and stop, generally unoutlined.
Die II. Clear white line separates numeral, etc. from background.

1958–60. No wmk. P 14½×14.

D132 ½d. carmine and deep green (I) (27.2.58) 4·75 4·75
a. Die II (6.59) 2·50 1·25
D133 1d. carmine and deep green (I) (25.2.58) 2·50 3·00
a. Die II (6.59) 2·50 75
D134 3d. carmine and deep green (II) (25.5.60) 2·00 3·00
D135 4d. carmine and deep green (I) (27.2.58) 10·00 7·00
a. Die II (6.59) 2·75 4·00
D136 5d. carmine and deep green (I) (27.2.58) 11·00 22·00
a. Die II (6.59) 60·00 70·00
D137 6d. carmine and deep green (II) (25.5.60) 2·50 2·00
D138 8d. carmine and deep green (II) (25.2.58) 6·00 28·00
D139 10d. carmine and deep green (II) (9.12.59) 3·50 1·40
D140 1s. carmine and deep green (6.5.58) 5·50 1·50
a. Deep carmine and deep green (6.59) 6·50 1·00
D141 2s. deep carmine and deep green (8.3.60) 12·00 1·50
D132a/D141 *Set of* 10 45·00 60·00

Nos. D140*a* and D141. Value tablets are re-engraved and have thicker and sharper printed lines than before.

The use of Postage Due stamps ceased on 31 January 1963.

OFFICIAL STAMPS

From 1902 the departments of the Commonwealth government were issued with stamps of the various Australian States perforated 'OS' to denote official use. These were replaced in 1913 by Commonwealth of Australia issues with similar perforated initials as listed below.

During the same period the administrations of the Australian States used their own stamps and those of the Commonwealth perforated with other initials for the same purpose. These States issues are outside the scope of this catalogue.

Most shades listed under the postage issues also exist perforated 'OS'. Only those which are worth more than the basic colours are included below.

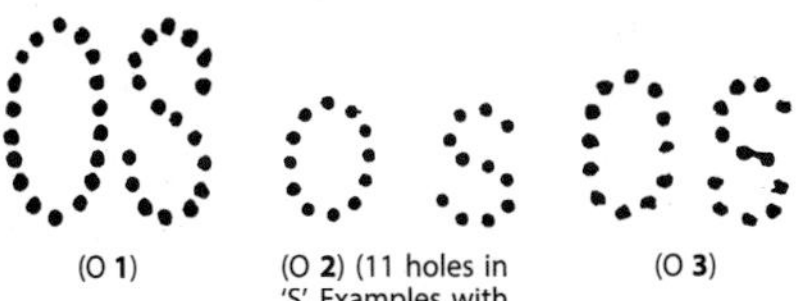

(O **1**) (O **2**) (11 holes in 'S'. Examples with 12 holes in 'S' are N.S.W. state issues) (O **3**)

1913 (Jan–Apr). Nos. 1/16 punctured as Type O **1**. W **2**. P 12.

O1 **1** ½d. green (Die I) 28·00 20·00
w. Wmk inverted † £150
O2 1d. red (Die I) 18·00 4·75
cw. Wmk inverted £160 27·00
d. Die II 45·00 16·00
da. Wmk sideways † £1200
dw. Wmk inverted £160 25·00
O3 2d. grey (Die I) 60·00 23·00
O4 2½d. indigo (Die II) £350 £140
O5 3d. olive (Die I) £225 50·00
ca. In pair with Die II £2000
dw. Wmk inverted £400 £150
e. Die II £750 £275
ew. Wmk inverted £1800 £500
O6 4d. orange (Die II) £275 22·00
a. Orange-yellow £700 £200
O7 5d. chestnut (Die II) £275 50·00
O8 6d. ultramarine (Die II) £225 20·00
w. Wmk inverted £1800 £750
O9 9d. violet (Die II) £325 65·00
w. Wmk inverted † £10000

O10		1s. emerald (Die II)	£375	28·00
		w. Wmk inverted	£2750	£1000
O11		2s. brown (Die II)	£650	£160
		a. Double print	†	£5000
O12		5s. grey and yellow	£1600	£700
O13		10s. grey and pink	£6000	£3250
O14		£1 brown and ultramarine	£11000	£8000
O15		£2 black and rose	£50000	£42000

1914. Nos. 1/16 punctured as Type O **2**. W **2**. P 12.

O16	**1**	½d. green (Die I)	27·00	10·00
		w. Wmk inverted	†	£180
O17		1d. red (Die I)	55·00	27·00
		d. Die II	45·00	3·75
		e. Die IIA	50·00	3·75
O18		2d. grey (Die I)	90·00	4·50
		w. Wmk inverted	£225	60·00
O19		2½d. indigo (Die II)	£400	£160
O20		3d. olive (Die I)	£180	16·00
		dw. Wmk inverted	£425	£100
		e. Die II	£800	£300
		ew. Wmk inverted	£1500	£550
O21		4d. orange (Die II)	£450	£100
		a. Orange-yellow	£950	£325
O22		5d. chestnut (Die II)	£350	65·00
O23		6d. ultramarine (Die II)	£250	14·00
		w. Wmk inverted	†	£1000
O24		9d. violet (Die II)	£325	50·00
O25		1s. emerald (Die II)	£325	22·00
O26		2s. brown (Die II)	£1000	£140
O27		5s. grey and yellow		
O28		10s. grey and pink	£12000	£8500
O29		£1 brown and ultramarine	£17000	£12000
O30		£2 black and rose	£45000	

1915. Nos. 24 and 26/30 punctured as Type O **2**. W **5**. P 12.

O31	**1**	2d. grey (Die I)	£200	12·00
O33		6d. ultramarine (Die II)	£425	22·00
		b. Die IIA	£7000	£3500
O34		9d. violet (Die II)	£900	£110
O35		1s. blue-green (Die II)	£900	£130
O36		2s. brown (Die II)	£1800	£160
O37		5s. grey and yellow	£2000	£225
		a. Yellow portion doubly printed	†	£4750
		w. Wmk inverted	£2100	£325

1914–21. Nos. 20/23 punctured as Type O **2**. W **5**. P 14¼×14 (comb).

O38	**5a**	½d. bright green	24·00	2·75
		a. Perf 14¼ (line)	†	£3750
		w. Wmk inverted	30·00	9·50
O39		1d. carmine-red (I) (No. 21c)	15·00	1·00
		gw. Wmk inverted	30·00	6·00
		h. Die II	£550	75·00
O41		4d. orange	90·00	3·50
		a. Yellow-orange	£100	7·50
		b. Pale orange-yellow	£200	18·00
		c. Lemon-yellow	£700	£100
		w. Wmk inverted	£150	30·00
O42		5d. brown (P 14¼ (line))	90·00	4·50
		aw. Wmk inverted	£1300	£700
		b. Printed on the gummed side (wmk inverted)	£9500	
		c. Perf 14¼×14 (comb)	90·00	4·00
		cw. Wmk inverted	£1200	£700

1915–28. Nos. 35/45 punctured as Type O **2**. W **6**. P 12.

O43	**1**	2d. grey (Die I)	65·00	14·00
		bw. Wmk inverted	£170	80·00
		d. Die IIA	90·00	27·00
		da. Printed double	†	£3750
O44		2½d. deep blue (Die II)	£100	35·00
		w. Wmk inverted	—	£140
O45		3d. yellow-olive (Die I)	70·00	5·50
		cw. Wmk inverted	£140	75·00
		d. Die II	£375	£120
		dw. Wmk inverted	£650	£325
		e. Die IIB	85·00	30·00
		ew. Wmk inverted	£250	£120
O46		6d. ultramarine (Die II)	80·00	11·00
		a. Die IIA	£6000	£1800
		d. Die IIB	£160	48·00
		dw. Wmk inverted	£300	£150
O47		9d. violet (Die II)	95·00	35·00
		b. Die IIB	£110	40·00
		bw. Wmk inverted	†	£140
O48		1s. blue-green (Die II)	65·00	3·50
		aw. Wmk inverted	£1200	£800
		b. Die IIB	60·00	6·50
O49		2s. brown (Die II)	£475	17·00
		b. Red-brown (aniline)	£2250	£750
		w. Wmk inverted	£4250	£850
O50		5s. grey and yellow	£700	70·00
		w. Wmk inverted	£2000	£1300
O51		10s. grey and pink	£1200	75·00
O52		£1 chocolate and dull blue	£9500	£6000
		ab. Wmk sideways. Chestnut and bright blue	£170000	
		aw. Wmk inverted	£11000	£7000
O53		£2 black and rose	£5500	£2500

1916–20. Nos. 47/47f and 5d. as No. 23 punctured as Type O **2**. Rough paper. W **5**. P 14.

O54	**5a**	1d. scarlet (Die I)	50·00	7·00
		a. Deep red	50·00	7·00
		b. Rose-red	50·00	7·00
		c. Rosine	£130	22·00
		dw. Wmk inverted	£110	21·00
		e. Die II. Rose-red	£500	38·00
		f. Die II. Rosine	£800	£130
		gw. Die II. Wmk inverted	£1100	£160
O60		5d. bright chestnut (P 14¼ (line)) (9.20)	£5500	£180

All examples of the 5d. on this paper were perforated 'OS'.

1918–20. Nos. 48/52 punctured as Type O **2**. W **6a**. P 14.

O61	**5a**	½d. green	30·00	2·00
		w. Wmk inverted	50·00	20·00
O62		1d. carmine-pink (I)	†	£2250
O63		1d. carmine (I)	£200	75·00
O64		1½d. black-brown	20·00	14·00
		a. Very thin paper	£150	65·00
		w. Wmk inverted	£130	60·00
O65		1½d. red-brown	42·00	2·50
		w. Wmk inverted	£130	60·00
O61/O65 *Set of 4*			£250	80·00

1918–23. Nos. 56/59 and 61/66 punctured as Type O **2**. W **5**. P 14.

O66	**5a**	½d. orange	17·00	10·00
O67		1d. violet	50·00	15·00
		w. Wmk inverted	†	£25000
O68		1½d. black-brown	50·00	7·50
		w. Wmk inverted	£110	35·00
O69		1½d. deep red-brown	50·00	2·50
		aw. Wmk inverted	£130	60·00
O69*b*		1½d. bright red-brown	—	£120
O70		1½d. green	42·00	3·75
O71		2d. brown-orange	16·00	3·75
		w. Wmk inverted	£325	85·00
O72		2d. bright rose-scarlet	42·00	4·00
		w. Wmk inverted	£1300	£200
O73		4d. violet	90·00	13·00
O74		4d. ultramarine	80·00	11·00
O75		1s.4d. pale blue	£110	18·00
		b. Deep turquoise	£4250	£3500
O66/O75 *Set of 10*			£450	75·00

1923–24. Nos. 73/75 punctured as Type O **2**. W **6**. P 12.

O76	**1**	6d. chestnut (Die IIB)	45·00	2·50
O77		2s. maroon (Die II)	£180	12·00
O78		£1 grey (Die IIB)	£1900	£1100
O76/O78 *Set of 3*			£2000	£1100

1924. Nos. 76/84 punctured as Type O **2**. P 14.

*(a) W **5***

O79	**5a**	1d. sage-green	24·00	6·00
O80		1½d. scarlet	15·00	1·00
		w. Wmk inverted	£130	30·00
		wa. Printed on the gummed side	£375	
O81		2d. red-brown	24·00	18·00
		a. Bright red-brown	85·00	38·00
O82		3d. dull ultramarine	55·00	6·00
O83		4d. olive-yellow	60·00	6·00
O84		4½d. violet	£300	17·00
		w. Wmk inverted	†	£15000

*(b) W **6a***

O85	**5a**	1d. sage-green	45·00	35·00

(c) No wmk

O86	**5a**	1d. sage-green	85·00	85·00
O87		1½d. scarlet	90·00	85·00
O79/O87 *Set of 9*			£550	£225

1926–30. Nos. 85/104 punctured as Type O **2**. W **7**.

(a) P 14

O88	**5a**	½d. orange	£400	£160
O89		1d. sage-green	12·00	3·50
O90		1½d. scarlet	45·00	5·00
		a. Golden scarlet	50·00	9·00
		w. Wmk inverted	60·00	12·00
O92		2d. red-brown (Die I)	£275	45·00
O93		3d. dull ultramarine	£100	13·00
		w. Wmk inverted	£120	90·00
O94		4d. yellow-olive	£300	50·00
O95		4½d. violet	£275	40·00
O96		1s.4d. pale greenish blue	£800	£275
O88/O96 *Set of 8*			£1900	£500

(b) P 13½×12½

O97	**5a**	½d. orange	12·00	1·25
O98		1d. sage-green (Die I)	7·00	1·75
		b. Die II	£160	£160
O100		1½d. scarlet	20·00	2·50
		a. Golden scarlet	20·00	5·00
		w. Wmk inverted	22·00	5·50
O102		1½d. red-brown	40·00	5·00
O103		2d. red-brown (Die II)	55·00	16·00
O104		2d. golden scarlet (Die II)	25·00	4·50
		a. Die III	30·00	7·00
		aw. Wmk inverted	40·00	12·00
O106		3d. dull ultramarine (Die I)	50·00	7·00
		b. Die II. Deep ultramarine	24·00	1·50
		bw. Wmk inverted	£16000	£13000
O108		4d. yellow-olive	42·00	3·75
O109		4½d. violet	£250	£170
O110		5d. orange-brown (Die II)	90·00	7·00
O111		1s.4d. turquoise	£550	40·00
O97/O111 *Set of 11*			£900	£225

1927 (9 May). Opening of Parliament House, Canberra. No. 105 punctured as Type O **3**.

O112	**8**	1½d. brownish lake	24·00	9·50

1928 (29 Oct). National Stamp Exhibition, Melbourne. No. 106 punctured as Type O **2**.

O113		3d. blue	15·00	9·50

1929–30. Nos. 107/114 punctured as Type O **2**. W **7**. P 12.

O114	**1**	6d. chestnut (Die IIB)	45·00	7·50
O115		9d. violet (Die IIB)	£100	7·00
O116		1s. blue-green (Die IIB)	25·00	11·00
O117		2s. maroon (Die II)	£225	8·50
O118		5s. grey and yellow	£800	45·00
O118*a*		10s. grey and pink	£14000	£14000
O118*b*		£2 black and rose	£32000	£30000

1929 (20 May). Air. No. 115 punctured as Type O **3**.

O119	**9**	3d. green	35·00	12·00

1929 (28 Sept). Centenary of Western Australia. No. 116 punctured as Type O **3**.

O120	**10**	1½d. dull scarlet	26·00	22·00

1930 (2 June). Centenary of Exploration of River Murray by Captain Sturt. Nos. 117/118 punctured as Type O **2**.

O121	**11**	1½d. scarlet	23·00	8·50
O122		3d. blue	32·00	8·50

(O **4**)

1931 (4 May). Nos. 121/122 optd with Type O **4**.

O123	**13**	2d. rose-red	85·00	27·00
O124		3d. blue	£275	27·00

For No. 139 overprinted with Type O **4**, see No. 139*a*.

1932 (Feb)–**33**. Optd as Type O **4**.

*(a) W **7***

(i) P 13½×12½

O125	**5a**	2d. golden scarlet (Die III)	27·00	1·50
		a. Opt inverted	†	£75000
		w. Wmk inverted	£4750	£3250
O126		4d. yellow-olive (3.32)	26·00	3·00

(ii) P 12

O127	**1**	6d. chestnut (3.32)	55·00	55·00

*(b) W **15***

(i) P 13½×12½

O128	**5a**	½d. orange (11.7.32)	12·00	1·50
		a. Opt inverted	£30000	£22000
O129		1d. green (3.32)	4·25	45
		w. Wmk inverted	£1300	£800
		x. Wmk reversed	£2250	£900
O130		2d. golden scarlet (Die III)	25·00	55
		a. Opt inverted	†	£50000
O131		3d. ultramarine (Die II) (2.33)	7·50	4·75
O132		5d. orange-brown (7.32)	50·00	27·00

(ii) P 12

O133	**1**	6d. chestnut (9.32)	42·00	20·00
		a. Opt inverted	†	£75000

(c) Recess. No wmk. P 11

O134	**18**	2d. scarlet (3.32)	12·00	2·00
O135		3d. blue (3.32)	18·00	5·00
O136	**17**	1s. green (4.32)	50·00	30·00

No. O128a and probably the other inverted overprints were caused by the insertion of a stamp upside down into sheets repaired before surcharging.

Issue of overprinted official stamps ceased in February 1933 and remaining supplies were withdrawn from sale on 1 October 1935. Thereafter mail from the federal administration was carried free.

BRITISH COMMONWEALTH OCCUPATION FORCE (JAPAN)

Nos. J1/J7 were used by the Australian forces occupying Japan after the Second World War. Initially their military post offices supplied unoverprinted Australian stamps, but it was decided to introduce the overprinted issue to prevent currency speculation.

B.C.O.F.
JAPAN
1946
(**1**)

B.C.O.F.
JAPAN
1946
(**2**)

1946 — Wrong fount '6' (left pane R. 9/4)

.F. AN — Normal

.F. AN — Narrow 'N' (right pane R. 1/8)

1946 (12 Oct)–**47**. Stamps of Australia optd as T **1** (1d., 3d.,) or T **2** (others) at Hiroshima Printing Co, Japan.

J1	**27**	½d. orange (No. 179)	9·00	14·00
		a. Wrong fount '6'	£190	£200
		b. Narrow 'N'	£200	£225
		c. Stop after 'JAPAN' (right pane R. 5/5)	£300	£325
J2	**46**	1d. brown-purple (No. 203)	8·00	8·50
		a. Blue-black overprint	60·00	£110
J3	**31**	3d. purple-brown (No. 187)	3·00	5·50
		a. Opt double	£1200	£1300
J4	**34**	6d. purple-brown (No. 190*a*) (8.5.47)	29·00	23·00
		a. Wrong fount '6'	£300	£325
		b. Stop after 'JAPAN' (right pane R. 5/5)	£425	£425
		c. Narrow 'N'	£300	£325
J5	**36**	1s. grey-green (No. 192) (8.5.47)	20·00	25·00
		a. Wrong fount '6'	£350	£425
		b. Stop after 'JAPAN' (right pane R. 5/5)	£550	£600
		c. Narrow 'N'	£350	£425
		d. Roller flaw	£250	£275
J6	**1**	2s. maroon (No. 212) (8.5.47)	45·00	65·00
J7	**38**	5s. claret (No. 176) (8.5.47)	£140	£180
		a. Thin rough paper (No. 176a)	£110	£180
J1/J7a *Set of 7*			£190	£275

The ½d., 1d. and 3d. values were first issued on 12 October 1946, and withdrawn two days later, but were re-issued together with the other values on 8 May 1947.

The following values with T **2** in the colours given were from proof sheets which, however, were used for postage: ½d. (red) 1d. (red or black) and 3d. (gold, red or black). (*Prices for black opts £100, each, and for red or gold from £325 each, all un*).

The use of B.C.O.F. stamps ceased on 12 February 1949.

AUSTRALIAN ANTARCTIC TERRITORY

For use at the Antarctic bases of Casey (opened early 1969: used Wilkes postmark until early 1970), Davis (closed from 1965 until early 1969), Heard Island (seasonal occupation only), Macquarie Island, Mawson and Wilkes (closed January 1969). Stamps of Australia were used from the bases before 27 March 1957 and remained valid for use there after the introduction of Australian Antarctic Territory issues.

The following are also valid for use in Australia, where they are put on sale for a limited period when first issued.

DATES OF ISSUE. The dates given refer to release dates in Australia. Local release dates are usually later and where known they are given in footnotes.

1 1954 Expedition at Vestfold Hills and Map

(Des. T. Lawrence: adapted by artist of the Printing Branch. Recess)

1957 (27 Mar). P 14½.

1	**1**	2s. ultramarine	1·00	65

Issued Macquarie Island 11.12.57, Davis 6.2.58, Mawson 18.2.58, Wilkes 1.2.59.

2 Members of Shackleton Expedition at South Magnetic Pole, 1909

3 Weazel and Team

4 Dog team and iceberg

5 Map of Antarctica and Emperor Penguins

1959 (16 Dec). T **2/4.** T **3.** Recess; new values surch typo (5d., 8d.). P 14½ (5d.), 14½×14 (8d.) or 14×14½ (others).

2	**2**	5d. on 4d. black and sepia	60	15
3	**3**	8d. on 7d. black and indigo	1·75	2·25
4	**4**	1s. deep green	2·25	2·00
5	**5**	2s.3d. green	7·00	3·00
2/5 *Set of 4*			10·50	6·75

Issued Macquarie Island 26.12.59, Davis 30.1.60, Mawson 10.2.60, Wilkes 13.2.60.

6

7 Sir Douglas Mawson (Expedition leader)

Normal

Weak entry

Weak entry at left (R. 1/5 and 2/5)

1961 (5 July). Recess. P 14½.

6	**6**	5d. deep blue	1·60	20
		a. Weak entry	32·00	

Issued Macquarie Island 6.12.61, Wilkes 10.1.62, Davis 20.1.62, Mawson 30.1.62.

1961 (18 Oct). 50th Anniversary of 1911–1914 Australasian Antarctic Expedition. Recess. P 14½.

7	**7**	5d. myrtle-green	55	20

Issued Macquarie Island 6.12.61, Wilkes 10.1.62, Davis 20.1.62, Mawson 30.1.62.

(New Currency. 100 cents = 1 Australian dollar)

8 Aurora and Camera Dome

9 Bell 47G Trooper Helicopter

(Des J. Mason. Photo)

1966 (28 Sept)–**68**. Vert designs as T **8** (1c. to 15c.) or horiz as T **9** (20c. to $1). Multicoloured. Helecon paper (5c.). P 13½.

8	1c. Type **8** (*shades*)	70	30
9	2c. Emperor Penguins (*shades*)	3·00	80
10	4c. Ship and iceberg	1·00	90
11	5c. Banding Elephant Seals (25.9.68)	1·75	1·75
12	7c. Measuring snow strata	80	80
13	10c. Wind gauges	1·00	1·10
14	15c. Weather balloon	4·00	2·00
15	20c. Type **9**	9·50	2·50
16	25c. Radio operator	1·50	2·25
17	50c. Ice compression tests	2·25	4·00
18	$1 Parahelion ('mock sun')	16·00	12·00
8/18 *Set of 11*		38·00	25·00

Nos. 13/15 and 17 have parts of the designs printed in bright orange fluorescent ink.

Nos. 8/10 and 12/18 placed on sale locally at Macquarie Island on 11.12.66, Wilkes 9.2.67 and Mawson 16.2.67.

No. 11 issued Macquarie Island 4.12.68, Mawson 13.1.69, Wilkes/Casey 9.2.69 and Davis 20.2.69.

CHRISTMAS ISLAND

Formerly a part of the Straits Settlements and then of the Colony of Singapore, Christmas Island was occupied by the Japanese from 31 March, 1942, until September, 1945. It reverted to Singapore after liberation, but subsequently became an Australian territory on 15 October 1958.

Stamps of the STRAITS SETTLEMENTS were used on Christmas Island from 1901 until 1942. Following liberation issues of MALAYA (BRITISH MILITARY ADMINISTRATION) and then SINGAPORE were used from 1946 to 1958.

(Currency. 100 cents = 1 Malayan dollar)

1 Queen Elizabeth II

(Des G. Lissenden. Recess with name and value typo in black. Note Printing Branch, Commonwealth Bank, Melbourne)

1958 (15 Oct). No wmk. P 14½.

1	**1**	2c. yellow-orange	55	80
2		4c. brown	60	30
3		5c. deep mauve	60	50
4		6c. grey-blue	1·00	30
5		8c. black-brown	1·75	50
6		10c. violet	1·00	30
7		12c. carmine	1·75	1·75
8		20c. blue	1·00	1·75
9		50c. yellow-green	2·00	1·75
10		$1 deep bluish green	2·00	1·75
1/10 *Set of 10*			11·00	8·75

PRINTERS. Nos. 11/32 were printed by the Note Printing Branch, Reserve Bank of Australia, Melbourne. Nos. 33/82 were printed in photogravure by Harrison and Sons, Ltd, London.

2 Map

3 Moonflower

4 Robber crab

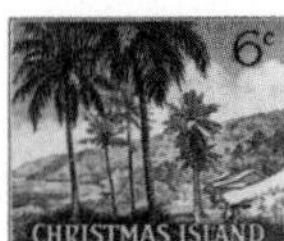

5 Island scene

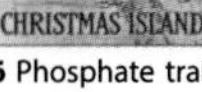

6 Phosphate train

7 Raising phosphate

8 Flying Fish Cove

9 Loading cantilever

10 Christmas Island Frigatebird

11 White-tailed Tropicbird

(Des G. Lissenden (2, 8c.), P. Morriss (4, 5, 10, 20c.), B. Stewart (others). Recess)

1963 (28 Aug). T **2/11.** P 14½ × 14 ($1) or 14½ (others).

11	**2**	2c. orange	1·25	35
12	**3**	4c. red-brown	50	15
13	**4**	5c. purple	50	20
14	**5**	6c. indigo	30	35
15	**6**	8c. black	2·50	35
16	**7**	10c. violet	40	15
17	**8**	12c. brown-red	40	25
18	**9**	20c. blue	1·00	20
19	**10**	50c. green	1·00	20
20	**11**	$1 yellow	1·75	35
11/20 *Set of 10*			8·50	2·25

I Thick lettering

II Thinner lettering

1965. 50th Anniversary of Gallipoli Landing. As T **184** of Australia but slightly larger (22×34½ *mm*) and colour changed. Photo. P 13½.

21	10c. sepia, black and emerald (I) (14.4)	30	1·75
	a. Black-brown, black and light emerald (II) (24.4)	2·50	2·75

(New Currency. 100 cents = 1 Australian dollar)

12 Golden-striped Grouper

13 Angel (mosaic)

(Des G. Hamori. Photo)

1968 (6 May)–**70.** Fish. T **12** and similar horiz designs. Multicoloured. P 13½.

22	1c. Type **12**	45	45
23	2c. Moorish Idol	60	20
24	3c. Long-nosed Butterflyfish	60	30
25	4c. Pink-tailed Triggerfish	60	20
	a. Deep blue (face value) omitted	£3000	
26	5c. Regal Angelfish	60	20
27	9c. White-cheeked Surgeonfish	60	40
28	10c. Lionfish	60	20
28*a*	15c. Saddle Butterflyfish (14.12.70)	2·25	2·50
29	20c. Ornate Butterflyfish	1·50	55
29*a*	30c. Giant Ghost Pipefish (14.12.70)	2·25	2·50
30	50c. Clown Surgeonfish	2·75	2·75
31	$1 Meyer's Butterflyfish	2·75	2·75
22/31 *Set of 12*		14·00	11·50

(Des G. Hamori. Photo)

1969 (10 Nov). Christmas. P 13½.

32	**13**	5c. red, deep blue and gold	20	30

14 *The Ansidei Madonna* (Raphael)

(Des Harrison)

1970 (26 Oct). Christmas. Paintings. T **14** and similar vert design. Multicoloured. P 14×14½.

33	3c. Type **14**	20	15
34	5c. *The Virgin and Child, St. John the Baptist and an Angel* (Morando)	20	15

COCOS (KEELING) ISLANDS

The Cocos (Keeling) Islands, which had been settled by the Clunies Ross family in the 1820s, were annexed by Great Britain in 1857. In 1878 the group was attached to Ceylon, but was transferred to the Straits Settlements on 7 February 1886. During the Second World War the islands were under British military control exercised from Ceylon. At the end of hostilities administration from Singapore was continued until the islands were transferred to Australia on 23 November 1955.

> The stamps of the STRAITS SETTLEMENTS were used by a postal agency operating on Cocos (Keeling) Islands from 1 April 1933 until 1 March 1937. The postal agency reopened on 2 September 1952 and used the stamps of SINGAPORE until the islands were transferred to Australia in 1955. From 1955 until 1963 stamps of AUSTRALIA were in use.
>
> Nos. 1/31 were also valid for use in Australia.

> **PRINTERS.** All the following stamps to No. 31 were printed by the Note Printing Branch, Reserve Bank of Australia, Melbourne.

1 Copra Industry

2 Super Constellation

3 Map of islands

4 Palms

5 Dukong (sail boat)

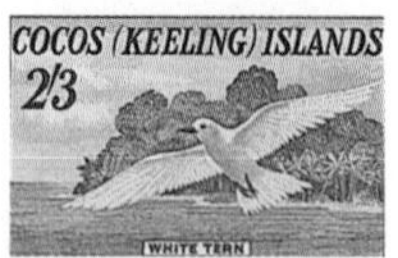

6 White Tern

(Des K. McKay and E. Jones (5d.), E. Jones (others). Eng E. Jones. Recess)

1963 (11 June). T **1/6**. P 14½×14 (5d., 2s.3d.) or 14½ (others).

No.	Description	Unused	Used
1	3d. chocolate	1·50	1·50
2	5d. ultramarine	2·25	80
3	8d. scarlet	1·00	1·75
4	1s. green	1·00	75
5	2s. deep purple	8·00	2·00
6	2s.3d. deep green	9·00	1·75
1/6	*Set of 6*	20·00	7·50

I Thick lettering

II Thinner lettering

1965 (14 Apr). 50th Anniversary of Gallipoli Landing. As T **184** of Australia, but slightly larger (22×34½ *mm*) and colour changed. Photo. P 13½.

No.	Description	Unused	Used
7	5d. sepia, black and emerald (I)	60	45
	a. Black-brown, black and light emerald (II)	3·00	2·25

No. 7*a* comes from a second printing, using a new black cylinder, which was available from the end of April.

With the introduction of decimal currency on 14 February 1966, Australian stamps were used in Cocos Islands, until the appearance of the new definitives on 9 July 1969.

(New Currency. 100 cents = 1 Australian dollar)

7 Reef Clam (*Tridacna derasa*)

8 Great Frigatebird

(Des L. Annois (1c. to 6c.), P. Jones (10c. to $1). Photo)

1969 (9 July). Decimal Currency. T **8** or designs as T **7**. Multicoloured. P 13½.

No.	Description	Unused	Used
8	1c. Lajonkaines Turbo shell (*Turbo lajonkairii*) (*vert*)	30	60
9	2c. Elongate or Small Giant Clam (*Tridacna maxima*) (*vert*)	60	80
10	3c. Type **7**	40	20
11	4c. Floral Blenny (fish)	30	50
	a. Salmon-pink omitted	£2750	
12	5c. *Porites cocosensis* (coral)	35	30
13	6c. Atrisignis Flyingfish	60	75
14	10c. Buff-banded Rail	60	70
15	15c. Java Sparrow	60	30
16	20c. Red-tailed Tropicbird	60	30
17	30c. Sooty Tern	60	30
18	50c. Eastern Reef Heron (*vert*)	60	30
19	$1 Type **8**	1·25	75
8/19	*Set of 12*	6·00	5·25

NEW GUINEA

> Stamps of Germany and later of GERMAN NEW GUINEA were used in New Guinea from 1888 until 1914.
>
> During the interim period between the 'G.R.I.' surcharges and the 'N.W. PACIFIC ISLANDS' overprints, stamps of AUSTRALIA perforated 'OS' were utilised.

PRICES FOR STAMPS ON COVER TO 1945

Nos. 1/30	*from* × 3
Nos. 31/32	—
Nos. 33/49	*from* × 3
Nos. 50/59	*from* × 2
Nos. 60/62	—
Nos. 63/64	*from* × 2
Nos. 64*c*/64*q*	—
Nos. 65/81	*from* × 5
Nos. 83/85	—
Nos. 86/97	*from* × 5
No. 99	—
Nos. 100/116	*from* × 4
Nos. 117/118	—
Nos. 119/124	*from* × 4
Nos. 125/203	*from* × 2
Nos. 204/205	—
Nos. 206/211	*from* × 8
Nos. 212/225	*from* × 2
Nos. O1/O54	*from* × 8

AUSTRALIAN OCCUPATION

Stamps of German New Guinea surcharged

G.R.I. 2d. (1)   G.R.I. 1s. (2)   1 (3)

SETTINGS. The 'G.R.I.' issues of New Guinea were surcharged on a small hand press which could only accommodate one horizontal row of stamps at a time. In addition to complete sheets the surcharges were also applied to multiples and individual stamps which were first lightly affixed to plain paper backing sheets. Such backing sheets could contain a mixture of denominations, some of which required different surcharges.

Specialists recognise 12 settings of the low value surcharges (1d. to 8d.):

Setting 1	(Nos. 1/4, 7/11) shows the bottom of the 'R' 6 mm from the top of the 'd'
Setting 2	(Nos. 16/19, 22/26) shows the bottom of the 'R' 5 mm from the top of the 'd'
Setting 3	was used for the Official stamps (Nos. O1/O2)
Setting 4, Setting 5	which included the 2½d. value for the first time, and showed individual stamps with either 6 mm or 5 mm spacing.

These five settings were for rows of ten stamps, but the remaining seven, used on odd stamps handed in for surcharging, were applied as strips of five only. One has, so far, not been reconstructed, but of the remainder three show the 6 mm spacing, two the 5 mm and one both.

On the shilling values the surcharges were applied as horizontal rows of four and the various settings divide into two groups, one with 3½ to 4½ mm between the bottom of the 'R' and the top of numeral, and the second with 5½ mm between the 'R' and numeral. The first group includes the very rare initial setting on which the space is 4 to 4½ mm.

G.R.I. 2d. '1' for 'I' (Setting 1)   G.R.I. 1d. Short '1' (Setting 1)   G.R.I. 1s. Large 'S' (Setting 1)

1914 (17 Oct)–**15**. Stamps of 1901 surch.

(a) As T **1**. *'G.R.I.' and value 6 mm apart*

No.	Description	Unused	Used
1	1d. on 3pf. brown	£750	£850
	a. '1' for 'I'	£2000	£2250
	b. Short '1'	£2000	£2250
	c. '1' with straight top serif (Setting 6)	£2000	
	d. 'I' for '1' (Setting 12)	£3500	
2	1d. on 5pf. green	85·00	£110
	a. '1' for 'I'	£350	£425
	b. Short '1'	£350	£425
	c. '1' with straight top serif (Settings 6 and 9)	£475	£550
3	2d. on 10pf. carmine	90·00	£120
	a. '1' for 'I'	£400	£500
4	2d. on 20pf. ultramarine	90·00	£110
	a. '1' for 'I'	£375	£425
	e. Surch double, one 'G.R.I.' albino	£5500	
	f. Surch inverted	£16000	
5	2½d. on 10pf. carmine (27.2.15)	95·00	£200
	a. Fraction bar omitted (Setting 9)	£3500	£3500
6	2½d. on 20pf. ultramarine (27.2.15)	£110	£225
	a. Fraction bar omitted (Setting 9)	†	£9500
7	3d. on 25pf. black and red/*yellow*	£375	£450
	a. '1' for 'I'	£1100	£1300
8	3d. on 30pf. black and orange/*buff*	£475	£500
	a. '1' for 'I'	£1300	£1500
	e. Surch double	£15000	£15000
9	4d. on 40pf. black and carmine	£475	£500
	a. '1' for 'I'	£1500	
	e. Surch double	£4000	£4750
	f. Surch inverted	£16000	
10	5d. on 50pf. black and purple/*buff*	£850	£1000
	a. '1' for 'I'	£2250	£3000
	e. Surch double	£16000	
	f. Surch inverted	£16000	
11	8d. on 80pf. black and carmine/*rose*	£1000	£1500
	a. '1' for 'I'	£3250	£4250
	d. No stop after 'd'	£4250	
	e. Error. Surch 'G.R.I. 4d.'	£15000	

(b) As T **2**. *'G.R.I.' and value 3½ to 4 mm apart*

No.	Description	Unused	Used
12	1s. on 1m. carmine	£3500	£4250
	a. Large 's'	£13000	£13000
13	2s. on 2m. blue	£3250	£4000
	a. Large 's'	£12000	£14000
	c. Error. Surch 'G.R.I. 5s.'	£45000	
	d. Error. Surch 'G.R.I. 2d.' corrected by handstamped 'S'	£50000	
14	3s. on 3m. violet-black	£5500	£7000
	a. Large 's'	£16000	
	b. No stop after 'I' (Setting 3)	£13000	£13000
15	5s. on 5m. carmine and black	£14000	£16000
	a. Large 's'	£29000	
	b. No stop after 'I' (Setting 3)	£18000	£20000
	c. Error. Surch 'G.R.I. 1s.'	£85000	

G.R.I. 3d. Thick '3' (Setting 2)   G.R.I. 5d. Thin '5' (Setting 2)

1914 (16 Dec)–**15**. Stamps of 1901 surch.

(a) As T **1**. *'G.R.I.' and value 5 mm apart*

No.	Description	Unused	Used
16	1d. on 3pf. brown	£100	£110
	a. 'I' for '1' (Setting 11)	£750	
	b. Short '1' (Setting 2)	£325	
	c. '1' with straight top serif (Settings 2 and 6)	£150	£180
	e. Surch double	£1500	£1800
	f. Surch double, one inverted	£8000	
	g. Surch inverted	£6000	
	h. Error. Surch 'G.R.I. 4d.'	£17000	
17	1d. on 5pf. green	35·00	50·00
	b. Short '1' (Setting 2)	£130	£190
	c. '1' with straight top serif (Setting 2)	50·00	80·00
	e. 'd' inverted	†	£3750
	f. '1d' inverted	†	£11000
	g. 'G.R.I.' without stops or spaces	£11000	
	ga. 'G.R.I.' without stops, but with normal spaces	—	£11000
	h. 'G.I.R.' instead of 'G.R.I.'	£13000	£14000
	i. Surch double	£5000	£6000
18	2d. on 10pf. carmine	50·00	60·00
	e. No stop after 'd' (Setting 2)	£180	£250
	f. Stop before, instead of after, 'G' (Settings 4 and 5)	£11000	
	g. Surch double	£16000	£16000
	h. Surch double, one inverted	—	£13000
	i. In vert pair with No. 20	£20000	
	j. In horiz pair with No. 20	£28000	
	k. Error. Surch 'G.R.I. 1d.'	£12000	£12000
	l. Error. Surch 'G.I.R. 3d.'	£13000	
19	2d. on 20pf. ultramarine	50·00	70·00
	e. No stop after 'd' (Setting 2)	£130	£190
	f. No stop after 'I' (Setting 11)	£1500	
	g. 'R' inverted (Settings 4 and 5)	—	£9000
	h. Surch double	£3500	£5000
	i. Surch double, one inverted	£4750	£7000
	j. Surch inverted	£10000	
	k. Albino surch (in horiz pair with normal)	£23000	
	l. In vert pair with No. 21	£18000	£21000
	m. Error. Surch 'G.R.I. 1d.'	£13000	£15000
20	2½d. on 10pf. carmine (27.2.15)	£225	£350
21	2½d. on 20pf. ultramarine (27.2.15)	£2000	£2500
	a. Error. Surch 'G.R.I. 3d.' (in vert pair with normal)	£40000	
22	3d. on 25pf. black and red/*yellow*	£190	£250
	e. Thick '3'	£600	£750
	f. Surch double	£11000	£13000
	g. Surch inverted	£11000	£13000
	h. Surch omitted (in horiz pair with normal)	£13000	
	i. Error. Surch 'G.R.I. 1d.'	£20000	
23	3d. on 30pf. black and orange/*buff*	£170	£225
	e. No stop after 'd' (Setting 2)	£800	
	f. Thick '3'	£550	
	g. Surch double	£4000	£4500
	h. Surch double, one inverted	£4500	£5500
	i. Surch double, both inverted	£13000	£14000
	j. Surch inverted	£10000	
	k. Albino surch	£12000	
	l. Surch omitted (in vert pair with normal)	£13000	
	m. Error. Surch 'G.R.I. 1d.'	£12000	£15000
24	4d. on 40pf. black and carmine	£180	£275
	e. Surch double	£3500	
	f. Surch double, one inverted	£5000	
	g. Surch double, both inverted	£13000	
	h. Surch inverted	£9500	
	i. Error. Surch 'G.R.I. 1d.'	£9000	
	ia. Surch 'G.R.I. 1d.' inverted	£19000	
	j. Error. Surch 'G.R.I. 3d.' double	£27000	
	k. No stop after 'I' (Setting 11)	£3250	

25 5d. on 50pf. black and purple/*buff* £325 £400
e. Thin '5' £1400 £3250
f. Surch double £4500 £5500
g. Surch double, one inverted £10000 £10000
h. Surch double, both inverted £13000 £14000
i. Surch inverted £10000
j. Error. Surch 'G.I.R. 3d.' £22000
26 8d. on 80pf. black and carmine/*rose* £425 £600
e. Surch double £7000 £8000
f. Surch double, one inverted £7000 £8000
g. Surch triple £9500 £10000
h. Surch inverted £14000
i. Error. Surch 'G.R.I. 3d.' £18000

(b) As T **2**. *'G.R.I.' and value 5½ mm apart*
27 1s. on 1m. carmine £5000 £8000
a. No stop after 'I' (Setting 7) £12000
28 2s. on 2m. blue £5500 £8000
a. No stop after 'I' (Setting 7) £12000
29 3s. on 3m. violet-black £10000 £15000
a. 'G.R.I.' double £45000
30 5s. on 5m. carmine and black £42000 £48000

1915 (1 Jan). Nos. 18 and 19 further surch with T **3**.
31 1d. on 2d. on 10pf. £28000 £28000
32 1d. on 2d. on 20pf. £28000 £17000

German New Guinea Registration Labels surcharged

4

4a

G.R.I.

3d.

Sans serif 'G'
and different '3'

1915 (Jan). Registration Labels surch 'G.R.I. 3d.' in settings of five or ten and used for postage. Each black and red on buff. Inscr '(Deutsch Neuguinea)' spelt in various ways as indicated. P 14 (No. 43) or 11½ (others).

I. With name of town in sans-serif letters as T **4**
33 **Rabaul** '(Deutsch Neuguinea)' £275 £325
a. 'G.R.I. 3d.' double £5000 £6500
b. No bracket before 'Deutsch' £900 £1300
ba. No bracket and surch double £16000
d. '(Deutsch-Neuguinea)' £425 £550
da. 'G.R.I. 3d.' double £16000 £16000
db. No stop after 'I' £900
dc. 'G.R.I. 3d' inverted £16000
dd. No bracket before 'Deutsch' £1500 £2000
de. No bracket after 'Neuguinea' £1500 £2000
34 **Deulon** '(Deutsch Neuguinea)' £32000 £35000
35 **Friedrich-Wilhelmshafen** '(Deutsch Neuguinea)' £250 £800
a. No stop after 'd' £450
b. 'G' omitted £7500
c. Sans-serif 'G' £16000
d. Sans-serif 'G' and different '3' £14000
e. Surch inverted † £16000
f. '(Deutsch-Neuguinea)' £275 £800
fa. No stop after 'd' £475
36 **Herbertshohe** '(Deutsch Neuguinea)' £300 £850
a. No stop after 'd' £500
b. No stop after 'I' £900 £1800
c. 'G' omitted £8500
d. Surch omitted (in horiz pair with normal) £18000
e. '(Deutsch Neu-Guinea)' £500 £1000
f. '(Deutsch-Neuguinea)'
37 **Kawieng** '(Deutsch-Neuguinea)' £1000
a. No bracket after 'Neuguinea' £3750
b. 'Deutsch Neu-Guinea' £325 £650
ba. No stop after 'd' £550
bb. 'G.R.I.' double £8000
bc. '3d.' double £8000
bd. 'G' omitted £8500
38 **Kieta** '(Deutsch-Neuguinea)' £450 £800
a. No bracket before 'Deutsch' £1600 £2750
b. No stop after 'd' £850
c. Surch omitted (right hand stamp of horiz pair) £16000
e. No stop after 'I' £1300
f. 'G' omitted £8000
39 **Manus** '(Deutsch Neuguinea)' £325 £900
a. 'G.R.I. 3d.' double £9000
b. No bracket before 'Deutsch' £1500 £2500
40 **Stephansort** '(Deutsch Neu-Guinea)' — £4500
a. No stop after 'd' † £8500

II. With name of town in letters with serifs as T **4a**
41 **Friedrich Wilhelmshafen** '(Deutsch-Neuguinea)' £275 £750
b. No stop after 'd' £450 £1100
c. No stop after 'I' £850 £1600
d. No bracket before 'Deutsch' £1600 £2250
e. No bracket after 'Neuguinea' £1600 £2250
42 **Kawieng** '(Deutsch Neuguinea)' £250 £650
a. No stop after 'd' £475
b. No stop after 'I'
43 **Manus** '(Deutsch-Neuguinea)' £4500 £5500
a. No stop after 'I' £9000 £8500

Examples of Nos. 33db, 36b, 38e, 41c and 43a also show the stop after 'R' either very faint or missing completely.

Stamps of Marshall Islands surcharged

SETTINGS. The initial supply of Marshall Islands stamps, obtained from Nauru, was surcharged with Setting 2 (5 *mm* between 'R' and 'd') on the penny values and with the 3½ to 4 setting on the shilling stamps.

Small quantities subsequently handed in were surcharged, often on the same backing sheet as German New Guinea values, with Settings 6, 7 or 12 (all 6 *mm* between 'R' and 'd') for the penny values and with a 5½ mm setting for the shilling stamps.

1914 (16 Dec). Stamps of 1901 surch.

(a) As T **1**. *'G.R.I.' and value 5 mm apart*
50 1d. on 3pf. brown £110 £170
c. '1' with straight top serif (Setting 2) £180 £300
d. 'G.R.I.' and '1' with straight top serif (Settings 4 and 5) † £14000
e. Surch inverted £9000
51 1d. on 5pf. green 80·00 85·00
c. '1' with straight top serif (Settings 2 and 11) £140 £160
d. 'I' for '1' (Setting 11) £1200
e. '1' and 'd' spaced £300 £325
f. Surch double £3750
g. Surch inverted £5000
52 2d. on 10pf. carmine 27·00 50·00
e. No stop after 'G' (Setting 2) £850
f. Surch double £3750
g. Surch double, one inverted £5500
h. Surch inverted £7000
i. Surch sideways £10000
53 2d. on 20pf. ultramarine 27·00 50·00
e. No stop after 'd' (Setting 2) 70·00 £110
g. Surch double £4000 £5000
h. Surch double, one inverted £10000 £10000
i. Surch inverted £11000 £11000
54 3d. on 25pf. black and red/*yellow* £450 £550
e. No stop after 'd' (Settings 2 and 11) £850 £1100
f. Thick '3' £1000 £1400
g. Surch double £4250 £4750
h. Surch double, one inverted £4750
i. Surch inverted £13000
55 3d. on 30pf. black and orange/*buff* £475 £600
e. No stop after 'd' (Setting 2) £900 £1200
f. Thick '3' £1100
g. Surch inverted £9000
h. Surch double £7000
56 4d. on 40pf. black and carmine £170 £250
e. No stop after 'd' (Setting 2) £425 £650
f. 'd' omitted (Setting 2) † £7000
g. Surch double £7000 £8000
h. Surch triple £14000
i. Surch inverted £10000
j. Error. Surch 'G.R.I. 1d.' £17000
k. Error. Surch 'G.R.I. 3d.' £17000
57 5d. on 50pf. black and purple/*buff* £300 £375
e. Thin '5' £3750
f. 'd' omitted (Setting 2) £2000
g. Surch double £10000
h. Surch inverted £16000
58 8d. on 80pf. black and carmine/*rose* £475 £700
e. Surch double £10000
f. Surch double, both inverted £13000 £14000
g. Surch triple £16000
h. Surch inverted £11000

(b) As T **2**. *'G.R.I.' and value 3½–4 mm apart*
59 1s. on 1m. carmine £4000 £5000
b. No stop after 'I' £6000 £9000
e. Surch double £45000
f. Error. Additional surch '1d.' £45000
60 2s. on 2m. blue £1900 £4000
b. No stop after 'I' £3500 £6000
e. Surch double £45000
f. Surch double, one inverted £42000 £42000
61 3s. on 3m. violet-black £6500 £9500
b. No stop after 'I' £8500
e. Surch double £40000 £45000
62 5s. on 5m. carmine and black £14000 £15000
e. Surch double, one inverted † £65000

1915 (Jan). Nos. 52 and 53 further surch with T **3**.
63 1d. on 2d. on 10pf. carmine £200 £275
a. '1' double £16000
b. '1' inverted £19000 £19000
c. Small '1' £650
64 1d. on 2d. on 20pf. ultramarine £4000 £2500
a. On No. 53e £9000 £4000
b. '1' inverted £19000 £19000

The surcharged '1' on No. 63c is just over 4 mm tall. Type **3** is 6 mm tall.

1915. Stamps of 1901 surch.

(a) As T **1**. *'G.R.I.' and value 6 mm apart*
64*c* 1d. on 3pf. brown £3500
cc. '1' with straight top serif (Setting 6)
cd. 'I' for '1' (Setting 12) £4250
ce. Surch inverted £16000
64*d* 1d. on 5pf. green £3500
dc. '1' with straight top serif (Setting 6) £4250
dd. 'I' for '1' (Setting 12) £4250
de. Surch inverted £16000
df. Surch double £16000
64*e* 2d. on 10pf carmine £4500
ea. Surch sideways £16000
64*f* 2d. on 20pf. ultramarine £4000
fe. Surch inverted £16000
64*g* 2½d. on 10pf. carmine £27000
64*h* 2½d. on 20pf. ultramarine £40000
64*i* 3d. on 25pf. black and red/*yellow* £6500
64*j* 3d. on 30pf. black and orange/*buff* £6500
je. Error. Surch 'G.R.I. 1d.' £18000
64*k* 4d. on 40pf. black and carmine £6500
ke. Surch double £18000
kf. Surch inverted £18000
64*l* 5d. on 50pf. black and purple/*buff* £6000
le. Surch double £18000
64*m* 8d. on 80pf. black and carmine/*rose* £7500
me. Surch inverted £18000

(b) As T **2**. *'G.R.I.' and value 5½ mm apart*
64*n* 1s. on 1m. carmine £17000
na. Large 's' (Setting 5) £21000
nb. No stop after 'I' (Setting 7) £21000
64*o* 2s. on 2m. blue £14000
a. Large 's' (Setting 5) £19000
b. Surch double, one inverted £55000
64*p* 3s. on 3m. violet-black £27000
pa. Large 's' (Setting 5) £38000
pb. No stop after 'I' (Setting 7) £38000
pe. Surch inverted £65000
64*q* 5s. on 5m. carmine and black £38000
qa. Large 's' (Setting 5) £50000

Stamps of Australia overprinted

N. W. PACIFIC ISLANDS.	N. W. PACIFIC ISLANDS.	N. W. PACIFIC ISLANDS.
(a)	(b)	(c)

(6)

1915–16. Stamps of Australia optd in black as T **6** (a), (b) or (c).

(i) T **5a**. *W* **5** *of Australia. P 14¼×14 (4 Jan–15 Mar 1915)*
65 ½d. green 3·00 9·00
a. Bright green 3·00 10·00
aw. Wmk inverted £2250 £2500
67 1d. pale rose (Die I) (4.1) 7·00 6·50
a. Dull red 7·00 6·50
b. Carmine-red 7·00 6·50
ba. Substituted cliché (Pl 2 right pane R. 6/5) £1900 £1500
bb. Dot before '1' £130 £140
bc. 'Secret mark' £130 £140
bd. Flaw under neck £130 £140
be. 'RA' joined £130 £140
c. Die II. *Carmine-red* £110 £140
ca. Substituted cliché (Pl 2 right pane R. 6/4) £1900 £1500
70 4d. yellow-orange 4·00 15·00
a. Pale orange-yellow 35·00 55·00
b. Chrome-yellow £250 £275
c. Line through 'FOUR PENCE' (PL 2 right pane R. 2/6) *(all shades)* ...*from* £425 £700
72 5d. brown (P 14¼ (line)) 3·00 17·00

(ii) T **1**. *W* **2** *of Australia. P 12 (4 Jan 1915–March 1916)*
73 2d. grey (Die I) 20·00 65·00
74 2½d. indigo (Die II) (4.1.15) 2·75 16·00
76 3d. yellow-olive (Die I) 21·00 55·00
a. Die II £350 £550
ab. In pair with Die I £800 £1200
c. Greenish olive £200 £275
ca. Die II £1300
cb. In pair with Die I £2250
78 6d. ultramarine (Die II) £110 £120
a. Retouched 'E' £7500 £8500
w. Wmk inverted £300 £400
79 9d. violet (Die II) 55·00 65·00
81 1s. green (Die II) 60·00 70·00
83 5s. grey and yellow (Die II) (3.16) £2750 £3750
84 10s. grey and pink (Die II) (12.15) £150 £180
85 £1 brown and ultramarine (Die II) (12.15) £550 £700

(iii) T **1**. *W* **5** *of Australia. P 12 (Oct 1915–July 1916)*
86 2d. grey (Die I) 18·00 48·00
87 2½d. indigo (Die II) (7.16) £28000 £28000
88 6d. ultramarine (Die II) 10·00 12·00
89 9d. violet (Die II) (12.15) 16·00 21·00
90 1s. emerald (Die II) (12.15) 11·00 24·00
91 2s. brown (Die II) (12.15) £110 £130
92 5s. grey and yellow (Die II) (12.15) 75·00 £110

(iv) T **1**. *W* **6** *of Australia. P 12 (Dec 1915–1916)*
94 2d. grey (Die I) 6·50 32·00
96 3d. yellow-olive (Die I) 5·50 11·00
a. Die II £110 £170
ab. In pair with Die I £325
97 2s. brown (Die II) (8.16) 35·00 50·00
w. Wmk inverted 30·00 90·00
99 £1 chocolate and dull blue (Die II) (8.16) £350 £450

Dates for Nos. 67 and 74 are issue dates at Rabaul. The stamps were in use from 2 January 1915 on Nauru. All other dates are those of despatch. Nos. 65/66, 68/73, 76/81 were despatched on 15 March 1915.

For Die IIA of 2d. see note below Australia No. 45.

SETTINGS. T **6** exists in three slightly different versions, illustrated above as (a), (b), and (c). These differ in the letters 'S' of 'ISLANDS' as follows:

(a) Both 'SS' normal.
(b) First 'S' with small head and large tail and second 'S' normal.
(c) Both 'SS' with small head and large tail.

T **11**, which also shows the examples of 'S' as the normal version, can be identified from T **6** *(a)* by the relative position of the second and third lines of the overprint. On T **6** *(a)* the 'P' of 'PACIFIC' is exactly over the first 'S' of 'ISLANDS'. On T **11** the 'P' appears over the space between 'I' and 'S'.

It has been established, by the study of minor variations, that there are actually six settings of the 'N.W. PACIFIC ISLANDS' overprint, including that represented by T **11**, but the following are the different arrangements of T **6** (a), (b), and (c) which occur.

A. Horizontal rows 1 and 2 all Type (a). Row 3 all Type (b). Rows 4 and 5 all Type (c).
B. (½d. green only). As A, except that the types in the bottom row run (c) (c) (c) (c) (b) (c).
C. As A, but bottom row now shows types (a) (c) (c) (c) (b) (c).

Horizontal strips and pairs showing varieties (a) and (c), or (b) and (c) *se-tenant* are scarce.

The earliest printing of the 1d. and 2½d. values was made on sheets with margin attached on two sides, the later printings being on sheets from which the margins had been removed. In this printing the vertical distances between the overprints are less than in later printings, so that in the lower horizontal rows of the sheet the overprint is near the top of the stamp.

The settings used on King George stamps and on the Kangaroo type are similar, but the latter stamps being smaller the overprints are closer together in the vertical rows.

PURPLE OVERPRINTS. We no longer differentiate between purple and black overprints in the above series. In our opinion the two colours are nowadays insufficiently distinct to warrant separation.

PRICES. The prices quoted for Nos. 65 to 101 apply to stamps with opts T **6** (a) or **6** (c). Stamps with opt T **6** (b) are worth a 25 per cent premium. Vertical strips of three, showing (a), (b) and (c), are worth from four times the prices quoted for singles as T **6** (a) or **6** (c).

One Penny (10)

N. W. PACIFIC ISLANDS. (11)

1918 (23 May). Nos. 72 and 81 surch locally with T **10**.

100 1d. on 5d. brown 90·00 80·00
101 1d. on 1s. green £100 80·00

T **6** (a), (b), (c) occur on these stamps also.

1918–22. Stamps of Australia optd with T **11** ('P' of 'PACIFIC' over space between 'I' and 'S' of 'ISLANDS').

*(i) T **5a**. W **5** of Australia. P 14¼×14*

102 ½d. green 1·75 3·50
w. Wmk inverted £3500
103 1d. carmine-red (Die I) 3·75 1·60
a. Substituted cliché (Pl 2 right pane R. 6/5) £1000 £650
ab. Dot before '1' 95·00 85·00
ac. 'Secret mark' 95·00 85·00
ad. Flaw under neck 95·00 85·00
ae. 'RA' joined 95·00 85·00
b. Die II £110 80·00
ba. Substituted cliché (Pl 2 right pane R. 6/4) £1000 £650
104 4d. yellow-orange (1919) 4·75 16·00
a. Line through 'FOUR PENCE' (Pl 2 right pane R. 2/6) £850 £1300
105 5d. brown (1919) 4·00 12·00

*(ii) T **1**. W **6** of Australia. P 12*

106 2d. grey (Die I) (1919) 7·50 25·00
a. Die II 12·00 50·00
107 2½d. indigo (Die II) (1919) 5·50 16·00
a. '1' of '½' omitted £14000 £17000
b. Blue (1920) 15·00 48·00
109 3d. greenish olive (Die I) (1919) 23·00 26·00
a. Die II 75·00 85·00
ab. In pair with Die I £425 £700
110 6d. ultramarine (Die II) (1919) 4·75 14·00
a. Greyish ultramarine (1922) 42·00 65·00
b. Die IIB. *Greyish ultramarine* — £750
112 9d. violet (Die IIB) (1919) 9·00 50·00
113 1s. emerald (Die II) 6·50 30·00
a. Pale blue-green (Die IIB) 14·00 32·00
115 2s. brown (Die II) (1919) 21·00 38·00
116 5s. grey and yellow (Die II) (1919) 65·00 70·00
117 10s. grey and bright pink (Die II) (1919) £170 £250
118 £1 bistre-brown and grey-blue (Die II) (1922) £4500 £6000

*(iii) T **5a**. W **6a**. of Australia (Mult Crown A). P 14*

119 ½d. green (1919) 5·50 7·50
w. Wmk inverted £130 £275

*(iv) T **5a**. W **5** of Australia. Colour changes and new value*

120 1d. violet (*shades*) (1922) 2·50 6·50
a. Dot before '1' 80·00 £140
b. 'Secret mark' 80·00 £140
c. Flaw under neck 80·00 £140
d. 'RA' joined 80·00 £140
121 2d. orange (1921) 9·50 2·50
122 2d. rose-scarlet (1922) 9·50 2·00
123 4d. violet (1922) 20·00 40·00
a. 'FOUR PENCE' in thinner letters (Pl 2 right pane R. 2/6) £800 £1400
124 4d. ultramarine (1922) 11·00 60·00
a. 'FOUR PENCE' in thinner letters (Pl 2 right pane R. 2/6) £900 £1800
120/124 *Set of 5* 45·00 £100

T **11** differs from T **6** (*a*) in the position of the 'P' of 'PACIFIC', which is further to the left in T **11**.

For 1d. rosine Dies I and II on rough unsurfaced paper see Nos. O16/O16b.

MANDATED TERRITORY OF NEW GUINEA

A civil administration for the Mandated Territory of New Guinea was established on 9 May 1921.

PRINTERS. See note at the beginning of Australia.

12 Native Village

(**13**)

(Des R. Harrison. Eng T. Harrison. Recess Note Printing Branch, Treasury, Melbourne, from 1926 Note Ptg Branch, Commonwealth Bank of Australia, Melbourne)

1925 (23 Jan)–**27**. P 11.

125 **12** ½d. orange 2·50 7·00
126 1d. green 2·50 5·50
126*a* 1½d. orange-vermilion (1926) 3·25 2·75
127 2d. claret 7·00 4·50
128 3d. blue 8·50 4·00
129 4d. olive-green 13·00 26·00
130 6d. brown-ochre 20·00 50·00
a. Bistre (1.25) 6·00 50·00
b. Yellow-brown (7.27) 15·00 48·00
131 9d. dull purple (*to violet*) 13·00 45·00
132 1s. dull blue-green (6.4.25) 15·00 27·00
133 2s. brown-lake (6.4.25) 30·00 48·00
134 5s. bistre (6.4.25) 50·00 65·00
135 10s. dull rose (6.4.25) £120 £180
136 £1 dull olive-green (6.4.25) £190 £300
125/136 *Set of 13* £400 £650

1931 (8 June). Air. Optd with T **13**. P 11.

137 **12** ½d. orange 1·50 9·50
138 1d. green 1·60 5·00
139 1½d. orange-vermilion 1·25 8·50
140 2d. claret 1·25 7·00
141 3d. blue 1·75 13·00
142 4d. olive-green 1·25 9·00
143 6d. light brown 1·75 14·00
144 9d. violet 3·00 17·00
145 1s. dull blue-green 3·00 17·00
146 2s. brown-lake 7·00 48·00
147 5s. olive-bistre 20·00 65·00
148 10s. bright pink 85·00 £110
149 £1 olive-grey £160 £250
137/149 *Set of 13* £250 £500

14 Raggiana Bird of Paradise (Dates either side of value)

AIR MAIL

(**15**)

(Recess John Ash, Melbourne)

1931 (2 Aug). Tenth Anniversary of Australian Administration. T **14** (with dates). P 11.

150 **14** 1d. green 4·25 7·50
151 1½d. vermilion 5·00 10·00
152 2d. claret 5·00 2·25
153 3d. blue 5·00 4·75
154 4d. olive-green 7·00 30·00
155 5d. deep blue-green 9·00 24·00
156 6d. bistre-brown 5·00 19·00
157 9d. violet 8·50 19·00
158 1s. pale blue-green 6·00 15·00
159 2s. brown-lake 10·00 48·00
160 5s. olive-brown 42·00 55·00
161 10s. bright pink £120 £140
162 £1 olive-grey £250 £275
150/162 *Set of 13* £425 £550

1931 (2 Aug). Air. Optd with T **15**.

163 **14** ½d. orange 3·25 3·25
164 1d. green 4·00 7·00
165 1½d. vermilion 3·75 10·00
166 2d. claret 3·75 3·00
167 3d. blue 6·00 6·50
168 4d. olive-green 6·00 6·00
169 5d. deep blue-green 6·00 11·00
170 6d. bistre-brown 7·00 26·00
171 9d. violet 8·00 15·00
172 1s. pale blue-green 7·50 15·00
173 2s. dull lake 16·00 50·00
174 5s. olive-brown 42·00 70·00
175 10s. bright pink 80·00 £120
176 £1 olive-grey £150 £250
163/176 *Set of 14* £300 £500

1932 (30 June)–**34.** T **14** (redrawn without dates). P 11.

177 1d. green 7·50 20
178 1½d. claret 7·50 21·00
179 2d. vermilion 5·50 20
179*a* 2½d. green (14.9.34) 6·50 28·00
180 3d. blue 8·00 1·25
180*a* 3½d. aniline carmine (14.9.34) 13·00 23·00
181 4d. olive-green 6·50 6·50
182 5d. deep blue-green 7·00 70
183 6d. bistre-brown 7·50 5·50
184 9d. violet 9·50 26·00
185 1s. blue-green 6·50 10·00
186 2s. dull lake 5·00 17·00
187 5s. olive 32·00 48·00
188 10s. pink 55·00 70·00
189 £1 olive-grey £120 £100
177/189 *Set of 15* £250 £300

The ½d. orange redrawn without dates exists without overprint, but it is believed that this was not issued (*Price* £110 *un*).

1932 (30 June)–**34**. Air. T **14** (redrawn without dates), optd with T **15**. P 11.

190 ½d. orange 60 1·50
191 1d. green 1·25 3·50
192 1½d. claret 1·75 11·00
193 2d. vermilion 1·75 30
193*a* 2½d. green (14.9.34) 8·50 2·50
194 3d. blue 3·25 3·00
194*a* 3½d. aniline carmine (14.9.34) 4·75 3·25
195 4d. olive-green 4·50 10·00
196 5d. deep blue-green 7·00 7·50
197 6d. bistre-brown 4·50 15·00
198 9d. violet 6·00 9·00
199 1s. pale blue-green 6·00 12·00
200 2s. dull lake 15·00 50·00
201 5s. olive-brown 50·00 60·00
202 10s. pink 95·00 85·00
203 £1 olive-grey 85·00 55·00
190/203 *Set of 16* £250 £275

16 Bulolo Goldfields

(Recess John Ash, Melbourne)

1935 (1 May). Air. P 11.

204 **16** £2 bright violet £350 £140
205 £5 emerald-green £750 £450

HIS MAJESTY'S JUBILEE. 1910 — 1935

(**17**)

18

1935 (27 June). Silver Jubilee. As Nos. 177 and 179, but shiny paper. Optd with T **17**.

206 1d. green 1·00 65
207 2d. vermilion 4·50 65

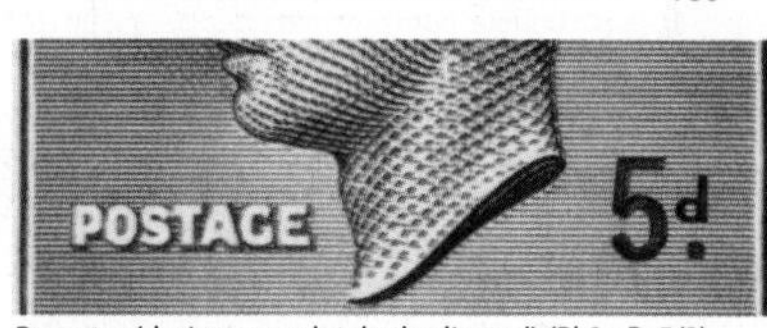

Re-entry (design completely duplicated) (Pl 2a R. 5/2)

(Recess John Ash, Melbourne)

1937 (18 May). Coronation. P 11.

208 **18** 2d. scarlet 50 1·50
209 3d. blue 50 1·75
210 5d. green 50 1·75
a. Re-entry 75·00 £130
211 1s. purple 50 2·25
208/211 *Set of 4* 1·75 6·50

(Recess John Ash, Melbourne)

1939 (1 Mar). Air. Inscr 'AIRMAIL POSTAGE' at foot. P 11.

212 **16** ½d. orange 4·00 9·50
213 1d. green 3·25 4·50
214 1½d. claret 4·00 19·00
215 2d. vermilion 9·50 3·00
216 3d. blue 18·00 18·00
217 4d. yellow-olive 15·00 8·50
218 5d. deep green 14·00 4·00
219 6d. bistre-brown 45·00 32·00
220 9d. violet 45·00 45·00
221 1s. pale blue-green 45·00 32·00
222 2s. dull lake 90·00 75·00
223 5s. olive-brown £190 £160
224 10s. pink £600 £425
225 £1 olive-green £140 £150
212/225 *Set of 14* £1100 £850

OFFICIAL STAMPS

O. S. G.R.I. 1d. (O 1)

O S (O 2)

O S (O 3)

1915 (27 Feb). Stamps of 1901 surch as T O **1**. 'G.R.I.' and value 3½ mm apart.

O1 1d. on 3pf. brown 35·00 75·00
a. '1' and 'd' spaced 85·00 £170
b. Surch double £5500
O2 1d. on 5pf. green £100 £140
a. '1' and 'd' spaced £200 £300

1919–23. Stamps of Australia optd with T **11** and punctured 'O S' as T O **2** of Australia (8×15½ *mm* with 11 holes in the perforated 'S').

*(i) T **5a**. of Australia. W **5**. P 14¼×14*

O3 1d. carmine-red (Die I) £275 55·00
ab. Dot before '1' — £300
ac. 'Secret mark' — £300
ad. Flaw under neck £900 £300
O4 4d. yellow-orange (19.5.19) £375 £130
a. Line through 'FOUR PENCE' (Pl 2 right pane R. 2/6) — £4250
O5 5d. brown (1921) £450 £100

*(ii) T **1** of Australia. W **6**. P 12*

O6 2d. grey (Die I) £400 80·00
O7 2½d. indigo (Die II) £600 £425
O8 3d. greenish olive (Die I) (1921) £650 £140
O9 6d. ultramarine (Die II) (1921) £700 £200
a. Greyish ultramarine £600 £200
b. Die IIB. *Greyish ultramarine* — £250
O10 9d. violet (Die IIB) (1921) £300 £150
O11 1s. emerald (Die II) (1921) £400 £160
a. Pale blue-green £450 £170
O12 2s. brown (Die II) (1922) £750 £375
O13 5s. grey and yellow (Die II) (1922) — £1600
O14 10s. grey and bright pink (Die II) (1921)

*(iii) T **5a** of Australia. W **5**. Rough unsurfaced paper, locally gummed. P 14*

O16 1d. rosine (Die I) (1920) £1200 £190
b. Die II £5000 £950

*(iv) T **5a** of Australia. W **5**. Colour changes and new value. P 14*

O17 1d. violet (*shades*) (1923) £350 50·00
O18 2d. orange (1921) £150 48·00
O19 2d. rose-scarlet (1923) £350 35·00
O20 4d. violet (23.7.21) £250 £120
a. 'FOUR PENCE' in thinner letters (Pl 2 right pane R. 2/6) — £4250
O21 4d. ultramarine (1.23) £375 £160

Dates quoted for Nos. O3/O21 are those of despatch from Australia. The earliest postmark date recorded is 2 April 1919 on No. O3. Their continued use on mail from government departments after the establishment of the civil administration is confirmed by a notice in the official *New Guinea Gazette* of 1 August 1921.

Australian postal archives indicate that nine sheets of the £1 T **1** perforated 'O S' were sent to New Guinea in September 1921. There is a pane of 30 of this stamp in the Royal Collection, but as no other examples are known it may not have been issued for postal purposes.

1925 (6 Apr)–**31**. Optd with Type O **2**. P 11.

O22 **12** 1d. green 5·50 4·50
O23 1½d. orange-vermilion (1931) 5·50 17·00
O24 2d. claret 3·00 3·75
O25 3d. blue 6·00 10·00
O26 4d. olive-green 4·50 8·50
O27 6d. bistre 27·00 35·00
a. Yellow-brown (4.31) 7·50 35·00
O28 9d. violet 4·25 35·00
O29 1s. dull blue-green 5·50 35·00
O30 2s. brown-lake 42·00 65·00
O22/O30 *Set of 9* 75·00 £190

1931 (2 Aug). Optd with T O **3**. P 11.

O31	**14**	1d. green	12·00	13·00
O32		1½d. vermilion	12·00	12·00
O33		2d. claret	12·00	7·00
O34		3d. blue	7·00	6·00
O35		4d. olive-green	7·50	8·50
O36		5d. deep blue-green	10·00	12·00
O37		6d. bistre-brown	14·00	17·00
O38		9d. violet	16·00	28·00
O39		1s. pale blue-green	16·00	28·00
O40		2s. brown-lake	40·00	70·00
O41		5s. olive-brown	£110	£180
O31/O41 *Set of* 11			£225	£350

1932 (30 June)–**34**. T **14** (redrawn without dates), optd with T O **3**. P 11.

O42		1d. green	19·00	21·00
O43		1½d. claret	19·00	21·00
O44		2d. vermilion	19·00	3·25
O45		2½d. green (14.9.34)	11·00	13·00
O46		3d. blue	11·00	42·00
		a. Double opt, one albino	£1000	
O47		3½d. aniline carmine (14.9.34)	9·00	9·00
O48		4d. olive-green	20·00	32·00
O49		5d. deep blue-green	9·00	30·00
O50		6d. bistre-brown	25·00	55·00
O51		9d. violet	15·00	48·00
O52		1s. pale blue-green	15·00	30·00
O53		2s. dull lake	30·00	75·00
O54		5s. olive-brown	£120	£180
O42/O54 *Set of* 13			£275	£475

Civil Administration in New Guinea was suspended in 1942, following the Japanese invasion.

Various New Guinea stamps exist overprinted with an anchor and three Japanese characters in a style similar to the Japanese Naval Control Area overprints found on the stamps of Netherlands Indies. These overprints on New Guinea are bogus. Two different versions are known, one produced in Japan during 1947 and the other in Australia during the late 1980s.

On resumption, after the Japanese defeat in 1945, Australian stamps were used until the appearance of the issue for the combined territories of Papua & New Guinea.

NORFOLK ISLAND

Norfolk Island, first settled in 1788 from New South Wales, was transferred to Tasmania on 29 September 1844. It became a separate settlement on 1 November 1856 under the control of the Governor of New South Wales. The island was declared an Australian Territory on 1 July 1914. Unlike the other External Territories it retains an independent postal administration.

> A Post Office was opened on Norfolk Island in 1832. The stamps of TASMANIA were used on Norfolk Island from July 1854 until May 1855, such use being identified by the '72' numeral cancellation. Stamps of NEW SOUTH WALES were first used on the island in 1877, but were not regularly available until 1898. The first 'NORFOLK ISLAND' cancellation was supplied in 1892, but not used until 1898. Stamps of AUSTRALIA were in use from 1913 to 1947.

1 Ball Bay

(Des and eng F. Manley. Recess Note Printing Branch, Reserve Bank of Australia)

1947 (10 June)–**59**. Toned paper. P 14.

1	**1**	½d. orange	85	60
		a. White paper (11.56)	3·25	17·00
2		1d. bright violet	50	60
		a. White paper (8.57)	5·00	38·00
3		1½d. emerald-green	50	70
		a. White paper (11.56)	9·00	28·00
4		2d. reddish violet	55	40
		a. White paper (11.56)	£130	£200
5		2½d. scarlet	80	30
6		3d. chestnut	70	70
6*a*		3d. emerald-green (*white paper*) (6.7.59)	15·00	12·00
7		4d. claret	1·75	40
8		5½d. indigo	70	30
9		6d. purple-brown	70	30
10		9d. magenta	1·25	40
11		1s. grey-green	70	40
12		2s. yellow-bistre	1·25	2·00
12*a*		2s. deep blue (*white paper*) (6.7.59)	16·00	12·00
1/12*a* *Set of* 14			35·00	28·00

Stamps as T **1**, in different colours, perforated 11 were prepared in 1940 but never issued. Examples of the 1d. emerald, 2d. scarlet, 3d. ultramarine, 6d. chocolate and 1s. slate-green exist from sheets stolen prior to the destruction of these stocks.

2 Warder's Tower

3 Airfield

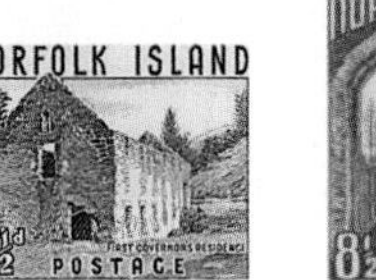

4 Old Stores (Crankmill)

5 Barracks entrance

6 Salt House

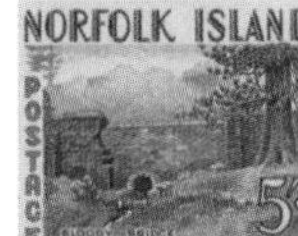

7 Bloody Bridge

(Des B. Stewart, eng. G. Lissenden (3½d.), D. Cameron (7½d.). Des and eng D. Cameron (6½d.), P. Morriss (8½d., 10d.) or G. Lissenden (5s.))

1953 (10 June). T **2/7**. P 14½×15 (vert) or 15×14½ (horiz).

13	**2**	3½d. brown-lake	1·00	90
14	**3**	6½d. deep green	2·25	4·25
15	**4**	7½d. deep blue	1·50	3·00
16	**5**	8½d. chocolate	1·75	4·75
17	**6**	10d. reddish violet	1·00	75
18	**7**	5s. sepia	35·00	8·50
13/18 *Set of* 6			38·00	20·00

8 Norfolk Island Seal and Pitcairners Landing

Two types of 2s.:

Type I

Type II

Alternate stamps on each horizontal row are with or without a dot in bottom right corner.

(Des and eng F. Manley)

1956 (8 June). Centenary of Landing of Pitcairn Islanders on Norfolk Island. P 15×14½.

19	**8**	3d. deep bluish green	1·00	40
20		2s. violet (I)	1·75	1·00
		a. Type II	1·75	1·00
		b. Deep violet (I)	2·75	1·75
		ba. Type II	2·75	1·75

NORFOLK ISLAND

(9)

(10)

(11)

1958 (1 July). Nos. 15/16 surch with T **9/10**.

21	7d. on 7½d. deep blue	1·25	1·00
22	8d. on 8½d. chocolate	1·25	1·00

1959 (7 Dec). 150th Anniversary of Australian Post Office. No. 331 of Australia surch with T **11**.

23	5d. on 4d. slate (R.)	35	30

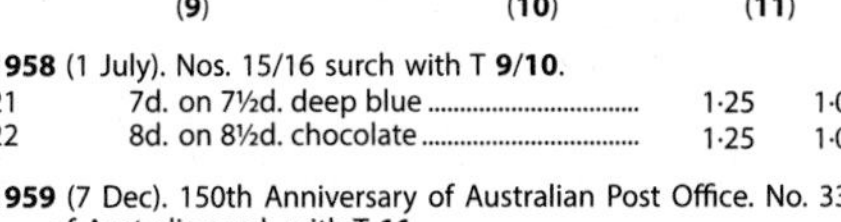

12 *Hibiscus insularis*

13 *Lagunaria patersonii*

14 White Tern

15 Lantana

16 Red Hibiscus

17 Queen Elizabeth II and Cereus

18 Fringed Hibiscus

19 Solander's Petrel

20 Passion Flower

21 Rose Apple

22 Red-tailed Tropicbird

(Des G. Lissenden, eng P. Morriss (5s.). Des and eng G. Lissenden (10s.), P. Morriss (others). Recess and typo (2s.8d.), recess (others))

1960–62. T **6/7** and **12/22**. P 14½ or 14½×14 (10s.).

24	**12**	1d. bluish green (23.5.60)	15	10
25	**13**	2d. rose and myrtle-green (23.5.60)	20	10
26	**14**	3d. green (1.5.61)	70	15
27	**15**	5d. bright purple (20.6.60)	55	20
28	**16**	8d. red (20.6.60)	80	50
29	**17**	9d. ultramarine (23.5.60)	80	45
30	**6**	10d. brown and reddish violet (as No. 17) (27.2.61)	2·00	1·00
31	**18**	1s.1d. carmine-red (16.10.61)	80	35
32	**19**	2s. sepia (1.5.61)	4·00	1·00
33	**20**	2s.5d. deep violet (5.2.62)	1·00	40
34	**21**	2s.8d. cinnamon and deep green (9.4.62)	2·25	55
35	**7**	5s. sepia and deep green (as No. 18) (27.2.61)	3·00	75
36	**22**	10s. emerald-green (14.8.61)	26·00	38·00
		s. Optd 'SPECIMEN'	42·00	
24/36 *Set of* 13			38·00	38·00

Nos. 30 and 35 are redrawn.

The SPECIMEN overprint on No. 36 is from sets sold by the Australian Post Office.

For Nos. 25 and 28 with face values in decimal currency see Nos. 600/601.

2/8

(23) (24) (25)

1960. As Nos. 13/15 but colours changed, surch with T **23/5**.

37	1s.1d. on 3½d. deep ultramarine (26.9.60)	2·00	1·50
38	2s.5d. on 6½d. bluish green (26.9.60)	3·00	2·50
39	2s.8d. on 7½d. sepia (29.8.60)	7·00	9·00
37/39 *Set of* 3		11·00	11·50

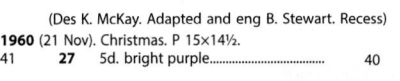

26 Queen Elizabeth II and Map

27 Open Bible and Candle

(Des and eng P. Morriss)

1960 (24 Oct). Introduction of Local Government. P 14.

40	**26**	2s.8d. reddish purple	4·00	7·00

(Des K. McKay. Adapted and eng B. Stewart. Recess)

1960 (21 Nov). Christmas. P 15×14½.

41	**27**	5d. bright purple	40	1·00

28 Open Prayer Book and Text

29 Stripey (*Atypichthys latus*)

(Des G. Lissenden. Eng P. Morriss. Recess)

1961 (20 Nov). Christmas. P 14½×14.

42	**28**	5d. slate-blue	30	70

> **PRINTERS.** All the following issues to No. 233 were printed in photogravure by Harrison and Sons, Ltd, London, *except where otherwise stated.*

1962–63. Fish. Horiz designs as T **29**. P 14½×14.

43	6d. sepia, yellow and deep bluish green (16.7.62)	60	25
44	11d. red-orange, brown and blue (25.2.63)	75	80
45	1s. blue, pink and yellow-olive (17.9.62)	60	25
46	1s.3d. blue, red-brown and green (15.7.63)	1·00	2·50
47	1s.6d. sepia, violet and light blue (6.5.63)	1·25	80
48	2s.3d. deep blue, red and greenish yellow (23.9.63)	1·50	1·25
43/48 *Set of* 6		5·00	5·00

Designs: 6d. T **29**; 11d. Gold-mouthed Emperor (*Lethrinus chrysostomus*); 1s. Surge Wrasse ('Po'ov'); 1s.3d. Seachub ('Dreamfish'); 1s.6d. Giant Grouper (*Promicrops lanceolatus*); 2s.3d. White Trevally (*Carangidae*).

30 Madonna and Child

31 'Peace on Earth...'

(Des and eng G. Lissenden. Recess Note Ptg Branch, Reserve Bank of Australia)

1962 (19 Nov). Christmas. P 14½.
49 **30** 5d. ultramarine 45 80

(Des R. Warner. Eng B. Stewart. Recess Note Ptg Branch, Reserve Bank of Australia)

1963 (11 Nov). Christmas. P 14½.
50 **31** 5d. red 40 70

32 Overlooking Kingston

33 Norfolk Pine

1964 (24 Feb–28 Sept). Views. Horiz designs as T **32**. Multicoloured. P 14½×14.
51 5d. Type **32** .... 60 1·25
52 8d. Kingston .... 1·00 1·50
53 9d. The Arches (Bumboras) (11.5) .... 1·00 30
54 10d. Slaughter Bay (28.9) .... 1·00 30
51/54 *Set of 4* .... 3·25 3·00

(Photo Note Ptg Branch, Reserve Bank of Australia, Melbourne)

1964 (1 July). 50th Anniversary of Norfolk Island as Australian Territory. P 13½.
55 **33** 5d. black, red and orange 40 15
56 8d. black, red and grey-green .... 40 1·10

34 Child looking at Nativity Scene

35 Nativity Scene

(Des P. Morriss and J. Mason. Photo Note Ptg Branch, Reserve Bank of Australia)

1964 (9 Nov). Christmas. P 13½.
57 **34** 5d. green, blue, buff and violet 30 40

1965 (14 Apr). 50th Anniversary of Gallipoli Landing. As T **22** of Nauru. P 13½.
58 5d. sepia, black and emerald 15 10

(Des J. Mason. Photo Note Ptg Branch, Reserve Bank of Australia)

1965 (25 Oct). Christmas. Helecon paper. P 13½.
59 **35** 5d. multicoloured 15 10

(New Currency. 100 cents = 1 Australian dollar)

38 *Hibiscus insularis*

39 Headstone Bridge

1966 (14 Feb). Decimal currency. Various stamps surch in black on silver tablets, which vary slightly in size, obliterating old value as in T **38**. Surch typo.
60 **38** 1c. on 1d. bluish green (*value tablet* 4×5 *mm*) 20 10
a. Value tablet larger, 5½×5½ mm 40 30
61 **13** 2c. on 2d. rose and myrtle-green (No. 25) 20 10
a. Surch omitted (in pair with normal) £3000
62 **14** 3c. on 3d. green .... 1·50 1·00
a. Silver tablet omitted £700
63 **15** 4c. on 5d. bright purple (No. 27) 25 10
64 **16** 5c. on 8d. red 30 10
65 **6** 10c. on 10d. brown and reddish violet (No. 30) .... 1·00 15
66 **18** 15c. on 1s.1d. carmine-red (No. 31) .... 50 1·25
67 **19** 20c. on 2s. sepia (No. 32) .... 2·75 3·75
68 **20** 25c. on 2s.5d. deep violet (No. 33) .... 1·00 40
69 **21** 30c. on 2s.8d. cinnamon and deep green .... 1·00 50
70 **7** 50c. on 5s. sepia and deep green (No. 35) .... 1·75 75
71 **22** $1 on 10s. emerald-green (*value tablet* 7×6½ *mm*) .... 2·50 2·50
a. Value tablet smaller, 6½×4 mm .... 2·00 3·25
60/71a *Set of 12* (*cheapest*) .... 11·00 9·00

No. 61a shows the black figure of value omitted, but the silver tablet is present.

1966 (27 June). Horiz designs as T **39**. Multicoloured. P 14½×14.
72 7c. Type **39** 40 15
73 9c. Cemetery Road 40 15

41 St. Barnabas' Chapel (interior)

42 St. Barnabas' Chapel (exterior)

1966 (23 Aug). Centenary of Melanesian Mission. P 14×14½.
74 **41** 4c. multicoloured 10 10
75 **42** 25c. multicoloured 20 20

43 Star over Philip Island

44 HMS *Resolution*, 1774

(Des B. G. W. McCoy)

1966 (24 Oct). Christmas. P 14½.
76 **43** 4c. multicoloured 10 10

(Des V. Whiteley)

1967 (17 Apr)–**68**. T **44** and similar horiz designs showing ships. Multicoloured. P 14×14½.
77 1c. Type **44** 10 10
78 2c. *La Boussole and L'Astrolabe*, 1788 .... 15 10
79 3c. HMS *Supply*, 1788 .... 15 10
80 4c. HMS *Sirius*, 1790 .... 75 10
81 5c. *Norfolk* (sloop), 1798 (14.8.67) 20 10
82 7c. HMS *Mermaid* (survey cutter), 1825 (14.8.67) 20 10
83 9c. *Lady Franklin*, 1853 (14.8.67) 20 10
84 10c. *Morayshire*, 1856 (14.8.67) 20 50
85 15c. *Southern Cross*, 1866 (18.3.68) 50 30
86 20c. *Pitcairn*, 1891 (18.3.68) 60 40
87 25c. *Black Billy* (Norfolk Island whaleboat), 1895 (18.3.68) .... 1·50 75
88 30c. *Iris* (cable ship), 1907 (18.6.68) .... 1·50 2·00
89 50c. *Resolution*, 1926 (18.6.68) .... 2·50 2·75
90 $1 *Morinda*, 1931 (18.6.68) .... 3·00 2·75
77/90 *Set of 14* .... 10·50 9·00

45 Lions Badge and 50 Stars

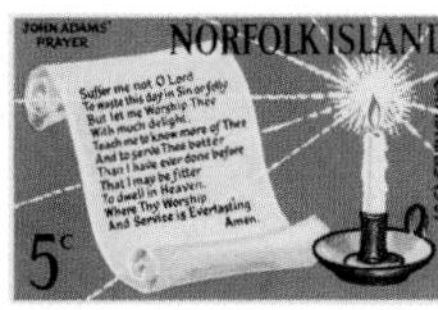

46 Prayer of John Adams and Candle

(Des M. Ripper. Photo Note Ptg Branch, Reserve Bank of Australia)

1967 (7 June). 50th Anniversary of Lions International. P 13½.
91 **45** 4c. black, bluish green and olive-yellow 10 10

(Des B. G. W. McCoy)

1967 (16 Oct). Christmas. P 14.
92 **46** 5c. black, light yellow-olive and red 10 10

47 Queen Elizabeth II

(Photo Note Ptg Branch, Reserve Bank of Australia)

1968 (5 Aug)–**71**. Coil stamps. P 15×imperf.
93 **47** 3c. black, light brown and vermilion 10 10
94 4c. black, light brown and blue-green 10 10
95 5c. black, light brown and deep violet 10 10
95*a* 6c. black, light brown and lake-brown (25.8.71) 30 60
93/95*a* *Set of 4* 55 80

59 Avro Type 691 Lancastrian and Douglas DC-4 Aircraft

60 Bethlehem Star and Flowers

(Des Harrison)

1968 (25 Sept). 21st Anniversary of QANTAS Air Service, Sydney-Norfolk Island. P 14.
96 **59** 5c. bluish black, carmine-red and light blue 15 10
97 7c. blackish brown, carmine-red and turquoise 15 10

(Des Betty Laing)

1968 (24 Oct). Christmas. P 14×14½.
98 **60** 5c. multicoloured 10 10

61 Captain Cook, Quadrant and Chart of Pacific Ocean Island

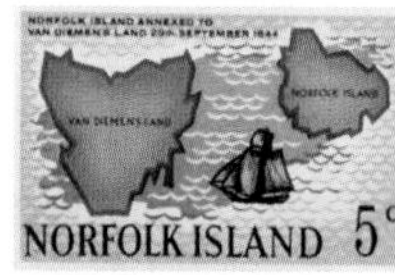

62 Van Diemen's Land, Norfolk and Sailing Cutter

(Des V. Whiteley from sketch by J. Cowap)

1969 (3 June). Captain Cook Bicentenary (1st issue). Observation of the transit of Venus across the Sun, from Tahiti. P 14.
99 **61** 10c. multicoloured 10 10

See also Nos. 118/119. Further sets were issued in subsequent years.

(Des Mrs. A. Bathie and Mrs. M. J. McCoy)

1969 (29 Sept). 125th Anniversary of the Annexation of Norfolk Island to Van Diemen's Land. P 14×14½.
100 **62** 5c. multicoloured 10 10
101 30c. multicoloured .... 50 1·00
a. Inscr 'VAN DIFMEN'S LAND' (R. 8/5) .... 16·00

63 The Nativity (carved mother-of-pearl plaque)

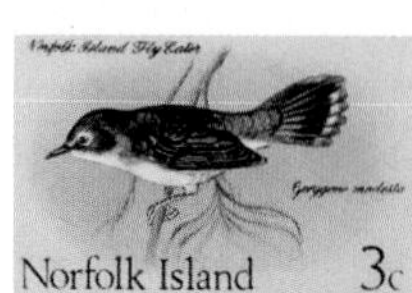

64 New Zealand Grey Flyeater

(Des J. Cowap)

1969 (27 Oct). Christmas. P 14½×14.
102 **63** 5c. multicoloured 10 10

(Des G. Mathews)

1970–71. Birds. T **64** and similar multicoloured designs. Chalk-surfaced paper. P 14.
103 1c. Scarlet Robins (22.7.70) 30 10
104 2c. Golden Whistler (24.2.71) 30 40
105 3c. Type **64** (25.2.70) 30 10
106 4c. Long-tailed Koels (25.2.70) 60 10
107 5c. Red-fronted Parakeet (24.2.71) .... 1·50 75
108 7c. Long-tailed Triller (22.7.70) 45 10
109 9c. Island Thrush (25.2.70) 70 10
110 10c. Boobook Owl (22.7.70) .... 1·50 2·75
111 15c. Norfolk Island Pigeon (24.2.71) .... 1·00 65
112 20c. White-chested White Eye .... 5·00 3·25
113 25c. Norfolk Island Parrots (22.7.70) .... 1·00 40
a. Error. Glazed, ordinary paper £475
114 30c. Collared Grey Fantail (16.6.71) .... 5·00 1·75
115 45c. Norfolk Island Starlings (25.2.70) 70 60
116 50c. Crimson Rosella (24.2.71) .... 1·00 2·25
117 $1 Sacred Kingfisher (16.6.71) .... 6·50 9·50
103/117 *Set of 15* .... 23·00 20·00

Nos. 105, 106, 109, 112, 114, 115 and 117 are horizontal, and the remainder vertical designs.

It is believed that only one sheet of No. 113a was issued.

65 Captain Cook and Map of Australia

66 First Christmas Service, 1788

(Des R. Bates)

1970 (29 Apr). Captain Cook Bicentenary (2nd issue). Discovery of Australia's East Coast. T **65** and similar horiz design. Multicoloured. P 14.
118 5c. Type **65** 15 10
119 10c. HMS *Endeavour* and aborigine 40 10

(Des R. Bates)

1970 (15 Oct). Christmas. P 14.
120 **66** 5c. multicoloured 10 10

PAPUA (BRITISH NEW GUINEA)

Stamps of QUEENSLAND were used in British New Guinea (Papua) from at least 1885 onwards. Post Offices were opened at Daru (1894), Kulumadau (Woodlarks) (1899), Nivani (1899), Port Moresby (1885), Samarai (1888), Sudest (1899) and Tamata (1899). Stamps were usually cancelled 'N.G.' (at Port Moresby from 1885) or 'BNG' (without stops at Samarai or with stops at the other offices) from 1888. Queensland stamps were replaced in Papua by the issue of 1901.

PRICES FOR STAMPS ON COVER TO 1945

Nos. 1/7	*from* × 15
No. 8	—
Nos. 9/15	*from* × 20
No. 16	—
Nos. 17/27	*from* × 6
No. 28	—
Nos. 34/45a	*from* × 5
Nos. 47/71	*from* × 8
Nos. 72/74	—
Nos. 75/92*a*	*from* × 8
Nos. 93/103	*from* × 6
Nos. 104/105	—
Nos. 106/111	*from* × 10
Nos. 112/114	*from* × 6
No. 115	—
Nos. 116/128	*from* × 5
Nos. 130/153	*from* × 4
Nos. 154/157	*from* × 12
Nos. 158/167	*from* × 4
No. 168	*from* × 3
Nos. O1/O54	*from* × 10
Nos. O55/O66*a*	*from* × 7
No. F1	*from* × 8

BRITISH NEW GUINEA

1 Lakatoi (trading canoe) with Hanuabada Village in Background

2 (Horizontal)

Normal   Thin 'd' at left (R. 4/2)

Deformed 'd' at left (R. 4/3)

(Recess D.L.R.)

1901 (1 July)–**05.** Wmk Mult Rosettes, W **2**. P 14.

A. Wmk horizontal. Thick paper. Line perf

No.	Type	Description	Unused	Used
1	1	½d. black and yellow-green	24·00	26·00
		a. Thin paper	£350	£275
2		1d. black and carmine	20·00	19·00
3		2d. black and violet	28·00	10·00
4		2½d. black and ultramarine	40·00	10·00
		a. Thin paper	£400	£225
		ab. Black and dull blue	£900	£475
		b. Thin 'd' at left	£400	£150
5		4d. black and sepia	65·00	35·00
		a. Deformed 'd' at left	£800	£500
6		6d. black and myrtle-green	65·00	35·00
7		1s. black and orange	75·00	70·00
8		2s.6d. black and brown (1.1.05)	£650	£550
1/8 *Set of 8*			£850	£650

B. Wmk vertical. Medium to thick paper. Line or comb perf

No.	Type	Description	Unused	Used
9	1	½d. black and yellow-green	23·00	3·75
		a. Thin paper (*comb perf*) (1905)	28·00	42·00
10		1d. black and carmine	13·00	2·00
11		2d. black and violet	13·00	4·25
		a. Thin paper (*comb perf*) (1905)	65·00	16·00
12		2½d. black and ultramarine (*shades*)	38·00	12·00
		a. Thin 'd' at left	£375	£160
13		4d. black and sepia	48·00	55·00
		a. Deformed 'd' at left	£700	£800
		b. Thin paper (*comb perf*) (1905)	£350	£1300
		ba. Deformed 'd' at left	£3500	
14		6d. black and myrtle-green	65·00	90·00
		a. Thin paper (*comb perf*) (1905)	£1200	
15		1s. black and orange	65·00	£100
		a. Thin paper (*comb perf*) (1905)	£950	£4250
16		2s.6d. black and brown (1905)	£6000	£4000
		a. Thin paper (*comb perf*)	£600	£1400
9/16a *Set of 8 (cheapest)*			£750	£1500

The paper used for Nos. 1/8 is white, of consistent thickness and rather opaque. The thin paper used for the horizontal watermark printings is of variable thickness, readily distinguishable from the thick paper by its greater transparency and by the gum which is thin and smooth.

Nos. 9/16 were initially printed on the same thick paper as the stamps with horizontal watermark and were line perforated. Values from ½d. to 2½d. were subsequently printed on medium paper on which the watermark was more visible. These were comb perforated. The thin paper with vertical watermark, produced in 1905, is much more transparent and has smooth gum. Printings were made on this paper for all values except the 2½d., but only the ½d. and 2d. were issued in Papua although used examples of the 4d., 1s. and 2s.6d. are also known. The entire printing of the 1d. on thin paper with vertical watermark was used for subsequent overprints.

The sheets of the ½d., 2d. and 2½d. show a variety known as 'white leaves' on R. 4/5, while the 2d. and 2½d. (both R. 6/2) and the ½d. and 1s. (both R. 6/3) show what is known as the 'unshaded leaves' variety.

TERRITORY OF PAPUA

Papua. (3)   **Papua.** (4)

1906 (8 Nov). I. Optd with T **3** (large opt), at Port Moresby.

A. Wmk horizontal. Thick paper. Line perf

No.	Type	Description	Unused	Used
16*b*		2½d. black and ultramarine	†	—
17	1	4d. black and sepia	£250	£170
		a. Deformed 'd' at left	£2500	£1800
18		6d. black and myrtle-green	60·00	48·00
19		1s. black and orange	30·00	48·00
20		2s.6d. black and brown	£170	£190

B. Wmk vertical. Thin paper (½d., 1d., 2d.) or medium to thick paper (others). Comb perf (½d. to 2½d.) or line perf (others)

No.	Type	Description	Unused	Used
21	1	½d. black and yellow-green	13·00	20·00
22		1d. black and carmine	21·00	19·00
23		2d. black and violet	21·00	5·50
24		2½d. black and ultramarine	13·00	15·00
		a. Thin 'd' at left	£150	£180
25		4d. black and sepia	£225	£160
		a. Deformed 'd' at left	£2250	£1700
26		6d. black and myrtle-green	48·00	60·00
27		1s. black and orange	£1800	£1400
28		2s.6d. black and brown	£18000	£12000
19/26 *Set of 8*			£450	£450

1907 (May–June). Optd with T **4** (small opt), at Brisbane.

A. Wmk horizontal. Thick paper. Line perf

No.	Type	Description	Unused	Used
34	1	½d. black and yellow-green	—	
		a. Thin paper	75·00	90·00
35		2½d. black and ultramarine	£2000	
		a. Thin paper	80·00	85·00
		ac. Black and dull blue	£325	£350
		b. Thin 'd' at left	£800	£850
36		1s. black and orange	£325	£400
37		2s.6d. black and brown	50·00	75·00
		a. Opt reading downwards	£7500	
		c. Opt double (*horiz*)	†	£6000
		d. Opt triple (*horiz*)	†	£4500

B. Wmk vertical. Thin paper (½d., 1d., 2d., 4d., 6d.) or medium to thick paper (2½d., 1s., 2s.6d.). Line or comb perf (2½d.), line perf (1s., 2s.6d.) or comb perf (others)

No.	Type	Description	Unused	Used
38	1	½d. black and yellow-green	23·00	30·00
		a. Opt double	£3500	
39		1d. black and carmine	11·00	5·00
		a. Opt reading upwards	£8000	£4500
40		2d. black and violet	7·50	2·25
		a. Opt double	£4250	
41		2½d. black and ultramarine	22·00	20·00
		a. Thin 'd' at left	£225	£225
42		4d. black and sepia	50·00	70·00
		a. Deformed 'd' at left	£750	£850
43		6d. black and myrtle-green	50·00	45·00
		a. Opt double	£7000	£13000
44		1s. black and orange	80·00	90·00
		b. Thin paper (*comb perf*)	50·00	42·00
		ba. Opt double, one diagonal	£21000	£14000
45		2s.6d. black and brown	£19000	£10000
		a. Thin paper (*comb perf*)	55·00	90·00
38/45a *Set of 8*			£225	£250

In the setting of this overprint Nos. 10, 16, and 21 have the 'p' of 'Papua' with a defective foot or inverted 'd' for 'p', and in No. 17 the 'pua' of 'Papua' is a shade lower than the first 'a'.

No. 37a comes from a single sheet on which the overprints were sideways. Examples exist showing one, two or four complete or partial overprints.

PRINTERS. All the following issues were printed at Melbourne by the Stamp Ptg Branch (to 1928) or Note Ptg Branch.

WATERMARK VARIETIES. The lithographed issues Nos. 47/83 were printed using a 'print-and-turn' technique. Thus, after one half of the sheet had been printed it was turned 180 degrees and the second half printed. As a result, upright and inverted (or sideways and sideways-inverted) watermarks were produced in equal quantities. Nos. 51/3, 55, 57, 62 and 69 are known with watermark reversed and others may well exist.

5 Large 'PAPUA'

B

C

Three types of the 2s.6d.: A. Thin top to '2' and small ball. Thin '6' and small ball. Thick uneven stroke.

B. Thin top to '2' and large, round ball. Thin '6' and large ball. Very thick uneven stroke. Every stamp in Type B varies slightly.

C. Thick uniform figures with large oval balls Thin even stroke.

Type A is not illustrated as the stamp is distinguishable by perf and watermark.

The litho stones were prepared from the engraved plates of the 1901 issue, value for value except the 2s.6d. for which the original plate was mislaid. No. 48 containing Type A was prepared from the original ½d. plate with the value inserted on the stone and later a fresh stone was prepared from the 1d. plate and this contained Type B. Finally, the original plate of the 2s.6d. was found and a third stone was prepared from this, and issued in 1911. These stamps show Type C.

6 Small 'PAPUA'

2s.6d. 'POSTAGIE' at top left (R. 1/5)

2d. 'C' for 'O' in 'POSTAGE' (R. 4/3)

(Litho Stamp Ptg Branch, Melbourne, from transfers taken from original engraved plates)

1907–10. A. Large 'PAPUA'. Wmk Crown over double-lined A, W w **11**.

(a) Wmk upright. P 11

No.	Type	Description	Unused	Used
47	5	½d. black and yellow-green (11.07)	4·50	3·50

(b) Wmk sideways. P 11

No.	Type	Description	Unused	Used
48	5	2s.6d. black and chocolate (A) (12.09)	75·00	90·00
		a. 'POSTAGIE' at left (R.1/5)	£1700	£2250

B. Small 'PAPUA' I. Wmk upright

(a) P 11 (1907–1908)

No.	Type	Description	Unused	Used
49	6	1d. black and rose (6.08)	6·50	5·00
50		2d. black and purple (10.08)	27·00	4·50
51		2½d. black and bright ultramarine (7.08)	30·00	35·00
		a. Black and pale ultramarine	17·00	7·00
		b. Thin 'd' at left	£180	£110
52		4d. black and sepia (20.11.07)	7·00	17·00
		a. Deformed 'd' at left	£150	£275
53		6d. black and myrtle-green (4.08)	17·00	16·00
54		1s. black and orange (10.08)	55·00	21·00

(b) P 12½ (1907–1909)

No.	Type	Description	Unused	Used
55	6	2d. black and purple (10.08)	42·00	10·00
56		2½d. black and bright ultramarine (7.08)	£180	£190
		a. Black and pale ultramarine	65·00	85·00
		b. Thin 'd' at left	£650	£750
57		4d. black and sepia (20.11.07)	9·50	8·00
		a. Deformed 'd' at left	£190	£170
58		1s. black and orange (10.08)	75·00	£100

II. Wmk sideways

(a) P 11 (1909–1910)

No.	Type	Description	Unused	Used
59	6	½d. black and yellow-green (12.09)	2·50	3·00
		a. Black and deep green (1910)	28·00	42·00
60		1d. black and carmine (1.10)	9·50	8·00
61		2d. black and purple (1.10)	27·00	8·00
62		2½d. black and dull blue (1.10)	4·50	26·00
		a. Thin 'd' at left	£100	£225
63		4d. black and sepia (1.10)	4·75	9·00
		a. Deformed 'd' at left	£150	£180
64		6d. black and myrtle-green (11.09)	10·00	22·00
65		1s. black and orange (3.10)	55·00	75·00

(b) P 12½ (1909–1910)

No.	Type	Description	Unused	Used
66	6	½d. black and yellow-green (12.09)	4·00	4·00
		a. Black and deep green (1910)	32·00	45·00
67		1d. black and carmine (1.10)	7·50	12·00
68		2d. black and purple (1.10)	10·00	15·00
69		2½d. black and dull blue (1.10)	10·00	45·00
		a. Thin 'd' at left	£140	£300
70		6d. black and myrtle-green (11.09)	£5500	£14000
71		1s. black and orange (3.10)	19·00	65·00

(c) Perf compound of 11 and 12½

No.	Type	Description	Unused	Used
72	6	½d. black and yellow-green (12.09)	£5500	£5500
73		2d. black and purple (1.10)	£1700	

(d) Mixed perfs 11 and 12½

No.	Type	Description	Unused	Used
74	6	4d. black and sepia (1.10)	£16000	

Compound perforations on the 4d. are fakes.

The only known examples of No. 74 come from the top row of a sheet perforated 11 and with an additional line perf 12½ in the top margin.

Note that Nos. 59*a* and 66*a* are a strong shade of deep green, without any hint of yellow. They should not be confused with darker shades of the yellow-green, Nos. 59 and 66.

(Litho Stamp Ptg Branch, Melbourne, by J. B. Cooke, from new stones made by fresh transfers)

1910 (Sept)–**11.** Large 'PAPUA'. Wmk Crown over double-lined A, W w **11** (upright). P 12½.

No.	Type	Description	Unused	Used
75	5	½d. black and green (12.10)	4·75	15·00
76		1d. black and carmine	15·00	17·00
77		2d. black and dull purple (*shades*) (12.10)	6·50	5·00
		a. 'C' for 'O' in 'POSTAGE' (R. 4/3)	£150	£130
78		2½d. black and blue-violet (10.10)	14·00	18·00
		a. Thin 'd' at left	£150	£200
79		4d. black and sepia (10.10)	13·00	11·00
		a. Deformed 'd' at left	£225	£200
80		6d. black and myrtle-green	8·50	14·00
81		1s. black and deep orange (12.10)	14·00	21·00
82		2s.6d. black and brown (B)	60·00	60·00
83		2s.6d. black and brown (C) (1911)	75·00	75·00
75/82 *Set of 8*			£120	£140

A variety showing a white line or 'rift' in clouds occurs on R. 5/3 in Nos. 49/74 and the 'white leaves' variety mentioned below No. 16 occurs on the 2d. and 2½d. values in both issues. They are worth about three times the normal price.

8

ONE PENNY (9)

(Eng S. Reading. Typo J. B. Cooke)

1911–15. Printed in one colour. Wmk Crown over single-lined A, W **8** (sideways*).

No.	Type	Description	Unused	Used
		(a) P 12½ (1911–1912)		
84	**6**	½d. yellow-green	2·25	3·75
		a. Green	70	2·25
		w. Wmk Crown to right of A	25·00	
85		1d. rose-pink	2·00	75
		w. Wmk Crown to right of A	75·00	75·00
86		2d. bright mauve	4·25	75
		w. Wmk Crown to right of A	£200	£130
87		2½d. bright ultramarine	6·50	8·50
		a. Dull ultramarine	8·50	8·50
		aw. Wmk Crown to right of A	£200	
88		4d. pale olive-green	2·25	11·00
		w. Wmk Crown to right of A	£250	£200
89		6d. orange-brown	3·75	5·00
		w. Wmk Crown to right of A	£275	
90		1s. yellow	9·50	15·00
		w. Wmk Crown to right of A	£300	
91		2s.6d. rose-carmine	42·00	50·00
		w. Wmk Crown to right of A	£550	£850
84/91 *Set of 8*			60·00	85·00
		(b) P 14		
92	**6**	1d. rose-pink (6.15)	42·00	7·00
		a. Pale scarlet	23·00	2·00
		w. Wmk Crown to right of A	—	£250

*The normal sideways watermark shows Crown to left of A, *as seen from the back of the stamp.*

(Typo J. B. Cooke (1916–1918), T. S. Harrison (1918–1926), A. J. Mullett (No. 95*b* only) (1926–1927), or John Ash (1927–1931))

1916 (Aug)–**31.** Printed in two colours. Wmk Crown over single-lined A, W **8** (sideways*). P 14.

No.	Type	Description	Unused	Used
93	**6**	½d. myrtle and apple green (Harrison) (1919)	80	1·00
		a. Myrtle and pale olive-green (Ash) (1927)	1·75	3·50
		w. Wmk Crown to right of A	30·00	35·00
94		1d. black and carmine-red	1·75	1·25
		aw. Wmk Crown to right of A		
		b. Grey-black and red (1918)	1·75	1·25
		bw. Wmk Crown to right of A	5·50	50
		c. Intense black and red (Harrison) (*wmk Crown to right of A*) (1926)	2·50	2·50
95		1½d. pale grey-blue (*shades*) and brown (1925)	1·50	80
		aw. Wmk Crown to right of A	22·00	8·00
		b. Cobalt and light brown (Mullett) (*wmk Crown to right of A*) (1927)	10·00	3·25
		c. Bright blue and bright brown (1929)	3·00	2·00
		d. 'POSTACE' at right (R.1/1) (all printings) ... *From*	40·00	40·00
96		2d. brown-purple and brown-lake (1919)	1·75	75
		a. Deep brown-purple and lake (1931)	25·00	1·75
		aw. Wmk Crown to right of A	45·00	6·00
		b. Brown-purple and claret (1931)	2·00	75
97		2½d. myrtle and ultramarine (1919)	4·75	12·00
98		3d. black and bright blue-green (12.16)	4·50	1·75
		a. Error. Black and deep greenish Prussian blue†	£1300	£1300
		b. Sepia-black and bright blue-green (Harrison)	22·00	21·00
		c. Black and blue-green (1927)	4·50	8·00
99		4d. brown and orange (1919)	2·50	5·00
		a. Light brown and orange (1927)	21·00	18·00
		aw. Wmk Crown to right of A	17·00	30·00
100		5d. bluish slate and pale brown (1931)	4·25	16·00
101		6d. dull and pale purple (*wmk Crown to right of A*) (1919)	4·75	9·50
		aw. Wmk Crown to left of A	35·00	
		b. Dull purple and red-purple (*wmk Crown to left of A*) (1927)	16·00	25·00
		c. 'POSTACE' at left (R. 6/2) (all printings) ... *From*	95·00	£140
102		1s. sepia and olive (1919)	6·00	7·00
		a. Brown and yellow-olive (1927)	8·50	14·00
103		2s.6d. maroon and pale pink (1919)	23·00	40·00
		a. Maroon and bright pink (*shades*) (1927)	20·00	55·00
104		5s. black and deep green (12.16)	55·00	48·00
105		10s. green and pale ultramarine (1925)	£180	£190
93/105 *Set of 13*			£250	£300

* The normal sideways watermark shows Crown to left of A, *as seen from the back of the stamp.*

† Beware of similar shades produced by removal of yellow pigment. No 98a is a colour trial, prepared by Cooke, of which, it is believed, five sheets were sold in error.

The printers of various shades can be determined by their dates of issue. The Ash printings are on whiter paper.

For 9d. and 1s.3d. values, see Nos. 127/128.

1917 (Oct). Nos. 84, 86/89 and 91 surch with T **9** by Govt Ptg Office, Melbourne.

No.	Type	Description	Unused	Used
106	**6**	1d. on ½d. yellow-green	1·50	1·60
		a. Green	1·00	1·25
		w. Wmk Crown to right of A	8·00	11·00
107		1d. on 2d. bright mauve	12·00	15·00
		w. Wmk Crown to right of A	£325	
108		1d. on 2½d. ultramarine	1·25	3·75
109		1d. on 4d. pale olive-green	1·75	4·50
		w. Wmk Crown to right of A	£200	£160
110		1d. on 6d. orange-brown	8·50	24·00
111		1d. on 2s.6d. rose-carmine	3·75	6·00
		a. Wmk upright (inverted)	£2500	
106/111 *Set of 6*			25·00	48·00

AIR MAIL (10)

(11)

1929 (Oct)–**30.** Air. Optd with T **10** by Govt Printer, Port Moresby.

No.	Type	Description	Unused	Used
		(a) Cooke printing. Yellowish paper		
112	**6**	3d. black and bright blue-green	3·25	20·00
		a. Opt omitted in vert pair with normal	£8500	
		(b) Harrison printing. Yellowish paper		
113	**6**	3d. sepia-black and bright blue-green	50·00	75·00
		a. Opt double	£4500	
		b. Opt double, one albino	£2500	
		(c) Ash printing. White paper		
114	**6**	3d. black and blue-green	2·00	11·00
		aa. Opt double (one albino)	£2500	
		a. Opt omitted (in horiz pair with normal)	£8000	
		b. Ditto, but vert pair	£7500	
		c. Opt vertical, on back	£6500	
		d. Opts *tête-bêche* (vert pair)	£13000	

1930 (15 Sept). Air. Optd with T **11**, in carmine by Govt Printer, Port Moresby.

No.	Type	Description	Unused	Used
		(a) Harrison printings. Yellowish paper		
115	**6**	3d. sepia-black and bright blue-green	£4000	£6000
116		6d. dull and pale purple (Wmk Crown to right of A)	3·00	12·00
		a. 'POSTACE' at left (R. 6/2)	80·00	£160
117		1s. sepia and olive	7·00	20·00
		a. Opt inverted	£15000	
		(b) Ash printings. White paper		
118	**6**	3d. black and blue-green	2·25	6·00
119		6d. dull purple and red-purple	5·50	20·00
		a. 'POSTACE' at left (R. 6/2)	£100	£200
120		1s. brown and yellow-olive	5·50	13·00
118/120 *Set of 3*			12·00	35·00

The rare Harrison printing with this overprint, No. 115, should not be confused with examples of the Ash printing, No. 118, which have been climatically toned.

5d.

TWO PENCE (12) FIVE PENCE (13)

1931 (1 Jan). Surch with T **12** by Govt Printer, Port Moresby.

No.	Type	Description	Unused	Used
		(a) Mullett printing		
121	**6**	2d. on 1½d. cobalt and light brown	12·00	24·00
		a. 'POSTACE' at right (R. 1/1)	£150	£225
		(b) Ash printing		
122	**6**	2d. on 1½d. bright blue and bright brown	1·00	2·00
		a. 'POSTACE' at right (R. 1/1)	28·00	42·00

1931. Surch as T **13** by Govt Printer, Port Moresby.

No.	Type	Description	Unused	Used
		(a) Cooke printing		
123	**6**	1s.3d. on 5s. black and deep green	7·50	15·00
		(b) Harrison printing. Yellowish paper		
124	**6**	9d. on 2s.6d. maroon and pale pink (12.31)	6·00	27·00
		(c) Ash printings. White paper		
125	**6**	5d. on 1s. brown and yellow-olive (26.7)	1·25	2·00
126		9d. on 2s.6d. maroon and bright pink	5·50	9·00

(Typo J. Ash)

1932. W **15** of Australia (Mult 'C of A'). P 11.

No.	Type	Description	Unused	Used
127	**5**	9d. lilac and violet	10·00	38·00
128		1s.3d. lilac and pale greenish blue	12·00	38·00
127s/128s Optd 'SPECIMEN' *Set of 2*			£750	

15 Motuan girl

16 A Chieftain's son

17 Tree houses

18 Raggiana Bird of Paradise

19 Papuan dandy

20 Native mother and child

21 Masked dancer

22 Papuan motherhood

23 Papuan shooting fish

24 *Dubu*—or ceremonial platform

25 'Lakatoi'

26 Papuan art

27 Pottery making

28 Native policeman

29 Lighting a fire

30 Delta house

(Des F. E. Williams (2s., £1 and frames of other values), E. Whitehouse (2d., 4d., 6d., 1s., and 10s.); remaining centres from photos by Messrs F. E. Williams and Gibson. Recess J. Ash (all values) and W. C. G. McCracken (½d., 1d., 2d., 4d.))

1932 (14 Nov)–**40.** T **15/30**. No wmk. P 11.

No.	Type	Description	Unused	Used
130	**15**	½d. black and orange	4·50	3·75
		a. Black and buff (McCracken) (1940)	19·00	42·00
131	**16**	1d. black and green	3·50	60
132	**17**	1½d. black and lake	4·50	8·00
133	**18**	2d. red	12·00	30
134	**19**	3d. black and blue	4·50	6·50
135	**20**	4d. olive-green	12·00	9·50
136	**21**	5d. black and slate-green	7·00	3·00
137	**22**	6d. bistre-brown	7·50	5·50
138	**23**	9d. black and violet	12·00	21·00
139	**24**	1s. dull blue-green	9·50	8·50
140	**25**	1s.3d. black and dull purple	20·00	28·00
141	**26**	2s. black and slate-green	15·00	24·00
142	**27**	2s.6d. black and rose-mauve	25·00	30·00
143	**28**	5s. black and olive-brown	70·00	55·00
144	**29**	10s. violet	£150	£120
145	**30**	£1 black and olive-grey	£275	£180
130/145 *Set of 16*			£550	£450

31 Hoisting the Union Jack

32 Scene on HMS *Nelson*

(Recess J. Ash)

1934 (6 Nov). 50th Anniversary of Declaration of British Protectorate. P 11.

No.	Type	Description	Unused	Used
146	**31**	1d. green	2·50	3·50
147	**32**	2d. scarlet	2·25	3·00

148 **31** 3d. blue .... 2·50 3·00
149 **32** 5d. purple .... 11·00 23·00
146/149 *Set of 4* .... 16·00 29·00

HIS MAJESTY'S JUBILEE.

HIS MAJESTY'S
JUBILEE.
1910 1935 1910 — 1935
(33) (34)

MAJESTY'S MAJESTY'S
Normal 'Accent' flaw (R.5/4)

1935 (9 July). Silver Jubilee. Nos. 131, 133/134 and 136 optd with T **33** or **34** (2d.).
150 **16** 1d. black and green .... 1·50 3·25
a. 'Accent' flaw .... 48·00 85·00
151 **18** 2d. scarlet .... 8·50 7·00
152 **19** 3d. black and blue .... 5·00 3·75
a. 'Accent' flaw £100 £120
153 **21** 5d. black and slate-green .... 5·00 3·50
a. 'Accent' flaw £100 £120
150/153 *Set of 4* .... 18·00 16·00

35

Normal

1d. 'Halo' flaw (Pl 1a. R. 5/2)

(Recess J. Ash)

1937 (14 May). Coronation. P 11.
154 **35** 1d. green 45 20
a. 'Halo' .... 40·00 50·00
155 2d. scarlet .... 45 1·25
156 3d. blue .... 45 1·25
157 5d. purple .... 45 1·75
154/157 *Set of 4* .... 1·60 4·00
Some covers franked with these stamps and posted on 2 June 1937 were postmarked 2 April 1937 in error.

36 Port Moresby

(Recess J. Ash)

1938 (6 Sept). Air. 50th Anniversary of Declaration of British Possession. P 11.
158 **36** 2d. rose-red .... 3·00 3·50
159 3d. bright blue .... 3·00 2·50
160 5d. green .... 3·00 3·75
161 8d. brown-lake .... 6·00 24·00
162 1s. mauve .... 25·00 27·00
158/162 *Set of 5* .... 35·00 55·00

37 Natives poling Rafts

(Recess J. Ash)

1939 (6 Sept). Air. P 11.
163 **37** 2d. rose-red .... 4·25 8·50
164 3d. bright blue .... 4·25 14·00
165 5d. green .... 3·50 2·50
166 8d. brown-lake .... 8·00 6·00
167 1s. mauve .... 14·00 10·00

(Recess W. C. G. McCracken)

1941 (2 Jan). Air. P 11½.
168 **37** 1s.6d. olive-green .... 30·00 42·00
163/168 *Set of 6* .... 55·00 75·00

OFFICIAL STAMPS

1908 (Oct). Punctured 'OS' as T O **3** of Australia.
O1 **1** 2s.6d. black and brown (No. 37) .... £1200 38·00
O2 2s.6d. black and brown (No. 45) £6500 £3750
a. Thin paper (No. 45a) £1700 £1700

1908 (Dec)–**10**. Nos. 49/71 punctured 'OS' as T O **3** of Australia.

I. Wmk upright

(a) P 11
O4 **6** 1d. black and rose .... 60·00 16·00
O5 2d. black and purple .... 70·00 5·00
O6 2½d. black and bright ultramarine .... £110 40·00
a. Black and pale ultramarine .... 65·00 5·00
b. Thin 'd' at left £600 £130
O7 4d. black and sepia .... 65·00 5·00
a. Deformed 'd' at left £600 £160
O8 6d. black and myrtle-green .... £150 55·00
O9 1s. black and orange .... £150 21·00
O4/O9 *Set of 6* .... £500 95·00

(b) P 12½
O10 **6** 2d. black and purple .... £120 30·00
O11 2½d. black and bright ultramarine £375 £140
a. Black and pale ultramarine .... £190 95·00
b. Thin 'd' at left £1400 £800
O12 4d. black and sepia .... £130 9·50
a. Deformed 'd' at left £1000 £225
O13 1s. black and orange £350 £110
O10/O13 *Set of 4* £700 £200

II. Wmk sideways

(a) P 11
O14 **6** ½d. black and yellow-green .... 55·00 4·75
a. Black and deep green .... 90·00 38·00
O15 1d. black and carmine .... £110 28·00
O16 2d. black and purple .... 35·00 2·50
O17 2½d. black and dull blue .... 80·00 6·00
a. Thin 'd' at left £700 £120
O18 4d. black and sepia .... 60·00 11·00
a. Deformed 'd' at left £550 £250
O19 6d. black and myrtle-green .... £100 6·00
O20 1s. black and orange .... £350 95·00
O14/O20 *Set of 7* £700 £140

(b) P 12½
O21 **6** ½d. black and yellow-green .... 50·00 2·25
a. Black and deep green .... 80·00 32·00
O22 1d. black and carmine .... 95·00 4·25
O23 2d. black and purple .... 60·00 3·25
O24 2½d. black and dull blue .... £100 15·00
a. Thin 'd' at left £900 £200
O25 6d. black and myrtle-green .... — £1400
O26 1s. black and orange .... £150 40·00
No. O7 is known with watermark reversed.

1910. Nos. 47/48 punctured 'OS' as T O **3** of Australia.
O27 **5** ½d. black and yellow-green (wmk upright) .... 55·00 16·00
O28 2s.6d. black and chocolate (wmk sideways) £350 £160
a. 'POSTAGIE' at left .... — £4250

1910–11. Nos. 75/83 punctured 'OS' as T O **3** of Australia.
O29 **5** ½d. black and green .... 60·00 27·00
O30 1d. black and carmine .... £130 22·00
O31 2d. black and purple .... 60·00 27·00
a. 'C' for 'O' in 'POSTAGE' £550 £300
O32 2½d. black and blue-violet .... 80·00 8·00
a. Thin 'd' at left £650 £170
O33 4d. black and sepia .... 80·00 7·00
a. Deformed 'd' at left £800 £170
O34 6d. black and myrtle-green .... 90·00 7·00
O35 1s. black and deep orange .... £140 10·00
O36 2s.6d. black and brown (B) .... £170 35·00
O37 2s.6d. black and brown (C) .... £190 80·00
O29/O36 *Set of 8* £750 £130

1911–12. Nos. 84/91 punctured 'OS' as T O **3** of Australia.
O38 **6** ½d. yellow-green .... 30·00 2·25
w. Wmk Crown to right of A .... — 85·00
O39 1d. rose-pink .... 35·00 1·50
O40 2d. bright mauve .... 35·00 1·50
w. Wmk Crown to right of A .... — £130
O41 2½d. bright ultramarine .... 45·00 26·00
O42 4d. pale olive-green .... 60·00 35·00
O43 6d. orange-brown .... 60·00 7·00
O44 1s. yellow .... £100 19·00
O45 2s.6d. rose-carmine £170 £120
O38/O45 *Set of 8* £475 £190

1930. Nos. 93/96a and 98c/103 punctured 'OS' as T O **3** of Australia.
O46 **6** ½d. myrtle and apple green .... 26·00 40·00
O47 1d. intense black and red .... 45·00 13·00
O48 1½d. bright blue and bright brown .... 29·00 42·00
a. 'POSTACE' at right £275 £325
O49 2d. deep brown-purple and lake .... 50·00 55·00
O50 3d. black and blue-green £130 £150
O51 4d. light brown and orange .... 65·00 65·00
O52 6d. dull purple and pale purple .... 40·00 55·00
a. 'POSTACE' at left £450 £650
O53 1s. brown and yellow-olive .... 90·00 95·00
O54 2s.6d. maroon and pale pink £225 £275
O46/O54 *Set of 9* £650 £700

O S
(O 1)

(Typo T. S. Harrison (1d. and 2s.6d.) and J. Ash)

1931 (29 July)–**32**. Optd with T O **1**. W **7** or W **15** of Australia (9d., 1s.3d.). P 14 or 11 (9d., 1s.3d.).
O55 **6** ½d. myrtle and apple-green .... 3·00 4·75
O56 1d. Intense black and red .... 10·00 20·00
O57 1½d. bright blue and bright brown .... 2·00 12·00
a. 'POSTACE' at right .... 75·00 £200
O58 2d. brown-purple and claret .... 9·50 22·00
O59 3d. black and blue-green .... 2·75 22·00
O60 4d. light brown and orange (No. 99aw) .... 3·75 22·00
w. Wmk Crown to left of A .... 4·25 26·00
O61 5d. bluish slate and pale brown .... 6·00 38·00
O62 6d. dull purple and red-purple .... 4·50 8·50
a. 'POSTACE' at left £170 £325
O63 9d. lilac and violet (1932) .... 30·00 48·00
O64 1s. brown and yellow-olive .... 9·00 30·00
O65 1s.3d. lilac and pale greenish blue (1932) .... 30·00 48·00
O66 2s.6d. maroon and pale pink (Harrison) .... 48·00 95·00
a. Maroon and bright pink (Ash) .... 55·00 95·00
O55/O66 *Set of 12* £130 £325
Civil Administration in Papua was suspended in 1942. On resumption, after the Japanese defeat in 1945, Australian stamps were used until the appearance of the issue of the combined territories of Papua & New Guinea.

POSTAL FISCAL STAMP

Stamp Duty.
F 1

1912 (May) No. 85 Optd with T F **1** by Govt Printer, Port Moresby.
F1 1d. rose-pink .... 55·00 70·00
a. Pair, one without opt £4000
b. Opt double £1700 £1700
c. 'Samp' for 'Stamp' (R. 1/1) £1400
The use of No. F1 was authorised at Samarai in May 1912 and in early 1913 during shortages of 1d. stamps. Other values, including the 1d. with a curved sans-serif overprint are known used at other offices and at other times, but such use was not authorised.

PAPUA NEW GUINEA

AUSTRALIAN TRUST TERRITORY

Stamps of Australia were used in the combined territory following the defeat of the Japanese in 1945. They remained valid for postal purposes from Papua and New Guinea until 1 March 1953.

The name of the combined territory was changed from 'Papua and New Guinea' to 'Papua New Guinea' at the beginning of 1972.

SPECIMEN OVERPRINTS. These come from specimen sets in which the lower values were cancelled-to-order, but stamps above the value of 10s. were overprinted 'SPECIMEN'. These overprints are listed as they could be purchased from the Post Office.

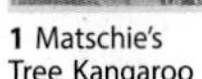
1 Matschie's Tree Kangaroo

2 Buka Head-dresses

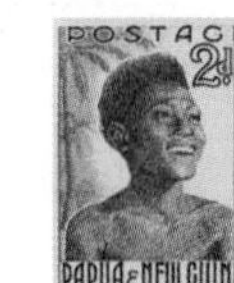

3 Native Youth

4 Greater Bird of Paradise

5 Native policeman

6 Papuan Headdress

7 Kiriwana Chief house

8 Kiriwana Yam house

9 Copra making

10 Lakatoi

11 Rubber tapping

12 Sepik dancing masks

13 Native shepherd and flock

14 Map of Papua and New Guinea

15 Papuan shooting Fish

(Recess Note Printing Branch, Commonwealth Bank, Melbourne)

1952 (30 Oct)–**58**. T **1/15**. P 14.

No.	Type	Description	Unused	Used
1	**1**	½d. emerald	30	10
2	**2**	1d. deep brown	20	10
3	**3**	2d. blue	35	10
4	**4**	2½d. orange	3·00	50
5	**5**	3d. deep green	50	10
6	**6**	3½d. carmine-red	50	10
6a		3½d. black (2.6.58)	5·00	1·25
7	**7**	6½d. dull purple	1·25	10
		a. Maroon (1956)	9·00	25
8	**8**	7½d. blue	2·50	1·00
9	**9**	9d. brown	2·75	40
10	**10**	1s. yellow-green	1·50	10
11	**11**	1s.6d. deep green	2·75	60
12	**12**	2s. indigo	2·50	10
13	**13**	2s.6d. brown-purple	2·75	40
14	**14**	10s. blue-black	32·00	13·00
15	**15**	£1 deep brown	45·00	15·00
1/15 *Set of* 16			90·00	29·00
14s/15s Optd 'SPECIMEN' *Set of* 2			90·00	

(**16**) (**17**)

1957 (29 Jan). Nos. 4 and 10 surch with T **16** or T **17**.

No.	Type	Description	Unused	Used
16		4d. on 2½d. orange	1·25	10
17		7d. on 1s. yellow-green	40	10

18 Cacao Plant

19 Klinki Plymill

20 Cattle

21 Coffee Beans

(Recess Note Ptg Branch, Commonwealth Bank, Melbourne)

1958 (2 June)–**60**. New values. P 14.

No.	Type	Description	Unused	Used
18	**18**	4d. vermilion	60	10
19		5d. green (10.11.60)	60	10
20	**19**	7d. bronze-green	2·00	10
21		8d. deep ultramarine (10.11.60)	60	1·00
22	**20**	1s.7d. red-brown	7·00	3·25
23		2s.5d. vermilion (10.11.60)	1·50	1·00
24	**21**	5s. crimson and olive-green	2·00	1·00
18/24 *Set of* 7			13·00	5·50

(**22**)

23 Council Chamber, Port Moresby

1959 (1 Dec). No. 1 surch with T **22**.

No.	Type	Description	Unused	Used
25	**1**	5d. on ½d. emerald	75	10

(Photo Harrison)

1961 (10 Apr). Reconstitution of Legislative Council. P 15×14.

No.	Type	Description	Unused	Used
26	**23**	5d. deep green and yellow	75	25
27		2s.3d. deep green and light salmon	2·00	2·75

24 Female, Goroka, New Guinea

25 Tribal elder, Tari, Papua

26 Female Dancer

27 Male Dancer

28 Traffic Policeman

(Des Pamela M. Prescott, Recess Note Ptg Branch, Reserve Bank of Australia, Melbourne)

1961 (26 July)–**62**. T **24/28**. P 14½×14 (1d., 3d., 3s.) or 14×14½ (others).

No.	Type	Description	Unused	Used
28	**24**	1d. lake	70	10
29	**25**	3d. indigo	30	10
30	**26**	1s. bronze-green	1·00	15
31	**27**	2s. maroon	45	15
32	**28**	3s. deep bluish green (5.9.62)	1·00	2·00
28/32 *Set of* 5			3·00	2·25

29 Campaign Emblem

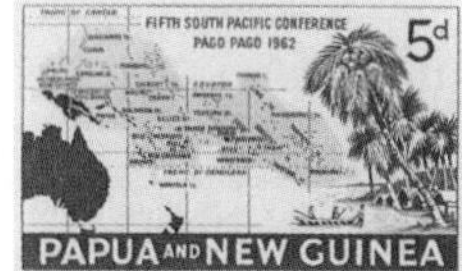

30 Map of South Pacific

(Recess Note Ptg Branch, Reserve Bank of Australia, Melbourne)

1962 (7 Apr). Malaria Eradication. P 14.

No.	Type	Description	Unused	Used
33	**29**	5d. carmine-red and light blue	30	15
34		1s. red and sepia	50	25
35		2s. black and yellow-green	60	1·25
33/35 *Set of* 3			1·25	1·50

(Des Pamela M. Prescott. Recess Note Ptg Branch, Reserve Bank of Australia, Melbourne)

1962 (9 July). Fifth South Pacific Conference, Pago Pago. P 14½×14.

No.	Type	Description	Unused	Used
36	**30**	5d. scarlet and light green	50	15
37		1s.6d. deep violet and light yellow	85	1·40
38		2s.6d. deep green and light blue	85	1·40
36/38 *Set of* 3			2·00	2·75

31 Throwing the Javelin

33 Runners

(Des G. Hamori. Photo Courvoisier)

1962 (24 Oct). Seventh British Empire and Commonwealth Games, Perth. T **31**, **33** and similar design. P 11½.

No.	Type	Description	Unused	Used
39	**31**	5d. brown and light blue	20	10
		a. Pair. Nos. 39/40	40	50
40		5d. brown and orange	20	10
41	**33**	2s.3d. brown and light green	70	75
39/41 *Set of* 3			1·00	85

Design: (As T **31**)—5d. High jump.

Nos. 39/40 are arranged together *se-tenant* in sheets of 100.

34 Raggiana Bird of Paradise

35 Common Phalanger

36 Rabaul

37 Queen Elizabeth II

(Des S. T. Cham (10s.), A. Buckley (photo) (£1). Photo Harrison (£1), Courvoisier (others))

1963 (13 Feb–3 July). P 14½ (£1) or 11½ (others).

No.	Type	Description	Unused	Used
42	**34**	5d. yellow, chestnut and sepia (27.3)	70	10
43	**35**	6d. red, yellow-brown and grey (27.3)	50	1·00
44	**36**	10s. multicoloured (13.2)	8·50	4·50
45	**37**	£1 sepia, gold and blue-green (3.7)	1·25	1·75
		a. Gold ptd double		
42/45 *Set of* 4			10·00	6·50
44s/45s Optd 'SPECIMEN' *Set of* 2			90·00	

38 Centenary Emblem

39 Waterfront, Port Moresby

39a Piaggio P-166B Portofino aircraft landing at Tapini

(Des G. Hamori. Photo Note Ptg Branch, Reserve Bank of Australia, Melbourne)

1963 (1 May). Red Cross Centenary. P 13½×13.

No.	Type	Description	Unused	Used
46	**38**	5d. red, grey-brown and bluish green	75	10

(Des J. McMahon (8d.), Pamela M. Prescott (2s.3d.). Recess Note Ptg Branch, Reserve Bank of Australia, Melbourne)

1963 (8 May). T **39** and similar horiz design. P 14×13½.

No.	Type	Description	Unused	Used
47	**39**	8d. green	30	15
48	**39a**	2s.3d. ultramarine	30	30

40 Games Emblem

41 Watam Head

(Des Pamela M. Prescott. Recess Note Ptg Branch, Reserve Bank of Australia, Melbourne)

1963 (14 Aug). First South Pacific Games, Suva. P 13½×14½.

No.	Type	Description	Unused	Used
49	**40**	5d. bistre	10	10
50		1s. deep green	30	60

(Des Pamela M. Prescott. Photo Courvoisier)

1964 (5 Feb). Native Artefacts. T **41** and similar vert designs. Multicoloured. P 11½.

No.	Type	Description	Unused	Used
51		11d. Type **41**	25	10
52		2s.5d. Watam Head (*different*)	30	1·75
53		2s.6d. Bosmun Head	30	10
54		5s. Medina Head	35	20
51/54 *Set of* 4			1·10	1·75

45 Casting Vote

46 'Health Centres'

(Photo Courvoisier)

1964 (4 Mar). Common Roll Elections. P 11½.

No.	Type	Description	Unused	Used
55	**45**	5d. brown and drab	10	10
56		2s.3d. brown and pale blue	20	25

(Recess Note Ptg Branch, Reserve Bank of Australia, Melbourne)

1964 (5 Aug). Health Services. T **46** and similar vert designs. P 14.

No.	Type	Description	Unused	Used
57		5d. violet	10	10
58		8d. bronze-green	10	10
59		1s. blue	15	10
60		1s.2d. brown-red	20	35
57/60 *Set of* 4			50	60

Designs: 8d. 'School health'; 1s. 'Infant, child and maternal health'; 1s.2d. 'Medical training'.

50 Striped Gardener Bowerbird

51 Adelbert Bowerbird

52 Blue Bird of Paradise

53 Lawes's Parotia

54 Black-billed Sicklebill

55 Emperor of Germany Bird of Paradise

56 Brown Sicklebill

57 Lesser Bird of Paradise

58 Magnificent Bird of Paradise

59 Twelve-wired Bird of Paradise

60 Magnificent Riflebird

(Photo Courvoisier)

1964 (28 Oct)–**65**. Birds. T **50/60**. Multicoloured; background colours given. P 11½ (1d. to 8d.) or 12×11½ (1s. to 10s.).

61	**50**	1d. pale olive-yellow (20.1.65)	40	10
62	**51**	3d. light grey (20.1.65)	40	30
63	**52**	5d. pale red (20.1.65)	40	10
64	**53**	6d. pale green	50	10
65	**54**	8d. lilac	1·00	20
66	**55**	1s. salmon	1·25	10
67	**56**	2s. light blue (20.1.65)	50	30
68	**57**	2s.3d. light green (20.1.65)	50	85
69	**58**	3s. pale yellow (20.1.65)	50	1·25
70	**59**	5s. cobalt (20.1.65)	5·00	1·00
71	**60**	10s. pale drab	1·25	6·50
		s. Optd 'SPECIMEN'	85·00	
61/71 *Set of* 11			10·00	9·50

61 Canoe Prow

(Des Pamela M. Prescott. Photo Courvoisier)

1965 (24 Mar). Sepik Canoe Prows in Port Moresby Museum. T **61** and similar horiz designs showing carved prows. P 11½.

72	4d. multicoloured	30	10
73	1s.2d. multicoloured	1·00	1·75
74	1s.6d. multicoloured	30	10
75	4s. multicoloured	40	80
72/75 *Set of* 4		1·75	2·50

1965 (14 Apr). 50th Anniversary of Gallipoli Landing. As T **22** of Nauru. P 13½.

76	2s.3d. sepia, black and emerald	20	10

65 Urban Plan and Native House

(Des G. Hamori. Photo Courvoisier)

1965 (7 July). Sixth South Pacific Conference, Lae. T **65** and similar horiz design. P 11½.

77	6d. multicoloured	10	10
78	1s. multicoloured	10	10

No. 78 is similar to T **65** but with the plan on the right and the house on the left. Also 'URBANISATION' reads downwards.

66 Mother and Child

67 Globe and UN Emblem

(Photo Courvoisier)

1965 (13 Oct). 20th Anniversary of UNO T **66/67** and similar vert design. P 11½.

79	**66**	6d. sepia, blue and pale turquoise-blue	10	10
80	**67**	1s. orange-brown, blue and reddish violet	10	10
81	–	2s. blue, blue-green and light yellow-olive	10	10
79/81 *Set of* 3			25	25

Design: 2s. UN Emblem and globes.

(New Currency. 100 cents = 1 Australian dollar)

69 *Papilio ulysses*

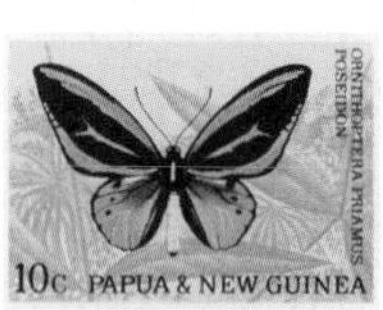

71 *Ornithoptera priamus*

$1 Plate I

Black line through left blue patch on wing consists of two dots only. There are two blue lines extending from upper right edge of right wing towards two small patches of blue.

$1 Plate II

The black line through left blue patch on wing is continuous. Blue lines at upper right edge of wing are omitted. There is an extra short faint blue line extending from edge of lower right wing which is absent in Plate I.

$2 Plate I

In the lower left of the butterfly there are two short black lines from the edge to the yellow part.

In the lower part of the upper right wing there is a series of indeterminate short lines and dots.

$2 Plate II

The two black lines at lower left are lacking.
There are clear fine lines of shading in place of the thicker lines.

There are numerous other minor differences between the two plates of each value and also slight variations in the shades.

(Photo Courvoisier)

1966 (14 Feb)–**67**. Decimal Currency. Butterflies. Vert designs as T **69** (1 to 5c.), or horiz as T **71** (others). Multicoloured. P 11½.

82	1c. Type **69**	40	75
83	3c. *Cyrestis acilia*	40	1·00
84	4c. *Graphium weiskei*	40	1·00
85	5c. *Terinos alurgis*	40	10
86	10c. Type **71**	40	30
86*a*	12c. *Euploea callithoe* (12.10)	4·50	2·25
87	15c. *Papilio euchenor*	1·00	80
88	20c. *Parthenos sylvia*	40	10
89	25c. *Delias aruna*	50	1·00
90	50c. *Apaturina erminea*	8·00	1·00
91	$1 *Doleschallia dascylus* (Plate I)	2·50	2·00
	a. Plate II (8.67)	4·50	2·50
92	$2 *Ornithoptera paradises* (Plate I)	3·50	10·00
	a. Plate II (8.67)	8·50	10·00
82/92 *Set of* 12		20·00	18·00

80 'Molala Harai'

84 Throwing the Discus

(Des Rev. H. A. Brown. Photo Courvoisier)

1966 (8 June). Folklore. Elema Art (1st series). T **80** and similar vert designs. P 11½.

93	2c. black and carmine	10	10
94	7c. black, light yellow and light blue	10	65
95	30c. black, carmine and apple-green	15	15
96	60c. black, carmine and yellow	40	65
93/96 *Set of* 4		65	1·40

Designs: 2c. T **80**; 7c. 'Marai'; 30c. 'Meavea Kivovia'; 60c. 'Toivita Tapaivita'.

Nos. 93/96 were supplementary values to the decimal currency definitive issue.

See also Nos. 152/155. A further set was issued in 1977.

(Photo Courvoisier)

1966 (31 Aug). South Pacific Games, Nouméa. T **84** and similar vert designs. Multicoloured. P 11½.

97	5c. Type **84**	10	10
98	10c. Football	15	10
99	20c. Tennis	20	40
97/99 *Set of* 3		40	55

87 *Mucuna novoguineensis*

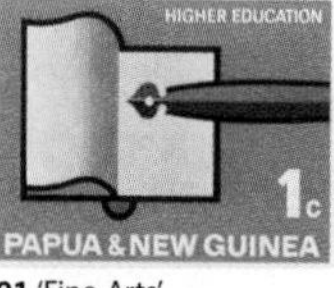

91 'Fine Arts'

(Des Mrs. D. Pearce. Photo Courvoisier)

1966 (7 Dec). Flowers. T **87** and similar vert designs. Multicoloured. P 11½.

100	5c. Type **87**	15	10
101	10c. *Tecomanthe dendrophila*	15	10
102	20c. *Rhododendron macgregoriae*	20	10
103	60c. *Rhododendron konori*	50	1·40
100/103 *Set of* 4		90	1·50

(Des G. Hamori. Photo Courvoisier)

1967 (8 Feb). Higher Education. T **91** and similar horiz designs. Multicoloured. P 12½×12.

104	1c. Type **91**	10	10
105	3c. 'Surveying'	10	15
106	4c. 'Civil Engineering'	10	15
107	5c. 'Science'	10	10
108	20c. 'Law'	15	10
104/108 *Set of* 5		45	45

96 *Sagra speciosa* **100** Laloki River

(Des Pamela M. Prescott. Photo Courvoisier)

1967 (12 Apr). Fauna Conservation (Beetles). T **96** and similar vert designs. Multicoloured. P 11½.

109 5c. Type **96** ... 15 10
110 10c. *Eupholus schoenherri* ... 15 10
111 20c. *Sphingnotus albertisi* ... 25 10
112 25c. *Cyphogastra albertisi* ... 25 10
109/112 *Set of 4* ... 70 35

(Des G. Wade. Photo Courvoisier)

1967 (28 June). Laloki River Hydro-Electric Scheme, and 'New Industries'. T **100** and similar vert designs. Multicoloured. P 12½.

113 5c. Type **100** ... 10 10
114 10c. Pyrethrum ... 10 10
115 20c. Tea Plant ... 15 10
116 25c. Type **100** ... 15 10
113/116 *Set of 4* ... 45 35

103 Air Attack at Milne Bay **107** Papuan Lory

(Des R. Hodgkinson (2c.), F. Hodgkinson (5c.), G. Wade (20c., 50c.). Photo Courvoisier)

1967 (30 Aug). 25th Anniversary of the Pacific War. T **103** and similar multicoloured designs. P 11½.

117 2c. Type **103** ... 10 50
118 5c. Kokoda Trail (*vert*) ... 10 10
119 20c. The Coast Watchers ... 25 10
120 50c. Battle of the Coral Sea ... 80 70
117/120 *Set of 4* ... 1·10 1·25

(Des T. Walcot. Photo Courvoisier)

1967 (29 Nov). Christmas. Territory Parrots. T **107** and similar vert designs. Multicoloured. P 12½.

121 5c. Type **107** ... 20 10
122 7c. Pesquet's Parrot ... 25 90
123 20c. Dusky Lory ... 30 10
124 25c. Edward's Fig Parrot ... 35 10
121/124 *Set of 4* ... 1·00 1·10

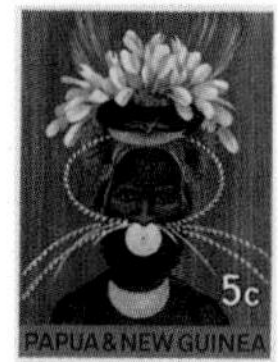

111 Chimbu Headdresses **112**

(Des P. Jones. Photo Courvoisier)

1968 (21 Feb). 'National Heritage'. T **111/112** and similar multicoloured designs. P 12×12½ (5, 60c.) or 12½×12 (10, 20c.).

125 5c. Type **111** ... 10 10
126 10c. Southern Highlands Headdress (*horiz*) ... 15 10
127 20c. Western Highlands Headdress (*horiz*) ... 15 10
128 60c. Type **112** ... 40 45
125/128 *Set of 4* ... 70 65

115 *Hyla thesaurensis* **119** Human Rights Emblem and Papuan Headdress (abstract)

(Des and photo Courvoisier)

1968 (24 Apr). Fauna Conservation (Frogs). T **115** and similar horiz designs. Multicoloured. P 11½.

129 5c. Type **115** ... 15 10
130 10c. *Hyla iris* ... 15 20
131 15c. *Ceratobatrachus guentheri* ... 15 30
132 20c. *Nyctimystes narinosa* ... 20 60
129/132 *Set of 4* ... 60 1·10

(Des G. Hamori. Litho Enschedé)

1968 (26 June). Human Rights Year. T **119** and similar horiz design. Multicoloured. P 13½×12½.

133 5c. Type **119** ... 10 10
134 10c. Human Rights in the World (abstract) ... 10 10

121 Leadership (abstract) **123** Common Egg Cowrie (*Ovula ovum*)

(Des G. Hamori. Litho Enschedé)

1968 (26 June). Universal Suffrage. T **121** and similar horiz design. Multicoloured. P 13½×12½.

135 20c. Type **121** ... 15 20
136 25c. Leadership of the community (abstract) ... 15 30

(Des P. Jones. Photo Courvoisier)

1968–69. Sea Shells. Multicoloured designs as T **123**. P 12×12½ ($2), 12½×12 (1c. to 20c.) or 11½ (others).

137 1c. Type **123** (29.1.69) ... 10 10
138 3c. Laciniate Conch (*Strombus sinuatus*) (30.10.68) ... 30 1·25
139 4c. Lithograph Cone (*Conus litoglyphus*) (29.1.69) ... 20 1·25
140 5c. Marbled Cone (*Conus marmoreus marmoreus*) (28.8.68) ... 25 10
141 7c. Episcopal Mitre (*Mitra mitra*) (29.1.69) ... 35 10
142 10c. *Cymbiola rutila ruckeri* (30.10.68) ... 45 10
143 12c. Checkerboard Bonnet (*Phalium areola*) (29.1.69) ... 1·25 1·50
144 15c. Scorpion Conch (*Lambis scorpius*) (30.10.68) ... 45 75
145 20c. Fluted Giant Clam or Scale Tridacna (*Tridacna sqamosa*) (28.8.68) ... 50 10
146 25c. Camp Pitar Venus (*Lioconcha castrensis*) (28.8.68) ... 50 1·40
147 30c. Ramose Murex (*Murex ramosus*) (28.8.68) ... 50 75
148 40c. Chambered or Pearly Nautilus (*Nautilus pompilius*) (30.10.68) ... 50 1·00
149 60c. Trumpet Triton (*Charonia tritonis*) (28.8.68) ... 50 35
150 $1 Manus Green Papuina (*Papuina pulcherrima*) (30.10.68) ... 1·00 45
151 $2 Glory of the Sea Cone (*Conus gloriamaris*) (*vert*) (29.1.69) ... 7·00 1·00
137/151 *Set of 15* ... 12·00 9·00

The 1, 5, 7, 15, 40, 60c. and $1 exist with PVA gum as well as gum arabic.

138 Tito Myth **139** Iko Myth

140 Luvuapo Myth **141** Miro Myth

(Des from native motifs by Revd. H. A. Brown. Litho Enschedé)

1969 (9 Apr). Folklore. Elema Art (2nd series). P 12½×13½×Roul 9 between *se-tenant* pairs.

152 **138** 5c. black, yellow and red ... 10 60
a. Pair. Nos. 152/153 ... 20 1·10
153 **139** 5c. black, yellow and red ... 10 60
154 **140** 10c. black, grey and red ... 15 60
a. Pair. Nos. 154/155 ... 30 1·10
155 **141** 10c. black, grey and red ... 15 60
152/155 *Set of 4* ... 45 2·00

Nos. 152/153 and 154/155 were issued in vertical *se-tenant* pairs, separated by a line of roulette.

142 Fireball class Dinghy **145** *Dendrobium ostrinoglossum*

(Des J. Fallas. Recess Note Ptg Branch, Reserve Bank of Australia)

1969 (25 June). Third South Pacific Games, Port Moresby. T **142** and similar designs. P 14×14½ (5c.) or 14½×14 (others).

156 5c. black ... 10 10
157 10c. deep bluish violet ... 10 20
158 20c. myrtle-green ... 15 30
156/158 *Set of 3* ... 30 50

Designs: Horiz—5c. T **142**; 10c. Swimming pool, Boroko; 20c. Games arena, Konedobu.

(Des P. Jones. Photo Courvoisier)

1969 (27 Aug). Flora conservation (Orchids). T **145** and similar vert designs. Multicoloured. P 11½.

159 5c. Type **145** ... 25 10
160 10c. *Dendrobium lawesii* ... 25 70
161 20c. *Dendrobium pseudofrigidum* ... 30 90
162 30c. *Dendrobium conanthum* ... 30 70
159/162 *Set of 4* ... 1·00 2·25

149 Bird of Paradise **150** Native Potter

(Des G. Hamori. Photo Note Ptg Branch, Reserve Bank of Australia)

1969 (24 Sept)–**71**. Coil stamps. P 15×imperf.

162*a* **149** 2c. blue, black and red (1.4.71) ... 10 65
163 5c. bright green, brown and red-orange ... 10 10

(Des G. Hamori. Photo Courvoisier)

1969 (24 Sept). 50th Anniversary of International Labour Organisation. P 11½.

164 **150** 5c. multicoloured ... 10 10

151 Tareko **155** Prehistoric Ambun Stone

(Des G. Hamori. Photo Courvoisier)

1969 (29 Oct). Musical Instruments. T **151** and similar horiz designs. P 12½×12.

165 5c. multicoloured ... 10 10
166 10c. black, olive-green and pale yellow ... 10 10
167 25c. black, yellow and brown ... 15 15
168 30c. multicoloured ... 25 15
165/168 *Set of 4* ... 55 45

Designs: 5c. T **151**; 10c. Garamut; 25c. Iviliko; 30c. Kundu.

(Des R. Bates. Photo Courvoisier)

1970 (11 Feb). 'National Heritage'. T **155** and similar horiz designs. Multicoloured. P 12½×12.

169 5c. Type **155** ... 10 10
170 10c. Masawa canoe of Kula circuit ... 10 10
171 25c. Torres' Map, 1606 ... 40 15
172 30c. HMS *Basilisk* (paddle-sloop), 1873 ... 65 25
169/172 *Set of 4* ... 1·10 55

159 King of Saxony Bird Paradise

(Des T. Walcot. Photo Courvoisier)

1970 (13 May). Fauna Conservation (Birds of Paradise). T **159** and similar vert designs. Multicoloured. P 12.

173 5c. Type **159** ... 40 15
174 10c. King Bird of Paradise ... 40 45
175 15c. Raggiana Bird of Paradise ... 55 80
176 25c. Sickle-crested Bird of Paradise ... 65 50
173/176 *Set of 4* ... 1·75 1·75

163 Douglas Dc-6B and Mt Wilhelm **164** Lockheed L.188 Electra and Mt. Yule

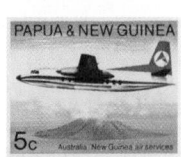

165 Boeing 727-100 and Mt. Giluwe **166** Fokker F.27 Friendship and Manam Island

(Des D. Gentleman. Photo Harrison)

1970 (8 July). Australian and New Guinea Air Services. T **163/166** and similar horiz designs. Multicoloured. P 14½×14.

177 5c. Type **163** ... 25 30
a. Block of 4. Nos. 177/180 ... 1·00 2·00

178	5c. Type **164**	25	30
179	5c. Type **165**	25	30
180	5c. Type **166**	25	30
181	25c. Douglas DC-3 and Matupi Volcano	35	40
182	30c. Boeing 707 and Hombrom's Bluff	35	60
177/182 *Set of 6*		1·50	2·50

Nos. 177/180 were issued together, *se-tenant*, in blocks of four throughout the sheet.

169 N. Miklouho-Maclay (scientist) and Effigy

(Des D. Gentleman. Photo Courvoisier)

1970 (19 Aug). 42nd ANZAAS (Australian—New Zealand Association for the Advancement of Science) congress, Port Moresby. T **169** and similar horiz designs. P 11½.

183	5c. multicoloured	10	10
184	10c. multicoloured	15	10
185	15c. multicoloured	60	25
186	20c. multicoloured	25	25
183/186 *Set of 4*		1·00	60

Designs: 5c. T **169**; 10c. B. Malinowski (anthropologist) and native hut; 15c. T. Salvadori (ornithologist) and Double-wattled Cassowary; 20c. FRR Schlechter (botanist) and flower.

170 Wogeo Island Food Bowl

(Des P. Jones. Photo Courvoisier)

1970 (28 Oct). Native Artefacts. T **170** and similar multicoloured designs. P 12½×12 (30c.) or 12×12½ (others).

187	5c. Type **170**	10	10
188	10c. Lime Pot	20	10
189	15c. Aibom Sago Storage Pot	20	10
190	30c. Manus Island Bowl (*horiz*)	25	30
187/190 *Set of 4*		65	55

STAMP BOOKLETS

B **1**

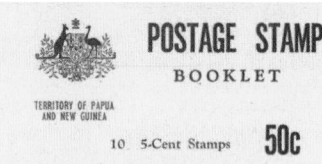

1970 (28 Jan). Green on olive-yellow cover, 120×52 mm, as T B **1**, but 'POSTAGE STAMP' in seriffed type. Stamps attached by selvedge.

SB1 50c. booklet containing 5c. (No. 140) in block of 10 .... £375

1970 (25 May). Green on cream cover as T B **1** with 'POSTAGE STAMP' without serifs. Stamps attached by selvedge.

SB2 50c. booklet containing 5c. (No. 140) in block of 10 .... 15·00

No. SB2 shows 'GP-P&NG/B112' imprint on reverse.

An example of No. SB2 has been reported containing No. 187 in block of 10.

POSTAGE DUE STAMPS

POSTAL
CHARGES

6d.

IXIXIXIXIX

(D **1**)

POSTAL
CHARGES

3s.

(D **2**)

1960 (1 Mar). Postage stamps surcharged.

*(a) No. 8 with T D **1***

D1	6d. on 7½d. blue (R.)	£850	£450
	a. Surch double	£4250	£2500

*(b) Nos. 1, 4, 6a, 7/8 as T D **2***

D2	1d. on 6½d. maroon	2·50	4·00
D3	3d. on ½d. emerald (B.)	5·00	1·25
	a. Surch double	£1100	
D4	6d. on 7½d. blue (R.)	40·00	5·50
	a. Surch double	£1200	
D5	1s. 3d. on 3½d. black (O.)	2·50	1·25
D6	3s. on 2½d. orange	10·00	2·25
D2/D6 *Set of 5*		55·00	13·00

Genuine used examples of No. D1a should be postmarked at Goroko or Kawieng.

Examples of Nos. D1, D1a, D3a and D4a should only be purchased if accompanied by an expert committee's certificate.

D **3**

(Typo Note Ptg Branch, Reserve Bank of Australia, Melbourne)

1960 (2 June). W **15** of Australia. P 14.

D7	D **3**	1d. orange	40	50
D8		3d. yellow-brown	40	40
D9		6d. blue	45	20
D10		9d. deep red	45	1·50
D11		1s. light emerald	45	20
D12		1s.3d. violet	60	65
D13		1s.6d. pale blue	2·50	3·75
D14		3s. yellow	60	20
D7/D14 *Set of 8*			5·25	6·75

The use of Postal Charge stamps was discontinued on 12 February 1966, but they remained on sale at the Philatelic Bureau until 31 August 1966.

Bahamas

The British Post Office at Nassau was established during the early days of the West Indies packet system, and was certainly operating by 1733. The first known local postmark dates from 1802.

The crowned-circle handstamp No. CC1 was issued in 1846 and was generally replaced, for the public mails, by various stamps of Great Britain in 1858.

Local mail deliveries were rudimentary until 1859 when Nos. 1/2 were issued by the colonial authorities for interisland mails. Examples used for this purpose are usually cancelled in manuscript or with a '27' postmark. The 'local' 1d. stamp became valid for overseas mails in May, 1860, when the colonial authorities took over this service from the British GPO.

For illustrations of the handstamp and postmark types see BRITISH POST OFFICES ABROAD notes, following GREAT BRITAIN.

NASSAU

CROWNED-CIRCLE HANDSTAMPS

CC1 CC **2** BAHAMAS (Nassau) (18.5.1846) (R.) .... *Price on cover* £2250

No. CC1 was later struck in black and used as an Official Paid mark in 1865 and between 1897 and 1937. Handstamps as Types CC **1** and CC **3** (only three known) struck in black were used for the same purpose from 1933 until 1953; but it is believed that these were never employed during the pre-stamp period. *Price on cover from £50.*

Stamps of GREAT BRITAIN cancelled 'A05' as Type **2**.

1858–60.

Z1	1d. rose-red (1857), perf 14	£2500
Z2	2d. blue (1858) (Plate Nos. 7, 8)	£1600
Z3	4d. rose (1857)	£475
Z3*a*	6d. purple (1854), embossed	£5500
Z4	6d. lilac (1856)	£375
Z5	1s. green (1856)	£2750

PRICES FOR STAMPS ON COVER TO 1945

No. 1	*from* × 10
No. 2	—
Nos. 3/6	*from* × 8
No. 7	—
Nos. 8/11	*from* × 10
Nos. 12/15	*from* × 4
Nos. 16/19*a*	*from* × 6
Nos. 20/25	*from* × 15
Nos. 26/28	*from* × 4
No. 29	—
Nos. 30/32	*from* × 15
No. 33	*from* × 30
Nos. 35/37	*from* × 6
Nos. 38/39	*from* × 10
No. 39*b*	*from* × 30
No. 40	*from* × 50
No. 41	*from* × 6
No. 42	*from* × 15
No. 43	*from* × 5
Nos. 44/44*a*	*from* × 10
No. 45	*from* × 40
Nos. 47/57	*from* × 4
Nos. 58/89	*from* × 2
Nos. 90/130	*from* × 3
Nos. 131/132	*from* × 10
Nos. 141/145	*from* × 4
Nos. 146/148	*from* × 6
Nos. 149/157	*from* × 3
Nos. 158/160	*from* × 4
No. 161	*from* × 8
Nos. 162/175	*from* × 5
Nos. S1/53	*from* × 20

CROWN COLONY

1

2

3

(Eng and recess P.B.)

1859 (10 June)–**60**. No wmk. Imperf.

(a) Thick, opaque paper

1	**1**	1d. reddish lake (*shades*)	£5000	£2250

(b) Thin paper

2	**1**	1d. dull lake (4.60)	65·00	£1500

No. 1, the printing on thick opaque paper, is very rare in unused condition. Unused remainders, on medium to thick, but slightly transparent, paper are worth about £250.

Collectors are warned against false postmarks upon the remainder stamps of 1d., imperf, on thin paper.

1860 (Oct). No wmk. Clean-cut perf 14 to 16.

3	**1**	1d. lake (H/S 'CANCELLED' in oval £8500)	£5500	£750

For notes on 'CANCELLED' examples see Catalogue Introduction. Examples with this handstamp on No. 3 are imperforate horizontally.

1861 (June)–**62**. No wmk.

(a) Rough perf 14 to 16

4	**1**	1d. lake	£650	£325
5	**2**	4d. dull rose (12.61)	£1400	£400
		a. Imperf between (pair)	£38000	
6		6d. grey-lilac (12.61)	£4250	£600
		a. Pale dull lilac	£3250	£500

(b) P 11 to 12½ (1862)

7	**1**	1d. lake	£2250	

No. 7 was a perforation trial on a new machine at Perkins Bacon. It was not sent out to the Colony and is also known part perforated.

(Recess D.L.R.)

1862. No wmk.*

No.	Type	Description	Unused	Used
		(a) P 11½, 12 (July)		
8	1	1d. carmine-lake	£1000	£190
9		1d. lake	£1600	£275
10	2	4d. dull rose	£3750	£425
11		6d. lavender-grey	£11000	£500
		(b) P 11½, 12, compound with 11		
12	1	1d. carmine-lake	£2250	£850
13		1d. lake	£2500	£950
14	2	4d. dull rose	£21000	£2000
15		6d. lavender-grey	£21000	£1900
		(c) P 13 (Oct)		
16	1	1d. lake	£900	£170
17		1d. brown-lake	£750	£140
18	2	4d. dull rose	£2750	£375
19		6d. lavender-grey	£3250	£475
		a. Lilac	£2750	£450

* Stamps exist with part of papermaker's sheet wmk ('T. H. SAUNDERS 1860').

The compound perfs Nos. 12/15 usually show Perf 11 on one side only, from the margins of sheets. The 1d. value is recorded Perf 11 at top or left, the 4d. Perf 11 at bottom and the 6d. Perf 11 at top, but examples of the 1d. are recorded Perf 11 at both top and bottom.

1863 (May)–**77**. Wmk Crown CC.

No.	Type	Description	Unused	Used
		(a) P 12½		
20	1	1d. brown-lake	£100	70·00
		w. Wmk inverted	£190	£120
		x. Wmk reversed		
		y. Wmk inverted and reversed	—	£180
21		1d. carmine-lake	£120	70·00
		w. Wmk inverted	£190	£100
		x. Wmk reversed	£130	70·00
22		1d. carmine-lake (aniline)	£150	75·00
		w. Wmk inverted	£250	
		x. Wmk reversed		
23		1d. rose-red	70·00	45·00
		w. Wmk inverted	£140	
		x. Wmk reversed	70·00	45·00
24		1d. red	70·00	45·00
		w. Wmk inverted		
		x. Wmk reversed	—	45·00
25		1d. vermilion 1875	75·00	45·00
		w. Wmk inverted	£130	80·00
		x. Wmk reversed	75·00	45·00
		y. Wmk inverted and reversed	£190	£100
26	2	4d. bright rose	£300	60·00
		w. Wmk inverted	—	£250
		x. Wmk reversed	—	85·00
27		4d. dull rose	£400	60·00
		w. Wmk inverted	—	£250
		x. Wmk reversed	£375	60·00
		y. Wmk inverted and reversed	£1000	£250
28		4d. brownish rose (*wmk reversed*)	£475	80·00
		w. Wmk inverted	—	£275
29		6d. rose-lilac	—	£2250
		w. Wmk inverted	£6500	
30		6d. lilac (*shades*)	£425	75·00
		w. Wmk inverted	—	£250
		x. Wmk reversed		
31		6d. deep violet	£160	60·00
		w. Wmk inverted	£650	£250
		x. Wmk reversed	£180	65·00
		y. Wmk inverted and reversed	—	£250
32		6d. violet (aniline)	£250	90·00
		x. Wmk reversed	£250	95·00
		(b) P 14		
33	1	1d. scarlet-vermilion (1877)	70·00	15·00
		x. Wmk reversed	85·00	23·00
34		1d. scarlet (or scarlet-vermilion) (aniline)	£1000	
		x. Wmk reversed		
35	2	4d. bright rose (1876)	£400	40·00
		w. Wmk inverted	£950	£225
36		4d. dull rose	£1500	40·00
		w. Wmk inverted		
37		4d. rose-lake	£450	40·00

No. 29 is believed to be the shade of the first printing only and should not be confused with other lilac shades of the 6d.

No. 34 is not known postally used, although manuscript fiscal cancellations on this shade do exist.

(Typo D.L.R.)

1863–80. Wmk Crown CC.

No.	Type	Description	Unused	Used
		(a) P 12½		
38	3	1s. blue-green (1865)	£2750	£300
		(b) P 14		
39	3	1s. deep green	£400	50·00
		aw. Wmk inverted		
		b. Green	£120	30·00
		ba. Thick paper (1880)	9·00	11·00
		bw. Wmk inverted (thick paper)	—	£150

1882 (Mar). Wmk Crown CA.

No.	Type	Description	Unused	Used
		(a) P 12		
40	1	1d. scarlet-vermilion	60·00	14·00
		x. Wmk reversed	—	65·00
41	2	4d. rose	£550	45·00
		(b) P 14		
42	1	1d. scarlet-vermilion	£475	60·00
		x. Wmk reversed	£600	
43	2	4d. rose	£850	60·00
		x. Wmk reversed	£950	70·00

1882 (Mar)–**98**. Wmk Crown CA. P 14.

No.	Type	Description	Unused	Used
44	3	1s. green	50·00	14·00
44*a*		1s. blue-green (1898)	38·00	48·00

FOURPENCE

(4)

5

1883.* No. 31 surch with T **4**.

No.	Type	Description	Unused	Used
45	2	4d. on 6d. deep violet	£550	£400
		a. Surch inverted	£18000	£10000
		x. Wmk reversed	£600	£450

* The only recorded date of use is 4 June.

T **4** was applied by handstamp and occurs in various positions. Caution is needed in buying Nos. 45/45x.

2½d. Sloping '2' (R. 10/6)

6d. Malformed 'E'

(Typo D.L.R.)

1884–90. Wmk Crown CA. P 14.

No.	Type	Description	Unused	Used
47	5	1d. pale rose	90·00	14·00
48		1d. carmine-rose	8·50	2·00
49		1d. bright carmine (aniline)	6·50	5·50
50		2½d. dull blue (1888)	90·00	18·00
51		2½d. blue	50·00	8·00
		a. Sloping '2'	£450	£120
52		2½d. ultramarine	16·00	1·75
		a. Sloping '2'	£160	70·00
		s. Optd 'SPECIMEN'	65·00	
		w. Wmk inverted	£250	£120
53		4d. deep yellow	9·50	4·75
54		6d. mauve (1890)	7·00	38·00
		a. Malformed 'E' (R. 6/6)	£200	£400
		s. Optd 'SPECIMEN'	65·00	
56		5s. sage-green	90·00	£100
57		£1 Venetian red	£275	£225
47/57 *Set of 6*			£350	£325

Examples of Nos. 54/57 are known showing a forged Bahamas postmark dated 'AU 29 94'.

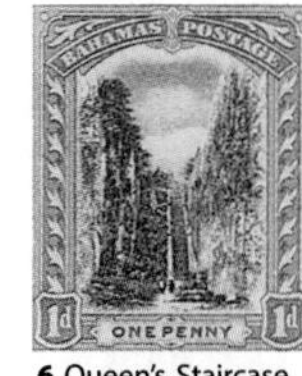

6 Queen's Staircase, Nassau

7

8

(Recess D.L.R.)

1901 (23 Sept)–**03**. Wmk Crown CC. P 14.

No.	Type	Description	Unused	Used
58	6	1d. black and red	15·00	2·00
		w. Wmk inverted	£170	£170
		y. Wmk inverted and reversed	£300	£325
59		5d. black and orange (1.03)	9·50	50·00
		x. Wmk reversed	£300	
		y. Wmk inverted and reversed	£225	£350
60		2s. black and blue (1.03)	29·00	60·00
		x. Wmk reversed	£425	
61		3s. black and green (1.03)	50·00	65·00
		w. Wmk inverted		
		y. Wmk inverted and reversed	£140	£140
58/61 *Set of 4*			90·00	£160
58s/61s Optd 'SPECIMEN' *Set of 4*			£150	

For stamps in this design, but with Mult Crown CA or Mult Script CA watermarks see Nos. 75/80 and 111/114.

(Typo D.L.R.)

1902 (18 Dec)–**07**. Wmk Crown CA. P 14.

No.	Type	Description	Unused	Used
62	7	1d. carmine	1·75	1·50
63		2½d. ultramarine	13·00	1·25
		a. Sloping '2'	£250	£120
64		4d. orange	15·00	60·00
65		4d. deep yellow	29·00	75·00
66		6d. brown	8·50	35·00
		a. Malformed 'E' (R. 6/6)	£170	£300
67		1s. grey-black and carmine	22·00	55·00
68		1s. brownish grey and carmine (6.07)	22·00	55·00
69		5s. dull purple and blue	80·00	95·00
70		£1 green and black	£300	£350
62/70 *Set of 7*			£375	£550
62s/70s Optd 'SPECIMEN' *Set of 7*			£300	

Examples of most values are known showing a forged Nassau postmark dated '2 MAR 10'.

1906 (Apr)–**11**. Wmk Mult Crown CA. P 14.

No.	Type	Description	Unused	Used
71	7	½d. pale green (5.06)	5·50	3·75
		s. Optd 'SPECIMEN'	55·00	
72		1d. carmine-rose	27·00	1·25
73		2½d. ultramarine (4.07)	27·00	26·00
		a. Sloping '2'	£350	£400
		w. Wmk inverted	£170	£170
74		6d. bistre-brown (8.11)	17·00	48·00
		a. Malformed 'E' (R. 6/6)	£275	£475
71/74 *Set of 4*			65·00	70·00

1911 (Feb)–**19**. Wmk Mult Crown CA. P 14.

No.	Type	Description	Unused	Used
75	6	1d. black and red	25·00	2·75
		a. Grey-black and scarlet (1916)	6·00	2·75
		b. Grey-black and deep carmine-red (1919)	11·00	7·00
76		3d. purple/*yellow* (*thin paper*) (18.5.17)	7·00	45·00
		a. Reddish purple/buff (thick paper) (1.19)	7·50	14·00
		s. Optd 'SPECIMEN'	50·00	
		x. Wmk reversed	†	£500
77		3d. black and brown (23.3.19)	3·25	2·25
		s. Optd 'SPECIMEN'	50·00	
		w. Wmk inverted		
		x. Wmk reversed	†	£500
78		5d. black and mauve (18.5.17)	4·00	5·50
		s. Optd 'SPECIMEN'	50·00	
79		2s. black and blue (11.16)	38·00	55·00
		w. Wmk inverted	£500	
		x. Wmk reversed	†	£500
80		3s. black and green (8.17)	70·00	55·00
		w. Wmk inverted	£350	£350
		y. Wmk inverted and reversed	£170	£160
75*a*/80 *Set of 6*			£110	£110

(Typo D.L.R.)

1912–19. Wmk Mult Crown CA. Chalk-surfaced paper (1s. to £1). P 14.

No.	Type	Description	Unused	Used
81	8	½d. green	80	12·00
		a. Yellow-green	2·75	17·00
82		1d. carmine (aniline)	3·50	30
		a. Deep rose	8·00	2·25
		b. Rose	11·00	3·00
		w. Wmk inverted	£350	£140
		y. Wmk inverted and reversed	†	£350
83		2d. grey (1919)	2·25	3·00
84		2½d. ultramarine	4·75	35·00
		a. Deep dull blue	18·00	45·00
		b. Sloping '2'	£275	£425
85		4d. orange-yellow	5·50	27·00
		a. Yellow	2·50	22·00
86		6d. bistre-brown	1·75	9·00
		a. Malformed 'E' (R. 6/6)	£130	£225
87		1s. grey-black and carmine	1·75	9·00
		a. Jet-black and carmine	15·00	22·00
88		5s. dull purple and blue	42·00	70·00
		a. Pale dull purple and deep blue	55·00	80·00
89		£1 dull green and black	£200	£350
		a. Green and black	£275	£375
81/89 *Set of 9*			£225	£425
81s/89s Optd 'SPECIMEN' *Set of 9*			£325	

1.1.17. (9) **WAR TAX** (10)

Long stroke to '7' (R. 4/6)

1917 (18 May). No. 75*b* optd with T **9** in red by D.L.R.

No.	Type	Description	Unused	Used
90	6	1d. grey-black and deep carmine-red	40	2·75
		a. Long stroke to '7'	40·00	75·00
		s. Optd 'SPECIMEN'	65·00	

It was originally intended to issue No. 90 on 1 January 1917, but the stamps were not received in the Bahamas until May. Half the proceeds from their sale were donated to the British Red Cross Society.

1918 (21 Feb–10 July). Nos. 75/76, 81/82 and 87 optd at Nassau with T **10**.

No.	Type	Description	Unused	Used
91	8	½d. green	15·00	50·00
92		1d. carmine (aniline)	1·00	1·25
		w. Wmk inverted	£300	
		x. Wmk reversed	£400	
93	6	1d. black and red (10.7)	5·00	12·00
		a. Opt double, one inverted	£850	
		b. Opt double	£1700	£1800
		c. Opt inverted	£1500	£1600
		x. Wmk reversed	£350	
94		3d. purple/*yellow* (*thin paper*)	3·25	3·50
		a. Opt double	£1600	£1700
		b. Opt inverted	£1100	£1200
		c. 'W' of 'WAR' inserted by hand	£5000	
95	8	1s. grey-black and carmine	£110	£160
91/95 *Set of 5*			£120	£200

No. 93 was only on sale for ten days.

No. 94c occurred on R. 1/1 of one sheet, the original 'W' having been omitted as a result of a paper fold.

Examples of Nos. 91/92 with overprint inverted, and of Nos. 91/92 and 95 with overprint double, are now considered to be forgeries.

WAR TAX (11) **WAR TAX** (12) **WAR CHARITY 3.6.18.** (13)

1918 (20 July). Optd by D.L.R. in London with T **11** or **12** (3d).

No.	Type	Description	Unused	Used
96	8	½d. green	1·75	1·75
		w. Wmk inverted		
		x. Wmk reversed		
97		1d. carmine	4·75	65
		a. Wmk sideways	£200	
		w. Wmk inverted		
		y. Wmk inverted and reversed	£325	
98	6	3d. purple/*yellow*	1·00	1·50
		w. Wmk inverted	£170	
		x. Wmk reversed	£200	
99	8	1s. grey-black and carmine (R.)	15·00	8·00
96/99 *Set of 4*			20·00	10·50
96s/99s Optd 'SPECIMEN' *Set of 4*			£170	

1919 (21 Mar). No. 77 optd with T **12** by D.L.R.

No.	Type	Description	Unused	Used
100	6	3d. black and brown	2·25	7·50
		a. 'C' and 'A' missing from wmk	£1800	
		s. Optd 'SPECIMEN'	50·00	
		w. Wmk inverted	70·00	

No. 100a shows the 'C' omitted from one impression and the 'A' missing from the next one to the right (*as seen from the front of the stamp*). The 'C' is badly distorted in the second watermark.

1919 (1 Jan). No. 75*b* optd with T **13** by D.L.R.

No.	Type	Description	Unused	Used
101	6	1d. grey-black and deep carmine-red (R.)	30	2·50
		a. Opt double	£2000	
		s. Optd 'SPECIMEN'	55·00	
		w. Wmk inverted	80·00	

		x. Wmk reversed	85·00	95·00
		y. Wmk inverted and reversed	£160	

The date is that originally fixed for the issue of the stamp. The year 1918 was also the bicentenary of the appointment of the first Royal Governor.

WAR TAX (14) **WAR TAX** (15)

1919 (14 July).

(a) Optd with T **14** *by D.L.R.*

102	8	½d. green (R.)	30	1·50
103		1d. carmine	1·50	2·50
104	–	1s. grey-black and carmine (R.)	27·00	60·00

(b) No. 77 optd with T **15**

105	6	3d. black and brown	2·25	10·00
		w. Wmk inverted	70·00	
		ws. Ditto. Optd 'SPECIMEN'	£100	
		x. Wmk reversed	75·00	
		y. Wmk inverted and reversed	£130	
102/105 *Set of 4*			27·00	65·00
102s/105s Optd 'SPECIMEN' *Set of 4*			£170	

16

17 Great Seal of the Bahamas.

(Recess D.L.R.)

1920 (1 Mar). Peace Celebration. Wmk Mult Crown CA (sideways*). P 14.

106	16	½d. green	1·00	6·00
		a. 'A' of 'CA' missing from wmk	£850	
		x. Wmk sideways reversed	£350	£350
107		1d. carmine	2·75	1·25
		a. 'A' of 'CA' missing from wmk	†	£650
		b. 'C' of 'CA' missing from wmk	£850	
		x. Wmk sideways reversed	£375	
		y. Wmk Crown to right of CA and reversed	£375	
108		2d. slate-grey	2·75	9·00
		a. 'C' of 'CA' missing from wmk	£850	
109		3d. deep brown	2·75	9·00
		a. 'C' of 'CA' missing from wmk	£950	
		b. 'A' of 'CA' missing from wmk	£950	
		w. Wmk Crown to right of CA	£300	
110		1s. deep myrtle-green	15·00	38·00
		a. Substituted crown in wmk	£1800	
		b. 'C' of 'CA' missing from wmk	£1800	
		x. Wmk sideways reversed	£650	
106/110 *Set of 5*			22·00	55·00
106s/110s Optd 'SPECIMEN' *Set of 5*			£170	

* The normal sideways watermark shows Crown to left of CA, *as seen from the back of the stamp.*

For illustration of the substituted watermark crown see Catalogue Introduction.

1921 (29 Mar)–**29**. Wmk Script CA. P 14.

111	6	1d. grey and rose-red	3·75	5·00
		x. Wmk reversed	£350	
112		5d. black and purple (8.29)	3·75	45·00
113		2s. black and blue (11.22)	22·00	22·00
114		3s. black and green (9.24)	55·00	70·00
111/114 *Set of 4*			75·00	£130
111s/114s Optd or Perf (5d.) 'SPECIMEN' *Set of 4*			£225	

Examples of all values are known showing a forged Nassau postmark dated '2 MAR 10'.

½d. Elongated 'E' (left pane R. 9/6)

1921 (8 Sept)–**37**. Wmk Mult Script CA. Chalk-surfaced paper (3d., 1s., 5s., £1). P 14.

115	8	½d. green (1924)	50	40
		a. Elongated 'E'	£100	£110
116		1d. carmine	1·00	15
117		1½d. brown-red (1934)	13·00	1·00
118		2d. grey (1927)	1·50	2·00
119		2½d. ultramarine (1922)	1·00	1·40
		y. Wmk inverted and reversed	†	£800
120		3d. purple/*pale yellow* (1931)	6·50	9·50
		a. Purple/orange-yellow (1937)	16·00	28·00
121		4d. orange-yellow (1924)	1·50	2·25
122		6d. bistre-brown (1922)	70	1·25
		a. Malformed 'E' (R.6/6)	£100	£160
123		1s. black and carmine (1926)	10·00	5·50
124		5s. dull purple and blue (1924)	42·00	65·00
125		£1 green and black (1926)	£180	£375
115/125 *Set of 11*			£225	£425
115s/125s Optd or Perf (1½d., 3d.) 'SPECIMEN' *Set of 11*			£550	

(Recess B.W.)

1930 (2 Jan). Tercentenary of Colony. Wmk Mult Script CA. P 12.

126	17	1d. black and scarlet	4·00	2·75
127		3d. black and deep brown	5·50	15·00
128		5d. black and deep purple	5·50	18·00
129		2s. black and deep blue	18·00	50·00
130		3s. black and green	48·00	85·00
126/130 *Set of 5*			70·00	£150
126s/130s Perf 'SPECIMEN' *Set of 5*			£180	

18

(Recess B.W.)

1931 (14 July)–**46**. Wmk Mult Script CA. P 12.

131	18	2s. slate-purple and deep ultramarine	27·00	35·00
		a. Slate-purple and indigo (9.42)	£110	50·00
		b. Brownish black and indigo (13.4.43)	15·00	9·50
		c. Brownish black and steel-blue (6.44)	19·00	3·75
132		3s. slate-purple and myrtle-green	38·00	32·00
		a. Brownish black and green (13.4.43)	13·00	4·50
		ab. 'A' of 'CA' missing from wmk	£1800	
		b. Brownish black and myrtle-green (1.10.46)	8·00	9·00
131s/132s Perf 'SPECIMEN' *Set of 2*			95·00	

Most of the stamps from the September 1942 printing (No. 131*a* and further stocks of the 3s. similar to No. 132) were used for the 1942 'LANDFALL' overprints.

1935 (6 May). Silver Jubilee. As Nos. 91/94 of Antigua.

141		1½d. deep blue and carmine	1·00	3·50
		h. Dot by flagstaff	£130	£200
		i. Dash by turret	£325	
142		2½d. brown and deep blue	5·00	9·50
		f. Diagonal line by turret	£180	£250
		g. Dot to left of chapel	£375	£450
143		6d. light blue and olive-green	7·00	16·00
		g. Dot to left of chapel	£250	£375
		h. Dot by flagstaff	£350	
144		1s. slate and purple	7·00	15·00
		h. Dot by flagstaff	£325	£400
		i. Dash by turret	£500	£600
141/144 *Set of 4*			18·00	40·00
141s/144s Perf 'SPECIMEN' *Set of 4*			£140	

For illustrations of plate varieties see Omnibus section following Zanzibar.

19 Greater Flamingos in flight

20 King George VI

(Recess Waterlow)

1935 (22 May). Wmk Mult Script CA. P 12½.

145	19	8d. ultramarine and scarlet	9·00	3·75
		s. Perf 'SPECIMEN'	85·00	

1937 (12 May). Coronation. As Nos. 95/97 of Antigua. P 14.

146		½d. green	15	15
147		1½d. yellow-brown	40	1·10
148		2½d. bright blue	55	1·10
146/148 *Set of 3*			1·00	2·10
146s/148s Perf 'SPECIMEN' *Set of 3*			£120	

½d. Accent flaw (right pane R. 1/5) (1938 ptg only)

2d. Short 'T' in 'TWO' (right pane R. 3/6) (Retouched on No. 152*c*, although bottom of letter is still pointed)

3d. 'RENCE' flaw (Right pane R. 9/3. Later corrected)

(Typo D.L.R.)

1938 (11 Mar)–**52**. Wmk Mult Script CA. Chalk-surfaced paper (1s. to £1). P 14.

149	20	½d. green	3·50	1·25
		a. Elongated 'E'	£200	£225
		b. Accent flaw	£550	£275
		c. Bluish green (11.9.42)	3·75	3·50
		ca. Elongated 'E'	£250	
		d. Myrtle-green (11.12.46)	12·00	13·00
		da. Elongated 'E'	£425	
149*e*		½d. brown-purple (18.2.52)	1·00	4·00
		ea. Error. Crown missing	£15000	
		eb. Error. St Edward's Crown	£4250	£3250
		ec. Elongated 'E'	£180	£300
150		1d. carmine	8·50	1·50
150*a*		1d. olive-grey (17.9.41)	3·50	3·50
		ab. Pale slate (11.9.42)	60	70
151		1½d. red-brown (19.4.38)	1·50	1·25
		a. Pale red-brown (19.4.48)	11·00	3·00
152		2d. pale slate (19.4.38)	19·00	3·50
		a. Short 'T'	£950	£375
152*b*		2d. scarlet (17.9.41)	1·00	65
		ba. Short 'T'	£140	£130
		bb. 'TWO PENCE' printed double	†	£17000
		bc. Dull rose-red (19.4.48)	8.00	3·25
152*c*		2d. green (1.5.51)	2·50	80
153		2½d. ultramarine	3·25	1·50
153*a*		2½d. violet (1.7.43)	1·50	1·75
		ab. '2½ PENNY' printed double	£6000	
154		3d. violet (19.4.38)	16·00	3·00
154*a*		3d. blue (4.43)	2·75	1·25
		aa. 'RENCE' flaw	£3750	
		ab. Bright ultramarine (19.4.48)	10·00	6·50
154*b*		3d. scarlet (1.2.52)	2·75	3·25
154*c*		10d. yellow-orange (18.11.46)	2·50	20
155		1s. grey-black and carmine (*thick paper*) (15.9.38)	38·00	6·50
		a. Brownish grey and scarlet (thin striated paper) (4.42)	£1000	£110
		b. Ordinary paper. *Black and carmine* (9.42)	28·00	7·00
		c. Ordinary paper. *Grey-black and bright crimson* (6.3.44)	20·00	75
		d. Pale brownish grey and crimson (19.4.48)	20·00	1·50
156		5s. lilac and blue (*thick paper*) (19.4.38)	£170	£100
		a. Reddish-lilac and blue (thin striated paper) (4.42)	£5000	£700
		b. Ordinary paper. *Purple and blue* (9.42)	40·00	25·00
		c. Ordinary paper. *Dull mauve and deep blue* (11.46)	£130	75·00
		d. Brown-purple and deep bright blue (19.4.48)	45·00	19·00
		e. Red-purple and deep bright blue (8.51)	24·00	24·00
157		£1 deep grey-green and black (*thick paper*) (15.9.38)	£250	£150
		a. Ordinary paper. *Blue-green and black* (13.4.43)	60·00	55·00
		b. Ordinary paper. *Grey-green and black* (3.44)	£200	£140
149/157*a* *Set of 17*			£150	85·00
149s/157s Perf 'SPECIMEN' *Set of 14*			£600	

The ½d. green, 1d. carmine, 1d. grey, 3d. blue and 1s. exist in coils, constructed from normal sheets by Waterlow.

No. 149eb occurs on a row in the watermark in which the crowns and letters 'CA' alternate.

The thick chalk-surfaced paper, used for the initial printing of the 1s., 5s. and £1, was usually toned and had streaky gum. The April 1942 printing for the 1s. and 5s., which was mostly used for the 'LANDFALL' overprints, was on thin striated paper. Printings of the three values between September 1942 and November 1946 were on a thick, smooth, opaque ordinary paper.

21 Sea Garden, Nassau

22 Fort Charlotte

23 Greater Flamingos in flight

3d. (24)

(Recess Waterlow)

1938 (1 July). Wmk Mult Script CA. P 12½.

158	21	4d. light blue and red-orange	1·25	1·00
159	22	6d. olive-green and light blue	1·75	1·00
160	23	8d. ultramarine and scarlet	16·00	3·75
158/160 *Set of 3*			17·00	5·25
158s/160s Perf 'SPECIMEN' *Set of 3*			£150	

1940 (28 Nov). No. 153 surcharged with T **24** by *The Nassau Guardian.*

161	20	3d. on 2½d. blue	1·50	3·25

1492 LANDFALL OF COLUMBUS 1942
(25)

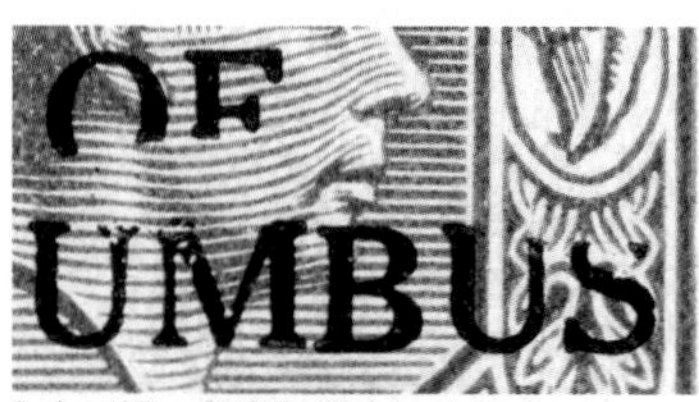

Broken 'OF' and 'US' (R. 2/6, late printing)

1942 (12 Oct). 450th Anniversary of Landing of Columbus in New World. Optd as T **25** by *The Nassau Guardian.*

162	20	½d. bluish green	30	60
		a. Elongated 'E'	80·00	
		b. Opt double	£2250	
		c. Accent flaw	£600	
163		1d. pale slate	30	60
164		1½d. red-brown	40	60
165		2d. scarlet	50	65
		a. Short 'T'	£130	
166		2½d. ultramarine	50	65
167		3d. ultramarine	30	65
		a. 'RENCE' flaw	£3500	
		sa. Opt double, Perf 'SPECIMEN'	£1000	
168	21	4d. light blue and red-orange	40	90
		a. 'COIUMBUS' (R. 5/2)	£1200	£1400
169	22	6d. olive-green and light blue	40	1·50
		a. 'COIUMBUS' (R. 5/2)	£1200	£1500
170	23	8d. ultramarine and scarlet	3·50	70
		a. 'COIUMBUS' (R. 5/2)	£13000	£4250
171	20	1s. brownish grey and scarlet (thin striated paper)	12·00	5·00

		a. Ordinary paper. *Black and carmine*	12·00	16·00
		b. Ordinary paper. *Grey-black and bright crimson*	24·00	16·00
		c. Broken 'OF' and 'US'	£375	
172	**18**	2s. slate-purple and indigo	21·00	30·00
		a. Brownish black and indigo	9·00	11·00
		b. Brownish black and steel-blue	42·00	35·00
		c. Stop after 'COLUMBUS' (R. 2/12)	£5000	£5000
173		3s. slate-purple and myrtle-green	10·00	6·50
		a. Brownish black and green	55·00	50·00
		b. Stop after 'COLUMBUS' (R. 2/12)	£2500	
174	**20**	5s. reddish lilac and blue (thin striated paper)	50·00	26·00
		a. Ordinary paper. *Purple and blue*	23·00	16·00
		b. Broken 'OF' and 'US'	£750	
175		£1 deep grey-green and black (*thick paper*)	80·00	£150
		a. Ordinary paper. *Grey-green and black*	30·00	25·00
		b. Broken 'OF' and 'US'	£1000	
162/175*a* *Set of 14*			80·00	60·00
162s/175s Perf 'SPECIMEN' *Set of 14*			£600	

These stamps replaced the definitive series for a period of six months. Initially stocks of existing printings were used, but when further supplies were required for overprinting a number of new printings were produced, some of which, including the new colour of the 3d., did not appear without overprint until much later.

1946 (11 Nov). Victory. As Nos. 110/111 of Antigua.

176	1½d. brown	10	60
177	3d. blue	10	60
176s/177s Perf 'SPECIMEN' *Set of 2*		90·00	

26 Infant Welfare Clinic

27 Agriculture (combine-harvester)

28 Sisal

29 Straw work

30 Dairy farm

31 Fishing fleet

32 Hatchet Bay, Eleuthera

33 Tuna fishing

34 Paradise Beach

35 Modern hotels

36 Yacht racing

37 Watersports–skiing

38 Shipbuilding

39 Transportation

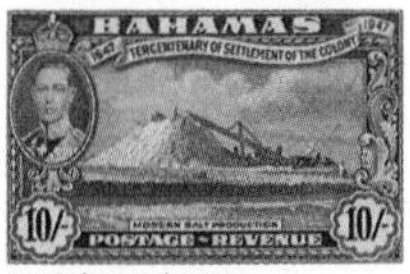

40 Salt production

41 Parliament buildings

(Recess C.B.N.)

1948 (11 Oct). Tercentenary of Settlement of Island of Eleuthera. T **26/41**. P 12.

178	**26**	½d. orange	40	1·75
179	**27**	1d. sage-green	60	35
180	**28**	1½d. yellow	40	80
181	**29**	2d. scarlet	60	40
182	**30**	2½d. brown-lake	70	75
183	**31**	3d. ultramarine	2·50	85
184	**32**	4d. black	60	70
185	**33**	6d. emerald-green	2·50	80
186	**34**	8d. violet	1·25	70
187	**35**	10d. carmine	1·25	35
188	**36**	1s. sepia	3·00	50
189	**37**	2s. magenta	6·00	8·50
190	**38**	3s. blue	13·00	8·50
191	**39**	5s. mauve	20·00	6·00
192	**40**	10s. grey	17·00	13·00
193	**41**	£1 vermilion	17·00	17·00
178/193 *Set of 16*			75·00	55·00

1948 (1 Dec). Royal Silver Wedding. As Nos. 112/113 of Antigua.

194	1½d. red-brown	20	25
195	£1 slate-green	45·00	35·00

1949 (10 Oct). 75th Anniversary of Universal Postal Union. As Nos. 114/117 of Antigua.

196	2½d. violet	35	75
197	3d. deep blue	2·25	3·50
198	6d. greenish blue	55	3·25
199	1s. carmine	55	75
196/199 *Set of 4*		3·25	7·50

(Des and eng B.W. Recess D.L.R.)

1953 (3 June). Coronation. As No. 120 of Antigua.

200	6d. black and pale blue	1·75	60

42 Infant Welfare Clinic

43 Queen Elizabeth II

(Recess B.W.)

1954 (1 Jan)–**63**. Designs previously used for King George VI issue, but bicoloured with portrait of Queen Elizabeth II as in T **42**, and commemorative inscr omitted. Wmk Mult Script CA. P 11×11½.

201	**42**	½d. black and red-orange	10	1·50
202	**27**	1d. olive-green and brown	10	30
203	**32**	1½d. blue and black	15	80
204	**29**	2d. yellow-brown and myrtle-green	15	30
		a. Yellow-brown and deep myrtle-green (23.1.62)	13·00	12·00
205	**31**	3d. black and carmine-red	65	1·25
206	**37**	4d. turquoise-green and deep reddish purple	30	30
		a. Turquoise-blue and deep reddish purple (23.1.62)	28·00	24·00
207	**30**	5d. red-brown and deep bright blue	1·40	2·25
208	**39**	6d. light blue and black	2·50	20
		w. Wmk inverted	—	£1200
209	**34**	8d. black and reddish lilac	2·00	40
		a. Black and deep reddish lilac (21.11.56)	9·00	2·75
210	**35**	10d. black and ultramarine	55	10
		a. Black and deep ultramarine (8.1.63)	8·50	2·75
211	**36**	1s. ultramarine and olive-brown	2·75	10
		a. Ultramarine and deep olive-sepia (19.2.58)	8·50	1·00
212	**28**	2s. orange-brown and black	5·50	70
		a. Chestnut and black (19.2.58)	20·00	2·00
213	**38**	2s.6d. black and deep blue	3·50	1·00
214	**33**	5s. bright emerald and orange	23·00	75
		a. Bright emerald and reddish orange (14.1.59)	90·00	11·00
215	**40**	10s. black and slate-black	40·00	2·50
216	**41**	£1 slate-black and violet	32·00	9·00
201/216 *Set of 16*			£100	19·00

Nos. 201/202, 205, 208 and 211 exist in coils, constructed from normal sheets.

See also No. 246.

(Recess Waterlow)

1959 (10 June). Centenary of First Bahamas Postage Stamp. W w **12**. P 13½.

217	**43**	1d. black and scarlet	50	20
218		2d. black and blue-green	50	1·00
219		6d. black and blue	60	40
220		10d. black and chocolate	60	1·00
217/220 *Set of 4*			2·00	2·40

44 Christ Church Cathedral

(Photo Enschedé)

1962 (30 Jan). Nassau Centenary. T **44** and similar horizontal design. P 14×13.

221	8d. green	65	65
222	10d. bluish violet	65	35

Design: 8d. T **44**; 10d. Nassau Public Library.

1963 (4 June). Freedom from Hunger. As No. 146 of Antigua.

223	8d. sepia	40	40
	a. Name and value omitted	£1200	£2000

BAHAMAS TALKS 1962 (**46**)

NEW CONSTITUTION 1964 (**47**)

1963 (15 July). Bahamas Talks, 1962. Nos. 209/210 optd with T **46**.

224	8d. black and reddish lilac	65	75
225	10d. black and deep ultramarine	65	75

1963 (2 Sept). Red Cross Centenary. As Nos. 147/148 of Antigua.

226	1d. red and black	40	75
227	10d. red and blue	85	2·50

SELF GOVERNMENT

1964 (7 Jan). New Constitution. As Nos. 201/216 but W w **12**, optd with T **47**, by B.W.

228	½d. black and red-orange	15	1·75
229	1d. olive-green and brown	15	15
230	1½d. blue and black	70	1·50
231	2d. yellow-brown and deep myrtle-green	15	20
232	3d. black and carmine-red	2·00	1·75
233	4d. turquoise-blue and deep reddish purple	70	55
234	5d. red-brown and deep bright blue	70	1·50
235	6d. light blue and black	3·50	30
236	8d. black and reddish lilac	70	30
237	10d. black and deep ultramarine	30	15
238	1s. ultramarine and olive-brown	1·50	15
239	2s. chestnut and black	2·00	1·75
240	2s.6d. black and deep blue	3·00	3·00
241	5s. bright emerald and orange	7·00	3·25
242	10s. black and slate black	7·00	5·50
243	£1 slate-black and violet	7·50	27·00
228/243 *Set of 16*		32·00	42·00

1964 (23 Apr). 400th Birth Anniversary of William Shakespeare. As No. 164 of Antigua.

244	6d. turquoise	30	10
	w. Wmk inverted	65·00	

8d (**48**)

1964 (1 Oct). Olympic Games, Tokyo. As No. 211 but W w **12**, surch with T **48**.

245	8d. on 1s. ultramarine and olive-brown	45	15

1964 (6 Oct). As No. 204*a*, but wmk w **12**.

246	2d. yellow-brown and deep myrtle-green	1·75	30

49 Colony's Badge

50 Out Island regatta

51 Hospital

52 High School

53 Greater Flamingo

54 RMS *Queen Elizabeth*

55 'Development'

56 Yachting

57 Public square

58 Sea Gardens

59 Old cannons at Fort Charlotte

60 Sikorsky S-38 flying boat, 1929 and Boeing 707 airliner

61 Williamson Film Project, 1914 and Undersea Post Office, 1939

62 Queen or Pink Conch

63 Columbus's flagship

(Queen's portrait by Anthony Buckley. Litho and recess (portrait and 'BAHAMAS') B.W.)

1965 (7 Jan–14 Sept). Horizontal designs as T **49/63**. W w **12**. P 13½.

247 **49** ½d. multicoloured ... 15 2·50
248 **50** 1d. slate, light blue and orange ... 1·00 1·25
249 **51** 1½d. rose-red, green and brown ... 15 4·00
250 **52** 2d. slate, green and turquoise-blue ... 15 10
251 **53** 3d. red, light blue and purple ... 4·50 20
252 **54** 4d. green, blue and orange-brown ... 5·00 3·75
253 **55** 6d. dull green, light blue and rose ... 1·75 10
254 **56** 8d. reddish purple, light blue and bronze green ... 50 30
255 **57** 10d. orange-brown, green and violet ... 25 10
256 **58** 1s. red, yellow, turquoise-blue and deep emerald ... 2·75 20
a. *Red, yellow, dull blue and emerald* (14.9.65) ... 2·25 10
257 **59** 2s. brown, light blue and emerald ... 1·25 1·25
258 **60** 2s.6d. yellow-olive, blue and carmine ... 2·50 3·00
259 **61** 5s. orange-brown, ultramarine and green ... 2·75 1·00
260 **62** 10s. rose, blue and chocolate ... 16·00 3·50
261 **63** £1 chestnut, blue and rose-red ... 22·00 11·00
247/261 *Set of* 15 ... 50·00 28·00

Nos. 247/248, 251, 253 and 256 exist in coils, constructed from normal sheets.

1965 (17 May). ITU Centenary. As Nos. 166/167 of Antigua.

262 1d. light emerald and orange ... 15 30
w. Wmk inverted ... £120
263 2s. purple and yellow-olive ... 65 1·60
w. Wmk inverted ... 13·00

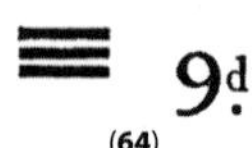

(64)

1965 (12 July). No. 254 surch with T **64**.

264 9d. on 8d. reddish purple, light blue and bronze-green ... 30 15

1965 (25 Oct). International Co-operation Year. As Nos. 168/169 of Antigua.

265 ½d. reddish purple and turquoise-green ... 10 1·60
266 1s. deep bluish green and lavender ... 30 40

1966 (24 Jan). Churchill Commemoration. As Nos. 170/173 of Antigua.

267 ½d. new blue ... 10 75
w. Wmk inverted ... 60·00
268 2d. deep green ... 50 30
269 10d. brown ... 85 85
270 1s. bluish violet ... 85 1·40
267/270 *Set of* 4 ... 2·00 3·00

1966 (4 Feb). Royal Visit. As Nos. 174/175 of Antigua, but inscr 'to the Caribbean' omitted.

271 6d. black and ultramarine ... 75 50
272 1s. black and magenta ... 1·00 1·25

(New Currency. 100 cents = 1 Bahamas dollar)

(65) **(66)**

1966 (25 May). Decimal Currency. Nos. 247/261 variously surch as T **65/66**, by B.W.

273 1c. on ½d. multicoloured ... 10 30
274 2c. on 1d. slate, light blue and orange ... 75 30
275 3c. on 2d. slate, green and turquoise-blue ... 10 10
276 4c. on 3d. red, light blue and purple ... 2·00 20
277 5c. on 4d. green, blue and orange-brown ... 2·00 3·00
a. Surch omitted (vert strip of 10) ... £3250
278 8c. on 6d. dull green, light blue and rose ... 20 20
279 10c. on 8d. reddish purple, light blue and bronze-green ... 30 75
280 11c. on 1½d. rose-red, green and brown ... 15 30
281 12c. on 10d. orange-brown, green and violet ... 15 10
282 15c. on 1s. multicoloured ... 25 10
283 22c. on 2s. brown, light blue and emerald ... 60 1·25
284 50c. on 2s.6d. yellow-olive, blue and carmine ... 1·00 1·40
285 $1 on 5s. orange-brown, ultramarine and green ... 1·75 1·50
286 $2 on 10s. rose, blue and chocolate ... 7·50 4·50
287 $3 on £1 chestnut, blue and rose-red ... 7·50 4·50
273/287 *Set of* 15 ... 22·00 16·00

The above were made on new printings, some of which vary slightly in shade, and in No. 273 the shield appears as vermilion and green instead of carmine and blue-green due to a different combination of the printing colours.

No. 277a. One sheet exists and the stamp can be distinguished from No. 252 when in a vertical strip of ten as these were printed in sheets of 100 whereas No. 252 was printed in sheets of 60 (six rows of ten across).

1966 (1 July). World Cup Football Championship. As Nos. 176/177 of Antigua.

288 8c. violet, yellow-green, lake and yellow-brown ... 35 15
289 15c. chocolate, blue-green, lake and yellow-brown ... 40 25

1966 (20 Sept). Inauguration of WHO Headquarters, Geneva. As Nos. 178/179 of Antigua.

290 11c. black, yellow-green and light blue ... 50 90
291 15c. black, light purple and yellow-brown ... 50 50

1966 (1 Dec). 20th Anniversary of UNESCO As Nos. 196/198 of Antigua.

292 3c. slate-violet, red, yellow and orange ... 10 10
293 15c. orange-yellow, violet and deep olive ... 35 20
294 $1 black, bright purple and orange ... 1·10 2·00
292/294 *Set of* 3 ... 1·40 2·00

67 *Oceanic*

68 Conch Shell

(Portrait by Anthony Buckley. Litho and recess (portrait, 'BAHAMAS' and value), B.W.)

1967 (25 May)–**71**. As T **49/63** and additional design (T **67**) but values in decimal currency, as T **68** and colours changed. Toned paper. W w **12**. P 13½.

295 **49** 1c. multicoloured (as ½d.) ... 10 3·25
a. Whiter paper (1970) ... 45 4·75
296 **50** 2c. slate, light blue and deep emerald (as 1d.) ... 50 60
a. Whiter paper (1970) ... 1·40 12·00
297 **52** 3c. slate, green and violet (as 2d.) ... 10 10
a. Whiter paper (1970) ... 42·00 5·00
298 **53** 4c. red, light blue and ultramarine (as 3d.) ... 4·75 50
a. Whiter paper (9.70*) ... 10·00 18·00
299 **67** 5c. black, greenish blue and purple ... 1·00 3·50
a. Whiter paper (1970) ... 2·25 12·00
300 **55** 8c. dull green, light blue and sepia (as 6d.) ... 3·25 10
a. Whiter paper (1970) ... £160 20·00
301 **56** 10c. reddish purple, greenish blue and carmine (as 8d.) ... 30 70
a. Whiter paper (1970) ... 1·00 4·50
302 **51** 11c. rose-red, green and blue (as 1½d.) ... 25 80
a. Whiter paper (1970) ... 1·00 2·50
303 **57** 12c. orange-brown green and olive (as 10d.) ... 25 10
a. Whiter paper (4.71) ... 12·00 29·00
304 **58** 15c. red, yellow, turquoise-blue and carmine (as 1s.) ... 55 10
a. Whiter paper (1970) ... £250 27·00
305 **59** 22c. brown, new blue and rose-red (as 2s.) ... 70 65
a. Whiter paper (1970) ... 1·50 11·00
306 **60** 50c. yellow-olive, new blue and emerald (as 2s.6d.) ... 3·00 1·00
a. Whiter paper (1970) ... 2·25 7·50
307 **61** $1 orange-brown ultramarine and slate-purple (as 5s.) ... 2·00 60
a. Whiter paper (4.71) ... 20·00 85·00
308 **68** $2 multicoloured ... 13·00 3·00
a. Whiter paper (4.71) ... 35·00 £100
309 **63** $3 chestnut, new blue and purple (as £1) ... 3·75 2·00
a. Whiter paper (4.71) ... 35·00 £100
295/309 *Set of* 15 ... 30·00 15·00
295a/309a *Set of* 15 (whiter paper) ... £500 £375

* This is the earliest known date recorded in the Bahamas.

The 3c. has the value at right instead of at left as on No. 250.

The 1970–1971 printings on whiter paper were released as needed, the 12c., $1, $2 and $3 only a week or two before the issue was withdrawn. Due to the marked difference in paper and the use of some new plates there are marked differences in shade in nearly all values.

69 Bahamas Crest

(Des R. Granger Barrett. Photo Enschedé)

1967 (1 Sept). Diamond Jubilee of World Scouting. T **69** and similar horizontal design. Multicoloured. W w **12** (sideways*). P 14×13.

310 3c. Type **69** ... 35 15
w. Wmk Crown to left of CA ... 42·00
311 15c. Scout badge ... 40 15

* The normal sideways watermark shows Crown to right of CA, *as seen from the back of the stamp.*

71 Globe and Emblem

74 Golf

(Des R. Granger Barrett, Litho D.L.R.)

1968 (13 May). Human Rights Year. T **71** and similar horizontal designs. Multicoloured. W w **12** (sideways*). P 14×13½.

312 3c. Type **71** ... 10 10
313 12c. Scales of Justice and emblem ... 20 10
314 $1 Bahamas Crest and emblem ... 70 80
312/314 *Set of* 3 ... 90 85

* The normal sideways watermark shows Crown to right of CA on the 12c. and Crown to left of CA on the others, *each when seen from the back of the stamp.*

(Litho B.W.)

1968 (20 Aug). Tourism. T **74** and similar vert designs. Multicoloured. P 13.

315 5c. Type **74** ... 1·25 1·50
316 11c. Yachting ... 75 40
317 15c. Horse-racing ... 1·25 40
318 50c. Water-skiing ... 1·75 6·50
315/318 *Set of* 4 ... 4·50 8·00

78 Racing Yacht and Olympic Monument

(Photo Harrison)

1968 (29 Sept). Olympic Games, Mexico City. T **78** and similar horiz designs. No wmk. P 14½×13½.

319 5c. red-brown, orange-yellow and blue-green ... 40 60
320 11c. multicoloured ... 40 15
321 50c. multicoloured ... 60 60
322 $1 olive-grey, greenish blue and violet ... 2·00 1·50
319/322 *Set of* 4 ... 3·00 2·50

Designs: 5c., $1 Type **78**; 11c. Long-jumping and Olympic Monument; 50c. Running and Olympic Monument.

It is understood that the above were released by the Philatelic Agency in the USA on 1st September.

81 Legislative Building

(Des J. Cooter, Litho Format)

1968 (1 Nov). 14th Commonwealth Parliamentary Conference. T **81** and similar multicoloured designs. P 14.

323 3c. Type **81** ... 10 30
324 10c. Bahamas Mace and Westminster Clock Tower (*vert*) ... 15 30
325 12c. Local straw market (*vert*) ... 15 25
326 15c. Horse-drawn Surrey ... 20 35
323/326 *Set of* 4 ... 55 1·10

85 Obverse and reverse of $100 Gold Coin

(Recess D.L.R.)

1968 (2 Dec). Gold Coins commemorating the first General Election under the New Constitution. T **85** and similar 'boomerang' shaped designs. P 13½.

327 3c. red/*gold* ... 40 40
328 12c. blue-green/*gold* ... 45 50
329 15c. dull purple/*gold* ... 50 60
330 $1 black/*gold* ... 1·25 5·00
327/330 *Set of* 4 ... 2·40 6·00

Designs: 3c. T **85**; 12c. Obverse and reverse of $50 gold coin; 15c. Obverse and reverse of $20 gold coin; $1 Obverse and reverse of $10 gold coin.

89 First Flight Postcard of 1919

90 Sikorsky S-38 Flying Boat of 1929

(Des V. Whiteley. Litho Format)

1969 (30 Jan). 50th Anniversary of Bahamas Airmail Service. P 14.

331	**89**	12c. multicoloured	50	50
332	**90**	15c. multicoloured	60	1·75

91 Game-fishing Boats

92 *The Adoration of the Shepherds* (Louis le Nain)

(Des J. Cooter. Litho Format)

1969 (26 Aug). Tourism. One Millionth Visitor to Bahamas. T **91** and similar horizontal designs. Multicoloured. W w **12** (sideways). P 14½.

333	3c. Type **91**	25	10
334	11c. Paradise Beach	35	15
335	12c. 'Sunfish' sailing boats	35	15
336	15c. Rawson Square and Parade	45	25
333/336	*Set of 4*	1·25	60
MS337	130×96 mm. Nos. 333/336	2·75	4·00

(Des G. Drummond. Litho D.L.R.)

1969 (15 Oct). Christmas. T **92** and similar vertical designs. W w **12**. P 12.

338	3c. Type **92**	20	20
339	11c. *The Adoration of the Shepherds* (Poussin)	30	30
340	12c. *The Adoration of the Kings* (Gerard David)	30	20
341	15c. *The Adoration of the Kings* (Vincenzo Foppa)	30	65
338/341	*Set of 4*	1·00	1·25

93 Badge of Girl Guides

(Des Mrs. R. Sands. Litho Harrison)

1970 (23 Feb). Girl Guides Diamond Jubilee. T **93** and similar designs. Multicoloured. W w **12**. P 14½.

342	3c. Type **93**	30	30
	w. Wmk inverted		
343	12c. Badge of Brownies	45	40
344	15c. Badge of Rangers	50	50
	w. Wmk inverted	17·00	
342/344	*Set of 3*	1·10	1·10

94 UPU Headquarters and Emblem

(Des L. Curtis, Litho J.W.)

1970 (20 May). New UPU Headquarters Building. W w **12** (sideways). P 14.

345	**94**	3c. multicoloured	10	40
346		15c. multicoloured	20	60

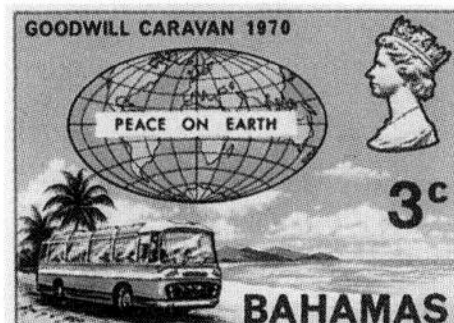

95 Coach and Globe

(Des G. Drummond. Litho B.W.)

1970 (14 July). 'Goodwill Caravan'. T **95** and similar horizontal designs. Multicoloured. W w **12** (sideways*). P 13½×13.

347	3c. Type **95**	85	20
	w. Wmk Crown to right of CA		
348	11c. Diesel train and globe	1·60	60
349	12c. *Canberra* (liner), yacht and globe	1·60	60
	w. Wmk Crown to right of CA	3·00	
350	15c. BAC One Eleven airliner and globe	1·60	1·75
347/350	*Set of 4*	5·00	2·75
MS351	165×125 mm. Nos. 347/350	9·50	17·00

* The normal sideways watermark shows Crown to left of CA, *as seen from the back of the stamp.*

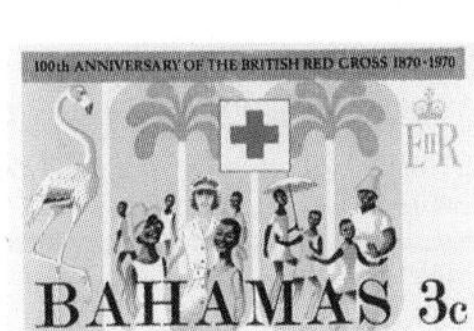

96 Nurse, Patients and Greater Flamingo

97 *The Nativity* (detail, Pittoni)

(Photo Harrison)

1970 (1 Sept). Centenary of British Red Cross. T **96** and similar horizontal design. Multicoloured. W w **12** (sideways*). P 14½.

352	3c. Type **96**	1·00	50
	a. Gold ('EIIR', etc) omitted	£750	
	w. Wmk Crown to right of CA	35·00	
353	15c. Hospital and Blue Marlin	1·00	1·75
	w. Wmk Crown to right of CA	—	£150

* The normal sideways watermark shows Crown to left of CA, *as seen from the back of the stamp.*

(Des G. Drummond. Litho D.L.R.)

1970 (3 Nov). Christmas. T **97** and similar vertical designs. Multicoloured. W w **12**. P 13.

354	3c. Type **97**	15	15
355	11c. *The Holy Family* (detail, Anton Raphael Mengs)	20	25
356	12c. *The Adoration of the Shepherds* (detail, Giorgione)	20	20
357	15c. *The Adoration of the Shepherds* (detail, School of Seville)	30	75
354/357	*Set of 4*	75	1·25
MS358	114×140 mm. Nos. 354/357 plus two labels	1·40	4·25

STAMP BOOKLETS

1938. Black on pink cover with map and 'BAHAMAS ISLES OF JUNE' on reverse. Stapled.

SB1	2s. booklet containing 12×1d. (No. 150) in blocks of 6 and 8×1½d. (No. 151) in folded block of 8	£11000

1961. (15 Aug). Brown-purple cover (3s.) or green cover (6s.) Stitched.

SB2	3s. booklet containing 8×1d., 8×1½d. and 8×2d. (Nos. 202/204) in blocks of 4	28·00
SB3	6s. booklet containing 4×4d., 4×6d. and 4×8d. (Nos. 206, 208/209) in blocks of 4	35·00

1965. (23 Mar). Pink cover (3s.) or green cover (6s.).

SB4	3s. booklet containing 8×1d., 8×1½d. and 8×2d. (Nos. 248/250) in blocks of 4	19·00
SB5	6s. booklet containing 4×4d., 4×6d. and 4×8d. (Nos. 252/254) in blocks of 4	19·00

SPECIAL DELIVERY STAMPS

SPECIAL
DELIVERY
(S **1**)

1916 (1 May). No. 59 optd with T S **1** by *The Nassau Guardian*.

S1	**6**	5d. black and orange	7·50	45·00
		a. Opt double	£800	£1200
		b. Opt double, one inverted	£950	£1300
		c. Opt inverted	£1300	£1400
		d. Pair, one without opt	£27000	£35000
		x. Wmk reversed	£850	

No. S1 was issued as a result of a reciprocal arrangement between the Bahamas and Canadian Post Offices, whereby the application of a special delivery stamp from the country of destination would ensure special treatment on arrival. Canadian special delivery stamps were supplied to the Bahamas Post Office, but, there being no equivalent in Bahamas, the current 5d. definitive was overprinted 'SPECIAL DELIVERY' and sent to Canada.

There were three printings from similar settings of 30 (6×5), and each sheet had to pass through the press twice. The first printing of 600 was on sale from March 1916 at four post offices in Canada; Ottawa, Toronto, Westmount (Montreal) and Winnipeg; and was used in combination with Canadian stamps and cancelled in Canada. Towards the end of 1916, however, the Canadian authorities decided to leave the Bahamas stamps to be cancelled on arrival in Nassau.

The second printing of 6000 was released in February 1917 and the third, estimated to be 1200 to 1800, in March the same year. They were both on sale only in the Bahamas. In August 1917 the Canadian Post Office became aware of the later printings and ordered all remaining stocks at the four offices in Canada to be sold off, bringing the facility to an end.

It is not possible to identify the three printings with certainty without plating both the basic stamp and the overprint. The first printing was applied to stamps from vignette plate 1 only, while the second and third were applied to stamps from both plate 1 and plate 2. In general, the word 'SPECIAL' is further to the right in relation to 'DELIVERY' in the second printing than the first or third, but this alone should not be considered conclusive.

Our prices for No. S1 are for the second printing and any stamps which can be positively identified as being from the first or third would be worth about ten times (first) or four times (third) as much, either unused or used. Examples on cover, posted at one of the four eligible Canadian offices and with the special delivery stamp cancelled in Canada, are very scarce.

All the errors appear to be from the second printing.

SPECIAL
DELIVERY
(S **2**)

SPECIAL
DELIVERY
(S **3**)

1917 (2 July). As No. 59, but Wmk Mult Crown CA. Optd with T S **2** by D.L.R.

S2	**6**	5d. black and orange	60	10·00
		s. Optd 'SPECIMEN'	70·00	

1918. No. 78 optd with T S **3** by D.L.R.

S3	**6**	5d. black and mauve (R.)	40	4·25
		s. Optd 'SPECIMEN'	70·00	

Nos. S2/S3 were only on sale in the Bahamas.

Bahrain

An independent sheikhdom, with an Indian postal administration from 1884. A British postal administration operated from 1 April 1948 to 31 December 1965.

The first, and for 62 years the only, post office in Bahrain opened at the capital, Manama, on 1 August 1884 as a sub-office of the Indian Post Office at Bushire (Iran), both being part of the Bombay Postal Circle.

Unoverprinted postage stamps of India were supplied to the new office, continuing on sale there until 1933.

Z 1

Z 2

Stamps of INDIA cancelled with T Z **1** (this was normally struck elsewhere on the envelope with the stamps obliterated with 'B' enclosed in a circular background of horizontal bars) (1884–1886)

1882–90. Queen Victoria (Nos. 84/101).
Z1 ½a. deep blue-green £650
Z2 2a. pale blue £650

Stamps of INDIA cancelled with T Z **2** (squared-circle) (1886–1909)

1882–90. Queen Victoria (Nos. 84/101).
Z5 ½a. deep blue-green 16·00
Z5*a* ½a. blue-green 17·00
Z6 1a. brown-purple 18·00
Z6*a* 1a. plum 18·00
Z7 1a.6p. sepia 65·00
Z8 2a. pale blue 24·00
Z8*a* 2a. blue 25·00
Z9 3a. orange 70·00
Z9*a* 3a. brown-orange 27·00
Z10 4a. olive-green 55·00
Z10*a* 4a. slate-green 50·00
Z11 8a. dull mauve 80·00
Z11*a* 8a. magenta 75·00

1891. Surch on Queen Victoria (No. 102).
Z12 2½a. on 4a.6p. yellow-green 55·00

1892–97. Queen Victoria (Nos. 103/106).
Z13 2a.6p. yellow-green 20·00
Z13*a* 2a.6p. pale blue-green 22·00
Z14 1r. green and aniline carmine £100

1900–02. Queen Victoria (Nos. 112/118).
Z15 ½a. pale yellow-green 23·00
Z15*a* ½a. yellow-green 25·00
Z16 1a. carmine 24·00
Z17 2½a. ultramarine 45·00

OFFICIAL STAMPS

1883–99. Queen Victoria (Nos. O37*a*/O48).
Z18 ½a. blue-green 95·00
Z19 1a. brown-purple £100

Z 3

Z 4

Stamps of INDIA cancelled with T Z **3** (single circle, principally intended for use as a backstamp) (1897–1920)

1882–90. Queen Victoria (Nos. 84/101).
Z21 ½a. blue-green 42·00
Z22 3a. brown-orange 48·00

1892–97. Queen Victoria (Nos. 103/106).
Z23 1r. green and aniline carmine £120

1899. Queen Victoria (No. 111).
Z24 3p. aniline carmine 45·00

1900–02. Queen Victoria (Nos. 112/118).
Z24a 3p. grey £140
Z25 ½a. pale yellow-green 35·00
Z25*a* ½a. yellow-green 38·00
Z26 1a. carmine 35·00
Z26*a* 2a. pale violet 85·00
Z27 2a.6p. ultramarine 60·00

1902–11. King Edward VII (Nos. 119/147).
Z28 ½a. green 32·00
Z29 2a. mauve 38·00
Z30 2a.6p. ultramarine 27·00

1906–07. King Edward VII (Nos. 149/150).
Z31 ½a. green 20·00
Z32 1a. carmine 22·00

1911–22. King George V. Wmk Star (Nos. 151/191).
Z33 3p. grey 27·00
Z34 ½a. light green 22·00
Z35 2a. purple 45·00
Z36 2a.6p. ultramarine (No. 171) 45·00

OFFICIAL STAMPS

1902–09. King Edward VII (Nos. O54/O65).
Z37 2a. mauve £100

1906–07. King Edward VII (Nos. O66/O67).
Z38 1a. carmine 95·00

Stamps of INDIA cancelled with T Z **4** (double circle with date band and black lines in centre) (1902–1924)

1876. Queen Victoria (Nos. 80/82).
Z40 6a. pale brown 95·00

1882–90. Queen Victoria (Nos. 84/101).
Z40*a* ½a. blue-green 30·00
Z41 3a. brown-orange 42·00
Z42 4a. slate-green 50·00
Z43 8a. dull mauve 70·00
Z44 12a. purple/*red* £140

1892–97. Queen Victoria (Nos. 103/106).
Z44*b* 1r. green and aniline carmine £140

1895. Queen Victoria (Nos. 107/109).
Z45 2r. carmine and yellow-brown £425
Z45*a* 3r. brown and green £450
Z46 5r. ultramarine and violet £450

1899. Queen Victoria (No. 111).
Z47 3p. aniline carmine 24·00

1900–02. Queen Victoria (Nos. 112/118).
Z48 ½a. pale yellow-green 20·00
Z48*a* ½a. yellow-green 22·00
Z49 1a. carmine 24·00
Z50 2a. pale violet 65·00
Z51 2a.6p. ultramarine 48·00

1902–11. King Edward VII (Nos. 119/147).
Z52 3p. grey 15·00
Z52*a* 3p. slate-grey 17·00
Z53 ½a. yellow-green 9·50
Z53*a* ½a. green 9·50
Z54 1a. carmine 12·00
Z55 2a. violet 27·00
Z55*a* 2a. mauve 27·00
Z56 2a.6p. ultramarine 15·00
Z57 3a. orange-brown 35·00
Z58 4a. olive 40·00
Z59 6a. olive-bistre 65·00
Z60 8a. purple 85·00
Z60*a* 12a. purple/*red* £140
Z60*b* 1r. green and carmine £120
Z61 2r. rose-red and yellow-brown £275

1905. Surcharged on King Edward VII (No. 148).
Z62 ¼a. on ½a. green 40·00

1906–07. King Edward VII (Nos. 149/150).
Z63 ½a. green 12·00
Z64 1a. carmine 19·00

1911–22. King George V. Wmk Star (Nos. 151/191).
Z65 3p. grey 21·00
Z66 ½a. light green 12·00
Z67 1a. carmine 14·00
Z67*a* 1a. rose-carmine 14·00
Z68 1½a. chocolate (Type A) 55·00
Z69 2a. purple 30·00
Z70 2a.6p. ultramarine (No. 171) 22·00
Z71 3a. orange 40·00
Z72 6a. yellow-bistre 55·00

1922–26. King George V. Wmk Star (Nos. 197/200).
Z73 1a. chocolate 25·00
Z73*b* 3a. ultramarine 70·00

OFFICIAL STAMPS

1902–09. King Edward VII (Nos. O54/O65).
Z74 2a. mauve 75·00
Z74*a* 4a. olive £140

1906. King Edward VII (Nos. O66/O67).
Z75 1a. carmine 60·00

1912–13. King George V (No. O85).
Z77 1a. carmine 55·00

1921. King George V (No. O97).
Z78 9p. on 1a. rose-carmine 85·00

Z 5

Stamps of INDIA cancelled with T Z **5** (double circle without arc) (previously intended for use as a backstamp) (1915–1933)

1911–22. King George V. Wmk Star (Nos. 151/191).
Z79 3p. grey 30·00
Z80 ½a. light green 19·00
Z80*a* ½a. emerald 20·00
Z81 1a. aniline carmine 22·00
Z81*a* 1a. pale rose-carmine 23·00
Z82 1½a. chocolate (Type A) 70·00
Z83 2a. purple 32·00
Z83*a* 2a. reddish purple 32·00
Z83*b* 2a. bright reddish violet 32·00
Z84 2a.6p. ultramarine (No. 171) 24·00
Z85 3a. orange 48·00
Z86 6a. yellow-bistre 70·00
Z87 1r. brown and green (*shades*) 95·00

1922–26. King George V. Wmk Star (Nos. 197/200).
Z88 1a. chocolate 28·00
Z89 3a. ultramarine 55·00

1926–33. King George V. Wmk Multiple Star (Nos. 201/219).
Z90 3p. slate 15·00
Z91 ½a. green 14·00
Z92 1a. chocolate 12·00
Z93 2a. bright purple (No. 205) 90·00
Z94 2a. purple (No. 206) 24·00
Z95 3a. ultramarine 45·00
Z95*a* 3a. blue 40·00
Z96 4a. sage-green (No. 211) 30·00
Z97 8a. reddish purple 48·00
Z98 1r. chocolate and green 60·00
Z99 2r. carmine and orange £110
Z100 5r. ultramarine and purple £200

The 1a. is known with inverted watermark.

1929. Air (Nos. 220/225).
Z101 2a. deep blue-green 40·00
Z102 3a. blue 38·00
Z103 4a. olive-green 42·00
Z104 6a. bistre 55·00

1931. Inauguration of New Delhi (Nos. 226/231).
Z105 ¼a. olive-green and orange-brown 60·00
Z105a ¼a. violet and green 48·00
Z106 1a. mauve and chocolate 35·00

Nos. Z101/Z106 come with watermark sideways to left or right.

OFFICIAL STAMPS

1902–09. King Edward VII (Nos. O54/O65).
Z107 2a. mauve 75·00

1912–13. King George V. Wmk Star (Nos. O73/O96).
Z108 ½a. light green 42·00
Z109 1a. rose-carmine 42·00
Z110 2a. reddish purple 60·00

Z 6

Stamps of INDIA cancelled with T Z **6** (double circle with black arc in lower segment) (1924–33)

1911–22. King George V. Wmk Star (Nos. 151/191).
Z115 3p. grey 28·00
Z116 ½a. light green 17·00
Z117 1a. aniline carmine 19·00
Z118 2a. purple 30·00
Z119 6a. yellow-bistre 45·00

1921. King George V. (No. 192).
Z119*a* 9p. on 1a. rose-carmine 60·00

1922–26. King George V. Wmk Star (Nos. 197/200).
Z120 1a. chocolate 18·00
Z120*a* 2½a. orange 60·00
Z121 3a. ultramarine 38·00

1926–33. King George V. Wmk Multiple Star (Nos. 201/219).
Z122 3p. slate 9·00
Z123 ½a. green 10·00
Z124 1a. chocolate 9·00
a. Tête-bêche (pair)
Z125 1½a. rose-carmine 60·00
Z126 2a. bright purple (No. 205) 65·00
Z127 2a. purple (No. 206) 16·00
Z128 3a. blue 20·00
Z130 4a. sage-green (No. 211) 22·00
Z131 8a. reddish purple 35·00
Z131*a* 12a. claret 75·00
Z131*b* 1r. chocolate and green 60·00

The ½a. and 1a. are known with watermark inverted.

1929. Air (Nos. 220/225).
Z132 2a. deep blue-green 24·00
Z133 3a. blue 25·00
Z134 4a. olive-green 29·00
Z135 6a. bistre 32·00

1931. Inauguration of New Delhi (Nos. 226/231).
Z136 ½a. violet and green 38·00
Z137 2a. green and blue 42·00
Z137*a* 3a. chocolate and carmine 70·00

Nos. Z132/Z135 and Z136/Z137*a* exist with watermark showing stars pointing left or right.

1932–36. King George V. Wmk Multiple Star (Nos. 232/239).
Z138 1a. chocolate 22·00
Z139 1a.3p. mauve 19·00
Z140 2a. vermilion 35·00
Z141 3a. carmine 40·00

OFFICIAL STAMPS

1926–31. King George V (Nos. O109/O120).

Z145	1a. chocolate		50·00

PRICES FOR STAMPS ON COVER TO 1945	
Nos. 1/14	*from* × 5
Nos. 15/19	*from* × 6
Nos. 20/37	*from* × 2
Nos. 38/50	*from* × 6

(Currency. 12 pies = 1 anna; 16 annas = 1 rupee)

BAHRAIN (1) BAHRAIN (2)

Stamps of India overprinted with T 1 or T 2 (rupee values).

1933 (10 Aug)–**37**. King George V. Wmk Mult Star. T **69**.

No.	Type		Unused	Used
1	**55**	3p. slate (11.33)	4·25	45
2	**56**	½a. green	8·00	6·50
		w. Wmk inverted	85·00	50·00
3	**80**	9p. deep green (*litho*)	5·00	6·50
		a. Typo ptg (1937)	25·00	24·00
4	**57**	1a. chocolate	14·00	4·00
		w. Wmk inverted	48·00	12·00
5	**82**	1a.3p. mauve	19·00	4·75
		w. Wmk inverted	19·00	4·75
6	**70**	2a. vermilion	10·00	22·00
		w. Wmk inverted	23·00	22·00
7	**62**	3a. blue	19·00	75·00
8	**83**	3a.6p. ultramarine	3·75	40
		w. Wmk inverted	21·00	60
9	**71**	4a. sage-green	19·00	75·00
10	**65**	8a. reddish purple	6·00	30
		w. Wmk inverted	†	£150
11	**66**	12a. claret	7·50	3·75
		w. Wmk inverted	†	£150
12	**67**	1r. chocolate and green	16·00	15·00
13		2r. carmine and orange	35·00	48·00
14		5r. ultramarine and purple	£300	£275
		w. Wmk inverted	£170	£200
1/14w *Set of* 14			£300	£425

1934–37. King George V. Wmk Mult Star. T **69**.

No.	Type		Unused	Used
15	**79**	½a. green (1935)	13·00	3·50
		w. Wmk inverted	21·00	3·00
16	**81**	1a. chocolate	14·00	40
		w. Wmk inverted (*from booklets*)	35·00	70·00
17	**59**	2a. vermilion (1935)	50·00	7·50
17*a*		2a. vermilion (*small die*) (1937)	£100	25
18	**62**	3a. carmine	7·00	60
19	**63**	4a. sage-green (1935)	7·00	40
15/19 *Set of* 6			£170	11·00

1938–41. King George VI.

No.	Type		Unused	Used
20	**91**	3p. slate (5.38)	23·00	9·50
21		½a. red-brown (5.38)	12·00	20
22		9p. green (5.38)	18·00	18·00
23		1a. carmine (5.38)	19·00	20
24	**92**	2a. vermilion (1939)	5·00	9·00
26	**94**	3a. yellow-green (1941)	12·00	17·00
27	**95**	3a.6p. bright blue (7.38)	6·00	16·00
28	**96**	4a. brown (1941)	£190	75·00
30	**98**	8a. slate-violet (1940)	£350	35·00
31	**99**	12a. lake (1940)	£170	55·00
32	**100**	1r. grey and red-brown (1940)	10·00	3·50
33		2r. purple and brown (1940)	23·00	12·00
34		5r. green and blue (1940)	15·00	13·00
35		10r. purple and claret (1941)	95·00	70·00
36		15r. brown and green (1941)	£350	£400
		w. Wmk inverted	90·00	90·00
37		25r. slate-violet and purple (1941)	£130	£110
20/37 *Set of* 16			£1000	£450

1942–45. King George VI on white background.

No.	Type		Unused	Used
38	**100a**	3p. slate	3·50	2·75
39		½a. purple	5·50	6·00
40		9p. green	18·00	26·00
41		1a. carmine	8·00	1·25
42	**101**	1a.3p. bistre	10·00	24·00
43		1½a. dull violet	7·00	8·50
44		2a. vermilion	7·00	1·50
45		3a. bright violet	22·00	7·50
46		3½a. bright blue	6·50	25·00
47	**102**	4a. brown	12·00	2·00
48		6a. turquoise-green	20·00	12·00
49		8a. slate-violet	17·00	9·00
50		12a. lake	24·00	10·00
38/50 *Set of* 13			£140	£120

Unoverprinted India Victory stamps, Nos. 278/281, were placed on sale in Bahrain on 2 January 1946 (1½a. and 3½a.) and 8 February (9p. and 12a.).

Although the stamps of Pakistan were never placed on sale in Bahrain examples of the 1947 'PAKISTAN' overprints on India can be found cancelled in Bahrain from air mail originating at Dubai or Sharjah.

Stamps of Great Britain surcharged

For similar surcharges without the name of the country, see BRITISH POSTAL AGENCIES IN EASTERN ARABIA.

BAHRAIN 1 ANNA (3) BAHRAIN 5 RUPEES (4)

1948 (1 Apr)–**49**. Surch as T **3**, **4** (2r. and 5r.) or similar surch with bars at foot (10r.).

No.	Type		Unused	Used
51	**128**	½a. on ½d. pale green	50	1·25
52		1a. on 1d. pale scarlet	50	3·50
53		1½a. on 1½d. pale red-brown	50	6·00
54		2a. on 2d. pale orange	50	20
55		2½a. on 2½d. light ultramarine	50	6·50
56		3a. on 3d. pale violet	50	10
57	**129**	6a. on 6d. purple	50	10
58	**130**	1r. on 1s. bistre-brown	1·25	10
59	**131**	2r. on 2s.6d. yellow-green	5·50	5·50
60		5r. on 5s. red	5·50	5·50
60*a*	**132**	10r. on 10s. ultramarine (4.7.49)	95·00	80·00
51/60*a* *Set of* 11			£100	95·00

BAHRAIN 2½ ANNAS (5) BAHRAIN 15 RUPEES (6)

1948 (26 Apr). Silver Wedding, surch as T **5** or **6**.

No.	Type		Unused	Used
61	**137**	2½a. on 2½d. ultramarine	1·00	2·75
62	**138**	15r. on £1 blue	32·00	50·00

1948 (29 July). Olympic Games, surch as T **5**, but in one line (6a.) or two lines (others); the 1r. also has a square of dots as T **7**.

No.	Type		Unused	Used
63	**139**	2½a. on 2½d. ultramarine	1·50	4·75
		a. Surch double	£3500	£4250
64	**140**	3a. on 3d. violet	1·00	4·25
65	**141**	6a. on 6d. bright purple	1·50	4·25
66	**142**	1r. on 1s. brown	2·75	4·25
63/66 *Set of* 4			6·00	16·00

15 used examples of No. 63a are known, of which 13, including a block of 4, were postmarked at Experimental P.O. K-121 (Muharraq), one on cover from F.P.O. 756 (Shaibah) on 25 October 1948 and one apparently cancelled-to-order at Bahrain on 10 October 1949.

BAHRAIN 3 ANNAS 

(7)

1949 (10 Oct). 75th Anniversary of UPU, surch as T **7**, in one line (2½a.) or in two lines (others).

No.	Type		Unused	Used
67	**143**	2½a. on 2½d. ultramarine	60	3·00
		a. Lake in India	£150	£300
68	**144**	3a. on 3d. violet	70	5·50
69	**145**	6a. on 6d. bright purple	60	3·00
70	**146**	1r. on 1s. brown	1·25	4·00
67/70 *Set of* 4			2·75	14·00

BAHRAIN 2 RUPEES (7a) Type I — BAHRAIN 2 RUPEES Type II

BAHRAIN

5r. Extra bar (R. 6/1)

Three Types of 2r.:

Type I. As Type **7a** showing '2' level with 'RUPEES' and 'BAHRAIN' sharp. 15 mm between 'BAHRAIN' and '2 RUPEES'.

Type II. '2' raised. 'BAHRAIN' worn. 15 mm between 'BAHRAIN' and '2 RUPEES'.

Type III. As Type II, but 16 mm between 'BAHRAIN' and '2 RUPEES'. Value is set more to the left of 'BAHRAIN'.

1950 (2 Oct)–**55**. Surch as T **3** or **7a** (rupee values).

No.	Type		Unused	Used
71	**128**	½a. on ½d. pale orange (3.5.51)	2·75	4·50
72		1a. on 1d. light ultramarine (3.5.51)	3·25	20
73		1½a. on 1½d. pale green (3.5.51)	5·00	14·00
74		2a. on 2d. pale red-brown (3.5.51)	1·50	30
75		2½a. on 2½d. pale scarlet (3.5.51)	5·00	18·00
76	**129**	4a. on 4d. light ultramarine	5·50	1·50
77	**147**	2r. on 2s.6d. yellow-green (3.5.51)	45·00	17·00
		a. Surch Type II (1953)	£160	55·00
		b. Surch Type III (1955)	£1700	£140
		ba. 'I' inverted and raised (R. 2/1)	£9000	£1200
78	**148**	5r. on 5s. red (3.5.51)	16·00	8·00
		a. Extra bar	£900	£700
79	**149**	10r. on 10s. ultramarine (3.5.51)	42·00	11·00
71/79 *Set of* 9			£110	60·00

1952 (5 Dec)–**54**. Q.E. II (W **153**), surch as T **3** (in two lines on 2½ and 6a.).

No.	Type		Unused	Used
80	**154**	½a. on ½d. orange-red (31.8.53)	10	1·00
		a. Fraction '½' omitted	£200	£400
81		1a. on 1d. ultramarine (31.8.53)	15	10
82		1½a. on 1½d. green	10	30
83		2a. on 2d. red-brown (31.8.53)	30	10
84	**155**	2½a. on 2½d. carmine-red	20	1·75
85		3a. on 3d. deep lilac (B.) (18.1.54)	3·00	10
86	**156**	4a. on 4d. ultramarine (2.11.53)	18·00	30
87	**157**	6a. on 6d. reddish purple (18.1.54)	3·75	10
88	**160**	12a. on 1s.3d. green (2.11.53)	3·25	20
89	**159**	1r. on 1s.6d. grey-blue (2.11.53)	3·25	10
80/89 *Set of* 10			29·00	3·25

The word BAHRAIN is in taller letters on the 1½a., 2½a., 3a. and 6a.

In early printings of No. 80 the '½' was printed in a separate operation to 'BAHRAIN' and 'ANNA'. Later printings of the ½a. and all printings of other values were printed in a single operation.

2½ BAHRAIN ANNAS (8)

1953 (3 June). Coronation. Surch as T **8**, or similarly.

No.	Type		Unused	Used
90	**161**	2½a. on 2½d. carmine-red	1·25	75
91	**162**	4a. on 4d. ultramarine	2·25	8·00
92	**163**	12a. on 1s.3d. deep yellow-green	6·00	6·50
93	**164**	1r. on 1s.6d. deep grey-blue	7·50	50
90/93 *Set of* 4			15·00	14·00

BAHRAIN 2 RUPEES (9) I

BAHRAIN 2 RUPEES (9) II

BAHRAIN 2 RUPEES (9) III

BAHRAIN 5 RUPEES (10) I

BAHRAIN 5 RUPEES (10) II

BAHRAIN 10 RUPEES (11) I

BAHRAIN 10 RUPEES (11) II

TYPE I (T **9/11**). Type-set surch by Waterlow. Bold thick letters with sharp corners and straight edges.

TYPE II (T **9/11**). Plate-printed surch by Harrison. Thinner letters, rounded corners and rough edges. Bars wider apart.

TYPE III (T **9**). Plate-printed surch by Harrison. Similar to Type II as regards the position of the bars on all 40 stamps of the sheet, but the letters are thinner and with more rounded corners than in II, while the ink of the surcharge is less black.

The general characteristics of Type II of the 2r. are less pronounced than in the other values, but a distinguishing test is in the relative position of the bars and the 'U' of 'RUPEES'. In Type II (except for the 1st stamp, 5th row) the bars start immediately beneath the left-hand edge of the 'U'. In Type I they start more to the right.

In the 10r. the '1' and the '0' are spaced 0.9 mm in Type I and only 0.6 mm in Type II.

1955 (23 Sept)–**60**. T **166/168** (Waterlow ptgs) surch as T **9/11**.

No.	Type		Unused	Used
94		2r. on 2s.6d. black-brown (Type I)	5·50	2·25
		a. Type II (13.5.58)	14·00	21·00
		b. Type III (No. 536a, D.L.R.) (29.1.60)	26·00	70·00
95		5r. on 5s. rose-red (Type I)	20·00	2·75
		a. Type II (19.8.57)	8·00	7·00
96		10r. on 10s. ultramarine (Type I)	20·00	2·75
		a. Type II (13.5.58)	50·00	£120
		ab. Type II. Surch on No. 538a (D.L.R. ptg) (1960)	£100	
94/96 *Set of* 3			40·00	7·00
94a/96a *Set of* 3			65·00	£130

Designs: No. 94, Carrickfergus Castle; No. 95, Caernarvon Castle; No. 96, Edinburgh Castle.

1956–57. Q.E. II (W **165**), surch as T **3** (in two lines on 6a.).

No.	Type		Unused	Used
97	**154**	½ a. on ½d. orange-red (20.3.57)	10	15
98	**156**	4a. on 4d. ultramarine (8.6.56)	5·50	24·00
99	**155**	6a. on 6d. reddish purple (5.12.56)	50	75
100	**160**	12a. on 1s.3d. green (2.8.56)	7·50	11·00
101	**159**	1r. on 1s.6d. grey-blue (1.4.57)	11·00	10
		a. Surch double	†	£5000
97/101 *Set of* 5			22·00	32·00

The two surcharges on No. 101a are almost coincident.

New Currency. 100 naye paise = 1 rupee.

BAHRAIN 1 NP NP (12) — BAHRAIN 3 NP NP (13) — BAHRAIN 75 NP (14)

1957 (1 Apr)–**59**. Q.E. II (W **165**), surch as T **12** (1n.p., 15n.p., 25n.p., 40n.p., and 50n.p.), T **14** (75n.p.) or T **13** (others).

No.	Type		Unused	Used
102	**157**	1n.p. on 5d. brown	10	15
103	**154**	3n.p. on ½d. orange-red	1·00	3·00

No.	Type	Description	Unused	Used
104		6n.p. on 1d. ultramarine	1·00	3·00
105		9n.p. on 1½d. green	50	3·25
106		12n.p. on 2d. light red-brown	30	70
107	155	15n.p. on 2½d. carmine-red (Type I)	30	15
		a. Type II (1959)	1·00	5·50
108		20n.p. on 3d. deep lilac (B.)	30	10
109	156	25n.p. on 4d. ultramarine	1·25	2·50
110	157	40n.p. on 6d. reddish purple	40	10
		a. Deep claret (1959)	65	10
111	158	50n.p. on 9d. bronze-green	3·75	4·50
112	160	75n.p. on 1s.3d. green	2·50	50
102/112 *Set of 11*			10·00	16·00

BAHRAIN
15 NP

(15)

1957 (1 Aug). World Scout Jubilee Jamboree. Surch in two lines as T **15** (15n.p.), or in three lines (others).

No.	Type	Description	Unused	Used
113	170	15n.p. on 2½d. carmine-red	35	35
114	171	25n.p. on 4d. ultramarine	35	35
115	172	75n.p. on 1s.3d. green	40	45
113/115 *Set of 3*			1·00	1·00

1960 (24 May). QE. II (W **179**), surch as T **12**.

No.	Type	Description	Unused	Used
116	155	15n.p. on 2½d. carmine-red (Type II)	2·25	8·00

16 Sheikh Salman bin Hamed al-Khalifa

17

(Des M. Farrar Bell. Photo Harrison (T **16**). Des O. C. Meronti. Recess D.L.R. (T **17**))

1960 (1 July). P 15×14 (T **16**) or 13½×13 (T **17**).

No.	Type	Description	Unused	Used
117	16	5n.p. bright blue	20	10
118		15n.p. red-orange	20	10
119		20n.p. reddish violet	20	10
120		30n.p. bistre-brown	20	10
121		40n.p. grey	20	10
122		50n.p. emerald-green	20	10
123		75n.p. chocolate	30	15
124	17	1r. black	3·00	30
125		2r. rose-red	3·00	2·50
126		5r. deep blue	5·00	3·50
127		10r. bronze-green	16·00	6·00
117/127 *Set of 11*			25·00	11·00

Sheikh Isa bin Salman al-Khalifa
2 November 1961–6 March 1999

18 Sheikh Isa bin Salman al-Khalifa

19 Air Terminal, Muharraq

20 Deep Water Harbour

(Des M. Farrar Bell. Photo Harrison (5 to 75n.p.). Des D. C. Rivett. Recess B.W. (others))

1964 (22 Feb). P 15×14 (T **18**) or 13½×13 (T **19/20**).

No.	Type	Description	Unused	Used
128	18	5n.p. bright blue	10	10
129		15n.p. orange red	15	1·00
130		20n.p. reddish violet	15	10
131		30n.p. olive-brown	15	10
132		40n.p. slate	15	10
133		50n.p. emerald-green	15	1·50
134		75n.p. brown	25	10
135	19	1r. black	11·00	2·25
136		2r. carmine-red	11·00	6·50
137	20	5r. ultramarine	15·00	21·00
138		10r. myrtle-green	15·00	21·00
128/138 *Set of 11*			48·00	48·00

LOCAL STAMPS

The following stamps were issued primarily for postage within Bahrain, but apparently also had franking value when used on external mail.

L **1** Sheikh Salman bin Hamed al-Khalifa

L **2** Sheikh Salman bin Hamed al-Khalifa

(Types L **1/2**. Recess De La Rue)

1953–56. P 12×12½.

No.	Type	Description	Unused	Used
L1	L 1	½a. deep green (1.10.56)	2·75	1·00
L2		1a. deep blue (1.10.56)	2·75	1·00
L3		1½a. carmine (15.2.53)	50	2·50
L1/L3 *Set of 3*			5·50	4·00

1957 (16 Oct). As Nos. L1/L3 but values in new currency.

No.	Type	Description	Unused	Used
L4		3p. deep green	3·00	1·25
L5		6p. carmine	3·00	1·25
L6		9p. deep blue	3·00	1·25
L4/L6 *Set of 3*			8·00	3·25

1961 (20 Mar). P 12×12½.

No.	Type	Description	Unused	Used
L7	L 2	5p. green	1·25	30
L8		10p. carmine-red	3·75	30
L9		15p. grey	1·50	25
L10		20p. blue	2·50	25
L11		30p. sepia	2·00	25
L12		40p. ultramarine	9·50	30
L7/L12 *Set of 6*			18·00	1·50

STAMP BOOKLET

1934. Red and black on tan cover. Mysore Sandal Soap advertisement on front.

SB1 1r. booklet containing 16×1a. (Nos. 16 and/or 16w) in blocks of 4 .... £2750

The Bahrain Post Department took over the postal services on 1 January 1966. Later stamp issues wil be found in Stanley Gibbons *Arabia Catalogue*.

Barbados

Regular mails between Barbados and Great Britain were established at an early date in the island's development and it is believed that the British Mail Packet Agency at Bridgetown was opened in 1688 as part of the considerable expansion of the Packet Service in that year.

From 1 August 1851 the colonial authorities were responsible for the internal post system, but the British GPO did not relinquish control of the overseas post until 1858.

For illustrations of the handstamp types see BRITISH POST OFFICES ABROAD notes, following GREAT BRITAIN.

CROWNED-CIRCLE HANDSTAMPS

CC1 CC **1** *BARBADOES (3.10.1849) (R.)...... Price on cover* £475

Combination covers exist with the local postage paid by a Barbados 1d. stamp and the overseas fee by an example of No. CC1.

During shortages of ½d. stamps in 1893 (17 February to 15 March) and of the ¼d. in 1896 (23 January to 4 May) No. CC1 was utilised, struck in black, on local mail. *Price on cover from* £100.

PRICES FOR STAMPS ON COVER TO 1945

Nos.	Price
Nos. 1/35	*from* × 5
Nos. 43/63	*from* × 4
Nos. 64/66	*from* × 10
Nos. 67/83	*from* × 5
Nos. 86/88	*from* × 3
Nos. 89/103	*from* × 4
No. 104	*from* × 20
Nos. 105/115	*from* × 4
Nos. 116/124	*from* × 8
Nos. 125/133	*from* × 5
Nos. 135/144	*from* × 4
Nos. 145/152	*from* × 6
No. 153	*from* × 8
Nos. 158/162	*from* × 5
Nos. 163/169	*from* × 3
Nos. 170/196	*from* × 4
Nos. 197/8	*from* × 10
Nos. 199/212	*from* × 6
Nos. 213/239	*from* × 3
No. 240	*from* × 10
Nos. 241/244	*from* × 5
Nos. 245/247	*from* × 6
Nos. 248/256*a*	*from* × 4
Nos. 257/261	*from* × 5
Nos. D1/D3	*from* × 25

PERKINS BACON 'CANCELLED'. For notes on these handstamps, showing 'CANCELLED' between horizontal bars forming an oval, see Catalogue Introduction.

CROWN COLONY

1 Britannia

2 Britannia

(Recess Perkins Bacon & Co)

1852 (15 Apr)–**55**. Paper blued. No wmk. Imperf.

No.	Type	Description	Unused	Used
1	1	(½d.) yellow-green (1855)	—	£700
2		(½d.) deep green	£150	£325
3		(1d.) blue	60·00	£190
4		(1d.) deep blue	42·00	70·00
4*a*		(2d.) greyish slate	£300	£1400
		b. Bisected (1d.) (*on cover*) (1854)	†	£8500
5		(4d.) brownish red (1855)	£120	£275

The bisect, No. 4b was authorised for use between 4 August and 21 September 1854 during a shortage of 1d. stamps.

Prepared for use but not issued.

No.	Type	Description	Unused	Used
5*a*	1	(No value), slate-blue (*shades*)	28·00	
5*b*		(No value), deep slate	£250	

Nos. 5*a*/5*b* were never sent to Barbados and come from the Perkins Bacon remainders sold in the 1880's.

Apart from the shade, which is distinctly paler, No. 4*a* can be distinguished from No. 5*b* by the smooth even gum, the gum of No. 5*b* being yellow and patchy, giving a mottled appearance to the back of the stamp. No. 5*a* also has the latter gum.

1855 (Feb)–**58**. White paper. No wmk. Imperf.

No.	Type	Description	Unused	Used
7	1	(½d.) yellow-green (1857)	£500	£110
8		(½d.) green (*shades*) (1858)	£190	£150
9		(1d.) pale blue	£180	70·00
10		(1d.) deep blue (H/S 'CANCELLED' in oval £12000)	£110	60·00

No. 8 exists in a yellowish green shade which should not be confused with No. 7.

1858 (10 Nov). No wmk. Imperf.

No.	Type	Description	Unused	Used
11	2	6d. pale rose-red	£750	£120
11*a*		6d. deep rose-red	£750	£180
12		1s. brown-black	£250	£110
12*a*		1s. black	£225	75·00

BISECTS. The various 1d. bisects recorded between Nos. 14a and 73a were principally used for the ½d. inland rate, covering newspapers from 1854 onwards. Prices for Nos. 24a, 52a, 66a and 73a are for examples on dated piece, undated pieces being worth considerably less. Nos. 14a, 15a and 19a are only known on undated piece and the prices for these bisects are for items in this condition.

1860. No wmk.

(a) Pin-perf 14

No.	Type	Description	Unused	Used
13	1	(½d.) yellow-green	£2750	£425
14		(1d.) pale blue	£2250	£150
		a. Bisected (½d.) (*on piece*)	†	£750
15		(1d.) deep blue	£2500	£180
		a. Bisected (½d.) (*on piece*)	†	£750

(b) Pin-perf 12½

No.	Type	Description	Unused	Used
16	1	(½d.) yellow-green	£9000	£650
16*a*		(1d.) blue	—	£1600

(c) Pin-perf 14×12½

No.	Type	Description	Unused	Used
16*b*	1	(½d.) yellow-green	—	£7500

1861. No wmk. Clean-cut perf 14 to 16.

No.	Type	Description	Unused	Used
17	1	(½d.) deep green (H/S 'CANCELLED' in oval £12000)	£180	22·00
18		(1d.) pale blue	£750	85·00
19		(1d.) blue	£850	90·00
		a. Bisected (½d.) (*on piece*)	†	£550

1861–70. No wmk.

(a) Rough perf 14 to 16

No.	Type	Description	Unused	Used
20	1	(½d.) deep green	35·00	50·00
21		(½d.) green	29·00	38·00
21*a*		(½d.) blue-green	55·00	75·00
		b. Imperf (pair)	£750	
22		(½d.) grass-green	42·00	50·00
		a. Imperf (pair)	£850	
23		(1d.) blue (1861)	80·00	2·25
		a. Imperf (pair) (pale blue, worn plate)	£800	
24		(1d.) deep blue	75·00	4·00
		a. Bisected diag (½d.) (*on piece*) (1863)	†	£500
25		(4d.) dull rose-red (1861)	£160	70·00
		a. Imperf (pair)	£1100	
26		(4d.) dull brown-red (1865)	£190	80·00
		a. Imperf (pair)	£1600	
27		(4d.) lake-rose (1868)	£190	£100
		a. Imperf (pair)	£1700	
28		(4d.) dull vermilion (1869)	£350	£110
		a. Imperf (pair)	£1500	
29	2	6d. rose-red (1861) (Handstamped 'CANCELLED' in oval £12000)	£375	24·00
30		6d. orange-red (1864)	£180	32·00
31		6d. bright orange-vermilion (1868)	£160	35·00
32		6d. dull orange-vermilion (1870)	£180	29·00
		a. Imperf (pair)	£750	
33		6d. orange (1870)	£200	50·00
34		1s. brown-black (1863)	75·00	11·00
		a. Error. Blue	£18000	
35		1s. black (1866)	65·00	11·00
		a. Imperf between (horiz pair)	£9000	

(b) Prepared for use, but not issued. P 11 to 12½

No.	Type	Description	Unused	Used
36	1	(½d.) grass-green	£15000	
37		(1d.) blue	£2000	

The (1d.) deep blue No. 24, also exists imperforate, from a new plate introduced in 1867, but examples cannot readily be distinguished from No. 10.

The bisect, No. 24a, was first authorised for use in April 1863 and further examples have been reported up to January 1869 during shortages of ½d. stamps.

No. 34a was an error on the part of the printer who supplied the first requisition of the 1s. value in the colour of the 1d. The 1s. blue stamps were never placed on sale, but the Barbados Colonial Secretary circulated some samples which were defaced by a manuscript corner-to-corner cross. A number of these samples subsequently had the cross removed.

Nos. 36/37 were never sent to Barbados and come from the Perkins Bacon remainders. It is believed that the imperforate pairs came from the same source.

1870–71. Wmk Large Star, T w **1**. Rough perf 14 to 16.

No.	Type	Description	Unused	Used
43	1	(½d.) green	£170	10·00
43*b*		(½d.) yellow-green (1871)	£225	50·00
44		(1d.) blue	£2500	70·00
		a. Blue paper	£4500	£140
		b. Wmk sideways	†	£1400
45		(4d.) dull vermilion	£1600	£120
46	2	6d. orange-vermilion	£1000	90·00
47		1s. black	£450	20·00

No. 43 exists imperforate (*Price £1300, unused pair*).

1871. Wmk Small Star, T w **2**. Rough perf 14 to 16.

No.	Type	Description	Unused	Used
48	1	(1d.) blue	£180	4·25
49		(4d.) dull rose-red	£1300	70·00
50	2	6d. orange-vermilion	£700	28·00
51		1s. black	£250	18·00

1872. Wmk Small Star, T w **2**.

(a) Clean-cut perf 14½ to 15½

No.	Type	Description	Unused	Used
52	1	(1d.) blue	£325	3·00
		a. Bisected diag (½d.) (*on piece*)	†	£750
53	2	6d. orange-vermilion	£950	90·00
54		1s. black	£190	18·00

(b) P 11 to 13×14½ to 15½

No.	Type	Description	Unused	Used
56	1	(½d.) green	£375	65·00
57		(4d.) dull vermilion	£800	£110

1873. Wmk Large Star, T w **1**.

(a) Clean-cut perf 14½ to 15½

No.	Type	Description	Unused	Used
58	1	(½d.) green	£450	29·00
59		(4d.) dull rose-red	£1400	£250
60	2	6d. orange-vermilion	£900	95·00
		a. Imperf between (horiz pair)	£10000	
		b. Imperf (pair)	£100	
61		1s. black	£180	24·00
		a. Imperf between (horiz pair)	£9000	

(b) Prepared for use, but not issued. P 11 to 12

No.	Type	Description	Unused	Used
62	2	6d. orange-vermilion	£10000	

Only eight mint examples, in two strips of four, are known of No. 62. Two used singles of No. 60b have been seen.

1873 (June). Wmk Small Star, T w **2** (sideways = two points upwards). P 14.

No.	Type	Description	Unused	Used
63	2	3d. brown-purple	£325	£110

3

1873 (June). Wmk Small Star, T w **2** (sideways). P 15½×15.

No.	Type	Description	Unused	Used
64	3	5s. dull rose	£950	£300
		s. Handstamped 'SPECIMEN'	£375	

1874 (May)–**75.** Wmk Large Star, T w **1**.

(a) Perf 14

No.	Type	Description	Unused	Used
65	2	½d. deep green	60·00	18·00
66		1d. deep blue	£140	5·50
		a. Bisected (½d.) (*on piece*) (5.75)	†	£600

(b) Clean-cut perf 14½ to 15½

No.	Type	Description	Unused	Used
66*b*	2	1d. deep blue	†	£25000
		c. Imperf (pair)		

(Recess D.L.R.)

1875–81. Wmk Crown CC (sideways* on 6d., 1s.).

(a) P 12½

No.	Type	Description	Unused	Used
67	2	½d. bright green	90·00	9·00
		x. Wmk reversed	£110	13·00
		y. Wmk inverted and reversed		
68		4d. deep red	£350	28·00
		w. Wmk inverted	£475	55·00
		x. Wmk reversed	£350	30·00
69		6d. bright yellow (aniline)	£950	£100
70		6d. chrome-yellow	£650	70·00
		a. Wmk upright	†	£3000
		w. Wmk Crown to right of CC	£750	80·00
		x. Wmk sideways reversed		
71		1s. violet (aniline)	£500	4·50
		x. Wmk sideways reversed	£500	4·00
		y. Wmk sideways inverted and reversed	—	13·00

(b) P 14

No.	Type	Description	Unused	Used
72	2	½d. bright green (1876)	28·00	50
		s. Handstamped 'SPECIMEN' in red	£110	
		sa. Handstamped 'SPECIMEN' in black	£130	
		w. Wmk inverted	—	25·00
		x. Wmk reversed	28·00	75
		y. Wmk inverted and reversed	£180	
73		1d. dull blue	£140	2·00
		a. Bisected (½d.) (*on piece*) (3.77)	†	£300
		s. Handstamped 'SPECIMEN' in red	£110	
		sa. Handstamped 'SPECIMEN' in black	£140	
		w. Wmk inverted		
		x. Wmk reversed	£150	2·50
74		1d. grey-blue	£140	1·50
		a. Wmk sideways	†	£750
		w. Wmk inverted	£225	30·00
		x. Wmk reversed	£150	1·75
		y. Wmk inverted and reversed	—	55·00
75		3d. mauve-lilac (shades) (1878)	£170	16·00
		s. Handstamped 'SPECIMEN' in black	£150	
		w. Wmk inverted	†	£150
76		4d. red (1878)	£150	14·00
		s. Handstamped 'SPECIMEN' in black	£150	
		x. Wmk reversed	£180	18·00
77		4d. carmine (1879)	£225	4·25
		w. Wmk inverted	†	£100
		x. Wmk reversed	£225	6·50
78		4d. crimson-lake (1881)	£500	4·50
79		6d. chrome-yellow (1876)	£150	2·25
		s. Handstamped 'SPECIMEN' in black	£150	
		w. Wmk Crown to right of CC	£160	3·00
		x. Wmk sideways reversed	£190	3·00
80		6d. yellow (1878)	£350	12·00
		w. Wmk Crown to right of CC	—	15·00
81		1s. purple (4.78)	£170	9·00
		s. Handstamped 'SPECIMEN' in red	£150	
		w. Wmk Crown to right of CC	£150	9·00
		x. Wmk sideways reversed	—	12·00
82		1s. violet (aniline) (1876)	£4250	40·00
		w. Wmk Crown to right of CC	—	40·00
		x. Wmk sideways reversed	—	45·00
83		1s. dull mauve (1879)	£500	5·50
		a. Bisected (6d.) (*on piece*) (1.80)	†	—
		x. Wmk sideways reversed	—	13·00

(c) P 14×12½

No.	Type	Description	Unused	Used
84	2	4d. red	£5000	

* The normal sideways watermark shows Crown to left of CC, *as seen from the back of the stamp.*

Only two examples, both used, of No. 70a have been reported.

Nos. 72sa/73sa were from postal stationery and are without gum.

About 20 examples of No. 84 have been found unused and only one used example is known.

1D. 1D. 1D.

(**3a**) (**3b**) (**3c**)

1878 (28 Mar). No. 64 surch by *West Indian Press* with T **3a/3c** sideways twice on each stamp and then divided vertically by 11½ to 13 perforations. The lower label, showing the original face value, was removed before use.

(a) With T **3a**. *Large numeral '1', 7 mm high with curved serif, and large letter 'D', 2¾ mm high*

No.	Type	Description	Unused	Used
86	3	1d. on half 5s. dull rose	£5000	£650
		a. No stop after 'D'	£16000	£2000
		b. Unsevered pair (both No. 86)	£26000	£2500
		c. Ditto, Nos. 86 and 87	—	£5000
		ca. Pair without dividing perf	†	£40000
		d. Ditto, Nos. 86 and 88	£42000	£8500

(b) With T **3b**. *As last, but numeral with straight serif*

No.	Type	Description	Unused	Used
87	3	1d. on half 5s. dull rose	£7500	£950
		a. Unsevered pair	†	£4250

(c) With T **3c**. *Smaller numeral '1', 6 mm high and smaller 'D', 2½ mm high*

No.	Type	Description	Unused	Used
88	3	1d. on half 5s. dull rose	£9000	£1000
		a. Unsevered pair	£38000	£5000

All types of the surcharge were applied reading upwards and downwards in equal quantities, and there are minor varieties of the type.

4

HALF-PENNY
(5)

(Typo D.L.R.)

1882 (28 Aug)–**86.** Wmk Crown CA. P 14.

No.	Type	Description	Unused	Used
89	4	½d. dull green (1882)	35·00	2·25
		w. Wmk inverted	†	£275
90		½d. green	40·00	2·25
91		1d. rose (1882)	90·00	2·50
		a. Bisected (½d.) (*on cover*)	†	£2250
		w. Wmk inverted	†	£225
92		1d. carmine	60·00	1·25
93		2½d. ultramarine (1882)	£120	1·75
		w. Wmk inverted	—	£140
94		2½d. deep blue	£140	1·75
95		3d. deep purple (1885)	£120	50·00
96		3d. reddish purple	10·00	35·00
97		4d. grey (1882)	£350	4·50
		a. Value doubly printed	†	£4500
98		4d. pale brown (1885)	32·00	5·00
		w. Wmk inverted	—	£140
		x. Wmk reversed	†	£275
		y. Wmk inverted and reversed	†	£425
99		4d. deep brown	18·00	2·00
100		6d. olive-black (1886)	75·00	48·00
102		1s. chestnut (1886)	29·00	21·00
103		5s. bistre (1886)	£170	£200
89/103 *Set of 9*			£750	£275
96s/103s (ex 4d. grey) Optd 'SPECIMEN' *Set of 5*			£475	

1892 (11 July). No. 99 surch with T **5** by *West Indian Press.*

No.	Type	Description	Unused	Used
104	4	½d. on 4d. deep brown	2·25	6·00
		a. No hyphen	20·00	40·00
		b. Surch double (R.+Bk.)	£900	£1200
		ba. Surch double (R.+Bk.) both without hyphen	£3500	£4000
		c. Surch double, one albino		
		d. Surch 'PENNY HALF'	£375	£225

Nos. 104b/104ba come from a sheet with a trial surcharge in red which was subsequently surcharged again in black and put back into stock.

No. 104c is known in a horizontal pair (*Price, £2500, unused*) with the left hand stamp showing the first two letters of the second impression inked. The right hand stamp shows a complete albino surcharge.

The 'No hyphen' variety occurs in several positions in the setting of 60.

6 Seal of Colony

7

(Typo D.L.R.)

1892 (July)–**1903.** Wmk Crown CA. P 14.

No.	Type	Description	Unused	Used
105	6	¼d. slate-grey and carmine (5.5.96)	2·50	10
		w. Wmk inverted		
106		½d. dull green	2·50	10
		w. Wmk inverted	£150	£150
107		1d. carmine	4·75	10
108		2d. slate-black and orange (5.99)	15·00	75
109		2½d. ultramarine	17·00	20
110		5d. grey-olive	8·00	4·50
111		6d. mauve and carmine	18·00	2·25
112		8d. orange and ultramarine	5·00	32·00
113		10d. dull blue-green and carmine	13·00	10·00
114		2s.6d. blue-black and orange	50·00	65·00
		w. Wmk inverted	£170	£200
115		2s.6d. violet and green (29.5.03)	£150	£300
105/115 *Set of 11*			£250	£375
105s/115s Optd 'SPECIMEN' *Set of 11*			£275	

See also Nos. 135/144 and 163/169.

(Typo D.L.R.)

1897 (16 Nov)–**98.** Diamond Jubilee. T **7**. Wmk Crown CC. P 14.

(a) White paper

No.	Type	Description	Unused	Used
116		¼d. grey and carmine	10·00	1·25
		sa. Opt 'SPECIMEN' double	£325	
117		½d. dull green	10·00	60
118		1d. rose	15·00	60
119		2½d. ultramarine	18·00	1·50
		w. Wmk inverted	—	£200
120		5d. olive-brown	42·00	20·00
121		6d. mauve and carmine	48·00	25·00
122		8d. orange and ultramarine	25·00	27·00
123		10d. blue-green and carmine	75·00	55·00
124		2s.6d. blue-black and orange	£110	65·00
		w. Wmk inverted		
116/124 *Set of 9*			£300	£170
116s/124s Optd 'SPECIMEN' *Set of 9*			£250	

(b) Paper blued

No.	Type	Description	Unused	Used
125		¼d. grey and carmine	30·00	30·00
126		½d. dull green	30·00	30·00
127		1d. carmine	40·00	40·00
128		2½d. ultramarine	42·00	45·00
129		5d. olive-brown	£225	£250
130		6d. mauve and carmine	£140	£140
131		8d. orange and ultramarine	£140	£150
132		10d. dull green and carmine	£200	£225
133		2s.6d. blue-black and orange	£150	£150

1905. Wmk Mult Crown CA. P 14.

No.	Type	Description	Unused	Used
135	6	¼d. slate-grey and carmine	13·00	3·25
136		½d. green (*shades*)	29·00	10
137		1d. carmine	30·00	10

139		2½d. blue (*shades*)	35·00	15
141		6d. mauve and carmine	48·00	38·00
142		8d. orange and ultramarine	65·00	£130
144		2s.6d. violet and green	65·00	£150
135/144 *Set of 7*			£250	£275

See also Nos. 163/169.

8 Nelson Monument

(Des Mrs. G. Goodman. Recess D.L.R.)

1906 (1 Mar). Nelson Centenary. Wmk Crown CC. P 14.

145	**8**	¼d. black and grey	18·00	1·75
		w. Wmk inverted	55·00	65·00
146		½d. black and pale green	11·00	15
		w. Wmk inverted	£100	
		x. Wmk reversed	£225	£120
		y. Wmk inverted and reversed	£300	
147		1d. black and red	12·00	15
		w. Wmk inverted	£100	£100
		x. Wmk reversed	†	£120
148		2d. black and yellow	4·00	4·50
149		2½d. black and bright blue	4·50	1·25
		w. Wmk inverted	£350	£300
150		6d. black and mauve	19·00	28·00
151		1s. black and rose	23·00	50·00
145/151 *Set of 7*			75·00	75·00
145s/151s Optd 'SPECIMEN' *Set of 7*			£160	

Two sets may be made of the above: one on thick, opaque, creamy white paper; the other on thin, rather transparent, bluish white paper.

See also Nos. 158/162*a*.

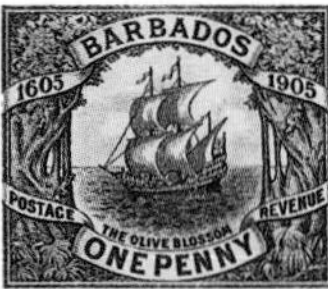

9 *Olive Blossom*, 1605

Kingston Relief Fund. 1d.

(**10**)

(Des Lady Carter. Recess D.L.R.)

1906 (15 Aug). Tercentenary of Annexation. Wmk Multiple Crown CA (sideways). P 14.

152	**9**	1d. black, blue and green	19·00	25
		s. Optd 'SPECIMEN'	70·00	

1907 (25 Jan–25 Feb). Kingston Relief Fund. No. 108 surch with T **10** by T. E. King & Co., Barbados.

153	**6**	1d. on 2d. slate-black and orange (R.)	10·00	16·00
		a. Surch inverted (25.2.07)	1·75	6·50
		b. Surch double	£850	£950
		c. Surch double, both inverted	£850	
		d. Surch *tête-bêche* (vert pair)	£1800	
		e. No stop after '1d.'	70·00	£110
		ea. Do., surch inverted (25.2.07)	45·00	£100
		eb. Do., surch double	—	£2250
		f. Vert pair, one normal, one surch double	—	£1200

The above stamp was sold for 2d. of which 1d. was retained for the postal revenue, and the other 1d. given to a fund for the relief of the sufferers from the earthquake in Jamaica.

An entire printing as No. 153a was created after a sheet of inverted surcharges was found in the initial supply.

1907 (6 July). Nelson Centenary. Wmk Mult Crown CA. P 14.

158	**8**	¼d. black and grey	6·00	13·00
161		2d. black and yellow	32·00	48·00
		x. Wmk reversed	£325	
162		2½d. black and bright blue	8·00	50·00
		a. Black and indigo	£700	£800
158/162 *Set of 3*			42·00	£100

1909 (July)–**10**. Wmk Mult Crown CA. P 14.

163	**6**	¼d. brown	11·00	30
165		1d. red	30·00	10
166		2d. greyish slate (8.10)	12·00	25·00
168		6d. dull and bright purple (1910)	30·00	42·00
169		1s. black/*green* (8.10)	20·00	21·00
163/169 *Set of 5*			90·00	80·00
163s/169s Optd 'SPECIMEN' *Set of 5*			£140	

11

12

13

(Typo D.L.R.)

1912 (23 July)–**16**. Wmk Mult Crown CA. P 14.

170	**11**	¼d. brown	2·25	1·50
		a. Pale brown (1916)	4·50	3·75
		aw. Wmk inverted		
171		½d. green	3·75	10
		a. Wmk sideways	†	£2000
172		1d. red (13.8.12)	11·00	10
		a. Scarlet (1915)	45·00	4·00
173		2d. greyish slate (13.8.12)	7·50	24·00
174		2½d. bright blue (13.8.12)	1·75	1·75
175	**12**	3d. purple/*yellow* (13.8.12)	3·00	14·00
176		4d. black and red/*yellow* (13.8.12)	5·50	26·00
177		6d. dull purple and purple (13.8.12)	12·00	12·00
178	**13**	1s. black/*green* (13.8.12)	17·00	28·00
179		2s. purple and blue/*blue* (13.8.12)	65·00	70·00
180		3s. green and violet (13.8.12)	£120	£130
170/180 *Set of 11*			£225	£275
170s/180s Optd 'SPECIMEN' *Set of 11*			£180	

14

WAR TAX

(15)

(Recess D.L.R.)

1916 (16 June)–**19**. Wmk Mult Crown CA. P 14.

181	**14**	¼d. deep brown	75	40
		a. Chestnut-brown (9.17)	1·50	35
		b. Sepia-brown (4.18)	4·25	3·00
		w. Wmk inverted	17·00	18·00
		y. Wmk inverted and reversed	50·00	60·00
182		½d. green	4·25	15
		a. Deep green (9.17)	1·60	15
		b. Pale green (4.18)	2·25	80
		w. Wmk inverted	40·00	
		x. Wmk reversed	£130	
		y. Wmk inverted and reversed	75·00	80·00
183		1d. deep red	17·00	6·00
		a. Bright carmine-red (4.17)	2·50	15
		b. Pale carmine-red (9.17)	6·00	65
		w. Wmk inverted	42·00	50·00
		x. Wmk reversed	£130	
		y. Wmk inverted and reversed	45·00	60·00
184		2d. grey	15·00	42·00
		a. Grey-black (9.19)	60·00	80·00
		x. Wmk reversed	—	£750
		y. Wmk inverted and reversed		
185		2½d. deep ultramarine	8·00	3·50
		a. Royal blue (11.17)	13·00	4·50
		w. Wmk inverted		
		y. Wmk inverted and reversed	50·00	50·00
186		3d. purple/*yellow* (thin paper)	15·00	19·00
		a. Deep purple/yellow (thick paper) (9.19)	45·00	60·00
187		4d. red/*yellow*	1·50	14·00
188		6d. purple	15·00	10·00
189		1s. black/*green*	17·00	12·00
190		2s. purple/*blue*	22·00	7·50
		y. Wmk inverted and reversed	£250	
191		3s. deep violet	75·00	£180
		w. Wmk inverted		
		y. Wmk inverted and reversed	£1700	£2250
181/191 *Set of 11*			£140	£250
181s/191s 'SPECIMEN' *Set of 11*			£275	

Dates quoted for shades are those of despatch from Great Britain.

Examples of the ½d. and 1d. values can be found perforated either by line or by comb machines.

See also Nos. 199/200*a*.

1917 (10 Oct)–**18**. War Tax. Optd in London with T **15**.

197	**11**	1d. bright red	50	15
		s. Optd 'SPECIMEN'	55·00	
		w. Wmk inverted	—	£250
198		1d. pale red (*thicker bluish paper*) (4.18)	7·50	70

1918 (18 Feb)–**20**. Colours changed. Wmk Mult Crown CA. P 14.

199	**14**	4d. black and red	2·50	4·00
		x. Wmk reversed	£325	
		y. Wmk inverted and reversed	†	£500
200		3s. green and deep violet	32·00	£110
		a. Green and bright violet (1920)	£250	£375
199s/200s Optd 'SPECIMEN' *Set of 2*			£130	

The centres of these are from a new die having no circular border line.

16 Winged Victory from the Louvre

17 Victory from Victoria Memorial, London

(Recess D.L.R.)

1920 (9 Sept)–**21**. Victory. P 14.

(a) Wmk Mult Crown CA (sideways on T* **17***)*

201	**16**	¼d. black and bistre-brown	30	70
		a. 'C' of 'CA' missing from wmk	£400	
		c. Substituted crown in wmk	£450	£450
		w. Wmk inverted	£160	
		x. Wmk reversed	75·00	
		y. Wmk inverted and reversed	80·00	
202		½d. black and bright yellow-green	2·25	15
		a. 'C' of 'CA' missing from wmk	£450	£400
		b. 'A' of 'CA' missing from wmk	£450	
		c. Substituted crown in wmk	£650	
		w. Wmk inverted	£200	£170
		x. Wmk reversed	£160	
		y. Wmk inverted and reversed	£150	£150
203		1d. black and vermilion	4·00	10
		a. 'A' of 'CA' missing from wmk	£600	£500
		b. 'C' of 'CA' missing from wmk	£600	
		c. Substituted crown in wmk	†	£500
		w. Wmk inverted	55·00	65·00
		wa. Substituted crown in wmk	£1200	
		x. Wnk reversed	£200	
		y. Wmk inverted and reversed	£150	£150
204		2d. black and grey	3·00	18·00
		a. 'C' of 'CA' missing from wmk	£500	
205		2½d. indigo and ultramarine	2·75	29·00
		a. 'C' of 'CA' missing from wmk	£500	
		b. 'A' of 'CA' missing from wmk	£500	
		w. Wmk inverted	—	£180
		y. Wmk inverted and reversed	£160	£180
206		3d. black and purple	4·25	6·50
		a. 'C' of 'CA' missing from wmk	£500	
		w. Wmk inverted	35·00	55·00
207		4d. black and blue-green	4·25	7·00
208		6d. black and brown-orange	6·50	27·00
		w. Wmk inverted	80·00	£150
		wa. 'C' of 'CA' missing from wmk	£1800	
		wb. Substituted crown in wmk	£1800	
209	**17**	1s. black and bright green	21·00	55·00
		a. 'C' of 'CA' missing from wmk	£1300	
		w. Wmk Crown to left of CA	£150	
		x. Wmk sideways reversed	£225	
		y. Wmk sideways inverted and reversed	£250	£350
210		2s. black and brown	50·00	75·00
		w. Wmk Crown to left of CA	80·00	£160
		x. Wmk sideways reversed	£250	
		y. Wmk sideways inverted and reversed	£225	
211		3s. black and dull orange	55·00	95·00
		a. 'C' of 'CA' missing from wmk	£1500	£1500
		c. Substituted crown in wmk	£1500	
		w. Wmk Crown to left of CA	£160	
		x. Wmk sideways reversed	£300	£300
		y. Wmk sideways inverted and reversed		

(b) Wmk Mult Script CA

212	**16**	1d. black and vermilion (22.8.21)	17·00	30
201/212 *Set of 12*			£150	£275
201s/212s Optd 'SPECIMEN' *Set of 12*			£275	

* The normal sideways watermark on Nos. 209/211 shows Crown to right of CA, *as seen from the back of the stamp*.

For illustration of the substituted watermark crown see Catalogue Introduction.

18

19

(Recess D.L.R.)

1921 (14 Nov)–**24**. P 14.

(a) Wmk Mult Crown CA

213	**18**	3d. purple/*pale yellow*	2·00	13·00
		a. 'A' of 'CA' missing from wmk	†	£600
		x. Wmk reversed	£325	£325
214		4d. red/*pale yellow*	1·75	26·00
215		1s. black/*emerald*	7·50	25·00
		w. Wmk inverted	†	£475
		x. Wmk reversed	£425	£375

(b) Wmk Mult Script CA

217	**18**	¼d. brown	25	10
		x. Wmk reversed	30·00	
		y. Wmk inverted and reversed	75·00	£120
219		½d. green	1·50	10
220		1d. red	80	10
		aw. Wmk inverted	25·00	32·00
		ax. Wmk reversed	—	£180
		ay. Wmk inverted and reversed	—	£180
		b. Bright rose-carmine	9·50	1·00
		bw. Wmk inverted	27·00	
221		2d. grey	1·75	20
		y. Wmk inverted and reversed	†	£500
222		2½d. ultramarine	1·50	9·00
225		6d. reddish purple	3·50	9·00
226		1s. black/*emerald* (18.9.24)	55·00	£150
		sa. Opt 'SPECIMEN' double	£225	
227		2s. purple/*blue*	10·00	26·00
228		3s. deep violet	29·00	85·00
		y. Wmk inverted and reversed		
213/228 *Set of 12*			£100	£300
213s/228s Optd 'SPECIMEN' *Set of 12*			£225	

1925 (1 Apr)–**35**. Wmk Mult Script CA. P 14.

229	**19**	¼d. brown	25	10
230		½d. green	60	10
		a. Perf 13½×12½ (2.32)	12·00	10
231		1d. scarlet	60	10
		a. 'A' of 'CA' missing from wmk	†	£1000
		bx. Wmk reversed	†	£500
		c. Perf 13½×12½ (2.32)	15·00	50
231*d*		1½d. orange (1933)	15·00	3·25
		da. Perf 13½×12½ (15.8.32)	9·00	1·00
232		2d. grey	75	3·25
233		2½d. blue	50	80
		a. Bright ultramarine (1933)	21·00	2·50
		ab. Perf 13½×12½ (2.32)	21·00	10·00
234		3d. purple/*pale yellow*	1·50	45
		a. Reddish purple/yellow (1935)	6·50	7·50
235		4d. red/*pale yellow*	1·00	1·75
236		6d. purple	1·00	90
237		1s. black/*emerald*	3·25	9·00
		a. Perf 13½×12½ (8.32)	70·00	50·00
		b. Brownish black/bright yellow-green (1934)	9·00	10·00
238		2s. purple/*blue*	7·00	10·00
238*a*		2s.6d. carmine/*blue* (1.9.32)	32·00	50·00
239		3s. deep violet	11·00	24·00
229/239 *Set of 13*			60·00	90·00
229s/239s Optd or Perf (1½d., 2s.6d.) 'SPECIMEN' *Set of 13*			£225	

Nos. 230/231 exist in coils constructed from normal sheets.

Later printings (from 1932) of the ½d., 1d., 2½d. and 6d. and all printings of the 1½d. and 2s.6d. were produced from curved plates, resulting in the width of the design increasing from less than 20.5mm to 21mm.

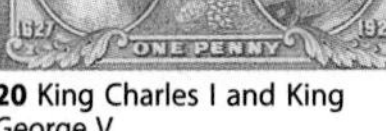

20 King Charles I and King George V

21 Badge of the Colony

(Des and Recess B.W.)

1927 (17 Feb). Tercentenary of Settlement of Barbados. Wmk Mult Script CA. P 12½.

No.	Type	Description	Unused	Used
240	**20**	1d. carmine	2·00	80
		a. Perf 12×12½	5·00	3·50
		s. Optd 'SPECIMEN'	55·00	

1935 (6 May). Silver Jubilee. As Nos. 91/94 of Antigua, but ptd by Waterlow. P 11×12.

No.	Description	Unused	Used
241	1d. deep blue and scarlet	2·50	20
	j. Damaged turret	£700	£375
242	1½d. ultramarine and grey	5·50	8·50
	j. Damaged turret	£850	
243	2½d. brown and deep blue	3·00	6·50
	m. 'Bird' by turret	£300	£400
244	1s. slate and purple	25·00	35·00
	l. Kite and horizontal log	£750	£800
241/244 *Set of 4*		32·00	45·00
241s/244s Perf 'SPECIMEN' *Set of 4*		£140	

For illustrations of plate varieties see Omnibus section following Zanzibar.

1937 (14 May). Coronation. As Nos. 95/97 of Antigua, but printed by D.L.R. P 14.

No.	Description	Unused	Used
245	1d. scarlet	30	15
246	1½d. yellow-brown	1·00	75
247	2½d. bright blue	1·40	75
245/247 *Set of 3*		2·40	1·50
245s/247s Perf 'SPECIMEN' *Set of 3*		90·00	

½d. Recut line (R. 10/6)

2d. Extra frame line (R. 11/9) (corrected on Aug 1949 ptg)

2½d. Mark on central ornament (R. 1/3, 2/3, 3/3)

3d. Vertical line over horse's head (R. 4/10) (corrected on Dec 1947 ptg)

4d. 'Flying mane' (R. 4/1) (corrected on Dec 1947 ptg)

4d. Curved line at top right (R. 7/8) (corrected on Dec 1947 ptg)

4d. Scratched plate (extends to top right ornament) (R. 6/10)

(Recess D.L.R.)

1938 (3 Jan)–**47**. Wmk Mult Script CA. P 13½×13.

No.	Type	Description	Unused	Used
248	**21**	½d. green	6·00	15
		a. Recut line	£150	40·00
		b. Perf 14 (8.42)	70·00	2·25
		ba. Recut line	£650	95·00
248*c*		½d. yellow-bistre (16.10.42)	15	30
		ca. 'A' of 'CA' missing from wmk	£1100	
		cb. Recut line	23·00	35·00
249		1d. scarlet (9.39)	£275	5·00
		a. Perf 14 (3.1.38)	19·00	10
249*b*		1d. blue-green (16.10.42)	5·00	1·50
		c. Perf 14 (16.10.42)	15	10
		ca. 'A' of 'CA' missing from wmk	£1100	£1100
		cb. Printed double, one albino	£900	£1000
250		1½d. orange	20	40
		a. 'A' of 'CA' missing from wmk	£1100	
		b. Perf 14 (11.41)	9·50	1·00
250*c*		2d. claret (3.6.41)	1·50	2·00
		ca. Extra frame line	80·00	£140
250*d*		2d. carmine (20.9.43)	1·75	70
		da. Extra frame line	60·00	65·00
		db. 'A' of 'CA' missing from wmk	†	—
		e. Perf 14 (11.9.44)	60	2·25
		ea. Extra frame line	50·00	£120
251		2½d. ultramarine	1·00	60
		a. Mark on central ornament	55·00	55·00
		b. Blue (17.2.44)	2·50	6·00
		ba. 'A' of 'CA' missing from wmk	£1000	
		bb. Mark on central ornament	85·00	£160
252		3d. brown	2·25	4·50
		a. Vertical line over horse's head	£150	£275
		ab. 'A' of 'CA' missing from wmk	£1000	
		b. Perf 14 (4.41)	30	60
		ba. Vertical line over horse's head	£110	£140
252*c*		3d. blue (1.4.47)	1·25	1·75
		ca. Vertical line over horse's head	£130	£170
253		4d. black	30	10
		a. Flying mane	£160	70·00
		b. Curved line at top right	£140	70·00
		c. Scratched plate	£160	80·00
		d. Perf 14 (11.9.44)	2·00	6·50
		da. Flying mane	£180	£375
		db. Curved line at top right	£170	£350
		dc. Scratched plate	£150	£375
254		6d. violet	1·00	40
254*a*		8d. magenta (9.12.46)	1·00	2·00
		ab. 'A' of 'CA' missing from wmk	£1200	
255		1s. olive-green	16·00	2·50
		a. Deep brown-olive (19.11.45)	2·00	10
256		2s.6d. purple	12·00	1·50
256*a*		5s. indigo (3.6.41)	12·00	14·00
		ab. 'A' of 'CA' missing from wmk	£2250	
248/256*a* *Set of 16*			50·00	22·00
248s/256as Perf 'SPECIMEN' *Set of 16*			£450	

No. 249a was perforated by two machines, one gauging 13.8×14.1 line (1938), the other 14.1 comb (October 1940).

Nos. 248/248*c* and 249/249*c* exist in coils constructed from normal sheets.

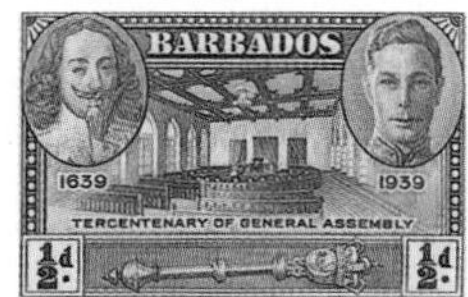

22 Kings Charles I, George VI, Assembly Chamber and Mace

(Recess D.L.R.)

1939 (27 June). Tercentenary of General Assembly. Wmk Mult Script CA. P 13½×14.

No.	Type	Description	Unused	Used
257	**22**	½d. green	3·00	1·00
258		1d. scarlet	3·00	1·25
259		1½d. orange	3·25	60
260		2½d. bright ultramarine	5·00	8·50
261		3d. brown	5·00	5·50
257/261 *Set of 5*			17·00	15·00
257s/261s Perf 'SPECIMEN' *Set of 5*			£180	

1½d. Two flags on tug (R. 5/2)

3d. 'Kite' (R.10/4)

1946 (18 Sept). Victory. As Nos. 110/111 of Antigua.

No.	Description	Unused	Used
262	1½d. red-orange	15	50
	a. Two flags on tug	27·00	42·00
263	3d. brown	15	50
	a. Kite flaw	45·00	60·00
262s/263s Perf 'SPECIMEN' *Set of 2*		85·00	

ONE
PENNY
(**23**)

NY PEN

Short 'Y' (R. 6/2) Broken 'E' (R. 7/4 and 11/4)

ONE
PENNY

Broken 'N's (R. 2/8, later sheets only)

(Surch by Barbados Advocate Co.)

1947 (21 Apr). Surch with T **23**.

(a) P 14

No.	Type	Description	Unused	Used
264	**21**	1d. on 2d. carmine (No. 250e)	2·25	7·00
		a. Extra frame line	£110	£190
		b. Broken 'N's	£180	
		c. Short 'Y'	£110	£190
		d. Broken 'E'	70·00	£110

(b) P 13½×13

No.	Type	Description	Unused	Used
264*e*	**21**	1d. on 2d. carmine (No. 250*d*)	3·00	8·50
		ea. Extra frame line	£200	£325
		eb. Broken 'N's	£325	£600
		ec. Short 'Y'	£200	£325
		ed. Broken 'E'	£140	£225
		f. Surch double	£3000	

The relationship of the two words in the surcharge differs on each position of the sheet.

1948 (24 Nov). Royal Silver Wedding. As Nos. 112/113 of Antigua.

No.	Description	Unused	Used
265	1½d. orange	30	50
266	5s. indigo	17·00	14·00

1949 (10 Oct). 75th Anniversary of Universal Postal Union. As Nos. 114/17 of Antigua.

No.	Description	Unused	Used
267	1½d. red-orange	50	2·00
268	3d. deep blue	2·75	8·00
269	4d. grey	50	4·00
270	1s. olive	50	1·50
267/270 *Set of 4*		3·75	14·00

(New Currency. 100 cents = 1 West Indian, later Barbados, dollar)

24 Dover Fort

25 Sugar cane breeding

26 Public buildings

27 Statue of Nelson

28 Casting net

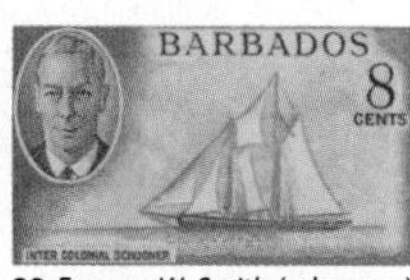

29 *Frances W. Smith* (schooner)

30 Four-winged Flying Fish

31 Old Main Guard Garrison

32 St Michael's Cathedral

33 Careenage

34 Map of Barbados and wireless mast

35 Seal of Barbados

(Recess B.W.)

1950 (1 May). T **24/35**. Wmk Mult Script CA. P 11×11½ (horizontal), 13½ (vertical).

No.	Type	Description	Unused	Used
271	**24**	1c. indigo	35	4·50
272	**25**	2c. emerald-green	15	3·00
273	**26**	3c. reddish brown and blue-green	1·25	4·00
274	**27**	4c. carmine	15	40
275	**28**	6c. light blue	15	2·25
276	**29**	8c. bright blue and purple-brown	2·75	3·75
277	**30**	12c. greenish blue and brown-olive	1·00	1·75
278	**31**	24c. scarlet and black	1·00	50
279	**32**	48c. violet	13·00	7·00
280	**33**	60c. green and claret	11·00	14·00
281	**34**	$1.20 carmine and olive-green	13·00	5·00
282	**35**	$2.40 black	26·00	42·00
271/282 *Set of 12*			55·00	75·00

1951 (16 Feb). Inauguration of BWI University College. As Nos. 118/119 of Antigua.

No.	Description	Unused	Used
283	3c. brown and blue-green	30	40
284	12c. blue-green and brown-olive	1·25	2·25

36 King George VI and Stamp of 1852

(Recess Waterlow)

1952 (15 Apr). Barbados Stamp Centenary. Wmk Mult Script CA. P 13½.

285	**36**	3c. green and slate-green	40	40
286		4c. blue and carmine	40	1·40
287		12c. slate-green and bright green	40	1·00
288		24c. red-brown and brownish black	50	55
285/288 *Set of 4*			1·50	3·00

37 Harbour Police

(Recess B.W.)

1953 (13 Apr)–**61**. Designs previously used for King George VI issue, but with portrait or cypher ($2.40) of Queen Elizabeth II, as in T **37**. Wmk Mult Script CA. P 11×11½ (horizontal) or 13½ (vertical).

289	**24**	1c. indigo	10	80
290	**25**	2c. orange and deep turquoise (15.4.54)	15	1·50
291	**26**	3c. black and emerald (15.4.54)	1·00	1·00
292	**27**	4c. black and orange (15.4.54)	20	20
		a. Black and reddish orange (18.3.59)	5·50	2·25
293	**37**	5c. blue and deep carmine-red (4.1.54)	1·25	60
294	**28**	6c. red-brown (15.4.54)	3·25	60
		w. Wmk inverted		
295	**29**	8c. black and blue (15.4.54)	2·00	40
296	**30**	12c. turquoise-blue and brown-olive (15.4.54)	1·00	10
		a. Turquoise-green and brown-olive (18.3.59)	17·00	3·00
		b. Turquoise-blue and bronze-green (13.6.61)	19·00	2·00
297	**31**	24c. rose-red and black (2.3.56)	1·50	10
298	**32**	48c. deep violet (2.3.56)	8·00	1·00
299	**33**	60c. blue-green and brown-purple (3.4.56)	40·00	5·50
		a. Blue-green and pale maroon (17.5.60)	70·00	11·00
300	**34**	$1.20 carmine and bronze-green (3.4.56)	19·00	6·50
301	**35**	$2.40 black (1.2.57)	7·50	1·75
289/301 *Set of 13*			75·00	18·00

See also Nos. 312/319.

1953 (4 June). Coronation. As No. 120 of Antigua.

302		4c. black and red-orange	1·00	20

1958 (23 Apr). Inauguration of British Caribbean Federation. As Nos. 135/137 of Antigua.

303		3c. deep green	80	20
304		6c. blue	1·00	2·25
305		12c. scarlet	1·00	30
303/305 *Set of 3*			2·50	2·50

38 Deep Water Harbour, Bridgetown

(Recess B.W.)

1961 (6 May). Opening of Deep Water Harbour, Bridgetown. W w **12**. P 11×12.

306	**38**	4c. black and red-orange	55	50
307		8c. black and blue	55	60
308		24c. carmine-red and black	60	60
306/308 *Set of 3*			1·50	1·50

SELF-GOVERNMENT

39 Scout Badge and Map of Barbados

(Recess B.W.)

1962 (9 Mar). Golden Jubilee of Barbados Boy Scout Association. W w **12**. P 11½×11.

309	**39**	4c. black and orange	85	10
310		12c. blue and olive-brown	1·40	15
311		$1.20 carmine and olive-green	2·00	3·75
309/311 *Set of 3*			3·75	3·75

1964 (14 Jan)–**65**. As Nos. 289, etc., but wmk w **12**.

312	**24**	1c. indigo (6.10.64)	50	6·00
313	**27**	4c. black and orange	30	50
314	**29**	8c. black and blue (29.6.65)	70	35
315	**30**	12c. turquoise-blue and brown-olive (29.6.65)	50	50
316	**31**	24c. rose-red and black (6.10.64)	2·25	70
317	**32**	48c. deep violet	6·00	1·50
318	**33**	60c. blue-green and brown-purple (6.10.64)	10·00	4·00
319	**35**	$2.40 black (29.6.65)	1·25	1·75
312/319 *Set of 8*			19·00	14·00

The above dates are for Crown Agents releases. The 14.1.64 printings were not released in Barbados until April 1964, the 6.10.64 printings until December 1964 and of the stamps released in London on 29 June 1965 the 8c. and $2.40 were released from about 15 June 1965, but the 12c. value was never put on sale in Barbados.

1965 (17 May). ITU Centenary. As Nos. 166/167 of Antigua.

320		2c. lilac and red	20	40
321		48c. yellow and grey-brown	45	1·00

40 Deep Sea Coral

41 Lobster

42 Lined Seahorse

43 Sea Urchin

44 Staghorn Coral

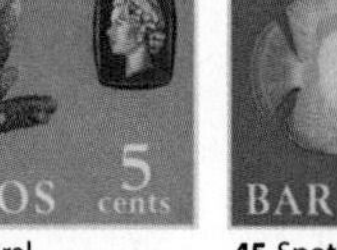

45 Spot-finned Butterflyfish

46 Rough File Shell

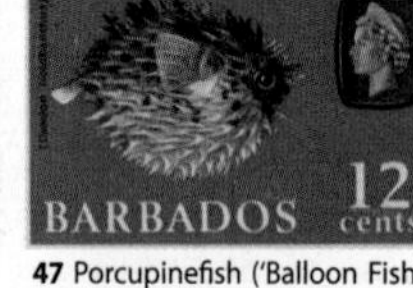

47 Porcupinefish ('Balloon Fish')

48 Grey Angelfish

49 Brain Coral

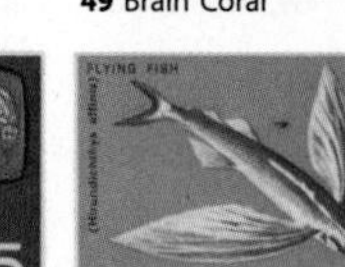

50 Brittle Star

51 Four-winged Flyingfish

52 Queen or Pink Conch Shell

53 Fiddler Crab

(Des V. Whiteley, from drawings by Mrs. J. Walker. Photo Harrison)

1965 (15 July). Marine Life. T **40/53**. W w **12** (upright). P 14×13½.

322	**40**	1c. black, pink and blue	20	30
323	**41**	2c. olive-brown, yellow and magenta	20	15
324	**42**	3c. olive-brown and orange	45	60
325	**43**	4c. deep blue and olive-green	15	10
		a. Imperf (pair)	£325	£250
		w. Wmk inverted	—	25·00
326	**44**	5c. sepia, rose and lilac	30	20
327	**45**	6c. multicoloured	45	20
		w. Wmk inverted	1·25	1·00
328	**46**	8c. multicoloured	25	10
		w. Wmk inverted	5·50	
329	**47**	12c. multicoloured	35	10
		a. Grey printing double	65·00	
		w. Wmk inverted	†	£160
330	**48**	15c. black, greenish yellow and red	4·00	30
331	**49**	25c. ultramarine and yellow-ochre	1·00	30
332	**50**	35c. brown-red and deep green	1·50	15
		w. Wmk inverted	†	85·00
333	**51**	50c. bright blue and apple-green	2·00	40
334	**52**	$1 multicoloured	3·50	2·00
335	**53**	$2.50 multicoloured	2·75	9·00
322/335 *Set of 14*			15·00	12·00

The 3c. value is wrongly inscribed 'Hippocanpus', the correct spelling 'Hippocampus' was used for subsequent printings, see No. 344.

See also Nos. 342, etc.

1966 (24 Jan). Churchill Commemoration. As Nos. 170/173 of Antigua.

336		1c. new blue	10	3·75
		w. Wmk inverted	42·00	
337		4c. deep green	60	10
338		25c. brown	1·50	50
339		35c. bluish violet	1·50	70
336/339 *Set of 4*			3·25	4·50

1966 (4 Feb). Royal Visit. As Nos. 174/175 of Antigua.

340		3c. black and ultramarine	75	1·00
341		35c. black and magenta	2·25	1·00

53a Dolphinfish

54 Arms of Barbados

1966 (15 Mar)–**69**. As Nos. 322/335 but wmk w **12** (sideways*). New value and design (as T **53a**).

342	**40**	1c. black, pink and blue	10	20
		w. Wmk Crown to right of CA		
343	**41**	2c. olive-brown, yellow and magenta (16.5.67)	30	80
344	**42**	3c. olive-brown and orange (4.12.67)	30	2·75
345	**43**	4c. deep blue and olive-green	50	10
		w. Wmk Crown to right of CA	70·00	
346	**44**	5c. sepia, rose and lilac (23.8.66)	45	10
347	**45**	6c. multicoloured (31.1.67)	70	10
348	**46**	8c. multicoloured (19.9.67)	75	10
349	**47**	12c. multicoloured (31.1.67)	45	10
350	**48**	15c. black, greenish yellow and red	2·25	10
351	**49**	25c. ultramarine and yellow-ochre	2·25	40
		aw. Wmk Crown to right of CA	9·50	9·50
		b. Deep ultramarine and yellow-ochre (26.9.66)	12·00	2·25
352	**50**	35c. brown-red and deep green (23.8.66)	5·00	65
		a. Chestnut and deep green (26.11.68)	18·00	3·50
353	**51**	50c. bright blue and apple-green	2·00	4·25
		w. Wmk Crown to right of CA	85·00	
354	**52**	$1 multicoloured (23.8.66)	6·00	1·00
355	**53**	$2.50 multicoloured (23.8.66)	7·00	3·00
355*a*	**53a**	$5 multicoloured (9.1.69)	21·00	20·00
342/355*a* *Set of 15*			42·00	30·00

* The normal sideways watermark shows Crown to left of CA, *as seen from the back of the stamp.*

The 3c. value is correctly inscribed 'Hippocampus'.

All values except the 50c. exist with PVA gum as well as gum arabic but the $5 exists with PVA gum only.

The $5 was released by the Crown Agents on 6 January but was not put on sale locally until 9 January.

INDEPENDENT

(Des. V. Whiteley. Photo Harrison)

1966 (2 Dec). Independence. T **54** and similar multicoloured designs. P 14.

356		4c. Type **54**	10	10
357		25c. Hilton Hotel (*horiz*)	15	10
358		35c. G. Sobers (Test cricketer)	1·50	65
359		50c. Pine Hill Dairy (*horiz*)	50	1·10
356/359 *Set of 4*			2·00	1·75

1967 (6 Jan). 20th Anniversary of UNESCO As Nos. 196/198 of Antigua.

360		4c. slate-violet, red, yellow and orange	20	10
361		12c. orange-yellow, violet and deep olive	45	50
362		25c. black, bright purple and orange	75	1·25
360/362 *Set of 3*			1·25	1·60

58 Policeman and Anchor

62 Governor-General Sir Winston Scott, G.C.M.G.

(Des V. Whiteley. Litho D.L.R.)

1967 (16 Oct). Centenary of Harbour Police. T **58** and similar multicoloured designs. P 14.

363		4c. Type **58**	25	10
364		25c. Policeman with telescope	40	15
365		35c. *BP1* (police launch) (*horiz*)	45	15
366		50c. Policeman outside HQ	60	1·60
363/366 *Set of 4*			1·50	1·75

(Des V. Whiteley. Photo Harrison)

1967 (4 Dec). First Anniversary of Independence. T **62** and similar multicoloured designs. P 14½×14 (4c.) or 14×14½ (others).

367		4c. Type **62**	15	10
368		25c. Independence Arch (*horiz*)	25	10
369		35c. Treasury Building (*horiz*)	30	10
370		50c. Parliament Building (*horiz*)	40	90
367/370 *Set of 4*			1·00	1·00

66 UN Building, Santiago, Chile

BARBADOS 3c RADAR ANTENNA WORLD METEOROLOGICAL DAY 1968

67 Radar Antenna

(Des G. Vasarhelyi. Photo Harrison)

1968 (27 Feb). 20th Anniversary of the Economic Commission for Latin America. P 14½.
371 **66** 15c. multicoloured 10 10

(Des G. Vasarhelyi. Photo Harrison)

1968 (4 June). World Meteorological Day. T **67** and similar multicoloured designs. P 14×14½ (25c.) or 14½×14 (others).
372 3c. Type **67** 10 10
373 25c. Meteorological Institute (*horiz*) 25 10
374 50c. Harp Gun and Coat of Arms 30 90
372/374 *Set of 3* .... 55 1·00

70 Lady Baden-Powell, and Guide at Camp Fire

(Des. V. Whiteley (from local designs). Photo Harrison)

1968 (29 Aug). 50th Anniversary of Girl Guiding in Barbados. T **70** and similar horizontal designs. P 14.
375 3c. ultramarine, black and gold 20 45
376 25c. turquoise-blue, black and gold 30 45
377 35c. orange-yellow, black and gold 35 45
375/377 *Set of 3* .... 75 1·25

Designs: 3c. T **70**; 25c. Lady Baden-Powell and Pax Hill; 35c. Lady Baden-Powell and Guide Badge.

73 Hands breaking Chain, and Human Rights Emblem

(Des V. Whiteley. Litho B.W.)

1968 (10 Dec*). Human Rights Year. T **73** and similar horizontal designs. P 11×12.
378 4c. violet, brown and light green 10 20
379 25c. black, blue and orange-yellow 10 25
380 35c. multicoloured 15 25
378/380 *Set of 3* 30 60

Designs: 4c. T **73**; 25c. Human Rights emblem and family enchained; 35c. Shadows of refugees beyond opening fence.

* This was the local release date but the Crown Agents issued the stamps on 29 October.

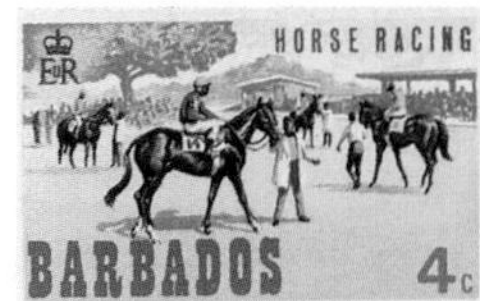

76 Racehorses in the Paddock

(Des J. Cooter. Litho Format)

1969 (20 Mar*). Horse-Racing. T **76** and similar horizontal designs. Multicoloured. P 14.
381 4c. Type **76** 25 15
382 25c. Starting-gate 25 15
383 35c. On the flat 30 15
384 50c. Winning post .... 35 2·40
381/384 *Set of 4* .... 1·00 2·50
MS385 117×85 mm. Nos. 381/384 .... 2·00 2·75

* This was the local release date but the Crown Agents issued the stamps on 15 March.

80 Map showing CARIFTA Countries

81 Strength in Unity

(Des J. Cooter. Photo Harrison)

1969 (6 May). First Anniversary of CARIFTA (Caribbean Free Trade Area). W w **12** (sideways on T **80**). P 14.
386 **80** 5c. multicoloured 10 10
387 **81** 12c. multicoloured 10 10
388 **80** 25c. multicoloured 10 10
389 **81** 50c. multicoloured 15 20
386/389 *Set of 4* 30 30

82 ILO Emblem and '1919–1969'.

ONE CENT

(83)

(Des Sylvia Goaman. Litho Enschedé)

1969 (12 Aug). 50th Anniversary of International Labour Organisation. P 14×13.
390 **82** 4c. black, emerald and turquoise-blue 10 10
391 25c. black, cerise and brown-red 20 10

Although released by the Crown Agents on 5 August, the above were not put on sale in Barbados until 12 August.

1969 (30 Aug). No. 363 surch with T **83**.
392 1c. on 4c. Type **58** 10 10
a. Surch double £100

84 National Scout Badge

(Des J. Cooter. Litho Enschedé)

1969 (16 Dec). Independence of Barbados Boy Scouts Association and 50th Anniversary of Barbados Sea Scouts. T **84** and similar horizontal designs. Multicoloured. P 13×13½.
393 5c. Type **84** 15 10
394 25c. Sea Scouts rowing 30 10
395 35c. Scouts around camp fire 35 10
396 50c. Scouts and National Scout Headquarters .... 60 1·25
393/396 *Set of 4* .... 1·25 1·40
MS397 155×115 mm. Nos. 393/396 .... 15·00 13·00

4 X

(88)

89 Lion at Gun Hill

1970 (11 Mar). No. 346 surch locally with T **88**.
398 4c. on 5c. sepia, rose and lilac 10 10
a. Vert pair, one without surch .... 60·00 70·00
b. Surch double .... 30·00 38·00
c. Vert pair, one normal, one surch double .... 85·00 95·00
d. Surch triple £300 £160
e. Surch normal on front, inverted on back .... 22·00
f. Surch omitted on front, inverted on back .... 30·00

(Des J.W. Photo D.L.R.)

1970 (4 May)–**71**. Multicoloured designs as T **89**. W w **12** (sideways on 12c. to $5). Chalk-surfaced paper. P 12½.
399 1c. Type **89** .... 10 2·50
a. Glazed, ordinary paper (15.3.71) .... 10 1·50
400 2c. Trafalgar Fountain .... 30 1·25
a. Glazed, ordinary paper (15.3.71) .... 10 1·75
401 3c. Montefiore Drinking Fountain .... 1·50 1·00
a. Glazed, ordinary paper (15.3.71) .... 10 1·75
aw. Wmk inverted .... 9·50
402 4c. St. James' Monument .... 1·00 15
a. Glazed, ordinary paper (15.3.71) 30 10
403 5c. St. Anne's Fort 10 10
a. Glazed, ordinary paper (15.3.71) 10 10
404 6c. Old Sugar Mill, Morgan Lewis .... 35 3·00
405 8c. Cenotaph 10 10
a. Glazed, ordinary paper (15.3.71) 10 10
406 10c. South Point Lighthouse .... 3·50 50
a. Glazed, ordinary paper (15.3.71) .... 1·25 15
407 12c. Barbados Museum (*horiz*) .... 1·75 10
a. Glazed, ordinary paper (13.12.71) .... 9·00 30
408 15c. Sharon Moravian Church (*horiz*) 30 15
a. Glazed, ordinary paper (13.12.71) .... 2·75 30
409 25c. George Washington House (*horiz*) 25 15
a. Glazed, ordinary paper (15.3.71) 50 35
410 35c. Nicholas Abbey (*horiz*) 30 85
a. Glazed, ordinary paper (15.3.71) 45 70
411 50c. Bowmanston Pumping Station (*horiz*) .... 40 1·00
a. Glazed, ordinary paper (15.3.71) .... 70 4·50
412 $1 Queen Elizabeth Hospital (*horiz*) .... 70 2·50
a. Glazed, ordinary paper (15.3.71) .... 4·00 11·00
413 $2.50 Modern sugar factory (*horiz*) .... 1·50 4·00
a. Glazed, ordinary paper (13.12.71) .... 32·00 16·00
414 $5 Seawell International Airport (*horiz*) .... 6·00 11·00
a. Glazed, ordinary paper (15.3.71) .... 13·00 15·00
399/414 *Set of 16* .... 14·00 24·00
399a/414a *Set of 15* .... 55·00 48·00

Stamps in this set were re-issued between 1972 and 1974 with watermark *w* **12** sideways on 4c. to 10c.; upright on 12c. to $5.

105 Primary Schoolgirl

(Des V. Whiteley. Litho J.W.)

1970 (26 June). 25th Anniversary of United Nations. T **105** and similar horizontal designs. Multicoloured. W w **12**. P 14.
415 4c. Type **108** 10 10
416 5c. Secondary Schoolboy 10 10
417 25c. Technical Student 40 10
418 50c. University Buildings .... 55 1·50
415/418 *Set of 4* .... 1·00 1·60

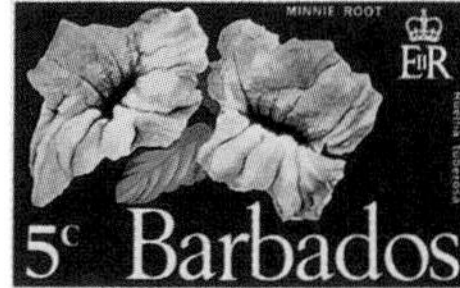

106 Minnie Root

(Des and litho J.W.)

1970 (24 Aug). Flowers of Barbados. T **106** and similar designs. Multicoloured. W w **12** (sideways on horiz designs). P 14½.
419 1c. Barbados Easter Lily (*vert*) .... 10 3·25
420 5c. Type **106** 30 10
421 10c. Eyelash Orchid .... 1·60 30
422 25c. Pride of Barbados (*vert*) .... 1·00 75
423 35c. Christmas Hope .... 1·00 85
419/423 *Set of 5* .... 3·50 4·75
MS424 162×101 mm. Nos. 419/423. Imperf .... 2·00 6·50

STAMP BOOKLETS

1906 (Feb).
SB1 2s.0½d. booklet containing 24×1d. (No. 137) in blocks of 6 ....

1909. Black on red cover. Stapled.
SB1*a* 1s.6d. booklet containing 18×1d. (No. 165) in blocks of 6 ....

1913 (June). Black on red cover. Stapled.
SB2 2s. booklet containing 12×½d. and 18×1d. (Nos. 171/172) in blocks of 6 .... £3000

1916 (16 June). Black on red cover. Stapled.
SB3 2s. booklet containing 12×½d. and 18×1d. (Nos. 182/183) in pairs £1000

1920 (Sept). Black on red cover. Stapled.
SB4 2s. booklet containing 12×½d. and 18×1d. (Nos. 202/203) in pairs £3000

1932 (12 Nov). Black on pale green cover. Austin Cars and Post Office Guide advertisements on front. Stapled.
SB5 2s. booklet containing ½d. and 1d. (Nos. 230a, 231a) each in block of 10 and 1½d. (No. 231da) in block of 6 .... £2250

1933 (4 Dec). Black on pale green cover. Advocate Co. Ltd. advertisement on front. Stapled.
SB6 2s. booklet containing ½d. and 1d. (Nos. 230/201) each in block of 10 and 1½d. (No. 231*d*) in block of 6 .... £2500

1938 (3 Jan). Black on light blue cover. Advocate Co. Ltd. advertisement on front. Stapled.
SB7 2s. booklet containing ½d. and 1d. (Nos. 248, 249a) each in block of 10 and 1½d. (No. 250) in block of 6 .... £2750

POSTAGE DUE STAMPS

D **1**

Missing top serif on 'c' (R. 2/4)

(Typo D.L.R.)

1934 (2 Jan)–**47**. Wmk Mult Script CA. P 14.
D1 D **1** ½d. green (10.2.35) .... 1·25 10·00
D2 1d. black .... 2·25 1·25
a. Bisected (½d.) (*on cover*) .... † £1800
D3 3d. carmine (11.3.47) .... 20·00 24·00
D1/D3 *Set of 3* .... 21·00 32·00
D1s/D3s Perf 'SPECIMEN' *Set of 3* £110

The bisected 1d. was officially authorised for use between March 1934 and February 1935. Some examples had the value '½d.' written across the half stamp in red or black ink (*Price on cover* £2250).

(Typo D.L.R.)

1950 (8 Dec)–**53**. Values in cents. Wmk Mult Script CA. Ordinary paper. P 14.

D4	D **1**	1c. green	5·50	45·00
		a. Chalk-surfaced paper. *Deep green* (29.11.51)	30	3·00
		ab. Error. Crown missing, W **9a**	£900	
		ac. Error. St Edward's Crown, W **9b**	£450	£650
D5		2c. black	7·50	20·00
		a. Chalk-surfaced paper (20.1.53)	1·00	6·50
		ac. Error. St Edward's Crown, W **9b**	£800	
D6		6c. carmine	23·00	23·00
		a. Chalk-surfaced paper (20.1.53)	1·00	8·50
		ab. Error. Crown missing, W **9a**	£325	
		ac. Error. St Edward's Crown, W **9b**	£180	
D4/D6 *Set of* 3			32·00	80·00
D4a/D6a *Set of* 3			2·10	16·00

The 1c. has no dot below 'c'.

1965 (3 Aug)–**68**. As Nos. D4/D6 but wmk w **12** (upright). Chalk-surfaced paper.

D7	D **1**	1c. deep green	30	4·00
		a. Missing top serif on 'C' (R. 2/4)	8·00	45·00
		b. *Green*	3·00	8·50
		c. Centre inverted	£26000	
D8		2c. black	30	5·00
D9		6c. carmine	50	7·00
		a. *Carmine-red* (14.5.68)	1·40	12·00
D7/D9 *Set of* 3			1·00	13·50

Barbuda (*see after* Antigua)

Basutoland

Stamps of CAPE OF GOOD HOPE were used in Basutoland from about 1876, initially cancelled by upright oval with framed number type postmarks of that colony. Cancellation numbers known to have been used in Basutoland are 133 (Quthing), 156 (Mafeteng), 210 (Mohaleshoek), 277 (Morija), 281 (Maseru), 317 (Thlotse Heights) and 688 (Teyateyaneng).

From 1910 until 1933 the stamps of SOUTH AFRICA were in use. Stamps of the Union provinces are also known used in Basutoland during the early years of this period and can also be found cancelled-to-order during 1932–1933.

The following post offices and postal agencies existed in Basutoland before December 1933. Stamps of Cape of Good Hope or South Africa with recognisable postmarks from them are worth a premium. For a few of the smaller offices or agencies there are, as yet, no actual examples recorded. Dates given are those generally accepted as the year in which the office was first opened.

Bokong (1931)
Butha Buthe (1907)
Jonathan's (1927)
Khabos (1927)
Khetisas (1930)
Khukhune (1933)
Kolonyama (1914)
Kueneng (1914)
Leribe (1890)
Mafeteng (1874)
Majara (1912)
Makhoa (1932)
Makoalis (1927)
Mamathes (1919)
Mapoteng (1925)
Marakabeis (1932)
Maseru (1872)
Maseru Rail (1915?)
Mashai (1929)
Matsaile (1930)
Mekading (1914)
Mofokas (1915)
Mohaleshoek (1873)
Mokhotlong (1921)
Morija (1884)
Motsekuoa (1915)
Mount Morosi (1918)
Mphotos (1914)
Peka (1908)
Phamong (1932)
Pitseng (1921)
Qachasnek (1895)
Qalo (1923?)
Quthing (1882)
Rankakalas (1933)
Roma Mission (1913)
Sebapala (1930)
Seforong (1924)
Sehlabathebe (1921)
Sekake (1931)
Teyateyaneng (1886)
Thaba Bosigo (1913)
Thabana Morena (1922)
Thabaneng (1914)
Thaba Tseka (1929)
Thlotse Heights (1872)
Tsepo (1923)
Tsoelike (1927)
Tsoloane (1918)

For further details of the postal history of Basutoland see *The Cancellations and Postal Markings of Basutoland/Lesotho* by A. H. Scott, published by Collectors Mail Auctions (Pty) Ltd, Cape Town, from which the above has been, with permission, extracted.

PRICES FOR STAMPS ON COVER TO 1945	
Nos. 1/19	*from* × 5
Nos. 11/14	*from* × 6
Nos. 15/17	*from* × 10
Nos. 18/28	*from* × 6
Nos. 29/31	*from* × 10
Nos. O1/O4	*from* × 4
Nos. D1/D2	*from* × 25

CROWN COLONY

1 King George V, Nile Crocodile and Mountains

(Recess Waterlow)

1933 (1 Dec). Wmk Mult Script CA. P 12½.

1	**1**	½d. emerald	1·25	1·75
2		1d. scarlet	1·50	1·25
3		2d. bright purple	1·50	80
4		3d. bright blue	1·50	1·25
5		4d. grey	3·50	8·00
6		6d. orange-yellow	2·25	1·75
7		1s. red-orange	4·25	4·50
8		2s.6d. sepia	45·00	55·00
9		5s. violet	80·00	95·00
10		10s. olive-green	£225	£250
1/10 *Set of* 10			£325	£375
1s/10s Perf 'SPECIMEN' *Set of* 10			£350	

1935 (4 May). Silver Jubilee. As Nos. 91/94 of Antigua. P 13½×14.

11	1d. deep blue and carmine	1·25	3·50
	f. Diagonal line by turret	£180	£275
	h. Dot by flagstaff	—	£700
12	2d. ultramarine and grey	1·25	3·75
	f. Diagonal line by turret	£180	£275
	g. Dot to left of chapel	£350	£450
	i. Dash by turret	£425	
13	3d. brown and deep blue	4·50	8·00
	g. Dot to left of chapel	£375	£450
	h. Dot by flagstaff	£450	£550
	i. Dash by turret	£550	
14	6d. slate and purple	4·50	8·00
	g. Dot to left of chapel	£650	
	h. Dot by flagstaff	£425	£475
	i. Dash by turret	£600	£700
11/14 *Set of* 4		10·50	21·00
11s/14s Perf 'SPECIMEN' *Set of* 4		£150	

For illustrations of plate varieties see Omnibus section following Zanzibar.

1937 (12 May). Coronation. As Nos. 95/97 of Antigua, but printed by D.L.R. P 14.

15	1d. scarlet	35	1·25
16	2d. bright purple	50	1·25
17	3d. bright blue	60	1·25
15/17 *Set of* 3		1·25	3·25
15s/17s Perf 'SPECIMEN' *Set of* 3		£130	

2 King George VI, Nile Crocodile and Mountains

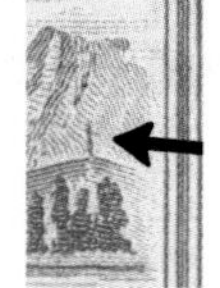
1d. Tower flaw (R. 2/4)

(Recess Waterlow)

1938 (1 Apr). Wmk Mult Script CA. P 12½.

18	**2**	½d. green	30	1·25
19		1d. scarlet	1·50	70
		a. Tower flaw	£170	£275
20		1½d. light blue	1·00	50
21		2d. bright purple	75	60
22		3d. bright blue	75	1·25
23		4d. grey	3·00	3·75
24		6d. orange-yellow	3·50	1·50
25		1s. red-orange	3·50	1·00
26		2s.6d. sepia	20·00	8·50
27		5s. violet	45·00	9·50
28		10s. olive-green	48·00	25·00
18/28 *Set of* 11			£110	48·00
18s/28s Perf 'SPECIMEN' *Set of* 11			£375	

Basutoland
(**3**)

1945 (3 Dec). Victory. Stamps of South Africa, optd with T **3**, inscr alternately in English and Afrikaans.

			Un pair	*Used pair*	*Used single*
29	**55**	1d. brown and carmine	50	80	10
		a. Barbed wire flaw	15·00		
30	**56**	2d. slate-blue and violet	50	60	10
31	**57**	3d. deep blue and blue	50	85	15
29/31 *Set of* 3			1·40	2·00	30

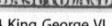

4 King George VI

5 King George VI and Queen Elizabeth

6 Queen Elizabeth II as Princess, and Princess Margaret

7 The Royal Family

(Recess Waterlow)

1947 (17 Feb). Royal Visit. Wmk Mult Script CA. P 12½.

32	**4**	1d. scarlet	10	10
33	**5**	2d. green	10	10
34	**6**	3d. ultramarine	10	10
35	**7**	1s. mauve	15	10
32/35 *Set of* 4			40	30
32s/35s Perf 'SPECIMEN' *Set of* 4			£140	

1948 (1 Dec). Royal Silver Wedding. As Nos. 112/113 of Antigua.

36	1½d. ultramarine	20	10
37	10s. grey-olive	50·00	50·00

1949 (10 Oct). 75th Anniversary of Universal Postal Union. As Nos. 114/117 of Antigua.

38	1½d. blue	20	1·50
39	3d. deep blue	2·00	2·00
40	6d. orange	1·00	5·50
41	1s. red-brown	50	1·40
38/41 *Set of* 4		3·25	9·50

1953 (3 June). Coronation. As No. 120 of Antigua.

42	2d. black and reddish purple	65	40

8 Qiloane

9 Orange River

10 Mosuto horseman

11 Basuto household

12 Maletsunyane Falls

13 Herd-boy playing lesiba

14 Pastoral scene

15 Aeroplane over Lancers Gap

16 Old Fort, Leribe

17 Mission Cave House

18 Mohair (Shearing Angora Goats)

(Recess D.L.R.)

1954 (18 Oct)–**58**. T **8/18** Wmk Mult Script CA. P 11½ (10s.) or 13½ (others).

No.	Type	Description	Unused	Used
43	**8**	½d. grey-black and sepia	65	10
44	**9**	1d. grey-black and bluish green	60	10
45	**10**	2d. deep bright blue and orange	1·25	10
46	**11**	3d. yellow-green and deep rose-red	2·25	30
		a. Yellow-green and rose (27.11.58)	17·00	2·50
47	**12**	4½d. indigo and deep ultramarine	1·50	15
48	**13**	6d. chestnut and deep grey-green	2·75	15
49	**14**	1s. bronze-green and purple	2·50	30
50	**15**	1s.3d. brown and turquoise-green	28·00	10·00
51	**16**	2s.6d. deep ultramarine and crimson	30·00	15·00
		a. Bright ultramarine and crimson-lake (27.11.58)	£110	27·00
52	**17**	5s. black and carmine-red	15·00	15·00
53	**18**	10s. black and maroon	40·00	32·00
43/53 *Set of* 11			£110	65·00

½d. ▬
(19)

1959 (1 Aug). No. 45 surch with T **19**, by South African Govt Ptr, Pretoria.

No.	Description	Unused	Used
54	½d. on 2d. deep bright blue and orange.	35	20

20 *Chief Moshoeshoe I* (engraving by Delangle)

21 Council house

22 Mosuto horseman

(Des from drawings by James Walton. Recess Waterlow)

1959 (15 Dec). Basutoland National Council. T **20/2**. W w **12**. P 13×13½.

No.	Description	Unused	Used
55	3d. black and yellow-olive	75	20
56	1s. carmine and yellow-green	75	90
57	1s.3d. ultramarine and red-orange	1·00	90
55/57 *Set of* 3		2·25	1·75

(New Currency. 100 cents = 1 rand)

½c. (23) 1c. (24) 2c (25)

2½c (I) 2½c (II) 3½c (I) 3½c (II)

5c (I) 5c (II) 10c (I) 10c (II)

12½c (I) 12½c (II) 50c (I) 50c (II)

25c (I) 25c (II) 25c (III)

R1 (I) R1 (II) R1 (III)

1961 (14 Feb). Nos. 43/53 surch with T **23** (½c.), **24** (1c.) or as T **25** (others) by South African Govt Printer, Pretoria.

No.	Description	Unused	Used
58	½c. on ½d. grey-black and sepia	10	30
	a. Surch double	£1250	
	b. Surch omitted		
59	1c. on 1d. grey-black and bluish green	30	10
60	2c. on 2d. deep bright blue and orange	1·50	2·25
	a. Surch inverted	£300	
61	2½c. on 3d. yellow-green and rose (Type I)	15	10
	a. Type II (central on vignette)	15	10
	ab. Type II (higher to left, fraction dropped)	30	15
	b. Type II inverted	†	£4750
62	3½c. on 4½d. indigo and deep ultramarine (Type I)	45	20
	a. Type II	5·50	13·00
63	5c. on 6d. chestnut and deep grey-green (Type I)	1·00	10
	a. Type II	50	10
64	10c. on 1s. bronze-green and purple (Type I)	50	10
	a. Type II	£225	£275
65	12½c. on 1s.3d. brown and turquoise-green (Type I)	18·00	7·00
	a. Type II	7·00	2·50
66	25c. on 2s.6d. bright ultramarine and crimson-lake (Type I)	2·25	1·00
	a. Type II	75·00	20·00
	b. Type III	3·00	3·75
67	50c. on 5s. black and carmine-red (Type I)	11·00	8·00
	a. Type II	6·00	8·00
68	1r. on 10s. black and maroon (Type I)	75·00	32·00
	a. Type II	38·00	75·00
	b. Type III	38·00	32·00
58/68b *Set of* 11 (*cheapest*)		50·00	42·00

Examples of the 2c. surcharge are known in a fount similar to T **24** (*Price £325 unused*).

No. 58b was caused by a paper fold affecting a single sheet.

All known examples of No. 61b are postmarked Mokhotlong on 2 or 3 July 1962.

26 Basuto Household

(Recess D.L.R.)

1961–63. As Nos. 43/53 but values in cents as in T **26**. Wmk Mult Script CA. P 13½ or 11½ (1r.).

No.	Description	Unused	Used
69	½c. grey-black and sepia (as ½d.) (25.9.62)	50	20
	a. Imperf (pair)	£425	
70	1c. grey-black and bluish green (as 1d.) (25.9.62)	1·50	40
71	2c. deep bright blue and orange (as 2d.) (25.9.62)	3·00	2·25
72	2½c. yellow-green and deep rose-red (14.2.61)	2·00	1·00
	a. Pale yellow-green and rose-red (22.5.62)	20·00	2·00
73	3½c. indigo and deep ultramarine (as 4½d.) (25.9.62)	1·00	2·25
74	5c. chestnut and deep grey-green (as 6d.) (10.8.62)	70	75
75	10c. bronze-green and purple (as 1s.) (22.10.62)	50	40
76	12½c. brown and turquoise-green (as 1s.3d.) (17.12.62)	27·00	16·00
77	25c. deep ultramarine and crimson (as 2s.6d.) (25.9.62)	6·50	6·50
78	50c. black and carmine-red (as 5s.) (22.10.62)	23·00	29·00
79	1r. black and maroon (as 10s.) (4.2.63)	55·00	32·00
	a. Black and light maroon (16.12.63)	90·00	50·00
69/79 *Set of* 11		£100	80·00

1963 (4 June). Freedom from Hunger. As No. 146 of Antigua.

No.	Description	Unused	Used
80	12½c. reddish violet	40	15

1963 (2 Sept). Red Cross Centenary. As Nos. 147/148 of Antigua.

No.	Description	Unused	Used
81	2½c. red and black	30	10
82	12½c. red and blue	80	90

1964 (10 Mar–10 Nov). As Nos. 70, 72, 74, 76 and 78, but W w **12**.

No.	Description	Unused	Used
84	1c. grey-black and bluish green (11.8.64)	10	20
86	2½c. pale yellow-green and rose-red (10.3.64)	25	25
88	5c. chestnut and deep grey-green (10.11.64)	60	65
90	12½c. brown and turquoise-green (10.11.64)	17·00	3·75
92	50c. black and carmine-red (29.9.64)	7·25	19·00
84/92 *Set of* 5		23·00	21·00

SELF-GOVERNMENT

28 Mosotho Woman and Child

29 Maseru Border Post

1965 (10 May). New Constitution. T **28/29** and similar horizontal designs. Multicoloured. W w **12**. P 14×13½.

No.	Description	Unused	Used
94	2½c. Type **28**	50	10
	w. Wmk inverted	£100	50·00
95	3½c. Type **29**	90	70
96	5c. Mountain scene	90	70
	w. Wmk inverted	30·00	22·00
97	12½c. Legislative Buildings	90	1·25
94/97 *Set of* 4		2·75	2·50

1965 (17 May). ITU Centenary. As Nos. 166/167 of Antigua.

No.	Description	Unused	Used
98	1c. orange-red and bright purple	15	10
99	20c. light blue and orange-brown	50	30

1965 (25 Oct). International Co-operation Year. As Nos. 168/169 of Antigua.

No.	Description	Unused	Used
100	½c. reddish purple and turquoise-green	10	2·00
101	12½c. deep bluish green and lavender	45	35

1966 (24 Jan). Churchill Commemoration. Printed in black, cerise, gold and background in colours stated. As Nos. 170/173 of Antigua.

No.	Description	Unused	Used
102	1c. new blue	15	2·25
103	2½c. deep green	75	10
104	10c. brown	1·10	60
105	22½c. bluish violet	1·75	2·00
102/105 *Set of* 4		3·25	4·50

OFFICIAL STAMPS

OFFICIAL
(O **1**)

1934 (Feb). Nos. 1/3 and 6 optd with T O **1**, by Govt printer, Pretoria.

No.	Type	Description	Unused	Used
O1	**1**	½d. emerald	£16000	£8000
O2		1d. scarlet	£6000	£4000
O3		2d. bright purple	£6500	£1400
O4		6d. orange-yellow	£16000	£5000
O1/O4 *Set of* 4			£40000	£17000

Collectors are advised to buy these stamps only from reliable sources. They were not sold to the public.

300 of each value were supplied in January 1934 for use by the Secretariat in Maseru. Limited usage is recorded between 28 Feb 1934 and 8 June 1934. The issue was then withdrawn and the remainders destroyed. Only the following numbers appear to have been issued: ½d. 24, 1d. 34, 2d. 54, 6d. 27, from which a maximum of ten mint sets exist.

POSTAGE DUE STAMPS

D **1**

2d Normal

2d Large 'd.' (R. 9/6, 10/6)

2d. Serif on 'd' (R. 1/6)

(Typo D.L.R.)

1933 (1 Dec)–**52**. Ordinary paper. Wmk Mult Script CA. P 14.

No.	Type	Description	Unused	Used
D1	D **1**	1d. carmine	4·25	17·00
		a. Scarlet (1938)	50·00	60·00
		b. Chalk-surfaced paper. Deep carmine (24.10.51)	2·25	11·00
		ba. Error. Crown missing, W **9a**	£425	
		bb. Error. St Edward's Crown, W **9b**	£170	
D2		2d. violet	12·00	25·00
		aa. Large 'd'	70·00	
		a. Chalk-surfaced paper (6.11.52)	30	25·00
		ab. Error. Crown missing, W **9a**	£450	
		ac. Error. St Edward's Crown, W **9b**	£180	
		ad. Large 'd'	8·50	£120
		ae. Serif on 'd'	12·00	
D1s/D2s Perf 'SPECIMEN' *Set of* 2			75·00	

D 2

(Typo D.L.R.)

1956 (1 Dec). Wmk Mult Script CA. P 14.

D3 **D 2** 1d. carmine ... 30 3·00
D4 2d. deep reddish violet ... 30 6·00

5c (I) 5c (II)

1961 (14 Feb). Surch as T **24**, but without stop.

D5 **D 2** 1c. on 1d. carmine ... 10 35
D6 1c. on 2d. deep reddish violet ... 10 1·25
D7 5c. on 2d. deep reddish violet (Type I) ... 15 45
a. Type II ... 16·00 60·00
D5/D7 *Set of 3* ... 30 1·90

1961 (1 June). No. D2a surch as T **24** (without stop).

D8 **D 1** 5c. on 2d. violet ... 1·00 7·50
a. Error. Missing Crown, W **9a** ... £2000
b. Error. St Edward's Crown, W **9b** ... £375
c. Large 'd' ... 22·00

1964. As No. D3/D4 but values in cents and W w **12** (sideways on 1c.).

D9 **D 2** 1c. carmine ... 4·75 26·00
D10 5c. deep reddish violet ... 5·50 26·00

POSTAL FISCAL

In July 1961 the 10s. stamp, T **9**, surcharged 'R1 Revenue', was used for postage at one post office at least, but such usage was officially unauthorised.

Basutoland attained independence on 4 October 1966 as the Kingdom of Lesotho.

Batum

Batum, the outlet port on the Black Sea for the Russian Transcaucasian oilfields, was occupied by the Turks on 15 April 1918.

Under the terms of the armistice signed at Mudros on 30 October 1918 the Turks were to withdraw and be replaced by an Allied occupation of Batum, the Baku oilfields and the connecting Transcaucasia Railway. British forces arrived off Batum in early December and the oblast, or district, was declared a British military governorship on 25 December 1918. The Turkish withdrawal was complete five days later.

The provision of a civilian postal service was initially the responsibility of the Batum Town Council. Some form of mail service was in operation by February 1919 with the postage prepaid in cash. Letters are known showing a framed oblong handstamp, in Russian, to this effect. The Town Council was responsible for the production of the first issue, Nos. 1/6, but shortly after these stamps were placed on sale a strike by Council employees against the British military governor led to the postal service being placed under British Army control.

SURCHARGES. Types **2** and **4/8** were all applied by handstamp. Most values from No. 19 to 40 are known showing the surcharge inverted, surcharge double or in pairs with surcharge *tête-bêche*. Inverted surcharges are worth from 2×normal, *tête-bêche* pairs from four times the price of a single stamp.

FORGERIES. Collectors are warned that all the stamps, overprints and surcharges of Batum have been extensively forged. Even the T **1** stamps should be purchased with caution, and rarities should not be acquired without a reliable guarantee.

BRITISH OCCUPATION

(Currency. 100 kopeks = 1 rouble)

PRICES FOR STAMPS ON COVER TO 1945	
Nos. 1/6	*from* × 50
Nos. 7/10	*from* × 15
Nos. 11/18	*from* × 50
Nos. 19/20	*from* × 15
Nos. 21/44	—
Nos. 45/53	*from* × 75

1 Aloe Tree

БАТУМ. ОБ.

Руб 10 Руб.

(**2**)

1919 (4 Apr). Litho. Imperf.

1 **1** 5k. green ... 7·50 27·00
2 10k. ultramarine ... 9·50 27·00
3 50k. yellow ... 9·00 15·00
4 1r. chocolate ... 13·00 9·50
5 3r. violet ... 11·00 20·00
6 5r. brown ... 10·00 45·00
1/6 *Set of 6* ... 55·00 £130

Nos. 1/6 were printed in sheets of 198 (18×11).

1919 (13 Apr). Russian stamps (Arms types) handstamped with T **2**.

7 10r. on 1k. orange (imperf) ... 80·00 90·00
8 10r. on 3k. carmine-red (imperf) ... 35·00 42·00
9 10r. on 5k. brown-lilac (perf) ... £500 £600
10 10r. on 10 on 7k. deep blue (perf) ... £750 £750

A similar handstamped surcharge, showing the capital letters without serifs, is bogus.

BRITISH
OCCUPATION

(**3**)

1919 (10 Nov). Colours changed and new values. Optd with T **3**.

11 **1** 5k. yellow-green ... 32·00 18·00
12 10k. bright blue ... 16·00 23·00
13 25k. orange-yellow ... 32·00 26·00
14 1r. pale blue ... 9·50 24·00
15 2r. pink ... 1·00 8·50
16 3r. bright violet ... 1·00 10·00
17 5r. brown ... 1·25 10·00
a. 'CCUPATION' (R. 5/1) ... £400
18 7r. brownish red ... 7·00 14·00
11/18 *Set of 8* ... 90·00 £120

Nos. 11/18 were printed in sheets of 432 (18×24).

(**4**)

БАТУМЪ
BRITISH
Р.15 Р.
OCCUPATION
ОБЛ.

(**5**)

1919 (27 Nov)–**20**. Russian stamps (Arms types) handstamped with T **4** or **5**. Imperf.

19 10r. on 3k. carmine-red ... 30·00 32·00
20 15r. on 1k. orange ... £110 £130
a. Red surch ... 90·00 £110
b. Violet surch (10.3.20) ... £130 £160

Nos. 20a/20b have the handstamp in soluble ink.

1920 (12 Jan). Russian stamps (Arms types) handstamped as T **4**.

(a) Imperf

21 50r. on 1k. orange ... £650 £850
22 50r. on 2k. yellow-green (R.) ... £900 £1200

(b) Perf

23 50r. on 2k. yellow-green ... £900 £1200
24 50r. on 3k. carmine-red ... £1500 £1600
25 50r. on 4k. red ... £1000 £1100
26 50r. on 5k. brown-lilac ... £450 £600
27 50r. on 10k. deep blue (R.) ... £3500 £3250
28 50r. on 15k. blue and red-brown ... £900 £1200

(**6**)

1920 (30 Jan–21 Feb). Russian stamps (Arms types) handstamped as T **6**.

(a) Perf

29 25r. on 5k. brown-lilac (21.2) ... 55·00 75·00
a. Blue surch ... 55·00 70·00
30 25r. on 10 on 7k. blue (21.2) ... £150 £160
a. Blue surch ... 90·00 £110
31 25r. on 20 on 14k. deep carmine and blue (21.2) ... £100 £130
a. Blue surch ... £100 £130
32 25r. on 25k. deep violet and light green (21.2) ... £180 £200
a. Blue surch ... £120 £150
33 25r. on 50k. green and copper-red (21.2) ... £130 £140
a. Blue surch ... 95·00 £130
34 50r. on 2k. yellow-green ... £140 £190
35 50r. on 3k. carmine-red ... £140 £190
36 50r. on 4k. red ... £130 £160
37 50r. on 5k. brown-lilac ... £100 £140

(b) Imperf

38 50r. on 2k. yellow-green ... £450 £500
39 50r. on 3k. carmine-red ... £550 £650
40 50r. on 5k. brown-lilac ... £1800 £1900

1920 (10 Mar). Romanov issue, as T **25** of Russia, handstamped with T **6**.

41 50r. on 4k. rose-carmine (B.) ... £150 £180

руб 25 лей

25 руб. 25

(**7**)

R.50R.
BRITISH
OCCUPATION
РУБ.

(**8**)

1920 (1 Apr). Nos. 3, 11 and 13 handstamped with T **7** (Nos. 42/43) or **8** (No. 44).

42 25r. on 5k. yellow-green ... 55·00 75·00
a. Blue surch ... 75·00 £100
43 25r. on 25k. orange-yellow ... 42·00 45·00
a. Blue surch ... £170 £200
44 50r. on 50k. yellow ... 35·00 42·00
a. '50' cut ... 23·00 26·00
b. Blue surch ... £120 £150
ba. '50' cut ... £300 £350

Nos. 44a and 44ba show the figures broken by intentional file cuts applied as a protection against forgery. The '5' is cut at the base and on the right side of the loop. The '0' is chipped at top and foot, and has both vertical lines severed.

1920 (19 June). Colours changed and new values. Optd with T **3**. Imperf.

45 **1** 1r. chestnut ... 2·25 18·00
a. 'BPITISH' ... 90·00
46 2r. pale blue ... 2·25 18·00
a. 'BPITISH' ... £110
47 3r. pink ... 2·25 18·00
a. 'BPITISH' ... £110
48 5r. black-brown ... 2·25 18·00
a. 'BPITISH' ... £110
49 7r. yellow ... 2·25 18·00
a. 'BPITISH' ... £110
50 10r. myrtle-green ... 2·25 18·00
a. 'BPITISH' ... £110
51 15r. violet ... 2·75 23·00
a. 'BPITISH' ... £250
52 25r. scarlet ... 2·50 22·00
a. 'BPITISH' ... £190
53 50r. deep blue ... 2·75 25·00
a. 'BPITISH' ... £450
45/53 *Set of 9* ... 19·00 £160

Nos. 45/53 were printed in sheets of 308 (22×14). The 'BPITISH' error occurs on R. 1/19 of the overprint.

POSTCARD STAMPS

When Nos. 7/10 were issued on 13 April 1919 a similar 35k. surcharge was applied to stocks of various Russian postcards held by the post office. The majority of these had stamp impressions printed directly on to the card, but there were also a few cards, originally intended for overseas mail, on which Russia 4k. stamps had been affixed.

PRICES. Those in the left-hand column are for unused examples on complete postcard; those on the right for used examples off card. Examples used on postcard are worth more.

1919 (13 Apr). Russian stamps handstamped as T **2**.

P1 35k. on 4k. red (Arms type) ... £10000 £10000
P2 35k. on 4k. carmine-red (Romanov issue) £18000 £18000

Batum was handed over to the National Republic of Georgia on 7 July 1920.

Bechuanaland

Before the 1880s the only Europeans in the area which became Bechuanaland were scattered hunters and traders, together with the missionaries who were established at Kuruman as early as 1816.

Tribal conflicts in the early years of the decade led to the intervention of Boers from the Transvaal who established the independent republics of Goshen and Stellaland.

STELLALAND

The Boer republic of Stellaland was proclaimed towards the end of 1882. A postal service was organised from the capital, Vryburg, and stamps were ordered from a firm in Cape Town. These were only valid within the republic. Until June 1885 mail to other parts of South Africa was sent through Christiana, in the Transvaal, and was franked with both Stellaland and Transvaal stamps.

No date stamps or obliterators were used by the Stellaland Post Office. Stamps were initially pen-cancelled with the date only and from August 1884 to May 1885 by the date and the postmaster's initials. After May 1885 they were generally cancelled by a pen stroke or cross or left uncancelled. Postmarks found on Stellaland stamps were applied in transit; those known being '3' (Rustenburg), '6' (Christiana) and '8' (Zeerust) of Transvaal, '27' (Hoopstad, Orange Free State) or '232' (Barkly West, Cape Colony).

PRICES FOR STAMPS ON COVER TO 1945

The issues of Stellaland are very rare on cover.

1 Arms of the Republic

(Litho by Van der Sandt, de Villiers & Co., Cape Town)

1884 (29 Feb). P 12.

1	1	1d. red	£225	£325
		a. Imperf between (horiz pair)	£4500	
		b. Imperf between (vert pair)	£5000	
2		3d. orange	38·00	£375
		a. Imperf between (horiz pair)	£1000	
		b. Imperf between (vert pair)	£2250	
		c. Imperf vert (horiz pair)	£1400	
3		4d. olive-grey	32·00	£400
		a. Imperf between (horiz pair)	£800	
		b. Imperf between (vert pair)	£2500	
4		6d. lilac-mauve	38·00	£400
		a. Imperf between (horiz pair)	£1700	
		b. Imperf between (vert pair)	£1900	
5		1s. green	90·00	£800
		a. Imperf between (vert pair)		

In 1884 the British Government, following appeals from local chiefs for protection, decided to annex both Goshen and Stellaland. A force under Sir Charles Warren from the Cape reached Vryburg on 7 February 1885 and continued to Mafeking, the principal town of Goshen.

On 30 September 1885 Stellaland and other territory to the south of the Molopo River was constituted the Crown Colony of British Bechuanaland. A protectorate was also proclaimed over a vast tract of land to the north of the Molopo.

Stellaland stamps continued to be used until 2 December 1885 with external mail, franked with Stellaland and Cape of Good Hope stamps, postmarked at Barkly West and Kimberley in Griqualand West.

1885 (Oct). Handstamped "Twee" sideways in violet-lake.

6	1	2d. on 4d. olive-grey	£3500

On 2 December 1885 Cape of Good Hope stamps overprinted 'British Bechuanaland' were placed on sale at the Vryburg post office.

BRITISH BECHUANALAND

CROWN COLONY

PRICES FOR STAMPS ON COVER TO 1945

Nos. 1/8	*from* × 12
No. 9	*from* × 80
Nos. 10/21	*from* × 8
Nos. 22/28	*from* × 10
No. 29	*from* × 10
No. 30	*from* × 10
Nos. 31/32	*from* × 12
Nos. 33/37	*from* × 20
Nos. 38/39	*from* × 25

BRITISH

British

Bechuanaland (1)

BECHUANALAND (2)

1885 (2 Dec)–**87**. Stamps of Cape of Good Hope ('Hope' seated) optd with T **1**, by W. A. Richards & Sons, Cape Town.

(a) Wmk Crown CC (No. 3) or Crown CA (others)

1	½d. grey-black (No. 40*a*) (R.)	35·00	45·00
	a. Opt in lake	£5000	£5500
	b. Opt double (Lake+Black)	£750	
2	3d. pale claret (No. 43)	60·00	70·00
	a. No dot to 1st 'i' of 'British'	£800	
3	4d. dull blue (No. 30) (2.6.87)	95·00	85·00

(b) Wmk Anchor (Cape of Good Hope. T **13***)*

4	½d. grey-black (No. 48*a*) (24.12.86)	17·00	30·00
	a. Error. 'ritish'	£2750	
	b. Opt double	£3500	
	w. Wmk inverted		
5	1d. rose-red (No. 49)	27·00	9·00
	a. Error. 'ritish'	£4250	£2250
	b. No dot to 1st 'i' of 'British'	£475	£300
	c. Opt double	†	£2250
6	2d. pale bistre (No. 50)	55·00	8·00
	a. Error. 'ritish'	£8000	£4000
	b. No dot to 1st 'i' of 'British'	£850	£275
	c. Opt double	†	£2250
	w. Wmk inverted	†	£800
7	6d. reddish purple (No. 52)	£200	38·00
	a. No dot to 1st 'i' of 'British'	£2250	£750
8	1s. green (No. 53) (26.11.86)	£375	£190
	a. Error. 'ritish'	£24000	£15000

Nos. 1/8 were overprinted from settings of 120. The missing 'B' errors are believed to have occurred on one position for one of these settings only. The 'No dot to 1st 'i'' variety occurs on R. 10/3 of the left pane.

Overprints with stop after 'Bechuanaland' are forged, as are overprints on the 1s. Wmk Crown CC and the 5s. Cape of Good Hope stamps.

1888 (19 Jan). No. 197 of Great Britain optd with T **2**, by D.L.R.

9	½d. vermilion	2·75	1·50
	a. Opt double	£2500	
	s. Handstamped 'SPECIMEN'	85·00	

3

4

5

(Typo D.L.R.)

1888 (19 Jan).

(a) Wmk Orb (Great Britain T **48***). P 14*

10	3	1d. lilac and black	28·00	4·75
11		2d. lilac and black	£120	2·25
		a. Pale dull lilac and black	£120	25·00
12		3d. lilac and black	8·50	8·50
		a. Pale reddish lilac and black	80·00	25·00
13		4d. lilac and black	65·00	2·50
14		6d. lilac and black	80·00	2·50

(b) Wmk Script 'V R' (sideways, reading up). P 13½

15	4	1s. green and black	30·00	13·00
16		2s. green and black	70·00	60·00
17		2s.6d. green and black	80·00	80·00
18		5s. green and black	£130	£170
19		10s. green and black	£275	£400

(c) Two Orbs (sideways). P 14×13½

20	5	£1 lilac and black (f.c. £50)	£900	£800
21		£5 lilac and black (f.c. £200)	£4000	£1700
10s/21s		H/S 'SPECIMEN' *Set of* 12	£1000	

Nos. 10/21 were produced by overprinting a series of 'Unappropriated Die' designs originally produced by the Board of Inland Revenue for use as Great Britain fiscal stamps.

Several values are known on blued paper. No. 11*a* is the first printing of the 2d. (on safety paper?) and has a faded appearance.

When purchasing Nos. 20/21 in used condition beware of copies with fiscal cancellations cleaned off and bearing forged postmarks.

For No. 15 surcharged '£5' see No. F2.

1d. (6) 1s. (7) 2d. Curved foot to '2'

1888 (Sept–20 Nov). Nos. 10/11 and 13/15 surch as T **6** or **7**, by P. Townshend & Co., Vryburg.

22	3	1d. on 1d. lilac and black	8·00	8·00
23		2d. on 2d. lilac and black (R.)	65·00	4·00
		a. Pale dull lilac and black (No. 11*a*)	£150	65·00
		b. Curved foot to '2'	£350	£150
		c. Surch in green	†	£4000
25		4d. on 4d. lilac and black (R.) (20.11)	£425	£750
26		6d. on 6d. lilac and black	£150	12·00
		a. Surch in blue	†	£13000
28	4	1s. on 1s. green and black	£250	90·00

Nos. 23c and 26a are from two sheets of surcharge trials subsequently put into stock and used at Vryburg (2d.) or Mafeking (6d.) during 1888–1889.

It should be noted that, in addition to its curved foot, the '2' on No. 23b is distinctly shorter than the 'd'.

A single example of No. 23c with the 'curved foot to '2'' variety has been recorded (*Price, £18,000, used*).

One Half-Penny

(8)

1888 (8 Dec). No. 12*a* surch with T **8**, by P. Townshend & Co, Vryburg.

29	3	½d. on 3d. pale reddish lilac and black	£275	£325
		a. Broken 'f' in 'Half'	£17000	£12000

No. 29 was produced from a setting of 60 (12×5).

No. 29a shows the letter 'f' almost completely missing and occurs on R. 5/11 of the setting. Five unused examples are known, one being in the Royal Collection. A single used example is also known.

Errors of spelling on this surcharge are bogus. The normal surcharge has also been extensively forged.

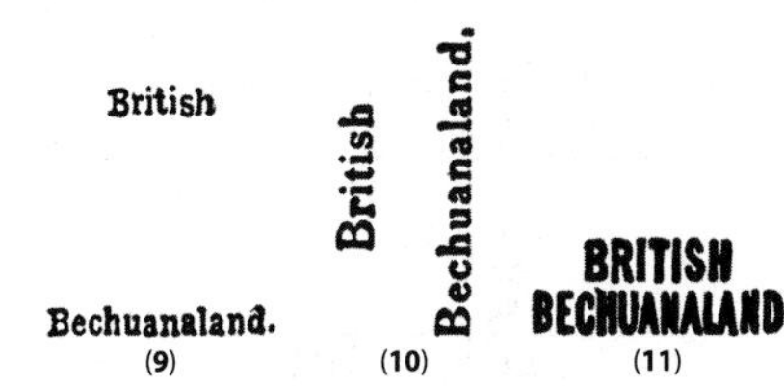

(9) (10) (11)

1888 (27 Dec). No. 48*a* of Cape of Good Hope (wmk Anchor) optd with T **9**, by P. Townshend & Co, Vryburg.

30	½d. grey-black (G.)	3·25	35·00
	a. Opt 'Bechuanaland British'	£3000	
	ab. 'British' omitted	£7000	
	b. Opt double, one inverted, inverted opt 'Bechuanaland British'	£3000	
	ba. Opt double, one inverted, inverted 'British' omitted	£7500	
	c. Opt double, one vertical	£850	
	ca. *Se-tenant* with stamp without opt	£10000	

No. 30 was produced using a setting of 30 (6×5).

The overprint was misplaced upwards on at least one pane, giving the overprint 'Bechuanaland British' (No. 30a) on rows 1 to 4 and 'British' omitted on row 5 (No. 30ab). 'British' was also omitted on R. 5/1 of the setting on some sheets only.

On one pane on which the overprint was applied double, one inverted, the inverted overprint was misplaced downwards, giving No. 30b on rows 7 to 10 and 'British' omitted (No. 30ba) on row 6.

n n

Normal 'n' Inverted 'u'

1891 (Nov). Nos. 49*a*/50 of Cape of Good Hope (wmk Anchor), optd with T **10**, reading upwards.

31	1d. carmine-red	13·00	21·00
	a. Horiz pair, one without opt	£26000	
	b. Optd 'Bechuanaland. British'		
	c. 'Bechuanaland' omitted	£3500	
	d. Inverted 'u' for 2nd 'n'	£225	£275
32	2d. bistre (*shades*)	8·50	2·25
	a. No stop after 'Bechuanaland'	£350	£350
	b. Inverted 'u' for 2nd 'n'	£300	£300
31s/32s	H/S 'SPECIMEN' *Set of* 2	£130	

The overprint on Nos. 31 and 32 was of 120 impressions in two panes of 60 (6×10). That on No. 32 was applied both by a stereo plate and by a forme made up from loose type. No. 31 was overprinted only with the latter. No. 32a is from the stereo overprinting (left pane, R. 3/3), 31d and 32b are from the typeset overprinting (left pane, R. 10/4).

A single example of No. 31 with 'British' omitted is known; it is in the Royal Philatelic Collection.

See also Nos. 38 and 39.

1891 (1 Dec)–**1904**. Nos. 172, 200, 205, 208 and 211 of Great Britain optd with T **11**, by D.L.R.

33	1d. lilac	7·00	1·50
34	2d. grey-green and carmine	25·00	4·00
35	4d. green and purple-brown	4·50	1·00
	a. Bisected (2d.) (*on cover*) (11.99)	†	£2500
36	6d. purple/*rose-red*	9·50	2·25
37	1s. dull green (7.94)	13·00	20·00
	a. Bisected (6d.) (*on cover*) (12.04)	†	—
33/37	*Set of* 5	55·00	26·00
33s/36s	H/S 'SPECIMEN' *Set of* 4	£170	

No. 35a was used at Palapye Station and No. 37a at Kanye, both in the Protectorate.

1893 (Dec)–**95**. As Nos. 31/32, but T **10** reads downwards.

38	1d. carmine-red	4·75	2·25
	b. 'British' omitted	£4250	£4250
	c. Optd 'Bechuanaland. British'	£1500	£1600
	d. Inverted 'u' for 2nd 'n'	£160	£160
	e. No dots to 'i' of 'British'	£160	£160
	f. 's' omitted	£700	£700
	g. Opt reading up, no dots to 'i' of 'British'	£4500	
39	2d. bistre (12.3.95)	16·00	4·00
	a. Opt double	£1400	£700
	b. 'British' omitted	£850	£500
	c. 'Bechuanaland' omitted	—	£700
	d. Optd 'Bechuanaland. British'	£500	£300
	e. Inverted 'u' for 2nd 'n'	£275	£170
	f. No dots to 'i' of 'British'	£275	£170
	g. Opt reading up, no dots to 'i' of 'British'	£4750	

The same typeset overprint was used for Nos. 38 and 39 as had been employed for Nos. 31 and 32 but applied the other way up; the inverted 'u' thus falling on the right pane, R. 1/3. The no dots to 'i' variety only occurs on this printing (right pane, R. 1/4). Some sheets of both values were overprinted the wrong way up, resulting in Nos. 38g. and 39g.

No. 38f. developed gradually on right pane R. 10/8. The variety is not known on Nos. 31, 32 or 39.

On 16 November 1895 British Bechuanaland was annexed to the Cape of Good Hope and ceased to have its own stamps, but they remained in use in the Protectorate until superseded in 1897. The Postmaster-General of Cape Colony had assumed control of the Bechuanaland postal service on 1 April 1893 and the Cape, and subsequently the South African, postal authorities continued to be responsible for the postal affairs of the Bechuanaland Protectorate until 1963.

BECHUANALAND PROTECTORATE

PRICES FOR STAMPS ON COVER TO 1945	
Nos. 40/51	*from* × 10
Nos. 52/71	*from* × 6
Nos. 72/82	*from* × 5
Nos. 83/98	*from* × 4
Nos. 99/110	*from* × 6
Nos. 111/117	*from* × 10
Nos. 118/128	*from* × 4
Nos. 129/131	*from* × 10
Nos. D1/D3	*from* × 50
Nos. D4/D6	*from* × 60
No. F1	*from* × 5
No. F2	—
No. F3	*from* × 5

This large area north of the Molopo River was proclaimed a British Protectorate on 30 September 1885 at the request of the native chiefs.

A postal service using runners was inaugurated on 9 August 1888 and Nos. 40 to 55 were issued as a temporary measure with the object of assessing the cost of this service.

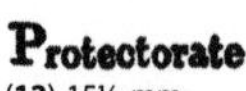
(**12**) 15½ mm

Protectorate 1d
(**13**)

13a Small figure '1' (R. 7/2)

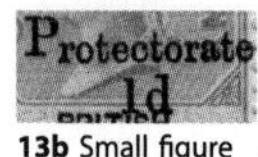
13b Small figure '1' (R. 10/2)

2 — Normal '2'

2 — Curved foot to '2' (42b)

1888 (Aug). No. 9 optd with T **12** and Nos. 10/19 surch or optd only as T **13** by P. Townshend & Co. Vryburg.

40	–	½d. vermilion	13·00	55·00
		a. 'Protectorate' double	£350	
		s. Handstamped 'SPECIMEN'	90·00	
41	3	1d. on 1d. lilac and black	20·00	16·00
		a. Small figure '1' (R. 7/2, 10/2)	£425	£500
		b. Space between '1' and 'd' (R. 10/9)	£650	
42		2d. on 2d. lilac and black	50·00	18·00
		b. Curved foot to '2'	£950	£550
43		3d. on 3d. pale reddish lilac and black	£200	£275
44		4d. on 4d. lilac and black	£475	£500
		a. Small figure '4' (R. 7/12)	£6000	£6000
45		6d. on 6d. lilac and black	£120	55·00
46	4	1s. green and black	£140	60·00
		a. First 'o' omitted	£6500	£3750
		s. Handstamped 'SPECIMEN'	£130	
47		2s. green and black	£750	£1200
		a. First 'o' omitted	£18000	
48		2s.6d. green and black	£600	£950
		a. First 'o' omitted	£20000	
49		5s. green and black	£1300	£2250
		a. First 'o' omitted	£25000	
50		10s. green and black	£5000	£7500

Nos. 40/45 were produced from a basic setting of 120 (12×10) on which a faulty first 'o' in 'Protectorate' occurred on R. 5/12. For Nos. 46/50 the setting was reduced to 84 (12×7) and on many sheets the first 'o' on R. 5/12 failed to print.

There were two distinct printings made of No. 40, the first in 1888 and the second in 1889. The overprint setting used for the first printing was broken up and had to be remade for the second. The first printing used a matt ink which produces a cleaner impression than the second, which is printed with a black glossy ink giving a distinctly muddy appearance.

There are a number of smaller than normal '1's in the setting, usually identifiable by the upper serif of the '1' which is pointed and slopes sharply downwards at the left. R. 7/2 and 10/2 are quite distinct and are as shown.

The normal space between '1' and 'd' measures 1 mm. On No. 41b it is 1.7 mm.

It should be noted that, like No. 23b, the '2' on No. 42b is distinctly shorter than the 'd' and has a distinctive curl to the upper part of the '2', not present on No. 23.

The height of the '4' on No. 44a is 2.15 mm, as opposed to 2.4-2.5 mm for the normal surcharge. Other identifying features of the genuine variety are the '4' positioned below the first 't' of 'Protectorate' and the top of the second 't' being missing.

A single example of No. 50 with the first 'o' omitted is known; it is in the Royal Philatelic Collection.

Nos. 40/50 were first placed on sale in Vryburg on 23 June 1888. The August issue date refers to the start of the Runner Post.

See also Nos. 54/55.

1888 (10 Dec). No. 25 optd with T **12** by P. Townshend & Co., Vryburg.

51	3	4d. on 4d. lilac and black	£150	60·00
		a. Opt (T **12**) double	†	£2750

Bechuanaland

Protectorate

Protectorate — (**14**)

Fourpence — (**15**)

1888 (27 Dec). No. 48*a* of Cape of Good Hope (wmk Anchor), optd with T **14** by P. Townshend & Co., Vryburg.

52	½d. grey-black (G.)	6·50	55·00
	a. Opt double	£500	£750
	ab. Ditto, one reading 'Protectorate Bechuanaland'	£1200	
	ac. Ditto, one reading 'Bechuanaland' only	£2500	
	b. 'Bechuanaland' omitted	£2000	
	c. Optd 'Protectorate Bechuanaland'	£1100	£1100

1889 (Mar). No. 9 surch with T **15** by P. Townshend & Co., Vryburg.

53	4d. on ½d. vermilion	50·00	6·00
	a. 'rpence' omitted (R. 9/2)	†	£6000
	b. 'ourpence' omitted (R. 9/2)	£10000	
	c. Surch (T **15**) inverted	†	£4000
	cb. Ditto. 'ourpence' omitted	†	£17000
	s. Handstamped 'SPECIMEN'	£150	

The lines of the surcharge are normally 6 mm apart, but 5 mm and 4.5 mm spacings are known.

Examples of No. 53c are postmarked '679' (Tati).

The surcharge is known printed in green, due to faulty cleaning of the inking roller. All examples known were cancelled at Shoshong. (*Price £1500 used*).

Protectorate — (**16**) 15 mm

Protectorate — (**17**) 19 mm

1890. No. 9 optd.

54	16	½d. vermilion	£225	£250
		a. Type **16** inverted	85·00	£120
		b. Type **16** double	£130	£180
		c. Type **16** double and inverted	£750	£850
		d. Optd 'Portectorate' inverted	£20000	
		w. Wmk inverted		
55	17	½d. vermilion	£275	£450
		a. Type **17** double	£1600	£1700
		b. Optd 'Protectorrte'		
		c. Optd 'Protectorrte' double	£20000	

These were trial printings made in June 1888 (No. 55) and subsequently (No. 54) which were later issued.

The 15 mm measurement of the overprint on No. 54 should not be relied on as a sole diagnostic, since the overprint on a few positions within the setting of No. 40 similarly measure 15 mm. No. 54 is a cleaner, more even overprint and the out of line letters so frquently encountered on No. 40, especially the raised 'P' of 'Protectorate' and its consequent greater separation from the first 'r' are not found on this stamp.

In June 1890 the Bechuanaland Protectorate and the Colony of British Bechuanaland came under one postal administration and the stamps of British Bechuanaland were used in the Protectorate until 1897.

BRITISH

BECHUANALAND — (**18**)

BECHUANALAND PROTECTORATE — (**19**)

1897. No. 61 of Cape of Good Hope (wmk Anchor), optd as T **18**.

(a) Lines 13 mm apart, bottom line 16 mm long, by Taylor & Marshall, Cape Town

56	½d. yellow-green (7.97?)	2·50	20·00

(b) Lines 13½ mm apart bottom line 15 mm long, by P. Townshend & Co, Vryburg

57	½d. yellow-green (4.97)	45·00	£120

(c) Lines 10½ mm apart, bottom line 15 mm long, by W. A. Richards & Sons, Cape Govt Printers

58	½d. yellow-green (7.97?)	20·00	75·00

Although issued only in the Protectorate, the above were presumably overprinted 'BRITISH BECHUANALAND' because stamps bearing this inscription were in use there at the time.

Examples of No. 57 are known with an addional reversed albino overprint due to the sheet having been folded during overprinting.

1897 (Oct)–**1902.** Nos. 172, 197, 200, 202, 205 and 208 of Great Britain (Queen Victoria) optd with T **19** by D.L.R.

59	½d. vermilion	3·00	2·25
60	½d. blue-green (25.2.02)	1·40	3·50
61	1d. lilac	4·00	75
62	2d. grey-green and carmine	15·00	3·50
63	3d. purple/*yellow* (12.97)	6·00	15·00
64	4d. green and purple-brown	28·00	25·00
65	6d. purple/*rose-red*	24·00	15·00
59/65 *Set of 7*		70·00	60·00
59s/65s Optd or H/S (No. 60s) 'SPECIMEN' *Set of 7*		£275	

BECHUANALAND PROTECTORATE — (**20**)

BECHUANALAND PROTECTORATE — (**21**)

1904 (29 Nov)–**13.** Nos. 216, 218/219, 230 and 313/314 (Somerset House ptgs) of Great Britain (King Edward VII) optd with T **20**, by D.L.R.

66	½d. blue-green (3.06)	2·75	4·25
67	½d. yellowish green (11.08)	3·75	3·75
68	1d. scarlet (4.05)	11·00	30
	s. Optd 'SPECIMEN'	65·00	
69	2½d. ultramarine	12·00	11·00
	a. Stop after 'P' in 'PROTECTORATE'	£1000	£1300
70	1s. deep green and scarlet (10.12)	55·00	£170
	a. Opt double, one albino	£225	
71	1s. green and carmine (1913)	60·00	£140
	s. Optd 'SPECIMEN'	£110	

No. 69a occurs on R. 5/9 of the lower pane.

1912 (Sept)–**14.** No. 342 of Great Britain (King George V, wmk Crown) optd with T **20.**

72	1d. scarlet	3·75	60
	a. No cross on crown	£150	75·00
	b. *Aniline scarlet* (No. 343) (1914)	£190	95·00

1913 (1 July)–**24.** Stamps of Great Britain (King George V) optd.

(a) Nos. 351, 357, 362, 367, 370/371, 376, 379, 385 and 395 (wmk Simple Cypher, T **100***) optd with T* **20**

73	½d. green (*shades*)	1·25	1·50
74	1d. scarlet (*shades*) (4.15)	2·75	75
	a. Carmine-red (1922)	40·00	4·00
75	1½d. red-brown (12.20)	7·00	2·50
	a. Opt double, one albino	£325	
76	2d. reddish orange (Die I)	13·00	3·25
	a. Orange (Die I) (1921)	25·00	3·00
	aw. Wmk inverted		
77	2d. orange (Die II) (1924)	50·00	2·75
78	2½d. cobalt-blue	3·50	30·00
	a. Blue (1915)	27·00	25·00
79	3d. bluish violet	6·00	19·00
80	4d. grey-green	6·50	42·00
81	6d. reddish purple (*shades*)	9·50	29·00
	a. Opt double, one albino	£325	
82	1s. bistre	23·00	45·00
	a. Bistre-brown (1923)	55·00	32·00
	b. Opt double, one albino	£350	
	s. Optd '*SPECIMEN*'	£100	
73/82 *Set of 9*		65·00	£140

(b) With T **21**

(i) Waterlow printings (Nos. 399 and 401) (1914–1915)

83	2s.6d. deep sepia-brown (1.15)	£140	£275
	a. Re-entry (R. 2/1)	£1400	£2000
	b. Opt double, one albino	£300	
84	5s. rose-carmine (1914)	£160	£375
	a. Opt double, one albino	£375	
83s/84s Optd '*SPECIMEN*' *Set of 2*		£275	

(ii) D.L.R. printings (Nos. 407/408 and 409) (1916–1919)

85	2s.6d. pale brown (7.16)	£120	£250
	a. Re-entry (R. 2/1)	£1200	£1800
86	2s.6d. sepia (1917)	£130	£225
	a. Opt treble, two albino		
	b. Re-entry (R. 2/1)	£1400	£1700
87	5s. bright carmine (8.19)	£300	£425
	a. Opt double, one albino	£450	

(iii) B.W. printings (Nos. 414 and 416) (1920–1923)

88	2s.6d. chocolate-brown (7.23)	90·00	£160
	a. Major re-entry (R. 1/2)	£2500	
	b. Opt double, one albino	£550	
	c. Opt treble, two albino	£550	
89	5s. rose-carmine (7.20)	£110	£275
	a. Opt treble, two albino	£375	
	b. Opt double, one albino		

Examples of Nos. 83/89 are known showing a forged Lobatsi postmark dated '6 MAY 35' or '6 MAY 39'.

1925 (July)–**27.** Nos. 418/419, 421, 423/424, 426/426*a* and 429 of Great Britain (wmk Block Cypher, T **111**) optd with T **20.**

91	½d. green (1927)	1·50	1·75
92	1d. scarlet (8.25)	2·00	70
	w. Wmk inverted	£400	
93	2d. orange (Die II)	2·25	1·00
94	3d. violet (10.26)	4·75	29·00
	a. Opt double, one albino	£200	
	w. Wmk inverted	£200	
95	4d. grey-green (10.26)	9·00	55·00
	a. Printed on the gummed side		
96	6d. reddish purple (*chalk-surfaced paper*) (12.25)	75·00	£110
97	6d. purple (*ordinary paper*) (1926)	50·00	55·00
98	1s. bistre-brown (10.26)	9·00	26·00
	w. Wmk inverted	£350	£300
91/98 *Set of 8*		£140	£250

No. 94w. also usually shows the variety, opt double, one albino.

22 King George V, Baobab Tree and Cattle

23 King George VI, Baobab Tree and Cattle

(Des from photo by Resident Commissioner, Ngamiland, Recess Waterlow)

1932 (12 Dec). Wmk Mult Script CA. P 12½.

99	22	½d. green	2·75	1·00
		a. Imperf between (horiz pair)	£35000	
100		1d. scarlet	2·75	40
101		2d. brown	2·75	45
102		3d. ultramarine	5·00	5·50
103		4d. orange	5·00	15·00
104		6d. purple	7·50	10·00
105		1s. black and olive-green	6·50	10·00
106		2s. black and orange	27·00	75·00
107		2s.6d. black and scarlet	27·00	55·00
108		3s. black and purple	48·00	65·00
109		5s. black and ultramarine	£130	£130
110		10s. black and brown	£325	£325
99/110 *Set of 12*			£500	£600
99s/110s Perf 'SPECIMEN' *Set of 12*			£450	

Examples of most values are known showing a forged Lobatsi postmark dated '6 MAY 35' or '6 MAY 39'.

1935 (4 May). Silver Jubilee. As Nos. 91/94 of Antigua but ptd by B.W. P 11×12.

111	1d. deep blue and scarlet	1·75	7·00
	a. Extra flagstaff	£275	£500
	b. Short extra flagstaff	£550	
	c. Lightning conductor	£400	
	d. Flagstaff on right-hand turret	£650	
	e. Double flagstaff	£650	£700
112	2d. ultramarine and grey-black	3·75	7·00
	a. Extra flagstaff	£140	£225
	b. Short extra flagstaff	£200	£300
	c. Lightning conductor	£170	£275

113 3d. brown and deep blue .... 4·25 13·00
a. Extra flagstaff £180 £350
b. Short extra flagstaff £275
c. Lightning conductor £200 £350
114 6d. slate and purple .... 9·50 14·00
a. Extra flagstaff £200 £300
b. Short extra flagstaff £250
c. Lightning conductor £225 £300
111/114 *Set of 4* .... 17·00 38·00
111s/114s Perf 'SPECIMEN' *Set of 4* £140

For illustrations of plate varieties see Omnibus section following Zanzibar.

1937 (12 May). Coronation. As Nos. 95/97 of Antigua, but printed by D.L.R. P 14.
115 1d. scarlet 45 40
116 2d. yellow-brown .... 60 1·00
117 3d. bright blue .... 60 1·25
115/117 *Set of 3* .... 1·50 2·40
115s/117s Perf 'SPECIMEN' *Set of 3* £140

(Recess Waterlow)

1938 (1 Apr)–**52**. Wmk Mult Script CA. P 12½.
118 **23** ½d. green .... 4·25 3·75
a. Light yellowish green (1941) .... 15·00 13·00
b. Yellowish green (4.43) .... 20·00 6·00
c. Deep green (4.49) .... 5·00 14·00
119 1d. scarlet 75 50
120 1½d. dull blue .... 16·00 2·50
a. Light blue (4.43) .... 1·00 1·00
121 2d. chocolate-brown 75 50
122 3d. deep ultramarine .... 1·00 2·50
123 4d. orange .... 2·00 3·50
124 6d. reddish purple .... 12·00 3·00
a. Purple (1944) .... 6·50 2·50
ab. 'A' of 'CA' missing from wmk .... † —
125 1s. black and brown-olive .... 5·50 9·50
a. Grey-black and olive-green (21.5.52) .... 28·00 50·00
126 2s.6d. black and scarlet .... 14·00 20·00
127 5s. black and deep ultramarine .... 48·00 32·00
a. Grey-black and deep ultramarine (10.46) .... 90·00 75·00
128 10s. black and red-brown .... 30·00 40·00
118/128 *Set of 11* £110 £100
118s/128s Perf 'SPECIMEN' *Set of 11* £375

Bechuanaland

(24)

1945 (3 Dec). Victory. Stamps of South Africa optd with T **24**. Inscr alternately in English and Afrikaans.

			Un pair	*Used pair*	*Used single*
129	**55**	1d. brown and carmine	75	1·50	10
		a. Barbed wire flaw	15·00		
130	**56**	2d. slate-blue and violet	50	1·50	10
131	**57**	3d. deep blue and blue	50	1·75	10
		a. Opt omitted (in vert pair with normal)	£17000		
129/131 *Set of 3*			1·60	4·25	25

No. 131a comes from a sheet on which the overprint was displaced downwards so that it is omitted from stamps in the top row and shown on the sheet margin at foot.

(Recess Waterlow)

1947 (17 Feb). Royal Visit. As Nos. 32/35 of Basutoland. Wmk Mult Script CA. P 12½.
132 1d. scarlet 10 10
133 2d. green 10 10
134 3d. ultramarine 10 10
135 1s. mauve 10 10
132/135 *Set of 4* 35 30
132s/135s Perf 'SPECIMEN' *Set of 4* £150

1948 (1 Dec). Royal Silver Wedding. As Nos. 112/113 of Antigua.
136 1½d. ultramarine 30 10
137 10s. black .... 42·00 50·00

1949 (10 Oct). 75th Anniversary of Universal Postal Union. As Nos. 114/117 of Antigua.
138 1½d. blue .... 30 1·25
139 3d. deep blue .... 1·50 2·50
140 6d. magenta .... 60 4·75
141 1s. olive .... 60 1·50
138/141 *Set of 4* .... 2·75 9·00

1953 (3 June). Coronation. As No. 120 of Antigua.
142 2d. black and brown .... 1·50 30

25 Queen Elizabeth II, Baobab Tree and Cattle

26 Queen Victoria, Queen Elizabeth II and Landscape

(Des from photo by Resident Commissioner, Ngamiland. Recess Waterlow)

1955 (3 Jan)–**58**. Wmk Mult Script CA. P 13½×14.
143 **25** ½d. green 50 30
144 1d. rose-red 80 10
145 2d. red-brown .... 1·25 30
146 3d. ultramarine .... 3·00 2·50
a. Bright ultramarine (16.1.57) .... 19·00 5·50
146*b* 4d. red-orange (1.12.58) .... 13·00 15·00
147 4½d. blackish blue .... 1·50 35
148 6d. purple .... 1·25 60
149 1s. black and brown-olive .... 1·25 1·00
150 1s.3d. black and lilac .... 18·00 9·50
151 2s.6d. black and rose-red .... 13·00 10·00
152 5s. black and violet-blue .... 21·00 20·00
153 10s. black and red-brown .... 45·00 20·00
143/153 *Set of 12* .... £100 70·00

(Photo Harrison)

1960 (21 Jan). 75th Anniversary of Bechuanaland Protectorate. W w **12**. P 14½×14.
154 **26** 1d. sepia and black 50 50
155 3d. magenta and black 50 30
156 6d. bright blue and black 55 50
154/156 *Set of 3* .... 1·40 1·10

(New Currency. 100 cents = 1 rand)

1c (27) 1c (I) 1c (II) 2½c (I) 2½c (II)

3 (I) 3 (II) 3 (III) 5c (I) 5c (II) R1 (I) R1 (II)

2½c Spaced 'c' (R. 10/3)

3½c Normal 3½c Bold 'c'

The Bold 'c' variety occurs on the Type II surcharge (R. 9/3) and Type III (R. 7/3).

1961 (14 Feb–26 July). Nos. 144/146*a* and 148/153 surch as T **27** by South African Govt Printer, Pretoria.
157 **25** 1c. on 1d. rose-red (Type I) 30 10
a. Type II (6.6) 40 10
158 2c. on 2d. red-brown 30 10
159 2½c. on 2d. red-brown (Type I) 30 10
a. Type II (26.7) .... 2·50 3·75
b. Vert pair, one without surch £16000
160 2½c. on 3d. bright ultramarine .... 12·00 17·00
a. Spaced 'c' (R. 10/3) £300
161 3½c. on 4d. red-orange (Type I) .... 50 4·25
a. Wide surch (I) .... 18·00 48·00
b. Type II .... 3·00 16·00
ba. Bold 'c' (Type II) £120 £180
c. Wide surch (II) .... 65·00 £100
d. Type III (6.6) 20 60
da. Bold 'c' (Type III) .... 10·00 19·00
162 5c. on 6d. purple (Type I) .... 2·25 3·50
a. Type II (12.5) 20 10
163 10c. on 1s. black and brown-olive 20 10
a. Horiz pair, righthand stamp without surch £13000
164 12½c. on 1s.3d. black and lilac 65 20
165 25c. on 2s.6d. black and rose-red .... 1·50 1·00
166 50c. on 5s. black and violet-blue .... 2·00 3·75
167 1r. on 10s. black and red-brown (Type I) £275 £170
a. Type II (surch at bottom left) (17.3) .... 32·00 48·00
b. Type II (surch at foot, either to right or central) (4.61) .... 29·00 27·00
157/167b *Set of 11* (*cheapest*) .... 42·00 45·00

Nos. 161/161c occur from the same printing, each sheet containing 33 examples of Type I, five of Type I with wide spacing, 19 of Type II and three of Type II with wide spacing. The wide surcharge measures 9½ mm overall (with 'C' spaced 1½ *mm* from '½') and comes on eight of the ten stamps in the last vertical row. The surcharge on the remainder of the sheet varies between 8½ and 9½ mm.

No. 163a was caused by a shift of the surcharge so that the last vertical row on the sheet is without '10 c'.

A later printing of the 12½c. on 1s.3d. was from a fresh setting of type, but is insufficiently different for separate listing. Later printings of the 10c. and 25c. were identical to the originals.

Examples of No.167 with the surcharge central at foot are believed to originate from the Botswana Post archive.

28 African Golden Oriole

29 Hoopoe

30 Scarlet-chested Sunbird

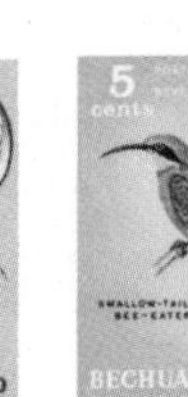

31 Yellow-rumped Bishop

32 Swallow-tailed Bee-eater

33 African Grey Hornbill

34 Red-headed Weaver

35 Brown-hooded Kingfisher

36 Woman Musician

37 Baobab Tree

38 Woman grinding maize

39 Bechuana Ox

40 Lion

41 Police Camel Patrol

(Des P. Jones (1c. to 12½c.). Photo Harrison)

1961 (2 Oct). T **28**/**41**. W w **12**. P 14½×14 (25c., 50c.) or 14×14½ (others).
168 **28** 1c. yellow, red, black and lilac .... 1·50 50
169 **29** 2c. orange, black and yellow-olive .... 2·00 4·50
170 **30** 2½c. carmine, green, black and bistre .... 1·75 10
171 **31** 3½c. yellow, black, sepia and pink .... 2·50 5·00
172 **32** 5c. yellow, blue, black and buff .... 3·25 1·00
173 **33** 7½c. brown, red, black and apple-green .... 2·25 2·25
174 **34** 10c. red, yellow, sepia and turquoise-green .... 2·25 60
175 **35** 12½c. buff, blue, red and grey-black .... 18·00 6·00
176 **36** 20c. yellow-brown and drab .... 4·75 5·00
177 **37** 25c. deep brown and lemon .... 5·00 3·00
178 **38** 35c. deep blue and orange .... 4·50 7·00
179 **39** 50c. sepia and olive .... 3·50 2·75
180 **40** 1r. black and cinnamon .... 11·00 2·75
181 **41** 2r. brown and turquoise-blue .... 32·00 18·00
168/181 *Set of 14* .... 80·00 50·00

1963 (4 June). Freedom from Hunger. As No. 146 of Antigua.
182 12½c. bluish green 30 15

1963 (2 Sept). Red Cross Centenary. As Nos. 147/148 of Antigua.
183 2½c. red and black 30 10
184 12½c. red and blue 70 50

1964 (23 Apr). 400th Birth Anniversary of William Shakespeare. As No. 164 of Antigua.
185 12½c. light brown 15 15

INTERNAL SELF–GOVERNMENT

42 Map and Gaberones Dam

Bay flaw (R. 4/1) Lake flaw (R. 5/5)

(Des Mrs. M. Townsend, adapted V. Whiteley. Photo Harrison)

1965 (1 Mar). New Constitution. W w **12**. P 14½×14.
186 **42** 2½c. red and gold 40 10
a. Bay flaw .... 13·00 10·00
b. Lake flaw .... 13·00 10·00
w. Wmk inverted .... 24·00 2·50
187 5c. ultramarine and gold 40 40
a. Bay flaw .... 13·00 13·00
b. Lake flaw .... 13·00 13·00

188 12½c. brown and gold 55 40
a. Bay flaw .... 15·00 14·00
b. Lake flaw .... 15·00 14·00
189 25c. green and gold 65 55
a. Bay flaw .... 16·00 16·00
b. Lake flaw .... 16·00 16·00
186/189 *Set of 4* .... 1·75 1·25

1965 (17 May). ITU Centenary. As Nos. 166/167 of Antigua.
190 2½c. red and bistre-yellow 20 10
191 12½c. mauve and brown 45 30

1965 (25 Oct). International Co-operation Year. As Nos. 168/169 of Antigua.
192 1c. reddish purple and turquoise-green .... 10 1·00
193 12½c. deep bluish green and lavender 60 55

1966 (24 Jan). Churchill Commemoration. As Nos. 170/173 of Antigua.
194 1c. new blue .... 30 3·00
195 2½c. deep green 40 10
196 12½c. brown 75 35
197 20c. bluish violet 75 55
194/197 *Set of 4* .... 2·00 3·50

43 Haslar Smoke Generator

(Des V. Whiteley. Photo Harrison)

1966 (1 June). Bechuanaland Royal Pioneer Corps. T **43** and similar horiz designs. W w **12**. P 14½.
198 2½c. Prussian blue, red and light emerald 25 10
199 5c. brown and light blue 30 20
200 15c. Prussian blue, rosine and emerald .... 1·75 25
201 35c. buff, blackish brown, red and green .... 30 2·00
198/201 *Set of 4* .... 2·40 2·25

Designs: 2½c. T **43**; 5c. Bugler; 15c. Gun-site; 35c. Regimental cap badge.

POSTAGE DUE STAMPS

BECHUANALAND PROTECTORATE (D **1**)

BECHUANALAND PROTECTORATE (D **2**)

1926 (1 Jan). Nos. D9/D10 and D13 of Great Britain, optd with Types D **1** or D **2** (2d.).
D1 ½d. emerald (wmk sideways - inverted) .... 15·00 £130
D2 1d. carmine .... 15·00 80·00
D3 2d. agate .... 15·00 90·00
D1/D3 *Set of 3* .... 40·00 £275

The watermark shows Crown to the left of GvR on D1 and to the right of GvR of D2/D3, *as seen from the back of the stamp.*

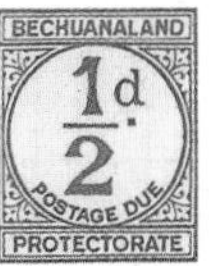
D **3**

Normal

Large 'd.' (R. 9/6, 10/6)

2d. Serif on 'd' (R. 1/6)

(Typo D.L.R.)

1932 (12 Dec)–**58**. Ordinary paper. Wmk Mult Script CA. P 14.
D4 D **3** ½d. sage-green .... 5·00 48·00
D5 1d. carmine .... 7·00 9·00
a. Chalk-surfaced paper (27.11.58) .... 1·50 30·00
D6 2d. violet .... 9·00 48·00
a. Large 'd' £160 £225
b. Serif on 'd' £250
c. Chalk-surfaced paper (27.11.58) .... 1·75 22·00
ca. Large 'd' .... 50·00 £150
cb. Serif on 'd' .... 70·00
D4/D6c *Set of 3 (cheapest)* .... 7·50 70·00
D4s/D6s Perf 'SPECIMEN' *Set of 3* £110

Nos. D6a/D6b first occurred on the 1947 printing.

1c I (Small) — 1c II (Large) — c Narrow 'C' (R.3/6)

1961 (14 Feb–Apr). Surch as T **27**. Chalk-surfaced paper (Nos. D7/D8).
D7 D **3** 1c. on 1d. (Type I) 25 50
a. Type II (4.61) .... 15 1·75
ab. Double surch £375
ac. Ordinary paper .... 21·00 65·00
ad. Narrow 'c' .... 12·00
D8 2c. on 2d. (Type I) .... 25 1·50
a. Large 'd' .... 12·00
b. Serif on 'd' .... 23·00
c. Type II .... 15 2·00
ca. Large 'd' .... 8·50 27·00
cb. Serif on 'd' .... 17·00
d. Ordinary paper. Type II £180 £200
da. Large 'd' £800
D9 5c. on ½d. 20 60
D7/D9 *Set of 3* .... 45 2·40

Normal

1c. Bold 'c' and larger dot (R. 2/6)

1961 (15 Nov). As Type D **3** but values in cents. Chalk-surfaced paper. Wmk Mult Script CA. P 14.
D10 1c. carmine .... 30 2·00
a. Bold 'c' and larger dot .... 12·00
D11 2c. violet .... 30 2·00
D12 5c. green .... 50 2·00
D10/D12 *Set of 3* .... 1·00 5·50

POSTAL FISCAL STAMPS

The following stamps issued for fiscal purposes were each allowed to be used for postal purposes for a short time. No. F2 was used by the public because the word 'POSTAGE' had not been obliterated and No. F3 because the overprint did not include the words 'Revenue only' as did the contemporary fiscal overprints for Basutoland and Swaziland.

Bechuanaland Protectorate (F **1**)

£5 (F **2**)

Bechuanaland Protectorate. (F **3**)

1910 (July). No. 266a of Transvaal optd with Type F **1** by Transvaal Govt Ptg Wks, Pretoria.
F1 6d. black and brown-orange (Bl.-Blk.) £190 £375

No. F1 was supplied to Assistant Commissioners in January 1907 for revenue purposes. The 'POSTAGE' inscription was not obliterated, however, and the stamp is known postally used for a period of a year from July 1910.

1918. No. 15 surch with Type F **2** at top.
F2 **4** £5 on 1s. green and black (F.C. £1000) £60000

1921. No. 4*b* of South Africa optd with Type F **3**, in varying positions.
F3 1d. scarlet .... 50·00 £150
a. Opt double, one albino £180

Bechuanaland became the independent republic of Botswana, within the Commonwealth, on 30 September 1966.

MILITARY TELEGRAPH STAMPS

Military Telegraph Stamps were provided for the pre-payment of non-official messages sent via the army telegraph system. They were used by army personnel for private communications, newspaper reporters and the local population when the army was in control of the telegraph system. They were supplied to the Bechuanaland Expedition in late November 1884.

T **1**

T **2**

T **3**

(Typo D.L.R.)

1884.

(a) Wmk Orb. P 14
MT1 T **1** 1d. lilac and black £100 £300
MT2 3d. lilac and brown £100 £300
MT3 6d. lilac and green £100 £300

(b) Wmk script 'VR', sideways reading up. P 13½
MT4 T **2** 1s. green and black £100 £475
MT5 2s. green and blue £150 £600
MT6 5s. green and mauve £200 £750
MT7 10s. green and red £375 £850

(c) Wmk Two Orbs (sideways). P 14×13½
MT8 T **3** £1 lilac and black £700 £1400

For use of Nos. MT1/MT8 in Egypt and Sudan see Egypt (British Forces) Nos. MT1/MT8.

For similar stamps inscribed 'ARMY TELEGRAPHS' see South Africa (VIII, British Army Field Offices During South African War) Nos. AT3/AT15.

The stamps were either cancelled in manuscript or by an 'ARMY TELEGRAPHS' datestamp incorporating a code letter at either end of the date to identify the office of despatch. The codes used were:

B L Barkley	**B K** Bank's Drift	**B R** Brussels Farm
D H Dry Hartz	**G C** Groot Choing	**G L** Barkley West
G U Gunning's Store	**L P** Leeuw Pan	**M F** Mafeking
M L Muller's Store	**M Z** Maritzani	**S A** Saanies
S H Setlagoli	**T S** Taungs	**V R** Vryburg

Military

Telegraphs

(T **4**)

1885. Nos 52 and 26 of Cape of Good Hope optd with Type T **4**.
MT9 6d. purple .... 70·00 35·00
MT10 1s. green .... 85·00 40·00

The above were overprinted in Cape Town for use in Vryburg, following its occupation by Sir Charles Warren's forces on 7 February 1885.

MT9/MT10 can be found with or without stop after 'Telegraphs'.

1885. (July–Aug). Nos. MT1, MT7, MT6 and MT8 surch in manuscript.
MT11 '6d' on 1d. lilac and black .... † —
MT12 '6d' on 10s. green and red .... † —
MT13 '1/-' on 5s. green and mauve .... † —
MT14 '1/-' on £1 lilac and black .... † —

Bermuda

The first internal postal system for Bermuda was organised by Joseph Stockdale, the proprietor of the *Bermuda Gazette*, in January 1784. This service competed with that of the colonial post office, set up in May 1812, until 1818.

Control of the overseas postal services passed to the British GPO in 1818. The internal delivery system was discontinued between 1821 and 1830. The overseas posts became a colonial responsibility in September 1859.

For illustrations of the handstamp types see BRITISH POST OFFICES ABROAD notes, following GREAT BRITAIN.

CROWNED-CIRCLE HANDSTAMPS

CC1	CC **1**	ST GEORGES BERMUDA (R.) (1.8.1845) ... *Price on cover*	£8500
CC2		IRELAND ISLE BERMUDA (R.) (1.8.1845) ... *Price on cover*	£7500
CC3		HAMILTON BERMUDA (R.) (13.11.1846) ... *Price on cover*	£4000

For Nos. CC1 and CC3 used as adhesive Postmasters' Stamps see Nos. O7 and O6.

PRICES FOR STAMPS ON COVER TO 1945

Nos. 1/11	*from* × 5
Nos. 12/17	*from* × 10
Nos. 19/29*a*	*from* × 8
Nos. 30/30a	*from* × 10
Nos. 31/34	*from* × 4
Nos. 34/55	*from* × 3
Nos. 56/58	*from* × 10
Nos. 59/76	*from* × 4
Nos. 76a/93	*from* × 3
Nos. 94/97	*from* × 4
Nos. 98/106	*from* × 3
Nos. 107/115	*from* × 4
Nos. 116/121	*from* × 5
No. 122	*from* × 20

COLONY

O 1

O 2

1848–61. Postmasters' Stamps. Adhesives prepared and issued by the postmasters at Hamilton and St Georges. Dated as given in brackets.

(a) By W. B. Perot at Hamilton

O1	O **1**	1d. black/*bluish grey* (1848)	—	£200000
O2		1d. black/*bluish grey* (1849)	—	£225000
O3		1d. red/*thick white* (1853)	—	£200000
O4		1d. red/*bluish wove* (1854)	—	£450000
O5		1d. red/*bluish wove* (1856)	—	£275000
O6	O **2**	(1d.) carmine-red/*bluish laid* (1861)	£150000	£110000

(b) By J. H. Thies at St Georges. As T O **2** *but inscr 'ST. GEORGES'*

O7	–	(1d.) carmine-red/*buff* (1860)	†	£85000

Stamps of T O **1** bear manuscript value and signature, the dates being those shown on the 11 known examples. The stamps are distributed between the dates as follows: 1848 three examples, 1849 two examples, 1853 three examples, 1854 two examples, 1856 one example.

It is believed that the franking value of Nos. O6/O7 was 1d., although this is not shown on the actual stamps. Four examples are known of this type used from Hamilton, from March 1861 (and one unused), and five used from St Georges between July 1860 and January 1863, both issues being cancelled by pen.

Prices shown reflect our estimation of value based on known copies. For instance of the two copies known of No. O4, one is in the Royal collection and the other is on entire.

It is possible that a fourth postmaster's provisional was used by Robert Ward at Hamilton in late 1862 when two examples of T O **2** on laid paper are known cancelled by blue crayon.

1 2 3 4 5

(Typo D.L.R.)

1865–1903. Wmk Crown CC.

(a) P 14

1	**1**	1d. rose-red (25.9.65)	£100	1·25
		a. Imperf	£75000	£27000
		w. Wmk inverted	£550	£200
2		1d. pale rose	£140	7·50
		w. Wmk inverted	£600	£300
3	**2**	2d. dull blue (14.3.66)	£475	42·00
		w. Wmk inverted	£1800	£750
4		2d. bright blue (1877)	£475	21·00
		w. Wmk inverted	£1800	£750
5	**3**	3d. orange (10.3.73)	£2250	£170
5*a*		3d. yellow-buff (8.74)	£475	65·00
		aw. Wmk inverted	£1400	£350
		ax. Wmk reversed	£2500	£1200
6	**4**	6d. dull purple (25.9.65)	£1000	75·00
		w. Wmk inverted	—	£1600
7		6d. dull mauve (2.7.74)	23·00	12·00
		w. Wmk inverted	£180	£275
8	**5**	1s. green (25.9.65)	£350	70·00
		w. Wmk inverted	£900	£350

(b) P 14×12½

10	**3**	3d. yellow-buff (12.81)	£180	60·00
10*a*	**4**	6d. bright mauve (1903)	17·00	22·00
		w. Wmk inverted	£1500	£1600
11	**5**	1s. green (11.93)	17·00	£120
		a. Imperf between (vert strip of 3)	£12000	
		w. Wmk inverted	£1400	

No. 11a occurs from Rows 8, 9, and 10 of four panes, possibly from a single sheet. Some of the stamps have become partially separated. One *used* vertical pair is known (*Price* £18000).

Although they arrived in Bermuda in March 1880, stamps perforated 14×12½ were not issued until the dates given above.

THREE PENCE (6) THREE PENCE (6a)

THREE PENCE (7) One Penny. (8)

1874 (12 Mar–19 May). Nos. 1 and 8 surch diagonally.

(a) With T **6** *('P' and 'R' different type)*

12	**1**	3d. on 1d. rose-red	£18000	
13	**5**	3d. on 1s. green	£2500	£850

(b) With T **6a** *('P' same type as 'R')*

13*b*	**5**	3d. on 1s. green	£2000	£800

(c) With T **7** *(19 May)*

14	**5**	3d. on 1s. green	£1500	£650

The 3d. on 1d. was a trial surcharge which was not regularly issued, though a few examples were postally used before 1879. Nos. 13, 13*b* and 14, being handstamped, are found with double or partial double surcharges.

(Surch by Queens Printer, Donald McPhee Lee)

1875 (March–May). Surch with T **8**.

15	**2**	1d. on 2d. (No. 3) (23.4)	£700	£375
		a. No stop after 'Penny'	£25000	£13000
16	**3**	1d. on 3d. (No. 5*a*) (8.5)	£450	£350
17	**5**	1d. on 1s. (No. 8) (11.3)	£500	£250
		a. Surch inverted	—	£50000
		b. No stop after 'Penny'	£40000	£18000

It is emphasised that the prices quoted for Nos. 12/17 are for fine examples. The many stamps from these provisional issues which are in inferior condition are worth much less.

9

10

11

(Typo D.L.R.)

1880 (25 Mar). Wmk Crown CC. P 14.

19	**9**	½d. stone	8·50	4·75
		w. Wmk inverted	£130	£225
		y. Wmk inverted and reversed	£2250	
20	**10**	4d. orange-red	21·00	1·75
		w. Wmk inverted	—	£1600
		x. Wmk reversed		

(Typo D.L.R.)

1883–1904. Wmk Crown CA. P 14.

21	**9**	½d. dull green (10.92)	9·00	4·50
21*a*		½d. deep grey-green (1893)	5·00	80
22	**1**	1d. dull rose (12.83)	£170	4·75
		w. Wmk inverted	£750	£400
23		1d. rose-red	90·00	3·25
		w. Wmk inverted	—	£375
24		1d. carmine-rose (3.86)	60·00	1·00
		w. Wmk inverted	—	£375
24*a*		1d. aniline carmine (1889)	22·00	20
		aw. Wmk inverted	£500	£200
25	**2**	2d. blue (12.86)	75·00	7·50
		x. Wmk reversed	†	£1500
26		2d. aniline purple (7.93)	17·00	5·50
26*a*		2d. brown purple (1898)	6·50	2·50
27	**11**	2½d. deep ultramarine (10.11.84)	40·00	3·75
		aw. Wmk inverted	£1000	£300
27*b*		2½d. pale ultramarine	25·00	40
		bw. Wmk inverted	£600	£250
28	**3**	3d. grey (20.1.86)	23·00	11·00
28*a*	**10**	4d. orange-brown (18.1.04)	35·00	60·00
		ax. Wmk reversed	£500	£750
29	**5**	1s. yellow-brown (1893)	24·00	25·00
		ax. Wmk reversed	£1800	£1100
29*b*		1s. olive-brown	14·00	25·00
		bx. Wmk reversed	£1800	£1200
21/29*b* *Set of 8* (*cheapest*)			£180	95·00
21s, 26s & 29s Optd 'SPECIMEN' *Set of 3*			£375	

1893 PROVISIONAL POSTCARD. Following the reduction of the overseas postcard rate to 1d. in 1893 existing stocks of postal stationery postcards, including some from the September 1880 issue franked with Nos. 19 and 22, were surcharged 'One Penny'. This surcharge was applied by the *Royal Gazette* press. It is generally believed that an individual in the Post Office acquired all the examples showing Nos. 19 and 22, but provisional postcards are known used to Europe or locally (*Price from £600 unused, £1600 used).*

ONE FARTHING

(12)

13 Dry Dock

14

1901. As Nos. 29/29*b* but colour changed, surch with T **12** by D.L.R.

30	**5**	¼d. on 1s. dull grey (11.1.01)	5·00	1·00
		as. Optd 'SPECIMEN'	80·00	
30*b*		¼d. on 1s. bluish grey (18.3.01)	5·50	1·50
		ba. 'F' in 'FARTHING' inserted by handstamp	£8000	£10000

Ten examples of No. 30ba are known, eight unused (one being in the Royal Philatelic Collection) and two used (one on postcard). It would appear that the 'F' in position 1 of an unspecified horizontal row was damaged and an additional impression of the letter was then inserted by a separate handstamp.

(Typo D.L.R.)

1902 (Nov)–**03.** Wmk Crown CA. P 14.

31	**13**	½d. black and green (12.03)	14·00	4·50
32		1d. brown and carmine	8·00	10
33		3d. magenta and sage-green (9.03)	6·00	2·50
31/33 *Set of 3*			25·00	6·25
31s/33s Optd 'SPECIMEN' *Set of 3*			£150	

1906–10. Wmk Mult Crown CA. P 14.

34	**13**	¼d. brown and violet (9.08)	1·75	1·50
35		½d. black and green (12.06)	21·00	65
36		½d. green (3.09)	27·00	5·00
37		1d. brown and carmine (4.06)	45·00	20
		w. Wmk inverted	£700	£350
		y. Wmk inverted and reversed	£1200	
38		1d. red (5.08)	26·00	10
39		2d. grey and orange (10.07)	7·50	10·00
40		2½d. brown and ultramarine (12.06)	35·00	7·00
41		2½d. blue (14.2.10)	28·00	9·50
42		4d. blue and chocolate (11.09)	3·00	16·00
34/42 *Set of 9*			£170	45·00
34s, 36s, 38s/42s Optd 'SPECIMEN' *Set of 7*			£400	

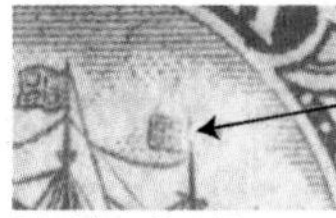

'Flag' flaw (R. 1/8)

(Recess D.L.R.)

1910–25. Wmk Mult Crown CA. P 14.

44	**14**	¼d. brown (26.3.12)	1·75	1·50
		a. Pale brown	2·50	1·25
45		½d. green (4.6.10)	3·75	25
		a. Deep green (1918)	15·00	1·25
		w. Wmk inverted	†	—
		x. Wmk reversed	£1000	£550
46		1d. red (I) (15.10.10)	21·00	30
		a. Rose-red (1916)	26·00	30
		b. Carmine (12.19)	60·00	8·00
		ba. 'Flag' flaw	£400	85·00
		w. Wmk inverted	£750	£500
		x. Wmk reversed	£1300	£950
		y. Wmk inverted and reversed	£850	£850
47		2d. grey (1.13)	7·00	21·00
48		2½d. blue (27.3.12)	3·50	60
		w. Wmk inverted	£700	£550
		x. Wmk reversed	—	£600
		y. Wmk inverted and reversed	£475	£325
49		3d. purple/*yellow* (1.13)	3·75	6·00
49*a*		4d. red/*yellow* (1.9.19)	14·00	18·00
50		6d. purple (26.3.12)	19·00	20·00
		a. Pale claret (2.6.24)	11·00	8·50
51		1s. black/*green* (26.3.12)	6·50	4·75
		a. Jet black/olive (1925)	6·50	23·00
		ax. Wmk reversed	£1700	
44/51 *Set of 9*			60·00	50·00
44s/51s Optd 'SPECIMEN' *Set of 9*			£475	

Nos. 44 to 51*a* are comb-perforated 13.8×14 or 14. No. 45 exists also line-perforated 14 probably from the printing dispatched to Bermuda on 13 March 1911.

See also Nos. 77/87*a*.

15

HIGH VALUE KEY TYPES. The reign of King Edward VII saw the appearance of the first in a new series of 'key type' designs, initially for Nyasaland, to be used for high value denominations where a smaller design was felt to be inappropriate. The system was extended during the reign of King George V, using the portrait as Bermuda T **15**, to cover Bermuda, Ceylon, Leeward Islands, Malaya – Straits Settlements, Malta and Nyasaland. A number of these territories continued to use the key type concept for high value King George VI stamps and one, Leeward Islands, for stamps of Queen Elizabeth II.

In each instance the King George V issues were printed in sheets of 60 (12×5) on various coloured papers. The system utilised a common 'head' plate used with individual 'duty' plates which printed the territory name and face value.

Many of the major plate flaws on the King George V head plate occur in different states, having been repaired and then damaged once again, perhaps on several occasions. Later printings of R. 1/12 show additional damage to the crown and upper scrolls. The prices quoted in the listings are for examples approximately as illustrated.

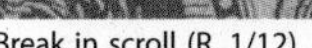

Break in scroll (R. 1/12)

Broken crown and scroll (R. 2/12)

Nick in top right scroll (R. 3/12) (Some printings from 1920 onwards show attempts at repair)

Break through scroll (R. 1/9. Ptgs from June 1929. Some show attempts at repair)

Break in lines below left scroll (R. 4/9. Ptgs from May 1920)

Damaged leaf at bottom right (R. 5/6. Ptgs from April 1918)

Gash in fruit and leaf (R. 5/12. Ptgs from November 1928)

(Typo D.L.R.)

1918 (1 Apr)–**22**. Wmk Mult Crown CA. Chalk-surfaced paper. P 14.

No.	Type	Description	Unused	Used
51*b*	**15**	2s. purple and blue/*blue* (19.6.20)	23·00	55·00
		ba. Break in scroll	£275	£350
		bb. Broken crown and scroll	£225	£350
		bc. Nick in top right scroll	£275	
		be. Break in lines below left scroll	£275	£400
		bf. Damaged leaf at bottom right	£275	
		bx. Wmk reversed	£2000	£2500
52		2s.6d. black and red/*blue*	40·00	80·00
		a. Break in scroll	£325	£400
52*b*		4s. black and carmine (19.6.20)	60·00	£160
		ba. Break in scroll	£300	£650
		bb. Broken crown and scroll	£300	£650
		bc. Nick in top right scroll	£325	£650
		be. Break in lines below left scroll	£350	£650
		bf. Damaged leaf at bottom right	£350	
53		5s. deep green and deep red/*yellow*	75·00	£140
		a. Break in scroll	£425	
		c. Nick in top right scroll	£425	£550
		d. Green and carmine-red/pale yellow (1920)	60·00	£120
		da. Break in scroll	£375	£550
		db. Broken crown and scroll	£375	£550
		de. Break in lines below left scroll	£400	
		df. Damaged leaf at bottom right	£400	
		dw. Wmk inverted	£475	£650
		dx. Wmk reversed	£8000	
		dy. Wmk inverted and reversed	£6000	
54		10s. green and carmine/*pale bluish green*	£180	£350
		a. Break in scroll	£750	
		c. Green and red/pale bluish green (10.22)	£275	£425
		ca. Break in scroll	£950	
		cb. Broken crown and scroll	£950	
		ce. Break in lines below left scroll	£1000	
		cf. Damaged leaf at bottom right	£1000	
		cw. Wmk inverted	†	—
55		£1 purple and black/*red*	£275	£550
		a. Break in scroll	£850	
		b. Broken crown and scroll	£1000	
		c. Nick in top right scroll	£1000	
		d. Break through scroll	£2250	
		e. Break in lines below left scroll	£1600	
		f. Damaged leaf at bottom right	£1200	
		g. Gash in fruit and leaf	£2250	
		w. Wmk inverted	£2000	£2750
51*b*/55 *Set of* 6			£600	£1100
51*bs*/55s Optd 'SPECIMEN' *Set of* 6			£900	

Beware of cleaned copies of the 10s. with faked postmarks.

Examples of Nos. 51*b*/55 are known showing a forged Hamilton double ring postmark dated '22 JAN 13'.

See also Nos. 88/93.

WAR TAX (**16**) **WAR TAX** (**17**)

1918 (4 May). Nos. 46 and 46*a* optd with T **16** by the Bermuda Press.

No.	Type	Description	Unused	Used
56	**14**	1d. red	50	1·25
		a. Rose-red	1·25	2·00
		ay. Wmk inverted and reversed	£3000	£2000

1920 (5 Feb). No. 46*b* optd with T **17** by the Bermuda Press.

No.	Type	Description	Unused	Used
58	**14**	1d. carmine	4·00	3·50
		a. 'Flag' flaw	£140	£180

The War Tax stamps represented a compulsory levy on letters to Great Britain and often Empire Countries in addition to normal postal fees until 31 Dec 1920. Subsequently they were valid for ordinary postage.

18

19

(Des by the Governor (Gen. Sir James Willcocks). Typo D.L.R.)

1920 (11 Nov)–**21**. Tercentenary of Representative Institutions (1st issue). Chalk-surfaced paper (3d. to 1s.). P 14.

(a) Wmk Mult Crown CA (sideways) (19.1.21)*

No.	Type	Description	Unused	Used
59	**18**	¼d. brown	3·50	28·00
		a. 'C' of 'CA' missing from wmk	£800	
		b. 'A' of 'CA' missing from wmk	£800	
		w. Wmk Crown to right of CA	£300	£350
		x. Wmk sideways reversed	£400	£450
		y. Wmk sideways inverted and reversed	£450	£600
60		½d. green	9·50	20·00
		a. 'C' of 'CA' missing from wmk	£1100	
		b. 'A' of 'CA' missing from wmk	£1300	
		w. Wmk Crown to right of CA	£450	£500
		x. Wmk sideways reversed	£475	£500
		y. Wmk sideways inverted and reversed	£550	£550
61		2d. grey	18·00	55·00
		a. 'C' of 'CA' missing from wmk	£1100	
		w. Wmk Crown to right of CA	£650	
		y. Wmk sideways inverted and reversed	£850	£900
62		3d. dull and deep purple/*pale yellow*	12·00	55·00
		w. Wmk Crown to right of CA	£1100	
		x. Wmk sideways reversed	£1200	£1200
63		4d. black and red/*pale yellow*	12·00	40·00
		a. 'C' of 'CA' missing from wmk	£1800	
		x. Wmk sideways reversed	£1100	
64		1s. black/*blue-green*	18·00	48·00

(b) Wmk Mult Script CA (sideways)*

No.	Type	Description	Unused	Used
65	**18**	1d. carmine	4·50	30
		w. Wmk Crown to right of CA	†	£750
		y. Wmk sideways inverted and reversed	†	£750
66		2½d. bright blue	20·00	20·00
67		6d. dull and bright purple (19.1.21)	32·00	95·00
59/67 *Set of* 9			£110	£325
59s/67s Optd 'SPECIMEN' *Set of* 9			£375	

* The normal sideways watermark shows Crown to left of CA, *as seen from the back of the stamp.*

(Des J. H. Dale. Recess D.L.R.)

1921 (12 May). Tercentenary of Representative Institutions (2nd issue). P 14.

(a) Wmk Mult Crown CA (sideways)*

No.	Type	Description	Unused	Used
68	**19**	2d. slate-grey	13·00	55·00
		a. 'C' of 'CA' missing from wmk	£1000	£1000
		w. Wmk Crown to left of CA	£750	
69		2½d. bright ultramarine	15·00	7·00
		a. 'C' of 'CA' missing from wmk	£1000	
		b. 'A' of 'CA' missing from wmk	£1000	
		w. Wmk Crown to left of CA	—	£750
		x. Wmk sideways reversed	£1100	£700
70		3d. purple/*pale yellow*	5·50	21·00
		w. Wmk Crown to left of CA		
71		4d. red/*pale yellow*	19·00	45·00
		x. Wmk sideways reversed	£300	£425
72		6d. purple	19·00	65·00
		a. 'C' of 'CA' missing from wmk	£1400	
		b. 'A' of 'CA' missing from wmk	£1500	
		c. Substituted crown in wmk	†	£2750
73		1s. black/*green*	25·00	65·00

(b) Wmk Mult Script CA (sideways)*

No.	Type	Description	Unused	Used
74	**19**	¼d. brown	4·25	4·25
		w. Wmk Crown to left of CA	£550	£550
		x. Wmk sideways reversed	£750	£700
		y. Wmk sideways inverted and reversed	—	£750
75		½d. green	3·50	9·50
		w. Wmk Crown to left of CA	£250	£325
		x. Wmk sideways reversed	£750	£650
		y. Wmk sideways inverted and reversed	£475	
		ys. Optd 'SPECIMEN'	£225	
76		1d. deep carmine	13·00	35
		a. 'C' of 'CA' missing from wmk	£750	
		w. Wmk Crown to left of CA	£700	£600
		x. Wmk sideways reversed	£500	£650
		y. Wmk sideways inverted and reversed	£1000	£700
68/76 *Set of* 9			£100	£225
68s/76s Optd 'SPECIMEN' *Set of* 9			£350	

* The normal sideways watermark shows Crown to right of CA, *as seen from the back of the stamp.*

For illustration of the substituted watermark crown see Catalogue Introduction.

Examples of most values of Nos. 59/76 are known showing part strikes of the forged Hamilton postmark mentioned below Nos. 51*b*/55.

I II III

Three Types of the 1d.

I. Scroll at top left very weak and figure '1' has pointed serifs.
II. Scroll weak. '1' has square serifs and '1d' is heavy.
III. Redrawn. Scroll is completed by a strong line and '1' is thinner with long square serifs.

I II

Two Types of the 2½d.

I. Short, thick figures, especially of the '1', small 'd'.
II. Figures taller and thinner, 'd' larger.

1922–34. Wmk Mult Script CA. P 14.

No.	Type	Description	Unused	Used
77	**14**	¼d. brown (7.28)	1·50	2·50
77*a*		½d. green (11.22)	1·50	15
		aw. Wmk inverted	£850	£500
		ax. Wmk reversed	£900	£500
78		1d. scarlet (I) (11.22)	17·00	60
		aa. 'Flag' flaw	£180	42·00
		a. Carmine (7.24)	18·00	60
		ab. 'Flag' flaw	£180	42·00
		bx. Wmk reversed	£600	£500
78*c*		1d. carmine (II) (12.25)	55·00	8·50
		d. Scarlet (8.27)	35·00	4·25
79		1d. scarlet (III) (10.28)	17·00	30
		a. Carmine-lake (1934)	25·00	2·25
79*b*		1½d. red-brown (27.3.34)	10·00	35
80		2d. grey (12.23)	1·50	1·50
		x. Wmk reversed	75·00	£150
81		2½d. pale sage-green (12.22)	3·75	1·50
		a. Deep sage-green (1924)	3·75	1·50
		aw. Wmk inverted	—	£750
		ax. Wmk reversed	£800	£500
		ay. Wmk inverted and reversed	£800	£500
82		2½d. ultramarine (I) (1.12.26)	5·50	50
		aw. Wmk inverted	£300	£325
82*b*		2½d. ultramarine (II) (3.32)	2·00	70
83		3d. ultramarine (12.24)	19·00	26·00
		w. Wmk inverted	£160	£200
84		3d. purple/*yellow* (10.26)	4·00	1·00
		sa. Opt 'SPECIMEN' double, one albino	£250	
85		4d. red/*yellow* (8.24)	2·50	1·00
		x. Wmk reversed	£550	£600
86		6d. purple (8.24)	1·50	1·00
87		1s. black/*emerald* (10.27)	9·00	9·00
		a. Brownish black/yellow-green (1934)	35·00	50·00
77/87 *Set of* 12			65·00	40·00
77s/87s Optd or Perf (1½d.) 'SPECIMEN' *Set of* 12			£650	

Both comb and line perforations occur on Nos. 77/87*a*.

Detailed gauges are as follows:

13.7×13.9 comb	—	Nos. 77*a*, 78/78*a*, 80, 81/81*a*, 83, 84, 85, 86, 87
13.75 line	—	Nos. 77*a*, 77, 78*c*/78*d*, 79/79*a*, 79*b*, 80, 82, 82*b*, 84, 85, 86, 87/87*a*
13.75×14 line	—	Nos. 77*a*, 78*c*/78*d*, 79*b*, 80, 82*b*, 86, 87*a*
14×13.75 line	—	Nos. 79/79*a*
14 line	—	Nos. 81/81*a*

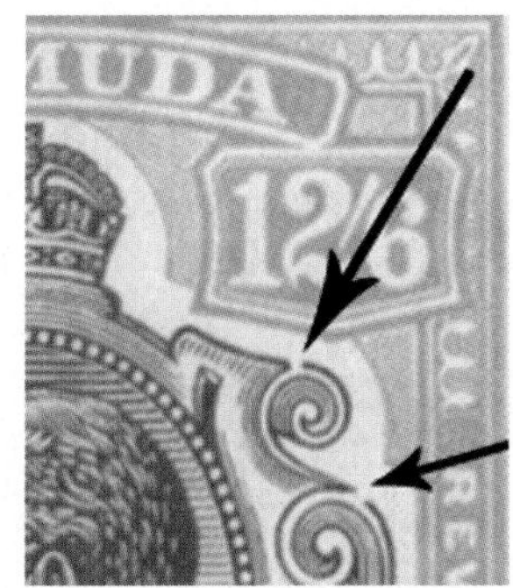

Breaks in scrolls at right (R. 1/3. Ptgs of 12s.6d. from July 1932)

1924–32. Wmk Mult Script CA. Chalk-surfaced paper. P 14.

88 **15** 2s. purple and bright blue/*pale blue* (1.9.27) 50·00 75·00
a. Break in scroll £250
b. Broken crown and scroll £250 £350
c. Nick in top right scroll £275
e. Break in lines below left scroll £275
f. Damaged leaf at bottom right £275
g. Purple and blue/grey-blue (1931) 65·00 85·00
ga. Break in scroll £300 £500
gb. Broken crown and scroll £300
gd. Break through scroll £350 £550
ge. Break in lines below left scroll £350
gf. Damaged leaf at bottom right £350
gg. Gash in fruit and leaf £350

89 2s.6d. black and carmine/*pale blue* (4.27) 60·00 £100
a. Break in scroll £300
b. Broken crown and scroll £300
d. Break through scroll £450
e. Break in lines below left scroll £350
f. Damaged leaf at bottom right £350
g. Black and red/blue to deep blue (6.29) 75·00 £110
ga. Break in scroll £350
gb. Broken crown and scroll £350
gd. Break through scroll £400
ge. Break in lines below left scroll £400
gf. Damaged leaf at bottom right £400
gg. Gash in fruit and leaf £400
h. Grey-black and pale orange-vermilion/grey-blue (3.30) £2750 £2750
ha. Break in scroll £5500
hb. Broken crown and scroll £5500
hd. Break through scroll £5500
he. Break in lines below left scroll £5500
hf. Damaged leaf at bottom right £5500
hg. Gash in fruit and leaf £5500
i. Black and carmine-red/deep grey-blue (8.30) £100 £140
ia. Break in scroll £500
ib. Broken crown and scroll £500
id. Break through scroll £600
ie. Break in lines below left scroll £600
if. Damaged leaf at bottom right £600
ig. Gash in fruit and leaf £600
j. Black and scarlet-vermilion/ deep blue (9.31) 90·00 £130
ja. Break in scroll £450
jb. Broken crown and scroll £450
jc. Nick in top right scroll £500 £600
jd. Break through scroll £550
je. Break in lines below left scroll £550
jf. Damaged leaf at bottom right £550
jg. Gash in fruit and leaf £550
k. Black and bright orange-vermilion/deep blue (8.32) £3250 £3000
kb. Broken crown and scroll £6000
kc. Nick in top right scroll £6000
kd. Break through scroll £6000
ke. Break in lines below left scroll £6000
kf. Damaged leaf at bottom right £6000
kg. Gash in fruit and leaf £6000

92 10s. green and red/*pale emerald* (12.24) £140 £250
a. Break in scroll £800 £1000
b. Broken crown and scroll £700 £1000
e. Break in lines below left scroll £800
f. Damaged leaf at bottom right £800
g. Green and red/deep emerald (1930) £150 £275
ga. Break in scroll £800 £1000
gb. Broken crown and scroll £700 £900
gc. Nick in top right scroll £750
gd. Break through scroll £850 £1000
ge. Break in lines below left scroll £850
gf. Damaged leaf at bottom right £750
gg. Gash in fruit and leaf £750

93 12s.6d. grey and orange (8.32) £250 £375
a. Break in scroll £700 £900
b. Broken crown and scroll £750 £950
c. Nick in top right scroll £800 £950
d. Break through scroll £900
e. Break in lines below left scroll £900
f. Damaged leaf at bottom right £800
g. Gash in fruit and leaf £800
h. Break in scrolls at right £900 £1100
i. Error. Ordinary paper

88/93 *Set of 4* £450 £700
88s/93s Optd or Perf (12s.6d) 'SPECIMEN' *Set of 4* £600

The true No. 89*h* is the only stamp on grey-blue paper, other deeper orange-vermilion shades exist on different papers. No. 89*k* was despatched to Bermuda in July/August 1932, but is not known used before 1937.

Beware of fiscally used 2s.6d. 10s. and 12s.6d. stamps cleaned and bearing faked postmarks. Large quantities were used for a 'head tax' levied on travellers leaving the country.

For 12s.6d. design inscribed 'Revenue' at both sides see No. F1 under POSTAL FISCAL.

1935 (6 May). Silver Jubilee. As Nos. 91/94 of Antigua, but ptd by Waterlow. P 11×12.

94 1d. deep blue and scarlet 1·25 2·50
j. Damaged turret £1000
m. 'Bird' by turret £200 £225
95 1½d. ultramarine and grey 1·25 3·50
m. 'Bird' by turret £200 £275
96 2½d. brown and deep blue 1·50 2·50
m. 'Bird' by turret £275 £325
97 1s. slate and purple 22·00 50·00
k. Kite and vertical log £275 £425
l. Kite and horizontal log £700 £900
94/7 *Set of 4* 23·00 50·00
94s/7s Perf 'SPECIMEN' *Set of 4* £225

For illustrations of plate varieties see Omnibus section following Zanzibar.

20 Red Hole, Paget

21 South Shore

22 *Lucie* (yacht)

23 Grape Bay, Paget Parish

24 Point House, Warwick Parish

25 Gardener's Cottage, Par-la-Ville, Hamilton

(Recess B.W.)

1936 (14 Apr)–**47**. T **12**. Wmk Mult Script CA (sideways on horizontal designs).

98 **20** ½d. bright green 10 10
99 **21** 1d. black and scarlet 65 30
100 1½d. black and chocolate 1·25 50
101 **22** 2d. black and pale blue 5·00 1·75
102 **23** 2½d. light and deep blue 1·00 25
103 **24** 3d. black and scarlet 7·50 2·75
104 **25** 6d. carmine-lake and violet 80 10
a. Claret and dull violet (6.47) 8·00 2·75
105 **23** 1s. green 21·00 24·00
106 **20** 1s.6d. brown 50 10
98/106 *Set of 9* 32·00 26·00
98s/106s Perf 'SPECIMEN' *Set of 9* £325

All are line-perf 11.9, except printings of the 6d. from July 1951 onwards, which are comb-perf 11.9×11.75.

1937 (14 May). Coronation. As Nos. 95/97 of Antigua, but printed by D.L.R. P 14.

107 1d. scarlet 90 1·50
108 1½d. yellow-brown 60 1·75
109 2½d. bright blue 70 1·75
107/109 *Set of 3* 2·00 4·50
107s/109s Perf 'SPECIMEN' *Set of 3* £225

26 Ships in Hamilton Harbour

27 St David's Lighthouse

28 White-tailed Tropicbird, Arms of Bermuda and Native Flower

29 King George VI

(Des Miss Higginbotham (T **28**). Recess B.W.)

1938 (20 Jan)–**52**. T **22**, T **23** (but with portrait of King George VI) and T **26** to **28**. Wmk Mult Script CA. P 12.

110 **26** 1d. black and red (*a*) (*b*) 2·75 20
111 1½d. deep blue and purple-brown (*a*) (*b*) 12·00 1·50
a. Blue and brown (*a*) (3.43) 19·00 10·00
b. Light blue and purple-brown (*a*) (*b*) (9.45) 2·75 2·00
ba. 'A' of 'CA' missing from wmk £1800
112 **22** 2d. light blue and sepia (*a*) 50·00 10·00
112*a* 2d. ultramarine and scarlet (*a*) (*b*) (8.11.40) 3·75 2·25
113 **23** 2½d. light and deep blue (*a*) 14·00 1·25
113*a* 2½d. light blue and sepia-black (*a*) (18.12.41) 6·50 7·00
b. Pale blue and sepia-black (*a*) (3.43) 4·50 4·00
c. Bright blue and deep sepia-black (*b*) (23.9.52) 6·50 10·00
114 **27** 3d. black and rose-red (*a*) 50·00 6·00
114*a* 3d. black and deep blue (*a*) (*b*) (16.7.41) 3·50 40
114*b* **28** 7½d. black, blue and bright green (*a*) (18.12.41) 12·00 4·75
c. Black, blue and yellow-green (*a*) (3.43) 8·50 2·75

115 **23** 1s. green (*a*) (*b*) 2·50 50
a. Bluish green (*b*) (20.6.52) 15·00 7·50

Perforations. Two different perforating machines were used on the various printings of these stamps: (*a*) the original 11.9 line perforation; (*b*) 11.9×11.75 comb perforation, introduced in July 1950. These perforations occur as indicated above.

Shading omitted from top right scroll (R. 1/1. March 1943 ptgs of 2s. and £1)

Lower right scroll with broken tail (R. 2/10. Line perforated printings only)

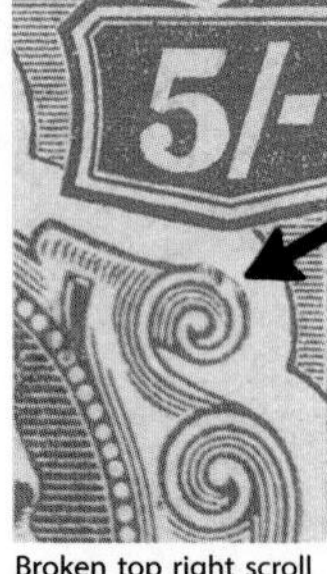
Broken top right scroll (R. 5/11. Line perforated ptgs only. A retouched state of the flaw is visible in later ptgs up to March 1943)

Broken lower right scroll (R. 5/12. Occurs on printings made between May 1941 and March 1943)

Gash in chin (R. 2/5. Ptgs between May 1941 and March 1943)

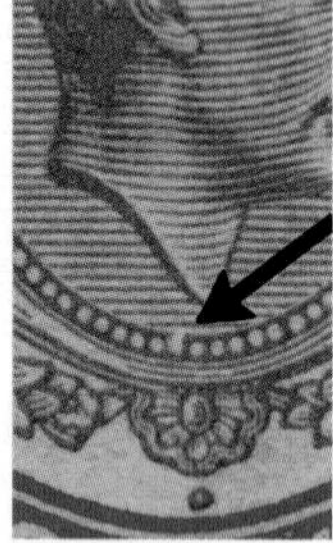
Missing pearl (R. 5/1, Nov 1945 ptg of 5s. only)

'ER' joined (R. 1/2. Occurs in its complete state on 1938 ptg only. Subsequent ptgs show it incomplete)

Damaged left value tablet (R. 1/11. Part of 1951 ptg only)

(Typo D.L.R.)

1938 (20 Jan)–**53**. T **29**. Wmk Mult Crown CA (£1) or Mult Script CA (others). Chalk-surfaced paper. P 14 (comb).

116 2s. deep purple and ultramarine/*grey-blue* £110 18·00
a. Deep reddish purple and ultramarine/grey-blue (21.11.40)* £350 50·00
b. Perf 14¼ line. *Deep purple and ultramarine/grey-blue* (14.11.41)* £350 £100
bc. Lower right scroll with broken tail £4000 £1800
bd. Broken top right scroll £2000 £900
be. Broken lower right scroll £2000 £900
bf. Gash in chin £2750 £1300
c. Ordinary paper. *Purple and blue/deep blue* (7.6.42) 11·00 1·50
ce. Broken lower right scroll £225 £120
cf. Gash in chin £325 £150
d. Ordinary paper. *Purple and deep blue/pale blue* (5.3.43) 15·00 2·00
db. Shading omitted from top right scroll £2000 £2000
de. Broken lower right scroll £700 £700
df. Gash in chin £850 £850

	e. Perf 13. Ordinary paper. *Dull purple and blue/pale blue* (15.2.50)	14·00	18·00
	f. Perf 13. Ordinary paper. *Reddish purple and blue/pale blue* (10.10.50)	19·00	40·00
117	2s.6d. black and red/*grey-blue*	70·00	14·00
	a. Perf 14¼ line. *Black and red/grey-blue* (21.2.42)*	£600	£120
	ac. Lower right scroll with broken tail	£4250	£1900
	ad. Broken top right scroll	£2750	£1100
	ae. Broken lower right scroll	£2750	£1100
	af. Gash in chin	£3250	£1500
	b. Ordinary paper. *Black and red/pale blue* (5.3.43)	22·00	13·00
	be. Broken lower right scroll	£650	£650
	bf. Gash in chin	£850	£750
	c. Perf 13. Ordinary paper. *Black and orange-red/pale blue* (10.10.50)	17·00	11·00
	d. Perf 13. Ordinary paper. *Black and red/pale blue* (18.6.52)	18·00	27·00
118	5s. green and red/*yellow*	£150	48·00
	a. Pale green and red/yellow (14.3.39)*	£375	85·00
	b. Perf 14¼ line. *Dull yellow-green and red/yellow* (11.10.42)*	£300	40·00
	bc. Lower right scroll with broken tail	£3500	£1100
	bd. Broken top right scroll	£1300	£550
	be. Broken lower right scroll	£1300	£550
	bf. Gash in chin	£1600	£750
	c. Ordinary paper. *Bronze-green and carmine-red/pale yellow* (5.42)*	£1500	£180
	ce. Broken lower right scroll	£9000	£2750
	cf. Gash in chin	£9500	£2750
	d. Ordinary paper. *Pale bluish green and carmine-red/pale yellow* (5.3.43)	£100	50·00
	de. Broken lower right scroll	£1100	£800
	df. Gash in chin	£1200	£800
	e. Ordinary paper. *Green and red/pale yellow* (5.45)*	50·00	27·00
	ea. Missing pearl	£1000	
	f. Perf 13. Ordinary paper. *Yellow-green and red/pale yellow* (15.2.50)	35·00	40·00
	g. Perf 13. *Green and scarlet/yellow* (*chalk-surfaced*) (10.10.50)	60·00	75·00
119	10s. green and deep lake/*pale emerald*	£450	£325
	a. Bluish green and deep red/green (8.39)*	£225	£130
	b. Perf 14¼ line. Ordinary paper. *Yellow green and carmine/green* (1942)*	£550	£130
	bc. Lower right scroll with broken tail	£5000	£2250
	bd. Broken top right scroll	£2500	£1300
	be. Broken lower right scroll	£2500	£1300
	bf. Gash in chin	£3250	£1400
	c. Ordinary paper. *Yellowish green and deep carmine-red/green* (5.3.43)	70·00	65·00
	ce. Broken lower right scroll	£2750	
	cf. Gash in chin	£3000	
	d. Ordinary paper. *Deep green and dull red/green* (*emerald back*) (11.12.46)	85·00	70·00
	e. Perf 13. Ordinary paper. *Green and vermilion/green* (19.9.51)	48·00	50·00
	f. Perf 13. Ordinary paper. *Green and dull red/green* (16.4.53)	50·00	65·00
120	12s.6d. deep grey and brownish orange	£550	£450
	a. Grey and brownish orange (*shades*)	£225	75·00
	b. Grey and pale orange (9.11.40)*	£110	55·00
	c. Ordinary paper (2.3.44)*	£120	70·00
	ce. Broken lower right scroll	£2250	£2500
	cf. Gash in chin	£2500	
	d. Ordinary paper. *Grey and yellow*† (17.9.47)*	£700	£500
	e. Perf 13. *Grey and pale orange* (*chalk surfaced*) (10.10.50)	£100	85·00
121	£1 purple and black/*red*	£275	£100
	a. 'ER' joined	£1100	£600
	b. Pale purple and black/pale red (13.5.43)*	90·00	80·00
	ba. 'ER' joined	£700	£600
	be. Broken lower right scroll	£2000	£1500
	bf. Gash in chin	£2250	£1700
	c. Deep reddish purple and black/pale red (5.3.43)*	60·00	75·00
	ca. 'ER' joined	£650	£700
	cb. Shading omitted from top right scroll	£4000	
	ce. Broken lower right scroll	£1800	£1500
	cf. Gash in chin	£2000	
	d. Perf 13. *Violet and black/scarlet* (7.12.51)	55·00	85·00
	da. Damaged left value tablet	£4500	
	e. Perf 13. *Bright violet and black/scarlet* (10.12.52)	£180	£300
110/121*d*	*Set of 16*	£350	£225
110s/121s	Perf 'SPECIMEN' *Set of 16*	£2000	

Following extensive damage to their printing works on 29 December 1940 much of De La Rue's work was transferred to other firms operating under their supervision. It is understood that Williams Lea & Co produced those new printings ordered for the Bermuda high value stamps during 1941. The first batch of these printings showed the emergency use, by Williams Lea, of a 14¼ line perforating machine (exact gauge 14.15) instead of the comb perforation (exact gauge 13.9×13.8).

Dates marked * are those of earliest known use.

In No. 116*c* the coloured surfacing of the paper is mottled with white specks sometimes accompanied by very close horizontal lines. In Nos. 116*d*, 117*b* and 118*c*/118*d* the surfacing is the same colour as the back, sometimes applied in widely spaced horizontal lines giving the appearance of laid paper.

† No. 120*d* is the so-called 'lemon' shade.

HALF PENNY

X X

30

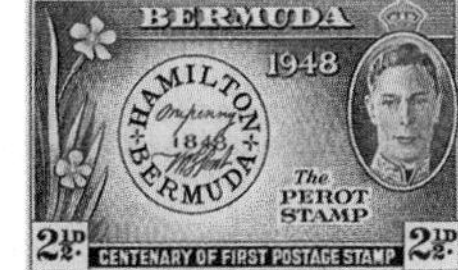

31 Postmaster Perot's Stamp

1940 (20 Dec). No. 110 surch with T **30** by *Royal Gazette*, Hamilton.

122	**26**	½d. on 1d. black and red (*shades*)	1·75	3·75

The spacing between 'PENNY' and 'X' varies from 12½ mm to 14 mm.

1946 (6 Nov). Victory. As Nos. 110/111 of Antigua.

123	1½d. brown	15	15
124	3d. blue	40	65
123s/124s	Perf 'SPECIMEN' *Set of 2*	£170	

1948 (1 Dec). Royal Silver Wedding. As Nos. 112/113 of Antigua.

125	1½d. red-brown	30	50
126	£1 carmine	45·00	55·00

(Recess B.W.)

1949 (11 Apr). Centenary of Postmaster Perot's Stamp. Wmk Mult Script CA. P 13½.

127	**31**	2½d. blue and brown	35	35
128		3d. black and blue	35	15
129		6d. violet and green	40	15
127/129		*Set of 3*	1·00	60

1949 (10 Oct). 75th Anniversary of Universal Postal Union. As Nos. 114/117 of Antigua.

130	2½d. blue-black	30	2·25
	a. 'C' of 'CA' missing from watermark	£1200	
131	3d. deep blue	2·25	1·50
132	6d. purple	40	1·00
133	1s. blue-green	1·00	1·75
130/133	*Set of 4*	3·50	6·00

1953 (4 June). Coronation. As No. 200 of Bahamas, but ptd by B. W.

134	1½d. black and blue	1·25	75

32 Easter Lilies

33 Postmaster Perot's stamp

34 Easter Lily

35 *Victory II* (racing dinghy)

36 Sir George Somers and *Sea Venture*

37 Map of Bermuda

38 *Sea Venture* (galleon), coin and Perot stamp

39 White-tailed Tropicbird

40 Early Bermudan coinage

41 Arms of St Georges

42 Warwick Fort

43 1 tog coin

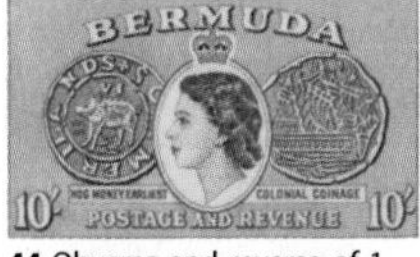

44 Obverse and reverse of 1 tog coin

45 Arms of Bermuda

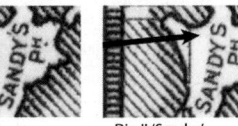

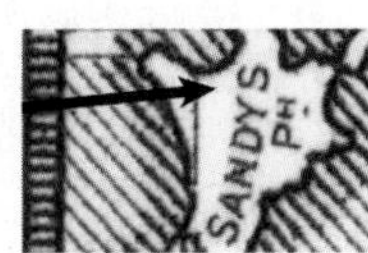

Die I 'Sandy's'

Die II 'Sandys'

(Des C. Deakins (½d., 3d., 1s.3d., 5s.), J. Berry (1d., 1½d., 2½d., 4d., 1s.). B. Brown (2d., 6d., 8d.), D. Haig (4½d., 9d.), Pamela Braley-Smith (2s.6d.) and E. C. Leslie (10s.) all adapted by W. Harrington Recess (except £1, centre typo), B.W.)

1953 (9 Nov)–**62**. T **32/45**. Wmk Mult Script CA. P 13½.

135	**32**	½d. olive-green	1·00	5·00
		a. Yellow-olive (19.5.54)	40	2·75
136	**33**	1d. black and red	2·25	1·00
		a. Black and deep red (19.5.54)	9·00	1·50
137	**34**	1½d. green	30	10
138	**35**	2d. ultramarine and brown-red	50	40
139	**36**	2½d. rose-red	2·00	50
140	**37**	3d. deep purple (I)	30	10
140*a*		3d. deep purple (II) (2.1.57)	1·00	20
141	**33**	4d. black and bright blue	55	1·75
142	**38**	4½d. emerald	2·00	1·00
143	**39**	6d. black and deep turquoise	6·50	60
143*a*		8d. black and red (16.5.55)	3·25	30
143*b*	**38**	9d. violet (6.1.58)	14·00	2·50
144	**40**	1s. orange	50	15
145	**37**	1s.3d. blue (I)	3·75	30
		a. Greenish blue (21.9.54)	14·00	1·50
145*b*		1s.3d. blue (II) (2.1.57)	7·00	50
		bc. Bright blue (14.8.62)	25·00	9·50
146	**41**	2s. brown	4·50	85
147	**42**	2s.6d. scarlet	11·00	45
148	**43**	5s. carmine	23·00	1·00
149	**44**	10s. deep ultramarine	23·00	9·50
		a. Ultramarine (13.2.57)	80·00	19·00
150	**45**	£1 brown, blue, red, green and bronze-green	48·00	21·00
135/150		*Set of 18*	£130	40·00

Nos. 136, 138 and 143 exist in coils, constructed from normal sheets.

1953 (26 Nov). Royal Visit. As No. 143 but inscr 'ROYAL VISIT 1953' in top left corner.

151	6d. black and deep turquoise	1·25	20

Three Power Talks
December, 1953.
(**46**)

Three Power Talks
December, 1953.
(**46a**)

First setting (T **46**). First line 24½ mm long.
Second setting (T **46a**). First line 25¼ mm long.

1953 (8 Dec). Three Power Talks. Nos. 140 and 145 optd with T **46** by *Royal Gazette*, Hamilton.

152	**37**	3d. deep purple (T **46**) (B.)	20	10
		a. Optd with T **46a**	2·00	30
153		1s.3d. blue (T **46**) (R.)	20	10
		a. Optd with T **46a**	9·00	8·00

50TH ANNIVERSARY
U S – BERMUDA
OCEAN RACE 1956
(**47**)

48 Perot's Post Office

1956 (22 June). 50th Anniversary of United States–Bermuda Yacht Race. Nos. 143*a* and 145*a* optd with T **47** by the *Bermuda Press*.

154	8d. black and red (Bk.)	30	45
155	1s.3d. greenish blue (R.)	30	55

(Des W. Harrington. Recess B.W.)

1959 (1 Jan). Wmk Mult Script CA. P 13½.

156	**48**	6d. black and deep mauve	1·75	15

49 Arms of King James I and Queen Elizabeth II

3d. and **8d.** A horizontal red registration line shows in the SW section of the right garter (R. 4/8)

(Des W. Harrington. Recess; Arms litho D.L.R.)

1959 (29 July). 350th Anniversary of First Settlement. Arms, red, yellow and blue; frame colours below. W w **12**. P 13.

157	**49**	1½d. grey-blue	35	10
158		3d. drab-grey	40	50
		a. Registration line	25·00	
159		4d. reddish purple	45	55
160		8d. slate-violet	45	15
		a. Registration line	25·00	
161		9d. olive-green	45	1·25
162		1s.3d. brown	45	30
157/162		*Set of 6*	2·25	2·50

50 The Old Rectory, St George's, *circa* 1730

51 Church of St Peter, St George's

52 Government House, 1892

53 The Cathedral, Hamilton, 1894

54 HM Dockyard, 1811

55 Perot's Post Office, 1848

56 GPO Hamilton, 1869

57 Library, Par-la-Ville

58 Bermuda cottage, *circa* 1705

59 Christ Church, Warwick, 1719

60 City Hall Hamilton, 1960

61 Town of St George

62 Bermuda house, *circa* 1710

63 Bermuda house, early 18th-century

64 Colonial Secretariat, 1833

65 Old Post Office, Somerset, 1890

66 The House of Assembly, 1815

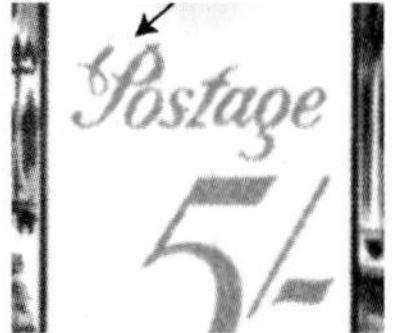
5s. Top loop of 'P' of 'Postage' broken. (Pl. 1A-1A, R. 1/1). Corrected on No. 246

(Des W. Harrington. Photo Harrison)

1962 (26 Oct)–**68**. T **50/66**. W w **12** (upright). P 12½.

163	**50**	1d. reddish purple, black and orange	10	75
		w. Wmk inverted	—	£750
164	**51**	2d. lilac, indigo, yellow and green	1·00	35
		a. Lilac omitted	£1000	£1000
		b. Green omitted	†	£7500
		c. Imperf (pair)	£2250	
		d. *Pale lilac, indigo, yellow and green* (22.10.68)	9·00	4·50
		w. Wmk inverted	—	£350
165	**52**	3d. yellow-brown and light blue	10	10
166	**53**	4d. red-brown and magenta	20	40
167	**54**	5d. grey-blue and rose	1·25	3·25
168	**55**	6d. grey-blue, emerald and light blue	30	30
		w. Wmk inverted	£275	£275
169	**56**	8d. bright blue, bright green and orange	30	35
170	**57**	9d. light blue and brown	30	60
170*a*	**58**	10d. violet and ochre (8.2.65)	15·00	2·50
		aw. Wmk inverted	£1500	£1100
171	**59**	1s. black, emerald, bright blue and orange	30	10
172	**60**	1s.3d. lake, grey and bistre	75	15
		w. Wmk inverted	†	£2500
173	**58**	1s.6d. violet and ochre	75	1·00
174	**61**	2s. red-brown and orange	3·00	1·25
175	**62**	2s.3d. bistre-brown and yellow-green	1·00	7·00
176	**63**	2s.6d. bistre-brown, bluish green and olive-yellow	55	50
177	**64**	5s. brown-purple and blue-green	1·75	1·50
		a. Broken 'P'	40·00	
		w. Wmk inverted	£350	£325
178	**65**	10s. magenta, deep bluish green and buff	5·50	7·00
		w. Wmk inverted	£800	£750
179	**66**	£1 black, yellow-olive and yellow-orange	14·00	15·00
163/179 *Set of 18*			40·00	35·00

Three examples of No. 164b are known, all used *on piece*. The 3d. value with the yellow-brown omitted, previously No. 165a, is no longer listed as this is believed to be a dry print. All reported examples show traces of the yellow-brown.

See also Nos. 195/200 and 246a.

1963 (4 June). Freedom from Hunger. As No. 146 of Antigua.

180	1s.3d. sepia	60	40

1963 (2 Sept). Red Cross Centenary. As Nos. 147/148 of Antigua.

181	3d. red and black	50	25
182	1s.3d. red and blue	1·00	2·50

67 *Tsotsi in the Bundu* (Finn class dinghy)

(Des V. Whiteley. Photo D.L.R.)

1964 (28 Sept). Olympic Games, Tokyo. W w **12**. P 14×13½.

183	**67**	3d. red, violet and blue	10	10

1965 (17 May). ITU Centenary. As Nos. 166/167 of Antigua.

184	3d. light blue and emerald	35	25
185	2s. yellow and ultramarine	65	1·50

68 Scout Badge and St Edward's Crown

(Des W. Harrington. Photo Harrison)

1965 (24 July). 50th Anniversary of Bermuda Boy Scouts Association. W w **12**. P 12½.

186	**68**	2s. multicoloured	50	50
		w. Wmk inverted	55·00	65·00

1965 (25 Oct). International Co-operation Year. As Nos. 168/169 of Antigua.

187	4d. reddish purple and turquoise-green	40	20
188	2s.6d. deep bluish green and lavender	60	80

1966 (24 Jan). Churchill Commemoration. As Nos. 170/173 of Antigua.

189	3d. new blue	25	20
190	6d. deep green	60	1·25
191	10d. brown	65	75
192	1s.3d. bluish violet	75	2·50
189/192 *Set of 4*		2·00	4·25

1966 (1 July). World Cup Football Championship. As Nos. 176/177 of Antigua.

193	10d. violet, yellow-green, lake and yellow-brown	40	15
194	2s.6d. chocolate, blue-green, lake and yellow-brown	60	1·25

1966 (25 Oct)–**69**. Designs as Nos. 164, 167 (1s.6d.), 169, 170*a*/171 and 174 but W w **12** (sideways*).

195	**51**	2d. lilac, indigo, yellow and green (20.5.69)	6·50	8·50
		w. Wmk Crown to right of CA	—	£400
196	**56**	8d. bright blue, bright green and orange (14.2.67)	50	1·50
197	**58**	10d. violet and ochre (1.11.66)	1·25	60
		w. Wmk Crown to right of CA	£1400	£1400
198	**59**	1s. black, emerald, bright blue and orange (14.2.67)	1·75	1·40
199	**54**	1s.6d. grey-blue and rose (1.11.66)	1·00	30
		w. Wmk Crown to right of CA	£150	£160
200	**61**	2s. red-brown and orange	1·50	60
195/200 *Set of 6*			11·00	11·50

* The normal sideways watermark shows Crown to left of CA, *as seen from the back of the stamp.*

The 2d. value exists with PVA gum only, and the 8d. exists with PVA gum as well as gum arabic.

1966 (1 Dec). 20th Anniversary of UNESCO As Nos. 196/198 of Antigua.

201	4d. slate-violet, red, yellow and orange	35	15
202	1s.3d. orange-yellow, violet and deep olive	60	65
203	2s. black, bright purple and orange	75	1·75
201/203 *Set of 3*		1·50	2·25

69 GPO Building

(Des G. Vasarhelyi. Photo Harrison)

1967 (23 June). Opening of New General Post Office, Hamilton. W w **12**. P 14½.

204	**69**	3d. multicoloured	10	10
205		1s. multicoloured	15	10
206		1s.6d. multicoloured	30	25
207		2s.6d. multicoloured	35	1·00
204/207 *Set of 4*			75	1·25

70 *Mercury* (cable ship) and Chain Links

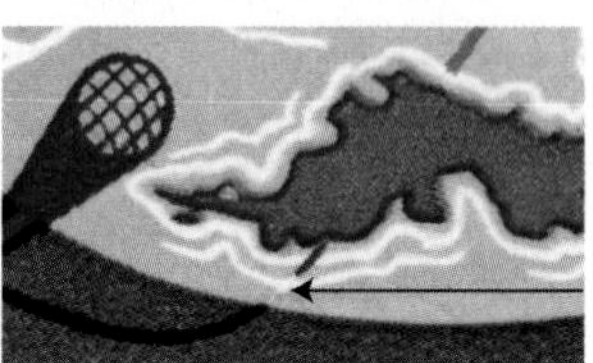
1s. Broken cable above 'R' of 'BERMUDA' (R. 12/1)

(Des V. Whiteley. Photo Harrison)

1967 (14 Sept). Inauguration of Bermuda–Tortola Telephone Service. T **70** and similar horizontal designs. Multicoloured. W w **12**. P 14½×14.

208	3d. Type **70**	15	10
209	1s. Map, telephone and microphone	25	10
	a. Broken cable	12·00	
210	1s.6d. Telecommunications media	25	25
211	2s.6d. *Mercury* (cable ship) and marine fauna	40	1·25
208/211 *Set of 4*		1·00	1·50

74 Human Rights Emblem and Doves

(Des M. Farrar Bell. Litho Harrison)

1968 (1 Feb). Human Rights Year. W w **12**. P 14×14½.

212	**74**	3d. indigo, blue and dull green	10	10
213		1s. yellow-brown, blue and light blue	10	10
214		1s.6d. black, blue and rose	10	15
215		2s.6d. grey-green, blue and yellow	15	25
212/215 *Set of 4*			30	55

REPRESENTATIVE GOVERNMENT

75 Mace and Queen's Profile

(Des R. Granger Barrett. Photo Harrison)

1968 (1 July). New Constitution. T **75** and similar horizontal design. W w **12**. P 14.

216	**75**	3d. multicoloured	10	10
217		1s. multicoloured	10	10
218	–	1s.6d. greenish yellow, black and turquoise-blue	10	20
219	–	2s.6d. lilac, black and orange-yellow	15	75
216/219 *Set of 4*			30	1·00

Design: 1s.6d., 2s.6d. Houses of Parliament and House of Assembly, Bermuda.

77 Football, Athletics and Yachting

(Des V. Whiteley. Photo Harrison)

1968 (24 Sept). Olympic Games, Mexico. W w **12**. P 12½.

No.	Type	Description	Unused	Used
220	**77**	3d. multicoloured	15	10
		a. Red-brown ('BERMUDA' and value) omitted	£4750	£5000
221		1s. multicoloured	25	10
222		1s.6d. multicoloured	50	30
223		2s.6d. multicoloured	50	1·40
220/223 *Set of 4*			1·25	1·75

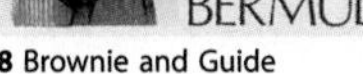

78 Brownie and Guide

80 Emerald-studded Gold Cross and Seaweed

(Des Harrison. Litho Format)

1969 (17 Feb). 50th Anniversary of Bermuda Girl Guides. P 14.

No.	Type	Description	Unused	Used
224	**78**	3d. multicoloured	10	10
225		1s. multicoloured	20	10
226	–	1s.6d. multicoloured	25	40
227	–	2s.6d. multicoloured	35	1·40
224/227 *Set of 4*			80	1·75

Design: 1s.6d., 2s.6d. Guides and badge.

(Des K. Giles adapted by V. Whiteley. Photo Harrison)

1969 (29 Sept). Underwater Treasure. T **80** and similar vert design. Multicoloured. W w **12** (sideways). P 14½×14.

No.	Description	Unused	Used
228	4d. Type **80**	20	10
229	1s.3d. Emerald-studded gold cross and seabed	35	15
	a. Green (jewels) omitted		
230	2s. Type **80**	45	90
231	2s.6d. As 1s.3d.	45	1·75
228/231 *Set of 4*		1·25	2·50

(New Currency. 100 cents = 1 Bermuda dollar)

1c

2c

(82)

Tall '2' (Pl 1A. R. 2/2)

1970 (6 Feb). Decimal Currency. As Nos. 163, 165/166, 168, 170, 172, 175/179 and 195/200 surch as T **82**. W w **12** (sideways* on 2, 5, 10, 12, 15, 18, 24, 30, 60c., $1.20 and $2.40).

No.	Description	Unused	Used
232	1c. on 1d. reddish purple, black and orange	10	1·75
	w. Wmk inverted	50·00	50·00
233	2c. on 2d. lilac, indigo, yellow and green	10	10
	a. Lilac omitted	£1100	
	b. Vert pair, one without surch	£7500	
	c. Tall '2'	10·00	
	d. Surch double, one albino		
	ew. Wmk Crown to right of CA	£140	£160
	f. Wmk upright (No. 164)	3·00	7·00
	fa. Tall '2'	45·00	
	g. Wmk upright (No. 164*d*)	7·50	10·00
	ga. Tall '2'	75·00	
234	3c. on 3d. yellow-brown and light blue	10	30
235	4c. on 4d. red-brown and magenta (Br.)	10	10
236	5c. on 8d. bright blue, bright green and orange	15	2·25
237	6c. on 6d. grey-blue, emerald and light blue	15	1·75
	a. Horiz pair, one with albino surch, the other with albino bar	£5500	
	w. Wmk inverted	£325	£190
238	9c. on 9d. light blue and brown (Br.)	30	2·75
239	10c. on 10d. violet and ochre	30	25
240	12c. on 1s. black, emerald, bright blue and orange	30	1·25
241	15c. on 1s.3d. lake, grey and bistre	2·00	1·75
242	18c. on 1s.6d. grey-blue and rose	80	65
243	24c. on 2s. red-brown and orange	85	4·50
	w. Wmk Crown to right of CA	£170	£225
244	30c. on 2s.6d. bistre-brown, bluish green and olive-yellow	1·00	3·00
245	36c. on 2s.3d. bistre-brown and yellow-green	1·75	8·00
246	60c. on 5s. brown-purple and blue-green	2·25	4·00
	a. Surch omitted †	£1500	
247	$1.20 on 10s. magenta, deep bluish green and buff	3·50	12·00
248	$2.40 on £1 black, yellow-olive and yellow-orange	4·50	15·00
232/248 *Set of 17*		16·00	50·00

* The normal sideways watermark shows Crown to left of CA, *as seen from the back of the stamp*.

† No. 246a differs from the normal No. 177 by its watermark, which is sideways, and its gum, which is PVA.

The surcharge was applied typo on the lc., 2c., 3c., 6c. and 36c. and photo on the remaining values.

83 *Spathiphyllum*

(Des W. Harrington. Photo D.L.R.)

1970 (6 July)–**75**. Flowers. Multicoloured designs as T **83**. W w **12** (sideways on horizontal designs). P 14.

No.	Description	Unused	Used
249	1c. Type **83**	10	20
250	2c. Bottlebrush	20	25
251	3c. Oleander (*vert*)	15	10
252	4c. Bermudiana	15	10
253	5c. Poinsettia	2·75	20
254	6c. Hibiscus	30	30
255	9c. Cereus	20	45
256	10c. Bougainvillea (*vert*)	20	15
257	12c. Jacaranda	60	45
258	15c. Passion-Flower	90	70
258*a*	17c. As 15c. (2.6.75)	2·75	6·00
259	18c. Coralita	1·75	70
259*a*	20c. As 18c. (2.6.75)	2·75	4·75
260	24c. Morning Glory	1·50	5·00
260*a*	25c. As 24c. (2.6.75)	2·75	4·50
261	30c. Tecoma	1·00	1·00
262	36c. Angel's Trumpet	1·00	1·00
262*a*	40c. As 36c. (2.6.75)	2·75	5·50
263	60c. Plumbago	1·50	1·00
263*a*	$1 As 60c. (2.6.75)	3·25	6·50
264	$1.20 Bird of Paradise flower	1·75	1·00
264*a*	$2 As $1.20 (2.6.75)	11·00	11·00
265	$2.40 Chalice Cup	4·00	1·25
265*a*	$3 As $2.40 (2.6.75)	13·00	11·00
249/265*a* *Set of 24*		50·00	50·00

The 5c., 6c., 12c. and 30c. were reissued on upright watermark paper in 1974-1976.

84 The State House, St George's

(Des G. Drummond. Litho Questa)

1970 (12 Oct). 350th Anniversary of Bermuda Parliament. T **84** and similar horizontal designs. Multicoloured. W w **12** (sideways). P 14.

No.	Description	Unused	Used
266	4c. Type **84**	10	10
267	15c. The Sessions House, Hamilton	30	20
268	18c. St Peter's Church, St George's	30	25
269	24c. Town Hall, Hamilton	40	1·00
266/269 *Set of 4*		1·00	1·40
MS270 131×95 mm. Nos. 266/269		1·10	1·50

STAMP BOOKLETS

1948 (5 Apr–10 May). Pink (No. SB1), or light blue (No. SB2) covers. Stapled.

No.	Description	Price
SB1	5s. booklet containing 6×1d., 6×1½d., 6×2d., 6×2½d. and 6×3d. (Nos. 110, 111*b*, 112*a*, 113*b*, 114*a*) in blocks of 6 (10.5)	£140
SB2	10s.6d. booklet containing 6×3d. and 18×6d. (Nos. 114*a*, 104) in blocks of 6 with 12 air mail labels	£150

POSTAL FISCAL

1937 (1 Feb). As T **15**, but inscr 'REVENUE' at each side. Wmk Mult Script CA. Chalk-surfaced paper. P 14

No.	Description	Unused	Used
F1	12s.6d. grey and orange	£1100	£1500
	a. Break in scroll (R. 1/12)	£4250	£6500
	b. Broken crown and scroll (R. 2/12)	£4250	
	d. Break through scroll (R. 1/9)	£4250	
	e. Break in lines below left scroll	£4250	
	f. Damaged leaf at bottom right	£4250	
	g. Gash in fruit and leaf	£4250	
	h. Breaks in scrolls at right (R. 1/3)	£4250	

No. F1 was issued for fiscal purposes towards the end of 1936. Its use as a postage stamp was authorised from 1 February to April 1937. The used price quoted above is for examples postmarked during this period. Later in the same year postmarks with other dates were obtained by favour.

For illustrations of No. F1a/F1h see above Nos. 51*b* and 88.

Botswana

INDEPENDENCE

47 National Assembly Building

(Des R. Granger Barrett. Photo Harrison)

1966 (30 Sept). Independence. T **47** and similar horiz designs. Multicoloured. P 14½.

No.	Description	Unused	Used
202	2½c. Type **47**	15	10
	a. Imperf (pair)	£450	
203	5c. Abattoir Lobatsi	20	10
204	15c. National Airways Douglas DC-3	65	20
205	35c. State House, Gaberones	40	30
202/205 *Set of 4*		1·25	55

REPUBLIC OF BOTSWANA

(**51**)

52 Golden Oriole

1966 (30 Sept). Nos. 168/181 of Bechuanaland optd as T **51**.

No.	Description	Unused	Used
206	1c. yellow, red, black and lilac	25	10
207	2c. orange, black and yellow-olive	30	1·75
208	2½c. carmine, green, black and bistre	30	10
209	3½c. yellow, black, sepia and pink	1·50	40
	a. Yellow, black, sepia and flesh	12·00	2·25
210	5c. yellow, blue, black and buff	2·00	1·50
211	7½c. brown, red, black and apple-green	50	1·75
	a. Yellow background	—	£1000
212	10c. red, yellow, sepia and turquoise-green	1·00	20
213	12½c. buff, blue, red and grey-black	2·00	4·00
214	20c. yellow-brown and drab	20	1·00
215	25c. deep brown and lemon	20	2·00
216	35c. deep blue and orange	30	3·00
217	50c. sepia and olive	20	70
218	1r. black and cinnamon	40	1·25
219	2r. brown and turquoise-blue	1·00	3·75
206/219 *Set of 14*		9·00	19·00

No. 209*a* was a special printing produced to make up quantities. It does not exist without the overprint.

No. 211a shows the background in yellow instead of apple-green and may have come from a trial printing. Most known examples come from first day covers but eight unused examples have also been reported.

(Des D. M. Reid-Henry. Photo Harrison)

1967 (3 Jan). Birds. Vertical designs as T **52**. Multicoloured. P 14×14.

No.	Description	Unused	Used
220	1c. Type **52**	30	15
	a. Error. Wmk **105** of Malta	†	£850
221	2c. Hoopoe	60	70
222	3c. Groundscraper Thrush	55	10
223	4c. Cordon-bleu ('Blue Waxbill')	55	10
224	5c. Secretary Bird	55	10
225	7c. Yellow-billed Hornbill	60	1·00
226	10c. Burchell's Gonolek ('Crimson-breasted Shrike')	60	15
227	15c. Malachite Kingfisher	8·50	3·25
228	20c. African Fish Eagle	8·50	2·25
229	25c. Go-away Bird ('Grey Loerie')	4·00	1·50
230	35c. Scimitar-bill	6·00	4·00
231	50c. Comb Duck	2·75	2·75
232	1r. Levaillant's Barbet	5·00	3·50
233	2r. Didric Cuckoo	7·00	17·00
220/233 *Set of 14*		40·00	32·00

A used copy of the 20c. has been seen with the pale brown colour missing, resulting in the value (normally shown in white) being omitted.

The 1, 2, 4, 7 and 10c. values exist with PVA gum as well as gum arabic.

66 Students and University

(Des V. Whiteley. Photo Harrison)

1967 (7 Apr). First Conferment of University Degrees. P 14×14½.

No.	Type	Description	Unused	Used
234	**66**	3c. sepia, ultramarine and light orange-yellow	10	10
235		7c. sepia, ultramarine and light greenish blue	10	10
236		15c. sepia, ultramarine and rose	10	10
237		35c. sepia, ultramarine and light violet	20	20
234/237 *Set of 4*			30	30

67 Bushbuck

(Des G. Vasarhelyi. Photo Harrison)

1967 (2 Oct). Chobe Game Reserve. T **67** and similar horizontal designs. Multicoloured. P 14.

238		3c. Type **67**	10	20
239		7c. Sale Antelope	15	30
240		35c. Fishing on Chobe River	90	1·10
238/240 *Set of 3*			1·00	1·40

70 Arms of Botswana and Human Rights Emblem

(Litho D.L.R.)

1968 (8 Apr). Human Rights Year. T **70** and similar horizontal designs showing Anniversary of Botswana and Human Rights emblem arranged differently. P 13½×13.

241		3c. multicoloured	10	10
242		15c. multicoloured	25	45
243		25c. multicoloured	25	60
241/243 *Set of 3*			50	1·00

73 Eland and Giraffe Rock Paintings, Tsodilo Hills

75 *Baobab Trees* (Thomas Baines)

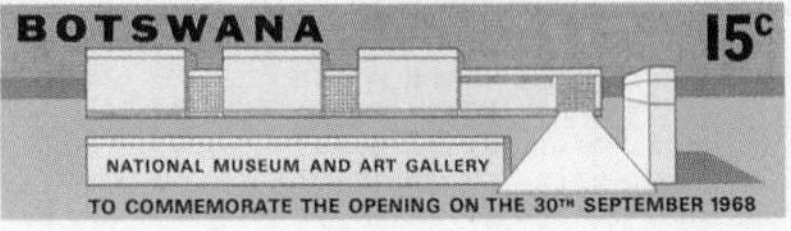

76 National Museum and Art Gallery

(Litho D.L.R.)

1968 (30 Sept). Opening of National Museum and Art Gallery. T **73/76** and similar multicoloured design. P 12½ (7c.), 12½×13½ (15c.), or 13×13½ (others).

244		3c. Type **73**	20	20
245		7c. Girl wearing ceremonial beads (30×48 *mm*)	25	40
246		10c. Type **75**	25	30
247		15c. Type **76**	40	1·50
244/247 *Set of 4*			1·00	2·25
MS248		132×82 mm. Nos. 244/247. P 13	1·00	2·25

77 African Family, and Star over Village

(Des Mrs M. E. Townsend, adapted J. Cooter. Litho Enschedé)

1968 (11 Nov). Christmas. P 13×14.

249	**77**	1c. multicoloured	10	25
250		2c. multicoloured	10	25
251		5c. multicoloured	10	10
252		25c. multicoloured	15	50
249/252 *Set of 4*			30	1·00

78 Scout, Lion and Badge in Frame

(Des D.L.R. Litho Format)

1969 (21 Aug). 22nd World Scout Conference, Helsinki. T **78** and similar multicoloured designs. P 13½.

253		3c. Type **78**	35	30
254		15c. Scouts cooking over open fire (*vert*)	35	1·00
255		25c. Scouts around camp fire	40	1·00
253/255 *Set of 3*			1·00	2·00

81 Woman, Child and Christmas Star

82 Diamond Treatment Plant, Orapa

(Des A. Vale, adapted V. Whiteley. Litho Harrison)

1969 (6 Nov). Christmas. P 14½×14.

256	**81**	1c. pale blue and chocolate	10	20
257		2c. pale yellow-olive and chocolate	10	20
258		4c. yellow and chocolate	10	10
259		35c. chocolate and bluish violet	35	20
256/259 *Set of 4*			50	60
MS260		86×128 mm. Nos. 256/259. P 14½ (*shades*).	1·00	1·10

(Des J.W. Litho Harrison)

1970 (23 Mar). Developing Botswana. T **82** and similar designs. Multicoloured. P 14½×14 (3c., 7c.) or 14×14½ (others).

261		3c. Type **82**	80	20
262		7c. Copper-nickel mining	1·00	20
263		10c. Copper-nickel mine, Selebi-Pikwe (*horiz*)	1·25	15
264		35c. Orapa diamond mine, and diamonds (*horiz*)	3·00	1·25
261/264 *Set of 4*			5·50	1·60

83 Mr. Micawber (*David Copperfield*)

(Des V. Whiteley. Litho Walsall)

1970 (6 July). Death Centenary of Charles Dickens. T **83** and similar horizontal designs. Multicoloured. P 11.

265		3c. Type **83**	25	10
266		7c. Scrooge (*A Christmas Carol*)	25	10
267		15c. Fagin (*Oliver Twist*)	45	40
268		25c. Bill Sykes (*Oliver Twist*)	70	60
265/268 *Set of 4*			1·50	1·00
MS269		114×81 mm. Nos. 265/268	2·75	4·00

84 UN Building and Emblem

(Des J. Cooter. Litho Walsall)

1970 (24 Oct). 25th Anniversary of United Nations. P 11.

270	**84**	15c. bright blue, chestnut and silver	70	50

85 Crocodile

(Des A. Vale. Litho Questa)

1970 (3 Nov). Christmas. T **85** and similar horizontal designs. Multicoloured. P 14.

271		1c. Type **85**	10	10
272		2c. Giraffe	10	10
273		7c. Elephant	15	15
274		25c. Rhinoceros	60	80
271/274 *Set of 4*			80	1·00
MS275		128×90 mm. Nos. 271/274	1·00	3·00

POSTAGE DUE STAMPS

REPUBLIC OF

BOTSWANA

(D **4**)

1967 (1 Mar). Nos. D10/D12 of Bechuanaland optd with Type D **4**.

D13		1c. carmine	15	1·75
		a. Bold 'c' and larger dot	8·00	
D14		2c. violet	15	1·75
D15		5c. green	20	1·75
D13/D15 *Set of 3*			45	4·75

British Antarctic Territory

1963. 12 pence (d.) = 1 shilling; 20 shillings = £1
1971. 100 pence (p.) = £1

For use at the following bases:

- Adelaide Island (Graham Land) (*closed* 1977)
- Argentine Islands ('Faraday' *from* 1981), (Graham Land) (*closed* 8 February 1996 *and transferred to Ukraine*)
- Brabant Island (Graham Land) (*opened* 1984, *closed* 1985)
- Deception Island (South Shetlands) (*closed* December 1967, *opened* 4 December 1968, *closed* 23 February 1969)
- Halley Bay (Coats Land)
- Hope Bay (Graham Land) (*closed* 12 February 1964)
- Port Lockroy (Graham Land) (*opened* 25 November 1996)
- Rothera Point (Graham Land) (*opened* 1977)
- Signy Island (South Orkneys)
- Stonington Island (Graham Land) (*closed* February 1975)

1 MV *Kista Dan*

2 Manhauling

3 Muskeg (tractor)

4 Skiing

5 de Havilland DHC-2 Beaver

6 RRS *John Biscoe II*

7 Camp scene

8 HMS *Protector*

9 Sledging

10 de Havilland DHC-3 Otter

11 Huskies

12 Westland Whirlwind

13 Snocat

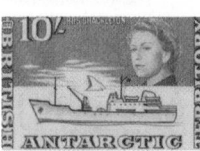

14 RRS *Shackleton*

15 Antarctic map

16 HMS *Endurance*

(Des B.W. (No. 15*a*), M. Goaman (others). Recess B.W.)

1963 (1 Feb)–**69**. T **1/16**. W w **12**. P 11×11½.

1	**1**	½d. deep blue	1·25	1·75
2	**2**	1d. brown	1·25	80
3	**3**	1½d. orange-red and brown-purple	1·25	1·50
4	**4**	2d. purple	1·50	80
5	**5**	2½d. myrtle-green	2·00	1·25
6	**6**	3d. deep blue	2·50	1·50
7	**7**	4d. sepia	1·75	1·50
8	**8**	6d. olive and deep ultramarine	5·00	2·50
9	**9**	9d. olive-green	3·00	2·00
10	**10**	1s. deep turquoise-blue	2·75	1·50
11	**11**	2s. deep violet and orange-sepia	20·00	10·00

12 **12** 2s.6d. blue ... 22·00 15·00
13 **13** 5s. red-orange and rose-red ... 22·00 19·00
14 **14** 10s. deep ultramarine and emerald ... 45·00 26·00
15 **15** £1 black and light blue ... 48·00 48·00
15*a* **16** £1 red and brownish black (1.12.69) ... £130 £120
1/15*a* *Set of* 16 ... £275 £225

1966 (24 Jan). Churchill Commemoration. As Nos. 223/226 of Falkland Islands.
16 ½d. new blue ... 80 3·25
17 1d. deep green ... 3·25 3·25
18 1s. brown ... 13·00 5·00
19 2s. bluish violet ... 14·00 5·50
16/19 *Set of* 4 ... 28·00 15·00

17 Lemaire Channel and Icebergs

(Des R. Granger Barrett. Litho Format)

1969 (6 Feb). 25th Anniversary of Continuous Scientific Work. T **17** and similar horizontal designs. W w **12** (sideways). P 14.
20 3½d. black, pale blue and ultramarine ... 2·50 2·50
21 6d. multicoloured ... 75 1·75
22 1s. black, pale blue and vermilion ... 75 1·50
23 2s. black, orange and turquoise-blue ... 75 2·25
20/23 *Set of* 4 ... 4·25 7·25

Designs: 3½d. T **17**; 6d. Radio Sonde balloon; 1s. Muskeg pulling tent equipment; 2s. Surveyors with theodolite.

British Columbia and Vancouver Island *see* Canada

British East Africa *see* Kenya, Uganda and Tanganyika

British Guiana

The postal service from what was to become British Guiana dates from 1796, being placed on a more regular basis after the final British occupation.

An inland postal system was organised in 1850, using the adhesive stamps of British Guiana, but, until 1 May 1860, overseas mails continued to be the province of the British GPO. The stamps of Great Britain were supplied for use on such letters from 11 May 1858 and examples of their use in combination with British Guiana issues have been recorded.

For illustration of the handstamp and postmark type see BRITISH POST OFFICES ABROAD notes, following GREAT BRITAIN.

CROWNED-CIRCLE HANDSTAMPS

The provision of a handstamp, probably as T CC **1**, inscribed 'DEMERARA', is recorded in the GPO proof book under 1 March 1856. No examples have been reported. A further handstamp, as T CC **6**, recorded in the proof book on 17 February 1866, is known used as a cancellation in at least three instances, including one on cover dated 8 November 1868.

GEORGETOWN (DEMERARA)

Stamps of GREAT BRITAIN cancelled 'A03' as T **2**.

1858–60.
Z1 1d. rose-red (1857), *perf* 14 ... £350
Z2 4d. rose (1857) ... £180
Z3 6d. lilac (1856) ... £120
a. Azure paper ...
Z4 1s. green (1856) ... £1800

NEW AMSTERDAM (BERBICE)

Stamps of GREAT BRITAIN cancelled 'A04' as T **2**.

1858–60.
Z5 1d. rose-red (1857), *perf* 14 ... £850
Z6 2d. blue (1858) (Plate Nos. 7, 8) ... £1300
Z7 4d. rose (1857) ... £450
Z8 6d. lilac (1856) ... £325
Z9 1s. green (1856) ... £2250

PRICES FOR STAMPS ON COVER TO 1945

No. 1	*from* × 1
Nos. 2/8	*from* × 4
Nos. 9/21	*from* × 3
No. 23	†
Nos. 24/27	*from* × 3
Nos. 29/115	*from* × 5
Nos. 116/124	*from* × 20
Nos. 126/136	*from* × 7
Nos. 137/159	*from* × 8
Nos. 162/165	*from* × 15
Nos. 170/174	*from* × 8
Nos. 175/189	*from* × 10
No. 192	*from* × 30
Nos. 193/210	*from* × 5
Nos. 213/215	*from* × 8
Nos. 216/221	*from* × 5
Nos. 222/224	*from* × 10
Nos. 233/250	*from* × 4
No. 251	—
Nos. 252/257	*from* × 4
Nos. 259/282	*from* × 5
Nos. 283/287	*from* × 8
Nos. 288/300	*from* × 5
Nos. 301/304	*from* × 6
Nos. 305/307	*from* × 8
Nos. 308/319	*from* × 5
Nos. D1/D4	*from* × 15
Nos. O1/O12	—

CROWN COLONY
(Currency. 100 cents = 1 dollar)

1

2

(Set up and printed at the office of the *Royal Gazette*, Georgetown, British Guiana)

1850 (1 July)–**51**. Type-set. Black impression on coloured paper.

(a) Medium wove paper. Prices are for—I. Cut square. II. Cut round

I Used II Used
1 **1** 2c. *rose* (1.3.51) ... — £325000
2 4c. *orange* ... £100000 £16000
3 4c. *lemon-yellow* (1851) ... £130000 £24000
4 8c. *green* ... £70000 £16000
5 12c. *blue* ... £35000 £11000
6 12c. *indigo* ... £45000 £13000
7 12c. *pale blue* (1851) ... £40000 £13000
a. '2' of '12' with straight foot ... £110000 £25000
b. '1' of '12' omitted ... † £250000

(b) Pelure paper (1851)
8 **1** 4c. *pale yellow* ... £130000 £24000

These stamps were usually initialled by the postmaster, or the Post Office clerks, before they were issued. The initials are–E. T. E. D(alton), E. D. W(ight), J. B. S(mith), H. A. K(illikelly), and W. H. L(ortimer). There are several types of each value and it seems likely that the setting contained one horizontal row of four slightly different impressions.

Ten examples of No. 1 have been recorded, including three pairs on separate covers.

(Litho Waterlow)

1852 (1 Jan). Surface-coloured paper. Imperf.
9 **2** 1c. black/*magenta* ... £15000 £5500
10 4c. black/*deep blue* ... £25000 £12000

There are two types of each value, which can be distinguished by differences in the waves at left, the length and shape of the curlique on the 'Q' of 'QUE' and in the outline of the upper sail. A sub-type of the 1c. exists without stop after 'CENT'.

Reprints on thicker paper, and perf 12½, were made in 1865 (*Price £24 either value*).

Such reprints with the perforations removed are sometimes offered as genuine originals.

CONDITION. Prices for Nos. 9 to 27 are for fine copies. Poor to medium specimens can be supplied when in stock at much lower rates.

3

4

5

(Dies eng and stamps litho Waterlow)

1853–59. Imperf.

(a) Original printing
11 **3** 1c. vermilion ... £7500 £1700

This 1c. in reddish brown is probably a proof (*Price* £1700).

ONE CENT
A

ONE CENT
B

ONE CENT
C

ONE CENT
D

A. 'O' large and 1 mm from left corner.
B. 'O' small and ¾ mm from left corner.
C. 'O' small and ¾ mm from left corner. 'NT' widely spaced.
D. 'ONE' close together, 'O' 1¼ mm from left corner.

(b) Fresh lithographic transfers from the 4c. with varying labels of value. White line above value (1857–1859).
12 **3** 1c. dull red (A) ... £7500 £2000
13 1c. brownish red (A) ... £15000 £2500
14 1c. dull red (B) ... £8500 £2250
15 1c. brownish red (B) ... £16000 £2750
16 1c. dull red (C) ... £10000 £2500
16*a* 1c. brownish red (C) ... — £3500
17 1c. dull red (D) ... † £25000

The four types (A to D) occurred within the same sheet and exist *se-tenant* (*Prices, for se-tenant pair from £26000 unused, £7500 used*).

1853–55. Imperf.
18 **4** 4c. deep blue ... £5500 £1100
a. Retouched ... £8000 £1600
19 4c. blue (1854) ... £3000 £800
a. Retouched ... £4500 £1000
20 4c. pale blue (1855) ... £2250 £700
a. Retouched ... £3250 £1000

The 4c. value was produced from transfers from the original 1c., with the bottom inscription removed, teamed with a new face value. The join often shows as a white line or traces of it above the label of value and lower corner figures. In some stamps on the sheet this line is missing, owing to having been retouched, and in these cases a line of colour usually appears in its place.

The 1c. and 4c. stamps were reprinted in 1865 from fresh transfers of five varieties. These are on thin paper and perf 12½ (*Price £21 each unused*).

1860 (May). Figures in corners framed. Imperf
21 **5** 4c. blue ... £7000 £800

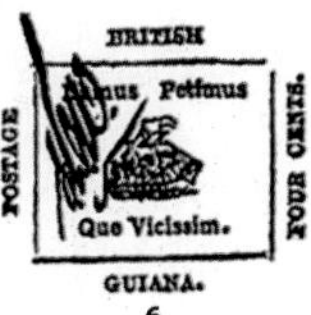

6

(Type-set and printed at the *Official Gazette* by Baum and Dallas, Georgetown).

1856.

(a) Surface-coloured paper
23 **6** 1c. black/*magenta* ... † —
24 4c. black/*magenta* (1.56) ... £100000 £25000
25 4c. black/*rose-carmine* (8.56) ... † £40000
26 4c. black/*blue* (9.56) ... † £150000

(b) Paper coloured through
27 **6** 4c. black/*deep blue* (8.56) ... † £225000

Since only one example of No. 23 is known, no market price can be given. This celebrated stamp, frequently termed 'the world's rarest', was last sold in New York in June 2014 for nearly £6 million. It is initialled by E. D. Wight and postmarked at Demerara on 4 April 1856.

These stamps, like those of the first issue, were initialled before being issued; the initials are–E.T.E.D(alton), E.D.W (ight), C.A.W(atson), and W.H.L(ortimer). C.A.W. only appears on stamps postmarked between 14 March and 4 April and also 16–20 May. E.T.E.D. is only known on stamps between 1–5 July and on 1 August. All examples on the rose-carmine or blue papers show E.D.W.

Stamps as T **6** were printed in sheets of four (2×2) each stamp differing slightly in the position of the inscriptions. There is evidence that the setting was re-arranged at some point before August, *possibly* to accommodate the production of the 1c.

PAPERMAKERS' WATERMARKS. Seven different papermakers' watermarks were used in the period 1860 to 1875 and stamps bearing portions of these are worth a premium.

7

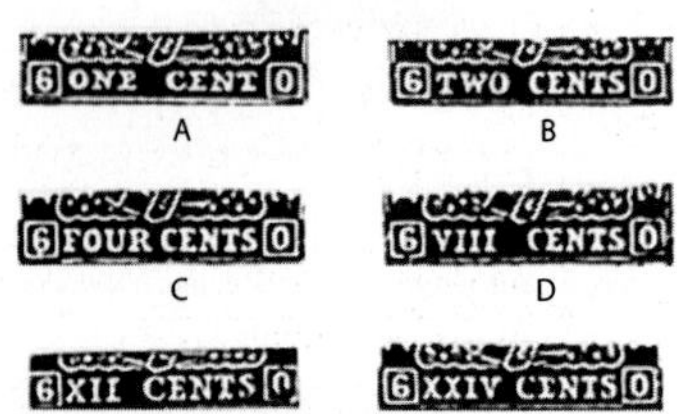

A B C D E F

(Dies eng and litho Waterlow)

1860 (July)–**63**. Tablets of value as illustrated. Thick paper. P 12.

29 **7** 1c. pale rose £3500 £275
30 2c. deep orange (8.60) £350 55·00
31 2c. pale orange £375 60·00
32 4c. deep blue (8.60) £900 £120
33 4c. blue £500 75·00
34 8c. brownish rose £1300 £160
35 8c. pink £900 90·00
36 12c. lilac £1000 50·00
37 12c. grey-lilac £850 50·00
38 24c. deep green (6.63) £2500 £150
39 24c. green £1800 80·00

The 1c. was reprinted in 1865 on *thin* paper, P 12½–13, and in a different shade. *Price* £22.

The 12c. in both shades is frequently found surcharged with a large '5d' in *red*; this is to denote the proportion of postage repayable by the colony to Great Britain for overseas letters.

1861 (3 Aug*). Colour changed. Thick paper. P 12.

40 **7** 1c. reddish brown £550 £110

* Earliest known postmark date.

1862–65.

(a) Thin paper. P 12

41 **7** 1c. brown £1000 £250
42 1c. black (1863) £180 60·00
43 2c. orange £170 60·00
44 4c. blue £190 50·00
45 4c. pale blue £170 38·00
46 8c. pink (1863) £350 85·00
47 12c. dull purple (1863) £425 35·00
48 12c. purple £450 40·00
49 12c. lilac £450 50·00
50 24c. green £2000 £100

(b) Thin paper. P 12½–13 (1863)

51 **7** 1c. black 85·00 24·00
52 2c. orange £100 26·00
53 4c. blue £110 18·00
54 8c. pink £400 90·00
55 12c. brownish lilac £1400 £140
56 24c. green £900 65·00

Copies are found on *pelure* paper.

(c) Medium paper. P 12½–13

57 **7** 1c. black (1864) 75·00 50·00
58 2c. deep orange (1864) 95·00 29·00
59 2c. orange £100 27·00
60 4c. greyish blue (1864) £120 22·00
61 4c. blue £140 29·00
62 8c. pink (1864) £350 75·00
63 12c. brownish lilac (1865) £1200 £130
64 24c. green (1864) £475 50·00
65 24c. deep green £550 85·00

(d) Medium paper. P 10 (Nov. 1865)

65*a* **7** 12c. grey-lilac £900 90·00

8 9

G H

I K

New transfers for the 1c., 2c., 8c., and 12c. with the spaces between values and the word 'CENTS' about 1 mm.

1863–76. Medium paper.

(a) P 12½–13 (1863–1868)

66 **8** 1c. black (1866) 95·00 38·00
67 2c. orange-red (1865) £100 9·50
68 2c. orange £100 9·50
69 **9** 6c. blue (1865) £250 65·00
70 6c. greenish blue £250 70·00
71 6c. deep blue £325 £100
72 6c. milky blue £250 65·00
73 **8** 8c. pink (1868) £500 25·00
74 8c. carmine £600 27·00
75 12c. grey-lilac (1867) £700 48·00
76 12c. brownish purple £800 50·00
77 **9** 24c. green (*perf* 12) £375 21·00
78 24c. yellow-green (*perf* 12) £300 14·00
79 24c. yellow-green (*perf* 12½–13) £275 14·00
80 24c. green (*perf* 12½–13) (1864) £300 14·00
81 24c. blue-green (*perf* 12½–13) £400 22·00
82 48c. pale red £400 75·00
83 48c. deep red £450 75·00
84 48c. carmine-rose £450 75·00

The 4c. corresponding to this issue can only be distinguished from that of the previous issue by minor plating flaws.

There is a variety of the 6c. with stop before 'VICISSIM'.

Varieties of most of the values of issues of 1863–1864 and 1866 are to be found on both very thin and thick papers.

(b) P 10 (1866–1871)

85 **8** 1c. black (1869) 28·00 8·00
86 1c. grey-black 30·00 16·00
87 2c. orange (1868) 70·00 4·75
88 2c. reddish orange 90·00 6·50
89 4c. slate-blue £170 13·00
90 4c. blue £150 9·00
a. Bisected (*on cover*) † £7500
b. Ditto. Imperf (*on cover*) † —
91 4c. pale blue £130 9·50
92 **9** 6c. milky blue (1867) £225 35·00
93 6c. ultramarine £275 60·00
94 6c. dull blue £225 38·00
95 **8** 8c. pink (5.71) £325 45·00
96 8c. brownish pink £400 50·00
96*a* 8c. carmine £500 55·00
97 12c. pale lilac (1867) £375 27·00
98 12c. grey-lilac £350 26·00
99 12c. brownish grey £350 28·00
100 12c. lilac £350 28·00
101 **9** 24c. deep green £400 9·50
102 24c. bluish green £375 8·00
103 24c. yellow-green £325 7·50
104 48c. crimson (1867) £475 48·00
s. Handstamped 'SPECIMEN' £350
as. Perf 'SPECIMEN' £300
105 48c. red £450 40·00

(c) P 15 (1875–1876)

106 **8** 1c. black 70·00 7·50
107 2c. orange-red £200 16·00
108 2c. orange £200 16·00
109 4c. bright blue £350 £100
111 **9** 6c. ultramarine £1200 £150
112 **8** 8c. deep rose (1876) £400 £110
113 12c. lilac £950 95·00
114 **9** 24c. yellow-green £750 35·00
115 24c. deep green £1700 £120

There is a variety of the 48c. with stop after 'P' in 'PETIMUSQUE'.

Imperforate stamps of this and of the previous issue are considered to be proofs, although examples of the 24c. imperforate from the 1869–1873 period are known commercially used.

NOTE: Prices for stamps of the 1862 issue are for good average copies. Copies with roulettes on all sides very seldom occur and do not exist in marginal positions.

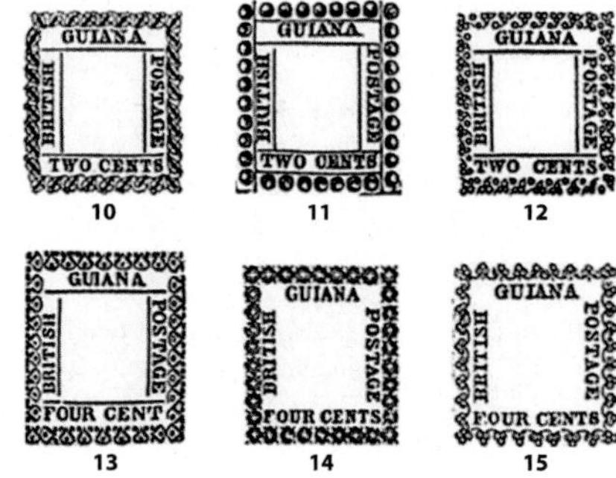

10 11 12

13 14 15

(Type-set and printed at the Office of the *Royal Gazette*, Georgetown)

1862 (Sept). Black on coloured paper. Roul 6.

116 **10** 1c. *rose* £5500 £850
a. Unsigned £700
b. Wrong ornament (as T **13**) at left (R. 1/1) — £1400
c. '1' for 'I' in 'BRITISH' (R. 1/5) — £1400
d. Wrong ornament (as T **13**) at right (R. 2/6) £10000 £1400
117 **11** 1c. *rose* £7000 £1000
a. Unsigned £800
b. Narrow 'T' in 'CENT' (R. 3/1) — £1400
c. Wrong ornament (as T **15**) at top (R. 3/3) — £1400
d. '1' for 'I' in 'BRITISH' and italic 'S' in 'POSTAGE' (R. 3/5) — £1400
118 **12** 1c. *rose* £10000 £1500
a. Unsigned £1300
b. '1' for 'I' in 'GUIANA' (R. 4/4) — £1500
c. Wrong ornament (as T **15**) at left (R. 4/5) — £1500
d. 'C' for 'O' in 'POSTAGE' (R. 4/6) — £1500
119 **10** 2c. *yellow* £5500 £450
a. Unsigned £2500
b. Wrong ornament (as T **13**) at left (R. 1/1) — £850
c. '1' for 'I' in 'BRITISH' (R. 1/5) — £850
120 **11** 2c. *yellow* £7500 £600
a. Unsigned £2750
b. 'C' for 'O' in 'TWO' and narrow 'T' in 'CENTS' (R. 3/1) — £850
c. Wrong ornament (as T **15**) at top (R. 3/3) — £850
d. Italic 'S' in 'CENTS' (R. 3/4) £9500 £850
e. '1' for 'I' in 'BRITISH' and italic 'S' in 'POSTAGE' (R. 3/5) £9500 £850
f. Italic 'T' in 'TWO' (R. 3/6) — £850
121 **12** 2c. *yellow* £10000 £900
a. Unsigned £3500
b. '1' for 'I' in 'GUIANA' (R. 4/4) — £900
c. Wrong ornament (as T **15**) at left (R. 4/5) — £900
d. 'C' for 'O' in 'POSTAGE' (R. 4/6) — £900
122 **13** 4c. *blue* £6000 £1000
a. Unsigned £1200
b. Wrong ornament (as T **15**) at left (R. 1/6) £9000 £1600
c. Wrong ornament (as T **15**) at top and italic 'S' in 'CENTS' (R. 2/2) — £1600
d. Ornament omitted at right (R. 2/4) — £1600
123 **14** 4c. *blue* £8000 £1400
a. Unsigned £1300
b. With inner frame lines (as in T **10/13**) (R. 2/5–6) £11000 £1900
ba. '1' for 'I' in 'BRITISH' (R. 2/5) £11000 £1900
c. '1' for 'I' in 'BRITISH' and 'GUIANA' (R. 4/1) — £1600
124 **15** 4c. *blue* £8500 £1400
a. Unsigned £1400
b. Wrong ornament (as T **12**) at foot (R. 3/1) — £1600
c. Italic 'S' in 'CENTS' (R. 3/2) — £1600
d. Italic 'S' in 'BRITISH' (R. 3/3) — £1600

Stamps were initialled across the centre before use by the Acting Receiver-General, Robert Mather. Black was used on the 1c., red for the 2c. and an ink which appears white for the 4c.

The three values of this provisional were each printed in sheets of 24 (6×4). The 1c. and 2c. were produced from the same setting of the border ornaments which contained 12 examples as T **10** (Rows 1 and 2), eight as T **11** (R. 3/1 to R. 4/2) and four as T **12** (R. 4/3-6).

The setting of the 4c. contained ten examples as T **13** (R. 1/1 to R. 2/4), eight as T **14** (R. 2/5–6 and Row 4) and six as T **15** (Row 3).

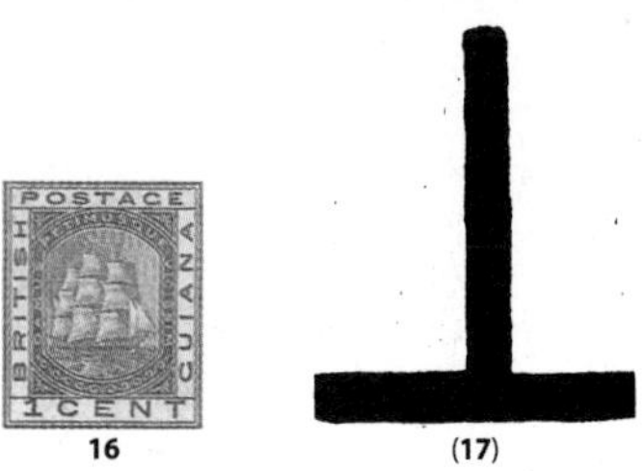

16 (17)

(Typo D.L.R.)

1876 (1 July)–**79**. Wmk Crown CC.

(a) P 14

126 **16** 1c. slate 2·75 1·40
w. Wmk inverted £250 £250
127 2c. orange 85·00 4·00
w. Wmk inverted † £300
128 4c. blue £140 9·00
129 6c. brown £100 13·00
w. Wmk inverted † £400
130 8c. rose £150 75
w. Wmk inverted † £300
131 12c. pale violet 75·00 2·50
w. Wmk inverted † £550
132 24c. emerald-green 80·00 3·50
w. Wmk inverted † £550
133 48c. red-brown £150 45·00
134 96c. olive-bistre £475 £250
126/134 *Set of* 9 £1100 £275
126s/132s, 134s Handstamped 'SPECIMEN' *Set of* 8 £1200
131sa/132sa Perf 'SPECIMEN' *Set of* 2 £300

(b) P 12½ (1877)

135 **16** 4c. blue £1200 £200

(c) Perf compound of 14×12½ (1879)

136 **16** 1c. slate — £200

1878. Provisionals. Various stamps with old values ruled through with thick bars, in black ink, the bars varying in depth of colour.

(a) With two horiz bars (17 Apr)

137 **16** (1c.) on 6c. brown 50·00 £130

(b) Official stamps with horiz bars across 'OFFICIAL' (end Aug)

138 **8** 1c. black £300 80·00
a. Imperf between (horiz pair) † £30000
139 **16** 1c. slate £200 75·00
140 2c. orange £450 75·00

*(c) With horiz and vert bars as T **17** (6 Nov)*

141 **9** (1c.) on 6c. ultramarine (No.93) £225 75·00
142 **16** (1c.) on 6c. brown £425 £110
a. Optd with vert bar only † £8500

(d) Official stamps with bars across 'OFFICIAL' (23 Nov)

(i) With two horiz bars and one vert

144 **16** (1c.) on 4c. blue £400 £110
145 (1c.) on 6c. brown £700 £110
146 **8** (2c.) on 8c. rose £5000 £400

(ii) With one horiz bar and one vert

147 **16** (1c.) on 4c. blue † £5500
148 (2c.) on 8c. rose £550 £140

1 2 2

(18) (19) (20)

1881 (21 Dec). No. 134 with old value ruled through with bar in black ink and surch.

149 **18** 1 on 96c. olive-bistre 5·50 14·00
a. Bar in red
b. Bar omitted
150 **19** 2 on 96c. olive-bistre 24·00 28·00
a. Bar in red
b. Bar omitted
151 **20** 2 on 96c. olive-bistre 85·00 £160
a. Bar in red

In the setting of 60 T **19** occurs on the first five vertical rows and T **20** on the sixth.

1 2 2

(21) (23) (24)

1881 (28 Dec). Various stamps with old value ruled with bar and surch.

(a) On No. 105

152 **21** 1 on 48c. red 50·00 5·50
a. Bar omitted — £600

(b) On Official stamps (including unissued 48c. optd with T O 2)

153	**21**	1 on 12c. brownish purple (No. O4)	£140	75·00
154		1 on 48c. red-brown	£200	£130
155	**23**	2 on 12c. pale violet (No. O11)	90·00	50·00
		a. Pair. Nos. 155/156	£1600	£1800
		b. Surch double	£850	£475
		c. Surch double (T **23** + **24**)	£6000	£3750
		d. Extra bar through 'OFFICIAL'		
156	**24**	2 on 12c. pale violet (No. O11)	£700	£475
157	**23**	2 on 24c. emerald-green (No. O12)	£100	65·00
		a. Pair. Nos. 157/158	£1900	£2000
		b. Surch double	£1100	
158	**24**	2 on 24c. emerald-green (No. O12)	£900	£900
159	**19**	2 on 24c. green (No. O5)	£375	£180

On Nos. 149/159 the bar is found in various thicknesses ranging from 1 to 4 mm.

It is believed that the same composite surcharge setting of 60 (6×10) was used for Nos. 155/156 and 157/158. T **24** occurs on R. 7/2, 4-6 and R. 8/1.

26

27

(Type-set, Baldwin & Co. Georgetown)

1882 (9 Jan). Black impression. P 12. Perforated with the word 'SPECIMEN' diagonally.

162	**26**	1c. *magenta*	75·00	30·00
		a. Imperf between (horiz pair)	†	—
		b. Without 'SPECIMEN'	£1500	£550
		c. '1' with foot	£180	85·00
163		2c. *yellow*	£110	55·00
		a. Without 'SPECIMEN'	£1300	£700
		b. Small '2'	£110	55·00
164	**27**	1c. *magenta*	75·00	30·00
		a. Without 'SPECIMEN'	£1500	£550
		b. '1' with foot	£275	£110
		c. Imperf between (horiz pair)	†	£10000
165		2c. *yellow*	95·00	50·00
		a. Bisected diagonally (1c.) (*on cover*)	†	—
		b. Without 'SPECIMEN'	£1300	£700
		c. Small '2'	£180	£100

These stamps were perforated 'SPECIMEN' as a precaution against fraud. The letters may be upright, inverted, reversed or inverted and reversed and stamps are known with 'SPECIMEN' double or treble.

The 2c. is known printed double, one albino.

The 1c. and 2c. stamps were printed in separate sheets, but utilising the same clichés, these being altered according to the face value required. Two settings were used, common to both values:—

First setting. Four rows of three, T **26** being Nos. 5, 6, 7, 8, 11 and 12, and T **27** the remainder.

From this setting there were two printings of the 2c., but only one of the 1c.

Second setting. Six rows of two, T **26** being Nos. 3, 7, 8, 9, 11 and 12, and T **27** the remainder.

There were two printings of each value from this setting.

Se-tenant pairs are worth about 20% more.

The '1' with foot occurs on T **27** on No. 9 in the first setting and on T **26** on No. 7 in the first printing only of the second setting.

The small '2' appears on T **26** in the first setting on Nos. 6, 7, 8 and 12 in the first printing and on Nos. 7, 8 and 12 only in the second printing: in the second setting it comes on Nos. 3, 9 and 12 in the first printing and on Nos. 9, 11 and 12 in the second printing. On T **27** the variety occurs in the first setting on No. 9 of the second printing only and in the second setting on No. 10 in both printings.

(Typo D.L.R.)

1882. Wmk Crown CA. P 14.

170	**16**	1c. slate (27.1)	19·00	30
		w. Wmk inverted		
		x. Wmk reversed	—	£275
171		2c. orange (27.1)	60·00	15
		a. Value doubly printed	†	£10000
		w. Wmk inverted	£400	£325
		x. Wmk reversed	—	£325
172		4c. blue	£110	5·00
173		6c. brown	5·00	6·50
		w. Wmk inverted		
174		8c. rose	£140	40
		x. Wmk reversed	—	£300
170/174 *Set of 5*			£300	11·00
170s/174s Perf 'SPECIMEN' *Set of 5*			£500	

INLAND

2 CENTS

REVENUE

(**28**)

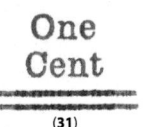

4 CENTS (*a*) **4 CENTS** (*b*)

Two types of '4'

6 (*c*) **6** (*d*)

Two types of '6'

1888–89. T **16** (without value in lower label) optd 'INLAND REVENUE', and surch with value as T **28**, by D.L.R. Wmk Crown CA. P 14.

175	1c. dull purple (8.89)	2·75	20
176	2c. dull purple (25.5.89)	3·25	3·50
177	3c. dull purple	2·25	20
178	4c. dull purple (*a*)	12·00	30
	a. Larger figure '4' (*b*)	21·00	6·50
179	6c. dull purple (*c*)	18·00	7·50
	a. Figure 6 with straight top (*d*)	21·00	11·00
180	8c. dull purple (8.89)	2·50	1·25
181	10c. dull purple	8·00	2·50
182	20c. dull purple	27·00	26·00
183	40c. dull purple	50·00	42·00
184	72c. dull purple (1.10.88)	80·00	65·00
185	$1 green (1.10.88)	£500	£650
186	$2 green (1.10.88)	£250	£325
187	$3 green (1.10.88)	£275	£325
188	$4 green (*a*) (1.10.88)	£600	£750
	a. Larger figure '4' (*b*)	£2250	£2750
189	$5 green (1.10.88)	£400	£475
175/189 *Set of 15*		£2000	£2250

Nos. 175/189 were surcharged in settings of 60 (6×10). No. 178a occurs on all stamps in the third vertical column, No. 179a in the fourth and sixth vertical columns and No. 188a in the second vertical column.

2 (**29**)

30

One Cent (**31**)

1889 (6 June). No. 176 surch with T **29** in red by Official Gazette.

192	'2' on 2c. dull purple	7·00	1·00

The varieties with figure '2' *inverted* or *double* were made privately by a postal employee in Demerara.

1889 (Sept). Wmk Crown CA. P 14.

193	**30**	1c. dull purple and slate-grey	10·00	3·75
194		2c. dull purple and orange	8·50	10
		w. Wmk inverted	—	£300
195		4c. dull purple and ultramarine	4·50	4·00
		w. Wmk inverted	£300	
196		4c. dull purple and cobalt	21·00	4·00
197		6c. dull purple and brown	35·00	30·00
198		6c. dull purple and maroon	7·50	28·00
199		8c. dull purple and rose	24·00	4·25
		w. Wmk inverted	—	£300
200		12c. dull purple and bright purple	18·00	4·50
200*a*		12c. dull purple and mauve	8·50	4·25
201		24c. dull purple and green	6·00	3·75
202		48c. dull purple and orange-red	42·00	12·00
		w. Wmk inverted	£750	
		x. Wmk reversed	£700	
		xs. Ditto. Optd 'SPECIMEN'	£275	
203		72c. dull purple and red-brown	28·00	50·00
204		72c. dull purple and yellow-brown	65·00	75·00
205		96c. dull purple and carmine	65·00	70·00
		x. Wmk reversed	£650	£650
206		96c. dull purple and rosine	75·00	80·00
193/205 *Set of 10*			£170	£150
193s/205s Optd 'SPECIMEN' *Set of 10*			£200	

1890 (15 July). Stamps of 1888-1889 surch locally 'One Cent', in red, as in T **31**.

207	1c. on $1 (No. 185)	3·25	35
	a. Surch double	£275	£150
208	1c. on $2 (No. 186)	2·25	1·25
	a. Surch double	£110	
209	1c. on $3 (No. 187)	4·00	1·25
	a. Surch double	£150	
210	1c. on $4 (No. 188)	7·00	16·00
	a. Surch double	£140	
	b. Larger figure '4' (*b*)	15·00	48·00
207/210 *Set of 4*		15·00	17·00

1890–91. Colours changed. Wmk Crown CA. P 14

213	**30**	1c. sea-green (12.90)	1·00	10
		w. Wmk inverted	†	£225
214		5c. ultramarine (1.91)	6·00	10
215		8c. dull purple and greenish black (10.90)	13·00	3·25
213/215 *Set of 3*			18·00	3·25
213s/215s Optd 'SPECIMEN' *Set of 3*			85·00	

32 Mount Roraima

33 Kaieteur Falls

(Recess D.L.R.)

1898 (18 July). Queen Victoria's Jubilee. Wmk Crown CC (sideways* on T **32**). P 14.

216	**32**	1c. blue-black and carmine-red	9·50	2·25
		w. Wmk Crown to left of CC	11·00	2·50
		x. Wmk sideways reversed		
		y. Wmk sideways inverted and reversed		
217	**33**	2c. brown and indigo	35·00	4·25
		a. Imperf between (horiz pair)	£16000	
		w. Wmk inverted	£500	
		x. Wmk reversed	£425	£225
		y. Wmk inverted and reversed	£475	
218		2c. brown and blue	42·00	4·25
219	**32**	5c. deep green and sepia	55·00	6·00
		a. Imperf between (horiz pair)		
		w. Wmk Crown to left of CC	48·00	5·00
220	**33**	10c. blue-black and brown-red	27·00	30·00
		x. Wmk reversed	£650	
221	**32**	15c. red-brown and blue	32·00	27·00
		x. Wmk sideways reversed	£700	
216/221 *Set of 5*			£130	60·00
216s/221s Optd 'SPECIMEN' *Set of 5*			£160	

* The normal sideways watermark on T **32** shows Crown to right of CC, *as seen from the back of the stamp.*

A second plate was later used for the 1c. on which the lines of shading on the mountains in the background are strengthened, and those along the ridge show distinct from each other, whereas, in the original, they are more or less blurred. In the second plate the shading of the sky is less pronounced.

TWO CENTS. (**34**)

CE Shaved 'E'

35

(Surch at Printing Office of *The Daily Chronicle*, Georgetown)

1899 (24 Feb–15 June). Surch with T **34**.

222	**32**	2c. on 5c. (No. 219) (15.6)	4·75	4·50
		a. No stop after 'CENTS'	£180	£160
		b. Comma after 'CENTS' (R. 7/2)	75·00	
		c. 'CINTS' (R. 4/1)	£180	£200
		d. Shaved 'E' (R. 6/2)	70·00	70·00
		w. Wmk Crown to left of CC	6·00	4·50
223	**33**	2c. on 10c. (No. 220)	4·25	2·25
		a. No stop after 'CENTS' (R. 5/5 or 2/9)	22·00	60·00
		b. 'GENTS' for 'CENTS' (R. 5/7)	65·00	£100
		c. Surch inverted	£700	£800
		ca. Surch inverted and stop omitted	£7500	
		d. Shaved 'E' (R. 4/2 or 3/8)	42·00	
		x. Wmk reversed	£200	
		y. Wmk inverted and reversed	£350	
224	**32**	2c. on 15c. (No. 221)	5·00	1·25
		a. No stop after 'CENTS' (R. 9/2)	75·00	75·00
		b. Surch double	£1000	£1300
		ba. Surch double, one without stop	£12000	
		d. Surch inverted	£800	£950
		da. Surch inverted and stop omitted	£10000	
		f. Shaved 'E' (R. 6/2)	60·00	
222/224 *Set of 3*			12·50	7·25

No. 222c was caused by damage to the first 'E' of 'CENTS' which developed during surcharging. The listing is for an example with only the upright stroke of the letter visible.

There were two settings of No. 223 with the no stop and shaved 'E' varieties occurring on R. 5/5 and R. 4/2 of the first and on R. 2/9 and R. 3/8 of the second.

No. 224b occurred on the first five vertical columns of one sheet, the surcharges on the right hand vertical column being normal.

Only two examples of No. 224ba are known.

There is only one known example of No. 224da.

1900–03. Wmk Crown CA. P 14.

233	**30**	1c. grey-green (1902)	2·00	6·50
234		2c. dull purple and carmine	3·25	30
		x. Wmk reversed	—	£325
235		2c. dull purple and black/*red* (1901)	3·25	10
		w. Wmk inverted	—	£150
236		6c. grey-black and ultramarine (1902)	7·50	11·00
237		48c. grey and purple-brown (1901)	50·00	50·00
		a. Brownish grey and brown	35·00	32·00
238		60c. green and rosine (1903)	70·00	£250
233/238 *Set of 6*			£110	£275
233s/238s Optd 'SPECIMEN' *Set of 6*			£140	

No. 233 is a reissue of No. 213 in non-fugitive ink.

1905–07. Wmk Multiple Crown CA. Ordinary paper (1c. to 60c.) or chalk-surfaced paper (72, 96c.).

240	**30**	1c. grey-green	10·00	30
		aw. Wmk inverted	—	£250
		b. Chalk-surfaced paper	12·00	1·25
		c. Blue-green (1907)	16·00	2·75
241		2c. purple and black/*red*	22·00	10
		a. Chalk-surfaced paper	8·00	10
242		4c. dull purple and ultramarine	20·00	25·00
		a. Chalk-surfaced paper	8·00	14·00
243		5c. dull purple and blue/*blue* (1.5.05)	26·00	27·00
		a. Chalk-surfaced paper	3·50	8·00
		s. Optd 'SPECIMEN'	27·00	
244		6c. grey-black and ultramarine	24·00	48·00
		aw. Wmk inverted	£400	£350
		b. Chalk-surfaced paper	15·00	42·00
		bw. Wmk inverted		
245		12c. dull and bright purple	38·00	50·00
		a. Chalk-surfaced paper	22·00	50·00
246		24c. dull purple and green (1906)	17·00	24·00
		a. Chalk-surfaced paper	3·75	7·00
247		48c. grey and purple-brown	40·00	50·00
		a. Chalk-surfaced paper	14·00	25·00
248		60c. green and rosine	26·00	£110
		a. Chalk-surfaced paper	14·00	95·00
249		72c. purple and orange-brown (1907)	45·00	75·00
250		96c. black and vermilion/*yellow* (20.11.05)	38·00	50·00
		s. Optd 'SPECIMEN'	40·00	
240/250 *Set of 11*			£160	£325

1905. Optd 'POSTAGE AND REVENUE'. Wmk Multiple Crown CA. Chalk-surfaced paper. P 14.

251	**35**	$2.40, green and violet	£190	£450
		s. Optd 'SPECIMEN'	85·00	

No. 253

No. 253a

1907–10. Colours changed. Wmk Mult Crown CA. P 14

253	**30**	2c. rose-red	23·00	1·00
		a. Redrawn (1910)	8·50	10

254 4c. brown and purple 6·50 1·75
255 5c. ultramarine 21·00 7·50
256 6c. grey and black 13·00 7·00
257 12c. orange and mauve 4·50 6·50
253a/257 *Set of* 5 48·00 20·00
253s/257s Optd 'SPECIMEN' *Set of* 5 £110

In No. 253a the flag at the main truck is close to the mast, whereas in the original type it appears to be flying loose from halyards. There are two background lines above the value '2 CENTS' instead of three and the 'S' is further away from the end of the tablet.

37

War
Tax
(38)

(Typo D.L.R.)

1913–21. Wmk Mult Crown CA. Chalk-surfaced paper (4c. and 48c. to 96c.). P 14.

259 **37** 1c. yellow-green 5·50 80
a. Blue-green (1917) 3·00 25
ay. Wmk inverted and reversed † £375
w. Wmk inverted † £450
260 2c. carmine 1·50 10
a. Scarlet (1916) 3·50 10
b. Wmk sideways † £3000
w. Wmk inverted † £475
261 4c. brown and bright purple (1914) 9·00 25
aw. Wmk inverted £275
b. Deep brown and purple 3·75 25
262 5c. bright blue 2·00 1·00
263 6c. grey and black 4·00 3·75
264 12c. orange and violet 1·50 1·00
265 24c. dull purple and green (1915) 3·25 6·50
266 48c. grey and purple-brown (1914) 23·00 17·00
267 60c. green and rosine (1915) 17·00 65·00
268 72c. purple and orange-brown (1915) 55·00 £100
269 96c. black and vermilion/*yellow* (1915) 30·00 60·00
a. White back (1914) 28·00 50·00
b. On lemon (1916) 20·00 50·00
bs. Optd 'SPECIMEN' 38·00
c. On pale yellow (1921) 23·00 60·00
cs. Optd 'SPECIMEN' 40·00
259/269*a* *Set of* 11 £120 £225
259s/269as Optd 'SPECIMEN' *Set of* 11 £250

The 1c. and 2c. exist from coils made up from normal sheets.

Examples of Nos. 267/269*c* are known with part strikes of forged postmarks of Grove dated '29 OCT 1909' and of Georgetown dated '30 OCT 1909'.

1918 (4 Jan). No. 260*a* optd with T **38**, by *The Daily Chronicle*, Georgetown.

271 **37** 2c. scarlet 1·50 15

The relative position of the words 'WAR' and 'TAX' vary considerably in the sheet.

1921–27. Wmk Mult Script CA. Chalk-surfaced paper (24c. to 96c.). P 14.

272 **37** 1c. green (1922) 4·75 30
273 2c. rose-carmine 7·00 20
w. Wmk inverted † £375
274 2c. bright violet (1923) 2·50 10
275 4c. brown and bright purple (1922) 4·75 10
276 6c. bright blue (1922) 3·00 30
277 12c. orange and violet (1922) 2·75 1·50
278 24c. dull purple and green 2·00 4·50
279 48c. black and purple (1926) 9·50 3·50
280 60c. green and rosine (1926) 10·00 60·00
281 72c. dull purple and orange-brown (1923) 38·00 80·00
282 96c. black and red/*yellow* (1927) 32·00 50·00
272/282 *Set of* 11 £100 £180
272s/282s Optd 'SPECIMEN' *Set of* 11 £250

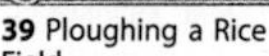
39 Ploughing a Rice Field

40 Indian shooting Fish

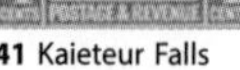
41 Kaieteur Falls

42 Public buildings, Georgetown

(Recess Waterlow)

1931 (21 July). Centenary of County Union. T **39/42**. Wmk Mult Script CA. P 12½.

283 **39** 1c. emerald-green 2·50 1·25
284 **40** 2c. brown 2·00 10
285 **41** 4c. carmine 2·50 45
286 **42** 6c. blue 2·50 1·25
287 **41** $1 violet 55·00 65·00
283/287 *Set of* 5 60·00 65·00
283s/287s Perf 'SPECIMEN' *Set of* 5 £140

43 Ploughing a Rice Field

44 Gold Mining

45 Shooting logs over falls

46 Stabroek Market

47 Sugar canes in punts

48 Forest road

49 *Victoria Regia* Lilies

50 Mount Roraima

51 Sir Walter Raleigh and his son

52 Botanical Gardens

(Recess Waterlow)

1934 (1 Oct)–**51.** T **40** (without dates at top of frame) and **43/52.** Wmk Mult Script CA (sideways on horiz designs). P 12½.

288 **43** 1c. green 60 2·00
289 **40** 2c. red-brown 1·50 1·75
290 **44** 3c. scarlet 30 10
aa. Wmk error. Crown missing £4000 £2500
a. Perf 12½×13½ (30.12.43) 1·00 1·00
b. Perf 13×14 (28.4.49) 2·00 1·00
291 **41** 4c. slate-violet 2·00 3·50
a. Imperf between (vert pair) † £40000
b. Imperf horiz (vert pair) £22000 £23000
292 **45** 6c. deep ultramarine 8·00 7·00
293 **46** 12c. red-orange 45 20
a. Perf 14×13 (16.4.51) 50 1·00
294 **47** 24c. purple 3·75 14·00
295 **48** 48c. black 12·00 10·00
296 **41** 50c. green 17·00 25·00
297 **49** 60c. red-brown 28·00 35·00
298 **50** 72c. purple 2·00 3·25
299 **51** 96c. black 40·00 48·00
300 **52** $1 bright violet 50·00 50·00
288/300 *Set of* 13 £140 £180
288s/300s Perf 'SPECIMEN' *Set of* 13 £250

Examples of Nos. 295/300 are known with forged Georgetown postmarks dated '24 JY 31' or '6 MY 35'.

1935 (6 May). Silver Jubilee. As Nos. 91/94 of Antigua.

301 2c. ultramarine and grey 40 20
f. Diagonal line by turret 50·00 40·00
g. Dot to left of chapel — £275
h. Dot by flagstaff £130 £130
i. Dash by turret £225
302 6c. brown and deep blue 2·00 5·50
f. Diagonal line by turret £120
g. Dot to left of chapel £140 £200
h. Dot by flagstaff £180
303 12c. green and indigo 9·50 10·00
f. Diagonal line by turret £160 £200
g. Dot to left of chapel £375
h. Dot by flagstaff £300 £325
i. Dash by turret £400
304 24c. slate and purple 15·00 23·00
h. Dot by flagstaff £350 £550
i. Dash by turret £475 £600
301/304 *Set of* 4 24·00 35·00
301s/304s Perf 'SPECIMEN' *Set of* 4 £130

For illustrations of plate varieties see Omnibus section following Zanzibar.

1937 (12 May). Coronation. As Nos. 95/97 of Antigua, but ptd by D.L.R. P 14.

305 2c. yellow-brown 15 10
306 4c. grey-black 60 1·00
307 6c. bright blue 75 2·00
305/307 *Set of* 3 1·40 2·75
305s/307s Perf 'SPECIMEN' *Set of* 3 £120

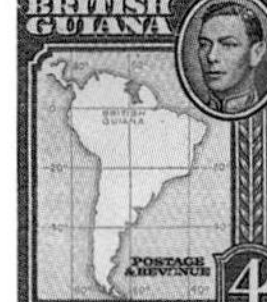
53 South America

54 *Victoria Regia*, water-lilies

(Recess Waterlow)

1938 (1 Feb)–**52.** As earlier types but with portrait of King George VI as in T **53/54.** Wmk Mult Script CA. P 12½.

308 **43** 1c. yellow-green 23·00 1·75
a. Green (1940) 30 10
ab. 'A' of 'CA' missing from Wmk — £1200
b. Perf 14×13 (1949) 1·75 80
309 **41** 2c. slate-violet 60 10
a. Perf 13×14 (28.4.49) 55 10
310 **53** 4c. scarlet and black 1·25 30
a. Imperf horiz (vert pair) £40000 £32000
b. Perf 13×14 (1952) 1·75 15
311 **40** 6c. deep ultramarine 2·75 10
a. Perf 13×14 (24.10.49) 3·25 30
312 **47** 24c. blue-green 26·00 10·00
a. Wmk sideways 4·25 10
313 **41** 36c. bright violet (7.3.38) 7·50 20
a. Perf 13×14 (13.12.51) 3·25 30
314 **48** 48c. orange 2·50 1·00
a. Perf 14×13 (8.5.51*) 2·25 3·00
315 **45** 60c. red-brown 23·00 9·50
316 **51** 96c. purple 18·00 2·75
a. Perf 12½×13½ (1944) 18·00 18·00
b. Perf 13×14 (8.2.51) 7·00 14·00
317 **52** $1 bright violet 28·00 35
a. Perf 14×13 (1951) £550 £600
318 **50** $2 purple (11.6.45) 22·00 27·00
a. Perf 14×13 (9.8.50) 28·00 42·00
319 **54** $3 red-brown (2.7.45) 38·00 45·00
a. Bright red-brown (12.46) 60·00 32·00
b. Perf 14×13. *Red-brown* (29.10.52) 42·00 50·00
308a/319 *Set of* 12 £110 65·00
308s/319s Perf 'SPECIMEN' *Set of* 12 £375

* Earliest known postmark date.

1946 (21 Oct). Victory. As Nos. 110/111 of Antigua.

320 3c. carmine 25 40
321 6c. blue 75 85
320s/321s Perf 'SPECIMEN' *Set of* 2 £100

1948 (20 Dec). Royal Silver Wedding. As Nos. 112/113 of Antigua, but $3 in recess.

322 3c. scarlet 10 40
323 $3 red-brown 22·00 30·00

1949 (10 Oct). 75th Anniversary of Universal Postal Union. As Nos. 114/117 of Antigua.

324 4c. carmine 20 60
325 6c. deep blue 1·75 2·00
326 12c. orange 30 75
327 24c. blue-green 30 70
324/327 *Set of* 4 2·25 3·50

1951 (16 Feb). University College of BWI. As Nos. 118/119 of Antigua.

328 3c. black and carmine 50 50
329 6c. black and blue 50 65

1953 (2 June). Coronation. As No. 120 of Antigua.

330 4c. black and scarlet 60 10

55 GPO, Georgetown

56 Botanical Gardens

57 *Victoria Regia* Water-lilies

58 Amerindian shooting fish

59 Map of Caribbean

60 Rice combine-harvester

61 Sugar cane entering factory

62 Felling Greenheart

63 Mining for bauxite

64 Mount Roraima

65 Kaieteur Falls

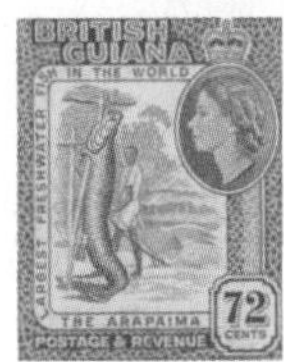

66 Arapaima

67 Channel-billed Toucan

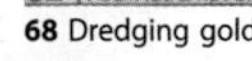

68 Dredging gold

69 Arms of British Guiana

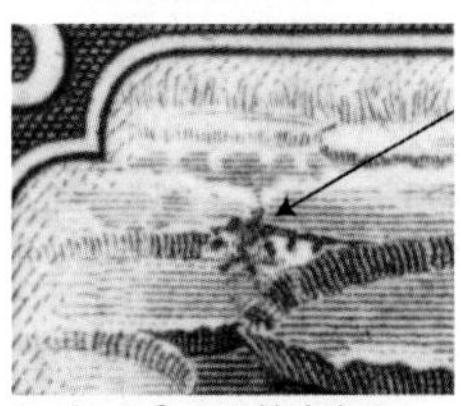

3c. Green flaw on lily below second 'I' of 'BRITISH' resembling weed (R. 3/10)

3c. Green spot on claw of right-hand bird appearing as clubbed foot (R. 4/1)

(Centre litho, frame recess ($1); recess (others). Waterlow (until 1961), then D.L.R.)

1954 (1 Dec)–**63**. T **55/69**. Wmk Mult Script CA. P 12½×13* (horiz) or 13 (vert).

331	**55**	1c. black	20	10
332	**56**	2c. myrtle-green	20	10
333	**57**	3c. brown-olive and red-brown	4·00	20
		a. 'Weed' flaw	65·00	
		b. 'Clubbed foot'	65·00	
		w. Wmk inverted		
334	**58**	4c. violet	1·75	10
		a. D.L.R. ptg (5.12.61)	13·00	4·00
		ab. Deep violet (3.1.63)	25·00	4·50
335	**59**	5c. scarlet and black	1·75	10
		w. Wmk inverted		
336	**60**	6c. yellow-green	1·50	10
		a. D.L.R. ptg. *Green* (22.5.62)	4·75	5·00
337	**61**	8c. ultramarine	1·50	20
		a. D.L.R. ptg. *Blue* (19.9.61)	21·00	2·50
338	**62**	12c. black and reddish brown	1·50	40
		a. Black and light brown (13.6.56)	1·50	10
		b. D.L.R. ptg. *Black and brown* (11.7.61)	40·00	4·25
339	**63**	24c. black and brownish orange	6·00	10
		a. Black and orange (13.6.56)	9·50	10
340	**64**	36c. rose-carmine and black	12·00	1·25
		w. Wmk inverted		
341	**65**	48c. ultramarine and brown-lake	2·25	1·00
		a. Bright ultramarine and pale brown-lake (13.6.56)	2·25	1·00
		ab. D.L.R. ptg (19.9.61)	42·00	28·00
342	**66**	72c. carmine and emerald	23·00	2·75
		a. D.L.R. ptg (17.7.62)	18·00	26·00
343	**67**	$1 pink. yellow. green and black	20·00	4·00
344	**68**	$2 deep mauve	35·00	9·00
		a. D.L.R. ptg. *Reddish mauve* (11.7.61)	75·00	15·00
345	**69**	$5 ultramarine and black	27·00	40·00
		a. D.L.R. ptg (19.9.61)	50·00	50·00
331/345 *Set of* 15			£110	50·00

On the Waterlow printings there is *always* a single wide-tooth perforation on each side at the top of the stamps. For the De La Rue stamps these teeth can occur *either* at the top or the bottom and, where not distinguishable by shade, can be identified by the quality of the printing, which is characterised by finer lines of shading and less intense colour than the Waterlow versions. Those listed De La Rue printings, which do not differ in shade, are for examples with the wide-tooth perforation at the bottom.

* All the Waterlow printings and early De La Rue printings of the horizontal designs are perforated 12.3×12.8, but De La Rue printings from 22 May 1962 (including those on the Block CA watermark) are perf 12.3×12.6.

The 1c. and 2c., printed by Waterlow, exist in coils constructed from normal sheets.

See also Nos. 354/365.

SELF-GOVERNMENT

70 **71** Weightlifting

(Photo Harrison)

1961 (23 Oct). History and Culture Week. W w **12**. P 14½×14.

346	**70**	5c. sepia and orange-red	25	10
347		6c. sepia and blue-green	25	15
348		30c. sepia and yellow-orange	60	45
346/348 *Set of* 3			1·00	60

1963 (14 July). Freedom from Hunger. As No. 146 of Antigua.

349		20c. reddish violet	30	60

1963 (2 Sept). Red Cross Centenary. As Nos. 147/148 of Antigua.

350		5c. red and black	20	20
351		20c. red and blue	55	35

1963–65. As Nos. 333/344, but wmk w **12**.

354	**57**	3c. brown-olive and red-brown (12.65)	5·50	2·00
356	**59**	5c. scarlet and black (28.5.64)	1·25	10
		w. Wmk inverted		
359	**62**	12c. black and yellowish brown (6.10.64)	2·50	10
360	**63**	24c. black and bright orange (10.12.63)	4·00	10
361	**64**	36c. rose-carmine and black (10.12.63)	1·75	60
362	**65**	48c. bright ultramarine and Venetian red (25.11.63)	2·75	1·50
		w. Wmk inverted		
363	**66**	72c. carmine and emerald (25.11.63)	5·00	25·00
364	**67**	$1 pink, yellow, green and black (10.12.63)	11·00	1·00
365	**68**	$2 reddish mauve (10.12.63)	18·00	14·00
354/365 *Set of* 9			45·00	40·00

There was no London release of No. 354.

The 5c. exists in coils constructed from normal sheets.

For 1c. value with wmk w **12**, see Guyana No. 429a (error opt omitted).

(Photo D.L.R.)

1964 (1 Oct). Olympic Games, Tokyo. W w **12**. P 13×13½.

367	**71**	5c. orange	10	10
368		8c. blue	15	35
369		25c. magenta	25	40
367/369 *Set of* 3			45	75

1965 (17 May). ITU Centenary. As Nos. 166/167 of Antigua.

370		5c. emerald and yellow-olive	10	15
371		25c. light blue and magenta	20	15

1965 (25 Oct). International Co-operation Year. As Nos. 168/169 of Antigua.

372		5c. reddish purple and turquoise-green	15	10
373		25c. deep bluish green and lavender	30	20

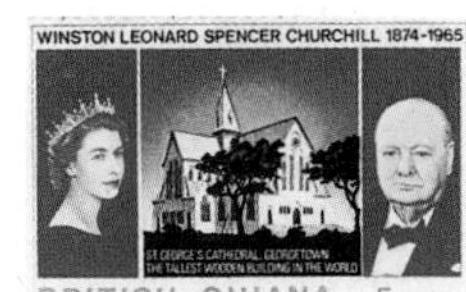

72 St George's Cathedral, Georgetown

(Des Jennifer Toombs, Photo Harrison)

1966 (24 Jan). Churchill Commemoration. W w **12**. P 14×14½.

374	**72**	5c. black, crimson and gold	1·25	10
375		25c. black, blue and gold	2·75	50

1966 (3 Feb). Royal Visit. As Nos. 174/175 of Antigua.

376		3c. black and ultramarine	75	15
377		25c. black and magenta	1·50	60

STAMP BOOKLETS

1909 (14 June). Black on pink cover without face value. Stapled.

SB1	49c. booklet containing 12×1c. and 18×2c. (Nos. 252/253) in blocks of 6	£2750

1923. Black on pink cover without face value. Stapled.

SB2	30c. booklet containing 6×1c. and 12×2c. (Nos. 272, 274) in blocks of 6	

1923. Black on pink without face value. Stapled.

SB3	48c. booklet containing 12×1c. and 18×2c. (Nos. 272, 274) in blocks of 6	£2000
	a. With face value on front cover	

1923. Black on red cover without face value. Stapled.

SB4	72c. booklet containing 12×1c., 6×2c. and 12×4c. (Nos. 272, 274/275) in blocks of 6	£3000

1934. Black on orange cover. Stitched.

SB5	24c. booklet containing 8×1c. and 8×2c. (Nos. 288/289) in blocks of 4	

1934. Black on orange cover. Stitched.

SB6	36c. booklet containing 4×1c., 8×2c. and 4×4c. (Nos. 288/289, 291) in blocks of 4	

1938. Black on orange cover. Stitched.

SB7	36c. booklet containing 4×1c., 8×2c. and 4×4c. (Nos. 308/310) in blocks of 4	£850

1944. Black on red cover. Stitched.

SB8	24c. booklet containing 8×1c. and 8×2c. (Nos. 308a/309) in blocks of 4	£600

1945–49. Black on red cover. Stitched.

SB9*a*	24c. booklet containing 1c., 2c. and 3c., each in block of 4 (Nos. 290, 308*a*, 309)	70·00
	b. Containing Nos. 290, 308*a*, 309a	70·00
	c. Containing Nos. 290a, 308*a*, 309	75·00
	d. Containing Nos. 290b, 308*a*, 309	95·00
	e. Containing Nos. 290b, 308*a*, 309a	90·00
	f. Containing Nos. 290b, 308b, 309a	£110

POSTAGE DUE STAMPS

D 1

(Typo D.L.R.)

1940 (Mar)–**55**. Wmk Mult Script CA. Chalk-surfaced paper (4c.). P 14.

D1	D **1**	1c. green	6·50	16·00
		a. Chalk-surfaced paper. *Deep green*, (30.4.52)	2·00	22·00
		ab. W **9a** (Crown missing)	£600	
		ac. W **9b** (St Edward's Crown)	£150	
D2		2c. black	28·00	2·00
		a. Chalk-surfaced paper (30.4.52)	4·50	12·00
		ab. W **9a** (Crown missing)	£425	
		ac. W **9b** (St Edward's Crown)	£160	
D3		4c. bright blue (1.5.52)	1·00	14·00
		a. W **9a** (Crown missing)	£400	
		b. W **9b** (St Edward's Crown)	£160	
D4		12c. scarlet	38·00	7·50
		a. Chalk-surfaced paper (19.7.55)	20·00	48·00
D1, D2, D4 *Set of 3*			65·00	23·00
D1*a*/D4a *Set of* 4			25·00	85·00
D1s, D2s and D4s Perf 'SPECIMEN' *Set of* 3			£100	

OFFICIAL STAMPS

OFFICIAL (O **1**) OFFICIAL (O **1a**) **OFFICIAL** (O **2**)

1875. Optd with T O **1** (1c.) or O **1a** (others) by litho. P 10.

O1	**8**	1c. black (R.)	75·00	27·00
		a. Imperf between (horiz pair)	†	£30000
O2		2c. orange	£475	14·00
O3		8c. rose	£375	£150
O4	**7**	12c. brownish purple	£3500	£500
O5	**9**	24c. green	£2750	£275

Two types of the word 'OFFICIAL' are found on each value. On the 1c. the word is either 16 or 17 mm long. On the other values the chief difference is in the shape and position of the letter 'o' in 'OFFICIAL'. In one case the 'o' is upright, in the other it slants to the left.

1877. Optd with T O **2** by typo. Wmk Crown CC. P 14.

O6	**16**	1c. slate	£375	65·00
		a. Imperf between (vert pair)	†	£30000
O7		2c. orange	£180	15·00
O8		4c. blue	£150	28·00
O9		6c. brown	£5500	£600
O10		8c. rose	£2000	£450

Prepared for use, but not issued.

O11	**16**	12c. pale violet	£1800	
O12		24c. green	£2250	

The 'OFFICIAL' overprints have been extensively forged.

The use of Official stamps was discontinued in June 1878.

British Guiana became independent as Guyana on 25 May 1966.

British Honduras

It is recorded that the first local post office was established by the inhabitants in 1809, but Belize did not become a regular packet port of call until December 1829. The post office came under the control of the British GPO in April 1844 and the stamps of Great Britain were supplied for use on overseas mail from May 1858.

The colonial authorities took over the postal service on 1 April 1860, the Great Britain stamps being withdrawn at the end of the month. There was no inland postal service until 1862.

For illustrations of the handstamp and postmark types see BRITISH POST OFFICES ABROAD notes, following GREAT BRITAIN.

BELIZE

CROWNED-CIRCLE HANDSTAMPS

CC1 CC **1** BELIZE (R.) (13.11.1841) *Price on cover* £4000

Stamps of GREAT BRITAIN cancelled 'A06' as Type **2**.

1858–60.

Z1 1d. rose-red (1857), *perf* 14 £1200
Z2 4d. rose (1857) £425
Z3 6d. lilac (1856) £375
Z4 1s. green (1856) £2500

PRICES FOR STAMPS ON COVER TO 1945

Nos. 1/4	*from* × 50
Nos. 5/16	*from* × 30
Nos. 17/22	*from* × 20
Nos. 23/26	*from* × 10
Nos. 27/30	*from* × 15
Nos. 35/42	*from* × 20
Nos. 43/44	*from* × 30
Nos. 49/50	*from* × 25
Nos. 51/69	*from* × 15
Nos. 80/100	*from* × 6
Nos. 101/110	*from* × 5
Nos. 111/120	*from* × 15
Nos. 121/122	*from* × 8
No. 123	*from* × 10
Nos. 124/137	*from* × 6
Nos. 138/142	*from* × 10
Nos. 143/149	*from* × 8
Nos. 150/161	*from* × 5
Nos. D1/D3	*from* × 30

CROWN COLONY

1

(Typo D.L.R.)

1865 (1 Dec). No wmk. P 14.

1 **1** 1d. pale blue 70·00 65·00
a. Imperf between (pair)
2 1d. blue £100 75·00
3 6d. rose £425 £170
4 1s. green £400 £130
a. In horiz pair with 6d. £50000
b. In vert pair with 1d. £65000

In the first printing all three values were printed in the same sheet separated by horizontal and vertical gutter margins. The sheet comprised two panes of 60 of the 1d. at the top with a pane of 60 of the 1s. at bottom left and another of 6d. at bottom right. Copies of 1d. *se-tenant* with the 6d. are not known. There were two later printings of the 1d. but they were in sheets without the 6d. and 1s.

1872–79. Wmk Crown CC.

(a) P 12½

5 **1** 1d. pale blue 95·00 38·00
w. Wmk inverted £350
y. Wmk inverted and reversed £450
6 1d. deep blue (1874) £120 32·00
7 3d. red-brown £170 80·00
8 3d. chocolate (1874) £190 £100
9 6d. rose £450 55·00
9*a* 6d. bright rose-carmine (1874) £600 65·00
10 1s. green £700 48·00
10*a* 1s. deep green (1874) £550 30·00
b. Imperf between (horiz pair) † £26000
w. Wmk inverted — £250

(b) P 14 (1877–1879)

11 **1** 1d. pale blue (1878) 85·00 35·00
12 1d. blue 90·00 27·00
a. Imperf between (horiz strip of 3) £28000
13 3d. chestnut £170 32·00
14 4d. mauve (1879) £300 9·50
x. Wmk reversed
15 6d. rose (1878) £475 £200
w. Wmk inverted — £550
16 1s. green £325 14·00
a. Imperf between (pair)

1882–87. Wmk Crown CA. P 14.

17 **1** 1d. blue (4.84) 75·00 25·00
18 1d. rose (1884) 23·00 17·00
a. Bisected (½d.) (*on cover*) † —
s. Optd 'SPECIMEN' £275
19 1d. carmine (1887) 60·00 32·00
20 4d. mauve (7.82) 95·00 4·75
w. Wmk inverted — £200
21 6d. yellow (1885) £275 £225
22 1s. grey (1.87) £250 £160
s. Optd 'SPECIMEN' 75·00

(New Currency. 100 cents = 1 British Honduras dollar)

2 CENTS (2) TWO (3) 2 CENTS (4)

1888 (1 Jan). Stamps of 1872–1879 (wmk Crown CC), surch locally as T **2**.

(a) P 12½

23 **1** 2c. on 6d. rose £350 £275
24 3c. on 3d. chocolate £18000 £6000

(b) P 14

25 **1** 2c. on 6d. rose £190 £170
a. Surch double £2500
b. Bisected (1c.) (*on cover*) † £300
c. Slanting '2' with curved foot £3250
w. Wmk inverted — £650
26 3c. on 3d. chestnut £110 £110

There are very dangerous forgeries of these surcharges, particularly of No. 24.

No. 25c may be a trial.

1888. Stamps of 1882–1887 (wmk Crown CA), surch locally as T **2**, P 14.

27 **1** 2c. on 1d. rose 15·00 50·00
a. Surch inverted £7500 £5500
b. Surch double £900 £900
c. Bisected (1c.) (*on cover*) † £200
28 10c. on 4d. mauve 70·00 19·00
29 20c. on 6d. yellow 30·00 50·00
30 50c. on 1s. grey £475 £700
a. Error. '5' for '50' £17000

Various settings were used for the surcharges on Nos. 23/30, the most common of which was of 36 (6×6) impressions. For No. 29 this setting was so applied that an albino surcharge occurs in the margin above each stamp in the first horizontal row.

The same setting was subsequently amended, by altering the '2' to '1', to surcharge the 4d. value. As this was in sheets of 30 it was only necessary to alter the values on the bottom five rows of the setting. Albino surcharges once again occur in the top margin of the sheet, but, as the type in the first horizontal row remained unaltered, these read '20 CENTS' rather than the '10 CENTS' on the actual stamps.

1888 (Mar). No. 30 further surch locally with T **3**.

35 **1** 'TWO' on 50c. on 1s. grey (R.) 60·00 £100
a. Bisected (1c.) (*on cover*) † £300
b. Surch in black £16000 £15000
c. Surch double (R.+Blk.) £16000 £16000

1888 (May)–**91**. Surch in London as T **4**. Wmk Crown CA. P 14.

36 **1** 1c. on 1d. dull green (?12.91) 1·00 1·50
37 2c. on 1d. carmine 75 2·25
a. Bisected (1c.) (*on cover*) † £110
w. Wmk inverted £325
38 3c. on 3d. red-brown 6·50 1·40
39 6c. on 3d. ultramarine (?4.91) 7·50 27·00
40 10c. on 4d. mauve 27·00 50
a. Surch double £3250
41 20c. on 6d. yellow (2.89) 19·00 14·00
42 50c. on 1s. grey (11.88) 38·00 85·00
36/42 *Set of 7* 85·00 £110
36s/42s Optd 'SPECIMEN' *Set of 7* £375

(5)

FIVE (6) 15 (7)

1891. Stamps of 1888–1889 surch locally.

*(a) With T **5** (May)*

43 **1** 6c. on 10c. on 4d. mauve (R.) 1·50 2·50
a. '6' and bar inverted £600 £600
b. '6' only inverted † £6500
44 6c. on 10c. on 4d. mauve (Blk.) 3·75 1·50
a. '6' and bar inverted £4500 £1100
b. '6' only inverted † £6500

Of variety (b) only six copies of each can exist, as one of each of these errors came in the first six sheets, and the mistake was then corrected. Of variety (a) more copies exist.

Essays are known with 'SIX' in place of '6' both with and without bars (*price* £140 *and* £550 *respectively*). Although not issued we mention them, as three contemporary covers franked with them are known.

*(b) With T **6/7** (23 Oct)*

49 **1** 5c. on 3c. on 3d. red-brown 1·25 1·40
a. Wide space between 'I' and 'V' 60·00 75·00
b. 'FIVE' and bar double £375 £425
50 15c. on 6c. on 3d. ultramarine (R.) 19·00 28·00

8

9

10

11

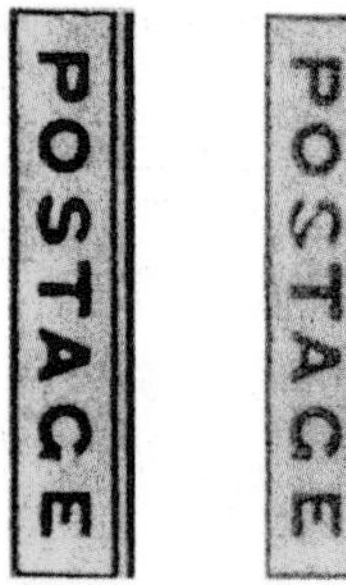

Normal

Malformed 'S'

Repaired 'S'

The Malformed and Repaired 'S' occur on R. 7/3 of the left pane from Key Plate 2.

(Typo D.L.R.)

1891 (July)–**1901**. Wmk Crown CA. P 14.

51 **8** 1c. dull green (4.95) 3·00 2·00
a. Malformed 'S' £400 £250
w. Wmk inverted † £300
52 2c. carmine-rose 4·25 20
a. Malformed 'S' £450 £180
b. Repaired 'S' £375 £150
53 3c. brown 10·00 5·00
w. Wmk inverted £300
54 5c. ultramarine (4.95) 12·00 1·75
a. Malformed 'S' £650 £225
55 **11** 5c. grey-black and ultramarine/*blue* (10.00) 23·00 4·25
56 **8** 6c. ultramarine 15·00 2·00
57 **9** 10c. mauve and green (4.95) 14·00 22·00
58 **10** 10c. dull purple and green (1901) 12·00 12·00
59 **9** 12c. reddish lilac and green 2·50 4·50
60 24c. yellow and blue 7·00 26·00
a. Orange and blue 30·00 55·00
61 25c. red-brown and green (3.98) £100 £160
62 **10** 50c. green and carmine (3.98) 30·00 75·00
63 **11** $1 green and carmine (12.99) £100 £170
64 $2 green and ultramarine (12.99) £160 £325
65 $5 green and black (12.99) £325 £475
51/65 *Set of 15* £700 £1100
51s/65s Optd 'SPECIMEN' *Set of 15* £400

Most values are known with a forged Belize postmark dated 'OC 23 09'.

1899 (1 July). Optd 'REVENUE' 12 mm long.

66 **8** 5c. ultramarine 28·00 3·25
a. 'BEVENUE' £180 £180
b. Malformed 'S' at right £700 £350
d. Opt 11 mm long 35·00 12·00
67 **9** 10c. mauve and green 22·00 25·00
a. 'BEVENUE' £350 £425
b. 'REVENU' £700
c. Opt 11 mm long 26·00 50·00
cb. 'REVENU' £800 £900
68 25c. red-brown and green 5·50 45·00
a. 'BEVENUE' £200 £425
b. 'REVE UE' £2500
c. Repaired 'S' at right £750
d. Opt 11 mm long 7·00 65·00
69 **1** 50c. on 1s. grey £275 £425
a. 'BEVENUE' £5500 £6500
c. Opt 11 mm long £425 £650

Two minor varieties, a small 'U' and a tall, narrow 'U' are found in the word 'REVENUE'.

The overprint setting of 60 (6×10) contained 43 examples of the 12 mm size and 17 of the 11 mm. The smaller size overprints occur on R. 8/1, R. 8/3 to 6 and on all positions in Rows 9 and 10.

The 'BEVENUE' error appears on R. 6/4 and, it is believed, 'REVE UE' comes from R. 6/6. Both occur on parts of the printing only. The missing 'E' developed during the overprinting and damage to this letter can be observed on at least eight positions in the setting.

14

15

(Typo D.L.R.)

1902 (10 Oct)–**04**. Wmk Crown CA. P 14.

80 **14** 1c. grey-green and green (28.4.04) 3·00 28·00
81 2c. purple and black/*red* (18.3.03) 3·50 25
w. Wmk inverted £200 £110
82 5c. grey-black and blue/*blue* 22·00 30
w. Wmk inverted
83 **15** 20c. dull and bright purple (28.4.04) 15·00 20·00
80/83 *Set of 4* 40·00 45·00
80s/83s Optd 'SPECIMEN' *Set of 4* 80·00

1904 (Dec)–**07**. Wmk Mult Crown CA. Ordinary paper (1, 2c.) or chalk-surfaced paper (others). P 14.

84 **14** 1c. grey-green and green (8.05) 22·00 21·00
a. Chalk-surfaced paper (1906) 5·50 2·50
85 2c. purple and black/*red* 3·50 30
a. Chalk-surfaced paper (1906) 3·50 20
86 5c. grey-black and blue/*blue* (5.2.06) 2·50 20
87 **15** 10c. dull purple and emerald-green (20.9.07) 4·00 20·00
89 25c. dull purple and orange (20.9.07) 12·00 60·00
90 50c. grey-green and carmine (20.9.07) 38·00 £110
91 **14** $1 grey-green and carmine (20.9.07) 80·00 £130
92 $2 grey-green and blue (20.9.07) £160 £275
93 $5 grey-green and black (20.9.07) £375 £450
84a/93 *Set of 9* £600 £900
87s/93s Optd 'SPECIMEN' *Set of 6* £250

Examples of most values are known showing a forged Belize postmark dated 'OC 23 09'.

1908 (7 Dec)–**11**. Colours changed. Wmk Mult Crown CA. Chalk-surfaced paper (25c.). P 14.

95	**14**	1c. blue-green (1.7.10)	24·00	50
96		2c. carmine	19·00	10
		w. Wmk inverted		
97		5c. ultramarine (1.6.09)	4·50	10
100	**15**	25c. black/*green* (14.10.11)	9·50	48·00
95/100 *Set of 4*			50·00	48·00
96s/100s Optd 'SPECIMEN' *Set of 3*			95·00	

16

17

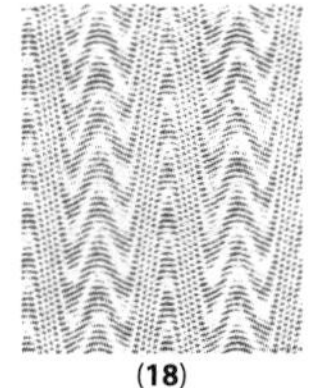
(18)

1913–21. Wmk Mult Crown CA. Chalk-surfaced paper (10c. to $5). P 14.

101	**16**	1c. blue-green	7·00	1·50
		a. Yellow-green (13.3.17)	13·00	2·75
		w. Wmk inverted	£275	
102		2c. red	7·00	1·00
		a. Bright scarlet (1915)	12·00	1·00
		b. Dull scarlet (8.17)	9·00	1·50
		c. Red/bluish	15·00	8·00
		w. Wmk inverted	†	£400
103		3c. orange (16.4.17)	2·75	20
104		5c. bright blue	4·25	85
105	**17**	10c. dull purple and yellow-green	8·00	6·50
		a. Dull purple and bright green (1917)	26·00	25·00
		ax Wmk reversed	£550	
106		25c. black/*green*	2·00	12·00
		a. On blue-green, olive back (8.17)	5·00	11·00
		b. On emerald back (1921)	2·00	35·00
107		50c. purple and blue/*blue*	35·00	17·00
108	**16**	$1 black and carmine	38·00	70·00
109		$2 purple and green	90·00	£130
110		$5 purple and black/*red*	£275	£350
101/110 *Set of 10*			£400	£500
101s/110s Optd 'SPECIMEN' *Set of 10*			£275	

1915–16. Optd with T **18**, in violet.

111	**16**	1c. green (30.12.15)	4·75	26·00
		a. Yellow-green (6.6.16)	50	22·00
112		2c. scarlet (3.11.15)	3·50	50
113		5c. bright blue (29.7.15)	30	6·00
111s/113s Optd 'SPECIMEN' *Set of 3*			£140	

These stamps were shipped early in the 1914–1918 war, and were thus overprinted, so that if seized by the enemy, they could be distinguished and rendered invalid.

WAR
(19)

WAR
(20)

21

1916 (23 Aug). No. 111 optd locally with T **19**.

114	**16**	1c. green	10	3·00
		a. Opt inverted	£300	£350

1917–18. Nos. 101 and 103 optd with T **19**.

116	**16**	1c. blue-green (6.17)	1·50	9·00
		aw. Wmk inverted	£250	
		ax. Wmk reversed	£300	
		b. Yellow-green (3.3.17)	20	5·00
118		3c. orange (12.3.18)	5·50	19·00
		a. Opt double	£400	

1918. Nos. 101 and 103 optd with T **20**.

119	**16**	1c. blue-green (25.4.18)	20	40
		a. Yellow-green	4·50	6·50
120		3c. orange (9.18)	80	4·50
		y. Wmk inverted and reversed	£225	
119s/120s Optd 'SPECIMEN' *Set of 2*			£120	

(Recess D.L.R.)

1921 (28 Apr). Peace Commemoration. Wmk Mult Crown CA (sideways). P 14.

121	**21**	2c. rose-red	7·00	50
		a. 'C' of 'CA' missing from wmk	£400	
		s. Optd 'SPECIMEN'	60·00	

1921 (26 Nov). Wmk Mult Script CA. P 14.

122	**16**	1c. green	10·00	13·00
		s. Optd 'SPECIMEN'	55·00	

1922 (4 Jan). As T **21** but with words 'PEACE' omitted. Wmk Mult Script CA (sideways). P 14.

123		4c. slate	14·00	50
		s. Optd 'SPECIMEN'	50·00	

22

BELIZE
RELIEF FUND
PLUS
3 CENTS
(23)

(Typo D.L.R.)

1922 (1 Aug)–**33**. Ordinary paper (1c. to 5c.) or chalk-surfaced paper (others). P 14.

(a) Wmk Mult Crown CA

124	**22**	25c. black/*emerald*	10·00	50·00
125		$5 purple and black/*red* (1.10.24)	£225	£300

(b) Wmk Mult Script CA

126	**22**	1c. green (2.1.29)	20·00	6·50
127		2c. brown (1.3.23)	1·50	1·50
128		2c. rose-carmine (10.12.26)	12·00	1·50
129		3c. orange (1933)	38·00	4·00
130		4c. grey (1.10.29)	22·00	85
131		5c. ultramarine	1·75	55
		a. Milky blue (1923)	5·50	4·25
132		10c. dull purple and sage-green (1.12.22)	4·50	30
133		25c. black/*emerald* (1.10.24)	3·25	8·50
134		50c. purple and blue/*blue* (1.11.23)	8·00	16·00
136		$1 black and scarlet (2.1.25)	23·00	38·00
137		$2 yellow-green and bright purple	50·00	£140
124/137 *Set of 13*			£350	£500
124s/137s Optd or Perf (1c., 3c., 4c.) 'SPECIMEN' *Set of 13*			£375	

1932 (2 May). Belize Relief Fund. Surch as T **23**. Wmk Mult Script CA. P 14.

138	**22**	1c.+1c. green	3·00	17·00
139		2c.+2c. rose-carmine	3·00	17·00
140		3c.+3c. orange	3·50	35·00
141		4c.+4c. grey (R.)	18·00	38·00
142		5c.+5c. ultramarine	9·50	14·00
138/142 *Set of 5*			32·00	£110
138s/142s Perf 'SPECIMEN' *Set of 5*			£150	

1935 (6 May). Silver Jubilee. As Nos. 91/94 of Antigua, but ptd by B.W. & Co. P 11×12.

143	3c. ultramarine and grey-black	2·25	1·00
	a. Extra flagstaff	80·00	£100
	b. Short extra flagstaff	£140	£170
	c. Lightning conductor	90·00	£110
	d. Flagstaff on right-hand turret	£250	
	e. Double flagstaff	£275	
144	4c. green and indigo	5·00	4·75
	a. Extra flagstaff	£180	£225
	c. Lightning conductor	£200	£225
	d. Flagstaff on right-hand turret	£375	
	e. Double flagstaff	£400	£425
145	5c. brown and deep blue	2·50	3·25
146	25c. slate and purple	14·00	17·00
	a. Extra flagstaff	£250	£375
	b. Short extra flagstaff	£500	
	c. Lightning conductor	£325	£475
	d. Flagstaff on right-hand turret	£450	
	e. Double flagstaff	£475	
143/146 *Set of 4*		21·00	23·00
143s/146s Perf 'SPECIMEN' *Set of 4*		£120	

For illustrations of plate varieties see Omnibus section following Zanzibar.

1937 (12 May). Coronation. As Nos. 95/97 of Antigua, but printed by D.L.R. P 14.

147	3c. orange	30	30
148	4c. grey-black	70	30
149	5c. bright blue	80	1·90
147/149 *Set of 3*		1·60	2·25
147s/149s Perf 'SPECIMEN' *Set of 3*		95·00	

24 Maya Figures

25 Chicle Tapping

26 Cohune palm

27 Local products

28 Grapefruit

29 Mahogany logs in river

30 Sergeant's Cay

31 Dorey

32 Chicle industry

33 Court House Belize

34 Mahogany felling

35 Arms of Colony

(Recess B.W.)

1938 (10 Jan)–**47**. T **24/35**. Wmk Mult Script CA (sideways on horizontal stamps). P 11½×11 (horizontal designs) or 11×11½ (vertical designs).

150	**24**	1c. bright magenta and green (14.2.38)	70	1·50
151	**25**	2c. black and scarlet (14.2.38)	1·50	1·00
		a. Perf 12 (1947)	3·75	1·50
152	**26**	3c. purple and brown	2·25	1·75
153	**27**	4c. black and green	2·00	70
154	**28**	5c. mauve and dull blue	3·50	1·75
155	**29**	10c. green and reddish brown (14.2.38)	4·75	60
156	**30**	15c. brown and light blue (14.2.38)	8·50	1·50
157	**31**	25c. blue and green (14.2.38)	5·00	2·00
158	**32**	50c. black and purple (14.2.38)	40·00	4·75
159	**33**	$1 scarlet and olive (28.2.38)	50·00	10·00
160	**34**	$2 deep blue and maroon (28.2.38)	55·00	42·00
161	**35**	$5 scarlet and brown (28.2.38)	50·00	60·00
150/161 *Set of 12*			£190	£110
150s/161s Perf 'SPECIMEN' *Set of 12*			£300	

1946 (9 Sept). Victory. As Nos. 110/111 of Antigua.

162	3c. brown	10	20
163	5c. blue	10	20
162s/163s Perf 'SPECIMEN' *Set of 2*		95·00	

1948 (1 Oct). Royal Silver Wedding. As Nos. 112/113 of Antigua.

164	4c. green	15	60
165	$5 brown	28·00	50·00

36 Island of St George's Cay

37 HMS *Merlin*

(Recess Waterlow)

1949 (10 Jan). 150th Anniversary of Battle of St George's Cay. Wmk Mult Script CA. P 12½.

166	**36**	1c. ultramarine and green	30	1·50
167		3c. blue and yellow-brown	30	1·50
168		4c. olive and violet	30	1·75
169	**37**	5c. brown and deep blue	2·25	75
170		10c. green and red-brown	2·25	30
171		15c. emerald and ultramarine	2·25	30
166/171 *Set of 6*			7·00	5·50

1949 (10 Oct). 75th Anniversary of UPU. As Nos. 114/117 of Antigua.

172	4c. blue-green	30	1·50
173	5c. deep blue	1·50	50
174	10c. red-brown	40	4·00
175	25c. blue	35	50
172/175 *Set of 4*		2·25	6·00

1951 (16 Feb). Inauguration of BWI University College. As Nos. 118/119 of Antigua.

176	3c. reddish violet and brown	45	1·75
177	10c. green and brown	45	30

1953 (2 June). Coronation. As No. 120 of Antigua.

178	4c. black and green	75	30

38 Arms of British Honduras

39 Baird's Tapir ('Mountain Cow')

40 Mace and Legislative Council Chamber

41 Pine industry

42 Spiny Lobster

43 Stanley Field Airport

44 Maya frieze, Xunantunich

45 *Morpho peleides*

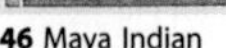

46 Maya Indian

47 Nine-banded Armadillo

48 Hawkesworth Bridge

49 Mountain Orchid

(Recess Waterlow (until 20.6.1961), then D.L.R.)

1953 (2 Sept)–**62**. T **38/39**. Wmk Mult Script CA. P 13½.

179	**38**	1c. green and black	10	40
		a. Perf 13½×13 (3.10.61)	3·50	2·75
180	**39**	2c. yellow-brown and black	1·75	3·00
		a. Perf 14 (18.9.57)	2·75	65
		b. Perf 13½×13 (20.6.61)	3·50	2·25
181	**40**	3c. reddish violet and bright purple	75	45
		a. Perf 14 (18.9.57)	50	10
		b. Perf 13½×13 (20.6.61)	16·00	28·00
		ba. Reddish lilac and pale magenta (19.1.62)	3·25	3·50
182	**41**	4c. brown and green	1·50	30
183	**42**	5c. deep olive-green and scarlet	1·00	20
		a. Perf 14 (15.5.57)	2·75	10
		ab. D.L.R. ptg (3.10.61)	16·00	28·00
		aba. Imperf three sides (horiz pair)	£9000	
184	**43**	10c. slate and bright blue	2·25	10
		a. Perf 13½×13 (19.1.62)	2·25	10
185	**44**	15c. green and violet	65	10
186	**45**	25c. bright blue and yellow-brown	7·50	3·75
187	**46**	50c. yellow-brown and reddish purple	20·00	4·00
		a. Pale yellow-brown and pale purple (22.3.60)	70·00	15·00
188	**47**	$1 slate-blue and red-brown	11·00	5·00
189	**48**	$2 scarlet and grey	11·00	4·50
190	**49**	$5 purple and slate	48·00	17·00
179/190 *Set of* 12			90·00	30·00

Nos. 179/190 were released a day earlier by the Crown Agents in London.

Stamps from the Waterlow printings perforated 13½×13 or 14 have a very fine perforation tooth at the *top* of each vertical side. On the De La Rue printings this tooth is at the *bottom*. Stamps perforated 13½ have 'normal' perforation teeth at top and bottom.

50 *Belize from Fort George, 1842* (C. J. Hullmandel)

51 Public Seals, 1860 and 1960

52 Tamarind Tree, Newtown Barracks

(Recess B.W.)

1960 (1 July). Post Office Centenary. W w **12**. P 11½×11.

191	**50**	2c. green	75	1·50
192	**51**	10c. deep carmine	75	10
193	**52**	15c. blue	75	35
191/193 *Set of* 3			2·00	1·75

NEW CONSTITUTION
1960
(53)

HURRICANE
HATTIE
(54)

1961 (1 Mar). New Constitution. Nos. 180a, 181a and 184/185 optd with T **53** by Waterlow.

194	2c. yellow-brown and black	25	40
195	3c. reddish violet and bright purple	30	40
196	10c. slate and bright blue	60	10
197	15c. green and violet	40	20
194/197 *Set of* 4		1·40	1·00

1962 (15 Jan). Hurricane Hattie Relief Fund. Nos. 179a, 184a, 186 and 187 optd with T **54** by D.L.R.

198	1c. green and black	10	1·75
199	10c. slate and bright blue	30	10
200	25c. bright blue and yellow-brown	1·75	80
201	50c. yellow-brown and reddish purple	75	1·75
198/201 *Set of* 4		2·50	4·00

55 Great Curassow

(Des D. R. Eckelberry. Photo Harrison)

1962 (2 Apr). Horizontal designs on T **55**. Multicoloured. W w **12** (upright). P 14×14½.

202	1c. Type **55**	1·50	75
	a. Orange-yellow (knob) omitted	£800	
	w. Wmk inverted		
203	2c. Red-legged Honey-creeper	2·00	10
	a. Turquoise-blue (bird's head) omitted	£800	
204	3c. Northern Jacana	4·50	3·50
	a. Blue-green (legs) omitted	£700	
205	4c. Great Kiskadee	3·75	4·25
206	5c. Scarlet-rumped Tanager	2·75	10
	w. Wmk inverted		
207	10c. Scarlet Macaw	4·50	10
	a. Blue omitted	£850	
	w. Wmk inverted	†	—
208	15c. Slaty-tailed Trogon	1·50	10
	w. Wmk inverted	45·00	17·00
209	25c. Red-footed Booby	4·50	30
	w. Wmk inverted		
210	50c. Keel-billed Toucan	6·00	35
	a. Pale blue (claw and beak) omitted	£1200	£1200
211	$1 Magnificent Frigatebird	9·00	2·50
212	$2 Rufous-tailed Jacamar	24·00	8·00
	*a. Shade**	70·00	21·00
	w. Wmk inverted	£140	
213	$5 Montezuma Oropendola	28·00	21·00
202/213 *Set of* 12		80·00	35·00

* On No. 212*a*, the bird is myrtle-green and red-brown instead of yellow-green and orange-brown.

Nos. 202, 206 and 207 exist in coils, constructed from normal sheets. See also Nos. 239/245.

1963 (4 June). Freedom from Hunger. As No. 146 of Antigua.

214	22c. bluish green	30	15

1963 (2 Sept). Red Cross Centenary. As Nos. 147/148 of Antigua.

215	4c. red and black	20	1·40
216	22c. red and blue	40	1·40

SELF-GOVERNMENT

SELF GOVERNMENT
1964
(56)

DEDICATION OF SITE
NEW CAPITAL
9th OCTOBER 1965
(57)

1964. New Constitution. Nos. 202, 204/205, 207 and 209 optd with T **56**.

217	1c. Type **55** (20.4)	10	30
	a. Opt inverted	£800	
	b. Orange-yellow (knob) omitted	£300	
218	3c. Northern Jacana (20.4)	45	30
219	4c. Great Kiskadee (3.2)	45	30
220	10c. Scarlet Macaw (20.4)	45	10
221	25c. Red-footed Booby (3.2)	55	30
217/221 *Set of* 5		1·75	1·10

1965 (17 May). ITU Centenary. As Nos. 166/167 of Antigua.

222	2c. orange-red and light green	10	10
223	50c. yellow and light purple	35	25

1965 (25 Oct). International Co-operation Year. As Nos. 168/169 of Antigua.

224	1c. reddish purple and turquoise-green	10	15
225	22c. deep bluish green and lavender	20	15

1966 (24 Jan). Churchill Commemoration. As Nos. 170/173 of Antigua.

226	1c. new blue	10	75
227	4c. deep green	70	10
228	22c. brown	1·10	10
229	25c. bluish violet	1·25	45
226/229 *Set of* 4		2·75	1·10

1966 (1 July). Dedication of New Capital Site. As Nos. 202, 204/205, 207 and 209, but wmk sideways, optd with T **57** by Harrison.

230	1c. Type **55**	15	40
	a. Orange-yellow (knob) omitted	£400	
	w. Wmk Crown to right of CA	70	
231	3c. Northern Jacana	60	40
232	4c. Great Kiskadee	60	40
233	10c. Scarlet Macaw	60	10
234	25c. Red-footed Booby	85	35
230/234 *Set of* 5		2·50	1·50

* The normal sideways watermark shows Crown to left of CA, *as seen from the back of the stamp.*

58 Citrus Grove

(Des V. Whiteley. Photo Harrison)

1966 (1 Oct). Stamp Centenary*. T **58** and similar horizontal designs. Multicoloured. W w **12**. P 14×14½.

235	5c. Type **58**	10	10
236	10c. Half Moon Cay	10	10
237	22c. Hidden Valley Falls	10	10
238	25c. Maya Ruins, Xunantunich	15	45
235/238 *Set of* 4		30	65

* It is now known that the first stamps were issued in December 1865.

1967. As Nos. 202, etc, but W w **12** (sideways).

239	1c. Type **55** (16.2)	10	50
240	2c. Red-legged Honey-creeper (28.11)	30	1·00
241	4c. Great Kiskadee (16.2)	3·50	3·00
242	5c. Scarlet-rumped Tanager (16.2)	60	10
243	10c. Scarlet Macaw (28.11)	40	10
244	15c. Slaty-tailed Trogon (28.11)	40	10
245	50c. Keel-billed Toucan (16.2)	2·50	3·50
239/245 *Set of* 7		7·00	7·50

The 15c. value exists with PVA gum as well as gum arabic.

59 Sailfish

60 *Schomburgkia tibicinis*

(Des R. Granger Barrett. Photo Harrison)

1967 (1 Dec). International Tourist Year. T **59** and similar horizontal designs. W w **12**. P 12½.

246	5c. deep violet-blue black and light yellow	20	30
247	10c. brown, black and orange-red	20	10
248	22c. yellow-orange, black and bright green	35	10
249	25c. light greenish blue, black and greenish yellow	35	60
246/249 *Set of* 4		1·00	1·00

Designs: 5c. T **59**; 10c. Red Brocket; 22c. Jaguar; 25c. Atlantic Tarpon.

(Des Sylvia Goaman. Photo Harrison)

1968 (16 Apr). 20th Anniversary of Economic Commission for Latin America. T **60** and similar vertical designs showing orchids. Multicoloured. W w **12** (sideways). P 14½×14.

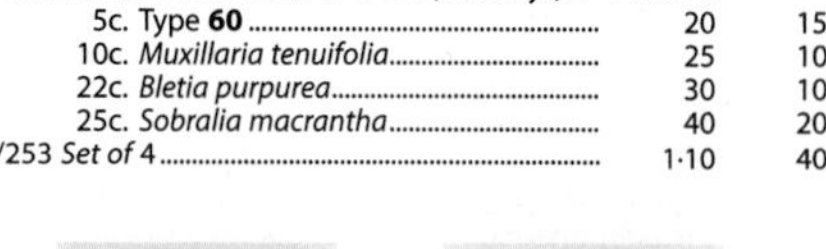

250	5c. Type **60**	20	15
251	10c. *Maxillaria tenuifolia*	25	10
252	22c. *Bletia purpurea*	30	10
253	25c. *Sobralia macrantha*	40	20
250/253 *Set of* 4		1·10	40

61 Monument to Belizean Patriots

62 Monument at Site of New Capital

(Des G. Vasarhelyi. Litho B.W.)

1968 (15 July). Human Rights Year. W w **12**. P 13½.

254	**61**	22c. multicoloured	15	10
255	**62**	50c. multicoloured	15	20

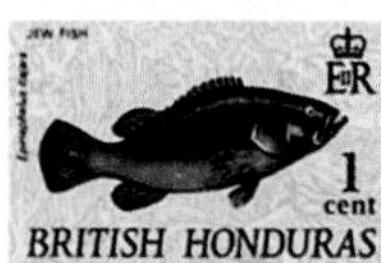

63 Spotted Jewfish

(Des J. W. Litho D.L.R.)

1968 (15 Oct). Wildlife. Horiz designs as T **63**. Multicoloured. No wmk. P 13×12½.

256	1c. Type **63**	30	10
257	2c. White-Tipped Peccary ('Warree')	10	10
258	3c. Misty Grouper	20	10
259	4c. Collared Anteater	15	1·25
260	5c. Bonefish	15	1·25
261	10c. Para ('Gibnut')	15	10
262	15c. Dolphinfish	2·00	20
263	25c. Kinkajou ('Night Walker')	30	20
264	50c. Mutton Snapper	70	1·25
265	$1 Tayra ('Bush Dog')	2·50	1·25
266	$2 Great Barracuda	2·50	2·00
267	$5 Puma	14·00	6·50
256/267 *Set of* 12		21·00	12·00

See also Nos. 276/278.

The 3c., 5c. and 10c. were re-issued in 1972 with watermark W **12** upright.

64 *Rhyncholaelia digbyana*

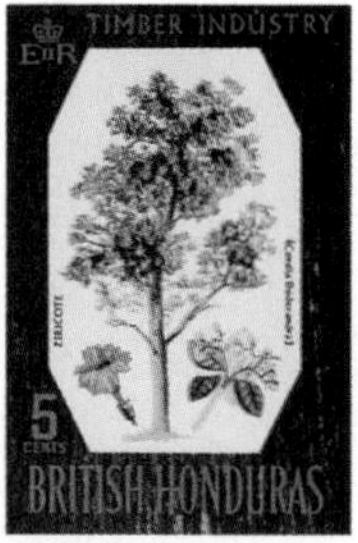

65 Ziricote Tree

(Des Sylvia Goaman. Photo Harrison)

1969 (9 Apr). Orchids of Belize (1st series). T **64** and similar vertical designs. Multicoloured. W w **12** (sideways). P 14½×14.

268	5c. Type **64**	60	20
269	10c. *Cattleya bowringiana*	65	15
270	22c. *Lycaste cochleatum*	95	15
271	25c. *Coryanthes speciosum*	1·10	1·10
268/271 *Set of 4*		3·00	1·40

See also Nos. 287/290.

(Des V. Whiteley. Litho D.L.R.)

1969 (1 Sept). Indigenous Hardwoods (1st series). T **65** and similar vertical designs. Multicoloured. W w **12**. P 14.

272	5c. Type **65**	10	50
273	10c. Rosewood	10	10
274	22c. Mayflower	20	20
275	25c. Mahogany	20	85
272/275 *Set of 4*		45	1·50

See also Nos. 291/294.

1969–72. As Nos. 257/258, 261, 267 and new value and design (½ c.), but W w **12** (sideways*).

276	½c. Mozambique Mouthbrooder ('Crana') (ultramarine background) (1.9.69)	10	30
277	½c. Mozambique Mouthbrooder ('Crana') (yellow-olive background) (1.2.71)	2·50	3·25
	a. Black (inscr and value) omitted	£500	
	bw. Wmk Crown to right of CA	4·00	
277*c*	2c. White-tipped Peccary (5.5.72)	7·00	6·00
277*d*	3c. Misty Grouper (5.5.72)	7·00	6·00
277*e*	10c. Paca (5.5.72)	7·00	6·00
278	$5 Puma (12.5.70)	2·50	10·00
276/278 *Set of 6*		23·00	28·00

* The normal sideways watermark shows Crown to left of CA, *as seen from the back of the stamp.*

66 *The Virgin and Child* (Bellini)

POPULATION CENSUS 1970

(**68**)

(Des adapted by G. Drummond. Litho Format)

1969 (1 Nov). Christmas. Paintings. T **66** and similar vertical design. Multicoloured. W w **12**. P 14×14½.

279	5c. Type **66**	10	10
280	15c. Type **66**	10	10
281	22c. *The Adoration of the Kings* (Veronese)	10	10
282	25c. As 22c.	10	20
279/282 *Set of 4*		30	30

Although released by the Crown Agents on 1 October this issue was not put on sale locally until 1 November.

1970 (2 Feb). Population Census. As Nos. 260 and 262/263 but W w **12** (sideways) and No. 277*e* optd with T **68**.

283	5c. Bonefish	10	10
284	10c. Paca	15	10
285	15c. Dolphinfish	20	10
286	25c. Kinkajou	20	15
283/286 *Set of 4*		55	30

(Des G. Drummond. Litho Format)

1970 (2 Apr). Orchids of Belize (2nd series). As T **64**. Multicoloured. W w **12**. P 14.

287	5c. Black Orchid	35	15
288	15c. White Butterfly Orchid	50	10
289	22c. Swan Orchid	70	10
290	25c. Butterfly Orchid	70	40
287/290 *Set of 4*		2·00	60

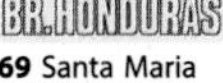

69 Santa Maria

70 *The Nativity* (A. Hughes).

(Des Jennifer Toombs, Litho Questa)

1970 (7 Sept). Indigenous Hardwoods (2nd series). T **69** and similar vertical designs. Multicoloured. W w **12** (sideways). P 14×14½.

291	5c. Type **69**	25	10
292	15c. Nargusta	40	10
293	22c. Cedar	45	10
294	25c. Sapodilla	45	35
291/294 *Set of 4*		1·40	55

(Des J. Cooter Litho J.W.)

1970 (7 Nov*). Christmas. T **70** and similar vertical design. Multicoloured. W w **12**. P 14.

295	½c. Type **70**	10	10
296	5c. *The Mystic Nativity* (Botticelli)	10	10
297	10c. Type **70**	15	10
298	15c. As 5c.	25	10
299	22c. Type **70**	30	10
300	50c. As 5c.	40	85
295/300 *Set of 6*		1·00	1·10

* These stamps were released by the Crown Agents in London on 2 November.

STAMP BOOKLETS

1920. Black on pink cover inscr 'British Honduras–100–Two Cent Stamps'. Stapled.

SB1 $2 booklet containing 100×2c. (No. 102*b*) in blocks of 10 (5×2) £4000

1920. Grey-blue cover inscr 'British Honduras–100–Three Cent Stamps'. Stapled.

SB2 $3 booklet containing 100×3c. (No. 103) in blocks of 10 (5×2)

1923. Black on pink cover inscr 'British Honduras–100–Two Cent Stamps'. Stapled.

SB3 $2 booklet containing 100×2c. brown (No. 127) in blocks of 10 (5×2) £5000

1927. Black on pink cover inscr 'British Honduras–100–Two Cent Stamps'. Stapled.

SB4 $2 booklet containing 100×2c. rose-carmine (No. 128) in blocks of 10 (5×2)

POSTAGE DUE STAMPS

D **1**

(Typo D.L.R.)

1923–64. Wmk Mult Script CA. Ordinary paper. P 14.

D1	D **1**	1c. black	2·25	13·00
		a. Chalk-surfaced paper (25.9.56)	50	27·00
		b. White uncoated paper (9.4.64)	18·00	45·00
D2		2c. black	2·25	7·50
		a. Chalk-surfaced paper (25.9.56)	50	22·00
D3		4c. black	1·25	6·00
		a. Missing top serif on 'C' (R. 6/6)	55·00	
		bw. Wmk inverted	£300	
		c. Chalk-surfaced paper (25.9.56)	1·00	22·00
		ca. Missing top serif on 'C' (R. 6/6)	45·00	
D1/D3 *Set of 3*			5·25	24·00
D1a/D3c *Set of 3*			1·75	65·00
D1s/D3s Optd 'SPECIMEN' *Set of 3*			85·00	

The early ordinary paper printings were yellowish and quite distinct from No. D1b.

1965 (3 Aug)–**72.** As Nos. D2a and D3c, but Wmk w **12** (sideways on 2c.). P 13½×13 (2c.) or 13½×14 (4c.).

D4	D **1**	2c. black (10.1.72)	3·75	9·50
D5		4c. black	2·25	9·50

The missing top serif on 'C' variety of R. 6/6 was corrected before No. D5 was printed.

Although the design size is the same, No. D4 measures 22×26 mm, while D2/D2a and D5 are 21×24½ mm.

British Indian Ocean Territory

This Crown Colony was created on 8 November 1965 when it comprised the Chagos Archipelago, previously administered by Mauritius, together with the islands of Aldabra, Farquhar and Desroches, previously administered by Seychelles.

(Currency. 100 cents = 1 rupee).

B.I.O.T.

(**1**)

1968 (17 Jan). As Nos. 196/200, 202/204 and 206/212 of Seychelles, optd with T **1**. W w **12** (sideways* on 5, 10, 15, 20, 25, 50, 75c. and 10r.).

1	5c. multicoloured	1·00	1·50
	a. No stop after 'I'	19·00	22·00
	b. No stop after 'O'	6·50	10·00
	w. Wmk Crown to right of CA	90·00	
2	10c. multicoloured	10	15
	a. No stop after 'I'	45·00	40·00
	b. No stop after 'O'	5·50	13·00
3	15c. multicoloured	25	40
	a. No stop after 'I'	16·00	20·00
	b. No stop after 'O'	5·50	10·00
4	20c. multicoloured	20	15
	a. No stop after 'I'	18·00	18·00
	b. No stop after 'O'	7·50	8·50
5	25c. multicoloured	20	15
	a. No stop after 'I'	12·00	17·00
	b. No stop after 'O'	5·50	10·00
6	40c. multicoloured	20	20
	a. No stop after 'I'	20·00	20·00
	b. No stop after 'O'	8·50	13·00
7	45c. multicoloured	20	30
	a. No stop after 'I'	25·00	20·00
	b. No stop after 'B'	50·00	30·00
	c. No stop after 'O'	90·00	60·00
8	50c. multicoloured	20	30
	a. No stop after 'I'	20·00	19·00
	b. No stop after 'O'	7·50	9·50
9	75c. multicoloured	3·00	35
10	1r. multicoloured	2·00	35
	a. No stop after 'I'	27·00	24·00
	b. No stop after 'O'	8·00	11·00
11	1r.50 multicoloured	2·00	1·50
	a. No stop after 'I'	50·00	50·00
	b. No stop after 'O'	30·00	17·00
12	2r.25 multicoloured	3·00	3·75
	a. No stop after 'I'	£110	£120
	b. No stop after 'O'	80·00	80·00
13	3r.50 multicoloured	3·00	4·50
	a. No stop after 'I'	£100	£100
	b. No stop after 'O'	45·00	42·00
14	5r. multicoloured	10·00	6·50
	a. No stop after 'I'	£150	£140
	b. No stop after 'O'	60·00	55·00
15	10r. multicoloured	20·00	15·00
	a. No stop after 'B'	£190	£180
	b. No stop after 'I'	£250	£250
	c. No stop after 'O'	£110	£110
1/15 *Set of 15*		40·00	30·00

* The normal sideways watermark shows Crown to left of CA, *as seen from the back of the stamp.*

These were issued by the Crown Agents on 15 January but owing to shipping delays they were not put on sale locally until 17 January.

The positions of the 'no stop' varieties are as follows:

After 'I': R. 2/4 on horiz stamps except 45c. where it occurs on R. 3/3, and R. 8/5 on vert stamps except 10r. where it occurs on R. 4/3.

After 'O': R. 3/2 and 5/1 on vert stamps, R. 2/1 and 4/4 on horiz stamps (only occurs on R. 2/1 for 45c.), and R. 2/7 and 5/9 on 10r. value.

After 'B': R. 10/4 (45c.) or R. 1/8 (10r.).

As sheets of all values from 5c. to 50c. are known with all stops in place the no stop varieties either developed during printing or their omission was discovered and replacements inserted.

2 Lascar

(Des G. Drummond, based on drawings by Mrs. W. Veevers-Cartor. Litho D.L.R.)

1968 (23 Oct)–**70.** Marine Life. Multicoloured designs as T **2**. White paper (Nos. 20*a*, 23*a*, 24*a*) or cream paper (others). W w **12** (sideways on horizontal, inverted on vertical designs). P 14.

16	5c. Type **2**	1·00	2·50
17	10c. Smooth Hammerhead (*vert*)	30	1·25
18	15c. Tiger Shark	30	1·75
19	20c. Spotted Eagle Ray ('Bat Ray')	30	1·00
20	25c. Yellow-finned Butterflyfish and Earspotted Angelfish (*vert*)	80	1·00
20*a*	30c. Robber Crab (7.12.70)	2·50	2·75
21	40c. Blue-finned Trevally ('Caranx')	2·00	40
22	45c. Crocodile Needlefish ('Garfish') (*vert*)	1·75	2·00
23	50c. Pickhandle Barracuda	2·00	30
23*a*	60c. Spotted Pebble Crab (7.12.70)	2·50	4·00
24	75c. Indian Ocean Steep-headed Parrotfish	2·00	1·75
24*a*	85c. Rainbow Runner ('Dorado') (7.12.70)	2·75	2·50
	b. Magenta omitted	£1100	
25	1r. Giant Hermit Crab	1·75	35
26	1r.50 Parrotfish ('Humphead')	2·00	2·75

27	2r.25 Yellow-edged Lyretail and Areolate Grouper ('Rock Cod')	6·00	9·00
28	3r.50 Black Marlin	2·75	3·50
29	5r. black, blue-green and greenish blue (Whale Shark) (*vert*)	24·00	16·00
30	10r. Lionfish	4·00	6·50
	a. Imperf (pair)	£1100	
16/30 *Set of* 18		50·00	50·00

The 5c. was re-issued in 1973 on white paper with watermark w **12** upright.

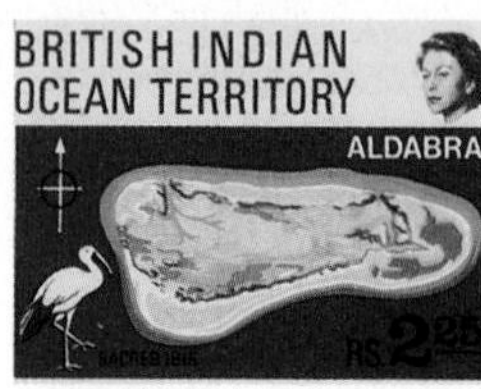

3 Sacred Ibis and Aldabra Coral Atoll

(Des and litho D.L.R.)

1969 (10 July). Coral Atolls. W w **12** (sideways). P 13½×13.

31	**3**	2r.25 multicoloured	1·50	1·00

4 Outrigger Canoe

(Des Mrs. M. Hayward adapted by V. Whiteley. Litho D.L.R.)

1969 (15 Dec). Ships of the Islands. T **4** and similar horizontal designs. Multicoloured. W w **12** (sideways). P 13½×14.

32	45c. Type **4**	45	75
33	75c. Pirogue	45	80
34	1r. MV *Nordvaer*	50	90
35	1r.50 *Isle of Farquhar*	55	1·00
32/35 *Set of* 4		1·75	3·00

British Levant

The term 'British Levant' is used by stamp collectors to describe the issues made by various British Post Offices within the former Turkish Empire.

Arrangements for the first such service were included amongst the terms of a commercial treaty between the two countries in 1832, but the system did not start operations until September 1857 when a post office for civilian use was opened in Constantinople, replacing the Army Post Office which had existed there since June 1854.

Eventually the number of British Post Offices grew to five:

Beyrout (Beirut, Lebanon). Opened March 1873, closed 30 September 1914.

Constantinople (Istanbul). Opened 1 July 1857, closed 30 September 1914, re-opened 4 February 1919, finally closed 27 September 1923.

Salonica (Thessalonika, Greece). Opened 1 May 1900, closed October 1914. The city was captured by Greek troops on 7 November 1912 and incorporated into Greece by the Treaty of London (July 1913).

Smyrna (Izmir). Opened December 1872, closed 30 September 1914, re-opened 1 March 1919, finally closed 13 September 1922. Between 15 May 1919 and 8 September 1922 the city was under Greek occupation.

Stamboul (a sub-office of Constantinople). Opened April 1885, closed 25 August 1896, re-opened 10 February 1908, finally closed 30 September 1914.

Stamps from the two British Post Offices in Egypt still technically part of the Turkish Empire, are listed under EGYPT.

A. BRITISH POST OFFICES IN TURKISH EMPIRE, 1857–1914

Z 1 Z 2 Z 3 Z 4 Z 5 Z 6 Z 7 Z 8

From 1 August 1885 letter and registered charges were prepaid with surcharged stamps (No. 1 onwards). Until 14 August 1905 postcards and parcels continued to be franked with unoverprinted Great Britain stamps. Only a limited range of values were stocked for this purpose and these are listed. Other values exist with Levant postmarks, but these stamps did not originate from the local post offices.

After 15 August 1905 the post offices were supplied with Great Britain stamps overprinted 'LEVANT'. Subsequent examples of unoverprinted stamps with Levant postmarks are omitted from the listing. Such stamps used during 1919–1922 at Constantinople and Smyrna are listed as Z176/Z201 and Z282/Z295.

BEYROUT (BEIRUT)

Between 1873 and 1876 much of the mail from the British Post Office in Beyrout sent to European addresses was forwarded through the French or Italian Post Offices at Alexandria. Such covers show Great Britain stamps used in combination with those of French or Italian PO's in the Turkish Empire.

Stamps of GREAT BRITAIN cancelled 'G06' T Z **4** or with circular postmark inscr 'BEYROUT' as Types Z **6** or Z **8**.

1873–81.

Z1	½d. rose-red (1870–1879) *From* Plate Nos. 12, 13, 14, 19, 20.	65·00
Z2	1d. rose-red (1864–1879) *From* Plate Nos. 107, 118, 130, 140, 145, 148, 155, 157, 162, 167, 177, 179, 180, 184, 185, 186, 187, 195, 198, 200, 203, 204, 211, 213, 215, 218, 220, 222.	27·00
Z3	1½d. lake-red (1870–1874) (Plate 3)	£400
Z4	2d. blue (1858–1869) *From* Plate Nos. 13, 14, 15.	32·00
Z5	2½d. rosy mauve (1875) (*blued paper*) Plate No. 1.	80·00
Z6	2½d. rosy mauve (1875–1876) *From* Plate Nos. 1, 2, 3.	35·00
Z7	2½d. rosy mauve (1876–1879) *From* Plate Nos. 3, 4, 5, 6, 7, 8, 9, 10, 11, 12, 13, 14, 15, 16, 17.	26·00
Z8	2½d. blue (1880) *From* Plate Nos. 17, 18, 19, 20.	16·00
Z9	2½d. blue (1881) *From* Plate Nos. 21, 22, 23.	12·00
Z10	3d. rose (1867–1873) (Plate No. 10)	
Z11	3d. rose (1873–1876) Plate Nos. 12, 15, 16, 18, 19, 20.	65·00
Z12	3d. rose (1881) (Plate Nos. 20, 21)	
Z13	4d. vermilion (1865–1873) *From* Plate Nos. 11, 12, 13, 14.	48·00
Z14	4d. vermilion (1876) (Plate No. 15)	£190
Z15	4d. sage-green (1877) Plate Nos. 15, 16.	£130
Z16	4d. grey-brown (1880) wmk Large Garter (Plate No. 17)	
Z17	4d. grey-brown (1880) wmk Crown Plate Nos. 17, 18.	75·00
Z18	6d. mauve (1870) (Plate Nos. 8, 9)	
Z19	6d. buff (1872–1873) *From* Plate Nos. 11, 12.	95·00
Z20	6d. chestnut (1872) (Plate No. 11)	50·00
Z21	6d. grey (1873) (Plate No. 12)	£160
Z22	6d. grey (1874–1880) *From* Plate Nos. 13, 14, 15, 16, 17.	42·00
Z23	8d. orange (1876)	£550
Z24	10d. red-brown (1867)	£170
Z25	1s. green (1867–1873) Plate Nos. 6, 7.	50·00
Z26	1s. green (1873–1877) *From* Plate Nos. 8, 9, 10, 12, 13.	65·00
Z27	1s. orange-brown (1880) (Plate No. 13)	£275
Z28	1s. orange-brown (1881) Plate Nos. 13, 14.	90·00
Z29	2s. blue (1867)	£180
Z30	5s. rose (1867) (Plate Nos. 1, 2) *From*	£800

1880.

Z31	½d. deep green	16·00
Z32	½d. pale green	17·00
Z33	1d. Venetian red	26·00
Z34	1½d. Venetian red	£250
Z35	2d. pale rose	80·00
Z36	2d. deep rose	80·00
Z37	5d. indigo	£140

1881.

Z38	1d. lilac (14 dots)	
Z39	1d. lilac (16 dots)	7·50

1884.

Z40	½d. slate-blue	23·00
Z41	1½d. lilac	£140
Z42	2d. lilac	£100
Z43	2½d. lilac	12·00
Z44	4d. dull green	£275
Z45	5d. dull green	£120
Z46	1s. dull green	£450

1887–92.

Z47	½d. vermilion	11·00
Z48	1½d. dull purple and green	
Z51	3d. purple/*yellow*	
Z54	6d. purple/*rose-red*	30·00
Z55	1s. dull green	£225

1900.

Z56	½d. blue-green	13·00
Z57	1s. green and carmine	£225

1902–04. De La Rue ptgs.

Z58	½d. blue-green	6·00
Z59	½d. yellowish green	6·50
Z60	1d. scarlet	5·50
Z61	1½d. dull purple and green	
Z62	3d. dull purple/*yellow*	
Z63	6d. pale dull purple	
Z64	1s. dull green and carmine	48·00

CONSTANTINOPLE

Stamps of GREAT BRITAIN cancelled 'C' or circular postmark, T Z **1/2**, as T Z **3** or Z **7**.

1857–83.

Z68	½d. rose-red (1870–1879) *From* Plate Nos. 4, 5, 6, 10, 11, 12, 13, 14, 15, 20.	28·00
Z69	1d. red-brown (1854), Die I, wmk Small Crown, perf 16	
Z70	1d. red-brown (1855), Die II, wmk Small Crown, perf 14	
Z71	1d. red-brown, (1855), Die II, wmk Large Crown, perf 14	22·00
Z72	1d. rose-red (1857)	8·50
Z73	1d. rose-red (1861) Alphabet IV	
Z74	1d. rose-red (1864–1879) *From* Plate Nos. 71, 72, 73, 74, 76, 78, 79, 80, 81, 83, 85, 87, 89, 90, 92, 93, 94, 95, 96, 97, 99, 101, 102, 105, 106, 108, 109, 110, 111, 113, 116, 118, 119, 120, 121, 122, 123, 124, 125, 127, 129, 130, 131, 134, 135, 136, 137, 138, 140, 141, 143, 144, 145, 146, 147, 148, 149, 150, 151, 152, 155, 156, 157, 158, 159, 160, 161, 162, 163, 164, 165, 166, 167, 170, 171, 172, 173, 174, 175, 176, 177, 178, 179, 180, 181, 183, 184, 186, 187, 188, 189, 190, 191, 192, 193, 194, 195, 196, 197, 198, 199, 200, 201, 203, 204, 205, 206, 207, 208, 210, 211, 212, 214, 215, 216, 220, 222, 224.	12·00
Z75	1½d. rose-red (1870) (Plate 1)	£250
Z76	2d. blue (1855), wmk Large Crown, perf 14. (Plate Nos. 5, 6)	

Z77 2d. blue (1858–1869) From 15·00
Plate Nos. 7, 8, 9, 12, 13, 14, 15.
Z78 2½d. rosy mauve (1875–1876) (*blued paper*) (Plate Nos. 1, 2) From 60·00
Z79 2½d. rosy mauve (1875–1876) From 32·00
Plate Nos. 1, 2, 3.
Z80 2½d. rosy mauve (*Error of Lettering*)
Z81 2½d. rosy mauve (1876–1879) From 24·00
Plate Nos. 3 to 17.
Z82 2½d. blue (1880–1881) From 12·00
Plate Nos. 17, 18, 19, 20.
Z83 2½d. blue (1881) (Plate Nos. 21, 22, 23) 8·00
Z84 3d. carmine-rose (1862) (Plate No. 2) £150
Z85 3d. rose (1865) (Plate No. 4) 90·00
Z86 3d. rose (1867–1873) (Plate Nos. 4 to 10) 85·00
Z87 3d. rose (1873–1876) 32·00
Plate Nos. 11, 12, 15, 16, 17, 18, 19.
Z88 3d. rose (1881) (Plate No. 21)
Z89 3d. on 3d. lilac (1883) (Plate No. 21)
Z90 4d. rose (1857) 48·00
a. Rose-carmine
Z91 4d. red (1862) (Plate Nos. 3, 4) From 40·00
Z92 4d. vermilion (1865–1873) From 27·00
Plate Nos. 7 to 14.
Z93 4d. vermilion (1876) (Plate No. 15) £160
Z94 4d. sage-green (1877) £110
Plate Nos. 15, 16.
Z95 4d. grey-brown (1880) wmk Large Garter (Plate No. 17)
Z96 4d. grey-brown (1880) wmk Crown (Plate Nos. 17, 18) From 60·00
Z97 6d. lilac (1856) 65·00
Z98 6d. lilac (1862) (Plate Nos. 3, 4) From 40·00
Z99 6d. lilac (1865–1867) 38·00
Plate Nos. 5, 6.
Z100 6d. lilac (1867) (Plate No. 6) 42·00
Z101 6d. violet (1867–1870) From 35·00
Plate Nos. 6, 8, 9.
Z102 6d. buff (1872–1873) 60·00
Plate Nos. 11, 12.
Z103 6d. chestnut (1872) (Plate No. 11) 32·00
Z104 6d. grey (1873) (Plate No. 12) 80·00
Z105 6d. grey (1874–1876) From 35·00
Plate Nos. 13, 14, 15, 16, 17.
Z106 6d. grey (1881–1882) (Plate Nos. 17, 18) 42·00
Z107 6d. on 6d. lilac (1883) £100
a. Dots slanting (Letters MI or SJ) £225
Z108 8d. orange (1876) £500
Z109 10d. red-brown (1867), wmk Emblems £35000
Z110 10d. red-brown (1867) £170
Z111 1s. green (1856) £120
Z112 1s. green (1862) 65·00
Z113 1s. green (1862) ('K' variety)
Z114 1s. green (1862) (*thick paper*)
Z115 1s. green (1865) (Plate No. 4) 70·00
Z116 1s. green (1867–1873) From 24·00
Plate Nos. 4, 5, 6, 7.
Z117 1s. green (1873–1877) From 32·00
Plate Nos. 8, 9, 10, 11, 12, 13.
Z118 1s. orange-brown (1880) (Plate No. 13) £200
Z119 1s. orange-brown (1881) From 55·00
Plate Nos. 13, 14.
Z120 2s. blue (1867) £100
Z121 5s. rose (1867–1874) From £275
Plate Nos. 1, 2.
Z122 5s. rose (1882) (*white paper*) £900
Z123 5s. rose (1882) (*blued paper*) £1600

1880.
Z124 ½d. deep green 10·00
Z125 ½d. pale green 12·00
Z126 1d. Venetian red 17·00
Z127 2d. pale rose 48·00
Z128 2d. deep rose 48·00
Z129 5d. indigo

1881.
Z130 1d. lilac (14 *dots*) 75·00
Z131 1d. lilac (16 *dots*) 3·00

1883–84.
Z132 ½d. slate-blue 10·00
Z133 1½d. lilac £150
Z134 2d. lilac 80·00
Z135 2½d. lilac 7·50
Z136 3d. lilac £200
Z137 4d. dull green £300
Z138 5d. dull green 95·00
Z139 6d. dull green £250
Z140 9d. dull green £550
Z141 1s. dull green £350
Z142 2s.6d. lilac (*blued paper*) £750
Z143 2s.6d. lilac (*white paper*) 95·00
Z144 5s. rose (*blued paper*)
Z145 5s. rose (*white paper*)

1887–92.
Z146 ½d. vermilion 3·75
Z147 1½d. dull purple and green
Z148 2d. grey-green and carmine
Z150 3d. purple/*yellow*
Z154 6d. purple/*rose-red* 15·00
Z157 1s. dull green £120

1900.
Z158 ½d. blue-green 7·00
Z159 1s. green and carmine £180

1902–04. De La Rue ptgs.
Z160 ½d. blue-green 3·50
Z161 ½d. yellowish green 4·00
Z162 1d. scarlet 3·00
Z163 1½d. dull purple and green
Z166 3d. purple/*yellow*
Z169 6d. purple 15·00
Z172 1s. green and carmine 25·00
Z173 2s.6d. lilac
Z174 5s. carmine

POSTAL FISCALS

Z175 1d. purple (wmk Anchor) (1868)
Z175*a* 1d. purple (wmk Orb) (1881) £600

SALONICA

Stamps of GREAT BRITAIN cancelled with circular postmark as in T Z **6** or double-circle datestamp.

1881.
Z202 ½d. vermilion (1887) 26·00
Z203 ½d. blue-green (1900) 28·00
Z204 1d. lilac (1881) 26·00
Z205 6d. purple/*red* (1887) 42·00
Z206 1s. green and carmine (1900) £300
Z207 5s. rose (white paper) (1883) £1300

1902.
Z208 ½d. blue-green 30·00
Z209 ½d. yellow-green 24·00
Z209*a* 1d. scarlet 24·00
Z209*c* 1s. green and carmine 75·00

SMYRNA (IZMIR)

Stamps of GREAT BRITAIN cancelled 'F87' or circular postmark as T Z **4**, Z **5** or Z **6**.

1858–83.
Z210 ½d. rose-red (1870–1879) From 40·00
Plates 11, 12, 13, 14, 15.
Z211 1d. rose-red (1864–1879) From 17·00
Plate Nos. 120, 124, 134, 137, 138, 139, 140, 142, 143, 145, 146, 148, 149, 150, 151, 152, 153, 155, 156, 157, 158, 159, 160, 161, 162, 163, 164, 166, 167, 168, 169, 170, 171, 172, 173, 174, 175, 176, 177, 178, 183, 184, 185, 186, 187, 188, 191, 193, 194, 195, 196, 198, 200, 201, 204, 210, 212, 215, 217, 218.
Z212 1½d. lake-red (1870–1874) (Plate Nos. 1, 3) From £275
Z214 2d. blue (1858–1869) From 22·00
Plate Nos. 13, 14, 15.
Z215 2½d. rosy mauve (1875) (*blued paper*) 65·00
Plate No. 1.
Z216 2½d. rosy mauve (1875–1876) From 29·00
Plate Nos. 1, 2, 3.
Z217 2½d. rosy mauve (*Error of lettering*)
Z218 2½d. rosy mauve (1876–1879) From 23·00
Plate Nos. 3, 4, 5, 6, 7, 8, 9, 10, 11, 12, 13, 14, 15, 16, 17.
Z219 2½d. blue (1880) From 12·00
Plate Nos. 17, 18, 19, 20.
Z220 2½d. blue (1881) 10·00
Plate Nos. 21, 22, 23.
Z221 3d. rose (1867–1873) 55·00
Plate Nos. 5, 7, 9, 10.
Z222 3d. rose (1873–1876) (Plate No. 14)
Z223 4d. vermilion (1865–1873) 28·00
Plate Nos. 12, 13, 14.
Z224 4d. vermilion (1876) (Plate No. 15) £160
Z225 4d. sage-green (1877) £100
Plate Nos. 15, 16.
Z226 4d. grey-brown (1880) wmk Large Garter (Plate No. 17)
Z227 4d. grey-brown (1880) wmk Crown (Plate Nos. 17, 18) From 50·00
Z228 6d. buff (1872–1873) From 75·00
Plate Nos. 11, 12.
Z229 6d. chestnut (1872) (Plate No. 11)
Z230 6d. grey (1873) (Plate No. 12) 80·00
Z231 6d. grey (1874–1880) From 28·00
Plate Nos. 13, 14, 15, 16, 17.
Z232 6d. grey (1881–1882) (Plate Nos. 17, 18) 65·00
Z233 6d. on 6d. lilac (1883) £130
Z234 8d. orange (1876)
Z235 9d. straw (1867) £450
Z236 10d. red-brown (1867) £160
Z237 1s. green (1867–1873) (Plate Nos. 6, 7)
Z238 1s. green (1873–1877) From 42·00
Plate Nos. 8, 9, 10, 11, 12, 13.
Z239 1s. orange-brown (1880) (Plate No. 13) £200
Z240 1s. orange-brown (1881) (Plate Nos. 13, 14) 60·00
Z241 5s. rose (1867–1874) (Plate No. 2)

1880.
Z242 ½d. deep green 12·00
Z243 ½d. pale green 12·00
Z244 1d. Venetian red 20·00
Z245 1½d. Venetian red £150
Z246 2d. pale rose 50·00
Z247 2d. deep rose 50·00
Z248 5d. indigo 90·00

1881.
Z249 1d. lilac (16 dots) 5·00

1884.
Z250 ½d. slate-blue 20·00
Z251 2d. lilac 95·00
Z252 2½d. lilac 11·00
Z253 4d. dull green £300
Z254 5d. dull green £110
Z255 1s. dull green £450

1887.
Z256 ½d. vermilion 7·00
Z257 1½d. dull purple and green
Z260 3d. purple/*yellow*
Z263 6d. purple/*rose-red* 21·00
Z263*a* 9d. purple and blue
Z264 1s. dull green £160

1900.
Z265 ½d. blue-green 9·00
Z266 1s. green and carmine

1902–04. De La Rue ptgs.
Z267 ½d. blue-green 5·00
Z268 ½d. yellowish green 6·00
Z269 1d. scarlet 4·50
Z270 1½d. dull purple and green
Z273 3d. purple/*yellow*
Z276 6d. purple 18·00
Z279 1s. green and carmine 35·00
Z280 2s.6d. purple
Z281 5s. carmine

STAMBOUL (CONSTANTINOPLE)

Stamps of GREAT BRITAIN cancelled 'S' as T Z **3**, or circular postmarks inscribed either 'BRITISH POST OFFICE CONSTANTINOPLE S' or 'BRITISH POST OFFICE STAMBOUL' as T Z **6**.

1884.
Z296 ½d. slate-blue 30·00
Z297 1d. lilac 13·00
Z298 2d. lilac
Z299 2½d. lilac 16·00
Z300 5d. dull green £160

1887–92.
Z306 ½d. vermilion 16·00
Z314 6d. purple/*rose-red* 38·00
Z317 1s. dull green

The 'S' cancellation was in use from 1885 to 1891 and the 'Stamboul' mark from 1892 to 1896, when the office was closed, and from its reopening in 1908 to 1914. The 'CONSTANTINOPLE S' handstamp was normally used as a back stamp, but can be found cancelling stamps in the period 1885 to 1892.

PRICES FOR STAMPS ON COVER TO 1945	
Nos. 1/3a	*from* × 8
Nos. 4/6*a*	*from* × 5
Nos. 7/40	*from* × 3
Nos. L1/L10	*from* × 6
Nos. L11/L17	*from* × 3

I. TURKISH CURRENCY
(40 paras = 1 piastre)

Following the depreciation of the Turkish piastre against sterling in 1884 it was decided to issue stamps surcharged in Turkish currency to avoid speculation. During the early period unsurcharged stamps of Great Britain remained on sale from the British Post Offices at the current rate of exchange until replaced by 'LEVANT' overprints.

80 PARAS (1) **4 PIASTRES** (2) **12 PIASTRES** (3)

PRINTERS. Nos. 1/24 were surcharged or overprinted by De La Rue, *unless otherwise stated.*

Stamps of Great Britain (Queen Victoria) surch as T 1 to 3

1885 (1 Aug)–**88**.
1 **64** 40pa. on 2½d. lilac £160 1·25
2 **62** 80pa. on 5d. green £225 9·50
3 **58** 12pi. on 2s.6d. lilac/*bluish* £550 £300
a. On white paper (4.88) 65·00 26·00

Nos. 3, 11 and 33 were surcharged from a horizontal setting of eight clichés of which three showed a small final 'S'.

4 PIASTRES
Large wide '4' (R. 1/2, R. 1/4)

1887 (June)–**96**.
4 **74** 40pa. on 2½d. purple/*blue* 21·00 10
a. Surch double £1900 £2500
5 **78** 80pa. on 5d. purple and blue (7.90) 18·00 30
a. Small '0' in '80' £375 95·00
w. Wmk inverted — £650
6 **81** 4pi. on 10d. dull purple and carmine (10.10.96) 45·00 8·50
a. Dull purple and deep bright carmine 45·00 11·00
b. Large, wide '4' (R. 1/2, 1/4) £225 70·00

No. 5a first appeared on the June 1895 printing when the size of the surcharge plate was increased from 60 to 120. On the Victorian stamp the variety comes on R. 4/1 and 4/7. The same setting was used for the first printing of the Edward VII surcharge, but here the sheet size was further increased to 240 so that No. 9a occurs on R. 4/1, 4/7, 14/1 and 14/7.

1893 (25 Feb). Roughly handstamped at Constantinople, as T **1**.
7 **71** 40pa. on ½d. vermilion £425 £100

This provisional was in use for five days only at the Constantinople and Stamboul offices. As fraudulent copies were made with the original handstamp, and can be found 'used' on piece cancelled by fraudulent use of the usual canceller, this stamp should only be purchased from undoubted sources.

The handstamp became damaged during use so that by 1 March the top of the 'S' was broken. Used examples dated 25 or 26 February showing the broken 'S' *must* be fraudulent. It is also known with genuine handstamp inverted (*Price* £850 *unused*, £325 *used*).

1902–05. Stamps of King Edward VII surch as T **1** to **3**.
8 **86** 40pa. on 2½d. ultramarine (3.02) 24·00 10
a. Pale ultramarine 26·00 10
ab. Surch double † £2500
9 **89** 80pa. on 5d. dull purple and ultramarine (5.6.02) 19·00 2·00
a. Small '0' in '80' £325 £200
10 **92** 4pi. on 10d. dull purple and carmine (6.9.02) 27·00 4·50
a. No cross on crown £180 90·00
b. Chalk-surfaced paper 6·00 10·00
ba. Chalk-surfaced paper. No cross on crown £100 £120

11 **94** 12pi. on 2s.6d. lilac (29.8.03) 42·00 38·00
a. Chalk-surfaced paper. *Pale dull purple* 75·00 80·00
b. Chalk-surfaced paper. *Dull purple* 42·00 38·00
12 **95** 24pi. on 5s. bright carmine (15.8.05) 32·00 42·00
8/12 *Set of* 5 £110 75·00
9s/11s Optd 'SPECIMEN' *Set of* 3 £160

No. 9a only occurs on the first printing of 80pa. on 5d.

1 PIASTRE
(4)

1905–08. Surch in 'PIASTRES' instead of 'PARAS' as T **4** and **2**.

13 **86** 1pi. on 2½d. ultramarine (17.4.06) 32·00 10
a. Surch double † £2000
w. Wmk inverted £750 £750
14 **89** 2pi. on 5d. dull purple and ultramarine (11.11.05) 50·00 2·50
a. Chalk-surfaced paper (1.08) 30·00 5·00
ab. Slate-purple and ultramarine 50·00 9·50

1 Piastre (5) 1 PIASTRE 10 PARAS (6)

1906 (2 July). Issued at Beyrout. No. L4 surch with T **5** by American Press, Beyrout.

15 **85** 1pi. on 2d. grey-green and carmine £1500 £700

1909 (16 Nov–Dec). Stamps of King Edward VII surch as T **1** (30pa.) **6**, and **2** (5pi). Ordinary paper (No. 19) or chalk-surfaced paper (others).

16 **84** 30pa. on 1½d. pale dull purple and green 20·00 1·25
a. Surch double, one albino
17 **87** 1pi.10pa. on 3d. dull purple/*orange-yellow* 12·00 50·00
18 **88** 1pi.30pa. on 4d. green and chocolate-brown 5·00 21·00
19 1pi.30pa. on 4d. brown-orange (16.12.09) 22·00 70·00
20 **83** 2pi.20pa. on 6d. dull purple 26·00 70·00
21 **93** 5pi. on 1s. dull green and carmine 4·25 17·00
s. Optd 'SPECIMEN' 80·00
16/21 *Set of* 6 75·00 £200

Examples of Nos. 17/21 are known showing forged Constantinople postmarks dated 'MR 1 10', 'AP 1 10' and 'AP 18 10', or a forged Smyrna registered oval dated '24 OC 10'.

1¾ PIASTRE (7) — **4** Normal '4' — **4** Pointed '4'

1910 (24 Jan). Stamps of King Edward VII surch as T **7**. Chalk-surfaced paper (Nos. 22 and 24).

22 **87** 1¼pi. on 3d. dull purple/*orange-yellow* 1·00 1·00
23 **88** 1¾pi. on 4d. pale orange 50 60
a. Orange-red 7·00 7·50
b. Thin, pointed '4' in fraction 5·50 26·00
24 **83** 2½pi. on 6d. dull purple 4·00 65
22/24 *Set of* 3 5·00 2·00

No. 23b occurs in the first and seventh vertical rows of the sheet. The variety also occurs on No. 38, but not on No. 38*b*.

1 PIASTRE (8) **1 PIASTRE** (9)

TYPE DIFFERENCES. In T **4** the letters are tall and narrow and the space enclosed by the upper part of the 'A' is small.

In T **8** the opening of the 'A' is similar but the letters are shorter and broader, the 'P' and the 'E' being particularly noticeable.

In T **9** the letters are short and broad, but the 'A' is thin and open.

1911–13. Stamps of King Edward VII, Harrison or Somerset House ptgs, surch at Somerset House.

(a) Surch with T **4** *(20 July)*

25 **86** 1pi. on 2½d. bright blue (perf 14) 27·00 11·00
a. Surch double, one albino £225
26 1pi. on 2½d. bright blue (perf 15×14) (14.10.11) 40·00 4·75
a. Dull blue 32·00 4·25
b. Surch double, one albino

(b) Surch with T **8**

27 **86** 1pi. on 2½d. bright blue (perf 15×14) (3.12) 28·00 7·00
a. Dull blue 32·00 7·50

(c) Surch with T **9** *(7.12)*

28 **86** 1pi. on 2½d. bright blue (perf 15×14) 90·00 75
a. Dull blue 90·00 75

(d) Surch with T **1** *to* **3** *(1911–1913)*

29 **84** 30pa. on 1½d. reddish purple and bright green (22.8.11) 6·50 1·00
a. Slate-purple and green 12·00 2·50
b. Surch double, one albino 55·00
30 **89** 2pi. on 5d. dull reddish purple and bright blue (13.5.12) 28·00 3·25
a. Deep dull reddish purple and bright blue 32·00 3·25
31 **92** 4pi. on 10d. dull purple and scarlet (26.6.12) 60·00 27·00
a. Dull reddish purple and aniline pink £325 £140
b. Dull reddish purple and carmine 20·00 11·00
c. No cross on crown
32 **93** 5pi. on 1s. green and carmine (2.13) 23·00 13·00
a. Surch double, one albino £250
33 **94** 12pi. on 2s.6d. dull reddish purple (3.2.12) 65·00 40·00
a. Dull greyish purple 65·00 40·00
34 **95** 24pi. on 5s. carmine (1912) 80·00 £100
a. Surch double, one albino £325
29/34 *Set of* 6 £200 £140

1913 (Apr)–**14**. Stamps of King George V, wmk Royal Cypher, surch as T **1** (30pa.), **9** (1pi.) **7** or **2** (4 and 5pi.).

35 **105** 30pa. on 1½d. red-brown (4.13) 3·50 14·00
a. Surch double, one albino £120
36 **104** 1pi. on 2½d. cobalt-blue (6.13) 16·00 10
a. Bright blue 14·00 15
37 **106** 1¼pi. on 3d. dull reddish violet (9.13) 9·00 4·25
a. Violet 14·00 7·50
b. Surch double, one albino £300
38 1¾pi. on 4d. deep grey-green (7.13) 4·50 9·00
a. Thin, pointed '4' in fraction 45·00 90·00
b. Grey-green 15·00 7·00
39 **108** 4pi. on 10d. turquoise-blue (12.13) 14·00 29·00
40 5pi. on 1s. bistre-brown (1.14) 48·00 80·00
35/40 *Set of* 6 80·00 £120

II. BRITISH CURRENCY

Stamps overprinted 'LEVANT' were for use on parcels, with the ½d. and 1d. principally used for printed paper and postcards. They replaced unoverprinted Great Britain stamps, Nos. Z58/Z64, Z160/Z174, Z208/Z209c and Z267/Z281, which had previously been used for these purposes.

From October 1907 the three lowest values were also used for certain other amended postal rates until Nos. 16/21 were introduced.

LEVANT
(L 1)

1905 (15 Aug)–**12**. Stamps of King Edward VII optd with T L **1**.

(a) De La Rue ptgs

L1 **83** ½d. pale yellowish green 8·50 15
a. Yellowish green 8·50 15
L2 1d. scarlet 14·00 15
a. Bright scarlet 14·00 90
L3 **84** 1½d. dull purple and green 6·50 2·50
a. Chalk-surfaced paper. *Pale dull purple and green* 25·00 3·50
L4 **85** 2d. grey-green and carmine-red 19·00 50·00
a. Chalk-surfaced paper. *Pale grey-green and carmine-red* 4·25 8·50
ab. Dull blue-green and carmine 4·25 8·50
L5 **86** 2½d. ultramarine 8·50 20·00
L6 **87** 3d. dull purple/*orange-yellow* 7·00 12·00
L7 **88** 4d. green and grey-brown 10·00 70·00
a. Green and chocolate-brown 26·00 75·00
L8 **89** 5d. dull purple and ultramarine 16·00 38·00
L9 **83** 6d. slate-purple 12·00 25·00
L10 **93** 1s. dull green and carmine 42·00 55·00
a. Chalk-surfaced paper 42·00 55·00
L1/L10 *Set of* 10 £110 £200

(b) Harrison ptgs optd at Somerset House

L11 **83** ½d. dull yellow-green (P 14) (1.12) 50·00 50·00
a. Dull green 50·00 50·00
b. Deep dull green 65·00 55·00

On 28 December 1909 all values, except for the ½d., 1d. and 2d. were withdrawn from sale. Subsequently dated cancellations on the withdrawn values are philatelic, being worth much less than the used prices quoted.

ANT
Distorted 'N' (R. 2/12, 12/12)

1911–13. Stamps of King George V optd with T L **1** at Somerset House.

(a) Die A. Wmk Crown

L12 **98** ½d. green (No. 322) (12.9.11) 3·50 4·75
a. Distorted 'N' 50·00
L13 **99** 1d. carmine-red (No. 327) (1.1.12) 75 8·50
a. No cross on crown £150
b. Opt double, one albino £100
c. Distorted 'N' 21·00

(b) Redrawn types. Wmk Crown

L14 **101** ½d. green (No. 339) (19.3.12) 4·00 20
a. Yellow-green 5·00 1·25
b. Distorted 'N' 45·00
L15 **102** 1d. bright scarlet (No. 341) (24.2.12) 3·25 1·60
a. Scarlet (No. 342) 3·25 1·60
b. Opt triple, two albino 45·00
c. Distorted 'N' 40·00

(c) New types. Wmk Royal Cypher (7.13)

L16 **105** ½d. green (No. 351) 2·25 3·50
a. Yellow-green 4·50 4·75
b. Distorted 'N' 30·00
L17 **104** 1d. scarlet (No. 357) 40 7·50
a. Vermilion 22·00 21·00
b. Distorted 'N' 18·00

Similar overprints were issued when the British Post Offices reopened in 1919, and are listed below.

B. BRITISH POST OFFICES IN CONSTANTINOPLE AND SMYRNA, 1919–1923

CONSTANTINOPLE

Following the occupation of Constantinople by Allied forces a British Military Post Office was opened for civilian use on 4 February 1919. During the period of its existence stamps of Great Britain with face values to 10s. were available and such use can be identified by the following cancellations:

'FIELD POST OFFICE H12' (4 February 1919 to 18 March 1919)
'ARMY POST OFFICE Y' (20 March 1919 to June 1920)
'ARMY POST OFFICE S.X.3' (March 1919 to April 1920)
'British A.P.O. CONSTANTINOPLE' (July 1919 to July 1920).

Of these four marks the first two types were also used for military mail.

The office reverted to civilian control on 29 July 1920, Nos. 41/50 and L18/L24 being intended for its use.

Z 9 Z 10 Z 11 Z 12

1919–20. Used at the Army Post Office. Stamps of GREAT BRITAIN cancelled with T Z **9**, Z **10**, Z **11**, Z **12**.

Z176 ½d. green 2·50
Z177 1d. scarlet 2·50
Z178 1½d. brown 3·75
Z179 2d. orange (Die I) 3·00
Z180 2½d. blue 4·50
Z181 4d. grey-green 12·00
Z181*a* 5d. yellow-brown
Z182 6d. purple 6·50
Z183 9d. agate 30·00
Z184 1s. bistre 7·00
Z185 2s.6d. brown 70·00
Z186 5s. rose-carmine £110
Z187 10s. dull grey-blue £190

1920–21. Used at the Civilian Post Office. Stamps of GREAT BRITAIN cancelled as T Z **7** or double-circle datestamp.

Z188 ½d. green 2·50
Z189 1d. scarlet 2·50
Z190 1½d. brown 3·75
Z191 2d. orange (Die I) 3·00
Z192 2½d. blue 4·50
Z193 3d. violet 8·50
Z194 4d. grey-green 12·00
Z195 5d. brown 18·00
Z196 6d. purple 6·50
Z197 10d. turquoise-blue 30·00
Z198 1s. bistre 7·00
Z199 2s.6d. brown 70·00
Z200 5s. rose-carmine £110
Z201 10s. dull grey-blue £190

PRICES FOR STAMPS ON COVER TO 1945	
Nos. 41/50	*from* × 2
Nos. L18/L24	*from* × 5

Stamps of Great Britain surch at Somerset House

I. TURKISH CURRENCY

1½ PIASTRES (10) **15 PIASTRES** (11)

18¾
Short fraction bar (R. 4/12, 14/12)

1921 (Aug). Stamps of King George V, wmk Royal Cypher, surch as T **1** (30pa.), **10** and **11** (15 and 18¾pi.).

41 **105** 30pa. on ½d. green 75 17·00
a. Yellow-green 4·75 19·00
42 **104** 1½pi. on 1d. bright scarlet 1·75 2·00
a. Vermilion 26·00 9·00
b. Scarlet-vermilion 23·00 10·00
43 3¾pi. on 2½d. blue 1·25 25
a. Dull Prussian blue 60·00 4·00
44 **106** 4½pi. on 3d. violet 2·00 3·75
a. Bluish violet 8·00 3·75
45 **107** 7½pi. on 5d. brown 50 10
a. Yellow-brown 3·50 50
46 **108** 15pi. on 10d. turquoise-blue 70 15
47 18¾pi. on 1s. bistre-brown 4·25 5·50
a. Short fraction bar 65·00
b. Olive-bistre 10·00 7·50
ba. Short fraction bar £110

No. 41 is known with inverted surcharge, but the status of this variety is uncertain.

45 PIASTRES (12) **45** Joined figures (second stamp in each horiz row)

1921. Stamps of King George V (Bradbury Wilkinson printing) surch as *T* **12**.

48 **109** 45pi. on 2s.6d. chocolate-brown 22·00 45·00
a. Joined figures 35·00 70·00
b. Olive-brown 55·00 65·00

		ba. Joined figures	75·00	95·00
		c. Pale brown	£250	£250
49		90pi. on 5s. rose-carmine	25·00	30·00
		a. Surch double, one albino	£250	
50		180pi. on 10s. dull grey-blue	45·00	40·00
		a. Surch double, one albino	£250	
41/50 *Set of* 10			90·00	£130
47s/50s Optd 'SPECIMEN' *Set of* 4			£275	

II. BRITISH CURRENCY

1921. Stamps of King George V optd as *T* L **1**.

L18	**106**	2d. reddish orange (Die I)	2·75	45·00
		a. Bright orange	2·25	45·00
L19		3d. bluish violet	7·50	10·00
L20		4d. grey-green	5·00	28·00
L21	**107**	5d. yellow-brown	12·00	28·00
L22		6d. dull purple (*chalk-surfaced paper*)	24·00	42·00
		a. Reddish purple	45·00	8·50
L23	**108**	1s. bistre-brown	21·00	8·50
		a. Olive-bistre	21·00	8·50
		s. Optd 'SPECIMEN'	80·00	
L24	**109**	2s.6d. chocolate-brown	38·00	£100
		a. Olive-brown	65·00	£130
		b. Pale brown	£250	£150
		s. Optd 'SPECIMEN'	£140	
L18/L24 *Set of* 7			£100	£200

On No. L24 the letters of the overprint are shorter, being only 3 mm high.

Nos. 41/50 and L18/L24 were used at the Constantinople office only.

SMYRNA

When the office re-opened on 1 March 1919 existing stocks of surcharged or overprinted issues were utilised until they were exhausted in mid-1920. During this period examples of Nos. 24, 29*a*, 30*a*, 33*a*/37, 39/40, L4*ab*, L14/L17 are known with commercial postmarks. These stamps were supplemented and finally replaced in mid-1920 by ordinary stamps of Great Britain.

1919–22. Stamps of GREAT BRITAIN cancelled with circular postmark as *T* Z **7** or with 'REGISTERED' oval.

Z282	½d. green	3·00
Z283	1d. scarlet	3·00
Z284	1½d. brown	4·00
Z285	2d. orange (Die I)	3·50
Z286	2d. orange (Die II)	35·00
Z287	2½d. blue (*shades*)	5·50
Z288	2½d. dull Prussian blue	£500
Z289	4d. grey-green	13·00
Z290	6d. purple	9·00
Z290*a*	8d. black/*yellow-buff*	
Z291	10d. turquoise-blue	42·00
Z292	1s. bistre	10·00
Z293	2s.6d. brown	£110
Z294	5s. rose-carmine	£180
Z295	10s. dull grey-blue	£325

Turkish forces entered Smyrna on 9 September 1922 and the British postal service was suspended shortly afterwards.

C. BRITISH FIELD OFFICE IN SALONICA

These overprints were originally prepared for use by a civilian post office to be set up on Mt. Athos, Northern Greece. When the project was abandoned they were placed on sale at the Army Field Office in Salonica.

PRICES FOR STAMPS ON COVER TO 1945	
Nos. S1/S8	*from* × 3

Levant

(S 1)

1916 (end Feb–9 Mar). Stamps of Gt. Britain, optd with *T* S **1** by Army Printing Office, Salonica.

S1	**105**	½d. green	70·00	£325
		a. Opt double	£4500	£5000
		b. Vert pair, one without opt	£2250	£3000
S2	**104**	1d. scarlet	70·00	£325
		a. Opt double	£3000	£3500
S3	**106**	2d. reddish orange (Die I)	£200	£475
S4		3d. bluish violet	£160	£475
S5		4d. grey-green	£190	£475
S6	**107**	6d. reddish purple (*chalk-surfaced paper*)	£110	£400
		a. Vert pair, one without opt	£2250	£3250
S7	**108**	9d. agate	£400	£750
		a. Opt double	£17000	£12000
S8		1s. bistre-brown	£350	£650
S1/S8 *Set of* 8			£1400	£3500

There are numerous forgeries of this overprint.

All values can be found with an additional albino overprint, inverted on the gummed side. These are worth a 25% premium.

British New Guinea
see **Papua** *after* **Australia**

British Occupation of Iraq *see* **Iraq**

British Occupation of Italian Colonies

PRICES FOR STAMPS ON COVER TO 1945	
Nos. M1/M21	*from* × 4
Nos. MD1/MD5	*from* × 10
Nos. S1/S9	*from* × 4

The above prices refer to covers from the territories concerned, not examples used in Great Britain.

MIDDLE EAST FORCES

For use in territory occupied by British Forces in Eritrea (1942), Italian Somaliland (from 13 April 1942), Cyrenaica (1943), Tripolitania (1943), and some of the Dodecanese Islands (1945).

PRICES. Our prices for used stamps with 'M.E.F.' overprints are for examples with identifiable postmarks of the territories in which they were issued. These stamps were also used in the United Kingdom with official sanction, from the summer of 1950 onwards, and with UK postmarks are worth considerably less.

PRINTERS. Considerable research has been undertaken to discover the origins of Nos. M1/M10. It is now suggested that Nos. M1/M5, previously assigned to Harrison and Sons, were produced by the Army Printing Services, Cairo, and that the smaller printing, Nos. M6/M10, previously identified as the work of the Army Printing Services, Cairo, was from GHQ, Middle East Land Forces, Nairobi.

M.E.F. (M **1**) Opt. 14 mm long. Regular lettering and upright oblong stops.

M.E.F. (M **2**) Opt. 13½ mm long. Regular lettering and square stops.

M.E.F. (M **2a**) Opt. 13½ mm long. Rough lettering and round stops.

M.E.F. Sliced 'M' (R. 6/10)

(Illustrations twice actual size)

1942 (2 Mar). Stamps of Great Britain optd. W **127**. P 15×14.

(a) With T M **1**

M1	**128**	1d. scarlet (No. 463)	3·50	4·75
		a. Sliced 'M'	£170	£200
M2		2d. orange (No. 465)	3·00	6·00
		a. Sliced 'M'	£130	£250
M3		2½d. ultramarine (No. 466)	3·25	2·00
		a. Sliced 'M'	£170	£190
M4		3d. violet (No. 467)	2·75	30
		a. Sliced 'M'		
M5	**129**	5d. brown	2·75	1·00
		a. Sliced 'M'	£160	£170

(b) With T M **2**

M6	**128**	1d. scarlet (No. 463)	55·00	26·00
		a. Optd with Type M **2a**	48·00	25·00
		b. Nos. M6/M6a *se-tenant* vert	£200	£160
M7		2d. orange (No. 465)	90·00	£160
		a. Optd with Type M **2a**	80·00	£160
		b. Nos. M7/M7a *se-tenant* vert	£425	£700
M8		2½d. ultramarine (No. 466)	70·00	12·00
		a. Optd with Type M **2a**	65·00	15·00
		b. Nos. M8/M8a *se-tenant* vert	£325	95·00
M9		3d. violet (No. 467)	£140	60·00
		aa. Opt double	†	£6500
		a. Optd with Type M **2a**	£130	75·00
		ab. Opt double	†	£6500
		b. Nos. M9/M9a *se-tenant* vert	£600	£350
M10	**129**	5d. brown	£500	£130
		a. Optd with Type M **2a**	£450	£130
		b. Nos. M10/M10a *se-tenant* vert	£1800	£1000

See note after No. M21.

Nos. M6/M10 were issued in panes of 60 (6×10), rows 2, 3, and 7 being overprinted with T M **2** and the other seven rows with T M **2a**.

M.E.F.

(M **3**) Optd 13½ mm long. Regular lettering and upright oblong stops.

(Illustration twice actual size)

1943 (1 Jan)–**47**. Stamps of Great Britain optd with T M **3** by Harrison & Sons. W **127**, P 15×14 (1d. to 1s.); W **133**, P 14 (others).

M11	**128**	1d. pale scarlet (No. 486)	1·50	10
M12		2d. pale orange (No. 488)	2·25	1·25
M13		2½d. light ultramarine (No. 489)	2·25	10
M14		3d. pale violet (No. 490)	1·50	10
M15	**129**	5d. brown	4·00	10
M16		6d. purple	65	10
M17	**130**	9d. deep olive-green	85	10
M18		1s. bistre-brown	50	10
M19	**131**	2s.6d. yellow-green	7·00	1·00
M20		5s. red (27.1.47)	32·00	15·00
M21	**132**	10s. ultramarine (27.1.47)	45·00	8·00
M11/M21 *Set of* 11			85·00	23·00
M18s/M21s Optd 'SPECIMEN' *Set of* 4			£650	

The overprint on No. M15 should not be confused with the other overprints on the 5d. value. It can be distinguished from No. M5 by the ½ mm difference in length; and from No. M10 by the more intense colour, thicker lettering and larger stops.

POSTAGE DUE STAMPS

M.E.F.

(MD **1**)

1942 (2 Mar). Postage Due stamps of Great Britain Nos. D27/D30 and D33 optd with T MD **1**, in blue-black.

MD1	D **1**	½d. emerald	40	13·00
MD2		1d. carmine	40	1·75
		w. Wmk sideways inverted*	—	£110
MD3		2d. agate	2·00	1·25
MD4		3d. violet	50	4·25
MD5		1s. deep blue	4·00	13·00
		s. Optd *'SPECIMEN'*	£190	
MD1/MD5 *Set of* 5			6·50	30·00

* No. MD2w shows the Crown pointing to the left, *as seen from the back of the stamp.*

CYRENAICA

In June 1949 the British authorities recognised the leader of the Senussi, Amir Mohammed Idris Al-Senussi, as Amir of Cyrenaica with autonomy in internal affairs.

(Currency. 10 millièmes = 1 piastre, 100 piastres = 1 Egyptian pound)

24 Mounted Warrior

25 Mounted Warrior

(Recess Waterlow)

1950 (16 Jan). P 12½.

136	**24**	1m. brown	6·00	10·00
137		2m. carmine	6·00	10·00
138		3m. orange-yellow	6·00	7·50
139		4m. blue-green	6·00	10·00
140		5m. grey-black	6·00	10·00
141		8m. orange	6·00	4·75
142		10m. violet	6·00	2·75
143		12m. scarlet	6·00	4·25
144		20m. blue	6·00	2·75
145	**25**	50m. ultramarine and purple-brown	22·00	11·00
146		100m. carmine and black	35·00	13·00
147		200m. violet and deep blue	45·00	48·00
148		500m. orange-yellow and green	70·00	£110
136/148 *Set of* 13			£200	£225

POSTAGE DUE STAMPS

D **26**

(Recess Waterlow)

1950 (16 Jan). P 12½.

D149	D **26**	2m. brown	60·00	£110
D150		4m. blue-green	60·00	£110
D151		8m. scarlet	60·00	£120
D152		10m. orange	60·00	£120
D153		20m. orange-yellow	60·00	£140
D154		40m. blue	60·00	£180
D155		100m. grey-brown	60·00	£200
D149/D155 *Set of* 7			£375	£900

On 24 December 1951 Cyrenaica united with Tripolitania, Fezzan and Ghadames to form the independent Kingdom of Libya, whose issues are listed in our *Africa since Independence F—M* catalogue.

ERITREA

From early 1950 examples of Nos. E1/E32 exist precancelled in manuscript by a black or blue horizontal line for use on non-concession rate mail.

BRITISH MILITARY ADMINISTRATION
(Currency. 100 cents = 1 shilling)

B. M. A.
ERITREA
10
CENTS
(E 1)

B. M. A.
ERITREA
5 SHILLINGS
(E 2)

SH. 50 Normal

SH .50 Misplaced Stop

Two settings of the 5s. on 5s.
I 1.8mm between obliterating bars
II 1mm between obliterating bars

1948 (27 May)–**49**. Stamps of Great Britain surch as T E **1** or E **2**.

E1	**128**	5c. on ½d. pale green	2·75	65
E2		10c. on 1d. pale scarlet	2·00	2·50

E3 20c. on 2d. pale orange 3·00 2·25
E4 25c. on 2½d. light ultramarine 2·00 60
E5 30c. on 3d. pale violet 2·50 4·50
E6 **129** 40c. on 5d. brown 2·75 4·25
E7 50c. on 6d. purple 2·25 1·00
E7*a* **130** 65c. on 8d. bright carmine (1.2.49) 7·00 2·00
E8 75c. on 9d. deep olive-green 3·75 75
E9 1s. on 1s. bistre-brown 2·50 50
E10 **131** 2s.50c. on 2s.6d. yellow-green 13·00 12·00
a. Misplaced stop (R. 4/7) £180 £225
E11 5s. on 5s. red 14·00 24·00
a. Second setting (1.49) £250 £250
E12 **132** 10s. on 10s. ultramarine 30·00 24·00
E1/E12 *Set of* 13 75·00 70·00

BRITISH ADMINISTRATION

1950 (6 Feb). As Nos. E1/E12, but surch 'B.A. ERITREA' and new values instead of 'B.M.A.' etc.

E13 **128** 5c. on ½d. pale green 1·75 8·00
E14 10c. on 1d. pale scarlet 40 3·00
E15 20c. on 2d. pale orange 1·75 80
E16 25c. on 2½d. light ultramarine 1·00 60
E17 30c. on 3d. pale violet 40 2·25
E18 **129** 40c. on 5d. brown 3·00 1·75
E19 50c. on 6d. purple 40 20
E20 **130** 65c. on 8d. bright carmine 6·50 1·50
E21 75c. on 9d. deep olive-green 2·00 25
E22 1s. on 1s. bistre-brown 40 15
E23 **131** 2s.50c. on 2s.6d. yellow-green 10·00 5·50
E24 5s. on 5s. red 10·00 12·00
E25 **132** 10s. on 10s. ultramarine 80·00 70·00
E13/E25 *Set of* 13 £100 95·00

1951 (28 May*). Nos. 503/504, 506/507 and 509/511 of Great Britain surch 'B.A. ERITREA' and new values.

E26 **128** 5c. on ½d. pale orange 3·75 6·00
E27 10c. on 1d. light ultramarine 2·75 75
E28 20c. on 2d. pale red-brown 3·75 30
E29 25c. on 2½d. pale scarlet 3·75 30
E30 **147** 2s.50c. on 2s.6d. yellow-green 22·00 35·00
E31 **148** 5s. on 5s. red 23·00 40·00
E32 10s. on 10s. ultramarine 30·00 40·00
E26/E32 *Set of* 7 75·00 £110

* This is the local release date. The stamps were placed on sale in London on 3 May.

POSTAGE DUE STAMPS

B. M. A.
ERITREA
10 CENTS
(ED **1**)

1948 (27 May). Postage Due stamps of Great Britain Nos. D27/D30 and D33 surch as T ED **1**.

ED1 **D 1** 5c. on ½d. emerald 10·00 22·00
a. No stop after 'A' — £475
ED2 10c. on 1d. carmine 10·00 24·00
a. No stop after 'B' (R. 1/9) £190 £375
ED3 20c. on 2d. agate 17·00 16·00
a. No stop after 'A' 70·00
b. No stop after 'B' (R. 1/9) £225 £300
ED4 30c. on 3d. violet 13·00 17·00
ED5 1s. on 1s. deep blue 21·00 32·00
a. No stop after 'A' — £650
ED1/ED5 *Set of* 5 65·00 £100

1950 (6 Feb). As Nos. ED1/ED5, but surch 'B.A. ERITREA' and new values instead of 'B.M.A.' etc.

ED6 **D 1** 5c. on ½d. emerald 16·00 65·00
ED7 10c. on 1d. carmine 16·00 22·00
a. 'C' of 'CENTS' omitted £5000
ab. 'C' omitted and vertical oblong for 'E' of 'CENTS' £8500
ED8 20c. on 2d. agate 16·00 25·00
a. No stop after 'A' £450
ED9 30c. on 3d. violet 20·00 50·00
w. Wmk sideways-inverted* — 75·00
ED10 1s. on 1s. deep blue 21·00 50·00
a. No stop after 'A' (R. 2/13) £650
ED6/ED10 *Set of* 5 80·00 £180

No. ED7a, and probably No. ED7ab, occurred on R. 7/17, but the error was quickly corrected.

* No. ED9w shows the Crowns pointing to the left, *as seen from the back of the stamp.*

Stamps of Ethiopia were used in Eritrea after 15 September 1952 following federation with Ethiopia.

SOMALIA

BRITISH OCCUPATION

E.A.F.
(S **1** 'East Africa Forces')

1943 (15 Jan)–**46**. Stamps of Great Britain optd with T S **1**, in blue.

S1 **128** 1d. pale scarlet 1·50 3·00
S2 2d. pale orange 1·75 1·75
S3 2½d. light ultramarine 2·00 3·50
S4 3d. pale violet 1·75 15
S5 **129** 5d. brown 2·50 40
S6 6d. purple 2·25 1·50
S7 **130** 9d. deep olive-green 2·75 4·25
S8 1s. bistre-brown 3·75 15
S9 **131** 2s.6d. yellow-green (14.1.46) 42·00 14·00
S1/S9 *Set of* 9 55·00 25·00
S8s/S9s Optd 'SPECIMEN' *Set of* 2 £350

The note *re* used prices above T M **1** of Middle East Forces also applies to the above issue.

BRITISH MILITARY ADMINISTRATION

(Currency. 100 cents = 1 shilling)

1948 (27 May). Stamps of Great Britain surch 'B.M.A./SOMALIA' and new values, as T E **1** and E **2** of Eritrea.

S10 **128** 5c. on ½d. pale green 1·25 2·75
S11 15c. on 1½d. pale red-brown 1·75 15·00
S12 20c. on 2d. pale orange 3·00 7·00
S13 25c. on 2½d. light ultramarine 2·25 4·50
S14 30c. on 3d. pale violet 2·25 9·00
S15 **129** 40c. on 5d. brown 1·25 20
S16 50c. on 6d. purple 50 2·00
S17 **130** 75c. on 9d. deep olive-green 2·00 28·00
S18 1s. on 1s. bistre-brown 1·25 20
S19 **131** 2s.50c. on 2s.6d. yellow-green 11·00 25·00
a. Misplaced stop (R. 4/7) £150 £300
S20 5s. on 5s. red 22·00 65·00
S10/S20 *Set of* 11 42·00 £140

For illustration of No. S19a, see above No. E1 of Eritrea.

BRITISH ADMINISTRATION

1950 (2 Jan). As Nos. S10/S20, but surch 'B.A./SOMALIA' and new values, instead of 'B.M.A.' etc.

S21 **128** 5c. on ½d. pale green 20 3·50
S22 15c. on 1½d. pale red-brown 75 17·00
S23 20c. on 2d. pale orange 75 7·50
S24 25c. on 2½d. light ultramarine 50 14·00
S25 30c. on 3d. pale violet 1·25 12·00
S26 **129** 40c. on 5d. brown 60 3·25
S27 50c. on 6d. purple 60 1·00
S28 **130** 75c. on 9d. deep olive-green 2·00 15·00
S29 1s. on 1s. bistre-brown 70 2·25
S30 **131** 2s.50c. on 2s.6d. yellow-green 8·50 38·00
S31 5s. on 5s. red 23·00 55·00
S21/S31 *Set of* 11 35·00 £140

Somalia reverted to Italian Administration on 1 April 1950 later becoming independent. Later issues will be found listed in our *Italy and Switzerland* catalogue.

TRIPOLITANIA

BRITISH MILITARY AUTHORITY

(Currency. 100 centesimi = 1 Military Authority lira)

4 M.A.L. — Normal
4 M.A.L. — Misaligned surcharge (R. 8/8, 18/8)

1948 (1 July). Stamps of Great Britain surch 'B.M.A./TRIPOLITANIA' and new values, as T E **1** and E **2** of Eritrea, but expressed in M(ilitary) A(uthority) L(ire).

T1 **128** 1l. on ½d. pale green 1·00 6·00
T2 2l. on 1d. pale scarlet 50 15
T3 3l. on 1½d. pale red-brown 50 50
a. Misaligned surch 65·00 75·00
T4 4l. on 2d. pale orange 50 1·00
a. Misaligned surch 65·00 85·00
T5 5l. on 2½d. light ultramarine 50 20
T6 6l. on 3d. pale violet 50 40
T7 **129** 10l. on 5d. brown 50 15
T8 12l. on 6d. purple 50 20
T9 **130** 18l. on 9d. deep olive-green 1·50 1·75
T10 24l. on 1s. bistre-brown 2·75 3·25
T11 **131** 60l. on 2s.6d. yellow-green 9·50 17·00
T12 120l. on 5s. red 29·00 30·00
T13 **132** 240l. on 10s. ultramarine 32·00 £150
T1/T13 *Set of* 13 70·00 £180

BRITISH ADMINISTRATION

1950 (6 Feb). As Nos. T1/T13, but surch 'B.A. TRIPOLITANIA' and new values, instead of 'B.M.A.' etc.

T14 **128** 1l. on ½d. pale green 6·00 13·00
T15 2l. on 1d. pale scarlet 5·00 40
T16 3l. on 1½d. pale red-brown 4·50 13·00
a. Misaligned surch £140 £350
T17 4l. on 2d. pale orange 4·25 4·50
a. Misaligned surch £150 £180
T18 5l. on 2½d. light ultramarine 2·25 70
T19 6l. on 3d. pale violet 3·75 3·25
T20 **129** 10l. on 5d. brown 3·75 4·00
T21 12l. on 6d. purple 5·00 50
T22 **130** 18l. on 9d. deep olive-green 8·00 2·75
T23 24l. on 1s. bistre-brown 7·50 3·75
T24 **131** 60l. on 2s.6d. yellow-green 21·00 12·00
T25 120l. on 5s. red 42·00 48·00
T26 **132** 240l. on 10s. ultramarine 55·00 90·00
T14/T26 *Set of* 13 £140 £170

1951 (3 May). Nos. 503/507 and 509/511 of Great Britain surch 'B.A. TRIPOLITANIA' and new values.

T27 **128** 1l. on ½d. pale orange 55 10·00
T28 2l. on 1d. light ultramarine 55 1·00
T29 3l. on 1½d. pale green 55 8·00
T30 4l. on 2d. pale red-brown 55 1·25
T31 5l. on 2½d. pale scarlet 1·25 7·50
T32 **147** 60l. on 2s.6d. yellow-green 21·00 40·00
T33 **148** 120l. on 5s. red 21·00 48·00
T34 **149** 240l. on 10s. ultramarine 50·00 85·00
T27/T34 *Set of* 8 80·00 £170

POSTAGE DUE STAMPS

1948 (1 July). Postage Due stamps of Great Britain Nos. D27/D30 and D33 surch 'B.M.A./TRIPOLITANIA' and new values, as T ED **1** of Eritrea, but expressed in M(ilitary) A(uthority) L(ire).

TD1 **D 1** 1l. on ½d. emerald 6·00 65·00
a. No stop after 'A' 90·00
TD2 2l. on 1d. carmine 2·75 55·00
a. No stop after 'A' 50·00
b. No stop after 'M' (R. 1/17) £160
TD3 4l. on 2d. agate 13·00 50·00
a. No stop after 'A' (R. 2/12, R. 3/8) £170
b. No stop after 'M' (R. 1/17) £325
TD4 6l. on 3d. violet 7·50 27·00
TD5 24l. on 1s. deep blue 29·00 £110
TD1/TD5 *Set of* 5 50·00 £275

1950 (6 Feb). As Nos. TD1/TD5, but surch 'B.A. TRIPOLITANIA' and new values, instead of 'B.M.A.' etc.

TD6 **D 1** 1l. on ½d. emerald 17·00 £110
a. No stop after 'B' (R. 11/10) £250
TD7 2l. on 1d. carmine 11·00 38·00
a. No stop after 'A' (R.11/2) £250
b. No stop after 'B' (R. 11/10) £130
TD8 4l. on 2d. agate 13·00 50·00
a. No stop after 'B' (R. 11/10) £140
TD9 6l. on 3d. violet 19·00 80·00
a. No stop after 'B' (R. 11/10) £275
w. Wmk sideways-inverted* 35·00 £150
TD10 24l. on 1s. deep blue 55·00 £180
a. No stop after 'A' (R. 11/2) £700
b. No stop after 'B' (R. 11/10) £700
TD6/TD10 *Set of* 5 £100 £400

* No. TD9w shows the Crowns pointing to the left, *as seen from the back of the stamp.*

Tripolitania became part of the independent kingdom of Libya on 24 December 1951.

British POs in Crete

BRITISH ADMINISTRATION OF CANDIA PROVINCE (HERAKLEION)

Crete, formerly part of the Turkish Empire, was made autonomous, under Turkish suzerainty, in November 1898 with British, French, Italian and Russian troops stationed in separate zones to keep the peace.

Overseas mail franked with Nos. B1/B5 was forwarded through the Austrian post office at Canea, being additionally franked with stamps of the Austro-Hungarian Post Offices in the Turkish Empire.

(Currency. 40 paras = 1 piastre)

PRICES FOR STAMPS ON COVER TO 1945	
No. B1	*from* × 8
Nos. B2/B5	—

B 1

B 2

1898 (25 Nov). Handstruck locally. Imperf.

B1	B **1**	20pa. bright violet	£450	£225

1898 (3 Dec). Litho by M. Grundmann, Athens. P 11½.

B2	B **2**	10pa. blue	11·00	25·00
		a. Imperf (pair)	£250	
B3		20pa. green	20·00	23·00
		a. Imperf (pair)	£250	

1899. P 11½.

B4	B **2**	10pa. brown	11·00	35·00
		a. Imperf (pair)	£250	
B5		20pa. rose	20·00	19·00
		a. Imperf (pair)	£250	

Forgeries exist of Nos. B1/B5. Note that genuine examples of T B **2** show a full circle in the ornament above the figures of value. Forgeries with a broken circle in this position are frequently met with.

The British postal service closed at the end of 1899.

British PO in Siam

(Bangkok)

An overseas postal service for foreign residents was operated by the British Consulate at Bangkok from 1858. Mail was despatched by steamer to Singapore and from 1876 onwards was increasingly franked with Straits Settlements stamps. These were initially cancelled on arrival at Singapore, but later an oval postmark inscribed 'BRITISH CONSULATE BANGKOK' was used. In 1883 a circular 'BANGKOK' datestamp was introduced for use with Nos. 1/23. Both cancellations can also be found used on Hong Kong stamps between 1881 and 1885.

(Currency. 100 cents = 1 Straits dollar)

Stamps of Straits Settlements (see Malaysia) cancelled with oval postmark inscribed 'BRITISH CONSULATE BANGKOK' around Royal Arms.

1882. Wmk Crown CC (Nos. 11/15, 33, 35).

Z1	2c. brown	£450
Z2	4c. rose	£500
Z3	6c. dull lilac	£500
Z4	8c. orange-yellow	£450
Z5	10c. on 30c. claret (thin '0') (No. 33)	£1300
Z6	10c. on 30c. claret (thick '10') (No. 34)	£1300
Z7	10c. on 30c. claret (thin '1', thick '0') (No. 35)	£1600
Z8	12c. blue	£700

Subsequent Straits Settlements values to 8c. watermarked Crown CA are known used at Bangkok in 1883 and 1884. During this period the stamps overprinted 'B' were on sale at the British Post Office.

PRICES FOR STAMPS ON COVER TO 1945
The issues of the British Post Offices in Siam are worth *from* × 100 the prices quoted for used stamps when on cover.

B (1) B (2)

1882 (May)–**85**. Stamps of Straits Settlements optd with T **1**.

(a) On No. 9 of 1867

1	32c. on 2a. yellow (1885)	£35000	

(b) On Nos. 11/13, 14a, 15/17 and 19 of 1867–1872 and Nos. 48/49 of 1882. Wmk Crown CC

2	2c. brown	£4000	£1600
3	4c. rose	£3750	£1400
	a. Opt double	—	£7500
4	5c. purple-brown	£475	£550
5	6c. lilac	£325	£150
	a. Opt Type **2**	†	£1800
6	8c. orange	£3750	£275
7	10c. slate	£750	£200
	a. Opt double	†	£4750
	b. Opt Type **2**	†	£1700
8	12c. blue	£1500	£550
	a. Opt Type **2**	†	£1000
9	24c. green	£800	£170
	a. Opt Type **2**	†	£1500
10	30c. claret	£45000	£30000
11	96c. grey	£7500	£3000

(c) On Nos. 59/60 of April 1883

12	2c. on 32c. pale red (*Wide* 'S')	£3250	£3250
13	2c. on 32c. pale red (*Wide* 'E')	£4250	£4250

(d) On Nos. 50/53 of 1882 and Nos. 63/67 of 1883–1884. Wmk Crown CA

14	2c. brown	£750	£400
	a. Opt Type **2**	†	£1600
15	2c. pale rose (1883)	75·00	55·00
	a. Opt inverted	†	£16000
	b. Opt double	£2750	£2750
	c. Opt treble	£10000	
16	4c. rose (1883)	£900	£375
	a. Opt Type **2**	†	£1500
17	4c. pale brown (1883)	£100	85·00
	a. Opt double	£3500	
	b. Broken oval	£1800	£1600
18	5c. blue (1884)	£400	£200
19	6c. lilac (1884)	£325	£160
20	8c. orange (1883)	£250	75·00
	a. Opt inverted	£30000	£16000
	b. Opt Type **2**	†	£1400
	c. Opt double	†	£4250
21	10c. slate (1883)	£250	95·00
22	12c. brown-purple (1883)	£425	£180
23	24c. yellow-green (1884?)	£8000	£3250

B (1) B (2)

Opt T **2** differs from T **1** in having the two loops of the 'B' almost equal in size with wider internal dimensions. The T **2** overprints are generally placed higher than T **1**. It is believed that the two types were both supplied to Bangkok in May 1882.

The prices quoted for the overprint double errors, Nos. 3a, 15b, 17a and 20c, are for stamps showing two clear impressions of the overprint. Examples showing partial doubling, on these and other values, are worth a small premium over the price quoted for normal stamps.

No. 17b shows the edge of the central oval broken above the 'O' of 'POSTAGE'. It occurs on R. 10/5 of the lower right pane.

The use of these stamps ceased on 30 June 1885. Siam joined the Universal Postal Union on 1 July 1885.

British Postal Agencies in Eastern Arabia

Certain Arab States in Eastern Arabia, whilst remaining independent, had British postal administrations replacing Bahrain, and subsequently Indian, post offices at Dubai and Muscat.

Bahrain and Kuwait (from 1948) and Qatar (from 1957) used British stamps overprinted and surcharged in local currency. Abu Dhabi (from 1964) and Trucial States (from 1961 and used only in Dubai) had definitive issues made under the auspices of the British Agencies.

In addition, British stamps were surcharged with value only for use in Muscat and certain other states. They were formerly listed under Muscat as they were first put on sale there, but in view of their more extended use, the list has been transferred here, retaining the same numbering.

The stamps were used in Muscat from 1 April 1948 to 29 April 1966; in Dubai from 1 April 1948 to 6 January 1961; in Qatar: Doha from August 1950, Umm Said from February 1956, to 31 March 1957; and in Abu Dhabi from 30 March 1963 (Das Island from December 1960) to 29 March 1964.

Nos. 21/22 were placed on sale in Kuwait Post Offices in April and May 1951 and from February to November 1953 due to shortages of stamps with 'KUWAIT' overprint. Isolated examples of other values can be found commercially used from Bahrain or Kuwait.

(Currency. 12 pies = 1 anna; 16 annas = 1 rupee)

Stamps of Great Britain surcharged

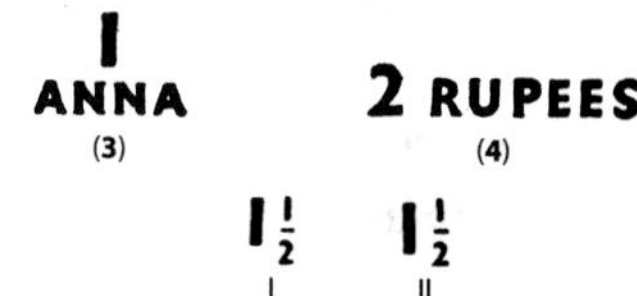

(3) (4)

I II

Two types of 1½a. surcharge:

I. '1' 3¼ mm high and aligns with top of '2' in '½' (Rows 1 to 10).

II. '1' 3½ mm high with foot of figure below top of '2' (Rows 11 to 20).

1948 (1 Apr). Surch with *T* **3** (½a. to 1r.) or **4** (2r.).

16	**128**	½a. on ½d. pale green	3·00	10·00
17		1a. on 1d. pale scarlet	3·00	30
18		1½a. pale red-brown (I)	21·00	12·00
		a. 1½a. on 1½d. Type II	21·00	12·00
		b. Vert pair. Nos. 18/18a	£550	
19		2a. on 2d. pale orange	2·25	3·25
20		2½a. on 2½d. light ultramarine	3·50	11·00
21		3a. on 3d. pale violet	3·50	10
22	**129**	6a. on 6d. purple	5·00	10
23	**130**	1r. on 1s. bistre-brown	7·50	1·75
24	**131**	2r. on 2s.6d. yellow-green	13·00	50·00
16/24 *Set of* 9			55·00	80·00

One example of No. 22 is known with the surcharge almost completely omitted from position R. 20/2 in the sheet.

(5) (6)

1948 (26 Apr). Royal Silver Wedding. Nos. 493/494 surch with T **5** or **6**.

25	**137**	2½a. on 2½d. ultramarine	2·75	6·00
26	**138**	15r. on £1 blue	25·00	35·00

1948 (29 July). Olympic Games. Nos. 495/498 surch with new values in 'ANNAS' or '1 RUPEE', as T **5**/**6**, but in one line on 2½a. (vert) or 6a. and 1r. (horiz) and grills obliterating former values of all except 2½a.

27	**139**	2½a. on 2½d. ultramarine	45	2·50
28	**140**	3a. on 3d. violet	55	2·50
		a. Crown flaw	£110	
29	**141**	6a. on 6d. bright purple	65	2·75
30	**142**	1r. on 1s. brown	1·40	5·50
		a. Surch double	£1800	
27/30 *Set of* 4			2·75	12·00

1949 (10 Oct). 75th Anniversary of Universal Postal Union. Nos. 499/502 surch with new values in 'ANNAS' or '1 RUPEE' as T **3**/**4**, but all in one line, with grills obliterating former values.

31	**143**	2½a. on 2½d. ultramarine	60	3·25
		a. Lake in India	£130	
32	**144**	3a. on 3d. violet	60	4·25
33	**145**	6a. on 6d. bright purple	60	2·75
34	**146**	1r. on 1s. brown	2·25	7·50
31/34 *Set of* 4			3·50	16·00

(6a) (6b)

Type **6a**. '2' and 'RUPEES' level and in line with lower of the two bars.

Type **6b**. '2' raised in relation to 'RUPEES' and whole surcharge below the lower bar.

1950 (2 Oct)–**55**. Nos. 503/508 surch as T **3** and No. 509 with T **6a**.

35	**128**	½a. on ½d. pale orange (3.5.51)	1·00	9·00
36		1a. on 1d. light ultramarine (3.5.51)	40	7·50

37		1½a. on 1½d. pale green (I) (3.5.51)	19·00	48·00
		a. Type II	19·00	48·00
		b. Vert pair. Nos. 37/37a	£500	
38		2a. on 2d. pale red-brown (3.5.51)	40	8·50
39		2½a. on 2½d. pale scarlet (3.5.51)	40	16·00
40	**129**	4a. on 4d. light ultramarine	1·25	3·50
41	**147**	2r. on 2s.6d. yellow-green (3.5.51)	50·00	8·50
		a. Surch with Type **6b** (1955)	£400	65·00
35/41 *Set of 7*			65·00	90·00

1952 (5 Dec)–**54**. Stamps of Queen Elizabeth II. Wmk Tudor Crown, surch as T **3** (in one line on 2½a. and 6a.).

42	½a. on ½d. orange-red (31.8.53)	10	3·50
43	1a. on 1d. ultramarine (31.8.53)	20	2·25
44	1½a. on 1½d. green	10	2·25
45	2a. on 2d. red-brown (31.8.53)	20	10
46	2½a. on 2½d. carmine-red	10	10
47	3a. on 3d. deep lilac (B.) (13.1.54)	20	1·25
48	4a. on 4d. ultramarine (2.11.53)	3·00	4·00
49	6a. on 6d. reddish purple (18.1.54)	35	10
50	12a. on 1s.3d. green (2.11.53)	9·00	30
51	1r. on 1s.6d. grey-blue (2.11.53)	2·25	10
42/51 *Set of 10*		14·00	12·00

In early printings of No. 42 the '½' was printed in a separate operation to 'ANNA'. Later printings and all printings of other values were printed in a single operation.

1953 (10 June). Coronation. Nos. 532/535 surch with new values.

52	2½a. on 2½d. carmine-red	1·75	5·25
53	4a. on 4d. ultramarine	1·75	1·25
54	12a. on 1s.3d. deep yellow-green	5·50	1·25
55	1r. on 1s.6d. deep grey-blue	5·50	50
52/55 *Set of 4*		13·00	7·50

2 RUPEES

2 RUPEES

2 RUPEES

(**7**)

5 RUPEES

5 RUPEES

(**8**)

Types of surcharges

2 rupees.

Type I. On *Waterlow ptg*. Top of 'R' level with top of '2' and other letters of 'RUPEES'. Bars 7 mm long.

Type II. On *Waterlow ptg* by Harrison: 'R' dropped out of alignment with 2' and other letters of RUPEES'. Bars 6½ mm long.

Type III. On *De La Rue ptg* by Harrison. Top of 'R' below level of top of '2'. Bars 7–7¼ mm long and with left sides aligned with 'S'.

5 rupees.

Type I. On *Waterlow ptg* by Harrison. Ends of letters square and sharp. There were two printings made in March and May 1957.

Type II. On *De La Rue ptg* by Harrison. Type is thicker and ends of letters are relatively rounded.

For differences between Waterlow and De La Rue printings of the basic stamps see notes in Great Britain after No. 539.

1955–60. T **166/167** (Waterlow ptgs) (W **165**, St Edward's Crown) surch with T **7/8**.

56	2r. on 2s.6d. black-brown (Type I) (23.9.55)	10·00	70
	a. Type II (2.57)	10·00	5·50
	b. Type III (No. 536a D.L.R.) (6.60)	28·00	80·00
57	5r. on 5s. rose-red (Type I) (1.3.57)	10·00	2·25
	a. Wide surcharge	£550	£425
	b. Type II (No. 537a D.L.R.) (27.1.60)	20·00	65·00

Designs: No. 56, Carrickfergus Castle; No. 57, Caernarvon Castle.

No. 57a ('5' and 'R' spaced 2¼ *mm* instead of 1¼ *mm*) occurred on R. 8/4 of the first surcharging of No. 57 only.

1956–57. Stamps of Queen Elizabeth II, W **165**, St Edward's Crown, surch as T **3** (in one line on 2½a and 6a.).

58	1a. on 1d. ultramarine (20.3.57)	35	1·00
58*a*	1½a. on 1½d. green (1956)	£8000	£1200
59	2a. on 2d. red-brown (8.6.56)	70	2·50
60	2½a. on 2½d. carmine-red (8.6.56)	80	7·50
61	3a. on 3d. deep lilac (B.) (3.2.57)	1·00	11·00
62	4a. on 4d. ultramarine (9.12.56)	7·00	25·00
63	6a. on 6d. red-purple (10.2.57)	1·25	7·00
64	1r. on 1s.6d. grey-blue (2.8.56)	18·00	15
58/64 (*ex 58a*) *Set of 7*		26·00	48·00

No. 58*a* came from a few sheets of the St Edward's Crown watermark included, in error, with a printing of No. 44. Most examples were used in Dubai, but two are known from Muscat, a pair and a single on separate covers from Bahrain and a single postmarked FPO 936 (Sharjah). A single mint example also exists.

NP 1 NP (**9**) **3 NP NP** (**10**) **75 NP** (**11**)

1957 (1 Apr)–**59**. Value in naye paise. Stamps of Queen Elizabeth II, W **165**, St Edward's Crown, surch as T **9** (1, 15, 25, 40, 50n.p.), **11** (75n.p.) or **10** (others).

65	1n.p. on 5d. brown	10	1·00
66	3n.p. on ½d. orange-red	20	2·75
67	6n.p. on 1d. ultramarine	20	2·75
68	9n.p. on 1½d. green	1·25	2·50
69	12n.p. on 2d. light red-brown	30	3·00
70	15n.p. on 2½d. carmine-red (Type I)	30	10
	a. Type II (4.59)	30	4·25
71	20n.p. on 3d. deep lilac (B.)	20	10
72	25n.p. on 4d. ultramarine	70	12·00
73	40n.p. on 6d. reddish purple	30	10
	a. Deep claret (3.59)	35	10
74	50n.p. on 9d. bronze-green	1·25	2·75
75	75n.p. on 1s.3d. green	3·75	40
65/75 *Set of 11*		7·75	24·00

15 NP

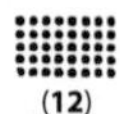

(**12**)

1957 (1 Aug). World Scout Jubilee Jamboree. Nos. 557/559 surch in one line as T **12** (15np.) or in two lines (others).

76	15n.p. on 2½d. carmine-red	35	85
77	25n.p. on 4d. ultramarine	35	85
78	75n.p. on 1s.3d. green	40	85
76/78 *Set of 3*		1·00	2·25

Designs: No. 76, Scout badge and 'Rolling Hitch'; No. 77, 'Scouts coming to Britain'; No. 78, Globe within a compass.

1960 (26 Apr)–**61**. Stamps of Queen Elizabeth II. W **179**, Mult Crown, surch as T **9** (1, 15, 30, 40, 50n.p.), **11** (75n.p.), **3** (1r.), **7** (2r., 5r.) or **10** (others).

79	1n.p. on 5d. brown (30.8.60)	10	20
80	3n.p. on ½d. orange-red (21.6.60)	55	80
81	5n.p. on 1d. ultramarine (8.4.61)	2·50	6·50
82	6n.p. on 1d. ultramarine (21.6.60)	1·25	1·00
83	10n.p. on 1½d. green (8.4.61)	1·50	3·00
84	12n.p. on 2d. light red-brown (21.6.60)	2·00	2·50
85	15n.p. on 2½d. carmine-red (Type II)	25	10
86	20n.p. on 3d. deep lilac (B.) (28.9.60)	25	10
87	30n.p. on 4½d. chestnut (8.4.61)	40	1·00
88	40n.p. on 6d. deep claret (28.9.60)	45	10
89	50n.p. on 9d. bronze-green (8.4.61)	1·25	2·50
90	75n.p. on 1s.3d. green (8.4.61)	6·50	2·00
91	1r. on 1s.6d. grey-blue (8.4.61)	38·00	12·00
92	2r. on 2s.6d. black-brown (No. 595) (8.4.61)	17·00	55·00
93	5r. on 5s. rose-red (No. 596) (8.4.61)	32·00	75·00
79/93 *Set of 15*		90·00	£140

Designs: Nos. 79/91, Queen Elizabeth II; No. 92, Carrickfergus Castle; No. 93, Caernarvon Castle.

The '5' on No. 93 differs from that on Nos. 57/57b, being the same height as 'RUPEES'.

British Solomon Islands

The first British Resident Commissioner, Charles Woodford, was appointed in 1896 and an administrative centre established at Tulagi.

Mail was initially sent unstamped by sealed bag to Sydney where New South Wales stamps were applied and cancelled. Later the Resident Commissioner kept a stock of New South Wales stamps which were still not cancelled until arrival at Sydney. From April 1906 Mr. Woodford used a vertical oblong 'BRITISH SOLOMON ISLANDS PAID' handstamp in place of New South Wales stamps which were then added to many of the covers by the postal authorities in Sydney.

PRICES FOR STAMPS ON COVER TO 1945

Nos. 1/7	*from* × 12
Nos. 8/17	*from* × 25
Nos. 18/36	*from* × 6
Nos. 37/38	—
Nos. 39/51	*from* × 6
No. 52	—
Nos. 53/56	*from* × 2
Nos. 57/59	*from* × 6
Nos. 60/72	*from* × 2
Nos. D1/D8	*from* × 5

BRITISH PROTECTORATE

1

2

(Des C. M. Woodford. Litho W. E. Smith & Co. Sydney)

1907 (14 Feb). No wmk. P 11.

1	**1**	½d. ultramarine	9·00	14·00
2		1d. rose-carmine	23·00	25·00
3		2d. indigo	48·00	32·00
		a. Imperf between (horiz pair)	£15000	
4		2½d. orange-yellow	32·00	50·00
		a. Imperf between (vert pair)	£7500	
		b. Imperf between (horiz pair)	£12000	£7000
5		5d. emerald-green	60·00	70·00
6		6d. chocolate	55·00	70·00
		a. Imperf between (vert pair)	£7000	
7		1s. bright purple	80·00	85·00
1/7 *Set of 7*			£275	£300

Nos. 1/7 did not become valid for international postage until early September 1907. Overseas covers before that date show additional New South Wales values.

Three types exist of the ½d. and 2½d., and six each of the other values, differing in minor details.

Forgeries of Nos. 1/7 show different perforations and have the boat paddle touching the shore. Genuine stamps show a gap between the paddle and the shore.

(Recess D.L.R.)

1908 (1 Nov)–**11**. Wmk Mult Crown CA (sideways). P 14.

8	**2**	½d. green	1·50	1·00
9		1d. red	1·25	1·50
10		2d. greyish slate	1·25	1·00
11		2½d. ultramarine	3·75	2·25
11*a*		4d. red/*yellow* (6.3.11)	3·50	9·00
12		5d. olive	10·00	5·00
13		6d. claret	10·00	5·50
14		1s. black/*green*	8·50	5·00
15		2s. purple/*blue* (7.3.10)	50·00	55·00
16		2s.6d. red/*blue* (7.3.10)	60·00	70·00
17		5s. green/*yellow* (7.3.10)	90·00	£110
8/17 *Set of 11*			£200	£225
8s/17s Optd 'SPECIMEN' *Set of 11*			£325	

The ½d. and 1d. were issued in 1913 on rather thinner paper and with brownish gum.

3

4

(T **3** and **4**. Typo D.L.R.)

1913. Inscribed 'POSTAGE POSTAGE'. Wmk Mult Crown CA. P 14.

18	**3**	½d. green (1.4)	1·00	3·50
19		1d. red (1.4)	8·50	20·00
20		3d. purple/*yellow* (27.2)	2·00	4·00
		a. On orange-buff	12·00	24·00
21		11d. dull purple and scarlet (27.2)	3·00	12·00
18/21 *Set of 4*			13·00	35·00
18s/21s Optd 'SPECIMEN' *Set of 4*			85·00	

1914 (Mar)–**23**. Inscribed 'POSTAGE REVENUE'. Chalk-surfaced paper (3d. to £1). Wmk Mult Crown CA. P 14.

22	**4**	½d. green	2·50	12·00
23		½d. yellow-green (1917)	7·00	20·00
24		1d. carmine-red	1·75	1·25
25		1d. scarlet (1917)	8·00	6·50
26		2d. grey (7.14)	4·75	9·00
27		2½d. ultramarine (7.14)	4·75	4·00
28		3d. purple/*pale yellow* (3.23)	30·00	£140
29		4d. black and red/*yellow* (7.14)	2·00	2·50
30		5d. dull purple and olive-green (7.14)	24·00	30·00

31		5d. brown-purple and olive-green (7.14)	24·00	30·00
32		6d. dull and bright purple (7.14)	6·00	12·00
33		1s. black/*green* (7.14)	4·75	7·00
		a. On blue-green, olive back (1923)	7·50	22·00
34		2s. purple and blue/*blue* (7.14)	10·00	10·00
35		2s.6d. black and red/*blue* (7.14)	10·00	15·00
36		5s. green and red/*yellow* (7.14)	48·00	48·00
		a. On orange-buff (1920)	55·00	70·00
37		10s. green and red/*green* (7.14)	95·00	65·00
38		£1 purple and black/*red* (7.14)	£250	£120
22/38 *Set of* 14			£425	£425
22s/38s Optd 'SPECIMEN' *Set of* 14			£425	

Variations in the coloured papers are mostly due to climate and do not indicate separate printings.

1922–31. Chalk-surfaced paper (4d. and 5d. to 10s). Wmk Mult Script CA. P 14.

39	**4**	½d. green (10.22)	50	3·50
40		1d. scarlet (4.23)	6·00	11·00
41		1d. dull violet (2.27)	1·00	7·50
42	**3**	1½d. bright scarlet (7.24)	2·25	60
43	**4**	2d. slate-grey (4.23)	6·50	15·00
44		3d. pale ultramarine (11.23)	70	4·50
45		4d. black and red/*yellow* (7.27)	3·50	26·00
45*a*		4½d. red-brown (1931)	3·00	20·00
46		5d. dull purple and olive-green (12.27)	3·25	30·00
47		6d. dull and bright purple (12.27)	3·75	30·00
48		1s. black/*emerald* (12.27)	2·75	12·00
49		2s. purple and blue/*blue* (2.27)	30·00	55·00
50		2s.6d. black and red/*blue* (12.27)	9·50	60·00
51		5s. green and red/*pale yellow* (12.27)	45·00	60·00
52		10s. green and red/*emerald* (1.25)	£140	£110
39/52 *Set of* 15			£200	£375
39s/52s Optd or Perf (4½d.) 'SPECIMEN' *Set of* 16			£425	

1935 (6 May). Silver Jubilee. As Nos. 91/94 of Antigua. P 13½×14.

53		1½d. deep blue and carmine	1·00	1·00
		a. Frame printed double, one albino		
		f. Diagonal line by turret	90·00	£100
		h. Dot by flagstaff	£200	
		i. Dash by turret	£300	£300
54		3d. brown and deep blue	6·50	7·50
		f. Diagonal line by turret	£160	£200
		h. Dot by flagstaff	£300	£350
55		6d. light blue and olive-green	16·00	12·00
		a. Frame printed double, one albino		
		b. Frame printed triple, two albino	£1300	
		h. Dot by flagstaff	£425	£425
		i. Dash by turret	£650	
56		1s. slate and purple	7·50	27·00
		a. Frame printed double, one albino	£1800	£1800
		f. Diagonal line by turret	£300	
		h. Dot by flagstaff	£425	£550
		i. Dash by turret	£600	
53/56 *Set of* 4			28·00	42·00
53s/56s Perf 'SPECIMEN' *Set of* 4			£130	

The second albino impression on No. 55b is sometimes almost coincidental with the inked impression of the frame.

For illustrations of plate varieties see Omnibus section following Zanzibar.

1937 (13 May). Coronation. As Nos. 95/97 of Antigua. P 11×11½.

57		1d. violet	30	1·25
58		1½d. carmine	30	60
59		3d. blue	50	50
57/59 *Set of* 3			1·00	2·10
57s/59s Perf 'SPECIMEN' *Set of* 3			£120	

5 Spears and Shield

6 Native Constable and Chief

7 Artificial Island, Malaita

8 Canoe House

9 Roviana Canoe

10 Roviana Canoes

11 Native House, Reef Islands

12 Coconut Plantation

13 Breadfruit

14 Tinakula Volcano

15 Bismarck Scrub Fowl

16 Malaita Canoe

(Recess D.L.R. (2d., 3d., 2s. and 2s.6d.), Waterlow (others))

1939 (1 Feb)–**51.** T **5/16**. Wmk Mult Script CA. P 13½ (2d., 3d., 2s. and 2s.6d.) or 12½ (others).

60	**5**	½d. blue and blue-green	15	1·75
61	**6**	1d. brown and deep violet	30	1·50
62	**7**	1½d. blue-green and carmine	2·25	1·75
63	**8**	2d. orange-brown and black	3·75	2·00
		a. Perf 12 (7.11.51)	75	1·50
64	**9**	2½d. magenta and sage-green	4·00	2·25
		a. Imperf horiz (vert pair)	£26000	
65	**10**	3d. black and ultramarine	3·75	2·00
		a. Perf 12 (29.11.51)	1·50	2·50
66	**11**	4½d. green and chocolate	5·50	13·00
67	**12**	6d. deep violet and reddish purple	2·75	1·00
68	**13**	1s. green and black	2·75	1·00
		a. 'A' of 'CA' missing from wmk	£1200	
69	**14**	2s. black and orange	14·00	6·50
70	**15**	2s.6d. black and violet	32·00	4·50
71	**16**	5s. emerald-green and scarlet	32·00	13·00
72	**11**	10s. sage-green and magenta (27.4.42)	4·00	8·50
60/72 *Set of* 13			90·00	50·00
60s/72s Perf 'SPECIMEN' *Set of* 13			£500	

Examples of No. 64a from the first two rows of the only known sheet are perforated between stamp and top margin.

1946 (15 Oct). Victory. As Nos. 110/101 of Antigua.

73		1½d. carmine	15	1·25
74		3d. blue	15	20
73s/74s Perf 'SPECIMEN' *Set of* 2			£110	

Pocket handkerchief flaw (R. 1/6)

1949 (14 Mar). Royal Silver Wedding. As Nos. 112/113 of Antigua.

75		2d. black	50	50
		a. Pocket handkerchief flaw	60·00	60·00
76		10s. magenta	10·00	9·50

1949 (10 Oct). 75th Anniversary of UPU. As Nos. 114/117 of Antigua.

77		2d. red-brown	50	1·00
78		3d. deep blue	2·25	2·25
79		5d. deep blue-green	50	1·75
80		1s. blue-black	50	1·75
77/80 *Set of* 4			3·25	6·00

1953 (2 June). Coronation. As No. 120 of Antigua.

81		2d. black and grey-black	1·50	1·25

17 Ysabel Canoe

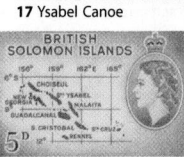

18 Roviana Canoe

19 Map

20 *Miena* (schooner)

21 Henderson Airfield

22 Voyage of HMS *Swallow*

23 Mendaña and *Todos los Santos*

24 Native Constable and Malaita Chief

25 Arms of the Protectorate

(Des Miss I. R. Stinson (½d.), R. Bailey (2½d.), R. A. Sweet (5d., 1s., 1s.3d.), Capt. J. Brett Hilder (6d., 8d., 9d., 5s.). Recess B.W. (½d., 2½d., 5d., 6d., 8d., 9d., 1s., 1s.3d., 5s.), D.L.R. (1d., 2d., 2s.), Waterlow (1½d., 3d., 2s.6d., 10s., £1), until 1962, then D.L.R.)

1956 (1 Mar)–**63.** T **17/25** and similar horiz designs. Wmk Mult Script CA. P 12 (1d., 2d., 2s.), 13 (1½d., 3d., 2s.6d., 10s., £1) or 11½ (others).

82	**17**	½d. orange and purple	15	50
83	**10**	1d. yellow-green and red-brown	15	15
84	**7**	1½d. slate-green and carmine-red	15	1·25
		a. Slate-green and brown-red (31.7.63)	4·00	75
85	**8**	2d. deep brown and dull green	30	30
86	**18**	2½d. black and blue	1·50	60
87	**16**	3d. blue-green and red	85	15
88	**19**	5d. black and blue	60	55
89	**20**	6d. black and turquoise-green	60	25
90	**21**	8d. bright blue and black	1·50	30
90*a*		9d. emerald and black (28.1.60)	3·25	80
91	**22**	1s. slate and yellow-brown	3·00	50
		a. Slate and orange-brown (13.6.61)	10·00	3·75
91*b*	**19**	1s.3d. black and blue (28.1.60)	6·00	1·75
		ba. Black and pale ultramarine (11.12.62)	15·00	3·75
92	**14**	2s. black and carmine	16·00	7·00
93	**11**	2s.6d. emerald and bright purple	7·50	45
		a. Emerald and reddish purple (19.2.63)	27·00	4·00
94	**23**	5s. red-brown	15·00	5·50
95	**24**	10s. sepia	27·00	9·00
96	**25**	£1 black and blue (5.11.58)	35·00	42·00
82/96 *Set of* 17			£100	60·00

See also Nos. 103/111.

LEGISLATIVE COUNCIL

32 Great Frigatebird

(Litho Enschedé)

1961 (19 Jan). New Constitution, 1960. W w **12** (sideways*). P 13×12½.

97	**32**	2d. black and turquoise-green	10	30
		w. Wmk Crown to right of CA	10	30
98		3d. black and rose-carmine	10	10
		w. Wmk Crown to right of CA	10	10
99		9d. black and reddish purple	15	30
		w. Wmk Crown to right of CA	15	30
97/99 *Set of* 3			30	60

* This issue with watermark sideways exists in almost equal quantities with the watermark showing Crown to left or right of CA.

1963 (4 June). Freedom from Hunger. As No. 146 of Antigua.

100		1s.3d. ultramarine	75	35

1963 (2 Sept). Red Cross Centenary. As Nos. 147/148 of Antigua.

101		2d. red and black	25	20
102		9d. red and blue	50	1·75

1963–64. As Nos. 83/85, 87, 89, 90*a* and 91*a*/93, but wmk w **12**.

103	**10**	1d. yellow-green and red-brown (9.7.64)	25	30
104	**7**	1½d. slate-green and red (9.7.64)	3·00	1·00
105	**8**	2d. deep brown and dull green (9.7.64)	25	20
106	**16**	3d. light blue-green and scarlet (16.11.63)	3·00	15
		a. Yellowish green and red (9.7.64)	6·00	4·00
107	**20**	6d. black and turquoise (7.7.64)	60	40
108	**21**	9d. emerald and black (7.7.64)	1·25	35
109	**19**	1s.3d. black and blue (7.7.64)	60	70
110	**14**	2s. black and carmine (9.7.64)	1·00	5·50
111	**11**	2s.6d. emerald and reddish purple (9.7.64)	16·00	15·00
103/111 *Set of* 9			23·00	21·00

33 Makira Food Bowl

2 c

(**48**)

(Des M. Farrar-Bell. Litho D.L.R.)

1965 (24 May). Horiz designs as T **33**. W w **12**. P 13×12½.
112 ½d. black, deep slate-blue and light blue 10 1·40
113 1d. black, orange and yellow 70 60
114 1½d. black, blue and yellow-green 35 65
115 2d. black, ultramarine and light blue 60 1·75
116 2½d. black, light brown and pale yellow-brown 10 1·25
117 3d. black, green and light green 10 10
118 6d. black, magenta and yellow-orange 35 80
119 9d. brownish black, deep bluish green and pale yellow 40 15
120 1s. black, chocolate and magenta 1·00 15
121 1s.3d. black and rose-red 4·50 2·25
122 2s. black, bright purple and lilac 7·50 2·75
123 2s.6d. black, olive-brown and light brown 1·00 70
124 5s. black, ultramarine and violet 13·00 4·50
125 10s. black, olive-green and yellow 18·00 3·00
126 £1 black, deep reddish violet and pink 11·00 4·50
112/126 *Set of* 15 50·00 22·00

Designs: 1d. *Dendrobium veratrifolium* (orchid); 1½d. Chiragra Spider Conch; 2d. Blyth's Hornbill; 2½d. Ysabel shield; 3d. Rennellese club; 6d. Moorish Idol; 9d. Lesser Frigatebird; 1s. *Dendrobium macrophyllum* (orchid); 1s.3d. *Dendrobium spectabilis* (orchid); 2s. Sanford's Sea Eagle; 2s.6d. Malaita belt; 5s. *Ornithoptera victoreae* (butterfly); 10s. Ducorp's Cockatoo; £1, Western canoe figurehead.

1965 (28 June). ITU Centenary. As Nos. 166/167 of Antigua.
127 2d. orange-red and turquoise-blue 20 15
128 3d. turquoise-blue and olive-brown 20 15

1965 (25 Oct). International Co-operation Year. As Nos. 168/169 of Antigua.
129 1d. reddish purple and turquoise-green 10 55
130 2s.6d. deep bluish green and lavender 45 70

1966 (24 Jan). Churchill Commemoration. As Nos. 170/173 of Antigua.
131 2d. new blue 15 10
132 9d. deep green 25 10
133 1s.3d. brown 35 10
134 2s.6d. bluish violet 40 55
131/134 *Set of* 4 1·00 70

(New Currency. 100 cents = 1 Australian, later Solomon Islands dollar)

8 c. Normal '8'

8 c. Inverted '8' (No. 142Aa) (R. 9/2. Later corrected)

1966 (14 Feb)–**67**. Decimal Currency. Nos. 112/126 variously surch as T **48** by De La Rue.

A. Wmk upright
135A 1c. on ½d. black, deep slate-blue and light blue 10 10
136A 2c. on 1d. black, orange and yellow 10 10
137A 3c. on 1½d. black, blue and yellow-green 10 10
138A 4c. on 2d. black, ultramarine and light blue 15 10
139A 5c. on 6d. black, magenta and yellow-orange 15 10
140A 6c. on 2½d. black, light brown and pale yellow-brown 15 10
141A 7c. on 3d. black, green and light green 15 10
142A 8c. on 9d. brownish black, deep bluish green and pale yellow 25 10
a. Inverted '8' 55·00 20·00
b. Surch omitted (vert pair with normal) £5000
143A 10c. on 1s. black, chocolate and magenta 30 10
145A 13c. on 1s.3d. black and rose-red 2·50 15
147A 20c. on 2s. black, bright purple and lilac 2·50 25
148A 25c. on 2s.6d. black, olive-brown and light brown 60 40
150A 50c. on 5s. black, ultramarine and violet (R.) 4·50 1·50
151A $1 on 10s. black, olive-green and yellow 3·50 1·50
152A $2 on £1 black, deep reddish violet and pink 2·25 3·00
135A/152A *Set of* 15 15·00 7·00

B. Wmk sideways
135B 1c. on ½d. black, deep slate-blue and light blue (6.66) 10 10
136B 2c. on 1d. black, orange and yellow (6.66) 10 10
137B 3c. on 1½d. black, blue and yellow-green (6.66) 15 10
138B 4c. on 2d. black, ultramarine and light blue (6.66) 15 10
139B 5c. on 6d. black, magenta and yellow-orange (6.66) 15 10
140B 6c. on 2½d. black, light brown and pale yellow-brown (6.66) 10 10
141B 7c. on 3d. black, green and light green (6.66) 10 10
142B 8c. on 9d. brownish black, deep bluish green and pale yellow (6.66) 15 10
143B 10c. on 1s. black, chocolate and magenta (6.66) 40 10
144B 12c. on 1s.3d. black and rose-red (1.3.67) 65 10
145B 13c. on 1s.3d. black and rose-red (6.66) 4·50 1·75
146B 14c. on 3d. black, green and light green (1.3.67) 40 10
147B 20c. on 2s. black, bright purple and lilac (6.66) 3·25 30
148B 25c. on 2s.6d. black, olive-brown and light brown (6.66) 2·50 35
149B 35c. on 2d. black, ultramarine and light blue (1.3.67) 2·75 25
a. Surch omitted (horiz pair with normal) £4250
b. Surch value only omitted
150B 50c. on 5s. black, ultramarine and violet (R.) (6.66) 12·00 4·00
151B $1 on 10s. black, olive-green and yellow (6.66) 9·00 1·25
152B $2 on £1 black, deep reddish violet and pink (6.66) 9·50 2·00
135B/152B *Set of* 18 40·00 9·00

The positions of the bars in the surcharge vary considerably from stamp to stamp within the sheets.

The stamps with sideways watermark are all from new printings and in some instances there are marked shade variations from Nos. 112/126 which were used for making Nos. 135A/152A.

No. 142Ab comes from the bottom left-hand corner of the sheet and was covered by a paper fold. The bottom stamp in the pair is completely without surcharge and the upper has the surcharge value and one bar missing.

1966 (1 July). World Cup Football Championship. As Nos. 176/177 of Antigua.
153 8c. violet, yellow-green, lake and yellow-brown 15 15
154 35c. chocolate, blue-green, lake and yellow-brown 30 15

1966 (20 Sept). Inauguration of WHO Headquarters, Geneva. As Nos. 178/179 of Antigua.
155 3c. black, yellow-green and light blue 20 10
156 50c. black, light purple and yellow-brown 60 20

1966 (1 Dec). 20th Anniversary of UNESCO As Nos. 196/198 of Antigua.
157 3c. slate-violet, red, yellow and orange 15 10
158 25c. orange-yellow, violet and deep olive 30 15
159 $1 black, bright purple and orange 75 70
157/159 *Set of* 3 1·10 85

49 Henderson Field

(Des V. Whiteley. Photo Harrison)

1967 (28 Aug). 25th Anniversary of Guadalcanal Campaign (Pacific War). T **49** and similar horiz design. Multicoloured. W w **12**. P 14×14½.
160 8c. Type **49** 15 15
161 35c. Red Beach landings 15 15

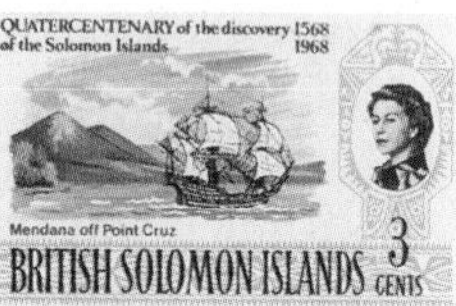

51 Mendaña's *Todos los Santos* off Point Cruz

(Des V. Whiteley. Photo Harrison)

1968 (7 Feb). Quatercentenary of the Discovery of Solomon Islands. T **51** and similar horiz designs. Multicoloured. W w **12**. P 14.
162 3c. Type **51** 20 10
163 8c. Arrival of missionaries 20 10
164 35c. Pacific Campaign, World War II 40 30
165 $1 Proclamation of the Protectorate 60 1·75
162/165 *Set of* 4 1·25 2·00

55 Vine Fishing

(Des R. Granger Barrett. Photo Harrison)

1968 (20 May)–**71**. Horiz designs as T **55**. Chalk-surfaced paper. W w **12**. P 14½.
166 1c. turquoise-blue, black and brown 10 10
a. Glazed, ordinary paper (9.8.71) 1·00 1·00
aw. Wmk inverted 1·00
167 2c. apple-green, black and brown 10 10
aw. Wmk inverted. Glazed, ordinary paper (9.8.71) 1·75 1·00
168 3c. green, myrtle-green and black 10 10
a. Glazed, ordinary paper (9.8.71) 1·00 1·00
169 4c. bright purple, black and brown 15 10
a. Glazed, ordinary paper (9.8.71) 1·00 1·00
170 6c. multicoloured 30 10
171 8c. multicoloured 25 10
a. Glazed, ordinary paper (9.8.71) 1·50 1·60
172 12c. yellow-ochre, brown-red and black 50 50
a. Glazed, ordinary paper (9.8.71) 2·25 2·50
aw. Wmk inverted 3·00
173 14c. orange-red, chocolate and black 2·00 3·50
174 15c. multicoloured 80 80
a. Glazed, ordinary paper (9.8.71) 2·50 3·75
175 20c. bright blue, red and black 4·00 3·00
a. Glazed, ordinary paper (9.8.71) 4·75 8·00
176 24c. rose-red, black and yellow 1·50 3·25
177 35c. multicoloured 1·50 30
178 45c. multicoloured 1·00 30
179 $1 violet-blue light green and black 2·00 1·50
180 $2 multicoloured 8·00 3·50
w. Wmk inverted £140
166/180 *Set of* 15 20·00 15·00
166a/175a *Set of* 8 14·00 18·00

Designs: 2c. Kite fishing; 3c. Platform fishing; 4c. Net fishing; 6c. Gold Lip shell diving; 8c. Night fishing; 12c. Boat building; 14c. Cocoa; 15c. Road building; 20c. Geological survey; 24c. Hauling timber; 35c. Copra; 45c. Harvesting rice; $1, Honiara Port; $2, Internal air service.

The stamps on glazed, ordinary paper exist with PVA gum only. The 1c. to 12c. and 20c. on chalk-surfaced paper exist with PVA gum as well as gum arabic, but the others exist with gum arabic only.

70 Map of Australasia and Diagram **71** Basketball Player

(Des R. Gates. Litho Enschedé)

1969 (10 Feb). Inaugural Year of the South Pacific University. P 12½×12.
181 **70** 3c. multicoloured 10 10
182 12c. multicoloured 10 10
183 35c. multicoloured 15 10
181/183 *Set of* 3 30 25

(Des J. Cooter. Photo Harrison)

1969 (13 Aug). Third South Pacific Games, Port Moresby. T **71** and similar vert designs. Multicoloured. W w **12** (sideways*). P 14½×14.
184 3c. Type **71** 10 10
w. Wmk Crown to right of CA 65 80
185 8c. Footballer 10 10
186 14c. Sprinter 10 10
187 45c. Rugby player 20 15
184/187 *Set of* 4 45 40
MS188 126×120 mm. Nos. 184/187 2·75 8·00

* The normal sideways watermark shows Crown to left of CA, *as seen from the back of the stamp*.

Stamps from the miniature sheets differ slightly from those in the ordinary sheets, particularly the 14c. value, which has a shadow below the feet on the runner. The footballer and rugby player on the 8c. and 45c. values also have shadows below their feet, but these are more pronounced than on the stamps from the ordinary sheets.

75 South Sea Island with Star of Bethlehem **76** Southern Cross, 'PAX' and Frigatebird (stained glass window)

(Des L. Curtis. Photo Harrison)

1969 (21 Nov). Christmas. W w **12** (sideways). P 14½×14.
189 **75** 8c. black, violet and turquoise-green 10 10
190 **76** 35c. multicoloured 20 20

77 'Paid' Stamp, New South Wales 1896–1906 2d. Stamp and 1906–1907 Tulagi Postmark

(Des G. Drummond. Litho B.W.)

1970 (15 Apr). Inauguration of New GPO Honiara. T **77** and similar horiz designs. W w **12** (sideways). P 13.
191 7c. light magenta, deep blue and black 15 15
192 14c. sage-green, deep blue and black 20 15
193 18c. multicoloured 20 15
194 23c. multicoloured 20 20
191/194 *Set of* 4 65 60

Designs: 7c. T **77**; 14c. 1906–1907 2d. stamp and C. M. Woodford; 18c. 1910–1914 5s. stamp and Tulagi postmark, 1913; 23c. New GPO, Honiara.

81 Coat of Arms **83** British Red Cross HQ, Honiara

(Des V. Whiteley. Photo Harrison)

1970 (15 June). New Constitution. T **81** and similar design. W w **12** (sideways on 18c.). P 14½×14 (18c.) or 14×14½ (35c.).
195 18c. multicoloured 15 10
196 35c. pale apple-green, deep blue and ochre 35 20

Designs: Vert—18c. T **81**. Horiz—35c. Map.

(Des L. Curtis. Litho Questa)

1970 (17 Aug). Centenary of British Red Cross. T **83** and similar horiz design. W w **12** (sideways). P 14×14½.

197		3c. multicoloured	10	10
198		35c. blue, vermilion and black	25	20

Designs: 3c. T **83**; 35c. Wheelchair and map.

86 Reredos (Altar Screen)

(Des L. Curtis. Litho J.W.)

1970 (19 Oct). Christmas. T **86** and similar design. W w **12** (sideways on 45c.). P 14×13½ (8c.) or 13½×14 (45c.).

199		8c. ochre and bluish violet	10	10
200		45c. chestnut, yellow-orange and blackish brown	25	20

Design: Vert—8c. Carved Angel. Horiz—45c. T **86**.

STAMP BOOKLETS

1959 (1 Apr). Black on buff (No. SB1) or grey (No. SB2) covers. Stapled.

SB1	4s. booklet containing 8×1d., 8×2d. and 8×3d. (Nos. 83, 85, 87) in blocks of 4	30·00
SB2	11s. booklet containing 8×1d. and 8×8d., and 4×3d. and 4×1s. (Nos. 83, 87, 90/91) in blocks of 4	40·00

1960 (1 May)–**64**. Black on green (No. SB3) or orange (No. SB4) covers. Stapled.

SB3	5s. booklet containing 8×1d., 8×1½d., 8×2d. and 8×3d. (Nos. 83/85, 87) in blocks of 4	50·00
SB4	£1 booklet containing 8×1d., 8×2d., 8×3d., 8×9d. and 8×1s.3d. (Nos. 83, 85, 87, 90*a*, 91*a*) in blocks of 4	80·00
	a. Contents as No. SB4, but Nos. 103, 85, 106*a*, 108/109 (1964)	

POSTAGE DUE STAMPS

D **1**

(Typo B.W.)

1940 (1 Sept). Wmk Mult Script CA. P 12.

D1	D **1**	1d. emerald-green	6·50	7·00
D2		2d. scarlet	7·00	7·00
D3		3d. brown	7·00	11·00
D4		4d. blue	11·00	11·00
D5		5d. grey-green	12·00	21·00
D6		6d. purple	12·00	16·00
D7		1s. violet	14·00	29·00
D8		1s.6d. turquoise-green	38·00	48·00
D1/D8 *Set of* 8			95·00	£130
D1s/D8s Perf 'SPECIMEN' *Set of* 8			£250	

British Virgin Islands

CROWN COLONY

Apart from the 1951 Legislative Council issue, the word 'BRITISH' did not appear regularly on the stamps until 1968 when it was introduced to avoid confusion with the nearby Virgin Islands of the United States (the former Danish West Indies).

Most mail from the early years of the islands' history was sent via the Danish island of St. Thomas.

It is not known exactly when the first post office, or agency, was established on Tortola, but an entry in a GPO account book suggest that it was operating by 1787 and the earliest letter postmarked 'TORTOLA' dates from June of that year. The stamps of Great Britain were used from 1858 to May 1860, when the colonial authorities assumed responsibility for the overseas mails from the British GPO.

For illustrations of the handstamp and postmark types see BRITISH POST OFFICES ABROAD notes, following GREAT BRITAIN.

TORTOLA

CROWNED-CIRCLE HANDSTAMPS

CC1	CC **1** TORTOLA (R.) (15.12.1842) *Price on cover*	£6500
CC2	CC **5** TORTOLA (R.) (21.6.1854) *Price on cover*	£22000

No. CC2 is known used as an Official Paid mark during the years 1900 to 1918. *Price on cover* £750.

Stamps of GREAT BRITAIN cancelled 'A13' as Type **2**.

1858–60.

Z1	1d. rose-red (1857), perf 14	£4250
Z2	4d. rose (1857)	£5500
Z3	6d. lilac (1856)	£1800
Z4	1s. green (1856)	

PRICES FOR STAMPS ON COVER TO 1945

Nos. 1/7	*from* × 30
Nos. 8/9	*from* × 40
No. 10	—
No. 11	*from* × 10
No. 12	*from* × 30
No. 13	—
Nos. 14/14*b*	*from* × 10
Nos. 15/17	*from* × 30
Nos. 18/19	*from* × 40
No. 20	—
Nos. 21/21*b*	*from* × 20
Nos. 22/22b	*from* × 30
Nos. 24/31	*from* × 25
Nos. 32/34	*from* × 50
Nos. 35/37	*from* × 30
Nos. 38/41	*from* × 15
No. 42	*from* × 30
Nos. 43/50	*from* × 8
Nos. 54/77	*from* × 6
Nos. 78/81	*from* × 6
Nos. 82/101	*from* × 3
Nos. 103/106	*from* × 4
Nos. 107/109	*from* × 6
Nos. 110/121	*from* × 2

1 St Ursula

2 St Ursula

(Litho Nissen & Parker from original dies by Waterlow)

1866 (Dec). No wmk. P 12.

(a) White wove paper

1	**1**	1d. green	50·00	60·00
2		1d. deep green	55·00	65·00
3	**2**	6d. rose	90·00	£110
		a. Large 'V' in 'VIRGIN' (R. 2/1)	£375	£475
4		6d. deep rose	£130	£140
		a. Large 'V' in 'VIRGIN' (R. 2/1)	£425	£500

(b) Toned paper

5	**1**	1d. green	50·00	60·00
		a. Perf 15×12	£5500	£7000
6		1d. deep green	£100	£120
7	**2**	6d. rose-red	60·00	90·00
		a. Large 'V' in 'VIRGIN' (R. 2/1)	£275	£375

The above were printed in sheets of 25.

6d. stamps showing part of the papermaker's watermark ('A. Cowan & Sons Extra Superfine A. C. & S.') are worth 50% more.

Beware of fakes of No. 5a made from perf 12 stamps.

3

4

Normal

Variety

1s. Long-tailed 'S' in 'ISLANDS' (R. 3/1)

(Litho and typo (figure of the Virgin) (1s.) or litho (others) Nissen and Parker from original dies by Waterlow)

1867–70. No wmk. P 15. 1s. with double-lined frame.

(a) White wove paper

8	**1**	1d. yellow-green (1868)	80·00	80·00
9		1d. blue-green (1870)	65·00	70·00
10	**2**	6d. pale rose	£600	£600
11	**4**	1s. black and rose-carmine	£275	£375
		a. Long-tailed 'S'	£900	£1100

(b) Greyish (No. 14) or toned paper (others)

12	**1**	1d. yellow-green (1868)	85·00	80·00
13	**2**	6d. dull rose (1868)	£300	£350
14	**4**	1s. black and rose-carmine (*greyish paper*)	£275	£375
		a. Long-tailed 'S'	£900	£1100
14*b*		1s. black and rose-carmine (*toned paper*)	£325	£375
		ba. Long-tailed 'S'	£900	£1100

(c) Pale rose paper

15	**3**	4d. lake-red	55·00	75·00

(d) Buff paper

16	**3**	4d. lake-red	45·00	60·00
17		4d. lake-brown	45·00	60·00

The thin lines of the frame on the 1s. are close together and sometimes merge into one.

The 1d. from the 1868 printing was in sheets of 20 (5×4) with narrow margins between the stamps. Later printings were in sheets of 12 (3×4) with wider margins. The 4d. was in sheets of 25; and the remaining two values in sheets of 20 (5×4).

The greyish paper used for Nos. 14 and 20 often shows traces of blue.

1867. Nos. 11 and 14/14*b* with crimson frames superimposed extending into margins. P 15.

18	**4**	1s. black and rose-carmine (*white paper*)	90·00	£100
		a. Long-tailed 'S'	£300	£350
		b. Figure of Virgin omitted	£150000	
19		1s. black and rose-carmine (*toned paper*)	75·00	85·00
		a. Long-tailed 'S'	£225	£275
20		1s. black and rose-carmine (*greyish paper*)	£750	£900
		a. Long-tailed 'S'	£2000	£2250

1868. Nos. 11 and 14*b* with frame lines retouched so as to make them single lines. Margins remain white. P 15.

21	**4**	1s. black and rose-carmine (*white paper*)	£160	£190
		a. Long-tailed 'S'	£500	£600
21*b*		1s. black and rose-carmine (*toned paper*)	£160	£190
		ba. Long-tailed 'S'	£500	£600

(Litho D.L.R.)

1878. Wmk Crown CC (sideways). P 14.

22	**1**	1d. green	85·00	£100
		a. Yellow-green	£170	£130
		b. Wmk upright	£100	£130

6 (Die I)

4D

(7)

(Typo D.L.R.)

1879–80. Wmk Crown CC. P 14.

24	**6**	1d. emerald-green (1880)	75·00	90·00
25		2½d. red-brown	£120	£130

1883 (June)–**84.** Wmk Crown CA. P 14.

26	**6**	½d. yellow-buff	85·00	85·00
		x. Wmk reversed		
27		½d. dull green (*shades*) (11.83)	6·50	18·00
		b. Top left triangle detached	£325	£475
29		1d. pale rose (15.9.83)	50·00	50·00
		a. Deep rose (1884)	65·00	70·00
31		2½d. ultramarine (9.84)	4·25	16·00
		b. Top left triangle detached	£300	
		w. Wmk inverted	£180	

For illustration of 'top left triangle detached' variety see above No. 21 of Antigua.

(Litho D.L.R.)

1887–89. Wmk Crown CA. P 14.

32	**1**	1d. red (5.89)	3·75	9·00
		x. Wmk reversed	£225	
33		1d. rose-red	3·25	8·50
34		1d. rose	5·50	14·00
35	**3**	4d. chestnut	35·00	65·00
		x. Wmk reversed	£300	
36		4d. pale chestnut	35·00	65·00
37		4d. brown-red	45·00	70·00
38	**2**	6d. dull violet	19·00	50·00
39		6d. deep violet	19·00	50·00
40	**4**	1s. sepia (2.89)	80·00	£100
41		1s. brown *to* deep brown	45·00	70·00
34s/40s Optd 'SPECIMEN' *Set of* 4			£300	

The De La Rue transfers of T **1** to **4** are new transfers and differ from those of Messrs. Nissen and Parker, particularly T **4**.

1888 (July). Nos. 18/19. Surch with T **7**, in violet, in Antigua.

42	**4**	4d. on 1s. black and rose-carmine (*toned paper*)	£140	£160
		a. Surch double	£8500	
		b. Surch inverted (in pair with normal)	£55000	
		c. Long-tailed 'S'	£500	£600
42*d*		4d. on 1s. black and rose-carmine (*white paper*)	£180	£225
		dc. Long-tailed 'S'	£600	£750

The special issues for Virgin Islands were superseded on 31 October 1890, by the general issue for Leeward Islands. In 1899, however, a new special issue, Nos. 43/50, appeared; it did not supersede the general issue for Leeward Islands, but was used concurrently, as were all subsequent issues, until 1 July 1956 when the general Leeward Islands stamps were withdrawn.

8

9

10

(Recess D.L.R.)

1899 (Jan). Wmk Crown CA. P 14.

43	**8**	½d. yellow-green	4·00	55
		a. Error. 'HALFPFNNY' (R. 10/1)	85·00	£120
		b. Error. 'HALΓPENNY' (R. 8/2)	85·00	£120
		c. Imperf between (horiz pair)	£13000	
44		1d. brick-red	6·00	2·00
45		2½d. ultramarine	12·00	2·75
46		4d. brown	6·00	22·00
		a. Error 'FOURPENCF' (R.10/3)	£750	£1100
47		6d. dull violet	8·50	3·00
48		7d. deep green	13·00	6·00
49		1s. brown-yellow	23·00	35·00
50		5s. indigo	80·00	90·00
43/50 *Set of* 8			£130	£140
43s/50s Optd 'SPECIMEN' *Set of* 8			£190	

Nos. 43a/43b and 46a were corrected after the first printing.

(Typo D.L.R.)

1904 (1 June). Wmk Mult Crown CA. P 14.

54	**9**	½d. dull purple and green	1·00	40
55		1d. dull purple and scarlet	2·50	35
56	**10**	2d. dull purple and ochre	7·50	3·50
57	**9**	2½d. dull purple and ultramarine	4·50	2·25
58	**10**	3d. dull purple and black	6·50	2·50
59	**9**	6d. dull purple and brown	4·50	2·50
60	**10**	1s. green and scarlet	8·00	7·50
61		2s.6d. green and black	40·00	55·00
62	**9**	5s. green and blue	50·00	70·00
54/62 *Set of* 9			£110	£130
54s/62s Optd 'SPECIMEN' *Set of* 9			£160	

11

12

(Typo D.L.R.)

1913 (Feb)–**19**. Die I. Chalk-surfaced paper (3d. to 5s.). Wmk Mult Crown CA. P 14.

69	**11**	½d. green	4·00	6·50
		a. Yellow-green (8.16)	5·00	15·00
		b. Blue-green and deep green (3.19)	1·25	6·00
70		1d. deep red	9·00	11·00
		a. Deep red and carmine (10.17)	2·25	14·00
		b. Scarlet (10.17)	2·25	14·00
		c. Carmine-red (3.19)	50·00	27·00
71	**12**	2d. grey	8·50	30·00
		a. Slate-grey (1919)	9·50	45·00
72	**11**	2½d. bright blue	9·00	9·00
73	**12**	3d. purple/*yellow*	2·75	6·50
74	**11**	6d. dull and bright purple	10·00	22·00
75	**12**	1s. black/*blue-green*	3·25	11·00
76		2s.6d. black and red/*blue*	50·00	55·00
77	**11**	5s. green and red/*yellow*	45·00	£130
69/77 *Set of* 9			£110	£250
69s/77s Optd 'SPECIMEN' *Set of* 9			£200	

Stock of the original printing of the ½d., No. 69 was exhausted by January 1916 and Leeward Islands ½d. stamps were used until the yellow-green printing, No. 69*a*, arrived in August 1916.

WAR STAMP

(**13**)

14

1916 (20 Oct)–**19**. Optd with T **13** by D.L.R.

78	**11**	1d. carmine	1·75	24·00
		a. Watermark sideways	£1100	
		b. Pale red/bluish	50	7·00
		bw. Wmk inverted	75·00	
		by. Wmk inverted and reversed	£150	
		c. Scarlet (11.3.19)	2·50	6·00
		d. Short opt (right pane R.10/1)	25·00	
79	**12**	3d. purple/*yellow*	7·00	38·00
		a. Purple/lemon (12.3.17)	8·50	23·00
		b. Purple/buff-yellow (11.3.19)	9·00	30·00
		bw. Wmk inverted	10·00	50·00
		by. Wmk inverted and reversed		
		c. Short opt (right pane R. 10/1)	60·00	
78s/79s Optd 'SPECIMEN' *Set of* 2			75·00	

Nos. 78d and 79c show the overprint 2 mm high instead of 2½ mm.

No. 78*c* is known with the 'A' of the 'CA' watermark sideways.

1921 (18 Nov). As 1913–1919, but Die II and wmk Mult Script CA.

80	**11**	½d. green	16·00	60·00
		w. Wmk inverted		
81		1d. scarlet and deep carmine	11·00	35·00
80s/81s Optd 'SPECIMEN' *Set of* 2			85·00	

(Typo D.L.R.)

1922 (Mar)–**28**. P 14.

(a) Wmk Mult Crown CA. Chalk surfaced paper

82	**14**	3d. purple/*pale yellow* (15.6.22)	65	17·00
83		1s. black/*emerald* (15.6.22)	75	17·00
84		2s.6d. black and red/*blue* (15.6.22)	5·50	11·00
85		5s. green and red/*pale yellow* (15.6.22)	48·00	£110
82/85 *Set of* 4			50·00	£140
82s/85s Optd 'SPECIMEN' *Set of* 4			£100	

(b) Wmk Mult Script CA. Chalk-surfaced paper (5d. to 5s.)

86	**14**	½d. dull green	85	2·75
87		1d. rose-carmine	60	60
88		1d. bright violet (1.27)	1·75	7·50
89		1d. scarlet (12.28)	28·00	14·00
90		1½d. carmine-red (1.27)	1·75	3·25
91		1½d. Venetian red (11.28)	2·50	1·50
92		2d. grey	1·25	6·00
93		2½d. pale bright blue	6·50	23·00
94		2½d. dull orange (1.9.23)	1·25	2·75
95		2½d. bright blue (1.27)	19·00	3·50
96		3d. purple/*pale yellow* (2.28)	2·25	11·00
97		5d. dull purple and olive (6.22)	5·50	48·00
98		6d. dull and bright purple (6.22)	1·75	6·50
99		1s. black/*emerald* (2.28)	2·50	17·00
100		2s.6d. black and red/*blue* (2.28)	19·00	55·00
101		5s. green and red/*yellow* (1.9.23)	24·00	75·00
86/101 *Set of* 16			£100	£225
86s/101s Optd or Perf (Nos. 89, 91) 'SPECIMEN' *Set of* 16			£350	

In the 1½d. stamps the value is in colour on a white ground.

1935 (6 May). Silver Jubilee. As Nos. 91/94 of Antigua but printed by Waterlow. P 11×12.

103		1d. deep blue and scarlet	1·25	9·00
		k. Kite and vertical log	£160	
		l. Kite and horizontal log	£160	£275
104		1½d. ultramarine and grey	1·25	7·50
		k. Kite and vertical log	£170	
		l. Kite and horizontal log	£170	£275
		m. 'Bird' by turret	£200	£300
105		2½d. brown and deep blue	4·75	8·00
		k. Kite and vertical log	£190	
		l. Kite and horizontal log	£200	£275
106		1s. slate and purple	21·00	40·00
		k. Kite and vertical log	£425	
		l. Kite and horizontal log	£400	£500
103/106 *Set of* 4			25·00	55·00
103s/106s Perf 'SPECIMEN' *Set of* 4			£140	

For illustrations of plate varieties see Omnibus section following Zanzibar.

1937 (12 May). Coronation. As Nos. 95/97 of Antigua. P 11×11½.

107		1d. carmine	1·00	3·75
108		1½d. yellow-brown	75	3·00
109		2½d. blue	60	1·50
107/109 *Set of* 3			2·10	7·50
107s/109s Perf 'SPECIMEN' *Set of* 3			£110	

15 King George VI and Badge of Colony

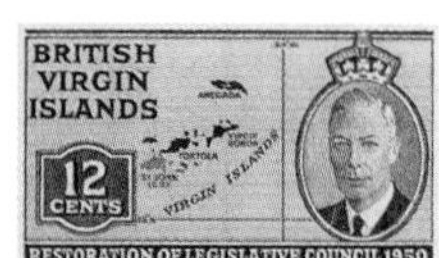

16 Map

(Photo Harrison)

1938 (1 Aug)–**47**. Chalk-surfaced paper. Wmk Mult Script CA. P 14.

110	**15**	½d. green	3·75	4·00
		a. Ordinary paper (10.43)	1·50	1·00
111		1d. scarlet	6·50	2·50
		a. Ordinary paper (10.43)	2·50	1·75
112		1½d. red-brown	8·00	8·00
		a. Ordinary paper (10.43)	3·25	1·75
		w. Wmk inverted	†	£2250
113		2d. grey	8·00	3·25
		a. Ordinary paper (10.43)	3·25	1·75
114		2½d. ultramarine	4·75	2·50
		a. Ordinary paper (10.43)	3·75	2·75
115		3d. orange	9·00	1·50
		a. Ordinary paper (10.43)	2·25	1·00
116		6d. mauve	14·00	3·50
		a. Ordinary paper (10.43)	6·00	2·25
117		1s. olive-brown	24·00	6·00
		a. Ordinary paper (8.42)	6·00	2·25
118		2s.6d. sepia	70·00	13·00
		a. Ordinary paper (8.42)	17·00	6·50
119		5s. carmine	70·00	15·00
		a. Ordinary paper (8.42)	20·00	7·50
120		10s. blue (1.12.47)	9·00	10·00
121		£1 black (1.12.47)	11·00	24·00
110a/121 *Set of* 12			75·00	55·00
110s/121s Perf 'SPECIMEN' *Set of* 12			£400	

The ordinary paper, used as a substitute for the chalk-surfaced for printings between 1942 and 1945, is thick, smooth and opaque.

1946 (1 Nov). Victory. As Nos. 110/111 of Antigua.

122		1½d. lake-brown	10	10
123		3d. orange	10	60
122s/123s Perf 'SPECIMEN' *Set of* 2			90·00	

1949 (3 Jan). Royal Silver Wedding. As Nos. 112/113 of Antigua.

124		2½d. ultramarine	10	10
125		£1 black	16·00	24·00

1949 (10 Oct). 75th Anniversary of UPU. As Nos. 114/117 of Antigua.

126		2½d. ultramarine	30	3·25
127		3d. orange	1·50	2·75
128		6d. magenta	45	75
129		1s. olive	35	50
126/129 *Set of* 4			2·40	6·50

(New Currency. 100 cents = 1 BWI dollar)

1951 (16 Feb–10 Apr). Inauguration of BWI University College. As Nos. 118/119 of Antigua.

130		3c. black and brown-red (10.4)	40	2·50
131		12c. black and reddish violet	60	1·75

Issue of the 3c. value was delayed when the supplies were sent to Puerto Rico by mistake.

(Recess Waterlow)

1951 (2 Apr). Restoration of Legislative Council. Wmk Mult Script CA. P 14½×14.

132	**16**	6c. orange	1·00	2·25
133		12c. purple	1·25	1·00
134		24c. olive	1·00	1·25
135		$1.20 carmine	3·50	2·00
132/135 *Set of* 4			6·00	6·00

17 Sombrero Lighthouse

18 Map of Jost Van Dyke

19 Sheep industry

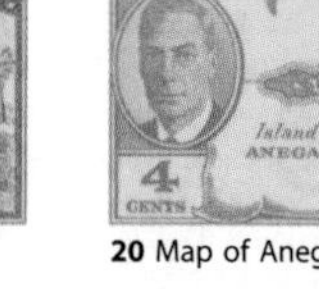

20 Map of Anegada

21 Cattle industry

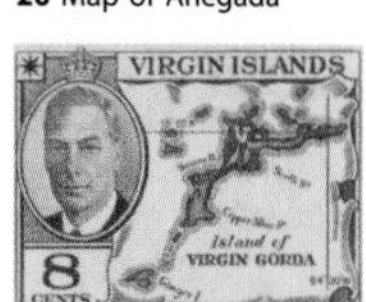

22 Map of Virgin Gorda

23 Map of Tortola

24 Badge of the Presidency

25 Dead Man's Chest

26 Sir Francis Drake Channel

27 Road Town

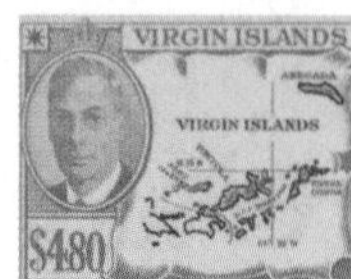

28 Map of Virgin Islands

(Recess D.L.R.)

1952 (15 Apr). T **17/28**. Wmk Mult Script CA. P 12½×13 (vert) or 13×12½ (horiz).

136	**17**	1c. black	80	4·00
137	**18**	2c. deep green	70	30
138	**19**	3c. black and brown	80	2·75
139	**20**	4c. carmine-red	70	3·00
140	**21**	5c. claret and black	1·50	50
141	**22**	8c. bright blue	1·00	2·25
142	**23**	12c. dull violet	1·00	2·25
143	**24**	24c. deep brown	70	50
144	**25**	60c. yellow-green and blue	6·50	11·00
145	**26**	$1.20 black and bright blue	5·50	12·00
146	**27**	$2.40 yellowish green and red-brown	17·00	19·00
147	**28**	$4.80 bright blue and carmine	22·00	21·00
136/147 *Set of* 12			50·00	65·00

1953 (2 June). Coronation. As No. 120 of Antigua.

148		2c. black and green	30	1·25

29 Map of Tortola

30 Virgin Islands sloop

31 Nelthrop Red Poll bull

32 Road Harbour

33 Mountain travel

34 Badge of the Presidency

35 Beach scene

36 *New Idea* (sloop) under construction

37 White Cedar tree

38 Skipjack Tuna ('Bonito')

39 Coronation celebrations, Treasury Square

40 Brown Pelican

41 Magnificent Frigatebird

(Recess D.L.R.)

1956 (1 Nov)–**62**. T **29/41**. Wmk Mult Script CA. P 13×12½ (½c. to $1.20) or 12×11½ ($2.40 and $4.80).

149	**29**	½c. black and reddish purple	1·25	30
		a. Black and deep reddish purple (19.4.60)	3·25	4·75
150	**30**	1c. turquoise-blue and slate	1·50	2·00
		a. Turquoise and slate-violet (26.11.62)	23·00	28·00
151	**31**	2c. vermilion and black	30	10
152	**32**	3c. blue and deep olive	30	30
153	**33**	4c. deep brown and turquoise-green	1·00	30
154	**34**	5c. grey-black	50	10
155	**35**	8c. yellow-orange and deep blue	2·50	40
156	**36**	12c. ultramarine and rose-red	4·00	75
157	**37**	24c. myrtle-green and brown-orange	1·00	65
158	**38**	60c. indigo and yellow-orange	8·50	8·00
159	**39**	$1.20 deep yellow-green and carmine-red	7·00	13·00
160	**40**	$2.40 lemon and deep dull purple	48·00	17·00
161	**41**	$4.80 blackish brown and turquoise-blue	48·00	17·00
149/161 *Set of 13*			£110	50·00

(New Currency. 100 cents = 1 US dollar)

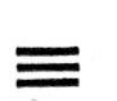
1¢

(**42**)

1962 (10 Dec). As Nos. 149/153 and 155/161, but W w **12**, surch in US currency as T **42** by D.L.R.

162	1c. on ½c. black and deep reddish purple	30	20
163	2c. on 1c. turquoise and slate-violet	1·75	15
164	3c. on 2c. vermilion and black	70	15
165	4c. on 3c. black and deep olive	50	15
166	5c. on 4c. deep brown and turquoise-green	30	15
167	8c. on 8c. yellow-orange and deep blue	30	15
168	10c. on 12c. ultramarine and rose-red	2·00	15
169	12c. on 24c. myrtle-green and brown-orange	30	15
170	25c. on 60c. indigo and yellow-orange	2·75	45
171	70c. on $1.20 deep yellow-green and carmine-red	35	45
	a. Stop to right of C in surcharge instead of beneath it (in pair with normal)	4·00	3·50
172	$1.40 on $2.40 lemon and deep dull purple	9·50	4·50
173	$2.80 on $4.80 blackish brown and turquoise-blue	9·50	4·50
162/173 *Set of 12*		25·00	10·00

No. 171a occurs on the first stamp on Rows 1 to 10.

1963 (4 June). Freedom from Hunger. As No. 146 of Antigua.

174	25c. reddish violet	20	10

1963 (2 Sept). Red Cross Centenary. As Nos. 147/148 of Antigua.

175	2c. red and black	15	1·60
176	25c. red and blue	50	20

1964 (23 Apr). 400th Birth Anniversary of William Shakespeare. As No. 164 of Antigua.

177	10c. bright blue	20	10

43 Skipjack Tuna

44 Soper's Hole

45 Brown Pelican

46 Dead Man's Chest

47 Road Harbour

48 Fallen Jerusalem

49 The Baths, Virgin Gorda

50 Map of Virgin Islands

51 *Youth of Tortola,* Tortola-St Thomas ferry

52 The Towers, Tortola

53 Beef Island Airfield

54 Map of Tortola

55 Virgin Gorda

56 Yachts at anchor

57 Badge of the Colony

(Des and recess D.L.R.)

1964 (2 Nov)–**68**. T **43/57**. W w **12**. P 11½×12 ($2.80), 13×13½ (70c., $1, $1.40), or 13×12½ (others).

178	**43**	1c. blue and olive-green	30	2·25
179	**44**	2c. yellow-olive and rose-red	15	30
180	**45**	3c. sepia and turquoise-blue	4·75	2·75
181	**46**	4c. black and carmine-red	80	3·25
182	**47**	5c. black and deep bluish green	2·25	2·25
183	**48**	6c. black and brown-orange	30	85
184	**49**	8c. black and magenta	30	1·00
185	**50**	10c. lake and deep lilac	6·00	1·50
		a. Bright lake and reddish lilac (26.11.68)	20·00	4·25
186	**51**	12c. deep bluish green and deep violet-blue	2·50	3·50
187	**52**	15c. yellow-green and grey-black	1·50	2·25
188	**53**	25c. green and purple	14·00	2·50
189	**54**	70c. black and yellow-brown	4·25	8·50
190	**55**	$1 yellow-green and chestnut	4·25	3·50
191	**56**	$1.40 light blue and rose	24·00	14·00
192	**57**	$2.80 black and bright purple	28·00	15·00
178/192 *Set of 15*			80·00	55·00

1965 (17 May). ITU Centenary. As Nos. 166/167 of Antigua.

193	4c. yellow and turquoise	20	10
194	25c. light blue and orange-buff	45	20

1965 (25 Oct). International Co-operation Year. As Nos. 168/169 of Antigua.

195	1c. reddish purple and turquoise-green	10	15
196	25c. deep bluish green and lavender	30	15

1966 (24 Jan). Churchill Commemoration. As Nos. 170/173 of Antigua.

197	1c. new blue	10	40
198	2c. deep green	50	40
199	10c. brown	1·10	10
200	25c. bluish violet	1·50	25
197/200 *Set of 4*		2·75	1·00

1966 (22 Feb). Royal Visit. As Nos. 174/175 of Antigua.

201	4c. black and ultramarine	30	10
202	70c. black and magenta	1·10	45

58 *Atrato I* (paddle-steamer), 1866

(Des R. Granger Barrett. Litho B.W.)

1966 (25 Apr). Stamp Centenary. T **58** and similar horiz designs. W w **12** (sideways). P 13.

203	5c. black, red, yellow and emerald	35	10
204	10c. black, green and rose-red/*cream*	35	10
205	25c. black, rose-red and blue/*pale green*	55	10
206	60c. black, red and green/*pale blue*	1·00	2·50
203/206 *Set of 4*		2·00	2·50

Design: 5c. T **58**; 10c. 1d. and 6d. stamps of 1866; 25c. Air mail transport, Beef Island, and 6d. stamp of 1866; 60c. Landing mail at Roadtown, 1866 and 1d. stamp of 1866.

50c.

═══

(**62**)

1966 (15 Sept). As Nos. 189 and 191/192 but wmk sideways, surch as T **62**.

207	50c. on 70c. black and yellow-brown	1·25	90
208	$1.50 on $1.40 light blue and rose	2·25	2·00
209	$3 on $2.80 black and bright purple	2·25	2·75
207/209 *Set of 3*		5·00	5·00

1966 (1 Dec). 20th Anniversary of UNESCO. As Nos. 196/198 of Antigua.

210	2c. slate-violet, red, yellow and orange	10	10
211	12c. orange-yellow, violet and deep olive	45	10
212	60c. black, bright purple and orange	1·25	45
210/212 *Set of 3*		1·60	60

63 Map of Virgin Islands

(Des G. Vasarhelyi. Photo Harrison)

1967 (18 Apr). New Constitution. W w **12**. P 14½.

213	**63**	2c. multicoloured	10	10
214		10c. multicoloured	15	10
		w. Wmk inverted	25·00	
215		25c. multicoloured	15	10
		w. Wmk inverted	9·00	
216		$1 multicoloured	55	40
213/216 *Set of 4*			75	55

64 *Mercury* (cable ship) and Bermuda–Tortola Link

(Des G. Drummond, Photo Harrison)

1967 (14 Sept). Inauguration of Bermuda–Tortola Telephone Service. T **64** and similar horiz designs. Multicoloured. W w **12**. P 14½.

217	4c. Type **64**	30	10
218	10c. Chalwell Telecommunications Station	20	10
219	50c. *Mercury* (cable ship)	60	30
217/219 *Set of 3*		1·00	40

67 Blue Marlin

(Des V. Whiteley. Photo Enschedé)

1968 (2 Jan). Game Fishing. T **67** and similar horiz designs. W w **12** (sideways). P 12½×12.

220	2c. multicoloured	10	1·75
221	10c. multicoloured	25	10
222	25c. black, blue and bright violet	55	10
223	40c. multicoloured	85	85
220/223	*Set of 4*	1·60	2·50

Designs: 2c. T **67**; 10c. Cobia; 25c. Wahoo; 40c. Fishing launch and map.

(**71**)

72 Dr. Martin Luther King, Bible, Sword and Armour Gauntlet

1968 (29 July). Human Rights Year. Nos. 185 and 188 optd with T **71**.

224	10c. lake and deep lilac	20	10
225	25c. green and purple	30	40

29 July was the date of issue in the islands. The Crown Agents supplies went on sale in London on 1 July, the local consignment being delayed in transit.

(Des V. Whiteley. Litho Format)

1968 (15 Oct). Martin Luther King Commemoration. W w **12** (sideways). P 14.

226	**72** 4c. multicoloured	25	20
227	25c. multicoloured	40	40

73 de Havilland DHC-6 Twin Otter 100

(Des R. Granger Barrett. Litho Format)

1968 (16 Dec). Opening of Beef Island Airport Extension. T **73** and similar horiz designs. Multicoloured. P 14.

228	2c. Type **73**	25	1·50
229	10c. Hawker Siddeley H.S.748 airliner	30	10
230	25c. de Havilland DH.114 Heron 2	35	10
231	$1 Royal Engineers cap badge	35	2·00
228/231	*Set of 4*	1·10	3·25

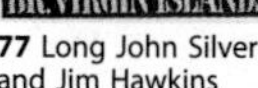

77 Long John Silver and Jim Hawkins

78 Jim Hawkins escaping from the Pirates

(Des Jennifer Toombs. Photo Enschedé)

1969 (18 Mar). 75th Death Anniversary of Robert Louis Stevenson. Scenes from *Treasure Island*. T **77/8** and similar designs. W w **12** (sideways on 10c., $1). P 13½×13 (4c., 40c.) or 13×13½ (others).

232	4c. indigo, pale yellow and carmine-red	25	15
233	10c. multicoloured	25	10
234	40c. brown, black and blue	30	30
235	$1 multicoloured	60	1·00
232/235	*Set of 4*	1·25	1·40

Designs: Vert—4c. T **77**; 40c. The fight with Israel Hands. Horiz—10c. T **78**; $1 Treasure trove.

82 Yachts in Road Harbour, Tortola

(Des J. Cooter, Litho P.B.)

1969 (20 Oct). Tourism. T **82** and similar multicoloured designs. W w **12** (sideways on 2c., $1). P 12½.

236	2c. Tourist and Yellow-finned Grouper (fish) (*vert*)	15	50
237	10c. Type **82**	30	10
238	20c. Sun-bathing at Virgin Gorda National Park	40	20
239	$1 Tourist and Pipe Organ Cactus at Virgin Gorda (*vert*)	90	1·50
236/239	*Set of 4*	1·60	2·00

85 Carib Canoe

(Des and litho J.W.)

1970 (16 Feb)–**74**. Horiz designs as T **85**. W w **12** (sideways*). P 14.

240	½c. buff, red-brown and sepia	10	1·75
241	1c. new blue, apple-green and chalky blue	15	75
	a. Perf 13½ (12.11.74)	1·25	2·00
242	2c. yellow-orange, red-brown and slate	40	1·00
243	3c. orange-red, cobalt and sepia	30	1·25
244	4c. greenish blue, chalky blue and bistre-brown	30	50
	w. Wmk Crown to right of CA	£170	
245	5c. emerald, pink and black	30	10
246	6c. reddish violet mauve and myrtle-green	40	2·25
247	8c. apple-green, greenish yellow and sepia	50	6·00
248	10c. greenish blue, yellow-brown and red-brown	50	15
	a. Perf 13½ (12.11.74)	2·00	2·25
249	12c. yellow, crimson and brown	65	1·50
	a. Perf 13½ (12.11.74)	2·00	3·25
250	15c. turquoise-green, orange and bistre-brown	5·00	85
	a. Perf 13½ (12.11.74)	2·75	3·25
251	25c. grey-green, steel-blue and plum	3·50	1·75
252	50c. magenta, dull green and purple-brown	2·75	1·50
253	$1 salmon, olive-green and red-brown	3·50	3·75
254	$2 buff, slate and grey	7·50	7·00
255	$3 ochre, deep blue and sepia	2·25	4·50
256	$5 violet and grey	2·25	5·00
240/256	*Set of 17*	26·00	35·00

Designs: ½c. T **85**; 1c. *Santa Maria*. (Columbus' flagship); 2c. *Elizabeth Bonaventure* (Drake's flagship); 3c. Dutch Buccaneer, *circa* 1660; 4c. *Thetis*, 1827 (after etching by E. W. Cooke); 5c. Henry Morgan's ship (17th-century); 6c. HMS *Boreas* (Captain Nelson, 1784); 8c. HMS *Eclair*, 1804; 10c. HMS *Formidable*, 1782; 12c. HMS *Nymph*, 1778; 15c. *Windsor Castle* (sailing packet) engaging *Jeune Richard* (French brig), 1807; 25c. HMS *Astrea*, 1808; 50c. Wreck of RMS *Rhone*, 1867; $1 Tortola sloop; $2 HMS *Frobisher*; $3 *Booker Viking* (cargo liner), 1967; $5 Hydrofoil *Sun Arrow*.

* The normal sideways watermark shows Crown to left of CA, *as seen from the back of the stamp.*

The ½c., 3c., 4c., 5c., 10c., and 12c. were reissued in 1973 with W w **12** upright.

102 *A Tale of Two Cities*

(Des W. G. Brown. Litho D.L.R.)

1970 (4 May). Death Centenary of Charles Dickens. T **102** and similar horiz designs showing original book illustrations. W w **12** (sideways). P 14.

257	5c. black, light rose and grey	30	1·00
258	10c. black, light blue and pale green	40	10
259	25c. black, light green and pale yellow	70	25
257/259	*Set of 3*	1·25	1·00

Designs: 5c. T **102**; 10c. *Oliver Twist*; 25c. *Great Expectations*.

103 Hospital Visit

(Des R. Granger Barrett. Litho Questa)

1970 (10 Aug). Centenary of British Red Cross. T **103** and similar horiz designs. Multicoloured. W w **12** (sideways*). P 14.

260	4c. Type **103**	20	45
261	10c. First Aid Class	20	10
262	25c. Red Cross and Coat of Arms	50	55
	w. Wmk Crown to right of CA	75·00	
260/262	*Set of 3*	1·00	1·00

* The normal sideways watermark shows Crown to left of CA, *as seen from the back of the stamp.*

104 Mary Read

(Des and litho J.W.)

1970 (16 Nov). Pirates. T **104** and similar vert designs. Multicoloured. W w **12**. P 14×14½.

263	½c. Type **104**	10	15
264	10c. George Lowther	30	10
265	30c. Edward Teach (Blackbeard)	60	25
266	60c. Henry Morgan	80	1·00
263/266	*Set of 4*	1·50	1·40

Brunei

Sultan Hashim Jalil-ul-alam Akamudin, 1885–1906

(Currency. 100 cents = 1 Straits, later Malayan and Brunei, dollar)

For many years the status of the 1895 issue remained uncertain to such an extent that the 1906 provisionals on Labuan were taken to be the first issue of Brunei.

The 1895 'Star and Crescent' design stamps were, from their first appearance, considered bogus or, at best, as an issue made purely for philatelic purposes. Research into the background of the events surrounding the set led to the publication, in 1933, of the original agreement between Sultan Hashim and J. C. Robertson, dated 20 August 1894, which made clear that the stamps fulfilled a genuine postal purpose. Although Robertson and his partners intended to exploit the philatelic sales for their own benefit, the agreement testifies, as does other evidence, to the use of the stamps by the Sultan for his postal service. As Brunei did not, at that time, belong to any local or international postal union, the stamps were only valid within the state or on mail to Labuan or Sarawak. Items for further afield required franking with Labuan stamps in addition. Although most covers surviving are addressed to Robertson's associates, enough commercial covers and cards exist to show that there was, indeed, a postal service.

PRICES FOR STAMPS ON COVER TO 1945	
Nos. 1/10 are rare used on cover.	
Nos. 11/22	*from* × 30
Nos. 23/33	*from* × 25
Nos. 34/50	*from* × 10
Nos. 51/59	*from* × 12
Nos. 60/78	*from* × 8

The Sarawak Government maintained a post office at the coal mining centre of Brooketon, and the stamps of SARAWAK were used there from 1893 until the office was handed over to Brunei in February 1907.

1 Star and Local Scene

(Litho in Glasgow)

1895 (22 July). P 13–13½.

No.	Type	Description	Unused	Used
1	**1**	½c. brown	8·00	23·00
2		1c. brown-lake	7·50	16·00
3		2c. black	5·00	21·00
4		3c. deep blue	7·00	14·00
5		5c. deep blue-green	6·50	23·00
6		8c. plum	6·50	50·00
7		10c. orange-red	8·00	50·00
		a. Imperf (pair)	£3000	
8		25c. turquoise-green	85·00	£100
9		50c. yellow-green	27·00	£100
10		$1 yellow-olive	28·00	£120
1/10 *Set of* 10			£170	£450

BRUNEI. BRUNEI.

BRUNEI. (2) TWO CENTS. (3) 25 CENTS. (4)

Line through 'B' (R. 5/10)

(Optd by Govt Printer, Singapore)

1906 (1 Oct). Nos. 117, 119, 121 and 123/124 of Labuan (see North Borneo), optd with T **2**, or surch as T **3** or **4** (25c.), in red. P 13½ or 14 (1c.).

No.	Type	Description	Unused	Used
11		1c. black and purple	50·00	55·00
		a. Error. Opt in black	£2500	£3000
		b. Line through 'B'	£900	
		c. Perf 13½–14, comp 12–13	£325	
12		2c. on 3c. black and sepia	7·00	23·00
		a. 'BRUNEI' double	£3750	£2500
		b. 'TWO CENTS' double	£5000	
		c. Line through 'B'	£325	£600
13		2c. on 8c. black and vermilion	27·00	80·00
		a. 'TWO CENTS' double	£14000	
		b. 'TWO CENTS' omitted (in vert pair with normal)	£15000	
		c. Line through 'B'	£800	
14		3c. black and sepia	38·00	85·00
		a. Line through 'B'	£850	
15		4c. on 12c. black and yellow	8·50	5·00
		a. Line through 'B'	£350	
16		5c. on 16c. green and brown	48·00	75·00
		a. Line through 'B'	£950	
17		8c. black and vermilion	15·00	32·00
		a. Line through 'B'	£500	£750
18		10c. on 16c. green and brown	7·00	22·00
		a. Line through 'B'	£450	£600
19		25c. on 16c. green and brown	£110	£120
		a. Line through 'B'	£1700	
20		30c. on 16c. green and brown	£120	£130
		a. Line through 'B'	£1700	
21		50c. on 16c. green and brown	£120	£130
		a. Line through 'B'	£1700	
22		$1 on 8c. black and vermilion	£120	£130
		a. Line through 'B'	£1700	£2000
11/22 *Set of* 12			£600	£800

Only one sheet of the 1c. received the black overprint.

The surcharges were applied in settings of 50. Nos. 13a/13b occur from one sheet on which the surcharge from the second impression of the setting was misplaced to give two surcharges on row five and none on row ten.

Examples of all values are known showing a forged Brunei postmark dated '13 JUL'.

Sultan Mohamed Jemal-ul-Alam, 1906–1924

PRINTERS. All Brunei stamps from Nos. 23 to 113 were recess-printed by De La Rue.

5 View on Brunei River

1907 (26 Feb)–**10**. Wmk Mult Crown CA. P 14.

No.	Type	Description	Unused	Used
23	**5**	1c. grey-black and pale green	2·25	11·00
		x. Wmk reversed	15·00	25·00
24		2c. grey-black and scarlet	2·50	3·25
		x. Wmk reversed	32·00	42·00
		xs. Ditto, opt 'SPECIMEN'	50·00	
25		3c. grey-black and chocolate	10·00	22·00
		x. Wmk reversed	40·00	55·00
26		4c. grey-black and mauve	7·50	6·00
		a. Grey-black and reddish purple (1910)	50·00	40·00
		w. Wmk inverted	£300	
		x. Wmk reversed	85·00	£100
27		5c. grey-black and blue	50·00	95·00
		x. Wmk reversed	£120	£180
		y. Wmk inverted and reversed	£275	
28		8c. grey-black and orange	7·50	23·00
29		10c. grey-black and deep green	4·50	4·00
30		25c. pale blue and ochre-brown	32·00	48·00
31		30c. violet and black	29·00	20·00
		x. Wmk reversed	£425	
32		50c. green and deep brown	15·00	20·00
33		$1 red and grey	60·00	90·00
23/33 *Set of* 11			£200	£300
23xs/33s Optd 'SPECIMEN' *Set of* 11			£325	

The 1c. 'SPECIMEN' is normally found with wmk reversed.

I

II

I Double plate. Lowest line of shading on water is dotted.
II Single plate. Dotted line of shading removed.
Stamps printed in two colours are as I.

1908 (12 June)–**22**. Colours changed. Double or single plates. Wmk Mult Crown CA. P 14.

No.	Type	Description	Unused	Used
34	**5**	1c. green (I)	80	2·25
35		1c. green (II) (1911)	60	2·00
		a. 'A' missing from wmk	£225	
		b. 'C' missing from wmk	£225	
36		2c. black and brown (5.4.11)	4·25	1·25
		w. Wmk inverted	£130	
37		3c. scarlet (I)	8·00	1·25
		a. Substituted crown in wmk	£700	
38		3c. scarlet (II) (1916)	£130	38·00
39		4c. claret (II) (17.4.12)	8·00	75
		a. 'C' of 'CA' missing from wmk	£375	
		x. Wmk reversed	£350	
40		5c. black and orange (1916)	7·00	7·00
41		8c. blue and indigo-blue (10.08)	7·00	11·00
42		10c. purple/*yellow* (II) (11.12)	10·00	1·75
		a. On pale yellow (1922)	7·50	4·00
		as. Optd 'SPECIMEN'	60·00	
		w. Wmk inverted	£225	
		x. Wmk reversed	£190	
		y. Wmk inverted and reversed	£450	£450
43		25c. deep lilac (II) (30.5.12)	11·00	32·00
		a. Deep dull purple (1920)	20·00	32·00
44		30c. purple and orange-yellow (18.3.12)	19·00	21·00
45		50c. black/*green* (II) (1912)	38·00	65·00
		a. On blue-green (1920)	11·00	42·00
46		$1 black and red/*blue* (18.3.12)	28·00	48·00
47		$5 carmine/*green* (I) (1910)	£190	£350
48		$25 black/*red* (I) (1910)	£650	£1300
34/47 *Set of* 12			£250	£450
34s/48s Optd 'SPECIMEN' *Set of* 13			£700	

The used price for No. 48 is for a cancelled-by-favour example, dated before December 1941; there being no actual postal rate for which this value could be used. Examples dated after 1945 are worth much less.

For illustration of the substituted watermark crown see Catalogue Introduction.

Retouch

Normal

MALAYA-
BORNEO
EXHIBITION.
1922.
(6)

RETOUCHES. We list the very distinctive 5c. Retouch (top left value tablet, R. 1/8), but there are others of interest, notably in the clouds.

1916. Colours changed. Single plates. Wmk Mult Crown CA. P 14.

No.	Type	Description	Unused	Used
49	**5**	5c. orange	27·00	23·00
		a. '5c.' retouch	£600	£700
50		8c. ultramarine	8·00	32·00
49s/50s Optd 'SPECIMEN' *Set of* 2			£120	

MALAYA-BORNEO EXHIBITION OVERPRINTS. These were produced from a setting of 30 examples, applied twice to overprint the complete sheet of 60 stamps. Three prominent overprint flaws exist, each occurring on all the stamps in two vertical rows of the sheet.

HI	EX	NE
Short 'I' (all stamps in 2nd and 8th vertical rows)	Broken 'E' (all stamps in 4th and 10th vertical rows)	Broken 'N' (all stamps in 6th and 12th vertical rows)

(Optd by Govt Printer, Singapore)

1922 (31 Mar). Optd with T **6**, in black.

No.	Type	Description	Unused	Used
51	**5**	1c. green (II)	12·00	60·00
		a. Short 'I'	15·00	80·00
		b. Broken 'E'	15·00	80·00
		c. Broken 'N'	15·00	80·00
52		2c. black and brown	14·00	55·00
		a. Short 'I'	17·00	75·00
		b. Broken 'E'	17·00	75·00
		c. Broken 'N'	17·00	75·00
53		3c. scarlet (II)	14·00	65·00
		a. Short 'I'	17·00	90·00
		b. Broken 'E'	17·00	90·00
		c. Broken 'N'	17·00	90·00
54		4c. claret (II)	20·00	60·00
		a. Short 'I'	25·00	85·00
		b. Broken 'E'	25·00	85·00
		c. Broken 'N'	25·00	85·00
55		5c. orange (II)	26·00	70·00
		a. '5c.' retouch (and short 'I')	£600	£1100
		b. Short 'I'	32·00	£100
		c. Broken 'E'	32·00	£100
		d. Broken 'N'	32·00	£100
56		10c. purple/*yellow* (II)	11·00	65·00
		a. Short 'I'	14·00	95·00
		b. Broken 'E'	14·00	95·00
		c. Broken 'N'	14·00	95·00
57		25c. deep dull purple (II)	14·00	85·00
		a. Short 'I'	30·00	£140
		b. Broken 'E'	30·00	£140
		c. Broken 'N'	30·00	£140
		d. 'C' of 'CA' missing from wmk	£1300	
		x. Wmk reversed	£425	
58		50c. black/*blue-green* (II)	45·00	£160
		a. Short 'I'	80·00	£250
		b. Broken 'E'	80·00	£250
		c. Broken 'N'	80·00	£250
59		$1 black and red/*blue*	75·00	£200
		a. Short 'I'	£130	£300
		b. Broken 'E'	£130	£300
		c. Broken 'N'	£130	£300
51/59 *Set of* 9			£200	£750

The used prices quoted for Nos. 51/59 are for examples with verifiable contemporary postmarks. Forged postmarks are frequently met with, in a wide variety of types.

Sultan Ahmed Tajudin Akhazul Khairi Wadin, 1924–1950

7 Native houses, Water Village

1924 (Feb)–**37**. Printed from single plates as Type II, except 30c. and $1 as Type I. Wmk Mult Script CA. P 14.

No.	Type	Description	Unused	Used
60	**5**	1c. black (9.26)	1·00	75
		a. 'A' of 'CA' missing from wmk	£800	
61		2c. brown (3.24)	1·25	11·00
62		2c. green (3.33)	2·00	1·00
63		3c. green (3.24)	1·75	6·50
64		4c. maroon (3.24)	3·75	1·25
65		4c. orange (1929)	2·00	1·00
66		5c. orange-yellow* (3.24)	17·00	2·00
		a. '5c.' retouch	£325	£130
67		5c. grey (1931)	25·00	12·00
		a. '5c.' retouch	£550	£425
68		5c. chocolate (1933)	25·00	1·00
		a. '5c.' retouch	£325	70·00
69	**7**	6c. intense black** (3.24)	15·00	10·00
		x. Wmk reversed	£500	
70		6c. scarlet (1931)	12·00	11·00
71	**5**	8c. ultramarine (9.27)	6·00	4·50
72		8c. grey-black (1933)	16·00	75
73		10c. purple/*yellow* (3.37)	42·00	30·00
		s. Perf 'SPECIMEN'†	£170	
74	**7**	12c. blue (*shades*)	4·50	8·00
75	**5**	25c. slate-purple (1931)	24·00	13·00
76		30c. purple and orange-yellow (1931)	26·00	16·00
77		50c. black/*emerald* (1931)	19·00	15·00
78		$1 black and red/*blue* (1931)	29·00	80·00
60/78 *Set of* 19			£225	£200
60s/78s (*ex* 10c.) Optd (Nos. 60/61, 63/64, 66, 69, 71, 74) or Perf 'SPECIMEN' *Set of* 18			£600	

* For 5c, orange, see No. 82. No. 66 is a 'Wet' printing and No. 82a 'Dry'.

** For 6c. black, see No. 83. Apart from the difference in shade there is a variation in size, No. 69 being 37¾ mm long and No. 83 39 mm.

The 2c. orange and 3c. blue-green in Type **5**, and the 6c. greenish grey (Perf 14×11½), 8c. red and 15c. ultramarine in Type **7** were not issued without the Japanese Occupation overprint, although unoverprinted examples exist. It is believed that these 1941 printings were produced and possibly perforated, by other firms in Great Britain following bomb damage to the De La Rue works at the end of 1940 (*Prices* 2c., 8c., *each* £75, 15c. £100, 6c. £130, 3c. £250 *unused*).

During the life of this issue De La Rue changed the method of production from a 'Wet' to a 'Dry' process. Initially the stamps were printed on ungummed paper which was dampened before being put on the press. Once the paper had dried, and contracted in the process, the gum was then applied. 'Dry' printings, introduced around 1934, were on pre-gummed paper. The contraction of the 'Wet' printings was considerable and usually involves a difference of between 0.5 mm and 1 mm when compared with the larger 'Dry' printings. The following stamps occur from both 'Wet' and 'Dry' versions: 1c., 2c. green, 4c. orange, 5c. chocolate, 6c. scarlet, 8c. grey-black, 10c. and 25c.

Stamps of this issue can be found either line or comb perforated.

† The 10c. perforated 'SPECIMEN' (No 73s) is listed separately due to its later distribution by the UPU.

Brunei was occupied by the Japanese Army in January 1942 and remained under Japanese administration until liberated by the 9th Australian Division in June 1945.

After the cessation of hostilities with the Japanese, postal services were re-introduced by the British Military Administration. From 6 November, military post offices using Australian stamps were opened for civilian use, until offices under B.M.A. control were opened at Brunei Town and Kuala Belait on 17 December 1945 where B.M.A. overprints on the stamps of NORTH BORNEO and SARAWAK were used until the reappearance of Brunei issues on 2 January 1947.

Redrawn clouds (R. 1/1 of No. 80*ab* only)

1947 (2 Jan)–**51**. Colours changed and new values. Wmk Mult Script CA. P 14.

79	5	1c. chocolate	50	2·00
		a. 'A' of 'CA' missing from wmk	£1200	
80		2c. grey	60	11·00
		a. Perf 14½×13½ (25.9.50)	2·00	4·75
		ab. Black (27.6.51)	2·00	6·50
		ac. Redrawn clouds	85·00	
81	7	3c. green	1·50	8·00
82	5	5c. orange*	80	2·00
		a. '5c.' retouch	70·00	£100
		b. Perf 14½×13½ (25.9.50)	4·00	23·00
		c. Ditto '5c.' retouch	£140	£275
83	7	6c. black*	1·25	7·50
84	5	8c. scarlet	50	2·50
		a. Perf 13 (25.1.51)	55	13·00
85		10c. violet	2·25	30
		a. Perf 14½×13½ (25.9.50)	4·00	5·50
86		15c. ultramarine	1·75	70
87		25c. deep claret	2·75	3·75
		a. 'A' of 'CA' missing from wmk	—	£1200
		b. Perf 14½×13½ (25.1.51)	4·75	19·00
88		30c. black and orange	2·50	1·00
		aw. Wmk inverted	—	£1500
		b. Perf 14½×13½ (25.1.51)	3·50	23·00
89		50c. black	6·50	1·50
		a. Perf 13 (25.9.50)	1·90	24·00
90		$1 black and scarlet	19·00	3·00
91		$5 green and red-orange (2.2.48)	25·00	28·00
92		$10 black and purple (2.2.48)	£120	30·00
79/92 *Set of* 14			£160	80·00
79s/92s Perf 'SPECIMEN' *Set of* 14			£350	

* See also Nos. 66 and 69.

The 1, 2, 3, 5, 6, 10 and 25c. values utilised the plates of the pre-war issue and were line perforated until the introduction of the 14½×13½ comb machine for some values in 1950–1951. The 8, 15, 50c., $1, $5 and $10 were from new plates with the sheets comb perforated. The 30c. was initially a pre-war plate, but it is believed that a new plate was introduced in 1951.

8 Sultan Ahmed Tajudin and Water Village

1949 (22 Sept). Sultan's Silver Jubilee. Wmk Mult Script CA. P 13.

93	8	8c. black and carmine	1·50	1·25
94		25c. purple and red-orange	1·50	1·60
95		50c. black and blue	1·50	1·60
93/95 *Set of* 3			4·00	4·00

1949 (10 Oct). 75th Anniversary of Universal Postal Union. As Nos. 114/117 of Antigua.

96	8c. carmine	1·00	3·00
97	15c. deep blue	3·50	1·50
98	25c. magenta	1·00	1·50
99	50c. blue-black	1·00	1·25
96/99 *Set of* 4		6·00	6·50

Sultan Sir Omar Ali Saifuddin-Wasa'adul Khairi Wadin, 1950-1967

9 Sultan Omar Ali Saifuddin

10 Native houses, Water Village

1952 (1 Mar)–**58**. Wmk Mult Script CA. P 13.

100	9	1c. black	10	50
101		2c. black and orange	15	50
102		3c. black and lake-brown	25	30
103		4c. black and green	30	20
104		6c. black and grey	2·50	10
105		8c. black and crimson	1·25	60
		a. Black and crimson-lake (15.2.56)	19·00	20
106		10c. black and sepia	30	10
107		12c. black and violet	6·00	10
108		15c. black and pale blue	5·00	10
109		25c. black and purple	2·50	10
		a. Black and reddish purple (8.10.53)	12·00	1·00
110		50c. black and ultramarine	6·00	10
		a. Black and blue (22.6.55)	16·00	10
111	10	$1 black and green	6·00	1·60
		a. Black and bronze-green (23.7.58)	13·00	3·50
112		$2 black and scarlet	7·00	3·00
113		$5 black and maroon	38·00	12·00
		a. Black and brown-purple (15.2.56)	55·00	14·00
100/113 *Set of* 14			65·00	16·00

No. 106 exists in coils constructed from normal sheets.

See also Nos. 118/131.

11 Brunei Mosque and Sultan Omar

(Recess B.W.)

1958 (24 Sept). Opening of Brunei Mosque. W w **12**. P 13½.

114	11	8c. black and myrtle-green	20	90
115		15c. black and carmine	25	15
116		35c. black and deep lilac	30	90
114/116 *Set of* 3			65	1·75

12 'Protein Foods'

(Des M. Goaman. Photo Harrison)

1963 (4 June). Freedom from Hunger. W w **12**. P 14×14½.

117	12	12c. sepia	2·75	1·00

1964–72. As Nos. 100/113, but W w **12**. Glazed paper ($2, $5) or ordinary paper (others).

118	9	1c. black (17.3.64)	50	70
		a. Glazed paper. Grey (28.11.69)	2·75	4·50
		ab. Slate grey (30.6.72)	15	2·75
119		2c. black and orange (17.3.64)	1·50	20
		a. Glazed paper (27.5.70)	2·50	10
120		3c. black and lake-brown (10.11.64)	1·50	60
		a. Glazed paper (27.5.70)	2·50	10
121		4c. black and green (12.5.64)	40	10
		a. Glazed paper (6.3.70)	50	10
		ab. Black and emerald (19.11.71)	2·50	4·00
122		6c. black and grey (12.5.64)	4·00	10
		a. Black (28.11.69)	12·00	12·00
		b. Glazed paper (28.11.69)	50	30
		ba. Light grey (19.11.71)	2·00	3·75
123		8c. black and crimson-lake (12.5.64)	1·50	10
		a. Glazed paper (27.5.70)	1·00	15
		ab. Black and brown-red (19.11.71)	5·00	4·50
124		10c. black and sepia (12.5.64)	1·25	10
		a. Glazed paper (31.3.70)	2·25	10
		ab. Grey and pale brown (coil) (11.10.71)	4·00	6·50
125		12c. black and violet (12.5.64)	1·50	10
		a. Glazed paper (5.11.70)	15·00	1·00
126		15c. black and pale blue (12.5.64)	55	10
		a. Glazed paper (28.11.69)	65	20
127		25c. black and purple (12.5.64)	7·50	10
		a. Glazed paper (18.5.70)	14·00	9·00
		ab. Glazed paper. Black and reddish violet (30.4.71)	17·00	1·25
128		50c. black and ultramarine (10.11.64)	2·50	10
		a. Black and bright ultramarine (17.3.69)	8·50	2·25
		b. Glazed paper (5.11.70)	19·00	4·00
		ba. Grey and indigo (21.12.71)	22·00	6·50
129	10	$1 black and bronze-green (14.5.68)	3·00	6·00
		a. Glazed paper (5.11.70)	9·00	6·00
130		$2 black and scarlet (5.11.70)	45·00	20·00
131		$5 black and maroon (5.11.70)	45·00	35·00
118/129 *Set of* 12			23·00	7·00
118ab/129a, 130/1 *Set of* 14			£140	65·00

Printings of the 6 and 15c. issued on 28 November 1969 were on both ordinary and glazed paper, the 6c. on ordinary producing a distinct shade.

No. 124a exists in coils constructed from normal sheets.

The 2c., 3c., 4c., 6c., 8c., 10c., 12c. and 15c. were reissued between 1972 and 1974 with W w **12** sideways.

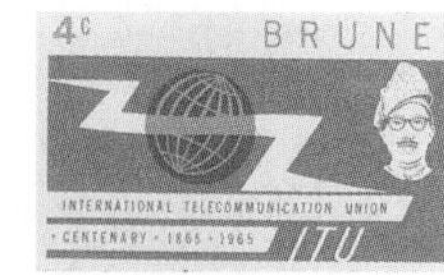

13 ITU Emblem

(Des M. Goaman. Litho Enschedé)

1965 (17 May). ITU Centenary. W w **12**. P 11×11½.

132	13	4c. mauve and orange-brown	35	10
133		75c. orange-yellow and light emerald	1·00	75

14 ICY Emblem

(Des V. Whiteley. Litho Harrison)

1965 (25 Oct). International Co-operation Year. W w **12**. P 14.

134	14	4c. reddish purple and turquoise-green	20	10
135		15c. deep bluish green and lavender	55	35

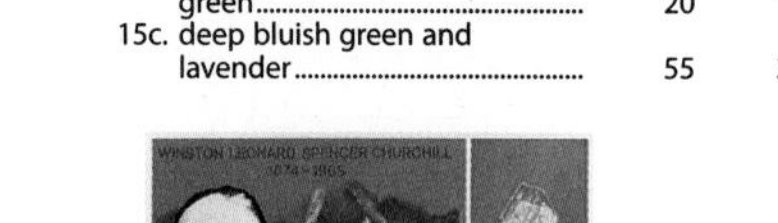

15 Sir Winston Churchill and St Paul's Cathedral in Wartime

(Des Jennifer Toombs. Photo Harrison)

1966 (24 Jan). Churchill Commemoration. W w **12**. P 14.

136	15	3c. black, cerise, gold and new blue	30	2·75
137		10c. black, cerise, gold and deep green	1·25	20
138		15c. black, cerise, gold and brown	1·50	35
139		75c. black, cerise, gold and bluish violet	3·75	5·50
136/139 *Set of* 4			6·00	8·00

16 Footballer's Legs, Ball and Jules Rimet Cup

(Des V. Whiteley. Litho Harrison)

1966 (4 July). World Cup Football Championship. W w **12** (sideways). P 14.

140	16	4c. violet, yellow-green, lake and yellow-brown	20	15
141		75c. chocolate, blue-green, lake and yellow-brown	80	60

17 WHO Building

(Des M. Goaman. Litho Harrison)

1966 (20 Sept). Inauguration of WHO Headquarters, Geneva. W w **12** (sideways). P 14.

142	17	12c. black, yellow-green and light blue	40	65
143		25c. black, light purple and yellow-brown	60	1·50

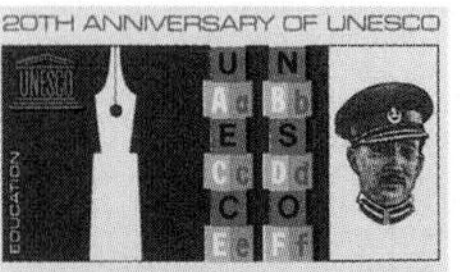

18 'Education'

19 'Science'

20 'Culture'

(Des Jennifer Toombs. Litho Harrison)

1966 (1 Dec). 20th Anniversary of UNESCO. W w **12** (sideways). P 14.

144	**18**	4c. slate-violet, red, yellow and orange	35	10
145	**19**	15c. orange-yellow, violet and deep olive	75	50
146	**20**	75c. black, bright purple and orange	2·50	6·50
144/146 *Set of 3*			3·25	6·50

Sultan Sir Hassanal Bolkiah Mu'izzadin Waddaulah, 1967

21 Religious Headquarters Building

(Des and photo Harrison)

1967 (19 Dec). 1400th Anniversary of Revelation of the Koran. W w **12** (sideways). P 12½.

147	**21**	4c. multicoloured	10	10
148		10c. multicoloured	15	10
149	–	25c. multicoloured	20	30
150	–	50c. multicoloured	35	1·50
147/150 *Set of 4*			70	1·75

Nos. 149/150 are as T **21** but have sprigs of laurel flanking the main design (which has a smaller circle) in place of flagpoles.

22 Sultan of Brunei, Mosque and Flags

(Des V. Whiteley. Photo Enschedé)

1968 (9 July). Installation of YTM Seri Paduka Duli Pengiran Temenggong. T **22** and similar multicoloured design. P 14×13 (12c.) or 13×14 (others)

151	4c. Type **22**	15	80
152	12c. Sultan of Brunei, Mosque and Flags (*horiz*)	40	1·60
153	25c. Type **22**	55	2·00
151/153 *Set of 3*		1·00	4·00

23 Sultan of Brunei **24** Sultan of Brunei

(Des V. Whiteley. Litho D.L.R.)

1968 (15 July). Sultan's Birthday. W w **12** (sideways). P 12.

154	**23**	4c. multicoloured	10	50
155		12c. multicoloured	20	85
156		25c. multicoloured	30	1·40
154/156 *Set of 3*			55	2·50

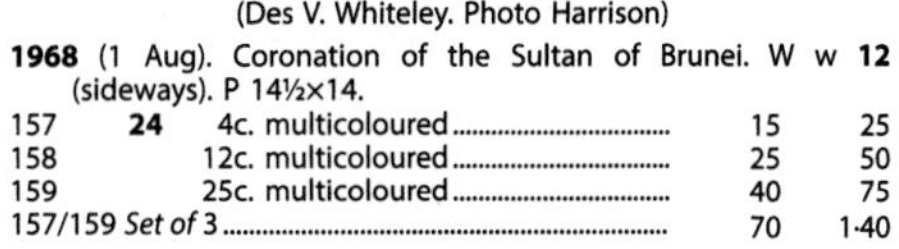

(Des V. Whiteley. Photo Harrison)

1968 (1 Aug). Coronation of the Sultan of Brunei. W w **12** (sideways). P 14½×14.

157	**24**	4c. multicoloured	15	25
158		12c. multicoloured	25	50
159		25c. multicoloured	40	75
157/159 *Set of 3*			70	1·40

25 New Building and Sultan's Portrait

26 New Building and Sultan's Portrait

(Photo Enschedé)

1968 (29 Sept). Opening of Language and Literature Bureau. W w **12** (sideways). P 13½ (10c.) or 12½×13½ (others).

160	**25**	10c. multicoloured	20	1·75
		a. *Tête-bêche* (pair)	40	3·50
161	**26**	15c. multicoloured	20	35
162		30c. multicoloured	45	90
160/162 *Set of 3*			75	2·75

The above were scheduled for release in 1967, and when finally issued had the year altered by overprinting.

27 Human Rights Emblem and struggling Man **28** Sultan of Brunei and WHO Emblem

(Des V. Whiteley. Litho Harrison)

1968 (16 Dec). Human Rights Year. W w **12**. P 14.

163	**27**	12c. black, yellow and green	10	20
164		25c. black, yellow and blue	15	25
165		75c. black, yellow and dull purple	45	1·75
163/165 *Set of 3*			65	2·00

(Des V. Whiteley. Litho Format)

1968 (19 Dec). 20th Anniversary of World Health Organisation. P 14.

166	**28**	4c. yellow, black and cobalt	30	1·25
167		15c. yellow, black and deep bluish violet	55	65
168		25c. yellow, black and pale yellow-olive	65	1·25
166/168 *Set of 3*			1·40	2·75

29 Deep Sea Oil-Rig, Sultan of Brunei and inset portrait of Pengiran Di-Gadong

(Des adapted by V. Whiteley. Photo Enschedé)

1969 (10 July). Installation (9th May, 1968) of Pengiran Shahbandar as YTM Seri Paduka Duli Pengiran Di-Gadong Sahibol Mal. W w **12**. P 14×13.

169	**29**	12c. multicoloured	85	50
170		40c. multicoloured	1·25	2·50
171		50c. multicoloured	1·25	2·50
169/171 *Set of 3*			3·00	5·00

30 Aerial View of Parliament Buildings

(Des Harrison. Litho D.L.R.)

1969 (23 Sept). Opening of Royal Audience Hall and Legislative Council Chamber. P 15.

172	**30**	12c. multicoloured	20	25
173		25c. multicoloured	30	45
174	–	50c. rose-red and bluish violet	60	3·50
172/174 *Set of 3*			1·00	3·75

Design: 50c. Elevation of new buildings.

32 Youth Centre and Sultan's Portrait

(Des V. Whiteley. Litho D.L.R.)

1969 (20 Dec). Opening of the New Youth Centre. W w **12**. P 15×14½.

175	**32**	6c. flesh, slate-lilac and black	20	1·00
176		10c. olive-yellow, grey-green and blackish brown	25	10
177		30c. yellow-olive, yellow-brown and black	70	1·00
175/177 *Set of 3*			1·00	1·90

JAPANESE OCCUPATION OF BRUNEI

Japanese forces landed in Northern Borneo on 15 December 1941 and the whole of Brunei had been occupied by 6 January 1942.

Brunei, North Borneo, Sarawak and, after a short period, Labuan, were administered as a single territory by the Japanese. Until September-October 1942, previous stamp issues, without overprint, continued to be used in conjunction with existing postmarks. From the Autumn of 1942 onwards unoverprinted stamps of Japan were made available and examples can be found used from the area for much of the remainder of the War. Japanese Occupation issues for Brunei, North Borneo and Sarawak were equally valid throughout the combined territory but not, in practice, equally available.

PRICES FOR STAMPS ON COVER TO 1945	
Nos. J1/J16	*from* × 8
Nos. J17/J20	—

(1) ('Imperial Japanese Government') **(2)** ('Imperial Japanese Postal Service $3')

1942 (Oct)–**44**. Stamps of Brunei handstamped with T **1** in violet to blue. Wmk Mult Script CA (except Nos. J18/J19, Mult Crown CA). P 14.

J1	**5**	1c. black	10·00	23·00
		a. Red opt	£225	£250
J2		2c. green	50·00	£110
J3		2c. orange (1943)	6·00	9·00
J4		3c. blue-green	32·00	75·00
		a. Opt omitted (in pair with normal)	£4250	
J5		4c. orange	4·00	13·00
J6		5c. chocolate	6·50	13·00
		a. '5c.' retouch	£160	£400
J7	**7**	6c. greenish grey (P 14×11½) (1944)	40·00	£325
J8		6c. scarlet	£600	£600
J9	**5**	8c. grey-black	£850	£900
J10	**7**	8c. red	10·00	12·00
		a. Opt omitted (in pair with normal)	£2750	
J11	**5**	10c. purple/*yellow*	10·00	26·00
J12	**7**	12c. blue	35·00	26·00
		a. Red opt	£650	£750
J13		15c. ultramarine (1944)	25·00	26·00
J14	**5**	25c. slate-purple	26·00	50·00
		a. Red opt	£850	£1000
J15		30c. purple and orange-yellow	95·00	£180
J16		50c. black/*emerald*	38·00	60·00
		a. Red opt	£900	£900
J17		$1 black and red/*blue* (1944)	55·00	70·00
		a. Red opt	—	£1800
J18		$5 carmine/*green* (1944)	£1000	£3500
J19		$25 black/*red* (1944)	£1000	£3500

The overprint varies in shade from violet to blue, and being handstamped, exists inverted, double, double one inverted and treble.

Nos. J3, J4, J7, J10 and J13 were not issued without the overprint (See footnote below Brunei No. 78).

1944 (11 May). No. J1 surch with T **2** in orange-red.

J20	**5**	$3 on 1c. black	£9000	£10000
		a. Surch on No. 60 of Brunei	£11000	

Three separate handstamps were used to apply T **2**, one for the top line, one for the bottom and the third for the two central characters.

Burma

(Currency. 12 pies = 1 anna; 16 annas = 1 rupee)

Stamps of India were used in Burma from 1854 and, after 1856, individual examples can be identified by the use of the concentric octagonal postmarks of the Bengal Postal Circle of which the following were supplied to Burmese post offices:

Type A No. B156 (Rangoon)

Type B No. B5 (Akyab)

B5	Akyab	B146	Pegu
B12*	Bassein	B150	Prome
B22	Nga Thine Khyoung	B156*	Rangoon
B56	Amherst	B159	Sandoway
B108	Kyouk Phyoo	B165	Sarawah (*to* 1860)
B111	Meeaday	B165	Henzada (*from* 1861)
B112	Mengyee	B171	Shoay Gyeen
B127	Moulmein	B173	Sittang
B128	Mergui	B179	Thayetmyo
B129	Tavoy	B181	Toungoo
B133	Myanoung	B227	Port Blair
B136	Namayan		

* Exists in black or blue. Remainder in black only.

Akyab, Moulmein and Rangoon used postmarks as both Type A and Type B, Port Blair as Type B only and the remainder as Type A only.

From 1860 various types of duplex cancellations were introduced and Burmese examples can be identified when sufficient of the left-hand portion is visible on the stamp. Such marks were issued for the following offices:

Akyab	Rangoon
Bassein	Rangoon C.R.H. (Cantonment Receiving House)
Mandalay	Thayetmyo
Moulmein	Toungoo
Port Blair	
Prome	

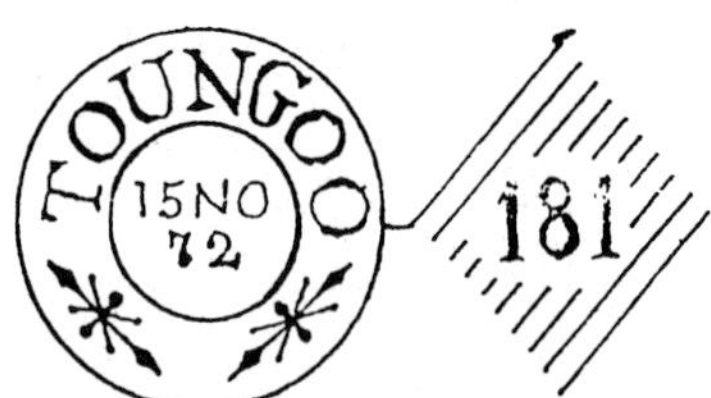

1862 Duplex from Toungoo

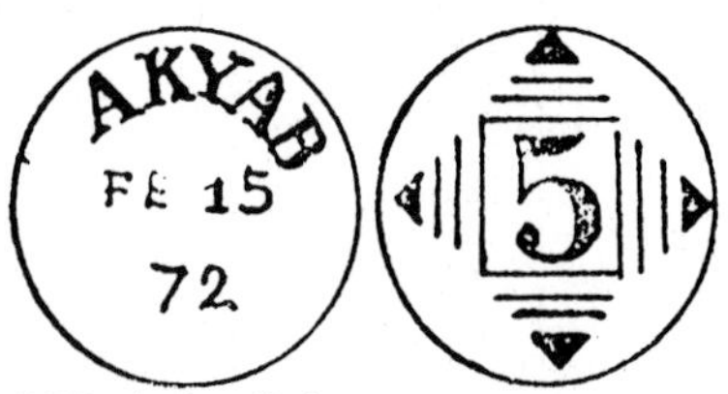

1865 Duplex from Akyab

During 1875, a further series of duplex marks was introduced in which the right-hand portion of the cancellation included the office code number, prefixed by the letter 'R' for Rangoon:

R-1	Rangoon	R-9	Myanoung
R-1/1	Rangoon Cantonment	R-10	Port Blair
R-2	Akyab	1/R-10	Nancowry
R-3	Bassein	R-11	Prome
R-4	Henzada	R-12	Sandoway
R-5	Kyouk Phyoo	R-13	Shwegyeen
R-6	Mandalay	R-14	Tavoy
R-7	Mergui	R-15	Thayetmyo
R-8	Moulmein	R-16	Tounghoo
1/R-8	Amherst		

1875 type from Rangoon

1875 type from Rangoon Cantonment Receiving House

From 1886 the whole of Burma was united under the Crown and the post offices were supplied with circular date stamps giving the name of the town.

Most Indian stamps, both postage and official, issued during the period were supplied to post offices in Burma. None of the imperforates printed by De La Rue have been seen however, and from the later issues the following have not been recorded with Burma postmarks:

Nos. 39a, 66a, 68, 85a, 92a, 110a/110b, 148a, 165, 192a/192c, 195a/195b, O15, O38, O40b, O50a/O50b, O74a, O101*a*, O102, O103/O103a, O104/O105 and O142.

The value of most Indian stamps used in Burma coincides proportionately with the used prices quoted for India, but some, especially the provisional surcharges, are extremely rare with Burmese postmarks. Stamps of the face value of 2r. and above from the reigns of Victoria and Edward VII are more common with telegraph cancellations than with those of the postal service.

PRICES FOR STAMPS ON COVER TO 1945

Nos. 1/18	*from* × 6
Nos. 18*a*/33	*from* × 4
No. 34	*from* × 5
Nos. 35/50	*from* × 8
Nos. O1/O27	*from* × 15

BRITISH ADMINISTRATION

From 1 January 1886 Burma was a province of the Indian Empire but was separated from India and came under direct British administration on 1 April 1937.

BURMA (**1**)   **BURMA** (**1a**)

1937 (1 Apr). Stamps of India. (King George V inscr 'INDIA POSTAGE') optd with T **1** or **1a** (rupee values). W **69**. P 14.

1	3p. slate	2·75	10
	w. Wmk inverted	22·00	3·25
2	½a. green	1·25	10
	w. Wmk inverted	20·00	3·25
3	9p. deep green (*typo*)	1·50	10
	w. Wmk inverted	14·00	3·25
4	1a. chocolate	5·50	10
	w. Wmk inverted	16·00	3·25
5	2a. vermilion (*small die*)	1·00	10
6	2½a. orange	75	10
	w. Wmk inverted	17·00	3·25
7	3a. carmine	5·00	30
	w. Wmk inverted	35·00	4·25
8	3½a. deep blue	9·00	10
	aw. Wmk inverted	10·00	30
	b. Dull blue	30·00	14·00
	bw. Wmk inverted	21·00	4·00
9	4a. sage-green	1·25	10
	w. Wmk inverted	—	£130
10	6a. bistre	1·50	35
	w. Wmk inverted	£200	£130
11	8a. reddish purple	4·25	10
	w. Wmk inverted	£200	
12	12a. claret	20·00	4·50
	w. Wmk inverted	42·00	10·00
13	1r. chocolate and green	70·00	7·00
14	2r. carmine and orange	50·00	28·00
	w. Wmk inverted	80·00	40·00
15	5r. ultramarine and purple	70·00	40·00
	w. Wmk inverted	—	£325
16	10r. green and scarlet	£275	£100
	w. Wmk inverted	†	—
17	15r. blue and olive (wmk inverted)	£800	£275
18	25r. orange and blue	£1700	£600
	aw. Wmk inverted	£1700	£600
1/18	*Set of* 18	£2750	£900

The opt is at top on all values except the 3a.

The 1a. has been seen used from Yenangyaung on 22 Mar 1937.

It is necessary to emphasis that the unused prices quoted for Nos. 1/18 are for unmounted examples, as they were issued within the reign of King George VI.

2 King George VI and 'Chinthes'

3 King George VI and 'Nagas'

4 *Karaweik* (royal barge)

5 Burma teak

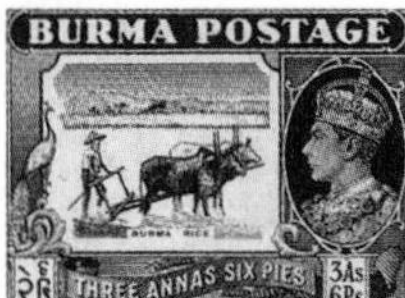

6 Burma rice

7 River Irrawaddy

8 King George VI and Peacock

9 King George VI and 'Nats'

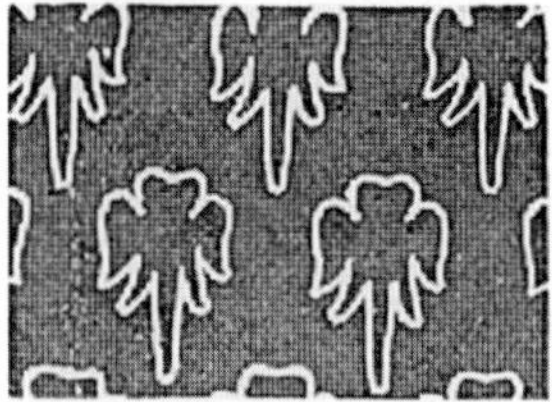
10 Elephants' Heads

6p. 'Medallion' flaw (R. 14/3)

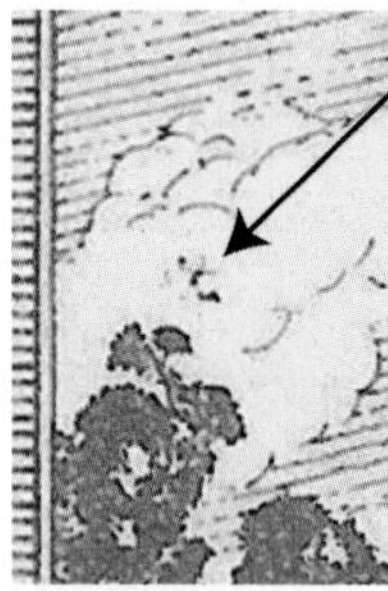
2a.6p. 'Birds over trees at left (R. 15/3)

3a.6p. Extra trees flaw (R. 11/8)

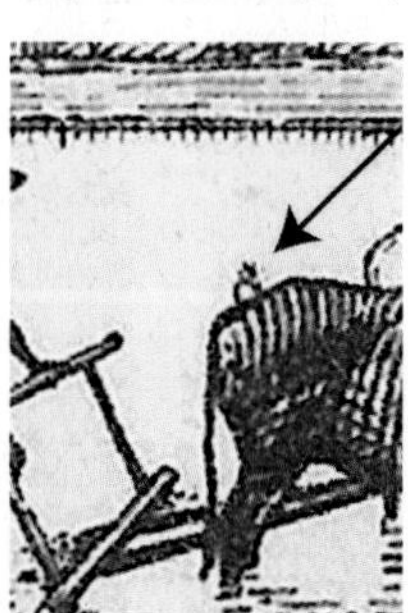
3a.6p. 'Tick bird' flaw (R. 9/5)

(Des Maung Kyi (2a.6p.), Maung Hline (3a.), Maung Ohn Pe (3a.6p.) and N. K. D. Naigamwalla (8a.). Litho Security Ptg Press, Nasik)

1938 (15 Nov)–**40**. T **2/9**. W **10**. P 14 (vert) or 13½ × 13 (horiz).

18*b*	**2**	1p. red-orange (1.8.40)	3·50	2·50
19		3p. bright violet	30	3·00
20		6p. bright blue	2·00	10
		a. Medallion flaw	80·00	24·00
21		9p. yellow-green	3·50	2·75

22	3	1a. purple-brown	30	10
23		1½a. turquoise-green	3·00	4·00
24		2a. carmine	4·50	1·00
25	4	2a.6p. claret	17·00	3·75
		a. Birds over trees	£300	95·00
26	5	3a. dull violet	21·00	4·00
27	6	3a.6p. light blue and blue	4·50	10·00
		a. Extra trees flaw	£160	£200
		b. Tick bird flaw	£160	£200
28	3	4a. greenish blue	4·75	20
29	7	8a. myrtle-green	4·00	55
30	8	1r. purple and blue	4·00	1·00
31		2r. brown and purple	28·00	7·50
32	9	5r. violet and scarlet	80·00	70·00
33	9	10r. brown and myrtle	85·00	£100
18*b*/33 *Set of* 16			£225	£180

The 1a. exists lithographed or typographed, the latter having a 'Jubilee' line in the sheet margin.

COMMEMORATION POSTAGE STAMP 6th MAY 1840

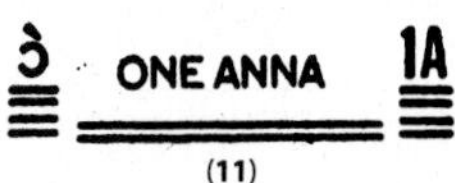

(**11**)

Broken bar (R. 7/8)

1940 (6 May). Centenary of First Adhesive Postage Stamps. No. 25 surch with T **11**.

34	4	1a. on 2a.6p. claret	4·25	2·00
		a. Birds over trees	90·00	80·00
		b. Broken bar	90·00	80·00

For stamps issued in 1942–1945 see under Japanese Occupation.

CHIN HILLS DISTRICT. This area, in the far north-west of the country, remained in British hands when the Japanese overran Burma in May 1942.

During the period July to December 1942 the local officials were authorised to produce provisional stamps and the letters 'OHMS' are known overprinted by typewriter on Nos. 3, 20, 22/24, 28/29 and 31 of Burma or handstamped, in violet, on Nos. 25, 27 and 29. The two types can also occur together or in combination with a handstamped 'SERVICE'.

From early in 1943 ordinary postage stamps of India were used from the Chin Hills post offices of Falam, Haka, Fort White and Tiddim, this expedient continuing until the fall of Falam to the Japanese on 7 November 1943.

The provisional stamps should only be collected on Official cover (*Price, from* £2250) where dates and the sender's handwriting can be authenticated.

BRITISH MILITARY ADMINISTRATION

Preparations for the liberation of Burma commenced in February 1943 when the Civil Affairs Service (Burma) (CAS(B)) was set up at Delhi as part of the proposed military administration structure. One of the specific tasks assigned to CAS(B) was the operation of a postal service for the civilian population.

Operations against the Japanese intensified during the second half of 1944. The port of Akyab in the Arakan was reoccupied in January 1945. The 14th Army took Mandalay on 29 March and Rangoon was liberated from the sea on 3 May.

Postal services for the civilian population started in Akyab on 13 April 1945, while post offices in the Magwe Division around Meiktila were operating from 4 March. Mandalay post offices opened on 8 June and those in Rangoon on 16 June, but the full network was only completed in December 1945, just before the military administration was wound up.

MILY ADMN (**12**) MILY ADMN (**13**)

1945 (from 11 Apr). Nos. 18*b* to 33 optd with T **12** (small stamps) or **13** (others) by Security Printing Press, Nasik.

35	2	1p. red-orange	10	10
		a. Opt omitted (in pair with normal)	£1600	
		w. Wmk inverted	£150	
36		3p. bright violet	20	2·00
37		6p. bright blue	20	30
		a. Medallion flaw	35·00	40·00
38		9p. yellow-green	30	2·00
39	3	1a. purple-brown (16.6)	20	10
40		1½a. turquoise-green (16.6)	20	15
41		2a. carmine	20	15
42	4	2a.6p. claret	2·25	3·75
		a. Birds over trees	70·00	90·00
43	5	3a. dull violet	1·50	30
44	6	3a.6p. light blue and blue	20	1·00
		a. Extra trees flaw	40·00	55·00
45	3	4a. greenish blue	20	70
46	7	8a. myrtle-green	20	2·00
47	8	1r. purple and blue	50	50
48		2r. brown and purple	50	1·50
49	9	5r. violet and scarlet	50	1·50
50		10r. brown and myrtle	50	1·50
35/50 *Set of* 16			7·00	16·00

Only the typographed version of the 1a., No. 22, received this overprint.

The missing overprints on the 1p. occur on the stamps from the bottom row of one sheet. A further block with two examples of the variety caused by a paper fold also exists.

The exact dates of issue for Nos. 35/50 are difficult to establish.

The initial stock of overprints is known to have reached CAS(B) headquarters, Imphal, at the beginning of April 1945. Postal directives issued on 11 April refer to the use of the overprints in Akyab and in the Magwe Division where surcharged pre-war postal stationery envelopes had previously been in use. The 6p., 1a., 1½a. and 2a. values were placed on sale at Mandalay on 8 June and the 1a. and 2a. at Rangoon on 16 June. It has been suggested that only a limited service was initially available in Rangoon. All values were on sale by 9 August 1945.

BRITISH CIVIL ADMINISTRATION

3a.6p. Curved plough handle (R. 8/4)

1946 (1 Jan). As Nos. 19/33, but colours changed.

51	2	3p. brown	15	4·00
52		6p. deep violet	1·50	30
		a. Medallion flaw	80·00	
53		9p. green	1·75	7·00
54	3	1a. blue	1·50	20
55		1½a. orange	1·50	10
56		2a. claret	60	50
57	4	2a.6p. greenish blue	2·75	10·00
		aa. Birds over trees	80·00	£100
57*a*	5	3a. blue-violet	6·50	13·00
57*b*	6	3a.6p. black and ultramarine	4·50	6·50
		ba. Curved plough handle	£120	£130
58	3	4a. purple	70	1·50
59	7	8a. maroon	1·75	7·50
60	8	1r. violet and maroon	3·25	3·75
61		2r. brown and orange	10·00	9·50
62	9	5r. green and brown	12·00	32·00
63		10r. claret and violet	25·00	45·00
51/63 *Set of* 15			60·00	£120

No. 54 was printed in typography only.

14 Burman

(Des A. G. I. McGeogh. Litho Nasik)

1946 (2 May). Victory. T **14** and similar vert designs. W **10** (sideways). P 13.

64	9p. turquoise-green	20	40
65	1½a. violet	30	15
66	2a. carmine	30	15
67	3a.6p. ultramarine	1·00	40
64/67 *Set of* 4		1·60	1·00

Designs: 9p. T **14**; 1½a. Burmese woman; 2a. Chinthe; 3a.6p. Elephant.

INTERIM BURMESE GOVERNMENT

ကြားဖြတ် အစိုးရ။ (**18** *Trans.* 'Interim Government') — ားဖြတ်ကြ အစိုးရ။ (**18a**) — တ်ကြားဖြ အစိုးရ။ (**18b**)

Type **18a** shows the first character transposed to the end of the top line (R. 6/15).

Type **18b** shows the last two characters transposed to the front of the top line (R. 14/14).

Some sheets of the 3p. show both errors corrected by a handstamp as Type **18**.

1947 (1 Oct). Stamps of 1946 optd with T **18** (small stamps) or larger opt (others).

68	2	3p. brown	1·75	70
		a. Opt Type **18a**	75·00	
		ab. Corrected by handstamp as Type **18**	£200	
		b. Opt Type **18b**	85·00	
		ba. Corrected by handstamp as Type **18**	£200	
69		6p. deep violet	20	30
		a. Opt Type **18a**	70·00	
		b. Medallion flaw	40·00	
70		9p. green	20	30
		a. Opt inverted	25·00	40·00
71	3	1a. blue	40	30
		a. Vert pair, one with opt omitted	£1600	
72		1½a. orange	3·00	10
73		2a. claret	40	15
		a. Horiz pair, one with opt omitted	£1700	
		b. Opt Type **18a**	90·00	
74	4	2a.6p. greenish blue	1·75	1·00
		a. Birds over trees	60·00	60·00
75	5	3a. blue-violet	2·75	1·75
76	6	3a.6p. black and ultramarine	2·75	4·00
77	3	4a. purple	1·75	30
78	7	8a. maroon	1·75	3·50
79	8	1r. violet and maroon	9·50	4·25
80		2r. brown and orange	11·00	12·00
81	9	5r. green and brown	11·00	12·00
82		10r. claret and violet	10·00	12·00
68/82 *Set of* 15			50·00	45·00

The 3p., 6p., 2a., 2a.6p., 3a.6p. and 1r. are also known with overprint inverted.

OFFICIAL STAMPS

BURMA SERVICE (O **1**) BURMA SERVICE (O **1a**)

1937 (Apr–June). Stamps of India. (King George V inscr 'INDIA POSTAGE') optd with Type O **1** or O **1a** (rupee values). W **69**. P 14.

O1	3p. slate	4·50	10
	w. Wmk inverted	£150	50·00
O2	½a. green	19·00	10
	w. Wmk inverted	†	£120
O3	9p. deep green	5·00	3·00
O4	1a. chocolate	9·50	10
O5	2a. vermilion (*small die*)	20·00	45
	w. Wmk inverted	—	55·00
O6	2½a. orange	13·00	5·50
O7	4a. sage-green	13·00	10
O8	6a. bistre	11·00	23·00
O9	8a. reddish purple (1.4.37)	13·00	4·75
O10	12a. claret (1.4.37)	14·00	23·00
O11	1r. chocolate and green (1.4.37)	40·00	14·00
	w. Wmk inverted	£250	
O12	2r. carmine and orange	55·00	85·00
	w. Wmk inverted	55·00	85·00
O13	5r. ultramarine and purple	£225	£100
O14	10r. green and scarlet	£650	£350
O1/O14 *Set of* 14		£950	£550

For the above issue the stamps were either overprinted 'BURMA' and 'SERVICE' at one operation or had the two words applied separately. Research has yet to establish if all values exist with both forms of overprinting.

An example of the 4a. in orange is known cancelled at Moulmein.

SERVICE (O **2**) SERVICE (O **3**)

1939 (1 Apr). Nos. 19/24 and 28 optd with Type O **2** (typo) and Nos. 25 and 29/33 optd with Type O **3** (litho).

O15	2	3p. bright violet	20	20
O16		6p. bright blue	20	20
		a. Medallion flaw	42·00	42·00
O17		9p. yellow-green	4·00	8·00
O18	3	1a. purple-brown	20	15
O19		1½a. turquoise-green	3·50	3·75
O20		2a. carmine	2·50	20
O21	4	2a.6p. claret	35·00	27·00
		a. Birds over trees	£425	£300
O22	3	4a. greenish blue	4·50	2·50
O23	7	8a. myrtle-green	24·00	4·50
O24	8	1r. purple and blue	16·00	5·50
O25		2r. brown and purple	35·00	23·00
O26	9	5r. violet and scarlet	26·00	50·00
O27		10r. brown and myrtle	£140	55·00
O15/O27 *Set of* 13			£250	£150

Both versions of the 1a. value exist with this overprint.

1946 (1 Jan). British Civil Administration. Nos. 51/56 and 58 optd with Type O **2** (typo) and Nos. 57 and 59/63 optd with Type O **3** (litho).

O28	2	3p. brown	4·25	8·50
O29		6p. deep violet	3·25	2·25
O30		9p. green	3·00	9·50
O31	3	1a. blue	40	2·00
O32		1½a. orange	3·00	20
O33		2a. claret	40	2·00
O34	4	2a.6p. greenish blue	4·50	17·00
		a. Birds over trees	90·00	
O35	3	4a. purple	1·75	1·00
O36	7	8a. maroon	7·00	9·50
O37	8	1r. violet and maroon	4·50	14·00
O38		2r. brown and orange	8·50	55·00
O39	9	5r. green and brown	23·00	70·00
O40		10r. claret and violet	23·00	80·00
O28/O40 *Set of* 13			75·00	£250

1947 (1 Oct). Interim Burmese Government. Nos. O28/O40 optd with T **18** (small stamps) or larger opt (others).

O41	2	3p. brown	4·25	40
O42		6p. deep violet	7·00	15
O43		9p. green	9·50	90
O44	3	1a. blue	9·50	80
O45		1½a. orange	17·00	30
O46		2a. claret	10·00	15
O47	4	2a.6p. greenish blue	45·00	26·00
		a. Birds over trees	£450	£275
O48	3	4a. purple	30·00	40
O49	7	8a. maroon	30·00	5·50
O50	8	1r. violet and maroon	18·00	5·00
O51		2r. brown and orange	22·00	26·00
O52	9	5r. green and brown	23·00	28·00
O53		10r. claret and violet	23·00	48·00
O41/O53 *Set of* 13			£225	£130

TELEGRAPH STAMPS

Indian telegraph stamps were used in Burma up to 1910 and subsequently Indian and then Burmese postage stamps, prior to the issue of the first Burmese telegraph stamps in 1946.

T 1

(Litho Nasik)

1946 (1 Oct?). Type **T 1**. W **10**. P 14.

T 1	**1**	1a. carmine-red	3·00	45·00
T 2		2a. deep dull blue	3·00	45·00
T 3		8a. grey-green	4·00	
T 4		12a. bluish grey	5·00	
T 5		1r. brown	6·00	55·00
T 6		2r. deep dull purple	7·00	55·00
T 7		10r. turquoise-blue	8·00	
T1/T7 *Set of 7*			32·00	

Nos. T1/T7 also exist with a one-line 'Service' overprint in Burmese script, for official use (*Price, £75, for set of 7, unused*). Their date of issue is unknown.

Later stamp issues will be found listed in Stanley Gibbons *South-East Asia Catalogue*.

JAPANESE OCCUPATION OF BURMA

PRICES FOR STAMPS ON COVER TO 1945	
Nos. J1/J44	—
Nos. J45/J46	*from* × 6
Nos. J47/J56	*from* × 8
No. J56*g*	—
Nos. J57/J72	*from* × 6
Nos. J73/J75	*from* × 25
No. J76	*from* × 8
No. J77	*from* × 20
Nos. J78/J81	*from* × 25
Nos. J82/J84	*from* × 10
Nos. J85/J87	*from* × 40
No. J88	*from* × 12
Nos. J89/J97	*from* × 30
Nos. J98/J104	*from* × 50
Nos. J105/J111	*from* × 30

BURMA INDEPENDENCE ARMY ADMINISTRATION

The Burma Independence Army, formed by Aung San in 1941, took control of the Delta area of the Irrawaddy in May 1942. They reopened a postal service in the area and were authorised by the Japanese to overprint local stocks of stamps with the Burmese emblem of a peacock.

Postage and Official stamps with the peacock overprints or handstamps were used for ordinary postal purposes with the probable exception of No. J44.

DISTINGUISHING FEATURES. Type **1**. Body and head of Peacock always clearly outlined by broad uncoloured band. There are four slightly different sub-types of overprint Type **1**.

Type **2**. Peacock with slender neck and more delicately detailed tail. Clear spur on leg at right. Heavy fist-shaped blob of ink below and parallel to beak and neck.

Type **4**. No basic curve. Each feather separately outlined. Straight, short legs.

Type **5**. Much fine detail in wings and tail in clearly printed overprints. Thin, long legs ending in claws which, with the basic arc, enclose clear white spaces in well printed copies. Blob of colour below beak shows shaded detail and never has the heavy fist-like appearance of this portion in Type **2**.

Two sub-types may be distinguished in Type **5**, the basic arc of one having a chord of 14–15 mm and the other 12½–13 mm.

Type **6**. Similar to Type **5**, but with arc deeply curved and reaching nearly to the top of the wings. Single diagonal line parallel to neck below beak.

Collectors are warned against forgeries of these overprints, often in the wrong colours or on the wrong values.

(**1**)

(**2**)

(**3**)

1942 (May). Stamps of Burma overprinted with the national device of a Peacock.

I. Overprinted at Myaungmya

A. With T **1** *in black*

On Postage Stamps of King George V.

J1		9p. deep green (No. 3)	£110	
J2		3½a. deep blue (No. 8)	80·00	

On Official Stamp of King George V

J3		6a. bistre (No. O8)	80·00	

On Postage Stamps of King George VI

J4	**2**	9p. yellow-green	£160	
J5	**3**	1a. purple-brown	£550	
J6		4a. greenish blue (opt black on red)	£160	
		a. Triple opt, black on double red	£475	

On Official Stamps of King George VI

J7	**2**	3p. bright violet	42·00	90·00
J8		6p. bright blue	27·00	65·00
J9	**3**	1a. purple-brown	28·00	55·00
J9*a*		1½a. turquoise-green	£950	£1400
J10		2a. carmine	40·00	£100
J11		4a. greenish blue	40·00	80·00

The overprint on No. J6 was apparently first done in red in error, and then corrected in black. Some stamps have the black overprint so accurately superimposed that the red hardly shows. These are rare.

Nos. J5 and J9 exist with the Peacock overprint on both the typographed and the litho printings of the original stamps.

B. With T **2** *or* **3** *(rupee values), in black*

On Postage Stamps of King George VI

J12	**2**	3p. bright violet	22·00	75·00
J13		6p. bright blue	50·00	£110
J14		9p. yellow-green	27·00	70·00
J15	**3**	1a. purple-brown	17·00	65·00
J16		2a. carmine	28·00	85·00
J17		4a. greenish blue	60·00	£120
		a. Opt double		
		b. Opt inverted	£850	
		c. Opt double, one inverted	£475	
		d. Opt double, both inverted	£750	
J18	**8**	1r. purple and blue	£450	£750
J19		2r. brown and purple	£275	£550

The Myaungmya overprints (including No. J44) are usually clearly printed.

(**4**)

(**5**)

(**6**)

Type **5** generally shows the details of the peacock much less clearly and, due to heavy inking, or careless impression, sometimes appears as almost solid colour.

Type **6** was officially applied only to postal stationery. However, the handstamp remained in the possession of a postal official who used it on postage stamps after the war. These stamps are no longer listed.

II. Handstamped (at Pyapon?) with T **4**, *in black (so-called experimental type)*

On Postage Stamps of King George VI.

J19*a*	**2**	6p. bright blue	75·00	
J19*b*	**3**	1a. purple-brown	£100	£250
J20		2a. carmine	£130	£300
J21		4a. greenish blue	£700	£700

Unused specimens of Nos. J20/J21 are usually in poor condition.

III. Overprinted at Henzada with T **5** *in blue, or blue-black*

On Postage Stamps of King George V

J22		3p. slate (No. 1)	4·00	23·00
		a. Opt double	10·00	55·00
J23		9p. deep green (No. 3)	27·00	70·00
		a. Opt double	80·00	
J24		2a. vermilion (No. 5)	£130	£225

On Postage Stamps of King George VI

J25	**2**	1p. red-orange	£250	£400
J26		3p. bright violet	48·00	80·00
J27		6p. bright blue	25·00	55·00
		a. Opt double	£100	£150
		b. Clear opt, on back and front	£350	
J28		9p. yellow-green	£1200	
J29	**3**	1a. purple-brown	9·00	42·00
		a. Opt inverted	£2750	£1300
J30		1½a. turquoise-green	23·00	70·00
		a. Opt omitted (in pair with normal)	£4250	
J31		2a. carmine	23·00	70·00
		a. Opt double	£2750	
J32		4a. greenish blue	45·00	£100
		a. Opt double	£250	
		b. Opt inverted	£3750	

On Official Stamps of King George VI

J33	**2**	3p. bright violet	£140	£275
J34		6p. bright blue	£160	£275
J35	**3**	1½a. turquoise-green	£180	£325
J35*a*		2a. carmine	£375	£450
J36		4a. greenish blue	£1000	

(**6a**) ('Yon Thon' = 'Office use')

V. Official Stamp of King George VI optd at Myaungmya with T **6a** *in black.*

J44	**7**	8a. myrtle-green	£110	£300

No. J44 was probably for official use.

There are two types of T **6a**, one with base of peacock 8 mm long and the other with base about 5 mm long. The neck and other details also vary. The two types are found *se-tenant* in the sheet. Stocks of the peacock types were withdrawn when the Japanese Directorate-General took control of the postal services in the Delta in August 1942.

JAPANESE ARMY ADMINISTRATION

7

8 Farmer

1942 (1 June). Impressed by hand. Thick yellowish paper. No gum. P 12×11.

J45	**7**	(1a.) red	50·00	70·00

This device was the personal seal of Yano Sitza, the Japanese official in charge of the Posts and Telegraphs department of the Japanese Army Administration. It was impressed on paper already perforated by a line machine. Some stamps show part of the papermaker's watermark, either 'ABSORBO DUPLICATOR' or 'ELEPHANT BRAND', each with an elephant.

Other impressions of this seal on different papers, and showing signs of wear, were not valid for postal purposes.

(Des T. Kato. Typo *Rangoon Gazette* Press)

1942 (15 June). Value in annas. P 11 or 11×11½. Laid bâtonné paper. No gum.

J46	**8**	1a. scarlet	23·00	25·00

Some stamps show part of the papermaker's watermark, either 'ELEPHANT BRAND' or 'TITAGHUR SUPERFINE', each with an elephant.

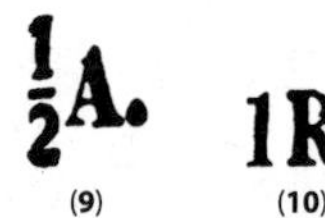

(**9**) (**10**)

1942 (22 Sept).

(a) Nos. 314/317, 320/322, 325, 327 and 396 of Japan surch as T **9**/**10**.

J47	**9**	¼a. on 1s. chestnut (Rice harvesting)	50·00	50·00
		a. Surch inverted	£150	£150
		b. Surch double, one inverted	£190	
J48		½a. on 2s. bright scarlet (General Nogi)	55·00	50·00
		a. Surch inverted	£140	£150
		b. Surch double, one inverted	£190	
J49		¾a. on 3s. green (Power station)	80·00	80·00
		a. Surch inverted	£170	£170
		b. Surch double, one inverted	—	£200
J50		1a. on 5s. claret (Admiral Togo)	80·00	70·00
		a. Surch inverted	£250	£250
		b. Surch double, one inverted	£300	£275
		c. Surch omitted (in pair with normal)	£450	£400
J51		3a. on 7s. green (Diamond Mts)	£130	£150
		a. Surch inverted	£325	
J52		4a. on 4s. emerald (Togo)	60·00	65·00
		a. Surch inverted	£225	
J53		8a. on 8s. violet (Meiji Shrine)	£150	£150
		a. Surch inverted	£325	£325
		b. Surch double, one inverted	£425	
		c. Surch in red	£275	£300
		d. Red surch inverted	£450	
		e. Surch double (black and red)	£1100	
J54	**10**	1r. on 10s. deep carmine (Yomei Gate)	29·00	38·00
		a. Surch inverted	95·00	£110
		b. Surch double	80·00	£100
		c. Surch double (black and red)	£500	£500
		d. Surch omitted (in pair with normal)	£400	£400
		e. Surch omitted (in pair with inverted surch)	£550	
J55		2r. on 20s. ultramarine (Mt Fuji)	55·00	55·00
		a. Surch inverted	£150	£150
		b. Surch double, one inverted	£170	
		c. Surch omitted (in pair with normal black surch)	£275	£275
		d. Surch in red	55·00	55·00
		e. Red surch inverted	£150	£150
		f. Red surch double	£140	£140
		g. Surch omitted (in pair with normal red surch)	£350	£350
		ga. Surch omitted (in pair with double red surch)		
		h. Surch double (black and red)	£500	
J56	**9**	5r. on 30s. turquoise (Torii Shrine)	19·00	27·00
		a. Surch inverted	90·00	
		b. Surch double	£120	
		c. Surch double, one inverted	£160	
		d. Surch omitted (in pair with normal surch)	£325	£325
		e. Surch omitted (in pair with inverted black surch)	£425	
		f. Surch in red	30·00	32·00
		fa. Red surch inverted	95·00	95·00
		fb. J56a and J56fa *se-tenant*	£650	£650
		fc. Surch omitted (in pair with normal red surch)	£325	£325

(b) No. 386 of Japan commemorating the fall of Singapore similarly surch

J56*g*	**9**	4a. on 4+2s. green and red	£180	£190
		h. Surch omitted (in pair with normal)	£750	
		ha. Surch omitted (in pair with inverted surch)	£800	
		i. Surch inverted	£450	

(New Currency. 100 cents = 1 rupee)

15 C. 15 C. 15 C.

(**11**) (**12**) (**13**)

1942 (15 Oct). Previous issues, with 'anna' surcharges obliterated, handstamped with new value in cents, as T **11** or **12.** (No. J57 handstamped with new value only).

(a) On No. J46

J57	5c. on 1a. scarlet	26·00	30·00
	a. Surch omitted (in pair with normal)	£2000	

(b) On Nos. J47/J53

J58	1c. on ¼a. on 1s. chestnut	55·00	55·00
	a. '1 c.' omitted (in pair with normal)	£900	
	b. '¼ a.' inverted	£275	
J59	2c. on ½a. on 2s. bright scarlet	55·00	55·00
J60	3c. on ¾a. on 3s. green	60·00	60·00
	a. Surch in blue	£225	
J61	5c. on 1a. on 5s. claret	85·00	65·00
J62	10c. on 3a. on 7s. green	£170	£140
J63	15c. on 4a. on 4s. emerald	50·00	55·00
J64	20c. on 8a. on 8s. violet	£900	£700
	a. Surch on No. J53c (surch in red)	£350	£170

The 'anna' surcharges were obliterated by any means available, in some cases by a bar or bars, and in others by the butt of a pencil dipped in ink. In the case of the fractional surcharges, the letter 'A' and one figure of the fraction, were sometimes barred out, leaving the remainder of the fraction to represent the new value, e.g. the '1' of '½' deleted to create the 2c. surcharge or the '4' of '¾' to create the 3c. surcharge.

1942. Nos. 314/317, 320/321 and 396 of Japan surcharged in cents only as T **13**.

J65	1c. on 1s. chestnut (Rice harvesting)	40·00	20·00
	a. Surch inverted	£140	£140
J66	2c. on 2s. bright scarlet (General Nogi)	60·00	45·00
J67	3c. on 3s. green (Power station)	£100	65·00
	a. Pair, with and without surch	—	£375
	b. Surch inverted	£170	
	c. Surch in blue	£110	£120
	d. Surch in blue inverted	£325	£350
J68	5c. on 5s. claret (Admiral Togo)	£100	55·00
	a. Pair, with and without surch	£450	
	b. Surch in violet	£180	£190
	ba. Surch inverted	—	£350
J69	10c. on 7s. green (Diamond Mts)	£140	80·00
J70	15c. on 4s. emerald (Togo)	29·00	29·00
	a. Surch inverted	£170	£180
	b. Pair, with and without surch	—	£350
J71	20c. on 8s. violet (Meiji Shrine)	£200	95·00
	a. Surch double	£425	

Nos. J67c and J68b were issued for use in the Shan States.

BURMESE GOVERNMENT

On 1 November 1942 the Japanese Army Administration handed over the control of the postal department to the Burmese Government. On 1 August 1943 Burma was declared by the Japanese to be independent.

14 Burma State Crest

15 Farmer

(Des U Tun Tin and Maung Tin from drawing by U Ba Than. Typo Rangoon)

1943 (15 Feb). No gum. P 11.

J72	**14**	5c. scarlet	29·00	35·00
		a. Imperf	29·00	35·00
		ab. Printed on both sides	95·00	

No. J72 was usually sold affixed to envelopes, particularly those with the embossed 1a. King George VI stamp, which it covered. Unused specimens off cover are not often seen and blocks are scarce.

1943. Typo. No gum. P 11½.

J73	**15**	1c. orange (22.3)	6·00	9·00
		a. Brown-orange	5·00	10·00
J74		2c. yellow-green (24.3)	1·50	1·00
		a. '3' for '2' in face value (R. 2/10)	£350	
		b. Blue-green	15·00	
J75		3c. light blue (25.3)	5·00	1·00
		a. On laid paper	23·00	40·00
		b. Imperf between (horiz pair)	—	£350
J76		5c. carmine (small 'c') (17.3)	32·00	21·00
J77		5c. carmine (large 'C')	3·50	8·00
		a. Imperf (pair)	£110	
		b. 'G' for 'C' (R. 2/6)	£180	
J78		10c. grey-brown (25.3)	9·50	9·50
		a. Imperf (pair)	£110	
		b. Imperf between (horiz pair)	—	£350
J79		15c. magenta (26.3)	30	4·50
		b. On laid paper	6·00	23·00
		ba. Inverted 'C' in value (R. 2/3)	£200	
J80		20c. grey-lilac (29.3)	30	1·00
J81		30c. deep blue-green (29.3)	1·25	3·00

The 1c., 2c. and 3c. have large 'C' in value as illustrated. The 10c. and higher values have small 'c'. Nos. J73/J81 had the face values inserted individually into the plate used for No. J46 with the original face value removed. There were a number of printings for each value, often showing differences such as missing stops, various founts of figures or 'c', etc., in the value tablets.

The face value error, No. J74a, was later corrected.

Some sheets of No. J75a show a sheet watermark of Britannia seated within a crowned oval spread across 15 stamps in each sheet. This paper was manufactured by T. Edmonds and the other half of the sheet carried the watermark inscription 'FOOLSCAP LEDGER'. No stamps have been reported showing letters from this inscription, but a block of 25 is known on laid paper showing a different sheet watermark 'HERTFORDSHIRE LEDGER MADE IN ENGLAND'. Examples showing parts of these sheet watermarks are rare.

There are marked varieties of shade in this issue.

16 Soldier carving word 'Independence'

17 Rejoicing Peasant

18 Boy with National Flag

Normal

Skyline flaw (R. 5/6)

(Des Maung Ba Thit (**16**), Naung Ohn Maung (**17**), and Maung Soi Yi (**18**). Typo State Press, Rangoon)

1943 (1 Aug). Independence Day. No gum.

(a) P 11

J82	**16**	1c. orange	15·00	20·00
J83	**17**	3c. light blue	15·00	20·00
J84	**18**	5c. carmine	23·00	11·00
		a. Skyline flaw	£140	
J82/J84 *Set of 3*			48·00	45·00

(b) Rouletted

J85	**16**	1c. orange	1·50	1·75
		b. Perf×roul	£150	£150
		c. Imperf (pair)	45·00	55·00
J86	**17**	3c. light blue	2·50	4·00
		b. Perf×roul	£120	£120
		c. Imperf (pair)	45·00	55·00
J87	**18**	5c. carmine	3·50	4·25
		b. Perf×roul	70·00	70·00
		c. Imperf (pair)	45·00	55·00
		d. Skyline flaw	32·00	38·00
J85/J87 *Set of 3*			6·50	9·00

The stamps perf×rouletted may have one, two or three sides perforated.

The rouletted stamps often appear to be roughly perforated owing to failure to make clean cuts. These apparent perforations are very small and quite unlike the large, clean holes of the stamps perforated 11.

A few imperforate sets, mounted on a special card folder and cancelled with the commemorative postmark were presented to officials. These are rare.

19 Burmese Woman

20 Elephant carrying Log

21 Watch Tower, Mandalay

(Litho G. Kolff & Co, Batavia)

1943 (1 Oct). P 12½.

J88	**19**	1c. red-orange	20·00	15·00
J89		2c. yellow-green	50	2·00
J90		3c. deep violet	50	2·25
		a. Bright violet	1·75	5·50
J91	**20**	5c. carmine	75	60
J92		10c. blue	2·25	1·10
J93		15c. red-orange	1·00	3·00
J94		20c. yellow-green	1·00	1·75
J95		30c. olive-brown	1·00	2·00
J96	**21**	1r. red-orange	30	2·00
J97		2r. bright violet	30	2·25
J88/J97 *Set of 10*			26·00	29·00

22 Bullock Cart

23 Shan Woman

ဗမာနိုင်ငံတော်

၂၀ ဆင့်

(**24** 'Burma State' and value)

(Litho G. Kolff & Co, Batavia)

1943 (1 Oct). Issue for Shan States. P 12½.

J98	**22**	1c. olive-brown	45·00	40·00
J99		2c. yellow-green	50·00	40·00
J100		3c. bright violet	8·00	14·00
J101		5c. ultramarine	3·50	8·50
J102	**23**	10c. blue	17·00	18·00
J103		20c. carmine	48·00	22·00
J104		30c. olive-brown	27·00	48·00
J98/J104 *Set of 7*			£180	£170

The Shan States, except for the frontier area around Keng Tung which was ceded to Thailand on 20 August 1943, were placed under the administration of the Burmese Government on 24 December 1943, and these stamps were later overprinted as T **24** for use throughout Burma.

1944 (1 Nov). Optd as T **24** (the lower characters differ for each value).

J105	**22**	1c. olive-brown	5·00	10·00
J106		2c. yellow-green	60	6·50
		a. Opt inverted	£425	£700
J107		3c. bright violet	2·50	7·00
J108		5c. ultramarine	3·00	4·00
J109	**23**	10c. blue	3·25	2·25
J110		20c. carmine	65	1·50
J111		30c. olive-brown	1·50	1·75
J105/J111 *Set of 7*			15·00	30·00

Bushire

BRITISH OCCUPATION

(Currency. 20 chahis = 1 kran; 10 kran = 1 toman)

Bushire, a seaport town of Persia, was occupied by the British on 8 August 1915. The Persian postal authorities resumed control on 18 October 1915. British forces returned to Bushire during 1916, but mail from this period was carried by Indian Army F.P.O. No. 319.

FORGERIES. Collectors are warned that the Bushire type **1** opt has been extensively forged. These stamps should not be purchased without a reliable guarantee.

PRICES FOR STAMPS ON COVER TO 1945	
Nos. 1/29	*from* × 5
No. 30	—

Types of Iran (Persia) overprinted

57

66

67

68

BUSHIRE
Under British
Occupation.
(1)

1915 (16 Aug). Nos. 361/363, 365, 367/370, 372, 374/376 and 378/379 of Iran optd with T **1** at the British Residency.

No.	Type	Description	Unused	Used
1	57	1ch. orange and green	£100	£100
		a. No stop	£325	£325
2		2ch. sepia and carmine	90·00	£100
		a. No stop	£300	£350
3		3ch. green and grey	£110	£110
		a. No stop	£425	£425
4		5ch. carmine and brown	£850	£800
5		6ch. brown-lake and green	90·00	60·00
		a. No stop	£325	£275
		b. Opt double	†	£10000
6		9ch. indigo-lilac and brown	£110	£120
		a. No stop	£400	£500
		b. Opt double		
7		10ch. brown and carmine	95·00	£100
		a. No stop	£425	£425
8		12ch. blue and green	£120	£100
		a. No stop	£475	£550
9		24ch. green and purple	£225	£120
		a. No stop	£900	£450
10		1kr. carmine and blue	£200	70·00
		a. Opt double	£10000	
		b. No stop	£800	£250
11		2kr. claret and green	£600	£350
		a. No stop	£1800	£900
12		3kr. black and lilac	£500	£475
		a. No stop	£1700	£1300
13		5kr. blue and red	£500	£300
		a. No stop	£1500	£1200
14		10kr. rose and bistre-brown	£475	£275
		a. No stop	£1500	£900

Nos. 1/3 and 5/14 were overprinted in horizontal strips of ten and No. 4 in horizontal strips of five. Eight different settings are recognised with the 'No stop' variety occurring on stamp 9 from four settings with 3 mm between 'Under' and 'British' and on stamp 10 from one setting where the gap is 2 mm.

1915 (11 Sept). Nos. 426/440 and 441 of Iran optd with T **1**.

No.	Type	Description	Unused	Used
15	66	1ch. deep blue and carmine	£1300	£1000
16		2ch. carmine and deep blue	£20000	£20000
17		3ch. deep green	£1300	£1200
18		5ch. vermilion	£17000	£17000
19		6ch. carmine and green	£13000	£13000
20		9ch. deep violet and brown	£2000	£1400
21		10ch. brown and deep green	£3250	£3250
22		12ch. ultramarine	£3500	£3500
23		24ch. sepia and brown	£1600	£1200
24	67	1kr. black, brown and silver	£1800	£1400
25		2kr. carmine, slate and silver	£1700	£1600
26		3kr. sepia, dull lilac and silver	£1800	£1800
27		5kr. slate, sepia and silver	£1700	£1800
		a. Opt inverted	—	£27000
28	68	1t. black, violet and gold	£1400	£1400
29		3t. red, crimson and gold	£10000	£8000

Nos. 15/29 were overprinted in strips of five.

1915. No. 414 of Iran ('1 CH 1915' provisional) optd with T **1**.

No.	Type	Description	Unused	Used
30	57	1ch. on 5ch. carmine and brown	£15000	

Cameroon

Allied operations against the German protectorate of Kamerun commenced in September 1914 and were completed in 18 February 1916. The territory was divided, under an Anglo-French agreement, on 31 March 1916, with the British administering the area in the west along the Nigerian border. League of Nations mandates were issued for the two sections of Cameroon on 20 July 1922, which were converted into United Nations trusteeships in 1946.

Supplies of Kamerun stamps were found on the German steamer *Professor Woermann*, captured at Freetown, and these were surcharged, probably in Sierra Leone, and issued by the Cameroons Expeditionary Force at Duala in July 1915.

A French post office opened in Duala on 10 November 1915 using stamps of Gabon overprinted 'Corps Expeditionnaire Franco Anglais Cameroun'. Although under the overall control of the British combined force commander, this office remained part of the French postal system.

PRICES FOR STAMPS ON COVER TO 1945
The stamps of British Occupation of Cameroons are rare used on cover.

I. CAMEROONS EXPEDITIONARY FORCE

A

B

C.E.F. 1d. (1)   C.E.F. 1s. (2)

SETTINGS. Nos. B1/B3 were surcharged from a setting of 100 (10×10) with the face value changed for the 1d.

Nos. B4 and B6/B9 were surcharged from a common setting of 50 (5×10) with the face value amended.

No. B5 was surcharged from a setting of ten in a vertical strip repeated across the sheet. The figures of the surcharge on this are in a different style from the remainder of the pence stamps.

Nos. B10/B13 were surcharged from a common setting of 20 (4×5) with the face value amended.

d. Normal   d. Different fount 'd' (R. 2/10, 6/9, 10/10)

1d. '1' with thin serifs (R. 5/1)

Short '4' (R. 10/2, 10/7)

5s 's' broken at top (R. 3/1)   5s. 's' inverted (R. 3/4)

1915 (12 July). Stamps of German Kamerun. Types A and B, surch as T **1** (Nos. B1/B9) or **2** (Nos. B10/B13) in black or blue.

No.	Type	Description	Unused	Used
B1	A	½d. on 3pf. brown (No. K7) (B.)	13·00	55·00
		a. Different fount 'd'	£180	£425
B2		½d. on 5pf. green (No. K21 wmk lozenges) (B.)	7·00	10·00
		a. Different fount 'd'	85·00	£140
		b. Surch double	†	£1000
		ba. Surch double, one albino	£400	
B3		1d. on 10pf. carmine (No. K22 wmk lozenges) (B.)	1·25	9·50
		a. '1' with thin serifs	13·00	70·00
		b. Surch double	£425	
		ba. Surch double, one albino	£160	
		c. '1d.' only double	£2000	
		d. Surch triple, two albino	£400	
		e. Surch in black	12·00	55·00
		ea. '1' with thin serifs	£275	
B4		2d. on 20pf. ultramarine (No. K23 wmk lozenges)	3·50	22·00
		a. Surch double, one albino	£400	
B5		2½d. on 25pf. black and red/*yellow* (No. K11)	21·00	55·00
		a. Surch double	£13000	
		ab. Surch double, one albino	£1500	
B6		3d. on 30pf. black and orange/*buff* (No. K12)	13·00	60·00
		a. Large '3' (R. 3/5, 3/10)	£1500	
		b. Surch triple, two albino	£475	
B7		4d. on 40pf. black and carmine (No. K13)	14·00	60·00
		a. Short '4'	£1000	£1800
		b. Surch triple, two albino	£375	
		c. Surch quadruple, three albino	£1500	
B8		6d. on 50pf. black and purple/*buff* (No. K14)	13·00	60·00
		a. Surch double, one albino	£375	
B9		8d. on 80pf. black and carmine/*rose* (No. K15)	13·00	60·00
		a. Surch triple, two albino	£1600	
B10	B	1s. on 1m. carmine (No. K16)	£200	£900
		a. 's' inverted	£1000	£3750
B11		2s. on 2m. blue (No. K17)	£225	£1000
		a. 's' inverted	£1000	£3750
		b. Surch double, one albino	£2750	
B12		3s. on 3m. violet-black (No. K18)	£225	£1000
		a. 's' inverted	£1000	£4000
		b. 's' broken at top	£900	
		c. Surch double	£15000	
		ca. Surch triple, two albino	£2750	
B13		5s. on 5m. carmine and black (No. K25a wmk lozenges)	£275	£1100
		a. 's' inverted	£1300	£4500
		b. 's' broken at top	£1200	
B1/B13 *Set of 13*			£900	£4000

The 1d. on 10pf. was previously listed with 'C.E.F.' omitted. This was due to misplacement, so that all stamps (except for a pair in the Royal Collection) from the bottom row show traces of the overprint on the top perforations.

Examples of all values exist showing a forged Duala, Kamerun postmark dated '11 10 15'. Another forged cancel dated '16 11 15' is also known. This can be identified by the lack of a serif on the index letter 'b'.

The stamps of Nigeria were subsequently used in British Cameroons and the area was administered as part of Nigeria from February 1924.

For issues of Cameroun under French administration see Stanley Gibbons *French Colonies Catalogue*.

II. CAMEROONS TRUST TERRITORY

Following the independence of the French Trust Territory of Cameroun on 1 January 1960 the United Nations directed that a plebiscite should be held in the British Trust Territory whose postal service continued, for the time being, to be run by Nigeria. The northern area voted to join Nigeria, but the southern part of the territory decided to join the Cameroun Republic.

The following issue, although ordered by the Southern Cameroons authorities, was also on sale in Northern Cameroons, until the latter joined Nigeria on 1 June 1961. The stamps therefore can be found with Nigerian postmarks.

CAMEROONS
U.K.T.T.
(1)

6d. Major re-touch consisting of heavy diagonal shading (Pl. 2-1, R. 2/10)

1960 (1 Oct)–**61**. Nos. 69/71, 72*cd*/72*f* and 73/80 of Nigeria optd with T **1**, in red.

No.	Type	Description	Unused	Used
T1	18	½d. black and orange	10	2·75
T2	–	1d. black and bronze-green	10	70
		a. Grey-black and dull bronze-green (19.9.61)	1·00	2·25
T3	–	1½d. blue-green	10	20
T4	21	2d. grey (Type B)	75	3·75
		aa. Extra figure		
		a. Slate-blue (Type A)	£1100	£400
		b. Bluish grey (Type B)	95·00	29·00
		c. Pale grey (Type B) (19.9.61)	3·25	6·00
T5	–	3d. black and deep lilac	20	10
T6	–	4d. black and blue	30	3·00
T7	24	6d. orange-brown and black (P 14)	40	20
		a. Perf 13×13½ (19.9.61)	30	2·50
		ab. Major retouch	35·00	
T8	–	1s. black and maroon	40	10
T9	26	2s.6d. black and green	2·50	1·00
T10	–	5s. black and red-orange	3·50	3·75
T11	–	10s. black and red-brown	4·50	7·50
T12	29	£1 black and violet	21·00	38·00
T1/T12 *Set of 12*			30·00	55·00

Nos. T2 and T4/T4*b* were overprinted on stamps printed by Waterlows' subsidiary, Imprimerie Belge de Securité.

Nos. T2*a*, T4*c* and T7*a* were from new printings produced by De La Rue instead of Waterlow.

As well as being a paler shade, No. T4*c* is much less deeply engraved than T4/T4*b*, clearly evident in the shading in the hills and sky.

The above stamps were withdrawn on 30 September 1961, when Southern Cameroons became part of the Cameroun Republic, although some post offices had been using unoverprinted Nigerian stamps for some months previously.

Canada

Separate stamp issues appeared for British Columbia and Vancouver Island, Canada, New Brunswick, Newfoundland, Nova Scotia and Prince Edward Island before these colonies joined the Dominion of Canada.

BRITISH COLUMBIA & VANCOUVER ISLAND

Vancouver Island was organised as a Crown Colony in 1849 and the mainland territory was proclaimed a separate colony as British Columbia in 1858. The two colonies combined, as British Columbia, on 19 November 1866.

PRICES FOR STAMPS ON COVER TO 1945	
Nos. 2/3	*from* × 6
Nos. 11/12	*from* × 2
Nos. 13/14	*from* × 6
Nos. 21/22	*from* × 10
Nos. 23/27	*from* × 6
Nos. 28/29	*from* × 10
No. 30	—
No. 31	*from* × 10
Nos. 32/33	—

1

(Typo D.L.R.)

1860. No wmk. P 14.

2	**1**	2½d. deep reddish rose	£425	£200
3		2½d. pale reddish rose	£425	£200

When Vancouver Island adopted the dollar currency in 1862 the 2½d. was sold at 5c. From 18 May until 1 November 1865 examples of Nos. 2/3 were used to prepay mail from Vancouver Island to British Columbia at the price of 15 cents a pair.

From 20 June 1864 to 1 November 1865, the 2½d. was sold in British Columbia for 3d. and was subsequently used for the same purpose during a shortage of 3d. stamps in 1867.

Imperforate plate proofs exist in pale dull red (*Price £10,000 un*).

VANCOUVER ISLAND

(New Currency. 100 cents = 1 dollar)

2

3

(Typo D.L.R.)

1865 (19 Sept). Wmk Crown CC.

(a) Imperf (1866)

11	**2**	5c. rose	£32000	£9000
12	**3**	10c. blue	£2000	£900

(b) P 14

13	**2**	5c. rose	£350	£200
		w. Wmk inverted	£1900	£900
		x. Wmk reversed	†	£1100
14	**3**	10c. blue	£250	£170
		w. Wmk inverted	£800	£600

Medium or poor examples of Nos. 11 and 12 can be supplied at much lower prices, when in stock.

After the two colonies combined Nos. 13/14 were also used in British Columbia.

BRITISH COLUMBIA

4

(Typo D.L.R.)

1865 (1 Nov)–**67**. Wmk Crown CC. P 14.

21	**4**	3d. deep blue	£120	85·00
22		3d. pale blue (19.7.67)	£110	85·00
		w. Wmk inverted	£500	£275
		y. Wmk inverted and reversed	†	£550

British Columbia changed to the dollar currency on 1 January 1866. Remaining stocks of No. 21 and the supply of No. 22, when it finally arrived, were sold at 12½c. a pair.

(New Currency. 100 cents = 1 dollar)

TWO CENTS (5) 5.CENTS.5 (6)

1868–71. T **4** in various colours. Surch as T **5** *or* **6**. Wmk Crown CC.

(a) P 12½ (3.69)

23	5c. red (Bk.)	£1600	£1200
24	10c. lake (B.)	£900	£700
25	25c. yellow (V.)	£600	£600
26	50c. mauve (R.)	£850	£700
27	$1 green (G.)	£1300	£1400

(b) P 14

28	2c. brown (Bk.) (1.68)	£170	£140
29	5c. pale red (Bk.) (5.69)	£250	£160
30	10c. lake (B.)	£1400	
31	25c. yellow (V.) (21.7.69)	£250	£160
	w. Wmk inverted	†	£1200
32	50c. mauve (R.) (23.2.71)	£650	£1100
	w. Wmk inverted	£1100	
33	$1 green (G.)	£1100	

Nos. 30 and 33 were not issued.

British Columbia joined the Dominion of Canada on 20 July 1871.

COLONY OF CANADA

The first British post offices in what was to become the Colony of Canada were opened at Quebec, Montreal and Trois Rivières during 1763. These, and subsequent, offices remained part of the British GPO system until 6 April 1851.

The two provinces of Upper Canada (Ontario) and Lower Canada (Quebec) were united in 1840.

For illustration of the handstamp types see BRITISH POST OFFICES ABROAD notes, following GREAT BRITAIN.

QUEBEC

CROWNED-CIRCLE HANDSTAMPS

CC1	CC **1**	QUEBEC L.C. (R.) (13.1.1842)... *Price on cover*	£160

PRICES FOR STAMPS ON COVER TO 1945	
Nos. 1/23	*from* × 2
Nos. 25/28	*from* × 3
Nos. 29/43*a*	*from* × 3
Nos. 44/45	*from* × 8

1 American Beaver (Designed by Sir Sandford Fleming)

2 Prince Albert

3

Major re-entry: Line through 'EE PEN' (Upper pane R. 5/7)

(T **1/6**. Eng and recess Rawdon, Wright, Hatch and Edson, New York)

1851. Laid paper. Imperf.

1	**1**	3d. red (23.4)	£38000	£1100
1*a*		3d. orange-vermilion	£38000	£1100
		b. Major re-entry	—	£3750
2	**2**	6d. slate-violet (15.5)	£50000	£1300
3		6d. brown-purple	£50000	£1400
		a. Bisected (3d.) *on cover*	†	£38000
4	**3**	12d. black (14.6)	£200000	£100000

There are several re-entries on the plate of the 3d. in addition to the major re-entry listed. All re-entries occur in this stamp on all papers.

Forgeries of the 3d. are known without the full stop after 'PENCE'. They also omit the foliage in the corners, as do similar forgeries of the 6d.

4

5

6 Jacques Cartier

Re-entry (R. 10/12)

1852–57. Imperf.

A. Handmade wove paper, varying in thickness (1852–1857)

5	**1**	3d. red	£2750	£225
		a. Bisected (1½d.) *on cover* (1856)	†	£38000
6		3d. deep red	£3000	£275
7		3d. scarlet-vermilion	£3500	£275
8		3d. brown-red	£3000	£275
		a. Bisected (1½d.) *on cover* (1856).	†	£38000
		b. Major re-entry (*all shades*) *from*	£7500	£950
9	**2**	6d. slate-violet	£45000	£1100
		a. Bisected (3d.) *on cover*	†	£20000
10		6d. greenish grey	£45000	£1200
11		6d. brownish grey	£48000	£1400
12	**5**	7½d. yellow-green (*shades*) (2.6.57)	£13000	£2500
13	**6**	10d. bright blue (1.55)	£14000	£1800
14		10d. dull blue	£13000	£1700
15		10d. blue *to* deep blue	£14000	£1800
		a. Major re-entry (*all shades*) *from*	—	£3250
16	**3**	12d. black		† £150000

B. Machine-made medium to thick wove paper of a more even hard texture with more visible mesh. Clearer impressions (1857)

17	**4**	½d. deep rose (1.8.57)	£1000	£600
		a. Re-entry	£3250	£1500
18	**1**	3d. red	£3500	£450
		a. Bisected (1½d.) *on cover*	†	£38000
		b. Major re-entry	—	£1500
19	**2**	6d. grey-lilac	£48000	£2500
20	**6**	10d. blue *to* deep blue	£16000	£2250
		a. Major re-entry	£27000	£3500

C. Thin soft horizontally ribbed paper (1857)

21	**4**	½d. deep rose	£9500	£2250
		a. Vertically ribbed paper	£10000	£3250
22	**1**	3d. red	£4750	£450
		a. Major re-entry	—	£1600

D. Very thick soft wove paper (1857)

23	**2**	6d. reddish purple	£48000	£4000
		a. Bisected (3d.) *on cover*	†	£35000

Bisected examples of the 3d. value were used to make up the 7½d. Canadian Packet rate to England from May 1856 until the introduction of the 7½d. value on 2 June 1857.

The 7½d. and 10d. values can be found in wide and narrow versions. These differences are due to shrinkage of the paper, which was wetted before printing and then contracted unevenly during drying. The width of these stamps varies between 17 and 18 mm.

The listed major re-entry on the 10d. occurs on R. 3/5 and shows strong doubling of the top frame line and the left-hand '8d. stg.' with a line through the lower parts of 'ANAD' and 'ENCE'. Smaller re-entries occur on all values.

Examples of the 12d. on wove paper come from a proof sheet used for postal purposes by the postal authorities.

The 3d. is known perforated 14 and also *percé en scie* 13. Both are contemporary, but were unofficial.

1858–59. P 11¾.

A. Machine-made medium to thick wove paper with a more even hard texture

25	**4**	½d. deep rose (12.58)	£4750	£1000
		a. Lilac-rose	£4750	£1100
		b. Re-entry (R. 10/10)	£8500	£2500
26	**1**	3d. red (1.59)	£13000	£375
		a. Major re-entry	—	£1500
27	**2**	6d. brownish grey (1.59)	£18000	£4250
		a. Slate-violet	£18000	£4000

B. Thin soft horizontally ribbed paper

27*b*	**4**	½d. deep rose-red	—	£4500
28	**1**	3d. red	—	£1800
		a. Major re-entry		

The re-entry on the imperforate and perforated ½d sheets was the same, but occurred on R. 10/10 of the perforated sheets because the two left-hand vertical rows were removed prior to perforation.

(New Currency. 100 cents = 1 dollar)

7

8 American Beaver

9 Prince Albert

10

11 Jacques Cartier

5c. Major re-entry showing as doubling of oval frame lines and lettering, particularly at the left of the design (R. 3/8)

(On 1 May 1858, Messrs. Rawdon, Wright, Hatch and Edson joined with eight other firms to form 'The American Bank Note Co' and the 'imprint' on sheets of the following stamps has the new title of the firm with 'New York' added.)

(Recess A.B.N. Co)

1859 (1 July). P 12.

29	**7**	1c. pale rose (*to* rose-red)	£425	50·00
30		1c. deep rose (*to* carmine-rose)	£500	70·00
		a. Imperf (pair)	£4750	
		b. Imperf×perf		
31	**8**	5c. pale red	£450	20·00
32		5c. deep red	£450	22·00
		a. Re-entry* (R. 3/8)	£4000	£450
		b. Imperf (pair)	£18000	
		c. Bisected (2½c.) with 10c. *on cover*	†	£7500
33	**9**	10c. black-brown	£18000	£2500
		a. Bisected (5c.), *on cover*	†	£12000
33*b*		10c. deep red-purple	£4250	£700
		ba. Bisected (5c.), *on cover*	†	£7000
34		10c. purple (*shades*)	£1500	80·00
		a. Bisected (5c.), *on cover*	†	£6500

35		10c. brownish purple	£1400	85·00
36		10c. brown (*to pale*)	£1400	80·00
		a. Bisected (5c.), *on cover*	†	£7500
37		10c. dull violet	£1500	85·00
38		10c. bright red-purple	£1500	80·00
		a. Imperf (pair)	£15000	
39	**10**	12½c. deep yellow-green	£1300	70·00
40		12½c. pale yellow-green	£1200	70·00
41		12½c. blue-green	£1500	85·00
		a. Imperf (pair)	£7000	
		b. Imperf between (vert pair)		
42	**11**	17c. deep blue	£1600	95·00
		a. Imperf (pair)	£6500	
43		17c. slate-blue	£1900	£130
43*a*		17c. indigo	£1800	£100

* Slighter re-entries are worth from £40 upwards in used condition.

As there were numerous PO Dept. orders for the 10c., 12½c. and 17c. and some of these were executed by more than one separate printing, with no special care to ensure uniformity of colour, there is a wide range of shade, especially in the 10c., and some shades recur at intervals after periods during which other shades predominated. The colour-names given in the above list therefore represent groups only.

It has been proved by leading Canadian specialists that the perforations may be an aid to the approximate dating of a particular stamp, the gauge used measuring 11¾×11¾ from mid-July 1859 to mid-1863, 12×11¾ from March 1863 to mid-1865 and 12×12 from April 1865 to 1868. Exceptionally, in the 5c. value many sheets were perforated 12×12 between May and October, 1862, whilst the last printings of the 12½c. and 17c. perf 11¾×11¾ were in July 1863, the perf 12×11¾ starting towards the end of 1863.

12

(Recess A.B.N. Co)

1864 (1 Aug). P 12.

44	**12**	2c. rose-red	£600	£170
45		2c. bright rose	£600	£170
		a. Imperf (pair)	£3500	

The Colony of Canada became part of the Dominion of Canada on 1 July 1867.

NEW BRUNSWICK

New Brunswick, previously part of Nova Scotia, became a separate colony in June 1784. The colony became responsible for its postal service on 6 July 1851.

PRICES FOR STAMPS ON COVER TO 1945

Nos. 1/4	*from* × 2
Nos. 5/6	*from* × 3
Nos. 7/9	*from* × 10
Nos. 10/12	*from* × 30
No. 13	—
Nos. 14/17	*from* × 2
No. 18	*from* × 5
No. 19	*from* × 100

1 Royal Crown and Heraldic Flowers of the United Kingdom

(Recess P.B.)

1851 (5 Sept)–**60**. Blue paper. Imperf.

1	**1**	3d. bright red	£4000	£425
2		3d. dull red	£3500	£350
		a. Bisected (1½d.) (1854) (*on cover*)	†	£3000
2*b*		6d. mustard-yellow	£7500	£1500
3		6d. yellow	£5000	£900
4		6d. olive-yellow	£5000	£800
		a. Bisected (3d.) (1854) (*on cover*)	†	£3000
		b. Quartered (1½d.) (1860) (*on cover*)	†	£42000
5		1s. reddish mauve	£18000	£4500
6		1s. dull mauve	£21000	£5000
		a. Bisected (6d.) (1855) (*on cover*)	†	£24000
		b. Quartered (3d.) (1860) (*on cover*)	†	£38000

Reprints of all three values were made in 1890 on thin, hard, white paper. The 3d. is bright orange, the 6d. and 1s. violet-black.

Nos. 2a and 4b were to make up the 7½d. rate to Great Britain, introduced on 1 August 1854.

(New Currency. 100 cents = 1 dollar)

2 Locomotive

3

3a Charles Connell

4

5

6 Paddle-steamer *Washington*

7 King Edward VII when Prince of Wales

(Recess A.B.N. Co)

1860 (15 May)–**63**. No wmk. P 12.

7	**2**	1c. brown-purple	85·00	60·00
8		1c. purple	70·00	50·00
9		1c. dull claret	70·00	50·00
		a. Imperf vert (horiz pair)	£650	
10	**3**	2c. orange (1863)	35·00	29·00
11		2c. orange-yellow	42·00	29·00
12		2c. deep orange	45·00	29·00
		a. Imperf horiz (vert pair)	£475	
13	**3a**	5c. brown	£10000	
14	**4**	5c. yellow-green	28·00	18·00
15		5c. deep green	28·00	18·00
16		5c. sap-green (deep yellowish green)	£300	40·00
17	**5**	10c. red	65·00	75·00
		a. Bisected (5c.) (*on cover*) (1860)	†	£600
18	**6**	12½c. indigo	70·00	42·00
19	**7**	17c. black	42·00	90·00

Beware of forged cancellations.

No. 13 was not issued due to objections to the design showing Charles Connell, the Postmaster-General. Most of the printing was destroyed.

New Brunswick joined the Dominion of Canada on 1 July 1867 and its stamps were withdrawn in March of the following year.

NEWFOUNDLAND

Newfoundland became a self-governing colony in 1855 and a Dominion in 1907. In 1934 the adverse financial situation led to the suspension of the constitution, with a reversion to colonial status.

The first local postmaster, at St John's, was appointed in 1805, the overseas mails being routed via Halifax, Nova Scotia. A regular packet service was established between these two ports in 1840, the British GPO assuming control of the overseas mails at the same time.

The responsibility for the overseas postal service reverted to the colonial administration on 1 July 1851.

ST JOHN'S

CROWNED-CIRCLE HANDSTAMPS

CC **1a**

CC1	CC **1a**	ST JOHN'S NEWFOUNDLAND (R.) (27.6.1846)	*Price on cover*	£1000

PRICES FOR STAMPS ON COVER TO 1945

No. 1	*from* × 30
Nos. 2/4	*from* × 3
No. 5	*from* × 20
No. 6	*from* × 10
No. 7	*from* × 3
No. 8	*from* × 30
No. 9	*from* × 8
No. 10	—
No. 11	*from* × 8
No. 12	*from* × 3
Nos. 13/14	*from* × 20
Nos. 15/17	—
Nos. 18/20	*from* × 20
No. 21	*from* × 15
Nos. 22/23	—
No. 25	*from* × 30
No. 26	*from* × 5
No. 27	*from* × 8
No. 28	*from* × 3
Nos. 29/30	*from* × 10
No. 31	*from* × 30
No. 32	*from* × 8
No. 33	*from* × 5
Nos. 34/39	*from* × 8
Nos. 40/41	*from* × 5
Nos. 42/43	*from* × 30
Nos. 44/48	*from* × 8
No. 49	*from* × 50
Nos. 50/53	*from* × 10
No. 54	*from* × 4
Nos. 55/58*b*	*from* × 10
No. 59	*from* × 100
No. 59*a*	*from* × 10
Nos. 60/61	*from* × 4
Nos. 62/65	*from* × 8

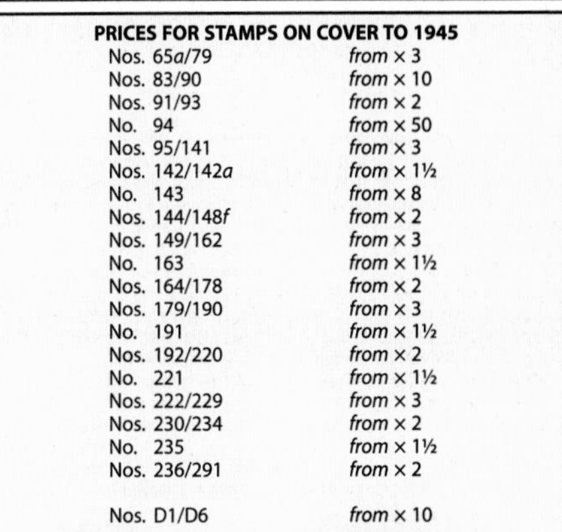

PRICES FOR STAMPS ON COVER TO 1945

Nos. 65*a*/79	*from* × 3
Nos. 83/90	*from* × 10
Nos. 91/93	*from* × 2
No. 94	*from* × 50
Nos. 95/141	*from* × 3
Nos. 142/142*a*	*from* × 1½
No. 143	*from* × 8
Nos. 144/148*f*	*from* × 2
Nos. 149/162	*from* × 3
No. 163	*from* × 1½
Nos. 164/178	*from* × 2
Nos. 179/190	*from* × 3
No. 191	*from* × 1½
Nos. 192/220	*from* × 2
No. 221	*from* × 1½
Nos. 222/229	*from* × 3
Nos. 230/234	*from* × 2
No. 235	*from* × 1½
Nos. 236/291	*from* × 2
Nos. D1/D6	*from* × 10

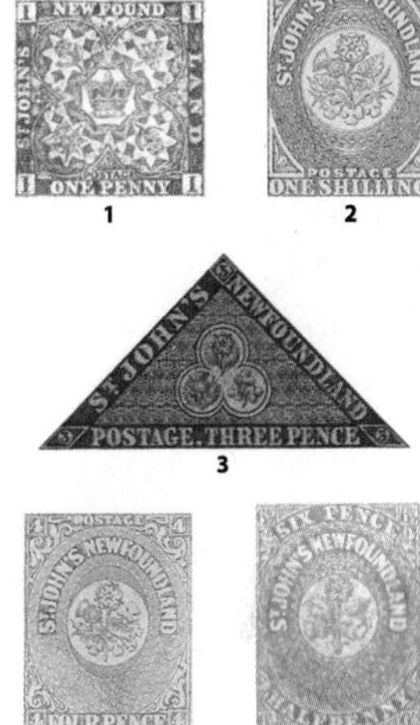

1 2 3 4 5

Royal Crown and Heraldic flowers of the United Kingdom

(Recess P.B.)

1857 (1 Jan)–**64**. Thick, machine-made paper with a distinct mesh. No wmk. Imperf.

1	**1**	1d. brown-purple	£160	£250
		a. Bisected (½d.) (1864) (*on cover*)	†	£40000
2	**2**	2d. scarlet-vermilion (15.2)	£25000	£6500
3	**3**	3d. yellowish green (H/S 'CANCELLED' in oval £12000)	£2000	£425
4	**4**	4d. scarlet-vermilion	£15000	£3500
5	**1**	5d. brown-purple	£350	£500
6	**4**	6d. scarlet-vermilion	£28000	£4750
7	**5**	6½d. scarlet-vermilion	£4500	£4750
8	**4**	8d. scarlet-vermilion	£400	£950
		a. Bisected (4d.) (1859) (*on cover*).	†	£4250
9	**2**	1s. scarlet-vermilion	£27000	£9000
		a. Bisected (6d.) (1860) (*on cover*).	†	£17000

The 6d. and 8d. differ from the 4d. in many details, as does also the 1s. from the 2d.

PERKINS BACON 'CANCELLED'. For notes on these handstamps, showing 'CANCELLED' between horizontal bars forming an oval, see Catalogue Introduction.

1860 (15 Aug–Dec). Medium, hand-made paper without mesh. Imperf.

10	**2**	2d. orange-vermilion	£600	£700
11	**3**	3d. green *to* deep green* (H/S 'CANCELLED' in oval £11000)	£110	£190
12	**4**	4d. orange-vermilion (H/S 'CANCELLED' in oval £14000)	£4500	£1100
		a. Bisected (2d.) (12.60) (*on cover*).	†	£20000
13	**1**	5d. Venetian red (H/S 'CANCELLED' in oval £13000)	£140	£400
14	**4**	6d. orange-vermilion	£5000	£800
15	**2**	1s. orange-vermilion (H/S 'CANCELLED' in oval £17000)	£35000	£11000
		a. Bisected (6d.) (12.60) (*on cover*).	†	£45000

* No. 11 includes stamps from the July and November 1861 printings which are very difficult to distinguish.

The 1s. on horizontally or vertically *laid* paper is now considered to be a proof (*Price* £21000).

Stamps of this and the following issue may be found with part of the paper-maker's watermark 'STACEY WISE 1858'.

BISECTS. Collectors are warned against buying bisected stamps of these issues without a reliable guarantee.

1862–64. New colours. Hand-made paper without mesh. Imperf.

16	**1**	1d. chocolate-brown	£350	£450
		a. Red-brown	£8500	
17	**2**	2d. rose-lake	£300	£500
18	**4**	4d. rose-lake (H/S 'CANCELLED' in oval £13000)	50·00	£110
		a. Bisected (2d.) (1864) (*on cover*).	†	£38000
19	**1**	5d. chocolate-brown (*shades*)	£100	£325
		a. Red-brown (shades)	90·00	£200
20	**4**	6d. rose-lake (H/S 'CANCELLED' in oval £11000)	35·00	£100
		a. Bisected (3d.) (1863) (*on cover*).	†	£9500
21	**5**	6½d. rose-lake (H/S 'CANCELLED' in oval £11000)	£100	£450

22	**4**	8d. rose-lake	£130	£650
23	**2**	1s. rose-lake (H/S 'CANCELLED' in oval £12000)	50·00	£300
		a. Bisected (6d.) (1863) (*on cover*)	†	£22000

Nos. 16/23 come from printings made in July (2d., 4d., 6d., 6½d., and 1s. only) or November 1861 (all values), which were received in Newfoundland in January 1862. The paper used was from the same manufacturer as that for Nos. 10/15, but was of more variable thickness and texture, ranging from a relatively soft medium paper, which can be quite opaque, to a thin hard transparent paper. The rose-lake stamps also show a considerable variation in shade ranging from pale to deep. The extensive remainders of this issue were predominantly in pale shades on thin hard paper, but it is not possible to distinguish between stamps from the two printings with any certainty. Deep shades of the 2d., 4d., 6d., 6½d. and 1s. on soft opaque paper do, however, command a considerable premium.

Beware of buying used examples of the stamps which are worth much less in unused condition, as many unused stamps have been provided with faked postmarks. A guarantee should be obtained.

(New Currency. 100 cents = 1 dollar)

6 Atlantic Cod

7 Common Seal on Ice-floe

8 Prince Consort

9 Queen Victoria

10 Schooner

11 Queen Victoria

(Recess A.B.N. Co, New York)

1865 (15 Nov)–**70.** P 12.

(a) Thin yellowish paper

25	**6**	2c. yellowish green	£170	£110
		a. Bisected (1c.) (*on cover*) (1870)	†	£8500
26	**7**	5c. brown	£600	£180
		a. Bisected (2½c.) (*on cover*)	†	£10000
27	**8**	10c. black	£375	£110
		a. Bisected (5c.) (*on cover*) (1869)	†	£7000
28	**9**	12c. red-brown	£650	£150
		a. Bisected (6c.) (*on cover*) (1869)	†	£5000
29	**10**	13c. orange-yellow	£120	£140
30	**11**	24c. blue	50·00	38·00

(b) Medium white paper

31	**6**	2c. bluish green (*to deep*) (1870)	£120	50·00
32	**8**	10c. black (1870)	£275	48·00
33	**9**	12c. chestnut (1870)	60·00	48·00

The inland postage rate was reduced to 3c. on 8 May, 1870. Until the 3c. value became available examples of No. 25 were bisected to provide 1c. stamps.

For the 12c. value in deep brown, see No. 61.

12 King Edward VII when Prince of Wales

14 Queen Victoria

I

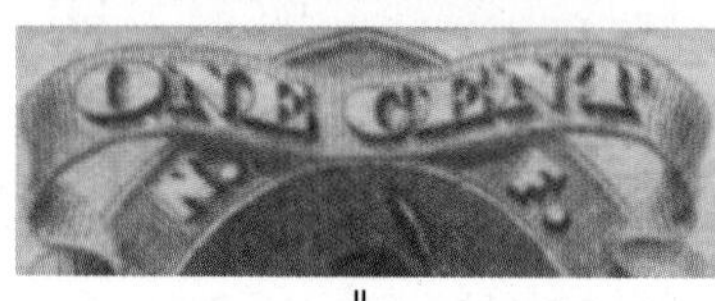

II

In Type II the white oval frame line is unbroken by the scroll containing the words 'ONE CENT', the letters 'N.F.' are smaller and closer to the scroll, and there are other minor differences.

(Recess National Bank Note Co, New York)

1868 (Nov). P 12.

34	**12**	1c. dull purple (I)	75·00	60·00

(Recess A.B.N. Co)

1868 (Nov)–**73.** P 12.

35	**12**	1c. brown-purple (II) (3.71)	£130	70·00
36	**14**	3c. vermilion (7.70)	£300	£100
37		3c. blue (1.4.73)	£275	27·00
38	**7**	5c. black	£325	£110
39	**14**	6c. rose (7.70)	17·00	30·00

1876–79. Rouletted.

40	**12**	1c. lake-purple (II) (1877)	£120	55·00
41	**6**	2c. bluish green (1879)	£170	50·00
42	**14**	3c. blue (1877)	£325	6·00
43	**7**	5c. blue	£200	4·00
		a. Imperf (pair)		

15 King Edward VII when Prince of Wales

16 Atlantic Cod

17

18 Common Seal on Ice-floe

(Recess British American Bank Note Co, Montreal)

1880–82. P 12.

44	**15**	1c. dull grey-brown	50·00	17·00
		a. Dull brown	50·00	17·00
		b. Red-brown	55·00	20·00
46	**16**	2c. yellow-green (1882)	60·00	32·00
47	**17**	3c. pale dull blue	£150	9·50
		a. Bright blue	85·00	6·50
48	**18**	5c. pale dull blue	£350	10·00

19 Newfoundland Dog

20 Atlantic Brigantine

21 Queen Victoria

(Recess British American Bank Note Co, Montreal)

1887 (1 Nov). New colours and values. P 12.

49	**19**	½c. rose-red	16·00	11·00
50	**15**	1c. blue-green	21·00	14·00
		a. Green	7·00	4·50
		b. Yellow-green	13·00	11·00
51	**16**	2c. orange-vermilion	27·00	7·50
		a. Imperf (pair)	£375	
52	**17**	3c. deep brown	85·00	2·75
53	**18**	5c. deep blue	£120	5·50
54	**20**	10c. black	75·00	75·00
49/54 *Set of* 6			£300	95·00

For reissues in similar colours, see Nos. 62/65*a*.

(Recess B.A.B.N. Co)

1890 (Nov). P 12.

55	**21**	3c. deep slate	55·00	3·50
		a. Imperf (pair)		
56		3c. slate-grey (*to grey*)	50·00	3·75
		a. Imperf horiz (vert pair)	£550	
57		3c. slate-violet	70·00	8·00
58		3c. grey-lilac	70·00	3·75
58*a*		3c. brown-grey	75·00	9·00
58*b*		3c. purple-grey	75·00	9·00

There is a very wide range of shades in this stamp, and those given only cover the main groups.

Stamps on pink paper are from a consignment recovered from the sea and which were affected by the salt water.

(Recess British American Bank Note Co, Montreal)

1894 (Aug–Dec). Changes of colour. P 12.

59	**19**	½c. black (11.94)	10·00	9·50
59*a*	**18**	5c. bright blue (12.94)	80·00	5·50
60	**14**	6c. crimson-lake (12.94)	32·00	28·00
61	**9**	12c. deep brown	90·00	90·00

The 6c. is printed from the old American Bank Note Company's plates.

1896 (Jan)–**98.** Reissues. P 12.

62	**19**	½c. orange-vermilion	65·00	55·00
63	**15**	1c. deep brown	90·00	55·00
63*a*		1c. deep green (1898)	35·00	27·00
64	**16**	2c. green	£120	70·00
65	**17**	3c. deep blue	90·00	30·00
65*a*		3c. chocolate-brown	£120	95·00
62/65*a Set of* 6			£450	£300

The above were *reissued* for postal purposes. The colours were generally brighter than those of the original stamps.

22 Queen Victoria

23 John Cabot

24 Cape Bonavista

25 Caribou hunting

26 Mining

27 Logging

28 Fishing

29 *Matthew* (Cabot)

30 Willow Grouse

31 Group of Grey Seals

32 Salmon-fishing

33 Seal of the Colony

34 Iceberg off St John's

35 Henry VII

(Des R. O. Smith. Recess A.B.N. Co)

1897 (24 June). 400th Anniversary of Discovery of Newfoundland and 60th year of Queen Victoria's reign. P 12.

66	**22**	1c. green	8·50	13·00
67	**23**	2c. bright rose	2·75	2·75
		a. Bisected (1c.) *on cover*	†	£325
68	**24**	3c. bright blue	4·00	1·00
		a. Bisected (1½c.) *on cover*	†	£325
69	**25**	4c. olive-green	14·00	9·50
70	**26**	5c. violet	14·00	4·50
71	**27**	6c. red-brown	9·50	3·25
		a. Bisected (3c.) *on cover*	†	£350
72	**28**	8c. orange	21·00	9·50
73	**29**	10c. sepia	45·00	15·00
74	**30**	12c. deep blue	42·00	12·00
75	**31**	15c. bright scarlet	26·00	26·00
76	**32**	24c. dull violet-blue	32·00	38·00
77	**33**	30c. slate-blue	55·00	£110
78	**34**	35c. red	70·00	95·00
79	**35**	60c. black	27·00	22·00
66/79 *Set of* 14			£325	£325

The 60c. surcharged 'TWO—2—CENTS' in three lines is an essay made in December 1918 (*Price* £450).

ONE CENT

(36)

ONE CENT

(37)

ONE CENT

(38)

1897 (19 Oct). T **21** surch with T **36/38** by *Royal Gazette*, St John's, on stamps of various shades.

80	**36**	1c. on 3c. grey-purple	80·00	40·00
		a. Surch double, one diagonal	£1300	
		d. Vert pair, one without lower bar and 'ONE CENT'	£4000	
81	**37**	1c. on 3c. grey-purple	£170	£120
82	**38**	1c. on 3c. grey-purple	£600	£500

Nos. 80/82 occur in the same setting of 50 (10×5) applied twice to each sheet. T **36** appeared in the first four horizontal rows, T **37** on R. 5/1–8 and T **38** on R. 5/9 and 10.

Trial surcharges in red or red and black were not issued. (*Price:* T **36** *in red* £1000, *in red and black* £1000: T **37** *in red* £3000, *in red and black* £3000: T **38** *in red* £7500, *in red and black* £8000).

These surcharges exist on stamps of various shades, but those on brown-grey are clandestine forgeries, having been produced by one of the printers at the *Royal Gazette*.

39 Prince Edward later Duke of Windsor

40 Queen Victoria

41 King Edward VII when Prince of Wales

42 Queen Alexandra when Princess of Wales

43 Queen Mary when Duchess of York

44 King George V when Duke of York

(Recess A.B.N. Co)

1897 (4 Dec)–**1918**. P 12.

83	**39**	½c. olive (8.98)	2·25	1·50
		a. Imperf (pair)	£650	
84	**40**	1c. carmine	8·00	9·00
85		1c. blue-green (6.98)	19·00	20
		a. Yellow-green	21·00	20
		b. Imperf horiz (vert pair)	£275	
86	**41**	2c. orange	10·00	10·00
		a. Imperf (pair)	—	£500
87		2c. scarlet (6.98)	22·00	75
		a. Imperf (pair)	£375	£375
		b. Imperf between (pair)	£650	
88	**42**	3c. orange (6.98)	32·00	30
		a. Imperf horiz (vert pair)	£450	
		b. Imperf (pair)	£375	£375
		c. Red-orange/bluish (6.18)	50·00	3·50
89	**43**	4c. violet (21.10.01)	35·00	11·00
		a. Imperf (pair)	£600	
90	**44**	5c. blue (6.99)	50·00	3·00
83/90 *Set of 8*			£150	32·00

No. 88*c* was an emergency war-time printing made by the American Bank Note Co from the old plate, pending receipt of the then current 3c. from England.

The imperforate errors of this issue are found used, but only as philatelic 'by favour' items. It is possible that No. 86*a* only exists in this condition.

45 Map of Newfoundland

(Recess A.B.N. Co)

1908 (31 Aug). P 12.

94	**45**	2c. lake	30·00	1·00

46 King James I

47 Arms of Colonisation Co

48 John Guy

49 *Endeavour* (immigrant ship), 1610

50 Cupids

51 Sir Francis Bacon

52 View of Mosquito

53 Logging Camp, Red Indian Lake

54 Paper Mills, Grand Falls

55 King Edward VII

56 King George V

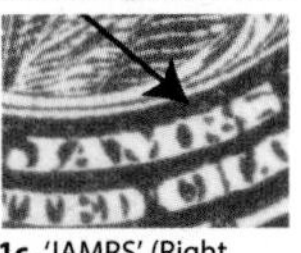
1c. 'NFWFOUNDLAND' (Right pane, R. 5/1)

1c. 'JAMRS' (Right pane, R. 5/2)

6c. (A) 'Z' in 'COLONIZATION' reversed. (B) 'Z' correct.

(Litho Whitehead, Morris & Co Ltd)

1910 (15 Aug).

		(a) P 12		
95	**46**	1c. green	19·00	3·75
		a. 'NFWFOUNDLAND'	85·00	£110
		b. 'JAMRS'	85·00	£110
		c. Imperf between (horiz pair)	£350	£375
96	**47**	2c. rose-carmine	27·00	2·50
97	**48**	3c. olive	14·00	27·00
98	**49**	4c. violet	27·00	21·00
99	**50**	5c. bright blue	50·00	15·00
100	**51**	6c. claret (A)	60·00	£170
100*a*		6c. claret (B)	38·00	£110
101	**52**	8c. bistre-brown	70·00	£130
102	**53**	9c. olive-green	70·00	£110
103	**54**	10c. purple-slate	75·00	£140
104	**55**	12c. pale red-brown	70·00	£100
		a. Imperf (pair)	£325	
105	**56**	15c. black	70·00	£130
95/105 *Set of 11*			£475	£700
		(b) P 12×14		
106	**46**	1c. green	9·00	18·00
		a. 'NFWFOUNDLAND'	70·00	£160
		b. 'JAMRS'	70·00	£160
		c. Imperf between (horiz pair)	£700	£750
107	**47**	2c. rose-carmine	9·50	40
		a. Imperf between (horiz pair)	£700	
108	**50**	5c. bright blue (P 14×12)	12·00	3·00
		(c) P 12×11		
109	**46**	1c. green	3·25	30
		a. Imperf between (horiz pair)	£325	
		b. Imperf between (vert pair)	£375	
		c. 'NFWFOUNDLAND'	45·00	60·00
		e. 'JAMRS'	45·00	60·00
		(d) P 12×11½		
110	**47**	2c. rose-carmine	£450	£300

(Dies eng Macdonald & Sons. Recess A. Alexander & Sons, Ltd)

1911 (7 Feb). As T **51** to **56**, but recess printed. P 14.

111	6c. claret (B)	18·00	50·00
112	8c. yellow-brown	50·00	80·00
	a. Imperf between (horiz pair)	£1100	
113	9c. sage-green	50·00	£150
	a. Imperf between (horiz pair)	£1100	
114	10c. purple-black	90·00	£150
	a. Imperf between (horiz pair)	£1100	
115	12c. red-brown	70·00	70·00
116	15c. slate-green	65·00	£130
111/116 *Set of 6*		£300	£550

The 9c. and 15c. exist with papermaker's watermark 'E. TOWGOOD FINE'.

Nos. 111/116 exist imperforate. (*Price* £250, *unused, for each pair*).

57 Queen Mary

58 King George V

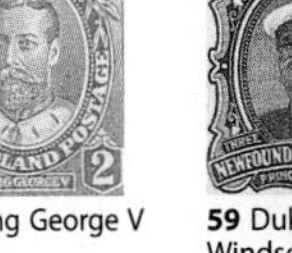
59 Duke of Windsor when Prince of Wales

60 King George VI when Prince Albert

61 Princess Mary, the Princess Royal

62 Prince Henry, Duke of Gloucester

63 Prince George, Duke of Kent

64 Prince John

65 Queen Alexandra

66 Duke of Connaught

67 Seal of Newfoundland

(1c. to 5c., 10c. eng and recess D.L.R.; others eng Macdonald & Co, recess A. Alexander & Sons)

1911 (19 June)–**16**. Coronation. P 13½×14 (comb) (1c. to 5c., 10c.) or 14 (line) (others).

117	**57**	1c. yellow-green	10·00	30
		a. Blue-green (1915)	25·00	30
118	**58**	2c. carmine	12·00	20
		a. Rose-red (*blurred impression*). Perf 14 (1916)	17·00	1·00
119	**59**	3c. red-brown	26·00	50·00
120	**60**	4c. purple	25·00	45·00
121	**61**	5c. ultramarine	8·00	2·25
122	**62**	6c. slate-grey	15·00	27·00
123	**63**	8c. aniline blue	60·00	85·00
		a. Greenish blue	95·00	£130
124	**64**	9c. violet-blue	35·00	55·00
125	**65**	10c. deep green	42·00	50·00
126	**66**	12c. plum	32·00	50·00
127	**67**	15c. lake	29·00	50·00
117/127 *Set of 11*			£250	£350

The 2c. rose-red, No. 118*a* is a poor war-time printing by Alexander & Sons.

Although No. 123 has a typical aniline appearance it is believed that the shade results from the thinning of non-aniline ink.

Nos. 117/118, 121 and 126/127 exist imperforate, without gum. (*Prices for* 1c., 2c., 5c., 12c., £250, *for* 15c. £75, *unused, per pair*).

68 Caribou

FIRST TRANS-ATLANTIC AIR POST April, 1919.

(**69**)

(Des J. H. Noonan. Recess D.L.R.)

1919 (2 Jan). Newfoundland Contingent, 1914–1918. P 14.

130	**68**	1c. green (*a*) (*b*)	3·75	20
131		2c. scarlet (*a*) (*b*)	3·75	85
		a. Carmine-red (*b*)	25·00	80
132		3c. brown (*a*) (*b*)	8·50	20
		a. Red-brown (*b*)	16·00	60
133		4c. mauve (*a*)	13·00	80
		a. Purple (*b*)	28·00	50
134		5c. ultramarine (*a*) (*b*)	18·00	1·25
135		6c. slate-grey (*a*)	19·00	70·00
136		8c. bright magenta (*a*)	19·00	70·00
137		10c. deep grey-green (*a*)	9·00	8·00
138		12c. orange (*a*)	22·00	75·00
139		15c. indigo (*a*)	17·00	90·00
		a. Prussian blue (*a*)	£110	£150
140		24c. bistre-brown (*a*)	32·00	42·00
141		36c. sage-green (*a*)	24·00	50·00
130/141 *Set of 12*			£160	£350

Each value bears with 'Trail of the Caribou' the name of a different action: 1c. Suvla Bay; 3c. Gueudecourt; 4c. Beaumont Hamel; 6c. Monchy; 10c. Steenbeck; 15c. Langemarck; 24c. Cambrai; 36c. Combles; 2c., 5c., 8c., and 12c. inscribed 'Royal Naval Reserve-Ubique'.

Perforations. Two perforating heads were used: (*a*) comb 14×13.9; (*b*) line 14.1×14.1.

Nos. 130/141 exist imperforate, without gum. (*Price* £350 *unused, for each pair*).

1919 (12 Apr). Air. No. 132 optd with T **69**, by Robinson & Co Ltd, at the offices of the *Daily News*.

142	**68**	3c. brown	£22000	£12000

These stamps franked correspondence carried by Lieut. H. Hawker on his Atlantic flight. 18 were damaged and destroyed, 95 used on letters, 11 given as presentation copies, and the remaining 76 were sold in aid of the Marine Disasters Fund.

1919 (19 Apr). Nos. 132 inscribed in MS. 'Aerial Atlantic Mail. J.A.R.'.

142*a*	**68**	3c. brown	£70000	£20000

This provisional was made by W. C. Campbell, the Secretary of the Postal Department, and the initials are those of the Postmaster, J. A. Robinson, for use on correspondence intended to be carried on the abortive Morgan-Raynham Trans-Atlantic flight. The mail was eventually delivered by sea.

In addition to the 25 to 30 used examples, one unused, no gum, example of No. 142*a* is known.

Single examples of a similar overprint on the 2c., (No. 131) and 5c. (No. 134) are known used on cover, the former with an unoverprinted example of the same value.

Trans-Atlantic AIR POST, 1919. ONE DOLLAR.

(**70**)

THREE CENTS

(**71**)

1919 (9 June). Air. No. 75 surch with T **70** by *Royal Gazette*, St John's.

143	**31**	$1 on 15c. bright scarlet	£130	£150
		a. No comma after 'AIR POST'	£160	£180
		b. As var a and no stop after '1919'	£375	£450
		c. As var a and 'A' of 'AIR' under 'a' of 'Trans'	£375	£450

These stamps were issued for use on the mail carried on the first successful flight across the Atlantic by Captain J. Alcock and Lieutenant A. Brown, and on other projected Trans-Atlantic flights (Alcock flown cover, *Price* £3000).

The surcharge was applied in a setting of which 16 were normal, 7 as No. 143a, 1 as No. 143b and 1 as No. 143c.

1920 (Sept). Nos. 75 and 77/78 surch as T **71**, by *Royal Gazette* (2c. with only one bar, at top of stamp).

A. Bars of surch 10½ mm apart. B. Bars 13½ mm apart.

144	**33**	2c. on 30c. slate-blue (24.9)	8·00	38·00
		a. Surch inverted	£1400	£1600
145	**31**	3c. on 15c. bright scarlet (A.) (13.9)	£250	£275
		a. Surch inverted	£3000	
146		3c. on 15c. bright scarlet (B.) (13.9)	40·00	42·00

147	**34**	3c. on 35c. red (15.9)	18·00	27·00
		a. Surch inverted	£2750	
		b. Lower bar omitted	£180	£225
		c. 'THREE' omitted	£1200	

Our prices for Nos. 147b and 147c are for stamps with lower bar or 'THREE' entirely missing. The bar may be found in all stages of incompleteness and stamps showing broken bar are not of much value.

On the other hand, stamps showing either only the top or bottom of the letters 'THREE' are scarce, though not as rare as No. 147c.

The 6c. T **27** surcharged 'THREE CENTS', in red or black, is an essay (*Price* £950). The 2c. on 30c. with red surcharge is a colour trial (*Price* £1300).

AIR MAIL to Halifax, N.S. 1921.

(**72**)

1921 (16 Nov). Air. No. 78 optd with T **72** by *Royal Gazette*.

		I. 2¾ mm between 'AIR' and 'MAIL'		
148	**34**	35c. red	£150	£100
		a. No stop after '1921'	£130	90·00
		b. No stop and first '1' of '1921' below 'f' of 'Halifax'	£375	£275
		c. As No. 148, inverted	£7000	
		d. As No. 148a, inverted	£5000	
		e. As No. 148b, inverted	£27000	
		II. 1½ mm between 'AIR' and 'MAIL'		
148*f*	**34**	35c. red	£180	£120
		g. No stop after '1921'	£225	£150
		h. No stop and first '1' of '1921' below 'f' of 'Halifax'	£375	£275
		i. As No. 148*f*, inverted	£9000	
		k. As No. 148g, inverted	£16000	
		l. As No. 148h, inverted	£27000	

T **72** was applied as a setting of 25 which contained ten stamps as No. 148a, seven as No. 148, four as No. 148*f*, two as No. 148g, one as No. 148b and one as No. 148h.

73 Twin Hills, Tor's Cove

74 South-West Arm, Trinity

75 Statue of the Fighting Newfoundlander St John's

76 Humber River

77 Coast at Trinity

78 Upper Steadies, Humber River

79 Quidi Vidi, near St John's

80 Caribou crossing lake

81 Humber River Canyon

82 Shell Bird Island

83 Mount Moriah, Bay of Islands

84 Humber River nr. Little Rapids

85 Placentia

86 Topsail Falls

(Recess D.L.R.)

1923 (9 July)–**24**. T **73/86**. P 14 (comb or line).

149	**73**	1c. green	2·25	20
150	**74**	2c. carmine	1·00	10
		a. Imperf (pair)	£170	
151	**75**	3c. brown	3·75	10
152	**76**	4c. deep purple	1·00	30
153	**77**	5c. ultramarine	6·50	1·75
154	**78**	6c. slate	12·00	20·00
155	**79**	8c. purple	19·00	4·25
156	**80**	9c. slate-green	21·00	38·00
157	**81**	10c. violet	17·00	11·00
		a. Purple	26·00	3·50
158	**82**	11c. sage-green	7·00	40·00
159	**83**	12c. lake	8·00	19·00
160	**84**	15c. Prussian blue	8·00	40·00
161	**85**	20c. chestnut (28.4.24)	32·00	21·00
162	**86**	24c. sepia (22.4.24)	70·00	£100
149/162 *Set of* 14			£180	£250

Perforations. Three perforating heads were used: comb 13.8×14 (all values); line 13.7 and 14, and combinations of these two (for all except 6, 8, 9 and 11c.).

Nos. 149 and 151/160 also exist imperforate, but these are usually without gum. (*Price per pair from £200, unused*)

Air Mail DE PINEDO 1927

(**87**)

1927 (18 May). Air. No. 79 optd with T **87**, by Robinson & Co, Ltd.

163	**35**	60c. black (R.)	£42000	£13000

For the mail carried by De Pinedo to Europe 300 stamps were overprinted, 230 used on correspondence, 66 presented to De Pinedo, Government Officials, etc., and four damaged and destroyed. Stamps without overprint were also used.

88 Newfoundland and Labrador

89 SS *Caribou*

90 King George V and Queen Mary

91 Duke of Windsor when Prince of Wales

92 Express Train

93 Newfoundland Hotel, St John's

94 Heart's Content

95 Cabot Tower, St John's

96 War Memorial, St John's

97 GPO, St John's

98 Vickers Vimy Aircraft

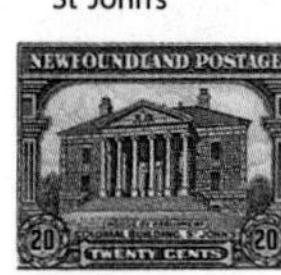

99 Parliament House, St John's

100 Grand Falls, Labrador

(Recess D.L.R.)

1928 (3 Jan)–**29**. Publicity issue. P 14 (1c.) 13½×13 (2, 3, 5, 6, 10, 14, 20c.), 13×13½ (4c.) (all comb), or 14–13½* (line) (others).

164	**88**	1c. deep green	5·00	1·50
165	**89**	2c. carmine	6·00	50
166	**90**	3c. brown	13·00	2·50
		a. Perf 14–13½ (line)	5·50	2·25
167	**91**	4c. mauve	7·50	4·25
		a. Rose-purple (1929)	14·00	14·00
168	**92**	5c. slate-grey	16·00	19·00
		a. Perf 14–13½ (line)	48·00	16·00
169	**93**	6c. ultramarine	16·00	55·00
		a. Perf 14–13½ (line)	35·00	50·00
170	**94**	8c. red-brown	12·00	55·00
171	**95**	9c. deep green	3·25	27·00
172	**96**	10c. deep violet	27·00	35·00
		a. Perf 14–13½ (line)	7·50	35·00
173	**97**	12c. carmine-lake	3·25	27·00
174	**95**	14c. brown-purple (8.28)	45·00	16·00
		a. Perf 14–13½ (line)	26·00	12·00
175	**98**	15c. deep blue	14·00	50·00
176	**99**	20c. grey-black	32·00	20·00
		a. Perf 14–13½ (line)	9·50	13·00
177	**97**	28c. deep green (11.28)	28·00	70·00
178	**100**	30c. sepia	8·00	25·00
164/178 (*cheapest*) *Set of* 15			£140	£350

* Exact gauges for the various perforations are: 14 comb = 14×13.9; 13½×13 comb = 13.5×12.75; 14–13½ line = 14–13.75.

See also Nos. 179/187 and 198/208.

Differences between De La Rue and Perkins Bacon Printings of Types **88-100**

De La Rue | **Perkins Bacon**

1c. 'C. NORMAN' is below 'C.BAULD'

1c. 'C. NORMAN' is above 'C.BAULD'

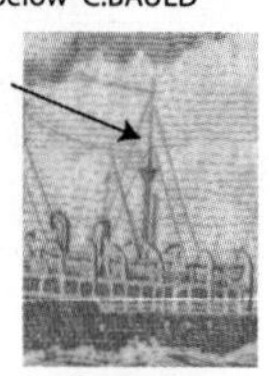

2c. Two wires to left of rear mast

2c. One wire to left of rear mast

3c. The jewels in the band of the crown are colourless

3c. The jewels are represented by dark dashes

4c. The shading of the '4' is cross-hatched

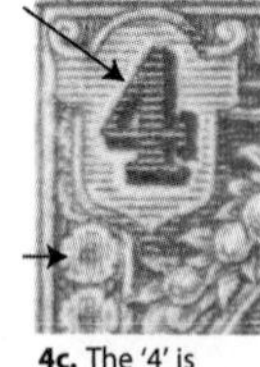

4c. The '4' is shaded horizontally

5c. The tips of the leaves framing the value tablets are rounded

5c. The tips of the leaves are pointed

6c. The lower leaves in the corner ornaments do not curl upwards at the end. Full stop after 'ST. JOHNS'

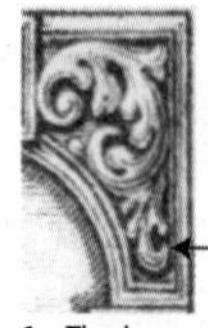

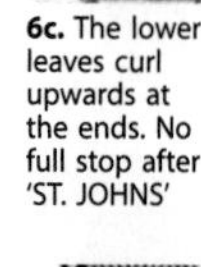

6c. The lower leaves curl upwards at the ends. No full stop after 'ST. JOHNS'

10c. The torch at left is topped by a single flame. Full stop after 'ST. JOHNS'

10c. The torch is topped by a double flame. No full stop after 'ST. JOHNS'

15c. 'L' of 'LEAVING' under 'AI' of 'AIRPLANE' in inscription

15c. 'L' of 'LEAVING' under 'T' of 'FIRST'

20c. The points at the foot of the 'W' of 'NEWFOUNDLAND' are flattened

20c. The points of the 'W' are sharp

There are many other differences between the work of the two printers.

1929 (10 Aug)–**31**. Perkins Bacon printing. Former types re-engraved. No wmk. P 14 (comb) (1c.), 13½ (comb) (2, 6c.), 14–13½ (line) (20c.) or 13½×14 (comb) (others)*.

179	**88**	1c. green (26.9.29)	8·00	1·50
		a. Perf 14–13½ (line)	8·50	30
		b. Imperf between (vert pair)	£225	
		c. Imperf (pair)	£160	
180	**89**	2c. scarlet	1·75	40
		a. Imperf (pair)	£170	
		b. Perf 14–13½ (line)	6·00	1·25
181	**90**	3c. red-brown	1·00	20
		a. Imperf (pair)	£160	
182	**91**	4c. reddish purple (26.8.29)	2·75	80
		a. Imperf (pair)	£180	
183	**92**	5c. deep grey-green (14.9.29)	13·00	5·00
184	**93**	6c. ultramarine (8.11.29)	17·00	28·00
		a. Perf 14–13½ (line)	3·50	32·00
185	**96**	10c. violet (5.10.29)	10·00	5·50
186	**98**	15c. blue (1.30)	22·00	£100
187	**99**	20c. black (1.1.31)	65·00	60·00
179/187 *Set of 9*			£110	£170

* Exact gauges for the various perforations are: 14 comb = 14×13.9; 13½ comb = 13.6×13.5; 14–13½ line = 14–13.75; 13½ ×14 comb = 13.6×13.8.

THREE
CENTS

(**101**)

(Surch by Messrs D. R. Thistle, St John's)

1929 (23 Aug). No. 154 surch with T **101**.

188	3c. on 6c. slate (R.)	3·75	13·00
	a. Surch inverted	£950	£1400
	b. Surch in black	£1000	

The issued surcharge shows 3 mm. space between 'CENTS' and the bar. The black surcharge also exists with 5 mm. space, from a trial setting (*Price*, £900).

Trans-Atlantic
AIR MAIL
By B. M.
"Columbia"
September
1930
Fifty Cents

(**102**)

1930 (25 Sept). Air. No. 141 surch with T **102** by Messrs D. R. Thistle.

191	**68**	50c. on 36c. sage-green	£6500	£6500

103 Aeroplane and Dog-team

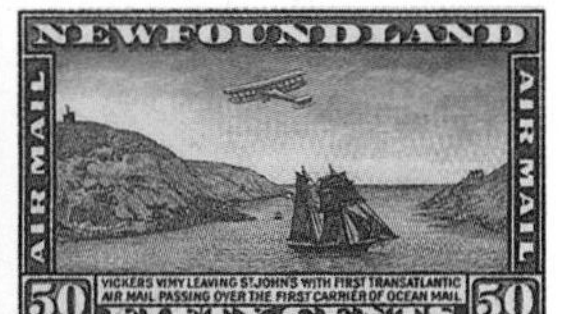

104 Vickers-Vimy Biplane and early Sailing Packet

105 Routes of historic Transatlantic Flights

106

(Des A. B. Perlin. Recess P.B.)

1931. Air. P 14.

(a) Without wmk (2.1.31)

192	**103**	15c. chocolate	9·00	18·00
		a. Imperf between (horiz pair)	£1000	
		b. Imperf between (vert pair)	£1200	
		c. Imperf (pair)	£550	
193	**104**	50c. green	38·00	55·00
		a. Imperf between (horiz pair)	£1300	£1200
		b. Imperf between (vert pair)	£1700	
		c. Imperf (pair)	£850	
194	**105**	$1 deep blue	50·00	95·00
		a. Imperf between (horiz pair)	£1300	
		b. Imperf between (vert pair)	£1400	
		c. Imperf (pair)	£900	
192/194 *Set of 3*			85·00	£150

(b) Wmk W **106**, *(sideways*) (13.3.31)*

195	**103**	15c. chocolate	13·00	32·00
		a. Pair, with and without wmk	42·00	
		b. Imperf between (horiz pair)	£1000	
		c. Imperf between (vert pair)	£1200	
		ca. Ditto, one without wmk (vert pair)	£1700	
		d. Imperf (pair)	£600	
		e. Wmk Cross (pair)	£160	
196	**104**	50c. green	35·00	75·00
		a. Imperf between (horiz pair)	£1100	
		b. Imperf between (vert pair)	£1600	
		c. Imperf (pair)		
		d. Pair, with and without wmk	£550	
		w. Wmk top of shield to right	90·00	
197	**105**	$1 deep blue	80·00	£150
		a. Imperf between (horiz pair)	£1400	
		b. Imperf between (vert pair)	£1200	
		c. Imperf horiz (vert pair)	£800	
		d. Pair, with and without wmk	£900	
		e. Imperf (pair)	£800	
195/197 *Set of 3*			£110	£225

The normal sideways wmk on this issue shows the top of the shield to right on the 15c., but top of the shield to left on the 50c. and $1.

'WITH AND WITHOUT WMK' PAIRS listed in the issues from No. 195a onwards must have one stamp *completely* without any trace of watermark.

1931 (25 March–July). Perkins Bacon printing (re-engraved types). W **106** (sideways on 1c., 4c., 30c.). P 13½ (1c.) or 13½×14 (others), both comb*.

198	**88**	1c. green (7.31)	17·00	3·00
		a. Imperf between (horiz pair)	£650	
199	**89**	2c. scarlet (7.31)	11·00	6·00
		w. Wmk inverted	75·00	
200	**90**	3c. red-brown (7.31)	8·50	4·75
		w. Wmk inverted	75·00	
201	**91**	4c. reddish purple (7.31)	8·50	1·25
202	**92**	5c. deep grey-green (7.31)	7·00	23·00
203	**93**	6c. ultramarine	7·00	40·00
		w. Wmk inverted	90·00	
204	**94**	8c. chestnut (1.4.31)	48·00	55·00
		w. Wmk inverted	95·00	£110
205	**96**	10c. violet (1.4.31)	40·00	48·00
206	**98**	15c. blue (1.7.31)	21·00	85·00
207	**99**	20c. black (1.7.31)	60·00	27·00
208	**100**	30c. sepia (1.7.31)	40·00	55·00
198/208 *Set of 11*			£225	£300

* Exact gauges for the two perforations are: 13½ = 13.6×13.5; 13½×14 = 13.6×13.8.

107 Atlantic Cod

108 King George V

109 Queen Mary

110 Duke of Windsor when Prince of Wales

111 Caribou

112 Queen Elizabeth II when Princess

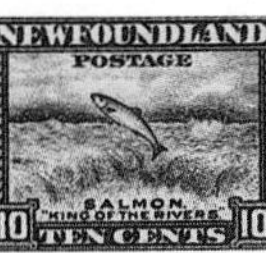

113 Atlantic Salmon

114 Newfoundland Dog

115 Harp Seal

116 Cape Race

117 Sealing Fleet

118 Fishing Fleet

(Recess P.B.)

1932 (2 Jan). W **106** (sideways* on vert designs). P 13½ (comb).

209	**107**	1c. green	3·75	30
		a. Imperf (pair)	£180	
		b. Perf 13 (line)	23·00	55·00
		ba. Imperf between (vert pair)	£130	
		w. Wmk top of shield to right	70·00	
210	**108**	2c. carmine	1·50	20
		a. Imperf (pair)	£180	
		c. Perf 13 (line)	23·00	45·00
		w. Wmk top of shield to right	70·00	
211	**109**	3c. orange-brown	1·50	20
		a. Imperf (pair)	£100	
		c. Perf 13 (line)	27·00	55·00
		ca. Imperf between (vert pair)	£250	
		d. Perf 14 (line). Small holes	35·00	55·00
		w. Wmk top of shield to right	70·00	
212	**110**	4c. bright violet	13·00	2·25
		w. Wmk top of shield to right		
213	**111**	5c. maroon	10·00	8·00
		a. Imperf (pair)	£180	
		w. Wmk top of shield to right	75·00	
214	**112**	6c. light blue	4·00	15·00
215	**113**	10c. black-brown	1·00	65
		a. Imperf (pair)	70·00	
		w. Wmk inverted	10·00	
216	**114**	14c. black	5·50	6·00
		a. Imperf (pair)	£160	
217	**115**	15c. claret	1·25	2·00
		a. Imperf (pair)	£180	
		b. Perf 14 (line)	8·00	11·00
218	**116**	20c. green	1·00	1·00
		a. Imperf (pair)	£180	
		b. Perf 14 (line)	£150	£150
		w. Wmk inverted	48·00	
219	**117**	25c. slate	2·00	2·50
		a. Imperf (pair)	£180	
		b. Perf 14 (line)	75·00	90·00
		ba. Imperf between (vert pair)	£500	
220	**118**	30c. ultramarine	55·00	45·00
		a. Imperf (pair)	£600	
		b. Imperf between (vert pair)	£1600	
		c. Perf 14 (line)	£500	
209/220 *Set of 12*			85·00	75·00

The Caribou shown on T **111** is taken from the monument to the Royal Newfoundland Regiment, near Beaumont Hamel, France.

* The normal sideways watermark shows the top of the shield to left, *as seen from the back of the stamp.*

Nos. 209b, 210c and 211c were only issued in stamp booklets.

For similar stamps in different perforations see Nos. 222/228*c* and 276/289.

TRANS-ATLANTIC
WEST TO EAST
Per Dornier DO-X
May, 1932.
One Dollar and Fifty Cents

(**119**)

1932 (19 May). Air. No. 197 surch as T **119**, by Messrs. D. R. Thistle. P 14.

221	**105**	$1.50 on $1 deep blue (R.)	£250	£225
		a. Surch inverted	£21000	

120 Queen Mother, when Duchess of York

121 Corner Brook Paper Mills

122 Loading Iron Ore, Bell Island

(Recess P.B.)

1932 (15 Aug)–**38**. W **106** (sideways* on vert designs). P 13½ (comb).

222	**107**	1c. grey	3·25	10
		a. Imperf (pair)	48·00	
		c. Perf 14 (line)	8·50	23·00
		d. Perf 14 (line). Small holes	30·00	55·00
		e. Pair, with and without wmk	95·00	
		w. Wmk top of shield to right	65·00	50·00
223	**108**	2c. green	2·50	10
		a. Imperf (pair)	40·00	
		c. Perf 14 (line)	8·50	23·00
		ca. Imperf between (horiz pair)	£275	
		d. Perf 14 (line). Small holes	23·00	50·00
		e. Pair, with and without wmk	95·00	
		w. Wmk top of shield to right	50·00	
224	**110**	4c. carmine (21.7.34)	6·50	40
		a. Imperf (pair)	70·00	
		b. Perf 14 (line)	8·00	15·00
		ba. Imperf between (horiz pair)	£350	
		bb. Imperf between (vert pair)	£140	
		c. Pair, with and without wmk	£100	
		w. Wmk top of shield to right	70·00	
225	**111**	5c. violet (Die I)	6·00	1·75
		a. Imperf (pair)	75·00	
		b. Perf 14 (line). Small holes	27·00	55·00
		c. Die II	1·00	30
		ca. Imperf (pair)	70·00	
		cb. Perf 14 (line)	25·00	50·00
		cbw. Wmk top of shield to right	80·00	
		cc. Imperf between (horiz pair)	£275	
		cd. Pair, with and without wmk	£180	
		cw. Wmk top of shield to right	75·00	
226	**120**	7c. red-brown	3·00	4·25
		b. Perf 14 (line)	£250	
		ba. Imperf between (horiz pair)	£650	
		c. Imperf (pair)	£190	
		w. Wmk top of shield to right		
227	**121**	8c. brownish red	3·75	2·00
		a. Imperf (pair)	£110	
		w. Wmk inverted		
228	**122**	24c. bright blue	1·25	3·25
		a. Imperf (pair)	£350	
		b. Doubly printed	£1600	
		w. Wmk inverted	75·00	

228c **118** 48c. red-brown (1.1.38) 13·00 10·00
ca. Imperf (pair) £140
222/228c *Set of* 8 30·00 18·00

* The normal sideways watermark shows the top of the shield to left, *as seen from the back of the stamp.*

No. 223. Two dies exist of the 2c., Die I was used for No. 210 and both dies for No. 223. The differences, though numerous, are very slight.

No. 225. There are also two dies of the 5c., Die I only being used for No. 213 and both dies for the violet stamp. In Die II the antler pointing to the 'T' of 'POSTAGE' is taller than the one pointing to the 'S' and the individual hairs on the underside of the caribou's tail are distinct.

For similar stamps in a slightly larger size and perforated 12½ or 13½ (5c.) see Nos. 276/289.

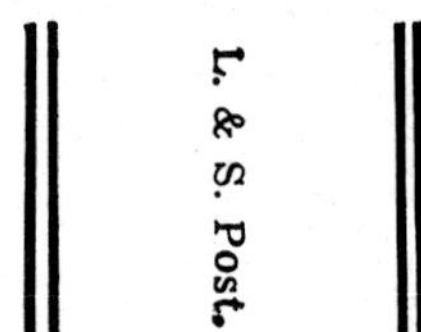

(**123**) 'L. & S.'—Land and Sea

1933 (9 Feb). No. 195 optd with T **123** for ordinary postal use, by Messrs D. R. Thistle. W **106** (sideways top of shield to right from back). P 14.

229 **103** 15c. chocolate 6·50 23·00
a. Pair, one without wmk 26·00
b. Opt reading up £5000
c. Vertical pair, one without opt £7000

124 Put to Flight

125 Land of Heart's Delight

126 Spotting the Herd

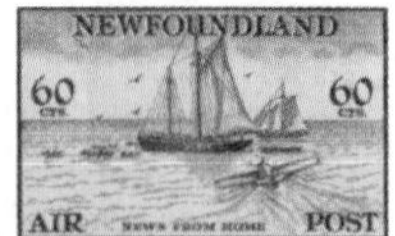

127 News from Home

128 Labrador

(Des J. Scott. Recess P.B.)

1933 (9 June). Air. T **124/128** and similar horiz designs. W **106** (sideways*). P 14 (5c., 30c., 75c.) or 11½ (10c., 60c.).

230 **124** 5c. red-brown 22·00 22·00
a. Imperf (pair) £190
b. Imperf between (horiz pair) £1000
c. Imperf between (vert pair) £1200
231 **125** 10c. orange-yellow 18·00 35·00
a. Imperf (pair) £160
232 **126** 30c. light blue 40·00 50·00
a. Imperf (pair) £600
233 **127** 60c. green 50·00 £120
a. Imperf (pair) £600
234 **128** 75c. yellow-brown 50·00 £120
a. Imperf (pair) £550
b. Imperf between (horiz or vert pair) £6000
w. Wmk top of shield to left £150
230/234 *Set of* 5 £160 £325

* The normal sideways watermark shows the top of the shield to right, *as seen from the back of the stamp.*

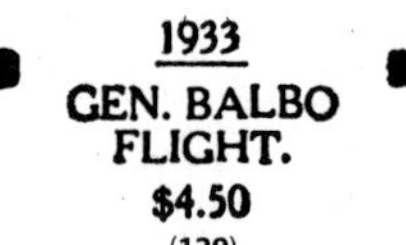

(**129**)

(Surch by Robinson & Co, St John's)

1933 (24 July). Air. Balbo Transatlantic Mass Formation Flight. No. 234 surch with T **129**. W **106**. P 14.

235 $4.50 on 75c. yellow-brown £275 £350
a. Surch inverted £90000
b. Surch on 10c. (No. 231) £75000
w. Wmk top of shield to left £2250

No. 235a. When this error was discovered the stamps were ordered to be officially destroyed but four copies which had been torn were recovered and skilfully repaired. In addition, four undamaged examples exist and the price quoted is for one of these (*Price for repaired example, £20000, unused*).

130 Sir Humphrey Gilbert

131 Compton Castle, Devon

132 Gilbert Coat of Arms

133 Eton College

134 Anchor token

135 Gilbert commissioned by Elizabeth I

136 Fleet leaving Plymouth, 1583

137 Arrival at St John's

138 Annexation, 5th August, 1583

139 Royal Arms

140 Gilbert in the *Squirrel*

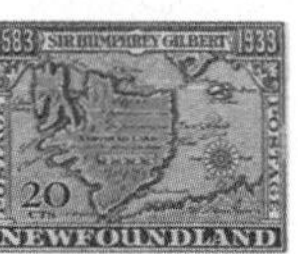

141 Map of Newfoundland, 1626

142 Queen Elizabeth I

143 Gilbert's statue at Truro

(Recess P.B.)

1933 (3 Aug). 350th Anniversary of the Annexation by Sir Humphrey Gilbert. T **130/143**. W **106** (sideways* on vert designs). P 13½ (comb†).

236 **130** 1c. slate 1·25 1·50
a. Imperf (pair) 60·00
237 **131** 2c. green 2·00 70
a. Imperf (pair) 50·00
b. Doubly printed £500
238 **132** 3c. chestnut 2·50 1·25
239 **133** 4c. carmine 1·00 50
a. Imperf (pair) 55·00
240 **134** 5c. violet 2·00 1·00
241 **135** 7c. greenish blue 18·00 24·00
a. Perf 14 (line) 21·00 60·00
242 **136** 8c. vermilion 9·50 25·00
a. Brownish red £500
b. Bisected (4c.) (*on cover*) † £425
243 **137** 9c. ultramarine 7·50 26·00
a. Imperf (pair) £300
b. Perf 14 (line) 85·00 £110
244 **138** 10c. brown-lake 8·50 21·00
a. Imperf (pair) £300
b. Perf 14 (line) £120 £150
245 **139** 14c. grey-black 22·00 50·00
a. Perf 14 (line) 25·00 70·00
aw. Wmk top of shield to right £100
246 **140** 15c. claret 26·00 50·00
w. Wmk top of shield to right 9·50 35·00
247 **141** 20c. grey-green 20·00 25·00
a. Perf 14 (line) 38·00 70·00
w. Wmk inverted 90·00
248 **142** 24c. maroon 22·00 35·00
a. Imperf (pair) £140
b. Perf 14 (line) 42·00 55·00
w. Wmk top of shield to right 45·00
249 **143** 32c. olive-black 20·00 75·00
a. Perf 14 (line) 22·00 95·00
w. Wmk top of shield to right 18·00 80·00
236/249 *Set of* 14 £110 £275

* The normal sideways watermark shows the top of the shield to left, *as seen from the back of the stamp.*

† Exact gauges for the two perforations are: 13½ comb = 13.4; 14 line = 13.8.

1935 (6 May). Silver Jubilee. As Nos. 91/94 of Antigua, but ptd by B.W. P 11×12.

250 4c. rosine 1·00 1·75
251 5c. bright violet 1·25 4·25
252 7c. blue 4·75 7·00
253 24c. olive-green 5·00 28·00
250/253 *Set of* 4 11·00 38·00
250s/253s Perf 'SPECIMEN' *Set of* 4 £190

1937 (12 May). Coronation Issue. As Nos. 95/97 of Antigua, but name and value uncoloured on coloured background. P 11×11½.

254 2c. green 1·00 3·00
255 4c. carmine 1·60 4·00
256 5c. purple 3·00 4·00
254/256 *Set of* 3 5·00 10·00
254s/256s Perf 'SPECIMEN' *Set of* 3 £150

144 Atlantic Cod

145 Map of Newfoundland

146 Caribou

147 Corner Brook Paper Mills

148 Atlantic Salmon

149 Newfoundland Dog

150 Harp Seal

151 Cape Race

152 Bell Island

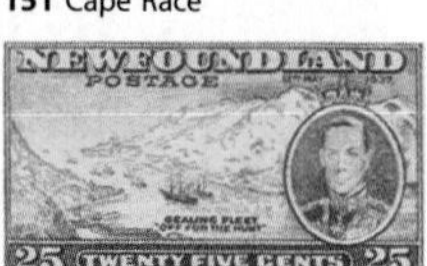

153 Sealing Fleet

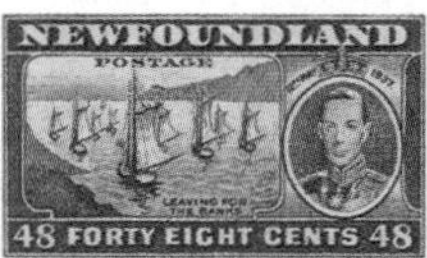

154 The Banks Fishing Fleet

Die I

Die II

No. 258. In Die II the shading of the King's face is heavier and dots have been added down the ridge of the nose. The top frame line is thicker and more uniform.

1c. Fish-hook flaw (R. 1/7 or 3/3)

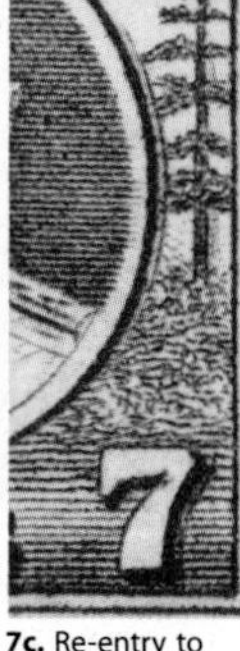

7c. Re-entry to right of design (inscr oval, tree and value) (R. 4/8)

20c. Extra chimney (R. 6/5)

(Des and eng J. B. Dickinson & Co. Recess P.B.)

1937 (12 May). Additional Coronation Issue. T **144/154**. W **106**. P 14 (line)*.

257 **144** 1c. grey 3·50 30
a. Pair, with and without wmk 32·00
b. Fish-hook flaw 32·00 20·00
cw. Wmk inverted 70·00
d. Perf 13½ (line) 5·00 1·25
da. Pair, with and without wmk 45·00
db. Fish-hook flaw 45·00 30·00
e. Perf 13 (comb) 38·00 80·00
ea. Pair, with and without wmk
eb. Fish-hook flaw £200 £425

No.	Type	Description	Unused	Used
258	**145**	3c. orange-brown (I)	38·00	7·50
		a. Pair, with and without wmk	£250	
		b. Imperf between (horiz pair)	£500	
		c. Perf 13½ (line)	38·00	11·00
		ca. Pair, with and without wmk	£250	
		cb. Imperf between (vert pair)	£650	
		d. Perf 13 (comb)	22·00	4·00
		e. Die II (P 14, line)	18·00	13·00
		ea. Pair, with and without wmk	£200	
		ec. Perf 13½ (line)	15·00	14·00
		eca. Pair, with and without wmk	£200	
		ecb. Imperf between (vert pair)	£750	
		ed. Perf 13 (comb)	9·50	5·00
		eda. Pair, with and without wmk	£180	
259	**146**	7c. bright ultramarine	4·00	1·25
		a. Pair, with and without wmk	£150	
		b. Re-entry at right	85·00	85·00
		c. Perf 13½ (line)	4·25	1·75
		ca. Pair, with and without wmk	£160	
		cb. Re-entry at right	85·00	
		d. Perf 13 (comb)	£700	£800
		db. Re-entry at right	£4000	
260	**147**	8c. scarlet	5·50	4·00
		a. Pair, with and without wmk	£130	
		b. Imperf between (horiz pair)	£1200	
		c. Imperf between (vert pair)	£1300	
		d. Imperf (pair)	£450	
		e. Perf 13½ (line)	7·50	8·00
		ea. Pair, with and without wmk	£160	
		eb. Imperf between (vert pair)		
		f. Perf 13 (comb)	24·00	29·00
261	**148**	10c. blackish brown	7·50	9·00
		a. Pair, with and without wmk	£170	
		b. Perf 13½ (line)	9·50	13·00
		ba. Pair, with and without wmk	£170	
		c. Perf 13 (comb)	3·25	20·00
		cw. Wmk inverted	£110	
262	**149**	14c. black	3·00	4·00
		a. Pair, with and without wmk	£150	
		b. Perf 13½ (line)	3·75	6·00
		ba. Pair, with and without wmk	£150	
		c. Perf 13 (comb)	£25000	£16000
263	**150**	15c. claret	21·00	9·00
		a. Pair, with and without wmk	£180	
		bw. Wmk inverted	£150	
		c. Perf 13½ (line)	26·00	13·00
		ca. Pair, with and without wmk	£200	
		cb. Imperf between (vert pair)	£1600	
		d. Perf 13 (comb)	48·00	75·00
		da. Pair, with and without wmk	£325	
264	**151**	20c. green	11·00	21·00
		a. Pair, with and without wmk	£160	
		c. Extra chimney	£130	
		dw. Wmk inverted	£180	
		e. Perf 13½ (line)	11·00	23·00
		ea. Pair, with and without wmk	£250	
		eb. Imperf between (vert pair)	£2500	
		ec. Extra chimney	£130	£200
		f. Perf 13 (comb)	7·50	10·00
		fc. Extra chimney	£120	
		fw. Wmk inverted	£275	
265	**152**	24c. light blue	2·75	3·00
		a. Pair, with and without wmk	£275	
		c. Perf 13½ (line)	2·75	3·00
		ca. Pair, with and without wmk	£275	
		cb. Imperf between (vert pair)	£4000	
		d. Perf 13 (comb)	50·00	70·00
266	**153**	25c. slate	5·00	4·50
		a. Pair, with and without wmk	£225	
		b. Perf 13½ (line)	8·00	6·00
		ba. Pair, with and without wmk	£250	
		c. Perf 13 (comb)	50·00	£120
267	**154**	48c. slate-purple	11·00	6·50
		a. Pair, with and without wmk	£350	
		b. Imperf between (vert pair)	£3750	
		c. Perf 13½ (line)	17·00	14·00
		ca. Pair, with and without wmk	£400	
		cb. Imperf between (vert pair)	£3750	
		cw. Wmk inverted	£350	
		d. Perf 13 (comb)	65·00	£150
257/267 *Set of* 11			60·00	50·00

The line perforations measure 14.1 (14) or 13.7 (13½). The comb perforation measures 13.3×13.2. The 1c., 7c. and 14c. values are known with compound perforations of 13½ and 14.

The paper used had the watermarks spaced for smaller format stamps. In consequence, the individual watermarks are out of alignment so that for instance stamps from the second vertical column or the bottom horizontal row were sometimes without watermark.

155 King George VI

156 Queen Mother

157 Queen Elizabeth II as princess

158 Queen Mary

(Recess P.B.)

1938 (12 May). T **155/158**. W **106** (sideways*). P 13½ (comb).

No.	Type	Description	Unused	Used
268	**155**	2c. green	5·50	1·75
		a. Pair, with and without wmk	£250	
		b. Imperf (pair)	£130	
		w. Wmk top of shield to right	£100	
269	**156**	3c. carmine	1·00	1·00
		a. Perf 14 (line)	£1000	£650
		b. Pair, with and without wmk	£375	
		c. Imperf (pair)	£130	
270	**157**	4c. light blue	4·25	1·00
		a. Pair, with and without wmk	£150	
		b. Imperf (pair)	£120	
		w. Wmk top of shield to right	£100	
271	**158**	7c. deep ultramarine	1·50	12·00
		a. Pair, with and without wmk	£225	
		b. Imperf (pair)	£190	
268/271 *Set of* 4			11·00	14·00

* The normal sideways watermark shows the top of the shield to left, *as seen from the back of the stamp.*

For similar designs, perf 12½, see Nos. 277/281.

159 King George VI and Queen Elizabeth

(Recess B.W.)

1939 (17 June). Royal Visit. No wmk. P 13½.

No.	Type	Description	Unused	Used
272	**159**	5c. deep ultramarine	4·00	1·00

2

▲ **CENTS** ▲

(**160**)

'CENTL' (R. 5/3)

1939 (20 Nov). No. 272 surch as T **160**, at St John's.

No.	Type	Description	Unused	Used
273	**159**	2c. on 5c. deep ultramarine (Br.)	2·50	50
274		4c. on 5c. deep ultramarine (C.)	2·00	2·25
		a. 'CENTL'	55·00	55·00

161 Grenfell on the *Strathcona* (after painting by Gribble)

162 Memorial University College

(Recess C.B.N.)

1941 (1 Dec). 50th Anniversary of Sir Wilfred Grenfell's Labrador Mission. P 12.

No.	Type	Description	Unused	Used
275	**161**	5c. blue	30	1·00

Damaged 'A' (R. 5/9)

(Recess Waterlow)

1941 (Oct)–**44**. W **106** (sideways* on vert designs). P 12½ (line).

No.	Type	Description	Unused	Used
276	**107**	1c. grey (14.8.42)	20	2·75
		w. Wmk top of shield to right	75·00	
277	**155**	2c. green (11.41)	40	75
		w. Wmk top of shield to right	55·00	
278	**156**	3c. carmine (10.41)	40	30
		a. Pair, with and without wmk	£140	
		b. Damaged 'A'	90·00	50·00
		w. Wmk top of shield to right	55·00	
279	**157**	4c. blue (As No. 270) (10.41)	4·50	40
		a. Pair, with and without wmk	£250	
		w. Wmk top of shield to right	70·00	
280	**111**	5c. violet (Die I) (P 13½ comb) (11.41)	£180	
		a. Perf 12½ (line) (6.42)	2·75	1·00
		ab. Pair, with and without wmk	£225	
		ac. Printed double, one albino	£750	
		ad. Imperf vert (horiz pair)	£650	
		b. Imperf (pair)	£225	
281	**158**	7c. deep ultramarine (As No. 271) (3.43)	14·00	29·00
		a. Pair, with and without wmk	£350	
282	**121**	8c. rose-red (9.42)	2·25	4·50
		a. Pair, with and without wmk	£225	
283	**113**	10c. black-brown (4.43)	1·75	2·25
284	**114**	14c. black (1.44)	9·00	14·00
285	**115**	15c. claret (7.43)	6·00	8·50
286	**116**	20c. green (1.44)	6·00	8·50
287	**122**	24c. blue (4.43)	3·25	25·00
		w. Wmk inverted	90·00	
288	**117**	25c. slate (4.43)	11·00	21·00
289	**118**	48c. red-brown (1.43)	5·00	9·50
276/289 *Set of* 14			55·00	£110

* The normal sideways watermark shows the top of the shield to left, *as seen from the back of the stamp.*

Nos. 279 and 281 were printed from the original Perkins Bacon plates. New plates were made for the other values, using the original dies of Nos. 282/287 and 289, but new (1c., 25c.) or re-engraved (2c., 3c., 5c.) dies for the remaining values. Note that the 5c. measures 21 mm in width as opposed to the 20.4 mm of the Perkins Bacon printings.

No. 280. For Die I see note relating to No. 225.

(Recess C.B.N.)

1943 (1 Jan). P 12.

No.	Type	Description	Unused	Used
290	**162**	30c. carmine	2·50	5·50

163 St John's

TWO

CENTS

(**164**)

(Recess C.B.N.)

1943 (1 June). Air. P 12.

No.	Type	Description	Unused	Used
291	**163**	7c. ultramarine	50	1·25

1946 (21 Mar). No. 290 surch locally with T **164**.

No.	Type	Description	Unused	Used
292	**162**	2c. on 30c. carmine	30	2·50

165 Queen Elizabeth II when Princess

166 Cabot off Cape Bonavista

(Recess Waterlow)

1947 (21 Apr). Princess Elizabeth's 21st Birthday. W **106** (sideways). P 12½.

No.	Type	Description	Unused	Used
293	**165**	4c. light blue	40	1·00
		a. Imperf vert (horiz pair)	£475	

(Recess Waterlow)

1947 (24 June). 450th Anniversary of Cabot's Discovery of Newfoundland. W **106** (sideways). P 12½.

No.	Type	Description	Unused	Used
294	**166**	5c. mauve	50	1·00
		w. Wmk top of shield to right	50·00	

STAMP BOOKLETS

1926. Black on pink cover with Ayre and Sons advertisement on front. Stapled.

SB1 40c. booklet containing 8×1c. and 16×2c. (Nos. 149/150) in blocks of 8 .... £1900

B **1**

1932 (2 Jan). Black on buff cover as Type B **1**. Stapled.

SB2 40c. booklet containing 4×1c., 12×2c. and 4×3c. (Nos. 209b, 210c, 211c) in blocks of 4 .... £500

a. Contents as No. SB2, but containing Nos. 209b, 210 and 211c £550

b. Contents as No. SB2, but containing Nos. 222d, 223d and 211d £500

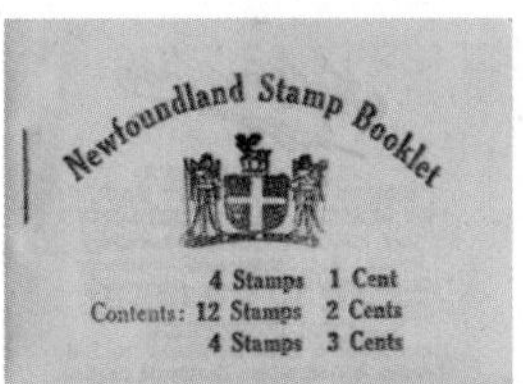

B **2**

1932. Black on cream cover as Type B **2**. Stapled.

SB3 40c. booklet containing 4×1c., 12×2c. and 4×3c. (Nos. 222, 223, 211) in blocks of 4 .... £500

POSTAGE DUE STAMPS

D 1

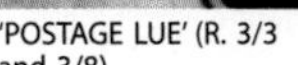

'POSTAGE LUE' (R. 3/3 and 3/8)

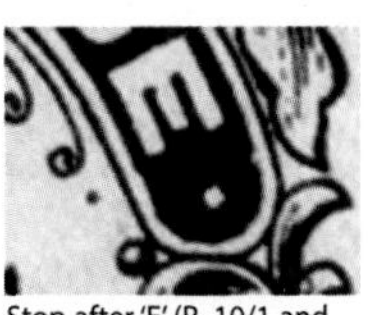

Stop after 'E' (R. 10/1 and 10/6)

(Litho John Dickinson & Co, Ltd)

1939 (1 May)–**49**. No Wmk. P 10.

D1	D **1**	1c. green	2·25	23·00
		a. Perf 11 (1949)	3·25	28·00
D2		2c. vermilion	20·00	8·50
		a. Perf 11×9 (1946)	14·00	29·00
D3		3c. ultramarine	5·00	40·00
		a. Perf 11×9 (1949)	13·00	65·00
		b. Perf 9	£4750	
D4		4c. orange	9·00	30·00
		a. Perf 11×9 (5.48)	16·00	70·00
D5		5c. brown	13·00	45·00
D6		10c. violet	13·00	30·00
		a. Perf 11 (W **106**) (1949)	18·00	£100
		ab. Ditto. Imperf between (vert pair)	£1400	
		ac. 'POSTAGE LUE'	£150	£475
		ad. Stop after 'E'	£150	£475
D1/D6 *Set of 6*			50·00	£160

Newfoundland joined the Dominion of Canada on 31 March 1949.

NOVA SCOTIA

Organised postal services in Nova Scotia date from April 1754 when the first of a series of Deputy Postmasters was appointed, under the authority of the British GPO. This arrangement continued until 6 July 1851 when the colony assumed responsibility for its postal affairs.

For illustrations of the handstamp types see BRITISH POST OFFICES ABROAD notes, following GREAT BRITAIN.

AMHERST

CROWNED-CIRCLE HANDSTAMPS

CC1	CC **1**	AMHERST. N.S.(R) (25.2.1845)...*Price on cover*	£1000

ST MARGARETS BAY

CROWNED-CIRCLE HANDSTAMPS

CC2	CC **1**	ST MARGARETS BAY. N.S.(R) (30.6.1845) *Price on cover*	£10000

Nos. CC1/2 were later used during temporary shortages of stamps, struck in red or black.

PRICES FOR STAMPS ON COVER

No. 1	*from* × 5
Nos. 2/4	*from* × 2
Nos. 5/8	*from* × 4
Nos. 9/10	*from* × 10
Nos. 11/13	*from* × 2
Nos. 14/15	—
No. 16	*from* × 4
Nos. 17/19	*from* × 10
Nos. 20/25	*from* × 2
No. 26	*from* × 50
Nos. 27/28	*from* × 4
No. 29	*from* × 10

1

2

Crown and Heraldic Flowers of United Kingdom and Mayflower of Nova Scotia.

(Recess P.B.)

1851 (1 Sept)–**60**. Bluish paper. Imperf.

1	**1**	1d. red-brown (12.5.53)	£3000	£475
		a. Bisected (½d.) (*on cover*) (1857)	†	£50000
2	**2**	3d. deep blue	£1300	£170
		a. Bisected (1½d.) (*on cover*)	†	£2500
3		3d. bright blue	£1100	£150
		a. Bisected (1½d.) (*on cover*)	†	£2500
4		3d. pale blue (1857)	£1000	£150
		a. Bisected (1½d.) (*on cover*)	†	£2500
5		6d. yellow-green	£4750	£550
		a. Bisected (3d.) (*on cover*)	†	£3250
		b. Quartered (1½d.) (*on cover*) (1860)	†	£60000
6		6d. deep green (1857)	£10000	£1000
		a. Bisected (3d.) (*on cover*)	†	£5000
7		1s. cold violet	£25000	£5500
7*c*		1s. deep purple (1851)	£18000	£4000
		d. Watermarked	£25000	£6000
8		1s. purple (1857)	£18000	£3500
		a. Bisected (6d.) (*on cover*) (1860)	†	£38000
		b. Quartered (3d.) (*on cover*) (1858)	†	£90000

The watermark on No. 7d consists of the whole or part of a letter from the name 'T. H. SAUNDERS' (the papermakers).

The stamps formerly catalogued on almost white paper are probably some from which the bluish paper has been discharged.

Reprints of all four values were made in 1890 on thin, hard, white paper. The 1d. is brown, the 3d. blue, the 6d. deep green, and the 1s. violet-black.

The 3d. bisects, which were authorised on 19 October 1854, are usually found used to make up the 7½d. rate.

(New Currency. 100 cents = 1 dollar)

3

4

5

(Recess American Bank Note Co, New York)

1860–63. P 12.

(a) Yellowish paper

9	**3**	1c. jet black	4·25	18·00
		a. Bisected (½c.) (*on cover*)	†	£8000
10		1c. grey-black	4·25	18·00
11		2c. grey-purple	11·00	16·00
11*a*		2c. purple	17·00	15·00
12		5c. blue	£475	25·00
13		5c. deep blue	£475	25·00
14	**4**	8½c. deep green	5·00	65·00
15		8½c. yellow-green	4·00	65·00
16		10c. scarlet	25·00	42·00
17	**5**	12½c. black	38·00	30·00
17*a*		12½c. greyish black	—	30·00

(b) White paper

18	**3**	1c. black	4·25	21·00
		a. Imperf vert (horiz pair)	£170	
19		1c. grey	4·25	21·00
20		2c. dull purple	4·75	14·00
21		2c. purple	4·75	14·00
22		2c. grey-purple	4·75	14·00
		a. Bisected (1c.) (*on cover*)	†	£3500
23		2c. slate-purple	4·75	13·00
24		5c. blue	£550	29·00
25		5c. deep blue	£550	29·00
26	**4**	8½c. deep green	23·00	65·00
27		10c. scarlet	8·50	42·00
28		10c. vermilion	5·50	42·00
		a. Bisected (5c.) (*on cover*)	†	£750
29	**5**	12½c. black	60·00	32·00

Nova Scotia joined the Dominion of Canada on 1 July 1867.

PRINCE EDWARD ISLAND

Prince Edward Island, previously administered as part of Nova Scotia, became a separate colony in 1769.

PRICES FOR STAMPS ON COVER

Nos. 1/4	*from* × 4
No. 5	—
No. 6	*from* × 5
Nos. 7/8	*from* × 10
Nos. 9/11	*from* × 8
Nos. 12/18	*from* × 6
Nos. 19/20	*from* × 10
Nos. 21/26	*from* × 4
Nos. 27/31	*from* × 8
Nos. 32/33	*from* × 40
Nos. 34/37	*from* × 8
No. 38	*from* × 30
Nos. 39/41	*from* × 20
No. 42	*from* × 50
Nos. 43/47	*from* × 8

1 2 3 4 5 6

Two Dies of 2d.:

Die I. Left-hand frame and circle merge at centre left (all stamps in the sheet of 60 (10×6) except R. 2/5)

Die II. Left-hand frame and circle separate at centre left (R. 2/5). There is also a break in the top frame line.

(Typo Charles Whiting, London)

1861 (1 Jan). Yellowish toned paper.

(a) P 9

1	**1**	2d. rose (I)	£500	£190
		a. Imperf between (horiz pair)	£11000	
		b. Imperf horiz (vert pair)		
		c. Bisected (1d.) (*on cover*)	†	£8000
		d. Die II		
2		2d. rose-carmine (I)	£550	£200
		a. Die II	—	£1000
3	**2**	3d. blue	£1100	£450
		a. Bisected (1½d.) (*on cover*)	†	£8000
		b. Double print	£4000	
4	**3**	6d. yellow-green	£1700	£750

(b) Rouletted

5	**1**	2d. rose (I)	†	£25000

The 2d. and 3d., perf 9, were authorised to be bisected and used for half their normal value.

1862–69. Yellowish toned paper.

(a) P 11 (1862) or 11¼ (1869)

6	**4**	1d. brown-orange	£120	90·00
6*a*		2d. rose (I) (1869)	†	£550
7	**6**	9d. bluish lilac (29.3.62)	£170	£100
8		9d. dull mauve	£170	£100

(b) P 11½–12 (1863-1869)

9	**4**	1d. yellow-orange (1863)	55·00	70·00
		a. Bisected (½d.) (*on cover*)	†	£5500
		b. Imperf between (horiz pair)	£550	
10		1d. orange-buff	60·00	70·00
11		1d. yellow	70·00	70·00
12	**1**	2d. rose (I) (1863)	26·00	19·00
		a. Imperf vert (horiz pair)		
		b. Bisected (1d.) (*on cover*)	†	£3750
		c. Die II	£110	£100
13		2d. deep rose (I)	28·00	23·00
		a. Die II	£120	£110
14	**2**	3d. blue (1863)	48·00	32·00
		a. Imperf horiz (vert pair)		
		b. Bisected (1½d.) (*on cover*)	†	—
15		3d. deep blue	48·00	32·00
16	**5**	4d. black (1869)	32·00	65·00
		a. Imperf vert (horiz pair)	£350	
		b. Bisected (2d.) (*on cover*)	†	£2000
		c. Imperf between (horiz strip of 3)	£550	
17	**3**	6d. yellow-green (15.12.66)	£170	£120
		a. Bisected (3d.) (*on cover*)	†	£6500
18		6d. blue-green (1868)	£170	£120
19	**6**	9d. lilac (1863)	£120	£100
20		9d. reddish mauve (1863)	£120	£100
		a. Imperf vert (horiz pair)	£950	
		b. Bisected (4½d.) (*on cover*)	†	£6000

A new perforator, gauging exactly 11¼, was introduced in 1869. Apart from No. 6*a*, it was used in compound with the perf 11½–12 machine.

(c) Perf compound of 11 or 11¼ (1869) and 11½–12

21	**4**	1d. yellow-orange	£250	90·00
22	**1**	2d. rose (I)	£225	70·00
		a. Die II		
23	**2**	3d. blue	£275	70·00
24	**5**	4d. black	£325	£250
25	**3**	6d. yellow-green	£375	£300
26	**6**	9d. reddish mauve	£475	£325

1870. Coarse, wove bluish white paper. P 11½–12.

27	**1**	2d. rose (I)	17·00	21·00
		a. Die II	95·00	£110
28		2d. rose-pink (I)	9·50	19·00
		a. Die II	70·00	85·00
		b. 'TWC' (R. 6/4)	90·00	£130
		c. Imperf between (horiz pair)	£275	
		d. Imperf horiz (vert pair)	£275	
29	**2**	3d. pale blue	16·00	23·00
30		3d. blue	11·00	23·00
		a. Imperf between (horiz pair)	£375	
31	**5**	4d. black	7·00	45·00
		a. Imperf between (horiz pair)	£225	
		b. Bisected (2d.) (*on cover*)	†	£2000

(New Currency. 100 cents = 1 dollar)

7

(Recess British-American Bank Note Co., Montreal and Ottawa)

1870 (1 June). P 12.

32	**7**	4½d. (3d. stg), yellow-brown	75·00	85·00
33		4½d. (3d. stg), deep brown	75·00	95·00

8 9 10 11 12 13

(Typo Charles Whiting, London)

1872 (1 Jan).

(a) P 11½–12

34	**8**	1c. orange	10·00	35·00
35		1c. yellow-orange	13·00	30·00
36		1c. brown-orange	9·00	35·00
37	**10**	3c. rose	42·00	48·00
		a. Stop between 'PRINCE. EDWARD'	85·00	£110
		b. Bisected (1½c.) (*on cover*)		
		c. Imperf horiz (vert pair)	£550	

(b) Perf 12 to 12¼ large holes

38	9	2c. blue	27·00	65·00
		a. Bisected (1c.) (*on cover*)	†	£4000
39	11	4c. yellow-green	12·00	38·00
40		4c. deep green	14·00	38·00
		a. Bisected (2c.) (*on cover*)	†	£4750
41	12	6c. black	8·50	38·00
		a. Bisected (3c.) (*on cover*)	†	£2000
		b. Imperf between (horiz pair)	£300	
		c. Imperf vert (horiz pair)		
42	13	12c. reddish mauve	10·00	85·00

(c) P 12½–13, smaller holes

43	8	1c. orange	24·00	
44		1c. brown-orange	9·50	40·00
45	10	3c. rose	40·00	50·00
		a. Stop between 'PRINCE. EDWARD'.	85·00	£130
45*b*	12	6c. black	—	£250

(d) Perf compound of (a) and (c) 11½–12×12½–13

46	8	1c. orange	90·00	65·00
47	10	3c. rose	£120	70·00
		a. Stop between 'PRINCE. EDWARD'.	£300	£275

The Stop between 'PRINCE. EDWARD' variety listed as Nos. 37a, 45a, 47a occurred at R. 1/2 in the master block of ten clichés (5×2), which was repeated ten times to construct the plate of 100 (10×10). It therefore appears ten times in each sheet at R. 1/2, 1/7, 3/2, 3/7, 5/2, 5/7, 7/2, 7/7, 9/2 and 9/7.

Prince Edward Island joined the Dominion of Canada on 1 July 1873.

DOMINION OF CANADA

On 1 July 1867, Canada, Nova Scotia and New Brunswick were united to form the Dominion of Canada.

The provinces of Manitoba (1870), British Columbia (1871), Prince Edward Island (1873), Alberta (1905), Saskatchewan (1905), and Newfoundland (1949) were subsequently added, as were the Northwest Territories (1870) and Yukon Territory (1898).

PRICES FOR STAMPS ON COVER TO 1945

Nos. 46/67	*from* × 2
Nos. 68/71	*from* × 10
Nos. 72/89	*from* × 3
Nos. 90/100	*from* × 2
Nos. 101/102	*from* × 5
Nos. 103/111	*from* × 3
Nos. 115/120	*from* × 6
Nos. 121/149	*from* × 3
Nos. 150/165	*from* × 2
Nos. 166/172	*from* × 3
Nos. 173/187	*from* × 5
Nos. 188/195	*from* × 2
Nos. 196/215	*from* × 3
Nos. 219/224*b*	*from* × 4
Nos. 225/245	*from* × 2
Nos. 246/255	*from* × 8
Nos. 256/310	*from* × 2
No. 312	*from* × 20
No. 313	*from* × 10
Nos. 315/318	*from* × 2
Nos. 319/328	*from* × 3
Nos. 329/340	*from* × 2
Nos. 341/400	*from* × 1
Nos. R1/R7*a*	*from* × 5
Nos. R8/R9	*from* × 50
Nos. R10/R11	*from* × 20
Nos. S1/S3	*from* × 8
No. S4	*from* × 6
No. S5	*from* × 5
Nos. S6/S11	*from* × 3
Nos. S12/S14	*from* × 5
Nos. D1/D8	*from* × 4
Nos. D9/D13	*from* × 5
Nos. D14/D24	*from* × 4

13

14

15

Large types

PRINTERS. Nos. 46/120 were recess-printed by the British American Bank Note Co at Ottawa or Montreal.

1868 (1 Apr)**–90.** As T **13/15** (various frames).

I. Ottawa printings. P 12

(a) Thin rather transparent crisp paper

46	13	½c. black (1.4.68)	£120	85·00
47	14	1c. red-brown (1.4.68)	£750	85·00
48		2c. grass-green (1.4.68)	£850	65·00
49		3c. red-brown (1.4.68)	£1600	38·00
50		6c. blackish brown (1.4.68)	£1800	£170
51		12½c. bright blue (1.4.68)	£1200	£130
52		15c. deep reddish purple	£1300	£180

In these first printings the impression is generally blurred and the lines of the background are less clearly defined than in later printings.

(b) Medium to stout wove paper (1868–1871)

53	13	½c. black	80·00	70·00
54		½c. grey-black	80·00	70·00
		a. Imperf between (pair)		
		b. Watermarked	£25000	£9500
55	14	1c. red-brown	£550	65·00
		a. Laid paper	£25000	£4000
		b. Watermarked (1868)	£2750	£325
56		1c. deep orange (1.1869)	£1600	£130
56*a*		1c. orange-yellow (5(?).1869)	£1100	£100
56*b*		1c. pale orange-yellow	£1200	£110
		ba. Imperf		
57		2c. deep green	£750	55·00
57*a*		2c. pale emerald-green (1871)	£950	85·00
		ab. Bisected (1c. with 2c. to make 3c. rate) *on cover*	†	£5500
		ac. Laid paper	†	£150000
57*d*		2c. bluish green	£800	55·00
		da. Watermarked (1868)	£2750	£300
58		3c. brown-red	£1300	25·00
		a. Laid paper	£16000	£600
		b. Watermarked (1868)	£3750	£250
59		6c. blackish brown (*to chocolate*)	£1400	75·00
		a. Watermarked (1868)	£9500	£1300
59*b*		6c. yellow-brown (1870)	£1300	65·00
		ba. Bisected (3c.), *on cover*	†	£3250
60		12½c. bright blue	£950	60·00
		a. Imperf horiz (vert pair)	†	£25000
		b. Watermarked (1868)	£5000	£300
60*c*		12½c. pale dull blue (milky)	£1000	75·00
61		15c. deep reddish purple	£850	70·00
61*a*		15c. pale reddish purple	£650	65·00
		ab. Watermarked (1868)	—	£1400
61*b*		15c. dull violet-grey	£250	35·00
		ba. Watermarked (1868)	£5500	£800
61*c*		15c. dull grey-purple	£325	35·00

The official date of issue was 1 April 1868. Scattered examples of most values can be found used in the second half of March.

The watermark on the stout paper stamps consists of the words 'E & G BOTHWELL CLUTHA MILLS,' in large double-lined capitals which can be found upright, inverted or reversed. Portions of one or two letters only may be found on these stamps, which occur in the early printings of 1868.

The paper may, in most cases, be easily divided if the stamps are laid face downwards and carefully compared. The thin hard paper is more or less transparent and shows the design through the stamp; the thicker paper is softer to the feel and more opaque.

Of the 2c. laid paper No. 57ac three examples only are known.

No. 60a is only known as a vertical strip of six.

II. Montreal printings. Medium to stout wove paper

(a) P 11½×12 or 11¾×12

62	13	½c. black (1873)	£110	85·00
63	15	5c. olive-green (28.9.75)	£850	85·00
		a. Perf 12	£6000	£800
64	14	15c. dull grey-purple (1874)	£1200	£225
65		15c. lilac-grey (3.77)	£1300	£225
		a. Script watermark	£24000	£3750
		b. 'BOTHWELL' watermark	†	£850
66		15c. slate	£1300	£300

(b) P 12

67	14	15c. clear deep violet (*thick paper*) (1879)	£4000	£700
68		15c. deep slate (1881)	£160	35·00
69		15c. slaty blue (1887)	£180	35·00
70		15c. slate-purple (*shades*) (7.88–92)	75·00	20·00

No. 63a gauges 12 or above on all four sides.

The watermark on No. 65a is part of 'Alexr Pirie & Sons' which appeared diagonally as script letters once per sheet in a small batch of the paper used for the 1877 printing. For a description of the sheet watermark on No. 65b, see note after No. 61*c*.

Several used examples of the 12½c. have been reported perforated 11½×12 or 11¾×12.

The last printing of the 15c. slate-purple, No. 70, took place at Ottawa.

III. Ottawa printings. Thinnish paper of poor quality, often toned grey or yellowish. P 12

71	14	15c. slate-violet (*shades*) (5.90)	75·00	22·00
		a. Imperf (pair). *Brown-purple*	£1400	

Examples of No. 71 are generally found with yellowish streaky gum.

21 *Small type*

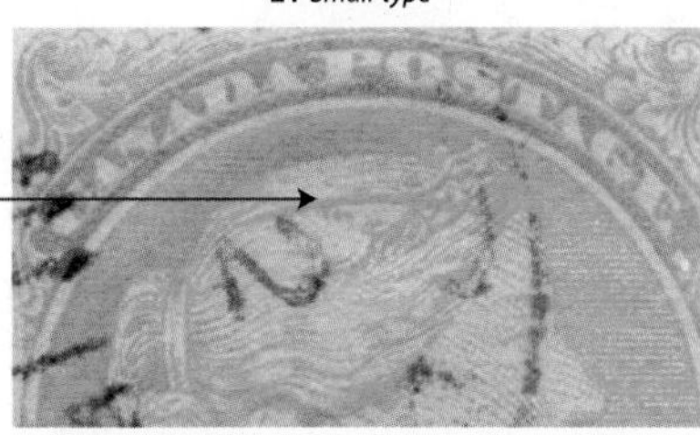

1c. Strand of hair

5c. Straw in hair

6c. Major re-entry (Pl. A, R. 7/7)

1870–90. As T **21** (various frames). Ottawa (1870–1873) and Montreal printings. P 12 (or slightly under).

Papers	(*a*)	1870–1880. Medium to stout wove.
	(*b*)	1870–1872. Thin, soft, very white.
	(*c*)	1878–1897. Thinner and poorer quality.

72	21	1c. bright orange (*a, b*) (2.1870–1873)	£225	45·00
		a. Thick soft paper (1871)	£800	£160
73		1c. orange-yellow (*a*) (1876–1879)	90·00	7·00
74		1c. pale dull yellow (*a*) (1877–1879)	65·00	4·75
75		1c. bright yellow (*a, c*) (1878–1897)	48·00	2·25
		a. Imperf (pair) (*c*)	£600	
		b. Bisected (½c.) (on *Railway News*)	†	£4500
		c. Printed both sides	£2000	
		d. Strand of hair	£1000	£325
76		1c. lemon-yellow (*c*) (1880)	£110	20·00
77		2c. deep green (*a, b*) (2.72–73 and 1876–1878)	90·00	6·00
78		2c. grass-green (*c*) (1878–1888)	60·00	2·50
		a. Imperf (pair)	£700	
		b. Bisected (1c.) *on cover*	†	£2500
		c. Stamp doubly printed	†	£5000
79		3c. Indian red (*a*) (1.70)	£1100	50·00
		a. Perf 12½ (2.70)	£8000	£700
80		3c. pale rose-red (*a*) (9.70)	£350	17·00
81		3c. deep rose-red (*a, b*) (1870–1873)	£375	17·00
		a. Thick soft paper (1.71)	£2000	£150
82		3c. dull red (*a, c*) (1876–1888)	£100	3·50
83		3c. orange-red (*shades*) (*a, c*) (1876–1888)	75·00	3·00
84		3c. rose-carmine (*c*) (10.88.–4.89)	£375	18·00
85		5c. olive-green (*a, c*) (2.76–88)	£425	17·00
		a. Straw in hair	£2000	£650
86		6c. yellowish brown (*a, b, c*) (1.72–73 and 1876–1890)	£350	24·00
		a. Major re-entry	£1300	£300
		b. Bisected (3c.) *on cover*	†	£1400
		c. Perf 12×11½* (1873)	†	—
		d. Perf 12×12½	†	£2500
87		10c. pale lilac-magenta (*a*) (1876–?)	£700	55·00
88		10c. deep lilac-magenta (*a, c*) (3.76–88)	£800	65·00
89		10c. lilac-pink (3.88)	£350	50·00

Nos. 75 and 78 were printed in the same shades during the second Ottawa period. Nos. 75a and 78a date from *circa* 1894–1895.

There are four variants of the Strand of Hair, with the strand in the same position but varying in length. R. 2/13 and R. 3/16 have been identified. The illustration shows the 'Long Strand'.

Examples of paper (*a*) can often be found showing traces of ribbing, especially on the 2c. value.

No. 79a was issued in New Brunswick and Nova Scotia.

* The exact perforation measurement on No. 86c is 11.85×11.6.

6c. Neck flaw ('A' Plate, R. 5/1)

27

1873–79. Montreal printings. Medium to stout wove paper. P 11½×12 or 11¾×12.

90	21	1c. bright orange	£300	50·00
91		1c. orange-yellow (1873–1879)	£250	17·00
92		1c. pale dull yellow (1877–1879)	£250	21·00
93		1c. lemon-yellow (1879)	£300	21·00
94		2c. deep green (1873–1878)	£400	24·00
95		3c. dull red (1875–1879)	£300	24·00
96		3c. orange-red (1873–1879)	£300	24·00
97		5c. olive-green (1.2.76–79)	£650	38·00
98		6c. yellowish brown (1873–1879)	£550	55·00
		a. Neck flaw	£1800	£275
99		10c. very pale lilac-magenta (11.74)	£1500	£350
100		10c. deep lilac-magenta (1876–1879)	£1100	£200

1882–97. Montreal (to March 1889) and Ottawa printings. Thinnish paper of poor quality. P 12.

101	27	½c. black (7.82–97)	22·00	13·00
102		½c. grey-black	22·00	13·00
		ab. Imperf (pair) (1891–1893?)	£700	
		ac. Imperf between (horiz pair)	£950	

2c. Latent entries (R. 9, above, R. 10/8, below)

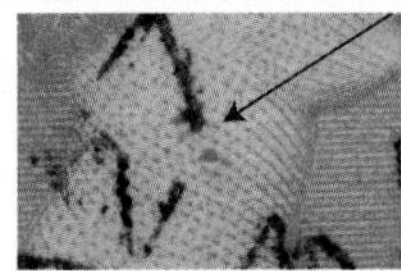

3c. 'Vampire bite'

5c. on **6c.** re-entry (R. 3/5)

6c. Major re-entry (Pane B, R. 9/7)

1889–97. Ottawa printings. Thinnish paper of poor quality, often toned grey or yellowish. P 12.

No.	Type	Description	Unused	Used
103	**21**	2c. dull sea-green	75·00	2·50
104		2c. blue-green (7.89–91)	60·00	3·50
		a. Latent entries	£750	£250
105		3c. bright vermilion (4.89–97)	55·00	1·50
		a. Vampire bite	£550	£180
		b. Imperf (pair) (1891–1893?)	£550	
106		5c. brownish grey (5.89)	£110	1·75
		a. Imperf (pair) (1891–1893)	£700	
107		6c. deep chestnut (10.90)	50·00	20·00
		a. '5c.' re-entry*	£4500	£1800
		b. Major re-entry	£500	£150
		c. Imperf (pair) (1891–1893?)	£750	
108		6c. pale chestnut	65·00	20·00
109		10c. salmon-pink	£325	£110
110		10c. carmine-pink (4.90)	£275	45·00
		a. Imperf (pair) (1891–1893?)	£850	
111		10c. brownish red (1894?)	£250	42·00
		a. Imperf (pair)	£750	

On No. 107a the top portion of the 5c. design cuts across 'CANADA POSTAGE', the white circle surrounding the head, and can be seen on the top of the head itself. Lesser re-entries are visible on R. 2/10 and R. 3/1 from another plate.

There are two latent entries recognised on the 2c. The stamp with the partial image in the upper margin has been identified as being R. 10/8, that with the image in the lower margin is from a position in row 9. The plates are not known.

The 1c. showed no change in the Ottawa printings, so is not included. The 2c. reverted to its previous grass-green shade in 1891.

28

29

(Recess B.A.B.N.)

1893 (17 Feb). P 12.

No.	Type	Description	Unused	Used
115	**28**	20c. vermilion	£250	65·00
		a. Imperf (pair)	£1700	
116		50c. blue	£275	45·00
		a. Imperf (*Prussian blue*) (pair)	£1800	

1893 (1 Aug). P 12.

No.	Type	Description	Unused	Used
117	**29**	8c. pale bluish grey	£180	10·00
		a. Imperf (pair)	£950	
118		8c. bluish slate	£150	10·00
119		8c. slate-purple	£130	10·00
120		8c. blackish purple	£110	10·00
		a. Imperf (pair)	£900	

PRINTERS. The following stamps to No. 287 were recess-printed by the American Bank Note Co, Ottawa, which in 1923 became the Canadian Bank Note Co.

30

(Des L. Pereira and F. Brownell)

1897 (19 June). Jubilee issue. P 12.

No.	Type	Description	Unused	Used
121	**30**	½c. black	75·00	75·00
122		1c. orange	13·00	6·50
123		1c. orange-yellow	13·00	6·50
		a. Bisected (½c.) (on *Railway News*)	†	£5500
124		2c. green	26·00	11·00
125		2c. deep green	26·00	11·00
126		3c. carmine	12·00	2·25
127		5c. slate-blue	55·00	20·00
128		5c. deep blue	55·00	20·00
129		6c. brown	£140	£140
130		8c. slate-violet	55·00	42·00
131		10c. purple	90·00	70·00
132		15c. slate	£140	£120
133		20c. vermilion	£140	£100
134		50c. pale ultramarine	£190	£110
135		50c. bright ultramarine	£200	£120
136		$1 lake	£550	£550
137		$2 deep violet	£1000	£425
138		$3 bistre	£1500	£800
139		$4 violet	£1400	£700
140		$5 olive-green	£1400	£700
121/140 *Set of* 16			£6000	£3500
133s/140s Handstamped 'SPECIMEN' *Set of* 7			£2500	

No. 123a was used on issues of the *Railway News* of 5, 6 and 8 November 1897 and must be on a large part of the original newspaper with New Glasgow postmark.

31

32

(From photograph by W. & D. Downey, London)

1897–98. P 12.

No.	Type	Description	Unused	Used
141	**31**	½c. grey-black (9.11.97)	18·00	7·50
142		½c. black	15·00	5·00
		a. Imperf (pair)	£475	
143		1c. blue-green (12.97)	30·00	1·00
		a. Imperf (pair)	£450	
144		2c. violet (12.97)	26·00	2·00
		a. Imperf (pair)	£475	
145		3c. carmine (1.98)	55·00	2·25
		a. Imperf (pair)	£800	
146		5c. deep blue/*bluish* (12.97)	70·00	3·00
		a. Imperf (pair)	£475	
147		6c. brown (12.97)	60·00	38·00
		a. Imperf (pair)	£750	
148		8c. orange (12.97)	85·00	11·00
		a. Imperf (pair)	£475	
149		10c. brownish purple (1.98)	£140	55·00
		a. Imperf (pair)	£550	
141/149 *Set of* 8			£425	£100

BOOKLET PANES. Most definitive booklets issued from 1900 onwards had either the two horizontal sides or all three outer edges imperforate. Stamps from the panes show one side or two adjacent sides imperforate.

Two types of the 2c.

Die Ia. Frame consists of four fine lines.
Die Ib. Frame has one thick line between two fine lines.

The die was retouched in 1900 for Plates 11 and 12, producing weak vertical frame lines and then retouched again in 1902 for Plates 15 to 20 resulting in much thicker frame lines. No. 155*b* covers both states of the retouching.

1898–1902. P 12.

No.	Type	Description	Unused	Used
150	**32**	½c. black (9.98)	8·50	1·10
		a. Imperf (pair)	£475	
151		1c. blue-green (6.98)	35·00	1·00
152		1c. deep green/*toned paper*	45·00	3·25
		a. Imperf (pair)	£1100	
153		2c. dull purple (Die Ia) (9.98)	48·00	1·00
		a. Thick paper (6.99)	£120	10·00
154		2c. violet (Die Ia)	30·00	30
154*a*		2c. reddish purple (Die Ia)	70·00	2·25
155		2c. rose-carmine (Die Ia) (20.8.99)	38·00	30
		a. Imperf (pair)	£475	
155*b*		2c. rose-carmine (Die Ib) (1900)	80·00	2·25
		ba. Booklet pane of 6 (11.6.00)	£750	
156		3c. rose-carmine (6.98)	80·00	1·00
157		5c. slate-blue/*bluish*	£110	4·00
		a. Imperf (pair)	£1000	
158		5c. Prussian blue/*bluish*	£120	4·00
159		6c. brown (9.98)	£100	65·00
		a. Imperf (pair)	£1000	
160		7c. greenish yellow (23.12.02)	70·00	26·00
161		8c. orange-yellow (10.98)	£130	45·00
162		8c. brownish orange	£120	45·00
		a. Imperf (pair)	£1000	
163		10c. pale brownish purple (11.98)	£170	15·00
164		10c. deep brownish purple	£170	15·00
		a. Imperf (pair)	£1000	
165		20c. olive-green (29.12.00)	£325	50·00
150/165 *Set of* 11			£950	£180

The 7c. and 20c. also exist imperforate, but unlike the values listed in this condition, they have no gum. (*Price*, 7c. £450, 20c. £3500 *pair, un*).

33

(Des R. Weir Crouch, G. Hahn, A. H. Howard and R. Holmes. Eng C. Skinner. Design recess, colours added by typo)

1898 (7 Dec). Imperial Penny Postage. Design in black. British possessions in red. Oceans in colours given. P 12.

No.	Type	Description	Unused	Used
166	**33**	2c. lavender	30·00	7·00
		a. Imperf (pair) (*no gum*)	£400	
167		2c. greenish blue	38·00	7·50
		a. Imperf (pair) (*no gum*)	£450	
168		2c. blue	42·00	7·50
		a. Imperf (pair) (*no gum*)	£475	

Forgeries of T **33** are without horizontal lines across the continents and have a forged Montreal postmark of 24.12.98.

1899 (4 Jan). Provisionals used at Port Hood, Nova Scotia. No. 156 divided vertically and handstamped.

No.	Type	Description	Unused	Used
169	**32**	'1' in blue, on 1/3 of 3c.	—	£3500
170		'2' in violet, on 2/3 of 3c.	—	£3000

Nos. 169/170 were prepared by the local postmaster during a shortage of 2c. stamps caused by a change in postage rates.

2 CENTS

(**34**)

35 King Edward VII

1899. Surch with T **34**, by Public Printing Office.

No.	Type	Description	Unused	Used
171	**31**	2c. on 3c. carmine (8.8)	22·00	8·00
		a. Surch inverted	£350	
172	**32**	2c. on 3c. rose-carmine (28.7)	19·00	4·25
		a. Surch inverted	£350	

(Des King George V when Prince of Wales and J. A. Tilleard)

1903 (1 July)–**12.** P 12.

No.	Type	Description	Unused	Used
173	**35**	1c. pale green	42·00	50
174		1c. deep green	35·00	50
175		1c. green	35·00	50
176		2c. rose-carmine	20·00	50
		a. Booklet pane of 6	£800	£950
177		2c. pale rose-carmine	20·00	50
		a. Imperf (pair) (18.7.09)	30·00	45·00
178		5c. blue/*bluish*	90·00	2·75
179		5c. indigo/*bluish*	90·00	2·75
180		7c. yellow-olive	90·00	2·75
181		7c. greenish bistre	£110	2·75
181*a*		7c. straw (1.12)	£120	65·00
182		10c. brown-lilac	£160	27·00
183		10c. pale dull purple	£160	27·00
184		10c. dull purple	£160	27·00
185		20c. pale olive-green (27.9.04)	£300	38·00
186		20c. deep olive-green	£325	38·00
		s. Handstamped 'SPECIMEN'	£110	
187		50c. deep violet (19.11.08)	£500	£130
173/187 *Set of* 7			£1100	£180

The 1c., 5c., 7c. and 10c. exist imperforate but are believed to be proofs. (*Prices per pair*, 1c. £550, 5c. £1000, 7c. £650, 10c. £1000, *without gum*).

Between 1905 and 1907 experimental printings of the 2c. value were made on dry paper (see note above No. 196). The resulting stamps are slightly wider with a sharper impression.

IMPERFORATE AND PART-PERFORATED SHEETS. Prior to 1946 many Canadian issues exist imperforate, or with other perforation varieties, in the colours of the issued stamps and, usually, with gum. In the years before 1927 such examples are believed to come from imprimatur sheets, removed from the Canadian Post Office archives. From 1927 until 1946 it is known that the printers involved in the production of the various issues submitted several imperforate plate proof sheets of each stamp to the Post Office authorities for approval. Some of these sheets or part sheets were retained for record purposes, but the remainder found their way on to the philatelic market.

Part-perforated sheets also occur from 1927–1929 issues.

From 1908 until 1946 we now only list and price such varieties of this type which are known to be genuine errors, sold from post offices. Where other imperforate or similar varieties are known they are recorded in footnotes.

It is possible, and in some cases probable, that some imperforate varieties listed before 1908 may have also been removed from the archives as mentioned above, but it is far harder to be explicit over the status of this earlier material.

36 King George V and Queen Mary when Prince and Princess of Wales

37 Jacques Cartier and Samuel Champlain

Re-entry (R. 5/4)

38 King Edward VII and Queen Alexandra

39 Champlain's house in Quebec

40 Generals Montcalm and Wolfe

41 Quebec in 1700

42 Champlain's departure for the West

43 Cartier's arrival before Quebec

(Des Machado)

1908 (16 July). Quebec Tercentenary. T **36/43.** P 12.

No.	Type	Description	Unused	Used
188	**36**	½c. sepia	6·00	3·50
		a. Re-entry	75·00	75·00
189	**37**	1c. blue-green	38·00	3·00
190	**38**	2c. carmine	28·00	1·00
191	**39**	5c. indigo	65·00	40·00

192 **40** 7c. olive-green 90·00 65·00
193 **41** 10c. violet £100 85·00
194 **42** 15c. brown-orange £120 95·00
195 **43** 20c. dull brown £160 £130
188/195 *Set of 8* £550 £375

Some values exist on both toned and white papers.

Nos. 188/195 exist imperforate. (*Price £650, un, for each pair*).

WET AND DRY PRINTINGS. Until the end of December 1922 all Canadian stamps were produced by the 'wet' method of recess-printing in which the paper was dampened before printing, dried and then gummed.

In late December 1922 the Canadian Bank Note Co. began to use the 'dry' process in which the paper was gummed before printing. Late printings of the 3c. brown were the first stamps to be produced by this method, but the changeover was not completed until January 1926.

'Dry' printings have a sharper appearance and can often be found with a degree of embossing showing on the reverse. Stamps from 'wet' printings shrink during drying and are narrower than 'dry' examples. In many cases the difference can be as great as 0.5 mm. On some early booklet panes the difference is in the vertical, rather than the horizontal, measurement.

On Nos. 196/215 all values only exist from 'wet' printings, except the 3c., 20c. and 50c. which come from both types of printing.

44 King George V

1c. Major re-entry

1911–22. P 12.

196 **44** 1c. yellow-green (22.12.11) 14·00 75
197 1c. bluish green 5·50 50
a. Major re-entry £5000 £1500
b. Booklet pane of 6 (1.5.13) 50·00
198 1c. deep bluish green 8·00 50
a. With fine horiz lines across stamp 50·00 10·00
199 1c. deep yellow-green 8·00 1·00
a. Booklet pane of 6 18·00
200 2c. rose-red (15.12.11) 12·00 50
201 2c. deep rose-red 7·00 50
a. Booklet pane of 6 (1.12) 32·00
202 2c. pale rose-red 9·00 50
a. With fine horiz lines across stamp 26·00 18·00
203 2c. carmine 11·00 50
204 3c. brown (6.8.18) 7·50 50
205 3c. deep brown 7·50 50
a. Booklet pane of 4+2 labels (2.22) 55·00
205*b* 5c. deep blue (17.1.12) 70·00 75
206 5c. indigo £120 10·00
206*a* 5c. grey-blue £110 5·00
206*b* 7c. straw (12.1.12) 95·00 20·00
207 7c. pale sage-green (1914) £275 55·00
208 7c. olive-yellow (1915) 26·00 4·25
209 7c. yellow-ochre (1916) 26·00 4·25
210 10c. brownish purple (12.1.12) £100 2·75
211 10c. reddish purple £140 7·00
212 20c. olive-green (23.1.12) 45·00 1·50
213 20c. olive 45·00 1·75
214 50c. grey-black (26.1.12) £140 12·00
215 50c. sepia 50·00 3·75
196/215 *Set of 8* £275 12·00

The 20c. and 50c. values exist imperforate (*Price £3500 un, for each pair*).

The major re-entry on the 1c. (No. 197a) shows as a distinct doubling of the lower right corner of the stamp on Plate 12, lower right pane, R. 4/5.

1912 (Oct)–**21**. For use in coil-machines.

(a) Perf 12×imperf

216 **44** 1c. yellow-green (1914) 3·50 16·00
217 1c. blue-green (1914) 28·00 28·00
a. Two large holes at top and bottom (vert pair) (7.18) 80·00 90·00
218 2c. deep rose-red (1914) 45·00 26·00
218*a* 3c. brown (1921) 5·00 10·00

No. 217a has two large holes about 3½ mm in diameter in the top and bottom margins. They were for experimental use in a vending machine at Toronto in July 1918 and were only in use for two days.

The 1c. and 2c. also exist with two small 'V' shaped holes about 9.5 mm apart at top which are gripper marks due to modifications made in vending machines in 1917.

(b) Imperf×perf 8

219 **44** 1c. yellow-green (10.12) 25·00 8·00
220 1c. blue-green 32·00 7·50
a. With fine horiz lines across stamp 75·00
221 2c. carmine (10.12) 23·00 2·25
222 2c. rose-red 24·00 2·75
223 2c. scarlet 48·00 6·50
224 3c. brown (8.18) 5·00 2·00

(c) Perf 8×imperf

224*a* **44** 1c. blue-green (13.2.13) 65·00 50·00
224*b* 2c. carmine (15.2.13) 65·00 50·00

The stamps imperf×perf 8 were sold in coils over the counter; those perf 8×imperf were on sale in automatic machines. Varieties showing perf 12 on 2 or 3 adjacent sides and 1 or 2 sides imperf are from booklets, or the margins of sheets.

(45)

46

47

1915 (12 Feb). Optd with T **45**.

225 **44** 5c. blue £130 £200
226 20c. olive-green 60·00 £100
227 50c. sepia (R.) £140 £180
225/227 *Set of 3* £300 £425

These stamps were intended for tax purposes, but owing to ambiguity in an official circular dated 16 April 1915, it was for a time believed that their use for postal purposes was authorised. The position was clarified by a further circular on 20 May 1916 which made clear that Nos. 225/227 were for fiscal use only.

1915. P 12.

228 **46** 1c. green (15.4.15) 7·00 50
229 2c. carmine-red (16.4.15) 28·00 3·50
230 2c. rose-carmine 35·00 4·75

Die I Die II

In Die I there is a long horizontal coloured line under the foot of the 'T', and a solid bar of colour runs upwards from the '1' to the 'T'.

In Die II this solid bar of colour is absent, and there is a short horizontal line under the left side of the 'T', with two short vertical dashes and a number of dots under the right-hand side.

1916 (1 Jan). P 12.

231 **47** 2c. +1c. rose-red (Die I) 65·00 1·25
232 2c. +1c. bright carmine (Die I) 50·00 1·25
233 2c. +1c. scarlet (Die I) 60·00 2·25

1916 (Feb). Coil stamps. Imperf×perf 8.

234 **47** 2c. +1c. rose-red (Die I) 70·00 12·00

1916 (July). P 12×8.

235 **47** 2c. +1c. carmine-red (Die I) 38·00 60·00
236 2c. +1c. bright rose-red (Die I) 45·00 60·00

1916 (Aug). P 12.

237 **47** 2c. +1c. carmine-red (Die II) £170 28·00

1916 (Aug). Colour changed.

(a) P 12

238 **47** 2c. +1c. brown (Die I) £375 27·00
239 2c. +1c. yellow-brown (Die II) 7·50 50
a. Imperf (pair) £1500
240 2c. +1c. deep brown (Die II) 22·00 50

(b) Coil stamps. Imperf×perf 8

241 **47** 2c. +1c. brown (Die I) £110 13·00
a. Pair, 241 and 243 £350
243 2c. +1c. deep brown (Die II) 60·00 4·75

No. 239a, which is a genuine error, should not be confused with ungummed proofs of the Die I stamp, No. 238 (*Price per pair*, £140).

This value also exists P 12×imperf or imperf×perf 12, but was not issued with these perforations (*Price, in either instance, £350, un, per pair*).

48 Quebec Conference, 1864, from painting *The Fathers of Confederation*, by Robert Harris

1917 (15 Sept). 50th Anniversary of Confederation. P 12.

244 **48** 3c. bistre-brown 24·00 3·50
245 3c. deep brown 26·00 4·25

No. 244 exists imperforate, without gum (*Price per pair, £500 un*).

Die I (top). Space between top of 'N' and oval frame line and space between 'CENT' and lower frame line.

Die II (bottom). 'ONE CENT' appears larger so that 'N' touches oval and 'CENT' almost touches frame line. There are other differences but this is the most obvious one.

Die I (top). The lowest of the three horizontal lines of shading below the medals does not touch the three heavy diagonal lines; three complete white spaces over both 'E's' of 'THREE'; long centre bar to figures '3'. Vertical spandrel lines fine.

Die II (bottom). The lowest horizontal line of shading touches the first of the three diagonal lines; two and a half spaces over first 'E' and spaces over second 'E' partly filled by stem of maple leaf; short centre bar to figures '3'. Vertical spandrel lines thick. There are numerous other minor differences.

WET AND DRY PRINTINGS. See notes above No. 196.

On Nos. 246/263 all listed items occur from both 'wet' and 'dry' printings except Nos. 246aa/246ab, 248aa, 256, 259, 260 and 262 which come 'wet' only, and Nos. 246a, 248/248a, 252/254a, 256b and 263 which are 'dry' only.

1922–31. As T **44**.

(a) P 12

246 **44** 1c. chrome-yellow (Die I) (7.6.22) 3·25 60
aa. Booklet pane of 4+2 labels (7.22) 60·00
ab. Booklet pane of 6 (12.22) 40·00
a. Die II (1925) 9·00 30
247 2c. deep green (6.6.22) 2·25 10
aa. Booklet pane of 4+2 labels (7.22) 55·00
ab. Booklet pane of 6 (12.22) £325
b. Thin paper (9.24) 3·00 6·00
248 3c. carmine (Die I) (18.12.23) 3·75 10
aa. Booklet pane of 4+2 labels (12.23) 50·00
a. Die II (11.24) 45·00 80
249 4c. olive-yellow (7.7.22) 8·00 3·50
a. Yellow-ochre 8·00 3·50
250 5c. violet (2.2.22) 5·00 1·75
a. Thin paper (9.24) 5·00 9·50
b. Reddish violet (1925) 12·00 2·00
251 7c. red-brown (12.12.24) 12·00 9·00
a. Thin paper £170 50·00
252 8c. blue (1.9.25) 23·00 11·00
253 10c. blue (20.2.22) 15·00 3·25
254 10c. bistre-brown (1.8.25) 29·00 4·00
a. Yellow-brown 18·00 5·00
255 $1 brown-orange (22.7.23) 55·00 9·50
246/255 *Set of 10* £130 38·00

The $1 differs from T **44** in that the value tablets are oval.

Nos. 249/252 and 254/255 exist imperforate (*Prices per un pair* 4c. *to* 10c. £2500 *each*, $1 £3000).

(b) Coil stamps. Imperf×perf 8

256 **44** 1c. chrome-yellow (Die I) (1922) 4·00 11·00
a. Imperf horiz (vert pair) (1924) £180
b. Die II (1925) 4·50 7·00
c. Do. Imperf horiz (vert pair) (1927) 8·00 27·00
257 2c. deep green (26.7.22) 7·00 2·25
b. Imperf horiz (vert pair) (1927) 9·00 27·00
258 3c. carmine (Die I) (9.4.24) 80·00 19·00
a. Imperf horiz (vert pair) (1924) £250
b. Die II (1925) £100 38·00
256/258 *Set of 3* 85·00 25·00

Nos. 256a, 256c, 257b and 258a come from coil printings sold in sheet form. Those issued in 1924 were from 'wet' printings and those in 1927 from 'dry'. A 'wet' printing of No. 257b, issued in 1924, also exists (*Price £180 mint*), but cannot be identified from that issued in 1927 except by the differences between 'wet' and 'dry' stamps.

(c) Imperf (pairs)

259 **44** 1c. chrome-yellow (Die I) (6.10.24) 50·00 70·00
260 2c. deep green (6.10.24) 50·00 70·00
261 3c. carmine (Die I) (31.12.23)† 32·00 55·00

(d) Coil stamp. Perf 12×imperf

262 **44** 2c. deep green (9.24) 65·00 65·00

(e) P 12×8

263 **44** 3c. carmine (Die II) (24.6.31) 5·50 4·00

† Earliest known postmark.

Nos. 259 to 261 were on sale only at the Philatelic Branch, PO Dept, Ottawa.

No. 263 was produced by adding horizontal perforations to unused sheet stock of No. 258b. The stamps were then issued in 1931 pending the delivery of No. 293.

2 CENTS **2 CENTS**
(49) (50)

1926. No. 248 surch.

*(a) With T **49**, by the Govt Printing Bureau*

264 **44** 2c. on 3c. carmine (12.10.26) 50·00 65·00
a. Pair, one without surch £450
b. On Die II £400

*(b) With T **50**, by the Canadian Bank Note Co*

265 **44** 2c. on 3c. carmine (4.11.26) 20·00 35·00
a. Surch double (partly treble) £200

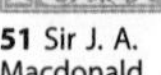

51 Sir J. A. Macdonald

52 *The Fathers of Confederation*

53 Parliament Buildings, Ottawa

54 Sir W. Laurier

55 Canada, Map 1867–1927

1927 (29 June). 60th Anniversary of Confederation. P 12.

I. Commemorative Issue. Inscr '1867–1927 CANADA CONFEDERATION'

266	**51**	1c. orange	2·50	1·50
267	**52**	2c. green	2·25	30
268	**53**	3c. carmine	11·00	5·00
269	**54**	5c. violet	7·00	4·75
270	**55**	12c. blue	35·00	8·00
266/270 *Set of 5*			50·00	18·00

Nos. 266/270 exist imperforate, imperf×perf or perf×imperf (*Prices from £120, un, per pair*).

56 Darcy McGee

57 Sir W. Laurier and Sir J. A. Macdonald

58 R. Baldwin and L. H. Lafontaine

II. Historical Issue

271	**56**	5c. violet	3·00	2·50
272	**57**	12c. green	17·00	5·50
273	**58**	20c. carmine	17·00	15·00
271/273 *Set of 3*			32·00	21·00

Nos. 271/273 exist imperforate, imperf×perf or perf×imperf (*Prices from £120, un, per pair*).

59

(Des H. Schwartz)

1928 (21 Sept). Air. P 12.

274	**59**	5c. olive-brown	8·00	6·50

No. 274 exists imperforate, imperf×perf or perf×imperf (*Price per pair, £275, un*).

60 King George V

61 Mt. Hurd and Indian Totem Poles

62 Quebec Bridge

63 Harvesting with Horses

64 *Bluenose* (fishing schooner)

65 Parliament Buildings, Ottawa

1928–29.

(a) P 12

275	**60**	1c. orange (25.10.28)	2·75	3·00
		a. Booklet pane of 6	19·00	
276		2c. green (16.10.28)	1·25	20
		a. Booklet pane of 6	19·00	
277		3c. lake (12.12.28)	20·00	23·00
278		4c. olive-bistre (16.8.29)	13·00	13·00
279		5c. violet (12.12.28)	6·50	5·50
		a. Booklet pane of 6 (6.1.29)	£130	
280		8c. blue (21.12.28)	7·50	7·50
281	**61**	10c. green (5.12.28)	8·50	2·25
282	**62**	12c. grey-black (8.1.29)	26·00	20·00
283	**63**	20c. lake (8.1.29)	38·00	20·00
284	**64**	50c. blue (8.1.29)	£150	55·00
285	**65**	$1 olive-green (8.1.29)	£150	85·00
		a. Brown-olive	£225	£100
275/285 *Set of 11*			£375	£200

(b) Coil stamps. Imperf×perf 8 (5.11.28)

286	**60**	1c. orange	15·00	27·00
287		2c. green	20·00	9·00

Slight differences in the size of many Canadian stamps, due to paper shrinkage, are to be found.

Nos. 275/285 exist imperforate, imperf×perf or perf×imperf (*Prices per unused pair*, 1c. to 8c., *from* £110, 10c. to 20c., *from* £200, 50c. and $1, *from* £650). *Tête-bêche* horizontal pairs of the 1c., 2c. and 5c. are also known from uncut booklet sheets (*Prices per pair*, £325, *un*).

PRINTERS. The following stamps to No. 334 were recess-printed by the British American Bank Note Co, Ottawa.

66 King George V

67 Parliamentary Library, Ottawa

68 The Old Citadel, Quebec

69 Harvesting with Tractor

70 Acadian Memorial Church and Statue of *Evangeline*, Grand Pre, Nova Scotia

71 Mt. Edith Cavell, Canadian Rockies

Die I

Die II

1c.

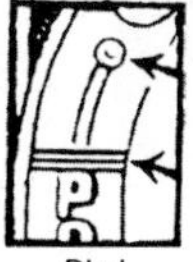

Die I

Die II

2c.

1c. Die I. Three thick coloured lines and one thin between 'P' and ornament, at right. Curved line in ball-ornament short.

Die II. Four thick lines. Curved line longer.

2c. Die I. Three thick coloured lines between 'P' and ornament, at left. Short line in ball.

Die II. Four thick lines. Curved line longer.

Normal

2c. 'Cockeyed King' (Retouch on coil stamps)

1930–31.

(a) P 11

288	**66**	1c. orange (I) (17.7.30)	1·75	1·75
289		1c. green (I) (6.12.30)	4·00	10
		b. Booklet pane of 6 (21.7.31)	35·00	
		d. Die II (8.31)	3·75	10
		da. Imperf (pair)	£2000	
		db. Booklet pane of 4+2 labels (13.11.31)	£100	
290		2c. green (I) (6.6.30)	1·75	10
		a. Booklet pane of 6 (17.6.30)	45·00	
291		2c. scarlet (I) (17.11.30)	3·00	3·50
		a. Booklet pane of 6 (17.11.30)	27·00	
		b. Die II	1·00	10
292		2c. deep brown (I) (4.7.31)	3·00	6·00
		a. Booklet pane of 6 (23.7.31)	55·00	
		b. Die II (4.7.31)	2·00	10
		ba. Booklet pane of 4+2 labels (13.11.31)	£140	
293		3c. scarlet (13.7.31)	2·50	10
		a. Booklet pane of 4+2 labels	55·00	
294		4c. yellow-bistre (5.11.30)	12·00	4·50
295		5c. violet (18.6.30)	2·75	8·00
296		5c. deep slate-blue (13.11.30)	5·50	20
		a. Dull blue	25·00	1·50
297		8c. blue (13.8.30)	11·00	16·00
298		8c. red-orange (5.11.30)	11·00	5·50
299	**67**	10c. olive-green (15.9.30)	23·00	2·25
		a. Imperf (pair)	£1800	
300	**68**	12c. grey-black (4.12.30)	14·00	7·00
301	**69**	20c. red (4.12.30)	22·00	2·50
302	**70**	50c. blue (4.12.30)	90·00	17·00
303	**71**	$1 olive-green (4.12.30)	£130	40·00
288/303 *Set of 16*			£275	90·00

(b) Coil stamps. Imperf×perf 8½

304	**66**	1c. orange (I) (14.7.30)	12·00	21·00
305		1c. green (I) (4.2.31)	6·00	7·00
306		2c. green (I) (27.6.30)	4·00	13·00
		a. Cockeyed King	65·00	95·00
307		2c. scarlet (I) (19.11.30)	4·50	11·00
		a. Cockeyed King	70·00	95·00
308		2c. deep brown (I) (4.7.31)	9·00	1·50
		a. Cockeyed King	80·00	65·00
309		3c. scarlet (13.7.31)	14·00	2·00
304/309 *Set of 6*			45·00	50·00

Nos. 300/303 exist imperforate (*Prices per unused pair*, 12c. £900, 20c. £900, 50c. £950, $1 £1000).

Some low values in the above and subsequent issues have been printed by both Rotary and 'Flat plate' processes. The former can be distinguished by the gum, which has a striped appearance.

For 13c. bright violet, T **68**, see No. 325.

72 Mercury and Western Hemisphere

73 Sir Georges Étienne Cartier

(Des H. Schwartz)

1930 (4 Dec). Air. P 11.

310	**72**	5c. deep brown	26·00	27·00

1931 (30 Sept). P 11.

312	**73**	10c. olive-green	14·00	20

No. 312 exists imperforate (*Price per pair, £500, un*).

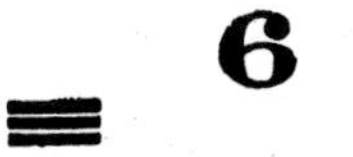

(**74**)  (**75**)

1932 (22 Feb). Air. No. 274 surch with T **74**.

313	**59**	6c. on 5c. olive-brown	3·00	3·00

Examples of this stamp with surcharge inverted, surcharge double, surcharge triple or surcharge omitted in pair with normal are not now believed to have been regularly issued. Such 'errors' have also been forged and collectors are warned against forged examples, some of which bear unauthorised markings which purport to be the guarantee of Stanley Gibbons Ltd.

1932 (21 June). Nos. 291/291b surch with T **75**.

314	**66**	3c. on 2c. scarlet (I)	6·00	5·00
		a. Die II	1·00	60

76 King George V

77 Duke of Windsor when Prince of Wales

78 Allegory of British Empire

(**79**)

1932 (12 July). Ottawa Conference. P 11.

(a) Postage stamps

315	**76**	3c. scarlet	1·00	80
316	**77**	5c. blue	14·00	5·50
317	**78**	13c. green	14·00	6·00

(b) Air. No. 310 surch with T **79**

318	**72**	6c. on 5c. deep brown (B.)	16·00	25·00
315/318 *Set of 4*			40·00	32·00

80 King George V

'3' level Die I

'3' raised Die II

1932 (1 Dec)–**33**.

(a) P 11

319	**80**	1c. green	60	10
		a. Booklet pane of 6 (28.12.33)	16·00	
		b. Booklet pane of 4+2 labels (19.9.33)	85·00	
320		2c. sepia	70	10
		a. Booklet pane of 6 (7.9.33)	22·00	
		b. Booklet pane of 4+2 labels (19.9.33)	95·00	
321		3c. scarlet (Die I)	2·75	10
		a. Booklet pane of 4+2 labels (22.8.33)	60·00	
		b. Die II (29.11.32)	85	10
		ba. Booklet pane of 4+2 labels (19.9.33)	45·00	

322		4c. yellow-brown	50·00	15·00
323		5c. blue	13·00	10
		a. Imperf vert (horiz pair)	£1800	
324		8c. red-orange	45·00	4·25
325	**68**	13c. bright violet	85·00	3·00
319/325 *Set of 7*			£170	20·00

Nos. 319/325 exist imperforate (*Prices per unused pair*, 1c. to 8c. £225, 13c. £800).

(b) Coil stamps. Imperf×perf 8½ (1933)

326	**80**	1c. green (3.11.33)	24·00	6·50
327		2c. sepia (15.8.33)	24·00	5·50
328		3c. scarlet (Die II) (16.8.33)	12·00	3·25
326/328 *Set of 3*			55·00	13·50

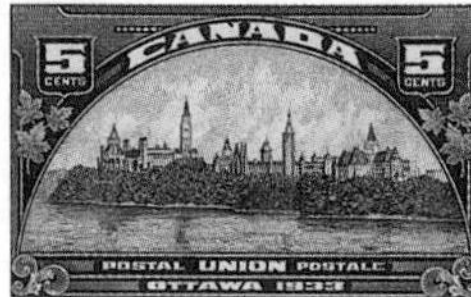
81 Parliament Buildings, Ottawa

1933 (18 May). UPU Congress Preliminary Meeting. P 11.

329	**81**	5c. blue	13·00	4·25

No. 329 exists imperforate (*Price per pair £850, un*).

WORLD'S
GRAIN EXHIBITION &
CONFERENCE

REGINA 1933

(**82**)

1933 (24 July). World's Grain Exhibition and Conference, Regina. No. 301 optd with T **82** in blue.

330	**69**	20c. red	22·00	15·00

No. 330 exists imperforate (*Price per pair £850, un*).

83 SS *Royal William* (after S. Skillett)

84 Jacques Cartier approaching Land

1933 (17 Aug). Centenary of First Trans-Atlantic Steamboat Crossing. P 11.

331	**83**	5c. blue	20·00	5·50

No. 331 exists imperforate (*Price per pair £850, un*).

1934 (1 July). 400th Anniversary of Discovery of Canada. P 11.

332	**84**	3c. blue	7·50	1·50

No. 332 exists imperforate (*Price per pair £800, un*).

85 UEL Statue, Hamilton

86 Seal of New Brunswick

1934 (1 July). 150th Anniversary of Arrival of United Empire Loyalists. P 11.

333	**85**	10c. olive-green	16·00	12·00

No. 333 exists imperforate (*Price per pair £1600, un*).

1934 (16 Aug). 150th Anniversary of Province of New Brunswick. P 11.

334	**86**	2c. red-brown	1·50	3·50

No. 334 exists imperforate (*Price per pair £850, un*).

PRINTERS. The following stamps were recess-printed (except where otherwise stated) by the Canadian Bank Note Co, Ottawa, until No. 616.

87 Queen Elizabeth II when Princess

88 King George VI when Duke of York

89 King George V and Queen Mary

90 King Edward VIII when Prince of Wales

91 Windsor Castle

92 Royal Yacht *Britannia*

'Weeping Princess' (Pl 1 upper right pane R. 3/1)

'Shilling mark' (Pl 1 upper right pane R. 8/8)

1935 (4 May). Silver Jubilee. T **87/92**. P 12.

335	**87**	1c. green	1·50	80
		a. Weeping Princess	£160	£100
336	**88**	2c. brown	1·00	80
337	**89**	3c. carmine-red	4·50	2·25
338	**90**	5c. blue	9·00	9·00
339	**91**	10c. green	13·00	10·00
340	**92**	13c. blue	16·00	10·00
		a. Shilling mark	£500	£500
335/340 *Set of 6*			40·00	30·00

Nos. 335/340 exist imperforate (*Prices per unused pair*, 1c to 5c. *each* £300, 10c. and 13c. *each* £350).

93 King George V

94 Royal Canadian Mounted Policeman

95 Confederation Conference, Charlottetown, 1864

96 Niagara Falls

97 Parliament Buildings, Victoria, British Columbia

98 Champlain Monument, Quebec

99 Daedalus

10c. Broken leg (Pl. 1, R. 5/8)

50c. Major re-entry (Pl. 1 upper right pane, R. 5/5)

1c. Normal

1c. Narrow '1'

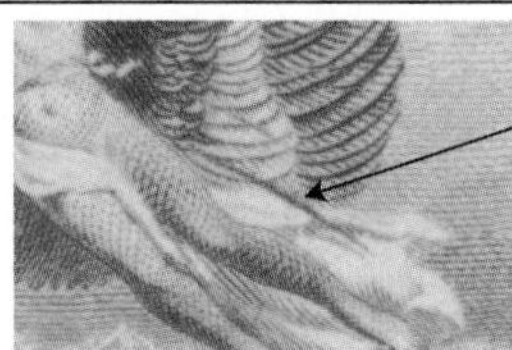
6c. Moulting wing (Pl. 1, lower right pane, R. 3/4)

1935 (1 June–16 Nov). T **93/99**.

(a) Postage

(i) P 12

341	**93**	1c. green	1·75	10
		a. Booklet pane of 6 (19.8.35)	28·00	
		b. Booklet pane of 4+2 labels (22.7.35)	70·00	
342		2c. brown	1·75	10
		a. Booklet pane of 6 (16.11.35)	29·00	
		b. Booklet pane of 4+2 labels (22.7.35)	70·00	
343		3c. scarlet	1·75	10
		a. Booklet pane of 4+2 labels	42·00	
		b. Printed on the gummed side	£325	
344		4c. yellow	3·50	3·00
345		5c. blue	3·50	10
		a. Imperf vert (horiz pair)	£225	
346		8c. orange	4·25	5·00
347	**94**	10c. carmine	6·50	50
		a. Broken leg	£1900	£1400
348	**95**	13c. purple	7·50	65
349	**96**	20c. olive-green	25·00	1·75
350	**97**	50c. deep violet	26·00	8·50
		a. Major re-entry	£140	85·00
351	**98**	$1 bright blue	42·00	11·00
341/351 *Set of 11*			£110	27·00

(ii) Coil stamps. Imperf×perf 8

352	**93**	1c. green (5.11.35)	21·00	15·00
		a. Narrow '1'	80·00	65·00
353		2c. brown (14.10.35)	14·00	6·50
354		3c. scarlet (20.7.35)	9·00	1·75
352/354 *Set of 3*			40·00	21·00

(b) Air. P 12

355	**99**	6c. red-brown	4·25	1·00
		a. Imperf vert (horiz pair)	£8500	
		b. Moulting wing	£110	70·00

Nos. 341/351 (*Prices per pair*, 1c. to 8c. *each* £170, 10c. to 50c. *each* £300, $1 £350, *un*) and 355 (*Price per pair £750, un*) exist imperforate.

100 King George VI and Queen Elizabeth

1937 (10 May). Coronation. P 12.

356	**100**	3c. carmine	2·00	1·50

No. 356 exists imperforate (*Price per pair £900, un*).

101 King George VI

102 Memorial Chamber, Parliament Buildings, Ottawa

103 Entrance to Halifax Harbour

104 Fort Garry Gate, Winnipeg

105 Entrance, Vancouver Harbour

106 Château de Ramezay, Montréal

107 Fairchild 45-80 Sekani Seaplane over *Distributor* on River Mackenzie

Crease on collar (Pl 2 upper right pane R. 9/5)

(T **101**. Photograph by Bertram Park)

1937–38. T **101/107**.

(a) Postage

(i) P 12

No.	Type	Description	Unused	Used
357	**101**	1c. green (1.4.37)	2·50	10
		a. Booklet pane of 4+2 labels (14.4.37)	30·00	
		b. Booklet pane of 6 (18.5.37)	8·50	
358		2c. brown (1.4.37)	3·25	10
		a. Booklet pane of 4+2 labels (14.4.37)	60·00	
		b. Booklet pane of 6 (3.5.38)	11·00	
359		3c. scarlet (1.4.37)	1·75	10
		a. Booklet pane of 4+2 labels (14.4.37)	4·25	
		b. Crease on collar	£100	40·00
360		4c. yellow (10.5.37)	5·50	1·75
361		5c. blue (10.5.37)	8·00	10
362		8c. orange (10.5.37)	6·50	3·75
363	**102**	10c. rose-carmine (15.6.38)	6·50	60
		a. Red	5·00	10
364	**103**	13c. blue (15.11.38)	35·00	3·00
365	**104**	20c. red-brown (15.6.38)	25·00	2·75
366	**105**	50c. green (15.6.38)	50·00	16·00
367	**106**	$1 violet (15.6.38)	65·00	16·00
		a. Imperf horiz (vert pair)	£7500	
357/367 *Set of* 11			£180	40·00

Nos. 357/367 exist imperforate (*Prices per pair* 1c. to 8c. *each* £375, 10c. to 50c. *each* £700, $1 £900 *un*).

(ii) Coil stamps. Imperf×perf 8

No.	Type	Description	Unused	Used
368	**101**	1c. green (15.6.37)	4·50	7·00
369		2c. brown (18.6.37)	3·75	6·50
370		3c. scarlet (15.4.37)	35·00	2·50
368/370 *Set of* 3			38·00	14·50

(b) Air. P 12

No.	Type	Description	Unused	Used
371	**107**	6c. blue (15.6.38)	20·00	2·25

No. 371 exists imperforate (*Price per pair* £850, *un*).

108 Queen Elizabeth II when Princess and Princess Margaret

109 National War Memorial

110 King George VI and Queen Elizabeth

1939 (15 May). Royal Visit. P 12.

No.	Type	Description	Unused	Used
372	**108**	1c. black and green	2·50	25
373	**109**	2c. black and brown	3·00	2·00
374	**110**	3c. black and carmine	2·00	25
372/374 *Set of* 3			6·75	2·25

Nos. 372/374 exist imperforate (*Price* £850, *un, for each pair*).

111 King George VI in Naval uniform

112 King George VI in Military uniform

113 King George VI in Air Force uniform

114 Grain Elevator

115 Farm Scene

116 Parliament Buildings

117 Ram Tank

118 Launching of Corvette HMCS *La Malbaie*, Sorel

119 Munitions Factory

120 HMS *Cossack* (destroyer)

121 Air Training Camp

1942 (1 July)–**48**. War Effort. T **111/121** and similar designs.

(a) Postage

(i) P 12

No.	Type	Description	Unused	Used
375	**111**	1c. green	1·50	10
		a. Booklet pane of 4+2 labels (12.9.42)	35·00	
		b. Booklet pane of 6 (24.11.42)	2·50	
376	**112**	2c. brown	1·75	10
		a. Booklet pane of 4+2 labels (12.9.42)	42·00	
		b. Booklet pane of 6 (6.10.42)	32·00	
377	**113**	3c. carmine-lake	1·25	60
		a. Booklet pane of 4+2 labels (20.8.42)	4·25	
378		3c. purple (30.6.43)	1·75	10
		a. Booklet pane of 4+2 labels (28.8.43)	6·50	
		b. Booklet pane of 6 (24.11.47)	16·00	
379	**114**	4c. slate	5·50	3·75
380	**112**	4c. carmine-lake (9.4.43)	70	10
		a. Booklet pane of 6 (3.5.43)	3·50	
381	**111**	5c. blue	3·50	10
382	**115**	8c. red-brown	5·50	1·25
383	**116**	10c. brown	16·00	10
384	**117**	13c. dull green	13·00	13·00
385		14c. dull green (16.4.43)	29·00	1·00
386	**118**	20c. chocolate	22·00	45
387	**119**	50c. violet	26·00	7·00
388	**120**	$1 blue	50·00	15·00
375/388 *Set of* 14			£150	38·00

Nos. 375/388 exist imperforate (*Prices per pair* 1c. to 8c. *each* £375, 10c. to 20c. *each* £750, 50c. and $1 *each* £850, *un*).

(ii) Coil stamps. Imperf×perf 8

No.	Type	Description	Unused	Used
389	**111**	1c. green (9.2.43)	1·00	1·50
390	**112**	2c. brown (24.11.42)	2·25	3·50
391	**113**	3c. carmine-lake (23.9.42)	2·00	11·00
392		3c. purple (19.8.43)	12·00	11·00
393	**112**	4c. carmine-lake (13.5.43)	13·00	2·25
389/393 *Set of* 5			27·00	26·00

(iii) Booklet stamps. Imperf×perf 12 (1.9.43)

No.	Type	Description	Unused	Used
394	**111**	1c. green	6·50	1·50
		a. Booklet pane of 3	17·00	
395	**113**	3c. purple	6·50	2·00
		a. Booklet pane of 3	17·00	
396	**112**	4c. carmine-lake	6·50	2·50
		a. Booklet pane of 3	17·00	
394/396 *Set of* 3			17·00	5·50

Nos. 394/396 are from booklets in which the stamps are in strips of three, imperforate at top and bottom and right-hand end.

(iv) Coil stamps. Imperf×perf 9½

No.	Type	Description	Unused	Used
397	**111**	1c. green (13.7.48)	4·25	5·00
397*a*	**112**	2c. brown (1.10.48)	8·00	19·00
398	**113**	3c. purple (2.7.48)	5·00	6·00
398*a*	**112**	4c. carmine-lake (22.7.48)	9·00	7·00
397/398*a* *Set of* 4			24·00	32·00

(b) Air. P 12

No.	Type	Description	Unused	Used
399	**121**	6c. blue (1.7.42)	32·00	14·00
400		7c. blue (16.4.43)	5·50	50

Nos. 399/400 exist imperforate (*Price* £1000, *un, for each pair*).

122 Ontario Farm Scene

123 Great Bear Lake

124 St Maurice River Power Station

125 Combine-Harvester

126 Lumbering in British Columbia

127 *Abegweit* (train ferry), Prince Edward Is.

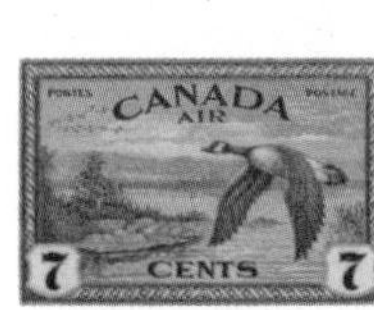

128 Canada Geese in Flight

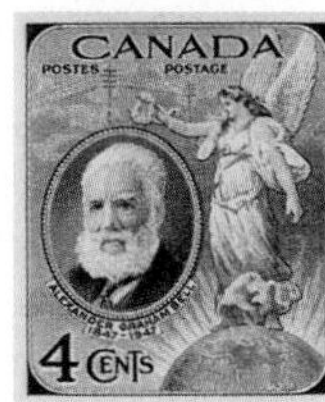

129 Alexander Graham Bell and 'Fame'

1946 (16 Sept)–**47**. Peace Re-conversion. T **122/128**. P 12.

(a) Postage

No.	Type	Description	Unused	Used
401	**122**	8c. brown	3·25	3·00
402	**123**	10c. olive-green	2·75	10
403	**124**	14c. sepia	6·50	3·50
404	**125**	20c. slate	5·00	10
405	**126**	50c. green	12·00	6·50
406	**127**	$1 purple	23·00	6·50

(b) Air

No.	Type	Description	Unused	Used
407	**128**	7c. blue	6·00	40
		a. Booklet pane of 4 (24.11.47)	9·00	
401/407 *Set of* 7			50·00	18·00

1947 (3 Mar). Birth Centenary of Bell (inventor of telephone). P 12.

No.	Type	Description	Unused	Used
408	**129**	4c. blue	15	50

130 'Canadian Citizenship'

131 Queen Elizabeth II when Princess

1947 (1 July). Advent of Canadian Citizenship and 18th Anniversary of Confederation. P 12.

No.	Type	Description	Unused	Used
409	**130**	4c. blue	10	40

(From photograph by Dorothy Wilding)

1948 (16 Feb). Princess Elizabeth's Marriage. P 12.

No.	Type	Description	Unused	Used
410	**131**	4c. blue	15	30

132 Queen Victoria, Parliament Building, Ottawa, and King George VI

133 Cabot's Ship *Matthew*

1948 (1 Oct). 100 Years of Responsible Government. P 12.

No.	Type	Description	Unused	Used
411	**132**	4c. grey	10	10

1949 (1 Apr). Entry of Newfoundland into Canadian Confederation. P 12.

No.	Type	Description	Unused	Used
412	**133**	4c. green	30	10

134 *Founding of Halifax, 1749* (C. W. Jefferys)

1949 (21 June). Bicentenary of Halifax, Nova Scotia. P 12.

No.	Type	Description	Unused	Used
413	**134**	4c. violet	45	20

135

136

137

138 King George VI

139 King George VI

(From photographs by Dorothy Wilding)

1949 (15 Nov)–**51**.

(i) P 12

No.	Type	Description	Unused	Used
414	**135**	1c. green	50	10
415	**136**	2c. sepia	2·25	45
415*a*		2c. olive-green (25.7.51)	1·40	10
416	**137**	3c. purple	30	10
		a. Booklet pane of 4+2 labels (12.4.50)	2·25	
417	**138**	4c. carmine-lake	20	10
		a. Booklet pane of 6 (5.5.50)	22·00	
417*b*		4c. vermilion (2.6.51)	60	10
		ba. Booklet pane of 6	6·00	
418	**139**	5c. blue	1·50	60
414/418 *Set of* 7			6·00	1·00

(ii) Coil stamps. Imperf×perf 9½

No.	Type	Description	Unused	Used
419	**135**	1c. green (18.5.50)	3·00	3·25
420	**136**	2c. sepia (18.5.50)	9·50	6·00
420*a*		2c. olive-green (9.10.51)	1·75	5·00
421	**137**	3c. purple (18.5.50)	2·25	3·75
422	**138**	4c. carmine-lake (20.4.50)	14·00	12·00
422*a*		4c. vermilion (27.11.51)	3·25	3·00
419/422*a* *Set of* 6			30·00	30·00

(iii) Booklet stamps. Imperf×perf 12

No.	Type	Description	Unused	Used
422*b*	**135**	1c. green (18.5.50)	1·25	3·25
		ba. Booklet pane of 3	3·25	
423	**137**	3c. purple (18.5.50)	1·40	1·00
		a. Booklet pane of 3	3·75	

No.	Type	Description	Unused	Used
423*b*	**138**	4c. carmine-lake (18.5.50)	18·00	12·00
		ba. Booklet pane of 3	50·00	
423*c*		4c. vermilion (25.10.51)	13·00	12·00
		ca. Booklet pane of 3	35·00	
422*b*/423*c* *Set of 4*			29·00	25·00

These booklet panes are imperforate at top, bottom and right-hand end.

140 King George VI

141 Oil Wells in Alberta

(From photograph by Dorothy Wilding)

1950 (19 Jan). As T **135/139** but without 'POSTES POSTAGE', as T **140**.

(i) P 12

No.	Type	Description	Unused	Used
424		1c. green	70	2·25
425		2c. sepia	1·00	5·50
426		3c. purple	70	1·00
427		4c. carmine-lake	70	30
428		5c. blue	70	3·75
424/428 *Set of 5*			3·50	11·00

(ii) Coil stamps. Imperf×perf 9½

No.	Type	Description	Unused	Used
429		1c. green	30	1·75
430		3c. purple	80	2·75

1950 (1 Mar). P 12.

No.	Type	Description	Unused	Used
431	**141**	50c. green	7·50	1·00

142 Drying Furs

143 Fisherman

1950 (2 Oct). P 12.

No.	Type	Description	Unused	Used
432	**142**	10c. brown-purple	3·50	10

1951 (1 Feb). P 12.

No.	Type	Description	Unused	Used
433	**143**	$1 ultramarine	35·00	6·00

144 Sir R. L. Borden

145 W. L. Mackenzie King

1951 (25 June). Prime Ministers (1st issue). P 12.

No.	Type	Description	Unused	Used
434	**144**	3c. blue-green	30	1·50
435	**145**	4c. rose-carmine	80	25

See also Nos. 444/445, 475/476 and 483/484.

146 Mail Trains, 1851 and 1951

147 SS *City of Toronto* and SS *Prince George*

148 Mail Coach and DC-4M North Star

149 Reproduction of 3d., 1851

1951 (24 Sept). Canadian Stamp Centenary. P 12.

No.	Type	Description	Unused	Used
436	**146**	4c. black	75	10
437	**147**	5c. violet	2·00	3·50
438	**148**	7c. blue	75	1·90
439	**149**	15c. scarlet	1·60	10
436/439 *Set of 4*			4·50	5·00

150 Queen Elizabeth II when Princess and Duke of Edinburgh

151 Forestry Products

1951 (26 Oct). Royal Visit. P 12.

No.	Type	Description	Unused	Used
440	**150**	4c. violet	20	30

(Des A. L. Pollock)

1952 (1 Apr). P 12.

No.	Type	Description	Unused	Used
441	**151**	20c. grey	2·75	10

152 Red Cross Emblem

1952 (26 July). 18th International Red Cross Conference, Toronto. Design recess; cross litho. P 12.

No.	Type	Description	Unused	Used
442	**152**	4c. scarlet and blue	15	10

153 Canada Goose

154 Pacific Coast Indian House and Totem Pole

(Des E. Hahn)

1952 (3 Nov). P 12.

No.	Type	Description	Unused	Used
443	**153**	7c. blue	1·25	10

1952 (3 Nov). Prime Ministers (2nd issue). Various portraits as T **144**. P 12.

No.	Type	Description	Unused	Used
444		3c. reddish purple	35	75
445		4c. orange-red	25	35

Portraits: 3c. Sir John J. C. Abbott; 4c. A. Mackenzie.

(Des E. Hahn)

1953 (2 Feb). P 12.

No.	Type	Description	Unused	Used
446	**154**	$1 black	3·25	20

155 Polar Bear

156 Elk

157 American Bighorn

(Des J. Crosby (2c.), E. Hahn (others))

1953 (1 Apr). National Wild Life Week. P 12.

No.	Type	Description	Unused	Used
447	**155**	2c. blue	15	10
448	**156**	3c. sepia	15	70
449	**157**	4c. slate	15	10
447/449 *Set of 3*			40	70

158 Queen Elizabeth II

159 Queen Elizabeth II

(From photograph by Karsh, Ottawa)

1953 (1 May–3 Sept).

(a) Sheet stamps. P 12

No.	Type	Description	Unused	Used
450	**158**	1c. purple-brown	10	10
451		2c. green	15	10
452		3c. carmine	15	15
		a. Booklet pane of 4+2 labels (17.7)	1·90	
453		4c. violet	20	10
		a. Booklet pane of 6 (6.7)	5·00	
454		5c. ultramarine	25	10
450/454 *Set of 5*			75	30

(b) Coil stamps. Imperf×perf 9½

No.	Type	Description	Unused	Used
455	**158**	2c. green (30.7)	2·25	2·00
456		3c. carmine (27.7)	2·25	1·00
457		4c. violet (3.9)	2·25	1·25
455/457 *Set of 3*			6·00	3·75

(c) Booklet stamps. Imperf×perf 12

No.	Type	Description	Unused	Used
458	**158**	1c. purple-brown (12.8)	2·25	1·50
		a. Booklet pane of 3	6·00	
459		3c. carmine (17.7)	2·25	1·50
		a. Booklet pane of 3	6·00	
460		4c. violet (6.7)	2·25	1·50
		a. Booklet pane of 3	6·00	
458/460 *Set of 3*			6·00	4·00

These booklet stamps have top and bottom or top, bottom and right-hand sides imperforate.

(Des E. Hahn)

1953 (1 June). Coronation. P 12.

No.	Type	Description	Unused	Used
461	**159**	4c. violet	10	10

160 Textile Industry

161 Queen Elizabeth II

(Des A. L. Pollock)

1953 (2 Nov). P 12.

No.	Type	Description	Unused	Used
462	**160**	50c. deep bluish green	1·75	10

(From photograph by Dorothy Wilding)

1954–62.

(i) P 12

No.	Type	Description	Unused	Used
463	**161**	1c. purple-brown (10.6.54)	10	10
		a. Booklet pane. 5 stamps plus printed label (1.6.56)	1·50	
		p. 2 phosphor bands (13.1.62)	1·00	3·75
464		2c. green (10.6.54)	20	10
		a. Pack. 2 blocks of 25 (12.61)	9·00	
		p. 2 phosphor bands (13.1.62)	1·00	4·50
465		3c. carmine (10.6.54)	1·00	10
		a. Imperf vert (horiz pair)	£1800	
		p. 2 phosphor bands (13.1.62)	1·50	3·50
466		4c. violet (10.6.54)	30	10
		a. Booklet pane of 6 (7.7.55)	4·75	
		b. Booklet pane. 5 stamps plus printed label (1.6.56)	2·25	
		p. 1 phosphor band (13.1.62)	2·25	11·00
467		5c. bright blue (1.4.54)	30	10
		a. Booklet pane. 5 stamps plus printed label (14.7.54)	2·75	
		b. Pack. 1 block of 20 (12.61)	6·00	
		c. Imperf vert (horiz pair)*	£6000	
		p. 2 phosphor bands (13.1.62)	3·50	8·00
468		6c. red-orange (10.6.54)	1·75	55
463/468 *Set of 6*			3·25	70
463p/467p *Set of 5*			8·25	27·00

(ii) Coil stamps. Imperf×perf 9½

No.	Type	Description	Unused	Used
469	**161**	2c. green (9.9.54)	1·50	75
470		4c. violet (23.8.54)	55	1·60
471		5c. bright blue (6.7.54)	1·75	45
469/471 *Set of 3*			3·50	2·50

* No. 467c is from the left side of a sheet and shows perforations between the stamps and the sheet margin.

Nos. 464a and 467b are blocks with the outer edges imperf. These come from 'One Dollar Plastic Packages' sold at post offices.

WINNIPEG PHOSPHOR BANDS. In 1962 facer-cancelling machines were introduced in Winnipeg which were activated by phosphor bands on the stamps. Under long or short wave ultra-violet light the phosphor glows and there is also a short after-glow when the lamp is turned off. This should not be confused with the fluorescent bands introduced in Ottawa in 1971.

162 Walrus

163 American Beaver

164 Northern Gannet

(Des E. Hahn)

1954 (1 Apr). National Wild Life Week. P 12.

No.	Type	Description	Unused	Used
472	**162**	4c. slate-black	45	30
473	**163**	5c. ultramarine	35	10
		a. Booklet pane. 5 stamps plus 1 printed label	2·00	

(Des L. Hyde)

1954 (1 Apr). P 12.

No.	Type	Description	Unused	Used
474	**164**	15c. black	1·50	10

1954 (1 Nov). Prime Ministers (3rd issue). Various portraits as T **144**. P 12.

No.	Type	Description	Unused	Used
475		4c. violet	20	1·00
476		5c. bright blue	20	60

Portraits: 4c. Sir John Thompson; 5c. Sir Mackenzie Bowell.

165 Inuit Hunter

(Des H. Beament)

1955 (21 Feb). P 12.

No.	Type	Description	Unused	Used
477	**165**	10c. purple-brown	1·25	10

166 Musk Ox

167 Whooping Cranes

(Des E. Hahn (4c.), Dr. W. Rowan (5c.))

1955 (4 Apr). National Wild Life Week. P 12.

No.	Type	Description	Unused	Used
478	**166**	4c. violet	30	10
479	**167**	5c. ultramarine	1·00	20

168 Dove and Torch

169 Pioneer Settlers

(Des W. Lohse)

1955 (1 June). Tenth Anniversary of International Civil Aviation Organisation. P 12.

No.	Type	Description	Unused	Used
480	**168**	5c. ultramarine	40	20

(Des L. Hyde)

1955 (30 June). 50th Anniversary of Alberta and Saskatchewan Provinces. P 12.
481 **169** 5c. ultramarine 20 30

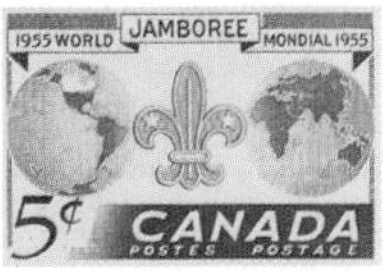

170 Scout Badge and Globe

173 Ice-hockey Players

(Des L. Hyde)

1955 (20 Aug). Eighth World Scout Jamboree, Niagara-on-the-Lake. P 12.
482 **170** 5c. orange-brown and green........ 30 10

1955 (8 Nov). Prime Ministers (4th issue). Various portraits as T **144**. P 12.
483 4c. violet 25 70
484 5c. bright blue 25 10
Portraits: 4c. R. B. Bennett; 5c. Sir Charles Tupper.

(Des J. Simpkins)

1956 (23 Jan). Ice-hockey Commemoration. P 12.
485 **173** 5c. ultramarine 20 20

174 Reindeer

175 Mountain Goat

(Des E. Hahn)

1956 (12 Apr). National Wild Life Week. P 12.
486 **174** 4c. violet 20 15
487 **175** 5c. bright blue 20 10

176 Pulp and Paper Industry

177 Chemical Industry

(Des A. J. Casson (20c.), A. L. Pollock (25c.))

1956 (7 June). P 12.
488 **176** 20c. green 75 10
489 **177** 25c. red 75 10

178

(Des A. Price)

1956 (9 Oct). Fire Prevention Week. P 12.
490 **178** 5c. red and black 30 10

179 Fishing

180 Swimming

(Des L. Hyde)

1957 (7 Mar). Outdoor Recreation. T **179/180** and similar horiz designs. P 12.
491 **179** 5c. ultramarine 40 15
a. Block of 4. Nos. 491/494 .... 1·40 1·50
492 **180** 5c. ultramarine 40 15
493 – 5c. ultramarine 40 15
494 – 5c. ultramarine 40 15
491/494 *Set of 4* .... 1·40 55
Designs: No. 493, Hunting. No. 494, Skiing.
Nos. 491/494 are printed together in sheets of 50 (5×10). In the first, second, fourth and fifth vertical rows the four different designs are arranged in *se-tenant* blocks, whilst the central row is made up as follows (reading downwards): Nos. 491/494, 491/492 (or 493/494), 491/494.

183 White-billed Diver

184 Thompson with Sextant, and North American Map

(Des L. Hyde)

1957 (10 Apr). National Wild Life Week. P 12.
495 **183** 5c. black 50 20

(Des G. A. Gundersen)

1957 (5 June). Death Centenary of David Thompson (explorer). P 12.
496 **184** 5c. ultramarine 45 30

185 Parliament Buildings, Ottawa

186 Globe within Posthorn

(Des Carl Mangold)

1957 (14 Aug). 14th UPU Congress, Ottawa. P 12.
497 **185** 5c. grey-blue 15 10
498 **186** 15c. blackish blue .... 55 1·75

187 Miner

188 Queen Elizabeth II and Duke of Edinburgh

(Des A. J. Casson)

1957 (5 Sept). Mining Industry. P 12.
499 **187** 5c. black 35 20

(From photographs by Karsh, Ottawa)

1957 (10 Oct). Royal Visit. P 12.
500 **188** 5c. black 30 10

189 'A Free Press'

190 Microscope

(Des A. L. Pollock)

1958 (22 Jan). The Canadian Press. P 12.
501 **189** 5c. black 20 70

(Des A. L. Pollock)

1958 (5 Mar). International Geophysical Year. P 12.
502 **190** 5c. blue 20 10

191 Miner panning for Gold

192 La Vérendrye (statue)

(Des J. Harman)

1958 (8 May). Centenary of British Columbia. P 12.
503 **191** 5c. deep turquoise-green 20 10

(Des G. Trottier)

1958 (4 June). La Vérendrye (explorer) Commemoration. P 12.
504 **192** 5c. ultramarine 20 10

193 Samuel de Champlain and the Heights of Québec

194 Nurse

(Des G. Trottier)

1958 (26 June). 350th Anniversary of Founding of Québec. P 12.
505 **193** 5c. brown-ochre and deep green... 30 10

(Des G. Trottier)

1958 (30 July). National Health. P 12.
506 **194** 5c. reddish purple 30 10

195 'Petroleum 1858–1958'

196 Speaker's Chair and Mace

(Des A. L. Pollock)

1958 (10 Sept). Centenary of Canadian Oil Industry. P 12.
507 **195** 5c. scarlet and olive 30 10

(Des G. Trottier and C. Dair)

1958 (2 Oct). Bicentenary of First Elected Assembly. P 12.
508 **196** 5c. deep slate 30 10

197 John McCurdy's *Silver Dart* Biplane

198 Globe showing NATO Countries

1959 (23 Feb). 50th Anniversary of First Flight of the *Silver Dart* in Canada. P 12.
509 **197** 5c. black and ultramarine 30 10

(Des P. Weiss)

1959 (2 Apr). Tenth Anniversary of North Atlantic Treaty Organisation. P 12.
510 **198** 5c. ultramarine 40 10

199

200 Queen Elizabeth II

(Des Helen Fitzgerald)

1959 (13 May). 'Associated Country Women of the World' Commemoration. P 12.
511 **199** 5c. black and yellow-olive 15 10

(Des after painting by Annigoni)

1959 (18 June). Royal Visit. P 12.
512 **200** 5c. lake-red 30 10

201 Maple Leaf linked with American Eagle

202 Maple Leaves

(Des A. L. Pollock, G. Trottier (of Canada); W. H. Buckley, A. J. Copeland, E. Metzl (of the United States))

1959 (26 June). Opening of St Lawrence Seaway. P 12.
513 **201** 5c. ultramarine and red 20 10
a. Centre inverted £9000 £6500
It is believed that No. 513a occurred on two printer's sheets, each of 200 stamps. About 230 examples have been discovered, but many have slight imperfections. The prices quoted are for examples in very fine condition.

(Des P. Weiss)

1959 (10 Sept). Bicentenary of Battle of Plains of Abraham (Québec). P 12.
514 **202** 5c. deep green and red 30 10

203

204 Dollard des Ormeaux

(Des Helen Fitzgerald)

1960 (20 Apr). Golden Jubilee of Canadian Girl Guides Movement. P 12.
515 **203** 5c. ultramarine and orange-brown 20 10

(Des P. Weiss)

1960 (19 May). Tercentenary of Battle of the Long Sault. P 12.
516 **204** 5c. ultramarine and light brown..... 20 10

205 Surveyor, Bulldozer and Compass Rose

206 E. Pauline Johnson

(Des B. J. Reddie)

1961 (8 Feb). Northern Development. P 12.
517 **205** 5c. emerald and red 15 10

(Des B. J. Reddie)

1961 (10 Mar). Birth Centenary of E. Pauline Johnson (Mohawk poetess). P 12.
518 **206** 5c. green and red 15 10

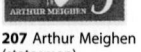

207 Arthur Meighen (statesman)

208 Engineers and Dam

1961 (19 Apr). Arthur Meighen Commemoration. P 12.
519 **207** 5c. ultramarine 15 10

(Des B. J. Reddie)

1961 (28 June). Tenth Anniversary of Colombo Plan. P 12.
520 **208** 5c. blue and brown 30 10

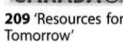

209 'Resources for Tomorrow'

210 'Education'

(Des A. L. Pollock)

1961 (12 Oct). Natural Resources. P 12.
521 **209** 5c. blue-green and brown 15 10

(Des Helen Fitzgerald)

1962 (28 Feb). Education Year. P 12.
522 **210** 5c. black and orange-brown 15 10

211 Lord Selkirk and Farmer

212 Talon bestowing Gifts on Married Couple

(Des Phillips-Gutkin Ltd)

1962 (3 May). 150th Anniversary of Red River Settlement. P 12.
523 **211** 5c. chocolate and green 20 10

(Des P. Weiss)

1962 (13 June). Jean Talon Commemoration. P 12.
524 **212** 5c. blue 20 10

213 Br. Columbia & Vancouver Is. 2½d. stamp of 1860, and Parliament Buildings, BC

214 Highway (map version) and Provincial Arms

(Des Helen Bacon)

1962 (22 Aug). Centenary of Victoria, BC. P 12.
525 **213** 5c. red and black 30 10

(Des A. L. Pollock)

1962 (31 Aug). Opening of Trans-Canada Highway. P 12.
526 **214** 5c. black and orange-brown 15 20

215 Queen Elizabeth II and Wheat (agriculture) Symbol

216 Sir Casimir Gzowski

(From drawing by Ernst Roch)

1962–64. Horiz designs as T **215** showing Queen Elizabeth II and industry symbols.

(i) P 12

527 1c. chocolate (4.2.63) 10 10
 a. Booklet pane. 5 stamps plus 1 printed label (15.5.63) .... 5·00
 p. 2 phosphor bands (15.5.63) 15 70
528 2c. green (2.5.63) 15 20
 a. Pack. 2 blocks of 25 .... 12·00
 p. 2 phosphor bands (15.5.63) .... 40 3·00
529 3c. reddish violet† (2.5.63) 15 10
 p. 2 phosphor bands (15.5.63) .... 40 1·00
530 4c. carmine-red (4.2.63) 20 10
 a. Booklet pane. 5 stamps plus 1 printed label (15.5.63) .... 5·00
 b. Pack. 1 block of 25 .... 11·00
 p. 1 centre phosphor band (*narrow*)* (2.63) .... 50 3·25
 pa. 1 centre phosphor band (*wide*) (8.64) .... 6·00 14·00
 pb. 1 side phosphor band (12.64) .... 1·75 6·50
531 5c. ultramarine (3.10.62) 50 10
 a. Booklet pane. 5 stamps plus 1 printed label (5.63) .... 8·00
 b. Pack. 1 block of 20 .... 14·00
 c. Imperf horiz (vert pair) £3250 £750
 p. 2 phosphor bands (31.1.63?) .... 50 1·75
 pa. Pack. 1 block of 20 .... 18·00
 pb. Imperf (pair) £3250
527/531 *Set of 5* .... 1·00 25
527p/531p *Set of 5* .... 1·75 8·75

(ii) Coil stamps. Perf 9½×imperf

532 2c. green (2.5.63) .... 8·00 10·00
532*a* 3c. reddish violet (2.5.63) .... 4·75 3·50
533 4c. carmine-red (4.4.63) .... 3·00 3·50
 a. Imperf (vert pair) £3250
534 5c. ultramarine (3.10.62) .... 4·50 1·50
532/534 *Set of 4* .... 18·00 17·00

Symbols: 1c. Crystals (Mining); 2c. Tree (Forestry); 3c. Fish (Fisheries); 4c. Electricity pylon (Industrial power); 5c. T **215**.

Nos. 528a, 530b, 531b and 531pa are blocks with the outer edges imperf. These come from One Dollar Plastic Packages sold at post offices.

† This is a fugitive colour which tends to become reddish on drying. In successive printings the violet colour became more and more reddish as the printer tried to match the shade of each previous printing instead of referring back to the original shade. A deep reddish violet is also known from Plate 3. As there is such a range of shades it is not practical to list them.

* On No. 530p the band is 4 mm wide as against 8 mm on No. 530pa. No. 530pb exists with the band at either left or right side of the stamp, the bands being applied across alternate vertical perforations.

Postal forgeries are known of the 4c. showing a coarser background and lack of shading on the Queen's face.

(Des P. Weiss)

1963 (5 Mar). 150th Birth Anniversary of Sir Casimir Gzowski (engineer). P 12.
535 **216** 5c. reddish purple 15 10

217 Export Trade

218 Frobisher and barque *Gabriel*

(Des A. L. Pollock)

1963 (14 June). P 12.
536 **217** $1 carmine .... 4·25 1·50

(Des P. Weiss)

1963 (21 Aug). Sir Martin Frobisher Commemoration. P 12.
537 **218** 5c. ultramarine 30 10

219 Horseman and Map

220 Canada Geese

(Des B. J. Reddie)

1963 (25 Sept). Bicentenary of Québec–Trois-Rivieres–Montréal Postal Service. P 12.
538 **219** 5c. red-brown and deep green 20 25

(Des A. Short and P. Arthur)

1963 (30 Oct). P 12.
539 **220** 15c. blue .... 1·00 10

221 Douglas DC-9 Airliner and Uplands Airport, Ottawa

222 'Peace on Earth'

1964. P 12.
540 **221** 7c. blue (11.3) 35 80
540*a* 8c. blue (18.11) 50 50

1964 (8 Apr). 'Peace'. Litho and recess. P 12.
541 **222** 5c. ochre, blue and turquoise-blue 15 10

223 Maple Leaves

1964 (14 May). Canadian Unity. P 12.
542 **223** 5c. lake-red and light blue 10 10

224 White Trillium and Arms of Ontario

225 Madonna Lily and Arms of Quèbec

226 Purple Violet and Arms of New Brunswick

227 Mayflower and Arms of Nova Scotia

228 Dogwood and Arms of British Columbia

229 Prairie Crocus and Arms of Manitoba

230 Lady's Slipper and Arms of Prince Edward Island

231 Wild Rose and Arms of Alberta

232 Prairie Lily and Arms of Saskatchewan

233 Pitcher Plant and Arms of Newfoundland

234 Mountain Avens and Arms of Northwest Territories

235 Fireweed and Arms of Yukon Territory

236 Maple Leaf and Arms of Canada

1964–66. Provincial Emblems. T **224/236**. Recess (No. 555) or litho and recess (others). P 12.
543 5c. green, brown and orange (30.6.64) 35 20
544 5c. green, orange-brown and yellow (30.6.64) 35 20
545 5c. carmine-red, green and bluish violet (3.2.65) 25 20
546 5c. blue, red and green (3.2.65) 25 20
547 5c. purple, green and yellow-brown (28.4.65) 25 20
548 5c. red-brown, deep bluish green and mauve (28.4.65) 25 20
549 5c. slate-lilac, green and light reddish purple (21.7.65) 40 20
550 5c. green, yellow and rose-red (19.1.66) 25 20
551 5c. sepia, orange and green (19.1.66) 25 20
552 5c. black, green and red (23.2.66) 25 20
553 5c. drab, green and yellow (23.3.66) 25 20
554 5c. blue, green and rose-red (23.3.66) 25 20
555 5c. red and blue (30.6.66) 25 20
543/555 *Set of 13* .... 3·25 2·40

(237)

238 Fathers of the Confederation Memorial, Charlottetown

1964 (15 July). No. 540 surch with T **237**.
556 **221** 8c. on 7c. blue 25 30
 a. Surch omitted (left-hand stamp of horiz pair) £11000

(Des P. Weiss)

1964 (29 July). Centenary of Charlottetown Conference. P 12.
557 **238** 5c. black 10 10

239 Maple Leaf and Hand with Quill Pen

240 Queen Elizabeth II

(Des P. Weiss)

1964 (9 Sept). Centenary of Québec Conference. P 12.

558	**239**	5c. light red and chocolate	15	10

(Portrait by Anthony Buckley)

1964 (5 Oct). Royal Visit. P 12.

559	**240**	5c. reddish purple	15	10

241 'Canadian Family'

242 'Co-operation'

1964 (14 Oct). Christmas. P 12.

560	**241**	3c. scarlet	10	10
		a. Pack. 2 blocks of 25	7·00	
		p. 2 phosphor bands	60	2·50
		pa. Pack. 2 blocks of 25	16·00	
561		5c. ultramarine	10	10
		p. 2 phosphor bands	90	5·00

Nos. 560a and 560pa are blocks with the outer edges imperf. These come from $1.50 Plastic Packages sold at post offices.

1965 (3 Mar). International Co-operation Year. P 12.

562	**242**	5c. grey-green	35	10

243 Sir W. Grenfell

244 National Flag

1965 (9 June). Birth Centenary of Sir Wilfred Grenfell (missionary). P 12.

563	**243**	5c. deep bluish green	20	10

1965 (30 June). Inauguration of National Flag. P 12.

564	**244**	5c. red and blue	15	10

245 Sir Winston Churchill

246 Peace Tower, Parliament Buildings, Ottawa

(Des P. Weiss from photo by Karsh. Litho)

1965 (12 Aug). Churchill Commemoration. P 12.

565	**245**	5c. purple-brown	15	10

(Des Philips-Gutkin)

1965 (8 Sept). Inter-Parliamentary Union Conference, Ottawa. P 12.

566	**246**	5c. deep green	10	10

247 Parliament Buildings, Ottawa, 1865

248 Gold, Frankincense and Myrrh

(Des G. Trottier)

1965 (8 Sept). Centenary of Proclamation of Ottawa as Capital. P 12.

567	**247**	5c. brown	10	10

(Des Helen Fitzgerald)

1965 (13 Oct). Christmas. P 12.

568	**248**	3c. olive-green	10	10
		a. Pack. 2 blocks of 25	5·00	
		p. 2 phosphor bands	10	2·00
		pa. Pack. 2 blocks of 25	6·50	
569		5c. ultramarine	10	10
		p. 2 phosphor bands	30	50

Nos. 568a and 568pa are blocks with the outer edges imperf. These come from $1.50 Plastic Packages sold at post offices.

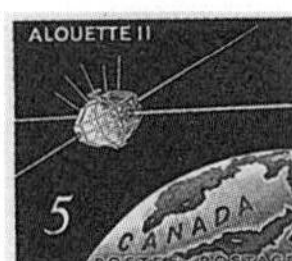
249 *Alouette 2* over Canada

250 La Salle

1966 (5 Jan). Launching of Canadian Satellite, *Alouette 2*. P 12.

570	**249**	5c. ultramarine	15	10

(Des Brigdens Ltd., Toronto)

1966 (13 Apr). 300th Anniversary of La Salle's Arrival in Canada. P 12.

571	**250**	5c. deep bluish green	15	10

251 Road Signs

252 Canadian Delegation and Houses of Parliament

(Des Helen Fitzgerald)

1966 (2 May). Highway Safety. Invisible gum. P 12.

572	**251**	5c. yellow, blue and black	15	10

(Des P. Pederson (Brigdens Ltd.))

1966 (26 May). London Conference Centenary. P 12.

573	**252**	5c. red-brown	10	10

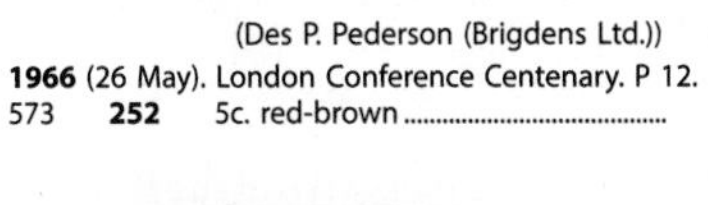

253 Douglas Point Nuclear Power Station

254 Parliamentary Library, Ottawa

(Des A. L. Pollock)

1966 (27 July). Peaceful Uses of Atomic Energy. P 12.

574	**253**	5c. ultramarine	10	10

(Des Brigdens Ltd.)

1966 (8 Sept). Commonwealth Parliamentary Association Conference, Ottawa. P 12.

575	**254**	5c. purple	10	10

255 *Praying Hands*, after Dürer

256 Flag and Canada on Globe

(Des G. Holloway)

1966 (12 Oct). Christmas. P 12.

576	**255**	3c. carmine	10	10
		a. Pack. 2 blocks of 25	4·50	
		p. 2 phosphor bands	1·25	1·25
		pa. Pack. 2 blocks of 25	8·00	
577		5c. orange	10	10
		p. 2 phosphor bands	1·25	1·25

Nos. 576a and 576pa are blocks with the outer edges imperf. These come from $1.50 Plastic Packages sold at post offices.

(Des Brigdens Ltd.)

1967 (11 Jan). Canadian Centennial. Invisible gum. P 12.

578	**256**	5c. scarlet and blue	10	10
		p. 2 phosphor bands	40	2·00

257 Northern Lights and Dog-team

258 Totem pole

259 Combine-harvester and oil derrick

260 Ship in lock

261 Harbour scene

261a Transport

262 *Alaska Highway* (A.Y. Jackson)

263 *The Jack Pine* (T. Thomson)

264 *Bylot Island* (L. Harris)

265 *Québec Ferry* (J. W. Morrice)

266 *The Solemn Land* (J. E. H. MacDonald)

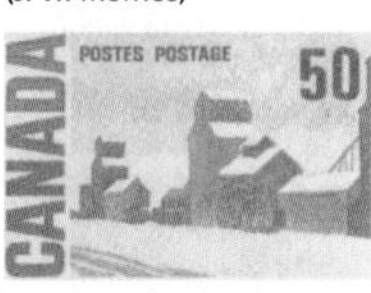
267 *Summer's Stores* (grain elevators) (J. Ensor)

268 *Oilfield* (near Edmonton) (H. G. Glyde)

268a Library of Parliament

(Des H. T. Prosser (lc.–6c.), Rapid Grip and Batten Ltd (8c.–$1), Eng A. A. Carswell (8c.–50c.), Y. Baril (1c.–6c. and $1))

1967 (8 Feb)–**73**. T **257/268a**.

A. Recess C.B.N.

(i) P 12

579	1c. brown	10	10
	a. Booklet pane. 5 stamps plus 1 printed label (2.67)	1·25	
	b. Printed on the gummed side	£850	
	c. White paper (10.71)	10	
	ca. White fluorescent paper (6.71)	1·00	
	p. 2 phosphor bands	60	1·00
	pa. Centre phosphor band (12.68)	30	2·00
	pac. Centre phosphor band, white paper (9.71)	30	
	paca. Centre phosphor band, white fluorescent paper (10.71)	3·00	
	q. 2 fluorescent bands (11.71)	60	75
580	2c. green	10	20
	a. Glazed fluorescent paper (booklets) (26.10.70)	25	
	b. Booklet pane. No. 580a×4 *se-tenant* with No. 581a×4 with gutter margin between	1·75	
	c. White paper (3.72)	10	
	p. 2 phosphor bands	1·50	4·00
	pa. Centre phosphor band (12.68)	30	1·00
	pac. Centre phosphor band, white paper (3.72)	60	
	q. 2 fluorescent bands (12.72)	75	1·00
581	3c. slate-purple	30	50
	a. Glazed fluorescent paper (booklets) (26.10.70)	25	
	p. 2 phosphor bands	30	3·00
	q. 2 fluorescent bands (1972?)	2·00	3·50
582	4c. red	20	10
	a. Booklet pane. 5 stamps plus 1 printed label (2.67)	1·75	
	b. Pack. 1 block of 25 (8.2.67)	13·00	
	c. White paper (5.72)	20	
	p. 1 side phosphor band	1·25	4·00
	pa. Centre phosphor band (3.69)	30	1·00
	pac. Centre phosphor band, white paper (5.72)	50	
	paca. Centre phosphor band, white fluorescent paper (1972)	2·00	
	q. 2 fluorescent bands (4.73)	55	1·75
583	5c. blue	20	10
	a. Booklet pane. 5 stamps plus 1 printed label (3.67)	6·00	
	b. Pack. 1 block of 20 (2.67)	22·00	
	c. White paper (12.71?)	40	
	ca. White fluorescent paper (12.71)	1·00	
	p. 2 phosphor bands	75	3·25
	pa. Pack. 1 block of 20 (8.2.67)	35·00	
	pb. Centre phosphor band (12.68)	30	2·50
	pbc. Centre phosphor band, white paper (4.72)	1·00	
	pbca. Centre phosphor band, white fluorescent paper (12.71)	1·00	
583*r*	6c. black (*white paper*) (1.72)	2·50	30
	ra. Printed on the gummed side	12·00	
	rp. Centre phosphor band (1.72)	4·75	6·50
	rq. 2 fluorescent bands (1.72)	1·00	1·75
584	8c. purple-brown	25	1·00
	c. White fluorescent paper (7.71)	12·00	
585	10c. olive-green	25	10
	c. White paper (3.71)	80	
	ca. White fluorescent paper (12.71)	80	
	p. 2 phosphor bands (9.12.69)	1·50	3·50
	pc. 2 phosphor bands, white paper (11.72)	1·00	
	pca. 2 phosphor bands, white fluorescent paper (1.72)	4·50	
	q. 2 fluorescent bands (1.72)	1·00	1·00
	qa. 2 fluorescent bands, white fluorescent paper (2.72)	4·50	

No.	Description	Mint	Used
586	15c. dull purple	30	10
	c. White paper (3.72)	65	
	ca. White fluorescent paper (3.71)	2·00	
	p. 2 phosphor bands (9.12.69)	1·50	2·75
	pc. 2 phosphor bands, white paper (3.72)	2·00	
	q. 2 fluorescent bands (2.72)	1·00	2·00
587	20c. deep blue	2·00	10
	c. White paper (5.72)	1·60	
	ca. White fluorescent paper (8.71)	2·00	
	p. 2 phosphor bands (9.12.69)	2·50	6·00
	pc. 2 phosphor bands, white paper (5.72)	2·00	
588	25c. myrtle-green	2·00	10
	ca. White fluorescent paper (10.71)	2·25	
	p. 2 phosphor bands (9.12.69)	4·25	8·00
	pca. 2 phosphor bands, white fluorescent paper (12.71)	16·00	
589	50c. cinnamon	2·00	10
	c. White paper (12.71)	2·50	
	ca. White fluorescent paper (3.71)	3·00	
590	$1 scarlet	1·50	1·25
	c. White paper (12.71)	3·00	
	ca. White fluorescent paper (3.71)	3·00	
579/590	*Set of 13*	8·50	3·00
579pa/588p	*Set of 10*	13·50	29·00
	(ii) Coil stamps. Perf 9½×imperf		
591	3c. slate-purple (3.67)	2·00	5·50
592	4c. red (3.67)	2·00	2·75
593	5c. blue (2.67)	2·00	4·00
	(iii) Coil stamps. Perf 10×imperf		
594	6c. orange-red (1.69)	90	35
	a. Imperf (vert pair)	£225	
	c. White fluorescent paper (12.69)	11·00	
	ca. Imperf (vert pair)	£2000	
595	6c. black (*white fluorescent paper*) (8.70)	35	3·00
	a. Imperf (vert pair)	£2000	
596	7c. green (*white fluorescent paper*) (30.6.71)	40	3·00
	a. Imperf (vert pair)	£850	
597	8c. black (*white paper*) (30.12.71)	1·75	2·75
	a. Imperf (vert pair)	£425	
	q. 2 fluorescent bands (7.72)	40	40
	qa. 2 fluorescent bands, white fluorescent paper	1·00	
	qb. Imperf (vert pair)	£800	
	B. Recess B.A.B.N.		
	(i) P 10 (sheets (601/601p) or booklets)		
598	1c. brown (9.68)	30	2·50
	a. Booklet pane. No. 598×5 *se-tenant* with No. 599×5 (9.68)	1·75	
	b. Booklet pane. No. 601×4 *se-tenant* with No. 598 plus one printed label (10.68)	2·00	
	c. White fluorescent paper (11.69)	10·00	
	cb. Booklet pane. No. 601c×4 *se-tenant* with No. 598c plus 1 printed label (11.69)	16·00	
599	4c. red (9.68)	20	2·50
	a. Booklet pane. 25 stamps plus 2 printed labels	6·50	
600	5c. blue (9.68)	30	2·50
	a. Booklet pane of 20	4·50	
601	6c. orange-red (10.68)	45	10
	a. Booklet pane. 25 stamps plus 2 printed labels (10.68)	10·00	
	c. White fluorescent paper (11.69)	1·50	
	p. 2 phosphor bands (1.11.68)	1·00	1·00
602	6c. black (1.70)	1·00	2·25
	a. Booklet pane. 25 stamps plus 2 printed labels	16·00	
	c. White fluorescent paper (11.69)	60·00	
	ca. Booklet pane. 25 stamps plus 2 printed labels	£1200	
603	6c. black (*re-engraved die*) (8.70)	3·50	4·50
	a. Booklet pane of 4	12·00	
	(ii) P 12½×12 (sheets (606/610) or booklets)		
604	1c. brown (30.6.71)	50	3·00
	a. Booklet pane. Nos. 604×4, 605×4 and 609×12 *se-tenant*	13·00	
	b. Booklet pane. Nos. 604/605 and 609×3 *se-tenant* plus 1 printed label	4·00	
	c. Booklet pane. Nos. 604×3, 608 and 610×2 *se-tenant* (30.12.71)	1·50	
	d. Booklet pane. Nos. 604×6, 608 and 610×11 *se-tenant* (30.12.71)	6·50	
	e. Booklet pane. Nos. 604×4, 608 and 610×5 *se-tenant* (8.72)	4·50	
	f. White fluorescent paper (30.12.71)	40	1·00
	fa. Booklet pane. No. 604f×4, 608 and 610×5 *se-tenant* (30.12.71)	1·75	
	q. 2 fluorescent bands (30.12.71)	40	2·25
	qc. Booklet pane. Nos. 604q×3, 608q and 610q×2 *se-tenant*	2·00	
	qd. Booklet pane. Nos. 604q×6, 608q and 610q×11 *se-tenant*	5·00	
	qe. Booklet pane. Nos. 604q×4, 608q and 610q×5 *se-tenant* (8.72)	4·50	
	qf. 2 fluorescent bands, white fluorescent paper (30.12.71)	40	
	qfa. Booklet pane. No. 604qfa×4, 608 and 610×5 *se-tenant* (30.12.71)	2·50	
605	3c. slate-purple (30.6.71)	4·50	8·00
606	6c. orange-red (3.69)	60	1·00
	f. White fluorescent paper (12.69)	17·00	
	p. 2 phosphor bands (4.69)	2·00	2·00
	pf. 2 phosphor bands, white fluorescent paper (12.69)	£850	
607	6c. black (7.1.70)	30	10
	a. Booklet pane. 25 stamps plus 2 printed labels (8.70)	20·00	
	f. White fluorescent paper (1.70)	14·00	
	p. 2 phosphor bands (1.70)	2·50	3·25
608	6c. black (*re-engraved die*) (9.70)	1·00	10
	a. Booklet pane of 4 (11.70)	4·00	
	f. White fluorescent paper	1·25	
	p. One centre phosphor band (9.71)	3·75	5·00
	q. 2 fluorescent bands (30.12.71)	1·75	45
	qf. 2 fluorescent bands, white fluorescent paper (12.71)	1·00	
609	7c. myrtle-green (30.6.71)	30	1·25
	p. 2 phosphor bands	1·25	3·75
610	8c. slate-black (30.12.71)	30	10
	c. White paper (7.72)	30	
	cf. White fluorescent paper (11.72)	2·75	
	p. 2 phosphor bands	60	1·00
	pf. 2 phosphor bands, white paper (7.72)	50	
	pfa. 2 phosphor bands, white fluorescent paper (11.72)	4·50	
	q. 2 fluorescent bands (30.12.71)	45	15
	qf. 2 fluorescent bands, white paper	75	
	qfa. 2 fluorescent bands, white fluorescent paper (12.72)	1·50	

No. 581q only exists as a pre-cancel.

Nos. 582b, 583b, 583pa are blocks with the outer edges imperf. These come from One Dollar Plastic Packages sold at post offices.

No. 582p comes with the band to the left or right of the stamp, the phosphor having been applied across alternate vertical perforations.

Postal forgeries exist of the 6c. orange printed in lithography and perforated 12½.

Normal

Re-engraved

When the basic postal rate was changed to 6c. the C.B.N. lent their die to B.A.B.N. who made a duplicate die from it by transfer. Parts of this proved to be weak, but it was used for Nos. 601/602 and 606/607. B.A.B.N. later re-engraved their die to make fresh plates which were used for Nos. 603 and 608. No. 608 first appeared on sheets from Plate 4. The engraving is much more deeply etched and the side frame lines are noticeably thicker. The Canadian Bank Note printings, Nos. 583r and 595 are more clearly engraved than the first B.A.B.N. issue, but lack the heavy side frames of the re-engraved version.

There are no records of dates of issue of the booklets, packs and coils, but supplies of these were distributed to depots in the months indicated.

IMPERF BETWEEN PAIRS FROM COIL STAMPS. Nos. 594/597 are known in blocks or horizontal pairs imperf between vertically. Coils are supplied to post offices in batches of ten coils held together by roulettes between every fourth stamp so that they can easily be split apart. If two or more unsplit coils are purchased it is possible to obtain blocks or pairs imperf between vertically.

Vertical coil stamps are also known imperf between horizontally or with some stamps apparently completely imperf. These can result from blind perforations identifiable by slight indentations.

WHITE PAPERS. Original printings of the sheet and coil stamps were made on toned paper. From the later part of 1969 experimental printings were made on white fluorescent paper, as referred to in the note below No. 620; this paper is distinct from the glazed type used for the 'Opal' booklet (see Nos. 580a and 581a).

During 1971 a further type of paper, white but non-fluorescent, was introduced. This later white (non-fluorescent) paper typically has PVA gum, readily distinguishable from the shiny 'Dextrine' gum of the white fluorescent paper. Exceptions are 582paca and 610/610qfa, which have PVA gum. Identification of fluorescent papers can be confirmed with the use of a UV lamp. Particular care is needed in the cases of Nos. 602c/602ca and 606pf, where the listings refer to examples on the 'hybrite' paper.

FLUORESCENT BANDS. During the second half of 1971 new sorting machines were installed in the Ottawa area which were activated by stamps bearing fluorescent bands. These differ from the Winnipeg phosphor bands in that they react green and have no after-glow. To the naked eye the fluorescent bands appear shiny when compared with the remainder of the stamp when looking along its surface. Winnipeg phosphor bands appear matt.

The experiments were successful and what was at first called 'Ottawa tagging' has since come into more general use and the Winnipeg phosphor was phased out. However, the substance at first used (known as OP-4) was found to migrate to envelopes, documents, album pages, etc. as well as to adjoining stamps. Late in 1972 this fault was cured by using another substance (called OP-2). The migrating bands were used on early printings of Nos. 604q, 608q and 610q as well as certain stamps referred to in a footnote after No. 692. It is most advisable to use plastic mounts for housing stamps with migrating bands or else clear acetate should be affixed to the album leaves.

269 Canadian Pavilion

270 Allegory of 'Womanhood' on Ballot-box

(Des C.B.N.)

1967 (28 Apr). World Fair, Montreal. P 12.

611	**269**	5c. blue and red	10	10

(Des Helen Fitzgerald. Litho)

1967 (24 May). 50th Anniversary of Women's Franchise. P 12.

612	**270**	5c. reddish purple and black	10	10

271 Queen Elizabeth II and Centennial Emblem

272 Athlete

(Portrait from photo by Anthony Buckley)

1967 (30 June). Royal Visit. P 12.

613	**271**	5c. plum and orange-brown	15	10

(Des Brigdens Ltd.)

1967 (19 July). Fifth Pan-American Games, Winnipeg. P 12.

614	**272**	5c. rose-red	10	10

273 World News

274 Governor-General Vanier

(Des W. McLauchlan)

1967 (31 Aug). 50th Anniversary of the Canadian Press. P 12.

615	**273**	5c. blue	10	10

(Des from photo by Karsh)

1967 (15 Sept). Vanier Commemoration. P 12.

616	**274**	5c. black	10	10

PRINTERS. The following were printed either by the Canadian Bank Note Co, Ottawa (C.B.N.) or the British American Bank Note Co, Ottawa (B.A.B.N.), *except where otherwise stated*.

275 People of 1867 and Toronto, 1967

276 Carol Singers

(Des and recess C.B.N.)

1967 (28 Sept). Centenary of Toronto as Capital City of Ontario. P 12.

617	**275**	5c. myrtle-green and vermilion	10	10

(Des and recess B.A.B.N.)

1967 (11 Oct). Christmas. P 12.

618	**276**	3c. scarlet	10	10
		a. Pack. 2 blocks of 25	4·50	
		p. 2 phosphor bands	20	1·75
		pa. Pack. 2 blocks of 25	5·50	
619		5c. emerald-green	10	10
		p. 2 phosphor bands	70	1·50

Nos. 618a and 618pa are blocks with the outer edges imperf. These come from $1.50 Plastic Packs sold at post offices.

277 Grey Jays

278 Weather Map and Instruments

(Des M. G. Loates. Litho C.B.N.)

1968 (15 Feb). Wild Life. P 12.

620	**277**	5c. multicoloured	30	10

See also Nos. 638/640.

WHITE FLUORESCENT PAPER. Different papers with varying degrees of whiteness have been used for Canadian stamps and it is understood that much of the paper contained a high percentage of recycled pulp. The fluorescent content of this paper varies, but during 1968–1970 a distinctive very white and highly fluorescent paper was used known by the trade-name 'hybrite'; this fluoresces on the back and front. Some issues were wholly printed on this paper, and these can be used for distinguishing those which appeared on ordinary paper as well, both being listed.

See also notes following No. 610qfa.

(Des and litho B.A.B.N.)

1968 (13 Mar). Bicentenary of First Meteorological Readings. P 11.

621	**278**	5c. multicoloured	15	10
		a. White fluorescent paper	1·00	

279 Narwhal

280 Globe, Maple Leaf and Rain Gauge

(Des J. A. Crosby. Litho B.A.B.N.)

1968 (10 Apr). Wildlife. White fluorescent paper. P 11.
622 **279** 5c. multicoloured 15 10
a. Ordinary paper .... 2·00

No. 622 has a background of yellow-green and pale blue but copies are known with the yellow-green apparently missing. This 'yellow-green' is produced by an overlay of yellow on the blue but we have not come across any examples where the yellow is completely missing and the wide range of colour variation is due to technical difficulties in maintaining an exact blend of the two colours.

(Des I. von Mosdossy. Litho B.A.B.N.)

1968 (8 May). International Hydrological Decade. P 11.
623 **280** 5c. multicoloured 15 10
a. White fluorescent paper 40

IMPERF EDGES. On Nos. 624/654, 657 and 659 (stamps printed by the B.A.B.N. Co.) the outer edges of the sheets were guillotined to remove the imprints for PO stock so that single stamps may, therefore, be found with either one, or two adjacent sides imperforate.

281 *Nonsuch*

282 Lacrosse Players

(Recess and photo B.A.B.N.)

1968 (5 June). 300th Anniversary of Voyage of the *Nonsuch*. P 10.
624 **281** 5c. multicoloured 20 20

(Des J. E. Aldridge. Recess and photo B.A.B.N.)

1968 (3 July). Lacrosse. P 10.
625 **282** 5c. black, red and lemon 15 10

283 Front Page of *The Globe*, George Brown and Legislative Building

284 H. Bourassa

(Des N. Sabolotny. Recess and photo B.A.B.N.)

1968 (21 Aug). 150th Birth Anniversary of George Brown (politician and journalist). P 10.
626 **283** 5c. multicoloured 10 10

(Des, recess and litho C.B.N.)

1968 (4 Sept). Birth Centenary of Henri Bourassa (journalist and politician). White fluorescent paper. P 12.
627 **284** 5c. black, red and pale cream 10 10

285 John McCrae, Battlefield and First Lines of *In Flanders Fields*

286 Armistice Monument, Vimy

(Des I. von Mosdossy. Litho C.B.N.)

1968 (15 Oct). 50th Death Anniversary of John McCrae (soldier and poet). White fluorescent paper. P 12.
628 **285** 5c. multicoloured 10 10

(Des and recess C.B.N.)

1968 (15 Oct). 50th Anniversary of 1918 Armistice. P 12.
629 **286** 15c. slate-black 30 50

287 Inuit Family (carving)

288 Mother and Child (carving)

(Designs from Inuit carvings by Munamee (6c.) and unknown carver (5c.). Photo C.B.N.)

1968. Christmas. White fluorescent paper. P 12.
630 **287** 5c. black and new blue (1.11.68) 10 10
a. Booklet pane of 10 (15.11.68) .... 2·25
p. 1 centre phosphor band .... 10 1·75
pa. Booklet pane of 10 (15.11.68) .... 3·00
631 **288** 6c. black and ochre (15.11.68) 10 10
p. 2 phosphor bands .... 20 2·00

289 Curling

290 Vincent Massey

(Des D. Eales. Recess and photo B.A.B.N.)

1969 (15 Jan). Curling. P 10.
632 **289** 6c. black, new blue and scarlet 15 25

(Des I. von Mosdossy. Recess and litho C.B.N.)

1969 (20 Feb). Vincent Massey, First Canadian-born Governor-General. White fluorescent paper. P 12.
633 **290** 6c. sepia and yellow-ochre 10 10

291 *Return from the Harvest Field* (Suzor-Côté)

292 Globe and Tools

(Photo C.B.N.)

1969 (14 Mar). Birth Centenary of Marc Aurèle de Foy Suzor-Côté (painter). White fluorescent paper. P 12.
634 **291** 50c. multicoloured .... 1·50 3·25

(Des J. Hébert. Recess B.A.B.N.)

1969 (21 May). 50th Anniversary of International Labour Organisation. White fluorescent paper. P 12½×12.
635 **292** 6c. bronze-green 10 10
a. Ordinary paper .... 1·00

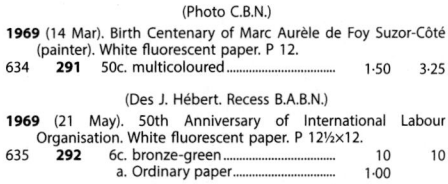

293 Vickers FB-27 Vimy Aircraft over Atlantic Ocean

294 *Sir William Osler* (J. S. Sargent)

(Des R. W. Bradford. Recess and photo B.A.B.N.)

1969 (13 June). 50th Anniversary of First Non-stop Transatlantic Flight. White fluorescent paper. P 12×12½.
636 **293** 15c. chocolate, bright green and pale blue .... 40 1·50

(Des, recess and photo B.A.B.N.)

1969 (23 June). 50th Death Anniversary of Sir William Osler (physician). P 12½×12.
637 **294** 6c. deep blue, light blue and chestnut 20 10
a. White fluorescent paper 80

295 White-throated Sparrows

298 Flags of Winter and Summer Games

(Des M. G. Loates. Litho C.B.N.)

1969 (23 July). Birds. T **295** and similar multicoloured designs. White fluorescent paper. P 12.
638 6c. Type **295** 25 10
639 10c. Savannah Sparrow ('Ipswich Sparrow') (*horiz*) .... 35 1·25
640 25c. Hermit Thrush (*horiz*) .... 1·10 3·75
638/640 *Set of 3* .... 1·50 4·50

(Des C. McDiarmid. Recess and litho C.B.N.)

1969 (15 Aug). Canadian Games. White fluorescent paper. P 12.
641 **298** 6c. emerald, scarlet and blue 10 10

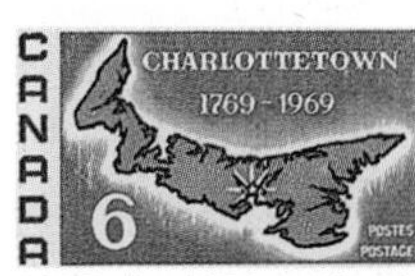

299 Outline of Prince Edward Island showing Charlottetown

300 Sir Isaac Brock and Memorial Column

(Des L. Fitzgerald. Recess and photo B.A.B.N.)

1969 (15 Aug). Bicentenary of Charlottetown as Capital of Prince Edward Island. White fluorescent paper. P 12×12½.
642 **299** 6c. yellow-brown, black and blue 20 20
a. Ordinary paper 80

(Des I. von Mosdossy. Recess and litho C.B.N.)

1969 (12 Sept). Birth Bicentenary of Sir Isaac Brock. P 12.
643 **300** 6c. orange, bistre and bistre-brown 10 10

301 Children of the World in Prayer

302 Stephen Butler Leacock, Mask and 'Mariposa'

(Des Rapid Grip and Batten Ltd. Litho C.B.N.)

1969 (8 Oct). Christmas. White fluorescent paper. P 12.
644 **301** 5c. multicoloured 10 10
a. Booklet pane of 10 .... 1·50
p. 1 centre phosphor band .... 10 1·75
pa. Booklet pane of 10 .... 2·50
645 6c. multicoloured 10 10
a. Black (inscr, value and frame omitted) £1700 £1300
p. 2 phosphor bands .... 20 1·75

(Des, recess and photo B.A.B.N.)

1969 (12 Nov). Birth Centenary of Stephen Butler Leacock (humorist). P 12×12½.
646 **302** 6c. multicoloured 10 10

303 Symbolic Cross-roads

304 'Enchanted Owl' (Kenojuak)

(Des K. C. Lochhead. Litho C.B.N.)

1970 (27 Jan). Centenary of Manitoba. P 12.
647 **303** 6c. ultramarine, lemon and vermilion 15 10
p. 2 phosphor bands .... 15 1·75

(Des N. E. Hallendy and Miss S. Van Raalte. Recess C.B.N.)

1970 (27 Jan). Centenary of Northwest Territories. White fluorescent paper. P 12.
648 **304** 6c. carmine, red and black 10 10

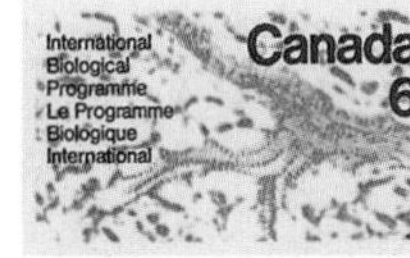

305 Microscopic View of Inside of Leaf

306 Expo 67 Emblem and Stylised Cherry Blossom

(Des I. Charney. Recess and photo B.A.B.N.)

1970 (18 Feb). International Biological Programme. P 12×12½.
649 **305** 6c. emerald, orange-yellow and ultramarine 15 10

(Des E. R. C. Bethune. Litho C.B.N.)

1970 (18 Mar). World Fair, Osaka. T **306** and similar horiz designs. Multicoloured; colour of Cherry Blossom given. P 12.
650 25c. red .... 1·50 2·25
a. Block of 4. Nos. 650/653 .... 5·50 8·00
p. 2 phosphor bands .... 1·50 2·75
pa. Block of 4. Nos. 650p/653p .... 5·50 10·00
651 25c. violet .... 1·50 2·25
p. 2 phosphor bands .... 1·50 2·75
652 25c. green .... 1·50 2·25
p. 2 phosphor bands .... 1·50 2·75
653 25c. blue .... 1·50 2·25
p. 2 phosphor bands .... 1·50 2·75
650/653 *Set of 4* .... 5·50 8·00
650p/653p *Set of 4* .... 5·50 10·00

Designs: No. 650, T **306**; No. 651, Dogwood and stylised cherry blossom; No. 652, White Trillium and stylised cherry blossom; No. 653, White Garden Lily and stylised cherry blossom.

Nos. 650/653 and 650p/653p are printed together in sheets of 50 (5×10). In the first, second, fourth and fifth vertical rows the four different designs are arranged in *se-tenant* blocks, whilst the centre row is composed as follows (reading downwards): 650(p)/653(p), 650(p)×2, 653(p), 651(p), 652(p) and 650(p).

310 Henry Kelsey **311** 'Towards Unification'

(Des D. Burton. Recess and photo B.A.B.N.)

1970 (15 Apr). 300th Birth Anniversary of Henry Kelsey (explorer). P 12×12½.

654 **310** 6c. multicoloured 10 10

(Des B. Fisher. Litho B.A.B.N.)

1970 (13 May). 25th Anniversary of United Nations. P 11.

655 **311** 10c. blue .... 40 1·75
p. 2 phosphor bands .... 60 3·25
656 15c. magenta and bluish lilac 40 50
p. 2 phosphor bands .... 60 3·00

312 Louis Riel (Métis leader) **313** Mackenzie's Inscription, Dean Channel

(Des R. Derreth. Photo B.A.B.N.)

1970 (19 June). Louis Riel Commemoration. P 12½×12.

657 **312** 6c. greenish blue and vermilion 10 10

(Design from Government Archives photo. Recess C.B.N.)

1970 (25 June). Sir Alexander Mackenzie (explorer). White fluorescent paper. P 12×11½.

658 **313** 6c. bistre-brown 15 10

314 Sir Oliver Mowat (statesman) **315** *Isles of Spruce* (A. Lismer)

(Des E. Roch. Recess and photo B.A.B.N.)

1970 (12 Aug). Sir Oliver Mowat Commemoration. P 12×12½.

659 **314** 6c. vermilion and black 10 10

(Litho Ashton-Potter)

1970 (18 Sept). 50th Anniversary of 'Group of Seven' (artists). P 11.

660 **315** 6c. multicoloured 10 10

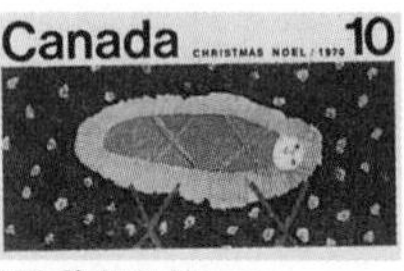

316 *Horse-drawn Sleigh* (D. Niskala) **317** *Christ in Manger* (C. Fortier)

(Des from children's drawings. Litho C.B.N.)

1970 (7 Oct). Christmas. Horiz designs as T **316/317**, showing children's drawings. Multicoloured. White fluorescent paper. P 12.

661 5c. Type **316** 30 20
a. Strip of 5. Nos. 661/665 .... 1·40 2·50
p. 1 centre phosphor band .... 55 1·25
pa. Strip of 5. Nos. 661p/665p .... 2·50 5·00
662 5c. *Stable and Star of Bethlehem* (L. Wilson) (26×21 *mm*) 30 20
p. 1 centre phosphor band .... 55 1·25
663 5c. *Snowmen* (M. Lecompte) (26×21 *mm*) 30 20
p. 1 centre phosphor band .... 55 1·25
664 5c. *Skiing* (D. Durham) (26×21 *mm*) 30 20
p. 1 centre phosphor band .... 55 1·25
665 5c. *Santa Claus* (A. Martin) (26×21 *mm*) 30 20
p. 1 centre phosphor band .... 55 1·25
666 6c. *Santa Claus* (E. Bhattacharya) (26×21 *mm*) 30 20
a. Strip of 5. Nos. 666/670 .... 1·40 2·50
p. 2 phosphor bands .... 55 1·25
pa. Strip of 5. Nos. 666p/670p .... 2·50 5·00
667 6c. *Christ in Manger* (J. McKinney) (26×21 *mm*) 30 20
p. 2 phosphor bands .... 55 1·25
668 6c. *Toy Shop* (N. Whateley) (26×21 *mm*) 30 20
p. 2 phosphor bands .... 55 1·25
669 6c. *Christmas Tree* (J. Pomperleau) (26×21 *mm*) 30 20
p. 2 phosphor bands .... 55 1·25
670 6c. *Church* (J. McMillan) (26×21 *mm*) 30 20
p. 2 phosphor bands .... 55 1·25
671 10c. Type **317** 25 30
p. 2 phosphor bands .... 45 1·25
672 15c. *Trees and Sledge* (J. Dojcak) (35×21 *mm*) 35 60
p. 2 phosphor bands .... 55 1·75
661/672 *Set of* 12 .... 3·25 2·50
661p/672p *Set of* 12 .... 6·00 12·50

The designs of the 5c. and 6c. were each issued with the various designs *se-tenant* in a diamond-shaped arrangement within the sheet. This generally results in *se-tenant* pairs both vert and horiz, but due to the sheet arrangement vert and horiz pairs of the same design exist from the two centre vert and horiz rows.

328 Sir Donald A. Smith

(Des Dora de Pédery-Hunt. Litho C.B.N.)

1970 (4 Nov). 150th Birth Anniversary of Sir Donald Alexander Smith. P 12.

673 **328** 6c. yellow, brown and bronze-green 15 10

STAMP BOOKLETS

Booklet Nos. SB1/SB60 are stapled.

All booklets up to and including No. SB41 contain panes consisting of two rows of three (3×2).

B 1

1900 (11 June). Red on pink cover. Two panes of 6×2c. (No. 155ba).
SB1 25c. booklet. Cover as Type B **1** with English text £2000

1903 (1 July). Red on pink cover. Two panes of 6×2c. (No. 176a).
SB2 25c. booklet. Cover as Type B **1** with English text £2500

1912 (Jan)–**16**. Red on pink cover. Two panes of 6×2c. (No. 201a).
SB3 25c. booklet. Cover as Type B **1** with English text .... 65·00
a. Cover handstamped 'NOTICE Change in Postal Rates For New Rates See Postmaster'. 65·00
b. French text (4.16) £160
ba. Cover handstamped 'AVIS Changement des tarifs Postaux Pour les nouveaux tarifs consulter le maitre de poste' £120

1913 (1 May)–**16**. Green on pale green cover. Four panes of 6×1c. (No. 197a).
SB4 25c. booklet. Cover as Type B **1** with English text £450
a. Containing pane No. 199a .... 90·00
ab. Cover handstamped 'NOTICE Change in Postal Rates For New Rates See Postmaster'. 90·00
b. French text (28.4.16) £700
ba. Containing pane No. 199a £225
bb. Cover handstamped 'AVIS Changement des tarifs Postaux Pour les nouveaux tarifs consulter le maitre de poste' £750

1922 (Mar). Black on brown cover. Two panes of 4×3c. and two labels (No. 205a).
SB5 25c. booklet. Cover as Type B **1** with English text £350
a. French text £700

1922 (July–Dec). Black on blue cover. Panes of 4×1c., 4×2c. and 4×3c. each. (Nos. 246aa, 247aa, 205a) and two labels.
SB6 25c. booklet. Cover as Type B **1** with English text £350
a. French text (12.22) £650

1922 (Dec). Black on orange cover. Four panes of 6×1c. (No. 246ab).
SB7 25c. booklet. Cover as Type B **1** with English text £140
a. French text £170

1922 (Dec). Black on green cover. Two panes of 6×2c. (No. 247ab).
SB8 25c. booklet. Cover as Type B **1** with English text £600
a. French text £700

1923 (Dec). Black on blue cover. Panes of 4×1c., 4×2c. and 4×3c. each. (Nos. 246aa, 247aa, 248aa) and 2 labels.
SB9 25c. booklet. Cover as Type B **1** with English text £250
a. French text £650

1923 (Dec)–**24**. Black on brown cover. Two panes of 4×3c. (No. 248aa) and two labels.
SB10 25c. booklet. Cover as Type B **1** with English text £200
a. French text (5.24) £375

B 2

1928 (16 Oct). Black on green cover. Two panes of 6×2c. (No. 276a).
SB11 25c. booklet. Cover as Type B **2** with English text 65·00
a. French text £150

1928 (25 Oct). Black on orange cover. Four panes of 6×1c. (No. 275a).
SB12 25c. booklet. Cover as Type B **2** with English text £120
a. French text £300

1929 (6 Jan). Plain manilla cover. Three panes of 6×1c., two panes of 6×2c. and one pane of 6×5c. (Nos. 275a, 276a, 279a).
SB13 72c. booklet. Plain cover £400
a. With 'Philatelic Div., Fin. Br. P.O. Dept., Ottawa' circular cachet on front cover £1400
b. With '1928' in the centre of the circular cachet £1500

1930 (17 June). Black on green cover. Two panes of 6×2c. (No. 290a).
SB14 25c. booklet. Cover as Type B **2** with English text £110
a. French text £200

1930 (17 Nov). Black on red cover. Two panes of 6×2c. (No. 291a).
SB15 25c. booklet. Cover as Type B **2** with English text 65·00
a. French text £160

1931 (13 July). Black on red cover. Two panes of 4×3c. (No. 293a) and two labels.
SB16 25c. booklet. Cover as Type B **2** with English text 85·00
a. French text £130

1931 (21 July). Black on green cover. Four panes of 6×1c. (No. 289b).
SB17 25c. booklet. Cover as Type B **2** with English text £130
a. French text £200

1931 (23 July). Black on brown cover. Two panes of 6×2c. (No. 292a).
SB18 25c. booklet. Cover as Type B **2** with English text £140
a. French text £450

1931 (13 Nov). Black on blue cover. Panes of 4×1c., 4×2c. and 4×3c. each. (Nos. 289db, 292ba, 293a) and 2 labels.
SB19 25c. booklet. Cover as Type B **2** with English text £300
a. French text £500

1933 (22 Aug–13 Nov). Black on red cover. Two panes of 4×3c. (No. 321a) and two labels.
SB20 25c. booklet. Cover as Type B **2** with English text (13.11) .... 90·00
a. French text (22.8) £170

1933 (7 Sept). Black on brown cover. Two panes of 6×2c. (No. 320a).
SB21 25c. booklet. Cover as Type B **2** with English text £225
a. French text £450

1933 (19 Sept–5 Dec). Black on blue cover. Panes of 4×1c., 4×2c. and 4×3c. each. (Nos. 319b, 320b, 321ba) and two labels.
SB22 25c. booklet. Cover as Type B **2** with English text £200
a. French text (5.12) £300

1933 (28 Dec)–**34**. Black on green cover. Four panes of 6×1c. (No. 319a).
SB23 25c. booklet. Cover as Type B **2** with English text £150
a. French text (26.3.34) £225

B 3

1935 (1 June–8 Aug). Red on white cover. Two panes of 4×3c. (No. 343a) and two labels.
SB24 25c. booklet. Cover as Type B **3** with English text (8.8) .... 65·00
a. French text (1.6) £110

1935 (22 July–1 Sept). Blue on white cover. Panes of 4×1c., 4×2c. and 4×3c. each. (Nos. 341b, 342b, 343a) and two labels.
SB25 25c. booklet. Cover as Type B **3** with English text £150
a. French text (.9) £190

1935 (19 Aug–18 Oct). Green on white cover. Four panes of 6×1c. (No. 341a).
SB26 25c. booklet. Cover as Type B **3** with English text 90·00
a. French text (18.10) £130

1935 (16–18 Mar). Brown on white cover. Two panes of 6×2c. (No. 342a).
SB27 25c. booklet. Cover as Type B **3** with English text .... 70·00
a. French text (18.3) £120

B 4

1937 (14 Apr)–**38**. Blue and white cover. Panes of 4×1c., 4×2c. and 4×3c. each. (Nos. 357a, 358a, 359a) and two labels.
SB28 25c. booklet. Cover as Type B **3** with English text .... 85·00
a. French text (4.1.38) £150
SB29 25c. booklet. Cover as Type B **4** with English text 57 mm wide .... 70·00
a. English text 63 mm wide £120
b. French text 57 mm wide (4.1.38) .... 95·00
ba. French text 63 mm wide £190

1937 (23–27 Apr). Red and white cover. Two panes of 4×3c. (No. 359a) and two labels.
SB30 25c. booklet. Cover as Type B **3** with English text (27.4) .... 50·00
a. French text (23.4) .... 65·00

SB31 25c. booklet. Cover as Type B **4** with English text 57 mm wide (27.4) 10·00
a. English text 63 mm wide 65·00
b. French text 57 mm wide (23.4) 13·00
ba. French text 63 mm wide £180

1937 (18 May)–**38**. Green and white cover. Four panes of 6×1c. (No. 357b).
SB32 25c. booklet. Cover as Type B **3** with English text 60·00
a. French text (14.10.38) 75·00
SB33 25c. booklet. Cover as Type B **4** with English text 57 mm wide 42·00
a. English text 63 mm wide 75·00
b. French text 57 mm wide (14.10.38) 22·00
ba. French text 63 mm wide £170

1938 (3 May)–**39**. Brown and white cover. Two panes of 6×2c. (No. 358b).
SB34 25c. booklet. Cover as Type B **3** with English text 60·00
a. French text (3.3.39) 85·00
SB35 25c. booklet. Cover as Type B **4** with English text 57 mm wide 27·00
a. English text 63 mm wide 85·00
b. French text 57 mm wide 35·00
ba. French text 63 mm wide £120

1942 (20–29 Aug). Red and white cover. Two panes of 4×3c. (No. 377a) and two labels.
SB36 25c. booklet. Cover as Type B **4** with English text 8·50
a. French text (29.8) 12·00

1942 (12–14 Sept). Violet and white cover. Panes of 4×1c., 4×2c. and 4×3c. each. (Nos. 375a, 376a, 377a), each with two labels.
SB37 25c. booklet. Cover as Type B **4** with English text (14.9) 48·00
a. French text (12.9) 90·00

1942 (6 Oct)–**43**. Brown and white cover. Two panes of 6×2c. (No. 376b).
SB38 25c. booklet. Cover as Type B **4** with English text 55·00
a. French text (6.4.43) 70·00

1942 (24 Nov)–**46**. Green and white cover. Four panes of 6×1c. (No. 375b).
SB39 25c. booklet. Cover as Type B **4** with English text 11·00
a. French text (16.2.43) 17·00
b. Bilingual text (8.1.46) 45·00

1943 (3 May)–**46**. Orange and white cover. One pane of 6×4c. (No. 380a).
SB40 25c. booklet. Cover as Type B **4** with English text 4·00
a. French text (12.5.43) 15·00
b. Bilingual text (8.1.46) 18·00

1943 (28 Aug)–**46**. Purple and white cover. Two panes of 4×3c. (No. 378a) and two labels.
SB41 25c. booklet. Cover as Type B **4** with English text 10·00
a. French text (7.9.43) 28·00
b. Bilingual text (8.1.46) 22·00

B **5**

1943 (1 Sept)–**46**. Black and white cover. Panes of 3×1c., 3×3c. and 3×4c. each. (Nos. 394a, 395a, 396a) (3×1).
SB42 25c. booklet. Cover as Type B **5** with English text 55·00
a. French text (18.9.43) 70·00
c. Bilingual text (23.1.46) 65·00

B **6**

1947 (24 Nov). Brown on orange cover. Panes of 6×3c. and 6×4c. each. (3×2) and two panes of 4×7c. (2×2) (Nos. 378b, 380a, 407a).
SB43 $1 booklet. Cover as Type B **6** with English text 25·00
a. French text 40·00

1950 (12 Apr–18 May). Purple and white cover. Two panes of 4×3c. (No. 416a) and two labels (3×2).
SB44 25c. booklet. Cover as Type B **4** with English text 5·00
a. Bilingual text (18.5) 5·00

1950 (5–10 May). Orange and white cover. One pane of 6×4c. (No. 417a) (3×2).
SB45 25c. booklet. Cover as Type B **4** with English text 38·00
a. Stitched 60·00
b. Bilingual text (10.5) 55·00

1950 (18 May). Black and white cover. Panes of 3×1c., 3×3c. and 3×4c. each (Nos. 422ba, 423a, 423ba) (3×1).
SB46 25c. booklet. Cover as Type B **5** with English text 55·00
a. Bilingual text 75·00

1951 (2 June). Orange and white cover. One pane of 6×4c. (No. 417ba) (3×2).
SB47 25c. booklet. Cover as Type B **4** with English text 6·00
a. Stitched 12·00
b. Bilingual text 12·00

1951 (25 Oct)–**52**. Black and white cover. Panes of 3×1c., 3×3c. and 3×4c. each (Nos. 422ba, 423a, 423ca) (3×1).
SB48 25c. booklet. Cover as Type B **5** with English text 55·00
a. Bilingual text (9.7.52) 70·00

1953 (6 July–19 Aug). Orange cover. One pane of 6×4c. (No. 453a) (3×2).
SB49 25c. booklet. Cover as Type B **4** with English text 5·00
a. Bilingual text (19.8) 12·00

1953 (17 July–20 Oct). Purple cover. Two panes of 4×3c. (No. 452a) and two labels (3×2).
SB50 25c. booklet. Cover as Type B **4** with English text 4·50
a. Bilingual text (20.10) 19·00

1953 (12 Aug). Grey cover. Panes of 3×1c., 3×3c. and 3×4c. each (Nos. 458a, 459a, 460a) (3×1).
SB51 25c. booklet. Cover as Type B **5** with English text 17·00
a. Bilingual text 42·00

All the following booklets are bilingual

1954 (1 Apr–Nov). Blue cover as Type B **4**.
SB52 25c. booklet containing pane of 5×5c. and one label (No. 473a) (3×2) 2·25
a. Stitched (11.54) 3·25

1954 (14 July–Nov). Blue cover as Type B **4**.
SB53 25c. booklet containing pane of 5×5c. and one label (No. 467a) (3×2) 2·75
a. Stitched (11.54) 6·00

1955 (7 July). Violet cover as Type B **4**.
SB54 25c. booklet containing pane of 6×4c. (No. 466a) (3×2) 4·75

B **7**

1956 (1 June). Red and white cover as Type B **7**.
SB55 25c. booklet containing two panes of 5×1c. and 5×4c., each with one label (Nos. 463a, 466b) (3×2) 3·50

1956 (July). Blue and white cover as Type B **7**.
SB56 25c. booklet containing pane of 5×5c. and one label (No. 467a) (3×2) 2·75

B **8**

1963 (May)–**67**. Blue and white cover as Type B **7**.
SB57 25c. booklet containing pane of 5×5c. and one label (No. 531a) (2×3) 8·00
a. Cover Type B **8** (1.67) 48·00

1963 (15 May). Red and white cover as Type B **7**.
SB58 25c. booklet containing two panes of 5×1c. and 5×4c., each with one label (Nos. 527a, 530a) (2×3) 10·00

1967 (Feb). Red cover as Type B **8**.
SB59 25c. booklet containing two panes of 5×1c. and 5×4c., each with one label (Nos. 579a, 582a) (2×3) 3·00

1967 (Mar). Blue cover as Type B **8**.
SB60 25c. booklet containing pane of 5×5c. and one label (No. 583a) (2×3) 6·00

B **9**

1968 (Sept). Brown and cream cover, 70×48 mm, as Type B **9**.
SB61 25c. booklet containing *se-tenant* pane of 5×1c. and 5×4c. (No. 598a) (2×5) 1·75

1968 (Sept). Red and cream cover as Type B **9**.
SB62 $1 booklet containing pane of 25×4c. and two labels (No. 599a) (3×9) 6·50

1968 (Sept). Blue and cream cover, 82×48 mm, as Type B **9**.
SB63 $1 booklet containing pane of 20×5c. (No. 600a) (2×10) 4·50

1968 (Oct). Orange and cream cover, 70×48 mm, as Type B **9**, but without border.
SB64 25c. booklet containing *se-tenant* pane of 1×1c., 4×6c. and one label (No. 598b) (2×3) 2·00

B **10** (*Illustration reduced. Actual size* 128×60 *mm*)

1968 (15 Nov). Christmas. Red and green cover as Type B **10**.
SB65 $1 booklet containing two panes of 10×5c. (No. 630a) (5×2) 4·50
p. Phosphor (No. 630pa) 6·00

Nos. SB65/SB65p exist with left or right opening (i.e. with selvedge at left or right of pane).

1969 (Jan). Orange-red on cream cover as Type B **9**, but without border.
SB66 $1.50, booklet containing pane of 25×6c. and two labels (No. 601a) (3×9) 10·00

1969 (8 Oct). Christmas. Red cover size as Type B **10**.
SB67 $1 booklet containing two panes of 10×5c. (No. 644a) (5×2) 3·00
p. Phosphor (No. 644pa) 5·00

1970 (Jan). Black on cream cover as Type B **9**, but without border.
SB68 $1.50 booklet containing pane of 25×6c. and two labels (No. 602a) (3×9) 16·00

1970 (Aug). Black on cream cover, 70×48 mm, as Type B **9**, but without border.
SB69 25c. booklet containing pane of 4×6c. (No. 603a) (2×2) 12·00

1970 (Aug). Black on cream cover as Type B **9**, but without border.
SB70 $1.50 booklet containing pane of 25×6c. and two labels (No. 607a) (3×9) 20·00

1970 (26 Oct). Indigo on cream cover, 70×50mm. Inscr 'CANADIAN POSTAGE STAMPS ... MADE EXPRESSLY FOR OPAL MANUFACTURING CO. LIMITED'.
SB71 25c. booklet containing 4×2c. and 4×3c. (No. 580b) (2×2) with gutter margin between 1·75

No. SB71 was produced by the Canadian Bank Note Co for use in the private stamp-vending machines owned by the Opal Manufacturing Co Ltd, Toronto. To cover the cost of manufacture and installation these booklets were sold at 25c. each. They were not available from the Canadian Post Office.

1970 (Nov). Black on cream cover, 70×48 mm, as Type B **9**, but without border.
SB72 25c. booklet containing pane of 4×6c. (No. 608a) (2×2) 4·00

REGISTRATION STAMPS

R **1**

(Eng and recess-printed British-American Bank Note Co, Montreal and Ottawa)

1875 (15 Nov)–**92**. White wove paper.

		(*a*) *P* 12 (*or slightly under*)		
R1	R **1**	2c. orange (1876)	65·00	1·00
R2		2c. orange-red (1889)	75·00	6·00
R3		2c. vermilion	90·00	10·00
		a. Imperf (pair)	†	£4500
R4		2c. rose-carmine (1888)	£150	55·00
R5		5c. yellow-green (12.1.76)	£120	1·50
R6		5c. deep green	90·00	1·25
		a. Imperf (pair)	£950	
R7		5c. blue-green (1889)	95·00	1·50
R7*a*		5c. dull sea-green (1892)	£150	3·50
R8		8c. bright blue	£450	£300
R9		8c. dull blue	£425	£275
		(*b*) *P* 12×11½ *or* 12×11¾		
R10	R **1**	2c. orange	£350	60·00
R11		5c. green (*shades*)	£1000	£150

SPECIAL DELIVERY STAMPS

PRINTERS. The following Special Delivery and Postage Due Stamps were recess-printed by the American Bank Note Co (to 1928), the British American Bank Note Co (to 1934), and the Canadian Bank Note Co (1935 onwards).

S **1**

1898–1920. P 12.

S1	S **1**	10c. blue-green (28.6.98)	90·00	16·00
S2		10c. deep green (12.13)	70·00	16·00
S3		10c. yellowish green (8.20)	70·00	18·00

The differences between Types I and II (figures '10' with and without shading) formerly illustrated were due to wear of the plate. There was only one die.

S 2

S 3 Mail-carrying, 1867 and 1927

1922 (21 Aug). P 12.

S4	**S 2**	20c. carmine-red	40·00	6·50

No. S4 exists in two slightly different sizes due to the use of 'wet' or 'dry' printing processes. See note below No. 195.

1927 (29 June). 60th Anniversary of Confederation. P 12.

S5	**S 3**	20c. orange	13·00	21·00

No. S5 exists imperforate, imperf×perf or perf×imperf (*Price, in each instance, £190 per pair, un*).

S 4

1930 (2 Sept). P 11.

S6	**S 4**	20c. brown-red	42·00	11·00

1932 (24 Dec). Type as S **4**, but inscr 'CENTS' in place of 'TWENTY CENTS'. P 11.

S7		20c. brown-red	45·00	20·00

No. S7 exists imperforate (*Price per pair £700, un*).

S **5** Allegory of Progress

(Des A. Foringer)

1935 (1 June). P 12.

S8	**S 5**	20c. scarlet	5·00	5·00

No. S8 exists imperforate (*Price per pair £750, un*).

S **6** Canadian Coat of Arms

1938–39. P 12.

S9	**S 6**	10c. green (1.4.39)	24·00	4·00
S10		20c. scarlet (15.6.38)	42·00	29·00

Nos. S9/S10 exist imperforate (*Price £800, un, for each pair*).

≡10   10≡

(S 7)

1939 (1 Mar). Surch with Type S **7**.

S11	**S 6**	10c. on 20c. scarlet	10·00	20·00

S **8** Coat of Arms and Flags

S **9** Lockheed L.18 Lodestar

1942 (1 July)–**43**. War Effort. P 12.

(a) Postage

S12	**S 8**	10c. green	14·00	1·00

(b) Air

S13	**S 9**	16c. ultramarine	6·00	45
S14		17c. ultramarine (1.4.43)	4·50	55

Nos. S12/S14 exist imperforate (*Prices per un pair 10c. £750, 16c. £900, 17c. £900*).

S **10** Arms of Canada and Peace Symbols

S **11** Canadair DC-4M North Star

1946 (16 Sept–5 Dec). P 12.

(a) Postage

S15	**S 10**	10c. green	13·00	1·75

(b) Air

(i) Circumflex accent in 'EXPRÊS'

S16	**S 11**	17c. ultramarine	4·50	10·00

(ii) Grave accent in 'EXPRÈS'

S17	**S 11**	17c. ultramarine (5.12.46)	12·00	7·50

POSTAGE DUE STAMPS

PRINTERS. See note under 'Special Delivery Stamps'.

D **1**

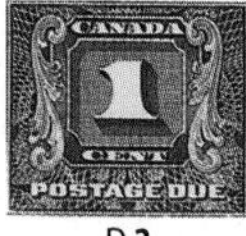
D **2**

1906 (1 July)–**28.** P 12.

D1	**D 1**	1c. dull violet	10·00	2·75
D2		1c. red-violet (1916)	18·00	4·25
		a. Thin paper (10.24)	16·00	23·00
D3		2c. dull violet	38·00	1·00
D4		2c. red-violet (1917)	35·00	2·25
		a. Thin paper (10.24)	32·00	23·00
D5		4c. violet (3.7.28)	50·00	65·00
D6		5c. dull violet	40·00	4·25
D7		5c. red-violet (1917)	50·00	6·00
		a. Thin paper (10.24)	20·00	40·00
D8		10c. violet (3.7.28)	32·00	26·00
D1/D8 *Set of 5*			£130	90·00

The 1c., 2c. and 5c. values exist imperforate, without gum (*Price £375 for each un pair*).

Printings up to October 1924 used the 'wet' method, those from mid 1925 onwards the 'dry'. For details of the differences between these two methods, see above No. 196.

1930–32. P 11.

D9	**D 2**	1c. bright violet (14.7.30)	8·50	11·00
D10		2c. bright violet (21.8.30)	7·50	2·25
D11		4c. bright violet (14.10.30)	15·00	6·50
D12		5c. bright violet (12.12.31)	16·00	42·00
D13		10c. bright violet (24.8.32)	65·00	45·00
D9/D13 *Set of 5*			£100	95·00

No. D13 exists imperf×perf (*Price for vertical pair £1200, un*).

D **3**

D **4**

1933–34. P 11.

D14	**D 3**	1c. violet (5.5.34)	14·00	19·00
D15		2c. violet (20.12.33)	9·00	6·00
D16		4c. violet (12.12.33)	17·00	15·00
D17		10c. violet (20.12.33)	30·00	48·00
D14/D17 *Set of 4*			60·00	80·00

No. D14 exists imperforate (*Price per pair £400, un*).

1935–65. P 12.

D18	**D 4**	1c. violet (14.10.35)	80	10
D19		2c. violet (9.9.35)	3·75	10
D20		3c. violet (4.65)	6·00	5·00
D21		4c. violet (2.7.35)	1·50	10
D22		5c. violet (12.48)	6·00	6·50
D23		6c. violet (1957)	2·00	1·40
D24		10c. violet (16.9.35)	70	10
D18/D24 *Set of 7*			19·00	11·50

The 1c., 2c., 4c. and 10c. exist imperforate (*Price £225 for each un pair*).

D **5**

1967–78. Litho. P 12½×12 (20c., 24c., 50c.) or 12 (others).

(a) Size 20×17½ mm

D25	**D 5**	1c. scarlet (3.67)	2·00	6·00
D26		2c. scarlet (3.67)	1·50	1·00
D27		3c. scarlet (3.67)	3·00	7·00
D28		4c. scarlet (2.67)	2·75	1·25
D29		5c. scarlet (3.67)	4·25	7·50
D30		6c. scarlet (2.67)	1·60	3·75
D31		10c. scarlet (1.67)	2·00	2·50
D25/D31 *Set of 7*			15·00	26·00

(b) Size 19½×16 mm

D32	**D 5**	1c. scarlet (12.69)	2·00	1·00
		a. White paper (1.74)	75	1·50
		b. White fluorescent paper	4·00	
		c. Perf 12½×12 (*white paper*) (9.12.77)	15	2·00
D33		2c. scarlet (*white paper*) (1973)	1·00	3·00
		a. White fluorescent paper	7·50	
D34		3c. scarlet (*white paper*) (1.74)	3·50	6·50
		a. White fluorescent paper	5·00	
D35		4c. scarlet (4.69)	2·00	60
		a. White paper (1.74)	60	60
		b. White fluorescent paper	2·00	
		ba. Printed on the gummed side	£750	
		c. Perf 12½×12 (*white paper*) (9.12.77)	30	1·00
D36		5c. scarlet (2.69)	25·00	35·00
		a. Perf 12½×12 (*white paper*) (9.12.77)	30	2·00
D37		6c. scarlet (*white paper*) (1973)	2·75	3·75
		a. White fluorescent paper	5·00	
D38		8c. scarlet (1.69)	30	45
		a. White paper (1.74)	1·00	45
		b. White fluorescent paper	75	
		c. Perf 12½×12 (*white paper*) (28.6.78)	75	1·40
D39		10c. scarlet (4.69)	1·75	45
		a. White paper (1973)	40	45
		b. Perf 12½×12 (*white paper*) (9.77)	40	60
D40		12c. scarlet (1.69)	30	50
		a. White paper (1973)	30	1·00
		b. White fluorescent paper	1·00	
		c. Perf 12½×12 (*white paper*) (9.77)	80	1·50
D41		16c. scarlet (*white paper*) (1.74)	5·50	7·00
D42		20c. scarlet (*white paper*) (9.12.77)	30	1·25
D43		24c. scarlet (*white paper*) (9.12.77)	30	1·50
D44		50c. scarlet (*white paper*) (9.12.77)	40	2·00
D32/D44 *Set of 13*			14·00	27·00

There are no records of dates of issue of the above but supplies were distributed to depots in the months indicated.

The original 1969 printings of the 1, 4, 5, 8, 10 and 12c. on ordinary paper, and the 8c. and 12c. on white fluorescent paper (Nos. D38b, D40b), have shiny 'Dextrine' gum. Later issues on white and white fluorescent ('hybrite') papers have PVA gum.

OFFICIAL STAMPS

Stamps perforated 'O H M S' were introduced in May 1923 for use by the Receiver General's department in Ottawa and by the Assistant Receiver Generals' offices in provincial cities. From 1 July 1939 this use was extended to all departments of the federal government and such stamps continued to be produced until replaced by the 'O.H.M.S.' overprinted issue of 1949.

The perforated initials can appear either upright, inverted or sideways on individual stamps. The prices quoted are for the cheapest version. Stamps perforated with T O **1** are only priced used. Only isolated examples are known mint and these are very rare.

A number of forged examples of the perforated 'O.H.M.S.' are known, in particular of T O **1**. Many of these forged perforated initials were applied to stamps which had already been used and this can aid their detection. Genuine examples, postmarked after the perforated initials were applied, often show the cancellation ink bleeding into the holes.

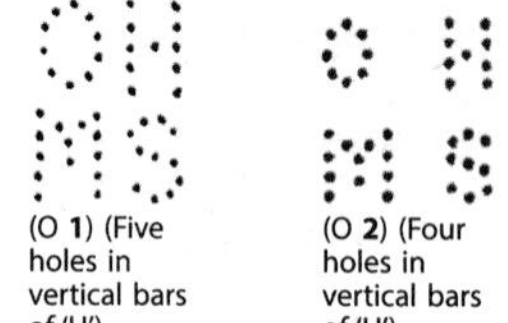
(O **1**) (Five holes in vertical bars of 'H')

(O **2**) (Four holes in vertical bars of 'H')

1923 (May). Nos. 196/215 punctured as T O **1**.

O1	**44**	1c. yellow-green	—	50·00
O2		2c. carmine	—	40·00
O3		3c. deep brown	—	35·00
O4		5c. deep blue	—	45·00
O5		7c. yellow-ochre	—	70·00
O6		10c. reddish purple	—	60·00
O7		20c. olive	—	50·00
O8		50c. sepia	—	75·00
O1/O8 *Set of 8*			—	£375

1923 (May). 50th Anniversary of Confederation. No. 244 punctured as T O **1**.

O9	**48**	3c. bistre-brown	—	£275

1923 (May)–**31**. Nos. 246/255 and 263 punctured as T O **1**.

(a) P 12

O10	**44**	1c. chrome-yellow (Die I)	—	40·00
		a. Die II (1925)	—	40·00
O11		2c. deep green	—	32·00
O12		3c. carmine (Die I) (12.23)	—	32·00
		a. Die II (1924)	—	35·00
O13		4c. olive-yellow	—	48·00
O14		5c. violet	—	42·00
		a. Thin paper (1924)	—	48·00
O15		7c. red-brown (1924)	—	50·00
O16		8c. blue (1925)	—	65·00
O17		10c. blue	—	48·00
O18		10c. bistre-brown (1925)	—	35·00
O19		$1 brown-orange (7.23)	—	£110
O10/O19 *Set of 10*			—	£450

(b) P 12×8

O20	**44**	3c. carmine (Die II) (1931)	—	90·00

1927 (29 June). 60th Anniversary of Confederation. Nos. 266/273 punctured as T O **1**.

(a) Commemorative issue

O21	**51**	1c. orange	—	75·00
O22	**52**	2c. green	—	85·00
O23	**53**	3c. carmine	—	£100
O24	**54**	5c. violet	—	65·00
O25	**55**	12c. blue	—	£275
O21/O25 *Set of 5*			—	£550

(b) Historical issue

O26	**56**	5c. violet	—	70·00

O27	**57**	12c. green	—	£250
O28	**58**	20c. carmine	—	£180
O26/O28 *Set of 3*			—	£450

1928 (21 Sept). Air. No. 274 punctured as T O **1**.

O29	**59**	5c. olive-brown	—	£190

1928–29. Nos. 275/285 punctured as T O **1**.

O30	**60**	1c. orange	—	42·00
O31		2c. green	—	30·00
O32		3c. lake	—	75·00
O33		4c. olive-bistre	—	£100
O34		5c. violet	—	35·00
O35		8c. blue	—	85·00
O36	**61**	10c. green	—	28·00
O37	**62**	12c. grey-black	—	£275
O38	**63**	20c. lake	—	75·00
O39	**64**	50c. blue	—	£450
O40	**65**	$1 olive-green	—	£375
O30/O40 *Set of 11*			—	£1400

1930–31. Nos. 288/297 and 300/305 punctured as T O **1**.

O41	**66**	1c. orange (Die I)	—	45·00
O42		1c. green (Die I)	—	26·00
		a. Die II	—	24·00
O43		2c. green (Die I)	—	£110
O44		2c. scarlet (Die I)	—	35·00
		a. Die II	—	30·00
O45		2c. deep brown (Die I)	—	35·00
		a. Die II	—	32·00
O46		3c. scarlet	—	24·00
O47		4c. yellow-bistre	—	75·00
O48		5c. violet	—	50·00
O49		5c. deep slate-blue	—	42·00
O50		8c. blue	—	90·00
O51		8c. red-orange	—	65·00
O52	**67**	10c. olive-green	—	35·00
O53	**68**	12c. grey-black	—	£200
O54	**69**	20c. red	—	90·00
O55	**70**	50c. blue	—	£140
O56	**71**	$1 olive-green	—	£275
O41/O56 *Set of 15*			—	£1100

1930 (4 Dec). Air. No. 310 punctured as T O **1**.

O57	**72**	5c. deep brown	—	£275

1931 (30 Sept). No. 312 punctured as T O **1**.

O58	**73**	10c. olive-green	—	48·00

1932 (22 Feb). Air. No. 313 punctured as T O **1**.

O59	**59**	6c. on 5c. olive-brown	—	£200

1932 (21 June). Nos. 314/314a punctured as T O **1**.

O60	**66**	3c. on 2c. scarlet (Die I)	—	48·00
		a. Die II	—	40·00

1932 (12 July). Ottawa Conference. Nos. 315/318 punctured as T O **1**.

(a) Postage

O61	**76**	3c. scarlet	—	35·00
O62	**77**	5c. blue	—	75·00
O63	**78**	13c. green	—	£300

(b) Air

O64	**72**	6c. on 5c. deep brown	—	£250
O61/O64 *Set of 4*			—	£600

1932–33. Nos. 319/325 punctured as T O **1**.

O65	**80**	1c. green	—	24·00
O66		2c. sepia	—	24·00
O67		3c. scarlet	—	24·00
O68		4c. yellow-brown	—	£100
O69		5c. blue	—	45·00
O70		8c. red-orange	—	£100
O71	**68**	13c. bright violet	—	90·00
O65/O71 *Set of 7*			—	£375

1933 (18 May). UPU Congress Preliminary Meeting. No. 329 punctured as T O **1**.

O72	**81**	5c. blue	—	£100

1933 (24 July). World's Grain Exhibition and Conference, Regina. No. 330 punctured as T O **1**.

O73	**69**	20c. red	—	£130

1933 (17 Aug). Centenary of First Trans-Atlantic Steamboat Crossing. No. 331 punctured as T O **1**.

O74	**83**	5c. blue	—	£100

1934 (1 July). Fourth Centenary of Discovery of Canada. No. 332 punctured as T O **1**.

O75	**84**	3c. blue	—	£110

1934 (1 July). 150th Anniversary of Arrival of United Empire Loyalists. No. 333 punctured as T O **1**.

O76	**85**	10c. olive-green	—	£140

1934 (16 Aug). 150th Anniversary of Province of New Brunswick. No. 334 punctured as T O **1**.

O77	**86**	2c. red-brown	—	£140

1935 (4 May). Silver Jubilee. Nos. 335/340 punctured as T O **1**.

O78	**87**	1c. green	—	75·00
O79	**88**	2c. brown	—	90·00
O80	**89**	3c. carmine-red	—	£100
O81	**90**	5c. blue	—	£120
O82	**91**	10c. green	—	£250
O83	**92**	13c. blue	—	£275
O78/O83 *Set of 6*			—	£850

1935. Nos. 341/351 and 355 punctured as T O **1**.

(a) Postage

O84	**93**	1c. green	—	28·00
O85		2c. brown	—	50·00
O86		3c. scarlet	—	48·00
O87		4c. yellow	—	90·00
O88		5c. blue	—	55·00
O89		8c. orange	—	90·00
O90	**94**	10c. carmine	—	75·00
O91	**95**	13c. purple	—	80·00
O92	**96**	20c. olive-green	—	90·00
O93	**97**	50c. deep violet	—	60·00
O94	**98**	$1 bright blue	—	£180

(b) Air

O95	**99**	6c. red-brown	—	£200
O84/O95 *Set of 12*			—	£950

1937 (10 May). Coronation. No. 356 punctured as T O **1**.

O96	**100**	3c. carmine	—	£100

1937–38. Nos. 357/367, 370 and 371 punctured as T O **1**.

(a) Postage

O97	**101**	1c. green	—	5·00
O98		2c. brown	—	6·00
O99		3c. scarlet	—	5·00
O100		4c. yellow	—	20·00
O101		5c. blue	—	14·00
O102		8c. orange	—	35·00
O103	**102**	10c. rose-carmine	—	40·00
		a. Red	—	45·00
O104	**103**	13c. blue	—	55·00
O105	**104**	20c. red-brown	—	65·00
O106	**105**	50c. green	—	£130
O107	**106**	$1 violet	—	£225
O97/O107 *Set of 11*			—	£550

(b) Coil stamp

O108	**101**	3c. scarlet	—	£130

(c) Air

O109	**107**	6c. blue	—	60·00

1939 (15 May). Royal Visit. Nos. 372/374 punctured as T O **1**.

O110	**108**	1c. black and green	—	90·00
O111	**109**	2c. black and brown	—	95·00
O112	**110**	3c. black and carmine	—	90·00
O110/O112 *Set of 3*			—	£250

1939 (1 July). Air. No. 274 punctured as T O **2**.

O113	**59**	5c. olive-brown	32·00	22·00

1939 (1 July). Nos. 347/350 and 355 punctured as T O **2**.

(a) Postage

O114	**94**	10c. carmine	£120	55·00
O115	**95**	13c. purple	£130	55·00
O116	**96**	20c. olive-green	£140	65·00
O117	**97**	50c. deep violet	£130	55·00

(b) Air

O118	**99**	6c. red-brown	£110	90·00
O114/O118 *Set of 5*			£550	£275

1939 (1 July). Coronation. No. 356 punctured as T O **2**.

O119	**100**	3c. carmine	£110	70·00

1939 (1 July). Nos. 357/367, 369/370 and 371 punctured as T O **2**.

(a) Postage

O120	**101**	1c. green	3·25	1·00
O121		2c. brown	4·00	1·00
O122		3c. scarlet	4·25	1·00
O123		4c. yellow	9·50	5·50
O124		5c. blue	6·00	1·50
O125		8c. orange	23·00	7·50
O126	**102**	10c. rose-carmine	75·00	3·75
		a. Red	17·00	1·00
O127	**103**	13c. blue	30·00	3·25
O128	**104**	20c. red-brown	50·00	4·00
O129	**105**	50c. green	75·00	13·00
O130	**106**	$1 violet	£150	48·00
O120/O130 *Set of 11*			£325	75·00

(b) Coil stamps

O131	**101**	2c. brown	£100	65·00
O132		3c. scarlet	£100	65·00

(c) Air

O133	**107**	6c. blue	5·50	2·00

1939 (1 July). Royal Visit. Nos. 372/374 punctured as T O **2**.

O134	**108**	1c. black and green	£130	60·00
O135	**109**	2c. black and brown	£130	60·00
O136	**110**	3c. black and carmine	£130	60·00
O134/O136 *Set of 3*			£350	£160

1942–43. War Effort. Nos. 375/388 and 399/400 punctured as T O **2**.

(a) Postage

O137	**111**	1c. green	2·00	50
O138	**112**	2c. brown	2·00	20
O139	**113**	3c. carmine-lake	4·50	2·50
O140		3c. purple	3·50	30
O141	**114**	4c. slate	13·00	4·00
O142	**112**	4c. carmine-lake	2·50	30
O143	**111**	5c. blue	4·00	1·25
O144	–	8c. red-brown	16·00	4·00
O145	**116**	10c. brown	11·00	30
O146	**117**	13c. dull green	17·00	14·00
O147		14c. dull green	18·00	2·50
O148	**118**	20c. chocolate	25·00	2·00
O149	**119**	50c. violet	55·00	8·50
O150	**120**	$1 blue	£120	35·00

(b) Air

O151	**121**	6c. blue	7·00	8·50
O152		7c. blue	7·00	2·00
O137/O152 *Set of 16*			£250	75·00

1946. Peace Re-conversion. Nos. 401/407 punctured as T O **2**.

(a) Postage

O153	**122**	8c. brown	48·00	8·00
O154	**123**	10c. olive-green	5·00	20
O155	**124**	14c. sepia	17·00	3·00
O156	**125**	20c. slate	17·00	75
O157	**126**	50c. green	50·00	19·00
O158	**127**	$1 purple	85·00	25·00

(b) Air

O159	**128**	7c. blue	5·50	3·75
O153/O159 *Set of 7*			£200	50·00

1949. Nos. 415 and 416 punctured as T O **2**.

O160	**136**	2c. sepia	4·00	6·50
O161	**137**	3c. purple	4·00	6·00

O.H.M.S.

(O **3**)

1949. Nos. 375/376, 378, 380 and 402/407 optd as T O **3** by typography.

(a) Postage

O162	**111**	1c. green	7·00	9·50
		a. Missing stop after 'S'	£250	£150
O163	**112**	2c. brown	12·00	12·00
		a. Missing stop after 'S'	£225	£150
O164	**113**	3c. purple	6·00	6·50
O165	**112**	4c. carmine-lake	7·00	6·00
O166	**123**	10c. olive-green	9·00	20
		a. Missing stop after 'S'	£200	85·00
O167	**124**	14c. sepia	20·00	10·00
		a. Missing stop after 'S'	£275	£150
O168	**125**	20c. slate	14·00	1·75
		a. Missing stop after 'S'	£250	£110
O169	**126**	50c. green	£180	£170
		a. Missing stop after 'S'	£1300	£1100
O170	**127**	$1 purple	45·00	70·00
		a. Missing stop after 'S'	£6500	£6500

(b) Air

O171	**128**	7c. blue	24·00	16·00
		a. Missing stop after 'S'	£275	£140
O162/O171 *Set of 10*			£275	£275

Forgeries exist of this overprint. Genuine examples are 2.3×15 mm and show the tops of all letters aligned, as are the stops. The serifs are well defined and, in the case of the 'S', they are vertical. The crossbar of the 'H' is slightly above centre. Overprints applied by lithography are forgeries.

Only a few sheets of the $1 showed the variety, No. O170a.

MISSING STOP VARIETIES. These occur on R. 6/2 of the lower left pane (Nos. O162a, O163a, O175a and O176a) or R. 10/2 of the lower left pane (O166a, O167a, O168a, O169a, O170a and O171a). No. O176a also occurs on R. 8/8 of the upper left pane in addition to R. 6/2 of the lower left pane.

1949–50. Nos. 414/415, 416/417, 418 and 431 optd as T O **3** by typography.

O172	**135**	1c. green	6·00	4·25
O173	**136**	2c. sepia	3·50	6·50
O174	**137**	3c. purple	2·75	4·00
O175	**138**	4c. carmine-lake	2·75	50
		a. Missing stop after 'S'	£250	£110
O176	**139**	5c. blue (1949)	8·00	4·00
		a. Missing stop after 'S'	£150	75·00
O177	**141**	50c. green (1950)	48·00	60·00
O172/O177 *Set of 6*			65·00	70·00

G (O **4**) **G** (O **5**) **G** (O **6**)

Variations in thickness are known in T O **4** these are due to wear and subsequent cleaning of the plate. All are produced by typography. Examples showing the 'G' applied by lithography are forgeries.

1950 (2 Oct)**–52.** Nos. 402/404, 406/407, 414/418 and 431 optd with T O **4** (1 to 5c.) or O **5** (7c. to $1).

(a) Postage

O178	**135**	1c. green	1·50	10
O179	**136**	2c. sepia	7·50	8·50
O180		2c. olive-green (11.51)	1·75	10
O181	**137**	3c. purple	2·25	10
O182	**138**	4c. carmine-lake	8·00	2·00
O183		4c. vermilion (1.5.52)	3·00	60
O184	**139**	5c. blue	8·00	3·00
O185	**123**	10c. olive-green	3·00	10
O186	**124**	14c. sepia	23·00	15·00
O187	**125**	20c. slate	60·00	2·00
O188	**141**	50c. green	20·00	28·00
O189	**127**	$1 purple	80·00	85·00

(b) Air

O190	–	7c. blue	24·00	15·00
O178/O190 *Set of 13*			£200	£130

1950–51. Nos. 432/433 optd with T O **5**.

O191	**142**	10c. brown-purple	4·00	1·00
		a. Opt omitted in pair with normal	£950	£650
O192	**143**	$1 ultramarine (1.2.51)	80·00	90·00

On a small number of sheets of 10c. the opt was omitted from R7/1.

1952–53. Nos. 441, 443 and 446 optd with T O **5**.

O193	**153**	7c. blue (3.11.52)	2·00	3·50
O194	**151**	20c. grey (1.4.52)	3·00	20
O195	**154**	$1 black (2.2.53)	5·50	13·00
O193/O195 *Set of 3*			9·50	15·00

1953 (1 Sept)**–61.** Nos. 450/454 and 462 optd with T O **4** (1 to 5c.) or O **5** (50c.).

O196	**158**	1c. purple-brown	15	10
O197		2c. green	20	10
O198		3c. carmine	20	10
O199		4c. violet	30	10
O200		5c. ultramarine	30	10
O201	**160**	50c. deep bluish green (2.11.53)	3·25	6·00
		a. Opt Type O **6** (24.4.61*)	2·50	7·50
O196/O201 *Set of 6*			3·25	6·00

*Earliest recorded date.

1955–56. Nos. 463/464 and 466/467 optd with T O **4**.

O202	**161**	1c. purple-brown (12.11.56)	65	20
O203		2c. green (19.1.56)	15	20
O204		4c. violet (23.7.56)	40	1·00
O205		5c. bright blue (11.1.55)	15	10
O202/O205 *Set of 4*			1·25	1·25

1955–62. Nos. 477 and 488 optd with T O **5**.

O206	**165**	10c. purple-brown (21.2.55)	70	80
		a. Opt Type O **6** (28.3.62*)	40	2·75
O207	**176**	20c. green (4.12.56)	3·25	30
		a. Opt Type O **6** (10.4.62*)	6·00	2·75

*Earliest recorded date.

1963 (15 May). Nos. 527/528 and 530/531 optd as T O **4**.

O208	1c. chocolate	50	7·00
	a. Opt double	£750	
O209	2c. green	1·00	7·00
	a. Type O **4** omitted (vert pair with normal)	£900	
O210	4c. carmine-red	60	2·25
O211	5c. ultramarine	50	2·50
O208/O211 *Set of 4*		2·40	17·00

No. O209a comes from the top row of an upper pane on which the overprint was misplaced downwards by one row. Owing to the margin between the panes the top row of the bottom pane had the overprint at the top of the stamp.

OFFICIAL SPECIAL DELIVERY STAMPS

1923 (May). Nos. S3/S4 punctured as T O **1**.

OS1	S **1**	10c. yellowish green	—	£300
OS2	S **2**	20c. carmine-red	—	£300

1927 (29 June). 60th Anniversary of Confederation. No. S5 punctured as T O **1**.

OS3	S **3**	20c. orange	—	£300

1930 (2 Sept). Inscr 'TWENTY CENTS' at foot. No. S6 punctured as T O **1**.

OS4	S **4**	20c. brown-red	—	£250

1932 (24 Dec). Inscr 'CENTS' at foot. No. S7 punctured as T O **1**.

OS5	S **4**	20c. brown-red	—	£225

1935 (1 June). No. S8 punctured as T O **1**.

OS6	S **5**	20c. scarlet	—	£225

1938–39. Nos. S9/S10 punctured as T O **1**.

OS7	S **6**	10c. green	—	80·00
OS8		20c. scarlet	—	£150

1939 (1 Mar). No. S11 punctured as T O **1**.

OS9	S **6**	10c. on 20c. scarlet	—	£140

1939 (1 July). Inscr 'CENTS' at foot. No. S7 punctured as T O **2**.

OS10	S **4**	20c. brown-red	£300	£150

1939 (1 July). No. S8 punctured as T O **2**.

OS11	S **5**	20c. scarlet	£150	65·00

1939 (1 July). No. S9 punctured as T O **2**.

OS12	S **6**	10c. green	14·00	14·00

1939 (1 July). No. S11 punctured as T O **2**.

OS13	S **6**	10c. on 20c. scarlet	£180	75·00

1942–43. Nos. S12/S14 punctured as T O **2**.

(a) Postage

OS14	S **8**	10c. green	17·00	15·00

(b) Air

OS15	S **9**	16c. ultramarine	26·00	32·00
OS16		17c. ultramarine	20·00	18·00

1946–47. Nos. S15/S17 punctured as T O **2**.

(a) Postage

OS17	S **10**	10c. green	16·00	11·00

(b) Air

OS18	S **11**	17c. ultramarine (circumflex accent)	60·00	45·00
OS19		17c. ultramarine (grave accent)	95·00	85·00

1950. No. S15 optd as T O **3**, but larger.

OS20	S **10**	10c. green	15·00	40·00

1950 (2 Oct). No. S15 optd as T O **4**, but larger.

OS21	S **10**	10c. green	26·00	30·00

The use of official stamps was discontinued on 31 December 1963.

Cape of Good Hope *see* South Africa

Cayman Islands

The first post office was opened at Georgetown in April 1889. The stamps of Jamaica with the following cancellations were used until 19 February 1901. At some stage, probably around 1891, a supply of the Jamaica 1889 1d., No. 27, was overprinted 'CAYMAN ISLANDS', but these stamps were never issued. Two surviving examples are known, one unused and the other cancelled at Richmond in Jamaica.

Types of Jamaica

2

3

4

8

11

13

PRICES OF NOS. Z1/Z27. These are for a single stamp showing a clear impression of the postmark. Nos. Z1, Z2, Z6/Z8, Z11/Z13, Z18, Z22, Z25 and Z26 are known used on cover and these are worth considerably more.

GEORGETOWN, GRAND CAYMAN

Z 1

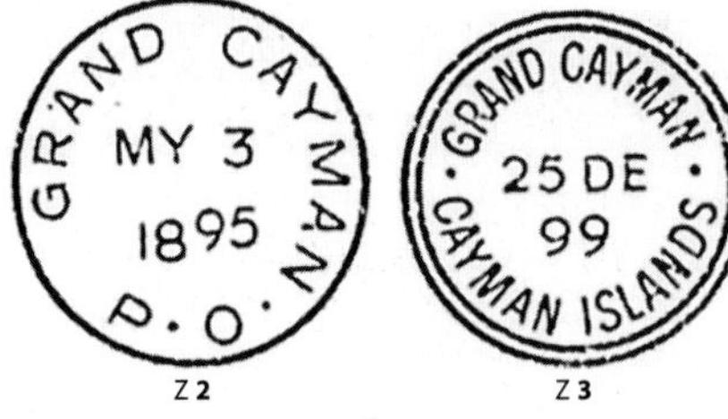

Z 2 Z 3

Stamps of JAMAICA cancelled with T Z **1** in purple.

1889–94.

Z1	**8**	½d. yellow-green (No. 16)	£600
Z2	**11**	1d. purple and mauve (No. 27)	£600
Z2*a*	**2**	2d. slate (No. 20*a*)	£7500
Z3	**11**	2d. green (No. 28)	£950
Z4		2½d. dull purple and blue (No. 29)	£1300
Z5	**4**	4d. red-brown (No. 22*b*)	£4250

Stamps of JAMAICA cancelled with T Z **2** in purple or black.

1895–98.

Z6	**8**	½d. yellow-green (No. 16)	£700
Z7	**11**	1d. purple and mauve (No. 27)	£600
Z8		2½d. dull purple and blue (No. 29)	£1000
Z9	**3**	3d. sage-green (No 21)	£6500

Stamps of JAMAICA cancelled with T Z **3**

1898–1901.

Z10	**8**	½d. yellow-green (No. 16)	£600
		a. Green (No. 16*a*)	£600
Z11	**11**	1d. purple and mauve (No. 27)	£600
Z12	**13**	1d. red (No. 31) (1900)	£650
Z13	**11**	2½d. dull purple and blue (No. 29)	£850

OFFICIAL STAMPS

Stamps of JAMAICA cancelled with T Z **1** in purple.

1890–94.

Z14	**8**	½d. green (No. O1) (*opt 17–17½ mm long*)	£1400
Z15		½d. green (No. O3) (*opt 16 mm long*) (1893)	£3750
Z16	**11**	1d. rose (No. O4)	£1500
Z17		2d. grey (No. O5)	£6500

Stamps of JAMAICA cancelled with T Z **2** in purple or black.

1895–98.

Z18	**8**	½d. green (No. O3)	£4250
Z19	**11**	1d. rose (No. O4)	£6500
Z20		2d. grey (No. O5)	£7500

STAKE BAY, CAYMAN BRAC

Z 4

Z 5

Stamps of JAMAICA cancelled with T Z **4**.

1898–1900.

Z21	**8**	½d. yellow-green (No. 16)	£4500
Z22	**11**	1d. purple and mauve (No. 27)	£4250
Z23		2d. green (No. 28)	£7500
Z24		2½d. dull purple and blue (No. 29)	£4250

Stamps of JAMAICA cancelled with T Z **5**.

1900–01.

Z25	**8**	½d. yellow-green (No. 16)	£5500
Z26	**11**	1d. purple and mauve (No. 27)	£5500
Z27	**13**	1d. red (No. 31)	£6000
Z28	**11**	2½d. dull purple and blue (No. 29)	£5500

PRICES FOR STAMPS ON COVER TO 1945

Nos. 1/2	*from* × 25
Nos. 3/12	*from* × 5
Nos. 13/16	*from* × 4
Nos. 17/19	*from* × 12
Nos. 25/34	*from* × 5
Nos. 35/52*b*	*from* × 4
Nos. 53/67	*from* × 5
Nos. 69/83	*from* × 4
Nos. 84/95	*from* × 6
Nos. 96/99	*from* × 5
Nos. 100/111	*from* × 4
Nos. 112/114	*from* × 6
Nos. 115/126	*from* × 2

DEPENDENCY OF JAMAICA

1

2

3

(T **1/3**, **8/9** and **12/13** typo D.L.R.)

1900 (1 Nov). Wmk Crown CA. P 14.

1	**1**	½d. deep green	21·00	28·00
		a. Pale green	15·00	24·00
2		1d. rose-carmine	17·00	4·75
		a. Pale carmine	21·00	16·00
1s/2s Optd 'SPECIMEN' *Set of 2*			£170	

(Dented frame under 'A' (R. 1/6 of left pane). (The variety is believed to have occurred at some point between 9 January and 9 April 1902 and is then present on all subsequent printings of the 'POSTAGE POSTAGE' design)

1902 (1 Jan)–**03**. Wmk Crown CA. P 14.

3	**2**	½d. green (15.9.02)	6·50	29·00
		a. Dented frame	£300	
4		1d. carmine (6.3.03)	10·00	13·00
		a. Dented frame	£375	£400
5		2½d. bright blue	11·00	21·00
		a. Dented frame	£425	
6		6d. brown	35·00	70·00
		a. Dented frame	£750	£1100
7	**3**	1s. orange	60·00	£120
		a. Dented frame	£950	£1400
3/7 *Set of 5*			£110	£225
3s/7s Optd 'SPECIMEN' *Set of 5*			£250	

1905 (Feb–Oct). Wmk Mult Crown CA. P 14.

8	**2**	½d. green	12·00	19·00
		a. Dented frame	£375	£425
9		1d. carmine (18.10)	25·00	17·00
		a. Dented frame	£550	£500
10		2½d. bright blue	13·00	6·00
		a. Dented frame	£375	£350
11		6d. brown	19·00	42·00
		a. Dented frame	£450	£600
12	**3**	1s. orange	29·00	48·00
		a. Dented frame	£650	
8/12 *Set of 5*			85·00	£110

1907 (13 Mar). Wmk Mult Crown CA. P 14.

13	**3**	4d. brown and blue	40·00	60·00
		a. Dented frame	£800	£1000

14 **2** 6d. olive and rose 48·00 75·00
a. Dented frame £800 £1000
15 **3** 1s. violet and green 60·00 90·00
a. Dented frame £950
16 5s. salmon and green £200 £350
a. Dented frame £5000 £6000
13/16 *Set of 4* £300 £500
13s/16s Optd 'SPECIMEN' *Set of 4* £225

One Halfpenny. (4) ½D (5) 1D (6)

1907 (30 Aug). No. 9 surch at Govt Printing Office, Kingston, with T **4**.
17 **2** ½d. on 1d. carmine 60·00 85·00
a. Dented frame £1100 £1400

1907 (Nov). No. 16 handstamped at Georgetown PO with T **5** or **6**.
18 **3** ½d. on 5s. salmon and green (25.11) £300 £450
a. Surch inverted £100000
b. Surch double £12000 £11000
c. Surch double, one inverted
d. Surch omitted (in pair with normal) £100000
e. Dented frame £5000
19 1d. on 5s. salmon and green (23.11) £275 £400
a. Surch double £22000
b. Surch inverted £150000
c. Dented frame £5000 £6000

The ½d. on 5s. may be found with the figures '1' or '2' omitted, owing to defective handstamping.

8

9

2½D (10)

1907 (27 Dec)–**09**. Chalk-surfaced paper (3d. to 10s.). P 14.

(a) Wmk Mult Crown CA
25 **8** ½d. green 5·00 4·00
26 1d. carmine 1·75 75
27 2½d. ultramarine (30.3.08) 7·50 2·50
28 **9** 3d. purple/*yellow* (30.3.08) 3·25 2·75
29 4d. black and red/*yellow* (30.3.08) 60·00 80·00
30 **8** 6d. dull purple and violet-purple (2.10.08) 28·00 35·00
a. Dull and bright purple 32·00 55·00
31 **9** 1s. black/*green* (5.4.09) 9·00 22·00
32 5s. green and red/*yellow* (30.3.08) 40·00 75·00

(b) Wmk Crown CA (30.3.08)
33 **9** 1s. black/*green* 65·00 £100
34 **8** 10s. green and red/*green* £180 £250
25/34 *Set of 10* £350 £500
25s/30s, 32s/4s Optd 'SPECIMEN' *Set of 9* £350

1908 (12 Feb). No. 13 handstamped by J. H. O'Sullivan, Inspector of Police, with T **10**.
35 **3** 2½d. on 4d. brown and blue £1800 £3500
a. Surch double £50000 £30000
b. Dented frame £24000

No. 35 should only be purchased when accompanied by an expert committee's certificate or similar form of guarantee.

MANUSCRIPT PROVISIONALS. During May and June 1908 supplies of ½d. and 1d. stamps became exhausted, and the payment of postage was indicated by the postmistress, Miss Gwendolyn Parsons, using a manuscript endorsement. Such endorsements were in use from 12 May to 1 June.

MP1 '(Postage Paid G.A.P.)' (12.5 to 1.6) £6000
MP1*a* '(Postage Paid G.A.P.)½' (23.5 to 1.6) £8500
MP1*b* '(Postage Paid G.A.P.)1' (23.5 to 1.6) £7500

In October of the same year there was a further shortage of ¼d. stamps and the manuscript endorsements were again applied by either the new Postmaster, William Graham McCausland or by Miss Parsons who remained as his assistant.

MP2 'Pd ¼d.W.G. McC' (4.10 to 27.10) £250
MP2*a* ¼d. Pd. W.G. McC' (14.10) £1500
MP2*b* 'Pd ¼d.W.G. McC' (6.10) £2000
MP3 'Paid' (7.10) £13000
MP4 'Pd ¼d.' (8.10) £8500
MP5 'Paid ¼d./ GAP. asst.' (15.10) £11000

No. MP2 exists in different inks and formats. Nos. MP2 and MP2*a* show the endorsement in two lines, whereas it is in one line on No. MP2*b*.

Manuscript endorsement for the 2½d. rate is also known, but this is thought to have been done by oversight.

A 1d. surcharge on 4d. (No. 29), issued in mid-May, was intended as a revenue stamp and was never authorised for postal use (*price* £250 *un.*). Used examples were either cancelled by favour or passed through the post in error. Exists with surcharge inverted (*price* £2000 *un.*), surcharge double (*price* £2750 *un.*) or surcharge double, both inverted (*price* £3000 *un.*).

11

12

13

1908 (30 June)–**09**. Wmk Mult Crown CA. Litho. P 14.
38 **11** ¼d. brown 5·50 60
a. Grey-brown (2.09) 7·00 1·00
s. Optd 'SPECIMEN' 95·00

1912 (24 Apr)–**20**. Die I. Wmk Mult Crown CA. Chalk-surfaced paper (3d. to 10s.). P 14.
40 **13** ¼d. brown (10.2.13) 1·00 40
41 **12** ½d. green 2·75 5·00
w. Wmk inverted † £1400
42 1d. red (25.2.13) 3·25 2·50
43 **13** 2d. pale grey 1·00 10·00
44 **12** 2½d. bright blue (26.8.14) 6·00 7·50
a. Deep bright blue (9.11.17) 14·00 25·00
45 **13** 3d. purple/*yellow* (26.11.14) 15·00 45·00
a. White back (19.11.13) 3·50 8·00
b. On lemon (12.3.18) 4·25 18·00
bs. Optd 'SPECIMEN' 70·00
c. On orange-buff (1920) 10·00 32·00
d. On buff (1920)
e. On pale yellow (1920) 4·50 30·00
46 4d. black and red/*yellow* (25.2.13) 1·00 10·00
47 **12** 6d. dull and bright purple (25.2.13) 5·50 8·00
48 **13** 1s. black/*green* (15.5.16) 3·50 27·00
as. Optd 'SPECIMEN' 65·00
b. White back (19.11.13) 3·50 3·50
49 2s. purple and bright blue/*blue* 16·00 65·00
50 3s. green and violet 19·00 75·00
51 5s. green and red/*yellow* (26.8.14) 85·00 £180
52 **12** 10s. deep green and red/*green* (26.11.14) £150 £250
as. Optd 'SPECIMEN' £110
b. White back (19.11.13) £130 £200
c. On blue-green, olive back (5.10.18) £120 £250
40/52*b Set of 13* £225 £500
40s/44s, 45*as*, 46s/47s, 48*bs*, 49s/51s, 52*bs* Optd 'SPECIMEN' *Set of 13* £425

WAR STAMP. 1½d (14) WAR STAMP. 1½d (15) 1½d Straight serif (Left-hand pane R. 10/2)

1917 (26 Feb). T **12** surch with T **14** or **15** at Kingston, Jamaica.
53 **14** 1½d. on 2½d. deep blue 21·00 27·00
a. No fraction bar £275 £300
b. Missing stop after 'STAMP' (R. 1/4) £850
54 **15** 1½d. on 2½d. deep blue 1·75 6·00
a. No fraction bar 75·00 £140
b. Straight serif 95·00 £180

On No. 53 'WAR STAMP' and '1½d.' were applied separately.

WAR STAMP 1½d (16) WAR STAMP 1½d (17) WAR STAMP 1½d. (18)

1917 (4 Sept). T **12** surch with T **16** or **17** by D.L.R.
55 **16** 1½d. on 2½d. deep blue £750 £2000
56 **17** 1½d. on 2½d. deep blue 30 60
s. Optd 'SPECIMEN' £120
x. Wmk reversed £170

De La Rue replaced surcharge T **16** by T **17** after only a few sheets as it did not adequately obliterate the original face value. A small quantity, said to be 3½ sheets, of T **16** was included in the consignment in error.

1919–20. T **12** and **13** (2½d. special printing), optd only, or surch in addition at Kingston (No. 58) or by D.L.R. (others).
57 — ½d. green (4.2.19) 60 2·50
a. Short opt (right pane R. 10/1) 27·00
58 **18** 1½d. on 2d. grey (10.3.20) 5·00 9·00
59 **17** 1½d. on 2½d. orange (4.2.19) 80 1·25
57s, 59s Optd 'Specimen' *Set of 2* £120

No. 57 was overprinted with T **13** of British Virgin Islands.

The ½d. stamps on *buff* paper, and later consignments of the 2d. T **13** on *pinkish*, derived their colour from the paper in which they were packed for despatch from England.

No. 57a shows the overprint 2 mm high instead of 2½ mm.

A further surcharge as No. 58, but in red, was prepared in Jamaica during April 1920, but these were not issued.

19

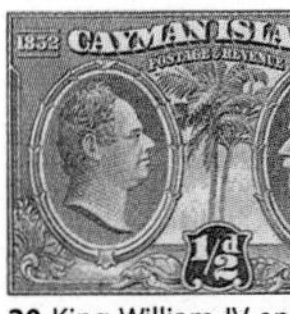
20 King William IV and King George V

1921 (4 Apr)–**26**. P 14.

(a) Wmk Mult Crown CA
60 **19** 3d. purple/*orange-buff* 1·50 8·00
aw. Wmk inverted £250 £325
ay. Wmk inverted and reversed £160 £200
b. Purple/pale yellow 45·00 60·00
bw. Wmk inverted £375
62 4d. red/*yellow* (1.4.22) 1·00 7·00
63 1s. black/*green* 1·25 10·00
x. Wmk reversed £550
64 5s. yellow-green/*pale yellow* 16·00 70·00
a. Deep green/pale yellow £100 £160
b. Blue-green/pale yellow £110 £180
c. Deep green/orange-buff (19.11.21) £160 £225
67 10s. carmine/*green* (19.11.21) 75·00 £120
60/67 *Set of 5* 85·00 £190
60s/67s Optd 'SPECIMEN' *Set of 5* £225

(b) Wmk Mult Script CA
69 **19** ¼d. yellow-brown (1.4.22) 50 1·50
y. Wmk inverted and reversed £325
70 ½d. pale grey-green (1.4.22) 50 30
w. Wmk inverted
y. Wmk inverted and reversed
71 1d. deep carmine-red (1.4.22) 1·75 85
72 1½d. orange-brown 1·75 30
73 2d. slate-grey (1.4.22) 1·75 4·75
74 2½d. bright blue (1.4.22) 50 50
x. Wmk reversed £500
75 3d. purple/*yellow* (29.6.23) 4·00 6·00
y. Wmk inverted and reversed £500
76 4½d. sage-green (29.6.23) 4·50 3·75
77 6d. claret (1.4.22) 5·50 35·00
a. Deep claret 19·00 40·00
79 1s. black/*green* (15.5.25) 9·50 32·00
80 2s. violet/*blue* (1.4.22) 14·00 38·00
81 3s. violet (1.4.22) 23·00 16·00
82 5s. green/*yellow* (15.2.25) 32·00 55·00
83 10s. carmine/*green* (5.9.26) 70·00 £100
69/83 *Set of 14* £140 £250
69s/83s Optd 'SPECIMEN' *Set of 14* £450

An example of the 4d, No. 62, is known with the 'C' missing from the watermark in the top sheet margin.

'A.S.R.' PROVISIONAL. On the night of 9/10 November 1932 the Cayman Brac Post Office at Stake Bay, and its contents, was destroyed by a hurricane. Pending the arrival of replacement stamp stocks and cancellation the Postmaster, Mr A. S. Rutty, initialled covers to indicate that postage had been paid. Those destined for overseas addresses additionally received a 'Postage Paid' machine postmark in red when they passed through Kingston, Jamaica.

MP6 Endorsed 'A.S.R.' in manuscript £11000
MP7 Endorsed 'A.S.R.' in manuscript and 'Postage Paid' machine postmark in red £16000

These emergency arrangements lasted until 19 December.

(Recess Waterlow)

1932 (5 Dec). Centenary of the 'Assembly of Justices and Vestry'. Wmk Mult Script CA. P 12½.
84 **20** ¼d. brown 1·50 1·00
a. 'A' of 'CA' missing from wmk £1500 £1500
85 ½d. green 2·75 11·00
a. 'A' of 'CA' reversed in wmk £1600
86 1d. scarlet 2·75 15·00
87 1½d. red-orange 2·75 2·75
a. 'A' of 'CA' missing from wmk £1800
88 2d. grey 2·75 3·50
89 2½d. ultramarine 2·75 1·50
90 3d. olive-green 8·50 7·00
91 6d. purple 14·00 25·00
92 1s. black and brown 17·00 32·00
93 2s. black and ultramarine 50·00 85·00
94 5s. black and green £100 £160
95 10s. black and scarlet £350 £450
84/95 *Set of 12* £500 £750
84s/95s Perf 'SPECIMEN' *Set of 12* £600

The design of Nos. 92/95 differs slightly from T **20**.

No. 85a shows one 'A' of the watermark reversed so that its head points to right when seen from the back. It is believed that this stamp may also exist with 'A' missing.

Examples of all values are known showing a forged George Town postmark dated 'DE 31 1932'.

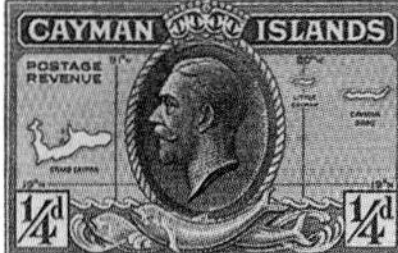
21 Cayman Islands

22 Cat Boat

23 Red-footed Booby

24 Queen or Pink Conch Shells

25 Hawksbill Turtles

(Recess Waterlow)

1935 (1 May). T **21**/**25**. Wmk Mult Script CA. P 12½.
96 **21** ¼d. black and brown 50 1·00
97 **22** ½d. ultramarine and yellow-green 1·00 1·00
98 **23** 1d. ultramarine and scarlet 4·00 2·25
99 **24** 1½d. black and orange 1·50 1·75
100 **22** 2d. ultramarine and purple 3·75 1·10
101 **25** 2½d. blue and black 3·25 1·25
102 **21** 3d. black and olive-green 2·50 3·00
103 **25** 6d. bright purple and black 8·50 4·75
104 **22** 1s. ultramarine and orange 6·00 6·50
105 **23** 2s. ultramarine and black 50·00 38·00
106 **25** 5s. green and black 65·00 65·00
107 **24** 10s. black and scarlet £100 £100
96/107 *Set of 12* £200 £200
96s/107s Perf 'SPECIMEN' *Set of 12* £350

Examples of all values are known showing a forged George Town postmark dated 'AU 23 1936'.

1935 (6 May). Silver Jubilee. As Nos. 91/94 of Antigua.

No.	Description	Unused	Used
108	½d. black and green	15	1·00
	f. Diagonal line by turret	70·00	£100
	g. Dot to left of chapel	£160	
	h. Dot by flagstaff	£130	
	i. Dash by turret	£180	
109	2½d. brown and deep blue	7·00	1·00
110	6d. light blue and olive-green	1·75	10·00
	h. Dot by flagstaff	£350	£475
	i. Dash by turret	£400	
111	1s. slate and purple	13·00	10·00
	h. Dot by flagstaff	£450	£450
	i. Dash by turret	£650	
108/111 *Set of 4*		20·00	20·00
108s/111s Perf 'SPECIMEN' *Set of 4*		£160	

For illustrations of plate varieties see Omnibus section following Zanzibar.

1937 (13 May). Coronation Issue. As Nos. 95/97 of Antigua. P 11 × 11½.

No.	Description	Unused	Used
112	½d. green	30	1·90
113	1d. carmine	50	50
114	2½d. blue	95	40
112/114 *Set of 3*		1·60	2·50
112s/114s Perf 'SPECIMEN' *Set of 3*		£150	

26 Beach View

27 Dolphinfish (*Coryphaena hippurus*)

28 Cayman Islands map

29 Hawksbill Turtles

30 *Rembro* (schooner)

(Recess D.L.R. (½d., 2d., 6d., 1s., 10s.), Waterlow (others))

1938 (5 May)–**48**. T **26/30**. Wmk Mult Script CA (sideways on ¼d., 1d., 1½d., 2½d., 3d., 2s., 5s.). Various perfs.

No.	Type	Description	Unused	Used
115	**26**	¼d. red-orange (P 12½)	70	55
		a. Perf 13½×12½ (16.7.43)	10	1·75
116	**27**	½d. green (P 13×11½)	1·00	55
		a. Perf 14 (16.7.43)	2·50	1·40
		ab. 'A' of 'CA' missing from wmk	£1700	
117	**28**	1d. scarlet (P 12½)	30	75
118	**26**	1½d. black (P 12½)	30	10
119	**29**	2d. violet (P 11½×13)	3·00	40
		a. Perf 14 (16.7.43)	60	30
120	**30**	2½d. bright blue (P 12½)	40	20
120*a*		2½d. orange (P 12½) (25.8.47)	3·50	50
121	**28**	3d. orange (P 12½)	40	15
121*a*		3d. bright blue (P 12½) (25.8.47)	3·00	30
122	**29**	6d. olive-green (P 11½×13)	15·00	4·50
		a. Perf 14 (16.7.43)	3·25	1·25
		b. Brownish olive (P 11½×13) (8.7.47)	3·00	1·50
123	**27**	1s. red-brown (P 13×11½)	6·50	2·25
		a. Perf 14 (16.7.43)	7·00	2·00
		ab. 'A' of 'CA' missing from wmk	£2500	
124	**26**	2s. yellow-green (*shades*) (P 12½)	55·00	14·00
		a. Deep green (16.7.43)	25·00	9·00
125	**30**	5s. carmine-lake (P 12½)	42·00	15·00
		a. Crimson (1948)	75·00	27·00
126	**29**	10s. chocolate (P 11½×13)	38·00	9·00
		a. Perf 14 (16.7.43)	30·00	9·00
		aw. Wmk inverted		
115/126a *Set of 14*			£100	35·00
115s/126s Perf 'SPECIMEN' *Set of 14*			£500	

3d. Stop after '1946' (Plate B1 R. 2/1)

1946 (26 Aug). Victory. As Nos. 110/111 of Antigua.

No.	Description	Unused	Used
127	1½d. black	65	40
128	3d. orange-yellow	65	40
	a. Stop after '1946'	40·00	50·00
127s/128s Perf 'SPECIMEN' *Set of 2*		£130	

1948 (29 Nov). Royal Silver Wedding. As Nos. 112/113 of Antigua.

No.	Description	Unused	Used
129	½d. green	10	1·00
130	10s. violet-blue	24·00	32·00

1949 (10 Oct). 75th Anniversary of Universal Postal Union. As Nos. 114/117 of Antigua.

No.	Description	Unused	Used
131	2½d. orange	30	1·50
132	3d. deep blue	1·50	3·75
133	6d. olive	60	3·75
134	1s. red-brown	60	70
131/134 *Set of 4*		2·75	8·75

31 Cat Boat

32 Coconut Grove, Cayman Brac

33 Green Turtle

34 Thatch Rope Industry

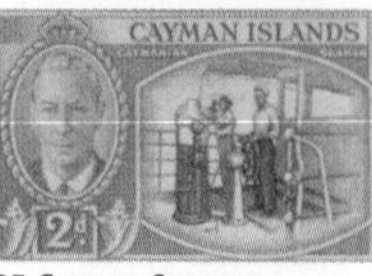

35 Cayman Seamen

36 Map of Cayman Islands

37 Parrotfish

38 Bluff, Cayman Brac

39 Georgetown Harbour

40 Turtle in 'crawl'

41 *Ziroma* (schooner)

42 Boat-building

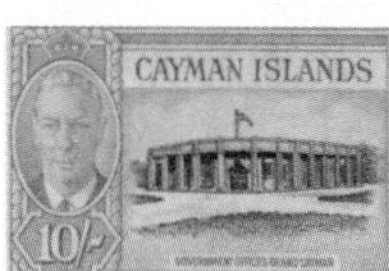

43 Government Offices, Grand Cayman

(Recess B.W.)

1950 (2 Oct). T **31/43**. Wmk Mult Script CA. P 11½ × 11.

No.	Type	Description	Unused	Used
135	**31**	¼d. bright blue and pale scarlet	15	60
136	**32**	½d. reddish violet and emerald-green	15	1·50
137	**33**	1d. olive-green and deep blue	60	1·00
138	**34**	1½d. green and brown	40	75
139	**35**	2d. reddish violet and rose-carmine	1·25	1·50
140	**36**	2½d. turquoise and black	1·25	60
141	**37**	3d. bright green and light blue	1·40	1·50
142	**38**	6d. red-brown and blue	2·00	1·25
143	**39**	9d. scarlet and grey-green	13·00	2·00
144	**40**	1s. brown and orange	3·25	2·75
145	**41**	2s. violet and reddish purple	14·00	11·00
146	**42**	5s. olive-green and violet	24·00	8·00
147	**43**	10s. black and scarlet	29·00	26·00
135/147 *Set of 13*			80·00	50·00

44 South Sound Lighthouse, Grand Cayman

45 Queen Elizabeth II

1953 (2 Mar)–**62**. Designs previously used for King George VI issue but with portrait of Queen Elizabeth II as in T **44/45**. Wmk Mult Script CA. P 11½×11 or 11×11½ (4d., £1).

No.	Type	Description	Unused	Used
148	**31**	¼d. deep bright blue and rose-red (21.2.55)	1·00	60
		a. Bright blue and bright rose-red (5.12.56)	4·75	2·50
149	**32**	½d. purple and bluish green (7.7.54)	75	50
150	**33**	1d. brown-olive and indigo (7.7.54)	70	40
151	**34**	1½d. deep green and red-brown (7.7.54)	60	20
152	**35**	2d. reddish violet and cerise (2.6.54)	3·00	85
153	**36**	2½d. turquoise-blue and black (2.6.54)	3·50	80
154	**37**	3d. bright green and blue (21.2.55)	4·00	60
155	**44**	4d. black and deep blue	2·00	40
		a. Black and greenish blue (13.10.54)	27·00	24·00
		b. Black and deep bright blue (10.7.62)	15·00	15·00
156	**38**	6d. lake-brown and deep blue (7.7.54)	1·75	30
157	**39**	9d. scarlet and bluish green (2.6.54)	7·50	30
158	**40**	1s. brown and red-orange (21.2.55)	3·75	20
159	**41**	2s. slate-violet and reddish purple (21.2.55)	13·00	9·50
160	**42**	5s. olive-green and slate-violet (21.2.55)	15·00	11·00
161	**43**	10s. black and rose-red (21.2.55)	24·00	11·00
161*a*	**45**	£1 blue (6.1.59)	45·00	17·00
148/161*a* *Set of 15*			£110	45·00

1953 (2 June). Coronation. As No. 120 of Antigua, but printed by B.W.

No.	Description	Unused	Used
162	1d. black and emerald	30	2·00

46 Arms of the Cayman Islands

(Photo D.L.R.)

1959 (4 July). New Constitution. Wmk Mult Script CA. P 12.

No.	Type	Description	Unused	Used
163	**46**	2½d. black and light blue	45	2·50
164		1s. black and orange	55	50

CROWN COLONY

47 Cuban Amazon

48 Cat Boat

49 *Schomburgkia thomsoniana* (orchid)

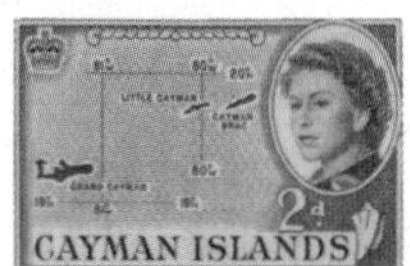

50 Map of Cayman Islands

51 Fisherman casting net

52 West Bay Beach

53 Green Turtle

54 *Kirk B* (schooner)

55 Angler with King Mackerel

56 Iguana

57 Swimming pool, Cayman Brac

58 Water sports

59 Fort George

60 Coat of Arms **61** Queen Elizabeth II

(Recess B.W.)

1962 (28 Nov)–**64.** T **47/61.** W w **12.** P 11×11½ (vert) or 11½×11 (horiz).

165 **47** ¼d. emerald and red 55 2·50
a. Emerald and rose (18.2.64) 4·00 6·00
166 **48** 1d. black and yellow-olive 80 20
167 **49** 1½d. yellow and purple 2·75 1·25
168 **50** 2d. blue and deep brown 1·50 30
169 **51** 2½d. violet and bluish green 85 1·00
170 **52** 3d. bright blue and carmine 30 10
171 **53** 4d. deep green and purple 3·75 60
172 **54** 6d. bluish green and sepia 3·25 30
173 **55** 9d. ultramarine and purple 4·00 40
174 **56** 1s. sepia and rose-red 2·25 10
175 **57** 1s.3d. bluish green and orange-brown 7·50 3·75
176 **58** 1s.9d. deep turquoise and violet 21·00 1·25
177 **59** 5s. plum and deep green 14·00 18·00
178 **60** 10s. olive and blue 23·00 18·00
179 **61** £1 carmine and black 23·00 32·00
165/179 *Set of 15* 95·00 65·00

1963 (4 June). Freedom from Hunger. As No. 146 of Antigua.
180 1s.9d. carmine 30 15

1963 (2 Sept). Red Cross Centenary. As Nos. 147/148 of Antigua.
181 1d. red and black 30 1·25
182 1s.9d. red and blue 70 1·75

1964 (23 Apr). 400th Birth Anniversary of William Shakespeare. As No. 164 of Antigua.
183 6d. magenta 20 10

1965 (17 May). ITU Centenary. As Nos. 166/167 of Antigua.
184 1d. blue and light purple 15 35
185 1s.3d. bright purple and green 55 90

1965 (25 Oct). International Co-operation Year. As Nos. 168/169 of Antigua.
186 1d. reddish purple and turquoise-green 20 10
187 1s. deep bluish green and lavender 80 25

1966 (24 Jan). Churchill Commemoration. As Nos. 170/173 of Antigua.
188 ¼d. new blue 10 2·25
w. Wmk inverted 60·00
189 1d. deep green 60 15
190 1s. brown 1·00 15
w. Wmk inverted 2·00 3·75
191 1s.9d. bluish violet 1·00 75
188/191 *Set of 4* 2·40 3·00

1966 (4 Feb). Royal Visit. As Nos. 174/175 of Antigua.
192 1d. black and ultramarine 50 35
193 1s.9d. black and magenta 2·00 1·50

1966 (1 July). World Cup Football Championships. As Nos. 176/177 of Antigua.
194 1½d. violet, yellow-green, lake and yellow-brown 25 10
195 1s.9d. chocolate, blue-green, lake and yellow-brown 1·00 25

1966 (20 Sept). Inauguration of WHO Headquarters, Geneva. As Nos. 178/179 of Antigua.
196 2d. black, yellow-green and light blue 75 15
197 1s.3d. black, light purple and yellow-brown 1·75 60

62 Telephone and Map

(Des V. Whiteley. Litho Harrison)

1966 (5 Dec). International Telephone Links. W w **12.** P 14½×14.
198 **62** 4d. red, black, greenish blue and olive-green 20 20
199 9d. violet-blue, black, brown-red and light green 20 30

1966 (12 Dec*). 20th Anniversary of UNESCO. As Nos. 196/198 of Antigua.
200 1d. slate-violet, red, yellow and orange 15 10
201 1s.9d. orange-yellow, violet and deep olive 75 10
202 5s. black, bright purple and orange 1·60 1·40
200/202 *Set of 3* 2·25 1·40

* This is the local date of issue; the Crown Agents released the stamps on 1 December.

63 BAC One Eleven 200/400 Airliner over *Ziroma* (Cayman schooner)

(Des V. Whiteley. Photo Harrison)

1966 (17 Dec). Opening of Cayman Jet Service. W w **12.** P 14½.
203 **63** 1s. black, new blue and olive-green 35 30
204 1s.9d. deep purple-brown, ultramarine and emerald 40 35

64 Water-skiing

(Des G. Vasarhelyi. Photo Harrison)

1967 (1 Dec). International Tourist Year. T **64** and similar horiz designs. Multicoloured. W w **12.** P 14½×14.
205 4d. Type **64** 35 10
a. Gold omitted £375 £325
206 6d. Skin diving 35 30
207 1s. Sport fishing 35 30
208 1s.9d. Sailing 40 75
205/208 *Set of 4* 1·25 1·25

A used copy of No. 207 is known with yellow omitted.

68 Former Slaves and Emblem

(Des and photo Harrison)

1968 (3 June). Human Rights Year. W w **12.** P 14½×14.
209 **68** 3d. deep bluish green, black and gold 10 10
w. Wmk inverted 60 80
210 9d. brown, gold and myrtle-green 10 10
211 5s. ultramarine, gold and myrtle-green 30 90
209/211 *Set of 3* 40 1·00

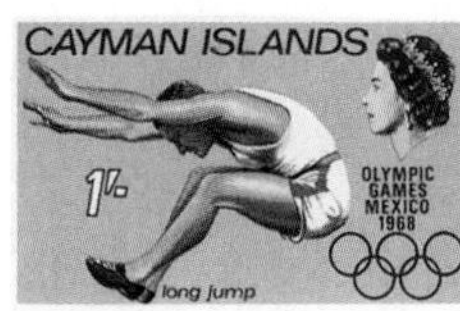

69 Long jumping

(Des R. Granger Barrett. Litho P.B.)

1968 (1 Oct). Olympic Games, Mexico. T **69** and similar multicoloured designs. W w **12.** P 13½.
212 1s. Type **69** 15 10
213 1s.3d. High jumping 20 25
214 2s. Pole vaulting (*vert*) 20 75
212/214 *Set of 3* 50 1·00

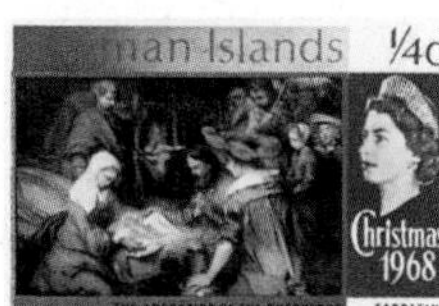

72 *The Adoration of the Shepherds* (Fabritius)

(Des and photo Harrison)

1968–69. Christmas. T **72** and similar horiz design. Centres multicoloured; country name and frames in gold; value and background in colours given. P 14×14½.

(a) W w **12.** *(18.11.68)*

215 **72** ¼d. brown 10 20
a. Gold omitted £275
216 – 1d. bluish violet 10 10
217 **72** 6d. bright blue 20 10
218 – 8d. cerise 20 15
219 **72** 1s.3d. bright green 30 25
220 – 2s. grey 35 35

(b) No wmk (8.1.69)

221 **72** ¼d. bright purple 20 20
215/221 *Set of 7* 1·25 1·10

Design: 1d., 8d., 2s. *The Adoration of the Shepherds* (Rembrandt).

74 Grand Cayman Thrush

76 Arms of the Cayman Islands

(Des G. Vasarhelyi. Litho Format)

1969 (5 June). Designs as T **74** and T **76** in black, ochre and red (£1) or multicoloured (others). No wmk. P 14.
222 ¼d. Type **74** 10 75
223 1d. Brahmin Cattle (*horiz*) 10 10
224 2d. Blowholes on the coast (*horiz*) 10 10
225 2½d. Map of Grand Cayman (*horiz*) 15 10
226 3d. Georgetown scene (*horiz*) 10 10
227 4d. Royal Poinciana (*horiz*) 15 10
228 6d. Cayman Brac and Little Cayman on Chart (*horiz*) 20 10
229 8d. Motor vessels at berth (*horiz*) 25 10
230 1s. Basket-making (*horiz*) 15 10
231 1s.3d. Beach scene (*horiz*) 35 1·00
232 1s.6d. Straw-rope making (*horiz*) 35 1·00
233 2s. Great Barracuda (*horiz*) 1·25 80
234 4s. Government House (*horiz*) 35 80
235 10s. Type **76** 1·00 1·50
236 £1 Queen Elizabeth II (*vert*) 1·25 2·00
222/236 *Set of 15* 5·00 7·00

1969 (11 Aug). As No. 222, but wmk w **12** (sideways).
237 **74** ¼d. multicoloured 30 65

(New Currency. 100 cents = 1 dollar.)

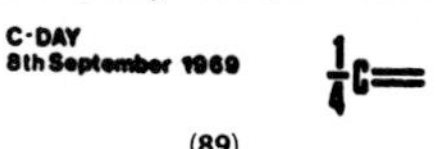

(89)

1969 (8 Sept). Decimal Currency. No. 237, and as Nos. 223/236, but wmk w **12** (sideways on horiz designs), surch as T **89.**
238 ¼c. on ¼d. Type **74** 10 75
239 1c. on 1d. Brahmin Cattle 10 10
240 2c. on 2d. Blowholes on the coast 10 10
241 3c. on 4d. Royal Poinciana 10 10
242 4c. on 2½d. Map of Grand Cayman 10 10
243 5c. on 6d. Cayman Brac and Little Cayman on Chart 10 10
244 7c. on 8d. Motor vessels at berth 10 10
245 8c. on 3d. Georgetown scene 15 10
246 10c. on 1s. Basket-making 25 10
247 12c. on 1s.3d. Beach scene 35 1·75
248 15c. on 1s.6d. Straw-rope making 45 2·00
249 20c. on 2s. Great Barracuda 1·25 1·75
250 40c. on 4s. Government House 35 85
251 $1 on 10s. Type **76** 1·50 2·50
w. Wmk inverted £400
252 $2 on £1 Queen Elizabeth II 1·50 3·25
238/252 *Set of 15* 5·50 11·00

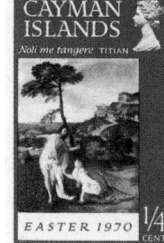

90 *Virgin and Child* (Vivarini) **92** *Noli me tangere* (Titian)

(Des adapted by G. Drummond. Photo Harrison)

1969 (14 Nov*). Christmas. Multicoloured; background colours given. W w **12** (sideways on 1, 7 and 20c.). P 14½.
253 **90** ¼c. orange-red 10 10
w. Wmk inverted 2·75 7·00
254 ¼c. magenta 10 10
w. Wmk inverted 2·75 7·00
255 ¼c. emerald 10 10
a. Gold frame omitted £250
w. Wmk inverted 1·00 2·00
256 ¼c. new blue 10 10
w. Wmk inverted 2·75 7·00
257 – 1c. ultramarine 10 10
258 **90** 5c. orange-red 10 10
259 – 7c. myrtle-green 10 10
260 **90** 12c. emerald 15 15
261 – 20c. brown-purple 20 25
253/261 *Set of 9* 45 45

Design: 1, 7, 20c. *The Adoration of the Kings* (Gossaert).

* This is the local release date. The Crown Agents released the stamps on 4 November.

(Des L. Curtis. Litho D.L.R.)

1970 (23 Mar). Easter. Paintings multicoloured; frame colours given. P 14.
262 **92** ¼c. carmine-red 10 10
263 ¼c. deep green 10 10
264 ¼c. yellow-brown 10 10
265 ¼c. pale violet 10 10
266 10c. chalky blue 30 10
267 12c. chestnut 30 10
268 40c. plum 40 60
262/268 *Set of 7* 1·00 75

93 Barnaby (*Barnaby Rudge*)

97 Grand Cayman Thrush

(Des Jennifer Toombs. Photo Harrison)

1970 (17 June). Death Centenary of Charles Dickens. T **93** and similar vert designs. W w **12** (sideways*). P 14½×14.

No.	Type	Description	Unused	Used
269		1c. black, olive-green and greenish yellow	10	10
		w. Wmk Crown to right of CA	—	2·25
270		12c. black, lake-brown and red	40	15
271		20c. black, ochre-brown and gold	45	15
272		40c. black, bright ultramarine and new blue	55	35
269/272 *Set of 4*			1·25	65

Designs: 1c. T **93**; 12c. Sairey Gamp (*Martin Chuzzlewit*); 20c. Mr. Micawber and David (*David Copperfield*); 40c. The 'Marchioness' (*The Old Curiosity Shop*).

* The normal sideways watermark shows Crown to left of CA, *as seen from the back of the stamp.*

1970 (8 Sept). Decimal Currency. Designs as Nos. 223/237, but with values inscr in decimal currency as T **97**. W w **12** (sideways* on cent values).

No.	Type	Description	Unused	Used
273		¼c. Type **97**	65	1·50
274		1c. Brahmin Cattle	10	10
275		2c. Blowholes on the coast	10	10
276		3c. Royal Poinciana	20	10
277		4c. Map of Grand Cayman	20	10
278		5c. Cayman Brac and Little Cayman on Chart	35	10
		w. Wmk Crown to right of CA	20·00	
279		7c. Motor vessels at berth	30	10
280		8c. Georgetown scene	30	10
281		10c. Basket-making	30	10
282		12c. Beach scene	90	1·25
283		15c. Straw-rope making	1·25	4·00
284		20c. Great Barracuda	3·25	1·50
285		40c. Government House	85	75
286		$1 Type **76**	1·25	4·75
		w. Wmk inverted	11·00	9·00
287		$2 Queen Elizabeth II	2·25	5·00
273/287 *Set of 15*			10·50	17·00

* The normal sideways watermark shows Crown to left of CA, *as seen from the back of the stamp.*

98 The Three Wise Men

(Des G. Drummond. Litho Format)

1970 (8 Oct). Christmas. T **98** and similar horiz design. W w **12** (sideways*). P 14.

No.	Type	Description	Unused	Used
288	**98**	¼c. apple-green, grey and emerald	10	85
		w. Wmk Crown to right of CA	4·00	5·50
289	–	1c. black, lemon and turquoise-green	10	10
290	**98**	5c. grey, red-orange and crimson	10	10
291	–	10c. black, lemon and orange-red	10	10
292	**98**	12c. grey, pale turquoise and ultramarine	15	10
293	–	20c. black, lemon and green	20	15
288/293 *Set of 6*			55	1·25

Design: 1, 10, 20c. Nativity scene and Globe.

* The normal sideways watermark shows Crown to left of CA, *as seen from the back of the stamp.*

Ceylon

PRICES FOR STAMPS ON COVER TO 1945

No. 1	*from* × 5
Nos. 2/12	*from* × 4
Nos. 16/17	*from* × 5
Nos. 18/59	*from* × 8
Nos. 60/62	*from* × 15
Nos. 63/72	*from* × 8
Nos. 121/138	*from* × 6
Nos. 139/141	†
Nos. 142/143	*from* × 10
Nos. 146/151	*from* × 6
Nos. 151*a*/152	†
Nos. 153/193	*from* × 8
Nos. 195/201	*from* × 12
Nos. 202/243	*from* × 6
Nos. 245/249	*from* × 4
Nos. 250/255	*from* × 5
Nos. 256/264	*from* × 4
Nos. 265/276	*from* × 3
Nos. 277/288	*from* × 4
Nos. 289/300	*from* × 8
Nos. 301/318	*from* × 2
Nos. 319/323	—
Nos. 330/337b	*from* × 4
Nos. 338/356	*from* × 2
Nos. 357/360	—
Nos. 361/362	*from* × 5
Nos. 363/367	*from* × 3
Nos. 368/378	*from* × 2
Nos. 379/382	*from* × 4
Nos. 383/385	*from* × 3
Nos. 386/397	*from* × 2
Nos. 398/399	*from* × 8
Nos. O1/O7	†
Nos. O11/O27	*from* × 30

CROWN COLONY

PRICES. The prices of the imperf stamps of Ceylon vary greatly according to condition. The following prices are for fine copies with four margins.

Poor to medium specimens can be supplied at much lower prices.

1

2

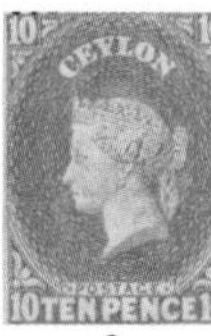

3

NOTE. Beware of stamps of T **2** which are often offered with corners added.

(Recess P.B.)

1857 (1 Apr). Blued paper. Wmk Star W w **1**. Imperf.

No.	Type	Description	Unused	Used
1	**1**	6d. purple-brown	£12000	£450

Collectors should beware of proofs with faked watermark, often offered as originals.

PERKINS BACON 'CANCELLED'. For notes on these handstamps, showing 'CANCELLED' between horizontal bars forming an oval, see Catalogue Introduction.

1857 (2 July)–**59**. Wmk Star, W w **1**. White paper.

No.	Type	Description	Unused	Used
		(a) Imperf		
2	**1**	1d. deep turquoise-blue (24.8.57)	£1100	45·00
		a. Blue	£1200	80·00
		b. Blued paper	—	£225
3		2d. green (*shades*) (24.8.57)	£200	65·00
		a. Yellowish green	£500	90·00
4	**2**	4d. dull rose (23.4.59)	£70000	£4500
5	**1**	5d. chestnut	£1600	£150
6		6d. purple-brown (1859)	£2750	£140
		a. Brown	£11000	£550
		b. Deep brown	£12000	£1000
		c. Light brown	—	£1500
7	**2**	8d. brown (23.4.59)	£28000	£1500
8		9d. purple-brown (23.4.59)	£60000	£900
9	**3**	10d. dull vermilion	£900	£325
10		1s. slate-violet	£5500	£200
11	**2**	1s.9d. green (H/S 'CANCELLED' in oval £9500)	£800	£800
		a. Yellow-green	£5500	£3000
12		2s. dull blue (23.4.59)	£6500	£1300
		(b) Unofficial perf 7½ (1s.9d.) or roul (others)		
13	**1**	1d. blue	£10000	
14		2d. green	£5000	£2750
15	**2**	1s.9d. green	£16000	

Nos. 13/15 were privately produced, probably by commercial firms for their own convenience.

The 10d. also exists with 'CANCELLED' in oval, but no examples are believed to be in private hands.

4

(Typo D.L.R.)

1857 (Oct)–**64**. No wmk. Glazed paper.

No.	Type	Description	Unused	Used
		(a) Imperf		
16	**4**	½d. reddish lilac (*blued paper*)	£4250	£650
17		½d. dull mauve (1858)	£190	£250
		a. Private roul	£8000	
		(b) P 12½		
18	**4**	½d. dull mauve (1864)	£225	£180

(Recess P.B.)

1861–64. Wmk Star, W w **1**.

No.	Type	Description	Unused	Used
		(a) Clean-cut and intermediate perf 14 to 15½		
19	**1**	1d. light blue	£2500	£300
		a. Dull blue (H/S 'CANCELLED' in oval £11000)	£200	16·00
20		2d. green (*shades*)	£275	28·00
		a. Imperf between (vert pair)	†	—
		b. Yellowish green (H/S 'CANCELLED' in oval £12000)	£275	25·00
21	**2**	4d. dull rose (H/S 'CANCELLED' in oval £12000)	£2250	£325
22	**1**	5d. chestnut (H/S 'CANCELLED' in oval £8000)	£120	8·50
23		6d. brown (H/S 'CANCELLED' in oval £9000)	£3000	£180
		a. Bistre-brown	—	£275
24	**2**	8d. brown (H/S 'CANCELLED' in oval £10000)	£2500	£500
25		9d. purple-brown	£15000	£250
26	**3**	1s. slate-violet (H/S 'CANCELLED' in oval £11000)	£140	13·00
27	**2**	2s. dull blue	£4750	£900
		(b) Rough perf 14 to 15½		
28	**1**	1d. dull blue	£160	13·00
		a. Blued paper	£800	27·00
29		2d. green	£475	85·00
30	**2**	4d. rose-red	£600	£130
		a. Deep rose-red	£700	£160
31	**1**	6d. deep brown	£1300	£130
		a. Light brown	£2250	£200
		b. Olive-sepia	£1200	£120
32	**2**	8d. brown	£1700	£650
		a. Yellow-brown	£1600	£425
33		9d. deep brown (H/S 'CANCELLED' in oval £9000)	£160	£130
		a. Light brown	£1300	£130
		b. Olive-sepia	£850	85·00
34	**3**	10d. dull vermilion	£300	28·00
		a. Imperf vert (horiz pair)	†	—
35		1s. slate-violet	£225	18·00
36	**2**	1s.9d. light green (*prepared for use, but not issued*)	£750	
37		2s. dull blue (H/S 'CANCELLED' in oval £11000)	£750	£160
		a. Deep dull blue	£1100	£200
		(c) P 12½ by D.L.R.		
38	**3**	10d. dull vermilion (9.64)	£325	22·00

The line machine used for Nos. 19/37 produced perforations of variable quality due to wear, poor cleaning and faulty servicing, but it is generally accepted that the clean-cut and intermediate versions occurred on stamps perforated up to March 1861 and the rough variety when the machine was used after that date.

(Recess D.L.R.)

1862. No wmk. Smooth paper.

No.	Type	Description	Unused	Used
		(a) P 13		
39	**1**	1d. dull blue	£180	7·00
40		5d. lake-brown	£1800	£150
41		6d. brown	£200	29·00
		a. Deep brown	£200	29·00
42	**2**	9d. brown	£1300	£120
43	**3**	1s. slate-purple	£1800	£110
		(b) P 11½, 12		
44	**1**	1d. dull blue	£1800	£130
		a. Imperf between (horiz pair)	†	£18000

Nos. 39/44 were printed on paper showing a papermaker's watermark of 'T H SAUNDERS 1862', parts of which can be found on individual stamps. Examples are rare and command a premium.

The 1s. is known imperforate, but was not issued in this condition (*Price, £4000, unused*).

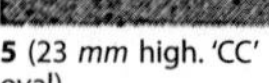

5 (23 *mm* high. 'CC' oval)

6 (21½ *mm* high. 'CC' round and smaller)

(Typo (½d.) or recess (others) D.L.R.)

1863–66. W **5**. Paper medium thin and slightly soft.

No.	Type	Description	Unused	Used
		(a) P 11½, 12		
45	**1**	1d. deep blue	£3500	£325
		x. Wmk reversed	£4750	£550
		(b) P 13		
46	**1**	6d. sepia	£2750	£250
		x. Wmk reversed	£3250	£300
		y. Wmk inverted and reversed	£4000	£700
47	**2**	9d. sepia	£6500	£1000
		(c) P 12½		
48	**4**	½d. dull mauve (1864)	80·00	50·00
		aw. Wmk inverted	£500	£180
		b. Reddish lilac	90·00	65·00
		c. Mauve	55·00	55·00
49	**1**	1d. deep blue	£180	9·00
		a. Imperf		
		w. Wmk inverted	†	70·00
		x. Wmk reversed	£250	9·50
		y. Wmk inverted and reversed	†	£110
50		2d. grey-green (1864)	£100	15·00
		a. Imperf	†	£5000
		bw. Wmk inverted	£400	£110
		by. Wmk inverted and reversed	†	£225
		c. Bottle-green	†	£4000
		d. Yellowish green	£9000	£400

		dx. Wmk reversed	†	£1100
		e. Emerald (wmk reversed)	£190	£110
		ew. Wmk inverted	£950	£500
51		2d. ochre (*wmk reversed*) (1866)	£325	£275
		w. Wmk inverted	£950	£800
		y. Wmk inverted and reversed	£850	£600
52	2	4d. rose-carmine (1865)	£900	£275
		ax. Wmk reversed	£1300	
		b. Rose	£550	£130
		bx. Wmk reversed	£750	£170
53	1	5d. red-brown (*shades*) (1865)	£325	£110
		w. Wmk inverted	†	£350
		x. Wmk reversed	£450	85·00
54		5d. grey-olive (1866)	£2000	£425
		ax. Wmk reversed	£1600	£350
		b. Yellow-olive	£900	£275
		bx. Wmk reversed	£850	£300
55		6d. sepia	£250	4·50
		aw. Wmk inverted	†	£130
		ax. Wmk reversed		
		b. Reddish brown	£350	15·00
		c. Blackish brown	£300	11·00
		ca. Double print	†	£4250
		cw. Wmk inverted	£450	£120
		cx. Wmk reversed	£375	75·00
		cy. Wmk inverted and reversed	†	£225
56	2	8d. reddish brown (*shades*) (1864)	£150	80·00
		x. Wmk reversed	£275	£130
		y. Wmk inverted and reversed	£650	£225
57		9d. sepia	£350	50·00
		x. Wmk reversed	£850	£130
58	3	10d. vermilion (1866)	£5000	70·00
		ax. Wmk reversed	†	£170
		b. Orange-red	£7500	£450
		bx. Wmk reversed	†	£650
59	2	2s. steel-blue (*shades*) (1864)	£375	42·00
		x. Wmk reversed	£750	£130
		y. Wmk inverted and reversed	£1000	£350

Watermarks as T **5** were arranged in four panes, each of 60, with the words 'CROWN COLONIES' between the panes. Parts of this marginal watermark often appear on the stamps.

De La Rue had considerable difficulty matching the standard Crown CC watermark to the plates received from Perkins Bacon with the result that the watermark W **5** is frequently found misplaced.

A further aid to identifying the two watermarks is the distance between the top of the cross and the foot of 'CC', which measures 2 mm on W **5** and 6.5 mm on W **6**.

The ½d. dull mauve, 2d. ochre and 5d. grey-olive with this watermark also exist imperforate, but are not known used. The 6d. sepia and 2s. steel-blue also exist imperforate on wove paper without watermark.

One used example of the 2d. grey-green is known showing private roulettes added to an imperforate stamp (*Price* £5000).

7

8

(Typo D.L.R.)

1866–68. Wmk Crown CC.

(a) P 12½

60	7	3d. rose	£275	£100

(b) P 14

61	8	1d. blue (*shades*) (1868)	26·00	13·00
		w. Wmk inverted	†	£275
62	7	3d. carmine-rose (1867)	90·00	50·00
		a. Bright rose	95·00	55·00

Nos. 60/61 exist imperforate.

(Recess D.L.R.)

1867–70. W **6**. Specially produced hand-made paper. P 12½.

63	1	1d. dull blue	£325	18·00
		aw. Wmk inverted	£700	£160
		ax. Wmk reversed	£325	18·00
		ay. Wmk inverted and reversed	†	£275
		b. Deep blue	£275	17·00
		bw. Wmk inverted	—	£170
		bx. Wmk reversed	£450	45·00
64		2d. ochre	£170	15·00
		aw. Wmk inverted		
		ax. Wmk reversed	£300	45·00
		b. Bistre	£100	9·50
		bw. Wmk inverted	£160	
		c. Olive-bistre	£170	20·00
		cw. Wmk inverted	£170	
		d. Yellow	£130	9·00
		dx. Wmk reversed	85·00	22·00
65	2	4d. rose	£300	55·00
		ax. Wmk reversed	£275	45·00
		b. Rose-carmine	90·00	24·00
		bw. Wmk inverted	†	£160
		bx. Wmk reversed	£120	26·00
		by. Wmk inverted and reversed	£700	£225
66	1	5d. yellow-olive	£160	25·00
		ax. Wmk reversed	£150	27·00
		ay. Wmk inverted and reversed	†	£160
		b. Olive-green	£150	30·00
		bx. Wmk reversed	†	75·00
		c. Bronze-green	65·00	60·00
67		6d. deep brown (1869)	£140	13·00
		ax. Wmk reversed	£250	
		b. Blackish brown	£190	10·00
		bw. Wmk inverted	†	£180
		bx. Wmk reversed	£225	19·00
		c. Red-brown	65·00	42·00
68	2	8d. chocolate	£130	80·00
		ax. Wmk reversed	—	£150
		b. Lake-brown	£140	85·00
		bx. Wmk reversed	£325	£150
69		9d. bistre-brown (12.68)	£950	38·00
		ax. Wmk reversed	£500	25·00
		b. Blackish brown	70·00	8·50
70	3	10d. dull vermilion (*wmk reversed*)	£6000	£150
		ay. Wmk inverted and reversed	†	£350
		b. Red-orange	90·00	18·00
		bx. Wmk reversed	£190	19·00
		by. Wmk inverted and reversed	£1000	
		c. Orange	£150	20·00
71		1s. reddish lilac (1870)	£300	30·00
		ax. Wmk reversed	£500	85·00
		b. Reddish violet	£150	13·00
		bw. Wmk inverted	†	£275
		bx. Wmk reversed	£450	85·00
72	2	2s. steel-blue	£275	22·00
		ax. Wmk reversed	†	55·00
		b. Deep blue	£170	20·00
		bx. Wmk reversed	£200	25·00

Watermarks as T **6** were arranged in one pane of 240 (12×20) with the words 'CROWN COLONIES' twice in each side margin.

Unused examples of the 1d. dull blue, 1d. deep blue, 5d. yellow-olive, 6d. deep brown, 9d. blackish brown and 10d. red orange with this watermark exist imperforate.

Nos. 73 to 120 are vacant.

PRINTERS. All stamps from No. 121 to 367 were typographed by De La Rue & Co. Ltd, London.
A wide variety of shades may be found on stamps of this period. We only list the most significant.

(New Currency. 100 cents = 1 rupee)

9 10 11 12 13 14 15 16 17 18 19

1872–80. Wmk Crown CC.

(a) P 14

121	9	2c. pale brown (*shades*)	38·00	4·25
		w. Wmk inverted	£190	£100
122	10	4c. grey	55·00	2·00
		w. Wmk inverted	£450	£100
123		4c. rosy-mauve (1880)	80·00	1·50
		w. Wmk inverted	£400	£225
124	11	8c. orange-yellow	65·00	7·00
		a. Yellow	50·00	8·00
		w. Wmk inverted	†	£250
126	12	16c. pale violet	£150	2·75
		w. Wmk inverted	†	£225
127	13	24c. green	90·00	2·50
		w. Wmk inverted	†	£180
128	14	32c. slate (1877)	£190	15·00
		w. Wmk inverted	£600	£200
129	15	36c. blue	£200	30·00
		x. Wmk reversed	£425	£170
130	16	48c. rose	£120	9·50
		w. Wmk inverted	—	95·00
131	17	64c. red-brown (1877)	£300	75·00
132	18	96c. drab	£275	30·00
		w. Wmk inverted	—	£250
121/132 *Set of* 11			£1300	£150

(b) P 14×12½

133	9	2c. brown	£425	70·00
134	10	4c. grey	£2500	42·00
135	11	8c. orange-yellow	£475	55·00
		w. Wmk inverted	†	£400

(c) P 12½

136	9	2c. brown	£4500	£250
		w. Wmk inverted	†	£650
137	10	4c. grey	£3000	£325

(d) P 12½×14

138	19	2r.50 dull-rose (1879)	£800	£425

(e) Prepared for use and sent out to Ceylon, but not issued unsurcharged

139	14	32c. slate (P 14×12½)	£1400
140	17	64c. red-brown (P 14×12½)	£1600
141	19	2r.50 dull rose (P 12½)	£3250

FORGERIES—Beware of forged overprint and surcharge varieties on Victorian issues.

SIXTEEN

16

CENTS

(20)

1882 (Oct). Nos. 127 and 131 surch as T **20** by Govt Printer.

142	13	16c. on 24c. green	48·00	10·00
		a. Surch inverted		
143	17	20c. on 64c. red-brown	15·00	9·00
		a. Surch double	†	£1800

1883–98. Wmk Crown CA.

(a) P 14

146	9	2c. pale brown	75·00	3·75
147		2c. dull green (1884)	3·75	15
		s. Optd 'SPECIMEN'	£475	
		w. Wmk inverted	£275	£120
148	10	4c. rosy mauve	7·00	50
		w. Wmk inverted	†	£275
		x. Wmk reversed	†	£400
149		4c. rose (1884)	7·50	13·00
		s. Optd 'SPECIMEN'	£475	
150	11	8c. orange-yellow	8·50	14·00
		a. Yellow (1898)	6·00	12·00
151	12	16c. pale violet	£2000	£180

(b) Trial perforation. P 12

151*a*	9	2c. dull green	£7000
151*b*	10	4c. rose	£7000
151*c*	13	24c. brown-purple	£7500

(c) Prepared for use and sent out to Ceylon, but not issued unsurcharged. P 14

152	13	24c. brown-purple	£1700
		s. Optd 'SPECIMEN'	£800

Although delivered in 1884 it is believed that the 4c. rose, No. 149, was not used until the early 1890s.

See also Nos. 246, 256 and 258 for the 2c. and 4c. in different colours.

Postage &

FIVE CENTS

Revenue

(21)

TEN CENTS

(22)

Twenty Cents

(23)

One Rupee Twelve Cents

(24)

1885 (1 Jan–Mar). T **10/19** surch locally as T **21/24**.

I. Wmk Crown CC

(a) P 14

153	21	5c. on 16c. pale violet	†	£3000
154		5c. on 24c. green	£6500	£110
155		5c. on 32c. slate	70·00	15·00
		a. Surch inverted	†	£2750
		b. Dark grey	£225	48·00
156		5c. on 36c. blue	£300	13·00
		a. Surch inverted	†	£2750
		x. Wmk reversed	†	£200
157		5c. on 48c. rose	£2500	75·00
158		5c. on 64c. red-brown	£140	13·00
		a. Surch double	†	£3500
159		5c. on 96c. drab	£550	70·00
161	22	10c. on 16c. pale violet	£12000	£3000
162		10c. on 24c. green	£550	£140
163		10c. on 36c. blue	£500	£300
164		10c. on 64c. red-brown	£450	£250
165		20c. on 24c. green	90·00	35·00
166	23	20c. on 32c. slate	£100	80·00
		a. Dark grey	£130	65·00
		aw. Wmk inverted	£475	
167		25c. on 32c. slate	30·00	11·00
		a. Dark grey	32·00	12·00
168		28c. on 48c. rose	40·00	13·00
		a. Surch double	†	£3000
		w. Wmk inverted	†	£450
		x. Wmk reversed	†	£550
169	22	30c. on 36c. blue	27·00	19·00
		x. Wmk reversed	18·00	15·00
		xa. Surch inverted	£325	£150
170		56c. on 96c. drab	35·00	27·00

(b) P 14×12½

172	21	5c. on 32c. slate	£850	55·00
173		5c. on 64c. red-brown	£950	55·00
		w. Wmk inverted	†	£650
174	22	10c. on 64c. red-brown	£100	£170
		a. Imperf between (vert pair)	£7000	
175	24	1r.12 on 2r.50 dull rose (P 12½)	£700	£110
176		1r.12 on 2r.50 dull rose (P 12½×14)	£110	50·00

II. Wmk Crown CA. P 14

178	21	5c. on 4c. rose (3.85)	27·00	5·50
		a. Surch inverted	†	£325
179		5c. on 8c. orange-yellow	£100	11·00
		a. Surch double	†	£3750
		b. Surch inverted	†	£4250
180		5c. on 16c. pale violet	£190	19·00
		a. Surch inverted	†	£250
182		5c. on 24c. brown-purple	—	£500
184	22	10c. on 16c. pale violet	£13000	£1700
185		10c. on 24c. brown-purple	20·00	12·00
186		15c. on 16c. pale violet	16·00	11·00

The 5c. on 4c. rosy mauve and 5c. on 24c. green, both watermarked Crown CA, previously catalogued are now known to be forgeries.

REVENUE AND POSTAGE

5 CENTS

(25)

10 CENTS

(26)

1 R. 12 C.

(27)

1885. T **11/15**, **18** and **19** surch with T **25/27** by D.L.R. P 14.

(a) Wmk Crown CA

No.	Type	Description	Unused	Used
187	**25**	5c. on 8c. lilac	28·00	1·50
		w. Wmk inverted	†	£160
		x. Wmk reversed	£425	£375
188	**26**	10c. on 24c. brown-purple	15·00	8·50
189		15c. on 16c. orange-yellow	60·00	15·00
190		28c. on 32c. slate	29·00	2·50
191		30c. on 36c. olive-green	29·00	16·00
192		56c. on 96c. drab	50·00	17·00
		(b) Wmk Crown CC (sideways)		
193	**27**	1r.12 on 2r.50 dull rose	60·00	£160
187/193 *Set of 7*			£225	£200
187s/193s Optd 'SPECIMEN' *Set of 7*			£1300	

28

29

1886. Wmk Crown CA. P 14.

No.	Type	Description	Unused	Used
195	**28**	5c. dull purple	3·75	10
		w. Wmk inverted	£275	£160
196	**29**	15c. sage-green	9·00	2·50
		w. Wmk inverted	£350	£275
197		15c. olive-green	11·00	2·75
198		25c. yellow-brown	7·00	2·00
		a. Value in yellow	£150	90·00
199		28c. slate	26·00	2·00
195s, 197s/199s Optd 'SPECIMEN' *Set of 4*			£300	

Six plates were used for the 5c., No. 195, between 1885 and 1901, each being replaced by its successor as it became worn. Examples from the worn plates show thicker lines in the background and masses of solid colour under the chin, in front of the throat, at the back of the neck and at the base.

30

1887. Wmk Crown CC (sideways). White or blued paper. P 14.

No.	Type	Description	Unused	Used
201	**30**	1r.12 dull rose	35·00	35·00
		aw. Wmk Crown to left of CC	£120	£120
		b. Wmk upright	70·00	80·00
		bw. Wmk inverted	£750	£375
		s. Optd 'SPECIMEN'	£200	

The normal sideways watermark shows Crown to right of CC, *as seen from the back of the stamp.*

TWO CENTS (31) Two (32) 2 Cents (33)

Two Cents (34) 2 Cents (35)

1888–90. Nos. 148/149 surch with T **31/35**.

No.	Type	Description	Unused	Used
202	**31**	2c. on 4c. rosy mauve	1·75	80
		a. Surch inverted	27·00	24·00
		b. Surch double, one inverted	—	£400
203		2c. on 4c. rose	2·50	40
		a. Surch inverted	22·00	23·00
		b. Surch double	—	£425
204	**32**	2(c). on 4c. rosy mauve	1·00	30
		a. Surch inverted	45·00	45·00
		b. Surch double	£130	£140
		c. Surch double, one inverted	£100	£100
205		2(c). on 4c. rose	9·00	20
		a. Surch inverted	£450	
		b. Surch double	£120	£140
		c. Surch double, one inverted	£120	£140
206	**33**	2c. on 4c. rosy mauve	85·00	32·00
		a. Surch inverted	£180	42·00
		b. Surch double, one inverted	£250	
207		2c. on 4c. rose	4·50	75
		a. Surch inverted	20·00	11·00
		b. Surch double	£200	£160
		c. Surch double, one inverted	8·50	16·00
		w. Wmk inverted	£250	
208	**34**	2c. on 4c. rosy mauve	65·00	28·00
		a. Surch inverted	£200	30·00
209		2c. on 4c. rose	3·25	1·10
		a. Surch inverted	20·00	11·00
		b. Surch double	£160	£150
		c. Surch double, one inverted	20·00	14·00
210	**35**	2c. on 4c. rosy mauve	70·00	38·00
		a. Surch inverted	£100	42·00
		b. Surch double, one inverted	£150	£150
		c. Surch double	—	£450
		d. 's' of 'Cents' inverted (R. 3/5)	—	£750
		e. As d. Whole surch inverted		
211		2c. on 4c. rose	15·00	1·00
		a. Surch inverted	26·00	10·00
		b. Surch double	£150	£150
		c. Surch double, one inverted	27·00	17·00
		d. 's' of 'Cents' inverted (R. 3/5)	£650	£375
		x. Wmk reversed	†	£400
209s, 211s Optd 'SPECIMEN' *Set of 2*			65·00	

The 4c. rose and the 4c. rosy mauve are found surcharged 'Postal Commission 3 (or 'Three') Cents'. They denote the extra commission charged by the Post Office on postal orders which had not been cashed within three months of the date of issue. For a short time the Post Office did not object to the use of these stamps on letters.

POSTAGE

Five Cents

REVENUE

(36)

FIFTEEN

CENTS

(37)

1890. No. 197 surch locally with T **36**.

No.	Type	Description	Unused	Used
233		5c. on 15c. olive-green	4·50	3·00
		a. Surch inverted	65·00	75·00
		b. Surch double	£120	£140
		c. 'Flve' for 'Five' (R. 1/1)	£140	95·00
		d. Variety as c, inverted	—	£1800
		e. 'REVENUE' omitted	£225	£200
		f. Inverted 's' in 'Cents' (R. 10/2)	£140	£120
		g. Variety as f, and whole surch inverted	£2250	
		h. 'REVENUE' omitted and inverted 's' in 'Cents'	£1800	
		i. 'POSTAGE' spaced between 'T' and 'A' (R. 1/5)	90·00	90·00
		j. Variety as i, and whole surch inverted	£2250	£1800
		s. Optd 'SPECIMEN'	35·00	

1891. Nos. 198/199 surch locally with T **37**.

No.	Type	Description	Unused	Used
239	**29**	15c. on 25c. yellow-brown	20·00	22·00
240		15c. on 28c. slate	21·00	9·00
		w. Wmk inverted	†	£375

3 Cents

(38) 39

1892. Nos. 148/149 and 199 surch locally with T **38**.

No.	Type	Description	Unused	Used
241	**10**	3c. on 4c. rosy mauve	2·25	3·25
242		3c. on 4c. rose	9·00	13·00
		s. Optd 'SPECIMEN'	42·00	
		w. Wmk inverted	£200	
		ws. Optd 'SPECIMEN'	£150	
243	**29**	3c. on 28c. slate	6·50	6·50
		a. Surch double	£170	
241/243 *Set of 3*			16·00	20·00

1893–99. Wmk Crown CA. P 14.

No.	Type	Description	Unused	Used
245	**39**	3c. terracotta and blue-green	7·00	45
246	**10**	4c. carmine-rose (1898)	13·00	17·00
247	**29**	30c. bright mauve and chestnut	5·00	3·25
		a. Bright violet and chestnut	6·50	3·50
249	**19**	2r.50 purple/*red* (1899)	45·00	70·00
245/249 *Set of 4*			65·00	80·00
245s, 247s/249s Optd 'SPECIMEN' *Set of 3*			85·00	

Six Cents (40) 2 R. 25 C. (41)

1898 (Dec)–**99**.

No.	Type	Description	Unused	Used
		(a) No. 196 surch locally with T **40**		
250	**29**	6c. on 15c. sage-green	1·25	75
		(b) As No. 138, but colour changed and perf 14, surch as T **41** *by D.L.R. (1899)*		
254	**19**	1r.50 on 2r.50 slate	21·00	55·00
		w. Wmk inverted	£325	£400
255		2r.25 on 2r.50 yellow	50·00	85·00
250s/255s Optd 'Specimen' (Nos. 250s) or 'SPECIMEN' *Set of 3*			85·00	

43

1899–1900. Wmk Crown CA (1r.50, 2r.25 wmk Crown CC). P 14.

No.	Type	Description	Unused	Used
256	**9**	2c. pale orange-brown	5·00	30
257	**39**	3c. deep green	5·00	55
258	**10**	4c. yellow	4·25	3·75
259	**29**	6c. rose and black	3·25	45
		w. Wmk inverted	†	£300
260	**39**	12c. sage-green and rose (1900)	6·50	9·50
261	**29**	15c. blue	8·50	1·25
262	**39**	75c. black and red-brown	11·00	10·00
263	**43**	1r.50 rose	35·00	55·00
		w. Wmk inverted	£425	£425
264		2r.25 dull blue	38·00	55·00
256/264 *Set of 9*			£100	£120
256s/264s Optd 'SPECIMEN' *Set of 9*			£225	

44

45

46

47

48

1903 (29 May)–**05**. Wmk Crown CA. P 14.

No.	Type	Description	Unused	Used
265	**44**	2c. red-brown (21.7.03)	2·00	20
266	**45**	3c. green (11.6.03)	2·25	1·00
267		4c. orange-yellow and blue	2·25	6·00
268	**46**	5c. dull purple (2.7.03)	3·25	60
		sa. Opt 'SPECIMEN' double, one albino	£225	
269	**47**	6c. carmine (5.11.03)	9·50	1·50
		w. Wmk inverted	£140	£150
270	**45**	12c. sage-green and rosine (13.8.03)	5·00	11·00
271	**48**	15c. blue (2.7.03)	6·50	3·50
272		25c. bistre (11.8.03)	6·50	12·00
273		30c. dull violet and green	3·25	4·00
274	**45**	75c. dull blue and orange (31.3.05)	4·50	24·00
275	**48**	1r.50 greyish slate (7.4.04)	70·00	70·00
276		2r.25 brown and green (12.4.04)	95·00	65·00
265/276 *Set of 12*			£190	£180
265s/276s Optd 'SPECIMEN' *Set of 12*			£190	

1904 (13 Sept)–**05**. Wmk Mult Crown CA. Ordinary paper. P 14.

No.	Type	Description	Unused	Used
277	**44**	2c. red-brown (17.11.04)	2·75	10
278	**45**	3c. green (17.11.04)	1·75	15
279		4c. orange and ultramarine	3·00	1·50
		w. Wmk inverted	—	£275
280	**46**	5c. dull purple (29.11.04)	4·00	1·25
		a. Chalk-surfaced paper (5.10.05)	7·50	70
		ay. Wmk inverted and reversed	—	£350
281	**47**	6c. carmine (11.10.04)	6·00	15
		w. Wmk inverted	†	£325
282	**45**	12c. sage-green and rosine (29.9.04)	1·75	1·75
283	**48**	15c. blue (1.12.04)	3·75	60
284		25c. bistre (5.1.05)	6·00	3·75
		w. Wmk inverted	†	£375
285		30c. violet and green (7.9.05)	2·50	3·00
286	**45**	75c. dull blue and orange (25.5.05)	5·25	8·00
287	**48**	1r.50 grey (5.1.05)	35·00	15·00
288		2r.25 brown and green (22.12.04)	22·00	32·00
277/288 *Set of 12*			80·00	55·00

50

51

1908. Wmk Mult Crown CA. P 14.

No.	Type	Description	Unused	Used
289	**50**	5c. deep purple (26.5)	7·50	10
290		5c. dull purple	10·00	30
291	**51**	6c. carmine (6.6)	3·50	10
289s, 291s Optd 'SPECIMEN' *Set of 2*			70·00	

1910 (1 Aug)–**11**. Wmk Mult Crown CA. P 14.

No.	Type	Description	Unused	Used
292	**44**	2c. brown-orange (20.5.11)	1·50	50
293	**48**	3c. green (5.7.11)	1·00	75
294		10c. sage-green and maroon	2·50	3·50
295		25c. grey	2·50	3·00
296		50c. chocolate	4·00	7·50
297		1r. purple/*yellow*	8·50	13·00
298		2r. red/*yellow*	15·00	30·00
299		5r. black/*green*	48·00	£120
300		10r. black/*red*	£140	£325
292/300 *Set of 9*			£200	£450
292s/300s Optd 'SPECIMEN' *Set of 9*			£300	

Examples of Nos. 298/300 are known showing a forged Colombo registered postmark dated '27.1.10'.

52

53

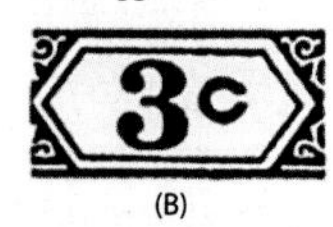

(A) (B)

Most values in T **52** were produced by two printing operations, using 'Key' and 'Duty' plates. Differences in the two Dies of the Key plate are described in the introduction to this catalogue.

In the Ceylon series, however, the 1c. and 5c. values, together with later printings of the 3c. and 6c., were printed from special plates at one operation. These plates can be identified by the large 'C' in the value tablet (see illustration A). Examples of these values from Key and Duty plates printing have value tablet as illustration B. The 3c. and 5c. stamps from the single plates *resemble* Die I, and the 1c. and 6c. Die II, although in the latter case the inner top corners of the side panels are square and not curved.

1912–25. Wmk Mult Crown CA. Chalk-surfaced paper (30c. to 100r.). P 14.

(a) Printed from single plates. Value tablet as A

No.	Type	Description	Unused	Used
301	**52**	1c. brown (1919)	1·00	10
		w. Wmk inverted	25·00	
302		3c. blue-green (1919)	5·50	45
		w. Wmk inverted	21·00	45·00
		y. Wmk inverted and reversed	28·00	65·00
303		5c. purple	12·00	2·75
		a. Wmk sideways (Crown to right of CA)	£500	
		x. Wmk reversed	†	£300
		y. Wmk inverted and reversed	£140	
304		5c. bright magenta	1·00	60

No.	Type	Description	Unused	Used
		w. Wmk inverted	£180	£150
305		6c. pale scarlet (1919)	14·00	85
		a. Wmk sideways (Crown to left of CA)	45·00	£100
		w. Wmk inverted	32·00	60·00
306		6c. carmine	19·00	1·25
		a. Wmk sideways (Crown to right of CA)	55·00	
		aw. Wmk sideways (Crown to left of CA)	95·00	
		w. Wmk inverted	70·00	
		y. Wmk inverted and reversed	50·00	
		(b) Printed from Key and Duty plates. Die I. 3c. and 6c. have value tablet as B		
307	52	2c. brown-orange	40	30
		a. Deep orange-brown	30	20
308		3c. yellow-green	6·50	2·25
		a. Deep green (1917)	4·50	1·10
309		6c. scarlet (*shades*)	1·10	50
		a. Wmk sideways	†	—
310		10c. sage-green	3·00	1·75
		a. Deep sage-green (1917)	7·00	2·50
		w. Wmk inverted	£200	
311		15c. deep bright blue	3·25	1·25
		a. Ultramarine (1918)	1·75	1·25
		aw. Wmk inverted	25·00	
312		25c. orange and blue	8·00	4·50
		a. Yellow and blue (1917)	1·75	1·75
		aw. Wmk inverted	£200	£200
313		30c. blue-green and violet	4·00	3·25
		a. Yellow-green and violet (1915)	7·00	4·00
		ab. Wmk sideways (Crown to right of CA)	35·00	
		abw. Wmk Crown to left of CA	35·00	
		aw. Wmk inverted	55·00	
		awa. Ditto. Duty plate ('CEYLON' and '30c') printed double, one albino and inverted	£375	
314		50c. black and scarlet	1·75	1·75
		w. Wmk inverted	21·00	45·00
315		1r. purple/*yellow*	6·00	4·50
		a. White back (1913)	6·00	5·00
		as. Optd 'SPECIMEN'	55·00	
		b. On lemon (1915)	4·25	8·00
		bs. Optd 'SPECIMEN'	45·00	
		c. On orange-buff (1918)	28·00	35·00
		cw. Wmk inverted	80·00	
		d. On pale yellow (1922)	6·50	11·00
		ds. Optd 'SPECIMEN'	45·00	
316		2r. black and red/*yellow*	4·50	16·00
		a. White back (1913)	2·75	16·00
		as. Optd 'SPECIMEN'	50·00	
		b. On lemon (1915)	28·00	30·00
		bs. Optd 'SPECIMEN'	45·00	
		c. On orange-buff (1919)	45·00	48·00
		cw. Wmk inverted	65·00	
		d. On pale yellow (1921)	45·00	45·00
317		5r. black/*green*	20·00	48·00
		a. White back (1914)	25·00	42·00
		as. Optd 'SPECIMEN'	48·00	
		b. On blue-green (olive back) (1917)	26·00	48·00
		bs. Optd 'SPECIMEN'	£110	
		bw. Wmk inverted	£100	£150
		c. Die II. *On emerald back* (1923)	48·00	£120
		cs. Optd 'SPECIMEN'	65·00	
318		10r. purple and black/*red*	70·00	90·00
		aw. Wmk inverted	£300	
		b. Die II (1923)	90·00	£180
		bw. Wmk inverted	£750	
319		20r. black and red/*blue*	£150	£160
320	53	50r. dull purple (f.c. £60)	£650	£1400
		a. Break in scroll	£1800	
		b. Broken crown and scroll	£1800	
		f. Damaged leaf at bottom right	£1800	
		s. Optd 'SPECIMEN'	£225	
321		100r. grey-black (f.c. £120)	£3250	
		a. Break in scroll	£6000	
		b. Broken crown and scroll	£6000	
		f. Damaged leaf at bottom right	£6000	
		s. Optd 'SPECIMEN'	£425	
		w. Wmk inverted	£7000	
322		500r. dull green (f.c. £350)	£8500	
		a. Break in scroll	£17000	
		b. Broken crown and scroll	£17000	
		f. Damaged leaf at bottom right		
		s. Optd 'SPECIMEN'	£750	
323		1000r. purple/*red* (1925) (f.c. £3000)	£35000	
		b. Broken crown and scroll	£48000	
		e. Break in lines below left scroll		
		f. Damaged leaf at bottom right		
		s. Optd 'SPECIMEN'	£1600	
301/318 *Set of 14*			£100	£140
301s/319s Optd 'SPECIMEN' *Set of 15*			£425	

For illustrations of the varieties on Nos. 320/323 see above No. 51*b* of Bermuda.

The 2c. and 5c. exist in coils, constructed from normal sheets, used in stamp-affixing machines introduced in 1915.

Sideways watermark varieties are described *as seen from the back of the stamp.*

The 'substituted crown' watermark variety is known on the sheet margin of the 1c., No. 301.

An example of the 1000r. optd 'SPECIMEN' is known with the break in scroll variety (R. 1/12).

WAR STAMP
(54)

WAR STAMP ONE CENT
(55)

1918 (18 Nov)–**19**.

(a) Optd with T **54** *by Govt Printer, Colombo*

No.	Type	Description	Unused	Used
330	52	2c. brown-orange	20	40
		a. Opt inverted	70·00	80·00
		b. Opt double	32·00	45·00
331		3c. blue-green (No. 302) (1919)	3·75	40
		a. Opt double	£140	
332		3c. deep green (No. 308*a*)	20	50
		a. Opt double	£100	£120
		w. Wmk inverted	†	£200
333		5c. purple	50	30
		a. Opt double	70·00	80·00
		w. Wmk inverted	£120	
334		5c. bright magenta	4·50	3·25
		a. Opt inverted	70·00	80·00
		b. Opt double	50·00	60·00
		(b) Surch with T **55**		
335	52	1c. on 5c. purple	50	40
		w. Wmk inverted	£160	
		y. Wmk inverted and reversed	£120	
336		1c. on 5c. bright magenta	3·25	20
330s, 332s/333s, 335s Optd 'SPECIMEN' *Set of 4*			£130	

Collectors are warned against forgeries of the errors in the 'WAR STAMP' overprints.

1918. Surch as T **55**, but without 'WAR STAMP'.

No.	Type	Description	Unused	Used
337	52	1c. on 5c. purple	15	25
		a. Surch double	£200	
		bs. Optd 'SPECIMEN'	42·00	
		by. Wmk inverted and reversed	£160	
337*c*		1c. on 5c. bright magenta	3·25	4·25

1921–32. Wmk Mult Script CA. Chalk-surfaced paper (30c. to 100r.). P 14.

(a) Printed from single plates. Value tablet as A

No.	Type	Description	Unused	Used
338	52	1c. brown (1927)	1·00	35
339		3c. green (5.5.22)	5·50	75
		w. Wmk inverted	20·00	50·00
340		3c. slate-grey (1923)	75	20
		a. Wmk sideways	£1700	
		w. Wmk inverted	48·00	
341		5c. purple (1927)	60	15
342		6c. carmine-red (3.8.21)	4·00	75
		w. Wmk inverted	22·00	50·00
		y. Wmk inverted and reversed	75·00	
343		6c. bright violet (1922)	2·75	15
		w. Wmk inverted	50·00	
		y. Wmk inverted and reversed	75·00	
		(b) Printed from Key and Duty plates		
344	52	2c. brown-orange (Die II) (1927)	70	25
345		9c. red/*pale yellow* (Die II) (1926)	3·00	30
346		10c. sage-green (Die I) (16.9.21)	1·40	40
		aw. Wmk inverted	50·00	
		ay. Wmk inverted and reversed	45·00	70·00
		b. Die II (1924)	2·00	60
		c. Vert gutter pair. Die I and Die II. Nos. 346 and 346b	£375	
347		12c. rose-scarlet (Die I) (1925)	10·00	5·50
		a. Die II	1·25	2·25
		as. Optd 'SPECIMEN'	£110	
		b. Vert gutter pair. Die I and Die II. Nos. 347 and 347a	£160	
348		15c. ultramarine (Die I) (30.5.22)	3·75	22·00
349		15c. green/*pale yellow* (Die I) (1923)	5·50	1·25
		a. Die II (1924)	4·75	1·00
		aw. Wmk inverted	50·00	
		b. Vert gutter pair. Die I and Die II. Nos. 349 and 349a	£325	
350		20c. bright blue (Die I) (1922)	6·00	6·00
		aw. Wmk inverted	70·00	
		b. Die II (1924)	3·50	45
		c. Vert gutter pair. Die I and Die II. Nos. 350 and 350b	£375	
351		25c. orange-yellow and blue (Die I) (17.10.21)	3·00	1·90
		aw. Wmk inverted	75·00	
		b. Die II (1924)	5·50	1·25
		c. Vert gutter pair. Die I and Die II. Nos. 351 and 351b	£200	
352		30c. yellow-green and violet (Die I) (15.3.22)	1·60	6·50
		a. Die II (1924)	6·00	1·25
		b. Vert gutter pair. Die I and Die II. Nos. 352 and 352a	£750	
353		50c. black and scarlet (Die II) (1922)	2·00	80
		a. Die I (1932)	60·00	95·00
354		1r. purple/*pale yellow* (Die I) (1923)	15·00	50·00
		a. Die II (1925)	25·00	45·00
		b. Vert gutter pair. Die I and Die II. Nos. 354 and 354a	£400	
355		2r. black and red/*pale yellow* (Die II) (1923)	7·00	14·00
356		5r. black/*emerald* (Die II) (1924)	50·00	95·00
357		20r. black and red/*blue* (Die II) (1924).	£325	£400
358	53	50r. dull purple (1924) (f.c. £70)	£800	£1400
		a. Break in scroll	£1500	
		b. Broken crown and scroll	£1500	
		e. Break in lines below left scroll	£1500	
		f. Damaged leaf at bottom right	£1500	
		g. Gash in fruit and leaf	£1500	
		s. Optd 'SPECIMEN'	£200	
359		100r. brownish grey (1924) (f.c. £140).	£3250	
		a. Break in scroll	£5500	
		b. Broken crown and scroll	£5500	
		c. Nick in top right scroll	£5500	
		e. Break in lines below left scroll	£5500	
		f. Damaged leaf at bottom right	£5500	
		h. Grey-black	£3250	
		ha. Break in scroll	£5500	
		hb. Broken crown and scroll	£5500	
		he. Break in lines below left scroll	£5500	
		hf. Damaged leaf at bottom right	£5500	
		s. Optd 'SPECIMEN'	£475	
360		100r. dull purple and blue (24.10.27) (f.c. £180)	£2750	
		a. Break in scroll	£4750	
		b. Broken crown and scroll	£4750	
		e. Break in lines below left scroll	£4750	
		f. Damaged leaf at bottom right	£4750	
		g. Gash in fruit and leaf	£4750	
		s. Optd 'SPECIMEN'	£550	
338/356 *Set of 19*			£100	£170
338s/357s Optd 'SPECIMEN' *Set of 20*			£650	

The 2c. to 30c. and 1r. values produced from Key and Duty plates were printed in sheets of 240 using two plates one above the other. Nos. 346c, 347b, 349b, 350c, 351c, 352b and 354b come from printings in 1924 and 1925 which combined Key Plate 7 (Die I) with Key Plate 12 (Die II).

No. 353a, from Key Plate 23, was a mistake; the 'retired' Die I being issued in error when it became necessary to replace Key Plate 21.

For illustrations of the varieties on Nos. 358/360 see above No. 51*b* of Bermuda.

2 Cents.
(56)

57

(Surch at Ceylon Govt Printing Works)

1926 (27 Nov). Surch as T **56**.

No.	Type	Description	Unused	Used
361	52	2c. on 3c. slate-grey	3·50	1·00
		a. Surch double	70·00	
		b. Bar omitted	80·00	90·00
362		5c. on 6c. bright violet	1·00	40
361s/362s Optd 'SPECIMEN' *Set of 2*			80·00	

No. 361b comes from the bottom horizontal row of the sheet which was often partially obscured by the selvedge during surcharging.

1927 (27 Nov)–**29**. Wmk Mult Script CA. Chalk-surfaced paper. P 14.

No.	Type	Description	Unused	Used
363	57	1r. dull and bright purple (1928)	2·50	1·25
364		2r. green and carmine (1929)	3·75	2·75
365		5r. green and dull purple (1928)	17·00	32·00
366		10r. green and brown-orange	70·00	£180
367		20r. dull purple and blue	£300	£475
363/367 *Set of 5*			£350	£600
363s/367s Optd 'SPECIMEN' *Set of 5*			£275	

No. 364. Collectors are warned against faked 2r. stamps, showing what purports to be a double centre.

58 Tapping Rubber

59 Adam's Peak

60 Colombo Harbour

61 Plucking tea

62 Hill paddy (rice)

63 River scene

64 Coconut Palms

65 Temple of the Tooth, Kandy

66 Ancient irrigation tank

67 Wild elephants

68 Trincomalee

(Recess D.L.R. (2, 3, 20, 50c.), B.W. (others))

1935 (1 May)–**36**. T **58/68**. Wmk Mult Script CA (sideways on 10, 15, 25, 30c. and 1r.). Various perfs.

No.	Type	Description	Unused	Used
368	58	2c. black and carmine (P 12×13)	30	40
		a. Perf 14	9·00	40
369	59	3c. black and olive-green (P 13×12) (1.10.35)	1·25	40
		a. Perf 14	40·00	35
370	60	6c. black and blue (P 11×11½) (1.1.36)	30	30
371	61	9c. green and orange (P 11×11½) (1.1.36)	1·50	65
372	62	10c. black and purple (P 11½×11) (1.6.35)	1·25	3·00
373	63	15c. red-brown and green (P 11½×11)	2·25	50
374	64	20c. black and grey-blue (P 12×13) (1.1.36)	2·75	3·50

375	**65**	25c. deep blue and chocolate (P 11½×11)	2·00	1·75
376	**66**	30c. carmine and green (P 11½×11) (1.8.35)	2·75	3·50
377	**67**	50c. black and mauve (P 14) (1.1.36)	17·00	1·75
378	**68**	1r. violet-blue and chocolate (P 11½×11) (1.7.35)	40·00	32·00
368/378 *Set of* 11			60·00	42·00
368s/378s Perf 'SPECIMEN' *Set of* 11			£350	

1935 (6 May). Silver Jubilee. As Nos. 91/94 of Antigua. P 13½×14.

379		6c. ultramarine and grey	75	30
		f. Diagonal line by turret	80·00	32·00
		g. Dot to left of chapel	£130	50·00
		h. Dot by flagstaff	£110	50·00
		i. Dash by turret	£180	90·00
380		9c. green and indigo	75	2·75
		f. Diagonal line by turret	95·00	£130
		g. Dot to left of chapel	£200	£225
		h. Dot by flagstaff	£170	£200
381		20c. brown and deep blue	4·25	2·75
		f. Diagonal line by turret	£200	£130
		g. Dot to left of chapel	£350	£200
382		50c. slate and purple	5·25	16·00
		f. Diagonal line by turret	£400	£450
		h. Dot by flagstaff	£400	£450
379/382 *Set of* 4			10·00	20·00
379s/382s Perf 'SPECIMEN' *Set of* 4			£140	

For illustrations of plate varieties, see Omnibus section following Zanzibar.

1937 (12 May). Coronation. As Nos. 95/97 of Antigua. P 11×11½.

383		6c. carmine	65	1·00
384		9c. green	2·50	4·50
385		20c. blue	3·50	4·00
383/385 *Set of* 3			6·00	8·50
383s/385s Perf 'SPECIMEN' *Set of* 3			£120	

69 Tapping Rubber

70 Sigiriya (Lion Rock)

70b Plucking Tea

71 Ancient Guard-stone, Anuradhapura

72 King George VI

Comma flaw (Pl 2A R. 5/6)

5c. Apostrophe flaw (Frame Pl 1A R. 6/6) (ptg of 1 Jan 1943 only)

(Recess B.W. (6, 10, 15, 20, 25, 30c., 1r., 2r. (both)), D.L.R (others) T **72** typo D.L.R.)

1938–49. T **69/72** and designs as 1935–1936, but with portrait of King George VI instead of King George V, 'POSTAGE & REVENUE' omitted and some redrawn. Wmk Mult Script CA (sideways on 10, 15, 25, 30c. and 1r.). Chalk-surfaced paper (5r.). P 11×11½ (6, 20c., 2r. (both)), 11½×11 (10, 15, 25, 30c., 1r.), 11½×13 (2c.), 13×11½ (3, 50c.), 13½ (5c.) or 14 (5r.).

386	**69**	2c. black and carmine (25.4.38)	26·00	4·00
		aa. Comma flaw	£600	£170
		a. Perf 13½×13 (1938)	£120	1·75
		ab. Comma flaw	£1600	£140
		b. Perf 13½ (25.4.38)	4·00	10
		ba. Comma flaw	£180	80·00
		c. Perf 11×11½ (17.2.44)	1·75	2·00
		cw. Wmk inverted	—	£1600
		d. Perf 12 (22.4.49)	2·75	6·00

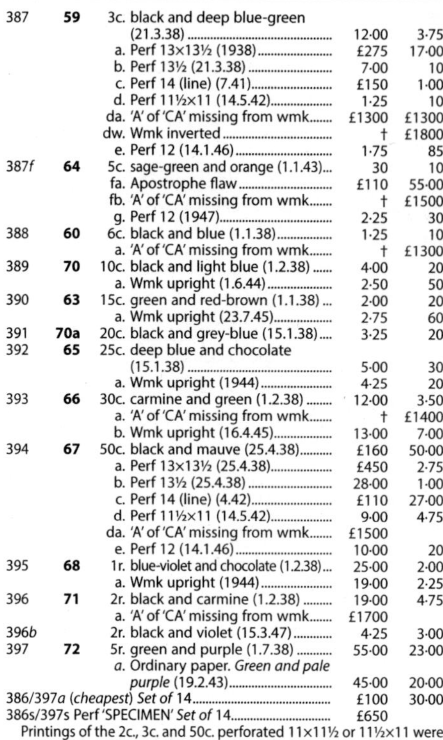

387	**59**	3c. black and deep blue-green (21.3.38)	12·00	3·75
		a. Perf 13×13½ (1938)	£275	17·00
		b. Perf 13½ (21.3.38)	7·00	10
		c. Perf 14 (line) (7.41)	£150	1·00
		d. Perf 11½×11 (14.5.42)	1·25	10
		da. 'A' of 'CA' missing from wmk	£1300	£1300
		dw. Wmk inverted	†	£1800
		e. Perf 12 (14.1.46)	1·75	85
387*f*	**64**	5c. sage-green and orange (1.1.43)	30	10
		fa. Apostrophe flaw	£110	55·00
		fb. 'A' of 'CA' missing from wmk	†	£1500
		g. Perf 12 (1947)	2·25	30
388	**60**	6c. black and blue (1.1.38)	1·25	10
		a. 'A' of 'CA' missing from wmk	†	£1300
389	**70**	10c. black and light blue (1.2.38)	4·00	20
		a. Wmk upright (1.6.44)	2·50	50
390	**63**	15c. green and red-brown (1.1.38)	2·00	20
		a. Wmk upright (23.7.45)	2·75	60
391	**70a**	20c. black and grey-blue (15.1.38)	3·25	20
392	**65**	25c. deep blue and chocolate (15.1.38)	5·00	30
		a. Wmk upright (1944)	4·25	20
393	**66**	30c. carmine and green (1.2.38)	12·00	3·50
		a. 'A' of 'CA' missing from wmk	†	£1400
		b. Wmk upright (16.4.45)	13·00	7·00
394	**67**	50c. black and mauve (25.4.38)	£160	50·00
		a. Perf 13×13½ (25.4.38)	£450	2·75
		b. Perf 13½ (25.4.38)	28·00	1·00
		c. Perf 14 (line) (4.42)	£110	27·00
		d. Perf 11½×11 (14.5.42)	9·00	4·75
		da. 'A' of 'CA' missing from wmk	£1500	
		e. Perf 12 (14.1.46)	10·00	20
395	**68**	1r. blue-violet and chocolate (1.2.38)	25·00	2·00
		a. Wmk upright (1944)	19·00	2·25
396	**71**	2r. black and carmine (1.2.38)	19·00	4·75
		a. 'A' of 'CA' missing from wmk	£1700	
396*b*		2r. black and violet (15.3.47)	4·25	3·00
397	**72**	5r. green and purple (1.7.38)	55·00	23·00
		a. Ordinary paper. *Green and pale purple* (19.2.43)	45·00	20·00
386/397*a* (*cheapest*) *Set of* 14			£100	30·00
386s/397s Perf 'SPECIMEN' *Set of* 14			£650	

Printings of the 2c., 3c. and 50c. perforated 11×11½ or 11½×11 were produced by Bradbury Wilkinson after the De La Rue works had been bombed in December 1940.

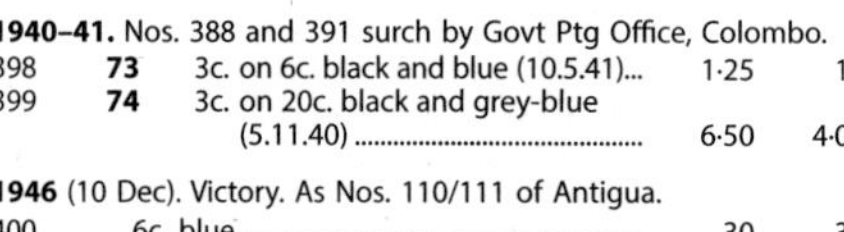

(**73**) (**74**)

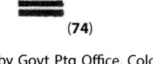

1940–41. Nos. 388 and 391 surch by Govt Ptg Office, Colombo.

398	**73**	3c. on 6c. black and blue (10.5.41)	1·25	10
399	**74**	3c. on 20c. black and grey-blue (5.11.40)	6·50	4·00

1946 (10 Dec). Victory. As Nos. 110/111 of Antigua.

400		6c. blue	30	35
401		15c. brown	30	1·75
400s/401s Perf 'SPECIMEN' *Set of* 2			£110	

75 Parliament Building

76 Adam's Peak

77 Temple of the Tooth

78 Anuradhapura

(Des R. Tenison and M. S. V. Rodrigo. Recess B.W.)

1947 (25 Nov). Inauguration of New Constitution. T **75/78**. Wmk Mult Script CA. P 11×12 (horiz) or 12×11 (vert).

402	**75**	6c. black and blue	40	15
403	**76**	10c. black, orange and carmine	35	40
404	**77**	15c. green and purple	35	80
405	**78**	25c. ochre and emerald-green	35	1·75
402/405 *Set of* 4			1·25	2·75
402s/405s Perf 'SPECIMEN' *Set of* 4			£130	

DOMINION

79 Lion Flag of Dominion

80 D. S. Senanayake

81 Lotus Flowers and Sinhalese Letters 'Sri'

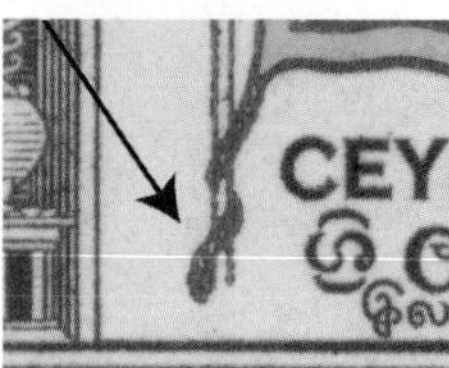
4c. Normal

4c. 'Short rope' (Pl 1 R. 10/9)

(Recess (flag typo) B.W.)

1949 (4 Feb–5 Apr). First Anniversary of Independence.

(a) Wmk Mult Script CA (sideways on 4c.). P 12½×12 (4c.) or 12×12½ (5c.)

406	**79**	4c. yellow, carmine and brown	20	20
		a. 'Short rope'	30·00	25·00
407	**80**	5c. brown and green	10	10

*(b) W **81** (sideways on 15c.). P 13×12½ (15c.) or 12×12½ (25c.) (5 Apr)*

408	**79**	15c. yellow, carmine and vermilion	1·00	1·50
409	**80**	25c. brown and blue	15	1·00
406/409 *Set of* 4			1·25	2·50

The 15c. is larger, measuring 28×12 mm.

82 Globe and Forms of Transport

83

84

(Recess D.L.R.)

1949 (10 Oct). 75th Anniversary of Universal Postal Union. W **81**. P 13 (25c.) or 12 (others).

410	**82**	5c. brown and bluish green	75	10
411	**83**	15c. black and carmine	1·10	3·00
412	**84**	25c. black and ultramarine	1·10	75
410/412 *Set of* 3			2·75	3·50

85 Kandyan Dancer

86 Kiri Vehera Polonnaruwa

87 Vesak Orchid

88 Sigiriya (Lion Rock)

89 Octagon Library, Temple of the Tooth

90 Ruins at Madirigiriya

(Recess B.W.)

1950 (4 Feb). T **85/90**. W **81**. P 11×11½ (75c.), 11½×11 (1r.), 12×12½ (others).

413	**85**	4c. purple and scarlet	15	10
414	**86**	5c. green	15	10
415	**87**	15c. blue-green and violet	3·00	50
416	**88**	30c. carmine and yellow	30	70
417	**89**	75c. ultramarine and orange	9·50	20
418	**90**	1r. deep blue and brown	1·75	30
413/418 *Set of 6*			13·50	1·50

These stamps were issued with redrawn inscriptions in 1958/1959. See Nos. 448/465.

91 Sambars, Ruhuna National Park

92 Ancient Guard-stone, Anuradhapura

93 Harvesting rice

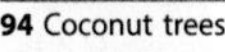

94 Coconut trees

95 Sigiriya fresco

96 Star Orchid

97 Rubber Plantation

98 Outrigger canoe

99 Tea Plantation

100 River Gal Dam

101 Bas-relief, Anuradhapura

102 Harvesting rice

35c. I. No. 424

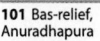

35c. II. No. 424a (Dot added)

(Photo Courvoisier)

1951 (1 Aug)–**54**. T **91/102**. No wmk. P 11½.

419	**91**	2c. brown and blue-green (15.5.54)	10	1·25
420	**92**	3c. black and slate-violet (15.5.54)	10	1·00
421	**93**	6c. brown-black and yellow-green (15.5.54)	15	30
422	**94**	10c. green and blue-grey	1·00	65
423	**95**	25c. orange-brown and bright blue (15.3.54)	20	20
424	**96**	35c. red and deep green (I) (1.2.52)	1·50	1·50
		a. Type II (1954)	7·00	60
425	**97**	40c. deep brown (15.5.54)	5·00	1·00
426	**98**	50c. indigo and slate-grey (15.3.54)	30	10
427	**99**	85c. black and deep blue-green (15.5.54)	3·50	30
428	**100**	2r. blue and deep brown (15.5.54)	12·00	1·50
429	**101**	5r. brown and orange (15.3.54)	18·00	1·75
430	**102**	10r. red-brown and buff (15.3.54)	60·00	27·00
419/430 *Set of 12*			85·00	32·00

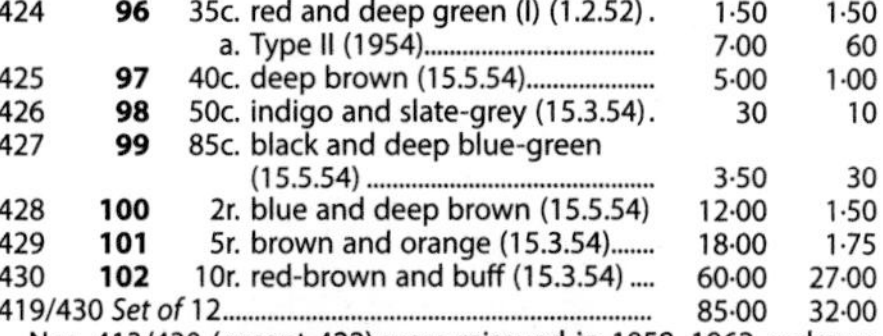

Nos. 413/430 (except 422) were reissued in 1958–1962, redrawn with 'CEYLON' much smaller and other inscriptions in Sinhalese. See Nos. 448/465.

103 Ceylon Mace and symbols of Progress

(Photo Harrison)

1952 (23 Feb). Colombo Plan Exhibition. Chalk-surfaced paper. W **81** (sideways). P 14½×14.

431	**103**	5c. green	30	10
432		15c. ultramarine	30	60

104 Queen Elizabeth II

105 Ceremonial Procession

(Recess B.W.)

1953 (2 June). Coronation. W **81**. P 12×13.

433	**104**	5c. green	1·75	10

(Recess D.L.R.)

1954 (10 Apr). Royal Visit. W **81** (sideways). P 13×12½.

434	**105**	10c. deep blue	1·50	10

106 King Coconuts

107 Farm Produce

(Photo Courvoisier)

1954 (1 Dec). No wmk. P 11½.

435	**106**	10c. orange, bistre-brown and buff	70	10

For this design with redrawn inscription see No. 453.

(Photo Harrison)

1955 (10 Dec). Royal Agricultural and Food Exhibition. W **81** (sideways). P 14×14½.

436	**107**	10c. brown and orange	10	10

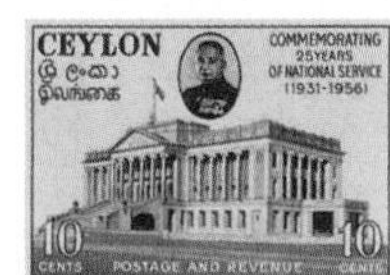

108 Sir John Kotelawala and House of Representatives

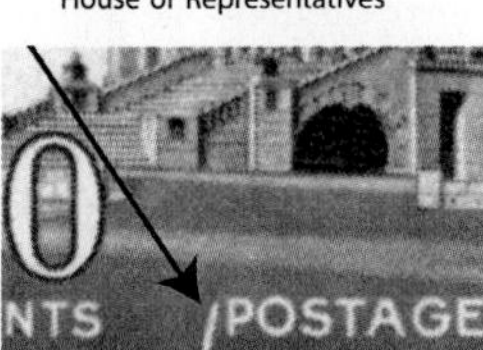

White stroke to left of 'POSTAGE' (R. 2/6)

(Photo Courvoisier)

1956 (26 Mar). Prime Minister's 25 Years of Public Service. P 11½.

437	**108**	10c. deep bluish green	10	10
		a. White stroke	1·50	

109 Arrival of Vijaya in Ceylon

110 Lampstand and Dharmachakra

111 Hand of Peace and Dharmachakra

112 Dharmachakra encircling the Globe

(Photo Courvoisier)

1956. Buddha Jayanti. P 11½.

438	**109**	3c. blue and brownish grey (23.5)	1·00	15
439	**110**	4c. +2c. greenish yellow and deep blue (10.5)	20	75
440	**111**	10c. +5c. carmine, yellow and grey (10.5)	20	1·00
441	**112**	15c. bright blue (23.5)	25	10
438/441 *Set of 4*			1·50	1·75

113 Mail Transport

114 Stamp of 1857

(Photo Enschedé (4c., 10c.), Courvoisier (others))

1957 (1 Apr). Centenary of First Ceylon Postage Stamp. P 12½×13 (4c., 10c.) or 11½ (others).

442	**113**	4c. orange-red and deep bluish green	60	50
443		10c. vermilion and blue	60	10
444	**114**	35c. brown, yellow and blue	30	35
445		85c. brown, yellow and grey-green	60	1·25
442/445 *Set of 4*			1·90	2·00

(115) **(116)**

117 Kandyan Dancer

1958 (15 Jan). Nos. 439/440 with premium obliterated as T **115** (4c.) or T **116** (10c.).

446	**110**	4c. greenish yellow and deep blue	10	10
		a. Opt inverted	20·00	38·00
		b. Opt double	35·00	50·00
447	**111**	10c. carmine, yellow and grey	10	10
		a. Opt inverted	14·00	19·00
		b. Narrower square (R. 2/3 and R. 10/1)	1·25	

The 4c. exists with opt misplaced to right so that some stamps show the vertical bar on the left (*Price £20 un.*).

On No. 447b the obliterating square is 3 mm. wide instead of 4 mm.

(Recess B.W. (4c., 5c., 15c., 30c., 75c., 1r.). Photo Courvoisier (others))

1958 (14 May)–**62**. As earlier types, but inscriptions redrawn as in T **117**. W **81** (4, 5, 15, 30, 75c., 1r.) or no wmk (others). P 11×11½ (75c.), 11½×11 (1r.), 12×12½ (4, 5, 15, 30c.), or 11½ (others).

448	**91**	2c. brown and blue-green	10	50
449	**92**	3c. black and slate-violet	10	70
450	**117**	4c. purple and scarlet	10	10
451	**86**	5c. green (1.10.58)	10	1·60
		a. Yellow-green (13.6.61)	1·00	2·50
		b. Deep green (19.6.62)	9·00	4·00
452	**93**	6c. brown-black and yellow-green	50	1·00
453	**106**	10c. orange, bistre-brown and buff (1.10.58)	10	10
454	**87**	15c. blue-green and violet (1.10.58)	3·00	1·00
455	**95**	25c. orange-brown and bright blue	25	10
456	**88**	30c. carmine and yellow (1.5.59)	25	1·40
457	**96**	35c. red and deep green (II) (15.7.58)	2·00	30
459	**98**	50c. indigo and slate-grey (15.7.58)	30	10
460	**89**	75c. ultramarine and orange (1.5.59)	9·00	5·50
		a. Ultramarine and brown-orange (3.4.62)	12·00	4·00
461	**99**	85c. black and deep blue-green (1.5.59)	3·75	13·00
462	**90**	1r. deep blue and brown (1.10.58)	60	10
463	**100**	2r. blue and deep brown	8·50	30
464	**101**	5r. brown and orange	19·00	30
465	**102**	10r. red-brown and buff	19·00	1·00
448/465 *Set of 17*			60·00	22·00

118 'Human Rights'

119 Portraits of Founders and University Buildings

(Photo Enschedé)

1958 (10 Dec). Tenth Anniversary of Declaration of Human Rights. P 13×12½.
466 **118** 10c. vermilion and dull purple 10 10
467 85c. vermilion and deep blue-green 30 1·25

(Photo Enschedé)

1959 (31 Dec). Institution of Pirivena Universities. P 13×12½.
468 **119** 10c. red-orange and ultramarine 10 10

120 Uprooted Tree

121 S. W. R. D. Bandaranaike

(Des W. A. Ariyasena. Photo Courvoisier)

1960 (7 Apr). World Refugee Year. P 11½.
469 **120** 4c. red-brown and gold 10 85
470 25c. blackish violet and gold 10 15

(Photo Courvoisier)

1961 (8 Jan). Prime Minister Bandaranaike Commemoration. P 11½.
471 **121** 10c. deep blue and greenish blue 10 10
a. Portrait redrawn (15.6.61)* 10 10

* Earliest known postmark date.

No. 471a can be identified by Mr. Bandaranaike's dark hair at temples.

122 Ceylon Scout Badge

123 Campaign Emblem

(Des W. A. Ariyasena. Photo Courvoisier)

1962 (26 Feb). Golden Jubilee of Ceylon Boy Scouts Association. P 11½.
472 **122** 35c. buff and blue 15 10

(Photo Harrison)

1962 (7 Apr). Malaria Eradication. W **81**. P 14½×14.
473 **123** 25c. red-orange and sepia 10 10

124 de Havilland DH.85 Leopard Moth and Hawker Siddeley Comet 4

125 'Produce' and Campaign Emblem

(Photo Courvoisier)

1963 (28 Feb). 25th Anniversary of Airmail. P 11½.
474 **124** 50c. black and light blue 50 50

(Photo Courvoisier)

1963 (21 Mar). Freedom from Hunger. P 11½.
475 **125** 5c. vermilion and blue .... 1·50 2·00
476 25c. brown and yellow-olive .... 3·50 30

ශත
2
சதம்

(126)

127 'Rural Life'

1963 (1 June). No. 450 surch with T **126**.
477 **117** 2c. on 4c. purple and scarlet 10 10
a. Surch inverted .... 17·00
b. Surch double.................................. 50·00
c. Surch omitted (in pair with normal) £300

(Photo Harrison)

1963 (5 July). Golden Jubilee of Ceylon Co-operative Movement (1962). W **81**. P 14×14½.
478 **127** 60c. rose-red and black .... 1·50 50

128 S. W. R. D. Bandaranaike

129 Terrain, Elephant and Tree

(Recess Courvoisier)

1963 (26 Sept). P 11½.
479 **128** 10c. light blue 10 10

(Photo Harrison)

1963 (9 Dec). National Conservation Week. W **81** (sideways). P 14×14½.
480 **129** 5c. sepia and blue 60 40

130 S. W. R. D. Bandaranaike

131 Anagarika Dharmapala (Buddhist missionary)

(Photo Courvoisier)

1964 (1 July). P 11½
481 **130** 10c. deep violet-blue and greenish grey 10 10

(Photo Courvoisier)

1964 (16 Sept). Birth Centenary of Anagarika Dharmapala (founder of Maha Bodhi Society). P 11½.
482 **131** 25c. sepia and olive-yellow 10 10

134 Southern Grackle

135 D. S. Senanayake

136

137 Common Peafowl

138 Ruins at Madirigiriya

139 Ceylon Junglefowl

140 Asian Black-headed Oriole

146 Tea Plantation

147 Girls transplanting rice

149 Map of Ceylon

(Des A. Dharmasiri (5r.); P. A. Miththapala (10r.). Photo Courvoisier (10c. (486), 20c.), Harrison (10c. (487), 60c., 1r., 5r., 10r.), D.L.R. (others incl sheet))

1964 (1 Oct)–**72**. T **134/140**, **146**, **149** and similar designs. No wmk (Nos. 486, 489). W **81** (others; sideways on Nos. 487, 494 499). P 11½ (Nos. 486, 489), 14½×14 (No. 494) or 14 (others).
485 **134** 5c. multicoloured (5.2.66) .... 2·00 1·00
486 **135** 10c. myrtle-green (22.3.66) 80 10
487 **136** 10c. myrtle-green (23.9.68) 10 10
a. Imperf (pair) .... 48·00
b. Horiz pair, one stamp imperf 3 sides £150
488 **137** 15c. multicoloured (5.2.66) .... 4·50 30
489 **138** 20c. brown-purple and buff 30 25
494 **139** 60c. multicoloured (5.2.66) .... 5·50 1·25
a. Red omitted .... 55·00
b. Blue and green omitted* .... 45·00
495 **140** 75c. multicoloured (5.2.66) .... 3·00 70
a. No wmk (8.6.72) .... 12·00 16·00
497 **146** 1r. brown and bluish green .... 1·75 30
a. Brown (tea picker, etc) omitted £1500
b. Bluish green omitted £1600
499 **147** 5r. multicoloured (15.8.69) .... 12·00 11·00
500 **149** 10r. multicoloured (1.10.69) .... 29·00 3·00
485/500 *Set of* 10 .... 50·00 16·00
MS500*a* 148×174 mm. As Nos. 485, 488, 494 and 495. Imperf .... 8·00 14·00

* Actually only the blue printing is omitted on this sheet, but where this was printed over the yellow to form the leaves it appeared as green.

The 5c., 75c. and 1r. exist with PVA gum as well as gum arabic.

No. 487b comes from a sheet which showed stamps in the third vertical row imperforate at top, bottom and at right.

In the miniature sheet the inscriptions on the 60c. have been rearranged to conform with the style of the other values.

150 Exhibition Buildings and Cogwheels

151 Trains of 1864 and 1964

(Photo State Printing Works, Budapest)

1964 (1 Dec). Industrial Exhibition. T **150** and similar horiz design. No wmk. P 11.
501 **150** 5c. multicoloured 10 75
a. Pair. Nos. 501/502.......................... 35 2·50
502 5c. multicoloured 10 75

No. 501 is inscribed 'INDUSTRIAL EXHIBITION' in Sinhala and Tamil, No. 502 in Sinhala and English. The stamps were issued together *se-tenant* in alternate vertical rows, producing horizontal pairs.

(Photo Harrison)

1964 (21 Dec). Centenary of Ceylon Railways. T **151** and similar horiz design. W **81** (sideways). P 14×14½.
503 **151** 60c. blue, reddish purple and yellow-green .... 2·75 40
a. Vert pair. Nos. 503/504 .... 5·50 5·50
504 60c. blue, reddish purple and yellow-green .... 2·75 40

No. 503 is inscribed 'RAILWAY CENTENARY' in Sinhala and Tamil, No. 504 in Sinhala and English. The stamps were issued together *se-tenant* in alternate horizontal rows, producing vertical pairs.

152 ITU Emblem and Symbols

153 ICY Emblem

(Photo Harrison)

1965 (17 May). ITU Centenary. W **81** (sideways). P 14½.
505 **152** 2c. bright blue and red .... 1·00 1·10
506 30c. brown and red .... 3·25 45
a. Value omitted £190

No. 506a was caused by the misplacement of the red.

(Photo Courvoisier)

1965 (26 June). International Co-operation Year. T **153** and similar horiz design. P 11½.
507 3c. deep blue and rose-carmine .... 1·25 1·00
508 50c. black, rose-carmine and gold .... 3·25 50

No. 508 is similar to T **153** but has the multilingual inscription 'CEYLON' rearranged.

154 Town Hall, Colombo

5

(155)

(Photo Courvoisier)

1965 (29 Oct). Centenary of Colombo Municipal Council. P 11×11½.
509 **154** 25c. myrtle-green and sepia 60 30

1965 (18 Dec). No. 481 surch with T **155**.
510 **130** 5c. on 10c. deep violet-blue and greenish grey .... 10 2·00

157 Kandy and Council Crest

158 WHO Building

(Photo Harrison)

1966 (15 June). Kandy Municipal Council Centenary. W **81**. P 14×13½.
512 **157** 25c. multicoloured 20 20

(Litho D.L.R.)

1966 (8 Oct). Inauguration of WHO Headquarters. Geneva. P 14.
513 **158** 4c. multicoloured .... 3·50 3·00
514 1r. multicoloured .... 8·50 1·50

159 Rice Paddy and Map of Ceylon

160 Rice Paddy and Globe

(Photo Courvoisier)

1966 (25 Oct). International Rice Year. P 11½.

515 **159** 6c. multicoloured 20 1·00
516 **160** 30c. multicoloured 30 15

161 UNESCO Emblem **162** Water-resources Map

(Litho State Ptg Wks, Vienna)

1966 (3 Nov). 20th Anniversary of UNESCO. P 12.

517 **161** 3c. multicoloured 2·75 3·75
518 50c. multicoloured 8·00 50

(Litho D.L.R.)

1966 (1 Dec). International Hydrological Decade. P 14.

519 **162** 2c. orange-brown, greenish yellow and blue 30 85
520 2r. orange-brown, greenish yellow, blue and yellow-green.. 2·25 2·25

163 Devotees at Buddhist Temple **167** Galle Fort and Clock Tower

(Photo State Ptg Wks, Vienna)

1967 (2 Jan). Poya Holiday System. T **163** and similar horiz designs. Multicoloured. P 12.

521 5c. Type **163** 20 60
522 20c. Mihintale 30 10
523 35c. Sacred Bo-tree, Anuradhapura 30 15
524 60c. Adam's Peak 30 10
521/524 *Set of 4* 1·00 85

(Litho Rosenbaum Brothers, Vienna)

1967 (5 Jan). Centenary of Galle Municipal Council. P 13½.

525 **167** 25c. multicoloured 70 20

168 Field Research

(Litho Rosenbaum Bros, Vienna)

1967 (1 Aug). Centenary of Ceylon Tea Industry. T **168** and similar horiz designs. Multicoloured. P 13½.

526 4c. Type **168** 50 80
527 40c. Tea-tasting equipment 1·00 1·50
528 50c. Leaves and bud 1·00 20
529 1r. Shipping tea 1·00 10
526/529 *Set of 4* 3·25 2·25

169 Elephant Ride **170** Ranger, Jubilee Emblem and Flag

(Litho Rosenbaum Bros, Vienna)

1967 (15 Aug). International Tourist Year. P 13½.

530 **169** 45c. multicoloured 2·25 80

1967 (16 Sept). First National Stamp Exhibition. No. **MS**500*a* optd 'FIRST NATIONAL STAMP EXHIBITION 1967'.

MS531 148×174 mm. Nos. 485, 488, 494/495. Imperf 4·75 6·00

(Litho D.L.R.)

1967 (19 Sept). Golden Jubilee of Ceylon Girl Guides Association. P 12½×13.

532 **170** 3c. multicoloured 50 20
533 25c. multicoloured 75 10

171 Col. Olcott and Buddhist Flag

(Litho Rosenbaum Bros, Vienna)

1967 (8 Dec). 60th Death Anniversary of Colonel H. S. Olcott (theosophist). P 13½.

534 **171** 15c. multicoloured 30 20

172 Independence Hall **173** Lion Flag and Sceptre

(Photo Harrison)

1968 (2 Feb). 20th Anniversary of Independence. W **81** (sideways). P 14.

535 **172** 5c. multicoloured 25 55
536 **173** 1r. multicoloured 50 10

174 Sir D. B. Jayatilleke **175** Institute of Hygiene

(Litho D.L.R.)

1968 (14 Feb). Birth Centenary of Sir Baron Jayatilleke (scholar and statesman). P 14.

537 **174** 25c. yellow-brown and sepia 10 10

(Litho B.W.)

1968 (7 Apr). 20th Anniversary of World Health Organisation. W **81**. P 12.

538 **175** 50c. multicoloured 10 10

176 Vickers Super VC-10 Aircraft over Terminal Building **177** Open Koran and '1400'

(Des and litho B.W.)

1968 (5 Aug). Opening of Colombo Airport. W **81**. P 13½.

539 **176** 60c. grey-blue, chestnut, red and yellow 1·00 10

(Des M. I. M. Mohideen. Photo Harrison)

1968 (14 Oct). 1400th Anniversary of the Holy Koran. W **81**. P 14.

541 **177** 25c. multicoloured 10 10

178 Human Rights Emblem **179** All Ceylon Buddhist Congress Headquarters

(Photo Pakistan Security Printing Corp)

1968 (10 Dec). Human Rights Year. P 12½×13½.

542 **178** 2c. multicoloured 10 30
543 20c. multicoloured 10 10
544 40c. multicoloured 10 10
545 2r. multicoloured 80 4·75
542/545 *Set of 4* 1·00 4·75

(Des A. Dharmasiri. Litho Rosenbaum Bros, Vienna)

1968 (19 Dec). Golden Jubilee of All Ceylon Buddhist Congress. P 13½.

546 **179** 5c. multicoloured 10 50

A 50c. value showing a footprint was prepared but its release was stopped the day before it was due for issue. However, some are known to have been released in error at rural offices and examples are known on first day cover (*Price* £38 *mint*).

180 E. W. Perera (patriot)

181 Symbols of Strength in Savings

(Photo Harrison)

1969 (17 Feb). E. W. Perera Commemoration. W **81**. P 14×13½.

547 **180** 60c. brown 10 30

(Des A. Dharmasiri. Photo Harrison)

1969 (20 Mar). Silver Jubilee of National Savings Movement. W **81**. P 14.

548 **181** 3c. multicoloured 10 30

182 Seat of Enlightenment under Sacred Bodhi Tree **183** Buduresmala (Six fold Buddha-Rays)

(Des L. T. P. Manjusree. Litho D.L.R.)

1969 (10 Apr). Vesak Day (inscr 'Wesak'). W **81** (sideways). P 15.

549 **182** 4c. multicoloured 10 50
550 **183** 6c. multicoloured 10 50
551 **182** 35c. multicoloured 10 10
549/551 *Set of 3* 25 1·00

No. 549 exists with the gold apparently omitted. Normally the gold appears (without a seperate plate number) over an underlay of olive-green on carmine. In one sheet we have seen, the gold only shows as tiny specks under a strong magnifying glass and as there may be intermediate stages of faint printing we do not list this.

184 A. E. Goonesinghe **185** ILO Emblem

(Des and photo Harrison)

1969 (29 Apr). Commemoration of Goonesinghe (founder of Labour Movement in Ceylon). W **81**. P 14.

552 **184** 15c. multicoloured 10 10

(Photo Harrison)

1969 (4 May). 50th Anniversary of International Labour Organisation. W **81** (sideways). P 14.

553 **185** 5c. black and turquoise-blue 10 10
554 25c. black and carmine-red 10 10

186 Convocation Hall, University of Ceylon **187** Uranium Atom

(Des Ahangama Edward (35c.); L. D. P. Jayawardena (50 c.); A. Dharmasiri (60c.); 4c. from photograph. Litho Rosenbaum Bros, Vienna)

1969 (1 Aug). Educational Centenary. T **186**, **187** and similar multicoloured designs. P 13½.

555 4c. Type **186** 10 80
556 35c. Lamp of Learning, Globe and flags (*horiz*) 20 10
557 50c. Type **187** 20 10
558 60c. Symbols of Scientific education 30 10
555/558 *Set of 4* 70 1·00

188 Ath Pana (Elephant Lamp)

189 Rock Fortress of Sigiriya

(Des from photographs. Litho Rosenbaum Bros, Vienna)

1969 (1 Aug). Archaeological Centenary. P 13½.

559 **188** 6c. multicoloured 25 1·50
560 **189** 1r. multicoloured 25 10

190 Leopard

191 Emblem and Symbols

(Litho Rosenbaum Bros, Vienna)

1970 (11 May). Wildlife Conservation. T **190** and similar horiz designs. Multicoloured. P 13½.

561 5c. Water Buffalo 1·00 1·25
a. Magenta omitted £160

562		15c. Slender Loris	1·75	1·25
		a. Magenta omitted	£200	
563		50c. Spotted Deer	1·10	1·25
		a. Imperf (in vert pair with stamp perf 3 sides)	£600	
564		1r. Type **190**	1·10	1·75
561/564 *Set of 4*			4·50	5·00

In No. 561a the Buffalo are predominantly green instead of brown and in No. 562a the sky is blue instead of violet and the animal is in green and yellow only.

(Des A. Dharmasiri. Litho Rosenbaum Bros, Vienna)

1970 (17 June). Asian Productivity Year. P 13½.

565	**191**	60c. multicoloured	10	10

192 New UPU HQ Building

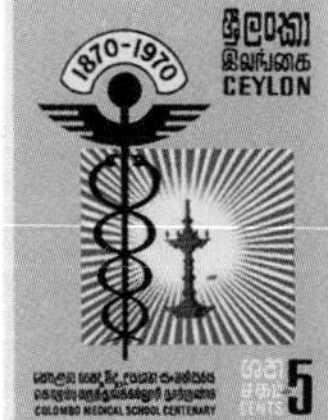

193 Oil Lamp and Caduceus

(Litho Rosenbaum Bros, Vienna)

1970 (14 Aug). New UPU Headquarters Building. P 13½.

566	**192**	50c. yellow-orange, black and new blue	50	10
		a. New blue (Building) omitted	£200	
567		1r.10 vermilion, black and new blue	4·00	40

(Des A. Dharmasiri. Litho Rosenbaum Bros, Vienna)

1970 (1 Sept). Centenary of Colombo Medical School. P 13½.

568	**193**	5c. multicoloured	1·25	80
		a. Vert pair, bottom stamp imperf	£500	
569		45c. multicoloured	1·50	60

194 Victory March and S. W. R. D. Bandaranaike

195 UN Emblem and Dove of Peace

(Des A. Dharmasiri. Litho D.L.R.)

1970 (25 Sept). Definitive issue marking establishment of United Front Government. P 13½.

570	**194**	10c. multicoloured	10	10

(Des A. Dharmasiri. Photo Pakistan Security Printing Corp)

1970 (24 Oct). 25th Anniversary of United Nations. P 12½×13½.

571	**195**	2r. multicoloured	2·00	4·25

196 Keppetipola Dissawa

197 Ola Leaf Manuscript

(Des A. Dharmasiri. Litho Harrison)

1970 (26 Nov). 152nd Death Anniversary of Keppetipola Dissawa (Kandyan patriot). P 14×14½.

572	**196**	25c. multicoloured	10	10

(Des A. Dharmasiri. Photo Pakistan Security Printing Corp)

1970 (21 Dec). International Education Year. P 13.

573	**197**	15c. multicoloured	2·75	1·25

STAMP BOOKLETS

1905 (Oct). Black on grey (No. SB1) or black on buff (No. SB1a) covers. Stapled.

SB1	1r.21, booklet containing 24×5c. (No. 280) in blocks of 12	
SB1*a*	1r.45, booklet containing 24×6c. (No. 281) in blocks of 6	£5000

1908. Black on grey cover. Advertisement on back cover. Stapled.

SB2	1r.20, booklet containing 24×5c. (No. 289) in blocks of 12	

1912. Black on grey cover. Advertisement on back cover, Stapled.

SB2*a*	1r.20, booklet containing 24×5c. (No. 304) in blocks of 12	

1919. Black on orange covers. Telegraph details on back cover. Stapled.

SB3	1r.44, booklet containing 24×6c. (No. 309) in blocks of 6	
	a. Advertisement on back cover	
	b. Black on grey cover. Advertisement on back cover	
SB4	1r.44, booklet containing 24×3c. and 12×6c. (Nos. 308/309) in blocks of 6	
	a. Advertisement on back cover	

1919 (?). Black on cream cover. Advertisement on back. Stapled.

SB4*b*	1r.45, booklet containing 24×3c. (No. 302) and 12×6c. (No. 305)	

1922. Black on green covers. 'Fiat' advertisement on back cover. Stapled.

SB5	1r.44, booklet containing 24×6c. (No. 343) in blocks of 6	
SB6	1r.46, booklet containing 24×6c. (No. 343) in blocks of 6	£3750
SB6*a*	1r.46, booklet containing 24×3c. and 12×6c. (Nos. 340/343) in blocks of 6	£4000
	b. Black on orange cover. 'Colombo Jewelry Store' advertisement on back cover	

1926. Black on green covers. Kennedy & Co. (No. SB7) or Fiat (No. SB8) advertisements on back cover. Stapled.

SB7	2r.06, booklet containing 12×3c., 12×5c. on 6c. and 12×9c. each (Nos. 340, 362 and 345) in blocks of 6	£3500
SB8	2r.16, booklet containing 24×9c. (No. 345) in blocks of 6	

1932. Black on green covers. Stapled.

SB9	1r.80, booklet containing 30×6c. (No. 343) in blocks of 6 and pane of three airmail labels	£1600
SB10	2r.70, booklet containing 30×9c. (No. 345) in blocks of 6 and pane of three airmail labels	£2000

1935 (May). Silver Jubilee of King George V. Black on light blue (No. SB11) or light green (No. SB12) covers. Stapled.

SB11	1r.80, booklet containing 30×6c. (No. 379) in blocks of 6	£1400
SB12	2r.70, booklet containing 30×9c. (No. 380) in blocks of 6	£1800

1935 (Dec)–**36.** Black on blue (No. SB13) or green (No. SB14) covers. Stapled.

SB13	1r.80, booklet containing 30×6c. (No. 370) in blocks of 6 and pane of four airmail labels	£900
	a. Stamps in blocks of 10	£900
SB14	2r.70, booklet containing 30×9c. (No. 371) in blocks of 6 and pane of four airmail labels	£1100
	a. Stamps in blocks of 10 (1936)	£1100

1937 (May). Coronation of King George VI. Black on blue (No. SB15) or olive-green (No. SB16) covers. Stapled.

SB15	1r.80, booklet containing 30×6c. (No. 383) in blocks of 10 and pane of four airmail labels	£1200
SB16	2r.70, booklet containing 30×9c. (No. 384) in blocks of 10 and pane of four airmail labels	£1300

1938. Black on blue (No. SB17) or grey (No. SB18) covers. Stapled.

SB17	1r.80, booklet containing 30×6c. (No. 388) in blocks of 10 and pane of four airmail labels	£1400
SB18	3r. booklet containing 15×20c. (No. 391) in blocks of 5 or 10 and pane of four airmail labels	£1500

1941. Black on pink cover, with contents amended in manuscript. Stapled.

SB19	1r.80, booklet containing 60×3c. on 6c. (No. 398) in blocks of 10	
	a. Black on blue cover	

1951 (5 Dec). Black on buff cover. Stitched.

SB20	1r. booklet containing 20×5c. (No. 414) in blocks of four and pane of airmail labels	20·00
	a. Containing two blocks of 10×5c. stamps and no airmail labels	50·00

1952 (21 Jan). Black on green cover. Stitched.

SB21	6r. booklet containing 8×75c. (No. 417) in blocks of 4 and two panes of four airmail labels	20·00

OFFICIAL STAMPS

1869. Issues of 1867–1868 overprinted 'SERVICE' in block letters. Although these stamps were prepared for use and sent out to the colony, they were never issued.

SERVICE

(O **1**)

Optd with T O **1** by D.L.R. Wmk **6**. P 12½.

O1	**1**	2d. yellow	75·00
		x. Wmk reversed	£225
O2		6d. deep brown (R.)	75·00
O3	**2**	8d. chocolate	75·00
O4	**1**	1s. pale lilac	£170
O5	**2**	2s. deep blue	£120
		a. Imperf	£1100

SERVICE

(O **2**)

Optd with T O **2** by D.L.R. Wmk Crown CC. P 14.

O6	**8**	1d. blue	75·00
O7	**7**	3d. carmine-rose	£150

Until 1 October 1895 all Official mail was carried free. After that date postage was paid on Official letters to the general public, on certain interdepartmental mail and on all packets over 1lb in weight. Nos. O11/O27 were provided for this purpose.

On

Service

(O **3**)

1895. Optd with T O **3** by the Govt Printer, Colombo.

O11	**9**	2c. green (No. 147)	21·00	70
		w. Wmk inverted	†	£400
O12	**39**	3c. terracotta and blue-green (No. 245)	12·00	2·75
O13	**28**	5c. dull purple (No. 195)	5·50	30
O14	**29**	15c. sage-green (No. 196)	24·00	65
		x. Wmk reversed	†	£375
O15		25c. yellow-brown (No. 198)	13·00	3·25
O16		30c. bright mauve and chestnut (No. 247)	13·00	60
O17	**30**	1r.12 dull rose (*wmk sideways*) (No. 201)	95·00	65·00
		a. Opt double, one albino	£300	
		b. Wmk upright	£100	80·00
O11/O17 *Set of 7*			£160	65·00

1899 (June)–**1900.** Nos. 256/257 and 261/262 optd with T O **3**.

O18	**9**	2c. pale orange-brown (3.00)	12·00	60
O19	**39**	3c. deep green (9.00)	13·00	4·75
O20	**29**	15c. blue (9.00)	27·00	60
O21	**39**	75c. black and red-brown (R.)	10·00	10·00
O18/O21 *Set of 4*			55·00	14·00

1903 (26 Nov)–**04.** Nos. 265/266, 268 and 271/273 optd with T O **3**.

O22	**44**	2c. red-brown (4.1.04)	23·00	1·00
O23	**45**	3c. green	16·00	2·00
O24	**46**	5c. dull purple	32·00	1·50
O25	**48**	15c. blue	42·00	2·50
O26		25c. bistre (15.7.04)	38·00	18·00
O27		30c. dull violet and green (14.3.04)	21·00	1·50
O22/O27 *Set of 6*			£150	25·00

Stamps overprinted 'On Service' were withdrawn on 1 October 1904.

POSTAL FISCAL

1952 (1 Dec). As T **72** but inscr 'REVENUE' at sides. Chalk-surfaced paper.

F1	10r. dull green and yellow-orange	£100	50·00

This revenue stamp was on sale for postal use from 1 December 1952 until 14 March 1954. Earlier printings were on ordinary paper.

Used price for stamp with identifiable postal cancellation.

The 20r. purple and blue in the same design is also known postally used during this period, but such usage is not known to have been officially authorised.

TELEGRAPH STAMPS

Telegraph Stamps of INDIA used in Ceylon

1869 (1 July)–**78.** Telegraph stamps of India (Nos. T5/T20) used in Ceylon.

ZT1	2a. maroon	6·50
ZT2	4a. blue	4·50
ZT3	8a. brown	3·50
	a. Imperf (10.78)	£1100
ZT4	1r. grey (Die I)	85·00
ZT5	1r. grey (Die II)	3·00
ZT6	2r.8a. orange-yellow (Die I)	6·00
ZT7	2r.8a. orange (Die II) (1878)	50·00
ZT8	5r. orange-brown	6·50
ZT9	10r. green (Die I)	6·00
ZT10	10r. green (Die II) (1878)	38·00
ZT11	14r.4a. lilac (1870)	48·00
ZT12	25r. violet (Die I)	16·00
ZT13	25r. violet (Die II) (1878)	38·00
ZT14	28r.8a. yellow-green (1870)	48·00
ZT15	50r. rose (Die I)	48·00

The prices quoted above are for used upper halves with clearly identifiable cancels of offices in Ceylon. The large block letters used in these straight-line cancels are such that only three or four letters usually appear on a single stamp, and multiples or examples on piece may be needed to confirm identification. Usage is recorded at the following offices, with Colombo being the most frequently seen : ANURADHAPURA, BADULLA, BATTICALOA, COLOMBO, GALLE, GAMPOLA, JAFFNA (or JAFFRA, in error), KALATURA, KANDY, MANAAR, MATALLE, NAWALAPITYA, NEWARAELIYA or NEWARAELLYA, PANADURE and TRINCOMALEE.

The Tapling Collection (British Library) includes a pair of the India 1a yellow-green (No. T4) used at Colombo.

The use of Indian telegraph stamps in Ceylon ceased with the release of the following optd issue (Nos. T1/T9).

PRICES. For Nos. T1/T164 prices are quoted for unused whole stamps and used upper halves. Used lower halves (often with punched holes) are worth from ×2. Used whole stamps are rare and for many issues unknown.

(T **1**)

1880 (1 July). Telegraph stamps of India (1869–1878 issue) optd with Type T **1** twice (on upper and lower halves).

T1	2a. maroon	†	60·00
T2	4a. blue	£1400	48·00
T3	8a. brown	†	24·00
T4	1r. grey (Die II)	†	15·00
T5	2r.8a. orange (Die II)	†	40·00
T6	5r. orange-brown	†	50·00
T7	10r. green (Die II)	†	35·00
T8	25r. violet (Die II)	—	45·00
T9	50r. rose-carmine (Die II)	†	£750

The Type T **1** opt has been extensively forged.

T 2 T 3 T 4

T 5 T 6 T 7

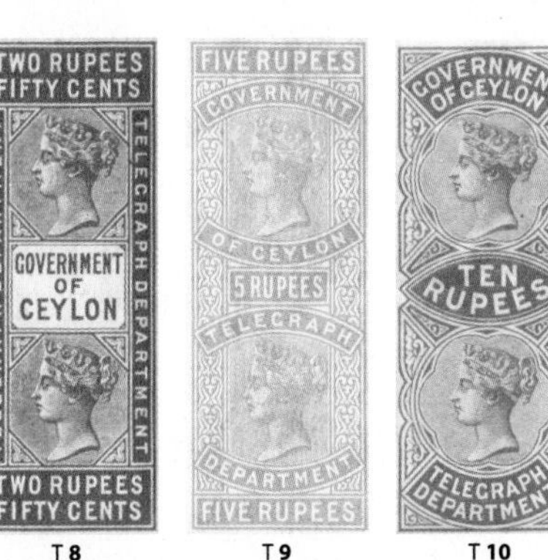

T 8 T 9 T 10

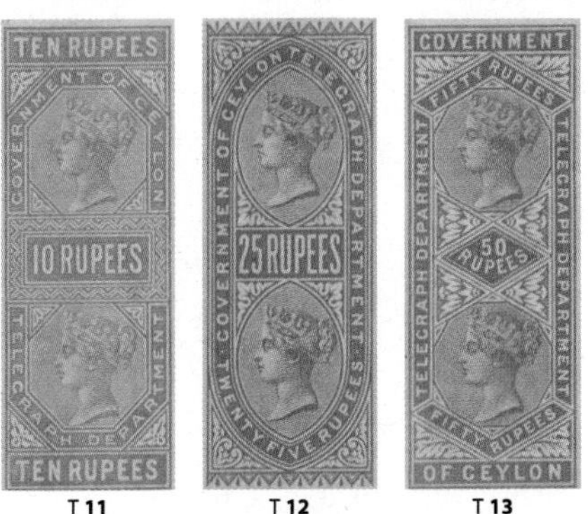

T 11 T 12 T 13

T 14 ('CA' in narrow letters)

(Typo, De La Rue)

1881 (14 Feb)–82. W T **14**. Perf 14.

T10	T **2**	12c. bistre	22·00	1·00
		w. Wmk inverted	80·00	11·00
T11	T **3**	25c. blue-green	£350	25·00
T12	T **4**	25c. green (3.82)	20·00	50
		w. Wmk inverted	—	55·00
T13	T **5**	50c. blue	24·00	50
		w. Wmk inverted	80·00	14·00
T14	T **6**	1r. red-brown	£200	7·50

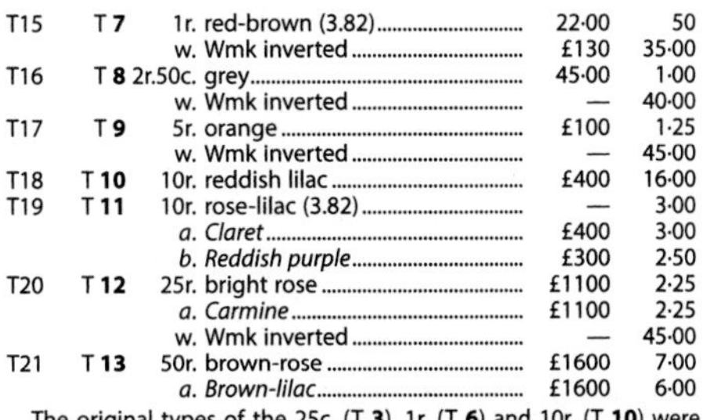

T15	T **7**	1r. red-brown (3.82)	22·00	50
		w. Wmk inverted	£130	35·00
T16	T **8**	2r.50c. grey	45·00	1·00
		w. Wmk inverted	—	40·00
T17	T **9**	5r. orange	£100	1·25
		w. Wmk inverted	—	45·00
T18	T **10**	10r. reddish lilac	£400	16·00
T19	T **11**	10r. rose-lilac (3.82)	—	3·00
		a. Claret	£400	3·00
		b. Reddish purple	£300	2·50
T20	T **12**	25r. bright rose	£1100	2·25
		a. Carmine	£1100	2·25
		w. Wmk inverted	—	45·00
T21	T **13**	50r. brown-rose	£1600	7·00
		a. Brown-lilac	£1600	6·00

The original types of the 25c. (T **3**), 1r. (T **6**) and 10r. (T **10**) were withdrawn and replaced after it was found that the face value could become difficult to determine after horizontal bisection in use. In the other designs the face value was clearly stated on both top and bottom halves.

For later printings in these types, but wmk T **129**, see Nos. T139/T147.

(T **15**)

1882 (7 Feb). Fiscal stamp inscr 'STAMP DUTY' opt as Type T **15**. Wmk T **14**. Perf 14.

T22	T **15**	25c. lilac	†	£850

Alternate horizontal rows were optd 'TELE' and 'GRAPH', to provide vertical pairs for separation. No unused examples, or used examples with 'TELE', have been reported.

(T **16**)

(T **17**)

(T **18**)

(T **19**)

(T **20**)

(T **21**)

(T **22**)

1882 (1 Jan)–**94**. Nos. T12/T17 and T19/T21 surch with new values by Ceylon Govt Printer, as Types T **16**/T **121**.

(a) Surch 12c.

T23	T **16**	12c. on 25c. green (20.4.87)	£350	60·00
T24	T **17**	12c. on 25c. green (16.1.89)	£400	22·00
		a. Small '12', '2' with straight foot (Type T **18**)	—	65·00
T25	T **19**	12c. on 50c. blue (20.4.87)	£140	5·00
T26	T **20**	12c. on 50c. blue (7.5.88)	75·00	5·00
T27	T **21**	12c. on 50c. blue (16.1.89)	—	28·00
		a. Small '12', '2' with straight foot (Type T **22**)	—	75·00

(T **23**)

(T **24**)

(T **25**)

(T **26**)

(T **27**)

(T **28**)

(T **29**)

(T **30**)

(T **31**) (T **32**)

(b) Surch 20c.

T28	T **23**	20c. on 25c. green (9.7.86)	£160	6·00
		a. Surch double	†	£500
T29	T **24**	20c. on 25c. green (7.4.87)	£160	6·50
T30	T **25**	20c. on 25c. green (13.4.88)	£100	10·00
T31	T **26**	20c. on 25c. green (1.4.92)	£200	15·00
		a. '2' in upper '20 cents' with straight foot	†	85·00
T32	T **27**	20c. on 50c. blue (7.4.87)	£140	5·00
		a. Surch double	†	£550
		w. Wmk inverted	—	65·00
T33	T **28**	20c. on 50c. blue (16.1.89)	£100	5·50
T34	T **29**	20c. on 50c. blue (2.8.89)	£100	5·00
T35	T **30**	20c. on 50c. blue (18.1.90)	85·00	5·50
T36	T **31**	20c. on 50c. blue (26.9.90)	80·00	5·50
T37	T **32**	20c. on 1r. red-brown (2.92)	£150	6·00

(T **33**)

(T **34**)

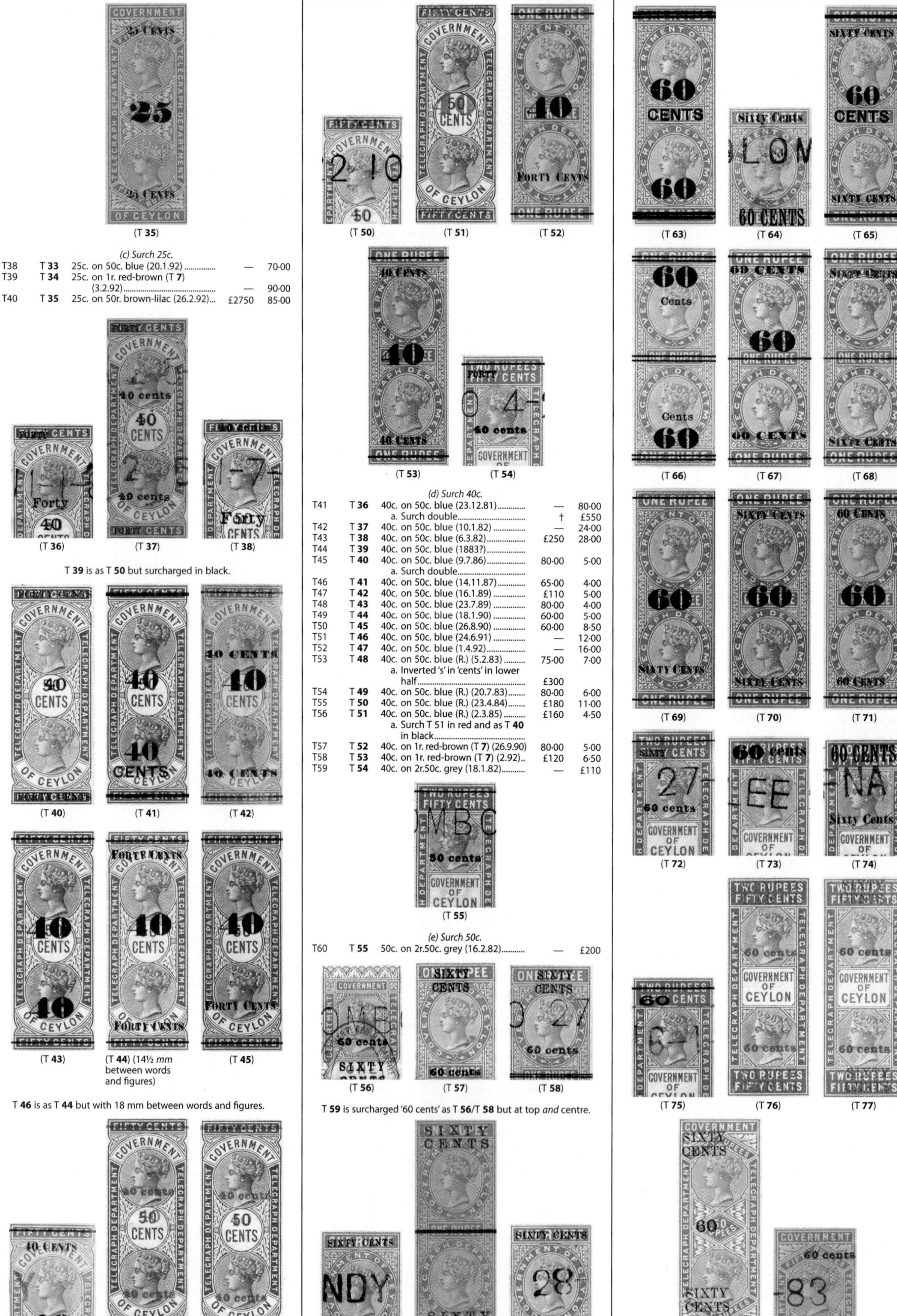

(T 35)

(c) Surch 25c.

T38	T **33**	25c. on 50c. blue (20.1.92)	—	70·00
T39	T **34**	25c. on 1r. red-brown (T **7**) (3.2.92)	—	90·00
T40	T **35**	25c. on 50r. brown-lilac (26.2.92)	£2750	85·00

(T 36) (T 37) (T 38)

T **39** is as T **50** but surcharged in black.

(T 40) (T 41) (T 42)

(T 43) (T 44) (14½ *mm* between words and figures) (T 45)

T **46** is as T **44** but with 18 mm between words and figures.

(T 47) (T 48) (single bar) (T 49) (double bar)

(T 50) (T 51) (T 52)

(T 53) (T 54)

(d) Surch 40c.

T41	T **36**	40c. on 50c. blue (23.12.81)	—	80·00
		a. Surch double	†	£550
T42	T **37**	40c. on 50c. blue (10.1.82)	—	24·00
T43	T **38**	40c. on 50c. blue (6.3.82)	£250	28·00
T44	T **39**	40c. on 50c. blue (1883?)		
T45	T **40**	40c. on 50c. blue (9.7.86)	80·00	5·00
		a. Surch double		
T46	T **41**	40c. on 50c. blue (14.11.87)	65·00	4·00
T47	T **42**	40c. on 50c. blue (16.1.89)	£110	5·00
T48	T **43**	40c. on 50c. blue (23.7.89)	80·00	4·00
T49	T **44**	40c. on 50c. blue (18.1.90)	60·00	5·00
T50	T **45**	40c. on 50c. blue (26.8.90)	60·00	8·50
T51	T **46**	40c. on 50c. blue (24.6.91)	—	12·00
T52	T **47**	40c. on 50c. blue (1.4.92)	—	16·00
T53	T **48**	40c. on 50c. blue (R.) (5.2.83)	75·00	7·00
		a. Inverted 's' in 'cents' in lower half	£300	
T54	T **49**	40c. on 50c. blue (R.) (20.7.83)	80·00	6·00
T55	T **50**	40c. on 50c. blue (R.) (23.4.84)	£180	11·00
T56	T **51**	40c. on 50c. blue (R.) (2.3.85)	£160	4·50
		a. Surch T 51 in red and as T **40** in black		
T57	T **52**	40c. on 1r. red-brown (T **7**) (26.9.90)	80·00	5·00
T58	T **53**	40c. on 1r. red-brown (T **7**) (2.92)	£120	6·50
T59	T **54**	40c. on 2r.50c. grey (18.1.82)	—	£110

(T 55)

(e) Surch 50c.

T60	T **55**	50c. on 2r.50c. grey (16.2.82)	—	£200

(T 56) (T 57) (T 58)

T **59** is surcharged '60 cents' as T **56**/T **58** but at top *and* centre.

(T 60) (T 61) (T 62)

(T 63) (T 64) (T 65)

(T 66) (T 67) (T 68)

(T 69) (T 70) (T 71)

(T 72) (T 73) (T 74)

(T 75) (T 76) (T 77)

(T 78) (T 79)

(f) Surch 60c.

T61	T **56**	60c. on 1r. red-brown (T **6**) (23.12.81)	—	17·00
T62	T **57**	60c. on 1r. red-brown (T **7**) (6.3.82)	£180	11·00
		a. Surch inverted	†	£800
		w. Wmk inverted	†	90·00
T63	T **58**	60c. on 1r. red-brown (T **7**) (18.10.82)	—	12·00
T64	T **59**	60c. on 1r. red-brown (T **7**) (1883?)		
T65	T **60**	60c. on 1r. red-brown (T **7**) (2.3.85)	—	18·00
		w. Wmk inverted	—	75·00
T66	T **61**	60c. on 1r. red-brown (T **7**) (6.7.85)	£180	7·00
		w. Wmk inverted	†	90·00
T67	T **62**	60c. on 1r. red-brown (T **7**) (9.7.86)	—	10·00
		a. Surch double, one inverted		
		b. Surch double	†	£700
T68	T **63**	60c. on 1r. red-brown (T **7**) (7.4.87)	£160	11·00
T69	T **64**	60c. on 1r. red-brown (T **7**) (10.8.87)	—	16·00
T70	T **65**	60c. on 1r. red-brown (T **7**) (21.12.87)	£150	6·00
T71	T **66**	60c. on 1r. red-brown (T **7**) (13.4.88)	90·00	7·00
T72	T **67**	60c. on 1r. red-brown (T **7**) (16.1.89)	75·00	4·50
		w. Wmk inverted	—	70·00
T73	T **68**	60c. on 1r. red-brown (T **7**) (12.12.89)	80·00	6·00
T74	T **69**	60c. on 1r. red-brown (T **7**) (26.9.90)	80·00	6·50
T75	T **70**	60c. on 1r. red-brown (T **7**) (24.6.91)	85·00	5·00
T76	T **71**	60c. on 1r. red-brown (T **7**) (2.92)	£130	7·50
		w. Wmk inverted	†	90·00
T77	T **72**	60c. on 2r.50c. grey (16.2.82)	—	£120
T78	T **73**	60c. on 2r.50c. grey (25.2.87)	£140	7·50
T79	T **74**	60c. on 2r.50c. grey (10.8.87)	—	35·00
T80	T **75**	60c. on 2r.50c. grey (29.10.88)	—	12·00
T81	T **76**	60c. on 2r.50c. grey (R.) (20.7.83)	80·00	6·00
		a. Inverted 's' in 'cents' in lower half	£325	
T82	T **77**	60c. on 2r.50c. grey (R.) (23.4.84)	90·00	9·00
T83	T **78**	60c. on 50r. brown-lilac (5.2.83)	90·00	12·00
T84	T **79**	60c. on 50r. brown-lilac (1883?)	—	£200

(T **80**)  (T **81**)  (T **82**)

(T **83**)  (T **84**)  (T **85**)

(T **86**)  (T **87**)  (T **88**)

(T **89**)  (T **90**)  (T **91**)

(T **92**)  (T **93**)  (T **94**)

(T **95**)  (T **96**)  (T **97**)

(T **98**)  (T **99**)  (T **100**)

(T **101**)  (T **102**)  (T **103**)

(T **104**)

T **105** is surcharged '80 Cents' similar to T **87**, but at top *and* centre.

(T **106**)  (T **107**)  (T **108**)

(T **109**)  (T **110**)  (T **111**)

(T **112**)  (T **113**)  (T **114**)

(T **115**)  (T **116**)  (T **117**)

(T **118**)  (T **119**)

(g) Surch 80c.

T85	T **80**	80c. on 1r. red-brown (T **6**) (10.1.82)	—	14·00
T86	T **81**	80c. on 1r. red-brown (T **7**) (6.3.82)	£250	18·00
T87	T **82**	80c. on 1r. red-brown (T **7**) (18.10.82)	£120	16·00
T88	T **83**	80c. on 1r. red-brown (T **7**) (6.7.85)	£190	6·00
		a. Surch double	†	£500
T89	T **84**	80c. on 1r. red-brown (T **7**) (13.4.88)	£100	8·00
T90	T **85**	80c. on 1r. red-brown (T **7**) (16.1.89)	95·00	7·00
		w. Wmk inverted	£170	32·00
T91	T **86**	80c. on 1r. red-brown (T **7**) (16.1.89)	—	18·00
T92	T **87**	80c. on 1r. red-brown (T **7**) (2.8.89)	—	11·00
		a. 's' in upper 'Cents' inverted	†	75·00
T93	T **88**	80c. on 1r. red-brown (T **7**) (18.1.90)	£100	4·50
T94	T **89**	80c. on 1r. red-brown (T **7**) (3.92)	£130	13·00
T95	T **90**	80c. on 2r.50c. grey (2.3.85)	£250	28·00
T96	T **91**	80c. on 2r.50c. grey (9.7.86)	£170	6·00
		a. Surch double	†	£425
T97	T **92**	80c. on 2r.50c. grey (26.9.88)	—	8·00
		a. 'S' in upper 'CENTS' inverted	†	65·00
T98	T **93**	80c. on 2r.50c. grey (16.1.89)	£160	10·00
T99	T **94**	80c. on 2r.50c. grey (18.1.90)	£100	8·00

T100	**T 95**	80c. on 2r.50c. grey (16.9.90)	£375	10·00
T101	**T 96**	80c. on 2r.50c. grey (3.2.92)	—	16·00
T102	**T 97**	80c. on 5r. orange (3.9.84)	—	50·00
T103	**T 98**	80c. on 5r. orange (7.4.87)	£250	40·00
		w. Wmk inverted	†	90·00
T104	**T 99**	80c. on 5r. orange (10.8.87)	—	42·00
		w. Wmk inverted	—	42·00
T105	**T 100**	80c. on 5r. orange (21.12.87)	—	22·00
T106	**T 101**	80c. on 5r. orange (26.9.90)	£180	12·00
		a. '00' for '80'	£5500	£375
T107	**T 102**	80c. on 10r. rose-lilac (T **11**) (3.9.84)	—	90·00
T108	**T 103**	80c. on 10r. rose-lilac (T **11**) (7.4.87)	—	11·00
		w. Wmk inverted	£375	
T109	**T 104**	80c. on 10r. rose-lilac (T **11**) (10.8.87)	—	22·00
T110	**T 105**	80c. on 10r. rose-lilac (T **11**) (1887?)		
T111	**T 106**	80c. on 10r. rose-lilac (T **11**) (21.12.87)	£200	21·00
T112	**T 107**	80c. on 10r. reddish purple (T **11**) (26.9.90)	£170	12·00
		a. '00' for '80'	£6000	£450
T113	**T 108**	80c. on 25r. bright rose (5.2.83)	£100	13·00
		a. Inverted 's' in '80 cents' on lower half	£375	
T114	**T 109**	80c. on 25r. bright rose (20.7.83)	£225	19·00
T115	**T 110**	80c. on 25r. bright rose (23.4.84)	£150	16·00
T116	**T 111**	80c. on 25r. bright rose (10.8.87)	£200	21·00
T117	**T 112**	80c. on 25r. bright rose (21.12.87)	—	15·00
T118	**T 113**	80c. on 25r. carmine (26.9.90)	—	16·00
T119	**T 114**	80c. on 25r. carmine (3.92)	—	48·00
T120	**T 115**	80c. on 50r. brown-rose (20.7.83)	—	42·00
T121	**T 116**	80c. on 50r. brown-lilac (3.9.84)	—	£120
T122	**T 117**	80c. on 50r. brown-lilac (7.4.87)	—	£170
T123	**T 118**	80c. on 50r. brown-lilac (21.12.87)	—	20·00
T124	**T 119**	80c. on 50r. brown-lilac (3.92)	—	55·00

(T **120**)

(T **121**)

(h) Surch 5r.

T125	**T 120**	5r. on 25r. carmine (1.4.92)	£350	11·00
		a. Small 's' in 'RUPEES' on upper half	—	75·00
T126	**T 121**	5r. on 50r. brown-lilac (13.8.94)	—	£225

The dates quoted above for Nos. T23/T126 refer to printing dates, where known. For stamps similar to Nos. T125/T126, but wmk T **129**, see Nos. T148/T149.

T **122**

T **123**

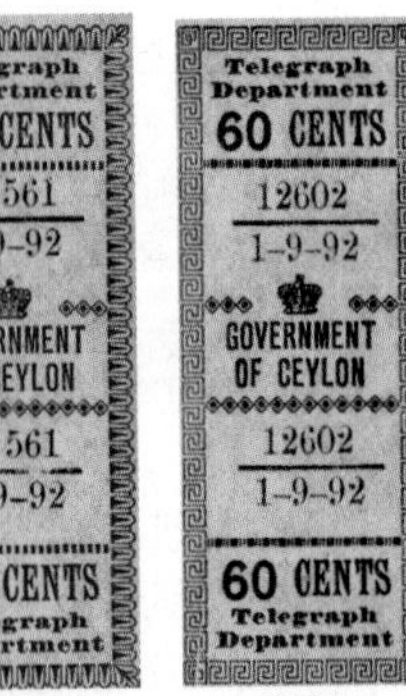
T **124**

T **125**

T **126**

T **127**

T **128**

T **129** ('CA' in wide letters)

(Typo, Govt Printer, Colombo)

1892 (1 Apr)–**1903**. Types T **122**/T **128** (different frame ornaments for each value). No wmk. Date and control figures in black. Perf 12.

(a) Date numerals separated by oblique lines. Large control figures

T127	**T 122**	20c. green (1/4/92)	—	12·00
		a. Small control figures	£400	4·00
T128	**T 123**	40c. blue (1/4/92)	—	8·50
		a. Small control figures	£400	3·00
T129	**T 124**	60c. brown (1/4/92)	—	12·00
		a. Small control figures	£425	4·00
T130	**T 125**	80c. olive (1/4/92)	—	12·00
		a. Small control figures	£400	4·00

The 80c. exists imperforate, with date '1/4/92', and the 40c. and 80c. also imperforate with date '1/5/92' but the latter were not issued.

(b) Date numerals separated by dashes

T131	**T 126**	5c. lilac-rose (1-4-97)	95·00	3·00
		a. Date 1-11-97	80·00	3·00
		b. Date 1-7-98	—	5·00
		c. Date 1-12-98	90·00	3·00
		d. Date 1-12-99	£110	2·50
T132		5c. deep purple (1-12-00)	85·00	2·50
		a. Date 1-12-01	90·00	3·00
		b. Date 1-12-02	—	3·00
		c. Bluish paper. Date 18-5-03	—	6·00
T133	**T 127**	10c. yellow (1-4-97)	£110	3·00
		a. Date 1-11-97	£100	3·00
		b. Date 1-12-98	—	3·00
		c. Date 1-12-99	£100	2·50
		d. Date 1-12-00	£120	8·00
		e. Date 1-12-01	95·00	3·00
		f. Bluish paper. Date 18-5-03	—	6·00
T134	**T 122**	20c. green (1-9-92)	£100	5·00
		a. Date 9-1-93	£110	3·00
		b. Date 1-5-94	95·00	3·00
		c. Date 1-11-94	90·00	3·00
		d. Date 1-11-95	—	3·00
		e. Date 1-9-96	—	3·00
		f. Date 1-11-97	90·00	2·50
		g. Date 1-12-98	£225	3·00
		h. Date 1-12-99	85·00	3·00
		i. Date 1-12-00	£110	4·50
		j. Date 1-12-01	95·00	4·50
		k. Bluish paper. Date 18-5-03	—	6·00
T135	**T 128**	25c. deep olive (1-12-97. Date in blue, without control figures)	£475	8·00
T136	**T 123**	40c. blue (1-9-92)	£110	3·00
		a. Date 9-1-93	95·00	3·00
		b. Date 1-5-94	85·00	2·50
		c. Date 1-11-94	95·00	2·00
		d. Date 1-11-95	—	3·00
		e. Date 1-9-96	80·00	2·00
		f. Date 1-12-99	—	6·00
		g. Date 1-12-00	£110	4·50
		h. Date 1-12-01	£110	6·00
		i. Bluish paper. Date 18-5-03	—	7·00
T137	**T 124**	60c. dark brown (1-9-92)	£100	5·00
		a. Date 9-1-93	—	3·00
		b. Date 1-5-94	£170	8·00
		c. Date 1-11-94	95·00	3·00
		d. Date 1-11-95	—	3·00
		e. Date 1-9-96	95·00	3·00
		f. Date 1-7-98	85·00	3·00
		g. Date 1-12-98	—	8·00
		h. Date 1-12-99	—	6·00
		i. Date 1-12-00	—	5·00
		j. Date 1-12-01	£110	5·00
		k. Date 1-12-02	—	6·00
		l. Bluish paper. Date 18-5-03	—	6·00
T138	**T 125**	80c. olive (1-9-92)	£110	5·00
		a. Date 9-1-93	—	3·00
		b. Date 1-5-94	—	3·50
		c. Date 1-11-94	90·00	3·00
		d. Date 1-11-95	—	3·00
		e. Date 1-9-96	£100	2·50
		f. Date 1-7-98	£100	3·00
		g. Date 1-12-98	—	12·00
		h. Date 1-12-99	—	6·00
		i. Date 1-12-00	£100	5·00
		j. Date 1-12-01	£100	4·00
		k. Date 1-12-02	—	6·00
		l. Bluish paper. Date 18-5-03	—	8·00

The plates used to print the 5c., 10c. and 25c. values (Nos. T131/T133, T135) each included two different 'dies', which can be found in *se-tenant* pairs.

1894. Typo, De La Rue. As Nos. T10, T12/T13, T15/T17, T19/T21, but wmk T **129**. Perf 14.

T139	**T 2**	12c. olive-bistre	25·00	1·25
T140	**T 4**	25c. green	25·00	75
T141	**T 5**	50c. blue	25·00	1·00
T142	**T 7**	1r. red-brown	30·00	75
T143	**T 8**	2r.50c. slate	55·00	1·00
T144	**T 9**	5r. orange	85·00	1·25
T145	**T 11**	10r. purple	£275	2·50
		a. Claret	—	2·50
		b. Dull magenta	—	2·50
T146	**T 12**	25r. carmine	£1100	2·00
T147	**T 13**	50r. lake	£1600	15·00

(T **130**)

T **131**

T **132**

1894. Nos. T146/T147 surch with new values as Types T **121** and T **130** by Ceylon Govt Printer, Colombo.

T148	**T 130**	5r. on 25r. carmine (26.11.94)	—	42·00
T149	**T 121**	5r. on 50r. lake (13.8.94)	—	24·00

(Typo, De La Rue)

1903 (June)–**04**. Types T **131** or T **132** (25c.). Wmk T **129**. Perf 14.

T150	**T 131**	5c. brown and green	£160	2·50
T151		10c. bluish green and ochre	£160	3·50
T152		12c. olive-bistre and green (1.04)	£250	7·00
T153		20c. drab and purple	£160	4·00
T154	**T 132**	25c. green (1.04)	£160	2·50
		w. Wmk inverted	†	48·00
T155	**T 131**	40c. purple and brown	£160	5·50
T156		50c. blue and purple	£160	3·00
T157		60c. olive and ochre	£160	4·00
T158		75c. pale blue and blue	£160	3·00
T159		1r. red-brown	£160	1·00
T160		2r.50c. slate and ochre	£425	5·00
T161		5r. orange and carmine	£425	8·00
T162		10r. reddish purple and green	£650	15·00
T163		25r. carmine and scarlet	£1800	10·00
T164		50r. claret and blue	£3000	90·00

1905. As Nos. T150/T164, but Wmk Mult Crown CA (sideways)*.

			Unused	*Used whole*	*Used upper half*
T165	**T 131**	5c. brown and green	13·00	2·50	50
T166		10c. bluish green and ochre	18·00	3·00	50
T167		12c. olive-bistre and green	17·00	10·00	75
T168		20c. drab and purple	15·00	5·50	75
T169	**T 132**	25c. green	19·00	3·00	50
T170	**T 131**	40c. purple and brown	17·00	8·50	60
T171		50c. blue and purple	22·00	7·00	75
T172		60c. olive and ochre	20·00	7·50	75
T173		75c. pale blue and blue	21·00	7·50	75
T174		1r. red-brown	20·00	4·00	75
T175		2r.50c. slate and ochre	40·00	8·00	1·00
		w. Wmk Crown to right of CA	†	—	70·00
T176		5r. orange and carmine	£110	11·00	1·00
T177		10r. reddish purple and green	£200	15·00	1·50
T178		25r. carmine and scarlet	£700	£110	5·00
T179		50r. claret and blue	£1000	£325	38·00

* The normal sideways watermark shows Crown to left of CA, *as seen from the back of the stamp.*

During the currency of Nos. T165/T179 changes in administrative practice meant that horizontal bisection of the stamps largely ceased. Prices are accordingly quoted both for used whole stamps and used upper halves.

(T **133**)

(T **134**)

1910 (May–July). Nos T167, T169 and T174 surch with new values in words as Types T **133** or T **134** (No. T181) by Ceylon Govt Printer, Colombo.

T180	**T 133**	20c. on 12c. olive-bistre and green	90·00
T181	**T 134**	20c. on 25c. green (7.10)	90·00
T182	**T 133**	40c. on 12c. olive-bistre and green	90·00
T183		40c. on 1r. red-brown (7.10)	90·00
T184		60c. on 12c. olive-bistre and green	90·00
T185		5r. on 12c. olive-bistre and green	£3750
T186		5r. on 1r. red-brown (7.10)	£3750
T187		10r. on 12c. olive-bistre and green	£3750

No used examples of Nos. T180/T187 have been seen. Forged surcharges exist.

The telegraph stamps of Ceylon were withdrawn from use on 1 August 1910.

Cook Islands

COOK ISLANDS

A British Protectorate was declared over this group of 15 islands by the local Vice-Consul on 20 September 1888.

Before the introduction of the Cook Islands Post Office, mail was forwarded via Auckland, New Zealand.

PRICES FOR STAMPS ON COVER TO 1945	
Nos. 1/4	*from* × 5
Nos. 5/74	*from* × 4
Nos. 75/145	*from* × 3

BRITISH PROTECTORATE

1

2 Queen Makea Takau

3 White Tern or Torea

(Des F. Moss. Typo Govt Printing Office, Wellington)

1892 (19 Apr). No wmk. Toned or white paper. P 12½.

1 **1** 1d. black ... 35·00 26·00
a. Imperf between (vert pair) ... £10000
2 1½d. mauve ... 48·00 38·00
a. Imperf (pair) ... £17000
3 2½d. blue ... 48·00 38·00
4 10d. carmine ... £140 £130
1/4 *Set of 4* ... £225 £200

Nos. 1/4 were printed in sheets of 60 (6×10) from plates constructed from a matrix of six slightly different types.

(Eng A. E. Cousins. Typo Govt Printing Office, Wellington)

1893 (28 July)–**1900**. W **12b** of New Zealand (N Z and Star wide apart) (sideways on T **3**).

(a) P 12×11½

5 **2** 1d. brown ... 50·00 55·00
6 1d. blue (3.4.94) ... 13·00 2·00
a. Perf 12×11½ and 12½ mixed ... † £2250
7 1½d. mauve ... 20·00 6·00
8 2½d. rose ... 55·00 23·00
a. Rose-carmine ... 65·00 48·00
ab. Perf 12×11½ and 12½ mixed ... £3000
9 5d. olive-black ... 23·00 15·00
10 10d. green ... 85·00 50·00
5/10 *Set of 6* ... £200 £130

(b) P 11 (July 1896–1900)

11 **3** ½d. steel blue (1st setting) (11.99) ... 35·00 48·00
a. Upper right 'd' omitted ... £1500
b. Second setting ... 23·00 23·00
ba. Deep blue (1900) ... 5·50 15·00
12 **2** 1d. blue ... 5·00 5·50
13 1d. deep brown/*cream* (4.99) ... 30·00 21·00
a. Wmk sideways ... £1600
b. Bistre-brown (1900) ... 30·00 23·00
14 1½d. deep lilac ... 18·00 7·00
a. Deep mauve (1900) ... 12·00 7·00
15 **3** 2d. brown/*thin toned* (7.98) ... 19·00 6·50
a. Deep brown (1900) ... 16·00 8·50
16 **2** 2½d. pale rose ... 55·00 38·00
a. Deep rose (1900) ... 25·00 14·00
17 5d. olive-black ... 29·00 19·00
18 **3** 6d. purple/*thin toned* (7.98) ... 45·00 42·00
a. Bright purple (1900) ... 24·00 27·00
19 **2** 10d. green ... 18·00 55·00
20 **3** 1s. red/*thin toned* (7.98) ... 65·00 75·00
a. Deep carmine (1900) ... 48·00 48·00
11ba/20a *Set of 10* ... £190 £200

Examples of the 1d., 1½d., 2½d. and 5d. perforated 11 and on laid paper are perforation trials. On the first setting of the ½d. the face values are misplaced in each corner. As corrected in the second setting the face values are correctly positioned in each corner.

ONE
HALF
PENNY
(4)

(5)

1899 (24 Apr). No. 12 surch with T **4** by Govt Printer, Rarotonga.

21 **2** ½d. on 1d. blue ... 32·00 48·00
a. Surch inverted ... £850 £900
b. Surch double ... £1000 £900

NEW ZEALAND TERRITORY

On 8 and 9 October 1900 the chiefs of all the main islands, except Aitutaki, ceded their territory to the British Crown. On 11 June 1901 all the islands, including Aitutaki, were transferred by Great Britain to New Zealand control.

1901 (8 Oct). No. 13 optd with T **5** by Govt Printer, Rarotonga.

22 **2** 1d. brown ... £180 £140
a. Crown inverted ... £2250 £1700
c. Optd with crown twice ... £1600 £1600

1902. No wmk. P 11.

(a) Medium white Cowan paper (Feb)

23 **3** ½d. blue-green ... 10·00 10·00
a. Imperf horiz (vert pair) ... £1300
24 **2** 1d. dull rose ... 16·00 22·00

(b) Thick white Pirie paper (May)

25 **3** ½d. yellow-green ... 11·00 4·25
26 **2** 1d. rose-red ... 20·00 11·00
a. Rose-lake ... 18·00 6·50
27 2½d. dull blue ... 13·00 21·00

NEW ZEALAND WATERMARKS. In W **43** the wmk units are in vertical columns widely spaced and the sheet margins are unwatermarked or wmkd 'NEW ZEALAND POSTAGE' in large letters.

In W **98** the wmk units are arranged alternately in horizontal rows closely spaced and are continued into the sheet margins. Stamps with W **98** sideways show the star to the left of NZ, *as seen from the back*. Sideways inverted varieties have the star to the right, *as seen from the back*.

1902 (Sept). W **43** of New Zealand (single-lined NZ and Star, close together; sideways on T **2**). P 11.

28 **3** ½d. yellow-green ... 4·75 3·25
a. Grey-green ... 30·00 70·00
29 **2** 1d. rose-pink ... 4·00 3·00
30 1½d. deep mauve ... 5·50 8·50
31 **3** 2d. deep brown ... 10·00 10·00
a. No figures of value ... £2250 £3500
b. Perf 11×14 ... £2500
32 **2** 2½d. deep blue ... 3·75 7·00
33 5d. olive-black ... 35·00 48·00
34 **3** 6d. purple ... 38·00 30·00
35 **2** 10d. green ... 50·00 £110
36 **3** 1s. carmine ... 50·00 80·00
a. Perf 11×14 ... £3000
28/36 *Set of 9* ... £170 £275

Stamps in T **3** were printed from a master plate with the value added by a series of separate duty plates. One sheet of the 2d. missed this second pass through the press and was issued without value.

For Nos. 28/36 T **3** exists with the watermark in equal quantities either upright or inverted and for T **2**, on which the watermark is sideways, in equal quantities with the star to the right or left of NZ.

1909–11. W **43** of New Zealand.

37 **3** ½d. green (P 14½×14) (1911) ... 13·00 8·00
38 **2** 1d. deep red (P 14) ... 45·00 32·00
a. Wmk sideways (24.12.09) ... 14·00 2·50

For Nos. 37/38 the watermark is either upright or inverted. For No. 38a it is sideways, either with star to right or left of NZ.

1913–19. W **43** of New Zealand (sideways on T **3**). Chalk-surfaced paper.

39 **3** ½d. deep green (P 14) (1915) ... 11·00 15·00
a. Wmk upright ... 15·00 25·00
40 **2** 1d. red (P 14) (7.13) ... 13·00 4·50
41 1d. red (P 14×14½) (1914) ... 11·00 6·00
42 1½d. deep mauve (P 14) (1915) ... 90·00 18·00
43 1½d. deep mauve (P 14×15) (1916) ... 21·00 4·00
44 **3** 2d. deep brown (P 15×14) (1919) ... 5·00 48·00
45 **2** 10d. green (P 14×15) (1918) ... 38·00 £120
46 **3** 1s. carmine (P 15×14) (1919) ... 27·00 £110
39/46 *Set of 6* ... £100 £275

RAROTONGA

APA PENE
(8)

1919 (Apr–July). Stamps of New Zealand surch as T **8**.

(a) T **53**. *W* **43**. *De La Rue chalk-surfaced paper. P 14×15*

47 1d. carmine (No. 405) (B.) (6.19) ... 1·75 5·50

(b) T **60** *(recess). W* **43**. *Cowan unsurfaced paper. P 14×13½*

48 2½d. blue (No. 419) (R.) (6.19) ... 2·75 6·50
a. Perf 14×14½ ... 2·00 2·25
b. Vert pair. Nos. 48/48a ... 20·00 50·00
49 3d. chocolate (No. 420) (B.) ... 3·75 8·00
a. Perf 14×14½ ... 3·75 4·25
b. Vert pair. Nos. 49/49a ... 22·00 60·00
50 4d. bright violet (No. 422) (B.) ... 2·25 5·50
a. Re-entry (Pl 20 R. 1/6) ... 60·00
b. Re-entry (Pl 20 R. 4/10) ... 60·00
c. Perf 14×14½ ... 1·75 4·25
d. Vert pair (Nos. 50 and 50c) ... 20·00 65·00
51 4½d. deep green (No. 423) (B.) ... 3·00 8·00
a. Perf 14×14½ ... 1·75 8·00
b. Vert pair. Nos. 51/51a ... 20·00 75·00
52 6d. carmine (No. 425) (B.) (6.19) ... 4·25 8·50
a. Perf 14×14½ ... 1·75 5·50
b. Vert pair. Nos. 52/52a ... 38·00 90·00
53 7½d. red-brown (No. 426a) (B.) ... 1·50 5·50
54 9d. sage-green (No. 429) (R.) ... 4·25 15·00
a. Perf 14×14½ ... 3·25 15·00
b. Vert pair. Nos. 54/54a ... 40·00 £120
55 1s. vermilion (No. 430) (B.) (6.19) ... 12·00 30·00
a. Perf 14×14½ ... 2·75 28·00
b. Vert pair. Nos. 55/55a ... 48·00 £140

(c) T **61** *(typo). W* **43**. *De La Rue chalk-surfaced paper. P 14×15*

56 ½d. green (No. 435) (R.)(6.19) ... 40 1·00
57 1½d. orange-brown (No. 438) (R.) (6.19) ... 50 75
58 2d. yellow (No. 439) (R.) ... 2·00 2·25
59 3d. chocolate (No. 440) (B.) (7.19) ... 2·75 13·00
47/59 *Set of 13* ... 23·00 80·00

9 Captain Cook landing

10 Wharf at Avarua

11 *Captain Cook (Dance)*

12 Palm Tree

13 Huts at Arorangi

14 Avarua Harbour

R. 2/8

R. 3/6 Double derrick flaws

R. 5/2

(Des, eng and recess Perkins Bacon & Co)

1920 (23 Aug). No wmk. P 14.

70 **9** ½d. black and green ... 4·00 28·00
71 **10** 1d. black and carmine-red ... 4·75 28·00
a. Double derrick flaw (R. 2/8, 3/6 or 5/2) ... 13·00
72 **11** 1½d. black and dull blue ... 8·50 8·50
73 **12** 3d. black and chocolate ... 2·25 5·50
74 **13** 6d. brown and yellow-orange ... 5·00 8·50
75 **14** 1s. black and violet ... 9·00 17·00
70/75 *Set of 6* ... 30·00 85·00

Examples of the 1d. and 1s. with centre inverted were not supplied to the Post Office (*Price £850 each, unused)*.

RAROTONGA
(15)

RAROTONGA

Trimmed overprint (R. 1/6 and R. 3/7)

1921 (Oct)–**23**. Postal Fiscal stamps as T F **4** of New Zealand optd with T **15**. W **43** (sideways). Chalk-surfaced 'De La Rue' paper. P 14½×14.

76 2s. deep blue (No. F111) (R.) ... 27·00 55·00
a. Trimmed opt ... £120
b. Carmine opt (1923) ... £200 £225
ba. Trimmed opt ... £600 £650
c. Optd on 'Jones' chalk-surfaced paper ... — £650
77 2s.6d. grey-brown (No. F112) (B.) ... 19·00 50·00
a. Trimmed opt ... 90·00
78 5s. yellow-green (No. F115) (R.) ... 29·00 70·00
a. Trimmed opt ... £120
79 10s. maroon (No. F120) (B.) ... 85·00 £140
a. Trimmed opt ... £275
80 £1 rose-carmine (No. F123) (B.) ... £140 £250
a. Trimmed opt ... £375
76/80 *Set of 5* ... £275 £500

For details of the 'Jones' paper, see below No. 385 of New Zealand.

See also Nos. 85/89.

16 Te Po, Rarotongan Chief

17 Harbour, Rarotonga and Mt. Ikurangi

(2½d. from a print; 4d. des A. H. Messenger. Plates by P.B. Recess Govt Ptg Office, Wellington)

1924–27. W **43** of New Zealand (sideways on 4d.). P 14.

81 **9** ½d. black and green (13.5.26) ... 4·50 8·50
82 **10** 1d. black and deep carmine (10.11.24) ... 6·00 2·25
a. Double derrick flaw (R. 2/8, 3/6 or 5/2) ... 16·00 10·00
x. Wmk reversed ... £225
83 **16** 2½d. red-brown and steel blue (15.10.27) ... 13·00 38·00
84 **17** 4d. green and violet (15.10.27) ... 21·00 17·00
81/84 *Set of 4* ... 40·00 60·00

1926 (Feb–May). As Nos. 76/80, but on thick, opaque white chalk-surfaced 'Cowan' paper.

85 2s. blue (No. F131) (C.) ... £200 £325
a. Trimmed opt ... £600
86 2s.6d. deep grey-brown (No. F132) (B.) ... 95·00 £180
87 5s. yellow-green (No. F135) (R.) (5.26) ... £110 £180
a. Trimmed opt ... £325
88 10s. brown-red (No. F139) (B.) (5.26) ... £140 £250
a. Trimmed opt ... £350
89 £1 rose-pink (No. F142) (B.) (5.26) ... £190 £375
a. Trimmed opt ... £550
85/89 *Set of 5* ... £650 £1200

1926 (Oct)–**28**. T **72** of New Zealand, overprinted with T **15**.

(a) Jones chalk-surfaced paper

90 2s. deep blue (No. 466) (R.) ... 10·00 40·00
w. Wmk inverted

(b) Cowan thick, opaque chalk-surfaced paper

91 2s. light blue (No. 469) (R.) (18.6.27) ... 19·00 40·00
92 3s. pale mauve (No. 470) (R.) (30.1.28) ... 16·00 50·00
90/92 *Set of 3* ... 40·00 £120

TWO PENCE
(18)

COOK ISLANDS.
(19)

1931 (1 Mar). Surch with T **18**. P 14.

(a) No wmk

93	**11**	2d. on 1½d. black and blue (R.)	9·50	4·75

(b) W 43 of New Zealand

94	**11**	2d. on 1½d. black and blue (R.)	4·75	11·00

1931 (12 Nov)–**32**. Postal Fiscal stamps as T F **6** of New Zealand. W **43**. Thick, opaque, white chalk-surfaced 'Cowan' paper. P 14.

(a) Optd with T **15**

95	2s.6d. deep brown (No. F147) (B.)	15·00	22·00
96	5s. green (No. F149) (R.)	26·00	55·00
97	10s. carmine-lake (No. F155) (B.)	38·00	£110
98	£1 pink (No. F158) (B.)	£120	£190

(b) Optd with T **19** *(3.32)*

98*a*	£3 green (No. F164) (R.)	£500	£900
98*b*	£5 indigo-blue (No. F168) (R.)	£250	£400

The £3 and £5 values were mainly used for fiscal purposes.

20 Captain Cook landing

21 Captain Cook

22 Double Maori Canoe

23 Natives working Cargo

24 Port of Avarua

25 RMS *Monowai*

26 King George V

(Des L. C. Mitchell. Recess P.B.)

1932 (15 Mar–2 May). No wmk. P 13.

99	**20**	½d. black and deep green	3·50	16·00
		a. Perf 14	28·00	95·00
100	**21**	1d. black and lake	10·00	4·50
		a. Centre inverted	£8500	£8500
		b. Perf compound of 13 and 14	£225	£275
		c. Perf 14	15·00	32·00
101	**22**	2d. black and brown	3·00	8·50
		a. Perf 14	9·00	20·00
102	**23**	2½d. black and deep blue	26·00	60·00
		a. Perf 14	19·00	60·00
103	**24**	4d. black and bright blue	32·00	70·00
		a. Perf 14	11·00	55·00
		b. Perf 14×13	30·00	£110
		c. Perf compound of 14 and 13	50·00	£120
104	**25**	6d. black and orange	29·00	48·00
		a. Perf 14	4·25	15·00
105	**26**	1s. black and violet (P 14) (2.5)	23·00	23·00
99/105 *Set of 7*			65·00	£160

Nos. 100b and 103c come from sheets reperforated 14 on arrival at Wellington. No. 100b comes from the first vertical column of a sheet and has 14 at left and No. 103c from the third or fourth vertical column with 13 at left or right.

Other major errors exist on this issue, but these are not listed as they originated from printer's waste which appeared on the market in 1935. They include the ½d. in vertical pair, imperforate horizontally (*price £425, unused*), and the ½d. 2d. and 2½d. with centre inverted (*prices ½d. £950, 2d. £500 and 2½d. £300, unused*).

(Recess from P.B. plates at Govt Printing Office, Wellington)

1933–36. W **43** of New Zealand (Single N Z and Star). P 14.

106	**20**	½d. black and deep green	1·25	4·50
		w. Wmk inverted	—	£120
107	**21**	1d. black and scarlet (1935)	1·50	2·00
		y. Wmk inverted and reversed		
108	**22**	2d. black and brown (1936)	1·50	50
		w. Wmk inverted	—	£425
109	**23**	2½d. black and deep blue	1·50	2·25
110	**24**	4d. black and bright blue	1·50	50
111	**25**	6d. black and orange-yellow (1936)	1·75	2·25
112	**26**	1s. black and violet (1936)	22·00	42·00
106/112 *Set of 7*			28·00	48·00

SILVER JUBILEE
OF
KING GEORGE V.
1910 - 1935.

(**27**)

Normal Letters

B K E N

B K E N

Narrow Letters

1935 (7 May). Silver Jubilee. Optd with T **27** (wider vertical spacing on 6d.). Colours changed. W **43** of New Zealand. P 14.

113	**21**	1d. red-brown and lake	60	1·40
		a. Narrow 'K' in 'KING'	2·75	5·50
		b. Narrow 'B' in 'JUBILEE'	19·00	22·00
114	**23**	2½d. dull and deep blue (R.)	3·75	3·50
		a. Narrow first 'E' in 'GEORGE'	3·75	6·00
115	**25**	6d. green and orange	10·00	7·00
		a. Narrow 'N' in KING'	11·00	20·00
113/115 *Set of 3*			13·00	10·50

1936 (15 July)–**44**. Stamps of New Zealand optd with T **19**. W **43**. P 14.

(a) T **72**. *Cowan thick, opaque chalk-surfaced paper*

116	2s. light blue (No. 469)	14·00	45·00
117	3s. pale mauve (No. 470)	15·00	70·00

(b) T F **6**. *Cowan thick, opaque chalk-surfaced paper*

118	2s.6d. deep brown (No. F147)	48·00	£110
119	5s. green (No. F149) (R.)	50·00	£130
120	10s. carmine-lake (No. F155)	90·00	£250
121	£1 pink (No. F158)	£120	£275
118/121 *Set of 4*		£250	£700

(c) T F **6**. *Thin, hard, chalk-surfaced Wiggins Teape paper*

122	2s.6d. dull brown (No. F170) (12.40)	£180	£160
123	5s. green (No. F172) (R.) (10.40)	£600	£500
123*a*	10s. pale carmine-lake (No. F177) (11.44)	£150	£200
123*b*	£3 green (No. F183) (R.) (date?)	£450	£700
122/123*b* *Set of 4*		£1200	£1400

COOK
IS'DS.

(**28**)

IS'DS.

Small second 'S' (R. 1/2 and R. 8/4, first printing, and R. 6/10, second printing)

1937 (1 June). Coronation. Nos. 599/601 of New Zealand (inscr '12th MAY 1937') optd with T **28**.

124	1d. carmine	40	80
	a. Small second 'S'	16·00	18·00
125	2½d. Prussian blue	80	1·40
	a. Small second 'S'	27·00	30·00
126	6d. red-orange	80	60
	a. Small second 'S'	27·00	27·00
124/126 *Set of 3*		1·75	2·50

The 'Small second 'S" was corrected for the third printing.

29 King George VI

30 Native Village

31 Native Canoe

32 Tropical Landscape

(Des J. Berry (2s., 3s., and frame of 1s.). Eng B.W. Recess Govt Ptg. Office, Wellington)

1938 (2 May). W **43** of New Zealand. P 14.

127	**29**	1s. black and violet	9·00	14·00
128	**30**	2s. black and red-brown	22·00	14·00
		w. Wmk inverted		
129	**31**	3s. greenish blue and green	65·00	55·00
127/129 *Set of 3*			85·00	70·00

(Recess B.W.)

1940 (2 Sept). Surch as in T **32**. W **98** of New Zealand. P 13½×14.

130	**32**	3d. on 1½d. black and purple	75	60

T **32** was not issued without surcharge but archival examples exist (*Price, £250, unused*).

1943–54. Postal Fiscal stamps as T F **6** of New Zealand optd with T **19**. W **98**. Wiggins Teape chalk-surfaced paper. P 14.

131	2s.6d. dull brown (No. F193) (3.46)	£140	£140
	w. Wmk inverted (2.4.51)	55·00	55·00
132	5s. green (No. F195) (R.) (11.43)	19·00	40·00
	w. Wmk inverted (5.54)	65·00	65·00
133	10s. pale carmine-lake (No. F201) (10.48)	£110	£150
	w. Wmk inverted (10.51)	80·00	£120
134	£1 pink (No. F203) (11.47)	75·00	£130
	w. Wmk inverted (19.5.54)	£140	£190
135	£3 green (No. F208) (R.) (1946?)	£1700	£1800
	w. Wmk inverted (28.5.53)	70·00	£180
136	£5 indigo-blue (No. F211) (R.) (25.10.50)	£375	£500
	w. Wmk inverted (19.5.54)	£325	£425
131w/136w *Set of 6*		£550	£850

The £3 and £5 were mainly used for fiscal purposes.

(Recess Govt Ptg Office, Wellington)

1944–46. W **98** of New Zealand (sideways on ½d. 1d., 1s., and 2s.). P 14.

137	**20**	½d. black and deep green (11.44)	1·75	4·25
		w. Wmk sideways inverted	6·50	11·00
138	**21**	1d. black and scarlet (3.45)	2·00	2·75
		w. Wmk sideways inverted	9·00	4·00
		x. Wmk sideways reversed		
139	**22**	2d. black and brown (2.46)	4·50	20·00
140	**23**	2½d. black and deep blue (5.45)	1·50	4·00
141	**24**	4d. black and blue (4.44)	6·00	28·00
		y. Wmk inverted and reversed	42·00	80·00
142	**25**	6d. black and orange (6.44)	5·00	4·25
143	**29**	1s. black and violet (9.44)	5·50	4·75
144	**30**	2s. black and red-brown (8.45)	38·00	60·00
145	**31**	3s. greenish blue and green (6.45)	42·00	35·00
		w. Wmk inverted	£130	
137/145 *Set of 9*			95·00	£140

The normal sideways watermark shows the star to the left of NZ *as seen from the back of the stamp.*

COOK
ISLANDS

(**33**)

1946 (4 June). Peace. Nos. 668, 670, 674/675 of New Zealand optd with T **33** (reading up and down at sides on 2d.).

146	1d. green (Parliament House)	30	10
147	2d. purple (Royal Family) (B.)	30	50
148	6d. chocolate and vermilion (Coat of Arms, foundry and farm)	1·00	1·25
149	8d. black and carmine ('St George') (B.).	60	1·25
146/149 *Set of 4*		2·00	2·75

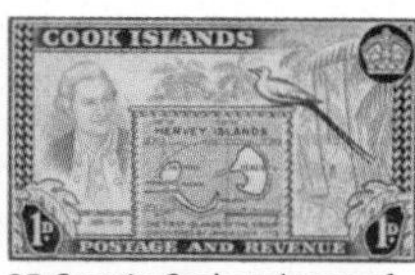

34 Ngatangiia Channel, Rarotonga

35 Captain Cook and map of Hervey Islands

36 Raratonga and Revd. John Williams

37 Aitutaki and palm trees

38 Rarotonga Airfield

39 Penrhyn village

40 Native hut

41 Map and Statue of Captain Cook

42 Native hut and palms

43 *Matua* (inter-island freighter)

(Des J. Berry. Recess Waterlow)

1949 (1 Aug)–**61**. T **34/43**. W **98** of New Zealand (sideways on shilling values). P 13½×13 (horiz) or 13×13½ (vert).

150	**34**	½d. violet and brown	10	1·75
151	**35**	1d. chestnut and green	3·75	3·75
152	**36**	2d. reddish brown and scarlet	2·25	3·75
153	**37**	3d. green and ultramarine	7·00	2·00
		aw. Wmk inverted	£100	
		b. Wmk sideways (white opaque paper) (22.5.61)	8·00	4·00
154	**38**	5d. emerald-green and violet	8·50	1·50
155	**39**	6d. black and carmine	5·50	3·00
156	**40**	8d. olive-green and orange	70	3·75
		w. Wmk inverted	£150	80·00
157	**41**	1s. light blue and chocolate	4·50	3·75
158	**42**	2s. yellow-brown and carmine	7·50	13·00
		w. Wmk sideways inverted		
159	**43**	3s. light blue and bluish green	21·00	32·00
150/159 *Set of 10*			50·00	60·00

43a Queen Elizabeth II

(Des J. Berry. Photo Harrison)

1953 (25 May). Coronation. T **43a** and similar vert design. W **98**. P 14×14½.

160	3d. brown	1·50	85
161	6d. slate-grey	1·50	1·50

Designs: 3d. T **43**; 6d. Westminster Abbey.

IMPERFORATE STAMPS: Imperforate examples of many Cook Islands stamps formerly in the Islands' philatelic archives, were put on sale from mid-2013. These include Nos. 160/161 and numerous issues from 1966 onwards. Such material is outside the scope of this catalogue.

1/6

(44)

1960 (1 Apr). No. 154 surch with T **44**.
162 1s.6d. on 5d. emerald-green and violet.... 75 1·25

45 Tiare Maori

46 Fishing God

47 Frangipani

48 White Tern

49 Hibiscus

50 Long-tailed Tuna

51 Oranges

52 Queen Elizabeth II

53 Island Scene

54 Administration Centre, Mangaia

55 Rarotonga

(Des J. Berry. Recess (1s.6d.), litho (others) B.W.)

1963 (4 June). T **45/55**. W **98** of New Zealand (sideways). P 13½×13 (1d., 2d., 8d.), 13×13½ (3d., 5d., 6d., 1s.) or 13½ (others).
163 **45** 1d. emerald-green and yellow 75 75
164 **46** 2d. brown-red and yellow.............. 30 65
165 **47** 3d. yellow, yellow-green and reddish violet.............................. 70 75
166 **48** 5d. blue and black........................ 8·00 2·25
167 **49** 6d. red, yellow and green................ 1·00 60
168 **50** 8d. black and blue.......................... 4·25 1·50
169 **51** 1s. orange-yellow and yellow-green.. 1·00 1·00
170 **52** 1s.6d. bluish violet............................ 2·75 2·00
171 **53** 2s. bistre-brown and grey-blue...... 2·75 1·75
172 **54** 3s. black and yellow-green............. 2·00 3·50
173 **55** 5s. bistre-brown and blue .... 20·00 8·50
163/173 *Set of 11*.. 40·00 21·00

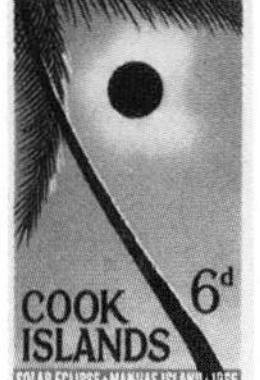
56 Eclipse and Palm

57 NZ Ensign and Map

(Des L. C. Mitchell. Litho B.W.)

1965 (31 May). Solar Eclipse Observation, Manuae Island. W **98** of New Zealand. P 13½.
174 **56** 6d. black, yellow and light blue....... 20 10

The Cook Islands became a self-governing territory in 'free association' with New Zealand on 16 September 1965.

SELF-GOVERNMENT

(Des R. M. Conly (4d.), L. C. Mitchell (10d., 1s.), J. Berry (1s.9d.). Litho B.W.)

1965 (16 Sept). Internal Self-Government. T **57** and similar horiz designs. W **98** of New Zealand (sideways). P 13½.
175 4d. red and blue.......................... 45 10
176 10d. multicoloured....................... 20 15
177 1s. multicoloured........................ 20 15
178 1s.9d. multicoloured..................... 50 1·25
175/178 *Set of 4*.. 1·25 1·50
Designs: 4d. T **57**; 10d. London Missionary Society Church; 1s. Proclamation of Cession, 1900; 1s.9d. Nikao School.

In Memoriam
SIR WINSTON CHURCHILL
1874 - 1965
(61)

Airmail
(62)

1966 (24 Jan). Churchill Commemoration. Nos. 171/173 and 175/177 optd with T **61**, in red.
179 4d. red and blue......................... 1·50 30
a. 'l' for '1' in '1874'......................... 14·00
180 10d. multicoloured...................... 2·50 80
a. Opt inverted.............................. £225
b. 'l' for '1' in '1874'......................... 16·00
181 1s. multicoloured........................ 2·75 1·25
a. Opt inverted.............................. £170
b. 'l' for '1' in '1874'......................... 16·00
182 2s. bistre-brown and grey-blue............... 2·75 2·25
a. 'l' for '1' in '1874'......................... 8·00
183 3s. black and yellow-green..................... 2·75 2·25
a. 'l' for '1' in '1874'......................... 8·00
184 5s. bistre-brown and blue...................... 3·00 2·25
a. 'l' for '1' in '1874'......................... 11·00
179/184 *Set of 6*.. 13·50 8·25
The lower case 'l' for '1' in '1874' occurred on R. 6/5 for all values and additionally on R. 12/5 for the 2s., 3s. and 5s.

1966 (22 Apr). Air. Various stamps optd with T **62** or surch also.
185 6d. red, yellow and green (No. 167)........ 1·25 20
186 7d. on 8d. black and blue (No. 168)........ 2·00 25
187 10d. on 3d. yellow, yellow-green and reddish violet (No. 165)..................... 1·00 15
188 1s. orange-yellow and yellow-green (No. 169).. 1·00 15
189 1s.6d. bluish violet (No. 170)...................... 2·00 1·25
190 2s.3d. on 3s. black and yellow-green (No. 172).. 1·00 65
191 5s. bistre-brown and blue (No. 173)....... 1·75 1·50
192 10s. on 2s. bistre-brown and grey-blue (No. 171).. 1·75 14·00
193 £1 pink (No. 134)............................ 13·00 20·00
a. Aeroplane omitted.......................... 35·00 55·00
w. Wmk inverted................................. 17·00 23·00
wa. Aeroplane omitted.......................... 38·00 60·00
185/193 *Set of 9*.. 22·00 35·00
No. 193a occurred in all stamps of the last vertical row as insufficient aeroplane symbols were available. There are also numerous other varieties on all values, notably aeroplanes of different sizes and broken first 'i' with dot missing owing to damaged type.

PRINTERS. The following stamps were printed by Heraclio Fournier, Spain, except *where otherwise stated.* The process used was photogravure.

63 *Adoration of the Magi* (Fra Angelico)

1966 (28 Nov). Christmas. T **63** and similar multicoloured designs. P 13×12 (horiz) or 12×13 (vert).
194 1d. Type **63**...................................... 50 1·00
a. Perf 13×14½................................ 10 10
195 2d. *The Nativity* (Memling) (*vert*)............ 13·00 23·00
a. Perf 14½×13................................ 20 10
196 4d. *Adoration of the Magi* (Velazquez).... 1·00 1·00
a. Perf 13×14½................................ 30 15
197 10d. *Adoration of the Magi* (Bosch)........... 2·00 7·00
a. Perf 13×14½................................ 30 20
198 1s.6d. *Adoration of the Shepherds* (J. de Ribera) (*vert*)................................ 45·00 10·00
a. Perf 14½×13................................ 40 35
194/198 *Set of 5*.. 55·00 38·00
194a/198a *Set of 5*...................................... 1·10 80

68 Tennis, and Queen Elizabeth II

(Des V. Whiteley)

1967 (12 Jan). Second South Pacific Games, Nouméa. T **68** and similar horiz designs in orange-brown, black and new blue (1d.) or multicoloured (others). P 13½.

(a) Postage
199 ½d. Type **68**.. 10 10
200 1d. Netball and Games emblem............... 10 10
201 4d. Boxing and Cook Islands' team badge 10 10
202 7d. Football and Queen Elizabeth II........ 20 15

(b) Air
203 10d. Running and Games emblem............ 20 15
204 2s.3d. Running and Cook Islands' team badge.. 25 65
199/204 *Set of 6*.. 70 1·00

(New Currency, 100 cents = 1 dollar)

1c (74) 2½c (I) 2½c (II)

1c Condensed 'c'
1c Thin 'c'
1c Thin numeral
1c Thin numeral and 'c'
.7c Thin numeral and 'c' with stop

1967 (3 Apr–6 June). Decimal Currency. Nos. 134, 135w, 136, 163/170 and 172/175 surch as T **74** by the Government Printer. Sterling values obliterated except No. 218.
205 1c. on 1d. emerald-green and yellow (4.5.67).. 45 1·50
a. Condensed 'c' (R. 2/4, 3/8, 6/2, 8/4). 3·50
b. Thin 'c' (R. 3/5, 8/1)......................... 4·50
c. Thin '1' (R. 3/6, 8/2)......................... 4·50
d. Thin '1c' (R. 3/7, 8/3)...................... 4·50
206 2c. on 2d. brown-red and yellow............ 10 10
a. Thin '2c' (R. 2/1, 8/8)...................... 2·00
b. Condensed 'c' (R. 4/8, 5/4)................ 2·00
207 2½c. on 3d. yellow, yellow-green and reddish violet (I).. 20 10
a. Horiz pair. Nos. 207/208.................. 60 75
b. Thin '2½c' (R. 6/5)............................ 4·00
208 2½c. on 3d. yellow, yellow-green and reddish violet (II)...................................... 20 10
a. Thin '2½c' and stop to left (R. 3/4).... 4·00
b. Thin '2½c' and stop to right (R. 9/2).. 4·00
209 3c. on 4d. red and blue.......................... 15 10
a. Thin '3c' (R. 3/6, 4/10, 5/7, 6/3)......... 2·00
210 4c. on 5d. blue and black (4.5.67)........... 12·00 30
a. Thin '4c' (R. 5/4, 7/5)........................ 45·00
b. Thin '4c' and stop (R. 2/8).................. 75·00
211 5c. on 6d. red, yellow and green............. 15 10
a. Thin '5c' (R. 2/8, 8/7)........................ 3·00
b. Thin '5c' and stop (R. 6/4)................. 6·50
212 5c. on 6d. black, yellow and light blue... 5·00 2·75
a. Thin '5c' (R. 5/10, 6/6)...................... 25·00
b. Thin '5c' and stop (R. 4/5)................. 45·00
c. Condensed 'c' (R. 2/4, 3/9)................ 25·00
213 7c. on 8d. black and blue........................ 30 10
a. Thin '7c' (R.7/1, 8/5)........................ 5·00
b. Thin '7c' and stop (R. 3/8, 6/4).......... 5·00
214 10c. on 1s. orange-yellow and yellow-green.. 15 10
a. Thin '10c' (R. 3/4, 5/5, 9/8)............... 3·00
215 15c. on 1s.6d. bluish violet (R.) (4.5.67).... 2·25 1·00
216 30c. on 3s. black and yellow-green (R.) (4.5.67).. 32·00 9·00
a. Thin '30c' (R. 3/10)........................... 85·00
217 50c. on 5s. bistre-brown and blue (R.) (4.5.67).. 4·00 3·25
a. Thin '50c' (R. 2/1, 3/7, 5/4, 4/10)......... 13·00
218 $1 and 10s. on 10d. mult (R.) (4.5.67).... 19·00 5·50
219 $2 on £1 pink (R.) (6.6.67)..................... 65·00 85·00
220 $6 on £3 green (R.) (6.6.67)................... £120 £160
221 $10 on £5 blue (R.) (6.6.67).................... £170 £200
w. Wmk inverted................................. £150 £200
205/218 *Set of 14*.. 65·00 21·00
The two types of the 2½c. occur on alternate vertical rows within the sheet.
The surcharge on No. 218 is $1 and its equivalent 10s. in the old currency. The '10d.' is obliterated by three bars.

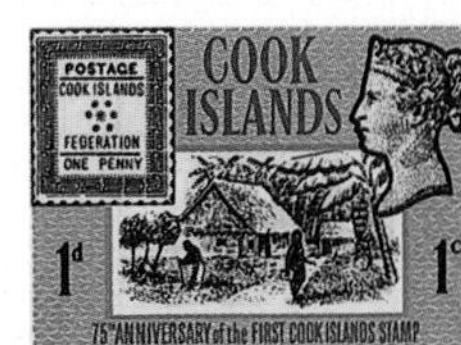
75 Village Scene. Cook Islands 1d. Stamp of 1892 and Queen Victoria (from 'Penny Black')

(Des V. Whiteley)

1967 (3 July). 75th Anniversary of First Cook Islands Stamps. T **75** and similar horiz designs. Multicoloured. P 13½.
222 1c. (1d.) Type **75**.................................. 10 35
223 3c. (4d.) Post Office, Avarua, Rarotonga and Queen Elizabeth II......................... 15 20
224 8c. (10d.) Avarua, Rarotonga and Cook Islands 10d. stamp of 1892................. 30 15
225 18c. (1s.9d.) *Moana Roo* (inter-island ship), Douglas DC-3 aircraft, map and Captain Cook.............................. 1·40 1·25
222/225 *Set of 4*.. 1·75 1·75
MS226 134×109 mm. Nos. 222/225............................. 1·75 2·75
The face values are expressed in decimal currency and in the sterling equivalent.
Each value was issued in sheets of eight stamps and one label.

79 Hibiscus

80 Queen Elizabeth II

81 Queen Elizabeth and Flowers

Two types of $4

I. Value 32½ mm long. Coarse screen.
II. Value 33½ mm long. Finer screen.

(Floral designs from paintings by Kay Billings)

1967 (31 July)–**71**. Multicoloured designs as T **79/81**. P 14×13½.

A. Without fluorescent security markings

227A	½c. Typa **79**	10	10
228A	1c. *Hibiscus syriacus* (27×37 *mm*)	10	10
229A	2c. Frangipani (27×37 *mm*)	10	10
230A	2½c. *Clitoria ternatea* (27×37 *mm*)	20	10
231A	3c. *Suva Queen* (27×37 *mm*)	55	10
232A	4c. Water Lily ('WALTER LILY') (27×37 *mm*)	70	1·00
233A	4c. Water Lily (27×37 *mm*)	2·00	2·00
234A	5c. *Bauhinia bipianata rosea* (27×37 *mm*)	35	10
235A	6c. Hibiscus (27×37 *mm*)	40	10
236A	8c. *Allamanda cathartica* (27×37 *mm*)	40	10
237A	9c. Stephanotis (27×37 *mm*)	40	10
238A	10c. *Poinciana regia flamboyant* (27×37 *mm*)	40	10
239A	15c. Frangipani (27×37 *mm*) (11.8.67)	40	10
240A	20c. Thunbergia (27×37 *mm*) (11.8.67)	4·50	1·50
241A	25c. Canna Lily (27×37 *mm*) (11.8.67)	80	30
242A	30c. *Euphorbia pulcherrima poinsettia* (27×37 *mm*) (11.8.67)	65	50
243A	50c. *Gardenia taitensis* (27×37 *mm*) (11.8.67)	1·00	55
244A	$1 Type **80** (31.8.67)	2·25	80
245A	$2 Type **80** (31.8.67)	4·75	1·50
246A	$4 Type **81** (I) (30.4.68)	1·50	4·25
247A	$6 Type **81** (30.4.68)	1·75	7·00
247cA	$8 Type **81** (21.4.69)	6·00	17·00
248A	$10 Type **81** (12.7.68)	3·25	14·00
227A/248A	*Set of 22*	27·00	42·00

B. With fluorescent security markings

227B	½c. Type **78** (9.2.70)	20	10
228B	1c. *Hibiscus syriacus* (27×37 *mm*) (9.2.70)	20	10
229B	2c. Frangipani (27×37 *mm*) (9.2.70)	20	10
230B	2½c. *Clitoria ternatea* (27×37 *mm*) (9.2.70)	20	10
231B	3c. *Suva Queen* (27×37 *mm*) (9.2.70)	40	10
233B	4c. Water Lily (27×37 *mm*) (9.2.70)	2·50	10
234B	5c. *Bauhinia bipirsnata roses* (27×37 *mm*) (9.2.70)	30	10
235B	6c. Hibiscus (27×37 *mm*) (9.2.70)	30	10
236B	8c. *Allemanda cathartica* (27×37 *mm*) (9.2.70)	30	10
237B	9c. Stephanotis (27×37 *mm*) (9.2.70)	30	10
238B	10c. *Poinciana regia flamboyant* (27×37 *mm*) (9.2.70)	30	10
239B	15c. Frangipani (27×37 *mm*) (9.2.70)	40	10
240B	20c. Thunbergia (27×37 *mm*) (9.2.70)	3·50	1·75
241B	25c. Canna Lily (27×37 *mm*) (9.2.70)	1·00	15
242B	30c. *Euphorbia pulcherrima poinsettia* (27×37 *mm*) (9.2.70)	1·25	40
243B	50c. *Gardenia taitensis* (27×37 *mm*) (9.2.70)	1·25	40
244B	$1 Type **80** (12.10.70)	1·25	80
245B	$2 Type **80** (12.10.70)	2·25	2·50
246B	$4 Type **81** (I) (11.11.70)	35·00	55·00
	a. Type II (14.7.71)	5·50	8·50
247B	$6 Type **81** (12.2.71)	11·00	6·00
247cB	$8 Type **81** (3.5.71)	12·00	10·00
248B	$10 Type **81** (14.6.71)	16·00	12·00
227B/248B	*Set of 22*	55·00	38·00

The 'WALTER' spelling error occurred on all stamps in one of the four post office sheets which went to make up the printing sheet and this was corrected in later supplies.

FLUORESCENT PAPER. This is on paper treated with fluorescent security markings, in the form of faint multiple Coats of Arms. Stamps exist with these markings inverted. In addition an invisible synthetic gum has been used which prevents curling and is suitable for use in the tropics without interleaving the sheets.

Some of the above are known with these markings omitted and can be distinguished when in unused condition from the original printings without markings by their synthetic invisible gum.

97 *Ia Oraria Maria*

1967 (24 Oct). Gauguin's Polynesian Paintings. T **97** and similar designs. Multicoloured. P 13.

249	1c. Type **97**	10	10
250	3c. *Riders on the Beach*	10	10
251	5c. *Still Life with Flowers*	15	10
252	8c. *Whispered Words*	20	10
253	15c. *Maternity*	30	15
254	22c. *Why are you angry?*	35	20
249/254	*Set of 6*	1·00	65
MS255	156×132 mm. Nos. 249/254	1·40	1·50

The 5c. includes an inset portrait of Queen Elizabeth.

98 *The Holy Family* (Rubens)

HURRICANE
RELIEF
PLUS 5c

(**99**)

1967 (4 Dec). Christmas. Renaissance Paintings. T **98** and similar designs. Multicoloured. P 12×13.

256	1c. Type **98**	10	10
257	3c. *Adoration of the Magi* (Dürer)	10	10
258	4c. *The Lucca Madonna* (J. van Eyck)	10	10
259	8c. *The Adoration of the Shepherds* (J. da Bassano)	20	15
260	15c. *Adoration of the Shepherds* (El Greco)	35	15
261	25c. *Madonna and Child* (Correggio)	40	15
256/261	*Set of 6*	1·10	65

1968 (12 Feb). Hurricane Relief. Nos. 231A, 233A, 251, 238A, 241A and 243A/244A surch as T **99** by Govt Printer, Rarotonga.

262	3c.+1c. *Suva Queen*	15	25
263	4c.+1c. Water Lily	15	25
264	5c.+2c. *Still Life with Flowers*	15	25
	a. Black surch albino		
265	10c.+2c. *Poinciana regia flamboyant*	15	25
266	25c.+5c. Canna Lily	20	30
267	50c.+10c. *Gardenia taitensis*	25	40
268	$1+10c. Type **80**	35	60
262/268	*Set of 7*	1·25	2·00

The surcharge on No. 268 is as T **99**, but with seriffed letters. On No. 264 silver blocking obliterates the design area around the lettering.

100 *Matavai Bay, Tahiti* (J. Barralet)

101 *Resolution and Discovery* (J. Webber)

(Des J. Berry)

1968 (12 Sept). Bicentenary of Captain Cook's First Voyage of Discovery. Multicoloured. Invisible gum. P 13.

(a) Postage. Vert designs as T **100**

269	½c. Type **100**	10	20
270	1c. *Island of Huaheine* (John Cleveley)	15	20
271	2c. *Town of St Peter and St Paul, Kamchatka* (J. Webber)	25	25
272	4c. *The Ice Islands* (Antarctica: W. Hodges)	35	20

(b) Air. Horiz designs as T **101**

273	6c. Type **101**	35	25
274	10c. *The Island of Tahiti* (W. Hodges)	35	25
275	15c. *Karakakooa, Hawaii* (J. Webber)	35	35
276	25c. *The Landing at Middleburg* (J. Shemin)	45	55
269/276	*Set of 8*	2·00	2·00

Each value was issued in sheets of ten stamps and two labels.

FLUORESCENT PAPER. From No. 277, *unless otherwise stated*, all issues are printed on paper treated with fluorescent security markings with invisible synthetic gum. These markings may be inverted or omitted in error.

102 Dinghy-sailing

103 *Madonna and Child* (Titian)

1968 (21 Oct). Olympic Games, Mexico. T **102** and similar horiz designs. Multicoloured. P 13.

277	1c. Type **102**	10	10
278	5c. Gymnastics	10	10
279	15c. High jumping	15	10
280	20c. High-diving	15	10
281	30c. Cycling	60	20
282	50c. Hurdling	35	25
277/282	*Set of 6*	1·25	75

Each value was issued in sheets of ten stamps and two labels.

1968 (2 Dec). Christmas. Paintings. T **103** and similar vert designs. Multicoloured. P 13½.

283	1c. Type **103**	10	10
284	4c. *The Holy Family with Lamb* (Raphael)	15	10
285	10c. *The Virgin of the Rosary* (Murillo)	20	10
286	20c. *Adoration of the Kings* (Memling)	30	10
287	30c. *Adoration of the Magi* (Ghirlandaio)	40	10
283/287	*Set of 5*	1·00	45
MS288	114×177 mm. Nos. 283/287 plus label	1·25	1·60

104 Camp-fire Cooking

1969 (6 Feb). Diamond Jubilee of New Zealand Scout Movement and Fifth National (New Zealand) Jamboree. T **104** and similar square designs. Multicoloured. P 13½.

289	½c. Type **104**	10	10
290	1c. Descent by rope	10	10
291	5c. Semaphore	15	10
292	10c. Tree-planting	20	10
293	20c. Constructing a shelter	25	15
294	30c. Lord Baden-Powell and island scene	45	25
289/294	*Set of 6*	1·00	50

Each value was issued in sheets of ten stamps and two labels.

105 High Jumping

1969 (7 July). Third South Pacific Games, Port Moresby. T **105** and similar triangular designs. Multicoloured. Without fluorescent security markings. P 13×13½.

295	½c. Type **105**	10	40
296	½c. Footballer	10	40
297	1c. Basketball	50	40
298	1c. Weightlifter	50	40
299	4c. Tennis-player	50	50
300	4c. Hurdler	50	50
301	10c. Javelin-thrower	55	50
302	10c. Runner	55	50
303	15c. Golfer	1·75	1·50
304	15c. Boxer	1·75	1·50
295/304	*Set of 10*	6·00	5·75
MS305	174×129 mm. Nos. 295/304 plus two labels	8·00	7·00

Each value was issued in sheets containing five *se-tenant* pairs of both designs and two labels.

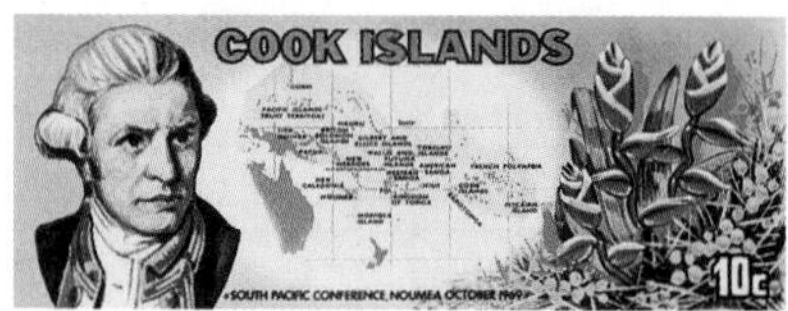

106 Flowers, Map and Captain Cook

1969 (8 Oct). South Pacific Conference, Nouméa. T **106** and similar horiz designs. Multicoloured. Without fluorescent security markings. P 13.

306	5c. Flowers, map and Premier Albert Henry	20	20
307	10c. Type **106**	80	40
308	25c. Flowers, map and NZ Arms	30	40
309	30c. Queen Elizabeth II, map and flowers	30	40
306/309	*Set of 4*	1·40	1·25

107 *Virgin and Child with Saints Jerome and Dominic* (Lippi)

108 *The Resurrection of Christ* (Raphael)

1969 (21 Nov). Christmas. Paintings. T **107** and similar designs. Multicoloured. Without fluorescent security markings. P 13.

310	1c. Type **107**	10	10
311	4c. *The Holy Family* (Fra Bartolomeo)	10	10
312	10c. *The Adoration of the Shepherds* (A. Mengs)	15	10

313 20c. *Madonna and Child with Saints* (R. Campin) 25 20
314 30c. *The Madonna of the Basket* (Correggio) 25 30
310/314 *Set of 5* 75 70
MS315 132×97 mm. Nos. 310/314 1·00 1·50
Each value was issued in sheets of nine stamps and one label.

1970 (12 Mar). Easter. Paintings. T **108** and similar vert designs showing *The Resurrection of Christ* by the artists named. Multicoloured. P 13.
316 4c. Type **108** 10 10
317 8c. Dirk Bouts 10 10
318 20c. Altdorfer 15 10
319 25c. Murillo 20 10
316/319 *Set of 4* 50 35
MS320 132×162 mm. Nos. 316/319 1·25 1·25
Each value was issued in sheets of eight stamps and one label.

KIA ORANA
APOLLO 13
ASTRONAUTS
Te Atua to
Tatou Irinakianga
(**109**)

1970 (17–30 Apr). *Apollo 13*. Nos. 233, 236, 239/240, 242 and 245/246 optd with T **109** (4c. to $2) or with first three lines only in larger type ($4), by Govt Printer. Without fluorescent security markings.
321 4c. Water Lily 10 15
a. Opt albino 26·00
322 8c. *Allamanda cathartics* 10 15
323 15c. Frangipani 10 15
324 20c. Thunbergia 40 20
325 30c. *Euphorbia pulcherrima poinsettia* 20 25
326 $2 Type **80** 50 1·00
327 $4 Type **81** (30.4) 29·00 45·00
a. With fluorescent security markings 1·25 2·75
ab. Opt double, one albino † —
321/327a *Set of 7* 2·25 4·25

110 The Royal Family

(Des V. Whiteley (5c.), J. Berry ($1))

1970 (12 June). Royal Visit to New Zealand. T **110** and similar horiz designs. Multicoloured. P 13.
328 5c. Type **110** 75 30
329 30c. Captain Cook and HMS *Endeavour* 1·75 1·75
330 $1 Royal Visit commemorative coin 2·25 3·00
328/330 *Set of 3* 4·25 4·50
MS331 145×97 mm. Nos. 328/330 8·50 10·00
Each value was issued in sheets of eight stamps and one label.

FOUR
DOLLARS

FIFTH ANNIVERSARY SELF-GOVERNMENT AUGUST 1970 (**113**)
$4.00 (**114**)

1970 (27 Aug). Fifth Anniversary of Self-Government. Nos. 328/330 optd with T **113** (30c. and $1), or in single line in silver around frame of stamp (5c.).
332 5c. Type **110** 40 15
333 30c. Captain Cook and HMS *Endeavour* 80 35
334 $1 Royal Visit commemorative coin 1·00 90
332/334 *Set of 3* 2·00 1·25

1970 (11 Nov). Nos. 247c and 248 surch with T **114** by Govt Printer, Rarotonga. Without fluorescent security markings.
335 **81** $4 on $8 multicoloured 32·00 28·00
a. With fluorescent security markings 1·25 1·75
336 $4 on $10 multicoloured 32·00 48·00
a. With fluorescent security markings 1·25 1·50
There are variations in the setting of this surcharge and also in the rule.

115 Mary, Joseph and Christ in Manger

(Des from De Lisle Psalter)

1970 (30 Nov). Christmas. T **115** and similar square designs. Multicoloured. P 13.
337 1c. Type **115** 10 10
338 4c. Shepherds and Apparition of the Angel 20 10
339 10c. Mary showing Child to Joseph 25 10
340 20c. The Wise Men bearing Gifts 30 20
341 30c. Parents wrapping Child in swaddling clothes 30 35
337/341 *Set of 5* 1·00 75
MS342 100×139 mm. Nos. 337/341 plus label 1·00 1·50
Each value was issued in sheets of five stamps and one label. Stamps from the miniature sheet are smaller, since they do not have the buff parchment border as on the stamps from the sheets.

AITUTAKI

The island of Aitutaki, under British protection from 1888, was annexed by New Zealand on 11 June 1901.

NEW ZEALAND DEPENDENCY

Stamps of COOK ISLANDS were used in Aitutaki from 1892 until 1903.

PRICES FOR STAMPS ON COVER TO 1945

Nos. 1/7	*from* × 4
Nos. 9/14	*from* × 3
Nos. 15/29	*from* × 4
Nos. 30/32	*from* × 6

Stamps of New Zealand overprinted or surcharged. For illustrations of watermarks and definitive types see New Zealand.

AITUTAKI. (**1**)
Ava Pene. (**2**) ½d.
Tai Pene. (**3**) 1d.
Rua Pene Ma Te Ava. (**4**) 2½d.
Toru Pene. (**5**) 3d.
Ono Pene. (**6**) 6d.
Tai Tiringi. (**7**) 1s.

1903 (29 June)–**11**. T **23**, **27/28**, **31**, **34** and **42** surch with T **1** at top and T **2** to **7** at foot. Thin, hard 'Cowan' paper. W **43**.
(a) P 14
1 ½d. green (No. 302) (R.) 4·75 6·50
2 1d. carmine (No. 303) (B.) 5·00 5·50
3 2½d. deep blue (No. 320*a*) (R.) (9.11) 8·00 18·00
a. 'Ava' without stop £150 £250
1/3 *Set of 3* 16·00 27·00
(b) P 11
4 2½d. blue (No. 308) (R.) 20·00 12·00
5 3d. yellow-brown (No. 309) (B.) 18·00 15·00
6 6d. rose-red (No. 312*a*) (B.) 32·00 25·00
7 1s. bright red (No. 315*a*) (B.) 55·00 90·00
a. 'Tiringi' without stop (R. 7/12) £650 £950
b. Orange-red 70·00 £100
ba. 'Tiringi' without stop (R. 7/12) £850 £1100
4/7 *Set of 4* £110 £130
Nos. 1/2 and 4/7 were placed on sale in Auckland on 12 June 1903. There were four states of the overprint used for No. 3. On the first the 'no stop' variety (No. 3a) occurs on R. 6/8, on the second it appears on R. 1/4, 2/4 and 6/8, on the third on R. 5/8 and 6/8, and on the fourth all stops are present.

AITUTAKI.

Ono Pene.
(**8**)

1911–16. T **51** and **53** surch with T **1** at top and T **2** or **3** at foot and T **52** surch as T **8**. P 14×15 (½d., 1d.) or 14×14½ (others).
9 ½d. green (No. 387) (R.) (9.11) 1·00 8·50
10 1d. carmine (No. 405) (B.) (2.13) 3·00 13·00
11 6d. carmine (No. 392) (B.) (23.5.16) 50·00 £140
12 1s. vermilion (No. 394) (B.) (9.14) 60·00 £150
9/12 *Set of 4* £100 £275

1916–17. T **60** (recess) surch as T **8**. W **43**. P 14×13½.
13 6d. carmine (No. 425) (B.) (6.6.16) 9·00 50·00
a. Perf 14×14½ 7·50 29·00
b. Vert pair. Nos. 13/13a 50·00 £180
14 1s. vermilion (No. 430) (B.) (3.17) 10·00 90·00
a. Perf 14×14½ 12·00 90·00
ab. 'Tai' without dot (R. 8/9, 9/12, 10/12) £225 £750
ac. 'Tiringi' without dot on second 'i' (R. 8/12, 10/7) £300 £850
ad. 'Tiringi' without dot on third 'i' (R. 8/11) £425 £1100
b. Vert pair. Nos. 14/14a £100 £400

1917–18. T **60** (recess) optd 'AITUTAKI' only, as in T **8**. W **43**. P 14×13½.
15 2½d. blue (No. 419) (R.) (12.18) 2·00 25·00
a. Perf 14×14½ 1·75 16·00
b. Vert pair. Nos. 15/15a 30·00 £150
16 3d. chocolate (No. 420) (B.) (1.18) 1·75 40·00
a. Perf 14×14½ 1·50 32·00
b. Vert pair. Nos. 16/16a 30·00 £170
17 6d. carmine (No. 425) (B.) (11.17) 6·00 23·00
a. Perf 14×14½ 4·75 21·00
b. Vert pair. Nos. 17/17a 40·00 £150
18 1s. vermilion (No. 430) (B.) (11.17) 14·00 48·00
a. Perf 14×14½ 10·00 32·00
b. Vert pair. Nos. 18/18a 65·00 £225
15/18 *Set of 4* 21·00 £120
15a/18a *Set of 4* 16·00 90·00

1917–20. T **53** and **61** (typo) optd 'AITUTAKI' only, as in T **8**. W **43**. P 14×15.
19 ½d. green (No. 435) (R.) (2.20) 1·00 6·00
20 1d. carmine (No. 405) (B.) (5.20) 6·00 35·00
21 1½d. slate (No. 437) (R.) (11.17) 4·75 30·00
22 1½d. orange-brown (No. 438) (R.) (2.19) 80 7·00
23 3d. chocolate (No. 440) (B.) (6.19) 3·50 22·00
19/23 *Set of 5* 14·50 90·00

(Des and recess Perkins Bacon & Co)

1920 (23 Aug). T **9/14** of Cook Islands, but inscr 'AITUTAKI'. No wmk. P 14.
24 ½d. black and green 3·50 25·00
25 1d. black and dull carmine 3·50 17·00
a. Double derrick flaw (R. 2/8, 3/6 or 5/2) 11·00
26 1½d. black and sepia 6·00 13·00
27 3d. black and deep blue 2·50 15·00
28 6d. red-brown and slate 5·50 15·00
29 1s. black and purple 9·50 16·00
24/29 *Set of 6* 27·00 90·00
Examples of the 6d. with centre inverted (*price* £900, *unused*) and the 1s. with frame printed double (*price* £225, *unused*) come from printer's waste and were not issued.

(Recess Govt Printing Office, Wellington)

1924–27. T **9/10** and **16** of Cook Islands, but inscr 'AITUTAKI'. W **43** of New Zealand. P 14.
30 ½d. black and green (5.27) 2·00 24·00
31 1d. black and deep carmine (10.24) 6·00 13·00
a. Double derrick flaw (R. 2/8, 3/6 or 5/2) 16·00 29·00
32 2½d. black and dull blue (10.27) 7·50 85·00
30/32 *Set of 3* 14·00 £110
Cook Islands stamps superseded those of Aitutaki on 15 March 1932.

PENRHYN ISLAND

Stamps of COOK ISLANDS were used on Penrhyn Island from late 1901 until the issue of the surcharged stamps in May 1902.

PRICES FOR STAMPS ON COVER TO 1945

No. 1	*from* × 25
No. 3	—
Nos. 4/5	*from* × 25
Nos. 6/8	—
Nos. 9/10	*from* × 50
Nos. 11/13	—
Nos. 14/18	*from* × 3
Nos. 19/23	*from* × 2
Nos. 24/37	*from* × 3
Nos. 38/40	*from* × 5

NEW ZEALAND DEPENDENCY The island of Penrhyn, under British protection from 20 September 1888, was annexed by New Zealand on 11 June 1901.

Stamps of New Zealand overprinted or surcharged. For illustrations of New Zealand watermarks and definitive types see New Zealand.

PENRHYN ISLAND. ½ PENI. (**1**)
PENRHYN ISLAND. TAI PENI. (**2**) 1d.
PENRHYN ISLAND. 2½ PENI. (**3**)

1902 (5 May). T **23**, **27** and **42** surch with T **1**, **2** and **3**.
(a) Thick, soft Pirie paper. No wmk. P 11
1 2½d. blue (No. 260) (R.) 15·00 15·00
a. '½' and 'P' spaced (all stamps in 8th vert row) 30·00 32·00
(b) Thin, hard Basted Mills paper. W 38 of New Zealand
(i) P 11
3 1d. carmine (No. 286) (Br.) £850 £1200
(ii) P 14
4 ½d. green (No. 287) (R.) 1·00 14·00
a. No stop after 'ISLAND' £150 £325
5 1d. carmine (No. 288) (Br.) 3·25 28·00
(iii) Perf compound of 11 and 14
6 1d. carmine (No. 290) (Br.) £1200 £1400
(iv) Mixed perfs
7 ½d. green (No. 291) (R.) £2250
8 1d. carmine (No. 292) (Br.) £2500
(c) Thin, hard Cowan paper. W 43 of New Zealand
(i) P 14
9 ½d. green (No. 302) (R.) 4·75 16·00
a. No stop after 'ISLAND' (R. 10/6) £180 £375
10 1d. carmine (No. 303) (B.) 1·25 9·50
a. No stop after 'ISLAND' (R. 10/6) 60·00 £170
(ii) Perf compound of 11 and 14
11 1d. carmine (No. 305) (B.) £15000
(iii) Mixed perfs
12 ½d. green (No. 306) (R.) £2250 £2500
13 1d. carmine (No. 307) (B.) £800 £1000

PENRHYN ISLAND. (**4**)
Toru Pene. (**5**) 3d.
Ono Pene. (**6**) 6d.
Tahi Silingi. (**7**) 1s.

1903 (28 Feb). T **28**, **31** and **34** surch with name at top, T **4**, and values at foot, T **5/7**. Thin, hard 'Cowan' paper. W **43** (sideways) of New Zealand. P 11.
14 3d. yellow-brown (No. 309) (B.) 10·00 45·00
15 6d. rose-red (No. 312*a*) (B.) 15·00 50·00

16 1s. brown-red (No. 315) (B.) 60·00 60·00
a. *Bright red* 42·00 42·00
b. *Orange-red* 65·00 65·00
14/16*a Set of 3* 60·00 £120

1914 (May)–**15**. T **51/52** surch with T **1** (½d.) or optd with T **4** at top and surch with T **6/7** at foot.
19 ½d. yellow-green (No. 387) (C.) (5.14) 80 12·00
a. No stop after 'ISLAND' 25·00 £110
b. No stop after 'PENI' (R. 3/17) £110 £350
c. Vermilion opt (1.15) 80 8·50
ca. No stop after 'ISLAND' 10·00 75·00
cb. No stop after 'PENI' (R. 3/5, 3/17) 55·00 £190
22 6d. carmine (No. 393) (B.) (8.14) 23·00 75·00
23 1s. vermilion (No. 394) (B.) (8.14) 50·00 £100
19/23 *Set of 3* 65·00 £160

The 'no stop after ISLAND' variety occurs on R. 1/4, 1/10, 1/16, 1/22, 6/4, 6/10, 6/16 and 6/22 of the carmine surcharge, No. 19, and on these positions plus R. 1/12, 1/24, 6/12 and 6/24 for the vermilion, No. 19c.

PENRHYN ISLAND. — Normal.
PENRHYN ISLAND. — Narrow spacing.

1917 (Nov)–**20**. Optd as T **4**.

*(a) T **60** (recess). W **43** of New Zealand. P 14×13½*
24 2½d. blue (No. 419) (R.) (10.20) 3·00 18·00
a. Perf 14×14½ 2·00 12·00
ab. No stop after 'ISLAND' (R. 10/8) £190 £500
b. Vert pair. Nos. 24/24a 45·00 £110
25 3d. chocolate (No. 420) (B.) (6.18) 12·00 70·00
a. Perf 14×14½ 9·50 70·00
b. Vert pair. Nos. 25/25a 70·00 £275
26 6d. carmine (No. 425) (B.) (1.18) 8·00 26·00
a. Perf 14×14½ 5·00 21·00
ab. No stop after 'ISLAND' (R. 10/8) £450 £900
b. Vert pair. Nos. 26/26a 55·00 £160
27 1s. vermilion (No. 430) (B.) (12.17) 15·00 45·00
a. Perf 14×14½ 12·00 35·00
ab. No stop after 'ISLAND' (R. 10/8) £550 £1000
b. Vert pair. Nos. 27/27a £100 £275
24/27 *Set of 4* 35·00 £140
24a/27a *Set of 4* 26·00 £120

*(b) T **61** (typo). W **43** of New Zealand. P 14×15*
28 ½d. green (No. 435) (R.) (2.20) 1·00 2·00
a. No stop after 'ISLAND' (R. 2/24) £150 £225
b. Narrow spacing 7·50 16·00
29 1½d. slate (No. 437) (R.) 7·00 28·00
a. Narrow spacing 18·00 65·00
30 1½d. orange-brown (No. 438) (R.) (2.19) 1·00 28·00
a. Narrow spacing 7·50 65·00
31 3d. chocolate (No. 440) (B.) (6.19) 4·50 45·00
a. Narrow spacing 17·00 £100
28/31 *Set of 4* 12·00 90·00

The narrow spacing variety occurs on R. 1/5–8, 4/21–4, 7/5–8 and 9/21–4.

(Recess P.B.)

1920 (23 Aug). As T **9/14** of Cook Islands, but inscr 'PENRHYN'. No wmk. P 14.
32 ½d. black and emerald 1·50 25·00
a. Part imperf block of 4 £1500
33 1d. black and deep red 1·50 17·00
a. Double derrick flaw (R. 2/8, 3/6 or 5/2) 5·50 48·00
34 1½d. black and deep violet 6·50 19·00
35 3d. black and red 2·50 19·00
36 6d. red-brown and sepia 3·25 20·00
37 1s. black and slate-blue 10·00 28·00
32/37 *Set of 6* 22·00 £110

No. 32a comes from sheets on which two rows were imperforate between horizontally and the second row additionally imperforate vertically.

Examples of the ½d. and 1d. with centre inverted were not supplied to the Post Office (*Price £1000 each, unused*).

(Recess Govt Printing Office, Wellington)

1927–29. As T **9/10** and **16** of Cook Islands, but inscr 'PENRHYN'. W **43**. P 14.
38 ½d. black and green (5.29) 5·50 25·00
39 1d. black and deep carmine (14.3.28) 5·50 25·00
a. Double derrick flaw (R. 2/8, 3/6 or 5/2) 16·00
40 2½d. red-brown and dull blue (10.27) 19·00 50·00
38/40 *Set of 3* 27·00 90·00

Cook Islands stamps superseded those of Penrhyn Island on 15 March 1932.

Cyprus

Cyprus was part of the Turkish Ottoman Empire from 1571.

The first records of an organised postal service date from 1871 when a post office was opened at Nicosia (Lefkosa) under the jurisdiction of the Damascus Head Post Office. Various stamps of Turkey from the 1868 issue onwards are known used from this office, cancelled 'KIBRIS', in Arabic, within a double-lined oblong. Manuscript cancellations have also been reported. The records report the opening of a further office at Larnaca (Tuzla) in 1873, but no cancellation for this office has been identified.

To provide an overseas postal service the Austrian Empire opened a post office in Larnaca during 1845. Stamps of the Austrian Post Offices in the Turkish Empire were placed on sale there from 1 June 1864 and were cancelled with an unframed straight-line mark or circular date stamp. This Austrian post office closed on 6 August 1878.

BRITISH ADMINISTRATION

Following the convention with Turkey, Great Britain assumed the administration of Cyprus on 11 July 1878 and the first post office, as part of the British GPO. system, was opened at Larnaca on 27 July 1878. Further offices at Famagusta, Kyrenia, Limassol, Nicosia and Paphos followed in September 1878.

The stamps of Great Britain were supplied to the various offices as they opened and continued to be used until the Cyprus Administration assumed responsibility for the postal service on 1 April 1880. With the exception of '969' (Nicosia) similar numeral cancellations had previously been used at offices in Great Britain.

Numeral postmarks for Headquarters Camp, Nicosia ('D48') and Polymedia (Polemidhia) Camp, Limassol ('D47') were supplied by the GPO in London during January 1881. These cancellations had three bars above and three bars below the numeral. Similar marks, but with four bars above and below, had previously been used in London on newspapers and bulk mail.

Although both three bar cancellations subsequently occur on Cyprus issues only, isolated examples have been found on loose Great Britain stamps and there are no known covers or pieces which confirm such usage in Cyprus.

For illustrations of the postmark types see BRITISH POST OFFICES ABROAD notes, following GREAT BRITAIN.

FAMAGUSTA

Stamps of GREAT BRITAIN cancelled '982' as T **9**.

1878–80.
Z1 ½d. rose-red (1870–1879) (Plate Nos. 11, 13) £750
Z2 1d. rose-red (1864–1879) £600
Plate Nos. 145, 174, 181, 193, 202, 204, 206, 215, 217.
Z3 2d. blue (1858–1869) (Plate Nos. 13, 14, 15) £1200
Z4 2½d. rosy mauve (1876) (Plate Nos. 13, 16) £1300
Z5 6d. grey (1874–1880) (Plate No. 15) £3250
Z6 1s. green (1873–1877) (Plate No. 12)

KYRENIA

Stamps of GREAT BRITAIN cancelled '974' as T **9**.

1878–80.
Z8 ½d. rose-red (1870–1879) (Plate No. 13) £1100
Z9 1d. rose-red (1864–1879) *From* £700
Plate Nos. 168, 171, 193, 196, 206, 207, 209, 220.
Z10 2d. blue (1858–1869) (Plate Nos. 13, 15) *From* £1200
Z11 2½d. rosy mauve (1876–1879) (Plate Nos. 12, 13, 14, 15) *From* £1200
Z12 4d. sage-green (1877) (Plate No. 16)
Z13 6d. grey (1874–1880) (Plate No. 16)

LARNACA

Stamps of GREAT BRITAIN cancelled '942' as T **9**.

1878–80.
Z14 ½d. rose-red (1870–1879) *From* £250
Plate Nos. 11, 12, 13, 14, 15, 19, 20.
Z15 1d. rose-red (1864–1879) *From* £180
Plate Nos. 129, 131, 146, 154, 170, 171, 174, 175, 176, 177, 178, 179, 181, 182, 183, 184, 187, 188, 190, 191, 192, 193, 194, 195, 196, 197, 198, 199, 200, 201, 202, 203, 204, 205, 206, 207, 208, 209, 210, 212, 213, 214, 215, 216, 217, 218, 220, 221, 222, 225.
Z16 1½d. lake-red (1870) (Plate No. 3) £2250
Z17 2d. blue (1858–1869) (Plate Nos. 9, 13, 14, 15) £300
Z18 2½d. rosy mauve (1876–1879) *From* 75·00
Plate Nos. 4, 5, 6, 8, 9, 10, 11, 12, 13, 14, 15, 16, 17.
Z19 2½d. blue (1880) (Plate Nos. 17, 18) £500
Z21 4d. sage-green (1877) (Plate Nos. 15, 16) £550
Z22 6d. grey (1874–1876) (Plate Nos. 15, 16, 17) £600
Z23 6d. pale buff (1872–1873) (Plate No. 11) £3750
Z24 8d. orange (1876) £8500
Z25 1s. green (1873–1877) (Plate Nos. 12, 13) £1000
Z27 5s. rose (1874) (Plate No. 2) £8500

LIMASSOL

Stamps of GREAT BRITAIN cancelled '975' as T **9**.

1878–80.
Z28 ½d. rose-red (1870–1879) (Plate Nos. 11, 13, 15, 19) £450
Z29 1d. rose-red (1864–1879) *From* £300
Plate Nos. 159, 160, 171, 173, 174, 177, 179, 184, 187, 190, 193, 195, 196, 197, 198, 200, 202, 206, 207, 208, 209, 210, 213, 215, 216, 218, 220, 221, 222, 225.
Z30 1½d. lake-red (1870–1874) (Plate No. 3) £2750
Z31 2d. blue (1858–1869) (Plate Nos. 14, 15) *From* £550
Z32 2½d. rosy-mauve (1876–1880) *From* £250
Plate Nos. 11, 12, 13, 14, 15, 16.
Z33 2½d. blue (1880) (Plate No. 17) £1200
Z34 4d. sage-green (Plate No. 16) £1100

NICOSIA

Stamps of GREAT BRITAIN cancelled '969' as T **9**.

1878–80.
Z35 ½d. rose-red (1870–1879) £475
Plate Nos. 12, 13, 14, 15, 20.
Z36 1d. rose-red (1864–1879) *From* £300
Plate Nos. 170, 171, 174, 189, 190, 192, 193, 195, 196, 198, 200, 202, 203, 205, 206, 207, 210, 212, 214, 215, 218, 221, 222, 225.
Z36*a* 1½d. lake red (1870) (Plate No. 3) £3250
Z37 2d. blue (1858–1869) (Plate Nos. 14, 15) £550
Z38 2½d. rosy mauve (1876–1879) *From* £200
Plate Nos. 10, 11, 12, 13, 14, 15, 16.
Z39 2½d. blue (1880) (Plate No. 17) £800
Z42 4d. sage-green (1877) (Plate No. 16) £850
Z43 6d. grey (1873) (Plate No. 16) £1000

PAPHOS

Stamps of GREAT BRITAIN cancelled '981' as T **9**.

1878–80.
Z44 ½d. rose-red (1870–1879) (Plate Nos. 13, 15)
Z45 1d. rose-red (1864–1879) *From* £700
Plate Nos. 196, 201, 202, 204, 206, 213, 217.
Z46 2d. blue (1858–1869) (Plate No. 15) £1200
Z47 2½d. rosy mauve (1876–1879) *From* £650
Plate Nos. 13, 14, 15, 16.

PRICES FOR STAMPS ON COVER TO 1945

Nos. 1/4	*from* × 50
Nos. 5/6	—
Nos. 7/10	*from* × 100
Nos. 11/15	*from* × 12
No. 16	—
Nos. 16*a*/22	*from* × 20
Nos. 23/25	*from* × 100
No. 26	—
No. 27	*from* × 25
No. 28	—
No. 29	*from* × 200
Nos. 31/35*a*	*from* × 10
Nos. 36/37	—
Nos. 40/49	*from* × 8
Nos. 50/71	*from* × 5
Nos. 74/99	*from* × 4
Nos. 100/102	—
Nos. 103/117	*from* × 4
No. 117*a*	—
Nos. 118/131	*from* × 8
No. 132	—
Nos. 133/143	*from* × 5
Nos. 144/147	*from* × 6
Nos. 148/163	*from* × 5

PERFORATION. Nos. 1/122 are perf 14.

Stamps of Great Britain overprinted

CYPRUS (1) CYPRUS (2)

(Optd by D.L.R.)

1880 (1 Apr).
1 1 ½d. rose £120 £110
a. Opt double (Plate 15) † £45000

Plate No.	*Un.*	*Used.*	*Plate No.*	*Un.*	*Used*
12.	£225	£250	19.	£5000	£700
15.	£120	£110			

2 2 1d. red 23·00 48·00
a. Opt double (Plate 208) £27000 †
aa. Opt double (Plate 218) £4250 †
b. Vert pair, top stamp without opt (Plate 208) £27000 †

Plate No.	*Un.*	*Used.*	*Plate No.*	*Un.*	*Used*
174.	£1400	£1400	208.	£130	55·00
181.	£500	£190	215.	23·00	60·00
184.	£20000	£3500	216.	24·00	48·00
193.	£800	†	217.	24·00	65·00
196.	£700	†	218.	30·00	70·00
201.	27·00	55·00	220.	£350	£375
205.	90·00	55·00			

3 2 2½d. rosy mauve 4·50 18·00
a. Large thin 'C' (Plate 14) (BK, JK) £110 £375
b. Large thin 'C' (Plate 15) (BK, JK) £225 £1000
w. Wmk inverted (Plate 15) £650

Plate No.	*Un.*	*Used.*	*Plate No.*	*Un.*	*Used*
14.	4·50	18·00	15.	8·00	50·00

4 2 4d. sage-green (Plate 16) £140 £225
a. Opt double, one albino £1500
5 6d. grey (Plate 16) £500 £650
6 1s. green (Plate 13) £850 £475

HALF-PENNY (**3**) 18 mm
HALF-PENNY (**4**) 16 or 16½ mm
HALF-PENNY (**4a**) 17 mm
HALF-PENNY (**5**) 13 mm
30 PARAS (**6**)

(Optd by Govt Ptg Office, Nicosia)

1881 (Feb–June). No. 2 surch.
7 3 ½d. on 1d. red (2.81) 80·00 90·00
a. 'HALFPENN' (BG, LG) (*all plates*) *From* £3000 £2750
b. Surch double (Plate 220) £2750

Plate No.	Un.	Used.	Plate No.	Un.	Used
174.	£250	£375	215.	£800	£950
181.	£225	£250	216.	80·00	95·00
201.	£110	£130	217.	£900	£850
205.	80·00	90·00	218.	£500	£650
208.	£200	£350	220.	£325	£400

8 **4** ½d. on 1d. red (2.81) £130 £160
a. Surch double (Plates 201 and 216) £3750 £2500

Plate No.	Un.	Used.	Plate No.	Un.	Used
201.	£130	£160	218.	—	£15000
216.	£350	£425			

8*b* **4a** ½d. on 1d. red (2.81) — £800

Plate No.	Un.	Used.	Plate No.	Un.	Used
201.	—	£800	216.	—	£1100

The most noticeable difference between T **4** (16½ *mm*) and T **4a** (17 *mm*) is the space between the 'F' of 'HALF' and the 'P' of 'PENNY'. This measures 1 mm on T **4**, but 2 mm on T **4a**.

9 **5** ½d. on 1d. red (1 June) 50·00 70·00
aa. Surch double (Plate 205) £800
ab. Surch double (Plate 215) £450 £650
b. Surch treble (Plate 205) £4500
ba. Surch treble (Plate 215) £800
bc. Surch treble (Plate 218) £4500
c. Surch quadruple (Plate 205) £7000
ca. Surch quadruple (Plate 215) £7000

Plate No.	Un.	Used.	Plate No.	Un.	Used
205.	£400	—	217.	£160	£110
215.	50·00	70·00	218.	90·00	£120

The surcharges on Nos. 8 and 8*b* were handstamped; the others were applied by lithography.

(New Currency: 40 paras = 1 piastre, 180 piastres = £1)

1881 (June). No. 2 surch with T **6** by lithography.
10 **6** 30 paras on 1d. red £150 90·00
a. Surch double, one invtd (Plate 216) £7500
aa. Surch double, one invtd (Plate 220) £1900 £1400

Plate No.	Un.	Used.	Plate No.	Un.	Used
201.	£180	£110	217.	£200	£200
216.	£150	90·00	220.	£170	£180

7

'US' damaged at foot (R. 5/5 of both panes)

(Typo D.L.R.)

1881 (1 July). Die I. Wmk Crown CC.
11 **7** ½pi. emerald-green £180 45·00
w. Wmk inverted £1200 £650
12 1pi. rose £375 32·00
13 2pi. blue £450 35·00
w. Wmk inverted — £1800
14 4pi. pale olive-green £950 £275
15 6pi. olive-grey £1800 £475

Stamps of Queen Victoria initialled 'J.A.B.' or overprinted 'POSTAL SURCHARGE' with or without the same initials were employed for accounting purposes between the Chief Post Office and sub-offices, the initials are those of the then Postmaster, Mr. J. A. Bulmer.

1882 (May)–**86**. Die I*. Wmk Crown CA.
16 **7** ½pi. emerald-green (5.82) £5000 £500
a. Dull green (4.83) 25·00 3·00
ab. Top left triangle detached £1400 £275
17 30pa. pale mauve (7.6.82) 80·00 28·00
a. Top left triangle detached £2500 £1000
b. Damaged 'US' £1300 £500
18 1pi. rose (3.83) £110 4·25
a. Top left triangle detached — £325
19 2pi. blue (4.83) £160 3·75
a. Top left triangle detached — £375
20 4pi. pale olive-green (10.83) £350 38·00
a. Deep olive-green £550 50·00
b. Top left triangle detached £5000 £1200
21 6pi. olive-grey (7.82) 75·00 17·00
a. Top left triangle detached — £1200
22 12pi. orange-brown (1886) £200 42·00
s. Optd 'SPECIMEN' £2250
16*a*/22 *Set of 7* £900 £120

* For description and illustrations of Dies I and II see Introduction.

For illustration of 'top left triangle detached' variety see above No. 21 of Antigua.

No. 21 with manuscript 'Specimen' endorsement is known with 'CYPRUS' and value double.

See also Nos. 31/37.

½ (8) ½ 30 PARAS (9)

Spur on '1' (position 3 in setting)

(Surch litho by Govt Ptg Office, Nicosia)

1882. Surch with T **8**/**9**.

(a) Wmk Crown CC
23 **7** ½ on ½pi. emerald-green (6.82) £700 75·00
c. Spur on '1' £1500 £140
w. Wmk inverted
24 30pa. on 1pi. rose (22.5.82) £1600 £110

(b) Wmk Crown CA
25 **7** ½ on ½pi. emerald-green (22.5.82) £170 9·00
a. Surch double † £2750
b. '½' inserted by hand † £5000
c. Spur on '1' £325 16·00

Nos. 23 and 25 were surcharged by a setting of six arranged as a horizontal row.

No. 25b shows an additional handstamped '½' applied to examples on which the surcharge was so misplaced as to almost omit one of the original '½'s.

½ ½ (10)

11

Varieties of numerals:

1 Normal 1 Large 1 Small

2 Normal 2 Large

1886 (Apr). Surch with T **10** (fractions approx 6 *mm* apart) in typography.

(a) Wmk Crown CC
26 **7** ½ on ½pi. emerald-green £22000 †

(b) Wmk Crown CA
27 **7** ½ on ½pi. emerald-green £300 70·00
a. Large '2' at right £3000 £750

No. 27a occured at R. 10/1 and another unknown position in the setting of 60.

1886 (27 May–June). Surch with T **10** (fractions approx 8 *mm* apart) in typography.

(a) Wmk Crown CC
28 **7** ½ on ½pi. emerald-green £8000 £425
a. Large '1' at left — £1900
b. Small '1' at right £16000 £2250
c. Large '2' at left — £2250
d. Large '2' at right † £2250

(b) Wmk Crown CA
29 **7** ½ on ½pi. emerald-green (1 June) £550 17·00
a. Large '1' at left £4000 £275
b. Small '1' at right £3500 £275
c. Large '2' at left £4000 £350
d. Large '2' at right £4000 £350

Nos. 28/29 were surcharged in a setting of 60. The large '1' at left occurs at R. 4/4, the large '2' at left at R. 2/5 and the large '2' at right at R. 3/4. The position of the small '1' at right (as illustrated) may be R. 1/2, but this awaits confirmation.

A third type of this surcharge is known with the fractions spaced approximately 10 mm apart on CA paper with postmarks from August 1886. This may be due to the shifting of type.

1892–94. Die II. Wmk Crown CA.
31 **7** ½pi. dull green 16·00 2·75
w. Wmk inverted
32 30pa. mauve 12·00 14·00
a. Damaged 'US' £350 £350
33 1pi. carmine 15·00 10·00
34 2pi. ultramarine 14·00 2·00
35 4pi. olive-green 50·00 50·00
a. Pale olive-green 18·00 42·00
36 6pi. olive-grey (1894) £250 £750
37 12pi. orange brown (1893) £190 £450
31/37 *Set of 7* £450 £1100

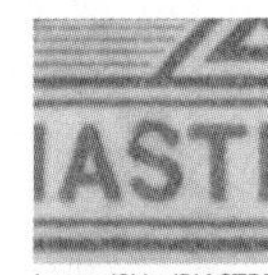

Large 'S' in 'PIASTRE'

1894 (14 Aug)–**96**. Colours changed and new values. Die II. Wmk Crown CA.
40 **7** ½pi. green and carmine (1896) 4·25 1·25
a. Large 'S' in 'PIASTRE' £190 90·00
w. Wmk inverted † £2500
41 30pa. bright mauve and green (1896) 5·00 5·50
a. Damaged 'US' £200 £200
42 1pi. carmine and blue (1896) 8·50 2·00
43 2pi. blue and purple (1896) 18·00 1·50
44 4pi. sage-green and purple (1896) 22·00 17·00
45 6pi. sepia and green (1896) 22·00 40·00
46 9pi. brown and carmine 29·00 40·00
47 12pi. orange-brown and black (1896) 24·00 70·00
48 18pi. greyish slate and brown 55·00 65·00
49 45pi. grey-purple and blue £120 £160
40/49 *Set of 10* £250 £325
40s/49s Optd 'SPECIMEN' *Set of 10* £350

The large 'S' in 'PIASTRE' was a retouch to correct a damaged letter (R. 1/4, both panes). It was corrected when a new duty plate (120-set) was introduced in 1905.

LIMASSOL FLOOD HANDSTAMP. Following a flood on 14 November 1894, which destroyed the local stamp stocks, the postmaster of Limassol produced a temporary handstamp showing '½C.P.' which was applied to local letters with the usual c.d.s.

(Typo D.L.R.)

1902–04. Wmk Crown CA.
50 **11** ½pi. green and carmine (12.02) 15·00 1·25
a. Large 'S' in 'PIASTRE' £225 60·00
w. Wmk inverted £170 90·00
51 30pa. violet and green (2.03) 26·00 5·00
a. Mauve and green 30·00 10·00
b. Damaged 'US' £450 £160
52 1pi. carmine and blue (9.03) 42·00 7·50
53 2pi. blue and purple (2.03) 85·00 17·00
54 4pi. olive-green and purple (9.03) 60·00 26·00
55 6pi. sepia and green (9.03) 50·00 £150
56 9pi. brown and carmine (5.04) £120 £275
57 12pi. chestnut and black (4.03) 25·00 85·00
58 18pi. black and brown (5.04) 90·00 £170
59 45pi. dull purple and ultramarine (10.03) £200 £500
50/59 *Set of 10* £600 £1100
50sw/59s Optd 'SPECIMEN' *Set of 10* £450

The ½pi 'SPECIMEN' is only known with watermark inverted.

Broken top left triangle (Left pane R. 7/5)

1904–10. Wmk Mult Crown CA.
60 **11** 5pa. bistre and black (14.1.08) 1·00 2·00
a. Broken top left triangle 95·00 £150
w. Wmk inverted £1900
61 10pa. orange and green (12.06) 6·00 1·75
aw. Wmk inverted — £160
b. Orange-yellow and green 45·00 5·50
bw. Wmk inverted — £180
c. Broken top left triangle £170 80·00
62 ½pi. green and carmine (1.7.04) 12·00 1·50
a. Broken top left triangle £225 60·00
b. Large 'S' in 'PIASTRE' £275 75·00
w. Wmk inverted £225 £150
y. Wmk inverted and reversed † £1700
63 30pa. purple and green (1.7.04) 21·00 2·50
a. Violet and green (1910) 28·00 2·50
b. Broken top left triangle £400 £120
c. Damaged 'US' £325 90·00
w. Wmk inverted † £1800
64 1pi. carmine and blue (11.04) 17·00 1·00
a. Broken top left triangle £300 85·00
65 2pi. blue and purple (11.04) 22·00 1·75
a. Broken top left triangle £375 £110
w. Wmk inverted † £2500
66 4pi. olive-green and purple (2.05) 32·00 20·00
a. Broken top left triangle £475 £325
67 6pi. sepia and green (17.7.04) 32·00 15·00
a. Broken top left triangle £475 £375
68 9pi. brown and carmine (30.5.04) 60·00 9·50
a. Yellow-brown and carmine 60·00 24·00
aw. Wmk inverted £325 £120
b. Broken top left triangle £750 £325
69 12pi. chestnut and black (4.06) 38·00 65·00
a. Broken top left triangle £750 £950
70 18pi. black and brown (16.6.04) 55·00 14·00
a. Broken top left triangle £850 £375
71 45pi. dull purple and ultram (15.6.04) £120 £160
a. Broken top left triangle £1800
60/71 *Set of 12* £350 £250
60s/61s Optd 'SPECIMEN' *Set of 2* £130

12

13

Broken bottom left triangle (Right pane R. 10/6)

(Typo D.L.R.)

1912 (July)–**15**. Wmk Mult Crown CA.
74 **12** 10pa. orange and green (11.12) 7·50 2·50
a. Wmk sideways † £3500
b. Broken bottom left triangle £200 85·00
c. Orange-yellow and bright green (8.15) 2·25 1·25
ca. Broken bottom left triangle £130 65·00
75 ½pi. green and carmine 4·50 30
a. Broken bottom left triangle £160 75·00
b. Yellow-green and carmine 7·50 1·90
ba. Broken bottom left triangle £200 90·00
w. Wmk inverted † £2000
76 30pa. violet and green (12.12) 3·00 2·25
a. Broken bottom left triangle £150 75·00
w. Wmk inverted
77 1pi. rose-red and blue (9.12) 8·50 1·75
a. Broken bottom left triangle £225 80·00
b. Carmine and blue (1.15?) 15·00 4·25
ba. Broken bottom left triangle £375 £120
78 2pi. blue and purple (7.13) 6·50 2·00
a. Broken bottom left triangle £225 85·00

79 4pi. olive-green and purple 4·50 6·00
a. Broken bottom left triangle £190 £225
80 6pi. sepia and green 8·50 11·00
a. Broken bottom left triangle £275 £325
81 9pi. brown and carmine (3.15) 42·00 27·00
a. Yellow-brown and carmine 48·00 38·00
b. Broken bottom left triangle £750 £600
82 12pi. chestnut and black (7.13) 25·00 55·00
b. Broken bottom left triangle £450 £750
83 18pi. black and brown (12.14) 50·00 50·00
a. Broken bottom left triangle £750 £750
84 45pi. dull purple and ultramarine (3.15) £130 £160
a. Broken bottom left triangle £1800 £2000
74/84 *Set of* 11 £250 £275
74s/84s Optd 'SPECIMEN' *Set of* 11 £550

1921–23.

(a) Wmk Mult Script CA

85 **12** 10pa. orange and green 15·00 19·00
a. Broken bottom left triangle £300 £350
w. Wmk inverted £3250 £3250
86 10pa. grey and yellow (1923) 15·00 11·00
a. Broken bottom left triangle £275 £190
87 30pa. violet and green 4·00 2·75
a. Broken bottom left triangle £160 85·00
w. Wmk inverted £3000 £3000
y. Wmk inverted and reversed † £2750
88 30pa. green (1923) 7·50 1·75
a. Broken bottom left triangle £200 75·00
w. Wmk inverted † £2500
89 1pi. carmine and blue 25·00 50·00
a. Broken bottom left triangle £375
90 1pi. violet and red (1922) 3·75 4·00
a. Broken bottom left triangle £160 £180
91 1½pi. yellow and black (1922) 13·00 11·00
a. Broken bottom left triangle £250 £200
92 2pi. blue and purple 32·00 30·00
a. Broken bottom left triangle £475 £425
93 2pi. carmine and blue (1922) 15·00 27·00
a. Broken bottom left triangle £325 £550
94 2¾pi. blue and purple (1922) 12·00 9·00
a. Broken bottom left triangle £250 £275
95 4pi. olive-green and purple 18·00 25·00
a. Broken bottom left triangle £350 £450
w. Wmk inverted † £2750
96 6pi. sepia and green (1923) 38·00 95·00
a. Broken bottom left triangle £475
97 9pi. brown and carmine (1922) 50·00 95·00
a. Yellow-brown and carmine £120 £160
b. Broken bottom left triangle £650 £950
98 18pi. black and brown (1923) 90·00 £180
a. Broken bottom left triangle £1000
99 45pi. dull purple and ultramarine (1923) £275 £275
a. Broken bottom left triangle £2500 £2750
85/99 *Set of* 15 £550 £750
85s/99s Optd 'SPECIMEN' *Set of* 15 £700

A ½pi. black was prepared for use but not issued. One example exists, opt 'SPECIMEN'.

(b) Wmk Mult Crown CA (1923)

100 **12** 10s. green and red/*pale yellow* £400 £900
a. Broken bottom left triangle £4750
101 £1 purple and black/*red* £1400 £3500
a. Broken bottom left triangle £8500 £14000
100s/101s Optd 'SPECIMEN' *Set of* 2 £600

Examples of Nos. 96/101 are known showing a forged Limassol postmark dated '14 MR 25'.

1924–28. Chalk-surfaced paper.

(a) Wmk Mult Crown CA

102 **13** £1 purple and black/*red* £300 £850

(b) Wmk Mult Script CA

103 **13** ¼pi. grey and chestnut 2·00 50
w. Wmk inverted † £2500
104 ½pi. brownish black and black 6·00 14·00
105 ¾pi. green 4·00 1·00
106 1pi. purple and chestnut 3·25 1·00
107 1½pi. orange and black 6·50 18·00
108 2pi. carmine and green 6·50 23·00
109 2¾pi. bright blue and purple 3·25 5·00
110 4pi. sage-green and purple 5·00 5·00
111 4½pi. black and orange/*emerald* 3·50 5·00
112 6pi. olive-brown and green 5·00 12·00
113 9pi. brown and purple 9·00 5·50
114 12pi. chestnut and black 18·00 65·00
115 18pi. black and orange 32·00 5·00
116 45pi. purple and blue 70·00 50·00
117 90pi. green and red/*yellow* £130 £275
117*a* £5 black/*yellow* (1928) (F.C. £350) £3750 £8000
as. Optd 'SPECIMEN' £1000

Examples of No. 102 are known showing a forged Limassol postmark dated '14 MR 25' and of No. 117*a* showing a forged Registered Nicosia postmark dated '6 MAY 35'.

CROWN COLONY

1925. Wmk Mult Script CA. Chalk-surfaced paper (½, ¾ and 2pi.).

118 **13** ½pi. green 5·00 1·00
119 ¾pi. brownish black and black 6·50 1·00
120 1½pi. scarlet 10·00 1·50
121 2pi. yellow and black 15·00 3·25
122 2½pi. bright blue 11·00 1·75
102/122 (*ex* £5) *Set of* 21 £550 £1200
102s/122s (*ex* £5) Optd 'SPECIMEN' *Set of* 21 £1100

In the above set the fraction bar in the value is horizontal. In Nos. 91, 94, 107 and 109 it is diagonal.

14 Silver Coin of Amathus, 6th-cent BC

15 Zeno (philosopher)

16 Map of Cyprus

17 Discovery of body of St Barnabas

18 Cloister, Abbey of Bellapaise

19 Badge of Cyprus

20 Tekke of Umm Haram

21 Statue of Richard I, Westminster

22 St Nicholas Cathedral (now Lala Mustafa Pasha Mosque), Famagusta

23 King George V

(Recess B.W.)

1928 (1 Feb). 50th Anniversary of British Rule. T **14/23**. Wmk Mult Script CA. P 12.

123 **14** ¾pi. deep dull purple 3·75 1·50
124 **15** 1pi. black and greenish blue 4·00 1·50
125 **16** 1½pi. scarlet 8·50 2·00
126 **17** 2½pi. light blue 4·25 2·25
127 **18** 4pi. deep brown 11·00 11·00
128 **19** 6pi. blue 14·00 40·00
129 **20** 9pi. maroon 11·00 19·00
130 **21** 18pi. black and brown 30·00 45·00
131 **22** 45pi. violet and blue 42·00 50·00
132 **23** £1 blue and bistre-brown £225 £300
123/132 *Set of* 10 £300 £400
123s/132s Optd 'SPECIMEN' *Set of* 10 £700

24 Ruins of Vouni Palace

25 Small Marble Forum, Salamis

26 Church of St Barnabas and St Hilarion, Peristerona

27 Roman Theatre, Soli

28 Kyrenia Harbour

29 Kolossi Castle

30 St Sophia Cathedral, Nicosia (now Selimiye Mosque)

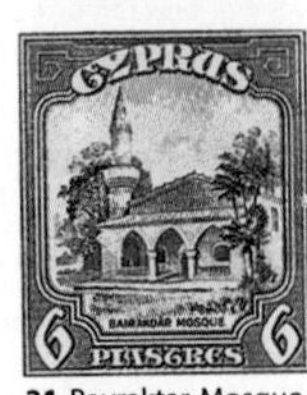

31 Bayraktar Mosque, Nicosia

32 Queen's window, St Hilarion Castle

33 Buyuk Khan, Nicosia

34 Forest scene, Troodos

(Recess Waterlow)

1934 (1 Dec). T **24/34**. Wmk Mult Script CA (sideways on ½pi., 1½pi., 2½pi., 4½pi., 6pi., 9pi. and 18pi.). P 12½.

133 **24** ¼pi. ultramarine and orange-brown 2·00 1·00
a. Imperf between (vert pair) £55000 £32000
134 **25** ½pi. green 3·75 1·00
a. Imperf between (vert pair) £18000 £20000
135 **26** ¾pi. black and violet 4·00 40
a. Imperf between (vert pair) £60000
136 **27** 1pi. black and red-brown 5·00 2·25
a. Imperf between (vert pair) £25000 £25000
b. Imperf between (horiz pair) £21000
137 **28** 1½pi. carmine 6·00 2·00
138 **29** 2½pi. ultramarine 7·00 1·75
139 **30** 4½pi. black and crimson 8·50 6·50
140 **31** 6pi. black and blue 12·00 24·00
141 **32** 9pi. sepia and violet 22·00 8·50
142 **33** 18pi. black and olive-green 55·00 55·00
143 **34** 45pi. green and black £120 90·00
133/143 *Set of* 11 £200 £170
133s/143s Perf 'SPECIMEN' *Set of* 11 £650

1935 (6 May). Silver Jubilee. As Nos. 91/94 of Antigua, but ptd by Waterlow & Sons. P 11×12.

144 ¾pi. ultramarine and grey 4·00 1·50
145 1½pi. deep blue and scarlet 6·00 2·75
l. Kite and horizontal log £950 £750
146 2½pi. brown and deep blue 5·00 2·25
147 9pi. slate and purple 23·00 30·00
144/147 *Set of* 4 35·00 32·00
144s/147s Perf 'SPECIMEN' *Set of* 4 £200

For illustration of plate variety see Omnibus section following Zanzibar.

1937 (12 May). Coronation. As Nos. 95/97 of Antigua. P 11×11½.

148 ¾pi. grey 3·00 1·00
149 1½pi. carmine 3·50 3·00
150 2½pi. blue 3·50 3·25
148/150 *Set of* 3 9·00 6·50
148s/150s Perf 'SPECIMEN' *Set of* 3 £225

35 Vouni Palace

36 Map of Cyprus

37 Othello's Tower, Famagusta

38 King George VI

(Recess Waterlow)

1938 (12 May)–**51**. T **35** to **38** and other designs as 1934, but with portrait of King George VI. Wmk Mult Script CA. P 12½.

151 **35** ¼pi. ultramarine and orange-brown 1·75 60
152 **25** ½pi. green 2·75 50
152*a* ½pi. violet (2.7.51) 4·50 75
153 **26** ¾pi. black and violet 22·00 1·75
154 **27** 1pi. orange 3·25 40
a. Perf 13½×12½ (4.44) £550 27·00
155 **28** 1½pi. carmine 6·00 1·50
155*a* 1½pi. violet (15.3.43) 3·00 75
155*ab* 1½pi. green (2.7.51) 7·00 1·25
155*b* **26** 2pi. black and carmine (2.2.42) 3·25 40
c. Perf 12½×13½ (10.44) 4·25 17·00
156 **29** 2½pi. ultramarine 45·00 2·50
156*a* 3pi. ultramarine (2.2.42) 3·50 60
156*b* 4pi. ultramarine (2.7.51) 7·00 1·25
157 **36** 4½pi. grey 3·00 40
158 **31** 6pi. black and blue 4·50 1·00
159 **37** 9pi. black and purple 3·75 75
160 **33** 18pi. black and olive-green 16·00 1·75
a. Black and sage-green (19.8.47) 24·00 2·50
161 **34** 45pi. green and black 55·00 4·75
162 **38** 90pi. mauve and black 38·00 8·50
163 £1 scarlet and indigo 65·00 32·00
151/163 *Set of* 19 £250 55·00
151s/163s Perf 'SPECIMEN' *Set of* 16 £800

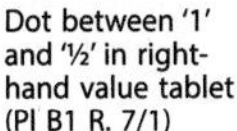
Dot between '1' and '½' in right-hand value tablet (Pl B1 R. 7/1)

Extra decoration (R. 3/5)

1946 (21 Oct). Victory. As Nos. 110/111 of Antigua.

164		1½pi. deep violet	50	10
		a. Dot between '1' and '½'	70·00	65·00
165		3pi. blue	50	40
164s/165s		Perf 'SPECIMEN' *Set of 2*	£190	

1948 (20 Dec). Royal Silver Wedding. As Nos. 112/113 of Antigua.

166		1½pi. violet	1·50	50
		a. Extra decoration	55·00	65·00
167		£1 indigo	60·00	75·00

1949 (10 Oct). 75th Anniversary of Universal Postal Union. As Nos. 114/117 of Antigua but inscr 'CYPRUS' (recess).

168		1½pi. violet	60	1·50
169		2pi. carmine-red	1·50	1·50
		a. 'C' of 'CA' missing from wmk	£1600	
170		3pi. deep blue	1·00	1·50
171		9pi. purple	1·00	6·50
168/171		*Set of 4*	3·50	10·00

1953 (2 June). Coronation. As No. 120 of Antigua.

172		1½pi. black and emerald	2·00	10

(New Currency = 1000 mils = £1)

39 Carobs

40 Grapes

41 Oranges

42 Mavrovouni Copper Pyrites Mine

43 Troodos Forest

44 Beach of Aphrodite

45 5th-century BC coin of Paphos

46 Kyrenia

47 Harvest in Mesaoria

48 Famagusta Harbour

49 St Hilarion Castle

50 Hala Sultan Tekke

51 Kanakaria Church

52 Coins of Salamis, Paphos, Citium and Idalium

53 Arms of Byzantium, Lusignan, Ottoman Empire and Venice

1955 (1 Aug)–**60**. T **39/53**. Wmk Mult Script CA. P 13½ (Nos. 183/5) or 11½ (others).

173	**39**	2m. blackish brown	1·00	40
174	**40**	3m. blue-violet	65	15
175	**41**	5m. brown-orange	3·25	10
		a. Orange-brown (17.9.58)	13·00	1·00
176	**42**	10m. deep brown and deep green	3·25	10
177	**43**	15m. olive-green and indigo	5·50	45
		aa. Yellow-olive and indigo (17.9.58)	42·00	6·00
		a. Bistre and indigo (14.6.60)	35·00	17·00
178	**44**	20m. brown and deep bright blue	2·50	15
179	**45**	25m. deep turquoise-blue	5·00	60
		a. Greenish blue (17.9.58)	29·00	5·50
180	**46**	30m. black and carmine-lake	3·75	10
181	**47**	35m. orange-brown and deep turquoise-blue	3·25	40
182	**48**	40m. deep green and sepia	3·25	60
183	**49**	50m. turquoise-blue and reddish brown	3·25	30
184	**50**	100m. mauve and bluish green	14·00	60
185	**51**	250m. deep grey-blue and brown	17·00	13·00
186	**52**	500m. slate and purple	38·00	15·00
187	**53**	£1 brown-lake and slate	30·00	55·00
173/187		*Set of 15*	£110	75·00

ΚΥΠΡΙΑΚΗ ΔΗΜΟΚΡΑΤΙΑ KIBRIS CUMHURIYETI

(**54** 'Cyprus Republic')

55 Map of Cyprus

(Recess B.W.)

1960 (16 Aug)–**61**. Nos. 173/187 optd as T **54** in blue by B.W. Opt larger on Nos. 191/197 and in two lines on Nos 198/202.

188		2m. blackish brown	20	75
189		3m. blue-violet	20	15
190		5m. brown-orange	2·25	10
		a. Orange-brown (15.8.61)	10·00	1·00
191		10m. deep brown and deep green	1·00	10
192		15m. yellow-bistre and indigo	3·50	40
		a. Olive-green and indigo	£160	85·00
		b. Brownish bistre and deep indigo (10.10.61)	22·00	5·50
193		20m. brown and deep bright blue	1·75	1·50
		a. Opt double	†	£12000
194		25m. deep turquoise-blue	1·75	1·75
		a. Greenish blue (7.2.61)	50·00	16·00
195		30m. black and carmine-lake	1·75	30
		a. Opt double	†	£45000
196		35m. orange-brown and deep turquoise-blue	1·75	70
197		40m. deep green and sepia	2·00	2·50
198		50m. turquoise-blue and reddish brown	2·00	60
199		100m. mauve and bluish green	9·00	2·50
200		250m. deep grey-blue and brown	30·00	5·50
201		500m. slate and purple	45·00	27·00
202		£1 brown-lake and slate	48·00	65·00
188/202		*Set of 15*	£130	95·00

Only three used examples of No. 195a are known.

(Recess B.W.)

1960 (16 Aug). Constitution of Republic. W w **12**. P 11½.

203	**55**	10m. sepia and deep green	25	10
204		30m. ultramarine and deep brown	50	10
205		100m. purple and deep slate	1·75	2·00
203/205		*Set of 3*	2·25	2·00

PRINTERS. All the following stamps were designed by A. Tassos and lithographed by Aspioti-Elka, Athens, unless otherwise stated.

56 Doves

(Des T. Kurpershoek)

1962 (19 Mar). Europa. P 14×13.

206	**56**	10m. purple and mauve	10	10
207		40m. ultramarine and cobalt	20	15
208		100m. emerald and pale green	20	20
206/208		*Set of 3*	45	40

57 Campaign Emblem

1962 (14 May). Malaria. Eradication. P 14×13½.

209	**57**	10m. black and olive-green	15	15
210		30m. black and brown	30	15

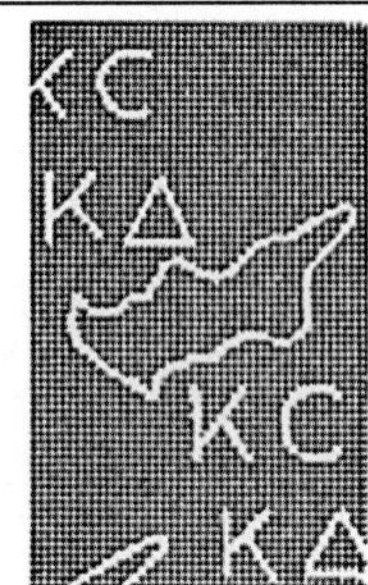
58 Mult K C K Δ and Map

WATERMARK VARIETIES. The issues printed by Aspioti-Elka with W **58** are known with the vertical stamps having the watermark normal or inverted and the horizontal stamps with the watermark reading upwards or downwards. Such varieties are not given separate listing.

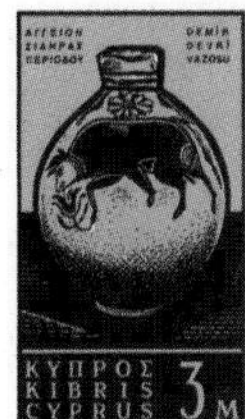
59 Iron Age Jug

60 Grapes

61 Bronze head of Apollo

62 Selimiye Mosque, Nicosia

63 St Barnabas's Church

64 Temple of Apollo, Hylates

65 Head of Aphrodite

66 Skiing, Troodos

67 Salamis Gymnasium

68 Hala Sultan Tekke

69 Bellapaise Abbey

70 Mouflon

71 St Hilarion Castle

1962 (17 Sept). T **59/71**. W **58** (sideways) on 25, 30, 40, 50, 250m., £1). P 13½×14 (vert) or 14×13½ (horiz).

211	**59**	3m. deep brown and orange-brown	10	30
212	**60**	5m. purple and grey-green	10	10
213	**61**	10m. black and yellow-green	15	10
214	**62**	15m. black and reddish purple	50	15
215	**63**	25m. deep brown and chestnut	60	20
216	**64**	30m. deep blue and light blue	20	10
217	**65**	35m. light green and blue	35	10
218	**66**	40m. black and violet-blue	1·25	1·75

No.	Type	Description	Unused	Used
219	67	50m. bronze-green and bistre	50	10
220	68	100m. deep brown and yellow-brown	3·50	30
221	69	250m. black and cinnamon	17·00	1·75
222	70	500m. deep brown and light green	22·00	9·00
223	71	£1 bronze-green and grey	15·00	28·00
211/223		*Set of* 13	55·00	38·00

72 Europa 'Tree'

(Des L. Weyer)

1963 (28 Jan). Europa. W **58** (sideways). P 14×13½.

No.	Type	Description	Unused	Used
224	**72**	10m. bright blue and black	1·50	20
225		40m. carmine-red and black	4·50	1·50
226		150m. emerald-green and black	15·00	5·00
224/226		*Set of* 3	19·00	6·00

73 Harvester

75 Wolf Cub in Camp

1963 (21 Mar). Freedom from Hunger. T **73** and similar vert design. W **58**. P 13½×14.

No.	Type	Description	Unused	Used
227		25m. ochre, sepia and bright blue	1·00	25
228		75m. grey, black and lake	2·75	2·50

Designs: 25m, T **73**; 75m. Demeter, Goddess of Corn.

1963 (21 Aug). 50th Anniversary of Cyprus Scout Movement and Third Commonwealth Scout Conference, Platres. T **75** and similar vert designs. Multicoloured. W **58**. P 13½×14.

No.	Type	Description	Unused	Used
229		3m. Type **75**	10	20
230		20m. Sea Scout	35	10
231		150m. Scout with Mouflon	1·00	2·50
229/231		*Set of* 3	1·25	2·50
MS231*a*		110×90 mm. Nos. 229/231 (*sold at* 250m.). Imperf	£110	£180

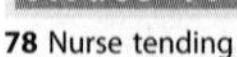

78 Nurse tending Child

79 Children's Centre, Kyrenia

1963 (9 Sept). Centenary of Red Cross. W **58** (sideways on 100m.). P 13½×14 (10m.) or 14×13½ (100m.).

No.	Type	Description	Unused	Used
232	**78**	10m. red, blue, grey-blue, chestnut and black	50	15
233	**79**	100m. red, green, black and blue	3·00	4·50

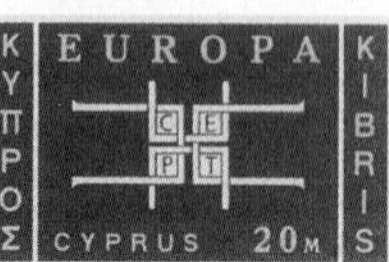

80 'Co-operation' (emblem)

(**81**)

(Des A. Holm)

1963 (4 Nov). Europa. W **58** (sideways). P 14×13½.

No.	Type	Description	Unused	Used
234	**80**	20m. buff, blue and violet	1·75	40
235		30m. grey, yellow and blue	1·75	40
236		150m. buff, blue and orange-brown	15·00	9·00
234/236		*Set of* 3	17·00	9·00

1964 (5 May). UN Security Council's Cyprus Resolutions, March, 1964. Nos. 213, 216, 218/220 optd with T **81** in blue by Govt Printing Office, Nicosia.

No.	Type	Description	Unused	Used
237	**61**	10m. black and yellow-green	15	10
238	**64**	30m. deep blue and light blue	20	10
239	**66**	40m. black and violet-blue	25	30
240	**67**	50m. bronze-green and bistre	25	10
241	**68**	100m. deep brown and yellow-brown	25	50
237/241		*Set of* 5	1·00	1·00

82 Soli Theatre

1964 (15 June). 400th Birth Anniversary of Shakespeare. T **82** and similar horiz designs. Multicoloured. W **58**. P 13½×13.

No.	Type	Description	Unused	Used
242		15m. Type **82**	90	15
243		35m. Curium Theatre	90	15
244		50m. Salamis Theatre	90	15
245		100m. Othello Tower and scene from *Othello*	1·50	2·25
242/245		*Set of* 4	3·75	2·50

86 Running

89 Europa 'Flower'

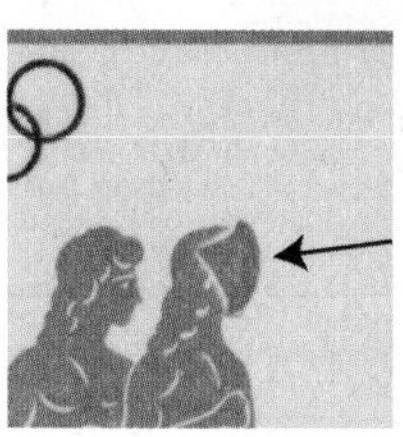

10m. Brown flaw covering face of right-hand runner gives the appearance of a mask (R. 9/2).

As these stamps were printed in sheets of 400, divided into four post office sheets of 100, the variety was only constant on one sheet in four. Moreover, it was quickly discovered and many were removed from the sheets by post office clerks.

1964 (6 July). Olympic Games, Tokyo. T **86** and similar designs. W **58** (sideways, 25m., 75m.). P 13½×14 (10m.) or 14×13½ (others).

No.	Type	Description	Unused	Used
246		10m. brown, black and yellow	10	10
		a. Blind runner	£900	
247		25m. brown, blue and blue-grey	20	10
248		75m. brown, black and orange-red	35	65
246/248		*Set of* 3	60	75
MS248*a*		110×90 mm. Nos. 246/248 (*sold at* 250m.). Imperf	4·75	15·00

Designs: Vert—10m. T **86**. Horiz—25m. Boxing; 75m. Charioteers.

(Des G. Bétemps)

1964 (14 Sept). Europa. W **58**. P 13½×14.

No.	Type	Description	Unused	Used
249	**89**	20m. chestnut and light ochre	1·25	10
250		30m. ultramarine and light blue	1·25	10
251		150m. olive and light blue-green	9·00	4·75
249/251		*Set of* 3	10·00	4·75

90 Dionysus and Acme

91 Silenus (satyr)

1964 (26 Oct). Cyprus Wines. T **90/91** and similar multicoloured designs. W **58** (sideways, 10m. or 100m.). P 14×13½ (horiz) or 13½×14 (vert).

No.	Type	Description	Unused	Used
252		10m. Type **90**	25	10
253		40m. Type **91**	55	75
254		50m. Commandaria Wine (*vert*)	55	10
255		100m. Wine factory (*horiz*)	1·10	1·50
252/255		*Set of* 4	2·25	2·00

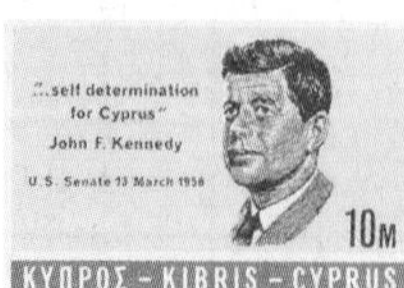

94 President Kennedy

1965 (16 Feb). President Kennedy Commemoration. W **58** (sideways). P 14×13½.

No.	Type	Description	Unused	Used
256	**94**	10m. ultramarine	10	10
257		40m. green	25	35
258		100m. carmine-lake	30	35
256/258		*Set of* 3	60	70
MS258*a*		110×90 mm. Nos. 256/258 (*sold at* 250m.). Imperf	2·25	7·00

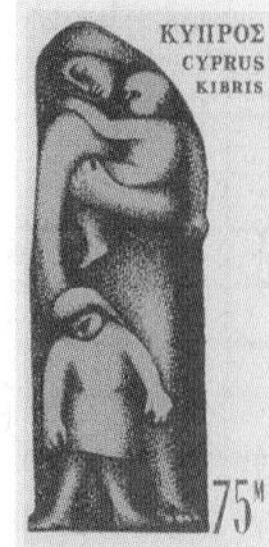

95 'Old Age'

96 'Maternity'

1965 (12 Apr). Introduction of Social Insurance Law. T **95/96** and similar design. W **58**. P 13½×12 (75m.) or 13½×14 (others).

No.	Type	Description	Unused	Used
259		30m. drab and dull green	15	10
260		45m. light grey-green, blue and deep ultramarine	20	10
261		75m. red-brown and flesh	1·25	1·50
259/261		*Set of* 3	1·40	1·50

Designs: 30m. T **95**. Vert as T **95**—45m. 'Accident'. 75m. T **96**.

98 ITU Emblem and Symbols

1965 (17 May). ITU Centenary. W **58** (sideways). P 14×13½.

No.	Type	Description	Unused	Used
262	**98**	15m. black, brown and yellow	75	20
263		60m. black, green and light green	6·50	3·25
264		75m. black, indigo and light blue	7·50	4·75
262/264		*Set of* 3	13·00	7·25

99 ICY Emblem

1965 (17 May). International Co-operation Year. W **58** (sideways). P 14×13½.

No.	Type	Description	Unused	Used
265	**99**	50m. brown, deep green and light yellow-brown	75	10
266		100m. purple, deep green and light purple	1·25	50

100 Europa 'Sprig'

U. N.
Resolution
on Cyprus
18 Dec. 1965

(**101**)

(Des H. Karlsson)

1965 (27 Sept). Europa. W **58** (sideways). P 14×13½.

No.	Type	Description	Unused	Used
267	**100**	5m. black, orange-brown and orange	50	10
268		45m. black, orange-brown and light emerald	3·00	2·00
269		150m. black, orange-brown and light grey	7·50	4·50
267/269		*Set of* 3	10·00	6·00

1966 (31 Jan). UN General Assembly's Cyprus Resolution, 18 December 1965. Nos. 211, 213, 216 and 221 optd with T **101** in blue by Govt Printing Office, Nicosia.

No.	Type	Description	Unused	Used
270	**59**	3m. deep brown and orange-brown	10	50
271	**61**	10m. black and yellow-green	10	10
272	**64**	30m. deep blue and light blue	15	15
273	**69**	250m. black and cinnamon	80	2·25
270/273		*Set of* 4	1·00	2·75

102 Discovery of St Barnabas's Body

104 St Barnabas (icon)

103 St Barnabas's Chapel

105 *Privileges of Cyprus Church* (*Actual size* 102×82 *mm*)

1966 (25 Apr). 1900th Death Anniversary of St Barnabas. W **58** (sideways on 15m., 100m., 250m.). P 14×13 (25m.) or 13×14 (others).

274	**102**	15m. multicoloured	10	10
275	**103**	25m. drab, black and blue	15	10
276	**104**	100m. multicoloured	45	2·00
274/276		*Set of 3*	60	2·00
MS277		110×91 mm. Type **105** 250m. mult. Imperf	2·25	10·00

5 M

Ξ

(**106**)

107 General K. S. Thimayya and UN Emblem

1966 (30 May). No. 211 surch with T **106** by Govt Printing Office, Nicosia.

278	5m. on 3m. deep brown and orange-brown	10	10

1966 (6 June). General Thimayya Commemoration. W **58** (sideways). P 14×13.

279	**107**	50m. black and light orange-brown	30	10

108 Europa 'Ship'

(Des G. and J. Bender)

1966 (26 Sept). Europa. W **58**. P 13½×14.

280	**108**	20m. green and blue	30	10
281		30m. bright purple and blue	30	10
282		150m. bistre and blue	2·25	2·50
280/282		*Set of 3*	2·50	2·50

110 Church of St James, Trikomo

119 Vase of 7th-century BC

120 Bronze Ingot-stand

1966 (21 Nov)–**69**. T **110**, **119/120** and similar designs. W **58** (sideways on 3, 15, 25, 50, 250, 500m., £1. P 12×13 (3m.), 13×12 (5, 10m.), 14×13½ (15, 25, 50m.), 13½×14 (20, 30, 35, 40, 100m.) or 13×14 (others).

283	3m. grey-green, buff, black and light blue	40	10
284	5m. bistre, black and steel-blue	10	10
	a. Brownish bistre, black and steel-blue (18.4.69)	75	20
285	10m. black and bistre	15	10
286	15m. black, chestnut and light orange-brown	15	10
287	20m. black, slate and brown	1·25	1·00
288	25m. black, drab and lake-brown	30	10
289	30m. black, yellow-ochre and turquoise	50	20
290	35m. yellow, black and carmine-red	50	30
291	40m. black, grey and new blue	70	30
	a. Grey (background) omitted		
292	50m. black, slate and brown	90	10
293	100m. black, red, pale buff and grey	4·00	15
294	250m. olive-green, black and light yellow-ochre	1·00	40
295	500m. multicoloured	2·75	70
296	£1 black, drab and slate	2·25	6·50
283/296	*Set of 14*	13·00	8·50

Designs: Horiz (as T **110**)—3m. Stavrovouni Monastery. (As T **119**)—15m. *Minoan wine ship of 700 BC* (painting); 25m. *Sleeping Eros* (marble statue); 50m. Silver coin of Alexander the Great. Vert 5m. T **110.** (As T **110**)—10m. *Zeno of Cibium* (marble bust). (As T **119**)—20m. Silver coin of Evagoras I; 30m. St Nicholas Cathedral, Famagusta; 35m. Gold sceptre from Curium; 40m. Silver dish from 7th-century. 100m. T **119.** 250m. T **120.** (As T **120**)—500m. *The Rape of Ganymede* (mosaic); £1 Aphrodite (marble statue).

123 Power Station, Limassol

124 Cogwheels

1967 (10 Apr). First Development Programme. T **123** and similar designs but horiz. Multicoloured. W **58** (sideways on 15 to 100m.). P 13½×14 (10m.) or 14×13½ (others).

297	10m. Type **123**	10	10
298	15m. Arghaka-Maghounda Dam	15	10
299	35m. Troodos Highway	30	10
300	50m. Hilton Hotel, Nicosia	20	10
301	100m. Famagusta Harbour	35	1·10
297/301	*Set of 5*	1·00	1·25

(Des O. Bonnevalle)

1967 (2 May). Europa. W **58**. P 13½×14.

302	**124**	20m. olive-green, green and pale yellow-green	25	10
303		30m. reddish violet, lilac and pale lilac	25	10
304		150m. brown, light reddish brown and pale yellow-brown	1·75	2·25
302/304		*Set of 3*	2·00	2·25

125 Throwing the Javelin

126 Running (amphora) and Map of Eastern Mediterranean (*Actual size 97×77 mm*)

1967 (4 Sept). Athletic Games, Nicosia. T **125** and similar designs and T **126**. Multicoloured. W **58**. P 13½×13.

305	15m. Type **125**	20	10
306	35m. Running	20	35
307	100m. High jumping	30	1·00
305/307	*Set of 3*	60	1·25
MS308	110×90 mm. Type **126**. 250m. (wmk sideways). Imperf	1·25	6·50

127 Ancient Monuments

128 St Andrew Mosaic

1967 (16 Oct). International Tourist Year. T **127** and similar horiz designs. Multicoloured. W **58**. P 13×13½.

309	10m. Type **127**	10	10
310	40m. Famagusta Beach	20	90
311	50m. Hawker Siddeley Comet 4 at Nicosia Airport	40	10
312	100m. Skier and youth hostel	45	95
309/312	*Set of 4*	1·00	1·75

1967 (8 Nov). Centenary of St Andrew's Monastery. W **58** (sideways). P 13×13½.

313	**128**	25m. multicoloured	10	10

129 *The Crucifixion* (icon)

130 The Three Magi

(Photo French Govt Ptg Wks, Paris)

1967 (8 Nov). Cyprus Art Exhibition, Paris. P 12½×13½.

314	**129**	50m. multicoloured	10	10

1967 (8 Nov). 20th Anniversary of UNESCO W **58** (sideways). P 13×13½.

315	**130**	75m. multicoloured	35	35

131 Human Rights Emblem over Stars

132 Human Rights and UN Emblems

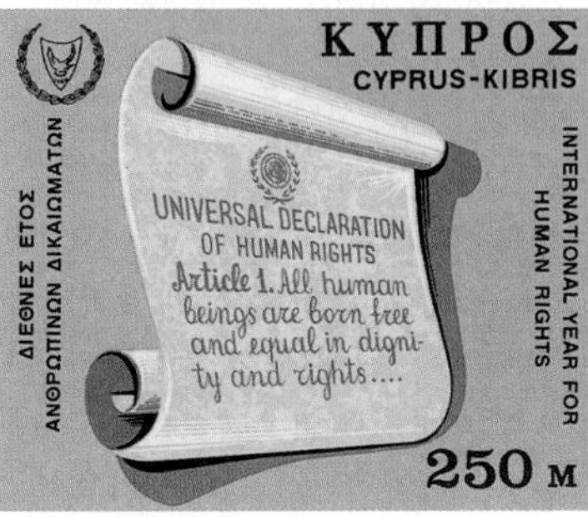

133 Scroll of Declaration (*Actual size 95×75½ mm*)

1968 (18 Mar). Human Rights Year. W **58**. P 13×14.

316	**131**	50m. multicoloured	10	10
317	**132**	90m. multicoloured	30	70
MS318		95×75½ mm. Type **133** 250m. multicoloured. W **58** (sideways). Imperf	60	4·75

134 Europa 'Key'

(Des H. Schwarzenbach)

1968 (29 Apr). Europa. W **58** (sideways). P 14×13.

319	**134**	20m. multicoloured	25	10
320		30m. multicoloured	25	10
321		150m. multicoloured	1·00	2·25
319/321		*Set of 3*	1·40	2·25

135 UN Children's Fund Symbol and Boy drinking Milk

136 Aesculapius

1968 (2 Sept). 21st Anniversary of UNICEF W **58** (sideways). P 14×13.

322	**135**	35m. yellow-brown, carmine-red and black	10	10

1968 (2 Sept). 20th Anniversary of WHO W **58**. P 13×14.

323	**136**	50m. black, green and light olive	10	10

137 Throwing the Discus

138 ILO Emblem

1968 (24 Oct). Olympic Games, Mexico. T **137** and similar designs. Multicoloured. W **58** (sideways on 100m.). P 14×13 (100m.) or 13×14 (others).

324	10m. Type **137**	10	10
325	25m. Sprint finish	10	10
326	100m. Olympic Stadium (*horiz*)	20	1·25
324/326	*Set of 3*	35	1·25

1969 (3 Mar). 50th Anniversary of International Labour Organisation. W **58**. P 12×13½.

327	**138**	50m. yellow-brown, blue and light blue	15	10
328		90m. yellow-brown, black and pale grey	15	55

139 Mercator's Map of Cyprus, 1554

140 Blaeu's Map of Cyprus, 1635

1969 (7 Apr). First International Congress of Cypriot Studies. W **58** (sideways). P 14×14½.

329	**139**	35m. multicoloured	20	30
330	**140**	50m. multicoloured	20	10
		a. Wmk upright	5·00	2·75
		ab. Grey (shading on boats and cartouche) omitted	£450	

141 Europa Emblem

142 European Roller

(Des L. Gasbarra and G. Belli)

1969 (28 Apr). Europa. W **58** (sideways). P 14×13½.

331	**141**	20m. multicoloured	30	10
332		30m. multicoloured	30	10
333		150m. multicoloured	1·00	2·00
331/333 *Set of 3*			1·40	2·00

1969 (7 July). Birds of Cyprus. T **142** and similar designs. Multicoloured. W **58** (sideways on horiz designs). P 13½×12 (horiz designs) or 12×13½ (vert designs).

334	5m. Type **142**	35	15
335	15m. Audouin's Gull	40	15
336	20m. Cyprus Warbler	40	15
337	30m. Jay (*vert*)	40	15
338	40m. Hoopoe (*vert*)	45	30
339	90m. Eleanora's Falcon (*vert*)	80	3·50
334/339 *Set of 6*		2·50	4·00

The above were printed on glazed Samuel Jones paper with very faint watermark.

143 *The Nativity* (12th-century Wall Painting)

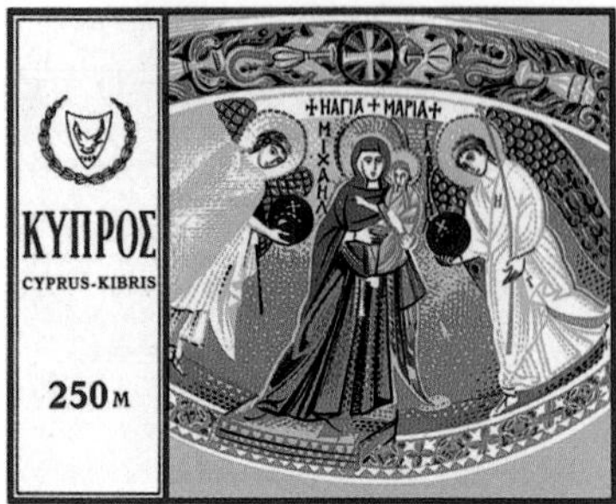

145 *Virgin and Child between Archangels Michael and Gabriel* (6th/7th-century Mosaic) (*Actual size 102×81 mm*)

1969 (24 Nov). Christmas. T **143** and similar horiz design, and T **145**. Multicoloured. W **58** (sideways). P 13½×13.

340	20m. Type **143**	15	10
341	45m. *The Nativity* (14th-century wall painting)	15	20
MS342	110×90 mm. Type **145**. 250m. Imperf	3·00	12·00
	a. Grey and light brown omitted	£3500	

146 Mahatma Gandhi

1970 (26 Jan). Birth Centenary of Mahatma Gandhi. W **58** (sideways). P 14×13½.

343	**146**	25m. ultramarine, drab and black	50	10
344		75m. yellow-brown, drab and black	75	65

147 *'Flaming Sun'*

148 Gladioli

(Des L. le Brocquy)

1970 (4 May). Europa. W **58** (sideways). P 14×13.

345	**147**	20m. brown, greenish yellow and orange	30	10
346		30m. new blue, greenish yellow and orange	30	10
347		150m. bright purple, greenish yellow and orange	1·00	2·50
345/347 *Set of 3*			1·40	2·50

1970 (3 Aug). European Conservation Year. T **148** and similar vert designs. Multicoloured. W **58**. P 13×13½.

348	10m. Type **148**	10	10
349	50m. Poppies	15	10
350	90m. Giant Fennel	50	1·10
348/350 *Set of 3*		65	1·10

149 IEY Emblem

150 Mosaic

151 Globe, Dove and UN Emblem

(Des G. Simonis (75m.))

1970 (7 Sept). Anniversaries and Events. W **58** (sideways on horiz designs). P 13×14 (5m.) or 14×13 (others).

351	**149**	5m. black, red-brown and light yellow-brown	10	10
352	**150**	15m. multicoloured	10	10
353	**151**	75m. multicoloured	15	75
351/353 *Set of 3*			30	85

Events:—5m. International Education Year; 15m. 50th General Assembly of International Vine and Wine Office; 75m. 25th anniversary of United Nations.

152 Virgin and Child

(Photo Harrison)

1970 (23 Nov). Christmas. Wall-painting from Church of Panayia Podhythou, Galata. T **152** and similar multicoloured designs. P 14×14½.

354	25m. Archangel (facing right)	15	20
	a. Horiz strip of 3. Nos. 354/356	40	55
355	25m. Type **152**	15	20
356	25m. Archangel (facing left)	15	20
357	75m. Virgin and Child between Archangels	15	30
354/357 *Set of 4*		55	80

The 75m. is horiz, size 42×30 mm, and the 25m. values are vert, size as T **152**.

Nos. 354/356 were issued in *se-tenant* strips of three, throughout the sheet. The triptych thus formed is depicted in its entirety on the 75m. value.

STAMP BOOKLETS

Booklet vending machines, originally fitted to provide stamps to the value of 50m., were introduced by the Cyprus Post Office in 1962.

The stamps contained in these booklets were a haphazard selection of low values to the required amount, attached by their sheet margins to the cardboard covers. From 1968 these covers carried commercial advertising and details of postage rates.

Dominica

CROWN COLONY

A British packet agency was operating on Dominica from about 1778, the date of the earliest known use of a postal marking. This was replaced by a branch office of the British GPO which opened at Roseau on 8 May 1858. The stamps of Great Britain were used from that date until 1 May 1860, after which the colonial authorities assumed responsibility for the postal service. Until the introduction of Nos. 1/3 in 1874 No. CC1 and later handstamps were utilised.

For illustrations of handstamp and postmark types see BRITISH POST OFFICES ABROAD notes, following GREAT BRITAIN.

ROSEAU

CROWNED/CIRCLE HANDSTAMPS

CC1	CC **1**	DOMINICA (Black or R.) (17.5.1845) *Price on cover*	£550

No. CC1 is also known struck in black on various adhesive stamps as late as 1883.

Stamps of GREAT BRITAIN cancelled 'A07' as T **2**.

1858–60.

Z1	1d. rose-red (1857), *perf* 14	£350
Z2	2d. blue (1858) (Plate No. 7)	£1100
Z3	4d. rose (1857)	£325
Z4	6d. lilac (1856)	£300
Z5	1s. green	£2000

PRICES FOR STAMPS ON COVER TO 1945

Nos. 1/3	*from* × 25
No. 4	*from* × 40
No. 5	*from* × 100
No. 6	*from* × 40
Nos. 7/8	*from* × 100
No. 9	*from* × 40
Nos. 10/12	*from* × 15
Nos. 13/15	*from* × 100
No. 17	*from* × 50
Nos. 18/18a	—
No. 19	*from* × 40
Nos. 20/25	*from* × 30
No. 26	—
Nos. 27/90	*from* × 5
No. 91	—
Nos. 92/98	*from* × 10
Nos. 99/109	*from* × 3
Nos. R1/R3	*from* × 15
No. R4	*from* × 50
No. R6	*from* × 3

1 (2) (3) (4)

(Typo D.L.R.)

1874 (4 May). Wmk Crown CC. P 12½.

1	**1**	1d. lilac	£150	55·00
		a. Bisected vert (½d.) (*on cover*)	†	£9000
2		6d. green	£550	£100
3		1s. dull magenta	£325	70·00

NCE Normal — NCE Malformed 'CE' (R. 10/6)

1877–79. Wmk Crown CC. P 14.

4	**1**	½d. olive-yellow (1879)	20·00	60·00
5		1d. lilac	22·00	3·75
		a. Bisected vert or diag (½d.) (*on cover or card*)	†	£2500
		w. Wmk inverted	£130	
6		2½d. red-brown (1879)	£250	45·00
		w. Wmk inverted	†	£180
7		4d. blue (1879)	£130	3·00
		a. Malformed 'CE' in 'PENCE'	£1600	£130
8		6d. green	£170	20·00
9		1s. magenta	£130	50·00

1882 (25 Nov)–**83**. No. 5 bisected vertically and surch.

10	**2**	½(d.), in *black*, on half 1d.	£225	55·00
		a. Surch inverted	£1100	£800
		b. Surcharges *tête-bêche* (pair)	£2500	
11	**3**	½(d.), in *red*, on half 1d. (12.82)	38·00	19·00
		a. Surch inverted	£1100	£475
		c. Surch double	£1600	£650
12	**4**	½d. in *black*, on half 1d. (3.83)	70·00	42·00
		b. Surch double	£800	

T **4** is found reading up or down.

1883–86. Wmk Crown CA. P 14.

13	**1**	½d. olive-yellow	7·00	11·00
14		1d. lilac (1886)	60·00	15·00
		a. Bisected (½d.) (*on cover*)	†	£2250
15		2½d. red-brown (1884)	£140	4·75
		w. Wmk inverted	£500	

Half Penny (5) — One Penny (6)

1886 (1 Mar). Nos. 8 and 9 surch locally.
17 **5** ½d. on 6d. green 12·00 14·00
w. Wmk inverted † £450
18 **6** 1d. on 6d. green £35000 £10000
a. Thick bar (approx 1 *mm*) † £18000
19 1d. on 1s. magenta 23·00 20·00
a. Surch double £11000 £4000

It is believed that only two sheets of the 1d. on 6d. were surcharged. On one of these sheets the six stamps in the top row showed the thick bar variety, No. 18a.

1886–90. Wmk Crown CA. P 14.
20 **1** ½d. dull green 5·50 5·50
22 1d. rose (1887) 17·00 26·00
a. Deep carmine (1889) 5·50 15·00
b. Bisected (½d.) (*on cover*) † £1900
w. Wmk inverted £200 £200
23 2½d. ultramarine (1888) 4·00 8·50
24 4d. grey 8·50 7·50
a. Malformed 'CE' in 'PENCE' £160 £275
25 6d. orange (1888) 22·00 90·00
26 1s. dull magenta (1890) £200 £400
20/26 *Set of 6* £200 £475
20s/25s Optd 'SPECIMEN' *Set of 5* £225

The stamps of Dominica were superseded by the general issue for Leeward Islands on 31 October 1890, but the sets following were in concurrent use with the stamps inscribed 'LEEWARD ISLANDS' until 31 December 1939, when the island came under the administration of the Windward Islands.

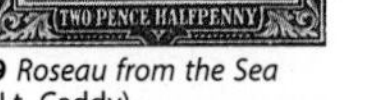

9 Roseau from the Sea (Lt. Caddy)

10

(T **9** to **11** typo D.L.R.)

1903 (1 Sept)–**07**. Wmk Crown CC (sideways* on T **9**). Ordinary paper. P 14.
27 **9** ½d. green and grey-green 4·50 4·75
a. Chalk-surfaced paper (1906) 28·00 26·00
28 1d. grey and red 17·00 75
a. Chalk-surfaced paper (1906) 50·00 8·00
29 2d. green and brown 6·50 8·50
a. Chalk-surfaced paper (1906) 48·00 55·00
30 2½d. grey and bright blue 12·00 4·00
a. Chalk-surfaced paper (3.9.07) 32·00 60·00
31 3d. dull purple and grey-black 12·00 3·25
ay. Wmk sideways inverted and reversed £275
b. Chalk-surfaced paper (1906) 50·00 38·00
32 6d. grey and chestnut 15·00 18·00
33 1s. magenta and grey-green 40·00 50·00
a. Chalk-surfaced paper (1906) 75·00 £150
34 2s. grey-black and purple 40·00 32·00
ws. Wmk Crown to left of CC, optd 'SPECIMEN' £120
35 2s.6d. grey-green and maize 19·00 75·00
w. Wmk Crown to left of CC
36 **10** 5s. black and brown £110 £170
27/36 *Set of 10* £225 £325
27s/36s Optd 'SPECIMEN' *Set of 10* £180

* The normal sideways watermark shows Crown to right of CC, *as seen from the back of the stamp.*

1907–08. Wmk Mult Crown CA (sideways* on T **9**). Chalk-surfaced paper. P 14.
37 **9** ½d. green 15·00 11·00
x. Wmk sideways reversed £200
38 1d. grey and red 2·25 40
39 2d. green and brown 15·00 24·00
40 2½d. grey and bright blue 6·00 21·00
41 3d. dull purple and grey-black 4·00 20·00
42 6d. black and chestnut 55·00 85·00
43 1s. magenta and grey-green (1908) 3·75 55·00
44 2s. grey-black and purple (1908) 29·00 32·00
45 2s.6d. grey-green and maize (1908) 29·00 70·00
46 **10** 5s. black and brown (1908) 75·00 75·00
37/46 *Set of 10* £200 £350

* The normal sideways watermark shows Crown to right of CA, *as seen from the back of the stamp.*

Examples of Nos. 27/36 and 37/46 are known showing a forged General Post Office Dominica postmark dated 'JU 1 11'.

11

WAR TAX

ONE HALFPENNY

(12)

1908–20. Wmk Mult Crown CA (sideways* on T **9**). Chalk-surfaced paper (3d., 6d., 1s.). P 14.
47 **9** ½d. blue-green 14·00 10·00
aw. Wmk Crown to left of CA 7·00 4·50
ay. Wmk sideways inverted and reversed
b. Deep green (wmk Crown to left of CA) 3·50 2·25
by. Wmk sideways inverted and reversed £225
48 1d. carmine-red 3·00 30
aw. Wmk Crown to left of CA 6·50 40
b. Scarlet (1916) 1·50 40
bw. Wmk Crown to left of CA 2·75 70
49 2d. grey (1909) 4·75 5·00
aw. Wmk Crown to left of CA 5·50 16·00
b. Slate (wmk Crown to left of CA) (1918) 3·50 12·00
50 2½d. blue 8·50 3·50
aw. Wmk Crown to left of CA 9·00 9·00
b. Bright blue (1918) 5·00 9·00
bw. Wmk Crown to left of CA 12·00 16·00
51 3d. purple/*yellow* (1909) 3·00 2·50
a. Ordinary paper (wmk Crown to left of CA) (1912) 3·00 4·00
ab. *On pale yellow* (1920) 8·50 19·00
52 6d. dull and bright purple (1909) 10·00 6·00
a. Ordinary paper. *Dull purple* (wmk Crown to left of CA) (1915) 4·50 18·00
53 1s. black/*green* (1910) 4·00 2·75
a. Ordinary paper (wmk Crown to left of CA) (1912) 5·50 4·00
as. Optd 'SPECIMEN' in red 70·00
asa. Ditto. Opt double, one albino £200
53*b* 2s. purple and deep blue/*blue* (wmk Crown to left of CA) (1919) 26·00 90·00
53*c* 2s.6d. black and red/*blue* (wmk Crown to left of CA) (1920) 26·00 £100
54 **11** 5s. red and green/*yellow* (1914) 60·00 £100
47/54 *Set of 10* £120 £275
48s/54s Optd 'SPECIMEN' (1s. optd in blk) *Set of 9* £200

The watermark orientation differs according to the printings. *Unless otherwise stated* the watermark shows the Crown to right of CA *as seen from the back of the stamp.*

1916 (Sept). No. 47*b* surch with T **12** by De La Rue.
55 **9** ½d. on ½d. deep green (R.) 3·75 75
a. Small 'O' in 'ONE' 7·50 9·50
x. Wmk sideways reversed £150

No. 55a occurs on ten stamps within each sheet of 60.

1918 (18 Mar). No. 47b optd with T **12** locally, from D.L.R. plate, but with 'ONE HALFPENNY' blanked out.
56 **9** ½d. deep green (Blk.) 9·50 6·00
w. Wmk Crown to right of CA £160

The blanking out of the surcharge was not completely successful so that it almost always appears as an albino to a greater or lesser extent.

WAR TAX

(14)

1918 (1 June)–**19**. Nos. 47*b* and 51a optd with T **14** by De La Rue.
57 **9** ½d. deep green 15 50
w. Wmk Crown to right of CA £150
x. Wmk sideways reversed £160
y. Wmk sideways inverted and reversed £180
58 3d. purple/*yellow* (R.) (1919) 5·50 4·00

WAR TAX
1½D.

(15)

1 ½D.

Short Fraction Bar (R. 6/4)

1919. As No. 50aw, but colour changed, surch with T **15** by De La Rue.
59 **9** 1½d. on 2½d. orange (R.) 15 55
a. Short fraction bar 9·00 38·00
b. 'C' and 'A' missing from wmk £550

No. 59b shows the 'C' omitted from one impression with the 'A' missing from the next one to the left (*as seen from the back of the stamp*). The 'C' is badly distorted in the second watermark.

1920 (1 June). As No. 59, but without 'WAR TAX'.
60 **9** 1½d. on 2½d. orange (Blk.) 8·00 4·50
a. Short fraction bar 60·00 70·00
b. 'A' of 'CA' missing from wmk £600
55s/60s Optd 'SPECIMEN' or '*Specimen*.' (Nos. 56s) *Set of 6* £200

An example of No. 60 is known with 'C' of 'CA' missing from wmk in the sheet margin.

1921–22. Wmk Mult Script CA (sideways*). Chalk-surfaced paper (6d.). P 14.
62 **9** ½d. blue-green 2·50 24·00
63 1d. carmine-red 3·00 3·75
w. Wmk Crown to right of CA — 60·00
64 1½d. orange 3·00 21·00
65 2d. grey 2·75 3·25
66 2½d. bright blue 3·25 18·00
67 6d. purple 5·00 48·00
69 2s. purple and blue/*blue* (1922) 50·00 £160
70 2s.6d. black and red/*blue* 42·00 £160
62/70 *Set of 8* £100 £400
62s/70s Optd 'SPECIMEN' *Set of 8* £160

* The normal sideways watermark shows Crown to left of CA, *as seen from the back of the stamp.*

The 1½d. has figures of value in the lower corner and no ornamentation below words of value.

Examples of some values are known showing a forged GPO Dominica postmark dated 'MY 19 27'.

16

(Typo D.L.R.)

1923 (1 Mar)–**33**. Chalk-surfaced paper. P 14.

(a) Wmk Mult Script CA (sideways)*
71 **16** ½d. black and green 1·75 60
72 1d. black and bright violet 7·00 1·75
73 1d. black and scarlet (1933) 17·00 1·00
74 1½d. black and scarlet 6·50 65
75 1½d. black and red-brown (1933) 15·00 70
76 2d. black and grey 4·25 50
77 2½d. black and orange-yellow 4·00 9·00
78 2½d. black and ultramarine (1927) 7·50 2·00
79 3d. black and ultramarine 4·25 19·00
80 3d. black and red/*yellow* (1927) 4·75 1·00
81 4d. black and brown 4·75 5·50
82 6d. black and bright magenta 5·50 7·00
83 1s. black/*emerald* 3·50 4·25
84 2s. black and blue/*blue* 26·00 40·00
85 2s.6d. black and red/*blue* 28·00 40·00
86 3s. black and purple/*yellow* (1927) 4·75 15·00
sa. Opt 'SPECIMEN' double £450
87 4s. black and red/*emerald* 23·00 40·00
88 5s. black and green/*yellow* (1927) 42·00 60·00

(b) Wmk Mult Crown CA (sideways)*
89 **16** 3s. black and purple/*yellow* 4·25 70·00
90 5s. black and green/*yellow* 9·00 55·00
91 £1 black and purple/*red* £225 £350
71/91 *Set of 21* £375 £600
71s/91s Optd or Perf (Nos. 73s, 75s) 'SPECIMEN' *Set of 21* £425

* The normal sideways watermark shows Crown to left of CA, *as seen from the back of the stamp.*

Examples of most values are known showing a forged GPO Dominica postmark dated 'MY 19 27'.

1935 (6 May). Silver Jubilee. As Nos. 91/94 of Antigua.
92 1d. deep blue and carmine 1·50 30
f. Diagonal line by turret 70·00 70·00
g. Dot to left of chapel £110
h. Dot by flagstaff £120 90·00
i. Dash by turret £160
93 1½d. ultramarine and grey 6·00 3·50
f. Diagonal line by turret £100 £130
h. Dot by flagstaff £130 £160
94 2½d. brown and deep blue 7·00 5·50
95 1s. slate and purple 7·00 14·00
h. Dot by flagstaff £160 £275
i. Dash by turret £300 £425
92/95 *Set of 4* 20·00 21·00
92s/95s Perf 'SPECIMEN' *Set of 4* £110

For illustrations of plate varieties see Omnibus section following Zanzibar.

1937 (12 May). Coronation. As Nos. 95/97 of Antigua. P 11×11½.
96 1d. carmine 40 10
97 1½d. yellow-brown 60 10
98 2½d. blue 1·00 1·75
96/98 *Set of 3* 1·75 1·75
96s/98s Perf 'SPECIMEN' *Set of 3* £100

17 Fresh Water Lake

18 Layou River

19 Picking limes

20 Boiling Lake

(Recess Waterlow)

1938 (15 Aug)–**47**. T **17/20**. Wmk Mult Script CA. P 12½.
99 **17** ½d. brown and green 10 15
100 **18** 1d. grey and scarlet 25 25
101 **19** 1½d. green and purple 1·00 70
102 **20** 2d. carmine and grey-black 50 2·25
103 **19** 2½d. purple and bright blue 6·00 1·75
a. Purple and bright ultramarine (8.42) 30 2·25
104 **18** 3d. olive-green and brown 30 50
104*a* **19** 3½d. ultramarine and purple (15.10.47) 2·75 2·75
105 **17** 6d. emerald-green and violet 1·75 1·50
105*a* 7d. green and yellow-brown (15.10.47) 2·25 2·00
106 **20** 1s. violet and olive-green 6·00 1·50
106*a* **18** 2s. slate and purple (15.10.47) 10·00 17·00
107 **17** 2s.6d. black and vermilion 23·00 5·50
108 **18** 5s. light blue and sepia 18·00 13·00
108*a* **20** 10s. black and brown-orange (15.10.47) 22·00 25·00

21 King George VI

(Photo Harrison)

1940 (15 Apr)–**42**. Wmk Mult Script CA. Chalk-surfaced paper. P 15×14.
109 **21** ¼d. chocolate 1·50 1·00
a. Ordinary paper (1942) 40 2·25
99/109a *Set of 15* 75·00 65·00
99s/109s Perf 'SPECIMEN' *Set of 15* £350

1946 (14 Oct). Victory. As Nos. 110/111 of Antigua.
110 1d. carmine 30 10
111 3½d. blue 30 10
110s/111s Perf 'SPECIMEN' *Set of 2* 80·00

1948 (1 Dec). Royal Silver Wedding. As Nos. 112/113 of Antigua.
112 1d. scarlet 15 10
113 10s. red-brown 25·00 45·00

(New Currency. 100 cents = 1 BWI, later East Caribbean dollar)

1949 (10 Oct). 75th Anniversary of Universal Postal Union. As Nos. 114/17 of Antigua.

No.		Description	Unused	Used
114		5c. blue	20	15
115		6c. brown	1·25	3·25
116		12c. purple	45	2·75
		a. 'A' of 'CA' missing from wmk	—	£750
117		24c. olive	30	40
114/117		*Set of 4*	2·00	6·00

1951 (16 Feb). Inauguration of BWI University College. As Nos. 118/119 of Antigua.

No.		Description	Unused	Used
118		3c. yellow-green and reddish violet	50	1·25
119		12c. deep green and carmine	75	40

22 King George VI

23 Drying Cocoa

24 Making Carib baskets

25 Lime plantation

26 Picking oranges

27 Bananas

28 Botanical Gardens

29 Drying vanilla beans

30 Fresh Water Lake

31 Layou River

32 Boiling Lake

33 Picking oranges

(Photo Harrison (½c.). Recess B.W. (others))

1951 (1 July). T **22/33**. Wmk Mult Script CA. Chalk-surfaced paper (½c.). P 15×14 (½c.), 13½×13 ($2.40), 13×13½ (others).

No.	Type	Description	Unused	Used
120	**22**	½c. chocolate	10	30
121	**23**	1c. black and vermilion	10	30
		b. 'A' of 'CA' missing from wmk	£400	
		c. 'JA' for 'CA' in wmk	£450	
122	**24**	2c. red-brown and deep green	15	1·50
		a. 'C' of 'CA' missing from wmk	£450	£475
		b. 'A' of 'CA' missing from wmk	£450	
		c. 'JA' for 'CA' in wmk	—	£475
123	**25**	3c. green and reddish violet	25	3·50
		a. 'C' of 'CA' missing from wmk	£425	
		c. 'JA' for 'CA' in wmk	£450	
124	**26**	4c. brown-orange and sepia	70	4·00
		a. 'C' of 'CA' missing from wmk	£475	£475
		b. 'A' of 'CA' missing from wmk	£475	
125	**27**	5c. black and carmine	85	30
		a. 'C' of 'CA' missing from wmk	£600	£500
		b. 'A' of 'CA' missing from wmk	£600	
		c. 'JA' for 'CA' in wmk	£650	
126	**28**	6c. olive and chestnut	1·00	30
		a. 'C' of 'CA' missing from wmk	£475	
		b. 'A' of 'CA' missing from wmk	£600	
127	**29**	8c. blue-green and blue	3·25	2·25
		b. 'A' of 'CA' missing from wmk		
128	**30**	12c. black and bright green	70	1·25
		a. 'C' of 'CA' missing from wmk	£950	
129	**31**	14c. blue and violet	1·25	3·50
		a. 'C' of 'CA' missing from wmk	£1000	
		b. 'A' of 'CA' missing from wmk	—	£650
		c. 'JA' for 'CA' in wmk	£850	
130	**32**	24c. reddish violet and rose-carmine	75	40
		a. 'C' of 'CA' missing from wmk	£1000	£850
131	**25**	48c. bright green and red-orange	7·00	16·00
		a. 'C' of 'CA' missing from wmk	£1000	
		b. 'A' of 'CA' missing from wmk	£1000	
		c. 'JA' for 'CA' in wmk		
132	**24**	60c. carmine and black	4·50	11·00
		c. 'JA' for 'CA' in wmk	£800	
133	**30**	$1.20 emerald and black	9·00	8·00
		a. 'C' of 'CA' missing from wmk	£1200	
		b. 'A' of 'CA' missing from wmk	£1200	
134	**33**	$2.40 orange and black	30·00	55·00
120/134		*Set of 15*	50·00	95·00

Nos. 121b, 122b, 124b, 125b, 126b, 127b, 129b, 131b and 133b must show no trace of the letter 'A'. Examples with part of the left leg of the 'A' still present are worth much less.

Nos. 121c, 122c, 123c, 125c, 129c, 131c and 132c may represent an attempt to repair the missing 'C' variety.

NEW CONSTITUTION 1951

(34)

1951 (15 Oct). New Constitution. Nos. 123, 125, 127 and 129 optd with T **34** by B.W.

No.	Type	Description	Unused	Used
135	**25**	3c. green and reddish violet	25	70
		a. 'C' of 'CA' missing from wmk	£475	£500
		c. 'JA' for 'CA' in watermark	£475	£500
136	**27**	5c. black and carmine	25	2·25
		a. 'JA' for 'CA' in wmk	£550	£650
137	**29**	8c. blue-green and blue (R.)	25	20
		a. 'JA' for 'CA' in wmk	£600	
138	**31**	14c. blue and violet (R.)	2·50	1·75
		a. 'C' of 'CA' missing from wmk		
		b. 'A' of 'CA' missing from wmk	£750	
135/138		*Set of 4*	3·00	4·50

1953 (2 June). Coronation. As No. 120 of Antigua.

No.		Description	Unused	Used
139		2c. black and deep green	30	10

35 Queen Elizabeth II

36 Mat Making

37 Canoe Making

38 Cutting bananas

(Photo Harrison (½c.). Recess B.W. (others))

1954 (1 Oct)–**62**. Designs previously used for King George VI issue, but with portrait of Queen Elizabeth II as in T **35/38**. Wmk Mult Script CA. P 15×14 (½c.), 13½×13 ($2.40), 13×13½ (others).

No.	Type	Description	Unused	Used
140	**35**	½c. brown	10	1·75
141	**23**	1c. black and vermilion	30	20
142	**24**	2c. chocolate and myrtle-green	1·25	2·75
		a. Chocolate and grey-green (13.3.62)	16·00	15·00
143	**25**	3c. green and purple	1·50	40
144	**36**	3c. black and carmine (15.10.57)	6·50	2·50
145	**26**	4c. brown-orange and sepia	30	10
146	**27**	5c. black and carmine-red	3·50	1·00
147	**37**	5c. light blue and sepia-brown (15.10.57)	16·00	2·00
		a. Blue and sepia (13.3.62)	45·00	10·00
148	**28**	6c. bronze-green and red-brown	50	10
149	**29**	8c. deep green and deep blue	1·75	10
150	**38**	10c. green and brown (15.10.57)	9·00	3·75
		a. Green and deep brown (17.7.62)	20·00	9·00
151	**30**	12c. black and emerald	60	10
152	**31**	14c. blue and purple	60	10
153	**32**	24c. purple and carmine	60	10
154	**25**	48c. green and red-orange	3·50	19·00
155	**36**	48c. deep brown and violet (15.10.57)	5·50	4·00
156	**24**	60c. rose-red and black	4·50	1·00
157	**30**	$1.20 emerald and black	22·00	9·00
158	**33**	$2.40 yellow-orange and black	22·00	14·00
140/158		*Set of 19*	85·00	50·00

1958 (22 Apr). Inauguration of British Caribbean Federation. As Nos. 135/137 of Antigua.

No.		Description	Unused	Used
159		3c. deep green	90	15
160		6c. blue	1·00	1·75
161		12c. scarlet	1·10	20
159/161		*Set of 3*	2·75	1·90

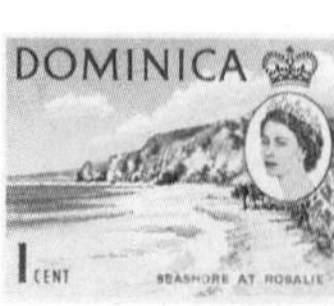

40 Seashore at Rosalie

41 Queen Elizabeth II

42 Sailing canoe

43 Sulphur springs

44 Road-making

45 Dug-out canoe

46 Crapaud (Toad)

47 Scott's Head

48 Traditional Costume

49 Bananas

50 Imperial Amazon

51 Goodwill

52 Cocoa tree

53 Coat of Arms

54 Trafalgar Falls

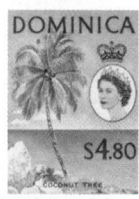

55 Coconut Palm

Two types of 14c.

I. Eyes of model looking straight ahead.
II. Eyes looking to her right.

(Des S. Scott. Photo Harrison)

1963 (16 May)–**65**. T **40/55**. W w **12** (upright). P 14×14½ (vert) or 14½×14 (horiz).

No.	Type	Description	Unused	Used
162	**40**	1c. green, blue and sepia	10	85
163	**41**	2c. bright blue	30	10
		w. Wmk inverted	—	19·00
164	**42**	3c. blackish brown and blue	1·75	1·25
165	**43**	4c. green, sepia and slate-violet	10	10
166	**41**	5c. magenta	30	10
167	**44**	6c. green, bistre and violet	15	80
168	**45**	8c. green, sepia and black	30	20
169	**46**	10c. sepia and pink	20	20
170	**47**	12c. green, blue and blackish brown	1·00	10
171	**48**	14c. multicoloured (I)	1·00	10
171*a*		14c. multicoloured (II) (1.4.65)	2·50	1·40
172	**49**	15c. yellow, green and brown	1·50	10
		w. Wmk inverted	—	32·00
173	**50**	24c. multicoloured	9·00	20
174	**51**	48c. green, blue and black	1·00	1·50
175	**52**	60c. orange, green and black	1·00	70
176	**53**	$1.20 multicoloured	6·50	2·00
177	**54**	$2.40 blue, turquoise and brown	6·50	4·75
178	**55**	$4.80 green, blue and brown	27·00	38·00
162/178		*Set of 17*	50·00	45·00

See also Nos. 200/204.

1963 (4 June). Freedom from Hunger. As No. 146 of Antigua.

No.		Description	Unused	Used
179		15c. reddish violet	15	10

1963 (2 Sept). Red Cross Centenary. As Nos. 147/148 of Antigua.

No.		Description	Unused	Used
180		5c. red and black	20	40
181		15c. red and blue	40	60

1964 (23 Apr). 400th Birth Anniversary of William Shakespeare. As No. 164 of Antigua.

No.		Description	Unused	Used
182		15c. bright purple	10	10
		w. Wmk inverted	1·00	

1965 (17 May). ITU Centenary. As Nos. 166/167 of Antigua.

No.		Description	Unused	Used
183		2c. light emerald and blue	10	10
184		48c. turquoise-blue and grey	45	20

1965 (25 Oct). International Co-operation Year. As Nos. 168/169 of Antigua.

No.		Description	Unused	Used
185		1c. reddish purple and turquoise-green	10	20
186		15c. deep bluish green and lavender	75	10

1966 (24 Jan). Churchill Commemoration. As Nos. 170/173 of Antigua.

No.	Type	Description	Unused	Used
187		1c. new blue	10	1·60
		a. Gold omitted	£2500	
188		5c. deep green	45	10
189		15c. brown	95	10
190		24c. bluish violet	1·00	20
		w. Wmk inverted	£160	
187/190 *Set of 4*			2·25	1·75

No. 187a occurred on five stamps in the bottom two rows of one sheet.

An example of the 1c. is known showing the gold face value printed double.

1966 (4 Feb). Royal Visit. As Nos. 174/175 of Antigua.

No.	Type	Description	Unused	Used
191		5c. black and ultramarine	75	40
192		15c. black and magenta	1·00	60

1966 (1 July). World Cup Football Championship. As Nos. 176/177 of Antigua.

No.	Type	Description	Unused	Used
193		5c. violet, yellow-green, lake and yellow-brown	25	15
194		24c. chocolate, blue-green, lake and yellow-brown	85	15

1966 (20 Sept). Inauguration of WHO Headquarters, Geneva. As Nos. 178/179 of Antigua.

No.	Type	Description	Unused	Used
195		5c. black, yellow-green and light blue	15	15
196		24c. black, light purple and yellow-brown	30	15

1966 (1 Dec). 20th Anniversary of UNESCO As Nos. 196/198 of Antigua.

No.	Type	Description	Unused	Used
197		5c. slate-violet, red, yellow and orange	20	15
198		15c. orange-yellow, violet and deep olive	50	10
199		24c. black, bright purple and orange	60	15
197/199 *Set of 3*			1·10	30

1966 (30 Dec)–**67**. As Nos. 165, 167/169 and 172 but wmk w **12** sideways.

No.	Type	Description	Unused	Used
200	**43**	4c. green, sepia and slate-violet (16.5.67)	1·00	90
201	**44**	6c. green, bistre and violet	20	15
202	**45**	8c. green, sepia and black	40	10
203	**46**	10c. sepia and pink (16.5.67)	50	10
204	**49**	15c. yellow, green and brown (16.5.67)	50	10
200/204 *Set of 5*			2·40	1·25

ASSOCIATED STATEHOOD

56 Children of Three Races

(Des and photo Harrison)

1967 (2 Nov). National Day. T **56** and similar horiz designs. Multicoloured. W w **12**. P 14½.

No.	Type	Description	Unused	Used
205		5c. Type **56**	10	10
206		10c. The *Santa Maria* and motto	40	15
207		15c. Hands holding motto ribbon	15	15
208		24c. Belaire dancing	15	20
205/208 *Set of 4*			70	45

57 John F. Kennedy

(Des G. Vasarhelyi. Litho D.L.R.)

1968 (20 Apr). Human Rights Year. T **57** and similar horiz designs. Multicoloured. W w **12** (sideways). P 14×13½.

No.	Type	Description	Unused	Used
209		1c. Type **57**	10	30
210		10c. Cecil A. E. Rawle	10	10
		a. Imperf (pair)	90·00	
211		12c. Pope John XXIII	45	15
212		48c. Florence Nightingale	20	25
213		60c. Albert Schweitzer	35	30
209/213 *Set of 5*			1·00	1·00

ASSOCIATED STATEHOOD
(**58**)

NATIONAL DAY 3 NOVEMBER 1968
(**59**)

1968 (8 July). Associated Statehood. As Nos. 162, 170 and 174, but wmk sideways, or Nos. 163/164, 166, 170, 171*a*, 173, 175/178 and 200/204 optd with T **58**.

No.	Type	Description	Unused	Used
214	**40**	1c. green, blue and sepia (Sil.)	10	10
215	**41**	2c. bright blue (Sil.)	10	10
216	**42**	3c. blackish brown and blue (Sil.)	10	10
217	**43**	4c. green, sepia and slate-violet (Sil.)	10	10
218	**41**	5c. magenta (Sil.)	10	10
219	**44**	6c. green, bistre and violet	10	10
220	**45**	8c. green, sepia and black	10	10
221	**46**	10c. sepia and pink (Sil.)	55	10
222	**47**	12c. green, blue and blackish brown (Sil.) (wmk sideways)	10	60
		a. Wmk upright	10	10
224	**48**	14c. multicoloured (II) (Sil.)	10	10
225	**49**	15c. yellow, green and brown (Sil.)	10	10
226	**50**	24c. multicoloured (Sil.)	4·50	10
227	**51**	48c. green, blue and black (Sil.) (wmk sideways)	55	3·00
		a. Wmk upright	65	1·00
228	**52**	60c. orange, green and black	1·00	70
229	**53**	$1.20 multicoloured	1·00	3·25
230	**54**	$2.40 blue, turquoise and brown (Sil.)	1·00	2·50
231	**55**	$4.80 green, blue and brown (Sil.)	1·25	9·00
214/231 *Set of 17*			9·00	15·00

The 2, 5, 6, 8 and 10c. values exist with PVA gum as well as gum arabic.

1968 (3 Nov). National Day. Nos. 162/164, 171 and 176 optd with T **59**.

No.	Type	Description	Unused	Used
232	**40**	1c. green, blue and sepia	10	10
		a. Opt inverted	48·00	
		b. Opt double		
233	**41**	2c. bright blue	10	10
		a. Opt double	35·00	
234	**42**	3c. blackish brown and blue	10	10
		a. Opt inverted	35·00	
235	**48**	14c. multicoloured (I)	10	10
		a. Opt double	75·00	
236	**53**	$1.20 multicoloured	55	40
		a. Opt double	35·00	
		b. Vert pair, one opt omitted, other opt double	£650	
232/236 *Set of 5*			60	40

The above set was put on sale by the New York Agency on 1 November but not sold locally until the 3 November.

60 Forward shooting at Goal

(Des M. Shamir (1c., 60c.), K. Plowitz (5c., 48c.). Litho B.W.)

1968 (25 Nov). Olympic Games, Mexico. T **60** and similar horiz designs. Multicoloured. P 11½×11.

No.	Type	Description	Unused	Used
237		1c. Type **60**	10	10
		a. Horiz pair. Nos. 237/238	10	10
238		1c. Goalkeeper trying to save goal	10	10
239		5c. Swimmers about to dive	10	10
		a. Horiz pair. Nos. 239/240	10	10
240		5c. Swimmers diving	10	10
241		48c. Javelin-throwing	15	15
		a. Horiz pair. Nos. 241/242	30	30
242		48c. Hurdling	15	15
243		60c. Basketball	90	25
		a. Horiz pair. Nos. 243/244	1·75	50
244		60c. Basketball players	90	25
237/244 *Set of 8*			2·00	85

Nos. 237/244 were issued in sheets of 40 containing two panes of *se-tenant* pairs.

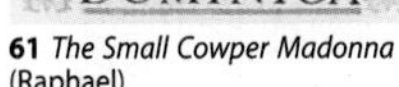

61 *The Small Cowper Madonna* (Raphael)

62 *Venus and Adonis* (Rubens)

(Photo Delrieu, Paris)

1968 (23 Dec). Christmas. P 12½×12.

No.	Type	Description	Unused	Used
245	**61**	5c. multicoloured	10	50

Three other values were issued: 12c. *Madonna of the Chair* (Raphael); 24c. *Madonna and Child* (Italo-Byzantine, 16th-century); $1.20 *Madonna and Child* (Byzantine, 13th-century). Sizes as T **61**.

These only come from miniature sheets, containing two *se-tenant* strips of each value.

(Litho D.L.R.)

1969 (30 Jan). 20th Anniversary of World Health Organisation. Paintings. T **62** and similar vert designs. Multicoloured. W w **12**. P 15.

No.	Type	Description	Unused	Used
246		5c. Type **62**	20	10
247		15c. *The Death of Socrates* (J.-L. David)	30	10
248		24c. *Christ and the Pilgrims of Emmaus* (Velázquez)	30	10
249		50c. *Pilate washing his Hands* (Rembrandt)	50	40
246/249 *Set of 4*			1·10	50

66 Picking Oranges

67 'Strength in Unity' Emblem and Fruit Trees

(Des K. Plowitz. Litho Harrison)

1969 (10 Mar). Tourism. T **66** and similar horiz designs. Multicoloured. W w **12**. P 14½.

No.	Type	Description	Unused	Used
250		10c. Type **66**	15	15
		a. Horiz pair. Nos. 250/251	30	30
251		10c. Woman, child and ocean scene	15	15
252		12c. Fort Yeoung Hotel	50	15
		a. Horiz pair. Nos. 252/253	1·00	30
253		12c. Red-necked Amazons	50	15
254		24c. Calypso band	30	20
		a. Horiz pair. Nos. 254/255	60	40
		w. Wmk inverted	45·00	
255		24c. Women dancing	30	20
		w. Wmk inverted	45·00	
256		48c. Underwater life	30	25
		a. Horiz pair. Nos. 256/257	60	50
257		48c. Skin-diver and Turtle	30	25
250/257 *Set of 8*			2·25	1·25

Each denomination was printed *se-tenant* throughout the sheet. The 12c. values are on cream coloured paper.

(Litho B.W.)

1969 (July). First Anniversary of CARIFTA (Caribbean Free Trade Area). T **67** and similar horiz designs. Multicoloured. P 13½×13.

No.	Type	Description	Unused	Used
258		5c. Type **67**	10	10
259		8c. Hawker Siddeley H.S.748 aircraft, emblem and island	30	20
260		12c. Chart of Caribbean Sea and emblem	30	25
261		24c. Steamship unloading, tug and emblem	40	25
258/261 *Set of 4*			1·00	70

71 *Spinning*

72 Mahatma Gandhi Weaving and Clock Tower, Westminster

(Litho B.W.)

1969 (10 July). 50th Anniversary of International Labour Organisation. T **71** and similar vert designs showing paintings of people at work by J. Millet, bordered by flags of member nations of the ILO Multicoloured. No wmk. P 13×13½.

No.	Type	Description	Unused	Used
262		15c. Type **71**	10	10
263		30c. *Threshing*	15	15
264		38c. *Flax-pulling*	15	15
262/264 *Set of 3*			30	30

(Des G. Vasarhelyi. Litho Format)

1969 (20 Oct). Birth Centenary of Mahatma Gandhi. T **72** and similar horiz designs. Multicoloured. P 14½.

No.	Type	Description	Unused	Used
265		6c. Type **72**	45	10
266		38c. Gandhi, Nehru and Mausoleum	65	15
267		$1.20 Gandhi and Taj Mahal	1·00	1·00
265/267 *Set of 3*			1·90	1·00

Nos. 265/267 are incorrectly inscribed 'Ghandi'.

75 *Saint Joseph*

(Des G. Vasarhelyi. Litho Govt Printer, Jerusalem)

1969 (3 Nov). National Day. Stained Glass Windows. T **75** and similar vert designs. Multicoloured. P 14.

No.	Type	Description	Unused	Used
268		6c. Type **75**	10	10
269		8c. *Saint John*	10	10
270		12c. *Saint Peter*	10	10
271		60c. *Saint Paul*	30	50
268/271 *Set of 4*			40	60

Nos. 268/271 were printed in sheets of 16 (4×4) containing 12 stamps and four printed labels in the top row. The labels each contain two lines of a patriotic poem by W. O. M. Pond, the first letter from each line spelling 'DOMINICA'.

79 Queen Elizabeth II

80 Purple-throated Carib and Flower

81 Government Headquarters

82 Coat of Arms

(Photo D.L.R.)

1969 (26 Nov)–**72**. T **79/82** and similar horiz designs. Multicoloured. W **41** of Singapore (Half-check Pattern) (60c. to $4.80) or no wmk (others). Chalk-surfaced paper. P 13½×14 (½c.), 14×13½ (1 to 50c.) or 14 (60c. to $4.80).

272	½c. Type **79**	10	2·75
	a. Glazed paper (1972)	75	2·50
273	1c. Type **80**	1·00	3·00
	a. Glazed paper (1972)	1·50	1·50
274	2c. Poinsettia	15	10
	a. Glazed paper (1972)	50	40
275	3c. Red-necked Pigeon	3·00	3·25
	a. Glazed paper (1972)	4·25	1·50
276	4c. Imperial Amazon	3·00	3·25
	a. Glazed paper (1972)	4·25	1·50
277	5c. *Battus polydamas* (butterfly)	2·75	3·00
	a. Glazed paper (1972)	2·75	1·75
278	6c. *Dryas julia* (butterfly)	2·75	4·25
	a. Glazed paper (1972)	2·75	2·75
279	8c. Shipping Bananas	20	10
	a. Glazed paper (1972)	40	50
280	10c. Portsmouth Harbour	20	10
	a. Glazed paper (1972)	35	20
281	12c. Copra processing plant	20	10
	a. Glazed paper (1972)	35	20
282	15c. Straw workers	20	10
	a. Glazed paper (1972)	35	25
283	25c. Timber plant	30	10
	a. Glazed paper (1972)	40	25
284	30c. Pumice mine	1·50	90
	a. Glazed paper (1972)	1·50	70
285	38c. Grammar school and playing field	14·00	1·75
	a. Glazed paper (1972)	8·50	15·00
286	50c. Roseau Cathedral	50	45
	a. Glazed paper (1972)	80	1·00
287	60c. Type **81**	55	1·50
288	$1.20 Melville Hall Airport (40×27 *mm*)	1·50	1·75
289	$2.40 Type **82**	1·00	4·00
290	$4.80 Type **79** (26×39 *mm*)	1·75	7·00
272/290 *Set of* 19		30·00	32·00
272a/286a *Set of* 15		25·00	27·00

99 *Virgin and Child with St John* (Perugino)

101 Astronaut's First Step onto the Moon

(Des G. Vasarhelyi. Litho B.W.)

1969 (19 Dec). Christmas. Paintings. T **99** and similar perf designs. Multicoloured. P 14×14½.

291	6c. *Virgin and Child with St John* (Lippi)	10	10
292	10c. *Holy Family with the Lamb* (Raphael)	10	10
293	15c. Type **99**	10	10
294	$1.20 *Madonna of the Rose Hedge* (Botticelli)	35	40
291/294 *Set of* 4		35	40
MS295 89×76 mm. Nos. 293/294. Imperf		75	1·00

(Des G. Vasarhelyi. Photo Banknote Printing Office, Helsinki)

1970 (6 Feb*). Moon Landing. T **101** and similar horiz designs. Multicoloured. P 12½.

296	½c. Type **101**	10	10
297	5c. Scientific Experiment on the Moon, and Flag	15	10
298	8c. Astronauts collecting Rocks	15	10
299	30c. Module over the Moon	20	15
300	50c. Moon Plaque	30	25
301	60c. Astronauts	30	30
296/301 *Set of* 6		1·00	80
MS302 116×112 mm. Nos. 298/301. Imperf		1·75	2·25

* This is the date of release in Dominica, but the above were released by the Philatelic Agency in the USA on 2 February.

107 Giant Green Turtle

(Des G. Drummond. Litho Kyodo Printing Co, Tokyo)

1970 (7 Sept). Flora and Fauna. T **107** and similar horiz designs. Multicoloured. P 13.

303	6c. Type **107**	25	20
304	24c. Atlantic Flyingfish	30	45
305	38c. Anthurium Lily	35	65
306	60c. Imperial and Red-necked Amazons	3·75	5·50
303/306 *Set of* 4		4·25	6·00
MS307 160×111 mm. Nos. 303/306		5·50	8·00

108 18th-century National Costume

(Des G. Drummond from local designs. Litho Questa)

1970 (30 Oct). National Day. T **108** and similar horiz designs. Multicoloured. P 14.

308	5c. Type **108**	10	10
309	8c. Carib Basketry	10	10
310	$1 Flag and Chart of Dominica	30	40
308/310 *Set of* 3		30	40
MS311 150×85 mm. Nos. 308/310 plus three labels		50	1·75

109 Scrooge and Marley's Ghost

(Des R. Granger Barrett. Litho Questa)

1970 (23 Nov). Christmas and Charles Dickens' Death Centenary. T **109** and similar vert designs showing scenes from *A Christmas Carol*. Multicoloured. P 14×14½.

312	2c. Type **109**	10	10
313	15c. Fezziwig's Ball	25	10
314	24c. Scrooge and his Nephew's Party	25	10
315	$1.20 Scrooge and the Ghost of Christmas Present	80	90
312/315 *Set of* 4		1·25	1·00
MS316 142×87 mm. Nos. 312/315		1·25	3·75

110 *The Doctor* (Sir Luke Fildes)

(Des G. Vasarhelyi. Litho Questa)

1970 (28 Dec). Centenary of British Red Cross. T **110** and similar horiz designs. Multicoloured. P 14½×14.

317	8c. Type **110**	10	10
318	10c. Hands and Red Cross	10	10
319	15c. Flag of Dominica and Red Cross Emblem	30	10
320	50c. *The Sick Child* (E. Munch)	60	1·25
317/320 *Set of* 4		1·00	1·25
MS321 108×76 mm. Nos. 317/320		1·00	3·00

POSTAL FISCALS

REVENUE (R **1**) **Revenue** (R **2**)

1879–88. Optd with T R **1** by De La Rue. P 14.

(a) Wmk Crown CC

R1	1	1d. lilac	80·00	8·00
		a. Bisected vert (½d.) *on cover*	†	£2750
R2		6d. green	3·00	24·00
		w. Wmk inverted	£130	
R3		1s. magenta	17·00	16·00
R1/R3 *Set of* 3			90·00	42·00
		(b) Wmk Crown CA		
R4	1	1d. lilac (1888)	6·50	10·00

1888. Optd with T R **2** locally. Wmk Crown CA.

R6	1	1d. rose	£250	70·00

East Africa (G.E.A.) *see* Tanganyika

East Africa and Uganda Protectorates *see* Kenya, Uganda and Tanganyika

Egypt

TURKISH SUZERAINTY

In 1517 Sultan Selim I added Egypt to the Ottoman Empire, and it stayed more or less under Turkish rule until 1805, when Mohammed Ali became governor. He established a dynasty of governors owing nominal allegiance to the Sultan of Turkey until 1914.

Khedive Ismail

18 January 1863–26 June 1879

He obtained the honorific title of Khedive (viceroy) from the Sultan in 1867.

The operations of British Consular Post Offices in Egypt date from August 1839 when the first packet agency, at Alexandria, was opened. Further agencies at Suez (1 January 1847) and Cairo (1856) followed. Alexandria became a post office on 17 March 1858 with Cairo following on 23 February 1859 and Suez on 1 January 1861.

Great Britain stamps were issued to Alexandria in March 1858 and to the other two offices in August/September 1859. 'BO1' cancellations as T **2** were issued to both Alexandria and Cairo. Cancellations with this number as T **8**, **12** and **15** were only used at Alexandria.

Before 1 July 1873 combination covers showing Great Britain stamps and the first issue of Egypt exist with the latter paying the internal postage to the British Post Office at Alexandria.

The Cairo office closed on 30 June 1873 and the other two on 30 March 1878. Suez continued to function as a transit office for a number of years.

Stamps issued after 1877 can be found with the Egyptian cancellation 'Port Said', but these are on letters posted from British ships.

For cancellations used during the 1882 and 1885 campaigns, see BRITISH FORCES IN EGYPT at the end of the listing.

For illustrations of the handstamp and postmark types see BRITISH POST OFFICES ABROAD notes following GREAT BRITAIN.

ALEXANDRIA

CROWNED-CIRCLE HANDSTAMPS

CC1	CC **1b** ALEXANDRIA (R.) (13.5.1843) *Price on cover*	£3250

Stamps of GREAT BRITAIN cancelled 'B01' as in T **2** (also used at Cairo), **8**, **12** or **15**.

1858 (Mar)–**79**.

Z1	½d. rose-red (1870–1879) *From* Plate Nos. 5, 6, 8, 10, 13, 14, 15, 19, 20.	22·00
Z2	1d. rose-red (1857)	7·50
Z3	1d. rose-red (1861) (Alph IV)	
Z4	1d. rose-red (1864–1879) *From* Plate Nos. 71, 72, 73, 74, 76, 78, 79, 80, 81, 82, 83, 84, 85, 86, 87, 88, 89, 90, 91, 92, 93, 94, 95, 96, 97, 98, 99, 101, 102, 103, 104, 106, 107, 108, 109, 110, 111, 112, 113, 114, 115, 117, 118, 119, 120, 121, 122, 123, 124, 125, 127, 129, 130, 131, 133, 134, 136, 137, 138, 139, 140, 142, 143, 144, 145, 146, 147, 148, 149, 150, 152, 154, 156, 157, 158, 159, 160, 162, 163, 165, 168, 169, 170, 171, 172, 174, 175, 177, 179, 180, 181, 182, 183, 185, 188, 190, 198, 200, 203, 206, 210, 220.	11·00
Z5	2d. blue (1858–1869) *From* Plate Nos. 7, 8, 9, 13, 14, 15.	13·00
Z6	2½d. rosy mauve (1875) (blued *paper*) *From* Plate Nos. 1, 2.	65·00
Z7	2½d. rosy mauve (1875–1876) (Plate Nos. 1, 2, 3)	35·00
Z8	2½d. rosy mauve (*Error of Lettering*)	£1800
Z9	2½d. rosy mauve (1876–1879) *From* Plate Nos. 3, 4, 5, 6, 7, 8, 9.	25·00
Z10	3d. carmine-rose (1862)	£120
Z11	3d. rose (1865) (Plate No. 4)	60·00
Z12	3d. rose (1867–1873) Plate Nos. 4, 5, 6, 7, 8, 9.	25·00
Z13	3d. rose (1873–1876) *From* Plate Nos. 11, 12, 14, 15, 16, 18, 19.	27·00
Z15	4d. rose (1857)	42·00
Z16	4d. red (1862) (Plate Nos. 3, 4) *From*	42·00
Z17	4d. vermilion (1865–1873) *From* Plate Nos. 7, 8, 9, 10, 11, 12, 13, 14.	29·00
Z18	4d. vermilion (1876) (Plate No. 15)	£160
Z19	4d. sage-green (1877) (Plate No. 15)	£110
Z20	6d. lilac (1856)	50·00
Z21	6d. lilac (1862) (Plate Nos. 3, 4) *From*	45·00
Z22	6d. lilac (1865–1867) (Plate Nos. 5, 6) *From*	32·00
Z23	6d. lilac (1867) (Plate No. 6)	42·00
Z24	6d. violet (1867–1870) (Plate Nos. 6, 8, 9) *From*	38·00
	a. Imperf (Plate No. 8)	£4500
Z25	6d. buff (1872–1873) (Plate Nos. 11, 12) *From*	55·00
Z26	6d. chestnut (1872) (Plate No. 11)	27·00
Z27	6d. grey (1873) (Plate No. 12)	80·00
Z28	6d. grey (1874–1876) Plate Nos. 13, 14, 15. *From*	24·00
Z29	9d. straw (1862)	£160
Z30	9d. bistre (1862)	
Z31	9d. straw (1865)	
Z32	9d. straw (1867)	
Z33	10d. red-brown (1867)	£140
Z34	1s. green (1856)	£130
Z35	1s. green (1862)	75·00
Z36	1s. green (1862) ('K' *variety*)	
Z37	1s. green (1865) (Plate No. 4)	35·00
Z38	1s. green (1867–1873) Plate Nos. 4, 5, 6, 7. *From*	18·00
Z39	1s. green (1873–1877) *From* Plate Nos. 8, 9, 10, 11, 12, 13.	30·00
Z40	2s. blue (1867)	£110
Z41	5s. rose (1867–1874) (Plate Nos. 1, 2) *From*	£250

CAIRO

CROWNED-CIRCLE HANDSTAMPS

CC2	CC **6** CAIRO (R. or Blk.) (23.3.1859) *Price on cover*	£5000

Cancellation 'B01' as T **2** (also issued at Alexandria) was used to cancel mail franked with Great Britain stamps between April 1859 and June 1873.

SUEZ

CROWNED-CIRCLE HANDSTAMPS

CC3 CC **1** SUEZ (B. or Black) (16.7.1847) *Price on cover* £6000

Stamps of GREAT BRITAIN cancelled 'B02' as in T **2** and **8**, or with circular date stamp as T **5**.

1859 (Aug)–**79**.

No.	Description	Price
Z42	½d. rose-red (1870–1879) Plate Nos. 6, 10, 11, 12, 13, 14.	40·00
Z43	1d. rose-red (1857)	12·00
Z44	1d. rose-red (1864–1879) *From* Plate Nos. 73, 74, 78, 79, 80, 81, 83, 84, 86, 87, 90, 91, 93, 94, 96, 97, 100, 101, 106, 107, 108, 110, 113, 118, 119, 120, 121, 122, 123, 124, 125, 129, 130, 131, 134, 136, 137, 138, 140, 142, 143, 144, 145, 147, 148, 149, 150, 151, 152, 153, 154, 156, 158, 159, 160, 161, 162, 163, 164, 165, 166, 167, 168, 170, 174, 176, 177, 178, 179, 180, 181, 182, 184, 185, 186, 187, 189, 190, 205.	15·00
Z45	2d. blue (1858–1869) *From* Plate Nos. 8, 9, 13, 14, 15.	20·00
Z46	2½d. rosy mauve (1875) (blued *paper*) *From* Plate Nos. 1, 2, 3.	75·00
Z47	2½d. rosy mauve (1875–1876) *From* Plate Nos. 1, 2, 3.	40·00
Z48	2½d. rosy mauve (*Error of Lettering*)	£2250
Z49	2½d. rosy mauve (1876–1879) *From* Plate Nos. 3, 4, 5, 6, 7, 8, 9, 10.	30·00
Z50	3d. carmine-rose (1862)	£150
Z51	3d. rose (1865) (Plate No. 4)	80·00
Z52	3d. rose (1867–1873) (Plate Nos. 5, 6, 7, 8, 10)	
Z53	3d. rose (1873–1876) (Plate Nos. 12, 16) *From*	35·00
Z54	4d. rose (1857)	65·00
Z55	4d. red (1862) (Plate Nos. 3, 4) *From*	55·00
Z56	4d. vermilion (1865–1873) *From* Plate Nos. 7, 8, 9, 10, 11, 12, 13, 14.	32·00
Z57	4d. vermilion (1876) (Plate No. 15)	
Z58	4d. sage-green (1877) (Plate No. 15)	£150
Z59	6d. lilac (1856)	65·00
Z60	6d. lilac (1862) (Plate Nos. 3, 4) *From*	50·00
Z61	6d. lilac (1865–1867) (Plate Nos. 5, 6) *From*	42·00
Z62	6d. lilac (1867) (Plate No. 6)	55·00
Z63	6d. violet (1867–1870) (Plate Nos. 6, 8, 9) *From*	42·00
Z64	6d. buff (1872–1873) (Plate Nos. 11, 12) *From*	70·00
Z65	6d. pale chestnut (Plate No. 12) (1872)	£3000
Z66	6d. chestnut (1872) (Plate No. 11)	38·00
Z67	6d. grey (1873) (Plate No. 12)	£100
Z68	6d. grey (1874–1876) *From* Plate Nos, 13, 14, 15, 16.	32·00
Z69	8d. orange (1876)	
Z70	9d. straw (1862)	£250
	a. Thick paper	
Z71	9d. bistre (1862)	£300
Z72	9d. straw (1867)	£300
Z73	10d. red-brown (1867)	£225
Z74	1s. green (1856)	£170
Z75	1s. green (1862)	95·00
Z76	1s. green (1862) ('K' *variety*)	
Z77	1s. green (1865) (Plate No. 4)	55·00
Z78	1s. green (1867–1873) Plate Nos. 4, 5, 6, 7. *From*	26·00
Z79	1s. green (1873–1877) *From* Plate Nos. 8, 9, 10, 11, 12.	38·00
Z80	2s. blue (1867)	£190
Z81	5s. rose (1867–1874) (Plate Nos. 1, 2) *From*	£375

PRICES FOR STAMPS ON COVER TO 1945

Nos. 1/41	*from* × 10
Nos. 42/43	*from* × 1000
Nos. 44/83	*from* × 5
Nos. 84/97	*from* × 2
Nos. D57/D70	*from* × 20
Nos. D71/D76	*from* × 50
Nos. D84/D103	*from* × 10
Nos. O64/O87	*from* × 5
Nos. O88/O101	*from* × 2

(Currency: 40 paras = 1 piastre)

1

2

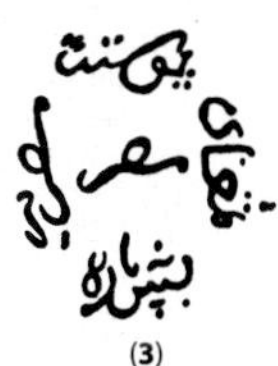
(3)

(Typo (1pi) or litho (others) Pellas Brothers, Genoa. Inscr (T **3**) applied typo (1, 2pi.) or litho (others))

1866 (1 Jan). Various designs as T **1** with black inscriptions as T **3**. The lowest group of characters indicates the value. 1pi. no wmk, others W **2** (inverted). P 12½.

No.	Description	Unused	Used
1	5pa. grey	65·00	35·00
	a. Greenish grey	65·00	35·00
	b. Imperf (pair)	£225	
	c. Imperf between (pair)	£400	
	d. Perf 12½×13 and compound	85·00	60·00
	e. Perf 13	£350	£400
	w. Wmk upright	£450	£275
2	10pa. brown	75·00	35·00
	a. Imperf (pair)	£200	
	b. Imperf between (pair)	£500	
	c. Perf 12½×13 and compound	£110	60·00
	d. Perf 12½×15	£300	£325
	e. Perf 13	£275	£300
	w. Wmk upright	90·00	38·00
3	20pa. pale blue	90·00	38·00
	a. Greenish blue	90·00	38·00
	b. Imperf (pair)	£300	
	c. Imperf between (pair)	£500	
	d. Perf 12½×13 and compound	£140	80·00
	e. Perf 13	£550	£350
	w. Wmk upright	90·00	38·00
4	1pi. claret	80·00	5·00
	a. Imperf (pair)	£130	
	b. Imperf between (pair)	£500	
	c. Perf 12½×13 and compound	£120	20·00
	d. Perf 13	£425	£275
	e. Perf 12½×15	£350	
5	2pi. yellow	£120	50·00
	a. Orange-yellow	£120	50·00
	b. Imperf (pair)	£500	
	c. Imperf between (pair)	£600	£500
	d. Bisected diag (1pi.) (*on cover*)	†	£2750
	e. Perf 12½×13 and compound	£190	70·00
	f. Perf 12½×15	£200	
	w. Wmk upright	£120	50·00
6	5pi. rose	£325	£190
	a. Imperf (pair)	£2000	
	b. Imperf between (pair)	£1200	
	c. Perf 12½×13 and compound	£375	
	d. Error. Inscr 10pi., perf 12½×15	£1000	£900
	da. Imperf	£750	
	e. Perf 13	£800	
	w. Wmk upright	£325	£190
7	10pi. slate	£375	£300
	a. Imperf (pair)	£750	
	b. Imperf between (pair)	£2250	
	c. Perf 12½×13 and compound	£550	£475
	d. Perf 13	£1900	
	w. Wmk upright	£350	£300

The 2pi. bisected was authorised for use between 16 and 31 July 1867 at Alexandria or Cairo.

Stamps perforated 12½, 12½×13 and compound, and 13 occur in the same sheets with the 13 gauge usually used on the top, left-hand, right-hand or bottom rows. Each sheet of 200 contained one stamp perforated 13 all round, two 13 on three sides, one 13 on two adjacent sides, 18 13×12½, eight 12½×13, eight 13 on one side and 18 13 at top or bottom. So many sheets were received imperforate or part-perforated that some stock was passed to V. Penasson of Alexandria who applied the 12½×15 gauge.

The two halves of each background differ in minor details of the ornamentation. All values can be found with either half at the top.

Proofs of all values exist on smooth paper, without watermark. Beware of forgeries.

All values also exist with the watermark reversed (*same price as upright*) or inverted and reversed (*same price as inverted*).

4

5

6

(Des F. Hoff. Litho V. Penasson, Alexandria)

1867 (1 Aug)–**71**. W **6** (impressed on reverse). P 15×12½.

No.	Description	Unused	Used
11	**4** 5pa. orange-yellow	50·00	9·00
	a. Imperf (pair)		
	b. Imperf between (horiz pair)	£200	
	x. Wmk impressed on face		
12	10pa. dull lilac	90·00	14·00
	b. Bright mauve (7.69)	65·00	9·00
	ba. Bisected diag (5pa.) (*on piece*) (17.11.71)	†	£750
	w. Wmk inverted	£300	£200
	x. Wmk impressed on face		
13	20pa. deep blue-green	£130	13·00
	a. Pale blue-green	£130	13·00
	b. Yellowish green (7.69)	£130	12·00
	x. Wmk impressed on face		
14	**5** 1pi. dull rose-red *to* rose	32·00	1·00
	a. Lake	£170	
	b. Imperf (pair)	£110	
	c. Imperf between (horiz pair)	£200	
	d. Bisected diag (20pa.) (*on piece*)	†	£750
	e. Rouletted	65·00	
	w. Wmk inverted	60·00	30·00
	x. Wmk impressed on face		
15	2pi. bright blue	£140	17·00
	a. Pale blue	£140	17·00
	b. Imperf (pair)	£650	
	c. Imperf between (pair)	£550	£750
	d. Bisected diag (1pi.) (*on cover*)	†	—
	e. Perf 12½	£250	
16	5pi. brown	£300	£180
	x. Wmk impressed on face		

Each value was engraved four times, the resulting blocks being used to form sheets of 200. There are therefore four types showing minor variations for each value.

No. 12ba was used on newspapers from Alexandria between 17 November 1871 and 20 January 1872.

Stamps printed both sides, both imperf and perf, come from printer's waste. The 1pi. rose without watermark is a proof.

7

8 (Side panels transposed and inverted)

8a (I) 8a (II)

WATERMARK 8a. There are two types of this watermark which, as they are not always easy to distinguish, we do not list separately. Type II is slightly wider and less deep and the crescent is flatter than in Type I. The width measurement for Type I is generally about 14 mm and for Type II about 15 mm, but there is some variation within the sheets for both types.

Nos. 26/43, 45/47*a*, 49/49*a*, 50/51 and 57 come with Type I only. Nos. 44*a*, 48/48*a*, 52, 54*b*, 73/77 and 78 exist with both types of watermark (but No. 83 and official overprints on these stamps still require research); our prices are generally for Type II. Other watermarked issues between 1888 and 1907 have Type II watermarks only.

1872 (1 Jan)–**75**. T **7** (the so-called 'Penasson' printing*). Thick opaque paper. W **8a**. P 12½×13½.

No.	Description	Unused	Used
	A. LITHOGRAPHED		
26	**7** 20pa. blue (*shades*)	£180	65·00
	a. Imperf (pair)		
	b. Imperf between (pair)	—	£2250
	c. Perf 13½	£300	70·00
	w. Wmk inverted	£300	85·00
27	1pi. red (*shades*)	£325	19·00
	a. Perf 13½	£850	40·00
	w. Wmk inverted	£650	35·00
	B. TYPOGRAPHED		
28	**7** 5pa. brown (*shades*)	12·00	8·00
	a. Perf 13½	32·00	9·50
	w. Wmk inverted	£100	50·00
29	10pa. mauve	6·00	3·00
	a. Perf 13½	6·00	3·25
	w. Wmk inverted	40·00	25·00
30	20pa. blue (*shades*)	65·00	5·00
	a. Perf 13½	90·00	20·00
	w. Wmk inverted	60·00	30·00
31	1pi. rose-red	70·00	1·50
	a. Bisected (20pa.) (*on piece* with No. 31) (7.75)	†	£850
	b. Perf 13½	90·00	3·50
	w. Wmk inverted	65·00	25·00
32	2pi. chrome-yellow	90·00	4·00
	a. Bisected (1pi.) (*on piece*) (4.73)	†	£950
	b. Perf 13½	26·00	5·50
	w. Wmk inverted		
33	2½pi. violet	90·00	28·00
	a. Perf 13½	£800	£200
	w. Wmk inverted	£100	32·00
34	5pi. yellow-green	£200	50·00
	a. *Tête-bêche* (pair)	£11000	
	b. Perf 13½	£300	60·00
	w. Wmk inverted	£225	90·00

* It is now accepted that stamps in both processes were printed by the Government Printing Works at Bûlâq, Cairo, although Penasson may have been involved in the production of the dies.

The lithographed and typographed stamps each show the characteristic differences between these two processes:—

The typographed stamps show the coloured lines of the design impressed into the paper and an accumulation of ink along the margins of the lines.

The lithographed stamps are essentially flat in appearance, without the heaping of the ink. Many of the 20pa. show evidence of retouching, particularly of the outer frame lines.

The 1p. bisected was used at Gedda, on 5 July 1875, or Scio, and the 2pi. vertically bisected at Gallipoli or Scio. The price quoted for No. 31a is for usage at Scio, with usage at Gedda worth double.

See also footnote below No. 41.

1874 (Nov)–**75**. Typo from new stereos at Bûlâq, on thinner paper. W **8a**. P 12½.

No.	Description	Unused	Used
35	**8** 5pa. brown (3.75)	35·00	4·00
	a. *Tête-bêche* (vert pair)	60·00	60·00
	b. *Tête-bêche* (horiz pair)	£275	£300
	c. Imperf (pair)		
	d. Imperf between (pair)	£110	£130
	ew. Wmk inverted	35·00	4·00
	f. Perf 13½×12½	38·00	4·00
	fa. *Tête-bêche* (vert pair)	70·00	70·00
	fb. *Tête-bêche* (horiz pair)	£325	£350
	fw. Wmk inverted	38·00	4·00
36	**7** 10pa. grey-lilac (*shades*) (8.75)	17·00	5·00
	a. *Tête-bêche* (vert pair)	£150	£170
	b. *Tête-bêche* (horiz pair)		
	c. Imperf (pair)		
	dw. Wmk inverted	17·00	5·00
	e. Perf 13½×12½	50·00	4·50
	ea. *Tête-bêche* (vert pair)	£160	£180
	eb. *Tête-bêche* (horiz pair)		
	ew. Wmk inverted	50·00	4·75
37	20pa. grey-blue (*shades*) (2.75)	£110	3·00
	b. Bisected diag (10pa.) (*on cover*)	†	—
	cw. Wmk inverted	£110	3·00
	d. Perf 13½×12½	17·00	3·75
	da. Imperf between (pair)	£325	
	dw. Wmk inverted	17·00	3·75
38	1pi. red (*shades*) (4.75)	11·00	65
	a. *Tête-bêche* (vert pair)	90·00	90·00
	b. *Tête-bêche* (horiz pair)	£300	£300
	c. Imperf (pair)	£200	
	d. Imperf between (pair)	£400	£400
	ew. Wmk inverted	13·00	1·50
	f. Perf 13½×12½	85·00	1·25
	fa. *Tête-bêche* (vert pair)	£450	£450
	fb. *Tête-bêche* (horiz pair)	—	£450
	fw. Wmk inverted	90·00	7·50
39	2pi. yellow (12.74)	85·00	4·75
	a. *Tête-bêche* (pair)	£400	£400
	bw. Wmk inverted	£100	7·50
	c. Perf 13½×12½	5·50	6·50
	ca. *Tête-bêche* (pair)	£450	£400
	cb. Bisected diag (1pi.) (*on cover*) (13.4.75)	†	£4500
	cw. Wmk inverted	7·50	7·00
	d. Perf 12½×13½	75·00	16·00
	da. *Tête-bêche* (pair)	£950	£650
	dw. Wmk inverted	95·00	19·00

40		2½pi. violet	8·50	8·00
		a. *Tête-bêche* (pair)	£400	£400
		bw. Wmk inverted	12·00	9·00
		c. Perf 12½×13½	75·00	19·00
		ca. *Tête-bêche* (pair)	£1000	£1000
		cw. Wmk inverted	65·00	25·00
41		5pi. green	60·00	20·00
		a. Imperf (pair)	†	—
		bw. Wmk inverted	£100	50·00
		c. Perf 12½×13½	£350	£275

The 2pi. bisected was used at Gedda and are all postmarked 13 April.

The 1872 printings have a thick line of colour in the top margin of the sheet and the other margins are all plain, an exception being the 5pa., which on the majority of the sheets has the line at the right-hand side of the sheet. The 1874–1875 printings have a wide fancy border all round every sheet.

The 1872 printings are on thick opaque paper, with the impressions sharp and clear. The 1874–1875 printings are on thinner paper, often semi-transparent and oily in appearance, and having the impressions very blurred and badly printed. These are only general distinctions and there are a number of exceptions.

The majority of the 1874–1875 stamps have blind or defective perforations, while the 1872 stamps have clean-cut perfs.

The two printings of the 5pa. to 1pi. values can be identified by their perforation gauges, which are always different; the 5pa. also differs in the side panels (T **7** and **8**). Only the perf 12½×13½ varieties of the three higher values may need to be distinguished. As well as the general points noted above the following features are also helpful:

2pi. In the 1872 issue the left-hand Arabic character in the top inscription is one complete shape, resembling an inverted 'V' with a horizontal line on top. In the 1874 issue the character has three separate components, a line with two dots below.

2½pi. There is a distinct thinning of the frame line in the top right-hand corner of the 1872 issue. This sometimes takes the form of a short white line within the frame.

5pi. In the 1872 issue the top frame line is split for its entire length; in the 1874 issue the line is solid for all or most of its length. The 1872 printing always has a white dot above the 'P' of 'PIASTRE'; this dot appears on only a few positions of the 1874 printing.

There seem to be many different compositions of the sheets containing the *tête-bêche* varieties, settings being known with one, three, nine and ten inverted stamps in various sheets. Sheets of the 5pa. are known with nine of the 20 horizontal rows inverted, giving vertical *tête-bêche* pairs; four stamps were inverted within their row giving four horizontal *tête-bêche* pairs.

Examples of some values exist without watermark due to the paper being misplaced on the press.

PARAS 5   PARAS 10

(9)   (9a)

1878 (Dec). No. 40 surch as T **9** at Bûlâq. P 12½.

42	**7**	5pa. on 2½pi. violet	6·50	6·00
		a. Surch inverted	70·00	70·00
		b. *Tête-bêche* (pair)	£5000	
		c. Imperf (pair)	£900	
		d. Surch as Type **9a**	£100	£120
		dw. Wmk inverted	7·50	7·50
		e. Perf 12½×13½	6·50	8·00
		ea. Surch inverted	£140	£140
		eb. *Tête-bêche* (pair)	£5000	
		ed. Surch as Type **9a**	£100	£120
		ew. Wmk inverted	7·50	7·50
43		10pa. on 2½ pi. violet	11·00	10·00
		a. Surch inverted	75·00	75·00
		b. *Tête-bêche* (pair)	£2250	
		c. Surch as Type **9a**	£100	£120
		dw. Wmk inverted	15·00	15·00
		e. Perf 12½×13½	16·00	15·00
		ea. Surch inverted	£110	£110
		eb. *Tête-bêche* (pair)	£2750	
		ed. Surch as Type **9a**	£100	£120
		ew. Wmk inverted	25·00	25·00

Surcharge T **9a**, with guide marks in the corners, is assumed to be from an early printing. Guide marks are also known on stamps with the surcharge inverted.

10   11   12

13   14   15

(Typo De La Rue)

1879 (1 Apr). Ordinary paper. W **8a** (inverted on 10pa.). P 14.

44	**10**	5pa. deep brown	6·50	2·50
		a. Pale brown	6·50	2·50
		w. Wmk inverted	£120	£100
45	**11**	10pa. reddish lilac	75·00	3·00
		w. Wmk upright	†	£100
46	**12**	20pa. pale blue	80·00	3·00
		w. Wmk inverted	95·00	15·00
47	**13**	1pi. rose	50·00	20
		a. Pale rose	50·00	20
		w. Wmk inverted	65·00	10·00
48	**14**	2pi. orange	50·00	50
		a. Orange-yellow	50·00	1·25
		w. Wmk inverted	50·00	2·00
49	**15**	5pi. green	70·00	19·00
		a. Blue-green	70·00	18·00
		w. Wmk inverted	65·00	19·00

See also Nos. 50/56.

Khedive Tewfik

26 June 1879–7 January 1892

British troops were landed in Egypt in 1882 to secure the Suez Canal against a nationalist movement led by Arabi Pasha. Arabi was defeated at Tel-el-Kebir and British troops remained in Egypt until 1954. A British resident and consul-general advised the Khedive. Holders of this post were Sir Evelyn Baring (Lord Cromer), 1883–1907; Sir Eldon Gorst, 1907–1911; and Lord Kitchener, 1911–1914.

1881–1902. Colours changed. Ordinary paper. W **8a** (inverted on No. 50). P 14.

50	**11**	10pa. claret (1.81)	70·00	15·00
51		10pa. bluish grey (25.1.82)	30·00	2·25
		w. Wmk inverted	50·00	3·25
52		10pa. green (15.12.84)	4·25	3·50
		w. Wmk inverted	30·00	10·00
53	**12**	20pa. rose-carmine (15.12.84)	30·00	1·00
		a. Bright rose	30·00	1·00
		w. Wmk inverted	42·00	7·00
54	**13**	1pi. blue (15.12.84)	16·00	1·00
		a. Deep ultramarine	16·00	1·00
		b. Pale ultramarine	8·50	70
		cw. Wmk inverted	27·00	10·00
		d. Chalk-surfaced paper. *Ultramarine* (1902)	3·00	10
		da. Blue	3·00	10
		dw. Wmk inverted	75·00	40·00
55	**14**	2pi. orange-brown (1.8.93)	12·00	30
		aw. Wmk inverted	80·00	40·00
		b. Chalk-surfaced paper (1902)	12·00	10
		ba. Orange	23·00	1·50
		bw. Wmk inverted	—	30·00
56	**15**	5pi. pale grey (15.12.84)	26·00	50
		a. Slate	26·00	50
		bw. Wmk inverted		
		c. Chalk-surfaced paper. *Slate-grey* (1902)	16·00	15
		cw. Wmk inverted	—	£100

(17)

1884 (1 Feb). Surch with T **17** at Bûlâq.

57	**15**	20pa. on 5pi. green	7·50	2·25
		a. Surch inverted	65·00	60·00
		w. Wmk inverted	50·00	30·00

(New Currency: 1000 milliemes = 100 piastres = £1 Egyptian)

18   19   20

21   22

1888 (1 Jan)–**1909**. Ordinary paper. W **8a**. P 14.

58	**18**	1m. pale brown	4·00	10
		a. Deep brown	4·00	10
		bw. Wmk inverted	25·00	4·00
		c. Chalk-surfaced paper. *Pale brown* (1902)	4·00	10
		ca. Deep brown	4·00	10
		cw. Wmk inverted	40·00	5·00
59	**19**	2m. blue-green	4·00	30
		a. Green	1·75	10
		bw. Wmk inverted	40·00	5·00
		c. Chalk-surfaced paper. *Green* (1902)	1·75	10
		cw. Wmk inverted	40·00	5·00
60	**20**	3m. maroon (1.1.92)	12·00	3·75
61		3m. yellow (1.8.93)	10·00	1·00
		a. Orange-yellow	5·00	15
		bw. Wmk inverted	45·00	15·00
		c. Chalk-surfaced paper. *Orange-yellow* (1902)	4·50	10
		cw. Wmk inverted	75·00	30·00
62	**21**	4m. vermilion (*chalk-surfaced paper*) (1906)	5·50	10
		a. Bisected (2m.) (*on cover*) (11.09)	†	£2500
		w. Wmk inverted	—	60·00
63		5m. rose-carmine	12·00	55
		a. Bright rose	5·50	10
		b. Aniline rose	5·50	10
		cw. Wmk inverted	—	75·00
		d. Chalk-surfaced paper. *Rose* (1902)	3·00	10
		da. Deep aniline rose	6·00	35
64	**22**	10p. mauve (1.1.89)	15·00	2·00
		a. Aniline mauve	18·00	2·00
		bw. Wmk inverted	—	50·00
		c. Chalk-surfaced paper. *Mauve* (1902)	22·00	50

No. 62a was used at Gizira in conjunction with the 1m. value and the Official, No. O64.

No. 63d exists in coils constructed from normal sheets.

Khedive Abbas Hilmi

7 January 1892–19 December 1914

A set of three values, in a common design showing Cleopatra and a Nile boat, was prepared in 1895 for the Nile Winter Fête, but not issued. Examples survive from the De La Rue archives.

29 Nile Feluccas

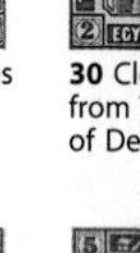

30 Cleopatra from Temple of Dendera

31 Ras-el-Tin Palace, Alexandria

32 Pyramids of Giza

33 Sphinx

34 Colossi of Amenophis III at Thebes

35 Archway of Ptolemy III, Karnak

36 Citadel, Cairo

37 Rock Temple of Abu Simbel

38 Aswân Dam

(Typo D.L.R.)

1914 (8 Jan). W **8a**. P 13½×14 (1m. to 10m.) or 14 (20m. to 200m.).

73	**29**	1m. sepia	1·50	40
		w. Wmk inverted	—	75·00
74	**30**	2m. green	4·00	20
		w. Wmk inverted	—	40·00
75	**31**	3m. yellow-orange	3·75	35
		a. Double impression		
		w. Wmk inverted	—	40·00
76	**32**	4m. vermilion	6·50	65
		w. Wmk inverted	—	40·00
77	**33**	5m. lake	4·25	10
		a. Wmk sideways star to right* (booklets)	10·00	26·00
		aw. Wmk sideways star to left	10·00	26·00
		w. Wmk inverted	15·00	10·00
78	**34**	10m. dull blue	9·50	10
		w. Wmk inverted	25·00	25·00
79	**35**	20m. olive	9·50	30
		w. Wmk inverted	60·00	40·00
80	**36**	50m. purple	26·00	2·50
		w. Wmk inverted	—	50·00
81	**37**	100m. slate	26·00	2·25
82	**38**	200m. maroon	35·00	6·00
73/82 *Set of* 10			£110	11·50

* The normal sideways watermark shows the star to the right of the crescent, *as seen from the back of the stamp.*

All the above exist imperforate, but imperforate stamps without watermark are proofs.

See also Nos. 84/97.

BRITISH PROTECTORATE

On 18 December 1914, after war with Turkey had begun, Egypt was declared to be a British protectorate. Abbas Hilmi was deposed, and his uncle, Hussein Kamil, was proclaimed Sultan of Egypt.

Sultan Hussein Kamil

19 December 1914–9 October 1917

(39)

1915 (15 Oct). No. 75 surch with T **39**, at Bûlâq.

83	**31**	2m. on 3m. yellow-orange	1·25	2·75
		a. Surch inverted	£225	£200
		b. Surch double, one albino	£150	
		w. Wmk inverted	—	75·00

Sultan Ahmed Fuad
9 October 1917–15 March 1922

40

(A)

(B)

41 Statue of Rameses II, Luxor

42

(Typo Harrison)

1921–22. As Nos. 73/82 and new designs (15m.). W **40**. P 14 (20, 50, 100m.) or 13½×14 (others).

84 **29** 1m. sepia (A) ... 1·50 4·75
a. Two dots omitted (B) (R. 10/10) 35·00 55·00
w. Wmk inverted ... 10·00 8·50
85 **30** 2m. green ... 10·00 6·50
w. Wmk inverted ... 16·00 10·00
86 2m. vermilion (1922) ... 7·50 3·50
w. Wmk inverted ... 16·00 10·00
87 **31** 3m. yellow-orange ... 11·00 7·50
w. Wmk inverted ... 17·00 10·00
88 **32** 4m. green (1922) ... 10·00 8·50
w. Wmk inverted ... — 10·00
89 **33** 5m. lake (1.21) ... 8·50 2·25
w. Wmk inverted ... 15·00 10·00
90 5m. pink (11.21) ... 17·00 20
w. Wmk inverted ... 21·00 10·00
91 **34** 10m. dull blue ... 14·00 1·25
w. Wmk inverted ... — 10·00
92 10m. lake (9.22) ... 4·50 1·25
w. Wmk inverted ... — 10·00
93 **41** 15m. indigo (3.22) ... 13·00 20
w. Wmk inverted ... — 8·00
94 **42** 15m. indigo ... 55·00 6·50
w. Wmk inverted ... 60·00 11·00
95 **35** 20m. olive ... 13·00 30
w. Wmk inverted ... 21·00 10·00
96 **36** 50m. purple ... 13·00 1·75
w. Wmk inverted ... 20·00 12·00
97 **37** 100m. slate (1922) ... 90·00 7·50
84/97 *Set of* 14 ... £225 45·00

The 15m. T **42** was printed first; but because the Arabic inscription at right was felt to be unsuitable the stamps were withheld and the corrected T **41** printed and issued. T **42** was released later.

STAMP BOOKLETS

1903 (1 Jan). Black on pink cover inscr 'Egyptian Post Office' in English and French. Stapled.
SB1 121m. booklet containing 24×5m. (No. 63/63*d*) in blocks of 6 ... £5000

1903 (1 July). Black on blue cover inscr 'Egyptian Post Office' in English and French. Stapled.
SB2 73m. booklet containing 24×3m. (No. 61/61bw) in blocks of 6 ... £8500

1911 (1 July). Black on pink cover inscr 'Egyptian Post Office' in English and Arabic. Stapled.
SB3 120m. Contents as No. SB1 ... £4500

1914 (8 Jan). Black on pink cover inscr 'Egyptian Post Office' in English and Arabic. Stapled.
SB4 125m. booklet containing 24×5m. (No. 77a) in blocks of 6 ... £4500

1919 (1 Jan). Black on pink cover inscr 'Egyptian Post Office' in English and Arabic. Stapled.
SB5 120m. Contents as No. SB4 ... £3250

1921 (12 June). Deep blue on pink cover inscr 'POST OFFICE' in English and Arabic. Stapled.
SB6 120m. booklet containing 24×5m. (No. 89) in blocks of 6 ...
a. Stitched ... £2500

1921 (Nov). Deep blue or pink cover inscr 'POST OFFICE' in English and Arabic. Stapled.
SB7 120m. booklet containing 24×5m. (No. 90) in blocks of 6 ... £2250

POSTAGE DUE STAMPS

D 16

D 23

D 24

(Des L. Barkhausen. Litho V. Penasson, Alexandria)

1884 (1 Jan). W **6** (impressed on reverse). P 10½.
D57 D **16** 10pa. red ... 65·00 9·00
a. Imperf (pair) ... £120
b. Imperf between (pair) ... £140
x. Wmk impressed on face ...
D58 20pa. red ... £130 50·00
x. Wmk impressed on face ...
D59 1pi. red ... £150 50·00
x. Wmk impressed on face ...
D60 2pi. red ... £225 12·00
w. Wmk inverted ... £325 22·00
x. Wmk impressed on face ...
D61 5pi. red ... 15·00 50·00
x. Wmk impressed on face ...

1886 (1 Aug)–**87**. No wmk. P 10½.
D62 D **16** 10pa. rose-red (1887) ... 80·00 24·00
a. Imperf between (pair) ... £120
D63 20pa. rose-red ... £250 50·00
a. Imperf between (pair) ...
D64 1pi. rose-red ... 42·00 12·00
a. Imperf between (pair) ... £150 £150
D65 2pi. rose-red ... 48·00 4·00
a. Imperf between (pair) ... £150

Specialists distinguish four types of each value in both these issues.

(Litho V. Penasson, Alexandria)

1888 (1 Jan). No wmk. P 11½.
D66 D **23** 2m. green ... 30·00 40·00
a. Imperf between (pair) ... £225 £225
b. Imperf (pair) ...
D67 5m. rose-carmine ... 50·00 32·00
a. Imperf (pair) ...
D68 1p. blue ... £150 35·00
a. Imperf between (pair) ... £200
D69 2p. orange ... £160 19·00
D70 5p. grey ... £250 £225
a. With stop after left-hand 'PIASTRES' ... £325 £250

Specialists distinguish four types of each value. No. D70a occurs on all examples of one of these types in the sheet except that on R. 2/1. Beware of forgeries of the 5p.

(Typo De La Rue)

1889 (Apr)–**1907**. Ordinary paper. W **8a**. P 14.
D71 D **24** 2m. green ... 14·00 65
a. Bisected (1m.) (*on cover with unbisected 2m.*) (2.98) ... † £500
bw. Wmk inverted ... 15·00 3·00
c. Chalk-surfaced paper (1906) ... 20·00 65
D72 4m. maroon ... 7·50 50
aw. Wmk inverted ... 8·00 1·00
b. Chalk-surfaced paper (1906) ... 7·50 50
D73 1p. ultramarine ... 5·50 50
aw. Wmk inverted ... 8·50 3·00
b. Chalk-surfaced paper (1906) ... 6·50 50
D74 2p. orange ... 5·50 70
bw. Wmk inverted ... 5·00 70
c. Chalk-surfaced paper (1907) ... 5·00 70

No. D71a was authorised for use on Egyptian Army letters from the Sudan campaign which were only charged 3m. postage due.

See also Nos. 84/86 for stamps with watermark sideways.

(D **26**)

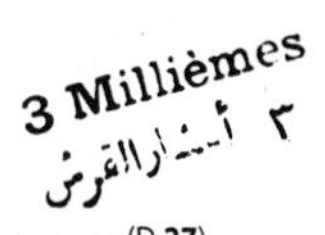

(D **27**)

Slanting 'I' (R. 5/2)

Type D **26**

The Arabic figure at right is less than 2 mm from the next character, which consists of a straight stroke only.

Type D **27**

The distance is 3 mm and the straight character has a comma-like character above it. There are other minor differences.

1898 (7 May)–**1907**. No. D74 surch at Bûlâq. Ordinary paper.

*(a) With T D **26***
D75 D **24** 3m. on 2p. orange ... 3·50 9·00
a. Surch inverted ... 60·00 75·00
b. Pair, one without surch ... £200
c. Arabic '2' for '3' ... 60·00
d. Arabic '3' over '2' ... £100

No. D75c occurred in the first printing on positions 10, 20, 30, 40, 50 and 60 of the pane of 60 (the Arabic figure is the right-hand character of the second line—see illustration on page xxxi). In the second printing the correct figure was printed on top to form No. D75d. The error was corrected in subsequent printings.

*(b) With T D **27** (11.04)*
D76 D **24** 3m. on 2p. orange ... 7·00 22·00
a. Surch inverted ... 50·00 60·00
b. Chalk-surfaced paper (1907) ... 7·00 22·00
ba. Surch inverted ... 60·00 70·00
bb. Surch double ... £250
bc. Slanting 'I' ... 50·00

1914–15. As Nos. D71/D73 but wmk sideways*.
D84 D **24** 2m. bright green (1915) ... 30·00 5·50
w. Wmk star to left of crescent ... 40·00 16·00
D85 4m. maroon ... 30·00 24·00
w. Wmk star to left of crescent ... 42·00
D86 1p. dull ultramarine ... 45·00 14·00
w. Wmk star to left of crescent ... 40·00 15·00

* The normal sideways watermark shows star to right of crescent, *as seen from the back of the stamp.*

D **43**

D **44**

(Typo Harrison)

1921 (Apr)–**22**. Chalk-surfaced paper. W **40** (sideways*). P 14×13½.
D98 D **43** 2m. green ... 4·00 11·00
w. Wmk stars below crescents ... 13·00 11·00
D99 2m. scarlet (1922) ... 2·75 4·25
w. Wmk stars below crescents ... 10·00 7·00
D100 4m. scarlet ... 9·00 27·00
D101 4m. green (1922) ... 9·50 3·75
w. Wmk stars below crescents ... 16·00 8·50
D102 D **44** 10m. deep slate-blue (11.21) ... 15·00 38·00
D103 10m. lake (1922) ... 9·00 3·00
w. Wmk stars below crescents ... 14·00 5·50
D98/D103 *Set of* 6 ... 45·00 75·00

* The normal sideways watermark shows the stars above the crescents.

OFFICIAL STAMPS

O **25**

O.H.H.S. اميرى
(O **28**)

"O.H.H.S."
(O **29**)

(Typo De La Rue)

1893 (1 Jan)–**1914**. Ordinary paper. W **8a**. P 14.
O64 O **25** (–) chestnut ... 4·50 10
a. Chalk-surfaced paper (1903) ... 7·00 50
bw. Wmk inverted ... 9·50
c. Wmk sideways star to right. Chalk-surfaced paper (1914) ... 12·00 12·00
cw. Wmk sideways star to left ...

From January 1907 No. O64 was used on most official mail to addresses within Egypt. In 1907 it was replaced by Nos. O73/O78, but the use of No. O64 for unregistered official mail to Egyptian addresses was resumed on 1 January 1909.

After No. O64c was withdrawn in 1915 the remaining stock was surcharged 1p., 2p., 3p. or 5p. for fiscal use.

1907 (1 Feb–Aug). Nos. 54*da*, 56*c*, 58*c*, 59*c*, 61*c* and 63*d* optd with T O **28** by De La Rue.
O73 **18** 1m. pale brown ... 2·00 30
O74 **19** 2m. green ... 4·25 10
a. Opt double ...
O75 **20** 3m. orange-yellow ... 8·50 1·25
O76 **21** 5m. rose ... 16·00 10
O77 **13** 1p. blue ... 6·50 20
O78 **15** 5p. slate-grey (8.07) ... 16·00 13·00
O73/O78 *Set of* 6 ... 48·00 13·00

Nos. O73/O78 were used on all official mail from February 1907 until 1 January 1909 after which their use was restricted to registered items and those sent to addresses overseas.

1913 (Nov). No. 63*d* optd at Bûlâq.

*(a) With T O **29***
O79 **21** 5m. rose ... — £750
a. Opt inverted ... — £6000

*(b) As T O **29** but without inverted commas*
O80 **21** 5m. rose ... 13·00 70
a. No stop after 'S' (R. 11/10) ... 60·00 16·00
b. Opt inverted ... — 75·00

O.H.H.S. اميرى
(O **38**)

O.H.H.S. أميرى
(O **39**)

O.H.H.S. أميرى
(O **43**)

1914 (Dec)–**15**. Stamps of 1902–1906 and 1914 optd with T O **38** at Bûlâq.
O83 **29** 1m. sepia (1.15) ... 2·75 6·50
a. No stop after 'S' (R. 10/10) ... 15·00 30·00
w. Wmk inverted ... † —
O84 **19** 2m. green (3.15) ... 8·00 16·00
a. No stop after 'S' ... 19·00 32·00
b. Opt inverted ... 35·00 40·00
c. Opt double ... £500
O85 **31** 3m. yellow-orange (3.15) ... 5·00 8·50
a. No stop after 'S' (R. 10/10) ... 16·00 30·00
O86 **21** 4m. vermilion (12.14) ... 11·00 8·50
a. Opt inverted ... £190 £140
b. Pair, one without opt ...
O87 **33** 5m. lake (1.15) ... 4·25 4·00
a. No stop after 'S' (R. 10/10) ... 16·00 23·00
O83/O87 *Set of* 5 ... 28·00 38·00

No. O84a occurs on three positions from the first printing and on two different positions from the second. Nos. O83a, O85a and O87a usually show a faint trace of the stop.

1915 (Oct). Nos. 59c, 62 and 77 optd lithographically with T O **39** at Bûlâq.
O88 **19** 2m. green ... 7·00 7·00
a. Opt inverted ... 20·00 20·00
b. Opt double ... 25·00
O89 **21** 4m. vermilion ... 15·00 16·00
O90 **33** 5m. lake ... 19·00 2·25
a. Pair, one without opt ... £275

1922. Nos. 84, etc optd lithographically with T O **43** at Bûlâq.
O98 **29** 1m. sepia (A) (28.6) ... 3·50 21·00
a. Two dots omitted (B) ... £200
w. Wmk inverted ...
O99 **30** 2m. vermilion (16.6) ... 14·00 32·00
O100 **31** 3m. yellow-orange (28.6) ... 65·00 £140
O101 **33** 5m. pink (13.3) ... 29·00 7·50

Egypt was declared to be an independent kingdom on 15 March 1922, and Sultan Ahmed Fuad became king.

Later stamp issues will be found listed in the Stanley Gibbons *North-East Africa catalogue*.

ANDREW PROMOTING PHILATELY ON THE ALAN TITCHMARSH SHOW ITV

Selling Your Stamps?

Summary Tip #19: 5 Different Ways to Sell your Stamps: Choose with Care

by Andrew McGavin

Dear Colleague,

Following the first article (page 42) in the 'Selling your Stamps?' series we present the advantages and disadvantages inherent in each of the 5 different ways to sell your stamps.

1. Direct Sale: To a Dealer – or Stamp Auction buying on their own account.

The merits of 'direct sale' are often under-estimated by collectors. Direct sale, intelligently handled, may yield considerable benefits. For example we recently purchased a modest collection at a major London auction which was estimated at £4,000 to £5,000. Remember in our last article #18 when we talked about 'know the strength of your collection' ... this collection was the kind that no public auction house could afford to 'break' on behalf of the owner – so it was offered intact as one lot. Inevitably no collector would purchase such a diverse collection – so the 'trade' was bidding against each other in order to purchase. Finally we purchased the collection for £8,158 including 20% buyer's premium. The collection actually sold for £6,800. The auction's commission charged to the buyer was £1,358.

But that's not the end of the story. Did the seller receive £6,800? ... NO. The seller received £6,800 less the seller's commission which unless specially negotiated was a further 17.62% inclusive of VAT. That's a further £1,198 to be deducted from the £6,800 sale price. The owner will have received £5,602 upon a collection sold to us for which we paid £8,158 !

I can hear you saying that Auctions exist so that buyers compete to pay more for your stamps – it's true – but some collections simply are not suited to being sold via public auction. All you are doing is paying an auction to ensure that dealers compete to purchase your collection ...

45% MORE was paid for the public auction to sell the collection to a stamp dealer. £2,556 more was paid that the collector did not receive.

BUT – there are imaginative ways that you can obtain more from dealers without going to auction – and have the benefit of certainty too, whilst not waiting up to 6 months for your money ... for example – ... a valuable collection was offered to us earlier this year. We're allowed to write what happened without revealing any confidences. Unfortunately the Father had died leaving one of his two Daughters £25,000 and the other Daughter his Stamp Collection – a very difficult situation as you might imagine. Believing the collection may be valuable, unusually, 3 different dealers visited to value it. All 3 dealers incurred costs – in our case 6 travelling hours and 260 miles – so none was happy to leave an offer on the 'table' for the next dealer to pay £50 more and purchase the collection – what was the client to do allowing fair play to all? We suggested an 'auction' monitored by the owner of the collection – not hard to conduct in the age of landline and mobile phones... and opened the bidding with a £20,000 bid.

The 3rd Dealer dropped out – the 2nd dealer had just finished viewing the collection so was actually on the client's premises. He bid £21,000, we bid £22,000 ... and so it went on until bidding 'narrowed' to £500 increments and finally we purchased the collection for £27,500 and travelled 260 miles again to collect it and pay for it. The client thanked the 2nd dealer for his time and participation with a small ex-gratia payment. Fortunately a happy ending for the client – amazingly, more than her Sister ... it could so easily have been a different outcome.

But what if that collection had been auctioned as one lot or 7 volumes + residue? For the client to have been better off – the trade would have had to pay more than £40,000 ... an unlikely scenario. The moral – know the strength of your collection and 'pick' the right people to participate in its purchase.

In our next article we'll discuss alternatives

Happy collecting from us all,

PS. If you find this 'tip' interesting please forward it to a philatelic friend.

Andrew McGavin

Managing Director: Universal Philatelic Auctions, Omniphil & Avon Approvals, Avon Mixtures, Universal Philatelic (Ebay)

To read the rest of this series 'SELLING YOUR STAMPS?' see the relevant pages listed below:

Summary Tip 18 – page 42 (Australia)

Summary Tip 19 – page 206 (Egypt)

Summary Tip 20 – page 266 (India)

To read the final instalment, Summary Tips 21 and 22 – 'Selling via Online Auction' simply e-mail and request to: *info@upastampauctions.co.uk*

Also, at the back of this catalogue to see how UPA can pay you upto 36% more for your collectio

EGYPTIAN POST OFFICES ABROAD

From 1865 Egypt operated various post offices in foreign countries. No special stamps were issued for these offices and use in them of unoverprinted Egyptian stamps can only be identified by the cancellation. Stamps with such cancellations are worth more than the used prices quoted in the Egypt listings.

Such offices operated in the following countries. An * indicates that details will be found under that heading elsewhere in the catalogue.

ETHIOPIA

A B C D

MASSAWA. *Open* Nov 1867 to 5 Dec 1885. *Postmark types* A (*also without* REGIE), B, C, D. *An Arabic seal type is also known on stampless covers.*

SENHIT (near Keren). *Open* 1878 *to* April 1885. *Only one cover, cancelled* 'Mouderie Senhit' *in* 1879, *is known, together with one showing possible hand-drawn cancellation.*

A post office is also recorded at Harar in 1878, but no postal marking has so far been reported.

SOMALILAND*

Unoverprinted stamps of Egypt used from 1876 until 1884.

SUDAN*

Unoverprinted stamps of Egypt used from 1867 until 1897.

TURKISH EMPIRE

E F G H I J K L

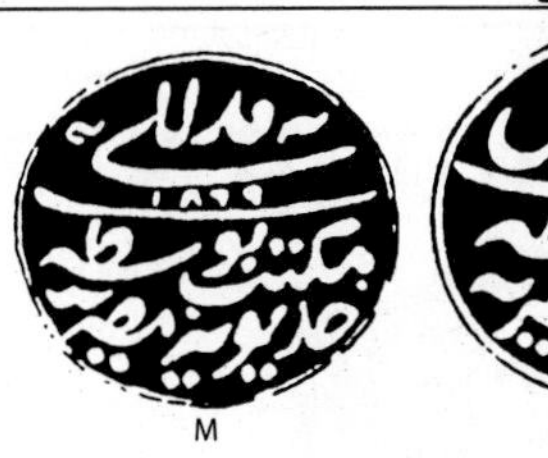

M

N

O

The offices are listed according to the spelling on the cancellation. The present-day name (if different) and country are given in brackets.

ALESSANDRETTA (Iskenderun, Turkey). *Open* 14 July 1870 *to* Feb 1872. *Postmark types* E, I.

BAIROUT (Beirut, Lebanon). *Open* 14 July 1870 *to* Feb 1872. *Postmark types* E, J.

CAVALA (Kavala, Greece). *Open* 14 July 1870 *to* Feb 1872. *Postmark type* E.

COSTANTINOPOLI (Istanbul, Turkey). *Open* 13 June 1865 *to* 30 June 1881. *Postmark types* E, F, O.

DARDANELLI (Canakkle, Turkey). *Open* 10 June 1868 *to* 30 June 1881. *Postmark types* H, K.

DJEDDAH, *see* GEDDA.

GALIPOLI (Gelibolu, Turkey). *Open* 10 June 1868 *to* 30 June 1881. *Postmark types* E, L.

GEDDA, DJEDDAH (Jeddah, Saudi Arabia). *Open* 8 June 1865 *to* 30 June 1881. *Postmark types* F, G (*also with year replacing solid half-circle*), O (*all spelt* GEDDA), D (*spelt* DJEDDAH).

JAFFA (Jaffa, Israel). *Open* 14 July 1870 *to* Feb 1872. *Postmark type* E.

LAGOS (Port Logo, Greece). *Open* 14 July 1870 *to* Feb 1872. *Postmark type* E.

LATAKIA (Syria). *Open* 14 July 1870 *to* Feb 1872. *Postmark type* E.

LEROS (Aegean Is). *Open* July 1873 *to* January 1874 *and* May *to* October 1874. *Postmark type* E.

MERSINA (Mersin, Turkey). *Open* 14 July 1870 *to* Feb 1872. *Postmark type* E.

METELINO (Lesbos, Greece). *Open* 14 July 1870 *to* 30 June 1881. *Postmark types* E, M.

RODI (Rhodes, Greece). *Open* 13 Aug 1872 *to* 30 June 1881. *Postmark type* E.

SALONNICCHI (Thessaloniki, Greece). *Open* 14 July 1870 *to* Feb 1872. *Postmark type* E.

SCIO (Chios, Aegean Is.). *Open* 14 July 1870 *to* 30 June 1881. *Postmark types* E, N.

SMIRNE (Izmir, Turkey). *Open* 14 Nov 1865 *to* 30 June 1881. *Postmark types* E (*also without* 'V. R.'), F.

TENEDOS (Bozcaada, Turkey). *Open* 14 July 1870 *to* March 1871. *Postmark type* E.

TRIPOLI (Lebanon). *Open* 14 July 1870 *to* Feb 1872. *Postmark type* E.

VOLO (Volos, Greece). *Open* 14 July 1870 *to* Feb 1872. *Postmark type* E.

BRITISH FORCES IN EGYPT

Following the rise of a nationalist movement led by Arabi Pasha, and serious disturbances in Alexandria, British troops landed at Ismalia in August 1882 and defeated the nationalists at Tel-el-Kebir on 13 September. A British Army Post Office detachment landed at Alexandria on 21 August and provided a postal service for the troops, using Great Britain stamps, from various locations until it was withdrawn on 7 October.

During the Gordon Relief Expedition of 1884–1885 a postal detachment was sent to Suakin on the Red Sea. This operated between 25 March and 30 May 1885 using Great Britain stamps.

ZA **1**

Stamps of GREAT BRITAIN cancelled with Type ZA **1**.

1882 (Aug–Oct).

ZA1	½d. rose-red (Plate No. 20)	
ZA2	½d. green (1880)	£300
ZA3	1d. Venetian red (1880)	£600
ZA4	1d. lilac (1881)	£175
ZA5	2½d. blue (1881) (Plate Nos. 21, 22, 23)	£100

1885. Used at Suakin.

ZA6	½d. slate-blue (1884)	£500
ZA7	1d. lilac (1881)	£300
ZA8	2½d. lilac (1884)	£225
ZA9	5d. dull green (1884)	£500

From 1 November 1932 to 29 February 1936 members of the British Forces in Egypt and their families were allowed to send letters to the British Isles at reduced rates. Special seals, which were on sale in booklets at NAAFI Institutes and Canteens, were used instead of Egyptian stamps. These seals were stuck on the back of the envelopes, letters bearing the seals being franked on the front with a hand-stamp inscribed 'EGYPT POSTAGE PREPAID' in a double circle surmounted by a crown.

PRICES FOR STAMPS ON COVER TO 1945	
Nos. A1/A9	*from* × 5
No. A10	*from* × 1·5
No. A11	*from* × 5
No. A12	*from* × 75
No. A13	*from* × 20
No. A14	*from* × 100
No. A15	*from* × 20

A **1**

A **2**

(Des Lt-Col. C. Fraser. Typo Hanbury, Tomsett & Co. Ltd, London)

1932 (1 Nov)–**33**. P 11.

(a) Inscr 'POSTAL SEAL'

A1	A **1**	1p. deep blue and red	95·00	6·00

(b) Inscr 'LETTER SEAL'

A2	A **1**	1p. deep blue and red (8.33)	50·00	1·25

(Des Sgt. W. F. Lait. Litho Walker & Co, Amalgamated Press, Cairo)

1932 (26 Nov)–**35**. Christmas Seals. P 11½.

A3	A **2**	3m. black/*azure*	50·00	70·00
A4		3m. brown-lake (13.11.33)	7·50	50·00
A5		3m. deep blue (17.11.34)	8·00	35·00
A6		3m. vermilion (23.11.35)	1·25	50·00
		a. Pale vermilion (19.12.35)	15·00	40·00

A **3**

(Des Miss Waugh. Photo Harrison)

1934 (1 June)–**35**.

(a) P 14½×14

A7	A **3**	1p. carmine	55·00	85
A8		1p. green (5.12.34)	8·50	8·00

(b) P 13½×14

A9	A **3**	1p. carmine (24.4.35)	7·50	5·50

JUBILEE
COMMEMORATION
1935

(A **4**)

1935 (6 May). Silver Jubilee. As No. A9, but colour changed and optd with T A **4**, in red.

A10	A **3**	1p. ultramarine	£375	£180

Xmas 1935
3 Milliemes

(A **5**)

1935 (16 Dec). Provisional Christmas Seal. No. A9 surch with T A **5**.

A11	A **3**	3m. on 1p. carmine	18·00	70·00

The seals and letter stamps were replaced by the following Army Post stamps issued by the Egyptian Postal Administration. No. A9 was accepted for postage until 15 March 1936.

A **6** King Fuad I

A **7** King Farouk

W **48** of Egypt

(Photo Survey Dept, Cairo)

1936. W **48** of Egypt. P 13½ × 14.

A12	A **6**	3m. green (1.12.36)	1·00	3·25
A13		10m. carmine (1.3.36)	9·00	10
		w. Wmk inverted		

(Photo Survey Dept, Cairo)

1939 (16 Dec). W **48** of Egypt. P 13×13½.

A14	A **7**	3m. green	9·00	12·00
A15		10m. carmine	12·00	10
		w. Wmk inverted		

These stamps were withdrawn in April 1941 but the concession, without the use of special stamps, continued until October 1951 when the postal agreement was abrogated.

MILITARY TELEGRAPH STAMPS

Military Telegraph stamps were provided for the pre-payment of non-official messages sent by the army telegraph system. They were used by army personnel for private communications, newspaper reporters and the local population (when the army was in control of the telegraph system).

The 'unadopted die' stamps, (Type T **1/3** of Bechuanaland inscribed 'MILITARY TELEGRAPHS') were supplied for use in Bechuanaland, Egypt and Sudan.

Operations in Egypt commenced in 1884 and on 1 May 1885 the telegraph system in upper Egypt was transferred to military control.

1885. Nos. MT1/MT8 of Bechuanaland.

(a) Wmk Orb. P 14

MT1	1d. lilac and black		£300
MT2	3d. lilac and brown		
MT3	6d. lilac and green		

(b) Wmk script 'VR' (sideways). P 13½

MT4	1s. green and black		
MT5	2s. green and blue		
MT6	5s. green and mauve		
MT7	10s. green and red		£750

(c) Wmk Two Orbs (sideways). P 14×13½

MT8	£1 lilac and black		

The survival rate of unsurcharged military telegraph stamps used in Egypt is very low.

Used prices for Nos. MT1/MT8 are for stamps with identifiable Egypt cancellations. For usage in Sudan, see Sudan Nos. MT1/MT8. For mint prices see Bechuanaland Nos. MT1/MT8.

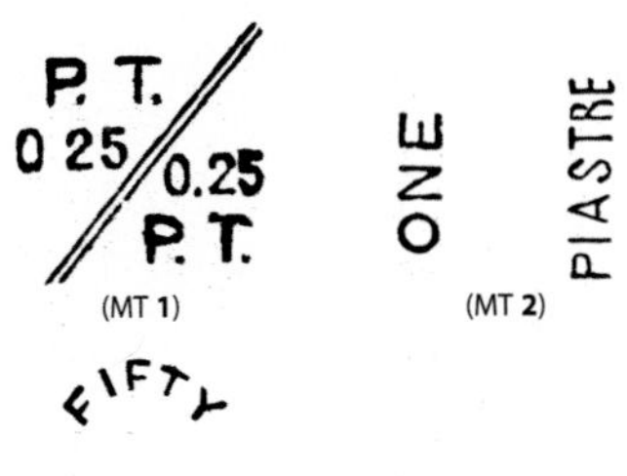

(MT **1**)

ONE PIASTRE

(MT **2**)

(MT **3**)

HUNDRED PIASTRES

(MT **4**)

1886 (July). Nos. MT1/MT8 handstamped locally as T MT **1/4**.

MT9	MT **1**	'0.1 P.T.' on 1d. lilac and black	£100	
		a. bisected (0.05pt) (*on piece*)	†	—
MT10		'0.25 P.T.' on 3d. lilac and brown	£100	
		a. bisected (0.125pt) (*on piece*)	†	—
MT11	MT **2**	'ONE PIASTRE' on 6d. lilac and green	£100	
MT12	MT **3**	'FIVE PIASTRES' on 1s. green and black	£100	
MT13		'TEN PIASTRES' on 2s. green and blue	£275	
MT14		'TWENTY FIVE PIASTRES' on 5s. green and mauve	£375	
MT15		'FIFTY PIASTRES' on 10s. green and red	£750	
MT16	MT **4**	'HUNDRED PIASTRES' on £1 lilac and black	£1600	

TWENTY-FIVE

(MT **5**)

PIASTRES

(MT **6**)

ONE HUNDRED

PIASTRES

(MT **7**)

1887 (Feb). Nos. MT1/MT8 and additional values surch in London as T MT **5/7**.

MT17	MT **5**	'ONE DIME' on 1d. lilac and black	50·00
MT18		'TWO DIMES' on 2d. lilac and blue	50·00
MT19		'FIVE DIMES' on 3d. lilac and brown	50·00
MT20		'ONE PIASTRE' on 6d. lilac and green	75·00
MT21		'TWO PIASTRES' on 8d. lilac and carmine	75·00
MT22	MT **6**	'FIVE PIASTRES' on 1s. green and black	75·00
MT23		'TEN PIASTRES' on 2s. green and blue	£110
MT24		'TWENTY-FIVE PIASTRES' on 5s. green and mauve	£225
MT25		'FIFTY PIASTRES' on 10s. green and red	£375
MT26	MT **7**	'ONE HUNDRED PIASTRES' on £1 lilac and black	£650

Nos. MT 18 and 21 were surcharged on 2d and 8d values which were not issued without surcharge.

The London surcharges were withdrawn in Spring 1890. The usage was limited as nearly all the stamps were returned to England and destroyed.

SUEZ CANAL COMPANY

PRICES FOR STAMPS ON COVER	
Nos. 1/4	*from* × 25

100 Centimes = 1 Franc

On 30 November 1855 a concession to construct the Suez Canal was granted to Ferdinand de Lesseps and the Compagnie Universelle du Canal Maritime de Suez was formed. Work began in April 1859 and the canal was opened on 17 November 1869. In November 1875 the Khedive sold his shares in the company to the British Government, which then became the largest shareholder.

The company transported mail free of charge between Port Said and Suez from 1859 to 1867, when it was decided that payment should be made for the service and postage stamps were introduced in July 1868. Letters for destinations beyond Port Said or Suez required additional franking with Egyptian or French stamps.

The imposition of charges for the service was not welcomed by the public and in August the Egyptian Government agreed to take it over.

1

(Litho Chezaud, Aine & Tavernier, Paris)

1868 (8 July). Imperf.

1	**1**	1c. black	£250	£1500
2		5c. green	85·00	£1000
3		20c. blue	75·00	£500
4		40c. pink	£130	£1200

Shades of all values exist.

Stamps can be found showing parts of the papermaker's watermark 'LA+-F' (La Croix Frères).

These stamps were withdrawn from sale on 16 August 1868 and demonetised on 31 August.

Many forgeries exist, unused and cancelled. The vast majority of these forgeries show vertical lines, instead of cross-hatching, between 'POSTES' and the central oval. It is believed that other forgeries, which do show cross-hatching, originate from the plate of the 40c. value which is missing from the company's archives. These are, however, on thin, brittle paper with smooth shiny gum.

Falkland Islands

PRICES FOR STAMPS ON COVER TO 1945	
No. 1	*from* × 125
No. 2	*from* × 70
Nos. 3/4	*from* × 10
No. 5	—
Nos. 6/10	*from* × 30
Nos. 11/12	*from* × 15
Nos. 13/14	*from* × 20
Nos. 15/17	*from* × 20
Nos. 17*b*/17*c*	*from* × 100
Nos. 18/21	*from* × 10
Nos. 22/22*b*	*from* × 30
Nos. 23/24	*from* × 100
Nos. 25/26	*from* × 30
No. 27	*from* × 20
No. 28	*from* × 40
No. 29	*from* × 5
Nos. 30/30*b*	*from* × 50
No. 30*c*	*from* × 15
No. 31	*from* × 5
Nos. 32/38	*from* × 15
Nos. 41/42	—
Nos. 43/48	*from* × 12
Nos. 49/50	—
Nos. 60/65	*from* × 10
Nos. 66/69	—
Nos. 70/71	*from* × 10
Nos. 72/72*b*	—
Nos. 73/79	*from* × 4
No. 80	—
No. 115	*from* × 2
Nos. 116/119	*from* × 20
Nos. 120/122	*from* × 6
Nos. 123/126	—
Nos. 127/134	*from* × 5
Nos. 135/138	—
Nos. 139/145	*from* × 50
Nos. 146/163	*from* × 5

CROWN COLONY

1 2

1869–76. The Franks.

FR1	**1** In black, *on cover*	£17000
FR2	**2** In red, *on cover* (1876)	£26000

On piece, No. FR1 on white or coloured paper £110; No. FR2 on white £190.

The first recorded use of No. FR1 is on a cover to London date stamped 4 January 1869. The use of these franks ceased when the first stamps were issued.

3

½d.

(4)

In the ½d., 2d., 2½d. and 9d. the figures of value in the lower corners are replaced by small rosettes and the words of value are in colour.

NOTE. Nos. 1, 2, 3, 4, 8, 10, 11 and 12 exist with one or two sides imperf from the margin of the sheets.

(Recess B.W.)

1878–79. No wmk. P 14, 14½.

1	**3**	1d. claret (19.6.78)	£750	£425
2		4d. grey-black (9.79)	£1400	£150
		a. On wmkd paper	£3750	£500
3		6d. blue-green (19.6.78)	£120	80·00
4		1s. bistre-brown (1878)	85·00	70·00

No. 2a shows portions of the papermaker's watermark—'R. TURNER, CHAFFORD MILLS'—in ornate double-lined capitals.

NOTES. The dates shown for Nos. 5/12 and 15/38 are those on which the printer delivered the various printings to the Crown Agents. Several months could elapse before the stamps went on sale in the Colony, depending on the availability of shipping.

The plates used for these stamps did not fit the paper so that the watermark appears in all sorts of positions on the stamp. Well centred examples are scarce. Examples can also be found showing parts of the marginal watermarks, either 'CROWN AGENTS' horizontally in letters 12 mm high or 'CROWN AGENTS FOR THE COLONIES' vertically in 7 mm letters. Both are in double-lined capitals.

1882 (22 Nov). Wmk Crown CA (upright). P 14, 14½.

5	**3**	1d. dull claret	£325	£190
		a. Imperf vert (horiz pair)	£90000	
		x. Wmk reversed	£1400	
		y. Wmk inverted and reversed	£600	£475
6		4d. grey-black	£850	95·00
		w. Wmk inverted	£1600	£350

For later printings with upright wmk, in different shades, see Nos. 11/12, 18/24 and 31/32.

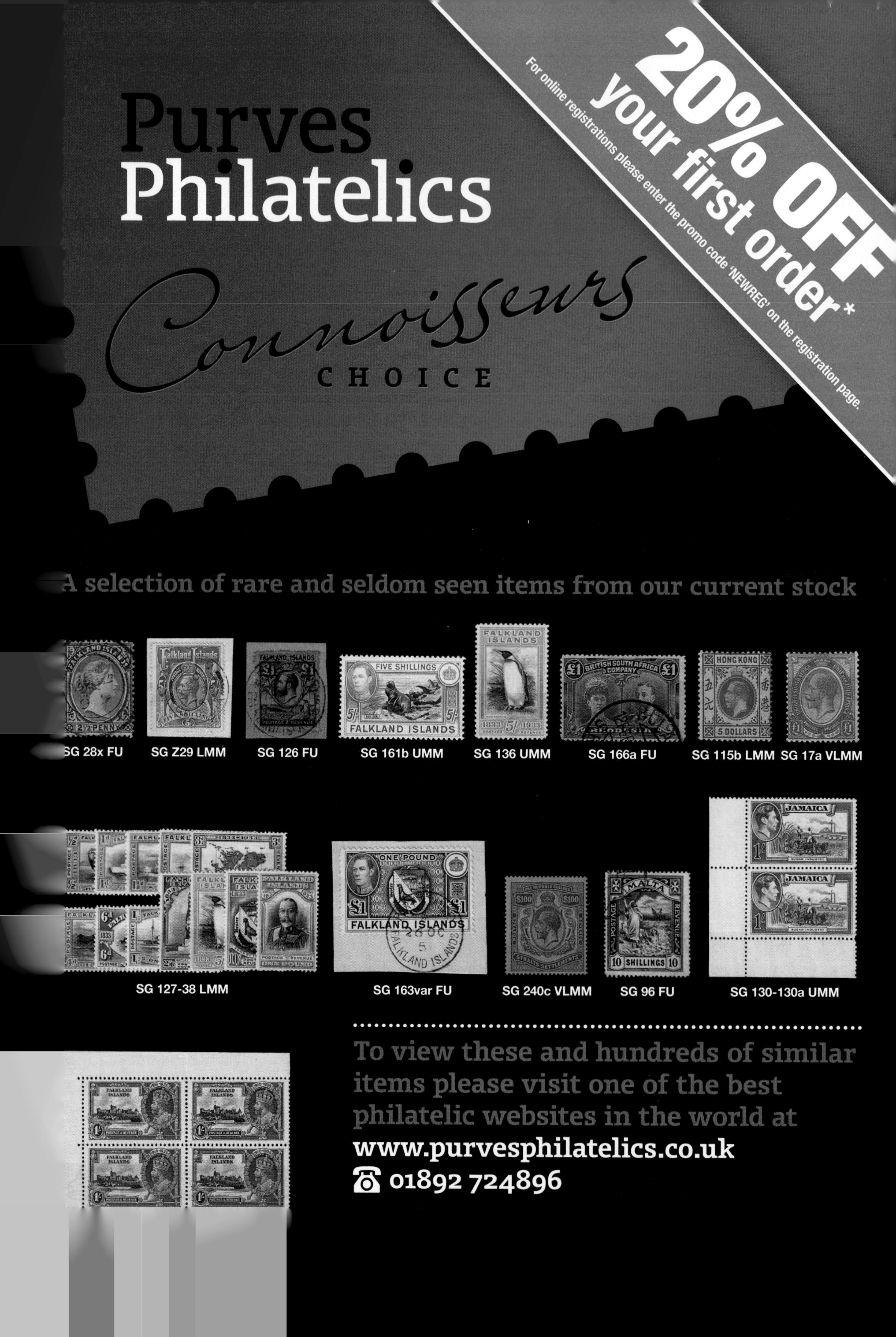

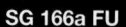

1885 (23 Mar)–**91**. Wmk Crown CA (sideways*). P 14, 14½.

7	3	1d. pale claret	95·00	65·00
		w. Wmk Crown to right of CA	£120	80·00
		x. Wmk sideways reversed	£300	£160
		y. Wmk Crown to right of CA and reversed	£275	£170
8		1d. brownish claret (3.10.87)	£120	55·00
		a. Bisected (*on cover*) (1.91)	†	£4000
		w. Wmk Crown to right of CA	£150	55·00
		x. Wmk sideways reversed	£350	£130
		y. Wmk Crown to right of CA and reversed	£350	£180
9		4d. pale grey-black	£850	85·00
		w. Wmk Crown to right of CA	£850	£120
		x. Wmk sideways reversed	£1000	£225
		y. Wmk Crown to right of CA and reversed	£900	£160
10		4d. grey-black (3.10.87)	£450	50·00
		w. Wmk Crown to right of CA	£450	55·00
		x. Wmk sideways reversed	£1300	£150
		y. Wmk Crown to right of CA and reversed	£1100	£120

* The normal sideways watermark shows Crown to left of CA, *as seen from the back of the stamp*.

For No. 8a see note below No. 14.

1889 (26 Sept)–**91**. Wmk Crown CA (upright). P 14, 14½.

11	3	1d. red-brown (21.5.91)	£350	90·00
		a. Bisected (*on cover*) (7.91)	†	£4500
		x. Wmk reversed	£800	£300
12		4d. olive grey-black	£200	60·00
		w. Wmk inverted	£1400	£475
		x. Wmk reversed	£500	£190

For No. 11a see note below No. 14.

1891 (Jan–11 July). Nos. 8 and 11 bisected diagonally and each half handstamped with T **4**.

13	3	½d. on half of 1d. brownish claret (No. 8)	£600	£300
		a. Unsevered pair	£4000	£1100
		b. Unsevered pair *se-tenant* with unsurcharged whole stamp	£40000	
		c. Bisect *se-tenant* with unsurcharged whole stamp	†	£2250
14		½d. on half of 1d. red-brown (No. 11) (11.7)	£700	£275
		a. Unsevered pair	£5000	£1600
		b. Bisect *se-tenant* with unsurcharged whole stamp	£3500	£2000

1891 PROVISIONALS. In 1891 the postage to the United Kingdom and Colonies was reduced from 4d. to 2½d. per half ounce. As no ½d. or 2½d. stamps were available the bisection of the 1d. was authorised from 1 January 1891. This authorisation was withdrawn on 11 January 1892, although bisects were accepted for postage until July of that year. The ½d. and 2½d. stamps were placed on sale from 10 September 1891.

Cork Cancel used in 1891

The T **4** surcharge was not used regularly; unsurcharged bisects being employed far more frequently. Genuine bisects should be cancelled with the cork cancel illustrated above. The use of any other postmark, including a different cork cancel or an 'F.I.' obliterator, requires date evidence linked to known mail ship sailings to prove authenticity.

After 10 September 1891 the post office supplied 'posthumous' examples of the surcharged bisects to collectors. These were without postal validity and differ from T **4** by showing a large full stop, long fraction bar or curly tail to '2' (*Prices from £50 each, unused or used*). Some of the posthumous surcharges were applied to No. 18 which was not used for the original bisects. Examples are also known showing the surcharge double, inverted or sideways.

1891 (10 Sept)–**1902**. Wmk Crown CA (upright). P 14, 14½.

15	3	½d. blue-green (10.9–11.1891)	28·00	27·00
		x. Wmk reversed	£700	£650
		y. Wmk inverted and reversed	£750	£750
16		½d. green (20.5.92)	16·00	15·00
		ax. Wmk reversed	£325	£300
		ay. Wmk inverted and reversed	£550	£550
		b. Deep dull green (15.4.96)	40·00	30·00
17		½d. deep yellow-green (1894–1895)	18·00	21·00
		ay. Wmk inverted and reversed	£325	£300
		b. Yellow-green (19.6.99)	3·50	3·25
		c. Dull yellowish green (13.1.1902)	7·50	4·75
		cx. Wmk reversed	£650	£600
18		1d. orange red-brown (14.10.91)	£130	85·00
		a. Brown	£180	90·00
		w. Wmk inverted	£1800	£750
		x. Wmk reversed	£375	£375
19		1d. reddish chestnut (20.4.92)	50·00	42·00
20		1d. orange-brown (wmk reversed) (18.1.94)	65·00	50·00
21		1d. claret (23.7.94)	£130	80·00
		x. Wmk reversed	85·00	50·00
22		1d. Venetian red (pale *to* deep) (1895–1896)	25·00	17·00
		ax. Wmk reversed	13·00	12·00
		b. Venetian claret (1898?)	38·00	18·00
23		1d. pale red (19.6.99)	8·50	2·75
		x. Wmk reversed	£325	£500
24		1d. orange-red (13.1.1902)	17·00	4·25
25		2d. purple (pale *to* deep) (1895–1898)	7·00	12·00
		x. Wmk reversed	£800	£800
		xs. Ditto, optd 'SPECIMEN.'	£750	
26		2d. reddish purple (15.4.96)	6·50	11·00
27		2½d. pale chalky ultramarine (10.9.91)	£275	55·00
28		2½d. dull blue (19.11.91)	£300	35·00
		x. Wmk reversed	£750	£500
29		2½d. Prussian blue (18.1.94)	£250	£130
30		2½d. ultramarine (1894–1896)	50·00	13·00
		ax. Wmk reversed	£130	18·00
		ay. Wmk inverted and reversed	£1600	
		b. Pale ultramarine (10.6.98)	70·00	17·00
		bx. Wmk reversed	£160	75·00
		c. Deep ultramarine (18.9.1901)	50·00	42·00
		cx. Wmk reversed	£600	£600
31		4d. brownish black (wmk reversed) (18.1.94)	£800	£350
32		4d. olive-black (11.5.95)	16·00	21·00
33		6d. orange-yellow (19.11.91)	£325	£225
		x. Wmk reversed	85·00	55·00
34		6d. yellow (15.4.96)	55·00	48·00
35		9d. pale reddish orange (15.11.95)	60·00	60·00
		x. Wmk reversed	£700	£750
		y. Wmk inverted and reversed	£1000	£1000
36		9d. salmon (15.4.96)	65·00	65·00
		x. Wmk reversed	£700	£750
37		1s. grey-brown (15.11.95)	80·00	55·00
		x. Wmk reversed	£225	£225
38		1s. yellow-brown (15.4.96)	75·00	48·00
		x. Wmk reversed	£225	£225
17b/38 *Set of 8*			£225	£180
15s, 26s, 28s, 33s, 35s Optd 'SPECIMEN.' *Set of 5*			£700	

The ½d. and 2½d. were first placed on sale in the Falkland Islands on 10 September 1891. Such stamps came from the August 1891 printing. The stock of the May printings sent to the Falkland Islands was lost at sea.

The 2½d. ultramarine printing can sometimes be found in a violet shade, but the reason for this is unknown.

5

6

(Recess B.W.)

1898 (5 Oct). Wmk Crown CC. P 14, 14½.

41	5	2s.6d. deep blue	£275	£275
42	6	5s. red	£250	£250
41s/42s Optd 'SPECIMEN.' *Set of 2*			£550	

7

8

(Recess D.L.R.)

1904 (16 July)–**12**. Wmk Mult Crown CA. P 14.

43	7	½d. yellow-green	9·00	1·50
		aw. Wmk inverted	£700	£425
		ax. Wmk reversed	£1800	
		b. Pale yellow-green (on thick paper) (6.08)	21·00	7·50
		by. Wmk inverted and reversed	—	£2000
		c. Deep yellow-green (7.11)	17·00	3·00
44		1d. vermilion	17·00	1·50
		aw. Wmk inverted	£600	£425
		ax. Wmk reversed	£900	£650
		b. Wmk sideways (7.06)	1·50	4·50
		c. Thick paper (1908)	27·00	2·50
		cw. Wmk inverted	£900	£700
		cx. Wmk reversed	£1000	£750
		d. Dull coppery red (on thick paper) (3.08)	£200	30·00
		dx. Wmk reversed	£1600	£750
		e. Orange-vermilion (7.11)	40·00	2·75
		ex. Wmk reversed	£1100	£800
45		2d. purple (27.12.04)	25·00	21·00
		ax. Wmk reversed	£225	£225
		b. Reddish purple (13.1.12)	£225	£275
46		2½d. ultramarine (*shades*)	29·00	7·50
		aw. Wmk inverted	£750	£425
		aws. Ditto, optd 'SPECIMEN'	£800	
		ay. Wmk inverted and reversed	£1600	£1400
		b. Deep blue (13.1.12)	£275	£130
47		6d. orange (27.12.04)	45·00	48·00
48		1s. brown (27.12.04)	45·00	32·00
49	8	3s. green	£180	£160
		aw. Wmk inverted	£4000	£3250
		axs. Wmk reversed, optd 'SPECIMEN'.	£3000	
		b. Deep green (4.07)	£150	£130
		bx. Wmk reversed	£4500	£3000
50		5s. red (27.12.04)	£225	£150
43/50 *Set of 8*			£475	£350
43s/50s Optd 'SPECIMEN' *Set of 8*			£600	

Examples of Nos. 41/50 and earlier issues are known with a forged Falkland Islands postmark dated 'OCT 15 10'.

For details of South Georgia underprint, South Georgia provisional handstamps and Port Foster handstamp see under FALKLAND ISLANDS DEPENDENCIES.

9

10

(Des B. MacKennal. Eng J. A. C. Harrison. Recess D.L.R.)

1912 (3 July)–**20**. Wmk Mult Crown CA. P 13¾×14 (comb) (½d. to 1s.) or 14 (line) (3s. to £1).

60	9	½d. yellow-green	2·75	3·50
		a. Perf 14 (line). *Deep yellow-green* (1914)	18·00	38·00
		b. Perf 14 (line). *Deep olive* (1918)	24·00	£170
		c. Deep olive (4.19)	3·50	50·00
		ca. Printed both sides	†	£7000
		d. Dull yellowish green (on thick greyish paper) (1920)	4·50	40·00
61		1d. orange-red	5·00	2·50
		a. Perf 14 (line). *Orange-vermilion* (1914, 1916)	50·00	2·50
		b. Perf 14 (line). *Vermilion* (1918)	†	£900
		c. Orange-vermilion (4.19)	7·50	3·00
		d. Orange-vermilion (on thick greyish paper) (1920)	8·00	2·00
		dx. Wmk reversed	£425	£700
62		2d. maroon	30·00	23·00
		a. Perf 14 (line). *Deep reddish purple* (1914)	£375	£160
		b. Perf 14 (line). *Maroon* (4.18)	£400	£170
		c. Deep reddish purple (4.19)	8·50	16·00
63		2½d. deep bright blue	27·00	24·00
		a. Perf 14 (line). *Deep bright blue* (1914)	42·00	50·00
		b. Perf 14 (line). *Deep blue* (1916, 4.18)	50·00	60·00
		c. Deep blue (4.19)	7·00	17·00
64		6d. yellow-orange (6.7.12)	15·00	20·00
		aw. Wmk inverted	£1000	£800
		b. Brown-orange (4.19)	15·00	42·00
		by. Wmk inverted and reversed		
65		1s. light bistre-brown (6.7.12)	32·00	30·00
		a. Pale bistre-brown (4.19)	95·00	£130
		b. Brown (on thick greyish paper) (1920)	38·00	£170
66	10	3s. slate-green	95·00	£100
67		5s. deep rose-red	£120	£120
		a. Reddish maroon (1914)	£300	£300
		b. Maroon (1916)	£130	£150
		bx. Wmk reversed	£7000	£5000
68		10s. red/*green* (11.2.14)	£190	£275
69		£1 black/*red* (11.2.14)	£550	£600
60/69 (*inc 67b*) *Set of 11*			£1000	£1200
60s/69s (*inc both 67s and 67as*) Optd 'SPECIMEN' *Set of 11*			£1900	

The exact measurement of the comb perforation used for T **9** is 13.7×13.9. The line perforation, used for the 1914, 1916 and 1918 printings and for all the high values in T **10**, measured 14.1×14.1.

It was previously believed that all examples of the 1d. in vermilion with the line perforation were overprinted to form No. 71, but it has now been established that some unoverprinted sheets of No. 61*b* were used during 1919.

Many of the sheets showed stamps from the left-hand side in a lighter shade than those from the right. It is believed that this was due to the weight of the impression. Such differences are particularly noticeable on the 2½d. 1916 and 1918 printings where the lighter shades, approaching milky blue in appearance, are scarce.

All 1919 printings show weak impressions of the background either side of the head caused by the poor paper quality.

Examples of all values are known with forged postmarks, including one of Falkland Islands dated '5 SP 19' and another of South Shetlands dated '20 MR 27'.

WAR STAMP

(11)

2½D

(12)

1918 (22 Oct*)–**20**. Optd by Govt Printing Press, Stanley, with T **11**.

70	9	½d. deep olive (line perf) (No. 60b)	1·00	13·00
		a. Yellow-green (No. 60) (4.19)	30·00	£700
		ab. Albino opt	£2500	
		b. Deep olive (comb perf) (No. 60*c*) (4.19)	50	6·50
		c. Dull yellowish green (on thick greyish paper) (No. 60*d*) (5.20)	8·00	55·00
		cx. Wmk reversed	£550	
71		1d. vermilion (line perf) (No. 61*b*)	2·00	18·00
		a. Opt double, one albino	£425	
		b. Orange-vermilion (line perf) (No. 61*a*) (4.19)	32·00	†
		c. Orange-vermilion (comb perf) (No. 61*c*) (4.19)	50	3·75
		ca. Opt double	£4500	
		cx. Wmk reversed	£750	
		d. Orange-vermilion (on thick greyish paper) (No. 61*d*) (5.20)	£120	£200
72		1s. light bistre-brown (No. 65)	55·00	90·00
		a. Pale bistre-brown (No. 65*a*) (4.19)	4·50	50·00
		ab. Opt double, one albino	£2250	
		ac. Opt omitted (in pair with normal)	£20000	
		b. Brown (on thick greyish paper) (No. 65*b*) (5.20)	6·00	48·00
		ba. Opt double, one albino	£1900	
		bw. Wmk inverted	£425	£500
		bx. Wmk reversed	£3500	

* Earliest known postal use. Cancellations dated 8 October were applied much later.

There were five printings of the 'WAR STAMP' overprint, but all, except that in May 1920, used the same setting. Composition of the five printings was as follows:

October 1918. Nos. 70, 71 and 72.
January 1919. Nos. 70, 71 and 72.
April 1919. Nos. 70/70*b*, 71*b*/71*c* and 72*a*.
October 1919. Nos. 70*b*, 71*c* and 72*a*.
May 1920. Nos. 70*c*, 71*d* and 72*b*.

It is believed that the entire stock of No. 70*a* was sold to stamp dealers. Only a handful of used examples are known which may have subsequently been returned to the colony for cancellation.

No. 71ca exists in a block of 12 (6×2) from the bottom of a sheet on which the first stamp in the bottom row shows a single overprint, but the remainder have overprint double.

Examples of Nos. 70/72 are known with a forged Falkland Islands postmark dated '5 SP 19'.

1921–28. Wmk Mult Script CA. P 14.

73	**9**	½d. yellowish green	3·00	4·00
		a. Green (1925)	3·00	4·00
74		1d. dull vermilion (1924)	6·00	2·00
		aw. Wmk inverted	†	£4500
		ay. Wmk inverted and reversed	£850	
		b. Orange-vermilion (shades) (1925)	5·50	1·25
75		2d. deep brown-purple (8.23)	26·00	8·00
		aw. Wmk inverted	—	£4500
		ax. Wmk reversed	£3750	
		b. Purple-brown (1927)	50·00	27·00
		c. Reddish maroon (1.28)	10·00	24·00
76		2½d. deep blue	24·00	16·00
		a. Indigo (28.4.27)	27·00	21·00
		b. Deep steel-blue (1.28)	16·00	16·00
77		2½d. deep purple/*pale yellow* (8.23)	5·00	38·00
		a. Pale purple/pale yellow (1925)	5·00	38·00
		ay. Wmk inverted and reversed	£950	
78		6d. yellow-orange (1925)	11·00	38·00
		w. Wmk inverted	£600	
		x. Wmk reversed	£3750	
79		1s. deep ochre	23·00	48·00
80	**10**	3s. slate-green (8.23)	£100	£160
73/80 *Set of 8*			£150	£275
73s/80s (*inc both 76s and 76as*) Optd 'SPECIMEN' *Set of 9*			£850	

Dates quoted above are those of despatch from Great Britain.

No. 76*b* includes the so-called 'Prussian blue' shades (formerly listed as No. 76*c*) which formed part of a second printing in Oct 1928.

1928 (7 Feb). No. 75*b* surch with T **12**.

115	**9**	2½d. on 2d. purple-brown	£1300	£1300
		a. Surch double	£60000	

No. 115 was produced on South Georgia during a shortage of 2½d. stamps. The provisional was withdrawn on 22 February 1928.

13 Fin Whale and Gentoo Penguins

14

(Recess P.B.)

1929 (2 Sept)–**37**. P 14 (comb).

(a) Wmk Mult Script CA

116	**13**	½d. green	1·25	4·00
		a. Line perf (1936)	3·25	8·50
117		1d. scarlet	4·50	80
		a. Line perf. *Deep red* (1936)	8·00	14·00
118		2d. grey	6·00	4·00
119		2½d. blue	6·00	2·25
120	**14**	4d. orange (line perf) (18.2.32)	23·00	13·00
		a. Line perf 13½. *Deep orange* (7.37)	£100	70·00
121	**13**	6d. purple	24·00	19·00
		a. Line perf. *Reddish purple* (1936)	50·00	25·00
122		1s. black/*emerald*	27·00	35·00
		a. Line perf. *On bright emerald* (1936)	35·00	27·00
123		2s.6d. carmine/*blue*	70·00	70·00
124		5s. green/*yellow*	£100	£110
125		10s. carmine/*emerald*	£225	£275

(b) Wmk Mult Crown CA

126	**13**	£1 black/*red*	£325	£425
116/126 *Set of 11*			£700	£850
116s/126s Perf 'SPECIMEN' *Set of 11*			£1000	

Three kinds of perforation exist:

A. Comb perf 13.9:—original values of 1929.

B. Line perf 13.9, 14.2 or compound (small holes)— 1931 printing of 4d. (Issued Feb 1932) and 1936 printings of ½d., 1d., 6d. and 1s. On some sheets of the former the last vertical row of perforations shows larger holes.

C. Line perf 13.7 (large holes) — 1937 printing of 4d.

Examples of most values are known with forged postmarks, including one of Port Stanley dated '14 JY 31' and another of South Georgia dated 'AU 30 31'.

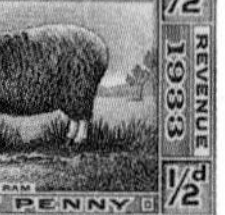

15 Romney Marsh Ram

16 Iceberg

17 Whale-catcher *Bransfield*

18 Port Louis

19 Map of Falkland Islands

20 South Georgia

21 Fin Whale

22 Government House, Stanley

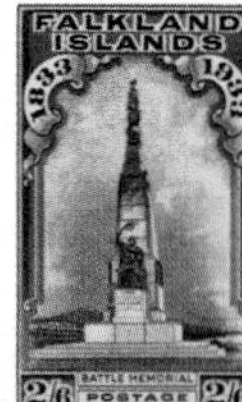

23 Battle Memorial

24 King Penguin

25 Coat of Arms

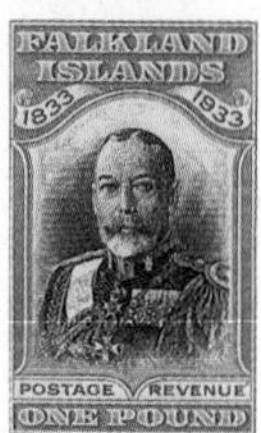

26 King George V

Thick serif to '1' at left (R. 1/3, first printing only)

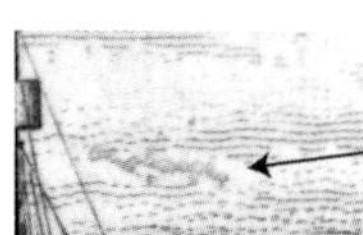
1½d. Break in cloud (R. 9/3)

(Des (except 6d.) by G. Roberts. Eng and recess B.W.)

1933 (2 Jan–Apr). Centenary of British Administration. T **15/26**. Wmk Mult Script CA. P 12.

127	**15**	½d. black and green	4·00	13·00
128	**16**	1d. black and scarlet	3·50	3·00
		a. Thick serif to '1' at left	£500	£350
129	**17**	1½d. black and blue	22·00	26·00
		a. Break in cloud	£1500	£1600
130	**18**	2d. black and brown	17·00	30·00
131	**19**	3d. black and violet	28·00	38·00
132	**20**	4d. black and orange	25·00	28·00
133	**21**	6d. black and slate	75·00	95·00
134	**22**	1s. black and olive-green	70·00	£100
135	**23**	2s.6d. black and violet	£250	£400
136	**24**	5s. black and yellow	£950	£1500
		a. Black and yellow-orange (4.33)	£3250	£3750
137	**25**	10s. black and chestnut	£850	£1500
138	**26**	£1 black and carmine	£2500	£3500
127/138 *Set of 12*			£4250	£6500
127s/138s Perf 'SPECIMEN' *Set of 12*			£4250	

Examples of all values are known with forged Port Stanley postmarks dated '6 JA 33'. Some values have also been seen with part strikes of the forged Falkland Islands postmark mentioned below Nos. 60/69 and 70/72.

(Des H. Fleury. Recess B.W.)

1935 (7 May). Silver Jubilee. As Nos. 91/94 of Antigua, but printed by B.W. P 11×12.

139	1d. deep blue and scarlet	3·25	40
	b. Short extra flagstaff	£1100	£1000
	d. Flagstaff on right-hand turret	£450	£350
	e. Double flagstaff	£550	£400
140	2½d. brown and deep blue	12·00	1·75
	b. Short extra flagstaff	£3500	£3500
	d. Flagstaff on right-hand turret	£500	£425
	e. Double flagstaff	£900	£500
	l. Re-entry on value tablet (R. 8/1)	£200	£120
141	4d. green and indigo	24·00	8·00
	b. Short extra flagstaff	£1200	£1000
	d. Flagstaff on right-hand turret	£850	£500
	e. Double flagstaff	£1000	£600
142	1s. slate and purple	15·00	3·75
	a. Extra flagstaff	£3500	£2500
	b. Short extra flagstaff	£900	£550
	c. Lightning conductor	£3500	£1800
	d. Flagstaff on right-hand turret	£1600	£850
	e. Double flagstaff	£1700	£900
139/142 *Set of 4*		48·00	12·50
139s/142s Perf 'SPECIMEN' *Set of 4*		£500	

For illustrations of plate varieties see Omnibus section following Zanzibar.

1937 (12 May). Coronation. As Nos. 95/97 of Antigua. P 11×11½.

143	½d. green	30	10
144	1d. carmine	1·00	50
145	2½d. blue	1·50	1·40
143/145 *Set of 3*		2·50	1·75
143s/145s Perf 'SPECIMEN' *Set of 3*		£425	

27 Whale's Jawbones

28 Black-necked Swan

29 Battle Memorial

30 Flock of sheep

31 Magellan Goose

32 *Discovery II* (polar supply vessel)

33 *William Scoresby* (supply ship)

34 Mount Sugar Top

34a Turkey Vultures

35 Gentoo Penguins

36 Southern Sealion

37 Deception Island

38 Arms of the Falkland Islands

(Des G. Roberts (Nos. 146, 148/149, 158 and 160/163), K. Lellman (No. 159). Recess B.W.)

1938 (3 Jan)–**50**. T **27/38**. Wmk Mult Script CA. P 12.

146	**27**	½d. black and green (*shades*)	30	75
147	**28**	1d. black and carmine	35·00	80
		a. Black and vermilion	3·75	85
148	**29**	1d. black and violet (14.7.41)	2·75	3·75
		a. Black and purple-violet	10·00	4·00
149		2d. black and deep violet	1·25	50
150	**28**	2d. black and carmine-red (14.7.41)	3·00	4·50
		a. Black and red	3·50	3·00
151	**30**	2½d. black and bright blue	1·25	30
152	**31**	2½d. black and blue (15.6.49)	8·50	8·00
153	**30**	3d. black and blue (14.7.41)	7·50	8·50
		a. Black and deep blue	17·00	4·75
154	**31**	4d. black and purple	3·25	2·00
155	**32**	6d. slate-black and deep brown	11·00	2·50
		a. Black and sepia (shades)	6·00	2·00
156		6d. black (15.6.49)	8·50	6·50
157	**33**	9d. black and grey-blue	28·00	6·50
158	**34**	1s. light dull blue	75·00	19·00
		a. Dull greenish blue	60·00	6·00
		b. Dull blue (greyish paper)	38·00	£160
		c. Deep dull blue (thin paper) (1948)	75·00	£130
159	**34a**	1s.3d. black and carmine-red (11.12.46)	3·00	1·75
160	**35**	2s.6d. slate	60·00	21·00
161	**36**	5s. blue and chestnut	£150	95·00
		b. Indigo and pale yellow-brown	£1100	90·00
		c. Dull blue and yellow brown (greyish paper) (1949)	£120	£600
		d. Steel blue and buff-brown (thin paper) (9.50)	£425	£500
162	**37**	10s. black and orange-brown	£200	65·00
		a. Black and orange (1942?)	£350	65·00
		b. Black and red-orange (greyish paper) (1949)	£120	£500
		c. Black and deep reddish orange (thin paper) (1950)	£850	£650
163	**38**	£1 black and violet	£130	60·00
146/163 *Set of 18*			£475	£225
146s/151s, 153s/155s, 157s/163s Perf 'SPECIMEN' *Set of 16*			£2500	

The 'thin paper' referred to will aid identification of Nos. 158*c*, 161*d* and 162*c*. It is more transparent than previous papers and has white gum.

Examples of values issued before 1946 are known with forged Port Stanley postmarks dated '14 JY 41' and '28 JY 43'.

Crown flaw and re-entry (Pl 1, R. 8/5)

1946 (7 Oct). Victory. As Nos. 110/111 of Antigua. P 13½×14.

164	1d. dull violet	30	75
165	3d. blue	45	50
	a. Crown flaw and re-entry	65·00	70·00
164s/165s Perf 'SPECIMEN' *Set of 2*		£400	

The re-entry, which shows as a doubling of the shadow lines to 'LANDS', the tower of Big Ben and the King's face, also exists without the Crown flaw and is scarcer in this form.

1948 (1 Nov). Royal Silver Wedding. As Nos. 112/113 of Antigua.

166		2½d. ultramarine	2·00	1·00
167		£1 mauve	90·00	60·00

1949 (10 Oct). 75th Anniversary of Universal Postal Union. As Nos. 114/117 of Antigua.

168		1d. violet	1·75	1·00
169		3d. deep blue	5·00	6·50
170		1s.3d. deep blue-green	3·25	2·25
171		2s. blue	3·00	8·00
168/171 *Set of 4*			11·50	16·00

39 Sheep

40 *Fitzroy* (supply ship)

41 Magellan Goose

42 Map of Falkland Islands

43 Arms of the Colony

44 Auster Autocrat Aircraft

45 *John Biscoe* (research ship)

46 View of the Two Sisters

47 Gentoo Penguins

48 Kelp Goose and Gander

49 Sheep shearing

50 Battle Memorial

51 Southern Sealion and South American Fur Seal

52 Hulk of *Great Britain*

(Des from sketches by V. Spencer. Recess Waterlow)

1952 (2 Jan). T **39/52**. Wmk Mult Script CA. P 13×13½ (vert) or 13½×13 (horiz).

172	**39**	½d. green	1·25	70
173	**40**	1d. scarlet	2·50	40
174	**41**	2d. violet	4·50	2·50
175	**42**	2½d. black and light ultramarine	2·00	50
176	**43**	3d. deep ultramarine	2·25	1·00
177	**44**	4d. reddish purple	13·00	1·50
178	**45**	6d. bistre-brown	12·00	1·00
179	**46**	9d. orange-yellow	9·00	2·00
180	**47**	1s. black	24·00	1·00
181	**48**	1s.3d. orange	18·00	7·00
182	**49**	2s.6d. olive-green	22·00	12·00
183	**50**	5s. purple	20·00	11·00
184	**51**	10s. grey	30·00	20·00
185	**52**	£1 black	40·00	27·00
172/185 *Set of 14*			£180	75·00

1953 (4 June). Coronation. As No. 120 of Antigua.

186		1d. black and scarlet	80	1·50

53 Sheep

(Recess Waterlow)

1955–57. Designs previously used for King George VI issue but with portrait of Queen Elizabeth II as in T **53**. Wmk Mult Script CA. P 13×13½ (vert) or 13½×13 (horiz).

187	**53**	½d. green (2.9.57)	1·25	1·25
188	**40**	1d. scarlet (2.9.57)	1·25	1·25
189	**41**	2d. violet (4.9.56)	3·25	4·50
190	**45**	6d. deep yellow-brown (1.6.55)	12·00	60
191	**46**	9d. orange-yellow (2.9.57)	11·00	17·00
192	**47**	1s. black (15.7.55)	16·00	2·75
187/192 *Set of 6*			40·00	24·00

54 Austral Thrush

55 Southern Black-backed Gull

56 Gentoo Penguins

57 Long-tailed Meadowlark

58 Magellan Geese

59 Falkland Islands Flightless Steamer Ducks

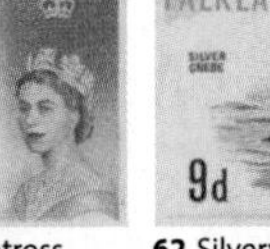

60 Rockhopper Penguin

61 Black-browed Albatross

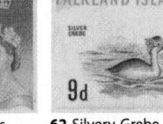

62 Silvery Grebe

63 Magellanic Oystercatchers

64 Chilean Teal

65 Kelp Geese

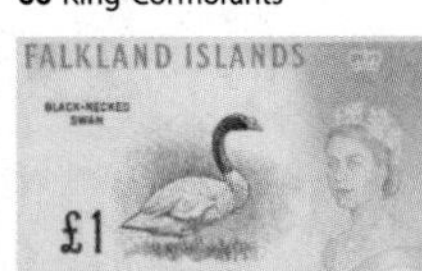

66 King Cormorants

67 Common Caracara

68 Black-necked Swan

½d. Extended cross-bar to first 'H' in 'THRUSH' (D.L.R. Pl. 1 (black), R. 2/2).

variety

normal

½d., 1d., 2d., 2s. Weak entry under 'FA' of 'FALKLAND' (D.L.R. Pl. 2, R. 12/5).

(Des from sketches by S. Scott. Recess Waterlow, then D.L.R. (from 9.1.62 onwards))

1960 (10 Feb)–**66**. T **54/68**. W w **12** (upright). P 13½.

193	**54**	½d. black and myrtle-green	5·00	2·25
		a. Black and green (D.L.R.) (9.1.62)	12·00	7·50
		ab. Weak entry	80·00	55·00
		ac. 'H' flaw	45·00	
		aw. Wmk inverted	£7500	£5500
194	**55**	1d. black and scarlet	4·50	2·00
		a. Black and carmine-red (D.L.R.) (15.7.63)	8·50	6·00
		ab. Weak entry	80·00	48·00
195	**56**	2d. black and blue	4·50	1·25
		a. Black and deep blue (D.L.R.) (25.10.66)	20·00	20·00
		ab. Weak entry	£140	£150
196	**57**	2½d. black and yellow-brown	2·50	1·00
197	**58**	3d. black and olive	1·25	50
198	**59**	4d. black and carmine	1·50	1·25
199	**60**	5½d. black and violet	3·25	2·50
200	**61**	6d. black and sepia	3·50	30
201	**62**	9d. black and orange-red	2·50	1·25
202	**63**	1s. black and maroon	1·25	40
203	**64**	1s.3d. black and ultramarine	13·00	14·00
204	**65**	2s. black and brown-red	32·00	2·50
		a. Black and lake-brown (D.L.R.) (25.10.66)	£225	70·00
		ab. Weak entry	£750	£350
205	**66**	5s. black and turquoise	28·00	11·00
206	**67**	10s. black and purple	48·00	25·00
207	**68**	£1 black and orange-yellow	48·00	27·00
193/207 *Set of 15*			£170	80·00

Waterlow

De La Rue

Waterlow printings were from frame plate 1 for all values except the 1d., 2½d., and 5s., where frame plate 2 was used. De La Rue used both frame plates for the ½d., 1d. and 6d. but only frame plate 2 for the 2d. and 2s. De La Rue printings can generally be distinguished by the finer lines of shading on the Queen's face (appearing as a white face), neck and shoulder and also the very faint cross-hatching left of the face. Typically the black vignette is also less intense on the De La Rue printings. The 6d. De La Rue shade varies little from the original, but for other values the shades are distinctive. The majority of the De La Rue 6d. stamps are from frame plate 1, plate 2 being rare. Perforation patterns and margin widths can also aid specialists in determining printers and printings.

Only one unused (without gum) and two used examples of No. 193aw have been reported.

For the ½d. watermark sideways see No. 227. An irreparable plate crack developed under R. 12/2 of the original vignette plate, so a new plate 2 had to be used for the final part of the 1968 printing.

69 Morse Key

70 One-valve Receiver

(Des M. Goaman. Photo Enschedé)

1962 (5 Oct). 50th Anniversary of Establishment of Radio Communications. T **69/70** and similar vert design. W w **12**. P 11½×11.

208	**69**	6d. carmine-lake and orange	75	40
209	**70**	1s. deep bluish green and yellow-olive	80	40
210	–	2s. deep violet and ultramarine	90	1·75
		w. Wmk inverted	£140	£350
208/210 *Set of 3*			2·25	2·25

Design: 2s. Rotary Spark Transmitter.

1963 (4 June). Freedom from Hunger. As No. 146 of Antigua.

211		1s. ultramarine	7·00	1·50

1963 (2 Sept). Red Cross Centenary. As Nos. 147/148 of Antigua.

212		1d. red and black	2·00	75
213		1s. red and blue	8·00	5·00

1964 (23 Apr). 400th Birth Anniversary of William Shakespeare. As No. 164 of Antigua.

214		6d. black	1·50	50

72 HMS *Glasgow*

73 HMS *Kent*

74 HMS *Invincible*

75 Battle Memorial

(Recess D.L.R.)

1964 (8 Dec). 50th Anniversary of the Battle of the Falkland Islands. T **72/75**. W w **12**. P 13×14 (2s.) or 13 (others).

215 2½d. black and red .... 9·00 3·75
216 6d. black and light blue 50 50
 a. Centre Type **72** £40000
217 1s. black and carmine-red .... 50 1·50
 w. Wmk inverted £4000
218 2s. black and blue 50 75
215/218 *Set of 4* .... 9·50 6·00

It is believed that No. 216a came from a sheet which was first printed with the centre of the 2½d. and then accidentally included among the supply of the 6d. value and thus received the wrong frame. About 25 examples of the 'Glasgow' error have been recorded.

1965 (26 May). ITU Centenary. As Nos. 166/167 of Antigua.

219 1d. light blue and deep blue 50 30
 w. Wmk inverted £3250 £3250
220 2s. lilac and bistre-yellow .... 2·50 1·75

1965 (25 Oct). International Co-operation Year. As Nos. 168/169 of Antigua.

221 1d. reddish purple and turquoise-green 40 40
222 1s. deep bluish green and lavender .... 1·60 1·10

1966 (24 Jan). Churchill Commemoration. As Nos. 170/173 of Antigua. Printed in black, cerise and gold with background in colours stated. W w **12**. P 14.

223 ½d. new blue .... 65 2·50
224 1d. deep green .... 1·50 30
 w. Wmk inverted .... 4·00 8·00
225 1s. brown .... 2·50 3·25
 w. Wmk inverted £100 £100
226 2s. bluish violet .... 1·75 4·00
223/226 *Set of 4* .... 6·00 9·00

1966 (25 Oct). As No. 193*a*, but wmk w **12** sideways.

227 **54** ½d. black and green 30 40
 a. Weak entry .... 38·00 40·00
 b. 'H' flaw .... 15·00

76 Globe and Human Rights Emblem

(Des M. Farrar Bell. Photo Harrison)

1968 (4 July). Human Rights Year. W w **12**. P 14×14½.

228 **76** 2d. multicoloured 40 20
 a. Yellow omitted ('1968' white) £2250
229 6d. muticoloured 40 20
230 1s. multicoloured 50 20
231 2s. multicoloured 65 30
228/231 *Set of 4* .... 1·75 80

77 Dusty Miller

78 Pig Vine

79 Pale Maiden

80 Dog Orchid

81 Sea Cabbage

82 Vanilla Daisy

83 Arrowleaf Marigold

85 Scurvy Grass

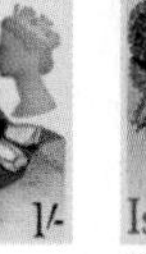

84 Diddle Dee

87 Fachine

86 Prickly Burr

89 Felton's Flower

90 Yellow Orchid

88 Lavender

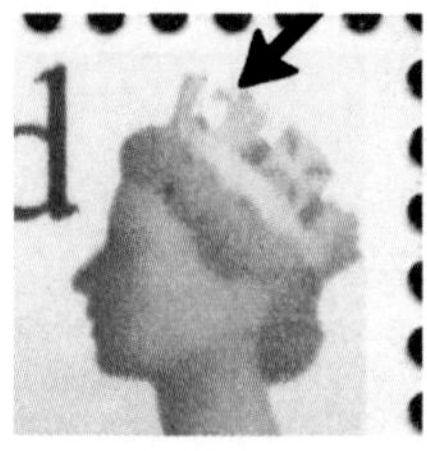

½d. Missing grey colour in diadem appears as a damaged crown (Pl. 1A, R. 2/2).

(Des Sylvia Goaman. Photo Harrison)

1968 (9 Oct). Flowers. T **77/90**. Chalk-surfaced paper. W w **12** (sideways on vert designs). P 14.

232 **77** ½d. multicoloured .... 15 1·75
 a. Crown damaged .... 9·00
233 **78** 1½d. multicoloured 40 15
234 **79** 2d. multicoloured 50 15
235 **80** 3d. multicoloured .... 6·00 1·00
236 **81** 3½d. multicoloured .... 30 1·75
237 **82** 4½d. multicoloured .... 1·50 2·00
238 **83** 5½d. olive-green, brown and yellow-green .... 1·50 2·50
239 **84** 6d. carmine, black and yellow-green 75 20
240 **85** 1s. multicoloured .... 1·00 1·50
 w. Wmk inverted £350
241 **86** 1s.6d. multicoloured .... 8·00 16·00
242 **87** 2s. multicoloured .... 5·50 6·50
243 **88** 3s. multicoloured .... 9·50 9·00
244 **89** 5s. multicoloured .... 30·00 14·00
245 **90** £1 multicoloured .... 12·00 3·75
232/245 *Set of 14* .... 65·00 48·00

A further printing of the £1 took place with the decimal surcharges issued 15 February 1971. It was for some time believed that stamps from this printing could be identified by the brown shading which extended to the foot of the design, instead of stopping short as on the original printing, but this test has now been shown to be inconsistent.

91 de Havilland DHC-2 Beaver Seaplane

(Des V. Whiteley. Litho Format)

1969 (8 Apr). 21st Anniversary of Government Air Services. T **91** and similar horiz designs. Multicoloured. W w **12** (sideways). P 14.

246 2d. Type **91** 80 30
247 6d. Noorduyn Norseman V 80 35
248 1s. Auster Autocrat 80 35
249 2s. Falkland Islands Arms .... 1·00 2·00
246/249 *Set of 4* .... 3·00 2·75

92 Holy Trinity Church, 1869

(Des G. Drummond. Litho Format)

1969 (30 Oct). Centenary of Bishop Stirling's Consecration. T **92** and similar horiz designs. W w **12** (sideways). P 14.

250 2d. black, grey and apple-green 40 60
251 6d. black, grey and orange-red 40 60
252 1s. black, grey and lilac 40 60
253 2s. multicoloured 50 75
250/253 *Set of 4* .... 1·50 2·25

Designs: 2d. T **92**; 6d. Christ Church Cathedral, 1969; 1s. Bishop Stirling; 2s. Bishop's Mitre.

96 Mounted Volunteer

97 SS *Great Britain* (1843)

(Des R. Granger Barrett. Litho B.W.)

1970 (30 Apr). Golden Jubilee of Defence Force. T **96** and similar designs. Multicoloured. W w **12** (sideways on 2d. and 1s.). P 13.

254 2d. Type **96** .... 1·00 70
255 6d. Defence Post (*horiz*) .... 1·00 70
256 1s. Corporal in Number One Dress Uniform .... 1·00 70
257 2s. Defence Force Badge (*horiz*) .... 1·00 75
254/257 *Set of 4* .... 3·50 2·50

(Des V. Whiteley. Litho J.W.)

1970 (30 Oct). Restoration of SS *Great Britain*. T **97** and views of the ship at different dates. Multicoloured. W w **12** (sideways*). P 14½×14.

258 2d. Type **97** 65 40
259 4d. In 1845 .... 65 75
 w. Wmk Crown to right of CA .... 19·00 3·00
260 9d. In 1876 .... 65 75
261 1s. In 1886 .... 65 75
 w. Wmk Crown to right of CA £1900
262 2s. In 1970 .... 1·00 75
258/262 *Set of 5* .... 3·25 3·00

* The normal sideways watermark shows Crown to left of CA, *as seen from the back of the stamp*.

FALKLAND ISLANDS DEPENDENCIES

PRICES FOR STAMPS ON COVER TO 1945
Nos. A1/D8 *from* × 20

A. GRAHAM LAND

For use at Port Lockroy (established 1 February 1944) and Hope Bay (established 12 February 1945) bases.

Falkland Islands definitive stamps with face values of 1s.3d. and above were valid for use from Graham Land in conjunction with Nos. A1/A8 and subsequently Nos. G1/G16.

Z 1

Z 2

Stamps of FALKLAND ISLANDS cancelled as T Z **1** or Z **2** at Port Lockroy or Hope Bay with Graham Land circular datestamps between12 February 1944 and 31 January 1954. Further offices were opened at Stonington Island (13.3.46–8.2.50) and Argentine Islands (from 25.1.47).

1938–50. King George VI (Nos. 159/163).

Z1 1s.3d. black and carmine-red £250
Z2 2s.6d. slate .... 90·00

Z3 5s. indigo and yellow-brown £140
Z4 10s. black and orange £100
Z5 £1 black and violet £110

1952. King George VI (Nos. 181/185).
Z6 1s.3d. orange £190
Z7 2s.6d. olive-green £225
Z8 5s. purple £225
Z9 10s. grey £250
Z10 £1 black £250

GRAHAM LAND

DEPENDENCY OF

(A **1**)

1944 (12 Feb)–**45.** Falkland Islands Nos. 146, 148, 150, 153/155, 157 and 158*a* optd with T A **1**, in red, by B.W.

A1	½d. black and green	30	2·25
	a. Blue-black and green	£3000	£1100
A2	1d. black and violet	30	1·00
A3	2d. black and carmine-red	50	1·00
A4	3d. black and blue	50	1·00
A5	4d. black and purple	2·00	1·75
A6	6d. black and brown	18·00	2·25
	a. Blue-black and brown (24.9.45)	18·00	
A7	9d. black and grey-blue	2·50	1·50
A8	1s. deep blue	2·50	1·50
A1/A8 *Set of* 8		24·00	11·00
A1s/A8s Perf 'SPECIMEN' *Set of* 8		£650	

B. SOUTH GEORGIA

The stamps of Falkland Islands were used at the Grytviken whaling station on South Georgia from 3 December 1909.

Mr. J. Innes Wilson, the Stipendary Magistrate whose duties included those of postmaster, was issued with a stock of stamps, values ½d. to 5s., together with an example of the current 'FALKLAND ISLANDS' circular datestamp. This was used to cancel the stamps, but, as it gave no indication that mail had originated at South Georgia, a straight-line handstamp inscribed 'SOUTH GEORGIA' was also supplied. A second handstamp, inscribed 'South Georgia' was sent on 17 February 1910. It was intended that these should be struck directly on to each letter or card below the stamp, but they can sometimes be found struck across the stamp instead.

The use of the 'South Georgia' handstamps continued after the introduction of the 'SOUTH GEORGIA' circular datestamp in June 1910 apparently for philatelic purposes, but no example has been reported used after June 1912.

SOUTH GEORGIA.

Z 1

South Georgia.

Z 2

		On piece	On cover/ card
ZU1	Example of T Z **1** used in conjunction with 'FALKLAND ISLANDS' postmark (22 Dec 1909 to 30 March 1910) *Price from*	£2000	£10000
ZU2	Example of T Z **2** used in conjunction with 'FALKLAND ISLANDS' postmark (May 1910) *Price from*	£1300	£6000
ZU3	Example of T Z **2** used in conjunction with 'SOUTH GEORGIA' postmark (June 1910 to June 1912) *Price from*	£300	£1000

Stamps of FALKLAND ISLANDS cancelled at Grytviken with South Georgia circular datestamps between 27 June 1910 and 31 January 1954.

1891–1902. Queen Victoria (Nos. 17/38).
Z11 ½d. yellow-green £250
Z11*a* 1d. pale red £200
Z11*b* 2d. purple £325
Z11*c* 2½d. deep ultramarine £400
Z12 4d. olive-black £475
Z12*a* 6d. yellow £475
Z12*b* 9d. salmon £475
Z12*d* 1s. yellow-brown £475

1898. Queen Victoria (No. 42).
Z13 5s. red £1000

1904–12. King Edward VII (Nos. 43/50).
Z14 ½d. green 24·00
Z15 1d. vermilion 23·00
b. Wmk sideways 70·00
d. Dull coppery red (on thick paper) 60·00
Z16 2d. purple 85·00
b. Reddish purple £325
Z17 2½d. ultramarine 35·00
b. Deep blue £200
Z18 6d. orange £200
Z19 1s. brown £200
Z20 3s. green £550
Z21 5s. red £650

SOUTH GEORGIA PROVISIONAL HANDSTAMPS

During October 1911 the arrival of the German South Polar Expedition at Grytviken, South Georgia, resulted in the local supply of stamps becoming exhausted. The Acting Magistrate, Mr. E. B. Binnie, who was also responsible for the postal facilities, produced a handstamp reading 'Paid at (or At) SOUTH GEORGIA' which, together with a manuscript indication of the postage paid and his signature, was used on mail from 18 October 1911 to January 1912, the handstamp being overstruck by the 'SOUTH GEORGIA' double-ring datestamp. Further examples, signed by John Innes Wilson, are known from February 1912.

1911 (18 Oct)–**12.**
PH1 'Paid 1 at SOUTH GEORGIA EBB' *Price on cover* £9500
PH1*a* 'Paid 1 At SOUTH GEORGIA EBB' (16.12.11) *Price on cover* £8500
PH2 'Paid 2½ at SOUTH GEORGIA EBB' *Price on cover* £7500
PH2*a* 'Paid 2½ At SOUTH GEORGIA EBB' (16.12.11) *Price on cover* £9500
PH3 'Paid 1 At SOUTH GEORGIA JIW' (14.2.12) *Price on cover* £14000
PH4 'Paid 2½ At SOUTH GEORGIA JIW' (14.2.12) *Price on cover* £12000

1912–23. King George V. Wmk Mult Crown CA (Nos. 60/69).
Z22 ½d. green 21·00
a. Perf 14 (line). *Deep yellow-green* 38·00
d. Dull yellowish green (on thick greyish paper) 50·00
Z23 1d. orange-red 14·00
a. Perf 14 (line). *Orange-vermilion* 14·00
d. Orange-vermilion 14·00
Z24 2d. maroon 65·00
Z25 2½d. deep bright blue 48·00
c. Deep blue 45·00
Z26 6d. yellow-orange 90·00
b. Brown-orange £100
ba. Bisected (diag) (3d.) (*on cover*) (3.23) £25000
Z27 1s. light bistre-brown £180
a. Pale bistre-brown £200
b. Brown (on thick greyish paper) £250
Z28 3s. slate-green £375
Z29 5s. deep rose-red £425
a. Reddish maroon £550
b. Maroon £500
Z30 10s. red/*green* £700
Z31 £1 black/*red* £1000

1918–20. 'WAR STAMP' opts (Nos. 70/72).
Z32 ½d. deep olive 32·00
Z33 1d. vermilion 32·00
Z34 1s. light bistre-brown £160

1921–28. King George V. Wmk Mult Script CA (Nos. 73/80).
Z35 ½d. yellowish green 8·50
Z36 1d. dull vermilion 7·00
Z37 2d. deep brown-purple 38·00
Z38 2½d. deep blue 32·00
a. Bisected (diag) (1d.) (*on cover*) (3.23) £18000
Z39 2½d. deep purple/*pale yellow* 65·00
Z40 6d. yellow-orange 75·00
Z41 1s. deep ochre 85·00
Z42 3s. slate-green £325

1928 PROVISIONAL. For listing of the 2½d. on 2d. surcharge issued at Grytviken on 7 February 1928 see No. 115 of Falkland Islands.

1929–37. King George V. Whale and Penguins design (Nos. 116/126).
Z43 ½d. green 9·00
Z44 1d. scarlet 7·50
Z45 2d. grey 18·00
a. Bisected (diag) (1d.) (*on postcard*) £15000
Z46 2½d. blue 9·00
Z47 4d. orange 38·00
Z48 6d. purple 55·00
Z49 1s. black/*emerald* 75·00
Z50 2s.6d. carmine/*blue* £160
Z51 5s. green/*yellow* £275
Z52 10s. carmine/*emerald* £500
Z53 £1 black/*red* £850

Examples of most values are known with forged postmarks dated 'Au 30' in 1928, 1930 and 1931.

1933. Centenary of British Administration (Nos. 127/138).
Z54 ½d. black and green 18·00
Z55 1d. black and scarlet 7·50
Z56 1½d. black and blue 48·00
Z57 2d. black and brown 55·00
Z58 3d. black and violet 60·00
Z59 4d. black and orange 45·00
Z60 6d. black and slate £180
Z61 1s. black and olive-green £200
Z62 2s.6d. black and violet £700
Z63 5s. black and yellow £2250
a. Black and yellow-orange £4750
Z64 10s. black and chestnut £2250
Z65 £1 black and carmine £4750

1935. Silver Jubilee (Nos. 139/142).
Z66 1d. deep blue and scarlet 8·00
Z67 2½d. brown and deep blue 9·00
Z68 4d. green and indigo 11·00
Z69 1s. slate and purple 11·00

1937. Coronation (Nos. 143/145).
Z70 ½d. green 4·25
Z71 1d. carmine 4·25
Z72 2½d. blue 4·25

1938–50. King George VI (Nos. 146/163).
Z73 ½d. black and green 8·00
Z74 1d. black and carmine 13·00
a. Black and vermilion 7·00
Z75 1d. black and violet 15·00
Z76 2d. black and deep violet 14·00
Z77 2d. black and carmine-red 20·00
Z78 2½d. black and bright blue (No. 151) 7·50
Z79 3d. black and blue 22·00
Z80 4d. black and purple 16·00
Z81 6d. black and brown 18·00
Z82 9d. black and grey-blue 27·00
Z83 1s. light dull blue 70·00
a. Dull greenish blue 75·00
Z84 1s.3d. black and carmine-red 85·00
Z85 2s.6d. slate 55·00
Z86 5s. blue and chestnut £225
a. Indigo and yellow-brown £140
b. Dull blue and yellow-brown £850
c. Steel blue and buff-brown £650
Z87 10s. black and orange-brown £180
a. Black and orange 85·00
b. Black and red-orange £700
Z88 £1 black and violet 95·00

From 6 April 1944 the post office on South Georgia ceased to sell Falkland Islands stamps with values up to 1s. Stamps of 1s.3d. and above continued to be valid from South Georgia after the introduction of Nos. B1/B8 and subsequently Nos. G1/G16. Forged South Georgia postmarks exist dated '30 MR 49'.

1952. King George VI (Nos. 181/185).
Z89 1s.3d. orange £100
Z90 2s.6d. olive-green £190
Z91 5s. purple £190
Z92 10s. grey £200
Z93 £1 black £225

1944 (24 Feb)–**45.** Falkland Islands Nos. 146, 148, 150, 153/155, 157 and 158*a* optd 'SOUTH GEORGIA/DEPENDENCY OF', in red, as T A **1** of Graham Land.

B1	½d. black and green	30	2·25
	a. Wmk sideways	£4750	
B2	1d. black and violet	30	1·00
B3	2d. black and carmine-red	50	1·00
B4	3d. black and blue	50	1·00
B5	4d. black and purple	2·00	1·75
B6	6d. black and brown	18·00	2·25
	a. Blue-black and brown (24.9.45)	18·00	
B7	9d. black and grey-blue	2·50	1·50
B8	1s. deep blue	2·50	1·50
B1/B8 *Set of* 8		24·00	11·00
B1s/B8s Perf 'SPECIMEN' *Set of* 8		£650	

C. SOUTH ORKNEYS

Used from the *Fitzroy* in February 1944 and at Laurie Island (established January 1946).

Falkland Islands definitive stamps with face values of 1s.3d. and above were valid for use from the South Orkneys in conjunction with Nos. C1/C8 and subsequently Nos. G1/G16.

Z **3** Z **4**

Stamps of FALKLAND ISLANDS cancelled on the *Fitzroy*, at Laurie Island or at Signy Island with South Orkneys circular datestamps as T Z **3** or Z **4** between 21 February 1944 and 31 January 1954.

1938–50. King George VI (Nos. 159/163).
Z94 1s.3d. black and carmine-red £325
Z95 2s.6d. slate 90·00
Z96 5s. indigo and yellow-brown £140
Z97 10s. black and orange £100
Z98 £1 black and violet £110

1952. King George VI (Nos. 181/185).
Z99 1s.3d. orange £200
Z100 2s.6d. olive-green £225
Z101 5s. purple £225
Z102 10s. grey £250
Z103 £1 black £250

1944 (21 Feb)–**45.** Falkland Islands Nos. 146, 148, 150, 153/155, 157 and 158*a* optd 'SOUTH ORKNEYS/DEPENDENCY OF', in red, as T A **1** of Graham Land.

C1	½d. black and green	30	2·25
C2	1d. black and violet	30	1·00
	w. Wmk inverted	£8000	
C3	2d. black and carmine-red	50	1·00
C4	3d. black and blue	50	1·00
C5	4d. black and purple	2·00	1·75
C6	6d. black and brown	18·00	2·25
	a. Blue-black and brown (24.9.45)	18·00	
C7	9d. black and grey-blue	2·50	1·50
C8	1s. deep blue	2·50	1·50
C1/C8 *Set of* 8		24·00	11·00
C1s/C8s Perf 'SPECIMEN' *Set of* 8		£650	

D. SOUTH SHETLANDS

Postal facilities were first provided at the Port Foster whaling station on Deception Island for the 1912–1913 whaling season and were available each year between November and the following April until March 1931.

No postmark was provided for the 1912–1913 season and the local postmaster was instructed to cancel stamps on cover with a straight-line 'PORT FOSTER' handstamp. Most letters so cancelled subsequently received a 'FALKLAND ISLANDS' circular postmark dated between 19 and 28 March 1913. It is known that only low value stamps were available at Port Foster. Higher values, often with other 'FALKLAND ISLANDS' postmark dates, were, it is believed, subsequently 'made to order'.

Stamps of FALKLAND ISLANDS cancelled at Port Foster, Deception Island with part of 'PORT FOSTER' straightline handstamp.

1904–12. King Edward VII (Nos. 43*c*, 44*e*).
Z104 ½d. deep yellow-green £1800
Z105 1d. orange-vermilion £1800

1912. King George V. Wmk Mult Crown CA (Nos. 60/61).
Z106 ½d. yellow-green £1800
Z107 1d. orange-red £1800

Stamps of FALKLAND ISLANDS cancelled at Port Foster with part of oval 'DECEPTION ISLAND SOUTH SHETLANDS' postmark in black or violet between 1914 and 1927.

1904–12. King Edward VII (No. 43*c*).
Z108 ½d. deep yellow-green £550

1912–20. King George V. Wmk Mult Crown CA (Nos. 60/69).
Z110 ½d. yellow-green £170
Z111 1d. orange-red £170
Z112 2d. maroon £225
Z113 2½d. deep bright blue £225
Z114 6d. yellow-orange £325
Z115 1s. light bistre-brown £400
a. Brown (on thick greyish paper) £475
Z116 3s. slate-green £750
Z117 5s. maroon £900
Z118 10s. red/*green* £1200
Z119 £1 black/*red* £1600

1918–20. 'WAR STAMP' opts (Nos. 70/72).
Z120 ½d. deep olive £200
a. Dull yellowish green (on thick greyish paper) £225

Z121	1d. vermilion	£200
Z122	1s. light bistre-brown	£500

1921–28. King George V. Wmk Mult Script CA (Nos. 73/80).

Z123	½d. yellowish green	£200
Z126	2½d. deep blue	£250
Z129	1s. deep ochre	£350

Stamps of FALKLAND ISLANDS cancelled at Port Foster with 'SOUTH SHETLANDS' circular datestamp between 1923 and March 1931.

1912–20. King George V. Wmk Mult Crown CA (Nos. 60/69).

Z129*a*	½d. dull yellowish green (on thick greyish paper)	£150
Z130	1d. orange-vermilion	£100
Z131	2d. deep reddish purple	£130
Z132	2½d. deep bright blue	£170
	c. Deep blue	£170
Z133	6d. brown-orange	£200
Z134	1s. bistre-brown	£300
Z135	3s. slate-green	£450
Z136	5s. maroon	£550
Z137	10s. red/*green*	£850
Z138	£1 black/*red*	£1400

Examples of all values are known with forged postmarks dated '20 MR 27'.

1918–20. 'WAR STAMP' ovpts (Nos. 70/72).

Z138*a*	½d. deep olive	£180
Z139	1d. vermilion	£160
Z140	1s. light bistre-brown	£400

1921–28. King George V. Wmk Mult Script CA (Nos. 73/80).

Z141	½d. yellowish green	55·00
Z142	1d. dull vermilion	55·00
Z143	2d. deep brown-purple	85·00
Z144	2½d. deep blue	80·00
Z145	2½d. deep purple/*pale yellow*	95·00
Z146	6d. yellow-orange	£150
Z147	1s. deep ochre	£160
Z148	3s. slate-green	£475

1929. King George V. Whale and Penguins design (Nos. 116/126).

Z149	½d. green	85·00
Z150	1d. scarlet	85·00
Z151	2d. grey	£130
Z152	2½d. blue	£110
Z153	6d. purple	£160
Z154	1s. black/*emerald*	£190
Z155	2s.6d. carmine/*blue*	£375
Z156	5s. green/*yellow*	£425
Z157	10s. carmine/*emerald*	£750
Z158	£1 black/*red*	£1300

The whaling station at Port Foster was abandoned at the end of the 1930–1931 season.

It was reoccupied as a Falkland Islands Dependencies Survey base on 3 February 1944.

Falkland Islands definitive stamps with face values of 1s.3d. and above were valid for use from the South Shetlands in conjunction with Nos. D1/D8 and subsequently Nos. G1/G16.

Z 5

Z 6

Stamps of FALKLAND ISLANDS cancelled at Port Foster (from 5.2.44) or Admiralty Bay (from 7.1.47) with South Shetlands circular datestamps as T Z **5** or Z **6** between 5 February 1944 and 31 January 1954.

1938–50. King George VI (Nos. 159/163).

Z158*a*	1s.3d. black and carmine-red	£325
Z159	2s.6d. slate	90·00
Z160	5s. indigo and yellow-brown	£140
Z161	10s. black and orange	£100
Z162	£1 black and violet	£110

1952. King George VI (Nos. 181/185).

Z163	1s.3d. orange	£180
Z164	2s.6d. olive-green	£200
Z165	5s. purple	£200
Z166	10s. grey	£225
Z167	£1 black	£225

1944 (5 Feb)–**45.** Falkland Islands Nos. 146, 148, 150, 153/155, 157 and 158*a* optd 'SOUTH SHETLANDS/DEPENDENCY OF', in red, as T A **1** of Graham Land.

D1	½d. black and green	30	2·25
D2	1d. black and violet	30	1·00
D3	2d. black and carmine-red	50	1·00
D4	3d. black and blue	50	1·00
D5	4d. black and purple	2·00	1·75
D6	6d. black and brown	18·00	2·25
	a. Blue-black and brown (24.9.45)	18·00	
D7	9d. black and grey-blue	2·50	1·50
D8	1s. deep blue	2·50	1·50
D1/D8 *Set of* 8		24·00	11·00
D1s/D8s Perf 'SPECIMEN' *Set of* 8		£650	

From 12 July 1946 to 16 July 1963, Graham Land, South Georgia, South Orkneys and South Shetlands used FALKLAND ISLANDS DEPENDENCIES stamps.

E. FALKLAND ISLANDS DEPENDENCIES

For use at the following bases:

Admiralty Bay (South Shetlands) (opened January 1948, closed January 1961)
Argentine Islands (Graham Land) (opened 1947)
Deception Island (South Shetlands)
Grytviken (South Georgia)
Hope Bay (Graham Land) (closed 4 February 1949, opened February 1952)
Laurie Island (South Orkneys) (*closed* 1947)
Port Lockroy (Graham Land) (*closed* 16 January 1962)
Signy Island (South Orkneys) (*opened* 1946)
Stonington Island (Graham Land) (*opened* 1946, *closed* 1950, *opened* 1958, *closed* 1959, *opened* 1960)

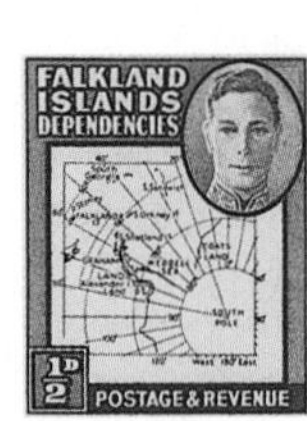

G 1

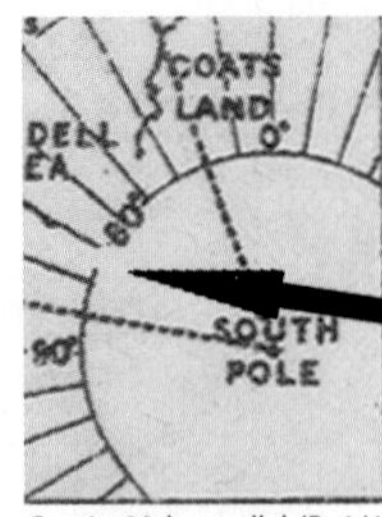

Gap in 80th parallel (R. 1/4, 1/9, 3/4, 3/9, 5/4 and 5/9)

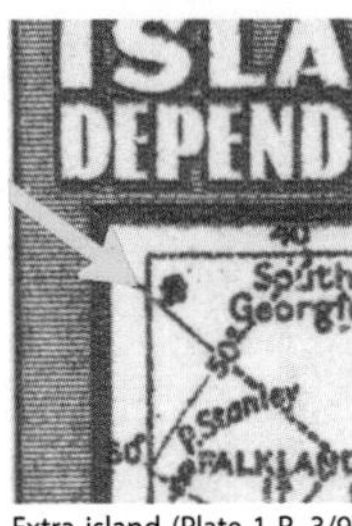

Extra island (Plate 1 R. 3/9)

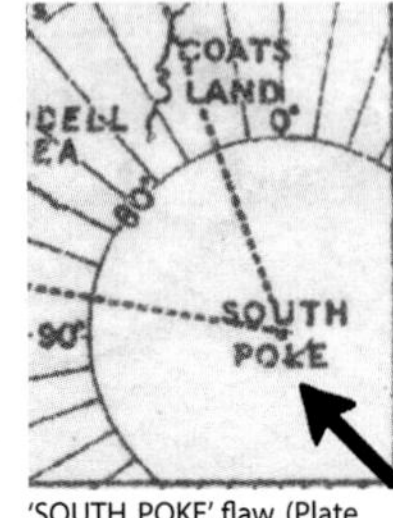

'SOUTH POKE' flaw (Plate 2 R. 6/8)

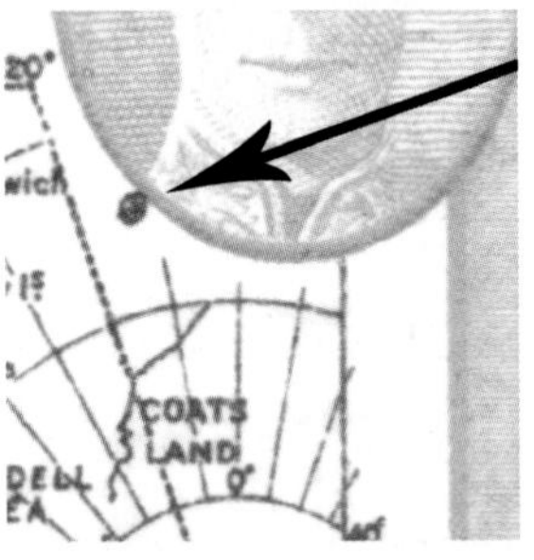

Missing 'I' in 'S. Shetland Is.' (Plate 1 R. 1/2)

Extra dot by oval (Plate 1 R. 4/6)

3d. 'Teardrop' flaw (Frame plate '1A', R. 6/7)

(Des. L.J. Newell. Map litho, frame recess D.L.R.)

1946 (12 July*)–**49.** Wmk Mult Script CA (sideways). P 12.

(a) Map thick and coarse

G1	G **1**	½d. black and green	1·00	3·50
		a. Gap in 80th parallel	3·00	10·00
		aa. Extra island	£325	£325
		b. Missing 'I'	£325	£325
		c. 'SOUTH POKE'	£225	£375
		d. Extra dot by oval	£325	£325
G2		1d. black and violet	1·25	2·00
		a. Gap in 80th parallel	3·50	6·50
		aa. Extra island	£170	£200
		b. Missing 'I'	£170	£200
		d. Extra dot by oval	£180	£200
G3		2d. black and carmine	1·25	2·50
		a. Gap in 80th parallel	3·50	6·00
		aa. Extra island	£350	£350
		b. Missing 'I'	£350	£350
		d. Extra dot by oval	£375	£375
G4		3d. black and blue	1·25	5·00
		a. Gap in 80th parallel	3·50	11·00
		aa. Extra island	£225	£350
		b. Missing 'I'	£200	£325
		d. Extra dot by oval	£250	£375
		e. 'Teardrop'	£110	£160
G5		4d. black and claret	2·50	4·75
		a. Gap in 80th parallel	6·50	14·00
		c. 'SOUTH POKE'	£325	£400
G6		6d. black and orange	3·50	5·00
		a. Gap in 80th parallel	7·50	14·00
		aa. Extra island	£275	£325
		b. Missing 'I'	£250	£325
		c. 'SOUTH POKE'	£180	£400
		d. Extra dot by oval	£275	£350
		e. Black and ochre	55·00	95·00
		ea. Gap in 80th parallel	90·00	£160
		eaa. Extra island	£750	
		eb. Missing 'I'	£750	
		ec. 'SOUTH POKE'	£700	
		ed. Extra dot by oval	£750	£950
G7		9d. black and brown	2·00	3·75
		a. Gap in 80th parallel	5·50	12·00
		c. 'SOUTH POKE'	£170	£275
G8		1s. black and purple	2·00	4·25
		a. Gap in 80th parallel	5·50	13·00
		c. 'SOUTH POKE'	£150	£300
G1/G8 *Set of* 8			13·00	27·00
G1s/G8s Perf 'SPECIMEN' *Set of* 8			£1100	

* This is the date of issue for South Georgia. Nos. G1/G8 were released in London on 11 February.

Nos. G1/G8

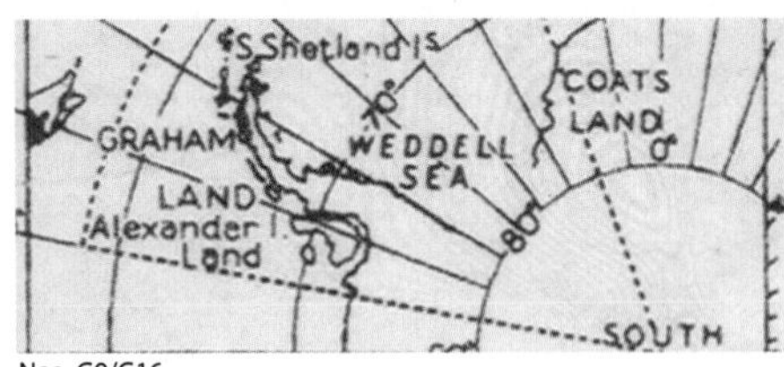

Nos. G9/G16

On Nos. G9 to G16 the map is redrawn; the '0°' meridian does not pass through the 'S' of 'COATS', the 'n' of 'Alexander' is not joined to the 'L' of 'Land' below, and the loops of letters 's' and 't' are generally more open.

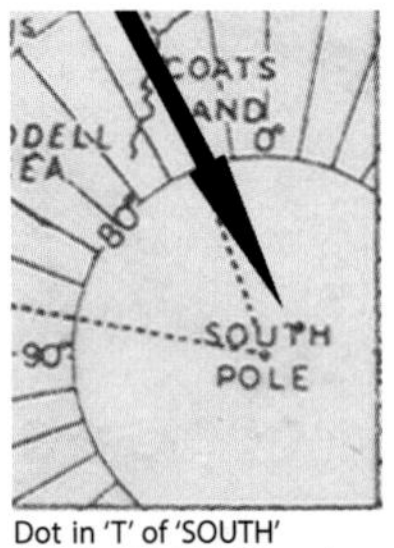

Dot in 'T' of 'SOUTH' (R. 5/2, 5/4, 5/6, 5/8 and 5/10)

(b) Map thin and clear (16.2.48)

G9	G **1**	½d. black and green	2·25	18·00
		a. Recess frame printed double, one albino and inverted	£2500	
		b. Dot in 'T'	7·50	50·00
G10		1d. black and violet	1·50	22·00
		a. Dot in 'T'	7·00	65·00
G11		2d. black and carmine	2·75	28·00
		a. Dot in 'T'	9·00	85·00
G11*b*		2½d. black and deep blue (6.3.49)	6·50	4·00
G12		3d. black and blue	2·75	4·00
		a. Dot in 'T'	9·00	15·00
		b. 'Teardrop'	£160	£190
G13		4d. black and claret	17·00	32·00
		a. Dot in 'T'	45·00	95·00
G14		6d. black and orange	26·00	7·00
		a. Dot in 'T'	55·00	23·00
G15		9d. black and brown	26·00	7·00
		a. Dot in 'T'	55·00	23·00
G16		1s. black and purple	26·00	7·00
		a. Dot in 'T'	55·00	23·00
G9/G16 *Set of* 9			£100	£110

Nos. G11, G12 and G13 are known with the map apparently printed double. These are not true 'double prints', in that they were not the result of two impressions of the inked printing plate, but were caused by incorrect tension in the rubber 'blanket' which transferred ink from the cylinder to the paper. Such varieties are outside the scope of this catalogue.

1946 (4 Oct*). Victory. As Nos. 110/111 of Antigua.

G17	1d. deep violet	50	50
G18	3d. blue	75	50
G17s/G18s Perf 'SPECIMEN' *Set of* 2		£375	

* This is the date of issue for South Georgia. The stamps were placed on sale from the South Orkneys on 17 January 1947, from the South Shetlands on 30 January 1947 and from Graham Land on 10 February 1947.

1948 (6 Dec). Royal Silver Wedding. As Nos. 112/113 of Antigua, but 1s. country name in recess.

G19	2½d. ultramarine	1·75	3·00
G20	1s. violet-blue	1·75	2·50

1949 (10 Oct). 75th Anniversary of UPU As Nos. 114/117 of Antigua.

G21	1d. violet	1·00	4·00
G22	2d. carmine-red	5·00	4·00
G23	3d. deep blue	3·50	1·25
G24	6d. red-orange	4·00	3·00
G21/G24 *Set of 4*		12·00	11·00

1953 (4 June). Coronation. As No. 120 of Antigua.

G25	1d. black and violet	1·10	1·25

G **2** *John Biscoe I*, 1947–1952

G **3** *Trepassey*, 1945–1947

G **4** *Wyatt Earp*, 1934–1936

G **5** *Eagle*, 1944–1945

G **6** *Penola*, 1934–1937

G **7** *Discovery II*, 1929–1937

G **8** *William Scoresby*, 1926–1946

G **9** *Discovery*, 1925–1927

G **10** *Endurance*, 1914–1916

G **11** *Deutschland*, 1910–1912

G **12** *Pourquoi-pas?*, 1908–1910

G **13** *Français*, 1903–1905

G **14** *Scotia*, 1902–1904

G **15** *Antarctic*, 1901–1903

G **16** *Belgica* 1897–1999

Normal

Retouch (R 12/1)

1d. There are a number of retouches of the cross-hatching in the clouds where lines have been deepened. The one illustrated is on left pane R. 12/1 and other prominent retouches occur on left pane R. 8/1 and R. 10/1 but there are other less marked ones.

(Recess Waterlow, then D.L.R. (from 27.3.62))

1954 (1 Feb)–**62**. T G **2/16**. Wmk Mult Script CA. P 12½.

G26	G **2**	½d. black and bluish green	1·00	5·00
		a. Black and deep green (D.L.R.) (17.4.62)	10·00	42·00
G27	G **3**	1d. black and sepia-brown	1·75	3·00
		a. Retouches to cross-hatching *from*	12·00	
		b. Black and sepia (D.L.R.) (27.3.62)	17·00	42·00
		ba. Retouches to cross-hatching *from*	50·00	
G28	G **4**	1½d. black and olive	2·50	4·50
		a. Black and yellow-olive (D.L.R.) (21.9.62)	10·00	4·00
G29	G **5**	2d. black and rose-red	3·25	4·25
G30	G **6**	2½d. black and yellow-ochre	1·25	35
G31	G **7**	3d. black and deep bright blue	1·75	35
G32	G **8**	4d. black and bright reddish purple	6·00	3·75
G33	G **9**	6d. black and deep lilac	7·50	3·75
G34	G **10**	9d. black	6·50	5·00
G35	G **11**	1s. black and brown	5·00	4·00
G36	G **12**	2s. black and carmine	19·00	24·00
G37	G **13**	2s.6d. black and pale turquoise	24·00	12·00
G38	G **14**	5s. black and violet	42·00	14·00
G39	G **15**	10s. black and blue	65·00	28·00
G40	G **16**	£1 black	80·00	38·00
G26/G40 *Set of 15*			£225	£130

TRANS-ANTARCTIC EXPEDITION 1955-1958
(G **17**)

1956 (30 Jan). Trans-Antarctic Expedition. Nos. G27, G30/G31 and G33 optd with T G **17**.

G41	1d. black and sepia-brown	10	50
	a. Retouches to cross-hatching.... *from*	10·00	
G42	2½d. black and yellow-ochre	50	70
G43	3d. black and deep bright blue	50	30
G44	6d. black and deep lilac	50	30
G41/G44 *Set of 4*		1·40	1·60

The stamps of Falkland Islands Dependencies were withdrawn on 16 July 1963 after Coats Land, Graham Land, South Orkneys and South Shetlands had become a separate colony, known as British Antarctic Territory.

F. SOUTH GEORGIA

From 17 July 1963 South Georgia and South Sandwich Islands used stamps inscribed 'South Georgia'.

1 Reindeer

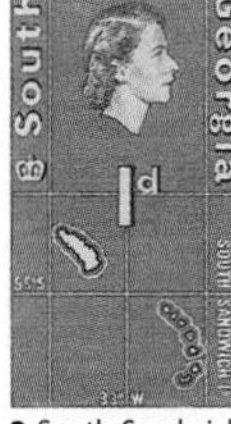
2 South Sandwich Islands

3 Sperm Whale

4 Chinstrap and King Penguins

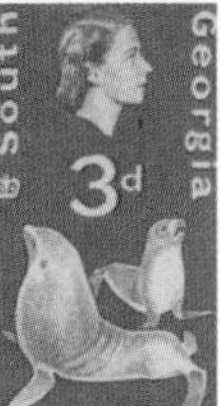
5 South American Fur Seal

6 Fin Whale

7 Southern Elephant-seal

8 Light-mantled Sooty Albatross

9 *R2* (Whale catcher)

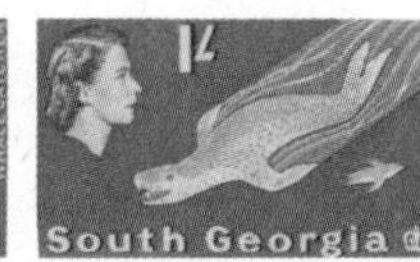
10 Leopard Seal

11 Shackleton's Cross

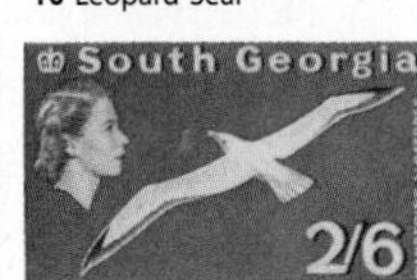
12 Wandering Albatross

13 Southern Elephant-seal and South American Fur Seal

14 Plankton and Krill

15 Blue Whale

16 King Penguins

(Des D.L.R. (No. 16), M. Goaman (others). Recess D.L.R.)

1963 (17 July)–**69**. T **1/16**. Ordinary or glazed paper (No. 16). W w **12**. P 15.

1	**1**	½d. brown-red	50	1·25
		a. Perf 14×15 (13.2.67)	70	1·50
2	**2**	1d. violet-blue	2·75	1·25
3	**3**	2d. turquoise-blue	1·25	1·25
4	**4**	2½d. black	6·00	2·50
5	**5**	3d. bistre	2·50	30
6	**6**	4d. bronze-green	5·50	1·50
7	**7**	5½d. deep violet	2·00	30
8	**8**	6d. orange	75	50
9	**9**	9d. blue	7·50	2·00
10	**10**	1s. purple	75	30
11	**11**	2s. yellow-olive and light blue	27·00	7·00
12	**12**	2s.6d. blue	25·00	4·00
13	**13**	5s. orange-brown	22·00	4·00
14	**14**	10s. magenta	48·00	15·00
15	**15**	£1 ultramarine	90·00	48·00
16	**16**	£1 grey-black (1.12.69)	8·00	13·00
1/16 *Set of 16*			£200	90·00

1970 (22 Jan). As No. 1, but wmk w **12** sideways and on glazed paper.

17	½d. brown-red	1·50	2·25

Faröe Islands
UNDER BRITISH OCCUPATION

The Faröe islands were under British administration from 12 April 1940 to 1945 to prevent their seizure by the Germans, who had occupied Denmark.

Types of Denmark overprinted

43

44

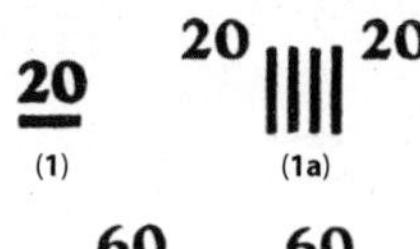

(1) (1a)

60 60

(1b)

1940 (2 Nov)–**41**. T **44** of Denmark, surch with T **1** by H. N. Jacobsen, Tórshavn.

1		20ö. on 15ö. scarlet (II)	60·00	10·00
		a. Surcharge bar omitted (4.41)	—	£650
		aa. Do. Surch double	—	£750

No. 1a is from proof sheets (200 stamps), later sold over PO counter. Nearly all copies were used.

1940–41. T **43** of Denmark, surch by H. N. Jacobsen, Tórshavn, with T **1a** (No. 3) or as T **1b** (others).

2		20ö. on 1ö. blackish green (B.) (2.5.41)	30·00	35·00
3		20ö. on 5ö. maroon (B.) (17.3.41)	20·00	12·00
4		50ö. on 5ö. maroon (6.12.40)	£200	35·00
5		60ö. on 6ö. orange (21.12.40)	90·00	£100

During a shortage of stamps in May and June 1941 circular post paid cancellations were used inscribed 'FAERØERNE FRANCO-BETALT' and the value in the centre: 5, 10 or 20 ØRE and also with the centre blank and a higher value inserted by hand. These are mainly seen on clippings from money order forms but are very rare on complete covers.

Fiji

PRICES FOR STAMPS ON COVER TO 1945

Nos. 1/9	*from* × 8
Nos. 10/34	*from* × 5
Nos. 35/59	*from* × 8
Nos. 60/63	—
Nos. 64/69	*from* × 20
Nos. 70/75	*from* × 5
Nos. 76/103	*from* × 8
Nos. 104/114	*from* × 5
Nos. 115/124	*from* × 4
Nos. 125/137	*from* × 3
Nos. 138/241	*from* × 4
Nos. 242/245	*from* × 3
Nos. 246/248	*from* × 8
Nos. 249/266*b*	*from* × 2
No. 267	*from* × 8
Nos. D1/D5c	*from* × 6
Nos. D6/D10	*from* × 20
Nos. D11/D18	*from* × 15

King Cakobau 1852–Oct 1874

Christian missionaries reached Fiji in 1835 and early letters are known to and from their mission stations, sent via Sydney, Hobart or Auckland.

In 1852 Cakobau, the chief of the island of Bau, declared himself King of Fiji and converted to Christianity two years later. Internal problems and difficulties with the American government led the king to offer to cede Fiji to Great Britain. The offer was refused, but resulted in the appointment of a British Consul in 1858. A Consular Post Office operated from September 1858 until 1872 and franked mail with New South Wales stamps from 1863.

The destruction of plantations in the Confederacy during the American Civil War led to an increased demand for Fijian cotton and this upsurge in commercial activity encouraged *The Fiji Times* newspaper on Levuka to establish a postal service on 1 November 1870.

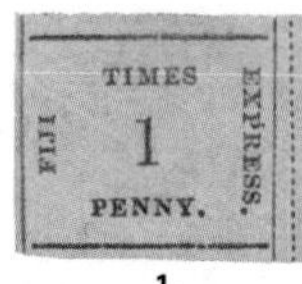

1

(Type-set and printed at the office of *The Fiji Times*, Levuka, Ovalau, Fiji)

1870 (1 Nov)–**71**. Rouletted in the printing.

(a) Thin Quadrillé paper

1	**1**	1d. black/*rose*	£4500	£4750
2		3d. black/*rose*	£5500	£5000
		a. Comma after 'EXPRESS' (R. 4/4)	£8000	£8000
3		6d. black/*rose*	£3000	£3000
4		1s. black/*rose*	£2250	£2500

(b) Thin vertically ribbed paper (1871)

5	**1**	1d. black/*rose*	£1100	£2000
		a. Vert strip of 4. Nos. 5, 7/9	£45000	
6		3d. black/*rose*	£1800	£3250
7		6d. black/*rose*	£1500	£2000
8		9d. black/*rose*	£3250	£3750
		a. Comma after 'EXPRESS' (R. 4/4)	£4250	
9		1s. black/*rose*	£1800	£1800

Nos. 1/4 were printed *se-tenant* as a sheet of 24 (6×4) with the 6d. stamps in the first horizontal row, the 1s. in the second, the 1d. in the third and the 3d. in the fourth. Nos. 5/9 were produced from the same plate on which three of the 3d. impressions had been replaced with three 9d. values.

The paper used for Nos. 1/4 shows a quadrillé watermark pattern comprising 3.7 mm squares. That used for Nos. 5/9 shows a pattern of vertical lines 1mm apart usually with thickened lines at 8.5 mm intervals. Stamps without the additional thickened lines are worth a premium.

The issued stamps showed the vertical frame lines continuous from top to bottom of the sheet with the horizontal rules broken and not touching the verticals. Used examples are cancelled in manuscript, by an Australian arrival mark or by the star cancellation used at Bua.

It should be noted that the initial rose colour of the papers has faded significantly in the majority of stamps found today.

There are no reprints of these stamps, but the 1d., 3d., 6d. and 1s. are known in the correct type on *yellow wove* paper and are believed to be proofs.

There are also three different sets of imitations made by the proprietors of *The Fiji Times* to meet the demands of collectors:—

The first was produced in 1876 on *white wove* paper, surfaced to simulate the appearance of vertically ribbed when viewed with light reflecting off its surface. Rouletted on dotted lines and arranged in sheets of 40 (5 rows of 8) comprising 1d., 3d., 6d., 9d. and 1s.; the horizontal frame lines are continuous and the vertical ones broken.

The second was produced before 1888 on *thick rosy mauve wove* paper, rouletted on dotted lines and arranged in sheets of 30 (5 rows of 6) comprising 1s., 9d., 6d., 3d. and 1d.; the vertical frame lines are continuous and the horizontal ones broken.

The third only came to light in the 1960s and is rare, only one complete sheet being recorded, which has since been destroyed. The sheet arrangement is the same as Nos. 1/4, which suggests that this was the first imitation to be produced. It is on *off-white wove* paper, rouletted on closely dotted or solid lines, with vertical frame lines continuous and the horizontal ones broken, as in the originals. These differ from the proofs mentioned above in that the lettering is slightly larger and the figures also differ.

King Cakobau established a formal government in June 1871 and stamps for the royal post office were ordered from Sydney. These arrived in October 1871 and the postal service was placed on a firm basis by the First Postal Act in December of that year. Under its terms *The Fiji Times* service closed on 17 January 1872 and the British Consular Post Office followed six months later.

2

3

Two

Cents

(4)

(Eng and electrotyped by A. L. Jackson. Typo Govt Printing Office, Sydney)

1871 (Oct). Wove paper. Wmk impressed 'FIJI POSTAGE' in small sans serif capitals across the middle row of stamps in the sheet. P 12½.

10	**2**	1d. blue	60·00	£120
11		3d. pale yellow-green	£120	£350
12	**3**	6d. rose	£160	£300

The 3d. differs from T **2** in having a white circle containing square dots surrounding the centre.

All three values are known *imperf*, but were not issued in that condition.

See notes after No. 33b.

1872 (13 Jan). Surch as T **4**, in local currency, by Govt Ptg Office, Sydney.

13	**2**	2c. on 1d. pale blue	60·00	65·00
		a. Deep blue	55·00	55·00
14		6c. on 3d. yellow-green	85·00	85·00
15	**3**	12c. on 6d. carmine-rose	£120	85·00

CROWN COLONY

King Cakobau renewed his offer to cede Fiji to Great Britain and this took place on 12 October 1874.

V.R. (5) V.R. (6) 2d. (7)

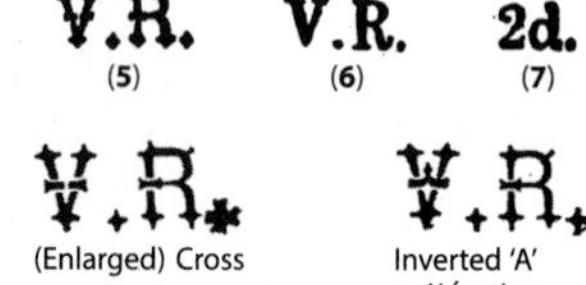

(Enlarged) Cross Inverted 'A' pattée stop

Cross pattée stop after 'R' (R. 3/6).
Round raised stop after 'V' (R. 3/8)
Round raised stops after 'V' and 'R' (R. 3/9).
Inverted 'A' for 'V' (R. 3/10).
No stop after 'R' (R. 2/3 on T **5**, R. 5/3 on T **6**).
Large stop after 'R' (R. 5/10).

(Optd at *Polynesian Gazette* Office, Levuka)

1874 (21 Oct). Nos. 13/15 optd.

*(a) With T **5***

16	**2**	2c. on 1d. blue	£1100	£300
		a. No stop after 'R'	£3250	£1000
		b. Cross pattée stop after 'R'	£3250	£1000
		c. Round raised stop after 'V'	£3250	£1000
		d. Round raised stops after 'V' and 'R'	£3250	£1000
		e. Inverted 'A' for 'V'	£3250	£1000
17		6c. on 3d. green	£2000	£700
		a. No stop after 'R'	£5500	£1800
		b. Cross pattée stop after 'R'	£5500	£1800
		c. Round raised stop after 'V'	£5500	£1800
		d. Round raised stops after 'V' and 'R'	£5500	£1800
		e. Inverted 'A' for 'V'	£5500	£1800
		f. Vert pair. Nos. 17 and 20	£14000	
18	**3**	12c. on 6d. rose	£900	£250
		a. No stop after 'R'	£3000	£1000
		b. Cross pattée stop after 'R'	£3000	£1000
		c. Round raised stop after 'V'	£3000	£1000
		d. Round raised stops after 'V' and 'R'	£3000	£1000
		e. Inverted 'A' for 'V'	£3000	£1000
		f. Opt inverted	—	£5500
		g. Vert pair. Nos. 18 and 21	£7500	

*(b) With T **6***

19	**2**	2c. on 1d. blue	£1200	£325
		a. No stop after 'R'	£3250	£1000
		f. Large stop after 'R'	—	£1000
20		6c. on 3d. green	£2500	£950
		a. No stop after 'R'	£5500	£1800
21	**3**	12c. on 6d. rose	£1000	£275
		a. No stop after 'R'	£3000	£1000
		b. Opt inverted	£7000	

Nos. 16/21 were produced in sheets of 50 (10×5) of which the top three rows were overprinted with T **5** and the lower two with T **6**.

1875. Stamps of 1874 surch at *Polynesian Gazette* Office, Levuka, with T **7**.

(a) In red (Apr)

22	**2**	2d. on 6c. on 3d. green (No. 17)	£750	£225
		a. No stop after 'R'	£2250	£800
		b. Cross pattée stop after 'R'	£2250	£800
		c. Round raised stop after 'V'	£2250	£800
		d. Round raised stops after 'V' and 'R'	£2250	£800
		e. Inverted 'A' for 'V'	£2250	£800
		f. No stop after '2d' (R. 1/2)	£2250	£800
		g. Vert pair. Nos. 22/23	£6500	
23		2d. on 6c. on 3d. green (No. 20)	£900	£275
		a. No stop after 'R'	£2250	£800
		b. Stop between '2' and 'd' (R. 5/7)	£2250	£800

(b) In black (30 Sept)

24	**2**	2d. on 6c. on 3d. green (No. 17)	£1900	£600
		a. No stop after 'R'	£4750	£1500
		b. Cross pattée stop after 'R'	£4750	£1500
		c. Round raised stop after 'V'	£4750	£1500
		d. Round raised stops after 'V' and 'R'	£4750	£1500
		e. Inverted 'A' for 'V'	£4750	£1500
		f. No stop after '2d' (R. 1/2)	£4750	£1500
		g. 'V.R.' double		
		h. Vert pair. Nos. 24/25	£13000	
25		2d. on 6c. on 3d. green (No. 20)	£2500	£800
		a. No stop after 'R'	£4750	£1500

		b. Stop between '2' and 'd' (R. 5/7)	£4750	£1500
		c. 'V.R.' double	£5500	£4500

1875 (20 Nov). No. 15 surch at *Polynesian Gazette* Office, Levuka, with T **7** and 'V.R.' at one operation.

(a) 'V.R.' T **5**

26	**3**	2d. on 12c. on 6d. rose	£2750	£850
		a. No stop after 'R'	—	£2250
		b. Round raised stop after 'R'	—	£1600
		c. Inverted 'A' for 'V' (R. 1/3, 2/8, 4/4)	£4250	£1300
		d. Do. and round raised stop after 'V' (R. 3/3, 3/6, 3/8, 3/10)	£4000	£1100
		e. As 'c' and round raised stops after 'R' and 'V' (R. 3/2, 3/9)	£4500	£1400
		f. Surch double	—	£4750
		g. Vert pair. Nos. 26/7	£14000	

(b) 'V.R.' T **6**

27	**3**	2d. on 12c. on 6d. rose	£3000	£900
		a. Surch double	—	£5500

The setting used for Nos. 26/27 was similar to that of Nos. 16/21, but the fourth stamp in the fourth row had a T **5** 'V.R.' instead of a T **6**.

The position of No. 26b is not known.

(8) **Two Pence** **(9)**

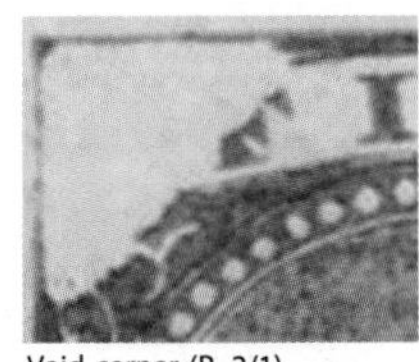
Void corner (R. 2/1)

(Typo Govt Printing Office, Sydney, from plates of 1871)

1876–77. On paper previously lithographed 'VR' as T **8**, the 3d. surch with T **9**. P 12½.

(a) Wove paper (31.1.76)

28	**2**	1d. grey-blue	55·00	55·00
		a. Dull blue	55·00	55·00
		b. Doubly printed	£550	
		c. Void corner	£750	£425
		d. Imperf vert (horiz pair)	£850	
29		2d. on 3d. pale green	60·00	60·00
		a. Deep green	55·00	60·00
30	**3**	6d. pale rose	70·00	70·00
		a. Dull rose	60·00	60·00
		b. Carmine-rose	60·00	60·00
		c. Doubly printed	£2500	

(b) Laid paper (5.1.77)

31	**2**	1d. blue	35·00	50·00
		a. Deep blue	35·00	50·00
		b. Void corner (R. 2/1)	£400	£350
		c. Imperf vert (horiz pair)	£700	
32		2d. on 3d. yellow-green	75·00	80·00
		a. Deep yellow-green	70·00	75·00
		b. Imperf between (pair)	£850	
		c. Perf 10	£375	
		ca. Imperf vert (horiz pair)	£950	
		d. Perf 11	£350	
33	**3**	6d. rose	55·00	38·00
		a. Carmine-rose	55·00	42·00
		b. Imperf vert (horiz pair)	£700	

The extent of the void area on Nos. 28c and 31b varies.

The 3d. *green* is known without the surcharge T **9** on wove paper and also without the surcharge and the monogram. In this latter condition it can only be distinguished from No. 11 by its colour, which is a fuller, deeper yellow-green.

Stamps on both wove and laid paper *imperf* are from printer's trial or waste sheets and were not issued.

All values are known on laid paper without the monogram 'VR' and the 3d. stamp also without the surcharge but these are also believed to be from printer's trial sheets which were never issued for postal purposes. Being on laid paper they are easily distinguishable from Nos. 10/12.

1877 (12 Oct). Optd with T **8** and surch as T **9**. Laid paper. P 12½.

34	**2**	4d. on 3d. mauve	£100	26·00
		a. Imperf vert (horiz pair)	£1000	

10

11

Four Pence
A

Four Pence
B

Type A: Length 12½ mm
Type B: Length 14 mm
Note also the different shape of the two 'e's.

(Typo from new plates made from original dies of 1871 with 'CR' altered to 'VR' at Govt Printing Office, Sydney. 2d. and 4d. made from old 3d. die.)

1878–99. Surcharges as T **9** or as Types A or B for 4d. value. Wove unwatermarked paper, or with paper-maker's name 'T. H. SAUNDERS', 'E. D. & Co. SUPERFINE', 'IMPERIAL LINEN' or 'SANDERSON' in double-lined capitals extending over a varying number of stamps in each full sheet, the last being accompanied by an ornamental crown and shield.

(a) P 12½ (1878–1880)

35	**10**	1d. pale ultramarine (19.2.79)	21·00	20·00
		a. Ultramarine	22·00	20·00
36		2d. on 3d. green (17.10.78)	12·00	45·00
37		2d. yellow-green (1.9.79)	48·00	21·00
		a. Blue-green	60·00	26·00
		b. Error. Ultramarine	£40000	
38	**11**	6d. rose (30.7.80)	£110	35·00

(b) P 10 (1881–1890)

39	**10**	1d. dull blue (11.5.82)	60·00	3·00
		a. Ultramarine	32·00	3·00
		b. Cambridge blue (12.7.83)	60·00	4·25
40		2d. yellow-green (20.10.81)	48·00	1·00
		a. Blue-green	55·00	5·50
41		4d. on 1d. mauve (29.1.90)	75·00	55·00
42		4d. on 2d. pale mauve (A) (23.5.83)	90·00	15·00
		a. Dull purple	90·00	15·00
43		4d. on 2d. dull purple (B) (7.11.88)	—	£140
44		4d. mauve (13.9.90)	80·00	
		a. Deep purple	80·00	75·00
45	**11**	6d. pale rose (11.3.85)	75·00	35·00
		a. Bright rose	32·00	32·00

(c) P 10×12½ (1881–1882)

46	**10**	1d. ultramarine (11.5.82)	£190	50·00
47		2d. green (20.10.81)	£160	60·00
48	**11**	6d. rose (20.10.81)	£350	55·00
		a. Pale rose	£350	55·00

(d) P 12½×10 (1888–1890)

49	**10**	1d. ultramarine (1890)	—	£350
49*a*		2d. green (1888)		
49*b*		4d. on 2d. dull purple (A)	†	—

(e) P 10×11¾ (3.9.86)

50	**10**	1d. dull blue	£100	25·00
		a. Ultramarine		
51		2d. yellow-green	70·00	15·00

(f) P 11¾×10 (1886–1888)

51*a*	**10**	1d. dull blue (7.11.88)	£225	55·00
		ab. Ultramarine		
51*b*		2d. yellow-green (3.9.86)	—	£550
52	**11**	6d. rose (1887)	†	£850

(g) P 11×10 (1892–1893)

53	**10**	1d. ultramarine (18.8.92)	35·00	23·00
54		4d. pale mauve (18.8.92)	24·00	38·00
55	**11**	6d. pale rose (14.2.93)	27·00	22·00
		a. Rose	25·00	28·00

(h) P 11 (1897–1899)

56	**10**	4d. mauve (14.7.96)	42·00	11·00
57	**11**	6d. dull rose (14.7.96)	50·00	60·00
		a. Printed both sides (12.99)	£2250	£1700
		b. Bright rose	75·00	80·00

*(i) P 11×11¾ (1896)**

58	**10**	4d. deep purple (14.7.96)	60·00	
		a. Bright purple	15·00	7·00
59	**11**	6d. rose (23.7.96)	50·00	
		a. Bright rose	15·00	3·75

(j) Imperf (pairs) (1882–1890)

60	**10**	1d. ultramarine		
61		2d. yellow-green		
62		4d. on 2d. pale mauve		
63	**11**	6d. rose	—	£1800

* Under this heading are included stamps from several perforating machines with a gauge varying between 11.6 and 12.

No. 37b was printed in the colour of the 1d. in error. Only four examples have been reported, one of which was subsequently destroyed.

In the absence of detailed information on dates of issue, printing dates are quoted for Nos. 35/63 and 76/103.

12

13

(Des T. Richards, Eng A. L. Jackson. Typo Govt Printing Office, Sydney)

1881–99. Paper-maker's name wmkd as previous issue.

(a) P 10 (19.10.81)

64	**12**	1s. pale brown	95·00	32·00
		a. Deep brown	95·00	35·00

(b) P 11×10 (1894)

65	**12**	1s. pale brown	60·00	55·00

(c) P 11 (1897)

66	**12**	1s. pale brown	55·00	15·00

(d) P 11×11¾ (5.99)

67	**12**	1s. pale brown	55·00	12·00
		a. Brown	55·00	12·00
		b. Deep brown	65·00	50·00

(e) P 11¾×11 (3.3.97)

68	**12**	1s. brown	70·00	55·00

Dates given of earliest known use.
Forgeries exist.

Red arc above 'FIJI' (R. 1/4)

(Centre typo, frame litho Govt Printing Office, Sydney)

1882 (23 May). Toned paper wmkd with paper-maker's name 'Cowan' in old English outline type once in each sheet. P 10.

69	**13**	5s. dull red and black	70·00	32·00
		a. Red arc above 'FIJI'	£550	£250

An unknown quantity of the 1s. and 264 sheets (13,200 stamps) of the 5s., both perf 10 and imperf, were cancelled by the Fiji Post Office and sold as remainders. A number of different 'SUVA' remainder cancellations have been recorded between '15 DEC 00' and '21 DE 1902'.

An electrotyped plate was also produced for the frame of the 5s. This printing was not used for postal purposes but examples were included among the remainders, all cancelled '15 DEC 00'. The electrotyped printing, in dull orange and black, is on paper watermarked 'NEW SOUTH WALES GOVERNMENT', either upright or sideways in double-line capitals and perforated 11½ - 11¾. Apart from the colour of the medallion, it differs in a number of respects from the original, most notably in the circular frame surrounding the Queen's head, which is notably thicker than the litho printing. Examples are rare.

2½d. **(14)** 2½d. **(15)**

Types **14** (fraction bar 1 *mm* from '2') and **15** (fraction bar 2 *mm* from '2') are from the same setting of 50 (10×5) with T **15** occurring on R. 1/2, 2/2, 3/2 and 4/2.

(Stamps typo in Sydney and surch at Govt Printing Office, Suva)

1891 (1 Jan). T **10** surch. P 10.

70	**14**	2½d. on 2d. green	50·00	50·00
71	**15**	2½d. on 2d. green	£130	£140

½d. **(16)** 5d **(17)**

FIVE PENCE **(18)** 2 mm spacing

FIVE PENCE **(19)** 3 mm spacing

1892 (1 Mar)–**93.** P 10.

(a) Surch on T **10**

72	**16**	½d. on 1d. dull blue	60·00	80·00
		a. Ultramarine	60·00	75·00
73	**17**	5d. on 4d. deep purple (25.7.92)	60·00	75·00
		a. Dull purple	60·00	75·00

(b) Surch on T **11**

74	**18**	5d. on 6d. brownish rose (30.11.92)	65·00	75·00
		a. Bright rose	60·00	70·00
		b. Perf 10×12½		
75	**19**	5d. on 6d. rose (4.1.93)	80·00	95·00
		a. Deep rose	70·00	85·00
		b. Brownish rose	75·00	

20

21 Native Canoe

22

(Typo in Sydney)

1891–8. Wmk in sheet, either 'SANDERSON' or 'NEW SOUTH WALES GOVERNMENT' in outline capitals.

(a) P 10 (1891–1894)

76	**20**	½d. slate-grey (26.4.92)	7·00	11·00
77	**21**	1d. black (19.9.94)	32·00	6·50
78		2d. pale green (19.9.94)	£140	23·00
79	**22**	2½d. chocolate (8.6.91)	60·00	29·00
80	**21**	5d. ultramarine (14.2.93)	£120	60·00

(b) P 11×10 (1892–1893)

81	**20**	½d. slate-grey (20.10.93)	17·00	35·00
82	**21**	1d. black (14.2.93)	21·00	9·00
83		2d. green (14.2.93)	35·00	10·00
84	**22**	2½d. chocolate (17.8.92)	35·00	50·00
		a. Brown	12·00	20·00
		b. Yellowish brown		
85	**21**	5d. ultramarine (14.2.93)	26·00	7·50

(c) P 11 (1893–1896)

86	**20**	½d. slate-grey (2.6.96)	4·00	6·50
		a. Greenish slate	2·50	6·50
87	**21**	1d. black (31.10.95)	23·00	8·00
88		1d. pale mauve (2.6.96)	23·00	1·00
		a. Rosy mauve	24·00	1·00
89		2d. dull green (17.3.94)	8·50	80
		a. Emerald-green	12·00	2·00
90	**22**	2½d. brown (31.10.95)	55·00	20·00
		a. Yellowish brown	30·00	35·00
91	**21**	5d. ultramarine (14.2.93)	£170	

(d) P 10×11¾ (1893–1894)

92	**20**	½d. greenish slate	£1000	£750
93	**21**	1d. black (20.7.93)	50·00	6·50
94		2d. dull green (19.9.94)	£800	£400

(e) P 11¾×10 (19.9.94)

94*a*	**20**	½d. greenish slate	—	£1000

(f) P 11¾ (1894–1898)

95	**20**	½d. greenish slate (19.9.94)	3·75	12·00
		a. Grey	50·00	
96	**21**	1d. black (19.9.94)	£225	50·00
97		1d. rosy mauve (4.5.98)	18·00	8·00
98		2d. dull green (19.9.94)	£120	55·00

(g) P 11×11¾ (1895–1897)

99	**20**	½d. greenish slate (8.10.97)	1·00	4·75
100	**21**	1d. black (31.10.95)	£3000	£1500
101		1d. rosy mauve (14.7.96)	12·00	1·00
		a. Pale rosy mauve	4·50	2·00
102		2d. dull green (26.7.97)	55·00	4·00
103	**22**	2½d. brown (26.7.97)	18·00	27·00
		a. Yellow-brown	9·00	5·00

(h) P 11¾×11 (1897–1898)

103*b*	**20**	½d. greenish slate (8.10.97)	9·50	20·00
103*c*	**21**	1d. rosy mauve (10.2.97)	28·00	7·00
103*d*		2d. dull green (4.5.98) (*shades*)	£375	£100

The 2½d. brown is known doubly printed, but only occurs in the remainders and with the special obliteration (*Price* £180 *cancelled-to-order*). It was never issued for postal use.

23

24

(Typo D.L.R.)

1903 (1 Feb). Wmk Crown CA. P 14.

104	23	½d. green and pale green	3·00	2·25
105		1d. dull purple and black/*red*	20·00	55
106	24	2d. dull purple and orange	3·75	1·25
107	23	2½d. dull purple and blue/*blue*	14·00	1·50
108		3d. dull purple and purple	1·50	2·25
109	24	4d. dull purple and black	1·50	2·25
110	23	5d. dull purple and green	1·50	2·00
111	24	6d. dull purple and carmine	1·50	1·75
112	23	1s. green and carmine	18·00	80·00
113	24	5s. green and black	80·00	£160
114	23	£1 grey-black and ultramarine (*shades*)	£375	£500
104/114 *Set of* 11			£450	£700
104s/114s Optd 'SPECIMEN' *Set of* 11			£325	

1904–09. Wmk Mult Crown CA. Chalk-surfaced paper (1s.). P 14.

115	23	½d. green and pale green	18·00	3·00
116		1d. purple and black/*red*	38·00	10
117		1s. green and carmine (1909)	30·00	40·00
115/117 *Set of* 3			75·00	40·00

1906–12. Colours changed. Wmk Mult Crown CA. Chalk surfaced paper (6d. to £1). P 14.

118	23	½d. green (1908)	12·00	3·25
119		1d. red (1906)	23·00	10
		w. Wmk inverted	†	—
120		2½d. bright blue (1910)	7·00	10·00
121	24	6d. dull purple (1910)	32·00	48·00
122	23	1s. black/*green* (1911)	11·00	17·00
123	24	5s. green and red/*yellow* (1911)	70·00	£100
124	23	£1 purple and black/*red* (1912)	£300	£275
118/124 *Set of* 7			£400	£400
119s/124s Optd 'SPECIMEN' *Set of* 6			£375	

Nos. 112/114, 117 and 120/124 are known with a forged registered postmark of Suva dated '10 DEC 1909'.

25

26

WAR STAMP
(27)

(Typo D.L.R.)

1912 (Oct)–**23.** Die I. Wmk Mult Crown CA. Chalk-surfaced paper (5d. to £1). P 14.

125	26	¼d. brown (21.3.16)	2·50	30
		a. Deep brown (1917)	1·50	40
		y. Wmk inverted and reversed		
126	25	½d. green	4·50	1·00
		a. Yellow-green (1916)	10·00	8·50
		b. Blue-green (1917)	4·50	50
		w. Wmk inverted	£225	
		y. Wmk inverted and reversed	£180	
127		1d. carmine	3·75	10
		a. Bright scarlet (1916)	2·25	75
		ax. Wmk reversed	†	—
		b. Deep rose (1916)	12·00	2·00
		bw. Wmk inverted	†	—
128	26	2d. greyish slate (5.14)	1·75	10
		a. Wmk sideways		
		b. 'C' of 'CA' missing from wmk	†	—
		w. Wmk inverted	—	£350
129	25	2½d. bright blue (5.14)	3·00	3·50
130		3d. purple/*yellow* (5.14)	4·25	13·00
		a. Wmk sideways	£350	£500
		b. On lemon (1915)	2·25	8·50
		c. On pale yellow (1921)	3·75	21·00
		ca. 'A' of 'CA' missing from wmk		
		cw. Wmk inverted		
		d. Die II. *On pale yellow* (1922)	3·25	24·00
131	26	4d. black and red/*yellow* (5.14)	23·00	21·00
		a. On lemon	3·00	16·00
		b. On orange-buff (1920)	50·00	65·00
		c. On pale yellow (1921)	6·50	14·00
		cw. Wmk inverted	£475	
		d. Die II. *On pale yellow* (1922)	3·00	35·00
		ds. Optd 'SPECIMEN'	50·00	
132	25	5d. dull purple and olive-green (5.14)	4·75	11·00
133	26	6d. dull and bright purple (5.14)	2·00	5·50
134	25	1s. black/*green*	1·50	14·00
		a. White back (4.14)	1·00	17·00
		b. On blue-green, olive back (1916)	3·00	10·00
		c. On emerald back (1921)	4·50	65·00
		cs. Optd SPECIMEN'	60·00	
		d. Die II. *On emerald back* (1922)	2·25	38·00
135	26	2s.6d. black and red/*blue* (19.1.16)	32·00	30·00
136		5s. green and red/*yellow*	32·00	35·00
137	25	£1 purple and black/*red* (5.14)	£275	£325
		a. Die II (1923)	£250	£325
125/137 *Set of* 13			£300	£400
125s/137s Optd 'SPECIMEN' *Set of* 13			£500	

Bold 'TA' (left pane, R. 5/4)

1915 (1 Dec)–**19.** Optd with T **27** by Govt Printer, Suva.

138	25	½d. green		
		a. Yellow-green (1916)	2·00	13·00
		b. Blue-green (1917)	1·50	6·00
		c. Opt inverted	£650	
		d. Opt double		
		e. Bold 'TA'	£130	
139		1d. carmine	45·00	26·00
		a. Bright scarlet	4·00	75
		ab. Horiz pair, one without opt	£6500	
		ac. Opt inverted	£700	
		d. Deep rose (1919)	8·50	3·25
		e. Bold 'TA'	£250	£225
138s/139s H/S 'SPECIMEN' *Set of* 2			£140	

No. 139ab occurred on one pane of 120 only, the overprint being so misplaced that all the stamps of the last vertical row escaped it entirely.

The bold 'TA' variety only occurs on later printings of Nos. 138/139.

Nos. 140/227 are no longer used.

1922–27. Die II. Wmk Mult Script CA. Chalk-surfaced paper (1s. to 5s.). P 14.

228	26	¼d. deep brown (1923)	3·75	24·00
229	25	½d. green (1923)	1·00	1·00
		w. Wmk inverted		
230		1d. carmine-red	6·50	50
231		1d. violet (6.1.27)	1·25	10
232	26	1½d. scarlet (6.1.27)	4·00	1·00
233		2d. grey	1·25	10
		a. Face value omitted	£28000	
234	25	3d. bright blue (1924)	2·75	1·00
235	26	4d. black and red/*yellow* (1924)	15·00	5·50
236	25	5d. dull purple and sage-green (1927)	1·50	1·50
237	26	6d. dull and bright purple	2·25	1·25
238	25	1s. black/*emerald* (1924)	14·00	1·50
		w. Wmk inverted		
		y. Wmk inverted and reversed		
239	26	2s. purple and blue/*blue* (6.1.27)	25·00	70·00
240		2s.6d. black and red/*blue* (1925)	11·00	32·00
241		5s. green and red/*pale yellow* (1926)	55·00	90·00
228/241 *Set of* 14			£120	£200
228s/241s Optd 'SPECIMEN' *Set of* 14			£400	

The 2d. imperforate with watermark T **10** of Ireland came from a trial printing and was not issued.

Only one example of No. 233a is known. It was caused by an obstruction during the printing of the duty plate.

1935 (6 May). Silver Jubilee. As Nos. 91/94 of Antigua. P 13½×14.

242	1½d. deep blue and carmine	1·00	9·50
	a. Deep blue and aniline red	11·00	29·00
	ab. Frame printed double, one albino	£1000	
	f. Diagonal line by turret	£150	
	g. Dot to left of chapel	£350	
	h. Dot by flagstaff	£275	
	i. Dash by turret	£375	£450
243	2d. ultramarine and grey	1·50	35
	f. Diagonal line by turret	£120	£120
	g. Dot to left of chapel	£275	
244	3d. brown and deep blue	2·75	6·00
	f. Diagonal line by turret	£225	£275
	h. Dot by flagstaff	£425	£475
	i. Dash by turret	£500	£550
245	1s. slate and purple	14·00	19·00
	a. Frame printed double, one albino	£1600	
	f. Diagonal line by turret	£350	£400
	h. Dot by flagstaff	£500	£550
	i. Dash by turret	£700	
242/245 *Set of* 4		17·00	32·00
242s/245s Perf 'SPECIMEN' *Set of* 4		£120	

For illustrations of plate varieties see Omnibus section following Zanzibar.

1937 (12 May). Coronation. As Nos. 95/97 of Antigua. P 11×11½.

246	1d. purple	60	1·25
247	2d. grey-black	60	2·25
248	3d. Prussian blue	60	2·25
246/248 *Set of* 3		1·60	5·25
246s/248s Perf 'SPECIMEN' *Set of* 3		£120	

28 Native sailing Canoe

29 Native Village

30 Camakua (canoe)

31 Map of Fiji Islands

Two Dies of T **30**:

Die I Empty Canoe

Die II Native in Canoe

Two Dies of T **31**:

Die I Without '180°'

Die II With '180°'

32 Government Offices

33 Canoe and Arms of Fiji

34 Sugar cane

35 Arms of Fiji

36 Spearing fish by torchlight

37 Suva Harbour

38 River scene

39 Chief's hut

40 Paw-paw tree

41 Police bugler

½d. Extra palm frond (R. 5/8)

Extra line (R. 10/2)

Scratch through value (R. 5/1)

2d. Scratched building (Pl. 1. R. 10/2)

2½d. Extra island (R. 10/5)

3d. Spur on Arms medallion
(Pl 2 R. 4/2) (ptg of 26 Nov 1945)

(Des V. E. Ousey (½d., 1s., 2s.6d.), Miss C. D. Lovejoy (1d., 1½d., 5d.), Miss I. Stinson (3d., 5s.) and A. V. Guy (2d. (Nos. 253/254), 2½d., 6d., 2s.). Recess De La Rue (½d., 1½d., 2d., (Nos. 253/255a), 2½d., 6d., 8d., 1s.5d., 1s.6d.), Waterlow (others))

1938 (5 Apr)–**55**. T **28/41**. Wmk Mult Script CA. Various perfs.

249	**28**	½d. green (P 13½)	20	75
		a. Perf 14 (5.41)	23·00	7·00
		b. Perf 12 (8.48)	1·50	3·00
		ba. Extra palm frond	£140	£200
250	**29**	1d. brown and blue (P 12½)	1·00	20
251	**30**	1½d. carmine (Die I) (P 13½)	18·00	35
252		1½d. carmine (Die II) (P 13½) (1.10.40)	3·75	3·00
		a. Deep carmine (10.42)	7·00	1·00
		b. Perf 14 (6.42)	32·00	19·00
		c. Perf 12 (21.7.49)	3·75	1·25
253	**31**	2d. brown and green (Die I) (P 13½)	40·00	40
		a. Extra line	£1000	95·00
		b. Scratch through value	£1000	95·00
254		2d. brown and green (Die II) (P 13½) (1.10.40)	25·00	16·00
255	**32**	2d. green and magenta (P 13½) (19.5.42)	65	60
		aa. Scratched building	60·00	50·00
		a. Perf 12 (27.5.46)	2·50	70
		ab. Scratched building	95·00	60·00
256	**31**	2½d. brown and green (Die II) (P 14) (6.1.42)	4·25	1·00
		a. Extra island	£160	60·00
		b. Perf 13½ (6.1.42)	3·25	80
		ba. Extra island	£140	60·00
		c. Perf 12 (19.1.48)	2·50	50
		ca. Extra island	£110	40·00
257	**33**	3d. blue (P 12½)	2·25	30
		a. Spur on Arms medallion	£750	£300
258	**34**	5d. blue and scarlet (P 12½)	42·00	12·00
259		5d. yellow-green and scarlet (P 12½) (1.10.40)	40	30
260	**31**	6d. black (Die I) (P 13×12)	60·00	10·00
261		6d. black (Die II) (P 13½) (1.10.40)	10·00	1·25
		a. Violet-black (1.44)	27·00	28·00
		b. Perf 12. *Black* (5.6.47)	4·50	1·00
261*c*	**35**	8d. carmine (P 14) (15.11.48)	3·75	3·50
		d. Perf 13 (7.6.50)	2·75	2·75
262	**36**	1s. black and yellow (P 12½)	3·25	80
263	**35**	1s.5d. black and carm (P 14) (13.6.40)	40	10
263*a*		1s.6d. ultramarine (P 14) (1.8.50)	4·25	2·75
		b. Perf 13 (16.2.55)	1·50	18·00
264	**37**	2s. violet and orange (P 12½)	4·50	40
265	**38**	2s.6d. green and brown (P 12½)	8·50	1·50
266	**39**	5s. green and purple (P 12½)	8·50	2·50
266*a*	**40**	10s. orange and emerald (P 12½) (13.3.50)	42·00	50·00
266*b*	**41**	£1 ultramarine and carmine (P 12½) (13.3.50)	55·00	60·00
249/266*b* *Set of 22*			£275	£140
249s/266s (*excl* 8d. *and* 1s.6d.) Perf 'SPECIMEN' *Set of 18*			£800	

2½d.

(**42**)

1941 (10 Feb). No. 254 surch with T **42** by Govt Printer, Suva.

267	**31**	2½d. on 2d. brown and green	2·50	1·00

1946 (17 Aug). Victory. As Nos. 110/111 of Antigua.

268	2½d. green	20	1·50
	a. Printed double, one albino	£550	
269	3d. blue	60	10
268s/269s Perf 'SPECIMEN' *Set of 2*		£110	

1948 (17 Dec). Royal Silver Wedding. As Nos. 112/13 of Antigua.

270	2½d. green	40	2·50
271	5s. violet-blue	14·00	8·00

1949 (10 Oct). 75th Anniversary of Universal Postal Union. As Nos. 114/117 of Antigua.

272	2d. bright reddish purple	30	75
273	3d. deep blue	2·00	7·00
274	8d. carmine-red	30	4·25
275	1s.6d. blue	35	3·00
272/275 *Set of 4*		2·75	13·50

43 Children Bathing

44 Rugby Football

(Recess B.W.)

1951 (17 Sept). Health Stamps. Wmk Mult Script CA. P 13½.

276	**43**	1d. +1d. brown	10	1·75
277	**44**	2d. +1d. green	50	1·00

(Des and eng B.W. Recess D.L.R.)

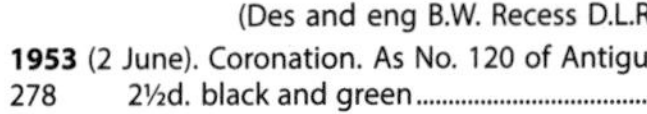

1953 (2 June). Coronation. As No. 120 of Antigua.

278	2½d. black and green	2·00	50

45 Arms of Fiji

(Recess D.L.R.)

1953 (16 Dec). Royal Visit. Wmk Mult Script CA. P 13.

279	**45**	8d. deep carmine-red	40	15

46 Queen Elizabeth II (after Annigoni)

47 Government Offices

48 Loading Copra

49 Sugar Cane Train

50 Preparing Bananas for Export

51 Gold Industry

(Des V. E. Ousey (½d., 1s., 2s.6d.), A. V. Guy (6d.). Recess D.L.R. (½d., 2d., 6d., 8d.), Waterlow (1s., 2s.6d., 10s., £1) B.W. (others))

1954 (1 Feb)–**59**. Types **46/51** and similar designs previously used for King George VI issue (but with portrait of Queen Elizabeth II as in T **47**). Wmk Mult Script CA. P 12 (2d.), 13 (8d.), 12½ (1s., 2s.6d., 10s., £1), 11½×11 (3d., 1s.6d., 2s., 5s.) or 11½ (½d. 1d., 1½d., 2½d, 6d.).

280	**28**	½d. myrtle-green (1.7.54)	1·00	1·50
281	**46**	1d. turquoise-blue (1.6.56)	1·75	10
282		1½d. sepia (1.10.56)	2·75	65
283	**47**	2d. green and magenta	1·25	40
284	**46**	2½d. blue-violet (1.10.56)	3·00	10
285	**48**	3d. brown and reddish violet (1.10.56)	4·75	20
		a. Brown and deep reddish violet (10.11.59)	21·00	1·00
287	**31**	6d. black (1.7.54)	2·50	1·00
288	**35**	8d. deep carmine-red (1.7.54)	8·50	1·75
		a. Carmine-lake (6.3.58)	18·00	2·00
289	**36**	1s. black and yellow	3·25	10
290	**49**	1s.6d. blue and myrtle-green (1.10.56)	16·00	1·00
291	**50**	2s. black and carmine (1.10.56)	4·75	1·00
292	**38**	2s.6d. bluish green and brown	2·75	50
		a. Bluish green and red-brown (14.9.54)	2·00	10
293	**51**	5s. ochre and blue (1.10.56)	8·00	1·25
294	**40**	10s. orange and emerald (1.7.54)	7·50	14·00
295	**41**	£1 ultramarine and carmine (1.7.54)	32·00	10·00
280/295 *Set of 15*			85·00	29·00

52 River Scene

53 Cross of Lorraine

(Recess B.W.)

1954 (1 Apr). Health Stamps. Wmk Mult Script CA. P 11×11½.

296	**52**	1½d. +½d. bistre-brown and green	15	1·00
297	**53**	2½d. +½d. orange and black	15	20

54 Queen Elizabeth II (after Annigoni)

55 Fijian beating Lali

56 Hibiscus

57 Yaqona ceremony

58 Location Map

59 Nadi Airport

60 Red Shining Parrot

61 Cutting Sugar-cane

62 Arms of Fiji

(Des M. Goaman: Photo Harrison (8d., 4s.). Recess. B.W. (others))

1959–63. Types **54/62**. Wmk Mult Script CA. P 11½ (Types **46** and **54**), 11½×11 (6d., 10d., 1s., 2s.6d., 10s. £1), 14½×14 (8d.) or 14×14½ (4s).

298	**46**	½d. emerald-green (14.11.61)	15	2·50
299	**54**	1d. deep ultramarine (3.12.62)	3·50	2·50
300		1½d. sepia (3.12.62)	3·50	2·50
301	**46**	2d. rose-red (14.11.61)	1·75	10
302		2½d. orange-brown (3.12.62)	3·50	5·00
303	**55**	6d. carmine and black (14.11.61)	1·75	10
304	**56**	8d. scarlet, yellow, green and black (1.8.61)	50	25
305	**57**	10d. brown and carmine (1.4.63)	2·50	60
306	**58**	1s. light blue and blue (14.11.61)	1·50	10
307	**59**	2s.6d. black and purple (14.11.61)	9·00	10
308	**60**	4s. red, green, blue and slate-green (13.7.59)	3·00	1·00
309	**61**	10s. emerald and deep sepia (14.11.61)	2·50	1·00
310	**62**	£1 black and orange (14.11.61)	5·50	3·00
298/310 *Set of 13*			32·00	16·00

Nos. 299 and 311 have turtles either side of 'Fiji' instead of shells.

63 Queen Elizabeth II

64 International Dateline

65 White Orchid

66 Orange Dove

(Des M. Goaman. Photo Harrison (3d., 9d., 1s.6d., 2s., 4s., 5s.). Recess B.W. (others))

1962 (3 Dec)–**67**. W w **12** (upright). P 11½ (1d., 2d.), 12½ (3d.), 11½×11 (6d., 10d., 1s., 2s.6d., 10s., £1), 14½×14 (9d., 2s.) or 14×14½ (1s.6d., 4s., 5s.).

311	**54**	1d. deep ultramarine (14.1.64)	1·25	3·75
312	**46**	2d. rose-red (3.8.65)	50	10
313	**63**	3d. multicoloured	25	10
		w. Wmk inverted		
314	**55**	6d. carmine and black (9.6.64)	1·50	10
315	**56**	9d. scarlet, yellow, green and ultramarine (1.4.63)	90	65
316	**57**	10d. brown and carmine (14.1.64)	60	50
317	**58**	1s. light blue and blue (24.1.66*)	2·50	45
318	**64**	1s.6d. red, yellow, gold, black and blue	1·50	60
		a. Error. Wmk sideways	£1100	
319	**65**	2s. yellow-green, green and copper	10·00	3·50
		a. Apple-green, green and copper (16.5.67)	25·00	4·50
320	**59**	2s.6d. black and purple (3.8.65)	6·00	1·25
		a. Black and deep purple (8.67)	9·50	3·50
321	**60**	4s. red, yellow-green, blue and green (1.4.64)	7·50	1·50
322		4s. red, green, blue and slate-green (1.3.66)	6·50	2·00

323 **66** 5s. red, yellow and grey ... 10·00 35
w. Wmk inverted ... £300 £160
324 **61** 10s. emerald and deep sepia (14.1.64) ... 8·00 2·00
325 **62** £1 black and orange (9.6.64) ... 14·00 6·00
311/325 *Set of* 15 ... 55·00 20·00

* This is the earliest known used date in Fiji and it was not released by the Crown Agents until 1 November.

The 3d. value exists with PVA gum as well as gum arabic.

For 4s. with watermark sideways see No. 359.

ROYAL VISIT

1963 **ROYAL VISIT 1963**

(**67**) (**68**)

1963 (1 Feb). Royal Visit. Nos. 313 and 306 optd with Types **67**/**68**.
326 **67** 3d. multicoloured ... 40 20
327 **68** 1s. light blue and blue ... 60 20

1963 (4 June). Freedom from Hunger. As No. 146 of Antigua.
328 2s. ultramarine ... 1·00 2·00

69 Running

(**73** CS *Retriever*.)

(Des M. Goaman. Photo Harrison)

1963 (6 Aug). First South Pacific Games, Suva. T **69** and similar designs. W w **12**. P 14½.
329 3d. red-brown, yellow and black ... 25 10
330 9d. red-brown, violet and black ... 25 1·50
331 1s. red-brown, green and black ... 25 10
332 2s.6d. red-brown, light blue and black ... 60 40
329/332 *Set of* 4 ... 1·25 1·75

Designs: Vert—9d. Throwing the discus; 1s. Hockey. Horiz—2s.6d. High-jumping.

1963 (2 Sept). Red Cross Centenary. As Nos. 147/148 of Antigua.
333 2d. red and black ... 35 10
334 2s. red and blue ... 75 2·50

1963 (3 Dec). Opening of COMPAC (Trans-Pacific Telephone Cable). No. 317 optd with T **73** by B.W.
335 1s. light blue and blue ... 55 20

74 Jamborette Emblem

75 Scouts of Three Races

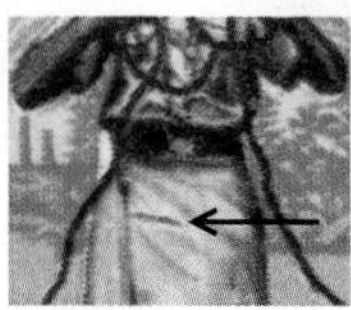
1s. 'Pocket in sulu' (R. 1/1)

(Des V. Whiteley assisted by Norman L. Joe Asst. D.C., Fiji Scouts for Jamboree emblem. Photo Harrison)

1964 (4 Aug). 50th Anniversary of Fijian Scout Movement. W w **12**. P 12½.
336 **74** 3d. multicoloured ... 20 25
337 **75** 1s. violet and yellow-brown ... 20 30
a. Pocket in sulu ... 9·00

76 Flying-boat *Aotearoa*

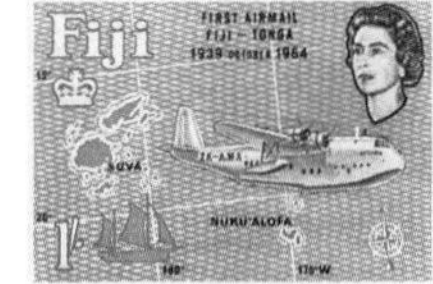
78 *Aotearoa* and Map

(Des V. Whiteley. Photo Harrison)

1964 (24 Oct). 25th Anniversary of First Fiji-Tonga Airmail Service. Types **76**, **78** and similar design. W w **12**. P 14½×14 (1s.) or 12½ (others).
338 3d. black and vermilion ... 50 10
339 6d. vermilion and bright blue ... 80 55
340 1s. black and turquoise-blue ... 80 55
338/340 *Set of* 3 ... 1·90 1·10

Design: Vert (as T **76**)—3d. T **76**; 6d. de Havilland DH.114 Heron 2. Horiz—1s. T **78**.

1965 (17 May). ITU Centenary. As Nos. 166/167 of Antigua.
341 3d. blue and rose-carmine ... 20 10
342 2s. orange-yellow and bistre ... 50 25

1965 (25 Oct). International Co-operation Year. As Nos. 168/169 of Antigua.
343 2d. reddish purple and turquoise-green ... 20 10
344 2s.6d. deep bluish green and lavender ... 80 25

1966 (24 Jan). Churchill Commemoration. As Nos. 170/173 of Antigua.
345 3d. new blue ... 40 10
346 9d. deep green ... 65 85
347 1s. brown ... 65 10
348 2s.6d. bluish violet ... 90 85
345/348 *Set of* 4 ... 2·40 1·60

1966 (1 July). World Cup Football Championship. As Nos. 176/177 of Antigua.
349 2d. violet, yellow-green, lake and yellow-brown ... 25 10
350 2s. chocolate, blue-green, lake and yellow-brown ... 1·25 30

79 HMS *Pandora* approaching Split Island, Rotuma

(Des V. Whiteley. Photo Enschedé)

1966 (29 Aug). 175th Anniversary of Discovery of Rotuma. T **79** and similar horiz designs. Multicoloured. W w **12** (sideways). P 14×13.
351 3d. Type **79** ... 30 10
352 10d. Rotuma Chiefs ... 30 10
353 1s.6d. Rotumans welcoming HMS *Pandora* ... 50 1·00
351/353 *Set of* 3 ... 1·00 1·00

1966 (20 Sept). Inauguration of WHO Headquarters, Geneva. As Nos. 178/179 of Antigua.
354 6d. black, yellow-green and light blue ... 1·25 25
355 2s.6d. black, light purple and yellow-brown ... 2·75 2·50

LEGISLATIVE ASSEMBLY

82 Running

(Des V. Whiteley. Photo Harrison)

1966 (5 Dec*). Second South Pacific Games, Nouméa. T **82** and similar designs. W w **12** (sideways on 9d.). P 14½×14 (9d.) or 14×14½ (others).
356 3d. black, chestnut and yellow-olive ... 10 10
357 9d. black, chestnut and greenish blue ... 15 15
358 1s. multicoloured ... 15 15
356/358 *Set of* 3 ... 30 35

Designs: Vert—9d. Putting the shot. Horiz— 3d. T **82**; 1s. Diving.

* These were not released in London until 8.12.66.

1967 (16 Feb). As No. 321 but wmk w **12** sideways.
359 **60** 4s. red, yellow-green, blue and green ... 4·50 1·00

85 Military Forces Band

(Des G. Vasarhelyi. Photo Enschedé)

1967 (20 Oct). International Tourist Year. T **85** and similar horiz designs. Multicoloured. W w **12** (sideways). P 14×13.
360 3d. Type **85** ... 40 10
361 9d. Reef diving ... 15 10
362 1s. Beqa fire walkers ... 15 10
363 2s. *Oriana* (cruise liner) at Suva ... 40 15
360/363 *Set of* 4 ... 1·00 30

89 Bligh (bust), HMS *Providence* and Chart

91 Bligh's Tomb

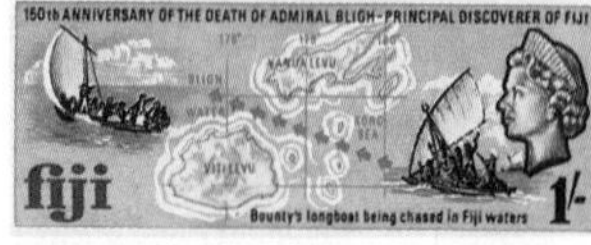

90 *Bounty's* longboat being chased in Fiji waters

(Des V. Whiteley. Photo Harrison)

1967 (11 Dec). 150th Death Anniversary of Admiral Bligh. W w **12** (sideways on 1s.). P 12½×13 (1s.) or 15×14 (others).
364 **89** 4d. multicoloured ... 10 10
365 **90** 1s. multicoloured ... 20 10
366 **91** 2s.6d. multicoloured ... 20 15
364/366 *Set of* 3 ... 45 30

92 Simmonds Spartan Seaplane

6d. White beacon on radio mast (R. 12/3)

(Des V. Whiteley. Photo Harrison)

1968 (5 June). 40th Anniversary of Kingsford Smith's Pacific Flight via Fiji. T **92** and similar horiz designs. W w **12**. P 14×14½.
367 2d. black and green ... 15 10
368 6d. greenish blue, black and lake ... 15 10
a. Radio mast flaw ... 9·00
369 1s. deep violet and turquoise-green ... 20 10
370 2s. orange-brown and blue ... 30 15
367/370 *Set of* 4 ... 70 30

Designs: 2d. T **92**; 6d. Hawker Siddeley H.S.748 and airline insignias; 1s. Fokker F.VIIa/3M *Southern Cross* and crew; 2s. Lockheed 8D Altair *Lady Southern Cross* monoplane.

96 Bure Huts

97 Eastern Reef Heron (after Belcher)

98 Sea Snake

99 Queen Elizabeth and Arms of Fiji

(Des G. Hamori (½d., 1d., 9d.), W. O. Cernohorsky (2d., 4s.) H. S. Robinson (4d., 10d.), D. W. Blair (6d., 5s.), P. D. Clarke (1s.), G. Vasarhelyi (2s.6d.), W. O. Cernohorsky and E. Jones (3s.), E. Jones and G. Hamori (10s.), E. Jones (£1) Adapted V. Whiteley. Photo D.L.R.)

1968 (15 July). Types **96**/**99** and similar designs. W w **12** (sideways on all vert designs). P 14×13½ (2s., 2s.6d., 5s., £1), 13½×14 (3d., 1s., 1s.6d., 4s., 10s.) or 13½×13 (others).
371 ½d. multicoloured ... 10 10
372 1d. deep greenish blue, red and yellow ... 10 10
373 2d. new blue, brown and ochre ... 10 10
374 3d. blackish green, blue and ochre ... 35 10
375 4d. multicoloured ... 80 2·00
376 6d. multicoloured ... 25 10
377 9d. multicoloured ... 15 2·00
378 10d. royal blue, orange and blackish brown ... 1·00 20
379 1s. Prussian blue and brown-red ... 20 10
380 1s.6d. multicoloured ... 4·00 4·50
381 2s. turquoise, black and rosine ... 60 2·00
382 2s.6d. multicoloured ... 60 30
383 3s. multicoloured ... 1·25 6·00
384 4s. yellow-ochre, black and olive ... 3·00 2·75
385 5s. multicoloured ... 1·50 1·50
386 10s. lake-brown, black and ochre ... 1·00 3·00
387 £1 multicoloured ... 1·25 3·00
371/387 *Set of* 17 ... 14·00 24·00

Designs: Horiz (as T **96**)—½d. T **96**; 1d. Passion Flowers; 2d. Chambered or Pearly Nautilus; 4d. *Psilogramma jordana* (moth); 6d. Pennant Coralfish; 9d. Bamboo raft; 10d. *Asota woodfordi* (moth); 3s. Golden Cowrie shell. Vert (as T **97**)—3d. T **97**; 1s. Black Marlin; 1s.6d. Orange-breasted Honeyeaters (after Belcher); 4s. Mining industry; 10s. Ceremonial whale's tooth. Horiz (as T **98**)—2s. T **98**; 2s.6d. Outrigger canoes; 5s. Bamboo Orchids. Horiz—£1 T **99**.

113 Map of Fiji, WHO Emblem and Nurses

(Des V. Whiteley. Litho D.L.R.)

1968 (9 Dec). 20th Anniversary of World Health Organisation. T **113** and similar horiz designs. Multicoloured. W w **12** (sideways). P 14.
388 3d. Type **113** ... 15 10
389 9d. Transferring patient to Medical Ship *Vuniwai* ... 20 25
390 3s. Recreation ... 25 30
388/390 *Set of* 3 ... 55 55

(New Currency. 100 cents = 1 dollar.)

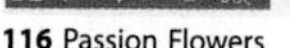

116 Passion Flowers

117 Fijian Soldiers overlooking the Solomon Islands

1969 (13 Jan)–**70**. Decimal Currency. Designs as Nos. 371/387, but with values inscr in decimal currency as T **116**. W w **12** (sideways on vert designs). Chalk-surfaced paper. P 14×13½ (20, 25, 50c. $2) 13½×14 (3, 10, 15, 40c., $1) or 13½×13 (others).

391 **116** 1c. deep greenish blue, red and yellow ... 10 10
392 – 2c. new blue, brown and ochre (as 2d.) ... 10 10
393 **97** 3c. blackish green, blue and ochre ... 1·25 1·00
394 – 4c. multicoloured (as 4d.) ... 1·50 1·00
395 – 5c. multicoloured (as 6d.) ... 20 10
396 **96** 6c. multicoloured ... 10 10
397 – 8c. multicoloured (as 9d.) ... 10 10
398 – 9c. royal blue, orange and blackish brown (as 10d.) ... 1·50 2·25
399 – 10c. Prussian blue and brown-red (as 1s.) ... 20 10
400 15c. multicoloured (as 1s.6d.) ... 6·50 6·00
401 **98** 20c. turquoise, black and rosine ... 1·25 80
402 – 25c. multicoloured (as 2s.6d.) ... 1·00 20
403 – 30c. multicoloured (as 3s.) ... 3·50 1·50
404 – 40c. yellow-ochre, black and olive (as 4s.) ... 7·50 4·00
405 – 50c. multicoloured (as 5s.) ... 1·50 20
a. Glazed, ordinary paper (3.9.70) ... 8·00 1·50
406 – $1 lake-brown, black and ochre (as 10s.) ... 1·50 40
a. Glazed, ordinary paper (3.9.70) ... 2·00 2·75
407 **99** $2 multicoloured ... 3·50 1·50
391/407 *Set of* 17 ... 27·00 17·00

(Des G. Drummond. Photo Harrison)

1969 (23 June). 25th Anniversary of Fijian Military Forces' Solomons Campaign. T **117** and similar horiz designs. W w **12**. P 14.

408 3c. yellow-brown, black and bright emerald ... 20 10
409 10c. multicoloured ... 25 10
410 25c. multicoloured ... 35 20
408/410 *Set of* 3 ... 70 30

Designs: 3c. T **117**; 10c. Regimental Flags and Soldiers in full dress and battledress; 25c. Corporal Sefanaia Sukanaivalu and Victoria Cross.

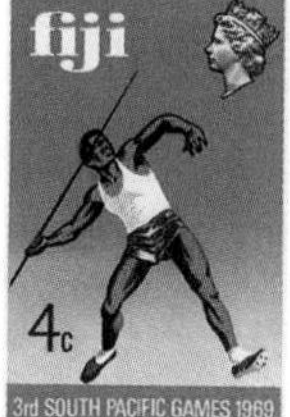

120 Javelin Thrower

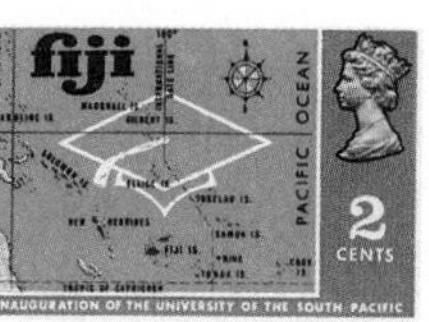

123 Map of South Pacific and 'Mortar-board'

(Des L. Curtis. Photo Harrison)

1969 (18 Aug). Third South Pacific Games. Port Moresby. T **120** and similar vert designs. W w **12** (sideways*). P 14½×14.

411 4c. black, brown and vermilion ... 10 10
w. Wmk Crown to right of CA ... 3·00
412 8c. black, grey and new blue ... 10 10
413 20c. multicoloured ... 20 20
411/413 *Set of* 3 ... 30 30

Designs: 4c. T **120**; 8c. Sailing dinghy; 20c. Games medal and winners' rostrum.

* The normal sideways watermark shows Crown to left of CA, *as seen from the back of the stamp.*

(Des G. Drummond. Photo Harrison)

1969 (10 Nov). Inauguration of University of the South Pacific. T **123** and similar horiz designs. Multicoloured. W w **12**. P 14×15.

414 2c. Type **123** ... 10 15
415 8c. RNZAF badge and Short S.25 Sunderland flying boat over Laucala Bay (site of University) ... 15 10
416 25c. Science students at work ... 25 15
w. Wmk inverted ... 2·00 1·50
414/416 *Set of* 3 ... 45 30

ROYAL VISIT 1970

(126)

127 Chaulmugra Tree, Makogai

1970 (4 Mar). Royal Visit. Nos. 392, 399 and 402 optd with T **126**.

417 2c. new blue, brown and ochre ... 10 20
418 10c. Prussian blue and brown-red ... 10 10
419 25c. multicoloured ... 20 10
417/419 *Set of* 3 ... 35 30

(Des G. Drummond. Photo Harrison)

1970 (25 May). Closing of Leprosy Hospital Makogai. T **127** and similar designs. W w **12** (sideways* on 10c.). P 14×14½.

420 2c. multicoloured ... 10 50
421 10c. pale turquoise-green and black ... 30 65
a. Pair. Nos. 421/422 ... 60 1·25
w. Wmk Crown to right of CA ... 6·00 6·00
422 10c. turquoise-blue, black and magenta ... 30 65
w. Wmk Crown to right of CA ... 6·00 6·00
423 30c. multicoloured ... 50 50
420/423 *Set of* 4 ... 1·10 2·10

Designs: Vert—No. 421, Cascade (Semisi Maya); No. 422, Sea Urchins (Semisi Maya). Horiz—No. 420 T **127**; No. 423, Makogai Hospital.

* The normal sideways watermark shows Crown to left of CA, *as seen from the back of the stamp.*

Nos. 421/422 were printed together, *se-tenant*, throughout the sheet.

131 Abel Tasman and Log, 1643

(Des V. Whiteley. Litho D.L.R.)

1970 (18 Aug). Explorers and Discoverers. T **131** and similar horiz designs. W w **12** (sideways*). P 13×12½.

424 2c. black, brown and turquoise ... 30 25
w. Wmk Crown to right of CA ... 85·00
425 3c. multicoloured ... 60 25
426 8c. multicoloured ... 60 15
427 25c. multicoloured ... 30 15
424/427 *Set of* 4 ... 1·60 70

Designs: 2c. T **131**; 3c. Captain Cook and HMS *Endeavour*, 1774; 8c. Captain Bligh and longboat, 1789; 25c. Fijian and ocean-going canoe.

* The normal sideways watermark shows Crown to left of CA, *as seen from the back of the stamp.*

INDEPENDENT

135 King Cakobau and Cession Stone

139 1d. and 6d. Stamps of 1870

(Des J. W. Litho Format)

1970 (10 Oct). Independence. T **135** and similar horiz designs. Multicoloured. W w **12** (sideways). P 14.

428 2c. Type **135** ... 10 10
429 3c. Children of the World ... 10 10
430 10c. Prime Minister and Fijian flag ... 1·00 10
431 25c. Dancers in costume ... 25 20
428/431 *Set of* 4 ... 1·25 30

The design for the 10c. value does not incorporate the Queen's head profile.

(Des V. Whiteley. Photo Harrison)

1970 (2 Nov). Stamp Centenary. T **139** and similar horiz designs. Multicoloured. W w **12** (sideways on 15c.). P 14½×14.

432 4c. Type **139** ... 15 10
433 15c. Fijian stamps of all reigns (61×21 *mm*) ... 40 15
434 20c. *Fiji Times* office and modern GPO ... 40 15
w. Wmk inverted ... 80·00
432/434 *Set of* 3 ... 85 35

STAMP BOOKLETS

1909. Black and pink cover. Stapled.

SB1 2s. booklet containing 11×½d. (No. 118) in blocks of 5 and 6, and 18×1d. (No. 119) in blocks of 6 ... £4000

1914. Black on red cover. Stapled.

SB2 2s. booklet containing 11×½d. (No. 126) in blocks of 5 and 6, and 18×1d. (No. 127) in blocks of 6 ... £3500

1939 (10 Mar)–**40**. Black on deep green covers. No advertising pages. Stapled.

SB3 3s. booklet containing 8×½d. and 8×1d. (Nos. 249/250) in blocks of 8 and 12×2d. (No. 253) in blocks of 6 ... £1400
a. Including four advertising pages (black on pale greenish buff cover) (1940) ... £1200
SB4 5s.9d. booklet containing10×½d. and 10×1d. (Nos. 249/250) in blocks of 10 and 27×2d. (No. 253) in blocks of 9 ... £4500
a. Including four advertising pages (black on pink cover) (1940) ... £4250

Nos. SB3/SB4 were produced locally and Nos. SB3a/SB4a by De La Rue.

1967 (23 Jan). Black on salmon cover. Stitched.

SB5 2s. booklet containing 8×3d. (No. 313) in blocks of four ... 9·50

The first printing was not released by the Crown Agents, but a second printing was released in London on 30.6.67. The first printing had 4d. as the surface-rate for letters to the British Commonwealth on the inside back cover (*Price* £12); in the second printing this was corrected to 3d.

1969 (27 Feb). Black on salmon cover. Stitched.

SB6 20c. booklet containing 10×2c. (No. 392) in two blocks of 4 and a vert pair ... 5·00

1970 (27 Oct). Black on salmon cover. Stitched.

SB7 20c. booklet containing 4×1c. and 8×2c. (Nos. 391/392) in blocks of 4 ... 6·50

POSTAGE DUE STAMPS

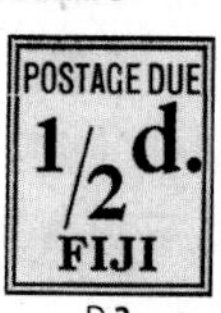

D **1** D **2**

(Typo Govt Printer, Suva)

1917 (1 Jan). Thick yellowish white laid paper with paper-maker's name 'DANVERS' and an ornamental device incorporating a crown and the figure of Britannia. No gum. P 11.

D1 D **1** ½d. black ... £1400 £500
a. Se-tenant strip of 4: 1d.+½d.+4d.+3d. ... £10000
D2 1d. black ... £550 £140
D3 2d. black ... £325 80·00
D4 3d. black ... £650 £120
D5 4d. black ... £1600 £550

Nos. D1/D2 and D4/D5 were printed, *se-tenant*, in sheets of 96 (8×12) with each horizontal row containing three 1d., one ½d., one 4d. and three 3d. in that order (*Price for complete horizontal strip of* 8, £18000, *unused*). Only 31 such sheets were issued. The 2d. was printed separately in sheets of 84 (7×12). On all these sheets marginal copies were imperforate on the outer edge.

1917 (21 Apr)–**18**. As Nos. D1/D3 but narrower setting, value in ½d. as T D **2**.

D5*a* ½d. black ... £500 £300
D5*b* 1d. black ... £350 £140
D5*c* 2d. black (5.4.18) ... £1300 £750

1d. and 2d. stamps must have wide margins (3½ to 4 *mm*) on the vertical sides to be Nos. D2 or D3. Stamps with narrow margins of approximately the same width on all four sides are Nos. D5*b* or D5*c*.

Nos. D5*a*/D5*c* were printed in separate sheets of 84 (7×12). The marginal copies are perforated on all sides.

D **3** D **4**

(Typo D.L.R.)

1918 (1 June). Wmk Mult Crown CA. P 14.

D6 D **3** ½d. black ... 3·00 32·00
D7 1d. black ... 3·50 5·50
D8 2d. black ... 3·25 7·50
D9 3d. black ... 3·25 55·00
sa. Wmk sideways, optd 'SPECIMEN' ... £750
D10 4d. black ... 6·00 30·00
D6/D10 *Set of* 5 ... 17·00 £110
D6s/D10s Optd 'SPECIMEN' *Set of* 5 ... £160

No. D9sa shows Wmk Crown to right of CA *as seen from the back of the stamp.*

No postage due stamps were in use between 31 August 1931 and 3 July 1940.

(Typo Waterlow)

1940 (3 July). Wmk Mult Script CA. P 12½.

D11 D **4** 1d. emerald-green ... 8·50 70·00
D12 2d. emerald-green ... 17·00 70·00
D13 3d. emerald-green ... 19·00 75·00
D14 4d. emerald-green ... 20·00 80·00
D15 5d. emerald-green ... 23·00 85·00
D16 6d. emerald-green ... 25·00 85·00
D17 1s. carmine-lake ... 25·00 £110
D18 1s.6d. carmine-lake ... 25·00 £160
D11/D18 *Set of* 8 ... £140 £650
D11s/D18s Perf 'SPECIMEN' *Set of* 8 ... £250

All values are known with forged postmarks, including one of Levuka dated '8 APR 41' and others of Suva dated '12 AUG 42', '14 AU 42' or '20 MR 45'.

The use of postage due stamps was discontinued on 30 April 1946.

Gambia

PRICES FOR STAMPS ON COVER TO 1945	
Nos. 1/4	*from* × 25
Nos. 5/8	*from* × 20
Nos. 10/20	*from* × 25
Nos. 21/31	*from* × 50
Nos. 32/36	*from* × 20
Nos. 37/44	*from* × 10
Nos. 45/68	*from* × 8
Nos. 69/70	*from* × 25
Nos. 72/85	*from* × 8
Nos. 86/142	*from* × 5
Nos. 143/146	*from* × 6
Nos. 147/149	*from* × 8
Nos. 150/161	*from* × 3

WEST AFRICAN SETTLEMENT

British traders were active in the River Gambia area from the beginning of the 17th-century, but it was not until 1808 that it was officially recognised as a Settlement. Administration passed from the merchants to the Governor of Freetown (Sierra Leone) in 1821 and in 1843 Gambia became a separate colony with a Protectorate declared over the banks of the river for 300 miles inland in 1857. A period of colonial retrenchment in 1865 saw a return to Settlement status under Sierra Leone, but Gambia once again became a Crown Colony in 1888.

There was no government postal service before 1858.

PRICES. The prices of Nos. 1 to 8 are for fine copies, with good margins and embossing. Brilliant or poor examples can be supplied at prices consistent with their condition.

DOUBLE EMBOSSING. The majority of the stamps of T **1** with so-called 'double embossing' are merely examples in which the printing and embossing do not register accurately and have no special value. We no longer list 'twice embossed' or 'twice embossed, once inverted' varieties as they are considered to be outside the scope of this catalogue.

1

(Typo and embossed by D.L.R.)

1869 (18 Mar)–**72**. No wmk. Imperf.

No.	Type	Description	Unused	Used
1	1	4d. brown	£600	£200
2		4d. pale brown (1871)	£500	£200
3		6d. deep blue	£550	£200
3*a*		6d. blue (*shades*)	£600	£180
4		6d. pale blue (4.1.72)	£3250	£1100

The 6d. pale blue shade, No. 4, is distinctive and rare. The date given is the earliest known postmark. It should not be confused with paler shades of the 'blue' group (No. 3*a*).

1874 (Aug). Wmk Crown CC. Imperf.

No.	Type	Description	Unused	Used
5	1	4d. brown	£400	£200
		w. Wmk inverted	£850	£400
		x. Wmk reversed	£950	£475
		y. Wmk inverted and reversed	£1000	£500
6		4d. pale brown	£425	£225
7		6d. deep blue	£350	£225
		w. Wmk inverted	£700	£400
		x. Wmk reversed	£900	£500
		y. Wmk inverted and reversed	£850	£475
8		6d. blue	£350	£200
		a. Sloping label	£850	£450
		b. Wmk sideways	†	—
		w. Wmk inverted	£700	£400

R. 1/1

R. 1/5

SLOPING LABEL VARIETIES. Traces of this flaw first occur in the 6d. imperforate on R. 1/1 and R. 1/5. In the perforated printings the variety on R. 1/5 is much more pronounced and appears as illustrated above. Our listings are these examples from R.1/5, the less noticeable varieties of this type from R. 1/1 being worth less. These varieties continued to appear until the introduction of a new 6d. plate in 1893, used for No. 34.

1880–81. Wmk Crown CC. P 14*.

A. Wmk sideways†

No.	Type	Description	Unused	Used
10A	1	½d. orange	£550	£425
		w. Wmk Crown to left of CC	£850	
12A		1d. maroon	£1700	£1200
		w. Wmk Crown to left of CC	£2500	
13A		2d. rose	£250	£100
		w. Wmk Crown to left of CC		
14A		3d. bright ultramarine	£500	£500
		w. Wmk Crown to left of CC		
15A		4d. brown	£800	£120
		w. Wmk Crown to left of CC	£600	65·00
16A		4d. pale brown	£750	£110
		w. Wmk Crown to left of CC	£550	65·00
17A		6d. deep blue	£300	£120
		c. Sloping label	£750	£350
18A		6d. blue	£225	£100
		c. Sloping label	£650	£325
		w. Wmk Crown to left of CC		
19A		1s. green	£500	£325
20A		1s. deep green	£650	£325
		w. Wmk Crown to left of CC	£900	
10A/20A *Set of 7*			£3750	£2500

B. Wmk upright

No.	Type	Description	Unused	Used
10B	1	½d. orange	19·00	28·00
11B		½d. dull orange	20·00	28·00
		w. Wmk inverted	£150	
12B		1d. maroon	12·00	6·00
		w. Wmk inverted	£225	£160
13B		2d. rose	65·00	11·00
		w. Wmk inverted	£700	£400
14B		3d. bright ultramarine	£100	45·00
14cB		3d. pale dull ultramarine	70·00	32·00
		w. Wmk inverted	85·00	60·00
15B		4d. brown	£325	23·00
		w. Wmk inverted	†	£300
16B		4d. pale brown	£325	24·00
17B		6d. deep blue	£130	45·00
		c. Sloping label	£350	£150
18B		6d. blue	£130	45·00
		c. Sloping label	£350	£150
		w. Wmk inverted	†	£600
19B		1s. green	£275	£150
		w. Wmk inverted	—	£700
20B		1s. deep green	£375	£180
10B/20B *Set of 7*			£800	£250

* There were three different printings of these stamps. The original supply, sent in June 1880 and covering all seven values, had watermark sideways and was perforated by a line machine. In October of the same year a further printing of the lowest five values had the watermark changed to upright, but was still with line perforation. The final printing, sent May 1881 and containing all values, also had watermark upright, but was perforated on a comb machine.

† The normal sideways watermark shows Crown to right of CC, *as seen from the back of the stamp.*

1886–93. Wmk Crown CA (sideways*). P 14.

No.	Type	Description	Unused	Used
21	1	½d. myrtle-green (1887)	6·00	2·25
		w. Wmk Crown to right of CA	£100	£150
22		½d. grey-green	5·00	3·25
23		1d. crimson (1887)	10·00	12·00
23*a*		1d. aniline crimson	8·50	14·00
23*b*		1d. pale carmine	8·50	14·00
24		2d. orange (1887)	15·00	5·00
25		2d. deep orange	4·50	10·00
		w. Wmk Crown to right of CA	†	£400
26		2½d. ultramarine (1887)	15·00	2·50
27		2½d. deep bright blue	12·00	2·25
		w. Wmk Crown to right of CA	£225	
28		3d. slate-grey (1886)	14·00	17·00
29		3d. grey	14·00	19·00
30		4d. brown (1887)	15·00	2·00
		w. Wmk Crown to right of CA	—	£150
31		4d. deep brown	12·00	2·25
		a. Wmk upright	†	£4250
		w. Wmk Crown to right of CA	£200	£140
32		6d. yellowish olive-green (1886)	£100	40·00
		a. Sloping label	£300	£100
		bw. Wmk Crown to right of CA	£425	
32*d*		6d. olive-green (1887)	80·00	70·00
		da. Sloping label	£250	£180
33		6d. bronze-green (1889)	45·00	70·00
		a. Sloping label	90·00	£170
		bw. Wmk Crown to right of CA	£425	
33*c*		6d. deep bronze-green (1889)	45·00	70·00
		ca. Sloping label	90·00	£170
34		6d. slate-green (1893)	19·00	65·00
35		1s. violet (1887)	4·25	20·00
36		1s. deep violet	10·00	22·00
36*b*		1s. aniline violet	£1100	
21/35 *Set of 8*			70·00	90·00
21s/24s, 32cs Optd 'SPECIMEN' *Set of 4*			£400	

* The normal sideways watermark shows Crown to left of CA, *as seen from the back of the stamp.*

The above were printed in panes of 15 on paper intended for larger panes. Hence the watermark is sometimes misplaced or omitted and letters from 'CROWN AGENTS FOR THE COLONIES' from the margin may appear on the stamps.

All values with watermark Crown CA are known imperforate (*price from £2250 each, unused*).

The previously listed 3d. 'pearl-grey' shade has been deleted as it is impossible to distinguish from other 3d. shades when it occurs on a single stamp. Sheets from this late printing can be identified by three coloured dots in the left sheet margin and one in the right, this being the reverse of the normal arrangement.

Only three used examples are known of the 4d. with upright watermark, No. 31a.

CROWN COLONY

2

Normal

Malformed 'S'

Repaired 'S'

The Malformed 'S' occurs on R. 7/3 of the left pane from Key Plate 2. This was used to print the initial supply of all values. Printings of the ½d., 1d. and 2½d. despatched on 24 September 1898 had the 'S' repaired as shown above. Subsequent printings of the ½d., 1d. and 3d. were from Key Plate 3.

(Typo D.L.R.)

1898 (2 May)–**1902**. Wmk Crown CA. P 14.

No.	Type	Description	Unused	Used
37	2	½d. dull green (*shades*)	2·75	1·75
		a. Malformed 'S'	£400	
		b. Repaired 'S'	£550	£400
38		1d. carmine (*shades*)	3·75	75
		a. Malformed 'S'	£425	
		b. Repaired 'S'	£550	£425
39		2d. orange and mauve	7·00	3·50
		a. Malformed 'S'	£500	£500
40		2½d. ultramarine	6·00	2·50
		a. Malformed 'S'	£475	£450
		b. Repaired 'S'	£650	
41		3d. reddish purple and blue	48·00	12·00
		a. Malformed 'S'	£750	£650
		b. Deep purple and ultramarine (1902)	£100	£100
42		4d. brown and blue	20·00	35·00
		a. Malformed 'S'	£550	£850
43		6d. olive-green and carmine	18·00	48·00
		a. Malformed 'S'	£600	£900
44		1s. violet and green	42·00	85·00
		a. Malformed 'S'	£800	£1000
37/44 *Set of 8*			£130	£170
37s/44s Optd 'SPECIMEN' *Set of 8*			£200	

3

4

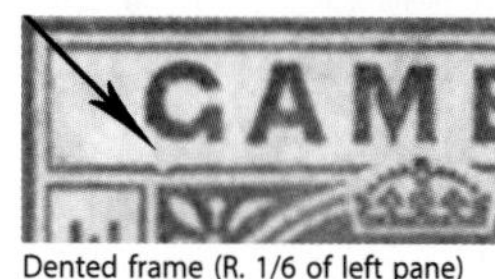

Dented frame (R. 1/6 of left pane)

1902 (13 Mar)–**05**. Wmk Crown CA. P 14.

No.	Type	Description	Unused	Used
45	3	½d. green (19.4.02)	7·50	2·50
		a. Dented frame	£180	£140
46		1d. carmine	16·00	1·00
		a. Dented frame	£275	£110
47		2d. orange and mauve (14.6.02)	3·25	2·00
		a. Dented frame	£225	£170
48		2½d. ultramarine (14.6.02)	50·00	18·00
		a. Dented frame	£650	£300
49		3d. purple and ultramarine (19.4.02)	24·00	3·50
		a. Dented frame	£450	£200
50		4d. brown and ultramarine (14.6.02)	10·00	42·00
		a. Dented frame	£300	£650
51		6d. pale sage-green and carmine (14.6.02)	19·00	14·00
		a. Dented frame	£375	£425
52		1s. violet and green (14.6.02)	48·00	90·00
		a. Dented frame	£700	
53	4	1s.6d. green and carmine/*yellow* (6.4.05)	13·00	26·00
		a. Dented frame	£400	£550
54		2s. deep slate and orange (14.6.02)	55·00	75·00
		a. Dented frame	£800	£1100
55		2s.6d. purple and brown/*yellow* (6.4.05)	15·00	70·00
		a. Dented frame	£500	
56		3s. carmine and green/*yellow* (6.4.05)	21·00	70·00
		a. Dented frame	£600	£1000
45/56 *Set of 12*			£250	£375
45s/56s Optd 'SPECIMEN' *Set of 12*			£250	

1904 (Aug)–**06**. Wmk Mult Crown CA. P 14.

No.	Type	Description	Unused	Used
57	3	½d. green (9.05)	4·50	30
		a. Dented frame	£170	95·00
58		1d. carmine	4·50	15
		a. Dented frame	£180	80·00
59		2d. orange and mauve (23.2.06)	13·00	2·25
		a. Dented frame	£375	£160
60		2½d. bright blue (8.05)	18·00	4·75
		a. Bright blue and ultramarine	25·00	26·00
		b. Dented frame	£375	£180
61		3d. purple and ultramarine (9.05)	21·00	2·00
		a. Dented frame	£375	£160
62		4d. brown and ultramarine (23.2.06)	26·00	48·00
		a. Dented frame	£550	
63	4	5d. grey and black (6.4.05)	20·00	32·00
		a. Dented frame	£475	£600
64	3	6d. olive-green and carmine (23.2.06)	27·00	70·00
		a. Dented frame	£550	
65	4	7½d. green and carmine (6.4.05)	22·00	60·00
		a. Dented frame	£500	
66		10d. olive and carmine (6.4.05)	35·00	50·00
		a. Dented frame	£600	£800
67	3	1s. violet and green (9.05)	45·00	65·00
		a. Dented frame	£750	
68	4	2s. deep slate and orange (7.05)	95·00	£120
		a. Dented frame	£1000	
57/68 *Set of 12*			£300	£400
63s, 65s/66s Optd 'SPECIMEN' *Set of 3*			75·00	

See also Nos. 72/85.

HALF PENNY

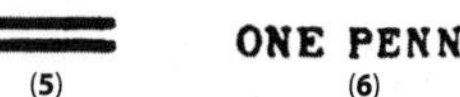

(5)

ONE PENNY

(6)

1906 (10 Apr). Nos. 55 and 56 surch with T **5** or T **6** by Govt Printer.

No.	Type	Description	Unused	Used
69		½d. on 2s.6d. purple and brown/*yellow*	55·00	65·00
		a. Dented frame	£900	£1000

70 1d. on 3s. carmine and green/*yellow* 60·00 30·00
a. Surch double £1800 £5000
b. Dented frame £1000 £1000

No. 69 was surcharged in a setting of 30 (6×5), the spacing between the words and the bars being 5 mm on rows 1, 2 and 5; and 4 mm on rows 3 and 4. Constant varieties occur on R. 2/1 (broken 'E') and R. 5/1 (dropped 'Y') of the setting.

No. 70 was surcharged in a setting of 60 (6×10) and a similar dropped 'Y' variety occurs on R. 6/3 and R. 8/4, the latter in conjunction with a dropped 'E'.

Both values were withdrawn on 24 April when fresh supplies of ½d. and 1d. definitives were received from London.

1909 (1 Oct). Colours changed. Wmk Mult Crown CA. P 14.

72 **3** ½d. blue-green 15·00 7·00
a. Dented frame £250 £200
73 1d. red 17·00 15
a. Dented frame £375 95·00
74 2d. greyish slate 2·50 11·00
a. Dented frame £200 £300
75 3d. purple/*yellow* 8·00 1·00
a. Purple/lemon-yellow 7·00 1·75
b. Dented frame £275 £160
76 4d. black and red/*yellow* 4·00 65
a. Dented frame £250 £150
77 **4** 5d. orange and purple 4·00 1·50
a. Dented frame £250 £200
78 **3** 6d. dull and bright purple 3·50 1·50
a. Dented frame £250 £250
79 **4** 7½d. brown and blue 5·50 2·50
a. Dented frame £275 £275
80 10d. pale sage-green and carmine 7·50 7·00
a. Dented frame £300 £350
81 **3** 1s. black/*green* 8·00 17·00
a. Dented frame £350
82 **4** 1s.6d. violet and green 30·00 75·00
a. Dented frame £550
83 2s. purple and bright blue/*blue* 16·00 20·00
a. Dented frame £450
84 2s.6d. black and red/*blue* 25·00 20·00
a. Dented frame £550
85 3s. yellow and green 48·00 48·00
a. Dented frame £750 £850
72/85 *Set of* 14 £160 £190
73s/85s Optd 'SPECIMEN' *Set of* 13 £300

Most values between Nos. 45 and 85 are known with forged postmarks. These include circular types of Bathurst, dated 'JA 2 97', and Macarthy Island, dated 'FE 17 10', and an oval registered Gambia postmark dated '22 JU 10'.

7

8

Split 'A' (R. 8/3 of left pane) (ptgs to 1918)

(Type D.L.R)

1912 (1 Sept)–**22**. Wmk Mult Crown CA. Chalk-surfaced paper (5s.) P 14.

86 **7** ½d. deep green 3·75 1·50
a. Green 3·75 1·50
b. Pale green (1916) 6·00 3·25
c. Split 'A' £150 £140
87 1d. red 2·75 80
a. Rose-red 4·50 30
b. Scarlet (1916) 10·00 90
c. Split 'A' £180 £130
88 **8** 1½d. olive-green and blue-green 75 30
a. Split 'A' £180 £275
89 **7** 2d. greyish slate 75 2·75
a. Split 'A' £170 £300
90 2½d. deep bright blue 6·50 3·50
a. Bright blue 4·50 2·50
b. Split 'A' £300 £275
91 3d. purple/*yellow* 2·25 30
a. On lemon (1917) 14·00 18·00
b. On orange-buff (1920) 10·00 8·50
c. On pale yellow 1·50 1·00
d. Split 'A' £190 £190
92 4d. black and red/*yellow* 1·00 10·00
a. On lemon (1917) 3·75 7·50
b. On orange-buff (1920) 9·00 14·00
c. On pale yellow 1·50 14·00
d. Split 'A' £225 £500
w. Wmk inverted £225
93 **8** 5d. orange and purple 1·75 2·00
a. Split 'A' £225 £275
94 **7** 6d. dull and bright purple 3·00 2·50
a. Split 'A' £250 £275
95 **8** 7½d. brown and blue 6·50 17·00
a. Split 'A' £350 £650
96 10d. pale sage-green and carmine 6·00 17·00
a. Deep sage-green and carmine 8·00 15·00
b. Split 'A' £425 £550
97 **7** 1s. black/*green* 4·50 1·00
a. On emerald back (1921) 3·50 27·00
b. Split 'A' £275 £350
98 **8** 1s.6d. violet and green 24·00 10·00
a. Split 'A' £700 £550
99 2s. purple and blue/*blue* 11·00 6·00
a. Split 'A' £650 £475
100 2s.6d. black and red/*blue* 11·00 14·00
a. Split 'A' £650 £750
101 3s. yellow and green 19·00 50·00
a. Split 'A' £850 £1100
102 5s. green and red/*pale yellow* (1922) £130 £200
86/102 *Set of* 17 £200 £300
86s/102s Optd 'SPECIMEN' *Set of* 17 £375

1921–22. Wmk Mult Script CA. Chalk-surfaced paper (4s.). P 14.

108 **7** ½d. dull green 30 21·00
x. Wmk reversed £200
109 1d. carmine-red 2·75 11·00
x. Wmk reversed £150 £150
110 **8** 1½d. olive-green and blue-green 2·75 25·00
111 **7** 2d. grey 1·50 3·25
x. Wmk reversed £170
112 2½d. bright blue 65 12·00
113 **8** 5d. orange and purple 1·75 26·00
x. Wmk reversed 50·00
114 **7** 6d. dull and bright purple 3·25 21·00
x. Wmk reversed 27·00
115 **8** 7½d. brown and blue 3·00 55·00
x. Wmk reversed 29·00
116 10d. pale sage-green and carmine 11·00 26·00
x. Wmk reversed £120
117 4s. black and red (1922) £100 £225
w. Wmk inverted 90·00 £250
108/117 *Set of* 10 £110 £375
108s/117s Optd 'SPECIMEN' *Set of* 10 £225

Forged postmarks of the types mentioned below No. 85 have also been seen on various values between No. 86 and No. 117. Collectors should beware of partial strikes which do not show the year date.

9

10

(Recess D.L.R.)

1922 (1 Sept)–**29**. Portrait and shield in black. P 14*.

(a) Wmk Mult Crown CA

118 **9** 4d. red/*yellow* (*a*) 8·00 7·00
119 7½d. purple/*yellow* (*a*) 10·00 11·00
120 **10** 1s. purple/*yellow* (*a*) 42·00 50·00
w. Wmk inverted £190 £225
121 5s. green/*yellow* (*c*) 75·00 £250
w. Wmk inverted
118/121 *Set of* 4 £120 £275
118s/121s Optd or H/S (5s.) 'SPECIMEN' *Set of* 4 £180

(b) Wmk Mult Script CA

122 **9** ½d. green (*abd*) 55 55
123 ½d. deep green (*bd*) (1925) 9·00 2·25
124 1d. brown (*abd*) 1·25 30
x. Wmk reversed † —
125 1½d. bright rose-scarlet (*abd*) 1·25 30
w. Wmk inverted † £750
126 2d. grey (*ab*) 2·25 5·00
127 2½d. orange-yellow (*b*) 3·50 14·00
w. Wmk inverted £200
128 3d. bright blue (*abd*) 1·00 20
a. 'C' of 'CA' missing from wmk £1100
129 4d. red/*yellow* (*bd*) (1.3.27) 29·00 42·00
130 5d. sage-green (*a*) 4·75 19·00
131 6d. claret (*ad*) 1·25 1·00
132 7½d. purple/*yellow* (*ab*) (1927) 26·00 95·00
133 10d. blue (*a*) 8·00 24·00
134 **10** 1s. purple/*yellow* (*aef*) (9.24) 5·50 2·25
a. Blackish purple/yellow-buff (*c*) (1929) 70·00 45·00
135 1s.6d. blue (*af*) 26·00 24·00
136 2s. purple/*blue* (*ac*) 16·00 8·50
137 2s.6d. deep green (*a*) 17·00 13·00
138 3s. bright aniline violet (*a*) 32·00 95·00
139 3s. slate-purple (*c*) (1928) £275 £475
140 4s. brown (*ace*) 19·00 26·00
141 5s. green/yellow (*acf*) (9.26) 55·00 85·00
142 10s. sage-green (*ce*) 85·00 £150
122/142 *Set of* 19 £300 £550
122s/142s Optd 'SPECIMEN' *Set of* 19 £600

Perforations. A number of different perforating machines were used for the various printings of these stamps and the following varieties are known: (*a*) the original 14 line perforation; (*b*) 14×13.8 comb perforation used for T **9**; (*c*) 13.8×13.7 comb perforation used for T **10**; (*d*) 13.7 line perforation used for T **9**; (*e*) 14×13.8 compound line perforation used for T **10**; (*f*) 13.8×14 compound line perforation used for T **10**. The occurrence of these perforations on the individual values is indicated by the letters shown after the colour descriptions above.

No. 139 has been faked, but note that this stamp is comb perf 13.8×13.7 whereas No. 138 is line perf 14 exactly. There are also shades of the slate-purple.

Most values of the above issue are known with a forged oval registered Gambia postmark dated '22 JU 10', often with the year date not shown. Collectors should exercise particular caution in buying used examples of No. 139.

1935 (6 May). Silver Jubilee. As Nos. 91/94 of Antigua, but printed by B.W. P 11×12.

143 1½d. deep blue and scarlet 70 4·50
a. Extra flagstaff £350 £475
b. Short extra flagstaff £350 £425
c. Lightning conductor £500 £500
d. Flagstaff on right-hand turret £600
e. Double flagstaff £600
144 3d. brown and deep blue 2·25 2·00
a. Extra flagstaff £200 £275
b. Short extra flagstaff £275 £325
c. Lightning conductor £275 £375
145 6d. light blue and olive-green 3·75 8·00
a. Extra flagstaff £190 £350
b. Short extra flagstaff £350 £400
c. Lightning conductor £300 £350
d. Flagstaff on right-hand turret £900
146 1s. slate and purple 15·00 15·00
a. Extra flagstaff £275 £375
b. Short extra flagstaff £425 £500
c. Lightning conductor £425 £475
d. Flagstaff on right-hand turret £1100
143/146 *Set of* 4 19·00 26·00
143s/146s Perf 'SPECIMEN' *Set of* 4 £130

For illustrations of plate varieties see Omnibus section following Zanzibar.

Sheets from the second printing of the 6d. and 1s. in November 1935 had the extra flagstaff partially erased with a sharp point.

1937 (12 May). Coronation. As Nos. 95/97 of Antigua. P 11×11½

147 1d. yellow-brown 30 1·25
148 1½d. carmine 30 1·25
149 3d. blue 55 2·00
147/149 *Set of* 3 1·00 4·00
147s/149s Perf 'SPECIMEN' *Set of* 3 £120

11 Elephant (from Colony Badge)

(Recess B.W.)

1938 (1 Apr)–**46**. Wmk Mult Script CA. P 12.

150 **11** ½d. black and emerald-green 15 70
151 1d. purple and brown 30 50
152 1½d. brown-lake and bright carmine £275 18·00
a. Brown-lake and scarlet 8·00 4·00
b. Brown-lake and vermilion 50 2·00
152*c* 1½d. blue and black (2.1.45) 30 1·50
153 2d. blue and black 15·00 3·25
153*a* 2d. lake and scarlet (1.10.43) 1·60 2·25
154 3d. light blue and grey-blue 30 10
154*a* 5d. sage-green and purple-brown (13.3.41) 75 50
155 6d. olive-green and claret 3·25 35
156 1s. slate-blue and violet 5·00 20
156*a* 1s.3d. chocolate and light blue (28.11.46) 4·00 2·00
157 2s. carmine and blue 16·00 3·50
158 2s.6d. sepia and dull green 20·00 3·00
159 4s. vermilion and purple 42·00 2·75
160 5s. blue and vermilion 42·00 4·25
161 10s. orange and black 42·00 13·00
150/161 *Set of* 16 £170 35·00
150s/161s Perf 'SPECIMEN' *Set of* 16 £550

1946 (6 Aug). Victory. As Nos. 110/111 of Antigua.

162 1½d. black 10 1·00
163 3d. blue 10 40
162s/163s Perf 'SPECIMEN' *Set of* 2 £110

1948 (24 Dec). Royal Silver Wedding. As Nos. 112/113 of Antigua.

164 1½d. black 25 10
165 £1 mauve 21·00 26·00

1949 (10 Oct). 75th Anniversary of Universal Postal Union. As Nos. 114/117 of Antigua.

166 1½d. blue-black 30 1·50
167 3d. deep blue 1·25 3·50
168 6d. magenta 75 5·00
169 1s. violet 45 60
166/169 *Set of* 4 2·50 9·50

1953 (2 June). Coronation. As No. 120 of Antigua, but ptd by B. W.

170 1½d. black and deep bright blue 80 1·50

12 Tapping for Palm Wine

13 Cutter

14 Wollof woman

15 Barra canoe

16 SS *Lady Wright*

17 James Island

18 Woman hoeing

19 Elephant and Palm (from colony badge)

(Des Mrs O. W. Meronti. Recess D.L.R.)

1953 (2 Nov)–**59**. Types **12/19**. Wmk Mult Script CA. P 13½.

171 **12** ½d. carmine-red and bluish green 80 30
a. Carmine and bluish green (7.1.59) 5·50 4·50

172	**13**	1d. deep ultramarine and deep brown	2·00	50
		a. Deep ultramarine and chocolate (22.8.56)	4·25	2·50
173	**14**	1½d. deep brown and grey-black	20	1·00
174	**15**	2½d. black and carmine-red	60	70
175	**16**	3d. deep blue and slate-lilac	45	10
176	**17**	4d. black and deep blue	1·75	3·00
177	**12**	6d. brown and reddish purple	1·50	15
178	**18**	1s. yellow-brown and yellow-green	1·50	60
179	**13**	1s.3d. ultramarine and pale blue	19·00	60
		a. Ultramarine and light blue (22.2.56)	25·00	1·00
180	**15**	2s. indigo and carmine	9·00	6·50
181	**13**	2s.6d. deep bluish green and sepia	11·00	3·25
182	**17**	4s. grey-blue and Indian red	17·00	4·75
183	**14**	5s. chocolate and bright blue	7·50	4·50
184	**16**	10s. deep blue and myrtle-green	30·00	17·00
185	**19**	£1 green and black	30·00	18·00
171/185 *Set of* 15			£110	50·00

20 Queen Elizabeth II and Palm

21 Queen Elizabeth II and West African Map

(Des J. R. F. Ithier (T **20**), A. W. Morley (T **21**). Recess B.W.)

1961 (2 Dec). Royal Visit. W w **12**. P 11½.

186	**20**	2d. green and purple	30	70
187	**21**	3d. turquoise-blue and sepia	75	15
188		6d. blue and cerise	75	70
189	**20**	1s.3d. violet and myrtle-green	75	2·25
186/189 *Set of* 4			2·25	3·50

1963 (4 June). Freedom from Hunger. As No. 146 of Antigua.

190	1s.3d. carmine	55	15

1963 (2 Sept). Red Cross Centenary. As Nos. 147/148 of Antigua.

191	2d. red and black	20	60
192	1s.3d. red and blue	40	2·25

SELF-GOVERNMENT

22 Beautiful Sunbird

23 Yellow-mantled Whydah

24 Cattle Egret

25 Senegal Parrot

26 Rose-ringed Parakeet

27 Violet Starling

28 Village Weaver

29 Rufous-crowned Roller

30 Red-eyed Dove

31 Double-spurred Francolin

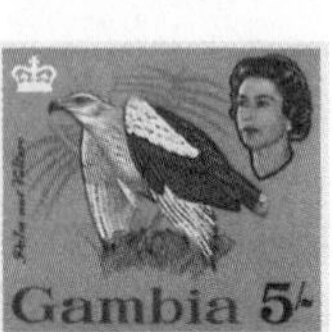

32 Palm-nut Vulture

33 Orange-cheeked Waxbill

34 African Emerald Cuckoo

SELF GOVERNMENT
1963

(**35**)

(Des V. Whiteley. Photo Harrison)

1963 (4 Nov). Birds. Horiz designs as Types **22/34**. Centres multicoloured, background colours given. W w **12**. P 12½×13.

193	**22**	½d. pale buff	75	1·50
194	**23**	1d. sage green	75	30
195	**24**	1½d. lilac	2·50	70
196	**25**	2d. pale yellow-ochre	2·50	70
197	**26**	3d. pale drab	2·50	1·00
198	**27**	4d. pale apple green	2·50	80
199	**28**	6d. pale turquoise-blue	2·50	10
200	**29**	1s. pale grey-green	2·50	10
201	**30**	1s.3d. pale blue	14·00	5·00
202	**31**	2s.6d. pale green	9·00	2·50
203	**32**	5s. light blue	9·00	3·50
204	**33**	10s. pale grey-green	14·00	11·00
205	**34**	£1 pale rose-pink	35·00	14·00
193/205 *Set of* 13			85·00	35·00

1963 (7 Nov). New Constitution. Nos. 194, 197, 200/201 optd with T **35**.

206	**23**	1d. Yellow-mantled Whydah	15	75
207	**26**	3d. Rose-ringed Parakeet	35	60
208	**29**	1s. Rufous-crowned Roller	35	20
		a. Opt double	†	£5000
209	**30**	1s.3d. Red-eyed Dove	35	70
206/209 *Set of* 4			1·10	2·00

1964 (23 Apr). 400th Birth Anniversary of William Shakespeare. As No. 164 of Antigua.

210	6d. bright blue	20	10
	w. Wmk inverted	50·00	55·00

INDEPENDENT

36 Gambia Flag and River

37 Arms

(Des V. Whiteley. Photo Harrison)

1965 (18 Feb). Independence. P 14½.

211	**36**	½d. multicoloured	10	40
212	**37**	2d. multicoloured	15	10
213	**36**	7½d. multicoloured	40	35
214	**37**	1s.6d. multicoloured	50	30
211/214 *Set of* 4			1·00	1·00

INDEPENDENCE
1965

(**38**)

39 ITU Emblem and Symbols

1965 (18 Feb). Nos. 193/205 optd with T **38** or with date centred (1d., 2d., 3d., 4d., 1s., 5s.).

215	**22**	½d. Beautiful Sunbird	30	1·00
216	**23**	1d. Yellow-mantled Whydah	40	20
217	**24**	1½d. Cattle Egret	60	1·00
218	**25**	2d. Senegal Parrot	70	30
219	**26**	3d. Rose-ringed Parakeet	70	15
220	**27**	4d. Violet Starling	70	1·75
221	**28**	6d. Village Weaver	70	10
222	**29**	1s. Rufous-crowned Roller	70	10
223	**30**	1s.3d. Red-eyed Dove	70	10
224	**31**	2s.6d. Double-spurred Francolin	70	60
225	**32**	5s. Palm-nut Vulture	70	75
226	**33**	10s. Orange-cheeked Waxbill	2·00	6·50
227	**34**	£1 African Emerald Cuckoo	11·00	9·00
215/227 *Set of* 13			18·00	19·00

(Des V. Whiteley. Photo Harrison)

1965 (17 May). ITU Centenary. P 14½.

228	**39**	1d. silver and Prussian blue	25	10
229		1s.6d. gold and bluish violet	1·00	40

THE GAMBIA. From this point onwards stamps are inscribed 'The Gambia'.

40 Sir Winston Churchill and Houses of Parliament

(Des Jennifer Toombs. Photo Harrison)

1966 (24 Jan). Churchill Commemoration. P 14×14½.

230	**40**	1d. multicoloured	15	40
231		6d. multicoloured	35	15
232		1s.6d. multicoloured	60	1·40
230/232 *Set of* 3			1·00	1·75

41 Red-cheeked Cordon Bleu

42 Pin-tailed Whydah

(Des V. Whiteley. Photo Harrison)

1966 (18 Feb). Birds. Horiz designs as T **41** and T **42**. Multicoloured. P 14×14½ (£1) or 12×13 (others).

233	½d. Type **41**	90	40
234	1d. White-faced Whistling Duck	30	50
235	1½d. Red-throated Bee-eater	30	40
236	2d. Lesser Pied Kingfisher	5·50	75
237	3d. Golden Bishop	30	10
238	4d. African Fish Eagle	50	30
239	6d. Yellow-bellied Green Pigeon	30	10
240	1s. Blue-bellied Roller	30	10
241	1s.6d. African Pygmy Kingfisher	40	30
242	2s.6d. Spur-winged Goose	40	70
243	5s. Cardinal Woodpecker	50	75
244	10s. Violet Turaco	65	2·75
245	£1 Type **42**	1·00	7·00
233/245 *Set of* 13		10·00	12·50

The ½d., 1d. and 2d. to 1s. values exist with PVA gum as well as gum arabic.

54 Arms, Early Settlement and Modern Buildings

(Photo, Arms die-stamped Harrison)

1966 (24 June). 150th Anniversary of Bathurst. P 14½×14.

246	**54**	1d. silver, brown and yellow-orange	10	10
247		2d. silver, brown and light blue	10	10
248		6d. silver, brown and light emerald	10	10
249		1s.6d. silver, brown and light magenta	15	15
		a. Silver omitted	†	£600
246/249 *Set of* 4			30	30

No. 249a shows an albino impression of the Arms.

55 ITY Emblem and Hotels

(Des and photo (emblem die-stamped) Harrison)

1967 (20 Dec). International Tourist Year. P 14½×14.

250	**55**	2d. silver, brown and apple-green	10	10
251		1s. silver, brown and orange	10	10
252		1s.6d. silver, brown and magenta	15	35
250/252 *Set of* 3			30	40

56 Handcuffs

(Des V. Whiteley. Photo Enschedé)

1968 (15 July). Human Rights Year. T **56** and similar horiz designs. Multicoloured. P 14×13.

253	1d. Type **56**	10	10
254	1s. Fort Bullen	10	10
255	5s. Methodist Church	30	1·00
253/255 *Set of* 3		35	1·00

59 Queen Victoria, Queen Elizabeth II and 4d. Stamp of 1869

(Des G. Drummond. Photo and embossing (cameo head) Harrison)

1969 (20 Jan). Gambia. Stamp Centenary. P 14½×13½.

256	**59**	4d. sepia and yellow-ochre	20	10
257		6d. Prussian blue and deep yellow-green	20	10

258 – 2s.6d. multicoloured 70 1·60
256/258 *Set of 3* 1·00 1·60
Design: 2s.6d. Queen Elizabeth II with 4d. and 6d. stamps of 1869. In the 6d. value the stamp illustrated is the 6d. of 1869.

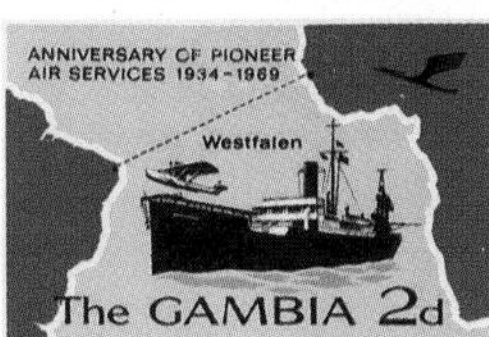

61 Catapult-Ship *Westfalen* launching Dornier DO-J II 10-t Wal

(Des L. Curtis. Litho Format)

1969 (15 Dec). 35th Anniversary of Pioneer Air Services. T **61** and similar horiz designs showing various forms of transport, map of South Atlantic and Lufthansa emblem. Multicoloured. P 13½×14.

259	2d. Type **61**	60	20
260	1s. Dornier Do-J II 10-t Wal *Boreas* flying boat	60	20
261	1s.6d. Airship LZ-127 *Graf Zeppelin*	70	1·60
259/261 *Set of 3*		1·75	1·75

REPUBLIC

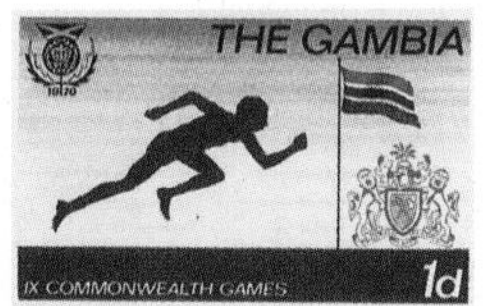

63 Athlete and Gambian Flag

(Des Jennifer Toombs. Litho Format)

1970 (16 July). Ninth British Commonwealth Games, Edinburgh. P 14.

262	**63**	1d. multicoloured	10	10
263		1s. multicoloured	10	10
264		5s. multicoloured	30	1·25
262/264 *Set of 3*			35	1·25

64 President Sir Dawda Kairaba Jawara and State House

(Des G. Vasarhelyi. Litho Questa)

1970 (2 Nov). Republic Day. T **64** and similar multicoloured designs. P 14.

265	2d. Type **64**	10	10
266	1s. President Sir Dawda Jawara	15	10
267	1s.6d. President and flag of Gambia	50	60
265/267 *Set of 3*		65	65

The 1s. and 1s.6d. are both vertical designs.

Ghana

DOMINION

***CANCELLED REMAINDERS.** In 1961 remainders of some issues of 1957 to 1960 were put on the market cancelled-to-order in such a way as to be indistinguishable from genuine postally used copies for all practical purposes. Our used quotations which are indicated by an asterisk are the same for cancelled-to-order or postally used copies.

29 Dr. Kwame Nkrumah, Palm-nut Vulture and Map of Africa

GHANA
INDEPENDENCE
6TH MARCH,
1957.
(**30**)

(Photo Harrison)

1957 (6 Mar). Independence. Wmk Mult Script CA. P 14×14½.

166	**29**	2d. scarlet	10	10*
167		2½d. green	10	15*
168		4d. brown	10	15*
169		1s.3d. deep blue	15	15*
166/169 *Set of 4*			40	45*

1957 (6 Mar)–**58**. Nos. 153*a*/164 of Gold Coast optd as T **30**.

170	½d. bistre-brown and scarlet	10	10*
	a. Olive-brown and scarlet	1·00	10*
171	1d. deep blue (R.)	10	10*
172	1½d. emerald-green	10	10*
173	2d. chocolate (26.5.58)	30	30
174	2½d. scarlet (26.5.58)	1·00	2·00
175	3d. magenta	30	10*
176	4d. blue (26.5.58)	6·50	13·00
177	6d. black and orange (R.)	10	10*
	a. Opt double	†	£750
178	1s. black and orange-red	10	10*
179	2s. brown-olive and carmine	60	10*
180	5s. purple and black	3·75	10*
181	10s. black and olive-green	3·75	70*
170/181 *Set of 12*		15·00	14·00*

Nos. 173/174 and 176 were officially issued on 26 May 1958 although, in error, small quantities were sold at certain post offices when the rest of the set appeared.

Nos. 170 and 171 exist in coils constructed from normal sheets.

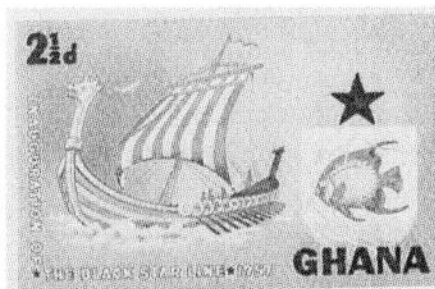

31 Viking Ship

(Des W. Wind. Recess E. A. Wright Bank Note Co., Philadelphia)

1957 (27 Dec). Inauguration of Black Star Shipping Line. T **31** and similar horiz designs. No wmk. P 12.

182	2½d. emerald-green	35	20
	a. Imperf between (vert pair)	£600	
	b. Imperf between (horiz pair)	£600	
183	1s.3d. deep blue	40	1·25
	a. Imperf horiz (vert pair)	£800	
184	5s. bright purple	60	3·00
	a. Imperf vert (horiz pair)	£850	
182/184 *Set of 3*		1·25	4·00

Designs: 2½d. T **31**; 1s.3d. Galleon; 5s. MV *Volta River*.

PRINTERS. Nos. 185/**MS**568 were printed in photogravure by Harrison & Sons *except where otherwise stated.*

34 Ambassador Hotel, Accra **35** Ghana Coat of Arms

1958 (6 Mar). First Anniversary of Independence. Types **34/35** and similar designs. Wmk Mult Script CA. P 14½×14 (2s.) or 14×14½ (others).

185	**34**	½d. black, red, yellow, green and carmine	10	40
186	–	2½d. black, red, green and yellow	10	10
187	–	1s.3d. black, red, yellow, green and blue	30	10
188	**35**	2s. red, yellow, blue, green, brown and black	45	50
185/188 *Set of 4*			75	1·00

Designs: Horiz as T **34**—2½d. State Opening of Parliament; 1s.3d. National Monument.

38 Map showing the Independent African States **39** Map of Africa and Flaming Torch

(Des R. Milton)

1958 (15 Apr). First Conference of Independent African States, Accra. Wmk Mult Script CA. P 13½×14½ (2½d., 3d) or 14½×13½ (others).

189	**38**	2½d. black, bistre and bright carmine-red	10	10
190		3d. black, bistre, brown and bright green	10	10
191	**39**	1s. black, yellow, red and dull blue	20	10
192		2s.6d. black, yellow, red and dull violet	40	90
189/192 *Set of 4*			60	1·00

40 Palm-nut Vulture over Globe **41** Bristol 175 Britannia 309 Airliner

(Des M. Goaman (2½d., 2s.6d.), R. Milton (1s.3d.), W. Wind (2s.))

1958 (15 July). Inauguration of Ghana Airways. Types **40/41** and similar designs. Wmk Mult Script CA. P 15×14 (2s.6d.) or 14×15 (others).

193	**40**	2½d. black, yellow-bistre and rose-carmine	35	10
194	**41**	1s.3d. multicoloured	55	20
195	–	2s. multicoloured	65	55
196	–	2s.6d. black and bistre	65	95
193/196 *Set of 4*			2·00	1·60

Designs: Horiz (as T **41**)—2s. Boeing 377 Stratocruiser and Yellow-nosed Albatross. (As T **40**)—2s.6d. Palm-nut Vulture and Vickers VC-10 aircraft.

PRIME
MINISTER'S
VISIT,
U.S.A. AND
CANADA
(**44**)

45

1958 (18 July). Prime Minister's Visit to the United States and Canada. Nos. 166/169 optd with T **44**.

197	**29**	2d. scarlet	10	40
198		2½d. green	10	30
199		4d. brown	10	50
200		1s.3d. deep blue	15	25
197/200 *Set of 4*			30	1·25

(Des W. Wind)

1958 (24 Oct). United Nations Day. Wmk Mult Script CA. P 14×14½.

201	**45**	2½d. purple-brown, green and black	10	10
202		1s.3d. purple-brown, blue and black	15	10
203		2s.6d. purple-brown, violet and black	15	35
201/203 *Set of 3*			30	40

46 Dr. Nkrumah and Lincoln Statue, Washington

47

(Des M. Goaman)

1959 (12 Feb). 150th Birth Anniversary of Abraham Lincoln. W **47**. P 14×14½.

204	**46**	2½d. pink and deep purple	10	10
205		1s.3d. light blue and blue	10	10
206		2s.6d. orange-yellow and deep olive-green	15	35
204/206 *Set of 3*			30	45
MS206*a* 102×77 mm. Nos. 204/206. Imperf			65	2·25

48 Kente Cloth and Traditional Symbols

(Des Mrs. T. Sutherland (½d.), M. Karoly (2½d.), K. Antubam (1s.3d.), A. M. Medina (2s.))

1959 (6 Mar). Second Anniversary of Independence. T **48** and similar multicoloured designs. W **47**. P 14½×14 (2s.) or 14×14½ (others).

207		½d. Type **48**	10	30
208		2½d. Talking drums and elephant-horn blower	10	10
209		1s.3d. 'Symbol of Greeting' (*vert*)	15	10
210		2s. Map of Africa, Ghana flag and palms	30	1·40
207/210 *Set of* 4			50	1·60

52 Globe and Flags

(Des Mrs. H. Potter)

1959 (15 Apr). Africa Freedom Day. W **47** (sideways). P 14½×14.

211	**52**	2½d. multicoloured	15	10
212		8½d. multicoloured	15	20

53 'God's Omnipotence'

54 Nkrumah Statue, Accra

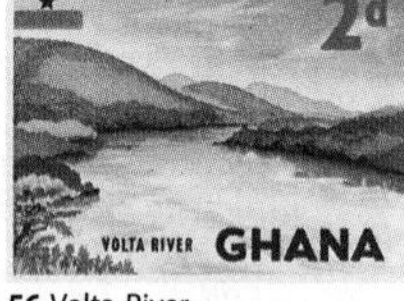

55 Ghana Timber

56 Volta River

57 Cocoa bean

58 'God's Omnipotence'

59 Diamond and mine

60 Red-crowned Bishop

61 Golden Spider Lily

62 Shell Ginger

63 Great Blue Turaco

64 Tiger Orchid

65 Jewel Cichlid

65a Red-fronted Gazelle

66 Pennant-winged Nightjar

67 Crowned Cranes

Two Types of ½d. and 3d:

I. Inscr 'GOD'S OMNIPOTENCE'
II. Inscr 'GYE NYAME'

(Des Mrs. T. Sutherland (½d., 3d.), Ghana Information Bureau (source of 1d. and 2d.), O. Haulkland (1½d.), A. Medina (2½d., 4d.), M. Goaman (6d., 1s.3d., 2s.6d.), W. Wind (11d., 1s., 2s., 5s.), W. H. Brown (10s), M. Shamir (£1))

1959 (5 Oct)–**61**. Types **53/67**. W **47** (sideways on horiz designs). P 11½×12 (½d.), 12×11½ (1d.), 14×14½ (½d., 11d., 1s., 2s., 5s., 10s. and £1) or 14½×14 (others).

		(a) Postage		
213	**53**	½d. Multicoloured (I)	10	10
		a. Type II (29.4.61)	30	10
214	**54**	1d. Multicoloured	10	10
215	**55**	1½d. Multicoloured	10	10
216	**56**	2d. Multicoloured	10	10
217	**57**	2½d. Multicoloured	1·75	10
218	**58**	3d. Multicoloured (I)	10	10
		a. Type II (29.4.61)	30	10
219	**59**	4d. Multicoloured	4·00	65
220	**60**	6d. Multicoloured	2·50	10
		a. Green (flag) omitted	£160	£180
221	**61**	11d. Multicoloured	25	10
222	**62**	1s. Multicoloured	25	10
223	**63**	2s.6d. Multicoloured	1·50	15
224	**64**	5s. Multicoloured	1·75	45
225	**65**	10s. Multicoloured	60	50
225*a*	**65a**	£1 Multicoloured (29.4.61)	2·75	2·75
		(b) Air		
226	**66**	1s.3d. Multicoloured	1·50	10
227	**67**	2s. Multicoloured	1·25	10
213/227 *Set of* 16			16·00	4·25

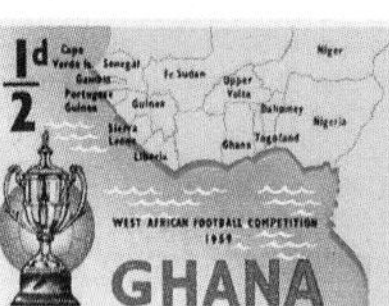

68 Gold Cup and West African Map

73 The Duke of Edinburgh and Arms of Ghana

(Des K. Lehmann (½d., 3d.), M. & G. Shamir (1d.), W. Wind (8d.), and K. Antubam (2s.6d.))

1959 (15 Oct). West African Football Competition, T **68** and similar multicoloured designs. W **47** (sideways on horiz designs). P 14×14½ (1d., 2s.6d) or 14½×14 (others).

228		½d. Type **68**	10	10*
229		1d. Footballers (*vert*)	10	10*
230		3d. Goalkeeper saving ball	10	10*
231		8d. Forward attacking goal	40	15*
232		2s.6d. 'Kwame Nkrumah' Gold Cup (*vert*)	50	15*
228/232 *Set of* 5			1·00	40*

(Des A. S. B. New)

1959 (24 Nov). Visit of the Duke of Edinburgh to Ghana. W **47** (sideways). P 15×14.

233	**73**	3d. black and magenta	30	10*

74 Ghana Flag and Talking Drums

75 Ghana Flag and UN Emblem

(Des K. Antubam (2e.6d.), A. Medina (others))

1959 (10 Dec). United Nations Trusteeship Council. Types **74/75** and similar multicoloured designs. W **47** (sideways on 3d). P 14½×14 (3d) or 14×14) (others).

234		3d. Type **74**	10	10*
235		6d. Type **75**	10	10*
236		1s.3d. Ghana flag and UN emblem (*vert*)	20	15*
237		2s.6d. 'Totem Pole' (*vert*)	25	15*
234/237 *Set of* 4			55	45*

78 Eagles in Flight

79 Fireworks

(Des A. Medina (½d), M. Goaman (3d), W. Wind (1s.3d., 2s.))

1960 (6 Mar). Third Anniversary of Independence. Types **78/79** and similar vert designs. Multicoloured. W **47**. P 14×14½.

238		½d. Type **78**	10	10*
239		3d. Type **79**	10	10*
240		1s.3d. 'Third Anniversary'	30	10*
241		2s. 'Ship of State'	30	15*
238/241 *Set of* 4			70	30*

82 'A' of National Flags

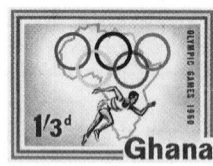

85 President Nkrumah

(Des W. Wind)

1960 (15 Apr). Africa Freedom Day. T **82** and similar horiz designs. Multicoloured. W **47** (sideways). P 14½×14.

242		3d. Type **82**	10	10*
243		6d. Letter 'f'	20	10*
244		1s. Letter 'd'	20	10*
242/244 *Set of* 3			40	20*

REPUBLIC

(Des A. Medina (3d., 10s.), W. Wind (1s.3d., 2s))

1960 (1 July). Republic Day. T **85** and similar multicoloured designs. W **47**. P 14½×14 (10s) or 14×14½ (others).

245		3d. Type **85**	10	10
246		1s.3d. Ghana flag	30	10
247		2s. Torch of Freedom	20	20
248		10s. Arms of Ghana (*horiz*)	50	1·10
245/248 *Set of* 4			1·00	1·25
MS248*a* 102×77 mm. Nos. 245/248. Imperf			40	1·50

89 Olympic Torch

90 Athlete

(Des A. Medina (T **89**), W. Wind (T **90**))

1960 (15 Aug). Olympic Games. W **47** (sideways on T **90**). P 14×14½ (T **89**) or 14½×14 (T **90**).

249	**89**	3d. multicoloured	10	10
250		6d. multicoloured	15	10
251	**90**	1s.3d. multicoloured	25	15
252		2s.6d. multicoloured	35	1·10
249/252 *Set of* 4			70	1·25

91 President Nkrumah

94 UN Emblem and Ghana Flag

(Des M. Goaman (3d., 6d.), W. Wind (1s.3d.))

1960 (21 Sept). Founder's Day. T **91** and similar multicoloured designs. W **47** (sideways on 3d.). P 14½×14 (3d.) or 14×14½ (others).

253		3d. Type **91**	10	10
254		6d. President Nkrumah (*vert*)	10	15
255		1s.3d. Flag-draped column over map of Africa (*vert*)	20	30
253/255 *Set of* 3			30	45

(Des M. Goaman (3d., 1s.3d.), W. Wind (6d.))

1960 (10 Dec). Human Rights Day. T **94** and similar vert designs. W **47**. P 14×14½.

256 3d. multicoloured 10 10
257 6d. yellow, black and blue 15 15
258 1s.3d. multicoloured 25 55
256/258 *Set of 3* 40 65

Designs: 3d. T **94**; 6d. UN emblem and Torch; 1s.3d. UN emblem.

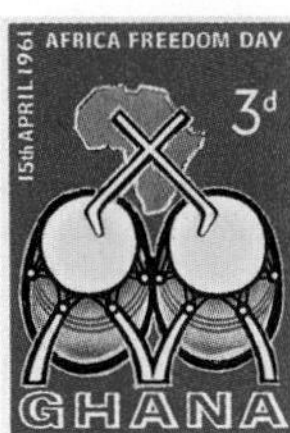

97 Talking Drums

100 Eagle on Column

(Des M. Goaman (3d.), A. S. B. New (6d.), W. Wind (2s.))

1961 (15 Apr). Africa Freedom Day. T **97** and similar designs. W **47** (sideways on 2s.). P 14½×14 (2s.) or 14×14½ (others).

259 3d. multicoloured 10 10
260 6d. red, black and green 20 10
261 2s. multicoloured 50 45
259/261 *Set of 3* 70 50

Designs: Vert—3d. T **97**; 6d. Map of Africa. Horiz—2s. Flags and map.

(Des A. S. B. New (3d.), M. Shamir (1s.3d.), W. Wind (2s.))

1961 (1 July). First Anniversary of Republic. T **100** and similar vert designs. Multicoloured. W **47**. P 14×14½.

262 3d. Type **100** 10 10
263 1s.3d. 'Flower' 10 10
264 2s. Ghana flags .... 20 1·25
262/264 *Set of 3* .... 30 1·25

103 Dove with Olive Branch

106 President Nkrumah and Globe

(Des V. Whiteley)

1961 (1 Sept). Belgrade Conference. T **103** and similar designs. W **47** (sideways on 1s.3d., 5s.). P 14×14½ (3d.) or 14½×14 (others).

265 3d. yellow-green 10 10
266 1s.3d. deep blue 15 10
267 5s. bright reddish purple .... 40 1·25
265/267 *Set of 3* .... 50 1·25

Designs: Vert—3d. T **103**. Horiz—1s.3d. World map, chain and olive branch; 5s. Rostrum, conference room.

(Des A. Medina (3d.), M. Goaman (1s.3d.), Miriam Karoly (5s.))

1961 (21 Sept). Founder's Day. T **106** and similar multicoloured designs. W **47** (sideways on 3d.). P 14½×14 (3d.) or 14×14½ (others).

268 3d. Type **106** 10 10
269 1s.3d. President and Kente Cloth (*vert*) 20 10
270 5s. President in National Costume (*vert*). .... 65 2·50
268/270 *Set of 3* .... 75 2·50

MS270*a* Three sheets 106×86 mm (3d.) or 86×106 mm (others) each with Nos. 268/270 in block of four. Imperf. *Three sheets* .... 2·50 14·00

The 1s.3d. Miniature Sheet is known with the brown colour omitted. (*Price, £2750, unused*)

109 Queen Elizabeth II and African Map

(Des M. Goaman)

1961 (9 Nov). Royal Visit. W **47**. P 14½×14.

271 **109** 3d. multicoloured 15 10
272 1s.3d. multicoloured 30 20
273 5s. multicoloured .... 65 4·00
271/273 *Set of 3* .... 1·00 4·00

MS273*a* 106×84 mm. No. 273 in block of four. Imperf .... 2·25 8·00

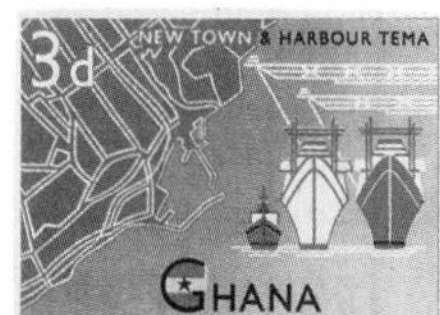

110 Ships in Tema Harbour

(Des C. Bottiau. Litho Enschedé & Sons)

1962 (10 Feb). Opening of Tema Harbour. T **110** and similar horiz designs. Multicoloured. No wmk. P 14×13.

(a) Postage

274 3d. Type **110** 15 10

(b) Air

275 1s.3d. Douglas DC-8 aircraft and ships at Tema 65 15
276 2s.6d. As 1s.3d .... 80 2·50
274/276 *Set of 3* .... 1·40 2·50

112 Africa and Peace Dove

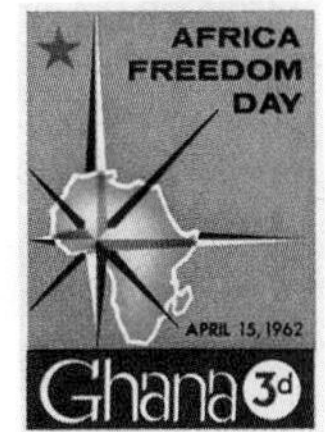

113 Compass over Africa

(Des R. Hegeman. Litho Enschedé)

1962 (6 Mar). First Anniversary of Casablanca Conference. No wmk. P 13×14.

(a) Postage

277 **112** 3d. multicoloured 10 10

(b) Air

278 **112** 1s.3d. multicoloured 20 15
279 2s.6d. multicoloured .... 30 2·00
277/279 *Set of 3* .... 55 2·00

(Des R. Hegeman)

1962 (24 Apr). Africa Freedom Day. W **47**. P 14×14½.

280 **113** 3d. sepia, blue-green and reddish purple 10 10
281 6d. sepia, blue-green and orange-brown 10 15
282 1s.3d. sepia, blue-green and red 15 15
280/282 *Set of 3* 30 30

114 Ghana Star and 'Five Continents'

115 Atomic Bomb-burst 'Skull'

(Des M. Goaman (3d.), M. Shamir (6d.), W. Wind (1s.3d))

1962 (21 June). Accra Assembly, Types **114**/**115** and similar vert design. W **47**. P 14×14½.

283 **114** 3d. black and lake-red 10 10
284 **115** 6d. black and scarlet 25 35
285 – 1s.3d. turquoise 30 50
283/5 *Set of 3* 55 80

Design: 1s.3d. Dove of Peace.

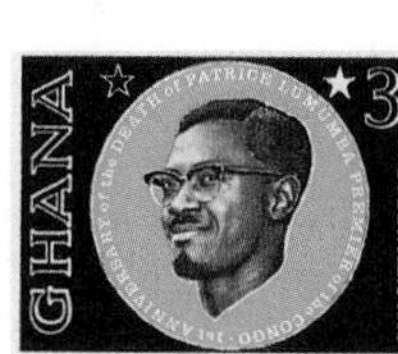

117 Patrice Lumumba

118 Star over Two Columns

(Des A. S. B. New)

1962 (30 June). First Death Anniversary of Lumumba. W **47**. P 14½×14.

286 **117** 3d. black and orange-yellow 10 10
287 6d. black, green and lake 10 30
288 1s.3d. black, pink and black-green 15 35
286/288 *Set of 3* 30 60

(Des A. S. B. New (3d.), A. Medina (6d), M. Goaman (1s.3d) Litho Enschedé)

1962 (1 July). Second Anniversary of Republic. T **118** and similar multicoloured designs. P 14×13½ (1s.3d) or 13½×14 (others).

289 3d. Type **118** 10 10
290 6d. Flaming torch 20 20
291 1s.3d. Eagle trailing flag (*horiz*) 40 40
289/291 *Set of 3* 60 60

121 President Nkrumah

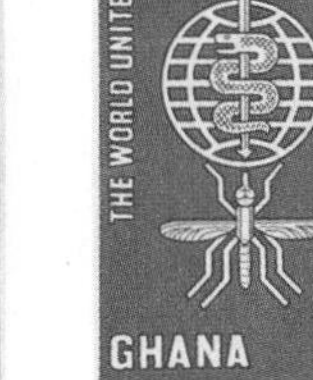

125 Campaign Emblem

(Litho Enschedé)

1962 (21 Sept). Founder's Day. T **121** and similar vert designs. P 13×14½.

292 1d. multicoloured 10 10
293 3d. multicoloured 10 10
294 1s.3d. black and bright blue 30 15
295 2s. multicoloured .... 30 1·75
292/295 *Set of 4* .... 70 1·75

Designs: 1d. T **121**; 3d. Nkrumah medallion; 1s.3d. President Nkrumah and Ghana Star; 2s. Laying 'Ghana' Brick.

1962 (3 Dec). Malaria Eradication. W **47**. P 14×14½.

296 **125** 1d. cerise 10 10
297 4d. yellow-green .... 20 1·50
298 6d. bistre 20 30
299 1s.3d. bluish violet 25 90
296/299 *Set of 4* .... 65 2·50

MS299*a* 90×115 mm. Nos. 296/299. Imperf .... 75 1·50

126 Campaign Emblem

129 Map of Africa

1963 (21 Mar). Freedom from Hunger. T **126** and similar designs. W **47** (sideways on 4d., 1s.3d.). P 14×14½ (1d.) or 14½×14 (others).

300 1d. multicoloured 25 25
301 4d. sepia, yellow and orange .... 1·25 2·00
302 1s.3d. ochre, black and green .... 1·90 1·25
300/302 *Set of 3* .... 3·00 3·25

Designs: Vert—1d. T **126**. Horiz—4d. Emblem in hands; 1s.3d. World map and emblem.

1963 (15 Apr). Africa Freedom Day. T **129** and similar designs. W **47** (sideways on 4d.). P 14½×14 (4d.) or 14×14½ (others).

303 1d. gold and red 10 10
304 4d. red, black and yellow 10 10
305 1s.3d. multicoloured 20 10
306 2s.6d. multicoloured .... 35 1·25
303/306 *Set of 4* .... 65 1·40

Designs: Horiz—4d. Carved stool. Vert—1d. T **129**; 1s.3d. Map and bowl of fire; 2s.6d. Topi (antelope) and flag.

133 Red Cross

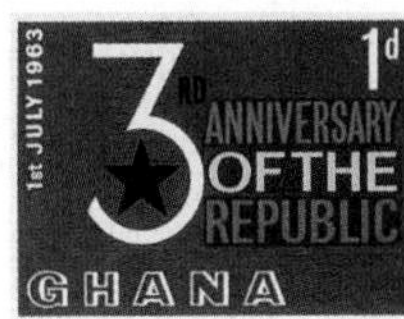

137 '3rd Anniversary'

(Des R. Hegeman (4d.), M. Shamir (others))

1963 (28 May). Red Cross Centenary. T **133** and similar multicoloured designs. W **47** (sideways on 1½d., 4d.). P 14½×14 (1d., 1s.3d.) or 14×14½ (others).

307 1d. Type **133** 50 15
308 1½d. Centenary emblem (*horiz*) .... 75 2·25
309 4d. Nurses and child (*horiz*) .... 1·25 20
310 1s.3d. Emblem, globe and laurel .... 1·75 2·00
307/310 *Set of 4* .... 3·75 4·25

MS310*a* 102×127 mm. Nos. 307/310. Imperf .... 2·75 12·00

(Des M. Goaman (1d., 4d.), R. Hegeman (others))

1963 (1 July). Third Anniversary of Republic. T **137** and similar multicoloured designs. W **47** (sideways on 1d., 4d.). P 14½×14 (horiz) or 14×14½ (vert).

311 1d. Type **137** 10 10
312 4d. Three Ghanaian flags 30 25
a. Black (stars on flag) omitted .... † £800
313 1s.3d. Map, flag and star (*vert*) 70 15
314 2s.6d. Flag and torch (*vert*) .... 70 2·50
311/314 *Set of 4* .... 1·60 2·75

141 President Nkrumah and Ghana Flag

145 Rameses II, Abu Simbel

(Des R. Hegeman (1d., 4d.), M. Shamir (1s.3d.), G. Rose (5s.))

1963 (21 Sept). Founder's Day. T **141** and similar designs. W **47** (sideways on 1s.3d., 5s.). P 14×14½ (vert) or 14½×14 (horiz).

315 1d. multicoloured 10 10
316 4d. multicoloured 15 10
317 1s.3d. multicoloured 30 10
a. Green omitted £400
318 5s. yellow and bright reddish purple 65 90
315/318 *Set of 4* .... 1·00 1·00

Designs: Vert—1d. T **141**; 4d. Nkrumah and flag. Horiz—1s.3d. Nkrumah and fireworks; 5s. Symbol of Wisdom.

(Des M. Farrar Bell and R. Hegeman. Litho (1½d., 2d.) or photo (others) Enschedé)

1963 (1 Nov). Nubian Monuments Preservation. T **145** and similar multicoloured designs. No wmk. P 11½×11 (vert) or 11×11½ (horiz).

319 1d. Type **145** 15 10
320 1½d. Rock paintings (*horiz*) 20 65

321 2d. Queen Nefertari (*horiz*) 20 10
322 4d. Sphinx, Selina 35 15
323 1s.3d. Rock Temple, Abu Simbel (*horiz*)........ 80 90
319/323 *Set of 5* .... 1·50 1·75

150 Class 248 Steam Locomotive and Diesel-electric Locomotive No. 1401

151 Eleanor Roosevelt and 'Flame of Freedom'

(Des H. L. W. Stevens)

1963 (1 Dec). 60th Anniversary of Ghana Railway. W **47** (sideways). P 14½×14.
324 **150** 1d. multicoloured 10 10
325 6d. multicoloured 40 10
326 1s.3d. multicoloured 45 40
327 2s.6d. multicoloured .... 75 1·90
324/327 *Set of 4* .... 1·50 2·25

(Des R. Hegeman and F. H. Savage. Photo Enschedé)

1963 (10 Dec). 15th Anniversary of Declaration of Human Rights. T **151** and similar multicoloured designs. No wmk. P 11×11½ (1s.3d.) or 11½×11 (others).
328 1d. Type **151** 10 10
329 4d. Type **151** 10 30
330 6d. Eleanor Roosevelt 10 10
331 1s.3d. Eleanor Roosevelt and emblems (*horiz*) 15 15
328/331 *Set of 4* 30 50
No. 329 differs from No. 328 in the arrangement of the trailing 'flame' and of the background within the circular emblem.

154 Sun and Globe Emblem

155 Harvesting Corn on State Farm

1964 (15 June). International Quiet Sun Years. W **47** (sideways). Each blue, yellow, red and green; background colours given. P 14½.
332 **154** 3d. pale brown 15 10
333 6d. pale grey 25 10
334 1s.3d. mauve 25 15
332/334 *Set of 3* 60 30
MS334*a* 90×90 mm. No. 334 in block of four. Imperf .... 75 2·50
Nos. 332/334 each exist in a miniature sheet of 12 in different colours (i.e. 3d. in colours of 6d.; 6d. in colours of 1s.3d.; 1s.3d. in colours of 3d.) but these were not generally available to the public.

(Des M. Shamir. Photo Govt Printer, Israel)

1964 (1 July). Fourth Anniversary of Republic. T **155** and similar horiz designs. P 13×14.
335 3d. olive brown and yellow-olive 10 10
336 6d. bluish green, brown and turquoise-green 10 10
337 1s.3d. brown-red, brown and salmon-red.. 10 10
338 5s. multicoloured .... 40 2·25
335/338 *Set of 4* .... 55 2·25
MS338*a* 126×100 mm. Nos. 335/338. Imperf .... 85 2·00
ab. Olive (central design and face value of 3d.) omitted £1000
ac. Green (face value of 5s.) omitted £1200
Designs: 3d. T **155**; 6d. Oil refinery, Tema; 1s.3d. 'Communal Labour'; 5s. Procession headed by flag.

159 Globe and Dove

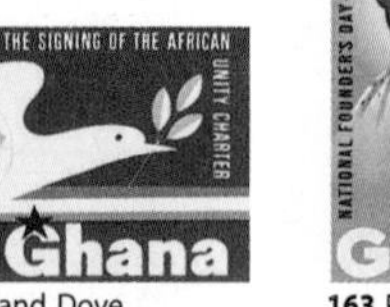

163 President Nkrumah and Hibiscus Flowers

(Des M. Shamir. Litho Lewin-Epstein Ltd, Bat Yam, Israel)

1964 (15 July). First Anniversary of African Unity Charter. T **159** and similar designs. P 14.
339 3d. multicoloured 10 10
340 6d. deep bronze-green and red 10 10
341 1s.3d. multicoloured 15 10
342 5s. multicoloured .... 45 1·00
339/342 *Set of 4* .... 65 1·00
Designs: Vert—6d. Map of Africa and quill pen; 5s. Planting flower. Horiz—3d. T **159**; 1s.3d. Hitched rope on map of Africa.

1964 (21 Sept). Founder's Day. W **47** (sideways). P 14×14½.
343 **163** 3d. sepia, red, deep green and light blue 10 10
344 6d. sepia, red, deep green and yellow 15 10
345 1s.3d. sepia, red, deep green and grey 25 10
346 2s.6d. sepia, red, deep green and light emerald .... 40 1·00
343/346 *Set of 4* .... 75 1·10
MS346*a* 90×122 mm. No. 346 in block of four. Imperf .... 70 2·50
ab. Deep green (face value) omitted £1700

IMPERFORATE STAMPS. Many issues, including miniature sheets, from here onwards exist imperforate, but these were not sold at post offices.

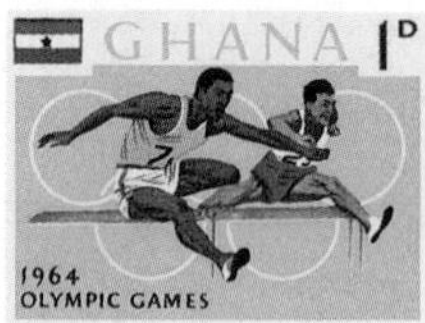

164 Hurdling

(Des A. S. B. New (No. 352))

1964 (25 Oct). Olympic Games, Tokyo. T **164** and similar multicoloured designs. W **47** (sideways on 1d., 2½d., 6d., 5s.). P 14½×14 (horiz) or 14×14½ (vert).
347 1d. Type **164** 10 10
348 2½d. Running .... 10 1·50
349 3d. Boxing (*vert*) 10 10
350 4d. Long-jumping (*vert*) 10 10
351 6d. Football (*vert*) 15 10
352 1s.3d. Athlete holding Olympic Torch (*vert*) 20 10
353 5s. Olympic Rings and flags .... 75 3·25
347/353 *Set of 7* .... 1·25 4·50
MS353*a* 128×102 mm. Nos. 351/353. Imperf .... 75 2·50
ab. Brown omitted £1000

171 G. Washington Carver (botanist) and Plant

173 African Elephant

(Des M. Shamir)

1964 (7 Dec). UNESCO Week. W **47**. P 14½.
354 **171** 6d. deep blue and green 15 10
355 – 1s.3d. reddish purple and greenish blue 30 10
w. Wmk inverted .... 11·00
356 **171** 5s. sepia and orange-red .... 50 4·25
354/356 *Set of 3* .... 85 4·25
MS356*a* 127×77 mm. Nos. 354/356. Imperf .... 75 2·00
Design: 1s.3d. Albert Einstein (scientist) and atomic symbol.

(Des A. S. B. New (No. 360). Photo Enschedé)

1964 (14 Dec). Multicoloured designs as T **173**. P 11½×11 (vert) or 11×11½ (horiz).
357 1d. Type **173** 40 50
358 1½d. Secretary Bird (*horiz*) .... 50 2·25
359 2½d. Purple Wreath (flower) .... 15 2·25
360 3d. Grey Parrot 50 50
361 4d. Blue-naped Mousebird (*horiz*) 50 70
362 6d. African Tulip Tree (*horiz*) 15 30
363 1s.3d. Violet Starling (*horiz*) 60 85
364 2s.6d. Hippopotamus (*horiz*) .... 60 5·00
357/364 *Set of 8* .... 3·00 11·00
MS364*a* (a) 150×86 mm. Nos. 357/359. (b) 150×110 mm. Nos. 360/364. Imperf *Set of 2 sheets*.. 3·00 14·00

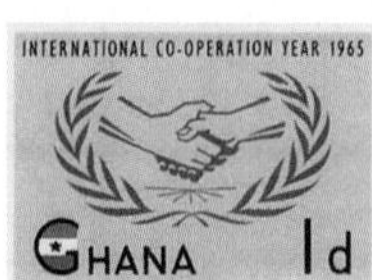

181 ICY Emblem

(Litho Enschedé)

1965 (22 Feb). International Co-operation Year. P 14×12½.
365 **181** 1d. multicoloured 35 70
366 4d. multicoloured .... 1·00 2·00
367 6d. multicoloured .... 1·00 70
368 1s.3d. multicoloured .... 1·25 2·75
365/368 *Set of 4* .... 3·25 5·50
MS368*a* 100×100 mm. No. 368 in block of four. Imperf .... 2·75 5·00

182 ITU Emblem and Symbols

(Litho Enschedé)

1965 (12 Apr). ITU Centenary. P 13½.
369 **182** 1d. multicoloured 15 15
370 6d. multicoloured 30 15
371 1s.3d. multicoloured 55 25
372 5s. multicoloured .... 1·25 3·25
369/372 *Set of 4* .... 2·00 3·50
MS372*a* 132×115 mm. Nos. 369/372. Imperf .... 8·00 12·00

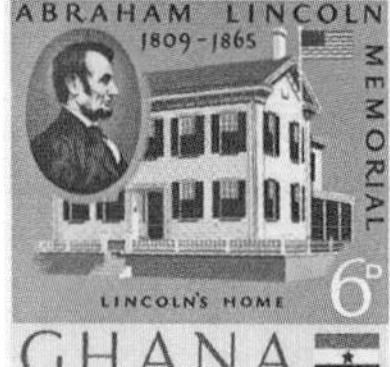

183 Lincoln's Home

(Des M. Farrar Bell (6d.), A. S. B. New (1s.3d., 5s.), R. Hegeman (2s.))

1965 (17 May). Death Centenary of Abraham Lincoln. T **183** and similar square-shaped designs. W **47** (sideways). P 12½.
373 6d. multicoloured 10 10
374 1s.3d. black, red and blue 15 15
375 2s. black, orange-brown and greenish yellow 15 35
376 5s. black and red .... 30 1·75
373/376 *Set of 4* .... 60 2·00
MS376*a* 115×115 mm. Nos. 373/376. Imperf .... 75 3·50
ab. Green (part of flag on 6d.) omitted ... £1100
Designs: 6d. T **183**; 1s.3d. Lincoln's Inaugural Address; 2s. Abraham Lincoln: 5s. Adaptation of US 90c Lincoln Stamp of 1899.

(New Currency. 100 pesewas = 1 cedi)

187 Obverse (President Nkrumah) and Reverse of 5p. Coin

(Photo Enschedé)

1965 (19 July). Introduction of Decimal Currency. T **187** and similar horiz designs. Multicoloured. P 11×13 (5p., 10p.), 13×12½ (25p.) or 13½×14 (50p.)
377 5p. Type **187** 20 10
378 10p. As Type **187** 25 10
379 25p. Size 63×39 mm .... 55 1·00
380 50p. Size 71×43½ mm .... 1·00 3·25
377/380 *Set of 4* .... 1·75 4·00
The coins in Nos. 378/380 are all circular and express the same denominations as on the stamps.

₵2·40
Ghana New Currency
19th July, 1965.

(188)

1965 (19 July). Nos. 214, 216 and 218a/227 surch as T **188** diagonally upwards, (D) or horizontally, (H), by Govt Printer, Accra.

(a) Postage
381 1p. on 1d. multicoloured (R.) (D) 10 10
a. Surch inverted .... 15·00
b. Surch double .... 70·00
382 2p. on 2d. multicoloured (Ultram.) (H) ... 10 10
a. Surch inverted .... 22·00
b. Surch double .... 18·00
c. Surch on back only £200
d. Surch on front and back £200
e. Red surch .... 28·00
f. Orange surch .... 38·00
g. Indigo surch .... 38·00
ga. Surch sideways ....
gb. Ditto. Pair, one without surch £200
383 3p. on 3d. multicoloured (II) (Br.) (H) .... 1·00 7·50
a. Surch inverted .... 22·00
b. Indigo surch ....
384 4p. on 4d. multicoloured (B.) (H) .... 5·00 45
a. Surch inverted .... 75·00 75·00
b. Surch double .... 60·00
c. Vert pair, one without surch £100
d. Red surch ....
385 6p. on 6d. multicoloured (Blk.) (H) 50 10
a. Surch inverted .... 8·50 10·00
b. Surch double .... 16·00
c. Horiz pair, one without surch £110
d. Green (flag) omitted £275
386 11p. on 11d. multicoloured (W.) (D) 25 10
a. Surch inverted .... 13·00 9·00
387 12p. on 1s. multicoloured (B.) (D) 25 10
a. Surch double .... 60·00
b. Surch double, one albino inverted ...
c. Pair, one without surch £100
d. Black surch .... 15·00 10·00
da. Surch inverted .... 14·00 7·00
388 30p. on 2s.6d. multicoloured (B.) (H) .... 6·50 12·00
389 60p. on 5s. multicoloured (B.) (D) .... 4·50 70
a. Surch double (G.+B.) .... 55·00
390 1c.20 on 10s. multicoloured (B.) (D) .... 75 2·25
a. Surch double (G.+B.) £170
391 2c.40 on £1 multicoloured (B.) (D) .... 1·00 6·50
a. Vert pair, one without surch £170

(b) Air
392 15p. on 1s.3d. multicoloured (W.) (H) .... 2·50 70
a. Surch inverted ....
393 24p. on 2s. multicoloured (G.) (D) .... 2·50 30
a. Surch on front and back .... 42·00
381/393 *Set of 13* .... 20·00 26·00
On the diagonal surcharges the values are horizontal.
The 30p. was not released in Ghana until 30 July and the 3p. sometime later.
Numerous minor varieties exist.

189 'OAU' and Flag

190 'OAU', Heads and Flag

191 'OAU' Emblem and Flag

192 African Map and Flag

1965 (21 Oct). OAU Summit Conference, Accra. Types **189/192** and similar horiz designs. Multicoloured. W **47** (sideways* except on 6p.). P 14 (Types **189/191**) or 14½×14 (others).

394	1p. Type **189**	20	40
	a. Red (part of flag) omitted	£275	
395	2p. Type **190**	20	40
396	5p. Type **191**	30	40
397	6p. Type **192**	30	10
398	15p. 'Sunburst', map and flag	40	30
399	24p. 'OAU' on map, and flag	55	70
	w. Wmk top of G to left		
394/399	*Set of 6*	1·75	2·00

* The 1p. also exists with the watermark facing left or right, but positional blocks are required to show the two types. The normal sideways watermark has top of G to right, *as seen from the back of the stamp.*

195 Goalkeeper saving Ball

198 President Kennedy and Grave Memorial

(Photo Enschedé)

1965 (15 Nov). African Soccer Cup Competition. T **195** and similar multicoloured designs. P 13×14 (15p.) or 14×13 (others).

400	6p. Type **195**	25	10
401	15p. Player with ball (*vert*)	40	30
402	24p. Players, ball and soccer cup	45	1·60
400/402	*Set of 3*	1·00	1·75

(Des A. S. B. New (No. 405))

1965 (15 Dec)–**66**. Second Anniversary of President Kennedy's Death. T **198** and similar square-shaped designs. W **47** (sideways). P 12½.

403	6p. multicoloured	15	10
404	15p. violet, red and green	20	35
405	24p. black and reddish violet	20	60
406	30p. dull purple and black	25	1·25
403/406	*Set of 4*	70	2·00
MS407	114½×114 mm. Nos. 403/406. Imperf (21.3.66)	1·50	4·00

Designs: 6p. T **198**; 15p. President Kennedy and Eternal Flame; 24p. President Kennedy and memorial inscription; 30p. President Kennedy.

202 Section of Dam and Generators

Black Stars Retain Africa Cup
21st Nov. 1965

(**206**)

(Des A. S. B. New (No. 411). Photo Enschedé)

1966 (22 Jan). Volta River Project. T **202** and similar horiz designs. P 11×11½.

408	6p. multicoloured	15	10
409	15p. multicoloured	20	15
410	24p. multicoloured	25	20
411	30p. black and new blue	35	1·50
408/411	*Set of 4*	85	1·75

Designs: 6p. T **202**; 15p. Dam and Lake Volta; 24p. Word 'GHANA' as dam; 30p. 'Fertility'.

1966 (7 Feb). 'Black Stars' Victory in African Soccer Cup Competition. Nos. 400/402 optd with T **206**, in black.

412	6p. Type **195**	50	20
	a. Green opt	22·00	
	b. Green opt double, one inverted	65·00	
	c. Stop after 'Nov' omitted (R. 5/1)	13·00	13·00
413	15p. Player with ball	70	40
414	24p. Players, ball and cup	75	1·40
	a. Opt inverted*	32·00	
	ab. Vert pair, one without opt, the other with opt inverted	£170	
	b. Error. Opt for 15p. on 24p. inverted*	32·00	
	c. Stop after 'Nov' omitted (R. 5/1)	17·00	
412/414	*Set of 3*	1·75	1·75

* In No. 414a the overprint reads downwards (top right to bottom left), but in No. 414b it reads upwards (bottom right to top left).

DATES OF ISSUE of miniature sheets are approximate as they are generally released some time after the related ordinary stamps, but it is known that the GPO sometimes applied first-day cancellations months after the dates shown on the cancellations.

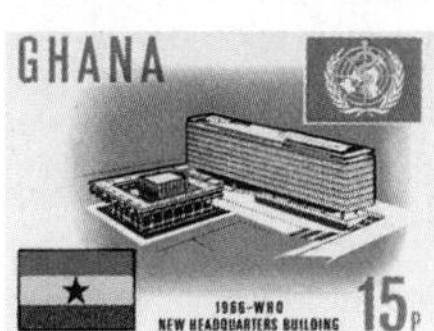

207 WHO Building and Ghana Flag

1966 (1 July–Nov). Inauguration of WHO Headquarters, Geneva. T **207** and similar horiz design. Multicoloured. W **47**. P 14½×14.

415	6p. Type **207**	1·25	10
416	15p. Type **207**	2·00	65
417	24p. WHO Building and emblem	2·00	2·25
418	30p. As 24p.	2·00	7·00
415/418	*Set of 4*	6·50	9·00
MS419	120×101 mm. Nos. 415/418. Imperf (11.66)	24·00	22·00

209 Atlantic Herring

(Des O. Hamann. Photo Enschedé)

1966 (10 Aug–Nov). Freedom from Hunger. T **209** and similar horiz designs. Multicoloured. P 14×13.

420	6p. Type **209**	20	10
421	15p. Turbot	40	15
422	24p. Spadefish	40	35
423	30p. Red Snapper	45	1·50
424	60p. Blue-finned Tuna	55	5·25
420/424	*Set of 5*	1·75	6·50
MS425	126×109 mm. No. 423 in block of four. Imperf (11.66)	5·50	13·00

214 African 'Links' and Ghana Flag

(Photo Enschedé)

1966 (11 Oct). Third Anniversary of African Charter. T **214** and similar multicoloured designs. P 13½.

426	6p. Type **214**	15	10
427	15p. Flags as 'Quill', and diamond (*horiz*)	35	55
428	24p. Ship's wheel, map and cocoa bean (*horiz*)	40	70
426/428	*Set of 3*	80	1·25

217 Player heading Ball, and Jules Rimet Cup

1966 (14 Nov). World Cup Football Championship, England. T **217** and similar horiz designs. Multicoloured. W **47**. P 14½×14.

429	5p. Type **217**	70	20
430	15p. Goalkeeper clearing ball	1·50	30
	w. Wmk inverted	1·60	1·60
431	24p. Player and Jules Rimet Cup (replica)	1·75	50
432	30p. Players and Jules Rimet Cup (replica)	2·00	1·75
433	60p. Players with ball	3·00	11·00
	w. Wmk inverted	12·00	
429/433	*Set of 5*	8·00	12·00
MS434	120×102 mm. 60p. (block of four). Imperf	25·00	26·00

222 UNESCO Emblem

1966 (23 Dec). 20th Anniversary of UNESCO. W **47** (sideways). P 14½.

435	**222** 5p. multicoloured	1·25	25
436	15p. multicoloured	2·50	60
437	24p. multicoloured	3·00	1·25
438	30p. multicoloured	3·00	3·75
439	60p. multicoloured	3·75	14·00
435/439	*Set of 5*	12·00	18·00
MS440	140×115 mm. Nos. 435/439. Imperf	25·00	30·00

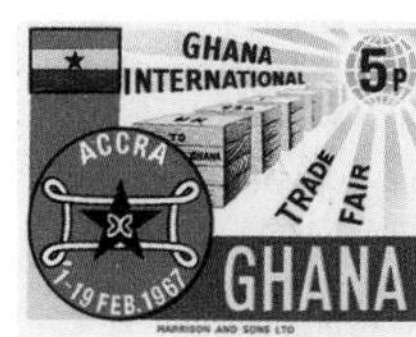

223 Fair Emblem and Crates

1967 (1 Feb). Ghana Trade Fair, Accra. T **223** and similar multicoloured designs. W **47** (sideways on 24p.). P 14×14½ (24p.) or 14½×14 (others).

441	5p. Type **223**	10	10
442	15p. Fair emblem and world map	15	20
443	24p. Shipping and flags (*vert*)	25	30
444	36p. Fair emblem and hand-held hoist	40	2·75
441/444	*Set of 4*	70	3·00

(New Currency. 100 new pesewae = 1 new cedi (1.2 old cedi))

1½Np N₵2.00

(**227**) (**228**)

1967 (23 Feb). Nos. 216, 219/223, 225/226 and 393 surch as Types **227/228**.

(a) Postage

445	1½n.p. on 2d. multicoloured (Blk.)	2·00	13·00
446	3½n.p. on 4d. multicoloured (R.)	9·00	6·00
	a. Surch double, one sideways		
	b. Surch double	—	70·00
447	5n.p. on 6d. multicoloured (R.)	5·50	2·25
448	9n.p. on 11d. multicoloured (W.)	30	1·00
449	10n.p. on 1s. multicoloured (W.)	30	2·25
450	25n.p. on 2s.6d. multicoloured (R.)	3·50	10·00
451	1n.c. on 10s. multicoloured (R.)	2·50	16·00
452	2n.c. on £1 multicoloured (R.)	4·00	24·00

(b) Air

453	12½n.p. on 1s.3d. multicoloured (W.)	5·00	7·50
454	20n.p. on 24p. on 2s. multicoloured (R.1)	6·00	10·00
445/454	*Set of 10*	32·00	80·00

Inverted surcharges in a different type face on the 3½, 5 and 25n.p. are fakes.

229 Ghana Eagle and Flag

(Des M. Shamir)

1967 (24 Feb). First Anniversary of February 24 Revolution. W **47** (sideways). P 14×14½.

455	**229** 1n.p. multicoloured	10	90
456	4n.p. multicoloured	10	10
457	12½n.p. multicoloured	35	60
458	25n.p. multicoloured	65	3·50
455/458	*Set of 4*	1·00	4·50
MS459	89×108 mm. Nos. 455/458. Perf or imperf	4·00	12·00

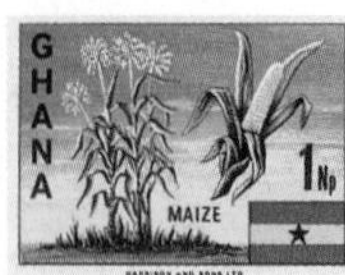

230 Maize

231 Forest Kingfisher

235 Rufous-crowned Roller

236 Akasombo Dam

1967 (1 June–Sept). Types **230/231**, **235/236** and similar designs. W **47** (1½, 2, 4, 50n.p. and 1n.c.) or sideways (others). P 11½×12 (1, 8n.p), 12×11½ (4n.p), 14×14½ (1½ 2, 2½, 20n.p., 2n.c. 50) or 14½×14 (others).

460	1n.p. multicoloured	10	10
	a. Salmon omitted**	£400	
461	1½n.p. multicoloured	1·00	2·75
	a. Blue omitted*	£275	
	b. Green printed double, once inverted†	†	£650
	c. Green omitted	†	£450
	d. Black omitted	†	£650
462	2n.p. multicoloured (4.9)	10	10
	a. Green (part of flag) omitted	£275	
	b. Gold (frame) omitted	£225	
	w. Wmk inverted	10·00	
463	2½n.p. multicoloured (4.9)	35	10
	a. Wmk upright	14·00	
	ab. Face value omitted	£450	
464	3n.p. multicoloured	20	40
	a. Green (part of flag) omitted	—	£700
465	4n.p. multicoloured	1·50	10
	a. Green (part of flag) omitted	£150	
	b. Red (part of flag) omitted	£700	
	c. Black (star, bird markings and shadow) omitted	£225	
466	6n.p. multicoloured	15	2·25
467	8n.p. multicoloured	15	1·00
468	9n.p. multicoloured (4.9)	75	10
469	10n.p. multicoloured	15	10
470	20n.p. deep blue and new blue (4.9)	20	10
471	50n.p. multicoloured	13·00	4·50
472	1n.c. multicoloured (4.9)	2·00	1·50
473	2n.c. multicoloured (4.9)	2·25	3·50
474	2n.c. 50 multicoloured	2·25	12·00
460/474 *Set of 15*		21·00	25·00

Designs:—Vert (as T **231**)—1½n.p. T **231**; 2n.p. The Ghana Mace; 2½n.p Commelina; 20n.p. Bush Hare; 2n.c. Frangipani; 2n.c. 50, Seat of State; 4n.p. T **235**. Horiz (as T **236**)—3n.p. West African Lungfish; 6n.p. T **236**; 9n.p. Chameleon; 10n.p Tema Harbour; 50n.p. Black-winged Stilt; 1n.c. Wooden Stool. (As T **230**)—1n.p. T **230**; 8n.p. Adomi Bridge.

* In this stamp the blue not only affects the bird but is printed over the yellow background to give the value in green, so that its omission results in the value also being omitted.

** This affects the maize flowers, corn and foreground.

† This affects the feather-tips and the flag.

The 2n.p. and 20n.p. were officially issued on 4 September but small quantities of both were released in error on 1 June. The 2½ n.p. is also known to have been released in error in June.

245 Kumasi Fort

(Des O. Hamann)

1967 (1 July). Castles and Forts. T **245** and similar designs. Multicoloured. W **47** (diagonal). P 14½.

475	4n.p. Type **245**	25	10
476	12½n.p. Cristiansborg Castle and British galleon	60	1·00
477	20n.p. Elmina Castle and Portuguese galleon	75	3·00
478	25n.p. Cape Coast Castle and Spanish galleon	75	3·75
475/478 *Set of 4*		2·10	7·00

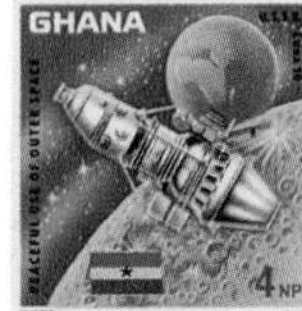

249 *Luna 10*

(Des M. Shamir. Photo Enschedé)

1967 (16 Aug). 'Peaceful Use of Outer Space'. T **249** and similar square designs. Multicoloured. P 13½×14.

479	4n.p. Type **249**	10	10
480	10n.p. *Orbiter 1*	10	60
481	12½n.p. Man in Space	20	1·10
479/481 *Set of 3*		35	1·60
MS482 140×90 mm. Nos. 479/481. Imperf		2·00	6·00

252 Scouts and Camp-fire

(Photo Enschedé)

1967 (18 Sept). 50th Anniversary of Ghanaian Scout Movement. T **252** and similar horiz designs. multicoloured. P 14½×13.

483	4n.p. Type **252**	20	10
484	10n.p. Scout on march	40	50
485	12½n.p. Lord Baden-Powell	50	1·75
483/485 *Set of 3*		1·00	2·00
MS486 167×95 mm. Nos. 483/485. Imperf		2·50	10·00

255 UN Headquarters Building

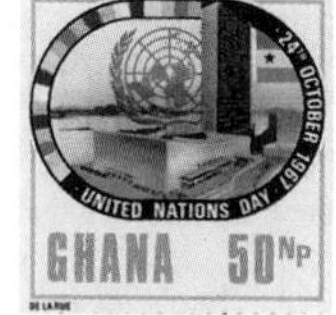

256 General View of UN HQ, Manhattan

(Litho D.L.R.)

1967 (20 Nov–4 Dec). United Nations Day (24 October). P 13½.

487	**255**	4n.p. multicoloured	10	10
488		10n.p. multicoloured	10	15
489	**256**	50n.p. multicoloured	20	70
490		2n.c.50 multicoloured	55	4·00
487/490 *Set of 4*			75	4·50
MS491 76×75 mm. No. 490. Imperf (4.12.67)			1·75	9·50

257 Leopard

1967 (28 Dec). International Tourist Year. T **257** and similar diamond-shaped designs. Multicoloured. W **47** (diagonal). P 12½.

492	4n.p. Type **257**	1·00	20
493	12½n.p. *Papilio demodocus* (butterfly)	2·50	1·50
494	20n.p. Carmine Bee-eater	3·50	3·75
495	50n.p. Waterbuck	2·50	9·00
492/495 *Set of 4*		8·50	13·00
MS496 126×126 mm. Nos. 493/495. Imperf		18·00	23·00

261 Revolutionaries entering Accra

(Litho D.L.R.)

1968 (24 Feb). Second Anniversary of February Revolution. T **261** and similar horiz designs. Multicoloured. P 14.

497	4n.p. Type **261**	10	10
498	12½n.p. Marching troops	20	20
499	20n.p. Cheering people	30	40
500	40n.p. Victory celebrations	50	3·25
497/500 *Set of 4*		1·00	3·50

265 Microscope and Cocoa Beans

1968 (18 Mar). Cocoa Reseach. T **265** and similar horiz design. Multicoloured. W **47** (sideways). P 14½×14.

501	2½n.p. Type **265**	10	1·25
502	4n.p. Microscope and cocoa tree, beans and pods	10	10
503	10n.p. Type **265**	15	30
504	25n.p. As 4n.p.	60	1·75
501/504 *Set of 4*		80	3·00
MS505 102×102 mm. Nos. 501/504. Imperf		2·25	5·50

267 Kotoka and Flowers

271 Tobacco

(Des A. S. B. New (No. 508) and F. Mate (others) Litho D.L.R.)

1968 (17 Apr). First Death Anniversary of Lieutenant General E. K. Kotoka. T **267** and similar multicoloured designs. P 14.

506	4n.p. Type **267**	10	10
507	12½n.p. Kotoka and wreath	20	30
508	20n.p. Kotoka in civilian clothes	35	75
509	40n.p. Lt.-Gen. Kotoka (*vert*)	50	3·00
506/509 *Set of 4*		1·00	3·75

(Des A. S. B. New (5n.p.))

1968 (19 Aug). Flora and Fauna. T **271** and similar vert designs. Multicoloured. W **47** (sideways). P 14×14½.

510	4n.p. Type **271**	15	10
511	5n.p. North African Crested Porcupine	15	1·25
512	12½n.p. Rubber	30	75
513	20n.p. *Cymothoe sangaris* (butterfly)	1·00	2·75
514	40n.p. *Charaxes ameliae* (butterfly)	1·25	5·00
510/514 *Set of 5*		2·50	8·50
MS515 88×114 mm. Nos. 510, 512/514. Imperf		2·50	9·00

276 Surgeons, Flag and WHO Emblem

277 Hurdling

(Photo Enschedé)

1968 (11 Nov). 20th Anniversary of World Health Organisation. P 14×13.

516	**276**	4n.p. multicoloured	20	10
517		12½n.p. multicoloured	40	40
518		20n.p. multicoloured	60	1·25
519		40n.p. multicoloured	1·00	3·75
516/519 *Set of 4*			2·00	5·00
MS520 132×110 mm. Nos. 516/519. Imperf			2·00	6·50

1969 (10–17 Jan). Olympic Games, Mexico (1968). T **277** and similar vert designs. Multicoloured. W **47** (sideways). P 14×14½.

521	4n.p. Type **277**	10	10
522	12½n.p. Boxing	20	30
523	20n.p. Torch, Olympic Rings and flags	40	75
524	40n.p. Football	70	3·25
521/524 *Set of 4*		1·25	4·00
MS525 89×114 mm. Nos. 521/524 Imperf (17.1.69)		3·00	8·00

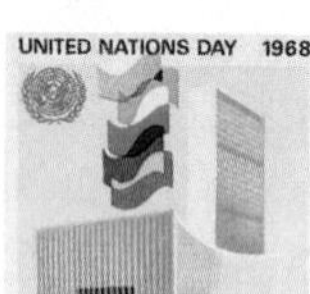

281 UN Building

(Litho D.L.R.)

1969 (1 Feb). United Nations Day (1968). T **281** and similar square-shaped designs. Multicoloured. P 13½.

526	4n.p. Type **281**	10	10
527	12½n.p. Native stool, staff and UN emblem	15	25
528	20n.p. UN building and emblem over Ghanaian flag	20	45
529	40n.p. UN emblem encircled by flags	40	2·75
526/529 *Set of 4*		75	3·25
MS530 127×117 mm. No. 526/529. Imperf		75	3·50

285 Dr. J. B. Danquah

1969 (7 Mar–17 Apr). Human Rights Year. T **285** and similar horiz design. Multicoloured. W **47** (sideways on **MS**535). P 14½×14.

531	4n.p. Type **285**	10	10
532	12½n.p. Dr. Martin Luther king	20	35
533	20n.p. As 12½n.p.	35	75
534	40n.p. Type **285**	50	3·00
531/534 *Set of 4*		1·00	3·75
MS535 116×50 mm. Nos. 531/534. Imperf (17.4.69)		80	4·25

287 Constituent Assembly Building

1969 (10 Sept). Third Anniversary of the Revolution. T **287** and similar horiz design. W **47** (sideways on **MS**540). P 14½×14.

536 4n.p. Type **287** 10 10
537 12½n.p. Arms of Ghana 10 15
538 20n.p. Type **287** 15 20
539 40n.p. As 12½n.p. 20 75
536/539 *Set of* 4 40 1·00
MS540 114×89 mm. Nos. 536/539. Imperf 70 3·00

NEW CONSTITUTION
1969
(289)

1969 (1 Oct). New Constitution. Nos. 460/474 optd with T **289** in various positions by Government Press, Accra.

541 1n.p. multicoloured (*horiz*) 10 2·75
a. Opt inverted 75·00
542 1½n.p. multicoloured (*vert down*) 4·25 7·50
aa. Opt omitted (*in horiz pair with normal*) £325
a. Opt vert up 4·50
b. Horiz opt 27·00
ba. Opt omitted (*in vert pair with normal*) £325
543 2n.p. multicoloured (*vert up*) 10 4·00
a. Opt vert up 5·00
b. Opt double 14·00
544 2½n.p. multicoloured (*vert up*) 40 2·50
a. Opt vert down 23·00
b. Opt omitted (*in horiz pair with normal*) £225
c. Opt double, one diagonal 65·00
545 3n.p. multicoloured (*horiz*) 1·75 2·75
a. Opt inverted 18·00
546 4n.p. multicoloured (Y.) (*vert down*) 2·50 1·25
a. Black opt (*vert down*) 4·00 1·75
b. Black opt (*vert up*) 23·00
c. Red opt (*vert down*) 20·00
d. Opt double (*White vert down+yellow vert up*) 30·00
547 6n.p. multicoloured (*horiz*) 15 3·25
548 8n.p. multicoloured (*horiz*) 15 4·75
549 9n.p. multicoloured (*horiz*) 15 3·75
550 10n.p. multicoloured (*horiz*) 2·50 4·50
551 20n.p. deep blue and new blue (*vert up*) 2·50 3·00
a. Opt vert down 24·00
552 50n.p. multicoloured (*horiz*) 7·00 8·50
a. Opt double 28·00
553 1n.c. multicoloured (*horiz*) 1·50 9·50
554 2n.c. multicoloured (R.) (*vert up*) 1·50 9·50
a. Opt double vert up and down 60·00
b. Opt triple (*Red vert up and down+yellow vert up*) 80·00
555 2n.c. 50 multicoloured (*vert down*) 1·50 10·00
541/555 *Set of* 15 23·00 65·00

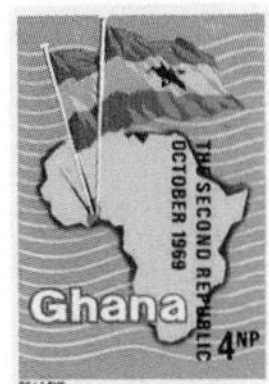

290 Map of Africa and Flags

(Litho D.L.R.)

1969 (4 Dec). Inauguration of Second Republic. T **290** and similar vert designs. Multicoloured. P 14.

556 4n.p. Type **290** 30 10
557 12½n.p. Figure '2', branch and Ghanaian colours 20 10
558 20n.p. Hands receiving egg 35 35
559 40n.p. Type **290** 1·10 1·75
556/559 *Set of* 4 1·75 2·00

293 ILO Emblem and Cog-wheels

1970 (5 Jan). 50th Anniversary of International Labour Organisation. W **47** (sideways). P 14½×14.

560 **293** 4n.p. multicoloured 10 10
561 12½n.p. multicoloured 20 55
562 20n.p. multicoloured 30 1·50
560/562 *Set of* 3 55 1·90
MS563 117×89 mm. Nos. 560/562. Imperf 70 3·00

294 Red Cross and Globe

298 General Kotoka, Vickers VC-10 and Airport

1970 (2 Feb). 50th Anniversary of League of Red Cross Societies. T **294** and similar multicoloured designs. W **47** (sideways on 4n.p.). P 14×14½ (4n.p) or 14½×14 (others).

564 4n.p. Type **294** 20 10
565 12½n.p. Henri Dunant and Red Cross emblem (*horiz*) 25 25
w. Wmk inverted
566 20n.p. Patient receiving medicine (*horiz*) 30 85
567 40n.p. Patient having arm bandaged (*horiz*) 35 3·50
564/567 *Set of* 4 1·00 4·25
MS568 114×89 mm. Nos. 564/567. Imperf 1·25 6·00

(Des G. Vasarhelyi. Litho D.L.R.)

1970 (17 Apr). Inauguration of Kotoka Airport. T **298** and similar horiz designs. Multicoloured. P 13×13½.

569 4n.p. Type **298** 15 10
570 12½n.p. Control tower and tail of Vickers VC-10 25 15
571 20n.p. Aerial view of airport 40 30
572 40n.p. Airport and flags 75 80
569/572 *Set of* 4 1·40 1·25

302 Lunar Module landing on Moon

306 Adult Education

(Des A. Medina (4n.p., 12½n.p), G. Vasarhelyi (others). Litho D.L.R.)

1970 (15 June). Moon Landing. T **302** and similar multicoloured designs. P 12½.

573 4n.p. Type **302** 25 10
574 12½n.p. Astronaut's first step onto the Moon 30 60
575 20n.p. Astronaut with equipment on Moon (*horiz*) 35 1·40
576 40n.p. Astronauts (*horiz*) 45 3·25
573/576 *Set of* 4 1·25 4·75
MS577 142×142 mm. Nos. 573/576. Imperf (with or without simulated perfs) 2·00 12·00

On 18 September 1970 Nos. 573/576 were issued overprinted 'PHILYMPIA LONDON 1970' but it is understood that only 900 sets were made available for sale in Ghana and we do not consider that this is sufficient to constitute normal postal use. The miniature sheet was also overprinted but not issued in Ghana.

(Litho D.L.R.)

1970 (10 Aug). International Education Year. T **306** and similar horiz designs. Multicoloured. P 13.

578 4n.p. Type **306** 10 10
579 12½n.p. International education 20 20
580 20n.p. 'Ntesie' and IEY symbols 35 30
581 40n.p. Nursery schools 60 1·40
578/581 *Set of* 4 1·10 1·75

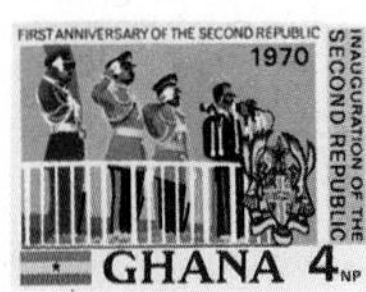

310 Saluting March-Past

(Litho D.L.R.)

1970 (1 Oct). First Anniversary of the Second Republic. T **310** and similar horiz designs. Multicoloured. P 13×13½.

582 4n.p. Type **310** 20 10
583 12½n.p. Busia declaration 15 15
584 20n.p. Doves symbol 25 30
585 40n.p. Opening of Parliament 50 1·00
582/585 *Set of* 4 1·00 1·40

314 *Crinum ornatum*

(Des G. Vasarhelyi. Photo Harrison)

1970 (2 Nov). Flora and Fauna. T **314** and similar horiz designs. Multicoloured. W **47** (sideways). P 14½×14.

586 4n.p. Type **314** 1·75 25
w. Wmk inverted 9·50
587 12½n.p. Lioness 1·25 85
588 20n.p. *Ansellia africana* (flower) 1·25 1·50
589 40n.p. African Elephant 2·00 6·00
586/589 *Set of* 4 5·50 7·75

315 Kuduo Brass Casket

(Des G. Vasarhelyi. Photo Harrison)

1970 (7 Dec)–**71**. Monuments and Archaeological Sites in Ghana. T **315** and similar horiz designs. Multicoloured. W **47**. P 14½×14.

590 4n.p. Type **315** 15 10
w. Wmk inverted 21·00
591 12½n.p. Akan traditional house 30 20
592 20n.p. Larabanga Mosque 35 55
593 40n.p. Funerary clay head 50 2·50
590/593 *Set of* 4 1·10 3·00
MS594 89×71 mm. Nos. 590, 592 and 12½n.p. Basilica of Pompeii, 40n.p. Pistrinum of Pompeii (wmk sideways). Imperf (2.71) 2·00 9·00

STAMP BOOKLETS

1961. Red (No. SB2), yellow (No. SB3) or green (No. SB4) covers. Stitched.

SB2 3s. booklet containing 12×3d. (No. 218a) in blocks of 4 6·50
SB3 6s. booklet containing 8×3d. and 8×6d. (Nos. 218a, 220) in blocks of 4 8·00
SB4 10s. booklet containing 4×3d., 8×6d. and 4×1s.3d. (Nos. 218a, 220, 226) in blocks of 4. 10·00

1963 (1 Jan). Black on red (No. SB5), black on yellow (No. SB6) or black on green (No. SB7) covers. Stitched.

SB5 4s. booklet containing 12×4d. (No. 219) in blocks of 4
SB6 6s. booklet containing 12×4d. and 4×6d. (Nos. 219/220) in blocks of 4
SB7 11s. booklet containing 12×4d., 4×6d. and 4×1s.3d. (Nos. 219/220, 226) in blocks of 4 ...
SB5/SB7 *Set of* 3 booklets £350

POSTAGE DUE STAMPS

GHANA
(D 2)

D 3

1958 (25 June). Nos. D5/D8 of Gold Coast and similar 1d. value optd with T D **2** in red.

D9 D **1** 1d. black 10 30
D10 2d. black 10 30
c. Large 'd' 2·25
D11 3d. black 10 30
a. Missing serif 4·50
D12 6d. black 15 65
D13 1s. black 20 1·50
c. Upright stroke 1·50
ca. Short upright stroke 5·00
D9/D13 *Set of* 5 50 2·75

(Typo De La Rue)

1958 (1 Dec). Chalk-surfaced paper. Wmk Mult Script CA. P 14.

D14 D **3** 1d. carmine 10 30
D15 2d. green 10 30
c. Large 'd' 2·25
D16 3d. orange 10 30
a. Missing serif 4·25
D17 6d. bright ultramarine 10 50
D18 1s. reddish violet 15 2·00
c. Upright stroke 1·50
ca. Short upright stroke 5·00
D14/D18 *Set of* 5 45 3·00

3p.
Ghana New Currency
19th July, 1965.
(D 4)

1½Np
(D 5)

1965 (19 July). Nos. D14/D18 surch as T D **4** diagonally upwards (D) or horiz (H), by Govt Printer, Accra.

D19 D **3** 1p. on 1d. (D) 10 75
a. Surch inverted 11·00
b. Surch double
c. Surch omitted (in horiz pair with normal) £110
D20 2p. on 2d. (B.) (H) 10 2·00
a. Surch inverted 9·00
c. Large 'd' 2·25
d. Surch omitted (in horiz pair with normal) 85·00
D21 3p. on 3d. (indigo) (H) 10 2·00
a. Surch inverted 12·00
b. Surch omitted (in horiz pair with normal)
c. Ultramarine surch 9·00
ca. Surch inverted 9·00
cb. Surch on front and back 15·00
d. Black surch
e. Missing serif 3·00
D22 6p. on 6d. (R.) (H) 10 3·25
a. Surch inverted 14·00
b. Purple-brown surch 11·00
ba. Surch double 26·00
c. Green surch 14·00

D23		12p. on 1s. (B.) (D)	15	3·50
		c. Upright stroke	1·50	
		ca. Short upright stroke	5·00	
D19/D23 *Set of 5*			45	10·50

On the diagonal surcharges the figures of value are horizontal.

No. D21b occurs in the first or second vertical row of one sheet which shows the surcharges shifted progressively to the right.

1968 (1 Feb)–**70**. Nos. D20/D22 additionally surch as T D **5**, in red (1½n.p., 5n.p.), or black (2½n.p.).

D24	D **3**	1½n.p. on 2p. on 2d.	7·00	4·25
		a. Type D **5** double, one albino		
		b. Albino surch (Type D **4**)		
		c. Large 'd'	23·00	
D25		2½n.p. on 3p. on 3d. (4.70?)	1·25	5·00
		a. Type D **5** double, one albino	5·50	
		b. Missing serif	5·50	
D26		5n.p. on 6p. on 6d. (1970)	3·25	
D24/D6 *Set of 3*			10·50	

The above were three in a series of surcharges, the others being 1n.p on 1p. and 10n.p. on 12p, which were prepared, but owing to confusion due to the two surcharges in similar currency it was decided by the authorities not to issue the stamps, however, Nos. D24/D26 were issued in error.

(Litho D.L.R.)

1970. Inscr in new currency. P 14½×14.

D27	D **3**	1n.p. carmine-red	1·75	6·50
D28		1½n.p. green	2·25	7·50
D29		2½n.p. yellow-orange	2·75	9·00
D30		5n.p. ultramarine	3·00	9·00
D31		10n.p. reddish violet	5·00	11·00
D27/D31 *Set of 5*			13·00	38·00

Gibraltar

CROWN COLONY

Early details of postal arrangements in Gibraltar are hard to establish, although it is known that postal facilities were provided by the Civil Secretary's Office from 1749. Gibraltar became a packet port in July 1806, although the Civil Secretary's office continued to be responsible for other mail. The two services were amalgamated on 1 January 1857 as a Branch Office of the British GPO, the control of the postal services not reverting to Gibraltar until 1 January 1886.

Spanish stamps could be used at Gibraltar from their introduction in 1850 and, indeed, such franking was required on letters weighing over ½ oz. sent to Spain after 1 July 1854. From 1 July 1856 until 31 December 1875 all mail to Spain required postage to be prepaid by Spanish stamps and these issues were supplied by the Gibraltar postal authorities, acting as a Spanish Postal Agent. The mail forwarded under this system was cancelled at San Roque with a horizontal barred oval, later replaced by a cartwheel type mark showing numeral 63. From 1857 combination covers showing the 2d. ship mail fee paid in British stamps and the inland postage by Spanish issues exist.

Stamps of Great Britain were issued for use in Gibraltar from 3 September 1857 (earliest recorded cover is dated 7 September 1857) to the end of 1885.

The initial supply contained 1d., 4d. and 6d. values. No supplies of the 2d. or 1s. were sent until the consignment of October 1857. No other values were supplied until early 1862.

Z 1 Z 2 Z 3 Z 4 Z 5 Z 6

Stamps of GREAT BRITAIN cancelled 'G' as Types Z **1** or Z **2** (3 Sept 1857 to 19 Feb 1859).

Z1	1d. red-brown (1841), imperf	£3250
Z1*a*	1d. red-brown (1854) Die I, *wmk* Small Crown, *perf* 16	£425
Z2	1d. red-brown (1855), Die II, *wmk* Small Crown, *perf* 16	£800
Z3	1d. red-brown (1855), Die II, *wmk* Small Crown *perf* 14	£375
Z4	1d. red-brown (1855), Die II, *wmk* Large Crown, *perf* 14	£100
Z5	1d. rose-red (1857), Die II, *wmk* Large Crown, *perf* 14	25·00
Z6	2d. blue (1855), *wmk* Small Crown, *perf* 14	£500
Z7	2d. blue (1855–1858), *wmk* Large Crown, *perf* 16	£400
Z8	2d. blue (1855), *wmk* Large Crown, *perf* 14 *From*	75·00
	Plate Nos. 5, 6.	
Z9	2d. blue (1858) (Plate No. 7)	£350
Z10	4d. rose (1857)	60·00
	a. Thick glazed paper	
Z11	6d. lilac (1856)	42·00
Z12	6d. lilac (1856) (blued *paper*)	£850
Z13	1s. green (1856)	£130
	a. Thick paper	
Z14	1s. green (1856) (blued *paper*)	£1500

Stamps of GREAT BRITAIN cancelled 'A26' as in Types Z **3**, Z **4**, Z **5**, Z **6** or similar or circular or oval datestamps (20 Feb 1859 to 31 Dec 1885).

Z15	½d. rose-red (1870–1879) *From*	42·00
	Plate Nos. 4, 5, 6, 8, 10, 11, 12, 13, 14, 15, 19, 20	
Z16	1d. red-brown (1841), *imperf*	£2500
Z17	1d. red-brown (1855), *wmk* Large Crown, *perf* 14	£250
Z18	1d. rose-red (1857), *wmk* Large Crown, *perf* 14	14·00
Z19	1d. rose-red (1864–1879) *From*	24·00
	Plate Nos. 71, 72, 73, 74 ,76, 78, 79, 80, 81, 82, 83, 84, 85, 86, 87, 88, 89, 90, 91, 92, 93, 94, 95, 96, 97, 98, 99, 100, 101, 102, 103, 104, 105, 106, 107, 108, 109, 110, 111, 112, 113, 114, 115, 116, 117, 118, 119, 120, 121, 122, 123, 124, 125, 127, 129, 130, 131, 132, 133, 134, 135, 136, 137, 138, 139, 140, 141, 142, 143, 144, 145, 146, 147, 148, 149, 150, 151, 152, 153, 154, 155, 156, 157, 158, 159, 160, 161, 162, 163, 164, 165, 166, 167, 168, 169, 170, 171, 172, 173, 174, 175, 176, 177, 178, 179, 180, 181, 182, 183, 184, 185, 186, 187, 188, 189, 190, 191, 192, 193, 194, 195, 196, 197, 198, 199, 200, 201, 202, 203, 204, 205, 206, 207, 208, 209, 210, 211, 212, 213, 214, 215, 216, 217, 218, 219, 220, 221, 222, 223, 224, 225.	
Z20	1½d. lake-red (1870) (Plate No. 3)	£750
Z21	2d. blue (1855), *wmk* Large Crown, *perf* 14.	£160
	Plate No. 6.	
Z22	2d. blue (1858–1869) *From*	24·00
	Plate Nos. 7, 8, 9, 12, 13, 14, 15.	
Z23	2½d. rosy mauve (1875) (blued *paper*) *From*	£100
	Plate Nos. 1, 2, 3.	
Z24	2½d. rosy mauve (1875–1876) *From*	32·00
	Plate Nos. 1, 2, 3.	
Z25	2½d. rosy mauve (*Error of Lettering*)	£3750
Z26	2½d. rosy mauve (1876–1879) *From*	21·00
	Plate Nos. 3, 4, 5, 6, 7, 8, 9, 10, 11, 12, 13, 14, 15, 16, 17.	
Z27	2½d. blue (1880–1881) *From*	13·00
	Plate Nos. 17, 18, 19, 20.	
Z28	2½d. blue (1881) (Plate Nos. 21, 22, 23) *From*	10·00
Z29	3d. carmine-rose (1862)	£350
Z30	3d. rose (1865) (Plate No. 4)	90·00
Z31	3d. rose (1867–1873) *From*	65·00
	Plate Nos. 4, 5, 6, 7, 8, 9, 10.	
Z32	3d. rose (1873–1876) *From*	85·00
	Plate Nos. 11, 12, 14, 15, 16, 17, 18, 19, 20.	
Z33	3d. rose (1881) (Plate Nos. 20, 21)	
Z34	3d. lilac (1883) (3d. *on* 3d.)	£225
Z35	4d. rose (1857)	£110
Z36	4d. red (1862) (Plate Nos. 3, 4) *From*	48·00
Z37	4d. vermilion (1865–1873) *From*	30·00
	Plate Nos. 7, 8, 9, 10, 11, 12, 13, 14.	
Z38	4d. vermilion (1876) (Plate No. 15)	£325
Z39	4d. sage-green (1877) (Plate Nos. 15, 16)	£140
Z40	4d. grey-brown (1880) *wmk* Large Garter	£425
	Plate No. 17.	
Z41	4d. grey-brown (1880) *wmk* Crown *From*	75·00
	Plate Nos. 17, 18.	
Z42	6d. lilac (1856)	42·00
Z43	6d. lilac (1862) (Plate Nos. 3, 4) *From*	40·00
Z44	6d. lilac (1865–1867) (Plate Nos. 5, 6) *From*	35·00
Z45	6d. lilac (1867) (Plate No. 6)	48·00
Z46	6d. violet (1867–1870) (Plate Nos. 6, 8, 9) *From*	32·00
Z47	6d. buff (1872–1873) (Plate Nos. 11, 12) *From*	£150
Z48	6d. chestnut (1872) (Plate No. 11)	38·00
Z49	6d. grey (1873) (Plate No. 12)	95·00
Z50	6d. grey (1874–1880) *From*	40·00
	Plate Nos. 13, 14, 15, 16, 17.	
Z51	6d. grey (1881) (Plate Nos. 17, 18)	£375
Z52	6d. lilac (1883) (6d. *on* 6d.)	£130
Z53	8d. orange (1876)	£750
Z54	9d. bistre (1862)	£450
Z55	9d. straw (1862)	£900
Z56	9d. straw (1865)	£850
Z57	9d. straw (1867)	£325
Z57a	10d. brown (1848), embossed	£5000
Z58	10d. red-brown (1867)	£150
Z59	1s. green (1856)	£110
Z60	1s. green (1862)	70·00
Z61	1s. green (1862) ('K' *variety*)	£2500
Z62	1s. green (1865) (Plate No. 4)	60·00
Z63	1s. green (1867–1873) (Plate Nos. 4, 5, 6, 7) *From*	40·00
Z64	1s. green (1873–1877) *From*	90·00
	Plate Nos. 8, 9, 10, 11, 12, 13.	
Z65	1s. orange-brown (1880) (Plate No. 13)	£475
Z66	1s. orange-brown (1881) *From*	£130
	Plate Nos. 13, 14.	
Z67	2s. blue (1867)	£350
Z68	5s. rose (1867) (Plate No. 1)	£1000

1880.

Z69	½d. deep green	30·00
Z70	½d. pale green	30·00
Z71	1d. Venetian red	30·00
Z72	1½d. Venetian red	£400
Z73	2d. pale rose	75·00
Z74	2d. deep rose	75·00
Z75	5d. indigo	£160

1881.

Z76	1d. lilac (14 *dots*)	45·00
Z77	1d. lilac (16 *dots*)	11·00

1884.

Z78	½d. slate-blue	35·00
Z79	2d. lilac	£140
Z80	2½d. lilac	19·00
Z81	3d. lilac	
Z82	4d. dull green	£200
Z83	6d. dull green	
Z83*a*	1s. dull green	£500

POSTAL FISCAL

Z83*b*	1d. purple (Die 4) (1878) *wmk* Small Anchor	£700
Z84	1d. purple (1881), *wmk* Orb	£1100

PRICES FOR STAMPS ON COVER TO 1945

Nos. 1/2	*from* × 25
No. 3	*from* × 10
No. 4	*from* × 25
Nos. 5/6	*from* × 8
Nos. 7/33	*from* × 6

PRICES FOR STAMPS ON COVER TO 1945

Nos. 39/45	*from* × 5
Nos. 46/109	*from* × 3
Nos. 110/113	*from* × 4
Nos. 114/117	*from* × 3
Nos. 118/120	*from* × 5
Nos. 121/131	*from* × 3

GIBRALTAR

(1)

1886 (1 Jan). Contemporary types of Bermuda optd with T **1** by D.L.R. Wmk Crown CA. P 14.

No.	Type	Description	Unused	Used
1	**9**	½d. dull green	23·00	12·00
2	**1**	1d. rose-red	85·00	6·00
3	**2**	2d. purple-brown	£140	85·00
		w. Wmk inverted		
4	**11**	2½d. ultramarine	£200	3·25
		a. Optd in blue-black	£500	£150
		w. Wmk inverted	—	£550
5	**10**	4d. orange-brown	£190	£110
6	**4**	6d. deep lilac	£300	£225
7	**5**	1s. yellow-brown	£450	£375
1/7 *Set of 7*			£1200	£700
1s/3s, 4as/7s Optd 'SPECIMEN' *Set of 7*			£5500	

Nos. 1/7 were overprinted on special printings of the underlying Bermuda stamps. The ½d., 2d. and 1s. values were not issued in these colours in Bermuda until 1893, while the 4d. was not issued on CA paper in Bermuda until 1904. The 6d. does not exist without opt. Collectors should be aware of Bermuda stamps with forged 'GIBRALTAR' overprints.

PRINTER. All Gibraltar stamps to No. 109 were typographed by De La Rue & Co, Ltd.

2

3

4

5

1886 (Nov)–**87**. Wmk Crown CA. P 14.

No.	Type	Description	Unused	Used
8	**2**	½d. dull green (1.87)	19·00	4·25
		w. Wmk inverted	†	£1000
9	**3**	1d. rose (2.87)	50·00	4·75
10	**4**	2d. brown-purple (12.86)	30·00	35·00
		w. Wmk inverted	£850	
11	**5**	2½d. blue	85·00	3·00
		w. Wmk inverted	£400	90·00
12	**4**	4d. orange-brown (16.4.87)	85·00	85·00
13		6d. lilac (16.4.87)	£140	£140
14		1s. bistre (2.87)	£250	£200
		w. Wmk inverted		
8/14 *Set of 7*			£600	£400
8s/14s Optd 'SPECIMEN' *Set of 7*			£500	

Examples of Nos. 3, 6/7 and 14 are known showing a forged Gibraltar postmark dated 'JU-13 87'.

See also Nos. 39/45.

5 CENTIMOS

(6)

5 — Normal

5 — '5' with short foot (all stamps in 1st, 5th and 6th vertical columns (5c. on ½d.) or all stamps in 2nd vertical column (25c. on 2d., 25c. on 2½d., 50c. on 6d. and 75c. on 1s.)

1889 (1 Aug). Surch as T **6**.

No.	Type	Description	Unused	Used
15	**2**	5c. on ½d. green	14·00	32·00
		a. '5' with short foot	14·00	32·00
16	**3**	10c. on 1d. rose	15·00	19·00
17	**4**	25c. on 2d. brown-purple	4·75	11·00
		a. '5' with short foot	10·00	22·00
		ab. Small 'I' (R. 6/2)	£100	£170
		b. Broken 'N' (R. 10/5)	£100	£170
18	**5**	25c. on 2½d. bright blue	29·00	2·50
		a. '5' with short foot	55·00	5·00
		ab. Small 'I' (R. 6/2)	£325	£100
		b. Broken 'N' (R. 10/5)	£325	£100
19	**4**	40c. on 4d. orange-brown	55·00	75·00
20		50c. on 6d. bright lilac	55·00	80·00
		a. '5' with short foot	£140	£170
21		75c. on 1s. bistre	55·00	65·00
		a. '5' with short foot	£150	£160
15/21 *Set of 7*			£200	£250
15s/21s Optd 'SPECIMEN' *Set of 7*			£375	

10c., 40c. and 50c. values from this issue and that of 1889–1896 are known bisected and used for half their value from various post offices in Morocco (*price on cover from* £500). These bisects were never authorised by the Gibraltar Post Office.

5c. Broken 'M' (Pls 1 & 2 R. 4/5)

7

20c. Flat top to 'C' (Pl 2 R. 4/4)

40c. Exclamation mark for 'I' (Pl 2 R. 8/4)

1889 (8 Oct*)–**96**. Issue in Spanish currency. Wmk Crown CA. P 14.

No.	Type	Description	Unused	Used
22	**7**	5c. green	6·50	1·00
		a. Broken 'M'	£190	85·00
		w. Wmk inverted	£300	£325
23		10c. carmine	4·50	50
		b. Value omitted	£7000	
24		20c. olive-green and brown (2.1.96)	27·00	24·00
		w. Wmk inverted	—	£850
25		20c. olive-green (8.7.96)	18·00	£100
		a. Flat top to 'C'	£350	
26		25c. ultramarine	27·00	70
		a. Deep ultramarine	38·00	1·00
27		40c. orange-brown	3·75	4·75
		a. Exclamation mark for 'I'	£150	£150
28		50c. bright lilac (1890)	3·25	2·75
29		75c. olive-green (1890)	32·00	32·00
30		1p. bistre (11.89)	75·00	20·00
31		1p. bistre and ultramarine (6.95)	5·00	8·50
32		2p. black and carmine (2.1.96)	12·00	30·00
33		5p. slate-grey (12.89)	42·00	£100
22/33 *Set of 12*			£225	£300
22s/24s, 26s/33s Optd 'SPECIMEN' *Set of 11*			£450	

* Earliest recorded postmark date.

Due to a shortage of 5c. and 10c. stamps between 13 and 21 February 1891, outgoing mail was paid for in cash and handstamped with the 'OFFICIAL PAID' datestamp in red.

1898 (1 Oct). Reissue in Sterling currency. Wmk Crown CA. P 14.

No.	Type	Description	Unused	Used
39	**2**	½d. grey-green	14·00	1·75
		w. Wmk inverted		
40	**3**	1d. carmine	14·00	50
		w. Wmk inverted	†	£1400
41	**4**	2d. brown-purple and ultramarine	29·00	2·50
42	**5**	2½d. bright ultramarine	45·00	50
		w. Wmk inverted	£350	90·00
43	**4**	4d. orange-brown and green	18·00	4·00
		a. 'FOUR PENCE' trimmed at top (Pl 2 R. 6/4 and 5, R. 8/4-6)	£500	
44		6d. violet and red	45·00	22·00
45		1s. bistre and carmine	45·00	8·00
		w. Wmk inverted		
39/45 *Set of 7*			£190	35·00
39s/45s Optd 'SPECIMEN' *Set of 7*			£275	

No. 39 is greyer than No. 8, No. 40 brighter and deeper than No. 9 and No. 42 much brighter than No. 11.

The degree of 'trimming' on No. 43a varies, but is most prominent on R. 6/4 and 5.

8

9

½ — Normal; ½ — Large '2'

2½d.

This occurs on R. 10/1 in each pane of 60. The diagonal stroke is also longer.

1903 (1 May). Wmk Crown CA. P 14.

No.	Type	Description	Unused	Used
46	**8**	½d. grey-green and green	14·00	11·00
47		1d. dull purple/*red*	35·00	60
48		2d. grey-green and carmine	32·00	42·00
49		2½d. dull purple and black/*blue*	8·50	60
		a. Large '2' in '½'	£325	£130
50		6d. dull purple and violet	40·00	21·00
51		1s. black and carmine	28·00	38·00
52	**9**	2s. green and blue	£200	£275
53		4s. dull purple and green	£150	£225
54		8s. dull purple and black/*blue*	£170	£200
55		£1 dull purple and black/*red*	£650	£750
46/55 *Set of 10*			£1200	£1400
46s/55s Optd 'SPECIMEN' *Set of 10*			£550	

1904–08. Wmk Mult Crown CA. Ordinary paper (½d. to 2d. and 6d. to 2s.) or chalk-surfaced paper (others). P 14.

No.	Type	Description	Unused	Used
56	**8**	½d. dull and bright green (4.4.04*)	24·00	4·25
		a. Chalk-surfaced paper (10.05)	15·00	8·50
57		1d. dull purple/*red* (6.9.04*)	32·00	50
		a. Bisected (½d.) (*on card or cover*)	†	£1800
		bw. Wmk inverted	†	£950
		c. Chalk-surfaced paper (16.9.05)	8·50	85
58		2d. grey-green and carmine (9.1.05)	40·00	17·00
		a. Chalk-surfaced paper (2.07)	10·00	18·00
59		2½d. purple and black/*blue* (4.5.07)	35·00	90·00
		a. Large '2' in '½'	£600	£1000
60		6d. dull purple and violet (19.4.06)	50·00	40·00
		a. Chalk-surfaced paper (4.08)	32·00	22·00
61		1s. black and carmine (13.10.05)	65·00	24·00
		a. Chalk-surfaced paper (4.06)	55·00	24·00
62	**9**	2s. green and blue (2.2.05)	£120	£140
		a. Chalk-surfaced paper (10.07)	£120	£150
63		4s. deep purple and green (6.08)	£350	£425
64		£1 deep purple and black/*red* (15.3.08)	£650	£700
56/64 *Set of 9*			£1100	£1300

* Earliest known date of use.

1906 (Oct)–**11**. Colours changed. Wmk Mult Crown CA. Chalk-surfaced paper (6d. to 8s.). P 14.

No.	Type	Description	Unused	Used
66	**8**	½d. blue-green (1907)	15·00	1·75
		x. Wmk reversed	†	£2000
67		1d. carmine	5·50	60
		a. Wmk sideways	£3750	£3500
		w. Wmk inverted	†	£550
68		2d. greyish slate (5.10)	10·00	11·00
69		2½d. ultramarine (6.07)	9·00	1·75
		a. Large '2' in '½'	£300	£120
70		6d. dull and bright purple (4.12.11)*	£150	£375
71		1s. black/*green* (1910)	23·00	21·00
72	**9**	2s. purple and bright blue/*blue* (4.10)	65·00	48·00
73		4s. black and carmine (4.10)	£170	£190
		x. Wmk reversed	£1800	£2000
74		8s. purple and green (1911)	£250	£250
66/74 *Set of 9*			£600	£800
67s/74s Optd 'SPECIMEN' *Set of 8*			£600	

* Earliest known date of use.

Examples of Nos. 54, 55, 64 and 73/74 are known showing a forged oval registered postmark dated '6 OC 10'.

10

11

1912 (17 July)–**24**. Wmk Mult Crown CA. Ordinary paper (½d. to 2½d) or chalk-surfaced paper (others). P 14.

No.	Type	Description	Unused	Used
76	**10**	½d. blue-green	3·25	70
		a. Yellow-green (4.17)	7·00	2·00
		w. Wmk inverted	†	£1200
		x. Wmk reversed	†	£1800
77		1d. carmine-red	4·50	75
		a. Scarlet (6.16)	9·00	1·25
		ay. Wmk inverted and reversed	†	£2000
78		2d. greyish slate	21·00	1·50
79		2½d. deep bright blue	10·00	3·00
		a. Large '2' in '½'	£300	£160
		b. Pale ultramarine (1917)	12·00	3·00
		ba. Large '2' in '½'	£300	£160
80		6d. dull purple and mauve	9·00	17·00
81		1s. black/*green*	19·00	3·25
		a. Ordinary paper (8.18)	£900	
		b. On blue-green, olive back (1919)	29·00	26·00
		c. On emerald surface (12.23)	30·00	70·00
		d. On emerald back (3.24)	32·00	£110
		ds. Optd 'SPECIMEN'	75·00	
82	**11**	2s. dull purple and blue/*blue* (*shades*)	29·00	4·25
		sa. Opt 'SPECIMEN' double	£650	
83		4s. black and carmine	38·00	55·00
84		8s. dull purple and green	£100	£130
85		£1 dull purple and black/*red*	£140	£275
76/85 *Set of 10*			£325	£425
76s/85s Optd 'SPECIMEN' *Set of 10*			£500	

WAR TAX

(12)

1918 (15 Apr). Optd with T **12** by Beanland, Malin & Co, Gibraltar.

No.	Type	Description	Unused	Used
86	**10**	½d. green	1·00	2·00
		a. Opt double	£900	
		w. Wmk inverted	£850	
		y. Wmk inverted and reversed	£550	

Two printings of this overprint exist, the second being in slightly heavier type on a deeper shade of green.

3 PENCE (I) — THREE PENCE (II)

1921–27. Wmk Mult Script CA. Chalk-surfaced paper (6d. to 8s.). P 14.

No.	Type	Description	Unused	Used
89	**10**	½d. green (25.4.27)	1·50	1·50
90		1d. carmine-red (2.21)	1·75	1·00
91		1½d. chestnut (1.12.22)	2·00	55
		a. Pale chestnut (7.24)	2·75	30
		w. Wmk inverted	†	£1300
93		2d. grey (17.2.21)	1·25	1·25
94		2½d. bright blue (2.21)	24·00	60·00
		a. Large '2' in '½'	£600	£850
95		3d. bright blue (I) (1.1.22)	3·50	4·50
		a. Ultramarine	2·50	1·50
97		6d. dull purple and mauve (1.23)	6·00	6·00
		a. Bright purple and magenta (22.7.26)	1·60	3·50
98		1s. black/*emerald* (20.6.24)	10·00	25·00
99	**11**	2s. grey-purple and blue/*blue* (20.6.24)	19·00	80·00
		a. Reddish purple and blue/blue (1925)	7·00	45·00
100		4s. black and carmine (20.6.24)	70·00	£130
101		8s. dull purple and green (20.6.24)	£325	£550
89/101 *Set of 11*			£400	£750
89s/101s Optd 'SPECIMEN' *Set of 11*			£600	

The ½d. exists in coils, constructed from normal sheets, first issued in February 1937.

1925 (15 Oct)–**32**. New values and colours changed. Wmk Mult Script CA. Chalk-surfaced paper. P 14.

No.	Type	Description	Unused	Used
102	**10**	1s. sage-green and black (8.1.29)	14·00	40·00
		a. Olive and black (1932)	14·00	20·00
103	**11**	2s. red-brown and black (8.1.29)	10·00	40·00
104		2s.6d. green and black	10·00	29·00
105		5s. carmine and black	20·00	75·00

106 10s. deep ultramarine and black....... 32·00 80·00
107 £1 red-orange and black (16.11.27)........ £190 £300
108 £5 violet and black........ £1600 £6000
s. Optd 'SPECIMEN'........ £800
102/107 *Set of 6*........ £250 £475
102s/107s Optd or Perf (1s., 2s.) 'SPECIMEN' *Set of 6* £500

Examples of Nos. 83/85, 99/101 and 102/108 are known showing forged oval registered postmarks dated '24 JA 25' or '6 MY 35'.

1930 (11 Apr). T **10** inscribed 'THREE PENCE'. Wmk Mult Script CA. P 14.
109 3d. ultramarine (II)........ 8·00 2·25
s. Perf 'SPECIMEN'........ 80·00

13 The Rock of Gibraltar

(Des Captain H. St. C. Garrood. Recess D.L.R.)

1931–33. Wmk Mult Script CA. P 14.
110 **13** 1d. scarlet (1.7.31)........ 2·50 2·50
a. Perf 13½×14........ 22·00 8·00
111 1½d. red-brown (1.7.31)........ 1·75 2·25
a. Perf 13½×14........ 17·00 4·00
112 2d. pale grey (1.11.32)........ 13·00 1·75
a. Perf 13½×14........ 24·00 4·50
113 3d. blue (1.6.33)........ 11·00 3·00
a. Perf 13½×14........ 42·00 42·00
110/113 *Set of 4*........ 25·00 8·50
110a/113a *Set of 4*........ 90·00 50·00
110s, 111as/113as Perf 'SPECIMEN' *Set of 4*........ £200

Figures of value take the place of both corner ornaments at the base of the 2d. and 3d.

1935 (6 May). Silver Jubilee. As Nos. 91/94 of Antigua but ptd by B.W. P 11×12.
114 2d. ultramarine and grey-black........ 1·60 2·50
a. Extra flagstaff........ 75·00 £130
b. Short extra flagstaff........ £160 £275
c. Lightning conductor........ £110 £170
d. Flagstaff on right-hand turret........ £425 £450
e. Double flagstaff........ £425 £450
115 3d. brown and deep blue........ 3·75 5·00
a. Extra flagstaff........ £325 £375
b. Short extra flagstaff........ £325 £375
c. Lightning conductor........ £350 £400
116 6d. green and indigo........ 14·00 19·00
a. Extra flagstaff........ £275 £325
b. Short extra flagstaff........ £500 £550
c. Lightning conductor........ £300 £350
117 1s. slate and purple........ 18·00 28·00
a. Extra flagstaff........ £225 £275
b. Short extra flagstaff........ £550 £550
c. Lightning conductor........ £275 £325
114/117 *Set of 4*........ 32·00 48·00
114s/117s Perf 'SPECIMEN' *Set of 4*........ £200

For illustrations of plate varieties see Omnibus section following Zanzibar.

1937 (12 May). Coronation. As Nos. 95/97 of Antigua. P 11×11½.
118 ½d. green........ 25 50
119 2d. grey-black........ 3·00 3·25
120 3d. blue........ 3·00 3·25
118/120 *Set of 3*........ 5·75 6·25
118s/120s Perf 'SPECIMEN' *Set of 3*........ £190

14 King George VI

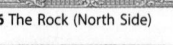

15 Rock of Gibraltar

16 The Rock (North Side)

17 Europa Point

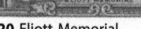

18 Moorish Castle

19 Southport Gate

20 Eliott Memorial

21 Government House

22 Catalan Bay

2d. Ape on rock (R. 1/5)

2s. Bird on memorial (R. 9/3)

Broken second 'R' in 'GIBRALTAR' (Frame Pl 2 R. 9/4)

(Des Captain H. St. C. Garrood. Recess D.L.R.)

1938 (25 Feb)–**51.** Types **14/22.** Mult Script CA.
121 **14** ½d. deep green (P 13½×14)........ 10 40
122 **15** 1d. yellow-brown (P 14)........ 30·00 2·25
a. Perf 13½ (1940)........ 30·00 2·25
ab. Perf 13½. Wmk sideways (1940)........ 6·50 7·00
b. Perf 13. Wmk sideways. *Red-brown* (1942)........ 2·25 60
c. Perf 13. Wmk sideways. *Deep brown* (1944)........ 3·25 3·50
d. Perf 13. *Red-brown* (1949)........ 6·00 1·50
123 1½d. carmine (P 14)........ 35·00 1·00
a. Perf 13½........ £275 18·00
123*b* 1½d. slate-violet (P 13) (1.1.43)........ 75 1·00
124 **16** 2d. grey (P 14)........ 32·00 40
aa. Ape on rock........ £700 £110
a. Perf 13½ (1940)........ 9·00 35
ab. Perf 13½. Wmk sideways (1940)........ £800 45·00
b. Perf 13. Wmk sideways (1943)........ 4·25 3·00
ba. 'A' of 'CA' missing from wmk........ £1700
124*c* 2d. carmine (P 13) (*wmk sideways*) (15.7.44)........ 2·00 60
125 **17** 3d. light blue (P 13½)........ 45·00 1·00
a. Perf 14........ £130 6·00
b. Perf 13 (1942)........ 4·50 30
ba. 'A' of 'CA' missing from wmk........ £2000
bb. Greenish blue (2.51)........ 8·50 1·00
125*c* 5d. red-orange (P 13) (1.10.47)........ 1·75 1·25
126 **18** 6d. carmine and grey-violet (P 13½) (16.3.38)........ 48·00 3·75
a. Perf 14........ £120 1·25
b. Perf 13 (1942)........ 11·00 1·40
c. Perf 13. *Scarlet and grey-violet* (1945)........ 13·00 3·75
127 **19** 1s. black and green (P 14) (16.3.38)........ 45·00 38·00
a. Perf 13½........ 75·00 6·00
b. Perf 13 (1942)........ 3·25 4·25
ba. Broken 'R'........ £950
128 **20** 2s. black and brown (P 14) (16.3.38)........ 65·00 23·00
a. Perf 13½........ £130 50·00
b. Perf 13 (1942)........ 15·00 6·50
ba. Broken 'R'........ £1300
bb. Bird on memorial........ £700 £500
129 **21** 5s. black and carmine (P 14) (16.3.38)........ £100 £170
a. Perf 13½........ 50·00 14·00
b. Perf 13 (1944)........ 42·00 17·00
ba. Broken 'R'........ £4000
130 **22** 10s. black and blue (P 14) (16.3.38)........ 70·00 £130
a. Perf 13 (1943)........ 42·00 25·00
ab. Broken 'R'........ £5000 £3250
131 **14** £1 orange (P 13½×14) (16.3.38)........ 42·00 55·00
121/131 Set of 14........ £180 £100
121s/131s Perf 'SPECIMEN' *Set of 14*........ £850

The ½d., 1d. and both colours of the 2d. exist in coils constructed from normal sheets. These were originally joined vertically, but, because of technical problems, the 1d. and 2d. grey were subsequently issued in horizontal coils. The 2d. carmine only exists in the horizontal version.

Examples of Nos. 129/131 are known showing forged oval registered postmarks dated '6 OC 43', '18 OC 43', '3 MR 44' and '4 AU 44'.

1946 (12 Oct). Victory. As Nos. 110/111 of Antigua.
132 ½d. green........ 30 1·50
133 3d. ultramarine........ 50 1·25
132s/133s Perf 'SPECIMEN' *Set of 2*........ £160

1948 (1 Dec). Royal Silver Wedding. As Nos. 112/113 of Antigua.
134 ½d. green........ 1·50 3·00
135 £1 brown-orange........ 60·00 80·00

1949 (10 Oct). 75th Anniversary of Universal Postal Union. As Nos. 114/117 of Antigua.
136 2d. carmine........ 1·00 1·25
137 3d. deep blue........ 2·00 1·50
138 6d. purple........ 1·75 2·00
139 1s. blue-green........ 1·75 5·00
136/139 *Set of 4*........ 6·60 8·75

No. 139 is known with the 'A' of 'CA' almost completely missing from the watermark.

NEW
CONSTITUTION
1950
(**23**)

1950 (1 Aug). Inauguration of Legislative Council. Nos. 124*c*, 125ba, 126b and 127b optd as T **23**.
140 **16** 2d. carmine........ 60 1·50
141 – 3d. greenish blue........ 65 1·00
142 – 6d. carmine and grey-violet........ 75 2·00
a. Opt double........ £1000 £1300
143 – 1s. black and green (R.)........ 75 2·25
a. Broken 'R'........ £130
140/143 *Set of 4*........ 2·50 6·00

Four sheets of No. 142 received double overprints. On some examples the two impressions are almost coincident.

Stop before '2' in '½' in right-hand value tablet (Pl. 1A–5A, R. 4/4)

1953 (2 June). Coronation. As No. 120 of Antigua.
144 ½d. black and bronze-green........ 75 2·25
a. Stop before '2' in '½'........ 16·00

24 Cargo and Passenger Wharves

25 South View from Straits

26 Gibraltar Fish Canneries

27 Southport Gate

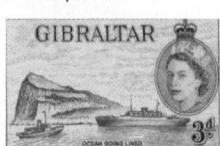

28 Sailing in the Bay

29 *Saturnia* (liner)

30 Coaling wharf

31 Airport

32 Europa Point

33 Straits from Buena Vista

34 Rosia Bay and Straits

35 Main Entrance, Government House

36 Tower of Homage, Moorish Castle

37 Arms of Gibraltar

5d. Major re-entry causing doubling of 'ALTA' in 'GIBRALTAR' (R. 4/6)

1s. Re-entry causing doubling of lines of sea wall and buildings (R. 6/3-5)

(Des D.L.R., based on photographs by N. Cummings. Recess (except £1, centre litho) De La Rue)

1953 (19 Oct)–**59**. Types **24/37**. Wmk Mult Script CA. P 13.

No.	Type	Description	Unused	Used
145	**24**	½d. indigo and grey-green	15	30
146	**25**	1d. bluish green	1·50	1·00
		a. Deep bluish green (31.12.57)	4·25	1·50
147	**26**	1½d. black	1·00	2·25
148	**27**	2d. deep olive-brown	3·00	1·25
		a. Sepia (18.6.58)	5·00	1·50
149	**28**	2½d. carmine	4·75	1·25
		a. Deep carmine (11.9.56)	8·50	1·50
		aw. Wmk inverted	£750	
150	**29**	3d. light blue	4·75	20
		a. Deep greenish blue (8.6.55)	11·00	55
		b. Greenish blue (18.6.58)	27·00	2·50
151	**30**	4d. ultramarine	7·00	3·50
		a. Blue (17.6.59)	35·00	13·00
152	**31**	5d. maroon	1·75	1·50
		a. Major re-entry	55·00	
		b. Deep maroon (31.12.57)	4·75	2·50
		ba. Major re-entry	£100	
153	**32**	6d. black and pale blue	7·50	2·00
		a. Black and blue (24.4.57)	10·00	3·00
		b. Black and grey-blue (17.6.59)	19·00	11·00
154	**33**	1s. pale blue and red-brown	1·25	2·25
		a. Re-entry	29·00	
		b. Pale blue and deep red-brown (27.3.56)	1·00	2·25
		ba. Re-entry	29·00	
155	**34**	2s. orange and reddish violet	50·00	16·00
		a. Orange and violet (17.6.59)	35·00	8·50
156	**35**	5s. deep brown	40·00	17·00
157	**36**	10s. reddish brown and ultramarine	45·00	45·00
158	**37**	£1 scarlet and orange-yellow	55·00	55·00
145/158 *Set of* 14			£180	£120

Nos. 145/146, 148 and 150 exist in coils, constructed from normal sheets by Harrison.

1954 (10 May). Royal Visit. As No. 150 but inscr 'ROYAL VISIT 1954' at top.

No.	Description	Unused	Used
159	3d. greenish blue	1·00	20

38 Gibraltar Candytuft

39 Moorish Castle

40 St George's Hall

41 The Keys

42 The Rock by moonlight

43 Catalan Bay

44 Map of Gibraltar

45 Air terminal

46 American War Memorial

47 Barbary Ape

48 Barbary Partridge

49 Blue Rock Thrush

50 Rock Lily (*Narcissus niveus*)

51 Rock and Badge of Gibraltar Regiment

1d. Retouch right of flag appears as an extra flag (Pl. 1B, R. 5/5)

1d. Jagged brown flaw in wall to right of gate appears as a crack (Pl. 1B, R. 2/5)

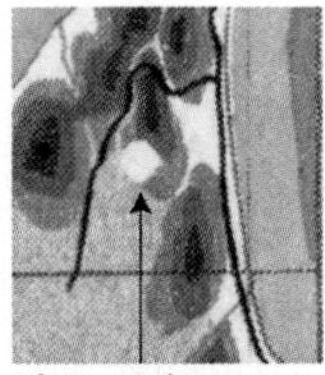

6d. Large white spot on map S.W. of 'CEUTA' (Pl. 1B, R. 4/5)

(Des J. Celecia (½d., 2d., 2½d., 2s., 10s.), N. A. Langdon frames of ½d. to 10s. and 1d., 3d., 6d., 7d., 9d., 1s.), M. Bonilla (4d.), L. V. Gomez (5s.), Sergeant T. A. Griffiths (£1). Recess (£1) or photo (others) D.L.R.)

1960 (29 Oct)–**62**. Designs as Types **38/51**. W w **12** (upright). P 14 (£1) or 13 (others).

No.	Type	Description	Unused	Used
160	**38**	½d. bright purple and emerald-green	15	50
161	**39**	1d. black and yellow-green	20	10
		a. Crack in wall	13·00	
		b. 'Phantom flag'	13·00	
162	**40**	2d. indigo and orange-brown	1·00	20
163	**41**	2½d. black and blue	1·75	80
		a. Black and grey-blue (16.10.62)	1·75	30
164	**42**	3d. deep blue and red-orange	1·75	10
165	**43**	4d. deep red-brown and turquoise	2·75	70
166	**44**	6d. sepia and emerald	1·00	70
		a. White spot on map	28·00	
167	**45**	7d. indigo and carmine-red	2·50	1·75
168	**46**	9d. grey-blue and greenish blue	1·25	1·00
169	**47**	1s. sepia and bluish green	1·50	70
170	**48**	2s. chocolate and ultramarine	20·00	3·25
171	**49**	5s. turquoise-blue and olive-brown	8·00	10·00
172	**50**	10s. yellow and blue	27·00	26·00
173	**51**	£1 black and brown-orange	22·00	26·00
160/173 *Set of* 14			80·00	60·00

New plates were made for all values other than the £1, incorporating a finer screen (250 dots per inch, rather than the original 200), giving clearer, deeper, better-defined impressions. No. 163*a* comes from the later plate of the 2½d.

Nos. 160/162, 164 and 166 exist in coils, constructed from normal sheets by Harrison.

See also No.199.

The 1d. imperforate comes from stolen printer's waste.

1963 (4 June). Freedom from Hunger. As No. 146 of Antigua.

No.	Description	Unused	Used
174	9d. sepia	2·50	2·50

1963 (2 Sept). Red Cross Centenary. As Nos. 147/148 of Antigua.

No.	Description	Unused	Used
175	1d. red and black	1·00	2·00
176	9d. red and blue	2·00	5·50

1964 (23 Apr). 400th Birth Anniversary of William Shakespeare. As No. 164 of Antigua.

No.	Description	Unused	Used
177	7d. bistre-brown	60	20

NEW CONSTITUTION 1964.

(**52**)

1964 (16 Oct). New Constitution. Nos. 164 and 166 optd with T **52**.

No.	Description	Unused	Used
178	3d. deep blue and red-orange	20	10
179	6d. sepia and emerald	20	60
	a. No stop after '1964' (R. 2/5)	19·00	50·00
	b. White spot on map	19·00	50·00

1965 (17 May). ITU Centenary. As Nos. 166/167 of Antigua.

No.	Description	Unused	Used
180	4d. light emerald and yellow	2·00	50
	w. Wmk inverted	38·00	
181	2s. apple-green and deep blue	5·50	5·00

1965 (25 Oct). International Co-operation Year. As Nos. 168/169 of Antigua.

No.	Description	Unused	Used
182	½d. deep bluish green and lavender	20	2·75
183	4d. reddish purple and turquoise-green	80	50

The value of the ½d. stamp is shown as '1/2'.

1966 (24 Jan). Churchill Commemoration. As Nos. 170/173 of Antigua. Printed in black, cerise and gold and with background in colours stated.

No.	Description	Unused	Used
184	½d. new blue	20	2·75
	w. Wmk inverted	75·00	
185	1d. deep green	30	10
186	4d. brown	1·50	10
187	9d. bluish violet	1·25	2·50
184/187 *Set of* 4		3·00	4·75

1966 (1 July). World Cup Football Championship. As Nos. 176/177 of Antigua.

No.	Description	Unused	Used
188	2½d. violet, yellow-green, lake and yellow and brown	75	2·25
189	6d. chocolate, blue-green, lake and yellow and brown	1·00	75

PRINTERS. All stamps from here to No. 239 were printed in photogravure by Harrison and Sons Ltd, London.

53 Red Seabream

4d. Break at top right corner of 'd' of value (R. 9/3).

(Des A. Ryman)

1966 (27 Aug). European Sea Angling Championships, Gibraltar. T **53** and similar designs. W w **12** (sideways on 1s.). P 13½×14(1s.) or 14×13½ (others).

No.	Description	Unused	Used
190	4d. rosine, bright blue and black	30	10
	a. Broken 'd'	6·00	
191	7d. rosine, deep olive-green and black	60	1·50
	a. Black (value and inscr) omitted	£1800	
	w. Wmk inverted	3·00	
192	1s. lake-brown, emerald and black	50	30
190/192 *Set of* 3		1·25	1·75

Designs: Horiz—4d. T **53**; 7d. Red Scorpionfish. Vert—1s. Stone Bass.

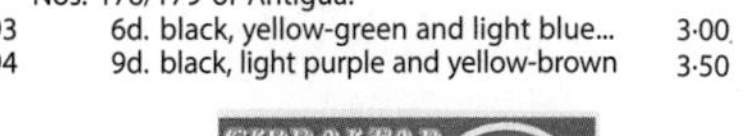

1966 (20 Sept). Inauguration of WHO Headquarters, Geneva. As Nos. 178/179 of Antigua.

No.	Description	Unused	Used
193	6d. black, yellow-green and light blue	3·00	1·50
194	9d. black, light purple and yellow-brown	3·50	4·75

56 'Our Lady of Europa'

(Des A. Ryman)

1966 (15 Nov). Centenary of Re-enthronement of 'Our Lady of Europa'. W w **12**. P 14×14½.

No.	Type	Description	Unused	Used
195	**56**	2s. bright blue and black	30	80

1966 (1 Dec). 20th Anniversary of UNESCO. As Nos. 196/198 of Antigua.

No.	Description	Unused	Used
196	2d. slate-violet, red, yellow and orange	60	10
197	7d. orange-yellow, violet and deep olive	2·25	10
198	5s. black, bright purple and orange	4·50	3·25
196/198 *Set of* 3		6·50	3·25

1966 (23 Dec). As No. 165 but wmk w **12** sideways.

No.	Description	Unused	Used
199	4d. deep red-brown and turquoise	30	2·75

57 HMS *Victory*

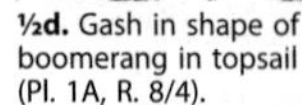

½d. Gash in shape of boomerang in topsail (Pl. 1A, R. 8/4).

½d. Grey mark in topsail resembling a stain (Pl. 1A, R. 8/6).

7d. Bold shading on sail appearing as patch (Pl. 1A, R. 10/5).

(Des A. Ryman)

1967 (3 Apr)–**69**. Horiz designs as T **57**. Multicoloured. W w **12**. P 14×14½.

No.		Description	Unused	Used
200		½d. Type **57**	10	20
		a. Grey (sails, etc) omitted	£800	
		b. Gash in sail	1·50	
		c. Stained sail	1·50	
201		1d. *Arab* (early steamer)	10	10
		w. Wmk inverted	3·25	4·75
202		2d. HMS *Carmania* (merchant cruiser)	15	10
		a. Grey-blue (hull) omitted	£8500	
203		2½d. *Mons Calpe* (ferry)	40	30
204		3d. *Canberra* (liner)	20	10
		w. Wmk inverted	45·00	9·00
205		4d. HMS *Hood* (battle cruiser)	1·50	10
		aw. Wmk inverted		
205*b*		5d. *Mirror* (cable ship) (7.7.69)	2·00	55
		bw. Wmk inverted	†	£1500
206		6d. *Xebec* (sailing vessel)	30	50
207		7d. *Amerigo Vespucci* (Italian cadet ship)	30	1·50
		a. Patched sail	14·00	
		w. Wmk inverted	19·00	
208		9d. *Raffaello* (liner)	30	1·75
209		1s. *Royal Katherine* (galleon)	30	35
210		2s. HMS *Ark Royal* (aircraft carrier), 1937	5·00	3·50
211		5s. HMS *Dreadnought* (nuclear submarine)	3·50	7·50
212		10s. *Neuralia* (liner)	12·00	23·00
213		£1 *Mary Celeste* (sailing vessel)	12·00	23·00
200/213 *Set of* 15			32·00	55·00

No. 202a results from the misaligning of the grey-blue cylinder. The bottom horizontal row of the sheet involved has this colour completely omitted except for the example above the cylinder numbers which shows the grey-blue '1A' towards the top of the stamp.

The ½d., 1d., 2d., 3d., 6d., 2s., 5s. and £1 exist with PVA gum as well as gum arabic, but the 5d. exists with PVA gum only.

Nos. 201/202, 204/205 and 206 exist in coils constructed from normal sheets.

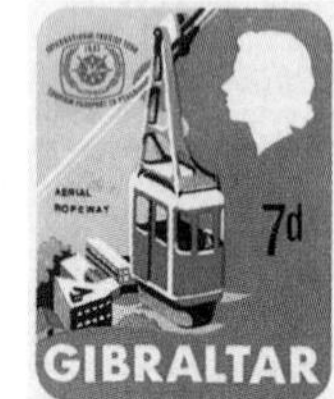

58 Aerial Ropeway

(Des A. Ryman)

1967 (15 June). International Tourist Year. T **58** and similar designs but horiz. Multicoloured. W w **12** (sideways on 7d.). P 14½×14 (7d.) or 14×14½ (others).

No.		Description	Unused	Used
214		7d. Type **58**	15	15
215		9d. Shark fishing	15	20
216		1s. Skin-diving	20	15
214/216 *Set of* 3			45	45

59 Mary, Joseph and Child Jesus

60 Church Window

1967 (1 Nov). Christmas. W w **12** (sideways* on 6d.). P 14.

No.		Description	Unused	Used
217	**59**	2d. multicoloured	15	10
		w. Wmk inverted	1·00	
218	**60**	6d. multicoloured	15	10
		w. Wmk Crown to right of CA	£475	

* The normal sideways watermark shows Crown to left of CA, *as seen from the back of the stamp.*

61 General Eliott and Route Map

62 Eliott directing Rescue Operations

(Des A. Ryman)

1967 (11 Dec). 250th Birth Anniversary of General Eliott. Multicoloured designs as T **61** (4d. to 1s.) or T **62**. W w **12** (sideways on horiz designs). P 14×15 (1s.) or 15×14 (others).

No.		Description	Unused	Used
219		4d. Type **61**	15	10
220		9d. Heathfield Tower and Monument, Sussex (38×22 *mm*)	15	10
221		1s. General Eliott (22×38 *mm*)	15	10
222		2s. Type **62**	25	50
219/222 *Set of* 4			65	70

65 Lord Baden-Powell

(Des A. Ryman)

1968 (27 Mar). 60th Anniversary of Gibraltar Scout Association. T **65** and similar horiz designs. W w **12**. P 14×14½.

No.		Description	Unused	Used
223		4d. buff and bluish violet	15	10
224		7d. ochre and blue-green	20	20
225		9d. bright blue, yellow-orange and black	20	30
226		1s. greenish yellow and emerald	20	30
223/226 *Set of* 4			65	75

Designs: 4d. T **65**; 7d. Scout Flag over the Rock; 9d. Tent, scouts and salute; 1s. Scout badges.

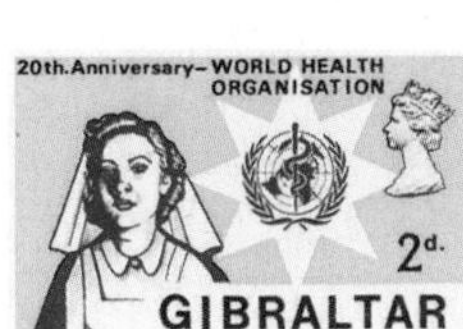

66 Nurse and WHO Emblem

68 King John signing *Magna Carta*

(Des A. Ryman)

1968 (1 July). 20th Anniversary of World Health Organisation. T **66** and similar horiz design. W w **12**. P 14×14½.

No.		Description	Unused	Used
227		2d. ultramarine, black and yellow	10	15
228		4d. slate, black and pink	10	10

Design: 2d. T **66**; 4d. Doctor and WHO emblem.

(Des A. Ryman)

1968 (26 Aug). Human Rights Year. T **68** and similar vert design. W w **12** (sideways). P 13½×14.

No.		Description	Unused	Used
229		1s. yellow-orange, brown and gold	15	10
230		2s. myrtle and gold	25	1·00

Designs: 1s. T **68**; 2s. 'Freedom' and Rock of Gibraltar.

70 Shepherd, Lamb and Star

72 Parliament Houses

(Des A. Ryman)

1968 (1 Nov). Christmas. T **70** and similar vert design. Multicoloured. W w **12**. P 14½×13½.

No.		Description	Unused	Used
231		4d. Type **70**	10	10
		a. Gold (star) omitted	£850	£850
232		9d. Mary holding Holy Child	15	20

(Des A. Ryman)

1969 (26 May). Commonwealth Parliamentary Association Conference. T **72** and similar designs. W w **12** (sideways on 2s.). P 14×14½ (2s.) or 14½×14 (others).

No.		Description	Unused	Used
233		4d. green and gold	10	10
234		9d. bluish violet and gold	10	10
235		2s. multicoloured	15	30
233/235 *Set of* 3			30	40

Designs: Horiz—4d. T **72**; 9d. Parliamentary emblem and outline of 'The Rock'. Vert—2s. Clock Tower, Westminster (Big Ben) and Arms of Gibraltar.

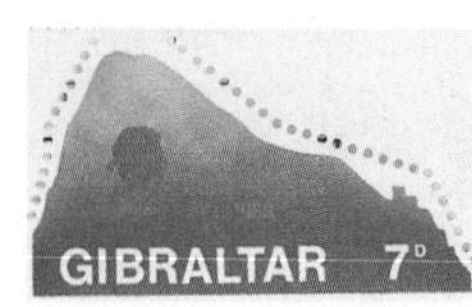

75 Silhouette of Rock, and Queen Elizabeth II

77 Soldier and Cap Badge, Royal Anglian Regiment, 1969

(Des A. Ryman)

1969 (30 July). New Constitution. W w **12**. P 14×13½ (in addition, the outline of the Rock is perforated).

No.		Description	Unused	Used
236	**75**	½d. gold and orange	10	10
237		5d. silver and bright green	20	10
		a. Portrait and inscr in gold and silver*		
238		7d. silver and bright purple	20	10
239		5s. gold and ultramarine	65	1·10
236/239 *Set of* 4			1·00	1·25

* No. 237a was first printed with the head and inscription in gold and then in silver but displaced slightly to lower left.

(Des A. Ryman. Photo D.L.R.)

1969 (6 Nov). Military Uniforms (1st series). T **77** and similar vert designs. Multicoloured. W w **12**. P 14.

No.		Description	Unused	Used
240		1d. Royal Artillery officer, 1758 and modern cap badge	15	10
241		6d. Type **77**	20	15
242		9d. Royal Engineers' Artificer, 1786 and modern cap badge	30	20
243		2s. Private, Fox's Marines, 1704 and modern Royal Marines cap badge	75	1·25
240/243 *Set of* 4			1·25	1·50

Nos. 240/243 have a short history of the Regiment printed on the reverse side over the gum, therefore, once the gum is moistened the history disappears.

See also Nos. 248/251.

80 *Madonna of the Chair* (detail, Raphael)

83 Europa Point

(Des A. Ryman. Photo Enschedé)

1969 (1 Dec). Christmas. T **80** and similar vert designs. Multicoloured. W w **12** (sideways). P 14×Roulette 9.

No.		Description	Unused	Used
244		5d. Type **80**	10	35
		a. Strip of 3. Nos. 244/246	45	1·00
		ab. Grey omitted		
245		7d. *Virgin and Child* (detail, Morales)	20	35
246		1s. *The Virgin of the Rocks* (detail, Leonardo da Vinci)	20	40
244/246 *Set of* 3			45	1·00

Nos. 244/246 were issued together in *se-tenant* strips of three throughout the sheet.

The grey omitted error affects the background tone of all three stamps. It is best collected with printer's check marks attached.

(Des A. Ryman. Photo Enschedé)

1970 (8 June). Europa Point. W w **12**. P 13½.

No.		Description	Unused	Used
247	**83**	2s. multicoloured	45	1·50
		w. Wmk inverted	2·00	3·25

(Des A. Ryman. Photo D.L.R.)

1970 (28 Aug). Military Uniforms (2nd series). Vert designs as T **77**. Multicoloured. W w **12**. P 14.

No.		Description	Unused	Used
248		2d. Royal Scots officer, 1839 and cap badge	25	10
249		5d. South Wales Borderers private, 1763 and cap badge	35	10
250		7d. Queens Royal Regiment private, 1742 and cap badge	35	10
251		2s. Royal Irish Rangers piper, 1969 and cap badge	1·00	1·25
248/251 Set of 4			1·75	1·25

Nos. 248/251 have a short history of the Regiment printed on the reverse side under the gum.

88 No. 191a and Rock of Gibraltar

(Des A. Ryman. Litho D.L.R.)

1970 (18 Sept). Philympia 1970 Stamp Exhibition, London. T **88** and similar horiz design. W w **12** (sideways). P 13.

252		1s. vermilion and bronze-green	15	10
253		2s. bright blue and magenta	25	65

Designs: 1s. T **88**; 2s. Victorian stamp (No. 23b) and Moorish Castle.

The stamps shown in the designs are well-known varieties with values omitted.

90 *The Virgin Mary* (stained-glass window by Gabriel Loire)

(Photo Enschedé)

1970 (1 Dec). Christmas. W w **12**. P 13×14.

254	**90**	2s. multicoloured	30	1·25

STAMP BOOKLETS

1906 (Oct). Black on red cover. Stapled.

SB1 2s.0½d. booklet containing 24×½d. and 12×1d. (Nos. 56a, 67) in blocks of 6

1912 (17 July). Black on red cover. Stapled.

SB2 2s.0½d. booklet containing 24×½d. and 12×1d. (Nos. 76/77) in blocks of 6 .... £7500

POSTAGE DUE STAMPS

D 1

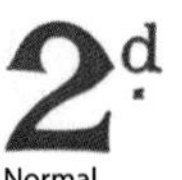

Normal

Large 'd.' (R. 9/6, 10/6)

4d. Ball of 'd' broken and serif at top damaged (R. 9/5). Other stamps in 5th vertical row show slight breaks to ball of 'd'.

(Typo D.L.R.)

1956 (1 Dec). Chalk-surfaced paper. Wmk Mult Script CA. P 14.

D1	D **1**	1d. green	1·50	4·25
D2		2d. sepia	2·25	2·75
		a. Large 'd' (R. 9/6, 10/6)	28·00	40·00
D3		4d. blue	1·75	5·00
		a. Broken 'd'	40·00	
D1/D3 *Set of 3*			5·00	11·00

Gilbert and Ellice Islands

No organised postal service existed in the Gilbert and Ellice Islands before the introduction of stamp issues in January 1911. A New Zealand Postal Agency was, however, provided on Fanning Island, one of the Line Islands, primarily for the use of the staff of the Pacific Cable Board cable station which was established in 1902. The agency opened on 29 November 1902 and although Fanning Island became part of the Gilbert and Ellice Islands colony on 27 January 1916, continued to operate until replaced by a Protectorate post office on 14 February 1939. The cable station closed on 16 January 1964. Fanning Island is now known as Tabuaeran.

Z 1

The following NEW ZEALAND stamps are known postmarked on Fanning Island with T Z **1** (in use from November 1902 until November 1936. The earliest known cover is postmarked 20 December 1902).

1882–1900 Q.V. (P 10) ½d. (No. 217) (P 11) ½d., 1d., 2d. (Nos. 236/238)
1898 Pictorials (*no wmk*) 1d., 2d., 2½d. (Nos. 247/248, 260)
1900 Pictorials (W **38**) ½d. 1½d., 2d. (Nos. 273, 275b, 276)
1901 1d. 'Universal' (W **38**) (Nos. 278, 280)
1902 ½d. Mt. Cook, 1d. 'Universal' (*no wmk*) (Nos. 294/295)
1902 ½d. Pictorial, 1d. 'Universal' (W **43**) (Nos. 302b, 303)
1902–1909 Pictorials (W **43**) 2d., 2½d., 3d., 5d., 6d., 8d., 9d., 1s., 2s., 5s. (Nos. 309, 312/317, 319/320, 322, 326, 328/329)
1907–1908 Pictorials (W **43**) 4d. (No. 379)
1908 1d. 'Universal' (*De La Rue paper*) 1d. (No. 386)
1909–1912 King Edward VII (*typo*) ½d. (No. 387)
1909–1916 King Edward VII (*recess*) 2d., 3d., 4d., 5d., 6d., 8d., 1s. (Nos. 388/391, 393/396, 397/398)
1909–1926 1d. 'Dominion' (W **43**) 1d. (Nos. 405, 410)
1915–1930 King George V (*recess*) 1½d., 2d. bright violet, 2½d., 3d., 4d. bright violet, 4½d., 5d., 6d., 7½d., 9d., 1s. (Nos. 416/417, 419/420, 422/426, 429/430)
1915–1934 King George V (*typo*) ½d., 1½d. (all 3), 2d., 3d. (Nos. 435/440, 446, 448/448b, 449/449b)
1915 'WAR STAMP' opt ½d. (No. 452)
1920 Victory 1d., 1½d. (Nos. 454/455)
1922 2d. on ½d. (No. 459)
1923–1925 Penny Postage 1d. (No. 460)
1926–1934 Admiral design 1d. (No. 468)
1935–1936 Pictorials ½d., 1d., 1½d., 2d., 4d., 8d., 1s. (Nos. 556, 557/557b, 558, 559, 562, 565, 567)
1935 Silver Jubilee ½d., 1d., 6d. (Nos. 573/575)
1936 Anzac ½d. + ½d., 1d. + 1d. (Nos. 591/592)
1899 1d. Postage due (D10)

Z 2

The following NEW ZEALAND stamps are known postmarked on Fanning Island with T Z **2** (in use from 7 December 1936 to 13 February 1939):

1935–1936 Pictorials (W **43**) 1d (No. 557)
1936–1939 Pictorials (W **98**) ½d., 1d., 1½d. (Nos. 577/579)
1936 Chambers of Commerce Congress ½d. (No. 593)
1936 Health 1d.+1d. (No. 598)
1937 Coronation 1d., 2½d., 6d. (Nos. 599/601)
1938–1939 King George VI ½d., 1d., 1½d. (Nos. 603, 605, 607)

The schooner which carried the mail from Fanning Island also called at Washington Island, another of the Line group. Problems arose, however, as the authorities insisted that mail from Washington must first pass through the Fanning Island Postal Agency before being forwarded which resulted in considerable delays. Matters were resolved by the opening of a New Zealand Postal Agency on Washington Island which operated from 1 February 1921 until the copra plantations were closed in early 1923. The postal agency was re-established on 15 May 1924, but finally closed on 30 March 1934. Covers from this second period occur with incorrectly dated postmarks. Manuscript markings on New Zealand Nos. 578, 599/600 and 692 are unofficial and were applied during the resettlement of the island between 1937 and 1948. Washington Island is now known as Teraina.

Z 3

The following NEW ZEALAND stamps are known postmarked on Washington Island with T Z **3**:

1909–1916 King Edward VII 5d., 8d. (Nos. 402, 404*b*)
1915–1930 King George V (*recess*) 6d., 7½d, 8d., 9d., 1s. (Nos. 425/427, 429/430)
1915–1934 King George V (*typo*) ½d., 1½d., 2d., 3d. (Nos. 435, 438/439, 449)
1915 'WAR STAMP' opt ½d (No. 452)
1920 Victory 1d., 1½d., 6d. (Nos. 454/455, 457)
1922 2d. on ½d. (No. 459)
1926–1934 Admiral design 1d. (No. 468/468*a*)

The above information is based on a special survey undertaken by members of the Kiribati & Tuvalu Philatelic Society and the Pacific Islands Study Circle, co-ordinated by Mr. Michael Shaw.

PRICES FOR STAMPS ON COVER TO 1945

Nos. 1/7	*from* × 5
Nos. 8/11	*from* × 10
Nos. 12/23	*from* × 6
No. 24	—
No. 26	*from* × 15
Nos. 27/30	*from* × 6
No. 35	—
Nos. 36/39	*from* × 4
Nos. 40/42	*from* × 12
Nos. 43/54	*from* × 4
Nos. D1/D8	*from* × 5

BRITISH PROTECTORATE

GILBERT& ELLICE

PROTECTORATE

(1)

2 Pandanus Pine

1911 (1 Jan). Stamps of Fiji optd with T **1**. Wmk Mult Crown CA. Chalk-surfaced paper (5d. to 1s.).

1	**23**	½d. green	6·00	50·00
2		1d. red	50·00	28·00
3	**24**	2d. grey	23·00	15·00
4	**23**	2½d. ultramarine	18·00	50·00
5		5d. purple and olive-green	65·00	95·00
6	**24**	6d. dull and bright purple	25·00	50·00
7	**23**	1s. black/*green* (R.)	26·00	75·00
1/7 *Set of 7*			£180	£325
1s/7s Optd 'SPECIMEN' *Set of 7*			£300	

The 2d. to 6d. are on special printings which were not issued without overprint.

Examples of Nos. 1/7 are known showing a forged Ocean Island postmark dated 'JY 15 11'.

(Recess D.L.R.)

1911 (Mar). Wmk Mult Crown CA. P 14.

8	**2**	½d. green	4·75	26·00
9		1d. carmine	2·00	13·00
		w. Wmk inverted	£650	
10		2d. grey	1·50	7·50
11		2½d. blue	12·00	16·00
8/11 *Set of 4*			18·00	55·00
8s/11s Optd 'SPECIMEN' *Set of 4*			£180	

3

WAR TAX

(5)

(Typo D.L.R.)

1912 (May)–**24**. Die I (½d. to 5s.) or Die II (£1). Wmk Mult Crown CA. Chalk-surfaced paper (3d. to £1). P 14.

12	**3**	½d. green (7.12)	70	6·00
		a. Yellow-green (1914)	5·00	14·00
13		1d. carmine (12.12)	2·25	17·00
		a. Scarlet (1915)	3·75	15·00
14		2d. greyish slate (1.16)	15·00	26·00
15		2½d. bright blue (1.16)	3·00	11·00
16		3d. purple/*yellow* (1918)	2·50	15·00
17		4d. black and red/*yellow* (10.12)	75	4·50
18		5d. dull purple and sage-green	1·75	5·50
19		6d. dull and bright purple	1·25	6·50
20		1s. black/*green*	1·25	4·00
21		2s. purple and blue/*blue* (10.12)	15·00	38·00
22		2s.6d. black and red/*blue* (10.12)	23·00	25·00
23		5s. green and red/*yellow* (10.12)	32·00	65·00
24		£1 purple and black/*red* (Die II) (3.24)	£550	£1600
12/24 Set of 13			£600	£1600
12s/24s Optd 'SPECIMEN' Set of 13			£600	

THE FUNAFUTI PROVISIONALS. In July 1916, during a shortage of stamps at the post office in Funafuti, a number of parcels were presented for despatch. The District Officer, who also acted as Postmaster, surcharged 1d. and 2½d. stamps by handstamping to meet the need for higher values, without first seeking authorisation from the Resident Commissioner on Ocean Island (a process which would have taken several weeks). Opinion as to the legitimacy of the provisionals has varied, but it seems that they were produced to meet a short-term need and there is no evidence that they were created for financial gain. The stamps concerned are the 1d. (No. 13), surcharged '2/-' (twice) in black and the 2½d. blue (No. 11) surcharged '2/-' in red and '3/-', also in red.

CROWN COLONY

1918 (June). Optd with T **5**.

26	**3**	1d. red	50	6·50
		s. Optd 'SPECIMEN'	70·00	

1922–27. Die II. Wmk Mult Script CA. Chalk-surfaced paper (10s.). P 14.

27 **3** ½d. green (1923) 4·25 3·25
28 1d. violet (1927) 4·75 9·50
29 1½d. scarlet (1924) 9·00 3·75
30 2d. slate-grey 7·50 45·00
35 10s. green and red/*emerald* (3.24) £160 £375
27s/35s Optd 'SPECIMEN' *Set of 5* £275

Examples of most values between Nos. 12 and 35 are known showing part strikes of the forged postmark mentioned below Nos. 1/7. Collectors should exercise particular caution when buying used examples of Nos. 24 and 35.

1935 (6 May). Silver Jubilee. As Nos. 91/94 of Antigua, but ptd by B.W. P 11×12.

36 1d. ultramarine and grey-black 2·25 17·00
c. Lightning conductor £2250
d. Flagstaff on right-hand turret £250 £450
e. Double flagstaff £475 £550
37 1½d. deep blue and scarlet 1·75 4·00
d. Flagstaff on right-hand turret £250
e. Double flagstaff £475
38 3d. brown and deep blue 6·50 26·00
d. Flagstaff on right-hand turret £375 £650
e. Double flagstaff £450 £700
39 1s. slate and purple 26·00 20·00
d. Flagstaff on right-hand turret £600 £600
e. Double flagstaff £600 £650
36/39 *Set of 4* 32·00 60·00
36s/39s Perf 'SPECIMEN' *Set of 4* £200

For illustrations of plate varieties see Omnibus section following Zanzibar.

1937 (12 May). Coronation. As Nos. 95/97 of Antigua, but ptd by D.L.R. P 14.

40 1d. violet 35 65
41 1½d. scarlet 35 65
42 3d. bright blue 40 70
40/42 *Set of 3* 1·00 1·75
40s/42s Perf 'SPECIMEN' *Set of 3* £170

6 Great Frigatebird

7 Pandanus Pine

8 Canoe crossing Reef

9 Canoe and boat-house

10 Native house

11 Seascape

12 Ellice Islands canoe

13 Coconut palms

14 Cantilever jetty, Ocean Island

15 HMCS *Nimanoa*

16 Gilbert Islands canoe

17 Coat of Arms

(Recess B.W. (½d., 2d., 2s.6d.), Waterlow (1d., 5d., 6d., 2s., 5s.), D.L.R. (1½d., 2½d., 3d., 1s.))

1939 (14 Jan)–**55**. Types **6/17**. Wmk Mult Script CA (sideways on ½d., 2d. and 2s.6d.). P 11½×11 (½d., 2d., 2s.6d.), 12½ (1d., 5d., 6d., 2s., 5s.) or 13½ (1½d., 2½d., 3d., 1s.).

43 **6** ½d. indigo and deep bluish green 60 1·00
a. 'A' of 'CA' missing from wmk £2000
44 **7** 1d. emerald and plum 30 1·50
45 **8** 1½d. brownish black and bright carmine 30 1·25
46 **9** 2d. red-brown and grey-black 1·25 1·00
47 **10** 2½d. brownish black and deep olive 1·50 1·00
a. Brownish black and olive-green (12.5.43) 9·00 7·50
48 **11** 3d. brownish black and ultramarine 60 1·00
a. Perf 12. *Black and bright blue* (24.8.55) 1·50 4·00
49 **12** 5d. deep ultramarine and sepia 7·00 2·75
a. Ultramarine and sepia (12.5.43). 19·00 25·00
b. Ultramarine and blackish brown (20.10.44) 12·00 9·00
50 **13** 6d. olive-green and deep violet 70 60
51 **14** 1s. brownish black and turquoise-green 40·00 3·75
a. Brownish black and turquoise-blue (12.5.43) 20·00 5·50
ab. Perf 12 (8.5.51) 4·50 20·00
52 **15** 2s. deep ultramarine and orange-red 10·00 12·00
53 **16** 2s.6d. deep blue and emerald 10·00 11·00
54 **17** 5s. deep rose-red and royal blue 13·00 17·00
43/54 *Set of 12* 42·00 48·00
43s/54s Perf 'SPECIMEN' *Set of 12* £600

1946 (16 Dec). Victory. As Nos. 110/111 of Antigua.

55 1d. purple 15 65
56 3d. blue 15 65
55s/56s Perf 'SPECIMEN' *Set of 2* £140

1949 (29 Aug). Royal Silver Wedding. As Nos. 112/113 of Antigua.

57 1d. violet 50 1·50
58 £1 scarlet 16·00 25·00

1949 (10 Oct). 75th Anniversary of UPU As Nos. 114/117 of Antigua.

59 1d. purple 50 2·75
60 2d. grey-black 2·50 4·50
61 3d. deep blue 1·00 4·50
62 1s. blue 75 2·75
59/62 *Set of 4* 4·25 13·00

1953 (2 June). Coronation. As No. 120 of Antigua.

63 2d. black and grey-black 1·50 2·25

18 Great Frigatebird

½d. Short line along top of 'Y' in 'PENNY' (Pl. 1, R. 10/1)

(Recess B.W. (½d., 2d., 2s.6d.), Waterlow (1d., 5d., 6d., 2s., 5s.), D.L.R. (2½d., 3d., 1s., 10s. and after 1962, 1d., 5d.))

1956 (1 Aug)–**62**. Designs previously used for King George VI issue; but with portrait of Queen Elizabeth II as in T **18**. Wmk Mult Script CA. P 11½×11 (½d., 2d., 2s.6d.), 12½ (1d., 5d., 6d., 2s., 5s.) or 12 (2½d., 3d., 1s., 10s.).

64 **18** ½d. black and deep bright blue 65 1·25
a. 'Y' flaw 23·00
65 **7** 1d. brown-olive and deep violet 60 1·25
66 **9** 2d. bluish green and deep purple 3·50 2·50
a. Bluish green and purple (30.7.62) 38·00 38·00
67 **10** 2½d. black and myrtle-green 50 60
68 **11** 3d. black and carmine-red 50 60
69 **12** 5d. ultramarine and red-orange 9·50 4·50
a. Ultramarine and brown-orange (D.L.R.) (30.7.62) 25·00 45·00
70 **13** 6d. chestnut and black-brown 70 2·75
71 **14** 1s. black and bronze-green 5·00 1·50
72 **15** 2s. deep bright blue and sepia 9·00 4·00
73 **16** 2s.6d. scarlet and deep blue 7·00 4·25
74 **17** 5s. greenish blue and bluish green 7·00 5·00
75 **8** 10s. black and turquoise 38·00 8·50
64/75 *Set of 12* 70·00 32·00

See also Nos. 85/86.

19 Loading Phosphate from Cantilever

(Des R. Turrell (2d.), M. Thoma (2½d.), M. A. W. Hook and A. Larkins (1s.). Photo D.L.R.)

1960 (1 May). Diamond Jubilee of Phosphate Discovery at Ocean Island. T **19** and similar horiz designs. W w **12**. P 12.

76 2d. green and carmine-rose 1·00 85
77 2½d. black and olive-green 1·00 85
78 1s. black and deep turquoise 1·00 85
76/78 *Set of 3* 2·75 2·40

Designs: 2d. T **19**; 2½d. Phosphate rock; 1s. Phosphate mining.

1963 (1 Aug). Freedom from Hunger. As No. 146 of Antigua.

79 10d. ultramarine 75 30

1963 (5 Oct). Red Cross Centenary. As Nos. 147/148 of Antigua.

80 2d. red and black 50 1·00
81 10d. red and blue 75 2·50

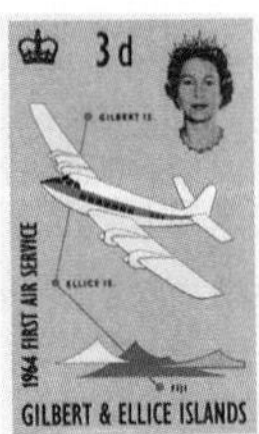

22 de Havilland DH.114 Heron 2 and Route Map

24 de Havilland DH.114 Heron 2 over Tarawa Lagoon

23 Eastern Reef Heron in Flight

(Des Margaret Barwick. Litho Enschedé)

1964 (20 July). First Air Service. W w **12** (sideways* on 3d., 3s.7d.). P 11×11½ (1s.) or 11½×11 (others).

82 **22** 3d. blue, black and light blue 70 30
w. Wmk Crown to right of CA 70 30
83 **23** 1s. light blue, black and deep blue 1·25 30
84 **24** 3s.7d. deep green, black and light emerald 1·75 1·50
82/84 *Set of 3* 3·25 1·90

* The normal sideways watermark shows Crown to left of CA, *as seen from the back of the stamp.*

(Recess B.W. (2d.), D.L.R. (6d.))

1964 (30 Oct)–**65**. As Nos. 66*a* and 70 but wmk w **12**.

85 **9** 2d. bluish green and purple 1·25 1·25
86 **13** 6d. chestnut and black-brown (26.4.65)* 1·25 1·25

* Earliest known postmark date.

1965 (4 June). ITU Centenary. As Nos. 166/167 of Antigua.

87 3d. red-orange and deep bluish green 15 10
88 2s.6d. turquoise-blue and light purple 45 20

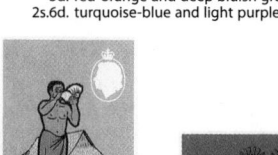

25 Maneaba and Gilbertese Man blowing Bu Shell

26 Gilbertese Women's Dance

(Des V. Whiteley from drawings by Margaret Barwick. Litho B.W.)

1965 (16 Aug). Vert designs as T **25** (½d. to 2s.) or horiz designs as T **26** (3s.7d. to £1). Centres multicoloured. W w **12**. P 12×11 (½d. to 2s.) or 11×12 (3s.7d. to £1).

89 ½d. turquoise-green 10 10
90 1d. deep violet-blue 10 10
91 2d. bistre 10 10
92 3d. rose-red 10 10
93 4d. purple 15 10
94 5d. cerise 20 10
95 6d. turquoise-blue 20 10
96 7d. bistre-brown 25 10
97 1s. bluish violet 1·00 10
98 1s.6d. lemon 1·00 1·00
99 2s. yellow-olive 1·00 1·40
100 3s.7d. new blue 1·75 65
101 5s. light yellow-olive 1·75 80
102 10s. dull green 2·75 1·00
103 £1 light turquoise-blue 3·50 1·75
89/103 *Set of 15* 12·00 6·00

Designs: ½d. T **25**; 1d. Ellice Islanders reef fishing by flare; 2d. Gilbertese girl weaving head garland; 3d. Gilbertese woman performing Ruoia; 4d. Gilbertese man performing Kamei; 5d. Gilbertese girl drawing water; 6d. Ellice islander performing a Fatele; 7d. Ellice youths performing spear dance; 1s. Gilbertese girl tending Ikaroa Babai plant; 1s.6d. Ellice islanders dancing a Fatele; 2s. Ellice islanders pounding Pulaka; 3s.7d. T **26**; 5s. Gilbertese boys playing stick game; 10s. Ellice youths beating the box for the Fatele; £1 Coat of Arms.

1965 (25 Oct). International Co-operation Year. As Nos. 168/169 of Antigua.

104 ½d. reddish purple and turquoise-green 10 10
105 3s.7d. deep bluish green and lavender 50 20

1966 (24 Jan). Churchill Commemoration. As Nos. 170/173 of Antigua.

106 ½d. new blue 10 10
107 3d. deep green 20 10
108 3s. brown 40 35
109 3s.7d. bluish violet 45 35
106/109 *Set of 4* 1·00 75

(New Currency, 100 cents = 1 Australian dollar)

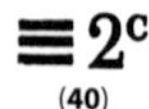

(40)

1966 (14 Feb). Decimal currency. Nos. 89/103 surch as T **40**.

110 1c. on 1d. deep violet-blue 10 10
111 2c. on 2d. bistre 10 10
112 3c. on 3d. rose-red 10 10
113 4c. on ½d. turquoise-green 10 10
114 5c. on 6d. turquoise-blue 15 10
115 6c. on 4d. purple 15 10
116 8c. on 5d. cerise 15 10
117 10c. on 1s. bluish violet 15 10
118 15c. on 7d. bistre-brown 60 1·00
119 20c. on 1s.6d. lemon 30 25
120 25c. on 2s. yellow-olive 30 20
121 35c. on 3s.7d. new blue 1·00 20
122 50c. on 5s. light yellow-olive 55 35
123 $1 on 10s. dull green 55 40
124 $2 on £1 light turquoise-blue 3·00 3·75
110/124 *Set of 15* 6·50 6·00

1966 (1 July). World Cup Football Championship. As Nos. 176/177 of Antigua.

125 3c. violet, yellow-green, lake and yellow-brown 20 10
126 35c. chocolate, blue-green, lake and yellow-brown 80 20

1966 (20 Sept). Inauguration of WHO Headquarters, Geneva. As Nos. 178/179 of Antigua.

127 3c. black, yellow-green and light blue 20 10
128 12c. black, light purple and yellow-brown 45 40

1966 (1 Dec). 20th Anniversary of UNESCO. As Nos. 196/198 of Antigua.

129 5c. slate-violet, red, yellow and orange. 25 90

130		10c. orange-yellow, violet and deep olive	35	20
131		20c. black, bright purple and orange	60	1·40
129/131 *Set of 3*			1·10	2·25

41 HMS *Royalist*

(Des V. Whiteley. Photo Harrison)

1967 (1 Sept). 75th Anniversary of the Protectorate. T **41** and similar horiz designs. W w **12**. P 14½.

132		3c. red, blue and myrtle-green	30	50
133		10c. multicoloured	15	15
134		35c. sepia, orange-yellow and deep bluish green	30	50
132/134 *Set of 3*			65	1·00

Designs: 3c. T **41**; 10c. Trading Post; 35c. Island family.

44 Gilbertese Women's Dance

1968 (1 Jan). Decimal Currency. Designs as Nos. 89/103 but with values inscr in decimal currency as T **44**. W w **12** (sideways on horiz designs). P 12×11 (vert) or 11×12 (horiz).

135		1c. deep violet-blue (as 1d.)	10	15
136		2c. bistre (as 2d.)	15	10
137		3c. rose-red (as 3d.)	15	10
138		4c. turquoise-green (as ½d.)	15	10
139		5c. turquoise-blue (as 6d.)	15	10
140		6c. purple (as 4d.)	20	10
141		8c. cerise (as 5d.)	20	10
142		10c. bluish violet (as 1s.)	20	10
143		15c. bistre-brown (as 7d.)	50	20
144		20c. lemon (as 1s.6d.)	65	15
		w. Wmk inverted	9·00	15·00
145		25c. yellow-olive (as 2s.)	1·25	20
146		35c. new blue	1·50	20
147		50c. light yellow-olive (as 5s.)	1·50	2·50
148		$1 dull green (as 10s.)	1·50	3·75
149		$2 light turquoise-blue (as £1)	5·50	6·00
135/149 *Set of 15*			12·00	12·00

45 Map of Tarawa Atoll

(Des V. Whiteley. Photo D.L.R.)

1968 (21 Nov). 25th Anniversary of the Battle of Tarawa. T **45** and similar designs. Multicoloured. W w **12** (sideways). P 14.

150		3c. Type **45**	20	30
151		10c. Marines landing	20	20
152		15c. Beach-head assault	20	35
153		35c. Raising US and British flags	25	50
150/153 *Set of 4*			75	1·25

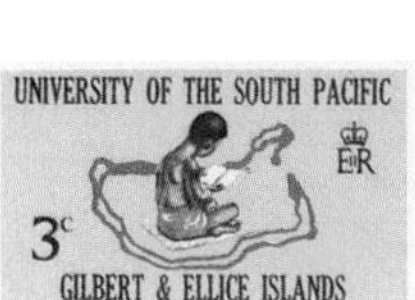

46 Young Pupil against outline of Abemama Island

47 *Virgin and Child* in Pacific Setting

(Des J.W. (from original designs by Mrs V. J. Anderson and Miss A. Loveridge) Litho D.L.R.)

1969 (2 June). End of Inaugural Year of South Pacific University. T **46** and similar horiz designs. W w **12** (sideways). P 12½.

154		3c. multicoloured	10	25
155		10c. multicoloured	10	10
156		35c. black, brown and grey-green	15	30
154/156 *Set of 3*			30	55

Designs: 3c. T **46**; 10c. Boy and girl students and Tarawa atoll; 35c. University graduate and South Pacific islands.

(Des Jennifer Toombs. Litho B.W.)

1969 (20 Oct). Christmas. W w **12** (sideways). P 11½.

157	–	2c. olive-green and multicoloured (*shades*)	15	20
158	**47**	10c. olive-green and multicoloured (*shades*)	15	10

Design: 2c. As T **47** but foreground has grass instead of sand.

48 'The Kiss of Life'

(Des Manate Tenang Manate. Litho J.W.)

1970 (9 Mar*). Centenary of British Red Cross. W w **12** (sideways). P 14.

159	**48**	10c. multicoloured	25	10
160	–	15c. multicoloured	35	45
161	–	35c. multicoloured	75	90
159/161 *Set of 3*			1·25	1·25

Nos. 160/161 are as T **48**, but arranged differently.

* The above were released by the Crown Agents on 2 March, but not sold locally until the 9 March.

49 Foetus and Patients

(Des Jennifer Toombs. Litho Enschedé)

1970 (26 June). 25th Anniversary of United Nations. T **49** and similar horiz designs. W w **12** (sideways). P 12½×13.

162		5c. multicoloured	20	30
163		10c. black, grey and red	20	15
164		15c. multicoloured	25	30
165		35c. new blue, black and turquoise-green	45	45
162/165 *Set of 4*			1·00	1·10

Designs: 5c. T **49**; 10c. Nurse and surgical instruments; 15c. X-ray plate and technician; 35c. UN emblem and map.

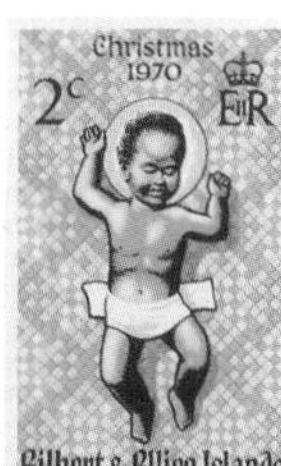

53 Map of Gilbert Islands

57 *Child with Halo* (T. Collis)

(Des G. Vasarhelyi. Litho Harrison)

1970 (1 Sept). Centenary of Landing in Gilbert Islands by London Missionary Society. T **53** and similar designs. W w **12** (sideways on vert designs). P 14½×14 (2c., 35c.) or 14×14½ (others).

166		2c. multicoloured	40	1·10
		w. Wmk inverted		
167		10c. black and pale green	50	15
168		25c. chestnut and cobalt	25	25
169		35c. turquoise-blue, black and red	60	70
166/169 *Set of 4*			1·60	2·00

Designs: Vert—10c. Sailing-ship *John Williams III*; 25c. Rev. S. J. Whitmee. Horiz—2c. T **53**; 35c. M V *John Williams VII*.

(Des L. Curtis. Litho Format)

1970 (3 Oct). Christmas. Sketches. T **57** and similar vert designs. Multicoloured. W w **12**. P 14½.

170		2c. Type **57**	10	60
171		10c. *Sanctuary, Tarawa Cathedral* (Mrs. A. Burroughs)	10	10
172		35c. *Three ships inside star* (Mrs. C. Barnett)	20	20
170/172 *Set of 3*			35	80

POSTAGE DUE STAMPS

D **1**

(Typo B.W.)

1940 (Aug). Wmk Mult Script CA. P 12.

D1	D **1**	1d. emerald-green	13·00	25·00
D2		2d. scarlet	14·00	25·00
D3		3d. brown	18·00	26·00
D4		4d. blue	20·00	35·00
D5		5d. grey-green	25·00	35·00
D6		6d. purple	25·00	35·00
D7		1s. violet	27·00	48·00
D8		1s.6d. turquoise-green	55·00	90·00
D1/D8 *Set of 8*			£180	£275
D1s/D8s Perf 'SPECIMEN' *Set of 8*			£250	

Examples of all values are known showing a forged Post Office Ocean Island postmark dated '16 DE 46'.

Gold Coast

Gold Coast originally consisted of coastal forts, owned by the Royal African Company, trading with the interior. In 1821, due to raids by the Ashanti king, the British Government took over the forts, together with some of the hinterland, and the Gold Coast was placed under the Governor of Sierra Leone.

The administration was handed back to a merchantile company in 1828, but the forts returned to British Government rule in 1843. The colony was reconstituted by Royal Charter on 24 July 1874, and at that time also included the settlement at Lagos which became a separate colony in January 1886.

Following the end of the final Ashanti War the whole of the territory was annexed in September 1901.

A postal service was established at Cape Coast Castle in 1853. There is no record of British stamps being officially issued in the Colony before 1875, apart from those used on board the ships of the West African Squadron, but examples do, however, exist cancelled by Gold Coast postmarks.

CROWN COLONY

PRICES FOR STAMPS ON COVER TO 1945	
Nos. 1/3	*from* × 125
Nos. 4/8	*from* × 40
Nos. 9/10	*from* × 15
Nos. 11/20	*from* × 30
Nos. 22/25	—
Nos. 26/34	*from* × 10
Nos. 35/36	*from* × 20
Nos. 38/69	*from* × 6
Nos. 70/98	*from* × 3
Nos. 100/102	—
Nos. 103/112	*from* × 5
Nos. 113/116	*from* × 3
Nos. 117/119	*from* × 4
Nos. 120/132	*from* × 3
No. D1	*from* × 6
No. D2	*from* × 20
Nos. D3/D4	*from* × 12

1

ONE PENNY.

(**2**)

(Typo D.L.R.)

1875 (1 July)–**76**. Wmk Crown CC. P 12½.

1	**1**	1d. blue	£550	95·00
		a. Bisected (½d.) (*on cover*) (1876)	†	—
2		4d. magenta	£475	£150
3		6d. orange	£750	80·00

1876–84. Wmk Crown CC. P 14.

4	**1**	½d. olive-yellow (1879)	95·00	42·00
		w. Wmk inverted	£475	
5		1d. blue	45·00	6·50
		a. Bisected (½d.) (*on cover*) (1877–1878 and 1882–1884)	†	£4500
		w. Wmk inverted	£700	£250
6		2d. green (1879)	£140	9·00
		a. Bisected (1d.) (*on cover*) (1882–1884)	†	£4250
		b. Quartered (½d.) (*on cover*) (1884)	†	£7500
		y. Wmk inverted and reversed	†	£500
7		4d. magenta	£275	6·00
		a. Bisected (2d.) (*on cover*) (1884).	†	£8000
		b. Quartered (1d.) (*on cover*) (1884)	†	£10000
		c. Tri-quadrisected (3d.) (*on cover*) (1884)	†	—
		w. Wmk inverted	£1200	£375
8		6d. orange	£325	28·00
		a. Bisected (3d.) (*on cover*) (1884)	†	£10000
		b. Sixth (1d.) (*on cover*) (1884)	†	£13000

In the period 1882–1884 some values were in short supply and the use of bisects and other divided stamps is known as follows:

No. 5a.	Used as part of 2½d. rate from Accra, Addah and Quittah
No. 6a.	Used as 1d. rate from Addah, Cape Coast Castle, Elmina, Quittah, Salt Pond, Secondee and Winnebah
No. 6b.	Used as part of 2½d. rate from Cape Coast Castle
No. 7a.	Used as 2d. or as part of 2½d. rate from Quittah
No. 7b.	Used as 1d. rate from Appam, Axim, Cape Coast Castle, Elmina and Winnebah
No. 7c.	Used as 3d. rate from Winnebah
No. 8a.	Used as 3d. rate from Secondee and Winnebah
No. 8b.	Used as 1d. rate from Cape Coast Castle and Winnebah.

Examples of bisects used *on piece* are worth about 10% of the price quoted for those *on cover*.

The 4d., No. 7, is known surcharged '1d'. This was previously listed as No. 8c, but there are now serious doubts as to its authenticity. The three examples reported of this stamp all show *different* surcharges!

1883. Wmk Crown CA. P 14.

9	**1**	½d. olive-yellow (1.83)	£275	85·00
10		1d. blue (5.83)	£900	85·00

Short 'P' and distorted 'E' (Pl 1 R. 5/6) ('P' repaired for Pl 2)

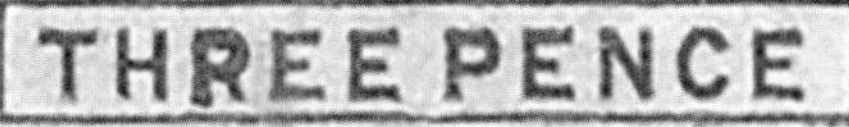

Large 'R' in 'THREE' (R. 10/4)

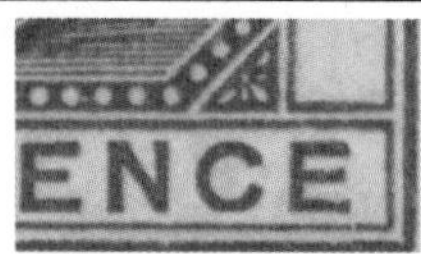

2d. Long centre bar to second 'E' in 'PENCE' (Pl 1, R. 2/6)

1884 (Aug)–**91**. Wmk Crown CA. P 14.

11	1	½d. green	5·00	1·50
		a. Dull green	5·00	1·50
		w. Wmk inverted	£300	£300
		x. Wmk reversed		
12		1d. rose-carmine	7·00	50
		a. Carmine	7·00	50
		b. Bisected (½d.) (*on cover*)	†	£5000
		c. Short 'P' and distorted 'E'	£300	70·00
		w. Wmk inverted	†	£600
13		2d. grey	50·00	7·00
		aw. Wmk inverted	£400	£400
		b. Slate	19·00	50
		c. Bisected (1d.) (*on cover*)	†	£5000
		d. Quartered (½d.) (*on cover*)	†	—
		e. Long centre bar to second 'E' in 'PENCE'	£300	70·00
14		2½d. ultramarine and orange (13.3.91)	15·00	70
		w. Wmk inverted	†	£375
15		3d. olive-yellow (9.89)	28·00	16·00
		a. Olive	28·00	14·00
		b. Large 'R' in 'THREE'	—	£500
16		4d. deep mauve (3.85)	29·00	4·50
		a. Rosy mauve	38·00	8·50
17		6d. orange (1.89)	28·00	7·00
		a. Orange-brown	28·00	7·00
		b. Bisected (3d.) (*on cover*)	†	£10000
18		1s. violet (1888)	50·00	16·00
		a. Bright mauve	17·00	3·50
19		2s. yellow-brown (1888)	£110	45·00
		a. Deep brown	60·00	16·00
11/19*a* *Set of* 9			£180	42·00
14s/15s, 18s/19s Optd 'SPECIMEN' *Set of* 4			£180	

During 1884 to 1886 and in 1889 some values were in short supply and the use of bisects and other divided stamps is known as follows:

No. 12b. Used as part of 2½d. rate from Cape Coast Castle
No. 13c. Used as 1d. or as part of 2d. rate from Cape Coast Castle, Chamah, Dixcove and Elmina
No. 13d. Used as part of 2½d. rate from Cape Coast Castle
No. 17b. Used as 3d. from Appam

The repaired 'P' in printings of the 1d. from plate 2 shows a slightly short and pointed foot to the letter.

1889 (Mar). No. 17 surch with T **2**.

20	1	1d. on 6d. orange	£150	55·00
		a. Surch double	†	£4750

In some sheets examples may be found with the bar and 'PENNY' spaced 8 mm, the normal spacing being 7 mm.

USED HIGH VALUES. Until the introduction of airmail in 1929 there was no postal use for values over 10s. Post Offices did, however, apply postal cancellations to high value stamps required for telegram fees.

3

4

1889 (Sept)–**94**. Wmk Crown CA. P 14.

22	3	5s. dull mauve and blue	80·00	30·00
23		10s. dull mauve and red	£140	18·00
		a. Dull mauve and carmine	£1100	£325
24		20s. green and red	£3500	
25		20s. dull mauve and black/*red* (4.94)	£170	35·00
		w. Wmk inverted	£650	£120
22s/25s Optd 'SPECIMEN' *Set of* 4			£450	

No. 24 was withdrawn from sale in April 1893 when a large part of the stock was stolen. No 20s. stamps were available until the arrival of the replacement printing a year later.

1898 (May)–**1902**. Wmk Crown CA. P 14.

26	3	½d. dull mauve and green	7·00	1·75
27		1d. dull mauve and rose	7·50	50
		aw. Wmk inverted	—	£225
27*b*	4	2d. dull mauve and orange-red (1902)	50·00	£160
28	3	2½d. dull mauve and ultramarine	10·00	13·00
29	4	3d. dull mauve and orange	10·00	4·75
30		6d. dull mauve and violet	15·00	3·75
31	3	1s. green and black (1899)	20·00	45·00
32		2s. green and carmine	38·00	45·00
33		5s. green and mauve (1900)	£100	60·00
34		10s. green and brown (1900)	£225	70·00
26/34 *Set of* 10			£400	£350
26s/34s Optd 'SPECIMEN' *Set of* 10			£300	

1901 (6 Oct). Nos. 28 and 30 surch with T **2**.

35	1d. on 2½d. dull mauve and ultramarine	13·00	8·50
	a. 'ONE' omitted	£1000	
36	1d. on 6d. dull mauve and violet	13·00	6·00
	a. 'ONE' omitted	£275	£550

6

7

8

1902. Wmk Crown CA. P 14.

38	6	½d. dull purple and green (8.02)	1·50	40
39		1d. dull purple and carmine (5.02)	1·50	15
		w. Wmk inverted	£275	£160
40	7	2d. dull purple and orange-red (4.02)	48·00	7·00
		w. Wmk inverted		
41	6	2½d. dull purple and ultramarine (8.02)	6·00	9·50
42	7	3d. dull purple and orange (8.02)	8·00	3·00
43		6d. dull purple and violet (8.02)	8·50	3·00
		w. Wmk inverted	—	£250
44	6	1s. green and black (8.02)	26·00	4·25
45		2s. green and carmine (8.02)	26·00	42·00
46		5s. green and mauve (8.02)	65·00	£120
47		10s. green and brown (8.02)	85·00	£160
48		20s. purple and black/*red* (8.02)	£190	£250
38/48 *Set of* 11			£400	£550
38s/48s Optd 'SPECIMEN' *Set of* 11			£275	

Examples of Nos. 45/48 are known showing a forged Accra postmark dated '25 MAR 1902'.

1904–06. Wmk Mult Crown CA. Ordinary paper (½d. to 6d.) or chalk-surfaced paper (2s.6d.).

49	6	½d. dull purple and green (3.06)	2·50	7·00
50		1d. dull purple and carmine (10.04)	26·00	1·50
		a. Chalk-surfaced paper (5.06)	17·00	3·00
		w. Wmk inverted		
51	7	2d. dull purple and orange-red (11.04)	16·00	2·50
		a. Chalk-surfaced paper (8.06)	38·00	4·25
52	6	2½d. dull purple and ultramarine (6.06)	65·00	85·00
53	7	3d. dull purple and orange (8.05)	90·00	9·50
		a. Chalk-surfaced paper (4.06)	29·00	1·50
54		6d. dull purple and violet (3.06)	90·00	8·00
		a. Chalk-surfaced paper (9.06)	50·00	3·50
57		2s.6d. green and yellow (3.06)	35·00	£140
		s. Optd SPECIMEN'	45·00	
49/57 *Set of* 7			£190	£200

1907–13. Wmk Mult Crown CA. Ordinary paper (½d. to 2½d. and 2s.) or chalk-surfaced paper (3d. to 1s., 2s.6d., 5s.). P 14.

59	6	½d. dull green (5.07)	12·00	30
		a. Blue-green (1909)	20·00	2·75
60		1d. red (2.07)	21·00	40
61	7	2d. greyish slate (4.09)	3·00	1·25
62	6	2½d. blue (4.07)	23·00	5·50
		w. Wmk inverted	£500	£400
63	7	3d. purple/*yellow* (16.4.09)	8·50	1·50
64		6d. dull and deep purple (12.08)	45·00	2·25
		a. Dull and bright purple (1911)	9·00	8·00
65	6	1s. black/*green* (10.09)	29·00	1·75
66		2s. purple and blue/*blue* (1910)	8·50	16·00
		a. Chalk-surfaced paper (1912)	18·00	16·00
67	7	2s.6d. black and red/*blue* (1911)	42·00	£100
68	6	5s. green and red/*yellow* (1913)	65·00	£250
59/68 *Set of* 10			£200	£325
59s/68s Optd 'SPECIMEN' *Set of* 10			£425	

Prepared for use but not issued.

69s	6	10s. green and red/*green* (optd 'SPECIMEN')	£350	

Although never actually issued, No. 69s was distributed by the Universal Postal Union to all member countries. One example exists without 'SPECIMEN' opt. A 20s. purple and black on *red*, T **6**, was also prepared, and exists with 'SPECIMEN' opt, but was not distributed by the UPU.

(Typo D.L.R.)

1908 (Nov). Wmk Mult Crown CA. P 14.

70	8	1d. red	9·50	10
		a. Wmk sideways	†	£3000
		s. Optd 'SPECIMEN'	60·00	

9

10

11

(Typo D.L.R.)

1913–21. Die I. Wmk Mult Crown CA. Chalk-surfaced paper (3d. to 20s.). P 14.

71	9	½d. green	2·50	2·25
		a. Yellow-green (1916)	3·75	2·50
72	10	1d. red	2·25	10
		a. Scarlet (1917)	4·00	50
		ab. 'A' of 'CA' missing from wmk	†	£700
		ac. 'C' of 'CA' missing from wmk	£750	
74	11	2d. grey	12·00	2·50
		a. Slate-grey (1920)	20·00	20·00
		w. Wmk inverted	†	£375
		x. Wmk reversed	†	£425
		y. Wmk inverted and reversed	†	£425
76	9	2½d. bright blue	15·00	3·00
		a. 'A' of 'CA' missing from wmk	£850	
		x. Wmk reversed	†	£400
77	11	3d. purple/*yellow* (8.15)	4·50	80
		as. Optd 'SPECIMEN'	40·00	
		aw. Wmk inverted	—	£225
		b. White back (9.13)	1·75	40
		c. On orange-buff (1919)	16·00	9·00
		cw. Wmk inverted	—	£225
		d. On buff (1920)		
		e. Die II. *On pale yellow* (1921)	65·00	6·50
		ew. Wmk inverted	†	£450
78		6d. dull and bright purple	13·00	2·75
79	9	1s. black/*green*	6·50	2·50
		bw. Wmk inverted		
		c. On blue-green, olive back (1916)	19·00	75
		ca. Wmk sideways	†	£2000
		cs. Optd 'SPECIMEN'	£100	
		cw. Wmk inverted	—	£300
		d. On emerald back (1920)	4·25	2·00
		ds. Optd 'SPECIMEN'	65·00	
		e. Die II. *On emerald back* (1921)	3·50	50
		es. Optd 'SPECIMEN'	45·00	
		ew. Wmk inverted	†	£375
80		2s. purple and blue/*blue*	15·00	5·00
		aw. Wmk inverted	—	£450
		b. Die II (1921)	£180	65·00
81	11	2s.6d. black and red/*blue*	15·00	13·00
		a. Die II (1921)	45·00	42·00
82	9	5s. green and red/*yellow* (1916)	30·00	70·00
		as. Optd 'SPECIMEN'	55·00	
		b. White back (10.13)	30·00	70·00
		c. On orange-buff (1919)	85·00	£100
		d. On buff (1920)		
		e. On pale yellow (1921)	£110	£160
		f. Die II. *On pale yellow* (1921)	50·00	£180
		fw. Wmk inverted	£475	
83		10s. green and red/*green*	70·00	£120
		a. On blue-green, olive back (1916)	48·00	£100
		aw. Wmk inverted	£1200	
		b. On emerald back (1921)	50·00	£200
84		20s. purple and black/*red*	£170	£120
71/84 *Set of* 12			£275	£275
71s/76s, 77bs, 78s/81s, 82bs/84s Optd 'SPECIMEN' *Set of* 12			£325	

The 10s. and 20s. were withdrawn locally from September 1920 and, in common with other Gold Coast stamps, were not available to stamp dealers from the Crown Agents in London.

WAR TAX

ONE PENNY

(**12**)

13 King George V and Christiansborg Castle

1918 (17 June). Surch with T **12**.

85	10	1d. on 1d. red	4·00	1·00
		s. Optd 'SPECIMEN'	65·00	

1921–24. Die I (15s., £2) or Die II (others). Wmk Mult Script CA. Chalk-surfaced paper (6d. to £2). P 14.

86	9	½d. green	1·75	1·00
87	10	1d. chocolate-brown (1922)	1·00	10
88	11	1½d. red (1922)	3·00	10
89		2d. grey	2·50	30
		x. Wmk reversed	†	£500
90	9	2½d. yellow-orange (1922)	3·50	16·00
91	11	3d. bright blue (1922)	1·75	1·75
94		6d. dull and bright purple	5·50	3·50
95	9	1s. black/*emerald* (1924)	12·00	4·25
96		2s. purple and blue/*blue* (1923)	4·25	4·25
97	11	2s.6d. black and red/*blue* (1924)	15·00	48·00
98	9	5s. green and red/*pale yellow* (1924)	29·00	85·00
100	11	15s. dull purple and green (Die I)	£200	£700
		a. Die II (1924)	£140	£700
		as. Optd 'SPECIMEN'	£110	
102		£2 green and orange (Die I)	£600	£2000
86/100a *Set of* 12			£180	£750
86s/102s Optd 'SPECIMEN' *Set of* 13			£475	

The Duty plate for the 1½d., 15s. and £2 has the words 'GOLD COAST' in distinctly larger letters.

Examples of Nos. 100/100a and 102 are known showing parts of forged Accra postmarks. These are dated '3 MAY 44' and '8 MAY 44', but are invariably positioned so that the year date is not shown.

(Des W. Palmer. Photo Harrison)

1928 (1 Aug). Wmk Mult Script CA. P 13½×14½.

103	13	½d. blue-green	1·50	40
104		1d. red-brown	1·00	10
105		1½d. scarlet	4·50	1·50
		w. Wmk inverted	†	£550
106		2d. slate	4·50	20
107		2½d. orange-yellow	4·75	3·50
108		3d. bright blue	4·25	40
109		6d. black and purple	5·50	40
110		1s. black and red-orange	8·50	1·75
111		2s. black and bright violet	35·00	7·00
112		5s. carmine and sage-green	65·00	55·00
103/112 *Set of* 10			£120	60·00
103s/112s Optd 'SPECIMEN.' *Set of* 10			£300	

1935 (6 May). Silver Jubilee. As Nos. 91/94 of Antigua, but printed by B.W. P 11×12.

113	1d. ultramarine and grey-black	60	50
	a. Extra flagstaff	£140	£130
	b. Short extra flagstaff	£275	£275
	c. Lightning conductor	£190	£200
	d. Flagstaff on right-hand turret	£550	£600
	e. Double flagstaff	£550	
114	3d. brown and deep blue	3·00	8·00
	a. Extra flagstaff	£170	£250
	b. Short extra flagstaff	£500	
	c. Lightning conductor	£275	
115	6d. green and indigo	18·00	32·00
	a. Extra flagstaff	£250	£375
	b. Short extra flagstaff	£550	£700
	c. Lightning conductor	£350	£475
	d. Flagstaff on right-hand turret	£850	
116	1s. slate and purple	5·50	42·00
	a. Extra flagstaff	£200	£475
	b. Short extra flagstaff	£375	£700
	c. Lightning conductor	£350	£650
113/116 *Set of* 4		24·00	75·00
113s/116s Perf 'SPECIMEN' *Set of* 4		£120	

For illustrations of plate varieties see Omnibus section following Zanzibar.

1937 (12 May). Coronation. As Nos. 95/97 of Antigua. P 11×11½.

117	1d. buff	1·75	2·50
118	2d. slate	2·25	7·00
119	3d. blue	3·75	3·00
117/119 *Set of* 3		7·00	11·00
117s/119s Perf 'SPECIMEN' *Set of* 3		£120	

14

15 King George VI and Christiansborg Castle, Accra

(Recess B.W.)

1938 (1 Apr)–**43**. Wmk Mult Script CA. P 11½×12 (comb) (1s.3d., 10s.) or 12 (line) (others).

No.	Type	Description	Unused	Used
120	**14**	½d. green	16·00	3·75
		a. Perf 12×11½ (1939)	40	50
121		1d. red-brown	20·00	30
		a. Perf 12×11½ (1939)	40	10
122		1½d. scarlet	19·00	8·00
		a. Perf 12×11½ (1940)	40	50
123		2d. slate	17·00	2·00
		a. Perf 12×11½ (1940)	40	10
124		3d. blue	12·00	1·50
		a. Perf 12×11½ (1940)	40	35
125		4d. magenta	10·00	4·50
		a. Perf 12×11½ (1942)	80	1·25
126		6d. purple	27·00	2·00
		a. Perf 12×11½ (1939)	80	20
127		9d. orange	9·50	3·25
		a. Perf 12×11½ (1943)	1·50	55
128	**15**	1s. black and olive-green	29·00	2·25
		a. Perf 11½×12 (1940)	1·50	65
129		1s.3d. brown and turquoise-blue (12.4.41)	2·00	50
130		2s. blue and violet	65·00	30·00
		a. Perf 11½×12 (1940)	6·50	21·00
131		5s. olive-green and carmine	£110	38·00
		a. Perf 11½×12 (1940)	13·00	24·00
132		10s. black and violet (7.40)	13·00	32·00
120a/132 *Set of* 13			35·00	70·00
120s/132s Perf 'SPECIMEN' *Set of* 13			£450	

The exact measurement of the comb perforated stamps is 12×11.8 (vertical designs) or 11.8×12 (horizontal designs).

The ½d. and 1d. values exist in coils constructed from normal sheets.

1946 (14 Oct). Victory. As Nos. 110/111 of Antigua. P 13½×14.

No.	Description	Unused	Used
133	2d. slate-violet	28·00	2·75
	a. Perf 13½	10	10
	aw. Wmk inverted	£2000	
134	4d. claret	5·50	4·00
	a. Perf 13½	1·50	3·25
133s/134as Perf 'SPECIMEN' *Set of* 2		£110	

16 Northern Territories Mounted Constabulary

17 Christiansborg Castle

18 Emblem of Joint Provincial Council

19 Talking drums

20 Map showing position of Gold Coast

21 Nsuta manganese mine

22 Lake Bosumtwi

23 Cocoa farmer

24 Breaking cocoa pods

25 Gold Coast Regt. Trooping the Colour

26 Surfboats

27 Forest

(Des B. A. Johnston (1½d.), M. Ziorkley and B. A. Abban (2d.), PO draughtsman (2½d.), C. Gomez (1s.), M. Ziorkley (10s.); others from photographs. Recess B.W.)

1948 (1 July). Types **16/27**. Wmk Mult Script CA. P 12×11½ (vert) or 11½×12 (horiz).

No.	Type	Description	Unused	Used
135	**16**	½d. emerald-green	20	60
136	**17**	1d. blue	15	15
137	**18**	1½d. scarlet	1·50	1·50
138	**19**	2d. purple-brown	55	10
139	**20**	2½d. yellow-brown and scarlet	2·00	6·00
140	**21**	3d. light blue	4·00	1·75
141	**22**	4d. magenta	4·75	6·50
142	**23**	6d. black and orange	1·00	30
143	**24**	1s. black and vermilion	3·50	30
		w. Wmk inverted	†	£4500
144	**25**	2s. sage-green and magenta	12·00	4·75
145	**26**	5s. purple and black	45·00	14·00
146	**27**	10s. black and sage-green	22·00	17·00
135/146 *Set of* 12			85·00	45·00
135s/146s Perf 'SPECIMEN' *Set of* 12			£450	

Nos. 135/136 exist in coils constructed from normal sheets.

1948 (20 Dec). Royal Silver Wedding. As Nos. 112/113 of Antigua.

No.	Description	Unused	Used
147	1½d. scarlet	30	70
148	10s. grey-olive	35·00	50·00

1949 (10 Oct). 75th Anniversary of UPU As Nos. 114/117 of Antigua.

No.	Description	Unused	Used
149	2d. red-brown	25	20
150	2½d. orange	1·50	8·25
151	3d. deep blue	35	1·75
152	1s. blue-green	35	30
	a. 'A' of 'CA' missing from wmk	—	£800
149/152 *Set of* 4		2·25	9·50

No. 149 is known with the 'A' of 'CA' almost completely missing from the watermark.

28 Northern Territories Mounted Constabulary

(Recess B.W.)

1952 (19 Dec)–**54**. Designs previously used for King George VI issue, but with portrait of Queen Elizabeth II, as in T **28**. Portrait faces left on ½d., 4d., 6d., 1s. and 5s. Wmk Mult Script CA. P 12×11½ (vert) or 11½×12 (horiz).

No.	Type	Description	Unused	Used
153	**20**	½d. yellow-brown and scarlet (1.4.53)	20	20
		a. Bistre-brown and scarlet (7.4.54)	1·00	30
154	**17**	1d. deep blue (1.3.54)	40	10
155	**18**	1½d. emerald-green (1.4.53)	30	1·50
156	**19**	2d. chocolate (1.3.54)	40	10
157	**28**	2½d. scarlet	45	1·50
158	**21**	3d. magenta (1.4.53)	1·25	10
159	**22**	4d. blue (1.4.53)	50	30
160	**23**	6d. black and orange (1.3.54)	1·00	15
161	**24**	1s. black and orange-red (1.3.54)	2·25	15
162	**25**	2s. brown-olive and carmine (1.3.54)	18·00	1·00
163	**26**	5s. purple and black (1.3.54)	32·00	8·00
164	**27**	10s. black and olive-green (1.3.54)	27·00	13·00
153/164 *Set of* 12			70·00	23·00

Nos. 153*a*/154 exist in coils constructed from normal sheets.

1953 (2 June). Coronation. As No. 120 of Antigua, but ptd by B. W.

No.	Description	Unused	Used
165	2d. black and sepia	1·50	10

STAMP BOOKLETS

1916 (Dec).

SB1 2s. booklet containing 12×½d. and 18×1d. (Nos. 70a, 72) in blocks of 6.

POSTAGE DUE STAMPS

D 1

(Typo D.L.R.)

1923 (6 Mar). Yellowish toned paper. Wmk Mult Script CA. P 14.

No.	Type	Description	Unused	Used
D1	D **1**	½d. black	20·00	£120
D2		1d. black	75	1·00
D3		2d. black	13·00	1·50
D4		3d. black	22·00	1·25
D1/D4 *Set of* 4			50·00	£120
D1s/D4s Optd 'SPECIMEN' *Set of* 4			90·00	

A bottom marginal strip of six of No. D2 is known showing the 'A' of 'CA' omitted from the watermark in the margin below the third vertical column.

3d Normal

3d Lower serif at left of '3' missing (R. 9/1)

1/- Column 4 (No. D8)

1/- Column 5 (No. D8c)

1/- Short upright stroke (R. 4/5)

The degree of inclination of the stroke on the 1s. value varies for each column of the sheet: Column 1, 2 and 6 104°, Column 3 108°, Column 4 107° and Column 5 (No. D8c) 100°.

1951–52. Wmk Mult Script CA. Chalk-surfaced paper. P 14.

No.	Type	Description	Unused	Used
D5	D **1**	2d. black (13.12.51)	4·00	35·00
		a. Error. Crown missing, W **9a**	£1600	
		b. Error. St Edward's Crown, W **9b**	£750	
		c. Large 'd' (R. 9/6, 10/6)	32·00	
		d. Serif on 'd' (R. 1/6)	60·00	
D6		3d. black (13.12.51)	4·50	32·00
		a. Error. Crown missing, W **9a**	£1500	
		b. Error. St Edward's Crown, W **9b**	£700	
		c. Missing serif	70·00	
D7		6d. black (1.10.52)	1·75	19·00
		a. Error. Crown missing, W **9a**	£2250	
		b. Error. St Edward's Crown, W **9b**	£1300	
D8		1s. black (1.10.52)	1·75	70·00
		b. Error. St Edward's Crown, W **9b**	£1700	
		c. Upright stroke	12·00	£250
		ca. Short upright stroke	35·00	
D5/D8 *Set of* 4			11·00	£140

For illustration of Nos. D5c/Dd see Nos. D4/D6 of Bechuanaland.

ARMY TELEGRAPHS

Nos. AT3/AT4, AT6 and AT8/AT12 listed under British Army Field Offices during the South African War were used in small quantities during the 1895 Ashanti Expedition.

Gold Coast became the Dominion of Ghana on 6 March 1957.

Grenada

The earliest recorded postmark of the British administration of Grenada dates from 1784, and, although details of the early period are somewhat sparse, it would appear that the island's postal service was operated at a branch of the British GPO. In addition to a Packet Agency at St George's, the capital, there was a further agency at Carriacou, in the Grenadines, which operated for a few years from 15 September 1847.

Stamps of Great Britain were supplied to the St George's office from April 1858 until the colony assumed responsibility for the postal service on 1 May 1860. Following the take-over the crowned-circle handstamp, No. CC2, was again used until the Grenada adhesives were issued in 1861.

There was no internal postal service before 1861.

For illustrations of the handstamp and postmark types see BRITISH POST OFFICES ABROAD notes, following GREAT BRITAIN.

CARRIACOU

CROWNED-CIRCLE HANDSTAMPS

A crowned-circle handstamp for Carriacou is recorded in the GPO proof book but no example has been reported used from Grenada.

ST GEORGE'S

CROWNED-CIRCLE HANDSTAMPS

CC2 CC 1 GRENADA (R.) (24.10.1850) .... *Price on cover* £2000

Stamps of GREAT BRITAIN cancelled 'A15' as T **2**.

1858–60.

Z1	1d. rose-red (1857), perf 14	£425
Z2	2d. blue (1858) (Plate No. 7)	£1200
Z3	4d. rose (1857)	£300
Z4	6d. lilac (1856)	£120
Z5	1s. green (1856)	£1800

PRICES FOR STAMPS ON COVER TO 1945

Nos. 1/3	*from* × 15
Nos. 4/23	*from* × 20
Nos. 24/26	*from* × 10
No. 27	*from* × 15
No. 28	—
No. 29	*from* × 10
Nos. 30/36	*from* × 20
Nos. 37/39	*from* × 15
No. 40	*from* × 40
Nos. 41/47	*from* × 20
Nos. 48/101	*from* × 4
Nos. 109/111	*from* × 8
Nos. 112/148	*from* × 4
Nos. 149/151	*from* × 10
No. 152/163	*from* × 4
Nos. D1/D3	*from* × 25
Nos. D4/D7	*from* × 12
Nos. D8/D14	*from* × 20

CROWN COLONY

PRINTERS. Types **1** and **5** recess-printed by Perkins Bacon and Co.

PERKINS BACON 'CANCELLED'. For notes on these handstamps, showing 'CANCELLED' between horizontal bars forming an oval, see Catalogue Introduction.

1

2 Small Star

(Eng C. Jeens)

1861 (3 June)–**62**. No wmk. Wove paper.

(a) Rough perf 14 to 16

1	1	1d. bluish green (H/S 'CANCELLED' in oval £10000)	£4500	£300
2		1d. green (5.62)	50·00	50·00
		a. Imperf between (horiz pair)		
3		6d. rose (*shades*) (H/S 'CANCELLED' in oval £10000)	£900	90·00

(b) Perf 11 to 12½

3*a*	1	6d. lake-red (6.62)	£750	†

No. 3*a* is only known unused, and may be the result of perforating machine trials undertaken by Perkins Bacon. It has also been seen on horizontally laid paper (*Price* £1200).

SIDEWAYS WATERMARK. W **2/3** when sideways show two points of star downwards.

1863–71. W **2** (Small Star). Rough perf 14 to 16.

4	1	1d. green (3.64)	£110	17·00
		a. Wmk sideways	—	30·00
5		1d. yellowish green	£130	27·00
6		6d. rose (*shades*) (5.63)	£600	13·00
		a. Wmk sideways	—	80·00
7		6d. orange-red (*shades*) (5.66)	£650	12·00
8		6d. dull rose-red (*wmk sideways*)	£3500	£225
9		6d. vermilion (5.71)	£750	12·00
		a. Double impression	—	£2000

1873 (Jan). W **2** (Small Star, sideways). Clean-cut perf 15.

10	1	1d. deep green	£130	50·00
		a. Bisected diag (*on cover*)	†	£9000
		b. Imperf between (pair)	—	£14000

No. 10a, and later bisected 1d. values, were authorised until 1881 to pay the island newspaper rate (½d.) or the newspaper rate to Great Britain (1½d.). Examples also exist on covers to France.

3 Large Star

4 Broad-pointed Star

1873 (Sept)–**74.** W **3** (Large Star). Intermediate perf 15.

11	1	1d. blue-green (*wmk sideways*) (2.74)	£110	27·00
		a. Double impression		
		b. Bisected diag (*on cover*)	†	£9000
12		6d. orange-vermilion	£700	26·00

5

POSTAGE

ONE SHILLING

(6)

NOTE. The early ½d., 2½d., 4d. and 1s. postage stamps were made by surcharging the undenominated T **5** design.

The surcharges were from two founts of type—one about 1½ mm high, the other 2 mm high—so there are short and tall letters on the same stamp; also the spacing varies considerably, so that the length of the words varies.

Examples of T **5** with surcharges, but without the 'POSTAGE' inscription, are revenue stamps.

1875 (July). Surch with T **6**. W **3**. P 14.

13	5	1s. deep mauve (B.)	£700	12·00
		a. 'SHLLIING'	£6500	£700
		b. 'NE SHILLING'	†	£3000
		c. Inverted 'S' in 'POSTAGE'	£4000	£500
		d. 'OSTAGE'	£7000	£2750

1875 (Dec). W **3** (Large Star, upright).

14	1	1d. green to yellow-green (P 14)	85·00	8·00
		a. Bisected diag (*on cover*)	†	£9000
15		1d. green (P 15)	£9000	£2250

No. 14 was comb perforated at Somerset House. 40 sheets of No. 15 were line perforated by Perkins Bacon to replace spoilages and to complete the order.

1878 (Aug). W **2** (Small Star, sideways). Intermediate perf 15.

16	1	1d. green	£250	50·00
		b. Bisected diag (*on cover*)	†	£9000
17		6d. deep vermilion	£850	38·00
		a. Double impression	—	£2000

1879 (Dec). W **2** (Small Star, upright). Rough perf 15.

18	1	1d. pale green (*thin paper*)	£300	30·00
		a. Double impression		
		b. Bisected diag (*on cover*)	†	—

1881 (Apr). W **2** (Small Star, sideways). Rough perf 14½.

19	1	1d. green	£160	9·50
		a. Bisected diag (*on cover*)	†	£9000

POSTAGE HALF-PENNY (7) — POSTAGE TWO PENCE HALF-PENNY (8) — POSTAGE FOUR PENCE (9)

1881 (Apr). Surch with Types **7/9**. P 14½.

*(a) W **3** (Large Star, sideways on ½d.)*

20	5	½d. pale mauve	40·00	11·00
21		½d. deep mauve	17·00	7·00
		a. Imperf (pair)	£300	
		ab. Ditto. 'OSTAGE' (R. 9/4)	£7000	
		b. Surch double	£325	
		c. 'OSTAGE' (R. 9/4)	£190	£130
		d. No hyphen	£190	£130
		e. 'ALF-PENNY'	£3750	
		f. Wmk upright	£300	£140
		g. Ditto. 'OSTAGE' (R. 9/4)	£2000	£800
22		2½d. rose-lake	75·00	9·00
		a. Imperf (pair)	£650	
		b. Imperf between (horiz pair)	£6500	
		c. No stop	£250	75·00
		d. 'PENCF' (R. 8/12)	£475	£180
23		4d. blue	£140	8·00
		a. Wmk sideways	£1200	£500
		b. Inverted 'S' in 'POSTAGE'		

*(b) W **4** (Broad-pointed Star)*

24	5	2½d. rose-lake	£160	50·00
		a. No stop	£550	£200
		b. 'PENCF' (R. 8/12)	£800	£275
25		2½d. claret	£425	£120
		a. No stop	£1100	£500
		b. 'PENCF' (R. 8/12)	£1600	£700
25*c*		2½d. deep claret	£650	£225
		d. No stop	£2250	£900
		e. 'PENCF' (R. 8/12)	£2750	£1100
26		4d. blue	£350	£190

Examples of the 'F' for 'E' error on the 2½d. value should not be confused with a somewhat similar broken 'E' variety. The latter is always without the stop and shows other damage to the 'E'. The authentic error always occurs with the full stop shown.

The 'no stop' variety occurs on R. 3/4, R. 6/2, R. 8/3 and R. 9/7.

ONE PENNY (10) — POSTAGE. (11) — POSTAGE POSTAGE (12)

1883 (Jan). Revenue stamps (T **5** with green surcharge as in T **10**) optd for postage. W **2** (Small Star). P 14½.

*(a) Optd horizontally with T **11***

27	5	1d. orange	£400	60·00
		a. 'POSTAGE' inverted	£3500	£2250
		b. 'POSTAGE' double	£1400	£1100
		c. Inverted 'S' in 'POSTAGE'	£1000	£600
		d. Bisected diag (*on cover*)	†	£3000

*(b) Optd diagonally with T **11** twice on each stamp, the stamp being cut and each half used as ½d*

28	5	Half of 1d. orange	£700	£225
		a. Unsevered pair	£3500	£1000
		b. 'POSTAGE' inverted	—	£1200

*(c) Optd with T **12**, the stamps divided diagonally and each half used as ½d*

29	5	Half of 1d. orange	£275	£110
		a. Unsevered pair	£1500	£450

Nos. 27/29 exist with wmk either upright or sideways.

1d. Revenue stamps with 'POSTAGE' added in black manuscript were used at Gouyave during February and March 1883 (*Price* £6500, *used*). Similar manuscript overprints, in red were also used at Grenville in June 1883 and in black or red at Sauteurs in September 1886 (*Price from* £10000, *used*).

13

Damaged value (R. 2/3)

d.
1
POSTAGE.
(14)

15

(Typo D.L.R.)

1883. Wmk Crown CA. P 14.

30	13	½d. dull green (2.83)	2·75	1·00
		a. *Tête-bêche* (vert pair)	5·50	21·00
31		1d. carmine (2.83)	90·00	3·25
		a. *Tête-bêche* (vert pair)	£325	£375
32		2½d. ultramarine (5.83)	14·00	1·00
		a. *Tête-bêche* (vert pair)	32·00	60·00
33		4d. greyish slate (5.83)	14·00	2·00
		a. *Tête-bêche* (vert pair)	35·00	65·00
34		6d. mauve (5.83)	4·75	4·25
		a. *Tête-bêche* (vert pair)	18·00	65·00
35		8d. grey-brown (2.83)	10·00	14·00
		a. *Tête-bêche* (vert pair)	40·00	90·00
		b. Damaged value	£150	£180
36		1s. pale violet (4.83)	£160	55·00
		a. *Tête-bêche* (vert pair)	£2000	£2250
30/36 *Set of 7*			£250	70·00

T **13** and T **15** were printed in rows *tête-bêche* in the sheets, so that 50% of the stamps have inverted watermarks.

No. 35b occurs on an inverted watermark stamp.

1886 (1 Oct–Dec). Revenue stamps (T **5** with green surch as T **10**), surch with T **14**. P 14.

*(a) Wmk Large Star, T **3***

37	5	1d. on 1½d. orange	60·00	50·00
		a. Surch inverted	£450	£300
		b. Surch double	£750	£300
		c. 'THRFE'	£300	£225
		d. 'PFNCE'	£300	£225
		e. 'HALH'	£300	£225
		f. Bisected diag (*on cover*)	†	£2250
38		1d. on 1s. orange (12.86)	50·00	48·00
		a. 'POSTAGE' (no stop)	£550	
		b. 'SHILLNG'	£550	£375
		c. Wide space (1¾ *mm*) between 'ONE' and 'SHILLING'	£375	£250
		d. Bisected diag (*on cover*)	†	£2250

*(b) Wmk Small Star, T **2***

39	5	1d. on 4d. orange (11.86)	£170	90·00

1887 (Jan). Wmk Crown CA. P 14.

40	15	1d. carmine	4·75	1·40
		a. *Tête-bêche* (vert pair)	11·00	30·00
		s. Optd 'SPECIMEN'	65·00	

Due to the sheet formation 50% of the stamps have inverted watermarks.

No. 40s can be found with the vertical 'SPECIMEN' opt reading either upwards or downwards.

4d. POSTAGE (16) — HALF PENNY POSTAGE (17)

1888 (31 Mar)–**91**. Revenue stamps (T **5** with green surch as T **10**) further surcharged. W **2** (sideways on 2s.). P 14½, and No. 35.

*I. Surch with T **16***

(a) 4 mm between value and 'POSTAGE'

41	5	4d. on 2s. orange	50·00	21·00
		a. Upright 'd' (R. 5/6)	£800	£475
		b. Wide space (2¼ *mm*) between 'TWO' and 'SHILLINGS'	£300	£160

No.	Type	Description	Unused	Used
		c. First 'S' in 'SHILLINGS' inverted	£500	£325
		d. Imperf between (horiz pair)	£10000	

(b) 5 mm between value and 'POSTAGE'

No.	Type	Description	Unused	Used
42	5	4d. on 2s. orange	70·00	38·00
		a. Wide space	£375	£225
		b. 'S' inverted	£750	£550

*II. Surch as T **17** (December 1889)*

No.	Type	Description	Unused	Used
43	5	½d. on 2s. orange	17·00	35·00
		a. Surch double	£325	£350
		b. Wide space	£130	£150
		c. 'S' inverted	£300	£325

POSTAGE d. AND 1 REVENUE **(18)**

POSTAGE AND REVENUE 1d. **(19)**

2½d. **(20)**

*III. Surch with T **18** (December 1890)*

No.	Type	Description	Unused	Used
44	5	1d. on 2s. orange	85·00	85·00
		a. Surch inverted	£750	
		b. Wide space	£375	£375
		c. 'S' inverted	£750	£700

*IV. Surch with T **19** (January 1891)*

No.	Type	Description	Unused	Used
45	5	1d. on 2s. orange	75·00	70·00
		a. No stop after '1d' (R. 3/8)	£500	£500
		b. Wide space	£300	£300
		c. 'S' inverted	£550	£550
46	13	1d. on 8d. grey-brown	12·00	21·00
		a. *Tête-bêche* (vert pair)	40·00	70·00
		b. Surch inverted	£325	£275
		c. No stop after '1d' (R. 6/5)	£250	£250
		d. Damaged value	£150	

*V. Surch with T **20** (December 1891)*

No.	Type	Description	Unused	Used
47	13	2½d. on 8d. grey-brown	23·00	11·00
		a. *Tête-bêche* (vert pair)	55·00	65·00
		b. Surch inverted		
		c. Surch double	£850	£800
		d. Surch double, one inverted	£550	£600
		e. Surch treble	—	£900
		f. Surch treble, two inverted	—	£1000
		g. Damaged value	£225	£150
		s. Optd '*Specimen*'	65·00	

The surcharges, Types **16/19**, were applied to half sheets as a setting of 60 (12×5).

The wide space between 'TWO' and 'SHILLINGS' occurs on R. 1/4 and 10/3 of the original 2s. Revenue stamp which was printed in sheets of 120 (12×10).

T **18** was a two-step surcharge comprising '1d./Revenue', followed by 'POSTAGE/AND'. An example of No. 44 is known with the 'POSTAGE' omitted due to faulty registration and the word applied by hand in a slightly different type style.

There are two varieties of fraction in T **20**, which each occur 30 times in the setting; in one the '1' has horizontal serif and the '2' commences in a ball; in the other the '1' has sloping serif and the '2' is without ball.

See also D4/D7.

21

22

23 Flagship of Columbus. (Columbus named Grenada 'La Concepcion')

(Typo D.L.R.)

1895 (6 Sept)–**99**. Wmk Crown CA. P 14.

No.	Type	Description	Unused	Used
48	22	½d. mauve and green (9.99)	5·00	1·75
49	21	1d. mauve and carmine (5.96)	7·00	75
50		2d. mauve and brown (9.99)	40·00	26·00
		x. Wmk reversed	£425	£325
51		2½d. mauve and ultramarine	13·00	1·50
52	22	3d. mauve and orange	6·50	16·00
53	21	6d. mauve and green	23·00	65·00
54	22	8d. mauve and black	12·00	50·00
55		1s. green and orange	23·00	65·00
48/55 *Set of* 8			£110	£200
48s/55s Optd 'SPECIMEN' *Set of* 8			£180	

(Recess D.L.R.)

1898 (15 Aug). 400th Anniversary of Discovery of Grenada by Columbus. Wmk Crown CC. P 14

No.	Type	Description	Unused	Used
56	23	2½d. ultramarine	22·00	6·00
		a. Bluish paper	40·00	40·00
		s. Optd 'SPECIMEN'	85·00	

24

25

(Typo D.L.R.)

1902. Wmk Crown CA. P 14.

No.	Type	Description	Unused	Used
57	24	½d. dull purple and green	6·00	1·25
58	25	1d. dull purple and carmine	10·00	30
59		2d. dull purple and brown	6·50	10·00
60		2½d. dull purple and ultramarine	8·00	2·75
61	24	3d. dull purple and orange	8·00	9·00
62	25	6d. dull purple and green	6·50	17·00
63	24	1s. green and orange	12·00	42·00
64		2s. green and ultramarine	38·00	65·00
65	25	5s. green and carmine	45·00	85·00
66	24	10s. green and purple	£160	£300
57/66 *Set of* 10			£250	£475
57s/66s Optd 'SPECIMEN' *Set of* 10			£200	

1904–06. Wmk Mult Crown CA. Ordinary paper. P 14.

No.	Type	Description	Unused	Used
67	24	½d. purple and green (1905)	23·00	50·00
68	25	1d. purple and carmine	24·00	2·50
69		2d. purple and brown (1905)	60·00	£130
70		2½d. purple and ultramarine (1905)	60·00	65·00
71	24	3d. purple and orange (1905)	6·50	14·00
		a. Chalk-surfaced paper	7·50	9·50
72	25	6d. purple and green (1906)	17·00	38·00
		a. Chalk-surfaced paper	18·00	45·00
73	24	1s. green and orange (1905)	6·00	42·00
74		2s. green and ultramarine (1906)	60·00	85·00
		a. Chalk-surfaced paper	50·00	80·00
75	25	5s. green and carmine (1906)	80·00	£120
76	24	10s. green and purple (1906)	£190	£300
67/76 *Set of* 10			£450	£750

Examples of most values between Nos. 57 and 76 are known showing a forged GPO Grenada BWI postmark dated 'OC 6 09'.

26 Badge of the Colony

27 Badge of the Colony

(Recess D.L.R.)

1906 (Jan). Wmk Mult Crown CA. P 14.

No.	Type	Description	Unused	Used
77	26	½d. green	4·50	30
		x. Wmk reversed	†	£400
78		1d. carmine	9·50	10
		y. Wmk inverted and reversed	—	£500
79		2d. orange	5·00	2·50
		w. Wmk inverted	£550	£400
		x. Wmk reversed	£600	
		y. Wmk inverted and reversed	£550	£550
80		2½d. blue	6·00	1·25
		a. Ultramarine	11·00	3·50

(Typo D.L.R.)

1908. Wmk Crown CA. Chalk-surfaced paper. P 14.

No.	Type	Description	Unused	Used
82	27	1s. black/*green*	50·00	80·00
83		10s. green and red/*green*	£160	£300

1908–11. Wmk Mult Crown CA. Chalk-surfaced paper. P 14.

No.	Type	Description	Unused	Used
84	27	3d. dull purple/*yellow*	8·50	1·75
85		6d. dull purple and purple	20·00	8·00
86		1s. black/*green* (1911)	7·00	4·00
87		2s. blue and purple/*blue*	38·00	14·00
88		5s. green and red/*yellow*	80·00	95·00
77/88 *Set of* 11			£350	£450
77s/80s, 82s/85s, 87s/88s Optd 'SPECIMEN' *Set of* 10			£250	

Examples of Nos. 82/88 are known showing a forged GPO Grenada BWI postmark dated 'OC 6 09'.

28

WAR TAX **(29)**

WAR TAX **(30)**

(Typo D.L.R.)

1913 (3 Jan)–**22**. Wmk Mult Crown CA. Chalk-surfaced paper (3d. to 10s.). P 14.

No.	Type	Description	Unused	Used
89	28	½d. yellow-green	1·75	1·60
90		½d. green	1·25	1·00
91		1d. red	2·25	30
92		1d. scarlet (1916)	14·00	2·00
		w. Wmk inverted		
93		2d. orange	1·75	30
94		2½d. bright blue	1·75	1·25
95		2½d. dull blue (1920)	5·50	6·00
96		3d. purple/*yellow*	65	85
		a. White back (3.14)	65	1·50
		as. Optd 'SPECIMEN'	35·00	
		b. On lemon (1917)	4·00	9·00
		c. On pale yellow (1921)	7·00	30·00
97		6d. dull and bright purple	1·50	9·00
98		1s. black/*green*	1·00	10·00
		a. White back (3.14)	1·25	7·50
		as. Optd 'SPECIMEN'	35·00	
		b. On blue-green, olive back (1917)	32·00	85·00
		c. On emerald surface	1·50	24·00
		d. On emerald back (6.22)	1·00	15·00
		ds. Optd 'SPECIMEN'	35·00	
		dw. Wmk inverted	£120	
99		2s. purple and blue/*blue*	6·50	12·00
100		5s. green and red/*yellow*	17·00	60·00
		a. On pale yellow (1921)	32·00	75·00
		as. Optd 'SPECIMEN'	50·00	
101		10s. green and red/*green*	70·00	£130
		a. On emerald back (6.22)	70·00	£190
		as. Optd 'SPECIMEN'	55·00	
89/101 *Set of* 10			95·00	£200
89s/101s Optd 'SPECIMEN' (1s. optd in red) *Set of* 10			£200	
98sa 1s. optd in black			48·00	

1916 (1 June). Optd with T **29** by Govt Press, St George's.

No.	Type	Description	Unused	Used
109	28	1d. red (*shades*)	2·25	1·75
		a. Opt inverted	£275	
		b. Triangle for 'A' in 'TAX'	55·00	70·00
		s. Handstamped 'SPECIMEN'	50·00	

A small 'A' in 'WAR', 2 mm high, is found on Nos. 29, 38 and 48 of the setting of 60 and a very small 'A' in 'TAX', 1½ mm high, on No. 11. Value about twice normal. The normal 'A' is 2¼ mm high.

No. 109b is on No. 56 of the setting.

1916 (1 Sept)–**18**. Optd with T **30** in London.

No.	Type	Description	Unused	Used
111	28	1d. scarlet	30	20
		a. Carmine-red/bluish (5.18)	4·00	1·50
		s. Optd 'SPECIMEN'	45·00	
		w. Wmk inverted	£130	

1921–31. Wmk Mult Script CA. Chalk-surfaced paper (3d. (No. 122) to 10s.) P 14.

No.	Type	Description	Unused	Used
112	28	½d. green	1·25	30
113		1d. carmine-red	80	75
114		1d. brown (1923)	1·50	30
115		1½d. rose-red (6.22)	2·25	1·00
116		2d. orange	1·25	30
117		2d. grey (1926)	2·50	2·75
117*a*		2½d. dull blue	8·50	8·50
118		2½d. grey (6.22)	1·00	9·00
119		2½d. bright blue (1926)	12·00	3·75
120		2½d. ultramarine (1931)	12·00	8·50
120*a*		2½d. chalky blue and blue (1928)	55·00	50·00
121		3d. bright blue (6.22)	1·25	11·00
122		3d. purple/*yellow* (1926)	3·00	3·00
123		4d. black and red/*yellow* (1926)	1·00	3·75
124		5d. dull purple and sage-green (27.12.22)	1·50	4·25
125		6d. dull and bright purple	1·25	30·00
126		6d. black and carmine (1926)	2·25	2·50
127		9d. dull purple and black (27.12.22)	2·25	9·50
128		1s. black/*emerald* (1923)	2·50	60·00
		y. Wmk inverted and reversed	£225	
129		1s. chestnut (1926)	3·00	6·00
130		2s. purple and blue/*blue* (1922)	6·00	17·00
131		2s.6d. black and carmine/*blue* (1929)	15·00	24·00
132		3s. green and violet (27.12.22)	13·00	27·00
133		5s. green and red/*pale yellow* (1923)	12·00	35·00
134		10s. green and red/*emerald* (1923)	55·00	£130
112/119, 121/134 *Set of* 22			£110	£350
112s/134s Optd or Perf (2s.6d.) 'SPECIMEN' *Set of* 23			£400	

Some values of Nos. 89/101 and 112/134 have been seen with part strikes of the forged postmark mentioned after Nos. 67/76 and 77/88.

31 Grand Anse Beach

32 Badge of the Colony

33 Grand Etang

34 St George's

(Recess Waterlow)

1934 (23 Oct)–**36**. Wmk Mult Script CA (sideways on T **32**). P 12½.

No.	Type	Description	Unused	Used
135	31	½d. green	15	1·25
		a. Perf 12½×13½ (1936)	12·00	70·00
136	32	1d. black and sepia	2·00	4·00
		a. Perf 13½×12½ (1936)	60	35
137	33	1½d. black and scarlet	10·00	7·50
		a. Perf 12½×13½ (1936)	1·25	40
138	32	2d. black and orange	1·00	75
139	34	2½d. blue	50	50
140	32	3d. black and olive-green	1·00	2·75
141		6d. black and purple	3·50	1·75
142		1s. black and brown	4·25	4·00
143		2s.6d. black and ultramarine	8·00	28·00
144		5s. black and violet	48·00	50·00
135/144 *Set of* 10			60·00	80·00
135s/144s Perf 'SPECIMEN' *Set of* 10			£190	

1935 (6 May). Silver Jubilee. As Nos. 91/94 of Antigua but ptd by Waterlow. P 11×12.

No.	Type	Description	Unused	Used
145		½d. black and green	1·00	1·25
		k. Kite and vertical log	85·00	£110
		l. Kite and horizontal log	£110	£180
146		1d. ultramarine and grey	1·25	1·75
		l. Kite and horizontal log	£150	£180
147		1½d. deep blue and scarlet	1·25	3·75
		l. Kite and horizontal log	£160	£250
148		1s. slate and purple	17·00	40·00
		l. Kite and horizontal log	£325	£475
145/148 *Set of* 4			18·00	42·00
145s/148s Perf 'SPECIMEN' *Set of* 4			£100	

For illustrations of plate varieties see Omnibus section following Zanzibar.

1937 (12 May). Coronation. As Nos. 95/97 of Antigua. P 11×11½.

No.	Type	Description	Unused	Used
149		1d. violet	40	1·75
150		1½d. carmine	40	50
151		2½d. blue	80	1·25
149/151 *Set of* 3			1·40	3·25
149s/151s Perf 'SPECIMEN' *Set of* 3			£100	

35 King George VI

(Photo Harrison)

1937 (12 July)–**50**. Wmk Mult Script CA. Chalk-surfaced paper. P 15×14.

152 **35** ¼d. brown 4·00 35
 a. Ordinary paper (11.42) 1·00 3·50
 b. Ordinary paper. *Chocolate* (1.45) 1·25 3·50
 c. Chalk-surfaced paper. *Chocolate* (8.50) 3·75 9·00

The ordinary paper is thick, smooth and opaque.

36 Grand Anse Beach

40 Badge of the Colony

Line on sail (Centre Pl 3 R. 1/1. Later partially retouched)

Colon flaw (R. 5/6. Corrected on ptg of Nov 1950)

Extra window and broken handrail (Centre Pl 2 R. 1/6)

(Recess D.L.R. (10s.), Waterlow (others))

1938 (16 Mar)–**50**. As Types **31/34** (but portrait of King George VI as in T **36**) and T **40**. Wmk Mult Script CA (sideways on T **32**). P 12½ or 12×13 (10s.).

153 **36** ½d. yellow-green 18·00 2·50
 a. Blue-green (10.9.43) 60 1·25
 b. Perf 12½×13½ (1938) 12·00 80
 ba. Blue-green 6·50 5·00
154 **32** 1d. black and sepia 1·00 20
 aa. Line on sail £190
 ab. Extra window and broken handrail £150 75·00
 b. Perf 13½×12½ (1938) 2·50 50
 ba. Line on sail £150
 bb. Extra window and broken handrail — 90·00
155 **33** 1½d. black and scarlet 50 2·00
 a. Perf 12½×13½ (1938) 4·00 30
156 **32** 2d. black and orange 40 50
 aa. Line on sail £250
 ab. Extra window and broken handrail £180 £100
 b. Perf 13½×12½ (1938) 3·00 85
 ba. Line on sail £250
 bb. Extra window and broken handrail £250 £200
157 **34** 2½d. bright blue 30 30
 a. Perf 12½×13½ (?3.50) £11000 £190
158 **32** 3d. black and olive-green 22·00 1·40
 a. Perf 13½×12½ (16.3.38) 15·00 1·00
 ab. Black and brown-olive (1942) 40 80
 ac. Line on sail £180
 ad. Extra window and broken handrail £275 £275
 b. Perf 12½. *Black and brown-olive* (16.8.50) 1·00 2·50
 ba. Colon flaw £170
 bb. Line on sail £170 £250
159 6d. black and purple 4·50 40
 a. Perf 13½×12½ (1942) 2·25 50
 ab. Extra window and broken handrail — £250
 b. Line on sail £375
160 1s. black and brown 5·50 40
 a. Perf 13½×12½ (1941) 5·50 2·75
 ab. Extra window and broken handrail £350
161 2s. black and ultramarine 45·00 3·00
 aa. Line on sail £1000
 a. Perf 13½×12½ (1941) 42·00 1·50
 ab. Extra window and broken handrail £1000 £250
162 5s. black and violet 11·00 7·50
 a. Perf 13½×12½ (1947) 7·00 9·50
163 **40** 10s. steel blue and carmine (*narrow*) (P 12×13) 60·00 18·00
 a. Perf 14. *Steel blue and bright carmine* (*narrow*) £225 60·00
 b. Perf 14. *Slate-blue and bright carmine* (*narrow*) (1943) £300 £160
 c. Perf 12. *Slate-blue and bright carmine* (*narrow*) (1943) £750 £1900
 d. Perf 14. *Slate-blue and carmine lake* (*wide*) (1944) £140 18·00
 e. Perf 14. *Blue-black and carmine* (*narrow*) (1943) 50·00 18·00
 ea. Frame printed double, one albino £4500
 f. Perf 14. *Blue-black and bright carmine* (*wide*) (1947) 35·00 48·00
152/163*e Set of* 12 80·00 27·00
152s/163s Perf 'SPECIMEN' *Set of* 12 £300

In the earlier printings of the 10s. the paper was dampened before printing and the subsequent shrinkage produced narrow frames 23½ to 23¾ mm wide. Later printings were made on dry paper producing wide frames 24¼ mm wide.

No. 163*a* is one of the earlier printings, line perf 13.8×14.1. Later printings of the 10s. are line perf 14.1.

Nos. 163*b*/163*c* show a blurred centre caused by the use of a worn plate.

Nos. 163*a* and 163*b* may be found with gum more or less yellow due to local climatic conditions.

The ½d. and 1d. in both perforations exist from coils made up from normal sheets.

Examples of No. 163*c* are known showing forged St George's postmarks dated '21 AU 42', '21 AU 43' or '2 OC 43'.

1946 (25 Sept). Victory. As Nos. 110/111 of Antigua.

164 1½d. carmine 10 50
165 3½d. blue 10 1·00
164s/165s Perf 'SPECIMEN' *Set of* 2 90·00

1948 (27 Oct). Royal Silver Wedding. As Nos. 112/113 of Antigua.

166 1½d. scarlet 15 10
167 10s. slate-green 24·00 20·00

(New Currency. 100 cents = 1 West Indian, later Eastern Caribbean, dollar)

1949 (10 Oct). 75th Anniversary of Universal Postal Union. As Nos. 114/117 of Antigua.

168 5c. ultramarine 15 20
169 6c. olive 1·50 3·00
170 12c. magenta 15 1·00
171 24c. red-brown 15 1·00
168/171 *Set of* 4 1·75 4·75

41 King George VI

42 Badge of the Colony

43 Badge of the Colony

(Recess B.W. (T **41**), D.L.R. (others))

1951 (8 Jan). Wmk Mult Script CA. P 11½ (T **41**), 11½×12½ (T **42**), and 11½×13 (T **43**).

172 **41** ½c. black and red-brown 15 1·60
173 1c. black and emerald-green 15 25
174 2c. black and brown 15 50
175 3c. black and rose-carmine 15 10
176 4c. black and orange 35 40
177 5c. black and violet 20 10
178 6c. black and olive 30 60
179 7c. black and light blue 1·75 10
180 12c. black and purple 2·25 30
181 **42** 25c. black and sepia 2·50 80
182 50c. black and blue 7·00 40
183 $1.50 black and yellow-orange 9·00 9·00
184 **43** $2.50 slate-blue and carmine 17·00 5·50
172/184 *Set of* 13 35·00 17·00

1951 (16 Feb). Inauguration of BWI University College. As Nos. 118/119 of Antigua.

185 3c. black and carmine 45 1·25
186 6c. black and olive 45 50

NEW CONSTITUTION

1951
(**44**)

1951 (21 Sept). New Constitution. Nos. 175/177 and 180 optd with T **44** by B.W.

187 **41** 3c. black and rose-carmine 55 70
188 4c. black and orange 60 70
189 5c. black and violet (R.) 60 90
190 12c. black and purple 75 1·25
187/190 *Set of* 4 2·25 3·25

1953 (3 June). Coronation. As No. 120 of Antigua.

191 3c. black and carmine-red 30 10

45 Queen Elizabeth II

46 Badge of the Colony

47 Badge of the Colony

(Recess B.W. (T **45**), D.L.R. (Types **46/47**))

1953 (15 June)–**59**. Wmk Mult Script CA. P 11½ (T **45**), 11½×12½ (T **46**), or 11½×13 (T **47**).

192 **45** ½c. black and brown (28.12.53) 10 1·00
193 1c. black and deep emerald 10 10
194 2c. black and sepia (15.9.53) 80 10
195 3c. black and carmine-red (22.2.54) 20 10
196 4c. black and brown-orange (22.2.54) 20 10
197 5c. black and deep violet (22.2.54) 20 10
198 6c. black and olive-green (28.12.53) 2·25 1·25
199 7c. black and blue (6.6.55) 2·75 10
200 12c. black and reddish purple 60 10
201 **46** 25c. black and sepia (10.1.55) 1·50 20
202 50c. black and deep blue (2.12.55) 5·50 1·00
203 $1.50 black and brown-orange (2.12.55) 18·00 15·00
204 **47** $2.50 slate-blue and carmine (16.11.59) 42·00 12·00
192/204 *Set of* 13 65·00 27·00

On 23 December 1965, No. 203 was issued surcharged '2' but this was intended for fiscal and revenue purposes and it was not authorised to be used postally, although some are known to have passed through the mail (*Price* £10, *unused*).

For stamps in Types **45/46** watermarked w **12** see Nos. 214/220.

1958 (22 Apr). Inauguration of British Caribbean Federation. As Nos. 135/137 of Antigua.

205 3c. deep green 50 10
206 6c. blue 65 90
207 12c. scarlet 80 10
205/207 *Set of* 3 1·75 1·00

48 Queen Victoria, Queen Elizabeth II, Mail Van and Post Office, St George's

(Photo Harrison)

1961 (1 June). Grenada Stamp Centenary. T **48** and similar horiz designs. W w **12**. P 14½×14.

208 3c. crimson and black 25 10
209 8c. bright blue and orange 55 25
210 25c. lake and blue 55 25
208/210 *Set of* 3 1·25 55

Designs: 3c. T **48**; 8c. Queen Victoria, Queen Elizabeth II and flagship of Columbus; 25c. Queen Victoria, Queen Elizabeth II, *Solent I* (paddle-steamer) and Douglas DC-3 aircraft.

1963 (4 June). Freedom from Hunger. As No. 146 of Antigua.

211 8c. bluish green 30 15

1963 (2 Sept). Red Cross Centenary. As Nos. 147/148 of Antigua.

212 3c. red and black 20 15
213 25c. red and blue 40 15

1964 (12 May)–**66**. As Nos. 194/198, 201/201, but wmk w **12**.

214 **45** 2c. black and sepia 1·50 20
215 3c. black and carmine-red 1·75 10
216 4c. black and brown-orange 60 1·25
217 5c. black and deep violet 60 10
218 6c. black and olive-green (4.1.66) £200 85·00
219 12c. black and reddish purple 2·00 70
220 **46** 25c. black and sepia 5·50 3·25
214/220 *Set of* 7 £200 85·00

1965 (17 May). ITU Centenary. As Nos. 166/167 of Antigua.

221 2c. red-orange and yellow-olive 10 10
222 50c. lemon and light red 25 20

1965 (25 Oct). International Co-operation Year. As Nos. 168/169 of Antigua.

223 1c. reddish purple and turquoise-green 10 15
224 25c. deep bluish green and lavender 45 15

1966 (24 Jan). Churchill Commemoration. As Nos. 170/173 of Antigua.

225 1c. new blue 10 30
226 3c. deep green 30 20
227 25c. brown 65 10
228 35c. bluish violet 70 15
225/228 *Set of* 4 1·50 65

1966 (4 Feb). Royal Visit. As Nos. 174/175 of Antigua.

229 3c. black and ultramarine 40 15
230 35c. black and magenta 1·40 15

52 Hillsborough, Carriacou

53 Bougainvillea

54 Flamboyant plant

55 Levera beach

56 Carenage, St George's

57 Annandale Falls

58 Cocoa pods

59 Inner Harbour

60 Nutmeg

61 St George's

62 Grand Anse beach

63 Bananas

64 Badge of the colony

65 Queen Elizabeth II

66 Map of Grenada

(Des V. Whiteley. Photo Harrison)

1966 (1 Apr). Designs as Types **52/66**. Multicoloured. W w **12**. P 14½ ($1, $2, $3) or 14½×13½ (others).

231	**52**	1c. Multicoloured	20	1·25
232	**53**	2c. carmine and myrtle green	20	10
233	**54**	3c. Multicoloured	1·00	1·00
234	**55**	5c. Multicoloured	1·25	10
235	**56**	6c. Multicoloured	1·00	10
236	**57**	8c. Multicoloured	1·00	10
		w. Wmk inverted		
237	**58**	10c. Multicoloured	1·25	10
		w. Wmk inverted	—	£160
238	**59**	12c. Multicoloured	30	1·25
239	**60**	15c. Multicoloured	30	1·25
240	**61**	25c. Multicoloured	30	10
241	**62**	35c. Multicoloured	30	10
242	**63**	50c. emerald and lavender	1·25	2·00
243	**64**	$1 Multicoloured	7·50	3·75
244	**65**	$2 Multicoloured	6·50	15·00
245	**66**	$3 Multicoloured	7·50	21·00
231/245 *Set of* 15			27·00	42·00

1966 (1 July). World Cup Football Championship. As Nos. 176/177 of Antigua.

246	5c. violet, yellow-green, lake and yellow-brown	10	10
247	50c. chocolate, blue-green, lake and yellow-brown	40	90

1966 (20 Sept). Inauguration of WHO Headquarters, Geneva. As Nos. 178/179 of Antigua.

248	8c. black, yellow-green and light blue	30	10
249	25c. black, light purple and yellow-brown	70	20

1966 (1 Dec). 20th Anniversary of UNESCO. As Nos. 196/198 of Antigua.

250	2c. slate-violet, red, yellow and orange	10	10
251	15c. orange-yellow, violet and deep olive	15	10
252	50c. black, bright purple and orange	50	90
250/252 *Set of* 3		65	1·00

ASSOCIATED STATEHOOD

(67) (68)

1967 (3 Mar). Statehood. Nos. 232/233, 236 and 240 optd with T **67**, in silver.

253	**53**	2c. Bougainvillea	10	20
254	**54**	3c. Flamboyant plant	10	15
255	**57**	8c. Annandale Falls	15	10
256	**61**	25c. St George's	15	15
253/256 *Set of* 4			30	50

1967 (1 June). World Fair, Montreal. Nos. 232, 237, 239 and 243/244 surch as T **68** or optd with Expo emblem only.

257	**60**	1c. on 15c. Nutmeg	10	20
		a. Surch and opt albino	16·00	
258	**53**	2c. Bougainvillea	10	20
259	**58**	3c. on 10c. Cocoa pods	10	20
		w. Wmk inverted	12·00	
260	**64**	$1 Badge of the Colony	30	25
261	**65**	$2 Queen Elizabeth II	45	30
257/261 *Set of* 5			70	1·00

ASSOCIATED STATEHOOD

(69)

70 Kennedy and Local Flower

1967 (1 Oct). Statehood. Nos. 231/245 optd with T **69**.

262	**52**	1c. Hillsborough, Carriacou	10	10
263	**53**	2c. Bougainvillea	10	10
264	**54**	3c. Flamboyant plant	10	10
265	**55**	5c. Levera beach	10	10
266	**56**	6c. Carenaga St George's	10	10
267	**57**	8c. Annandale Falls	10	10
268	**58**	10c. Cocoa pods	10	10
269	**59**	12c. Inner harbour	10	10
270	**60**	15c. Nutmeg	15	10
271	**61**	25c. St George's	20	10
272	**62**	35c. Grand Anse beach	55	10
273	**63**	50c. Bananas	1·00	20
274	**64**	$1 Badge of the Colony	1·50	60
275	**65**	$2 Queen Elizabeth II	1·25	3·75
276	**66**	$3 Map of Grenada	5·00	6·00
262/276 *Set of* 15			9·00	10·50

See also No. 295.

(Des M. Shamir. Photo Harrison)

1968 (13 Jan). 50th Birth Anniversary of President Kennedy. T **70** and similar horiz designs. Multicoloured. P 14½×14.

277	1c. Type **70**	10	25
278	15c. Type **70**	15	10
279	25c. Kennedy and strelitzia	20	10
280	35c. Kennedy and roses	20	10
281	50c. As 25c.	25	20
282	$1 As 35c.	30	60
277/282 *Set of* 6		1·00	1·00

73 Scout Bugler

76 *Near Antibes*

(Des K. Plowitz. Photo Govt Printer, Israel)

1968 (17 Feb). World Scout Jamboree, Idaho. T **73** and similar vert designs. Multicoloured. P 13×13½.

283	1c. Type **73**	10	10
284	2c. Scouts camping	10	10
285	3c. Lord Baden-Powell	10	10
286	35c. Type **73**	25	10
287	50c. As 2c.	35	20
288	$1 As 3c.	50	55
283/288 *Set of* 6		1·10	80

(Des G. Vasarhelyi. Photo Harrison)

1968 (23 Mar). Paintings by Sir Winston Churchill. T **76** and similar horiz designs. Multicoloured. P 14×14½.

289	10c. Type **76**	10	10
290	12c. *The Mediterranean*	15	10
291	15c. *St Jean Cap Ferratt*	15	10
292	25c. Type **76**	20	10
293	35c. As 15c.	25	10
294	50c. Sir Winston painting	35	25
289/294 *Set of* 6		1·10	45

(80) (81) (82)

1968 (18 May). No. 275 surch with T **80**.

295	**65**	$5 on $2 multicoloured	1·25	2·25

1968 (22 July–19 Aug). 'Children Need Milk'.

(a) Nos. 244/245 surch locally as T **81** *(22 July)*

296	**65**	2c. +3c. on $2 multicoloured	10	10
297	**66**	3c. +3c. on $3 multicoloured	10	10
		a. Surch inverted	55·00	21·00
		b. Surch double	28·00	
		c. Surch double, one albino		

(b) Nos. 243/244 surch locally as T **82** *(19 Aug)*

298	**64**	1c. +3c. on $1 multicoloured	10	40
		a. Surch on No. 274	75·00	75·00
		b. Surch double	38·00	
299	**65**	2c. +3c. on $2 multicoloured	24·00	60·00
		a. Surch on No. 275	85·00	
296/299 *Set of* 4			24·00	60·00

83 Edith McGuire (USA)

86 Hibiscus

(Des M. Shamir. Photo Harrison)

1968 (24 Sept). Olympic Games, Mexico. T **83** and similar square designs. P 12½.

300	1c. brown, black and blue	70	1·00
301	2c. orange, brown, blue and lilac	70	1·00
	a. Orange (badge, etc.) omitted		
302	3c. scarlet, brown and dull green	70	1·00
	a. Scarlet (rings, 'MEXICO' etc.) omitted	£1200	£1000
303	10c. brown, black, blue and vermilion	80	1·10
304	50c. orange, brown, blue and turquoise	80	1·10
305	60c. scarlet, brown and red-orange	80	1·10
300/305 *Set of* 6		4·00	5·50

Designs: 2, 50c. Arthur Wint (Jamaica); 3, 60c. Ferreira da Silva (Brazil); 1, 10c. T **83**.

Nos. 300/302 and 303/305 were issued in separate composite sheets containing three strips of three with three *se-tenant* labels showing Greek athlete (Nos. 300/302) or Discobolos (Nos. 303/305). (*Price for two sheets £8 mint, £12 used*).

(Des G. Vasarhelyi (No. 314*a*), V. Whiteley (75c.), M. Shamir (others). Litho Format (Nos. 314*a* and 317*a*). Photo Harrison (others))

1968 (1 Oct)–**71**. Multicoloured designs as T **86**. P 13½ (Nos. 314*a*. and 317*a*), 13½×14½ (vert except No. 314*a*) or 14½×13½ (horiz except No. 317*a*).

306	1c. Type **86**	10	10
307	2c. Strelitzia	10	10
308	3c. Bougainvillea (1.7.69)	10	10
309	5c. Rock Hind (*horiz*) (4.2.69)	10	10
310	6c. Sailfish	10	10
311	8c. Red Snapper (*horiz*) (1.7.69)	10	60
312	10c. Marine Toad (*horiz*) (4.2.69)	10	10
313	12c. Turtle	15	10
314	15c. Tree Boa (*horiz*)	1·00	60
314*a*	15c. Thunbergia (1970)	1·25	2·50
315	25c. Greater Trinidadian Murine Opossum (4.2.69)	30	10
316	35c. Nine-banded Armadillo (*horiz*) (1.7.69)	35	10
317	50c. Mona Monkey	45	25
317*a*	75c. Yacht in St George's Harbour (*horiz*) (9.10.71)	18·00	9·50
318	$1 Bananaquit	2·50	2·75
319	$2 Brown Pelican (4.2.69)	8·00	17·00
320	$3 Magnificent Frigatebird	3·75	10·00
321	$5 Bare-eyed Thrush (1.7.69)	14·00	27·00
306/321 *Set of* 18		45·00	60·00

Nos. 314*a*, 317*a* and the dollar values are larger—29×45½, 44×28½ and 25½×48 mm respectively.

No. 317*a* exists imperforate from stock dispersed by the liquidator of Format International Security Printers Ltd.

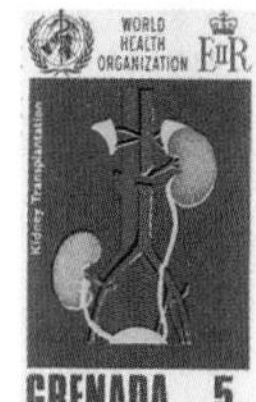

102 Kidney Transplant

106 *The Adoration of the Kings* (Veronese)

(Des M. Shamir. Litho B.W.)

1968 (25 Nov). 20th Anniversary of World Health Organisation. T **102** and similar vert designs. Multicoloured. P 13×13½.

322	5c. Type **102**	20	10
323	25c. Heart transplant	30	10
324	35c. Lung transplant	30	10
325	50c. Eye transplant	40	50
322/325 *Set of* 4		1·10	60

(Photo Harrison)

1968 (3 Dec). Christmas. T **106** and similar square designs. P 12½.

326	5c. multicoloured	10	10
327	15c. multicoloured	10	10
328	35c. multicoloured	10	10
329	$1 multicoloured	30	40
326/329 *Set of* 4		40	45

Designs: 5c. T **106**; 15c. *Madonna and Child with Sts John and Catherine* (Titian); 35c. *Adoration of the Kings* (Botticelli); $1 *A Warrior Adoring* (Catena).

VISIT CARIFTA EXPO '69
April 5-30
5c

(110)

1969 (1 Feb). Caribbean Free Trade Area Exhibition. Nos. 300/305 surch in red as T **110**.

330	5c. on 1c. brown, black and blue	20	30
	a. Surch double		
331	8c. on 2c. orange, brown, blue and lilac	20	30
	a. Surch double		

332 25c. on 3c. scarlet, brown and dull green 20 30
a. Surch double
333 35c. on 10c. brown, black, blue and vermilion 20 30
334 $1 on 50c. orange, brown, blue and turquoise 25 40
335 $2 on 60c. scarlet, brown and red-orange 35 60
a. Scarlet (rings, 'MEXICO' etc) omitted † —
330/335 *Set of 6* 1·25 2·00

The centre of the composite sheets is also overprinted with a commemorative inscription publicising CARIFTA EXPO 1969 (*Price for two sheets £4 mint, £7 used*).

111 Dame Hylda Bynoe (Governor) and Island Scene

(Des and litho D.L.R.)

1969 (1 May). Carifta Expo 1969. T **111** and similar horiz designs. Multicoloured. P 13×13½.
336 5c. Type **111** 10 10
337 15c. Premier E. M. Gairy and Island scene 10 10
338 50c. Type **111** 10 30
339 60c. Emblems of 1958 and 1967 World's Fairs 10 65
336/339 *Set of 4* 30 70

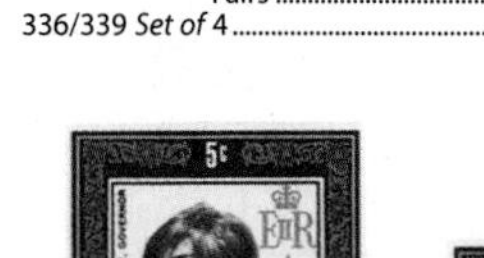

114 Dame Hylda Bynoe **115** *Balshazzar's Feast* (Rembrandt)

(Photo Enschedé)

1969 (8 June). Human Rights Year. Types **114/115** and similar multicoloured design. P 12½×13 ($1) or 13×12½ (others).
340 5c. Type **114** 10 10
341 25c. Dr Martin Luther King (*vert*) 15 10
342 35c. Type **114** 15 10
343 $1 Type **115** 30 45
340/343 *Set of 4* 55 55

117 Batsman and Wicket-keeper

(Des M. Shamir and L. W. Denyer. Photo Harrison)

1969 (1 Aug). Cricket. T **117** and similar horiz designs. P 14×14½.
344 3c. yellow, brown and ultramarine 75 1·25
a. Yellow (caps and wicket) omitted £1100
345 10c. multicoloured 75 40
346 25c. brown, ochre and myrtle-green 85 85
347 35c. multicoloured 1·00 90
344/347 *Set of 4* 3·00 3·00

Designs: 3c. T **117**; 10c. Batsman playing defensive stroke; 25c. Batsman sweeping ball; 35c. Batsman playing on-drive.

Nos. 344/347 were each issued in small sheets of nine (3×3) with decorative borders.

129 Astronaut handling Moon Rock

(Des G. Vasarhelyi. Photo)

1969 (24 Sept). First Man on the Moon. T **129** and similar multicoloured designs. P 13½ (½c.) or 12½ (others).
348 ½c. As Type **129** but larger (56×35 *mm*). 10 50
349 1c. Moon rocket and moon 10 50
350 2c. Module landing 10 50
351 3c. Declaration left on moon 10 50
352 8c. Module leaving rocket 20 10
353 25c. Rocket lifting-off (*vert*) 45 10
354 35c. Spacecraft in orbit (*vert*) 45 10
355 50c. Capsule with parachutes (*vert*) 60 30
356 $1 Type **129** 90 1·50
348/356 *Set of 9* 2·50 3·50
MS357 115×90 mm. Nos. 351 and 356. Imperf 1·25 3·00

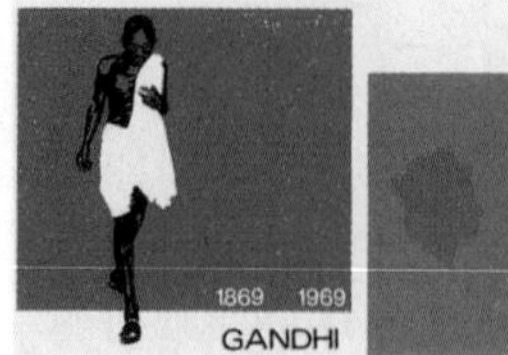

130 Gandhi

(Des A. Robledo. Litho B.W.)

1969 (8 Oct). Birth Centenary of Mahatma Gandhi. T **130** and similar designs. P 11½.
358 **130** 6c. multicoloured 55 30
359 – 15c. multicoloured 70 10
360 – 25c. multicoloured 75 10
361 – $1 multicoloured 1·00 65
358/361 *Set of 4* 2·75 1·00
MS362 155×122 mm. Nos. 358/361. Imperf 2·75 3·75

Designs: Vert—15c. Gandhi standing; 25c. Gandhi waking. Horiz—$1 Head of Gandhi.

1969

2c

(**134**)

135 'Blackbeard' (Edward Teach)

1969 (23 Dec). Christmas. Nos. 326/329 surch with T **134** in black (2c.) or optd with new date only in silver (others).
363 2c. on 15c. multicoloured 10 2·25
a. Surch inverted 50·00
364 5c. multicoloured 10 15
a. Opt double 50·00
365 35c. multicoloured 20 10
a. Opt inverted 50·00
b. Horiz pair, one with opt omitted £225
c. Opt double, one vertical 55·00
366 $1 multicoloured 80 2·25
a. Opt inverted 50·00
363/366 *Set of 4* 1·00 4·25

(Des K. Plowitz. Recess B.W.)

1970 (2 Feb). Pirates. T **135** and similar vert designs. P 13½.
367 15c. black 75 10
368 25c. dull green 1·00 10
369 50c. lilac 1·50 70
370 $1 carmine 2·25 3·00
367/370 *Set of 4* 5·00 3·50

Designs: 15c. T **135**; 25c. Anne Bonney; 50c. Jean Lafitte; $1 Mary Read.

(**139**) (**140**)

1970 (18 Mar). No. 348 surch with T **139**.
371 5c. on ½c. multicoloured 10 30
a. Surch double 27·00
b. Surch with T **140** 70 80
ba. Surch double, one inverted 48·00

141/2 *The Last Supper* (detail, Del Sarto)

(Des and litho B.W.)

1970 (13 Apr). Easter. Paintings. Types **141/142** and similar vert design. Mulicoloured. P 11½.
372 5c. Type **141** 20 50
a. Horiz pair. Nos. 372/373 40 1·00
373 5c. Type **142** 20 50
374 15c. *Christ crowned with Thorns* (detail, Van Dyck) 20 50
a. Horiz pair. Nos. 374/375 40 1·00
375 15c. As No. 374 20 50
376 25c. *The Passion of Christ* (detail, Memling) 20 50
a. Horiz pair. Nos. 376/377 40 1·00
377 25c. As No. 376 20 50
378 60c. *Christ in the Tomb* (detail, Rubens) 25 60
a. Horiz pair. Nos. 378/379 50 1·10
379 60c. As No. 378 25 60
372/379 *Set of 8* 1·50 3·75
MS380 120×140 mm. Nos. 376/379 1·00 1·75

Nos. 372/379 were issued with each design spread over two *se-tenant* stamps of the same denomination.

149 Girl with Kittens in Pram

(Des A. Robledo. Litho Questa)

1970 (27 May). Birth Bicentenary of William Wordsworth (poet). 'Children and Pets'. T **149** and similar horiz designs. Multicoloured. P 11.
381 5c. Type **149** 15 15
382 15c. Girl with puppy and kitten 25 15
383 30c. Boy with fishing rod and cat 30 40
384 60c. Boys and girls with cats and dogs 40 2·00
381/384 *Set of 4* 1·00 2·40
MS385 Two sheets each 114×126 mm. Nos. 381, 383 and Nos. 382, 384. Imperf 1·00 2·00

153 Parliament of India

(Des G. Vasarhelyi. Litho Questa)

1970 (15 June). Seventh Regional Conference of Commonwealth Parliamentary Association. T **153** and similar horiz designs. Multicoloured. P 14.
386 5c. Type **153** 10 10
387 25c. Parliament of Great Britain, Westminster 10 10
388 50c. Parliament of Canada 20 15
389 60c. Parliament of Grenada 20 15
386/389 *Set of 4* 50 35
MS390 126×90 mm. Nos. 386/389 50 1·00

157 Tower of the Sun

(Litho Kyodo Printing Co, Tokyo)

1970 (8 Aug). World Fair, Osaka. T **157** and similar multicoloured designs. P 13.
391 1c. Type **157** 10 65
392 2c. Livelihood and Industry Pavilion (*horiz*) 10 65
393 3c. Flower painting, 1634 10 65
394 10c. *Adam and Eve* (Tintoretto) (*horiz*) 15 10
395 25c. OECD (Organisation for Economic Co-operation and Development) Pavilion (*horiz*) 35 10
396 50c. San Francisco Pavilion 40 1·60
391/396 *Set of 6* 1·00 3·25
MS397 121×91 mm. $1 Japanese Pavilion (56×34 *mm*) 55 1·50

164 Roosevelt and 'Raising US Flag on Iwo Jima'

(Litho Questa)

1970 (3 Sept). 25th Anniversary of Ending of World War II. T **164** and similar horiz designs. Multicoloured. P 11.
398 ½c. Type **164** 10 3·00
399 5c. Zhukov and 'Fall of Berlin' 1·00 65
400 15c. Churchill and 'Evacuation at Dunkirk' 3·25 1·50
401 25c. De Gaulle and 'Liberation of Paris' 1·50 60
402 50c. Eisenhower and 'D-Day Landing' 1·75 2·50
403 60c. Montgomery and 'Battle of Alamein' 3·50 6·00
398/403 *Set of 6* 10·00 13·00
MS404 163×113 mm. Nos. 398, 400, 402/403 4·50 10·00
a. Brown (panel) on 60c. value omitted £1000

PHILYMPIA
LONDON 1970
(169)

170 UPU Emblem, Building and Transport

1970 (18 Sept). Philympia 1970 Stamp Exhibition, London. Nos. 353/6 optd with T **169**.

No.	Description	Unused	Used
405	25c. Rocket lifting-off	10	10
	a. Albino opt	5·00	
	b. Opt inverted	17·00	
406	35c. Spacecraft in orbit	10	10
	a. Opt inverted	55·00	
	b. Opt double, one albino, one inverted	75·00	
407	50c. Capsule with parachutes	15	15
	a. Albino opt	3·50	
408	$1 Type **129** (Sil.) (optd vert upwards)	20	30
	a. Albino opt	6·50	
	b. Opt inverted (vert downwards)		
405/408 *Set of 4*		40	50

The miniature sheet was also overprinted but we understand that only 300 of these were put on sale in Grenada.

(Litho Questa)

1970 (17 Oct). New UPU Headquarters Building. T **170** and similar multicoloured designs. P 14.

No.	Description	Unused	Used
409	15c. Type **170**	1·50	40
410	25c. As Type **170**, but modern transport	1·50	40
411	50c. Sir Rowland Hill and UPU Building	35	60
412	$1 Abraham Lincoln and UPU Building	45	3·25
409/412 *Set of 4*		3·50	4·25
MS413 79×85 mm. Nos. 411/412		1·00	3·75

The 50c. and $1 are both vertical designs.

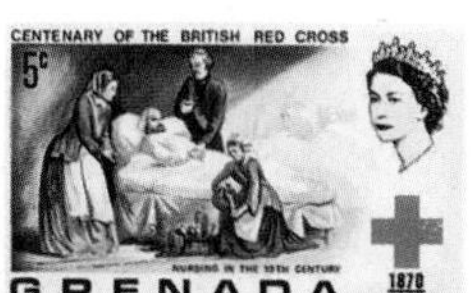

171 *The Madonna of the Goldfinch* (Tiepolo) **172** 19th-century Nursing

(Des G. Vasarhelyi. Litho Questa)

1970 (5 Dec). Christmas. T **171** and similar vert designs. Multicoloured. P 13½.

No.	Description	Unused	Used
414	½c. Type **171**	10	45
415	½c. *The Virgin and Child with St Peter and St Paul* (Bouts)	10	45
416	½c. *The Virgin and Child* (Bellini)	10	45
417	2c. *The Madonna of the Basket* (Correggio)	10	45
418	3c. Type **171**	10	45
419	35c. As No. 415	50	10
420	50c. As No. 417	60	40
421	$1 As No. 416	70	1·60
414/421 *Set of 8*		1·75	3·75
MS422 102×87 mm. Nos. 420/421		1·00	3·25

(Des G. Vasarhelyi. Litho Questa)

1970 (12 Dec). Centenary of British Red Cross. T **172** and similar horiz designs. Multicoloured. P 14½×14.

No.	Description	Unused	Used
423	5c. Type **172**	40	20
424	15c. Military Ambulance, 1918	1·00	20
425	25c. First-Aid Post, 1941	1·00	20
426	60c. Red Cross Transport, 1970	1·75	2·50
423/426 *Set of 4*		3·75	2·75
MS427 113×82 mm. Nos. 423/426		3·75	2·75
	a. Error. Imperf	30·00	

POSTAGE DUE STAMPS

D **1**

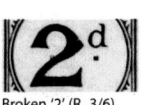

1d.
SURCHARGE
POSTAGE
(D **2**)

2d Broken '2' (R. 3/6)

(Typo D.L.R.)

1892 (18 Apr–Oct).

(a) T D **1**. *Wmk Crown CA. P 14*

No.	Type	Description	Unused	Used
D1	D **1**	1d. blue-black	42·00	1·50
D2		2d. blue-black	£250	1·50
		a. Broken '2'	—	50·00
D3		3d. blue-black	£250	2·50
D1/D3 *Set of 3*			£475	5·00

(b) Nos. 34 and 35 surch locally as T D **2**

No.	Type	Description	Unused	Used
D4	**13**	1d. on 6d. mauve (10.92)	£130	1·25
		a. *Tête-bêche* (vert pair)	£3500	£1500
		b. Surch double	†	£275
D5		1d. on 8d. grey-brown (8.92)	£3000	3·25
		a. *Tête-bêche* (vert pair)	£12000	£2750
		b. Damaged value	—	75·00
D6		2d. on 6d. mauve (10.92)	£200	2·50
		a. *Tête-bêche* (vert pair)	£4000	£1900
D7		2d. on 8d. grey-brown (8.92)	£5000	14·00
		a. *Tête-bêche* (vert pair)	—	£5500
		b. Damaged value	—	£150

Nos. D4/D7 were in use from August to November 1892. As supplies of Nos. D1/D3 were available from April or May of that year it would not appear that they were intended for postage due purposes. There was a shortage of 1d. postage stamps in July and August, but this was alleviated by Nos. 44/45 which were still available. The provisionals may have been intended for postal purposes, but the vast majority appear to have been used philatelically.

1906 (1 July)–**11**. Wmk Mult Crown CA. P 14.

No.	Type	Description	Unused	Used
D8	D **1**	1d. blue-black (1911)	5·00	7·50
D9		2d. blue-black	12·00	1·50
		a. Broken '2'	£150	50·00
D10		3d. blue-black (9.06)	19·00	5·00
D8/D10 *Set of 3*			32·00	12·50

1921 (1 Dec)–**22**. As T D **1**, but inscr 'POSTAGE DUE'. Wmk Mult Script CA. P 14.

No.	Description	Unused	Used
D11	1d. black	3·00	1·00
D12	1½d. black (15.12.22)	14·00	35·00
D13	2d. black	3·25	1·50
	a. Broken '2'	70·00	50·00
D14	3d. black	2·25	3·00
D11/D14 *Set of 4*		20·00	35·00
D11s/D14s Optd 'SPECIMEN' *Set of 4*		80·00	

1952 (1 Mar). As T D **1**, but inscr 'POSTAGE DUE'. Value in cents. Chalk-surfaced paper. Wmk Mult Script CA. P 14.

No.	Description	Unused	Used
D15	2c. black	30	12·00
	a. Error. Crown missing. W **9a**	£180	
	b. Error. St Edward Crown. W **9b**	55·00	
D16	4c. black	30	20·00
	a. Error. Crown missing. W **9a**	£180	
	b. Error. St Edward Crown. W **9b**	60·00	
D17	6c. black	45	12·00
	a. Error. Crown missing. W **9a**	£275	
	b. Error. St Edward Crown. W **9b**	£100	
D18	8c. black	75	17·00
	a. Error. Crown missing. W **9a**	£475	
	b. Error. St Edward Crown. W **9b**	£225	
D15/D18 *Set of 4*		1·60	55·00

Griqualand West *see* **South Africa**

Guyana

GUYANA
INDEPENDENCE
1966
(**73**)

1966 (26 May)–**67**. Various stamps of British Guiana as Nos. 331/345 optd with T **73** by De La Rue.

(a) Wmk Mult Script CA

No.	Description	Unused	Used
378	2c. myrtle-green	1·00	40
379	3c. brown-olive and red-brown	2·50	6·00
	a. 'Weed' flaw	50·00	
	b. 'Clubbed foot'	50·00	
380	4c. violet	3·25	75
381	6c. yellow-green	60	10
382	8c. ultramarine	3·25	2·00
	w. Wmk inverted	†	£450
383	12c. black and reddish brown	4·75	1·25
384	$5 ultramarine and black	27·00	60·00
378/384 *Set of 7*		38·00	65·00

(b) Wmk w **12** *(upright)*

No.	Description	Unused	Used
385	1c. black (28.2.67)	10	30
386	3c. brown-olive and red-brown	1·25	10
387	4c. violet (28.2.67)	20	2·75
388	5c. scarlet and black	40	10
389	6c. green (28.2.67)	10	20
390	8c. ultramarine (14.3.67)	3·25	2·00
391	12c. black and yellowish brown	10	10
392	24c. black and bright orange	8·50	1·25
393	36c. rose-carmine and black	30	30
394	48c. bright ultramarine and Venetian red	6·00	13·00
395	72c. carmine and emerald	1·00	1·50
396	$1 pink, yellow, green and black	11·00	35
397	$2 reddish mauve	1·50	2·00
398	$5 ultramarine and black	1·00	8·00
385/398 *Set of 14*		30·00	28·00

(c) Wmk w **12** *(sideways)*

No.	Description	Unused	Used
399	1c. black	10	10
400	4c. violet	10	10
401	8c. ultramarine	10	10
402	12c. black and yellowish brown (28.2.67)	10	10
403	24c. black and bright orange	2·00	60
404	36c. rose-carmine and black (28.2.67)	30	2·50
405	48c. bright ultramarine and Venetian red	30	30
406	72c. carmine and emerald (28.2.67)	3·25	7·50
407	$1 pink, yellow, green and black (14.3.67)	13·00	7·00
407*a*	$2 reddish mauve (28.2.67)	3·00	6·00
407*b*	$5 ultramarine and black (28.2.67)	1·50	6·00
399/407*b* *Set of 11*		21·00	27·00

See also Nos. 420/440.

74 Flag and Map

75 Arms of Guyana

(Des V. Whiteley. Photo Harrison)

1966 (26 May). Independence. P 14½.

No.	Type	Description	Unused	Used
408	**74**	5c. multicoloured	30	10
409		15c. multicoloured	40	10
410	**75**	25c. multicoloured	40	10
411		$1 multicoloured	1·10	1·25
408/411 *Set of 4*			2·00	1·25

76 Bank Building

(Des B. Granger Barrett. Photo Enschedé)

1966 (11 Oct). Opening of Bank of Guyana. P 13½×14.

No.	Type	Description	Unused	Used
412	**76**	5c. multicoloured	10	10
413		25c. multicoloured	10	10

CANCELLED REMAINDERS.* In 1969 remainders of some issues were put on the market cancelled-to-order in such a way as to be indistinguishable from genuine postally used copies for all practical purposes. Our used quotations which are indicated by an asterisk are the same for cancelled-to-order or postally used copies.

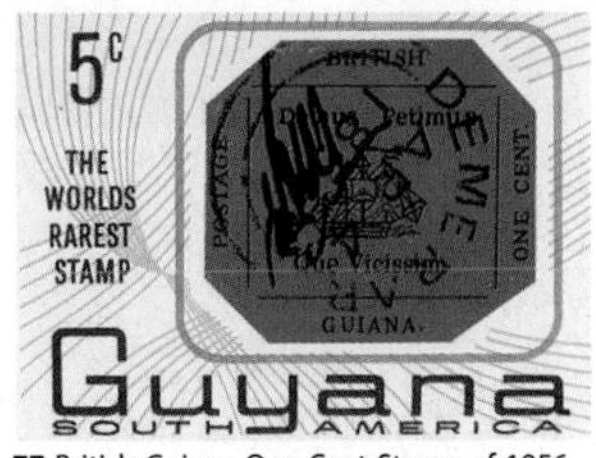

77 British Guiana One Cent Stamp of 1856

(Des V. Whiteley. Litho D.L.R.)

1967 (23 Feb). World's Rarest Stamp Commemoration. P 12½.

No.	Type	Description	Unused	Used
414	**77**	5c. black, magenta, silver and light ochre	10	10*
415		25c. black, magenta, gold and light green	10	10*

78 Chateau Margot

GUYANA INDEPENDENCE 1966

(**82**)

(Des R. Granger Barrett. Photo Harrison)

1967 (26 May). First Anniversary of Independence. T **78** and similar multicoloured designs. P 14 (6c.), 14½×14 (15c.) or 14×14½ (others).

No.	Type	Description	Unused	Used
416		6c. Type **78**	10	10*
417		15c. Independence Arch	10	10*
418		25c. Fort Island (*horiz*)	10	10*
419		$1 National Assembly (*horiz*)	35	15
416/419 *Set of 4*			50	20

1967 (3 Oct)–**68**. Stamps of British Guiana as Nos. 331/345 optd with T **82** locally.

(i) Wmk Mult Script CA

No.	Type	Description	Unused	Used
420		1c. black (3.10.67)	10	10
		a. Opt inverted	60·00	
		b. Date misplaced 5 mm	13·00	13·00
		c. Date misplaced 2 mm	13·00	13·00
421		2c. myrtle-green (3.10.67)	10	10
		a. '1966' for 'GUYANA'	18·00	20·00
		b. Date misplaced 5 mm	14·00	14·00
		c. Date misplaced 2 mm	14·00	14·00
422		3c. brown-olive and red-brown (3.10.67)	30	10
		a. '1966' for 'GUYANA'	15·00	15·00
		b. Vert pair, one without opt	£600	
		c. Date misplaced 2 mm	14·00	14·00
423		4c. violet (10.67)	10	10
		a. Deep violet	1·50	1·25
		b. Opt inverted	80·00	85·00
424		6c. yellow-green (11.67)	25	10
		a. '1966' for 'GUYANA'	28·00	42·00
		b. Opt inverted	65·00	70·00
		c. Opt double	85·00	90·00
425		8c. ultramarine (12.67)	10	10
426		12c. black and brown (12.67)	10	10
426*a*		24c. black and orange (date?)	£500	£170
427		$2 reddish mauve (12.67)	1·50	4·75
428		$5 ultramarine and black (12.67)	2·00	4·50

(ii) Wmk w **12** *(upright)*

No.	Type	Description	Unused	Used
429		1c. black (2.68)	10	2·75
		a. Opt omitted	£350	
430		2c. myrtle-green (2.68)	1·00	6·00
431		3c. brown-olive and red-brown (3.10.67)	30	10
		a. '1966' for 'GUYANA'	85·00	85·00
		b. Opt inverted	35·00	
432		4c. violet (2.68)	20	3·75
433		5c. scarlet and black (3.10.67)	2·00	4·25
		a. Deep scarlet and black	2·00	4·50
		aw. Wmk inverted	95·00	
		c. Date misplaced 2 mm	13·00	
434		6c. yellow-green (2.68)	30	3·25
		a. Opt double, one diagonal	95·00	
435		24c. black and bright orange (11.12.67)	12·00	10
		a. Opt double, one diagonal (horiz pair)	£200	
436		36c. rose-carmine and black (12.67)	3·50	10
437		48c. bright ultramarine and Venetian red (12.67)	2·75	2·75
		a. Opt inverted	£110	£130
438		72c. carmine and emerald (12.67)	5·00	1·50
439		$1 pink, yellow, green and black (12.67)	5·50	65
440		$2 reddish mauve (12.67)	6·00	4·00
420/440 (*excl. 426a*) *Set of 21*			38·00	35·00

The '1966' errors occurred on R. 7/10 and were later corrected. Nos. 425/428 and 436/440 were issued in mid-December, but some were cancelled-to-order with a November date in error.

On Nos. 420b and 421b the '1' of '1966' is below the second 'D' of 'INDEPENDENCE' (R. 6/3). On Nos. 420c, 421c, 422c and 433c it is below the second 'E' (R. 6/1). Lesser misplacements exist in other positions.

No. 433*a* is from a printing made specially for this overprint.

83 'Millie' (Blue and Yellow Macaw)

84 Wicket-keeping

(Des V. Whiteley. Photo Harrison)

1967 (6 Nov)–**68**. Christmas. P 14½×14.

(a) First issue (6 Nov 1967)

No.	Type	Description	Unused	Used
441	**83**	5c. yellow, new blue, black and bronze-green	10	10*
442		25c. yellow, new blue, black and violet	15	10*

(b) Second issue. Colours changed (22 Jan 1968)

No.	Type	Description	Unused	Used
443	**83**	5c. yellow, new blue, black and red	10	10*
444		25c. yellow, new blue, black and apple-green	15	10*

(Des V. Whiteley. Photo Harrison)

1968 (8 Jan). MCC's West Indies Tour. T **84** and similar vert designs. P 14.

No.	Type	Description	Unused	Used
445		5c. Type **84**	10	10*
		a. Strip of 3. Nos. 445/447	45	20*
446		6c. Batting	10	10*
447		25c. Bowling	30	10*
445/447 *Set of 3*			45	20*

Nos. 445/447 were issued in small sheets of nine containing three *se-tenant* strips.

87 Pike Cichlid

102 *Christ of St John of the Cross* (Salvador Dali)

(Des R. Granger Barrett. Photo Harrison)

1968 (4 Mar). Multicoloured designs as T **87**, showing fish (1 to 6c.), birds (10 to 40c.) or animals (others). No wmk. P 14×14½.

No.	Type	Description	Unused	Used
448		1c. Type **87**	10	10
449		2c. Red Piranha ('Pirai')	10	10
450		3c. Peacock Cichlid ('Lukunani')	10	10
451		5c. Armoured Catfish ('Hassar')	10	10
452		6c. Black Acara ('Patua')	55	10
453		10c. Spix's Guan (*vert*)	75	10
454		15c. Harpy Eagle (*vert*)	1·60	10
455		20c. Hoatzin (*vert*)	1·00	10
456		25c. Guianan Cock of the Rock (*vert*)	70	10
457		40c. Great Kiskadee (*vert*)	3·00	75
458		50c. Brazilian Agouti ('Accouri')	1·50	50
459		60c. White-lipped Peccary	1·50	10
460		$1 Paca ('Labba')	1·00	10
461		$2 Nine-banded Armadillo	2·00	2·00
462		$5 Ocelot	1·00	3·00
448/462 *Set of 15*			13·00	6·00

For Nos. 448/462 with W **106** see Nos. 485/499.

(Des and photo Harrison)

1968 (25 Mar). Easter. P 14.

No.	Type	Description	Unused	Used
463	**102**	5c. multicoloured	10	10*
464		25c. multicoloured	20	10*

103 'Efficiency Year'

104 'Savings Bonds'

(Des W. Starzmann. Litho B.W.)

1968 (22 July). 'Savings Bonds and Efficiency'. P 14.

No.	Type	Description	Unused	Used
465	**103**	6c. multicoloured	10	10*
466		25c. multicoloured	10	10*
467	**104**	30c. multicoloured	10	10*
468		40c. multicoloured	10	10*
465/468 *Set of 4*			30	15*

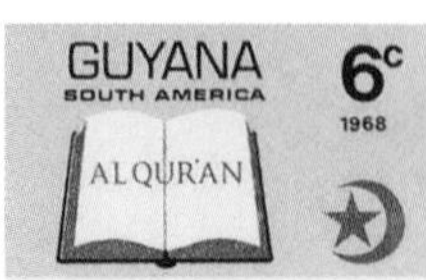

105 Open Book, Star and Crescent

(Des R. Gates. Photo D.L.R.)

1968 (9 Oct). 1400th Anniversary of the Holy Quran. P 14.

No.	Type	Description	Unused	Used
469	**105**	6c. black, gold and flesh	10	10*
470		25c. black, gold and lilac	10	10*
471		30c. black, gold and light apple-green	10	10*
472		40c. black, gold and cobalt	10	10*
469/472 *Set of 4*			30	15*

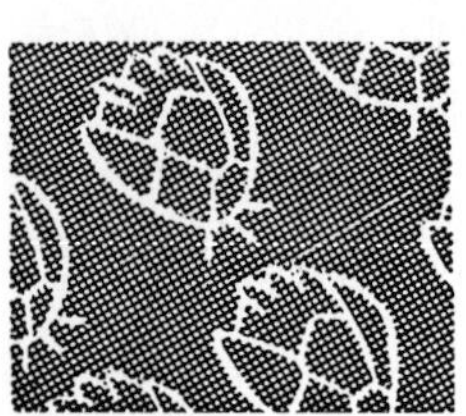

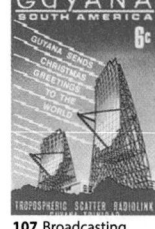

106 Lotus Blossoms

107 Broadcasting Greetings

(Des L. Pritchard; adapted G. Vasarhelyi. Litho D.L.R.)

1968 (11 Nov). Christmas. T **107** and similar vert design. W **106**. P 14.

No.	Type	Description	Unused	Used
473		6c. brown, blue and green	10	10*
474		25c. brown, reddish violet and green	10	10*
475		30c. blue-green and turquoise-green	10	10*
476		40c. red and turquoise-green	10	10*
473/476 *Set of 4*			30	15*

Designs: 6, 25c. Type **107**; 30, 40c. Map showing radio link, Guyana-Trinidad.

109 Festival Ceremony

(Des J. Cooter. Litho P.B.)

1969 (26 Feb). Hindu Festival of Phagwah. T **109** and similar horiz design. Multicoloured. W **106** (sideways). P 13½.

No.	Type	Description	Unused	Used
477		6c. Type **109**	10	10
478		25c. Ladies spraying scent	10	10
479		30c. Type **109**	10	10
480		40c. As 25c.	10	10
477/480 *Set of 4*			30	20

111 *Sacrament of the Last Supper* (Dali)

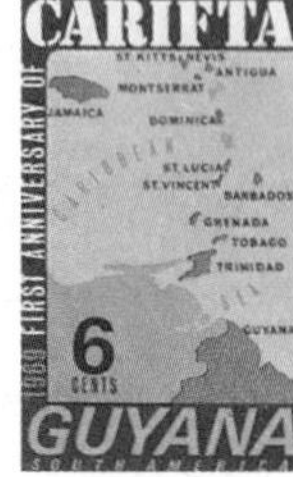

112 Map showing CARIFTA Countries

(Photo D.L.R.)

1969 (10 Mar). Easter. W **106** (sideways). P 13½×13.

No.	Type	Description	Unused	Used
481	**111**	6c. multicoloured	10	10
482		25c. multicoloured	10	10
483		30c. multicoloured	10	10
484		40c. multicoloured	10	10
481/484 *Set of 4*			30	15

1969–71. As Nos. 448/462, but Wmk **106** (sideways* on 1 to 6c. and 50c. to $5). Chalk-surfaced paper.

No.	Type	Description	Unused	Used
485		1c. Type **87**	10	10
486		2c. Red Piranha ('Pirai')	10	30
487		3c. Peacock Cichlid ('Lukunani')	10	75
488		5c. Armoured Catfish ('Hassar')	10	10
489		6c. Black Acara ('Patua')	10	1·00
490		10c. Spix's Guan	45	75
		a. Glazed paper (*wmk inverted*) (21.12.71)	1·00	7·00
491		15c. Harpy Eagle	60	10
		aw. Wmk inverted		
		b. Glazed paper (*wmk inverted*) (21.12.71)	1·25	6·00
492		20c. Hoatzin	50	80
493		25c. Guianan Cock of the Rock	45	10
		a. Glazed paper (*wmk inverted*) (21.12.71)	1·50	6·00
494		40c. Great Kiskadee	80	1·00
495		50c. Brazilian Agouti ('Accouri')	35	15
496		60c. White-lipped Peccary	35	1·00
497		$1 Paca ('Labba')	70	1·50
		a. Glazed paper (*wmk top of blossom to right*) (21.12.71)	1·75	14·00
498		$2 Nine-banded Armadillo	1·00	3·25
499		$5 Ocelot	1·00	5·00
485/499 *Set of 15*			5·75	14·00

* The normal sideways watermark shows the top of the blossom to the left, *as seen from the back of the stamp.*

These were put on sale by the Crown Agents on 25 March 1969 but although supplies were sent to Guyana in time they were not released there until needed as ample supplies remained of the stamps without watermark. It is understood that the 3c. and 5c. were put on sale in early May 1969 followed by the 25c. but there are no records of when the remainder were released.

(Des J. Cooter. Litho P.B.)

1969 (30 Apr). First Anniversary of CARIFTA (Caribbean Free Trade Area). T **112** and similar design. W **106** (sideways on 25c.). P 13½.

No.	Type	Description	Unused	Used
500		6c. rose-red, ultramarine and turquoise-blue	15	15
501		25c. lemon, brown and rose-red	15	15

Design: Vert—6c. T **112**. Horiz—25c. 'Strength in Unity'.

114 Building *Independence* (first aluminium ship)

116 Scouts raising Flag

(Des R. Gates. Litho B.W.)

1969 (30 Apr). 50th Anniversary of International Labour Organisation. T **114** and similar design. W **106** (sideways on 40c.). P 12×11 (30c.) or 11×12 (40c.).

502		30c. turquoise-blue, black and silver	40	25
503		40c. multicoloured	60	25

Design: Vert—30c. T **114**. Horiz—40c. Bauxite processing plant.

(Des Jennifer Toombs. Litho B.W.)

1969 (13 Aug). Third Caribbean Scout Jamboree and Diamond Jubilee of Scouting in Guyana. T **116** and similar horiz design. Multicoloured. W **106** (sideways). P 13.

504		6c. Type **116**	10	10
505		8c. Camp-fire cooking	10	10
506		25c. Type **116**	10	10
507		30c. As 8c.	10	10
508		50c. Type **116**	15	15
504/508 *Set of 5*			30	30

118 Gandhi and Spinning-wheel

119 'Mother Sally Dance Troupe'

(Des G. Drummond. Litho Format)

1969 (1 Oct). Birth Centenary of Mahatma Gandhi. W **106** (sideways). P 14½.

509	**118**	6c. black, brown and yellowish olive	1·00	65
510		15c. black, brown and lilac	1·00	65

(Des V. Whiteley (5, 25c.), J.W. (others). Litho B.W. (5, 25c.), D.L.R. (others))

1969 (17 Nov). Christmas. T **119** and similar vert designs. Multicoloured. No wmk (5, 25c.) or W **106** (others). P 13½ (5, 25c.) or 13×13½ (others).

511		5c. Type **119**	10	10
		a. Opt omitted	32·00	
		b. Opt double	28·00	
512		6c. City Hall, Georgetown	10	10
		a. Opt omitted	32·00	
		b. Opt inverted	35·00	
513		25c. Type **119**	10	10
		a. Opt omitted	35·00	
514		60c. As 6c.	20	25
511/514 *Set of 4*			30	30

Nos. 511/514 are previously unissued stamps optd as in T **119** by Guyana Lithographic Co, Ltd.

REPUBLIC

121 Forbes Burnham and Map

125 *The Descent from the Cross*

(Des L. Curtis. Litho D.L.R.)

1970 (23 Feb). Republic Day. T **121** and similar designs. W **106** (sideways on 15 and 25c.). P 14.

515		5c. sepia, ochre and pale blue	10	10
516		6c. multicoloured	10	10
517		15c. multicoloured	15	10
518		25c. multicoloured	20	15
515/518 *Set of 4*			40	30

Designs: Vert—5c. T **121**; 6c. 'Rural Self-help'. Horiz—15c. University of Guyana; 25c. Guyana House.

(Des J. Cooter. Litho Questa)

1970 (24 Mar). Easter. Paintings by Rubens. T **125** and similar vert design. Multicoloured. W **106** (inverted). P 14×14½.

519		5c. Type **125**	10	10
520		6c. *Christ on the Cross*	10	10
521		15c. Type **125**	20	15
522		25c. As 6c.	20	15
519/522 *Set of 4*			45	40

127 *Peace* and UN Emblem

128 *Mother and Child* (Philip Moore)

(Des and litho Harrison)

1970 (26 Oct). 25th Anniversary of United Nations. T **127** and similar horiz design. Multicoloured. W **106** (inverted). P 14.

523		5c. Type **127**	10	10
524		6c. UN Emblem, Gold-panning and Drilling	10	10
525		15c. Type **127**	10	10
526		25c. As 6c.	15	15
523/526 *Set of 4*			30	30

(Des Harrison. Litho J.W.)

1970 (8 Dec). Christmas. W **106**. P 13½.

527	**128**	5c. multicoloured	10	10
528		6c. multicoloured	10	10
529		15c. multicoloured	15	15
530		25c. multicoloured	15	15
527/530 *Set of 4*			30	30

POSTAGE DUE STAMPS

D **2**

(Typo D.L.R.)

1967–68. Chalk-surfaced paper. W w **12**. P 14.

D5	D **2**	2c. black (11.12.68)	1·75	18·00
D6		4c. deep ultramarine	30	6·00
D7		12c. reddish scarlet	30	6·00
D5/D7 *Set of 3*			2·10	27·00

Heligoland

Stamps of HAMBURG (see *Germany* of this catalogue) were used in Heligoland until 16 April 1867. The Free City of Hamburg ran the Heligoland postal service between 1796 and 1 June 1866. Its stamps continued in use on the island until replaced by Heligoland issues.

PRICES FOR STAMPS ON COVER
Nos. 1/19 *from* × 3

PRINTERS. All the stamps of Heligoland were typographed at the Imperial Printing Works, Berlin.

REPRINTS. Many of the stamps of Heligoland were subsequently reprinted at Berlin (between 1875 and 1885), Leipzig (1888) and Hamburg (1892 and 1895). Of these only the Berlin productions are difficult to distinguish from the originals so separate notes are provided for the individual values. Leipzig reprints can be identified by their highly surfaced paper and those from Hamburg by their 14 perforation. All of these reprints are worth much less than the original stamps priced below.

There was, in addition, a small reprinting of Nos. 13/19, made by the German government in 1890 for exchange purposes, but examples of this printing are far scarcer than the original stamps.

Forgeries, printed by lithography instead of typography, also exist for Nos. 1/4, 6 and 8 perforated 12½ or 13. Forged cancellations can also be found on originals and, on occasion, genuine postmarks on reprints.

1

(Currency. 16 schillings = 1 mark)

Three Dies of Embossed Head for Types **1** and **2**:

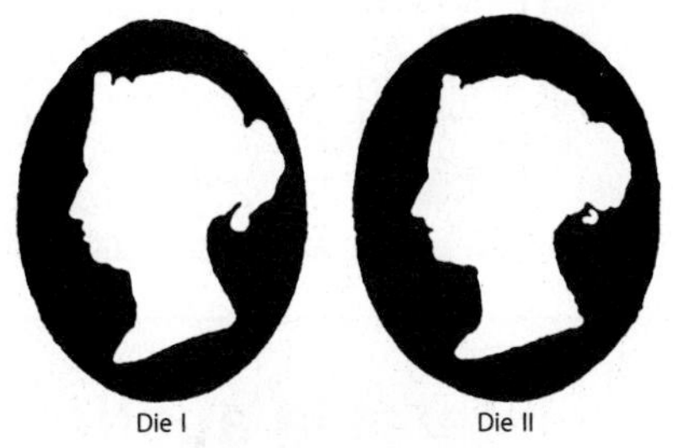

Die I. Blob instead of curl beneath the chignon. Outline of two jewels at top of diadem.
Die II. Curl under chignon. One jewel at top of diadem.
Die III. Shorter curl under chignon. Two jewels at top of diadem.

(Des Wedding. Die eng E. Schilling)

1867 (21 Mar)–**68**. Head Die I embossed in colourless relief. Roul.

1	**1**	½sch. blue-green and rose	£350	£850
		a. Head Die II (7.68)	£800	£1200
2		1sch. rose and blue-green	£180	£200
3		2sch. rose and grass-green	20·00	65·00
4		6sch. green and rose	21·00	£275

For Nos. 1/4 the second colour given is that of the spandrels on the ½ and 1sch., and of the spandrels and central background for the 2 and 6sch.

All four values exist from the Berlin, Leipzig and Hamburg reprintings. The following points are helpful in identifying originals from Berlin reprints; for Leipzig and Hamburg reprints see general note above:

½sch. – Reprints are all in yellowish green and show Head Die II
1sch. – All reprints are Head Die III
2sch. – Berlin reprints are in dull rose with a deeper blue-green
6sch. – Originals show white specks in green. Berlin reprints have a more solid bluish green

1869 (Apr)–**73**. Head embossed in colourless relief. P 13½×14½.

5	**1**	¼sch. rose and green (background) (I) (*quadrillé paper*) (8.73)	35·00	£1600
		a. Error. Green and rose (background) (9.73)	£190	£3250
		b. Deep rose and pale green (background) (11.73)	95·00	£1600
6		½sch. blue-green and rose (II)	£225	£250
		a. Yellow green and rose (7.71)	£160	£225
		b. Quadrillé paper (6.73)	£110	£170
7		¾sch. green and rose (I) (*quadrillé paper*) (12.73)	50·00	£1200
8		1sch. rose and yellow-green (III) (11.71)	£160	£200

		a. Quadrillé paper. *Rose and pale blue-green* (6.73)	£140	£200
9		1½sch. green and rose (I) (*quadrillé paper*) (9.73)	95·00	£275

For Nos. 5/9 the second colour given is that of the spandrels on the ½ and 1sch., of the central background on the ¼ and 1½sch., and of the central background, side labels and side marginal lines of the ¾sch.

No. 5a was a printing of the ¼sch. made in the colour combination of the 1½sch. by mistake.

A further printing of the ½sch. (Head die I) in deep rose-red and yellowish green (background), on non-*quadrillé* paper, was made in December 1874, but not issued (*Price £15, unused*).

All five values exist from the Berlin, Leipzig and Hamburg reprintings. The following points are helpful in identifying originals from Berlin reprints; for Leipzig and Hamburg reprints see general note above:

¼sch. – All Berlin and some Hamburg reprints are Head Die II
½sch. – Berlin reprints on thinner paper with solid colour in the spandrels
¾sch. – Berlin reprints on thinner, non-quadrillé paper
1sch. – Berlin reprints are on thinner paper or show many breaks in the rose line beneath 'SCHILLING' at the top of the design or in the line above it at the foot
1½sch. – All Berlin and some Hamburg reprints are Head Die II

Berlin, Leipzig and Hamburg reprints also exist of the 2 and 6sch., but these values do not come as perforated originals.

(New Currency. 100 pfennig = 1 mark)

2

3

4

5

(Des H. Gätke. Die eng E. Schilling (T **2**), A. Schiffner (others))

1875 (Feb)–**90**. Head Die II on T **2** embossed in colourless relief. P 13½×14½.

10	**2**	1pf. (¼d.) deep green and rose	20·00	£550
11		2pf. (½d.) deep rose and deep green	20·00	£650
12	**3**	3pf. (⅝d.) pale green, red and yellow (6.76)	£250	£1200
		a. Green, red and orange (6.77)	£170	£900
13	**2**	5pf. (¾d.) deep yellow-green and rose	23·00	20·00
		a. Deep green and rose (6.90)	27·00	55·00
14		10pf. (1½d.) deep rose and deep green	42·00	23·00
		a. Scarlet and pale blue-green (5.87)	17·00	24·00
15	**3**	20pf. (2½d.) rose, green and yellow (6.76)	£275	£120
		a. Rose-carmine, deep green and orange (4.80)	£180	55·00
		b. Dull red, pale green and lemon (7.88)	26·00	30·00
		c. Aniline vermilion, bright green and lemon (6.90)	16·00	55·00
16	**2**	25pf. (3d.) deep green and rose	24·00	29·00
17		50pf. (6d.) rose and green	26·00	42·00
18	**4**	1m. (1s.) deep green, scarlet and black (8.79)	£170	£200
		a. Perf 11½	£1400	
		b. Deep green, aniline rose and black (5.89)	£170	£200
19	**5**	5m. (5s.) deep green, aniline rose, black and yellow (8.79)	£225	£950
		a. Perf 11½	£1400	
		ab. Imperf between (horiz pair)	£6000	

For stamps as T **2** the first colour is that of the central background and the second that of the frame. On the 3pf. the first colour is of the frame and the top band of the shield, the second is the centre band and the third the shield border. The 20pf. is similar, but has the centre band in the same colour as the frame and the upper band on the shield in the second colour.

The 1, 2 and 3pf. exist from the Berlin, Leipzig and Hamburg reprintings. There were no such reprints for the other values. The following points are helpful in identifying originals from Berlin reprints; for Leipzig and Hamburg reprints see general note above:

1pf. – Berlin printings show a peculiar shade of pink
2pf. – All reprints are much lighter in shade than the deep rose and deep green of the originals
3pf. – Berlin reprints either show the band around the shield in brownish orange, or have this feature in deep yellow with the other two colours lighter

Heligoland was ceded to Germany on 9 August 1890.

Hong Kong

CROWN COLONY

Hong Kong island was formally ceded to Great Britain on 26 January 1841. The Hong Kong Post Office was established in October 1841, when much of the business previously transacted through the Macao postal agency was transferred to the island. The first cancellation is known from April 1842, but local control of the posts was short-lived as the Hong Kong Office became a branch of the British GPO on 15 April 1843.

The colonial authorities resumed control of the postal service on 1 May 1860 although the previously established postal agencies in the Chinese Treaty Ports remained part of the British GPO system until 1 May 1868.

CROWNED-CIRCLE HANDSTAMPS

CC **1**

CC **1b**

CC **3**

CC1	CC **1b** HONG KONG (R.) (17.10.1843)	*Price on cover*	£800
CC2	CC **1** HONG KONG (R.) (21.8.1844)	*Price on cover*	£1000
CC3	CC **3** HONG KONG (R.) (16.6.1852)	*Price on cover*	£475

We no longer list the Great Britain stamps with obliteration 'B62' within oval. The Government notification dated 29 November 1862 stated that only the Hong Kong stamps to be issued on 8 December would be available for postage and the stamps formerly listed were all issued in Great Britain later than the date of the notice.

(Currency. 100 cents = 1 Hong Kong dollar)

PRICES FOR STAMPS ON COVER TO 1945

Nos. 1/7	*from* × 6
Nos. 8/12	*from* × 15
No. 13	*from* × 6
Nos. 14/17	*from* × 15
No. 18	*from* × 50
No. 19	*from* × 15
Nos. 20/27	*from* × 10
Nos. 28/36	*from* × 8
Nos. 37/39	*from* × 10
Nos. 40/44	*from* × 8
Nos. 45/50	*from* × 10
No. 51	*from* × 20
No. 52	*from* × 10
Nos. 53/54	—
No. 55	*from* × 10
Nos. 56/61	*from* × 10
Nos. 62/99	*from* × 4
Nos. 100/132	*from* × 3
Nos. 133/136	*from* × 2
Nos. 137/139	*from* × 4
Nos. 140/168	*from* × 2
Nos. D1/D12	*from* × 10
Nos. P1/P3	*from* × 2
Nos. F1/F11	*from* × 20
No. F12	*from* × 4

PRINTERS. All definitive issues up to 1962 were typographed by De La Rue and Co., except for some printings between 1941 and 1945.

1

2

3

1862 (8 Dec)–**63**. No wmk. P 14.

1	**1**	2c. brown	£550	£120
		a. Deep brown (1863)	£750	£170
2		8c. yellow-buff	£750	85·00
3		12c. pale greenish blue	£650	60·00
4	**3**	18c. lilac	£650	55·00
5		24c. green	£1200	£120
6		48c. rose	£2750	£350
7		96c. brownish grey	£3750	£450

'GKON' of 'HONGKONG' damaged at foot (Pl 1 lower right pane R. 9/5)

1863 (Aug)–**71**. Wmk Crown CC. P 14.

8	**1**	2c. deep brown (11.64)	£350	35·00
		a. Brown	£130	8·00
		b. Pale yellowish brown	£160	13·00
		w. Wmk inverted	£750	£150
		x. Wmk reversed	—	£325
		y. Wmk inverted and reversed	†	£900
9	**2**	4c. grey	£160	22·00
		ay. Wmk inverted and reversed	†	£950
		b. Slate	£120	9·00
		bw. Wmk inverted	£600	£140
		c. Deep slate	£160	16·00
		d. Greenish grey	£350	50·00
		dw. Wmk inverted	†	£450
		e. Bluish slate	£475	26·00
		ew. Wmk inverted	£1400	£225
		f. Perf 12½. *Slate* (8.70)	£12000	£275
		fw. Wmk inverted	—	£900
10		6c. lilac	£450	20·00
		a. Mauve	£650	21·00
		w. Wmk inverted	£1500	£150
		x. Wmk reversed	£1800	£225
11	**1**	8c. pale dull orange (10.64)	£600	13·00
		a. Brownish orange	£500	16·00
		b. Bright orange	£475	16·00
		w. Wmk inverted	£1500	£180
		x. Wmk reversed	£1600	£325
12		12c. pale greenish blue (4.65)	£1100	40·00
		a. Pale blue	32·00	9·00
		b. Deep blue	£300	14·00
		w. Wmk inverted	—	£140
		x. Wmk reversed	—	£180
13	**3**	18c. lilac (1866)	£7000	£300
		w. Wmk inverted	£11000	£1100
		x. Wmk reversed	£18000	£1700
		y. Wmk inverted and reversed	†	£2750
14		24c. green (10.64)	£650	12·00
		a. Pale green	£800	18·00
		b. Deep green	£1300	35·00
		w. Wmk inverted	£2750	£180
		x. Wmk reversed	£2500	£275
15	**2**	30c. vermilion	£1000	16·00
		a. Orange-vermilion	£900	17·00
		b. 'GKON' of 'HONGKONG' damaged at foot	—	£1900
		w. Wmk inverted	£3000	£190
		x. Wmk reversed	—	£300
16		30c. mauve (14.8.71)	£275	5·50
		a. 'GKON' of 'HONGKONG' damaged at foot	—	£600
		w. Wmk inverted	£1400	£160
		x. Wmk reversed	—	£300
17		48c. pale rose (1.65)	£1500	70·00
		a. Rose-carmine	£950	35·00
		w. Wmk inverted	£2500	£200
		x. Wmk reversed	—	£350
18		96c. olive-bistre (1.65)	£80000	£750
		w. Wmk inverted	†	£5500
19		96c. brownish grey (1865)	£1500	65·00
		a. Brownish black	£2000	60·00
		w. Wmk inverted	£2000	£200
		y. Wmk inverted and reversed	†	£1900

There is a wide range of shades in this issue, of which we can only indicate the main groups.

No. 12 is the same shade as No. 3 without wmk, the impression having a waxy appearance.

A single used example of the 48c. in a bright claret shade is known. No other stamps in this shade, either mint or used, have been discovered.

See also Nos. 22 and 28/31.

16 cents.	28 cents.	5 cents.	10 cents.
(4)	(5)	(6)	(7)

No. 20b

1876 (Aug)–**77**. Nos. 13 and 16 surch with Types **4** or **5** by Noronha and Sons, Hong Kong.

20	**3**	16c. on 18c. lilac (1.4.77)	£2250	£150
		a. Space between 'n' and 't'	£8000	£900
		b. Space between 's' and stop	£8000	£900
		w. Wmk inverted	£6000	£1000
21	**2**	28c. on 30c. mauve	£1600	50·00
		a. 'GKON' of 'HONGKONG' damaged at foot	—	£1100

1877 (Aug). New value. Wmk Crown CC. P 14.

22	**3**	16c. yellow	£2000	65·00
		w. Wmk inverted	£4250	£500

1880 (1 Mar–Sept). Surch with Types **6** or **7** by Noronha and Sons.

23	**1**	5c. on 8c. bright orange (No. 11*b*) (9.80)	£1100	£110
		a. Surch inverted	†	£21000
		b. Surch double	†	£21000
24	**3**	5c. on 18c. lilac (No. 13)	£950	65·00
		x. Wmk reversed	£2500	£1100
		y. Wmk inverted and reversed	†	£3500

25	1	10c. on 12c. pale blue (No. 12*a*)	£1000	55·00
		a. Blue	£1700	£110
		b. Surch double	†	£50000
26	3	10c. on 16c. yellow (No. 22) (5.80)	£4250	£150
		a. Surch inverted	—	£95000
		b. Surch double	†	£75000
		w. Wmk inverted	†	£2000
27		10c. on 24c. green (No. 14) (6.80)	£1500	£100
		w. Wmk inverted	†	£700

Three examples of No. 26b are known, all used in Shanghai.

1880 (Mar–Dec). Colours changed and new values. Wmk Crown CC. P 14.

28	1	2c. dull rose	£275	40·00
		a. Rose	£300	40·00
		w. Wmk inverted	†	£500
29	2	5c. blue (12.80)	£800	55·00
		w. Wmk inverted	—	£500
30		10c. mauve (11.80)	£900	20·00
		w. Wmk inverted	—	£500
31	3	48c. brown	£1500	£110

1882 (May)–**96**. Wmk Crown CA. P 14.

32	1	2c. rose-lake (7.82)	£300	32·00
		a. Rose-pink	£225	32·00
		ab. Perf 12	£75000	£75000
		w. Wmk inverted	—	£275
		x. Wmk reversed	†	£700
33		2c. carmine (1884)	55·00	3·00
		a. Aniline carmine	55·00	3·00
		w. Wmk inverted	—	£180
34	2	4c. slate-grey (1.4.96)	38·00	3·00
		w. Wmk inverted	—	£275
35		5c. pale blue	50·00	1·25
		a. Blue	50·00	1·25
		aw. Wmk inverted	£500	£120
		x. Wmk reversed	—	£475
36		10c. dull mauve (8.82)	£1000	23·00
		w. Wmk inverted	—	£475
37		10c. deep blue-green (1884)	£1800	38·00
		a. Green (2.84)	£180	2·25
		aw. Wmk inverted	†	£750
38		10c. purple/*red* (1.1.91)	45·00	1·75
		w. Wmk inverted	£750	£120
		x. Wmk reversed	£1300	£225
		y. Wmk inverted and reversed		
39		30c. yellowish green (1.1.91)	£140	45·00
		a. Grey-green	£110	27·00
38s, 39*a*s Optd 'SPECIMEN' *Set of 2*			£400	

Examples of No. 39 should not be confused with washed or faded stamps from the grey-green shade which tend to turn to a very yellow-green when dampened.

For other stamps with this watermark, but in colours changed to the UPU scheme, see Nos. 56/61.

20 CENTS **(8)** 50 CENTS **(9)** 1 DOLLAR **(10)**

1885 (Sept). As Nos. 15, 19 and 31, but wmk Crown CA, surch with Types **8** to **10** by De La Rue.

40	2	20c. on 30c. orange-red	£200	8·00
		a. Surch double		
		w. Wmk inverted	£1600	£550
41	3	50c. on 48c. yellowish brown	£400	50·00
		w. Wmk inverted	£1600	£550
42		$1 on 96c. grey-olive	£750	85·00
40s/42s Optd 'SPECIMEN' *Set of 3*			£1300	

For the $1 on 96c. black and grey-black see Nos. 53/53*a*.

7 cents. **(11)** 14 cents. **(12)**

弍 **(13)** (20c.) 五十 **(14)** (50c.) 壹員 **(15)** ($1)

1891 (1 Jan–Mar).

(a) Nos. 16 and 37 surch with Types **11** *or* **12** *by Noronha and Sons, Hong Kong*

43	2	7c. on 10c. green	95·00	10·00
		a. Antique 't' in 'cents' (R. 1/1)	£700	£160
		b. Surch double	£7000	£1300
44		14c. on 30c. mauve (2.91)	£200	80·00
		a. Antique 't' in 'cents' (R. 1/1)	£2750	£950
		b. 'GKON' of 'HONGKONG' damaged at foot	£6000	£2000

(b) As Nos. 40/42 (surch with Types **8** *to* **10** *by De La Rue), but colours changed*

45	2	20c. on 30c. yellowish green (No. 39)	£170	£160
		a. Grey-green (No. 39*a*)	£110	£150
46	3	50c. on 48c. dull purple	£300	£325
47		$1 on 96c. purple/*red*	£800	£350
45*a*s/47s Optd 'SPECIMEN' *Set of 3*			£850	

(c) Nos. 45/47 with further surch, Types **13**/**15**, *in Chinese characters, handstamped locally (Mar)*

48	2	20c. on 30c. yellowish green	55·00	15·00
		a. Grey-green	42·00	14·00
		b. Surch double	£25000	£25000
49	3	50c. on 48c. dull purple	80·00	5·50
50		$1 on 96c. purple/*red*	£450	22·00
		w. Wmk inverted	£2000	

The true antique 't' variety (Nos. 43a and 44a) should not be confused with a small 't' showing a short foot. In the antique 't' the crossbar is accurately bisected by the vertical stroke, which is thicker at the top. The lower curve bends towards the right and does not turn upwards to the same extent as on the normal.

The handstamped surcharges on Nos. 48/50 were applied over the original Chinese face values. The single character for '2' was intended to convert '30c.' to '20c.'. There were six slightly different versions of the '2' handstamp and three for the '50c.'.

The errors of the Chinese surcharges previously listed on the above issue and also on Nos. 52 and 55 are now omitted as being outside the scope of the catalogue. While some without doubt possess philatelic merit, it is impossible to distinguish between the genuine errors and the clandestine copies made to order with the original chops. No. 55c is retained as this represents a distinctly different chop which was used for the last part of the printing.

1841 Hong Kong JUBILEE 1891 **(16)** 10 CENTS **(17)** 拾 **(18)** 拾 **(19)**

1891 (22 Jan). 50th Anniversary of Colony. Optd with T **16** by Noronha and Sons, Hong Kong.

51	1	2c. carmine (No. 33)	£475	£130
		a. Short 'J' in 'JUBILEE' (R. 1/6)	£800	£200
		b. Short 'U' in 'JUBILEE' (R. 1/1)	£800	£200
		c. Broken '1' in '1891' (R. 2/1)	£950	£300
		d. Tall narrow 'K' in 'Kong' (R. 1/3)	£1300	£475
		e. Opt double	£18000	£14000
		f. Space between 'O' and 'N' of 'Hong' (R. 1/5)	£1700	£750

Most of the supply of No. 51, which was only on sale for three days, was overprinted from a setting of 12 (6×2) applied five times to complete each pane. There were six printings from this setting, but a second setting, possibly of 30 or 60, was used for the seventh. Positions quoted are from the setting of 12. Most varieties only occur in some printings and many less marked overprint flaws also exist.

The prices quoted for No. 51e are for examples on which the two impressions are distinctly separated. Examples on which the two impressions are almost coincidental are worth considerably less.

1898 (1 Apr). Wmk Crown CA. P 14.

(a) Surch with T **10** *by D.L.R. and handstamped Chinese characters as T* **15**

52	3	$1 on 96c. black	£250	27·00
		a. Grey-black	£200	27·00

(b) Surch with T **10** *only*

53	3	$1 on 96c. black	£3250	£4000
		a. Grey-black	£2750	£3750
		as. Optd 'SPECIMEN'	£600	

Nos. 52/52*a* and 53/53*a* show considerable variation in shades, with some paler shades verging on grey. Nos. 53/53*a* should not be confused with the 1885 $1 on 96c. grey-olive (No. 42).

1898 (1 Apr).

(a) Surch with T **17** *by Noronha and Sons, Hong Kong*

54	2	10c. on 30c. grey-green (No. 39*a*)	£600	£1200
		a. Figures '10' widely spaced (1½ mm)	£7500	£10000
		b. Surch double		

(b) As No. 54, but with handstamped Chinese characters, T **18**, *in addition*

55	2	10c. on 30c. grey-green (No. 39*a*)	75·00	90·00
		a. Yellowish green	85·00	£110
		b. Figures '10' widely spaced (1½ mm)	£700	£900
		c. Chinese character large (Type **19**)	£900	£1000
		d. Surch Type **17** double	£12000	
		s. Handstamped 'SPECIMEN'	£140	

T **17** was applied in a horizontal setting of 12, Nos. 54a and 55b appearing on position 12 for the early printings only. The true 1½ mm wide spacing is not known on No. 55c. Examples showing spacing of 1.2-1.3 mm are worth a premium over the normal prices.

1900 (Aug)–**01**. Wmk Crown CA. P 14.

56	1	2c. dull green	28·00	85
		w. Wmk inverted	£325	£140
57	2	4c. carmine (1901)	21·00	85
		w. Wmk inverted	†	—
58		5c. yellow	30·00	10·00
		w. Wmk inverted	—	£700
59		10c. ultramarine	50·00	2·50
		w. Wmk inverted	—	£130
60	1	12c. blue (1901)	48·00	70·00
61	2	30c. brown (1901)	60·00	28·00
56/61 *Set of 6*			£200	£100
56s/59s, 61s Optd 'SPECIMEN' *Set of 5*			£600	

20

21

22

23

1903 (Jan–July). Wmk Crown CA. P 14.

62	20	1c. dull purple and brown	3·00	50
63		2c. dull green (7.03)	24·00	3·00
		w. Wmk inverted	†	£1300
		y. Wmk inverted and reversed	†	£1500
64	21	4c. purple/*red* (7.03)	30·00	40
65		5c. dull green and brown-orange (7.03)	25·00	11·00
66		8c. slate and violet (12.2.03)	18·00	2·25
67	20	10c. purple and blue/*blue* (7.03)	70·00	1·50
68	23	12c. green and purple/*yellow* (12.2.03)	16·00	7·00
69		20c. slate and chestnut (6.03)	65·00	6·00
70	22	30c. dull green and black (21.5.03)	65·00	27·00
71	23	50c. dull green and magenta (6.03)	65·00	70·00
72	20	$1 purple and sage-green (6.03)	£130	30·00
73	23	$2 slate and scarlet (7.03)	£375	£375
74	22	$3 slate and dull blue (7.03)	£450	£425
75	23	$5 purple and blue-green (6.03)	£650	£600
76	22	$10 slate and orange/*blue* (7.03)	£1400	£475
		w. Wmk inverted	†	—
62/76 *Set of 15*			£3000	£1800
62s/76s Optd 'SPECIMEN' *Set of 15*			£2000	

No. 63w is known used at Shanghai.

1904 (4 Oct)–**06**. Wmk Mult Crown CA. Chalk-surfaced paper (8, 12c., $3, $5) or ordinary paper (others). P 14.

77	20	2c. dull green	29·00	2·75
		a. Chalk-surfaced paper (1906)	30·00	5·50
		aw. Wmk inverted	†	£1100
78	21	4c. purple/*red*	42·00	40
		a. Chalk-surfaced paper (1906)	27·00	2·00
79		5c. dull green and brown-orange	75·00	22·00
		a. Chalk-surfaced paper (1906)	26·00	7·00
		aw. Wmk inverted		
80		8c. slate and violet (1906)	22·00	2·00
81	20	10c. purple and blue/*blue* (3.05)	40·00	1·50
82	23	12c. green and purple/*yellow* (1906)	26·00	9·00
83		20c. slate and chestnut	70·00	4·25
		a. Chalk-surfaced paper (1906)	65·00	3·75
		aw. Wmk inverted	†	£1100
84	22	30c. dull green and black	70·00	40·00
		a. Chalk-surfaced paper (1906)	70·00	24·00
85	23	50c. green and magenta	£110	18·00
		a. Chalk-surfaced paper (1906)	95·00	23·00
86	20	$1 purple and sage-green	£200	50·00
		a. Chalk-surfaced paper (1906)	£180	50·00
87	23	$2 slate and scarlet	£450	£170
		a. Chalk-surfaced paper (1905)	£350	£140
88	22	$3 slate and dull blue (1905)	£375	£350
89	23	$5 purple and blue-green (1905)	£550	£475
90	22	$10 slate and orange/*blue* (5.05)	£1900	£1500
		aw. Wmk inverted	†	—
		b. Chalk-surfaced paper (1906)	£2000	£1200
77/90 *Set of 14*			£3250	£2000

No. 77aw is known used at Shanghai in October 1908 and 83aw at Hoihow in March 1908.

1907–11. Colours changed and new value. Wmk Mult Crown CA. Chalk-surfaced paper (6c. and 20c. to $2). P 14.

91	20	1c. brown (9.10)	11·00	1·00
		x. Wmk reversed	†	£2000
92		2c. deep green	48·00	1·75
		a. Green	48·00	1·50
		w. Wmk inverted	£1500	£900
93	21	4c. carmine-red	21·00	40
		x. Wmk reversed	†	£2000
94	22	6c. orange-vermilion and purple (10.07)	45·00	9·00
95	20	10c. bright ultramarine	65·00	40
96	23	20c. purple and sage-green (3.11)	50·00	50·00
97	22	30c. purple and orange-yellow (3.11)	65·00	48·00
98	23	50c. black/*green* (3.11)	50·00	20·00
99		$2 carmine-red and black (1910)	£400	£425
91/99 *Set of 9*			£650	£475
91s, 93s/99s Optd 'SPECIMEN' *Set of 8*			£1200	

No. 91x is known used at Canton in December 1912 and January 1913, No. 92w at Shanghai in 1908 and 93x at Swatow in February 1911.

24

25

26

27

28

(A)

(B)

In Type A of the 25c. the upper Chinese character in the left-hand label has a short vertical stroke crossing it at the foot. In Type B this stroke is absent.

Crown broken at right (R. 9/2)

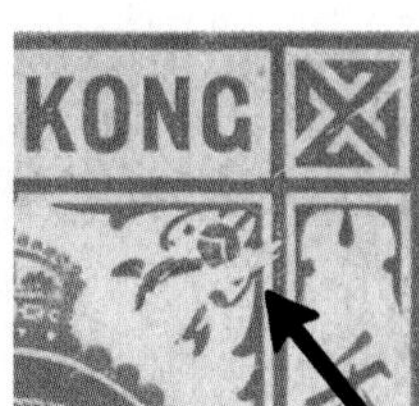

Broken flower at top right (Upper left pane R. 1/3)

1912 (9 Nov)–**21**. Wmk Mult Crown CA. Chalk-surfaced paper (12c. to $10). P 14.

100	24	1c. brown	7·50	55
		a. Black-brown	9·50	3·00
		b. Crown broken at right	£250	£180
101		2c. deep green	19·00	30
		a. Green	23·00	30
		w. Wmk inverted	†	£1500
		y. Wmk inverted and reversed	†	—

102	25	4c. carmine-red	13·00	30
		a. Scarlet (1914)	55·00	3·00
		aw. Wmk inverted		
		y. Wmk inverted and reversed	†	£2000
103	26	6c. yellow-orange	8·00	3·00
		a. Brown-orange	8·00	4·00
		w. Wmk inverted	£1200	£1100
104	25	8c. grey	35·00	11·00
		a. Slate (1914)	50·00	7·50
105	24	10c. ultramarine	55·00	30
		a. Deep bright ultramarine	32·00	30
106	27	12c. purple/*yellow*	15·00	16·00
		a. White back (1914)	17·00	20·00
		as. Optd 'SPECIMEN'	£160	
107		20c. purple and sage-green	19·00	1·75
108	28	25c. purple and magenta (Type A) (1.14)	48·00	45·00
109		25c. purple and magenta (Type B) (8.19)	£300	90·00
		a. Broken flower	£5000	
110	26	30c. purple and orange-yellow	65·00	14·00
		a. Purple and orange	42·00	9·00
		w. Wmk inverted		
111	27	50c. black/*blue-green*	29·00	3·50
		a. White back (5.14)	38·00	4·25
		as. Optd 'SPECIMEN'	£180	
		b. On blue-green, olive back (1917)	£1300	30·00
		c. On emerald surface (9.19)	45·00	8·00
		d. On emerald back (7.12.21)	38·00	11·00
		ds. Optd 'SPECIMEN'	£200	
		w. Wmk inverted	£4000	
		y. Wmk inverted and reversed	†	£3750
112	24	$1 purple and blue/*blue*	75·00	6·50
		w. Wmk inverted	£325	£200
113	27	$2 carmine-red and grey-black	£200	75·00
114	26	$3 green and purple	£300	£130
115	27	$5 green and red/*green*	£700	£425
		a. White back (5.14)	£600	£400
		as. Optd 'SPECIMEN'	£450	
		b. On blue-green, olive back (1917)	£1200	£400
		bs. Optd 'SPECIMEN'	£650	
		bw. Wmk inverted	£5500	
116	26	$10 purple and black/*red*	£600	£110
100/116 *Set of 17*			£2000	£800
100s/116s Optd 'SPECIMEN' *Set of 17*			£2250	

No. 100b occurred in 1916 on R. 9/2 of the lower right pane before being retouched.

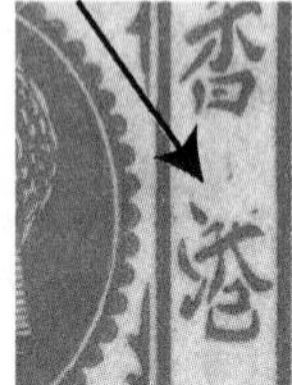

Top of lower Chinese characters at right broken off (R. 9/4, lower left pane).

1921 (Jan)–**37**. Wmk Mult Script CA. Chalk-surfaced paper (12c. to $5). P 14.

117	24	1c. brown	3·25	40
118		2c. blue-green	7·00	1·00
		a. Yellow-green (1932)	32·00	3·00
		bw. Wmk inverted	£110	
118*c*		2c. grey (14.4.37)	25·00	13·00
119	25	3c. grey (8.10.31)	15·00	2·00
120		4c. carmine-rose	8·00	70
		a. Carmine-red (1932)	16·00	30
		b. Top of lower Chinese characters at right broken off	£100	80·00
121		5c. violet (16.10.31)	24·00	30
122		8c. grey	26·00	38·00
123		8c. orange (7.12.21)	8·00	2·75
		w. Wmk inverted	£1400	£1000
124	24	10c. bright ultramarine	14·00	30
		aw. Wmk inverted	£475	
		b. 'A' of 'CA' missing from wmk	†	—
124*c*	27	12c. purple/*yellow* (3.4.33)	26·00	4·50
125		20c. purple and sage-green (7.12.21)	13·00	30
126	28	25c. purple and magenta (B) (7.12.21)	9·50	3·00
		a. Broken flower	50·00	70·00
		w. Wmk inverted	†	£900
127	26	30c. purple and chrome-yellow (7.12.21)	14·00	2·75
		a. Purple and orange-yellow	45·00	8·50
		w. Wmk inverted	£475	
128	27	50c. black/*emerald* (1924)	35·00	30
129	24	$1 purple and blue/*blue* (7.12.21)	50·00	1·00
130	27	$2 carmine-red and grey-black (7.12.21)	£140	10·00
131	26	$3 green and dull purple (1926)	£200	70·00
132	27	$5 green and red/*emerald* (1925)	£200	80·00
117/132 *Set of 18*			£1000	£200
117s/132s Optd or Perf (2c. grey, 3c., 5c., 12c.) 'SPECIMEN' *Set of 18*			£2000	

No. 120b occurs on R. 9/4 of the lower left pane.

1935 (6 May). Silver Jubilee. As Nos. 91/94 of Antigua, but ptd by B.W. P 11×12.

133	3c. ultramarine and grey-black	4·00	4·50
	c. Lightning conductor	£375	£275
	e. Double flagstaff	£1100	
134	5c. green and indigo	8·50	3·50
	a. Extra flagstaff	£325	£275
	b. Short extra flagstaff	£425	£425
	c. Lightning conductor	£400	£275
	d. Flagstaff on right-hand turret	£650	£400
	e. Double flagstaff	£750	£600
135	10c. brown and deep blue	18·00	1·75
136	20c. slate and purple	32·00	11·00
	b. Short extra flagstaff	£900	£400
	d. Flagstaff on right-hand turret	£950	£475
	e. Double flagstaff	£1100	£500
133/136 *Set of 4*		55·00	18·00
133s/136s Perf 'SPECIMEN' *Set of 4*		£500	

For illustrations of plate varieties see Omnibus section following Zanzibar.

1937 (12 May). Coronation. As Nos. 95/97 of Antigua. P 11×11½.

137	4c. green	4·50	7·50
138	15c. carmine	8·00	3·25
139	25c. blue	10·00	6·00
137/139 *Set of 3*		20·00	15·00
137s/139s Perf 'SPECIMEN' *Set of 3*		£350	

29 King George VI

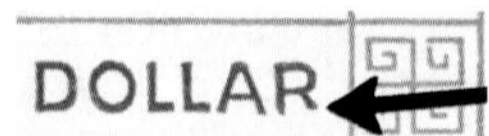

Short right leg to 'R' (Right pane R. 7/3, left pane R. 3/1)

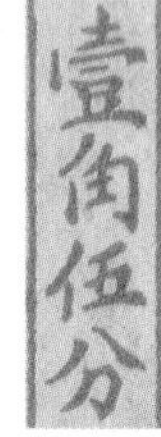

Normal

Broken character (left pane R. 6/6, later repaired)

Stop after 'CENTS' (Left pane R. 4/2)

1938–52. Wmk Mult Script CA. Chalk-surfaced paper (80c., $1 (No. 155), $2 (No. 157), $5 (No. 159), $10 (No. 161)). P 14.

140	29	1c. brown (24.5.38)	2·75	6·50
		aa. Doubly printed	£10000	
		a. Pale brown (4.2.52)	4·50	12·00
141		2c. grey (5.4.38)	2·00	50
		a. Perf 14½×14 (28.9.45)	1·75	7·00
142		4c. orange (5.4.38)	12·00	6·50
		a. Perf 14½×14 (28.9.45)	5·00	3·25
143		5c. green (24.5.38)	1·25	20
		a. Perf 14½×14 (28.9.45)	4·00	5·00
144		8c. red-brown (1.11.41)	1·75	3·50
		a. Imperf (pair)	£50000	
		b. Stop after 'CENTS'	£350	£225
145		10c. bright violet (13.4.38)	50·00	1·50
		a. Perf 14½×14. *Dull violet* (28.9.45)	9·50	20
		b. Dull reddish violet (8.4.46)	9·50	1·75
		c. Reddish lilac (9.4.47)	25·00	20
146		15c. scarlet (13.4.38)	2·00	30
		a. Broken character	£130	50·00
147		20c. black (1.2.46)	1·25	30
148		20c. scarlet-vermilion (1.4.48)	14·00	40
		a. Rose-red (25.4.51)	28·00	5·50
149		25c. bright blue (5.4.38)	29·00	4·75
150		25c. pale yellow-olive (24.9.46)	8·50	4·75
151		30c. yellow-olive (13.4.38)	£150	3·75
		a. Perf 14½×14. *Yellowish olive* (28.9.45)	28·00	13·00
152		30c. blue (27.12.46)	7·00	20
153		50c. purple (13.4.38)	55·00	70
		a. Perf 14½×14. *Deep magenta* (28.9.45)	30·00	1·25
		ab. Printed both sides, inverted on reverse	£1000	
		b. Reddish purple (9.4.46)	17·00	3·50
		c. Chalk-surfaced paper. *Bright purple* (9.4.47)	12·00	20
154		80c. carmine (2.2.48)	6·50	1·00
155		$1 dull lilac and blue (*chalk-surfaced paper*) (27.4.38)	9·50	4·25
		a. Short right leg to 'R'	£180	£190
		b. Ordinary paper. *Pale reddish lilac and blue* (28.9.45)	23·00	30·00
		ba. Short right leg to 'R'	£350	£400
156		$1 red-orange and green (8.4.46)	27·00	30
		a. Short right leg to 'R'	£275	65·00
		b. Chalk-surfaced paper (21.6.48)	55·00	1·25
		ba. Short right leg to 'R'	£450	90·00
		c. Chalk-surfaced paper. *Yellow-orange and green* (6.11.52)	90·00	15·00
		ca. Short right leg to 'R'	£750	£275
157		$2 red-orange and green (24.5.38)	80·00	42·00
158		$2 reddish violet and scarlet (8.4.46)	50·00	11·00
		a. Chalk-surfaced paper (9.4.47)	55·00	1·00
159		$5 dull lilac and scarlet (2.6.38)	70·00	50·00
160		$5 green and violet (8.4.46)	80·00	25·00
		a. Yellowish green and violet (8.4.46)	£600	42·00
		ab. Chalk-surfaced paper (9.4.47)	£120	5·00
161		$10 green and violet (2.6.38)	£700	£140
162		$10 pale bright lilac and blue (8.4.46)	£140	60·00
		a. Deep bright lilac and blue (8.4.46)	£300	75·00
		b. Chalk-surfaced paper. *Reddish violet and blue* (9.4.47)	£200	18·00
140/162 *Set of 23*			£1100	£250
140s/162s Perf 'SPECIMEN' *Set of 23*			£2750	

Following bomb damage to the De La Rue works on the night of 29 December 1940 various emergency arrangements were made to complete current requisitions for Hong Kong stamps:

Nos. 141a, 143a, 145*a*, 151*a* and 153*a* (all printings perforated 14½×14 except the 4c.) were printed and perforated by Bradbury Wilkinson & Co. Ltd. using De La Rue plates. These stamps are on rough-surfaced paper.

No. 142a was probably printed by Harrison & Sons, the major part of the printing being in undivided sheets of 120 (12×10) instead of the normal two panes of 60 (6×10).

Printings of the 1c. and dollar values and probably the 8c. were made by Williams, Lea & Co. using De La Rue plates.

With the exception of the 8c. it is believed that none of these printings were issued in Hong Kong before its occupation by the Japanese on 25 December 1941, although examples could be obtained in London from late 1941. The issue dates quoted are those on which the stamps were eventually released in Hong Kong following liberation in 1945.

Nos. 160/160*a* and 162/162*a* were separate printings released in Hong Kong on the same day.

No. 144a. One imperforate sheet was found and most of the stamps were sold singly to the public at a branch PO and used for postage.

30 Street Scene

31 *Empress of Japan* (liner) and Junk

32 The University

33 The Harbour

34 The Hong Kong Bank

35 *Falcon* (clipper) and Short S.23 Empire C class flying boat

(Des E. A. von Kobza Nagy and W. E. Jones. Recess B.W.)

1941 (26 Feb). Centenary of British Occupation. T **30/35**. Wmk Mult Script CA (sideways on horiz designs). P 13½×13 (2c. and 25c.) or 13×13½ (others).

163	2c. orange and chocolate	8·00	2·50
164	4c. bright purple and carmine	9·50	5·00
165	5c. black and green	3·50	50
166	15c. black and scarlet	9·50	3·00
167	25c. chocolate and blue	19·00	9·00
168	$1 blue and orange	50·00	13·00
163/168 *Set of 6*		90·00	30·00
163s/168s Perf 'SPECIMEN' *Set of 6*		£550	

Hong Kong was under Japanese occupation from 25 December 1941 until 30 August 1945. The Japanese post offices in the colony were closed from 31 August and mail was carried free, marked with cachets reading 'HONG KONG/1945/POSTAGE PAID'. Military administration lasted until 1 May 1946. Hong Kong stamps were re-introduced on 28 September 1945.

36 King George VI and Phoenix

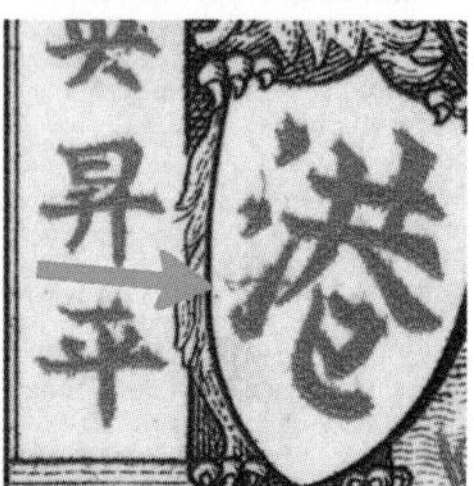

Extra stroke (R. 1/2)

(Des E. I. Wynne-Jones and W. E. Jones. Recess D.L.R.)

1946 (29 Aug). Victory. Wmk Mult Script CA. P 13.

169	**36**	30c. blue and red (*shades*)	2·75	2·25
		a. Extra stroke	£120	90·00
170		$1 brown and red	3·25	75
		a. Extra stroke	£130	70·00
169s/170s Perf 'SPECIMEN' *Set of 2*			£275	

Spur on 'N' of 'KONG' (R. 2/9)

1948 (22 Dec). Royal Silver Wedding. As Nos. 112/113 of Antigua.

171	10c. violet	3·75	1·50
	a. Spur on 'N'	£100	90·00
172	$10 carmine	£275	£130

Crack in rock (R. 12/5)

1949 (10 Oct). 75th Anniversary of Universal Postal Union. As Nos. 114/117 of Antigua.

173	10c. violet	4·00	1·00
174	20c. carmine-red	13·00	6·00
175	30c. deep blue	10·00	6·00
176	80c. bright reddish purple	30·00	4·00
	a. Crack in rock	£400	£180
173/176 *Set of 4*		50·00	15·00

1953 (2 June). Coronation. As No. 120 of Antigua.

177	10c. black and slate-lilac	2·50	30

37a Queen Elizabeth II

$2 Normal

$2 Short character

$2 The top stroke in the right-hand upper character is shortened (Pl. 1-1, R. 6/4)

Normal

$1.30 Short 'THI' (Pl. 1-1, R. 10/10)

1954 (5 Jan)–**62**. Ordinary paper (5c. to 15c.) or chalk-surfaced paper (others). Wmk Mult Script CA. P 14.

178	**37a**	5c. orange	1·75	20
		a. Imperf (pair)	£2250	
179		10c. lilac	2·50	10
		aw. Wmk inverted	£400	
		b. Reddish violet (25.1.61)	13·00	10
180		15c. green	3·50	3·50
		a. Pale green (6.12.55)	4·50	2·75
181		20c. brown	5·00	30
182		25c. scarlet	5·00	5·50
		a. Rose-red (26.6.58)	5·00	4·75
183		30c. grey	4·00	20
		a. Pale grey (26.2.58)	8·00	75
184		40c. bright blue	5·50	50
		a. Dull blue (10.1.61)	16·00	2·25
185		50c. reddish purple	5·50	20
186		65c. grey (20.6.60)	22·00	19·00
187		$1 orange and green	8·50	20
		a. Short right leg to 'R'	£150	23·00
188		$1.30 blue and red (20.6.60)	25·00	3·00
		a. Short 'THI'	£200	50·00
		b. Bright blue and red (23.1.62)	55·00	6·00
		ba. Short 'THI'	£400	90·00
189		$2 reddish violet and scarlet	12·00	1·00
		a. Short character	£170	50·00
		b. Light reddish violet and scarlet (26.2.58)	17·00	1·00
		ba. Short character	£225	50·00
190		$5 green and purple	80·00	4·25
		a. Yellowish green and purple (7.3.61)	£120	9·50
191		$10 reddish violet and bright blue	60·00	13·00
		a. Light reddish violet and bright blue (26.2.58)	85·00	14·00
178/191 *Set of 14*			£200	42·00

No. 178a exists from two sheets, each of which had 90 stamps imperforate and ten perforated on three sides only.

The 10c. exists in coils constructed from normal sheets.

The duty plates for the King George VI issue were reformatted to reduce the sheet size from 120 (two panes of 60) to 100. In doing so, one of the 'short 'R" clichés was discarded. The other occurs on R. 10/9 of No. 187.

On Nos. 188a/188ba the duty plate appears bolder than in other positions.

38 University Arms

39 Statue of Queen Victoria

(Des and photo Harrison)

1961 (11 Sept). Golden Jubilee of Hong Kong University. W w **12**. P 11½×12.

192	**38**	$1 multicoloured	3·25	2·00
		a. Gold ptg omitted	£3250	£3250

Normal

10c White spot over character in lower right corner (Pl. 1A-1A, R. 1/3)

(Des Cheung Yat-man. Photo Harrison)

1962 (4 May). Stamp Centenary. W w **12**. P 14½.

193	**39**	10c. black and magenta	45	10
		a. Spot on character	9·50	
194		20c. black and light blue	2·00	2·25
195		50c. black and bistre	2·75	40
193/195 *Set of 3*			4·75	2·50

40 Queen Elizabeth II (after Annigoni)

41 Queen Elizabeth II (after Annigoni)

Normal

Broken '5' 5c.

The horizontal bar of the '5' is missing (Pl. 1A, R. 3/1 and Pl. 1B, R. 2/2)

(Photo Harrison)

1962 (4 Oct)–**73**. Chalk-surfaced paper. W w **12** (upright). P 15×14 (5c. to $1) or 14×14½ (others).

196	**40**	5c. red-orange	75	60
		a. Broken '5'	21·00	
197		10c. bright reddish violet	1·50	10
		a. Reddish violet (19.11.71)	9·50	2·50
		ab. Glazed paper (14.4.72)	9·00	3·50
198		15c. emerald	3·25	4·25
199		20c. red-brown	2·50	2·00
		a. Brown (13.12.71)	7·00	7·00
		ab. Glazed paper (27.9.72)	14·00	18·00
200		25c. cerise	3·75	5·00
201		30c. deep grey-blue	2·50	10
		a. Chalky blue (19.11.71)	7·00	5·50
		ab. Glazed paper (27.9.72)	16·00	9·00
202		40c. deep bluish green	5·00	70
203		50c. scarlet	1·75	30
		a. Vermilion (13.12.71)	23·00	3·25
		ab. Glazed paper (27.9.72)	10·00	4·00
204		65c. ultramarine	18·00	2·50
205		$1 sepia	24·00	40
206	**41**	$1.30 multicoloured	2·75	20
		a. Pale yellow omitted	65·00	
		b. Pale yellow inverted (horiz pair)	£6500	
		c. Ochre (sash) omitted	60·00	
		d. Glazed paper (3.2.71)	22·00	3·00
		da. Ochre (sash) omitted	55·00	
		dw. Wmk inverted	40·00	
		dwa. Pale yellow omitted	£140	
207		$2 multicoloured	5·00	1·00
		a. Pale yellow omitted†	70·00	
		b. Ochre (sash) omitted	50·00	
		c. Pale yellow† and ochre (sash) omitted	£275	
		dw. Wmk inverted	11·00	
		e. Glazed paper (1973)*	£400	11·00
208		$5 multicoloured	14·00	1·75
		a. Ochre (sash) omitted	60·00	
		ab. Pale yellow and ochre omitted	£120	
		bw. Wmk inverted	42·00	
		c. Glazed paper (3.2.71)	35·00	13·00
		cw. Wmk inverted	70·00	50·00
209		$10 multicoloured	20·00	3·00
		a. Ochre (sash) omitted	£180	
		b. Pale yellow† and ochre (sash) omitted	£275	
		ba. Pale yellow† omitted	£200	
		cw. Wmk inverted	£150	
		d. Glazed paper (1973)*	£2250	£250
210		$20 multicoloured	60·00	26·00
		a. Ochre omitted	£325	
		w. Wmk inverted	£800	
196/210 *Set of 15*			£140	42·00

* These are from printings which were sent to Hong Kong in March 1973 but not released in London.

† This results in the Queen's face appearing pinkish.

No. 197 exists from coils.

It is believed that No. 206b comes from the last two vertical rows of a sheet, the remainder of which had the pale yellow omitted.

The $1.30 to $20 exist with PVA gum as well as gum arabic. The glazed paper printings are with PVA gum only.

See also Nos. 222/236.

1963 (4 June). Freedom from Hunger. As No. 146 of Antigua, but additionally inscr in Chinese characters.

211	$1.30 bluish green	28·00	4·00

1963 (2 Sept). Red Cross Centenary. As Nos. 147/148 of Antigua, but additionally inscr in Chinese characters at right.

212	10c. red and black	2·00	30
213	$1.30 red and blue	11·00	7·00

1965 (17 May). ITU Centenary. As Nos. 166/167 of Antigua.

214	10c. light purple and orange-yellow	1·50	25
	w. Wmk inverted	70·00	
215	$1.30 olive-yellow and deep bluish green	6·00	5·00

1965 (25 Oct). International Co-operation Year. As Nos. 168/169 of Antigua.

216	10c. reddish purple and turquoise-green	1·25	25
	w. Wmk inverted	1·25	2·50
217	$1.30 deep bluish green and lavender (*shades*)	5·50	3·50

1966 (24 Jan). Churchill Commemoration. As Nos. 170/173 of Antigua, but additionally inscr in Chinese characters.

218	10c. new blue	2·50	15
	w. Wmk inverted	26·00	
219	50c. deep green	3·25	30
	w. Wmk inverted	1·75	4·00
220	$1.30 brown	12·00	2·00
221	$2 bluish violet	22·00	9·00
	w. Wmk inverted	£225	
218/221 *Set of 4*		35·00	10·00

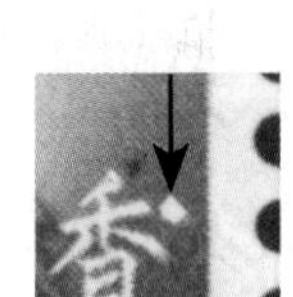
10c. Large white dot to right of upper white Chinese character (Pl. 2B, R. 3/4).

1966 (1 Aug)–**72**. As Nos. 196/208 and 210 but wmk W w **12** (sideways*). Chalk-surfaced paper (5c. to $1) or glazed, ordinary paper ($1.30 to $20).

222	**40**	5c. red-orange (6.12.66)	65	1·25
223		10c. reddish violet (31.3.67)†	70	70
		a. Imperf (horiz pair)	£1100	
		b. Dot beside character	10·00	
		w. Wmk Crown to right of CA	£200	£170
224		15c. emerald (31.3.67)†	2·00	4·50
225		20c. red-brown	2·25	2·75
		a. Glazed, ordinary paper (14.4.72)	8·50	16·00
226		25c. cerise (31.3.67)†	3·00	6·00
		aw. Wmk Crown to right of CA	42·00	
		b. Glazed, ordinary paper (14.4.72)	15·00	24·00
227		30c. deep grey-blue (31.3.70)	10·00	6·00
		a. Glazed, ordinary paper (14.4.72)	14·00	18·00
228		40c. deep bluish green (1967)	3·75	3·25
		a. Glazed, ordinary paper (14.4.72)	14·00	21·00
229		50c. scarlet (31.3.67)†	2·75	1·00
		w. Wmk Crown to right of CA (13.5.69)	4·00	3·00
230		65c. ultramarine (29.3.67)	6·50	13·00
		a. Bright blue (16.7.68)	12·00	17·00
231		$1 sepia (29.3.67)†	13·00	1·75
		w. Wmk Crown to right of CA	75·00	
232	**41**	$1.30 multicoloured (14.4.72)	15·00	3·25
		a. Pale yellow omitted	70·00	
		w. Wmk Crown to right of CA (17.11.72)	12·00	4·75
		wa. Ochre omitted	70·00	
233		$2 multicoloured (13.12.71)	25·00	3·25
		b. Pale yellow omitted	75·00	
		w. Wmk Crown to right of CA (17.11.72)	12·00	8·00
		wa. Ochre (sash) omitted	70·00	

234 $5 multicoloured (13.12.71) 75·00 32·00
a. Pale yellow omitted £170
236 $20 multicoloured (14.4.72) £160 85·00
222/236 *Set of 14* £275 £140

* The normal sideways watermark shows Crown to left of CA, *as seen from the back of the stamp*.

† Earliest known postmark dates.

The 5c. to 25c., 40c. and 50c. exist with PVA gum as well as gum arabic, but the 30c., and all stamps on glazed paper exist with PVA gum only. 223a also exists with both gums.

1966 (20 Sept). Inauguration of WHO Headquarters, Geneva. As Nos. 178/179 of Antigua.
237 10c. black, yellow-green and light blue 1·50 30
238 50c. black, light purple and yellow-brown 4·50 2·25

1966 (1 Dec). 20th Anniversary of UNESCO. As Nos. 196/198 of Antigua.
239 10c. slate-violet, red, yellow and orange 2·50 20
240 50c. orange-yellow, violet and deep olive 5·50 90
241 $2 black, light purple and orange 32·00 20·00
239/241 *Set of 3* 35·00 20·00

49 Rams' Heads on Chinese Lanterns

10c. White dot after '1967' (R. 2/2)

(Des V. Whiteley. Photo Harrison)

1967 (17 Jan). Chinese New Year. Year of the Ram. T **49** and similar horiz design. W w **12** (sideways). P 14½.
242 10c. rosine, olive-green and light yellow-olive 2·00 50
a. Dot after '1967' 14·00
243 $1.30 emerald, rosine and light yellow-olive 13·00 6·50
Design: 10c. T **49**; $1.30, Three rams.

50 Cable Route Map

(Des V. Whiteley. Photo Harrison)

1967 (30 Mar). Completion of Malaysia–Hong Kong Link of SEACOM Telephone Cable. W w **12**. P 12½.
244 **50** $1.30 new blue and red 5·00 1·50

51 Rhesus Macaques in Tree. Year of the Monkey

(Des R. Granger Barrett. Photo Harrison)

1968 (23 Jan). Chinese New Year. Year of the Monkey. T **51** and similar horiz design. W w **12** (sideways). P 14½.
245 10c. gold, black and scarlet 2·00 50
246 $1.30 gold, black and scarlet 13·00 6·50
Design: 10c. T **51**; $1.30, Family of Rhesus Macaques.

52 *Iberia* (liner) at Ocean Terminal

(Des and litho D.L.R.)

1968 (24 Apr). Sea Craft. T **52** and similar horiz design. P 13.
247 10c. multicoloured 1·75 15
a. Dull orange and new blue omitted £2750
248 20c. cobalt-blue, black and brown 2·50 1·75
249 40c. orange, black and mauve 7·50 14·00
250 50c. orange-red, black and green 5·00 75
a. Green omitted £1300
251 $1 greenish yellow, black and red 7·00 8·00
252 $1.30 Prussian blue, black and pink 21·00 3·25
247/252 *Set of 6* 40·00 25·00

Designs: 10c. T **52**; 20c. Pleasure launch; 40c. Car ferry, 50c. Passenger ferry; $1, Sampan; $1.30, Junk.

53 *Bauhinia blakeana* **54** Arms of Hong Kong

(Des V. Whiteley. Photo Harrison)

1968 (25 Sept)–**73**. W w **12**. P 14×14½.

(a) Upright wmk. Chalk-surfaced paper
253 **53** 65c. multicoloured 8·00 50
aw. Wmk inverted 32·00
b. Glazed, ordinary paper (3.73) £120 25·00
254 **54** $1 multicoloured 8·00 40
a. Glazed ordinary paper £160 40·00

(b) Sideways wmk. Glazed, ordinary paper
254*b* **53** 65c. multicoloured (27.9.72) 50·00 40·00
254*c* **54** $1 multicoloured (13.12.71) 8·00 2·50

Nos. 253/254 exist with PVA gum as well as gum arabic; Nos. 254*b*/254*c* with PVA gum only.

55 'Aladdin's Lamp' and Human Rights Emblem

(Des R. Granger Barrett. Litho B.W.)

1968 (20 Nov). Human Rights Year. W w **12** (sideways). P 13½.
255 **55** 10c. orange, black and myrtle-green 1·00 75
256 50c. yellow, black and deep reddish purple 2·00 2·50

56 Cockerel

(Des R. Granger Barrett. Photo Enschedé)

1969 (11 Feb). Chinese New Year. Year of the Cock. T **56** and similar multicoloured design. P 13½.
257 10c. Type **56** 2·50 1·00
a. Red omitted £400
258 $1.30 Cockerel (*vert*) 30·00 9·00

58 Arms of Chinese University **59** Earth Station and Satellite

(Des V. Whiteley. Photo Govt Ptg Bureau, Tokyo)

1969 (26 Aug). Establishment of Chinese University of Hong Kong. P 13½.
259 **58** 40c. violet, gold and pale turquoise-blue 1·75 2·25

(Des V. Whiteley. Photo Harrison)

1969 (24 Sept). Opening of Communications Satellite Tracking Station. W w **12**. P 14½.
260 **59** $1 multicoloured 4·00 2·00

60 Chow's Head

62 Expo '70 Emblem

(Des R. Granger Barrett. Photo D.L.R.)

1970 (28 Jan). Chinese New Year. Year of the Dog. T **60** and similar design. W w **12** (sideways on $1.30). P 14½×14 (10c.) or 14×14½ ($1.30).
261 10c. lemon-yellow, orange-brown and black 3·00 1·00
262 $1.30 multicoloured 35·00 10·00
Design: Vert—10c. T **60**. Horiz—$1.30, Chow standing.

(Des and litho B.W.)

1970 (14 Mar). World Fair Osaka. T **62** and similar multicoloured design. W w **12** (sideways on 25c.). P 13½×13 (15c.) or 13×13½ (25c.).
263 15c. Type **62** 65 85
264 25c. Expo '70 emblem and junks (*horiz*) 1·40 1·50

64 Plaque in Tung Wah Hospital **65** Symbol

(Des M. F. Griffith. Photo Harrison)

1970 (9 Apr). Centenary of Tung Wah Hospital. W w **12** (sideways*). P 14½.
265 **64** 10c. multicoloured 60 25
266 50c. multicoloured 1·40 1·50
w. Wmk Crown to right of CA 8·50

* The normal sideways watermark shows Crown to left of CA, *as seen from the back of the stamp*.

(Des J. Cooter. Litho B.W.)

1970 (5 Aug). Asian Productivity Year. W w **12**. P 14×13½.
267 **65** 10c. multicoloured 1·00 60

STAMP BOOKLETS

BOOKLET CONTENTS. In Nos. SB1/SB4 and SB6/SB7 the 1c. and 2c. were each in blocks of 12 and the 4c. in blocks of 12 and 4 or two blocks of 8, all having been taken from normal sheets. No. SB5 had both the 2c. and 4c. in blocks of 12 and 4 or as two blocks of 8. Other content formats exist.

The 'Metal fastener' used for SB2/SB2b, SB3 and SB7ca was a Hotchkiss 'Herringbone' stapler.

1904 (1 Jan). Black on cream cover showing contents and postage rates with 'K & W LD' imprint on front. Stapled.
SB1 $1 booket containing12×1c. (No. 62), 12×2c. (No. 56) and 16×4c. (No. 57)
a. 4c. No. 64 (King Edward VII) instead of No. 57 (Q.V.) £9000

1905 (May)–**07**. Black on cream cover showing contents and postage rates with 'Hongkong Printing Press' imprint on front. Metal fastener.
SB2 $1 booklet containing 12×1c., 12×2c. and 16×4c. (Nos. 62/64) £7000
a. 2c. and 4c. (Nos. 77/78) (MCA ordinary paper) instead of Nos. 63/64 (CA) (3.06) £9000
b. 2c. and 4c. (Nos. 77a/78a) (MCA chalk-surfaced paper) instead of Nos. 77/78 (MCA ordinary paper) (1.07) £10000

Some examples of No. SB2 show the reference to Australia on the front cover officially deleted in manuscript. No. SB2a has the rate information reset to omit 'EXCEPT AUSTRALIA'.

1907 (Nov)–**10**. Black on cream cover showing contents and postage rates for both Hong Kong and Agencies in China with 'Hongkong Printing Press' imprint. Metal fastener.
SB3 $1 booklet containing 12×1c. (No. 62), 12×2c. (No. 92) and 16×4c. (No. 93)
a. Stapled (6.10) £5500

1911 (Jan)–**12**. Black on cream cover showing contents, but no postage rates, with 'Hongkong Printing Press' imprint on front. Stapled.
SB4 $1 booklet containing 12×1c. (No. 62), 12×2c. (No. 92) and 16×4c. (No. 93)
a. 1c. No. 91 (MCA) instead of No. 62 (CA) (7.12) (off-white cover) £5500

1912 (July). Black on cream cover showing contents, but no postage rates, with 'Hongkong Printing Press' imprint on front. Stapled.
SB5 $1 booklet containing 4×1c., 16×2c. and 16×4c. (Nos. 91/93) £700

1913 (Mar). Black on cream cover showing contents, but no postage rates, with 'Hongkong Printing Press' imprint on front. Stapled.
SB6 $1 booklet containing 12×1c., 12×2c. and 16×4c. (Nos. 100/102) (MCA wmk) £4500

1922 (June). Black on cream cover showing contents, but no postage rates, with 'Hongkong Printing Press' imprint on front. Inscribed 'Price $1'. Stapled.
SB7 $1 booklet containing 12×1c., 12×2c. and 16×4c. (Nos. 117/118, 120) (Script wmk) £5000

1923 (Jan)–**25**. Black on grey cover showing contents but no postage rates, with 'Ye Olde Printerie' imprint on front. Inscribed 'Price $1'. Stapled.
SB7a $1 With 'Ye Olde Printerie' imprint (1.23) £6000
b. Imprint revised to 'Ye Older Printerie Ltd' (5.23)
c. Inscribed 'Price $' (9.24) £6000
ca. Bound with Metal fastener (2.25)

1965 (10 May). Orange-brown (No. SB8) or yellow-green (No. SB9) covers. Stitched.
SB8 $2 booklet containing 8×5c. and 16×10c. (Nos. 196/197) in blocks of 4 35·00
SB9 $5 booklet containing 12×5c., 8×10c., 8×20c. and 4×50c. (Nos. 196/197, 199, 203) in blocks of 4 £120

POSTAGE DUE STAMPS

PRINTERS. Nos. D1/D19 were typographed by De La Rue & Co.

D **1** Post-office Scales

1923 (1 Dec)–**56**. Wmk Mult Script CA. Ordinary paper. P 14.

D1	D **1**	1c. brown	2·50	65
		a. Wmk sideways (1931)	1·50	1·00
		ab. Chalk-surfaced paper (21.3.56)	30	1·00
D2		2c. green	45·00	11·00
		a. Wmk sideways (1928)	11·00	5·00
D3		4c. scarlet	50·00	7·00
		a. Wmk sideways (1928)	32·00	5·00
D4		6c. yellow	32·00	13·00
		a. Wmk sideways (1931)	90·00	38·00
D5		10c. bright ultramarine	27·00	9·00
		a. Wmk sideways (1934)	£130	5·00
D1/D5 *Set of 5*			£130	35·00
D1a/D5a *Set of 5*			£225	50·00
D1s/D5s Optd 'SPECIMEN' *Set of 5*			£425	

1938 (Feb)–**63**. Wmk Mult Script CA (sideways). Ordinary paper. P 14.

D6	D **1**	2c. grey	8·00	10·00
		a. Chalk-surfaced paper (21.3.56)	1·10	10·00
D7		4c. orange	12·00	3·25
		a. Chalk-surfaced paper. *Orange-yellow* (23.5.61)	2·50	12·00
D8		6c. scarlet	4·00	5·50
D9		8c. chestnut (26.2.46)	3·75	32·00
D10		10c. violet	25·00	50
		a. Chalk-surfaced paper (17.9.63)	14·00	26·00
D11		20c. black (26.2.46)	4·00	1·75
D12		50c. blue (7.47)	75·00	13·00
D6a/D12 *Set of 7*			95·00	60·00
D6s/D12s Perf 'SPECIMEN' *Set of 7*			£475	

1965 (15 Apr)–**72**. Chalk-surfaced paper. P 14.

(a) Wmk w **12** *(sideways)*

D13	D **1**	4c. yellow-orange	3·00	32·00
D14		5c. red (13.5.69)	2·75	4·50
		a. Glazed paper (17.11.72)	16·00	60·00
D15		10c. violet (27.6.67)	3·00	9·00
D16		20c. black (1965)	6·00	1·50
D17		50c. deep blue (1965)	32·00	8·00
		a. Blue (13.5.69)	20·00	2·00
D13/D17*a* *Set of 5*			32·00	45·00

(b) Wmk w **12** *(upright)*

D18	D **1**	5c. red (20.7.67)	2·00	4·75
D19		50c. deep blue (26.8.70)	38·00	10·00

The 5c. is smaller, 21×18 mm.

POSTCARD STAMPS

Stamps specially surcharged for use on Postcards.

PRICES. Those in the left-hand column are for unused examples on complete postcards; those on the right for used examples off card. Examples used on postcards are worth much more.

3 CENTS. (P **1**)

THREE (P **2**)

1879 (1 Apr). Nos. 22 and 13 surch as T P **1** by Noronha & Sons.

P1	**3**	3c. on 16c. yellow (No. 22)	£350	£450
P2		5c. on 18c. lilac (No. 13)	£375	£500

1879 (Nov). No. P2 handstamped with T P **2**.

P3	**3**	3c. on 5c. on 18c. lilac	£9000	£9000

POSTAL FISCAL STAMPS

I. Stamps inscribed 'STAMP DUTY'

NOTE. The dated circular 'HONG KONG' cancellation with 'PAID ALL' in lower segment was used for fiscal purposes, in black, from 1877. Previously it appears in red on mail to the USA, but is usually not used as a cancellation.

F **1**

F **2**

F **3**

1874–1902. Wmk Crown CC.

(a) P 15½×15

F1	F **1**	$2 olive-green	£425	70·00
F2	F **2**	$3 dull violet	£400	55·00
		b. Bluish paper		
F3	F **3**	$10 rose-carmine	£8500	£800

(b) P 14

F4	F **1**	$2 dull bluish green (10.97)	£450	£275
F5	F **2**	$3 dull mauve (3.02)	£700	£550
		a. Bluish paper	£2000	
F6	F **3**	$10 grey-green	£12000	£11000
F4s/F5s Optd 'SPECIMEN' *Set of 2*			£450	

Nos. F1/F3 and F7 exist on various papers, ranging from thin to thick.

All three of the values perforated 15½×15 were authorised for postal use in 1874. The $10 rose-carmine was withdrawn from such use in 1880, the $2 in September 1897 and the $3 in 1902.

The $2 and $3 perforated 14 were available for postal purposes until July 1903. The $10 in grey-green was issued for fiscal purposes in 1884 and is known with postal cancellations.

12 CENTS. (F **4**)

(F **5**)

1880. No. F3 surch with T F **4** by Noronha and Sons, Hong Kong.

F7	F **3**	12c. on $10 rose-carmine	£950	£350

1890 (24 Dec). Wmk Crown CA. P 14.

F8	F **5**	2c. dull purple	£200	50·00
		w. Wmk inverted	£2000	

No. F8 was authorised for postal use between 24 and 31 December 1890.

5 DOLLARS (F **6**)

ONE DOLLAR (F **7**)

(F **8**)

1891 (1 Jan). Surch with T F **6** by D.L.R. Wmk Crown CA. P 14.

F9	F **3**	$5 on $10 purple/*red*	£400	£120
		s. Optd 'SPECIMEN'	£250	

No. F9 was in use for postal purposes until June 1903.

1897 (Sept). Surch with T F **7** by Noronha and Sons, Hong Kong, and with the value in Chinese characters subsequently applied twice by handstamp as T **15**.

F10	F **1**	$1 on $2 olive-green (No. F1)	£225	£130
		a. Both Chinese handstamps omitted	£4250	£3000
		b. Diagonal Chinese handstamp omitted	£22000	
F11		$1 on $2 dull bluish green (No. F4)	£250	£150
		a. Both Chinese handstamps omitted	£2000	£1700
		b. Diagonal Chinese handstamp omitted	£40000	
		c. Vertical Chinese handstamp omitted		
		s. Handstamped 'SPECIMEN'	£150	

1938 (11 Jan). Wmk Mult Script CA. P 14.

F12	F **8**	5c. green	£100	17·00

No. F12 was authorised for postal use between 11 and 20 January 1938 due to a shortage of 5c., No 121.

Forged cancellations are known on this stamp inscribed 'VICTORIA 9.AM 11 JA 38 HONG KONG' without side bars between the rings.

II. Stamps overprinted 'S.O.' (Stamp Office) or 'S.D.' (Stamp Duty)

S. O. S. D.

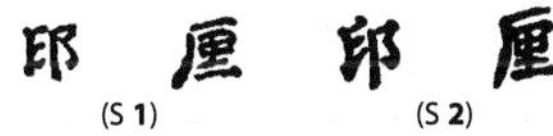

(S **1**) (S **2**)

1891 (1 Jan). Optd with Types S **1** or S **2**.

S1	S **1**	2c. carmine (No. 33)	£950	£375
S2	S **2**	2c. carmine (No. 33)	£425	£200
		a. Opt inverted	†	£9000
S3	S **1**	10c. purple/*red* (No. 38)	£1700	£450

Examples of No. S1 exist with the 'O' amended to 'D' in manuscript.

Other fiscal stamps are found apparently postally used, but there is no evidence that this use was authorised.

JAPANESE OCCUPATION OF HONG KONG

Hong Kong surrendered to the Japanese on 25 December 1941. The postal service was not resumed until 22 January 1942 when the GPO and Kowloon Central Office re-opened.

Japanese postmarks used in Hong Kong can be identified by the unique combination of horizontal lines in the central circle and three stars in the lower segment of the outer circle. Dates shown on such postmarks are in the sequence Year/Month/Day with the first shown as a Japanese regnal year number so that Showa 17 = 1942 and so on.

Initially six current Japanese definitives, 1, 2, 3, 4, 10 and 30s. (Nos. 297, 315/317, 322 and 327) were on sale, but the range gradually expanded to cover all values between ½s. and 10y. with Nos. 313/314, 318, 325, 328/331, 391, 395/396, 398/399 and 405 of Japan also available from Hong Kong post offices during the occupation. Philatelic covers exist showing other Japanese stamps, but these were not available from the local post offices. Supply of these Japanese stamps was often interrupted and, during the period between 28 July 1942 and 21 April 1943, circular 'Postage Paid' handstamps were sometimes used. A substantial increase in postage rates on 16 April 1945 led to the issue of the local surcharges, Nos. J1/J3.

PRICES FOR STAMPS ON COVER TO 1945	
Nos. J1/J3	*from* × 7

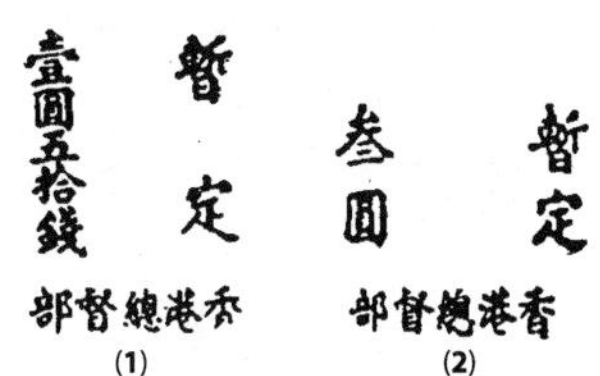

(**1**) (**2**)

1945 (16 Apr). Stamps of Japan surch with T **1** (No. J1) or as T **2**.

J1	1.50 yen on 1s. brown	38·00	32·00
J2	3 yen on 2s. scarlet	12·00	28·00
J3	5 yen on 5s. claret	£900	£150

Designs (18½×22 *mm*): 1s. Girl Worker; 2s. General Nogi; 5s. Admiral Togo.

No. J3 has four characters of value similarly arranged but differing from T **2**.

BRITISH POST OFFICES IN CHINA

Under the terms of the 1842 Treaty of Nanking, China granted Great Britain and its citizens commercial privileges in five Treaty Ports, Amoy, Canton, Foochow, Ningpo and Shanghai. British Consuls were appointed to each Port and their offices, as was usual during this period, collected and distributed mail for the British community. This system was formally recognised by a Hong Kong Government notice published on 16 April 1844. Mail from the consular offices was postmarked when it passed through Hong Kong.

The number of Chinese Treaty Ports was increased to 16 by the ratification of the Treaty of Peking in 1860 with British postal facilities being eventually extended to the Ports of Chefoo, Hankow, Kiungchow (Hoihow), Swatow, Tainan (Anping) and Tientsin.

As postal business expanded the consular agencies were converted into packet agencies or post offices which passed under the direct control of the Hong Kong postal authorities on 1 May 1868.

In May 1898 the British Government leased the territory of Wei Hai Wei from China for use as a naval station to counter the Russian presence at Port Arthur.

The opening of the Trans-Siberia Railway and the extension of Imperial Penny Postage to the Treaty Port agencies resulted in them becoming a financial burden on the colonial post office. Control of the agencies reverted to the GPO, London, on 1 January 1911.

The pre-adhesive postal markings of the various agencies are a fascinating, but complex, subject. Full details can be found in *Hong Kong & the Treaty Ports of China & Japan* by F. W. Webb (reprinted edition J. Bendon, Limassol, 1992) and in various publications of the Hong Kong Study Circle.

From 15 October 1864 the use of Hong Kong stamps on mail from the Treaty Ports became compulsory, although such stamps were, initially, not cancelled (with the exception of Amoy) until they reached Hong Kong where the 'B62' killer was applied. Cancellation of mail at the actual Ports commenced during 1866 at Shanghai and Ningpo, spreading to all the agencies during the next ten years. Shanghai had previously used a c.d.s. on adhesives during 1863 and again in 1865–1866.

The main types of cancellation used between 1866 and 1930 are illustrated below. The illustrations show the style of each postmark and no attempt has been made to cover differences in type letters or figures, arrangement, diameter or colour.

Until 1885 the vertical and horizontal killers were used to obliterate the actual stamps with an impression of one of the circular date stamps shown elsewhere on the cover. Many of the early postmarks were also used as backstamps or transit marks and, in the notes which follow, references to use are for the first appearance of the mark, not necessarily its first use as an obliterator.

Illustrations in this section are taken from *Hong Kong & the Treaty Ports of China & Japan* by F. W. Webb and are reproduced with the permission of the Royal Philatelic Society, London.

Details of the stamps known used from each post office are taken, with permission, from *British Post Offices in the Far East* by Edward B. Proud, published by Proud-Bailey Co. Ltd.

Postmark Types

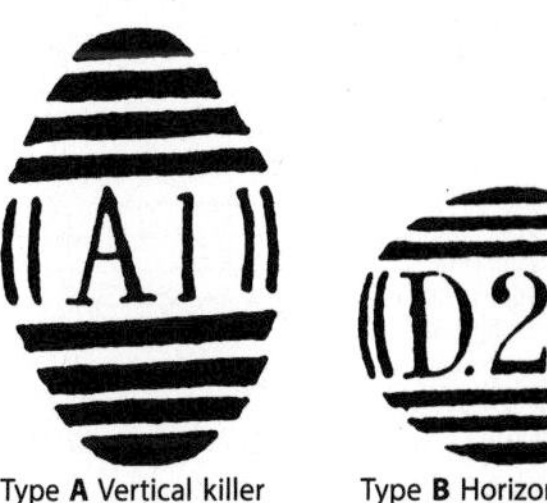

Type **A** Vertical killer Type **B** Horizontal killer

Type **C** Name horizontal

Type **D** Name curved

Type **E** Double circle Name at top

Type **F** Double circle Name at foot

Type **G** Single circle Name at top

PRICES. The prices quoted in this section are for fine used stamps which show a clear impression of a substantial part of the cancellation.

AMOY

One of the five original Treaty Ports, opened to British trade by the Treaty of Nanking in 1842. A consular postal agency was established in 1844 which expanded in 1876 into two separate offices, one on the off-shore island of Ku Lang Seu and the other in Amoy itself.

Amoy 'PAID' (*supplied* 1858) *used* 1859–1867
Type **A** ('A1') (*supplied* 1866) *used at Ku Lang Seu* 1869–1882
Type **D** (*supplied* 1866) *used* 1867–1922
Type **B** ('D.27') (*supplied* 1876) *used at Amoy* 1876–1884
Type **C** *used* 1876–1894
Type **F** (*supplied* 1913) *used* 1916–1922

Stamps of HONG KONG cancelled at Amoy between 1864 and 1916 with postmarks detailed above.

1862. No wmk (Nos. 1/7).
Z1 2c. brown £300
Z2 8c. yellow-buff £250
Z3 12c. pale greenish blue £225
Z4 18c. lilac £160
Z5 24c. green £275
Z6 48c. rose £1400
Z7 96c. brownish grey £1100

1863–71. Wmk Crown CC (Nos. 8/19).
Z8 2c. brown 40·00
Z9 4c. grey 45·00
a. Perf 12½
Z10 6c. lilac 75·00
Z11 8c. orange 55·00
Z12 12c. blue 25·00
Z13 18c. lilac £1100
Z14 24c. green 70·00
Z15 30c. vermilion £160
Z16 30c. mauve 21·00
Z17 48c. rose 85·00
Z18 96c. olive-bistre £3500
Z19 96c. brownish grey £350

1876–77. (Nos. 20/21).
Z20 16c. on 18c. lilac £350
Z21 28c. on 30c. mauve £150

1877. Wmk Crown CC (No. 22).
Z22 16c. yellow £140

1880. (Nos. 23/27).
Z23 5c. on 8c. orange £140
Z24 5c. on 18c. lilac £100
Z25 10c. on 12c. blue £100
Z26 10c. on 16c. yellow £225
Z27 10c. on 24c. green £150

1880. Wmk Crown CC (Nos. 28/31).
Z28 2c. rose 60·00
Z29 5c. blue 95·00
Z30 10c. mauve 75·00
Z31 48c. brown £325

1882–96. Wmk Crown CA (Nos. 32/39).
Z31*a* 2c. rose-lake 65·00
Z32 2c. carmine 5·00
Z33 4c. slate-grey 14·00
Z34 5c. blue 4·75
Z35 10c. dull mauve 50·00
Z36 10c. green 6·00
Z37 10c. purple/*red* 5·50
Z38 30c. green 50·00

1885. (Nos. 40/42).
Z39 20c. on 30c. orange-red 19·00
Z40 50c. on 48c. yellowish brown 90·00
Z41 $1 on 96c. grey-olive £150

1891. (Nos. 43/50).
Z42 7c. on 10c. green 27·00
Z43 14c. on 30c. mauve £140
Z44 20c. on 30c. green (No. 48) 19·00
Z45 50c. on 48c. dull purple (No. 49) 20·00
Z46 $1 on 96c. purple/*red* (No. 50) 60·00

1891. 50th Anniversary of Colony (No. 51).
Z47 2c. carmine £1100

1898. (No. 52).
Z48 $1 on 96c. black 75·00

1898. (No. 55).
Z49 10c. on 30c. green £275

1900–01. Wmk Crown CA (Nos. 56/61).
Z50 2c. dull green 5·00
Z51 4c. carmine 3·75
Z52 5c. yellow 24·00
Z53 10c. ultramarine 6·00
Z54 12c. blue £225
Z55 30c. brown 90·00

1903. Wmk Crown CA (Nos. 62/76).
Z56 1c. dull purple and brown 5·50
Z57 2c. dull green 5·00
Z58 4c. purple/*red* 3·25
Z59 5c. dull green and brown-orange 25·00
Z60 8c. slate and violet 8·50
Z61 10c. purple and blue/*blue* 4·50
Z62 12c. green and purple/*yellow* 19·00
Z63 20c. slate and chestnut 14·00
Z64 30c. dull green and black 70·00
Z65 50c. dull green and magenta £120
Z67 $2 slate and scarlet £550
Z68 $3 slate and dull blue £800

1904–06. Wmk Mult Crown CA (Nos. 77/90).
Z71 2c. dull green 5·00
Z72 4c. purple/*red* 3·25
Z73 5c. dull green and brown-orange 20·00
Z74 8c. slate and violet 12·00
Z75 10c. purple and blue/*blue* 4·75
Z76 12c. green and purple/*yellow* 23·00
Z77 20c. slate and chestnut 13·00
Z78 30c. dull green and black 45·00
Z79 50c. green and magenta 42·00
Z80 $1 purple and sage-green £110
Z81 $2 slate and scarlet £400
Z83 $5 purple and blue-green £700

1907–11. Wmk Mult Crown CA (Nos. 91/99).
Z85 1c. brown 5·50
Z86 2c. green 4·75
Z87 4c. carmine-red 3·25
Z88 6c. orange-vermilion and purple 20·00
Z89 10c. bright ultramarine 4·25
Z90 20c. purple and sage-green 80·00
Z91 30c. purple and orange-yellow 85·00
Z92 50c. black/*green* 80·00

1912–15. Wmk Crown CA (Nos. 100/116).
Z93 1c. brown 6·50
Z94 2c. green 6·00
Z95 4c. red 3·25
Z96 6c. orange 7·50
Z97 8c. grey 25·00
Z98 10c. ultramarine 4·50
Z99 12c. purple/*yellow* 35·00
Z100 20c. purple and sage-green 8·00
Z101 25c. purple and magenta (Type A) 95·00
Z102 30c. purple and orange-yellow 30·00
Z103 50c. black/*green* 17·00
Z104 $1 purple and blue/*blue* 30·00
Z105 $3 green and purple £250

POSTCARD STAMPS

1879. (Nos. P1/P2).
ZP106 3c. on 16c. yellow £1000
ZP107 5c. on 18c. lilac £1200

POSTAL FISCAL STAMPS

1874–1902. Wmk Crown CC. P 15½×15 (Nos. F1/F3)
ZF109 $2 olive-green £200
ZF110 $3 dull violet £200

1891. (No. F9).
ZF116 $5 on $10 purple/*red* £350

1897. (Nos. F10/F11).
ZF118 $1 on $2 olive-green
ZF119 $1 on $2 dull bluish green £425

ANPING

Anping is the port for Tainan, on the island of Formosa, opened to British trade in 1860. A British Vice-consulate operated in the port and mail is known postmarked there between 1889 and 1895. Formosa passed under Japanese control in 1895 and British Treaty Port rights then lapsed.

Type **D** *used* 1889–1895

Stamps of HONG KONG cancelled at Anping between 1889 and 1895 with postmark detailed above.

1882–91. Wmk Crown CA (Nos. 32/39).
Z120 2c. carmine £1100
Z121 5c. blue £950
Z123 10c. green £1000
Z124 10c. purple/*red* £1100

1885. (Nos. 40/42).
Z126 20c. on 30c. orange-red £1100
Z127 50c. on 48c. yellowish brown £3000

CANTON

A British postal service was organised in Canton from 1834, but was closed when the foreign communities were evacuated in August 1839. The city was one of the original Treaty Ports and a consular agency was opened there in 1844. The consulate closed during the riots of December 1856, being replaced by a temporary postal agency at Whampoa, further down the river. When British forces reached Canton a further temporary agency was set up on 23 March 1859, but both closed in July 1863 when the consulate was re-established.

Type **A** ('C1') (*supplied* 1866) *used* 1875–1884
Type **C** (*supplied* 1866) *used* 1870–1901
Type **D** *used* 1890–1922

Stamps of HONG KONG cancelled at Canton between 1870 and 1916 with postmarks detailed above.

1862. No wmk (Nos. 1/7).
Z135 18c. lilac £180

1863–71. Wmk Crown CC (Nos. 8/19).
Z136 2c. brown 42·00
Z137 4c. grey 45·00
Z138 6c. lilac 75·00
Z139 8c. orange 55·00
Z140 12c. blue 25·00
Z142 24c. green 80·00
Z143 30c. vermilion
Z144 30c. mauve 25·00
Z145 48c. rose £140
Z147 96c. brownish grey £325

1876–77. (Nos. 20/21).
Z148 16c. on 18c. lilac £300
Z149 28c. on 30c. mauve £120

1877. Wmk Crown CC (No. 22).
Z150 16c. yellow £170

1880. (Nos. 23/27).
Z151 5c. on 8c. orange £170
Z152 5c. on 18c. lilac £130
Z153 10c. on 12c. blue £120
Z154 10c. on 16c. yellow £275
Z155 10c. on 24c. green £170

1880. Wmk Crown CC (Nos. 28/31).
Z156 2c. rose 60·00
Z157 5c. blue 90·00
Z158 10c. mauve 65·00

1882–96. Wmk Crown CA (Nos. 32/39).
Z159 2c. rose-lake 45·00
Z160 2c. carmine 3·75
Z161 4c. slate-grey 15·00
Z162 5c. blue 5·50
Z163 10c. dull mauve 45·00
Z164 10c. green 10·00
Z165 10c. purple/*red* 5·00
Z166 30c. green 50·00

1885. (Nos. 40/42).
Z167 20c. on 30c. orange-red 18·00
Z168 50c. on 48c. yellowish brown 90·00
Z169 $1 on 96c. grey-olive £160

1891. (Nos. 43/50).
Z170 7c. on 10c. green 27·00
Z171 14c. on 30c. mauve £150
Z171*a* 20c. on 30c. green (No. 45) £300
Z172 20c. on 30c. green (No. 48) 22·00
Z173 50c. on 48c. dull purple (No. 49) 24·00
Z174 $1 on 96c. purple/*red* (No. 50) 75·00

1891. 50th Anniversary of Colony (No. 51).
Z175 2c. carmine £1100

1898. (No. 52).
Z176 $1 on 96c. black £160

1898. (No. 55).
Z177 10c. on 30c. grey-green £190

1900–01. Wmk Crown CA (Nos. 56/61)
Z178 2c. dull green 4·50
Z179 4c. carmine 4·25
Z180 5c. yellow 40·00
Z181 10c. ultramarine 4·50
Z182 12c. blue £160
Z183 30c. brown 80·00

1903. Wmk Crown CA (Nos. 62/76).
Z184 1c. dull purple and brown 4·75
Z185 2c. dull green 5·00
Z186 4c. purple/*red* 3·50
Z187 5c. dull green and brown-orange 26·00
Z188 8c. slate and violet 10·00
Z189 10c. purple and blue/*blue* 4·75
Z190 12c. green and purple/*yellow* 21·00
Z191 20c. slate and chestnut 12·00
Z192 30c. dull green and black 65·00
Z193 50c. dull green and magenta £100
Z194 $1 purple and sage-green £120

1904–06. Wmk Mult Crown CA (Nos. 77/90).
Z199 2c. dull green 4·75
Z200 4c. purple/*red* 3·50
Z201 5c. dull green and brown-orange 23·00

Z202 8c. slate and violet 15·00
Z203 10c. purple and blue/*blue* 4·50
Z204 12c. green and purple/*yellow* 27·00
Z205 20c. slate and chestnut 14·00
Z206 30c. dull green and black 45·00
Z207 50c. green and magenta 50·00
Z208 $1 purple and sage-green 90·00
Z209 $2 slate and scarlet £500
Z210 $3 slate and dull blue £650
Z212 $10 slate and orange/*blue* £1800

1907–11. Wmk Mult Crown CA (Nos. 91/99).
Z213 1c. brown 4·75
Z214 2c. green 4·75
Z215 4c. carmine-red 3·50
Z216 6c. orange-vermilion and purple 24·00
Z217 10c. bright ultramarine 4·25
Z218 20c. purple and sage-green 85·00
Z219 30c. purple and orange-yellow 75·00
Z220 50c. black/*green* 55·00
Z221 $2 carmine-red and black £600

1912–15. Wmk Mult Crown CA (Nos. 100/116).
Z222 1c. brown 4·75
Z223 2c. green 4·00
Z224 4c. red 3·00
Z225 6c. orange 7·50
Z226 8c. grey 23·00
Z227 10c. ultramarine 4·50
Z228 12c. purple/*yellow* 24·00
Z229 20c. purple and sage-green 7·00
Z230 25c. purple and magenta (Type A) £110
Z231 30c. purple and orange-yellow 25·00
Z232 50c. black/*green* 9·00
Z233 $1 purple and blue/*blue* 42·00
Z234 $2 carmine red and grey-black £150
Z235 $3 green and purple £250
Z235*b* $10 purple and black/*red* £400

POSTCARD STAMPS

1879. (Nos. P1/P2).
ZP236 3c. on 16c. yellow £850
ZP237 5c. on 18c. lilac £1000

POSTAL FISCAL STAMPS

1874–1902. Wmk Crown CC. Nos. F1/F5.
(a) P 15½×15
ZF238 $2 olive-green £200
(b) P 14
ZF242 $3 dull mauve £900

1891. (No. F9).
ZF246 $5 on $10 purple/*red* £450

1897. (No. F10).
ZF247 $1 on $2 olive-green

CHEFOO

Chefoo was opened to British trade in 1860. Although a consulate was established in 1863 no organised postal agency was provided until 1 January 1903 when one was opened at the premises of Curtis Brothers, a commercial firm.

Type **E** (*supplied* 1902) *used* 1903–1920
Type **D** (*supplied* 1907) *used* 1907–1913
Type **F** *used* 1916–1922

Stamps of HONG KONG cancelled at Chefoo between 1903 and 1916 with postmarks detailed above.

1882–96. Wmk Crown CA (Nos. 32/39).
Z249 5c. blue 42·00

1891. (Nos. 43/50).
Z250 20c. on 30c. grey-green (No. 48*a*) 65·00

1898. (No. 52).
Z251 $1 on 96c. black £150

1900–01. Wmk Crown CA (Nos. 56/61).
Z252 2c. dull green 30·00
Z253 4c. carmine 29·00
Z254 5c. yellow 85·00
Z255 10c. ultramarine 30·00
Z257 30c. brown £180

1903. Wmk Crown CA (Nos. 62/76).
Z258 1c. dull purple and brown 13·00
Z259 2c. dull green 11·00
Z260 4c. purple/*red* 10·00
Z261 5c. dull green and brown-orange 32·00
Z262 8c. slate and violet 22·00
Z263 10c. purple and blue/*blue* 14·00
Z264 12c. green and purple/*yellow* 42·00
Z265 20c. slate and chestnut 42·00
Z267 50c. dull green and magenta £150
Z268 $1 purple and sage-green £150

1904–06. Wmk Mult Crown CA (Nos. 77/90).
Z273 2c. dull green 11·00
Z274 4c. purple/*red* 9·00
Z275 5c. dull green and brown-orange 23·00
Z276 8c. slate and violet 20·00
Z277 10c. purple and blue/*blue* 11·00
Z278 12c. green and purple/*yellow* 38·00
Z279 20c. slate and chestnut 24·00
Z280 30c. dull green and black 75·00
Z281 50c. green and magenta 75·00
Z282 $1 purple and sage-green £130
Z283 $2 slate and scarlet £350
Z284 $3 slate and dull blue £650
Z285 $5 purple and blue-green £900

1907–11. Wmk Mult Crown CA (Nos. 91/99).
Z287 1c. brown 13·00
Z288 2c. green 12·00
Z289 4c. carmine-red 10·00
Z290 6c. orange-vermilion and purple 40·00
Z291 10c. bright ultramarine 11·00
Z292 20c. purple and sage-green £120
Z293 30c. purple and orange-yellow 90·00
Z294 50c. black/*green* 75·00
Z295 $2 carmine-red and black £700

1912–15. Wmk Mult Crown CA (Nos. 100/116).
Z296 1c. brown 10·00
Z297 2c. green 9·50
Z298 4c. red 7·50
Z299 6c. orange 20·00
Z300 8c. grey 42·00
Z301 10c. ultramarine 9·00
Z302 12c. purple/*yellow* 45·00
Z303 20c. purple and sage-green 15·00
Z305 30c. purple and orange-yellow 28·00
Z306 50c. black/*green* 15·00
Z307 $1 purple and blue/*blue* 23·00
Z308 $2 carmine-red and grey-black £120
Z309 $3 green and purple £200
Z310 $5 green and red/*green* £600
Z311 $10 purple and black/*red* £375

FOOCHOW

Foochow, originally known as Foochowfoo, was one of the original Treaty Ports opened to British trade in 1842. A British consulate and postal agency was established in June 1844.

Type **A** ('F1') (*supplied* 1866) *used* 1873–1884
Type **D** (inscr 'FOOCHOWFOO') (*supplied* 1866) *used* 1867–1905
Type **D** (inscr 'FOOCHOW') (*supplied* 1894) *used* 1894–1917
Type **E** (inscr 'B.P.O.') *used* 1906–1910
Type **F** *used* 1915–1922

Stamps of HONG KONG cancelled at Foochow between 1867 and 1916 with postmarks detailed above.

1862. No wmk (Nos. 1/7).
Z312 18c. lilac £200

1863–71. Wmk Crown CC (Nos. 8/19).
Z313 2c. brown 38·00
Z314 4c. grey 38·00
Z315 6c. lilac 60·00
Z316 8c. orange 55·00
Z317 12c. blue 22·00
Z318 18c. lilac £1000
Z319 24c. green 80·00
Z320 30c. vermilion £250
Z321 30c. mauve 20·00
Z322 48c. rose £140
Z324 96c. brownish grey £425

1876–77. (Nos. 20/21).
Z325 16c. on 18c. lilac £325
Z326 28c. on 30c. mauve £150

1877. Wmk Crown CC (No. 22).
Z327 16c. yellow £150

1880. (Nos. 23/27).
Z328 5c. on 8c. orange £350
Z329 5c. on 18c. lilac £130
Z330 10c. on 12c. blue £130
Z331 10c. on 16c. yellow
Z332 10c. on 24c. green £180

1880. Wmk Crown CC (Nos. 28/31).
Z333 2c. rose 48·00
Z334 5c. blue 95·00
Z335 10c. mauve 55·00
Z336 48c. brown £300

1882–96. Wmk Crown CA (Nos. 32/39).
Z336*a* 2c. rose-lake 42·00
Z337 2c. carmine 3·25
Z338 4c. slate-grey 9·00
Z339 5c. blue 3·75
Z340 10c. dull mauve 50·00
Z341 10c. green 11·00
Z342 10c. purple/*red* 4·50
Z343 30c. green 55·00

1885. (Nos. 40/42).
Z344 20c. on 30c. orange-red 20·00
Z345 50c. on 48c. yellowish brown 90·00
Z346 $1 on 96c. grey-olive £150

1891. (Nos. 43/50).
Z347 7c. on 10c. green 70·00
Z348 14c. on 30c. mauve £130
Z348*a* 20c. on 30c. green (No. 45) £275
Z349 20c. on 30c. green (No. 48) 23·00
Z350 50c. on 48c. dull purple 30·00
Z351 $1 on 96c. purple/*red* 75·00

1898. (No. 52).
Z353 $1 on 96c. black £110

1898. (No. 55).
Z354 10c. on 30c. green £250

1900–01. Wmk Crown CA (Nos. 56/61).
Z355 2c. dull green 4·50
Z356 4c. carmine 5·00
Z357 5c. yellow 26·00
Z358 10c. ultramarine 4·50
Z360 30c. brown £100

1903. Wmk Crown CA (Nos. 62/76).
Z361 1c. dull purple and brown 5·50
Z362 2c. dull green 4·75
Z363 4c. purple/*red* 3·25
Z364 5c. dull green and brown-orange 25·00
Z365 8c. slate and violet 14·00
Z366 10c. purple and blue/*blue* 4·75
Z367 12c. green and purple/*yellow* 25·00
Z368 20c. slate and chestnut 15·00
Z369 30c. dull green and black 60·00
Z370 50c. dull green and magenta 95·00
Z371 $1 purple and sage-green 85·00

1904–06. Wmk Mult Crown CA (Nos. 77/90).
Z376 2c. dull green 4·75
Z377 4c. purple/*red* 3·25
Z378 5c. dull green and brown-orange 19·00
Z379 8c. slate and violet 12·00
Z380 10c. purple and blue/*blue* 4·75
Z381 12c. green and purple/*yellow* 27·00
Z382 20c. slate and chestnut 13·00
Z383 30c. dull green and black 55·00
Z384 50c. green and magenta 45·00
Z385 $1 purple and sage-green 90·00

1907–11. Wmk Mult Crown CA (Nos. 91/99).
Z390 1c. brown 4·25
Z391 2c. green 4·25
Z392 4c. carmine-red 3·25
Z393 6c. orange-vermilion and purple 23·00
Z394 10c. bright ultramarine 4·00
Z395 20c. purple and sage-green 85·00
Z396 30c. purple and orange-yellow 75·00
Z397 50c. black/*green* 55·00

1912–15. Wmk Mult Crown CA (Nos. 100/116).
Z399 1c. brown 6·00
Z400 2c. green 4·50
Z401 4c. red 3·25
Z402 6c. orange 15·00
Z403 8c. grey 27·00
Z404 10c. ultramarine 4·50
Z405 12c. purple/*yellow* 38·00
Z406 20c. purple and sage-green 8·00
Z407 25c. purple and magenta (Type A) £110
Z408 30c. purple and orange-yellow 27·00
Z409 50c. black/*green* 24·00

POSTCARD STAMPS

1874–1902. (Nos. P1/P2).
ZP413 3c. on 16c. yellow £1100

POSTAL FISCAL STAMPS

1874–1902. Wmk Crown CC. P 15½×15 (Nos. F1/F3)
ZF415 $2 olive-green £180
ZF416 $3 dull violet £160

HANKOW

Hankow, on the Yangtse River 600 miles from the sea, became a Treaty Port in 1860. A British consulate opened the following year, but no organised British postal agency was established until 1872.

Type **D** (*supplied* 1874) *used* 1874–1916
Type **B** ('D.29') (*supplied* 1876) *used* 1878–1883
Type **F** *used* 1916–1922

Stamps of HONG KONG cancelled at Hankow between 1874 and 1916 with postmarks detailed above.

1862. No wmk (Nos. 1/7).
Z426 18c. lilac £400

1863–71. Wmk Crown CC (Nos. 8/19).
Z427 2c. brown £140
Z428 4c. grey £140
Z429 6c. lilac £180
Z430 8c. orange £170
Z431 12c. blue 55·00
Z432 18c. lilac £1400
Z433 24c. green £275
Z435 30c. mauve £140
Z436 48c. rose £375
Z438 96c. brownish grey

1876–77. (Nos. 20/21).
Z439 16c. on 18c. lilac £550
Z440 28c. on 30c. mauve £325

1877. Wmk Crown CC (No. 22).
Z441 16c. yellow £800

1880. (Nos. 23/27).
Z442 5c. on 8c. orange £350
Z443 5c. on 18c. lilac £250
Z444 10c. on 12c. blue £275
Z445 10c. on 16c. yellow £500
Z446 10c. on 24c. green £325

1880. Wmk Crown CC (Nos. 28/31).
Z447 2c. rose £110
Z448 5c. blue £130
Z449 10c. mauve £140
Z450 48c. brown £450

1882–96. Wmk Crown CA (Nos. 32/39).
Z450*a* 2c. rose-lake £100
Z451 2c. carmine 10·00
Z452 4c. slate-grey 22·00
Z453 5c. blue 11·00
Z454 10c. dull mauve £120
Z455 10c. green 14·00
Z456 10c. purple/*red* 12·00
Z457 30c. green 80·00

1885. (Nos. 40/42).
Z458 20c. on 30c. orange-red 42·00
Z459 50c. on 48c. yellowish brown £110
Z460 $1 on 96c. grey-olive £200

1891. (Nos. 43/50).
Z461 7c. on 10c. green 42·00
Z462 14c. on 30c. mauve £170
Z463 20c. on 30c. green 30·00
Z464 50c. on 48c. dull purple 32·00
Z465 $1 on 96c. purple/*red* 90·00

1898. (No. 52).
Z467 $1 on 96c. black £120

1898. (No. 55).
Z468 10c. on 30c. green £325

1900–01. Wmk Crown CA (Nos. 56/61).
Z469 2c. dull green 7·00
Z470 4c. carmine 7·50
Z471 5c. yellow 40·00
Z472 10c. ultramarine 9·00
Z473 12c. blue £190
Z474 30c. brown £110

1903. Wmk Crown CA (Nos. 62/76).
Z475 1c. dull purple and brown 7·50
Z476 2c. dull green 7·00
Z477 4c. purple/*red* 6·00
Z478 5c. dull green and brown-orange 28·00
Z479 8c. slate and violet 22·00
Z480 10c. purple and blue/*blue* 6·50
Z481 12c. green and purple/*yellow* 28·00
Z482 20c. slate and chestnut 19·00
Z483 30c. dull green and black 65·00
Z484 50c. dull green and magenta £110
Z485 $1 purple and sage-green 90·00

1904–06. Wmk Mult Crown CA (Nos. 77/90).
Z490 2c. dull green 6·50
Z491 4c. purple/*red* 5·50
Z492 5c. dull green and brown-orange 26·00
Z493 8c. slate and violet 13·00
Z494 10c. purple and blue/*blue* 6·50
Z495 12c. green and purple/*yellow* 30·00
Z496 20c. slate and chestnut 20·00
Z497 30c. dull green and black 55·00
Z498 50c. green and magenta 42·00
Z499 $1 purple and sage-green 90·00
Z500 $2 slate and scarlet £450
Z502 $5 purple and blue-green £850
Z503 $10 slate and orange/*blue* £2000

1907–11. Wmk Mult Crown CA (Nos. 91/99).
Z504 1c. brown 7·00
Z505 2c. green 6·00
Z506 4c. carmine-red 4·50
Z507 6c. orange-vermilion and purple 29·00
Z508 10c. bright ultramarine 6·50
Z509 20c. purple and sage-green £110
Z510 30c. purple and orange-yellow 95·00

1912–15. Wmk Mult Crown CA (Nos. 100/116).
Z513 1c. brown 8·00
Z514 2c. green 7·00
Z515 4c. red 5·50
Z516 6c. orange 16·00
Z517 8c. grey 35·00
Z518 10c. ultramarine 6·50
Z520 20c. purple and sage-green 16·00
Z522 30c. purple and orange-yellow 35·00
Z523 50c. black/*green* 20·00
Z524 $1 purple and blue/*blue* 80·00
Z526 $3 green and purple £275
Z527 $5 green and red/*green* £750

POSTCARD STAMPS

1879. (Nos. P1/P2).
ZP528 3c. on 16c. yellow £1600

POSTAL FISCAL STAMPS

1874–1902. Wmk Crown CC.

(a) P 15½×15 (Nos. F1/F3)
ZF529 $2 olive-green £300

(b) P 14 (Nos. F4/F6)
ZF532 $2 dull bluish green £500

1897. (No. F11).
ZF533 $1 on $2 dull bluish green £750

KIUNGCHOW (HOIHOW)

Kiungchow, a city on the island of Hainan, and its port of Hoihow was added to the Treaty Port system in 1860. A consular postal agency was opened at Kiungchow in 1876, being transferred to Hoihow in 1878. A second agency was opened at Kiungchow in 1879.

Type **B** ('D.28') (*supplied* 1876) *used* 1879–1883
Type **D** (inscr 'KIUNG-CHOW') (*supplied* 1878) *used* 1879–1881

A
28 JA85
KIUNG-CHOW

'REGISTERED KIUNG-CHOW' with 'REGISTERED' removed (*originally supplied* 1876) *used* 1883–1885
Type **D** (inscr 'HOIHOW') *used* 1885–1922

Stamps of HONG KONG cancelled at Kiungchow (Hoihow) between 1879 and 1916 with postmarks detailed above.

1863–71. Wmk Crown CC (Nos. 8/19).
Z540 2c. brown £1000
Z541 4c. grey £800
Z542 6c. lilac £1700
Z543 8c. orange £1700
Z544 12c. blue £550
Z546 24c. green £1700
Z547 30c. vermilion
Z548 30c. mauve £300
Z549 48c. rose £2750
Z551 96c. brownish grey £2750

1876–77. (Nos. 20/21).
Z552 16c. on 18c. lilac £1800
Z553 28c. on 30c. mauve £1400

1877. (No. 22).
Z554 16c. yellow £2750

1880. (Nos. 23/27).
Z555 5c. on 8c. orange £1200
Z556 5c. on 18c. lilac £1000
Z557 10c. on 12c. blue £1000
Z558 10c. on 16c. yellow £2000
Z559 10c. on 24c. green

1880. Wmk Crown CC (Nos. 28/31).
Z561 5c. blue £800
Z562 10c. mauve £950

1882–96. Wmk Crown CA (Nos. 32/39).
Z564 2c. carmine 60·00
Z565 4c. slate-grey 90·00
Z566 5c. blue 60·00
Z567 10c. dull mauve £800
Z568 10c. green 85·00
Z569 10c. purple/*red* 60·00
Z570 30c. green £150

1885. (Nos. 40/42).
Z571 20c. on 30c. orange-red £160
Z572 50c. on 48c. yellowish brown £180
Z573 $1 on 96c. grey-olive £350

1891. (Nos. 43/50).
Z574 7c. on 10c. green £200
Z576 20c. on 30c. green 65·00
Z577 50c. on 48c. dull purple 95·00
Z578 $1 on 96c. purple/*red* £190

1891. 50th Anniversary of Colony (No. 51).
Z579 2c. carmine £3000

1898. (No. 52).
Z580 $1 on 96c. black £375

1898. (No. 55).
Z581 10c. on 30c. green £550

1900–01. Wmk Crown CA (Nos. 56/61).
Z582 2c. dull green 80·00
Z583 4c. carmine 40·00
Z584 5c. yellow £120
Z585 10c. ultramarine 45·00
Z587 30c. brown £225

1903. Wmk Crown CA (Nos. 62/76).
Z588 1c. dull purple and brown 30·00
Z589 2c. dull green 30·00
Z590 4c. purple/*red* 21·00
Z591 5c. dull green and brown-orange 70·00
Z592 8c. slate and violet 55·00
Z593 10c. purple and blue/*blue* 26·00
Z594 12c. green and purple/*yellow* 75·00
Z595 20c. slate and chestnut 80·00
Z596 30c. dull green and black £150
Z597 50c. dull green and magenta £225
Z598 $1 purple and sage-green £300
Z599 $2 slate and scarlet £900

1904. Wmk Mult Crown CA (Nos. 77/90).
Z603 2c. dull green 27·00
Z604 4c. purple/*red* 21·00
Z605 5c. dull green and brown-orange 70·00
Z606 8c. slate and violet 38·00
Z607 10c. purple and blue/*blue* 24·00
Z608 12c. green and purple/*yellow* 75·00
Z609 20c. slate and chestnut 80·00
Z610 30c. dull green and black £100
Z612 $1 purple and sage-green £450

1907–11. Wmk Mult Crown CA (Nos. 91/99).
Z617 1c. brown 27·00
Z618 2c. green 26·00
Z619 4c. carmine-red 21·00
Z620 6c. orange-vermilion and purple 70·00
Z621 10c. bright ultramarine 24·00
Z622 20c. purple and sage-green £120
Z623 30c. purple and orange-yellow £100

1912–15. Wmk Mult Crown CA (Nos. 100/116).
Z625 1c. brown 25·00
Z626 2c. green 24·00
Z627 4c. red 21·00
Z628 6c. orange 40·00
Z629 8c. grey 95·00
Z630 10c. ultramarine 21·00
Z631 12c. purple/*yellow* 75·00
Z632 20c. purple and sage-green 48·00
Z633 25c. purple and magenta (Type A) £150
Z634 30c. purple and orange-yellow £100
Z635 50c. black/*green* 85·00
Z636 $1 purple and blue/*blue* 90·00

POSTAL FISCAL STAMPS

1874–1902. Wmk Crown CC.

(a) P 15½×15 (Nos. F1/F3)
ZF641 $2 olive-green £475

(b) P 14 (Nos. F4/F6)
ZF644 $2 dull bluish green £750

1897. (Nos. F10/F11).
ZF650 $1 on $2 olive-green £600

NINGPO

Ningpo was one of the 1842 Treaty Ports and a consular postal agency was established there in 1844.

Type **A** ('N1') (*supplied* 1866) *used* 1870–1882
Type **C** (*supplied* 1866) *used* 1870–1899
Type **D** *used* 1899–1922

Stamps of HONG KONG cancelled at Ningpo between 1866 and 1916 with postmarks detailed above.

1862. No wmk (Nos. 1/7).
Z652 18c. lilac £1200

1863–71. Wmk Crown CC (Nos. 8/19).
Z653 2c. brown £450
Z654 4c. grey £450
a. Perf 12½ £2750
Z655 6c. lilac £500
Z656 8c. orange £450
Z657 12c. blue £170
Z658 18c. lilac
Z659 24c. green £475
Z660 30c. vermilion £600
Z661 30c. mauve £150
Z662 48c. rose £850
Z663 96c. olive-bistre
Z664 96c. brownish grey £1000

1876–77. (Nos. 20/21).
Z665 16c. on 18c. lilac £700
Z666 28c. on 30c. mauve £400

1877. Wmk Crown CC (No. 22).
Z667 16c. yellow £550

1880. (Nos. 23/27).
Z668 5c. on 8c. orange £500
Z669 5c. on 18c. lilac £425
Z670 10c. on 12c. blue £450
Z672 10c. on 24c. green £500

1880. Wmk Crown CC (Nos. 28/31).
Z673 2c. dull rose £275
Z674 5c. blue £250
Z675 10c. mauve £250
Z676 48c. brown £950

1882–96. Wmk Crown CA (Nos. 32/39).
Z677 2c. carmine 50·00
Z678 4c. slate-grey 85·00
Z679 5c. blue 50·00
Z680 10c. dull mauve £250
Z681 10c. green 70·00
Z682 10c. purple/*red* 55·00
Z683 30c. green £160

1885. (Nos. 40/42).
Z685 50c. on 48c. yellowish brown £200

1891. (Nos. 43/50).
Z686 7c. on 10c. green 80·00
Z687 14c. on 30c. mauve £325
Z688 20c. on 30c. green 60·00
Z689 50c. on 48c. dull purple 95·00
Z690 $1 on 96c. purple/*red* £180

1898. (No. 52).
Z692 $1 on 96c. black £200

1898. (No. 55).
Z693 10c. on 30c. green £375

1900–01. Wmk Crown CA (Nos. 56/61).
Z694 2c. dull green 35·00
Z695 4c. carmine 30·00
Z697 10c. ultramarine 35·00

1903. Wmk Crown CA (Nos. 62/76).
Z700 1c. dull purple and brown 30·00
Z701 2c. dull green 30·00
Z702 4c. purple/*red* 23·00
Z703 5c. dull green and brown-orange 75·00
Z704 8c. slate and violet 40·00
Z705 10c. purple and blue/*blue* 25·00
Z706 12c. green and purple/*yellow* 85·00
Z709 50c. dull green and magenta £150

1904–06. Wmk Mult Crown CA (Nos. 77/90).
Z715 2c. dull green 28·00
Z716 4c. purple/*red* 25·00
Z718 8c. slate and violet 60·00
Z720 12c. green and purple/*yellow* 85·00
Z721 20c. slate and chestnut 75·00
Z722 30c. dull green and black £110
Z723 50c. green and magenta 95·00
Z724 $1 purple and sage-green £150

1907–11. Wmk Mult Crown CA (Nos. 91/99).

Z729	1c. brown	25·00
Z730	2c. green	25·00
Z731	4c. carmine-red	22·00
Z733	10c. bright ultramarine	25·00
Z734	20c. purple and sage-green	£140
Z735	30c. purple and orange-yellow	£130

1912–15. Wmk Mult Crown CA (Nos. 100/116).

Z738	1c. brown	26·00
Z739	2c. green	25·00
Z740	4c. red	23·00
Z742	8c. grey	85·00
Z743	10c. ultramarine	25·00
Z745	20c. purple and sage-green	65·00
Z747	30c. purple and orange-yellow	£100
Z749	$1 purple and blue/*blue*	90·00

POSTCARD STAMPS

1879. (Nos. P1/P2).

ZP751	3c. on 16c. yellow	£1800

POSTAL FISCAL STAMPS

1874–1902. Wmk Crown CC. P 15½×15 (Nos. F1/F3).

ZF754	$2 olive-green	£450

1880. (No. F7).

ZF760	12c. on $10 rose-carmine	

1897. (No. F10).

ZF763	$1 on $2 olive-green	

SHANGHAI

Shanghai was one of the original Treaty Ports of 1842 and a packet agency was opened at the British consulate in April 1844. It moved to a separate premise in 1861 and was upgraded to a Post Office in September 1867.

British military post offices operated in Shanghai from 1927 until 1940.

Type **D** (inscr 'SHANGHAE') (*supplied* 1861) *used* 1861–1899

Sunburst *used* 1864–1865
Type **A** ('S1') (*supplied* 1866) *used* 1866–1885
Type **D** (inscr 'SHANGHAI') (*supplied* 1885) *used* 1886-1906
Type **G** (inscr 'B.P.O.' at foot) (*supplied* 1904) *used* 1904–1921
Type **G** (inscr 'Br.P.O.' at foot) (*supplied* 1907) *used* 1907–1922
Type **E** (figures 'I' to 'VIII' at foot) *used* 1912–1922

Stamps of HONG KONG cancelled at Shanghai between 1863 and 1916 with postmarks detailed above.

1862. No wmk (Nos. 1/7).

Z765	2c. brown	£180
Z766	8c. yellow-buff	£200
Z767	12c. pale greenish blue	£160
Z768	18c. lilac	£130
Z769	24c. green	£250
Z770	48c. rose	£600
Z771	96c. brownish grey	£750

1863–71. Wmk Crown CC (Nos. 8/19).

Z772	2c. brown	12·00
Z773	4c. grey	11·00
	a. Perf 12½	£275
Z774	6c. lilac	24·00
Z775	8c. orange	19·00
Z776	12c. blue	11·00
Z777	18c. lilac	£375
Z778	24c. green	18·00
Z779	30c. vermilion	27·00
Z780	30c. mauve	8·50
Z781	48c. rose	42·00
Z782	96c. olive-bistre	£1400
Z783	96c. brownish grey	65·00

1876–77. (Nos. 20/21).

Z784	16c. on 18c. lilac	£170
Z785	28c. on 30c. mauve	55·00

1877. Wmk Crown CC (No. 22).

Z786	16c. yellow	75·00

1880. (Nos. 23/27).

Z787	5c. on 8c. orange	£110
Z788	5c. on 18c. lilac	70·00
Z789	10c. on 12c. blue	60·00
Z790	10c. on 16c. yellow	£190
Z791	10c. on 24c. green	£120

1880. Wmk Crown CC (Nos. 28/31).

Z792	2c. rose	45·00
Z793	5c. blue	70·00
Z794	10c. mauve	22·00
Z795	48c. brown	£150

1882–96. Wmk Crown CA (Nos. 32/39).

Z795*a*	2c. rose-lake	38·00
Z796	2c. carmine	3·25
Z797	4c. slate-grey	3·50
Z798	5c. blue	1·50
Z799	10c. dull mauve	28·00
Z800	10c. green	2·50
Z801	10c. purple/*red*	1·90
Z802	30c. green	40·00

1885. (Nos. 40/42).

Z803	20c. on 30c. orange-red	9·50
Z804	50c. on 48c. yellowish brown	60·00
Z805	$1 on 96c. grey-olive	£110

1891. (Nos. 43/50).

Z806	7c. on 10c. green	17·00
Z807	14c. on 30c. mauve	£100
Z807*a*	20c. on 30c. green (No. 45)	
Z807*b*	50c. on 48c. dull purple (No. 46)	£350
Z807*c*	$1 on 96c. purple/*red* (No. 47)	£400
Z808	20c. on 30c. green (No. 48)	10·00
Z809	50c. on 48c. dull purple (No. 49)	8·00
Z810	$1 on 96c. purple/*red* (No. 50)	30·00

1898. (No. 52).

Z812	$1 on 96c. black	45·00

1898. (No. 55).

Z813	10c. on 30c. green	£130

1900–01. Wmk Crown CA (Nos. 56/61).

Z814	2c. dull green	1·25
Z815	4c. carmine	1·25
Z816	5c. yellow	12·00
Z817	10c. ultramarine	2·75
Z818	12c. blue	£110
Z819	30c. brown	42·00

1903. Wmk Crown CA (Nos. 62/76).

Z820	1c. dull purple and brown	1·00
Z821	2c. dull green	3·00
Z822	4c. purple/*red*	85
Z823	5c. dull green and brown-orange	16·00
Z824	8c. slate and violet	3·25
Z825	10c. purple and blue/*blue*	2·00
Z826	12c. green and purple/*yellow*	10·00
Z827	20c. slate and chestnut	6·50
Z828	30c. dull green and black	40·00
Z829	50c. dull green and magenta	85·00
Z830	$1 purple and sage-green	42·00
Z831	$2 slate and scarlet	£425
Z832	$3 slate and dull blue	£600
Z833	$5 purple and blue-green	£700
Z834	$10 slate and orange/*blue*	£700

1904–06. Wmk Mult Crown CA (Nos. 77/90).

Z835	2c. dull green	3·00
Z836	4c. purple/*red*	85
Z837	5c. dull green and brown-orange	11·00
Z838	8c. slate and violet	3·50
Z839	10c. purple and blue/*blue*	1·75
Z840	12c. green and purple/*yellow*	13·00
Z841	20c. slate and chestnut	4·75
Z842	30c. dull green and black	32·00
Z843	50c. green and magenta	23·00
Z844	$1 purple and sage-green	50·00
Z845	$2 slate and scarlet	£180
Z846	$3 slate and dull blue	£450
Z847	$5 purple and blue-green	£600
Z848	$10 slate and orange/*blue*	£1600

1907–11. Wmk Mult Crown CA (Nos. 91/99).

Z849	1c. brown	1·75
Z850	2c. green	2·00
Z851	4c. carmine-red	85
Z852	6c. orange-vermilion and purple	11·00
Z853	10c. bright ultramarine	85
Z854	20c. purple and sage-green	65·00
Z855	30c. purple and orange-yellow	50·00
Z856	50c. black/*green*	28·00
Z857	$2 carmine-red and black	£550

1912–15. Wmk Mult Crown CA (Nos. 100/116).

Z858	1c. brown	1·25
Z859	2c. green	85
Z860	4c. red	70
Z861	6c. orange	3·75
Z862	8c. grey	12·00
Z863	10c. ultramarine	75
Z864	12c. purple/*yellow*	19·00
Z865	20c. purple and sage-green	2·25
Z867	30c. purple and orange-yellow	16·00
Z868	50c. black/*green*	6·50
Z869	$1 purple and blue/*blue*	10·00

POSTCARD STAMPS

1879. (Nos. P1/P2).

ZP871	3c. on 16c. yellow	£550
ZP872	5c. on 18c. lilac	£650

POSTAL FISCAL STAMPS

1874–1902. Wmk Crown CC.

(a) P 15½×15 (Nos. F1/F5)

ZF874	$2 olive-green	80·00
ZF875	$3 dull violet	60·00
ZF876	$10 rose-carmine	£750

(b) P 14

ZF877	$2 dull bluish green	£300
ZF878	$3 dull mauve	£600

1880. (No. F7).

ZF880	12c. on $10 rose-carmine	£350

1891. (No. F9).

ZF882	$5 on $10 purple/*red*	£170

1897. (No. F10/F11).

ZF883	$1 on $2 olive-green	£200
ZF884	$1 on $2 dull bluish green	£275

SWATOW

Swatow became a Treaty Port in 1860 and a consular packet agency was opened in the area made available for foreign firms during the following year. In 1867 the original agency was transferred to the Chinese city on the other side of the Han River, but a second agency was subsequently opened in the foreign concession during 1883.

Type **A** ('S2') (*supplied* 1866) *used* 1875–1885
Type **C** (*supplied* 1866) *used* 1866–1890
Type **D** (*supplied* 1883) *used* 1884–1922
Type **F** *used* 1916–1922

Stamps of HONG KONG cancelled at Swatow between 1866 and 1916 with postmarks detailed above.

1862. No wmk (Nos. 1/7).

Z885	18c. lilac	£450

1863–71. Wmk Crown CC (Nos. 8/19).

Z886	2c. brown	£170
Z887	4c. grey	£160
	a. Perf 12½	
Z888	6c. lilac	£600
Z889	8c. orange	£160
Z890	12c. blue	60·00
Z891	18c. lilac	£1300
Z892	24c. green	£200
Z893	30c. vermilion	
Z894	30c. mauve	60·00
Z895	48c. rose	£325
Z897	96c. brownish grey	£1000

1876–77. (Nos. 20/21).

Z898	16c. on 18c. lilac	£500
Z899	28c. on 30c. mauve	£275

1877. Wmk Crown CC (No. 22).

Z900	16c. yellow	£500

1880. (Nos. 23/27).

Z901	5c. on 8c. orange	£325
Z902	5c. on 18c. lilac	£275
Z903	10c. on 12c. blue	£300
Z904	10c. on 16c. yellow	£550
Z905	10c. on 24c. green	£375

1880. Wmk Crown CC (Nos. 28/31).

Z906	2c. rose	£150
Z907	5c. blue	£170
Z908	10c. mauve	£180

1882–96. Wmk Crown CA (Nos. 32/39).

Z910	2c. carmine	8·00
Z911	4c. slate-grey	26·00
Z912	5c. blue	8·50
Z913	10c. dull mauve	£140
Z914	10c. green	12·00
Z915	10c. purple/*red*	8·00
Z916	30c. green	75·00

1885. (Nos. 40/42).

Z917	20c. on 30c. orange-red	24·00
Z917*a*	50c. on 48c. yellowish brown	£180
Z918	$1 on 96c. grey-olive	£200

1891. (Nos. 43/50).

Z919	7c. on 10c. green	40·00
Z920	14c. on 30c. mauve	£160
Z920*a*	50c. on 48c. dull purple (No. 46)	£425
Z921	$1 on 96c. purple/*red* (No. 47)	£600
Z922	20c. on 30c. green	30·00
Z923	50c. on 48c. dull purple (No. 49)	32·00
Z924	$1 on 96c. purple/*red* (No. 50)	75·00

1891. 50th Anniversary of Colony (No. 51).

Z925	2c. carmine	£1300

1898. (No. 52).

Z926	$1 on 96c. black	£110

1898. (No. 55).

Z927	10c. on 30c. green	£300

1900–01. Wmk Crown CA (Nos. 56/61).

Z928	2c. dull green	8·50
Z929	4c. carmine	7·00
Z930	5c. yellow	32·00
Z931	10c. ultramarine	7·50
Z932	12c. blue	£225
Z933	30c. brown	80·00

1903. Wmk Crown CA (Nos. 62/76).

Z934	1c. dull purple and brown	8·00
Z935	2c. dull green	7·50
Z936	4c. purple/*red*	6·00
Z937	5c. dull green and brown-orange	25·00
Z938	8c. slate and violet	16·00
Z939	10c. purple and blue/*blue*	7·50
Z940	12c. green and purple/*yellow*	24·00
Z941	20c. slate and chestnut	12·00
Z942	30c. dull green and black	65·00
Z943	50c. dull green and magenta	£120
Z944	$1 purple and sage-green	£100

1904–06. Wmk Mult Crown CA (Nos. 77/90).

Z949	2c. dull green	8·00
Z950	4c. purple/*red*	6·00
Z951	5c. dull green and brown-orange	24·00
Z952	8c. slate and violet	15·00
Z953	10c. purple and blue/*blue*	7·00
Z954	12c. green and purple/*yellow*	25·00

Z955 20c. slate and chestnut 15·00
Z956 30c. dull green and black 60·00
Z957 50c. green and magenta 40·00
Z958 $1 purple and sage-green 95·00
Z959 $2 slate and scarlet £350
Z962 $10 slate and orange/*blue* £2000

1907–11. Wmk Mult Crown CA (Nos. 91/99).
Z963 1c. brown 9·00
Z964 2c. green 8·50
Z965 4c. carmine-red 6·00
Z966 6c. orange-vermilion and purple 21·00
Z967 10c. bright ultramarine 6·50
Z968 20c. purple and sage-green £110
Z969 30c. purple and orange-yellow 85·00
Z970 50c. black/*green* 55·00

1912–15. Wmk Mult Crown CA (Nos. 100/116).
Z972 1c. brown 7·00
Z973 2c. green 6·00
Z974 4c. red 5·00
Z975 6c. orange 11·00
Z976 8c. grey 29·00
Z977 10c. ultramarine 5·00
Z978 12c. purple/*yellow* 25·00
Z979 20c. purple and sage-green 7·50
Z980 25c. purple and magenta (Type A) 75·00
Z981 30c. purple and orange-yellow 32·00
Z982 50c. black/*green* 18·00
Z983 $1 purple and blue/*blue* 29·00

POSTCARD STAMP

1879. (Nos. P1/P2).
ZP986 3c. on 16c. yellow £1400

POSTAL FISCAL STAMPS

1874–1902. Wmk Crown CC.

(a) P 15½×15 (Nos. F1/F3)
ZF988 $2 olive-green £180
ZF989 $3 dull violet £160

(b) P 14
ZF991 $2 dull bluish green £500

TIENTSIN

Tientsin became a Treaty Port in 1860. A British consulate was established in 1861, but no formal postal agency was organised there until 1882. It was not, however, very successful and was closed during 1890. The British Post Office reopened on 1 October 1906 under the management of the Chinese Engineering and Mining Company.

British military post offices operated in Tientsin from 1927 until 1940.

Type **E** *used* 1906–1913
Type **G** (*supplied* 1907) *used* 1907–1922

Stamps of HONG KONG cancelled at Tientsin between 1906 and 1916 with postmarks detailed above.

1903. Wmk Crown CA (Nos. 62/76).
Z998 1c. dull purple and brown 17·00
Z998*b* 4c. purple/*red* 22·00
Z999 5c. dull green and brown-orange 42·00
Z1000 8c. slate and violet 18·00
Z1000*a* 12c. green and purple/*yellow* 60·00

1904–06. Wmk Mult Crown CA (Nos. 77/90).
Z1001 2c. dull green 7·50
Z1002 4c. purple/*red* 5·00
Z1003 5c. dull green and brown-orange 22·00
Z1004 8c. slate and violet 17·00
Z1005 10c. purple and blue/*blue* 6·50
Z1006 12c. green and purple/*yellow* 28·00
Z1007 20c. slate and chestnut 16·00
Z1008 30c. dull green and black 55·00
Z1009 50c. green and magenta 42·00
Z1010 $1 purple and sage-green 80·00
Z1011 $2 slate and scarlet £325
Z1012 $3 slate and dull blue £800
Z1013 $5 purple and blue-green £950
Z1014 $10 slate and orange/*blue* £2000

1907–11. Wmk Mult Crown CA (Nos. 91/99).
Z1015 1c. brown 8·00
Z1016 2c. green 6·00
Z1017 4c. carmine-red 4·50
Z1018 6c. orange-vermilion and purple 25·00
Z1019 10c. bright ultramarine 5·50
Z1020 20c. purple and sage-green £110
Z1021 30c. purple and orange-yellow 95·00
Z1022 50c. black/*green* 70·00
Z1023 $2 carmine-red and black £750

1912–15. Wmk Mult Crown CA (Nos. 100/116).
Z1024 1c. brown 7·00
Z1025 2c. green 6·00
Z1026 4c. red 4·25
Z1027 6c. orange 10·00
Z1028 8c. grey 40·00
Z1029 10c. ultramarine 6·50
Z1030 12c. purple/*yellow* 45·00
Z1031 20c. purple and sage-green 10·00
Z1033 30c. purple and orange-yellow 25·00
Z1034 50c. black/*green* 14·00
Z1035 $1 purple and blue/*blue* 20·00
Z1037 $3 green and purple £250
Z1038 $5 green and red/*green* £700

WEI HAI WEI

The territory of Wei Hai Wei was leased from the Chinese by the British Government from 24 May 1898 having been previously occupied by the Japanese. At that time there were no organised postal services from the area, although a private local post did operate between the port and Chefoo from 8 December 1898 until 15 March 1899. A Chinese Imperial post office opened in March 1899 to be followed by a British postal agency on the offshore island of Liu Kung Tau on 1 September 1899. A second British agency opened at Port Edward on 1 April 1904.

Liu Kung Tau oval *used* 1899–1901
Type **D** (inscr 'LIU KUNG TAU') (*supplied* 1899) *used* 1901–1930

Stamps of HONG KONG cancelled at Liu Kung Tau between 1899 and 1916 with postmarks detailed above.

1863–71. Wmk Crown CC (Nos. 8/19).
Z1039 12c. pale blue

1882–96. Wmk Crown CA (Nos. 32/39).
Z1040 2c. carmine 85·00
Z1041 4c. slate-grey £100
Z1042 5c. blue 85·00
Z1043 10c. purple/*red* 55·00
Z1044 30c. green 95·00

1891. (Nos. 48/50).
Z1045 20c. on 30c. green 70·00
Z1046 50c. on 48c. dull purple 75·00

1898. (No. 52).
Z1047 $1 on 96c. black £140

1900–01. Wmk Crown CA (Nos. 56/61).
Z1049 2c. dull green 13·00
Z1050 4c. carmine 13·00
Z1051 5c. yellow 40·00
Z1052 10c. ultramarine 13·00
Z1053 12c. blue £180
Z1054 30c. brown £110

1903. Wmk Crown CA (Nos. 62/76).
Z1055 1c. dull purple and brown 9·50
Z1056 2c. dull green 9·00
Z1057 4c. purple/*red* 8·00
Z1058 5c. dull green and brown-orange 28·00
Z1059 8c. slate and violet 20·00
Z1060 10c. purple and blue/*blue* 13·00
Z1061 12c. green and purple/*yellow* 45·00
Z1062 20c. slate and chestnut 21·00
Z1063 30c. dull green and black 75·00
Z1064 50c. dull green and magenta £130
Z1065 $1 purple and sage-green £100

1904–06. Wmk Mult Crown CA (Nos. 77/90).
Z1070 2c. dull green 9·50
Z1071 4c. purple/*red* 9·00
Z1073 8c. slate and violet 18·00
Z1076 20c. slate and chestnut 38·00
Z1077 30c. dull green and black £110
Z1078 50c. green and magenta 85·00
Z1079 $1 purple and sage-green £150

1907–11. Wmk Mult Crown CA (Nos. 91/99).
Z1084 1c. brown 10·00
Z1085 2c. green 10·00
Z1086 4c. carmine-red 7·50
Z1088 10c. bright ultramarine 9·00
Z1089 20c. purple and sage-green £130
Z1090 30c. purple and orange-yellow £100
Z1091 50c. black/*green* 85·00

1912–15. Wmk Mult Crown CA (Nos. 100/116).
Z1093 1c. brown 12·00
Z1094 2c. green 9·00
Z1095 4c. red 7·00
Z1096 6c. orange 18·00
Z1097 8c. grey 42·00
Z1098 10c. ultramarine 8·00
Z1104 $1 purple and blue/*blue* 42·00

POSTAL FISCAL STAMP

1874–1902. Wmk Crown CC. P 14 (Nos. F4/F6).
Z1106 $2 dull bluish green £1100

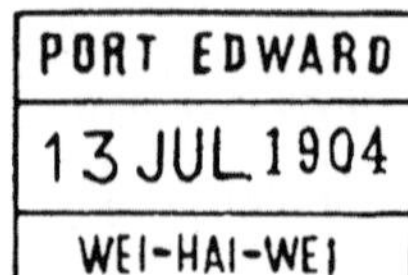

Port Edward rectangle used 1904–1908
Type **D** (inscr 'WEI-HAI-WEI' at top and 'PORT EDWARD' at foot) (*supplied* 1907) *used* 1907–1930

Stamps of HONG KONG cancelled at Port Edward between 1904 and 1916 with postmarks detailed above.

1900–01. Wmk Crown CA (Nos. 56/61).
Z1109 2c. dull green 95·00
Z1110 10c. ultramarine £120

1903. Wmk Crown CA (Nos. 62/76).
Z1111 1c. dull purple and brown 38·00
Z1112 2c. dull green 38·00
Z1113 4c. purple/*red* 32·00
Z1114 5c. dull green and brown-orange 55·00
Z1115 8c. slate and violet 50·00
Z1116 10c. purple and blue/*blue* 40·00
Z1117 12c. green and purple/*yellow* 75·00
Z1118 20c. slate and chestnut £100
Z1119 30c. dull green and black £100
Z1120 50c. dull green and magenta £140
Z1121 $1 purple and sage-green £110

1904–06. Wmk Mult Crown CA (Nos. 77/90).
Z1126 2c. dull green 21·00
Z1127 4c. purple/*red* 19·00
Z1128 5c. dull green and brown-orange 35·00
Z1129 8c. slate and violet 25·00
Z1132 20c. slate and chestnut 95·00
Z1133 30c. dull green and black 90·00
Z1134 50c. green and magenta 95·00
Z1135 $1 purple and sage-green £120

1907–11. Wmk Mult Crown CA (Nos. 91/99).
Z1140 1c. brown 20·00
Z1141 2c. green 20·00
Z1142 4c. carmine-red 14·00
Z1143 6c. orange-vermilion and purple 45·00
Z1144 10c. bright ultramarine 16·00
Z1145 20c. purple and sage-green £120
Z1146 30c. purple and orange-yellow £120
Z1148 50c. black/*green* 70·00

1912–15. Wmk Mult Crown CA (Nos. 100/116).
Z1151 1c. brown 18·00
Z1152 2c. green 13·00
Z1153 4c. red 8·00
Z1155 8c. grey 38·00
Z1156 10c. ultramarine 9·00
Z1157 12c. purple/*yellow* 48·00
Z1158 20c. purple and sage-green 24·00
Z1160 30c. purple and orange-yellow 42·00
Z1161 50c. black/*green* 32·00
Z1162 $1 purple and blue/*blue* 35·00

PRICES FOR STAMPS ON COVER	
Nos. 1/14	*from* × 50
Nos. 15/17	—
Nos. 18/28	*from* × 30

The overprinted stamps Nos. 1/17 were introduced on 1 January 1917 to prevent currency speculation in the Treaty Ports. They were used in the then-existing agencies of Amoy, Canton, Chefoo, Foochow, Hankow, Hoihow, Ningpo, Shanghai, Swatow, Tientsin and were also supplied to the British naval base of Wei Hai Wei.

CHINA

(1)

1917 (1 Jan)–**21.** Stamps of Hong Kong, 1912–1921 (wmk Mult Crown CA), optd with T **1**, at Somerset House.

No.	Description	Unused	Used
1	1c. brown	16·00	1·50
	a. Black-brown	9·50	2·50
	b. Crown broken at right	£400	£400
	c. Wmk sideways	†	£3000
	w. Wmk inverted	†	£1800
2	2c. green	20·00	30
	w. Wmk inverted	†	£2000
	x. Wmk reversed	†	£2250
3	4c. carmine-red	13·00	30
	a. Substituted crown in wmk	†	£1800
	w. Wmk inverted	†	£2500
4	6c. orange	10·00	1·75
	w. Wmk inverted	†	£1700
5	8c. slate	15·00	1·25
6	10c. ultramarine	21·00	30
	w. Wmk inverted	†	£2000
	y. Wmk inverted and reversed	†	£1200
7	12c. purple/*yellow*	18·00	11·00
8	20c. purple and sage-green	26·00	1·50
9	25c. purple and magenta (A)	15·00	15·00
11	30c. purple and orange-yellow	50·00	11·00
12	50c. black/*blue-green (olive back)*	75·00	1·50
	a. Emerald surface (1917?)	70·00	11·00
	b. On emerald back (1919)	55·00	5·50
	c. On white back (1920)	£1300	£180
13	$1 reddish purple and bright blue/*blue*	85·00	2·50
	a. Grey-purple and blue/blue (1921)	90·00	8·00
14	$2 carmine-red and grey-black	£225	80·00
15	$3 green and purple	£700	£275
16	$5 green and red/*blue-green (olive back)*	£350	£350
17	$10 purple and black/*red*	£700	£700
1/17 *Set of* 16		£2000	£1300
12s/17s H/S 'SPECIMEN' (50c.) or '*SPECIMEN*' *Set of* 6		£2250	

1922 (Mar)–**27.** As last, but wmk Mult Script CA.

No.	Description	Unused	Used
18	1c. brown	3·50	7·50
19	2c. green	9·00	2·25
	w. Wmk inverted	£475	
20	4c. carmine-rose	22·00	3·50
	a. Lower Chinese character at right broken at top	£325	£350
21	6c. orange-yellow	7·50	7·00
22	8c. grey	15·00	16·00
23	10c. bright ultramarine	24·00	4·50
	w. Wmk inverted	£300	
24	20c. purple and sage-green	22·00	5·00
25	25c. purple and magenta (B)	27·00	75·00
	a. Broken flower	£850	
26	50c. black/*emerald* (1927)	60·00	£350
	s. Handstamped '*SPECIMEN*'	£275	
27	$1 purple and blue/*blue*	80·00	80·00
28	$2 carmine-red and grey-black	£200	£250
18/28 *Set of* 11		£425	£750

STAMP BOOKLETS

1917. Black on red cover inscribed 'BRITISH POST OFFICE AGENCIES IN CHINA'. Stapled.

SB1	$1 booklet containing 8×2c., 6×4c. and 6×10c. (Nos. 2/3, 6)	£6500

Three settings of the front cover of No. SB1 are recognised.

1922. Cover as No. SB1. Stapled.

SB2	$1 booklet containing 8×2c., 6×4c., and 6×10c. (Nos. 19/20, 23)	£6000

The British PO's in the Treaty Ports closed by agreement with the Chinese on 30 November 1922, but the above over-printed issues continued in use at the Wei Hai Wei offices until they in turn closed on 30 September 1930. Under the terms of the Convention signed with China the Royal Navy continued to use the base at Wei Hai Wei until the mid-1930s.

BRITISH POST OFFICES IN JAPAN

Under the terms of the Anglo-Japanese Treaty of Yedo, signed on 26 August 1858, four Japanese ports were opened to British trade. British consulates were established at Decima (Nagasaki), Kanagawa (Yokohama), Hiogo (Kobe) and Hakodadi (Hakodate).The postage stamps of Hong Kong became available at the Yokohama and Nagasaki consulates during October 1864 and at Hiogo in 1869, although cancellation of mail did not commence until 1866 at Yokohama and Nagasaki or 1876 at Hiogo. Japan became a member of the UPUon 1 June 1877 and all of the British Postal Agencies were closed by the end of 1879.

For illustrations of postmark types see BRITISH POST OFFICES IN CHINA.

HAKODATE

A British consular office existed at Hakodate, but it was never issued with a c.d.s. obliterator or Hong Kong stamps. No British covers are recorded from this consulate prior to opening of the Japanese Post Office.

HIOGO

The Port of Hiogo (Kobe) was first opened to foreigners on 1 January 1868. The British Consular mail service at Hiogo commenced during 1869 to serve the foreigners at Hiogo, Kobe and Osaka. The cities of Hiogo and Kobe later merged to become the single city of Kobe. The consular office at Hiogo closed on 30 November 1879.

Type **B** ('D.30.') (*supplied* 1876) *used* 1876–1879
Type **D** (*supplied* 1876) *used* 1876–1879

Stamps of HONG KONG cancelled at Hiogo between 1876 and 1879 with postmarks detailed above.

1863–71. Wmk Crown CC (Nos. 8/19).

Z1	2c. brown	£6000
Z2	4c. grey	£4250
Z3	6c. lilac	£5500
Z4	8c. orange	£5000
Z5	12c. blue	£6000
Z6	18c. lilac	
Z7	24c. green	£4500
Z8	30c. vermilion	
Z9	30c. mauve	£6000
Z10	48c. rose	£9000
Z12	96c. brownish grey	£9000

1877. (Nos. 20/21).

Z13	16c. on 18c. lilac	

1877. Wmk Crown CC (No. 22).

Z15	16c. yellow	£7000

NAGASAKI

The British Consulate opened in Nagasaki on 14 June 1859, but, with few British residents at the port, the consular staff found it inconvenient to carry out postal duties so that few Nagasaki c.d.s. or 'N2' cancellations exist. The postal service was terminated on 30 September 1879.

Type **A** ('N2') (*supplied* 1866) *used* 1876–1879
Type **D** (*supplied* 1866) *used* 1876–1879

Stamps of HONG KONG cancelled at Nagasaki between 1876 and 1879 with postmarks detailed above.

1862. No wmk (Nos. 1/8).

Z15a	18c. lilac	£3750

1863–71. Wmk Crown CC (Nos. 8/19).

Z16	2c. brown	£2250
Z17	4c. grey	£2000
Z18	6c. lilac	£2000
Z19	8c. orange	£2000
Z20	12c. blue	£2000
Z21	18c. lilac	£7500
Z22	24c. green	£3500
Z24	30c. mauve	£3000
Z25	48c. rose	£4000
Z27	96c. brownish grey	

1876–77. (Nos. 20/21).

Z28	16c. on 18c. lilac	£3000
Z29	28c. on 30c. mauve	£2250

1877. Wmk Crown CC (No. 22).

Z30	16c. yellow	£3250

YOKOHAMA

The British Consulate opened in Kanagawa on 21 July 1859, but was relocated to Yokohama where it provided postal services from 1 July 1860 until a separate Post Office was established in July 1867. The British Post Office in Yokohama closed on 31 December 1879.

Type **A** ('YI') (*supplied* 1866) *used* 1867–1879
Type **D** (*supplied* 1866) *used* 1866–1879

Stamps of HONG KONG cancelled at Yokohama between 1866 and 1879 with postmarks detailed above.

1862. No wmk (Nos. 1/8).

Z30*a*	8c. yellow-buff	£425
Z31	18c. lilac	£140

1863–71. Wmk Crown CC (Nos. 8/19).

Z32	2c. brown	22·00
Z33	4c. grey	23·00
	a. Perf 12½	£550
Z34	6c. lilac	30·00
Z35	8c. orange	28·00
Z36	12c. blue	22·00
Z37	18c. lilac	£750
Z38	24c. green	26·00
Z39	30c. vermilion	75·00
Z40	30c. mauve	22·00
Z41	48c. rose	65·00
Z42	96c. olive-bistre	£5000
Z43	96c. brownish grey	85·00

1876–77. (Nos. 20/21).

Z44	16c. on 18c. lilac	£325
Z45	28c. on 30c. mauve	90·00

1877. Wmk Crown CC (No. 22).

Z46	16c. yellow	£140

POSTAL FISCAL STAMPS

1874. Wmk Crown CC. P 15½×15 (Nos. F1/F3).

ZF47	$2 olive-green	£160
ZF48	$3 dull violet	£150
ZF49	$10 rose-carmine	£1900

ANDREW PROMOTING PHILATELY ON THE ALAN TITCHMARSH SHOW ITV

Selling Your Stamps?

Summary Tip #20:
5 Different Ways to Sell your Stamps: Dealer 'runners'/ Private Treaty

by Andrew McGavin

Dear Colleague,

In Part 2 of 'Selling Your Stamps' (Page) we discussed the advantages of direct sale to dealers and how with careful handling and awareness of the 'strength of your collection' it is often possible to obtain more for your collection selling directly to dealers than by selling through auction.

In Part 4 of 'Selling your Stamps' we'll discuss the potential advantages and disadvantages of selling through auction on your own account .... but in this article we'll deal with two lesser known but nevertheless important aspects of selling your stamps .... the first being Dealers 'runners'.

Before you even start to try selling your stamps; preparation is all. Make some research:

1. Draw up a list of whom you consider as a possible target to sell / handle your collection. ..... then consider –
2. Why have I chosen those dealers/ organisations ?

Here's something to think about ... for the best part of 20 years I watched the same advertisements extolling the merits of selling to this or that particular dealer ... but try as I might – I never once saw an advertisement by those companies to sell stamps. This was in 'pre-internet' days ... nowadays people trade on the internet with all manner of weird and unusual trading names, sometimes to disguise who they actually are – but in those days traditional selling 'avenues' were shops, stamp fairs, auctions, approvals, and retail/mail-order lists ....

... so why was it impossible to find out how those dealers actually conducted their business? The answer was simple – they sold to other dealers – they rarely if ever sold to collectors – they were Dealers 'runners'. Now for you to part with your beloved collection to the first dealer that you contact does not necessarily mean that you have made a mistake ... but, if that dealer writes you out a cheque ... and almost before the ink has even dried on it – (probably before you have presented the cheque at your bank) ... he or she is at the nearest big dealer 50 miles away being paid a profit upon the price you sold your collection for – this is NOT in your best interest.

> ***...but try as I might – I never once saw an advertisement by those companies to sell stamps.***

So what should you be looking for? You should be looking for an organisation / dealer that you can see and understand how they conduct their business. Dealers that sell to other dealers are unlikely to be paying the best price.

Private Treaty: What is it?

The idea of Private Treaty is that collectors 'place' their collection with a dealer or auction that charges a small commission to sell their collection outright. Sometimes it is claimed that the Buyer will pay the commission so that the collector pays no charges whatsoever. Historically 'Private Treaty' has acquired notoriety as an excuse for the company handling the transaction to 'buy-in' the collection for themselves. Maybe collectors and dealers should forget the concept of private treaty in favour of an open approach whereby the dealer/auction explains that they are purchasing on their own account ... or will charge a small percentage for handling/ passing the collector/collection to a more appropriate buyer. In Part 4 of 'Selling your Stamps?' we'll discuss consigning your stamps for sale by auction.

Happy collecting from us all,

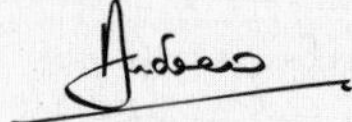

PS. If you find this 'tip' interesting please forward it to a philatelic friend.

Andrew McGavin

Managing Director: Universal Philatelic Auctions, Omniphil & Avon Approvals, Avon Mixtures, Universal Philatelic (Ebay)

To read the rest of this series 'SELLING YOUR STAMPS?' see the relevant pages listed below:

Summary Tip 18 – page 42 (Australia)
Summary Tip 19 – page 206 (Egypt)
Summary Tip 20 – page 266 (India)

To read the final instalment, Summary Tips 21 and 22 – 'Selling via Online Auction' simply e-mail and request to: *info@upastampauctions.co.uk*

Also, at the back of this catalogue to see how UPA can pay you upto 36% more for your collection

India

PRICES FOR STAMPS ON COVER TO 1945

Nos. S1/S3	*from* × 4
No. 1	†
Nos. 2/26	*from* × 5
Nos. 27/30	—
No. 31	*from* × 8
No. 34	†
Nos. 35/49	*from* × 3
No. 50	†
Nos. 51/53	*from* × 4
Nos. 54/65	*from* × 3
Nos. 66/68	*from* × 6
Nos. 69/82	*from* × 4
Nos. 84/277	*from* × 2
Nos. O1/O14	*from* × 8
Nos. O15/O18	—
No. O19	*from* × 5
Nos. O20/O30*a*	*from* × 12
No. O30*b*	†
Nos. O31/O133	*from* × 6
Nos. O135/O150	*from* × 3

(Currency. 12 pies = 1 anna; 16 annas = 1 rupee)

ISSUE FOR SIND PROVINCE

1

1852 (1 July). 'Scinde Dawk.' Embossed.

S1 **1** ½a. white £22000 £2500
S2 ½a. blue £50000 £11000
S3 ½a. scarlet .... — £32000

These stamps were issued under the authority of Sir Bartle Frere, Commissioner in Sind.

No. S3 is a sealing wax wafer (usually cracked). Perfect copies are very rare.

It is believed that examples in red were issued first followed, in turn, by those in white and blue. The latter, which shows an extra ring round the circumference, may have been produced by De La Rue. The Scinde Dawks were withdrawn in October 1854.

EAST INDIA COMPANY ADMINISTRATION

2 (*Much reduced*)

3

The ½a., 1a. and 4a. were lithographed in Calcutta at the office of the Surveyor-General. The die was engraved by Mr. Numerodeen (spelling uncertain, also reported as 'Maniruddin'). *Ungummed* paper watermarked as T **2** (the 'No. 4' paper) with the Arms of the East India Co in the sheet. The watermark is sideways on the ½a. and 1a., and upright on the 4a. where the paper was trimmed so that only the central portion showing the oval and the Arms was used. Imperforate.

1854 (1 Apr).

1 **3** ½a. vermilion .... £3250 †
a. Deep vermilion .... £4500 †

This stamp, with 9½ arches in the side border, was prepared for use and a supply was sent to Bombay, but was not officially issued.

The vermilion shade is normally found on toned paper and the deep vermilion on white.

ILLUSTRATIONS. Types **4/8** are shown twice actual size.

4

1854 (1 Oct)–**55**. Die I.

2 **4** ½a. blue .... £225 40·00
a. Printed on both sides .... † £40000
b. Printed double .... † £32000
3 ½a. pale blue .... £325 60·00
4 ½a. deep blue .... £250 45·00
5 ½a. indigo £700 £140

We give the official date of validity. Stamps were on sale to the public from mid September. Actual usage at Toungoo, Burma, is known from mid August.

These stamps were printed between 5 May and 29 July 1854 (Printing 30 millions).

4a

Die II.

6 **4a** ½a. blue £180 £130
7 ½a. indigo £190 £140

The bulk were printed between 1 and 12 August 1854, with some extra sheets on or before 2 November (Printing about 2 millions).

5

Die III (1855).

8 **5** ½a. pale blue .... £3250 95·00
8*a* ½a. blue .... £3000 85·00
9 ½a. greenish blue £4500 £250
10 ½a. deep blue £3750 £150

These stamps were printed between 3 July and 25 August 1855 (Printing about 4¾ millions).

THE THREE DIES OF THE ½ ANNA

DIE I. *Chignon shading* mostly solid blobs of colour. *Corner ornaments*, solid blue stars with long points, always conspicuous. *Band below diadem* always heavily shaded. *Diadem and jewels*. The middle and right-hand jewels usually show a clearly defined cross. *Outer frame lines*. Stamps with white or faintly shaded chignons and weak frame lines are usually Die I (worn state).

DIE II. *Chignon* normally shows much less shading. A strong line of colour separates hair and chignon. *Corner ornaments*. The right blue star is characteristic (see illustration) but tends to disappear. It never obliterates the white cross. *Band below diadem*. As Die I but heavier, sometimes solid. *Diadem and jewels*. As Die I but usually fainter. *Outer frame lines*. Always strong and conspicuous.

DIE III. *Chignon shading* shows numerous fine lines, often blurred. *Corner ornaments* have a small hollow blue star with short points, which tends to disappear as in Die II. *Band below diadem*, shows light shading or hardly any shading. *Diadem and jewels*. Jewels usually marked with a solid squat star. The ornaments between the stars appear in the shape of a characteristic white 'w'. *Frame lines* variable.

The above notes give the general characteristics of the three Dies, but there are a few exceptions due to retouching, etc.

6 (*See note below No. 14*)

Die I.

11 **6** 1a. deep red £1700 £110
12 1a. red .... £1200 80·00

Printing of these stamps commenced on 26 July 1854, and continued into August (Printing, see note below No. 14).

7

Die II: With more lines in the chignon than in Die I, and with white curved line where chignon joins head*.

13 **7** 1a. deep red £400 £120
14 1a. dull red .... £190 85·00

* Very worn printings of Die II may be found with chignon nearly as white as in Die I.

In stamps of Die I, however, the small blob of red projecting from the hair into the chignon is always visible.

These stamps were printed in August and September 1854 (Total printing, Dies I and II together, about 7¾ millions).

8

Die III. With pointed bust (1855).

15 **8** 1a. red £4000 £200
16 1a. dull red £4750 £250

These stamps were printed between 7 July and 25 August 1855 (Printing, about 1½ millions).

9

NOTE. Our catalogue prices for Four Annas stamps are for cut-square specimens, with clear margins and in good condition. Cut-to-shape copies are worth from 3% to 20% of these prices according to condition.

Four Dies of the Head:

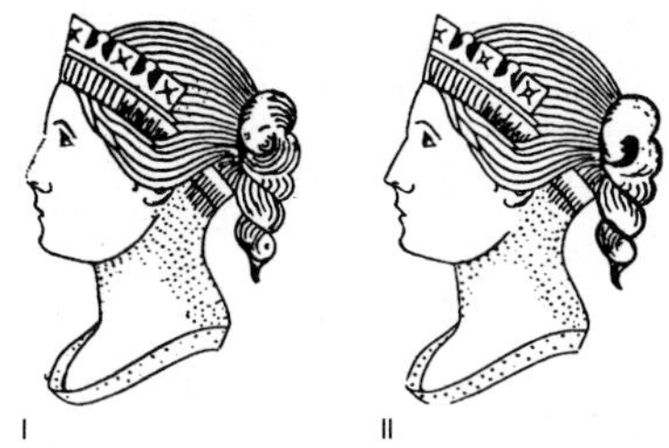

I II

DIE I. Band of diadem and chignon strongly shaded.

DIE II. Lines in band of diadem worn. Few lines in the upper part of the chignon, which, however, shows a strong drawn comma-like mark.

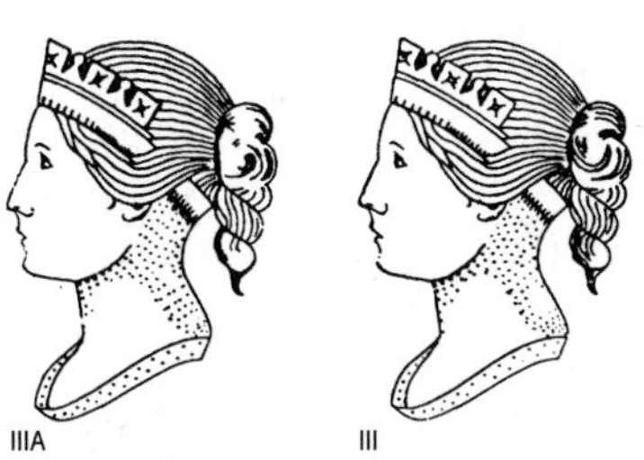

IIIA III

DIE IIIA. Upper part of chignon partly redrawn, showing two short, curved vertical lines in the NE corner. 'Comma' has disappeared.

DIE III. Upper part of chignon completely redrawn, but band of diadem shows only a few short lines.

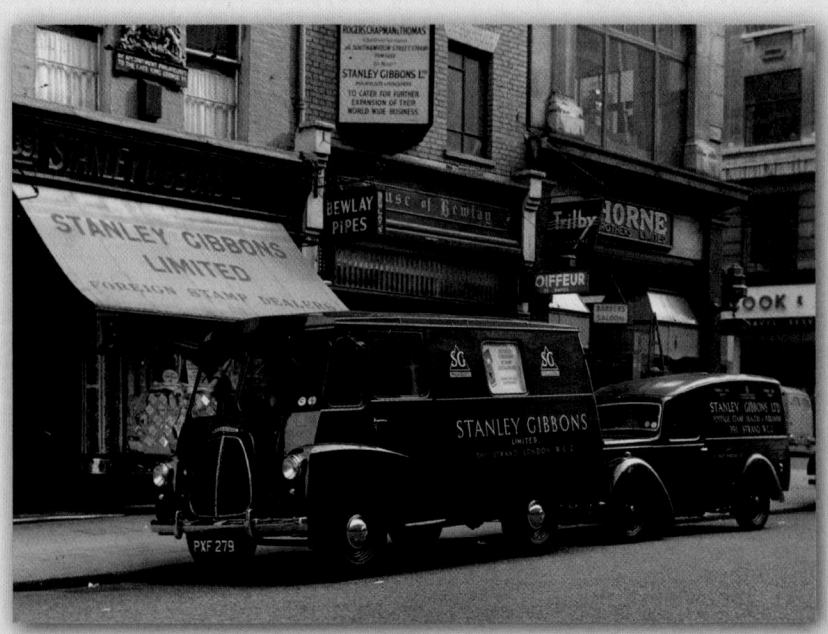

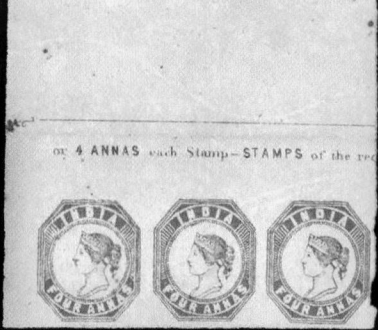

Two Dies of the Frame:

Die I. Outer frame lines weak. Very small dots of colour, or none at all, in the 'R' and 'A's'. The white lines to the right of 'INDIA' are separated, by a line of colour, from the inner white circle.

Die II. Outer frame lines strengthened. Dots in the 'R' and 'A's' strong. White lines to right of 'INDIA' break into inner white circle.

(Des Captain H. Thuillier)

1854 (15 Oct)–**55**. W **2** upright, central portion only. Imperf.

1st Printing, Head Die I. Frame Die I. Stamps widely spaced and separated by blue wavy line

			Un	Used	Us pr
17	9	4a. indigo and red	£22000	£1100	£5500
18		4a. blue and pale red	£22000	£1000	£5000
		a. Head inverted	†	£140000/ £450000	†

This printing was made between 13 and 28 Oct 1854 (Printing, 206,040).

27 confirmed examples of No. 18a are now known, only three of which are cut-square. The range of prices quoted reflects the difference in value between a sound and attractive cut-to-shape stamp and the finest example known. Several of the known examples are in poor condition, and these are worth much less.

2nd Printing. Head Die II. Frame Die I. Stamps widely spaced and separated by blue wavy line.

19	9	4a. blue and red	£20000	£700	£3750
		a. Blue (head) printed double	†	£40000	†
20		4a. indigo and deep red	£20000	£750	£4000

This printing was made between 1 and 13 Dec 1854 (Printing, 393,960).

No. 19a is only known used cut-to-shape.

3rd Printing. Head Dies II, IIIA and III. Frame Dies I and II. Stamps, often in bright shades, widely spaced and separated by wavy line (1855)

21	9	4a. blue and red shades (Head III, Frame I)	£42000	£2250	£11000
		a. Head II, Frame I	—	£2750	£14000
		b. Head IIIA, Frame I	—	£3250	£16000
		c. Head III, Frame II	—	—	£42000

This printing was made between 10 March and 2 April 1855 (Printing, 138,960).

Correct attribution of stamps to the scarce third printing requires careful study. Examples of Nos. 21/21c should only be purchased with a reliable guarantee.

4th Printing. Head Die III. Frame Die II. Stamps closely spaced 2 to 2½ mm without separating line (1855)

22	9	4a. deep blue and red	£13000	£650	£2250
23		4a. blue and red	£12000	£550	£2100
		a. Blue (head) printed double	†	£30000	†
24		4a. pale blue and pale red	£13000	£650	£2500

This printing was made between 3 April and 9 May 1855 (Printing, 540,960).

No. 23a is only known used cut-to-shape.

5th Printing. Head Die III. Frame Die II. Stamps spaced 4 to 6 mm without separating line (1855)

25	9	4a. blue and rose-red	£20000	£950	£4750
26		4a. deep blue and red	£20000	£1000	£4750

This printing was made between 4 Oct and 3 Nov 1855 (Printing, 380,064).

Serrated perf about 18, or pin-perf

27	½a. blue (Die I)	†	£18000
28	1a. red (Die I)	†	£11000
29	1a. red (Die II)	†	£10000
30	4a. blue and red (Die II)	†	£50000

This is believed to be an unofficial perforation. Most of the known specimens bear Madras circle postmarks (C122 to C126), but some are known with Bombay postmarks. Beware of fakes.

BISECTS. The bisected stamps for issues between 1854 and 1860 were used exclusively in the Straits Settlements during shortages of certain values. Prices quoted are for those with Singapore 'B 172' cancellations. Penang marks are considerably rarer.

10

11

10a (*Much reduced*)

(Plate made at Mint, Calcutta. Typo Stamp Office)

1854 (4 Oct). Sheet wmk sideways, similar to W **2** but with 'No. 3' at top left and more undulations in the frame. Imperf.

31	10	2a. green (*shades*)	£350	50·00
		a. Bisected (1a.) (1857) (*on cover*)	†	£250000
		b. Wmk **10a**	£1200	£800
34		2a. emerald-green	£2750	

The 2a. was also printed on paper with watermark W **10a** sideways. (Prices quoted are for examples with clearly identifiable portion of this watermark).

Apart from the rare emerald-green shade, there is a range of shades of No. 31 varying from bluish to yellowish green.

Many stamps show traces of lines external to the design shown in our illustration. Stamps with this frame on all four sides are scarce.

Many reprints of the ½, 1, 2, and 4a. exist.

PRINTERS. All Indian stamps from No. 35 to 200 were typographed by De La Rue & Co.

PRICES. It must be emphasised that the unused prices quoted for the early perforated stamps, especially Nos. 35/68, are for fine examples with fresh colour and original gum. Well-centred examples may command a premium.

1855 (1 Oct). Blue glazed paper. No wmk. P 14.

35	11	4a. black	£1400	22·00
		a. Imperf (pair)	£20000	£20000
		b. Bisected (2a.) (1859) (*on cover*)	†	£21000
36		8a. carmine (Die I)	£1100	21·00
		a. Imperf (pair)	£9500	
		b. Bisected (4a.) (1859) (*on cover*)	†	£130000

The first supply of the 4a. was on white paper, but it is difficult to distinguish it from No. 45.

In the 8a. the paper varies from deep blue to almost white.

For difference between Die I and Die II in the 8a., see illustrations above No. 73.

1856–64. Paper yellowish to white. No wmk. P 14.

37	11	½a. blue (Die I)	£160	6·00
		a. Imperf (pair)	£950	£4000
38		½a. pale blue (Die I)	£110	3·75
39		1a. brown	80·00	5·50
		a. Imperf between (vert pair)		
		b. Imperf (pair)	£1400	£4750
		c. Bisected (½a.) (1859) (*on cover*)	†	£130000
40		1a. deep brown	£160	7·00
41		2a. dull pink (1860)	£1400	50·00
		a. Imperf (pair)	£8000	
42		2a. yellow-buff (1859)	£950	45·00
		a. Imperf (pair)	£3750	£7500
43		2a. yellow (1863)	£1300	55·00
44		2a. orange (1858)	£1600	60·00
		a. Imperf (pair)		
45		4a. black	£1000	10·00
		a. Bisected diagonally (2a.) (1859) (*on cover*)	†	£65000
		b. Imperf (pair)	£8000	£8000
46		4a. grey-black	£900	5·50
47		4a. green (1864)	£5000	65·00
48		8a. carmine (Die I)	£1300	42·00
49		8a. pale carmine (Die I)	£1400	42·00
		a. Bisected (4a.) (1859) (*on cover*).	†	£130000
		Prepared for use, but not officially issued.		
50	11	2a. yellow-green	£3750	£4000
		a. Imperf (pair)	£9000	†

This stamp is known with trial obliterations, and a few are known postally used. It also exists *imperf*, but is not known used thus.

For difference between Die I and Die II in the ½a., see illustrations above No. 73.

CROWN COLONY

On 1 November 1858, Her Majesty Queen Victoria assumed the government of the territories in India 'heretofore administered in trust by the Honourable East India Company'.

12

13

1860 (9 May). No wmk. P 14.

51	12	8p. purple/*bluish*	£600	£140
52		8p. purple/*white*	90·00	7·50
		a. Bisected diagonally (4p.) (1862) (*on cover*)	†	£130000
		b. Imperf (pair)	£10000	£11000
53		8p. mauve	£180	16·00

1865. Paper yellowish to white. W **13**. P 14.

54	11	½a. blue (Die I)	35·00	2·50
		a. Imperf	†	£2000
		w. Wmk inverted	£650	60·00
55		½a. pale blue (Die I)	35·00	2·00
56	12	8p. purple	13·00	15·00
		w. Wmk inverted	55·00	£100
57		8p. mauve	27·00	20·00
58	11	1a. pale brown	19·00	2·00
59		1a. deep brown	17·00	2·00
		w. Wmk inverted	£180	85·00
60		1a. chocolate	22·00	2·25
61		2a. yellow	£475	8·50
62		2a. orange	£150	2·75
		a. Imperf (pair)	†	£8000
63		2a. brown-orange	48·00	2·75
		w. Wmk inverted	£160	90·00
64		4a. green	£1500	40·00
		w. Wmk inverted	†	£450
65		8a. carmine (Die I)	£4750	95·00
		w. Wmk inverted	£7000	£700

The 8p. mauve, No. 57, is found variously surcharged 'NINE' or 'NINE PIE' by local postmasters, to indicate that it was being sold for 9 pies, as was the case during 1874. Such surcharges were made without Government sanction. (*Price, from £850 unused*).

The stamps of India, wmk Elephant's Head, surcharged with a crown and value in 'CENTS', were used in the Straits Settlements.

14

POSTAGE (15)

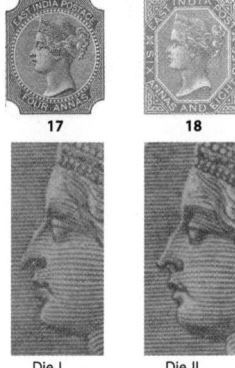

POSTAGE (16)

1866 (28 June). Fiscal stamps as T **14** optd. Wmk Crown over 'INDIA'. P 14 (at sides only).

(a) As T **15**

66	6a. purple (G.)	£2750	£150
	a. Overprint inverted	†	£30000

There are 20 different types of this overprint.

(b) With T **16**

68	6a. purple (G.)	£4750	£250

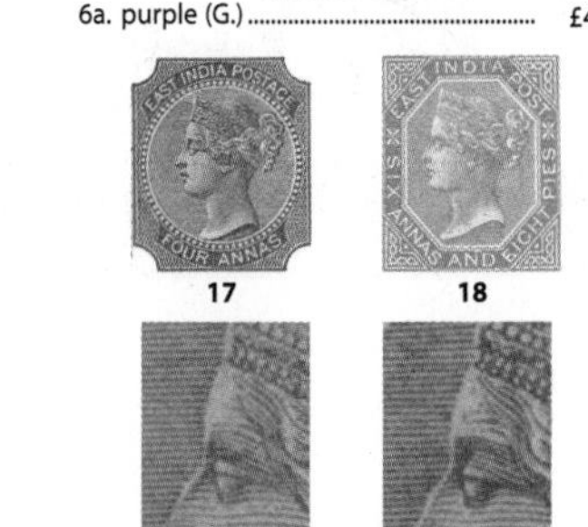
17 18

Die I Die II

Two Dies of 4a.:

Die I.—Mouth closed, line from corner of mouth downwards only. Pointed chin.

Die II.—Mouth slightly open; lips, chin, and throat defined by line of colour. Rounded chin.

1866 (1 Aug)–**78**. W **13**. P 14.

69	17	4a. green (Die I)	£150	5·00
70		4a. deep green (Die I)	£150	6·00
71		4a. blue-green (Die II) (1878)	50·00	3·75
		w. Wmk inverted	†	£475
72	18	6a.8p. slate (4.67)	£100	32·00
		a. Imperf (pair)	£10000	

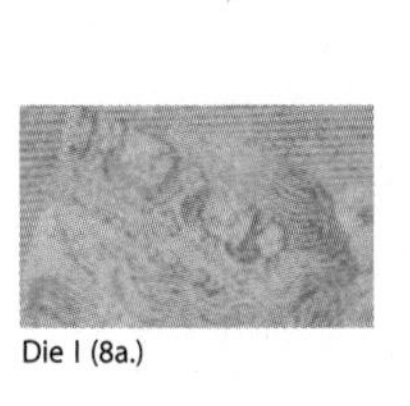
Die I (8a.)

Die I (½a.)

Die II (8a.)

Die II (½a.)

1868 (1 Jan). Die II. Profile redrawn and different diadem. W **13**. P 14.

73	11	8a. rose (Die II)	70·00	9·00
		w. Wmk inverted	£150	
74		8a. pale rose (Die II)	70·00	8·50

1873. Die II. Features, especially the mouth, more firmly drawn. W **13**. P 14.

75 **11** ½a. deep blue (Die II) 15·00 1·60
76 ½a. blue (Die II) 16·00 1·40
w. Wmk inverted £160 £110
y. Wmk inverted and reversed † £400

19

20

1874 (18 July–1 Sept). W **13**. P 14.

77 **19** 9p. bright mauve (18.7.74) 25·00 25·00
w. Wmk inverted — £550
78 9p. pale mauve 25·00 25·00
79 **20** 1r. slate (1.9.74) £100 38·00

21

22

1876 (19 Aug). W **13**. P 14.

80 **21** 6a. olive-bistre 9·00 2·50
w. Wmk inverted £190 £160
81 6a. pale brown 10·00 2·00
82 **22** 12a. Venetian red 22·00 42·00

EMPIRE

Queen Victoria assumed the title of Empress of India in 1877, and the inscription on the stamps was altered from 'EAST INDIA' to 'INDIA'.

23 **24** **25** **26** **27** **28** **29** **30** **31** **32** **33** **34**

1882 (1 Jan)–**90**. W **34**. P 14.

84 **23** ½a. deep blue-green (1883) 10·00 10
w. Wmk inverted — £160
85 ½a. blue-green 10·00 10
a. Double impression £1700 £3750
w. Wmk inverted — £160
86 **24** 9p. rose (1883) 2·75 4·25
87 9p. aniline carmine 3·00 4·25
w. Wmk inverted £700 £450
88 **25** 1a. brown-purple (1883) 12·00 30
89 1a. plum 12·00 30
w. Wmk inverted — £350
90 **26** 1a.6p. sepia 3·00 3·00
w. Wmk inverted — £475
91 **27** 2a. pale blue (1883) 12·00 60
92 2a. blue 12·00 60
a. Double impression £3500 £4000
93 **28** 3a. orange 38·00 10·00
94 3a. brown-orange (1890) 17·00 2·75
w. Wmk inverted — £450
95 **29** 4a. olive-green (6.85) 28·00 2·50
96 4a. slate-green 25·00 2·50
w. Wmk inverted £650 £375
97 **30** 4a.6p. yellow-green (1.5.86) 50·00 9·50
98 **31** 8a. dull mauve (1883) 48·00 2·75
99 8a. magenta 48·00 2·00
100 **32** 12a. purple/*red* (1.4.88) 18·00 5·50
w. Wmk inverted — £550
101 **33** 1r. slate (1883) 48·00 8·00
w. Wmk inverted — £400
84/101 *Set of* 11 £225 35·00
97s, 100s Handstamped 'SPECIMEN.' *Set of* 2 £120

No. 92a is from a sheet of 2a. stamps with a very marked double impression issued in Karachi in early 1898.

The discovery of postal forgeries of the 1r. slate (No. 101) at Bombay in 1890 led to its replacement by the T **37** bicoloured 1r. in a new design (Nos. 105/106.).

(**35**)

36

37

1891 (1 Jan). No. 97 surch with T **35** by Govt Press, Calcutta.

102 **30** 2½a. on 4½a. yellow-green 12·00 1·25
a. Surch double, one albino £400

There are several varieties in this surcharge due to variations in the relative positions of the letters and figures.

1892 (Jan)–**97**. W **34**. P 14.

103 **36** 2a.6p. yellow-green 8·00 40
104 2a.6p. pale blue-green (1897) 9·50 80
105 **37** 1r. green and rose 55·00 14·00
106 1r. green and aniline carmine 28·00 2·25

38

(**39**) Slanting serif (Lower pane R. 1/1) **40**

USED HIGH VALUES. It is necessary to emphasise that used prices quoted for the following and all later high value stamps are for postally used copies.

(Head of Queen from portrait by von Angeli)

1895 (1 Sept). W **34**. P 14.

107 **38** 2r. carmine and yellow-brown 95·00 21·00
107*a* 2r. carmine and brown £150 30·00
108 3r. brown and green 80·00 14·00
109 5r. ultramarine and violet £100 50·00
107/109 *Set of* 3 £250 75·00

1898 (1 Oct). No. 85 surch with T **39** by Govt Press, Calcutta.

110 **23** ¼a. on ½a. blue-green 20 1·00
a. Surch double £750
b. Double impression of stamp £750
c. Slanting serif on '1' £110

1899. W **34**. P 14.

111 **40** 3p. aniline carmine 40 20
w. Wmk inverted £325

1900 (1 Oct)–**02**. W **34**. P 14.

112 **40** 3p. grey 1·25 2·50
113 **23** ½a. pale yellow-green 3·50 70
114 ½a. yellow-green 6·00 1·00
w. Wmk inverted † £500
115 **25** 1a. carmine 6·50 30
116 **27** 2a. pale violet 11·00 4·25
117 2a. mauve (1902) 17·00 6·00
118 **36** 2a.6p. ultramarine 10·00 5·50
112/118 *Set of* 5 28·00 12·00

41 **42** **43** **44** **45** **46** **47** **48** **49**

50 **51** **52**

1902 (9 Aug)–**11**. W **34**. P 14.

119 **41** 3p. grey 1·00 10
120 3p. slate-grey (1904) 1·00 10
121 **42** ½a. yellow-green 5·00 20
122 ½a. green 5·00 20
123 **43** 1a. carmine 3·25 10
124 **44** 2a. violet (13.5.03) 11·00 50
125 2a. mauve 10·00 10
126 **45** 2a.6p. ultramarine (1902) 9·50 60
w. Wmk inverted † £600
127 **46** 3a. orange-brown (1902) 9·50 60
128 **47** 4a. olive (20.4.03) 4·50 80
129 4a. pale olive 9·50 80
130 4a. olive-brown 18·00 4·00
131 **48** 6a. olive-bistre (6.8.03) 25·00 4·75
132 6a. maize 21·00 4·50
133 **49** 8a. purple (*shades*) (8.5.03) 8·50 1·00
134 8a. claret (1910) 25·00 1·00
135 **50** 12a. purple/*red* (1903) 17·00 2·00
136 **51** 1r. green and carmine (1903) 11·00 70
137 1r. green and scarlet (1911) 80·00 7·50
138 **52** 2r. rose-red and yellow-brown (1903) £110 9·00
139 2r. carmine and yellow-brown £110 9·00
w. Wmk inverted £1700 £800
140 3r. brown and green (1904) 80·00 42·00
141 3r. red-brown and green (1911) £100 45·00
142 5r. ultramarine and violet (1904) £180 50·00
143 5r. ultramarine and deep lilac (1911) £300 70·00
144 10r. green and carmine (1909) (tel-c. 30·00) £400 50·00
146 15r. blue and olive-brown (1909) (tel-c. 30·00) £450 55·00
147 25r. brownish orange and blue (1909) (tel-c. £600) £3000 £1800
119/147 *Set of* 17 £3750 £1900

TELEGRAPH CANCELS. The high values of King Edward VII and King George V were widely used for telegraphic purposes. Such use can be identified by concentric arcs (rather than vertical bars, as on postal cancellations) above and below the date panel on double-ring cancellations, or the abbreviations 'T', 'TEL' or 'TELE' on other postal markings. Prices are now given for such use.

1905 (2 Feb). No. 122 surch with T **39**.

148 **42** ¼a. on ½a. green 55 10
a. Surch inverted — £2250

It is doubtful if No. 148a exists unused with genuine surcharge.

53

54

1906 (6 Dec)–**07**. W **34**. P 14.

149 **53** ½a. green 3·25 10
150 **54** 1a. carmine (7.1.07) 4·00 10

55 **56**

57

58 *

59 **60**

61

62

63

64

65

66

67

'Rs' flaw in right value tablet (R. 1/4)

* T **58**. Two types of the 1½a.; (A) As illustrated. (B) Inscribed '1½ As'. 'ONE AND A HALF ANNAS'.

1911 (1 Dec)–**23**. W **34**. P 14.

151 **55** 3p. grey (1912) 1·40 25
w. Wmk inverted 80·00
152 3p. pale grey 3·75 25

153		3p. bluish grey (1922)	4·25	50
		w. Wmk inverted	30·00	
154		3p. slate	3·75	35
		a. 'Rs' flaw	38·00	48·00
154*b*		3p. violet-grey	6·00	1·00
155	56	½a. light green (1912)	6·00	25
		w. Wmk inverted	£100	
156		½a. emerald	7·50	25
		w. Wmk inverted	†	£130
157		½a. bright green	8·00	15
159	57	1a. rose-carmine	6·50	20
160		1a. carmine	5·00	20
161		1a. aniline carmine	4·75	15
162		1a. pale rose-carmine (*chalk-surfaced paper*) (1918)	8·50	1·50
163	58	1½a. chocolate (Type A) (1919)	7·50	1·25
164		1½a. grey-brown (Type A)	15·00	5·50
165		1½a. chocolate (Type B) (1921)	9·00	10·00
		w. Wmk inverted	28·00	
166	59	2a. purple	10·00	80
167		2a. reddish purple	13·00	80
168		2a. deep mauve	14·00	70
		w. Wmk inverted	55·00	
169		2a. bright reddish violet (1923)	18·00	1·00
		a. Stop under 's' in right value tablet (R. 4/16)	£600	
170	60	2a.6p. ultramarine (1912)	4·50	3·50
171	61	2a.6p. ultramarine (1913)	4·50	20
172	62	3a. orange	4·50	20
173		3a. dull orange	12·00	45
174	63	4a. deep olive (1912)	7·00	1·00
175		4a. olive-green	7·00	1·00
		w. Wmk inverted	65·00	
177	64	6a. yellow-bistre (1912)	4·50	2·50
178		6a. brown-ochre	7·50	1·00
179	65	8a. deep magenta (1912)	6·50	2·75
180		8a. deep mauve	25·00	1·10
		w. Wmk inverted	£200	
181		8a. bright mauve (1918)	£110	14·00
182		8a. purple	42·00	3·75
183	66	12a. carmine-lake (1912)	6·50	2·50
		w. Wmk inverted	£450	£350
184		12a. claret	27·00	3·50
185	67	1r. red-brown and deep blue-green (1913)	32·00	3·25
		w. Wmk inverted	£160	
186		1r. brown and green (*shades*)	50·00	3·00
186*a*		1r. orange-brown and deep turquoise-green (1923)	85·00	9·00
187		2r. carmine and brown (1913)	35·00	2·50
		w. Wmk inverted	£180	
188		5r. ultramarine and violet (1913)	95·00	8·50
189		10r. green and scarlet (1913) (tel-c. 10·00)	£180	16·00
190		15r. blue and olive (1913) (tel-c. 25·00)	£300	42·00
		w. Wmk inverted	†	£750
191		25r. orange and blue (1913) (tel-c. 40·00)	£600	65·00
151/191 *Set of* 19			£1200	£140

Examples of the ½a. printed double are now believed to be forgeries.

FORGERIES. Collectors are warned against forgeries of all the later surcharges of India, and particularly the errors.

NINE

PIES

(68)

1921 (10 June). T **57** surch with T **68**.

192		9p. on 1a. rose-carmine	1·50	30
		a. Error. 'NINE NINE'	£130	£300
		b. Error. 'PIES PIES'	£130	£300
		c. Surch double	£300	£425
		w. Wmk inverted	†	£450
193		9p. on 1a. carmine-pink	4·00	60
194		9p. on 1a. aniline carmine	45·00	14·00

In the initial setting of the surcharge No. 192a occurred on R. 2/13–16 of the fourth pane and No. 192b on R. 4/13-16 of the third. For the second setting No. 192a was corrected. Examples of No. 192b still occur but on R. 2/13-16 of the third pane. Later printings showed this corrected also.

1922. T **56** surch with T **39**.

195		¼a. on ½a. bright green	1·40	35
		a. Surch inverted	12·00	
		b. Surch omitted (in horiz pair with normal)	£475	
		c. Slanting serif on '1'	80·00	
		w. Wmk inverted		
196		¼a. on ½a. emerald	12·00	3·25
		w. Wmk inverted		

1922–26. W **34**. P 14.

197	57	1a. chocolate	4·50	10
		w. Wmk inverted	48·00	
198	58	1½a. rose-carmine (Type B) (1926)	4·00	30
199	61	2a.6p. orange (1926)	5·00	2·50
200	62	3a. ultramarine (1923)	21·00	60
197/200 *Set of* 4			30·00	3·25

69

70

71

Stop under 's' in right value tablet (R. 4/16)

PRINTERS. The following issues of postage and contemporary official stamps were all printed by the Security Printing Press, Nasik, *unless otherwise stated.*

1926–33. Typo. W **69**. P 14.

201	55	3p. slate	1·75	10
		w. Wmk inverted	4·50	30
202	56	½a. green	4·75	10
		w. Wmk inverted	7·50	30
203	57	1a. chocolate	1·75	10
		a. *Tête-bêche* (vert pair) (1932)	4·25	12·00
		w. Wmk inverted	1·75	10
204	58	1½a. rose-carmine (Type B) (1929)	8·50	10
		a. Wmk sideways	†	£2500
		w. Wmk inverted	11·00	30
205	59	2a. bright purple	28·00	18·00
		a. Stop under 's'	£300	
		w. Wmk inverted	†	£160
206	70	2a. purple	5·50	10
		a. *Tête-bêche* (vert pair) (1933)	14·00	42·00
		w. Wmk inverted	6·00	30
207	61	2a.6p. orange (1929)	6·00	10
		w. Wmk inverted	6·50	40
208	62	3a. ultramarine	18·00	1·00
209		3a. blue (1928)	17·00	10
		w. Wmk inverted	17·00	75
210	63	4a. sage-green (*shades*)	2·50	10
		w. Wmk inverted	—	27·00
211	71	4a. sage-green (*shades*)	6·00	10
		w. Wmk inverted	18·00	50
212	65	8a. reddish purple	9·50	10
		w. Wmk inverted	11·00	40
213	66	12a. claret	9·00	30
		w. Wmk inverted	10·00	80
214	67	1r. chocolate and green	17·00	45
		a. Chocolate (head) omitted	£28000	
		w. Wmk inverted	21·00	1·00
215		2r. carmine and orange	30·00	80
		w. Wmk inverted	38·00	2·50
216		5r. ultramarine and purple	75·00	1·25
		w. Wmk inverted	£120	4·25
217		10r. green and scarlet (1927)	£140	9·00
		w. Wmk inverted	£300	14·00
218		15r. blue and olive (1928)	£100	40·00
		w. Wmk inverted	48·00	32·00
219		25r. orange and blue (1928)	£325	60·00
		w. Wmk inverted	£375	75·00
201/219 *Set of* 18			£650	£110

Examples of the ½a. printed double are believed to be forgeries.

Nos 203a and 206a come from surplus booklet sheets issued as normal stock.

72 de Havilland DH.66 Hercules

3a. '1' for second 'I' in 'INDIA' (R. 1/12)

6a. Scratch through tail of aircraft (R. 8/12)

8a. Missing tree-top (R. 11/6)

8a. Reversed serif on second 'I' of 'INDIA'

(Des R. Grant. Litho)

1929 (22 Oct). Air. W **69** (sideways*). P 14.

220	72	2a. deep blue-green	7·50	1·50
		w. Wmk stars pointing left	7·00	75
221		3a. blue	4·75	3·50
		a. 'Q' for 'O' in 'Postage' (R.11/4)	£650	£425
		b. '1' for second 'I' in 'INDIA'	£500	£325
		w. Wmk stars pointing left	4·75	3·00
222		4a. olive-green	6·50	1·50
		w. Wmk stars pointing left	7·50	1·25
223		6a. bistre	4·50	1·00
		a. Scratch through tail of aircraft	£250	£150
		w. Wmk stars pointing left	4·75	1·00
224		8a. purple	12·00	1·00
		a. Missing tree-top	£375	£250
		b. Reversed serif	£950	£475
		w. Wmk stars pointing left	13·00	1·00
225		12a. rose-red	25·00	9·50
		w. Wmk stars pointing left	26·00	9·50
220/225 *Set of* 6			50·00	15·00

* The normal sideways watermark shows the stars pointing right, *as seen from the back of the stamp.*

73 Purana Qila

74 War Memorial Arch

75 Council House

76 The Viceroy's House

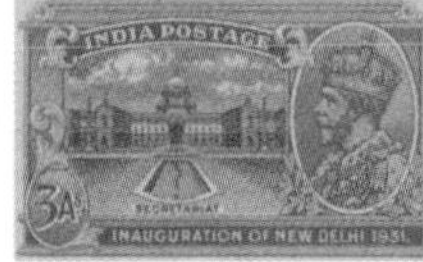

77 Government of India Secretariat

78 Dominion Columns and the Secretariat

¼a. 'F' for 'P' in 'PURANA' (R. 5/2)

(Des H. W. Barr. Litho)

1931 (9 Feb). Inauguration of New Delhi. Types **73/78**. W **69** (sideways*). P 13½×14.

226	73	¼a. olive-green and orange-brown	4·00	6·50
		a. 'F' for 'P' in 'PURANA'	£300	£350
		w. Wmk stars pointing left	3·00	6·50
227	74	½a. violet and green	2·75	40
		w. Wmk stars pointing left	2·00	40
228	75	1a. mauve and chocolate	1·50	20
		w. Wmk stars pointing left	3·00	45
229	76	2a. green and blue	3·75	4·50
		w. Wmk stars pointing left	2·00	1·25
230	77	3a. chocolate and carmine	8·00	3·25
		w. Wmk stars pointing left	5·00	3·00
231	78	1r. violet and green	26·00	48·00
		w. Wmk stars pointing left	25·00	48·00
226/231 *Set of* 6			35·00	50·00

* The normal sideways watermark shows the stars pointing to the right, *as seen from the back of the stamp.*

Collectors are warned against examples of No. 226a which have been provided with forged cancellations.

79

80

81

82

83

9p. litho. Heavier and longer lines on face. King's nose often shows six horizontal lines and always has lowest line long and thin

9p. typo. Lines lighter and shorter. Always five lines on King's nose with the lowest short and thick

(Types **82/83** des T. I. Archer. 9p. litho or typo; 1a.3p, 3a.6p. litho; others typo)

1932–36. W **69**. P 14.

232	79	½a. green (1934)	13·00	10
		w. Wmk inverted	—	4·00
233	80	9p. deep green (*litho*) (22.4.32)	7·50	10
		aw. Wmk inverted	8·00	3·75

No.	Type	Description	Unused	Used
233*b*		9p. deep green (*typo*) (27.8.34)	13·00	10
		bw. Wmk inverted		
234	**81**	1a. chocolate (1934)	8·00	10
		w. Wmk inverted	25·00	4·00
235	**82**	1a.3p. mauve (22.4.32)	2·25	10
		w. Wmk inverted	3·75	30
236	**70**	2a. vermilion	23·00	7·50
		aw. Wmk inverted	55·00	17·00
236*b*	**59**	2a. vermilion (1934)	3·75	50
		bw. Wmk inverted	—	50·00
236*c*		2a. vermilion (*small die*) (1936)	11·00	30
		cw. Wmk inverted	£200	20·00
237	**62**	3a. carmine	21·00	10
		w. Wmk inverted	£100	4·25
238	**83**	3a.6p. ultramarine (22.4.32)	8·50	20
		w. Wmk inverted	8·50	30
239	**64**	6a. bistre (1935)	18·00	1·50
		w. Wmk inverted	—	38·00
232/239 *Set of* 9			95·00	8·50

No. 236*b* measures 19×22.6 mm and No. 236*c* 18.4×21.8 mm.

'DOUBLE PRINTS'. Examples of Nasik litho-printed stamps showing doubling of all or part of the design or subsequent overprint are not uncommon. These are not true 'double prints', in that they were not the result of two impressions of the inked printing plate, but were caused by incorrect tension in the rubber 'blanket' which transferred ink from the cylinder to the paper. Such varieties are outside the scope of this catalogue.

84 Gateway of India, Bombay

85 Victoria Memorial, Calcutta

86 Rameswaram Temple, Madras

87 Jain Temple, Calcutta

88 Taj Mahal, Agra

89 Golden Temple, Amritsar

3½a. 'Bird' flaw (R. 9/3)

90 Pagoda in Mandalay

1935 (6 May). Silver Jubilee. Types **84/90**. W **69** (sideways*). P 13½×14.

No.	Type	Description	Unused	Used
240	**84**	½a. black and yellow-green	2·75	20
		w. Wmk stars pointing left	1·50	15
241	**85**	9p. black and grey-green	3·00	20
		w. Wmk stars pointing left	2·75	1·50
242	**86**	1a. black and brown	6·00	20
		w. Wmk stars pointing left	5·50	10
243	**87**	1¼a. black and bright violet	1·25	10
		w. Wmk stars pointing left	2·25	15
244	**88**	2½a. black and orange	12·00	1·60
		w. Wmk stars pointing left	10·00	1·00
245	**89**	3½a. black and dull ultramarine	8·00	13·00
		a. 'Bird' flaw	£375	£325
		w. Wmk stars pointing left	6·50	13·00
246	**90**	8a. black and purple	6·50	4·00
		w. Wmk stars pointing left	10·00	5·00
240/246 *Set of* 7			30·00	16·00

* The normal sideways watermark shows the stars pointing to the right, *as seen from the back of the stamp.*

91 King George VI

92 Dak Runner

93 Dak bullock cart

94 Dak tonga

95 Dak camel

96 Mail train

97 *Strathnaver* (liner)

98 Post truck

99 Armstrong Whitworth AW27 Ensign I mail plane (small head)

100 King George VI

1937 (23 Aug)–**40**. Types **91/100**. Typo. W **69**. P 13½×14 or 14×13½ (T **100**).

No.	Type	Description	Unused	Used
247	**91**	3p. slate (15.12.37)	2·75	10
		w. Wmk inverted	—	£120
248		½a. red-brown (15.12.37)	10·00	10
		w. Wmk inverted	—	£250
249		9p. green	8·50	75
		w. Wmk inverted	—	£120
250		1a. carmine	1·25	10
		a. *Tête-bêche* (vert pair) (1940)	3·25	3·00
		w. Wmk inverted (from booklets)	2·00	1·75
251	**92**	2a. vermilion (15.12.37)	13·00	30
		w. Wmk inverted		
252	**93**	2a.6p. bright violet (15.12.37)	1·50	20
		w. Wmk inverted	£375	95·00
253	**94**	3a. yellow-green (15.12.37)	13·00	30
		w. Wmk inverted	£375	95·00
254	**95**	3a.6p. bright blue (15.12.37)	11·00	60
		w. Wmk inverted	—	£250
255	**96**	4a. brown (15.12.37)	15·00	20
		w. Wmk inverted	—	95·00
256	**97**	6a. turquoise-green (15.12.37)	17·00	1·25
		w. Wmk inverted	—	£325
257	**98**	8a. slate-violet (15.12.37)	7·50	60
		w. Wmk inverted	—	£325
258	**99**	12a. lake (15.12.37)	18·00	1·40
		w. Wmk inverted		
259	**100**	1r. grey and red-brown (15.12.37)	3·50	15
		w. Wmk inverted	£120	90·00
260		2r. purple and brown (15.12.37)	14·00	30
		w. Wmk inverted	£130	
261		5r. green and blue (15.12.37)	48·00	50
		w. Wmk inverted	£190	£110
262		10r. purple and claret (15.12.37)	35·00	80
		w. Wmk inverted	£550	£200
263		15r. brown and green (15.12.37)	£180	£110
		w. Wmk inverted	£375	£300
264		25r. slate-violet and purple (15.12.37)	£275	45·00
		w. Wmk inverted	—	£300
247/264 *Set of* 18			£600	£140

No. 250a comes from surplus booklet sheets issued as normal stock following the rise in postal rates.

100a King George VI

101 King George VI

102 King George VI

103 Armstrong Whitworth A.W.27 Ensign I Mail Plane (large head)

1½a. and **3a.** Litho Lines thin and clean, particularly in the King's profile and the frames of the stamps. No Jubilee lines

1½a. and **3a.** Typo Lines thicker and more ragged. Value tablets and 'INDIA POSTAGE' panel unevenly inked. With Jubilee lines

(Types **100a/102** des T. I. Archer. Typo (1½a. and 3a. litho also))

1940 (15 Oct)–**43**. W **69**. P 13½×14.

No.	Type	Description	Unused	Used
265	**100a**	3p. slate (1.12.41)	30	10
		w. Wmk inverted	7·00	7·50
266		½a. purple (1.10.41)	1·50	10
		w. Wmk inverted	80·00	38·00
267		9p. green (16.8.41)	1·00	10
		w. Wmk inverted	—	48·00
268		1a. carmine (1.4.43)	1·75	10
		w. Wmk inverted	—	45·00
269	**101**	1a.3p. yellow-brown (15.5.41)	1·00	10
		aw. Wmk inverted	—	75·00
269*b*		1½a. dull violet (*litho*) (20.5.42)	4·50	30
		bw. Wmk inverted	—	40·00
269*c*		1½a. dull violet (*typo*) (1943)	2·25	10
		cw. Wmk inverted	—	40·00
270		2a. vermilion (15.5.41)	1·75	10
		w. Wmk inverted	65·00	40·00
271		3a. bright violet (*litho*) (5.1.41)	6·50	30
		aw. Wmk inverted	£150	50·00
271*b*		3a. bright violet (*typo*) (1943)	3·75	10
		bw. Wmk. inverted	—	35·00
272		3½a. bright blue (15.5.41)	1·25	1·00
		w. Wmk inverted	—	£110
273	**102**	4a. brown (15.5.41)	1·25	10
		w. Wmk inverted	—	90·00
274		6a. turquoise-green (15.5.41)	4·00	10
		w. Wmk inverted	†	£100
275		8a. slate-violet (15.5.41)	1·50	30
		w. Wmk inverted	—	£100
276		12a. lake (15.5.41)	14·00	1·00
		w. Wmk inverted	—	£180
277	**103**	14a. purple (15.10.40)	18·00	2·00
		w. Wmk inverted	—	£180
265/277 *Set of* 14			45·00	4·00

105 'Victory' and King George VI

1946 (2 Jan–8 Feb). Victory. Litho. W **69**. P 13.

No.	Type	Description	Unused	Used
278	**105**	9p. yellow-green (8.2.46)	1·00	1·50
		w. Wmk inverted	—	£160
279		1½a. dull violet	75	30
		w. Wmk inverted	—	£100
280		3½a. bright blue	2·25	2·50
		w. Wmk inverted	—	£160
281		12a. claret (8.2.46)	2·25	1·75
		w. Wmk inverted	—	£300
278/281 *Set of* 4			5·75	5·50

= =

3 PIES
(**106**)

1946 (8 Aug). Surch with T **106**.

No.	Type	Description	Unused	Used
282	**101**	3p. on 1a.3p. yellow-brown	20	15
		w. Wmk inverted	—	£100

DOMINION

301 Asokan Capital (Inscr reads 'Long Live India')

302 Indian National Flag

303 Douglas DC-4

'Teardrop' (R. 6/6)

(Des T. I. Archer. Litho)

1947 (21 Nov–15 Dec). Independence. W **69**. P 14×13½ (1½a.) or 13½×14 (others).

301	**301**	1½a. grey-green (15.12)	1·25	10
302	**302**	3½a. orange-red, blue and green	4·00	2·25
		a. Teardrop	60·00	70·00
		w. Wmk inverted	22·00	32·00
303	**303**	12a. ultramarine (15.12)	5·50	2·75
301/303 *Set of 3*			9·50	4·50

304 Lockheed Constellation

(Des T. I. Archer. Litho)

1948 (29 May). Air. Inauguration of India–UK Air Service. W **69**. P 13½×14.

304	**304**	12a. black and ultramarine	6·00	5·50

305 Mahatma Gandhi **306** Mahatma Gandhi

(Photo Courvoisier)

1948 (15 Aug). First Anniversary of Independence. P 11½.

305	**305**	1½a. brown	9·00	1·25
306		3½a. violet	15·00	5·50
307		12a. grey-green	28·00	10·00
308	**306**	10r. purple-brown and lake	£400	£140
305/308 *Set of 4*			£425	£140

307 Ajanta Panel **308** Konarak Horse **309** Trimurti

310 Bodhisattva **311** Nataraja **312** Sanchi Stupa, East Gate

313 Bodh Gaya Temple **314** Bhuvanesvara **315** Gol Gumbad, Bijapur

316 Kandarya Mahadeva Temple **317** Golden Temple, Amritsar

318 Victory Tower, Chittorgarh **319** Red Fort, Delhi

320 Taj Mahal, Agra **321** Qutb Minar, Delhi

322 Satrunjaya Temple, Palitana

(Des T. I. Archer and I. M. Das. Typo (low values), litho (rupee values))

1949 (15 Aug)–**52**. Types **307/322** W **69** (sideways* on 6p., 1r. and 10r.). P 14 (3p. to 2a.), 13½ (3a. to 12a.), 14×13½ (1r. and 10r.), 13½×14 (2r. and 5r.), 13 (15r.).

309	**307**	3p. slate-violet	15	10
		w. Wmk inverted	†	£100
310	**308**	6p. purple-brown	25	10
		w. Wmk stars pointing right	1·50	1·50
311	**309**	9p. yellow-green	40	10
		w. Wmk inverted	†	£160
312	**310**	1a. turquoise	60	10
		w. Wmk inverted	†	£110
313	**311**	2a. carmine	1·00	10
		w. Wmk inverted	£100	32·00
314	**312**	3a. brown-orange	2·25	10
		w. Wmk inverted	†	£225
315	**313**	3½a. bright blue	1·75	6·00
316	**314**	4a. lake	5·50	45
		w. Wmk inverted	£130	27·00
317	**315**	6a. violet	2·50	30
		w. Wmk inverted	15·00	17·00
318	**316**	8a. turquoise-green	2·25	10
		w. Wmk inverted	—	£250
319	**317**	12a. dull blue	12·00	30
		w. Wmk inverted	£110	26·00
320	**318**	1r. dull violet and green	45·00	10
		w. Wmk stars pointing left	40·00	1·25
321	**319**	2r. claret and violet	30·00	40
		w. Wmk inverted	£325	55·00
322	**320**	5r. blue-green and red-brown	70·00	2·75
		w. Wmk inverted	£350	60·00
323	**321**	10r. purple-brown and deep blue	£160	32·00
		aw. Wmk stars pointing left	£550	£170
		b. Purple-brown and blue (1952)	£275	18·00
		bw. Wmk stars pointing left	£375	£140
324	**322**	15r. brown and claret	26·00	29·00
		w. Wmk inverted	£325	
309/324 *Set of 16*			£325	50·00

* The normal sideways watermark has the stars pointing to the left on the 6p. value and to the right on the 1r. and 10r. *when seen from the back of the stamp.*

For T **310** with statue reversed see No. 333.

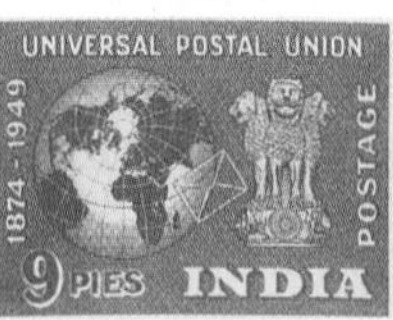

323 Globe and Asokan Capital

1949 (10 Oct). 75th Anniversary of UPU. Litho. W **69**. P 13.

325	**323**	9p. green	6·00	3·75
326		2a. rose	6·00	3·00
327		3½a. bright blue	7·00	3·00
328		12a. brown-purple	10·00	3·00
325/328 *Set of 4*			26·00	11·50

REPUBLIC

324 Rejoicing Crowds **325** Quill, ink-well and verse

326 Ear of corn and plough **327** Spinning-wheel and cloth

(Des D. J. Keymer & Co. Litho)

1950 (26 Jan). Inauguration of Republic. Types **324/327**. W **69** (sideways on 3½a.). P 13.

329		2a. scarlet	6·50	50
		w. Wmk inverted	£120	24·00
330		3½a. ultramarine	10·00	13·00
		w. Wmk stars pointing right	†	£120
331		4a. violet	10·00	1·50
332		12a. maroon	16·00	3·00
		w. Wmk inverted	£140	42·00
329/332 *Set of 4*			38·00	16·00

The normal sideways watermark shows the top of the stars to the left, *as seen from the back of the stamp.*

328 As T **310**, but statue reversed **329** Stegodon ganesa

1950 (15 July)–**51**. Typo. W **69**. P 14 (1a.), 13½ (others).

333	**328**	1a. turquoise	14·00	10
		aw. Wmk inverted	—	45·00
333*b*	**313**	2½a. lake (30.4.51)	3·50	3·25
333*c*	**314**	4a. bright blue (30.4.51)	6·00	10
		cw. Wmk inverted	—	£170
333/333*c* *Set of 3*			21·00	3·25

1951 (13 Jan). Centenary of Geological Survey of India. Litho. W **69**. P 13.

334	**329**	2a. black and claret	4·25	1·25

330 Torch **331** Kabir

1951 (4 Mar). First Asian Games, New Delhi. Litho. W **69** (sideways). P 14.

335	**330**	2a. reddish purple and brown-orange	3·00	1·00
		w. Wmk stars pointing right	†	£225
336		12a. chocolate and light blue	17·00	2·25

The normal sideways watermark shows the top of the stars to the left, *as seen from the back of the stamp.*

PROCESS. All the following issues were printed in photogravure, *except where otherwise stated.*

1952 (1 Oct). Indian Saints and Poets. T **331** and similar vert designs. W **69**. P 14.

337	9p. bright emerald-green	3·25	65
338	1a. carmine	3·25	20
339	2a. orange-red	3·50	50
340	4a. bright blue	18·00	60
341	4½a. bright mauve	2·00	1·25
342	12a. brown	20·00	1·25
337/342 *Set of 6*		45·00	4·00

Designs: 9p. T **331**; 1a. Tulsidas; 2a. Meera; 4a. Surdas; 4½a. Ghalib; 12a. Tagore.

332 Locomotives of 1853 and 1953 **333** Mount Everest

1953 (16 Apr). Railway Centenary. W **69**. P 14½×14.

343	**332**	2a. black	2·50	10

1953 (2 Oct). Conquest of Mount Everest. W **69**. P 14½×14.

344	**333**	2a. bright violet	2·50	10
345		14a. brown	14·00	25

334 Telegraph Poles of 1851 and 1951 **335** Postal Transport, 1854

1953 (1 Nov). Centenary of Indian Telegraphs. W **69**. P 14½×14.
346 **334** 2a. blue-green 3·50 10
347 12a. blue 12·00 40

1954 (1 Oct). Stamp Centenary. T **335** and similar horiz designs. W **69**. P 14½×14.
348 1a. reddish purple 3·00 20
349 2a. cerise 2·50 10
350 4a. orange-brown 10·00 1·00
351 14a. blue 4·50 40
348/351 *Set of* 4 17·00 1·50
Designs: 1a. T **335**; 2, 14a. 'Airmail'; 4a. Postal transport, 1954.

338 UN Emblem and Lotus

339 Forest Research Institute

1954 (24 Oct). United Nations Day. W **69** (sideways). P 13.
352 **338** 2a. turquoise-green 1·25 10

1954 (11 Dec). Fourth World Forestry Congress, Dehra Dun. W **69**. P 14½×14.
353 **339** 2a. ultramarine 1·25 10

340 Tractor

341 Power loom

342 Bullock-driven Well

343 Damodar Valley Dam

344 Woman Spinning

345 Naga woman weaving with hand loom

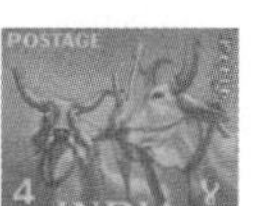
346 Bullocks

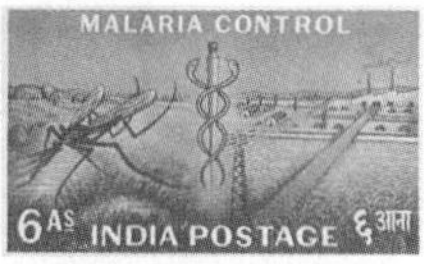

347 'Malaria Control' (Mosquito and Staff of Aesculapius)

348 Chittaranjan Locomotive Works

349 Marine Drive, Bombay

350 Hindustan Aircraft Factory, Bangalore

351 Kashmir Landscape

352 Telephone engineer

353 Cape Comorin

354 Mt Kangchenjunga

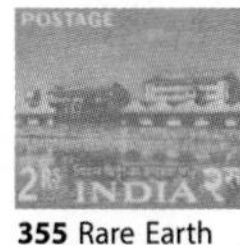
355 Rare Earth Factory, Alwaye

356 Sindri Fertiliser Factory

357 Steel Plant

1955 (26 Jan). Five Year Plan. Types **340/357**. W **69** (sideways on small horiz designs). P 14×14½ (small horiz) or 14½×14 (others).
354 **340** 3p. bright purple 30 10
355 **341** 6p. violet 30 10
356 **342** 9p. orange-brown 40 10
357 **343** 1a. blue-green 45 10
358 **344** 2a. light blue 30 10
359 **345** 3a. pale blue-green 1·00 20
360 **346** 4a. rose-carmine 60 10
361 **347** 6a. yellow-brown 2·75 10
362 **348** 8a. blue 13·00 10
363 **349** 10a. turquoise-green 6·00 3·25
364 **350** 12a. bright blue 6·00 10
365 **351** 14a. bright green 5·00 60
366 **352** 1r. deep dull green 7·00 10
367 **353** 1r.2a. grey 3·00 8·50
368 **354** 1r.8a. reddish purple 18·00 8·50
369 **355** 2r. cerise 4·50 10
370 **356** 5r. brown 28·00 2·25
371 **357** 10r. orange 21·00 4·75
354/371 *Set of* 18 £100 25·00
For stamps as Nos. 366, 369/371 but W **374** see Nos. 413/416.

358 Bodhi Tree

359 Round Parasol and Bodhi Tree

(Des C. Pakrashi (2a.), R. D'Silva (14a.))

1956 (24 May). Buddha Jayanti. W **69** (sideways on 14a.). P 13×13½ (2a.) or 13½×13 (14a.).
372 **358** 2a. sepia 2·50 10
373 **359** 14a. vermilion 10·00 3·75

360 Lokmanya Bal Gangadhar Tilak

361 Map of India

1956 (23 July). Birth Centenary of Tilak (journalist). W **69**. P 13×13½.
374 **360** 2a. chestnut 1·00 10

(New Currency. 100 naye paise = 1 rupee)

1957 (1 Apr)–**58**. W **69** (sideways). P 14×14½.
375 **361** 1n.p. blue-green 10 10
376 2n.p. light brown 10 10
377 3n.p. deep brown 10 10
378 5n.p. bright green 5·00 10
379 6n.p. grey 10 10
379*a* 8n.p. light blue-green (7.5.58) 3·00 75
380 10n.p. deep dull green 6·00 10
381 13n.p. bright carmine-red 1·25 10
381*a* 15n.p. violet (16.1.58) 4·25 10
382 20n.p. blue 1·00 10
383 25n.p. ultramarine 1·00 10
384 50n.p. orange 8·00 10
385 75n.p. reddish purple 2·75 10
385*a* 90n.p. bright purple (16.1.58) 4·00 75
375/385*a* *Set of* 14 32·00 1·50
The 8, 15 and 90n.p. have their value expressed as 'nP'.
For similar stamps but W **374** see Nos. 399/412.

362 The Rani of Jhansi

363 Shrine

1957 (15 Aug). Indian Mutiny Centenary. W **69**. P 14½×14 (15n.p.) or 13×13½ (90n.p.).
386 **362** 15n.p. brown 1·50 10
387 **363** 90n.p. reddish purple 8·00 1·00

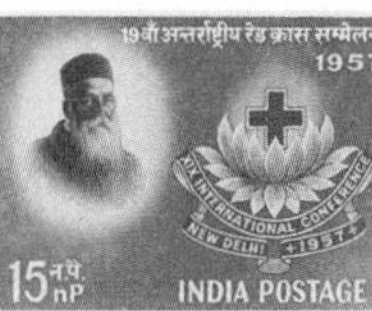

364 Henri Dunant and Conference Emblem

365 Nutrition

1957 (28 Oct). 19th International Red Cross Conference, New Delhi. W **69** (sideways). P 13½×13.
388 **364** 15n.p. deep grey and carmine 60 10

1957 (14 Nov). Children's Day. T **365** and similar designs. W **69** (sideways on 90n.p.). P 14×13½ (90n.p.) or 13½×14 (others).
389 8n.p. reddish purple 75 25
390 15n.p. turquoise-green 1·25 10
391 90n.p. orange-brown 1·25 15
389/391 *Set of* 3 3·00 45
Designs: Horiz—8n.p. T **365**; 15n.p. Education. Vert—90n.p. Recreation.

368 Bombay University

369 Calcutta University

1957 (31 Dec). Centenary of Indian Universities. Types **368/369** and similar design. W **69** (sideways on T **368**). P 14×14½ (No. 392) or 13½×14 (others).
392 **368** 10n.p. violet 2·00 60
393 **369** 10n.p. grey 1·25 60
394 – 10n.p. light brown 2·00 60
392/394 *Set of* 3 4·75 1·60
Design: Horiz as T **369**—No. 394, Madras University.

371 J. N. Tata (founder) and Steel Plant

372 Dr. D. K. Karve

1958 (1 Mar). 50th Anniversary of Steel Industry. W **69**. P 14½×14.
395 **371** 15n.p. orange-red 10 10

1958 (18 Apr). Birth Centenary of Karve (educationalist). W **69** (sideways). P 14.
396 **372** 15n.p. orange-brown 10 10

373 Westland Wapiti Biplane and Hawker Hunter

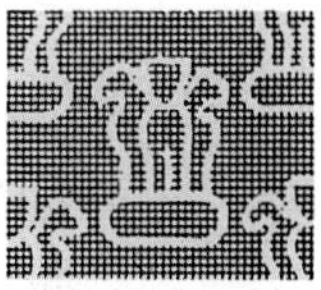

374 Asokan Capital

1958 (30 Apr). Silver Jubilee of Indian Air Force. W **69**. P 14½×14.
397 **373** 15n.p. blue 1·25 15
398 90n.p. ultramarine 3·50 55

1958–63. As Nos. 366, 369/371 and 375/385*a* but W **374**.
399 **361** 1n.p. blue-green (1960) 1·00 1·00
a. Imperf (pair) £700
400 2n.p. light brown (27.10.58) 10 10
401 3n.p. deep brown (1958) 10 10
402 5n.p. bright green (27.10.58) 10 10
403 6n.p. grey (1963) 55 3·25
404 8n.p. light blue-green (1958) 1·00 10
405 10n.p. deep dull green (27.10.58) 15 10
a. Imperf (pair) † £1100
406 13n.p. bright carmine-red (1963) 2·75 3·50
407 15n.p. violet (10.60) 75 10
408 20n.p. blue (27.10.58) 30 10
409 25n.p. ultramarine (27.10.58) 30 10
410 50n.p. orange (1959) 30 10
411 75n.p. reddish purple (1959) 40 10
412 90n.p. bright purple (1960) 5·50 10
413 **352** 1r. deep dull green (1959) 3·75 10
414 **355** 2r. cerise (1959) 9·00 10
415 **356** 5r. brown (1959) 9·00 50
416 **357** 10r. orange (1959) 50·00 15·00
399/416 *Set of* 18 75·00 21·00
The 5, 10, 15, 20, 25 and 50n.p. with serial numbers on the back are from coils of 810 stamps prepared from sheets for experimenting with vending machines. In the event the machines were not purchased and the stamps were sold over the counter.

375 Bipin Chandra Pal

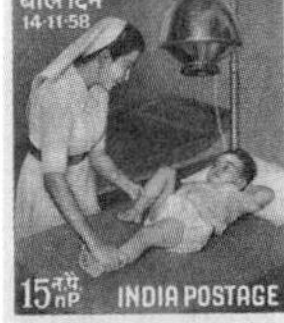

376 Nurse with Child Patient

1958 (7 Nov). Birth Centenary of Pal (patriot). W **374**. P 14×13½.
418 **375** 15n.p. deep dull green 10 10

1958 (14 Nov). Children's Day. W **374**. P 14×13½.
419 **376** 15n.p. violet 10 10

377 Jagadish Chandra Bose

378 Exhibition Gate

1958 (30 Nov). Birth Centenary of Bose (botanist). W **374**. P 14×13½.
420 **377** 15n.p. deep turquoise-green ... 20 10

1958 (30 Dec). India 1958 Exhibition, New Delhi. W **374** (sideways). P 14½×14.
421 **378** 15n.p. reddish purple ... 10 10

379 Sir Jamsetjee Jejeebhoy

380 *The Triumph of Labour* (after Chowdhury)

1959 (15 Apr). Death Centenary of Jejeebhoy (philanthropist). W **374**. P 14×13½.
422 **379** 15n.p. brown ... 10 10

1959 (15 June). 40th Anniversary of International Labour Organisation. W **374** (sideways). P 14½×14.
423 **380** 15n.p. dull green ... 10 10

381 Boys awaiting admission to Children's Home

382 Agriculture

1959 (14 Nov). Children's Day. W **374**. P 14×14½.
424 **381** 15n.p. deep dull green ... 10 10
a. Imperf (pair) ... £2500

1959 (30 Dec). First World Agricultural Fair, New Delhi. W **374**. P 13½×13.
425 **382** 15n.p. grey ... 30 10

383 Thiruvalluvar (philosopher)

1960 (15 Feb). Thiruvalluvar Commemoration. W **374**. P 14×13½.
426 **383** 15n.p. reddish purple ... 10 10

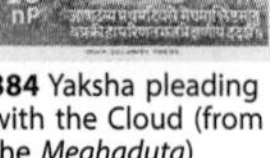

384 Yaksha pleading with the Cloud (from the *Meghaduta*)

385 Shakuntala writing a letter to Dushyanta (from the *Shakuntala*)

1960 (22 June). Kalidasa (poet) Commemoration. W **374**. P 13.
427 **384** 15n.p. grey ... 75 10
428 **385** 1r.3n.p. pale yellow and brown ... 4·25 1·50

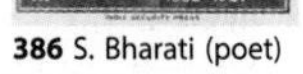

386 S. Bharati (poet)

387 Dr. M. Visvesvaraya

1960 (11 Sept). Subramania Bharati Commemoration. W **374**. P 14×13½.
429 **386** 15n.p. blue ... 10 10

1960 (15 Sept). Birth Centenary of Dr. M. Visvesvaraya (engineer). W **374**. P 13×13½.
430 **387** 15n.p. brown and bright carmine ... 10 10

388 Children's Health

1960 (14 Nov). Children's Day. W **374**. P 13½×13.
431 **388** 15n.p. deep dull green ... 10 10

389 Children greeting UN Emblem

390 Tyagaraja

1960 (11 Dec). UNICEF Day. W **374**. P 13½×13.
432 **389** 15n.p. orange-brown and olive-brown 10 10

1961 (6 Jan). 114th Death Anniversary of Tyagaraja (musician). W **374**. P 14×13½.
433 **390** 15n.p. greenish blue ... 10 10

391 'First Aerial Post' cancellation

392 Air India Boeing 707 Airliner and Humber Sommer Biplane

1961 (18 Feb). 50th Anniversary of First Official Airmail Flight, Allahabad–Naini. Types **391/392** and similar design. W **374**. P 14 (5n.p) or 13×13½ (others).
434 **391** 5n.p. olive-drab ... 3·00 30
435 **392** 15n.p. deep green and grey ... 1·10 30
436 – 1r. purple and grey ... 4·25 1·75
434/436 *Set of 3* ... 7·50 2·10
Design: Horiz as T **392**—1r. H. Pecquet flying Humber Sommer aeroplane and 'Aerial Post' cancellation.

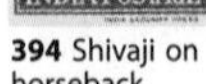

394 Shivaji on horseback

395 Motilal Nehru (politician)

1961 (17 Apr). Chatrapati Shivaji (Maratha ruler) Commemoration. W **374**. P 13×13½.
437 **394** 15n.p. brown and green ... 80 40

1961 (6 May). Birth Centenary of Pandit Motilal Nehru. W **374**. P 14.
438 **395** 15n.p. olive-brown and brown-orange 30 10

396 Tagore (poet)

397 All India Radio Emblem and Transmitting Aerials

1961 (7 May). Birth Centenary of Rabindranath Tagore. W **374**. P 13×13½.
439 **396** 15n.p. yellow-orange and blue-green. 1·50 40

1961 (8 June). Silver Jubilee of All India Radio. W **374**. P 13½×13.
440 **397** 15n.p. ultramarine ... 10 10

398 Prafulla Chandra Ray

399 V. N. Bhatkande

1961 (2 Aug). Birth Centenary of Ray (social reformer). W **374**. P 14×13½.
441 **398** 15n.p. grey ... 10 20

1961 (1 Sept). Birth Centenary of Bhatkande (composer) (1960). W **374**. P 13×13½.
442 **399** 15n.p. olive-brown ... 10 10

400 Child at Lathe

401 Fair Emblem and Main Gate

1961 (14 Nov). Children's Day. W **374**. P 14×13½.
443 **400** 15n.p. brown ... 10 20

1961 (14 Nov). Indian Industries Fair, New Delhi. W **374**. P 14×14½.
444 **401** 15n.p. blue and carmine ... 10 10

402 Indian Forest

1961 (21 Nov). Centenary of Scientific Forestry. W **374**. P 13×13½.
445 **402** 15n.p. green and brown ... 40 30

403 Pitalkhora: Yaksha

404 Kalibangan Seal

1961 (14 Dec). Centenary of Indian Archaeological Survey. W **374**. P 14×13½ (15 n.p.) or 13½×14 (90n.p.).
446 **403** 15n.p. orange-brown ... 1·25 10
447 **404** 90n.p. yellow-olive and light brown ... 5·25 30

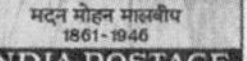

405 M. M. Malaviya

406 Gauhati Refinery

1961 (24 Dec). Birth Centenary of Malaviya (educationist). W **374**. P 14×13½.
448 **405** 15n.p. deep slate ... 10 20

1962 (1 Jan). Inauguration of Gauhati Oil Refinery. W **374**. P 13×13½.
449 **406** 15n.p. blue ... 1·00 20

407 Bhikaiji Cama

408 Village Panchayati and Parliament Building

1962 (26 Jan). Birth Centenary of Bhikaiji Cama (patriot). W **374**. P 14.
450 **407** 15n.p. reddish purple 10 10

1962 (26 Jan). Inauguration of Panchayati System of Local Government. W **374**. P 13×13½.
451 **408** 15n.p. bright purple 10 10

409 D. Saraswati (religious reformer)

410 G. S. Vidhyarthi (journalist)

1962 (4 Mar). Dayanard Saraswati Commemoration. W **374**. P 14.
452 **409** 15n.p. orange-brown 10 10

1962 (25 Mar). Ganesh Shankar Vidhyarthi Commemoration. W **374**. P 14×13½.
453 **410** 15n.p. red-brown 10 10

411 Malaria Eradication Emblem

412 Dr. R. Prasad

1962 (7 Apr). Malaria Eradication. W **374**. P 13×13½.
454 **411** 15n.p. yellow and claret 10 10

1962 (13 May). Retirement of President Dr. Rajendra Prasad. W **374**. P 13.
455 **412** 15n.p. bright purple (*shades*) 30 20

413 Calcutta High Court

416 Ramabai Ranade

1962. Centenary of Indian High Courts. T **413** and similar horiz designs. W **374**. P 14.

456	15n.p. dull green (1.7)	50	20
457	15n.p. red-brown (6.8)	50	20
458	15n.p. slate (14.8)	50	20
456/458	*Set of* 3	1·40	55

Designs: No. 456, T **413**; No. 457, Madras High Court; No. 458, Bombay High Court.

1962 (15 Aug). Birth Centenary of Ramabai Ranade (social reformer). W **374**. P 14×13½
459 **416** 15n.p. orange-brown 10 30

417 Indian Rhinoceros

418 'Passing the Flag to Youth'

1962 (1 Oct). Wild Life Week. W **374**. P 13½×14.
460 **417** 15n.p. red-brown and dp turquoise 55 15

INSCRIPTIONS. From No. 461 onwards all designs except No. 463 are inscribed 'BHARAT' in Devanagari in addition to 'INDIA' in English.

1962 (14 Nov). Children's Day. W **374**. P 13½×13.
461 **418** 15n.p. orange-red and turquoise-green 15 20

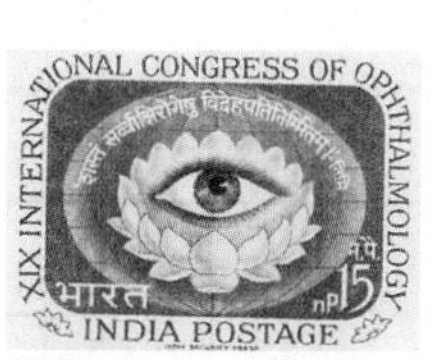

419 Human Eye within Lotus Blossom

420 S. Ramanujan

1962 (3 Dec). 19th International Ophthalmology Congress, New Delhi. W **374**. P 13½×13.
462 **419** 15n.p. deep olive-brown 45 10

1962 (22 Dec). 75th Birth Anniversary of Srinivasa Ramanujan (mathematician). W **374**. P 13½×14.
463 **420** 15n.p. deep olive-brown 70 40

Re.1

421 S. Vivekananda

(**422**)

1963 (17 Jan). Birth Centenary of Vivekananda (philosopher). W **374**. P 14×14½.
464 **421** 15n.p. orange-brown and yellow-olive 1·50 20

1963 (2 Feb). No. 428 surch with T **422**.
465 **385** 1r. on 1r.3n.p. pale yellow and brown .... 9·00 10

423 Hands reaching for FAO Emblem

424 Henri Dunant (founder) and Centenary Emblem

1963 (21 Mar). Freedom from Hunger. W **374**. P 13.
466 **423** 15n.p. grey-blue .... 3·00 30

1963 (8 May). Red Cross Centenary. W **374**. P 13.
467 **424** 15n.p. red and grey .... 3·00 40
a. Red (cross) omitted £25000

425 Artillery and Helicopter

1963 (15 Aug). Defence Campaign. T **425** and similar horiz design. W **374**. P 14.
468 15n.p. grey-green .... 1·50 10
469 1r. red-brown .... 6·00 65

Design: 15n.p. T **425**; 1r. Sentry and parachutists.

427 D. Naoroji (parliamentarian)

428 Annie Besant (patriot and theosophist)

1963 (4 Sept). Dadabhai Naoroji Commemoration. W **374**. P 13.
470 **427** 15n.p. grey 10 10

1963 (1 Oct). Annie Besant Commemoration. W **374**. P 13½×14.
471 **428** 15n.p. turquoise-green 15 10

No. 471 is incorrectly dated 1837. Mrs. Besant was born in 1847.

429 Gaur

430 Lesser Panda

1963 (7 Oct). Wild Life Preservation. Types **429/430** and similar designs. W **374**. P 13½×14 (10n.p.) or 13 (others).

472	10n.p. black and yellow-orange	2·50	1·50
473	15n.p. orange-brown and green	2·50	60
474	30n.p. slate and yellow-ochre	3·00	1·50
475	50n.p. orange and deep grey-green	3·75	80
476	1r. light brown and blue	4·75	50
472/476	*Set of* 5	15·00	4·50

Designs: Vert—15n.p. T **430**; 30n.p. Indian Elephant. Horiz—10n.p. T **429** (as T **430**) 50n.p. Tiger; 1r. Lion.

434 School Meals

435 Eleanor Roosevelt at Spinning-wheel

1963 (14 Nov). Children's Day. W **374**. P 14×13½.
477 **434** 15n.p. bistre-brown 10 10

1963 (10 Dec). 15th Anniversary of Declaration of Human Rights. W **374**. P 13½×13.
478 **435** 15n.p. reddish purple 10 15

436 Dipalakshmi (bronze)

437 Gopabandhu Das (social reformer)

1964 (4 Jan). 26th International Orientalists Congress, New Delhi. W **374**. P 13×13½.
479 **436** 15n.p. deep ultramarine 20 15

1964 (4 Jan). Gopabandhu Das Commemoration. W **374**. P 13×13½.
480 **437** 15n.p. deep dull purple 10 10

438 Purandaradasa

1964 (14 Jan). 400th Death Anniversary of Purandaradasa (composer). W **374**. P 13×13½.
481 **438** 15n.p. light brown 15 10

439 S. C. Bose and INA Badge

440 Bose and Indian National Army

1964 (23 Jan). 67th Birth Anniversary of Subhas Chandra Bose (nationalist). W **374**. P 13.
482 **439** 15n.p. yellow-bistre 50 20
483 **440** 55n.p. black, orange and orange-red .. 2·00 45

441 Sarojini Naidu

442 Kasturba Gandhi

1964 (13 Feb). 85th Birth Anniversary of Sarojini Naidu (poetess). W **374**. P 14.
484 **441** 15n.p. deep grey-green and purple 10 10

1964 (22 Feb). 20th Death Anniversary of Kasturba Gandhi. W **374**. P 14×13½.
485 **442** 15n.p. orange-brown 10 10

443 Dr. W. M. Haffkine (immunologist)

444 Jawaharlal Nehru (statesman)

1964 (16 Mar). Haffkine Commemoratian. W **374**. P 13.
486 **443** 15n.p. deep purple-brown/*buff* .... 1·25 10

(Value expressed as paisa instead of naye paise.)

1964 (12 June). Nehru Mourning Issue. No wmk. P 13½×13.
487 **444** 15p. deep slate 50 10

445 Sir Asutosh Mookerjee **446** Sri Aurobindo

1964 (29 June). Birth Centenary of Sir Asutosh Mookerjee (education reformer). W **374**. P 13½×13.
488 **445** 15p. bistre-brown and yellow-olive 10 10

1964 (15 Aug). 92nd Birth Anniversary of Sri Aurobindo (religious teacher). W **374**. P 13×13½.
489 **446** 15p. dull purple 20 10

447 Raja R. Roy (social reformer) **448** ISO Emblem and Globe

1964 (27 Sept). Raja Rammohun Roy Commemoration. W **374**. P 13×13½.
490 **447** 15n.p. brown 10 10

1964 (9 Nov). Sixth International Organisation for Standardisation General Assembly, Bombay. No wmk. P 13×13½.
491 **448** 15p. carmine 15 20

449 Jawaharlal Nehru (from 1r. commemorative coin) **450** St Thomas (after statue, Ortona Cathedral, Italy)

1964 (14 Nov). Children's Day. No wmk. P 14×13½.
492 **449** 15p. slate 10 10

1964 (2 Dec). St Thomas Commemoration. No wmk. P 14×13½.
493 **450** 15p. reddish purple 10 30
No. 493 was issued on the occasion of Pope Paul's visit to India.

451 Globe **452** J. Tata (industrialist)

1964 (14 Dec). 22nd International Geological Congress. W **374**. P 14×13½.
494 **451** 15p. blue-green 40 30

1965 (7 Jan). Jamsetji Tata Commemoration. No wmk. P 13½×13.
495 **452** 15p. dull purple and orange 30 20

453 Lala Lajpat Rai **454** Globe and Congress Emblem

1965 (28 Jan). Birth Centenary of Lala Lajpat Rai (social reformer). No wmk. P 13×13½.
496 **453** 15p. light brown 20 10

1965 (8 Feb). 20th International Chamber of Commerce Congress, New Delhi. No wmk. P 13½×13.
497 **454** 15p. grey-green and carmine 15 15

455 Freighter *Jalausha* and Visakhapatnam **456** Abraham Lincoln

1965 (5 Apr). National Maritime Day. W **374** (sideways). P 14½×14.
498 **455** 15p. blue 50 30

1965 (15 Apr). Death Centenary of Abraham Lincoln. W **374**. P 13.
499 **456** 15p. brown and yellow-ochre 15 10

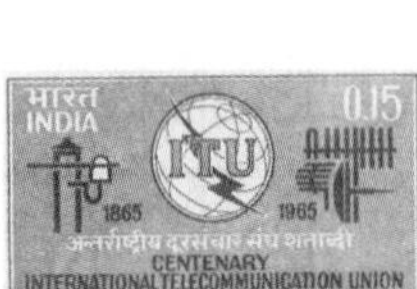

457 ITU Emblem and Symbols **458** 'Everlasting Flame'

1965 (17 May). ITU Centenary. W **374** (sideways). P 14½×14.
500 **457** 15p. reddish purple .... 1·00 30

1965 (27 May). First Anniversary of Nehru's Death. W **374**. P 13.
501 **458** 15p. carmine and blue 15 10

459 ICY Emblem **460** Climbers on Summit

1965 (26 June). International Co-operation Year. P 13½×13.
502 **459** 15p. deep olive and yellow-brown.... 1·25 1·25

1965 (15 Aug). Indian Mount Everest Expedition. P 13.
503 **460** 15p. deep reddish purple 45 20

461 Bidri Vase **462** Brass Lamp **463** Coffee berries

464 'Family Planning' **465** Konarak Elephant **465a** Spotted Deer ('Chital')

466 Electric Locomotive **467** Plucking Tea **468** Hindustan Aircraft Industries Ajeet jet fighter

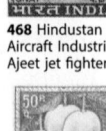

469 Indian dolls **470** Calcutta GPO **471** Mangoes

472 Somnath Temple **473** Hampi Chariot (sculpture) **474** Woman writing a Letter (medieval sculpture)

475 Dal Lake, Kashmir **476** Bhakra Dam, Punjab

477 Atomic reactor, Trombay

1965–75. Types **461/477**.

(a) W 374 (sideways on 2, 3, 5, 6, 8, 30, 50, 60p., 2, 5, 10r.). P 14×14½ (4, 10, 15, 20, 40, 70p., 1r.) or 14½×14 (others)

504	**461**	2p. red-brown (16.10.67)	10	1·00
505	**462**	3p. brown-olive (16.10.67)	1·00	4·00
505*a*	**463**	4p. lake-brown (15.5.68)	10	3·75
506	**464**	5p. cerise (16.10.67)	10	10
		a. Imperf (pair)	£180	
507	**465**	6p. grey-black (1.7.66)	30	4·25
508	**465a**	8p. red-brown (15.3.67)	40	4·25
509	**466**	10p. new blue (1.7.66)	60	10
510	**467**	15p. bronze-green (15.8.65)	8·50	10
511	**468**	20p. purple (16.10.67)	6·00	10
512	**469**	30p. sepia (15.3.67)	20	10
513	**470**	40p. maroon (2.10.68)	20	10
514	**471**	50p. blue-green (15.3.67)	20	10
515	**472**	60p. deep grey (16.10.67)	45	20
516	**473**	70p. chalky blue (15.3.67)	60	20
517	**474**	1r. red-brown and plum (1.7.66)	60	10
518	**475**	2r. new blue and deep slate-violet (15.3.67)	2·00	10
		w. Wmk capitals to right*	—	75·00
519	**476**	5r. deep slate-violet and brown (15.3.67)	3·00	90
520	**477**	10r. black and bronze-green (14.11.65)	32·00	80
504/520 *Set of 18*			50·00	17·00

(b) No wmk. P 14½×14

520*a*	**464**	5p. cerise (12.5.74)	2·25	10

(c) Wmk Large Star and 'INDIA GOVT'† in sheet. P 14½×14

521	**461**	2p. red-brown (1.3.75)	2·00	2·50
		aw. Wmk reversed	4·25	
521*b*	**464**	5p. cerise (1.3.75)	2·25	10

* The normal sideways watermark shows the heads of the capital to the left, *as seen from the back of the stamp*.

† The arrangement of this watermark in the sheet results in the words and the star appearing upright, inverted or sideways.

Two different postal forgeries exist of No. 511, both printed in lithography and without watermark. The cruder version is roughly perforated 15, but the more sophisticated is perforated 14×14½.

479 G. B. Pant (statesman) **480** V. Patel

1965 (10 Sept). Govind Ballabh Pant Commemoration. P 13.
522 **479** 15p. brown and deep green 10 20

1965 (31 Oct). 90th Birth Anniversary of Vallabhbhai Patel (statesman). P 14×13½.
523 **480** 15p. blackish brown 10 30

481 C. Das **482** Vidyapati (poet)

1965 (5 Nov). 95th Birth Anniversary of Chittaranjan Das (lawyer and patriot). P 13.
524 **481** 15p. yellow-brown 10 10

1965 (17 Nov). Vidyapati Commemoration. P 14×14½.
525 **482** 15p. yellow-brown 10 10

483 Sikandra, Agra **484** Soldier, Hindustan Aircraft Industries Ajeet jet fighters and Cruiser *Mysore*

1966 (24 Jan). Pacific Area Travel Association Conference, New Delhi. P 13½×14.
526 **483** 15p. slate 10 10

1966 (26 Jan). Indian Armed Forces. P 14
527 **484** 15p. violet .... 1·75 75

485 Lal Bahadur Shastri (statesman)
486 Kambar (poet) 

1966 (26 Jan). Shastri Mourning Issue. P 13×13½.
528 **485** 15p. black 80 10

1966 (5 Apr). Kambar Commemoration. P 14×14½.
529 **486** 15p. grey-green 10 10

487 B. R. Ambedkar
488 Kunwar Singh (patriot) 

1966 (14 Apr). 75th Birth Anniversary of Dr. Bhim Rao Ambedkar (lawyer). P 14×13½.
530 **487** 15p. purple-brown 10 10

1966 (23 Apr). Kunwar Singh Commemoration. P 14×13½.
531 **488** 15p. chestnut 10 10

489 G. K. Gokhale
490 Acharya Dvivedi (poet) 

1966 (9 May). Birth Centenary of Gopal Krishna Gokhale (patriot). P 13½×13.
532 **489** 15p. brown-purple and pale yellow .. 10 10

1966 (15 May). Dvivedi Commemoration. P 13½×14.
533 **490** 15p. drab 10 10

491 Maharaja Ranjit Singh (warrior)
492 Homi Bhabha (scientist) and Nuclear Reactor 

1966 (28 June). Maharaja Ranjit Singh Commemoration. P 14×13½.
534 **491** 15p. purple 60 30

1966 (4 Aug). Dr. Homi Bhabha Commemoration. P 14½×14.
535 **492** 15p. dull purple 15 30

493 A. K. Azad (scholar)
494 Swami Tirtha 

1966 (11 Nov). Abul Kalam Azad Commemoration. P 13½×14.
536 **493** 15p. chalky blue 15 15

1966 (11 Nov). 60th Death Anniversary of Swami Rama Tirtha (social reformer). P 13×13½.
537 **494** 15p. turquoise-blue 30 30

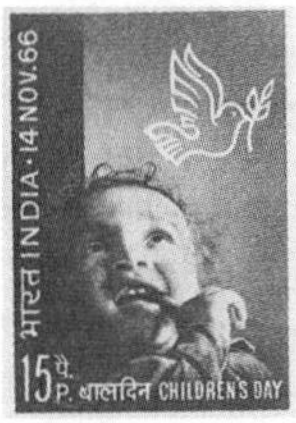

495 Infant and Dove Emblem
496 Allahabad High Court 

(Des C. Pakrashi)

1966 (14 Nov). Children's Day. P 13×13½.
538 **495** 15p. bright purple 60 20

1966 (25 Nov). Centenary of Allahabad High Court. P 14½×14.
539 **496** 15p. dull purple 70 30

497 Indian Family
498 Hockey Game 

1966 (12 Dec). Family Planning. P 13.
540 **497** 15p. brown 15 15

1966 (31 Dec). India's Hockey Victory in Fifth Asian Games. P 13.
541 **498** 15p. new blue .... 1·25 60

499 'Jai Kisan'
500 Voter and Polling Booth 

1967 (11 Jan). First Anniversary of Shastri's Death. P 13½×14.
542 **499** 15p. yellow-green 30 30

1967 (13 Jan). Indian General Election. P 13½×14.
543 **500** 15p. red-brown 15 15

501 Gurudwara Shrine, Patna
502 Taj Mahal, Agra 

1967 (17 Jan). 300th Birth Anniversary (1966) of Guru Gobind Singh (Sikh religious leader). P 14×13½.
544 **501** 15p. bluish violet .... 1·25 15

1967 (19 Mar). International Tourist Year. P 14½×14.
545 **502** 15p. bistre-brown and orange 30 15

503 Nandalal Bose and 'Garuda'
504 Survey Emblem and Activities 

1967 (16 Apr). First Death Anniversary of Nandalal Bose (painter). P 14×13½.
546 **503** 15p. bistre-brown 15 15

1967 (1 May). Survey of India Bicentenary. P 13½×13.
547 **504** 15p. reddish lilac .... 1·00 40

505 Basaveswara
506 Narsinha Mehta (poet) 

1967 (11 May). 800th Death Anniversary of Basaveswara (reformer and statesman). P 13½×14.
548 **505** 15p. orange-red 15 15

1967 (30 May). Narsinha Mehta Commemoration. P 14×13½.
549 **506** 15p. blackish brown 15 15

507 Maharana Pratap
508 Narayana Guru 

1967 (11 June). Maharana Pratap (Rajput leader) Commemoration. P 14×14½.
550 **507** 15p. red-brown 20 15

1967 (21 Aug). Narayana Guru (philosopher) Commemoration. P 14.
551 **508** 15p. brown 30 20

509 President Radhakrishnan
510 Martyrs' Memorial, Patna 

1967 (5 Sept). 75th Birth Anniversary of Sarvepalli Radhakrishnan (former President). P 13.
552 **509** 15p. claret 50 15

1967 (1 Oct). 25th Anniversary of 'Quit India' Movement. P 14½×14.
553 **510** 15p. lake 15 15

511 Route Map
512 Wrestling 

1967 (9 Nov). Centenary of Indo-European Telegraph Service. P 13½×14.
554 **511** 15p. black and light blue 70 20

1967 (12 Nov). World Wrestling Championships, New Delhi. P 13½×14.
555 **512** 15p. purple and light orange-brown 50 20

513 Nehru leading Naga Tribesmen
514 Rashbehari Basu (nationalist) 

1967 (1 Dec). Fourth Anniversary of Nagaland as a State of India. P 13×13½.
556 **513** 15p. ultramarine 15 15

1967 (26 Dec). Rashbehari Basu Commemoration. P 14.
557 **514** 15p. maroon 15 20

515 Bugle, Badge and Scout Salute

1967 (27 Dec). 60th Anniversary of Scout Movement in India. P 14½×14.
558 **515** 15p. chestnut .... 1·00 1·00

516 Men embracing Universe
517 Globe and Book of Tamil 

1968 (1 Jan). Human Rights Year. P 13.
559 **516** 15p. bronze-green 50 30

1968 (3 Jan). International Conference-Seminar of Tamil Studies, Madras. P 13.
560 **517** 15p. reddish lilac 60 15

518 UN Emblem and Transport
519 Quill and Bow Symbol

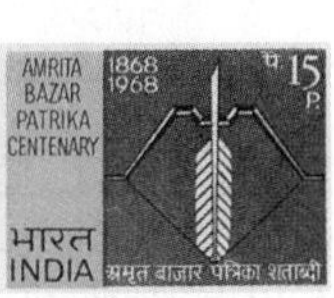

1968 (1 Feb). United Nations Conference on Trade and Development, New Delhi. P 14½×14.
561 **518** 15p. turquoise-blue................................ 60 15

1968 (20 Feb). Centenary of *Amrita Bazar Patrika* (newspaper). P 13½×14.
562 **519** 15p. sepia and orange-yellow............ 15 15

520 Maxim Gorky

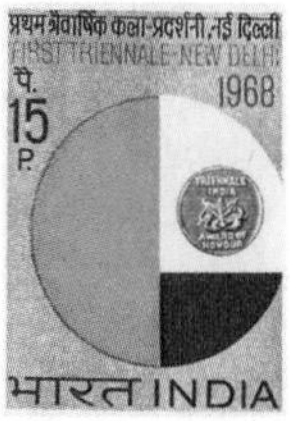

521 Emblem and Medal

1968 (28 Mar). Birth Centenary of Maxim Gorky. P 13½.
563 **520** 15p. plum................................ 15 50

1968 (31 Mar). First Triennale Art Exhibition, New Delhi. P 13.
564 **521** 15p. orange, royal blue and light blue................................ 30 20
a. Orange omitted................................ £10000

522 Letterbox and '100,000'

523 Stalks of Wheat, Agricultural Institute and Production Graph

(Des C. Pakrashi)

1968 (1 July). Opening of 100,000th Indian Post Office. P 13.
565 **522** 20p. red, blue and black........................ 40 15

1968 (17 July). Wheat Revolution. P 13.
566 **523** 20p. bluish green and orange-brown 30 15

524 *Self-portrait*

525 Lakshminath Bezbaruah

(Des from self-portrait)

1968 (17 Sept). 30th Death Anniversary of Gaganendranath Tagore (painter). P 13.
567 **524** 20p. brown-purple and ochre............ 50 15

1968 (5 Oct). Birth Centenary of Lakshminath Bezbaruah (writer). P 13½×14.
568 **525** 20p. blackish brown................................ 30 15

526 Athlete's Legs and Olympic Rings

527 Bhagat Singh and Followers

1968 (12 Oct). Olympic Games, Mexico. P 14½×14.
569 **526** 20p. brown and grey................................ 15 15
570 1r. sepia and brown-olive.................. 85 15

1968 (19 Oct). 61st Birth Anniversary of Bhagat Singh (patriot). P 13.
571 **527** 20p. yellow-brown................................ 1·00 1·00

528 Azad Hind Flag, Swords and Chandra Bose (founder)

529 Sister Nivedita

1968 (21 Oct). 25th Anniversary of Azad Hind Government. P 14×14½.
572 **528** 20p. deep blue................................ 1·25 15

1968 (27 Oct). Birth Centenary of Sister Nivedita (social reformer). P 14×14½.
573 **529** 20p. deep bluish green.......................... 30 30

530 Marie Curie and Radium Treatment

1968 (6 Nov). Birth Centenary of Marie Curie. P 14½×14.
574 **530** 20p. slate-lilac.. 1·40 1·25

531 Map of the World

532 Cochin Synagogue

1968 (1 Dec). 21st International Geographical Congress, New Delhi. P 13.
575 **531** 20p. new blue.. 15 15

1968 (15 Dec). 400th Anniversary of Cochin Synagogue. P 13.
576 **532** 20p. blue and carmine.......................... 1·00 40

533 INS *Nilgiri* (frigate)

534 Red-billed Blue Magpie

1968 (15 Dec). Navy Day. P 13.
577 **533** 20p. grey-blue.. 1·75 40

1968 (31 Dec). Birds. T **534** and similar designs. P 14×14½ (1r.) or 14½×14 (others).
578 20p. multicoloured.. 1·50 50
579 50p. scarlet, black and turquoise-green... 1·50 1·50
580 1r. deep blue, yellow-brown and pale blue.. 2·75 1·00
581 2r. multicoloured.. 2·25 2·75
578/581 *Set of 4*.. 7·25 5·25

Designs: Horiz—20p. T **534**; 50p. Brown-fronted Pied Woodpecker; 2r. Yellow-backed Sunbird. Vert—1r. Slaty-headed Scimitar Babbler.

538 Bankim Chandra Chatterjee

539 Dr. Bhagavan Das

1969 (1 Jan). 130th Birth Anniversary of Bankim Chandra Chatterjee (writer). P 13½.
582 **538** 20p. ultramarine...................................... 15 20

1969 (12 Jan). Birth Centenary of Dr. Bhagavan Das (philosopher). P 13½.
583 **539** 20p. pale chocolate................................ 15 50

540 Dr. Martin Luther King

541 Mirza Ghalib and Letter Seal

1969 (25 Jan). Martin Luther King Commemoration. P 13½.
584 **540** 20p. deep olive-brown.......................... 60 20

1969 (17 Feb). Death Centenary of Mirza Ghalib (poet). P 14½×14.
585 **541** 20p. sepia, brown-red and flesh......... 50 15

542 Osmania University

543 Rafi Ahmed Kidwai and Lockheed Constellation Mail Plane

1969 (15 Mar). 50th Anniversary of Osmania University. P 14½×14.
586 **542** 20p. olive-green.. 15 20

1969 (1 Apr). 20th Anniversary of 'ALL-UP' Air Mail Scheme. P 13.
587 **543** 20p. deep blue.. 1·50 30

544 ILO Badge and Emblem

545 Memorial, and Hands dropping Flowers

1969 (11 Apr). 50th Anniversary of International Labour Organisation. P 14½×14.
588 **544** 20p. chestnut.. 15 20

1969 (13 Apr). 50th Anniversary of Jallianwala Bagh Massacre, Amritsar. P 14×13½.
589 **545** 20p. rose-carmine.................................. 15 20

546 K. Nageswara Rao Pantulu (journalist)

547 Ardaseer Cursetjee Wadia, and Ships

1969 (1 May). Kasinadhuni Nageswara Rao Pantulu Commemoration. P 13½×14.
590 **546** 20p. brown.. 15 20

1969 (27 May). Ardaseer Cursetjee Wadia (ship-builder) Commemoration. P 14½×14.
591 **547** 20p. turquoise-green............................ 1·00 75

548 Serampore College

549 Dr. Zakir Husain

1969 (7 June). 150th Anniversary of Serampore College. P 13½.
592 **548** 20p. plum.. 15 20

1969 (11 June). President Dr. Zakir Husain Commemoration. P 13.
593 **549** 20p. sepia.. 15 20

550 Laxmanrao Kirloskar

1969 (20 June). Birth Centenary of Laxmanrao Kirloskar (agriculturalist). P 13.
594 **550** 20p. grey-black.. 15 15

551 Gandhi and his Wife

552 Gandhi's Head and Shoulders

553 Gandhi walking (woodcut)

554 Gandhi with Charkha

(Des Suraj Sadan (20p.), P. Chitnis (75p.), Indian Security Press (1r.) and C. Pakrashi (5r.))

1969 (2 Oct). Birth Centenary of Mahatma Gandhi. P 13½×14 (20p.), 14×14½ (1r.) or 13 (others).
595 **551** 20p. blackish brown.............................. 80 40
596 **552** 75p. cinnamon and drab...................... 2·50 3·50
597 **553** 1r. blue.. 2·50 65
598 **554** 5r. greyish brown and red-orange. 5·00 6·50
595/598 *Set of 4*.. 9·75 10·00

555 *Ajanta* (bulk carrier) and IMCO Emblem

1969 (14 Oct). Tenth Anniversary of Inter-Governmental Maritime Consultative Organisation. P 13.

599	**555**	20p. violet-blue	1·75	40

556 Outline of Parliament Building and Globe

557 Astronaut walking beside Space Module on Moon

1969 (30 Oct). 57th Inter-Parliamentary Conference, New Delhi. P 14½×14.

600	**556**	20p. new blue	15	20

1969 (19 Nov). First Man on the Moon. P 14×14½.

601	**557**	20p. olive-brown	60	30

558 Gurudwara Nankana Sahib (birthplace)

559 Tiger's Head and Hands holding Globe

1969 (23 Nov). 500th Birth Anniversary of Guru Nanak Dev (Sikh religious leader). P 13½.

602	**558**	20p. slate-violet	30	20

1969 (24 Nov). International Union for the Conservation of Nature and Natural Resources Conference, New Delhi. P 14½×14.

603	**559**	20p. orange-brown and bronze-green	1·00	45

560 Sadhu Vaswani

561 Thakkar Bapa

1969 (25 Nov). 90th Birth Anniversary of Sadhu Vaswani (educationist). P 14×14½.

604	**560**	20p. grey	15	15

1969 (29 Nov). Birth Centenary of Thakkar Bapa (humanitarian). P 13½.

605	**561**	20p. chocolate	15	20

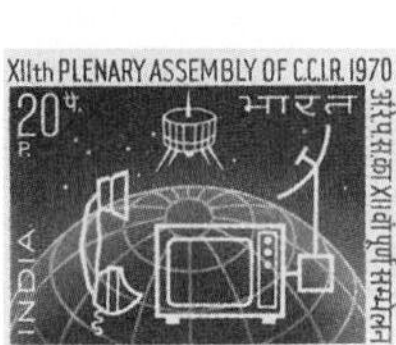

562 Satellite, Television, Telephone and Globe

563 C. N. Annadurai

1970 (21 Jan). 12th Plenary Assembly of International Radio Consultative Committee. P 13.

606	**562**	20p. Prussian blue	40	20

1970 (3 Feb). First Death Anniversary of Conjeevaram Natrajan Annadurai (statesman). P 13.

607	**563**	20p. reddish purple and royal blue	30	15

564 M. N. Kishore and Printing Press

565 Nalanda College

1970 (19 Feb). 75th Death Anniversary of Munshi Newal Kishore (publisher). P 13.

608	**564**	20p. lake	15	20

1970 (27 Mar). Centenary of Nalanda College. P 14½×14.

609	**565**	20p. brown	60	50

566 Swami Shraddhanand (social reformer)

567 Lenin

1970 (30 Mar). Swami Shraddhanand Commemoration. P 14×13½.

610	**566**	20p. yellow-brown	75	60

1970 (22 Apr). Birth Centenary of Lenin. P 13.

611	**567**	20p. orange-brown and sepia	40	20

568 New UPU HQ Building

569 Sher Shah Suri (15th-century ruler)

1970 (20 May). New UPU Headquarters Building, Berne. P 13.

612	**568**	20p. emerald, grey and black	15	20

1970 (22 May). Sher Shah Suri Commemoration. P 13.

613	**569**	20p. deep bluish green	30	70

570 V. D. Savarkar and Cellular Jail, Andaman Islands

571 'UN' and Globe

1970 (28 May). Vinayak Damodar Savarkar (patriot) Commemoration. P 13.

614	**570**	20p. orange-brown	65	30

1970 (26 June). 25th Anniversary of United Nations. P 13.

615	**571**	20p. light new blue	40	20

572 Symbol and Workers

1970 (18 Aug). Asian Productivity Year. P 14½×14.

616	**572**	20p. violet	20	20

573 Dr. Montessori and IEY Emblem

1970 (31 Aug). Birth Centenary of Dr. Maria Montessori (educationist). P 13.

617	**573**	20p. dull purple	30	30

574 J. N. Mukherjee (revolutionary) and Horse

575 V. S. Srinivasa Sastri

1970 (9 Sept). Jatindra Nath Mukherjee Commemoration. P 14½×14.

618	**574**	20p. chocolate	1·50	30

1970 (22 Sept). Srinivasa Sastri (educationalist) Commemoration. P 13×13½.

619	**575**	20p. yellow and brown-purple	30	30

576 I. C. Vidyasagar

577 Maharishi Valmiki

1970 (26 Sept). 150th Birth Anniversary of Iswar Chandra Vidyasagar (educationalist). P 13.

620	**576**	20p. brown and purple	40	30

1970 (14 Oct). Maharishi Valmiki (ancient author) Commemoration. P 13.

621	**577**	20p. purple	70	30

578 Calcutta Port

579 University Building

1970 (17 Oct). Centenary of Calcutta Port Trust. P 13½×13.

622	**578**	20p. greenish blue	1·50	70

1970 (29 Oct). 50th Anniversary of Jamia Millia Islamia University. P 14½×14.

623	**579**	20p. yellow-green	70	50

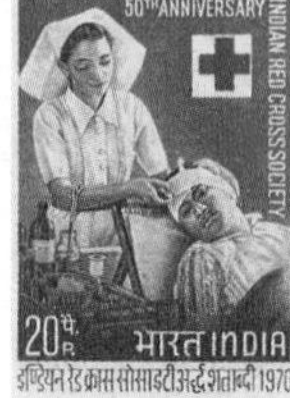

580 Jamnalal Bajaj

581 Nurse and Patient

1970 (4 Nov). Jamnalal Bajaj (industrialist) Commemoration. W **374**. P 13½×13.

624	**580**	20p. olive-grey	15	30

1970 (5 Nov). 50th Anniversary of Indian Red Cross. W **374** (sideways). P 13×13½.

625	**581**	20p. red and greenish blue	1·00	40

582 Sant Namdeo

583 Beethoven

1970 (9 Nov). 700th Birth Anniversary of Sant Namdeo (mystic). W **374**. P 13.

626	**582**	20p. orange	15	30

1970 (16 Dec). Birth Bicentenary of Beethoven. P 13.

627	**583**	20p. orange and greyish black	2·50	70

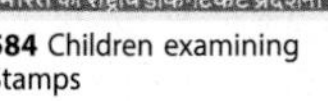

584 Children examining Stamps

585 Girl Guide

1970 (23 Dec). Indian National Philatelic Exhibition, New Delhi. T **584** and similar horiz design. P 13.

628	20p. orange and myrtle-green	50	10
629	1r. orange-brown and pale yellow-brown	6·00	1·00

Design: 20p. T **584**; 1r. Gandhi commemorative through magnifier.

1970 (27 Dec). Diamond Jubilee of Girl Guide Movement in India. P 13.

630	**585**	20p. maroon	60	30

STAMP BOOKLETS

1904. Black on green (No. SB1) or black on pink (No. SB2) covers. Stapled.

SB1 12¼a. booklet containing 24×½a. (No. 121) in blocks of 6 ... £2000
SB2 12¼a. booklet containing 12×1a. (No. 123) in blocks of 6 ... £2000

1906–11. Black on green (No. SB3), black on pink (No. SB4) or black on green and pink (No. SB5) match book type covers inscr 'Post Office of India' and royal cypher of King Edward VII. Stapled.

SB3 1r. booklet containing 32×½a. (No. 149) in blocks of 4 ... £1200
a. Without 'Post Office of India' inscr ... £1100
b. Ditto and showing royal cypher of King George V (1911) ... £1000
SB4 1r. booklet containing 16×1a. (No. 150) in blocks of 4 (1907) ... £1100
a. Without 'Post Office of India' inscr ... £1000
b. Ditto and showing royal cypher of King George V (1911) ... £1100
SB5 1r. booklet containing 16×½a. and 8×1a. (Nos. 149/150) in blocks of 4 (1907) ... £2250
a. Without 'Post Office of India' inscr ... £1900
b. Ditto and showing royal cypher of King George V (1911) ... £2000

1912–22. Black on green (Nos. SB6/SB7, SB12), black on pink (No. SB8), black on green and pink (No. SB9), black on purple (No. SB10) or black on blue (No. SB11) match book type covers with foreign postage rates on back. Stapled.

SB6 1r. booklet containing 64×3p. (No. 152) in blocks of 4 (blank back cover) ... £1600
SB7 1r. booklet containing 32×½a. (No. 155) in blocks of 4 ... £500
a. Blank back cover ... £500
b. Advertisement contractor's notice on back cover ... £700
c. Advertisement on back (1922) ... £700
SB8 1r. booklet containing 16×1a. (No. 159) in blocks of 4 ... £400
a. Blank back cover ... £400
b. Advertisements on front flap and back cover (1922) ... £500
SB9 1r. booklet containing 16×½a. and 8×1a. (Nos. 155, 159) in blocks of 4 (blank back cover) ... £350
a. Advertisement on back ... £400
b. Foreign postage rates on back ... £375
SB10 1r.8a. booklet containing 16×1½a. (No. 163) in blocks of 4 (1919) ... £800
a. Blank back cover (1921) ... £600
SB11 2r. booklet containing 16×2a. (No. 169) in blocks of 4 (blank back cover) (1921) ... £1400
a. Black on purple cover with postage rates on back (1922) ... £1400
SB12 2r. booklet containing 16×2a. (No. 166) in blocks of 4 (1922) ... £1400
a. Black on purple cover ... £1400

1921. Black on buff match book type cover. Stapled.

SB13 1r.2a. booklet containing 24×9p. on 1a. (No. 192) in blocks of 4 ... £200

1922. Black on brown (No. SB14) or black on green and pink (No. SB15) match book type covers with foreign postage rates on back. Stapled.

SB14 1r. booklet containing 16×1a. (No. 197) in blocks of 4 ... £475
a. Advertisement on back ... £500
b. Advertisements on front flap and back cover ... £700
c. Black on lilac cover with blank back ... £500
ca. Advertisements on front flap and back cover ... £700
d. Black on pink cover with blank back ... £650
SB15 1r. booklet containing 16×½a. and 8×1a. (Nos. 155, 197) in blocks of 4 (blank back cover) ... £1300

1926–28. Black on brown (No. SB16) or black on purple (No. SB17) match book type covers with foreign postage rates on back. Stapled.

SB16 1r. booklet containing 16×1a. (No. 203) in blocks of 4 ... £275
SB17 2r. booklet containing 16×2a. (No. 205) in blocks of 4 ... £600
a. Containing No. 206 (1928) ... £850

1929. Black on brown (No. SB18) or black on purple (No. SB19) separate leaf covers. Stitched.

SB18 1r. booklet containing 16×1a. (No. 203) in blocks of 4 (blank back cover) ... £275
a. Advertisement contractor's notice on back cover ... £275
b. Advertisements on front flap and back cover ... £300
c. Advertisement on back cover ... £300
SB19 2r. booklet containing 16×2a. (No. 205) in blocks of 4 (foreign postage rates on back cover) ... £800
a. Advertisement contractor's notice on back cover ... £800
b. Containing No. 206 (foreign postage rates on back cover) ... £1000
ba. Advertisement contractor's notice on back cover ... £1000

1932. Black on brown cover. Stitched.

SB20 1r.4a. booklet containing 16×1¼a. (No. 235) in blocks of 4 ... £850

1934. Black on buff cover. Stitched.

SB21 1r. booklet containing 16×1a. (No. 234) in blocks of 4 ... £450

1937. Black on red cover. Stamps with wmk upright or inverted. Stitched.

SB22 1r. booklet containing 16×1a. (No. 250) in blocks of 4 ... £500

OFFICIAL STAMPS

Stamps overprinted 'POSTAL SERVICE' or 'I.P.N.' were not used as postage stamps, and are therefore omitted.

Service.
(O 1)

(Optd by the Military Orphanage Press, Calcutta)

1866 (1 Aug)–**72.** Optd with T O **1**. P 14.

(a) No wmk

O1 **11** ½a. blue ... — £650
O2 ½a. pale blue ... £3750 £300
a. Opt inverted
O3 1a. brown ... — £425
O4 1a. deep brown ... — £325
O5 8a. carmine ... 55·00 £100

(b) Wmk Elephant's Head, T **13**

O6 **11** ½a. blue ... £800 30·00
w. Wmk inverted ... † £550
O7 ½a. pale blue ... £600 13·00
a. Opt inverted
b. No dot on 'i' (No. 50 on pane) ... — £800
c. No stop (No. 77 on pane) ... — £750
O8 **12** 8p. purple (1.72) ... 55·00 75·00
a. No dot on 'i' ... £800 £1000
b. No stop ... £800
O9 **11** 1a. brown ... £600 26·00
O10 1a. deep brown ... £700 55·00
a. No dot on 'i' ... — £1200
b. No stop ... — £1100
O11 2a. orange ... £400 £170
O12 2a. yellow ... £400 £180
a. Opt inverted
b. Imperf
c. Raised stop between 'c' and 'e' ... † £4500
w. Wmk inverted ... £475
y. Wmk inverted and reversed ... † £1000
O13 4a. green ... £550 £160
a. Opt inverted
O14 **17** 4a. green (Die I) ... £3000 £325

A variety with wide and more open capital 'S' occurs six times in sheets of all values except No. O8. Price four times the normal.

The first printing used a setting of 320 to overprint full sheets at one operation. A later printing in January 1872 of the ½a., 8p., and 1a. values only used a setting of 80 to overprint single panes. This included the 'No dot on i' and 'No stop' varieties.

Reprints exist of Nos. O6, O9 and O14; the latter is Die II instead of Die I.

Reprints of the overprint have also been made, in a different setting, on the 8 pies, purple, no watermark.

O 2 O 6

O 3 O 4

(No. O15 surch at Calcutta, others optd at Madras)

1866 (Oct). Fiscal stamps, Nos. O15/O18 with top and bottom inscrs removed, surch or optd. Wmk Crown over 'INDIA'.

(a) Surch as in T O **2**. *Thick blue glazed paper. Imperf×perf 14*

O15 O **2** 2a. purple ... £700 £600

(b) Optd 'SERVICE POSTAGE' in two lines as in Types O **3**/*O* **4** *and similar type. Imperf×perf 14*

O16 O **3** 2a. purple (G.) ... £3250 £1200
a. Optd on complete stamp (inscr 'FOREIGN BILL') ... † £28000
O17 O **4** 4a. purple (G.) ... £11000 £3500
O18 – 8a. purple (G.) ... £9500 £12000
a. Optd on complete stamp (inscr 'FOREIGN BILL') ... † £28000

(c) Optd 'SERVICE POSTAGE' in semi-circle. Wmk Large Crown. P 15½×15

O19 O **6** ½a. mauve/*lilac* (G.) ... £900 £160
a. Opt double ... £9000

So-called reprints of Nos. O15 to O18 are known, but in these the surcharge differs entirely in the spacing, etc., of the words; they are more properly described as Government imitations. The imitations of No. O15 have surcharge in *black* or in *green*. No. O19 exists with reprinted overprint which has a full stop after 'POSTAGE'.

PRINTERS. The following stamps up to No. O96 were overprinted by De La Rue.

Service. (O 7) **On H. S. M.** (O 8) **On H. S. M.** (O 9)

1867–73. Optd with T O **7**. Wmk Elephant's Head, T **13**. P 14.

O20 **11** ½a. blue (Die I) ... 80·00 50
w. Wmk inverted ... † £350
O21 ½a. pale blue (Die I) ... £100 3·50
O22 ½a. blue (Die II) (1873) ... £190 £110
O23 1a. brown ... 85·00 50
w. Wmk inverted ... † £400
O24 1a. deep brown ... 90·00 3·25
O25 1a. chocolate ... 95·00 3·25
O26 2a. yellow ... 50·00 2·50
O27 2a. orange ... 17·00 2·25
w. Wmk inverted ... — £425
O28 **17** 4a. pale green (Die I) ... 35·00 2·50
O29 4a. green (Die I) ... 6·00 1·50
O30 **11** 8a. rose (Die II) (1868) ... 7·50 1·50
O30*a* 8a. pale rose (Die II) ... 8·00 1·50
aw. Wmk inverted ... £150 75·00

Prepared for use, but not issued

O30*b* **18** 6a.8p. slate ... £700

1874–82. Optd with T O **8**.

(a) In black

O31 **11** ½a. blue (Die II) ... 29·00 20
O32 1a. brown ... 29·00 20
O33 2a. yellow ... £100 50·00
O33*a* 2a. orange ... 85·00 45·00
aw. Wmk inverted ... † £375
O34 **17** 4a. green (Die I) ... 45·00 3·00
O35 **11** 8a. rose (Die II) ... 9·00 14·00

(b) Optd in blue-black

O36 **11** ½a. blue (Die II) (1877) ... £1200 £100
w. Wmk inverted ... † £1600
O37 1a. brown (1882) ... £3500 £400

1883–99. Wmk Star, T **34**. Optd with T O **9**. P 14.

O37*a* **40** 3p. aniline carmine (1899) ... 20 10
O38 **23** ½a. deep blue-green ... 4·75 10
a. Opt double ... † £4750
b. Opt inverted ... † £1900
w. Wmk inverted ... † £375
O39 ½a. blue-green ... 2·75 10
O40 **25** 1a. brown-purple ... 8·00 50
a. Opt inverted ... £800 £900
aw. Opt inverted. Wmk inverted ... † £1400
b. Opt double ... † £5000
c. Opt omitted (in horiz pair with normal) ... £6500
w. Wmk inverted ... † £400
O41 1a. plum ... 1·75 10
O42 **27** 2a. pale blue ... 18·00 60
O43 2a. blue ... 19·00 60
O44 **29** 4a. olive-green ... 50·00 50
O44*a* 4a. slate-green ... 50·00 50
O45 **31** 8a. dull mauve ... 48·00 2·50
O46 8a. magenta ... 23·00 50
O47 **37** 1r. green and rose (1892) ... 80·00 9·50
O48 1r. green and carmine (1892) ... 48·00 40
O37*a*/O48 *Set of 7* ... £130 2·00

1900. Colours changed. Optd with T O **9**.

O49 **23** ½a. pale yellow-green ... 7·50 90
O49*a* ½a. yellow-green ... 9·50 50
ab. Opt double ... £2750
O50 **25** 1a. carmine ... 4·75 10
a. Opt inverted ... † £4250
b. Opt double ... † £4500
O51 **27** 2a. pale violet ... 55·00 1·50
O52 2a. mauve ... 55·00 50
O49/O52 *Set of 3* ... 60·00 1·00

1902–09. Stamps of King Edward VII optd with T O **9**.

O54 **41** 3p. grey (1903) ... 2·50 1·50
O55 3p. slate-grey (1905) ... 4·00 2·00
a. No stop after 'M' (R. 6/10) ... £750 £400
O56 **42** ½a. green ... 1·50 30
O57 **43** 1a. carmine ... 1·25 10
O58 **44** 2a. violet ... 4·50 50
O59 2a. mauve ... 4·00 10
w. Wmk inverted ... † £450
O60 **47** 4a. olive ... 32·00 30
O61 4a. pale olive ... 32·00 30
O62 **48** 6a. olive-bistre (1909) ... 2·00 15
O63 **49** 8a. purple (*shades*) ... 16·00 1·00
O64 8a. claret ... 17·00 85
O65 **51** 1r. green and carmine (1905) ... 4·25 80
O54/O65 *Set of 8* ... 60·00 3·50

1906. New types. Optd with T O **9**.

O66 **53** ½a. green ... 1·25 10
a. No stop after 'M' (R. 6/10) ... £350 £150
O67 **54** 1a. carmine ... 2·00 10
a. No stop after 'M' (R. 6/10) ... £550 £250
b. Opt albino (in pair with normal) ... £3000

On H. S. M.
(O **9a**)

1909. Optd with T O **9a**.

O68 **52** 2r. carmine and yellow-brown ... 25·00 1·50
O68*a* 2r. rose-red and yellow-brown ... 25·00 1·50
O69 5r. ultramarine and violet ... 16·00 1·50
O70 10r. green and carmine (tel-c. 25·00) ... 55·00 45·00
O70*a* 10r. green and scarlet (tel-c. 10·00) ... £200 17·00
O71 15r. blue and olive-brown (tel-c. 35·00) ... £150 65·00
O72 25r. brownish orange and blue (tel-c. 60·00) ... £325 £110
O68/O72 *Set of 5* ... £500 £170

NINE

SERVICE **SERVICE** **PIES**

(O **10**) (*14 mm*) (O **11**) (*21½ mm*) (O **12**)

1912–23. Stamps of King George V (wmk Single Star, T **34**) optd with Type O **10** or O **11** (rupee values).

O73 **55** 3p. grey ... 40 10
O73*a* 3p. pale grey ... 75 10
O74 3p. bluish grey ... 4·25 10
a. Opt omitted (in pair with normal) ...
O75 3p. slate ... 4·25 30
a. 'Rs' Flaw ...
O75*b* 3p. violet-grey ... 7·00 2·00
O76 **56** ½a. light green ... 50 10
O77 ½a. emerald ... 1·75 15
O78 ½a. bright-green ... 3·00 55
a. Opt double ... £130
O80 **57** 1a. rose-carmine ... 2·25 10
O81 1a. carmine ... 2·50 10
O82 1a. aniline carmine ... 1·75 10
a. Opt double ... † £2000
O83 **59** 2a. purple ... 3·75 30
O83*a* 2a. reddish purple ... 2·00 25
aw. Wmk inverted ... † £375
O84 2a. deep mauve ... 1·25 30
O84*a* 2a. bright reddish violet (1923) ... 9·50 2·50
ab. Stop under 's' in right value tablet (R. 4/16) ... £500
O85 **63** 4a. deep olive ... 1·25 10
O86 4a. olive-green ... 1·50 10
O87 **64** 6a. yellow-bistre ... 1·50 3·75
O88 6a. brown-ochre ... 9·00 6·00
O89 **65** 8a. deep magenta ... 4·00 1·50
O89*a* 8a. deep mauve ... 7·50 1·25
O90 8a. bright mauve (1918) ... 50·00 6·00
O91 **67** 1r. red-brown and deep blue-green (1913) ... 12·00 2·75
O91*a* 1r. brown and green ... 9·50 1·40
O92 2r. rose-carmine and brown (1913) ... 16·00 15·00
O93 5r. ultramarine and violet (1913) ... 40·00 50·00
O94 10r. green and scarlet (1913) (tel-c. 60·00) ... £130 £110
O95 15r. blue and olive (1913) (tel-c. £150) £225 £250
O96 25r. orange and blue (1913) (tel-c. £225) ... £375 £350
O73/O96 *Set of* 13 ... £700 £700

Used examples of Nos. O94/O96 should be purchased with caution, as the 'SERVICE' opt has been extensively forged.

1921. No. O80 surch at Calcutta with T O **12**.

O97 **57** 9p. on 1a. rose-carmine ... 2·25 2·00

1922. No. 197 optd by De La Rue with T O **10**.

O98 **57** 1a. chocolate ... 6·00 10

PRINTERS. The 1925-1926 provisional surcharges (Nos. O99/O108) were applied at Calcutta.

ONE RUPEE

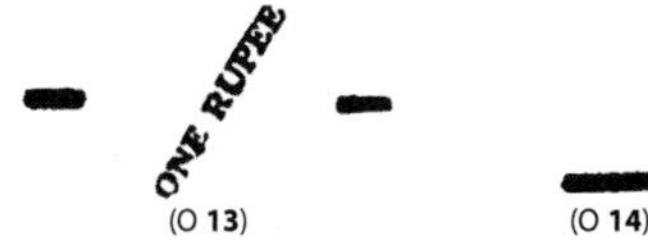

(O **13**) (O **14**)

1925. Official stamps surcharged.

(a) Issue of 1909, as T O **13**

O99 **52** 1r. on 15r. blue and olive ... 5·00 4·25
O100 1r. on 25r. chestnut and blue ... 42·00 £100
O101 2r. on 10r. green and scarlet ... 3·75 4·25
O101*a* 2r. on 10r. green and carmine ... £475 90·00

(b) Issue of 1912–1913 with T O **14**

O102 **67** 1r. on 15r. blue and olive ... 20·00 90·00
O103 1r. on 25r. orange and blue ... 11·00 12·00
a. Surch inverted ... £5000

(c) Issue of 1912–1913, as T O **13**

O104 **67** 2r. on 10r. green and scarlet ... £5000

Examples of the above showing other surcharge errors are believed to be of clandestine origin.

ONE ANNA **SERVICE** **ONE ANNA**

(O **15**) (O **16**)

1926. No. O62 surch with T O **15**.

O105 **48** 1a. on 6a. olive-bistre ... 45 30

1926. Postage stamps of 1911–1922 (wmk Single Star), surch as T O **16**.

O106 **58** 1a. on 1½a. chocolate (A) ... 20 10
O107 1a. on 1½a. chocolate (B) ... 8·00 4·50
a. Error. On 1a. chocolate (No. 197) £250
O108 **61** 1a. on 2a.6p. ultramarine ... 60 80

The surcharge on No. O108 has no bars at top.

Examples of Nos. O106/O107 with inverted or double surcharges are believed to be of clandestine origin.

PRINTERS. Official stamps from No. O109 were overprinted or printed by the Security Printing Press at Nasik, with the probable exception of No. O125.

SERVICE SERVICE **SERVICE**

(O **17a**) (*13½ mm*) (O **17b**) (*13½ mm*) (O **18**) (*19½ mm*)

Two types of the 13½ mm 'SERVICE' opt.
Type O **17a**: Small loop and long tail to 'R'
Type O **17b**: Large loop and shorter tail to 'R'

1926–31. Stamps of King George V (wmk Multiple Stars, T **69**) optd with Types O **17a** or O **18** (rupee values).

O109 **55** 3p. slate (1.10.29) ... 55 10
aw. Wmk inverted ... 7·00 3·00
b. Opt Type O **17b** ... — 50
O110 **56** ½a. green (1931) ... 21·00 60
aw. Wmk inverted ... 75·00 3·75
b. Opt Type O **17b** ... — 2·75
O111 **57** 1a. chocolate ... 20 10
aw. Wmk inverted ... 6·00 60
b. Opt Type O **17b** ... 1·75 30
bw. Wmk inverted ...
O112 **70** 2a. purple ... 30 10
w. Wmk inverted ... 7·00 2·00
O113 **71** 4a. sage-green ... 3·00 20
w. Wmk inverted ... 8·00 2·75
O115 **65** 8a. reddish purple ... 8·50 10
w. Wmk inverted ... 80 30
O116 **66** 12a. claret (1927) ... 70 2·50
w. Wmk inverted ... — 8·00
O117 **67** 1r. chocolate and green (1930) ... 16·00 1·00
w. Wmk inverted ... 18·00 5·50
O118 2r. carmine and orange (1930) ... 25·00 16·00
w. Wmk inverted ... — 25·00
O120 10r. green and scarlet (1931) ... £180 65·00
O109/O120 *Set of* 10 ... £225 80·00

1930. As No. O111, but optd as T O **10** (*14 mm*).

O121 **57** 1a. chocolate ... — 15·00
w. Wmk inverted ... £180 11·00

1932–36. Stamps of King George V (wmk Mult Stars, T **69**) optd with T O **17a**.

O122 **79** ½a. green (1935) ... 4·50 10
w. Wmk inverted ... — 17·00
O123 **80** 9p. deep green (*litho*) ... 30 15
aw. Wmk inverted ... — 13·00
O123*b* 9p. deep green (*typo*) ... 8·00 15
O124 **81** 1a. chocolate (1936) ... 2·50 10
cw. Wmk inverted ... 16·00 2·50
O125 **82** 1a.3p. mauve ... 30 10
w. Wmk inverted ... 1·00 40
O126 **70** 2a. vermilion ... 7·00 2·00
w. Wmk inverted ... — 17·00
O127 **59** 2a. vermilion (1935) ... 10·00 1·25
w. Wmk inverted ... — 20·00
O128 2a. vermilion (*small die*) (1936) ... 1·25 10
w. Wmk inverted ...
O129 **61** 2a.6p. orange (22.4.32) ... 60 10
w. Wmk inverted ... 7·50 2·25
O130 **63** 4a. sage-green (1935) ... 5·50 10
w. Wmk inverted ... — 27·00
O131 **64** 6a. bistre (1936) ... 40·00 10·00
O122/O131 *Set of* 9 ... 55·00 11·00

1937–39. Stamps of King George VI optd as Types O **17a** or O **18** (rupee values).

O132 **91** ½a. red-brown (1938) ... 17·00 1·25
w. Wmk inverted ... — 55·00
O133 9p. green (1937) ... 19·00 1·50
O134 1a. carmine (1937) ... 3·50 10
O135 **100** 1r. grey and red-brown (5.38) ... 75 50
w. Wmk inverted ... 95·00 60·00
O136 2r. purple and brown (5.38) ... 1·75 2·50
w. Wmk inverted ... — 85·00
O137 5r. green and blue (10.38) ... 16·00 7·50
w. Wmk inverted ... £140 £120
O138 10r. purple and claret (1939) ... 30·00 21·00
w. Wmk inverted ... £160 £110
O132/O138 *Set of* 7 ... 80·00 30·00

SERVICE 1A

(O **19**) O **20**

1939 (May). Stamp of King George V, surch with T O **19**.

O139 **82** 1a. on 1¼a. mauve ... 17·00 20
w. Wmk inverted ... — 10·00

(Des T. I. Archer)

1939 (1 June)–**42**. Typo. W **69**. P 14.

O140 O **20** 3p. slate ... 60 10
w. Wmk inverted ... — 55·00
O141 ½a. red-brown ... 13·00 10
w. Wmk inverted ... — 90·00
O142 ½a. purple (1.10.42) ... 30 10
w. Wmk inverted ... — 28·00
O143 9p. green ... 30 10
w. Wmk inverted ... — 70·00
O144 1a. carmine ... 30 10
w. Wmk inverted ... — 28·00
O145 1a.3p. yellow-brown (2.6.41) ... 9·00 70
w. Wmk inverted ... — 90·00
O146 1½a. dull violet (1.9.42) ... 65 10
w. Wmk inverted ... — 30·00
O147 2a. vermilion ... 60 10
w. Wmk inverted ... — 85·00
O148 2½a. bright violet ... 3·50 1·25
O149 4a. brown ... 60 10
w. Wmk inverted ... — 90·00
O150 8a. slate-violet ... 90 30
w. Wmk inverted ... — 85·00
O140/O150 *Set of* 11 ... 26·00 2·00

1948 (15 Aug). First Anniversary of Independence. Nos. 305/308 optd as T O **17a**.

O150*a* **305** 1½a. brown ... £110 £100
O150*b* 3½a. violet ... £7000 £2750
O150*c* 12a. grey-green ... £25000 £8500
O150*d* **306** 10r. purple-brown and lake ... £160000 †

Nos. O150*a*/O150*d* were only issued to the Governor-General's Secretariat. They have been extensively forged, and examples should only be acquired with a reliable guarantee.

O **21** Asokan Capital O **22**

(Des T.I. Archer)

1950 (2 Jan)–**51**. Typo (O **21**) or litho (O **22**). W **69**. P 14.

O151 O **21** 3p. slate-violet (1.7.50) ... 15 10
w. Wmk inverted ... £100
O152 6p. purple-brown (1.7.50) ... 30 10
w. Wmk inverted ... — £100
O153 9p. green (1.7.50) ... 1·25 10
O154 1a. turquoise (1.7.50) ... 1·25 10
w. Wmk inverted ...
O155 2a. carmine (1.7.50) ... 3·75 10
w. Wmk inverted ... — £100
O156 3a. red-orange (1.7.50) ... 8·00 2·00
O157 4a. lake (1.7.50) ... 15·00 20
O158 4a. ultramarine (1.10.51) ... 75 10
O159 6a. bright violet (1.7.50) ... 5·50 2·00
O160 8a. red-brown (1.7.50) ... 2·50 10
w. Wmk inverted ... 50·00 17·00
O161 O **22** 1r. violet ... 3·00 10
w. Wmk inverted ...
O162 2r. rose-carmine ... 1·00 1·00
O163 5r. bluish green ... 3·50 2·00
O164 10r. reddish brown ... 12·00 45·00
O151/O164 *Set of* 14 ... 50·00 45·00

Litho

Typo

Litho and typo printings: Apart from the shades, which in most cases are distinctive, unused typo stamps may be identified by the indentation of the design into the paper, as seen from the back of the stamp, whereas litho-printed versions are smooth on front and back. Marginal examples may also be allocated due to the fact that only the typo plates were surrounded by 'Jubilee' lines. On used stamps the fine lines are generally clearer and more even in the litho printings and the white border surrounding the value tablets appears wider than on typo versions.

1957 (1 Apr)–**58**. Values in naye paise. Typo (*t*) or litho (*l*). W **69**. P 14.

O165 O **21** 1n.p. slate (*l*) ... 1·50 10
a. Slate-black (l) ... 2·50 10
b. Greenish slate (t) ... 10 10
w. Wmk inverted ... 5·00 1·25
O166 2n.p. blackish violet (*t*) ... 10 10
w. Wmk inverted ...
O167 3n.p. chocolate (*t*) ... 20 10
O168 5n.p. green (*l*) ... 1·25 10
a. Deep emerald (t) ... 1·50 10
w. Wmk inverted ... — 50.00
O169 6n.p. turquoise-blue (*t*) ... 40 10
O170 13n.p. scarlet (*t*) ... 40 10
O171 15n.p. reddish violet (*l*) (6.58) ... 10·00 2·50
a. Reddish violet (t) ... 9·00 2·75
O172 20n.p. red (*l*) ... 1·25 1·25
a. Vermilion (t) ... 3·50 1·25
aw. Wmk inverted ...
O173 25n.p. violet-blue (*l*) ... 1·00 20
a. Ultramarine (t) ... 2·75 30
O174 50n.p. red-brown (*l*) ... 1·75 10
a. Reddish brown (t) ... 3·00 1·25
O165/O174 *Set of* 10 ... 13·50 3·75

1958–71. As Nos. O165/O174*a* and O161/O164 but W **374** (upright). Litho (*l*) or typo (*t*). P 14.

O175 O **21** 1n.p. slate-black (*t*) (1.59) ... 10 10
O176 2n.p. blackish violet (*t*) (1.59) ... 10 10
O177 3n.p. chocolate (*t*) (11.58) ... 10 10
w. Wmk inverted ... 4·00
O178 5n.p. deep emerald (*t*) (11.58) ... 10 10
O179 6n.p. turquoise-blue (*t*) (5.59) ... 10 10
O180 10n.p. deep grey-green (*l*) (1963) ... 50 50
a. Deep grey-green (t) (1966?) ... 2·50 3·50
O181 13n.p. scarlet (*t*) (1963) ... 1·00 3·75
O182 15n.p. deep violet (*t*) (11.58) ... 10 10
a. Light reddish violet (t) (1961) 3·50 10
O183 20n.p. vermilion (*t*) (5.59) ... 70 10
a. Red (t) (1966?) ... 13·00 1·00
O184 25n.p. ultramarine (*t*) (7.59) ... 10 10
O185 50n.p. reddish brown (*t*) (6.59) ... 70 10
a. Chestnut (l) (1966?) ... 14·00 1·50
O186 O **22** 1r. reddish violet (*l*) (2.59) ... 15 10
O187 2r. rose-carmine (*l*) (1960) ... 25 10
a. Wmk sideways*. *Pale rose-carmine (l) (1969?)* ... 2·50 3·75
aw. Wmk capitals to right ...

O188		5r. slate-green (*l*) (7.59)	40	1·75
		a. Wmk sideways*. *Deep grey-green* (*l*) (1969?)	90	2·25
O189		10r. brown-lake (*l*) (7.59)	1·00	2·75
		a. Wmk sideways* (*l*) (1971)	3·25	6·50
		ab. Printed on the gummed side	38·00	
		aw. Wmk capitals to right	3·75	
O175/O189 *Set of* 15			4·50	7·75

* The normal sideways watermark shows the head of the capitals pointing left, *as seen from the back of the stamp.*

O **23**

1967 (20 Mar)–**73**. Photo. W **374** (sideways). P 15×14.

O190	O **23**	2p. violet (1973?)	3·50	3·50
O191		5p. green (1973?)	3·25	1·50
O192		10p. myrtle-green (2.7.73)	3·25	25
O193		15p. plum (2.7.73)	3·50	55
O194		20p. red (2.7.73)	11·00	8·00
O195		30p. ultramarine (1973)	15·00	2·25
O196		50p. chestnut (2.7.73)	6·00	3·00
O197		1r. dull purple (20.3.67)	85	10
		a. Deep slate-purple (1969)	4·00	45
O190/O197 *Set of* 8			42·00	17·00

1967 (15 Nov)–**74**. Wmk Large Star and 'INDIA GOVT' in sheet*. Photo. P 15×14. No gum.

O200	O **23**	2p. violet	10	1·00
O201		3p. chocolate	40	1·25
O202		5p. green	10	10
		a. Yellowish green (1969)	10	10
		w. Wmk reversed	4·00	
O203		6p. turquoise-blue	1·25	1·50
O204		10p. myrtle-green	10	30
		a. Bronze-green (1969)	2·00	2·00
		w. Wmk reversed	4·00	
O205		15p. plum	10	30
		w. Wmk reversed		
O206		20p. red	10	30
		w. Wmk reversed	4·00	
O207		25p. carmine-red (1974?)	30·00	3·75
		w. Wmk reversed	30·00	
O208		30p. ultramarine	10	60
O209		50p. chestnut	10	60
		w. Wmk reversed	4·50	
O200/O209 *Set of* 10			30·00	8·75

* The arrangement of this watermark in the sheet results in the words and the star appearing upright, inverted or sideways.

TELEGRAPH STAMPS

PRINTERS. All Indian Telegraph stamps, including fiscal stamps optd or surch for provisional use, were typographed by De La Rue.

'SPECIMEN' and 'CANCELLED' overprints. Most Indian Telegraph stamps (with the exception of Nos. T1/T3, T21/T31, T53 and OT1/OT5) are known with 'SPECIMEN' or 'CANCELLED' overprints, for record purposes. In the case of the earlier issues up to 1890, and particularly the higher rupee values, these are usually worth considerably less than the prices quoted for unused examples.

T **1**

1860 (Jan). Inscr 'ELECTRIC TELEGRAPH'. Blue glazed paper. No wmk. Perf 14.

			Un	Used whole	Used half
T1	T **1**	4a. reddish purple	£3250	£2000	†
T2		1r. reddish purple	£7500	£5000	†
T3		4r. reddish purple	£30000	†	£8000

Imperforate examples are of proof status.

Used examples of this issue include whole stamps with punched holes and other forms of cancellation, but some left halves are known, indicating usage after 1869. Remainders were later optd 'COURT FEES' for fiscal use.

T **2**

T **3**

T **4**

T **5**

T **6**

T **7**

T **6** (Die I): Solid lines in spandrels.
T **7** (Die II): Hollow lines in spandrels.

T **8**

T **9**

T **10**

T **8** (Die I): Dark background in portrait ovals.
T **9** (Die II): Light background in portrait ovals.

T **11**

T **12**

T **13**

T **11** (Die I): Dark background in portrait ovals. Thin lettering in inscriptions.
T **12** (Die II): Light background in portrait ovals. Thicker lettering in inscriptions.

T **14**

T **15**

T **16**

T **14** (Die I): Diagonal '25 RUPEES' without ornaments. Dark background in portrait ovals. Tall lettering (round 'O').
T **15** (Die II): Diagonal '25 RUPEES' within ornaments. Light background in portrait ovals. Shorter lettering (oval 'O').

T **17**

T **18**

T **19**

T **17** (Die I): Solid lines in spandrels.
T **18** (Die II): Hollow lines in spandrels.

Watermarks:

T **19** Overall height 49mm. 'INDIA' 20 mm long, with wide 'D' and 'A'. Four horizontal lines in base of crown (max width of crown 18 *mm*).

T **25** Overall height 46mm. 'INDIA' 17 mm long, with narrow 'D' and 'A'. Three horizontal lines in base of crown (max width of crown 17 *mm*).

1869 (1 Feb)–**78**. Types T **2**/T **18**. Wmk T **19**. Perf 14.

			Un	Used half	Used whole
T4	T **2**	1a. yellow-green (1878)	50·00	6·00	—
		w. Wmk inverted	£300		
T5	T **3**	2a. maroon (1869)	38·00	1·00	£225
T6	T **4**	4a. light blue	42·00	1·00	
		w. Wmk inverted	£300	£100	†
T7	T **5**	8a. brown	55·00	1·00	£225
		a. Imperf	—	£1100	†
		w. Wmk inverted	†	£100	†
T8	T **6**	1r. grey (Die I)	£800	10·00	£425
		a. Imperf	—	£1400	†
T9	T **7**	1r. grey (Die II) (1869)	90·00	1·00	£150
		a. Double impression	†	—	†
T10	T **8**	2r.8a. orange-yellow (Die I)	£550	2·00	£225
T11	T **9**	2r.8a. orange (Die II) (1878)	£120	2·00	£170
		w. Wmk inverted	†	£150	†
T12	T **10**	5r. orange-brown	£120	3·00	—
		w. Wmk inverted	†	£160	†
T13	T **11**	10r. dull blue-green (Die I)	£850	3·00	—
T14	T **12**	10r. dull blue-green (Die II) (1878)	£1100	2·50	£225
T15	T **13**	14r.4a. bright lilac (Jan 1870)	£375	8·00	—
T16	T **14**	25r. reddish lilac (Die I)	£1400	7·00	—
T17	T **15**	25r. reddish lilac (Die II) (1878)	£550	3·50	£300
		w. Wmk inverted	†	£160	†
T18	T **16**	28r.8a. bright yellow-green (1.70)	£450	6·00	—
T19	T **17**	50r. rose (Die I)	£1500	19·00	—
T20	T **18**	50r. rose (Die II) (1874)	£850	8·00	—

The listed imperforate errors Nos. T7a and T8a were used respectively at Colombo (Ceylon) in Oct 1878 and at Bombay in May 1869. Other values also exist imperforate but are of proof status.

Several values, particularly the 2a., 4a. and 8a., exist on paper showing varying degrees of blueing.

Used prices for Nos. T4/T20 are quoted for both upper halves and whole stamps. The latter are usually found with additional punched holes. Lower halves, in this and subsequent issues, result from stamps being placed inverted on the telegraph form, against regulations, and are rare.

For later printings as Nos. T4/T7, T9, T11/T12, T14, T17 and T20, but wmk. T **25**, see Nos. T32/T41.

(T **20**)

(T **21**)

(T **22**)

(T **23**)

(T **24**)

1881 (Aug)–**82**. Fiscal stamps optd 'TELEGRAPH' as Types T **20**/T **24**. Wmk T **19** (sideways). Perf 14.

			Un	Used left half	Used right half
		(i) Opt Type T **20** *(28×3 mm with stop) at Calcutta*			
T21	T **20**	1a. dull lilac/*blued* (2.82)	£700	45·00	35.00
T22		2a. bright lilac (8.81)	£650	60·00	40.00
		a. Opt double, one albino	£1100	†	†
T23		4a. green (4.82)	£1400	45·00	35.00
		(ii) Opt Type T **21** *(24×2½ mm with stop) at Calcutta*			
T24	T **21**	1a. dull lilac/*blued* (2.82)	£700	50·00	35.00
T25		1a. pale lilac (2.82)	£300	45·00	35.00

The Calcutta opts Types T **20**/T **21** were intended to be applied at the top of the stamp, across the Queen's diadem.

(iii) Opt Type T **22** *(26×3 mm without stop) at Bombay*

T27	T **22**	2a. bright lilac (13.8.81)	†	£1100	£400

This first Bombay opt Type T **22** is of rough appearance, from worn type, and like Type T **23**, was applied to the centre of the stamp, across the portrait.

(iv) Opt Type T **23** *(24×2½ mm with stop) at Bombay*

T28	T **23**	2a. bright lilac (15.8.81).....	£1500	40·00	24·00

This second Bombay opt Type T **23** is of the same size as Type T **21** of Calcutta, but the 'G' is narrower, and there are other minor differences.

(v) Opt Type T **24** *(26×2¾ mm without stop) at Madras*

T29	T **24**	1a. pale lilac (20.3.82)........	£900	£150	£150
T30		2a. bright lilac (20.3.82).....	†	£1200	£1300
T31		4a. green (17.4.82).............	—	24·00	24·00

The Madras opt Type T **24** is from a bold fount, readily distinguishable from those used at Calcutta and Bombay for Type T **20**/T **23**. It was applied to the centre of the stamps, across the portrait.

Nos. T21/T31, being of horizontal format, were placed *vertically* on the telegraph forms and bisected in the usual way. Used prices are quoted for both left ('TELE(G)') and right ('(G)RAPH') halves, the former being scarcer in the case of Nos. T21/T28.

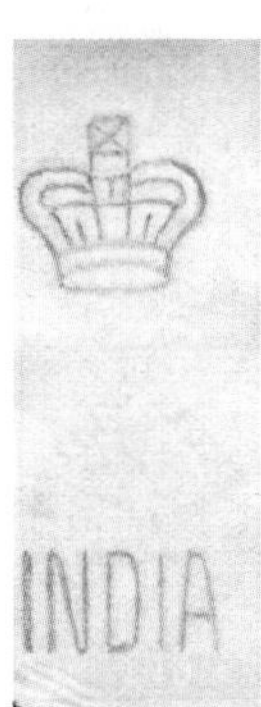

T **25**

1882. Designs as 1869–1878 issue, but wmk T **25**. Perf 14.

			Un	*Used half*	*Used whole*
T32	T **2**	1a. green..............................	28·00	2·00	95.00
T33	T **3**	2a. maroon............................	24·00	1·25	£100
T34	T **4**	4a. light blue........................	30·00	1·00	£120
T35	T **5**	8a. brown	30·00	1·00	£130
T36	T **7**	1r. grey (Die II)	38·00	1·00	£120
T37	T **9**	2r.8a. orange (Die II)...............	90·00	1·75	£180
T38	T **10**	5r. orange-brown	75·00	2·00	£130
		w. Wmk inverted	†	£150	†
T39	T **12**	10r. blue-green (Die II)........	£250	3·00	£120
T40	T **15**	25r. reddish lilac (Die II)......	£225	2·50	£160
T41	T **18**	50r. carmine (Die II).............	£425	1·75	£200

Used prices for whole stamps (often with additional punched holes), for this and subsequent issues, are quoted in the third price column.

T **26**

T **27**

T **28**

T **29**

T **30**

T **31**

T **32**

T **33**

T **34** T **35**

1890 (Aug)–**91**. New designs Type T **26**/T **35**. Wmk T **25**. Perf 14.

			Un	*Used half*	*Used whole*
T42	T **26**	1a. yellowish green............	20·00	1·50	45.00
T43	T **27**	2a. maroon (1.91)	22·00	1·25	45.00
T44	T **28**	4a. blue..................................	26·00	1·00	60.00
T45	T **29**	8a. brown	26·00	1·00	50.00
T46	T **30**	1r. grey..................................	30·00	1·00	50.00
T47	T **31**	2r.8a. orange (1.91).................	55·00	3·50	80.00
T48	T **32**	5r. brownish orange (1.91)	£130	2·50	80.00
T49	T **33**	10r. blue-green (1.91).........	£250	3·50	£140
T50	T **34**	25r. bright lilac (1.91)..........	£250	5·00	£110
T51	T **35**	50r. carmine (1.91)...............	£250	6·50	£110

Used upper halves of this issue (with the exception of No. T47) can be difficult to distinguish from the same values of the 1904 King Edward VII issue, unless they have pre-1904 cancels or show sufficient of the lower part of the design to confirm the absence of the King's crown.

(T **36**)

(T **37**)

1899 (4 Sep). No. T47 surch at Calcutta, as Type T **36**.

T52	T **36**	2r. on 2r.8a. orange...........	£300	10·00	—
		a. 'RUPLES' for 'RUPEES' in upper half..................	£600	75·00	—

1900 (24 Feb). Fiscal stamp of 1861 inscr 'FOREIGN BILL' optd as Type T **37** at Calcutta. Bluish glazed paper. Wmk T **2**. Perf 14.

T53	T **37**	2r. purple..............................	£500	£250	—

(T **38**)

T **39**

1900 (30 Apr). No. T47 surch by De La Rue, as Type T **38**.

T54	T **38**	2r. on 2r.8a. orange...........	£300	10·00	£275

1900 (14 Nov). New design Type T **39**. Wmk T **25**. Perf 14.

T55	T **39**	2r. yellow	£300	16·00	£300
		a. Red bar optd at foot ...	£325	†	£250
		b. Red line ruled by hand at foot..................	£550	†	£550

The colour chosen for No. T55 was found to be unsuitable, as it proved difficult to discern the design under artificial light. Stocks held at Calcutta were provided with a printed red bar at foot (No. T55a), while those at the Madras and Bombay offices were ruled with a red line by hand (No. T55b) before issue, to mark the bottom half of the stamp, and ensure that stamps were affixed to telegraph forms in the correct position.

T **40**

T **41**

T **42**

T **43**

T **44**

T **45**

T **46**

T **47**

T **48**

T **49**

1904. New designs with portrait of King Edward VII, Types T **40**/T **49**. Wmk T **25**. Perf 14.

			Unused	*Used half*	*Used whole*
T56	T **40**	1a. yellow-green..................	22·00	11·00	55.00
T57	T **41**	2a. maroon............................	24·00	10·00	48.00
T58	T **42**	4a. light blue.........................	24·00	9·00	38.00
T59	T **43**	8a. brown	28·00	9·00	42.00
T60	T **44**	1r. grey..................................	28·00	9·00	65.00
T61	T **45**	2r. brown-orange................	70·00	2·50	55.00
T62	T **46**	5r. orange-brown	85·00	12·00	60.00
T63	T **47**	10r. bluish green	£180	13·00	65.00
T64	T **48**	25r. bright lilac......................	£275	16·00	95.00
T65	T **49**	50r. carmine..........................	£350	19·00	95.00

With the exception of No. T61, used upper halves are only identifiable if they show sufficient of the lower part of the design to confirm the presence of the King's crown and our prices for used upper halves are for such examples. The designs are otherwise identical to Nos. T42/T46 and T48/T51.

Used whole stamps of this issue, usually without additional punched holes, result from changes in administrative practice, and often show special telegraphic circular datestamps, dated after 1 April 1908.

(T 50)

(T 51)

(T 52)

1904 (July). Nos. T46, T59 and 1861 fiscal stamp inscr 'FOREIGN BILL' (blue glazed paper, Wmk T **19**, perf 14) surch with new values at Calcutta, as Type T **50**/T **52**.

			Un	Used half
T66	T **50**	1a. on 4r. purple	16·00	3·50
		a. Numeral '1' of '1 ANNA' omitted from upper half	£425	£150
		b. 'h' for 'H' in 'TELEGRAPH' in upper half	£150	
		c. Small 'R' in 'TELEGRAPH' in upper half	£150	50·00
		d. 'C' for 'G' in 'TELEGRAPH' in lower half	£150	†
		w. Wmk inverted	50·00	20·00
T67	T **51**	2a. on 8a. brown	28·00	3·50
T68	T **52**	4a. on 1r. grey	23·00	3·50

No. T66a occurred once in the setting but was soon corrected.

OFFICIAL TELEGRAPH STAMPS

(OT **1**)

1908 (?). Nos. Type T **61**/**65** optd 'O H M S' as Type OT **1**. Perf 14.

OT1	2r. brown-orange	95·00	—
OT2	5r. orange-brown	£110	—
OT3	10r. bluish green	£140	—
OT4	25r. bright lilac	£250	—
OT5	50r. carmine	£350	—

No used examples of Nos. OT1/OT5 are known, but the upper halves remain identical to Nos. T61/T65, and it is possible that all lower halves were destroyed.

Separate Telegraph stamps were abolished on 1 April 1908, and replaced by postage stamps. Current issues remained valid for pre-payment of telegraph charges until stocks were exhausted.

INDIA USED ABROAD

In the years following 1858 the influence of the Indian Empire, political, military and economic, extended beyond its borders into neighbouring states, the Arabian Gulf, East Africa and the Far East. Such influence often led to the establishment of Indian civil and military post offices in the countries concerned where unoverprinted stamps of India were used.

Such offices operated in the following countries. An * indicates that details will be found under that heading elsewhere in the catalogue.

ABYSSINIA

Following the imprisonment of the British Consul by King Theodore of Abyssinia, an expedition under the command of Sir Robert Napier was dispatched from India to secure his release. The expedition landed on 28 November 1867 and, having achieved its objective, withdrew the following June. A detachment of the Indian Army Postal Corps accompanied the expedition and was in operation from January to June 1868.

Contemporary Indian stamps were cancelled with T AZ **1**.

AZ **1**

Stamps of India cancelled with T AZ **1**

1865. (Nos. 54/65).

AZ1	½a. pale blue	95·00
AZ2	8p. purple	95·00
AZ3	1a. brown	£110
AZ4	2a. yellow	£140
AZ5	8a. carmine	£200

1866-67. (Nos. 69/72).

AZ6	4a. green	£150
AZ7	6a.8p. slate	£140

ADEN*

Unoverprinted stamps of India used from 1854 until 1937.

BAHRAIN*

Unoverprinted stamps of India used from 1884 until 1933.

BRITISH EAST AFRICA (KENYA, UGANDA AND TANGANYIKA)*

Unoverprinted stamps of India used during August and September 1890.

FRENCH INDIAN SETTLEMENTS

The first Indian post office, at Chandernagore, was open in 1784 to be followed by offices in the other four Settlements. By an agreement with the French, dating from 1814, these offices handled mail destined for British India, Great Britain, the British Empire and most other foreign destinations except France and the French colonies. In later years the system was expanded by a number of sub-offices and it continued to operate until the French territories were absorbed into India on 2 May 1950 (Chandernagore) or 1 November 1954.

Chandernagore. Opened 1784. Used numeral cancellations 'B86' or '86'.

Sub-offices:

Gondalpara (opened 1906)
Lakhiganj (opened 1909)
Temata (opened 1891)

Karikal. Opened 1794. Used numeral cancellations in 'C147', '147' or '6/M-21'.

Sub-offices:

Ambagarattur (opened 1904)
Kottuchari (opened 1901)
Nedungaon (opened 1903)
Puraiyar Road (opened 1901)
Settur (opened 1905)
Tirumalrayapatnam (opened 1875) – used numeral cancellation '6/M-21/1'
Tiramilur (opened 1898)

Mahe. Opened 1795. Used numeral cancellations 'C192' or '9/M-14'.

Pondicherry. Opened 1787. Used numeral cancellations 'C111', '111' (also used elsewhere), '6/M-19' (also used elsewhere) or '6/M-20'.

Sub-offices:

Ariyankuppam (opened 1904)
Bahoor (opened 1885)
Mudaliarpet (opened 1897)
Muthialpet (opened 1885)
Pondicherry Bazaar (opened 1902)
Pondicherry Railway Station (opened 1895)
Olugarai (opened 1907)
Vallinur (opened 1875) – used numeral cancellation 'M-19/1'
Yanam. Opened 1876. Used numeral cancellation '5/M-4'.

IRAN

The British East India Company was active in the Arabian Gulf from the early years of the 17th-century with their first factory (trading centre) being established at Jask in 1619. After 1853 this commercial presence was converted into a political arm of the Indian Government culminating in the appointment of a Political Resident to Bushire in 1862.

The first Indian post office in Iran (Persia) opened at Bushire on 1 May 1864 with monthly mail services operating to the Resident there and to the British Legation at Tehran. Further offices in the other Gulf ports followed, but, unless otherwise stated below, all were closed on 1 April 1923.

Details of the stamps known used from each post office are taken with permission, from the listing published by the Iran Philatelic Study Circle.

Persian Expeditionary Force

Following the occupation of Herat, on the Afghan border, by Persia, Britain declared war on 1 Nov 1856 and the Indian Expeditionary Force took Bushire (occupied 12 Dec 1856 to 2 Oct 1857) and Mohammera (occupied 26 Mar 1857 to 16 May 1858) Kharg Island was used as a supply base (Dec 1856 to Feb 1858).

The expedition was accompanied by Field Post Offices using contemporary Indian stamps cancelled '131' in a diamond of lines. It should be noted that forgeries of this cancellation are known and the number was subsequently assigned to Billimoria in India.

Z **1**

Stamps of India cancelled with T Z **1**.

1854–55. (Nos. 2/26).

Z1	½a. blue (Die I)	£650
Z2	1a. red (Die I)	£600
	a. Die II	£700
Z3	4a. blue and red (Head die III, frame die II)	£2750

1854. (No. 31).

Z4	2a. green	£750

1856–64. (No. 37).

Z5	½a. blue (Die I)	£275

Abadan

An island at the mouth of the Shatt-el-Arab, the Anglo-Persian Oil Co. established an oil pipeline terminus there in 1909. An Indian post office was opened in 1917 and closed in 1923.

Z **2**

Z **3**

Postmark type	*Approx period of use*
Z **2**	1917–1923
Z **3**	1918–1922

1911–22. (Nos. 151/191).

Z6	3p. grey	22·00
Z7	½a. green	14·00
Z8	1a. carmine	16·00
Z9	1½a. chocolate (Type A)	35·00
Z10	2a. purple	18·00
Z11	2a.6p. ultramarine (1913)	14·00
Z12	3a. orange	16·00
Z13	4a. olive-green	21·00
Z14	6a. brown-ochre	22·00
Z15	8a. mauve	17·00
Z16	12a. carmine-lake	28·00
Z17	1r. brown and green	21·00
Z18	2r. carmine and brown	28·00
Z19	5r. ultramarine and violet	35·00
Z20	10r. green and scarlet	50·00

Prices quoted for Nos. Z6/Z20 are for stamps cancelled as T Z **2** or Z **3**. Stamps with telegraphic cancels of Abadan (showing concentric semi-circles above and below the date) are worth less.

Ahwaz

A city in south-west Iran, on the Karun River. An Indian post office was opened in 1915 and closed in 1923.

Z **4** 25 mm large date

Z **5**

Postmark type		*Approx period of use*
Z **4**	inscribed 'EXPERIMENTAL P.O./B504'	1915
Z **2**	inscribed 'AHWAZ'	1915–1922
Z **5**		1916–1923

Stamps of India cancelled at Ahwaz

1911–22. (Nos. 151/191).

Z21	3p. grey	35·00
Z22	½a. green	12·00
Z23	1a. carmine	12·00
Z25	2a. purple	20·00
Z26	2a.6p. ultramarine (1913)	14·00
Z27	3a. orange	18·00
Z28	4a. olive-green	32·00
Z30	8a. mauve	45·00
Z32	1r. brown and green	65·00

1922–26. (Nos. 197/200).

Z34	1a. chocolate	35·00

OFFICIAL STAMPS

1903–09. (Nos. O54/O65).

Z36	4a. olive	75·00

1906. (Nos. O66/O67).

Z38	½a. green	45·00

1912–13. (Nos. O73/O96).

Z43	2a. purple	

Bandar Abbas

Situated on the Strait of Hormuz, the British East India Company established a factory there in 1622. When a postal service between Bombay and Basra was established in 1862, Bandar Abbas was one of the regular ports of call but the Indian post office was not opened until 1 April 1867. It closed in 1923.

Z 6

Z 7

Z 8

Z 9 Nine lines in obliterator

Z 10 Eight lines in obliterator

Z 11

Z 12 Four thin lines in corners

Z 13

Postmark type		*Approx period of use*
Z 6		1870
Z 7		1871–1873
Z 8		1874–1888
Z 9		
Z 10	(inscr 'BANDARABAS')	
Z 10	(inscr 'BANDAR-ABAS')	
Z 11		1884
Z 12	(inscr 'BANDARABAS')	1886–1892
Z 12	(inscr 'BANDAR-ABAS')	1892–1893
Z 4	(inscr 'BANDAR-ABAS')	1905–1920
Z 4	(inscr 'BANDARABAS/PAR')	
Z 13		1907–1922

Stamps of India cancelled at Bandar Abbas

1865. (Nos. 54/65).
Z46 ½a. blue .... 20·00
Z48 1a. brown .... 22·00
Z49 2a. orange .... 42·00

1866–78. (Nos. 69/72).
Z49a 4a. green (Die I) .... 55·00
Z50 4a. blue-green (Die II) .... 60·00

1868–73. (Nos. 73/76).
Z51 8a. rose (Die II) .... 70·00
Z52 ½a. blue (Die II) .... 9·50

1882–90. (Nos. 84/101).
Z53 ½a. blue-green .... 6·00
Z55 1a. plum .... 9·50
Z57 2a. blue .... 15·00
Z58 3a. orange .... 28·00
Z59 4a. olive-green .... 22·00
Z60 4a.6p. yellow-green .... 32·00
Z63 1r. slate .... 55·00

1892–97. (Nos. 103/106).
Z64 2a.6p. yellow-green .... 14·00

1899. (No. 111).
Z66 3p. aniline-carmine .... 20·00

1900. (Nos. 112/118).
Z68 ½a. yellow-green .... 9·50
Z69 1a. carmine .... 9·50
Z70 2a. pale violet .... 22·00
Z71 2a.6p. ultramarine .... 14·00

1902–11. (Nos. 119/147).
Z72 3p. grey .... 8·00
Z73 ½a. green .... 6·00
Z74 1a. carmine .... 8·00
Z75 2a. mauve .... 7·00
Z76 2a.6p. ultramarine .... 6·00
Z78 4a. olive .... 21·00
Z82 1r. green and carmine .... 35·00
Z83 2r. carmine and yellow-brown .... 65·00

1906. (Nos. 149/150).
Z84 ½a. green .... 7·00
Z85 1a. carmine .... 8·00

1911–22. (Nos. 151/191).
Z86 3p. grey .... 12·00
Z87 ½a. green .... 6·00
Z88 1a. carmine .... 6·00
Z89 1½a. chocolate (Type A) .... 26·00
Z91 2a. purple .... 8·00
Z92 2a.6p. ultramarine (1912) .... 26·00
Z93 2a.6p. ultramarine (1913) .... 6·00
Z94 3a. orange .... 15·00
Z95 4a. olive-green .... 13·00
Z96 6a. brown-ochre .... 25·00

OFFICIAL STAMPS

1883–99. (Nos. O37*a*/O48).
Z102 4a. olive-green .... 45·00

1900. (Nos. O49/O52).
Z105 2a. mauve .... 45·00

1902–09. (Nos. O54/O65).
Z108 1a. carmine .... 20·00
Z109 2a. mauve .... 20·00

1906. (Nos. O66/O67).
Z112 1a. carmine .... 20·00

1912–13. (Nos. O73/O96).
Z113 3p. grey .... 30·00
Z114 ½a. green .... 19·00
Z115 1a. carmine .... 15·00

1921. (No. O97).
Z118 9p. on 1a. rose-carmine .... 55·00

Bushire

An Iranian Gulf port, the British East India Company's factory was transferred there from Bandar Abbas in 1762 and a political agency established. An Indian postal agency was established in 1857 and it was on the regular steamer service operated between Bombay and Basra in 1862. The Indian post office was opened on 1 May 1864 and closed in 1923.

Z 14 Three thick lines in corners

Z 15 (19 *mm*)

Z 16

Postmark type		*Approx period of use*
Z 1	('308' in diamond of bars)	1865–1870
Z 7	('26')	1870–1874
Z 8	(inscr 'BUSHIR'/K-5)	1874–1878
Z 8	(inscr 'BASHIR'/K-5)	1878–1880
Z 10	(inscr 'BUSHIRE')	1880–1882
Z 11	(inscr 'BUSHIRE')	1882–1885
Z 11	(c.d.s. only, inscr PAR/BUSHIRE)	?
Z 11	(c.d.s. only, inscr DEP/BUSHIRE)	?
Z 12	(inscr 'BUSHIRE')	1884–1899
Z 13	(inscr 'BUSHIRE')	1885–1904
Z 15		1887–1892
Z 14	(inscr 'BUSHIRE')	1889–1902
Z 16	(inscr 'BUSHIRE')	1892–1897
Z 16	(inscr 'BUSHIRF')	1897–1923
Z 15	(inscr BUSHIRE/REG)	1892–1915
Z 4	(inscr BUSHIRE)	1907–1915
Z 4	(inscr BUSHIRE/REG)	1902–1921

Stamps of India cancelled at Bushire

1854. (No. 14).
Z119 1a. dull red £800

1865. (Nos. 54/65).
Z120 ½a. blue .... 15·00
Z121 1a. brown .... 13·00
Z122 2a. orange .... 15·00
Z123 4a. green £120

1866–78. (Nos. 69/72).
Z125 4a. green (Die I) .... 38·00
Z126 4a. green (Die II) .... 16·00
Z127 6a.8p. slate £100

1868–73. (Nos. 73/76).
Z128 8a. rose (Die II) .... 40·00
Z129 ½a. blue (Die II) .... 5·50

1874–76. (Nos. 77/82).
Z130 1r. slate £130
Z131 6a. brown .... 23·00
Z132 12a. Venetian red .... 75·00

1882–90. (Nos. 84/101).
Z133 ½a. blue-green .... 3·25
Z135 1a. brown-purple .... 3·25
Z136 1½a. sepia .... 14·00
Z137 2a. blue .... 5·50
Z138 3a. orange .... 15·00
Z138*a* 3a. brown-orange .... 7·00
Z139 4a. olive-green .... 6·00
Z140 4a.6p. yellow-green .... 12·00
Z141 8a. magenta .... 9·00
Z142 12a. purple/*red* .... 35·00
Z143 1r. slate .... 25·00

1891. (No. 102).
Z144 2½a. on 4a.6p. yellow-green .... 9·00

1892–95. (Nos. 103/109).
Z145 2a.6p. yellow-green .... 4·25
Z146 1r. green and carmine .... 21·00
Z147 2r. carmine and yellow-brown .... 75·00
Z147*a* 3r. brown and green £100
Z147*b* 5r. ultramarine and violet £110

1898. (No. 110).
Z148 ¼ on ½a. blue-green .... 22·00

1899. (No. 111).
Z149 3p. aniline carmine .... 9·00

1900. (Nos. 112/118).
Z151 ½a. yellow-green .... 5·50
Z152 1a. carmine .... 8·00
Z153 2a. pale violet .... 10·00
Z154 2a.6p. ultramarine .... 7·50

1902–11. (Nos. 119/147).
Z155 3p. grey .... 10·00
Z156 ½a. green .... 6·50
Z157 1a. carmine .... 6·50
Z158 2a. mauve 7.00
Z159 2a.6p. ultramarine .... 3·25
Z160 3a. orange-brown .... 14·00
Z161 4a. olive .... 10·00
Z162 6a. maize .... 20·00
Z163 8a. purple .... 11·00
Z165 1r. green and carmine .... 30·00
Z170 15r. blue and olive-brown £150

1905. (No. 148).
Z171 ¼ on ½a green .... 18·00

1906. (Nos. 149/150).
Z172 ½a. green .... 4·25
Z173 1a. carmine .... 4·25

1911–22. (Nos. 151/191).
Z174 3p. grey .... 10·00
Z175 ½a. green .... 3·25
Z176 1a. carmine .... 3·25
Z177 1½a. chocolate (Type A) .... 19·00
Z178 1½a. chocolate (Type B) .... 45·00
Z179 2a. purple .... 6·50
Z180 2a.6p. ultramarine (1912) .... 20·00
Z181 2a.6p. ultramarine (1913) .... 4·25
Z182 3a. orange .... 5·50
Z183 4a. olive-green .... 12·00
Z184 6a. brown-ochre .... 16·00
Z185 8a. mauve .... 20·00
Z186 12a. carmine-lake .... 33·00
Z187 1r. brown and green .... 26·00
Z191 15r. blue and olive £140

1921. (No. 192).
Z192 9p. on 1a. rose-carmine .... 24·00

OFFICIAL STAMPS

1867–73. (Nos. O20/O30*a*).
Z193 ½a. blue (Die I) .... 25·00
Z194 1a. brown .... 25·00
Z195 8a. rose .... 22·00

1874–82. (Nos. O31/O35).

Z196	½a. blue	24·00
Z198	2a. orange	20·00
Z199	4a. green	20·00

1883–99. (Nos. O37*a*/O48).

Z202	½a. blue-green	15·00
Z203	1a. plum	15·00
Z204	2a. blue	19·00
Z205	4a. olive-green	20·00
Z207	1r. green and carmine	50·00

1900. (Nos. O49/O52).

Z208	½a. yellow-green	26·00
Z209	1a. carmine	19·00
Z210	2a. mauve	25·00

1902–09. (Nos. O54/O65).

Z212	½a. green	14·00
Z213	1a. carmine	9·00
Z214	2a. mauve	12·00
Z215	4a. olive	18·00

1906. (Nos. O66/O67).

Z218	½a. green	14·00
Z219	1a. carmine	12·00

1912–13. (Nos. O73/O96).

Z221	½a. green	12·00
Z222	1a. carmine	7·00
Z224	2a. purple	12·00

Bushire Camp

A sub-post office was opened in 1921 for troops of the South West Cordon Force. It closed in 1923.

Postmark type		*Approx period of use*
Z 3	(inscr 'BUSHIRE CAMP')	1921–1922

Stamps of India cancelled at Bushire Camp

1911–22. (Nos. 151/191).

Z229	1a. carmine	
Z232	2a.6p. ultramarine (1913)	55·00
Z233	3a. orange	60·00
Z235	6a. brown-ochre	

OFFICIAL STAMPS

1902. (Nos. O54/O65).

Z237	3p. grey	

1912–13. (Nos. O73/O96).

Z239	3p. grey	
Z240	½a. green	55·00
Z242	2a. mauve	

Chahbar

A port on the Gulf of Oman, the Indian post office was opened on 20 August 1913 and closed on 31 March 1923.

Postmark type		*Approx period of use*
Z 3	(inscr 'CHAHBAR/B.O./PERSIAN GULF')	1914–1923

Stamps of India cancelled at Chahbar

1902–11. (Nos. 119/147).

Z244	3p. grey	90·00

1906. (Nos. 149/150).

Z247	1a. carmine	£100

1911–22. (Nos. 151/191).

Z249	½a. green	90·00
Z250	1a. carmine	90·00
Z252	2a. mauve	£120

Duzdab

A small town near the frontier with India, an Indian exchange post office was opened in 1921 and closed in 1925.

Henjam

An island in the Straits of Hormuz, it was for a time a British Naval Station and telegraph relay station. The Indian post office opened on 21 June 1913 and closed in 1923.

Postmark type		*Approx period of use*
Z 3	(Inscr 'HENJAM/B.O./PERSIAN GULF')	1914–1922

Stamps of India cancelled at Henjam

1906. (Nos. 149/150).

Z254	½a. green	90·00

1911–22. (Nos. 151/191).

Z256	3p. grey	£100
Z257	½a. green	55·00
Z258	1a. carmine	85·00
Z260	2a. purple	£100
Z261	2a.6p. ultramarine (1913)	£110

OFFICIAL STAMPS

1912–13. (Nos. O73/O96).

Z268	4a. olive-green	£200

Jask

A port on the Gulf of Oman and site of the British East India Company's first factory in 1619, the Indian post office opened on 1 September 1880 and closed on 20 March 1923.

Z **17** As Z **9**/Z **10** but without obliterator

Postmark type		*Approx period of use*
Z 17		1884–1888
Z 14	(inscr JASK)	1889–1912
Z 3	(inscr JASK/B.O.PERSIAN GULF)	1914–1920

Stamps of India cancelled at Jask

1865. (Nos. 54/65).

Z270	½a. blue	50·00

1866–78. (Nos. 69/72).

Z273	4a. green	£100

1882–90. (Nos. 84/101).

Z276	½a. blue-green	24·00
Z278	1a. brown-purple	28·00
Z281	3a. orange	45·00
Z285	12a. purple/*red*	80·00

1891. (No. 102).

Z286	2½a. on 4a.6p. yellow-green	50·00

1892–97. (Nos. 103/109).

Z287	2a.6p. yellow-green	24·00

1898. (No. 110).

Z289	¼ on ½a. blue-green	65·00

1899. (No. 111).

Z290	3p. aniline-carmine	40·00

1900. (Nos. 112/118).

Z294	2a.6p. ultramarine	30·00

1902–11. (Nos. 119/147).

Z296	½a. green	27·00
Z297	1a. carmine	27·00
Z298	2a. mauve	30·00
Z299	2a.6p. ultramarine	21·00

1906–07. (Nos. 149/150).

Z303	½a. green	21·00
Z304	1a. carmine	21·00

1911–22. (Nos. 151/191).

Z306	½a. green	42·00
Z307	1a. carmine	28·00
Z310	2a. purple	32·00
Z311	2a.6p. ultramarine (1913)	42·00
Z315	8a. mauve	90·00
Z316	12a. carmine-lake	90·00

OFFICIAL STAMPS

1902–09. (Nos. O54/O69).

Z320	2a. mauve	55·00

1906. (Nos. O66/O67).

Z322	½a. green	32·00
Z323	1a. carmine	40·00

Kuh-Malik-Siah-Ziarat

A few miles north of Duzdab, where the frontiers of Iran, India and Afghanistan meet, an Indian exchange post office was open by January 1906. It closed in mid-1924.

Linga

A Persian Gulf port to the west of Bandar Abbas, the Indian post office there was opened on 1 April 1867. Linga was added to the regular ports of call of the Bombay–Basra steamer service in 1870. The post office closed in 1923.

Z **18** 25 mm small date

Postmark type		*Approx period of use*
Z 7	(numeral '21')	1872–1875
Z 8	(2/K-5)	1876–1880
Z 10	(inscr 'LINGA')	1880–1882
Z 11	(inscr LINGA)	1885
Z 14	(inscr LINGA)	1882–1905
Z 12	(inscr LINGA)	1900–1902
Z 13	(inscr LINGA)	1905–1922
Z 18		1912
Z 2	(inscr LINGA)	1920–1923
Z 3	(inscr LINGA)	1920

Stamps of India cancelled at Linga.

1865. (Nos. 54/65).

Z327	½a. blue	22·00
Z328	1a. brown	21·00
Z329	2a. orange	40·00

1866–78. (Nos. 69/72).

Z330	4a. green (Die I)	60·00
Z331	4a. green (Die II)	50·00

1868–76. (Nos. 73/82).

Z332	8a. rose	75·00
Z333	½a. blue (Die II)	11·00
Z334	6a. pale brown	42·00
Z335	12a. Venetian red	90·00

1882–90. (Nos. 84/101).

Z336	½a. blue-green	5·50
Z338	1a. plum	7·50
Z340	2a. blue	8·00
Z341	3a. orange	25·00
Z341*a*	3a. brown-orange	12·00
Z342	4a. olive-green	17·00
Z343	4a.6p. yellow-green	25·00
Z344	8a. mauve	30·00
Z345	12a. purple/*red*	42·00
Z346	1r. slate	42·00

1891. (No. 102).

Z347	2½a. on 4a.6p. yellow-green	25·00

1892–97. (Nos. 103/109).

Z348	2a.6p. yellow-green	8·50
Z349	1r. green and carmine	65·00
Z351	3r. brown and green	£130

1899. (No. 111).

Z352	3p. aniline carmine	11·00

1900–02. (Nos. 112/118).

Z353	3p. grey	55·00
Z354	½a. yellow-green	8·00
Z355	1a. carmine	13·00
Z356	2a. mauve	22·00
Z357	2a.6p. ultramarine	15·00

1902–11. (Nos. 119/147).

Z358	3p. grey	16·00
Z359	½a. green	6·00
Z360	1a. carmine	7·00
Z361	2a. mauve	7·50
Z362	2a.6p. ultramarine	6·00
Z363	3a. orange-brown	16·00
Z364	4a. olive	16·00
Z368	1r. green and carmine	28·00
Z369	2r. carmine and yellow-brown	70·00

1906. (Nos. 149/150).

Z372	½a. green	7·00
Z373	1a. carmine	9·00

1911–22. (Nos. 151/191).

Z374	3p. grey	18·00
Z375	½a. green	5·00
Z376	1a. carmine	6·00
Z377	1½a. chocolate (Type A)	24·00
Z378	2a. purple	9·50
Z379	2a.6p. ultramarine (1912)	24·00
Z380	2a.6p. ultramarine (1913)	7·00
Z381	3a. orange	11·00
Z382	4a. olive-green	16·00
Z383	6a. brown-ochre	20·00

OFFICIAL STAMPS

1883–99. (Nos. O37*a*/O48).

Z390	1a. plum	38·00

1906. (Nos. O66/O67).

Z399	1a. carmine	38·00

1912–13. (Nos. O73/O96).

Z401	½a. green	22·00
Z402	1a. carmine	24·00
Z403	2a. purple	38·00

Maidan-i-Naphtun

The site of the original oil find in Iran in the early part of the 20th-century, an Indian post office was opened during World War 1. It was closed in 1923.

Z **19**

Postmark type		*Approx period of use*
Z 19		1917–1920
Z 3	(inscr 'MAIADN-I-NAPHTUN/REG')*	1922–1923

Stamps of India cancelled at Maidan-i-Naphtun

1911–22. (Nos. 151/191).

Z406	½a. green	£100
Z407	1a. carmine	£110
Z409	2a. purple	£130
Z410	2½a. ultramarine (1913)	£120
Z411	3a. orange	£150

* The 'REG' c.d.s. (as T Z **3**) shows the 'MAIADN' spelling error.

Mirjawa

On the border with India (now Pakistan), an Indian post office was opened in 1921 to service the needs of a railway construction project. It was closed by 1931.

Postmark type		*Approx period of use*
Z 3	(inscr 'MIRJAWA')	1926

Stamps of India cancelled at Mirjawa

1911–22. (Nos. 151/191).

Z415	1½a. chocolate (Type A)	£120
Z418	2½a. ultramarine	
Z422	8a. mauve	

OFFICIAL STAMPS

1912–13. (Nos. O73/O96).

Z426	3p. grey	£120
Z428	1a. carmine	
Z429	2a. purple	£130

1922. (No. O98).

Z433	1a. chocolate	

Mohammera

Now known as Khorramshahr, Mohammerah was the chief port of Iran, on the Shatt-el-Arab. The first Indian post office was opened in 1892 and closed in 1923.

Postmark type		*Approx period of use*
Z 16	(inscr 'MAHOMMERAH')	1894–1911
Z 16	(inscr 'MOHAMMERAH')	1896–1904
Z 4	(inscr 'MOHAMMERA')	1904–1918
Z 4	(inscr 'MOHAMMERAH')	1910–1918
Z 13	(inscr 'MOHAMMERAH')	1905–1923
Z 3	(inscr 'MOHOMMERAH')	1919–1923

Stamps of India cancelled at Mohammera

1882–90. (Nos. 84/101).

Z434	½a. blue-green	8·50
Z435	1a. brown-purple	13·00
Z437	2a. blue	17·00
Z438	3a. brown-orange	26·00
Z439	4a. olive-green	30·00

1892–97. (Nos. 103/109).

Z440	2a.6p. yellow-green	8·50
Z441	1r. green and carmine	50·00
Z443	3r. brown and green	£140

1899. (No. 111).

Z444	3p. aniline carmine	18·00

1900. (Nos. 112/118).

Z445	½a. yellow-green	9·00
Z446	1a. carmine	13·00
Z447	2a. pale violet	18·00
Z448	2a.6p. ultramarine	15·00

1902–11. (Nos. 119/147).

Z449	3p. grey	14·00
Z450	½a. green	6·50
Z451	1a. carmine	7·50
Z452	2a. mauve	8·00
Z453	2a.6p. ultramarine	4·50
Z454	3a. orange-brown	18·00
Z455	4a. olive	14·00
Z456	6a. olive-bistre	35·00
Z457	8a. purple	35·00
Z458	1r. green and carmine	45·00

1905. (No. 148).

Z459	¼ on ½a. green	20·00

1906. (Nos. 149/150).

Z460	½a. green	6·50
Z461	1a. carmine	6·50

1911–22. (Nos. 151/191).

Z462	3p. grey	15·00
Z463	½a. green	3·25
Z464	1a. carmine	3·25
Z465	1½a. chocolate (Type A)	19·00
Z466	2a. purple	5·50
Z467	2a.6p. ultramarine (1912)	20·00
Z468	2a.6p. ultramarine (1913)	4·50
Z469	3a. orange	7·00
Z470	4a. olive-green	9·00
Z471	6a. yellow-bistre	32·00
Z472	8a. mauve	20·00
Z474	1r. brown and green	21·00
Z475	2r. carmine and brown	45·00

1922–26. (Nos. 197/200).

Z481	1a. chocolate	16·00

OFFICIAL STAMPS

1883–99. (Nos. O37*a*/O48).

Z482	1a. brown-purple	28·00

1902–09. (Nos. O54/O65).

Z485	1a. carmine	26·00
Z486	2a. mauve	
Z488	6a. olive-bistre	

1906. (Nos. O66/O67).

Z490	½a. green	16·00

1912–13. (Nos. O73/O96).

Z493	½a. green	15·00
Z494	1a. carmine	13·00
Z495	2a. purple	28·00

IRAQ*

Unoverprinted stamps of India used from 1868 until 1918.

KUWAIT*

Unoverprinted stamps of India used from 1904 until 1923.

MALAYA (STRAITS SETTLEMENTS)*

Unoverprinted stamps of India used from 1854 until 1867.

MUSCAT*

Unoverprinted stamps of India used from 1864 until 1947.

NEPAL

A post office was opened in the British Residency at Kathmandu in 1816 following the end of the Gurkha War. Stamps of India were used from 1854, initially with 'B137', '137' or 'C-37' numeral cancellations. The Residency Post Office continued to provide the overseas mail service after Nepal introduced its own issues in 1881.

In 1920 the Residency Post Office became the British Legation Post Office. On the independence of India in 1947 the service was transferred to the Indian Embassy and continued to function until 1965.

PORTUGUESE INDIA

A British post office was open in Damaun by 1823 and Indian stamps were used there until November 1883, some with '13' and '3/B-19' numeral cancellations.

No other British post offices were opened in the Portuguese territories, but from 1854 Indian stamps were sold by the local post offices. Between 1871 and 1877 mail intended for, or passing through, British India required combined franking of India and Portuguese India issues. After 1877 the two postal administrations accepted the validity of each other's stamps.

SOMALILAND PROTECTORATE*

Unoverprinted stamps of India used from 1887 until 1903.

TIBET

The first Indian post office in Tibet accompanied the Tibetan Frontier Commission in 1903. The Younghusband Military Expedition to Lhasa in the following year operated a number of Field Post Offices which were replaced by civil post offices at Gartok (opened 23 September 1906), Gyantse (opened March 1905), Pharijong (opened 1905) and Yatung (opened 1905). All Indian post offices in Tibet closed on 1 April 1955 except Gartok which, it is believed, did not operate after 1943. A temporary post office, C-622, operated at Gyantse between July 1954 and August 1955 following a flood disaster.

TRUCIAL STATES*

Unoverprinted stamps of India used at Dubai from 19 August 1909 until 1947.

ZANZIBAR*

Unoverprinted stamps of India used from 1875 until 1895.

CHINA EXPEDITIONARY FORCE

Following the outbreak of the Boxer Rising in North China the Peking Legations were besieged by the rebels in June 1900. An international force, including an Indian Army division, was assembled for their relief. The Legations were relieved on 14 August 1900, but operations against the Boxers continued in North China with Allied garrisons at key cities and along the Peking–Tientsin–Shanhaikwan railway. The last Indian Army battalion, and accompanying Field Post Offices, did not leave North China until 1 November 1923.

Field Post Offices accompanied the Indian troops and commenced operations on 23 July 1900 using unoverprinted Indian postage and official stamps. The unoverprinted postage issues were replaced in mid-August by stamps overprinted 'C.E.F.' to prevent currency speculation. The use of unoverprinted official stamps continued as they were not valid for public postage.

PRICES FOR STAMPS ON COVER TO 1945	
Nos. C1/C10	*from* × 15
No. C10*c*	†
Nos. C11/C22	*from* × 8
Nos. C23	*from* × 10
Nos. C24/C25	*from* × 20
Nos. C26/C28	*from* × 4
Nos. C29/C34	*from* × 3

C. E. F.
(C 1)

Stamps of India overprinted with T C **1**, in black

1900 (16 Aug). Stamps of Queen Victoria.

C1	**40**	3p. carmine	40	1·25
		a. No stop after 'F'	£300	
		b. Opt double, one albino	£180	
		c. No stop after 'C' (R. 1/2)		
C2	**23**	½a. blue-green	1·00	30
		a. No stop after 'F'	£325	
		b. Opt double		
C3	**25**	1a. plum	4·50	1·50
		a. No stop after 'F'	£475	
C4	**27**	2a. pale blue	3·50	9·00
		a. No stop after 'F'	£500	
C5	**36**	2a.6p. green	3·25	17·00
		a. No stop after 'F'	£700	
C6	**28**	3a. brown-orange	3·25	18·00
		a. No stop after 'F'	£700	
		b. Opt double, one albino	£150	
C7	**29**	4a. slate-green	3·25	9·50
		a. No stop after 'F'	£700	
		b. Opt double, one albino	£170	
C8	**31**	8a. magenta	3·25	27·00
		a. No stop after 'F'	£800	
		b. Opt double, one albino	£170	
C9	**32**	12a. purple/*red*	19·00	16·00
		a. No stop after 'F'	£950	
		b. Opt double, one albino	£190	
C10	**37**	1r. green and carmine	45·00	48·00
		a. No stop after 'F'	£1100	£1100
		b. Opt double, one albino	£275	
C1/C10 *Set of* 10			75·00	£130

Prepared, but not issued

C10*c*	**26**	1a.6p. sepia	£450	†

The missing stop after 'F' variety occurs in the ninth row of the upper pane on one printing only.

1904 (27 Feb).

C11	**25**	1a. carmine	50·00	8·00

1905 (16 Sept)–**11**. Stamps of King Edward VII.

C12	**41**	3p. grey (4.11)	12·00	9·50
		a. Opt double, one albino	£130	
		b. Opt triple, one albino	£450	
		c. Slate-grey	12·00	9·50
C13	**43**	1a. carmine	13·00	70
		a. Opt double, one albino	£100	
C14	**44**	2a. mauve (11.3.11)	15·00	6·00
		a. Opt double, one albino	£140	
C15	**45**	2a.6p. ultramarine (11.3.11)	4·00	5·00
C16	**46**	3a. orange-brown (11.3.11)	4·25	4·25
C17	**47**	4a. olive-green (11.3.11)	9·00	21·00
C18	**49**	8a. claret (11.3.11)	9·00	8·50
		a. Purple	85·00	65·00
C19	**50**	12a. purple/*red* (1909)	11·00	19·00
		a. No stop after 'E'	£850	
C20	**51**	1r. green and carmine (11.3.11)	17·00	48·00
C12/C20 *Set of* 9			85·00	£110

1908 (Dec)–**09**. 'POSTAGE & REVENUE'.

C21	**53**	½a. green (No. 149) (29.9.09)	1·75	1·50
		a. Opt double, one albino	£120	
C22	**54**	1a. carmine (No. 150)	7·50	30
		a. Opt double, one albino	£160	

1914 (5 May)–**22**. Stamps of King George V. Wmk Star.

C23	**55**	3p. grey (7.10.14)	10·00	48·00
		a. Opt double, one albino	£425	
C24	**56**	½a. light green	4·00	9·00
		a. Emerald	—	80·00
C25	**57**	1a. aniline carmine	5·00	4·00
C26	**58**	1½a. chocolate (Type A) (9.3.21)	40·00	£130
		a. Opt double, one albino	£250	
C27	**59**	2a. purple (11.19)	35·00	85·00
		a. Deep mauve	55·00	95·00
		ab. Opt triple	£700	
C28	**61**	2a.6p. bright blue (2.19)	24·00	29·00
C29	**62**	3a. orange (5.22)	48·00	£300
C30	**63**	4a. olive-green (5.22)	42·00	£250
		a. Opt double, one albino	£475	
C32	**65**	8a. deep mauve (12.21)	42·00	£475
C33	**66**	12a. carmine-lake (8.20)	42·00	£160
C34	**67**	1r. brown and green (10.21)	£120	£475
C23/C34 *Set of* 11			£350	£1800

Most dates quoted for Nos. C23/C34 are those of the earliest recorded postmarks.

On No. C27*a* two of the overprints are only lightly inked.

BRITISH RAILWAY ADMINISTRATION

As a vital communications link the North China Railway (Peking–Tientsin–Shanhaikwan) was captured by Russian forces during operations against the Boxers. Control of the line was subsequently, in February 1901, assigned to the China Expeditionary Force and a British Railway Administration was set up to run it. By international agreement the line was to provide postal services for the other national contingents and also, to a lesser extent, for the civilian population. Travelling post offices were introduced and, on 20 April 1901, a late letter service for which an additional fee of 5c. was charged.

T **32** of China

B.R.A.
5
Five Cents
(BR **35**)

1901 (20 Apr). No. 108 of China surch with T BR **35**.

BR133	**32**	5c. on ½c. brown (Bk.)	£450	£110
		a. Surch inverted	£10000	£2750
		b. Surch in green	£400	£150
		ba. Imperf between (horiz pair)	†	£20000

No. BR133 was used for the collection of the 5c. late letter fee and was affixed to correspondence by a postal official at the railway station. It was cancelled with a violet circular postmark showing 'RAILWAY POST OFFICE' at top and the name of the station (PEKING, TIENTSIN, TONGKU, TONGSHAN or SHANHAIKWAN) at foot. With the exception of official mail it could only be used in combination with Indian stamps overprinted 'C.E.F.', stamps from the other allied contingents or of the Chinese Imperial Post (*Price used on cover*: No. BR133 *from* £350. No. BR133b *from* £400).

It is suggested that stamps overprinted in black were used at Tientsin and Tongku with those in green being available at Peking, Tongshan and Shanhaikwan.

The late fee charge was abolished on 20 May 1901 and No. BR133 was then withdrawn. The British Railway Administration continued to run the line, and its travelling post offices, until it was returned to its private owners in September 1902.

INDIAN EXPEDITIONARY FORCES 1914–1921

Nos. E1/E13 were for use of Indian forces sent overseas during the First World War and its aftermath. Examples were first used in France during September 1914. Other areas where the stamps were used included East Africa, Mesopotamia and Turkey. 'I.E.F.' overprints ceased to be valid for postage on 15 October 1921.

PRICES FOR STAMPS ON COVER TO 1945	
Nos. E1/E13	*from* × 10

I. E. F.
(E 1)

1914 (Sept). Stamps of India (King George V) optd with T E **1**.

E1	**55**	3p. grey	15	30
		a. No stop after 'F'	27·00	45·00
		b. No stop after 'E'	£180	£180

c. Opt double ... 50·00 50·00
d. Opt double, one albino ... £130
E2 **56** ½a. light green ... 50 30
a. No stop after 'F' ... £120 £120
b. Opt double ... £140 £275
E3 **57** 1a. aniline carmine ... 1·25 30
a. No stop after 'F' ... 32·00 42·00
E4 1a. carmine ... 7·00 7·00
E5 **59** 2a. purple ... 1·25 30
a. No stop after 'F' ... 80·00 95·00
b. No stop after 'E' ... £425 £450
E6 **61** 2a.6p. ultramarine ... 1·50 3·50
a. No stop after 'F' ... £300 £325
E7 **62** 3a. orange ... 1·00 1·50
a. No stop after 'F' ... £275 £300
E8 **63** 4a. olive-green ... 1·00 1·50
a. No stop after 'F' ... £425 £450
E9 **65** 8a. deep magenta ... 1·25 2·50
a. No stop after 'F' ... £425 £450
E10 8a. deep mauve ... 11·00 19·00
E11 **66** 12a. carmine-lake ... 2·25 6·00
a. No stop after 'F' ... £500 £500
b. Opt double, one albino ... 60·00
E12 12a. claret ...
E13 **67** 1r. red-brown and deep blue-green ... 4·25 4·50
a. Opt double, one albino ... £100
b. Brown and green ... 3·50 5·00
E1/E13 *Set of* 10 ... 12·00 18·00

The 'no stop after F' variety occurred on R. 4/12 of the upper pane, in one printing.

No. E11b comes from a sheet issued at Basra in February 1916.

INDIAN CUSTODIAN FORCES IN KOREA

भारतीय
संरक्षा कटक
कोरिया
(K 1)

1953 (17 Oct). Stamps of India optd with T K **1**.
K1 **307** 3p. slate-violet ... 3·00 12·00
K2 **308** 6p. purple-brown ... 1·50 9·50
K3 **309** 9p. yellow-green ... 3·00 9·00
K4 **328** 1a. turquoise ... 1·50 4·75
K5 **311** 2a. carmine ... 1·50 4·75
K6 **313** 2½a. lake ... 1·50 6·00
K7 **312** 3a. brown-orange ... 1·50 9·00
K8 **314** 4a. bright blue ... 2·25 4·75
K9 **315** 6a. violet ... 12·00 9·00
K10 **316** 8a. turquoise-green ... 2·25 17·00
K11 **317** 12a. dull blue ... 2·25 17·00
K12 **318** 1r. dull violet and green ... 9·00 17·00
K1/K12 *Set of* 12 ... 38·00 £100

INDIAN UN FORCE IN CONGO

U.N.FORCE
(INDIA)
CONGO
(U 1)

1962 (15 Jan). Stamps of India optd with T U **1**. W **69** (sideways) (13n.p.) or W **374** (others).
U1 **361** 1n.p. blue-green ... 1·00 7·00
U2 2n.p. light brown ... 1·00 4·50
U3 5n.p. bright green ... 1·00 1·00
U4 8n.p. light blue-green ... 1·00 40
U5 13n.p. bright carmine-red ... 1·00 40
U6 50n.p. orange ... 1·00 70
U1/U6 *Set of* 6 ... 5·50 12·50

INDIAN UN FORCE IN GAZA (PALESTINE) UNEF

(G 1)

1965 (15 Jan). No. 492 of India optd with T G **1**.
G1 **449** 15p. slate (C.) ... 3·50 10·00

INTERNATIONAL COMMISSION IN INDO-CHINA

The International Control Commissions for Indo-China were established in August 1954 as part of the Geneva Declaration which partitioned Vietnam and sought to achieve stable settlements in Cambodia and Laos. The three supervisory commissions were chaired by India with Canada and Poland as the other members. Joint inspection teams of servicemen from the three countries were also provided.

The Indian contingent included a postal unit which handled mail for the three commissions and the inspection teams. The unit arrived in Indo-China on 3 September 1954 and opened field post offices at Saigon (F.P.O. 742), Hanoi (F.P.O. 743), Vientiane (F.P.O. 744) and Phnom Penh (F.P.O. 745).

अन्तर्राष्ट्रीय आयोग कम्बोज (N 1) — अन्तर्राष्ट्रीय आयोग लाओस (N 2) — अन्तर्राष्ट्रीय आयोग वियत नाम (N 3)

1954 (1 Dec). Stamps of India. W **69**.
(a) Optd as T N **1**, *for use in Cambodia*
N1 **307** 3p. slate-violet ... 2·75 15·00
N2 **328** 1a. turquoise ... 1·25 1·00
N3 **311** 2a. carmine ... 1·25 1·00
N4 **316** 8a. turquoise-green ... 1·75 4·00
N5 **317** 12a. dull blue ... 2·00 4·00
(b) Optd as T N **2**, *for use in Laos*
N6 **307** 3p. slate-violet ... 2·75 15·00
N7 **328** 1a. turquoise ... 1·25 1·00
N8 **311** 2a. carmine ... 1·25 1·00
N9 **316** 8a. turquoise-green ... 1·75 3·00
N10 **317** 12a. dull blue ... 2·00 3·00
(c) Optd as T N **3**, *for use in Vietnam*
N11 **307** 3p. slate-violet ... 2·75 9·00
N12 **328** 1a. turquoise ... 1·25 1·00
N13 **311** 2a. carmine ... 1·25 1·00
N14 **316** 8a. turquoise-green ... 1·75 3·00
N15 **317** 12a. dull blue ... 2·00 3·00
N1/N15 *Set of* 15 ... 24·00 55·00

1957 (1 Apr). Stamps of India. W **69** (sideways).
(a) Optd as T N **1**, *for use in Cambodia*
N16 **361** 2n.p. light brown ... 75 30
N17 6n.p. grey ... 50 30
N18 13n.p. bright carmine-red ... 70 40
N19 50n.p. orange ... 2·25 1·25
N20 75n.p. reddish purple ... 2·25 1·25
(b) Optd as T N **2**, *for use in Laos*
N21 **361** 2n.p. light brown ... 75 30
N22 6n.p. grey ... 50 30
N23 13n.p. bright carmine-red ... 70 40
N24 50n.p. orange ... 2·25 1·25
N25 75n.p. reddish purple ... 2·25 1·25
(c) Optd as T N **3**, *for use in Vietnam*
N26 **361** 2n.p. light brown ... 75 30
N27 6n.p. grey ... 50 30
N28 13n.p. bright carmine-red ... 70 40
N29 50n.p. orange ... 2·25 1·25
N30 75n.p. reddish purple ... 2·25 1·25
N16/N30 *Set of* 15 ... 17·00 9·50

F.P.O. 744 (Vientiane) was closed on 25 July 1958 and F.P.O. 745 (Phnom Penh) on 26 June 1958.

1960 (Sept)–**65**. Stamps of India. W **374**.
(a) Optd as T N **2** *for use in Laos*
N38 **361** 2n.p. light brown (15.1.62) ... 15 3·25
N39 3n.p. deep brown (1.8.63) ... 10 60
N40 5n.p. bright green (1.8.63) ... 10 20
N41 50n.p. orange (1965) ... 7·00 6·00
N42 75n.p. reddish purple (1965) ... 7·00 6·00
(b) Optd as T N **3**, *for use in Vietnam*
N43 **361** 1n.p. blue-green ... 10 25
N44 2n.p. light brown (15.1.62) ... 15 3·25
N45 3n.p. deep brown (1.8.63) ... 10 60
N46 5n.p. bright green (1.8.63) ... 10 20
N47 50n.p. orange (1965) ... 7·00 6·00
N48 75n.p. reddish purple (1965) ... 7·00 6·00
N38/N48 *Set of* 11 ... 25·00 29·00

F.P.O. 744 (Vientiane) re-opened on 22 May 1961.

Examples of the 2n.p. value overprinted as T N **1** for use in Cambodia exist, but were never placed on sale there as the Phnom Penh F.P.O. 745 was closed on 26 June 1958. Used examples appear to originate from unauthorised use of the F.P.O. 745 postmark which was in store at Saigon (*Price* 15p, *unused*).

ICC (N **4**) — ICC (N **5**)

1965 (15 Jan). No. 492 of India optd with T N **4**, for use in Laos and Vietnam.
N49 **449** 15p. slate (C.) ... 1·00 6·00

F.P.O. 743 (Hanoi) was closed on 13 July 1966.

1968 (2 Oct). Nos. 504/505, 506, 509/510, 515 and 517/518 etc of India optd as T N **5**, in red, for use in Laos and Vietnam.
N50 2p. red-brown ... 10 4·25
N51 3p. brown-olive ... 10 4·25
N52 5p. cerise ... 10 2·50
N53 10p. new blue ... 3·50 3·50
N54 15p. bronze-green ... 60 3·50
N55 60p. deep grey ... 35 2·50
N56 1r. red-brown and plum ... 50 3·50
N57 2r. new blue and deep slate-violet ... 1·50 13·00
N50/N57 *Set of* 8 ... 6·00 32·00

INDIAN NATIONAL ARMY

The following were prepared for use in the Japanese occupied areas of India during the drive on Imphal.

Genuine examples are inscribed 'PROVISIONAL GOVERNMENT OF FREE INDIA'. Forgeries also exist inscribed 'PROVISIONAL GOVT. OF FREE INDIA'.

Typo in Rangoon. No gum. Perf 11½ or imperf. 1p. violet, 1p. maroon, 1a. green. *Price from £70 each unused.*

Ten stamps, sharing six different designs, inscribed 'AZAD HIND', were produced in Germany during the Second World War, but did no postal duty.

JAPANESE OCCUPATION OF THE ANDAMAN AND NICOBAR ISLANDS

The Andaman Islands in the Bay of Bengal were occupied on the 23 March 1942 and the Nicobar Islands in July 1942. Civil administration was resumed in October 1945.

The following Indian stamps were surcharged with large figures preceded by a decimal point:

Postage stamps—.3 on ½a. (No. 248), .5 on 1a. (No. 250), .10 on 2a. (No. 236*b*), .30 on 6a. (No. 274).

Official stamps—.10 on 1a.3p. (No. O146*a*), .20 on 3p. (No. O143), .20 in red on 3p. (No. O143).

Prices from £450 each unused.

INDIAN CONVENTION STATES

The following issues resulted from a series of postal conventions agreed between the Imperial Government and the state administrations of Patiala (1 October 1884), Gwalior, Jind and Nabha (1 July 1885), and Chamba and Faridkot (1 January 1887).

Under the terms of these conventions the British Indian Post Office supplied overprinted British India issues to the state administrations which, in turn, had to conform to a number of conditions covering the issue of stamps, rates of postage and the exchange of mail.

Such overprinted issues were valid for postage within the state of issue, to other 'Convention States' and to destinations in British India.

Stamps of Chamba, Gwalior, Jind, Nabha and Patiala ceased to be valid for postage on 1 January 1951, when they were replaced by those of the Republic of India, valid from 1 April 1950.

RULERS OF INDIAN CONVENTION AND FEUDATORY STATES. Details of the rulers of the various states during the period when stamps were issued are now provided in a somewhat simplified form which omits reference to minor titles. Dates quoted are of the various reigns, extended to 1971 when the titles of the surviving rulers of the former princely states were abolished by the Indian Government.

During the absorption of the Convention and Feudatory States there was often an interim period during which the administration was handed over. In some instances it is only possible to quote the end of this interim period as the point of transfer.

STAMPS OF INDIA OVERPRINTED

In the Queen Victoria issues we omit varieties due to broken type, including the numerous small 'A' varieties which may have come about through damaged type. We do, however, list the small 'G', small 'R' and tall 'R' in 'GWALIOR' as these were definitely the result of the use of type of the wrong size.

Variations in the length of the words due to unequal spacing when setting are also omitted.

PRICES. Prices quoted for unused stamps are for examples with original fresh colour and gum (unmounted in the case of King George VI issues from 1937). Stamps which have become toned by climate are worth much less. Prices for used stamps are for stamps with clearly identifiable authentic postmarks, and collectors should exercise caution when acquiring any stamps where the used prices are significantly higher than those quoted for unused, as many forgeries are in circulation.

FORGERIES. The Convention States overprints have been extensively forged on both unused and previously used Indian stamps, and rarities, particularly the errors of the Queen Victoria period, should not be purchased without a reliable guarantee. Also, genuine unused stamps have often been provided with forged postmarks; this applies especially to the King George VI period, and such stamps should only be acquired from reputable sources.

CHAMBA

PRICES FOR STAMPS ON COVER TO 1945
Nos. 1/27 *from* × 20
Nos. 28/120 *from* × 12
Nos. O1/O86 *from* × 25

OVERPRINTS. From 1885 to 1926 these were applied typo by the Government of India Central Printing Press, Calcutta, and fom 1927 by litho at the Security Press, Nasik, *unless otherwise stated.*

Raja Sham Singh, 1873–1904

CHAMBA STATE (1) — CHAMBA (2)

1887 (1 Jan)–**95**. Queen Victoria. Optd with T **1**.
1 **23** ½a. blue-green ... 2·25 2·00
a. 'CHMABA' ... £850 £1300
b. '8TATE' ... £1100
c. Opt double ... £650
2 **25** 1a. brown-purple ... 4·25 4·75
a. 'CHMABA' ... £850 £1100
b. '8TATE' ... £2250
3 1a. plum ... 4·75 4·75
4 **26** 1a.6p. sepia (1895) ... 5·50 20·00
5 **27** 2a. dull blue ... 4·25 5·00
b. 'CHMABA' ... £3250 £4250
c. '8TATE' ... £3000
6 2a. ultramarine ... 3·50 3·75
7 **36** 2a.6p. green (1895) ... 50·00 £160
8 **28** 3a. orange (1887) ... 30·00 35·00
9 3a. brown-orange (1891) ... 4·25 8·50
a. 'CHMABA' ... £7500 £10000
b. Opt inverted ...
10 **29** 4a. olive-green ... 9·00 16·00
a. 'CHMABA' ... £2750 £4250
b. '8TATE' ... £7000
11 4a. slate-green ... 8·50 20·00
a. Opt double, one albino ... £130
12 **21** 6a. olive-bistre (1890) ... 10·00 28·00
a. Opt treble, two albino ... £160
b. Opt double, one albino ... £120
13 6a. bistre-brown ... 26·00 28·00
14 **31** 8a. dull mauve (1887) ... 15·00 20·00
a. 'CHMABA' ... £5500 £5500
15 8a. magenta (1895) ... 13·00 26·00
16 **32** 12a. purple/*red* (1890) ... 8·50 21·00
a. 'CHMABA' ... £16000
b. First 'T' in 'STATE' inverted ... £16000
c. Opt double, one albino ... 80·00
17 **33** 1r. slate (1887) ... 80·00 £200
a. 'CHMABA' ... £21000
18 **37** 1r. green and carmine (1895) ... 16·00 25·00
a. Opt double, one albino ... £120
19 **38** 2r. carmine and yellow-brown (1895) ... £200 £650
20 3r. brown and green (1895) ... £200 £500
21 5r. ultramarine and violet (1895) ... £225 £1000
a. Opt double, one albino ... £375
1/21 *Set of* 15 ... £750 £2250

The '8TATE' error occurred once per sheet in the October 1886 printing. The 'CHMABA' error occurred once per sheet in the July 1891 printing.

1900–04. Colours changed.

22	**40**	3p. carmine	1·25	1·75
		a. Opt double, one albino	70·00	
23		3p. grey (1904)	1·00	3·50
		a. Opt inverted	£100	
24	**23**	½a. pale yellow-green (1902)	4·00	6·50
25		½a. yellow-green (1903)	1·25	2·75
26	**25**	1a. carmine (1902)	2·50	60
27	**27**	2a. pale violet (1903)	19·00	50·00
22/27 *Set of 5*			22·00	50·00

Raja Bhuri Singh, 1904–1919

1903–05. King Edward VII. Optd with T **1**.

28	**41**	3p. pale grey	25	2·00
29		3p. slate-grey (1905)	75	2·25
30	**42**	½a. green	3·00	1·75
31	**43**	1a. carmine	2·75	2·25
32	**44**	2a. pale violet (1904)	3·50	6·00
33		2a. mauve	3·00	6·00
34	**46**	3a. orange-brown (1905)	8·00	10·00
		a. Opt double, one albino	80·00	
35	**47**	4a. olive (1904)	13·00	45·00
36	**48**	6a. olive-bistre (1905)	7·50	45·00
		a. Opt double, one albino	70·00	
37	**49**	8a. purple (*shades*) (1904)	11·00	45·00
		a. Opt double, one albino	£100	
38		8a. claret	28·00	55·00
39	**50**	12a. purple/*red* (1905)	13·00	60·00
		a. Opt double, one albino	75·00	
40	**51**	1r. green and carmine (1904)	12·00	42·00
		a. Opt double, one albino	£100	
28/40 *Set of 10*			65·00	£225

1908. Nos. 149/150 of India optd with T **1**.

41	**53**	½a. green	3·00	4·25
		a. Opt double, one albino	65·00	
42	**54**	1a. carmine	3·75	5·00

1913–23. King George V optd with T **1**.

43	**55**	3p. grey	40	1·50
		a. Pale grey	3·00	
		b. Bluish grey	4·00	
44	**56**	½a. light green	3·50	3·75
		a. Emerald	4·75	5·50
		b. Bright green	4·00	
		w. Wmk inverted		
45	**57**	1a. rose-carmine	20·00	22·00
		a. Aniline carmine	3·75	7·50
		ab. Opt double, one albino	85·00	
47	**59**	2a. purple	7·00	21·00
		a. Reddish purple	12·00	22·00
		b. Deep mauve	14·00	
		c. Bright reddish violet (1923)	18·00	
48	**62**	3a. orange	9·00	16·00
		a. Dull orange	—	15·00
49	**63**	4a. olive	4·50	9·00
50	**64**	6a. yellow-bistre	7·00	14·00
		a. Brown-ochre	9·00	11·00
51	**65**	8a. deep magenta	10·00	30·00
		a. Deep mauve	14·00	24·00
		b. Bright mauve (1918)	22·00	
		c. Purple	26·00	
52	**66**	12a. carmine-lake	6·50	23·00
		a. Claret	23·00	20·00
53	**67**	1r. red-brown and deep blue-green	30·00	65·00
		a. Opt double, one albino	65·00	
		b. Brown and green	38·00	55·00
		ba. Opt double, one albino	85·00	
		c. Orange-brown and deep turquoise-green (1923)	45·00	
43/53 *Set of 10*			75·00	£150

Raja Ram Singh, 1919–1935

1921. No. 192 of India optd with T **2**.

54	**57**	9p. on 1a. rose-carmine	1·00	20·00

1923–27. Optd with T **1**. New values, etc.

55	**57**	1a. chocolate	4·25	8·50
56	**58**	1½a. chocolate (Type A)	38·00	£225
57		1½a. chocolate (Type B) (1924)	5·00	9·50
58		1½a. rose-carmine (Type B) (1927)	1·75	28·00
59	**61**	2a.6p. ultramarine	1·00	7·00
60		2a.6p. orange (1927)	5·50	40·00
61	**62**	3a. ultramarine (1924)	6·00	35·00
		a. Opt double, one albino	£120	
55/61 *Set of 7*			55·00	£275

Nos. 58 and 60 with inverted overprint are of clandestine origin.

CHAMBA STATE (3) CHAMBA STATE (4)

1927–37. King George V (Nasik printing, wmk Mult Star). Optd at Nasik with Types **3** or **4** (1r.).

62	**55**	3p. slate (1928)	20	3·00
		w. Wmk inverted	9·00	
63	**56**	½a. green (1928)	30	3·75
		w. Wmk inverted	14·00	
64	**80**	9p. deep green (*litho*) (1932)	4·50	40·00
64*a*		9p. deep green (*typo*)	10·00	38·00
65	**57**	1a. chocolate	2·50	3·25
		w. Wmk inverted	10·00	3·75
66	**82**	1a.3p. mauve (1932)	4·00	9·50
		w. Wmk inverted	8·00	9·50
67	**58**	1½a. rose-carmine (B) (1932)	15·00	15·00
		w. Wmk inverted	8·00	8·00
68	**70**	2a. purple (1928)	2·50	7·00
69	**61**	2a.6p. orange (1932)	8·00	27·00
		w. Wmk inverted	5·50	30·00
70	**62**	3a. bright blue (1928)	2·00	28·00
71	**71**	4a. sage-green (1928)	1·25	12·00
72	**64**	6a. bistre (*wmk inverted*) (1937)	30·00	£225
73	**65**	8a. reddish purple (1928)	3·00	17·00
		w. Wmk inverted	1·50	15·00
74	**66**	12a. claret (1928)	1·75	17·00
75	**67**	1r. chocolate and green (1928)	21·00	48·00
		w. Wmk inverted	19·00	50·00
62/75 *Set of 14*			75·00	£400

Raja Lakshman Singh, 1935–1971

1935–36. New types and colours. Optd with T **3**.

76	**79**	½a. green	1·10	16·00
77	**81**	1a. chocolate	4·00	2·50
78	**59**	2a. vermilion (No. 236*b*)	1·40	35·00
79		2a. vermilion (*small die*, No. 236*c*)	£140	£170
80	**62**	3a. carmine	4·00	24·00
81	**63**	4a. sage-green (1936)	10·00	30·00
76/81 *Set of 6*			£150	£250

CHAMBA STATE (5) CHAMBA (6) CHAMBA (7)

1938. King George VI. Nos. 247/264 optd with T **3** (3p. to 1a.), T **5** (2a. to 12a.) or T **4** (rupee values).

82	**91**	3p. slate	12·00	38·00
83		½a. red-brown	5·00	26·00
84		9p. green	18·00	55·00
85		1a. carmine	11·00	8·00
86	**92**	2a. vermilion	15·00	40·00
87	**93**	2a.6p. bright violet	15·00	60·00
88	**94**	3a. yellow-green	18·00	50·00
89	**95**	3a.6p. bright blue	17·00	55·00
90	**96**	4a. brown	38·00	50·00
91	**97**	6a. turquoise-green	50·00	£150
92	**98**	8a. slate-violet	48·00	£100
93	**99**	12a. lake	35·00	£110
94	**100**	1r. grey and red-brown	55·00	£140
95		2r. purple and brown	90·00	£500
96		5r. green and blue	£160	£950
97		10r. purple and claret	£200	£1600
98		15r. brown and green	£180	£2250
		a. Opt double, one inverted	£2000	£3500
99		25r. slate-violet and purple	£350	£2250
		a. Optd front and back	£2000	
82/99 *Set of 18*			£1200	£7000

1942–47. Optd with T **6** (to 12a.), 'CHAMBA' only, as in T **5** (14a.) or T **7** (rupee values).

*(a) Stamps of 1937. W **69** (inverted on 15r.)*

100	**91**	½a. red-brown	85·00	80·00
101		1a. carmine	£160	85·00
102	**100**	1r. grey and red-brown	24·00	85·00
103		2r. purple and brown	24·00	£450
104		5r. green and blue	45·00	£500
105		10r. purple and claret	85·00	£800
106		15r. brown and green	£190	£1800
		w. Wmk upright	£850	£3000
107		25r. slate-violet and purple	£160	£1800
100/107 *Set of 8*			£700	£5000

(b) Stamps of 1940–1943

108	**100a**	3p. slate	1·00	8·00
109		½a. purple (1943)	1·00	8·00
110		9p. green	1·50	26·00
111		1a. carmine (1943)	2·75	6·50
112	**101**	1½a. dull violet (*typo*) (1943)	4·00	17·00
113		2a. vermilion (1943)	5·50	21·00
114		3a. bright violet (*litho*)	22·00	65·00
114*a*		3a. bright violet (*typo*)	15·00	60·00
115		3½a. bright blue	5·00	55·00
116	**102**	4a. brown	5·50	18·00
117		6a. turquoise-green	21·00	48·00
118		8a. slate-violet	24·00	65·00
119		12a. lake	27·00	80·00
120	**103**	14a. purple (1947)	18·00	5·00
108/120 *Set of 13*			£120	£375

OFFICIAL STAMPS

SERVICE

CHAMBA STATE (O 1)

1887 (1 Jan)–**98.** Queen Victoria. Optd with T O **1**.

O1	**23**	½a. blue-green	1·25	20
		a. 'CHMABA'	£500	£500
		b. 'SERV CE'		
		c. '8TATE'	£1800	
		d. Thin seriffed 'I' in 'SERVICE'	£400	
O2	**25**	1a. brown-purple	4·75	2·25
		a. 'CHMABA'	£800	£850
		b. 'SERV CE'	£5500	
		c. '8TATE'	£2500	
		d. 'SERVICE' double	£3750	£1400
		e. 'SERVICE' double, one albino	£110	
O3		1a. plum	4·00	30
		a. Thin seriffed 'I' in 'SERVICE'	£475	
O4	**27**	2a. dull blue	4·25	3·25
		a. 'CHMABA'	£1700	£3750
O5		2a. ultramarine (1887)	4·25	3·75
		a. Thin seriffed 'I' in 'SERVICE'	£550	
O7		3a. brown-orange (1890)	3·00	19·00
		a. 'CHMABA'	£5500	£5500
		b. Thin seriffed 'I' in 'SERVICE'		
		c. Opt double, one albino		
O8	**29**	4a. olive-green	6·50	12·00
		a. 'CHMABA'	£1700	£3750
		b. 'SERV CE'	£6000	
		c. '8TATE'	£4000	
O9		4a. slate-green	6·00	18·00
		a. Thin seriffed 'I' in 'SERVICE'	£900	
O10	**21**	6a. olive-bistre (1890)	8·50	24·00
		a. 'SERVICE' double, one albino	£100	
O12	**31**	8a. dull mauve (1887)	9·00	16·00
		a. 'CHMABA'	£14000	£14000
O13		8a. magenta (1895)	8·50	9·00
		a. Thin seriffed 'I' in 'SERVICE'	£1100	
O14	**32**	12a. purple/*red* (1890)	15·00	65·00
		a. 'CHMABA'	£13000	
		b. First 'T' in 'STATE' inverted	£16000	
		c. Thin seriffed 'I' in 'SERVICE'		
		d. 'SERVICE' double, one albino	£100	
		e. 'CHAMBA STATE' double, one albino	90·00	
O15	**33**	1r. slate (1890)	27·00	£300
		a. 'CHMABA'	£7000	
O16	**37**	1r. green and carmine (1898)	8·50	60·00
		a. Thin seriffed 'I' in 'SERVICE'		
O1/O16 *Set of 10*			75·00	£425

Printings up to and including that of December 1895 had the 'SERVICE' overprint applied to sheets of stamps already overprinted with T **1**. From the printing of September 1898 onwards both 'SERVICE' and 'CHAMBA STATE' were overprinted at the same time. Nos. O6, O8 and O12 only exist using the first method, and No. O16 was only printed using the second.

The thin seriffed 'I' in 'SERVICE' variety occurred on R. 19/12 of the September 1898 printing only.

1902–04. Colours changed. Optd as T O **1**.

O17	**40**	3p. grey (1904)	60	2·00
O18	**23**	½a. pale yellow-green	2·75	5·50
O19		½a. yellow-green	6·50	6·50
O20	**25**	1a. carmine	2·50	1·75
O21	**27**	2a. pale violet (1903)	16·00	48·00
O17/O21 *Set of 4*			20·00	50·00

1903–05. King Edward VII. Stamps of India optd as T O **1**.

O22	**41**	3p. pale grey	35	15
		a. Opt double, one albino	55·00	
O23		3p. slate-grey (1905)	50	65
O24	**42**	½a. yellow-green	35	10
O25	**43**	1a. carmine	1·50	30
O26	**44**	2a. pale violet (1904)	4·25	2·75
O27		2a. mauve	2·50	2·75
O28	**47**	4a. olive (1905)	3·75	25·00
O29	**49**	8a. purple (1905)	13·00	26·00
O30		8a. claret	19·00	32·00
		a. Opt double, one albino	70·00	
O31	**51**	1r. green and carmine (1905)	3·75	22·00
O22/O31 *Set of 7*			22·00	65·00

The 2a. mauve King Edward VII, overprinted 'On H.M.S.', was discovered in Calcutta in 1912, but was not sent to Chamba, and is an unissued variety (*Price un.* £45).

1908. Nos. 149/150 of India, optd with T O **1**.

O32	**53**	½a. green	50	75
		a. Opt inverted	£8500	£9500
		b. Opt double, one albino	55·00	
O33	**54**	1a. carmine	2·75	3·50

The inverted overprint, No. O32a, was due to an inverted cliché on R. 20/1 which was corrected after a few sheets had been printed.

1913–23. King George V Official stamps (wmk Single Star) optd with T **1**.

O34	**55**	3p. grey	20	50
		a. Pale grey	1·25	3·00
		b. Bluish grey	3·00	4·50
		c. Slate	1·50	3·00
O36	**56**	½a. light green	20	60
		a. Emerald	4·25	1·50
		b. Bright green	2·50	30
O38	**57**	1a. aniline carmine	20	10
		a. Rose-carmine	5·50	50
O40	**59**	2a. purple (1914)	1·10	24·00
		a. Reddish purple	22·00	
		b. Bright reddish violet (1923)	22·00	30·00
O41	**63**	4a. olive	1·75	28·00
O42	**65**	8a. deep magenta	3·75	40·00
		a. Deep mauve (1923)	17·00	40·00
O43	**67**	1r. red-brown and deep blue-green (1914)	13·00	60·00
		a. Opt double, one albino	80·00	
		b. Brown and green (1923)	16·00	60·00
O34/O43 *Set of 7*			18·00	£140

No. O36 with inverted overprint and No. O38*a* with double or inverted overprint (on gummed side) are of clandestine origin.

1914. King George V. Optd with T O **1**.

O44	**59**	2a. purple	15·00	
O45	**63**	4a. olive	13·00	

1921. No. O97 of India optd with T **2** at top.

O46	**57**	9p. on 1a. rose-carmine	20	10·00

1925. As 1913–1923. New colour.

O47	**57**	1a. chocolate	8·00	2·25

CHAMBA STATE SERVICE (O 2) CHAMBA STATE SERVICE (O 3)

1927–39. King George V (Nasik printing, wmk Mult Star), optd at Nasik with Types O **2** or O **3** (rupee values).

O48	**55**	3p. slate (1928)	50	40
		w. Wmk inverted	—	7·50
O49	**56**	½a. green (1928)	75	15
O50	**80**	9p. deep green (1932)	4·50	15·00
O51	**57**	1a. chocolate	30	10
		w. Wmk inverted	5·00	30
O52	**82**	1a.3p. mauve (1932)	9·50	1·00
		w. Wmk inverted		
O53	**70**	2a. purple (1928)	5·00	1·75
O54	**71**	4a. sage-green (1928)	3·50	4·25
O55	**65**	8a. reddish purple (1930)	24·00	20·00
		w. Wmk inverted	18·00	
O56	**66**	12a. claret (1928)	7·00	38·00
		w. Wmk inverted	25·00	
O57	**67**	1r. chocolate and green (1930)	16·00	65·00
O58		2r. carmine and orange (1939)	28·00	£375
O59		5r. ultramarine and purple (1939)	50·00	£475
O60		10r. green and scarlet (1939)	75·00	£425
O48/O60 *Set of 13*			£200	£1300

1935–39. New types and colours. Optd with T O **2**.

O61	**79**	½a. green	9·50	75
O62	**81**	1a. chocolate	6·50	45
O63	**59**	2a. vermilion	8·50	1·50
O64		2a. vermilion (*small die*) (1939)	18·00	30·00
O65	**63**	4a. sage-green (1936)	16·00	12·00
O61/O65 *Set of 5*			50·00	40·00

1938–40. King George VI. Optd with Types O **2** or O **3** (rupee values).

O66	**91**	9p. green	50·00	90·00
O67		1a. carmine	65·00	12·00
O68	**100**	1r. grey and red-brown (1940?)	£120	£850

O69 2r. purple and brown (1939) 42·00 £850
O70 5r. green and blue (1939) 60·00 £900
O71 10r. purple and claret (1939) 90·00 £1500
O66/O71 *Set of 6* £400 £3750

CHAMBA
SERVICE
(O **4**)

1940–43.

(a) Official stamps optd with T **6**

O72 **O 20** 3p. slate 70 1·40
O73 ½a. red-brown £100 6·00
O74 ½a. purple (1943) 70 5·00
O75 9p. green 3·00 16·00
w. Wmk inverted 40·00 35·00
O76 1a. carmine (1941) 2·25 3·50
O77 1a.3p. yellow-brown (1941) £160 24·00
O78 1½a. dull violet (1943) 11·00 12·00
O79 2a. vermilion 4·25 11·00
O80 2½a. bright violet (1941) 4·25 30·00
O81 4a. brown 4·25 24·00
O82 8a. slate-violet 10·00 90·00
w. Wmk inverted 12·00 £120

(b) Postage stamps optd with T O **4**

O83 **100** 1r. grey and red-brown (1942) 20·00 £350
O84 2r. purple and brown (1942) 35·00 £550
O85 5r. green and blue (1942) 70·00 £850
O86 10r. purple and claret (1942) 80·00 £1500
O72/O86 *Set of 15* £450 £2750

Chamba became part of Himachal Pradesh on 15 April 1948.

FARIDKOT

For earlier issues, see under INDIAN FEUDATORY STATES

PRICES FOR STAMPS ON COVER TO 1945
Nos. 1/17 *from* × 30

Nos. O1/O15 *from* × 40

Raja Bikram Singh, 1874–1898

FARIDKOT
STATE
(**1**)

1887 (1 Jan)–**1900**. Queen Victoria. Optd with T **1**.

1 **23** ½a. deep green 2·75 2·75
a. 'ARIDKOT'
b. 'FAR DKOT' — £4000
c. Opt double, one albino 95·00
2 **25** 1a. brown-purple 2·75 5·00
3 1a. plum 3·00 4·75
4 **27** 2a. blue 3·25 13·00
5 2a. deep blue 6·00 15·00
6 **28** 3a. orange 12·00 22·00
7 3a. brown-orange (1893) 5·50 12·00
8 **29** 4a. olive-green 14·00 23·00
a. 'ARIDKOT' £2500
9 4a. slate-green 11·00 45·00
10 **21** 6a. olive-bistre 55·00 £100
a. 'ARIDKOT' £3250
b. Opt double, one albino £100
11 6a. bistre-brown 4·00 28·00
12 **31** 8a. dull mauve 32·00 65·00
a. 'ARIDKOT' £4500
13 8a. magenta 32·00 £300
a. Opt double, one albino 65·00
14 **32** 12a. purple/*red* (1900) 60·00 £600
15 **33** 1r. slate 60·00 £450
a. 'ARIDKOT' £6500
16 **37** 1r. green and carmine (1893) 60·00 £140
a. Opt double, one albino £100
1/16 *Set of 10* £200 £1200

The ½a., 1a., 2a., 3a., 4a., 8a., 12a. and 1r. (No. 16) are known with broken 'O' (looking like a 'C') in 'FARIDKOT'. This variety occurred once per sheet (in the eleventh vertical column) in the February 1894 printing, and again at R. 4/2 in 1898-1900 printings.

Raja Balbir Singh, 1898–1906

1900. Optd with T **1**.

17 **40** 3p. carmine 3·25 75·00

OFFICIAL STAMPS

SERVICE

FARIDKOT
STATE
(O **1**)

1887 (1 Jan)–**98**. Queen Victoria. Optd with T O **1**.

O1 **23** ½a. deep green 75 1·75
a. 'SERV CE' £4250
b. 'FAR DKOT' £4750
c. Thin seriffed 'I' in 'SERVICE' £450
d. 'FARIDKOT STATE' double, one albino 85·00
e. 'ESRVICE' £5000
O2 **25** 1a. brown-purple 1·00 4·25
a. Thin seriffed 'I' in 'SERVICE' £475
b. Opt double, one albino 95·00
O3 1a. plum 3·25 3·50
a. 'SERV CE' £6000
O4 **27** 2a. dull blue 2·50 18·00
a. 'SERV CE' £6000
O5 2a. deep blue 6·00 26·00
O6 **28** 3a. orange 9·00 20·00
a. 'SERVICE' double, one albino
O7 3a. brown-orange (12.98) 9·00 70·00
a. Thin seriffed 'I' in 'SERVICE' £1100
O8 **29** 4a. olive-green 7·50 55·00
a. 'SERV CE' £5000
b. 'ARIDKOT'
c. 'SERVICE' treble, two albino £180
O9 4a. slate-green 30·00 90·00
a. 'SERVICE' double, one albino 55·00
O10 **21** 6a. olive-bistre 70·00 £190
a. 'ARIDKOT' £2000
b. 'SERVIC' £4500
c. 'SERVICE' double, one albino £110
d. 'FARIDKOT STATE' double, one albino £110
O11 6a. bistre-brown 45·00 48·00
O12 **31** 8a. dull mauve 18·00 48·00
a. 'SERV CE' £4500
O13 8a. magenta 27·00 £300
O14 **33** 1r. slate 75·00 £425
a. 'SERVICE' double, one albino £150
O15 **37** 1r. green and carmine (12.98) £120 £1200
a. Thin seriffed 'I' in 'SERVICE'
O1/O15 *Set of 9* £250 £1600

The ½a., 1a., 2a., 3a., 4a., 8a. and 1r. (No. O15) are known with the broken 'O'.

Printings up to and including that of November 1895 had the 'SERVICE' overprint applied to sheets already overprinted with T **1**. From December 1898 onwards 'SERVICE' and 'FARIDKOT STATE' were overprinted at one operation to provide fresh supplies of Nos. O1/O3, O7 and O15.

The thin seriffed 'I' variety occurs on the December 1898 overprinting only.

This State ceased to use overprinted stamps after 31 March 1901.

GWALIOR

PRICES FOR STAMPS ON COVER TO 1945
Nos. 1/3 *from* × 10
Nos. 4/11 —
Nos. 12/66 *from* × 5
Nos. 67/128 *from* × 4
Nos. 129/137 *from* × 5

Nos. O1/O94 *from* × 12

OVERPRINTS. From 1885 to 1926 these were applied typo by the Government of India Central Printing Press, Calcutta, and from 1927 by litho at the Security Press, Nasik, *unless otherwise stated.*

Maharaja Jayaji Rao Sindhia, 1843–1886

गवालियर

GWALIOR
(**1**)

GWALIOR
गवालियर
(**2**)

GWALIOR
Small 'G'

GWALIOR
Small 'R'

GWALIOR
Tall 'R' (original state)

GWALIOR
Tall 'R' (damaged state)

OVERPRINT VARIETIES OF TYPE 2.

Small 'G' — Occurs on R. 7/11 from June 1900 printing of ½, 1, 2, 3, 4a. and 3p. (No. 38), and on R. 3/1 of a left pane from May 1901 printing of 2, 3 and 5r.

Small 'R' — Occurs on R. 9/3 from June 1900 printing of 3p. to 4a. and on R. 2/3 from May 1901 printing of 2, 3 and 5r.

Tall 'R' — Occurs on R. 20/2 from printings between June 1900 and May 1907. The top of the letter is damaged on printings from February 1903 onwards.

1885 (1 July)–**97**. Queen Victoria.

I. Optd with T **1**.

(a) Space between two lines of overprint 13 mm. Hindi inscription 13 to 14 mm long (May 1885)

1 **23** ½a. blue-green £250 48·00
2 **25** 1a. brown-purple £150 48·00
3 **27** 2a. dull blue £130 25·00
1/3 *Set of 3* £475 £110

A variety exists of the ½a. in which the space between the two lines of overprint is only 9½ mm but this is probably from a proof sheet.

(b) Space between two lines of overprint 15 mm on 4a. and 6a. and 16 to 17 mm on other values (June 1885). Hindi inscription 13 to 14 mm long

4 **23** ½a. blue-green £110
a. Opt double, one albino £120
b. Hindi inscr 15 to 15½ mm long £225
ba. Opt double, one albino £275
c. Pair. Nos. 4/4b £1600
5 **25** 1a. brown-purple £110
a. Opt double, one albino £130
b. Hindi inscr 15 to 15½ mm long £225
ba. Opt double, one albino £275
c. Pair. Nos. 5/5b £1600
6 **26** 1a.6p. sepia £180
b. Hindi inscr 15 to 15½ mm long £400
c. Pair. Nos. 6/6b £1800
7 **27** 2a. dull blue £120
b. Hindi inscr 15 to 15½ mm long £190
c. Pair. Nos. 7/7b £550
8 **17** 4a. green £200
b. Hindi inscr 15 to 15½ mm long £400
c. Pair. Nos. 8/8b £1900
9 **21** 6a. olive-bistre £190
a. Opt double, one albino £200
b. Hindi inscr 15 to 15½ mm long £425
ba. Opt double, one albino £425
c. Pair. Nos. 9/9b £1900
10 **31** 8a. dull mauve £150
b. Hindi inscr 15 to 15½ mm long £300
c. Pair. Nos. 10/10b £1900
11 **33** 1r. slate £150
b. Hindi inscr 15 to 15½ mm long £300
c. Pair. Nos. 11/11b £1900
4/11 *Set of 8* £1100
4b/11b *Set of 8* £2250

The two types of overprint on these stamps occur in the same settings, with about a quarter of the stamps in each sheet showing the long inscription. Nos. 4/7 and 10/11 were overprinted in sheets of 240 and Nos. 8/9 in half-sheets of 160.

II. Optd with T **2**. *Hindi inscription 13 to 14 mm long*

(a) In red (Sept 1885)

12 **23** ½a. blue-green 2·50 20
b. Hindi inscr 15 to 15½ mm long 2·75 2·00
c. Pair. Nos. 12/12b 30·00 32·00
13 **27** 2a. dull blue 45·00 18·00
b. Hindi inscr 15 to 15½ mm long 80·00 65·00
c. Pair. Nos. 13/13b £500 £600
14 **17** 4a. green 65·00 32·00
aw. Wmk inverted £275
b. Hindi inscr 15 to 15½ mm long £400 £170
c. Pair. Nos. 14/14b £1800
15 **33** 1r. slate 15·00 42·00
aw. Wmk inverted 25·00 55·00
b. Hindi inscr 15 to 15½ mm long 50·00 £110
bw. Wmk inverted 75·00 £170
c. Pair. Nos. 15/15b £120 £200
cw. Wmk inverted £140
12/15 *Set of 4* £110 80·00
12b/15b *Set of 4* £475 £325

No. 14 was overprinted in half-sheets of 160, about 40 stamps having the Hindi inscription 15 to 15½ mm long. The remaining three values were from a setting of 240 containing 166 13 to 14 mm long and 74 15 to 15½ mm long.

Reprints have been made of Nos. 12 to 15, but the majority of the examples have the word 'REPRINT' overprinted upon them.

(b) In black (1885–1897)

16 **23** ½a. blue-green (1889) 6·50 3·00
b. Opt double, one albino 40·00
c. Hindi inscr 15 to 15½ mm long 1·25 10
ca. Opt double † £1700
cb. Opt double, one albino £140
cc. 'GWALICR' £110 £150
cd. Small 'G' 80·00 50·00
ce. Small 'R' £100
cf. Tall 'R' £130 £130
d. Pair. Nos. 16/16c £110 £120
17 **24** 9p. carmine (1891) 45·00 80·00
a. Opt double, one albino 70·00
c. Hindi inscr 15 to 15½ mm long 75·00 £110
ca. Opt double, one albino £100
d. Pair. Nos. 17/17c £375 £600
18 **25** 1a. brown-purple 3·50 20
c. Hindi inscr 15 to 15½ mm long 4·50 35
d. Pair. Nos. 18/18c 28·00 32·00
19 1a. plum (*Hindi inscr 15 to 15½ mm long*) 4·50 10
a. Small 'G' £110 60·00
b. Small 'R' £120
c. Tall 'R' £190
20 **26** 1a.6p. sepia 3·00 3·50
c. Hindi inscr 15 to 15½ mm long 2·25 2·50
d. Pair. Nos. 20/20c 27·00 38·00
w. Wmk inverted £250
21 **27** 2a. dull blue 18·00 1·25
c. Hindi inscr 15 to 15½ mm long 7·00 10
ca. 'R' omitted £700 £650
d. Pair. Nos. 21/21c £250 £275
22 2a. deep blue 25·00 4·50
c. Hindi inscr 15 to 15½ mm long 8·00 1·25
ca. Small 'G' £225 £250
cb. Small 'R' £275
cc. Tall 'R' £375 £425
d. Pair. Nos. 22/22c £325
23 **36** 2a.6p. yellow-green (*Hindi inscr 15 to 15½ mm long*) (1896) 15·00 28·00
a. 'GWALICR' £1000
24 **28** 3a. orange 28·00 32·00
a. Opt double, one albino £120
c. Hindi inscr 15 to 15½ mm long £130 85·00
ca. Opt double, one albino
d. Pair. Nos. 24/24c £500
25 3a. brown-orange 60·00 11·00
c. Hindi inscr 15 to 15½ mm long 8·50 15
ca. Opt double, one albino 65·00
cb. Small 'G' £375 £450
cc. Small 'R' £1600
cd. Tall 'R' £325 £325
d. Pair. Nos. 25/25c £375
26 **29** 4a. olive-green (1889) 20·00 4·00
c. Hindi inscr 15 to 15½ mm long 18·00 4·75
d. Pair. Nos. 26/26c £170
27 4a. slate-green 20·00 4·00
c. Hindi inscr 15 to 15½ mm long 9·50 1·75
ca. Opt double, one albino £100
cb. Small 'G' £800 £600
cc. Small 'R' £700
cd. Tall 'R' £550 £600
d. Pair. Nos. 27/27c 60·00
28 **21** 6a. olive-bistre 18·00 42·00
c. Hindi inscr 15 to 15½ mm long 11·00 32·00
ca. Opt double, one albino 65·00
d. Pair. Nos. 28/28c £150
29 6a. bistre-brown 8·00 14·00
c. Hindi inscr 15 to 15½ mm long 9·50 19·00
d. Pair. Nos. 29/29c 45·00
30 **31** 8a. dull mauve 25·00 70·00
c. Hindi inscr 15 to 15½ mm long 10·00 2·50
d. Pair. Nos. 30/30c £550
31 8a. magenta (*Hindi inscr 15 to 15½ mm long*) (1897) 15·00 17·00
32 **32** 12a. purple/*red* (1891) 11·00 9·50
c. Hindi inscr 15 to 15½ mm long 4·50 1·25
ca. Pair, one without opt £6000
cb. Tall 'R' £2000 £1100
d. Pair. Nos. 32/32c £110
33 **33** 1r. slate (1889) £190 £750
c. Hindi inscr 15 to 15½ mm long 8·00 6·00
d. Pair. Nos. 33/33c £1000

34	**37**	1r. green and carmine (*Hindi inscr 15 to 15½ mm long*) (1896)	16·00	9·50
		a. Opt double, one albino	£180	
		b. 'GWALICR'	£1700	£3500
35	**38**	2r. carmine and yellow-brown (*Hindi inscr 15 to 15½ mm long*) (1896)	6·50	3·25
		a. Small 'G'	£600	£275
		b. Small 'R'	£650	£300
		c. Opt double, one albino	£150	
		d. Opt triple, two albino	£180	
36		3r. brown and green (*Hindi inscr 15 to 15½ mm long*) (1896)	9·00	3·75
		a. Small 'G'	£700	£300
		b. Small 'R'	£750	£325
37		5r. ultramarine and violet (*Hindi inscr 15 to 15½ mm long*) (1896)	16·00	7·00
		a. Small 'G'	£700	£375
		b. Small 'R'	£850	£425
16c/37 *Set of 16*			£140	£140

Printings to 1891 continued to use the setting showing both types, but subsequently a new setting containing the larger overprint only was used.

The ½a., 1a., 2a. and 3a. exist with space between 'I' and 'O' of 'GWALIOR'.

The 'GWALICR' error occurs on R. 1/5 in the May 1896 printing only.

Maharaja Madhav Rao Sindhia, 1886–1925

1899–1911.

(a) Optd with T **2** *(Hindi inscr 15 to 15½ mm long)*

38	**40**	3p. carmine	50	20
		a. Opt inverted	£2500	£900
		b. Small 'G'	70·00	70·00
		d. Small 'R'	85·00	
		e. Tall 'R'	80·00	£100
		f. Opt double, one albino	65·00	
39		3p. grey (1904)	8·00	60·00
		e. Tall 'R'	£325	
		f. Opt double, one albino	75·00	
40	**23**	½a. pale yellow-green (1901)	3·50	2·50
		e. Tall 'R'	£120	
		f. Opt double, one albino	40·00	
40*g*		½a. yellow-green (1903)	5·00	2·25
		ge. Tall 'R'	£170	
41	**25**	1a. carmine (1901)	1·25	35
		e. Tall 'R'	£100	
		f. Opt double, one albino	80·00	
42	**27**	2a. pale violet (1903)	6·00	8·00
		e. Tall 'R'	£225	
43	**36**	2a.6p. ultramarine (1903)	4·25	12·00
		e. Tall 'R'	£350	
38/43 *Set of 6*			21·00	75·00

(b) Optd as T **2**, *but 'GWALIOR' 13 mm long. Opt spaced 2¾ mm*

44	**38**	3r. brown and green (1911)	£350	£350
45		5r. ultramarine and violet (1910)	£100	75·00
		a. Opt double, one albino	£180	

1903–11. King Edward VII. Optd as T **2**.

A. 'GWALIOR' 14 mm long. Overprint spaced 1¾ mm (1903–1906)

46A	**41**	3p. pale grey	1·50	20
		e. Tall 'R'	55·00	85·00
		f. Slate-grey (1905)	1·50	30
		fe. Tall 'R'	60·00	90·00
48A	**42**	½a. green	30	10
		e. Tall 'R'	55·00	80·00
49A	**43**	1a. carmine	20	10
		e. Tall 'R'	65·00	85·00
		f. Opt double, one albino	80·00	
50A	**44**	2a. pale violet (1904)	3·50	1·25
		e. Tall 'R'	£160	
		f. Mauve	5·00	20
		fe. Tall 'R'	£275	£180
52A	**45**	2a.6p. ultramarine (1904)	32·00	90·00
		e. Tall 'R'	£1800	
53A	**46**	3a. orange-brown (1904)	3·75	35
		e. Tall 'R'	£170	£200
54A	**47**	4a. olive	6·00	40
		e. Tall 'R'	£400	£325
		f. Pale olive	22·00	7·50
		fe. Tall 'R'	£800	
56A	**48**	6a. olive-bistre (1904)	3·75	4·50
		e. Tall 'R'	£1600	
57A	**49**	8a. purple (*shades*) (1905)	9·50	2·50
		e. Tall 'R'	£650	£550
59A	**50**	12a. purple/*red* (1905)	9·00	27·00
		e. Tall 'R'	£1700	
60A	**51**	1r. green and carmine (1905)	10·00	2·25
		e. Tall 'R'	£1200	£1100
61A	**52**	2r. carmine and yellow-brown (1906)	45·00	55·00
		a. Opt double, one albino	95·00	
46A/61A *Set of 12*			£110	£160

B. 'GWALIOR' 13 mm long. Overprint spaced 2¾ mm (1908–1911)

46B	**41**	3p. pale grey	4·75	10
		f. Slate-grey	5·50	50
49B	**43**	1a. carmine	12·00	4·00
50*f*B		2a. mauve	6·50	15
52B	**45**	2a.6p. ultramarine	3·25	15·00
53B	**46**	3a. orange-brown	7·50	20
54*f*B		4a. pale olive	6·00	60
56B	**48**	6a. olive-bistre	15·00	2·00
57B	**49**	8a. purple (*shades*)	17·00	1·60
		f. Claret	55·00	5·50
		fa. Opt double, one albino	£110	
59B	**50**	12a. purple/*red*	8·00	3·25
		f. Opt double, one albino	£150	
60B	**51**	1r. green and carmine	15·00	1·25
61B	**52**	2r. carmine and yellow-brown	9·00	11·00
		a. Opt double, one albino	£120	
62B		3r. brown and green (1910)	45·00	75·00
		a. Red-brown and green	80·00	85·00
63B		5r. ultramarine and violet (1911)	22·00	29·00
46B/63B *Set of 13*			£150	£130

1907–08. Nos. 149 and 150 of India optd as T **2**.

(a) 'GWALIOR' 14 mm long. Overprint spaced 1¾ mm

64	**53**	½a. green	20	70
		e. Tall 'R'	75·00	£110

(b) 'GWALIOR' 13 mm long. Overprint spaced 2¾ mm (1908)

65	**53**	½a. green	2·75	20
66	**54**	1a. carmine	1·50	20

1912–23. King George V. Optd as T **2**.

67	**55**	3p. grey	20	10
		a. Opt double	†	£1700
		b. Pale grey	2·50	10
		c. Bluish grey	—	1·75
		d. Slate (1922)	2·75	30
		da. 'Rs' flaw	75·00	85·00
68	**56**	½a. light green	1·00	10
		a. Emerald	4·50	35
		b. Bright green	2·50	10
		ba. Opt inverted	†	£500
69	**57**	1a. aniline carmine	40	10
		a. Opt double	25·00	
70	**59**	2a. purple	3·00	30
		a. Reddish purple	3·25	10
		aw. Wmk inverted	†	£275
		b. Deep mauve	8·50	2·50
		c. Bright reddish violet (1923)	10·00	3·00
71	**62**	3a. orange	1·75	15
		a. Dull orange (1922)	2·75	25
72	**63**	4a. olive (1913)	75	60
73	**64**	6a. yellow-bistre	3·50	1·75
		a. Brown-ochre	3·75	1·50
74	**65**	8a. deep magenta (1913)	5·00	1·50
		a. Deep mauve	8·00	30
		b. Bright mauve (1918)	25·00	5·00
75	**66**	12a. carmine-lake (1914)	2·50	4·00
		a. Claret	—	8·00
76	**67**	1r. red-brown and deep blue-green (1913)	18·00	1·75
		a. Opt double, one albino	24·00	
		b. Brown and green	24·00	40
		ba. Opt double	£750	
		c. Orange-brown and deep turquoise-green (1923)	38·00	9·00
77		2r. carmine-rose and brown (1913)	16·00	4·50
		a. Opt double, one albino	55·00	
78		5r. ultramarine and violet (1913)	40·00	6·50
		a. Opt double, one albino	85·00	
67/78 *Set of 12*			85·00	17·00

GWALIOR
(3)

1921. No. 192 of India optd with T **3**.

79	**57**	9p. on 1a. rose-carmine	10	50

No. 79 with inverted overprint is of clandestine origin.

1923–27. Optd as T **2**. New colours and values.

80	**57**	1a. chocolate	1·10	10
		a. Opt double, one albino	90·00	
81	**58**	1½a. chocolate (B) (1925)	5·00	1·00
82		1½a. rose-carmine (B) (1927)	20	20
83	**61**	2a.6p. ultramarine (1925)	4·25	1·75
84		2a.6p. orange (1927)	35	50
85	**62**	3a. ultramarine (1924)	6·00	75
80/85 *Set of 6*			15·00	3·75

No. 82 with inverted overprint is of clandestine origin.

Maharaja George Jivaji Rao Sindhia, 1925–1961

GWALIOR
गवालियर
(4)

GWALIOR
गवालियर
(5)

1928–36. King George V (Nasik printing, wmk Mult Star), optd at Nasik with T **4** or **5** (rupee values).

86	**55**	3p. slate (1932)	1·00	15
		w. Wmk inverted	3·50	1·25
87	**56**	½a. green (1930)	1·50	10
		w. Wmk inverted		
88	**80**	9p. deep green (*litho*) (1932)	5·50	30
		aw. Wmk inverted	5·50	80
88*b*		9p. deep green (*typo*)	3·50	50
89	**57**	1a. chocolate	85	10
		w. Wmk inverted	—	3·75
90	**82**	1a.3p. mauve (1936)	1·75	15
91	**70**	2a. purple	85	30
		w. Wmk inverted	75	30
92	**62**	3a. bright blue	1·75	40
93	**71**	4a. sage-green	3·50	1·10
		w. Wmk inverted	4·50	4·25
94	**65**	8a. reddish purple (*wmk inverted*)	4·50	1·10
95	**66**	12a. claret	6·00	4·00
96	**67**	1r. chocolate and green	8·00	6·50
		w. Wmk inverted	16·00	6·50
97		2r. carmine and orange	24·00	16·00
		w. Wmk inverted	8·00	4·50
98		5r. ultramarine and purple (*wmk inverted*) (1929)	38·00	32·00
99		10r. green and scarlet (1930)	£110	55·00
100		15r. blue and olive (*wmk inverted*) (1930)	£200	90·00
101		25r. orange and blue (1930)	£475	£275
86/101 *Set of 16*			£800	£425

1935–36. New types and colours. Optd with T **4**.

102	**79**	½a. green (1936)	75	20
		w. Wmk inverted	12·00	7·00
103	**81**	1a. chocolate	20	10
104	**59**	2a. vermilion (1936)	5·00	3·50
102/104 *Set of 3*			5·50	3·50

1938–48. King George VI. Nos. 247/250, 253, 255/256 and 259/264 optd with T **4** or **5** (rupee values).

105	**91**	3p. slate	15·00	10
106		½a. red-brown	15·00	10
107		9p. green (1939)	75·00	4·75
108		1a. carmine	15·00	15
109	**94**	3a. yellow-green (1939)	55·00	6·00
110	**96**	4a. brown	75·00	4·50
111	**97**	6a. turquoise-green (1939)	18·00	16·00
112	**100**	1r. grey and red-brown (1942)	13·00	1·75
113		2r. purple and brown (1948)	25·00	12·00
114		5r. green and blue (1948)	32·00	45·00
115		10r. purple and claret (1948)	32·00	48·00
116		15r. brown and green (1948)	90·00	£250
117		25r. slate-violet and purple (1948)	80·00	£200
105/117 *Set of 13*			£475	£500

1942–45. King George VI. Optd with T **4**.

118	**100a**	3p. slate	45	10
		w. Wmk inverted	—	45·00
119		½a. purple (1943)	1·00	10
120		9p. green	1·50	10
121		1a. carmine (1943)	1·00	10
		a. Opt double	—	£375
122	**101**	1½a. dull violet (*litho*)	11·00	1·25
122*a*		1½a. dull violet (1943) (*typo*)	6·00	30
123		2a. vermilion	1·75	20
		a. Opt double	†	£425
124		3a. bright violet (litho)	8·50	2·75
124*a*		3a. bright violet (1943) (*typo*)	6·00	2·25
		ab. Opt double	—	£400
125	**102**	4a. brown	5·00	20
126		6a. turquoise-green (1945)	14·00	27·00
127		8a. slate-violet (1944)	2·50	2·00
128		12a. lake (1943)	8·50	24·00
118/128 *Set of 11*			42·00	50·00

GWALIOR
गवालियर
(6)

1949 (Apr). King George VI. Optd Typo with T **6** at the Alizah Printing Press, Gwalior.

129	**100a**	3p. slate	5·00	60
130		½a. purple	5·00	50
131		1a. carmine	4·50	60
132	**101**	2a. vermilion	42·00	2·50
133		3a. bright violet (*typo*)	£100	35·00
134	**102**	4a. brown	17·00	3·50
135		6a. turquoise-green	75·00	85·00
136		8a. slate-violet	£150	75·00
137		12a. lake	£750	£300
129/137 *Set of 9*			£1000	£450

No. 137 has been extensively forged, and should not be purchased without a reliable guarantee.

OFFICIAL STAMPS

गवालियर
सरविस
(O 1)

गवालियर
सरविस
(O 2)

1895–96. Queen Victoria. Optd with T O **1**.

O1	**23**	½a. blue-green	1·75	10
		a. Hindi characters transposed	42·00	35·00
		b. 4th Hindi character omitted	£600	55·00
		c. Opt double	†	£1500
O2	**25**	1a. brown-purple	19·00	1·50
O3		1a. plum	6·00	10
		a. Hindi characters transposed	65·00	50·00
		b. 4th Hindi character omitted	£700	85·00
O4	**27**	2a. dull blue	6·50	50
O5		2a. deep blue	5·00	50
		a. Hindi characters transposed	£110	£150
		b. 4th Hindi character omitted	£130	£170
O6	**29**	4a. olive-green	7·50	2·50
		a. Hindi characters transposed	£700	£750
		b. 4th Hindi character omitted	£4000	£2500
O7		4a. slate-green	6·00	2·50
		a. Hindi characters transposed	£400	£600
O8	**31**	8a. dull mauve	8·50	5·00
		a. Opt double, one albino	80·00	
O9		8a. magenta	8·50	2·75
		a. Hindi characters transposed	£1600	£1900
		b. 4th Hindi character omitted		
O10	**37**	1r. green and carmine (1896)	13·00	3·50
		a. Hindi characters transposed	£3500	
O1/O10 *Set of 6*			35·00	8·50

In the errors listed above it is the last two Hindi characters that are transposed, so that the word reads 'Sersiv'. The error occurs on R. 19/1 in the sheet from the early printings up to May 1896.

1901–04. Colours changed.

O23	**40**	3p. carmine (1902)	2·75	50
O24		3p. grey (1904)	2·50	4·00
O25	**23**	½a. pale yellow-green	8·00	15
O26		½a. yellow-green	1·75	10
O27	**25**	1a. carmine	9·50	10
O28	**27**	2a. pale violet (1903)	3·75	3·50
O23/O28 *Set of 5*			18·00	7·50

1903–08. King Edward VII. Optd as T O **1**.

(a) Overprint spaced 10 mm (1903–1905)

O29	**41**	3p. pale grey	70	10
		a. Slate-grey (1905)	70	10
O31	**42**	½a. green	2·00	10
O32	**43**	1a. carmine	1·10	10
O33	**44**	2a. pale violet (1905)	6·50	1·00
		a. Mauve	5·00	30
O35	**47**	4a. olive (1905)	22·00	2·25
O36	**49**	8a. purple (1905)	17·00	70
		a. Claret	35·00	8·00
		ab. Opt double, one albino	90·00	
O38	**51**	1r. green and carmine (1905)	7·00	3·50
		a. Opt double, one albino	£140	
O29/O38 *Set of 7*			50·00	6·00

(b) Overprint spaced 8 mm (1907–1908)

O39 **41** 3p. pale grey 11·00 15
a. Slate-grey 20·00 2·25
b. 9mm spacing £100 2·50
O41 **42** ½a. green 8·00 15
a. 9mm spacing 75·00 2·50
O42 **43** 1a. carmine 5·50 10
a. 9mm spacing 50·00 2·50
O43 **44** 2a. mauve 20·00 75
a. 9mm spacing £150 7·50
O44 **47** 4a. olive 4·50 1·00
a. 9mm spacing 50·00 10·00
O45 **49** 8a. purple 10·00 3·75
a. 9mm spacing 90·00 30·00
O46 **51** 1r. green and carmine (1908) 65·00 13·00
a. 9mm spacing £450 £100
O39/O46 *Set of 7* £110 17·00

Three successive overprint formes, each a setting of 240 (20×12), were used to produce the King Edward VII official issues, Nos. O29/O50.

Printings up to Oct 1906 used a setting with 10mm space between the two lines, set up from loose type. The upper line varies in length from 14.5 to 15.5mm, and the two lines are often not well centred in relation to each other.

From March 1907 until Feb 1908 a new setting was employed, also from loose type but with 8mm space between lines, except for the 15th horizontal row, where the spacing is 9mm (exact measurement 8¾ mm). Vertical pairs showing the 8mm and 9mm spacing *se-tenant* are scarce.

Finally, during the Feb 1908 printing, a new stereotyped plate was introduced. The spacing between lines was again 10mm, but the overprints are now regular, with the upper line now consistently 14-14.5mm in length, and the two lines well centred in relation to each other. This plate remained in use until 1912.

Nos. O29/O38 can be found with both the type-set and stereo versions of the 10mm opt, except for No. O31 (type-set only) and No. O36*a* (stereo only). Nos. O47/O48 only occur with the second stereo opt.

1907–08. Nos. 149 and 150 of India optd as T O **1**.

(a) Overprint spaced 10 mm (1908)

O47 **53** ½a. green 14·00 10
O48 **54** 1a. carmine 13·00 15
a. Opt double, one albino 70·00

(b) Overprint spaced 8 mm (1907)

O49 **53** ½a. green 1·75 15
a. 9mm spacing 20·00 2·50
O50 **54** 1a. carmine 80·00 2·00
a. 9mm spacing £550 20·00

1913–23. King George V. Optd with Type O **1**.

O51 **55** 3p. grey 1·60 20
a. Pair, one without opt £2750
b. Pale grey 75 10
c. Bluish grey — 1·00
d. Slate 1·25 30
da. 'Rs' flaw £170
O52 **56** ½a. light green 20 10
b. Emerald — 20
ba. Opt double £130 £190
c. Bright green 50 20
O53 **57** 1a. rose-carmine 18·00 50
a. Aniline carmine 50 10
ab. Opt double 75·00
O54 1a. chocolate (1923) 7·50 30
O55 **59** 2a. purple 3·50 1·50
a. Reddish purple 1·75 20
b. Deep mauve 7·50
c. Bright reddish violet (1923) 2·00 75
O56 **63** 4a. olive 75 1·50
O57 **65** 8a. deep magenta 2·75 3·25
a. Deep mauve 4·50 1·60
b. Bright mauve (1918) 11·00
O58 **67** 1r. red-brown and deep blue-green 65·00 48·00
a. Opt double, one albino £130
b. Brown and green 55·00 30·00
c. Orange-brown and deep turquoise-green (1923) 65·00 45·00
O51/O58 *Set of 8* 60·00 30·00

1921. No. O97 of India optd with T **3**.

O59 **57** 9p. on 1a. rose-carmine 10 30

1927–35. King George V (Nasik printing, wmk Mult Star), optd at Nasik as T O **1** (but top line measures 13 *mm* instead of 14 *mm*) or with T O **2** (rupee values).

O61 **55** 3p. slate 30 10
w. Wmk inverted 10 60
O62 **56** ½a. green 10 15
w. Wmk inverted 6·00 6·00
O63 **80** 9p. deep green (1932) 20 15
O64 **57** 1a. chocolate 10 10
w. Wmk inverted 2·00 50
O65 **82** 1a.3p. mauve (1933) 50 15
w. Wmk inverted 8·50
O66 **70** 2a. purple 20 15
w. Wmk inverted 10·00
O67 **71** 4a. sage-green 2·00 30
w. Wmk inverted — 4·00
O68 **65** 8a. reddish purple (1928) 75 1·75
w. Wmk inverted 3·00 4·00
O69 **67** 1r. chocolate and green 1·25 2·00
w. Wmk inverted 1·90 3·25
O70 2r. carmine and orange (1935) 30·00 38·00
O71 5r. ultramarine and purple (1932) 45·00 £325
w. Wmk inverted 40·00
O72 10r. green and scarlet (1932) £250 £700
O61/O72 *Set of 12* £300 £950

1936–37. New types. Optd as T O **1** (13 *mm*).

O73 **79** ½a. green 15 15
w. Wmk inverted — 12·00
O74 **81** 1a. chocolate 15 15
O75 **59** 2a. vermilion 20 40
O76 2a. vermilion (*small die*) 6·50 1·25
O77 **63** 4a. sage-green (1937) 60 75
O73/O77 *Set of 5* 7·00 2·40

1938. King George VI. Optd as T O **1** (13 *mm*).

O78 **91** ½a. red-brown 7·50 30
O79 1a. carmine 3·75 20

ग्वालियर (O **3**) 1A 1A (O **4**)

1940–42. Official stamps optd with T O **3**.

O80 **O 20** 3p. slate 50 10
w. Wmk inverted — 70·00
O81 ½a. red-brown 15·00 25
O82 ½a. purple (1942) 1·50 10
O83 9p. green (1942) 1·25 70
O84 1a. carmine 2·25 10
O85 1a.3p. yellow-brown (1942) 70·00 1·75
w. Wmk inverted — 65·00
O86 1½a. dull violet (1942) 1·00 30
O87 2a. vermilion 1·00 30
O88 4a. brown (1942) 1·25 3·50
O89 8a. slate-violet (1942) 7·00 11·00
O80/O89 *Set of 10* 90·00 16·00

1941. Stamp of 1932 (King George V) optd with T O **1** and surch with T O **4**.

O90 **82** 1a. on 1a.3p. mauve 26·00 3·50
w. Wmk inverted 55·00 20·00

1942–47. King George VI. Optd with T O **2**.

O91 **100** 1r. grey and red-brown 15·00 28·00
O92 2r. purple and brown 18·00 £150
O93 5r. green and blue (1943) 30·00 £850
O94 10r. purple and claret (1947) 80·00 £2000
O91/O94 *Set of 4* £130 £2750

Gwalior became part of Madhya Bharat by 1 July 1948.

JIND

For earlier issues, see under INDIAN FEUDATORY STATES

PRICES FOR STAMPS ON COVER TO 1945

Nos. 1/4	*from* × 20
Nos. 5/16	—
Nos. 17/40	*from* × 15
Nos. 41/149	*from* × 8
Nos. O1/O86	*from* × 15

OVERPRINTS. From 1885 to 1926 these were applied typo by the Government of India Central Printing Press, Calcutta, and from 1927 by litho at the Security Press, Nasik, *unless otherwise stated.*

Raja Raghubir Singh, 1864–1887

JHIND STATE (**1**) JEEND STATE (**2**) JHIND STATE (**3**)

1885 (1 July). Queen Victoria. Optd with T **1**.

1 **23** ½a. blue-green 12·00 10·00
a. Opt inverted £170 £190
2 **25** 1a. brown-purple 80·00 £110
a. Opt inverted £1800 £2000
3 **27** 2a. dull blue 42·00 30·00
a. Opt inverted £1300 £1400
4 **17** 4a. green £120 £140
5 **31** 8a. dull mauve £700
a. Opt inverted £18000
6 **33** 1r. slate £700
a. Opt inverted £21000
1/6 *Set of 6* £1500

The overprint inverted errors occurred on R. 10/8 in the setting of 120, although it is believed that one pane of the ½a. had the overprint inverted on the entire pane. Examples of inverted overprints on the ½a., 1a. and 2a. with the lines much less curved are thought to come from a trial printing.

All six values exist with reprinted overprint. This has the words 'JHIND' and 'STATE' 8 and 9 mm in length respectively, whereas in the originals the words are 9 and 9½ mm.

1885. Optd with T **2**.

7 **23** ½a. blue-green (R.) £200
8 **25** 1a. brown-purple £200
9 **27** 2a. dull blue (R.) £225
10 **17** 4a. green (R.) £300
a. Opt double, one albino £425
11 **31** 8a. dull mauve £300
12 **33** 1r. slate (R.) £325
7/12 *Set of 6* £1400

1886. Optd with T **3**, in red.

13 **23** ½a. blue-green 70·00
a. 'JEIND' for 'JHIND' £2000
14 **27** 2a. dull blue 70·00
a. 'JEIND' for 'JHIND' £2000
b. Opt double, one albino £150
15 **17** 4a. green 90·00
a. Opt double, one albino 90·00
b. Opt treble, two albino £150
16 **33** 1r. slate £110
a. 'JEIND' for 'JHIND' £3000
13/16 *Set of 4* £300

Examples of No. 14a usually show an additional albino 'SERVICE' overprint as T O **16**.

1886–99. Optd with T **3**.

17 **23** ½a. blue-green 1·25 10
a. Opt inverted £275
18 **25** 1a. brown-purple 6·00 30
a. 'JEIND' for 'JHIND' £750
b. Opt double, one albino 85·00
19 1a. plum (1899) 11·00 1·00
20 **26** 1a.6p. sepia (1896) 5·50 6·00
a. Opt double, one albino 95·00
21 **27** 2a. dull blue 5·50 50
22 2a. ultramarine 5·50 1·00
a. Opt double, one albino 95·00
23 **28** 3a. brown-orange (1891) 7·50 1·75
24 **29** 4a. olive-green 8·50 4·75
25 4a. slate-green 15·00 9·00
26 **21** 6a. olive-bistre (1891) 16·00 45·00
a. Opt double, one albino 70·00
27 6a. bistre-brown 10·00 35·00
28 **31** 8a. dull mauve 20·00 42·00
a. 'JEIND' for 'JHIND' £2500
29 8a. magenta (1897) 26·00 55·00
a. Opt double, one albino 90·00
30 **32** 12a. purple/*red* (1896) 14·00 45·00
a. Opt double, one albino 90·00
31 **33** 1r. slate 20·00 85·00
32 **37** 1r. green and carmine (1897) 21·00 85·00
33 **38** 2r. carmine and yellow-brown (1896) £550 £2250
34 3r. brown and green (1896) £850 £1800
35 5r. ultramarine and violet (1896) £900 £1500
17/35 *Set of 14* £2100 £5000

Varieties exist in which the word 'JHIND' measures 10½ mm and 9¾ mm instead of 10 mm. Such varieties are to be found on Nos. 17, 18, 21, 24, 28 and 31.

Raja (Maharaja from 1911) Ranbir Singh, 1887–1959

1900–04. Colours changed.

36 **40** 3p. carmine 1·10 3·50
37 3p. grey (1904) 40 5·00
38 **23** ½a. pale yellow-green (1902) 8·00 10·00
39 ½a. yellow-green (1903) 12·00 21·00
40 **25** 1a. carmine (1902) 3·25 14·00
a. Opt double, one albino 60·00
36/40 *Set of 4* 11·50 30·00

1903–09. King Edward VII. Optd with T **3**.

41 **41** 3p. pale grey 60 20
a. Opt double, one albino 30·00
42 3p. slate-grey (1905) 80 80
43 **42** ½a. green 4·25 3·00
44 **43** 1a. carmine 3·25 2·50
45 **44** 2a. pale violet 8·00 3·25
46 2a. mauve (1906) 6·00 1·75
a. Opt double, one albino 75·00
47 **45** 2a.6p. ultramarine (1909) 3·00 11·00
a. Opt double, one albino 48·00
48 **46** 3a. orange-brown 7·50 1·25
a. Opt double £160 £325
49 **47** 4a. olive 17·00 17·00
a. Opt double, one albino 75·00
50 4a. pale olive 17·00 20·00
51 **48** 6a. bistre (1905) 14·00 45·00
a. Opt double, one albino 80·00
52 **49** 8a. purple (*shades*) 10·00 32·00
53 8a. claret 32·00 60·00
54 **50** 12a. purple/*red* (1905) 7·50 25·00
55 **51** 1r. green and carmine (1905) 10·00 42·00
a. Opt double, one albino £110
41/55 *Set of 11* 75·00 £160

1907–09. Nos. 149/150 of India optd with T **3**.

56 **53** ½a. green 1·75 30
57 **54** 1a. carmine (1909) 3·75 70

1913. King George V. Optd with T **3**.

58 **55** 3p. grey 10 2·50
59 **56** ½a. light green 10 75
60 **57** 1a. aniline carmine 10 60
61 **59** 2a. purple 15 4·75
62 **62** 3a. orange 1·50 17·00
63 **64** 6a. yellow-bistre 14·00 50·00
58/63 *Set of 6* 15·00 70·00

JIND STATE (**4**) JIND STATE (**5**) JIND STATE (**6**)

1914–27. King George V. Optd with T **4**.

64 **55** 3p. grey 2·75 1·25
a. Pale grey 3·00 20
b. Bluish grey 5·50 1·50
c. Slate 5·50
65 **56** ½a. light green 4·25 15
a. Emerald — 3·75
b. Bright green 2·75 30
66 **57** 1a. aniline carmine 3·00 15
67 **58** 1½a. chocolate (Type A) (1922) 7·00 9·50
68 1½a. chocolate (Type B) (1924) 1·60 2·50
69 **59** 2a. purple 4·50 2·00
a. Reddish purple 14·00 1·25
b. Bright reddish violet (1922) 6·50 1·75
70 **61** 2a.6p. ultramarine (1922) 75 7·00
71 **62** 3a. orange 75 7·50
72 **63** 4a. olive 3·25 13·00
73 **64** 6a. yellow-bistre 8·50 32·00
a. Brown-ochre 13·00 26·00
74 **65** 8a. deep magenta 8·00 32·00
a. Deep mauve (1925) 24·00 38·00
b. Bright mauve (1918) — 50·00
75 **66** 12a. carmine-lake 6·00 40·00
76 **67** 1r. red-brown and deep blue-green 18·00 48·00
a. Opt double, one albino 70·00
b. Brown and green 38·00
77 2r. carmine and yellow-brown (1927) 20·00 £200
78 5r. ultramarine and violet (1927) 80·00 £600
64/78 *Set of 15* £150 £900

No. 71 with inverted overprint is of clandestine origin.

1922. No. 192 of India optd 'JIND' in block capitals.

79 **57** 9p. on 1a. rose-carmine 1·25 17·00

1924–27. Optd with T **4**. New colours.

80 **57** 1a. chocolate 6·50 3·75
81 **58** 1½a. rose-carmine (Type B) (1927) 30 2·75
82 **61** 2a.6p. orange (1927) 2·00 12·00
83 **62** 3a. bright blue (1925) 4·00 9·00
80/83 *Set of 4* 11·50 25·00

Nos. 81/82 with inverted overprint are of clandestine origin.

1927–37. King George V (Nasik printing, wmk Mult Star), optd at Nasik with T **5** or **6** (rupee values).

84 **55** 3p. slate 10 10
w. Wmk inverted 9·00
85 **56** ½a. green (1929) 50 35

86 **80** 9p. deep green (1932) 2·25 40
87 **57** 1a. chocolate (1928) 15 10
w. Wmk inverted — 5·50
88 **82** 1a.3p. mauve (1932) 25 30
89 **58** 1½a. rose-carmine (Type B) (1930) 1·25 5·50
w. Wmk inverted 2·25 4·25
90 **70** 2a. purple (1928) 6·50 1·25
w. Wmk inverted 7·50 40
91 **61** 2a.6p. orange (1930) 4·50 20·00
w. Wmk inverted 1·25 18·00
92 **62** 3a. bright blue (1930) 10·00 29·00
w. Wmk inverted 11·00
93 **83** 3a.6p. ultramarine (1937) 6·50 40·00
w. Wmk inverted 75 28·00
94 **71** 4a. sage-green (1928) 10·00 5·50
w. Wmk inverted 2·50 4·50
95 **64** 6a. bistre (1937) 75 28·00
w. Wmk inverted 15·00
96 **65** 8a. reddish purple (1930) 13·00 4·00
w. Wmk inverted 14·00
97 **66** 12a. claret (1930) 22·00 45·00
w. Wmk inverted 13·00 35·00
98 **67** 1r. chocolate and green (1930) 14·00 16·00
w. Wmk inverted — 85·00
99 2r. carmine and orange (1930) 80·00 £225
w. Wmk inverted 38·00
100 5r. ultramarine and purple (1928) 20·00 55·00
w. Wmk inverted 60·00
101 10r. green and carmine (1928) 25·00 18·00
102 15r. blue and olive (*wmk inverted*) (1929) £190 £1500
103 25r. orange and blue (1929) £350 £2000
84/103 *Set of 20* £625 £3500

1934. New types and colours. Optd with T **5**.
104 **79** ½a. green 30 25
105 **81** 1a. chocolate 2·00 30
w. Wmk inverted — 14·00
106 **59** 2a. vermilion 7·00 70
107 **62** 3a. carmine 3·25 40
108 **63** 4a. sage-green 3·25 1·75
104/108 *Set of 5* 14·00 3·00

1937–38. King George VI. Nos. 247/264 optd with T **5** or T **6** (rupee values).
109 **91** 3p. slate 10·00 3·50
110 ½a. red-brown 1·00 7·00
111 9p. green (1937) 1·00 4·00
112 1a. carmine (1937) 75 75
113 **92** 2a. vermilion 3·50 30·00
114 **93** 2a.6p. bright violet 1·50 40·00
115 **94** 3a. yellow-green 7·00 38·00
116 **95** 3a.6p. bright blue 8·00 40·00
117 **96** 4a. brown 17·00 32·00
118 **97** 6a. turquoise-green 10·00 60·00
119 **98** 8a. slate-violet 14·00 45·00
120 **99** 12a. lake 5·00 55·00
121 **100** 1r. grey and red-brown 13·00 65·00
122 2r. purple and brown 15·00 £250
123 5r. green and blue 32·00 £150
124 10r. purple and claret 60·00 £130
125 15r. brown and green £110 £1600
126 25r. slate-violet and purple £1100 £2250
109/126 *Set of 18* £1300 £4250

JIND
(7)

1941–43. King George VI. Optd with T **7**.

(a) Stamps of 1937. W **69** *(inverted on 15r.)*
127 **91** 3p. slate 20·00 27·00
128 ½a. red-brown 1·25 3·75
129 9p. green 17·00 32·00
130 1a. carmine 1·00 8·00
131 **100** 1r. grey and red-brown 11·00 40·00
132 2r. purple and brown 20·00 55·00
133 5r. green and blue 45·00 £180
134 10r. purple and claret 60·00 £130
135 15r. brown and green £200 £300
136 25r. slate-violet and purple 60·00 £500
127/136 *Set of 10* £375 £1100

(b) Stamps of 1940–1943
137 **100a** 3p. slate (1942) 50 2·00
138 ½a. purple (1943) 50 2·50
139 9p. green (1942) 75 4·50
140 1a. carmine (1942) 1·00 1·50
141 **101** 1a.3p. yellow-brown 1·00 6·50
142 1½a. dull violet (*litho*) (1942) 10·00 7·00
142*a* 1½a. dull violet (*typo*) (1943) 3·00 8·00
143 2a. vermilion 1·00 7·00
144 3a. bright violet (*litho*) (1942) 10·00 9·00
144*a* 3a. bright violet (*typo*) (1943) 6·00 11·00
145 3½a. bright blue 9·00 17·00
146 **102** 4a. brown 2·75 8·50
147 6a. turquoise-green 9·00 22·00
148 8a. slate-violet 7·00 20·00
149 12a. lake 14·00 25·00
137/149 *Set of 13* 50·00 £120

STAMP BOOKLET

1929 (?). Black on brown covers (No. SB18a of India) with red opt 'JIND STATE' on front. Stitched.
SB1 1r. booklet containing 16×1a. (No. 87) in blocks of 4 £2750

OFFICIAL STAMPS

SERVICE

SERVICE (O 14) SERVICE (O 15) JHIND STATE (O 16)

1885 (1 July). Queen Victoria. Nos. 1/3 of Jind optd with T O **14**.
O1 **23** ½a. blue green 4·50 60
a. Opt Type **1** inverted £160 75·00
O2 **25** 1a. brown-purple 1·00 10
a. Opt Type **1** inverted 21·00 7·50
w. Wmk inverted † £550
O3 **27** 2a. dull blue 55·00 55·00
a. Opt Type **1** inverted £1600 £2250

The three values have had the overprint reprinted in the same way as the ordinary stamps of 1885. See note after No. 6.

1885. Nos. 7/9 of Jind optd with T O **15**.
O7 **23** ½a. blue-green (R.) £170
a. 'JEEND STATE' double, one albino £325
O8 **25** 1a. brown-purple £160
O9 **27** 2a. dull blue (R.) £150
O7/O9 *Set of 3* £450

1886. Optd with T O **16**, in red.
O10 **23** ½a. blue-green 55·00
a. 'ERVICE' £6000
b. 'JEIND' £950
c. 'JHIND STATE' double, one albino £130
O11 **27** 2a. dull blue 65·00
a. 'ERVICE' £3750
b. 'JEIND' £2250
c. 'SERVICE' double, one albino £120
d. 'JHIND STATE' double, one albino £120

1886–1902. Optd with T O **16**.
O12 **23** ½a. blue-green 6·00 10
a. 'JHIND STATE' double, one albino 85·00
O13 **25** 1a. brown-purple 60·00
a. 'ERVICE'
b. 'JEIND' £800
c. 'SERVICE' double, one albino 65·00
O14 1a. plum (1902) 24·00 1·75
O15 **27** 2a. dull blue 8·00 1·75
a. 'SERVICE' double, one albino 70·00
b. 'SERVICE' treble, two albino 85·00
O16 2a. ultramarine 5·50 40
a. 'JHIND STATE' double, one albino 90·00
O17 **29** 4a. olive-green (1892) 8·00 4·50
a. 'JHIND STATE' double, one albino 80·00
O18 4a. slate-green 10·00 6·50
O19 **31** 8a. dull mauve (1892) 12·00 9·00
O20 8a. magenta (1897) 12·00 14·00
a. 'JHIND STATE' double, one albino 80·00
O21 **37** 1r. green and carmine (1896) 12·00 75·00
a. 'SERVICE' double, one albino £120
b. 'JHIND STATE' treble, two albino £110
O12/O21 *Set of 6* 60·00 80·00

Varieties mentioned in note after No. 35 exist on Nos. O12, O15, O17 and O20.

Printings up to and including that of October 1897 had the 'SERVICE overprint. T O **15**, applied to sheets already overprinted with T **3**. From the printing of December 1899 onwards 'SERVICE' and 'JHIND STATE' were overprinted at one operation, as T O **16**, to provide fresh supplies of Nos. O12, O14 and O21.

1902. Colour changed. Optd with T O **16**.
O22 **23** ½a. yellow-green 5·00 40
a. 'V' of 'SERVICE' omitted £300 £130

No. O22a normally shows a tiny trace of the 'V' remaining. Examples showing the letter completely missing are worth much more.

1903–06. King Edward VII stamps of India optd with T O **16**.
O23 **41** 3p. pale grey 1·75 10
O24 3p. slate-grey (1906) 1·50 10
O25 **42** ½a. green 6·00 10
a. 'HIND' £4250 £450
b. Opt double, one albino 60·00
c. 'SERV CE' † £600
O26 **43** 1a. carmine 6·50 10
a. 'HIND' £6000 £450
b. Opt double, one albino 55·00
O27 **44** 2a. pale violet 6·00 1·50
O28 2a. mauve 3·75 10
O29 **47** 4a. olive 4·50 45
a. Opt double, one albino 90·00
O30 **49** 8a. purple (*shades*) 20·00 5·00
O31 8a. claret 13·00 1·50
O32 **51** 1r. green and carmine (1906) 3·25 2·25
O23/O32 *Set of 7* 35·00 4·00

The 'HIND' error Nos. O25a and O26a occurred on one position in the bottom row of the sheet.

1907. Nos. 149/150 of India optd with T O **16**.
O33 **53** ½a. green 2·25 10
O34 **54** 1a. carmine 3·50 10

1914–27. King George V. Official stamps of India optd with T **4**.
O35 **55** 3p. grey 10 10
a. 'JIND STATE' double, one albino 85·00
b. Pale grey 40 10
c. Bluish grey — 1·25
O36 **56** ½a. light green 10 10
a. Emerald 5·00 40
b. Bright green (1923) 2·00 30
O37 **57** 1a. aniline carmine 75 10
a. Pale rose-carmine 5·00 20
O39 **59** 2a. purple 40 30
a. Reddish purple — 20
b. Deep mauve 4·75 1·50
O40 **63** 4a. olive 2·00 20
O41 **64** 6a. brown-ochre (1926) 3·50 2·50
O42 **65** 8a. deep magenta 1·25 1·50
a. Deep mauve (1923) 7·50 2·25
O43 **67** 1r. red-brown and deep blue-green 8·00 2·25
a. 'JIND STATE' double, one albino 70·00
b. Brown and green (1923) 32·00
O44 2r. carmine and yellow-brown (1927) 21·00 75·00
O45 5r. ultramarine and violet (1927) 45·00 £500
O35/O45 *Set of 10* 75·00 £550

No. O40 with double overprint is of clandestine origin.

1924. As 1914–1927. New colour.
O46 **57** 1a. chocolate 60 10

JIND STATE SERVICE (O 17) JIND STATE SERVICE (O 18) JIND SERVICE (O 19)

1927–37. King George V (Nasik printing, wmk Mult Star), optd with Types O **17** or O **18** (rupee values).
O47 **55** 3p. slate (1928) 10 20
O48 **56** ½a. green (1929) 10 1·00
O49 **80** 9p. deep green (*litho*) (1932) 1·00 15
O49*a* 9p. deep green (*typo*) — 1·50
O50 **57** 1a. chocolate 10 10
w. Wmk inverted 1·00
O51 **82** 1a.3p. mauve (1932) 40 15
w. Wmk inverted 1·60 80
O52 **70** 2a. purple (1929) 25 15
O53 **61** 2a.6p. orange (1937) 2·00 23·00
O54 **71** 4a. sage-green (1929) 35 25
w. Wmk inverted 4·75 2·25
O55 **64** 6a. bistre (1937) 6·50 30·00
w. Wmk inverted 8·00 28·00
O56 **65** 8a. reddish purple (1929) — 3·25
w. Wmk inverted 75 2·00
O57 **66** 12a. claret (1928) 2·75 27·00
O58 **67** 1r. chocolate and green (1928) 9·00 11·00
O59 2r. carmine and orange (1930) 85·00 65·00
w. Wmk inverted 55·00
O60 5r. ultramarine and purple (1929) 14·00 £425
O61 10r. green and carmine (1928) 60·00 £190
w. Wmk inverted 95·00
O47/O61 *Set of 15* £140 £700

1934. Optd with Type O **17**.
O62 **79** ½a. green 20 15
O63 **81** 1a. chocolate 20 15
O64 **59** 2a. vermilion 30 15
w. Wmk inverted 3·50 6·50
O65 **63** 4a. sage-green 10·00 30
O62/O65 *Set of 4* 9·75 65

1937–40. King George VI. Optd with Types O **17** or O **18** (rupee values).
O66 **91** ½a. red-brown (1938) 85·00 30
O67 9p. green 6·50 28·00
O68 1a. carmine 6·00 30
O69 **100** 1r. grey and red-brown (1940) 75·00 85·00
O70 2r. purple and brown (1940) 85·00 £550
O71 5r. green and blue (1940) £150 £700
O72 10r. purple and claret (1940) £700 £2000
O66/O72 *Set of 7* £1000 £3000

1939–43.

(a) Official stamps optd with T **7**
O73 **O 20** 3p. slate 60 2·00
O74 ½a. red-brown 4·50 1·25
O75 ½a. purple (1943) 60 30
O76 9p. green 3·00 16·00
O77 1a. carmine 3·75 15
O78 1½a. dull violet (1942) 9·00 3·00
O79 2a. vermilion 8·50 30
w. Wmk inverted 10·00 9·00
O80 2½a. bright violet 5·00 13·00
O81 4a. brown 8·50 8·50
O82 8a. slate-violet 12·00 14·00

(b) Postage stamps optd with T O **19**
O83 **100** 1r. grey and red-brown (1942) 18·00 80·00
O84 2r. purple and brown (1942) 42·00 £325
O85 5r. green and blue (1942) 70·00 £800
O86 10r. purple and claret (1942) £225 £1300
O73/O86 *Set of 14* £350 £2250

Jind was absorbed into the Patiala and East Punjab States Union by 20 August 1948

NABHA

PRICES FOR STAMPS ON COVER TO 1945	
Nos. 1/3	*from* × 15
Nos. 4/6	—
Nos. 10/36	*from* × 12
Nos. 37/117	*from* × 7
Nos. O1/O68	*from* × 15

OVERPRINTS. From 1885 to 1926 these were applied typo by the Government of India Central Printing Press, Calcutta, and from 1927 by litho at the Security Press, Nasik, *unless otherwise stated.*

Raja Hira Singh, 1871–1911.

NABHA STATE (1) NABHA STATE (2)

1885 (1 July). Queen Victoria. Optd with T **1**.
1 **23** ½a. blue-green 8·00 13·00
2 **25** 1a. brown-purple 95·00 £375
3 **27** 2a. dull blue 45·00 £100
4 **17** 4a. green £140 £400
5 **31** 8a. dull mauve £600
6 **33** 1r. slate £600
1/6 *Set of 6* £1300

All six values have had the overprint reprinted. On the reprints the words 'NABHA' and 'STATE' both measure 9¼ mm in length, whereas on the originals these words measure 11 and 10 mm respectively. The varieties with overprint double come from the reprints.

1885 (Nov)–**1900.** Optd with T **2**.

(a) In red
10 **23** ½a. blue-green 4·75 3·00
11 **27** 2a. dull blue 6·00 5·00
a. Opt double, one albino £120

12 **17** 4a. green ... 80·00 £425
13 **33** 1r. slate ... £200 £600
a. Opt double, one albino ... £275
10/13 *Set of 4* ... £250 £900

(b) In black (Nov 1885–1897)

14 **23** ½a. blue-green (1888) ... 1·50 10
15 **24** 9p. carmine (1892) ... 3·50 7·50
16 **25** 1a. brown-purple ... 5·50 1·00
17 1a. plum ... 6·50 2·00
18 **26** 1a.6p. sepia (1891) ... 4·25 8·50
a. 'ABHA' for 'NABHA' ... £500
19 **27** 2a. dull blue (1888) ... 6·50 3·00
20 2a. ultramarine ... 6·00 3·25
21 **28** 3a. orange (1889) ... 30·00 48·00
a. Opt double, one albino ... 75·00
22 3a. brown-orange ... 10·00 3·50
23 **29** 4a. olive-green (1888) ... 11·00 6·50
24 4a. slate-green ... 11·00 5·50
25 **21** 6a. olive-bistre (1889) ... 24·00 27·00
26 6a. bistre-brown ... 4·50 7·50
27 **31** 8a. dull mauve ... 6·50 7·00
a. Opt double, one albino ... 90·00
28 **32** 12a. purple/*red* (1889) ... 6·00 10·00
a. Opt double, one albino ... 75·00
29 **33** 1r. slate (1888) ... 24·00 90·00
30 **37** 1r. green and carmine (1893) ... 27·00 22·00
a. 'N BHA' for 'NABHA' ...
b. Opt double, one albino ... 95·00
31 **38** 2r. carmine and yellow-brown (1897) ... £250 £425
a. Opt double, one albino ... £475
32 3r. brown and green (1897) ... £275 £650
33 5r. ultramarine and violet (1897) ... £275 £1000
14/33 *Set of 15* ... £800 £2000

(c) New value. In black (Nov 1900)

36 **40** 3p. carmine ... 30 20

1903–09. King Edward VII. Optd with T **2**.

37 **41** 3p. pale grey ... 75 15
a. 'NAB STA' for 'NABHA STATE' ... £1300
b. Opt double, one albino ... 45·00
37*c* 3p. slate-grey (1906) ... 75 15
38 **42** ½a. green ... 1·10 70
a. 'NABH' for 'NABHA' ... £1500
39 **43** 1a. carmine ... 3·00 2·00
40 **44** 2a. pale violet ... 8·00 5·00
40*a* 2a. mauve ... 7·00 35
40*b* **45** 2a.6p. ultramarine (1909) ... 19·00 £120
ba. Opt double, one albino ... 32·00
41 **46** 3a. orange-brown ... 2·75 40
a. Opt double, one albino ... 80·00
42 **47** 4a. olive ... 10·00 3·25
43 **48** 6a. olive-bistre ... 11·00 40·00
a. Opt double, one albino ... 60·00
44 **49** 8a. purple ... 12·00 50·00
44*a* 8a. claret ... 30·00 55·00
45 **50** 12a. purple/*red* ... 10·00 50·00
46 **51** 1r. green and carmine ... 12·00 32·00
37/46 *Set of 11* ... 80·00 £275

1907. Nos. 149/150 of India optd with T **2**.

47 **53** ½a. green ... 1·50 1·75
48 **54** 1a. carmine ... 2·25 70

Maharaja Ripudaman (Gurcharan) Singh, 1911–1928.

1913–23. King George V. Optd with T **2**.

49 **55** 3p. grey ... 2·00 1·60
a. Pale grey ... 1·75 40
b. Bluish grey ... 4·00 3·25
c. Slate ... 4·25
50 **56** ½a. light green ... 2·50 1·75
a. Emerald ... 5·50 1·25
b. Bright green ... 3·00 1·75
51 **57** 1a. aniline carmine ... 1·10 10
52 **59** 2a. purple ... 2·75 3·25
a. Reddish purple ... 6·50 3·00
b. Deep mauve ... 6·00 4·00
53 **62** 3a. orange ... 2·75 75
a. Dull orange ... 5·00 3·00
w. Wmk inverted ... £200
54 **63** 4a. olive ... 2·75 4·75
55 **64** 6a. yellow-bistre ... 6·00 9·00
a. Brown-ochre ... 6·50 13·00
56 **65** 8a. deep magenta ... 24·00 18·00
a. Deep mauve ... 19·00 10·00
b. Bright mauve (1918) ... 28·00
57 **66** 12a. carmine-lake ... 11·00 45·00
58 **67** 1r. red-brown and deep blue-green ... 23·00 25·00
a. Opt double, one albino ... 85·00
b. Brown and green ... 50·00 28·00
c. Orange-brown and deep turquoise-green (1923) ... 55·00
49/58 *Set of 10* ... 65·00 90·00

1924. As 1913. New colour.

59 **57** 1a. chocolate ... 16·00 9·00

No. 59 with inverted or double overprint is of clandestine origin.

NABHA STATE (**3**) NABHA STATE (**4**)

1927–36. King George V (Nasik printing, wmk Mult Star), optd as T **3** or **4** (rupee values).

60 **55** 3p. slate (1932) ... 1·75 15
w. Wmk inverted ... 9·00 5·00
61 **56** ½a. green (1928) ... 2·50 30
61*a* **80** 9p. deep green (*litho*) (1934) ... 11·00 12·00
61*b* 9p. deep green (*typo*) ... 6·00 1·40
62 **57** 1a. chocolate ... 2·25 15
w. Wmk inverted ... — 6·50
63 **82** 1a.3p. mauve (1936) ... 5·00 7·50
w. Wmk inverted ... 1·50
64 **70** 2a. purple (1932) ... 2·75 35
65 **61** 2a.6p. orange (1932) ... 4·00 17·00
66 **62** 3a. bright blue (1930) ... 7·00 3·50
67 **71** 4a. sage-green (1932) ... 10·00 4·75
71 **67** 2r. carmine and orange (1932) ... 60·00 £300
72 5r. ultramarine and purple (*wmk inverted*) (1932) ... £110 £800
60/72 *Set of 11* ... £190 £1000

Maharaja Partab Singh, 1928–1971

1936–37. New types and colours. Optd as T **3**.

73 **79** ½a. green ... 1·25 50
74 **81** 1a. chocolate ... 1·00 50
75 **62** 3a. carmine (1937) ... 4·25 23·00
76 **63** 4a. sage-green (1937) ... 12·00 6·00
73/76 *Set of 4* ... 17·00 27·00

NABHA STATE (**5**) NABHA (**6**)

1938. King George VI. Nos. 247/264 optd as T **3** (3p. to 1a.), T **5** (2a. to 12a.) or T **4** (rupee values). W **69** (inverted on 15r.).

77 **91** 3p. slate ... 13·00 2·75
78 ½a. red-brown ... 7·50 2·00
79 9p. green ... 18·00 5·50
80 1a. carmine ... 6·00 2·25
81 **92** 2a. vermilion ... 2·50 16·00
82 **93** 2a.6p. bright violet ... 3·50 22·00
83 **94** 3a. yellow-green ... 2·50 10·00
84 **95** 3a.6p. bright blue ... 7·50 48·00
85 **96** 4a. brown ... 13·00 8·00
86 **97** 6a. turquoise-green ... 7·00 50·00
87 **98** 8a. slate-violet ... 4·25 48·00
88 **99** 12a. lake ... 3·00 35·00
89 **100** 1r. grey and red-brown ... 16·00 50·00
90 2r. purple and brown ... 38·00 £200
91 5r. green and blue ... 48·00 £450
92 10r. purple and claret ... 65·00 £900
93 15r. brown and green ... £375 £1800
94 25r. slate-violet and purple ... £200 £1800
w. Wmk inverted ... £450 £2250
77/94 *Set of 18* ... £750 £5000

1941–45. King George VI. Optd with T **6**.

(a) Stamps of 1937

95 **91** 3p. slate (1942) ... 50·00 9·50
96 ½a. red-brown (1942) ... 90·00 10·00
97 9p. green (1942) ... 12·00 17·00
98 1a. carmine (1942) ... 15·00 6·50
95/98 *Set of 4* ... £150 38·00

(b) Stamps of 1940–1943

105 **100a** 3p. slate (1942) ... 1·25 1·25
106 ½a. purple (1943) ... 1·00 2·50
107 9p. green (1942) ... 1·00 2·75
108 1a. carmine (1945) ... 1·00 5·00
109 **101** 1a.3p. yellow-brown ... 1·00 4·50
110 1½a. dull violet (*litho*) (1942) ... 2·50 3·25
110*a* 1½a. dull violet (*typo*) (1943) ... 4·00 5·00
111 2a. vermilion (1943) ... 2·00 4·50
112 3a. bright violet (*typo*) (1943) ... 2·00 7·50
113 3½a. bright blue (1944) ... 10·00 £100
114 **102** 4a. brown ... 1·00 1·00
115 6a. turquoise-green (1943) ... 18·00 70·00
116 8a. slate-violet (1943) ... 17·00 60·00
117 12a. lake (1943) ... 16·00 90·00
105/117 *Set of 13* ... 65·00 £325

OFFICIAL STAMPS

SERVICE

SERVICE (**O 8**) NABHA STATE (**O 9**)

1885 (1 July). Nos. 1/3 of Nabha optd with T O **8**.

O1 **23** ½a. blue-green ... 12·00 3·00
O2 **25** 1a. brown-purple ... 70 20
a. Opt Type O **8** double ... † £3500
O3 **27** 2a. dull blue ... £140 £275
O1/O3 *Set of 3* ... £140 £275

The three values have had the overprint reprinted in the same way as the ordinary stamps of 1885.

1885 (Nov)**–97.** Optd with T O **9**.

(a) In red

O4 **23** ½a. blue-green ... 14·00 7·50
O5 **27** 2a. deep blue ... 2·75 55

(b) In black (Nov 1885–1897)

O6 **23** ½a. blue-green (1888) ... 40 10
a. 'SERVICE.' with stop ... £200 3·25
b. 'S ATE' for 'STATE' ...
c. 'SERVICE' double, one albino ... 85·00
O7 **25** 1a. brown-purple ... 4·00 60
O8 1a. plum ... 5·00 25
a. 'SERVICE.' with stop ... 15·00 75
ab. 'SERVICE.' with stop, and 'NABHA STATE' double ... £3500 £350
O9 **27** 2a. dull blue (1888) ... 7·50 3·25
O10 2a. ultramarine ... 8·00 3·75
O11 **28** 3a. orange (1889) ... 32·00 £160
O12 3a. brown-orange ... 45·00 £200
a. 'NABHA STATE' double, one albino ... £120
O13 **29** 4a. olive-green (1888) ... 8·00 2·50
O14 4a. slate-green ... 6·50 1·50
O15 **21** 6a. olive-bistre (1889) ... 32·00 55·00
a. 'SERVICE' double, one albino ... 85·00
O16 6a. bistre-brown ... £850
O17 **31** 8a. dull mauve (1889) ... 7·50 3·00
O18 **32** 12a. purple/*red* (1889) ... 9·00 30·00
a. SERVICE' double, one albino ... 90·00
b. 'NABHA STATE' double, one albino ... 75·00
O19 **33** 1r. slate (1889) ... 75·00 £600
O20 **37** 1r. green and carmine (1.97) ... 45·00 £130
O6/O20 *Set of 10* ... £200 £900

Printings up to and including that of August 1895 had the 'SERVICE' overprint applied to sheets of stamps already overprinted with T **2**. From the printing of January 1897 onwards the two parts of the overprint were applied at one operation. This method was only used for printings of the ½a., 1a. and 1r. (No. O20).

1903–06. King Edward VII stamps of India optd with T O **9**.

O24 **41** 3p. pale grey (1906) ... 12·00 42·00
O25 3p. slate-grey (1906) ... 7·00 28·00
a. Opt double, one albino ... 55·00
O26 **42** ½a. green ... 1·00 50
O27 **43** 1a. carmine ... 80 10
O28 **44** 2a. pale violet ... 5·50 2·25
O29 2a. mauve ... 6·00 40
a. Opt double, one albino ... 80·00
O30 **47** 4a. olive ... 3·50 50
O32 **49** 8a. purple (*shades*) ... 3·75 1·50
a. Opt double, one albino ... 60·00
O33 8a. claret ... 35·00 13·00
O34 **51** 1r. green and carmine ... 3·75 3·75
O24/O34 *Set of 7* ... 23·00 32·00

1907. Nos. 149/150 of India optd with T O **9**.

O35 **53** ½a. green ... 2·75 50
a. Opt double, one albino ... 29·00
O36 **54** 1a. carmine ... 1·50 30
a. Opt double, one albino ... 48·00

1913. King George V. Optd with T O **9**.

O37 **63** 4a. olive ... 10·00 80·00
O38 **67** 1r. red-brown and deep blue-green ... 85·00 £600
a. Opt double, one albino ... £150

1913–23. Official stamps of India optd with T **2**.

O39 **55** 3p. grey ... 3·00 14·00
a. Pale grey ... 2·25 11·00
b. Bluish grey ... 2·00 15·00
c. Slate ... 1·75 15·00
O40 **56** ½a. light green ... 1·00 50
a. Emerald ... 3·50 20
b. Bright green ... 3·50 15
O41 **57** 1a. aniline carmine ... 1·50 20
O42 **59** 2a. purple ... 2·50 1·75
a. Reddish purple ... 7·50 1·50
b. Deep mauve ... 7·00 50
c. Bright reddish violet (1923) ...
O43 **63** 4a. olive ... 2·00 1·00
O44 **65** 8a. deep magenta ... 4·50 2·25
a. Deep mauve ... 11·00
b. Bright mauve (1918) ... 18·00
O46 **67** 1r. red-brown and deep blue-green ... 11·00 8·00
a. Brown and green ... 15·00 9·00
O39/O46 *Set of 7* ... 22·00 21·00

NABHA STATE SERVICE (O **10**) NABHA SERVICE (O **11**)

1932–42?. King George V (Nasik printing, wmk Mult Star), optd at Nabha with T O **10**.

O47 **55** 3p. slate ... 10 15
O48 **81** 1a. chocolate (1935) ... 35 15
O49 **63** 4a. sage-green (1942?) ... 29·00 2·50
O50 **65** 8a. reddish purple (1937) ... 1·00 3·25
O47/O50 *Set of 4* ... 29·00 5·50

1938. King George VI. Optd as T O **10**.

O53 **91** 9p. green ... 12·00 4·00
O54 1a. carmine ... 18·00 1·10

1940–43.

(a) Official stamps optd with T **6**

O55 **O 20** 3p. slate (1942) ... 1·25 3·00
O56 ½a. red-brown (1942) ... 1·10 30
O57 ½a. purple (1943) ... 7·00 2·50
O58 9p. green ... 1·25 50
O59 1a. carmine (1942) ... 2·00 20
O61 1½a. dull violet (1942) ... 70 40
O62 2a. vermilion (1942) ... 2·25 1·50
w. Wmk inverted ... 13·00 6·00
O64 4a. brown (1942) ... 3·00 4·25
O65 8a. slate-violet (1942) ... 5·00 27·00

(b) Postage stamps optd with T O **11**

O66 **100** 1r. grey and red-brown (1942) ... 12·00 55·00
O67 2r. purple and brown (1942) ... 50·00 £450
O68 5r. green and blue (1942) ... £275 £1000
O55/O68 *Set of 12* ... £325 £1400

Nabha was absorbed into the Patiala and East Punjab States Union by 20 August 1948.

PATIALA

PRICES FOR STAMPS ON COVER TO 1945	
Nos. 1/6	*from* × 10
Nos. 7/34	*from* × 6
Nos. 35/45	*from* × 8
Nos. 46/115	*from* × 4
Nos. O1/O84	*from* × 15

OVERPRINTS. From 1885 to 1926 these were applied typo by the Government of India Central Printing Press, Calcutta, and from 1927 by litho at the Security Press, Nasik, *unless otherwise stated.*

Maharaja Rajindra Singh, 1876–1900

(**1**)

PUTTIALLA STATE (**2**) PATIALA STATE (**3**)

1884 (1 Oct). Queen Victoria. Optd with T **1**, in red.

1 **23** ½a. blue-green .... 8·00 4·75
a. Opt double, one sideways £5000 £1200
b. Opt double, one albino £150
2 **25** 1a. brown-purple .... 95·00 £140
a. Opt double ....
b. Optd in red and in black £1000
3 **27** 2a. dull blue .... 22·00 16·00
4 **17** 4a. green £160 £190
5 **31** 8a. dull mauve £600 £2000
a. Opt inverted £20000
b. Optd in red and in black £250 £950
ba. Ditto. Opts inverted £16000
c. Opt double, one albino £650
6 **33** 1r. slate £225 £1000
1/6 *Set of* 6 (*inclg No.*5) £1000 £3000

Nos. 5a and 5ba each occur once in the setting of 120. The 8a. value also exists with a trial overprint (showing the words more curved) reading downwards (*Price £800 unused*), which should not be confused with No. 5a.

1885. Optd with T **2**.

(a) In red

7 **23** ½a. blue-green .... 4·75 30
a. 'AUTTIALLA' .... 28·00 75·00
b. 'STATE' only ....
c. Wide spacing between lines .... 14·00 17·00
8 **27** 2a. dull blue .... 22·00 1·75
a. 'AUTTIALLA' £100
b. Wide spacing between lines .... 65·00 85·00
ba. Ditto 'AUTTIALLA' £2000
9 **17** 4a. green .... 10·00 4·25
a. Optd in red and in black £425
b. Wide spacing between lines £750
c. Opt double, one albino .... 90·00
10 **33** 1r. slate .... 65·00 £160
a. 'AUTTIALLA' £750
b. Wide spacing between lines £700

(b) In black

11 **25** 1a. brown-purple .... 1·50 60
a. Optd in red and in black .... 32·00 £170
b. 'AUTTIALLA' £130
ba. Ditto. Optd in red and in black £2750
c. Opt double £325 £375
d. Wide spacing between lines £550
12 **31** 8a. dull mauve .... 65·00 £140
a. 'AUTTIALLA' £650
b. Opt double, one albino £140
c. Wide spacing between lines £750
7/12 *Set of* 6 .... £150 £275

The ½, 2 and 4a. (T **29**), and 1r. (all overprinted in black), are proofs.

All six values exist with reprinted overprints, and the error 'AUTTIALLA STATE' has been reprinted in complete sheets on all values and in addition in black on the ½, 2, 4a. and 1r. Nearly all these however, are found with the word 'REPRINT' overprinted upon them. On the genuine 'AUTTIALLA' errors, which occur on R. 9/12 in the setting of 120, the word 'STATE' is 8½ mm long; on the reprints only 7¾ mm.

Nos. 7c, 8b, 9b, 10b, 11d and 12c show 1¼ mm spacing between the two lines of overprint. The normal spacing is ¾ mm.

Nos. 7/8 and 10/12 exist with error 'PUTTILLA', but their status is uncertain (*Price, from £1200, unused*).

1891–96. Optd with T **3**.

13 **23** ½a. blue-green (1892) .... 2·50 10
14 **24** 9p. carmine .... 2·00 3·25
15 **25** 1a. brown-purple .... 2·50 30
16 1a. plum .... 4·00 2·00
a. 'PATIALA' omitted £375 £600
b. 'PA' omitted ....
c. 'PATIA' omitted ....
d. 'PATIAL' omitted ....
17 **26** 1a.6p. sepia .... 3·00 3·00
18 **27** 2a. dull blue (1896) .... 4·00 40
19 2a. ultramarine .... 5·00 1·75
20 **28** 3a. brown-orange .... 3·75 1·50
21 **29** 4a. olive-green (1896) .... 7·50 1·50
a. 'PATIALA' omitted £800 £375
22 4a. slate-green .... 7·50 1·50
23 **21** 6a. bistre-brown .... 4·75 17·00
24 6a. olive-bistre .... 14·00 38·00
a. Opt double, one albino £110
25 **31** 8a. dull mauve ....
26 8a. magenta (1896) .... 7·50 18·00
27 **32** 12a. purple/*red* .... 6·00 19·00
28 **37** 1r. green and carmine (1896) .... 9·00 65·00
29 **38** 2r. carmine and yellow-brown (1895) £300 £1800
30 3r. brown and green (1895) £350 £1900
a. Opt double, one albino £425
b. Opt treble, two albino £350
31 5r. ultramarine and violet (1895) £400 £2000
13/31 *Set of* 14 .... £1000 £5250

The errors on the 1a. plum and 4a. olive-green occur on R. 19/1 in the December 1898 printing. Nos. 16b/16d are early stages of the error before the entire word was omitted.

1899–1902. Colours changed and new value. Optd with T **3**.

32 **40** 3p. carmine (1899) 30 15
a. Pair, one without opt £6500
b. Opt double, one albino .... 85·00
33 **23** ½a. pale yellow-green .... 1·10 1·75
34 **25** 1a. carmine .... 2·50 3·00
32/34 *Set of* 3 .... 3·50 4·25

Maharaja Bhupindra Singh, 1900–1938

1903–06. King Edward VII. Optd with T **3**.

35 **41** 3p. pale grey 40 10
a. Additional albino opt of Jind Type **3** £325
b. 'S' in 'STATE' sideways (R. 20/1) £1100 £1300
36 3p. slate-grey (1906) 75 10
37 **42** ½a. green .... 1·50 15
38 **43** 1a. carmine .... 3·75 10
a. Horiz pair, one without opt £1600
39 **44** 2a. pale violet .... 4·00 65
a. Mauve .... 18·00 1·25
40 **46** 3a. orange-brown .... 3·25 50
41 **47** 4a. olive (1905) .... 6·50 2·00
42 **48** 6a. olive-bistre (1905) .... 6·50 20·00
43 **49** 8a. purple (1906) .... 8·00 7·50
44 **50** 12a. purple/*red* (1906) .... 14·00 48·00
45 **51** 1r. green and carmine (1905) .... 8·00 13·00
35/45 *Set of* 10 .... 50·00 85·00

1912. Nos. 149/150 of India optd with T **3**.

46 **53** ½a. green 60 25
47 **54** 1a. carmine .... 1·75 1·50

1912–26. King George V. Optd with T **3**.

48 **55** 3p. grey .... 1·75 10
a. Pale grey .... 2·75 30
b. Bluish grey .... 2·50
c. Slate .... 6·50 2·25
ca. 'Rs' flaw .... 70·00
49 **56** ½a. light green .... 2·50 60
a. Emerald .... 6·50 1·25
b. Bright green .... 5·00 2·00
50 **57** 1a. aniline carmine .... 2·50 20
51 **58** 1½a. chocolate (Type A) (1922) 50 55
52 **59** 2a. purple .... 3·75 2·00
a. Reddish purple .... 9·00
b. Deep mauve .... 9·00
c. Bright reddish violet (1923) .... 12·00
53 **62** 3a. orange .... 5·50 2·50
54 **63** 4a. olive .... 6·00 3·75
55 **64** 6a. yellow-bistre .... 4·75 5·50
a. Brown-ochre (1921) .... 8·00 9·00
56 **65** 8a. deep magenta .... 7·50 5·00
a. Purple (1921) .... 11·00 7·00
57 **66** 12a. carmine-lake .... 8·00 12·00
58 **67** 1r. red-brown and deep blue-green .... 19·00 22·00
a. Opt double, one albino .... 75·00
b. Brown and green (1924) .... 35·00
59 2r. carmine and yell-brn (1926) .... 24·00 £160
60 5r. ultramarine and violet (1926) .... 60·00 £450

1923–26. As 1912–1926. New colours.

61 **57** 1a. chocolate .... 4·00 50
62 **62** 3a. ultramarine (1926) .... 7·00 18·00
48/62 *Set of* 15 .... £140 £600

PATIALA STATE (**4**) PATIALA STATE (**5**)

1928–34. King George V (Nasik printing, wmk Mult Star) optd at Nasik with Types **4** or **5** (rupee values).

63 **55** 3p. slate (1932) .... 2·00 10
w. Wmk inverted .... 7·50 3·75
64 **56** ½a. green 50 10
w. Wmk inverted .... 5·50 3·75
65 **80** 9p. deep green (*litho*) (1934) .... 2·25 1·00
aw. Wmk inverted .... — 12·00
65*b* 9p. deep green (*typo*) .... 4·50 50
66 **57** 1a. chocolate .... 1·75 25
w. Wmk inverted .... 7·50 3·50
67 **82** 1a.3p. mauve (1932) .... 4·25 15
w. Wmk inverted .... 7·50 4·00
68 **70** 2a. purple .... 2·25 40
w. Wmk inverted .... 6·50
69 **61** 2a.6p. orange (1934) .... 9·00 4·50
w. Wmk inverted .... 7·50
70 **62** 3a. bright blue (1929) .... 6·00 4·00
71 **71** 4a. sage-green .... 11·00 2·50
w. Wmk inverted .... 18·00
72 **65** 8a. reddish purple (1933) .... 12·00 6·00
73 **67** 1r. chocolate and green (1929) .... 13·00 18·00
w. Wmk inverted .... 30·00 32·00
74 2r. carmine and orange .... 55·00 £150
w. Wmk inverted .... 18·00 90·00
63/74w *Set of* 12 .... 70·00 £110

1935–37. Optd with Types **4**.

75 **79** ½a. blue-green (1937) .... 2·25 30
76 **81** 1a. chocolate (1936) .... 1·10 20
77 **59** 2a. vermilion (No. 236*b*) (1936) .... 40 1·50
78 **62** 3a. carmine .... 15·00 14·00
w. Wmk inverted .... 7·50 18·00
79 **63** 4a. sage-green .... 3·25 4·50
75/79 *Set of* 5 .... 13·00 19·00

PATIALA STATE (**6**) PATIALA (**7**) PATIALA (**8**)

1937–38. King George VI. Nos. 247/264 optd with T **4** (3p. to 1a.), T **6** (2a. to 12a.), or T **5** (rupee values).

80 **91** 3p. slate .... 15·00 35
81 ½a. red-brown .... 8·00 50
82 9p. green (1937) .... 5·00 1·00
83 1a. carmine (1937) .... 3·00 20
84 **92** 2a. vermilion .... 3·50 18·00
85 **93** 2a.6p. bright violet .... 14·00 50·00
86 **94** 3a. yellow-green .... 16·00 19·00
87 **95** 3a.6p. bright blue .... 14·00 50·00
88 **96** 4a. brown .... 38·00 32·00
89 **97** 6a. turquoise-green .... 45·00 £100
90 **98** 8a. slate-violet .... 50·00 85·00
91 **99** 12a. lake .... 32·00 £120
92 **100** 1r. grey and red-brown .... 38·00 60·00
93 2r. purple and brown .... 35·00 £180
94 5r. green and blue .... 45·00 £500
95 10r. purple and claret .... 70·00 £850
96 15r. brown and green £150 £1800
97 25r. slate-violet and purple £225 £1800
80/97 *Set of* 18 .... £750 £5000

Maharaja Yadavindra Singh, 1938–1971

1941–46. King George VI. Optd with T **7** or **8** (rupee value).

(a) Stamps of 1937

98 **91** 3p. slate .... 21·00 4·00
99 ½a. red-brown .... 6·50 3·25
100 9p. green .... £550 16·00
w. Wmk inverted ....
101 1a. carmine .... 40·00 3·50
102 **100** 1r. grey and red-brown (1946) .... 12·00 85·00
98/102 *Set of* 5 .... £600 £100

(b) Stamps of 1940–1943

103 **100a** 3p. slate (1942) .... 1·00 15
104 ½a. purple (1943) .... 1·00 15
a. Pair, one without opt £14000
105 9p. green (1942) .... 1·75 15
a. Vert pair, one without opt £6000
106 1a. carmine (1944) .... 2·00 10
107 **101** 1a.3p. yellow-brown .... 1·75 4·00
108 1½a. dull violet (*litho*) (1942) .... 4·00 4·25
108*a* 1½a. dull violet (*typo*) (1943) .... 6·00 6·00
109 2a. vermilion (1944) .... 2·00 50
110 3a. bright violet (*typo*) (1944) .... 2·00 3·75
111 3½a. bright blue (1944) .... 19·00 48·00
112 **102** 4a. brown (1944) .... 3·00 4·75
113 6a. turquoise-green (1944) .... 2·00 40·00
114 8a. slate-violet (1944) .... 2·00 15·00
115 12a. lake (1945) .... 25·00 £120
103/115 *Set of* 13 .... 60·00 £200

Only one example of No. 104a is known, resulting from a paper fold. No. 105a occurred on one sheet, the bottom row being without opt.

OFFICIAL STAMPS

SERVICE (**O 2**) SERVICE (**O 3**)

1884 (1 Oct). Nos. 1/3 of Patiala optd with T O **2**, in black.

O1 **23** ½a. blue-green .... 30·00 50
O2 **25** 1a. brown-purple .... 1·00 10
a. Opt Type **1** inverted £4000 £425
b. Opt Type **1** double .... † £170
c. 'SERVICE' double £3000 £900
d. 'SERVICE' inverted .... † £2500
w. Wmk inverted .... † £650
O3 **27** 2a. dull blue £11000 £150

Essays of No. O3 exist on which 'STATE' measures 10 mm long (normal 9 *mm*) and the words of the T **1** overprint are more curved. These are rare (*Price £1200 unused*).

1885–90.

(a) No. 7 of Patiala optd with T O **2**, *in black.*

O4 **23** ½a. blue-green .... 4·25 25
a. 'SERVICE' double .... † £900
b. 'AUTTIALLA' .... 90·00 22·00
ba. 'AUTTIALLA' and 'SERVICE' double .... † £8000

(b) No. 11 of Patiala optd with T O **2**, *in black*

O5 **25** 1a. brown-purple .... 2·50 10
a. 'SERVICE' double £4000
b. 'SERVICE' double, one inverted .... † £750
c. 'AUTTIALLA' .... £1200 65·00
d. 'PUTTIALLA STATE' double .... † £2500

(c) As No. 7 of Patiala, but optd in black, and No. 8, optd with T O **3**

O6 **23** ½a. blue-green (Bk.) (1890) .... 3·00 10
O7 **27** 2a. dull blue (R.) .... 1·00 40
a. 'SERVICE' double, one inverted .... 30·00 £200

Stamps as Nos. O4/O5, but with T O **3** (in red on the ½a.), were prepared for use but not issued, although some were erroneously overprinted 'REPRINT'. No. O7 with overprint in black is a proof. The ½a 'AUTTIALLA' has been reprinted in complete sheets, and can be found with 'AUTTIALLA' double.

No. O7 exists with error 'PUTTILLA', but its status is uncertain. (*Price £1500 unused*).

SERVICE

PATIALA STATE (**O 4**) PATIALA STATE SERVICE (**O 5**) PATIALA STATE SERVICE (**O 6**)

1891 (Nov)–**1900.** Optd with T O **4**, in black.

O8 **23** ½a. blue-green (9.95) .... 1·50 10
a. 'SERVICE' inverted .... 65·00
b. 'SERV CE' £2000
c. 'STA E' £900 £800
d. 'S ATE' ....
O9 **25** 1a. plum (10.1900) .... 9·00 10
a. 'SERVICE' inverted .... 65·00
O10 **27** 2a. dull blue (12.98) .... 7·00 4·50
a. Deep blue .... 5·50 4·00
b. 'SERVICE' inverted .... 65·00 £325
ba. 'SERV CE' inverted £4000
c. Thin seriffed 'I' in 'SERVICE' (R. 5/4) £425
O12 **28** 3a. brown-orange .... 4·75 4·50
a. 'SERV CE' £5000
O13 **29** 4a. olive-green .... 5·00 70
a. Slate-green (9.95) .... 5·50 30
b. 'SERV CE' ....
O15 **21** 6a. bistre-brown .... 3·75 45
a. Olive-bistre £1500
O16 **31** 8a. dull mauve .... 6·00 1·75
a. Magenta (12.98) .... 6·00 3·50
b. 'SERV CE' £6000
c. Thin seriffed 'I' in 'SERVICE' (R. 5/4) £750
O18 **32** 12a. purple/*red* .... 3·75 65
a. 'SERV CE' £8000
O19 **33** 1r. slate .... 4·25 70
a. 'SERV CE' ....
O8/O19 *Set of* 9 .... 38·00 11·00

Stamps from the first printing of November 1891 (Nos. O12/O13, O15/O16, O18/O19) had the 'SERVICE' overprint, as T O **3**, applied to sheets already overprinted with T **3**. Subsequent printings of Nos. O8/O10a, O13a and O16a had both overprints applied at one operation as shown on T O **4**.

The errors with 'SERVICE' inverted occur from a trial printing, in two operations, during 1894, which was probably not issued. Some of the 'SERV CE' varieties may also come from the same trial printing.

1902 (Jan)–**03.** Optd with T O **4**.

O20 **25** 1a. carmine .... 2·25 10
O21 **37** 1r. green and carmine (5.03) .... 7·50 10·00

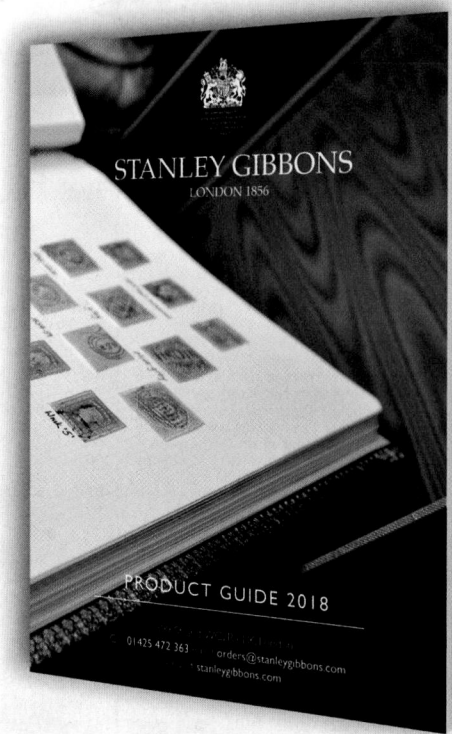

1903–10. King Edward VII stamps of India optd with T O **4**.

O22	**41**	3p. pale grey	50	10
		a. Slate-grey (1909)	50	15
O24	**42**	½a. green	1·50	10
O25	**43**	1a. carmine	60	10
O26	**44**	2a. pale violet (1905)	80	25
		a. Mauve	2·25	10
O28	**46**	3a. orange-brown	7·50	4·50
O29	**47**	4a. olive (1905)	4·25	20
		a. Opt double, one albino	90·00	
O30	**49**	8a. purple (*shades*)	3·25	75
		a. Claret (1910)	10·00	2·75
O32	**51**	1r. green and carmine (1906)	3·00	80
O22/O32 *Set of 8*			19·00	6·00

1907. Nos. 149/150 of India optd with T O **4**.

O33	**53**	½a. green	50	20
O34	**54**	1a. carmine	1·25	10

1913–26. King George V. Official stamps of India optd with T **3**.

O35	**55**	3p. grey	10	20
		a. Pale grey	1·25	75
		b. Slate (1926)	1·50	30
O36	**56**	½a. light green	10	20
		a. Emerald	6·00	1·00
		b. Bright green	3·50	60
O37	**57**	1a. aniline carmine	10	10
O38		1a. chocolate (1925)	11·00	1·25
O39	**59**	2a. purple	1·50	1·25
		a. Reddish purple	—	2·75
		b. Deep mauve	5·50	2·75
O40	**63**	4a. olive	50	35
O41	**64**	6a. brown-ochre (1926)	3·00	2·50
O42	**65**	8a. deep magenta	75	70
O43	**67**	1r. red-brown and deep blue-green	2·75	1·40
O44		2r. carmine and yellow-brown (1926)	23·00	60·00
		a. Opt double, one albino	£120	
O45		5r. ultramarine and violet (1926)	22·00	40·00
O35/O45 *Set of 11*			60·00	95·00

1927–36. King George V (Nasik printing, wmk Mult Star), optd at Nasik with T O **5** or T O **6** (rupee values).

O47	**55**	3p. slate	10	10
		a. Blue opt	3·50	2·50
		w. Wmk inverted	5·50	3·25
O48	**56**	½a. green (1932)	1·00	55
		w. Wmk inverted	—	6·00
O49	**57**	1a. chocolate	15	10
		w. Wmk inverted	4·50	50
O50	**82**	1a.3p. mauve (1932)	40	10
		w. Wmk inverted	5·50	20
O51	**70**	2a. purple	30	30
		w. Wmk inverted		
O52		2a. vermilion (1933)	1·00	35
O53	**61**	2a.6p. orange (1933)	5·00	35
		w. Wmk inverted	2·50	80
O54	**71**	4a. sage-green (1935)	50	30
		w. Wmk inverted	5·00	4·00
O55	**65**	8a. reddish purple (1929)	3·50	65
		w. Wmk inverted	1·60	80
O56	**67**	1r. chocolate and green (1929)	9·00	6·00
		w. Wmk inverted	3·00	4·00
O57		2r. carmine and orange (1936)	18·00	65·00
O47/O57 *Set of 11*			25·00	65·00

1935–39. New types. Optd with T O **5**.

O58	**79**	½a. green (1936)	75	10
O59	**81**	1a. chocolate (1936)	35	30
O60	**59**	2a. vermilion	15	30
O61		2a. vermilion (*small die*) (1939)	26·00	6·50
O62	**63**	4a. sage-green (1936)	5·50	1·75
O58/O62 *Set of 5*			30·00	8·00

1937–39. King George VI. Optd with T O **5** or T O **6** (rupee values).

O63	**91**	½a. red-brown (1938)	1·00	20
O64		9p. green (1938)	14·00	85·00
O65		1a. carmine	1·00	40
O66	**100**	1r. grey and red-brown (1939)	1·00	9·50
O67		2r. purple and brown (1939)	9·00	5·00
O68		5r. green and blue (1939)	19·00	85·00
O63/O68 *Set of 6*			42·00	£170

1A——1A (O **7**) 1A SERVICE 1A (O **8**) PATIALA SERVICE (O **9**)

1939–40. Stamp of 1932 (King George V).

(a) Optd with Types O 5 and O 7

O69	**82**	1a. on 1a.3p. mauve	22·00	5·50
		w. Wmk inverted	11·00	3·50

(b) Optd with T 4 and T O 8

O70	**82**	1a. on 1a.3p. mauve (1940)	18·00	6·00
		w. Wmk inverted	25·00	16·00

'SERVICE' measures 9¼ mm on No. O69 but only 8¾ mm on No. O70.

1939–44.

(a) Official stamps optd with T 7

O71	O **20**	3p. slate (1940)	1·00	10
O72		½a. red-brown	1·50	10
		w. Wmk inverted	—	60·00
O73		½a. purple (1942)	1·25	10
O74		9p. green	1·60	50
		w. Wmk inverted		
O75		1a. carmine	1·50	10
O76		1a.3p. yellow-brown (1941)	1·40	25
O77		1½a. dull violet (1944)	5·00	1·50
O78		2a. vermilion (1940)	5·00	35
		w. Wmk inverted	20·00	9·00
O79		2½a. bright violet (1940)	4·00	1·00
O80		4a. brown (1943)	2·00	2·50
O81		8a. slate-violet (1944)	5·50	7·00

(b) Postage stamps optd with T O 9

O82	**100**	1r. grey and red-brown (1943)	5·00	11·00
O83		2r. purple and brown (1944)	17·00	90·00
O84		5r. green and blue (1944)	29·00	£110
O71/O84 *Set of 14*			70·00	£200

TELEPHONE STAMPS

From about 1930 Patiala operated a Telephone message system, available through Post Offices, for the use of both the general public and Government departments. As with a telegraph service, charges were calculated according to the length and destination of the message, but transmission was by voice over the telephone. Charges were prepaid with specially overprinted 'Telephone' or 'Telephone Service' stamps, which were affixed to message forms. All overprints were applied typo.

DATES OF ISSUE. Precise dates of issue have not been established, but it is clear that remaining stocks of Queen Victoria and King Edward VII postage stamps were provided with Telephone overprints in the 1930s or even later. It seems certain that the large fount Type T1 and OT1 overprints are the earliest, with Type OT2 ('Service/Telephone') preceding Type OT3 ('Telephone/Service'). In the case of the later King George V and King George VI issues, the underlying postage stamps give a more reliable guide.

PRICES. Although stamps were often cancelled by circular or hooded datestamps inscribed 'TELEPHONES', manuscript cancels are also frequently met with, while a considerable proportion show no obliteration at all. In these circumstances no attempt has been made to provide separate prices for 'unused' or 'used' examples.

Telephone (T **1**) Telephone (T **2**)

(1) Overprinted 'Telephone' as Type T **1** *(14½ mm).*

On King George V postage stamp of 1912–1926. (No. 55a).

T1	6a. brown-ochre	7·50

(2) Overprinted 'Telephone' as Type T **2** *(12½ mm).*

On Queen Victoria postage stamps of 1891–1896. (Nos. 22/28).

T2	4a. slate-green	5·00
T3	6a. bistre-brown	5·00
T4	8a. magenta	7·50
T5	12a. purple/*red*	10·00
T6	1r. green and carmine	15·00

On King Edward VII postage stamps of 1903–1906. (Nos. 39/45).

T7	2a. pale violet	5·00
T8	3a. orange-brown	3·00
T9	12a. purple/*red*	15·00
T10	1r. green and carmine	20·00

On King George V postage stamp of 1912–1926. (No. 51).

T11	1½a. chocolate	10·00

On King George V postage stamps of 1928–1934. (Nos. 64/71).

T12	½a. green	3·00
T13	2a. purple	5·00
	w. Wmk inverted	5·00
T14	2a. 6p. orange (*wmk inverted*)	15·00
T15	4a. sage green	10·00

On King George V postage stamps of 1935–1937. (Nos. 75/79).

T16	½a. blue-green	3·00
T17	2a. vermilion	3·00
T18	4a. sage-green	5·00

On King George VI postage stamps of 1937–1938. (Nos. 81/83).

T19	½a. red-brown	10·00
T20	1a. carmine	10·00

On King George VI postage stamps of 1941–1946. (Nos. 99/101).

T21	½a. red-brown	7·00
T22	1a. carmine	5·00

On King George VI postage stamps of 1941–1946. (Nos. 104/113).

T23	½a. purple	4·00
T24	1a. carmine	4·00
T25	2a. vermilion	4·00
T26	3a. bright violet	5·00
T27	4a. brown	5·00
T28	6a. turquoise-green	5·00

OFFICIAL TELEPHONE STAMPS

Service Telephone (OT **1**) Service Telephone (OT **2**)

Telephone Service (OT **3**)

(1) Overprinted 'Service/Telephone' as Type OT **1**.

On King George V postage stamps of 1912–1926. (Nos. 52/55a).

OT1	2a. purple	5·00
OT2	6a. brown-ochre	7·50

On King George V postage stamps of 1928–1934. (No. 68).

OT3	2a. purple	10·00

(2) Overprinted 'Service/Telephone' as Type OT **2**.

On King George V postage stamps of 1928–1934. (Nos. 64/71).

OT4	½a. green	6·00
OT5	2a. purple	15·00
OT6	4a. sage-green	20·00

(3) Overprinted 'Telephone/Service' as Type OT **3**.

On Queen Victoria postage stamps of 1891–1896. (Nos. 22/23).

OT7	4a. slate-green	5·00
OT8	6a. bistre-brown	5·00

On King Edward VII postage stamps of 1903–1906. (Nos. 39/45).

OT9	2a. pale violet	3·00
OT10	3a. orange-brown	5·00
OT11	6a. olive-bistre	7·00
OT12	8a. purple	15·00
OT13	12a. purple/*red*	12·00
OT14	1r. green and carmine	25·00

On King George V postage stamps of 1912–1926. (Nos. 51/55a).

OT15	1½a. chocolate	10·00
OT16	6a. brown-ochre	12·00

On King George V postage stamps of 1928–1934. (Nos. 64/71).

OT17	½a. green	2·00
OT18	2a. purple	2·00
	w. Wmk inverted	3·00
OT19	2a. 6p. orange	10·00
	w. Wmk inverted	7·00
OT20	4a. sage green	5·00

On King George V postage stamps of 1935–1937. (Nos. 75/79).

OT21	½a. blue-green	3·00
OT22	2a. vermilion	3·00
OT23	4a. sage-green	3·00

On King George VI postage stamps of 1937–1938. (Nos. 81/83).

OT24	½a. red-brown	10·00
OT25	1a. carmine	7·00

On King George VI postage stamps of 1941–1946. (Nos. 104/113).

OT26	½a. purple	15·00
OT27	1a. carmine	15·00
OT28	2a. vermilion	15·00
OT29	6a. turquoise-green	15·00

(4) Overprinted 'Telephone' as Type T **2** **on** ***official*** **stamps.**

On Queen Victoria official stamp of 1891–1900. (No. O13*a*).

OT30	4a. slate-green	30·00

On King Edward VII official stamp of 1903–1910. (No. O32).

OT31	1r. green and carmine	25·00

On King George V official stamp of 1913–1926. No. O41).

OT32	6a. brown-ochre	25·00

On King George V official stamp of 1935–1939. (No. O60).

OT33	2a. vermilion	10·00

On King George VI official stamps of 1939–1944. (Nos. O72/O80).

OT34	½a. red-brown	10·00
OT35	1a. carmine	10·00
OT36	2a. vermilion	10·00
OT37	4a. brown	20·00

Patiala became part of the Patiala and East Punjab States Union by 20 August 1948.

INDIAN FEUDATORY STATES

These stamps were only valid for use within their respective states, *unless otherwise indicated.*

Postage stamps of the Indian States, current at that date, were replaced by those of the Republic of India on 1 April 1950.

Unless otherwise stated, all became obsolete on 1 May 1950 (with the exception of the 'Anchal' stamps of Travancore-Cochin which remained current until 1 July 1951 or Sept 1951 for the Official issues).

ALWAR

PRICES FOR STAMPS ON COVER TO 1945	
Nos. 1/2	*from* × 30
No. 3	*from* × 100
No. 4	—
No. 5	*from* × 100

Maharao Raja (Maharaja from 1889) Mangal Singh, 1874–1892.

1 (¼a.)

1877. Litho. Rouletted.

1	**1**	¼a. steel blue	27·00	9·50
		a. Bright greenish blue	15·00	9·50
		b. Ultramarine	6·00	1·10
		c. Grey-blue (shades)	5·00	1·10
2		1a. pale yellowish brown	22·00	9·00
		a. Brown (shades)	5·00	1·25
		b. Chocolate	10·00	8·00
		c. Pale reddish brown	3·25	1·50

Maharaja Jai Singh, 1892–1937

1899–1901. Redrawn. P 12.

(a) Wide margins between stamps

3	**1**	¼a. slate-blue	11·00	3·25
		a. Imperf between (horiz pair)	£650	£850
		b. Imperf between (vert pair)	£1600	£1700
4		¼a. emerald-green	£1100	£4000

(b) Narrower margins (1901)

5	**1**	¼a. emerald-green	8·50	2·50
		a. Imperf between (horiz pair)	£425	£550
		b. Imperf between (vert pair)	£475	£550
		c. Imperf horiz (vert pair)	£500	
		d. Imperf (pair)	£600	
		e. Pale yellow-green	10·00	2·75
		ea. Imperf (pair)	£1000	
		eb. Imperf between (horiz pair)	†	£1000

In the redrawn type only the bottom outer frameline is thick, whereas in the original 1877 issue the left-hand frameline is also thick, as shown in T 1.

The stamps of Alwar became obsolete on 1 July 1902.

BAHAWALPUR

See after PAKISTAN

BAMRA

PRICES FOR STAMPS ON COVER TO 1945	
Nos. 1/6	—
Nos. 8/40	*from* × 40

Raja Sudhal Deo, 1869–1903

GUM. The stamps of Bamra were issued without gum.

1 (¼a.) 1a 2 (½a.)

3 (1a.) 4 (2a.) 5 (4a.)

6 (8a.)

(illustrations actual size)

(Typo Jagannata Ballabh Press, Deogarh)

1888. Imperf.

1	1	¼a. black/*yellow*	£1000	
		a. 'g' inverted (R. 5/1)	£10000	
		b. Last native character inverted	£10000	
		c. Last native character as Type **1a**	£10000	
2	2	½a. black/*rose*	£160	
		a. 'g' inverted (R. 5/1)	£3000	
3	3	1a. black/*blue*	£130	
		a. 'g' inverted (R. 5/1)	£2750	
		b. Scroll inverted (R. 8/4)	£2500	
4	4	2a. black/*green*	£200	£750
		a. 'a' omitted (R. 8/3)	£3000	
		b. Scroll inverted (R. 8/4)	£2750	
5	5	4a. black/*yellow*	£160	£750
		a. 'a' omitted (R. 8/3)	£2750	
		b. Scroll inverted (R. 8/4)	£2500	
6	6	8a. black/*rose*	£100	
		a. 'a' omitted (R. 8/3)	£2250	
		b. Horiz pair, one printed on back	£1600	
		c. Scroll inverted (R. 8/4)	£2000	

These stamps were all printed from the same plate of 96 stamps, 12×8, but for some values only part of the plate was used. There are 96 varieties of the ½, 4 and 8a., 72 of the 1a., 80 of the 2a. and not less than 88 of the ¼a.

The scroll ornament can be found pointing to either the right or the left.

There are two forms of the third native character. In the first five horizontal rows it is as in T **1** and in the last three rows as in T **4**.

These stamps have been reprinted: the ¼a. and ½a. in blocks of eight varieties (all showing scroll pointing to right), and all the values in blocks of 20 varieties (all showing scroll pointing to left). On the reprints the fourth character is of a quite different shape.

8

1890 (July)–**93**. Black on coloured paper. Nos. 24/25 and 39/40 show face value as 'One Rupee'.

(a) 'Postage' with capital 'P'

8	8	¼a. on *rose-lilac*	8·00	15·00
		a. 'Eeudatory' (R. 2/4)	30·00	80·00
		b. 'Quatrer' (R. 1/3)	30·00	80·00
		c. Inverted 'e' in 'Postage' (R. 2/3)	30·00	80·00
9		¼a. on *bright rose*	3·25	3·25
10		¼a. on *reddish purple*	2·75	3·00
		a. First 'a' in 'anna' inverted (R. 3/3)	75·00	90·00
		b. 'AMRA' inverted (R. 4/4)	£100	£110
		c. 'M' and second 'A' in 'BAMRA' inverted (R. 4/4)	£180	£180
11		½a. on *dull green*	7·50	6·50
		a. 'Eeudatory' (R. 2/4)	£100	£150
12		½a. on *blue-green*	8·00	6·00
13		1a. on *bistre-yellow*	6·50	4·00
		a. 'Eeudatory' (R. 2/4)	£225	£300
14		1a. on *orange-yellow*	75·00	75·00
		a. 'annas' for 'anna' (R. 3/3)	£350	£375
15		2a. on *rose-lilac*	24·00	60·00
		a. 'Eeudatory' (R. 2/4)	£300	£600
16		2a. on *bright rose*	7·50	7·50
17		2a. on *dull rose*	21·00	11·00
18		4a. on *rose-lilac*	£1100	£1700
		a. 'Eeudatory' (R. 2/4)	£7500	
19		4a. on *dull rose*	26·00	16·00
		a. 'Eeudatory' (R. 2/4)	£2000	£2250
		b. 'BAMBA' (R. 2/1)	£2000	£2250
20		4a. on *bright rose*	9·50	11·00
20*a*		4a. on *deep pink*	21·00	15·00
		ab. Doubly printed	†	£2000
21		8a. on *rose-lilac*	45·00	£130
		a. 'Foudatory' and 'Postagc' (R. 1/2)	£450	£800
		b. 'BAMBA' (R. 2/1)	£450	£800
22		8a. on *bright rose*	16·00	24·00
23		8a. on *dull rose*	48·00	21·00
24		1r. on *rose-lilac*	£110	£225
		a. 'Eeudatory' (R. 2/4)	£1000	£1700
		b. 'BAMBA' (R. 2/1)	£850	£1400
		c. 'Postagc' (R. 1/2)	£850	£1400
25		1r. on *bright rose*	26·00	25·00
		a. Small 'r' in 'rupee'	£425	£425

(b) 'postage' with small 'p' (1891–1893)

26	8	¼a. on *bright rose*	2·50	3·75
27		¼a. on *reddish purple*	2·50	3·00
28		½a. on *dull green*	7·50	6·50
		a. First 'a' in 'anna' inverted (R. 3/3)	60·00	65·00
29		½a. on *blue-green*	6·00	6·00
		a. First 'a' in 'anna' inverted (R. 3/3)	65·00	65·00
30		1a. on *bistre-yellow*	6·50	3·75
31		1a. on *orange-yellow*	75·00	75·00
32		2a. on *bright rose*	9·00	7·00
33		2a. on *dull rose*	21·00	11·00
34		4a. on *dull rose*	28·00	17·00
35		4a. on *bright rose*	9·00	12·00
35*a*		4a. on *deep pink*	21·00	15·00
36		8a. on *rose-lilac*	£110	£225
37		8a. on *bright rose*	20·00	28·00
38		8a. on *dull rose*	48·00	23·00
39		1r. on *rose-lilac*	£170	£300
40		1r. on *bright rose*	26·00	25·00
		a. Small 'r' in 'rupee'	£450	£450
		b. Small 'r' in 'rupee' and native characters in the order 2, 3, 1, 4, 5 (R. 4/4)	£2750	£2750

There are ten settings of T **8**. The first setting (of 20 (4×5)) has capital 'P' throughout. The remaining settings (of 16 (4×4)) have capital 'P' and small 'p' mixed.

For the first setting the 8a. and 1r. values were printed within the same block, the ten left-hand stamps being 8a. values and the ten right-hand stamps 1r.

The various stamps were distributed between the settings as follows:

Setting I	—	Nos. 8/8c, 11/11a, 13/13a, 15/15a, 18/19a, 21, 24/24a
Setting II	—	Nos. 19, 19b, 21/21b, 24, 24b/24c, 34, 36, 39
Setting III	—	Nos. 9, 11, 13, 16, 26, 28, 30, 32
Setting IV	—	Nos. 20, 22, 25, 35, 37, 40
Setting V	—	Nos. 10, 10b/10c, 20*a*, 27, 35*a*
Setting VI	—	Nos. 11, 12, 28, 28a, 29/29a
Setting VII	—	Nos. 10/10a, 12, 17, 19, 23, 25a, 27, 29, 33/34, 38, 40a/40b
Setting VIII	—	Nos. 17, 33
Setting IX	—	Nos. 10/10a, 12, 14/14a, 17, 19, 23, 27, 29, 31, 33/34, 38
Setting X	—	Nos. 19, 34

There are four sizes of the central ornament, which represents an elephant's trunk holding a stick:—*(a)* 4 mm long; *(b)* 5 mm; *(c)* 6½ mm; *(d)* 11 mm. These ornaments are found pointing to right or left, either upright or inverted.

Ornaments *(a)* are found in all settings; *(b)* in all settings from Settings III to X; *(c)* in Settings I and II; and *(d)* only in Setting I.

The stamps of Bamra have been obsolete since 1 January 1895.

BARWANI

PRICES FOR STAMPS ON COVER TO 1945	
Nos. 1/2ab	*from* × 1.5
Nos. 3/43	*from* × 3

PROCESS. All Barwani stamps are typographed from clichés, and are in sheets of four, *unless otherwise indicated.*

Nos. 1/31 were printed by the Barwani State Printing Press. The 1932-1947 issues (Nos. 32A/43) were printed by the *Times of India* Press, Bombay.

GUM. Nos. 1/31 were issued without gum.

BOOKLET PANES. Those stamps which were printed in sheets of four were issued in stamp booklets, binding holes appearing in the side margin.

Rana Ranjit Singh, 1894–1930

1

2

3

1917 (May)–**21**. Blurred (Nos. 1 and 2) or clear impression. Medium wove paper. P 7 on two sides (No. 1) or all round (others).

1	1	¼a. light blue	†	£3000
		a. Imperf (pair)	†	£6000
		b. Blue-green (dull to deep) (1921)	£275	£750
2		½a. deep ultramarine	†	£5000
		a. Dull blue	£550	£1100
		ab. Imperf (pair)	†	£3000

The 'QUARTER ANNA' inscription on No. 1 is normally doubled. No. 1*b* also exists perforated on two sides only.

1921 (June?). Blurred impression. Soft wove paper. P 7 on two or three sides.

3	1	¼a. green (*shades*)	42·00	£300
4		½a. ultramarine (dull *to* pale)	26·00	£375

NOTE. As the small sheets of Barwani stamps were often not perforated all round, many of the earlier stamps are perforated on two or three sides only. Owing to the elementary method of printing, the colours vary greatly in depth, even within a single sheet.

1921. Clear impression. Vertically laid bâtonné paper. Imperf.

5	1	¼a. green (*shades*)	27·00	£170
6		½a. green (*shades*)	7·00	
		a. Perf 11 at top or bottom only	7·00	

It is suggested that No. 5 may be an error due to printing from the wrong plate.

1922. Clear impression. Thickish glazed wove paper. P 7 on two or three sides.

7	1	¼a. dull blue	£200	

1922. Smooth, soft medium wove paper. P 7 on two or three sides.

(a) Clear impression

8	1	¼a. deep grey-blue	£120	£275

(b) Poor impression

9	1	¼a. steel blue	23·00	

Examples of No. 9 exist with perforations on all four sides.

1922. P 11 on two or three sides.

(a) Thick, glazed white wove paper

10	2	1a. vermilion (*shades*)	4·50	35·00
		a. Imperf between (vert pair)	£750	
		b. Doubly printed	£2500	
11		2a. purple (*to* violet)	3·25	45·00
		a. Doubly printed	£500	
		b. Imperf between (horiz pair)	£475	£750
		c. Imperf between (vert pair)	£200	

(b) Thick, toned wove paper

12	2	2a. purple	22·00	90·00

1922. Poor impression. Thin, poor wove paper. Pin-perf 8½ on two or three sides.

13	1	¼a. grey (*to* grey-blue)	2·25	75·00
		a. Imperf (pair)	£700	
		b. Imperf between (vert pair)	£275	

1923. Thin, smooth, unglazed wove paper. P 11 on two or three sides.

14	1	½a. green (*pale to deep*)	2·00	30·00
		a. Imperf between (vert pair)	£1000	
15	2	1a. brown-red	£4000	£5000

1923. Poor impression. Thick, soft wove paper. P 7.

16	1	½a. green (pale *to* deep)	45·00	

No. 16 also exists perforated on two or three sides.

1923 (Mar?). Poor quality wove paper. P 7 on two or three sides.

17	1	¼a. black	90·00	£600
		a. Imperf between (horiz pair)	£4250	

1923 (May?). Horizontally laid bâtonné paper. P 12.

18	1	¼a. rose (*shades*)	4·25	22·00
		a. Imperf between (vert pair)	£850	
		ab. Imperf between (horiz pair)	£1800	
		b. Pin perf 6	£275	£120
		c. Perf compound of 12 and 6	75·00	£100
		d. Perf 7	£1600	£1800
		da. On wove paper	£5000	

No. 18 was issued in sheets of 12 (3 panes of 4) and was printed on paper showing a sheet watermark of Britannia and a double-lined inscription. No. 18d was only issued in booklet panes of four.

1925. Vertically laid bâtonné paper. P 11.

19	1	¼a. blue (pale *to* deep)	2·50	12·00
		a. *Tête-bêche* (horiz pair)	£4500	

No. 19 was issued in sheets of eight and was printed on paper with a sheet watermark of a shell and an inscription 'SHELL' in double-lined capitals.

1927. Very poor impression. Thin, brittle wove paper. P 7.

20	1	¼a. milky blue (*shades*)	9·00	60·00
21		½a. yellow-green (*shades*)	10·00	£130
		a. Imperf between (horiz pair)	£2250	
22	3	4a. orange-brown	£160	£750
		a. Imperf between (horiz pair)	£3250	
20/22 *Set of 3*			£170	£850

1927. Thick wove paper. Sewing machine perf 6-10.

23	3	4a. yellow-brown	£180	
		a. Imperf between (horiz pair)	£6000	
		b. Perf 7	20·00	£450
		c. Orange-brown	£200	£800

1928–32? Thick glazed paper.

(a) P 7

24	1	¼a. deep bright blue	13·00	
25		½a. bright yellow-green	40·00	

(b) P 10½ (rough) (Nov 1928)

26	1	¼a. ultramarine	10·00	
		a. *Tête-bêche* (horiz pair)	20·00	
		b. Horiz pair, one stamp printed on reverse	£4000	
27		½a. apple-green	6·50	
		a. *Tête-bêche* (vert pair)	12·00	

(c) P 11 (clean-cut) (1929–1932?)

28	1	¼a. bright blue	3·50	23·00
		a. Indigo	3·00	21·00
		ab. Imperf between (horiz pair)	£180	
		ac. Imperf between (horiz strip of 4)	£750	
		b. Deep dull blue	2·75	20·00
		ba. Imperf between (vert pair)	£600	
		c. Ultramarine	3·00	22·00
29		½a. myrtle-green	3·75	26·00
		a. Imperf between (horiz pair)	£550	
		b. Turquoise-green	4·50	24·00
		ba. Imperf between (vert pair)	£1000	£1200
30	2	1a. rose-carmine (1931)	20·00	70·00
		a. Imperf between (vert pair)	†	£4500
31	3	4a. salmon (*to* orange) (1931)	£110	£400
		a. Imperf between (horiz pair)	£4500	
28/31 *Set of 4*			£120	£475

No. 26 was printed in sheets of eight (4×2) with the two centre pairs *tête-bêche* while No. 27, in similar sheets, had the two horizontal rows *tête-bêche*. Both sheets are always found with one long side imperforate.

Nos. 28/31 were printed in sheets of eight, the two lower values existing either 4×2 or 2×4 and the two higher values 4×2 only. No *tête-bêche* pairs were included in these printings. It is believed that a small printing of No. 31 was produced in sheets of four, but details are uncertain.

Rana Devi Singh, 1930–1971

4 Rana Devi Singh

5 Rana Devi Singh

1932 (Oct)–**47**. Medium to thick wove paper.

A. Close setting (2½–4½ mm). P 11, 12 or compound (1932–1941)

32A **4** ¼a. slate ... 4·50 30·00
33A ½a. blue-green ... 6·00 32·00
34A 1a. brown ... 7·00 28·00
a. Imperf between (horiz pair) ... £2500
35A 2a. purple (*shades*) ... 5·50 70·00
36A 4a. olive-green ... 6·00 50·00
32A/36A *Set of 5* ... 26·00 £190

B. Wide setting (6–7 mm). P 11 (1945–1947)

32B **4** ¼a. slate ... 7·50 45·00
33B ½a. blue-green ... 8·00 35·00
34B 1a. brown ... 24·00 32·00
b. Chocolate. Perf 8½ (1947) ... 20·00 85·00
35*a*B 2a. rose-carmine ... £750 £1300
36B 4a. olive-green ... 32·00 70·00

The measurements given in the heading indicate the vertical spacing between impressions. There are eight settings of this interesting issue: four 'Close' where the overall stamp dimensions from centre to centre of perfs vary in width from 21½ to 23 mm and in height from 25 to 27½ mm; three 'Wide', width 23–23½ mm and height 29–30 mm and one 'Medium' (26½×31 *mm*) (No. 34B*b* only).

1933–47. P 11.

A. Close setting (3–4½ mm). Thick, cream-surfaced wove paper (1933 and 1941 (No. 38Aa))

37A **1** ¼a. black ... 9·00 £120
38A ½a. blue-green ... 14·00 48·00
a. Yellowish green (1941) ... 17·00 42·00
39A **2** 1a. brown (*shades*) ... 27·00 42·00
42A **3** 4a. sage-green ... 70·00 £180

B. Wide setting (7–10 mm). Medium to thick wove paper (1939–1947)

37B **1** ¼a. black (1945) ... 7·00 55·00
38*a*B ½a. yellowish green (1945) ... 7·00 60·00
39B **2** 1a. brown (*shades*) ... 17·00 42·00
a. Perf 8½ (*5 mm*) (1947) ... 12·00 80·00
40B 2a. bright purple ... £150 £500
41B 2a. rose-carmine (1945) ... 45·00 £190
42B **3** 4a. sage-green (1941) ... 55·00 £110
a. Pale sage-green (1939) ... 20·00 70·00

There were two 'Close' settings (overall stamp size 25×29 *mm*) and five 'Wide' settings with overall sizes 26½–31½ × 31–36½ mm. There was also one 'Medium' setting (26½×31 *mm*) but this was confined to the 1a. perf 8½, No. 39Ba.

1938. P 11.

43 **5** 1a. brown ... 55·00 90·00

Stamps printed in red with designs similar to Types **3** and **5** were intended for fiscal use.

STAMP BOOKLETS

Nos. 1/17, 18d/18da and 20/25 are believed to have been issued in sewn or stapled booklets, usually containing 32 examples of one value in blocks of four. All these early booklets had plain covers, often in shades of brown. Few complete booklets have survived from this period.

Nos. 32/47, produced by the *Times of India* Press in a series of nine printings between 1932 and 1947, were only issued in booklet form. Booklets from the 1932, 1933, 1937 and 1939 printings had plain card or paper covers in various colours, usually containing eight blocks of four, except for the 1933 printing, which contained 20 blocks of four. Booklets from the 1945 printing had plain white tissue covers from the same stock as the interleaving. All these booklets were stapled at left.

The following booklets, from a printing in 1941, and a series of three printings in 1947, had printed covers, produced by a handstamp in the case of Nos. SB14/SB15.

1941. Buff, green (No. SB3) or blue (No. SB7) card covers inscribed 'BARWANI STATE POSTAGE STAMPS', booklet value in brackets and number and value of stamps thus '(Rs 4) 32 2 Annas'. Panes of 4 with margin at left only. Stapled.

(a) Booklets 59×55 mm

SB1 8a. booklet containing 32×¼a. (No. 32A) ... £1800
SB2 1r. booklet containing 32×½a. (No. 33A) ... £2500
SB3 2r. booklet containing 32×1a. (No. 34A) ... £2000
SB4 4r. booklet containing 32×2a. (No. 35A) ... £900
SB5 8r. booklet containing 32×4a. (No. 36A) ... £1600

(b) Booklets 63×60 mm (No. SB6) or 73×72 mm (No. SB7)

SB6 1r. booklet containing 32×½a. (No. 38A*a*) ... £2000
SB7 8r. booklet containing 32×4a. (No. 42B) ... £2750

1947. Grey tissue covers inscribed '32 STAMPS VALUE ....' Panes of 4 with margins all round. Stapled at left.

(a) Booklets 70×95 mm

SB8 1r. booklet containing 32×½a. (No. 33B) ... £1000
SB9 2r. booklet containing 32×1a. (No. 34B) ... £2250
SB10 8r. booklet containing 32×4a. (No. 36B) ... £1600

(b) Booklets 76×95 mm

SB11 8a. booklet containing 32×¼a. (No. 37B) ... £1400
SB12 4r. booklet containing 32×2a. (No. 41B) ... £1600
SB13 8r. booklet containing 32×4a. (No. 42B*a*) ... £750

1947. Buff paper covers with violet handstamp inscribed '32 STAMPS VALUE Rs 2/-'. Panes of 4 with margins all round, Sewn with twine at left.

SB14 2r. booklets (71×69 *mm*) containing 32×1a. (No. 34B*b*) ... £850
SB15 2r. booklet (71×73 *mm*) containing 32×1a. (No. 39Ba) ... £500

1947. Grey tissue covers inscribed '32 STAMPS VALUE As 8'. Panes of 4 with margins all round. Stapled at left.

SB16 8a. booklet (70×75 *mm*) containing 32×¼a. (No. 32B) ... £325
SB17 8a. booklet (85×75 *mm*) containing 32×¼a. (No. 37B) ... £425

Barwani became part of Madhya Bharat by 1 July 1948.

BHOPAL

PRICES FOR STAMPS ON COVER TO 1945	
Nos. 1/100	*from* × 10
Nos. O301/O357	*from* × 15

The correct English inscription on these stamps is 'H.H. NAWAB SHAH JAHAN BEGAM'. In the case of Nos. 22 and 23 the normal stamps are spelt 'BEGAN' and examples with 'BEGAM' are 'errors'.

As the stamps were printed from lithographic stones on which each unit was drawn separately by hand, numerous errors of spelling occurred. These are constant on all sheets and are listed. Some of our illustrations inadvertently include errors of spelling.

ILLUSTRATIONS. Types **1/3a** and **6/12a** are shown actual size.

EMBOSSING. Nos. 1/99 were only valid for postage when embossed with the device, in Urdu, of the ruling Begam. On Types **1/3** and **6** to **12a**. this was intended to fill the central part of the design. Almost all varieties can be found with the embossing inverted or sideways, as well as upright.

Shah Jahan Sultan Jahan

(actual size)

The various basic types were often in concurrent use but for greater convenience the following list is arranged according to types instead of being in strict chronological order.

GUM. Nos. 1/99 were issued without gum.

Nawab Shah Jahan Begam, 16 November 1868–15 June 1901

1 (¼a.)

1872. Litho.

(a) Double frame. Sheets of 20 (5×4)

1 **1** ¼a. black ... £1800 £1100
a. 'BFGAM' (R. 3/1) ... £4500 £3250
b. 'BEGAN' (R. 2/2, R. 4/4) ... £3000 £1800
c. 'EGAM' (R. 4/5) ... £4500 £3250
2 ½a. red ... 21·00 75·00
a. 'BFGAM' (R. 3/1) ... 95·00 £300
b. 'BEGAN' (R. 2/2, R. 4/4) ... 60·00 £180
c. 'EGAM' (R. 4/5) ... 95·00 £300

2 (½a.)

(b) Single frame. Sheets of 20 (4×5)

3 **2** ¼a. black ... † £10000
4 ½a. red ... 70·00 £150
a. 'NWAB' (R. 2/2) ... £350 £650

3 (¼a.) **3a (¼a.)**

1878 (1 Jan). All lettered 'EEGAM' for 'BEGAM'. Sheets of 20 (4×5).

(a) Plate 1. Frame lines extend horiz and vert between stamps throughout sheet

5 **3** ¼a. black ... 8·00 25·00

(b) Plate 2. Frame lines normal

5*a* **3a** ¼a. black ... 19·00 30·00

Apart from the frame line difference between Types **3** and **3a** the stamps can also be distinguished by the differences in the value tablets, notably the thin vertical line in the centre in T **3a** compared with the slightly diagonal and heavier line in T **3**.

4 (¼a.) **5 (½a.)**

1878 (June?)–**79**. Value in parenthesis (Nos. 6/7). Sheets of 32 (4×8). Imperf.

6 **4** ¼a. green (1879) ... 17·00 45·00
7 ¼a. green (*perf*) (1879) ... 13·00 30·00
8 **5** ½a. red ... 7·00 27·00
a. 'JAHN' (R. 5/2) ... 65·00
b. 'NWAB' (R. 3/2, R. 4/2) ... 40·00
c. 'EEGAM' (R. 1/3) ... 65·00
9 ½a. brown ... 48·00 80·00
a. 'JAHN' (R. 5/2) ... £275 £375
b. 'NWAB' (R. 3/2, R. 4/2) ... £160 £250
c. 'EEGAM' (R. 1/3) ... £275 £375

The ¼a. shows the 'N' of 'NAWAB' reversed on R. 6/4 and the 'N' of 'JAHAN' reversed on R. 1/2–4 and R. 2/2-4.

1880. T **5** redrawn; value not in parenthesis. Sheets of 32 (4×8).

(a) Imperf

10 ¼a. blue-green ... 15·00 35·00
a. 'NAWA' (R. 2/2–4) ... 48·00 £110
b. 'CHAH' (R. 8/3) ... £140
11 ½a. brown-red ... 18·00 30·00

(b) Perf

12 ¼a. blue-green ... 18·00
a. 'NAWA' (R. 2/2–4) ... 70·00
b. 'CHAH' (R. 8/3) ... £170
13 ½a. brown-red ... 21·00

The ¼a. shows the 'N' of 'NAWAB' reversed on R. 8/4.

Nos. 12/13 sometimes come with gum.

1884. T **5** again redrawn. Sheets of 32 (4×8), some with value in parenthesis, others not. Perf.

14 ¼a. greenish blue ... 9·50 26·00
a. 'ANAWAB' (R. 8/1–4) ... 21·00

In this plate there is a slanting dash under and to left of the letters 'JA' of 'JAHAN', instead of a character like a large comma, as on all previous varieties of this design. With the exception of R. 1/1 all stamps in the sheet show 'N' of 'JAHAN' reversed.

1895. T **5** again redrawn. Sheets of eight (2×4). Laid paper.

15 ¼a. red (*imperf*) ... 7·00 5·50
16 ¼a. red (*perf*) ... — £1200

In these cases where the same design has been redrawn several times, and each time in a number of varieties of type, it is not easy to distinguish the various issues. Nos. 6 and 7 may be distinguished from Nos. 10 and 12 by the presence or absence of the parenthesis marks (); 8, 9 and 11 differ principally in colour; 8 and 15 are very much alike, but differ in the value as well as in paper.

6 (2a.)

1881. Sheets of 24 (4×6). Imperf.

17 **6** ¼a. black ... 6·00 40·00
a. 'NWAB' (R. 6/2–4) ... 17·00 95·00
18 ½a. red ... 6·50 32·00
a. 'NWAB' (R. 6/2–4) ... 18·00
19 1a. brown ... 4·50 32·00
a. 'NWAB' (R. 6/2–4) ... 14·00
20 2a. blue ... 4·50 32·00
a. 'NWAB' (R. 6/2–4) ... 14·00
21 4a. buff ... 38·00 £140
a. 'NWAB' (R. 6/2–4) ... 95·00
17/21 *Set of 5* ... 55·00 £250

In this issue all values were produced from the same drawing, and therefore show exactly the same varieties of type. The value at foot in this and all the following issues is given in only one form.

7 (½a.)

1886. Similar to T **6** but normally lettered (incorrectly) 'BEGAN'; larger lettering. Sheets of 32 (4×8).

(a) Imperf

22 **7** ½a. pale red ... 3·50 16·00
a. 'BEGAM' (R. 2/1) ... 17·00 55·00
b. 'NWAB' (R. 3/4) ... 17·00

(b) Perf

23 **7** ½a. pale red ... £1500
a. 'BEGAM' (R. 2/1) ... £2500
b. 'NWAB' (R. 3/4) ... £2500

8 (4a.)

1886. T **8**. T **6** redrawn. Sheets of 24 (4×6). The 'M' of 'BEGAM' is an inverted 'W'. The width of the stamps is rather greater than the height.

(a) Wove paper. Imperf

24 **8** 4a. yellow ... £1500
a. 'EEGAM' (R. 2/3–4, R. 3/3–4, R. 4/2, R. 4/4, R. 6/1) ... £1900

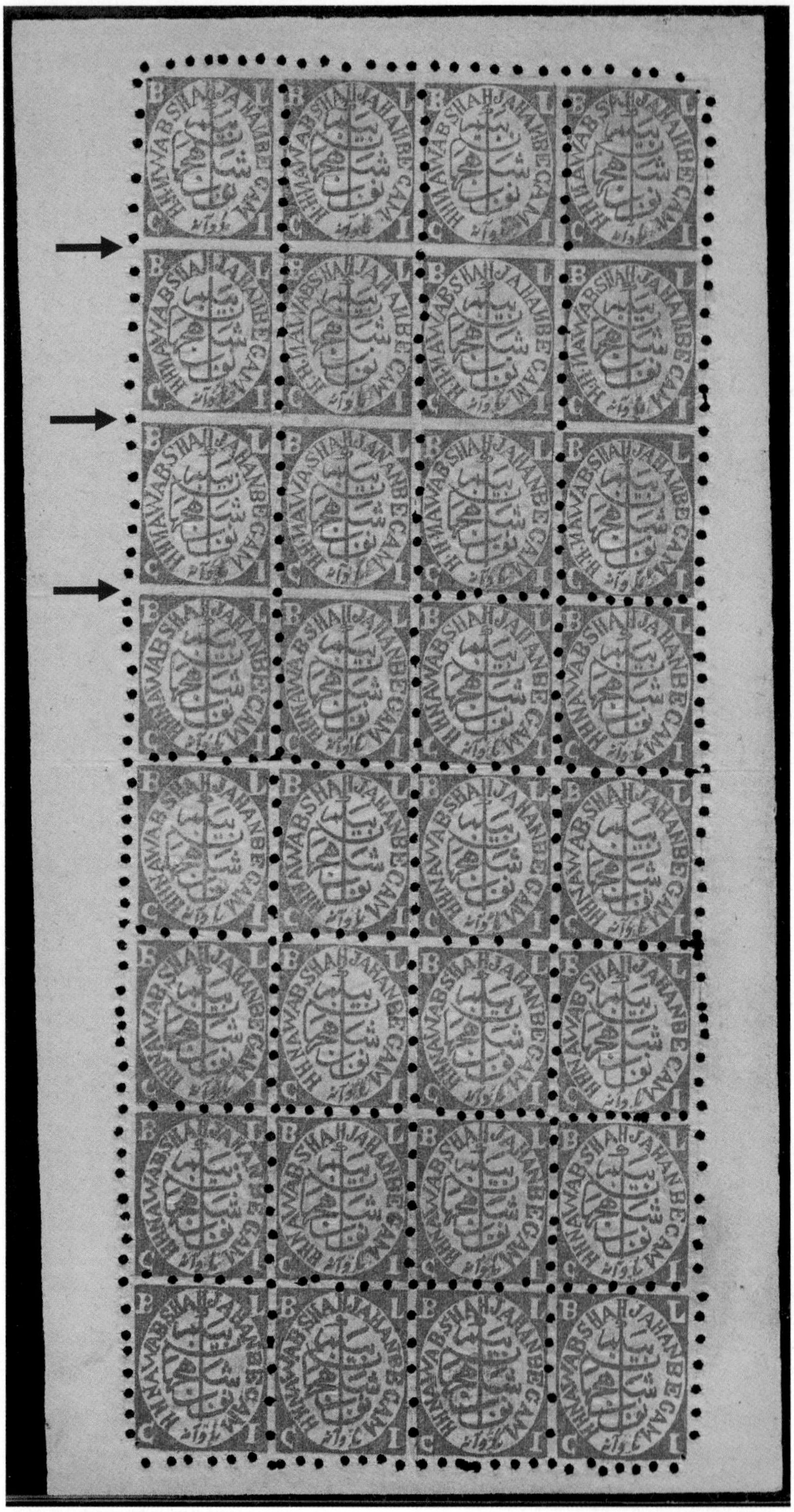

(b) Laid paper

25 **8** 4a. yellow (*imperf*) 22·00 70·00
a. 'EEGAM' (R. 2/3–4, R. 3/3–4, R. 4/2, R. 4/4, R. 6/1) 27·00
26 4a. yellow (*perf*) 7·00 35·00
a. 'EEGAM' (R. 2/3–4, R. 3/3–4, R. 4/2, R. 4/4, R. 6/1) 11·00 50·00

1889. T **6** again redrawn. Sheets of 32 (4×8) lettered 'BEGAN'.

27 ¼a. black (*perf*) 3·25 9·50
a. 'EEGAN' (R. 7/3) 25·00 55·00
b. Imperf between (horiz pair) £425
28 ¼a. black (*imperf*) 4·50 9·50
a. 'EEGAN' (R. 7/3) 30·00 55·00

9 (¼a.)

1889–90. T **9**. T **6** again redrawn. Sheets of 24 (4×6), all with 'M' like an inverted 'W'. Wove paper.

(a) Imperf

29 **9** ¼a. black 2·25 3·75
30 1a. brown 3·75 6·50
a. 'EEGAM' (R. 2/3) 25·00 42·00
b. 'BBGAM' (R. 3/1) 25·00 42·00
31 2a. blue 2·75 4·75
a. 'BBEGAM' (R. 1/2) 16·00 23·00
b. 'NAWAH' (R. 4/2) 16·00 23·00
32 4a. orange-yellow 3·25 4·25
29/32 *Set of 4* 11·00 17·00

(b) Perf

33 **9** ¼a. black 4·50 8·00
a. Imperf between (horiz pair) £475
34 1a. brown 5·50 13·00
a. 'EEGAM' (R. 2/3) 40·00 75·00
b. 'BBGAM' (R. 3/1) 40·00 75·00
35 2a. blue 2·75 6·00
a. 'BBEGAM' (R. 1/2) 18·00 28·00
b. 'NAWAH' (R. 4/2) 18·00 28·00
36 4a. orange-yellow 3·25 11·00
33/36 *Set of 4* 14·50 35·00

Nos. 32 and 36 are nearly square, in many cases rather larger in height than in width.

1891. As last, but sheets of 32 (4×8).

37 **9** ½a. red (*imperf*) 2·00 4·25
38 ½a. red (*perf*) 2·25 6·50

1894–98. T **6** again redrawn.

(a) Sheets of 24 (4×6), almost all showing a character inside the octagon below, as in T **9**. *Wove paper*

39 1a. deep brown (*imperf*) 7·50 5·50
a. Red-brown 60·00
b. Printed both sides — £1200
41 1a. deep brown (*perf*) 12·00 8·00

10 (1a.)

(b) As Nos. 39/41, but printed from a new stone showing the lines blurred and shaky. Wove paper. Imperf (1898)

42 **10** 1a. purple-brown 4·50 4·50
a. 'NAWAH' (R. 4/1) 28·00 40·00
43 1a. purple-brown/*buff* 4·50 5·00
a. 'NAWAH' (R. 4/1) 28·00 40·00
b. Printed on both sides

The above are known without embossing.

11 (¼a.)

1895. Sheets of eight (2×4), lettered 'EEGAM'. White laid paper.

44 **11** ¼a. black (*imperf*) 4·75 3·25
a. 'A' inserted (R. 4/2) 12·00 8·50
45 ¼a. black (*perf*) £150 50·00
a. 'NAW B' (R. 4/2) £500 £170

On the perf stamp the second 'A' in 'NAWAB' was missing on R. 4/2 in the setting. This letter was later inserted for the imperf printing varying progressively from small to large.

12 (½a.)

1895. Narrow label at bottom. Sheets of eight (2×4), lettered 'W W' for 'H H'. Laid paper.

46 **12** ½a. black (*imperf*) 2·75 2·00

12a

1896. Sheets of eight (2×4). Laid paper.

47 **12a** ½a. red (*imperf*) 3·50 2·25

No. 47 is a combination of Types **1** and **6**, having the double outer frame to the octagon and the value in one form only.

13 (¼a.)

14 (¼a.)

1884. Sheets of 32 (4×8). Perf.

48 **13** ¼a. blue-green £200 £250
a. 'JAN' (R. 2/1–2, R. 3/1, R. 3/3–4, R. 4/1–3, R. 5/1–3) £200 £250
b. 'BEGM' (R. 2/3–4) £600 £700
c. 'NWAB' and 'JAN' (R. 3/2) £1000
ca. 'NWAB' and 'JN' (R. 5/4) £1000
d. 'SHAHAN' (R. 4/4) £1000
e. 'JAHA' (R. 6/2–4) £450

1896. T **14**, double-lined frame round each stamp. Sheets of six (2×3), lettered 'JAN'. Laid paper.

49 **14** ¼a. bright green (*imperf*) 6·00 30·00

15 (½a.)

16 (¼a.)

1884. Sheets of 32 (4×8). Laid paper.

50 **15** ¼a. blue-green (*imperf*) £300 £325
a. 'NWAB' (R. 1/1) £800
b. 'SAH' (R. 1/4) £800
c. 'NAWA' and 'JANAN' (R. 3/2) £800
51 ¼a. blue-green (*perf*) 1·00 7·00
a. 'NWAB' (R. 1/1) 5·00
b. 'SAH' (R. 1/4) 5·00
c. 'NAWA' and 'JANAN' (R. 3/2) 5·00
d. Imperf between (vert pair) £500
52 ½a. black (*imperf*) 2·50 2·50
a. 'NWAB' (R. 1/1) 16·00 18·00
b. 'SAH' (R. 1/4) 16·00 18·00
c. 'NAWA' and 'JANAN' (R. 3/2) 16·00 18·00
53 ½a. black (*perf*) 1·00 3·50
a. 'NWAB' (R. 1/1) 4·75 16·00
b. 'SAH' (R. 1/4) 4·75 16·00
c. 'NAWA' and 'JANAN' (R. 3/2) 4·75 16·00

The ¼a. of this issue is in *blue-green*, or *greenish blue*. Both values were printed from the same stone, the value alone being altered. There are therefore the same varieties of each. These are the only stamps of this design on laid paper.

Both values show the 'N' of 'NAWAB' reversed on R. 1/1–4, R. 2/1–4, R. 3/1–4 and the 'N' of 'JAHAN' reversed on R. 1/1–4, R. 2/1–7, R. 3/4.

1886. T **15** redrawn. Sheets of 32 (4×8). Wove paper.

54 ¼a. green (*imperf*) 75 5·00
a. 'NAWA' (R. 6/3–4) 3·00 13·00
b. 'NWAB' (R. 1/1) 4·00 18·00
c. 'NWABA' (R. 7/4) 4·00 18·00
d. 'NAWAA' (R. 6/2) 4·00 18·00
e. 'BEGAAM' and 'NWABA' (R. 7/3) 4·00 18·00
55 ¼a. green (*perf*) 3·00 6·50
a. 'NAWA' (R. 6/3–4) 14·00
b. 'NWAB' (R. 1/1) 21·00
c. 'NWABA' (R. 7/4) 21·00
d. 'NAWAA' (R. 6/2) 21·00
e. 'BEGAAM' and 'NWABA' (R. 7/3) 21·00
f. Imperf between (horiz pair) £275
56 ½a. red (*imperf*) 1·00 1·75
a. 'SAH' (R. 1/4) 6·00 11·00
b. 'NAWABA' (R. 6/3–4) 4·00 8·50

The ¼a. varies from *yellow-green* to *deep green*.

All examples of the ¼a. value show the 'N' of 'NAWAB' reversed. On the same value the 'N' of 'JAHAN' is reversed on all positions except R. 3/2, R. 4/1, R. 4/3. On the ½a. both 'N's are always reversed.

1888. T **15** again redrawn. Sheets of 32 (4×8), letters in upper angles smaller. 'N' of 'NAWAB' correct. Wove paper.

57 ¼a. deep green (*imperf*) 1·00 2·00
a. 'SAH' (R. 6/2) 6·50 11·00
b. 'NAWA' (R. 4/4) 6·50 11·00
58 ¼a. deep green (*perf*) 2·00 3·50
a. 'SAH' (R. 6/2) 13·00 16·00
b. 'NAWA' (R. 4/4) 13·00 16·00
c. Imperf between (vert pair) £375

Nos. 50 to 58 have the dash under the letter 'JA' as in No. 14.

1891. T **15** again redrawn. Sheets of 32 (4×8), lettered 'NWAB'. Wove paper.

(a) Imperf

59 ½a. red 2·00 1·50
a. 'SAH' (R. 2/4) 8·50

(b) P 3 to 4½, or about 7

60 ½a. red 80 2·00
a. 'SAH' (R. 2/4) 7·00

Nos. 59 and 60 have the comma under 'JA'. The 'N' of 'JAHAN' is reversed on R. 1/1–3, R. 2/1–2.

1894. T **15** again redrawn; letters in corners larger than in 1888, value in very small characters. Sheets of 32 (4×8), all with 'G' in left-hand lower corner. Wove paper.

61 ¼a. green (*imperf*) 2·00 3·50
a. 'NAWAH' (R. 4/4) 13·00 16·00
b. Value in brackets (R. 1/1) 13·00 16·00
62 ¼a. green (*perf*) 3·00 3·75
a. 'NAWAH' (R. 4/4) 20·00 21·00
b. Value in brackets (R. 1/1) 20·00 21·00

Nos. 61 and 62 have neither the dash nor the comma under 'JA'.

1898. T **16**; oval narrower, stops after 'H.H.', space after 'NAWAB'. The line down the centre is under the first 'H' of 'SHAH' or between 'HA' instead of being under the second 'H' or between 'AH'. Sheets of 32 (4×8). Wove paper. Imperf.

63 **16** ¼a. bright green 75 80
a. 'SHAN' (R. 1/1) 5·00 5·00
64 ¼a. pale green 80 70
a. 'SHAN' (R. 1/1) 5·00 5·00
65 ¼a. black 75 50
a. 'SHAN' (R. 1/1) 5·00 5·00

1899. T **15** redrawn. Sheets of 32 (4×8), the first 'A' of 'NAWAB' always absent. Numerous defective and malformed letters. Wove paper. Imperf.

66 ½a. black 7·50 13·00
a. 'NWASBAHJANNI' (R. 2/4) 42·00 60·00
b. 'SBAH' (R. 3/3, R. 4/3–4, R.5/1–2, R. 6/4) 16·00 28·00
c. 'SBAN' (R. 8/2) 42·00 60·00
d. 'NWIB' (R. 3/2) 42·00 60·00
e. 'BEIAM' (R. 4/4) 42·00 60·00
f. 'SHH' (R. 6/3) 42·00 60·00
g. 'SBAH' and 'BBGAM' (R. 3/4) 42·00 60·00
h. 'BBGAM' (R. 1/3) 42·00 60·00

17 (8a.)

18 (¼a.)

1890. T **17**. Sheets of ten (2×5). Single-line frame to each stamp.

(a) Wove paper

67 **17** 8a. slate-green (*imperf*) 95·00 £190
a. 'HAH' (R. 3/1, R. 4/1, R. 5/1) £120 £250
b. 'JABAN' (R. 2/2) £140
68 8a. slate-green (*perf*) 95·00 £190
a. 'HAH' (R. 3/1, R. 4/1, R. 5/1) £120
b. 'JABAN' (R. 2/2) £140

(b) Thin laid paper

69 **17** 8a. green-black (*imperf*) £110 £275
a. 'HAH' (R. 3/1, R. 4/1, R. 5/1) £140
b. 'JABAN' (R. 2/2) £150
70 8a. green-black (*perf*) £110 £275
a. 'HAH' (R. 3/1, R. 4/1, R. 5/1) £150 £325
b. 'JABAN' (R. 2/2) £160

The 'N' of 'NAWAB' is reversed on R. 5/2 and the 'N' of 'JAHAN' on R. 1/1–2, R. 2/2, R. 3/2, R. 4/2 and R. 5/2.

1893. T **17** redrawn. No frame to each stamp, but a frame to the sheet. Sheets of ten (2×5).

(a) Wove paper

71 8a. green-black (*imperf*) 23·00 25·00
72 8a. green-black (*perf*) 42·00 55·00

(b) Thin laid paper. Imperf

73 8a. green-black £325 £475

1898. Printed from a new stone. Lettering irregular. Sheets of ten (2×5). Wove paper. Imperf.

74 8a. green-black 70·00 85·00
a. Reversed 'E' in 'BEGAM' (R. 1/2, R. 3/2) £140 £160
75 8a. black 65·00 85·00
a. Reversed 'E' in 'BEGAM' (R. 1/2, R. 3/2) £140 £160

1896–1901. Sheets of 32 (4×8).

(a) Wove paper. Imperf

76 **18** ¼a. black 2·75 1·50

(b) Printed from a new stone, lines shaky (1899)

77 **18** ¼a. black 4·50 5·00

(c) The same, on thick wove paper (1901)

78 **18** ¼a. black £550 £650

Nawab Sultan Jahan Begam, 16 June 1901–17 May 1926

19 (¼a.)

20

1902. T **19**. With the octagonal embossed device of the previous issues. Sheets of 16 (4×4) ¼a. or eight (2×4) others. Thin, yellowish wove paper. Imperf.
79 **19** ¼a. rose ... 6·50 12·00
80 ¼a. rose-red ... 4·50 8·50
81 ½a. black ... 6·00 9·00
a. Printed both sides ... £1400 £1400
82 1a. brown ... 14·00 21·00
83 1a. red-brown ... 10·00 17·00
84 2a. blue ... 16·00 27·00
85 4a. orange ... £100 £150
86 4a. yellow ... 38·00 85·00
87 8a. lilac ... £130 £325
88 1r. rose ... £425 £700
79/88 *Set of 7* ... £550 £1000

1903. With a circular embossed device. Sheets of 16 (4×4) ¼a. (two plates) or eight (2×4) (others). Wove paper.
89 **19** ¼a. rose-red ... 1·50 7·50
a. Laid paper ... 1·00 10·00
90 ¼a. red ... 1·50 7·50
a. Laid paper ... 30 7·50
91 ½a. black ... 1·75 5·50
a. Laid paper ... 1·00 11·00
92 1a. brown ... 8·00 15·00
a. Laid paper ... £130
93 1a. red-brown ... 12·00
a. Laid paper ...
94 2a. blue ... 15·00 38·00
a. Laid paper ... £250 £350
95 4a. orange (*laid paper*) ... £600 £600
96 4a. yellow ... 20·00 65·00
a. Laid paper ... £225 £160
97 8a. lilac ... 75·00 £160
a. Laid paper ... £2000
98 1r. rose ... £120 £325
a. Laid paper ... £1900
89/98 *Set of 7* ... £200 £550

1903. No. 71 optd with initial of the new Begam, either six or 11 mm long, in red.
99 8a. green-black ... £300 £325
a. Opt inverted ... £600 £650

Some of the previous stamps remained on sale (and probably in use) after the issue of the series of 1902, and some of these were afterwards put on sale with the new form of embossing; fresh plates were made of some of the old designs, in imitation of the earlier issues, and impressions from these were also sold with the new embossed device. We no longer list these doubtful items.

(Recess Perkins Bacon)

1908. P 13½.
100 **20** 1a. green ... 3·75 7·00
a. Printed both sides ... £180
b. Imperf (pair) ...

The ordinary postage stamps of Bhopal became obsolete on 1 July 1908.

OFFICIAL STAMPS

SERVICE (O **1**) **SERVICE** (O **2**)

(Recess and optd Perkins Bacon)

1908–11. As T **20**, but inscribed 'H.H. BEGUM'S SERVICE' at left. No wmk. P 13 to 14. Overprinted.

(a) With T O **1** *(typo)*
O301 ½a. yellow-green ... 3·25 10
a. Imperf (pair) ... £250
b. Pair, one without overprint ... £1100
c. Opt double, one inverted ... £140
ca. Ditto. Imperf (pair) ... £180
d. Opt inverted ... £275 £190
e. Imperf between (horiz pair) ... £1400
f. Imperf 3 sides (vert pair)* ... £1000
O302 1a. carmine-red ... 5·50 40
a. Opt inverted ... £190 £130
b. Imperf (pair) ... £200
c. Red ... 9·00 10
O303 2a. ultramarine ... 30·00 10
a. Imperf (pair) ... 80·00
O304 4a. brown (1911) ... 16·00 75
O301/O304 *Set of 4* ... 50·00 95

(b) With T O **2** *(litho)*
O305 ½a. yellow-green ... 13·00 2·25
O306 1a. carmine-red ... 16·00 90
O307 2a. ultramarine ... 6·00 1·00
a. Opt inverted ... 25·00
O308 4a. brown (1911) ... £100 1·50
a. Opt inverted ... 20·00 70·00
b. Opt double ... £225
c. Imperf (pair) ... 90·00
d. Imperf (pair) and opt inverted ... 90·00
O305/O308 *Set of 4* ... £120 5·00

The two overprints differ in the shape of the letters, noticeably in the 'R'.
* No. O301f occurs in a block of four with the other vertical pair imperf at left.

Nawab Mohammad Hamidullah. Khan
17 May 1928 to transfer of administration to India, 1 June 1949

(O **4**)

(Des T. I. Archer. Litho Indian Govt Ptg Wks, Nasik)

1930 (1 July)–**31**. T O **4** (25½×30½ *mm*). P 14.
O309 O **4** ½a. sage-green (1931) ... 21·00 1·75
O310 1a. carmine-red ... 22·00 15
O311 2a. ultramarine ... 16·00 45
O312 4a. chocolate ... 22·00 90
O309/O312 *Set of 4* ... 75·00 3·00

The 1a. is inscribed 'POSTAGE AND REVENUE' at left.

(Litho Perkins Bacon)

1932–34. As T O **4** (21×25 *mm*), but inscr 'POSTAGE' at left. Optd with T O **1**.

(a) 'BHOPAL STATE' at right. P 13
O313 ¼a. orange ... 2·50 1·25
a. Perf 11½ (1933) ... 12·00 20
b. Perf 14 (1934) ... 14·00 30
c. Perf 13½ (1934) ... 8·00 30
ca. Vert pair, one without opt ... £150

(b) 'BHOPAL GOVT' at right. P 13½
O314 ½a. yellow-green ... 11·00 10
O315 1a. carmine-red ... 14·00 15
a. Vert pair, one without opt ... £275
O316 2a. ultramarine ... 21·00 45
O317 4a. chocolate ... 17·00 1·00
a. Perf 14 (1934) ... 23·00 40
O313/O317 *Set of 5* ... 60·00 1·20

No. O317 is comb-perforated and No. O317a line-perforated.

1/4 A (O **5**) **THREE PIES** (O **6**) **ONE ANNA** (O **7**)

1935–36. Nos. O314, O316 and O317 surch as Types O **5** to O **7**.
O318 O **5** ¼a. on ½a. yellow-green (R.) ... 55·00 20·00
a. Surch inverted ... £425 £140
b. Vert pair. Nos. O318/O319 ... 80·00 32·00
ba. Ditto. Surch inverted ... £800 £300
O319 O **6** 3p. on ½a. yellow-green (R.) ... 6·00 4·75
a. Surch inverted ... £150 45·00
b. 'THEEE PIES' (R. 7/10) ... £140 80·00
ba. Ditto. Surch inverted ... £1700
c. 'THRFE' for 'THREE' (R. 10/6) ... £140 80·00
ca. Ditto. Surch inverted ... £1700
O320 O **5** ¼a. on 2a. ultramarine (R.) ... 50·00 30·00
a. Surch inverted ... £425 £120
b. Vert pair. Nos. O320/O321 ... 75·00 55·00
ba. Ditto. Surch inverted ... £800 £300
O321 O **6** 3p. on 2a. ultramarine (R.) ... 4·50 6·00
a. Surch inverted ... £150 45·00
b. 'THEEE PIES' (R. 7/10) ... £140 80·00
ba. Ditto. Surch inverted ... £1600 £1000
c. 'THRFE' for 'THREE' (R. 10/6) ... £140 80·00
ca. Ditto. Surch inverted ... £1600 £1000
O322 O **5** ¼a. on 4a. chocolate (R.) ... £2000 £600
a. Vert pair. Nos. O322 and O324 ... £3500 £1000
O323 ¼a. on 4a. chocolate (No. O317a) (Blk.) (25.5.36) ... £150 40·00
a. Vert pair. Nos. O323 and O325 ... £200 75·00
O324 O **6** 3p. on 4a. chocolate (R.) ... £350 £130
a. 'THEEE PIES' (R. 7/10) ... £1600 £1000
c. 'THRFE' for 'THREE' (R. 10/6) ... £1600 £1000
O325 3p. on 4a. chocolate (No. O317a) (Blk.) (25.5.36) ... 2·50 3·75
a. 'THRER' for 'THREE' (R. 8/2) ... £750 £425
b. 'FHREE' for 'THREE' (R. 3/10, R. 10/1) ... £850 £650
c. 'PISE' for 'PIES' (R. 10/10) ... £1400 £1000
d. 'PIFS' for 'PIES' (R. 7/9) ... £750 £425
O326 O **7** 1a. on ½a. yellow-green (V.) ... 5·00 1·50
a. Surch inverted ... £130 55·00
b. First 'N' in 'ANNA' inverted (R. 4/5) ... £160 75·00
ba. Ditto. Surch inverted ... £1500 £900
O327 1a. on 2a. ultramarine (R.) ... 2·25 3·00
a. Surch inverted ... £160 40·00
b. First 'N' in 'ANNA' inverted (R. 4/5) ... £110 75·00
ba. Ditto. Surch inverted ... £1600 £900
O327*d* 1a. on 2a. ultramarine (V.) ... 75·00 £120
da. Surch inverted ... £140 £170
db. First 'N' in 'ANNA' inverted (R. 4/5) ... £1300 £1600
dc. Ditto. Surch inverted ... £2000 £2250
O328 1a. on 2a. ultram (Blk.) (25.5.36) ... 70 2·50
a. 'ANNO' ... £3500
O329 1a. on 4a. chocolate (B.) ... 7·50 7·00
a. First 'N' in 'ANNA' inverted (R. 4/5) ... £180 £150
b. Perf 14 ... 28·00 10·00
ba. Ditto. First 'N' in 'ANNA' inverted (R. 4/5) ... £450 £170

Nos. O318 to O325 are arranged in composite sheets of 100 (10×10). The two upper horizontal rows of each value are surcharged as T O **5** and the next five rows as T O **6**. The remaining three rows are also surcharged as T O **6** but in a slightly narrower setting.

The surcharge on No. O323 differs from T O **5** in the shape of the figures and letter.

O **8**

(Des T. I. Archer. Litho Indian Govt Ptg Wks, Nasik (No. O330). Typo Bhopal Govt Ptg Wks (others))

1935–39. As T O **8**.

(a) Litho. Inscr 'BHOPAL GOVT POSTAGE'. Optd 'SERVICE' (13½ mm). P 13½
O330 1a.3p. blue and claret ... 3·50 2·25

(b) Typo. Inscr 'BHOPAL STATE POSTAGE'. Optd 'SERVICE' (11 mm). P 12
O331 1a.6p. blue and claret (1937) ... 2·50 1·75
a. Imperf between (pair) ... £325 £350
b. Opt omitted ... £275 £200
c. Opt double, one inverted ... £950 £1000
d. Imperf (pair) ... † £275
e. Blue printing double ... † £200
O332 1a.6p. claret (1939) ... 6·00 3·00
a. Imperf between (pair) ... £400 £425
b. Opt omitted ... — £800
c. Opt double, one inverted ... — £800
d. Opt double ... — £800
e. Bright rose-red ... — 20·00

PRINTERS. From No. O333 all issues were printed by the Bhopal Govt Ptg Wks in typography.

O **9**

O **10** The Moti Mahal

O **11** The Moti Masjid

O **12** Taj Mahal and Be-Nazir Palaces

O **13** Ahmadabad Palace

O **14** Rait Ghat

1936 (July)–**38**. Optd 'SERVICE'. P 12.
O333 O **9** ¼a. orange (Br.) ... 90 60
a. Imperf between (vert pair) ... £275
ab. Imperf between (horiz pair) ... † £800
b. Opt inverted ... £800 £650
c. Black opt ... 8·50 75
ca. Opt inverted ... † £500
cb. Opt double ... † £425
O334 ¼a. yellow (Br.) (1938) ... 13·00 2·50
O335 1a. scarlet ... 1·50 10
a. Imperf between (horiz pair) ... £275 £250
b. Imperf between (vert pair) ... † £550
c. Imperf between (block of 4) ... £800 £750
d. Imperf vert (horiz pair) ... † £300

1936–49. Types O **10**/O **14**. P 12.

(a) Optd 'SERVICE' (13½ mm)
O336 O **10** ½a. purple-brown and yellow-green ... 70 80
a. Imperf between (vert pair) ... † £425
ab. Imperf between (horiz pair) ... † £450
b. Opt double ... £350 £190
c. Frame double ... £120 15·00
d. Purple-brown and green (1938) ... 70 50

(b) Optd 'SERVICE' (11 mm)
O337 O **11** 2a. brown and blue (1937) ... 2·00 1·25
a. Imperf between (vert pair) ... † £600
ab. Imperf between (horiz pair) ... † £425
b. Opt inverted ... £300 £400
c. Opt omitted ... £500
d. Pair, one without opt ... £1000
e. As d. but opt inverted ... £1800
O338 2a. green and violet (1938) ... 19·00 40
a. Imperf between (vert pair) ... † £500
b. Imperf between (vert strip of 3) ... £275 £375
c. Frame double ... † £550
d. Centre double ... † £650
O339 O **12** 4a. blue and brown (1937) ... 3·75 50
a. Imperf between (horiz pair) ... † £1400
b. Opt omitted ... † £550
c. Opt double ... † £250
d. Centre double ... † £750
e. Blue and reddish brown (1938) ... 4·25 65
ea. Frame double ... † £550
O340 O **13** 8a. bright purple and blue (1938) ... 6·00 2·50
a. Imperf between (vert pair) ... † £800
b. Opt omitted ... † £325
c. Opt double ... † £275
d. Imperf vert (horiz pair) and opt omitted ... † £550
e. Imperf (pair) and opt omitted ... † £550
f. Frame double ... † £500
O341 O **14** 1r. blue and reddish purple (Br.) (1938) ... 30·00 11·00
a. Imperf horiz (vert pair) ... † £3500
b. Opt in black (1942) ... 25·00 4·50
ba. Light blue and bright purple ... 60·00 45·00
bb. Laid paper ... £1700 £1800
O336/O341b *Set of 6* ... 50·00 8·50

(c) Optd 'SERVICE' (11½ mm) with serifs
O342 O **14** 1r. dull blue and bright purple (Blk.) (1949) ... 75·00 £160

		a. 'SREVICE' for 'SERVICE' (R. 6/6)	£200	£475
		b. 'SERVICE' omitted	£1700	
		(d) Optd 'SERVICE' (13½ mm) with serifs		
O343	**O 13**	8a. bright purple and blue (1949)	£140	£200
		a. 'SERAICE' for 'SERVICE' (R. 6/5)	£800	£1200
		b. Fig '1' for 'I' in 'SERVICE' (R. 7/1)	£850	£1300

The ½a. is inscr 'BHOPAL GOVT' below the Arms, other values have 'BHOPAL STATE'.

O **15** Tiger

O **16** Spotted Deer

1940. Types O **15**/O **16**. P 12.

O344	**O 15**	¼a. bright blue	7·00	1·75
O345	**O 16**	1a. bright purple	55·00	4·75

1941. As T O **8** but coloured centre inscr 'SERVICE'; bottom frame inscr 'BHOPAL STATE POSTAGE'. P 12.

O346		1a.3p. emerald-green	3·50	3·25
		a. Imperf between (pair)	£700	£700

O **17** The Moti Mahal

O **18** The Moti Masjid

O **19** Be-Nazir Palaces

1944–47. Types O **17**/O **19**. P 12.

O347	**O 17**	½a. green	1·00	1·00
		a. Imperf (pair)	†	£130
		b. Imperf between (vert pair)	†	£375
		c. Doubly printed	†	£250
O348	**O 18**	2a. violet	26·00	4·25
		a. Imperf (pair)	†	£140
		c. Bright purple (1945)	8·50	3·75
		d. Mauve (1947)	15·00	15·00
		e. Error. Chocolate (imperf)	£375	£375
O349	**O 19**	4a. chocolate	13·00	2·25
		a. Imperf (pair)	†	£160
		b. Imperf vert (horiz pair)	†	£450
		c. Doubly printed	†	£300
O347/O349 *Set of 3*			20·00	6·25

Collectors are warned against faked perforation varieties of this issue, created by adding external perforations to genuine imperforate pairs (as Nos. O347a, O348a and O349a).

O **20** Arms of Bhopal

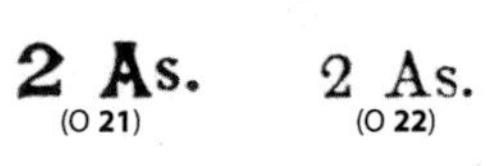

(O **21**) (O **22**)

1944–49. P 12.

O350	**O 20**	3p. bright blue	1·00	1·00
		a. Imperf between (vert pair)	£200	£225
		b. Imperf between (horiz pair)	†	£450
		c. Stamp doubly printed	95·00	
O351		9p. chestnut (*shades*) (1945)	11·00	4·25
		a. Imperf (pair)	†	£225
		b. Orange-brown	3·00	5·00
O352		1a. purple (1945)	11·00	1·75
		a. Imperf horiz (vert pair)	†	£750
		b. Violet (1946)	20·00	3·25
O353		1½a. claret (1945)	5·00	1·25
		a. Imperf between (horiz pair)	†	£600
		b. Imperf between (vert pair)	†	£650
O354		3a. yellow	26·00	26·00
		a. Imperf (pair)	†	£275
		b. Imperf horiz (vert pair)	†	£425
		c. Imperf vert (horiz pair)		
		d. Orange-brown (1949)	£160	£160
O355		6a. carmine (1945)	35·00	75·00
		a. Imperf (pair)	†	£425
		b. Imperf horiz (vert pair)	†	£550
		c. Imperf vert (horiz pair)	†	£550
O350/O355 *Set of 6*			75·00	£100

1949 (July). Surch with T O **21**. P 12.

O356	**O 20**	2a. on 1½a. claret	3·50	10·00
		a. Stop omitted	21·00	55·00
		b. Imperf (pair)	£425	£475
		ba. Ditto. Stop omitted (pair)	£1500	£1600
		c. '2' omitted (in pair with normal)	£2000	

The 'stop omitted' variety occurs on positions 60 and 69 in the sheet of 81.

1949. Surch with T O **22**. Imperf.

O357	**O 20**	2a. on 1½a. claret	£2250	£2250
		a. Perf 12	£2500	£2500

Three different types of '2' occur in the setting of T O **22**. This surcharge has been extensively forged, and should not be purchased without a reliable guarantee.

BHOR

PRICES FOR STAMPS ON COVER TO 1945

Nos. 1/2	*from* × 50
No. 3	*from* × 7

GUM. The stamps of Bhor were issued without gum.

Pandit Shankar Rao, 1871–1922

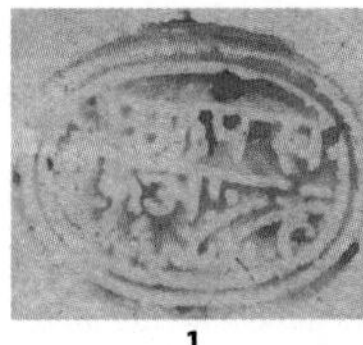
1

2

1879. Handstamped. Very thick to thin native paper. Imperf.

1	**1**	½a. carmine (*shades*)	5·50	8·00
		a. *Tête-bêche* (pair)	£1300	
2	**2**	1a. carmine (*shades*)	8·00	11·00

3

1901. Typo. Wove paper. Imperf.

3	**3**	½a. red	22·00	48·00

BIJAWAR

PRICES FOR STAMPS ON COVER TO 1945
The stamps of Bijawar are very rare used on cover.

Maharaja Sarwant Singh, 1899–1941

1

2

(Typo Lakshmi Art Ptg Works, Bombay)

1935 (1 July)–**36**.

		(a) P 11		
1	**1**	3p. brown	12·00	8·00
		a. Imperf (pair)	14·00	
		b. Imperf between (vert pair)	£110	
		c. Imperf horiz (vert pair)	70·00	
2		6p. carmine	11·00	8·00
		a. Imperf (pair)	£110	
		b. Imperf between (vert pair)	£100	
		c. Imperf between (horiz pair)	£110	£180
		d. Imperf horiz (vert pair)	£120	
3		9p. violet	15·00	9·00
		a. Imperf (pair)	£180	
		b. Imperf between (vert pair)	£130	
		c. Imperf between (horiz pair)	£110	
		d. Imperf horiz (vert pair)	£120	
4		1a. blue	18·00	8·00
		a. Imperf (pair)	£110	
		b. Imperf between (vert pair)	£120	
		c. Imperf between (horiz pair)	£190	
		d. Imperf horiz (vert pair)	£140	
		e. Imperf vert (horiz strip of 3)	£225	
5		2a. deep green	15·00	9·00
		a. Imperf (pair)	£140	
		b. Imperf horiz (vert pair)	18·00	
		c. Imperf between (vert pair)	45·00	
		d. Imperf between (horiz pair)	75·00	£120
1/5 *Set of 5*			65·00	38·00
		(b) Roul 7 (1936)		
6	**1**	3p. brown	9·50	13·00
		a. Printed on gummed side	£700	
7		6p. carmine	10·00	35·00
8		9p. violet	10·00	£200
9		1a. blue	11·00	£225
10		2a. deep green	20·00	£250
6/10 *Set of 5*			55·00	£650

1937 (May). Typo. P 9.

11	**2**	4a. orange	26·00	£170
		a. Imperf between (vert pair)	£170	
		b. Imperf (pair)	£225	
12		6a. lemon	27·00	£170
		a. Imperf between (vert pair)	£180	
		b. Imperf (pair)	£225	
13		8a. emerald-green	30·00	£225
		a. Imperf (pair)	£250	
14		12a. greenish blue	32·00	£250
		a. Imperf (pair)	£250	
15		1r. bright violet	55·00	£325
		a. '1 Rs' for '1 R' (R. 1/2)	75·00	£550
		b. Imperf (pair)	£300	
		ba. '1 Rs' for '1 R' (R. 1/2)	£850	
11/15 *Set of 5*			£160	£1000

The stamps of Bijawar were withdrawn in 1941.

BUNDI

PRICES FOR STAMPS ON COVER TO 1940

No. 1	*from* × 2
No. 2	*from* × 4
Nos. 3/53	*from* × 10
Nos. 54/63	*from* × 5
Nos. 64/78	*from* × 2
Nos. 79/92	*from* × 10
Nos. O1/O52	*from* × 15
Nos. O53/O57	*from* × 20
Nos. O58/O59	—

GUM. Nos. 1/17 were issued without gum.

ILLUSTRATIONS. Types **1/10** and the tablet inscriptions for T **11** are shown actual size.

In Nos. 1 to 17 characters denoting the value are below the dagger, except in Nos. 2a, 11 and 17.

All Bundi stamps until 1914 are lithographed and imperforate.

Maharao Raja Raghubir Singh, 1889–1927

1

1894 (May). Each stamp with a distinct frame and the stamps not connected by the framing lines. Three vertical lines on dagger. Laid paper.

1	**1**	½a. slate-grey	£21000	£4000
		a. Last two letters of value below the rest	†	£12000

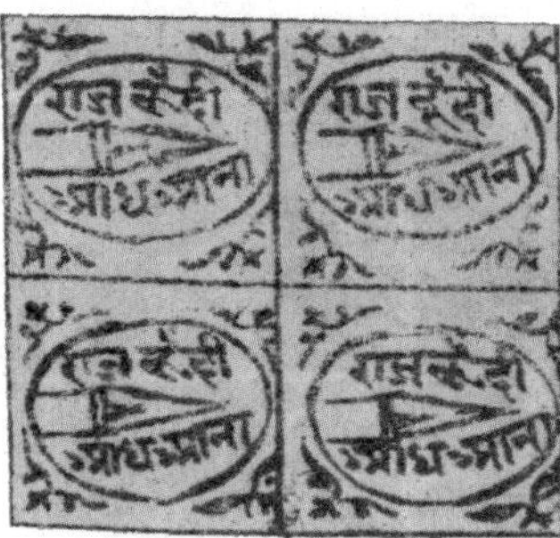
2 (Block of four stamps)

1894 (Dec). Stamps joined together, with no space between them. Two vertical lines on dagger. Thin wove paper.

2	**2**	½a. slate-grey	70·00	75·00
		a. Value at top, name below	£450	£700
		b. Right upper ornament omitted	£4250	£5500
		c. Last two letters of value below the rest	£2500	£2500
		d. Left lower ornament omitted	£4250	£5500

No. 2 was printed in sheets of 294, comprising two panes (10×14 and 11×14) side by side, in *tête-bêche* format. In the 10×14 pane No. 2a occurs on R1/1-10, No. 2b on R11/7 and No. 2d on R2/9. In the 11×14 pane No. 2c occurs on R2/11, 8/3 and 10/1.

3

1896 (Nov). Dagger shorter, lines thicker. Stamps separate. Laid paper.

3	**3**	½a. slate-grey	8·00	12·00
		a. Last two letters of value below the rest	£475	£700

No. 3 was printed in sheets of 168, comprising two panes (7×12) side by side.

4 (1 anna)

5 (4 annas)

6 (2 annas)

1897–98. No shading in centre of blade of dagger. The stamps have spaces between them, but are connected by the framing lines, both vertically and horizontally. Laid paper.

*I. Blade of dagger comparatively narrow, and either triangular, as in Types **4** and **6**, or with the left-hand corner not touching the bar behind it, as in T **5** (1897–1898)*

4	**4**	1a. Indian red	21·00	48·00
5	**5**	1a. red	26·00	42·00
6		2a. green	25·00	45·00
7	**6**	2a. yellow-green	25·00	50·00
8	**5**	4a. green	£120	£180
9		8a. Indian red	£200	£650
10		1r. yellow/*blue*	£700	£1100
4/10 *Set of 5*			£950	£1800

7

II. Blade varying in shape, but as a rule not touching the bar; value above and name below the dagger, instead of the reverse (Jan 1898)

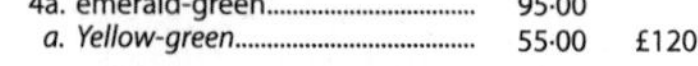

11	**7**	4a. emerald-green	95·00	
		a. Yellow-green	55·00	£120

8 (**½ anna**)

9 (**1 anna**)

III. Blade wider and (except on the ½a.) almost diamond shaped; it nearly always touches the bar (1898–1900)

12	**8**	½a. slate-grey (5.2.98)	8·00	8·00
13	**9**	1a. Indian red (7.98)	7·50	8·00
14		2a. pale green (9.11.98)	26·00	29·00
		a. First two characters of value (= two) omitted	£2750	£2750
15		8a. Indian red (7.98)	40·00	40·00
16		1r. yellow/*blue* (7.98)	50·00	£100
		a. On wove paper	38·00	55·00
12/16a *Set of 5*			£110	£130

10

IV. Inscriptions as on No. 11; point of dagger to left (9.11.98)

17	**10**	4a. green	95·00	£110
		a. Yellow-green	42·00	50·00

All the above stamps are lithographed in large sheets, containing as many varieties of type as there are stamps in the sheets.

11 Raja protecting Sacred Cows

T **11** was produced from separate clichés printed as a block of four. The same clichés were used for all values, but not necessarily in the same order within the block. The Devanagri inscriptions, 'RAJ BUNDI' at top and the face value at bottom, were inserted into the basic clichés as required so that various differences exist within the 58 settings which have been identified.

The denominations may be identified from the following illustrations. The ½a., 3a. and rupee values can be easily distinguished by their colours.

Bottom tablets:—

¼a. 1a. 2a. 2½a. 4a. 6a. 8a. 10a.

12a. 1r.

The nine versions of the inscriptions are as follows:

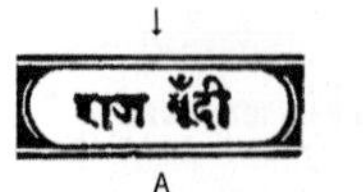

A

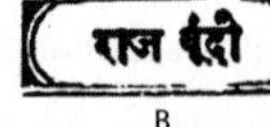

B

Top tablet

Type A. Top tablet has inscription in two separate words with a curved line over the first character in the second. The second word has three characters. Bottom tablet has short line above the first character in the second word.

Type B. Top tablet as Type A, but without the curved line over the first character in the second word. Bottom tablet as Type A.

C

Type C. Top tablet as Type B, but with large loop beneath the first character in the second word. This loop is usually joined to the main character, but is sometimes detached as in the illustration. Bottom tablet as Type A.

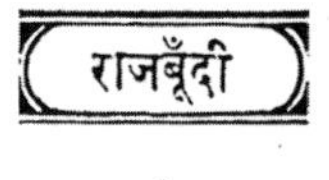

D

Top tablet

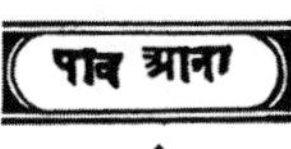

E

Bottom tablet

Type D. Top tablet in thinner lettering with the inscription shown as one word of six characters. The fourth character has a curved line above it, as in Type A, and a loop beneath, as in Type C. Bottom tablet as Type A, but thinner letters.

Type E. Top tablet as Type C. Bottom tablet shows a redrawn first character to the second word. This has the line at top extending over the entire character.

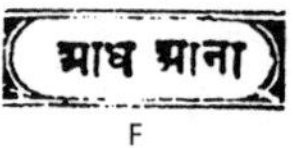

F

Bottom tablet

Type F. Top tablet as Type B. Bottom tablet as Type E, but first character in second word differs.

G

H

Type G. Top tablet as Type C, but without dot over first character in second word. There are now four characters in the second word. Bottom tablet as Type E.

Type H. Top tablet as Type G, but with characters larger and bolder. Bottom tablet as Type E, but with characters larger and bolder.

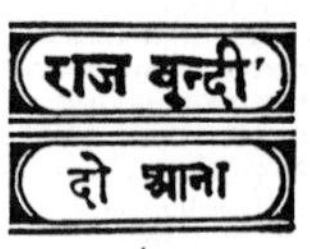

I

Type I. Top tablet as Type H. Bottom tablet as Type E.

Some settings contained more than one inscription type within the block of four so that *se-tenant* examples are known of Type B with Type C (¼, 1, 2, 4, 8, 10 and 12a.), Type C with Type E (¼, ½ and 4a.) and Type E with Type F (½ and 4a.). Type F only exists from this mixed setting.

1914 (Oct)–**41**. T **11**. Typo. Ungummed paper except for Nos. 73/78.

I. Rouletted in colour

(a) Inscriptions as Type A. Thin wove paper (1916–1923)

18	½a. black	3·50	12·00
19	1a. vermilion	12·00	35·00
20	2a. emerald	6·00	65·00
	a. Deep green (coarse ptg on medium wove paper) (1923)	7·00	10·00
21	2½a. chrome-yellow (*shades*) (1917)	24·00	75·00
	a. Printed both sides	£2000	
22	3a. chestnut (1917)	42·00	75·00
23	4a. yellow-green	21·00	
24	6a. cobalt (1917)	32·00	£160
25	1r. reddish violet (1917)	40·00	£160

A special printing of the 1a. took place in late 1917 in connection with the 'OUR DAY' Red Cross Society Fund. This had the 'RAJ BUNDI' inscription in the bottom tablet with the face value below it. The top tablet carried four Devanagri characters for 'OUR DAY'. No evidence has been found to suggest that this 1a. stamp was used for postal purposes (*Price, £250 unused*).

(b) Inscriptions as Type B. Thin wove or pelure paper (1914–1923)

25*a*	¼a. cobalt (1916)	5·00	32·00
	ab. Stamp doubly printed	£1100	
26	¼a. ultramarine (*shades*) (1917)	2·25	6·00
	a. Indigo (1923)	4·25	12·00
27	½a. black	3·00	8·50
28	1a. vermilion (1915)	6·00	20·00
	a. Carmine (1923)	17·00	22·00
	b. Red (shades) (1923)	6·50	20·00
29	2a. emerald (*shades*) (1915)	18·00	48·00
30	2½a. olive-yellow (1917)	22·00	40·00
31	3a. chestnut (1917)	18·00	75·00
32	4a. apple-green (1915)	4·50	55·00
32*a*	4a. olive-yellow (1917)	£200	£375
33	6a. pale ultramarine (*shades*) (1917)	21·00	£180
	a. Deep ultramarine (1917)	7·00	£160
34	8a. orange (1915)	7·50	£190
35	10a. olive-sepia (1917)	£250	£700
	a. Yellow-brown	£300	
36	12a. sage-green (1917)	£650	£900
36*a*	1r. lilac (*shades*) (1915)	25·00	

(c) Inscriptions as Type C. Thin to medium wove paper (1917–1941)

37	¼a. ultramarine (*shades*) (1923)	15·00	17·00
	a. Indigo (1923)	16·00	19·00
	c. Cobalt (medium wove paper) (1937)	40·00	32·00
38	½a. black	6·00	7·50
39	1a. orange-red	40·00	50·00
	a. Carmine (1923)	42·00	50·00
	b. Deep red (*medium wove paper*) (1936)	32·00	38·00
40	2a. emerald	22·00	42·00
	a. Sage-green	27·00	45·00
41	4a. yellow-green (*shades*)	£110	£250
	a. Olive-yellow	£160	£325
	b. Bright apple-green (medium wove paper) (1936)	£1200	£425
42	8a. reddish orange	10·00	90·00
43	10a. brown-olive	20·00	£180
	a. Olive-sepia	50·00	£225
	b. Yellow-brown	90·00	
44	12a. sage-green	24·00	£170
45	1r. lilac	40·00	£325
46	2r. red-brown and black	£120	£375
	a. Chocolate and black (medium wove paper) (1936)	70·00	£500
47	3r. blue and red-brown	£190	£550
	a. Grey-blue and chocolate (medium wove paper) (1941)	£120	
	ab. Chocolate (inscriptions) inverted	£32000	
48	4r. emerald and scarlet	£475	£600
49	5r. scarlet and emerald	£475	£600

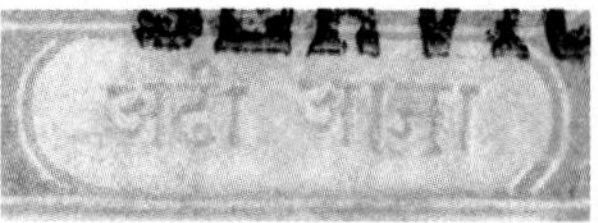

Type II (**2½a.**)

(d) Inscriptions as Type D. Thin wove paper (1918?)

50	2½a. buff (*shades*)	25·00	85·00
	a. Type II value		
51	3a. red-brown	42·00	48·00
	a. Semi-circle and dot omitted from 4th character	55·00	65·00
52	10a. bistre	45·00	£190
	a. 4th character turned to left instead of downwards	65·00	£300
53	12a. grey-olive	70·00	£200
	a. 4th character turned to left instead of downwards	£100	
	b. Blackish green	70·00	
	ba. 4th character turned to left instead of downwards	£100	

(e) Inscriptions as Type E

(i) Medium wove paper (1930–1937)

54	¼a. deep slate	23·00	35·00
54*a*	¼a. indigo (*thin wove paper*) (1935)	48·00	48·00
	b. Cobalt (1937)	42·00	32·00
55	½a. black	22·00	25·00
56	1a. carmine-red	28·00	48·00
57	3a. chocolate (*shades*) (1936)	11·00	55·00
58	4a. yellow-olive (1935)	£1300	£375
	a. Bright apple-green (1936)	£1300	£350
	ab. No tail to 4th character	£2000	£600

(ii) Very thick wove paper (1930–1932)

59	¼a. indigo (1932)	42·00	48·00
60	½a. black	£150	£160
61	1a. bright scarlet (1931)	25·00	40·00
	a. Carmine-red	£110	£120

(iii) Thin horizontally laid paper (1935)

62	¼a. indigo	5·50	28·00
63	1a. scarlet-vermilion	18·00	50·00

Nos. 62 and 63 exist in *tête-bêche* blocks of four on the same or opposite sides of the paper.

(f) Inscriptions as Type F. Medium wove paper (1935)

63*a*	½a. black	£190	£275
63*b*	4a. yellow-olive	£2500	£1100

(g) Inscriptions as Type G

(i) Horizontally laid paper (1935)

64	½a. black	£100	£100
	a. Vert laid paper	£100	£100
65	1a. scarlet	80·00	50·00
66	4a. bright green	20·00	50·00

(ii) Medium wove paper (1936)

66*a*	½a. black	6·00	38·00
66*b*	4a. yellow-green	£2000	£750

(h) Inscriptions as Type H. Medium wove paper (1935–1941)

67	¼a. ultramarine	2·50	7·00
68	½a. black (1938)	80·00	80·00
69	1a. deep red	8·50	45·00
	a. Rosine (1938)	28·00	50·00
70	4a. emerald (1938)	28·00	42·00
71	4r. yellow-green and vermilion (1941)	£190	
72	5r. vermilion and yellow-green (1941)	£250	

No. 70 shows the currency spelt as 'ANE' with the last letter missing and an accent over the Devanagri 'N'.

II. P 11

(a) Inscriptions as Type H. Medium wove paper with gum (1939–1941)

73	¼a. ultramarine	25·00	38·00
	a. Greenish blue (1941)	1·75	50·00
74	½a. black	42·00	45·00
75	1a. scarlet-vermilion (1940)	£200	65·00
	a. Rose (1940)	12·00	60·00
76	2a. yellow-green (1941)	16·00	90·00

(b) Inscriptions as Type I. Medium wove paper with gum (1940)

77	½a. black	£325	£180
78	2a. bright apple-green	75·00	80·00

FISCAL USE. Collectors are warned that the low values of the later settings of T **11** were extensively used for fiscal purposes. Stamps which have been fraudulently cleaned of pen-cancels, regummed or provided with forged postmarks are frequently met with. Particular care should be exercised with examples of Nos. 58/58a, 64/65, 68/70, 74/75a and 77.

Maharao Raja Ishwari Singh, 1927–1945

20

1941–44. Typo. P 11.

79	**20**	3p. bright blue	3·75	7·00
80		6p. deep blue	7·50	11·00
81		1a. orange-red	9·50	13·00
82		2a. chestnut	11·00	25·00
		a. Deep brown (no gum) (1944)	15·00	20·00
83		4a. bright green	17·00	80·00
84		8a. dull green	23·00	£400
85		1r. deep blue	48·00	£500
79/85 *Set of 7*			£110	£900

The first printing only of Nos. 79/85 is usually with gum; all further printings, including No. 82*a*, are without gum.

Maharao Raja Bahadur Singh, 1945–1971

21 Maharao Raja Bahadur Singh

22 Maharoa Raja Badahur Singh

23 Bundi

(Typo *Times of India* Press, Bombay)

1947. P 11.

86	**21**	¼a. blue-green	2·25	48·00
87		½a. violet	2·25	38·00
88		1a. yellow-green	2·25	40·00
89	**22**	2a. vermilion	2·25	85·00
90		4a. orange	3·50	£100
91	**23**	8a. ultramarine	3·50	
92		1r. chocolate	20·00	
86/92 *Set of 7*			30·00	

OFFICIAL STAMPS

PRICES. Prices for Nos. O1/O52 are for unused examples. Used stamps are generally worth a small premium over the prices quoted.

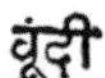

BUNDI

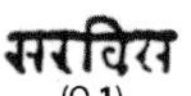

SERVICE

(O 1) (O 2)

BUNDI

SERVICE

(O 3)

1915–41. T **11** handstamped as Types O **1**/O **3**. Ungummed paper except Nos. O47/O52.

A. Optd with T O **1**. *B. Optd with T O* **2**.

C. Optd with T O **3**

I. Rouletted in colour

(a) Inscriptions as Type A. Thin wove paper

		A	B	C
O1	½a. black	£450	†	†
	a. Red opt	£400	†	†
O1*b*	2a. emerald	9·00	£375	†
	ba. Deep green (coarse ptg on medium wove paper)	6·50	15·00	£450
	bb. Red opt	35·00	25·00	†
O2	2½a. chrome-yellow (*shades*)	10·00	25·00	£500
	a. Red opt	£425	£475	†
O3	3a. chestnut	11·00	23·00	†
	a. Green opt	£375	†	†
	b. Red opt	£650	£700	†
O4	6a. cobalt	55·00	50·00	£550
	a. Red opt	£600	£650	£700
O5	1r. reddish violet	95·00	£100	†
	a. Red opt	£700	£800	†

(b) Inscriptions as Type B. Thin wove or pelure paper

		A	B	C
O6	¼a. ultramarine (*shades*)	1·75	5·50	7·50
	a. Red opt	1·25	4·00	£400
	b. Green opt	£200	†	†
O7	½a. black	16·00	7·50	50·00
	a. Red opt	5·50	16·00	£400
	b. Green opt	£180	†	†
O8	1a. vermilion	8·50	†	†
	a. Red opt	—	†	†
	b. Carmine	60·00	23·00	£170
	c. Red (shades)	8·50	7·00	£275
O9	2a. emerald (*shades*)	50·00	75·00	†
	a. Red opt	—	£300	†
O9*b*	3a. chestnut (R.)	—	†	†
O10	4a. apple-green	12·00	£130	£475
	a. Red opt	£600	†	†
O10*b*	4a. olive-yellow	£350	£500	†
	ba. Red opt	£850	£850	†
O11	6a. pale ultramarine (*shades*)	19·00	£375	†
	a. Red opt	£750	£750	†
	b. Deep ultramarine	80·00	90·00	†
	ba. Red opt	£250	£225	†
O12	8a. orange	90·00	£140	£750
	a. Red opt	£700	†	†
O13	10a. olive-sepia	£325	£350	£1000
	a. Red opt	£1300	£1500	£1600
O14	12a. sage-green	£200	£700	£1300
	a. Red opt	†	†	£1600
O14*b*	1r. lilac	£400	†	†

(c) Inscriptions as Type C. Thin to medium wove paper

		A	B	C
O15	¼a. ultramarine (*shades*)	9·50	4·75	23·00
	a. Red opt	1·50	5·50	£425
	b. Green opt	11·00	90·00	†
	c. Cobalt (medium wove paper)	80·00	80·00	£600
	ca. Red opt	55·00	40·00	£180
O16	½a. black	15·00	3·50	21·00
	a. Red opt	3·50	8·00	£400
	b. Green opt	5·50	†	†
O17	1a. orange-red	1·25	—	†
	a. Carmine	45·00	15·00	55·00
	b. Deep red (medium wove paper)	55·00	75·00	£170
	ba. Red opt	†	£350	†
O18	2a. emerald	14·00	28·00	£190
	a. Red opt	†	£250	†
	b. Sage-green	20·00	17·00	£140
O19	4a. yellow-green (*shades*)	20·00	£130	†
	b. Red opt	—	£550	†
	c. Olive-yellow	£180	£180	†
	ca. Red opt	£500	£650	†
	d. Bright apple-green (medium wove paper)	£2000	†	†
O20	8a. reddish orange	21·00	65·00	£425
	a. Red opt	£600	£600	†
O21	10a. brown-olive	£110	£170	£800
	a. Red opt	£850	£850	£1100
O22	12a. sage-green	90·00	£190	£900
	a. Red opt	£800	†	£1000
O23	1r. lilac	£200	†	†
	a. Red opt	£650	†	†
O24	2r. red-brown and black	£550	£225	†
	a. Red opt	†	£2000	†
	b. Green opt	£2000		
	c. Chocolate and black (medium wove paper)	£1300	£1300	†
O25	3r. blue and red-brown	£450	£250	†
	a. Red opt	£1900	†	†
	b. Grey-blue and chocolate (medium wove paper)	£2250	£2250	†
	ba. Red opt	£2500	†	†
O26	4r. emerald and scarlet	£425	£400	†
O27	5r. scarlet and emerald	£425	£400	†

(d) Inscriptions as Type D. Thin wove paper

		A	B	C
O28	2½a. buff (*shades*)	15·00	26·00	†
	a. Type II value	†	£850	†
	b. Red opt	£500	£650	†
O29	3a. red-brown	60·00	48·00	†
	a. Variety as No. 51a	80·00	75·00	†
	b. Red opt	†	£850	†
O30	10a. bistre	80·00	£120	£850
	a. Variety as No. 52a	£120	£190	£1300
	b. Red opt	£800	£750	†
	ba. Variety as No. 52a	£1100	†	†
O31	12a. grey-olive	£100	£160	£900
	a. Variety as No. 53a	£150	£250	£1400
	b. Red opt	£700	£1000	†
	ba. Variety as No. 53a	£950	†	†

(e) Inscriptions as Type E

(i) Medium wove paper

		A	B	C
O32	¼a. deep slate	50·00	20·00	†
	a. Red opt	40·00	70·00	†
O32*b*	¼a. indigo (*thin wove paper*)	80·00	55·00	†
	ba. Red opt	75·00	75·00	†
	bb. Green opt	£200	£275	†
	c. Cobalt	80·00	80·00	£600
	ca. Red opt	50·00	40·00	£170
O33	½a. black	65·00	13·00	†
	a. Red opt	35·00	13·00	†
	b. Green opt	£300	£375	†
O34	1a. carmine-red	70·00	75·00	£450
O35	3a. chocolate (*shades*)	£190	£140	£325
	a. Red opt	£1000	£1000	†
O35*b*	4a. yellow-olive	†	£2500	†
	ba. Bright apple-green	£2750	£2750	†

(ii) Very thick wove paper

		A	B	C
O36	¼a. indigo	14·00	20·00	†
	a. Red opt	40·00	90·00	†
	b. Green opt	£120	†	†
O37	½a. black	£300	£250	†
O38	1a. bright scarlet	22·00	21·00	£550
	a. Carmine-red	£170	£190	†

(iii) Thin horizontally laid paper

		A	B	C
O39	¼a. indigo	£120	£120	†
	a. Red opt	5·50	13·00	£350
O40	1a. scarlet-vermilion	90·00	50·00	†
	a. Red opt	£700	£750	†

Nos. O39/O40a exist in *tête-bêche* blocks of four on the same or opposite sides of the paper.

(f) Inscriptions as Type F. Medium wove paper

		A	B	C
O40*b*	½a. black	£600	£650	†
	ba. Red opt	£500	£550	†
	bb. Green opt	£800	†	†
O40*c*	4a. yellow-olive	†	£2750	†

(g) Inscriptions as Type G

(i) Horizontally laid paper

		A	B	C
O41	½a. black	£500	£650	†
	a. Red opt	£180	£275	†
	b. Vert laid paper	£275	£225	†
	ba. Red opt	£350	90·00	£750
O42	4a. bright green	£325	£325	†
	a. Red opt	£375	£450	†

(ii) Medium wove paper

		A	B	C
O42*b*	½a. black	£500	£600	†
	ba. Red opt	£425	£425	†

(h) Inscriptions as Type H. Medium wove paper

		A	B	C
O43	¼a. ultramarine	25·00	90·00	†
	a. Red opt	£225	£500	†
O44	½a. black	80·00	£130	†
	a. Red opt	70·00	†	£900
O45	1a. rosine	£275	£250	£900
	a. Deep red	£450	£450	†
O46	4a. emerald	£375	£400	£750
	a. Red opt	£1000	†	£1000

II. P 11

(a) Inscriptions as Type H. Medium wove paper with gum

		A	B	C
O47	¼a. ultramarine	50·00	65·00	£170
	a. Red opt	90·00	£120	†
	b. Greenish blue	75·00	75·00	£200
	ba. Red opt	£200	†	†
O48	½a. black	55·00	95·00	£475
	a. Red opt	£130	£650	£375
O49	1a. scarlet-vermilion	£425	£450	£950
	a. Stamp doubly printed	†	†	£2500
	b. Rose	£225	£180	£500
O50	2a. yellow-green	£850	£400	£500

(b) Inscriptions as Type I. Medium wove paper with gum

		A	B	C
O51	½a. black	£275	£450	£750
	a. Red opt	£1100	£1100	—
O52	2a. bright apple-green	£900	£800	£2750

Until 1941 it was the general practice to carry official mail free but some of the above undoubtedly exist postally used.

SERVICE

(O 4)

1941. Nos. 79 to 85 optd 'SERVICE' as T O **4**.

O53	**20**	3p. bright blue (R.)	11·00	22·00
O54		6p. deep blue (R.)	26·00	22·00
O55		1a. orange-red	20·00	22·00
O56		2a. brown	30·00	18·00
O57		4a. bright green	95·00	£250
O58		8a. dull green	£375	£1100
O59		1r. deep blue (R.)	£425	£1200
O53/O59 *Set of 7*			£900	£2250

Two different types of 'R' occur in the 'SERVICE' overprint. On five positions in the sheet of 12 the 'R' shows a larger loop and a pointed diagonal leg.

Bundi became part of the Rajasthan Union by 15 April 1948.

BUSSAHIR (BASHAHR)

PRICES FOR STAMPS ON COVER TO 1945

Nos. 1/21	*from* × 8
Nos. 22/23	*from* × 2
Nos. 24/43	*from* × 8

Raja Shamsher Singh, 1850–1914

1 2 3 4 5 6 7 8 (9)

The initials are those of the Tika Raghunath Singh, son of the then Raja, who was the organiser and former director of the State Post Office.

(Litho at the Bussahir Press by Maulvi Karam Bakhsh, Rampur)

1895 (20 June). Laid paper. Optd with T **9** in pale greenish blue (B.), rose (R.), mauve (M.) or lake (L.). With or without gum.

(a) Imperf

1	**1**	¼a. pink (M.) (1.9.95)	£4500
		a. Monogram in rose	£7500

2 2 ½a. grey (R.) £950 £1300
  a. Monogram in mauve
3 3 1a. vermilion (M.) £425
4 4 2a. orange-yellow (M.) £150 £375
  a. Monogram in rose £275 £400
  b. Monogram in lake £200
  c. Monogram in blue £550
5 5 4a. slate-violet (M.) £300
  a. Monogram in rose £325
  b. Monogram in lake £350
  c. Without monogram £550
  d. Thick paper £300
6 6 8a. red-brown (M.) £300 £425
  a. Monogram in blue £350
  b. Monogram in rose £400
  c. Monogram in lake
  d. Without monogram £425
  e. Thick paper £300
7 7 12a. green (L.) £400
  a. Monogram in mauve
8 8 1r. ultramarine (R.) £250
  a. Monogram in mauve £375
  b. Monogram in lake £325
  c. Without monogram £700 £900

(b) Perf with a sewing machine; gauge and size of holes varying between 7 and 11½

9 1 ¼a. pink (B.) £140 £180
  a. Monogram in mauve — £325
  b. Without monogram £850 £325
10 2 ½a. grey (R.) 35·00 £225
  a. Without monogram £1700
11 3 1a. vermilion (M.) 35·00 £160
  a. Without monogram
12 4 2a. orange-yellow (B.) 45·00 £160
  a. Monogram in rose
  b. Monogram in mauve £300
  c. Without monogram — £325
13 5 4a. slate-violet (B.) 42·00 £160
  a. Monogram in rose 60·00 £200
  b. Monogram in mauve 90·00
  c. Without monogram 60·00
14 6 8a. red-brown (M.) 30·00 £160
  a. Monogram in blue £110 £300
  b. Monogram in rose £225
  c. Without monogram £180 £475
15 7 12a. green (R.) £110 £225
  a. Monogram in mauve £275
  b. Monogram in lake £190
  c. Without monogram £375
16 8 1r. ultramarine (R.) 70·00 £180
  a. Monogram in mauve £225
  b. Without monogram £550 £750
9/16 *Set of 8* £450 £1300

1899. As 1895, but pin-perf or rouletted.

17 3 1a. vermilion (M.) £300 £325
18 4 2a. orange-yellow (M.) £130 £250
  a. Monogram in lake £140 £275
  b. Monogram in rose £170
  c. Monogram in blue £350
  d. Without monogram £700
19 5 4a. slate-violet (L.) £425
  a. Monogram in blue £700
  b. Monogram in rose £650
  c. Monogram in mauve £500
20 7 12a. green (R.) £600 £800
21 8 1r. ultramarine (R.) £600 £850

Nos. 1 to 21 were in sheets of 24. They seem to have been overprinted and perforated as required. Those first issued for use were perforated, but they were subsequently supplied imperf, both to collectors and for use. Nos. 17 to 21 were some of the last supplies. No rule seems to have been observed as to the colour of the overprinted monogram; pale blue, rose and mauve were used from the first. The pale blue varies to greenish blue or blue-green, and appears quite green on the yellow stamps. The lake is possibly a mixture of the mauve and the rose—it is a quite distinct colour and apparently later than the others. Examples without overprint are either remainders left in the Treasury or copies that have escaped accidentally; they have been found sticking to the backs of others that bore the overprint.

Varieties may also be found doubly overprinted, in two different colours.

10

11

12

T **11**. Lines of shading above and at bottom left and right of shield.
T **12**. White dots above shield and ornaments in bottom corners.

13 14 15 16

(Printed at the Bussahir Press by Maulvi Karam Bakhsh)

1896–97. Wove paper. Optd with monogram 'R.S.', T **9**, in rose. Recess singly from line-engraved dies. With or without gum. Various perfs.

22 10 ¼a. deep violet (1897) — £2500
23 11 ½a. grey-blue £1600 £600
23*a* ½a. deep blue (1897) — £850

No. 23 exists sewing-machine perf about 10 and also perf 14½–16. Nos. 22 and 23*a* are pin-perf.

1896–1900. As Nos. 22/23, but lithographed in sheets of various sizes. No gum.

(a) Imperf

24 10 ¼a. slate-violet (R.) 18·00
  a. Monogram in mauve 17·00
  b. Monogram in blue 20·00
  c. Monogram in lake 42·00
25 11 ½a. blue (*shades*) (R.) 21·00 30·00
  a. Monogram in mauve 16·00 30·00
  b. Monogram in lake 21·00
  c. Without monogram
  d. Laid paper (B.) £425
  da. Monogram in lake
26 13 1a. olive (*shades*) (R.) 28·00 75·00
  a. Monogram in mauve 85·00
  b. Monogram in lake 85·00

(b) Pin-perf or rouletted

27 10 ¼a. slate-violet (R.) 32·00 32·00
  a. Monogram in lake 30·00 30·00
  b. Monogram in mauve — 50·00
28 11 ½a. blue (*shades*) (R.) 26·00 50·00
  a. Monogram in mauve 23·00 50·00
  b. Monogram in lake 65·00 75·00
  c. Monogram in blue £275
  d. Laid paper (M.)
29 13 1a. olive (*shades*) (R.) 40·00
  a. Monogram in mauve £120 £120
  b. Monogram in lake 90·00 90·00
30 14 2a. orange-yellow (B.)* £2750 £2750

Originally printings of the ¼a. and ½a. were in sheets of eight (stone I), but this was subsequently increased to 24 (4×6). The 1a. and 2a. were always in sheets of four.

Nos. 25d/25da were printed from stone I and care is needed to distinguish this laid paper printing from some of the reprints on similar paper. Stamps from stone I are without marginal lines and are very clear impressions; reprints from stone IV have thick marginal lines and, in those shades similar to No. 25, show indistinct impressions.

* The prices quoted for No. 30 are for examples with a clear impression of the T **9** 'TRS' monogram. The T **14** 2a is often found as a remainder with the T **17** 'RNS' monogram, both imperf and pin-perf. (*Prices from £55, unused or c.t.o.*)

1900–01. ¼a., 1a, colours changed; ½a. redrawn type; 2a. with dash before 'STATE' and characters in lower left label; 4a. new value. No gum.

(a) Imperf

31 10 ¼a. vermilion (M.) 6·50 13·00
  a. Monogram in blue 8·50 20·00
  b. Without monogram
31*c* 12 ½a. blue (M.) 12·00 40·00
  ca. Monogram in rose 48·00
  cb. Without monogram 95·00
32 13 1a. vermilion (M.) 7·50 23·00
  a. Monogram in blue 12·00 20·00
  b. Monogram in lake
  c. Without monogram 95·00
33 15 2a. ochre (M.) (9.00) 80·00 £150
  a. Without monogram £150
34 2a. yellow (M.) (11.00) 95·00
  a. Monogram in blue 95·00 £170
  b. Without monogram £140
35 2a. orange (B.) (1.01) 95·00 £170
  a. Monogram in mauve 95·00 £150
  b. Without monogram 95·00
36 16 4a. claret (R.) 95·00 £200
  a. Monogram in mauve £110 £225
  b. Monogram in blue £160 £250
  c. Without monogram 60·00

(b) Pin-perf or rouletted

37 10 ¼a. vermilion (M.) 8·00 20·00
  a. Monogram in blue 8·00
  b. Without monogram
37*c* 12 ½a. blue (M.) £160 £225
38 13 1a. vermilion (M.) 16·00 27·00
  a. Monogram in blue 19·00 21·00
39 1a. brown-red (M.) (3.01) — £300
40 15 2a. ochre (M.) (9.00) £120
  a. Monogram in blue
41 2a. yellow (M.) (11.00) £100 £130
  a. Monogram in rose £110 £180
  b. Monogram in blue £150 £200
42 2a. orange (M.) (1.01) £110 £120
  a. Monogram in blue £150 £140
  b. Without monogram — £550
43 16 4a. claret (R.) £180
  a. Monogram in blue £180 £300
  b. Monogram in mauve £190

The ¼a., ½a. and 1a. are in sheets of 24; the 2a. in sheets of 50 differing throughout in the dash and the characters added at lower left; the 4a. in sheets of 28.

(**17**)

The stamps formerly catalogued with large overprint 'R.N.S.' (T **17**) are now believed never to have been issued for use.

Remainders are also found with overprint 'P.S.', the initials of Padam Singh who succeeded Raghunath Singh in the direction of the Post Office, and with the original monogram 'R.S.' in a damaged state, giving it the appearance of a double-lined 'R.'

The stamps of Bussahir have been obsolete since 1 April 1901. Numerous remainders were sold after this date, and all values were later reprinted in the colours of the originals, or in fancy colours, from the original stones, or from new ones. Printings were also made from new types, similar to those of the second issue of the 8a., 12a. and 1r. values, in sheets of eight.

Reprints are frequently found on laid paper.

Collectors are warned against obliterated copies bearing the Rampur postmark with date '19 MA 1900.' Many thousand remainders and reprints were thus obliterated for export after the closing of the State Post Office.

CHARKHARI

PRICES FOR STAMPS ON COVER TO 1945	
Nos. 1/2	*from* × 2
Nos. 3/4	—
Nos. 5/26	*from* × 20
Nos. 27/44	*from* × 3
Nos. 45/53	*from* × 100
Nos. 54/55	*from* × 5
No. 56	*from* × 2

Maharaja Malkhan Singh, 1880–1908

1

¼ ½ 1 2 4
¼ ½ 1 2 4

The top row shows the figures of value used in the stamps of 1894–1897, and the bottom row those for the 1904 issue. In the 4a. the figure slopes slightly to the right in the first issue, and to the left in the second.

1894. Typo from a single die. No gum. Imperf.

1 1 ¼ anna, rose £2750 £750
2 1 annas, dull green £4250 £4750
3 2 annas, dull green £5500
4 4 annas, dull green £3250

Nos. 1/2 are known pin-perforated.

1897. Inscr 'ANNA'. No gum. Imperf.

5 1 ¼a. magenta £160 £170
  a. Purple 4·25 4·50
  b. Violet 4·25 4·25
6 ½a. purple 4·25 5·00
  a. Violet 2·50 3·50
7 1a. blue-green 6·50 11·00
  a. Turquoise-blue 4·75 8·50
  b. Indigo 26·00 40·00
  c. Figure of value inverted £3000
8 2a. blue-green 10·00 17·00
  a. Turquoise-blue 7·00 13·00
  b. Indigo 26·00 40·00
9 4a. blue-green 13·00 22·00
  a. Turquoise-blue 8·50 19·00
  b. Indigo 55·00 80·00
  ba. Figure of value sideways £3000
5/9 *Set of 5* 24·00 42·00

Minor varieties may be found with the first 'A' in 'ANNA' not printed.

All values are known on various coloured papers, but these are proofs or trial impressions.

1902–04. Numerals changed as illustrated. No gum.

10 1 ¼a. violet 2·00 2·50
11 ½a. violet 5·50 6·00
12 1a. green 5·00 24·00
13 2a. green 38·00 45·00
14 4a. green 40·00 50·00
10/14 *Set of 5* 80·00 £110

Stamps of this issue can be found showing part of the papermaker's watermark. 'Mercantile Script Extra Strong John Haddon & Co.'

Maharaja Jujhar Singh, 1908–1914

2 (Right-hand sword over left)

POSTAGE STAMP
Type I

POSTAGE STAMP
Type II

Type I. 'P' of 'POSTAGE' in same size as other letters. 'E' small with long upper and lower arms. White dot often appears on one or both of the sword hilts.

Type II. 'P' larger than the other letters. 'E' large with short upper and lower arms. No dots occur on the hilts.

1909–19. Litho in Calcutta. Wove paper. P 11.

(a) Type I

15 2 1p. chestnut 80·00 80·00
  a. Pale chestnut 6·50 38·00
  b. Orange-brown 6·50 38·00
  c. 'CHARKHAPI' (R. 5/5) 90·00
16 1p. turquoise-blue 1·75 75
  a. Imperf between (horiz pair) £250
  b. Greenish blue (1911) 1·75 1·00
  c. Pale turquoise-green 2·00 1·25
17 ½a. vermilion 3·50 1·50
  a. Imperf (pair) £2000
  b. Deep rose-red 2·00 1·50
18 1a. sage-green 6·00 3·75
  a. Yellow-olive 4·50 3·25
19 2a. grey-blue 3·75 3·50
  a. Dull violet-blue 3·00 3·50
20 4a. deep green 4·25 5·50
21 8a. brown-red 8·00 25·00
22 1r. pale chestnut 13·00 70·00
15*a*/22 *Set of 8* 38·00 £130

(b) Type II

24 2 1p. turquoise-blue .... 6·50 4·50
25 ½a. vermilion .... 4·50 2·00
b. Deep rose-red .... 12·00 9·00
26 1a. yellow-olive (1919) .... 5·00 3·00
a. Sage-green .... 5·50 3·25
24/26 *Set of 3* .... 14·50 8·50

No. 15, from the original printing, shows an upstroke to the '1', not present on other brown printings of this value.

See also Nos. 31/44.

3 'JI' below Swords. Right sword overlaps left. Double framelines.

4 'JI' below Swords. Left sword overlaps right. Single frameline.

1912–17. Handstamped. Wove paper. No gum. Imperf.

27 3 1p. violet £1500 £130
a. Dull purple .... — £160
28 4 1p. violet (1917) .... 9·00 5·00
a. Dull purple .... 40·00 5·50
b. *Tête-bêche* (pair) £100 £100
c. Laid paper .... — £1300
d. Pair, one stamp sideways .... — £200

Maharaja Ganga Singh, 1914–1920
Maharaja Arimardan Singh, 1920–1942

5 *(actual size 63×25 mm)*

6 (Left-hand sword over right)

1921. Handstamped. No gum.

(a) Wove paper. Imperf

29 5 1a. violet £140 £160
a. Dull purple £150 £180

(b) Laid paper. P 11

30 5 1a. violet £140 £225
a. Imperf £275 £300

(Typo State Ptg Press, Charkhari)

1930–45. Wove paper. No gum. Imperf.

31 6 1p. deep blue .... 1·75 18·00
a. Vert pair, top ptd inverted on back, bottom normal upright .... 16·00
b. *Tête-bêche* (vert pair) £1800
c. Perf 11×imperf (horiz pair) (1939) £225 £180
d. Bluish slate (1944) .... 35·00 60·00
e. Laid paper (1944) .... — £600
ea. *Tête-bêche* (vert pair) £2750
32 1p. dull *to* light green (*pelure*) (1943) .... 85·00 £425
33 1p. violet (1943) .... 27·00 £275
a. *Tête-bêche* (vert pair) .... 75·00
34 ½a. deep olive .... 3·25 18·00
35 ½a. red-brown (1940) .... 6·50 32·00
a. *Tête-bêche* (vert pair) £1600
36 ½a. black (*pelure*) (1943) .... 85·00 £375
37 ½a. red (*shades*) (1943) .... 28·00 60·00
a. *Tête-bêche* (vert pair) .... 60·00
b. Laid paper (1944) .... — £600
38 ½a. grey-brown (*shades*) £150 £150
39 1a. green .... 3·75 24·00
a. Emerald (1938) £150 £160
b. Yellow-green £120 £160
40 1a. chocolate (*shades*) (1940) .... 17·00 35·00
a. *Tête-bêche* (vert pair) .... 90·00
b. Lake-brown .... — £110
41 1a. red (*shades*) (1940) £275 £120
a. Carmine .... — £120
b. Laid paper (1944) .... — £600
42 2a. light blue .... 2·25 23·00
a. *Tête-bêche* (vert pair) .... 15·00
43 2a. greenish grey (1941?) .... 90·00 £130
a. *Tête-bêche* (vert pair) £180
b. Laid paper (1944) .... — £600
c. Greyish green £160 £350
43*d* 2a. yellow-green (1945) £3250 £2000
44 4a. carmine .... 3·00 25·00
a. *Tête-bêche* (vert pair) .... 15·00

There are two different versions of No. 37a, one with the stamps *tête-bêche* base to base and the other showing them top to top.

The 1p. value is also known unused in deep olive (as No. 34), light blue (as No. 42) and carmine (as No. 44). These may be colour trials. (*Price, from £500 each*).

7 The Lake

8 Imlia Palace

9 Industrial School

10 Bird's-eye view of City

11 The Fort

12 Guest House

13 Palace Gate

14 Temples at Rainpur

15 Goverdhan Temple

½ As. **(16)**

(Typo Batliboi Litho Works, Bombay)

1931 (25 June). Types **7/15**. Thick, surfaced wove paper. P 11, 11½, 12 or compound.

45 7 ½a. blue-green (a) (b) (c) .... 2·50 10
a. Imperf between (horiz pair) (b) .... 60·00 12·00
b. Imperf between (vert pair) (b) .... 70·00 40·00
c. Imperf horiz (vert pair) (a) (b) .... 55·00
46 8 1a. blackish brown (a) (b) (c) .... 1·60 10
a. Imperf between (horiz pair) (b) .... 11·00 8·50
b. Imperf between (vert pair) (a) (b) .... 27·00 13·00
c. Imperf horiz (vert pair) (b) .... 18·00
d. Imperf (pair) .... 30·00
47 9 2a. violet (a) (b) (c) .... 2·00 10
a. Imperf vert (horiz pair) (a) (b) .... 38·00 40·00
b. Imperf between (vert pair) (b) .... 42·00 28·00
c. Imperf horiz (vert pair) (b) .... 24·00 24·00
d. Doubly printed (a) .... 11·00
e. Imperf (pair) .... 30·00
48 10 4a. olive-green (a) (b) (c) .... 2·50 20
a. Imperf between (vert pair) (b) .... 95·00 95·00
49 11 8a. magenta (a) (b) (c) .... 4·00 10
a. Imperf between (horiz pair) (b) (c) .... 90·00 35·00
b. Imperf between (vert pair) (b) .... 75·00 55·00
c. Imperf horiz (vert pair) .... 90·00 25·00
50 12 1r. green and rose (a) (b) .... 5·50 25
a. Imperf between (vert pair) (a) (b) £140 £120
b. Green (centre) omitted (b) .... — £350
c. Imperf horiz (vert pair) (a) £150
d. Imperf (pair) .... 80·00
51 13 2r. red and brown (a) (b) (c) .... 10·00 40
a. Imperf horiz (vert pair) (b) .... £300 32·00
52 14 3r. chocolate and blue-green (a) (b) .... 24·00 60
a. Imperf between (horiz pair) (b) .... — £350
b. *Tête-bêche* (pair) (a) (b) .... £700 20·00
c. Chocolate (centre) omitted (b) .... 22·00
53 15 5r. turquoise and purple (a) (b) .... 10·00 50
a. Imperf between (horiz pair) (a) £375
b. Centre inverted (b) .... £160 45·00
c. Centre doubly printed (b) .... — £300
45/53 *Set of 9* .... 55·00 2·00

Three different perforating heads were used for this issue: (a) perf 11; (b) perf 12; (c) perf 11½. Values on which each perforation occur are shown above. Nos. 46 and 53 are known perf compound of 11 and 12.

The *Tête-bêche* variety on the 3r. value (No. 52b) resulted from the inversion of the frame and vignette clichés at R. 11/9 on the sheet of 200 (10×20).

This issue was the subject of speculative manipulation, large stocks being thrown on the market cancelled-to-order at very low prices and unused at less than face value. The issue was an authorized one but was eventually withdrawn by the State authorities.

1939 (1 Dec)–**40**. Nos. 21/22 surch as T **16**.

54 2 ½a. on 8a. brown-red (1940) .... 55·00 £190
a. No space between '½' and 'As' .... 55·00 £190
b. Surch inverted £450 £650
c. '1' of '½' inverted £425
55 1a. on 1r. chestnut (1940) £200 £700
a. Surch inverted £500
56 '1 ANNA' on 1r. chestnut £2250 £1400

Maharaja Jaiendra Singh, 1942–1971

Charkhari became part of Vindhya Pradesh by 1 May 1948.

COCHIN

(6 puttans = 5 annas. 12 pies = 1 anna; 16 annas = 1 rupee)

Stamps of Cochin were also valid on mail posted to Travancore.

PRICES FOR STAMPS ON COVER TO 1945	
Nos. 1/3	*from* × 30
Nos. 4/5	*from* × 10
Nos. 6/6b	*from* × 3
Nos. 7/9	*from* × 20
Nos. 11/22	*from* × 15
Nos. 26/128	*from* × 8
Nos. O1/O105	*from* × 15

Raja Kerala Varma I, 1888–1895

1

2

(Dies eng P. Orr & Sons, Madras; typo Cochin Govt, Ernakulam)

1892 (13 Apr). No wmk, or wmk large Umbrella in the sheet. P 12.

1 1 ½ put. buff .... 3·50 3·00
a. Orange-buff .... 4·50 3·00
b. Yellow .... 3·75 3·50
c. Imperf (pair) ....
2 1 put. purple .... 3·75 3·00
a. Imperf between (vert pair) .... † £5000
3 2 2 put. deep violet .... 3·00 2·25
1/3 *Set of 3* .... 9·25 7·50

1893. Laid paper. P 12.

4 1 ½ put. orange-buff £1000 £180
a. Orange £1200 £225
b. Yellow £1200 £250

WATERMARKS. Prior to the 1911–1923 issue, printed by Perkins Bacon & Co, little attention was paid to the position of the watermark. Inverted and sideways watermarks are frequently found in the 1898 and 1902–1903 issues.

1894. Wmk small Umbrella on each stamp. P 12.

5 1 ½ put. buff .... 17·00 6·00
a. Orange .... 6·50 1·50
ab. Imperf (pair) ....
b. Yellow .... 9·00 1·00
6 1 put. purple .... 16·00 8·50
7 2 2 put. deep violet .... 12·00 4·50
a. Imperf (pair) ....
b. Doubly printed .... † £2750
c. Printed both sides £2750
d. *Tête-bêche* (pair) £8000
5/7 *Set of 3* .... 30·00 12·50

The paper watermarked with a small umbrella is more transparent than that of the previous issue. The wmk is not easy to distinguish.

The 1 put. in deep violet was a special printing for fiscal use only.

Raja Rama Varma I, 1895–1914

1896 (End). Similar to T **1**, but 28×33 mm. P 12.

(a) Wmk Arms and inscription in sheet

8 1 put. violet £140 £150

(b) Wmk Conch Shell to each stamp

9 1 put. deep violet .... 19·00 32·00

Nos. 8/9 were intended for fiscal use, but are also known used for postal purposes.

3

4

5

6

1898–1905. Thin yellowish paper. Wmk small Umbrella on each stamp. With or without gum. P 12.

11 3 3 pies. blue .... 1·40 1·10
a. Imperf between (horiz pair) £1000
b. Imperf between (vert pair) £1000
c. Doubly printed £1200
12 4 ½ put. green .... 1·75 1·50
a. Imperf between (horiz pair) £2250 £2250
b. Stamp sideways (in pair) .... † £5000
13 5 1 put. pink .... 6·50 1·75
a. *Tête-bêche* (pair) £8000 £4000
b. Laid paper (1905) .... † £2000
ba. Laid paper. *Tête-bêche* (pair) .... † £14000
c. Red .... 8·00 1·75
d. Carmine-red .... 9·00 2·50
14 6 2 put. deep violet .... 4·00 2·25
a. Imperf between (vert pair) £1000
b. Imperf between (vert strip of 3) £1400
11/14 *Set of 4* .... 12·00 5·50

1902–03. Thick white paper. Wmk small Umbrella on each stamp. With or without gum. P 12.

16 3 3 pies. blue .... 1·50 10
a. Doubly printed .... — £450
b. Imperf between (horiz pair) .... † £2250
17 4 ½ put. green .... 1·25 40
a. Stamp sideways (in pair) £1900 £1900
b. Doubly printed .... — £475
c. Imperf between (horiz pair) .... † £2250
18 5 1 put. pink (1903) .... 3·50 20
a. *Tête-bêche* (pair) .... † £6500
19 6 2 put. deep violet .... 3·75 50
a. Doubly printed £2500 £500
16/19 *Set of 4* .... 9·00 1·00

(7)

(7a)

2 **(7b)**

1909. T **3** (Paper and perf of 1903), surch with T **7**. Wmk is always sideways. No gum.

22 3 2 on 3 pies. rosy mauve 15 50
a. Surch Type **7** inverted £170 £170
b. Surch Type **7a** £1700 £850
c. Surch Type **7b** £190
d. Stamps *tête-bêche* £350 £400
e. Stamps and surchs *tête-bêche* £400 £475

Varieties a, d and e were caused by the inversion of one stamp (No. 7) in the plate and the consequent inversion of the corresponding surcharge to correct the error.

Types **7a** and **7b** were applied by handstamp to correct the omission of the surcharge on R. 3/2 in different settings. Other sheets show a handstamped version of T **7**.

8 Raja Rama Varma I

8a

(Recess Perkins Bacon)

1911–13. Currency in pies and annas. W **8a**. P 14.

No.	Type	Description	Unused	Used
26	**8**	2p. brown	50	10
		a. Imperf (pair)		
		w. Wmk inverted	†	£325
27		3p. blue	3·25	10
		a. Perf 14×12½	32·00	1·00
		w. Wmk inverted	—	£275
28		4p. green	4·00	10
		aw. Wmk inverted	—	£325
28*b*		4p. apple-green	4·25	40
		bw. Wmk inverted	†	£325
29		9p. carmine	3·75	10
		a. Wmk sideways		
30		1a. brown-orange	3·75	10
31		1½a. purple	12·00	45
32		2a. grey (1913)	8·00	40
33		3a. vermilion (1913)	75·00	48·00
26/33 *Set of 8*			£100	48·00

No. 27a is line perforated. Nos. 27 and 33 exist perforated 14 either from comb or line machines. The other values only come from the comb machine.

Raja (Maharaja from 1921) Rama Varma II, 1914–1932

9 Raja Rama Varma II

10 Raja Rama Varma II

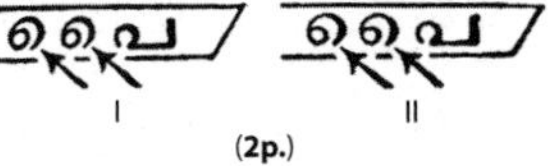
I II

(2p.)

I II

(1a.)

(Recess Perkins, Bacon)

1916–30. W **8a**. P 13½ to 14.

No.	Type	Description	Unused	Used
35	**10**	2p. brown (Die I) (*a*) (*b*) (*c*)	8·00	10
		a. Imperf (pair)	£850	
		b. Die II (*b*) (*c*) (1930)	1·60	10
36		4p. green (*a*) (*b*)	1·00	10
37		6p. red-brown (*a*) (*b*) (*c*) (*d*) (1922)	2·50	10
		w. Wmk inverted	—	£300
38		8p. sepia (*b*) (1923)	3·00	10
39		9p. carmine (*a*)	35·00	60
40		10p. blue (*b*) (1923)	10·00	10
41	**9**	1a. orange (Die I) (*a*)	32·00	4·75
		a. Die II (*a*) (*b*) (1922)	20·00	35
42	**10**	1½a. purple (*b*) (1923)	7·50	20
43		2a. grey (*a*) (*b*) (*d*)	4·50	10
44		2¼a. yellow-green (*a*) (*d*) (1922)	14·00	3·25
45		3a. vermilion (*a*) (*b*)	12·00	35
35/45 *Set of 11*			£100	4·75

Four different perforating heads were used for this issue: (*a*) comb 13.9; (*b*) comb 13.6; (*c*) line 13.8; (*d*) line 14.2. Values on which each perforation occur are shown above. Stamps with perforation (*a*) are on hand-made paper, while the other perforations are on softer machine-made paper with a horizontal mesh.

An unused example of the 9p. value (as No. 39, but perf (c)) has been seen with W **7** of Hyderabad. The status of this variety is uncertain.

2  

Two pies (11) Two pies (12) Two pies (13)

2 2

Two Pies (14) Two Pies (15)

1922–29. T **8** (P 14), surch with T **11/15**.

No.	Type	Description	Unused	Used
46	**11**	2p. on 3p. blue	1·00	30
		a. Surch double	£450	£450
47	**12**	2p. on 3p. blue	5·50	1·10
		a. Surch double	£1300	
		b. 'Pies' for 'pies' (R. 4/8)	75·00	22·00
		ba. Surch double		
		c. Perf 12½ at foot		
48	**13**	2p. on 3p. blue (6.24)	13·00	35
		a. 'Pies' for 'pies' (R. 4/8)	£110	16·00
		b. Perf 14×12½	15·00	18·00
		ba. Ditto. 'Pies' for 'pies' (R. 4/8)	£475	£600
49	**14**	2p. on 3p. blue (1929)	20·00	15·00
		a. Surch double	£600	
		b. Surch with Type **15**	£160	£250
		ba. Ditto. Surch double	£4250	

There are four settings of these surcharges. The first (July 1922) consisted of 39 stamps with T **11**, and nine with T **12**, and in T **11** the centre of the '2' is above the 'o' of 'Two'. In the second setting (March 1923) there were 36 of T **11** and 12 of T **12**, and the centre of the figure is above the space between 'Two' and 'Pies'. The third setting (June 1924) consists of stamps with T **13** only.

The fourth setting (1929) was also in sheets of 48. No. 49b being the first stamp in the fourth row.

No. 47c is from the bottom row of a sheet and was re-perforated 12½ line at foot as the bottom line of 14 perforations were too far from the design.

ONE ANNA
ഒരു അണ

Three Pies
൩ 3

ANCHAL & REVENUE (16)

മൂന്നു പൈ (17)

1928. Surch with T **16**.

No.	Type	Description	Unused	Used
50	**10**	1a. on 2¼a. yellow-green (*a*)	6·50	12·00
		a. 'REVENUF' for 'REVENUE'	90·00	£150
		b. Surch double		

1932–33. Surch as T **17**. W **8a**. P 13½.

No.	Type	Description	Unused	Used
51	**10**	3p. on 4p. green (*b*)	2·75	2·50
		a. 'r' in 'Three' inverted	†	£600
52		3p. on 8p. sepia (*b*)	3·00	3·25
53		9p. on 10p. blue (*b*)	2·75	3·25
51/53 *Set of 3*			7·75	8·00

Maharaja Rama Varma III, 1932–1941

18 Maharaja Rama Varma III

18a

(Recess Perkins Bacon & Co)

1933–38. Types **18** and **18a**. W **8a**. P 13×13½.

No.	Type	Description	Unused	Used
54	**18**	2p. brown (1936)	1·75	50
55		4p. green	60	10
56		6p. red-brown	70	10
57	**18a**	1a. brown-orange	2·75	30
		w. Wmk inverted	†	£375
58	**18**	1a.8p. carmine	3·00	8·00
59		2a. grey (1938)	12·00	2·25
60		2¼a. yellow-green	2·25	40
61		3a. vermilion (1938)	11·00	1·60
62		3a.4p. violet	1·75	2·00
63		6a.8p. sepia	1·75	20·00
64		10a. blue	3·00	20·00
54/64 *Set of 11*			35·00	50·00

For stamps in this design, but lithographed, see Nos. 67/71.

1934. Surcharged as T **14**. W **8a**. P 13½.

No.	Type	Description	Unused	Used
65	**10**	6p. on 8p. sepia (R.) (*b*)	1·00	60
66		6p. on 10p. blue (R.) (*b*)	1·75	2·00

'DOUBLE PRINTS'. The errors previously listed under this description are now identified as blanket offsets, a type of variety outside the scope of this catalogue. Examples occur on issues from 1938 onwards.

SPACING OF OVERPRINTS AND SURCHARGES. The typeset overprints and surcharges issued from 1939 onwards show considerable differences in spacing. Except for specialists, however, these differences have little significance as they occur within the same settings and do not represent separate printings.

(Litho The Associated Printers, Madras)

1938. W **8a**. P 11.

No.	Type	Description	Unused	Used
67	**18**	2p. brown	1·00	40
		aw. Wmk inverted	£350	£170
		b. Perf 13×13½	12·00	70
68		4p. green	1·00	35
		aw. Wmk inverted	†	£325
		b. Perf 13×13½	11·00	18·00
69		6p. red-brown	2·25	10
		aw. Wmk inverted	†	£275
		b. Perf 13×13½	†	£6500
70	**18a**	1a. brown-orange	£110	£130
		aw. Wmk inverted		
		b. Perf 13×13½	£170	£250
71	**18**	2¼a. sage-green	6·00	25
		a. Perf 13×13½	22·00	7·00
67/71 *Set of 5*			£110	£130

Most examples of Nos. 70/70b were used fiscally. Collectors are warned against examples which have been cleaned and regummed or provided with forged postmarks.

ANCHAL (19) ANCHAL (19a) THREE PIES (20)

SURCHARGED ANCHAL

ONE ANNA THREE PIES (21) ANCHAL

NINE PIES (22) ANCHAL

NINE PIES (23) SURCHARGED NINE PIES (24)

1939 (Jan). Nos. 57 and 70 optd with Types **19** or **19a**.

No.	Type	Description	Unused	Used
72	**18a**	1a. brown-orange (*recess*) (Type **19**)	10·00	2·00
		w. Wmk inverted	†	£325
73		1a. brown-orange (*litho*) (Type **19**)	£700	2·25
		aw. Wmk inverted	†	—
		b. Perf 13×13½	—	£500
74		1a. brown-orange (*litho*) (Type **19a**)	1·50	1·60
		a. Perf 13×13½	18·00	75

In 1939 it was decided that there would be separate 1a. stamps for revenue and postal purposes. The 'ANCHAL' overprints were applied to stamps intended for postal purposes.

1942–44. Types **18** and **18a** variously optd or surch.

No.	Description	Unused	Used
	I. Recess-printed stamp. No. 58		
75	3p. on 1a.8p. carmine (Type **20**)	£500	£225
76	3p. on 1a.8p. carmine (Type **21**)	13·00	17·00
77	6p. on 1a.8p. carmine (Type **20**)	6·00	27·00
78	1a.3p. on 1a.8p. carmine (Type **21**)	1·00	60
	II. Lithographed stamps. Nos. 68, 70 and 70b		
79	3p. on 4p. (Type **21**)	7·50	4·25
	a. Perf 13×13½	25·00	4·00
80	6p. on 1a. (Type **22**)	£1100	£375
	a. 'SIX PIES' double	†	£2250
81	6p. on 1a. (Type **23**)	£550	£300
	a. Perf 13×13½	£275	£100
82	9p. on 1a. (Type **22**)	£275	£170
83	9p. on 1a. (Type **23**) (P 13×13½)	£650	42·00
84	9p. on 1a. (Type **24**) (P 13×13½)	50·00	13·00

Maharaja Kerala Varma II, 1941–1943

26 Maharaja Kerala Varma II

27 (*The actual measurement of this wmk is 6¼×3⅝ in.*)

(Litho The Associated Printers, Madras)

1943. Frame of 1a. inscr 'ANCHAL & REVENUE'. P 13×13½.

No.	Type	Description	Unused	Used
		*(a) W **8a***		
85	**26**	2p. grey-brown	9·00	10·00
		a. Perf 11	†	£3750
85*b*		4p. green	£2750	£850
85*c*		1a. brown-orange	£170	£225
85/85*c* *Set of 3*			£2750	£1000
		*(b) W **27***		
86	**26**	2p. grey-brown	55·00	6·50
		a. Perf 11	†	£6000
87		4p. green	7·50	22·00
		a. Perf 11	4·75	6·00
88		6p. red-brown	9·50	10
		a. Perf 11	8·50	1·60
89		9p. ultramarine (P 11)	90·00	1·50
		a. Imperf between (horiz pair)	£4500	
90		1a. brown-orange	£225	£275
		a. Perf 11	26·00	75·00
91		2¼a. yellow-green	38·00	5·00
		a. Perf 11	38·00	9·00

Part of W **27** appears on many stamps in each sheet, while others are entirely without wmk. The watermark can appear upright, inverted or sideways.

In the above set Nos. 88a, 89, 90a and 91a (all Perf 11) are normally found without gum.

Although inscribed 'ANCHAL (= Postage) & REVENUE' most examples of Nos. 85c and 90/a were used fiscally. Collectors are warned against examples which have been cleaned and regummed or provided with forged postmarks.

Maharaja Ravi Varma, 1943–1946

1943. T **26** variously optd or surch. P 13×13½.

		(a) W **8a**		
92		3p. on 4p. (Type **21**)	£180	45·00
92*a*		9p. on 1a. (Type **23**)	14·00	6·50
		aw. Wmk inverted	†	£450
92*b*		9p. on 1a. (Type **24**)	14·00	4·50
92*c*		1a.3p. on 1a. (Type **21**)	†	£9000
		(b) W **27**		
93		2p. on 6p. (Type **20**)	75	5·00
		a. Perf 11	2·25	2·75
94		3p. on 4p. (Type **20**) (P 11)	13·00	10
95		3p. on 4p. (Type **21**)	9·00	10
96		3p. on 6p. (Type **20**)	3·50	20
		a. Perf 11	1·25	85
97		4p. on 6p. (Type **20**)	8·50	17·00

No. 92*c* is believed to be an error; one or more sheets of No. 85*c*, having been included in a stock of No. O70 intended to become No. O80.

28 Maharaja Ravi Varma

29 Maharaja Ravi Varma

I

II

(Litho The Associated Printers, Madras)

1944–48. W **27** No gum.

		(a) Type I. P 11		
98	**28**	9p. ultramarine (1944)	30·00	8·50
		(b) Type II. P 13		
98*a*	**28**	9p. ultramarine (1946)	40·00	8·00
		ab. Perf 13×13½	70·00	8·00
99		1a.3p. magenta (1948)	12·00	10·00
		a. Perf 13×13½	£600	£140
100		1a.9p. ultramarine (*shades*) (1948)	11·00	17·00
98*a*/100 *Set of 3*			55·00	32·00

Nos. 98*a*/100 are line-perforated, Nos. 98ab and 99a comb-perforated.

Maharaja Kerala Varma III, 1946–48

(Litho The Associated Printers, Madras)

1946–48. Frame of 1a. inscr 'ANCHAL & REVENUE'. W **27**. No gum (except for stamps perf 11). P 13.

101	**29**	2p. chocolate	4·00	20
		a. Imperf horiz (vert pair)	£5500	£5500
		c. Perf 11	11·00	60
		d. Perf 11×13	£500	£180
102		3p. carmine	1·00	40
103		4p. grey-green	£4000	85·00
104		6p. red-brown (1947)	28·00	11·00
		a. Perf 11	£300	9·00
105		9p. ultramarine	3·75	10
		a. Imperf between (horiz pair)	†	£5000
106		1a. orange (1948)	10·00	45·00
		a. Perf 11	£800	
107		2a. black	£180	12·00
		a. Perf 11	£225	10·00
108		3a. vermilion	£120	4·00
101/108 *Set of 8*			£4000	£140

Although inscribed 'ANCHAL (=Postage) & REVENUE' most examples of No. 106 were used fiscally.

The 1a.3p. magenta, 1a.9p. ultramarine and 2¼a. yellow-green in T **29** subsequently appeared surcharged or overprinted for official use. Examples of the 1a.3p. magenta exist without overprint, but may not have been issued in this state (*Price* £130 *unused*).

30 Maharaja Kerala Varma III

Die I

Die II

Two dies of **2p.**:

Die I. Back of headdress almost touches value tablet. Narrow strip of tunic visible below collar.

Die II. Back of headdress further away from tablet. Wider strip of tunic visible below collar.

Die I

Die II

Two dies of **3a.4p.**

Die I. Frame around head broken by value tablets. Two white lines below value inscription.

Die II. Continuous frame around head. Single white line below value inscription. (R. 6/1-2 on sheet 8×6).

Tail to turban flaw (R. 1/7)

(Litho The Associated Printers, Madras)

1948–50. W **27** (upright or inverted). P 11.

109	**30**	2p. grey-brown (I)	1·75	15
		a. Imperf vert (horiz pair)	†	£5000
		b. Imperf horiz (vert pair)	†	£5000
		c. Die II	80·00	4·50
110		3p. carmine	3·75	15
		a. Imperf between (vert pair)	—	£3250
111		4p. green	17·00	6·50
		a. Imperf vert (horiz pair)	£350	£475
112		6p. chestnut	26·00	25
		a. Imperf vert (horiz pair)	£950	
113		9p. ultramarine	2·50	1·25
114		2a. black	£110	3·25
115		3a. orange-red	£130	1·00
		a. Imperf vert (horiz pair)	£4750	
116		3a.4p. violet (1950)	70·00	£475
		a. Tail to turban flaw	£400	£1400
		b. Die II	£350	
109/116 *Set of 8*			£325	£475

Maharaja Rama Varma IV, 1948–1964

31 Chinese Nets

32 Dutch Palace

(Litho The Associated Printers, Madras)

1949. W **27**. P 11.

117	**31**	2a. black	9·00	15·00
		a. Imperf vert (horiz pair)	£800	
118	**32**	2¼a. green	3·50	15·00
		a. Imperf vert (horiz pair)	£800	

A used example of a 2¼a. value in a slightly different design exists showing a larger portrait of the ruler, the conch shell at upper right pointing to the right and with shading below 'DUTCH PALACE'. This may have come from a proof sheet subsequently used for postal purposes.

SIX PIES

ആറ പൈ

(**33**)

പൈ പൈ

Normal — Error (first character more open with longer tail)

Due to similarities between two Malayalam characters some values of the 1948 provisional issue exist with an error in the second word of the Malayalam surcharge. On Nos. 119, 122 and O103 this occurs twice in the setting of 48. No. 125 shows four examples and No. O104b one. Most instances are as illustrated above, but in two instances on the setting for No. 125 the error occurs on the second character.

1949. Surch as T **33**.

		(i) On 1944–1948 issue. P 13		
119	**28**	6p. on 1a.3p. magenta	11·00	7·50
		a. Incorrect character	70·00	50·00
120		1a. on 1a.9p. ultramarine (R.)	2·75	1·75
		(ii) On 1946–1948 issue		
121	**29**	3p. on 9p. ultramarine	12·00	26·00
122		6p. on 1a.3p. magenta	21·00	19·00
		a. Surch double	†	£900
		b. Incorrect character	£150	£130
123		1a. on 1a.9p. ultramarine (R.)	7·50	3·00
		a. Surch in black	†	£4750
		b. Black surch with smaller native characters 7½ mm instead of 10 mm long	†	£7500
		(iii) On 1948–1950 issue		
124	**30**	3p. on 9p. ultramarine	5·50	3·25
		a. Larger native characters 20 mm instead of 16½ mm long	2·75	50
		ab. Imperf between (vert pair)	†	£4000
		b. Surch double	£800	£900
		c. Surch both sides	£650	
125		3p. on 9p. ultramarine (R.)	10·00	3·50
		a. Incorrect character	60·00	40·00
126		6p. on 9p. ultramarine (R.)	2·50	1·00
119/126 *Set of 8*			65·00	55·00

The 9p. ultramarine (T **29**) with 6p. surcharge (T **33**) in red was prepared for use but not issued (*Price* £130 *unused*).

1949. Surch as T **20**. W **27**. P 13.

127	**29**	6p. on 1a. orange	£120	£275
128		9p. on 1a. orange	£200	£300

OFFICIAL STAMPS

On C S — (O **1**)

ON G C S — (O **2** Small 'ON')

ON G C S — (O **3** 'G' without serif)

1913. Optd locally by typography with T O **1** (3p.) or lithographically by Perkins Bacon with T O **2** (others).

O1	**8**	3p. blue (R.)	£170	10
		a. Black opt	†	£1900
		b. Inverted 'S'	—	60·00
		c. Opt double	†	£800
O2		4p. green (*wmk sideways*)	20·00	10
		a. Opt inverted	—	£350
O3		9p. carmine	£170	10
		a. Wmk sideways	24·00	10
		w. Wmk inverted	†	£325
O4		1½a. purple	80·00	10
		a. Opt double	—	£1100
O5		2a. grey	16·00	10
O6		3a. vermilion	85·00	45
O7		6a. violet	£100	2·25
O8		12a. ultramarine	50·00	7·50
O9		1½r. deep green	35·00	80·00
O1/O9 *Set of 9*			£500	85·00

1919–33. Optd by Perkins Bacon as T O **3** (*typo*).

O10	**10**	4p. green (*a*) (*b*)	10·00	10
		a. Opt double	—	£750
		w. Wmk inverted	†	£300
O11		6p. red-brown (*a*) (*b*) (1922)	23·00	10
		a. Opt double	—	£750
		w. Wmk inverted	†	£550
O12		8p. sepia (*b*) (1923)	12·00	10
		w. Wmk inverted	†	£550
O13		9p. carmine (*a*) (*b*)	95·00	10
O14		10p. blue (*b*) (1923)	27·00	10
		a. Opt double	†	£1000
O15		1½a. purple (*a*) (*b*) (1921)	5·50	10
		a. Opt double	†	£1000
O16		2a. grey (*b*) (1923)	55·00	30
O17		2¼a. yellow-green (*a*) (*b*) (1922)	23·00	10
		a. Opt double	†	£700
O18		3a. vermilion (*a*) (*b*) (*c*)	18·00	25
		a. Opt inverted	†	£650
O19		6a. violet (*a*) (*b*) (1924)	50·00	50
O19*a*		12a. ultramarine (*a*) (*b*) (1929)	25·00	7·50
O19*b*		1½r. deep green (*a*) (*b*) (1933)	30·00	£170
O10/O19*b* *Set of 12*			£325	£170

All values exist showing a straight-backed 'C' variety on R. 3/1.

8 Eight pies — (O **4** 27½ *mm high*)

ON C G S — (O **5** Straight back to 'C')

ON C G S — (O **6** Circular 'O'; 'N' without serifs)

1923 (Jan)**–24.** T **8** and T **10** surch locally with T O **4**.

O20		8p. on 9p. carmine (No. O3)	£450	2·00
		a. 'Pies' for 'pies' (R. 4/8)	£1800	60·00
		b. Wmk sideways	£130	20
		ba. 'Pies' for 'pies' (R. 4/8)	£550	18·00
		c. Surch double	†	£450
O21		8p. on 9p. carmine (*a*) (*b*) (No. O13) (7.24)	70·00	10
		a. 'Pies' for 'pies' (R. 4/8)	£225	12·00
		b. Surch double	†	£325
		c. Opt Type O **3** double	†	£475

Varieties with smaller 'i' or 't' in 'Eight' and small 'i' in 'Pies' are also known from a number of positions in the setting.

1925 (Apr). T **10** surch locally as T O **4**.

O22		10p. on 9p. carmine (*b*) (No. O13)	90·00	1·00
		b. Surch double	†	£450
		c. Surch 25 mm high (*a*)	£400	2·00
		ca. Surch double	†	£500

1929. T **8** surch locally as T O **4** (25 *mm* high).
O23 10p. on 9p. carmine (No. O3a) £3000 20·00
a. Surch double † £850
b. Wmk upright — 90·00

1929–31. Optd by Perkins Bacon with T O **5** (*typo*).
O24 **10** 4p. green (*b*) (1931) 30·00 3·25
a. Inverted 'S' £375 30·00
O25 6p. red-brown (*b*) (*c*) (*d*) (1930) 22·00 10
a. Inverted 'S' £200 4·75
O26 8p. sepia (*b*) (1930) 8·50 10
a. Inverted 'S' 90·00 5·00
O27 10p. blue (*b*) 6·50 10
a. Inverted 'S' 95·00 5·50
O28 2a. grey (*b*) (1930) 55·00 25
a. Inverted 'S' £450 14·00
O29 3a. vermilion (*b*) (1930) 13·00 20
a. Inverted 'S' £170 13·00
O30 6a. violet (*b*) (*d*) (1930) £130 3·25
a. Inverted 'S' £800 £110
O24/O30 *Set of* 7 £225 6·50

1933. Nos. O26/O27 surch locally as T **14**, in red.
O32 **10** 6p. on 8p. sepia (*b*) 4·00 10
a. Inverted 'S' 42·00 6·00
O33 6p. on 10p. blue (*b*) 4·00 10
a. Inverted 'S' 50·00 4·00

The inverted 'S' varieties occur on R. 2/1 of one setting of this overprint only.

1933–38. Recess-printed stamps of 1933–1938 optd.

(*a*) *With T O* **5**
O34 **18** 4p. green 10·00 10
O35 6p. red-brown (1934) 9·00 10
O36 **18a** 1a. brown-orange 35·00 10
O37 **18** 1a.8p. carmine 1·50 30
O38 2a. grey 45·00 10
O39 2¼a. yellow-green 14·00 10
O40 3a. vermilion 75·00 10
O41 3a.4p. violet 1·50 15
O42 6a.8p. sepia 1·50 20
O43 10a. blue 1·50 1·75
O34/O43 *Set of* 10 £180 2·75

(*b*) *With T O* **6** *(typo)*
O44 **18a** 1a. brown-orange (1937) 48·00 75
O45 **18** 2a. grey-black (1938) 38·00 3·00
O46 3a. vermilion (1938) 11·00 2·50
O44/O46 *Set of* 3 90·00 5·50

ON **C G S** — **ON** **C G S**
(O **7** Curved back to 'c') (O **8**)

ON C G S — **ON C G S** — **ON C G S**
(O **9** Circular 'O'; 'N' with serifs) (O **10** Oval 'O') (O **11**)

1938–44. Lithographed stamps of 1938. W **8a**, optd.

(*a*) *With Types O* **7** *or O* **8** *(1a). P 11*
O47 **18** 4p. green 45·00 3·00
a. Inverted 'S' 55·00 2·75
b. Perf 13×13½ 27·00 3·50
O48 6p. red-brown 45·00 40
a. Inverted 'S' 55·00 50
O49 **18a** 1a. brown-orange £475 2·50
O50 **18** 2a. grey-black 20·00 1·10
a. Inverted 'S' 24·00 1·25

(*b*) *With Types O* **9** *(litho) or O* **10** *(6p.)*
O51 **18** 6p. red-brown (P 13×13½) 20·00 7·00
O52 **18a** 1a. brown-orange 1·00 10
O53 **18** 3a. vermilion 4·25 3·25

(*c*) *With T O* **11**
O53*a* **18** 6p. red-brown £1600 £650

The inverted 'S' varieties, Nos. O47a, O48a and O50a, occur 21 times in the setting of 48.

1942–43. Unissued stamps optd with T O **10**. Litho. W **27**. P 11.
O54 **18** 4p. green £140 16·00
a. Perf 13×13½ 2·75 80
O55 6p. red-brown £300 12·00
a. Perf 13×13½ 20·00 1·00
ab. Optd both sides † £250
O56 **18a** 1a. brown-orange 16·00 5·00
a. Perf 13×13½ 5·50 4·25
ab. Optd both sides † £250
ac. Stamp printed both sides † £900
O56*b* **18** 2a. grey-black (1943) £130 1·25
ba. Opt omitted † £2500
O56*c* 2¼a. sage-green (1943) £4000 12·00
O56*d* 3a. vermilion (1943) 30·00 11·00

1943. Official stamps variously surch with T **20** or T **21**.

(*i*) *On 1½a. purple of 1919–1933*
O57 **10** 9p. on 1½a. (*b*) (Type **20**) £1300 40·00

(*ii*) *On recess printed 1a.8p. carmine of 1933–1944 (T O* **5** *opt)*
O58 3p. on 1a.8p. (Type **21**) 13·00 4·25
O59 9p. on 1a.8p. (Type **20**) £200 42·00
O60 1a.9p. on 1a.8p. (Type **20**) 5·50 4·00
O61 1a.9p. on 1a.8p. (Type **21**) 5·50 75

(*iii*) *On lithographed stamps of 1938–1944. P 11*

(*a*) *W* **8a**
O62 **18** 3p. on 4p. (Types O **7** and **20**) (P 13×13½) 70·00 19·00
a. Surch double £650 £275
O63 3p. on 4p. (Types O **7** and **21**) (P 13×13½) £375 90·00
O64 **18a** 3p. on 1a. (Types O **9** and **20**) 7·00 5·00
O65 9p. on 1a. (Types O **9** and **20**) £450 75·00
O66 1a.3p. on 1a. (Types O **9** and **21**) £500 £140

(*b*) *W* **27**
O67 **18** 3p. on 4p. (Types O **10** and **20**) (P 13×13½) £160 75·00
O67*a* 3p. on 4p. (Types O **10** and **21**) (P 13×13½) £3500
O67*b* **18a** 3p. on 1a. (Types O **10** and **20**) £275 £110
ba. Perf 13×13½ £180 £100

1943–44. Optd with T O **10**. W **27**. P 13×13½.
O68 **26** 4p. green £100 11·00
a. Perf 11 £300 7·50
b. Perf 13 £750 70·00
O69 6p. red-brown 7·00 10
a. Opt double — £100
b. Perf 11 3·00 10
ba. Opt double — £100
c. Perf 13 8·00 3·75
O70 1a. brown-orange £12000 75·00
O71 2a. black 7·00 1·25
O72 2¼a. yellow-green 6·50 1·10
a. Optd both sides † £225
O73 3a. vermilion 14·00 3·75
a. Perf 11 17·00 40

Stamps perforated 13×13½ are from a comb machine; those perforated 13 from a line perforator.

1944. Optd with T O **10** and variously surch as Types **20** and **21**. W **27**.
O74 **26** 3p. on 4p. (Type **20**) 6·50 10
a. Perf 11 16·00 60
ab. Optd Type O **10** on both sides † £200
O75 3p. on 4p. (Type **21**) 9·00 75
a. Perf 11 £500 £200
O76 3p. on 1a. (Type **20**) 48·00 13·00
O77 9p. on 6p. (Type **20**) 18·00 6·00
a. Stamp printed both sides † £800
O78 9p. on 6p. (Type **21**) 8·50 1·25
O79 1a.3p. on 1a. (Type **20**) 24·00 5·00
O80 1a.3p. on 1a. (Type **21**) 5·00 10
O74/O80 *Set of* 7 £110 24·00

1946–47. Stamps of 1944–1948 (Head Type II) optd with T O **10**. P 13.
O81 **28** 9p. ultramarine 4·25 10
a. Stamp printed both sides † £900
b. Perf 13×13½ 6·00 10
O82 1a.3p. magenta (1947) 1·60 20
a. Opt double 25·00 12·00
b. Optd on both sides £225
ba. Optd both sides, opt double and inverted on reverse £120 £120
O83 1a.9p. ultramarine (1947) 40 1·25
a. Opt double † £225
b. Pair, one without opt † £3250
O81/O83 *Set of* 3 5·50 1·40

1946–48. Stamps of 1946–1948 and unissued values optd with T O **2**. P 13.
O84 **29** 3p. carmine 2·75 10
a. Stamp printed both sides † £900
O85 4p. grey-green 38·00 8·00
O86 6p. red-brown 28·00 4·50
a. Stamp printed both sides † £900
O87 9p. ultramarine 1·25 10
a. Stamp printed both sides (one inverted) † £900
O88 1a.3p. magenta 7·50 2·00
O89 1a.9p. ultramarine 9·00 40
O90 2a. black 16·00 3·00
O91 2¼a. yellow-green 35·00 11·00
O84/O91 *Set of* 8 £120 26·00

1948–49. Stamps of 1948–1950 and unissued values optd with T O **7**.
O92 **30** 3p. carmine 1·25 15
a. 'C' for 'G' in opt 25·00 3·25
O93 4p. green 3·25 40
a. Imperf between (horiz pair) † £2250
b. Imperf between (vert pair) † £2500
c. Optd on both sides £160 £160
d. 'C' for 'G' in opt 32·00 7·00
O94 6p. chestnut 4·50 30
a. Imperf between (vert pair) † £4000
b. 'C' for 'G' in opt 45·00 4·00
O95 9p. ultramarine 5·00 10
a. 'C' for 'G' in opt 50·00 3·75
O96 2a. black 3·75 25
a. 'C' for 'G' in opt 45·00 4·25
O97 2¼a. yellow-green 5·50 9·00
a. 'C' for 'G' in opt 50·00 90·00
O98 3a. orange-red 1·10 1·50
a. 'C' for 'G' in opt 30·00 14·00
O99 3a.4p. violet (I) 80·00 70·00
a. 'C' for 'G' in opt £500 £500
b. Tail to turban flaw £500 £500
c. Die II £325 £325
O92/O99 *Set of* 8 95·00 75·00

The 'C' for 'G' variety occurs on R. 1/4. Nos. O92/O99, O103/O104 and O104b also exist with a flat back to 'G' which occurs twice in each sheet on R. 1/5 and R. 2/8.

No. O93 exists with watermark sideways, but can usually only be identified when in multiples.

1949. Official stamps surch as T **33**.

(*i*) *On 1946 issue*
O100 **28** 1a. on 1a.9p. ultramarine (R.) 60 70

(*ii*) *On 1948 issue*
O101 **29** 1a. on 1a.9p. ultramarine (R.) 42·00 17·00

(*iii*) *On 1949 issue*
O103 **30** 6p. on 3p. carmine 1·25 75
a. Imperf between (vert pair) † £2500
b. Surch double † £450
c. 'C' for 'G' in opt 25·00 13·00
d. Incorrect character 21·00 13·00
O104 9p. on 4p. green (18 *mm long*) 75 3·25
a. Imperf between (horiz pair) £1000 £1100
b. Larger native characters, 22 mm long 1·10 1·40
ba. Ditto. Imperf between (horiz pair) £950 £950
bb. Incorrect character 28·00 30·00
c. 'C' for 'G' in opt 28·00 32·00
ca. Ditto. Larger native characters, 22 mm long 30·00 32·00
O100/O104 *Set of* 4 42·00 18·00

No. O104 exists with watermark sideways, but can usually only be identified when in multiples.

SERVICE
(O **12**)

1949. No. 124a, but with lines of surch 17½ mm apart, optd 'SERVICE' as T O **12**.
O105 **30** 3p. on 9p. ultramarine 60 80
a. Imperf between (horiz pair) † £4000

From 1 July 1949 Cochin formed part of the new state of Travancore-Cochin. Existing stocks of Cochin issues continued to be used in conjunction with stamps of Travancore surcharged in Indian currency.

DHAR

PRICES FOR STAMPS ON COVER TO 1945	
Nos. 1/4	*from* × 50
No. 5	*from* × 30
No. 6	—
Nos. 7/9	*from* × 50
No. 10	—

Raja (Maharaja from 1877) Anand Rao Puar III, 1857–1898

1 (¼a.)

2

अर्धा बलड. अर्धा लबड. आर्धा डबल.
No. 1c No. 1d No. 2

1897–1900. Type-set. Colour-fugitive paper. With oval handstamp in black. No gum. Imperf.
1 **1** ½p. black/*red* (three characters at bottom left) 4·25 4·75
a. Handstamp omitted £750
b. Line below upper inscription (R. 2/2) 95·00 £100
c. Character transposed (R. 2/3) 42·00 50·00
d. Character transposed (R. 2/5) £110
2 ½p. black/*red* (four characters at bottom left) 4·25 7·00
a. Handstamp omitted £500
3 ¼a. black/*orange* 4·50 8·00
a. Handstamp omitted £600
4 ½a. black/*magenta* 5·50 8·50
a. Handstamp omitted £750 £550
b. Line below upper inscription (R. 2/2) £150 £180
5 1a. black/*green* 10·00 23·00
a. Handstamp omitted £1100
b. Printed both sides £1600
c. Line below upper inscription (R. 2/2) £475 £700
6 2a. black/*yellow* 48·00 90·00
e. Top right corner ornament transposed with one from top of frame (R. 2/5) £190 £300
1/6 *Set of* 6 70·00 £130

Nos. 1/6 were each issued in sheets of ten (5×2), but may, on the evidence of a single sheet of the ½ pice value, have been printed in sheets of 20 containing two of the issued sheets *tête-bêche*.

Research has identified individual characteristics for stamps printed from each position in the sheet.

The same research suggests that the type remained assembled during the entire period of production, being amended as necessary to provide the different values. Seven main settings have been identified with changes sometimes occurring during their use which form sub-settings.

The distribution of stamps between the main settings was as follows:

Setting I — ½p.
Setting II — ½a., 1a.
Setting III — 1a.
Setting IV — ½p., ½a., 1a.
Setting V — ½p.
Setting VI — ½p. (No. 2). ¼a.
Setting VII — 2a.

The listed constant errors all occurred during Setting IV.

In No. 1c the three characters forming the second word in the lower inscription are transposed to the order (2) (3) (1) and in No. 1d to the order (3) (2) (1).

On Nos. 1b, 4b and 5c the line which normally appears above the upper inscription is transposed so that it appears below the characters.

All values show many other constant varieties including mistakes in the corner and border ornaments, and also both constant and non-constant missing lines, dots and characters.

Examples of complete forgeries and faked varieties on genuine stamps exist.

Raja (Maharaja from 1918) Udaji Rao Puar II, 1898–1926

(Typo at Bombay)

1898–1900. P 11 to 12.
7 **2** ½a. carmine 9·00 9·50
a. Imperf (pair) 60·00
b. *Deep rose* 7·00 7·00
8 1a. claret 8·00 9·00
9 1a. reddish violet 7·50 21·00
a. Imperf between (horiz pair) £950
b. Imperf (pair) £200
10 2a. deep green 14·00 38·00
7/10 *Set of* 4 32·00 70·00

The stamps of Dhar have been obsolete since 31 March 1901

DUNGARPUR

PRICES FOR STAMPS ON COVER TO 1945
Nos. 1/15 *from* × 2

Maharawal Lakshman Singh, 1918–1971

1 State Arms

(Litho Shri Lakshman Bijaya Printing Press, Dungarpur)

1933–43. P 11.

No.	Type	Description	Unused	Used
1	1	¼a. bistre-yellow	—	£375
2		¼a. rose (1935)	£8500	£1500
		a. Salmon	—	£1400
3		¼a. red-brown (1937)	—	£750
4		1a. pale turquoise-blue	—	£300
5		1a. rose (1938)	—	£5500
6		1a.3p. deep reddish violet (1935)	—	£500
7		2a. deep dull green (1943)	£4500	£700
8		4a. rose (1934)	—	£1600

Nos. 2 and 5 are known in a *se-tenant* strip of three, the centre stamp being the 1a. value.

2 3 4

Maharawal Lakshman Singh

Three dies of ½a. (*shown actual size*):

Die I. Size 21×25½ mm. Large portrait (head 5 *mm* and turban 7½ *mm* wide), correctly aligned (sheets of 12 and left-hand stamps in subsequent blocks of four *se-tenant* horizontally with Die II)

Die II. Size 20×24½ mm. Large portrait (head 4¾ *mm* and turban 7 *mm* wide), but with less detail at foot and with distinct tilt to left (right-hand stamps in sheets of four horizontally *se-tenant* with Die I)

Die III. Size 21×25½ mm. Small portrait (head 4½ *mm* and turban 6½ *mm* wide) (sheets of four)

(Typo L. V. Indap & Co, Bombay)

1939–46. T **2** (various frames) and T **3**/T **4**. Various perfs.

No.	Type	Description	Unused	Used
9	2	¼a. orange-yellow (P 12)	—	£200
		a. No fraction bar at right	†	£800
		b. Perf 11. Yellow-orange (1940)	—	£225
		c. Perf 10½. *Yellow-orange* or *orange* (1941)	£2250	£180
		d. Perf 10. *Yellow-orange* or *orange* (1945)	£2250	£190
10		½a. vermilion (Die I) (P 12)	—	£225
		a. Perf 11. *Carmine-vermilion* (1943)	£1200	£200
		b. Perf 10½ (1944)	£800	£225
		c. Die II (P 10½) (1944)	£800	£225
		ca. Horiz pair Die I and Die II	£1900	£550
		d. Die III (P 10) (1945)	£1100	£130
		da. Imperf between (vert pair)	†	£6500
11		1a. deep blue (P 12)	—	£190
		a. Perf 11 (1941)	—	£190
		b. Perf 10½ (1940)	£1000	£140
		c. Perf 10 (1946)	£750	£140
12	3	1a.3p. bright mauve (P 10½) (1944)	£2500	£500
		a. Perf 10 (1945)	£2500	£550
13	4	1½a. deep violet (P 10) (1946)	£3000	£450
14	2	2a. bright green (P 12) (1943)	£4250	£1200
15		4a. brown (P 12) (1940)	—	£550
		a. Perf 10½ (1943)	—	£550
		b. Perf 10 (1945)	£3000	£550

Stamps perforated 12 and 11 were printed in sheets of 12 (4×3) which were imperforate along the top, bottom and, sometimes, at right so that examples exist with one or two adjacent sides imperforate. The ¼a, 1a., 1a.3p. and 4a. perf 10½ were printed in similar sheets of 12, but the ½a. perf 10½ (Nos. 10b, 10c, 10ca) was always in sheets of four, imperforate at top, bottom and right, comprising dies I (left vertical pair) and II (right vertical pair) *se-tenant*. Stamps perforated 10 were printed in sheets of four either imperforate at top, bottom and right-hand side or fully perforated.

Dungarpur became part of Rajasthan by 15 April 1948.

DUTTIA (DATIA)

PRICES FOR STAMPS ON COVER TO 1945

Nos. 1/7	—
Nos. 8/11	*from* × 5
Nos. 12/15	—
Nos. 16/40	*from* × 20

All the stamps of Duttia were impressed with a circular handstamp (usually in *blue*) before issue.

This handstamp shows the figure of Ganesh in the centre, surrounded by an inscription in Devanagari reading 'DATIYA STET POSTAJ 1893'. Stamps were not intended to be used for postage without this control mark.

PROCESS. Nos. 1/15 were type-set and printed singly. Nos. 16/40 were typo from plates comprising eight or more clichés.

GUM. The stamps of Duttia (*except* No. 25c) were issued without gum.

Maharaja Bhawani Singh, 1857–1907

Rectangular labels each showing a double hand-drawn frame (in black for the 1a. and in red for the others), face value in black and the Ganesh handstamp are known on thin cream (½a.), rose (1a.), orange (2a.) or pale yellow (4a.) paper. These are considered by some specialists to be the first stamps of Duttia, possibly issued during 1893, but the evidence for this is inconclusive (*Price for set of 4, £25,000, unused*).

1 (2a.) 2 (1a.) Ganesh 3 (¼a.)

1894? Rosettes in lower corners. Control handstamp in blue. Imperf.

No.	Type	Description	Unused	Used
1	1	½a. black/*green*	£30000	
2		2a. grey-blue/*yellow*	£10000	
		a. Handstamp in black	£12000	
		b. Handstamp in red	†	£45000

Only three examples of No. 1 have been reported. In each instance the Devanagari inscription was originally 8a., but was amended in manuscript to ½a.

1896. Control handstamp in blue. Imperf.

No.	Type	Description	Unused	Used
3	2	1a. red	£8000	£14000
		a. Handstamp in black	£10000	£14000
		b. Handstamp in brown	£16000	
3*c*		2a. deep blue (handstamp in black)	£35000	
		d. Handstamp in brown	£30000	

1896. Control handstamp in blue. Imperf.

No.	Type	Description	Unused	Used
4	3	¼a. black/*orange*	£12000	
		a. Without handstamp	£7500	
5		½a. black/*blue-green*	£26000	
		a. Without handstamp	£7500	£14000
6		2a. black/*yellow*	£7000	
		a. Without handstamp	£20000	
7		4a. black/*rose*	£2250	
		a. Without handstamp	£27000	

Two types of centre:

I II

Type I. Small Ganesh. Height 13 mm. Width of statue 11 mm. Width of pedestal 8 mm.

Type II. Large Ganesh. Height 13½ mm. Width of statue 11½ mm. Width of pedestal 11½ mm. 'Flag' in god's right hand; 'angle' above left. All stamps also show dot at top right corner.

1897–98. Imperf.

No.	Type	Description	Unused	Used
8	2	½a. black/*green* (I) (value in one group)	£130	£1000
		a. *Tête-bêche* (horiz pair)	£2000	
		b. Value in two groups	22·00	£750
		ba. *Tête-bêche* (vert pair)	£1900	
		bb. Doubly printed	£7000	
		bc. Type II (1898)	48·00	
9		1a. black/*white* (I)	£180	£800
		a. *Tête-bêche* (horiz pair)	£2000	
		b. Laid paper	32·00	
		ba. *Tête-bêche* (vert pair)	£1400	
		c. Type II (1898)	£225	
		ca. Laid paper	45·00	
		cb. Doubly printed	£7000	
10		2a. black/*yellow* (I)	55·00	£700
		a. On lemon	80·00	£750
		b. Type II (1898)	85·00	£800
11		4a. black/*rose* (I)	42·00	£250
		a. *Tête-bêche* (horiz pair)	£375	
		b. *Tête-bêche* (vert pair)	£200	£750
		d. Type II (1898)	70·00	
		da. Doubly printed	£7000	

A used example of the 4a. is known showing black roulettes at foot.

4 (2a.) 5 (2a.)

1897. Name spelt 'DATIA'. Imperf.

No.	Type	Description	Unused	Used
12	4	½a. black/*green*	£200	£1100
13		1a. black/*white*	£375	
14		2a. black/*yellow*	£225	£1100
		a. *Tête-bêche* (vert pair)	£10000	
15		4a. black/*rose*	£225	£1100
		a. *Tête-bêche* (vert pair)	£10000	
12/15 *Set of 4*			£900	

1899–1906.

(a) Rouletted in colour or in black, horizontally and at end of rows

No.	Type	Description	Unused	Used
16	5	¼a. vermilion	4·50	
		a. Rose-red	3·25	
		b. Pale rose	3·75	
		c. Lake	3·75	32·00
		d. Carmine	4·50	35·00
		e. Brownish red	11·00	
		ea. *Tête-bêche* (pair)	£4750	
17		½a. black/*blue-green*	3·00	32·00
		a. On deep green	6·50	
		b. On yellow-green (pelure)	5·50	35·00
		c. On dull green (1906)	4·25	
18		1a. black/*white*	4·25	32·00
19		2a. black/*lemon-yellow*	15·00	
		a. On orange-yellow	25·00	
		b. On buff-yellow	7·00	38·00
		ba. Handstamp in black	35·00	
		bb. Without handstamp	£900	
		c. On pale yellow (1906)	5·50	38·00
20		4a. black/*deep rose*	6·00	35·00
		a. *Tête-bêche* (pair)		
		b. Handstamp in black	45·00	
		c. Without handstamp	£750	

(b) Rouletted in colour between horizontal rows, but imperf at top and bottom and at ends of rows

No.	Type	Description	Unused	Used
20*d*	5	¼a. brownish red	65·00	£160
21		1a. black/*white*	21·00	90·00
		a. Without handstamp	£1100	
		b. Handstamp in black	£225	

One setting of 16 (8×2) of the ¼a. value (No. 16e) showed an inverted cliché at R. 1/2.

1904–05. Without rouletting.

No.	Type	Description	Unused	Used
22	5	¼a. red	7·00	55·00
		a. Without handstamp	£750	
23		½a. black/*green*	27·00	
24		1a. black (1905)	21·00	70·00

Maharaja Govind Singh, 1907–1955

1911. P 13½. Stamps very wide apart.

No.	Type	Description	Unused	Used
25	5	¼a. carmine	7·00	95·00
		a. Imperf horiz (vert pair)	£500	
		b. Imperf between (horiz pair)	£650	
		c. Stamps closer together (with gum)	13·00	80·00
		d. As c. Imperf vert (horiz pair)	£225	
		e. As c. imperf between (horiz strip of 5)	£750	
25*f*		1a. black	£2000	£2250

No. 25*f* was mainly used for fiscal purposes (*Price on piece*, £150).

1912? Printed close together.

(a) Coloured roulette×imperf

No.	Type	Description	Unused	Used
26	5	½a. black/*green*	10·00	45·00

(b) Printed wide apart. P 13½×coloured roulette (¼a.) or 13½×imperf (½a.)

No.	Type	Description	Unused	Used
27	5	¼a. carmine	5·50	70·00
		a. Without handstamp	£600	
28		½a. black/*dull green*	13·00	80·00

1916. Colours changed. Control handstamp in blue (Nos. 29/33) or black (No. 34). Imperf.

No.	Type	Description	Unused	Used
29	5	¼a. deep blue	5·50	42·00
30		½a. green	9·00	45·00
		a. Without handstamp	†	£2000
31		1a. purple	14·00	50·00
		a. *Tête-bêche* (vert pair)	27·00	
		ab. Without handstamp	£2500	
32		2a. brown	15·00	55·00
33		2a. lilac	9·50	30·00
		a. Handstamp in black	60·00	
		b. Without handstamp	£650	
34		4a. Venetian red (date?)	£110	
		a. Without handstamp	£1100	

1918. Colours changed.

(a) Imperf

No.	Type	Description	Unused	Used
35	5	½a. blue	5·00	27·00
36		1a. pink	5·00	25·00
		a. Handstamp in black	24·00	
		b. Without handstamp	£550	

(b) P 11½

No.	Type	Description	Unused	Used
37	5	¼a. black	8·00	42·00

1920. Rouletted.

No.	Type	Description	Unused	Used
38	**5**	¼a. blue	2·75	20·00
		a. Roulxperf 7	50·00	50·00
		b. Imperf between (vert pair)	£900	
		c. Without handstamp	£300	
		d. Handstamp in black	20·00	
39		½a. pink	4·50	20·00
		a. Roulxperf 7	£350	
		b. Without handstamp	£475	
		c. Handstamp in black	60·00	

1920. Rough perf about 7.

No.	Type	Description	Unused	Used
40	**5**	½a. dull red	24·00	70·00
		a. Handstamp in black	85·00	£180
		b. Without handstamp	£600	

The stamps of Duttia have been obsolete since 1 April 1921.

FARIDKOT

PRICES FOR STAMPS ON COVER TO 1945	
Nos. N1/N4	*from* × 10
Nos. N5/N6	*from* × 50
Nos. N7/N8	—

GUM. The stamps of Faridkot (Nos. N1/8) were issued without gum.

Raja Bikram Singh, 1874–1898

N **1** (1 folus = ¼a.)

N **2** (1 paisa = ¼a.)

N **3**

1879–86. Rough, handstamped impression. Imperf.

No.	Type	Description	Unused	Used
		(a) Native thick laid paper		
N1	N **1**	1f. ultramarine	70·00	75·00
N2	N **2**	1p. ultramarine	£300	£300
		(b) Ordinary laid paper		
N3	N **1**	1f. ultramarine	19·00	22·00
N4	N **2**	1p. ultramarine	£140	£170
		(c) Wove paper, thick to thinnish		
N5	N **1**	1f. ultramarine	3·25	4·75
		a. *Tête-bêche* (pair)	£275	
		b. Pair, one stamp sideways	£2500	
N6	N **2**	1p. ultramarine	6·50	17·00
		a. Pair, one stamp sideways	£3000	
		(d) Thin wove whitey brown paper		
N7	N **2**	1p. ultramarine	40·00	42·00

Faridkot signed a postal convention with the Imperial Government which led to the provision of India issues overprinted 'FARIDKOT STATE' from 1 January 1887. These are listed in the Convention States section.

Although the previous issues were no longer valid for postal purposes the state authorities continued to sell them to collectors for many years after 1887. Initially remaining stocks of Nos. N1/N7 were on offer, but these were soon supplemented by T N **1** handstamped in other colours, examples of a ½a., handstamped in various colours, which had originally been prepared in 1877 and by a replacement 1p, as T N **3**, (*Price* £2.00 *unused*, *tête-bêche pair*, £225, *unused*) which had not done postal duty before the convention came into force. The sale of such items was clearly an important source of revenue as the 1f. as T N **1**, yet another version of the 1p. and the ½a. subsequently appeared printed in sheets by lithography for sale to stamp collectors.

HYDERABAD

PRICES FOR STAMPS ON COVER TO 1945	
Nos. 1/3	*from* × 20
Nos. 4/12	—
Nos. 13/60	*from* × 5
Nos. O1/O53	*from* × 10

The official title of the State in English was The Dominions of the Nizam and in Urdu 'Sarkar-i-Asafia' (State of the successors of Asaf). This Urdu inscription appears in many of the designs.

Nawab Mir Mahbub Ali Khan Asaf Jah VI, 1869–1911

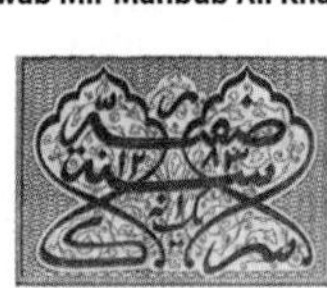
1

2

(Eng Mr. Rapkin. Plates by Nissen & Parker, London. Recess Mint, Hyderabad)

1869 (8 Sept). P 11½.

No.	Type	Description	Unused	Used
1	**1**	1a. olive-green	26·00	9·00
		a. Imperf between (horiz pair)	£350	
		b. Imperf horiz (vert pair)	£1100	£200
		c. Imperf (pair)	£750	£750
		d. Imperf vert (horiz pair)	†	£750

Reprints in the colour of the issue, and also in fancy colours, were made in 1880 on white wove paper, perforated 12½. Fakes of No. 1c are known created by the removal of the outer perforations from examples of Nos. 1a/1b.

1870 (16 May). Locally engraved; 240 varieties of each value; wove paper. Recess. P 11½.

No.	Type	Description	Unused	Used
2	**2**	½a. brown	4·00	4·25
3		2a. sage-green	85·00	60·00

Stamps exist showing traces of lines in the paper, but they do not appear to be printed on true laid paper.

Reprints of both values were made in 1880 on white wove paper, perforated 12½: the ½a. in grey-brown, yellow-brown, sea-green, dull blue and carmine and the 2a. in bright green and in blue-green.

3

A Normal

B Variety

2a.

In A the coloured lines surrounding each of the four labels join a coloured circle round their inner edge, in B this circle is missing.

C Normal

D Character ^ omitted

2a.

½a. Left side of central inscription omitted (Pl 4 R. 2/11)

½a., **1a.**, **2a.** Dot at top of central inscription omitted

1a. Second dot in bottom label omitted

2a. Centre dot in bottom label omitted

8a. Character at left of bottom label omitted

(Plates by Bradbury Wilkinson & Co. Recess Mint, Hyderabad)

1871–1909.

No.	Type	Description	Unused	Used
		(a) No wmk		
		(i) Rough perf 11½		
4	**3**	½a. red-brown	21·00	24·00
		a. Dot at top of central inscription omitted	£225	
5		1a. purple-brown	£170	£180
		a. Imperf horiz (vert pair)	†	£3500
		b. Dot at top of central inscription omitted	£1300	£1300
6		2a. green (A)	£3000	
7		3a. ochre-brown	70·00	£100
8		4a. slate	£225	£225
9		8a. deep brown		
10		12a. dull blue	£475	
		(ii) Pin perf 8-9		
11	**3**	½a. red-brown	£1500	£650
12		1a. drab	£450	£200
		(iii) P 12½		
13	**3**	½a. orange-brown	4·00	10
		a. Imperf vert (horiz pair)	†	£140
		ab. Imperf horiz (vert pair)	†	£1300
		b. *Orange*	4·00	10
		c. *Red-brown*	4·00	10
		d. *Brick-red*	4·00	10
		da. Imperf vert (horiz pair)	†	£140
		db. Doubly printed	£500	£180
		e. *Rose-red*	3·25	20
		ea. Doubly printed	†	£275
		f. Error. Magenta	65·00	8·00
		g. Left side of central inscription omitted	£500	£110
		h. Dot at top of central inscription omitted	£100	4·00
14		1a. purple-brown	16·00	9·50
		a. Doubly printed	£500	
		b. *Drab*	2·50	15
		ba. Imperf (pair)	—	£550
		bb. Doubly printed	£250	
		c. *Grey-black*	3·50	10
		ca. Imperf (pair)	†	£1400
		cb. Imperf between (vert pair)	†	£1500
		d. *Black* (1909)	3·50	10
		da. Doubly printed	£650	£300
		db. Imperf vert (horiz pair)	†	£1500
		dc. Imperf horiz (vert pair)	†	£1500
		e. Dot at top of central inscription omitted	—	£225
		f. Second dot in bottom label omitted	£200	55·00
15		2a. green (A)	4·50	15
		a. *Deep green* (A)	6·50	40
		b. *Blue-green* (A)	7·00	40
		ba. *Blue-green* (B)	£425	70·00
		c. *Pale green* (A)	4·50	15
		ca. *Pale green* (B)	£425	80·00
		d. *Sage-green* (A) (1909)	6·50	35
		da. *Sage-green* (B)	£300	55·00
		e. Dot at top of central inscription omitted	£600	£150
		f. Centre dot in bottom panel omitted	£300	60·00
		g. Perf 11½, 12 (*Blue-green*)	—	£800
16		3a. ochre-brown (C)	4·50	1·50
		a. Character omitted (D)	£375	85·00
		b. *Chestnut* (C)	3·75	1·50
		ba. Character omitted (D)	£325	70·00
17		4a. slate	13·00	3·50
		a. Imperf horiz (vert pair)	£1400	£1400
		b. *Greenish grey*	5·50	3·25
		ba. Imperf vert (horiz pair)	£2500	
		c. *Olive-green*	6·00	2·50
18		8a. deep brown	3·75	4·25
		a. Imperf vert (horiz pair)	£1200	
		b. Character omitted	£500	
19		12a. pale ultramarine	5·50	12·00
		a. *Grey-green*	8·00	9·00
13/19*a* *Set of 7*			26·00	16·00
		(b) W **7**. *P 12½*		
19*b*	**3**	1a. black (1909)	£200	26·00
19*c*		2a. sage-green (A) (1909)	£650	£160
19*d*		12a. bluish grey (1909)	£1600	

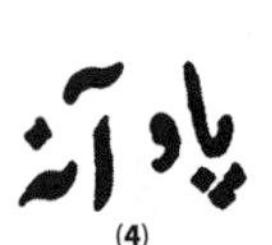

(4)

5

1898. Surch with T **4**. P 12½.

No.	Type	Description	Unused	Used
20	**3**	¼a. on ½a. orange-brown	50	85
		a. Surch inverted	50·00	28·00
		b. Pair, one without surcharge	£850	
		c. Left side of central inscription omitted	£275	

(Des Khusrat Ullah. Recess Mint, Hyderabad)

1900 (20 Sept). P 12½.

No.	Type	Description	Unused	Used
21	**5**	¼a. deep blue	7·00	4·50
		a. *Pale blue*	5·50	4·00

6

7

(Plates by Allan G. Wyon, London. Recess Mint, Hyderabad)

1905 (7 Aug). W **7**. P 12½.

No.	Type	Description	Unused	Used
22	**6**	¼a. dull blue	6·00	60
		a. Imperf (pair)	40·00	£200
		b. *Dull ultramarine*	5·00	80
		ba. Perf 11×12½	65·00	40·00
		c. *Pale blue-green*	28·00	3·00

23		½a. orange	9·00	35
		a. Perf 11	—	£250
		b. Vermilion	5·50	25
		ba. Imperf (pair)	38·00	£200
		c. Yellow	£130	17·00

1908–11. W **7**. P 12½.

24	**6**	¼a. grey	2·50	10
		a. Imperf between (horiz pair)	£800	£650
		b. Imperf between (vert pair)	†	£650
		c. Perf 11½, 12	2·75	35
		d. Perf 11	£130	30·00
25		½a. green	11·00	10
		a. Imperf between (vert pair)	£700	
		b. Perf 11½, 12	14·00	10
		c. Perf 13½	£250	60·00
		d. Pale green	12·00	20
		da. Perf 11½, 12	15·00	30
		e. Blue-green	14·00	1·00
26		1a. carmine	9·00	10
		a. Perf 11½, 12	17·00	1·00
		b. Perf 11	70·00	14·00
		c. Double impression (P 12½×11)		
27		2a. lilac	7·50	40
		a. Perf 11½, 12	10·00	1·10
		b. Perf 11	3·25	55
		c. Perf 13½	4·00	15
		ca. Imperf between (horiz pair)	†	£1000
		cb. Rose-lilac	3·50	10
28		3a. brown-orange (1909)	8·50	1·00
		a. Perf 11½, 12	13·00	2·50
		b. Perf 11	5·50	1·50
		c. Perf 13½	6·00	30
29		4a. olive-green (1909)	8·50	2·50
		a. Perf 11½, 12	14·00	7·00
		b. Perf 11	70·00	19·00
		ba. Imperf between (pair)	£1600	£1600
		c. Perf 13½	2·75	40
30		8a. purple (1911)	13·00	11·00
		a. Perf 11½, 12		
		b. Perf 11	3·50	7·00
		c. Perf 13½	2·75	2·25
31		12a. blue-green (1911)	£250	£150
		a. Perf 11½, 12	38·00	55·00
		b. Perf 11		
		c. Perf 13½	14·00	7·00
24/31c *Set of 8*			45·00	9·25

The above perforations also exist compound.

Nawab Mir Osman Ali Khan Asaf Jah VII, 1911–1967

1912. New plates engraved by Bradbury Wilkinson & Co. W **7**. P 12½.

32	**6**	¼a. grey-black	4·00	10
		a. Imperf horiz (vert pair)	†	£600
		b. Perf 11½, 12	3·50	35
		c. Perf 11	3·00	15
		ca. Imperf between (horiz pair)	†	£650
		cb. Imperf between (vert pair)	†	£650
		d. Perf 13½	2·75	10
33		¼a. brown-purple (*shades*) (P 13½).	4·00	10
		a. Imperf horiz (vert pair)	†	£650
34		½a. deep green	4·50	10
		a. Imperf between (pair)	†	£700
		b. Imperf (pair). Laid paper	£225	£160
		c. Perf 11½, 12	16·00	55
		d. Perf 11	11·00	10
		e. Perf 13½		

The above perforations also exist compound.

In Wyon's ¼a. stamp the fraction of value is closer to the end of the label than in the B.W. issue. In the Wyon ¼a. and ½a. the value in English and the label below are further apart than in the B.W.

Wyon's ¼a. measures 19½×20 mm and the ½a. 19½×20½ mm; both stamps from the Bradbury plates measure 19¾×21½ mm.

8 Symbols

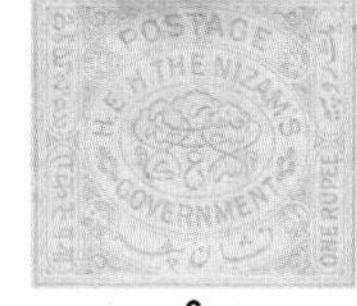
9

1915. Inscr 'Post & Receipt'. W **7**. P 13½.

35	**8**	½a. green	3·00	10
		a. Imperf between (pair)	£160	£170
		b. Emerald-green	4·50	20
		c. Perf 12½	13·00	35
		ca. Imperf between (pair)		
		d. Perf 11	75	10
		da. Imperf between (pair)	†	£550
		db. Imperf vert (horiz pair)	†	£550
		e. Imperf (pair)	£350	£200
36		1a. carmine	5·00	10
		a. Imperf between (pair)	£650	
		b. Scarlet	5·50	10
		ba. Imperf between (horiz pair)	†	£550
		bb. Imperf between (vert pair)	†	£550
		bc. Imperf vert (horiz pair)	†	£550
		c. Perf 12½	26·00	85
		ca. Imperf between (pair)		
		cc. Scarlet		
		d. Perf 11	1·25	20
		da. Scarlet	—	42·00
		e. Imperf (pair)	£400	£400

The above perforations also exist compound.

For ½a. claret, see No. 58.

1927 (1 Feb). As W **7**, but larger and sideways. P 13½.

37	**9**	1r. yellow	13·00	12·00

10 (4 pies) **11 (8 pies)**

1930 (6 May). Surch as Types **10** and **11**. W **7**. P 13½.

38	**6**	4p. on ¼a. grey-black (R.)	£140	32·00
		a. Perf 11	†	£200
		b. Perf 12½	†	85·00
		c. Perf 11½, 12	†	£450
39		4p. on ¼a. brown-purple (R.)	2·75	10
		a. Imperf between (pair)	£800	£800
		b. Surch double	†	£300
		c. Perf 11	†	£550
		d. Black surch	£650	£500
40	**8**	8p. on ½a. green (R.)	2·00	10
		a. Imperf between (horiz pair)	†	£400
		b. Perf 11	£325	£140
		c. Perf 12½	†	£275

12 Symbols

13 The Char Minar

14 High Court of Justice

15 Osman Sagar Reservoir

16 Entrance to Ajanta Caves

17 Bidar College

18 Victory Tower, Daulatabad

(Plates by De La Rue. Recess Stamps Office, Hyderabad)

1931 (12 Nov)–**47**. T **12/18**. W **7**. Wove paper. P 13½.

41	**12**	4p. black	40	10
		a. Laid paper (1947)	2·50	7·50
		b. Imperf (pair)	50·00	£180
		c. Imperf between (vert pair)	†	£1000
42		8p. green	1·50	10
		a. Imperf between (vert pair)	£1100	£950
		b. Imperf (pair)	60·00	£180
		c. Laid paper (1947)	3·00	4·50
43	**13**	1a. brown (*shades*)	1·50	10
		a. Imperf between (horiz pair)	—	£1000
		b. Perf 11	†	£1000
44	**14**	2a. violet (*shades*)	4·00	10
		a. Imperf (pair)	£140	£425
45	**15**	4a. ultramarine	3·50	70
		a. Imperf (pair)	£140	£475
46	**16**	8a. orange (*shades*)	12·00	4·50
		a. Yellow-orange (1944)	£100	35·00
47	**17**	12a. scarlet	14·00	12·00
48	**18**	1r. yellow	8·50	5·00
41/48 *Set of 8*			40·00	20·00

Nos. 41a and 42c have a large sheet watermark 'THE NIZAM'S GOVERNMENT HYDERABAD DECCAN' and Arms within a circle, but this does not appear on all stamps.

19 Unani General Hospital

20 Osmania General Hospital

21 Osmania University

22 Osmania Jubilee Hall

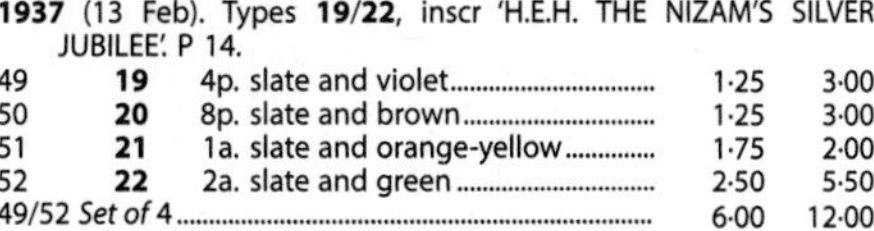

(Litho Indian Security Printing Press, Nasik)

1937 (13 Feb). Types **19/22**, inscr 'H.E.H. THE NIZAM'S SILVER JUBILEE'. P 14.

49	**19**	4p. slate and violet	1·25	3·00
50	**20**	8p. slate and brown	1·25	3·00
51	**21**	1a. slate and orange-yellow	1·75	2·00
52	**22**	2a. slate and green	2·50	5·50
49/52 *Set of 4*			6·00	12·00

23 Family Reunion

24 Town Hall

(Des T. I. Archer. Typo)

1945 (6 Dec). Victory. W **7** (very faint). Wove paper. P 13½.

53	**23**	1a. blue	10	10
		a. Imperf between (vert pair)	£1000	
		b. Laid paper	1·50	1·75

No. 53b shows the sheet watermark described beneath Nos. 41/48.

(Des. T. I. Archer. Litho Government Press)

1947 (17 Feb). Reformed Legislature. P 13½.

54	**24**	1a. black	2·50	1·90
		a. Imperf between (pair)	—	£1500

25 Power House, Hyderabad

26 Kaktyai Arch, Warangal Fort

27 Golkunda Fort

(Des T. I. Archer. Typo)

1947–49. As Types **25/27** (inscr 'H. E. H. THE NIZAM'S GOVT. POSTAGE'). W **7**. P 13½.

55	**25**	1a.4p. green	1·60	2·75
56	**26**	3a. greenish blue	3·50	7·00
		a. Bluish green	8·50	8·50
57	**27**	6a. sepia	4·50	26·00
		a. Red-brown (1949)	21·00	45·00
		ab. Imperf (pair)	£275	
55/57 *Set of 3*			8·50	32·00

1947. As 1915 issue but colour changed. P 13½.

58	**8**	½a. claret	3·00	75
		a. Imperf between (horizontal pair)	—	£475
		b. Imperf between (vert pair)	—	£900
		c. Doubly printed	†	£450

An Independence commemorative set of four, 4p., 8p., 1a. and 2a., was prepared in 1948, but not issued.

1948. As T **12** ('POSTAGE' at foot). Recess. W **7**. P 13½.

59		6p. claret	12·00	10·00

Following intervention by the forces of the Dominion of India during September 1948 the Hyderabad postal system was taken over by the Dominion authorities, operating as an agency of the India Post Office.

1949. T **12** ('POSTAGE' at top). Litho. W **7**. P 13½.

60	**12**	2p. bistre-brown	3·00	3·25
		a. Imperf between (horizontal pair)	†	£1200
		b. Imperf (pair)	£150	£500

No. 60 was produced from a transfer taken from a plate of the 4p., No. 41, with each impression amended individually.

OFFICIAL STAMPS

Official stamps became valid for postage to destinations within India from 1910.

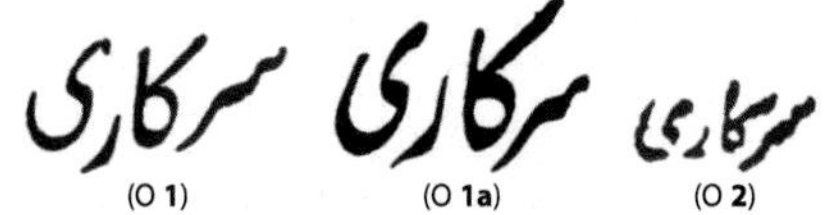
(O 1) **(O 1a)** **(O 2)**

1873.

I. Handstamped as T O **1** *in red*

O1	**1**	1a. olive-green	£200	55·00
		a. Black opt	—	£650
O2	**2**	½a. brown	—	£1400
		a. Black opt	—	£1100
O3		2a. sage-green	—	£1000
		a. Black opt	—	£350

At least ten different handstamps as T O **1** were used to produce Nos. O1/O17. These differ in the size, shape and spacing of the characters. The prices quoted are for the cheapest versions where more than one is known to exist on a particular stamp.

Imitations of these overprints on genuine stamps and on reprints are found horizontally or vertically in various shades of red, in magenta and in black.

II. T **3** *handstamped as T O* **1** *in red*

(a) Rough perf 11½

O4	½a. red-brown		
	a. Black opt	—	£1500
O5	1a. purple-brown	—	£2750
	a. Black opt	£200	£250
O6	2a. green (A)		
	a. Black opt	—	£2500
O7	4a. slate	—	£3000
	a. Black opt		
O8	8a. deep brown		
	a. Black opt	£2000	£1000
O8*b*	12a. dull blue	—	£3000

(b) Pin perf 8–9

O8*c*	1a. drab (*black opt*)	17·00	£130
	ca. Second dot in bottom label omitted	£300	

(c) P 12½

No.	Type	Description	Unused	Used
O9		½a. red-brown	50·00	14·00
		a. Black opt	21·00	5·50
		ab. Left side of central inscription omitted	—	£400
		ac. Dot at top of central inscription omitted	—	£110
O11		1a. purple-brown	£425	£170
		a. Black opt	—	90·00
O12		1a. drab	65·00	50·00
		aa. Dot at top of central inscription omitted	—	£275
		a. Black opt	7·50	4·50
		ab. Second dot in bottom label omitted	£200	£150
O13		2a. green (*to deep*) (A)	£180	80·00
		a. Black opt	20·00	13·00
		ab. Inner circle missing (B)	£700	
		ac. Centre dot in bottom label omitted	£375	£250
O14		3a. ochre-brown	£450	£350
		a. Black opt	£120	80·00
O15		4a. slate	£225	£120
		a. Black opt	65·00	50·00
O16		8a. deep brown	£225	£300
		a. Imperf vert (horiz pair)	£900	
		b. Black opt	£110	80·00
O17		12a. blue	£375	£400
		a. Black opt	£140	£180

Imitations and forgeries of these overprints are frequently met with. The prices quoted for Nos. O9/O17a are for genuine examples.

The use of Official Stamps (Sarkari) was discontinued in 1878, but was resumed in 1909, when the current stamps were overprinted from a new die.

1909–11. Optd with T O **1a**.

(a) On T **3**. *P 12½*

No.	Type	Description	Unused	Used
O18		½a. orange-brown	£225	10·00
		a. Opt inverted	†	£800
O19		1a. black	£140	50
		a. Second dot in bottom label omitted	—	12·00
O20		2a. sage-green (A)	£160	2·00
		a. Optd on No. 15*da* (B)	—	24·00
		b. Stamp doubly printed	†	£225
		c. Centre dot in bottom label omitted	—	24·00
		d. Opt double	†	£300
O20*e*		3a. ochre-brown	18·00	7·50
		ea. Character omitted (D)	—	£750
O20*f*		4a. olive-green	£600	13·00
		fa. Perf 11½, 12	—	£500
O20*g*		8a. deep brown	—	65·00
O20*h*		12a. grey-green	—	£120

(b) On T **6** *(Wyon ptgs). P 12½*

No.	Type	Description	Unused	Used
O21		½a. orange	—	4·50
		a. Vermilion	£250	40
		ab. Opt inverted	†	£650
		ac. Imperf horiz (vert pair)	†	£800
O22		½a. green	50·00	10
		a. Pale green	50·00	10
		b. Opt inverted	†	£130
		c. Imperf between (vert pair)	†	£650
		d. Imperf between (horiz pair)	†	£600
		e. Stamp doubly printed	†	£180
		f. Perf 11½, 12	42·00	30
		fa. Pale green	42·00	30
		fb. Opt inverted	†	£130
		g. Perf 11		
		ga. Pale green		
		h. Perf 13½	—	£140
O23		1a. carmine	£120	15
		a. Opt double	£450	
		b. Perf 11½, 12	£180	30
		ba. Stamp doubly printed	—	£200
		c. Perf 11	—	7·00
O24		2a. lilac	£120	60
		a. Perf 11½, 12	£200	5·50
		b. Perf 11	£550	
O25		3a. brown-orange	£400	32·00
		b. Perf 11½, 12	£550	42·00
		ba. Opt inverted	†	£325
		c. Perf 11	£650	85·00
		d. Perf 13½	—	£180
O26		4a. olive-green (1911)	70·00	3·00
		a. Perf 11½, 12	£200	4·50
		b. Perf 11	—	35·00
O27		8a. purple (1911)	26·00	3·50
		a. Perf 11½, 12	£225	21·00
		b. Perf 11	£600	£180
O28		12a. blue-green (1911)	30·00	5·00
		a. Imperf between (horiz pair)	†	£2500
		b. Perf 11½, 12	70·00	7·00
		c. Perf 11	†	£400

(c) On T **6** *(Bradbury Wilkinson ptgs). P 11*

No.	Type	Description	Unused	Used
O28*d*	**6**	¼a. grey-black	£1000	
O28*e*		½a. deep green	£1000	

1911–12. Optd with T O **2**.

(a) T **6** *(Wyon printings). P 13½ (8a, 12a.) or 12½ (others)*

No.	Type	Description	Unused	Used
O29		¼a. grey	£100	1·00
		a. Perf 11½, 12	50·00	75
		ab. Imperf between (vert pair)	†	£700
		b. Perf 11	£225	75·00
		c. Perf 13½		
O30		½a. pale green	90·00	2·00
		a. Perf 11½, 12	—	30
		ab. Imperf between (vert pair)	†	£750
		b. Perf 13½		
O31		1a. carmine	4·00	15
		a. Opt inverted	—	65·00
		b. Imperf horiz (vert pair)	†	£750
		c. Perf 11½, 12	5·50	15
		d. Perf 11	3·00	15
		e. Perf 13½		
O32		2a. lilac	22·00	1·75
		a. Perf 11½, 12	40·00	5·00
		b. Perf 11	6·00	1·25
		c. Perf 13½	15·00	10
		ca. Imperf between (horiz pair)	†	£800
		cb. Rose-lilac	4·25	10
O33		3a. brown-orange	60·00	9·00
		a. Opt inverted	†	£140
		b. Perf 11½, 12	75·00	9·00
		ba. Opt inverted	†	£150
		c. Perf 11	70·00	7·00
		ca. Opt inverted	†	£140
		d. Perf 13½	45·00	1·25
		da. Opt inverted	†	£120
O34		4a. olive-green	38·00	3·75
		a. Opt inverted	—	£140
		b. Perf 11½, 12	12·00	4·25
		ba. Opt inverted	—	£150
		c. Perf 11	12·00	1·75
		d. Perf 13½	9·00	15
		da. Opt inverted	†	£140
O35		8a. purple	16·00	30
		a. Perf 11½, 12		
		b. Perf 11	£650	£100
		c. Perf 12½	—	£425
O36		12a. blue-green	75·00	5·50
		a. Perf 11½, 12		
		b. Perf 11		
		c. Perf 12½		

(b) T **6** *(Bradbury Wilkinson printings). P 12½*

No.	Type	Description	Unused	Used
O37		¼a. grey-black	8·00	75
		a. Opt inverted	†	85·00
		b. Pair, one without opt		
		c. Imperf between (vert pair)	†	£600
		d. Perf 11½, 12	19·00	1·75
		da. Opt inverted	†	85·00
		db. Pair, one without opt		
		e. Perf 11	6·00	40
		ea. Opt sideways	†	£110
		eb. Blue opt	†	£110
		f. Perf 13½	8·50	10
		fa. Opt inverted	†	90·00
		fb. Pair, one without opt	†	£180
		fc. Imperf between (horiz pair)	†	£550
O38		¼a. brown-purple (*shades*) (P 13½)	4·75	10
		a. Imperf horiz (vert pair)	†	£550
		ab. Imperf between (vert pair)	†	£600
		b. Imperf between (horiz pair)	†	£600
		c. Perf 11		
O39		½a. deep green	12·00	25
		a. Opt inverted	—	40·00
		b. Perf 11½, 12	20·00	2·00
		ba. Pair, one without opt	†	£180
		c. Perf 11	13·00	15
		ca. Opt inverted	—	42·00
		cb. Imperf horiz (vert pair)	†	£600
		d. Perf 13½	7·00	10
		da. Imperf between (horiz pair)	†	£475
		db. Imperf between (vert pair)	†	£600
		dc. Yellow-green	—	70

1917–20. T **8** optd with T O **2**. P 13½.

No.	Type	Description	Unused	Used
O40		½a. green	3·50	10
		a. Opt inverted	†	40·00
		b. Pair, one without opt	†	£140
		c. Imperf between (horiz pair)	†	£350
		ca. Imperf vert (horiz pair)	†	£375
		d. Imperf between (vert pair)	†	£500
		e. Emerald-green	8·50	40
		f. Perf 12½	—	4·25
		g. Perf 11	18·00	30
		ga. Opt inverted	†	42·00
		gb. Pair, one without opt		
O41		1a. carmine	16·00	10
		a. Opt inverted	†	45·00
		b. Opt double	†	£140
		c. Imperf horiz (vert pair)	†	£550
		ca. Imperf between (horiz pair)	†	£650
		d. Stamp printed double		
		e. Scarlet (1920)	8·00	10
		ea. Stamp printed double	†	£275
		eb. Imperf between (horiz pair)	†	£600
		ec. Imperf between (vert pair)	†	£450
		ed. Imperf horiz (vert pair)	†	£500
		ee. Opt inverted	†	£140
		f. Perf 12½	—	3·50
		g. Perf 11	28·00	15
		ga. Opt inverted	†	32·00
		gb. Scarlet (1920)	—	35·00

1930–34. Types **6** and **8** optd as T O **2** and surch at top of stamp, in red, as Types **10** or **11**.

No.	Type	Description	Unused	Used
O42		4p. on ¼a. grey-black (No. O37*f*) (1934)	£850	28·00
O43		4p. on ¼a. brown-purple (No. O38)	4·75	10
		b. Imperf between (horiz pair)	†	£400
		c. Imperf between (vert pair)	†	£400
		d. Imperf horiz (vert pair)	†	£375
		e. Red surch double	†	£140
		f. Black opt double	†	£275
		g. Perf 11	†	£500
		h. Stamp doubly printed	†	£225
O44		8p. on ½a. green (No. O40)	4·75	10
		c. Imperf between (horiz pair)	†	£375
		ca. Imperf between (vert pair)	†	£425
		d. Red surch double	†	£140
		e. Stamp doubly printed	†	£225
		f. Black opt double	†	£275
O45		8p. on ½a. yellow-green (No. O39*dc*)	55·00	85·00

For Nos. O42/O45 the red surcharge was intended to appear on the upper part of the stamp, above the official overprint, T O **2**, but surcharge and overprint are not infrequently found superimposed on one another.

1934–44. Nos. 41/48 optd with T O **2**.

No.	Type	Description	Unused	Used
O46		4p. black	7·00	10
		a. Imperf (pair)	£120	
		b. Imperf between (vert pair)	£900	£700
		c. Imperf between (horiz pair)	—	£700
		d. Opt double	†	£300
O47		8p. green	2·75	10
		a. Opt inverted	†	£190
		b. Imperf between (horiz pair)	—	£750
		c. Opt double	†	£150
		d. Imperf (pair)	£275	£350
O48		1a. brown	7·00	10
		a. Imperf between (vert pair)	£800	£700
		b. Imperf between (horiz pair)	—	£600
		c. Imperf (pair)	£140	£250
		d. Opt double	—	£250
O49		2a. violet	16·00	10
		a. Imperf vert (horiz pair)	†	£2250
		b. Opt double	†	£500
O50		4a. ultramarine	16·00	25
		a. Opt double	†	£700
		b. Imperf between (vert pair)	†	£2750
O51		8a. orange (1935)	32·00	70
		a. Yellow-orange (1944)	—	45·00
O52		12a. scarlet (1935)	40·00	1·75
O53		1r. yellow (1935)	42·00	3·50
O46/O53		*Set of 8*	£150	6·00

1947. No. 58 optd with T O **2**.

No.	Type	Description	Unused	Used
O54	**8**	½a. claret	6·00	8·00

1949. No. 60 optd with T O **2**.

No.	Type	Description	Unused	Used
O55	**12**	2p. bistre-brown	7·00	12·00

1950. No. 59 optd with T O **2**.

No.	Type	Description	Unused	Used
O56		6p. claret	11·00	28·00

IDAR

PRICES FOR STAMPS ON COVER TO 1945

Nos. 1/2*b*	*from* × 2
Nos. 3/6	*from* × 3
Nos. F1/F5	*from* × 3

Maharaja Himmat Singh, 1931–1960

1 Maharaja Himmat Singh

2 Maharaja Himmat Singh

(Typo M. N. Kothari & Sons, Bombay)

1932–43. P 11*.

(a) White panels

No.	Type	Description	Unused	Used
1	**1**	½a. light green	£650	£100
		a. Pale yellow-green (thick paper) (1939)	38·00	38·00
		ab. Imperf between (horiz pair)	£3000	
		b. Emerald (1941)	35·00	38·00
		ba. Imperf between (pair)	£4500	
		c. Yellow-green (shades) (1943)	22·00	30·00

(b) Coloured panels

No.	Type	Description	Unused	Used
2	**1**	½a. pale yellow-green (*thick paper*) (1939)	55·00	40·00
		a. Emerald (1941)	32·00	35·00
		b. Yellow-green (shades) (1943)	15·00	30·00

In No. 2 the whole design is composed of half-tone dots. In No. 1 the dots are confined to the oval portrait.

* Two different perforating heads were used for Nos 1/2*b*. Nos. 1, 1*b* and 2*a* are P 11.3, whereas Nos. 1*a*, 1*c*, 2 and 2*b* are P 10.8. Apart from the difference in shade, No. 1 can be distinguished from No. 1*b* by the height of the stamp. No. 1 was printed in panes with wide outer imperforate margins, giving stamps 35-37 mm high. The average height of Nos. 1*a*/1*c* and 2/2*b* is only 28-30 mm.

(Typo P. G. Mehta & Co, Himatnagar)

1944 (21 Oct). P 12.

No.	Type	Description	Unused	Used
3	**2**	½a. blue-green	4·00	85·00
		a. Imperf between (vert pair)	£450	
		b. Yellow-green	4·50	85·00
		ba. Imperf between (vert pair)	15·00	
4		1a. violet	4·00	70·00
		a. Imperf (pair)	£225	
		b. Imperf vert (horiz pair)	£300	
5		2a. blue	3·50	£120
		a. Imperf between (vert pair)	£130	
		b. Imperf between (horiz pair)	£300	
6		4a. vermilion	4·50	£120
		a. Doubly printed	£2000	
3/6		*Set of 4*	14·50	£350

Nos. 1 to 6 are from booklet panes of four stamps, producing single stamps with one or two adjacent sides imperf.

The 4a. violet is believed to be a colour trial (*Price £650, unused*).

POSTAL FISCAL STAMPS

F 1

F 2

1936 (?). Typo. P 11½ on two or three sides.

No.	Type	Description	Unused	Used
F1	**F 1**	1a. reddish lilac and bright green	—	£1000

1940 (?)–**45**. Typo. P 12 on two or three sides.

No.	Type	Description	Unused	Used
F2	–	1a. violet (*shades*)	£325	£200
		a. Perf 11*	£200	£200
F3	**F 2**	1a. violet (1943)	£170	£200
F4		1¼a. on 1a. violet	£425	£550
F5		1¼a. yellow-green (1945)	26·00	
		a. Imperf between (vert pair)	55·00	
		b. Blue-green (1945)	£110	£180

No. F2 shows the portrait as T **1**. Used prices are for examples with postal cancellations. No. F4 shows a handstamped surcharge in Gujerati.

* No. F2a exists both P 10.8 and P 11.3. Fiscally used examples have been seen with a '1¼a' Gujerati handstamped surcharge, similar to No. F4.

Idar became part of Bombay Province on 10 June 1948.

INDORE

(HOLKAR STATE)

PRICES FOR STAMPS ON COVER TO 1945	
Nos. 1/2*a*	*from* × 20
No. 3	*from* × 3
Nos. 4/14	*from* × 20
No. 15	*from* × 10
Nos. 16/43	*from* × 6
Nos. S1/S7	*from* × 40

Maharaja Tukoji Rao Holkar II, 1843–1886

1 Maharaja Tukoji Rao Holkar II

(Litho Waterlow & Sons)

1886 (6 Jan). P 14½–15.

		(a) Thick white paper		
1	**1**	½a. bright mauve	38·00	30·00
		(b) Thin white or yellowish paper		
2	**1**	½a. pale mauve	8·00	3·50
		a. Dull mauve	7·50	4·25

Nos. 2 and 2*a* can be found with papermaker's watermark reading 'WATERLOW & SONS LIMITED LONDON'.

Maharaja Shivaji Rao Holkar, 1886–1903

2 Type I

2a Type II

TYPES 2 AND 2a. In addition to the difference in the topline character (marked by arrow), the two Types can be distinguished by the difference in the angles of the 6-pointed stars and the appearance of the lettering. In Type I the top characters are smaller and more cramped than the bottom; in Type II both are in the same style and similarly spaced.

1889 (Sept). Handstamped. No gum. Imperf.

3	**2**	½a. black/*pink*	50·00	38·00
4	**2a**	½a. black/*pink*	5·50	4·00
		a. *Tête-bêche* (pair)	£375	

3 Maharaja Shivaji Rao Holkar

4 Maharaja Tukoji Holkar III

5 Maharaja Tukoji Holkar III

(Recess Waterlow)

1889–92. Medium wove paper. P 14 to 15.

5	**3**	¼a. orange (9.2.92)	3·75	1·50
		a. Imperf between (horiz pair)	†	£950
		b. Very thick wove paper	4·75	4·75
		c. Yellow	5·00	4·25
6		½a. dull violet	6·50	1·75
		a. Brown-purple	5·00	25
		b. Imperf between (vert pair)	£1000	
7		1a. green (7.2.92)	7·50	2·50
		a. Imperf between (vert pair)	£1600	
		b. Very thick wove paper	75·00	
8		2a. vermilion (7.2.92)	13·00	3·00
		a. Very thick wove paper	14·00	3·75
5/8 *Set of 4*			26·00	6·50

Maharaja Tukoji Rao Holkar III, 1903–1926

(Recess Perkins Bacon)

1904–20. P 13½, 14.

9	**4**	¼a. orange	2·00	10
10	**5**	½a. lake (1909)	16·00	10
		a. Brown-lake (shades)	22·00	15
		b. Imperf (pair)	50·00	£850
11		1a. green	4·50	10
		a. Imperf (pair)	£160	
		b. Perf 12½ (1920)	£1400	£225
12		2a. brown	17·00	1·00
		a. Imperf (pair)	£130	
13		3a. violet	45·00	7·00
14		4a. ultramarine	32·00	6·50
		a. Dull blue	14·00	1·40
9/14*a Set of 6*			90·00	8·75

पाव आना.

(**6**)

7 Maharaja Yeshwant Rao Holkar II

1905 (June). No. 6*a* surch 'QUARTER ANNA' in Devanagari, as T **6**.

15	**3**	¼a. on ½a. brown-purple	13·00	30·00

On 1 March 1908 the Indore State postal service was amalgamated with the Indian Imperial system. Under the terms of the agreement stamps showing the Maharaja would still be used for official mail sent to addresses within the state. Initially Nos. 9/14 were used for this purpose, the 'SERVICE' overprints, Nos. S1/S7, being withdrawn.

Maharaja Yeshwant Rao Holkar II, 1926–1961

(Recess Perkins Bacon)

1927–37. P 13 to 14.

16	**7**	¼a. orange *(a) (d) (e)*	2·25	20
17		½a. claret *(a) (d) (e)*	4·50	20
18		1a. green *(a) (d) (e)*	5·50	10
19		1¼a. green *(c) (d)* (1933)	7·50	2·25
20		2a. sepia *(a)*	14·00	3·75
21		2a. bluish green *(d)* (1936)	15·00	2·25
		a. Imperf (pair)	27·00	£325
22		3a. deep violet *(a)*	7·00	11·00
23		3a. Prussian blue *(d)* (1935?)	27·00	
		a. Imperf (pair)	55·00	£900
24		3½a. violet *(d)* (1934)	7·00	15·00
		a. Imperf (pair)	£100	£900
25		4a. ultramarine *(a)*	16·00	5·50
26		4a. yellow-brown *(d)* (1937)	45·00	2·50
		a. Imperf (pair)	30·00	£550
27		8a. slate-grey *(a)*	13·00	4·50
28		8a. red-orange *(d)* (1937)	38·00	28·00
29		12a. carmine *(d)* (1934)	5·00	10·00
30	–	1r. black and light blue *(b)*	17·00	19·00
31	–	2r. black and carmine *(b)*	£100	£120
32	–	5r. black and brown-orange *(b)*	£180	£190

Nos. 30/32 are as T **7**, but larger, size 23×28 mm.

Five different perforating heads were used for this issue: *(a)* comb 13.6; *(b)* comb 13.9; *(c)* line 13.2; *(d)* line 13.8; *(e)* line 14.2. Values on which each perforation occur are indicated above.

Nos. 21a, 23a, 24a and 26a were specifically ordered by the state government in 1933 and are known used for postage *circa* 1938–1942. A plate proof of the 1r. in green and carmine is also known postally used (*Price of pair £45 unused, £500 used*).

Nos. 16/19 and 28/32 also exist as imperforate plate proofs, but these were never sent to India.

(**8**)

9

10

1940 (1 Aug). Surch in words as T **8** by *The Times of India* Press, Bombay.

33	**7**	¼a. on 5r. black and brown-orange *(b)*	28·00	1·75
		a. Surch double (Blk.+G.)	†	£550
34		½a. on 2r. black and carmine *(b)*	35·00	3·25
35		1a. on 1¼a. green *(c) (d) (e)*	45·00	1·00
		b. Surch inverted *(d)*	£120	
		c. Surch double *(c)*	£650	
33/35 *Set of 3*			95·00	5·50

(Typo *Times of India* Press, Bombay)

1940–46. P 11.

36	**9**	¼a. red-orange	2·25	20
37		½a. claret (1941)	7·00	10
38		1a. green (1941)	11·00	20
39		1¼a. yellow-green (1941)	22·00	3·25
		a. Imperf (pair)	£450	
40		2a. turquoise-blue (1941)	16·00	1·00
41		4a. yellow-brown (1946)	21·00	15·00
		Larger size (23×28 mm)		
42	**10**	2r. black and carmine (1943)	22·00	£275
43		5r. black and yellow-orange (1943)	22·00	£400
36/43 *Set of 8*			£110	£650

OFFICIAL STAMPS

SERVICE (S **1**)   **SERVICE** (S **2**)

1904–06.

		*(a) Optd with T S **1** (typo)*		
S1	**4**	¼a. orange (1906)	2·00	2·00
S2	**5**	½a. lake	75	10
		a. Opt inverted	55·00	95·00
		b. Opt double	60·00	
		c. Imperf (pair)	£150	
		d. Brown-lake	1·00	20
		da. Opt inverted	55·00	
		e. Pair, one without opt	£900	
S3		1a. green	25	25
S4		2a. brown (1905)	35	35
		a. Vert pair, one without opt	£1400	
S5		3a. violet (1906)	3·25	5·50
		a. Imperf (pair)	£450	
S6		4a. ultramarine (1905)	9·00	2·50
		*(b) Optd with T S **2** (litho)*		
S7	**5**	½a. lake	20	1·50
		a. Opt double	£700	
S1/S7 *Set of 7*			14·50	10·50

Types S **1** and S **2** differ chiefly in the shape of the letter 'R'.

Indore became part of Madhya Bharat by 1 July 1948.

JAIPUR

PRICES FOR STAMPS ON COVER TO 1945	
No. 1	*from* × 3
No. 2	*from* × 2
Nos. 3/5	*from* × 10
Nos. 6/70	*from* × 4
Nos. 71/80	*from* × 6
Nos. O1/O34	*from* × 8

Maharaja Sawai Madho Singh II, 1880–1922

1 (redrawn state)

1a

2

Chariot of the Sun God, Surya

Type **1** – Value at sides in small letters and characters. 'HALF ANNA', shown as one word except for R. 1/1 and 1/3, measuring between 13½ and 15 mm. Sheets of 12 (4×3) with stamps 2 to 2½ mm apart.

Type **1a** – Value in large letters and characters. 'HALF ANNA', always with a gap between the two words, measuring between 14½ and 15½ mm. Sheets of 24 (4×6) with stamps 3 to 4 mm apart.

Type **2** – Value in large letters and characters. 'HALF ANNA' measuring 16 to 17 mm. Both side inscriptions start below the inner frame line. Sheets of 24 (4×6) with stamps 1½ to 2 mm apart.

(Litho Durbar Press, Jaipur)

1904 (14 July). Roughly perf 14.

1	**1**	½a. pale blue	£275	£350
		a. Ultramarine	£400	£450
		b. Imperf, ultramarine	£550	
		*c. Pale slate-blue**	£2000	£2000
		*d. Imperf, pale slate-blue**	£1500	£1500
2	**1a**	½a. grey-blue	£4500	£300
		a. Imperf	£500	£900
		b. Ultramarine	—	£550
3	**2**	½a. pale blue	5·50	11·00
		a. Deep blue	6·00	11·00
		b. Ultramarine	6·50	11·00
		c. Imperf	£425	£425
4	**1**	1a. dull red	8·00	18·00
		a. Scarlet	8·00	18·00
5		2a. pale green	11·00	18·00
		a. Emerald-green	11·00	

Nos. 1*b*, 1*d*, 2*a* and 3*c* are on gummed paper. Imperforate plate proofs also exist for Nos. 1/5, but these are ungummed (*Prices, from £550 per pair*).

* Nos. 1*c*/1*d*, in pale slate-blue, were printed from the *original* state of the first stone of 12 (4×3), which was then extensively redrawn. Nos. 1/1*a*/1*b*, in pale blue or ultramarine, were printed from the second, redrawn state. In the original state the inner white lines are thin, and on all sheet positions there is a noticeable gap between the top of the umbrella and the inner frameline (below the 'U' of 'JAIPUR'). In the redrawn state the inner white lines are much thicker, and on all positions except R. 1/1 the top of the umbrella has been raised so that it touches or nearly touches the inner frameline. These differences can clearly be seen in the enlarged illustrations of R. 3/2 on the sheet in its original and redrawn states.

Type **I** (original state)

Type **I** (redrawn state)

3 Chariot of the Sun God, Surya

(Recess Perkins Bacon)

1904. P 12.

6	**3**	½a. blue	12·00	15·00
		a. Perf 12½	50·00	30·00
		b. Perf comp of 12 and 12½	23·00	32·00
7		1a. brown-red	75·00	75·00
		a. Perf 12½	£225	£225
		b. Perf comp of 12 and 12½	£150	£150
		c. Carmine	4·75	7·00
		ca. Imperf between (vert pair)	£800	£1100
		cb. Perf comp of 12 and 12½	15·00	24·00
8		2a. deep green	15·00	21·00
		a. Perf 12½	£375	£190
		b. Perf comp of 12 and 12½	29·00	50·00

Nos. 6b, 7b, 7cb and 8b occur on the bottom two rows of sheets otherwise perforated 12.

1905–09. Wmk 'JAs WRIGLEY & SON Ld. 219' 'SPECIAL POSTAGE PAPER LONDON' or 'PERKINS BACON & Co Ld LONDON' in sheet. P 13½

9	**3**	¼a. olive-yellow (1906)	2·75	2·50
10		½a. blue (1906)	10·00	3·75
		a. Indigo	4·25	1·75
11		1a. brown-red (1906)	16·00	7·00
		a. Bright red (1908)	8·00	1·75
12		2a. deep green (1906)	11·00	3·25
13		4a. chestnut	14·00	3·75
14		8a. bright violet	12·00	2·75

15		1r. orange-yellow	75·00	55·00
		a. Yellow (1909)	42·00	16·00
		b. Yellow-ochre	50·00	40·00
9/15*a* *Set of 7*			85·00	28·00

4 Chariot of the Sun God, Surya

३ आना
(5)

(Typo Jaipur State Press)

1911. Thin wove paper. No gum. Imperf.

16	**4**	¼a. green	5·00	6·00
		a. Printed double	15·00	
		ab. Ditto, one inverted		
		b. '¼' inverted in right upper corner (R. 1/2)	8·50	
		c. No stop after 'STATE' (R. 3/1)	8·50	
17		¼a. greenish yellow	40	2·50
		a. Printed double	2·75	
		b. Printed double, one sideways		
		c. '¼' inverted in right upper corner (R. 1/2)	1·50	
		d. No stop after 'STATE' (R. 3/1)	1·50	
18		½a. ultramarine	50	2·50
		a. Printed double	2·25	
		b. No stop after 'STATE' (R. 3/1)	1·00	
		c. Large 'J' in 'JAIPUR' (R. 1/2)	1·00	
		d. '⅓' for '½' at lower left (R. 3/1)	1·50	
		e. '1½a.' at lower right (R. 3/2)	1·50	
19		½a. grey-blue	6·00	6·00
		a. No stop after 'STATE' (R. 3/1)	10·00	
		b. Large 'J' in 'JAIPUR' (R. 1/2)	10·00	
		c. '⅓' for '½' at lower left (R. 3/1)	12·00	
		d. '1½a.' at lower right (R. 3/2)	13·00	
20		1a. rose-red	50	2·50
		a. Printed double	£300	
21		2a. greyish green	2·75	6·00
		a. Deep green	2·00	8·00
		ab. Printed double	£850	

Issued in sheets of six (2×3). There are three recognised settings. Nos. 18d/18e and 19c/19d come from Setting B, and Nos. 16b/16c, 17b/17c, 18b/18c and 19a/19b from Setting C.

One sheet of the ¼a. is known in blue.

(Typo Jaipur State Press)

1912–22. Paper-maker's wmk 'DORLING & CO. LONDON' in sheet. P 11.

22	**3**	¼a. pale olive-yellow	2·00	3·25
		a. Imperf horiz (vert pair)	£325	£325
		b. Imperf vert (horiz pair)	—	£225
23		¼a. olive	2·00	3·50
		a. Imperf between (horiz pair)	£300	£350
		b. Imperf vert (horiz pair)	£325	£350
		c. Imperf horiz (vert pair)	£325	
		d. *Tête-bêche* (pair)	£2500	
24		¼a. bistre	2·00	3·50
		a. Imperf between (horiz pair)	£400	
		b. Imperf between (vert pair)	†	£800
		c. Imperf horiz (vert pair)	†	£800
		d. Doubly printed	†	£1500
25		½a. pale ultramarine	4·00	3·25
		a. Imperf vert (horiz pair)	†	£1200
		ab. Imperf between (vert pair)	†	£1400
		b. Blue	2·75	3·00
		ba. Imperf between (horiz pair)	£750	
26		1a. carmine (1918)	13·00	13·00
		a. Imperf between (vert pair)	†	£1800
		b. Imperf horiz (vert pair)	†	£1800
		c. Imperf between (horiz pair)	£1800	£1800
27		1a. rose-red	13·00	18·00
		a. Imperf between (vert pair)	£1800	
28		1a. scarlet (1922)	8·50	7·50
		a. Imperf between (vert pair)	£1900	£1900
29		2a. green (1918)	10·00	12·00
30		4a. chocolate	14·00	21·00
31		4a. pale brown	14·00	21·00
		a. Imperf vert (horiz pair)	£1000	
22/31 *Set of 5*			32·00	42·00

Maharaja Sawai Man Singh II 1922–1970

1926. Surch with T **5**.

32	**3**	3a. on 8a. bright violet (R.)	5·00	6·00
		a. Surch inverted	£325	£200
33		3a. on 1r. yellow (R.)	6·00	10·00
		a. Surch inverted	£850	£300
		c. Yellow-ochre	28·00	32·00

1928. As 1912–1922 issue. Wmk 'DORLING & CO. LONDON' (½a., 1a., 2a.) or 'OVERLAND BANK' (all values) in sheet. No gum. P 12.

34	**3**	½a. ultramarine	4·25	4·00
		a. Perf comp of 12 and 11	21·00	12·00
35		1a. rose-red	42·00	22·00
		a. Imperf between (vert pair)	£1000	
36		1a. scarlet	65·00	15·00
		a. Perf comp of 12 and 11	£110	35·00
37		2a. green	£130	40·00
		a. Perf comp of 12 and 11	£375	85·00
39		1r. orange-vermilion	£1000	£1400

The 'OVERLAND BANK' paper has a coarser texture. The ½a. and 2a. values also exist on this paper perforated 11, but such stamps are difficult to distinguish from examples of Nos. 25 and 29.

6 Chariot of the Sun God, Surya

7 Maharaja Sawai Man Singh II

8 Elephant and State Banner

9 Sowar in Armour

10 Common Peafowl

11 Bullock carriage

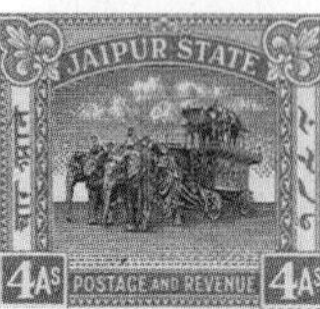
12 Elephant carriage

13 Albert Museum

14 Sireh Deorhi Gate

15 Chandra Mahal

16 Amber Palace

17 Maharajas Jai Singh and Man Singh

(Des T. I. Archer. Litho Indian Security Printing Press, Nasik)

1931 (14 Mar). Investiture of Maharaja. Types **6/17**. No wmk. P 14.

40	**6**	¼a. black and deep lake	7·00	4·75
41	**7**	½a. black and violet	75	20
42	**8**	1a. black and blue	20·00	18·00
43	**9**	2a. black and buff	18·00	16·00
44	**10**	2½a. black and carmine	50·00	70·00
45	**11**	3a. black and myrtle	35·00	65·00
46	**12**	4a. black and olive-green	50·00	95·00
47	**13**	6a. black and deep blue	15·00	80·00
48	**14**	8a. black and chocolate	32·00	£150
49	**15**	1r. black and pale olive	£130	£800
50	**16**	2r. black and yellow-green	£160	£950
51	**17**	5r. black and purple	£180	£1100
40/51 *Set of 12*			£650	£3000

18 of these sets were issued for presentation purposes with a special overprint 'INVESTITURE-MARCH 14,1931' in red (*Price for set of 12 £9000 unused, £10000 used*).

'DOUBLE PRINTS'. Examples of Nasik litho-printed stamps showing doubling of all or part of the design or subsequent overprint are not uncommon. These are not true 'double prints', in that they were not the result of two impressions of the inked printing plate, but were caused by incorrect tension in the rubber 'blanket' which transferred ink from the cylinder to the paper. Such varieties are outside the scope of this catalogue.

18 Maharaja Sawai Man Singh II

One Rupee
(19)

(Des T. I. Archer. Litho Indian Security Printing Press, Nasik)

1932–46. P 14.

(a) Inscr 'POSTAGE & REVENUE'

52	**18**	1a. black and blue	6·00	3·50
53		2a. black and buff	10·00	3·75
54		4a. black and grey-green	5·00	22·00
55		8a. black and chocolate	6·00	38·00
56		1r. black and yellow-bistre	48·00	£375
57		2r. black and yellow-green	£180	£1000
52/57 *Set of 6*			£225	£1300

(b) Inscr 'POSTAGE'

58	**7**	¼a. black and brown-lake	1·00	50
59		¾a. black and brown-red (1943?)	14·00	6·50
60		1a. black and blue (1943?)	18·00	9·00
61		2a. black and buff (1943?)	21·00	8·00
62		2½a. black and carmine	8·50	3·50
63		3a. black and green	5·00	1·00
64		4a. black and grey-green (1943?)	75·00	£275
65		6a. black and deep blue	13·00	60·00
		a. Black and pale blue (1946)	18·00	£130
66		8a. black and chocolate (1946)	55·00	£250
67		1r. black and yellow-bistre (1946)	20·00	£250
58/67 *Set of 10*			£200	£800

1936. Nos. 57 and 51 surch with T **19**.

68	**18**	1r. on 2r. black and yellow-green (R.)	18·00	£250
69	**17**	1r. on 5r. black and purple	20·00	£150

3 PIES

पाव आना
(20)

(21)

1938 (Nov). No. 41 surch 'QUARTER ANNA' in Devanagari, T **20**.

70	**7**	¼a. on ½a. black and violet (R.)	23·00	24·00

1947 (1 Dec). No. 41 surch with T **21**.

71	**7**	3p. on ½a. black and violet (R.)	22·00	38·00
		a. 'PIE' for 'PIES'	70·00	£200
		b. Bars at left vertical	£110	£250
		c. Surch inverted	70·00	65·00
		d. Surch inverted and 'PIE' for 'PIES'	£425	£375
		e. Surch double, one inverted	£110	80·00
		f. As variety e, but inverted surch showing 'PIE' for 'PIES'	£650	£550

There were three settings of T **21**, each applied to quarter sheets of 30 (6×5). No. 71a occurs in two of these settings on R. 5/5 and one of these settings also shows No. 71b on R. 6/1.

22 Palace Gate

23 Maharaja and Amber Palace

24 Map of Jaipur

25 Observatory

26 Wind Palace

27 Coat of Arms

28 Amber Fort Gate

29 Chariot of the Sun

30 Maharaja's portrait between State Flags

(Recess D.L.R.)

1948 (1 Mar–22 Nov). Silver Jubilee of Maharaja's Accession to Throne. Types **22/30**. P 13½×14.

72	**22**	¼a. red-brown and green (22.11)	3·50	7·50
73	**23**	½a. green and violet	50	4·50
74	**24**	¾a. black and lake (22.11)	4·00	11·00
75	**25**	1a. red-brown and ultramarine	1·50	4·75
76	**26**	2a. violet and scarlet	1·50	7·00
77	**27**	3a. green and black (22.11)	5·50	13·00
78	**28**	4a. ultramarine and brown	1·50	7·50
79	**29**	8a. vermilion and brown	1·50	7·50
80	**30**	1r. purple and green (22.11)	6·00	80·00
72/80 *Set of 9*			23·00	£130

OFFICIAL STAMPS

SERVICE
(O **1**)

SERVICE
(O **2**)

1928 (13 Nov)–**31**. T **3** typographed. No gum (except for Nos. O6/O6*a*). P 11, 12, or compound. Wmk 'DORLING & CO. LONDON' (4a.) or 'OVERLAND BANK' (others).

*(a) Optd with T O **1***

O1		¼a. olive	7·00	7·00
		a. Bistre	6·50	5·50
O2		½a. pale ultramarine (Blk.)	3·00	40
		a. Imperf between (horiz pair)	£750	£750
		b. Imperf between (vert pair)	†	£1600
		c. Opt inverted	†	£950
		d. Opt double (R. and Blk.)	†	£1300

O3		½a. pale ultramarine (R.) (13.10.30)	8·50	75
		a. Imperf horiz (vert pair)	£1600	
		b. Stamp doubly printed	†	£1200
O3c		1a. rose-red	6·50	1·50
		d. Imperf between (horiz pair)	†	£1800
O4		1a. scarlet	6·00	1·25
		a. Opt inverted	£2250	£2250
		b. Imperf between (horiz pair)	†	£1800
O5		2a. green	6·00	1·00
		a. Imperf between (vert pair)	†	£2750
		b. Imperf between (horiz pair)	£2750	£2750
O6		4a. pale brown (with gum)	12·00	1·75
		a. Chocolate (with gum)	7·50	1·75
O7		8a. bright violet (R.) (13.10.30)	18·00	80·00
O8		1r. orange-vermilion	55·00	£700
		(b) Optd with T O **2**		
O9		½a. ultramarine (Blk.) (11.2.31)	£250	75
		a. Imperf vert (horiz pair)	†	£2250
O10		½a. ultramarine (R.) (15.10.30)	£275	1·00
		a. Imperf between (vert pair)	†	£2250
O11		8a. bright violet (11.2.31)	£1100	£350
O12		1r. orange-vermilion (11.2.31)	£1300	£650

SERVICE (O **3**)   श्राध श्राना (O **4**)

1931–37. Nos. 41/43 and 46 optd at Nasik with T O **3**, in red.

O13	**7**	½a. black and violet	40	10
O14	**8**	1a. black and blue	£800	8·50
O15	**9**	2a. black and buff (1936)	10·00	10·00
O16	**12**	4a. black and olive-green (1937)	90·00	75·00
O13/O16 *Set of 4*			£850	85·00

1932. No. O5 surch with T O **4**.

O17	**3**	½a. on 2a. green	£325	6·00

1932–37. Nos. 52/56 optd at Nasik with T O **3**, in red.

O18	**18**	1a. black and blue	9·50	15
O19		2a. black and buff	14·00	15
O20		4a. black and grey-green (1937)	£450	18·00
O21		8a. black and chocolate	20·00	1·75
O22		1r. black and yellow-bistre	75·00	55·00
O18/O22 *Set of 5*			£500	65·00

1936–46. Stamps of 1932–1946, inscr 'POSTAGE'.

		(a) Optd at Nasik with T O **3**, *in red*		
O23	**7**	¼a. black and brown-lake (1936)	50	10
O24		¾a. black and brown-red (1944)	2·50	50
O25		1a. black and blue (1941?)	8·50	30
O26		2a. black and buff (date?)	6·50	3·25
O27		2½a. black and carmine (1946)	14·00	£110
O28		4a. black and grey-green (1942)	9·00	7·50
O29		8a. black and chocolate (1943)	5·00	10·00
O30		1r. black and yellow-bistre (date?)	35·00	
O23/O29 *Set of 7*			40·00	£120
		(b) Optd locally as T O **2** *(16 mm long), in black*		
O31	**7**	¼a. black and red-brown (1936)	£180	£120

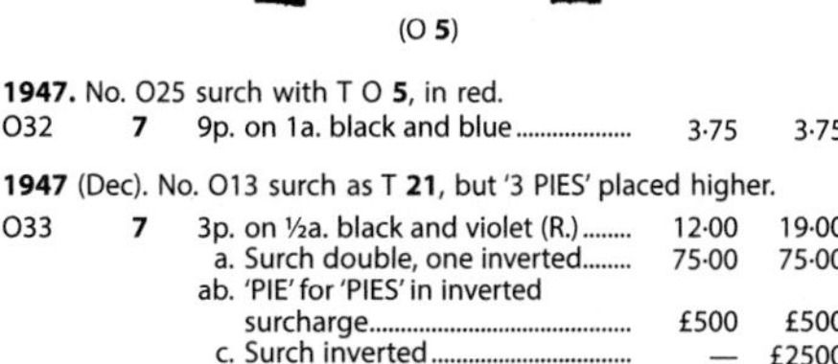

9 PIES

(O **5**)

1947. No. O25 surch with T O **5**, in red.

O32	**7**	9p. on 1a. black and blue	3·75	3·75

1947 (Dec). No. O13 surch as T **21**, but '3 PIES' placed higher.

O33	**7**	3p. on ½a. black and violet (R.)	12·00	19·00
		a. Surch double, one inverted	75·00	75·00
		ab. 'PIE' for 'PIES' in inverted surcharge	£500	£500
		c. Surch inverted	—	£2500

पौन आना

(O **6**) (No. O34)

पौन श्राना — Different Type 'A' (No. O34a)   पौत आना — 'Paut Ana' (No. O34b)

1948 (Dec). No. O13 surch with T O **6**, in red.

O34	**7**	¾a. on ½a. black and violet (R.)	35·00	25·00
		a. Different Type 'A'	45·00	32·00
		b. 'Paut Ana'	£150	£130
		c. Surch double	£2500	£1900

The surcharge, which reads 'Three Quarter Anna', or 'Paun Ana' in Devanagari, was applied in a setting of 30, repeated four times over a sheet of 120. Two different types of 'A' were used for the first letter of 'Ana', while the use of an incorrect character on one stamp in the setting altered 'Paun' to 'Paut'. No. O34 was present 19 times in the setting of 30, O34a ten times and O34b once (R. 5/2).

Jaipur became part of Rajasthan by 7 April 1949.

JAMMU AND KASHMIR

PRICES FOR STAMPS ON COVER TO 1945

Nos. 1/73	*from* × 3
Nos. 74/84	*from* × 2
No. 85	—
Nos. 86/89	*from* × 2
Nos. 90/101	*from* × 10
Nos. 101*b*/123	*from* × 5
Nos. 124/136	*from* × 10
Nos. 138/139	*from* × 100
Nos. 140/161*a*	*from* × 15
Nos. 162/168	*from* × 5
No. O1	*from* × 2
Nos. O2/O4	*from* × 4
No. O5	—
Nos. O6/O14	*from* × 30
Nos. O15/O18	—

ILLUSTRATIONS. Designs of Jammu and Kashmir are illustrated actual size.

Maharaja Ranbir Singh, 1857–1885

1 (**½a.**)

2 (**1a.**)

3 (**4a.**)

Characters denoting the value (on the circular stamps only) are approximately as shown in the central circles of the stamps illustrated above.

These characters were taken from Punjabi merchants' notation and were not familiar to most of the inhabitants of the state. T **1** was certainly the ½ anna value, but there has long been controversy over the correct face values of Types **2** and **3**.

The study of surviving material suggests that, to some extent, this confusion involved contemporary post office officials. Although covers posted at Jammu, where the stamps were in use for 12 years, show T **2** used as the 1a. value and T **3** as the 4a., those originating from Srinagar (Kashmir) during 1866–1868 show both Types **2** and **3** used as 1a. stamps.

In the following listing we have followed contemporary usage at Jammu and this reflects the prevailing opinion amongst modern authorities.

GUM. The stamps of Jammu and Kashmir were issued without gum.

PRICES. Prices for the circular stamps, Nos. 1/49, are for cut-square examples. In practice, stamps were often cut to shape before use, especially in the early period (1866-1867), and such examples are worth from 20% to 50% of the prices quoted, according to condition.

A. Handstamped in watercolours

1866 (23 Mar). Native paper, thick to thin, usually having the appearance of laid paper and tinted grey or brown. For Jammu and Kashmir.

1	**1**	½a. grey-black	£500	£200
2		½a. ultramarine	£8500	£8500
3	**2**	1a. royal blue	—	£1000
3*a*		1a. ultramarine	£1300	£300
4		1a. grey-black	£4000	£2750
5	**3**	4a. royal blue		
5*a*		4a. ultramarine	£2250	£850

No. 4 may be an error of colour. It is only known used in Kashmir.

1867–76. Reissued for use in Jammu only.

6	**3**	4a. grey-black	£4750	
7		4a. indigo	£5000	£3250
8		4a. red (1869)	£180	£250
9		4a. orange-red (1872)	£475	£600
10		4a. orange (1872)		
11		4a. carmine-red (1876)	£2500	

1874–76. Special Printings.

12	**1**	½a. red	£200	£475
12*a*		½a. orange-red	£1200	£1200
13	**2**	1a. red	£475	£500
13*a*		1a. orange-red	£1000	£1100
13*b*		1a. orange	£2500	
14	**1**	½a. deep black	60·00	£250
		a. *Tête-bêche* (pair)	£1800	
15	**2**	1a. deep black	£600	
16	**3**	4a. deep black	£550	
17	**1**	½a. bright blue (1876)	£750	£850
18	**2**	1a. bright blue (1876)	£250	£550
		a. *Tête-bêche* (pair)	£3750	
19	**3**	4a. bright blue (1876)	£475	
20	**1**	½a. emerald-green	£300	£450
21	**2**	1a. emerald-green	£325	£550
22	**3**	4a. emerald-green	£550	£900
23	**1**	½a. yellow	£1000	£1700
24	**2**	1a. yellow	£1800	
25	**3**	4a. yellow	£1000	
25*a*		4a. deep blue-black (1876)	£3500	£1800

These special printings were available for use, but little used.

B. Handstamped in oil colours. Heavy blurred prints

1877 (June)–**78.**

		(a) Native paper		
26	**1**	½a. red	75·00	£120
27	**2**	1a. red	95·00	£350
28	**3**	4a. red	£550	£750
29	**1**	½a. black	70·00	£130
		a. *Tête-bêche* (pair)	£4500	
32		½a. slate-blue	£325	£425
34	**2**	1a. slate-blue	75·00	£450
35	**1**	½a. sage-green	£200	
36	**2**	1a. sage-green	£250	
37	**3**	4a. sage-green	£250	
		(b) European laid paper, medium to thick		
38	**1**	½a. red	—	£2250
39	**3**	4a. red	£650	£850
41	**1**	½a. black	65·00	£130
		a. Printed both sides	£2000	
		b. *Tête-bêche* (pair)	£1500	
44		½a. slate-blue	£140	£475
45	**2**	1a. slate-blue	£150	£550
46	**3**	4a. slate-blue	£1400	£1400
47		4a. sage-green	£3000	£3500
48	**1**	½a. yellow	£250	
		(c) Thick yellowish wove paper		
49	**1**	½a. red (1878)	—	£1800

Forgeries exist of the ½a. and 1a. in types which were at one time supposed to be authentic.

Reprints and imitations (of which some of each were found in the official remainder stock) exist in a great variety of fancy colours, both on native paper, usually thinner and smoother than that of the originals, and on various thin European *wove* papers, on which the originals were never printed.

The imitations, which do not agree in type with the above illustrations, are also to be found on *laid* paper.

All the reprints, etc. are in oil colours or printer's ink. The originals in oil colour are usually blurred, particularly when on native paper. The reprints, etc. are usually clear.

FOR USE IN JAMMU

½a. ½a. 1a. ½a.

4

Types **4** to **11** have a star at the top of the oval band; the characters denoting the value are in the upper part of the inner oval. All are dated 1923, corresponding with AD 1866.

T **4**. Printed in blocks of four, three varieties of ½ anna and one of 1 anna.

1867 (Sept). In watercolour on native paper.

52	½a. grey-black	£2500	£750
53	1a. grey-black	£6000	£3750
54	½a. indigo	£900	£550
55	1a. indigo	£1800	£850
56	½a. deep ultramarine	£700	£350
57	1a. deep ultramarine	£1700	£800
58	½a. deep violet-blue	£475	£180
59	1a. deep violet-blue	£1800	£750

1868 (May)–**72.** In watercolour on native paper.

60	½a. red (*shades*)	20·00	11·00
61	1a. red (*shades*)	45·00	24·00
62	½a. orange-red	£425	£110
63	1a. orange-red	£1700	£700
64	½a. orange (1872)	£250	£300
65	1a. orange (1872)	£5500	£3500

1874–76. Special printings; in watercolour on native paper.

66	½a. bright blue (1876)	£3250	£700
67	1a. bright blue (1876)	£950	£950
68	½a. emerald-green	£4000	£2000
69	1a. emerald-green	£6500	£3250
69*a*	½a. jet-black	£325	£400
69*b*	1a. jet-black	£5000	£3750

1877 (June)–**78.** In oil colour.

	(a) Native paper		
70	½a. red	25·00	20·00
71	1a. red	75·00	50·00
72	½a. brown-red (1878)	—	85·00
73	1a. brown-red (1878)	—	£275
74	½a. black	†	£2250
75	1a. black	†	£4750
76	½a. deep blue-black	†	£3750
77	1a. deep blue-black	†	£7500
	(b) Laid paper (medium or thick)		
78	½a. red	—	£2250
	(c) Thick wove paper		
79	½a. red	†	£1000
80	1a. red		
	(d) Thin laid, bâtonné paper		
84	½a. red	†	£3500
85	1a. red	£7500	

The circular and rectangular stamps listed under the heading 'Special Printings' did not supersede those in *red*, which was the normal colour for Jammu down to 1878. It is not known for what reason other colours were used during that period, but these stamps were printed in 1874 or 1875 and were certainly put into use. The rectangular stamps were again printed in *black* (jet-black, as against the greyish black of the 1867 printings) at that time, and impressions of the two periods can also be distinguished by the obliterations, which until 1868 were in *magenta* and after that in *black*.

There are reprints of these, in *oil* colour, *brown-red* and *bright blue*, on native paper; they are very clearly printed, which is not the case with the originals in *oil* colour.

JAMMU & KASHMIR SOME ITEMS FROM OUR EVER CHANGING STOCK

SG T8 - **1 of only 2 known**

SG T9 - **1 of only 2 known**

SG T35 - **1 of only 3 known**

SG T35 - **1 of only 2 known**

Plate Proof of SG T65 - **2 of 6**

We have an in-depth stock of stamps, covers, postal stationery & collections by State from starter to gold medal winning exhibits. We look forward to working with you, whether it is to fill the gaps in your King George VI or your British Commonwealth collection, to form a world class exhibit, or simply because you find them exotic & fascinating. We are happy to **quote prices & availability against your want-list**.

I have collected Indian States for the past 33 years, given presentations, written articles and have exhibited them at the National & International level. I am also the immediately past editor of *"India Post"* - journal for the India Study Circle for philately in the UK. There is no need to worry about proper identification, reprints, forgeries etc. - our stock is backed by 33 years of knowledge, research & expertise as well as **full money back guarantee** if an item, sold by us, turns out to be improperly described. Furthermore, all Indian Feudatory States items priced over £500 can, upon request, be accompanied by a complimentary ISES "**Certificate of Authenticity**".

Naturally we are the biggest buyers of Indian States philatelic material - from individual rarities to exhibit collections to accumulations - no holding is too small or too large for us. You may be pleasantly surprised at the **record setting prices we are paying** for Indian States & British India Postal Stationery. I will gladly travel to you to discuss larger holdings.

Plate Proof of SG T56 - **4 of 6 known**

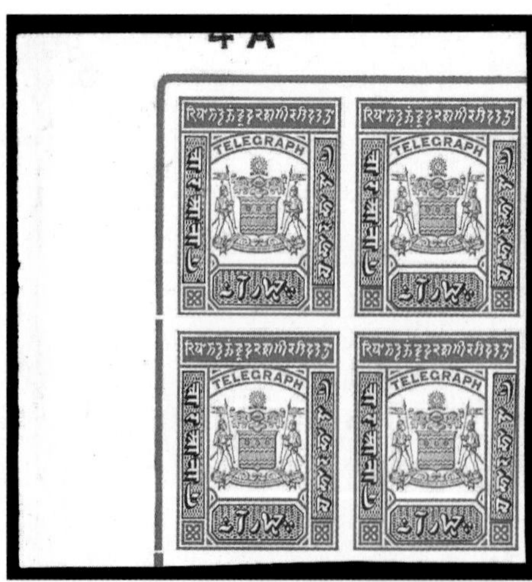

Plate Proof of SG T54 - **4 of 6 known**

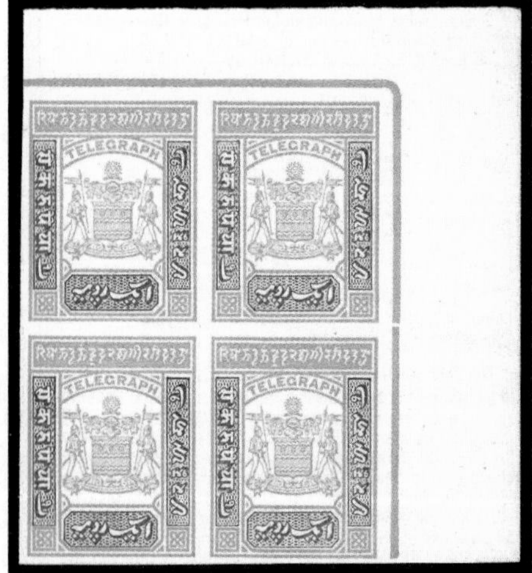

Plate Proof of SG T57 - **4 of 6 known**

PO Box 8689 Cranston, RI 02920 USA
Phone: (UK) 020 3002 3626
Phone: (USA) 1 401 688 9473
E-mail: **info@stampsinc.com**

4a

1877 (Sept). Provisional. Seal obliterator of Jammu handstamped in red watercolour on pieces of native paper, and used as a ½ anna stamp.

86	**4a**	(½a.) rose-red	—	£3000

FOR USE IN KASHMIR

5

1866 (Sept(?)). Printed from a single die. Native laid paper.

87	**5**	½a. black	£6500	£750

Forgeries of this stamp are commonly found, copied from an illustration in *Le Timbre-Poste*.

6 (½a.)

7 (1a.)

1867 (Apr). Native laid paper.

88	**6**	½a. black	£3500	£375
89	**7**	1a. black	£4750	£850

Printed in sheets of 25 (5×5), the four top rows being ½a. and the bottom row 1a.

8 (¼a.)

9 (2a.)

10 (4a.)

11 (8a.)

1867–77. Native laid paper.

90	**8**	¼a. black	9·50	10·00
		a. *Tête-bêche* (vert pair)	£10000	
91	**6**	½a. ultramarine (6.67)	12·00	5·50
		a. Bisected (¼a.) (*on cover*) (1877)	†	£14000
92		½a. violet-blue (1870)	30·00	13·00
93	**7**	1a. ultramarine (6.67)	£7500	£3500
94		1a. orange (7.67)	35·00	24·00
95		1a. brown-orange (1868)	35·00	24·00
96		1a. orange-vermilion (1876)	42·00	30·00
97	**9**	2a. yellow	45·00	50·00
98		2a. buff	70·00	60·00
99	**10**	4a. emerald-green	£110	90·00
		a. *Tête-bêche* (pair)	£2500	
		b. Stamp sideways (in pair)	£8000	
100		4a. sage-green	£650	£325
100*a*		4a. myrtle-green	£1800	£1500
101	**11**	8a. red (1868)	£120	95·00
		a. *Tête-bêche* (pair)	£10000	£10000

Of the above, the ½a. and 1a. were printed from the same plate of 25 as Nos. 88/89, the ¼a. and 2a. from a new plate of ten (5×2), the top row being ¼a. and the lower 2a., and the 4a. and 8a. from single dies. Varieties at one time catalogued upon European papers were apparently never put into circulation, though some of them were printed while these stamps were still in use.

Nos. 86 to 101 are in watercolour.

No. 91a was used at Srinagar, in conjunction with an India ½a., and was cancelled 'KASHMIR 5/L-6'.

FOR USE IN JAMMU AND KASHMIR

In the following issues there are 15 varieties on the sheets of the ⅛a., ¼a. and ½a.; 20 varieties of the 1a. and 2a. and eight varieties of the 4a. and 8a. The value is in the lower part of the central oval.

12 (¼a.)

13 (½a.)

14 (1a.)

15 (2a.)

16 (4a.)

17 (8a.)

1878 (May)–**79**. Provisional printings.

I. Ordinary white laid paper, of varying thickness

(a) Rough perf 10 to 12 (i) or 13 to 16 (ii)

101*b*	**12**	¼a. red (i)		
102	**13**	½a. red (i)	21·00	25·00
103	**14**	1a. red (i)	£2000	
104	**13**	½a. slate-violet (i)	£130	£130
104*a*	**14**	1a. violet (ii)		
104*b*	**15**	2a. violet (i)	£3000	

(b) Imperf

105	**13**	½a. slate-violet (*shades*)	29·00	25·00
106	**14**	1a. slate-purple	45·00	48·00
107		1a. mauve	90·00	80·00
108	**15**	2a. violet	55·00	60·00
109		2a. bright mauve	70·00	65·00
110		2a. slate-blue	£130	£130
111		2a. dull blue	£200	£200
112	**12**	¼a. red	42·00	42·00
113	**13**	½a. red	19·00	21·00
114	**14**	1a. red	19·00	22·00
115	**15**	2a. red	£150	£150
116	**16**	4a. red	£425	£350

II. Medium wove paper

(a) Rough perf 10 to 12

117	**13**	½a. red	—	£750

(b) Imperf

117*b*	**12**	¼a. red		
118	**13**	½a. red	27·00	25·00
119	**14**	1a. red	32·00	25·00
120	**15**	2a. red	£130	

III. Thick wove paper. Imperf

121	**13**	½a. red	65·00	90·00
122	**14**	1a. red	90·00	55·00
123	**15**	2a. red	45·00	55·00

Of the above stamps those in red were intended for use in Jammu and those in shades of violet and blue for use in Kashmir.

1879. Definitive issue. Thin wove paper, fine to coarse.

(a) Rough perf 10 to 12

124	**13**	½a. red	£900	£750

(b) Imperf

125	**12**	¼a. red	8·00	9·00
126	**13**	½a. red	2·75	2·75
		a. Bisected (¼a.) (*on cover* or *postcard*)	†	£9500
127	**14**	1a. red	5·50	7·50
		a. Bisected (½a.) (*on cover*)	†	£8500
128	**15**	2a. red	7·50	9·50
129	**16**	4a. red	28·00	22·00
130	**17**	8a. red	32·00	26·00

The plates were transferred from Jammu to Srinagar in early 1881 when further printings in red and all orange stamps were produced.

1880 (Mar). Provisional printing in watercolour on thin bâtonné paper. Imperf.

130*a*	**12**	¼a. ultramarine	£1600	£1000

1881–83. As Nos. 124 to 130. Colour changed.

(a) Rough perf 10 to 12

130*b*	**13**	½a. orange		

(b) Imperf

131	**12**	¼a. orange	30·00	35·00
132	**13**	½a. orange	32·00	28·00
		a. Bisected (¼a.) (*on cover*)		
133	**14**	1a. orange	50·00	32·00
		a. Bisected (½a.) (*on cover*)	†	£14000
134	**15**	2a. orange	42·00	32·00
135	**16**	4a. orange	85·00	90·00
136	**17**	8a. orange	£130	£130

Nos. 126a and 133a were used at Leh between April and July 1883.

Nos. 125/130 and 132/136 were re-issued between 1890 and 1894 and used concurrently with the stamps which follow. Such re-issues can be identified by the 'three circle' cancellations, introduced in December 1890.

18 (⅛a.)

1883–94. New colours. Thin wove papers, toned, coarse to fine, or fine white (1889). Imperf.

138	**18**	⅛a. yellow-brown	3·00	3·75
139		⅛a. yellow	3·00	3·75
140	**12**	¼a. sepia	2·75	1·25
141		¼a. brown	2·75	1·25
		a. Double impression	£1500	
142		¼a. pale brown	2·75	1·25
		a. Error. Green	£140	
143	**13**	½a. dull blue	20·00	
144		½a. bright blue	£100	
145		½a. vermilion	2·75	1·75
146		½a. rose	3·00	1·75
147		½a. orange-red	1·50	1·75
148	**14**	1a. greenish grey	2·50	2·75
149		1a. bright green	2·50	3·00
		a. Double impression		
150		1a. dull green	2·75	3·00
151		1a. blue-green	3·50	
152	**15**	2a. red/*yellow*	7·00	3·50
153		2a. red/*yellow-green*	8·50	11·00
154		2a. red/*deep green*	38·00	45·00
155	**16**	4a. deep green	6·50	7·50
156		4a. green	6·50	7·00
157		4a. pale green	6·50	4·50
158		4a. sage-green	8·00	
159	**17**	8a. pale blue	18·00	18·00
159*a*		8a. deep blue	25·00	29·00
160		8a. bright blue	18·00	21·00
161		8a. indigo-blue	24·00	27·00
161*a*		8a. slate-lilac	20·00	35·00

Well-executed forgeries of the ¼a. to 8a. have come from India, mostly postmarked; they may be detected by the type, which does not agree with any variety on the genuine sheets, and also, in the low values, by the margins being filled in with colour, all but a thin white frame round the stamp. The forgeries of the 8a. are in sheets of eight like the originals.

Other forgeries of nearly all values also exist, showing all varieties of type. All values are on thin, coarse wove paper.

In February 1890, a forgery, in watercolour, of the ½a. orange on thin wove or on thin laid paper appeared, and many have been found genuinely used during 1890 and 1891 (*Price* £7).

Nos. 143 and 144 were never issued.

Examples of the ¼a. brown, ½a. orange-red and 1a. green on wove paper exist with clean-cut perf 12.

There is a reference in the Jammu and Kashmir State Administration Report covering 1890–1891 to the re-introduction of perforating and the machine-gumming of paper at the Jammu printing works.

The few known examples, the ¼a. being only recorded used, the others unused or used, would appear to date from this period, but there is, as yet, no direct confirmation as to their status.

Maharaja Partap Singh, 1885–1925

1887–94. Thin creamy laid paper. Imperf.

162	**18**	⅛a. yellow	£120	£130
163	**12**	¼a. brown	13·00	9·50
164	**13**	½a. brown-red (3.87)	—	£140
165		½a. orange-red	19·00	13·00
166	**14**	1a. grey-green	£110	£110
168	**17**	8a. blue (*Printed in watercolour*)	£180	£180
		a. On wove paper	£120	£120

19

T **19** represents a ¼a. stamp, which exists in sheets of 12 varieties, in *red* and *black* on thin wove and laid papers, also in *red* on native paper, but which does not appear ever to have been issued for use. It was first seen in 1886.

The ¼a. *brown* and the 4a. *green* both exist on ordinary white laid paper and the ½a. *red* on native paper. None of these are known to have been in use.

OFFICIAL STAMPS

1878.

I. White laid paper

(a) Rough perf 10 to 12

O1	**13**	½a. black	—	£4000

(b) Imperf

O2	**13**	½a. black	£170	£160
O3	**14**	1a. black	£120	£120
O4	**15**	2a. black	90·00	95·00

II. Medium wove paper. Imperf

O5	**14**	1a. black	£700	

1880–94. Thin wove papers, toned, coarse to fine, or fine white (1889). Imperf.

O6	**12**	¼a. black	3·25	3·75
		a. Double print	£250	
O7	**13**	½a. black	50	1·75
		a. Printed both sides	£650	
O8	**14**	1a. black	1·50	2·25
O9	**15**	2a. black	75	85
O10	**16**	4a. black	3·00	3·50
O11	**17**	8a. black	4·75	3·00

1887–94. Thin creamy laid paper. Imperf.

O12	**12**	¼a. black	21·00	17·00

O13	**13**	½a. black	14·00	11·00
O14	**14**	1a. black	7·50	7·50
O15	**15**	2a. black	28·00	
O16	**16**	4a. black	90·00	£100
O17	**17**	8a. black	60·00	85·00

1889. Stout white wove paper. Imperf.

O18	**12**	¼a. black	£425	£275

The stamps of Jammu and Kashmir have been obsolete since 1 November 1894.

TELEGRAPH STAMPS

Telegraph lines from Srinagar to Jammu and to Gilgit were constructed according to a treaty of 1878 between the State Government and the Government of India. The lines were later extended along the State railway lines according to a further treaty of 1890.

PRICES. Unused prices quoted are always for whole stamps. The status of prices for used stamps is explained by the following note.

USED STAMPS. From 1884 until 1910 (Nos T1/T40 and OT1/OT15) stamps were intended to be affixed vertically to Telegraph forms, and were then bisected, with the upper halves on the receipt portion given to the sender, while the lower halves remained on the message portion retained by the authorities. Since Nos T1/T14 and OT1/OT15 are in horizontal format, used left and right halves survive in roughly equal quantities, and used whole stamps can be found. But Nos T15/T40, in 'double' vertical format, like the Telegraph stamps of India, were designed to be affixed to forms in such a way that only the upper halves remained on the receipt portion, and used lower halves are very rare.

After 1910, bisection in use ceased, and Nos T51/T82 were always used as whole stamps, although few examples survive.

T 1

T 2

T 3

T 4

T 5

T 6

T 7

1884. Design of State Arms, inscribed 'Jammu Kashmir Tibet Telegraphs' in Dogra script. Handstamped from single brass dies, with differing face values in Persian script at left and right, as Types T **1/7**. Thin white or toned wove paper. No gum. Imperf.

			Unused	*Used half*
T1	T **1**	1a. green	2·00	35·00
		a. yellow-green	2·50	35·00
		b. blue-green	2·50	—
		c. olive-green	3·00	35·00
T2	T **2**	2a. sepia	2·50	30·00
		a. dark brown	3·00	30·00
		b. yellow-brown	5·00	—
T3	T **3**	4a. ultramarine	3·00	30·00
T4	T **4**	8a. orange	6·00	50·00
		a. yellow	4·00	50·00
T5	T **5**	1r. scarlet	5·00	35·00
		a. brown-red	6·00	35·00
		b. vermilion	8·00	—
T6	T **6**	2r. blackish green	10·00	—
T7	T **7**	5r. brown	15·00	—
T8	–	10r. vermilion	£6000	—
T9	–	25r. violet	£6000	—

A contemporary forgery of the 1r. value was produced, apparently to defraud the authorities. It differs especially in the shield shape, which is much more narrow, and the supporters.

Cancellations on used stamps of the 1884 and 1887 issues take several forms, including manuscript, oval intaglio seals (in black or violet), and straight-line or circular datestamps. The straight-line datestamps are in Dogra script, but the circular datestamps include 'triple-ring' types with office name in English. Used examples are best collected on piece.

1887 (?). Handstamped from single brass dies. As 1884 issue, but thin toned laid paper. No gum. Imperf.

T10	T **1**	1a. yellow-green	6·00	—
T11	T **2**	2a. brown	5·00	50·00
T12	T **3**	4a. ultramarine	12·00	—
T13	T **4**	8a. brownish yellow	12·00	—
T14	T **5**	1r. scarlet	10·00	75·00

T 8 T 11

T 9

T 10

(Typo De la Rue)

1897. Double stamps as Type T **8**. Duty tablets in second colour, with face value in Persian script at centre on upper half and in English on lower half. Unwatermarked paper. Perf 14.

T15	T **8**	1a. bright blue and carmine	60·00	27·00
T16		2a. reddish violet and olive-brown	£120	38·00
T17		4a. rose-carmine and olive-brown	£130	55·00
T18		8a. yellow and bright blue	£120	55·00
T19		1r. brown-orange and reddish violet	£170	80·00
T20		2r. brown and light blue	£170	£120
T21		5r. blue-green and carmine	£170	—

Prices quoted for used examples of Nos T15/T21 and the subsequent 1899–1909 and 1906–1909 issues (Nos T22/T40) are for upper halves, usually with shield-shaped datestamps, although manuscript cancels and circular datestamps are also known. Dates follow the Samvat era, 57 years ahead of dates AD, so that '1963' is equivalent to 1906 AD Nos T22/T29 were also later used whole after a change in regulations in 1910, when bisection in use ceased, prior to their replacement by the 1911–1921 Type T **12** 'single' design.

(Typo De la Rue)

1899–1909. Double stamps. As 1897 issue, but wmk Multiple Rosettes (horiz. or vert.). Perf 14.

T22	T **8**	½a. blackish olive and blue-green (1909)	60·00	70·00
T23		1a. bright blue and carmine	60·00	27·00
T24		2a. reddish violet and olive-brown	£120	27·00
T25		4a. rose-carmine and olive-brown	£120	25·00
T26		6a. violet and sage-green (1909)	£325	—
T27		8a. yellow and bright blue	£120	55·00
T28		1r. brown-orange and reddish violet	£170	55·00
T29		2r. brown and light blue	£250	£110

The 5r. value was also printed on watermarked paper, but was apparently only issued with local surcharges.

1906–09. Type T **8** surcharged locally with new values in English as Types T **9/11**, in complete sheets.

a) On 1897 unwatermarked issue.

T31		1a. on 2r. brown and light blue		
T32		2a. on 2r. brown and light blue		
T33		4a. on 2r. brown and light blue		
T34		4a. on 5r. blue-green and carmine	—	£750

b) On 1899 watermarked issue, and similar 5r. value.

T35		½a. on 1a. bright blue and carmine	£2500	£500
T36		1a. on 2r. brown and light blue	£2500	£250
T37		2a. on 2r. brown and light blue	£2500	£250
T38		4a. on 1r. brown-orange and reddish violet	—	£750
T39		4a. on 2r. brown and light blue	—	£750
T40		8a. on 5r. blue-green and carmine	£170	£200

Different types of surcharges are known on most values, expressed as numeral + word (in one line) or as two words (usually in two lines, but in one line on No. T35) with whole unused examples often showing different styles on the upper and lower halves, and it seems likely that composite settings were used. At least eight varieties of the 8a. on 5r. have been recorded. A more detailed listing will be provided when fuller information is available.

T 12

T 13

T 14

(Typo De la Rue)

1911–21. Single stamps with trilingual face value, as Type T **12**. Duty tablets in second colour. Wmk Multiple Rosettes (horiz. or vert.). Perf 14.

			Unused	*Used*
T51	T **12**	½a. blackish olive and blue-green (1913)	£130	£130
T52		1a. bright blue and carmine	£180	£130
T53		2a. reddish violet and olive-brown (1913)	£180	£150
T54		4a. rose-carmine and olive-brown (1912)	£250	£150
T55		6a. violet and sage-green (1913)	£300	£190
T56		8a. yellow and bright blue (1912)	£300	£190
T57		1r. brown-orange and reddish violet (1916)	—	£325
T58		2r. brown and light blue (1921)		
T59		5r. blue-green and carmine (1921)		

Used examples of Nos T51/T59 and subsequent issues were cancelled by circular datestamps.

[?]. Local surcharges in English on 1911–1921 issue.

T60	–	1a. on 2a. reddish violet and olive-brown	£1500	
T61	T **13**	12a. on 6a violet and sage-green	†	£800

The only example seen of No. T60 shows the surcharge as 'ONE / ANNA.' (in two lines).

1930. Surcharged by De la Rue.

T65	T **14**	12a. on 1r. brown-orange and reddish violet	£550	

T 15

T 16

(Recess De la Rue)

1933–34. New design Type T **15** with portrait of Maharajah Sir Hari Singh, and differing face values in side tablets, in Devanagri at left and Persian script at right. Wmk mult rosettes (horiz.). Perf 14.

T66	T **15**	1a. deep blue	£100
T67		2a. chocolate (1934)	£160
T68		4a. bluish green	£160
T69		8a. reddish orange	£225
T70		12a. yellow-orange	£225
T71		1r. violet	£400
T72		2r. rose-carmine	£850
T73		5r. black	£1400

A similar 1a. stamp without 'TELEGRAPH' at foot was issued for fiscal purposes.

[?]. Local surcharges in English on 1933–1934 issue.

T74		8a. on 12a. yellow-orange	

The only example seen shows shows 'EIGHT ANNAS' at foot, with bars through the original face values at left and right.

1941 [?]. New design Type T**16** with bilingual face values as 1933–1934 issue. Litho, Security Press Nasik. No wmk. Perf 14.

T75	T **16**	1a. deep blue	75·00	
T76		2a. chocolate	£110	
T77		4a. deep green	£160	
T78		8a. red orange	£160	
T79		12a. yellow-orange	£225	
T80		1r. violet	£275	
T81		2r. rose-carmine	£1200	
T82		5r. black		

A similar 1a. stamp without 'TELEGRAPH' at foot was issued for fiscal purposes.

OFFICIAL TELEGRAPH STAMPS

1884. Handstamped from single brass dies. Thin white or toned wove paper. No gum. Imperf.

			Unused	Used half
OT1	T **1**	1a. black	6·00	50·00
OT2	T **2**	2a. black	6·00	50·00
OT3	T **3**	4a. black	6·00	50·00
OT4	T **4**	8a. black	20·00	
OT5	T **5**	1r. black	15·00	
OT6	T **6**	2r. black	30·00	
OT7	T **7**	5r. black	75·00	
OT8	–	10r. black	—	
OT9	–	25r. black	—	

1887 (?). Handstamped from single brass dies. As 1884 issue, but thin toned laid paper.

OT10	T **1**	1a. black	12·00	
OT11	T **2**	2a. black	20·00	
OT12	T **3**	4a. black	30·00	
OT14	T **5**	1r. black	75·00	
OT15	T **7**	5r. black		

JASDAN

PRICES FOR STAMPS ON COVER TO 1945	
Nos. 1/2	*from* × 2
No. 3	*from* × 3
Nos. 4/6	*from* × 4

Darbar Ala Khachar, 1919–1971

1 Sun

(Typo L. V. Indap & Co, Bombay)

1942 (15 Mar)–**47**. Stamps from booklet panes. Various perfs.

1	**1**	1a. deep myrtle-green (P 10½)	£3000	£1500
2		1a. light green (P 12)	£1800	£1500
3		1a. green (*shades*) (P 10½)	£275	£325
4		1a. pale yellow-green (P 8½–9) (1946)	25·00	£325
5		1a. dull yellow-green (P 10) (1945)..	50·00	£350
6		1a. bluish green (P 8½–9) (1947)	45·00	£325

Nos. 1/4 were issued in panes of four with the stamps imperforate on one or two sides; Nos. 5/6 were in panes of eight perforated all round.

No.3 exists in a variety of shades, from light to deep green, and comes from several printings. The evidence of dated covers suggests that some examples may pre-date the stamps currently listed as Nos. 1/2.

A 1a. rose with the Arms of Jasdan in the centre is a fiscal stamp.

Jasdan was merged with the United State of Kathiawar (later Saurashtra) by 15 April 1948.

JHALAWAR

PRICES FOR STAMPS ON COVER TO 1945	
Nos. 1/2	*from* × 30

Maharaj Rana Zalim Singh, 1875–1896

1 (**1 paisa**)

2 (**¼ anna**)

(Figure of an Apsara, 'RHEMBA', a dancing nymph of the Hindu Paradise)

1886–90. Typo in horizontal strips of 12. Laid paper. Imperf. No gum.

1	**1**	1p. yellow-green	6·50	24·00
		a. Blue-green	£275	£100
2	**2**	¼a. green (*shades*) (1890)	2·25	3·25

The stamps formerly listed as on wove paper are from sheets on laid paper, with the laid paper lines almost invisible. The laid lines are normally vertical, with stamps printed on horizontally laid paper scarce.

The Maharaj Rana was deposed in 1896 and much of the state's territory transferred to Kotah on 1 January 1899.

Raj (Maharaj from 1918) Rana Rhawani Singh, 1899–1929

The stamps of Jhalawar have been obsolete since 1 November 1900.

JIND

PRICES FOR STAMPS ON COVER TO 1945
The stamps of Jind are very rare used on cover.

ILLUSTRATIONS. Designs of Jind are illustrated actual size.

Raja Raghubir Singh, 1864–1887

J **1** (**½a.**)

J **2** (**1a.**)

J **3** (**2a.**)

J **4** (**4a.**)

J **5** (**8a.**)

(Litho Jind State Rajah's Press, Sungroor)

1874. Thin yellowish paper. Imperf.

J1	J **1**	½a. blue	17·00	9·00
		a. No frame to value. (Retouched all over) (R. 4/7)	£850	£500
J2	J **2**	1a. rosy mauve	11·00	9·00
J3	J **3**	2a. yellow	2·75	8·50
J4		2a. brown-buff	£550	£275
J5	J **4**	4a. green	40·00	6·00
J6	J **5**	8a. dull purple	£1300	£400
J6*a*		8a. bluish violet	£500	£225
J7		8a. slate-blue	£450	£200

Nos. J1/J7 were produced from two sets of stones. Those from the first set had rather blurred impressions, but those from the second are clearer with a conspicuous white frame around the value. Nos. J4 and J6*a*/J13 were only printed from the second set.

1876. Bluish laid card-paper. No gum. Imperf.

J8	J **1**	½a. blue	1·75	7·50
J9	J **2**	1a. purple	4·75	20·00
J10	J **3**	2a. brown	7·50	25·00
J11	J **4**	4a. green	4·25	25·00
J11*a*	J **5**	8a. bluish violet	14·00	30·00
J12		8a. slate-blue	11·00	13·00
J13		8a. steel-blue	13·00	20·00

Stocks of the ½a. (No. J8) and 2a. (No. J4) were perforated 12 in 1885 for use as fiscal stamps.

J **6** (**¼a.**)

J **7** (**½a.**)

J **8** (**1a.**)

J **9** (**2a.**)

J **10** (**4a.**)

J **11** (**8a.**)

(Litho Jind State Rajah's Press, Sungroor)

1882–85. Types J **6** to J **11**. No gum.

A. Imperf (1882–1884)

(a) Thin yellowish wove paper

J15	¼a. buff (*shades*)	40	1·50
J16	¼a. red-brown	50	1·50
	a. Doubly printed	£100	
J17	½a. lemon	4·00	3·50
J18	½a. buff	3·75	3·25
J19	½a. brown-buff	2·25	75
J20	1a. brown (*shades*)	2·25	3·25
J21	2a. blue	3·75	12·00
J22	2a. deep blue	4·75	3·50
J23	4a. sage-green	4·25	3·00
J24	4a. blue-green	4·75	6·00
J25	8a. red	9·50	5·00
	(b) Various thick laid papers		
J26	¼a. brown-buff	2·25	
J27	½a. lemon	1·25	
J28	½a. brown-buff		
J29	1a. brown	1·25	2·50
J30	2a. blue	24·00	21·00
J31	8a. red	2·50	13·00
	(c) Thick white wove paper		
J32	¼a. brown-buff	38·00	
J33	½a. brown-buff	60·00	
J34	1a. brown	9·00	
J35	8a. red	8·50	13·00
	B. Perf 12 (1885)		
	(a) Thin yellowish wove paper		
J36	¼a. buff (*shades*)	1·50	4·00
	a. Doubly printed	£180	
J37	¼a. red-brown	5·50	
J38	½a. lemon	£250	£250
J39	½a. buff	1·25	5·50
J40	½a. brown-buff	4·50	9·50
J41	1a. brown (*shades*)	2·75	10·00
J42	2a. blue	7·50	18·00
J43	2a. deep blue	5·50	8·00
J44	4a. sage-green	9·00	18·00
J45	4a. blue-green	5·50	
	a. Imperf vert (horiz pair)	£900	
J46	8a. red	21·00	
	(b) Various thick laid papers		
J47	¼a. brown-buff	11·00	
J48	½a. lemon	£200	35·00
J49	1a. brown	3·50	
J50	2a. blue	38·00	38·00
J51	8a. red	3·00	15·00
	(c) Thick white wove paper		
J52	1a. brown		
J53	8a. red	16·00	

The perforated stamps ceased to be used for postal purposes in July 1885, but were used as fiscals to at least the mid-1920s. Other varieties exist, but they must either be fiscals or reprints, and it is not quite certain that all those listed above were issued as early as 1885.

Jind became a Convention State and from 1 July 1885 used overprinted Indian stamps.

KISHANGARH

PRICES FOR STAMPS ON COVER TO 1945	
Nos. 1/3	—
Nos. 4/91	*from* × 8
Nos. O1/O32	*from* × 30

GUM. The stamps of Kishangarh were issued without gum, *except for* Nos. 42/50 and O17/O24.

Maharaja Sardul Singh, 1879–1900

1

1899–1900. Medium wove paper. Typo from a plate of eight (4×2).

1	**1**	1a. green (*imperf*)	25·00	85·00
2		1a. green (*pin-perf*) (1900)	£100	

1900. Thin white wove paper. Printed from a single die. Imperf.

3	**1**	1a. blue	£900

ILLUSTRATIONS. Types **2** to **10a** are shown actual size.

2 (**¼a.**)

3 (**½a.**)

4 (**1a.**)

5 (**2a.**) Maharaja Sardul Singh

6 (**4a.**)

7 (**1r.**)

8 (2r.)

9 (5r.)

1899 (Sept)–**1900**. Thin white wove paper.

(a) Imperf

4	**2**	¼a. yellow-green (1900)	£1000	£1300
5		¼a. carmine	14·00	
		a. Rose-pink	2·50	4·50
6		¼a. magenta	5·00	6·00
		a. Doubly printed	£275	
7	**3**	½a. lilac (1900)	£350	£600
8		½a. red (1899)	£5500	£2500
9		½a. green (1899)	40·00	45·00
10		½a. pale yellow-olive	65·00	65·00
11		½a. slate-blue (1900)	65·00	65·00
		b. Deep blue	10·00	11·00
		c. Light blue	2·50	1·75
		ca. Pair, one stamp sideways	£2500	
12	**4**	1a. slate	12·00	5·50
		a. Laid paper	80·00	
12*b*		1a. pink	£150	£450
13		1a. mauve	10·00	8·00
		a. Laid paper	60·00	
14		1a. brown-lilac	1·25	1·50
		a. Laid paper	40·00	
15	**5**	2a. dull orange	9·00	5·00
		a. Laid paper	£900	£750
16	**6**	4a. chocolate	8·00	
		a. Lake-brown	8·00	16·00
		b. Chestnut	7·50	16·00
		c. Laid paper (*shades*)	£170	£160
17	**7**	1r. dull green	32·00	48·00
18		1r. brown-lilac	21·00	28·00
19	**8**	2r. brown-red	£110	£180
		a. Laid paper	90·00	
20	**9**	5r. mauve	£110	£160
		a. Laid paper	£110	

(b) Pin-perf 12½ or 14 (from Nov 1899)

21	**2**	¼a. yellow-green	£550	£850
		a. Imperf between (pair)	£2250	
22		¼a. carmine	10·00	10·00
		a. Rose-pink	25	50
		ab. *Tête-bêche* (horiz pair)	£2500	
		ac. Doubly printed	£190	£200
		ad. Trebly printed	£500	
		ae. Imperf between (horiz pair)	£225	
		b. Rose		
23		¼a. magenta	5·00	7·00
		a. Bright purple		
		ab. Doubly printed		
24	**3**	½a. green	22·00	27·00
		a. Imperf between (pair)	£475	
25		½a. pale yellow-olive	13·00	16·00
		a. Imperf vert (horiz pair)	£400	
		b. Imperf between (horiz pair)	†	£900
26		½a. deep blue	6·00	3·50
		a. Light blue	2·00	50
		ab. Doubly printed	£275	£275
		ac. Imperf between (pair)	£475	
27	**4**	1a. slate	8·00	6·00
		a. Laid paper	80·00	35·00
27*b*		1a. pink	£180	£475
28		1a. mauve	2·25	3·00
		a. Laid paper	55·00	18·00
29		1a. brown-lilac	1·50	1·25
		a. Laid paper	45·00	14·00
		b. Pair, one stamp sideways	£3250	
30	**5**	2a. dull orange	5·00	5·00
		a. Laid paper	£850	£850
31	**6**	4a. chocolate	3·50	9·00
		a. Lake-brown	3·50	9·00
		b. Chestnut	3·50	9·00
		c. Laid paper (*shades*)	£100	85·00
32	**7**	1r. dull green	11·00	15·00
		a. Laid paper	£120	
		b. Imperf between (vert pair)	£1600	
33		1r. pale olive-yellow	£1500	
34	**8**	2r. brown-red	35·00	55·00
		a. Laid paper	50·00	
35	**9**	5r. mauve	35·00	70·00
		a. Laid paper	95·00	

All the above, both imperf and pin-perf, were printed singly, sometimes on paper with spaces marked in pencil. They exist in vertical *tête-bêche* pairs imperf between from the centre of the sheet. *Prices from 3×normal, unused.* No. 22ab is an error.

FISCAL STAMPS. Many of the following issues were produced in different colours for fiscal purposes. Such usage is indicated by the initials 'M.C.', punched hole or violet Stamp Office handstamp.

Maharaja Madan Singh, 1900–1926

10 (¼a.)

10a (1r.)

1901. Toned wove paper. Pin-perf.

36	**10**	¼a. dull pink	8·00	6·00
37	**4**	1a. violet	65·00	32·00
38	**10a**	1r. dull green	14·00	17·00
36/38 *Set of 3*			80·00	50·00

Nos. 36/38 were printed in sheets of 24. Sheets of the 1r. were always torn to remove R. 5/4 where the cliché is believed to have been defective.

The 1a. (No. 37) differs from T **4** in having an inscription in native characters below the words 'ONE ANNA'.

11 (½a.)

12 Maharaja Sardul Singh

1903. Litho. Thick white wove glazed paper. Imperf.

39	**11**	½a. pink	20·00	3·00
		a. Printed both sides	†	£3000
40	**12**	2a. dull yellow	3·50	8·00

12a (8a.)

1904. Printed singly. Thin paper. Pin-perf.

41	**12a**	8a. grey	5·00	9·00
		a. *Tête-bêche* (vert pair)	42·00	
		b. Doubly printed	£275	

13 Maharaja Madan Singh

14 Maharaja Madan Singh

(Recess Perkins Bacon)

1904–10. With gum. P 12½.

42	**13**	¼a. carmine	60	1·00
		a. Perf 13½ (1910)	1·75	1·00
		b. Perf 12×12½	£300	
43		½a. chestnut	4·25	2·00
		a. Perf 13½ (1906)	1·25	30
44		1a. blue	8·00	4·50
		a. Perf 13½ (1906)	4·00	2·75
45		2a. orange-yellow	15·00	8·50
		a. Perf 13½ (1907)	28·00	20·00
46		4a. brown	28·00	30·00
		a. Perf 13½ (1907)	15·00	22·00
		b. Perf 12	£200	£120
		c. Perf comp of 12 and 12½	£350	
47		8a. violet (1905)	32·00	65·00
48		1r. green	30·00	£100
49		2r. olive-yellow	50·00	£325
50		5r. purple-brown	28·00	£250
42/50 *Set of 9*			£160	£700

Stamps in other colours, all perforated 13½, were produced by Perkins Bacon as business samples.

1912. Printed from half-tone blocks. No ornaments to left and right of value in English; large ornaments on either side of value in Hindi. Small stop after 'STATE'.

(a) Thin wove paper. Rouletted

51	**14**	2a. deep violet ('TWO ANNA')	8·00	20·00
		a. *Tête-bêche* (vert pair)	16·00	85·00
		b. Imperf (pair)	£900	

No. 51 is printed in four rows, each inverted in respect to that above and below it.

(b) Thick white chalk-surfaced paper. Imperf

52	**14**	2a. lilac ('TWO ANNA')	£3500	£1200

(c) Thick white chalk-surfaced paper. Rouletted in colour (Medallion only in half-tone)

53	**14**	¼a. ultramarine	26·00	16·00

1913. No ornaments on either side of value in English. Small ornaments in bottom label. With stop after 'STATE'. Thick white chalk-surfaced paper. Rouletted.

54	**14**	2a. purple ('TWO ANNAS')	2·50	5·00

15

पाव आना
No. 59e. This occurs on R. 3/3 on one setting only

2 TWO ANNAS 2
No. 60. Small figures

2 TWO ANNAS 2
No. 60b. Large figures

(Typo Diamond Soap Works, Kishangarh)

1913 (Aug). Thick surfaced paper. Half-tone centre. Type-set inscriptions. Rouletted. Inscr 'KISHANGARH'.

59	**15**	¼a. pale blue	30	90
		a. Imperf (pair)	9·00	
		b. Roul×imperf (horiz pair)	48·00	
		ba. Imperf between (horiz pair)	80·00	
		c. 'OUARTER' (R. 4/4)	5·00	7·00
		ca. As last, imperf (pair)	42·00	
		cb. As last, roul×imperf (horiz pair)	£100	
		d. 'KISHANGAHR' (R. 2/3)	5·00	7·00
		da. As last, imperf (pair)	42·00	
		db. As last, roul×imperf (horiz pair)	£100	
		dc. As last, imperf between (horiz pair)	£160	
		e. Character omitted	7·00	7·00
		ea. As last, imperf (pair)	48·00	
60		2a. purple	16·00	35·00
		a. 'KISHANGAHR' (R. 2/3)	65·00	£180
		b. Large figures '2'	38·00	95·00

1913–16. Stamps printed far apart, horizontally and vertically, otherwise as No. 54, except as noted below.

63	**14**	¼a. blue	30	45
64		½a. green (1915)	30	1·75
		a. Printed both sides	£400	
		b. Imperf (pair)	£275	£300
		c. Emerald-green (1916)	1·75	4·00
65		1a. red	2·25	3·25
		a. Without stop*	1·75	8·00
		ab. Imperf (pair)	£275	
66		2a. purple ('TWO ANNAS') (1915)	6·50	8·00
67		4a. bright blue	6·00	8·00
68		8a. brown	7·00	65·00
69		1r. mauve	27·00	£275
		a. Imperf (pair)	£450	
70		2r. deep green	£160	£700
71		5r. brown	35·00	£700
63/71 *Set of 9*			£200	£1600

* For this issue, ornaments were added on either side of the English value (except in the ¼a.) and the inscription in the right label was without stop, except in the case of No. 65.

In Nos. 70 and 71 the value is expressed as 'RUPIES' instead of 'RUPEES'.

Initial printings of the ¼a., 1a. and 4a. values were in sheets of 20 containing two panes of ten separated by a central gutter margin. Stamps from these sheets measure 20×25½ mm and have heavier screening dots on the margins than on the designs. Subsequent printings of these stamps, and of other values in the set, were from single pane sheets of 20 on which the designs measured 19½×23¾ mm and with the screening dots uniform across the sheet.

Maharaja Yagyanarayan Singh, 1926–1939

16 Maharaja Yagyanarayan Singh

17 Maharaja Yagyanarayan Singh

1928–36. Thick surfaced paper. Typo. Pin-perf.

72	**16**	¼a. light blue	1·75	2·00
73		½a. yellow-green	4·00	2·50
		a. Deep green	7·00	3·00
		ab. Imperf (pair)	£300	£300
		ac. Imperf between (vert or horiz pair)	£375	£375
74	**17**	1a. carmine	2·00	2·00
		a. Imperf (pair)	£425	£275
75		2a. purple	3·00	8·50
75*a*		2a. magenta (1936)	8·50	13·00
		ab. Imperf (pair)	£700	£700
76	**16**	4a. chestnut	2·75	2·00
		a. Imperf (pair)		
77		8a. violet	7·00	40·00
78		1r. light green	21·00	95·00
79		2r. lemon-yellow (1929)	35·00	£475
80		5r. claret (1929)	70·00	£500
		a. Imperf (pair)	£350	
72/80 *Set of 9*			£130	£1000

The 4a. to 5r. are slightly larger than, but otherwise similar to, the ¼a. and ½a. The 8a. has a dotted background covering the whole design.

Maharaja Samar Singh, 1939–1971

1943–47. As last, but thick, soft, unsurfaced paper. Poor impression. Typo. Pin-perf.

81	**16**	¼a. pale dull blue (1945)	8·00	22·00
		a. Imperf (pair)	60·00	
82		¼a. greenish blue (1947)	5·00	25·00
		a. Imperf (pair)	55·00	
83		½a. deep green (1944)	4·75	3·75
		a. Imperf (pair)	45·00	38·00
84		½a. yellow-green (1946)	12·00	18·00
		a. Imperf (pair)	60·00	55·00
85	**17**	1a. carmine-red (1944)	12·00	6·50
		a. Double print	£475	
		b. Imperf (pair)	60·00	60·00
		d. Red-orange (1947)	£130	70·00
		da. Imperf (pair)	£250	£180
86		2a. bright magenta	18·00	13·00
		a. Imperf (pair)	£170	£190
87		2a. maroon (1947)	£225	45·00
		a. Imperf (pair)	90·00	£110
88	**16**	4a. brown (1944)	38·00	22·00
		a. Imperf (pair)		
89		8a. violet (1945)	38·00	£250

90 1r. green (1945) 90·00 £225
a. Imperf (pair) £425 £600
90b 2r. yellow (date?)
ba. Imperf (pair) £1300
91 5r. claret (1945) £1700 £1800
a. Imperf (pair) £750

Imperforate between pairs of the ½a., 1a., and 2a. values of this issue, formerly listed as Nos. 83b, 84b, 85c and 87b, are now considered to be faked.

OFFICIAL STAMPS

ON
K S
D
(O 1)

1917–18. Handstamped with O 1.

(a) Stamps of 1899–1901

(i) Imperf

O1 **2** ¼a. yellow-green — £400
O2 ¼a. rose-pink — 15·00
a. Pair, one without opt — £250
b. Stamp doubly printed † £200
O3 **4** 1a. mauve — £120
O3*a* 1a. brown-lilac £110 5·50
ab. Pair, one without opt £475 £225
O4 **6** 4a. chocolate — £250

(ii) Pin-perf

O5 **2** ¼a. yellow-green — £250
O6 ¼a. rose-pink 2·75 60
a. Pair, one without opt £250 £120
b. Stamp doubly printed £300 £160
O7 **3** ½a. light blue £800 80·00
O8 **4** 1a. mauve £110 1·50
a. Pair, one without opt † £250
O9 1a. brown-lilac 90·00 3·75
a. Pair, one without opt † £275
O10 **5** 2a. dull orange — £225
O11 **6** 4a. chocolate £130 16·00
a. Pair, one without opt — £250
O12 **7** 1r. dull green £275 £200
O13 **8** 2r. brown-red — £1400
O14 **9** 5r. mauve — £4000

(b) Stamp of 1901

O14*a* **10a** 1r. dull green — £1200

(c) Stamps of 1903 and 1904

O15 **12** 2a. dull yellow £170 5·00
a. Stamp printed both sides † £1500
b. Red opt £800 £500
O16 **12a** 8a. grey £160 30·00
a. Red opt — £550

(d) Stamps of 1904–1910. P 13½ (¼a. to 4a.) or 12½ (others)

O17 **13** ¼a. carmine — £500
O18 ½a. chestnut 3·25 1·75
a. Pair, one without opt £190 £130
O19 1a. blue 18·00 4·00
a. Red opt 32·00 11·00
b. Pair, one without opt — £180
O20 2a. orange-yellow — £1500
O21 4a. brown 90·00 18·00
a. Red opt £225 70·00
b. Pair, one without opt — £325
O22 8a. violet £550 £375
a. Red opt — £500
b. Pair, one without opt † £1400
O23 1r. green £1700 £1500
a. Red opt — £1100
O24 5r. purple-brown

(e) Stamps of 1913

O25 **15** ¼a. pale blue 15·00
a. Imperf (pair) £200
b. Roulximperf (horiz pair) £400
c. 'OUARTER' 60·00
ca. As last, imperf (pair) £350
d. 'KISHANGAHR' 60·00
da. As last, imperf (pair) £350
e. Character omitted 60·00
ea. As last, imperf (pair) £350
O26 **14** 2a. purple (No. 54) — £150
a. Red opt £350 20·00
O27 **15** 2a. purple £950 £1000
a. 'KISHANGAHR' £2750
b. Large figures '2' £1600 £1700

(f) Stamps of 1913–1916

O28 **14** ¼a. blue 3·50 1·50
a. Red opt 4·25 2·00
b. Imperf (pair) £600
O29 ½a. green 2·50 75
a. Pair, one without opt — £160
b. Red opt 7·50 1·60
ba. Pair, one without opt — £300
O30 1a. red 45·00 20·00
a. Without stop (No. 65a) 1·50 1·00
ab. Pair, one without opt £250 £250
ac. Red opt £225 £120
O31 2a. purple 24·00 12·00
a. Red opt £225 £110
b. Pair, one without opt — £200
O32 4a. bright blue 55·00 24·00
a. Red opt £225 55·00
O33 8a. brown £250 85·00
a. Red opt — £140
O34 1r. mauve £600 £500
O35 2r. deep green
O36 5r. brown £2500

This overprint is found inverted as often as it is upright; and many other 'errors' exist.

Kishangarh became part of Rajasthan by 15 April 1948.

LAS BELA

PRICES FOR STAMPS ON COVER TO 1945
Nos. 1/12 *from* × 8

Mir Kamal Khan, 1896–1926

1

2

(Litho Thacker & Co, Bombay)

1897–98. Thick paper. P 11½.
1 **1** ½a. black on *white* 60·00 28·00

1898–1900. P 11½.
2 **1** ½a. black on *greyish blue* (1898) 40·00 16·00
3 ½a. black on *greenish grey* (1899) 35·00 16·00
a. 'BFLA' for 'BELA' £425
4 ½a. black on *thin white surfaced paper* (1899) 60·00 £100
5 ½a. black on *slate* (1900) 55·00 60·00
a. Imperf between (horiz pair) £2000

1901–02. P 11½.
6 **1** ½a. black on *pale grey* 30·00 16·00
a. 'BFLA' for 'BELA' £375 £450
7 ½a. black on *pale green* (1902) 45·00 45·00
8 **2** 1a. black on *orange* 60·00 65·00

There are at least 14 settings of the above ½a. stamps, the sheets varying from 16 to 30 stamps.

No. 6a occurred on R. 3/2 of the July 1901 printing in sheets of 16 (4×4).

1904 (Feb–Nov). Stamps printed wider apart. P 11½.
11 **1** ½a. black on *pale blue* 28·00 14·00
a. Imperf between (pair) £1600
b. Imperf between (horiz strip of 3) £2250
c. Perf 12½ (11.04) 50·00 23·00
12 ½a. black on *pale green* 30·00 14·00
c. Perf 12½ (11.04) 50·00 23·00

There are five plates of the above two stamps, each consisting of 18 (3×6) varieties.

All the coloured papers of the ½a. show coloured fibres, similar to those in granite paper.

The stamps of Las Bela have been obsolete since 1 April 1907.

MORVI

PRICES FOR STAMPS ON COVER TO 1945
Nos. 1/17 *from* × 6
Nos. 18/19 *from* × 3

Thakur (Maharaja from 1926) Lakhdirji, 1922–1948

1 Maharaja Lakhdirji

2 Maharaja Lakhdirji

3 Maharaja Lakhdirji

1931 (1 Apr). Typo. P 12.

(a) Printed in blocks of four. Stamps 10 mm apart (Nos. 1/2) or 6½ mm apart (No. 3). Perf on two or three sides

1 **1** 3p. deep red 5·00 15·00
2 ½a. blue 35·00 70·00
3 2a. yellow-brown £200
1/3 *Set of 3* £225

(b) Printed in two blocks of four. Stamps 5½ mm apart. Perf on four sides

4 **1** 3p. bright scarlet 9·00 35·00
a. Error. Dull blue 5·00 35·00
b. Ditto. Double print £1000
c. Ditto. Printed on gummed side £1200
5 ½a. dull blue 10·00 35·00
a. Chalk-surfaced paper 10·00 27·00
6 1a. brown-red 3·50 45·00
7 2a. yellow-brown 5·00 60·00
4/7 *Set of 4* 25·00 £150

Nos. 1/3 were supplied to post offices in panes of four sewn into bundles with interleaving.

1932–33. Horizontal background lines wider apart and portrait smaller than in T 1. Typo. P 11.
8 **2** 3p. carmine-rose (*shades*) 5·00 21·00
9 6p. green 12·00 32·00
a. Imperf between (horiz pair) £4750
b. Emerald-green 9·00 25·00
10 1a. ultramarine (*to deep*) 11·00 25·00
a. Imperf between (vert pair) £4000
11 2a. bright violet (1933) 21·00 75·00
a. Imperf between (vert pair) £4250
8/11 *Set of 4* 42·00 £130

1934. Typo. London ptg. P 14.
12 **3** 3p. carmine 6·00 10·00
13 6p. emerald-green 4·50 12·00
14 1a. purple-brown 5·50 24·00
a. Imperf between (horiz pair) † £3500
15 2a. bright violet 6·00 48·00
12/15 *Set of 4* 20·00 80·00

1935–48. Typo. Morvi Press ptg. Rough perf 11.
16 **3** 3p. scarlet (*shades*) 3·00 7·50
a. Imperf between (horiz pair) £3500
17 6p. grey-green 7·00 8·50
a. Emerald-green 15·00 40·00
b. Yellow-green 21·00
18 1a. brown 12·00 22·00
a. Pale yellow-brown 16·00 35·00
b. Chocolate 26·00 42·00
19 2a. dull violet (*to deep*) 3·00 25·00
16/19 *Set of 4* 22·00 55·00

Nos. 17*a*, 18*a* and 18*b* were issued between 1944 and 1948.

Maharaja Mahendra Singh, 1948–1957

Morvi was merged with the United State of Kathiawar (later Saurashtra) by 15 April 1948.

NANDGAON

PRICES FOR STAMPS ON COVER TO 1945
The stamps of Nandgaon are very rare used on cover.

GUM. The stamps of Nandgaon were issued without gum.

Raja Mahant Balram Das, 1883–1897

1

2 (½a.)

(Litho at Poona)

1891. Imperf.
1 **1** ½a. blue 11·00 £250
a. Dull blue 11·00
2 2a. rose 38·00 £750

The few covers in existence franked with Nos. 1/2 have undated manuscript cancellations, but other forms are known on loose examples.

The state was under Imperial administration from January 1888 to November 1891 and it is possible that Nos. 1/2 may have appeared in late 1887.

Last character in top line omitted

(Typo Balram Press, Raj-Nandgaon)

1893 (1 Jan)–**94.** Printed in sheets of 16 (4×4). Imperf.

(a) Stamps printed wide apart (8 to 10 mm) without wavy lines between them. Thin, toned wove paper

3 **2** ½a. dull to deep green 16·00 £140
4 2a. red 20·00 £140
b. Dull rose 19·00 £140

(b) Stamps printed closer together (4 to 7 mm) with wavy lines between them. Thin, white wove paper (1894)

5 **2** ½a. green 45·00 £110
a. Last character in top line omitted (R. 4/3) £190
6 1a. rose £100 £180
ba. Laid paper £350

There were three settings of T **2** with a number of separate printings made from the third:
Setting I - Nos. 3, 4, 4*b*, O2
Setting II - Nos. 5, 6
Setting III - Nos. 5, 6ba, O3, O4, O4*a*, O5 and subsequent reprints.

The same clichés were used for all values with the face value inscriptions changed. These exist in two different sizes with both occurring on the ½a., the small on the 1a. and the large on the 2a. except for No. O5 which has the small type.

The ordinary postage stamps of Nandgaon became obsolete on 1 July 1894.

OFFICIAL STAMPS

(O **1**) ('M.B.D.' = Mahant Balram Das)

1893. Handstamped with ruler's initials in oval. T O **1**, in purple.
O1 **1** ½a. blue £550
O2 2a. rose £1500

1894. Handstamped with T O **1** in purple.

(a) Stamps printed wide apart (8 to 10 mm) without wavy lines between them. Thin, toned wove paper

O2*a* **2** ½a. dull green £800
O3 2a. red 50·00 £250

(b) Stamps printed closer together (4 to 7 mm) with wavy lines between them. Thin, white wove paper

O4 **2** ½a. yellow-green 10·00 20·00
a. Sage-green 11·00
O5 1a. rose (*shades*) 22·00 60·00
a. Thin laid paper 18·00 £140
O6 2a. rose (*shades*) 18·00 48·00

Further printings took place in 1895 after the Official stamps were withdrawn from postal use on 31 December 1894. These were all on thin, white wove paper with the ½a. and 2a. in slightly different shades and the 1a. in brown or ultramarine.

There is a forgery of the handstamp, T O **1**, which shows 8 mm between the two ornaments below the initials instead of the normal 4 mm.

NAWANAGAR

PRICES FOR STAMPS ON COVER TO 1945	
No. 1	*from* × 20
No. 2	*from* × 8
Nos. 3/4	*from* × 2
No. 5	—
Nos. 6/12	—
Nos. 13/15	*from* × 100
Nos. 16/18	—

GUM. The stamps of Nawanagar were issued without gum.

Jam Vibhaji 1882–1895

1 (1 docra)

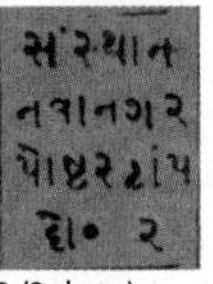
2 (2 docra)

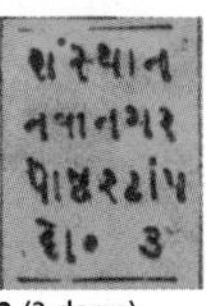
3 (3 docra)

1877. Typo in sheets of 32 (4×8 or 8×4). Laid paper.

(a) Imperf

1 **1** 1doc. blue (*shades*) 1·50 35·00
a. *Tête-bêche* (pair) £2500
b. Doubly printed £160

(b) Perf 12½ (line)

2 **1** 1doc. slate-blue £160 £300
a. Perf 11 (harrow) £190
ab. *Tête-bêche* (pair) £3750

The inverted clichés which cause the *tête-bêche* pairs come from different settings and occur on R. 3/2 (No. 1a) or R. 4/4 (No. 2ab) of sheets of 32 (4×8).

1877. Types **2** and **3**. Type-set in black. Wove paper. Thick horizontal and vertical frame lines. Stamp 19 mm wide.

3 1doc. deep mauve £6000 £475
a. Stamp 14½-15 mm wide † £900
b. Stamp 16 mm wide † £700
4 2doc. green £6000 £3000
5 3doc. yellow £5000 £2750

1880. As last, but thin frame lines, as illustrated. Stamp 15 to 18 mm wide.

6 1doc. deep mauve 5·00 20·00
a. On rose 6·00
ab. Stamp 14 mm wide 6·00 20·00
b. Error. Green
7 1doc. magenta (*stamp 14 mm wide*) 6·00
8 2doc. yellow-green 12·00 24·00
a. On blue-green 22·00
b. Error. Yellow £650
c. Stamp 14 mm wide 6·00 20·00
ca. On blue-green 18·00
9 3doc. orange-yellow 24·00
a. On yellow 10·00 32·00
ab. On laid paper £180
b. Stamp 14 mm wide. *On yellow* 7·00 17·00
ba. On laid paper 75·00

There are several different settings of each value of this series.

No. 8b occurs in the sheet of the 3 doc. value from one setting only.

4 (1 docra)

1893. Typo in sheets of 36. P 12.

(a) Thick paper

10 **4** 1doc. black 11·00
a. Imperf (pair) £1200
11 3doc. orange 12·00

(b) Thick laid paper

12 **4** 1doc. black £1200

(c) Thin wove paper

13 **4** 1doc. black *to* grey 2·75 13·00
a. Imperf between (pair) £900
b. Imperf (pair) £800
c. Imperf horiz (vert pair) £950
d. Imperf between (horiz strip of 6) £2500
14 2doc. green 4·50 20·00
a. Imperf (pair) £1100
b. Imperf between (vert pair) £1100
c. Imperf horiz (vert pair) £1100
15 3doc. orange-yellow 5·00 26·00
a. Imperf between (pair) £1400
b. Orange 4·50 23·00
ba. Imperf (pair) £1000
bb. Imperf vert (horiz pair) £1000
bc. Imperf between (horiz pair) £1000

(d) Thin, soft wove paper

16 **4** 1doc. black
17 2doc. deep green 8·50
18 3doc. brown-orange 11·00

Cancellations for postal purposes were intaglio seals, applied in black. Other forms of cancellation were only used on remainders.

The stamps of Nawanagar became obsolete on 1 January 1895.

NEPAL

Nepal being an independent state, its stamps will be found listed in the *South-East Asia* catalogue.

ORCHHA

PRICES FOR STAMPS ON COVER TO 1945	
Nos. 1/2	—
Nos. 3/7	*from* × 8
Nos. 8/30	*from* × 50
Nos. 31/45	*from* × 4

A set of four stamps, ½a. red, 1a. violet, 2a. yellow and 4a. deep blue-green, in a design similar to T **2**, was prepared in 1897 with State authority but not put into use. These exist both imperforate and pin-perforated. (*Price for set of 4, £30 unused or c.t.o.*)

Maharaja Partab Singh, 1874–1930

1

2

(Litho Shri Pratap Prabhakar)

1913. Background to Arms unshaded, Very blurred impression. Wove paper. No gum. Imperf.

1 **1** ½a. green 50·00 £180
2 1a. red 25·00 £300

(Litho Shri Pratap Prabhakar)

1914–35. Background shaded with short horizontal lines. Clearer impression. Wove paper. No gum. Imperf.

3 **2** ¼a. bright ultramarine 2·50 8·00
a. Grey-blue 40 5·50
b. Deep blue 1·60 4·00
ba. Laid paper £900
4 ½a. green (*shades*) 55 7·50
a. Dull green 2·50 10·00
b. Apple-green 4·00 5·00
5 1a. scarlet 2·50 13·00
a. Laid paper — £1100
b. Indian red 1·75 15·00
c. Carmine 3·50 8·50
ca. Laid paper (1935) £400 £450
6 2a. red-brown (1916) 4·50 24·00
a. Light brown 18·00 45·00
b. Chestnut 21·00 45·00
7 4a. ochre (1917) 11·00 65·00
a. Yellow-orange 12·00 65·00
b. Yellow 15·00 65·00
3/7 *Set of* 5 16·00 95·00

There are two sizes of T **2** in the setting of eight (4×2). In each value stamps from the upper row are slightly taller than those from the lower.

Maharaja Vir Singh II, 1930–1956

3 Maharaja Vir Singh II

4 Maharaja Vir Singh II

(Typo Lakshmi Art Ptg Wks, Bombay)

1935 (1 Apr). Thick, chalk-surfaced wove paper. Various perfs*.

8 **3** ¼a. purple and slate (P 11½) 2·75 9·00
a. Imperf between (vert pair)
b. Ordinary paper (P 11, 11½ or 12). 1·00 7·50
ba. Imperf between (vert pair) 18·00
bb. Imperf vert (horiz pair) 70·00
bc. Imperf horiz (vert pair) 65·00
9 ½a. olive-grey and emerald (P 11½ or 12) 2·00 4·50
a. Imperf (pair) 85·00
10 ¾a. magenta and deep myrtle-green (P 11½, 12 or compound with 11) 60 4·25
a. Imperf (pair) 80·00
11 1a. myrtle-green and purple-brown (P 12) 60 5·00
a. Imperf (pair) 90·00 £160
b. Imperf horiz (vert pair)
c. Imperf vert (horiz pair)
12 1¼a. slate and mauve (P 11½, 12 or compound) 60 5·00
a. Imperf (pair) 80·00 £500
b. Imperf between (horiz pair) 80·00
c. Frame doubly printed 75·00
13 1½a. brown and scarlet (P 12 or compound with 11½) 1·00 4·50
a. Imperf between (vert pair) 85·00
b. Imperf between (horiz pair) 80·00
14 2a. blue and red-orange (P 12 or compound with 11) 60 5·00

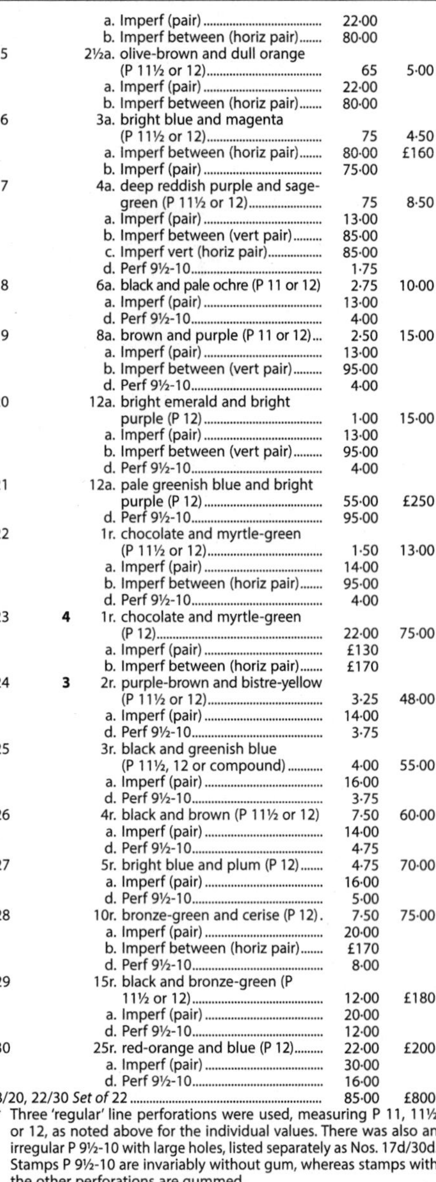
a. Imperf (pair) 22·00
b. Imperf between (horiz pair) 80·00
15 2½a. olive-brown and dull orange (P 11½ or 12) 65 5·00
a. Imperf (pair) 22·00
b. Imperf between (horiz pair) 80·00
16 3a. bright blue and magenta (P 11½ or 12) 75 4·50
a. Imperf between (horiz pair) 80·00 £160
b. Imperf (pair) 75·00
17 4a. deep reddish purple and sage-green (P 11½ or 12) 75 8·50
a. Imperf (pair) 13·00
b. Imperf between (vert pair) 85·00
c. Imperf vert (horiz pair) 85·00
d. Perf 9½-10 1·75
18 6a. black and pale ochre (P 11 or 12) 2·75 10·00
a. Imperf (pair) 13·00
d. Perf 9½-10 4·00
19 8a. brown and purple (P 11 or 12) 2·50 15·00
a. Imperf (pair) 13·00
b. Imperf between (vert pair) 95·00
d. Perf 9½-10 4·00
20 12a. bright emerald and bright purple (P 12) 1·00 15·00
a. Imperf (pair) 13·00
b. Imperf between (vert pair) 95·00
d. Perf 9½-10 4·00
21 12a. pale greenish blue and bright purple (P 12) 55·00 £250
d. Perf 9½-10 95·00
22 1r. chocolate and myrtle-green (P 11½ or 12) 1·50 13·00
a. Imperf (pair) 14·00
b. Imperf between (horiz pair) 95·00
d. Perf 9½-10 4·00
23 **4** 1r. chocolate and myrtle-green (P 12) 22·00 75·00
a. Imperf (pair) £130
b. Imperf between (horiz pair) £170
24 **3** 2r. purple-brown and bistre-yellow (P 11½ or 12) 3·25 48·00
a. Imperf (pair) 14·00
d. Perf 9½-10 3·75
25 3r. black and greenish blue (P 11½, 12 or compound) 4·00 55·00
a. Imperf (pair) 16·00
d. Perf 9½-10 3·75
26 4r. black and brown (P 11½ or 12) 7·50 60·00
a. Imperf (pair) 14·00
d. Perf 9½-10 4·75
27 5r. bright blue and plum (P 12) 4·75 70·00
a. Imperf (pair) 16·00
d. Perf 9½-10 5·00
28 10r. bronze-green and cerise (P 12). 7·50 75·00
a. Imperf (pair) 20·00
b. Imperf between (horiz pair) £170
d. Perf 9½-10 8·00
29 15r. black and bronze-green (P 11½ or 12) 12·00 £180
a. Imperf (pair) 20·00
d. Perf 9½-10 12·00
30 25r. red-orange and blue (P 12) 22·00 £200
a. Imperf (pair) 30·00
d. Perf 9½-10 16·00
8/20, 22/30 *Set of* 22 85·00 £800

* Three 'regular' line perforations were used, measuring P 11, 11½ or 12, as noted above for the individual values. There was also an irregular P 9½-10 with large holes, listed separately as Nos. 17d/30d. Stamps P 9½-10 are invariably without gum, whereas stamps with the other perforations are gummed.

Values to 5r. except the 1a., are inscribed 'POSTAGE', and the remaining values 'POSTAGE & REVENUE'.

The central portrait of T **3** is taken from a half-tone block and consists of large square dots. The portrait of T **4** has a background of lines.

Owing to a lack of proper State control considerable quantities of these stamps circulated at below face value and the issue was subsequently withdrawn, supplies being exchanged for the 1939–1942 issue. We are, however, now satisfied that the lower values at least did genuine postal duty until 1939.

Used prices are for stamps cancelled-to-order, postally used examples being worth considerably more.

5 Maharaja Vir Singh II

6 Maharaja Vir Singh II

(Litho Indian Security Printing Press, Nasik)

1939–42?. P 13½×14 (T **5**) or 14×13½ (T **6**).

31 **5** ¼a. chocolate 8·00 £140
32 ½a. yellow-green 7·50 90·00
33 ¾a. bright blue 8·50 £170
34 1a. scarlet 7·50 32·00
35 1¼a. blue 10·00 £170
36 1½a. mauve 8·00 £190
37 2a. vermilion 7·50 £110
38 2½a. turquoise-green 9·50 £425
39 3a. slate-violet 9·00 £180
40 4a. slate 11·00 42·00
41 8a. magenta 14·00 £400
42 **6** 1r. grey-green 42·00 £1000
43 2r. bright violet £120 £1500
44 5r. yellow-orange £375 £5500
45 10r. turquoise-green (1942) £1400 £8500
46 15r. slate-lilac (date ?) £30000
47 25r. claret (date ?) £22000

The used prices quoted for Nos. 31/45 are for stamps with identifiable authentic postal cancellations. This issue was extensively used for fiscal purposes, and forged postmarks are frequently met with.

Orchha became part of Vindhya Pradesh by 1 May 1948.

POONCH

PRICES FOR STAMPS ON COVER TO 1945	
No. 1	*from* × 3
Nos. 1*a*/2	*from* × 2
Nos. 3/63	*from* × 10
Nos. O1/O10	*from* × 30

Poonch was ruled by a junior branch of the Jammu and Kashmir princely family and by treaty, was subject to the 'advice and consent' of the Maharaja of that state.

The Poonch postal service operated an office at Kahuta in the Punjab which acted as the office of exchange between the state post and that of British India.

GUM. The stamps of Poonch were issued without gum, except for some examples of Nos. 7/10.

The stamps of Poonch are all imperforate, and handstamped in watercolours.

DATES OF ISSUE. Precise dates of issue are difficult to establish, with some papers of the 1885–1894 series reappearing after long intervals. It is, however, known that the 1 pice value (T **7**) was not issued until 1887.

ILLUSTRATIONS. Designs of Poonch are illustrated actual size.

Raja Moti Singh, 1852–1892

1

2

1876? T **1** (22×21 *mm*). Central face value in circle and five rosettes in outer frame. Yellowish white, wove paper.

1		6p. red	£20000	£275
		aa. Pair, one stamp sideways	†	£27000

Earliest recorded use of No. 1: July 20 1878.

1877? As T **1** (19×17 *mm*). Central face value in oval and two rosettes in outer frame. Same paper.

1*a*		½a. red	£27000	£13000

Earliest recorded use of No. 1*a*: May 1879.

1879? T **2** (21×19 *mm*). Central face value in oval and one rosette in outer frame. Same paper.

2		½a. red	—	£7000

Earliest recorded use of No. 2: April 16 1880.

3 (½a.)

4 (1a.)

5 (2a.)

6 (4a.)

1883. Yellowish white, wove paper.

3	**3**	½a. red	85·00	35·00
4	**4**	1a. red	£325	£160
5	**5**	2a. red	£750	£425
6	**6**	4a. red	£900	£550

1885. Toned wove bâtonné paper.

7	**3**	½a. red	15·00	10·00
8	**4**	1a. red	65·00	
9	**5**	2a. red	70·00	55·00
10	**6**	4a. red	£140	£140
		a. Pair, one stamp sideways	£5000	

These are sometimes found gummed.

7 (1 pice)

1885–94. Various papers.

(a) White laid bâtonné or ribbed bâtonné

11	**7**	1p. red (1887)	85·00	85·00
		a. Pair, one stamp sideways	£800	
		b. *Tête-bêche* (pair)	£850	
12	**3**	½a. red	7·50	7·50
		a. *Tête-bêche* (pair)	£5000	
13	**4**	1a. red	50·00	
		a. Pair, one stamp sideways	£3000	
14	**5**	2a. red	55·00	55·00
15	**6**	4a. red	65·00	
		a. Pair, one stamp sideways	£5000	

(b) Thick white laid paper (1885–1887)

22	**7**	1p. red	£550	
23	**3**	½a. red	£200	
24	**4**	1a. red	£200	
25	**5**	2a. red	£200	
26	**6**	4a. red	£250	

(c) Yellow wove bâtonné

27	**7**	1p. red	5·50	5·50
		a. Pair, one stamp sideways	75·00	
28	**3**	½a. red	25·00	25·00
29	**4**	1a. red	£160	
30	**5**	2a. red	27·00	28·00
		a. Pair, one stamp sideways	£3000	
31	**6**	4a. red	22·00	20·00

(d) Orange-buff wove bâtonné

32	**7**	1p. red	9·00	9·50
		a. Pair, one stamp sideways	55·00	75·00
		b. *Tête-bêche* (pair)	85·00	
33	**3**	½a. red	80·00	
34	**5**	2a. red	£250	
35	**6**	4a. red	75·00	

(e) Yellow laid paper

36	**7**	1p. red	5·00	5·50
		a. Pair, one stamp sideways	38·00	
		b. *Tête-bêche* (pair)	60·00	
37	**3**	½a. red	14·00	
38	**4**	1a. red	£160	
39	**5**	2a. red	£160	£170
40	**6**	4a. red	£150	

(f) Yellow laid bâtonné

41	**7**	1p. red	24·00	22·00

(g) Buff laid or ribbed bâtonné paper thicker than (d)

42	**4**	1a. red	£190	
43	**6**	4a. red	£180	

(h) Blue-green laid paper (1887)

44	**3**	½a. red	£110	
45	**4**	1a. red	14·00	14·00
46	**5**	2a. red	£120	
47	**6**	4a. red	£200	

(i) Yellow-green laid paper

48	**3**	½a. red		

(j) Blue-green wove bâtonné

49	**7**	1p. red	£120	£100
49*a*	**3**	½a. red	£2500	
50	**4**	1a. red	9·00	7·50

(k) Lavender wove bâtonné

51	**4**	1a. red	£180	£200
52	**5**	2a. red	10·00	10·00
		a. Pair, one stamp sideways	£4750	

(l) Blue wove bâtonné (1887)

53	**7**	1p. red	5·50	5·50
		a. Pair, one stamp sideways	55·00	75·00
		b. *Tête-bêche* (pair)	90·00	
53*c*		½a. red	£2500	
54	**4**	1a. red	£550	£600
54*a*		2a. red	£2500	

(m) Various coloured papers

55	**7**	1p. red/*grey-blue laid* (1894)	28·00	20·00
		a. *Tête-bêche* (pair)	£600	
56		1p. red/*lilac laid* (1894)	£110	£120
		a. Pair, one stamp sideways	£700	£700
		b. *Tête-bêche* (pair)	£650	

1887–94. Printed in aniline rose on various papers.

57	**7**	1p. on *blue wove bâtonné*	15·00	
		a. *Tête-bêche* (pair)	£140	
58		1p. on *buff laid*	30·00	
		a. *Tête-bêche* (pair)	£225	
		b. Pair, one stamp sideways	£225	
59	**3**	½a. on *white laid*	60·00	
60	**4**	1a. on *green laid*	35·00	42·00
61		1a. on *green wove bâtonné*	24·00	28·00
62	**5**	2a. on *lavender wove bâtonné*	24·00	24·00
63	**6**	4a. on *yellow laid*	38·00	45·00
		a. Pair, one stamp sideways	£2250	
		b. *Tête-bêche* (pair)	£2250	

Raja Baldeo Singh, 1892–1918

OFFICIAL STAMPS

1887.

(a) White laid bâtonné paper

O1	**7**	1p. black	7·00	7·00
		a. Pair, one stamp sideways	30·00	38·00
		b. *Tête-bêche* (pair)	40·00	
O2	**3**	½a. black	8·00	8·50
O3	**4**	1a. black	8·00	8·00
O4	**5**	2a. black	16·00	16·00
O5	**6**	4a. black	22·00	26·00

(b) White or toned wove bâtonné paper

O6	**7**	1p. black	5·00	
		a. Pair, one stamp sideways	38·00	45·00
		b. *Tête-bêche* (pair)	60·00	
O7	**3**	½a. black	7·00	8·00
		a. Pair, one stamp sideways	£4000	
O8	**4**	1a. black	22·00	22·00
O9	**5**	2a. black	15·00	16·00
O10	**6**	4a. black	20·00	

The stamps of Poonch became obsolete for postal purposes on 1 Jan 1895, but the 1a and 4a values continued in fiscal use until 1898.

RAJASTHAN

Rajasthan was formed in 1948–1949 from a number of States in Rajputana; these included Bundi, Jaipur and Kishangarh, whose posts continued to function more or less separately until ordered by the Indian Government to close on 1 April 1950.

PRICES FOR STAMPS ON COVER TO 1945	
Nos. 1/12	*from* × 4
Nos. 13/14	—
Nos. 15/25	*from* × 4
Nos. 26/42	*from* × 3

PRICES FOR STAMPS ON COVER TO 1945	
No. 43	*from* × 5
Nos. 44/60	*from* × 3
No. 61	*from* × 5
Nos. 62/65	—

FORGERIES. Collectors are warned that the Rajasthan T **1** opt on stamps of Bundi and especially Kishangarh has been extensively forged. The more expensive stamps should not be purchased without a reliable guarantee.

BUNDI

(1)

1948 (15 Oct)–**49**. Nos. 86/92 of Bundi.

(a) Handstamped with T **1** *in black*

1A	¼a. blue-green	11·00	£140
	a. Pair, one without opt	£650	
2A	½a. violet	10·00	90·00
	a. Pair, one without opt	£700	
3A	1a. yellow-green	10·00	65·00
4A	2a. vermilion	28·00	£180
5A	4a. orange	90·00	£300
6A	8a. ultramarine	18·00	

(b) Handstamped with T **1** *in violet*

1B	¼a. blue-green	9·50	£180
2B	½a. violet	9·50	70·00
	a. Pair, one without opt	£650	
3B	1a. yellow-green	28·00	80·00
	a. Pair, one without opt	£650	
4B	2a. vermilion	60·00	£170
5B	4a. orange	60·00	£180
6B	8a. ultramarine	18·00	
7B	1r. chocolate	£600	

(c) Handstamped with T **1** *in blue*

1C	¼a. blue-green	70·00	
2C	½a. violet	£100	
3C	1a. yellow-green	£100	£100
4C	2a. vermilion	—	£800
5C	4a. orange	£300	
6C	8a. ultramarine	£160	
7C	1r. chocolate	£180	

Many of these handstamps are known sideways, inverted or double.

It is believed that the blue handstamps (Nos. 1C/7C) were issued first, followed by violet and then black.

(d) Machine-printed as T **1** *in black (1949)*

11	2a. vermilion	22·00	£110
	a. Opt inverted	£500	
12	4a. orange	9·00	£110
	a. Opt double	£425	
13	8a. ultramarine	18·00	
	a. Opt inverted	£1100	
	b. Opt double	£550	
14	1r. chocolate	10·00	

JAIPUR

राजस्थान

RAJASTHAN

(2)

1950 (26 Jan). T **7** of Jaipur optd with T **2**.

15	¼a. black and brown-lake (No. 58) (B.)	13·00	32·00
16	½a. black and violet (No. 41) (R.)	13·00	32·00
17	¾a. black and brown-red (No. 59) (Blue-blk.)	13·00	42·00
	a. Opt in pale blue	22·00	60·00
18	1a. black and blue (No. 60) (R.)	13·00	85·00
19	2a. black and buff (No. 61) (R.)	13·00	£120
20	2½a. black and carmine (No. 62) (B.)	13·00	50·00
21	3a. black and green (No. 63) (R.)	14·00	£130
22	4a. black and grey-green (No. 64) (R.)	14·00	£160
23	6a. black and pale blue (No. 65*a*) (R.)	14·00	£200
24	8a. black and chocolate (No. 66) (R.)	18·00	£275
25	1r. black and yellow-bistre (No. 67) (R.)	28·00	£425
15/25 *Set of* 11		£150	£1400

Collectors are warned that the used prices quoted for Nos. 15/25 are for stamps with identifiable authentic cancellation. Forged postmarks on this issue are frequently seen.

KISHANGARH

1948 (Oct)–**49**. Various stamps of Kishangarh handstamped with T **1** in red.

(a) On stamps of 1899–1901

26	¼a. rose-pink (No. 5*a*) (B.)	£600	
26*a*	¼a. rose-pink (No. 22*a*)	—	£550
27	½a. deep blue (No. 26)	£1500	
28	1a. mauve (No. 28)	£160	£180
29	1a. brown-lilac (No. 29)	24·00	75·00
	a. *Tête-bêche* (horiz pair)	£2500	
	b. Imperf (pair)	70·00	£190
	c. Violet handstamp	£750	£750
	d. Black handstamp	—	£850
30	4a. chocolate (No. 31)	£140	£180
	a. Violet handstamp	—	£1000
31	1r. dull green (No. 32)	£650	£650
31*a*	2r. brown-red (No. 34)	£700	£700
32	5r. mauve (No. 35)	£700	£700

(b) On stamps of 1904–1910

33	13	½a. chestnut	—	£400
33*a*		1a. blue	—	£450
34		4a. brown	13·00	
		a. Blue handstamp	£275	
35	12a	8a. grey	£200	£350
36	13	8a. violet	11·00	
37		1r. green	12·00	
38		2r. olive-yellow	19·00	
39		5r. purple-brown	45·00	
		a. Blue handstamp	£750	

(c) On stamps of 1912–1916

40	14	½a. green (No. 64)	£650	£400
41		1a. red	—	£500
42		2a. deep violet (No. 51)	£1500	
43		2a. purple (No. 66)	8·00	17·00
		a. Pair, one without handstamp	£850	
44		4a. bright blue	—	£1300
45		8a. brown	5·00	
		a. Pair, one without handstamp	£850	
46		1r. mauve	10·00	
47		2r. deep green	10·00	
		a. Pair, one without handstamp	£1200	
48		5r. brown	£650	

(d) On stamps of 1928–1936

49	16	½a. yellow-green	£450	
49*a*		2a. magenta	—	£1000
50		4a. chestnut	£600	
51		8a. violet	6·50	90·00
		a. Pair, one without handstamp	£750	
52		1r. light green	29·00	
53		2r. lemon-yellow	17·00	
54		5r. claret	16·00	

(e) On stamps of 1943–1947

55	16	¼a. pale dull blue	£250	£250
56		¼a. greenish blue	90·00	90·00
		a. Imperf (pair)	£550	
57		½a. deep green	48·00	50·00
		a. Violet handstamp	—	£550
57*b*		½a. yellow-green	45·00	45·00
		ba. Imperf (pair)	£550	
		bb. Blue handstamp	—	£550
58	17	1a. carmine-red	£225	£200
		a. Violet handstamp	—	£550
58*b*		1a. orange-red (*imperf*)	£350	
		ba. Blue handstamp	£375	
59		2a. bright magenta	£450	£450
60		2a. maroon (*imperf*)	£600	
61	16	4a. brown	7·50	18·00
		a. Pair, one without handstamp	£650	
62		8a. violet	21·00	£130
63		1r. green	6·50	
64		2r. yellow	£180	
65		5r. claret	85·00	

A 1a. value in deep violet-blue was issued for revenue purposes, but is known postally used (*Price £160 used*).

RAJPIPLA

PRICES FOR STAMPS ON COVER TO 1945

No. 1	*from* × 50
Nos. 2/3	—

Maharana Ganbhir Singh, 1860–1897

The Rajpipla state post was opened to the public sometime in the late 1870s. Adhesive stamps were preceded by postal stationery lettersheets which were first reported in 1879.

1 (1 pice)

2 (2a.)

3 (4a.)

1880. Litho. With or without gum (1p.) or no gum (others). P 11 (1p.) or 12½.

1	1	1p. blue (1.6)	7·00	55·00
2	2	2a. green	38·00	£170
		a. Imperf between (horiz pair)	£1000	£1100
3	3	4a. red	20·00	£110
1/3 *Set of 3*			60·00	£300

No. 1 was produced in sheets of 64 (8×8) and the higher values in sheets of 20 (5×4).

These stamps became obsolete in 1886 when the Imperial postal service absorbed the Rajpipla state post.

SHAHPURA

PRICES FOR STAMPS ON COVER TO 1945

Nos. 1/4	*from* × 2
No. F1	*from* × 2

DATES. Those quoted are of first known use.

Rajadhiraj Nahar Singh, 1870–1932

RAJ
SHAHPURA
Postage 1 pice
1

RAJ
SHAHPURA
1 pice
2

1914–17. Typo.

1	1	1p. carmine/*bluish grey* (P 11)	—	£800
2		1p. carmine/*drab* (*imperf*) (1917)	—	£1100

Some examples of No. 1 are imperforate on one side or on two adjacent sides.

1920–28. Typo. Imperf.

3	2	1p. carmine/*drab* (1928)	—	£1300
4		1a. black/*pink*	—	£1500

Nos. 3/4 were also used for fiscal purposes. Manuscript cancellations must be assumed to be fiscal, unless on cover showing other evidence of postal use.

POSTAL FISCAL

Rajadhiraj Umaid Singh, 1932–1947
Rajadhiraj Sudarshan Deo, 1947–1971

F 1

1932–47. Typo. P 11, 11½ or 12.

F1	F 1	1a. red (*shades*)	75·00	£250
		a. Pin-perf 7 (1947)	—	£350
		ab. *Tête-bêche* (horiz pair)	—	£1000

Nos. F1/F1a were used for both fiscal and postal purposes. Manuscript cancellations must be assumed to be fiscal, unless on cover showing other evidence of postal use. The design was first issued for fiscal purposes in 1898.

Shahpura became part of Rajasthan by 15 April 1948.

SIRMOOR

PRICES FOR STAMPS ON COVER TO 1945
The stamps of Sirmoor are very rare used on cover.

Raja Shamsher Parkash, 1886–1898

1 (1 pice)

2

3 Raja Shamsher Parkash

1878 (June)–**80.** Litho. P 11½.

1	1	1p. pale green	38·00	£475
2		1p. blue (on *laid* paper) (1880)	9·00	£225
		a. Imperf between (pair)	£650	
		b. Imperf (pair)	£650	

(Litho at Calcutta)

1892. Thick wove paper. P 11½.

3	2	1p. yellow-green	1·75	1·75
		a. Imperf between (vert pair)	90·00	
		b. Imperf between (horiz pair)	£275	
		c. Deep green	1·25	1·25
		ca. Imperf between (vert pair)	90·00	£100
4		1p. blue	3·00	1·75
		a. Imperf between (vert pair)	80·00	90·00
		b. Imperf between (horiz pair)	80·00	90·00
		c. Imperf vert (horiz pair)	80·00	
		d. Imperf (pair)	90·00	

These were originally made as reprints, about 1891, to supply collectors, but there being very little demand for them they were put into use. The design was copied (including the perforations) from an illustration in a dealer's catalogue. Typographed forgeries, particularly of the perforation varieties, are frequently found.

A

B

C

D

There were seven printings of stamps as T **3**, all in sheets of 70 (10×7) and made up from groups of transfers which can be traced through minor varieties.

Printings I to V and VII of the 3p. and 6p. are as Types A and C (both with large white dots evenly spaced between the ends of the upper and lower inscriptions).

Printing VI is as Type B (small white dots and less space) and Type D (large white dots unevenly positioned between the inscriptions).

(Litho Waterlow)

1885–96. P 14 to 15.

5	3	3p. chocolate (A)	2·25	1·25
		a. Brown (B) (1896)	40	50
6		3p. orange (A) (1888)	3·50	1·25
		a. Type B (1896)	1·00	40
		ab. Imperf (pair)	£850	
7		6p. blue-green (C)	7·00	5·00
		a. Green (C) (1888)	3·50	2·25
		b. Bright green (C) (1891)	90·00	90·00
		c. Deep green (C) (1894)	75	60
		d. Yellowish green (D) (1896)	40	1·50
8		1a. bright blue	6·00	6·50
		a. Dull blue (1891)	16·00	9·00
		b. Steel-blue (1891)	£130	£130
		c. Grey-blue (1894)	2·50	1·50
		d. Slate-blue (1896)	50	3·00
9		2a. pink	10·00	18·00
		a. Carmine (1894)	3·50	3·00
		b. Rose-red (1896)	3·25	4·00

Composition of the various printings was as follows:

Printing I	— Nos. 5, 7, 8 and 9
Printing II	— Nos. 6 and 7*a*
Printing III	— Nos. 6, 7*b* and 8*a*
Printing IV	— Nos. 5, 6, 7*a*, and 8*b*
Printing V	— Nos. 6, 7*c*, 8*c* and 9*a*
Printing VI	— Nos. 5*a*, 6a, 7*d*, 8*d* and 9*b*
Printing VII	— Only exists overprinted 'On S. S. S.' (Nos. 78/81).

4 Indian Elephant

5 Raja Shamsher Parkash

(Recess Waterlow & Sons)

1894–99. P 12 to 15 and compounds.

22	4	3p. orange-brown	7·50	40
23		6p. green	3·75	1·00
		a. Imperf between (vert pair)	£4250	
24		1a. blue	12·00	3·25
25		2a. rose	11·00	3·50
26		3a. yellow-green	45·00	75·00
27		4a. deep green	32·00	45·00
28		8a. deep blue	40·00	50·00
29		1r. vermilion	65·00	£120
22/29 *Set of 8*			£190	£275

Raja Surindra Bikram Parkash, 1898–1911

(Recess Waterlow & Sons)

1899. P 13 to 15.

30	5	3a. yellow-green	11·00	22·00
31		4a. deep green	12·00	30·00
32		8a. deep blue	14·00	38·00
33		1r. vermilion	21·00	75·00
30/33 *Set of 4*			50·00	£150

OFFICIAL STAMPS

NOTE. The varieties occurring in the machine-printed 'On S.S.S.' overprints may, of course, also be found in the inverted and double overprints, and many of them are known thus.

Roman figures denote printings of the basic stamps (Nos. 6/9*b*). Where more than one printing was overprinted the prices quoted are for the commonest.

I. MACHINE-PRINTED

On
S. S.
S.
(11)

1890. Optd with T **11**.

(a) In black

50	3	6p. green (C)	£2250	£2250
		a. Stop before first 'S'		
51		2a. pink	£120	£375
		a. Stop before first 'S'	£275	

(b) In red

52	3	6p. green (C)	38·00	4·25
		a. Stop before first 'S'	80·00	25·00
53		1a. bright blue	£110	38·00
		a. Stop before first 'S'	£250	90·00
		b. Opt inverted	£2250	£1200

(c) Doubly optd in red and in black

53*c*	3	6p. green (C)	£1800	£1800
		ca. Stop before first 'S'	£4000	£4000

Nos. 50, 52 and 53*c* are from Printing II and the remainder from Printing I.

On
S. S.
S.
(12)

On
S. S.
S.
(13)

1891. Optd with T **12**.

(a) In black

54	3	3p. orange (A)	8·00	50·00
		a. Opt inverted	£900	
55		6p. green (C)	1·75	1·75
		a. Opt double	£300	
		b. No stop after lower 'S'	28·00	35·00
		c. Raised stop before lower 'S'	£300	£250
56		1a. bright blue	£650	£750
57		2a. pink	35·00	95·00

(b) In red

58	3	6p. green (C)	45·00	3·00
		a. Opt inverted	£425	£325
		b. Opt double	£425	£350
59		1a. bright blue	40·00	50·00
		a. Opt inverted	†	£900
		b. Opt double	†	£850
		c. No stop after lower 'S'	£325	£375

(c) In black and red

59*d*	3	6p. green (C)	£1800	

Nos. 54/55, 58 and 59*d* are from Printing II and the others from Printing I.

1892–97. Optd with T **13**.

(a) In black

No.	Type	Description	Unused	Used
60	3	3p. orange (A)	1·00	50
		a. Type B	5·00	60
		b. Opt inverted	£425	
		c. First 'S' inverted and stop raised	7·50	6·50
		d. No stop after lower 'S'	5·00	5·00
		e. Raised stop after second 'S'	65·00	22·00
		f. Vertical pair, Types **12** and **13**	£400	
61		6p. green (C)	15·00	2·50
		a. Deep green (C)	4·25	50
		b. First 'S' inverted and stop raised	70·00	22·00
		c. Raised stop after second 'S'	70·00	20·00
		d. No stop after lower 'S'	80·00	27·00
		e. Opt double	£900	
62		1a. steel-blue		
		a. Grey-blue	23·00	1·00
		b. Opt double	£650	
		c. First 'S' inverted and stop raised	80·00	10·00
		d. No stop after lower 'S'	£375	£140
		e. Raised stop after second 'S'	£140	12·00
63		2a. pink	23·00	28·00
		a. Carmine	10·00	7·00
		b. Opt inverted	£1500	£1500
		c. First 'S' inverted and stop raised	55·00	40·00
		d. No stop after lower 'S'	55·00	40·00
		e. Raised stop after second 'S'	£300	£180

(b) In red

No.	Type	Description	Unused	Used
64	3	6p. green (C)	12·00	50
		a. Bright green (C)	18·00	2·50
		b. Opt inverted	£250	£160
		c. First 'S' inverted and stop raised	40·00	5·00
		d. Vertical pair, Types **12** and **13**	£400	£400
65		1a. bright blue	26·00	6·50
		a. Steel-blue	28·00	1·00
		b. Opt inverted	£550	£375
		c. Opt double	£475	
		d. First 'S' inverted and stop raised	70·00	8·00
		e. No stop after lower 'S'	70·00	8·50

(c) Doubly overprinted in black and red

No.	Type	Description	Unused	Used
65*f*	3	6p. bright green (C)	—	£1800
		fa. Green (C). Red opt inverted	†	£2750

The printings used for this issue were as follows:

Printing I — Nos. 63 and 65
Printing II — Nos. 60, 64 and 65*fa*
Printing III — Nos. 60, 64*a* and 65*f*
Printing IV — Nos. 61, 62, 64 and 65*a*
Printing V — Nos. 60, 61*a*, 62*a* and 63*a*
Printing VI — No. 60a

There are seven settings of this overprint, the first of which was a composite setting of 20 (10×2), with examples of T **12** in the upper row. The inverted 'S' and the missing stop occur in the third and sixth settings with the latter also including the raised stop after second 'S'.

On S. S. S. (14) — On S. S. S. (15)

1896–97. Optd as T **14**.

No.	Type	Description	Unused	Used
66	3	3p. orange (B) (1897)	19·00	1·25
		a. Comma after first 'S'	70·00	35·00
		b. Opt inverted		
		c. Opt double	†	£1000
67		6p. deep green (C)	8·00	60
		a. Yellowish green (D)	—	11·00
		b. Comma after first 'S'	60·00	20·00
		c. Comma after lower 'S'	£400	24·00
		d. 'S' at right inverted	£400	80·00
68		1a. grey-blue	16·00	1·25
		a. Comma after first 'S'	75·00	22·00
		b. Comma after lower 'S'	£425	26·00
		c. 'S' at right inverted	—	90·00
69		2a. carmine (1897)	17·00	15·00
		a. Comma after first 'S'	£130	£130

Nos. 66 and 67*a* are from Printing VI and the remainder from Printing V.

There are four settings of this overprint, (1) 23 mm high, includes the comma after lower 'S'; (2) and (3) 25 mm high, with variety, comma after first 'S'; (4) 25 mm high, with variety, 'S' at right inverted.

1898 (Nov). Optd with T **15**.

No.	Type	Description	Unused	Used
70	3	6p. deep green (C)	£450	25·00
		a. Yellowish green (D)	£425	14·00
		b. Small 'S' at right	£700	28·00
		c. Comma after lower 'S'	—	80·00
		d. Lower 'S' inverted and stop raised	—	85·00
71		1a. grey-blue	£475	28·00
		a. Small 'S' at right	£750	65·00
		b. Small 'S' without stop	—	£300

No. 70*a* is from Printing VI and the others Printing V.

There are two settings of this overprint. Nos. 70b and 71a/71b occur in the first setting, and Nos. 70c/70d in the second setting.

On S. S. S. (16) — On S. S. S. (17)

1899 (July). Optd with T **16**.

No.	Type	Description	Unused	Used
72	3	3p. orange (B)	£600	16·00
73		6p. deep green (C)	—	35·00

No. 72 is from Printing VI and No. 73 from Printing V.

1899 (Dec)–**1900**. Optd as T **17**.

No.	Type	Description	Unused	Used
74	3	3p. orange (B)	—	20·00
		a. Raised stop after lower 'S'	†	£110
		b. Comma after first 'S'	†	£475
		c. No stop after first 'S'	†	£300
75		6p. deep green (C)	—	20·00
		a. Yellowish green (D)	†	15·00
		b. Raised stop after lower 'S'	†	£110
		c. Comma after first 'S'	†	£425
		d. No stop after first 'S'	†	£400
76		1a. bright blue	†	£400
		a. Grey-blue	†	32·00
		b. Slate-blue	—	38·00
		c. Raised stop after lower 'S'	†	£180
		d. Comma after first 'S'	†	£500
		e. No stop after first 'S'	†	£350
77		2a. carmine	—	£225
		a. Raised stop after lower 'S'	†	£750

There are two settings of this overprint: (1) 22 mm high, with raised stop variety; (2) 23 mm high, with 'comma' and 'no stop' varieties.

The printings used for this issue were as follows:

Printing I — No. 76
Printing V — Nos. 75, 76*a* and 77
Printing VI — Nos. 74, 75*a* and 76*b*

On S. S. S. (18) — On S S S (19)

(Optd by Waterlow & Sons)

1900. Optd with T **18**.

No.	Type	Description	Unused	Used
78	3	3p. orange	3·75	12·00
79		6p. green	2·00	60
80		1a. blue	35	70
81		2a. carmine	6·50	70·00

Nos. 78/81 were from Printing VII which was not issued without the overprint.

II. HANDSTAMPED

The words 'On' and each letter 'S' struck separately (except for T **22** which was applied at one operation).

1894. Handstamped with T **19**.

(a) In black

No.	Type	Description	Unused	Used
82	3	3p. orange (A)	3·25	3·75
		a. 'On' only	£100	
83		6p. green (C)	8·50	8·50
		a. Deep green (C)	21·00	23·00
		b. 'On' only	85·00	85·00
84		1a. bright blue	£140	90·00
		a. Dull blue	42·00	42·00
		b. Steel-blue		
		c. Grey-blue	55·00	45·00
		d. 'On' only	—	£130
85		2a. carmine	35·00	24·00
		a. 'On' only	£150	

(b) In red

No.	Type	Description	Unused	Used
86	3	6p. green (C)	£200	£225
86*a*		1a. grey-blue	£600	£600

The printings used for this issue were as follows:

Printing I — No. 84
Printing III — No. 84*a*
Printing IV — Nos. 83, 84*b* and 86
Printing V — Nos. 82, 83*a*, 84*c*, 85 and 86*a*

1896. Handstamped with letters similar to those of T **13**, with stops, but irregular.

No.	Type	Description	Unused	Used
87	3	3p. orange (A)	£140	£100
		a. Type B		
88		6p. green (C)		
		a. Deep green (C)	£110	85·00
		b. 'On' omitted	£225	
88*c*		1a. grey-blue	£170	£170
89		2a. carmine	£350	

Printings used for this issue were as follows:

Printing II — No. 88
Printing III — No. 87
Printing IV — No. 88
Printing V — Nos. 87, 88*a*, 88*c* and 89
Printing VI — No. 87a

1897. Handstamped with letters similar to those of T **14**, with stops, but irregular.

No.	Type	Description	Unused	Used
90	3	3p. orange (B)	24·00	28·00
91		6p. deep green (C)	£110	£120
		a. 'On' only	—	£140
92		1a. grey-blue	£550	£550
		a. 'On' only	—	£140
93		2a. carmine	£275	£275

No. 90 was from Printing VI and the remainder from Printing V.

1897. Handstamped with letters similar to those of T **16**, with stops, but irregular.

No.	Type	Description	Unused	Used
93*a*	3	6p. deep green (C)	£400	£325

No. 93*a* is from Printing V.

ON S S S (20) — on S S S (21)

1896.

(a) Handstamped with T **20**

No.	Type	Description	Unused	Used
94	3	3p. orange (A)	£140	£150
95		2a. carmine	£150	£160

(b) Handstamped with T **21**

No.	Type	Description	Unused	Used
96	3	3p. orange (A)	£325	£350
97		6p. bright green (C)		
98		1a. bright blue	£550	
		a. Dull blue		
98*b*		2a. carmine	£550	

No. 98 comes from Printing 1, No. 98*a* from Printing III, No. 97 possibly from Printing IV and the remainder from Printing V.

On S S S (22) — On S S S (23)

(c) Handstamped with T **22**

No.	Type	Description	Unused	Used
99	3	3p. orange (B)	£200	
100		6p. deep green	£325	
101		1a. grey-blue	£375	
101*a*		2a. carmine	£550	

No. 99 is from Printing VI and the others from Printing V.

1899. Handstamped with T **23**.

No.	Type	Description	Unused	Used
102	3	3p. orange (A)	—	£375
		a. Type B	32·00	7·00
103		6p. green (C)		
		a. Deep green (C)	48·00	30·00
		b. Yellowish green (D)	22·00	18·00
104		1a. bright blue	—	£300
		a. Grey-blue	75·00	65·00
105		2a. pink		
		a. Carmine	£100	48·00
		b. Rose-red	£130	80·00
		c. 'On' only	—	£190

Printings used for this issue were as follows:

Printing I — Nos. 104 and 105
Printing IV — Nos. 102 and 103
Printing V — Nos. 102, 103*a*, 104*a* and 105*a*
Printing VI — Nos. 102a, 103*b* and 105*b*

On S S S (24)

1901 (?). Handstamped with T **24**.

No.	Type	Description	Unused	Used
105*d*	3	6p. yellowish green (D)	—	£800

From Printing VI.

III. MIXED MACHINE-PRINTED AND HANDSTAMPED

1896.

(i) Handstamped 'On' as in T **19**, *and machine-printed opt T* **13** *complete*

No.	Type	Description	Unused	Used
106	3	6p. green (C)	—	£800

(ii) Handstamped opt as T **14**, *and machine-printed opt T* **13** *complete*

No.	Type	Description	Unused	Used
107	3	6p. deep green (C)		

No. 106 is from Printing IV and No. 107 from Printing V.

Various other types of these handstamps are known to exist, but in the absence of evidence of their authenticity we do not list them.

Stamps of T **4** (Nos. 22/25) exist with overprints similar to T **13** and T **22**. These are believed to have been produced for sale to collectors. The 6p. value is known in vertical pair, imperforate between (as No. 23a), with the former overprint. (*Price, £2000, unused*).

The stamps of Sirmoor have been obsolete since 1 April 1902.

SORUTH

PRICES FOR STAMPS ON COVER TO 1945

Nos. 1/2	*from* × 5
Nos. 4/4*a*	—
Nos. 5/7	*from* × 1
No. 8	*from* × 3
No. 9	*from* × 1
Nos. 10/11	*from* × 5
No. 11*e*	*from* × 1
No. 12	*from* × 4
No. 13	*from* × 5
Nos. 14/15	*from* × 3
Nos. 16/24	*from* × 20
Nos. 33/36	*from* × 50
Nos. 37/38	*from* × 10
Nos. 40/41	*from* × 50
Nos. 42/57	*from* × 10
Nos. O1/O13	*from* × 20
No. 58	*from* × 15
No. 59	*from* × 6
No. 60	*from* × 10
No. 61	*from* × 6

The name 'Saurashtra', corrupted to 'Sorath' or 'Soruth', was originally used for all the territory later known as Kathiawar. Strictly speaking the name should have been applied only to a portion of Kathiawar including the state of Junagadh. As collectors have known these issues under the heading of 'Soruth' for so long, we retain the name.

GUM. Nos. 1/47 of Soruth were issued without gum.

JUNAGADH

Nawab Mahabat Khan II, 1851–1882
(Currency 40 dokras or 16 annas = 1 koree)

1 (='Saurashtra Post 1864–65')

1864 (Nov). Handstamped in water-colour. Imperf.

1 **1** (1a.) black/*azure to grey* (laid) £850 £150
a. *Tête-bêche* (horiz pair) † £16000
2 (1a.) black/*azure to grey* (wove) — £300
3 (1a.) black/*cream* (laid) † £3500
4 (1a.) black/*cream* (wove) — £1600

ILLUSTRATIONS. Types **2** to **11** are shown actual size.

2 (**1a.**) (Devanagri numeral)

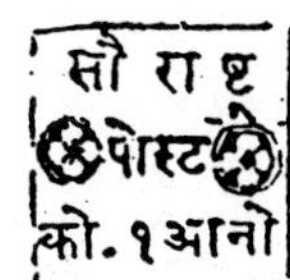

3 (**1a.**) (Gujarati numeral)

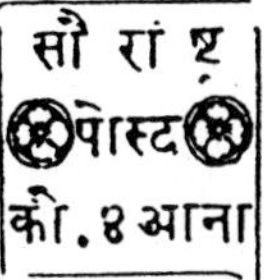

4 (**4a.**) (Devanagri numeral)

5 (**4a.**) (Gujarati numeral)

Differences in first character of bottom line on Nos. 8/*a*:

Type A 'ka' (correct)

Type B 'u' (error)

(Typeset Nitiprakash Ptg Press, Junagadh)

1868 (June)–**75**. Designs as Types **2** to **5**. Imperf.

A. Inscriptions in Gujarati characters. Wove paper

5 1a. black/*yellowish* † £35000

B. Inscriptions in Devanagri characters (as in the illustrations)

I. Accents over first letters in top and bottom lines. Wove paper

6 1a. red/*green* † £12000
7 1a. red/*blue* † £15000
7*a* 1a. red/*yellow* † £22000
8 1a. black/*pink* (first character in bottom line as Type A) £3250 £275
a. First character in bottom line as Type B (R. 1/3) † £6500
b. Bottom line with accent over second letter £6500 £1100
9 2a. black/*yellow* (1869) † £21000

II. Accents over second letters in top and bottom lines

(a) Wove paper

10 **2** 1a. black/*pink* (1869) £1000 £140
a. Printed both sides † £3750
b. First two characters in last word of bottom line omitted (R. 4/1) — £1400
c. *Se-tenant* pair. Nos. 8/10 † £2750

(b) Laid paper

11 **2** 1a. black/*azure* (1870) £190 15·00
a. Final character in both top and bottom lines omitted (R. 1/1) — £325
b. First two characters in last word of bottom line omitted (R. 4/1) — £250
c. Doubly printed † £1300
d. *Se-tenant* pair. Nos. 11/12 £1000 £325
11*e* 1a. black/*white* † £14000
12 **3** 1a. black/*azure* (1870) £550 38·00
a. Printed both sides † £1600
b. Final character in bottom line omitted (R. 1/1) £1400 £250
c. Accent omitted from last word in bottom line (R. 5/2, 5/4) — £180
d. Large numeral (R. 4/1) £1600 £325
e. First character in middle line omitted (R. 2/4) — £650
f. Central two characters in middle line omitted (R. 2/4) — £1100
13 1a. red/*white* (1875) 45·00 50·00
a. First two characters in bottom line omitted (R. 5/1) £200 £275
14 **5** 4a. black/*white* £550 £800
a. First two characters in last word of bottom line omitted (R. 4/1) £2500
b. Final character in bottom line omitted (R. 5/2) £6500
15 **4** 4a. black/*white* £350 £500
a. Final character in bottom line omitted (R. 1/1) £1100

The settings of Nos. 5/7*a* are unknown.

Nos. 10/15, and probably Nos. 8/9, were printed in sheets of 20 (4×5). The same type was used throughout, but changes occurred as the loose type was amended.

Specialists now recognise four main settings for the 1a., one of which was amended for the 2a. and another for the 4a. There are sub-settings within some of these groups:

1a. Setting I (pink wove paper) (No. 8 with No. 8a at R. 1/3)
Setting II (pink wove paper) (No. 8)
Setting III (pink wove paper) (No. 10)
Setting IV (Devanagri numerals only) (pink wove paper) (Nos. 10/10b)
Setting IVA (Devanagri numerals only) (azure vertical laid paper) (Nos. 11, 11b)
Setting IVB (Devanagri and Gujarati numerals mixed) (azure horizontal laid paper) (Nos. 11/11a, 11d, 12)
Setting IVC (Devanagri and Gujarati numerals mixed) (azure or white vertical laid paper) (Nos. 11, 11c/11d, 11e, 12/12b, 12e/12f)
Setting IVD (Devanagri and Gujarati numerals mixed) (azure vertical laid paper) (Nos. 11, 11d, 12, 12d)
Setting IVE (Gujarati numerals only) (white vertical laid paper) (Nos. 13/13a)
2a. Setting I (probably derived from 1a. Setting II) (yellow wove paper) (No. 9)
4a. Setting IA (Gujarati numerals only) (white vertical laid paper) (Nos. 14/14a)
Setting IB (Devanagri numerals only) (white horizontal laid paper) (No. 15)
Setting IC (Devanagri numerals only) (white vertical laid paper) (Nos. 15/15a)
Setting ID (only Gujarati numerals so far identified) (white vertical laid paper) (Nos. 14, 14b)

Settings IVA/D of the 1a. were subsequently adapted to form settings IA/D of the 4a.

Official imitations, consisting of 1a. carmine-red on white wove and white laid, 1a. black on blue wove, 4a. black on white wove, 4a. black on blue wove, 4a. red on white laid–all imperforate; 1a. carmine-red on white laid, 1a. black on blue wove, 4a. black on white laid and blue wove–all perforated 12, were made in 1890. Entire sheets of originals have 20 stamps (4×5), the imitations only 4 or 16.

6

7

(Typo Nitiprakash Ptg Press, Junagadh)

1878 (16 Jan)–**86**. Laid paper with the lines wide apart. Imperf

16 **6** 1a. green 1·00 1·25
a. Printed both sides £750 £800
b. Laid lines close together (1886) 1·00 50
17 **7** 4a. vermilion 2·75 1·75
a. Printed both sides £1100
b. Scarlet/bluish 7·50 7·50
18 4a. brown 35·00

Nawab Bahadur Khan III, 1882–1892

1886. P 12.

(a) On toned laid paper with the lines close together

19 **6** 1a. green 50 25
a. Imperf vert (horiz pair) £250
b. Imperf between (vert pair) † £600
c. Imperf horiz (vert pair) † £600
d. Doubly printed † £800
e. Error. Blue £650 £650
f. On bluish white laid paper 3·75 4·75
fa. Imperf between (vert pair) £425 £475
fb. Imperf vert (horiz pair) £375
g. Emerald-green 4·25 2·50
20 **7** 4a. red 3·25 2·75
a. On bluish white laid paper 20·00 26·00
ab. Printed both sides £800
b. Carmine 10·00 9·00
21 4a. brown 48·00

(b) Wove paper

22 **6** 1a. green 4·50 2·50
a. Imperf (pair) £160 £275
b. Error. Blue — £650
c. Imperf horiz (vert pair) £325
23 **7** 4a. red 14·00 20·00
a. Imperf (pair) £475 £650
b. Imperf between (horiz pair) £700
c. Imperf vert (horiz pair) £700
24 4a. brown 48·00

There is a very wide range of colours in both values. The laid paper, on which imperforate printings continued to appear until 1912, is found both vertical and horizontal.

The 1a. was originally issued in sheets of 15 (5×3), but later appeared in sheets of 20 (5×4) with marginal inscriptions. Stamps were sometimes printed in double sheets showing two impressions of the plate printed *tête-bêche* on the same or opposite sides of the paper.

The 4a. was in horizontal strips of five. No. 20 exists as a sheet of ten (5×2), with two impressions of the plate printed *tête-bêche*, and No. 23 in a similar sized sheet but with both impressions upright.

Nawab Rasul Khan 1892–1911
Nawab Mahabat Khan III, 1911–1959
(Indian currency)

Three pies.
ત્રણ પાઇ.
(**8**)

One anna.
એક આનો.
(**9**)

1913 (1 Jan). Surch in Indian currency with T **8** or **9**. P 12.

(a) On toned wove paper

33 **6** 3p. on 1a. emerald-green 25 40
a. Imperf (pair) £475
b. Imperf between (horiz pair) £475
c. Imperf vert (horiz pair) £475
d. Doubly printed £400
e. Imperf between (vert pair) £500
34 **7** 1a. on 4a. red 5·00 18·00
a. Imperf (pair) £1100
b. Capital 'A' in 'Anna' 11·00
c. Surch inverted £1100
d. Imperf between (horiz pair)

(b) On white wove paper

35 **6** 3p. on 1a. emerald-green 25 30
a. Imperf between (vert pair) £600

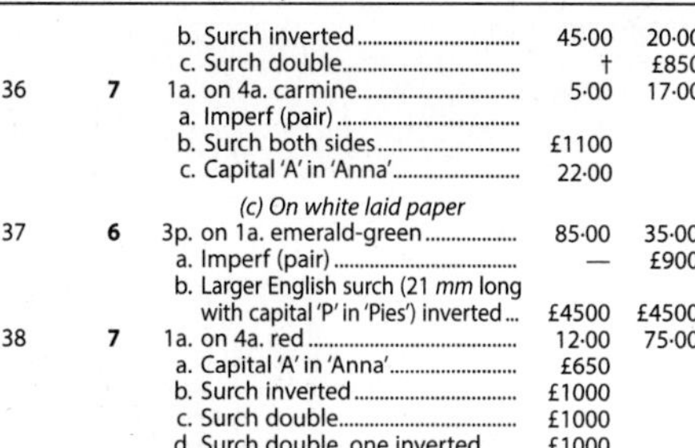

b. Surch inverted 45·00 20·00
c. Surch double † £850
36 **7** 1a. on 4a. carmine 5·00 17·00
a. Imperf (pair)
b. Surch both sides £1100
c. Capital 'A' in 'Anna' 22·00

(c) On white laid paper

37 **6** 3p. on 1a. emerald-green 85·00 35·00
a. Imperf (pair) — £900
b. Larger English surch (21 *mm* long with capital 'P' in 'Pies') inverted £4500 £4500
38 **7** 1a. on 4a. red 12·00 75·00
a. Capital 'A' in 'Anna' £650
b. Surch inverted £1000
c. Surch double £1000
d. Surch double, one inverted £1000

The 1a. surcharge with capital 'A' in 'Anna' comes from a separate setting.

10

11

(Dies eng Thacker & Co, Bombay. Typo Junagadh State Press)

1914 (1 Sept). New plates. Types **6/7** redrawn as Types **10/11**. Wove paper. P 12.

40 **10** 3p. green 3·50 35
a. Imperf (pair) 16·00 55·00
b. Imperf vert (horiz pair) £180
c. Laid paper 7·00 2·50
ca. Imperf (pair) 40·00 80·00
d. Error. Red (imperf) † £4250
41 **11** 1a. red 2·75 3·50
a. Imperf (pair) 38·00 £200
b. Imperf horiz (vert pair) £650
ba. Imperf vert (horiz pair) £650
c. Laid paper £250 £110

12 Nawab Mahabat Khan III

13 Nawab Mahabat Khan III

(Dies eng Popatlal Bhimji Pandya. Typo Junagadh State Press)

1923 (1 Sept). Blurred impression. Laid paper. Pin-perf 12.

42 **12** 1a. red 4·00 17·00

Sheets of 16 stamps (8×2).

This setting was later printed on wove paper, but single examples cannot readily be distinguished from No. 46b.

ત્રણ પાઇ
(**14**)

ત્રણ પાઈ
(**14a**)

1923 (1 Sept). Surch with T **14**.

43 **12** 3p. on 1a. red 8·50 12·00
a. Surch with T **14a** 10·00 15·00

Four stamps in the setting have surch. T **14a**, i.e. with top of last character curved to right.

1923 (Oct). Blurred impression. Wove paper. Pin-perf 12, small holes.

44 **13** 3p. mauve 60 50

Sheets of 16 (4×4).

1924. Clear impression. Wove paper. P 12, large holes.

45 **13** 3p. mauve (1.24) 4·75 35
a. Imperf (pair) £300
46 **12** 1a. red (4.24) 11·00 12·00
a. Imperf (pair) £100
b. Pin perf 4·50 5·50

The first plate of the 3p., which printed No. 44, produced unsatisfactory impressions, so it was replaced by a second plate, producing two panes of 16 (4×4), from which No. 45 comes. Sheets printed from the first plate had very large margins.

The 1a. is also from a new plate, giving a clearer impression. Sheets of 16 stamps (4×4).

1929. Clear impressions. Laid paper. P 12, large holes.

47 **13** 3p. mauve 5·50 7·50
a. Imperf (pair) 7·00 50·00
b. Perf 11 21·00 26·00
ba. Imperf between (horiz pair) 3·50 26·00

Sheets of two panes of 16 (4×4).

The laid paper shows several sheet watermarks.

No. 47ba was intentional to create a 6p. franking required by a rate change in October 1929.

15 Junagadh City

16 Gir Lion

17 Nawab Mahabat Khan III

18 Kathi Horse

(Des Amir Sheikh Mahamadbhai. Litho Indian Security Printing Press, Nasik)

1929 (1 Oct). Inscr 'POSTAGE'. P 14.

49	**15**	3p. black and blackish green	2·00	10
50	**16**	½a. black and deep blue	9·00	10
51	**17**	1a. black and carmine	10·00	2·00
52	**18**	2a. black and dull orange	16·00	2·25
		a. Grey and dull yellow	32·00	2·00
53	**15**	3a. black and carmine	8·00	23·00
54	**16**	4a. black and purple	14·00	45·00
55	**18**	8a. black and yellow-green	32·00	35·00
56	**17**	1r. black and pale blue	32·00	70·00
49/56 *Set of* 8			£110	£160

1935 (1 Jan). As T **17**, but inscr 'POSTAGE AND REVENUE'. P 14.

57	**17**	1a. black and carmine	10·00	1·00

OFFICIAL STAMPS

SARKARI
(O **1**)

1929 (1 Oct). Optd with T O **1**, in vermilion, at Nasik.

O1	**15**	3p. black and blackish green	2·75	15
		a. Red opt	4·25	10
O2	**16**	½a. black and deep blue	6·00	10
		a. Red opt	7·50	40
O3	**17**	1a. black and carmine (No. 51)	4·75	45
		a. Red opt	8·50	15
O4	**18**	2a. black and dull orange	3·25	1·25
		a. Grey and dull yellow	32·00	75
		b. Red opt	30·00	2·75
O5	**15**	3a. black and carmine	1·00	30
		a. Red opt	18·00	2·25
O6	**16**	4a. black and purple	7·00	45
		a. Red opt	32·00	4·00
O7	**18**	8a. black and yellow-green	7·50	3·25
O8	**17**	1r. black and pale blue	10·00	50·00
O1/O8 *Set of* 8			38·00	50·00

SARKARI (O **2**)   SARKARI (O **3**)

1932 (Jan)–**35**. Optd with T O **2**, in red, at Junagadh State Press.

O9	**15**	3a. black and carmine	26·00	18·00
		a. Optd with Type O **3** (1.35)	£160	4·00
O10	**16**	4a. black and purple	30·00	17·00
O11	**18**	8a. black and yellow-green	60·00	18·00
O12	**17**	1r. black and pale blue	70·00	£180
		a. Optd with Type O **3** (1.35)	£325	£250
O9/O12 *Set of* 4			£170	£200

1938. No. 57 optd with T O **1**, in vermilion.

O13	**17**	1a. black and carmine	35·00	2·25
		a. Brown-red opt	21·00	1·50

The state was occupied by Indian troops on 9 November 1947 following the flight of the Nawab to Pakistan.

UNITED STATE OF SAURASHTRA

The administration of Junagadh state was assumed by the Government of India on 9 November 1947. An Executive Council took office on 1 June 1948.

Under the new Constitution of India the United State of Saurashtra was formed on 15 February 1948, comprising 221 former states and estates of Kathiawar, including Jasdan, Morvi, Nawanagar and Wadhwan, but excluding Junagadh. A referendum was held by the Executive Council of Junagadh which then joined the United State on 20 January 1949. It is believed that the following issues were only used in Junagadh.

The following issues were surcharged at the Junagadh State Press.

POSTAGE & REVENUE

ONE ANNA
(**19**)

Postage & Revenue

ONE ANNA
(**20**)

1949. Stamps of 1929 surch.

(a) With T **19** *in red*

58	**16**	1a. on ½a. black and deep blue (5.49)	9·50	6·50
		a. Surch double	†	£750
		b. 'AFNA' for 'ANNA' and inverted 'N' in 'REVENUE'	£5000	£5000
		c. Larger first 'A' in 'ANNA' (R. 2/5)	90·00	60·00

(b) With T **20** *in green*

59	**18**	1a. on 2a. grey and dull yellow (2.49)	21·00	32·00
		a. 'evenue' omitted	—	£1200

No. 58b may have occurred on R. 2/5 with No. 58c being caused by its correction.

A number of other varieties occur on No. 58, including: small 'V' in 'REVENUE' (R. 2/3); small 'N' in 'REVENUE' (R. 2/4, 3/4); small 'E' in 'POSTAGE' (R. 3/2); thick 'A' in 'POSTAGE' (R. 4/4); inverted 'N' in 'REVENUE' and small second 'A' in 'ANNA' (R. 4/5); small 'O' in 'ONE' (R. 5/1); small 'V' and 'U' in 'REVENUE' (R. 6/3); small 'N' in 'ONE' (R. 7/2).

In No. 59 no stop after 'ANNA' is known on R. 1/4, 4/2, 7/4 and 8/3 and small 'N' in 'ONE' on R. 2/4.

21

(Typo Waterlow)

1949 (Sept). Court Fee stamps of Bhavnagar state optd 'SAURASHTRA' and further optd 'U.S.S. REVENUE & POSTAGE' as in T **21**, in black. P 11.

60	**21**	1a. purple	11·00	10·00
		a. 'POSTAGE' omitted (R. 1/2)	£650	£425
		b. Opt double	£550	£650

The Court Fee stamps were in sheets of 80 (8×10) and were overprinted in a setting of 40 applied twice to each sheet.

Minor varieties include small 'S' in 'POSTAGE' (R. 2/1 of the setting); small 'N' in 'REVENUE' (R. 2/7); small 'U' in 'REVENUE' (R. 3/2); small 'V' in 'REVENUE' (R. 3/8, 5/5); and small O' in 'POSTAGE' (R. 4/7).

Various missing stop varieties also occur.

POSTAGE & REVENUE
ONE ANNA
(**22**)

1950 (2 Mar). Stamp of 1929 surch with T **22**.

61	**15**	1a. on 3p. black and blackish green	40·00	75·00
		a. 'P' of 'POSTAGE' omitted (R. 8/1)	£500	£800
		b. 'O' of 'ONE' omitted (R. 6/1)	£750	

Other minor varieties include small second 'A' in 'ANNA' (R. 1/2); small 'S' in 'POSTAGE' with small 'V' in 'REVENUE' (R. 3/4, 6/1) and small 'V' in 'REVENUE' (R. 2/3, 3/1).

OFFICIAL STAMPS

1948 (July–Dec). Nos. O4/O7 surch 'ONE ANNA' (2¼ *mm* high) by Junagadh State Press.

O14	**18**	1a. on 2a. grey and dull yellow (B.)	£30000	26·00
O15	**15**	1a. on 3a. black and carmine (8.48)	£11000	£100
		a. Surch double	†	£7500
O16	**16**	1a. on 4a. black and purple (12.48)	£650	£100
		a. 'ANNE' for 'ANNA' (R. 5/4)	£6000	£700
		b. 'ANNN' for 'ANNA' (R. 7/5)	£6000	£700
O17	**18**	1a. on 8a. black and yellow-green (12.48)	£550	80·00
		a. 'ANNE' for 'ANNA' (R. 5/4)	£5500	£550
		b. 'ANNN' for 'ANNA' (R. 7/5)	£5500	£550

Numerous minor varieties of fount occur in this surcharge.

1948 (Nov). Handstamped 'ONE ANNA' (4 *mm* high).

O18	**17**	1a. on 1r. (No. O8)	£5500	90·00
O19		1a. on 1r. (No. O12)	£1600	85·00
		a. Optd on No. O12a	—	£130

A used copy of No. O12 is known surcharged in black as on Nos. O14/O17. This may have come from a proof sheet.

1949 (Jan). Postage stamps optd with T O **2**, in red.

O20	**15**	3p. black and blackish green	£325	27·00
O21	**16**	½a. black and deep blue	£800	19·00
O22	**18**	1a. on 2a. grey and dull yellow (No. 59)	£140	24·00

Various wrong fount letters occur in the above surcharges.

MANUSCRIPT OVERPRINTS. Nos. 49, 50, 57, 58, 59 and 60 are known with manuscript overprints reading 'Service' or 'SARKARI' (in English or Gujerati script), usually in red. Such provisionals were used at Gadhda and Una between June and December 1949 (*Price from £200 each, used on piece*).

The United State of Saurashtra postal service was incorporated into that of India on 30 March 1950.

TRAVANCORE

PRICES FOR STAMPS ON COVER TO 1945

Nos. 1/77	*from* × 10
Nos. O1/O108	*from* × 15

(16 cash = 1 chuckram; 28 chuckrams = 1 rupee)

'Anchel' or 'Anchal' = Post Office Department.

The stamps of Travancore were valid on mail posted to Cochin.

PRINTERS. All stamps of Travancore were printed by the Stamp Manufactory, Trivandrum, *unless otherwise stated.*

PRINTING METHODS. The dies were engraved on brass from which electrotypes were made and locked together in a forme for printing the stamps. As individual electrotypes became worn they were replaced by new ones and their positions in the forme were sometimes changed. This makes it difficult to plate the early issues. From 1901 plates were made which are characterised by a frame (or 'Jubilee' line) round the margins of the sheets.

Up to the 6 cash of 1910 the dies were engraved by Dharmalingham Asari.

SHADES. We list only the main groups of shades but there are many others in view of the large number of printings and the use of fugitive inks. Sometimes shade variation is noticeable within the same sheet.

Maharaja Rama Varma X, 1885–1924

1 Conch or Chank Shell

1888 (16 Oct). As T **1**, but each value differs slightly. Laid paper. P 12.

1	**1**	1ch. ultramarine (*shades*)	5·00	6·00
2		2ch. red	8·00	12·00
3		4ch. green	25·00	18·00
1/3 *Set of* 3			35·00	32·00

The paper bears a large sheet watermark showing a large conch shell surmounted by 'GOVERNMENT' in large outline letters, in an arch with 'OF TRAVANCORE' at foot in a straight line. Many stamps in the sheet are without watermark.

These stamps on laid paper in abnormal colours are proofs.

The paper is normally horizontally laid, but the 1ch. is also known on vertically laid paper.

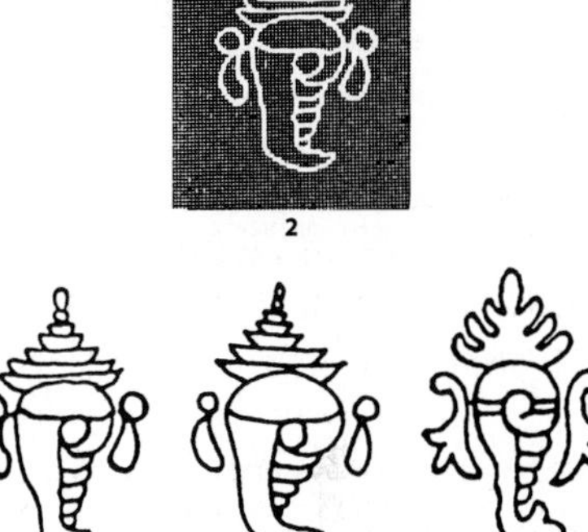

Three forms of watermark T **2**. (*as seen from the back of the stamp*)

WATERMARKS AND PAPERS.

Type A appeared upright on early printings of the 1, 2 and 4ch. values on odd-sized sheets which did not fit the number of shells. Later it was always sideways with 15 mm between the shells on standard-sized sheets of 84 (14×6) containing 60 shells (10×6). It therefore never appears centred on the stamps and it occurs on hand-made papers only.

Type B is similar in shape but can easily be distinguished as it is invariably upright, with 11 mm between the shells, and is well centred on the stamps. It also occurs only on handmade papers. It was introduced in 1904 and from 1914, when Type A was brought back into use, it was employed concurrently until 1924.

Type C is quite different in shape and occurs on machine-made papers. There are two versions. The first, in use from 1924 to 1939, has 84 shells 11 mm apart and is always upright and well centred. The second, introduced in 1929 and believed not to have been used after 1930, has 60 shells (12×5) 15 mm apart and is invariably badly centred so that some stamps in the sheet are without watermark. This second version is normally found upright, but a few sideways watermark varieties are known and listed as Nos. 35g, 37c, O31j and O32i. We do not distinguish between the two versions of Type C in the lists, but stamps known to exist in the second version are indicated in footnotes. The machine-made paper is generally smoother and of more even texture.

WATERMARK VARIETIES. Little attention seems to have been paid to the orientation of the watermark by the printers, with the result that inverted, reversed and inverted and reversed watermarks are frequently encountered. We do not list such varieties.

STAMPS WITHOUT WATERMARK. Some of these were formerly listed but we have now decided to omit them as they do not occur in full sheets. They arise in the following circumstances: (*a*) on sheets with wmk A; (*b*) on sheets with the wide-spaced form of wmk C; and (*c*) on late printings of the pictorial issues of 1939–1946. They are best collected in pairs, with and without watermark.

DATES OF ISSUE. In the absence of more definite information the dates noted usually refer to the first reported date of new printings on different watermarks but many were not noted at the time and the dates of these are indicated by a query. Dated postmarks on single stamps are difficult to find.

1889–1904. Wove paper. Wmk A (upright or sideways). P 12 (sometimes rough).

4	1	½ch. slate-lilac (1894)	3·25	50
		a. Doubly printed	†	£475
		b. *Reddish lilac*	75	25
		ba. Imperf between (vert pair)	£500	£500
		bb. Doubly printed	†	£475
		c. *Purple* (1899)	1·50	25
		ca. Doubly printed	†	£475
		d. *Dull purple* (1904)	1·50	25
5	5	¾ch. black (14.3.01)	2·00	1·40
6	1	1ch. ultramarine	1·50	15
		a. *Tête-bêche* (pair)	£4000	£3000
		b. Doubly printed	†	£650
		c. Imperf vert (horiz pair)	†	£700
		d. Imperf between (vert pair)	†	£650
		e. *Pale ultramarine* (1892)	3·00	20
		f. *Violet-blue* (1901)	3·75	40
7		2ch. salmon (1890)	4·00	1·00
		a. *Rose* (1891)	3·50	30
		ab. Imperf (pair)	†	£800
		b. *Pale pink* (1899)	3·00	35
		ba. Imperf between (vert pair)	£200	
		bb. Doubly printed	£300	
		c. *Red* (1904)	3·00	15
		ca. Imperf between (horiz pair)	£550	£550
8		4ch. green	3·25	70
		a. *Yellow-green* (1901)	2·50	55
		b. *Dull green* (1904)	7·00	1·00
		ba. Doubly printed	†	£700

Nos. 6, 6d, 7, 7c, 8 and 8a occur with the watermark upright and sideways. No. 7a is known only with the watermark upright. The remainder exist only with the watermark sideways.

The sheet sizes were as follows:

½ch. 56 (14×4) except for No. 4d which was 84 (14×6), initially without border, later with border.

¾ch. 84 (14×6) with border.

1ch. No. 6, 80 (10×8) and later 84 (14×6) without border and then with border; No. 6d, 96 (16×6); No. 6e, 84 (14×6) with border.

2ch. No. 7, 80 (10×8); No. 7a, 70 (10×7); Nos, 7b, 7c, 60 (10×6).

4ch. No. 8, 60 (10×6); Nos. 8a/8b, 84 (14×6) with border.

After 1904 all stamps in Types **3** to **8** were in standard-sized sheets of 84 (14×6) with border.

For later printings watermarked Type A, see Nos. 23/30.

1904–20. Wmk B, upright (centred). P 12, sometimes rough.

9	3	4ca. pink (11.08)	30	10
		a. Imperf between (vert pair)	£475	£475
10	1	6ca. chestnut (2.10)	30	10
		a. Imperf between (horiz pair)	†	£400
11		½ch. reddish lilac	2·25	10
		a. *Reddish violet* (6.10)	2·25	10
		ab. Doubly printed	†	£425
		b. *Lilac*	2·00	30
		c. 'CHUCRRAM' (R. 5/6)	13·00	6·00
		d. Imperf horiz (vert pair)	†	£375
		e. Printed both sides	†	£425
12	4	10ca. pink (1920)	42·00	5·50
13	5	¾ch. black	2·50	25
14	1	1ch. bright blue		
		a. *Blue*	5·50	1·00
		b. *Deep blue*	5·00	75
		c. *Indigo* (8.10)	1·00	10
		d. *Chalky blue* (1912)	6·00	1·00
15		1¼ch. claret (*shades*) (10.14)	55	55
		a. Imperf between (horiz pair)	£550	£550
16		2ch. salmon	23·00	7·00
		a. *Red* (8.10)	75	10
17	6	3ch. violet (11.3.11)	2·75	20
		a. Imperf between (vert pair)	£475	£375
		b. Imperf between (vert strip of 3)	†	£425
18	1	4ch. dull green	26·00	10·00
		a. *Slate-green*	4·50	45
19	7	7ch. claret (1916)	2·75	1·75
		a. Error. Carmine-red	—	50·00
20	8	14ch. orange-yellow (1916)	2·75	3·25
		a. Imperf vert (horiz strip of 3)	£750	

¼ (9)   1 C (10)

1906. Surch as T **9**. Wmk B.

21	1	¼ on ½ch. reddish lilac	1·25	30
		a. *Reddish violet*	1·25	20
		b. *Lilac*	2·25	50
		c. 'CHUCRRAM' (R. 5/6)	9·00	5·50
		d. Surch inverted	£130	75·00
22		⅜ on ½ch. reddish lilac	1·25	35
		a. *Reddish violet*	1·00	35
		b. *Lilac*	1·75	50
		c. 'CHUCRRAM' (R. 5/6)	9·50	7·00
		d. Surch inverted	—	£110
		e. Surch double		
		f. '8' omitted	—	65·00

1914–22. Reversion to wmk A (sideways). P 12 (sometimes rough).

23	3	4ca. pink (1915)	8·00	60
24	4	5ca. olive-bistre (30.10.21)	80	40
		a. Imperf between (horiz pair)	75·00	85·00
		b. Imperf between (horiz strip of 3)	£190	£200
		c. 'TRAVANCOPE' (R. 6/13)	30·00	18·00
25	1	6ca. orange-brown (2.15)	10·00	40
26		½ch. reddish violet (12.14)	4·50	75
		a. 'CHUCRRAM' (R. 5/6)	23·00	6·50
		b. Imperf between (horiz pair)	£375	
27	4	10ca. pink (26.10.21)	40	10
28	1	1ch. grey-blue (5.22)	24·00	4·50
		a. *Deep blue*	22·00	4·50
29		1¼ch. claret (12.19)	24·00	1·25
		a. Imperf between (horiz pair)	†	£550
30	6	3ch. reddish lilac (8.22)	30·00	1·50

1921 (Mar). Surch as T **10**. Wmk A (sideways).

31	3	1c. on 4ca. pink	15	20
		a. Surch inverted	45·00	22·00
		b. On wmk B (upright)		
32	1	5c. on 1ch. grey-blue (R.)	1·00	10
		a. *Deep blue*	1·00	10
		b. Stamp printed both sides		
		c. Imperf between (vert pair)	†	£425
		d. Surch inverted	13·00	8·50
		e. Surch double	£120	90·00
		f. On wmk B (upright). *Deep blue*.	38·00	27·00
		fa. Surch inverted	†	£200

ALBINO OVERPRINT VARIETIES. Stamps with overprint double, one albino are frequently found in the provisional and official issues of Travancore, and are only worth a small premium over the normal prices.

Maharaja Bala Rama Varma XI, 1924–1971

1924–39. Wmk C. Machine-made paper. P 12.

33	4	5ca. olive-bistre (18.6.25)	11·00	3·00
		a. Imperf between (horiz pair)	£250	
		b. 'TRAVANCOPE' (R. 6/13)	—	30·00
34		5ca. chocolate (1930)	3·75	60
		a. Imperf between (horiz pair)	50·00	
		b. Imperf between (vert pair)	†	£375
35	1	6ca. brown-red (3.24)	4·25	10
		a. Imperf between (horiz pair)	32·00	48·00
		b. Imperf between (vert pair)	£250	£250
		c. Printed both sides	50·00	
		d. Perf 12½	5·00	50
		e. Perf comp of 12 and 12½	6·50	4·00
		f. Perf 12½×11	—	£200
		g. Wmk sideways	—	35·00
36		½ch. reddish violet (date?)	5·00	5·50
		a. 'CHUCRRAM' (R. 5/6)	38·00	
37	4	10ca. pink (8.24)	2·50	10
		a. Imperf between (horiz pair)	£160	£170
		b. Imperf between (vert pair)	35·00	48·00
		c. Wmk sideways (16.9.28)	—	10·00
38	5	¾ch. black (4.10.32)	11·00	1·00
39		¾ch. mauve (16.11.32)	75	10
		a. Imperf between (horiz pair)	†	£350
		ab. Imperf between (vert pair)	†	£375
		b. Perf 12½ (8.37)	18·00	70
		ba. Imperf between (horiz pair)	£225	
		c. Perf comp of 12 and 12½	23·00	9·50
		ca. Imperf between (horiz pair)	£325	
40		¾ch. reddish violet (1939)	7·00	1·25
		a. Perf 12½	7·00	50
		b. Perf comp of 12 and 12½	11·00	2·50
		c. Perf 11	£375	£170
		d. Perf comp of 12 and 11	—	£170
		e. Perf 12½×11	—	£190
41	1	1ch. slate-blue (8.26)	3·00	30
		a. *Indigo*	5·50	20
		b. Imperf between (horiz pair)	†	£425
		c. Imperf between (vert pair)	†	£425
		d. Perf 12½	11·00	2·75
42		1½ch. rose (1932)	2·75	10
		a. Imperf between (horiz strip of 3)	£375	
		b. Perf 12½	23·00	2·75
		c. Perf comp of 12 and 12½	—	75·00
43		2ch. carmine-red (4.6.29)	3·00	30
44	6	3ch. violet (4.25)	7·00	15
		a. Imperf between (vert pair)	£100	£120
		b. Wmk sideways	—	75·00
		c. Perf 12½	—	12·00
		d. Perf comp of 12 and 12½	—	70·00
45	1	4ch. grey-green (5.4.34)	5·00	45
46	7	7ch. claret (1925)	15·00	2·00
		a. Doubly printed	†	£800
		b. *Carmine-red* (date?)	65·00	55·00
		c. *Brown-purple* (1932)	22·00	7·00
		ca. Perf 12½	9·00	22·00
		cb. Perf comb of 12 and 12½	9·00	22·00
46d	8	14ch. orange-yellow (date?)	48·00	
		da. Perf 12½	£275	

It is believed that the 12½ perforation and the perf 12 and 12½ compound were introduced in 1937 and that the 11 perforation came later, probably in 1939.

The 5ca. chocolate, 6ca., 10ca. and 3ch. also exist on the wide-spaced watermark (60 shells to the sheet of 84).

11 Sri Padmanabha Shrine

12 State Chariot

13 Maharaja Bala Rama Varma XI

(Des M. R. Madhawan Unnithan. Plates by Calcutta Chromotype Co. Typo Stamp Manufactory, Trivandrum)

1931 (6 Nov). Coronation. Cream or white paper. Wmk C. P 11½, 12.

47	11	6ca. black and green	1·60	1·75
		a. Imperf between (horiz pair)	£180	£250
48	12	10ca. black and ultramarine	1·25	70
		a. Imperf between (vert pair)	†	£900
49	13	3ch. black and purple	2·75	3·50
47/49 *Set of 3*			5·00	5·50

1 c (14)   1 C (15)

1932 (14 Jan).

(i) Surch as T **14**

(a) Wmk A (sideways)

50	1	1c. on 1¼ch. claret	15	50
		a. Imperf between (horiz pair)	£250	
		b. Surch inverted	4·25	9·00
		c. Surch double	48·00	60·00
		d. Pair, one without surch	£190	£225
		e. 'c' omitted	60·00	70·00
		f. '1' omitted	60·00	
51		2c. on 1¼ch. claret	15	30
		a. Surch inverted	4·25	7·00
		b. Surch double	42·00	
		c. Surch double, one inverted	95·00	
		d. Surch treble	90·00	
		e. Surch treble, one inverted	75·00	85·00
		f. Pair, one without surch	£170	£180
		g. '2' omitted	55·00	60·00
		h. 'c' omitted	55·00	60·00
		i. Imperf between (horiz pair)	£275	
		j. Imperf between (vert pair)	£275	

(b) Wmk B (upright)

52	1	1c. on 1¼ch. claret	2·75	1·75
		a. Surch inverted	28·00	21·00
		b. Surch double	50·00	
		c. 'c' omitted	85·00	
53		2c. on 1¼ch. claret	6·50	7·50
		a. Imperf between (horiz pair)	£275	

(c) Wmk C

54	1	1c. on 1¼ch. claret	18·00	26·00
		a. Surch inverted	£100	£130
		b. '1' omitted	£140	
		c. 'c' omitted	£140	
55		2c. on 1¼ch. claret	60·00	55·00

(ii) Surch as T **10**. *Wmk B*

56	1	2c. on 1¼ch. claret	5·50	18·00

1932 (5 Mar). Surch as T **15**. Wmk C.

57	4	1c. on 5ca. chocolate	15	15
		a. Imperf between (horiz pair)	£250	
		b. Surch inverted	7·50	10·00
		c. Surch inverted on back only	£150	
		d. Pair, one without surch	£250	
		e. '1' omitted	55·00	
		f. 'c' omitted	—	55·00
		g. 'TRAVANCOPE' (R. 6/13)	13·00	
58		1c. on 5ca. slate-purple	2·50	75
		a. Surch inverted	†	£425
		b. '1' inverted	£140	£140
59		2c. on 10ca. pink	15	15
		a. Imperf between (horiz pair)	£250	
		b. Surch inverted	5·00	9·00
		c. Surch double	32·00	35·00
		d. Surch double, one inverted	£150	£150
		e. Surch double, both inverted	65·00	

No. 58 was not issued without the surcharge.

16 Maharaja Bala Rama Varma XI and Subramania Shrine

17 Sri Padmanabha

18 Mahadeva

19 Kanyakumari

(Plates by Indian Security Printing Press, Nasik. Typo Stamp Manufactory, Trivandrum)

1937 (29 Mar). Temple Entry Proclamation. T **16/19**. Wmk C. P 12.

60	16	6ca. carmine	4·25	1·75
		a. Imperf between (horiz strip of 3).	£700	
		b. Perf 12½	3·25	2·75
		c. Compound perf	85·00	90·00
61	17	12ca. bright blue	6·00	1·25
		a. Perf 12½	7·00	1·25
		ab. Imperf between (vert pair)	£650	
		b. Compound perf	£120	
62	18	1½ch. yellow-green	1·75	3·50
		a. Imperf between (vert pair)	£500	
		b. Perf 12½	42·00	13·00
		c. Compound perf	—	£190
63	19	3ch. violet	7·50	3·00
		a. Perf 12½	8·00	5·00
60/63 *Set of 4*			16·00	8·50

COMPOUND PERFS. This term covers stamps perf compound of 12½ and 11, 12 and 11 or 12 and 12½, and where two or more combinations exist the prices are for the commonest. Such compounds can occur on values which do not exist perf 12 all round.

20 Lake Ashtamudi

21 Maharaja Bala Rama Varma XI

22

23

24 Sri Padmanabha Shrine

25 Cape Comorin

26 Pachipari Reservoir

(Des Nilakantha Pellai. Plates by Indian Security Printing Press, Nasik. Typo Stamp Manufactory, Trivandrum)

1939 (9 Nov). Maharaja's 27th Birthday. Types **20/26**. Wmk C. P 12½.

64 **20** 1ch. yellow-green 13·00 10
a. Imperf between (horiz pair) 45·00
b. Perf 11 18·00 10
ba. Imperf between (vert pair) 75·00 £110
bb. Imperf between (vert strip of 3) 40·00 80·00
c. Perf 12 42·00 3·50
ca. Imperf between (horiz pair) 35·00
cb. Imperf between (vert pair) 80·00 £140
d. Compound perf 50·00 6·00
da. Imperf between (vert pair) £300
65 **21** 1½ch. scarlet 7·00 7·00
a. Doubly printed £700
b. Imperf between (horiz pair) 55·00
c. Imperf between (vert pair) 48·00
d. Perf 11 8·00 42·00
da. Imperf horiz (vert pair) 11·00
e. Perf 12 80·00 9·00
f. Perf 13½ 30·00 £110
g. Compound perf £100 20·00
h. Imperf (pair) 38·00
66 **22** 2ch. orange 12·00 4·50
a. Perf 11 28·00 2·00
b. Perf 12 £200 9·00
c. Compound perf £225 8·00
67 **23** 3ch. brown 13·00 10
a. Doubly printed — £375
b. Imperf between (horiz pair) 70·00 £110
c. Perf 11 30·00 30
ca. Doubly printed 65·00 £100
d. Perf 12 75·00 7·00
da. Imperf between (vert pair) £200 £300
e. Compound perf 90·00 1·50
68 **24** 4ch. red 19·00 40
a. Perf 11 65·00 50
b. Perf 12 70·00 15·00
c. Compound perf £350 £275
69 **25** 7ch. pale blue 17·00 25·00
a. Perf 11 £170 70·00
ab. *Blue* £170 65·00
b. Compound perf £250 80·00
70 **26** 14ch. turquoise-green 8·00 85·00
a. Perf 11 16·00 £170
64/70 *Set of 7* 80·00 £110

27 Maharaja and Aruvikara Falls

2 CASH
(29)

28 Marthanda Varma Bridge, Alwaye

(Des Nilakantha Pellai. Plates by Indian Security Printing Press, Nasik. Typo Stamp Manufactory, Trivandrum)

1941 (20 Oct). Maharaja's 29th Birthday. Types **27/28**. Wmk C. P 12½.

71 **27** 6ca. blackish violet 7·50 10
a. Perf 11 6·50 10
ab. Imperf between (vert pair) 35·00
ac. Imperf horiz (vert pair) 80·00 £110
b. Perf 12 35·00 3·00
ba. Imperf between (horiz pair) 38·00
bb. Imperf between (vert pair) 95·00
bc. Imperf between (vert strip of 3) 40·00
c. Compound perf 14·00 3·50
72 **28** ¾ch. brown 9·50 30
a. Imperf between (vert pair) † £800
b. Perf 11 10·00 20
ba. Imperf between (horiz pair) £375
bb. Imperf between (vert pair) 32·00 75·00
bc. Imperf between (vert strip of 3) 42·00
bd. Block of four imperf between (horiz and vert) £425
c. Perf 12 75·00 15·00
d. Compound perf 20·00 1·10

1943 (17 Sept). Nos. 65, 71 (colour changed) and 72 surch as T **29**. P 12½.

73 2ca. on 1½ch. scarlet 1·75 1·75
a. Imperf between (vert pair) 85·00
b. '2' omitted £500 £500
c. 'CA' omitted £900
d. 'ASH' omitted £900
e. Perf 11 40 60
ea. 'CA' omitted £900
eb. Imperf between (horiz pair) † £475
f. Compound perf 1·25 2·50
fa. Imperf between (vert pair) £300
fb. '2' omitted £500
74 4ca. on ¾ch. brown 7·00 2·25
a. Perf 11 8·00 60
b. Perf 12 — £250
c. Compound perf 10·00 1·50
75 8ca. on 6ca. scarlet 5·00 30
a. Perf 11 5·00 10
ab. Imperf between (horiz pair) 55·00
b. Perf 12 — £150
c. Compound perf 25·00 13·00
73/75 *Set of 3* 11·00 1·00

30 Maharaja Bala Rama Varma XI

SPECIAL
(31)

(Des Nilakantha Pellai. Plates by Indian Security Printing Press, Nasik. Typo Stamp Manufactory, Trivandrum)

1946 (24 Oct). Maharaja's 34th Birthday. Wmk C. P 12½.

76 **30** 8ca. carmine 65·00 6·00
a. Perf 11 4·00 2·25
b. Perf 12 65·00 2·50
ba. Imperf between (horiz pair) 70·00 £110
bb. Imperf between (horiz strip of 3). £110
c. Compound perf

1946. No. O103 revalidated for ordinary postage with opt T **31**, in orange. P 12½.

77 **19** 6ca. blackish violet 8·50 5·00
a. Perf 11 65·00 10·00
b. Compound perf 8·50 9·50

OFFICIAL STAMPS

GUM. Soon after 1911 the Official stamps were issued without gum. Thus only the initial printings of the 1, 2, 3 and 4ch. values were gummed. As Nos. O38/O39, O41/O42 and O95 were overprinted on stamps intended for normal postage these, also, have gum.

PRINTINGS. Sometimes special printings of postage stamps were made specifically for overprinting for Official use, thus accounting for Official stamps appearing with watermarks or in shades not listed in the postage issues.

SETTINGS. These are based on the study of complete sheets of 84, and the measurements given are those of the majority of stamps on the sheet. Examples are known showing different measurements as each overprint was set individually in loose type, but these are not included in the listings.

On S. S (O **1**)   On S S (O **2**)
Rounded 'O'

1911 (16 Aug)–**30**. Contemporary stamps optd with T O **1** (13 *mm* wide). P 12, sometimes rough.

(a) Wmk B (upright) (16.8.11-1921)

O1 **3** 4ca. pink (1916) 20 10
a. Opt inverted † £110
b. Opt double £160 £120
c. 'S S' inverted 55·00 27·00
d. Imperf (pair) £500 £500
e. Stamp doubly printed † £500
f. Left 'S' inverted — 26·00
g. 'O' inverted — 40·00
O2 **1** 6ca. chestnut (date ?) 65·00 65·00
O3 ½ch. reddish lilac (R.) (1919) 4·00 35
a. 'CHUCRRAM' (R. 5/6) 25·00 8·50
O4 **4** 10ca. pink (1921) 50·00 8·00
a. 'O' inverted £180 28·00
b. Left 'S' inverted £180 28·00
c. Right 'S' inverted £180 28·00
d. Opt inverted † £225
O5 **1** 1ch. chalky blue (R.) 3·00 10
a. Imperf between (vert pair) † £300
b. Opt inverted 7·00 4·25
c. Opt double 90·00 50·00
d. 'nO' for 'On' (R. 5/7) £140 £110
e. 'O' inverted 18·00 3·25
f. Left 'S' inverted 18·00 3·00
g. Right 'S' inverted 18·00 3·25
h. 'S S' inverted — 85·00
O6 2ch. red 35 10
a. Opt inverted 9·00 9·00
b. 'O' inverted 16·00 1·25
c. Left 'S' inverted 16·00 1·25
d. Right 'S' inverted 16·00 2·50
e. Opt double † £120
O7 2ch. red (B.) (date ?) — £180
O8 **6** 3ch. violet 35 10
a. Imperf between (vert pair) £325 £375
b. Imperf vert (horiz pair) £190
c. Opt inverted 10·00 10·00
d. Opt double £110 70·00
e. Right 'S' inverted 7·50 1·00
f. Right 'S' omitted £275 £170
g. Left 'S' omitted £275 £160
O9 3ch. violet (B.) (date ?) £275 £120
O10 **1** 4ch. slate-green 55 10
a. Imperf between (horiz pair) — £475
b. Opt inverted 75·00 15·00
c. Opt double £150 90·00
d. 'O' inverted 20·00 3·50
e. Left 'S' inverted 21·00 6·00
f. Right 'S' inverted 23·00 7·00
g. Left 'S' omitted £275 £180
O11 4ch. slate-green (B.) (1921) — £100
a. 'O' inverted — £325
b. Left 'S' inverted — £325
c. Right 'S' inverted — £325

(b) Wmk A (sideways) (1919–1925)

O12 **3** 4ca. pink 6·50 15
a. Imperf (pair) £600 £600
b. Opt inverted £120 17·00
c. 'O' inverted 70·00 8·50
d. Left 'S' inverted 80·00 13·00
e. Right 'S' inverted 80·00 18·00
f. Stamp doubly printed † £500
g. Imperf between (horiz pair) † £550
O13 4ca. pink (B.) (1921) 65·00 75
a. 'O' inverted — 32·00
O14 **4** 5ca. olive-bistre (1921) 2·75 10
a. Opt inverted 24·00 9·50
b. 'O' inverted 14·00 4·00
c. Left 'S' inverted 16·00 4·00
d. Right 'S' inverted 16·00 4·00
O15 **1** 6ca. orange-brown (1921) 50 10
a. Imperf between (vert pair) † £425
b. Opt inverted 23·00 16·00
c. Opt double £120 £100
d. 'O' inverted 6·00 3·25
e. Left 'S' inverted 14·00 3·75
f. Right 'S' inverted 15·00 3·75
O16 6ca. orange-brown (B.) (1921) 27·00 3·25
a. Opt inverted £250 £180
b. 'O' inverted £110 22·00
c. Left 'S' inverted £110 22·00
d. Right 'S' inverted £110 22·00
O17 ½ch. reddish violet (R.) (date ?) 4·00 70
a. *Reddish lilac* (date ?) 3·50 70
b. Imperf between (horiz pair) £325 £225
c. Imperf between (vert pair) 95·00 £100
d. Stamp doubly printed 75·00
e. Opt inverted 21·00 9·00
f. Opt double, both inverted £250
g. 'CHUCRRAM' (R. 5/6) 24·00 9·00
h. 'On' omitted — £275
i. Right 'S' inverted — 48·00
j. Right 'S' omitted — £275
O18 **4** 10ca. pink (3.21) 3·25 10
a. *Scarlet* (1925?) — 22·00
b. Opt inverted — 19·00
c. Opt double £120 85·00
d. 'O' inverted 20·00 4·75
e. Left 'S' inverted 19·00 3·75
f. Right 'S' inverted 20·00 4·75
g. Imperf between (horiz pair) — £325
O19 10ca. pink (B.) (date ?) £150 42·00
a. Opt inverted — £140
b. 'O' inverted — £120
O20 **1** 1ch. grey-blue (R.) (date ?) 11·00 60
a. *Deep blue* 12·00 80
b. 'O' inverted 75·00 8·00
c. Left 'S' inverted 85·00 18·00
d. 'On' omitted
e. Opt inverted † £100
O21 1¼ch. claret (12.19) 75 10
a. Stamp doubly printed — £500
b. Opt inverted 16·00 8·00
c. Opt double 50·00
d. 'O' inverted 22·00 2·00
e. Left 'S' inverted 27·00 5·00
f. Right 'S' inverted 27·00 5·50
g. Error. Carmine 50·00
O22 1¼ch. claret (B.) (1921) — £140
a. 'O' inverted — £375
b. Left 'S' inverted — £375
c. Right 'S' inverted — £375

(c) Wmk C (1925–1930)

O23 **4** 5ca. olive-bistre (1926) 40 40
a. Imperf between (horiz pair) £425 £425
b. Opt inverted 48·00 38·00
c. 'O' inverted (R. 1/7) 11·00 5·50
d. Left 'S' inverted (R. 6/1, 6/8) 8·50 4·50
e. Right 'S' inverted (R. 6/7) 11·00 5·50
O24 10ca. pink (1926) 7·50 15
a. Imperf between (vert pair) — £325
b. Opt inverted 75·00 75·00
c. 'O' inverted (R. 1/7) 45·00 5·00
d. Left 'S' inverted (R. 6/1, 6/8) 38·00 4·50
e. Right 'S' inverted (R. 6/7) 45·00 5·00
f. Stamp doubly printed
g. Opt double † £170
O25 **1** 1¼ch. claret (1926) 26·00 1·00
a. 'O' inverted (R. 1/7) £120 10·00
b. Left 'S' inverted (R. 6/1, 6/8) £100 9·00
c. Right 'S' inverted (R. 6/7) £120 10·00
d. Opt double † £150
O26 **7** 7ch. claret 2·75 30
a. 'O' inverted (R. 1/7) 30·00 5·00
b. Left 'S' inverted (R. 6/1, 6/8) 24·00 3·50
c. Right 'S' inverted (R. 6/7) 30·00 5·00
d. *Carmine-red* 60·00
O27 **8** 14ch. orange-yellow 2·25 40
a. 'O' inverted (R. 1/7) 25·00 5·00
b. Left 'S' inverted (R. 6/1, 6/8) 14·00 3·00
c. Right 'S' inverted (R. 6/7) 25·00 5·00

1926–30. Contemporary stamps optd with T O **2** (16½ *mm* wide). Wmk C. P 12.

O28 **4** 5ca. olive-bistre 7·50 30
a. Right 'S' inverted (R. 4/9) 40·00 8·50
b. Left 'S' inverted 42·00 10·00
O29 5ca. chocolate (1930) 25 75
a. Imperf between (vert pair) † £475

b. Opt inverted 24·00
c. 'O' inverted 7·50 10·00
d. Left 'S' inverted 7·50 10·00
O30 1 6ca. brown-red (date ?) 4·75 1·00
a. 'O' inverted 38·00 10·00
b. Left 'S' inverted 45·00 13·00
c. Opt double † £200
O31 4 10ca. pink 40 10
a. Imperf between (horiz pair) £100 £110
b. Imperf between (vert pair) £110 £110
c. Imperf vert (horiz strip of 3) † £225
d. Opt inverted 9·00 11·00
e. 'Ou' for 'On' 65·00 50·00
f. 'O' inverted 9·00 3·25
g. Left 'S' inverted 8·50 3·00
h. Right 'S' inverted 8·00 1·75
i. Left 'S' omitted 65·00 55·00
j. Wmk sideways 30·00 16·00
O32 1 1¼ch. claret (*shades*) 3·50 30
a. Imperf between (horiz pair) £140 £150
b. Imperf between (vert pair) £190 £190
c. Opt inverted 30·00 35·00
d. 'O' inverted 30·00 7·00
e. Left 'S' inverted 30·00 7·00
f. Right 'S' inverted (R. 4/9) 30·00 7·00
g. Left 'S' omitted £225 £170
h. Right 'S' omitted £225 £170
i. Wmk sideways — 16·00
ia. Imperf between (vert pair) £250
O33 6 3ch. violet 21·00 80
a. Opt inverted † £170
b. 'O' inverted 80·00 22·00
c. 'O' omitted £150 95·00
d. 'Ou' for 'On' £250 £180
e. Left 'S' inverted — 42·00
O34 7 7ch. claret (date?) £160 7·50
O35 8 14ch. orange-yellow 65·00 85
a. Imperf between (vert pair) £800
b. 'O' inverted £170 12·00

The 5ca. olive-bistre, 3ch. and 7ch. exist only with the normal watermark spaced 11 mm; the 5ca. chocolate and 14ch. exist only with the wide 15 mm spacing; the 6ca., 10ca. and 1¼ch. exist in both forms.

On On On
S S S S S S
(O 3) (O 4) (O 5)
Italic 'S S'.

1930. Wmk C. P 12.

(a) Optd with T O 3

O36 4 10ca. pink £200 £150
O37 1 1¼ch. carmine-rose 10·00 3·25

(b) Optd with T O 4

O38 5 ¾ch. black (R.) 50 30
a. Left 'S' omitted £150 £150
b. Right 'S' omitted £150
c. Large Roman 'S' at left — £160

(c) Optd with T O 5

O39 5 ¾ch. black (R.) 35 15
a. Opt inverted † £325
b. 'n' omitted £170 £170
O40 1 4ch. slate-green (R.) 40·00 16·00

On On On
S S S S S S
(O 6) (O 7) (O 8)
Oval 'O'

1930–39? Contemporary stamps overprinted. P 12.

(a) With T O 6 (16 mm high)

(i) Wmk A (sideways)

O41 3 4ca. pink 45·00 £120
a. Large right 'S' as Type O 2 (R. 6/14) £325

(ii) Wmk B

O42 3 4ca. pink 28·00 £120
a. Large right 'S' as Type O 2 (R. 6/14) £250

(iii) Wmk C

O43 1 6ca. brown-red (1932) 35 10
a. Opt inverted 26·00
b. Opt double 50·00 50·00
c. 'O' inverted (R. 5/11-12) 15·00 9·50
d. Imperf between (vert pair) † £200
O44 4 10ca. pink 3·25 1·25
O45 5 ¾ch. mauve (1933) 6·50 10
a. Imperf between (horiz pair) £140 95·00
b. Imperf between (horiz strip of 3) † £225
c. Imperf between (vert pair) † £225
d. Stamp doubly printed † £325
e. Perf 12½ 7·50 50
f. Perf comp of 12 and 12½ 28·00 4·50
g. Right 'S' inverted — 50·00
O46 1 1¼ch. carmine-rose 19·00 1·75
a. Opt double £160 £120
b. Large right 'S' as Type O 2 (R. 6/14) £190 70·00
O47 4ch. grey-green 1·75 7·00
O48 4ch. grey-green (R.) (27.10.30) 70 20
a. Imperf between (horiz pair) £250 £200
b. Opt double 29·00 29·00
c. 'O' inverted (R. 5/11-12) 55·00 27·00
d. Large right 'S' as Type O 2 (R. 6/14) 75·00 40·00
e. Imperf between (vert pair) £325
O49 8 14ch. orange-yellow (1931) 17·00 2·25
a. Imperf between (vert pair) † £250

For the 1½ch. and 3ch., and for Nos. O43 and O48/O49 but perf 12½, see Nos. O66/O70 (new setting combining Types O **6** and O **8**).

(b) With T O 7 (14 mm high). Wmk C

O50 3 4ca. pink 12·00 70·00
a. 'O' inverted 75·00 £275
O51 4 5ca. chocolate (1932) 48·00 15·00
a. Opt inverted £110 £130
O52 1 6ca. brown-red 20 10
a. Imperf between (vert pair) £110 £110
b. Opt inverted 29·00
c. Opt double † 90·00
d. 'nO' for 'On' £275 £275
e. Right 'S' inverted 50·00 35·00
f. Left 'S' omitted — £150
g. Large 'n' as Type O **5** (R. 1/1, 1/14) 26·00 16·00
h. Large italic left 'S' as Type O **5** 38·00 27·00
i. Perf 12½ — 30·00
j. Perf compound of 12 and 12½. — 45·00
O53 ½ch. reddish violet (1932) 1·25 15
a. 'CHUCRRAM' (R. 5/6) 17·00 10·00
b. 'Ou' for 'On' £120 £110
c. Left 'S' omitted — £250
d. 'O' of 'On' omitted £375
O54 ½ch. reddish violet (R.) (1935) 20 10
a. Imperf between (vert pair) £170 £180
b. 'CHUCRRAM' (R. 5/6) 4·50 4·00
c. Left 'S' inverted 50·00 45·00
O55 4 10ca. pink (date ?) 7·50 5·00
a. Imperf between (horiz pair) 20·00 38·00
b. Imperf between (vert pair) 11·00 28·00
c. 'O' inverted 85·00 50·00
d. Right 'S' inverted 85·00 50·00
e. Right 'S' omitted † £250
O56 5 ¾ch. mauve (1933?) 75 15
a. Imperf between (vert pair) † £250
b. 'Ou' for 'On' £120 95·00
c. 'O' inverted 48·00 32·00
d. Right 'S' inverted — 42·00
e. Opt double † £200
f. Perf comp of 12 and 12½ 55·00 38·00
O57 1 1ch. deep blue (R.) (1935) 2·25 75
a. *Slate-blue* 1·50 50
b. Imperf between (horiz pair) £275 £275
c. Imperf between (vert pair) 30·00 60·00
d. Perf 12½ 19·00 11·00
e. Perf comp of 12 and 12½ 42·00 20·00
ea. Imperf between (vert pair) † £325
f. Left 'S' inverted — 65·00
O58 1¼ch. claret 2·50 2·00
O59 1½ch. rose (1933) 40 10
a. Imperf between (vert pair) † £225
b. Opt double 75·00 75·00
c. 'O' inverted 8·50 4·25
e. Large 'n' as Type O **5** (R. 1/1, 1/14) 55·00 25·00
f. Large italic left 'S' as Type O **5** 75·00 38·00
g. Left 'S' inverted — 48·00
h. Perf 12½ 60·00 20·00
i. Perf comp of 12 and 12½ — 55·00
ia. Stamp doubly printed — £400
O60 6 3ch. reddish violet (1933) 1·50 60
a. 'O' inverted 45·00 18·00
b. Opt double † £150
O61 3ch. violet (R.) (1934) 1·50 10
a. Imperf between (horiz pair) £170 80·00
b. Imperf between (vert pair) £110 65·00
c. Opt inverted † 85·00
d. 'O' inverted 42·00 20·00
e. Perf 12½ — 6·00
ea. Imperf between (vert pair) † £325
f. Perf comp of 12 and 12½ — 21·00
fa. Imperf between (horiz pair) † £325
g. 'Ou' for 'On' — £120
O63 4ch. grey-green (R.) (1935?) 4·75 20
a. 'Ou' for 'On' (R. 1/1) £100 55·00
O64 7 7ch. claret (*shades*) 2·25 30
a. Imperf between (vert pair) 50·00 65·00
b. 'O' inverted 70·00 20·00
c. Left 'S' inverted 90·00 45·00
d. Perf 12½ — 26·00
e. Perf comp of 12 and 12½ 60·00 16·00
ea. Imperf between (vert pair) † £190
eb. Imperf between (vert strip of 3) £225 £225
O65 8 14ch. orange (1933) 2·50 40
a. Imperf between (horiz pair) 60·00 85·00
b. Imperf between (vert pair) £325
c. Opt inverted £500 £500

(c) New setting combining T O 8 (18 mm high) in top row with T O 6 (16 mm high) for remainder. Wmk C (dates?)

A. T O 8

O66A 1 6ca. brown-red 15·00 8·00
a. Perf 12½ 15·00 8·00
b. Perf comp of 12 and 12½ — 85·00
O67A 1½ch. rose £100 9·00
a. Perf 12½ £150 17·00
ab. Imperf between (horiz pair) † £450
b. Perf comp of 12 and 12½ — £120
O68A 6 3ch. violet (R.) £140 14·00
a. Perf 12½ £250 50·00
b. Perf comp of 12 and 12½ £250 40·00
O69A 1 4ch. grey-green (R.) 55·00 45·00
a. Perf 12½ £150 45·00
O70A 8 14ch. orange-yellow £140 40·00
a. Perf 12½ £140 40·00

B. T O 6

O66Ba 1 6ca. brown-red (P 12½) 6·00 1·50
ab. Imperf between (vert pair) £275 £275
ac. 'O' inverted 30·00 17·00
c. Perf comp of 12 and 12½ 85·00 32·00
O67B 1½ch. rose 26·00 1·00
aa. 'O' inverted — 45·00
a. Perf 12½ 40·00 1·25
ab. 'O' inverted £150 35·00
c. Perf comp of 12 and 12½ — 48·00
O68B 6 3ch. violet (R.) 26·00 1·50
a. Perf 12½ 42·00 2·00
b. Perf comp of 12 and 12½ 65·00 14·00
O69Ba 1 4ch. grey-green (R.) (P 12½) 18·00 7·00
ab. Imperf between (horiz pair) † £375
ac. 'O' inverted £150 65·00
O70Ba 8 14ch. orange-yellow (P 12½) 25·00 1·50

Nos. O66/70A/70B in vertical *se-tenant* pairs are very scarce. As with the postage issues it is believed that the 12½ and compound perforations were issued between 1937 and 1939.

1 ch
8 c 1 ch
(O 9) Wrong fount '1 c' (R. 6/7)

1932. Official stamps surch as T **14** or with T O **9**. P 12.

(a) With opt T O 1

(i) Wmk A (sideways)

O71 4 6c. on 5ca. olive-bistre 85·00 48·00
a. 'O' inverted £375 £190
b. Left 'S' inverted £300 £160
c. Right 'S' inverted £375 £190
O71*d* 12c. on 10ca. pink † £550

(ii) Wmk C

O72 4 6c. on 5ca. olive-bistre 48·00 21·00
a. 'O' inverted £160 60·00
b. Left 'S' inverted £130 48·00
c. Right 'S' inverted £160 60·00
O73 12c. on 10ca. pink £275

(b) With opt T O 2. Wmk C

O74 4 6c. on 5ca. olive-bistre 2·00 2·00
a. Opt and surch inverted 95·00
b. Surch inverted £110
c. Left 'S' inverted 22·00 20·00
d. Right 'S' inverted 22·00 20·00
e. '6' omitted — £160
O75 6c. on 5ca. chocolate 1·00 1·00
a. Surch inverted 11·00 12·00
b. Surch double £140
c. Surch double, one inverted £120
d. 'O' inverted 7·50 8·00
e. Left 'S' inverted 9·00 9·00
f. Pair, one without surch £500
g. Right 'S' inverted 11·00
O76 12c. on 10ca. pink 3·75 1·50
a. Opt inverted 30·00 38·00
b. Surch inverted 7·00 10·00
c. Opt and surch inverted 75·00 85·00
d. Pair, one without surch £275
e. 'O' inverted 20·00 9·50
f. Left 'S' inverted 19·00 8·50
g. 'Ou' for 'On' £160 £160
h. Right 'S' inverted 19·00 9·50
i. 'c' omitted (R. 6/1) £130 £140
O77 1 1ch.8c. on 1¼ch. claret 4·50 1·50
a. Surch inverted † £170
b. 'O' inverted 23·00 9·00
c. Left 'S' inverted 23·00 9·00
d. Right 'S' inverted 23·00 9·00
e. Wrong fount '1 c' 55·00 28·00

(c) With opt T O 3. Wmk C

O78 4 12c. on 10ca. pink † £750
O79 1 1ch.8c. on 1¼ch. carmine-rose 65·00 48·00
a. 'n' omitted £450
b. Wrong fount '1 c' £400 £275

(d) With opt T O 6. Wmk C

O80 4 12c. on 10ca. pink £100 48·00
O81 1 1ch.8c. on 1¼ch. carmine-rose £200 32·00
a. Wrong fount '1 c' £650 £180
b. 'h' omitted
c. Large right 'S' as Type O2 (R. 6/14) † £225
d. *Brown-red* — 42·00

(e) With opt T O 7. Wmk C

O82 4 6c. on 5ca. chocolate 20 30
a. Opt inverted 90·00 90·00
b. Surch inverted 11·00 15·00
c. Right 'S' omitted £180 £180
d. Two quads for right 'S' £750
e. Right 'S' inverted 60·00
f. Surch double £120
O83 12c. on 10ca. pink 20 15
a. Opt inverted 11·00 13·00
b. Surch inverted 6·00 10·00
c. Opt and surch inverted 50·00 55·00
d. Opt double † £110
e. 'O' inverted 28·00 28·00
f. Right 'S' inverted 32·00 32·00
g. 'On' omitted — £225
h. 'n' omitted — £225
i. 'c' omitted (R. 6/1) 65·00 70·00
j. Surch double † £170
k. Surch on back and front £300
O84 1 1ch.8c. on 1¼ch. claret 35 25
a. Imperf between (vert pair) † £425
c. Surch inverted 14·00 15·00
d. Surch double 65·00
e. 'O' inverted 5·00 4·50
f. Wrong fount '1 c' 28·00 24·00
g. '1ch' omitted £150
h. Large left 'S' as Type O **2** — 50·00

SERVICE SERVICE SERVICE 8 CASH
(O 10) 13 mm ('R' with curved tail) (O 11) 13½ mm ('R' with straight tail) (O 12)

1939–41. Nos. 35 and 40 with type-set opt, T O **10**. P 12½.

O85 1 6ca. brown-red (1941) 1·00 40
a. Perf 11 1·75 1·00
b. Perf 12 70 30
c. Compound perf 70 1·10

O86 5 ¾ch. reddish violet £350 £180
a. Perf 12 42·00 2·50
b. Compound perf £325 £170

1939 (9 Nov). Maharaja's 27th Birthday. Nos. 64/70 with type-set opt, T O **10**. P 12½.
O87 1ch. yellow-green 13·00 1·00
O88 1½ch. scarlet 25·00 2·75
a. 'SESVICE' £200 45·00
b. Perf 12 £130 32·00
ba. 'SESVICE' — £300
bb. Imperf between (horiz pair) † £550
c. Compound perf 42·00 6·50
O89 2ch. orange 8·00 14·00
a. 'SESVICE' £170 £225
b. Compound perf £275 £275
O90 3ch. brown 8·50 20
a. 'SESVICE' £140 22·00
b. Perf 12 55·00 1·25
ba. 'SESVICE' £425 65·00
c. Compound perf 24·00 9·00
O91 4ch. red 27·00 9·00
O92 7ch. pale blue 30·00 7·00
O93 14ch. turquoise-green 48·00 13·00
O87/O93 *Set of 7* £140 42·00
The 'SESVICE' error occurs on the left pane, R. 6/5.

1940 (?)–**44**. Nos. 40a and 42b optd with T O **11** from stereos. P 12½.
O94 5 ¾ch. reddish violet 25·00 20
a. Imperf between (horiz pair) £225 £250
b. Perf 11 90·00 1·10
c. Perf 12 32·00 20
d. Compound perf 48·00 75
O95 1 1½ch. rose (1944) 18·00 8·50
a. Perf 12 8·50 1·00
b. Compound perf 27·00 15·00

1941 (?)–**42**. Nos. 64/70 optd with T O **11** from stereos. P 12½.
O96 1ch. yellow-green 1·50 10
a. Imperf between (vert pair) 85·00 90·00
b. Opt inverted † 65·00
c. Opt double 29·00
d. Perf 11 1·50 10
da. Imperf between (vert pair) 65·00
db. Opt double £225 £225
e. Perf 12 4·75 1·00
ea. Imperf between (vert pair) £130 £140
eb. Stamp doubly printed £180
ec. Opt inverted † £200
ed. Opt double 27·00 45·00
f. Compound perf 9·00 3·25
fa. Imperf between (vert pair) † £325
fb. Opt double £150
O97 1½ch. scarlet 7·00 10
a. Imperf between (horiz pair) £100
b. Perf 11 4·75 15
ba. Imperf between (vert pair) £300 £300
bb. Imperf between (vert strip of 3) £225
bc. Imperf between (horiz pair) † £300
c. Perf 12 12·00 1·75
ca. Imperf between (vert strip of 3) £350
d. Compound perf 6·50 75
da. Imperf between (vert strip of 3) £190
e. Imperf (pair) 32·00
O98 2ch. orange 7·00 30
a. Perf 11 25·00 5·00
ab. Imperf between (vert pair) † £1100
b. Perf 12 £275 £275
ba. Imperf between (vert pair) £1300 £1300
c. Compound perf £275 £275
O99 3ch. brown 4·50 10
a. Imperf between (vert pair) † £900
b. Perf 11 6·00 10
c. Perf 12 11·00 4·00
ca. Imperf between (vert pair) £1200 £1200
d. Compound perf 35·00 75
O100 4ch. red 7·50 1·00
a. Perf 11 7·00 50
b. Perf 12 32·00 11·00
c. Compound perf 80·00 40·00
O101 7ch. pale blue 11·00 35
a. Perf 11 11·00 6·00
b. Perf 12 38·00 18·00
c. Compound perf 30·00 5·00
d. *Blue* (P 11) 30·00 15·00
da. Perf 12 12·00 12·00
db. Compound perf 60·00 48·00
O102 14ch. turquoise-green 17·00 70
a. Perf 11 28·00 1·50
b. Perf 12 17·00 2·50
c. Compound perf £150 27·00
O96/O102 *Set of 7* 48·00 1·90

1942. Maharaja's 29th Birthday. Nos 71/72 optd with T O **11**. P 12½.
O103 6ca. blackish violet 60 50
a. Perf 11 70 10
b. Perf 12 £110 20·00
c. Compound perf 1·50 1·75
O104 ¾ch. brown 6·50 10
a. Imperf between (vert pair) † £700
b. Perf 11 8·50 10
c. Perf 12 £140 6·50
d. Compound perf 11·00 85

1943. Surch with T O **12**. P 12½.
O105 **27** 8ca. on 6ca. scarlet 3·50 30
a. Perf 11 2·00 10
ab. Surch inverted † £1800
b. Compound perf 9·00 1·25
c. 'SERVIC' † —

1943–45. Nos. 73/74 optd with T O **11**. P 12½.
O106 2ca. on 1½ch. scarlet 60 1·00
a. Perf 11 50 15
ab. Pair, one without surch £550
b. Compound perf 70 1·50
ba. '2' omitted £650 £650
c. Perf 12
O107 4ca. on ¾ch. brown (1945) 9·00 1·00
a. Perf 11 3·00 20
b. Compound perf 4·50 1·75

1946. Maharaja's 34th Birthday. Optd with T O **11**. P 11.
O108 **30** 8ca. carmine 5·50 2·00
a. Imperf between (horiz pair) 65·00
ab. Imperf between (vert pair) † £425
b. Opt double † £375
c. Perf 12½ 5·00 1·10
ca. Stamp doubly printed 60·00
d. Perf 12 4·00 1·40
da. Stamp doubly printed 75·00

From 1 July 1949 Travancore formed part of the new State of Travancore-Cochin and stamps of Travancore surcharged in Indian currency were used.

TRAVANCORE-COCHIN

On 1 July 1949 the United State of Travancore and Cochin was formed ('U.S.T.C.') and the name was changed to State of Travancore-Cochin ('T.C.') by the new constitution of India on 26 January 1950.

PRICES FOR STAMPS ON COVER TO 1945
Nos. 1/13 *from* × 8
Nos. O1/O17 *from* × 15

NO WATERMARK VARIETIES. These were formerly listed but we have now decided to omit them as they do not occur in full sheets. They are best collected in pairs, with and without watermarks.

COMPOUND PERFS. The notes above T **20** of Travancore also apply here.

VALIDITY OF STAMPS. From 6 June 1950 the stamps of Travancore-Cochin were valid on mail from both Indian and state post offices to destinations in India and abroad.

ONE ANNA
ഒരണ
(1)

രണ്ടു പൈസ Normal

രണ്ടു പൈസ **2p. on 6ca.** 1st character of 2nd group as 1st character of 1st group (Rt pane R. 14/2)

1949 (1 July). Stamps of Travancore surch in 'PIES' or 'ANNAS' as T **1**. P 12½.
1 **27** 2p. on 6ca. blackish violet (R.) 3·50 1·75
a. Surch inverted 65·00
b. Character error £275 £160
c. 'O' inverted (Rt pane R. 13/1) 60·00 22·00
d. Perf 11 2·25 40
da. Imperf between (vert pair) £400 £400
db. Pair, one without surch £170
dc. Character error £250 £160
dd. 'O' inverted (Rt pane R. 13/1) 75·00 30·00
e. Perf 12 1·00 20
ea. Imperf between (horiz pair) £120
eb. Imperf between (vert pair) 8·00 22·00
ec. Surch inverted £180
ed. Character error £250 £160
ee. Imperf between (vert strip of 3) 45·00
ef. Block of four imperf between (horiz and vert) 85·00
eg. 'O' inverted (Rt pane R. 13/1) 60·00 28·00
eh. Imperf between (horiz strip of 3) £110
f. Perf 14 † £850
g. Imperf (pair) 11·00
ga. Character error £350
h. Compound perf — 70·00
2 **30** 4p. on 8ca. carmine 1·75 40
a. Surch inverted 85·00
b. 'S' inverted (Rt pane R. 3/7) £120 50·00
c. Perf 11 2·75 30
ca. Imperf between (vert pair) £275 £300
cb. Surch inverted £180
cc. Pair, one without surch £300
cd. 'FOUP' for 'FOUR' £275 £160
ce. 'S' inverted (Rt pane R. 3/7) £120 55·00
d. Perf 12 1·50 30
da. Imperf between (vert pair) 28·00
db. Pair, one without surch £325
dc. 'FOUP' for 'FOUR' £225 £140
dd. 'S' inverted (Rt pane R. 2/4 and R. 3/7) £120 60·00
de. Surch inverted £250
e. Imperf (pair) £100
f. Compound perf £200 65·00
g. Perf 13½ † £900
3 **20** ½a. on 1ch. yellow-green 4·75 30
a. 'NANA' for 'ANNA' (Lt pane R. 3/3) £275 £110
b. Inverted 'H' in 'HALF' — £140
c. Imperf between (vert pair) † £300
d. Perf 11 3·75 30
da. Imperf between (vert pair) 48·00
db. Surch inverted † £325
dc. 'NANA' for 'ANNA' (Lt pane R. 3/3) £400 £170
dd. Inverted 'H' in 'HALF' — £140
e. Perf 12 1·00 40
ea. Imperf between (horiz pair) £120 £120
eb. Imperf between (vert pair) 6·50 18·00
ec. Surch inverted 5·00
ed. 'NANA' for 'ANNA' (Lt pane R. 3/3) £375 £180
ee. Block of four imperf between (horiz and vert) 65·00
f. Perf 14 † £700
g. Imperf (pair) 11·00 24·00
h. Compound perf — 65·00
4 **22** 1a. on 2ch. orange 4·75 30
a. Perf 11 1·50 30
ab. Surch double 60·00
b. Perf 12 5·00 50
ba. Imperf between (horiz pair) 15·00
bb. Imperf between (vert pair) 5·00 18·00
bc. Block of four imperf between (horiz and vert) 70·00
c. Perf 13½ £225 2·00
d. Imperf (pair) 13·00
e. Compound perf 70·00 28·00
5 **24** 2a. on 4ch. red (68) 5·00 60
a. Surch inverted † £400
b. 'O' inverted 70·00 23·00
c. Perf 11 4·50 60
ca. 'O' inverted — 25·00
d. Perf 12 6·00 55
da. 'O' inverted 80·00 25·00
e. Compound perf 80·00 50·00
6 **25** 3a. on 7ch. pale blue (69) 13·00 8·00
a. Perf 11 6·50 5·50
ab. Blue 90·00 5·50
ac. '3' omitted † £1500
b. Perf 12 13·00 4·50
c. Compound perf — £130
ca. Blue — £170
7 **26** 6a. on 14ch. turquoise-green (70) 28·00 60·00
a. Accent omitted from native surch (Rt pane R. 13/4) £650 £700
b. Perf 11 28·00 48·00
ba. Accent omitted from native surch (Rt pane R. 13/4) £650 £700
c. Perf 12 30·00 50·00
ca. Accent omitted from native surch (Rt pane R. 13/4) £650 £700
d. Compound perf 90·00 £100
da. Accent omitted from native surch (Rt pane R. 13/4) £950
e. Imperf (pair)
1/7 *Set of 7* 40·00 50·00
There are two settings of the ½a. surcharge. In one the first native character is under the second downstroke of the 'H' and in the other it is under the first downstroke of the 'A' of 'HALF'. They occur on stamps perf 12½, 11 and 12 equally commonly and also on the Official stamps.

U. S. T. C. (2) **T.-C.** (3) **SIX PIES** (4)

1949. No. 106 of Cochin optd with T **2**.
8 **29** 1a. orange 10·00 £110
a. No stop after 'S' (R. 1/6) 95·00
b. Raised stop after 'T' (R. 4/1) 95·00

1950 (1 Apr). No. 106 of Cochin optd with T **3**.
9 **29** 1a. orange 7·50 90·00
a. No stop after 'T' 65·00 £375
b. Opt inverted £300
ba. No stop after 'T' £2000
The no stop variety occurs on No. 5 in the sheet and again on No. 8 in conjunction with a short hyphen.

1950 (1 Apr). No. 9 surch as T **4**.
10 **29** 6p. on 1a. orange 4·75 75·00
a. No stop after 'T' (R. 1/5) 24·00
b. Error. Surch on No. 8 15·00
ba. No stop after 'S' £225
bb. Raised stop after 'T' £225
11 9p. on 1a. orange 4·50 75·00
a. No stop after 'T' (R. 1/5) 23·00
b. Error. Surch on No. 8 £225
ba. No stop after 'S' £950
bb. Raised stop after 'T' £950

5 Conch or Chank Shell **6** Palm Trees

(Litho Indian Security Printing Press, Nasik)

1950 (24 Oct). W **69** of India. P 14.
12 **5** 2p. rose-carmine 3·00 4·75
13 **6** 4p. ultramarine 5·00 18·00
The ordinary issues of Travancore-Cochin became obsolete on 1 July 1951.

OFFICIAL STAMPS

VALIDITY. Travancore-Cochin official stamps were valid for use throughout India from 30 September 1950.

SERVICE (O 1) **SERVICE** (O 2)

1949 (1 July)–**51**. Stamps of Travancore surch with value as T **1** and optd 'SERVICE'. No gum. P 12½.

(a) With T O 1

(i) Wmk C of Travancore

O1 **27** 2p. on 6ca. blackish violet (R.) 2·00 80
a. Imperf between (vert pair) £350 £350
b. Character error (Rt pane R. 14/2) 48·00 32·00
c. 'O' inverted (Rt pane R. 13/1) 35·00 22·00
d. Pair, one without surch £325
e. Perf 11 1·25 20
ea. Imperf between (vert pair) £450 £450
eb. Character error (Rt pane R. 14/2) 50·00 35·00
ec. 'O' inverted (Rt pane R. 13/1) 35·00 22·00
f. Perf 12 2·00 75
fa. Imperf between (horiz pair) 14·00 32·00
fb. Imperf between (vert pair) 6·50
fc. Character error (Rt pane R. 14/2) 48·00 35·00

fd. 'O' inverted (Rt pane R. 13/1) 38·00
fe. Block of four imperf between (horiz and vert) 28·00
g. Imperf (pair) 10·00 30·00
ga. Character error (Rt pane R. 14/2) £350
h. Compound perf £100
O2 **30** 4p. on 8ca. carmine 8·00 1·50
a. 'FOUB' for 'FOUR' (Lt pane R. 2/3) £350 £120
b. Perf 11 5·00 30
ba. 'FOUB' for 'FOUR' (Lt pane R. 2/3) £130 32·00
c. Perf 12 6·50 1·25
ca. 'FOUB' for 'FOUR' (Lt pane R. 2/3) £170 60·00
cb. 'FOUR PIES' omitted (in pair with normal) £1200
d. Compound perf 35·00 30·00
O3 **20** ½a. on 1ch. yellow-green 2·25 25
a. Pair, one without surch £140
b. Surch inverted 42·00
c. 'NANA' for 'ANNA' (Lt pane R. 3/3) £400 £110
d. Perf 11 3·25 25
da. Pair, one without surch £275
db. Surch inverted £100 £120
dc. 'NANA' for 'ANNA' (Lt pane R. 3/3) £400 £130
e. Perf 12 23·00 3·25
ea. 'NANA' for 'ANNA' (Lt pane R. 3/3) £750 £275
eb. Pair, one without surch £180
ec. Surch inverted on back only £500
f. Compound perf — 50·00
O4 **22** 1a. on 2ch. orange 18·00 8·00
a. Surch inverted £110
b. Pair, one without surch £900
c. Perf 11 16·00 7·50
ca. Pair, one without surch £1000
O5 **24** 2a. on 4ch. red (68) 4·50 1·00
a. 'O' inverted — £110
b. Perf 11 9·00 60
ba. Surch inverted £1700 †
bb. 'O' inverted — 75·00
c. Perf 12 12·00 6·00
ca. 'O' inverted — £150
cb. Pair, one without surch £475
d. Compound perf — 70·00
e. Imperf (pair) 15·00
O6 **25** 3a. on 7ch. pale blue (No. 69) 7·00 3·25
a. Imperf between (vert pair) 25·00
b. *Blue* 90·00 14·00
c. Perf 11 7·50 1·00
ca. *Blue* £110 24·00
d. Perf 12 5·00 8·50
da. Imperf between (horiz pair) 25·00
db. Imperf between (vert pair) 9·00
dc. Block of four imperf between (horiz and vert) 50·00
dd. *Blue* 90·00 7·50
dda. Imperf between (horiz pair) † £900
e. Imperf (pair) 13·00
O7 **26** 6a. on 14ch. turquoise-green (No. 70) 20·00 15·00
a. Imperf between (vert pair) 40·00
b. Perf 11 16·00 12·00
c. Perf 12 70·00 11·00
ca. Imperf between (horiz pair) 35·00
cb. Imperf between (vert pair) 40·00
cc. Block of four imperf between (horiz and vert) 70·00
d. Imperf (pair) 16·00
O1/O7 *Set of 7* 42·00 19·00

*(ii) W **27** of Cochin*

O8 **27** 2p. on 6ca. blackish violet (R.) 40 2·25
a. Type O **1** double 18·00
b. Perf 11 50 2·25
c. Perf 12 1·25 1·75
O9 **24** 2a. on 4ch. red (No. 68) 3·25 2·75
a. Perf 11 1·75 1·10
ab. Imperf between (vert pair) £500 £500
b. Perf 12 £120 £100
c. Compound perf 80·00 50·00

*(b) With T O **2***

(i) Wmk C of Travancore

O10 **30** 4p. on 8ca. carmine 1·25 20
a. 'FOUB' for 'FOUR' (Lt pane R. 2/3) £130 42·00
b. 2nd 'E' of 'SERVICE' in wrong fount £150 60·00
c. 'S' in 'PIES' inverted — 90·00
d. Imperf between (vert pair) † £300
e. Perf 11 50 20
ea. Imperf between (horiz pair) 5·00
eb. Imperf between (vert pair) 60·00
ec. 'FOUB' for 'FOUR' (Lt pane R. 2/3) £110 38·00
ed. 2nd 'E' of 'SERVICE' in wrong fount £140 70·00
ee. 'S' in 'PIES' inverted — £100
ef. Block of four imperf between (horiz and vert) 45·00
f. Perf 12 30 20
fa. Imperf between (horiz pair) 7·00
fb. Imperf between (vert pair) 2·25
fc. Block of four imperf between (horiz and vert) 16·00 42·00
fd. 'FOUB' for 'FOUR' (Lt pane R. 2/3) £130 45·00
ff. 2nd 'E' of 'SERVICE' in wrong fount £140 60·00
fg. 'FOUK' for 'FOUR' † £1000
fh. Imperf between (vert strip of 3) 50·00
fi. Imperf between (horiz strip of 3) 60·00
fj. 'S' in 'PIES' inverted £130
g. Perf 13½ 3·00 1·25
h. Compound perf 14·00 14·00
i. Imperf (pair) 6·00
ia. 2nd 'E' of 'SERVICE' in wrong fount £250
O11 **20** ½a. on 1ch. yellow-green 2·50 20
a. 'AANA' for 'ANNA' (Rt pane R. 13/1) £350 85·00
b. Perf 11 75 20
ba. Imperf between (horiz pair) £130 £130
bb. Imperf between (vert pair) 11·00
bc. Block of four imperf between (horiz and vert) 85·00
bd. 'AANA' for 'ANNA' (Rt pane R. 13/1) £110 42·00
c. Perf 12 1·25 15
ca. Imperf between (horiz pair) 3·50
cb. Imperf between (vert pair) 3·50 17·00
cc. 'AANA' for 'ANNA' (Rt pane R. 13/1) £140 65·00
cd. Block of four imperf between (horiz and vert) 35·00
d. Compound perf 60·00 30·00
da. 'AANA' for 'ANNA' (Rt pane R. 13/1) — £375
e. Imperf (pair) 9·00 25·00
O12 **22** 1a. on 2ch. orange 50 30
a. Imperf between (vert pair) † £350
ab. Imperf between (horiz pair) † £350
b. Perf 11 3·75 50
ba. Imperf between (horiz pair) 13·00 27·00
bb. Imperf between (vert pair) £180 £180
c. Perf 12 60 20
ca. Imperf between (horiz pair) 13·00
cb. Imperf between (vert pair) 4·50 20·00
cc. Block of four imperf between (horiz and vert) 28·00
d. Compound perf 35·00 28·00
e. Imperf (pair) 16·00
O13 **24** 2a. on 4ch. red (No. 68) 4·50 80
a. 'O' inverted (Lt pane R. 14/3) £120 42·00
b. Perf 11 1·50 1·10
ba. 'O' inverted (Lt pane R. 14/3) 85·00 42·00
c. Perf 12 17·00 1·10
ca. Imperf between (vert pair) £130 £140
cb. 'O' inverted (Lt pane R. 14/3) £250 60·00
cc. Pair, one without surch † £1600
d. Compound perf 35·00 24·00
O14 **25** 3a. on 7ch. pale blue (No. 69) 8·50 1·10
a. 'S' inverted in 'SERVICE' (Lt pane R. 6/3) 75·00 32·00
b. First 'E' inverted (Lt pane R. 7/4) £200 £140
c. 'C' inverted (Rt pane R.4/1 and 5/1) £110 80·00
d. Second 'E' inverted (Lt pane R. 3/2) £190 £130
e. Perf 11 1·50 1·10
ea. 'S' inverted in 'SERVICE' (Lt pane R. 6/3) 50·00 32·00
f. Perf 12 5·50 2·25
fa. 'S' inverted in 'SERVICE' (Lt pane R. 6/3) £130 80·00
g. Compound perf — 90·00
h. Imperf (pair) 55·00
O15 **26** 6a. on 14ch. turquoise-green (No. 70) 1·50 4·50
a. Accent omitted from native surch 16·00 14·00
b. 'S' inverted in 'SERVICE' (Lt pane R. 11/4) 85·00 45·00
c. Perf 11 14·00 7·00
ca. Accent omitted from native surch 60·00 26·00
cb. 'S' inverted in 'SERVICE' (Lt pane R. 11/4) £160 55·00
d. Perf 12 50·00 7·50
da. Accent omitted from native surch £150 30·00
db. 'S' inverted in 'SERVICE' (Lt pane R. 11/4) £375 65·00
e. Compound perf £160 £150
O10/O15 *Set of 6* 5·50 6·25

*(ii) W **27** of Cochin*

O16 **20** ½a. on 1ch. yellow-green 5·50 75
a. Perf 11 40 40
b. Perf 12 25·00 18·00
c. Compound perf 24·00 3·00
O17 **22** 1a. on 2ch. orange 1·00 1·00
a. Perf 11 50 40
b. Perf 12 13·00 4·00
c. Perf 13½ 1·50 1·00
d. Compound perf 8·00 3·00

Nos. O2, O10, O12 and O17 have the value at top in English and at bottom in native characters with 'SERVICE' in between. All others have 'SERVICE' below the surcharge.

T O **2** was overprinted at one operation with the surcharges.

Nos. O10b, O10ed, O10ff and O10ia, show the second 'E' of 'SERVICE' with serifs matching those on the surcharge. The variety occurred on Right pane R. 10/6 and R. 11/6, but was soon corrected.

The 'accent omitted' varieties on No. O15 occur on Left pane R. 5/1 and Right pane R. 1/4, 12/4, 14/1 and 13/4.

The Official stamps became obsolete in September 1951.

WADHWAN

PRICES FOR STAMPS ON COVER TO 1945

No. 1	*from* × 30
No. 2	—
Nos. 3/6	*from* × 30

Thakur Bal Singh, 1885–1910

1

(Litho Thacker & Co, Bombay)

1888–94.

(a) Thin toned wove paper

1 **1** ½ pice, black (I, III) (P 12½ *large holes*) 38·00 £120
a. Imperf between (vert pair) (I)
b. Pin-perf 6½ irregular (I) £160
c. Compound of 12½ and pin-perf 6½ (I) £300
2 ½ pice, black (II) (P 12½ *irregular small holes*) 65·00

(b) Medium toned wove paper

3 **1** ½ pice, black (III) (P 12½) 19·00 80·00
4 ½ pice, black (V) (P 12) 16·00 20·00

(c) Thick off-white or toned wove paper

5 **1** ½ pice, black (IV, VI) (P 12) (7.92) 13·00 14·00
a. Perf compound of 12 and 11 (IV) 29·00 70·00
6 ½ pice, black (VII) (*fine impression*) (P 12) (1894) 13·00 29·00

Sheets from the Stone IV printing had at least one horizontal line of perforations gauging 11, normally between the bottom two rows of the sheet.

These stamps were lithographed from seven different stones taken from a single die. Brief details of the individual stones are as follows:

Stone I – No. 1. Sheet size not known, but possibly 28 (4×7). Sheet margins imperforate
Stone II – No. 2. Sheets of 42 (7×6) with imperforate margins
Stone III – Nos. 1 (thin paper) and 3 (medium paper). Sheets of 40 (4×10) with imperforate margins
Stone IV – Nos. 5/5a. Sheets of 32 (4×8) with imperforate margins at top and right
Stone V – No. 4. Sheets of 20 (4×5) with imperforate margins at top, right and bottom
Stone VI – No. 5. Sheets of 30 (5×6) with all margins perforated
Stone VII – No. 6. Sheets of 32 (4×8) with all margins perforated. Much finer impression than the other stones

Stamps from stones I and II come with or without the dot before 'STATE'. Those from the later stones always show the dot. The shading on the pennant above the shield can also be used in stone identification. Stamps from stones I to III show heavy shading on the pennant, but this is less evident on stone IV and reduced further to a short line or dot on stones V to VII. There is a ')' hairline after 'HALF' on the majority of stamps from Stone III.

The stamps of Wadhwan became obsolete on 1 January 1895.

Ionian Islands

The British occupation of the Ionian Islands was completed in 1814 and the archipelago was placed under the protection of Great Britain by the Treaty of Paris of 9 November 1815. The United States of the Ionian Islands were given local self-government, which included responsibility for the postal services. Crowned-circle handstamps were, however, supplied in 1844, although it is believed these were intended for use on prepaid mail to foreign destinations.

Examples of the Great Britain 1855 1d. red-brown stamp are known used at Corfu, cancelled as No. CC2, but it is believed that these originate from mail sent by the British garrison.

For illustrations of the handstamp types see BRITISH POST OFFICES ABROAD notes, following GREAT BRITAIN.

CEPHALONIA

CROWNED-CIRCLE HANDSTAMPS

CC1	CC **1**	CEPHALONIA (19.4.1844).........*Price on cover*	£1800

CORFU

CROWNED-CIRCLE HANDSTAMPS

CC2	CC **1**	CORFU (19.4.1844)......................*Price on cover*	£650
CC3	CC **1**	CORFU (G. or B.) (1844)............*Price on cover*	—

ZANTE

CROWNED-CIRCLE HANDSTAMPS

CC4	CC **1**	ZANTE (G. or B.) (19.4.1844) ....*Price on cover*	£1400

Nos. CC1/CC2 were later, *circa* 1860/1861, struck in green (Cephalonia) or red (Corfu).

It is believed that examples of No. CC4 in black are from an unauthorised use of this handstamp which is now on display in the local museum. A similar handstamp, but without 'PAID AT' was introduced in 1861.

PRICES FOR STAMPS ON COVER TO 1945	
Nos. 1/3	*from* × 10

PERKINS BACON 'CANCELLED'. For notes on these handstamps, showing 'CANCELLED' between horizontal bars forming an oval, see Catalogue Introduction.

1

(Eng C. Jeens. Recess Perkins Bacon & Co)

1859 (15 June). Imperf.

1	**1**	(½d.) orange (no wmk) (H/S 'CANCELLED' in oval £12000).....	£140	£750
2		(1d.) blue (wmk '2') (H/S 'CANCELLED' in oval £12000).....	35·00	£300
3		(2d.) carmine (wmk '1') (H/S 'CANCELLED' in oval £12000).....	28·00	£300

On 30 May 1864, the islands were ceded to Greece, and these stamps became obsolete.

Great care should be exercised in buying used stamps, on or off cover, as forged postmarks are plentiful.

Iraq

(Currency. 16 annas = 1 rupee)

I. INDIAN POST OFFICES

Indian post offices were opened at Baghdad and Basra, then part of the Turkish Empire, on 1 January 1868. Unoverprinted stamps of India were used, cancels as detailed below.

Baghdad

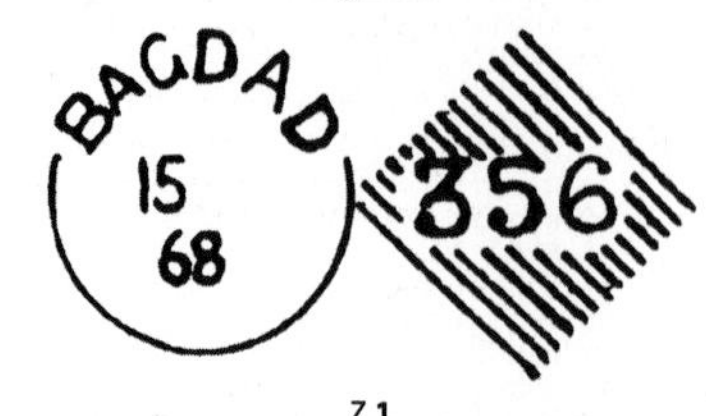

Z 1

Z 2

Z 3

BAGDAD. MR:22

Z 4

Z 5

Z 6

Z 7

Postmark Type	*Approx period of use*
Z **1**	1868–1869
Z **2**	1870–1875
Z **3**	1877–1880
Z **4**	1884–1885
Z **5**	1885–1886
Z **6**	1894–1914
Z **7**	1901–1914

Between 1881 and 1887 stamps were often cancelled with a 'B' in a square or circle of bars. Off cover, such stamps are indistinguishable from those used in other offices in the Bombay postal circle.

T Z **1** may be found with the numeral obliterator and datestamp applied separately.

T Z **4** exists with an acute accent over the first 'A' of 'BAGHDAD'.

Stamps of India cancelled at Baghdad between 1868 and 1914 with postmarks detailed above.

1856–64. (Nos. 37/49).

Z1	2a. yellow-buff	£110
Z2	4a. black	90·00

1865. (Nos. 54/65).

Z3	½a. blue (Die I)	12·00
Z4	1a. pale brown	15·00
Z5	2a. orange	26·00
Z7	8a. carmine (Die I)	£250

1866–78. (Nos. 69/72).

Z8	4a. green (Die I)	40·00
Z9	4a. blue-green (Die II)	42·00

1868. (Nos. 73/74).

Z10	8a. rose (Die II)	45·00

1873. (Nos. 75/76).

Z11	½a. blue (Die II)	9·00

1874. (Nos. 77/79).

Z12	9p. mauve	75·00

1876. (Nos. 80/82).

Z14	6a. olive-bistre	26·00
	a. Pale brown	26·00
Z15	12a. Venetian red	75·00

1882–90. (Nos. 84/101).

Z16	½a. blue-green	5·50
Z18	1a. brown-purple	5·50
Z19	1a.6p. sepia	14·00
Z20	2a. blue	7·00
Z21	3a. orange	16·00
	a. Brown-orange	8·50
Z22	4a. olive-green	9·00
Z23	4a.6p. yellow-green	30·00
Z24	8a. dull mauve	20·00
Z25	12a. purple/*red*	30·00
Z26	1r. slate	26·00

1891. (No. 102).

Z27	2½a. on 4a.6p. yellow-green	23·00

1892. (Nos. 103/106).

Z28	2a.6p. yellow-green	11·00
Z29	1r. green and aniline carmine	60·00

1895. (Nos. 107/109).

Z30	2r. carmine and yellow-brown	85·00
Z31	3r. brown and green	65·00
Z32	5r. ultramarine and violet	£110

1899. (No. 111).

Z34	3p. aniline carmine	21·00

1900. (Nos. 112/118).

Z36	½a. yellow-green	8·50
Z37	1a. carmine	10·00
Z38	2a. pale violet	13·00
Z39	2a.6p. ultramarine	13·00

1902–11. (Nos. 119/147).

Z40	3p. grey	16·00
Z41	½a. yellow-green	8·00
Z42	1a. carmine	8·00
Z43	2a. violet	11·00
Z44	2a. mauve	7·50
Z45	2a.6p. ultramarine	5·50
Z46	3a. orange-brown	26·00
Z47	4a. olive	10·00
Z49	8a. purple	17·00
Z51	1r. green and carmine	35·00
Z52	2r. rose-red and yellow-brown	65·00
Z54	5r. ultramarine and violet	£120

1905. (No. 148).

Z55	¼ on ½a. green	24·00

1906–07. (Nos. 149/150).

Z56	½a. green	5·50
Z57	1a. carmine	5·50

1911–22. (Nos. 151/191).

Z58	3p. grey	16·00
Z59	½a. light green	7·50
Z60	1a. carmine	7·50
Z61	2a. purple	9·50
Z62	2a.6p. ultramarine (No. 170)	14·00
Z63	2a.6p. ultramarine (No. 171)	11·00
Z64	3a. orange	20·00
Z67	8a. deep magenta	32·00
Z68	12a. carmine-lake	40·00

OFFICIAL STAMPS

1867–73. (Nos. O20/O30*a*).

Z76	4a. green (Die I)	50·00
Z77	8a. rose (Die II)	75·00

1874–82. (Nos. O31/O35).

Z80	2a. orange	45·00

1883–99. (Nos. O37*a*/O48).

Z84	½a. blue-green	20·00
Z85	1a. brown-purple	22·00
Z86	2a. blue	25·00

1900. (Nos. O49/O51).

Z90	½a. yellow-green	28·00
Z92	2a. pale violet	38·00

1902–09. (Nos. O54/O65).

Z95	1a. carmine	19·00
Z96	2a. mauve	15·00
Z97	4a. olive	15·00
Z98	6a. olive-bistre	30·00
Z99	8a. purple	45·00

1906. (Nos. O66/O67).

Z101	½a. green	15·00
Z102	1a. carmine	20·00

1912–13. (Nos. O73/O96).

Z108	½a. light green	14·00
Z109	1a. carmine	16·00
Z112	6a. yellow-bistre	32·00

The post office at Baghdad closed on 30 September 1914.

Basra

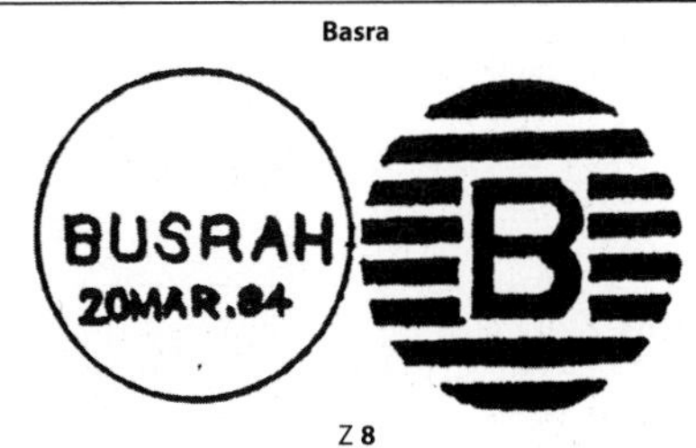

Z 8

Z 9

Z 10

Postmark Type	*Approx period of use*
Z **1** (inscr 'BUSSORAH/357')	1868–1873
Z **2** (inscr 'BUSREH/19')	1870–1873
Z **3** (inscr 'BUSREH/1/K-6')	1877–1879
Z **8**	1884
Z **4** (inscr 'BUSRAH')	1889–1892
Z **7**	1905–1918
Z **9**	1894–1916
Z **10**	1899–1903
Z **12** (inscr 'BUSRA')	1915–1918

Between 1881 and 1887 stamps were often cancelled with a 'B' in a square or circle of bars. As at Baghdad, such stamps are indistinguishable from those used at other offices in the Bombay postal circle.

Stamps of India cancelled at Basra between 1868 and 1918 with postmarks detailed above.

1865. (Nos. 54/65).
Z121 ½a. blue (Die I) 15·00
Z123 1a. pale brown 14·00
Z124 2a. orange 25·00
Z126 8a. carmine (Die I) £250

1866–78. (Nos. 69/72).
Z127 4a. green (Die I) 35·00
Z128 4a. blue-green (Die II) 42·00

1868. (Nos. 73/74).
Z129 8a. rose (Die II) 75·00

1873. (Nos. 75/76).
Z130 ½a. blue (Die II) 9·00

1876. (Nos. 80/82).
Z133 6a. pale brown 35·00
Z134 12a. Venetian red 95·00

1882–90. (Nos. 84/101).
Z135 ½a. blue-green 5·50
Z136 9p. rose 50·00
Z137 1a. brown-purple 5·50
Z138 1a.6p. sepia 12·00
Z139 2a. blue 7·00
Z140 3a. orange 16·00
a. Brown-orange 8·50
Z141 4a. olive-green 10·00
Z142 4a.6p. yellow-green 17·00
Z143 8a. dull mauve 16·00
Z145 1r. slate 38·00

1891. (No. 102).
Z146 2½a. on 4½a. yellow-green 13·00

1892–97. (Nos. 103/106).
Z147 2a.6p. yellow-green 6·50
Z148 1r. green and aniline carmine 80·00

1898. (No. 110).
Z152 ¼ on ½a. blue-green 30·00

1899. (No. 111).
Z153 3p. aniline carmine 11·00

1900. (Nos. 112/118).
Z155 ½a. yellow-green 8·50
Z156 1a. carmine 8·50
Z157 2a. pale violet 12·00
Z158 2a.6p. ultramarine 12·00

1902–11. (Nos. 119/147).
Z159 3p. grey 18·00
Z160 ½a. yellow-green 7·50
Z161 1a. carmine 9·50
Z162 2a. violet 10·00
a. Mauve 9·50
Z163 2a.6p. ultramarine 5·50
Z165 4a. olive 14·00
Z167 8a. purple 20·00
Z169 1r. green and carmine 50·00

1905. (No. 148).
Z172 ¼ on ½a. green 20·00

1906–07. (Nos. 149/150).
Z173 ½a. green 7·50
Z174 1a. carmine 9·50

1911–22. (Nos. 151/191).
Z175 3p. grey 19·00
Z176 ½a. light green 5·50
Z177 1a. carmine 5·50
Z178 2a. purple 7·50
Z179 2a.6p. ultramarine (No. 170) 15·00
Z180 2a.6p. ultramarine (No. 171) 8·00
Z181 3a. orange 23·00
Z182 4a. deep olive 14·00
Z186 1r. brown and green 40·00

OFFICIAL STAMPS

1867–73. (Nos. O20/O30*a*).
Z196 4a. green (Die I) 80·00
Z197 8a. rose (Die II) 85·00

1874–82. (Nos. O30/O35).
Z200 2a. orange 50·00

1883–99. (Nos. O37*a*/48).
Z204 ½a. blue-green 20·00
Z205 1a. brown-purple 20·00
Z206 2a. blue 27·00
Z207 4a. olive-green 32·00
Z208 8a. dull mauve 50·00

The post office at Basra closed on 30 September 1914. In November Basra was captured by the invading Indian Expeditionary Force and the post office was reopened the following month.

Basra City

Z 11 Z 12

The office at Basra City opened in March 1915

Postmark Type	*Approx period of use*
Z **11**	1915
Z **12**	1915–1918

1911–22. (Nos. 151/191).
Z222 ½a. light green 20·00
Z223 1a. carmine 25·00
Z229 8a. deep mauve 50·00
Z230 12a. carmine-lake 60·00
Z231 1r. brown and green 50·00

The sale of Indian stamps by these offices was forbidden from 1 September 1918, being replaced by issues for Iraq, Nos. 1-14 (ex.4). The Indian post offices closed on 30 April 1919.

Other offices opened in Iraq after 1914 are believed to have been operated by the Indian Army, using stamps overprinted 'I.E.F.'. Unoverprinted Indian stamps are also known cancelled at these offices (Amara, Ezra's Tomb, Fao, Magil and Naseriyeh) but their status is unclear.

II. ISSUES FOR BAGHDAD

PRICES FOR STAMPS ON COVER TO 1945	
Nos. 1/7	*from* × 8
No. 8	*from* × 4
Nos. 9/15	*from* × 8
No. 16	*from* × 3
Nos. 17/24	*from* × 8
No. 25	*from* × 5

BRITISH OCCUPATION

British and Indian troops took Baghdad from the Turks on 11 March 1917.

IN BRITISH BAGHDAD OCCUPATION
2 Ans
(1)

1917 (1 Sept). Stamps of Turkey, surch as T **1** in three operations.

(a) Pictorial designs of 1914. T ypes **32**, *etc., and* **31**
1 **32** ¼a. on 2pa. claret (Obelisk) £500 £550
a. 'IN BRITISH' omitted £18000
2 **34** ¼a. on 5pa. dull purple (Leander's Tower) £400 £425
b. 'IN BRITISH' double £2750
3 **36** ½a. on 10pa. green (Lighthouse garden) £2000 £2250
4 **31** ½a. on 10pa. green (Mosque of Selim) £4500 £4750
a. '½ An' double £9000
5 **37** 1a. on 20pa. red (Castle) £1300 £1400
a. 'BAGHDAD' double £3250
6 **38** 2a. on 1pi. bright blue (Mosque) £550 £600

(b) As (a), but overprinted with small five-pointed Star
7 **37** 1a. on 20pa. red (B.) £850 £900
b. 'BAGHDAD' double £3250
8 **38** 2a. on 1pi. bright blue (R.) £10000 £11000

(c) Postal Jubilee stamps (Old GPO). P 12½
9 **60** ½a. on 10pa. carmine £1600 £1700
a. Perf 13½ £5500
10 1a. on 20pa. blue £18000
a. Perf 13½ £3750 £4250
ab. Value omitted £22000
11 2a. on 1pi. black and violet £800 £850
a. Value omitted £20000
b. Perf 13½ £425 £450
ba. 'IN BRITISH' twice † £19000

(d) T **30** *(GPO, Constantinople) with opt T* **26**
12 **30** 2a. on 1pi. ultramarine £1600 £1800
a. 'IN BRITISH' omitted £20000

No. 11ba shows 'BAGHDAD' superimposed on a second impression of 'IN BRITISH' at the top of the stamp. The only known example is on cover.

The ¼a. on 5pa. value omitted, 1a. on 20pa. 'OCCUPATION' omitted and 2a. on 1pi. 'BAGHDAD' omitted, formerly listed as Nos. 2a, 7a and 11a, are all in the Royal Philatelic Collection.

(e) Stamps optd with six-pointed Star and Arabic date '1331' within Crescent. T **53** *(except No. 16, which has five-pointed Star and Arabic '1332', T* **57***)*
13 **30** ½a. on 10pa. green (R.) £400 £425
14 1a. on 20pa. rose £1300 £1400
a. Value omitted £13000 £9000
b. Optd with Type **26** (Arabic letter 'B') also £13000 £13000
15 **23** 1a. on 20pa. rose (No. 554a) £1400 £1500
a. Value omitted £22000
16 **21** 1a. on 20pa. carmine (No. 732) £12000 £15000
17 **30** 2a. on 1pi. ultramarine (R.) £425 £450
a. 'BAGHDAD' omitted † £20000
18 **21** 2a. on 1pi. dull blue (No. 543) (R.) £550 £600
a. 'OCCUPATION' omitted £19000

(f) Stamps with similar opt, but date between Star and Crescent (Nos. 19 and 22, T **54***; others T* **55** *five-pointed Star)*
19 **23** ½a. on 10pa. grey-green (No. 609a) (R.) £425 £475
a. 'OCCUPATION' omitted £18000
b. 'IN BRITISH' omitted £20000
20 **60** ½a. on 10pa. carmine (P 12½) (B.) £550 £600
a. Perf 13½ £1100 £1300
ab. 'BAGHDAD' double £6500
ac. Value double £6500
21 **30** 1a. on 20pa. rose £425 £475
22 **28** 1a. on 20pa. rose (Plate II) (No. 617) £1400 £1500
23 **15** 1a. on 10pa. on 20pa. claret (No. 630) £650 £700
a. 'OCCUPATION' omitted † £19000
24 **30** 2a. on 1pi. ultramarine (R.) £550 £650
a. 'OCCUPATION' omitted £19000
b. 'BAGHDAD' omitted £17000
25 **28** 2a. on 1pi. ultramarine (Pl. II) (No. 645) £5000 £5500

Each element of the overprint was applied separately using a small hand press, resulting in variable spacing between the lines.

The last group (*f*) have the Crescent obliterated by hand in violet-black ink, as this included the inscription, 'Tax for the relief of children of martyrs'.

No. 23a does exist unused, but the only example is in the Royal Philatelic Collection.

Other Ottoman stamps were also overprinted, but not issued due to the small quantities available; these include a ½a. on 10pa. green with five-pointed star and a 2a on 40pa. blue.

III. ISSUES FOR MOSUL

PRICES FOR STAMPS ON COVER TO 1945	
Nos. 1/8	*from* × 50

BRITISH OCCUPATION

A British and Indian force occupied Mosul on 1 November 1918.

As the status of the vilayet was disputed stocks of 'IRAQ IN BRITISH OCCUPATION' surcharges were withdrawn in early 1919 and replaced by Nos. 1/8.

1

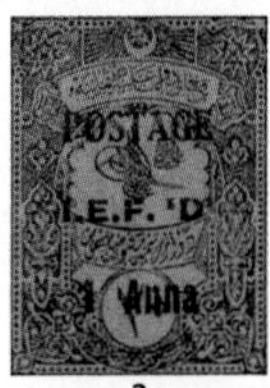

2

3

4

5

6

4 4
I II

Two types of tougra in central design:
(a) Large 'tougra' or sign-manual of El Ghazi 7 mm high.
(b) Smaller 'tougra' of Sultan Rechad 5½ mm high.

Two types of 4a. surcharge:
I. Normal '4'. Apostrophes on D 3½ mm apart.
II. Small '4'. Apostrophes on D 4½ mm apart.

1919 (1 Feb). Turkish Fiscal stamps surch as Types **1/6** by Govt Press, Baghdad. P 11½ (½a.), 12 (1a.), or 12½ (others).

No.	Type	Description	Unused	Used
1	**1**	½a. on 1pi. green and red	2·25	1·90
2	**2**	1a. on 20pa. black/*red* (*a*)	1·40	1·75
		a. Imperf between (horiz pair)	£1100	
		b. Surch double	£650	
		c. 'A' of 'Anna' omitted	£275	
3		1a. on 20pa. black/*red* (*b*)	4·00	3·00
		b. Surch double	£750	
4	**3**	2½a. on 1pi. mauve and yellow (*b*)	1·50	1·50
		a. No bar to fraction (R. 2/4)	90·00	£120
		b. Surch double	£1500	
5	**4**	3a. on 20pa. green (*a*)	1·60	4·00
		a. Surch double, one albino	£600	
6		3a. on 20pa. green and orange (*b*)	£100	£140
7	**5**	4a. on 1pi. deep violet (*a*) (I)	3·00	3·50
		a. '4' omitted	£1900	
		c. Surch double	£1200	
7*d*		4a. on 1pi. deep violet (*a*) (II)	21·00	28·00
		da. Surch double, one with '4' omitted	£3250	
8	**6**	8a. on 10pa. lake (*a*)	4·00	5·00
		a. Surch inverted	£900	£1000
		b. Surch double	£750	£850
		c. No apostrophe after 'D' (R. 1/5)	65·00	85·00
		d. Surch inverted. No apostrophe after 'D'		
		e. 'na' of 'Anna' omitted	£325	
		f. Error. 8a. on 1pi. deep violet	£3500	

The ½a. and 1a, are on unwatermarked paper. The 2½a. and 3a. (No. 6) are on paper with a sheet watermark of Turkish characters and the 3a. (No. 5), 4a. and 8a. are on paper watermarked with a series of parallel zig-zag lines.

No. 4a occurs on some sheets only. No. 8c comes from the first setting only.

Nos. 1/8 were replaced by 'IRAQ IN BRITISH OCCUPATION' surcharges during 1921 and invalidated on 1 September 1922.

In December 1925 the League of Nations awarded the vilayet of Mosul to Iraq.

IV. ISSUES FOR IRAQ

PRICES FOR STAMPS ON COVER TO 1945

Nos. 1/18	*from* × 6
Nos. 41/154	*from* × 2
Nos. O19/O171	*from* × 4

BRITISH OCCUPATION

1 Leander's Tower

1a Lighthouse Garden, Stamboul

1b Castle of Europe

1c Mosque of Sultan Ahmed

1d Martyrs of Liberty Monument

1e Fountains of Suleiman

1f Cruiser *Hamidiye*

1g Candilli, Bosphorus

1h Former Ministry of War

1i Sweet Waters of Europe

1j Suleiman Mosque

1k Bosphorus at Rumeli Hisar

1l Sultan Ahmed's Fountain

A

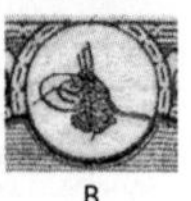

B

(Litho (¼a. and 1½a.) or recess (others), surch in litho. Bradbury Wilkinson)

1918 (1 Sept)–**21**. Turkish pictorial issue of 1914. P 12.

(a) No wmk. Tougra as A (1 Sept 1918–1920)

No.	Type	Description	Unused	Used
1	**1**	¼a. on 5pa. dull purple	1·25	1·00
2	**1a**	½a. on 10pa. green	1·00	20
3	**1b**	1a. on 20pa. red	1·00	10
4	**1**	1½a. on 5pa. dull purple (1920)	21·00	50
5	**1c**	2½a. on 1pi. bright blue	2·00	1·40
		a. Surch inverted	£12000	
6	**1d**	3a. on 1½pi. grey and rose	2·00	25
		a. Surch double (Bk.+R.)	£5000	£6000
7	**1e**	4a. on 1¾pi. red-brown and grey	2·00	25
		a. Centre inverted	†	£35000
8	**1f**	6a. on 2pi. black and green (32 *mm* surch)	3·25	1·75
		a. Centre omitted	£24000	
		b. Surch 27 mm wide	£150	1·75
9	**1g**	8a. on 2½pi. green and orange (30 *mm* surch)	4·75	2·00
		a. Surch inverted	†	£22000
		b. Surch 27 mm wide	22·00	70
10	**1h**	12a. on 5pi. deep lilac	2·75	6·00
11	**1i**	1r. on 10pi. red-brown	3·00	1·40
12	**1j**	2r. on 25pi. yellow-green	13·00	3·25
13	**1k**	5r. on 50pi. rose (32 *mm* surch)	32·00	30·00
		a. Surch 27 mm wide	80·00	42·00
14	**1l**	10r. on 100pi. indigo	£120	17·00
1/14 *Set of* 14			£190	55·00
1s/14s (ex 1½a. on 5pa.) Perf 'SPECIMEN' *Set of* 13			£900	

(b) No wmk. Tougra as B (one device instead of two) (1921)

No.	Type	Description	Unused	Used
15	**1i**	1r. on 10pi. red-brown	£350	27·00

(c) Wmk Mult Script CA (sideways on ½a., 1½a.) (1921)

No.	Type	Description	Unused	Used
16	**1a**	½a. on 10pa. green	7·50	2·75
17	**1**	1½a. on 5pa. dull purple	5·00	1·50
18	**1j**	2r. on 25pi. yellow-green	38·00	16·00
16/18 *Set of* 3			45·00	18·00
16s/18s Optd 'SPECIMEN.' *Set of* 3			£190	

The original settings of Nos. 1/18 showed the surcharge 27 mm wide, except for the 2½a. (24 *mm*), 4a. (26½ *mm*), 6a. (32 *mm*), 8a. (30½ *mm*), 12a. (33 *mm*), 1r. (31½ *mm*), 2r. (30 *mm*) and 5r. (32 *mm*). The 6a., 8a. and 5r. came from a subsequent setting with the surcharge 27 mm wide. Minor variations in the width of the surcharge on other values exist, but are not significant. On all surcharged values apart from the 2½a. and 12a. there is a stop after the 'An'. On these two values there is no stop.

Nos. 2, 3, 5, 6 and 7/9 are known bisected and used on philatelic covers. All such covers have Makinah or F.P.O. 339 cancellations.

During January 1923 an outbreak of cholera in Baghdad led to the temporary use for postal purposes of the above issue overprinted 'REVENUE'.

LEAGUE OF NATIONS MANDATE

On 25 April 1920 the Supreme Council of the Allies assigned to the United Kingdom a mandate under the League of Nations to administer Iraq.

The Emir Faisal, King of Syria in 1920, was proclaimed King of Iraq on 23 August 1921.

King Faisal I
23 August 1921–8 September 1933

2 Sunni Mosque, Muadhdham

3 Gufas on the Tigris

4 Winged Cherub

5 Bull from Babylonian wall-sculpture

6 Arch of Ctesiphon

7 Tribal Standard, Dulaim Camel Corps

8 Shiah Mosque, Kadhimain

9 Allegory of Date Palm

(Des Miss Edith Cheesman (½a., 1a., 4a., 6a., 8a., 2r., 5r., 10r.), Mrs. C. Garbett (Miss M. Maynard) (others). Typo (1r.) or recess (others) Bradbury, Wilkinson)

1923 (1 June)–**25**. Types **2/4** and similar designs. Wmk Mult Script CA (sideways on 2a., 3a., 4a., 8a., 5r.). P 12.

No.	Type	Description	Unused	Used
41	**2**	½a. olive-green	3·75	10
42	**3**	1a. brown	8·00	10
43	**4**	1½a. lake	2·50	10
44	**5**	2a. orange-buff	3·00	15
45	**6**	3a. grey-blue (1923)	6·50	15
46	**7**	4a. violet	7·50	30
		w. Wmk Crown to left of CA	£600	£250
47	**8**	6a. greenish blue	2·75	30
48	**7**	8a. olive-bistre	7·00	30
49	**9**	1r. brown and blue-green	38·00	1·75
50	**2**	2r. black	26·00	9·00
51		2r. olive-bistre (1925)	95·00	3·25
52	**7**	5r. orange	60·00	13·00
53	**8**	10r. lake	70·00	22·00
41/53 *Set of* 13			£300	45·00
41s/53s Optd 'SPECIMEN.' *Set of* 13			£850	

The normal sideways watermark on Nos. 44, 45, 46, 48 and 52 shows the crown to right of CA, *as seen from the back of the stamp*.

With the exception of Nos. 49 and 50, later printings of these stamps and of No. 78 are on a thinner paper.

10

11 King Faisal I

12

(Recess Bradbury Wilkinson)

1927 (1 Apr). Wmk Mult Script CA. P 12.

No.	Type	Description	Unused	Used
78	**10**	1r. red-brown	19·00	1·25
		s. Optd 'SPECIMEN.'	£110	

See note below No. 53.

(Recess Bradbury Wilkinson)

1931 (17 Feb). Wmk Mult Script CA (sideways on 1r. to 25r.). P 12.

No.	Type	Description	Unused	Used
80	**11**	½a. green	3·75	30
81		1a. red-brown	3·25	30
82		1½a. scarlet	3·75	50
83		2a. orange	3·25	10
84		3a. blue	3·25	20
85		4a. slate-purple	3·50	4·25
86		6a. greenish blue	3·50	80
87		8a. deep green	3·50	4·50
88	**12**	1r. chocolate	11·00	4·50
89		2r. yellow-brown	20·00	11·00
90		5r. orange	60·00	75·00
91		10r. scarlet	£170	£200
92	**10**	25r. violet	£2250	£3000
80/91 *Set of* 12			£250	£275
80s/92s Perf 'SPECIMEN' *Set of* 13			£1600	

(New Currency. 1000 fils = 1 dinar)

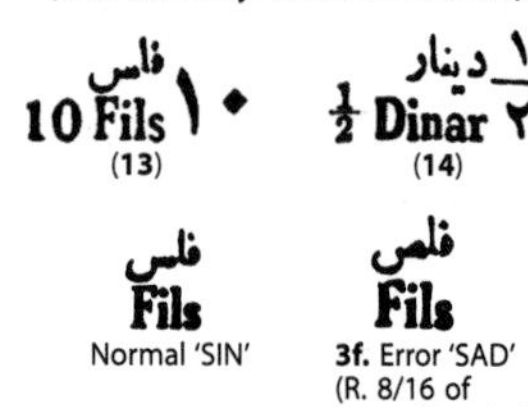

(**13**) (**14**)

Normal 'SIN'

3f. Error 'SAD' (R. 8/16 of second setting)

(Surcharged at Govt Ptg Wks, Baghdad)

1932 (1–21 Apr). Nos. 80/92 and 46 surch in Fils or Dinar as Types **13** or **14**.

No.	Type	Description	Unused	Used
106	**11**	2f. on ½a. green (21.4.32) (R.)	50	10
		a. Wide space between '2' and 'Fils'	55·00	32·00
107		3f. on ½a. green	1·50	10
		a. Surch double	£350	
		b. Surch inverted	£300	
		c. Arabic letter 'SAD' instead of 'SIN'	75·00	38·00
		d. Wide space between '3' and 'Fils'	55·00	32·00
		e. Horiz pair, one without surcharge	£1600	
108		4f. on 1a. red-brown (21.4.32) (G.)	3·25	25
		a. Wide space between '4' and 'Fils'	£130	50·00
109		5f. on 1a. red-brown	75	10
		a. Inverted Arabic '5' (R. 8/11)	85·00	60·00
		b. Surch inverted	£475	
110		8f. on 1½a. scarlet	1·00	50
		a. Surch inverted	£275	
111		10f. on 2a. orange	50	10
		a. Inverted Arabic '1' (R. 8/13)	65·00	38·00
		b. No space between '10' and 'Fils'	50	10
112		15f. on 3a. blue	1·50	1·00
113		20f. on 4a. slate-purple	3·75	3·75
		a. Surch inverted	£550	

114	–	25f. on 4a. violet (No. 46)	6·50	11·00
		a. 'Flis' for 'Fils' (R. 2/1, 10/8, 10/15)	£900	£1200
		b. Inverted Arabic '5' (R. 10/7, 10/14)	£1100	£1600
		c. Vars a and b in *se-tenant* pair	£2750	
		d. Error 20f. on 4a. violet (R. 10/1, 10/9)	£7000	
115	11	30f. on 6a. greenish blue	8·00	2·25
		a. Error 80f. on 6a. greenish blue	£7000	
116		40f. on 8a. deep green	4·75	9·00
117	12	75f. on 1r. chocolate	6·50	9·00
		a. Inverted Arabic '5'	£150	£170
118		100f. on 2r. yellow-brown	12·00	4·00
119		200f. on 5r. orange	60·00	55·00
120		½d. on 10r. scarlet	£150	£200
		a. No bar in English '½'	£2000	£2250
		b. Scarlet-vermilion	£180	£275
121	10	1d. on 25r. violet	£350	£475
106/121 *Set of* 16			£550	£700

Nos. 106/113 and 115/116 were in sheets of 160 (16×10) No. 114 sheets of 150 (15×10) and Nos. 117/121 sheets of 100 (10×10). There were three settings of the surcharge for the 3f. and two settings for the 5, 10, 25, 40, 100 and 200f. Nos. 109a and 111a come from the first setting and Nos. 107c, 111b and 114a/114b come from the second.

The 'wide space' varieties, Nos. 106a, 107a and 108a, show a 2 mm space between the numeral and 'Fils' instead of 1 mm. On No. 106a it occurs R. 8/5 and R. 8/13, on 107d on R. 10/5 and R. 10/10 of the first setting and R. 6/6 of the second and on No. 108a on R. 7/1 and R. 7/9, although R. 7/9 is also known with normal spacing.

No. 109a occurs in the first setting and can be easily identified as it shows the point of the Arabic numeral at the foot of the surcharge.

All 10f. stamps from the second setting are as No. 111b except for R. 4/7–8 and 15–16 where the spacing is the same as for the first setting (T **13**).

No. 114d shows '20' instead of '25'. Many examples of this error were removed from the sheets before issue. The Arabic value '25' was unaltered.

No. 115a shows the error in the English face value only.

No. 117a occurs on R. 1/2, 1/7 and a third position in the first vertical row not yet identified.

No. 120a occurs on R. 1/2, R. 2/3 and R. 10/1.

No. 120*b* was a special printing of No. 91 which does not exist unsurcharged.

15

1932 (9 May–June). T **10** to **12**, but with values altered to FILS or DINAR as in T **15**. Wmk Mult Script CA (sideways on 50f. to 1d.). P 12.

138	11	2f. ultramarine (6.32)	75	20
139		3f. green	50	10
140		4f. brown-purple (6.32)	2·25	10
141		5f. grey-green	1·50	10
142		8f. scarlet	3·25	10
143		10f. yellow	2·50	10
144		15f. blue	2·50	10
145		20f. orange	5·00	50
146		25f. mauve	5·50	50
147		30f. bronze-green	5·50	15
148		40f. violet	4·50	1·00
149	12	50f. brown	6·50	20
150		75f. dull ultramarine	15·00	6·00
151		100f. deep green	19·00	2·25
152		200f. scarlet	32·00	4·75
153	10	½d. deep blue	£100	80·00
154		1d. claret	£225	£180
138/154 *Set of* 17			£375	£250
138s/154s Perf 'SPECIMEN' *Set of* 17			£850	

OFFICIAL STAMPS

ON STATE SERVICE

(O 2)

1920 (16 May)–**23**. As Nos. 1/18, but surch includes additional wording 'ON STATE SERVICE' as T O **2** in black.

(a) No wmk. Tougra as A

O19	1a	½a. on 10pa. blue-green	32·00	2·00
O20	1b	1a. on 20pa. red	9·50	1·00
O21	1	1½a. on 5pa. purple-brown	75·00	3·25
O22	1c	2½a. on 1pi. blue	9·50	10·00
O23	1d	3a. on 1½pi. black and rose	28·00	1·50
O24	1e	4a. on 1¾pi. red-brown and grey-blue	60·00	6·00
O25	1f	6a. on 2pi. black and green	50·00	13·00
O26	1g	8a. on 2½pi. yellow-green and orange-brown	65·00	7·50
O27	1h	12a. on 5pi. purple	40·00	28·00
O28	1i	1r. on 10pi. red-brown	60·00	16·00
O29	1j	2r. on 25pi. olive-green	55·00	25·00
O30	1k	5r. on 50pi. rose-carmine	£100	80·00
O31	1l	10r. on 100pi. slate-blue	£160	£190
O19/O31 *Set of* 13			£700	£350

(b) No wmk. Tougra as B (No. 15) (1922)

O32	1i	1r. on 10pi. red-brown	50·00	7·00

(c) Wmk Mult Script CA (sideways on ½a. to 8a.) (1921–1923)

O33	1a	½a. on 10pa. green	2·00	1·00
O34	1b	1a. on 20pa. red	13·00	1·00
O35	1	1½a. on 5pa. purple-brown	2·75	1·50
O36	1e	4a. on 1¾pi. red-brown and grey-blue	2·50	3·25
O37	1f	6a. on 2pi. black and green (10.3.23)	48·00	£200
O38	1g	8a. on 2½pi. yellow-green and orange-brown	4·00	2·25
O39	1h	12a. on 5pi. purple (10.3.23)	45·00	£120
O40	1i	2r. on 25pi. olive-green (10.3.23)	£140	£190
O33/O40 *Set of* 8			£225	£475
O33s/O40s Optd 'SPECIMEN.' *Set of* 8			£550	

Nos. O25/O26, O30 and O37/O38 only exist from the setting with the surcharge 27½ mm wide.

On Nos. O19/O40 there is a stop after the 'An' on every value apart from the 2½a. (No. O22).

The 'SPECIMEN' opt on No. O34 is of a different type, without the full stop present on Nos. O33 and O35/O40.

ON STATE SERVICE (O 6) | ON STATE SERVICE (O 7)

1923. Optd with T O **6** (horiz designs) or T O **7** (vert designs).

O54	2	½a. olive-green	1·50	1·75
O55	3	1a. brown	1·75	30
O56	4	1½a. lake	1·75	3·25
O57	5	2a. orange-buff	2·00	55
O58	6	3a. grey-blue	2·50	1·50
O59	7	4a. violet	4·25	3·50
O60	8	6a. greenish blue	4·00	1·25
O61	7	8a. olive-bistre	4·00	5·00
O62	9	1r. brown and blue-green	22·00	4·75
O63	2	2r. black (R.)	38·00	17·00
O64	7	5r. orange	90·00	65·00
O65	8	10r. lake	£200	85·00
O54/O65 *Set of* 12			£325	£160
O54s/O65s Optd 'SPECIMEN.' *Set of* 12			£850	

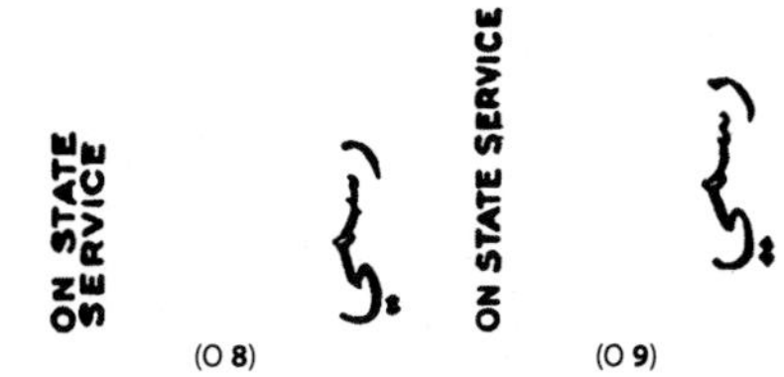

(O **8**) (O **9**)

1924–25. Optd with T O **8** (horiz designs) or T O **9** (vert designs).

O66	2	½a. olive-green	1·50	10
O67	3	1a. brown	1·25	10
O68	4	1½a. lake	1·25	30
O69	5	2a. orange-buff	1·50	10
O70	6	3a. grey-blue	2·00	10
O71	7	4a. violet	4·00	30
O72	8	6a. greenish blue	1·75	20
O73	7	8a. olive-bistre	3·75	35
O74	9	1r. brown and blue-green	24·00	4·50
O75	2	2r. olive-bistre (1925)	48·00	3·75
O76	7	5r. orange	£100	65·00
O77	8	10r. lake	£180	42·00
O66/O77 *Set of* 12			£325	£100
O66s/O77s Optd 'SPECIMEN.' *Set of* 12			£850	

1927 (1 Apr). Optd with T O **9**.

O79	10	1r. red-brown	17·00	3·00
		s. Optd 'SPECIMEN.'	£120	

ON STATE SERVICE

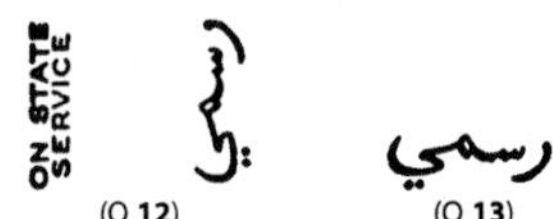

(O **12**) (O **13**)

1931. Optd.

(a) As T O **12**

O93	11	½a. green	65	2·75
O94		1a. red-brown	3·75	10
O95		1½a. scarlet	4·50	29·00
O96		2a. orange	80	10
O97		3a. blue	85	1·25
O98		4a. slate-purple	1·00	1·50
O99		6a. greenish blue	7·00	32·00
O100		8a. deep green	7·00	32·00

(b) As T O **13**, *horizontally*

O101	12	1r. chocolate	25·00	30·00
O102		2r. yellow-brown	42·00	95·00
O103		5r. orange	65·00	£180
O104		10r. scarlet	£225	£325

(c) As T O **13**, *vertically upwards*

O105	10	25r. violet	£2250	£3250
O93/O104 *Set of* 12			£350	£650
O93s/O105s Perf 'SPECIMEN' *Set of* 13			£1600	

1932 (1 Apr). Official issues of 1924–1925 and 1931 surch in FILS or DINAR, as Types **13** or **14**.

O122	11	3f. on ½a. green	8·50	4·75
		a. Pair, one without surch	£1200	
O123		4f. on 1a. red-brown (G.)	2·50	10
O124		5f. on 1a. red-brown	2·50	10
		a. Inverted Arabic '5' (R. 8/11)	£130	50·00
O125	4	8f. on 1½a. lake (No. O68)	16·00	50
O126	11	10f. on 2a. orange	6·50	10
		a. Inverted Arabic '1' (R. 8/13)	£140	45·00
		b. '10' omitted	†	£3250
		c. No space between '10' and 'Fils'	6·50	10
O127		15f. on 3a. blue	4·25	9·00
O128		20f. on 4a. slate-purple	6·50	6·00
O129		25f. on 4a. slate-purple	4·75	2·00
O130	8	30f. on 6a. greenish blue (No. O72)	17·00	1·75
O131	11	40f. on 8a. deep green	5·00	3·50
		a. 'Flis' for 'Fils' (R. 7/5, 7/13)	£900	£1000
O132	12	50f. on 1r. chocolate	23·00	5·50
		a. Inverted Arabic '5' (R. 1/2)	£350	£250
O133		75f. on 1r. chocolate	9·00	14·00
		a. Inverted Arabic '5'	£170	£190
O134	2	100f. on 2r. olive-bistre (surch at top)	50·00	3·75
		a. Surch at foot	50·00	15·00
O135	7	200f. on 5r. orange (No. O76)	29·00	26·00
O136	8	½d. on 10r. lake (No. O77)	£170	£190
		a. No bar in English '½' (R. 2/10)	£2250	£2750
O137	10	1d. on 25r. violet	£375	£550
O122/O137 *Set of* 16			£650	£750

Nos. O122/O124, O126/O129 and O131 were in sheets of 160 (16×10), Nos. O130, O134 and O136 150 (10×15), No. O135 150 (15×10) and Nos. O125, O132/O133 and O137 in sheets of 100 (10×10).

There was a second setting of the surcharge for the 3f. (equivalent to the third postage setting), 10f. to 25f., 40f. to 100f. and 1d. Nos. O126c, O131a and O134a come from the second setting.

All 100f. stamps from the second setting are as No. O134a.

For notes on other varieties see below No. 121.

1932 (9 May). Optd.

(a) As T O **12**

O155	11	2f. ultramarine	1·75	10
O156		3f. green	1·50	10
O157		4f. brown-purple	1·50	10
O158		5f. grey-green	1·50	10
O159		8f. scarlet	1·50	10
O160		10f. yellow	2·25	10
O161		15f. blue	2·50	10
O162		20f. orange	2·50	15
O163		25f. mauve	2·50	15
O164		30f. bronze-green	3·50	20
O165		40f. violet	4·50	30

(b) As T O **13**, *horizontally*

O166	12	50f. brown	3·25	20
O167		75f. dull ultramarine	3·50	1·00
O168		100f. deep green	11·00	4·25
O169		200f. scarlet	38·00	6·50

(c) As T O **13**, *vertically upwards*

O170	10	½d. deep blue	28·00	50·00
O171		1d. claret	£150	£170
O155/O171 *Set of* 17			£225	£200
O155s/O171s Perf 'SPECIMEN' *Set of* 17			£800	

The British Mandate was given up on 3 October 1932 and Iraq became an independent kingdom. Later issues will be found listed in the Stanley Gibbons *Middle East Catalogue*.

Ireland

All the issues of Ireland to 1970 are listed together here, in this section of the Gibbons Catalogue, purely as a matter of convenience to collectors.

PRICES FOR STAMPS ON COVER TO 1945

Nos. 1/15	*from* × 5
Nos. 17/21	*from* × 3
Nos. 26/29*a*	*from* × 5
Nos. 30/43	*from* × 4
Nos. 44/46	—
Nos. 47/63	*from* × 5
Nos. 64/66	*from* × 3
Nos. 67/70	*from* × 6
Nos. 71/82	*from* × 2
Nos. 83/88	*from* × 3
Nos. 89/98	*from* × 2
Nos. 99/104	*from* × 3
Nos. 105/137	*from* × 2
Nos. D1/D4	*from* × 7
Nos. D5/D14	*from* × 6

PROVISIONAL GOVERNMENT

16 January–6 December 1922

Stamps of Great Britain overprinted.

Types **104/108**, W **100;** T **109**, W **110**

Rialtas Sealadać na hÉireann 1922 (1)

Rialtas Sealadać na hÉireann 1922. (2)

Rialtas Sealadać na hÉireann 1922 (3)

('Provisional Government of Ireland, 1922')

1922 (17 Feb–July). Types **104** to **108** (W **100**) and **109** of Great Britain overprinted in black.

(a) With T **1**, *by Dollard Printing House Ltd. Optd in black**

No.	Type	Description	Unused	Used
1	**105**	½d. green	2·25	40
		a. Opt inverted	£475	£600
		w. Wmk inverted	—	£600
2	**104**	1d. scarlet	4·25	80
		a. Opt inverted	£275	£350
		b. Opt double, both inverted, one albino	£350	
		c. Opt double	†	£1600
		w. Wmk inverted	—	£450
3		1d. carmine-red	14·00	2·50
4		2½d. bright blue	2·50	11·00
		a. Opt double, one albino	£475	
		b. Red opt (1.4)	3·50	4·75
		ba. Opt double, one albino	£475	
5	**106**	3d. bluish violet	7·50	8·00
6		4d. grey-green	6·50	27·00
		a. Opt double, one albino	£475	
		b. Red opt (1.8)	11·00	16·00
		c. Carmine opt (7.22)	48·00	70·00
7	**107**	5d. yellow-brown	7·00	9·00
		x. Wmk reversed	—	£500
8	**108**	9d. agate	17·00	45·00
		a. Opt double, one albino	£375	
		b. Red opt (1.4)	19·00	19·00
		c. Carmine opt (7.22)	90·00	95·00
9		10d. turquoise-blue	11·00	65·00
1/9 *Set of* 8			50·00	£110

* All values except 2½d. and 4d. are known with greyish black overprint, but these are difficult to distinguish.

The carmine overprints on the 4d. and 9d. were produced by Alex Thom & Co. Ltd. There was a further overprinting of the 2½d. at the same time, but this is difficult to distinguish.

The ½d. with red overprint is a trial or proof printing (*Price* £160).

Bogus inverted T **1** overprints exist on the 2d., 4d., 9d and 1s. values.

(b) With T **2**, *by Alex Thom & Co Ltd*

No.	Type	Description	Unused	Used
10	**105**	1½d. red-brown (*shades*)	3·50	2·75
		a. Error. "PENCF"	£375	£325
		w. Wmk inverted	—	£375
		x. Wmk reversed	—	£400
12	**106**	2d. orange (Die I)	9·50	50
		a. Opt inverted	£200	£300
		w. Wmk inverted	—	£400
		x. Wmk reversed	£600	£375
13		2d. orange (Die II)	6·50	50
		a. Opt inverted	£400	£500
		w. Wmk inverted	£425	£375
		y. Wmk inverted and reversed	£400	
14	**107**	6d. reddish purple (*chalk-surfaced paper*)	23·00	32·00
		a. Deep reddish purple	28·00	38·00
		y. Wmk inverted and reversed	£500	
15	**108**	1s. bistre-brown	13·00	19·00
10/15 *Set of* 5			50·00	48·00

Varieties occur throughout the T **2** overprint in the relative positions of the lines of the overprint, the 'R' of 'Rialtas' being over either the 'Se' or 'S' of 'Sealadac' or intermediately.

(c) With T **3** *by Dollard Printing House Ltd*

No.	Type	Description	Unused	Used
17	**109**	2s.6d. sepia-brown	60·00	85·00
		a. Opt double, one albino	£1600	
18		2s.6d. reddish brown	75·00	95·00
		a. Opt double, one albino	£750	
19		5s. rose-carmine	90·00	£170
21		10s. dull grey-blue	£180	£375
17/21 *Set of* 3			£300	£550

1922 (19 June–Aug). Optd as T **2**, in black, by Harrison & Sons, for use in horiz and vert coils.

No.	Type	Description	Unused	Used
26	**105**	½d. green	3·00	24·00
27	**104**	1d. scarlet	3·75	11·00
28	**105**	1½d. red-brown (21.6)	4·00	55·00
29	**106**	2d. bright orange (Die I)	22·00	55·00
29*a*		2d. bright orange (Die II) (8.22)	22·00	48·00
		ay. Wmk inverted and reversed	—	£400
26/29*a* *Set of* 5			50·00	£170

The Harrison overprint measures 15×17 mm (maximum) against the 14½×16 mm of T **2** (Thom printing) and is a much bolder black than the latter, while the individual letters are taller, the 'i' of 'Rialtas' being specially outstanding as it extends below the foot of the 'R'.

The 'R' of 'Rialtas' is always over the 'Se' of 'Sealadac'.

1922. Optd by Thom.

(a) As T **2** *but bolder, in dull to shiny blue-black or red (June–Nov)*

No.	Type	Description	Unused	Used
30	**105**	½d. green	3·75	80
31	**104**	1d. scarlet	3·25	50
		a. 'Q' for 'O' (No. 357ab)	£1400	£1200
		b. Reversed 'Q' for 'O' (No. 357ac)	£375	£250
		w. Wmk inverted	†	£550
32	**105**	1½d. red-brown	4·00	4·75
		a. Chestnut	4·00	4·50
		y. Wmk inverted and reversed	†	£600
33	**106**	2d. orange (Die I)	18·00	1·50
34		2d. orange (Die II)	6·00	50
		y. Wmk inverted and reversed	£180	£150
35	**104**	2½d. blue (R.)	9·00	32·00
36	**106**	3d. violet	11·00	2·25
		a. Dull reddish violet	5·00	2·00
		y. Wmk inverted and reversed	£150	£150
37		4d. grey-green (R.)	4·50	14·00
38	**107**	5d. yellow-brown	6·50	15·00
39		6d. reddish purple (*chalk-surfaced paper*)	18·00	8·00
		a. Deep reddish purple	14·00	6·00
		w. Wmk inverted	£275	£140
		y. Wmk inverted and reversed	†	£375
40	**108**	9d. agate (R.)	14·00	30·00
41		9d. olive-green (R.)	6·50	55·00
42		10d. turquoise-blue	29·00	75·00
43		1s. bistre-brown	17·00	18·00
30/43 *Set of* 14			£110	£225

Both 2d. stamps exist with the overprint inverted but there remains some doubt as to whether they were issued.

These Thom printings are distinguishable from the Harrison printings by the size of the overprint, and from the previous Thom printings by the intensity and colour of the overprint, the latter being best seen when the stamp is looked through with a strong light behind it.

(b) As with T **3**, *but bolder, in shiny blue-black (17 Oct–Nov)*

No.	Type	Description	Unused	Used
44	**109**	2s.6d. sepia-brown	£250	£350
45		5s. rose-carmine (11.22)	£275	£375
46		10s. dull grey-blue	£1000	£1400
44/46 *Set of* 3			£1400	£1900

The above differ from Nos. 17/21 not only in the bolder impression and colour of the ink but also in the 'h' and 'e' of 'heireann' which are closer together and horizontally aligned at foot.

Rialtas Sealadać na hÉireann 1922. (4)

Saorstát Éireann 1922 (5 Wide date) ('Irish Free State 1922')

1922 (21 Nov–Dec). Optd by Thom with T **4** (wider setting) in shiny blue-black.

No.	Type	Description	Unused	Used
47	**105**	½d. green	1·00	2·75
		a. Opt in dull black	£100	90·00
48	**104**	1d. scarlet	6·00	3·75
		w. Wmk inverted	†	£275
49	**105**	1½d. red-brown (4.12)	3·00	14·00
50	**106**	2d. orange (Die II)	10·00	7·00
51	**108**	1s. olive-bistre (4.12)	50·00	95·00
47/51 *Set of* 5			60·00	£110

The overprint T **4** measures 15¾ × 16 mm (maximum).

IRISH FREE STATE

6 December 1922–29 December 1937

1922 (Dec)–**23**.

(a) Optd by Thom with T **5**, *in dull to shiny blue-black or red*

No.	Type	Description	Unused	Used
52	**105**	½d. green	2·00	30
		a. No accent in 'Saorstat'	£1400	£1000
		b. Accent inserted by hand	£110	£130
53	**104**	1d. scarlet	2·75	50
		aa. No accent in 'Saorstat'	£17000	£10000
		a. No accent and final 't' missing	£15000	£8000
		b. Accent inserted by hand	£160	£180
		c. Accent and 't' inserted	£250	£300
		d. Accent and 'at' inserted	£250	£300
		e. Reversed 'Q' for 'O' (No. 357ac)	£375	£250
		f. Opt triple, two albino	£600	
54	**105**	1½d. red-brown	3·50	8·50
55	**106**	2d. orange (Die II)	1·50	1·00
56	**104**	2½d. bright blue (R.) (6.1.23)	7·50	15·00
		a. No accent	£160	£200
57	**106**	3d. bluish violet (6.1.23)	7·00	11·00
		a. No accent	£325	£425
58		4d. grey-green (R.) (16.1.23)	6·50	16·00
		a. No accent	£180	£225
59	**107**	5d. yellow-brown	5·50	5·00
60		6d. reddish purple (*chalk-surfaced paper*) (*shades*)	3·75	2·00
		a. Accent inserted by hand	£850	£900
		y. Wmk inverted and reversed	85·00	70·00
61	**108**	9d. olive-green (R.)	12·00	5·50
		aa. Pale olive-green	16·00	12·00
		a. No accent	£275	£325
62		10d. turquoise-blue	24·00	75·00
63		1s. bistre-brown (*shades*)	8·00	11·00
		a. No accent	£12000	£12000
		b. Accent inserted by hand	£700	£800
64	**109**	2s.6d. chocolate-brown	50·00	70·00
		aa. Pale brown	50·00	70·00
		a. Major re-entry (R. 1/2)	£1200	£1400
		b. No accent	£450	£600
		c. Accent reversed	£700	£850
65		5s. rose-carmine	85·00	£160
		a. No accent	£600	£900
		b. Accent reversed	£900	£1200
66		10s. dull grey-blue	£190	£350
		a. No accent	£3000	£4000
		b. Accent reversed	£4500	£5500
52/66 *Set of* 15			£350	£650

The 'no accent' and 'accent inserted' varieties on the ½d. to 1s. values occur on R. 15/12. On the 2s.6d. to 10s. values the 'no accent' varieties occur on R. 3/2 and R. 8/2, the 'accent reversed' on R. 7/4.

The accents inserted by hand are in dull black. The reversed accents are grave (thus 'à') instead of acute ('á'). A variety with 'S' of 'Saorstát' directly over 'é' of 'éireann', instead of to left, may be found in all values except the 2½d. and 4d. In the 2s.6d., 5s. and 10s. it is very slightly to the left in the 'S' over 'é' variety, bringing the 'á' of 'Saorstát' directly above the last 'n' of 'éireann'.

(b) Optd with T **5**, *in dull or shiny blue-black, by Harrison, for use in horiz or vert coils (7.3.23)*

No.	Type	Description	Unused	Used
67		½d. green	1·75	11·00
		a. Long '1' in '1922'	20·00	55·00
		y. Wmk inverted and reversed	†	—
68		1d. scarlet	8·50	25·00
		a. Long '1' in '1922'	85·00	£140
69		1½d. red-brown	6·50	55·00
		a. Long '1' in '1922'	85·00	£225
70		2d. orange (Die II)	9·50	18·00
		a. Long '1' in '1922'	35·00	60·00
		w. Wmk inverted	—	£300
67/70 *Set of* 4			23·00	95·00

In the Harrison overprint the characters are rather bolder than those of the Thom overprint, and the foot of the '1' of '1922' is usually rounded instead of square. The long '1' in '1922' has a serif at foot. The second 'e' of 'éireann' appears to be slightly raised.

PRINTERS. The following and all subsequent issues to No. 148 were printed at the Government Printing Works, Dublin, *unless otherwise stated.*

6 'Sword of Light'

7 Map of Ireland

8 Arms of Ireland

9 Celtic Cross

10

(Des J. J. O'Reilly, T **6**; J. Ingram, T **7**; Miss M. Girling, T **8**; and Miss L. Williams, T **9**. Typo. Plates made by Royal Mint, London)

1922 (6 Dec)–**34**. W **10**. P 15×14.

No.	Type	Description	Unused	Used
71	**6**	½d. bright green (20.4.23)	3·00	90
		a. Imperf×perf 14, Wmk sideways (11.34)	23·00	50·00
		w. Wmk inverted	40·00	25·00
72	**7**	1d. carmine (23.2.23)	2·25	10
		aw. Wmk inverted	38·00	10·00
		b. Perf 15×imperf (single perf) (1933)	£100	£250
		bw. Ditto. Wmk inverted	£120	£250
		c. Perf 15×imperf (7.34)	12·00	42·00
		d. Booklet pane. Three stamps plus three printed labels (21.8.31)	£475	£600
		dw. Wmk inverted	£475	£600
73		1½d. claret (2.2.23)	3·75	2·00
		w. Wmk inverted	£1300	£1100
74		2d. grey-green (6.12.22)	2·25	10
		a. Imperf×perf 14, Wmk sideways (11.34)	40·00	85·00
		b. Perf 15×imperf (1934)	£13000	£1600
		w. Wmk inverted	35·00	10·00
		y. Wmk inverted and reversed	38·00	38·00
75	**8**	2½d. red-brown (7.9.23)	6·00	3·75
		w. Wmk inverted	60·00	27·00
76	**9**	3d. ultramarine (16.3.23)	3·25	2·00
		w. Wmk inverted	75·00	32·00
77	**8**	4d. slate-blue (28.9.23)	2·75	3·25
		w. Wmk inverted	£180	60·00
78	**6**	5d. deep violet (11.5.23)	10·00	6·50
79		6d. claret (21.12.23)	7·00	3·00
		w. Wmk inverted	£180	75·00
80	**8**	9d. deep violet (26.10.23)	15·00	5·50
81	**9**	10d. brown (11.5.23)	8·00	14·00
82	**6**	1s light blue (15.6.23)	16·00	4·50
		w. Wmk inverted	†	£1200
71/82 *Set of* 12			65·00	40·00

No. 72b is imperf vertically except for a single perf at each top corner. It was issued for use in automatic machines.

It is now thought that the initial printing of No. 74 may have been the work of De La Rue in London.

See also Nos. 111/122.

Saorstát Éireann 1922

(**11** Narrow Date)

12 Daniel O'Connell

1925 (Aug)–**28**. T **109** of Great Britain (Bradbury Wilkinson printing) optd at the Government Printing Works, Dublin or at Somerset House, London.

*(a) With T **11** in black or grey-black (25.8.25)*

83 2s.6d. chocolate-brown ... 40·00 £100
a. Wide and narrow date (pair) (1927). £300 £650
84 5s. rose-carmine ... 60·00 £150
a. Wide and narrow date (pair) (1927). £450 £1100
85 10s. dull grey-blue ... £150 £350
a. Wide and narrow date (pair) (1927). £1200 £2750
83/85 *Set of* 3 ... £225 £550

The varieties with wide and narrow date *se-tenant* are from what is known as the 'composite setting,' in which some stamps showed the wide date, as T **5**, while in others the figures were close together, as in T **11**.

Single examples of this printing with wide date may be distinguished from Nos. 64 to 66 by the colour of the ink, which is black or grey-black in the composite setting and blue-black in the Thom printing.

The type of the 'composite' overprint usually shows distinct signs of wear.

*(b) As T **5** (wide date) in black (1927–1928)*

86 2s.6d. chocolate-brown (9.12.27) ... 50·00 60·00
a. Circumflex accent over 'a' ... £275 £375
b. No accent over 'a' ... £450 £550
c. Flat accent on 'a' ... £550 £650
87 5s. rose-carmine (2.28) ... 80·00 £100
a. Circumflex accent over 'a' ... £425 £600
c. Flat accent on 'a' ... £750 £900
88 10s. dull grey-blue (15.2.28) ... £190 £225
a. Circumflex accent over 'a' ... £1000 £1400
c. Flat accent on 'a' ... £1700 £2000
86/88 *Set of* 3 ... £275 £350

This printing can be distinguished from the Thom overprints in dull black, by the clear, heavy impression (in deep black) which often shows in relief on the back of the stamp.

The variety showing a circumflex accent over the 'a' occurred on R. 9/2. The overprint in this position finally deteriorated to such an extent that some examples of the 2s.6d. were without accent (No. 86b). A new cliché was then introduced with the accent virtually flat and which also showed damage to the 'a' and the crossbar of the 't'.

(Des L. Whelan. Typo)

1929 (22 June). Catholic Emancipation Centenary. W **10**. P 15×14.

89 **12** 2d. grey-green ... 1·00 45
90 3d. blue ... 3·75 11·00
91 9d. bright violet ... 3·75 5·00
89/91 *Set of* 3 ... 7·50 15·00

13 Shannon Barrage

14 Reaper

(Des E. L. Lawrenson. Typo)

1930 (15 Oct). Completion of Shannon Hydro-Electric Scheme. W **10**. P 15×14.

92 **13** 2d. agate ... 1·25 55

(Des G. Atkinson. Typo)

1931 (12 June). Bicentenary of the Royal Dublin Society. W **10**. P 15×14.

93 **14** 2d. blue ... 1·00 30

15 The Cross of Cong

16 Adoration of the Cross

17 Hurler

(Des G. Atkinson. Typo)

1932 (12 May). International Eucharistic Congress. W **10**. P 15×14.

94 **15** 2d. grey-green ... 2·50 30
w. Wmk inverted ... † —
95 3d. blue ... 3·75 6·50

(Des R. J. King. Typo)

1933 (18 Sept). 'Holy Year.' W **10**. P 15×14.

96 **16** 2d. grey-green ... 2·50 15
w. Wmk inverted ... † £600
97 3d. blue ... 4·25 2·50

(Des R. J. King. Typo)

1934 (27 July). Golden Jubilee of the Gaelic Athletic Association. W **10**. P 15×14.

98 **17** 2d. green ... 2·25 55
w. Wmk inverted ... † £1000

1935 (Mar–July). T **109** of Great Britain (Waterlow re-engraved printings) optd as T **5** (wide date), at Somerset House, London.

99 **109** 2s.6d. chocolate (No. 450) ... 48·00 60·00
a. Flat accent on 'a' (R. 9/2) ... £300 £300
100 5s. bright rose-red (No. 451) ... 90·00 90·00
a. Flat accent on 'a' (R. 9/2) ... £425 £425
101 10s. indigo (No. 452) ... £300 £325
a. Flat accent on 'a' (R. 9/2) ... £1100 £1100
b. Opt double ... £8500 £6500
99/101 *Set of* 3 ... £400 £425

18 St Patrick

19 Ireland and New Constitution

(Des R. J. King. Typo)

1937 (8 Sept). W **10**. P 14×15.

102 **18** 2s.6d. emerald-green ... £160 70·00
w. Wmk inverted ... £1000 £450
103 5s. maroon ... £180 £120
w. Wmk inverted ... £900 £450
104 10s. deep blue ... £150 55·00
w. Wmk inverted ... £1400 £1600
102/104 *Set of* 3 ... £450 £200

See also Nos. 123/125.

EIRE

29 December 1937–17 April 1949

(Des R. J. King. Typo)

1937 (29 Dec). Constitution Day. W **10**. P 15×14.

105 **19** 2d. claret ... 2·00 20
w. Wmk inverted ... — £350
106 3d. blue ... 5·00 3·75

For similar stamps see Nos. 176/177.

20 Father Mathew

(Des S. Keating. Typo)

1938 (1 July). Centenary of Temperance Crusade. W **10**. P 15×14.

107 **20** 2d. agate ... 3·00 50
w. Wmk inverted ... † £400
108 3d. blue ... 10·00 5·50

21 George Washington, American Eagle and Irish Harp

22

(Des G. Atkinson. Typo)

1939 (1 Mar). 150th Anniversary of US Constitution and Installation of First US President. W **10**. P 15×14.

109 **21** 2d. scarlet ... 3·00 1·00
110 3d. blue ... 4·25 5·50

SIZE OF WATERMARK. T **22** can be found in various sizes from about 8 to 10 mm high. This is due to the use of two different dandy rolls supplied by different firms and to the effects of paper shrinkage and other factors such as pressure and machine speed.

White line above left value tablet joining horizontal line to ornament (R. 3/7)

1940–68. Typo. W **22**. P 15×14 or 14×15 (2s.6d. to 10s.).

111 **6** ½d. bright green (24.11.40) ... 4·00 40
w. Wmk inverted ... 60·00 18·00
112 **7** 1d. carmine (26.10.40) ... 50 10
aw. Wmk inverted ... 2·00 30
b. From coils. Perf 14×imperf (9.40) ... 60·00 65·00
c. From coils. Perf 15×imperf (20.3.46) ... 42·00 24·00
cw. Wmk inverted ... 42·00 24·00
d. Booklet pane. Three stamps plus three printed labels ... £3250
dw. Wmk inverted ... £3250
113 1½d. claret (1.40) ... 19·00 30
w. Wmk inverted ... 30·00 16·00
114 2d. grey-green (1.40) ... 50 10
w Wmk inverted ... 2·75 2·75
115 **8** 2½d. red-brown (3.41) ... 16·00 15
w. Wmk inverted ... 25·00 6·50
116 **9** 3d. blue (12.40) ... 85 10
w. Wmk inverted ... 4·00 2·00
117 **8** 4d. slate-blue (12.40) ... 55 10
w. Wmk inverted ... 24·00 6·50
118 **6** 5d. deep violet (7.40) ... 1·00 10
w. Wmk inverted ... 45·00 35·00
119 6d. claret (3.42) ... 3·25 50
aw. Wmk inverted ... 40·00 13·00
b. Chalk-surfaced paper (1967) ... 1·25 20
bw. Wmk inverted ... 11·00 3·50
119*c* 8d. scarlet (12.9.49) ... 80 1·50
cw. Wmk inverted ... 50·00 65·00
120 **8** 9d. deep violet (7.40) ... 1·50 80
w. Wmk inverted ... 14·00 7·00
121 **9** 10d. brown (7.40) ... 75 80
aw. Wmk inverted ... 16·00 13·00
121*b* 11d. rose (12.9.49) ... 2·25 3·50
122 **6** 1s. light blue (6.40) ... 70·00 18·00
w. Wmk inverted ... £1200 £300
123 **18** 2s.6d. emerald-green (10.2.43) ... 40·00 1·00
aw. Wmk inverted ... £100 48·00
b. Chalk-surfaced paper (1967) ... 1·50 3·25
bw. Wmk inverted ... 38·00 6·00
124 5s. maroon (15.12.42) ... 40·00 1·50
a. Line flaw ... £275 50·00
bw. Wmk inverted ... £225 55·00
c. Chalk-surfaced paper (1968?) ... 13·00 4·25
ca. Purple ... 4·00 9·50
cb. Line flaw ... £100 65·00
cw. Wmk inverted ... 38·00 10·00
125 10s. deep blue (7.45) ... 60·00 6·00
aw. Wmk inverted ... £375 £110
b. Chalk-surfaced paper (1968) ... 19·00 13·00
ba. Blue (shades) ... 4·00 16·00
bw. Wmk inverted
111/125*ba Set of* 17 ... £110 30·00

There is a wide range of shades and also variations in paper used in this issue.

See also Nos. 227/228.

1941 i gcuimhne aiséirghe 1916

(**23** Trans 'In memory of the rising of 1916')

24 Volunteer and GPO, Dublin

1941 (12 Apr). 25th Anniversary of Easter Rising (1916). Provisional issue. Types **7** and **9** (2d. in new colour), optd with T **23**.

126 **7** 2d. orange (G.) ... 2·50 1·00
127 **9** 3d. blue (V.) ... 27·00 12·00

(Des V. Brown. Typo)

1941 (27 Oct). 25th Anniversary of Easter Rising (1916). Definitive issue. W **22**. P 15×14.

128 **24** 2½d. blue-black ... 3·25 1·00

25 Dr. Douglas Hyde

26 Sir William Rowan Hamilton

27 Bro. Michael O'Clery

(Des S. O'Sullivan. Typo)

1943 (31 July). 50th Anniversary of Founding of Gaelic League. W **22**. P 15×14.

129 **25** ½d. green ... 1·25 70
130 2½d. claret ... 2·00 10
w. Wmk inverted ... † £425

(Des S. O'Sullivan from a bust by Hogan. Typo)

1943 (13 Nov). Centenary of Announcement of Discovery of Quaternions. W **22**. P 15×14.

131 **26** ½d. green ... 75 70
132 2½d. brown ... 2·25 20

(Des R. J. King. Typo)

1944 (30 June). Tercentenary of Death of Michael O'Clery. (Commemorating the *Annals of the Four Masters*). W **22** (sideways*). P 14×15.

133 **27** ½d. emerald-green ... 10 10
w. Wmk facing right ... 80 35
134 1s. red-brown ... 1·50 10
w. Wmk facing right ... 4·50 2·00

* The normal sideways watermark shows the top of the e facing left, *as seen from the back of the stamp.*

Although issued as commemoratives these two stamps were kept in use as part of the current issue, replacing Nos. 111 and 122.

28 Edmund Ignatius Rice

29 'Youth Sowing Seeds of Freedom'

(Des S. O'Sullivan. Typo)

1944 (29 Aug). Death Centenary of Edmund Rice (founder of Irish Christian Brothers). W **22**. P 15×14.

135 **28** 2½d. slate ... 1·75 45
w. Wmk inverted ... † £350

(Des R. J. King. Typo)

1945 (15 Sept). Centenary of Death of Thomas Davis (founder of Young Ireland Movement). W **22**. P 15×14.

136 **29** 2½d. blue ... 2·50 75
w. Wmk inverted ... — £350
137 6d. claret ... 7·00 10·00

30 'Country and Homestead'

(Des R. J. King. Typo)

1946 (16 Sept). Birth Centenaries of Davitt and Parnell (land reformers). W **22**. P 15×14.

138 **30** 2½d. scarlet .... 2·50 25
139 3d. blue .... 3·50 4·25

31 Angel Victor over Rock of Cashel  — **32** Over Lough Derg

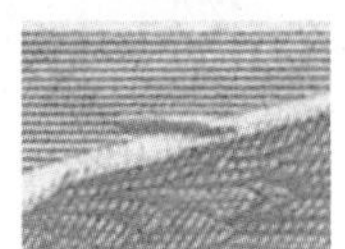

33 Over Croagh Patrick — **34** Over Glendalough

3d. Re-entry (R. 6/3) — **1s.3d.** 'Extra Feather' (R. 4/6)

(Des R. J. King. Recess Waterlow (1d. to 1s.3d. until 1961), D.L.R. (8d., 1s.3d. from 1961 and 1s.5d.))

1948 (7 Apr)–**65**. Air. Types **31/34**. W **22**. P 15 (1s.5d.) or 15×14 (others).

140 **31** 1d. chocolate (4.4.49) .... 3·00 7·00
141 **32** 3d. blue .... 3·00 3·50
a. Re-entry £150
142 **33** 6d. magenta .... 1·00 2·50
142*b* **32** 8d. lake-brown (13.12.54) .... 8·50 12·00
143 **34** 1s. green (4.4.49) .... 1·00 2·00
143*a* **31** 1s.3d. red-orange (13.12.54) .... 8·50 1·75
ab. 'Extra feather' £750 £500
aw. Wmk inverted £700 £425
143*b* 1s.5d. deep ultramarine *(shades)*(1.4.65) .... 4·00 2·75
140/143*b* *Set of 7* .... 26·00 28·00

35 Theobald Wolfe Tone

(Des K. Uhlemann. Typo)

1948 (19 Nov). 150th Anniversary of Insurrection. W **22**. P 15×14.

144 **35** 2½d. reddish purple .... 1·50 10
w. Wmk inverted .... † —
145 3d. violet .... 3·50 4·75

REPUBLIC OF IRELAND

18 April 1949

36 Leinster House and Arms of Provinces — **37** J. C. Mangan

(Des Muriel Brandt. Typo)

1949 (21 Nov). International Recognition of Republic. W **22**. P 15×14.

146 **36** 2½d. reddish brown .... 2·25 10
w. Wmk inverted .... † —
147 3d. bright blue .... 6·50 4·25

(Des R. J. King. Typo)

1949 (5 Dec). Death Centenary of James Clarence Mangan (poet). W **22**. P 15×14.

148 **37** 1d. green .... 1·50 35
w. Wmk inverted .... † —

38 Statue of St Peter, Rome

(Recess Waterlow & Sons)

1950 (11 Sept). Holy Year. W **22**. P 12½.

149 **38** 2½d. violet .... 1·00 40
150 3d. blue .... 6·00 12·00
151 9d. brown .... 7·50 15·00
149/151 *Set of 3* .... 13·00 25·00

PRINTERS. Nos. 152 to 200 were recess-printed by De La Rue & Co, Dublin, *unless otherwise stated.*

39 Thomas Moore — **40** Ireland at Home

(Eng W. Vacek)

1952 (10 Nov). Death Centenary of Thomas Moore (poet). W **22**. P 13.

152 **39** 2½d. reddish purple .... 1·00 10
w. Wmk inverted .... † —
153 3½d. deep olive-green .... 1·75 4·25

(Des F. O'Ryan. Typo Government Printing Works, Dublin)

1953 (9 Feb). 'An Tóstal' (Ireland at Home) Festival. W **22** (sideways). P 14×15.

154 **40** 2½d. emerald-green .... 2·00 35
155 1s.4d. blue .... 20·00 30·00

41 Robert Emmet — **42** *Madonna and Child* (Della Robbia) — **43** Cardinal Newman (first Rector)

(Eng L. Downey)

1953 (21 Sept). 150th Death Anniversary of Emmet (patriot). W **22**. P 13.

156 **41** 3d. deep bluish green .... 3·00 15
157 1s.3d. carmine .... 29·00 10·00

(Eng A. R. Lane)

1954 (24 May). Marian Year. W **22**. P 15.

158 **42** 3d. blue .... 1·00 10
159 5d. myrtle-green .... 1·75 3·25

(Des L. Whelan. Typo Govt Printing Works, Dublin)

1954 (19 July). Centenary of Founding of Catholic University of Ireland. W **22**. P 15×14.

160 **43** 2d. bright purple .... 2·25 10
w. Wmk inverted .... — £350
161 1s.3d. blue .... 13·00 7·00

44 Statue of Commodore Barry — **45** John Redmond — **46** Thomas O'Crohan

(Des and eng H. Woyty-Wimmer)

1956 (16 Sept). Barry Commemoration. W **22**. P 15.

162 **44** 3d. slate-lilac .... 1·00 10
163 1s.3d. deep blue .... 5·00 8·00

1957 (11 June). Birth Centenary of John Redmond (politician). W **22**. P 14×15.

164 **45** 3d. deep blue .... 1·25 10
165 1s.3d. brown-purple .... 10·00 16·00

1957 (1 July). Birth Centenary of Thomas O'Crohan (author). W **22**. P 14×15.

166 **46** 2d. maroon .... 1·00 20
w. Wmk inverted .... † £400
167 5d. violet .... 1·25 4·50

47 Admiral Brown — **48** *Father Wadding* (Ribera) — **49** Tom Clarke

(Des S. O'Sullivan. Typo Govt Printing Works, Dublin)

1957 (23 Sept). Death Centenary of Admiral William Brown. W **22**. P 15×14.

168 **47** 3d. blue .... 2·50 20
169 1s.3d. carmine .... 20·00 17·00

1957 (25 Nov). 300th Death Anniversary of Father Luke Wadding (theologian). W **22**. P 15.

170 **48** 3d. deep blue .... 2·00 10
171 1s.3d. lake .... 13·00 8·50

1958 (28 July). Birth Centenary of Thomas J. ('Tom') Clarke (patriot). W **22**. P 15.

172 **49** 3d. deep green .... 2·00 10
173 1s.3d. red-brown .... 4·00 11·00

50 Mother Mary Aikenhead — **51** Arthur Guinness

(Eng Waterlow. Recess Imprimerie Belge de Securité, Brussels subsidiary of Waterlow & Sons)

1958 (20 Oct). Death Centenary of Mother Mary Aikenhead (foundress of Irish Sisters of Charity). W **22**. P 15×14.

174 **50** 3d. Prussian blue .... 2·00 10
175 1s.3d. rose-carmine .... 11·00 8·00

(Typo Govt Printing Works, Dublin)

1958 (29 Dec). 21st Anniversary of the Irish Constitution. W **22**. P 15×14.

176 **19** 3d. brown .... 1·00 10
177 5d. emerald-green .... 1·00 4·50

1959 (20 July). Bicentenary of Guinness Brewery. W **22**. P 15.

178 **51** 3d. brown-purple .... 2·50 10
179 1s.3d. blue .... 10·00 8·00

52 'The Flight of the Holy Family'

(Des K. Uhlemann)

1960 (20 June). World Refugee Year. W **22**. P 15.

180 **52** 3d. purple 40 10
181 1s.3d. sepia .... 60 3·75

53 Conference Emblem

(Des P. Rahikainen)

1960 (19 Sept). Europa. W **22**. P 15.

182 **53** 6d. light brown .... 3·00 1·00
183 1s.3d. violet .... 14·00 20·00

The ink of No. 183 is fugitive.

54 Dublin Airport, de Havilland DH.84 Dragon Mk 2 *Iolar* and Boeing 720 — **55** St Patrick

(Des J. Flanagan and D. R. Lowther)

1961 (26 June). 25th Anniversary of Aer Lingus. W **22**. P 15.

184 **54** 6d. blue .... 1·75 3·75
w. Wmk inverted ....
185 1s.3d. green .... 2·25 5·50

(Recess B.W.)

1961 (25 Sept). 15th Death Centenary of St Patrick. W **22**. P 14½.

186 **55** 3d. blue .... 1·00 10
187 8d. purple .... 2·75 5·50
188 1s.3d. green .... 2·75 1·60
186/188 *Set of 3* .... 6·00 6·50

56 John O'Donovan and Eugene O'Curry

(Recess B.W.)

1962 (26 Mar). Death Centenaries of O'Donovan and O'Curry (scholars). W **22**. P 15.

189 **56** 3d. carmine 30 10
190 1s.3d. purple .... 1·25 2·25

57 Europa 'Tree'

(Des L. Weyer)

1962 (17 Sept). Europa. W **22**. P 15.

191	**57**	6d. carmine-red	70	1·00
192		1s.3d. turquoise	80	1·50

58 Campaign Emblem

(Des K. Uhlemann)

1963 (21 Mar). Freedom from Hunger. W **22**. P 15.

193	**58**	4d. deep violet	50	10
194		1s.3d. scarlet	3·25	2·75

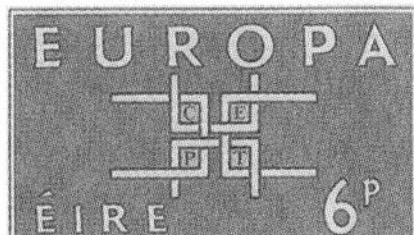

59 'Co-operation'

(Des A. Holm)

1963 (16 Sept). Europa. W **22**. P 15.

195	**59**	6d. carmine	1·00	75
196		1s.3d. blue	3·25	3·75

60 Centenary Emblem

(Des P. Wildbur. Photo Harrison & Sons)

1963 (2 Dec). Centenary of Red Cross. W **22**. P 14½×14.

197	**60**	4d. red and grey	40	10
198		1s.3d. red, grey and light emerald	1·10	2·00

61 Wolfe Tone

(Des P. Wildbur)

1964 (13 Apr). Birth Bicentenary of Wolfe Tone (revolutionary). W **22**. P 15.

199	**61**	4d. black	50	10
200		1s.3d. ultramarine	1·90	2·00

62 Irish Pavilion at Fair

(Des A. Devane. Photo Harrison & Sons)

1964 (20 July). New York World's Fair. W **22**. P 14½×14.

201	**62**	5d. blue-grey, brown, violet and yellow-olive	50	10
		a. Brown omitted*	£6000	
202		1s.5d. blue-grey, brown, turquoise blue and light yellow-green	2·00	2·00

* No 201a comes from the top row of the sheet and shows part of the brown cross which would appear in the sheet margin. As the second horizontal row was normal it would appear that the brown cylinder was incorrectly registered.

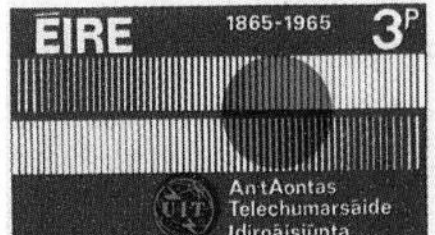

63 Europa 'Flower' **64** 'Waves of Communication'

(Des G. Bétemps. Photo Harrison)

1964 (14 Sept). Europa. W **22** (sideways). P 14×14½.

203	**63**	8d. olive-green and blue	1·50	1·50
204		1s.5d. red-brown and orange	5·00	4·50

(Des P. Wildbur. Photo Harrison)

1965 (17 May). ITU Centenary. W **22**. P 14½×14.

205	**64**	3d. blue and green	30	10
206		8d. black and green	1·25	1·60

PRINTERS Nos. 207 onwards were photogravure-printed by the Stamping Branch of the Revenue Commissioners, Dublin *unless otherwise stated.*

65 W. B. Yeats (poet) **66** ICY Emblem

(Des R. Kyne, from drawing by S. O'Sullivan)

1965 (14 June). Yeats' Birth Centenary. W **22** (sideways). P 15.

207	**65**	5d. black, orange-brown and deep green	50	10
208		1s.5d. black, grey-green and brown	2·75	2·00
		a. Brown omitted	£6000	

1965 (16 Aug). International Co-operation Year. W **22**. P 15.

209	**66**	3d. ultramarine and new blue	60	10
210		10d. deep brown and brown	1·00	3·25

67 Europa 'Sprig'

(Des H. Karlsson)

1965 (27 Sept). Europa. W **22**. P 15.

211	**67**	8d. black and brown-red	1·50	1·00
212		1s.5d. purple and light turquoise-blue	6·00	3·50

68 James Connolly **69** 'Marching to Freedom'

(Des E. Delaney (No. 216), R. Kyne, after portraits by S. O'Sullivan (others))

1966 (12 Apr). 50th Anniversary of Easter Rising. Types **68**/**69** and similar horiz portraits. W **22**. P 15.

213	3d. black and greenish blue	90	10
	a. Horiz pair. Nos. 213/214	1·75	3·00
214	3d. black and bronze-green	90	10
215	5d. black and yellow-olive	90	10
	a. Horiz pair. Nos. 215/216	1·75	2·50
216	5d. black, orange and blue-green	90	10
217	7d. black and light orange-brown	1·00	2·75
	a. Horiz pair. Nos. 217/218	2·00	10·00
218	7d. black and blue-green	1·00	2·75
219	1s.5d. black and turquoise	1·25	2·75
	a. Horiz pair. Nos. 219/220	2·50	10·00
220	1s.5d. black and bright green	1·25	2·75
213/220 *Set of 8*		7·25	10·00

Designs: No. 213, T **68**; No. 214, Thomas J. Clarke; No. 215, P. H. Pearse; No. 216, T **69**; No. 217, Eamonn Ceannt; No. 218, Sean MacDiarmada; No. 219, Thomas MacDonagh; No. 220, Joseph Plunkett.

Nos. 213/214, 215/216, 217/218 and 219/220 were each printed together, *se-tenant*, in horizontal pairs throughout the sheet.

76 R. Casement **77** Europa 'Ship'

(Des R. Kyne)

1966 (3 Aug). 50th Death Anniversary of Roger Casement (patriot). W **22** (sideways). P 15.

221	**76**	5d. black	15	10
222		1s. red-brown	40	50

(Des R. Kyne, after G. and J. Bender)

1966 (26 Sept). Europa. W **22** (sideways). P 15.

223	**77**	7d. emerald and orange	1·00	1·00
224		1s.5d. emerald and light grey	2·00	2·75

78 Interior of Abbey (from lithograph) **79** Cogwheels

1966 (8 Nov). 750th Anniversary of Ballintubber Abbey. W **22**. P 15.

225	**78**	5d. red-brown	10	10
226		1s. black	20	25

1966–67. As Nos. 116, 118 but photo. Smaller design (17×21 *mm*). Chalk-surfaced paper. W **22**. P 15.

227	**9**	3d. blue (1.8.67)	40	15
228	**6**	5d. bright violet (1.12.66)	30	15
		w. Wmk inverted (from booklets)	1·75	1·50

No. 228 was only issued in booklets (Nos. SB16/SB17) at first but was released in sheets on 1.4.68 in a slightly brighter shade. In the sheet stamps the lines of shading are more regular.

(Des O. Bonnevalle)

1967 (2 May). Europa. W **22** (sideways). P 15.

229	**79**	7d. light emerald, gold and pale cream	60	1·00
230		1s.5d. carmine-red, gold and pale cream	1·90	2·75

80 Maple Leaves

(Des P. Hickey)

1967 (28 Aug). Canadian Centennial. W **22**. P 15.

231	**80**	5d. multicoloured	10	10
232		1s.5d. multicoloured	20	1·25

81 Rock of Cashel (from photo by Edwin Smith)

1967 (25 Sept). International Tourist Year. W **22** (inverted). P 15.

233	**81**	7d. sepia	15	30
234		10d. slate-blue	15	70

82 1c. Fenian Stamp Essay **83** 24c. Fenian Stamp Essay

1967 (23 Oct). Centenary of Fenian Rising. W **22** (sideways). P 15.

235	**82**	5d. black and light green	10	10
236	**83**	1s. black and light pink	20	30

84 Jonathan Swift **85** Gulliver and Lilliputians

(Des M. Byrne)

1967 (30 Nov). 300th Birth Anniversary of Jonathan Swift. W **22** (sideways). P 15.

237	**84**	3d. black and olive-grey	10	10
238	**85**	1s.5d. blackish brown and pale blue	20	45

86 Europa 'Key'

(Des H. Schwarzenbach and M. Biggs)

1968 (29 Apr). Europa. W **22**. P 15.

239	**86**	7d. brown-red, gold and brown	50	50
240		1s.5d. new blue, gold and brown	75	1·00

87 St Mary's Cathedral, Limerick

(Des from photo by J. J. Bambury. Recess B.W.)

1968 (26 Aug). 800th Anniversary of St Mary's Cathedral, Limerick. W **22**. P 15.

241	**87**	5d. Prussian blue	10	10
242		10d. yellow-green	20	90

88 Countess Markievicz

89 James Connolly

1968 (23 Sept). Birth Centenary of Countess Markievicz (patriot). W **22** (inverted on 1s.5d.). P 15.

243	**88**	3d. black	10	10
244		1s.5d. deep blue and blue	70	1·75

1968 (23 Sept). Birth Centenary of James Connolly (patriot). W **22** (sideways). P 15.

245	**89**	6d. deep brown and chocolate	20	80
246		1s. blackish green, apple-green and myrtle-green	20	20

90 Stylised Dog (brooch)

91 Stag

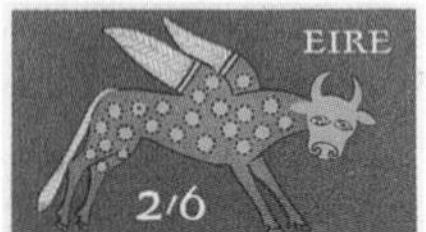

92 Winged Ox (Symbol of St Luke)

93 Eagle (Symbol of St John The Evangelist)

(Des H. Gerl)

1968–70. Pence values expressed with 'p'. W **22** (sideways* on ½d. to 1s.9d). P 15.

247	**90**	½d. red-orange (7.6.69)	10	30
248		1d. pale yellow-green (7.6.69)	15	30
		a. Coil stamp. Perf 14×15 (8.70?)	1·50	3·00
249		2d. light ochre (14.10.68)	50	10
		a. Coil stamp. Perf 14×15 (8.70?)	1·50	7·50
250		3d. blue (7.6.69)	35	10
		a. Coil stamp. Perf 14×15 (8.70?)	1·50	3·75
251		4d. deep brown-red (31.3.69)	30	10
252		5d. myrtle-green (31.3.69)	1·25	2·00
253		6d. bistre-brown (24.2.69)	30	10
		w. Wmk e facing right	5·50	3·25
254	**91**	7d. brown and yellow (7.6.69)	45	4·50
255		8d. chocolate and orange-brown (14.10.68)	45	3·50
256		9d. slate-blue and olive-green (24.2.69)	50	10
257		10d. chocolate and bluish violet (31.3.69)	1·50	3·50
258		1s. chocolate and red-brown (31.3.69)	40	10
259		1s.9d. black and light turquoise-blue (24.2.69)	4·00	3·50
260	**92**	2s.6d. multicoloured (14.10.68)	1·75	30
261		5s. multicoloured (24.2.69)	3·00	2·50
262	**93**	10s. multicoloured (14.10.68)	5·25	3·50
247/262 *Set of 16*			17·00	21·00

* The normal sideways watermark shows the top of the e facing left, *as seen from the back of the stamp.*

The 1d., 2d., 3d., 5d., 6d., 9d., 1s. and 2s.6d. exist with PVA gum as well as gum arabic. The coil stamps exist on PVA only, and the rest on gum arabic only.

Stamps in similar designs were issued from 1974 to 1983.

94 Human Rights Emblem

95 Dáil Éireann Assembly

1968 (4 Nov). Human Rights Year. W **22** (sideways). P 15.

263	**94**	5d. yellow, gold and black	15	10
264		7d. yellow, gold and red	15	40

(Des M. Byrne)

1969 (21 Jan). 50th Anniversary of Dáil Éireann (First National Parliament). W **22** (sideways). P 15×14½.

265	**95**	6d. myrtle-green	15	10
266		9d. Prussian blue	15	30

96 Colonnade

97 Quadruple ILO Emblems

(Des L. Gasbarra and G. Belli; adapted Myra Maguire)

1969 (28 Apr). Europa. W **22**. P 15.

267	**96**	9d. grey, ochre and ultramarine	1·00	1·40
268		1s.9d. grey, gold and scarlet	1·25	2·25

(Des K. C. Dabczewski)

1969 (14 July). 50th Anniversary of International Labour Organisation. W **22** (sideways). P 15.

269	**97**	6d. black and grey	20	10
270		9d. black and yellow	20	25

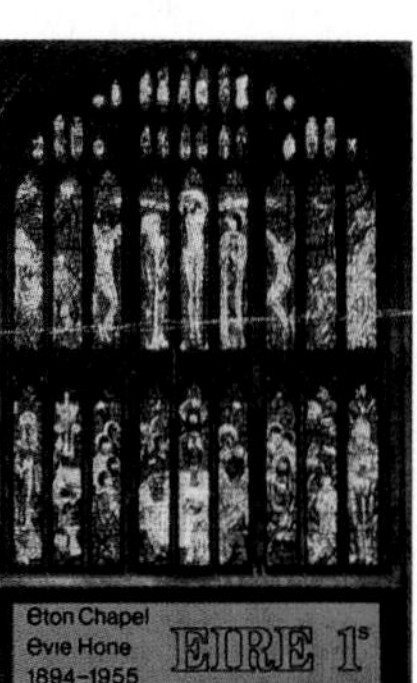

98 *The Last Supper and Crucifixion* (Evie Hone Window, Eton Chapel)

(Des R. Kyne)

1969 (1 Sept). Contemporary Irish Art (1st issue). W **22** (sideways). P 15×14½.

271	**98**	1s. multicoloured	30	1·50

See also No. 280.

99 Mahatma Gandhi

1969 (2 Oct). Birth Centenary of Mahatma Gandhi. W **22**. P 15.

272	**99**	6d. black and green	60	10
273		1s.9d. black and yellow	90	90

100 Symbolic Bird in Tree

(Des D. Harrington)

1970 (23 Feb). European Conservation Year. W **22**. P 15.

274	**100**	6d. bistre and black	20	10
275		9d. slate-violet and black	25	80

101 'Flaming Sun'

(Des L. le Brocquy)

1970 (4 May). Europa. W **22**. P 15.

276	**101**	6d. bright violet and silver	55	10
277		9d. brown and silver	90	1·25
278		1s.9d. deep olive-grey and silver	1·75	2·00
276/278 *Set of 3*			2·75	3·00

102 *Sailing Boats* (Peter Monamy)

103 *Madonna of Eire* (Mainie Jellett)

(Des P. Wildbur and P. Scott)

1970 (13 July). 250th Anniversary of Royal Cork Yacht Club. W **22**. P 15.

279	**102**	4d. multicoloured	15	10

1970 (1 Sept). Contemporary Irish Art (2nd issue) (sideways). W **22**. P 15.

280	**103**	1s. multicoloured	20	20

104 Thomas MacCurtain

106 Kevin Barry

(Des P. Wildbur)

1970 (26 Oct). 50th Death Anniversaries of Irish Patriots. T **104** and similar vert design. W **22** (sideways). P 15.

281	9d. black, bluish violet and greyish black	1·50	25
	a. Pair. Nos. 281/282	3·00	3·00
282	9d. black, bluish violet and greyish black	1·50	25
283	2s.9d. black, new blue and greyish black	2·00	4·00
	a. Pair. Nos. 283/284	4·00	11·00
284	2s.9d. black, new blue and greyish black	2·00	4·00
281/284 *Set of 4*		6·25	7·75

Designs: Nos. 281 and 283, T **104**; others, Terence MacSwiney.

Nos. 281/282 and 283/284 were each printed together, *se-tenant*, in horizontal and vertical pairs throughout the sheet.

(Des P. Wildbur)

1970 (2 Nov). 50th Death Anniversary of Kevin Barry (patriot). W **22** (inverted). P 15.

285	**106**	6d. olive-green	30	10
286		1s.2d. royal blue	40	1·10

STAMP BOOKLETS

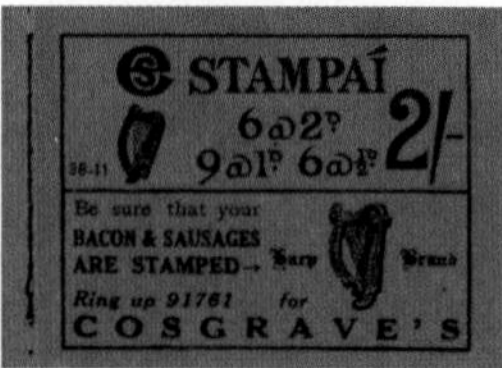

B **1** Harp and Monogram

B **2** Harp and 'EIRE'

1931 (21 Aug)–**40.** Black on red cover as T B **1**.

SB1	2s. booklet containing 6×½d., 6×2d. (Nos. 71, 74), each in block of 6, and 9×1d. (No. 72) in block of 6 and pane of 3 stamps and 3 labels (No. 72d or 72dw) *From*	£4000

Edition Nos.:—31-1, 31-2, 32-3, 33-4, 33-5, 34-6, 34-7, 35-8, 35-9, 36-10, 36-11, 37-12, 37-13, 37-14, 15-38, 16-38

	a. Cover as Type B **2** *From*	£4750

Edition Nos.:17-38,18-39, 19-39, 20-39, 21-40, 22-40

1940. Black on red cover as T B **2**.

SB2	2s. booklet containing 6×½d., 6×2d. (Nos. 71, 74), each in block of 6, and 9×1d. in block of 6 (No. 72) and pane of 3 stamps and 3 labels (No. 112d or 112dw)	£12000

Edition No.: 22-40

1940. Black on red cover as T B **2**.

SB3	2s. booklet containing 6×½d., 6×2d. (Nos. 111, 114), each in block of 6, and 9×1d. in block of 6 (No. 112) and pane of 3 stamps and 3 labels (No. 112d or 112dw)	£12000

Edition No.: 23-40

1941–44. Black on red cover as T B **2**.

SB4	2s. booklet containing 12×½d., 6×1d. and 6×2d. (Nos. 111/12, 114) in blocks of 6 *From*	£2500

Edition Nos.: 24-41, 25-42, 26-44

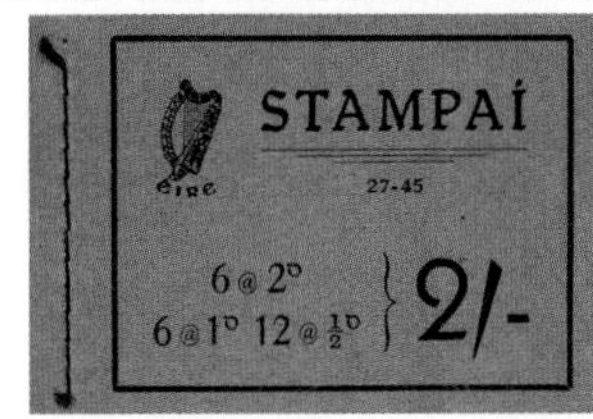

B 3

1945. Black on red cover as T B **3**.

SB5 — 2s. booklet containing 12×½d., 6×1d. and 6×2d. (Nos. 111/112, 114) in blocks of 6 .... £2500
Edition No.: 27–45

1946. Black on buff cover as T B **2**.

SB6 — 2s. booklet containing 12×½d., 6×1d. and 6×2d. (Nos. 111/112, 114) in blocks of 6 .... £1400
Edition No.: 28–46

1946–47. Black on buff cover as T B **2**.

SB7 — 2s. booklet containing 12×½d, 6×1d. and 6×2d. (Nos. 133, 112, 114) in blocks of 6 .... *From* £750
Edition Nos.: 29–46, 30–47

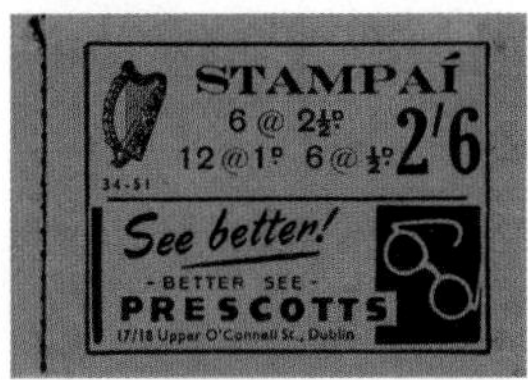

B **4** Harp only

1948–50. Black on orange-buff cover as T B **4**.

SB8 — 2s.6d. booklet containing 6×½d., 12×1d. and 6×2½d. (Nos. 133, 112, 115) in blocks of 6 .... *From* £325
Edition Nos.: 31–48, 32–49, 33–50

1951–53. Black on buff cover as T B **4**.

SB9 — 2s.6d. booklet containing 6×½d., 12×1d. and 6×2½d. (Nos. 133, 112, 115) in blocks of 6 .... *From* 70·00
Edition Nos.: 34–51, 35–52, 36–53

1954 (24 Nov). Black on buff cover as T B **4**.

SB10 — 4s. booklet containing 6×½d., 6×1½d. and 12×3d. (Nos. 133, 113, 116) in blocks of 6 .... £120
Edition No.: 37–54.

1956 (17 Dec). Black on buff cover as T B **4**.

SB11 — 4s. booklet containing 12×1d. and 12×3d. (Nos. 112, 116) in blocks of 6 .... £130
Edition No.: 38–56.

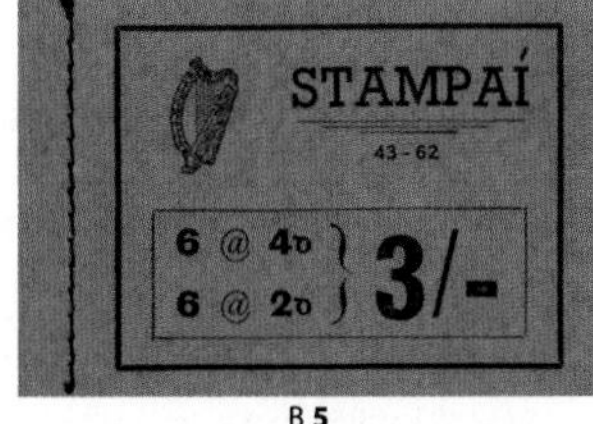

B **5**

1958–61. Black on buff cover as T B **5**.

SB12 — 4s. booklet containing 12×1d. and 12×3d. (Nos. 112, 116) in blocks of 6 .... £130
Edition Nos.: 39–58, 40–59, 41–60, 42–61.

1962 (23 Oct)–**63.** Black on buff cover as T B **5**.

SB13 — 3s. booklet containing 6×2d. and 6×4d. (Nos. 114, 117) in blocks of 6 .... *From* £110
Edition Nos.: 43–62, 44–63 (6.63).

B **6**

1964 (Sept). Red on yellow cover as T B **6**.

SB14 — 3s. booklet containing 12×1d. and 6×4d. (Nos. 112, 117) in blocks of 6 .... 60·00

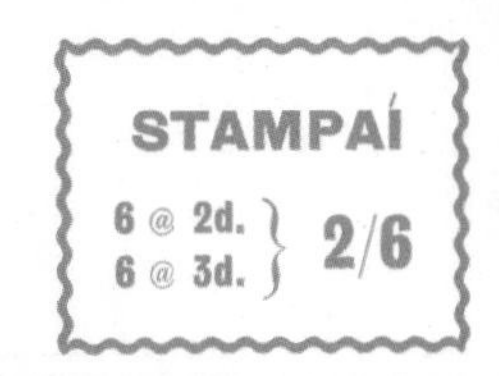

B **7**

1966 (1–9 Dec). Covers as T B **7** in red (No. SB15), blue (No. SB16) or green (No. SB17).

SB15 — 2s.6d. booklet containing 6×2d. and 6×3d. (Nos. 114, 116) in blocks of 6 (9.12) .... 19·00
SB16 — 2s.6d. booklet containing 6×5d. (No. 228) in block of 6 (9.12) .... 15·00
SB17 — 5s. booklet containing 12×5d. (No. 228) in blocks of 6 .... 30·00

B **8**

1969 (12 Sept). Plain blue-green cover as T B **8**.

SB18 — 6s. booklet containing 12×6d. (No. 253) in blocks of six .... 50·00

POSTAGE DUE STAMPS

From 1922 to 1925 Great Britain postage due stamps in both script and block watermarks were used without overprint.

D **1**

(Des Ruby McConnell. Typo Govt Printing Works, Dublin)

1925 (20 Feb). W **10**. P 14×15.

D1	D **1**	½d. emerald-green	12·00	16·00
D2		1d. carmine	15·00	3·50
		a. Wmk sideways	£1200	£600
		y. Wmk inverted and reversed	£170	£170
D3		2d. deep green	50·00	5·50
		a. Wmk sideways	55·00	17·00
		aw. Wmk sideways inverted	85·00	45·00
		w. Wmk inverted	90·00	35·00
D4		6d. plum	7·00	7·50
D1/D4 *Set of 4*			75·00	29·00

The normal sideways watermark shows the top of 'e' to the left, *as seen from the back of the stamp*.

1940–70. W **22**. P 14×15.

D5	D **1**	½d. emerald-green (1942)	35·00	23·00
		w. Wmk inverted	—	£500
D6		1d. carmine (1941)	1·50	70
		w. Wmk inverted	—	£475
D7		1½d. vermilion (1953)	4·00	13·00
		w. Wmk inverted	19·00	48·00
D8		2d. deep green (1940)	2·75	70
		w. Wmk inverted	£500	£100
D9		3d. blue (10.11.52)	5·00	5·50
		w. Wmk inverted	12·00	7·00
D10		5d. blue-violet (3.3.43)	6·00	2·25
		w. Wmk inverted	6·50	7·00
D11		6d. plum (21.3.60)	6·00	4·75
		a. Wmk sideways (1968)	15·00	15·00
		aw. Wmk sideways inverted	1·00	2·75
D12		8d. orange (30.10.62)	9·00	20·00
		w. Wmk inverted	17·00	40·00
D13		10d. bright purple (27.1.65)	7·50	7·50
D14		1s. apple-green (10.2.69)	8·50	11·00
		a. Wmk sideways (1970)	75·00	11·00
D5/D14 *Set of 10*			70·00	75·00

The normal sideways watermark shows the top of 'e' to the left, as seen from the back of the stamp.

Stamps in these designs but in different colours were issued between 1971 and 1978.

Jamaica

Records show that the first local Postmaster for Jamaica on a regular basis was appointed as early as 1671, although a reasonably organised service did not evolve until 1687–1688. In the early years of the 18th-century overseas mail was carried by the British packets, but between 1704 and 1711 this service was run on a commercial basis by Edmund Dummer. Following the collapse of the Dummer scheme Jamaica was virtually without a Post Office until 1720 and it was not until 1755 that overseas mail was again carried by British packets.

Stamps of Great Britain were used in Jamaica from 8 May 1858, initially on overseas mail only, but their use was extended to mail sent to Jamaican addresses from 1 February 1859. The island assumed responsibility for the postal service on 1 August 1860 and the use of Great Britain stamps then ceased.

KINGSTON

Z **1**

Stamps of GREAT BRITAIN cancelled 'A01' as T Z **1**.

1858–60.

Z1	1d. rose-red (1857), *perf* 16	£850
Z2	1d. rose-red (1857), *perf* 14	£120
Z4	4d. rose-carmine *or* rose (1857)	80·00
Z5	6d. lilac (1856)	85·00
Z6	1s. green (1856)	£425

Z **2**

Stamps of GREAT BRITAIN cancelled 'A01' as T Z **2**.

1859–60.

Z7	1d. rose-red (1857), *perf* 14	£400
Z9	4d. rose-carmine *or* rose (1857)	85·00
Z10	6d. lilac (1856)	90·00
Z11	1s. green (1856)	£850

Z **3**

Stamps of GREAT BRITAIN cancelled 'A01' as T Z **3**.

1859–60.

Z12	1d. rose-red (1857), *perf* 14	£600
Z14	4d. rose-carmine *or* rose (1857)	£375
	a. Thick *glazed* paper	£700
Z15	6d. lilac (1856)	£375
Z16	1s. green (1856)	

Cancellation 'A01' was later used by the London, Foreign Branch Office.

OTHER JAMAICA POST OFFICES

British stamps were issued to several District post offices between 8 May 1858 and 1 March 1859 (i.e. before the Obliterators A27—A78 were issued). These can only be distinguished (off the cover) when they have the Town's date-stamp on them. They are worth about three times the price of those with an obliteration number.

Stamps of GREAT BRITAIN cancelled 'A27' to 'A78'as T Z **1**.

1859–60.

'A27'. ALEXANDRIA

Z17	1d. rose-red (1857), *perf* 14	£1100
Z17*a*	2d. blue (1855) Large Crown, *perf* 14 (Plate 6)	£2000
Z18	4d. rose (1857)	£425
Z19	6d. lilac (1856)	£800

'A28'. ANNOTTO BAY

Z20	1d. rose-red (1857), *perf* 14	£550
Z21	4d. rose (1857)	£250
Z22	6d. lilac (1856)	£475

'A29'. BATH

Z23	1d. rose-red (1857), *perf* 14	£400
Z24	4d. rose (1857)	£250
Z25	6d. lilac (1856)	£700

'A30'. BLACK RIVER

Z26	1d. rose-red (1857), *perf* 14	£400
Z27	4d. rose (1857)	£180
Z28	6d. lilac (1856)	£350

'A31'. BROWN'S TOWN

Z29	1d. rose-red (1857), *perf* 14	£500
Z30	4d. rose (1857)	£425
Z31	6d. lilac (1856)	£425

'A32'. BUFF BAY

Z32	1d. rose-red (1857), *perf* 14	£450
Z33	4d. rose (1857)	£350
Z34	6d. lilac (1856)	£325

'A33'. CHAPELTON

Z35	1d. rose-red (1857), *perf 14*	£450
Z36	4d. rose (1857)	£300
Z37	6d. lilac (1856)	£400

'A34'. CLAREMONT

Z38	1d. rose-red (1857), *perf 14*	£750
Z39	4d. rose (1857)	£375
Z40	6d. lilac (1856)	£425

'A35'. CLARENDON

Z41	1d. rose-red (1857), *perf 14*	£500
Z42	4d. rose (1857)	£275
Z43	6d. lilac (1856)	£425

'A36'. DRY HARBOUR

Z44	1d. rose-red (1857), *perf 14*	£800
Z45	4d. rose (1857)	£550
Z46	6d. lilac (1856)	£475

'A37'. DUNCANS

Z47	1d. rose-red (1857), *perf 14*	£900
Z48	4d. rose (1857)	£700
Z49	6d. lilac (1856)	£550

'A38'. EWARTON

A38 was allocated to EWARTON but this office was closed towards the end of 1858 before the postmark arrived. A38 was re-issued to Falmouth in 1862.

'A39'. FALMOUTH

Z53	1d. rose-red (1857), *perf 14*	£300
Z54	4d. rose (1857)	£160
Z55	6d. lilac (1856)	£170
Z56	1s. green (1856)	£1600

'A40'. FLINT RIVER

Z57	1d. rose-red (1857), *perf 14*	£450
Z58	4d. rose (1857)	£325
Z59	6d. lilac (1856)	£375
Z60	1s. green (1856)	£1600

'A41'. GAYLE

Z61	1d. rose-red (1857), *perf 14*	£750
Z62	4d. rose (1857)	£250
Z63	6d. lilac (1856)	£350
Z64	1s. green (1856)	£1000

'A42'. GOLDEN SPRING

Z65	1d. rose-red (1857), *perf 14*	£550
Z66	4d. rose (1857)	£450
Z67	6d. lilac (1856)	£750
Z68	1s. green (1856)	£1400

'A43'. GORDON TOWN

Z69	1d. rose-red (1857), *perf 14*	
Z70	4d. rose (1857)	
Z71	6d. lilac (1856)	£900

'A44'. GOSHEN

Z72	1d. rose-red (1857), *perf 14*	£350
Z73	4d. rose (1857)	£300
Z74	6d. lilac (1856)	£170

'A45'. GRANGE HILL

Z75	1d. rose-red (1857), *perf 14*	£375
Z76	4d. rose (1857)	£150
Z77	6d. lilac (1856)	£180
Z77*a*	1s. green (1856)	£1500

'A46'. GREEN ISLAND

Z78	1d. rose-red (1857), *perf 14*	£500
Z79	4d. rose (1857)	£350
Z80	6d. lilac (1856)	£475
Z81	1s. green (1856)	£1500

'A47'. HIGHGATE

Z82	1d. rose-red (1857), *perf 14*	£400
Z83	4d. rose (1857)	£275
Z84	6d. lilac (1856)	£475

'A48'. HOPE BAY

Z85	1d. rose-red (1857), *perf 14*	£750
Z86	4d. rose (1857)	£375
Z87	6d. lilac (1856)	£800

'A49'. LILLIPUT

Z88	1d. rose-red (1857), *perf 14*	£350
Z89	4d. rose (1857)	£375
Z90	6d. lilac (1856)	£225

'A50'. LITTLE RIVER

A50 was allocated for use at LITTLE RIVER but this office was closed late in 1858, before the obliterator could be issued. Issued to Malvern in 1862.

'A51'. LUCEA

Z91	1d. rose-red (1857), *perf 14*	£500
Z92	4d. rose (1857)	£170
Z93	6d. lilac (1856)	£375

'A52'. MANCHIONEAL

Z94	1d. rose-red (1857), *perf 14*	£650
Z95	4d. rose (1857)	£375
Z96	6d. lilac (1856)	£700

'A53'. MANDEVILLE

Z97	1d. rose-red (1857), *perf 14*	£375
Z98	4d. rose (1857)	£160
Z99	6d. lilac (1856)	£350

'A54'. MAY HILL

Z100	1d. rose-red (1857), *perf 14*	£275
Z101	4d. rose (1857)	£225
Z102	6d. lilac (1856)	£160
Z102*a*	1s. green (1856)	£2000

'A55'. MILE GULLY

Z103	1d. rose-red (1857), *perf 14*	£475
Z104	4d. rose (1857)	£400
Z105	6d. lilac (1856)	£400

'A56'. MONEAGUE

Z106	1d. rose-red (1857), *perf 14*	£450
Z107	4d. rose (1857)	£425
Z108	6d. lilac (1856)	£800

'A57'. MONTEGO BAY

Z109	1d. rose-red (1857), *perf 14*	£375
Z110	4d. rose (1857)	£130
Z111	6d. lilac (1856)	£150
Z112	1s. green (1856)	£1400

'A58'. MONTPELIER

Z113	1d. rose-red (1857), *perf 14*	
Z114	4d. rose (1857)	
Z115	6d. lilac (1856)	£1300

'A59'. MORANT BAY

Z116	1d. rose-red (1857), *perf 14*	£600
Z117	4d. rose (1857)	£160
Z118	6d. lilac (1856)	£180

'A60'. OCHO RIOS

Z119	1d. rose-red (1857), *perf 14*	£1200
Z120	4d. rose (1857)	£200
Z121	6d. lilac (1856)	£425

'A61'. OLD HARBOUR

Z122	1d. rose-red (1857), *perf 14*	£400
Z123	4d. rose (1857)	£275
Z124	6d. lilac (1856)	£325

'A62'. PLANTAIN GARDEN RIVER

Z125	1d. rose-red (1857), *perf 14*	£325
Z126	4d. rose (1857)	£225
Z127	6d. lilac (1856)	£325

'A63'. PEAR TREE GROVE

No genuine specimen of A63 has been found on a British stamp.

'A64'. PORT ANTONIO

Z131	1d. rose-red (1857), *perf 14*	£650
Z132	4d. rose (1857)	£425
Z133	6d. lilac (1856)	£450

'A65'. PORT MORANT

Z134	1d. rose-red (1857), *perf 14*	£450
Z135	4d. rose (1857)	£225
Z136	6d. lilac (1856)	£450

'A66'. PORT MARIA

Z137	1d. rose-red (1857), *perf 14*	£450
Z138	4d. rose (1857)	£180
Z139	6d. lilac (1856)	£450

'A67'. PORT ROYAL

Z140	1d. rose-red (1857), *perf 14*	£700
Z140*a*	2d. blue (1858) (plate 9)	£3000
Z141	4d. rose (1857)	£750
Z142	6d. lilac (1856)	£750

'A68'. PORUS

Z143	1d. rose-red (1857), *perf 14*	£450
Z144	4d. rose (1857)	£225
Z145	6d. lilac (1856)	£650

'A69'. RAMBLE

Z146	1d. rose-red (1857), *perf 14*	£375
Z147	4d. rose (1857)	£350
	a. Thick *glazed* paper	£650
Z149	6d. lilac (1856)	£475

'A70'. RIO BUENO

Z150	1d. rose-red (1857), *perf 14*	£450
Z151	4d. rose (1857)	£350
Z152	6d. lilac (1856)	£275

'A71'. RODNEY HALL

Z153	1d. rose-red (1857), *perf 14*	£350
Z154	4d. rose (1857)	£225
Z155	6d. lilac (1856)	£275

'A72'. ST DAVID

Z156	1d. rose-red (1857), *perf 14*	£450
Z157	4d. rose (1857)	£600
Z158	6d. lilac (1856)	

'A73'. ST ANN'S BAY

Z159	1d. rose-red (1857), *perf 14*	£375
Z160	4d. rose (1857)	£200
Z161	6d. lilac (1856)	£325
Z161*a*	1s. green (1856)	£1800

'A74'. SALT GUT

Z162	1d. rose-red (1857), *perf 14*	£450
Z163	4d. rose (1857)	£300
Z164	6d. lilac (1856)	£400

'A75'. SAVANNAH-LA-MAR

Z165	1d. rose-red (1857), *perf 14*	£225
Z166	4d. rose (1857)	£160
Z167	6d. lilac (1856)	£350
Z168	1s. green (1856)	£1400

'A76'. SPANISH TOWN

Z169	1d. rose-red (1857), *perf 14*	£250
Z170	4d. rose (1857)	£140
Z171	6d. lilac (1856)	£180
Z172	1s. green (1856)	£1100

'A77'. STEWART TOWN

Z173	1d. rose-red (1857), *perf 14*	£700
Z174	4d. rose (1857)	£500
Z175	6d. lilac (1856)	£400

'A78'. VERE

Z176	1d. rose-red (1857), *perf 14*	£550
Z177	4d. rose (1857)	£225
Z178	6d. lilac (1856)	£160
Z179	1s. green (1856)	£1600

PRICES FOR STAMPS ON COVER TO 1945

Nos. 1/6	*from* × 4
Nos. 7/15	*from* × 6
Nos. 16/26	*from* × 8
Nos. 27/29	*from* × 6
No. 30	*from* × 5
Nos. 31/32	*from* × 15
Nos. 33/36	*from* × 5
Nos. 37/56	*from* × 3
No. 57	*from* × 4
Nos. 58/67	*from* × 3
Nos. 68/77	*from* × 6
Nos. 78/89	*from* × 3
Nos. 90/103	*from* × 4
Nos. 104/107	*from* × 5
Nos. 108/117	*from* × 3
Nos. 118/120	*from* × 5
Nos. 121/133*a*	*from* × 4
Nos. 134/140	*from* × 8
Nos. F1/F9	*from* × 3
Nos. O1/O5	*from* × 3

CROWN COLONY

PRINTERS. Until 1923, all the stamps of Jamaica were typographed by De La Rue & Co, Ltd, London, *unless otherwise stated.*

The official dates of issue are given, where known, but where definite information is not available the dates are those of earliest known use, etc.

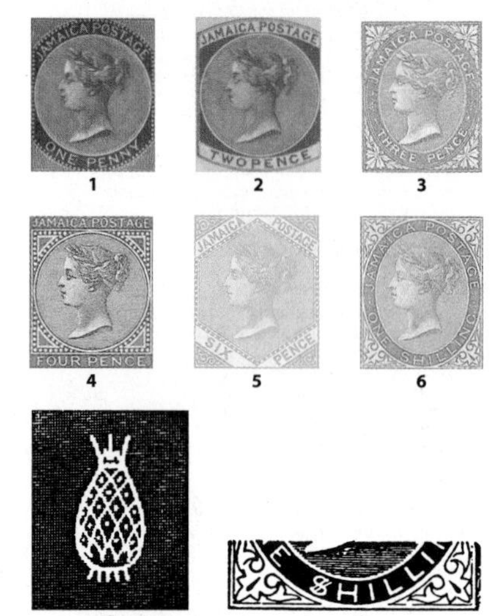

1860 (23 Nov)–**70.** W **7.** P 14.

1	**1**	1d. pale blue	75·00	15·00
		a. Pale greenish blue	£110	21·00
		b. Blue	70·00	12·00
		c. Deep blue (1865)	£140	35·00
		d. Bisected (½d.) (20.11.61) (*on cover*)	†	£650
		w. Wmk inverted	£180	55·00
2	**2**	2d. rose	£225	55·00
		a. Deep rose	£170	55·00
		w. Wmk inverted	—	£100
3	**3**	3d. green (10.9.63)	£160	25·00
		w. Wmk inverted	£200	50·00
4	**4**	4d. brown-orange	£275	50·00
		a. Red-orange	£225	22·00
		w. Wmk inverted		
5	**5**	6d. dull lilac	£200	22·00
		a. Grey-purple	£275	35·00
		b. Deep purple (1870)	£850	55·00
		w. Wmk inverted	—	£110
6	**6**	1s. yellow-brown	£500	25·00
		a. Purple-brown (1862)	£550	23·00
		b. Dull brown (1868)	£200	27·00
		c. '$' for 'S' in 'SHILLING' (A)	£3000	£600
		w. Wmk inverted	—	85·00

The diagonal bisection of the 1d. was authorised by a PO notice dated 20 November 1861 to pay the ½d. rate for newspapers or book post. Examples are only of value when on original envelope or wrapper. The authority was withdrawn as from 1 December 1872. Fakes are frequently met with. Other bisections were unauthorised.

The so-called 'dollar variety' of the 1s. occurs once in each sheet of stamps in all shades and in later colours, etc, on the second stamp in the second row of the left upper pane. The prices quoted above are for the dull brown shade, the prices for the other shades being proportionate to their normal value.

All values except the 3d. are known imperf, mint only.

There are two types of watermark in the 3d. and 1s., one being short and squat and the other elongated.

8

9

10

1870–83. Wmk Crown CC.

(a) P 14

7	**8**	½d. claret (29.10.72)	23·00	3·50
		a. Deep claret (1883)	29·00	5·50
		w. Wmk inverted	—	75·00

8	1	1d. blue (4.73)	£100	75
		a. Deep blue	£110	1·50
		w. Wmk inverted	£225	40·00
9	2	2d. rose (4.70)	£100	70
		a. Deep rose	£110	1·00
		w. Wmk inverted	£180	40·00
10	3	3d. green (1.3.70)	£160	11·00
		w. Wmk inverted	—	£120
11	4	4d. brown-orange (1872)	£325	12·00
		a. Red-orange (1883)	£425	6·00
		w. Wmk inverted	—	£100
12	5	6d. mauve (10.3.71)	95·00	5·50
		w. Wmk inverted	—	75·00
13	6	1s. dull brown (*to deep*) (23.2.73)	25·00	8·50
		a. '$' for 'S' in 'SHILLING' (A)	£1400	£600
		w. Wmk inverted	—	£110
		(b) P 12½		
14	9	2s. Venetian red (27.8.75)	45·00	38·00
		w. Wmk inverted	70·00	80·00
15	10	5s. lilac (27.8.75)	£120	£170
		w. Wmk inverted	£150	£225
7/15 *Set of 9*			£900	£200

The ½d., 1d., 4d., 2s. and 5s. are known imperforate.

1883–97. Wmk Crown CA. P 14.

16	8	½d. yellow-green (2.85)	12·00	1·50
		a. Green	3·75	10
		w. Wmk inverted	—	50·00
		x. Wmk reversed	—	£120
17	1	1d. blue (1884)	£325	8·50
		w. Wmk inverted	†	—
18		1d. rose (*to deep*) (3.3.85)	80·00	2·25
		a. Carmine (1886)	65·00	1·00
		w. Wmk inverted	—	65·00
19	2	2d. rose (*to deep*) (17.3.84)	£225	5·50
		w. Wmk inverted	—	85·00
20		2d. grey (1885)	£150	9·00
		a. Slate (1886)	£110	65
		w. Wmk inverted	—	42·00
21	3	3d. sage-green (11.86)	4·00	2·25
		a. Pale olive-green	2·75	3·00
22	4	4d. red-orange* (9.3.83)	£450	22·00
		aw. Wmk inverted		
		b. Red-brown (shades) (1885)	2·00	35
		bw. Wmk inverted	£100	42·00
23	5	6d. deep yellow (4.10.90)	38·00	8·00
		a. Orange-yellow	5·00	3·50
24	6	1s. brown (*to deep*) (3.97)	11·00	6·00
		a. '$' for 'S' in 'SHILLING' (A)	£800	£500
		b. Chocolate	17·00	12·00
25	9	2s. Venetian red (2.97)	32·00	38·00
26	10	5s. lilac (2.97)	65·00	95·00
16/26 *Set of 11*			£750	£130
16s, 18s, 20s/23s Optd 'SPECIMEN' *Set of 6*			£800	

* No. 22 is the same colour as No. 11*a*.

The 1d. carmine, 2d. slate, and 2s. are known imperf. All values to the 6d. inclusive are known perf 12. These are proofs.

11

TWO PENCE
HALF-PENNY
(12)

1889 (8 Mar)–**91**. Value tablet in second colour. Wmk Crown CA. P 14.

27	11	1d. purple and mauve	14·00	20
		w. Wmk inverted	—	50·00
28		2d. green	42·00	7·00
		a. Deep green (brown gum)	25·00	8·50
		aw. Wmk inverted	80·00	
29		2½d. dull purple and blue (25.2.91)	10·00	50
		w. Wmk inverted	£140	
27/29 *Set of 3*			45·00	7·00
27s/29s Optd 'SPECIMEN' *Set of 3*			£150	

A very wide range of shades may be found in the 1d. The headplate was printed in many shades of purple, and the duty plate in various shades of mauve and purple and also in carmine, etc. There are fewer shades for the other values and they are not so pronounced.

1d. stamps with the duty plate in blue are colour changelings.

1890 (4 June)–**91**. No. 22*b* surch with T **12** by C. Vendryes, Kingston.

30	4	2½d. on 4d. red-brown	40·00	17·00
		a. Spacing between lines of surch 1½ mm (2.91)	50·00	21·00
		b. Surch double	£325	£225
		c. 'PFNNY' for 'PENNY'	90·00	65·00
		ca. Ditto and broken 'K' for 'Y'	£160	£110
		w. Wmk inverted	£100	48·00

This provisional was issued pending receipt of No. 29 which is listed above for convenience of reference.

Three settings exist. (1) Ten varieties arranged in a single vertical row and repeated six times in the pane. (2) 12 varieties, in two horizontal rows of six, repeated five times, alternate rows show 1 and 1½ mm spacing between lines of surcharge. (3) Three varieties, arranged horizontally and repeated 20 times. All these settings can be reconstructed by examination of the spacing and relative position of the words of the surcharge and of the broken letters, etc, which are numerous.

A variety reading 'PFNNK', with the 'K' unbroken, is a forgery.

Surcharges misplaced either horizontally or vertically are met with, the normal position being central at the foot of the stamp with 'HALF-PENNY' covering the old value.

13 Llandovery Falls, Jamaica (photo by Dr. J. Johnston)

14 Arms of Jamaica

(Recess D.L.R.)

1900 (1 May)–**01**. Wmk Crown CC (sideways*). P 14.

31	13	1d. red	15·00	20
		w. Wmk Crown to left of CC	15·00	50
		x. Wmk reversed	—	90·00
		y. Wmk sideways inverted and reversed		
32		1d. slate-black and red (25.9.01)	14·00	20
		a. Blued paper	£110	£100
		b. Imperf between (vert pair)	£23000	
		w. Wmk Crown to left of CC	30·00	11·00
		x. Wmk reversed	—	90·00
		y. Wmk sideways inverted and reversed		
31s/32s Optd 'SPECIMEN' *Set of 2*			£140	

* The normal sideways wmk shows Crown to right of CC, *as seen from the back of the stamp.*

Many shades exist of both centre and frame of the bi-coloured 1d. which was, of course, printed from two plates and the design shows minor differences from that of the 1d. red which was printed from a single plate.

1903 (16 Nov)–**04**. Wmk Crown CA. P 14.

33	14	½d. grey and dull green	2·50	30
		a. 'SER.ET' for 'SERVIET'	40·00	45·00
		w. Wmk inverted	35·00	38·00
34		1d. grey and carmine (24.2.04)	4·75	10
		a. 'SER.ET' for 'SERVIET'	32·00	35·00
35		2½d. grey and ultramarine	9·00	30
		a. 'SER.ET' for 'SERVIET'	65·00	75·00
36		5d. grey and yellow (1.3.04)	18·00	23·00
		a. 'SER.ET' for 'SERVIET'	£800	£1000
		w. Wmk inverted	£150	
33/36 *Set of 4*			30·00	23·00
33s/36s Optd 'SPECIMEN' *Set of 4*			£100	

The 'SER.ET' variety occurs on R. 4/2 of the left upper pane. It was corrected by De La Rue in July 1905, following the printing of Nos. 37 and 43.

The centres of the above and later bi-coloured stamps in the Arms type vary in colour from grey to grey-black.

15 Arms type redrawn

16 Arms type redrawn

1905–11. Wmk Mult Crown CA. P 14.

		(a) Arms types. Chalk-surfaced paper		
37	14	½d. grey and dull green (20.11.05)	2·00	20
		a. 'SER.ET' for 'SERVIET'	26·00	40·00
		w. Wmk inverted		
		y. Wmk inverted and reversed	†	£200
38	15	½d. yellow-green (*ordinary paper*) (8.11.06)	12·00	50
		aw. Wmk inverted	†	£170
		b. Dull green	3·00	20
		c. Deep green	4·75	20
39	14	1d. grey and carmine (20.11.05)	18·00	1·75
		w. Wmk inverted	—	£150
40	16	1d. carmine (*ordinary paper*) (1.10.06)	1·50	10
		w. Wmk inverted	65·00	
41	14	2½d. grey and ultramarine (12.11.07)	7·50	9·00
42		2½d. pale ultramarine (*ordinary paper*) (21.9.10)	5·00	1·25
		a. Deep ultramarine	2·50	1·75
43		5d. grey and orange-yellow (24.4.07)	65·00	80·00
		a. 'SER.ET' for 'SERVIET'	£1400	£1600
44		6d. dull and bright purple (18.8.11)	14·00	23·00
45		5s. grey and violet (11.05)	55·00	55·00
37/45 *Set of 9*			£150	£150
38s, 40s, 42s, 44s/5s Optd 'SPECIMEN' *Set of 5*			£200	

See note below No. 36 concerning grey centres.

		(b) Queen Victoria types. Ordinary paper		
46	3	3d. olive-green (3.8.05)	13·00	4·50
		a. Sage-green (1907)	8·00	3·00
47		3d. purple/*yellow* (10.3.10)	12·00	3·50
		a. Chalk-surfaced paper. *Pale purple/yellow* (11.7.10)	2·00	1·50
		aw. Wmk inverted	55·00	65·00
48	4	4d. red-brown (6.6.08)	75·00	80·00
49		4d. black/*yellow* (*chalk-surfaced paper*) (21.9.10)	18·00	55·00
50		4d. red/*yellow* (3.10.11)	1·50	2·75
51	5	6d. dull orange (27.6.06)	17·00	25·00
		a. Golden yellow (9.09)	42·00	65·00
52		6d. lilac (19.11.09)	35·00	60·00
		a. Chalk-surfaced paper. *Purple* (7.10)	11·00	38·00
53	6	1s. brown (11.06)	27·00	50·00
		a. Deep brown	42·00	65·00
		b. '$' for 'S' in 'SHILLING' (A)	£1400	£1500
54		1s. black/*green* (*chalk-surfaced paper*) (21.9.10)	14·00	8·50
		a. '$' for 'S' in 'SHILLING' (A)	£950	£1200
55	9	2s. Venetian red (11.08)	£120	£170
56		2s. purple/*blue* (*chalk-surfaced paper*) (21.9.10)	16·00	8·00
46/56 *Set of 11*			£275	£375
47s, 49s, 50s, 52s, 54s, 56s Optd 'SPECIMEN' *Set of 6*			£325	

No. 38 exists in coils constructed from normal sheets.

17

18

(Typo D.L.R.)

1911 (3 Feb). Wmk Mult Crown CA. P 14.

57	17	2d. grey	10·00	13·00
		s. Optd 'SPECIMEN'	70·00	

(Typo D.L.R.)

1912–20. Wmk Mult Crown CA. Chalk-surfaced paper (3d. to 5s.). P 14.

58	18	1d. carmine-red (5.12.12)	1·50	10
		a. Scarlet (1916)	10·00	70
59		1½d. brown-orange (13.7.16)	2·00	40
		a. Yellow-orange	18·00	1·00
		b. Wmk sideways	†	£1700
		w. Wmk inverted	†	£200
60		2d. grey (2.8.12)	2·50	1·75
		a. Slate-grey	4·50	3·00
61		2½d. blue (13.2.13)	1·75	15
		a. Deep bright blue	80	1·00
62		3d. purple/*yellow* (6.3.12)	50	45
		a. White back (2.4.13)	55	40
		b. On lemon (25.9.16)	3·75	1·50
		bs. Optd 'SPECIMEN'	32·00	
		w. Wmk inverted		
63		4d. black and red/*yellow* (4.4.13)	50	2·25
		a. White back (7.5.14)	75	2·75
		b. On lemon (1916)	23·00	19·00
		bs. Optd 'SPECIMEN'	32·00	
		c. On pale yellow (1919)	22·00	15·00
64		6d. dull and bright purple (14.11.12)	4·50	10·00
		a. Dull purple and bright mauve (1915)	1·00	1·00
		b. Dull purple and bright magenta (1920)	7·00	2·25
65		1s. black/*green* (2.8.12)	2·25	1·50
		a. White back (4.1.15)	6·50	4·75
		b. On blue-green, olive back (1920)	4·75	13·00
66		2s. purple and bright blue/*blue* (10.1.19)	27·00	45·00
67		5s. green and red/*yellow* (5.9.19)	80·00	£100
		a. On pale yellow (1920)	£120	£130
		b. On orange-buff (1920)	£190	£225
58/67 *Set of 10*			£100	£130
58s/67s Optd 'SPECIMEN' *Set of 10*			£225	

No. 58 exists in coils constructed from normal sheets.

The paper of No. 67 is a bright yellow and the gum rough and dull. No. 67*a* is on practically the normal creamy 'pale yellow' paper, and the gum is smooth and shiny. The paper of No. 67*b* approaches the 'coffee' colour of the true 'orange-buff', and the colours of both head and frame are paler, the latter being of a carmine tone.

For the ½d. and 6d. with Script wmk see Nos. 92/93.

RED CROSS LABELS. A voluntary organisation, the Jamaica War Stamp League later the Jamaica Patriotic Stamp League, was founded in November 1915 by Mr. Lewis Ashenheim, a Kingston solicitor. The aims of the League were to support the British Red Cross, collect funds for the purchase of aircraft for the Royal Flying Corps and the relief of Polish Jews.

One fund-raising method used was the sale, from 1 December 1915, of ½d. charity labels. These labels, which were available from post offices, depicted a biplane above a cross and were printed in red by Dennison Manufacturing Company, Framingham, USA, the stamps being perforated 12 except for those along the edges of the sheet which have one side imperforate.

From 22 December 1915 supplies of the labels were overprinted 'JAMAICA' in red, the colour of this overprint being changed to black from 15 January 1916. Copies sold from 11 March 1916 carried an additional 'Half-Penny' surcharge, also in black.

Such labels had no postal validity when used by the general public, but, by special order of the Governor, were accepted for the payment of postage on the League's official mail. To obtain this concession the envelopes were to be inscribed 'Red Cross Business' or 'Jamaica Patriotic Stamp League' and the labels used endorsed with Mr. Ashenheim's signature. Such covers are rare.

WAR STAMP.	WAR STAMP.	WAR STAMP.
(19)	(20)	(21)

(Optd Govt Printing Office, Kingston)

1916 (1 Apr–Sept). Optd with T **19**.

68	15	½d. yellow-green	30	35
		a. No stop after 'STAMP' (R. 18/2)	17·00	27·00
		b. Opt double	£140	£160
		c. Opt inverted	£130	£150
		d. Space between 'W' and 'A' (R. 20/1)	20·00	35·00
		e. Blue-green	30	60
		ea. No stop after 'STAMP' (R. 3/11 or 11/1)	17·00	32·00
		eb. Space between 'W' and 'A' (R. 20/1)	20·00	40·00
		w. Wmk inverted		
69	18	3d. purple/*yellow* (white back)	38·00	50·00
		a. On lemon (6.16)	3·00	24·00
		ab. No stop after 'STAMP' (R. 8/6 or 9/6)	42·00	£100
		b. On pale yellow (9.16)	16·00	40·00

Minor varieties: ½d. (i) Small 'P'; (ii) 'WARISTAMP' (raised quad between words); (iii) Two stops after 'STAMP'. 3d. 'WARISTAMP'. There were several settings of the overprint used for each value. Where two positions are quoted for a variety these did not occur on the same sheet.

NOTE. The above and succeeding stamps with 'WAR STAMP' overprint were issued for payment of a special war tax on letters and postcards or on parcels. Ordinary unoverprinted stamps could also be used for this purpose.

(Optd Govt Printing Office, Kingston)

1916 (Sept–Dec). Optd with T **20**.

70	15	½d. blue-green (*shades*) (2.10.16)	10	30
		a. No stop after 'STAMP' (R. 5/7)	22·00	55·00
		b. Opt omitted (in pair with normal)	£6000	£5000
		c. 'R' inserted by hand (R. 1/10)	£1800	£1500
		w. Wmk inverted	75·00	
71	18	1½d. orange (1.9.16)	10	15
		aa. Wmk sideways	†	£2000
		a. No stop after 'STAMP' (R. 4/12, 8/6, 10/10, 11/1, 18/12, 19/12)	5·00	7·50

b. 'S' in 'STAMP' omitted (R. 6/12) (12.16) £200 £225
c. 'S' inserted by hand £425 £425
d. 'R' in 'WAR' omitted (R. 1/10) £3500 £3000
e. 'R' inserted by hand (R. 1/10) £1500 £1200
w. Wmk inverted .... 17·00 16·00

72 3d. purple/*lemon* (2.10.16) .... 7·00 1·00
aa. Opt inverted £325
a. No stop after 'STAMP' (R. 5/7) .... 70·00 75·00
b. 'S' in 'STAMP' omitted (R. 6/12) (12.16) £900 £900
c. 'S' inserted by hand £200 £200
e. On yellow (12.16) .... 16·00 10·00
ea. 'S' in 'STAMP' omitted (R. 6/12).. £1200 £1200
eb. 'S' inserted by hand £425 £375

Nos. 70c, 71c, 71e, 72c and 72eb show the missing 'R' or 'S' inserted by handstamp. The 3d. is known with this 'S' handstamp inverted or double.

Minor varieties, such as raised quads, small stop, double stop, spaced letters and letters of different sizes, also exist in this overprint. The setting was altered several times.

(Optd Govt Printing Office, Kingston)

1917 (Mar). Optd with T **21**.

73 **15** ½d. blue-green (*shades*) (25.3.17) .... 2·25 30
a. No stop after 'STAMP' (R. 2/5, 8/11, 8/12) .... 18·00 29·00
b. Stop inserted and 'P' impressed a second time (R. 7/6) £250
c. Optd on back only £250
d. Opt inverted .... 27·00 55·00

74 **18** 1½d. orange (3.3.17) 20 10
aa. Wmk sideways .... † £1700
a. No stop after 'STAMP' (R. 2/5, 8/11, 8/12) .... 3·00 18·00
b. Stop inserted and 'P' impressed a second time (R. 7/6) £250
c. Opt double .... 80·00 85·00
d. Opt inverted .... 80·00 75·00
e. 'WAP STAMP' (R. 6/2) ....
w. Wmk inverted .... 16·00 21·00

75 3d. purple/*yellow* (3.3.17) .... 2·50 1·40
a. No stop after 'STAMP' (R. 2/5, 8/11, 8/12) .... 26·00 50·00
b. Stop inserted and 'P' impressed a second time (R. 7/6) £225
c. Opt inverted £140 £180
d. Opt sideways (reading up) £425
da. Opt omitted (in horiz pair with No. 75d) £4000

Examples of No. 75d. exist showing parts of two or more overprints.

No. 75da shows the left-hand stamp as No. 75d and the right-hand stamp entirely without overprint.

There are numerous minor varieties in this overprint with the setting being altered several times.

WAR STAMP

(**22**)

1919 (4 Oct)–**20**. Optd with T **22** in red by D.L.R.

76 **15** ½d. green 20 15
77 **18** 3d. purple/*yellow* .... 15·00 4·00
a. Short opt (right pane R. 10/1) ...
b. Pale purple/buff (3.1.20) .... 6·00 1·75
c. Deep purple/buff (1920) .... 16·00 8·50
76s/77s Optd 'SPECIMEN' *Set of 2* .... 90·00

We list the most distinct variations in the 3d. The buff tone of the paper varies considerably in depth.

No. 77a shows the overprint 2 mm high instead of 2½ mm. The variety was corrected after the first overprinting. It is not found on the ½d.

23 Jamaica Exhibition, 1891

24 Arawak Woman preparing Cassava

25 War Contingent embarking, 1915

26 King's House, Spanish Town

Re-entry. Nos. 80a, 96a (R. 8/4)

The greater part of the design is re-entered, the hull showing in very solid colour and the people appear very blurred. There are also minor re-entries on stamps above (R. 7/4 and 6/4).

27 Return of War Contingent, 1919

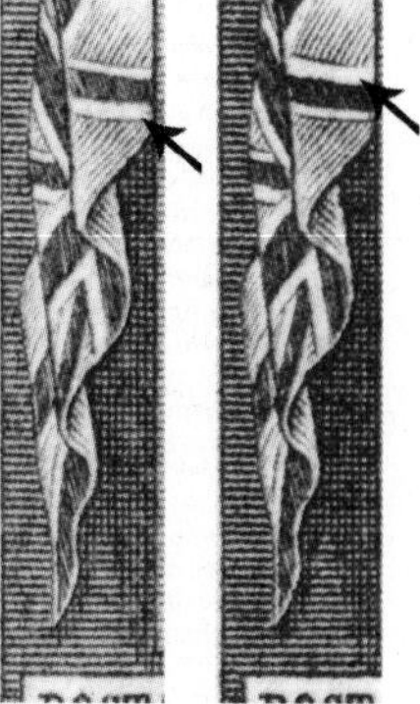
A B

28 Landing of Columbus, 1494

29 Cathedral, Spanish Town

30 Statue of Queen Victoria, Kingston

31 Admiral Rodney Memorial, Spanish Town

32 Sir Charles Metcalfe Statue, Kingston

33 Jamaican scenery

34

(Typo (½d., 1d.), recess (others) D.L.R.)

1919–21. Types **23/34**. Wmk Mult Crown CA (sideways* on 1d., 1½d. and 10s.). Chalk-surfaced paper (½d., 1d.). P 14.

78 **23** ½d. green and olive-green (12.11.20) .... 1·00 1·00
w. Wmk inverted ....
x. Wmk reversed ....
y. Wmk inverted and reversed ....

79 **24** 1d. carmine and orange (3.10.21) ... 1·75 1·75
w. Wmk Crown to left of CA ....

80 **25** 1½d. green (*shades*) (4.7.19) .... 40 1·00
a. Major re-entry (R. 8/4) £180
b. 'C' of 'CA' missing from wmk ...... † £350
c. 'A' of 'CA' missing from wmk £450 £350
w. Wmk Crown to left of CA .... 35·00 38·00
x. Wmk reversed .... — £120
y. Wmk sideways inverted and reversed .... £100 80·00

81 **26** 2d. indigo and green (18.2.21) .... 1·00 4·00
w. Wmk inverted .... 70·00
y. Wmk inverted and reversed .... 70·00

82 **27** 2½d. deep blue and blue (A) (18.2.21) .... 14·00 3·00
a. Blue-black and deep blue .... 2·00 1·75
b. 'C' of 'CA' missing from wmk £350 £300
c. 'A' of 'CA' missing from wmk £350
w. Wmk inverted .... 35·00
x. Wmk reversed .... 60·00
y. Wmk inverted and reversed .... 65·00

83 **28** 3d. myrtle-green and blue (8.4.21). 6·50 2·50
w. Wmk inverted .... 50·00 55·00
x. Wmk reversed .... † £250

84 **29** 4d. brown and deep green (21.1.21) 2·50 9·00
w. Wmk inverted ....
x. Wmk reversed ....

85 **30** 1s. orange-yellow and red-orange (10.12.20) .... 3·75 5·50
a. Frame inverted £40000 £25000
b. 'C' of 'CA' missing from wmk £1100
c. 'A' of 'CA' missing from wmk £1200 £1000
w. Wmk inverted .... † £150
x. Wmk reversed .... † £400

86 **31** 2s. light blue and brown (10.12.20) 9·00 38·00
b. 'C' of 'CA' missing from wmk £800
c. 'A' of 'CA' missing from wmk ....
w. Wmk inverted .... 45·00 75·00

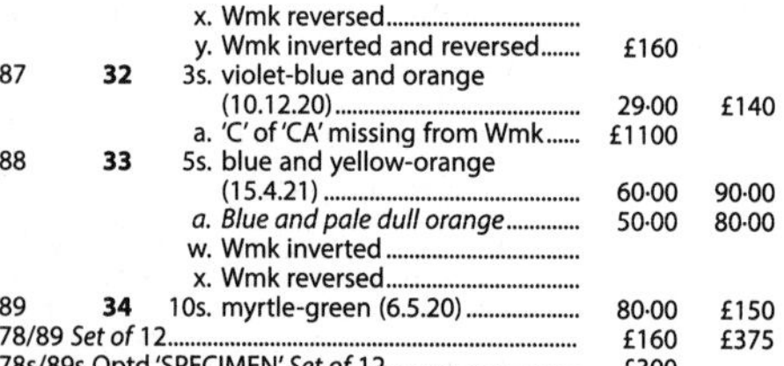

x. Wmk reversed ....
y. Wmk inverted and reversed £160

87 **32** 3s. violet-blue and orange (10.12.20) .... 29·00 £140
a. 'C' of 'CA' missing from Wmk £1100

88 **33** 5s. blue and yellow-orange (15.4.21) .... 60·00 90·00
a. Blue and pale dull orange .... 50·00 80·00
w. Wmk inverted ....
x. Wmk reversed ....

89 **34** 10s. myrtle-green (6.5.20) .... 80·00 £150
78/89 *Set of 12* £160 £375
78s/89s Optd 'SPECIMEN' *Set of 12* £300

* The normal sideways wmk on Nos. 79/80 shows Crown to right of CA, *as seen from the back of the stamp.*

The 2½d. of the above series showed the Union Jack at left, incorrectly, as indicated in illustration A. In the issue on paper with Script wmk the design was corrected (Illustration B).

An example of No. 80 has been reported with the 'A' inverted to the left of and above its normal position.

The 'C' omitted variety has been reported on an example of No. 88 overprinted 'SPECIMEN'.

34a 'Abolition of Slavery' 1st August 1838

Prepared for use but not issued

1921. Recess. P 14.

(a) Wmk Mult Crown CA

90 **34a** 6d. red and dull blue-green £60000
s. Optd 'SPECIMEN' £850
xs. Ditto, wmk reversed £1300

(b) Wmk Mult Script CA (Sideways)

91 6d. red and dull blue-green £38000
s. Optd 'SPECIMEN' £800

The 6d. stamps were prepared and sent out to Jamaica, but for political reasons were not issued, and the stocks destroyed. 'SPECIMEN' examples of both watermarks were distributed by the UPU in the normal way, but only one example of No. 90 and four examples of No. 91 exist in private hands without opt.

'Bow' flaw (R. 18/12)

1921 (21 Oct)–**27**. Wmk Mult Script CA. Chalk-surfaced paper (6d.). P 14.

92 **18** ½d. green (3.11.27) .... 4·00 10
a. Bow flaw .... £120 35·00
93 6d. dull purple and bright magenta 18·00 4·00
92s/93s Optd 'SPECIMEN' *Set of 2* £100

35 'POSTAGE & REVENUE' added

36 *Port Royal in 1853* (A. Duperly)

(Printing as before; the 6d. recess-printed)

1921–29. As Nos. 78/89. Wmk Mult Script CA (sideways* on 1d. and 1½d.). Chalk-surfaced paper (½d., 1d.). P 14.

94 **23** ½d. green and olive-green (5.2.22).. 50 50
a. Green and deep olive-green 50 50
w. Wmk inverted .... 60·00 60·00

95 **35** 1d. carmine and orange (5.12.22) ... 1·50 10
w. Wmk Crown to right of CA .... 3·00 10
x. Wmk reversed .... — £130

96 **25** 1½d. green (*shades*) (2.2.21) .... 3·50 45
a. Major re-entry (R. 8/4) £200
w. Wmk Crown to left of CA .... — 35·00
x. Wmk reversed .... 50·00 50·00
y. Wmk sideways inverted and reversed .... — 85·00

97 **26** 2d. indigo and green (4.11.21) .... 8·50 80
a. Indigo and grey-green (1925) ...... 17·00 1·00
w. Wmk inverted .... † —

98 **27** 2½d. deep blue and blue (B) (4.11.21) .... 6·00 1·75
a. Dull blue and blue (B) .... 6·50 60
w. Wmk inverted .... 40·00 40·00
x. Wmk reversed .... — £110
y. Wmk inverted and reversed ....

99 **28** 3d. myrtle-green and blue (6.3.22). 6·00 70
a. Green and pale blue .... 3·50 20
w. Wmk inverted ....
x. Wmk reversed .... — £250

100 **29** 4d. brown and deep green (5.12.21) .... 1·25 30
a. Chocolate and dull green .... 2·00 30
w. Wmk inverted .... 60·00
x. Wmk reversed .... 95·00

101 **36** 6d. black and blue (5.12.22) .... 17·00 1·50
a. Grey and dull blue .... 15·00 1·00
w. Wmk inverted .... † £600
x. Wmk reversed .... † £450

102 **30** 1s. orange and red-orange (4.11.21) 2·00 80
a. Orange-yellow and brown-orange 2·00 65
w. Wmk inverted
x. Wmk reversed — £250
103 **31** 2s. light blue and brown (5.2.22) 3·50 65
w. Wmk inverted 40·00 40·00
104 **32** 3s. violet-blue and orange (23.8.21) 20·00 9·00
105 **33** 5s. blue and yellow-brown (8.11.23) 30·00 25·00
a. Blue and pale dull orange 80·00 80·00
b. Blue and yellow-orange (1927) 45·00 23·00
c. Blue and pale bistre-brown (1929) 48·00 22·00
w. Wmk inverted — £400
x. Wmk reversed
106 **34** 10s. myrtle-green (3.22) 55·00 70·00
94/106 *Set of 13* £130 95·00
94s/106s Optd 'SPECIMEN' *Set of 13* £300

* The normal sideways wmk shows Crown to left of CA on No. 95 or Crown to right of CA on No. 96, *both as seen from the back of the stamp.*

The frame of No. 105*a* is the same colour as that of No. 88*a*.

The designs of all values of the pictorial series, with the exception of the 5s. and 10s. (which originated with the Governor, Sir Leslie Probyn), were selected by Mr. F. C. Cundall, F.S.A. The 1d. and 5s. were drawn by Miss Cundall, the 3d. by Mrs. Cundall, and the 10s. by De La Rue & Co. The 6d. is from a lithograph. The other designs are from photographs, the frames of all being the work of Miss Cundall and Miss Wood.

37

38

39

(Centres from photos by Miss V. F. Taylor. Frames des F. C. Cundall, F.S.A., and drawn by Miss Cundall. Recess B.W.)

1923 (1 Nov). Child Welfare. Wmk Mult Script CA. P 12.
107 **37** ½d. +½d. black and green 1·25 5·50
107*b* **38** 1d. +½d. black and scarlet 4·00 13·00
107*c* **39** 2½d. +½d. black and blue 23·00 19·00
107/107*c* *Set of 3* 25·00 32·00
107*a*s/107*c*s Optd 'SPECIMEN.' *Set of 3* £140

Sold at a premium of ½d. for the Child Welfare League, these stamps were on sale annually from 1 November to 31 January, until 31 January 1927, when their sale ceased, the remainders being destroyed on 21 February 1927.

40

41

42

Die I

Die II

(Recess D.L.R.)

1929–32. Wmk Mult Script CA. P 14.
108 **40** 1d. scarlet (Die I) (15.3.29) 16·00 20
a. Die II (1932) 16·00 10
109 **41** 1½d. chocolate (18.1.29) 9·50 15
110 **42** 9d. maroon (5.3.29) 9·50 1·00
108/110 *Set of 3* 32·00 1·10
108s/110s Perf 'SPECIMEN' *Set of 3* £110

In Die I the shading below JAMAICA is formed of thickened parallel lines, and in Die II of diagonal cross-hatching.

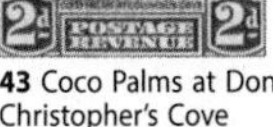
43 Coco Palms at Don Christopher's Cove

44 Wag Water River, St Andrew

45 Priestman's River, Portland

(Dies eng and recess Waterlow)

1932. Wmk Mult Script CA (sideways on 2d. and 2½d.). P 12½.
111 **43** 2d. black and green (4.11.32) 40·00 4·50
a. Imperf between (vert pair) £14000
112 **44** 2½d. turquoise-blue and ultramarine (5.3.32) 6·50 1·50
a. Imperf between (vert pair) £24000 £24000
113 **45** 6d. grey-black and purple (4.2.32) 35·00 6·00
111/113 *Set of 3* 70·00 11·00
111s/113s Perf 'SPECIMEN' *Set of 3* £120

1935 (6 May). Silver Jubilee. As Nos. 91/94 of Antigua, but ptd by B.W. P 11×12.
114 1d. deep blue and scarlet 50 15
b. Short extra flagstaff £1700
d. Flagstaff on right-hand turret £140 £160
e. Double flagstaff £140 £160
115 1½d. ultramarine and grey-black 60 1·50
a. Extra flagstaff 90·00 £130
b. Short extra flagstaff £130 £160
c. Lightning conductor £110 £140
116 6d. green and indigo 14·00 20·00
a. Extra flagstaff £200 £275
b. Short extra flagstaff £375
c. Lightning conductor £250 £325
117 1s. slate and purple 8·50 24·00
a. Extra flagstaff £250 £325
b. Short extra flagstaff £425 £550
c. Lightning conductor £300 £375
114/117 *Set of 4* 21·00 40·00
114s/117s Perf 'SPECIMEN' *Set of 4* £110

For illustrations of plate varieties see Omnibus section following Zanzibar.

1937 (12 May). Coronation. As Nos. 95/97 of Antigua, but printed by D.L.R. P 14.
118 1d. scarlet 30 15
119 1½d. grey-black 65 30
120 2½d. bright blue 1·00 70
118/120 *Set of 3* 1·75 1·00
118s/120s Perf 'SPECIMEN' *Set of 3* £100

46 King George VI

47 Coco Palms at Don Christopher's Cove

47a Wag Water River, St Andrew

48 Bananas

49 Citrus Grove

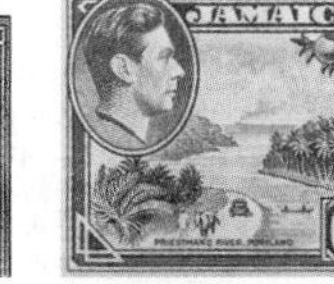

49a Priestman's River, Portland

50 Kingston Harbour

51 Sugar Industry

52 Bamboo Walk

52a Jamaican scenery

53 King George VI

53a Tobacco Growing and Cigar Making

2d. Extra branch (Centre plate (1) with frame Pl (1) to 7, R. 6/1)

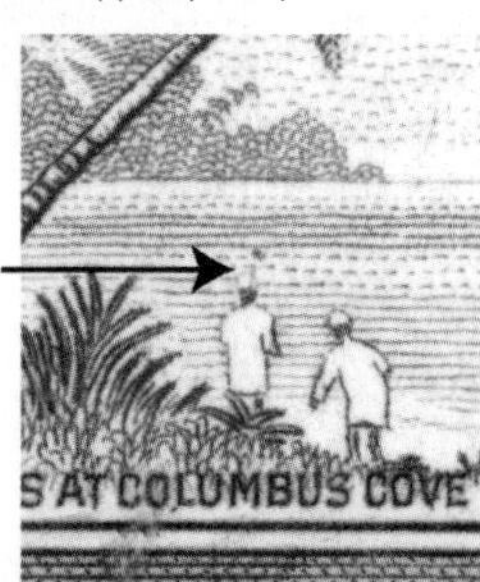

2d. Fishing rod (Centre plate (1) with frame Pl (1) to 7, R. 6/10)

6d. 'Exhaust pipe' variety (Centre plate (1), R. 6/1)

1s. Repaired chimney (Centre plate 1, R. 11/1)

(Recess D.L.R. (T **48**, 5s. and 10s.), Waterlow (others))

1938 (10 Oct)–**52**. Types **46/53a** and as Nos. 88, 112/113, but with inset portrait of King George VI, as in T **49**. Wmk Mult Script CA. P 13½×14 (½d., 1d., 1½d.), 14 (5s., 10s.) or 12½ (others).
121 **46** ½d. blue-green 2·00 10
a. Wmk sideways † £10000
121*b* ½d. orange (25.10.51) 3·25 30
122 1d. scarlet 1·25 10
122*a* 1d. blue-green (25.10.51) 4·75 10
123 1½d. brown 1·25 10
124 **47** 2d. grey and green (10.12.38) 1·25 1·00
a. Extra branch 60·00 30·00
b. Fishing rod 60·00 30·00
c. Perf 13×13½ (1939) 2·75 50
cb. 'C' of 'CA' missing from wmk £1500
d. Perf 12½×13 (1951) 1·25 10
125 **47a** 2½d. greenish blue and ultramarine (10.12.38) 9·50 2·75
126 **48** 3d. ultramarine and green (10.12.38) 1·00 1·50
a. 'A' of 'CA' missing from wmk £1500
126*b* 3d. greenish blue and ultramarine (15.8.49) 4·50 1·25
126*c* 3d. green and scarlet (1.7.52) 6·00 30
127 **49** 4d. brown and green (10.12.38) 1·00 10
128 **49a** 6d. grey and purple (10.12.38) 9·50 30
aa. 'Exhaust pipe' £350 50·00
a. Perf 13½×13 (10.10.50) 3·50 10
129 **50** 9d. lake (10.12.38) 1·00 50
a. 'A' of 'CA' missing from wmk £1600
130 **51** 1s. green and purple-brown (10.12.38) 16·00 20
a. Repaired chimney £650 £120
b. 'A' of 'CA' missing from wmk † £1400
131 **52** 2s. blue and chocolate (10.12.38) 35·00 1·00
a. 'A' of 'CA' missing from wmk † £1500
132 **52a** 5s. slate-blue and yellow-orange (10.12.38) 20·00 3·75
a. Perf 14, line (1941) £7000 £250
b. Perf 13 (24.10.49) 12·00 3·00
ba. Blue and orange (10.10.50) 12·00 3·00
133 **53** 10s. myrtle-green (10.12.38) 11·00 11·00
aa. Perf 13 (10.10.50) 18·00 7·00
133*a* **53a** £1 chocolate and violet (15.8.49) 60·00 38·00
121/133*a* *Set of 18* £150 50·00
121s/133s Perf 'SPECIMEN' *Set of 13* £350

No. 130a occurred in conjunction with Frame plate 2 on printings between 1942 and 1951.

No. 132a shows the emergency use of a line perforation machine, giving an irregular gauge of 14–14.15, after the De La Rue works were damaged in December 1940. The normal comb measures 13.8×13.7.

Nos. 121 and 122 exist in coils constructed from normal sheets.

SELF-GOVERNMENT

54 Courthouse, Falmouth

55 King Charles II and King George VI

56 Institute of Jamaica

57 House of Assembly

58 'Labour and Learning'

59 Scroll, flag and King George VI

(Recess Waterlow)

1945 (20 Aug)–**46**. New Constitution. Types **54/59**. Wmk Mult Script CA. P 12½.

134	**54**	1½d. sepia	30	30
		a. Perf 12½×13 (1946)	17·00	3·00
135	**55**	2d. green	17·00	2·25
		a. Perf 12½×13 (1945)	30	50
136	**56**	3d. ultramarine	30	50
		a. Perf 13 (1946)	3·25	2·75
137	**57**	4½d. slate	1·50	40
		a. Perf 13 (1946)	6·50	6·00
138	**58**	2s. red-brown	2·25	50
139	**59**	5s. indigo	4·50	2·25
140	**56**	10s. green	3·50	2·25
134/140 *Set of 7*			11·50	6·00
134s/140s Perf 'SPECIMEN' *Set of 7*			£200	

1946 (14 Oct). Victory. As Nos. 110/111 of Antigua.

141	1½d. purple-brown	3·00	10
	a. Perf 13½	1·00	4·50
142	3d. blue	9·00	3·00
	a. Perf 13½	1·00	9·00
141s/142s Perf 'SPECIMEN' *Set of 2*		90·00	

1948 (1 Dec). Royal Silver Wedding. As Nos. 112/113 of Antigua.

143	1½d. red-brown	30	10
144	£1 scarlet	28·00	75·00

1949 (10 Oct). 75th Anniversary of Universal Postal Union. As Nos. 114/117 of Antigua.

145	1½d. red-brown	20	15
	a. 'A' of 'CA' missing from wmk	£700	
146	2d. deep blue-green	1·25	8·00
147	3d. deep blue	50	1·75
148	6d. purple	50	2·50
145/148 *Set of 4*		2·25	11·00

(Recess Waterlow)

1951 (16 Feb). Inauguration of BWI University College. As Nos. 118/119 of Antigua.

149	2d. black and red-brown	30	50
150	6d. grey-black and purple	70	30

60 Scout Badge and Map of Caribbean

61 Scout Badge and Map of Jamaica

(Des. C. D'Souza. Litho B.W.)

1952 (5 Mar). First Caribbean Scout Jamboree. Wmk Mult Script CA. P 13½×13 (2d.) or 13×13½ (6d.).

151	**60**	2d. blue, apple-green and black	30	10
152	**61**	6d. yellow-green, carmine-red and black	70	60

1953 (2 June). Coronation. As No. 120 of Antigua.

153	2d. black and deep yellow-green	1·75	10

62 Coco Palms at Don Christopher's Cove

(Recess Waterlow)

1953 (25 Nov). Royal Visit. Wmk Mult Script CA. P 12½×13.

154	**62**	2d. grey-black and green	55	10

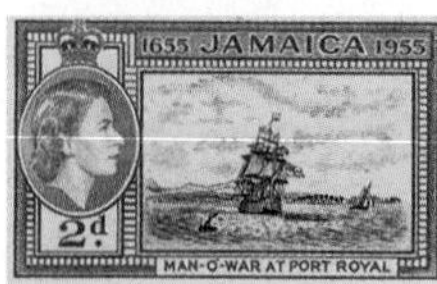

63 HMS *Britannia* (ship of the line) at Port Royal

64 Old Montego Bay

65 Old Kingston

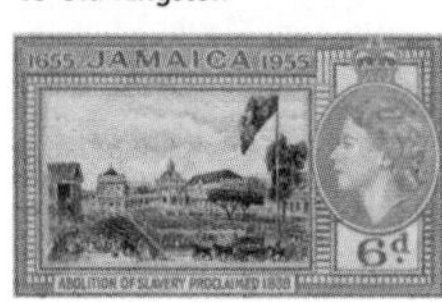

66 Proclamation of Abolition of Slavery, 1838

(Recess D.L.R.)

1955 (10 May). Tercentenary Issue. Types **63/66**. Wmk Mult Script CA. P 12½.

155	**63**	2d. black and olive-green	1·00	10
156	**64**	2½d. black and deep bright blue	15	60
157	**65**	3d. black and claret	15	50
158	**66**	6d. black and carmine-red	40	35
155/158 *Set of 4*			1·50	1·40

67 Coconut Palms

68 Sugar Cane

69 Pineapples

70 Bananas

71 Mahoe

72 Breadfruit

73 Ackee

74 Streamertail

75 Blue Mountain Peak

76 Royal Botanic Gardens, Hope

77 Rafting on the Rio Grande

78 Fort Charles

79 Arms of Jamaica

80 Arms of Jamaica

(Recess B.W. (Types **79/80**), D.L.R. (others))

1956 (1 May)–**58**. Types **67/80**. Wmk Mult Script CA. P 13 (½d. to 6d.), 13½ (8d. to 2s.) or 11½ (3s. to £1).

159	**67**	½d. black and deep orange-red	10	10
160	**68**	1d. black and emerald	10	10
161	**69**	2d. black and carmine-red (2.8.56)	15	10
162	**70**	2½d. black and deep bright blue (2.8.56)	1·75	50
163	**71**	3d. emerald and red-brown (17.12.56)	30	10
164	**72**	4d. bronze-green and blue (17.12.56)	1·50	10
		w. Wmk inverted	£350	£160
165	**73**	5d. scarlet and bronze-green (17.12.56)	1·75	3·00
166	**74**	6d. black and deep rose-red (3.9.56)	5·00	10
167	**75**	8d. ultramarine and red-orange (15.11.56)	2·50	10
168	**76**	1s. yellow-green and blue (15.11.56)	2·50	10
169	**77**	1s.6d. ultramarine and reddish purple (15.11.56)	1·25	10
170	**78**	2s. blue and bronze-green (15.11.56)	17·00	3·50
		a. *Grey-blue and bronze-green* (24.4.58)	35·00	4·50
171	**79**	3s. black and blue (2.8.56)	4·00	4·25
172		5s. black and carmine-red (15.8.56)	5·50	9·00
173	**80**	10s. black and blue-green (15.8.56)	35·00	23·00
174		£1 black and purple (15.8.56)	35·00	23·00
159/174 *Set of 16*			95·00	55·00

An earlier £1 value, in the design of No. 133*a* but showing the portrait of Queen Elizabeth II, was prepared, but not issued.

1958 (22 Apr). Inauguration of British Caribbean Federation. As Nos. 135/137 of Antigua.

175	2d. deep green	1·10	10
176	5d. blue	1·40	4·00
177	6d. scarlet	1·40	40
175/177 *Set of 3*		3·50	4·00

81 Bristol 175 Britannia 312 flying over *City of Berlin*, 1860

83 1s. Stamps of 1860 and 1956

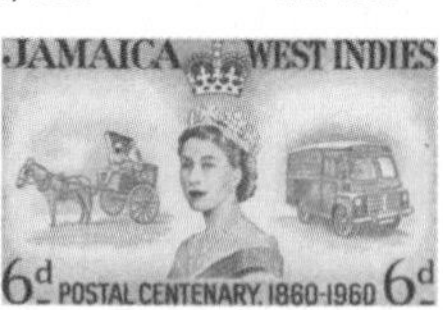

82 Postal mule-cart and motor van

(Recess Waterlow)

1960 (4 Jan). Stamp Centenary. T **81/83** and similar design. W w **12**. P 13×13½ (1s.) or 13½×14 (others).

178	**81**	2d. blue and reddish purple	85	10
179	**82**	6d. carmine and olive-green	85	70
180	**83**	1s. red-brown, yellow-green and blue	85	75
178/180 *Set of 3*			2·25	1·40

INDEPENDENT

1
9
6
2
INDEPENDENCE
(84)

1
9
6
2
INDEPENDENCE
1962
(85)

86 Military Bugler and Map

(Des V. Whiteley. Photo D.L.R. (2, 4d., 1s.6d., 5s.))

1962 (8 Aug)–**63**. Independence.

*(a) Nos. 159/160, 162, 171, 173/174 optd as T **84** and Nos. 163, 165/168, 170 optd with T **85***

181	**67**	½d. black and deep orange-red	10	1·00
182	**68**	1d. black and emerald	10	10
183	**70**	2½d. black and deep bright blue	15	1·25
184	**71**	3d. emerald and red-brown	15	10
185	**73**	5d. scarlet and bronze-green	25	80
186	**74**	6d. black and deep rose-red	4·50	10
187	**75**	8d. ultramarine and red-orange (opt at upper left)	30	10
		a. Opt at lower left (17.9.63?)	1·25	30

188	**76**	1s. yellow-green and blue	30	10
189	**78**	2s. blue and bronze-green	2·50	1·50
		a. Deep blue and deep bronze-green (20.8.63)	17·00	7·00
190	**79**	3s. black and blue	2·00	1·50
191	**80**	10s. black and blue-green	6·00	5·00
192		£1 black and purple	6·00	5·50
		(b) Horiz designs as T **86**. *W w* **12**. *P 13*		
193		2d. multicoloured	2·25	10
194		4d. multicoloured	1·50	10
195		1s.6d. black and red	6·00	85
196		5s. multicoloured	14·00	10·00
181/196 *Set of* 16			40·00	25·00

Designs: 2, 4d. T **86**; 1s.6d. Gordon House and banner; 5s. Map, factories and fruit.

For these overprints on stamps watermarked w **12** see Nos. 205/213.

89 Kingston Seal, Weightlifting, Boxing, Football and Cycling

90 Kingston Seal, diving, sailing, swimming and water polo

91 Kingston Seal, pole-vaulting, javelin throwing, discus throwing, relay racing and hurdling

92 Kingston Coat of Arms and athlete

(Photo Harrison)

1962 (11 Aug). Ninth Central American and Caribbean Games, Kingston. Types **89/92**. W w **12**. P 14½×14.

197	**89**	1d. sepia and carmine-red	40	10
198	**90**	6d. sepia and greenish blue	20	10
199	**91**	8d. sepia and bistre	20	10
200	**92**	2s. multicoloured	30	90
197/200 *Set of* 4			1·00	1·00

An imperf miniature sheet exists, but this was never available at face value or at any post office.

93 Farmer and Crops

(Des M. Goaman. Litho D.L.R.)

1963 (4 June). Freedom from Hunger. P 12½.

201	**93**	1d. multicoloured	40	10
202		8d. multicoloured	1·60	60

1963 (4 Sept). Red Cross Centenary. As Nos. 147/148 of Antigua.

203		2d. red and black	15	10
204		1s.6d. red and blue	50	1·50

1963–64. As Nos. 181/190, but wmk w **12**.

205	**67**	½d. black and deep orange-red (3.12.63*)	10	15
206	**68**	1d. black and emerald (3.4.64)	10	2·25
207	**70**	2½d. black and deep bright blue (3.4.64)	25	2·75
208	**71**	3d. emerald and red-brown (17.12.63*)	15	15
209	**73**	5d. scarlet and bronze-green (3.4.64)	40	2·75
210	**75**	8d. ultramarine and red-orange (3.4.64)	20	1·25
211	**76**	1s. yellow-green and blue (21.12.63*)	35	1·00
212	**78**	2s. deep blue and deep bronze-green (3.4.64)	60	8·00
213	**79**	3s. black and blue (5.2.64)	3·25	5·00
205/213 *Set of* 9			4·75	21·00

The overprint on the 8d., 1s. and 2s. is at lower left, the others are as before.

* These are the earliest known dates recorded in Jamaica.

95 Carole Joan Crawford ('Miss World 1963')

(Des and photo D.L.R.)

1964 (14 Feb–25 May). 'Miss World 1963' Commemoration. P 13.

214	**95**	3d. multicoloured	15	10
215		1s. multicoloured	20	10
216		1s.6d. multicoloured	30	50
214/216 *Set of* 3			60	60
MS216*a* 153×101 mm. Nos. 214/216. Imperf (25.5.64)			1·40	2·75

96 *Lignum Vitae*

97 Ackee

98 Blue Mahoe

99 Land shells

100 National Flag over Jamaica

101 Antillean Murex (*Murex formosus*) (shell)

102 *Papilio homerus* (butterfly)

103 Streamertail

104 Gypsum Industry

105 National Stadium

106 Palisadoes International Airport

107 Bauxite mining

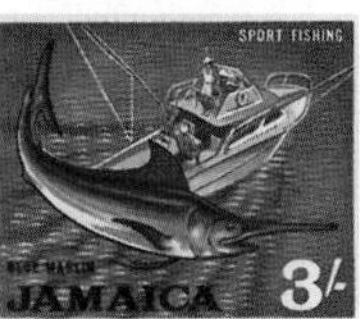

108 Blue Marlin (sport fishing)

109 Exploration of sunken city

110 Arms of Jamaica

110a Queen Elizabeth II and National Flag

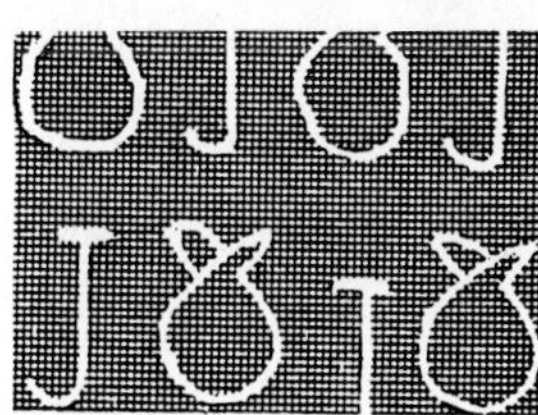
111 Multiple 'J' and Pineapple

(Des V. Whiteley. Photo Harrison)

1964 (4 May)–**68**. Types **96/110a**. W **111**. P 14½ (1d., 2d., 2½d., 6d., 8d.), 14×14½ (1½d., 3d., 4d., 10s.), 14½×14 (9d., 1s., 3s., 5s., £1) or 13½×14½ (1s.6d., 2s.).

217	1d. violet-blue, deep green and light brown (*shades*)	10	10
218	1½d. multicoloured	15	10
219	2d. red, yellow and grey-green	15	10
	w. Wmk inverted	14·00	
220	2½d. multicoloured	1·00	60
221	3d. yellow, black and emerald	25	10
222	4d. ochre and violet	50	10
223	6d. multicoloured	2·25	10
	a. Blue omitted	£100	
	b. Value omitted	£2250	
	w. Wmk inverted	18·00	
224	8d. mult (yellowish green background)	2·50	1·50
	a. Red (beak) omitted	£225	
	b. Greyish green background (16.7.68)	11·00	10·00
225	9d. blue and yellow-bistre	1·50	10
226	1s. black and light brown	20	10
	a. Light brown omitted	£3250	£3250
	ab. Value only omitted	£1600	
	b. Black omitted	£2250	
	ba. 'NATIONAL STADIUM' etc omitted	£1100	£1100
227	1s.6d. black, light blue and buff	4·00	15
228	2s. red-brown, black and light blue	2·75	15
229	3s. blue and dull green	1·00	80
	aw. Wmk inverted	13·00	
	b. Perf 13½×14½	35	65
230	5s. black, ochre and blue	1·25	1·25
	w. Wmk inverted	£100	
231	10s. multicoloured	1·50	1·25
	a. Blue ('JAMAICA', etc) omitted	£500	
232	£1 multicoloured	3·00	1·00
217/232 *Set of* 16		19·00	6·25

No. 223b. Two left half sheets are known with the black printing shifted downwards to such an extent that the value is omitted from the top row.

Nos. 226a/226ab came from a sheet on which the two bottom rows had the colour omitted with the next row showing it missing from the lower third of the stamps.

No. 226b comes from the bottom row of one sheet and rows seven and eight of a second sheet; the latter also being the source of No. 226ba.

112 Scout Belt

113 Globe, Scout Hat and Scarf

114 Scout Badge and Alligator

(Photo Harrison)

1964 (27 Aug). Sixth Inter-American Scout Conference, Kingston. W **111**. P 14 (1s.) or 14½×14 (others).

233	**112**	3d. red, black and pink	10	10
234	**113**	8d. bright blue, olive and black	15	25
		w. Wmk inverted	48·00	
235	**114**	1s. gold, deep blue and light blue	20	45
		w. Wmk inverted	20	45
233/235 *Set of* 3			40	70

115 Gordon House, Kingston

116 Headquarters House, Kingston

117 House of Assembly, Spanish Town

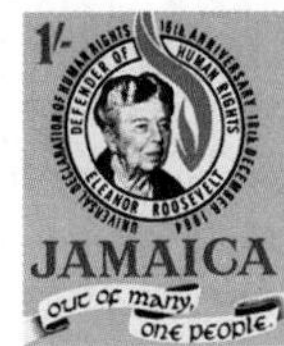

118 Eleanor Roosevelt

(Des V. Whiteley. Photo Harrison)

1964 (16 Nov). Tenth Commonwealth Parliamentary Conference, Kingston. Types **115/117**. W **111**. P 14½×14.

236	**115**	3d. black and yellow-green	10	10
237	**116**	6d. black and carmine-red	30	10
238	**117**	1s.6d. black and bright blue	50	30
236/238 *Set of* 3			80	40

(Des V. Whiteley. Photo Harrison)

1964 (10 Dec). 16th Anniversary of Declaration of Human Rights. W **111**. P 14½×14.

239	**118**	1s. black, red and light green	10	10

119 Guides' Emblem on Map

120 Guide Emblems

(Photo Harrison)

1965 (17 May). Golden Jubilee of Jamaica Girl Guides Association. W **111** (sideways on 3d.). P 14×14½ (3d.) or 14 (1s.).

240 **119** 3d. yellow, green and light blue 10 10
241 **120** 1s. yellow, black and apple-green.. 20 40
w. Wmk inverted 20 40

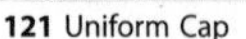
121 Uniform Cap

122 Flag-bearer and Drummer

(Photo Harrison)

1965 (23 Aug). Salvation Army Centenary. W **111**. P 14×14½ (3d.) or 14½×14 (1s.6d.).

242 **121** 3d. multicoloured 30 10
w. Wmk inverted .... 23·00
243 **122** 1s.6d. multicoloured .... 1·00 50
w. Wmk inverted .... 50·00

123 Paul Bogle, William Gordon and Morant Bay Court House

124 Abeng-blower, *Telstar*, Morse Key and ITU Emblem

(Photo Enschedé)

1965 (29 Dec). Centenary of Morant Bay Rebellion. No wmk. P 14×13.

244 **123** 3d. light brown, ultramarine and black 10 10
245 1s.6d. light brown, yellow-green and black 20 15
246 3s. light brown, rose and black .... 30 1·75
244/246 *Set of 3* .... 55 1·75

(Photo Harrison)

1965 (29 Dec). ITU Centenary. W **111**. P 14×14½.

247 **124** 1s. black, grey-blue and red 40 20

ROYAL VISIT
MARCH 1966
(125)

126 Sir Winston Churchill

1966 (3 Mar). Royal Visit. Nos. 221, 223, 226/227 optd with T **125**.

248 3d. yellow, black and emerald 15 15
249 6d. multicoloured .... 2·25 80
250 1s. black and light brown 55 15
251 1s.6d. black, light blue and buff .... 2·50 4·00
248/251 *Set of 4* .... 5·00 4·50

(Des Jennifer Toombs. Photo Harrison)

1966 (18 Apr). Churchill Commemoration. W **111**. P 14.

252 **126** 6d. black and olive-green 65 30
253 1s. bistre-brown and deep violet-blue 85 80

127 Statue of Athlete and Flags

131 Bolivar's Statue and Flags of Jamaica and Venezuela

(Des V. Whiteley. Photo Harrison)

1966 (4 Aug). Eighth British Empire and Commonwealth Games. T **127** and similar horiz designs. W **111**. P 14½×14.

254 3d. multicoloured 10 10
255 6d. multicoloured 60 10
w. Wmk inverted .... 42·00
256 1s. multicoloured 10 10
257 3s. bright gold and deep blue 35 45
w. Wmk inverted .... 42·00
254/257 *Set of 4* .... 1·00 55
MS258 128×103 mm. Nos. 254/257. Imperf .... 4·00 8·00

Designs: 3d. T **127** 6d. Racing cyclists; 1s. National Stadium, Kingston; 3s. Games emblem.

No. **MS**258 has been seen with the whole printing inverted except for the brown background.

(Des and photo Harrison)

1966 (5 Dec). 150th Anniversary of 'Jamaica Letter'. W **111**. P 14×15.

259 **131** 8d. multicoloured 20 10
w. Wmk inverted .... 38·00

132 Jamaican Pavilion

133 Sir Donald Sangster (Prime Minister)

(Des V. Whiteley. Photo Harrison)

1967 (28 Apr). World Fair, Montreal. W **111**. P 14½.

260 **132** 6d. multicoloured 10 15
261 1s. multicoloured 10 15
w. Wmk inverted .... 12·00

(Des and photo Enschedé)

1967 (28 Aug). Sangster Memorial Issue. P 13½.

262 **133** 3d. multicoloured 10 10
263 1s.6d. multicoloured 20 20

134 Traffic Duty

135 Personnel of the Force

(Des V. Whiteley. Photo Enschedé)

1967 (28 Nov). Centenary of the Constabulary Force. Types **134/135** and similar horiz design. Multicoloured. W **111**. P 13½×14.

264 3d. Type **134** 40 10
a. Wmk sideways .... 1·50 3·00
265 1s. Type **135** 40 10
266 1s.6d. Badge and Constables of 1867 and 1967 (as Type **134**) 50 75
264/266 *Set of 3* .... 1·10 85

136 Wicket-keeping

137 Sir Alexander and Lady Bustamante

(Des V. Whiteley. Photo Harrison)

1968 (8 Feb). MCC's West Indian Tour. T **136** and similar vert designs. Multicoloured. W **111** (sideways*). P 14.

267 6d. Type **136** 35 65
a. Horiz strip of 3. Nos. 267/269 .... 1·00 1·75
w. Wmk top of J to right 35 65
268 6d. Batting 35 65
w. Wmk top of J to right 35 65
269 6d. Bowling 35 65
w. Wmk top of J to right 35 65
267/269 *Set of 3* .... 1·00 1·75

* The normal sideways watermark shows the top of the 'J' to left, *as seen from the back of the stamp.*

Nos. 267/269 were issued in small sheets of nine comprising three *se-tenant* strips as No. 267a.

Nos. 267/269 exist on PVA gum as well as on gum arabic.

(Des and photo Harrison)

1968 (23 May). Labour Day. W **111**. P 14.

270 **137** 3d. rose and black 10 15
271 1s. olive and black 10 15

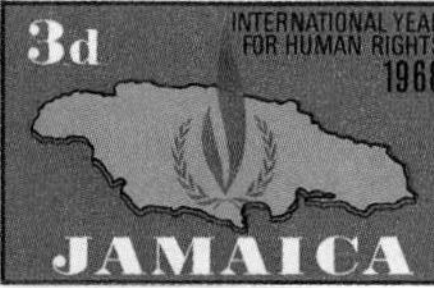

138 Human Rights Emblem over Map of Jamaica

(Photo Harrison)

1968 (3 Dec). Human Rights Year. T **138** and similar multicoloured designs. W **111**. P 14.

272 3d. Type **138** 10 10
a. Gold (flame) omitted £160
w. Wmk inverted .... 7·00
273 1s. Hands cupping Human Rights emblem (*vert*) 20 10
274 3s. Jamaican holding 'Human Rights' ..... 60 1·50
a. Gold (flame) omitted £180
272/274 *Set of 3* .... 75 1·50

Three designs, showing 3d. Bowls of Grain, 1s. Abacus, 3s. Hands in Prayer, were prepared but not issued (*Price for set of 3 mint* £200).

141 ILO Emblem

142 Nurse, and Children being weighed and measured

(Des V. Whiteley. Litho Format)

1969 (23 May). 50th Anniversary of International Labour Organisation. P 14.

275 **141** 6d. orange-yellow and blackish brown 10 10
276 3s. bright emerald and blackish brown 30 45

(Des and photo Harrison)

1969 (30 May). 20th Anniversary of WHO T **142** and similar designs. W **111**. P 14.

277 6d. grey, brown and orange 10 15
278 1s. black, sepia and blue-green 10 15
279 3s. grey-black, brown and pale bright blue .... 20 1·25
277/279 *Set of 3* .... 30 1·40

Designs: Horiz—6d. T **142**, 1s. Malaria eradication. Vert—3s. Trainee nurse.

(New Currency. 100 cents = 1 Jamaica dollar)

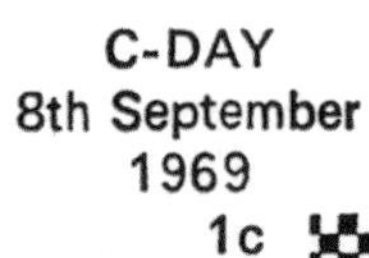

(145)

146 *The Adoration of the Kings* (detail, Foppa)

1969 (8 Sept). Decimal currency. Nos. 217, 219, 221/223 and 225/232 surch as T **145**. Sterling values unobliterated except 1c. to 4c. and 8c.

280 1c. on 1d. violet-blue, deep green and light brown 10 10
281 2c. on 2d. red, yellow and grey-green ... 10 10
w. Wmk inverted .... 3·25
282 3c. on 3d. yellow, black and emerald 10 10
283 4c. on 4d. ochre and violet .... 1·25 10
a. '8t' of '8th' omitted (R. 10/1) .... 70·00
284 5c. on 6d. multicoloured .... 1·25 10
a. Blue omitted £110
285 8c. on 9d. blue and yellow-bistre 10 10
286 10c. on 1s. black and light brown 10 10
287 15c. on 1s.6d. black, light blue and buff ... 50 90
288 20c. on 2s. red-brown, black and light blue .... 1·50 1·50
a. '8th' omitted £1800
289 30c. on 3s. blue and dull green .... 2·50 3·00
290 50c. on 5s. black, ochre and blue .... 1·25 3·00
291 $1 on 10s. multicoloured .... 1·25 6·50
w. Wmk inverted £130
292 $2 on £1 multicoloured .... 2·25 6·50
280/292 *Set of 13* .... 10·50 19·00

No. 281 exists with PVA gum as well as gum arabic.

Unlike the positional No. 283a the similar variety on the 20c. on 2s. was caused by a paper fold.

(Des J. Cooter. Litho D.L.R.)

1969 (25 Oct). Christmas. Paintings. T **146** and similar vert designs. Multicoloured. W **111**. P 13.

293 2c. Type **146** 20 40
294 5c. *Madonna, Child and St John* (Raphael) 25 40
295 8c. *The Adoration of the Kings* (detail, Dosso Dossi) 25 40
293/295 *Set of 3* .... 65 1·10

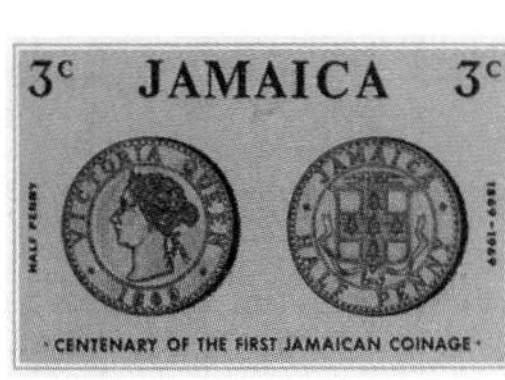
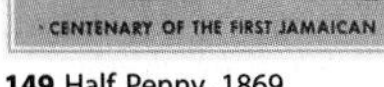

149 Half Penny, 1869 | **151** George William Gordon

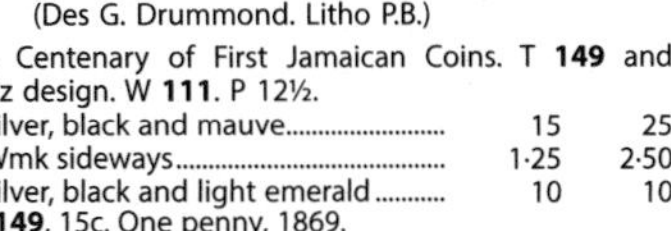

(Des G. Drummond. Litho P.B.)

1969 (27 Oct). Centenary of First Jamaican Coins. T **149** and similar horiz design. W **111**. P 12½.

296		3c. silver, black and mauve	15	25
		b. Wmk sideways	1·25	2·50
297		15c. silver, black and light emerald	10	10

Design: 3c. T **149**, 15c. One penny, 1869.

(Des G. Vasarhelyi. Litho Enschedé)

1970 (11 Mar). National Heroes. T **151** and similar vert designs. Multicoloured. P 12×12½.

298		1c. Type **151**	10	30
		a. Yellow (from flags) omitted	£400	
299		3c. Sir Alexander Bustamante	20	10
300		5c. Norman Manley	20	10
301		10c. Marcus Garvey	30	10
302		15c. Paul Bogle	35	25
298/302 *Set of 5*			1·00	60

156 *Christ appearing to St Peter* (Carracci)

2c (**159**)

(Des G. Drummond. Photo Enschedé)

1970 (23 Mar). Easter. T **156** and similar vert designs. Multicoloured. W **111**. P 12×12½.

303		3c. Type **156**	10	10
		w. Wmk inverted		
304		10c. *Christ Crucified* (Antonello da Messina)	10	10
		w. Wmk inverted		
305		20c. Easter Lily	20	60
303/305 *Set of 3*			30	70

1970 (16 July). No. 219 surch with T **159**.

306		2c. on 2d. red, yellow and grey-green	20	20

160 *Lignum Vitae*

1970 (7 Sept–2 Nov). Decimal Currency. Designs as Nos. 217/232 but inscr as T **160** in new currency. W **111** (sideways on 2, 4, 15, 20c. and $1). P 14½ (1, 5c.), 14×14½ (4c., $1), 13½×14½ (15, 20c.) or 14½×14 (others).

307		1c. violet-blue, deep green and light brown	75	2·25
308		2c. red, yellow and grey-green (as 2d.)	30	10
309		3c. yellow, black and emerald (as 3d.)	1·00	1·00
310		4c. ochre and violet (as 4d.)	3·00	30
311		5c. multicoloured (as 6d.)	3·00	65
312		8c. blue and yellow-bistre (as 9d.)	2·25	10
		a. Wmk sideways	2·00	45
313		10c. black and light brown (as 1s.)	60	20
314		15c. black, light blue and buff (as 1s.6d.) (2.11)	3·00	3·75
315		20c. red-brown, black and light blue (as 2s.) (2.11)	1·25	3·00
316		30c. blue and dull green (as 3s.) (2.11)	4·25	6·50
317		50c. black, ochre and blue (as 5s.) (2.11)	1·75	5·00
318		$1 multicoloured (as 10s.) (2.11)	1·00	5·50
319		$2 multicoloured (as £1) (2.11)	1·50	4·00
307/319 *Set of 13*			21·00	28·00

161 Cable Ship *Dacia*

(Des G. Drummond. Litho J.W.)

1970 (12 Oct). Centenary of Telegraph Service. T **161** and similar horiz designs. W **111** (sideways). P 14½×14.

320		3c. yellow, red and black	25	10
321		10c. black and turquoise	35	10
322		50c. multicoloured	80	1·00
320/322 *Set of 3*			1·25	1·10

Designs: 3c. T **161**; 10c. Bright's cable gear aboard *Dacia*; 50c. Morse key and chart.

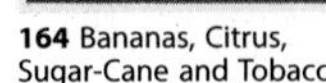

164 Bananas, Citrus, Sugar-Cane and Tobacco | **165** Locomotive *Projector* (1845)

(Des G. Drummond. Litho Questa)

1970 (2 Nov). 75th Anniversary of Jamaican Agricultural Society. W **111**. P 14.

323	**164**	2c. multicoloured	30	60
		w. Wmk inverted	8·50	
324		10c. multicoloured	70	10

(Des V. Whiteley. Litho Format)

1970 (21 Nov). 125th Anniversary of Jamaican Railways. T **165** and similar horiz designs. Multicoloured. W **111** (sideways). P 13½.

325		3c. Type **165**	30	10
326		15c. Steam locomotive No. 54 (1944)	65	30
327		50c. Diesel locomotive No. 102 (1967)	1·25	1·75
325/327 *Set of 3*			2·00	2·00

STAMP BOOKLETS

1912. Black on red covers. Stapled.

SB1	2s. booklet containing 24×1d. (No. 40) in blocks of 6 (9.3)	
SB2	2s. booklet containing 12×½d. and 18×1d. (Nos. 38, 58), each in blocks of 6 (5.12)	£1800

1923 (Dec). Black on red cover. Stapled.

SB3	2s. booklet containing 12×½d. (No. 94) in blocks of 4 and 18×1d. (No. 95) in blocks of 6	£1200

1928. Black on red cover. Stapled.

SB4	2s. booklet containing 12×½d. and 18×1d. (Nos. 92, 95) in blocks of 6	£2000

1928 (5 Sept). Black on red cover. Stapled.

SB5	1s.6d. booklet containing 12×½d. and 12×1d. (Nos. 92, 95), each in blocks of 6	

1929 (July)–**32.** Black on red cover. Stapled.

SB6	2s. booklet containing 6×½d., 12×1d. and 6×1½d. (Nos. 92, 108/109) in blocks of 6	£1500
	a. With 1d. Die II (No. 108a) (1932)	

1930–33. Black on red cover. Stapled.

SB7	2s. booklet containing 12×½d. and 18×1d. (Nos. 92, 108), each in blocks of 6	
	a. Black on pink cover with 1d. Die II (No. 108a) (1933)	£1300
	b. Black on blue cover (1936)	£1800

1935. Silver Jubilee. Black on pink cover. Stapled.

SB8	2s. booklet containing 24×1d. (No. 114) in blocks of 6	£1500
	a. In blocks of 4	£2250

1938–40. Black on green cover inscr 'JAMAICA POSTAGE STAMPS' in one line. Inland Postage Rates on interleaf. Stapled.

SB9	2s. booklet containing 12×½d. and 18×1d. (Nos. 121/122), each in blocks of 6 (inland letter rate 1d. per oz)	£500
	a. Inland letter rate 1½d. for first 2 oz (1940)	£550

1942–47. Black on blue cover inscr 'JAMAICA POSTAGE STAMPS' in three lines. Inland Postage Rates on inside front cover. Stapled.

SB10	2s. booklet containing 12×½d. and 18×1d. (Nos. 121/122), each in blocks of 6 (Inland letter rate 1½d. for first 2 oz)	£250
	a. Black on yellow cover (1947)	£110

1946. New Constitution. Black on blue cover. Stapled.

SB12	2s. booklet containing 16×1½d. (No. 134a) in blocks of 4	£225

1952. Black on yellow cover. Stapled.

SB13	2s. booklet containing 12×½d and 18×1d. (Nos. 121*b*, 122*a*), each in blocks of 6	25·00

1956. Black on green cover. Stitched.

SB14	3s. booklet containing ½d., 1d., 2d. and 2½d. (Nos. 159/162) in blocks of 6	11·00

1965 (15 Nov). Black on green cover. Stitched.

SB15	3s. booklet containing 1d., 2d. and 3d. (Nos. 217, 219, 221) in blocks of 6	5·00

POSTAL FISCALS

Revenue stamps were authorised for postal use by Post Office notice of 12 October 1887.

F **1**

(Typo D.L.R.)

1865–73. P 14.

(a) Wmk Pineapple (T 7)

F1	F **1**	1d. rose (1865)	£100	£110
		a. Imperf (pair)	£550	

(b) Wmk Crown CC

F2	F **1**	1d. rose (1871)	75·00	55·00

*(c) Wmk CA over Crown (T w **7** sideways, covering two stamps)*

F3	F **1**	1d. rose (1873)	60·00	7·00
		a. Imperf		

F **2** | F **3**

(Typo D.L.R.)

1855–74. (Issued). Glazed paper. P 14.

(a) No wmk

F4	F **2**	1½d. blue/*blue* (1857)	65·00	50·00
		a. Imperf (1855)		
		b. Blue on white	80·00	60·00
F5		3d. purple/*blue* (1857)	65·00	55·00
		a. Imperf (1855)		
		b. Purple on lilac (1857)	65·00	55·00
		ba. Imperf (1855)	£700	
		c. Purple on white (1857)	85·00	55·00

(b) Wmk Crown CC

F6	F **2**	3d. purple/*lilac* (1874)	30·00	30·00

All the above stamps *imperf* are exceedingly rare postally used.

1858 (1 Jan). (Issued). No wmk. P 15½×15.

F7	F **3**	1s. rose/*bluish*	£110	90·00
F8		5s. lilac/*bluish*	£500	£500
F9		10s. green/*bluish*	£650	£650

OFFICIAL STAMPS

OFFICIAL (O **1**) | **OFFICIAL** (O **2**)

1890 (1 Apr)–**91.** No. 16a optd with T O **1** by C. Vendryes, Kingston.

(a) 'OFFICIAL' 17 to 17½ mm long

O1	**8**	½d. green	18·00	2·25
		a. 'O' omitted	£800	
		b. One 'I' omitted		
		c. Both 'I's omitted	£900	£900
		d. 'L' omitted	£950	£950
		e. Opt inverted	£100	£110
		f. Opt double	£100	£110
		g. Opt double, one inverted	£550	£550
		h. Opt double, one vertical	£900	
		j. Pair, overprints *tête-bêche*		

(b) 'OFFICIAL' 15 to 16 mm long

O2	**8**	½d. green (3.91)	45·00	28·00
		a. Opt double	£800	

There were five settings of the locally-overprinted Officials. No. O1 occurred from settings I (2×10), II (3×6), IV and V (horizontal row of six each). No. O2 came from setting III (2×6). There are numerous minor varieties, due to broken type, etc. (*e.g.* a broken 'E' used for 'F').

Stamps with the 17–17½ mm opt were reissued in 1894 during a temporary shortage of No. O3.

1890 (1 Apr)–**91.** Optd with T O **2** by D.L.R. Wmk Crown CA. P 14.

O3	**8**	½d. green (1891)	10·00	1·75
O4	**11**	1d. rose	8·00	1·25
O5		2d. grey	32·00	1·25
O3/O5 *Set of 3*			45·00	3·75
O3s/O5s Optd 'SPECIMEN' *Set of 3*			£150	

Nos. O4/O5 were not issued without overprint.

The use of Official stamps ceased from 1 January 1898.

TELEGRAPH STAMPS

T **1** | T **2**

(Typo D.L.R.)

1879 (Oct). Wmk Crown CC (sideways on 3d.). P 14.

T1	T **1**	3d. lilac (*shades*)	50·00	10·00
T2	T **2**	1s. purple-brown (*shades*)	27·00	2·50
		s. Optd 'SPECIMEN'	70·00	

1889. Wmk Crown CA (sideways). P14.

T3	T **1**	3d. lilac (*shades*)	12·00	3·50
		s. Optd 'SPECIMEN'	70·00	

Nos. T2s and T3s were distributed to UPU member countries in March 1892.

1904. Wmk Mult Crown CA (sideways). P 14.

T4	T **1**	3d. lilac	42·00	25·00

Kenya

INDEPENDENT

(Currency. 100 cents = 1 East Africa, later Kenya Shilling)

1 Cattle Ranching

2 Wood-carving

3 National Assembly

(Des V. Whiteley. Photo Harrison)

1963 (12 Dec). Independence. Types **1/3** and similar designs. P 14×15 (small designs) or 14½ (others).

1	5c. brown, deep blue, green and bistre	10	55
2	10c. brown	10	10
3	15c. magenta	1·00	10
4	20c. black and yellow-green	15	10
5	30c. black and yellow	15	10
6	40c. brown and light blue	15	30
	a. Printed on the gummed side	£100	
7	50c. crimson, black and green	60	10
8	65c. deep turquoise-green and yellow	55	65
9	1s. multicoloured	20	10
10	1s.30 brown, black and yellow-green	5·00	30
11	2s. multicoloured	1·25	40
12	5s. brown, ultramarine and yellow-green	1·25	1·50
13	10s. brown and deep blue	9·00	3·00
14	20s. black and rose	4·00	11·00
1/14 *Set of* 14		21·00	16·00

Designs: As T **1/2**—5c. T **1**; 10c. T **2**; 15c. Heavy industry; 20c. Timber industry; 30c. Jomo Kenyatta and Mt Kenya; 40c. Fishing industry; 50c. Kenya flag 65c. Pyrethrum industry. As T **3**—1s. T **3**; 1s.30, Tourism (Treetops Hotel); 2s. Coffee industry; 5s. Tea industry; 10s. Mombasa Port; 20s. Royal College, Nairobi.

The 10c. was produced in coils of 1000 in addition to normal sheets.

4 Cockerel

(Des M. Goaman. Photo J. Enschedé)

1964 (12 Dec). Inauguration of Republic. T **4** and similar vert designs. Multicoloured. P 13×12½.

15	15c. Type **4**	15	15
16	30c. President Kenyatta	15	10
17	50c. Lion	15	10
18	1s.30 Hartlaub's Turaco	2·00	50
19	2s.50 Nandi flame	20	4·75
15/19 *Set of* 5		2·40	5·00

5 Thomson's Gazelle

6 Sable Antelope

7 Greater Kudu

15c. Grey flaw under snout of Aardvark resembles antheap (Pl. 1A, R. 10/5)

(Des Rena Fennessy. Photo Harrison)

1966 (12 Dec)–**71**. Various designs as Types **5/7**. Chalk-surfaced paper. P 14×14½ (5c. to 70c.) or 14½ (others).

20	5c. orange, black and sepia	20	20
21	10c. black and apple-green	10	10
	a. Glazed, ordinary paper (13.7.71)	1·00	5·00
22	15c. black and orange	10	10
	a. 'Antheap'	9·00	
	b. Glazed, ordinary paper (13.7.71)	1·25	1·00
23	20c. ochre, black and blue	10	15
	a. Glazed, ordinary paper (22.1.71)	1·00	1·50
24	30c. Prussian blue, blue and black	20	10
25	40c. black and yellow-brown	60	30
	a. Glazed, ordinary paper (19.2.71)	1·25	3·00
26	50c. black and red-orange	60	10
	a. Glazed, ordinary paper (19.2.71)	14·00	5·00
27	65c. black and light green	1·25	2·00
28	70c. black and claret (15.9.69)	4·00	1·75
	a. Glazed, ordinary paper (19.2.71)	38·00	16·00
29	1s. olive-brown, black and slate-blue	30	10
	a. Glazed, ordinary paper (22.1.71)	1·00	85
30	1s.30 indigo, light olive-green and black	4·00	20
31	1s.50 black, orange-brown and dull sage green (15.9.69)	1·50	3·00
	a. Glazed, ordinary paper (22.1.71)	1·50	6·00
32	2s.50 yellow, black and olive-brown	3·50	1·25
	a. Glazed, ordinary paper (22.1.71)	1·25	5·50
33	5s. yellow, black and emerald	75	70
	a. Glazed, ordinary paper (22.1.71)	1·50	12·00
34	10s. yellow-ochre, black and red-brown	3·50	3·00
35	20s. yellow-ochre, yellow-orange, black and gold	8·00	13·00
20/35 *Set of* 16		26·00	23·00
21a/33a *Set of* 10		50·00	50·00

Designs: As T **5/6**—5c. T **5**; 10c. T **6**; 15c. Aardvark ('Ant Bear'); 20c. Lesser Bushbaby; 30c. Warthog; 40c. Common Zebra; 50c. African Buffalo; 65c. Black Rhinoceros; 70c. Ostrich. As T **7**—1s. T **7**; 1s.30, African Elephant; 1s.50, Bat-eared Fox; 2s.50, Cheetah; 5s. Savanna Monkey ('Vervet Monkey'); 10s. Giant Ground Pangolin; 20s. Lion.

On chalk-surfaced paper, all values except 30c., 50c. and 2s.50 exist with PVA gum as well as gum arabic but the 70c. and 1s.50 exist with PVA gum only. The stamps on glazed, ordinary paper exist with PVA gum only.

Nos. 21 and 26 exist in coils constructed from normal sheets.

STAMP BOOKLETS

1964. Black on blue cover. Stitched.

SB1	5s. booklet containing 10c., 15c., 20c., 30c. and 50c. (Nos. 2/5, 7) in blocks of 4	20·00

1966 (12 Dec). Black on bluish grey (No. SB2) or buff (No. SB3) covers. Stitched.

SB2	3s. booklet containing 4×5c., 4×10c. and 8×30c. (Nos. 20/21, 24), each in blocks of 4	18·00
SB3	5s. booklet containing 4×5c., 4×10c., 4×50c. and 8×30c. (Nos. 20/21, 24, 26), each in blocks of 4	30·00

POSTAGE DUE STAMPS

The Postage Due stamps of Kenya, Uganda and Tanganyika were used in Kenya until 2 January 1967.

D **3**

1967 (3 Jan). Chalk-surfaced paper. P 14×13½.

D13	D **3**	5c. scarlet	15	2·75
		a. Perf 14. Ordinary paper. *Dull scarlet* (16.12.69)	40	7·50
D14		10c. green	20	2·50
		a. Perf 14. Ordinary paper (16.12.69)	55	4·25
D15		20c. blue	70	2·75
		a. Perf 14. Ordinary paper. *Deep blue* (16.12.69)	55	8·50
D16		30c. brown	80	3·25
		a. Perf 14. Ordinary paper. *Light red-brown* (16.12.69)	80	25·00
D17		40c. bright purple	65	5·00
		a. Perf 14. Ordinary paper. *Pale bright purple* (16.12.69)	65	25·00
D18		1s. bright orange	1·75	7·00
		a. Perf 14. Ordinary paper. *Dull bright orange* (18.2.70)	2·00	25·00
D13/D18 *Set of* 6			3·75	21·00
D13*a*/D18*a* *Set of* 6			4·50	85·00

OFFICIAL STAMPS

Intended for use on official correspondence of the Kenya Government only but there is no evidence that they were so used.

OFFICIAL
(O **4**)

(15c. 30c. opt typo; others in photogravure)

1964 (1 Oct). Nos. 1/5 and 7 optd with T O **4**.

O21	5c. brown, deep blue, green and bistre	10
O22	10c. brown	10
O23	15c. magenta	1·25
O24	20c. black and yellow-green	20
O25	30c. black and yellow	30
O26	50c. crimson, black and green	2·75
O21/O26 *Set of* 6		4·00

Kenya, Uganda and Tanganyika

BRITISH EAST AFRICA

The area which became British East Africa had been part of the domain of the Zanzibari Sultans since 1794. In 1887 the administration of the province was granted to the British East Africa Association, incorporated as the Imperial British East Africa Company the following year.

Company post offices were established at Lamu and Mombasa in May 1890, British mails having been previously sent via the Indian post office on Zanzibar, opened in 1875.

A German postal agency opened at Lamu on 22 November 1888 and continued to operate until 31 March 1891, using German stamps. These can be identified by the 'LAMU/OSTAFRIKA' cancellations and are listed under German East Africa in our *Germany* catalogue.

PRICES FOR STAMPS ON COVER TO 1945	
Nos. 1/3	*from* × 10
Nos. 4/19	*from* × 30
Nos. 20/21	*from* × 3
No. 22	—
No. 23	*from* × 3
No. 24	—
No. 25	*from* × 1
No. 26	*from* × 3
Nos. 27/28	*from* × 8
Nos. 29/30	*from* × 20
No. 31	*from* × 10
No. 32	—
Nos. 33/42	*from* × 10
Nos. 43/47	—
No. 48	*from* × 15
Nos. 49/64	*from* × 12
Nos. 65/79	*from* × 15
Nos. 80/91	*from* × 8
Nos. 92/96	*from* × 12
Nos. 97/99	—

(Currency. 16 annas = 1 rupee)

BRITISH EAST AFRICA COMPANY ADMINISTRATION

BRITISH
EAST AFRICA
COMPANY

HALF ANNA
(1)

BRITISH
EAST AFRICA
COMPANY

1 ANNA
(2)

(Surch D.L.R.)

1890 (23 May). Stamps of Great Britain (Queen Victoria) surch as T **1** or T **2** (1a. and 4a.).

1	½a. on 1d. deep purple (No. 173)	£275	£200
2	1a. on 2d. grey-green and carmine (No. 200)	£500	£275
3	4a. on 5d. dull purple and blue (No. 207*a*)	£600	£325

The second stamp of each horizontal row of the 4a. on 5d. had the 'BRITISH' shifted to the left, placing the 'B' directly over the 'S' of 'EAST'. In the normal overprint the 'B' is over 'ST' as shown in Type (**2**).

A copy of the ½a. with the short crossbar of 'F' in 'HALF' omitted exists in the Royal Collection but is the only known example.

Following the exhaustion of stocks of Nos. 1/3, stamps of India were used at Mombasa (and occasionally at Lamu) from late July 1890 until the arrival of Nos. 4/19. The following listing is for stamps clearly cancelled with the MOMBASA21 mm circular date stamp (code 'C'). Examples with LAMU circular date stamp are worth much more. Indian stamps used after October 1890, including other values, came from ship mail.

Stamps of INDIA1882–1890 (Nos. 84/101) cancelled at Mombasa between July and October 1890.

Z1	½a. blue-green	£600
Z2	1a. brown-purple	£500
Z3	1a.6p. sepia	£850
Z4	2a. blue	£950
Z5	3a. orange	£950
Z5*a*	4a. olive-green	£1000
Z6	4a.6p. yellow-green	£375
Z7	8a. dull mauve	£550
Z8	1r. slate	£950

3

4

5
ANNAS.
(5)

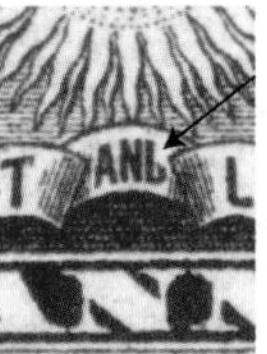
1a. 'ANL' (broken 'D') (R. 6/5)

(Litho B.W.)

1890 (13 Oct)–**95**. P 14.

4 3 ½a. dull brown 9·50 14·00
a. Imperf (pair) £1500 £700
b. Deep brown (21.10.93) 70 12·00
ba. Imperf (pair) £900 £375
bb. Imperf between (horiz pair) £1700 £650
bc. Imperf between (vert pair) £1400 £500
c. Pale brown (16.1.95) 1·00 17·00
5 1a. blue-green 9·50 16·00
aa. 'ANL' (broken 'D') £1000 £1100
a. Imperf (pair) £5000 £1300
ab. Ditto. 'ANL' (broken 'D') £20000
b. Deep blue-green (16.1.95) 1·00
6 2a. vermilion 7·00 8·00
a. Imperf (pair) £5000 £1400
7 3 2½a. black/*yellow-buff* (9.91) £100 35·00
aa. Imperf (pair) £6000
a. Imperf between (horiz pair) £8000
ab. Block of four imperf between (horiz and vert) £16000
b. Black/pale buff (9.92) £100 14·00
c. Black/bright yellow (21.10.93) 6·00 10·00
cb. Imperf (pair) £1200 £500
cc. Imperf between (horiz pair) £1400 £450
cd. Imperf between (vert pair) £1400 £600
8 3a. black/*dull red* (30.3.91) 26·00 27·00
a. Black/bright red (21.10.93) 4·00 19·00
ab. Imperf (pair) £1200 £450
ac. Imperf between (horiz pair) £900 £425
ad. Imperf between (vert pair) £700 £400
9 4a. yellow-brown 2·50 15·00
a. Imperf (pair) £5000 £1700
10 4a. grey (*imperf*) £1200 £1400
11 4½a. dull violet (30.3.91) 38·00 21·00
a. Brown-purple (21.10.93) 2·50 23·00
ab. Imperf (pair) £2000 £450
ac. Imperf between (horiz pair) £1500 £1000
ad. Imperf between (vert pair) £1100 £500
12 8a. blue 5·50 12·00
a. Imperf (pair) £10000 £1500
13 8a. grey £275 £225
14 1r. carmine 6·00 9·00
a. Imperf (pair) £15000 £1700
15 1r. grey £225 £225
16 4 2r. brick-red 14·00 50·00
17 3r. slate-purple 14·00 55·00
18 4r. ultramarine 12·00 55·00
19 5r. grey-green 30·00 75·00
4/9, 11/19 *Set of* 15 £550 £650

For the 5a. and 7½a. see Nos. 29/30.

The paper of Nos. 7, 7*b*, 7*c*, 8 and 8*a* is coloured on the surface only.

Printings of 1890/1892 are on thin paper having the outer margins of the sheets imperf and bearing sheet watermark 'PURE LINEN WOVE BANK' and 'W. C. S. & Co.' in a monogram, the trademark of the makers, Messrs. William Collins, Sons & Co.

1893/1894 printings are on thicker coarser paper with outer margins perforated through the selvedge and without watermark. Single specimens cannot always be distinguished by lack of watermark alone. Exceptions are the 1893 printings of the 2½a. and 3a. which were on Wiggins Teape paper showing a sheet watermark of '1011' in figures 1 centimetre high.

Nos. 7 (coloured through) and 16/19 on thick unwatermarked paper are from a special printing made for presentation purposes.

The printings of the 4a., 8a. and 1r. values in grey were intended for fiscal purposes, but in the event, were made available for postal use.

Forgeries of the 4a., 8a., 1r. grey and 2 to 5r. exist. The latter are common and can be distinguished by the scroll above 'LIGHT' where there are five vertical lines of shading in the forgeries and seven in the genuine stamps. Forged cancellations exist on the commoner stamps. Beware of 'imperf' stamps made by trimming margins of stamps from marginal positions.

1891. Mombasa Provisionals.

(a) New value handstamped in dull violet, with original face value obliterated and initials added in black manuscript

20 3 '½ Anna' on 2a. vermilion ('A.D.') (1.91) £11000 £1100
a. '½ Anna' double † £13000
b. Original face value not obliterated † £3750
21 '1 Anna' on 4a. brown ('A.B.') (2.91) £18000 £2250

(b) Manuscript value and initials in black

22 3 '½ Anna' on 2a. vermilion ('A.D.') (original face value not obliterated) (1.91) † £4750
23 '½ Anna' on 2a. vermilion ('A.B.') (2.91) £11000 £1100
a. Error. '½ Annas' ('A.B.') † £1200
24 '½ Anna' on 3a. black/*dull red* ('A.B.') (5.91) £18000 £2250
25 '1 Anna' on 3a. black/*dull red* ('V.H.M.') (6.91) £16000 £1400
26 '1 Anna' on 4a. brown ('A.B.') (3.91) £10000 £2000

A.D. = Andrew Dick, Chief Accountant.
A.B. = Archibald Brown, Cashier of the Company.
V.H.M. = Victor H. Mackenzie, Bank Manager.

Nos. 23 and 26 exist with manuscript surcharges in different hands. Examples with a heavy surcharge applied with a thick nib were mainly used at Lamu. Most of the surviving unused examples show this style, but used examples are worth a premium over the prices quoted.

(Surch B.W.)

1894 (1 Nov). Surch as T **5**.

27 3 5a. on 8a. blue 75·00 95·00
28 7½a. on 1r. carmine 75·00 95·00
27s/28s Handstamped 'SPECIMEN' *Set of* 2 95·00

Forgeries exist.

1895 (16 Jan). No wmk. P 14.

29 3 5a. black/*grey-blue* 1·25 13·00
30 7½a. black 1·25 19·00
29s/30s Handstamped 'SPECIMEN' *Set of* 2 75·00

The date quoted is that of earliest known use of stamps from this consignment.

These two stamps have 'LD' after 'COMPANY' in the inscription.

The paper of No. 29 is coloured on the surface only.

1895 (Feb). No. 8 surch with manuscript value and initials ('T.E.C.R.'). Original face value obliterated in manuscript.

31 3 '½ anna' on 3a. black/*dull red* (19.2) £600 55·00
32 '1 anna' on 3a. black/*dull red* (22.2) £10000 £7000

T.E.C.R. = T.E.C. Remington, Postmaster at Mombasa.

Similar manuscript surcharges on the black/*bright red* shade (No. 8*a*) are believed to be forgeries.

The Company experienced considerable financial problems during 1894 with the result that the British Government agreed to assume the administration of the territory, as a protectorate, on 1 July 1895.

IMPERIAL ADMINISTRATION

BRITISH
EAST
AFRICA
(6)

2½
(7)

(Handstamped at Mombasa)

1895 (9 July). Handstamped with T **6**.

33 3 ½a. deep brown 80·00 38·00
a. Pale brown £120 55·00
b. Dull brown † £3500
c. Double £475 £450
d. Inverted £7500
34 1a. blue-green £200 £130
a. Double £750 £500
b. 'ANL' (broken 'D') (R. 6/5) £3500 £3750
c. Deep blue-green † £4500
35 2a. vermilion £200 £100
a. Double £850 £550
36 2½a. black/*bright yellow* £200 70·00
a. Double £850 £500
b. Black/pale buff † £3000
37 3a. black/*dull red* £100 60·00
38 4a. yellow-brown 75·00 45·00
a. Double £600 £500
39 4½a. dull violet £225 £100
a. Double £900 £650
b. Brown-purple £1200 £1000
ba. Double £3250 £2250
40 5a. black/*grey-blue* £300 £150
a. Double £1100 £850
b. Inverted † £5000
41 7½a. black £140 90·00
a. Double £850 £650
42 8a. blue £100 80·00
a. Double £750 £650
b. Inverted £8000
43 1r. carmine 70·00 55·00
a. Double £700 £550
44 4 2r. brick-red £550 £350
45 3r. slate-purple £275 £170
a. Double £1200 £1000
b. Inverted
46 4r. ultramarine £225 £180
a. Double £1100 £900
47 5r. grey-green £450 £300
a. Double £1500 £1400
33/47 *Set of* 15 £2750 £1600

Forgeries exist.

The ½a. stamps used for this issue were mainly from the 1893–1894 printings on thicker paper, but three used examples are known on the 1890 thin paper printing with sheet watermark (No. 4). The 1a. stamps were mostly from the 1890 thin paper printing (No. 5), but one example is known from the 1895 printing on thick paper (No. 5*b*). The 2½a. stamps were mainly from the 1893 printing (No. 7*c*), but three used examples have been reported from the 1892 printing on thin pale buff paper (No. 7*b*).

1895 (29 Sept). No. 39 surch with T **7** by *The Zanzibar Gazette*.

48 3 2½a. on 4½a. dull violet (R.) £250 90·00
a. Opt (Type **6**) double £1200 £950

British
East
Africa
(8)

British
East
Africa
(9)

SETTING OF TYPE 8. This consisted of 120 impressions in ten horizontal rows of 12 stamps. This matched the size of the pane for all the Indian issues to 1r. with the exception of the 6a. The sheets of this value contained four panes, each 8×10, which meant that the outer vertical margins also received the overprint.

The setting of T **9** is not known.

Although only the one setting was used for the low values it is known that some of the overprint errors occurred, or were corrected, during the course of the various printings.

(Overprinted at the offices of *The Zanzibar Gazette*)

1895 (27 Oct)–**96**. Stamps of India (Queen Victoria) optd with T **8** or **9** (2r. to 5r.). W **13** (Elephant Head) (6a.) or W **34** (Large Star) (others) of India.

49 ½a. blue-green (No. 85) (8.11.95) 7·00 5·50
a. 'Britlsh' for 'British' £10000 £8000
b. 'Br1tish' for 'British' (R. 10/12) £600
c. 'Afr1ca' for 'Africa' (R. 1/11) £800
d. Opt double, one albino £225
e. 'Briti' for 'British' (R. 1/6) £4000
50 1a. plum (No. 89) (8.11.95) 7·00 6·00
a. 'Britlsh' for 'British' £18000 £5500
b. 'Br1tish' for 'British' (R. 10/12) £650 £700
c. 'Afr1ca' for 'Africa' (R. 1/11) £850
d. 'Briti' for 'British' (R. 1/6) £4250
51 1a.6p. sepia (No. 90) (23.11.95) 5·00 4·00
a. 'Br1tish' for 'British' (R. 10/12) £700 £550
b. 'Afr1ca' for 'Africa' (R. 1/11) £900
52 2a. blue (No. 92) (28.10.95) 9·50 3·75
a. 'Britlsh' for 'British' £10000 £8500
b. 'Br1tish' for 'British' (R. 10/12) £600 £275
c. 'Afr1ca' for 'Africa' (R. 1/11) £850 £375
d. 'h' of 'British' inserted by hand £3000
53 2a.6p. yellow-green (No. 103) 18·00 2·50
c. 'Britlsh' for 'British' † £5500
d. 'Eas' for 'East' (R. 2/12) £1300 £1500
e. 'Br1tish' for 'British' (R. 10/12) £800 £300
f. 'Afr1ca' for 'Africa' (R. 1/11) £1000 £400
g. 'Briti' for 'British' (R. 1/6) £4500
h. Opt double £1200
54 3a. brown-orange (No. 94) (18.12.95) 26·00 11·00
a. 'Br1tish' for 'British' (R. 10/12) £800 £550
b. 'Afr1ca' for 'Africa' (R. 1/11) £1100
c. Opt double, one albino £750
55 4a. olive-green (No. 95) (18.12.95) 50·00 48·00
a. 'Br1tish' for 'British' (R. 10/12) £1400
b. Slate-green 30·00 32·00
ba. 'Br1tish' for 'British' (R. 10/12) £1000 £650
bb. 'Afr1ca' for 'Africa' (R. 1/11) £1300 £850
56 6a. pale brown (No. 81) (18.12.95) 50·00 50·00
a. 'Br1tish' for 'British' (R. 10/8) £2000
b. 'Afr1ca' for 'Africa' (R. 1/7) £2500
c. 'E st' for 'East' † —
d. Opt double, one albino £300
57 8a. dull mauve (No. 98) (18.12.95) £100 70·00
a. 'Br1tish' for 'British' (R. 10/12)
b. 'Afr1ca' for 'Africa' (R. 1/11)
c. Magenta (1896) 35·00 55·00
ca. 'Br1tish' for 'British' (R. 10/12) £950 £900
cb. 'Afr1ca' for 'Africa' (R. 1/11) £1100 £950
cc. Inverted 'a' for 't' of 'East' (R. 2/12) † £25000
58 12a. purple/*red* (No. 100) (18.12.95) 22·00 42·00
a. 'Br1tish' for 'British' (R. 10/12) £900 £950
b. 'Afr1ca' for 'Africa' (R. 1/11) £1300 £1400
59 1r. slate (No. 101) (18.12.95) £100 70·00
a. 'Br1tish' for 'British' (R. 10/12)
b. 'Afr1ca' for 'Africa' (R. 1/11)
60 1r. green and aniline carmine (No. 106) (1896) 50·00 £130
a. Inverted 'a' for 't' of 'East' (R. 2/12) £18000
b. 'Br1tish' for 'British' (R. 10/12) £2250
c. 'Afr1ca' for 'Africa' (R. 1/11) £2250
d. Opt double, one sideways £425 £900
e. Opt double, one albino £750
61 2r. carmine and yellow-brown (No. 107) (18.12.95) £140 £200
a. 'B' handstamped £8500 £8500
62 3r. brown and green (No. 108) (18.12.95) £160 £200
a. 'B' handstamped £8500 £8500
b. Opt double, one albino £2000
63 5r. ultramarine and violet (No. 109) (18.12.95) £170 £225
a. Opt double £3500
b. 'B' handstamped £7500 £6500
c. Opt double, one albino £2000
49/63 *Set of* 15 £700 £900

The relative horizontal positions of the three lines of the overprint vary considerably but the distance vertically between the lines of the overprint is constant.

In both the 'Br1tish' and 'Afr1ca' errors the figure one is in a smaller type size.

There are other varieties, such as inverted 's' in 'British', wide and narrow 'B', and inverted 'V' for 'A' in 'Africa' (R. 1/1 and R. 6/7).

During the overprinting of Nos. 61/63 the 'B' of 'British' sometimes failed to print so that only traces of the letter appeared. It was replaced by a handstamped 'B' which is often out of alignment with the rest of the overprint. The handstamp is known double.

The 2, 3 and 5r., normally overprinted in larger type than the lower values, are also known with a smaller overprint, for use as specimen stamps for the UPU. These were not issued for postal purposes (*Price £500 un per set*). The lower values were reprinted at the same time using similar type to the original overprint.

Forgeries exist.

2½
(10)

11

1895 (19 Dec). No. 51 surch locally with T **10** in bright red.

64 2½ on 1½a. sepia £120 50·00
a. Inverted '1' in fraction (R. 5/7, 10/7) £1200 £700
b. 'Br1tish' for 'British' (R. 10/12) £1800
c. 'Afr1ca' for 'Africa' (R. 1/11) £1800

The setting of T **10** was in five horizontal rows of 12 stamps, repeated twice for each pane.

No. 51 also exists surcharged with Types **12**, **13** and **14** in brown-red. These stamps were sent to the Postal Union authorities at Berne, but were never issued to the public (*Price unused*: T **12** £110, T **13** £225, T **14** £150).

(Recess D.L.R.)

1896 (26 May)–**1901**. Wmk Crown CA. P 14.

65 11 ½a. yellow-green 6·50 1·00
x. Wmk reversed £450 £300
66 1a. carmine-rose 18·00 40
a. Bright rose-red 16·00 40
b. Rosine (1901) 32·00 4·50
w. Wmk inverted £250 £160
x. Wmk reversed £375 £225
y. Wmk inverted and reversed † £450
67 2a. chocolate 14·00 9·00
x. Wmk reversed † £200
68 2½a. deep blue 19·00 3·00
a. Violet-blue 27·00 3·75
b. Inverted 'S' in 'ANNAS' (R. 1/1) £250 85·00
w. Wmk inverted † £325
x. Wmk reversed £325 £200
69 3a. grey 12·00 17·00
x. Wmk reversed £180 £250
70 4a. deep green 9·50 6·00
71 4½a. orange-yellow 19·00 21·00
72 5a. yellow-bistre 8·50 8·50
73 7½a. mauve 14·00 28·00
w. Wmk inverted † £650
x. Wmk reversed † £550
74 8a. grey-olive 12·00 8·50
75 1r. pale dull blue 85·00 29·00
a. Ultramarine £150 70·00
76 2r. orange 70·00 35·00
77 3r. deep violet 70·00 40·00
78 4r. carmine-lake 70·00 80·00
79 5r. sepia 75·00 42·00

		a. Thin 'U' in 'RUPEES' (R. 3/2)	£1800	£1400
		x. Wmk reversed	†	£900
65/79 *Set of* 15			£450	£275
65s/79s Optd 'SPECIMEN' *Set of* 15			£350	

Examples of some values exist apparently without watermark or with double-lined lettering from the marginal watermark due to the paper being misplaced on the press.

(Overprinted at the offices of *The Zanzibar Gazette*)

1897 (2 Jan). Nos. 156/157, 159 and 165/167 of Zanzibar optd with T **8**. Wmk Single Rosette.

80		½a. yellow-green and red	60·00	50·00
81		1a. indigo and red	£100	95·00
82		2a. red-brown and red	50·00	26·00
83		4½a. orange and red	60·00	32·00
		a. No right serif to left-hand '4' (R. 1/1)	£1400	£850
		b. No fraction bar at right (R. 2/1)	£1400	£850
84		5a. bistre and red	65·00	50·00
		a. 'Bri' for 'British'	£2000	£2000
85		7½a. mauve and red	70·00	50·00
		a. 'Bri' for 'British'	£2500	
		b. Optd on front and back		
80/85 *Set of* 6			£375	£250

Nos. 84a and 85a appear to have occurred when the type was obscured during part of the overprinting.

The above six stamps exist with an overprint similar to T **8** but normally showing a stop after 'Africa'. These overprints (in red on the 1a.) were made officially to supply the UPU (*Price £300 un per set*). However, the stop does not always show. Pieces are known showing overprints with and without stop *se-tenant* (including the red overprint on the 1a.).

Stamps of Zanzibar, wmk 'Multiple Rosettes' and overprinted with T **8** are forgeries.

2½ 2½ 2½

(**12**) (**13**) (**14**)

SETTING OF TYPES 12/14. The setting of 60 (6×10) contained 26 examples of T **12**, 10 of T **13** and 24 of T **14**.

1897 (2 Jan). Nos. 157 and 162 of Zanzibar optd with T **8** and further surch locally, in red.

86	**12**	2½ on 1a. indigo and red	£130	70·00
		b. Opt Type **8** double	£7500	
87	**13**	2½ on 1a. indigo and red	£325	£120
88	**14**	2½ on 1a. indigo and red	£150	75·00
		a. Opt Type **8** double	£7500	
89	**12**	2½ on 3a. grey and red	£130	65·00
90	**13**	2½ on 3a. grey and red	£325	£120
91	**14**	2½ on 3a. grey and red	£150	70·00
86/91 *Set of* 6			£1100	£475

Both the notes after No. 85 also apply here.

A special printing for UPU requirements was made with the 2½ surcharge on the 1a. and 3a. stamps overprinted as T **8** but *with stop* after 'Africa' (*Price from £100 per stamp*). It also included a '2' over '1' error in T **14** (*Price, £2750, either value*) and a diagonal fraction bar variety in T **12**. The surcharge on the 3a. is known double, one albino.

15

(Recess D.L.R.)

1897 (Nov)–**1903**. Wmk Crown CC. P 14.

92	**15**	1r. grey-blue	£130	55·00
		a. Dull blue (1901)	£120	65·00
		b. Bright ultramarine (1903)	£550	£400
93		2r. orange	£150	£160
94		3r. deep violet	£180	£190
95		4r. carmine	£500	£550
		x. Wmk reversed	£850	£950
		y. Wmk inverted and reversed	£1800	
96		5r. deep sepia	£450	£550
97		10r. yellow-bistre	£450	£650
		s. Optd 'SPECIMEN'	85·00	
		x. Wmk reversed	£1700	
98		20r. pale green (f.c. £110)	£1200	£2750
		s. Optd 'SPECIMEN'	£180	
99		50r. mauve (f.c. £300)	£2500	£9000
		s. Optd 'SPECIMEN'	£400	
		x. Wmk reversed	£2750	£9000
		xs. Optd 'SPECIMEN'	£425	
92s/96s Optd 'SPECIMEN' *Set of* 5			£250	

On 1 April 1901 the postal administrations of British East Africa and Uganda were merged. Subsequent issues were inscribed 'EAST AFRICA AND UGANDA PROTECTORATES'.

EAST AFRICA AND UGANDA PROTECTORATES

For earlier issues see BRITISH EAST AFRICA and UGANDA.

For the issues of the Mandated Territory of Tanganyika and the war-time issues that preceded them, see TANGANYIKA.

PRICES FOR STAMPS ON COVER TO 1945

Nos. 1/43	*from* × 3
Nos. 44/75	*from* × 2
Nos. 76/95	*from* × 3
Nos. 96/105	—
Nos. 110/123	*from* × 2
Nos. 124/127	*from* × 3
Nos. 128/130	*from* × 5
Nos. 131/154	*from* × 3
Nos. D1/D12	*from* × 8

PRINTERS. All the stamps issued between 1903 and 1927 were typographed by De La Rue & Co. Ltd, London.

USED HIGH VALUES. Beware of cleaned fiscally cancelled examples with faked postmarks.

1

2

1903 (24 July)–**04**. P 14.

		(a) Wmk Crown CA		
1	**1**	½a. green (16.2.04)	7·00	23·00
2		1a. grey and red	2·75	2·00
3		2a. dull and bright purple (24.7.03)	8·50	2·50
		w. Wmk inverted	£250	£225
4		2½a. blue	12·00	55·00
5		3a. brown-purple and green	28·00	70·00
6		4a. grey-green and black	11·00	22·00
7		5a. grey and orange-brown	19·00	55·00
8		8a. grey and pale blue	28·00	50·00
		(b) Wmk Crown CC. Ordinary paper		
9	**2**	1r. green	27·00	65·00
		a. Chalk-surfaced paper	90·00	£140
10		2r. dull and bright purple	90·00	£100
11		3r. grey-green and black	£170	£300
12		4r. grey and emerald-green	£170	£325
13		5r. grey and red	£170	£350
14		10r. grey and ultramarine	£450	£650
		a. Chalk-surfaced paper	£600	£700
		w. Wmk inverted	£1200	
15		20r. grey and stone	£800	£1900
		s. Optd 'SPECIMEN'	£180	
16		50r. grey and red-brown (f.c. £225)	£2500	£4500
		s. Optd 'SPECIMEN'	£450	
		w. Wmk inverted (f.c. £500)	£5500	
1/13 *Set of* 13			£650	£1200
1s/14s Optd 'SPECIMEN' *Set of* 14			£475	

1904–07. Wmk Mult Crown CA. Ordinary paper (½a. to 8a.) or chalk-surfaced paper (1r. to 50r.).

17	**1**	½a. grey-green	8·50	3·00
		a. Chalk-surfaced paper	17·00	3·25
18		1a. grey and red	12·00	80
		a. Chalk-surfaced paper	18·00	1·75
19		2a. dull and bright purple	3·25	2·75
		a. Chalk-surfaced paper	3·50	2·75
20		2½a. blue	8·00	30·00
21		2½a. ultramarine and blue	7·50	17·00
22		3a. brown-purple and green	6·00	45·00
		a. Chalk-surfaced paper	6·50	48·00
23		4a. grey-green and black	7·50	18·00
		a. Chalk-surfaced paper	10·00	18·00
24		5a. grey and orange-brown	8·00	15·00
		a. Chalk-surfaced paper	6·50	32·00
25		8a. grey and pale blue	7·00	8·50
		a. Chalk-surfaced paper	7·00	23·00
26	**2**	1r. green (1907)	38·00	70·00
		w. Wmk inverted	£1300	£950
27		2r. dull and bright purple (1906)	55·00	75·00
28		3r. grey-green and black (1907)	£100	£150
29		4r. grey and emerald-green (1907)	£130	£200
		w. Wmk inverted	£1100	
30		5r. grey and red (1907)	£170	£225
31		10r. grey and ultramarine (1907)	£375	£425
		w. Wmk inverted	£1100	£1300
32		20r. grey and stone (1907)	£850	£1500
33		50r. grey and red-brown (1907) (f.c. £425)	£2750	£4500
17/30 *Set of* 13			£475	£750

(New Currency. 100 cents = 1 rupee)

1907–08. Wmk Mult Crown CA. Chalk-surfaced paper (10, 12, 25, 50, 75c.). P 14.

34	**1**	1c. brown	2·50	15
35		3c. grey-green	21·00	70
		a. Blue-green	26·00	4·00
36		6c. red	3·00	10
37		10c. lilac and pale olive	13·00	8·50
38		12c. dull and bright purple	10·00	2·75
39		15c. bright blue	32·00	8·50
40		25c. grey-green and black	25·00	7·00
41		50c. grey-green and orange-brown	19·00	17·00
42		75c. grey and pale blue (1908)	4·75	45·00
34/42 *Set of* 9			£110	80·00
34s/42s Optd 'SPECIMEN' *Set of* 9			£250	

Original

Redrawn

1910. T **1** redrawn. Printed from a single plate. Wmk Mult Crown CA. P 14.

43		6c. red	27·00	30

In the redrawn type a fine white line has been cut around the value tablets and above the name tablet separating the latter from the leaves above, EAST AFRICA AND UGANDA is in shorter and thicker letters and PROTECTORATES in taller letters than in No. 36

3

4

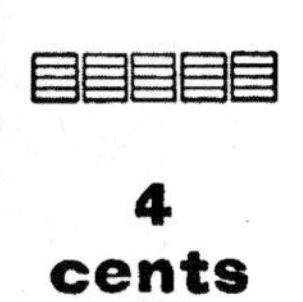

(**5**)

1912–21. Wmk Mult Crown CA. Chalk-surfaced paper (25c. to 500r.). P 14.

44	**3**	1c. black	30	1·75
		a. 'C' of 'CA' missing from wmk	†	£1000
		y. Wmk inverted and reversed	£800	£650
45		3c. green	2·00	60
		a. Deep blue-green (1917)	4·50	1·75
		w. Wmk inverted	†	—
46		6c. red	1·25	40
		a. Scarlet (1917)	25·00	3·00
		w. Wmk inverted	—	£700
		y. Wmk inverted and reversed	—	£700
47		10c. yellow-orange	2·00	50
		a. Orange (1921)	13·00	6·00
		w. Wmk inverted	£700	
48		12c. slate-grey	2·75	50
		a. Wmk sideways		
49		15c. bright blue	2·75	80
		w. Wmk inverted	£700	£700
50		25c. black and red/*yellow*	50	1·25
		a. White back (5.14)	50	4·50
		as. Optd 'SPECIMEN'	38·00	
		b. On lemon (1916)	11·00	11·00
		bs. Optd 'SPECIMEN'	42·00	
		c. On orange-buff (1921)	48·00	18·00
		d. On pale yellow (1921)	14·00	7·00
51		50c. black and lilac	1·50	1·75
52		75c. black/*green*	1·50	17·00
		a. White back (5.14)	1·00	16·00
		as. Optd 'SPECIMEN'	40·00	
		b. On blue-green, olive back	11·00	7·50
		bs. Optd 'SPECIMEN'	48·00	
		c. On emerald, olive back (1919)	45·00	£150
		d. On emerald back (1921)	12·00	60·00
53	**4**	1r. black/*green*	2·75	4·25
		aw. Wmk inverted	£850	
		b. On emerald back (1919)	5·00	50·00
54		2r. red and black/*blue*	26·00	45·00
		w. Wmk inverted	£500	
		x. Wmk reversed	†	—
55		3r. violet and green	32·00	£130
56		4r. red and green/*yellow*	60·00	£110
		a. On pale yellow	£140	£200
57		5r. blue and dull purple	65·00	£160
58		10r. red and green/*green*	£250	£350
59		20r. black and purple/*red*	£475	£450
60		20r. purple and blue/*blue* (1918)	£550	£850
61		50r. dull rose-red and dull greyish green (f.c. £75)	£900	£950
		a. Carmine and green	£1700	£1700
		s. Optd 'SPECIMEN'	£275	
62		100r. purple and black/*red* (f.c. £250)	£9500	£3750
		s. Optd 'SPECIMEN'	£700	
63		500r. green and red/*green* (f.c. £850)	£40000	
		s. Optd 'SPECIMEN'	£1500	
44/58 *Set of* 15			£400	£750
44s/60s Optd 'SPECIMEN' *Set of* 17			£900	

For values in this series overprinted 'G.E.A.' (German East Africa) see Tanganyika Nos. 45/62.

1919 (7 Apr). No. 46*a* surch with T **5** by the Swift Press, Nairobi.

64	**3**	4c. on 6c. scarlet (*shades*)	1·25	15
		a. Bars omitted	50·00	70·00
		b. Surch double	£160	£250
		c. Surch inverted	£350	£450
		d. Pair, one without surch	£2000	£2250
		e. Surch on back	£475	
		s. Handstamped 'SPECIMEN'	65·00	

1921. Wmk Mult Script CA. Chalk-surfaced paper (50c. to 50r.). P 14.

65	**3**	1c. black	80	1·75
		w. Wmk inverted	£425	£425
66		3c. green	6·00	17·00
		a. Blue-green	25·00	22·00
67		6c. carmine-red	10·00	22·00
68		10c. orange (12.21)	8·50	1·25
		w. Wmk inverted	†	£700
69		12c. slate-grey	12·00	£150
70		15c. bright blue	11·00	21·00
71		50c. black and dull purple	14·00	£130
72	**4**	2r. red and black/*blue*	75·00	£180
73		3r. violet and green	£150	£450
74		5r. blue and dull purple	£180	£375
75		50r. carmine and green (f.c. £450)	£3250	£9000
		s. Optd 'SPECIMEN'	£500	
65/74 *Set of* 10			£425	£1200
65s/74s Optd 'SPECIMEN' *Set of* 10			£400	

For values in this series overprinted 'G.E.A.' see Tanganyika Nos. 63/73.

KENYA AND UGANDA

(New Currency. 100 cents = 1 East Africa shilling)

On 23 July 1920, Kenya became a Crown Colony with the exception of the coastal strip, previously part of the Sultan of Zanzibar's territories, which remained a protectorate.

The northern province of Jubaland was ceded to Italy on 29 June 1925 and later incorporated into Italian Somaliland.

6

7

1922 (1 Nov)–**27**. Wmk Mult Script CA. P 14.

		(a) Wmk upright. Ordinary paper		
76	**6**	1c. pale brown	1·00	4·75
		a. Deep brown (1923)	1·50	3·50
		ax. Wmk reversed	£375	
77		5c. dull violet	7·50	75
		a. Bright violet	13·00	1·50
78		5c. green (1927)	2·00	30
		sa. Opt 'SPECIMEN' double	£550	

No.	Type	Description	Unused	Used
79		10c. green	1·50	30
		w. Wmk inverted		
80		10c. black (5.27)	4·00	20
81		12c. jet-black	15·00	38·00
		a. Grey-black	15·00	26·00
82		15c. rose-carmine	1·25	10
83		20c. dull orange-yellow	3·25	10
		a. Bright orange	6·50	10
84		30c. ultramarine	4·25	50
85		50c. grey	2·50	10
86		75c. olive	11·00	9·00
		(b) Wmk sideways. Chalk-surfaced paper*		
87	7	1s. green	7·00	2·50
88		2s. dull purple	9·00	21·00
		w. Wmk Crown to right of CA	£190	£275
89		2s.50 brown (1.10.25)	19·00	£120
90		3s. brownish grey	19·00	6·50
		a. Jet-black	55·00	50·00
91		4s. grey (1.10.25)	42·00	£130
		w. Wmk Crown to right of CA	80·00	£250
92		5s. carmine-red	24·00	22·00
		w. Wmk Crown to right of CA	—	£550
93		7s.50 orange-yellow (1.10.25)	£130	£350
94		10s. bright blue	80·00	75·00
		w. Wmk Crown to right of CA (f.c. £75)	£550	£550
95		£1 black and orange (f.c. £20)	£225	£325
96		£2 green and purple (1.10.25) (f.c. £170)	£1100	£2000
		s. Optd 'SPECIMEN'	£350	
97		£3 purple and yellow (1.10.25) (f.c. £300)	£1800	
		s. Optd 'SPECIMEN'	£400	
98		£4 black and magenta (1.10.25) (f.c. £300)	£3000	
		s. Optd 'SPECIMEN'	£550	
99		£5 black and blue (f.c. £120)	£3250	
		s. Optd 'SPECIMEN'	£650	
		w. Wmk Crown to right of CA	£3500	
100		£10 black and green (f.c. £325)	£14000	
		s. Optd 'SPECIMEN'	£900	
		w. Wmk Crown to right of CA (f.c. £375)	£22000	
101		£20 red and green (1.10.25) (f.c. £850)	£29000	
		s. Optd 'SPECIMEN'	£1600	
102		£25 black and red (f.c. £500)	£38000	
		s. Optd 'SPECIMEN'	£1700	
		w. Wmk Crown to right of CA	£48000	
103		£50 black and brown (f.c. £650)	£50000	
		s. Optd 'SPECIMEN'	£2250	
104		£75 purple and grey (1.10.25) (f.c. £3500)	£150000	
		s. Optd 'SPECIMEN'	£4250	
105		£100 red and black (1.10.25) (f.c. £2250)	£160000	
		s. Optd 'SPECIMEN'	£4750	
76/95 *Set of 20*			£500	£900
76s/95s Optd 'SPECIMEN' *Set of 20*			£850	

Nos. 87/94 were printed in two operations sometimes causing shade differences between the head and the frame.

* The normal sideways watermark shows Crown to left of CA, *as seen from the back of the stamp.*

KENYA, UGANDA AND TANGANYIKA

The postal administrations of Kenya, Tanganyika and Uganda were amalgamated on 1 January 1933. On the independence of the three territories the combined administration became the East African Posts and Telecommunications Corporation.

8 South African Crowned Cranes

9 Dhow on Lake Victoria

10 Lion

11 Kilimanjaro

12 Nile Railway Bridge, Ripon Falls

13 Mt. Kenya

14 Lake Naivasha

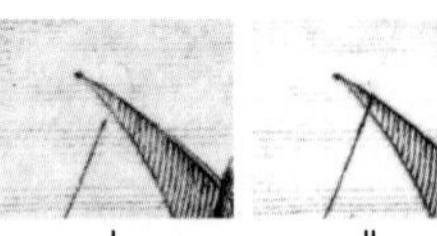
I II

(Des 1c., 20c., 10s., R. C. Luck, 10c., £1, A. Ross, 15c., 2s., G. Gill Holmes, 30c., 5s., R. N. Ambasana, 65c., L. R. Cutts. T **10** typo, remainder recess D.L.R.).

1935 (1 May)–**37**. Wmk Mult Script CA. Chalk-surfaced paper (10c., £1). P 12×13 (T **10**), 14 (T **9** and T **14**) and 13 (remainder).

No.	Type	Description	Unused	Used
110	**8**	1c. black and red-brown	1·00	1·50
111	**9**	5c. black and green (I)	4·00	20
		a. Rope joined to sail (II) (1937)	40·00	8·00
		b. Perf 13×12 (I)	£9500	£950
		ba. Rope joined to sail (II) (1937)	£850	£225
112	**10**	10c. black and yellow	7·50	60
113	**11**	15c. black and scarlet	4·50	10
		a. Frame double, one albino	†	—
114	**8**	20c. black and orange	3·50	20
115	**12**	30c. black and blue	5·00	1·00
116	**9**	50c. bright purple and black (I)	7·00	10
117	**13**	65c. black and brown	9·00	2·00
118	**14**	1s. black and green	5·50	1·50
		a. Frame double, one albino	†	£1200
		b. Perf 13×12 (1936)	£1500	£140
		ba. Frame treble, two albino	†	£1700
119	**11**	2s. lake and purple	12·00	4·50
120	**14**	3s. blue and black	20·00	15·00
		a. Perf 13×12 (1936)	£2500	
121	**12**	5s. black and carmine	25·00	27·00
122	**8**	10s. purple and blue	£100	£130
123	**10**	£1 black and red	£325	£425
110/123 *Set of 14*			£475	£550
110s/123s Perf 'SPECIMEN' *Set of 14*			£500	

Line through '0' of 1910 (R. 4/2)

(Des H. Fleury. Recess D.L.R.)

1935 (6 May). Silver Jubilee. As Nos. 91/94 of Antigua. Wmk Mult Script CA. P 13½×14.

No.	Description	Unused	Used
124	20c. light blue and olive-green	2·75	10
	f. Diagonal line by turret	£140	50·00
	g. Dot to left of chapel	£275	90·00
	h. Dot by flagstaff	£275	90·00
	i. Dash by turret	£350	£130
125	30c. brown and deep blue	3·50	3·00
	f. Diagonal line by turret	£225	£225
	g. Dot to left of chapel	£500	£450
	h. Dot by flagstaff	£500	£450
	i. Dash by turret	£550	
126	65c. green and indigo	2·00	3·00
	f. Diagonal line by turret	£250	£250
	g. Dot to left of chapel	£500	£550
127	1s. slate and purple	2·25	5·50
	f. Diagonal line by turret	£250	£325
	g. Dot to left of chapel	£550	£500
	h. Dot by flagstaff	£550	
	i. Dash by turret	£650	
	l. Line through '0' of 1910	£140	£180
124/127 *Set of 4*		9·50	10·50
124s/127s Perf 'SPECIMEN' *Set of 4*		£170	

For illustrations of the other plate varieties see Omnibus section following Zanzibar.

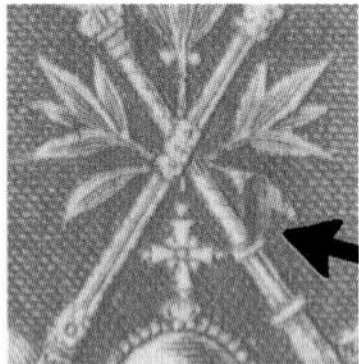
Broken leaf (R. 6/1)

(Des and recess D.L.R.)

1937 (12 May). Coronation. As Nos. 95/97 of Antigua but printed by D.L.R. Perf 14.

No.	Description	Unused	Used
128	5c. green	20	10
129	20c. orange	40	30
	a. Broken leaf	75·00	
130	30c. bright blue	60	1·75
128/130 *Set of 3*		1·10	1·90
128s/130s Perf 'SPECIMEN' *Set of 3*		£150	

15 Dhow on Lake Victoria

Damaged left-hand value tablet (Frame Pl 2–2, with Centre Pl 4A or 4B, R. 9/6)

Retouched value tablet (Frame Pl 2–2, with Centre Pls 4A, 4B, 5, 6 or 7, R. 9/6)

1c. 'Tadpole' flaw (Frame Pl 2–2, with centre Pl 4B R. 10/8)

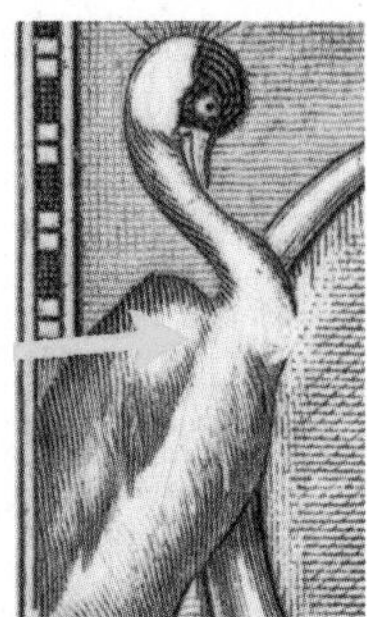
1c. Break in bird's breast (Frame Pl 2–2, with Centre Pls 4A or 4B, R. 2/5)

5c. Crecent-shaped 'shadow' on sail (Pl 2A, R.8/1)

Sky retouch (Pl 7A, R. 10/6)

1s., 3s. Damage on mountain (Pl 7B, R. 6/7. August 1948 ptg. Retouched in June 1949 for 10c. and 1s.)

10c., 1s. Mountain retouch (Covering the peak and the slopes to the left) (Pl 7B, R. 6/7)

10c., 1s. Mountain retouch (Covering the peak and the hills to its right) (Pl 7B, R. 5/10)

50c. With dot

Dot removed

In the 50c. printing of 14 June 1950 using Frame-plate 3, the dot was removed by retouching on all but five stamps (R. 5/2, 6/1, 7/2, 7/4 and 9/1). In addition, other stamps show traces of the dot where the retouching was not completely effective. Examples of the 10c. (135/135c and 136) and 1s. (145*a*) are known with the dot apparently removed, but these are due to random flaws on the plate rather than a deliberate attempt to retouch and are not listed.

PERFORATIONS. In this issue, to aid identification, the perforations are indicated to the nearest quarter.

(T **10** typo, others recess D.L.R.)

1938 (11 Apr)–**54**. As Types **8** to T **14** (but with portrait of King George VI in place of King George V, as in T **15**). Wmk Mult Script CA. Chalk-surfaced paper (£1).

No.	Type	Description	Unused	Used
131	**8**	1c. black and red-brown (P 13¼) (2.5.38)	4·75	85
		a. Perf 13¼×13¾. Black and chocolate-brown (1942)	30	50
		ab. 'A' of 'CA' missing from wmk	£225	
		ac. Damaged value tablet	£100	
		ad. Retouched value tablet	45·00	70·00
		ae. Break in bird's breast	90·00	
		af. 'Tadpole' flaw	£100	£200
		ag. Black and deep chocolate-brown (10.6.46)	2·25	3·50

No.	Type	Description	Unused	Used
		ah. Ditto. Retouched value tablet	50·00	80·00
		ai. Black and red-brown (26.9.51)	8·00	7·00
132	**15**	5c. black and green (II) (P 13×11¾)	7·00	50
		a. 'Shadow' on sail	£325	
133		5c. reddish brown and orange (P 13×11¾) (1.6.49)	2·75	8·50
		a. Perf 13×12½ (14.6.50)	4·75	5·50
134	**14**	10c. red-brown and orange (P 13×11¾) (2.5.38)	2·25	10
		a. 'A' of 'CA' missing from wmk	£1500	
		aw. Wmk inverted	†	£3000
		b. Perf 14 (22.4.41)	£130	8·50
135		10c. black and green (P 13×11¾) (1.6.49)	30	2·00
		a. Mountain retouch (R. 6/7)	95·00	£150
		ab. Mountain retouch (R. 5/10)	£500	£650
		b. Sky retouch	£300	
		c. Frame double, one albino	£1000	
		d. Perf 13×12½ (14.6.50)	5·50	10
136		10c. brown and grey (P 13×12½) (1.4.52)	1·75	55
137	**11**	15c. black and rose-red (P 13¼) (2.5.38)	32·00	55
		a. Perf 13¾×13¼ (2.43)	8·00	4·00
		ab. 'A' of 'CA' missing from wmk	£1700	
138		15c. black and green (P 13¾×13¼) (1.4.52)	3·00	6·00
139	**8**	20c. black and orange (P 13¼) (2.5.38)	42·00	30
		a. Perf 14 (19.5.41)	55·00	1·75
		b. Perf 13¼×13¾ (25.2.42)	9·50	10
		ba. Deep black and deep orange (21.6.51)	28·00	2·25
		bw. Wmk inverted	†	£5000
140	**15**	25c. black and carmine-red (P 13×12½) (1.4.52)	2·25	2·25
141	**12**	30c. black and dull violet-blue (P 13¼) (2.5.38)	55·00	40
		a. Perf 14 (3.7.41)	£160	11·00
		b. Perf 13¼×13¾ (10.5.42)	3·25	10
142		30c. dull purple and brown (P 13¼×13¾) (1.4.52)	1·75	40
		w. Wmk inverted	†	£4500
143	**8**	40c. black and blue (P 13¼×13¾) (1.4.52)	2·25	4·25
144	**15**	50c. purple and black (II) (P 13×11¾) (2.5.38)	23·00	1·00
		a. Rope not joined to sail (I) (R. 2/5)	£325	£250
		b. Dull claret and black (29.7.47)	£110	11·00
		c. Brown-purple and black (4.48)	£120	10·00
		d. Reddish purple and black (28.4.49)	50·00	6·50
		e. Ditto. Perf 13×12½ (10.49)	14·00	55
		ea. Dot removed (14.6.50)	32·00	55
		eb. Ditto. In pair with normal	£500	£150
		ew. Wmk inverted	†	£5000
145	**14**	1s. black and yellowish brown (P 13×11¾) (2.5.38)	38·00	30
		a. Black and brown (9.42)	23·00	30
		ab. Damage on mountain	—	£1500
		ac. Mountain retouch (R. 6/7)	£1400	£500
		ad. Mountain retouch (R. 5/10)	£4500	£700
		aw. Wmk inverted	†	£4000
		b. Perf 13×12½ (10.49)	23·00	60
		ba. Deep black and brown (clearer impression) (14.6.50)	48·00	2·25
146	**11**	2s. lake-brown and brown-purple (P 13¼) (*shades*) (2.5.38)	£140	3·50
		a. Perf 14 (1941)	80·00	20·00
		b. Perf 13¾×13¼ (24.2.44)	50·00	30
147	**14**	3s. dull ultramarine and black (P 13×11¾) (2.5.38)	50·00	9·00
		a. Deep violet-blue and black (29.4.47)	85·00	17·00
		ab. Damage on mountain	£7000	£2750
		ac. Perf 13×12½ (14.6.50)	50·00	9·00
148	**12**	5s. black and carmine (P 13¼) (2.5.38)	£150	22·00
		a. Perf 14 (1941)	50·00	3·25
		b. Perf 13¼×13¾ (24.2.44)	50·00	2·00
149	**8**	10s. purple and blue (P 13¼) (2.5.38)	£140	38·00
		a. Perf 14. Reddish purple and blue (1941)	50·00	25·00
		b. Perf 13¼×13¾ (24.2.44)	55·00	8·50
150	**10**	£1 black and red (P 11¾×13) (12.10.38)	£500	£160
		a. Perf 14 (1941)	42·00	25·00
		ab. Ordinary paper (24.2.44)	42·00	26·00
		b. Perf 12½ (21.1.54)	18·00	42·00
131/150b (*cheapest*) *Set of 20*			£250	50·00
131s/150s Perf 'SPECIMEN' *Set of 13*			£1000	

No. 131ab occurs once in some sheets, always in the sixth vertical row.

The two varieties described as 'Mountain retouch', Nos. 135a/135ab and 145ac/145ad, are found on printings from June 1949 onwards.

The first printing of the 50c. utilised the King George V centre plate on which each impression had been individually corrected to show the rope joined to sail. R. 2/5 was missed, however, and this continued to show Type I until replaced by a further printing from a new plate in September 1938.

Stamps perf 14, together with Nos. 131a, 137a, 139b, 141b, 146b, 148b and 149b, are the result of air raid damage to the De La Rue works which destroyed the normal perforators. Dates quoted for these stamps represent earliest known postmarks.

10c
KENYA
TANGANYIKA
UGANDA
(16)

70c. on 1s. A screw head in the surcharging forme appears as a crescent moon (R. 20/4)

1941 (1 July)–**42**. Pictorial Stamps of South Africa variously surch as T **16** by Government Printer, Pretoria. Inscr alternately in English and Afrikaans.

			Unused pair	Used pair	Used single
151		5c. on 1d. grey and carmine (No. 56)	1·75	1·75	15
152		10c. on 3d. ultramarine (No. 59)	6·00	9·00	30
153		20c. on 6d. green and vermilion (No. 61c)	4·00	3·50	20
154		70c. on 1s. brown and chalky blue (No. 62) (20.4.42)	22·00	5·00	45
		a. Crescent moon flaw	70·00	75·00	
151/154 *Set of 4*			30·00	17·00	1·00
151s/154s Handstamped 'SPECIMEN' *Set of 4 pairs*			£650		

1946 (11 Nov). Victory. As Nos. 110/111 of Antigua.

No.	Description	Unused	Used
155	20c. red-orange	50	10
156	30c. blue	50	75
155s/156s Perf 'SPECIMEN' *Set of 2*		£130	

Examples of Nos. 155/156 were pre-released at Lindi on 15 October 1946.

1948 (1 Dec). Royal Silver Wedding. As Nos. 112/113 of Antigua.

No.	Description	Unused	Used
157	20c. orange	1·00	50
158	£1 scarlet	50·00	70·00

1949 (10 Oct). 75th Anniversary of Universal Postal Union. As Nos. 114/117 of Antigua.

No.	Description	Unused	Used
159	20c. red-orange	15	10
	a. 'A' of 'CA' missing from wmk	†	£1000
160	30c. deep blue	1·75	2·25
	a. 'A' of 'CA' missing from wmk	£1100	
161	50c. grey	45	1·00
	a. 'A' of 'CA' missing from wmk	£1000	
162	1s. red-brown	50	60
159/162 *Set of 4*		2·50	3·50

17 Lake Naivasha

(Recess D.L.R.)

1952 (1 Feb). Visit of Princess Elizabeth and Duke of Edinburgh. Wmk Mult Script CA. P 13×12½.

No.	Type	Description	Unused	Used
163	**17**	10c. black and green	30	1·50
164		1s. black and brown	1·75	2·75

1953 (2 June). Coronation. As No 120 of Antigua.

No.	Description	Unused	Used
165	20c. black and red-orange	30	10

1954 (28 Apr). Royal Visit. As No. 171 but inscr 'ROYAL VISIT 1954' below portrait.

No.	Description	Unused	Used
166	30c. black and deep ultramarine	1·00	70

18 Owen Falls Dam

19 Giraffe

20 African Elephants

21 Lion

22 Mount Kilimanjaro

23 Royal Lodge, Sagana

24 Queen Elizabeth II

(Des G. Gill Holmes (10, 50c.), H. Grieme (15c., 1s.30, 5s.), R. McLellan Sim (10s.), De La Rue (65c., 2s., £1), O.C. Meronti (others). Recess D.L.R.)

1954 (1 June)–**59**. Designs as Types **18/24**. Wmk Mult Script CA. P 13 (£1); others, 12½×13 (vert) or 13×12½ (horiz).

No.	Type	Description	Unused	Used
167	**18**	5c. black and deep brown	1·75	50
		a. Vignette inverted	†	£60000
168	**19**	10c. carmine-red	2·75	10
169	**20**	15c. black and light blue (28.3.58)	2·75	1·50
		a. Redrawn. Stop below 'c' of '15 c' (29.4.59)	1·75	1·25
170	**21**	20c. black and orange	2·00	10
		a. Imperf (pair)	£1500	£1700
171	**18**	30c. black and deep ultramarine	1·50	10
		a. Vignette inverted	†	£30000
172	**21**	40c. bistre-brown (28.3.58)	1·50	1·00
		w. Wmk inverted		
173	**19**	50c. reddish purple	3·50	10
		a. Claret (23.1.57)	9·00	40
174	**22**	65c. bluish green and brown-purple (1.12.55)	2·75	1·50
175	**21**	1s. black and claret	3·75	10
176	**20**	1s.30 deep lilac and orange (1.12.55)	18·00	10
177	**22**	2s. black and green	16·00	1·50
		a. Black and bronze-green (19.4.56)	29·00	3·00
178	**20**	5s. black and orange	45·00	3·50
179	**23**	10s. black and deep ultramarine	48·00	5·50
180	**24**	£1 brown-red and black	19·00	22·00
		a. Venetian red and black (19.4.56)	65·00	28·00
167/180 *Set of 14*			£140	32·00

Only one example of No. 167a and three of No. 171a have been found, all being used.

The 5, 10 and 50c. exist from coils made up from normal sheets.

25 Map of E. Africa showing Lakes

(Recess Waterlow)

1958 (30 July). Centenary of Discovery of Lakes Tanganyika and Victoria by Burton and Speke. W w **12**. P 12½.

No.	Type	Description	Unused	Used
181	**25**	40c. blue and deep green	1·00	40
182		1s.30c. green and violet	1·00	1·60

26 Sisal

27 Cotton

28 Mt Kenya and Giant Plants

29 Queen Elizabeth II

5c. 'Snake' variety (Pl 2, R. 6/2)

15c. Serif at left of base of 'Y' in 'TANGANYIKA' (Pl 1, R. 2/7). This was later retouched but traces still remain

TANGANYIKA

1s. Re-entry. Whole of 'TANGANYIKA' is doubled (Pl 1-1 and 1-2, R. 9/4).

(Des M. Goaman. Photo (5c. to 65c.), recess (others) D.L.R.)

1960 (1 Oct)–**62**. Designs as Types **26/29**. W w **12**. P 15×14 (5c. to 65c.), 13 (20s.) or 14 (others).

No.	Description	Unused	Used
183	5c. Prussian blue	10	15
	a. 'Snake' variety (Pl 2, R. 6/2)	£275	
184	10c. yellow-green	10	10

No.	Type	Description	Unused	Used
185		15c. dull purple	30	10
		a. 'Serif' variety	16·00	10·00
		b. 'Serif' retouched	16·00	10·00
186		20c. magenta	20	10
187		25c. bronze-green	3·25	1·25
188		30c. vermilion	15	10
189		40c. greenish blue	15	20
190		50c. slate-violet	15	10
191		65c. yellow-olive	30	2·00
192		1s. deep reddish violet and reddish purple	2·50	10
		a. Blackish lilac and reddish purple (23.1.62)	18·00	1·50
		b. Re-entry	40·00	
193		1s.30 chocolate and brown-red	7·00	15
194		2s. deep grey-blue and greenish blue	10·00	40
195		2s.50 olive-green and deep bluish green	11·00	2·75
196		5s. rose-red and purple	5·00	60
197		10s. blackish green and olive-green	16·00	9·00
		a. Imperf (pair)	£1700	
198		20s. violet-blue and lake	30·00	30·00
183/198 *Set of 16*			70·00	40·00

Designs: Vert as Types **26/27**—5c. T **26**; 10c. T **27**; 15c. Coffee; 20c. Blue Wildebeest; 25c. Ostrich; 30c. Thomson's Gazelle; 40c. Manta; 50c. Common Zebra; 65c. Cheetah; 20s. T **29**. Horiz as T **28**—1s, T **28**; 1s.30, Murchison Falls and Hippopotamus; 2s. Mt Kilimanjaro and Giraffe; 2s.50, Candelabra Tree and Black Rhinoceros; 5s. Crater Lake and Mountains of the Moon; 10s. Ngorongoro Crater and African Buffalo.

The 10c. and 50c. exist in coils with the designs slightly shorter in height, a wider horizontal gutter every 11 stamps and, in the case of the 10c. only, printed with a coarser 200 screen instead of the normal 250. (*Price for* 10c., 10p. *unused.*) Plate 2 of 30c. shows coarser 200 screen. (*Price* 25p. *unused.*).

PRINTERS. All the following stamps were printed in photogravure by Harrison, *unless otherwise stated.*

30 Land Tillage

(Des V. Whiteley)

1963 (21 Mar). Freedom from Hunger. T **30** and similar horiz design. P 14½.

No.	Type	Description	Unused	Used
199	**30**	15c. blue and yellow-olive	50	10
200	–	30c. red-brown and yellow	65	10
201	**30**	50c. blue and orange-brown	85	10
202	–	1s.30 red-brown and light blue	1·40	1·75
199/202 *Set of 4*			3·00	1·75

Design: 30c., 1s.30, African with Corncob.

31 Scholars and Open Book

1963 (28 June). Founding of East African University. P 14½.

No.	Type	Description	Unused	Used
203	**31**	30c. lake, violet, black and greenish blue	10	10
204		1s.30 lake, blue, red and light yellow-brown	20	30

32 Red Cross Emblem

(Des V. Whiteley)

1963 (2 Sept). Centenary of Red Cross. P 14½.

No.	Type	Description	Unused	Used
205	**32**	30c. red and blue	1·75	30
206		50c. red and yellow-brown	2·25	1·25

33 Chrysanthemum Emblems

34

35 East African 'Flags'

(Des V. Whiteley)

1964 (21 Oct). Olympic Games. Tokyo. P 14½.

No.	Type	Description	Unused	Used
207	**33**	30c. yellow and reddish violet	15	10
208	**34**	50c. deep reddish violet and yellow	20	10
209	**35**	1s.30 orange-yellow, deep green and light blue	50	10
210		2s.50 magenta, deep violet-blue and light blue	60	3·00
207/210 *Set of 4*			1·25	3·00

KENYA, UGANDA AND TANZANIA

The following stamps were issued by the East African Postal Administration for use in Uganda, Kenya and Tanzania, excluding Zanzibar.

36 Rally Badge

37 Cars *en route*

1965 (15 Apr*). 13th East African Safari Rally. P 14.

No.	Type	Description	Unused	Used
211	**36**	30c. black, yellow and turquoise	10	10
212		50c. black, yellow and brown	10	10
		a. Imperf (pair)	£900	
213	**37**	1s.30 deep bluish green, yellow-ochre and blue	35	10
214		2s.50 deep bluish green, brown-red and light blue	60	3·00
211/214 *Set of 4*			1·00	3·00

* This is the local release date. The Crown Agents in London issued the stamps the previous day.

38 ITU Emblem and Symbols

1965 (17 May). ITU Centenary. P 14½.

No.	Type	Description	Unused	Used
215	**38**	30c. gold, chocolate and magenta	30	10
216		50c. gold, chocolate and grey	45	10
217		1s.30 gold, chocolate and blue	1·00	10
218		2s.50 gold, chocolate and turquoise-green	1·25	2·50
215/218 *Set of 4*			2·75	2·50

39 ICY Emblem

1965 (4 Aug). International Co-operation Year. P 14½×14.

No.	Type	Description	Unused	Used
219	**39**	30c. deep bluish green and gold	20	10
220		50c. black and gold	25	10
221		1s.30 ultramarine and gold	50	10
222		2s.50 carmine-red and gold	1·00	3·75
219/222 *Set of 4*			1·75	3·75

40 Game Park Lodge, Tanzania

(Des Rena Fennessy)

1966 (4 Apr). Tourism. T **40** and similar horiz designs. Multicoloured. P 14½.

No.	Type	Description	Unused	Used
223		30c. Type **40**	90	10
224		50c. Murchison Falls, Uganda	1·00	10
		a. Blue omitted	£425	
225		1s.30 Lesser Flamingoes, Lake Nakuru, Kenya	3·25	30
226		2s.50 Deep Sea Fishing, Tanzania	2·00	2·25
223/226 *Set of 4*			6·50	3·00

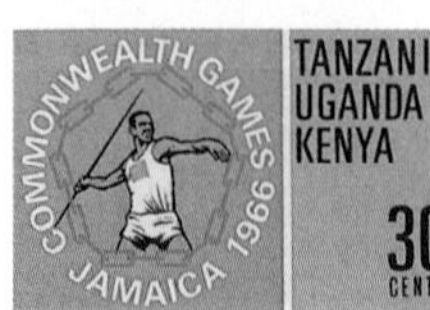

41 Games Emblem

(Des Harrison)

1966 (2 Aug). Eighth British Empire and Commonwealth Games Jamaica. P 14½.

No.	Type	Description	Unused	Used
227	**41**	30c. black, gold, turquoise-green and grey	10	10
228		50c. black, gold, cobalt and cerise	15	10
229		1s.30 black, gold, rosine and deep bluish green	20	10
230		2s.50 black, gold, lake and ultramarine	35	1·50
227/230 *Set of 4*			70	1·50

42 UNESCO Emblem

(Des Harrison)

1966 (3 Oct). 20th Anniversary of UNESCO. P 14½×14.

No.	Type	Description	Unused	Used
231	**42**	30c. black, emerald and red	80	10
232		50c. black, emerald and light brown	90	10
233		1s.30 black, emerald and grey	2·25	20
234		2s.50 black, emerald and yellow	2·75	6·50
231/234 *Set of 4*			6·00	6·50

43 de Havilland DH.89 Dragon Rapide

(Des R. Granger Barrett)

1967 (23 Jan). 21st Anniversary of East African Airways. T **43** and similar horiz designs. P 14½.

No.	Type	Description	Unused	Used
235		30c. slate-violet, greenish blue and myrtle-green	30	10
236		50c. multicoloured	40	10
		a. Red omitted	£800	
237		1s.30 multicoloured	85	30
238		2s.50 multicoloured	1·25	3·00
235/238 *Set of 4*			2·50	3·00

Designs: 30c. T **43**; 50c. Vickers Super VC-10; 1s.30, Hawker Siddeley Comet 4B; 2s.50, Fokker F.27 Friendship.

44 Pillar Tomb

45 Rock Painting

(Des Rena Fennessy)

1967 (2 May). Archaeological Relics. Types **44/45** and similar designs. P 14½.

No.	Type	Description	Unused	Used
239		30c. ochre, black and deep reddish purple	15	10
240		50c. orange-red, black and greyish brown	65	10
241		1s.30 black, greenish yellow and deep yellow-green	85	15
242		2s.50 black, ochre and brown-red	1·40	2·50
239/242 *Set of 4*			2·75	3·00

Designs: 30c. T **44**; 50c. T **45**; 1s.30, Clay head; 2s.50, Proconsul skull.

48 Unified Symbols of Kenya, Tanzania, and Uganda

(Des Rena Fennessy)

1967 (1 Dec). Foundation of East African Community. P 14½×14.

No.	Type	Description	Unused	Used
243	**48**	5s. gold, black and grey	40	1·50

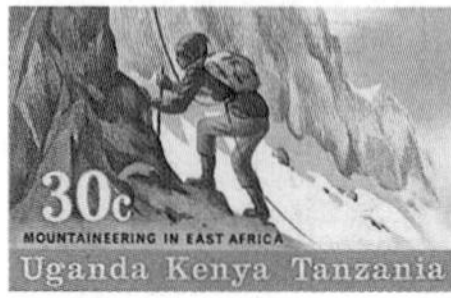

49 Mountaineering

(Des Rena Fennessy)

1968 (4 Mar). Mountains of East Africa. T **49** and similar horiz designs. Multicoloured. P 14.

No.	Type	Description	Unused	Used
244		30c. Type **49**	15	10
245		50c. Mount Kenya	25	10
246		1s.30 Mount Kilimanjaro	40	10
247		2s.50 Ruwenzori Mountains	60	2·25
244/247 *Set of 4*			1·25	2·25

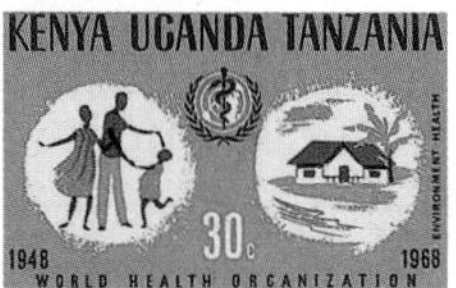

50 Family and Rural Hospital

(Des Rena Fennessy. Litho D.L.R.)

1968 (13 May). 20th Anniversary of World Health Organisation. T **50** and similar horiz designs. P 13½.

No.	Type	Description	Unused	Used
248		30c. deep yellow-green, lilac and chocolate	10	10

249		50c. slate-lilac, lilac and black	15	10
250		1s.30 yellow-brown, lilac and chocolate	20	15
251		2s.50 grey, black and reddish lilac	30	1·90
248/251 *Set of 4*			60	2·00

Designs: 30c. T **50**; 50c. Family and nurse; 1s.30, Family and microscope; 2s.50, Family and hypodermic syringe.

51 Olympic Stadium, Mexico City

(Des V. Whiteley)

1968 (14 Oct). Olympic Games, Mexico. T **51** and similar designs. P 14.

252		30c. light green and black	10	10
253		50c. black and blue-green	15	10
254		1s.30 carmine-red, black and grey	25	15
255		2s.50 blackish brown and yellow-brown	35	1·50
252/255 *Set of 4*			70	1·60

Designs: Horiz—30c. T **51**; 50c. High-diving boards; 1s.30, Running tracks. Vert—2s.50, Boxing ring.

52 *Umoja* (railway ferry)

(Des A. Grosart)

1969 (20 Jan). Water Transport. T **52** and similar horiz designs. P 14.

256		30c. deep blue, light blue and slate-grey	50	10
		a. Slate-grey omitted	60·00	
257		50c. multicoloured	60	10
258		1s.30 bronze-green, greenish blue and blue	1·00	20
259		2s.50 red-orange, deepp blue and pale blue	1·50	3·25
256/259 *Set of 4*			3·25	3·25

Designs: 30c. T **52**; 50c. SS *Harambee*; 1s.30, MV *Victoria*; 2s.50, *St Michael*.

53 ILO Emblem and Agriculture

54 Pope Paul VI and Ruwenzori Mountains

(Des Rena Fennessy)

1969 (14 Apr). 50th Anniversary of International Labour Organisation. T **53** and similar horiz designs. P 14.

260		30c. black, green and greenish yellow	10	10
261		50c. black, plum, cerise and rose	10	10
262		1s.30 black, orange-brown and yellow-orange	10	10
263		2s.50 black, ultramarine and turquoise-blue	20	90
260/263 *Set of 4*			35	1·00

Designs: 30c. T **53**; 50c. ILO emblem and building work; 1s.30, ILO emblem and factory workers; 2s.50, ILO emblem and shipping.

(Des Harrison)

1969 (31 July). Visit of Pope Paul VI to Uganda. P 14.

264	**54**	30c. black, gold and royal blue	15	10
265		70c. black, gold and claret	20	10
266		1s.50 black, gold and deep blue	25	20
267		2s.50 black, gold and violet	30	1·40
264/267 *Set of 4*			80	1·50

55 Euphorbia Tree shaped as Africa and Emblem

56 Marimba

(Des Rena Fennessy. Litho B.W.)

1969 (8 Dec). Fifth Anniversary of African Development Bank. P 13½.

268	**55**	30c. deep bluish green, gold and blue-green	10	10
269		70c. deep bluish green, gold and reddish purple	15	10
270		1s.50 deep bluish green, gold and light turquoise-blue	30	10
271		2s.50 deep bluish green, gold and orange-brown	35	2·00
268/271 *Set of 4*			75	2·00

(Des Rena Fennessy. Litho B.W.)

1970 (16 Feb). Musical Instruments. T **56** and similar horiz designs. P 11×12.

272		30c. buff, yellow-brown and bistre-brown	15	10
273		70c. olive-green, yellow-brown and yellow	25	10
274		1s.50 chocolate and yellow	40	10
275		2s.50 salmon, yellow and chocolate	60	2·50
272/275 *Set of 4*			1·25	2·50

Designs: 30c. T **56**; 70c. Amadinda; 1s.50, Nzomari; 2s.50, Adeudeu.

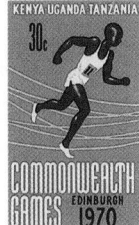

57 Satellite Earth Station

58 Athlete

(Des V. Whiteley. Litho J.W.)

1970 (18 May). Inauguration of East African Satellite Earth Station. T **57** and similar horiz designs. P 14½×14.

276		30c. multicoloured	10	10
277		70c. multicoloured	15	10
278		1s.50 black, slate-violet and pale orange	30	10
279		2s.50 multicoloured	60	2·50
276/279 *Set of 4*			1·00	2·50

Designs: 30c. T **57**; 70c. Transmitter in daytime; 1s.50, Transmitter at night; 2s.50, Earth and satellite.

(Des Rena Fennessy. Litho Walsall)

1970 (13 July). Ninth Commonwealth Games. P 14×14½.

280	**58**	30c. orange-brown and black	10	10
281		70c. olive-green and black	10	10
282		1s.50 slate-lilac and black	15	10
283		2s.50 turquoise-blue and black	20	1·25
280/283 *Set of 4*			40	1·40

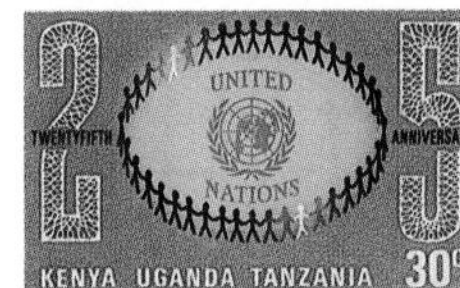

59 '25' and UN Emblem

(Des Rena Fennessy)

1970 (19 Oct). 25th Anniversary of United Nations. P 14½.

284	**59**	30c. multicoloured	10	10
285		70c. multicoloured	10	10
286		1s.50 multicoloured	20	10
287		2s.50 multicoloured	45	2·25
284/287 *Set of 4*			70	2·25

STAMP BOOKLETS

1912–17. Black on pink cover. Letter rate given as 6 cents per oz. Stapled.

SB1	1r.80, booklet containing 12×3c. and 24×6c. (Nos. 45/46), each in blocks of 6	£2500
	a. Letter rate 6 cents per ½oz. Contains Nos. 45*a*/46*a*	
SB2	2r. booklet containing 6×3c. and 30×6c. (Nos. 45/46), each in blocks of 6	£2500

1938. Black on pink cover. Stapled.

SB3	3s.40, booklet containing 12×15c. and 8×20c. (Nos. 137, 139), each in blocks of 4	£300

1950–52. Blue on yellow cover. Stapled.

SB4	1s. booklet containing 4×5c. and 8×10c. (Nos. 133a, 135c), each in blocks of 4	£750
	a. Contents as SB4, but 10c. changed to No. 136. Stitched (1952)	50·00

1954 (3 Sept). Blue on yellow cover. Stitched.

SB6	1s. booklet containing 4×5c. and 8×10c. (Nos. 167/168), each in blocks of 4	3·00

1958 (16 Jan). Black on yellow cover. Stitched.

SB7	5s. booklet containing 4×5c., 4×20c., 4×30c., 4×50c. and 8×10c. (Nos. 167/168, 170/171, 173), each in blocks of 4	21·00

1958 (16 Dec)–**59**. Black on rose-red cover. Stitched.

SB8	5s. booklet containing 10c., 15c., 20c., 30c. and 50c. (Nos. 168/169, 170/171, 173), in blocks of 4	85·00
	a. Contents as No. SB8, but 15c. changed to No. 169a (20.4.59)	50·00

1961 (1 Feb). Black on rose-red cover. Stitched.

SB9	5s. booklet containing 10c., 15c., 20c., 30c. and 50c. (Nos. 184/186, 188, 190) in blocks of 4	18·00

OFFICIAL STAMPS

For use on official correspondence of the Tanganyika Government.

OFFICIAL
(O 1)

OFFICIAL
£1 Broken 'O' in 'OFFICIAL' (R. 1/6).

1959 (1 July). Nos. 167/171, 173 and 175/180 optd as T O **1**.

O1	**18**	5c. black and deep brown	10	1·25
O2	**19**	10c. carmine-red	30	1·25
O3	**20**	15c. black and light blue (No. 169a)	75	1·25
O4	**21**	20c. black and orange	20	20
		a. Opt double	—	£1600
O5	**18**	30c. black and deep ultramarine	15	80
O6	**19**	50c. reddish purple	1·75	20
O7	**21**	1s. black and claret	20	75
O8	**20**	1s.30 orange and deep lilac	10·00	3·00
O9	**22**	2s. black and bronze-green	1·25	1·00
O10	**20**	5s. black and orange	14·00	4·00
O11	**23**	10s. black and deep ultramarine	3·25	7·50
		a. Opt at top	4·25	3·75
O12	**24**	£1 brown-red and black	7·00	25·00
		a. Broken 'O'	75·00	£180
O1/O12 *Set of 12*			32·00	35·00

The 30c., 50c., 1s. and 1s.30 exist with overprint double, but with the two impressions almost coincident.

OFFICIAL
(O 2)

OFFICIAL
(O 3)

1960 (18 Oct). Nos. 183/186, 188, 190, 192 and 196 optd with T O **2** (cents values) or O **3**.

O13		5c. Prussian blue	10	3·75
O14		10c. yellow-green	10	3·00
O15		15c. dull purple	10	3·75
		a. 'Serif' variety	15·00	
		b. 'Serif' retouched	15·00	
O16		20c. magenta	10	75
O17		30c. vermilion	10	10
O18		50c. slate-violet	30	1·00
O19		1s. deep reddish violet and reddish purple	30	10
		a. Re-entry	25·00	
O20		5s. rose-red and purple	22·00	65
O13/O20 *Set of 8*			22·00	11·50

The use of these overprints ceased on 8 December 1961.

POSTAGE DUE STAMPS

D 1

D 2

(Typo Waterlow)

1928 (Sept)–**33**. Wmk Mult Script CA. P 15×14.

D1	D **1**	5c. violet	2·50	1·00
D2		10c. vermilion	2·50	15
D3		20c. yellow-green	4·00	4·25
D4		30c. brown (1931)	28·00	19·00
D5		40c. dull blue	6·50	14·00
D6		1s. grey-green (1933)	70·00	£140
D1/D6 *Set of 6*			£100	£160
D1s/D6s Optd or Perf (30c., 1s.) 'SPECIMEN' *Set of 6*			£350	

(Typo D.L.R.)

1935 (1 May)–**60**. Wmk Mult Script CA. P 14.

D7	D **2**	5c. violet	2·75	1·75
D8		10c. scarlet	30	50
D9		20c. green	40	50
D10		30c. brown	1·50	50
		a. Bistre-brown (19.7.60)	3·00	10·00
D11		40c. ultramarine	1·50	3·00
D12		1s. grey	19·00	19·00
D7/D12 *Set of 6*			23·00	23·00
D7s/D12s Perf 'SPECIMEN' *Set of 6*			£300	

Kuwait

Kuwait, an independent Arab sheikhdom since 1756, placed itself under British protection in 1899 to counter the spread of Ottoman influence in the Arabian Gulf.

The first, somewhat limited, postal service, via Bushire, commenced with the appointment of a Political Agent to Kuwait in August 1904. Because of diplomatic problems this system continued until 21 January 1915 when a regular Indian post office was established.

Limited supplies of Indian stamps were used by the Political Agency postal service, but these became available to the general public from 21 January 1915. Stamps seen postally used from Kuwait before 1923 are usually ½a., 1a., 1r. or 5r. values, with the occasional Official issue. Much more common are values to 15r., both postage and Official, used telegraphically.

Before 1910 the name of the sheikhdom was spelt 'KOWEIT' and this spelling appears on various circular postmarks used between 1915 and 1923. The more modern version of the name was first used for a postal cancellation in 1923.

1915 'KOWEIT'

1923 'KUWAIT'

On 1 August 1921 responsibility for the Kuwait postal service passed to the Iraq Post Office.

Stamps of INDIA cancelled 'KOWEIT' as Z **1** or 'KUWAIT' as Z **2**.

1906-07. King Edward VII (inscr 'INDIA POSTAGE & REVENUE') (Nos. 149/150).

Z1	½a. green	£300

1911-22. King George V. Wmk Star (Nos. 151/191).

Z3	3p. grey	£250
Z4	½a. green	£180
Z5	1a. carmine	£200
Z6	1½a. chocolate (Type A)	£500
Z7	2a. purple	£225
Z8	2a.6p. ultramarine (No. 171)	£225
Z9	3a. orange	£225
Z10	4a. deep olive (T.C. £20)	£250
Z11	6a. brown ochre (T.C. £20)	£275
Z12	1r. brown and green (T.C. £20)	£350
Z13	2r. carmine and brown (T.C. £20)	£400
Z14	5r. ultramarine and violet (T.C. £30)	£550

This issue was extensively used for telegraphic purposes, with cancels inscribed 'KOWEIT/TELEGRAPHS M.E.F.' or 'KUWAIT/M.T.D.' showing concentric semi-circles above and below the date. The 8a.,12a., 10r. and 15r. values are also known thus.

OFFICIAL STAMPS

1902-09. King Edward VII (Nos. O54/65).

Z17	2a. mauve	£400

The 1909 Official 2r., 5r. and 15r. (Nos. O68/O69, O71) have been seen with telegraphic cancels of Kuwait (*Prices from* £500).

1912-13. King George V Wmk Single Star (O73/O96).

Z20	1a. carmine	£300
Z21	2a. purple	£400
Z24	4a. deep olive	£450

PRICES FOR STAMPS ON COVER TO 1945

Nos. 1/15	*from* × 6
Nos. 16/29	*from* × 4
Nos. 31/51	*from* × 3
Nos. 52/63	*from* × 4
Nos. O1/O27	*from* × 20

USED HIGH VALUES. It is necessary to emphasise that used prices quoted for high value stamps are for postally used examples. Nos. 12/15 and O10/O14 with telegraphic cancels are frequently met with and are worth about one-third of the prices quoted.

(Currency. 16 annas = 1 rupee)

KUWAIT (1) KUWAIT (2)

1923 (1 Apr)–**24.** Stamps of India (King George V), optd with TYPES **1** or **2** (rupee values, 15½ *mm*) by Indian Govt Ptg Wks. W **34** (Single Star) of India. P 14.

1	½a. emerald (No. 156)	4·50	17·00
	a. Opt double	£350	
	b. Vert pair, one without opt	£1800	
	c. Light green		
2	1a. chocolate (No. 197)	8·00	5·50
	a. Opt double	£500	
	b. Opt omitted (lower stamp of vert pair)	£2000	
3	1½a. chocolate (A) ('ANNA') (No. 163)	6·50	14·00
4	2a. bright reddish violet (No. 169)	5·50	10·00
	a. Reddish purple	15·00	
5	2a.6p. ultramarine (No. 171)	4·25	8·50
6	3a. dull orange (No. 173)	4·25	27·00
7	3a. ultramarine (No. 200) (1924)	11·00	4·50
8	4a. deep olive (No. 174)	11·00	27·00
	a. Olive-green	14·00	
9	6a. brown-ochre (No. 178)	8·50	13·00
10	8a. purple (No. 182)	8·00	55·00
11	12a. carmine-lake (No. 183)	14·00	60·00
	a. Claret	15·00	55·00
12	1r. brown and green (No. 186)	48·00	60·00
	a. Orange-brown and deep turquoise-green	60·00	75·00
13	2r. carmine and brown (No. 187)	65·00	£120
	a. Opt double, one albino	£700	
14	5r. ultramarine and violet (No. 188)	£140	£275
15	10r. green and scarlet (No. 189)	£275	£550
1/15 *Set of 15*		£550	£1100

Essays of the overprint using the obsolete spelling 'KOWEIT' were prepared in 1923 and can be found on the original 14 values of the postage stamps and on the 13 stamps of the Official series. (*Price for set of 27 unused £42000*).

Nos. 1/4 and 6/7 are all known with inverted overprint (*Price, from £35 each, unused*) and the overprint is also known (upright or inverted) on examples of India No. 165 ('ANNAS'). It is doubtful if such errors were actually sold at the Kuwait Post Office, although some are known on registered or ordinary covers.

KUWAIT (3) KUWAIT (4)

1929–37. Stamps of India (King George V, Nasik printing), optd with Types **3** or **4** (rupee values). W **69** (Mult Stars) of India. P 14.

16	½a. green (No. 202)	17·00	3·25
	aw. Wmk inverted	7·00	4·75
16*b*	½a. green (No. 232) (1934)	12·00	2·00
	bw. Wmk inverted	—	26·00
17	1a. chocolate (No. 203)	8·50	4·00
	aw. Wmk inverted	27·00	8·00
17*b*	1a. chocolate (No. 234) (1934)	18·00	1·50
18	2a. purple (No. 206)	10·00	2·25
19	2a. vermilion (No. 236)	20·00	95·00
	aw. Wmk inverted	20·00	£100
19*b*	2a. vermilion (No. 236*b*) (1934)	16·00	6·50
19*c*	2a. vermilion (*small die*) (No. 236*c*) (1937)	12·00	3·50
20	3a. blue (No. 209)	3·50	3·50
21	3a. carmine (No. 237)	5·50	4·25
22	4a. sage-green (*wmk inverted*) (No. 211w)	25·00	£100
	w. Wmk upright	80·00	
22*a*	4a. pale sage-green (No. 210) (1934)	20·00	14·00
22*b*	6a. bistre (No. 239) (1937)	29·00	70·00
23	8a. reddish purple (No. 212)	50·00	13·00
	w. Wmk inverted	9·00	22·00
24	12a. claret (*wmk inverted*) (No. 213w) (1933)	23·00	50·00
	w. Wmk upright	—	£140
25	1r. chocolate and green (No. 214)	85·00	55·00
	a. Extended 'T'	£1400	
	w. Wmk inverted	26·00	50·00
	wa. Extended 'T'	£800	
26	2r. carmine and orange (*wmk inverted*) (No. 215w)	26·00	70·00
	a. Extended 'T'	£800	£1300
	w. Wmk upright	£225	£225
27	5r. ultramarine and purple (No. 216) (1937)	£140	£325
	a. Extended 'T'	£1600	
28	10r. green and scarlet (No. 217) (1934)	£300	£550
	a. Extended 'T'	£3250	
29	15r. blue and olive (*wmk inverted*) (No. 218w) (1937)	£950	£1300
	a. Extended 'T'	£6500	
16/29 *Set of 20*		£1500	£2250

The 'T' of 'KUWAIT' shows a ¾ mm downward extension on R. 3/2, lower left pane.

Nos. 16, 17, 18/19 and 22 are inscribed 'INDIA POSTAGE & REVENUE'. The remainder are inscribed 'INDIA POSTAGE'.

No. 19*b* measures 19×22.6 mm and No. 19*c* 18.4×21.8 mm.

Examples of most values are known showing a forged Kuwait postmark dated '11 NOV 37'.

1933 (1 Feb)–**34.** Air. Nos. 220/223 of India optd as T **2** (16½ *mm*).

31	2a. deep blue-green	25·00	27·00
	w. Wmk stars to right	25·00	27·00
32	3a. blue	5·50	3·25
	a. 'Q' for 'O' in 'POSTAGE'	£1100	£550
	b. '1' for 'I' in 'INDIA'	£750	
	w. Wmk stars to right	5·50	3·25
33	4a. olive-green	£150	£225
34	6a. bistre (2.34)	10·00	5·50
	a. Scratch through aircraft	£350	£225
	w. Wmk stars to right	10·00	5·50
31/34 *Set of 4*		£180	£225

The normal sideways watermark on Nos. 31/34 shows stars pointing to left, *as seen from the back of the stamp*.

The 3a. value exists with a most pronounced lithography double print. *Price* £1000 *un.,* £1000 *used*. Examples of this and other stamps with slight double prints are of little additional value.

1939. Nos. 248, 250/251, 253, 255/263 of India (King George VI) optd with TYPES **3** or **4** (rupee values).

36	½a. red-brown	7·00	4·75
38	1a. carmine	8·00	3·75
39	2a. vermilion	10·00	6·00
41	3a. yellow-green	14·00	3·75
43	4a. brown	45·00	32·00
44	6a. turquoise-green	27·00	24·00
45	8a. slate-violet	29·00	40·00
46	12a. lake	20·00	95·00
47	1r. grey and red-brown	38·00	9·50
	a. Extended 'T'	£1100	£700
	b. Opt triple, one inverted	£4000	
48	2r. purple and brown	10·00	30·00
	a. Extended 'T'	£1100	£1200
49	5r. green and blue	19·00	35·00
	a. Extended 'T'	£1400	
50	10r. purple and claret	85·00	£110
	a. Opt double	£700	
	b. Extended 'T'	£2500	
51	15r. brown and green	£375	£425
	a. Extended 'T'	£4500	
	w. Wmk inverted	£120	£275
	wa. Extended 'T'	£3000	
36/51w *Set of 13*		£375	£600

On later printings the extended 'T' variety was corrected in two stages.

Examples of most values are known showing a forged Kuwait postmark dated '17 NOV 39'.

Following the rebellion in Iraq, control of the Kuwait postal service was assumed by the Indian authorities on 24 May 1941.

Stamps of INDIA cancelled 'EXPERIMENTAL P.O. K-79', 'KUWAIT/PERSIAN GULF' (double-ring datestamps) or 'KUWAIT' (circular datestamp with wavy lines at right).

1926-33. King George V Wmk Mult Star (Nos. 201/219).

Z31	3p. slate	25·00
Z32	½a. green	25·00
Z34	4a. sage-green	30·00
Z39	15r. blue and olive	£950

1932-36. King George V Wmk Mult Star (Nos. 232/239).

Z41	1a. chocolate	25·00
Z42	1a.3p. mauve	20·00

1937-40. King George VI (Nos. 247/264).

Z46	3p. slate	20·00
Z47	½a. red-brown	15·00
Z48	1a. carmine	15·00
Z49	2a. vermilion	30·00
Z50	2a.6p. bright violet	25·00
Z51	4a. brown	25·00
Z52	1r. grey and red-brown	30·00
Z53	2r. purple and brown	35·00
Z54	5r. green and blue	60·00
Z55	10r. purple and claret	75·00
Z56	15r. brown and green	£550

1940-43. King George VI (Nos. 265/277).

Z58	3p. slate	7·00
Z59	½a. purple	6·00
Z60	9p. green	10·00
Z61	1a. carmine	6·00
Z62	1a.3p. yellow-brown	8·00
Z63	1½a. dull violet (litho)	10·00
Z64	2a. vermilion	7·00
Z65	3a. bright violet (typo)	8·00
Z66	3½a. bright blue	10·00
Z67	4a. brown	10·00
Z68	6a. turquoise-green	12·00
Z69	8a. slate violet	14·00
Z70	12a. lake	40·00
Z71	14a. purple	30·00

1946. Victory (Nos. 278/281).

Z72	9p. yellow-green	60·00
Z73	1½a. dull violet	50·00
Z74	3½a. bright blue	60·00

The Victory issue of India was placed on sale in Kuwait alongside the 1945 overprinted issue.

Stamps of India Overprinted

1945. Nos. 265/268 and 269*b*/277 of India (King George VI, on white background) optd with T **3**.

52	3p. slate	4·00	13·00
53	½a. purple	4·00	7·00
54	9p. green	3·75	21·00
55	1a. carmine	4·00	2·75
56	1½a. dull violet	4·25	14·00
57	2a. vermilion	5·00	10·00
58	3a. bright violet	6·00	19·00
59	3½a. bright blue	6·50	20·00
60	4a. brown	6·50	5·50
60*a*	6a. turquoise-green	14·00	25·00
61	8a. slate-violet	7·00	19·00
62	12a. lake	8·50	10·00
63	14a. purple	17·00	25·00
52/63 *Set of 13*		75·00	£170

Following a short period of Pakistani control, from August 1947 the Kuwait postal service passed to British administration on 1 April 1948.

KUWAIT 1 ANNA (5) KUWAIT 5 RUPEES (6)

NOTE. From 1948 onwards, for stamps with similar surcharges, but without name of country, see British Postal Agencies in Eastern Arabia.

1948 (1 Apr)–**49.** Nos. 470, 475, 476*b*/477, 478*b* and 485/490 of Great Britain (King George VI), surch as TYPES **5** or **6** (rupee values).

64	½a. on ½d. pale green	3·75	4·25
65	1a. on 1d. pale scarlet	3·75	1·75
66	1½a. on 1½d. pale red-brown	4·00	1·75
67	2a. on 2d. pale orange	3·75	1·75
68	2½a. on 2½d. light ultramarine	4·00	1·00
69	3a. on 3d. pale violet	4·00	80
	a. Pair, one surch albino	£12000	
70	6a. on 6d. purple	4·00	75
71	1r. on 1s. bistre-brown	8·50	2·00
72	2r. on 2s. 6d. yellow-green	9·00	9·00
73	5r. on 5s. red	12·00	9·00
73*a*	10r. on 10s. ultramarine (4.7.49)	60·00	11·00
64/73*a* *Set of 11*		£100	38·00

KUWAIT 2½ ANNAS (7)

KUWAIT 15 RUPEES (8)

1948 (1 May). Royal Silver Wedding. Nos. 493/494 of Great Britain surch with Types **7** or **8**.

74	2½a. on 2½d. ultramarine	2·25	2·50
75	15r. on £1 blue	38·00	50·00
	a. Short bars (R. 3/4)	£250	£300

No. 75a has the bars cancelling the original face value 3 mm long. In other positions the bars measure between 3½ and 4 mm. R. 3/4 also exists with bars of normal length.

1948 (29 July). Olympic Games. Nos. 495/498 of Great Britain surch as T **7**, but in one line (6a.) or two lines (others).

76	2½a. on 2½d. ultramarine	1·75	5·00
77	3a. on 3d. violet	1·25	5·00
78	6a. on 6d. bright purple	1·50	4·50
79	1r. on 1s. brown	1·50	4·50
76/79 *Set of 4*		5·50	17·00

1949 (10 Oct). 75th Anniversary of UPU Nos. 499/502 of Great Britain surch 'KUWAIT' and new values.

80	2½a. on 2½d. ultramarine	1·50	3·50
	a. Lake in India	£100	£180
81	3a. on 3d. violet	1·25	5·50
82	6a. on 6d. bright purple	1·25	3·75
83	1r. on 1s. brown	1·25	1·75
80/83 *Set of 4*		4·75	13·00

KUWAIT KUWAIT

2 RUPEES Type I 2 RUPEES Type II

(8a)

KUWAIT 10 RUPEES Type I (8b)

KUWAIT 10 RUPEES Type II (8b)

2r. Type I. Type-set surcharge. '2' level with 'RUPEES'. Surcharge sharp.

Type II. Plate-printed surcharge. '2' raised. Surcharge worn.

Type III. Similar to Type II, but the space between the bars and the 'K' is 2½ mm rather than 3mm and the '2 RUPEES' is set slightly further to the left, with the 'S' directly below the 'T'.

10r. Type I. Type-set surcharge. '1' and 'O' spaced. Surcharge sharp and clean.

Type II. Plate-printed surcharge. '1' and 'O' closer together. Surcharge appears heavy and worn, see especially 'A', 'R' and 'P'.

KUWAIT Extra bar in centre (R. 7/2) KUWAIT Extra bar at top (R. 2/2)

1950 (2 Oct)–**55**. Nos. 503/511 of Great Britain (King George VI) surch as Types **5** or **8a/8b** (rupee values).

84	½a. on ½d. pale orange (3.5.51)	2·75	1·50
85	1a. on 1d. light ultramarine (3.5.51)	2·75	1·60
86	1½a. on 1½d. pale green (3.5.51)	3·50	2·25
87	2a. on 2d. pale red-brown (3.5.51)	3·50	1·50
88	2½a. on 2½d. pale scarlet (3.5.51)	3·50	2·75
89	4a. on 4d. light ultramarine	2·75	1·50
90	2r. on 2s.6d. yellow-green (I) (3.5.51)	26·00	9·00
	a. Extra bar in centre	£1400	£800
	b. Type II surch (1954)	£375	55·00
	c. Type III surch (1955)	£750	£275
91	5r. on 5s. red (3.5.51)	32·00	11·00
	a. Extra bar at top	£1100	£750
92	10r. on 10s. ultramarine (I) (3.5.51)	55·00	18·00
	a. Type II surch (1952)	£375	70·00
84/92 *Set of 9*		£110	45·00

No. 92a is known with surch spaced 10 mm apart instead of 9 mm.

1952 (10 Dec)–**54**. Nos. 515/521, 523 and 530/531 of Great Britain (Queen Elizabeth II. W **153**), surch as T **5** (in two lines only on 2½ and 6a.).

93	½a. on ½d. orange-red (31.8.53)	20	3·75
94	1a. on 1d. ultramarine (31.8.53)	20	10
95	1½a. on 1½d. green	15	2·00
96	2a. on 2d. red-brown (31.8.53)	35	10
97	2½a. on 2½d. carmine-red	15	1·75
98	3a. on 3d. deep lilac (B.) (18.1.54)	40	10
99	4a. on 4d. ultramarine (2.11.53)	1·25	1·00
100	6a. on 6d. reddish purple (18.1.54)	2·50	10
101	12a. on 1s.3d. green (2.11.53)	7·50	2·50
102	1r. on 1s.6d. grey-blue (2.11.53)	6·00	10
93/102 *Set of 10*		16·00	10·00

The word KUWAIT is in taller letters on the 1½a., 2½a., 3a. and 6a. In early printings of the ½a. the '½' was printed in a separate operation to 'KUWAIT' and 'ANNA'. Later printings of No. 93 and all printings of other values were printed in a single operation.

1953 (3 June). Coronation. Nos. 532/535 (Queen Elizabeth) of Great Britain surch 'KUWAIT' and new values.

103	2½a. on 2½d. carmine-red	3·50	3·50
104	4a. on 4d. ultramarine	4·50	3·50
105	12a. on 1s.3d. deep yellow-green	5·00	5·50
106	1r. on 1s.6d. deep grey-blue	4·00	1·25
103/106 *Set of 4*		15·00	12·50

KUWAIT 2 RUPEES I

KUWAIT 2 RUPEES II

(9)

KUWAIT 5 RUPEES I

KUWAIT 5 RUPEES II

(10)

KUWAIT 10 RUPEES I

KUWAIT 10 RUPEES II

(11)

Type I (Types **9/11**). Type-set overprints by Waterlow. Bold (generally thicker) letters with sharp corners and straight edges. Bars close together and usually slightly longer than in Type II.

Type II (Types **9/11**). Plate-printed overprints by Harrison. Thinner letters, rounder corners and rough edges. Bars wider apart.

1955 (23 Sept)–**57**. Nos. 536/538 of Great Britain ('Castles' high values) surch with Types **9/11**.

107	2r. on 2s.6d. black-brown (I)	11·00	3·50
	a. Type II (10.10.57)	75·00	8·50
108	5r. on 5s. rose-carmine (I)	11·00	9·50
	a. Type II (10.10.57)	£120	40·00
109	10r. on 10s. ultramarine (I)	11·00	6·00
	a. Type II (10.10.57)	£180	£140
107/109 *Set of 3*		30·00	17·00
107a/109a *Set of 3*		£350	£160

1956. Nos. 540/546, 548 and 555/556 of Great Britain (Queen Elizabeth II. W **165**) surch as T **5** (in two lines only on 2½ and 6a.).

110	½a. on ½d. orange-red	30	2·75
111	1a. on 1d. ultramarine (3.12.56)	50	4·75
112	1½a. on 1½d. green	40	1·00
113	2a. on 2d. red-brown	40	50
114	2½a. on 2½d. carmine-red	60	5·50
116	4a. on 4d. ultramarine (22.11.56)	4·75	3·25
117	6a. on 6d. reddish purple (3.12.56)	2·25	40
118	12a. on 1s.3d. green	12·00	8·00
119	1r. on 1s.6d. grey-blue (3.12.56)	17·00	30
110/119 *Set of 9*		35·00	24·00

KUWAIT NP 1 NP (12) KUWAIT 3 NP NP (13) KUWAIT 75 NP (14)

1957 (1 June)–**58**. Nos. 540/542, 543a/548, 551 and 555 of Great Britain (Queen Elizabeth II. W **165**) surch as T **12** (1, 15, 25, 40, 50n.p.), T **14** (75n.p.) or T **13** (others).

120	1n.p. on 5d. brown	10	70
121	3n.p. on ½d. orange-red	60	5·00
122	6n.p. on 1d. ultramarine	60	1·25
123	9n.p. on 1½d. green	60	4·75
124	12n.p. on 2d. light red-brown	60	5·50
125	15n.p. on 2½d. carmine-red (Type I)	60	7·00
	a. Type II (11.58)	50·00	£120
126	20n.p. on 3d. deep lilac (B.)	60	30
127	25n.p. on 4d. ultramarine	2·75	3·25
128	40n.p. on 6d. reddish purple	1·00	30
129	50n.p. on 9d. bronze-green	5·50	4·00
130	75n.p. on 1s.3d. green	6·00	9·50
120/130 *Set of 11*		17·00	38·00

20 Sheikh Abdullah

(Recess De La Rue)

1958 (1 Feb)–**59**. T **20** and similar designs. P 12½ (Nos. 131/136), 13½×13.

131	**20**	5n.p. bluish green	1·00	20
132		10n.p. rose-red	75	20
136		40n.p. maroon	4·75	1·50
131/136 *Set of 3*			6·00	1·75

Nos. 131/136 were only valid for internal use in Kuwait prior to 1 February 1959. Further values were added to this series following the closure of the British Agency Post Offices on 31 January 1959. Responsibility of the postal service then passed to the Kuwait Government and later issues are listed in the Stanley Gibbons *Arabia Catalogue*.

OFFICIAL STAMPS

KUWAIT SERVICE (O 1) KUWAIT SERVICE (O 2)

1923–24. Stamps of India (King George V), optd with Types O **1** or O **2** (rupee values, 15½–16 *mm*). W **34** (Large Star) of India. P 14.

O1	½a. light green (No. 155)	8·50	70·00
	a. Opt double, one albino	£170	
O2	1a. chocolate (No. 197)	7·50	29·00
	a. Opt double, one albino	£140	
O3	1½a. chocolate (A) (No. 163)	5·50	80·00
O4	2a. bright reddish violet (No. 169)	15·00	65·00
	a. Reddish purple	16·00	
O5	2a.6p. ultramarine (No. 171)	4·50	85·00
O6	3a. dull orange (No. 173)	6·50	90·00
O7	3a. ultramarine (No. 200) (1924)	5·00	90·00
O8	4a. olive-green (No. 175)	5·00	90·00
O9	8a. purple (No. 182)	6·00	£140
O10	1r. brown and green (No. 186)	45·00	£225
	a. Orange-brown and deep turquoise-green	50·00	£250
	b. Opt double, one albino	£200	
O11	2r. carmine and brown (No. 187)	45·00	£325
O12	5r. ultramarine and violet (No. 188)	£130	£500
	a. Opt double, one albino	£200	
O13	10r. green and scarlet (No. 189)	£275	£450
O14	15r. blue and olive (No. 190)	£425	£700
O1/O14 *Set of 14*		£850	£2750

1929–33. Nos. 203, 206, 209 and 211/218w of India (King George V, Nasik printing) optd as T O **1** (spaced 10 *mm*) or T O **2** (14½ *mm*×19–20 *mm* wide). W **69** (Mult Stars) of India. P 14.

O16	1a. chocolate		
	w. Wmk inverted	8·50	60·00
O17	2a. purple	70·00	£300
O19	3a. blue	4·50	70·00
O20	4a. sage-green	4·25	£110
	w. Wmk inverted		
O21	8a. reddish purple	7·00	£160
	w. Wmk inverted	10·00	£170
O22	12a. claret	50·00	£275
	w. Wmk inverted	70·00	
O23	1r. chocolate and green	16·00	£325
O24	2r. carmine and orange (*wmk inverted*)	21·00	£450
O25	5r. ultramarine and purple (*wmk inverted*)	55·00	£550
O26	10r. green and scarlet	95·00	£900
O27	15r. blue and olive (*wmk inverted*)	£325	£1600
O16w/O27 *Set of 11*		£600	£4500

Labuan *see* North Borneo

Lagos *see* Nigeria

Leeward Islands

The Federal Colony of the Leeward Islands was constituted in 1871 formalising links between Antigua, British Virgin Islands, Dominica, Montserrat and St Kitts-Nevis which stretched back to the 1670s. Issues for the individual islands were superseded by those inscribed 'LEEWARD ISLANDS', but were in concurrent use with them from 1903 (British Virgin Islands from 1899). Dominica was transferred to the Windward Islands on 31 December 1939.

PRICES FOR STAMPS ON COVER TO 1945

Nos. 1/8	*from* × 10
Nos. 9/16	*from* × 12
Nos. 17/19	*from* × 8
Nos. 20/28	*from* × 5
Nos. 29/35	*from* × 4
Nos. 36/45	*from* × 5
Nos. 46/57	*from* × 4
Nos. 58/87	*from* × 5
Nos. 88/91	*from* × 6
Nos. 92/94	*from* × 10
Nos. 95/114	*from* × 5

PRINTERS. All the stamps of Leeward Islands were typographed by De La Rue & Co, Ltd, London, *except where otherwise stated.*

1

2

4d. Damaged 'S' (R. ?/6, left pane)

1890 (31 Oct). Name and value in second colour. Wmk Crown CA. P 14.

1	1	½d. dull mauve and green	3·50	1·25
2		1d. dull mauve and rose	8·50	20
3		2½d. dull mauve and blue	9·50	30
		w. Wmk inverted	£450	£225
4		4d. dull mauve and orange	11·00	9·50
		a. Damaged 'S'	£300	
5		6d. dull mauve and brown	13·00	17·00
6		7d. dull mauve and slate	11·00	22·00
7	2	1s. green and carmine	23·00	60·00
8		5s. green and blue	£140	£325
1/8 *Set of* 8			£190	£375
1s/8s Optd 'SPECIMEN' *Set of* 8			£275	

The colours of this issue are fugitive.

(3)

One Penny

(4)

One Penny

(5)

1897 (22 July). Queen Victoria's Diamond Jubilee. Handstamped with T **3**.

9	1	½d. dull mauve and green	8·00	26·00
		a. Opt double	£1400	
		b. Opt triple	£6000	
10		1d. dull mauve and rose	9·00	26·00
		a. Opt double	£1000	
		b. Opt triple	£6000	
11		2½d. dull mauve and blue	9·50	26·00
		a. Opt double	£1200	
12		4d. dull mauve and orange	55·00	80·00
		a. Opt double	£1300	
13		6d. dull mauve and brown	60·00	£130
		a. Opt double	£1700	
14		7d. dull mauve and slate	60·00	£130
		a. Opt double	£1700	£2000
15	2	1s. green and carmine	£130	£275
		a. Opt double	£2250	
16		5s. green and blue	£450	£800
		a. Opt double	£6000	
9/16 *Set of* 8			£700	£1300

Beware of forgeries. The prices quoted above for overprint varieties are for certified examples showing two (or three) clear impressions of the handstamp. Stamps with slight or partial doubling are frequently encountered, and are worth little premium over the normal prices.

1902 (11 Aug). Nos. 4/6 surch locally.

17	4	1d. on 4d. dull mauve and orange	6·50	12·00
		a. Pair, one with tall narrow 'O' in 'One'	45·00	85·00
		b. Surch double	£6000	
		c. Damaged 'S'	£180	
18		1d. on 6d. dull mauve and brown	8·00	19·00
		a. Pair, one with tall narrow 'O' in 'One'	65·00	£150
19	5	1d. on 7d. dull mauve and slate	6·50	16·00
17/19 *Set of* 3			19·00	42·00

The tall narrow 'O' variety occurred on R. 1/1, 5/3, 5/5 and 7/4.

6

7

8

2½d. Wide 'A' (R. 6/1 of both panes. Replaced in 1912)

1s. Dropped 'R' (R. 1/1 of both panes from Pl 1 and 2

1902 (1 Sept–Oct). Wmk Crown CA. P 14.

20	6	½d. dull purple and green	6·00	1·00
21		1d. dull purple and carmine	11·00	20
22	7	2d. dull purple and ochre (10.02)	3·50	4·25
23	6	2½d. dull purple and ultramarine	7·00	2·25
		a. Wide 'A' in 'LEEWARD'	£275	£160
24	7	3d. dull purple and black (10.02)	12·00	7·50
25	6	6d. dull purple and brown	2·50	8·00
26	8	1s. green and carmine	11·00	30·00
		a. Dropped 'R' in 'LEEWARD'	£550	£850
27	7	2s.6d. green and black (10.02)	30·00	80·00
28	8	5s. green and blue	65·00	95·00
20/28 *Set of* 9			£120	£200
20s/28s Optd 'SPECIMEN' *Set of* 9			£190	

1905 (Apr)–**08**. Wmk Mult Crown CA. Ordinary paper (½d., 3d.) or chalk-surfaced paper (others).

29	6	½d. dull purple and green (2.06)	5·50	2·50
		a. Chalk-surfaced paper (25.7.08)	35·00	22·00
30		1d. dull purple and carmine (29.8.06)	11·00	80
31	7	2d. dull purple and ochre (25.7.08)	14·00	27·00
32	6	2½d. dull purple and ultramarine (23.7.06)	80·00	50·00
		a. Wide 'A' in 'LEEWARD'	£800	£550
33	7	3d. dull purple and black	26·00	60·00
		a. Chalk-surfaced paper (18.4.08)	60·00	£100
34	6	6d. dull purple and brown (15.7.08)	55·00	£100
35	8	1s. green and carmine (15.7.08)	50·00	£140
29/35 *Set of* 7			£200	£325

1907 (14 Apr)–**11**. Wmk Mult Crown CA. Chalk-surfaced paper (3d. to 5s.). P 14.

36	7	¼d. brown (7.8.09)	2·75	1·75
37	6	½d. dull green	6·50	2·00
		y. Wmk inverted and reversed	†	£800
38		1d. bright red (7.07)	16·00	80
		a. Rose-carmine (1910)	48·00	3·50
39	7	2d. grey (3.8.11)	6·00	15·00
40	6	2½d. bright blue (5.07)	9·50	4·25
		a. Wide 'A' in 'LEEWARD'	£300	£180
41	7	3d. purple/*yellow* (28.10.10)	3·50	7·50
42	6	6d. dull and bright purple (3.8.11)	10·00	12·00
43	8	1s. black/*green* (3.8.11)	9·50	21·00
44	7	2s.6d. black and red/*blue* (15.9.11)	42·00	55·00
45	8	5s. green and red/*yellow* (21.11.10)	48·00	65·00
36/45 *Set of* 10			£130	£160
36s/45s Optd 'SPECIMEN' *Set of* 10			£300	

10

11

12

13

1912 (23 Oct)–**22**. Die I (¼d. to 3d., 6d., 1s., 2s.6d. 5s.) or Die II (4d., 2s.). Wmk Mult Crown CA. Chalk-surfaced paper (3d. to 5s.). P 14.

46	10	¼d. brown	1·75	1·00
		a. Pale brown	6·00	2·75
47	11	½d. yellow-green (12.12)	5·50	2·00
		a. Deep green (1916)	8·00	1·50
48		1d. red	5·00	1·00
		a. Bright scarlet (8.15)	15·00	1·00
49	10	2d. slate-grey (9.1.13)	4·00	5·50
50	11	2½d. bright blue	3·25	7·00
		a. Deep bright blue (1914)	8·50	4·50
51	10	3d. purple/*yellow* (9.1.13)	4·00	26·00
		a. White back (11.13)	95·00	£180
		as. Optd 'SPECIMEN'	50·00	
		b. On lemon (11.14)	7·00	27·00
		c. On buff (1920)	35·00	50·00
		cs. Optd 'SPECIMEN'	45·00	
		d. On orange-buff (1920)	8·50	29·00
		dw. Wmk inverted	£475	£550
52		4d. black and red/*pale yellow* (Die II) (12.5.22)	7·50	24·00
53	11	6d. dull and bright purple (9.1.13)	4·50	9·50
54	12	1s. black/*green* (9.1.13)	4·00	8·00
		a. White back (11.13)	90·00	38·00
		as. Optd 'SPECIMEN'	50·00	
		b. On blue-green, olive back (1917)	18·00	8·00
		bs. Optd 'SPECIMEN'	£120	
55	10	2s. purple and blue/*blue* (Die II) (12.5.22)	19·00	65·00
56		2s.6d. black and red/*blue* (11.13)	23·00	55·00
57	12	5s. green and red/*yellow* (9.14)	65·00	£120
		a. White back (11.13)	55·00	90·00
		as. Optd 'SPECIMEN'	60·00	
		b. On lemon (1915)	50·00	85·00
		c. On orange-buff (1920)	£120	£200
46/57*b Set of* 12			£110	£250
46s/57s Optd 'SPECIMEN' *Set of* 12			£300	

Nos. 51*a*, 54*a* and 57*a* were only on sale from Montserrat.

1d., 1s. 'D I' shaved at foot 1d. R. 7/3 of left pane (printings from Sept 1947 until corrected during first printing in green in Oct 1948). 1s. R. 9/6 of right pane (all ptgs between 1932 and 1938). Less pronounced flaws, with the 'D' chamfered also exist on the 1s at R. 5/4 and R. 7/3 (right pane).

1921 (Oct)–**32**. Wmk Mult Script CA or Mult Crown CA (£1). Chalk-surfaced paper (3d. to £1). P 14.

(a) Die II (1921–1929)

58	10	¼d. brown (1.4.22)	2·25	1·00
59	11	½d. blue-green	1·25	75
60		1d. carmine-red	2·25	55
61		1d. bright violet (21.8.22)	2·25	1·00
62		1d. bright scarlet (1929)	19·00	2·25
63	10	1½d. carmine-red (10.9.26)	9·50	1·50
64		1½d. red-brown (1929)	2·50	10
65		2d. slate-grey (6.22)	3·00	1·00
		w. Wmk inverted	†	£375
		x. Wmk reversed	£550	
66	11	2½d. orange-yellow (22.9.23)	14·00	70·00
67		2½d. bright blue (1.3.27)	3·50	1·25
68	10	3d. light ultramarine (22.9.23)	18·00	42·00
		a. Deep ultramarine (1925)	70·00	60·00
69		3d. purple/*yellow* (1.7.27)	9·00	6·50
70		4d. black and red/*pale yellow* (2.24)	4·25	21·00
71		5d. dull purple and olive-green (12.5.22)	2·50	4·25
72	11	6d. dull and bright purple (17.7.23)	21·00	50·00
73	12	1s. black/*emerald* (17.7.23)	11·00	8·00
		a. 'DI' flaw		
74	10	2s. purple and blue/*blue* (12.5.22)	25·00	45·00
		a. Red-purple and blue/blue (1926)	14·00	48·00
		aw. Wmk inverted	£400	
75		2s.6d. black and red/*blue* (17.7.23)	14·00	28·00
76		3s. bright green and violet (12.5.22)	12·00	48·00
77		4s. black and red (12.5.22)	21·00	42·00
78	12	5s. green and red/*pale yellow* (17.7.23)	50·00	85·00
79	13	10s. green and red/*green* (1928)	80·00	£140
		a. Break in scroll	£300	£400
		b. Broken crown and scroll	£300	
		c. Nick in top right scroll	£300	
		e. Break in lines below left scroll	£300	
		f. Damaged leaf at bottom right	£300	
80		£1 purple and black/*red* (1928)	£225	£350
		a. Break in scroll	£550	
		b. Broken crown and scroll	£550	
		c. Nick in top right scroll	£550	
		e. Break in lines below left scroll	£550	
		f. Damaged leaf at bottom right	£550	
58/80 *Set of* 23			£450	£850
58s/80s Optd or Perf (1d. bright scarlet, 1½d. red-brown, 10s. £1) 'SPECIMEN' *Set of* 23			£700	

(b) Reversion to Die I (Plate 23) (1931–1932)

81	10	¼d. brown	20·00	27·00
82	11	½d. blue-green	25·00	75·00
83		1d. bright scarlet	45·00	1·50
84	10	1½d. red-brown	4·25	2·75
85	11	2½d. bright blue	7·00	3·50
86		6d. dull and bright purple	35·00	£100
87	12	1s. black/*emerald*	60·00	85·00
		a. 'D I' flaw	£600	
		b. 'A' of 'CA' missing from wmk	—	£2250
81/87 *Set of* 7			£170	£250

No. 66 was issued in Montserrat and 68*a* in St Kitts-Nevis.

Nos. 59, 62 and 82/83 exist in coils, constructed from normal sheets. No. 82 was only issued in this form.

For illustrations of varieties on Nos. 79/80 see above No. 51*b* of Bermuda.

Nos. 81/87 result from the use, in error, of Die I which had previously been 'retired' in late 1920, to produce Plate 23.

1935 (6 May). Silver Jubilee. As Nos. 91/94 of Antigua, but printed by Waterlow. P 11×12.

88	1d. deep blue and scarlet	1·90	3·50
89	1½d. ultramarine and grey	2·75	1·25
90	2½d. brown and deep blue	5·00	4·75
91	1s. slate and purple	28·00	48·00
	k. Kite and vertical log	£650	
	l. Kite and horizontal log	£650	£700
88/91 *Set of* 4		35·00	50·00
88s/91s Perf 'SPECIMEN' *Set of* 4		£140	

For illustrations of plate varieties see Omnibus section following Zanzibar.

1937 (12 May). Coronation. As Nos. 95/97 of Antigua, but printed by D.L.R. Perf 14

92	1d. scarlet	80	1·00
93	1½d. yellow-brown	80	1·50
94	2½d. bright blue	90	1·50
92/94 *Set of* 3		2·25	3·50
92s/94s Perf 'SPECIMEN' *Set of* 3		£120	

14

15

(Die A)

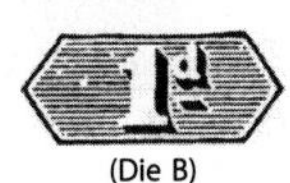
(Die B)

In Die B the figure '1' has a broader top and more projecting serif.

½d. 'ISI.ANDS' flaw (R. 1/2 of right pane) (Pl 2 ptg of May 1944)

6d. Broken second 'E' in 'LEEWARD' (R. 4/1 of right pane) (Pl 2 and 3 ptgs from March 1942 until corrected in June 1949) (The similar variety on the 5s. shows traces of the top bar)

5s. Damaged value tablet (R. 3/5 of left pane, first printing only)

Broken top right scroll (R. 5/11) (1942 ptg of 10s. only. Corrected on £1 value from same period)

Broken lower right scroll (R. 5/12. 1942 ptgs only)

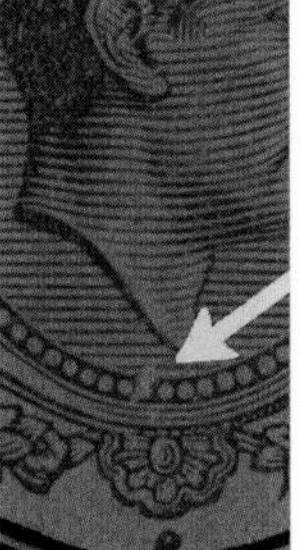
Missing pearl (R. 5/1. 1944 ptgs only)

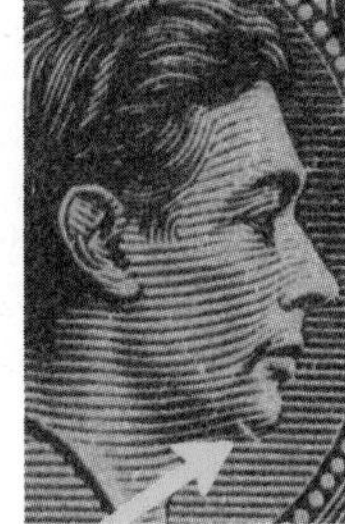
Gash in chin (R. 2/5. 1942 ptgs only)

1938 (25 Nov)–**51**. T **14** (and similar type, but shaded value tablet, ½d., 1d., 2½d., 6d.) and T **15** (10s., £1). Chalk-surfaced paper (3d. to £1). P 14.

(a) Wmk Mult Script CA

No.	Description	Unused	Used
95	¼d. brown	60	1·50
	a. Chalk-surfaced paper. *Deep brown* (13.6.49)	30	2·50
96	½d. emerald	2·00	70
	a. 'ISI.ANDS' flaw	£170	£250
97	½d. slate-grey (*chalk-surfaced paper*) (1.7.49)	2·00	1·50
98	1d. scarlet (Die A)	14·00	2·75
99	1d. scarlet (*shades*) (Die B) (1940)	2·25	1·75
	a. 'D I' flaw (9.47)	£200	
	b. Carmine (9.42)	3·00	16·00
	c. Red (13.9.48)	6·00	8·50
	ca. 'D I' flaw	£200	£275
100	1d. blue-green (*chalk-surfaced paper*) (1.7.49)	55	15
	a. 'D I' flaw	£200	£225
101	1½d. chestnut	1·00	50
102	1½d. yellow-orange and black (*chalk-surfaced paper*) (1.7.49)	1·75	40
103	2d. olive-grey	3·50	2·25
	a. Slate-grey (11.42)	6·50	4·00
104	2d. scarlet (*chalk-surfaced paper*) (1.7.49)	1·40	1·25
105	2½d. bright blue	35·00	4·00
	a. Light bright blue (11.42)	80	1·25
106	2½d. black and purple (*chalk-surfaced paper*) (1.7.49)	1·00	15
107	3d. orange	35·00	2·75
	a. Ordinary paper. *Pale orange* (3.42)	50	85
108	3d. bright blue (1.7.49)	1·00	15
109	6d. deep dull purple and bright purple	32·00	8·00
	a. Ordinary paper (3.42)	12·00	3·50
	ab. Broken 'E'	£550	£400
	b. Purple and deep magenta (29.9.47)	18·00	6·50
	ba. Broken 'E'	£750	£450
110	1s. black/*emerald*	18·00	2·00
	a. 'D I' flaw	£650	£400
	b. Ordinary paper (3.42)	5·50	1·00
	ba. Grey and black/emerald (8.42)	24·00	2·75
	bb. Black and grey/emerald (11.42)	£130	13·00
111	2s. reddish purple and blue/*blue*	35·00	3·00
	a. Ordinary paper (3.42)	16·00	2·00
	ab. Deep purple and blue/blue (29.9.47)	16·00	2·50
112	5s. green and red/*yellow*	50·00	25·00
	a. Broken 'E' (R. 4/3 of left pane)	£1700	£1000
	ab. Damaged value tablet	£1700	£1000
	b. Ordinary paper (12.43)	35·00	16·00
	ba. Broken 'E' (R. 4/3 of left pane)	£1200	
	c. Bright green and red/yellow (24.10.51)	65·00	£100
113	10s. bluish green and deep red/*green*	£200	£130
	a. Ordinary paper. *Pale green and dull red/green* (26.6.44*)	£850	£375
	ad. Broken top right scroll	£8000	
	ae. Broken lower right scroll	£8000	£4750
	af. Gash in chin	£8000	£4750
	b. Ordinary paper. *Green and red/green* (22.2.45*)	£150	90·00
	c. Ordinary paper. *Deep green and deep vermilion/green* (15.10.47*)	£120	£100
	ca. Missing pearl	£1700	

(b) Wmk Mult Crown CA

No.	Description	Unused	Used
114	£1 brown-purple and black/*red*	£375	£450
	a. Purple and black/carmine (21.9.42*)	90·00	55·00
	ae. Broken lower right scroll	£2000	£1300
	af. Gash in chin	£2250	£1300
	b. Brown-purple and black/salmon (5.2.45*)	45·00	32·00
	ba. Missing pearl	£1700	£1500
	c. Perf 13. *Violet and black/scarlet* (4.1.52*)	35·00	45·00
	ca. Wmk sideways	£7000	
	cw. Wmk inverted	£7000	
95/114*c*	*Set of* 19	£200	£140
95s/114s	Perf 'SPECIMEN' *Set of* 13	£750	

* Dates quoted for Nos. 113*a*/114*c* are earliest known postmark dates. Nos. 113*a* and 114*a* were despatched to the Leeward Islands in March 1942, Nos. 113*b* and 114*b* in December 1943, No. 113*c* in June 1944 and No. 114c on 13 December 1951.

Nos. 96, 98 and 99 exist in coils constructed from normal sheets.

Printings of the 10s. in March 1942 (No. 113*a*) and of the £1 in February and October 1942 (No. 114*a*) were made by Williams Lea & Co. Ltd. following bomb damage to the De La Rue works in 1940.

For illustrations of Nos. 99a, 99ca, 100a and 110a see above No. 58.

1946 (1 Nov). Victory. As Nos. 110/111 of Antigua.

No.	Description	Unused	Used
115	1½d. brown	15	75
116	3d. red-orange	15	75
115s/116s	Perf 'SPECIMEN' *Set of* 2	£100	

1949 (2 Jan). Royal Silver Wedding. As Nos. 112/113 of Antigua.

No.	Description	Unused	Used
117	2½d. ultramarine	10	10
118	5s. green	7·00	11·00

1949 (10 Oct). 75th Anniversary of Universal Postal Union. As Nos. 114/117 of Antigua.

No.	Description	Unused	Used
119	2½d. blue-black	15	3·00
120	3d. deep blue	2·00	3·00
121	6d. magenta	15	3·00
122	1s. blue-green	15	3·00
119/122	*Set of* 4	2·25	11·00

(New Currency. 100 cents = 1 BWI dollar)

1951 (16 Feb). Inauguration of BWI University College. As Nos. 118/119 of Antigua.

No.	Description	Unused	Used
123	3c. orange and black	30	2·00
124	12c. rose-carmine and reddish violet	1·00	2·00

1953 (2 June). Coronation. As No. 120 of Antigua.

No.	Description	Unused	Used
125	3c. black and green	1·00	2·25

16 Queen Elizabeth II

17

'Loop' flaw (R. 2/2)

Broken scroll (R. 4/3)

1954 (22 Feb). Chalk-surfaced paper. Wmk Mult Script CA. P 14 (T **16**) or 13 (T **17**).

No.	Type	Description	Unused	Used
126	**16**	½c. brown	10	60
		a. 'Loop' flaw	5·00	
127		1c. grey	1·25	1·25
		a. 'Loop' flaw	15·00	
128		2c. green	1·75	10
		a. 'Loop' flaw	20·00	
129		3c. yellow-orange and black	2·50	1·00
		a. 'Loop' flaw	25·00	
130		4c. rose-red	1·75	10
		a. 'Loop' flaw	20·00	
131		5c. black and brown-purple	2·25	1·00
		a. 'Loop' flaw	25·00	
132		6c. yellow-orange	2·25	60
		a. 'Loop' flaw	25·00	
133		8c. ultramarine	2·50	10
		a. 'Loop' flaw	25·00	
134		12c. dull and reddish purple	2·00	10
		a. 'Loop' flaw	25·00	
135		24c. black and green	2·00	20
		a. 'Loop' flaw	25·00	
136		48c. dull purple and ultramarine	8·00	2·75
		a. 'Loop' flaw	65·00	
137		60c. brown and green	6·00	2·25
		a. 'Loop' flaw	55·00	
138		$1.20 yellow-green and rose-red	7·00	4·25
		a. 'Loop' flaw	60·00	
139	**17**	$2.40 bluish green and red	15·00	8·50
		a. Broken scroll	£110	
140		$4.80 brown-purple and black	19·00	12·00
		a. Broken scroll	£140	
126/140		*Set of* 15	60·00	30·00

The 3c., 4c., 6c., 8c., 24c., 48c., 60c. and $1.20 have their value tablets unshaded.

The stamps of Leeward Islands were withdrawn and invalidated on 1 July 1956 when the federal colony was dissolved.

Lesotho

INDEPENDENT KINGDOM

King Moshoeshoe II, 4 October 1966–November 1990 (deposed)

33 Moshoeshoe I and Moshoeshoe II

(Des and photo Harrison)

1966 (4 Oct). Independence. P 12½×13.

No.	Type	Description	Unused	Used
106	**33**	2½c. light brown, black and red	10	10
107		5c. light brown, black and new blue	15	10
108		10c. light brown, black and emerald	20	10
109		20c. light brown, black and bright purple	25	30
106/109 *Set of* 4			60	45

LESOTHO

(**34**)

35 'Education Culture and Science'

1966 (1 Nov). Stamps of Basutoland optd as T **34**.

A. On Nos. 69/71 and 73/79 (Script CA wmk)

No.	Description	Unused	Used
110A	½c. grey-black and sepia	10	10
111A	1c. grey-black and bluish green	10	10
112A	2c. deep bright blue and orange	60	10
114A	3½c. indigo and deep ultramarine	30	10
115A	5c. chestnut and deep grey-green	10	10
116A	10c. bronze-green and purple	10	10
117A	12½c. brown and turquoise-green	4·75	35
118A	25c. deep ultramarine and crimson	30	20
119A	50c. black and carmine-red	1·00	2·25
120A	1r. black and maroon	3·25	7·50
	a. 'LSEOTHO' (R. 4/2)	85·00	
	b. Opt double	£300	
	ba. Ditto. 'LSEOTHO' (R. 4/2)		
110A/120A *Set of* 10		9·50	9·50

B. On Nos. 84/92 and unissued 1r. (wmk w **12***)*

No.	Description	Unused	Used
111B	1c. grey-black and bluish green	10	10
113B	2½c. pale yellow-green and rose-red	50	10
115B	5c. chestnut and deep grey-green	20	10
117B	12½c. brown and turquoise-green	30	20
119B	50c. black and carmine-red	70	50
120B	1r. black and maroon	65	1·25
	a. 'LSEOTHO' (R. 4/2)	50·00	70·00
111B/120B *Set of* 6		2·00	1·75

(Des V. Whiteley. Litho D.L.R.)

1966 (1 Dec). 20th Anniversary of UNESCO. P 14½×14.

No.	Type	Description	Unused	Used
121	**35**	2½c. orange-yellow and emerald-green	10	10
122		5c. light green and olive	15	10
123		12½c. light blue and red	35	15
124		25c. red-orange and deep greenish blue	60	85
121/124 *Set of* 4			1·10	1·00

36 Maize

37 Moshoeshoe II

(Des and photo Harrison)

1967 (1 Apr). Designs as Types **36/37**. No wmk. P 14½×13½ (2r.) or 13½×14½ (others).

No.	Description	Unused	Used
125	½c. bluish green and light bluish violet	10	10
126	1c. sepia and rose-red	10	10
127	2c. orange-yellow and light green	10	1·75
128	2½c. black and ochre	10	10
129	3½c. chalky blue and yellow	10	1·00
130	5c. bistre and new blue	20	10
131	10c. yellow-brown and bluish grey	10	10
132	12½c. black and red-orange	20	10
133	25c. black and bright blue	55	20
134	50c. black, new blue and turquoise	4·50	2·25
135	1r. multicoloured	65	75
136	2r. black, gold and magenta	1·00	1·75
125/136 *Set of* 12		6·25	7·00

Designs: Horiz as T **36**—½c. T **36**; 1c. Cattle; 2c. Agaves (wrongly inscr 'Aloes'); 2½c. Basotho Hat; 3½c. Merino Sheep ('Wool'); 5c. Basotho Pony; 10c. Wheat; 12½c. Angora Goat ('Mohair'); 25c. Maletsunyane Falls; 50c. Diamonds; 1r. Arms of Lesotho. Horiz—2r. T **37**.

See also Nos. 147/159.

46 Students and University

(Des V. Whiteley. Photo Harrison)

1967 (7 Apr). First Conferment of University Degrees. P 14×14½.

No.	Type	Description	Unused	Used
137	**46**	1c. sepia, ultramarine and light yellow-orange	10	10
138		2½c. sepia, ultramarine and light greenish blue	10	10
139		12½c. sepia, ultramarine and rose	10	10
140		25c. sepia, ultramarine and light violet	15	15
137/140 *Set of* 4			30	30

47 Statue of Moshoeshoe I

(Des and photo Harrison)

1967 (4 Oct). First Anniversary of Independence. T **47** and similar triangular designs. P 14½×14.

No.	Description	Unused	Used
141	2½c. black and light yellow-green	10	10
142	12½c. multicoloured	25	15
143	25c. black, green and light ochre	35	25
141/143 *Set of* 3		65	40

Designs: 2½c. T **47**; 12½c. Lesotho flag; 25c. Crocodile (National Emblem).

50 Lord Baden-Powell and Scout Saluting

(Des V. Whiteley. Photo Harrison)

1967 (1 Nov). 60th Anniversary of Scout Movement. P 14×14½.

No.	Type	Description	Unused	Used
144	**50**	15c. multicoloured	20	10

51 WHO Emblem and World Map

(Des G. Vasarhelyi. Photo Harrison)

1968 (7 Apr). 20th Anniversary of World Health Organisation. T **51** and similar horiz design. P 14×14½.

No.	Description	Unused	Used
145	2½c. blue, gold and carmine-red	15	10
	a. Gold (emblem) omitted	£850	
146	25c. multicoloured	45	60

Designs: 2½c. T **51**; 25c. Nurse and child.

53 Basotho Hat

54 Sorghum

1968–69. As Nos. 125/136 and T **54**, but wmk **53** (sideways on 2r.).

No.	Description	Unused	Used
147	½c. bluish green and light bluish violet (26.11.68)	10	10
	a. Blue-green and violet (30.9.69)	2·75	2·75
148	1c. sepia and rose-red (26.11.68)	10	10
149	2c. orange-yellow and light green (26.11.68)	10	10
	a. Orange-yellow and yellow-green (30.9.69)	1·00	1·75
150	2½c. black and ochre (21.10.68)	15	10
	a. Black and yellow-ochre (30.9.69)	1·00	1·00
151	3c. chocolate, green and yellow-brown (1.8.68)	15	15
152	3½c. chalky blue and yellow (26.11.68)	15	40
153	5c. bistre and new blue (22.7.68)	60	10
154	10c. yellow-brown and pale bluish grey (26.11.68)	15	10
155	12½c. black and red-orange (30.9.69)	60	35
156	25c. black and bright blue (30.9.69)	1·50	1·00
157	50c. black, new blue and turquoise (30.9.69)	11·00	5·50
158	1r. multicoloured (26.11.68)	1·50	2·25
159	2r. black, gold and magenta (30.9.69)	7·00	14·00
147/159 *Set of* 13		21·00	21·00

55 Running Hunters

(Des Jennifer Toombs. Photo Harrison)

1968 (1 Nov). Rock Paintings. T **55** and similar designs. W **53** (sideways on 5c., 15c.). P 14×14½ (5c., 15c.) or 14½×14 (others).

No.	Description	Unused	Used
160	3c. yellow-brown. light blue-green and blackish green	20	10
161	3½c. greenish yellow, yellow-olive and sepia	25	10
162	5c. Venetian red, yellow-ochre and blackish brown	25	10
163	10c. yellow, rose and deep maroon	35	10
164	15c. light buff, pale olive-yellow and blackish brown	50	30
165	20c. yellow-green, greenish yellow and blackish brown	60	55
166	25c. yellow, orange-brown and black	65	75
160/166 *Set of* 7		2·50	1·75

Designs: Horiz—3c. T **55**; 3½c. Baboons; 10c. Archers; 20c. Eland; 25c. Hunting scene. Vert—5c. Spear throwing; 15c. Blue Cranes.

62 Queen Elizabeth II Hospital

(Des C. R. Househam and G. Drummond. Litho P.B.)

1969 (11 Mar). Centenary of Maseru (capital). T **62** and similar horiz designs. Multicoloured. W **53** (sideways). P 14×13½.

No.	Description	Unused	Used
167	2½c. Type **62**	10	10
168	10c. Lesotho Radio Station	10	10
169	12½c. Leabua Jonathan Airport	35	10
170	25c. Royal Palace	25	15
167/170 *Set of* 4		65	30

66 Rally Car passing Mosotho Horseman

(Des P. Wheeler. Photo Harrison)

1969 (26 Sept). Roof of Africa Car Rally. T **66** and similar horiz designs. W **53**. P 14.

No.	Description	Unused	Used
171	2½c. yellow, mauve and plum	15	10
172	12½c. cobalt, greenish yellow and olive-grey	20	10
173	15c. blue, black and mauve	20	10
174	20c. black, red and yellow	20	10
171/174 *Set of* 4		65	30

Designs: 2½c. T **66**; 12½c. Rally car on mountain road; 15c. Chequered flags and mountain scenery; 20c. Map of rally route and Rally Trophy.

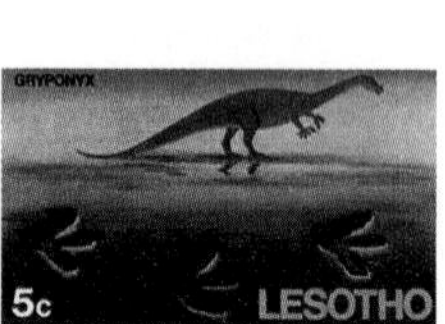

71 Gryponyx and Footprints

75 Moshoeshoe I, when a Young Man

(Des Jennifer Toombs. Photo Harrison)

1970 (5 Jan). Prehistoric Footprints. T **71** and similar designs. W **53** (sideways*). P 14×14½ (3c.) or 14½×14 (others).

No.	Description	Unused	Used
175	3c. pale brown, yellow-brown and sepia	90	70
176	5c. dull purple, pink and sepia	1·10	30
	w. Wmk hat pointing right	3·25	
177	10c. pale yellow, black and sepia	1·25	35
178	15c. olive-yellow, black and sepia	1·50	2·25
179	25c. cobalt and black	2·25	2·25
175/179 *Set of* 5		6·25	5·25

Designs: (60×23 *mm*)—3c. Dinosaur footprints at Moyeni. (40×24 *mm*)—5c. T **71**; 10c. Plateosauravus and footprints; 15c. Tritylodon and footprints; 25c. Massospondylus and footprints.

* The normal sideways watermark shows the hat pointing left, *when seen from the back of the stamp.*

(Des G. Vasarhelyi. Litho D.L.R.)

1970 (11 Mar). Death Centenary of King Moshoeshoe I. T **75** and similar vert design. W **53**. P 13½.

No.	Description	Unused	Used
180	2½c. pale green and magenta	10	10
181	25c. pale blue and chesnut	20	20

Designs: 2½c. T **75**; 25c. Moshoeshoe I as an old man.

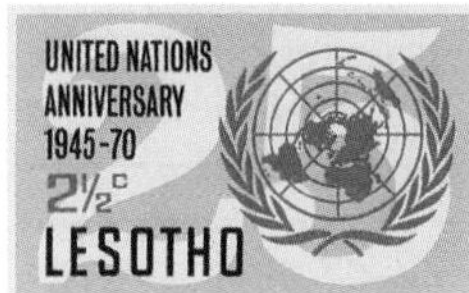

77 UN Emblem and '25'

(Des V. Whiteley. Litho Questa)

1970 (26 June). 25th Anniversary of United Nations. T **77** and similar horiz designs. W **53** (sideways). P 14½×14.

182	2½c. light pink, light blue and maroon	10	10
183	10c. multicoloured	10	10
184	12½c. brown-red, cobalt and drab	10	25
185	25c. multicoloured	15	65
182/185	*Set of 4*	30	60

Designs: 2½c. T **77**; 10c. UN Building; 12½c. 'People of the World'; 25c. Symbolic Dove.

78 Basotho Hat Gift Shop, Maseru

(Des G. Drummond. Litho Questa)

1970 (27 Oct). Tourism. T **78** and similar horiz designs. Multicoloured. W **53** (sideways). P 14.

186	2½c. Type **78**	10	10
187	5c. Trout fishing	20	10
188	10c. Pony trekking	25	10
189	12½c. Skiing	50	10
190	20c. Holiday Inn, Maseru	40	50
186/190	*Set of 5*	1·25	70

POSTAGE DUE STAMPS

D **3**

1966 (1 Nov). Nos. D9/D10 of Basutoland optd as T **34** but smaller.

D11	D **2**	1c. carmine	30	75
		a. 'LSEOTHO' (R. 4/7)	32·00	
D12		5c. deep reddish violet	30	90
		a. 'LSEOTHO' (R. 4/7)	50·00	

No. D11 exists with the overprint centred near the foot of the stamp (just above 'POSTAGE DUE') (*price* £50 *mint*). It is believed that this comes from proof sheets which were issued in the normal way. They contain the 'LSEOTHO' error, which only occurred in the first printing.

(Litho B.W.)

1967 (18 Apr). No wmk. P 13½.

D13	D **3**	1c. blue	15	3·00
D14		2c. brown-rose	15	3·50
D15		5c. emerald	20	3·50
D13/D15		*Set of 3*	45	9·00

Long Island

PRICES FOR STAMPS ON COVER TO 1945
Most covers from Long Island are philatelic, but these are worth from × 2 (Nos. 1/3) or from × 6 (Nos. 4/36).

The Turkish island of Chustan (or Keustan) in the Gulf of Smyrna was occupied by the Royal Navy during April 1916 and renamed Long Island.

The following stamps were provided by the Civil Administrator, Lieutenant Commander H. Pirie-Gordon, for the postal service inaugurated on 7 May 1916.

USED STAMPS. Stamps of Long Island were cancelled by hand-drawn circular date stamps in blue crayon for the Northend post office ('N') or in red crayon for Nikola post office ('S').

QUANTITIES ISSUED. The figures quoted do not include the remainders subsequently recorded as having been destroyed.

(1)

2

1916 (7 May). Turkish fiscal stamps surch by typewriter as in T **1**. No wmk. P 12.

1	½d. on 20pa. green and buff (new value in red, remainder of surch in black)	£8000	£10000
2	1d. on 10pa. carmine and buff	£9000	£10000
3	2½d. on 1pi. violet and buff (R.)	£8000	£10000

Quantities issued: ½d. 25; 1d. 20; 2½d. 25.

1916 (7 May). Typewritten as T **2** in various colours of ribbon and carbon. Each stamp initialled by the Civil Administrator. No gum. Imperf.

(a) On pale green paper with horizontal grey lines. No wmk. Sheets of 12 (4×3) or 16 (4×4) with stamps initialled in red ink

4	½d. black	£3000	£2500
	a. 'G.R.I.' double	£5500	
	b. '7' for '&'	£8500	
5	½d. blue	£2500	
	a. 'G.R.I.' double	£5500	
	b. '7' for '&'	£8500	
6	½d. mauve	£1000	£1200
	a. 'G.R.I.' double	£2750	
	b. '7' for '&'	£7000	

Quantity issued: 140 in all.

(b) On thin horiz laid paper with sheet wmk of 'Silver Linen' in double-lined letters. Sheets of 20 (4×5) or 16 (some ptgs of 1s.) with stamps initialled in red ink

7	½d. black	£1200	£1500
	a. 'postage' for 'Postage'	£6500	
	b. '7' for '&'	£6500	
8	½d. blue	£1700	£1800
	b. '7' for '&'	£6500	
9	½d. mauve	£600	£700
	a. 'postage' for 'Postage'	£3000	
	b. '7' for '&'	£4000	
10	1d. black	£450	£700
	a. '7' for '&'	£3750	
	b. 'Rvevue' for 'Revenue'	£3750	
	g. 'Postagg' for 'Postage'	£6000	
11	1d. blue	£600	£900
	a. '7' for '&'	£6000	
	c. 'postage' for 'Postage'	£6000	
	e. 'G.R?I?' for 'G.R.I.'	£6000	
	f. 'ONR' for 'ONE'	£3000	
12	1d. mauve	£325	£550
	a. '7' for '&'	£4250	
	b. 'Rvevue' for 'Revenue'	£6000	
	c. 'postage' for 'Postage'	£6000	
	e. 'G.R?I?' for 'G.R.I.'	†	£6000
	f. 'ONR' for 'ONE'	£2250	£3000
	g. 'Postagg' for 'Postage'	£4000	
13	1d. red	£375	£650
	a. '7' for '&'	£4000	
	c. 'postage' for 'Postage'	£6000	
	f. 'ONR' for 'ONE'	£3000	£3500
14	2½d. black	£3250	
15	2½d. blue	£3250	£3250
16	2½d. mauve	£7500	£3250
17	6d. black (inscr 'SIX PENCE')	£3750	£4500
	a. 'SIXPENCE' (one word)	£7000	
	b. Without red ink initials	†	£6500
19	6d. mauve (inscr 'SIX PENCE')	£1600	£2500
	a. 'SIXPENCE' (one word)	£5500	
20	1s. black	£325	£750
	a. 'ISLANA' for 'ISLAND'	£6000	
	b. 'Postge' for 'Postage'	£3000	£4500
	c. 'Rebenue' for 'Revenue'	£6000	
21	1s. blue	£3250	
22	1s. mauve	£325	£1000
	a. 'ISLANA' for 'ISLAND'	£4500	
	b. 'Postge' for 'Postage'	£6000	
	c. 'Rebenue' for 'Revenue'	£6000	

Quantities issued (all colours); ½d. 237; 1d. 881; 2½d. 80; 6d. 89; 1s. 383.

(c) On thin wove paper. No wmk. Sheets of 24 with stamps initialled in indelible pencil

23	½d. black	£700	£1100
25	½d. mauve	£1900	
26	1d. black	£1200	£1300
27	1d. red	£14000	£2500
30	2d. black	£550	£1100
	b. Error. 1d. and 2d. *se-tenant*	£14000	
	c. Initialled in red ink	£2500	£2750
31	2d. mauve	£550	£750
	a. Error. 1d. and 2d. *se-tenant*	£14000	
32	2½d. black	£1100	£1300
33	2½d. blue	£3250	
34	2½d. mauve	£3000	£3000
35	6d. black	£550	£1100
	a. 'Rvenne &' for 'Revenue'	£6000	
	b. Error. 2d. and 6d. *se-tenant*, also 'ISLND' for 'ISLAND'	£16000	£16000
	c. 'PENCC'	£5000	
36	6d. blue	£2500	
	a. 'Rvenne &' for 'Revenue'	£7000	
	b. Error. 2d. and 6d. *se-tenant*, also 'ISLND' for 'ISLAND'	£17000	
	c. 'PENCC'	£6000	

Quantities issued (all colours); ½d. 114; 1d. 120; 2d. 249; 2½d. 115; 6d. 200.

TOP SHEETS AND CARBONS. It is believed that the production sequence of the typewritten stamps was as follows:

½d. on pale green (Nos. 4/6)
Two black top sheets of 12 (4×3) and one of 16 (4×4)
Two blue carbon sheets of 12 (4×3) and one of 16 (4×4)
Five mauve carbon sheets of 12, two from one top sheet and three from the other
Varieties: '7' for '&' occurs on an unknown position from one of the sheets of 12 and 'G.R.I.' double occurs on R. 3/2-4 of the other

½d. on laid paper (Nos. 7/9) in sheets of 20 (4×5)
Three black top sheets
Three blue carbon sheets
Eight mauve carbon sheets, two or three from each top sheet
Varieties: 'postage' occurs on R. 3/2 of one top sheet and '7' for '&' on R. 4/2 of another

1d. on laid paper (Nos. 10/13) in sheets of 20 (4×5)
11 red top sheets
15 black carbon sheets, three each from five of the top sheets
Six blue carbon sheets, one each from six of the top sheets
22 mauve carbon sheets, probably two from each top sheet
Varieties: '7' for '&' on R. 3/3, 'postage' on R. 3/3, 'Rvevue' on R. 1/3 and 'Postagg' on R. 2/4, all from different top sheets
The position of 'G.R?I?' is not known. 'ONR' occurs from three different top sheets on R. 5/1, R. 5/2 and 4 or R. 4/1 and 5/2

2½d. on laid paper (Nos. 14/16) in sheets of 20 (4×5)
One black top sheet
One blue carbon sheet
Two mauve carbon sheets

6d. on laid paper (Nos. 17/19) in sheets of 20 (4×5)
One black top sheet
One blue carbon sheet*
Three mauve carbon sheets
Variety: 'SIXPENCE' occurs on R. 1/2-3

1s. on laid paper (Nos. 20/22)
Five black top sheets, four of 20 (4×5) and one of 16 (4×4)
Nine black carbon sheets three each from two of the top sheets of 20 and three from the top sheet of 16
Two blue carbon sheets, one each from two of the top sheets of 20
12 mauve carbon sheets, nine from various top sheets of 20 and three from the top sheet of 16
Varieties: 'ISLANA' occurs on R. 1/2 of one of the sheets of 20 and 'Postge' on R. 1/3 of the sheet of 16. 'Rebenue' comes from one of the other sheets of 20

½d. on wove paper (Nos. 23/25) in sheets of 24 (4×6)
One black top sheet
Three black carbon sheets
One blue carbon sheet*

One mauve carbon sheet 1d. on wove paper (Nos. 26/27) in sheets of 24 (4×6)
One red top sheet
Three black carbon sheets
One blue carbon sheet*
One mauve carbon sheet*

2d. on wove paper (Nos. 30/31) in sheets of 24 (4×6)
Two black top sheets
Six black carbon sheets, three from each top sheet. One initialled in red ink
Four mauve carbon sheets, two from each top sheet
Variety: the '1d.' error occurs on R. 5/2 from one top sheet

2½d. on wove paper (Nos. 32/34) in sheets of 24 (4×6)
One black top sheet
Three black carbon sheets
One blue carbon sheet
One mauve carbon sheet

6d. on wove paper (Nos. 35/36) in sheets of 24 (4×6)
Two black top sheets
Six black carbon sheets, three from each top sheet
Two blue carbon sheets, one from each top sheet
Varieties: the '2d.' error occurs on R. 5/3 from one top sheet which also showed 'PENCC' on R. 3/2, and 'Rvenne &' on R. 4/1 of the other

* These carbons are described in written records, but their existence has yet to be confirmed by actual examples.

Madagascar

PRICES FOR STAMPS ON COVER TO 1945	
Nos. 1/47	—
Nos. 50/56	*from* × 100
Nos. 57/62	*from* × 30

BRITISH CONSULAR MAIL

After May 1883 mail from the British community at Antananarivo, the capital, was sent by runner to the British Consulate at Tamatave for forwarding via the French Post Office.

In March of the following year the British Vice-Consul at Antananarivo, Mr. W. C. Pickersgill, reorganised this service and issued stamps for use on both local and overseas mail. Such stamps were only gummed at one of the top corners. This was to facilitate their removal from overseas mail where they were replaced by Mauritius stamps (at Port Louis) or by French issues (at the Vice-Consulate) for transmission via Tamatave and Réunion. Local mail usually had the stamps removed also, being marked with a 'PAID' or a Vice-Consular handstamp, although a few covers have survived intact.

CONDITION. Due to the type of paper used, stamps of the British Consular Mail are usually found with slight faults, especially thins and creases. Our prices are for fine examples.

USED STAMPS. Postmarks are not usually found on these issues. Cancellations usually take the form of a manuscript line or cross in crayon, ink or pencil or as five parallel horizontal bars in black, red or violet, approximately 15 mm long. Examples of Nos. 1/3, 5/8 and 11 showing a red diagonal line may have been pre-cancelled for accounting purposes.

1

2

1884 (Mar). Typo British Mission at Antananarivo. Rouletted vertically in colour. No gum, except on one upper corner. With circular consular handstamp reading 'BRITISH VICE-CONSULATE ANTANANARIVO' around Royal arms in black.

(a) Inscr 'LETTER'

No.	Type	Description	Unused	Used
1	1	6d. (½ oz) magenta	£475	£475
		a. Violet handstamp	£2750	
2		1s. (1 oz) magenta	£500	£450
3		1s.6d. (1½ oz) magenta	£500	£500
4		2s. (2 oz) magenta	£850	£900

(b) Inscr 'POSTAL PACKET'

No.	Type	Description	Unused	Used
5	1	1d. (1 oz) magenta	£550	£425
		a. Without handstamp	£10000	£10000
6		2d. (2 oz) magenta	£375	£300
7		3d. (3 oz) magenta	£400	£325
8		4d. (1 oz amended in ms to '4 oz') magenta	£1000	£700
		a. Without manuscript amendment	£6000	£5000
		ab. Violet handstamp	£1800	
		ac. Without handstamp	£9000	£9000

Nos. 1/8 were printed in horizontal strips of four, each strip containing two impressions of the setting. Each strip usually contained two stamps with normal stops after 'B.C.M.' and two with a hollow stop after 'B' (1d., 2d., 3d., 4d., 6d. and 2s.) or after 'M' (1s. and 1s.6d.), although the 2d. and 3d. have also been seen with a hollow stop after 'M' and the 6d. with hollow stops after both 'B' and 'C'.

Several values are known with the handstamp either inverted or double.

1886. Manuscript provisionals.

(a) No. 2 with 'SHILLING' erased and 'PENNY' written above in red ink

No.	Type	Description	Unused	Used
9	1	1d. on 1s. (1 oz) magenta	†	—

(b) No. 2 surch '4½d.' and 'W.C.P.' in red ink with a line through the original value

No.	Type	Description	Unused	Used
10	1	4½d. on 1s. (1 oz) magenta	†	—

1886. As No. 1, but colour changed. Handstamped with circular 'BRITISH VICE-CONSULATE ANTANANARIVO' in black.

No.	Type	Description	Unused	Used
11	1	6d. (½ oz) rose-red	£1400	£800

1886. As No. 8a, but handstamped 'BRITISH CONSULAR MAIL ANTANANARIVO' in black.

No.	Type	Description	Unused	Used
12	1	4d. (1 oz) magenta	£1600	
		a. Violet handstamp	£7500	

1886. Typo British Mission at Antananarivo. 'POSTAGE' and value in words printed in black. Rouletted vertically in colour. No gum, except on one upper corner.

I. 'POSTAGE' 29½ mm long. Stops after 'POSTAGE' and value

(a) Handstamped 'BRITISH VICE-CONSULATE ANTANANARIVO' in black

No.	Type	Description	Unused	Used
14	2	1d. rose	£140	£275
		a. Violet handstamp	£400	
15		1½d. rose	£3000	£1300
		a. Violet handstamp	£1500	£850
16		2d. rose	£200	
		a. Violet handstamp	£400	
17		3d. rose	£4000	£1400
		a. Violet handstamp	£550	£375
18		4½d. rose	£3750	£550
		a. Violet handstamp	£700	£325
19		8d. rose	£5000	£3000
		a. Violet handstamp	£2750	£1800
20		9d. rose	£4750	£2750
		a. Violet handstamp	£1300	

(b) Handstamped 'BRITISH CONSULAR MAIL ANTANANARIVO' in black.

No.	Type	Description	Unused	Used
21	2	1d. rose	£130	
22		1½d. rose	£160	£275
23		2d. rose	£190	
24		3d. rose	£160	£250
		a. Handstamp in red	†	£20000
25		4½d. rose	£180	£225
		a. Handstamp in red	†	£12000
26		8d. rose	£200	
		a. Handstamp in violet	£1700	
27		9d. rose	£225	£350
		a. Without handstamp	£8500	
		b. Handstamp in violet	£450	

II. 'POSTAGE' 29½ mm long. No stops after 'POSTAGE' or value.

(a) Handstamped 'BRITISH VICE-CONSULATE ANTANANARIVO' in violet

No.	Type	Description	Unused	Used
28	2	1d. rose	£1300	
29		1½d. rose	£3000	
30		3d. rose	£1300	
31		4½d. rose	£2250	
32		6d. rose	£1700	

(b) Handstamped 'BRITISH CONSULAR MAIL ANTANANARIVO' in black

No.	Type	Description	Unused	Used
33	2	1d. rose	£130	£225
		a. Without handstamp	£4750	
		b. Violet handstamp	£170	
34		1½d. rose	£140	£200
		a. Without handstamp	£5000	
		b. Violet handstamp	£275	
35		2d. rose	£150	£200
		b. Violet handstamp	£325	
36		3d. rose	£160	£225
		a. Without handstamp	£8000	
		b. Violet handstamp	£200	
37		4½d. rose	£150	£200
		a. Without handstamp	£9000	
		b. Violet handstamp	£225	
38		6d. rose	£160	£275
		a. Without handstamp	£9500	
		b. Violet handstamp	£500	

III. 'POSTAGE' 24½ mm long. No stop after 'POSTAGE', but stop after value

(a) Handstamped 'BRITISH VICE-CONSULATE ANTANANARIVO' in violet

No.	Type	Description	Unused	Used
39	2	4d. rose	£500	
40		8d. rose	£700	
40*a*		1s. rose	£22000	
41		1s.6d. rose	£12000	
42		2s. rose	£6500	
		a. Handstamp in black	£18000	

(b) Handstamped 'BRITISH CONSULAR MAIL ANTANANARIVO' in black

No.	Type	Description	Unused	Used
43	2	4d. rose	£375	
		a. Without handstamp	£6000	
		b. Violet handstamp	£450	
44		8d. rose	£2250	
		a. Without handstamp	£6000	
		b. Violet handstamp	£1400	
45		1s. rose	£600	
		a. Without handstamp	£8500	
		b. Violet handstamp	£1700	
46		1s.6d. rose	£750	
		a. Without handstamp	£7500	
		b. Violet handstamp	£1700	
47		2s. rose	£750	
		a. Without handstamp	£8500	
		b. Violet handstamp	£1700	

Nos. 14/47 were also printed in horizontal strips of four.

The stamps of the British Consular Mail were suppressed in 1887, but the postal service continued with the charges paid in cash.

BRITISH INLAND MAIL

In January 1895 the Malagasy government agreed that a syndicate of British merchants at Antananarivo, including the Vice-Consul, should operate an inland postal service during the war with France. Mail was sent by runner to the port of Vatomandry and forwarded via Durban where Natal stamps were added.

Nos. 50/62 were cancelled with dated circular postmarks inscribed 'BRITISH MAIL'.

4

5 Malagasy Runners

(Typeset London Missionary Society Press, Antananarivo)

1895 (1 Jan). Rouletted in black.

(a) Thick laid paper

No.	Type	Description	Unused	Used
50	4	4d. black	65·00	22·00
		a. 'FUOR' for 'FOUR' (R. 3/2)	—	£1200

(b) In black on coloured wove paper

No.	Type	Description	Unused	Used
51	4	1d. *blue-grey*	50·00	13·00
52		6d. *pale yellow*	50·00	13·00
53		8d. *salmon*	50·00	13·00
54		1s. *fawn*	60·00	13·00
55		2s. *bright rose*	75·00	30·00
		a. Italic '2' at left (R. 1/2)	£150	65·00
56		4s. *grey*	75·00	13·00
50/56 *Set of 7*			£375	£100

There are six types of each value, printed in blocks of six (2×3) separated by gutters, four times on each sheet; the upper and lower blocks being *tête-bêche*.

Nos. 51/56 have been reported on paper showing a sheet watermark in four lines, including a date and the words 'Tinted', 'Tul...' and 'Austria'.

(Typo John Haddon & Co, London)

1895 (Mar). The inscription in the lower label varies for each value. P 12.

No.	Type	Description	Unused	Used
57	5	2d. blue	14·00	60·00
		a. Imperf between (horiz pair)	£450	
		b. Imperf between (vert pair)	£750	
58		4d. rose	14·00	60·00
		a. Imperf between (horiz pair)	£250	
		b. Imperf between (vert pair)	£300	
		c. Imperf vert (horiz pair)	£275	
59		6d. green	14·00	75·00
		a. Imperf between (horiz pair)	£950	
60		1s. slate-blue	14·00	£120
		a. Imperf between (horiz pair)	£550	
61		2s. chocolate	35·00	£160
		a. Imperf between (horiz pair)	£700	
		b. Imperf between (vert pair)	£1000	
62		4s. bright purple	60·00	£225
		a. Imperf between (horiz pair)	£2250	
57/62 *Set of 6*			£140	£650

This post was suppressed when the French entered Antananarivo on 30 September 1895.

Malawi

INDEPENDENT

44 Dr. H. Banda (Prime Minister) and Independence Monument

(Des M. Goaman. Photo Harrison)

1964 (6 July). Independence. T **44** and similar horiz designs. P 14½.

No.	Type	Description	Unused	Used
211		3d. yellow-olive and deep sepia	10	10
212		6d. red, gold, blue, carmine and lake	10	10
213		1s.3d. red, green, black and bluish violet	45	10
214		2s.6d. multicoloured	45	1·25
		a. Blue omitted	£2750	
211/214 *Set of 4*			1·00	1·40

Designs: 3d. T **44**; 6d. Banda and rising sun; 1s.3d. Banda and Malawi flag; 2s.6d. Banda and Malawi Coat of Arms.

Six examples of No. 214a are known from the top horizontal row of an otherwise normal sheet.

48 Tung Tree

49 Christmas Star and Globe

(Des V. Whiteley. Photo Harrison)

1964 (6 July)–**65**. As Nos. 199/210 of Nyasaland, but inscr 'MALAWI' and T **48** (9d.). No wmk. P 14½.

No.	Type	Description	Unused	Used
215		½d. reddish violet	10	60
216		1d. black and green	10	10
217		2d. light red-brown	10	10
218		3d. red-brown, yellow-green and bistre-brown	15	10
219		4d. black and orange-yellow	85	15
220		6d. bluish violet, yellow-green and light blue	75	10
221		9d. bistre-brown, green and yellow	30	15
222		1s. brown, turquoise-blue and pale yellow	25	10
223		1s.3d. bronze-green and chestnut	50	60
224		2s.6d. brown and blue	1·10	1·00
225		5s. blue, green, yellow and sepia	65	3·25
225*a*		5s. blue, green, yellow and sepia (1.6.65)	14·00	1·00
226		10s. green, orange-brown and black	1·50	2·75
227		£1 deep reddish purple and yellow	4·00	5·50
215/227 *Set of 14*			22·00	13·00

No. 225*a* is inscribed 'LAKE MALAWI' instead of 'LAKE NYASA'.

See also Nos. 252/262.

(Des V. Whiteley. Photo Harrison)

1964 (1 Dec). Christmas. P 14½.

No.	Type	Description	Unused	Used
228	**49**	3d. blue-green and gold	10	10
		a. Gold (star) omitted	£650	
229		6d. magenta and gold	10	10
230		1s.3d. reddish violet and gold	10	10
231		2s.6d. blue and gold	20	50
228/231 *Set of 4*			45	70
MS231*a*		83×126 mm. Nos. 228/231. Imperf	1·00	1·75

No. 228a comes from a sheet on which 41 examples had the gold colour omitted due to a paper fold.

50 Coins

1/6

(**51**)

(Des V. Whiteley. Photo Enschedé)

1965 (1 Mar). Malawi's First Coinage. Coins in black and silver. P 13½.

No.	Type	Description	Unused	Used
232	**50**	3d. green	10	10
233		9d. magenta	20	10
		a. Silver omitted	†	—
234		1s.6d. purple	25	10
235		3s. blue	35	1·10
232/235 *Set of 4*			80	1·25
MS235*a*		126×104 mm. Nos. 232/235. Imperf	1·75	1·75

1965 (14 June). Nos. 223/224 surch as T **51**.

No.	Type	Description	Unused	Used
236		1s.6d. on 1s.3d. bronze-green and chestnut	10	10
237		3s. on 2s.6d. brown and blue	20	20

On No. 237 '3/-' is placed below the bars.

52 Chilembwe leading Rebels

(Des M. Goaman. Photo Harrison)

1965 (20 Aug). 50th Anniversary of 1915 Rising. P 14×14½.

No.	Type	Description	Unused	Used
238	**52**	3d. violet and light olive-green	10	10
239		9d. olive-brown and red-orange	10	10
240		1s.6d. red-brown and grey-blue	15	10
241		3s. turquoise-green and slate-blue	20	25
238/241 *Set of 4*			40	60
MS241*a*		127×83 mm. Nos. 238/241	5·00	6·00

53 'Learning and Scholarship'

(Des H. E. Baxter. Photo Harrison)

1965 (6 Oct). Opening of Malawi University. P 14½.

No.	Type	Description	Unused	Used
242	**53**	3d. black and emerald	10	10
243		9d. black and magenta	10	10
244		1s.6d. black and reddish violet	10	10
245		3s. black and blue	15	40
242/245 *Set of 4*			30	50
MS246		127×84 mm. Nos. 242/245	2·50	2·50

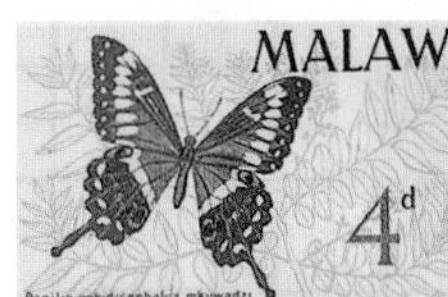

54 *Papilio ophidicephalus*

(Des V. Whiteley. Photo Enschedé)

1966 (15 Feb). Malawi Butterflies. T **54** and similar horiz designs. Multicoloured. P 13½.

No.	Type	Description	Unused	Used
247		4d. Type **54**	80	10
248		9d. *Papilio desmondi (magdae)*	1·00	10
249		1s.6d. *Epamera handmani*	1·50	30
250		3s. *Amauris crawshayi*	2·25	6·00
247/250 *Set of 4*			5·00	6·00
MS251		130×100 mm. Nos. 247/250	17·00	10·00

55 Cockerels

56 Burley Tobacco

£2
CYRESTIS CAMILLUS SUBLINEATUS
MALAWI

57 *Cyrestis camillus* (butterfly)

(New values des V. Whiteley (1s.6d.), M. Goaman (£2). Photo Harrison)

1966–67. As Nos. 215 etc. but W **55** (sideways on ½d., 2d.), and new values and designs (1s.6d., £2). P 14½.

No.	Type	Description	Unused	Used
252	–	½d. reddish violet (1.4.66)	10	10
253	–	1d. black and green (1.4.66)	15	10
254	–	2d. light red-brown (4.6.66)*	15	10
255	–	3d. red-brown, yellow-green and bistre-brown (4.3.67)*	20	35
256	–	6d. bluish violet, yellow-green and light blue (2.7.66)*	3·00	1·00
257	**48**	9d. bistre-brown, green and yellow (5.12.66)*	3·75	10
258	–	1s. brown, turquoise-blue and pale yellow (1.4.66)	25	10
259	**56**	1s.6d. chocolate and yellow-green (15.11.66)	55	10
260	–	5s. blue, green, yellow and sepia (6.10.66)*	8·50	5·50
261	–	10s. green, orange-brown and black (6.10.66)*	23·00	27·00
262	**57**	£2 black, orange-yellow, pale yellow and slate-violet (7.9.66)	27·00	24·00
252/262 *Set of 11*			55·00	50·00

* These are local dates of issue. The Crown Agents, in London, did not distribute these printings until some time later.

No. 260 is inscribed 'LAKE MALAWI'.

The 2d. exists with both PVA gum and gum arabic.

58 British Central Africa 6d. Stamp of 1891

4d REPUBLIC OF
6 JULY 1966
MALAWI 4d

59 President Banda

(Des V. Whiteley. Photo Harrison)

1966 (4 May–10 June). 75th Anniversary of Postal Services. W **55**. P 14½.

No.	Type	Description	Unused	Used
263	**58**	4d. grey-blue and yellow-green	10	10
264		9d. grey-blue and claret	15	10
265		1s.6d. grey-blue and reddish lilac	20	10
266		3s. grey-blue and new blue	30	70
263/266 *Set of 4*			60	80
MS267		83×127 mm. Nos. 263/266 (10.6)	4·50	3·25

REPUBLIC

(Des M. Goaman. Photo Harrison)

1966 (6 July). Republic Day. W **55**. P 14×14½.

No.	Type	Description	Unused	Used
268	**59**	4d. brown, silver and emerald	10	10
269		9d. brown, silver and magenta	10	10
270		1s.6d. brown, silver and violet	15	10
271		3s. brown, silver and blue	25	15
268/271 *Set of 4*			50	30
MS272		83×127 mm. Nos. 268/271	1·60	3·75

60 Bethlehem

(Des and photo Harrison)

1966 (12 Oct). Christmas. W **55**. P 14½.

No.	Type	Description	Unused	Used
273	**60**	4d. myrtle-green and gold	10	10
274		9d. brown-purple and gold	10	10
275		1s.6d. orange-red and gold	15	10
276		3s. blue and gold	40	80
273/276 *Set of 4*			65	1·00

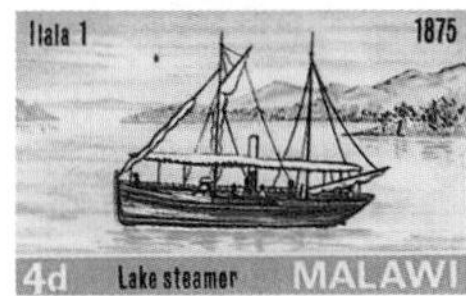

61 *Ilala I*

(Des Mrs. H. Breggar. Photo Harrison)

1967 (4 Jan). Lake Malawi Steamers. T **61** and similar horiz designs. W **55**. P 14½.

No.	Type	Description	Unused	Used
277		4d. black, yellow and bright green	25	10
		a. Yellow omitted	†	£850
278		9d. black, yellow and magenta	30	10
279		1s.6d. black, red and violet	40	20
280		3s. black, red and bright blue	60	1·75
277/280 *Set of 4*			1·40	1·90

Designs: 4d. T **61**; 9d. *Dove*; 1s.6d. *Chauncy Maples I* (wrongly inscr 'Chauncey'); 3s. *Gwendolen*.

No. 277*a* occurs on first day covers from Blantyre.

62 Golden Mbuna (female)

(Des R. Granger Barrett. Photo Enschedé)

1967 (3 May). Lake Malawi Cichlids. T **62** and similar horiz designs. Multicoloured. W **55** (sideways). P 12½×12.

No.	Type	Description	Unused	Used
281		4d. Type **62**	25	10
282		9d. Scraper-mouthed Mbuna	40	10
283		1s.6d. Zebra Mbuna	50	25
		a. Imperf (pair)	£400	
284		3s. Orange Mbuna	80	2·00
		a. Imperf (pair)	£400	
281/284 *Set of 4*			1·75	2·25

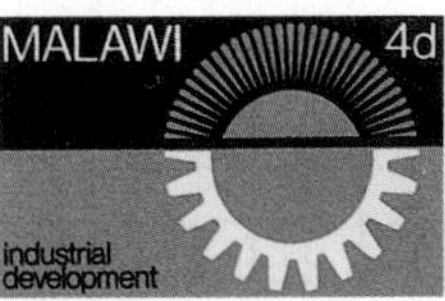

63 Rising Sun and Gearwheel

(Des Jennifer Toombs. Litho D.L.R.)

1967 (5 July). Industrial Development. P 13½×13.

No.	Type	Description	Unused	Used
285	**63**	4d. black and emerald	10	10

286	9d. black and carmine	10	10
287	1s.6d. black and reddish violet	10	10
288	3s. black and bright blue	15	30
285/288 *Set of 4*		30	50
MS289 134×108 mm. Nos. 285/288		1·25	2·75

64 Mary and Joseph beside Crib

(Des Jennifer Toombs. Photo Harrison)

1967 (21 Nov–1 Dec). Christmas. W **55**. P 14×14½.

290	**64**	4d. royal blue and turquoise-green	10	10
291		9d. royal blue and light red	10	10
292		1s.6d. royal blue and yellow	10	10
293		3s. royal blue and new blue	15	30
290/293 *Set of 4*			30	50
MS294 114×100 mm. Nos. 290/293. Wmk sideways. P 14×13½ (1.12)			1·00	3·00

65 *Calotropis procera*

(Des G. Drummond. Litho D.L.R.)

1968 (24 Apr). Wild Flowers. T **65** and similar horiz designs. Multicoloured. W **55** (sideways). P 13½×13.

295	4d. Type **65**	15	10
296	9d. *Borreria dibrachiata*	15	10
297	1s.6d. *Hibiscus rhodanthus*	15	10
298	3s. *Bidens pinnatipartita*	20	95
295/298 *Set of 4*		60	1·10
MS299 135×91 mm. Nos. 295/298		1·75	4·00

66 Bagnall Steam Locomotive No. 1, *Thistle*

(Des R. Granger Barrett. Photo Harrison)

1968 (24 July). Malawi Locomotives. T **66** and similar horiz designs. W **55**. P 14×14½.

300	4d. grey-green, slate-blue and red	20	10
301	9d. red, slate-blue and myrtle-green	25	15
302	1s.6d. multicoloured	35	30
303	3s. multicoloured	55	3·00
300/303 *Set of 4*		1·25	3·00
MS304 120×88 mm. Nos. 300/303. P 14½		1·50	6·00

Designs: 4d. T **66**; 9d. Class G steam locomotive No. 49; 1s.6d. Class Zambesi diesel locomotive No. 202; 3s. Diesel railcar No. DR1.

67 *The Nativity* (Piero della Francesca)

(Des and photo Harrison)

1968 (6 Nov). Christmas. Paintings. T **67** and similar horiz designs. Multicoloured. W **55** (sideways on 4d.). P 14×14½.

305	4d. Type **67**	10	10
306	9d. *The Adoration of the Shepherds* (Murillo)	10	10
307	1s.6d. *The Adoration of the Shepherds* (Reni)	10	10
308	3s. *Nativity with God the Father and Holy Ghost* (Pittoni)	15	15
305/308 *Set of 4*		30	30
MS309 115×101 mm. Nos. 305/308. P 14×13½		35	1·60

68 Scarlet-chested Sunbird

69 Nyasa Lovebird

70 Carmine Bee-eater

(Des V. Whiteley. Photo Harrison)

1968 (13 Nov). Birds. T **68/70** and similar designs. Multicoloured. W **55** (sideways on 1d. to 4d. and 3s. to £1). P 14½.

310	1d. Type **68**	15	65
311	2d. Violet Starling	30	40
312	3d. White-browed Robin Chat	30	10
313	4d. Red-billed Fire Finch	50	60
	a. Red omitted	†	—
314	6d. Type **69**	2·50	15
315	9d. Yellow-rumped Bishop	2·50	60
316	1s. Type **70**	1·00	15
317	1s.6d. Grey-headed Bush Shrike	2·50	7·00
318	2s. Paradise Whydah	2·50	7·00
319	3s. African Paradise Flycatcher	7·00	3·25
320	5s. Bateleur	2·50	4·00
321	10s. Saddle-bill Stork	2·50	7·00
322	£1 Purple Heron	6·00	16·00
323	£2 Knysna Turaco ('Livingstone's Loerie')	42·00	50·00
310/323 *Set of 14*		60·00	85·00

Sizes:—2d. to 4d. as T **68**; 9d. as T **69**; 1s.6d., 2s, £2 as T **70**; 3s. to £1 as T **70** but vertical.

No. 310 exists in coils, constructed from normal sheets.

An example of No. 313a is known used on local cover from Limbe in September 1970.

71 ILO Emblem

(Des G. Drummond. Photo, emblem die-stamped Harrison)

1969 (5 Feb). 50th Anniversary of the International Labour Organisation. W **55** (sideways on No. **MS**328). P 14.

324	**71**	4d. gold and myrtle-green	10	10
325		9d. gold and chocolate	10	10
326		1s.6d. gold and blackish brown	10	10
327		3s. gold and indigo	15	15
324/327 *Set of 4*			30	30
MS328 127×89 mm. Nos. 324/327			1·00	4·75

72 White-fringed Ground Orchid

73 African Development Bank Emblem

(Des J.W. Litho B.W.)

1969 (9 July). Orchids of Malawi. T **72** and similar horiz designs. Multicoloured. W **55**. P 13½×13.

329	4d. Type **72**	15	10
330	9d. Red Ground Orchid	20	10
331	1s.6d. Leopard Tree Orchid	30	20
332	3s. Blue Ground Orchid	60	2·00
329/332 *Set of 4*		1·10	2·00
MS333 118×86 mm. Nos. 329/332		1·10	4·00

(Des G. Vasarhelyi. Litho D.L.R.)

1969 (10 Sept). Fifth Anniversary of African Development Bank. W **55**. P 14.

334	**73**	4d. yellow, yellow-ochre and chocolate	10	10
335		9d. yellow, yellow-ochre and myrtle-green	10	10
336		1s.6d. yellow, yellow-ochre and blackish brown	10	10
337		3s. yellow, yellow-ochre and indigo	15	15
334/337 *Set of 4*			30	30
MS338 102×137 mm. Nos. 334/337			50	1·25

74 Dove over Bethlehem

75 *Zonocerus elegans* (Grasshopper)

(Des Jennifer Toombs. Photo Harrison)

1969 (5 Nov). Christmas. W **55**. P 14½×14.

339	**74**	2d. black and olive-yellow	10	10
340		4d. black and deep turquoise	10	10
341		9d. black and scarlet	10	10
342		1s.6d. black and deep bluish violet	10	10
343		3s. black and ultramarine	15	15
339/343 *Set of 5*			30	30
MS344 130×71 mm. Nos. 339/343			1·00	2·25
		a. Ultramarine (background of 3s.) omitted	£4000	

(Des V. Whiteley. Litho Format)

1970 (4 Feb). Insects of Malawi. T **75** and similar vert designs. Multicoloured. W **55**. P 14.

345	4d. Type **75**	15	10
346	9d. *Mylabris dicincta* (Beetle)	15	10
347	1s.6d. *Henosepilachna elaterii* (Ladybird)	20	15
348	3s. *Sphodromantis speculabunda* (Mantid)	35	1·60
345/348 *Set of 4*		75	1·75
MS349 86×137 mm. Nos. 345/348		1·25	3·25

Rand Easter Show
1970

(76)

1970 (18 Mar). Rand Easter Show. No. 317 optd with T **76**.

350	1s.6d. multicoloured	50	2·25

77 Runner

(Des J. Cooter. Litho B.W.)

1970 (3 June). Ninth British Commonwealth Games, Edinburgh. W **55**. P 13.

351	**77**	4d. royal blue and blue-green	10	10
352		9d. royal blue and carmine	10	10
353		1s.6d. royal blue and dull yellow	10	10
354		3s. royal blue and new blue	15	15
351/354 *Set of 4*			30	30
MS355 146×96 mm. Nos. 351/354			65	1·00

(New Currency, 100 tambalas = 1 kwacha)

10t

(78)

79 *Aegocera trimeni*

1970 (2 Sept). Decimal Currency. Nos. 316 and 318 surch as T **78**.

356	10t. on 1s. multicoloured	3·00	10
	a. Surch double	†	—
357	20t. on 2s. multicoloured	3·00	4·50

(Des R. Granger Barrett. Litho B.W.)

1970 (30 Sept). Moths. T **79** and similar horiz designs. Multicoloured. W **55**. P 11×11½.

358	4d. Type **79**	20	10
359	9d. *Faidherbia bauhiniae*	30	10
360	1s.6d. *Parasa karschi*	50	20
361	3s. *Teracotona euprepia*	1·25	3·50
358/361 *Set of 4*		2·00	3·50
MS362 112×92 mm. Nos. 358/361		3·75	6·50

80 Mother and Child

(Des Brother W. Meyer. Litho J.W.)

1970 (4 Nov). Christmas. W **55** (sideways). P 14.

363	**80**	2d. black and light yellow	10	10
364		4d. black and emerald	10	10
365		9d. black and orange-red	10	10
366		1s.6d. black and light purple	10	10
367		3s. black and blue	15	15
363/367 *Set of 5*			30	30
MS368 166×100 mm. Nos. 363/367			1·00	3·00

POSTAGE DUE STAMPS

REPUBLIC OF MALAWI
POSTAGE DUE
1D

D 2

(Litho Bradbury Wilkinson)

1967 (1 Sept). W **55**. P 11½.

D6	D **2**	1d. carmine	15	4·50
D7		2d. sepia	20	4·50
D8		4d. reddish violet	35	4·75
D9		6d. blue	25	5·00
D10		8d. emerald	60	5·50
D11		1s. black	70	6·00
D6/D11 *Set of 6*			2·00	27·00

Malaysia

The Federation of Malaya was formed on 1 February 1948 by the former Straits Settlements of Malacca and Penang, the four Federated Malay States and the five Unfederated States. It did not, however, issue any stamps until it became an independent member of the Commonwealth in 1957.

The philatelic history of the component parts of the federation is most complex.

The method adopted is to show the general issues for the area first, before dealing with the issues for the individual States. The section is divided as follows:

I. STRAITS SETTLEMENTS
II. FEDERATED MALAY STATES
III. MALAYAN POSTAL UNION
IV. MALAYA (BRITISH MILITARY ADMINISTRATION)
V. MALAYAN FEDERATION
VI. MALAYSIA
VII. MALAYAN STATES—Johore, Kedah, Kelantan, Malacca, Negri Sembilan (with Sungei Ujong), Pahang, Penang, Perak, Perlis, Sabah, Selangor, Trengganu
VIII. JAPANESE OCCUPATION OF MALAYA 1942–1945
IX. THAI OCCUPATION OF MALAYA 1943–1945

I. STRAITS SETTLEMENTS

The three original Settlements, Malacca, Penang (with Province Wellesley) and Singapore (with Christmas Island), were formed into a Crown Colony on 1 April 1867. The Cocos (Keeling) Islands were transferred to Straits Settlements on 7 February 1886. Labuan was attached to the Colony in 1896, becoming the fourth Settlement in 1906, but was transferred to North Borneo in 1946.

The first known prestamp cover with postal markings from Penang (Prince of Wales Island) is dated March 1806 and from Malacca, under British civil administration, February 1841. The civil post office at Singapore opened on 1 February 1823.

The stamps of India were used at all three post offices from late in 1854 until the Straits Settlements became a separate colony on 1 September 1867.

The Indian stamps were initially cancelled by dumb obliterators and their use in the Straits Settlements can only be identified from complete covers. In 1856 cancellations of the standard Indian octagonal type were issued, numbered 'B 109' for Malacca, 'B 147' for Penang and 'B 172' for Singapore.

CURRENCY. Before 1867 official accounts of the East India Company administration for the Straits Settlements were kept in rupees, although the vast majority of commercial transactions used Spanish American silver dollars, supplies of which reached Malaya via the Philippines.

This confusing situation was rapidly amended when the Straits Settlements became a Crown Colony on 1 April 1867 and Spanish American dollars were declared to be the only legal currency. In 1874 American trade dollars and Japanese yen were also accepted, but in 1890 recognition of the Spanish American dollars was restricted to those from the Mexican mints. A shortage of silver coinage led to the introduction of silver British trade dollars in 1895 which also circulated in Hong Kong and Labuan.

Dollar banknotes first appeared in 1899, but Mexican dollars were not finally replaced until the issue of silver Straits Settlements dollars in 1903, the gold value of which was set at 2s.4d. in January 1906.

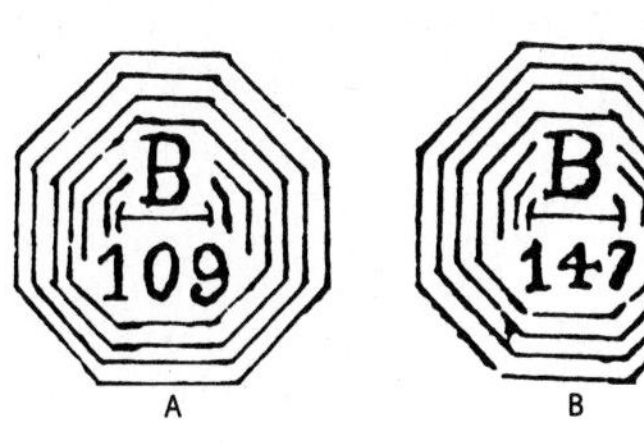

A B

C

The Penang and Singapore octagonals were replaced by a duplex type, consisting of a double-ringed datestamp and a diamond-shaped obliterator containing the office number, in 1863 and 1865 respectively.

D

E

PRICES. Catalogue prices in this section are for stamps with clearly legible, if partial, examples of the postmarks.

EAST INDIA COMPANY ADMINISTRATION

MALACCA

Stamps of INDIA cancelled with Type A.

1854. (Nos. 2/34).

Z1	½a. blue (Die I)	£3500
Z2	1a. red (Die I)	£3750
Z3	1a. dull red (Die II)	£4000
Z4	2a. green	£4000
Z4*a*	4a. blue and pale red (Head Die I) (*cut-to-shape*)	£5000
Z5	4a. blue and red (Head Die II) (*cut-to-shape*)	£5000
Z5*a*	4a. blue and red (Head Die III) (*cut-to-shape*)	£5000

1855. (Nos. 35/36).

Z6	8a. carmine (Die I)/*blue glazed*	£1000

1856–64. (Nos. 37/49).

Z7	½a. pale blue (Die I)	£700
Z8	1a. brown	£550
Z8*a*	2a. dull pink	£750
Z9	2a. yellow-buff	£600
Z10	2a. yellow	£650
Z10*a*	4a. black	£1000
Z11	4a. green	£950
Z12	8a. carmine (Die I)	£700

1860. (Nos. 51/53).

Z13	8p. purple/*bluish*	£1700
Z14	8p. purple/*white*	£900

1865. (Nos. 54/65).

Z15	4a. green	£1000

PENANG

Stamps of INDIA cancelled with Type B.

1854. (Nos. 2/34).

Z20	½a. blue (Die I)	£1100
Z21	1a. red (Die I)	£450
Z21*a*	1a. red (Die II)	£4000
Z22	2a. green	£550
Z23	4a. blue and pale red (Head Die I)	£4250
Z24	4a. blue and red (Head Die II)	£4250
Z25	4a. blue and red (Head Die III)	£2750

1855. (Nos. 35/36).

Z26	4a. black/*blue glazed*	£160
Z27	8a. carmine (Die I)/*blue glazed*	£150
	a. Bisected (4a.) (1860) (*on cover*)	£130000

1856–64. (Nos. 37/49).

Z28	½a. pale blue (Die I)	£160
Z29	1a. brown	90·00
Z30	2a. dull pink	£140
Z31	2a. yellow-buff	£130
Z32	2a. yellow	£130
Z33	2a. orange	£130
Z34	4a. black	90·00
Z35	8a. carmine (Die I)	£120

1860. (Nos. 51/53).

Z36	8p. purple/*white*	£325

Stamps of INDIA cancelled with Type D.

1854. (Nos. 2/34).

Z38	1a. red (Die I)	£5500

1856–64. (Nos. 37/49).

Z39	½a. pale blue (Die I)	£425
Z40	1a. brown	£100
Z40*a*	2a. yellow-buff	£150
Z41	2a. yellow	£120
Z42	4a. black	£110
Z43	4a. green	£350
Z44	8a. carmine (Die I)	£120

1860. (Nos. 51/53).

Z45	8p. purple/*white*	£180
Z46	8p. mauve	£200

1865. (Nos. 54/65).

Z47	8p. purple	
Z48	1a. deep brown	£110
Z49	2a. yellow	£120
Z50	4a. green	£375
Z51	8a. carmine (Die I)	

1866–67. (Nos. 69/72).

Z52	4a. green (Die 1)	£450

OFFICIAL STAMP

1866–67. (No. O2).

Z54	½a. pale blue	£1000

SINGAPORE

Stamps of INDIA cancelled with Type C.

1854. (Nos. 2/34).

Z60	½a. blue (Die I)	£450
Z61	1a. red (Die I)	£350
Z62	1a. dull red (Die II)	£325
Z63	1a. red (Die III)	£3500
Z64	2a. green	£150
	a. Bisected (1a.) (1857) (*on cover*)	£250000
Z65	4a. blue and pale red (Head Die I)	£3500
Z66	4a. blue and red (Head Die II)	£3250
Z67	4a. blue and red (Head Die III)	£1800

1855. (Nos. 35/36).

Z68	4a. black/*blue glazed*	60·00
	a. Bisected (2a.) (1859) (*on cover*)	£21000
Z69	8a. carmine/*blue glazed*	60·00
	a. Bisected (4a.) (1859) (*on cover*)	£130000

1856–66. (Nos. 37/49).

Z70	½a. pale blue (Die I)	80·00
Z71	1a. brown	38·00
	a. Bisected (½a.) (1859) (*on cover*)	£130000
Z72	2a. dull pink	75·00
Z73	2a. yellow-buff	65·00
Z74	2a. yellow	70·00
Z75	2a. orange	80·00
Z76	4a. black	40·00
	a. Bisected (2a.) (1859) (*on cover*)	£65000
Z77	4a. green	£225
Z78	8a. carmine (Die I)	60·00
	a. Bisected (4a.) (1866) (*on cover*)	£130000

1860–61. (Nos. 51/53).

Z79	8p. purple/*bluish*	£950
Z80	8p. purple/*white*	£110
	a. Bisected diagonally (4p.) (1861) (*on cover*)	£130000
Z81	8p. mauve	£130

1865. (Nos. 54/65).

Z82	½a. blue (Die I)	90·00
Z83	8p. purple	£275
Z84	1a. deep brown	75·00
Z85	2a. yellow	80·00
Z86	2a. orange	80·00
Z87	4a. green	£180
Z88	8a. carmine (Die I)	£325

1866–67. (Nos. 69/72).

Z89	4a. green (Die I)	£250
Z90	6a.8p. slate	£700

Stamps of INDIA cancelled with Type E.

1856–64. (Nos. 37/49).

Z100	1a. brown	£475
Z101	2a. yellow	£650
Z102	4a. black	£650
Z103	8a. carmine (Die I)	£650

1860. (Nos. 51/53).

Z104	8p. purple/*white*	£700

1865. (Nos. 54/65).

Z105	2a. yellow	£600
Z106	2a. orange	£600
Z107	4a. green	£750

OFFICIAL STAMPS

Stamps of INDIA cancelled with Type C.

1866–67. (Nos. O6/O14).

Z91	½a. pale blue	£950
Z92	2a. yellow	£1300

PRICES FOR STAMPS ON COVER TO 1945

Nos. 1/9	*from* × 20
No. 10	—
Nos. 11/19	*from* × 12
Nos. 20/21	*from* × 30
Nos. 22/39	*from* × 15
Nos. 41/46	*from* × 25
No. 47	—
Nos. 48/49	*from* × 12
Nos. 50/53	*from* × 20
Nos. 54/62	*from* × 30
Nos. 63/71	*from* × 15
No. 72	—
Nos. 73/80	*from* × 30
Nos. 82/87	*from* × 20
Nos. 88/94	*from* × 15
Nos. 95/105	*from* × 8
Nos. 106/109	*from* × 20
Nos. 110/121	*from* × 6
No. 122	—
Nos. 123/126	*from* × 5
Nos. 127/138	*from* × 4
Nos. 139/140	—
Nos. 141/151	*from* × 15
Nos. 152/167	*from* × 4
Nos. 168/169	—
Nos. 193/212	*from* × 3
Nos. 213/215	—
Nos. 216/217	*from* × 10
Nos. 218/240*a*	*from* × 3
Nos. 240*b*/240*d*	—
Nos. 241/255	*from* × 15
Nos. 256/259	*from* × 4
Nos. 260/298	*from* × 3
Nos. D1/D6	*from* × 20
No. F1	—

PRINTERS. All Straits Settlements issues were printed in typography by De La Rue & Co, Ltd, London, *unless otherwise stated*. All surcharges were applied by the Government Printer, Singapore, *unless otherwise stated.*

USED PRICES. The prices quoted for Nos. 1/9 are for fine used examples. Those showing parts of commercial 'chops' are worth less.

CROWN COLONY

(Currency. 100 cents = 1 Spanish American dollar)

THREE HALF CENTS (1) | 32 CENTS (2)

1867 (1 Sept). Nos. 54, 59, 61, 69 and 73 of India surch as Types **1** or **2** (24c., 32c.) by De La Rue. W **13** (Elephant's head) of India. P 14.

No.	Description	Unused	Used
1	1½c. on ½a. blue (Die I) (R.)	£140	£200
2	2c. on 1a. deep brown (R.)	£225	£100
3	3c. on 1a. deep brown (B.)	£200	95·00
4	4c. on 1a. deep brown (Bk.)	£350	£275
5	6c. on 2a. yellow (P.)	£950	£250
6	8c. on 2a. yellow (G.)	£375	42·00
7	12c. on 4a. green (R.)	£1600	£325
	a. Surch double	£4000	
8	24c. on 8a. rose (Die II) (B.)	£800	£100
9	32c. on 2a. yellow (Bk.)	£550	£110

The 32c. was re-issued for postal use in 1884.

No. 7a. is only known unused.

1869. (?) No. 1 with 'THREE HALF' deleted and '2' written above, in black manuscript.

No.	Description	Unused	Used
10	2 on 1½c. on ½a. blue	£20000	£6500

This stamp has been known from very early days and was apparently used at Penang, but nothing is known of its history.

5

6

7

8

9

6c. 'Slug' flaw (R. 2/4 of one pane)

1867 (Dec)–**72**. Ornaments in corners differ for each value. Wmk Crown CC. P 14.

No.	Type	Description	Unused	Used
11	5	2c. brown (6.68)	65·00	9·00
		a. Yellow-brown	70·00	9·00
		b. Deep brown	£160	19·00
		w. Wmk inverted	£650	£225
12		4c. rose (7.68)	£100	16·00
		a. Deep rose	£130	18·00
		w. Wmk inverted	£350	
13		6c. dull lilac (1.68)	£150	23·00
		a. Bright lilac	£180	23·00
		b. 'Slug' flaw	—	£325
		w. Wmk inverted	†	£350
		y. Wmk inverted and reversed	†	£450
14	6	8c. orange-yellow	£275	19·00
		a. Orange	£275	19·00
		w. Wmk inverted	£700	£200
15		12c. blue	£225	9·00
		a. Ultramarine	£250	11·00
		w. Wmk inverted	£700	
16	7	24c. blue-green	£200	8·00
		a. Yellow-green	£350	21·00
		w. Wmk inverted	†	£425
17	8	30c. claret (12.72)	£425	18·00
		w. Wmk inverted	†	£650
18	9	32c. pale red	£650	70·00
		w. Wmk inverted	†	£500
19		96c. grey	£400	55·00
		a. Perf 12½ (6.71)	£2500	£225

Five Cents. (10) | Seven Cents. (11)

1879 (May). Nos. 14*a* and 18 surch with Types **10** and **11**.

No.	Type	Description	Unused	Used
20	6	5c. on 8c. orange	£150	£190
		a. No stop after 'Cents'	£1100	£1300
		b. 'F i' spaced	£1200	£1400
21	9	7c. on 32c. pale red	£180	£200
		a. No stop after 'Cents'	£1800	£2500

The no stop variety occurred once in the setting.

10 cents. (12)

10 (*a*) 10 (*b*) 10 (*c*) 10 (*d*)

10 (*e*) 10 (*f*) 10 (*g*) 10 (*h*)

10 (*i*) 10 (*j*) 10 (*jj*) 10 (*k*) 10 (*l*)

(*a*) '1' thin curved serif and thin foot, '0' narrow.
(*b*) '1' thick curved serif and thick foot: '0' broad. Both numerals heavy.
(*c*) '1' as (*a*); '0' as (*b*).
(*d*) '1' as (*a*) but thicker; '0' as (*a*).
(*e*) As (*a*) but sides of '0' thicker.
(*f*) '1' as (*d*); '0' as (*e*).
(*g*) As (*a*) but '0' narrower.
(*h*) '1' thin, curved serif and thick foot; '0' as (*g*).
(*i*) '1' as (*b*); '0' as (*a*).
(*j*) '1' as (*d*); '0' as (*g*) but raised.
(*jj*) '1' as (*a*) but shorter, and with shorter serif and thicker foot; '0' as (*g*) but level with '1'.
(*k*) '1' as (*jj*); '0' as (*a*).
(*l*) '1' straight serif; '0' as (*g*).

1880 (Mar). No. 17 surch with T **12** (showing numerals (*a*) to (*jj*)).

No.	Description	Unused	Used
22	10c. on 30c. claret (*a*)	£650	£100
23	10c. on 30c. claret (*b*)	£600	95·00
24	10c. on 30c. claret (*c*)	£12000	£1100
25	10c. on 30c. claret (*d*)	£4500	£325
26	10c. on 30c. claret (*e*)	£23000	£2500
27	10c. on 30c. claret (*f*)	£23000	£2500
28	10c. on 30c. claret (*g*)	£7000	£650
29	10c. on 30c. claret (*h*)	£23000	£2500
30	10c. on 30c. claret (*i*)	£23000	£2500
31	10c. on 30c. claret (*j*)	£23000	£2500
32	10c. on 30c. claret (*jj*)	£23000	£2500

Nos. 22/32 come from the same setting of 60 (6×10) containing 20 examples of No. 22 (R. 1/1-2, 1/4, 1/6, 2/1-6, 3/1, 3/3, 3/5, 4/1, 4/3-4, 10/1, 10/3-5), 22 of No. 23 (R. 4/6, 5/1-6, 6/1-6, 7/1, 8/2-4, 9/1-5), six of No. 25 (R. 1/5, 3/2, 3/4, 4/2, 4/5, 10/2), four of No. 28 (R. 7/2-5), two of No. 24 (R. 9/6, 10/6) and one each of Nos. 26 (R. 3/6), 27 (R. 1/3), 29 (R. 7/6), 30 (R. 8/1), 31 (R. 8/6) and 32 (R. 8/5).

No. 23 is known with large stop after 'cents' and also with stop low.

1880 (Apr). No. 17 surch as T **12**, but without 'cents', showing numerals (*a*) to (*c*), (*g*) to (*i*), (*k*) and (*l*).

No.	Description	Unused	Used
33	10 on 30c. claret (*a*)	£300	60·00
	w. Wmk inverted	†	£550
34	10 on 30c. claret (*b*)	£325	60·00
	w. Wmk inverted	†	£550
35	10 on 30c. claret (*c*)	£900	£130
	w. Wmk inverted	†	£1000
36	10 on 30c. claret (*g*)	£2500	£375
	aw. Wmk inverted	†	£2000
36*b*	10 on 30c. claret (*h*)	†	£25000
37	10 on 30c. claret (*i*)	£8500	£1100
38	10 on 30c. claret (*k*)	£8500	£1100
39	10 on 30c. claret (*l*)	£8500	£1100

Nos. 33/39 were surcharged from an amended setting of 60 (6×10) of which 59 positions have been identified. Of those known No. 33 occurs on 24 (R. 6/1-6, 7/1-6, 8/1-6, 9/1-2, 9/6, 10/1-3), No. 34 on 21 (R. 1/2-6, 2/1-6, 3/1-6, 4/3-5, 5/6), No. 35 on eight (R. 1/1, 4/2, 4/6, 5/1-5), No. 36 on three (R. 9/3-5) and Nos. 37 (R. 10/6), 38 (R. 10/4) and 39 (R. 10/5) on one each. R. 4/1 remains unidentified.

However, the existence of No. 36*b*, known as a single example from the sixth vertical column, a stamp in the Royal Collection with '1' as (*b*) and '0' as (*g*), and a block of three comprising R. 9/4 and 10/4-5 with No. 38 (rather than 39) at R. 10/5, indicates that there must have been another setting or sub-setting.

5 cents. (13) | 5 cents. (14) | 5 cents. (15)

1880 (Aug). No. 14*a* surch with Types **13** to **15**.

No.	Type	Description	Unused	Used
41	13	5c. on 8c. orange	£200	£250
42	14	5c. on 8c. orange	£190	£225
43	15	5c. on 8c. orange	£750	£900

Surcharged in a setting of 60 (6×10) with T **13** on rows one to four, T **14** on rows five to nine and T **15** on row ten.

10 cents. (16) | 5 cents. (17)

1880 (Dec)–**81**. Nos. 13, 15/15*a* and 17 surch with T **16**.

No.	Description	Unused	Used
44	10c. on 6c. lilac (11.81)	90·00	6·00
	a. Surch double	—	£3000
	b. 'Slug' flaw	—	£200
	w. Wmk inverted	†	£700
45	10c. on 12c. ultramarine (1.81)	95·00	17·00
	a. Blue	75·00	9·00
46	10c. on 30c. claret (12.80)	£500	£100

A second printing of the 10c. on 6c. has the surcharge heavier and the '10' usually more to the left or right of 'cents'. This latter surcharge was applied individually to each stamp and a number of different overprinting units were employed.

1882 (Jan). No. 12 surch with T **17**.

No.	Description	Unused	Used
47	5c. on 4c. rose	£375	£400

18

19

1882 (Jan). Wmk Crown CC. P 14.

No.	Type	Description	Unused	Used
48	18	5c. purple-brown	£120	£140
49	19	10c. slate	£550	80·00
		s. Optd 'SPECIMEN'	£1000	

1882. Wmk Crown CA. P 14.

No.	Type	Description	Unused	Used
50	5	2c. brown (8.82)	£375	50·00
51		4c. rose (4.82)	£160	16·00
52	6	8c. orange (9.82)	7·50	1·00
		w. Wmk inverted	†	£500
53	19	10c. slate (10.82)	18·00	1·25
		w. Wmk inverted	£950	£500

For the 4c. in deep carmine see No. 98.

TWO CENTS — **20a** 'S' wide | TWO CENTS — **20b** 'E' and 'S' wide | TWO CENTS — **20c** 'N' wide

TWO CENTS — **20d** All letters narrow | TWO CENTS — **20e** 'EN' and 'S' wide | TWO CENTS — **20f** 'E' wide

1883 (Apr). Nos. 52 and 18 surch with Types **20a/20f.**

No.	Type	Description	Unused	Used
54	20a	2c. on 8c. orange	£350	£130
55	20b	2c. on 8c. orange	£350	£130
56	20c	2c. on 8c. orange	£350	£130
		w. Wmk inverted		
57	20d	2c. on 8c. orange	£180	90·00
		a. Surch double	£3500	£1300
58	20e	2c. on 8c. orange	£3250	£1000
		a. Surch double		
59	20a	2c. on 32c. pale red	£900	£250
		a. Surch double	£4500	£2250
60	20f	2c. on 32c. pale red	£1400	£350
		a. Surch double		

The 8c. was surcharged using one of two triplet settings, either 54 + 55 + 56 or 57 + 57 + 57, applied to rows 2 to 10. A single handstamp, either No. 57 or No. 58, was then used to complete row 1. The 32c. was surcharged in the same way with a triplet of 59 + 60 + 59 and a single handstamp as No. 60.

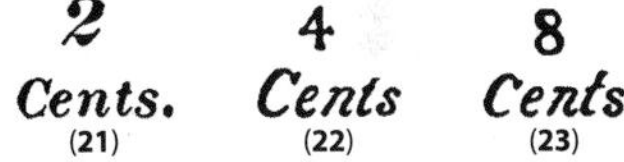
2 Cents. (21) | 4 Cents (22) | 8 Cents (23)

1883 (June–July). Nos. 51 and 15 surch with T **21**.

No.	Description	Unused	Used
61	2c. on 4c. rose	£100	£100
	a. 's' of 'Cents' inverted	£1700	£1800
62	2c. on 12c. blue (7.83)	£475	£170
	a. 's' of 'Cents' inverted	£8000	£3500

The inverted 'S' error occurred once in the first column of the setting of 60.

Broken oval above 'O' of 'POSTAGE' (Lower right pane R. 10/5)

1883 (July)–**91**. Wmk Crown CA. P 14.

No.	Type	Description	Unused	Used
63	5	2c. pale rose	50·00	4·75
		a. Bright rose (1889)	13·00	85
		aw. Wmk inverted	—	£550
64		4c. pale brown	55·00	7·00
		a. Broken oval	£650	£160
		b. Deep brown	70·00	8·50
		ba. Broken oval	£800	£200
		w. Wmk inverted	£325	£180
65	18	5c. blue (8.83)	19·00	1·25
		w. Wmk inverted	†	£500
66	5	6c. lilac (11.84)	26·00	26·00
		a. Violet	3·00	18·00
		b. 'Slug' flaw	£225	£325
		w. Wmk inverted	—	£350
67	6	12c. brown-purple	85·00	19·00
68	7	24c. yellow-green (2.84)	80·00	12·00
		a. Blue-green	13·00	6·50
		w. Wmk inverted	†	£450
69	8	30c. claret (9.91)	24·00	26·00
		w. Wmk inverted	£180	£100
70	9	32c. orange-vermilion (1.87)	18·00	5·50
		w. Wmk inverted	£100	£100

71 96c. olive-grey (7.88) 75·00 55·00
63*a*/71 *Set of 9* £275 £120
63s/65s, 67s Optd 'SPECIMEN' *Set of 4* £2500

Most examples of the 4c. in shades of olive-bistre are thought to be colour changelings.

For the 4c. in deep carmine and 12c. in claret see Nos. 98 and 102.

1884 (Feb–Aug). Nos. 65, 15 and 67 surch with Types **22** or **23**.

72 **18** 4c. on 5c. blue (8.84) £3500 £5500
73 4c. on 5c. blue (R.) (8.84) £200 £150
74 **6** 8c. on 12c. blue £1200 £160
w. Wmk inverted † £900
75 8c. on 12c. brown-purple (8.84) £750 £170
b. 's' of 'Cents' low (R. 5/1) £6500 £1800

1884 (Aug). No. 65 surch with Types **20d/20f.**

76 **20d** 2c. on 5c. blue £170 £180
a. Surch double † —
77 **20e** 2c. on 5c. blue £170 £180
a. Pair, with and without surch
b. Surch double
78 **20f** 2c. on 5c. blue £170 £180

Surcharged as a triplet, 77 + 76 + 78. On No. 76 'TS' are dropped below the line.

8 (24) 3 CENTS (25) THREE CENTS (26)

1884 (Sept). No. 75 additionally surch with large numeral as T **24** in red.

80 **6** 8 on 8c. on 12c. dull purple £550 £500
a. Surch Type **24** double £6000
b. Surch Type **23** in blue £11000
c. 's' of 'Cents' low £4500 £4750

Examples as No. 75, but with T **23** in blue, were further surcharged in error.

A similar '4' surcharge in red on No. 73 exists from a trial printing of which seven examples are known, all used on an official's correspondence (*Price* £42000 *used*).

1885. No. 65 and T **9** in new colour, wmk Crown CA, surch with Types **25** or **26**.

82 **25** 3c. on 5c. blue (9.85) £170 £275
a. Surch double £3250
83 **26** 3c. on 32c. pale magenta (12.85) 8·50 4·25
a. Deep magenta 3·50 1·00
s. Optd 'SPECIMEN' £375

The surcharge on No. 82 was applied locally by a triplet setting. No. 83 was surcharged by De La Rue in complete panes.

3 cents (27) 2 Cents (28)

1886 (Apr). No. 48 surch with T **27**.

84 **18** 3c. on 5c. purple-brown £325 £350

The surcharge on No. 84 was applied by a triplet setting.

1887 (July). No. 65 surch with T **28**.

85 **18** 2c. on 5c. blue 50·00 £100
a. 'C' of 'Cents' omitted — £4250
b. Surch double £1700 £1500

The surcharge on No. 85 was applied by a triplet setting.

10 CENTS (29) THIRTY CENTS (30)

1891 (Nov). Nos. 68 and 70 surch with Types **29** and **30**.

86 **7** 10c. on 24c. yellow-green 8·50 1·25
a. Narrow '0' in '10' (R. 4/6) 30·00 35·00
w. Wmk inverted £120 £130
87 **9** 30c. on 32c. orange-vermilion 18·00 3·50
w. Wmk inverted £225 £275

The 'R' of 'THIRTY' and 'N' of 'CENTS' are found wide or narrow and in all possible combinations.

ONE CENT (31) ONE CENT (32)

1892. Stamps of 1882–1891 (wmk Crown CA) surch with T **31**.

88 1c. on 2c. bright rose (3.92) 2·00 5·50
89 1c. on 4c. brown (4.92) 11·00 8·00
a. Surch double £1800
b. Broken oval £275 £275
w. Wmk inverted £325
90 1c. on 6c. lilac (2.92) 3·25 14·00
a. Surch double, one inverted £2250 £2000
b. 'Slug' flaw £140 £300
w. Wmk inverted £325 £375
91 1c. on 8c. orange (1.92) 1·00 4·50
92 1c. on 12c. brown-purple (3.92) 5·00 9·50
w. Wmk inverted £325
88/92 *Set of 5* 20·00 38·00

The three settings used for Nos. 88/92 contained various combinations of the following varieties: 'ON' of 'ONE' and 'N' of 'CENT' wide; 'O' wide, 'N' of 'ONE' narrow and 'N' of 'CENT' wide; 'O' narrow and both letters 'N' wide; 'ON' narrow and 'N' of 'CENT' wide; 'O' wide and both letters 'N' narrow; 'ON' wide and 'N' of 'CENT' narrow; 'ON' and 'N' of 'CENT' narrow; 'O' narrow; 'N' of 'ONE' wide and 'N' of 'CENT' narrow. Antique 'N' and 'E' letters also occur.

1892–94. Colours changed. Wmk Crown CA. P 14. Surch with Types **32** and **26** by De La Rue.

93 **6** 1c. on 8c. green (3.92) 1·00 1·50
94 **9** 3c. on 32c. carmine-rose (6.94) 2·25 70
a. Surch omitted £4500
93s/94s Optd 'SPECIMEN' *Set of 2* £170

No. 94a comes from a sheet found at Singapore on which all stamps in the upper left pane had the surcharge omitted. Five vertical inter-panneau pairs still exist with the surcharge omitted on the upper stamps (*Price* £45000 *unused*). The only used example of the error is on cover.

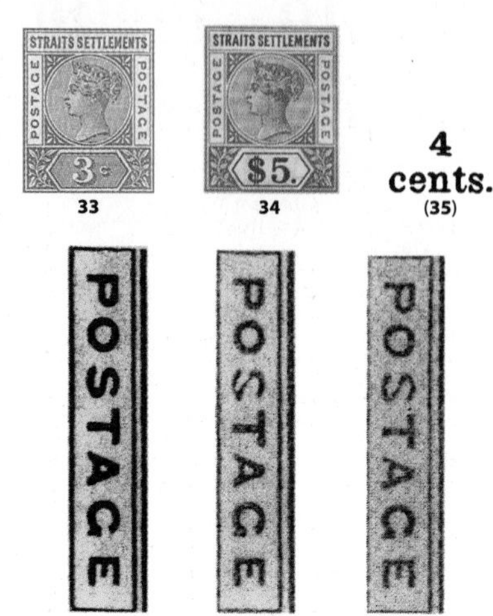

33 34 4 cents. (35)

Normal *Malformed 'S'* *Repaired 'S'*

The malformed 'S' occurs on R. 7/3 of the left pane from Key Plate 2. It is believed that the repair to it took place in mid-1898. Both states may occur on other stamps in Types **33** and **34**. Stamps subsequently printed from Key Plate 3 showed the 'S' normal.

1892 (Mar)–**99**. Wmk Crown CA. P 14.

95 **33** 1c. green (9.92) 9·00 70
a. Malformed 'S' £850 £275
b. Repaired 'S' £800 £250
w. Wmk inverted † £750
96 3c. carmine-rose (2.95) 12·00 40
a. Malformed 'S' £1100 £300
b. Repaired 'S' — £400
97 3c. brown (3.99) 19·00 1·50
a. Repaired 'S' £1100 £275
b. Yellow-brown 18·00 2·00
w. Wmk inverted £500
98 **5** 4c. deep carmine (7.99) 17·00 1·25
a. Broken oval £550 £170
99 **18** 5c. brown (6.94) 19·00 1·00
100 5c. magenta (7.99) 6·50 2·00
101 **6** 8c. ultramarine (6.94) 4·50 50
a. Bright blue 10·00 80
w. Wmk inverted † £400
102 12c. claret (3.94) 29·00 18·00
103 **33** 25c. purple-brown and green 50·00 9·00
a. Malformed 'S' £2000 £950
b. Repaired 'S' £1700 £750
c. Dull purple and green 35·00 9·00
104 50c. olive-green and carmine 29·00 3·75
a. Repaired 'S' £1800 £700
105 **34** $5 orange and carmine (10.98) £450 £325
a. Repaired 'S' £6500 £6500
95/105 *Set of 11* £550 £325
95s/101s, 103s/105s Optd 'SPECIMEN' *Set of 10* £1000

1898 (26 Dec). Types **18** and **6** surch with T **35** at Singapore.

106 4c. on 5c. brown (No. 99) 2·75 4·75
107 4c. on 5c. blue (No. 65) 15·00 35·00
a. Surch double † £3750
108 4c. on 8c. ultramarine (No. 101) 4·25 4·25
a. Surch double £1600 £1600
b. Bright blue (No. 101*a*) 4·25 2·50
106/108*b* *Set of 3* 20·00 38·00

Nos. 107 and 108*b* exist with stop spaced 1½ mm from the 'S' (R. 10/6).

FOUR CENTS (36)

37

38

1899 (Mar). T **18** (wmk Crown CA. P 14), surch with T **36** by De La Rue.

109 4c. on 5c. carmine 1·00 30
a. Surch omitted £40000
s. Optd 'SPECIMEN' 65·00
x. Wmk reversed £140

No. 109a is only known unused.

1902 (Apr)–**03**. Wmk Crown CA. P 14.

110 **37** 1c. grey-green (7.02) 2·75 5·50
a. Pale green 6·50 6·00
111 3c. dull purple and orange 3·50 20
w. Wmk inverted £900 £425
112 4c. purple/*red* (9.02) 4·75 30
113 **38** 5c. dull purple (8.02) 5·50 2·75
114 8c. purple/*blue* 4·50 20
115 10c. purple and black/*yellow* (9.02) 30·00 1·50
116 **37** 25c. dull purple and green (8.02) 18·00 14·00
117 **38** 30c. grey and carmine (7.02) 24·00 10·00
118 **37** 50c. deep green and carmine (9.02) 23·00 22·00
a. Dull green and carmine 23·00 24·00
119 **38** $1 dull green and black (9.02) 23·00 80·00
120 **37** $2 dull purple and black (9.02) 85·00 80·00
121 **38** $5 dull green and brown-orange (10.02) £225 £180
122 **37** $100 purple and green/*yellow* (3.03) (F.C. £250) £22000
s. Optd 'SPECIMEN' £750
110/121 *Set of 12* £400 £350
110s/121s Optd 'SPECIMEN' *Set of 12* £500

(Currency 100 cents = 1 Straits, later Malayan, dollar)

39 40 41 42

(Des N. Trotter and W. Egerton)

1903 (Dec)–**04**. Wmk Crown CA. P 14.

123 **39** 1c. grey-green 4·00 9·50
124 **40** 3c. dull purple (1.04) 11·00 4·50
125 **41** 4c. purple/*red* (4.04) 16·00 30
w. Wmk inverted † £475
126 **42** 8c. purple/*blue* (7.04) 55·00 1·25
123/126 *Set of 4* 75·00 14·00
123s/126s Optd 'SPECIMEN' *Set of 4* £225

1904 (Aug)–**10**. Wmk Multiple Crown CA. Ordinary paper (1c. to $1 and $5) or chalk-surfaced paper ($2, $25, $100). P 14.

127 **39** 1c. deep green (9.04) 5·50 10
a. Chalk-surfaced paper (12.05) 25·00 1·75
aw. Wmk inverted £200 £130
b. Blue-green (3.10) 23·00 1·10
128 **40** 3c. dull purple 3·00 30
a. Chalk-surfaced paper (8.06) 23·00 2·50
aw. Wmk inverted £225 £150
b. Plum (2.08) 15·00 1·75
129 **41** 4c. purple/*red* (11.04) 30·00 2·00
a. Chalk-surfaced paper (10.05) 27·00 1·25
aw. Wmk inverted £130 £100
130 **38** 5c. dull purple (12.06) 29·00 3·75
a. Chalk-surfaced paper (12.06) 42·00 15·00
ay. Wmk inverted and reversed † £700
131 **42** 8c. purple/*blue* (8.05) 55·00 1·50
a. Chalk-surfaced paper (12.05) 55·00 2·75
132 **38** 10c. purple and black/*yellow* (8.05) 8·50 80
a. Chalk-surfaced paper (11.05) 12·00 3·25
133 **37** 25c. dull purple and green (1.05) 60·00 50·00
a. Chalk-surfaced paper (11.05) 65·00 48·00
134 **38** 30c. grey and carmine (3.05) 50·00 4·25
a. Chalk-surfaced paper (3.06) 60·00 4·00
135 **37** 50c. dull green and carmine (10.05) 60·00 29·00
a. Chalk-surfaced paper (11.06) 35·00 21·00
136 **38** $1 dull green and black (3.05) 75·00 50·00
a. Chalk-surfaced paper (3.06) 65·00 29·00
137 **37** $2 dull purple and black (10.05) £120 90·00
138 **38** $5 dull green and brown-orange (10.05) £350 £200
a. Chalk-surfaced paper (1.08) £350 £180
139 **37** $25 grey-green and black (7.06) (F.C. £180) £3500 £3500
s. Optd 'SPECIMEN' £475
140 $100 purple and green/*yellow* (6.10) (F.C. £450) £22000
127/138a *Set of 12* £700 £350

STRAITS SETTLEMENTS. (43) Straits Settlements. (44)

STRAITS SETTLEMENTS.

FOUR CENTS. (45)

1906 (20 Dec)–**07**. T **18** of Labuan (Nos. 117 etc.) optd with Types **43** or **44** (10c.) or additionally surch with T **45**, in black (No. 145), vermilion (No. 148) or brown-red (others) at Singapore. P 13½–14.

141 1c. black and purple (P 14½–15) 70·00 £180
a. Perf 14 £425 £600
b. Line through 'B' £1100
c. Perf 13½–14 comp 12–13 — £1500
142 2c. black and green £425 £500
a. Perf 14½–15 £180 £325
b. Perf 13½–14 comp 12–13 £1400 £1400
c. Line through 'B' £2000
143 3c. black and sepia (1.07) 26·00 95·00
a. Line through 'B' £750
144 4c. on 12c. black and yellow 4·25 15·00
a. No stop after 'CENTS' (R. 1/8, 6/8) £650 £750
b. Line through 'B' £375 £600
145 4c. on 16c. green and brown (Blk.) 13·00 16·00
a. 'STRAITS SETTLEMENTS' in both brown-red and black £650 £1000
b. Ditto. In vert pair with normal £9000
c. Line through 'B' £450 £650
146 4c. on 18c. black and pale brown 2·75 15·00
a. No stop after 'CENTS' (R. 1/8, 6/8) £425 £650
b. 'FOUR CENTS' and bar double £17000

c. 'FOUR CENTS' and bar 1½ mm below normal position (pair with normal) £2750
d. Line through 'B' £350 £550
147 8c. black and vermilion 8·00 15·00
a. Line through 'B' £425 £650
148 10c. brown and slate 14·00 17·00
a. No stop after 'Settlements' (R. 1/4, 6/4) £750 £800
b. Line through 'B' £500 £650
149 25c. green and greenish blue (1.07) 40·00 50·00
a. Perf 14½–15 £110 £160
b. Perf 13½–14 comp 14½–15 £600
c. Line through 'B' £800
150 50c. dull purple and lilac (1.07) 25·00 70·00
a. Line through 'B' £800
151 $1 claret and orange (Claret) (1.07) 50·00 £120
a. Perf 14½–15 £1000
b. Line through 'B' £1200 £1900
141/151 *Set of 11* £375 £800

Nos. 141/151 were overprinted by a setting of 50 (10×5) applied twice to the sheets of 100. The 'FOUR CENTS' surcharges were applied separately by a similar setting.

No. 145a shows impressions of T **43** in both brown-red and black. It is known from one complete sheet and the top half of another. In the latter the two overprints are almost coincident, whereas in the former they are clearly separated.

No. 146b occurred on row 5 from one sheet only. No. 146c occurred on R. 4/10 and 9/10 of the first printing.

The line through 'B' flaw occurs on R. 5/10 of the basic stamp. For illustration see Labuan.

46 47

1906 (Sept)–**12**. Wmk Mult Crown CA. Ordinary paper (3c. to 10c.) or chalk-surfaced paper (21c. to $500). P 14.
153 **40** 3c. red (6.08) 8·00 10
154 **41** 4c. red (7.07) 9·50 2·50
155 4c. dull purple (2.08) 6·00 10
aw. Wmk inverted £400
b. Chalk-surfaced paper (1.12) 11·00 3·00
bs. Optd 'SPECIMEN' £180
156 4c. claret (9.11) 4·50 80
157 **38** 5c. orange (4.09) 2·75 2·50
158 **42** 8c. blue 4·25 60
159 **38** 10c. purple/*yellow* (7.08) 19·00 1·00
a. Chalk-surfaced paper (5.12) 32·00 23·00
160 **46** 21c. dull purple and claret (11.10) 6·50 40·00
161 **37** 25c. dull and bright purple (7.09) 32·00 13·00
162 **38** 30c. purple and orange-yellow (11.09) 55·00 4·25
163 **46** 45c. black/*green* (11.10) 3·00 4·00
164 **37** 50c. black/*green* (4.10) 12·00 5·00
165 **38** $1 black and red/*blue* (10.10) 15·00 8·50
166 **37** $2 green and red/*yellow* (12.09) 35·00 24·00
167 **38** $5 green and red/*green* (11.09) £150 75·00
w. Wmk inverted £1800 £850
168 **47** $25 purple and blue/*blue* (5.11) (F.C. £180) £3750 £2500
s. Optd 'SPECIMEN' £750
169 $500 purple and orange (5.10) (F.C. £900) £170000
s. Optd 'SPECIMEN' £4750
153/167 *Set of 15* £325 £160
153s/167s Optd 'SPECIMEN' *Set of 15* £1100

Beware of dangerous forgeries of No. 169 both 'unused' and 'used'. These are on watermarked paper, but the paper is not chalk-surfaced.

48 49 50
51 52 53
54

1912–23. $25, $100 and $500 as T **47**, but with head of King George V. Die I (5, 10, 25, 30, 50c., $1, $2, $5). Wmk Mult Crown CA. Ordinary paper (Nos. 193/196, 198/201, 203) or chalk-surfaced paper (others). P 14.
193 **48** 1c. green (9.12) 14·00 1·50
a. Pale green (1.14) 14·00 1·50
b. Blue-green (1917) 14·00 2·00
bw. Wmk inverted † £400
bx. Wmk reversed † £500
194 1c. black (2.19) 4·00 2·50
w. Wmk inverted † £500
y. Wmk inverted and reversed £750
195 **52** 2c. green (10.19) 2·25 50
w. Wmk inverted £750 £500
196 **49** 3c. red (2.13) 3·25 1·25
a. Scarlet (2.17) 3·00 10
y. Wmk inverted and reversed £500
197 **50** 4c. dull purple (3.13) 4·75 60
a. Wmk sideways † £3000
w. Wmk inverted † £550
y. Wmk inverted and reversed † £550
198 4c. rose-scarlet (2.19) 4·25 15
aw. Wmk inverted £550 £500
ay. Wmk inverted and reversed † £550
b. Carmine 2·00 20
199 **51** 5c. orange (8.12) 2·00 1·00
a. Yellow-orange 6·00 1·50
w. Wmk inverted † £550
x. Wmk reversed † £550
200 **52** 6c. dull claret (3.20) 2·00 50
a. Deep claret 7·50 2·75
aw. Wmk inverted £275 £300
201 8c. ultramarine (3.13) 3·50 80
w. Wmk inverted † £550
202 **51** 10c. purple/*yellow* (9.12) 1·50 1·00
aw. Wmk inverted † £550
b. White back (1913) 2·75 1·10
bs. Optd 'SPECIMEN' 65·00
bx. Wmk reversed † £800
by. Wmk inverted and reversed † £800
c. On lemon (1916) 18·00 1·25
cs. Optd 'SPECIMEN' £100
d. Wmk sideways † £4500
203 10c. deep bright blue (1918) 10·00 1·50
a. Bright blue (1919) 4·00 50
204 **53** 21c. dull and bright purple (11.13) 17·00 17·00
205 **54** 25c. dull purple and mauve (7.14) 16·00 14·00
aw. Wmk inverted £325 £325
ay. Wmk inverted and reversed £425
b. Dull purple and violet (1919) 75·00 24·00
207 **51** 30c. dull purple and orange (12.14) 8·50 7·00
w. Wmk inverted † £750
208 **53** 45c. black/*green (white back)* (12.14) 7·50 23·00
a. On blue-green, olive back (7.18) 13·00 35·00
ab. 'C' of 'CA' missing from wmk £1000
as. Optd 'SPECIMEN' 80·00
b. On emerald back (6.22) 9·00 13·00
209 **54** 50c. black/*green* (7.14) 6·00 5·50
aa. Wmk sideways † £5500
a. On blue-green, olive back (1918) 38·00 14·00
b. On emerald back (1921) 16·00 10·00
c. Die II. *On emerald back* (1922) 3·25 5·00
cs. Optd 'SPECIMEN' 80·00
cw. Wmk inverted £750 £750
210 **51** $1 black and red/*blue* (10.14) 21·00 18·00
w. Wmk inverted £275 £250
211 **54** $2 green and red/*yellow, white back* (1914) 16·00 55·00
a. Green and red/yellow (1915) 24·00 55·00
as. Optd 'SPECIMEN' 80·00
b. On orange-buff (1921) 80·00 90·00
c. On pale yellow (1921) 85·00 £100
212 **51** $5 green and red/*green, white back* (11.13) £130 55·00
a. Green and red/green (1915) £140 80·00
as. Optd 'SPECIMEN' £130
b. On blue-green, olive back (1918) £225 £110
bw. Wmk inverted
c. On emerald back (1920) £250 £130
d. Die II. *On emerald back* (1923) £140 85·00
ds. Optd 'SPECIMEN' £140
213 – $25 purple and blue/*blue* £2500 £650
a. Break in scroll £6500
b. Broken crown and scroll £6500
e. Break in lines below scroll £6500
f. Damaged leaf at bottom right £6500
s. Optd 'SPECIMEN' £550
214 – $100 black and carmine/*blue* (8.12) (F.C. £200) £12000
a. Break in scroll £25000
b. Broken crown and scroll £25000
e. Break in lines below scroll
f. Damaged leaf at bottom right
s. Optd 'SPECIMEN' £1300
215 – $500 purple and orange-brown (8.12) (F.C. £600) £100000
a. Break in scroll £130000
b. Broken crown and scroll £140000
f. Damaged leaf at bottom right
s. Optd 'SPECIMEN' £5500
193/212 *Set of 19* £225 £170
193s/212s Optd 'SPECIMEN' *Set of 19* £1200

The 6c. is similar to T **52**, but the head is in a beaded oval as in T **53**. The 2c., 6c. (and 12c. below) have figures of value on a circular ground while in the 8c. this is of oval shape.

For illustrations of the varieties on Nos. 213/215 see above No. 51*b* of Bermuda.

RED CROSS

2c.
(55)

MALAYA-
BORNEO
EXHIBITION.
(56)

1917 (1 May). Surch with T **55**.
216 **49** 3c. + 2c. scarlet 2·75 32·00
a. No stop (R. 2/3) £475 £1000
217 **50** 4c. + 2c. dull purple 3·75 32·00
a. No stop (R. 2/3) £550 £1000

Nos 216/217 were sold at face, plus 2c. on each stamp for Red Cross funds.

Nos. 216a and 217a occur in the first setting only.

Type I

Type II

The duty plate for the 25c. value was replaced in 1926. In Type II the solid shading forming the back of the figure 2 extends to the top of the curve; the upturned end of the foot of the 2 is short; two background lines above figure 5; c close to 5; STRAITS SETTLEMENTS in taller letters.

1921–33. Wmk Mult Script CA. Ordinary paper (1c. to 6c., 10c. (No. 230), 12c.) or chalk-surfaced paper (others). P 14.
218 **48** 1c. black (3.22) 60 10
219 **52** 2c. green (5.21) 60 10
w. Wmk inverted 55·00 75·00
x. Wmk reversed † £500
y. Wmk inverted and reversed £425
220 2c. brown (3.25) 7·00 5·00
221 **49** 3c. green (9.23) 1·50 80
w. Wmk inverted 55·00 85·00
222 **50** 4c. carmine-red (9.21) 2·00 6·50
y. Wmk inverted and reversed † £475
223 4c. bright violet (8.24) 60 10
w. Wmk inverted 50·00
224 4c. orange (8.29) 1·00 10
225 **51** 5c. orange (Die I) (5.21) 6·00 15
a. Wmk sideways † £4000
bw. Wmk inverted 50·00 75·00
bx. Wmk reversed † —
c. Die II (1922) 2·25 1·25
226 5c. brown (Die II) (1932) 3·00 10
a. Die I (1933) 5·00 10
ab. Face value omitted £30000
227 **52** 6c. dull claret (10.22) 2·25 15
w. Wmk inverted 45·00 60·00
228 6c. rose-pink (2.25) 35·00 9·50
229 6c. scarlet (1.27) 2·50 10
230 **51** 10c. bright blue (Die I) (1921) 1·75 4·00
w. Wmk inverted 55·00 £100
231 10c. purple/*pale yellow* (Die I) (1923) 3·25 17·00
a. Die II (11.26) 5·00 30
b. Purple/bright yellow (Die II) (1932) 38·00 3·25
ba. Die I (1933) 22·00 10
232 **52** 12c. bright blue (1.22) 1·25 20
w. Wmk inverted 70·00
233 **53** 21c. dull and bright purple (2.23) 6·00 55·00
234 **54** 25c. dull purple and mauve (Die I, Type I) (1921) 45·00 95·00
a. Die II, Type I (1923) 12·00 3·75
b. Die II, Type II (1927) 5·00 1·75
235 **51** 30c. dull purple and orange (Die I) (1921) 35·00 60·00
a. Die II (1922) 2·00 1·25
236 **53** 35c. dull purple and orange-yellow (8.22) 12·00 6·00
a. Dull purple and orange 3·50 2·25
237 35c. scarlet and purple (4.31) 10·00 2·25
238 **54** 50c. black/*emerald* (9.25) 1·75 40
239 **51** $1 black and red/*blue* (Die II) (1921) 6·00 2·25
240 **54** $2 green and red/*pale yellow* (Die II) (1923) 10·00 8·00
240*a* **51** $5 green and red/*green* (Die II) (1926) £120 45·00
240*b* – $25 purple and blue/*blue* (5.23) £1400 £200
ba. Break in scroll £3500
bb. Broken crown and scroll £3500 £1600
be. Break through lines below left scroll
bf. Damaged leaf at bottom right
bs. Optd 'SPECIMEN' £425
240*c* – $100 black and carmine/*blue* (5.23) (F.C. £150) £10000 £3000
ca. Break in scroll £19000
cb. Broken crown and scroll £19000
ce. Break through lines below left scroll
cf. Damaged leaf at bottom right
cs. Optd 'SPECIMEN' £1000
240*d* – $500 purple and orange-brown (4.23) (F.C. £600) £75000
da. Break in scroll £90000
db. Broken crown and scroll £95000
de. Break through lines below left scroll
df. Damaged leaf at bottom right
ds. Optd 'SPECIMEN' £5000
218/240*a* *Set of 24* £200 £120
218s/240as (*ex* 6c. rose-pink) Optd or Perf (Nos. 224s, 226s, 237s) 'SPECIMEN' *Set of 23* £1100

Prepared for use but not issued
240*e* **52** 8c. carmine
s. Optd 'SPECIMEN' £600

No. 240*e* was prepared in 1922 but never issued. 'SPECIMEN' examples were distributed through the UPU, and a few unoverprinted examples are known.

Nos. 240*b*/240*d* are as T **47**, but with portrait of George V.

No. 226ab was caused by a progressive inking failure, resulting in the value being completely omitted on R.10/10 of a single sheet.

The 2c. green was reissued in 1927, and exists with 'SPECIMEN' overprint 15.5×1.75 mm instead of the 14.5×2.5 mm of the original issue (*Price*, £75).

The paper of Nos. 231*b*/231ba is the normal *pale yellow* at the back, but with a bright yellow surface.

In 1926 new Key and Duty plates were made of 100 (10×10) instead of the usual 60 (6×10).

For illustrations of the varieties on Nos. 240*b*/240*d* see above No. 51*b* of Bermuda.

SETTINGS OF TYPE 56. Nos. 241/255 were produced using a typeset block of 12 (6×2) overprints from which ten stereos were taken to provide a forme for the complete sheet of 120. Two such formes were prepared of which the second was only used for a limited number of Straits Settlements sheets in addition to the Kedah and Trengganu issues.

Several constant varieties occur on the original typeset block of 12 and so appear ten times on sheets printed from both Settings I and II. These include:

Oval last 'O' in 'BORNEO' (R. 1/3 of typeset block of 12)
Raised stop after 'EXHIBITION' (R. 2/2 of typeset block of 12)
Small second 'A' in 'MALAYA' (R. 2/6 of typeset block of 12).

The two formes also produced constant varieties in each setting which include:

Setting I
No hyphen (Left pane. R. 7/1 or 9/2)
No stop (Left and right panes. Either on R. 10/4 (right pane) or, for some sheets, on other stamps from even numbered horizontal rows in the 4th vertical column (both panes))
Third 'I' in 'EXHIBITION' omitted (R. 8/5, 10/5 (left pane)). This must have occurred very late in the use of this setting and is only found on the 5c. and 10c.

Setting II
No stop (Left pane. R. 1/5)
'EXH.BITION' (Left pane. Stamps from even numbered horizontal rows in the 3rd vertical column)

1922 (31 Mar). Malaya-Borneo Exhibition, Singapore. Optd with T **56**.

(a) Wmk Mult Crown CA (Nos. 195, 198/199, 201, 205, 208a, 210, 211b and 212b)

241 **52** 2c. green ... 50·00 90·00
b. Oval last 'O' in 'BORNEO' ... £100 £160
c. Raised stop after 'EXHIBITION' ... £100 £160
d. Small second 'A' in 'MALAYA' ... £100 £160
e. No hyphen ... £325
f. No stop ... £140 £250
242 **50** 4c. rose-scarlet ... 11·00 29·00
b. Oval last 'O' in 'BORNEO' ... 21·00 55·00
c. Raised stop after 'EXHIBITION' ... 21·00 55·00
d. Small second 'A' in 'MALAYA' ... 21·00 55·00
e. No hyphen ... £100
f. No stop ... 28·00 65·00
h. 'EXH.BITION' ... £100
243 **51** 5c. orange ... 13·00 19·00
b. Oval last 'O' in 'BORNEO' ... 23·00 40·00
c. Raised stop after 'EXHIBITION' ... 23·00 40·00
d. Small second 'A' in 'MALAYA' ... 23·00 40·00
e. No hyphen ... 80·00
f. No stop ... 26·00 48·00
h. 'EXH.BITION' ... 75·00
244 **52** 8c. ultramarine ... 2·50 12·00
b. Oval last 'O' in 'BORNEO' ... 6·50 23·00
c. Raised stop after 'EXHIBITION' ... 6·50 23·00
d. Small second 'A' in 'MALAYA' ... 6·50 23·00
e. No hyphen ... 50·00
f. No stop ... 9·00 28·00
h. 'EXH.BITION' ... 50·00
245 **54** 25c. dull purple and mauve ... 6·00 50·00
b. Oval last 'O' in 'BORNEO' ... 12·00 95·00
c. Raised stop after 'EXHIBITION' ... 12·00 95·00
d. Small second 'A' in 'MALAYA' ... 12·00 95·00
e. No hyphen ... 70·00
f. No stop ... 15·00 £110
h. 'EXH.BITION' ... 65·00
246 **53** 45c. black/*blue-green (olive back)* ... 4·50 50·00
b. Oval last 'O' in 'BORNEO' ... 10·00 95·00
c. Raised stop after 'EXHIBITION' ... 10·00 95·00
d. Small second 'A' in 'MALAYA' ... 10·00 95·00
e. No hyphen ... 55·00
f. No stop ... 14·00 £100
247 **51** $1 black and red/*blue* ... £650 £1800
b. Oval last 'O' in 'BORNEO' ... £1200
c. Raised stop after 'EXHIBITION' ... £1200
d. Small second 'A' in 'MALAYA' ... £1200
e. No hyphen ... £2000
f. No stop ... £1400
248 **54** $2 green and red/*orange-buff* ... 26·00 £160
a. On pale yellow (No. 211c) ... 65·00 £190
b. Oval last 'O' in 'BORNEO' ... 60·00 £325
c. Raised stop after 'EXHIBITION' ... 60·00 £325
d. Small second 'A' in 'MALAYA' ... 60·00 £325
e. No hyphen ... £350
f. No stop ... 90·00 £400
h. 'EXH.BITION' ... £1100
249 **51** $5 green and red/*blue-green (olive-back)* ... £450 £800
b. Oval last 'O' in 'BORNEO' ... £800
c. Raised stop after 'EXHIBITION' ... £800
d. Small second 'A' in 'MALAYA' ... £800
e. No hyphen ... £2500
f. No stop ... £900
h. 'EXH.BITION' ...

(b) Wmk Mult Script CA (Nos. 218/219, 222, 225c, 230 and 239)

250 **48** 1c. black ... 3·00 26·00
b. Oval last 'O' in 'BORNEO' ... 8·00 50·00
c. Raised stop after 'EXHIBITION' ... 8·00 50·00
d. Small second 'A' in 'MALAYA' ... 8·00 50·00
e. No hyphen ... 55·00
f. No stop ... 11·00 55·00
h. 'EXH.BITION' ... 55·00
251 **52** 2c. green ... 2·50 16·00
b. Oval last 'O' in 'BORNEO' ... 6·50 30·00
c. Raised stop after 'EXHIBITION' ... 6·50 30·00
d. Small second 'A' in 'MALAYA' ... 6·50 30·00
e. No hyphen ... 45·00 £140
f. No stop ... 8·00 35·00
h. 'EXH.BITION' ... 45·00
252 **50** 4c. carmine-red ... 5·00 50·00
b. Oval last 'O' in 'BORNEO' ... 11·00 95·00
c. Raised stop after 'EXHIBITION' ... 11·00 95·00
d. Small second 'A' in 'MALAYA' ... 11·00 95·00
e. No hyphen ... 55·00
f. No stop ... 14·00 95·00
253 **51** 5c. orange (Die II) ... 2·75 50·00
b. Oval last 'O' in 'BORNEO' ... 8·00 95·00
c. Raised stop after 'EXHIBITION' ... 8·00 95·00
d. Small second 'A' in 'MALAYA' ... 8·00 95·00
e. No hyphen ... 55·00
f. No stop ... 10·00 £110
g. Third 'I' in 'EXHIBITION' omitted ... £4000
254 10c. bright blue ... 2·25 26·00
b. Oval last 'O' in 'BORNEO' ... 7·00 55·00
c. Raised stop after 'EXHIBITION' ... 7·00 55·00
d. Small second 'A' in 'MALAYA' ... 7·00 55·00
e. No hyphen ... 45·00
f. No stop ... 8·50 65·00
g. Third 'I' in 'EXHIBITION' omitted ... £850
255 $1 black and red/*blue* (Die II) ... 23·00 £160
b. Oval last 'O' in 'BORNEO' ... 60·00 £350
c. Raised stop after 'EXHIBITION' ... 60·00 £350
d. Small second 'A' in 'MALAYA' ... 60·00 £350
e. No hyphen ... £800
f. No stop ... 75·00 £425
h. 'EXH.BITION' ...
242/255 *Set of 11* ... £475 £1200

Examples of most values are known with part strikes of a forged Singapore postmark dated 'AU 1 1910'.

1935 (6 May). Silver Jubilee. As Nos. 91/94 of Antigua. but ptd by Waterlow & Sons. P 11×12.

256 5c. ultramarine and grey ... 3·00 30
m. 'Bird' by turret ... £1100 £750
257 8c. green and indigo ... 3·00 3·25
258 12c. brown and deep blue ... 3·00 8·00
j. Damaged turret ... £1100
259 25c. slate and purple ... 5·50 12·00
256/259 *Set of 4* ... 13·00 21·00
256s/259s Perf 'SPECIMEN' *Set of 4* ... £225

For illustration of plate varieties see Omnibus section following Zanzibar.

57

58

1936 (1 Jan)–**37**. Chalk-surfaced paper. Wmk Mult Script CA. P 14.

260 **57** 1c. black (1.1.37) ... 2·50 20
261 2c. green (1.2.36) ... 2·50 70
262 4c. orange (15.6.36) ... 2·25 70
263 5c. brown (1.8.36) ... 1·00 30
264 6c. scarlet (1.2.36) ... 1·50 1·10
265 8c. grey ... 3·75 70
266 10c. dull purple (1.7.36) ... 2·25 60
267 12c. bright ultramarine (1.9.36) ... 2·00 2·50
268 25c. dull purple and scarlet (1.2.36) ... 1·50 50
269 30c. dull purple and orange ... 1·50 3·25
270 40c. scarlet and dull purple ... 1·50 2·50
271 50c. black/*emerald* (1.9.36) ... 4·50 1·25
272 $1 black and red/*blue* (1.7.36) ... 20·00 1·75
273 $2 green and scarlet (1.4.36) ... 60·00 11·00
274 $5 green and red/*emerald* (1.1.37) ... £140 10·00
260/274 *Set of 15* ... £225 32·00
260s/274s Perf 'SPECIMEN' *Set of 15* ... £550

1937 (12 May). Coronation. As Nos. 95/97 of Antigua, but printed by D.L.R. Perf 14.

275 4c. orange ... 1·25 10
276 8c. grey-black ... 1·50 10
277 12c. bright blue ... 3·50 1·00
275/277 *Set of 3* ... 5·75 1·10
275s/277s Perf 'SPECIMEN' *Set of 3* ... £225

1937–41. Chalk-surfaced paper. Wmk Mult Script CA. P 14 or 15×14 (15c.).

(a) Die I (printed at two operations)

278 **58** 1c. black (1.1.38) ... 14·00 10
279 2c. green (6.12.37) ... 21·00 20
280 4c. orange (1.1.38) ... 35·00 1·75
281 5c. brown (19.11.37) ... 24·00 30
282 6c. scarlet (10.1.38) ... 11·00 60
283 8c. grey (26.1.38) ... 38·00 10
284 10c. dull purple (8.11.37) ... 16·00 10
285 12c. ultramarine (10.1.38) ... 16·00 50
286 25c. dull purple and scarlet (11.12.37) ... 48·00 1·10
287 30c. dull purple and orange (1.12.37) ... 20·00 2·00
288 40c. scarlet and dull purple (20.12.37) ... 19·00 2·25
289 50c. black/*emerald* (26.1.38) ... 16·00 10
290 $1 black and red/*blue* (26.1.38) ... 19·00 20
291 $2 green and scarlet (26.1.38) ... 48·00 17·00
292 $5 green and red/*emerald* (26.1.38) ... 29·00 9·50

(b) Die II (printed at one operation)

293 **58** 2c. green (28.12.38) ... 60·00 40
294 2c. orange (*thin striated paper*) (6.10.41) ... 2·00 19·00
295 3c. green (*ordinary paper*) (5.9.41) ... 13·00 4·00
296 4c. orange (29.10.38) ... 90·00 10
297 5c. brown (18.2.39) ... 48·00 10
298 15c. ultramarine (*ordinary paper*) (*shades*) (6.10.41) ... 12·00 10·00
278/298 *Set of 18* ... £350 55·00
278s/292s 294s/295s, 298s Perf 'SPECIMEN' *Set of 18* £900

Die I. Lines of background outside central oval touch the oval and the foliage of the palm tree is usually joined to the oval frame. The downward-pointing palm frond, opposite the King's eye, has two points.

Die II. Lines of background are separated from the oval by a white line and the foliage of the palm trees does not touch the outer frame. The palm frond has only one point.

Nos. 295 and 298 were printed by Harrison and Sons following bomb damage to the De La Rue works on 29 December 1940.

The 6c. grey, 8c. scarlet and $5 purple and orange were only issued with the BMA overprint, but the 8c. without overprint is known although in this state it was never issued (*Price* £15).

STAMP BOOKLETS

1914–19. Black on blue (No. SB1) or grey (No. SB1*b*) covers, Stapled.

SB1 $1 booklet containing 25×4c. dull purple (No. 197) in two blocks of 12 and one single.
a. Containing 4c. rose-scarlet (No. 198) (1919) ...
SB1*b* $1 booklet containing 4×1c., 16×3c. and 12×4c. (Nos. 193, 196/197) in blocks of four ...

1921. Black on blue cover. Stapled.

SB2 $1 booklet containing 25×4c. (No. 222) in two blocks of 12 and one single ...
a. Contents as SB2, but four blocks of 6 and one single ...

1922. Black on red cover. Stapled.

SB3 $1 booklet containing 5c. (No. 225) in block of 8 and 6c. (No. 227) in block of 10 ... £2250

1925–29. Black on red cover. Stapled.

SB4 $1.20 booklet containing 30×4c. bright violet (No. 223) in blocks of 10 ... £3500
a. Containing 4c. orange (No. 224) (1929) ... £3750

1927. Black on grey (No. SB5), green (No. SB6) or blue (No. SB7) covers. Stapled.

SB5 $1 booklet containing 4c. and 6c. (Nos. 223, 229) in blocks of 10 ... £3750
SB6 $1.20 booklet containing 20×6c. (No. 229) in blocks of 10 ... £3000
SB7 $1.20 booklet containing 2c., 4c. and 6c. (Nos. 219, 223, 229) in blocks of 10 ... £3750

1933. Black on buff cover. Stapled.

SB8 $1 booklet containing 20×5c. (No. 226a) in blocks of 10 ...

1936. Stapled.

SB9 $1 booklet containing 20×5c. (No. 263) in blocks of 10 ...
SB10 $1.30 booklet containing 5c. and 8c. (Nos. 263, 265) in blocks of 10 ...

1938. Black on buff (No. SB11) or black on green (No. SB12) covers. Stapled.

SB11 $1 booklet containing 20×5c. (No. 281) in blocks of 10 ... £4500
SB12 $1.30 booklet containing 5c. and 8c. (Nos. 281, 283) in blocks of 10 and pane of airmail labels ... £4750

POSTAGE DUE STAMPS

D 1

1924 (1 Jan)–**26**. Wmk Mult Script CA. P 14.

D1 **D 1** 1c. violet ... 14·00 5·50
D2 2c. black ... 3·25 1·00
D3 4c. green (5.26) ... 2·00 2·00
D4 8c. scarlet ... 4·50 55
D5 10c. orange ... 6·00 85
D6 12c. bright blue ... 7·00 65
sa. Opt 'SPECIMEN' double ... £550
D1/D6 *Set of 6* ... 32·00 9·50
D1s/D6s Optd 'SPECIMEN' *Set of 6* ... £350

For later issues of Postage Due stamps, see MALAYAN POSTAL UNION.

POSTAL FISCAL STAMPS

1938. T **47** but with head of King George VI and inscribed 'REVENUE' at each side. Wmk Mult Script CA. P 14.

F1 $25 purple and blue/*blue* ... £1400 £650

No. F1 was regularly used for postal purposes in 1941, although no specific authorisation for such use has been discovered.

The Straits Settlements were occupied by the Japanese in 1942.

After the Second World War the stamps of MALAYA (BRITISH MILITARY ADMINISTRATION) were used. In 1946 Singapore became a separate Crown Colony and Labuan was transferred to North Borneo. Separate stamps were issued for Malacca and Penang, which both joined the Malayan Federation on 1 February 1948.

II. FEDERATED MALAY STATES

On 1 July 1896, the States of Negri Sembilan, Pahang, Perak and Selangor were organised on a federal basis to be known as the Federated Malay States. For the time being each State continued with individual issues, although each state's issues were valid for use in the others from 27 January 1899. Stamps for the use of the Federation replaced these in 1900.

PRICES FOR STAMPS ON COVER TO 1945	
Nos. 1/13	*from* × 15
No. 14	—
Nos. 15/22	*from* × 10
Nos. 23/25	*from* × 3
No. 26	—
Nos. 27/50	*from* × 6
No. 51	—
Nos. 52/81	*from* × 5
No. 82	—
Nos. D1/D6	*from* × 10

PRINTERS. All issues of the Federated Malay States were printed in typography by De La Rue & Co, Ltd, London, *unless otherwise stated.*

FEDERATED MALAY STATES
(1)

FEDERATED MALAY STATES
(2)

1900. Optd with T **1** (cent values) or T **2** (dollar values).

(a) Stamps of Negri Sembilan (T **3***)*

1 1c. dull purple and green ... 3·00 14·00
2 2c. dull purple and brown ... 29·00 70·00
3 3c. dull purple and black ... 2·75 8·00
4 5c. dull purple and olive-yellow ... 75·00 £190
5 10c. dull purple and orange ... 17·00 65·00
6 20c. green and olive ... 90·00 £130
7 25c. green and carmine ... £275 £450
8 50c. green and black ... £110 £170
1/8 *Set of 8* ... £600 £1000
1s/8s Optd 'SPECIMEN' *Set of 8* ... £250

(b) Stamps of Perak (Types **44** *and* **45***)*

9	5c. dull purple and olive-yellow	30·00	75·00
10	10c. dull purple and orange	85·00	65·00
11	$1 green and pale green	£200	£275
	w. Wmk inverted	£1000	£1100
12	$2 green and carmine	£200	£325
13	$5 green and ultramarine	£550	£800
14	$25 green and orange (F.C. £600)	£17000	
	s. Optd 'SPECIMEN'	£550	
11s/13s Optd 'SPECIMEN' *Set of 3*		£200	

The Negri Sembilan 3c. dull purple and black does not exist without overprint T **1**.

Nos. 1/4 were never put on sale in Selangor, nor Nos. 1/3 in Perak.

The stamps of STRAITS SETTLEMENTS were used in Federated Malay States from 16 July 1900 until 31 December 1901.

3

4

1900–01. P 14.

(a) T **3**. *Wmk Crown CA, sideways (1901)*

15	1c. black and green	23·00	14·00
	a. Grey and green	6·50	1·50
	b. Grey-brown and green	15·00	45
16	3c. black and brown	28·00	8·50
	a. Grey and brown	8·00	35
	b. Grey-brown and brown	14·00	20
17	4c. black and carmine	26·00	15·00
	a. Grey and carmine	14·00	11·00
	b. Grey-brown and carmine	25·00	6·00
18	5c. green and carmine/*yellow*	2·50	4·00
19	8c. black and ultramarine	48·00	30·00
	a. Grey and ultramarine	25·00	11·00
	b. Grey-brown and ultramarine	27·00	3·75
20	10c. black and claret	£150	65·00
	a. Grey and claret	80·00	18·00
	b. Black and purple	£180	65·00
	c. Grey and purple	85·00	22·00
	d. Grey-brown and purple	90·00	11·00
21	20c. mauve and black	18·00	18·00
22	50c. black and orange-brown	£200	£160
	a. Grey and orange-brown	£100	65·00
	b. Grey-brown and orange-brown	£120	50·00
15/22b *Set of 8*		£200	80·00
15s/22s Optd 'SPECIMEN' *Set of 8*		£275	

Later printings in 1903–1904 show the two upper lines of shading in the background at the corner nearest to the 'S' of 'STATE' blurred and running into one another, whereas in earlier printings these lines are distinct. Two plates were used for printing the central design of T **3**. In Plate 1 the lines of background are regular throughout, but in Plate 2 they are lighter around the head and back of the tiger. The 5c. was the only value with single wmk to be printed from Plate 2. Stamps with multiple wmk were printed for a short time from Plate 1, and show the two blurred lines of background near 'S' of 'STATE,' but the majority of these stamps were printed from Plate 2 and later plates.

(b) T **4**. *Wmk Crown CC (1900)*

23	$1 green and pale green	£190	£190
	w. Wmk inverted	†	—
24	$2 green and carmine	£180	£200
25	$5 green and bright ultramarine	£450	£475
	a. Green and pale ultramarine	£425	£425
26	$25 green and orange (F.C. £110)	£5000	£2000
	s. Optd 'SPECIMEN'	£450	
23s/25s Optd 'SPECIMEN' *Set of 3*		£200	

Two dies for 1c. green and 4c. scarlet

Die I. 'Head' and duty plates. Thick frame line below 'MALAY' and in the 1c. the 'c' is thin whilst in the 4c. it is thick.

Die II. Single working plate. Thin frame line below 'MALAY' and in the 1c. the 'c' is thicker whilst in the 4c. it is thinner.

1904 (Aug)–**22**. T **3** and T **4** (dollar values). Wmk Mult Crown CA (sideways* on T **3**). Ordinary paper (1c. to 50c.) or chalk-surfaced paper ($1 to $25).

27	1c. grey and green (8.04)	85·00	10·00
	a. Grey-brown and green	48·00	70
28	1c. green (Die I) (8.7.06)	30·00	30
29	1c. green (Die II) (1908)	17·00	20
	a. Yellow-green	28·00	3·00
	aw. Wmk Crown to right of CA	95·00	12·00
	b. Blue-green	42·00	1·75
30	1c. deep brown (21.1.19)	2·25	90
	w. Wmk Crown to right of CA	†	£300
31	2c. green (18.2.19)	2·50	30
	w. Wmk Crown to right of CA	£100	18·00
32	3c. grey and brown (10.04)	75·00	2·00
	a. Grey-brown and brown (12.05)	55·00	1·75
	ab. Chalk-surfaced paper	48·00	2·75
33	3c. brown (11.7.06)	10·00	15
34	3c. carmine (2.2.09)	5·50	10
	aw. Wmk Crown to right of CA	38·00	50
	b. Scarlet (1.17)	35·00	50
	bw. Wmk Crown to right of CA	60·00	4·50
35	3c. grey (29.10.18)	2·50	20
	w. Wmk Crown to right of CA	95·00	18·00
36	4c. grey and scarlet (8.04)	70·00	10·00
	a. Chalk-surfaced paper. Grey and rose	50·00	6·00
	b. Grey-brown and scarlet	60·00	4·25
	c. Black and scarlet	32·00	3·50
	d. Black and rose	9·50	80
	dw. Wmk Crown to right of CA	16·00	1·00
	e. Black and deep rose (aniline) (1909)	60·00	6·00
	f. Jet black and rose (1914)	48·00	4·00
37	4c. scarlet (Die I) (11.2.19)	3·50	4·75
38	4c. scarlet (Die II) (15.4.19)	1·75	15
	aw. Wmk Crown to right of CA	70·00	6·50
	ay. Wmk Crown to right of CA and reversed	†	£650
	b. Wmk upright (2.22)	£900	£400
39	5c. green and carmine/*yellow* (5.06)	12·00	3·25
	aw. Wmk Crown to right of CA	£120	26·00
	b. Chalk-surfaced paper	50·00	8·50
	c. Deep green and carmine/yellow	15·00	4·00
	d. On orange-buff (1921)	24·00	19·00
	e. On pale yellow (4.22)	16·00	16·00
40	6c. orange (11.2.19)	2·75	3·75
41	8c. grey and ultramarine (2.05)	85·00	30·00
	aw. Wmk Crown to right of CA		
	b. Grey-brown and ultramarine (12.05)	21·00	6·00
	ba. Chalk-surfaced paper	95·00	23·00
	bb. Wmk upright (3.07)	9·00	7·00
42	8c. ultramarine (8.3.10)	13·00	1·25
	aw. Wmk Crown to right of CA	£150	42·00
	b. Deep blue (1918)	16·00	1·25
43	10c. grey-brown and claret (5.04)	90·00	15·00
	a. Chalk-surfaced paper (1905)	£140	23·00
	b. Black and claret	42·00	75
	bw. Wmk Crown to right of CA	65·00	1·50
	c. Grey-brown and purple (1905)	80·00	3·75
	d. Black and purple	50·00	3·50
	dy. Wmk Crown to right of CA and reversed	†	£450
	e. Jet-black and bright purple (1914)	£110	5·00
44	10c. deep blue (3.6.19)	8·00	2·00
	a. Bright blue	6·50	1·00
	ab. Wmk inverted	†	—
	ac. Substituted crown in wmk	†	£1100
	aw. Wmk Crown to right of CA	£120	25·00
45	20c. mauve and black (3.05)	23·00	1·25
	a. Chalk-surfaced paper	13·00	3·50
	w. Wmk Crown to right of CA	£160	32·00
46	35c. scarlet/*pale yellow* (25.8.22)	5·50	18·00
47	50c. grey and orange (3.05)	95·00	22·00
	aw. Wmk Crown to right of CA	£375	£100
	b. Wmk inverted (F.C. £150)	†	—
	c. Grey-brown and orange-brown (1906)	70·00	20·00
	caw. Wmk Crown to right of CA	†	—
	d. Chalk-surfaced paper. *Grey-brown and orange-brown*	75·00	9·00
	da. Grey and orange-brown	80·00	17·00
	db. Black and orange-brown	£130	38·00
	dc. Jet-black and orange-brown (1914)	£180	42·00
	dw. Wmk Crown to right of CA	†	£150
48	$1 grey-green and green (10.07)	£120	50·00
	a. Green and pale green	£160	50·00
	aw. Wmk inverted	£1100	
	ax. Wmk reversed	†	—
49	$2 green and carmine (4.12.07)	£130	£140
	a. Printed on the gummed side		
	w. Wmk inverted		
	y. Wmk inverted and reversed	†	£1200
50	$5 green and blue (1.08)	£325	£160
51	$25 green and orange (12.09) (F.C. £60)	£2250	£900
27/50 *Set of 22*		£800	£350
28s, 30s/31s, 33s/35s, 38s, 40s, 42s, 44s, 46s Optd 'SPECIMEN' *Set of 11*		£800	

* The normal sideways watermark shows Crown to left of CA, *as seen from the back of the stamp*. The watermark on No. 47b is vertical, inverted.

Nos. 29/29*b*, 30, 31, 33, 34/34*b* and 35 were printed from single working plates and all the rest from double plates.

Most examples of No. 47b have fiscal cancellations, but at least one is known postally used.

The 3c. scarlet (No. 34*b*) was surcharged '4/CENTS.' between horizontal lines in early 1918, but was never issued. The entire printing of five million stamps was sunk at sea, nevertheless a few examples do exist. *(Price, £5500, unused)*.

1922–34. Wmk Mult Script CA (sideways* on T **3**). Ordinary paper (1c. to 10c. (No. 66), 12c., 20c. (No. 69a), 35c. (No. 72)) or chalk-surfaced paper (others).

52	**3**	1c. deep brown (1.8.22)	1·50	5·00
		w. Wmk Crown to right of CA	£110	£110
53		1c. black (12.6.23)	75	20
54		2c. brown (5.8.25)	15·00	16·00
55		2c. green (15.6.26)	3·00	10
56		3c. grey (27.12.22)	1·75	7·50
		w. Wmk Crown to right of CA	£140	£140
57		3c. green (22.1.24)	1·25	1·50
58		3c. brown (31.5.27)	5·50	50
59		4c. carmine-red (Die II) (27.11.23)	4·00	70
		w. Wmk Crown to right of CA	55·00	22·00
60		4c. orange (9.11.26)	1·50	10
		a. No watermark	£375	£275
		c. 'A' of 'CA' missing from wmk	†	£900
61		5c. mauve/*pale yellow* (17.3.22)	1·00	20
		w. Wmk Crown to right of CA	£100	55·00
62		5c. brown (1.3.32)	3·50	10
63		6c. orange (2.5.22)	1·00	45
		w. Wmk Crown to right of CA	£180	
64		6c. scarlet (9.11.26)	1·50	10
65		10c. bright blue (23.10.23)	1·25	8·50
		w. Wmk Crown to right of CA		
66		10c. black and blue (18.1.24†)	2·00	75
67		10c. purple/*pale yellow* (14.7.31)	3·75	40
68		12c. ultramarine (12.9.22)	1·25	10
		w. Wmk Crown to right of CA	£120	40·00
		x. Wmk sideways reversed	£400	
69		20c. dull purple and black (*chalk-surfaced paper*) (3.4.23)	4·00	3·00
		a. Ordinary paper (29.12.26)	70·00	6·00
		b. Wmk inverted	†	£550
70		25c. purple and bright magenta (3.9.29)	2·75	3·75
71		30c. purple and orange-yellow (3.9.29)	3·25	5·50
72		35c. scarlet/*pale yellow* (6.11.28)	3·25	28·00
73		35c. scarlet and purple (29.9.31)	13·00	14·00
74		50c. black and orange (24.4.24)	13·00	21·00
		aw. Wmk Crown to right of CA	£180	
		b. Black and orange-brown	42·00	8·00
75		50c. black/*green* (16.6.31)	4·00	2·50
76	**4**	$1 pale green and green (2.2.26)	23·00	£100
		a. Grey-green and emerald (5.10.26)	23·00	55·00
		sa. Opt 'SPECIMEN' double	£500	
77	**3**	$1 black and red/*blue* (10.3.31)	12·00	5·00
78	**4**	$2 green and carmine (17.8.26)	48·00	£100
79	**3**	$2 green and red/*yellow* (6.2.34)	65·00	50·00
80	**4**	$5 green and blue (24.2.25)	£225	£300
		w. Wmk inverted	£1600	
81	**3**	$5 green and red/*green* (7.34)	£375	£300
82	**4**	$25 green and orange (14.2.28) (F.C. £180)	£2250	£2750
		s. Optd 'SPECIMEN'	£550	
52/81 *Set of 30*			£750	£800
52s/81s Optd or Perf (No. 62s, 67s, 70s/71s, 73s, 77s, 79s, 81s) 'SPECIMEN' *Set of 30*			£2000	

* The normal sideways watermark shows Crown to left of CA, *as seen from the back of the stamp*.

† No. 66 was released in London by the Crown Agents some months earlier but this is the official date of issue in the States.

The 2c. green (No. 55), 3c. brown (No. 58), 4c. orange (No. 60) and 6c. scarlet (No. 64) exist with wmk upright. These were formerly listed as Nos. 55a, 58a, 60b and 64a, but are now known to be colour trials, of unissued status. (Prices, £800 each).

Nos. 52, 56 and 59 were printed from single working plates and the rest from double plates.

No. 55 exists in coils constructed from normal sheets.

The 5c. mauve on white Script paper is the result of soaking early printings of No. 61 in water.

STAMP BOOKLETS

1909. Black on pink (Nos. SB1/SB2) or black on buff (No. SB3) covers. Stapled.

SB1	25c. booklet containing 4×1c. (No. 29) in blocks of 6	£2500
	a. Black on green cover (1917)	
	b. Black on blue cover	£2500
SB2	73c. booklet containing 24×3c. (No. 34) in blocks of 6	£2500
	a. Black on red cover (1917)	
	b. Black on blue cover	£2500
SB3	97c. booklet containing 24×4c. (No. 36*d*) in blocks of 6	£2750

1919. Black on green (No. SB4) or black on pink (No. SB5) covers. Stapled.

SB4	49c. booklet containing 24×2c. (No. 31) in blocks of 6	£5500
SB5	97c. booklet containing 24×4c. (No. 37) in blocks of 6	£2250

1922. Black on buff cover (No. SB7). Stapled.

SB6	$1.21 booklet containing 24×5c. (No. 61) in blocks of 6	£3250
SB7	$1.45 booklet containing 24×6c. (No. 63) in blocks of 6	£2750

1926. As Nos. SB4, SB3 and SB7, but sold at face value without premium. Black on green (No. SB8), black on pink (No. SB9) or black on buff (No. SB10) covers. Stapled.

SB8	48c. booklet containing 24×2c. (No. 55) in blocks of 6	
SB9	96c. booklet containing 24×4c. (No. 60) in blocks of 6	£2750
SB10	$1.44 booklet containing 24×6c. (No. 64) in blocks of 6	£2750

1926. Black on grey cover. Stapled.

SB11	$1 booklet containing 4c. and 6c. (Nos. 60, 64) each in block of 10	£2750

1927. Black on bluish green cover. Stapled.

SB12	$1.50 booklet containing 2c., 3c., 4c. and 6c. (Nos. 55, 58, 60, 64) each in block of 10	£3250

1927–30. Black on red (No. SB13), black on green (No. SB14) or black on blue (No. SB15) covers. Stapled.

SB13	$1.20 booklet containing 30×4c. (No. 60) in blocks of 10	£3000
	a. Black on orange cover (1930)	
SB14	$1.20 booklet containing 20×6c. (No. 64) in blocks of 10 (1928)	£3500
SB15	$1.20 booklet containing 2c., 4c. and 6c. (Nos. 55, 60, 64) each in block of 10 (1928)	£2750
	a. Black on white cover (1930)	

1934. Black on buff cover. Stapled.

SB16	$1 booklet containing 20×5c. (No. 62) in blocks of 10	£3250

POSTAGE DUE STAMPS

D **1**

(Typo Waterlow)

1924 (1 Dec)–**26**. Wmk Mult Script CA (sideways*). P 15×14.

D1	D **1**	1c. violet	4·75	55·00
		w. Wmk Crown to left of CA (1926)	28·00	48·00
D2		2c. black	1·75	12·00
		w. Wmk Crown to left of CA (1926)	4·00	3·25
D3		4c. green (wmk Crown to left of CA) (27.4.26)	2·25	5·00
D4		8c. red	4·75	48·00
		w. Wmk Crown to left of CA (1926)	15·00	18·00
D5		10c. orange	8·00	15·00
		w. Wmk Crown to left of CA (1926)	42·00	24·00
D6		12c. blue	8·00	27·00
		w. Wmk Crown to left of CA (1926)	15·00	6·00
D1/D6 *Set of 6*			27·00	85·00
D1s/D6s Optd 'SPECIMEN' *Set of 6*			£250	

* The normal sideways watermark shows Crown to right of CA, *as seen from the back of the stamp*.

The issues of the Federated Malay States were replaced by stamps for the individual States from 1935 onwards.

III. MALAYAN POSTAL UNION

The Malayan Postal Union was organised in 1934 and, initially, covered the Straits Settlements and the Federated Malay States. Stamps of the Straits Settlements together with issues for the individual States continued to be used, but Malayan Postal Union postage due stamps were introduced in 1936.

Following the end of the Second World War the use of these postage dues spread throughout Malaya and to Singapore.

PRICES FOR STAMPS ON COVER TO 1945	
Nos. D1/D6	*from* × 10
Nos. D7/D13	*from* × 4

POSTAGE DUE STAMPS

D **1**

10
cents
(D **2**)

(Typo Waterlow until 1961, then D.L.R.)

1936 (June)–**38**. Wmk Mult Script CA. P 15×14.

D1	D **1**	1c. slate-purple (4.38)	18·00	70
D2		4c. green (9.36)	40·00	1·00
D3		8c. scarlet	20·00	2·25
D4		10c. yellow-orange	26·00	30
D5		12c. pale ultramarine (9.36)	40·00	15·00
D6		50c. black (1.38)	30·00	4·50
D1/D6 *Set of 6*			£160	21·00
D1s/D6s Perf 'SPECIMEN' *Set of 6*			£275	

For use in Negri Sembilan, Pahang, Perak, Selangor and Straits Settlements including Singapore.

1945–49. New values and colours. Wmk Mult Script CA. P 15×14.

D7	D **1**	1c. purple	5·00	2·00
D8		3c. green	10·00	1·75
D9		5c. scarlet	6·00	1·75
D10		8c. yellow-orange (1949)	13·00	14·00
		s. Perf 'SPECIMEN'	90·00	
D11		9c. yellow-orange	40·00	50·00
D12		15c. pale ultramarine	£110	29·00
D13		20c. blue (1948)	10·00	5·00
		s. Perf 'SPECIMEN'	90·00	
D7/D13 *Set of 7*			£170	95·00

1951 (8 Aug)–**63**. Wmk Mult Script CA. P 14.

D14	D **1**	1c. violet (21.8.52)	70	1·60
D15		2c. deep slate-blue (16.11.53)	1·25	2·25
		a. Perf 12½ (15.11.60)	4·25	26·00
		ab. Chalk-surfaced paper (10.7.62)	2·00	17·00
		ac. Ditto. Imperf horiz (vert pair)	†	£10000
D16		3c. deep green (21.8.52)	40·00	23·00
D17		4c. sepia (16.11.53)	70	7·00
		a. Perf 12½ (15.11.60)	3·50	28·00
		ab. Chalk-surfaced paper. *Bistre-brown* (10.7.62)	1·00	21·00
D18		5c. vermilion	48·00	12·00
D19		8c. yellow-orange	2·50	11·00
D20		12c. bright purple (1.2.54)	1·25	6·00
		a. Perf 12½. Chalk-surfaced paper (10.7.62)	5·00	35·00
D21		20c. blue	11·00	6·50
		a. Perf 12½. *Deep blue* (10.12.57)	7·00	26·00
		ab. Chalk-surfaced paper (15.10.63)	12·00	50·00
D14/D21 *Set of 8*			90·00	60·00

Nos. D7 to D21ab were for use in the Federation and Singapore.

No. D15ac, the 2c. perforation error, is known only from a vertical strip of three *on piece* and a block of 20, used on a cover postmarked at Tanglin, Singapore on 21 May 1965.

1964 (14 Apr)–**65**. Chalk-surfaced paper. Wmk w **12** (sideways on 1c.). P 12½.

D22	D **1**	1c. maroon	30	21·00
		a. Perf 12. Wmk upright (4.5.65)	2·00	18·00
D23		2c. deep slate-blue	1·75	18·00
		a. Perf 12 (9.3.65)	1·25	24·00
D24		4c. bistre-brown	1·00	18·00
		a. Perf 12 (9.3.65)	2·50	18·00
D25		8c. yellow-orange (P 12) (4.5.65)	2·00	24·00
D27		12c. bright purple	1·50	22·00
		a. Perf 12 (4.5.65)	7·00	48·00
D28		20c. deep blue	2·50	40·00
		a. Perf 12 (4.5.65)	10·00	60·00
D22/D28 *Set of 6*			7·50	£130

1964 (1 Dec). As No. D19 surch locally with T D **2**.

D29	D **1**	10c. on 8c. yellow-orange	60	3·00

First supplies of this stamp differed from No. D19 in that they had been climatically affected, but later a fresh printing of No. D19 was surcharged.

1966. Unsurfaced paper. Wmk w **12**. P 15×14.

D30	D **1**	50c. black	£2250	£2000

Nos. D22/D29 were for use throughout Malaysia and Singapore. They were superseded on 15 August 1966 by the postage dues inscribed 'MALAYSIA', but continued in use, together with No. D30, for Singapore until 31 January 1968 when they were replaced by Singapore Postage Dues.

IV. MALAYA (BRITISH MILITARY ADMINISTRATION)

Following the Japanese surrender on 2 September 1945 British troops landed in Malaya which was placed under a British Military Administration. The Director of Posts was ashore at Singapore on 6 September and had reached Kuala Lumpur by 13 September. Postal services in Singapore and Johore resumed on 17 September and had spread to the remainder of the country by 5 October. No stamps were initially available so all mail up to 1 oz. was carried free until the first overprinted stamps appeared on 19 October.

De La Rue had overprinted available stocks of pre-war Straits Settlements stamps earlier in 1945 and initial supplies of these London overprints were placed on sale from 19 October (Nos. 1, 2a, 4, 6a, 7 and 8a) with the 15c. and 25c. (Nos. 11 and 13a) issued later. A second consignment contained dollar values including the $5 purple and orange. Duplicate plates were subsequently sent to the Government Printing Office at Kuala Lumpur, where the overprinting of surviving local stocks of the 1c., 5c., 10c., 15c. (overprinted in black) and $5 green and red on emerald took place, and to Australia for those shipments which had been diverted there in 1941.

The stamps were used throughout all Malay States and in Singapore. From 1948 this general issue was gradually replaced by individual issues for each state. The last usage was in Kelantan where B M A overprints were not withdrawn until 10 July 1951.

B M A
MALAYA
(**1**)

1945 (19 Oct)–**48**. T **58** of Straits Settlements from Die I (double-plate printing) or Die II (single-plate printing) optd with T **1**. Wmk Mult Script CA. Chalk-surfaced paper. P 14 or 15×14 (No. 11).

1	1c. black (I) (R.)	8·00	70
	aa. Opt double, one albino	£1500	
	ab. Magenta opt	£7000	£1400
	b. Ordinary paper	10	30
	c. Thin striated paper (8.46)	38·00	18·00
2	2c. orange (II) (8.7.47)	9·00	60
	a. Ordinary paper (19.10.45)	20	10
	b. Thin striated paper (7.46)	19·00	8·50
	w. Wmk inverted	†	£2000
3	2c. orange (I) (*ordinary paper*) (9.46)	30·00	7·50
4	3c. yellow-green (II) (*ordinary paper*)	9·00	50
	a. Blue-green (27.1.47)	13·00	8·50
	b. Chalk-surfaced paper. *Blue-green* (8.7.47)	27·00	1·00
5	5c. brown (II) (24.10.45)	70	1·00
6	6c. grey (II) (22.3.48)	30·00	7·00
	a. Ordinary paper (19.10.45)	30	20
	b. Thin striated paper (6.46)	20·00	12·00
7	8c. scarlet (II) (*ordinary paper*)	30	10
	a. Thin striated paper (6.46)	20·00	18·00
8	10c. purple (I) (12.45)	15·00	1·25
	a. Ordinary paper (19.10.45)	50	10
	b. Slate-purple (12.45)	11·00	30
	c. Magenta (22.3.48)	14·00	70
	d. Thin striated paper (8.46)	24·00	15·00
9	10c. purple (II) (28.7.48)	19·00	9·00
10	12c. bright ultramarine (I) (11.45)	1·75	22·00
11	15c. bright ultramarine (II) (*ordinary paper*) (11.45)	2·50	14·00
12	15c. bright ultramarine (II) (R.) (22.3.48)	50·00	2·50
	a. Ordinary paper (12.45)	75	20
	b. Blue (27.11.47)	75·00	85
	ba. Ordinary paper (8.7.47)	£150	22·00
13	25c. dull purple and scarlet (I) (22.3.48)	42·00	4·75
	a. Ordinary paper (12.45)	1·40	30
	ab. Opt double	£7000	
	ac. 'A' of 'CA' missing from watermark	†	£2750
	ad. Opt double, one albino	£1300	
	b. Thin striated paper (8.46)	25·00	8·00
14	50c. black/*emerald* (I) (*ordinary paper*) (R.) (12.45)	1·00	10
15	$1 black and red (I) (*ordinary paper*) (12.45)	2·00	10
	a. 'A' of 'CA' missing from watermark	†	£2750
16	$2 green and scarlet (I) (*ordinary paper*) (12.45)	2·75	1·00
17	$5 green and red/*emerald* (I) (11.45)	£110	£160
18	$5 purple and orange (I) (*ordinary paper*) (12.45)	6·50	3·00
1/18 *Set of 15*		£120	£170
1as/7s, 8as, 10s, 12as/16s, 18s Perf 'SPECIMEN' *Set of 14*		£850	

The 8c. grey with 'BMA' opt was prepared but not officially issued (*Price £550 unused*).

Nos. 3 and 9 do not exist without the overprint.

Initial printings on ordinary paper were produced by Harrison and Sons in 1941 following bomb damage to the De La Rue works on 29 December 1940.

For a description of the thin striated paper, see the introduction to this catalogue.

No. 8 with reddish purple medallion and dull purple frame is from a 1947 printing with the head in fugitive ink which discolours with moisture.

Postal forgeries of the 50c. value exist made by dyeing examples of the 1c. value and then altering the face value to 50c.

In 1946 8c. and 15c. stamps in the Crown Colony Victory design were prepared for the Malayan Union, but not issued. Examples of the 8c. carmine from this issue exist from unofficial leakages (Price £600 unused).

V. MALAYAN FEDERATION

The Malayan Federation, formed on 1 February 1948 by Malacca, Penang, the four Federated Malay States and the five Unfederated States, became an independent member of the British Commonwealth on 31 August 1957.

Commemoratives and a limited series of definitives were issued by the Federation and were used concurrently with the stamps from the individual States.

1 Tapping Rubber

2 Federation Coat of Arms

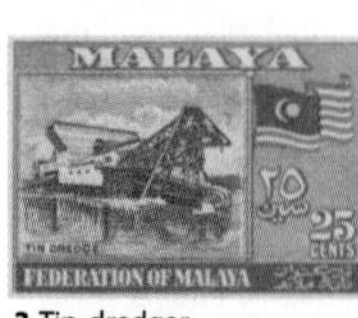

3 Tin dredger

4 Map of the Federation

(Centre recess, frame litho (6c., 25c.); centre litho, frame recess (12c.); recess (30c.), D.L.R.)

1957 (5 May)–**63**. Types **1**, **4** and similar designs. W w **12**. P 13×11½-12½* (No. 4) or 13 (others).

1	6c. deep blue, red, yellow and grey-blue	50	10
	a. Indigo, red, yellow and grey-blue (20.6.61)	10·00	1·25
	b. Indigo, red, yellow and slate-blue (12.2.63)	8·50	1·25
	c. Yellow (star and crescent) omitted	£140	
	w. Wmk inverted	†	£750
2	12c. red, yellow, blue, black and scarlet	2·25	1·00
3	25c. maroon, red, yellow and dull greenish blue	4·75	20
4	30c. orange-red and lake	2·00	20
	a. Perf 13. *Orange-red and deep lake* (20.6.61)	2·75	2·50
	ab. Orange-red and lake (10.7.62)	3·75	10
1/4 *Set of 4*		8·50	1·25

* On No. 4 the top five perforation holes measure 11½, with the remainder being perf 12½.

5 Prime Minister Tunku Abdul Rahman and Populace greeting Independence

(Des A. B. Seeman. Recess Imprimerie Belge de Sécurité SA)

1957 (31 Aug). Independence Day. Wmk Mult Script CA. P 12½.

5	**5**	10c. bistre-brown	80	10

6 United Nations Emblem

7 United Nations Emblem

(Recess D.L.R.)

1958 (5 Mar). UN Economic Commission for Asia and Far East Conference, Kuala Lumpur. W w **12**. P 13½ (12c.) or 13×11½-12½ (30c.).

6	**6**	12c. carmine-red	30	80
7	**7**	30c. maroon	40	80

8 Merdeka Stadium, Kuala Lumpur

9 The Yang di-Pertuan Agong (Tuanku Abdul Rahman)

(Photo Harrison)

1958 (31 Aug). First Anniversary of Independence. W w **12**. P 13½×14½ (10c.) or 14½×13½ (30c.).

8	**8**	10c. green, yellow, red and blue	15	10
9	**9**	30c. red, yellow, violet-blue and green	40	70

10 'Human Rights'

11 Malayan with Torch of Freedom

(Des J. P. Hendroff. Litho (10c.), photo (30c.) D.L.R.)

1958 (10 Dec). Tenth Anniversary of Declaration of Human Rights.

(a) W w **12**. *P 12½×13*

10	**10**	10c. blue, black, carmine and orange	15	10

(b) Wmk Mult Script CA. P 13×12½

11	**11**	30c. deep green	45	60

12 Mace and Malayan Peoples

(Photo Enschedé)

1959 (12 Sept). Inauguration of Parliament. No wmk. P 13×14.

No.	Type	Description	Unused	Used
12	12	4c. rose-red	10	10
13		10c. violet	10	10
14		25c. yellow-green	75	20
12/14 *Set of 3*			85	30

13

14

(Recess D.L.R.)

1960 (7 Apr). World Refugee Year. W w **12**. P 13½ (12c.) or 12½×13 (30c.)

No.	Type	Description	Unused	Used
15	13	12c. purple	15	60
16	14	30c. deep green	15	10

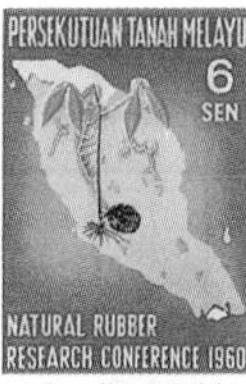

15 Seedling Rubber Tree and Map

16 The Yang di-Pertuan Agong (Tuanku Syed Putra)

(Photo Japanese Govt Ptg Wks)

1960 (19 Sept). Natural Rubber Research Conference and 15th International Rubber Study Group Meeting, Kuala Lumpur. T **15** and similar vert design. No wmk. P 13.

No.	Type	Description	Unused	Used
17		6c. yellow-green, black, orange and red-brown	20	1·25
18		30c. yellow-green, black, orange and bright blue	50	75

No. 18 is inscribed 'INTERNATIONAL RUBBER STUDY GROUP 15th MEETING KUALA LUMPUR' at foot.

(Photo Harrison)

1961 (4 Jan). Installation of Yang di-Pertuan Agong, Tuanku Syed Putra. W w **12**. P 14×14½.

No.	Type	Description	Unused	Used
19	16	10c. black and blue	10	10

17 Colombo Plan Emblem

18 Malaria Eradication Emblem

(Photo Japanese Govt Ptg Works)

1961 (30 Oct). Colombo Plan Conference, Kuala Lumpur. P 13.

No.	Type	Description	Unused	Used
20	17	12c. black and magenta	35	3·00
21		25c. black and apple-green	80	2·50
22		30c. black and turquoise-blue	70	1·00
20/22 *Set of 3*			1·75	6·00

(Photo Harrison)

1962 (7 Apr). Malaria. Eradication. W w **13**. P 14×14½.

No.	Type	Description	Unused	Used
23	18	25c. orange-brown	20	40
24		30c. deep lilac	20	15
25		50c. ultramarine	40	80
23/25 *Set of 3*			70	1·25

19 Palmyra Palm Leaf

20 'Shadows of the Future'

(Photo Harrison)

1962 (21 July). National Language Month. W w **13** (upright or inverted). P 13½.

No.	Type	Description	Unused	Used
26	19	10c. light brown and deep reddish violet	30	10
27		20c. light brown and deep bluish green	1·25	1·25
28		50c. light brown and magenta	2·50	1·75
26/28 *Set of 3*			3·50	2·75

Nos. 26/28 were printed *tête-bêche*.

(Photo Enschedé)

1962 (1 Oct). Introduction of Free Primary Education. W w **13**. P 13½.

No.	Type	Description	Unused	Used
29	20	10c. bright purple	10	10
		w. Wmk inverted	60·00	
30		25c. ochre	60	1·25
31		30c. emerald	3·00	10
29/31 *Set of 3*			3·25	1·25

21 Harvester and Fisherman

22 Dam and Pylon

(Photo Courvoisier)

1963 (21 Mar). Freedom from Hunger. P 11½.

No.	Type	Description	Unused	Used
32	21	25c. carmine and apple-green	3·25	3·50
33		30c. carmine and crimson	3·75	2·00
34		50c. carmine and bright blue	3·50	3·00
32/34 *Set of 3*			9·50	7·75

(Photo Harrison)

1963 (26 June). Cameron Highlands Hydro-Electric Scheme. W w **13**. P 14.

No.	Type	Description	Unused	Used
35	22	20c. green and reddish violet	60	10
36		30c. blue-green and ultramarine	1·00	1·50

The definitive general issue for Malaysia and the low value sets for the individual states superseded the stamps of the Malayan Federation by 15 November 1965.

VI. MALAYSIA

On 16 September 1963, the Malayan Federation, Sabah (North Borneo), Sarawak and Singapore formed the Federation of Malaysia. Singapore left the Federation on 9 August 1965, and became an independent republic. Stamps of Singapore continued to be valid in Malaysia, and those of Malaysia in Singapore, until 1 February 1967.

Individual issues for the component States continued, but were restricted to low value definitives and the occasional 'State' commemorative. The higher value definitives and the vast majority of commemoratives were issued on a 'National' basis.

NATIONAL ISSUES

General issues for use throughout the Malaysian Federation.

1 Federation Map

2 Bouquet of Orchids

(Photo Harrison)

1963 (16 Sept). Inauguration of Federation. W w **13**. P 14½.

No.	Type	Description	Unused	Used
1	1	10c. yellow and bluish violet	1·25	10
		a. Yellow omitted	£600	
2		12c. yellow and deep green	1·75	60
3		50c. yellow and chocolate	1·75	10
1/3 *Set of 3*			4·25	65

(Photo Enschedé)

1963 (3 Oct). Fourth World Orchid Conference, Singapore. No wmk. P 13×14.

No.	Type	Description	Unused	Used
4	2	6c. multicoloured	1·25	1·25
5		25c. multicoloured	1·25	25

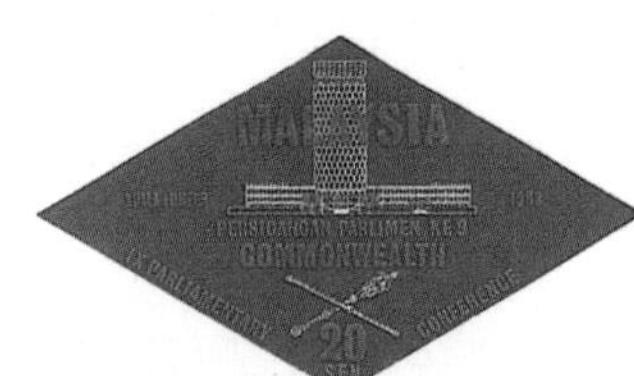
4 Parliament House, Kuala Lumpur

(Des V. Whiteley. Photo Harrison)

1963 (4 Nov). Ninth Commonwealth Parliamentary Conference, Kuala Lumpur. W w **13** (inverted). P 13½.

No.	Type	Description	Unused	Used
7	4	20c. deep magenta and gold	1·25	40
8		30c. deep green and gold	1·75	15

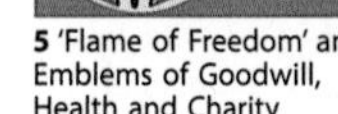

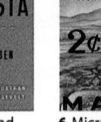

5 'Flame of Freedom' and Emblems of Goodwill, Health and Charity

6 Microwave Tower and ITU Emblem

(Photo Harrison)

1964 (10 Oct). Eleanor Roosevelt Commemoration. W w **13**. P 14½×13½.

No.	Type	Description	Unused	Used
9	5	25c. black, red and greenish blue	20	10
10		30c. black, red and deep lilac	20	15
11		50c. black, red and ochre-yellow	20	10
9/11 *Set of 3*			55	30

(Photo Courvoisier)

1965 (17 May). ITU Centenary. P 11½.

No.	Type	Description	Unused	Used
12	6	2c. multicoloured	75	3·25
13		25c. multicoloured	2·00	60
14		50c. multicoloured	2·75	10
12/14 *Set of 3*			5·00	3·50

7 National Mosque

8 Air Terminal

(Photo Harrison)

1965 (27 Aug). Opening of National Mosque, Kuala Lumpur. W w **13**. P 14×14½.

No.	Type	Description	Unused	Used
15	7	6c. carmine	10	10
16		15c. red-brown	20	10
17		20c. deep bluish green	20	15
15/17 *Set of 3*			45	30

(Photo Harrison)

1965 (30 Aug). Opening of International Airport, Kuala Lumpur. W w **13**. P 14½×14.

No.	Type	Description	Unused	Used
18	8	15c. black, yellow-green and new blue	40	10
		a. Yellow-green omitted	38·00	
19		30c. black, yellow-green and magenta	60	20

9 Crested Wood Partridge

17 Sepak Raga (ball game) and Football

75c. Extra stroke in Malay inscription above 'S' of 'MALAYSIA' (Pl. 1A, R. 9/4)

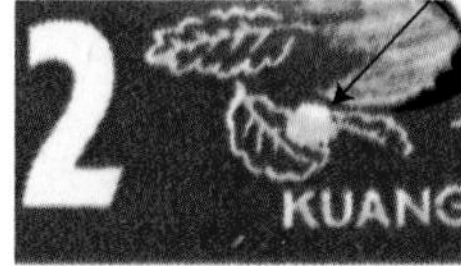
$2 Oval flaw above 'KU' of 'KUANG' resembles an egg (Pl. 1A, R.5/6)

(Des A. Fraser-Brunner. Photo Harrison)

1965 (9 Sept). T **9** and similar vert designs. Multicoloured. W w **13**. P 14½.

No.	Type	Description	Unused	Used
20		25c. Type **9**	50	10
		w. Wmk inverted	4·50	
21		30c. Blue-backed Fairy Bluebird	60	10
		a. Blue (plumage) omitted	£375	
		b. Yellow omitted	£550	
		w. Wmk inverted	13·00	
22		50c. Black-nailed Oriole	1·25	10
		a. Yellow omitted	£300	
		c. Scarlet (inscr and berries) omitted	£180	
		w. Wmk inverted	27·00	
23		75c. Rhinoceros Hornbill	1·00	10
		a. Inscription flaw	20·00	
24		$1 Zebra Dove	1·50	10
		w. Wmk inverted	50·00	
25		$2 Great Argus Pheasant	9·50	30
		b. 'Egg' flaw	65·00	
		w. Wmk inverted	16·00	
26		$5 Asiatic Paradise Flycatcher	20·00	3·25
		w. Wmk inverted	50·00	
27		$10 Blue-tailed Pitta	45·00	13·00
20/27 *Set of 8*			70·00	15·00

All values except the 75c. and $10 exist with PVA gum as well as gum arabic, 21a and 22c exist on both papers.

Nos 20/27 exist imperforate. The 50c., $2 and $10 were formerly listed as Nos 22b, 25a and 27a, but are now considered to be of proof status. (*Price for set of 8 imperforate pairs*, £1000).

(Des E. A. F. Anthony. Litho Japanese Govt Ptg Wks)

1965 (14 Dec). Third South East Asian Peninsular Games. T **17** and similar vert designs. P 13×13½.

No.	Type	Description	Unused	Used
28		25c. black and olive-green	40	1·25
29		30c. black and bright purple	40	20
30		50c. black and light blue	1·00	30
28/30 *Set of 3*			1·60	1·60

Designs: 25c. T **17**; 30c. Running; 50c. Diving.

20 National Monument

21 The Yang di-Pertuan Agong (Tuanku Ismail Nasiruddin Shah)

(Photo Harrison)

1966 (8 Feb). National Monument, Kuala Lumpur. W w **13**. P 13½.

31 **20** 10c. multicoloured 50 10
a. Blue omitted £225
32 20c. multicoloured .... 1·00 40

Nos. 31/32 were printed *tête-bêche*.

(Photo Japanese Govt Ptg Wks)

1966 (11 Apr). Installation of Yang di-Pertuan Agong, Tuanku Ismail Nasiruddin Shah. P 13½.

33 **21** 15c. black and light yellow 10 10
34 50c. black and greenish blue 20 20

22 School Building

23 'Agriculture'

(Photo D.L.R.)

1966 (21 Oct). 150th Anniversary of Penang Free School. W w **13** (sideways). P 13.

35 **22** 20c. multicoloured 70 10
36 50c. multicoloured 90 10

The 50c. is also inscr 'ULANG TAHUN KE-150' at foot and bears a shield at bottom left corner.

(Des Enche Ng Peng Nam. Photo Japanese Govt Ptg Wks)

1966 (1 Dec). First Malaysia Plan. T **23** and similar horiz designs. Multicoloured. P 13½.

37 15c. Type **23** 20 10
38 15c. 'Rural Health' 20 10
39 15c. 'Communications' .... 3·00 15
40 15c. 'Education' 20 10
41 15c. 'Irrigation' 20 10
37/41 *Set of 5* .... 3·50 50

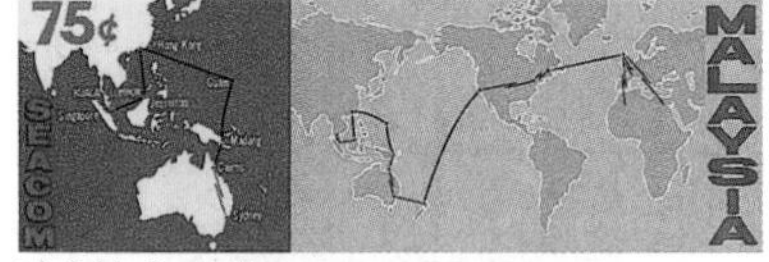

28 Cable Route Maps

(Des Enche Ng Peng Nam. Photo Japanese Govt Ptg Wks)

1967 (30 Mar). Completion of Malaysia–Hong Kong Link of SEACOM Telephone Cable. P 13½.

42 **28** 30c. multicoloured 80 50
43 75c. multicoloured .... 2·50 4·25

29 Hibiscus and Paramount Rulers

(Photo Harrison)

1967 (31 Aug). Tenth Anniversary of Independence. W w **13**. P 14½.

44 **29** 15c. multicoloured 20 10
w. Wmk inverted .... 4·00
45 50c. multicoloured .... 1·25 80

30 Mace and Shield

31 Straits Settlements 1867 8c. and Malaysia 1965 25c. Definitive

(Des Enche Ng Peng Nam. Photo Harrison)

1967 (8 Sept). Centenary of Sarawak Council. W w **13**. P 14½.

46 **30** 15c. multicoloured 10 10
47 50c. multicoloured 30 60

(Des Enche Ng Peng Nam. Photo Japanese Govt Ptg Works)

1967 (2 Dec). Stamp Centenary. T **31** and similar shaped designs. Multicoloured. P 11½.

48 25c. Type **31** .... 1·60 3·25
a. *Tête-bêche* (horiz pair) .... 3·00 6·50
49 30c. Straits Settlements 1867 24c. and Malaysia 1965 30c. definitive .... 1·60 2·75
a. *Tête-bêche* (horiz pair) .... 3·00 5·50
50 50c. Straits Settlements 1867 32c. and Malaysia 1965 50c. definitive .... 2·50 3·50
a. *Tête-bêche* (horiz pair) .... 5·00 7·00
48/50 *Set of 3* .... 5·25 8·50

Nos. 48/50 were each printed in sheets with the stamps arranged horizontally *tête-bêche*.

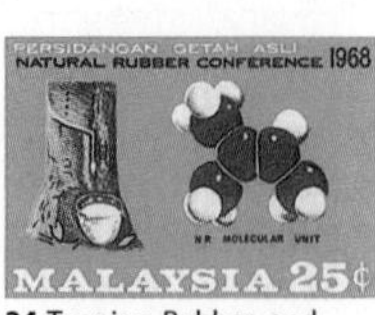

34 Tapping Rubber, and Molecular Unit

37 Mexican Sombrero and Blanket with Olympic Rings

(Litho B.W.)

1968 (29 Aug). Natural Rubber Conference, Kuala Lumpur. T **34** and similar horiz designs. Multicoloured. W w **13**. P 12.

51 25c. Type **34** 30 10
52 30c. Tapping rubber, and export consignment 40 20
53 50c. Tapping rubber, and aircraft tyres 40 10
51/53 *Set of 3* .... 1·00 35

(Litho B.W.)

1968 (12 Oct). Olympic Games Mexico. T **37** and similar vert design. Multicoloured. W w **13**. P 12×11½.

54 30c. Type **37** 20 10
55 75c. Olympic rings and Mexican embroidery 55 20

39 Tunku Abdul Rahman against background of Pandanus Weave

40 Tunku Abdul Rahman against background of Pandanus Weave

(Photo Japanese Govt Ptg Wks)

1969 (8 Feb). Solidarity Week. T **39/40** and similar multicoloured design. P 13½.

56 15c. Type **39** 15 10
57 20c. Type **40** .... 45 1·25
58 50c. Tunku Abdul Rahman with pandanus pattern (*horiz*) 50 20
56/58 *Set of 3* .... 1·00 1·40

42 Peasant Girl with Sheaves of Paddy

(Des Enche Hoessein Anas. Photo Harrison)

1969 (8 Dec). National Rice Year. W w **13**. P 13½.

59 **42** 15c. multicoloured 15 10
60 75c. multicoloured .... 55 1·50

43 Satellite tracking Aerial

44 *Intelsat III* in Orbit

(Photo Enschedé)

1970 (6 Apr). Satellite Earth Station. W w **13**. P 14×13 (15c.) or 13½×13 (30c.)

61 **43** 15c. multicoloured .... 1·00 15
a. *Tête-Bêche* (horiz pair) .... 2·00 2·50
62 **44** 30c. multicoloured* .... 1·00 2·75
63 30c. multicoloured* .... 1·00 2·75
61/63 *Set of 3* .... 2·75 5·00

No. 61 was issued horizontally and vertically *tête-bêche* in the sheets.

* Nos. 62/63 are of the same design, differing only in the lettering colours (No. 62 white; No. 63 gold).

45 *Euploea leucostictus*

46 Emblem

(Des V. Whiteley. Litho B.W. (to 1976) or Harrison)

1970 (31 Aug–16 Nov). Butterflies. T **45** and similar vert designs. Multicoloured. P 13×13½.

64 25c. Type **45** .... 1·00 10
65 30c. *Zeuxidia amethystus* .... 1·50 10
66 50c. *Polyura athamas* .... 2·00 10
67 75c. *Papilio memnon* .... 2·00 10
68 $1 *Appias nero* (16.11) .... 3·00 10
69 $2 *Trogonoptera brookiana* (16.11) .... 3·50 10
70 $5 *Narathura centaurus* (16.11) .... 5·00 3·75
71 $10 *Terinos terpander* (16.11) .... 17·00 5·00
64/71 *Set of 8* .... 32·00 8·50

There are considerable variations in the shades found on Nos. 64/71, with the Harrison printings appearing less green than the Bradbury Wilkinson.

(Litho Harrison)

1970 (7 Sept). 50th Anniversary of International Labour Organisation. P 14×13½.

72 **46** 30c. grey and new blue 10 20
73 75c. pink and new blue 20 30

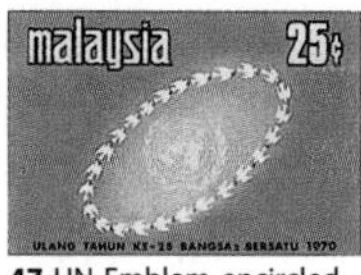

47 UN Emblem encircled by Doves

(Des Enche Ng Peng Nam. Litho D.L.R.)

1970 (24 Oct). 25th Anniversary of United Nations. T **47** and similar horiz designs. P 13×12½.

74 25c. gold, black and brown 35 40
75 30c. multicoloured 35 35
76 50c. black and dull yellow-green 40 75
74/76 *Set of 3* .... 1·00 1·40

Designs: 25c. T **47**; 30c. Line of doves and UN emblem; 50c. Doves looping UN emblem.

POSTAGE DUE STAMPS

Until 15 August 1966 the postage due stamps of MALAYAN POSTAL UNION were in use throughout MALAYSIA.

D **1**

(Litho Harrison)

1966 (15 Aug)–**71**. Ordinary paper. W w **13** (upright). P 14½×14.

D1 D **1** 1c. rose .... 20 7·00
D2 2c. indigo .... 25 2·75
D3 4c. apple-green .... 1·00 14·00
D4 8c. blue-green .... 2·00 25·00
a. Chalk-surfaced paper. *Bright blue green* (1.6.71) .... 4·50 20·00
D5 10c. bright blue .... 1·50 1·00
a. Chalk-surfaced paper (1.6.71) .... 4·50 14·00
D6 12c. reddish violet .... 60 4·75
D7 20c. red-brown .... 2·00 1·75
a. Chalk-surfaced paper. *Brown purple* (22.4.69) .... 2·75 15·00
D8 50c. brownish bistre .... 2·00 3·75
a. Chalk-surfaced paper. *Olive-bistre* (1.6.71) .... 4·50 16·00
D1/D8 *Set of 8* .... 8·50 50·00

Later issues in this design were printed on glazed or unwatermarked paper.

VII. MALAYSIAN STATES

PRINTERS. All Malaysian States stamps were printed in typography by De La Rue and Co. Ltd, London, *unless otherwise stated.*

JOHORE

A British adviser was appointed to Johore in 1914. The state joined the Federation of Malaya on 1 February 1948.

Until 1 January 1899 mail for addresses outside Malaya had the external postage paid by stamps of the STRAITS SETTLEMENTS.

PRICES FOR STAMPS ON COVER TO 1945	
Nos. 1/2	—
Nos. 3/5	*from* × 15
No. 6	*from* × 20
Nos. 7/8	—
Nos. 9/15	*from* × 25
No. 16	—
Nos. 17/20	*from* × 15
Nos. 21/31	*from* × 10
Nos. 32/38	*from* × 15

PRICES FOR STAMPS ON COVER TO 1945

Nos. 39/53	*from* × 8
Nos. 54/60	*from* × 6
Nos. 61/74	*from* × 8
Nos. 75/77	—
Nos. 78/87	*from* × 8
No. 88	*from* × 10
Nos. 89/102	*from* × 6
Nos. 103/125	*from* × 5
Nos. 126/128	—
Nos. 129/30	*from* × 6
Nos. D1/D5	*from* × 5

All overprints and surcharges were applied by the Government Printer, Singapore.

(**1**) (sideways)

1876 (July). No. 11 of Straits Settlements handstamped with T **1** (sideways or upright).

1		2c. brown	£25000	£8500

No. 1 is known with the handstamp double.

A single used example of the 4c. rose (Straits Settlements No. 12) exists with the T **1** handstamp.

From September 1878 to August 1884 no overprinted stamps were supplied by Singapore to Johore.

JOHORE
(**2**)

JOHORE (**3**) ('H' and 'E' wide. 'J' raised. Opt 16 *mm* long)
JOHORE (**4**) ('H' wide, 'E' narrow. Opt 16 *mm* long)
JOHORE (**5**) ('H' and 'E' wide. Opt 16¾ *mm* long)

JOHORE. (**6**)
JOHORE (**7**)
JOHORE (**8**)

1884 (June)–**86**. No. 63 of Straits Settlements optd with T **2/8**.

2	**2**	2c. pale rose	£10000	
3	**3**	2c. pale rose (8.84)	£3750	£800
		a. Opt double	£6500	£2500
4	**4**	2c. pale rose (8.84)	£3750	£1100
		a. Opt double		
5	**5**	2c. pale rose (8.84)	£3750	£800
		a. Opt double	—	£2500
6	**6**	2c. pale rose (3.85)	£225	£225
		a. Opt double	£1100	£1000
8	**8**	2c. pale rose (4.86)	£130	£140

Nos. 3 to 6 and 8 were from triplet settings, either 3+4+5 or three examples of the same overprint. No. 2 is probably a single unit handstamp.

The stamp formerly listed as No. 7, with 'JOHORE' opt in large seriffed capitals (illustrated as T **7**) is now considered to be bogus.

JOHOR (**9**) (All letters narrow)
JOHOR (**10**)
JOHOR (**11**) ('H' wide)

JOHOR (**12**)
JOHOR (**13**)
JOHOR. (**14**)

JOHOR (**15**)
JOHOR (**16**)
JOHOR Thin, narrow 'J'

1884 (Aug)–**91**. Nos. 63/63*a* of Straits Settlements optd with Types **9/16**.

9	**9**	2c. pale rose	28·00	20·00
		a. Opt double	£800	
		w. Wmk inverted	—	£500
10	**10**	2c. pale rose (10.84)	27·00	12·00
		a. Thin, narrow 'J' (R. 6/6)	£300	£180
		b. Opt double	£950	
		c. Bright rose (1890)	24·00	12·00
		ca. Thin, narrow 'J' (R. 6/6)	£275	£200
		cb. Opt double	£1200	
11	**11**	2c. pale rose (2.85)	£120	£110
		a. Opt double	£1500	
12	**12**	2c. pale rose (1886)	80·00	60·00
		a. Opt double	£750	
13	**13**	2c. pale rose (1886)	70·00	60·00
		a. Opt double	£750	
14	**14**	2c. pale rose (1888)	£225	75·00
		a. Thin, narrow 'J'	£1300	£450
		b. Opt double	£850	
15	**15**	2c. bright rose (9.90)	32·00	30·00
16	**16**	2c. bright rose (1891)	£9500	

Settings:

No. 9 – various triplets with the length of the overprint varying from 12 to 15 mm
No. 10 – triplet or 60 (6×10)
No. 11 – two types, length 13¼ mm and 14¼ mm, from separate printings, both triplets of 11+9+9
No. 12 – triplet
No. 13 – triplet
No. 14 – 30 (3×10)
No. 15 – 60 (6×10)
No. 16 – not known. As no used examples are known it is possible that this stamp was not issued.

JOHOR Two CENTS (**17**)
JOHOR Two CENTS (**18**)
JOHOR Two CENTS (**19**)
JOHOR Two CENTS (**20**)

1891 (May). No. 68 of Straits Settlements surch as Types **17/20**.

17	**17**	2c. on 24c. green	28·00	40·00
		a. 'CENST' (R. 5/4)	£950	£500
		b. Thin, narrow 'J' (R. 5/6)	£500	£500
		w. Wmk inverted	£250	£250
18	**18**	2c. on 24c. green	£140	£150
		a. Thin, narrow 'J' (R. 6/6)	£600	£600
		w. Wmk inverted	£700	
19	**19**	2c. on 24c. green	42·00	55·00
		w. Wmk inverted	£400	£400
20	**20**	2c. on 24c. green	£130	£140
		w. Wmk inverted	£700	£700

Nos. 17/20 come from the same setting of 60. T **17** occurs on horizontal rows 1 to 5, T **18** on row 6, T **19** on rows 7, 8 and 9 and T **20** on row 10.

The setting was altered to remove the 'CENST' error and in doing so the thin, narrow 'J' was moved from R. 5/6 to 6/6. Otherwise the two settings were the same.

One example of the 'CENST' error (No. 17a) has been recorded with inverted watermark (*Price*, £4000 *used*).

21 Sultan Abu Bakar

3 cents.
(**22**)

KEMAHKOTAAN
(**23**)

1891 (16 Nov)–**94**. No wmk. P 14.

21	**21**	1c. dull purple and mauve (7.94)	1·00	50
22		2c. dull purple and yellow	60	1·50
23		3c. dull purple and carmine (7.94)	60	60
24		4c. dull purple and black	2·75	21·00
25		5c. dull purple and green	7·00	21·00
26		6c. dull purple and blue	8·00	21·00
27		$1 green and carmine	85·00	£170
21/27 *Set of 7*			95·00	£200

1894 (Mar). Surch with T **22**.

28	**21**	3c. on 4c. dull purple and black	2·50	50
		a. No stop (R. 5/11)	£120	75·00
29		3c. on 5c. dull purple and green	2·00	5·00
		a. No stop (R. 5/11)	£140	£170
		b. '3 cents.' spaced 3½ mm from bar	£200	£110
30		3c. on 6c. dull purple and blue	3·50	9·00
		a. No stop (R. 5/11)	£200	£225
31		3c. on $1 green and carmine	12·00	75·00
		a. No stop (R. 5/11)	£475	£900
28/31 *Set of 4*			18·00	80·00

No. 29b shows the surcharge spaced 3½ mm from the bar instead of the normal 7½ mm. It appears to come from a separate setting as a cancelled-to-order block of eight is known.

1896 (16 Mar). Coronation of Sultan Ibrahim. Optd with T **23**.

32	**21**	1c. dull purple and mauve	50	1·00
		a. 'KETAHKOTAAN'	6·50	5·50
33		2c. dull purple and yellow	50	1·00
		a. 'KETAHKOTAAN'	8·50	9·00
34		3c. dull purple and carmine	55	1·00
		a. 'KETAHKOTAAN'	16·00	22·00
35		4c. dull purple and black	80	2·25
		a. 'KETAHKOTAAN'	2·75	22·00
36		5c. dull purple and green	5·50	7·50
		a. 'KETAHKOTAAN'	3·50	7·50
37		6c. dull purple and blue	3·50	6·50
		a. 'KETAHKOTAAN'	10·00	23·00
38		$1 green and carmine	65·00	£130
		a. 'KETAHKOTAAN'	38·00	£180
32/38 *Set of 7*			70·00	£140
32a/38a *Set of 7*			75·00	£225

Stamps overprinted 'KETAHKOTAAN' (= We mourn) come from the first overprinting. The overprint was subsequently changed to the intended 'KEMAHKOTAAN' (= Coronation), but both were issued together some months after the Coronation of Sultan Ibrahim had taken place.

24 Sultan Ibrahim

25 Sultan Ibrahim

26

27

1896 (26 Aug)–**99**. W **27**. P 14.

39	**24**	1c. green	80	3·25
40		2c. green and blue	50	1·50
41		3c. green and purple	4·00	5·50
		a. Green and dull claret	7·00	3·50
42		4c. green and carmine	1·00	4·00
43		4c. yellow and red (1899)	1·50	2·25
44		5c. green and brown	2·00	5·00
45		6c. green and yellow	2·00	7·50
46	**25**	10c. green and black (1898)	7·00	50·00
47		25c. green and mauve (1898)	9·00	50·00
48		50c. green and carmine (1898)	16·00	50·00
49	**24**	$1 dull purple and green (1898)	32·00	75·00
50	**26**	$2 dull purple and carmine (1898)	55·00	80·00
51		$3 dull purple and blue (1898)	50·00	£120
52		$4 dull purple and brown (1898)	50·00	85·00
53		$5 dull purple and yellow (1898)	£100	£130
39/53 *Set of 15*			£300	£600

Nos. 42 and 43 were reissued in 1918 to meet a shortage of 4c. stamps.

3 cents.
(**28**)

10 cents.
(**29**)

1903 (Apr). Surch with Types **28** or **29**.

54	**24**	3c. on 4c. yellow and red	60	1·10
		a. Original value uncancelled	3·75	27·00
55		10c. on 4c. green and carmine	3·75	18·00
		a. Tall '1' in '10' (R. 9/12)	80·00	£140
		b. Original value uncancelled	20·00	85·00
		ba. As b, with tall '1' in '10' (R. 9/12)	£1300	£1900

The bars on these stamps were ruled by hand with pen and ink.

50 Cents.
(**30**)

One Dollar
(**31**)

1903 (Oct). Surch with Types **30** or **31**.

56	**26**	50c. on $3 dull purple and blue	30·00	85·00
57		$1 on $2 dull purple and carmine	65·00	£120
		a. 'e' of 'One' inverted (R. 7/9)	£1900	

10 CENTS.
(**32**)

1904. Surch as T **32**.

58	**24**	10c. on 4c. yellow and red (4.04)	20·00	40·00
		a. Surcharge double	£8500	
59		10c. on 4c. green and carmine (8.04)	9·50	70·00
60	**26**	50c. on $5 dull purple and yellow (5.04)	80·00	£170
58/60 *Set of 3*			£100	£250

33

34

35 Sultan Sir Ibrahim

1904 (Sept)–**10**. W **27**. Ordinary paper. P 14.

61	**33**	1c. dull purple and green	2·00	40
		a. Chalk-surfaced paper (10.09)	24·00	13·00
62		2c. dull purple and orange	3·00	4·25
		a. Chalk-surfaced paper (10.10)	26·00	27·00
63		3c. dull purple and olive-black	4·75	60
		a. Chalk-surfaced paper	—	£120
64		4c. dull purple and carmine	8·00	5·00
65		5c. dull purple and sage-green	2·50	3·00
66	**35**	8c. dull purple and blue	4·25	22·00
67	**34**	10c. dull purple and black	50·00	11·00
		a. Chalk-surfaced paper (1910)	£120	80·00
68		25c. dull purple and green	8·50	40·00
69		50c. dull purple and red	40·00	17·00
70	**33**	$1 green and mauve	17·00	65·00
71	**35**	$2 green and carmine	35·00	50·00
72		$3 green and blue	48·00	85·00
73		$4 green and brown	48·00	£120
74		$5 green and orange	70·00	90·00
75	**34**	$10 green and black	£140	£200
76		$50 green and ultramarine (F.C. £50)	£475	£650
77		$100 green and scarlet (F.C. £50)	£650	£1000
61/75 *Set of 15*			£425	£650

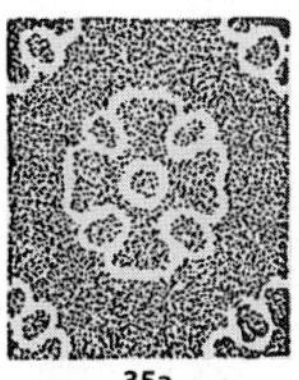

35a

3 CENTS.
(**36**)

1910–19. Wmk Mult Rosettes (vertical) W **35a**. Chalk-surfaced paper. P 14.

78	**33**	1c. dull purple and green (1912)	1·25	15
79		2c. dull purple and orange (1912)	6·00	1·00
80		3c. dull purple and olive-black (1912)	10·00	65
		a. Wmk horizontal (1910)	10·00	19·00
81		4c. dull purple and carmine (1912)	35·00	1·00
		a. Wmk horizontal (1910)	20·00	65·00
82		5c. dull purple and sage-green (1912)	11·00	3·25
83	**35**	8c. dull purple and blue (1912)	4·00	16·00
84	**34**	10c. dull purple and black (1912)	60·00	3·00
		a. Wmk horizontal (1911)	32·00	90·00
85		25c. dull purple and green (1912)	28·00	60·00
86		50c. dull purple and red (1919)	80·00	£150
87	**33**	$1 green and mauve (1917)	£120	£130
78/87 *Set of 10*			£275	£350

1912 (Mar). No. 66 surch with T **36**.

No.	Type	Description	Unused	Used
88		3c. on 8c. dull purple and blue	18·00	15·00
		a. 'T' of 'CENTS' omitted	£1700	
		b. Bars double	†	£5000

No. 88b shows the bars printed twice with the upper pair partly erased.

1918–20. Wmk Mult Crown CA. Chalk-surfaced paper. P 14.

No.	Type	Description	Unused	Used
89	**33**	2c. dull purple and green (1919)	50	3·00
		w. Wmk inverted	†	£500
90		2c. purple and orange (1919)	1·00	8·50
91		4c. dull purple and red	1·75	70
92		5c. dull purple and sage-green (1920)	2·00	17·00
		w. Wmk inverted	£200	
		ws. Ditto, optd 'SPECIMEN'	£100	
93	**34**	10c. dull purple and blue	2·00	1·40
		w. Wmk inverted	†	£500
94		21c. dull purple and orange (1919)	2·25	2·50
95		25c. dull purple and green (1920)	8·00	50·00
96		50c. dull purple and red (6.18)	24·00	65·00
97	**33**	$1 green and mauve	14·00	75·00
98	**35**	$2 green and carmine	23·00	65·00
99		$3 green and blue	75·00	£150
100		$4 green and brown	95·00	£225
101		$5 green and orange	£150	£250
102	**34**	$10 green and black	£450	£650
89/102 *Set of 14*			£750	£1400
89s/102s Optd 'SPECIMEN' *Set of 14*			£700	

1922–41. Wmk Mult Script CA. Chalk-surfaced paper. P 14.

No.	Type	Description	Unused	Used
103	**33**	1c. dull purple and black	30	20
104		2c. purple and sepia (1924)	1·25	4·25
105		2c. green (1928)	60	40
106		3c. green (1925)	2·00	8·00
107		3c. purple and sepia (1928)	1·40	2·00
108		4c. purple and carmine (1924)	2·50	20
109		5c. dull purple and sage-green	50	30
		w. Wmk inverted		
110		6c. dull purple and claret	50	50
111	**34**	10c. dull purple and blue	16·00	32·00
		w. Wmk inverted	†	£400
		ws. Ditto, opt 'SPECIMEN'	£140	
112		10c. dull purple and yellow	50	25
		a. Thin striated paper (1941)	£130	£190
113	**33**	12c. dull purple and blue	1·00	1·25
114		12c. ultramarine (1940)	55·00	1·75
115	**34**	21c. dull purple and orange (1928)	2·00	3·00
116		25c. dull purple and myrtle	6·50	1·00
117	**35**	30c. dull purple and orange (1936)	11·00	18·00
118		40c. dull purple and brown (1936)	12·00	19·00
119	**34**	50c. dull purple and red	4·00	1·60
		a. Thin striated paper (1941)	£375	£400
120	**33**	$1 green and mauve	3·75	1·25
		a. Thin striated paper (1941)	£225	£250
121	**35**	$2 green and carmine (1923)	10·00	4·75
		a. Thin striated paper (1941)	16·00	19·00
122		$3 green and blue (1925)	85·00	£110
123		$4 green and brown (1926)	£120	£200
		w. Wmk inverted	£1200	
124		$5 green and orange	70·00	50·00
		a. Thin striated paper (1941)	90·00	
125	**34**	$10 green and black (1924)	£350	£475
		a. Thin striated paper (1941)	£600	
126		$50 green and ultramarine (F.C. £100)	£1500	
		s. Optd 'SPECIMEN'	£300	
127		$100 green and scarlet (F.C. £150)	£2000	
		s. Optd 'SPECIMEN'	£375	
128	**35**	$500 blue and red (1926) (F.C. £425)	£24000	
		s. Optd 'SPECIMEN'	£1300	
103/125 *Set of 23*			£700	£850
103s/125s Optd or Perf (12c. ultramarine, 30c., 40c.) 'SPECIMEN' *Set of 23*			£1000	

For a description of the thin striated paper, see the introduction to this catalogue.

37 Sultan Sir Ibrahim and Sultana

(Recess Waterlow)

1935 (15 May). 50th Anniversary of Treaty Relations with Great Britain. Wmk Mult Script CA (sideways). P 12½.

No.	Type	Description	Unused	Used
129	**37**	8c. bright violet and slate	7·00	3·25
		s. Perf 'SPECIMEN'	85·00	

38 Sultan Sir Ibrahim

39 Sultan Sir Ibrahim

(Recess D.L.R.)

1940 (Feb). Wmk Mult Script CA. P 13½.

No.	Type	Description	Unused	Used
130	**38**	8c. black and pale blue	25·00	1·75
		s. Perf 'SPECIMEN'	£100	

Due to a stamp shortage in August and September 1941, meter stamps inscribed 'POSTAGE PAID JOHORE' but without a machine number in denominations of 80c., $1, $1.40 and $2 were printed onto strips of paper and affixed to the item being posted. They were subsequently postmarked in the normal way.

1948 (1 Dec). Royal Silver Wedding. As Nos. 112/113 of Antigua.

No.	Description	Unused	Used
131	10c. violet	20	75
132	$5 green	26·00	50·00

1949 (2 May)–**55**. Wmk Mult Script CA. Chalk-surfaced paper. P 17½×18.

No.	Type	Description	Unused	Used
133	**39**	1c. black	1·00	10
134		2c. orange	50	20
		a. Orange-yellow (22.1.52)	3·50	4·00
135		3c. green	2·75	1·00
		a. Yellow-green (22.1.52)	28·00	6·00
136		4c. brown	2·25	10
136*a*		5c. bright purple (1.9.52)	3·00	30
137		6c. grey	2·25	20
		a. Pale grey (22.1.52)	1·50	50
		ac. Error. St Edward's Crown W **9b**	£3250	£2250
138		8c. scarlet	7·00	1·25
138*a*		8c. green (1.9.52)	11·00	2·25
139		10c. magenta	1·50	10
		aa. Imperf (pair)	£5500	
139*a*		12c. scarlet (1.9.52)	13·00	9·00
140		15c. ultramarine	6·00	10
141		20c. black and green	5·00	1·00
141*a*		20c. bright blue (1.9.52)	2·00	10
142		25c. purple and orange	3·75	10
142*a*		30c. scarlet and purple (4.9.55)	3·25	2·75
142*b*		35c. scarlet and purple (1.9.52)	13·00	1·75
143		40c. red and purple	10·00	18·00
144		50c. black and blue	6·00	10
145		$1 blue and purple	14·00	2·00
146		$2 green and scarlet	32·00	13·00
147		$5 green and brown	50·00	17·00
133/147 *Set of 21*			£160	60·00

1949 (10 Oct). 75th Anniversary of UPU As Nos. 114/117 of Antigua.

No.	Description	Unused	Used
148	10c. purple	30	40
149	15c. deep blue	2·00	2·00
150	25c. orange	65	4·25
151	50c. blue-black	1·25	4·50
148/151 *Set of 4*		3·75	10·00

1953 (2 June). Coronation. As No. 120 of Antigua.

No.	Description	Unused	Used
152	10c. black and reddish purple	1·25	10

40 Sultan Sir Ibrahim

41 Sultan Sir Ismail and Johore Coat of Arms

(Recess D.L.R.)

1955 (1 Nov). Diamond Jubilee of Sultan. Wmk Mult Script CA. P 14.

No.	Type	Description	Unused	Used
153	**40**	10c. carmine-red	10	10

(Photo Courvoisier)

1960 (10 Feb). Coronation of Sultan. No wmk. P 11½.

No.	Type	Description	Unused	Used
154	**41**	10c. multicoloured	20	20

1960. As Types **9**/**19** of Kedah, but with portrait of Sultan Ismail. P 13½ ($1); others 12½×13 (vert) or 13×12½ (horiz).

No.	Description	Unused	Used
155	1c. black (7.10.60)	10	1·25
156	2c. orange-red (7.10.60)	10	2·25
157	4c. sepia (19.8.60)	10	10
158	5c. carmine-lake (7.10.60)	10	10
159	8c. myrtle-green (9.12.60)	4·25	5·50
160	10c. deep maroon (10.6.60)	30	10
161	20c. blue (9.12.60)	2·00	1·00
162	50c. black and bright blue (19.8.60)	50	20
163	$1 ultramarine and reddish purple (9.12.60)	8·50	8·50
164	$2 bronze-green and scarlet (9.12.60)	21·00	27·00
165	$5 brown and bronze-green (7.10.60)	42·00	48·00
155/165 *Set of 11*		70·00	80·00

In No. 161 there are only two figures in the boat, the steersman being missing. In the 20c. value for all the other dates there are three figures.

The 6, 12, 25 and 30c. values used with this issue were Nos. 1/4 of Malayan Federation.

42 *Vanda hookeriana* (Inset portrait of Sultan Ismail)

(Des A. Fraser-Brunner. Photo Harrison)

1965 (15 Nov). T **42** and similar horiz designs. W w **13** (upright). P 14½.

No.	Description	Unused	Used
166	1c. Type **42**	10	30
	a. Black (orchid's name and part of flower) omitted	£425	
	w. Wmk inverted	6·00	
167	2c. *Arundina graminifolia*	10	1·00
168	5c. *Paphiopedilum niveum*	10	10
	b. Yellow (flower) omitted	£110	
169	6c. *Spathoglottis plicata*	40	30
170	10c. *Arachnis flos-aeris*	40	20
	a. Green omitted	£200	
171	15c. *Rhyncostylis retusa*	1·50	10
	b. Green (face value and leaves) omitted	£750	
172	20c. *Phalaenopsis violacea*	1·75	75
	a. Bright purple (blooms) omitted	£325	
166/172 *Set of 7*		3·75	2·25

The 2c. to 15c. exist with both PVA gum and gum arabic.

The 2c. with black (name of State, Arms and head) omitted is listed under Sarawak No. 213a as there is some evidence that a sheet was issued there; if it also exists from any of the other states it would, of course, be identical.

The higher values used with this issue were Nos. 20/27 of Malaysia (National Issues).

1970. As No. 166 and 170 but W w **13** (sideways).

No.	Description	Unused	Used
173	1c. multicoloured (20.11)	1·75	9·50
174	10c. multicoloured (27.5)	1·75	2·50

STAMP BOOKLETS

1928. Black on white card. Interleaved with tissue. Stapled.

No.	Description	Price
SB1	$2 booklet containing 10×1c. and 10×2c. (Nos. 103, 105), 20×4c. (No. 108), each in blocks of 10 and 18×5c. (No. 109) in blocks of 6	£2750

1929. Black on pink cover. Stapled.

No.	Description	Price
SB2	$1 booklet containing 2c., 3c. and 5c. (Nos. 105, 107, 109) in blocks of 10	

1930. Black on buff cover. Stapled.

No.	Description	Price
SB3	$1 booklet containing 10×1c. and 10×5c. (Nos. 103, 109) and 20×2c. (Nos. 105) in blocks of 10	

POSTAGE DUE STAMPS

D **1**

(Typo Waterlow)

1938 (1 Jan). Wmk Mult Script CA. P 12½.

No.	Type	Description	Unused	Used
D1	D **1**	1c. carmine	22·00	50·00
D2		4c. green	45·00	40·00
D3		8c. orange	50·00	£160
D4		10c. brown	50·00	50·00
D5		12c. purple	55·00	£140
D1/D5 *Set of 5*			£200	£400
D1s/D5s Perf 'SPECIMEN' *Set of 5*			£160	

KEDAH

The Thai monarchy exercised suzereignty over Kedah and the other northern states of the Malay peninsula from the 16th-century onwards. The extent of Thai involvement in its internal affairs was very variable, being dependent on the strength, or otherwise, of the Bangkok administration and the degree of co-operation of the local ruler.

The Thai postal service, which had been inaugurated in 1883, gradually extended into the north of the Malay penninsula and an office was opened at Alor Star in Kedah during 1887 with the earliest known postmark being dated 27 October. Further post offices at Kuala Muda (3 Oct 1907), Kulim (7 July 1907) and Langkawi (16 Feb 1908) followed.

Stamps of Thailand used in Kedah

Types of Thailand (Siam)

1

2

9

๑ อัฐ 1 (12) ๒ อัฐ 2 (17) ๒ อัฐ 2 (18)

4 atts (24) 4 atts (25)

1 Atts.

ราคา ๑ อัฐ (27) 2 Atts. (28) 2 (33)

1 Att. 1 Att.

ราคา ๑ อัฐ (34) ราคา ๑ อัฐ (35) 1 Att. (36)

2 Atts. 10 Atts.

ราคา ๒ อัฐ (37) 2 Atts. (38) ราคา ๑๐ อัฐ (39)

4 Atts. (40) 4 Atts. (41)

1 Att.

ราคา ๑ อัฐ (42) 2 Atts. (44) 3 Atts. (45) 4 Atts. (46)

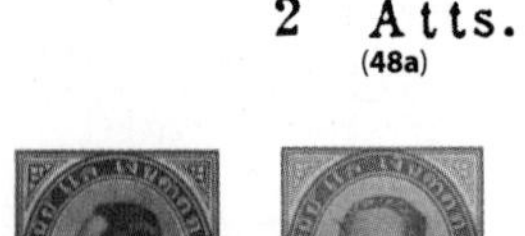

(48a)

49 50 (51)

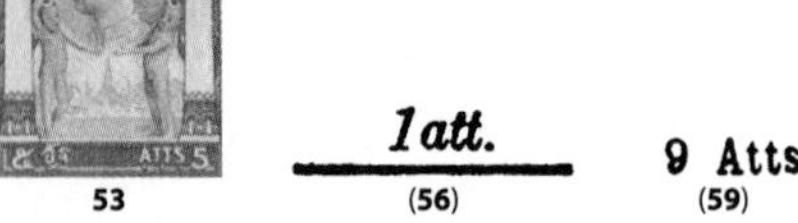

53 (56) (59)

The following types of postmark were used on Siamese stamps from the Malay tributary states:

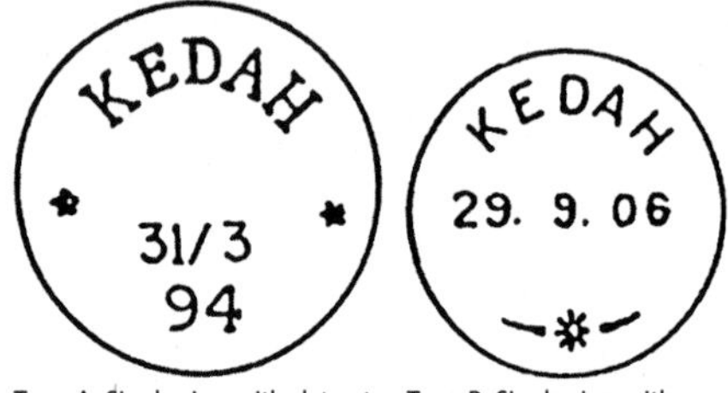

Type A. Single ring with date at foot (examples from 1900 show the year in manuscript)

Type B. Single ring with date in centre

Type C. Double ring. Bilingual

Type D. Double ring. English at top and ornament at foot

PRICES are for stamps showing a large part of the postmark with the inscription clearly visible.

The Siamese post office at Alor Star was opened during 1887 with the first known postmark being dated 27 October. Further post offices at Kuala Muda (3 Oct 1907), Kulim (7 July 1907) and Langkawi (16 Feb 1908) followed.

A straight-line obliteration showing 'KEDAH' between short vertical dashes is not believed to be genuine.

Alor Star

Stamps of SIAM cancelled as Type A inscribed 'KEDAH'.

1883. (Nos. 1/5).
Z2 **1** 1att. rose-carmine £500
Z3 1sio. red £750
Z4 **2** 1sik. yellow £750

1887–91. (Nos. 11/18).
Z6 **9** 1a. green £110
Z7 2a. green and carmine 95·00
Z8 3a. green and blue £120
Z9 4a. green and brown £100
Z10 8a. green and yellow £110
Z11 12a. purple and carmine 95·00
Z12 24a. purple and blue £120
Z13 64a. purple and brown £200

1889–91. Surch as T **12** (Nos. Z15, Z19), T **17** (No. Z21) or T **18** (No. Z22) (Nos. 20/30).
Z15 **9** 1a. on 2a. rose-carmine £130
Z19 1a. on 3a. red £150
Z21 2a. on 3a. yellow £200
Z22 2a. on 3a. green and blue £250

1892. Surch as Types **24/25** (with or without stop) and Siamese handstamp (Nos. 33/36).
Z28 **9** 4a. on 24a. purple and blue (Type **24**) £130
Z29 4a. on 24a. purple and blue (Type **25**) £150
Z30 4a. on 24a. purple and blue (Type **24** with stop) £150
Z31 4a. on 24a. purple and blue (Type **25** with stop) £150

1894. Surch as T **27** with variations of English figures as Types **28** and **33** (Nos. 37/44).
Z34 **9** 2a. on 64a. purple and brown (Type **28**) £130
Z39 2a. on 64a. purple and brown (Type **33**) £130

1894. Surch with T **34** (No. 45).
Z41 **9** 1a. on 64a. purple and brown £150

1894–95. Surch as T **35** with variations of English figures as Types **36/39** (Nos. 46/50).
Z42 **9** 1a. on 64a. purple and brown (Type **35**) £130
Z43 1a. on 64a. purple and brown (Type **36**) £130
Z44 2a. on 64a. purple and brown (Type **37**) £130
Z45 2a. on 64a. purple and brown (Type **38**) £130
Z46 10a. on 24a. purple and blue (Type **39**) £130

1896. Surch as T **39** (Siamese) and T **40** (English) (No. 51).
Z47 **9** 4a. on 12a. purple and carmine £120

1897. Surch as T **39** (Siamese) and T **41** (English) (No. 52).
Z48 **9** 4a. on 12a. purple and carmine £120

1898–99. Surch as T **42** with variations of English section as Types **44/46** (Nos. 53/62).
Z49 **9** 1a. on 12a. purple and carmine (Type **42**–11½ *mm long*) £170
Z52 2a. on 64a. purple and brown (Type **44**) £150
Z53 3a. on 12a. purple and carmine (Type **45**–13½ *mm long*) £130
Z54 3a. on 12a. purple and carmine (Type **45**–11½ to 11¾ *mm long*) £130
Z55 4a. on 12a. purple and carmine (Type **46**–8 *mm long*) £130
Z56 4a. on 12a. purple and carmine (Type **46**–8½ to 9 *mm long*) £130

1899. Surch in Siamese and English with T **48a** (Nos. 63/66).
Z62 **9** 2a. on 64a. purple and brown £140

1899–1904. (Nos. 67/81).
Z63 **49** 1a. olive-green (wide Siamese characters in face value) £130
Z64 2a. grass-green 95·00
Z65 3a. red and blue £100
Z66 4a. carmine 95·00
Z67 8a. deep green and orange 95·00
Z69 12a. brown-purple and carmine £150
Z70 24a. brown-purple and blue £250
Z71 64a. brown-purple and chestnut £190

1899. (Nos. 82/86).
Z72 **50** 1a. green £400
Z73 2a. green and red £600

Stamps of SIAM cancelled as Type B inscr 'KEDAH' (from March 1901).

1887–91. (Nos. 11/18).
Z74 **9** 12a. purple and carmine 90·00
Z75 24a. purple and brown 95·00

1898–99. Surch with T **42** with variations of English section as Types **45/46** (Nos. 53/62).
Z76 **9** 1a. on 12a. purple and carmine (Type **42**–11½ *mm long*) £130
Z81 3a. on 12a. purple and carmine (Type **45**–11½ to 11¾ *mm long*) 95·00
Z83 4a. on 12a. purple and carmine (Type **46**–8½ to 9 *mm long*) 95·00
Z84 4a. on 24a. purple and blue (Type **46**) £100

1899–1904. (Nos. 67/81).
Z86 **49** 1a. olive-green (wide Siamese characters in face value) 90·00
a. Narrow Siamese characters in face value 90·00
Z87 2a. grass-green 75·00
Z88 2a. scarlet and pale blue 80·00
Z89 3a. red and blue 85·00
Z90 3a. deep green 90·00
Z91 4a. carmine 75·00
Z92 4a. chocolate and pink 85·00
Z93 8a. deep green and orange 80·00
Z94 10a. ultramarine 75·00
Z95 12a. brown-purple and carmine 90·00
Z96 24a. brown-purple and blue £180
Z97 64a. brown-purple and chestnut £170

1905–09. (Nos. 92/105).
Z102 **53** 1a. green and orange 80·00
Z103 2a. grey and deep violet 75·00
Z104 3a. green 90·00
Z105 4a. pale red and sepia 75·00
Z106 5a. carmine 85·00
Z107 8a. olive-bistre and dull black 80·00
Z108 12a. blue 90·00
Z109 24a. red-brown £225
Z110 1t. bistre and deep blue £225

Stamps of SIAM cancelled as Type C inscr 'Kedah' at foot (from July 1907).

1887–91. (Nos. 11/18).
Z111 **9** 12a. purple and carmine £110

1899–1904. (Nos. 67/81).
Z112 **49** 1a. olive-green (wide Siamese characters in face value) 85·00
a. Narrow Siamese characters in face value 80·00
Z113 2a. scarlet and pale blue 80·00
Z114 3a. red and blue 90·00
Z116 8a. deep green and orange 85·00
Z117 10a. ultramarine 85·00
Z118 12a. brown-purple and carmine 85·00

1905–09. (Nos. 92/105).
Z128 **53** 1a. green and orange 75·00
Z129 2a. grey and deep violet 80·00
Z130 3a. green 85·00
Z131 4a. pale red and sepia 75·00
Z132 4a. scarlet 80·00
Z133 5a. carmine 80·00
Z134 8a. olive-bistre and dull black 75·00
Z135 9a. blue 75·00
Z136 18a. red-brown £130
Z137 24a. red-brown £225
Z138 1t. bistre and deep blue £225

1907. Surch with T **56** (No. 109).
Z139 **9** 1a. on 24a. purple and blue 90·00

Kuala Muda

Stamps of SIAM cancelled as Type B inscr 'KUALA MUDA' (from July 1907).

1887–91. (Nos. 11/18).
Z143 **9** 12a. purple and carmine £450

1899–1904. (Nos. 67/81).
Z144 **49** 2a. scarlet and pale blue £450
Z145 24a. brown-purple and blue £500

1905–09. (Nos. 92/105).
Z146 **53** 1a. green and orange £450
Z147 2a. grey and deep violet £450
Z148 3a. green £475
Z150 5a. carmine £475
Z151 8a. olive-bistre and dull black £450

Stamps of SIAM cancelled as Type C inscr 'Kwala Muda' at foot (from 1907).

1887–91. (Nos. 11/18).
Z155 **9** 12a. purple and carmine £250

1899–1904. (Nos. 67/81).
Z156 **49** 8a. deep green and orange £275
Z157 10a. ultramarine £300

1905–09. (Nos. 92/105).
Z158 **53** 1a. green and orange £300
Z159 2a. grey and deep violet £300
Z160 3a. green £325
Z161 4a. pale red and sepia £275
Z162 4a. scarlet £300
Z163 5a. carmine £350
Z164 8a. olive-bistre and dull black £300
Z165 9a. blue £250
Z166 24a. red-brown £500

1907. Surch with T **56** (No. 109).
Z167 **9** 1a. on 24a. purple and blue £250

Kulim

Stamps of SIAM cancelled as Type D inscr 'KULIM' (from July 1907).

1887–91. (Nos. 11/18).
Z173 **9** 12a. purple and carmine £450

1899–1904. (Nos. 67/81).
Z174 **49** 8a. deep green and orange £450

1905–09. (Nos. 92/105).
Z175 **53** 1a. green and orange £475
Z176 2a. grey and deep violet £475
Z177 3a. green £500
Z178 4a. pale red and sepia £450
Z179 4a. scarlet £425
Z180 5a. carmine £475
Z181 8a. olive-bistre and dull black £450
Z182 9a. blue £450

1907. Surch with T **56** (No. 109).
Z184 **9** 1a. on 24a. purple and blue £450

Stamps of SIAM cancelled as Type C inscr 'Kulim' at foot (from Feb 1908).

1887–91. (Nos. 11/18).
Z190 **9** 12a. purple and carmine £225

1899–1904. (Nos. 67/81).
Z191 **49** 8a. deep green and orange £200
Z192 10a. ultramarine £225

1905–09. (Nos. 92/105).
Z196 **53** 4a. pale red and sepia £200
Z197 4a. scarlet £200
Z198 5a. carmine £225
Z199 9a. blue £225
Z200 24a. red-brown £450
Z201 1t. bistre and deep blue £450

1907. Surch with T **56** (No. 109).
Z202 **9** 1a. purple and blue £225

Langkawi

Stamps of SIAM cancelled as Type D inscr 'LANGKAWI' (from Feb 1908).

1899–1904. (Nos. 67/81).
Z208 **49** 8a. deep green and orange £450
Z209 10a. ultramarine £450

1905–09. (Nos. 92/105).
Z211 2a. grey and deep violet £475
Z212 **53** 3a. green £475
Z213 4a. pale red and sepia £450
Z215 8a. olive-bistre and dull black £450

Stamps of SIAM cancelled as Type C inscr 'Langkawi' at foot (from Nov 1908).

1887–91. (Nos. 11/18).
Z219 **9** 12a. purple and carmine £225

1899–1904. (Nos. 67/81).
Z220 **49** 1a. olive-green (Type B) £250
Z221 8a. green and orange £200

1905–09. (Nos. 92/105).

No.	Type	Description	Price
Z222	**53**	2a. grey and deep violet	£225
Z223		3a. green	£300
Z224		4a. pale red and sepia	£225
Z225		4a. scarlet	£250
Z226		8a. olive-bistre and dull black	£225
Z228		24a. red-brown	£500
Z229		1t. bistre and deep blue	£500

1907. Surch with T **56** (No. 109).

No.	Type	Description	Price
Z230	**9**	1a. on 24a. purple and blue	£250

Suzerainty over Kedah was transferred by Thailand to Great Britain on 15 July 1909 and the following day stamps of the FEDERATED MALAY STATES were placed on sale in post offices in the state.

A Treaty of Friendship between Great Britain and Kedah was signed on 1 November 1923 and the state joined the Federation of Malaya on 1 February 1948.

Stamps of the Federated Malay States used in Kedah

Alor Star

Cancelled as Type C inscribed 'Kedah'

1909–12. (Nos. 29/49).

No.	Type	Description	Price
Z231	**3**	1c. green (Die II)	40·00
Z232		3c. carmine	45·00
Z233		4c. black and rose	48·00
Z234		5c. green and carmine/*yellow*	£110
Z235		8c. grey-brown and ultramarine	£110
		a. Wmk upright	70·00
Z236		10c. black and purple	85·00
Z237		20c. mauve and black (chalk-surfaced paper)	90·00
Z238		50c. grey-brown and orange-brown (chalk-surfaced paper)	£100
Z239	**4**	$1 grey-green and green	£225
Z240		$2 green and carmine	£450

Type F

Cancelled as Type F

1909–12. (No. 34).

No.	Type	Description	Price
Z241	**3**	3c. carmine	70·00

Type G

Cancelled as Type G

1909–12. (Nos. 34/47*dc*).

No.	Type	Description	Price
Z242	**3**	1c. green (Die II)	60·00
Z243		3c. carmine	60·00
Z244		4c. black and rose	85·00
Z245		8c. grey-brown and ultramarine	
		a. Wmk upright	85·00
Z246		10c. black and purple	90·00
Z247		50c. grey-brown and orange-brown (chalk-surfaced paper)	£100

Kulim

Type H

Cancelled as Type H

1909–12. (Nos. 34/45a).

No.	Type	Description	Price
Z248	**3**	1c. green (Die II)	75·00
Z249		3c. carmine	65·00
Z250		4c. black and rose	75·00
Z251		5c. green and carmine/*yellow*	£110
Z252		10c. black and purple	£110
Z253		20c. mauve and black (chalk-surfaced paper)	95·00

Type I

Cancelled as Type I

1909–12. (Nos. 34/43*d*).

No.	Description	Price
Z254	3c. carmine	65·00
Z255	4c. black and rose	75·00
Z255*a*	10c. black and purple	£120

Langkawi

Cancelled as Type H inscribed 'LANGKAWI'

1909–12. (Nos. 34/49).

No.	Type	Description	Price
Z256	**3**	3c. carmine	£100
Z256*a*		5c. green and carmine/*yellow*	£130
Z257		8c. grey-brown and ultramarine (wmk upright)	£110
Z258	**4**	$1 grey-green and green	£275
Z259		$2 green and carmine	£375

Cancelled as Type I inscribed 'LANGKAWI'

1909–12. (Nos. 29/43*d*).

No.	Type	Description	Price
Z260	**3**	1c. green (Die II)	£100
Z261		3c. carmine	55·00
Z262		10c. black and purple	£110

Kuala Muda

Cancelled as Type B inscribed 'KUALA MUDA'

1909–12. (Nos. 29/41bb).

No.	Type	Description	Price
Z263	**3**	1c. green (Die II)	85·00
Z264		3c. carmine	55·00
Z265		4c. black and rose	95·00
Z266		5c. green and carmine/*yellow*	95·00
Z267		8c. grey-brown and ultramarine (wmk upright)	90·00

Jitra

The post office in Jitra was opened in 1910.

Type J

Cancelled as Type J

1910–12. (No. 34).

No.	Type	Description	Price
Z268	**3**	3c. carmine	90·00

Cancelled as Type I inscribed 'JITRA'

1910–12. (Nos. 29/34).

No.	Type	Description	Price
Z269	**3**	1c. green (Die II)	55·00
Z270		3c. carmine	48·00

Lunas

The post office in Lunas was opened in 1910.

Type K

Cancelled as Type K

1910–12. (No. 34).

No.	Type	Description	Price
Z271	**3**	3c. carmine	£120

Cancelled as Type I inscribed 'LUNAS'

1910–12. (Nos. 29/36*d*).

No.	Type	Description	Price
Z272	**3**	1c. green (Die II)	75·00
Z273		3c. carmine	75·00
Z274		4c. black and rose	£100

Semiling

The post office in Semiling was opened in 1910.

Cancelled as Type I inscribed 'SEMILING'

1910–12. (Nos. 29/41*b*).

No.	Type	Description	Price
Z275	**3**	1c. green (Die II)	65·00
Z276		3c. carmine	£100
Z277		4c. black and rose	£100
Z278		8c. grey-brown and ultramarine (wmk upright)	£100

Sungei Patani

The post office in Sungei Patani was opened in 1911.

Cancelled as Type I inscribed 'SUNGEI PATANI'

1911–12. (Nos. 29/34).

No.	Type	Description	Price
Z279	**3**	1c. green (Die II)	£120
Z280		3c. carmine	£120

Yen

The post office in Yen was opened in 1910.

Cancelled as Type I inscribed 'YEN'

1910–12. (Nos. 29/34).

No.	Type	Description	Price
Z281	**3**	1c. green (Die II)	£130
Z282		3c. carmine	£130

PRICES FOR STAMPS ON COVER TO 1945

Nos.	Price
Nos. 1/14	*from* × 15
Nos. 15/23	*from* × 10
Nos. 24/40	*from* × 8
Nos. 41/48	*from* × 12
Nos. 49/51	—
Nos. 52/59	*from* × 4
Nos. 60/68	*from* × 3
Nos. 68*a*/69	*from* × 4

1 Sheaf of Rice

2 Malay ploughing

3 Council Chamber, Alor Star

'Feather in hat' flaw (Pl. 1, R. 9/5)

(Recess D.L.R.)

1912 (16 June). Wmk Mult Crown CA (sideways* on 10c. to $5). P 14.

No.	Type	Description	Unused	Used
1	**1**	1c. black and green	60	25
		y. Wmk inverted and reversed	£750	£450
2		3c. black and red	4·50	30
3		4c. rose and grey	10·00	25
4		5c. green and chestnut	2·25	3·00
5		8c. black and ultramarine	4·00	5·00
6	**2**	10c. blue and sepia	2·25	1·00
		a. 'Feather in hat'	£100	60·00
		w. Wmk Crown to left of CA	†	—
		y. Wmk Crown to left of CA and reversed	†	£450
7		20c. black and green	15·00	6·00
		x. Wmk reversed	£425	
8		30c. black and rose	3·50	11·00
9		40c. black and purple	3·50	26·00
		a. 'Feather in hat'	£130	
10		50c. brown and blue	9·00	13·00
11	**3**	$1 black and red/*yellow*	16·00	22·00
		w. Wmk Crown to left of CA	85·00	
		x. Wmk reversed	£500	
		y. Wmk Crown to left of CA and reversed		
12		$2 green and brown	28·00	85·00
13		$3 black and blue/*blue*	£130	£170
		a. 'A' of 'CA' missing from wmk	£2000	
14		$5 black and red	£130	£170
1/14 *Set of 14*			£325	£450
1s/14s Optd 'SPECIMEN' *Set of 14*			£375	

* The normal sideways watermark shows the Crown to right of CA, *as seen from the back of the stamp.*

The 'Feather in hat' variety was present on printings from 1919.

Due to an increase in postal rates 1c. and 4c. stamps of STRAITS SETTLEMENTS were used in Kedah for some months from March 1919.

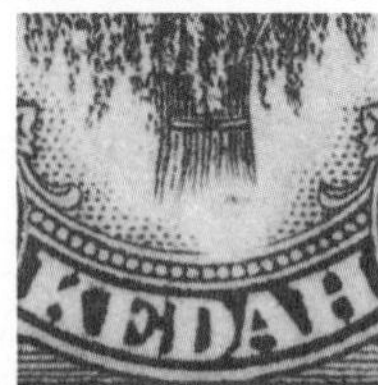

4c. Short sheaf (R. 10/1)

(i)

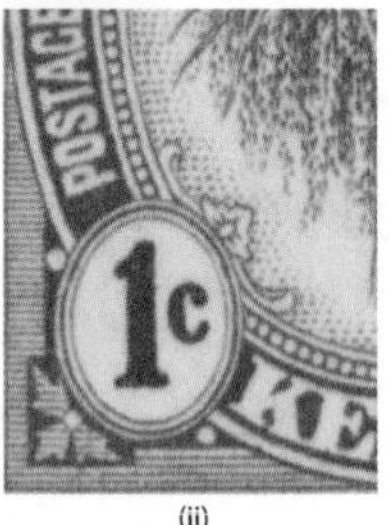

(ii)

DOUBLE AND SINGLE PLATES. (i) Printed from separate plates for frame and centre, with dotted shading extending close to the central sheaf. Soft impression of centre with little clear detail.

(ii) Printed from single plate, with white space around sheaf. Centre more deeply etched with sharp image.

1919 (June)–**21**. New colours and values. Wmk Mult Crown CA (sideways* on 21c., 25c.). P 14.

15	1	1c. brown (i) (18.8.19)	75	50
		w. Wmk inverted	£160	£200
		y. Wmk inverted and reversed	†	£550
18		2c. green (ii)	50	30
		x. Wmk reversed	†	£500
19		3c. deep purple (i) (1920)	65	4·50
		x. Wmk reversed	£400	
		y. Wmk inverted and reversed	90·00	£150
20		4c. rose (i)	12·00	2·25
21		4c. red (ii) (18.8.19)	6·50	1·00
		a. Short sheaf	£225	65·00
		w. Wmk inverted		
22	2	21c. mauve and purple (18.8.19)	5·50	70·00
		a. 'A' of 'CA' missing from wmk	—	£950
		c. 'Feather in hat'	£100	
		w. Wmk Crown to left of CA	£225	£300
		ws. Ditto, optd 'SPECIMEN'	£150	
		x. Wmk reversed	£400	
		y. Wmk Crown to left of CA and reversed	£425	
23		25c. blue and purple (1921)	1·75	38·00
		a. 'A' of 'CA' missing from wmk	£700	
		b. 'C' of 'CA' missing from wmk		
		c. 'Feather in hat'	50·00	
		x. Wmk reversed	£400	
15/23 *Set of 6*			14·00	£100
15s/23s Optd 'SPECIMEN' *Set of 6*			£170	

* The normal sideways watermark shows Crown to right of CA, *as seen from the back of the stamp.*

ONE

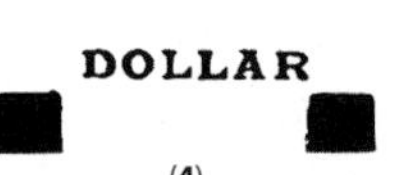

MALAYA-
BORNEO
EXHIBITION.

(**4**) (**5**)

(Surch by Ribeiro & Co, Penang)

1919 (Mar). Surch as T **4**.

24	3	50c. on $2 green and brown	70·00	80·00
		a. 'C' of 'CENTS' inserted by handstamp (R. 6/4)	£1300	£1500
25		$1 on $3 black and blue/*blue*	20·00	95·00

Nos. 24/25 were surcharged from settings of 30 (5×6).

Two types of centre plate for T **2** wmkd Mult Script CA:

Type I (Plate 1) (produced by electrotyping)

Type II (Plate 2) (produced by transfer die)

A new common centre plate, 2, was prepared from the original die in 1926. Stamps from Plate 2, produced using a transfer die, show considerably more detail of the ground and have the oxen, ploughman's hat and his clothing much more deeply cut as illustrated in Type II above.

1921–32. Wmk Mult Script CA (sideways* on 10c. to $5). P 14.

26	1	1c. brown (ii)	1·50	20
		w. Wmk inverted	†	£500
		y. Wmk inverted and reversed	†	£500
27		2c. dull green (ii) (Type I)	1·50	20
28		3c. deep purple (ii)	80	70
		w. Wmk inverted	£450	
29		4c. deep carmine (ii)	5·00	20
		a. Short sheaf	£225	40·00
30	2	10c. blue and sepia (I)	2·75	75
		a. 'Feather in hat'	60·00	30·00
		bx. Wmk reversed	£425	
		by. Wmk Crown to left of CA and reversed	£170	
		c. Type II (wmk Crown to left of CA) (1927)	65·00	1·25
		cy. Wmk Crown to right of CA and reversed	£550	£375
31		20c. black and yellow-green (I)	11·00	2·00
		a. 'Feather in hat'	£160	45·00
32		21c. mauve and purple (I)	2·25	13·00
		a. 'Feather in hat'	55·00	
33		25c. blue and purple (I)	2·25	9·00
		a. 'Feather in hat'	55·00	
		b. Type II (wmk Crown to left of CA) (1932)	£100	4·00
34		30c. black and rose (I) (1922)	4·00	11·00
		a. 'Feather in hat'	75·00	
		b. Type II (wmk Crown to left of CA) (1927)	65·00	3·00
35		40c. black and purple (I)	8·50	65·00
		a. 'Feather in hat'	£140	
		bw. Wmk Crown to left of CA (1924)	50·00	55·00
		c. Type II (wmk Crown to left of CA) (1932)	£130	35·00
36		50c. brown and grey-blue (I)	6·00	28·00
		a. 'Feather in hat'	£100	
		bw. Wmk Crown to left of CA (1924)	55·00	27·00
		c. Type II (wmk Crown to left of CA) (1932)	£130	9·50
37	3	$1 black and red/*yellow* (1924)	80·00	85·00
		w. Wmk Crown to left of CA	11·00	8·50
38		$2 myrtle and brown	13·00	£100
		w. Wmk Crown to left of CA (1924)	32·00	90·00
39		$3 black and blue/*blue*	80·00	£100
		w. Wmk Crown to left of CA (1924)	£140	90·00
40		$5 black and deep carmine	£110	£160
		w. Wmk Crown to left of CA (1926)	£170	£160
26/40 *Set of 15*			£225	£375
26s/40s Optd 'SPECIMEN' *Set of 15*			£400	

* The normal sideways watermark shows Crown to right of CA, *as seen from the back of the stamp.*

Nos. 26/40 were produced by De La Rue using the 'wet' method of recess-printing during which the stamps contracted when they were dried before gumming. From 1933 the firm adopted the 'dry' method, using pre-gummed paper, with the result that stamps were up to 0.5 mm larger in size. Of the low values as T **1** in this series only the 2c. was still current when the 'dry' method was introduced.

Stamps as T **1** can be found perforated either comb or line. The 1c. and 4c. come comb only, the 3c. line only and the 2c. either way.

Examples of Nos. 37/40 are known with part strikes of a forged Sungei Patang postmark dated '14 JY 1920'.

For the 2c. Type II see No. 69.

OVERPRINT SETTINGS FOR NOS. 41/51. The low values in T **1** were overprinted using Setting II as detailed under Straits Settlements. The three listed constant varieties from the original typeset block of 12 occur in the same positions for these Kedah stamps as does the No Stop variety from R. 1/5 of the left pane.

For the higher values in T **2**, which were in sheets of 60 (5×12), a further setting was prepared using the first four vertical rows of the typeset block with each horizontal row completed by a single random impression of the overprint. This means that, in addition to their positions in the truncated typeset block, the Oval last 'O' additionally occurs on R. 11/5 and the Raised stop on R. 5/5 of the sheet. In this setting, as for the low values, 'BORNEO' was 14 mm long.

Further supplies were subsequently required of the 21, 25 and 50c. values and these were produced using a completely different setting of 20 (5×4), applied three times to each sheet, on which 'BORNEO' was 15–15½ mm long. The small 'Y' in 'MALAYA' occurs on R. 4/2, 8/2 and 12/2.

1922 (Apr). Malaya-Borneo Exhibition, Singapore. Optd as T **5** at Singapore.

I. 'BORNEO' 14 mm long

(a) Wmk Mult Crown CA (Nos. 10, 18 and 22/23)

41	1	2c. green (ii)	5·50	30·00
		b. Oval last 'O' in 'BORNEO'	11·00	55·00
		c. Raised stop after 'EXHIBITION'	11·00	55·00
		d. Small second 'A' in 'MALAYA'	11·00	55·00
		f. No stop	48·00	
42	2	21c. mauve and purple	45·00	85·00
		b. Oval last 'O' in 'BORNEO'	75·00	£140
		c. Raised stop after 'EXHIBITION'	75·00	£140
43		25c. blue and purple	45·00	85·00
		a. Opt inverted	£1600	
		b. Oval last 'O' in 'BORNEO'	75·00	£140
		c. Raised stop after 'EXHIBITION'	75·00	£140
		d. 'Feather in hat'	£400	
44		50c. brown and blue	45·00	£100
		b. Oval last 'O' in 'BORNEO'	75·00	£160
		c. Raised stop after 'EXHIBITION'	75·00	£160
		d. 'Feather in hat'	£400	

(b) Wmk Mult Script CA (Nos. 26 and 28/30)

45	1	1c. brown (ii)	7·50	35·00
		b. Oval last 'O' in 'BORNEO'	15·00	60·00
		c. Raised stop after 'EXHIBITION'	15·00	60·00
		d. Small second 'A' in 'MALAYA'	15·00	60·00
		f. No stop	65·00	
46		3c. deep purple (ii)	6·00	50·00
		b. Oval last 'O' in 'BORNEO'	12·00	75·00
		c. Raised stop after 'EXHIBITION'	12·00	75·00
		d. Small second 'A' in 'MALAYA'	12·00	75·00
		f. No stop	50·00	
47		4c. deep carmine (ii)	6·50	25·00
		a. Short sheaf	£250	
		b. Oval last 'O' in 'BORNEO'	13·00	45·00
		c. Raised stop after 'EXHIBITION'	13·00	45·00
		d. Small second 'A' in 'MALAYA'	13·00	45·00
		f. No stop	50·00	
48	2	10c. blue and sepia (I)	15·00	50·00
		b. Oval last 'O' in 'BORNEO'	26·00	75·00
		c. Raised stop after 'EXHIBITION'	26·00	75·00
		d. 'Feather in hat'	£180	
41/48 *Set of 8*			£160	£400

II. 'BORNEO' 15–15½ mm long. Wmk Mult Crown CA (Nos. 10 and 22/23)

49	2	21c. mauve and purple	32·00	£110
		a. Small 'Y' in 'MALAYA'	90·00	
		b. 'Feather in hat'	£300	
50		25c. blue and purple	32·00	£130
		a. Small 'Y' in 'MALAYA'	90·00	
		b. 'Feather in hat'	£300	
51		50c. brown and blue	75·00	£180
		a. Small 'Y' in 'MALAYA'	£170	
		b. 'Feather in hat'	£475	
49/51 *Set of 3*			£120	£375

Examples of all values are known with part strikes of the forged postmark mentioned after Nos. 26/40.

1922–40. New colours, etc. Wmk Mult Script CA (sideways* on 12, 35c.). P 14.

52	1	1c. black (ii) (Type I)	1·00	10
53		3c. green (ii) (1924)	2·25	90
54		4c. violet (ii) (1926)	1·00	10
		a. Short sheaf	85·00	13·00
55		5c. yellow (ii)	3·50	10
		w. Wmk inverted	90·00	£110
		x. Wmk reversed	†	£425
		y. Wmk inverted and reversed	†	£425
56		6c. carmine (ii) (1926)	3·25	65
		a. Carmine-red (1940)	12·00	48·00
57		8c. grey-black (ii) (10.36)	24·00	10
58	2	12c. black and indigo (II) (1926)	12·00	3·50
59		35c. purple (II) (1926)	25·00	48·00
52/59 *Set of 8*			60·00	48·00
52s/59s Optd or Perf (8c.) 'SPECIMEN' *Set of 8*			£450	

* The normal sideways watermark shows Crown to left of CA, *as seen from the back of the stamp.*

With the exception of the 6c. and 8c. the printing plates for the T **1** values listed above were, as for the previous issue, produced by electrotyping with the face values added to the plates by pantograph. The plates for the 6c. and 8c. values were constructed by the more modern method of using a transfer die to enter each impression.

Printings after November 1933 were normally produced by the 'dry' method as described beneath Nos. 26/40. There were late 'wet' printings of the 1c. (No. 68*a*) and 2c. (No. 27) in August 1938. The 3c. only exists from a 'wet' printing, the 6c. (No. 56*a*) and 8c. from dry printings and the remainder from either method.

Stamps as T **1** can be found perforated either comb or line. The 3c. and 6c. (No. 56) come comb only, the 6c. (No. 56*a*) and 8c. line only and the 1, 4 and 5c. either way.

For the 1c. Type II see No. 68*a*.

6 Sultan Abdul Hamid Halimshah

(Recess Waterlow)

1937 (30 June). Wmk Mult Script CA. P 12½.

60	6	10c. ultramarine and sepia	8·00	2·25
61		12c. black and violet	70·00	3·25
		a. 'A' of 'CA' missing from wmk	£1800	
62		25c. ultramarine and purple	16·00	5·00
63		30c. green and scarlet	16·00	10·00
64		40c. black and purple	9·00	19·00
65		50c. brown and blue	16·00	6·00
66		$1 black and green	8·00	10·00
67		$2 green and brown	£130	75·00
68		$5 black and scarlet	42·00	£180
60/68 *Set of 9*			£275	£275
60s/68s Perf 'SPECIMEN' *Set of 9*			£325	

I

II

I

II

1938 (May)–**40**. As Nos. 52 and 27, but face values redrawn as Types II.

68*a*	1	1c. black	£160	1·40
69		2c. bright green (1940)	£350	5·50

1c. Type II. Figures '1' have square-cut corners instead of rounded, and larger top serif. Larger 'C'. Line perf. Produced from a new electrotyped Plate 2 with different engraved face values. Printings exist from either the 'wet' or 'dry' methods.

2c. Type II. Figures '2' have circular instead of oval drops and the letters 'c' are thin and tall instead of thick and rounded. Produced from a new plate, made from a transfer die, and printed by the 'dry' method.

1948 (1 Dec). Royal Silver Wedding. As Nos. 112/113 of Antigua.

70	10c. violet	20	40
71	$5 carmine	28·00	50·00

1949 (10 Oct). 75th Anniversary of UPU. As Nos. 114/117 of Antigua.

72	10c. purple	25	1·25
73	15c. deep blue	2·00	1·50
74	25c. orange	65	5·00
75	50c. blue-black	1·00	6·50
	a. 'A' of 'CA' missing from watermark	£1000	
72/75 *Set of 4*		3·50	13·00

7 Sheaf of Rice

8 Sultan Badlishah

1950 (1 June)–**55.** Wmk Mult Script CA. Chalk-surfaced paper. P 17½×18.

76	**7**	1c. black	1·00	30
77		2c. orange	50	15
78		3c. green	2·00	1·00
79		4c. brown	75	10
79*a*		5c. bright purple (1.9.52)	6·00	3·00
		ab. Bright mauve (24.9.53)	6·00	1·00
80		6c. grey	70	15
81		8c. scarlet	4·00	5·00
81*a*		8c. green (1.9.52)	7·50	4·00
		ab. Deep green (24.9.53)	27·00	26·00
82		10c. magenta	70	10
82*a*		12c. scarlet (1.9.52)	7·50	3·00
83		15c. ultramarine	6·50	35
84		20c. black and green	6·50	2·50
84*a*		20c. bright blue (1.9.52)	2·75	10
85	**8**	25c. purple and orange	1·50	30
85*a*		30c. scarlet and purple (4.9.55)	6·00	1·25
85*b*		35c. scarlet and purple (1.9.52)	8·00	1·50
86		40c. red and purple	9·00	10·00
87		50c. black and blue	6·50	35
88		$1 blue and purple	9·00	11·00
89		$2 green and scarlet	30·00	60·00
90		$5 green and brown	70·00	£100
76/90 *Set of 21*			£160	£180

1953 (2 June). Coronation. As No. 120 of Antigua.

91		10c. black and reddish purple	2·50	60

9 Copra

10 Pineapples

11 Ricefield

12 Alwi Mosque, Kangar

13 East Coast Railway

14 Tiger

15 Fishing Prau

16 Aborigines with Blowpipes

17 Government Offices

18 Bersilat

19 Weaving

(Recess D.L.R.)

1957. Inset portrait of Sultan Badlishah. W w **12**. P 13×12½ (1c. to 8c.), 12½×13 (10c., 20c.), 13×11½-12½ (50c.), 11½-12½×13 ($2, $5) or 13½ ($1).

92	**9**	1c. black (21.8)	10	60
93	**10**	2c. orange-red (25.7)	1·00	3·00
94	**11**	4c. sepia (21.8)	30	1·50
95	**12**	5c. carmine-lake (21.8)	30	1·50
96	**13**	8c. myrtle-green (21.8)	2·50	8·00
97	**14**	10c. deep brown (4.8)	80	40
98	**15**	20c. blue (26.6)	2·75	3·25
99	**16**	50c. black and blue (25.7)	3·75	4·25
100	**17**	$1 ultramarine and reddish purple (25.7)	16·00	26·00
101	**18**	$2 bronze-green and scarlet (21.8)	45·00	55·00
102	**19**	$5 brown and bronze-green (26.6)	60·00	60·00
92/102 *Set of 11*			£120	£140

The 6, 12, 25 and 30c. values used with this issue were Nos. 1/4 of Malayan Federation.

For a description of the compound perforations on Nos. 99, 101 and 102 see below Federation of Malaya No. 4. On horizontal stamps the perf 11½ section is at the left.

20 Sultan Abdul Halim Mu'Adzam Shah

21 Sultan Abdul Halim Shah

(Photo Harrison)

1959 (20 Feb). Installation of the Sultan. W w **12**. P 14×14½.

103	**20**	10c. multicoloured	1·00	10

1959 (1 July)–**62.** As Nos. 92/102 but with inset portrait of Sultan Abdul Halim Shah as in T **21**.

104	**21**	1c. black	10	75
105	**10**	2c. orange-red	10	2·00
106	**11**	4c. sepia	10	75
107	**12**	5c. carmine-lake	10	10
108	**13**	8c. myrtle-green	3·50	3·50
109	**14**	10c. deep brown	1·00	10
109*a*		10c. deep maroon (19.12.61)	18·00	1·50
110	**15**	20c. blue	1·00	1·00
111	**16**	50c. black and blue (P 12½)	30	1·75
		a. Perf 12½×13 (14.6.60)	30	60
112	**17**	$1 ultramarine and reddish purple	6·00	2·25
113	**18**	$2 bronze-green and scarlet	13·00	25·00
114	**19**	$5 brown and bronze-green (P 12½)	16·00	21·00
		a. Perf 13×12½ (26.11.62)	45·00	28·00
104/114 *Set of 12*			50·00	50·00

On Nos. 113/114 the perf 11½ section of the compound perforation is at the right of the stamp.

22 *Vanda hookeriana*

1965 (15 Nov). As Nos. 166/172 of Johore but with inset portrait of Sultan Abdul Halim Shah as in T **22**. W w **13** (upright).

115		1c. multicoloured	10	2·25
		a. Black omitted (orchid's name and part of flower)	£250	
116		2c. multicoloured	10	2·50
		b. Yellow (flower) omitted	£275	
		c. Dark green omitted	£325	
117		5c. multicoloured	10	55
		a. Black (country name and head) omitted	£325	
		c. Red omitted	£130	
118		6c. multicoloured	15	60
119		10c. multicoloured	30	50
		a. Red omitted	£800	
		b. Green (leaves) omitted	£1000	
120		15c. multicoloured	1·50	10
121		20c. multicoloured	2·00	2·00
		a. Bright purple (blooms) omitted	£550	
		b. Yellow (leaves) omitted	75·00	
115/121 *Set of 7*			3·75	7·50

The 1c. to 15c. exist with PVA gum as well as gum arabic.

The 6c. value exists with black (country name, Arms and head) omitted and is listed under Sarawak where it was issued.

The higher values used with this issue were Nos. 20/27 of Malaysia (National Issues).

1970 (27 May). As Nos. 115 and 119 but W w **13** (sideways).

122	**22**	1c. multicoloured	2·50	9·00
123	–	10c. multicoloured	1·00	4·50

KELANTAN

The Thai monarchy exercised suzeraity over Kelantan and the other northern states of the Malay peninsula from the 16th-century onwards.

The first Siamese post office in Kelantan opened at Kota Bharu in 1895. It appears that in the early years this office only accepted letters franked with stamps for delivery within Kelantan.

The initial cancellation, of which no complete example has been discovered, showed Thai characters only. Partial examples have been reported on the 1887–1891 8a. and 1896 4a. on 12a.

The operations of the Duff Development Company in Kelantan from 1903 led to a considerable expansion of the postal service based on the company's river steamers. A further post office opened at Batu Mengkebang in 1908, but may have been preceded by manuscript endorsements of 'B.M.' and date known from early 1907 onwards.

Type E. Double ring. English at top and bottom

For other stamps and postmark types, See under Kedah.

Kota Bharu

Stamps of SIAM cancelled as Type B inscr 'KALANTAN' (from March 1898).

1887–91. (Nos. 11/18).

Z301	**9**	2a. green and carmine	£150
Z302		3a. green and blue	£160
Z303		4a. green and brown	£160
Z304		8a. green and yellow	£160
Z305		12a. purple and carmine	£140
Z306		24a. purple and blue	£150

1894. Surch as T **27** with variation of English figures as T **33** (Nos. 37/44).

Z307	**9**	2a. on 64a. purple and brown	£225

1894–95. Surch as T **35** with variation of English figures as T **36** (Nos. 46/50).

Z308	**9**	1a. on 64a. purple and brown	£180

1896. Surch as T **39** (Siamese) and T **40** (English) (No. 51).

Z309	**9**	4a. on 12a. purple and carmine	£180

1897. Surch as T **39** (Siamese) and T **41** (English) (No. 52).

Z310	**9**	4a. on 12a. purple and carmine	£180

1898–99. Surch as T **42** with variation of English section as T **46** (Nos. 53/62).

Z311	**9**	3a. on 12a. (11½–11¾ *mm* long)	£190
Z312		4a. on 12a. purple and carmine (8 *mm* long)	£180

1899–1904. (Nos. 67/81).

Z313	**49**	1a. olive-green (wide Siamese characters in face value)	£150
Z314		2a. grass-green	£140
Z315		2a. scarlet and pale blue	£140
Z316		3a. red and blue	£160
Z317		4a. carmine	£140
Z318		4a. chocolate and pink	£160
Z319		8a. deep green and orange	£140
Z320		10a. ultramarine	£150
Z321		12a. brown-purple and carmine	£140
Z322		64a. brown-purple and chestnut	£350

1905–09. (Nos. 92/105).

Z323	**53**	1a. green and orange	£120
Z324		2a. grey and deep violet	£140
Z325		4a. pale red and sepia	£130
Z326		4a. scarlet	£140
Z327		5a. carmine	£160
Z328		8a. olive-bistre and dull black	£120
Z329		12a. blue	£160
Z330		24a. red-brown	£400
Z331		1t. bistre and deep blue	£400

1907. Surch with T **56** (No. 109).

Z332	**9**	1a. on 24a. purple and blue	£170

Stamps of SIAM cancelled as Type E inscr 'Kota Bahru/Kelantan' (from July 1908).

1887–91. (Nos. 11/18).

Z333	**9**	12a. purple and carmine	£130
Z334		24a. purple and blue	£170

1899–1904. (Nos. 67/81).

Z335	**49**	8a. deep green and orange	£140
Z336		64a. brown-purple and chestnut	£200

1905–09. (Nos. 92/105).

Z337	**53**	1a. green and orange	£140
Z338		2a. grey and deep violet	£140
Z339		2a. pale yellow-green	£140
Z340		4a. pale red and sepia	£140
Z341		4a. scarlet	£140
Z342		8a. olive-bistre and dull black	£140
Z343		9a. blue	£140
Z344		18a. red-brown	£225

1907. Surch with T **56** (No. 109).

Z345	**9**	1a. on 24a. purple and blue	£140

1908. Surch as T **59** (Nos. 110/112).

Z346	**9**	2a. on 24a. purple and blue	£200
Z347	**53**	4a. on 5a. carmine	£275
Z348	**49**	9a. on 10a. ultramarine	£150

Batu Mengkebang

Stamps of SIAM cancelled as Type E inscr 'Batu Menkebang/Kelantan' (from July 1908).

1887–91. (Nos. 11/18).

Z349	**9**	12a. purple and carmine	£275
Z349*a*		24a. purple and blue	£475

1899–1904. (Nos. 67/81).

Z350	**49**	8a. deep green and orange	£275

1905–09. (Nos. 92/105).

Z351	**53**	1a. green and orange	£250
Z352		2a. grey and deep violet	£250
Z353		2a. pale yellow-green	£275
Z354		4a. pale red and sepia	£275
Z355		4a. scarlet	£250
Z356		8a. olive-bistre and dull black	£200
Z357		9a. blue	£190
Z358		12a. blue	£325
Z359		24a. red-brown	£450
Z360		1t. bistre and deep blue	£475

1907. Surch with T **56** (No. 109).

Z361	**9**	1a. on 24a. purple and blue	£200

1908. Surch as T **59** (Nos. 110/112).

Z362	**49**	9a. on 10a. ultramarine	£325

Suzerainty over Kelantan was transferred by Thailand to Great Britain on 15 July 1909.

Siamese stamps were withdrawn from sale and replaced the following day by stamps of the Federated Malay States.

Stamps of the Federated Malay States used in Kelantan

Kota Bharu

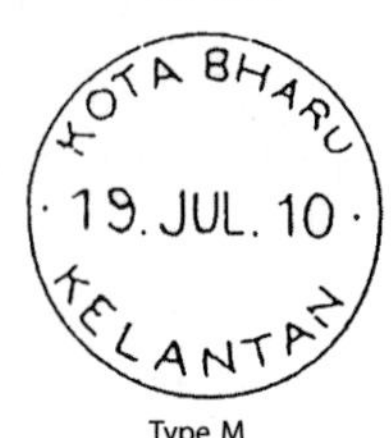

Type M

Cancelled as Type E

1909–11. (Nos. 29/49).

No.	Type	Description	Price
Z367	3	1c. green (Die II)	90·00
Z368		3c. carmine	75·00
Z369		4c. black and rose	90·00
Z370		8c. grey-brown and ultramarine	80·00
		a. Wmk upright	95·00
Z373	4	$2 green and carmine	£350

Cancelled as Type M

1909–11. (Nos. 29/45a).

No.	Type	Description	Price
Z375	3	1c. green (Die II)	70·00
Z376		3c. carmine	70·00
Z377		4c. black and rose	70·00
Z378		5c. green and carmine/*yellow*	£110
Z379		8c. grey-brown and ultramarine	90·00
		a. Wmk upright	£100
Z380		10c. black and purple	£120
Z381		20c. mauve and black (chalk-surfaced paper)	£120

Batu Menkebang

Cancelled as Type E inscribed 'Batu Menkebang'

1909–11. (Nos. 34/43*d*).

No.	Type	Description	Price
Z385	3	3c. carmine	£130
Z386		5c. green and carmine/*yellow*	£150
Z387		10c. black and purple	£150

Cancelled as Type M inscribed 'BATU MENKEBANG' at top

1909–11. (Nos. 29/45a).

No.	Type	Description	Price
Z391	3	1c. green (Die II)	95·00
Z392		3c. carmine	70·00
Z393		4c. black and rose	85·00
Z394		5c. green and carmine/*yellow*	£140
Z395		8c. grey-brown and ultramarine (wmk upright)	£110
Z396		10c. black and purple	£120
Z397		20c. mauve and black (chalk-surfaced paper)	£140

Federated Malay States stamps were replaced by those of Kelantan in January 1911.

A British adviser was appointed to Kelantan in 1923 and the state joined the Federation of Malaya on 1 February 1948.

PRICES FOR STAMPS ON COVER TO 1945

Nos.	Price
Nos. 1/11	*from* × 30
No. 12	—
Nos. 14/23	*from* × 30
Nos. 30/38	*from* × 15
Nos. 39/39a	*from* × 10
Nos. 40/48	*from* × 30
Nos. 49/52	*from* × 20
No. 53	*from* × 3
No. 54	—

1

MALAYA
BORNEO
EXHIBITION
(2)

1911 (Jan)–**15**. Wmk Mult Crown CA. Ordinary paper (1c. to 10c.) or chalk-surfaced paper (30c. to $25). P 14.

No.	Type	Description	Unused	Used
1	1	1c. yellow-green	7·00	1·00
		a. Blue-green	6·00	30
2		3c. red	4·25	15
3		4c. black and red	1·50	15
4		5c. green and red/*yellow*	10·00	2·25
		w. Wmk inverted	†	£750
5		8c. ultramarine	5·50	1·00
6		10c. black and mauve	30·00	75
7		30c. dull purple and red	11·00	2·00
		a. Purple and carmine	27·00	14·00
8		50c. black and orange	8·50	2·00
9		$1 green and emerald	50·00	35·00
9*a*		$1 green and brown (5.15)	75·00	2·00
10		$2 green and carmine	1·50	2·25
11		$5 green and blue	4·00	2·50
12		$25 green and orange	50·00	£120
1/12 *Set of* 13			£225	£150
1s/12s Optd 'SPECIMEN' *Set of* 13			£275	

1921 (5 May)–**28**. Wmk Mult Script CA. Ordinary paper (1c. to 10c.) or chalk-surfaced paper (30c. to $1). P 14.

No.	Type	Description	Unused	Used
14	1	1c. dull green (7.21)	4·25	60
15		1c. black (24.2.23)	1·00	50
16		2c. brown (29.7.22)	7·50	3·75
16*a*		2c. green (24.7.26)	5·50	40
16*b*		3c. brown (5.3.27)	5·00	1·00
		ba. 'C' of 'CA' missing from wmk		
17		4c. black and red (15.7.22)	3·50	10
18		5c. green and red/*pale yellow* (12.22)	1·75	10
19		6c. claret (29.7.22)	3·50	1·00
19*a*		6c. scarlet (26.5.28)	4·00	1·25
20		10c. black and mauve	3·00	10
21		30c. purple and carmine (24.7.26)	4·00	4·00
22		50c. black and orange (21.3.25)	6·50	45·00
23		$1 green and brown (9.2.24)	32·00	90·00
14/23 *Set of* 13			70·00	£130
14s/23s Optd 'SPECIMEN' *Set of* 13			£400	

Examples of Nos. 22/23 are known showing part strikes of a forged Kota Bharu postmark dated '27 JUL 11'.

For the 4c., 5c. and 6c. surcharged, see issues under 'Japanese Occupation'.

OVERPRINT SETTINGS FOR NOS. 30/38. All values were overprinted using a triplet of three slightly different types. It is not known if this was applied to the sheets three stamps at a time or if a forme to overprint a pane of 60 was constructed from it.

On the normal setting 'MALAYA' is 13 mm long. The 1c and 5c. only are also known with 'MALAYA' 14 mm from a different triplet setting. It has been suggested that this was a trial overprint which was subsequently included in postal stocks.

1922 (31 Mar). Malaya-Borneo Exhibition, Singapore. Optd with T **2** ('MALAYA' 13 *mm* long) by Govt Survey Office, Kota Bharu.

(a) Wmk Mult Crown CA

No.	Type	Description	Unused	Used
30	1	4c. black and red	7·00	50·00
		a. Opt double	£4250	
31		5c. green and red/*pale yellow*	7·00	50·00
		a. 'MALAYA' 14 mm long	£400	
32		30c. dull purple and red	7·00	80·00
33		50c. black and orange	10·00	85·00
34		$1 green and brown	32·00	£110
35		$2 green and carmine	£110	£275
36		$5 green and blue	£275	£500

(b) Wmk Mult Script CA

No.	Type	Description	Unused	Used
37	1	1c. green	4·50	55·00
		a. Opt double	£4250	
		b 'MALAYA' 14 mm. long	£750	
38		10c. black and mauve	7·50	75·00
30/38 *Set of* 9			£425	£1100

Nos. 30a and 37a show all three lines of the overprint double.

Examples of all values are known showing part strikes of the forged postmark mentioned below Nos. 14/23.

3 Sultan Ismail

4 Sultan Ismail

(Recess Harrison (No. 39) or D.L.R. (No. 39a))

1928–35. Wmk Mult Script CA. P 12.

No.	Type	Description	Unused	Used
39	3	$1 blue	15·00	90·00
		a. Perf 14 (1935)	75·00	50·00
		s. Perf 'SPECIMEN'	£130	

(Recess B.W.)

1937 (July)–**40**. Wmk Mult Script CA. P 12.

No.	Type	Description	Unused	Used
40	4	1c. grey-olive and yellow	2·75	55
41		2c. green	9·00	20
42		4c. scarlet	9·00	1·00
43		5c. red-brown	4·75	10
44		6c. lake (10.37)	27·00	16·00
45		8c. grey-olive	4·75	10
46		10c. purple (10.37)	42·00	2·75
47		12c. blue	8·50	8·00
48		25c. vermilion and violet	9·00	4·25
49		30c. violet and scarlet (10.37)	65·00	26·00
50		40c. orange and blue-green	12·00	48·00
51		50c. grey-olive and orange (10.37)	90·00	10·00
52		$1 violet and blue-green (10.37)	65·00	16·00
53		$2 red-brown and scarlet (3.40)	£425	£250
54		$5 vermilion and lake (3.40)	£1000	£1000
40/54 *Set of* 15			£1600	£1300
40s/54s Perf 'SPECIMEN' *Set of* 15			£1000	

For above issue surcharged see issues under 'Japanese Occupation'.

1948 (1 Dec). Royal Silver Wedding. As Nos. 112/113 of Antigua.

No.	Description	Unused	Used
55	10c. violet	75	2·75
56	$5 carmine	30·00	50·00

1949 (10 Oct). 75th Anniversary of UPU. As Nos. 114/117 of Antigua.

No.	Description	Unused	Used
57	10c. purple	25	30
58	15c. deep blue	2·25	4·50
59	25c. orange	40	8·50
60	50c. blue-black	70	3·75
57/60 *Set of* 4		3·25	15·00

Due to the exhaustion of certain B.M.A. values PERAK 2c., 3c., 4c., 6c., 15c., 20c. black and green, 25c., 40c. and 50c. stamps were used in Kelantan from 27 November 1950 until the issue of Nos. 61/81.

5 Sultan Ibrahim

Normal

No. 62a Tiny stop (R. 1/2)

1951 (11 July)–**55**. Chalk-surfaced paper. Wmk Mult Script CA. P 17½×18.

No.	Type	Description	Unused	Used
61	5	1c. black	50	30
62		2c. orange	1·25	35
		a. Tiny stop	32·00	42·00
		b. Orange-yellow (11.5.55)	15·00	6·00
63		3c. green	6·50	1·50
64		4c. brown	2·00	15
65		5c. bright purple (1.9.52)	1·50	50
		a. Bright mauve (9.12.53)	3·75	1·00
66		6c. grey	75	20
67		8c. scarlet	6·00	5·00
68		8c. green (1.9.52)	7·00	1·75
69		10c. magenta	65	10
70		12c. scarlet (1.9.52)	7·00	4·50
71		15c. ultramarine	9·00	60
72		20c. black and green	7·00	15·00
73		20c. bright blue (1.9.52)	2·00	25
74		25c. purple and orange	2·00	55
75		30c. scarlet and purple (4.9.55)	1·50	6·50
76		35c. scarlet and purple (1.9.52)	2·25	1·50
77		40c. red and purple	17·00	27·00
78		50c. black and blue	8·00	40
79		$1 blue and purple	9·50	18·00
80		$2 green and scarlet	50·00	70·00
81		$5 green and brown	75·00	85·00
		a. Green and sepia (8.12.53)	£160	£160
61/81 *Set of* 21			£200	£200

1953 (2 June). Coronation. As No. 120 of Antigua.

No.	Description	Unused	Used
82	10c. black and reddish purple	1·75	1·40

1957 (26 June)–**63**. As Nos. 92/102 of Kedah but with inset portrait of Sultan Ibrahim.

No.	Type	Description	Unused	Used
83	9	1c. black (21.8.57)	10	30
84	10	2c. orange-red (25.7.57)	75	1·50
		a. Red-orange (17.11.59)	18·00	9·00
85	11	4c. sepia (21.8.57)	40	10
86	12	5c. carmine-lake (21.8.57)	40	10
87	13	8c. myrtle-green (21.8.57)	4·00	4·50
88	14	10c. deep brown (4.8.57)	3·00	10
89		10c. deep maroon (19.4.61)	22·00	16·00
90	15	20c. blue	2·50	30
91	16	50c. black and blue (P 12½) (25.7.57)	50	2·50
		a. Perf 12½×13 (28.6.60)	1·00	1·75
92	17	$1 ultramarine and reddish purple (25.7.57)	13·00	1·50
93	18	$2 bronze-green and scarlet (P 12½) (21.8.57)	22·00	13·00
		a. Perf 13×12½ (9.4.63)	15·00	48·00
94	19	$5 brown and bronze-green (P 12½)	30·00	12·00
		a. Perf 13×12½ (13.8.63)	26·00	55·00
83/94 *Set of* 12			75·00	45·00

The 6, 12, 25 and 30c. values used with this issue were Nos. 1/4 of Malayan Federation.

6 Sultan Yahya Petra and Crest of Kelantan

(Photo Harrison)

1961 (17 July). Coronation of the Sultan. W w **12**. P 15×14.

No.	Type	Description	Unused	Used
95	6	10c. multicoloured	60	1·50

7 Sultan Yahya Petra

8 *Vanda hookeriana*

(Recess D.L.R.)

1961–63. As Nos. 92/98 of Kedah but with inset portrait of Sultan Yahya Petra as in T **7**. W w **13**. P 12½×13 (vert) or 13×12½ (horiz).

No.	Description	Unused	Used
96	1c. black (1.3.62)	25	3·00
97	2c. orange-red (1.3.62)	2·25	4·25
98	4c. sepia (1.3.62)	3·00	3·50
99	5c. carmine-lake (1.3.62)	3·00	1·25
100	8c. myrtle-green (1.3.62)	20·00	17·00
	a. Deep green (15.1.63)	30·00	18·00
101	10c. deep maroon (2.12.61)	1·75	75
102	20c. blue (1.3.62)	12·00	3·25
96/102 *Set of* 7		38·00	30·00

1965 (15 Nov). As Nos. 166/172 of Johore but with inset portrait of Sultan Yahya Petra as in T **8**. W w **13** (upright).

No.	Description	Unused	Used
103	1c. multicoloured	10	2·00
	b. Magenta omitted	£400	
104	2c. multicoloured	10	1·75
105	5c. multicoloured	15	30
106	6c. multicoloured	70	3·00
107	10c. multicoloured	30	25
	a. Red omitted	£225	
108	15c. multicoloured	1·50	25
109	20c. multicoloured	2·75	3·50
	a. Bright purple (blooms) omitted	£400	
	b. Yellow (leaves) omitted	£100	
103/109 *Set of* 7		5·00	10·00

The 5c. and 10c. exist with PVA as well as gum arabic.

A used example of No. 104 has been reported with yellow omitted.

The higher values used with this issue were Nos. 20/27 of Malaysia (National Issues).

1970 (20 Nov). As Nos. 103 and 107 but W w **13** (sideways).

No.	Type	Description	Unused	Used
110	8	1c. multicoloured	1·50	10·00
111	–	10c. multicoloured	3·75	7·00

STAMP BOOKLETS

1927 (June). Black on white (No. SB1) or black on grey (No. SB2) covers. Stapled.

No.	Description	Price
SB1	36c. booklet containing 36×1c. (No. 15) in blocks of 6	£3750
SB2	96c. booklet containing 24×4c. (No. 17) in blocks of 6	£3750

1927 (Dec). Black on white (No. SB3) or on grey (No. SB4) covers. Stapled.

SB3	40c. booklet containing 40×1c. (No. 15) in blocks of 10	£3750	
SB4	80c. booklet containing 20×4c. (No. 17) in blocks of 10	£3750	

MALACCA

One of the Straits Settlements which joined the Federation of Malaya on 1 February 1948.

1948 (1 Dec). Royal Silver Wedding. As Nos. 112/113 of Antigua.

1	10c. violet	30	1·75
2	$5 brown	35·00	50·00

1949 (1 Mar)–**52**. As T **58** of Straits Settlements, but inscr 'MALACCA' at foot. Wmk Mult Script CA. Chalk-surfaced paper. P 17½×18.

3	1c. black	30	70
4	2c. orange	80	45
5	3c. green	30	1·75
6	4c. brown	30	10
6*a*	5c. bright purple (1.9.52)	7·00	1·50
7	6c. grey	75	85
8	8c. scarlet	75	7·50
8*a*	8c. green (1.9.52)	9·00	8·00
9	10c. purple	30	10
9*a*	12c. scarlet (1.9.52)	9·00	18·00
10	15c. ultramarine	3·50	60
11	20c. black and green	1·00	8·50
11*a*	20c. bright blue (1.9.52)	11·00	3·00
12	25c. purple and orange	1·00	70
12*a*	35c. scarlet and purple (1.9.52)	12·00	3·00
13	40c. red and purple	1·50	11·00
14	50c. black and blue	1·50	1·25
15	$1 blue and purple	21·00	35·00
16	$2 green and scarlet	32·00	35·00
17	$5 green and brown	65·00	60·00
3/17 *Set of* 20		£150	£160

1949 (10 Oct). 75th Anniversary of UPU. As Nos. 114/117 of Antigua.

18	10c. purple	30	50
19	15c. deep blue	2·00	3·50
20	25c. orange	40	13·00
21	50c. blue-black	60	4·75
18/21 *Set of* 4		3·00	19·00

1953. Coronation. As No. 120 of Antigua.

22	10c. black and reddish purple	1·75	1·50

1 Queen Elizabeth II

2 Copra

1954 (9 June)–**57**. Chalk-surfaced paper. Wmk Mult Script CA. P 17½×18.

23	1	1c. black (27.4.55)	10	60
24		2c. yellow-orange (27.4.55)	30	1·25
25		4c. brown	2·00	10
		a. Pale brown (24.4.57)	20·00	4·75
26		5c. bright mauve (12.7.54)	30	2·50
27		6c. grey	10	40
28		8c. green (5.1.55)	40	2·75
29		10c. brown-purple (1.7.54)	2·25	10
		a. Reddish purple (27.3.57)	11·00	2·25
30		12c. rose-red (5.1.55)	30	3·00
31		20c. bright blue (5.1.55)	30	1·25
32		25c. brown-purple and yellow-orange (27.4.55)	30	1·50
33		30c. rose-red and brown-purple (5.9.55)	30	30
34		35c. rose-red and brown-purple (8.9.54)	30	1·50
35		50c. black and bright blue (5.1.55)	5·50	2·50
36		$1 bright blue and brown-purple (8.9.54)	7·00	18·00
37		$2 emerald and scarlet (27.4.55)	26·00	50·00
38		$5 emerald and brown (27.4.55)	26·00	55·00
23/38 *Set of* 16			60·00	£120

1957. As Nos. 92/102 of Kedah but with inset portrait of Queen Elizabeth II.

39	9	1c. black (21.8)	10	50
40	10	2c. orange-red (25.7)	10	50
41	11	4c. sepia (21.8)	50	10
42	12	5c. carmine-lake (21.8)	50	10
43	13	8c. myrtle-green (21.8)	3·00	2·50
44	14	10c. deep brown (4.8)	40	10
45	15	20c. blue (26.6)	2·75	2·50
46	16	50c. black and blue (25.7)	1·50	2·25
47	17	$1 ultramarine and reddish purple (25.7)	10·00	10·00
48	18	$2 bronze-green and scarlet (21.8)	27·00	48·00
49	19	$5 brown and bronze-green (26.6)	29·00	50·00
39/49 *Set of* 11			65·00	£100

The 6, 12, 25 and 30c. values used with this issue were Nos. 1/4 of Malayan Federation.

(Recess D.L.R.)

1960 (15 Mar)–**62**. As Nos. 39/49, but with inset picture of Melaka tree and Pelandok (mouse deer) as in T **2**. W w **12**. P 13×12½ (1c. to 8c., $2, $5), 12½×13 (10c. to 50c.) or 13½ ($1).

50	1c. black	10	30
51	2c. orange-red	10	65
52	4c. sepia	10	10
53	5c. carmine-lake	10	10
54	8c. myrtle-green	5·00	3·00
55	10c. deep maroon	40	10
56	20c. blue	3·00	80
57	50c. black and blue	2·25	1·00
	a. Black and ultramarine (9.1.62)	8·00	2·00
58	$1 ultramarine and reddish purple	7·00	3·00
59	$2 bronze-green and scarlet	7·00	17·00
60	$5 brown and bronze-green	17·00	14·00
50/60 *Set of* 11		35·00	35·00

3 *Vanda hookeriana*

1965 (15 Nov)–**68**. As Nos. 166/172 of Johore but with Arms of Malacca inset and inscr 'MELAKA' as in T **3**. W w **13** (upright).

61	1c. multicoloured	10	2·50
62	2c. multicoloured	10	2·50
63	5c. multicoloured	1·00	40
	b. Yellow (flower) omitted	75·00	
	c. Red omitted	£150	
64	6c. multicoloured	1·00	1·00
65	10c. multicoloured	30	10
66	15c. multicoloured	1·75	40
67	20c. multicoloured (purple-brown background)	2·25	1·00
	a. Red-brown background (2.4.68)	5·00	4·25
	b. Yellow (shading in leaves and flowers) omitted		
61/67 *Set of* 7		6·00	7·00

The 5c., 6c., 10c. and 20c. exist with PVA gum as well as gum arabic.

The higher values used with this issue were Nos. 20/27 of Malaysia (National Issues).

1970. As Nos. 61 and 65 but W w **13** (sideways)

68	**3**	1c. multicoloured (27.5.70)	1·75	11·00
69	–	10c. multicoloured (20.11.70)	5·50	9·00

NEGRI SEMBILAN

A federation of smaller states reconstituted in 1886. Sungei Ujong, taken under British protection in 1874, was absorbed into Negri Sembilan by Treaty of 8 August 1895. The Negri Sembilan federation joined the Federated Malay States in 1896.

A. SUNGEI UJONG

Until 1 January 1899, when the Federated Malay States joined the UPU, mail for addresses outside Malaya was franked with the stamps of the STRAITS SETTLEMENTS.

PRICES FOR STAMPS ON COVER

Nos. 1/14	—
Nos. 15/27	*from* × 25
Nos. 28/36	*from* × 8
Nos. 37/49	*from* × 10
Nos. 50/55	*from* × 25

Overprints and surcharges were applied by the Government Printer, Singapore, *unless otherwise stated.*

(1)

1878. No. 11 of Straits Settlements handstamped with T **1**.

1	2c. brown	£4750	£5000

This overprint on India No. 54 is bogus.

SUNGEI (**2**) (Narrow letters) — SUNGEI (**3**) ('N' wide) — SUNGEI (**4**) ('S' wide)

UJONG (**5**) ('N' wide) — UJONG (**6**) (Narrow letters, 'UJ' close together) — UJONG (**7**) (Narrow letters, evenly spaced)

1881. No. 11 of Straits Settlements optd with Types **2/7**.

2	**2+5**	2c. brown	£6000	£4000
3	**3+5**	2c. brown	£4250	£3000
4	**2+6**	2c. brown	£475	
		a. Opt Type **6** double	£1800	
5	**4+6**	2c. brown	£1600	
6	**2+7**	2c. brown	£425	

The two lines of this surcharge were applied as separate operations. On Nos. 2/3 'SUNGEI' was printed as a triplet, probably 2+3+3 'UJONG' being added by a single unit handstamp. Nos. 4 and 5 come from a similar triplet, 4+4+5, completed by another single unit handstamp. No. 6 comes from a single type triplet with the second line added as a triplet instead of by a single unit handstamp.

The 10c. slate overprinted Types **2** + **7** is bogus.

SUNGEI (**8**) ('N' and 'E' wide) — SUNGEI (**9**) ('SUN' and 'E' wide) — SUNGEI (**10**) ('SUN' wide)

SUNGEI (**11**) ('S' wide) — SUNGEI (**12**) (Narrow letters)

UJONG (**13**) ('U' and 'NG' wide) — UJONG (**14**) (Narrow letters)

1881. No. 11 of Straits Settlements optd with Types **8/14**.

7	**8+13**	2c. brown	£400	
8	**9+13**	2c. brown	£400	
9	**10+13**	2c. brown	£400	
10	**11+14**	2c. brown	£400	
		a. 'S' inverted	£4250	
11	**12+14**	2c. brown	£250	

Nos. 7/11 also had the two lines of the overprint applied at separate operations. 'SUNGEI' as a triplet, either 7+8+9 or 10+11+11, and 'UJONG' as a single unit.

S.U.
(**15**)

1882. Nos. 50/51 of Straits Settlements optd as T **15**.

12	2c. brown (with stops)	£325	
	a. Opt double	£3750	
13	2c. brown (without stops)	£275	£325
14	4c. rose (with stops)	£6000	£6500

Each of the above was applied by a triplet setting.

Examples of Straits Settlements No. 11 with a similar overprint, including stops, are trials which were not issued.

SUNGEI (**16**) ('S' and 'E' wide) — SUNGEI (**17**) ('E' wide) — UJONG (**18**) ('N' wide)

1882 (Dec)–**84**. Nos. 12, 50, 52/53 and 63 of Straits Settlements optd with Types **11/12**, **14** and **16/18**.

15	**12+14**	2c. brown	£1800	£800
16	**11+14**	2c. brown	£2750	£1200
17	**12+14**	2c. pale rose (1884)	£300	£300
18	**11+14**	2c. pale rose (1884)	£300	£300
		a. Opt Type **14** double		
19	**16+14**	2c. pale rose (1884)	£140	£140
		a. Opt Type **16** double	†	£1200
20	**17+14**	2c. pale rose (1884)	£150	£160
21	**12+18**	2c. pale rose (1884)	£150	£160
		a. Opt Type **18** double	£1200	
22	**12+14**	4c. rose	£1800	£2000
		a. Opt Type **12** double	†	£4750
23	**11+14**	4c. rose	£2750	£3250
24	**12+14**	8c. orange	£1900	£1700
25	**11+14**	8c. orange	£3250	£3000
26	**12+14**	10c. slate	£650	£475
27	**11+14**	10c. slate	£900	£750

Nos. 15/27 had the two lines of the overprint applied by separate triplets. Settings so far identified are Nos. 15+16+15, 17+18+19, 19+20+21, 22+23+22, 24+25+24 and 26+27+26.

The 4c. rose overprinted Types **16** + **14** is now believed to be a trial.

UJONG. (**19**) (With stop. Narrow letters) — UJONG. (**20**) (With stop. 'N' wide) — UJONG (**21**) (Without stop. Narrow letters)

1883–84. Nos. 50 and 63/64 of Straits Settlements optd with Types **12**, **16/17** and **19/21**.

28	**12+19**	2c. brown	65·00	£190
29	**16+19**	2c. brown	65·00	£190
30	**12+20**	2c. brown	65·00	£190
		a. Opt Type **12** double	£1200	
31	**16+21**	2c. pale rose (1884)	£140	£150
32	**17+21**	2c. pale rose (1884)	£140	£150
33	**12+21**	2c. pale rose (1884)	£140	£150
		a. Opt Type **21** double	£1200	
34	**16+21**	4c. brown (1884)	£300	£425
		a. Opt Type **16** double		
		b. Opt Type **21** double	£2750	
35	**17+21**	4c. brown (1884)	£300	£425
36	**12+21**	4c. brown (1884)	£300	£425
		a. Opt Type **21** double	£4000	

Nos. 28/36 had the two lines of the overprint applied by separate triplets. Settings were Nos. 28+29+30, 31+32+33, 33+31+32 and 34+35+36.

The 8c. orange overprinted Types **12** + **19** is now believed to be a trial (*Price* £1000 *unused*).

Sungei Ujong (**22**) — SUNGEI UJONG (**23**) — SUNGEI UJONG (**24**)

SUNGEI UJONG (**25**) — SUNGEI UJONG (**26**) — SUNGEI UJONG (**27**)

SUNGEI UJONG (**28**) — SUNGEI UJONG. (**29**) — SUNGEI UJONG (**30**)

Antique 'G' in 'SUNGEI' (R. 6/1)

1885–90. Nos. 63/63*a* of Straits Settlements optd with Types **22/30**.

37	**22**	2c. pale rose	90·00	£100
		a. Opt double	£850	£950
38	**23**	2c. pale rose	60·00	65·00
		a. Opt double	£750	
39	**24**	2c. pale rose (1886)	£110	£130
40	**25**	2c. pale rose (1886)	£140	£150
		a. Opt double		
41	**26**	2c. pale rose (1886)	£110	£110
		a. Opt double		
42	**27**	2c. pale rose (1887)	27·00	50·00

43	**28**	2c. pale rose (1889)	16·00	18·00
		a. Narrow 'E' (2 *mm* wide) (R. 3/4 and 4/3)	£160	
		c. Opt double	£1400	
		d. Bright rose (1890)	22·00	15·00
		da. Narrow 'E' (2 *mm* wide) (R. 3/4 and 4/3)	£200	
		db. Antique 'N' in 'UJONG' (R. 10/6)	£350	
44	**29**	2c. pale rose (1889)	£100	70·00
		a. 'UNJOG' (R. 7/3)	£5000	£3500
45	**30**	2c. bright rose (1890)	50·00	29·00
		a. Antique 'G' in 'SUNGEI' (R. 6/1)	£900	
		b. Antique 'G' in 'UJONG' (R. 8/3)	£900	
		c. Pale rose		

All the above overprints had both lines applied at the same operation. Nos. 37/42 were from different triplet settings. The first printing of T **28** was from a triplet (No. 43) but this was followed by two further settings of 60 (6×10), the first containing No. 43a and the second Nos. 43*d*/43db. Nos. 44/45 were both from settings of 60.

The antique letter varieties on Types **28** and **30** are similar in style to those on Types **25** and **26**.

SUNGEI UJONG Two CENTS **(31)**

SUNGEI UJONG Two CENTS **(32)**

SUNGEI UJONG *Two* CENTS **(33)**

SUNGEI UJONG *Two* CENTS **(34)**

1891. No. 68 of Straits Settlements surch with Types **31**/**34**.

46	**31**	2c. on 24c. green	£1100	£1100
		w. Wmk inverted	£2750	£2750
47	**32**	2c. on 24c. green	£475	£475
		w. Wmk inverted	£1100	£1200
48	**33**	2c. on 24c. green	£1100	£1100
		w. Wmk inverted	£2750	£2750
49	**34**	2c. on 24c. green	£275	£275
		a. Antique 'G' in 'SUNGEI' (R. 6/1)	£1900	
		b. Antique 'G' in 'UJONG' (R. 8/3)	£1900	
		w. Wmk inverted	£700	£800

Nos. 46/49 come from the same setting of 60 on which 'SUNGEI UJONG' was from the same type as No. 45. No. 46 occurs in row 1. No. 47 from rows 2 to 4, No. 48 from row 5 and No. 49 from rows 6 to 10.

35

3 CENTS

(36)

37

1891 (Nov)–**94**. Wmk Crown CA. P 14.

50	**35**	2c. rose	42·00	24·00
		a. 'S.UJONG' and '2c.' doubly printed	†	£2500
51		2c. orange (12.94)	1·75	4·25
52		5c. blue (3.93)	11·00	6·50
50/52 *Set of 3*			50·00	30·00
50s/52s Optd 'SPECIMEN' *Set of 3*			90·00	

1894 (Dec). Surch as T **36** by De La Rue. Wmk Mult Crown CA. P 14.

53	**35**	1c. on 5c. green	1·00	70
54		3c. on 5c. rose	2·50	9·50

1895 (Oct). Wmk Crown CA. P 14.

55	**37**	3c. dull purple and carmine	27·00	9·00
53s/55s Optd 'SPECIMEN' *Set of 3*			90·00	

B. NEGRI SEMBILAN

Stamps of the STRAITS SETTLEMENTS were used in Negri Sembilan during 1891, until replaced by the stamps listed below. Until the Federated Malay States joined the UPU on 1 January 1899 Straits Settlements stamps continued to be used for mail to addresses outside Malaya.

PRICES FOR STAMPS ON COVER TO 1945

No. 1	*from* × 200
Nos. 2/4	*from* × 10
Nos. 5/14	*from* × 8
Nos. 15/20	*from* × 10
Nos. 21/49	*from* × 4

(1)

2

3

1891 (Aug?). No. 63*a* of Straits Settlements optd with T **1**.

1		2c. bright rose	3·00	14·00

N.SEMBILAN

2c. Short 'N' in 'SEMBILAN' (Top left pane R. 8/3)

1891 (Nov)–**94**. Wmk Crown CA. P 14.

2	**2**	1c. green (6.93)	3·25	1·00
3		2c. rose	3·25	19·00
		a. Short 'N'	£120	
4		5c. blue (11.94)	30·00	48·00
2/4 *Set of 3*			32·00	60·00
2s/4s Optd 'SPECIMEN' *Set of 3*			95·00	

1895–99. Wmk Crown CA. P 14.

5	**3**	1c. dull purple and green (1899)	27·00	15·00
6		2c. dull purple and brown (1898)	35·00	£130
7		3c. dull purple and carmine	18·00	3·75
8		5c. dull purple and olive-yellow (1897)	18·00	20·00
9		8c. dull purple and ultramarine (1898)	29·00	27·00
10		10c. dull purple and orange (1897)	27·00	14·00
11		15c. green and violet (1896)	50·00	90·00
12		20c. green and olive (1897)	75·00	40·00
13		25c. green and carmine (1896)	80·00	£100
14		50c. green and black (1896)	95·00	70·00
5/14 *Set of 10*			£400	£450
5s/14s Optd 'SPECIMEN' *Set of 10*			£300	

Four cents.

(4)

Four cents.

(5)

1898 (Dec)–**1900**.

(a) Surch as T **4**

15	**3**	1c. on 15c. green and violet (1900)	£110	£350
		a. Raised stop (R. 5/1 and R. 10/1 of each pane)	£500	£1400
		b. Surch double, one albino	£450	
16	**2**	4c. on 1c. green	3·50	27·00
17	**3**	4c. on 3c. dull purple and carmine	7·50	29·00
		a. Horiz pair, one without surch	£15000	£7500
		b. Surch double	£2500	£1000
		ba. Ditto. 'Four cents' albino	†	£1000
		c. Surch inverted	£2500	£1600
		d. 'cents' repeated at left	£4500	£3750
		e. 'Four' repeated at right	£4500	£3750
		f. Without bar	£800	£650
		g. Bar double	†	£900
18	**2**	4c. on 5c. blue	1·50	15·00

On Nos. 15 and 17 the bar is at the top of the stamp.

The surcharges were applied as a setting of 30 (6×5).

(b) Surch as T **5**

19	**3**	4c. on 8c. dull purple and ultramarine (G.) (12.98)	16·00	4·25
		a. Vert pair, one without surch	£10000	£5500
		b. Surch double	£3000	£2500
		c. Surch double (G.+R.)	£850	£950
20		4c. on 8c. dull purple and ultramarine (Blk.)	£1500	£1600

Care should be taken in distinguishing the true black surcharge, No. 20, from very deep shades of the green surcharge, No. 19.

Pending the arrival of the permanent Federated Malay States issue the stamps of SELANGOR, FEDERATED MALAY STATES provisional overprints, STRAITS SETTLEMENTS and PERAK were used at various times between October 1899 and April 1901.

The general issues for FEDERATED MALAY STATES were used in Negri Sembilan from 29 April 1901 until 1935.

6 Arms of Negri Sembilan

7 Arms of Negri Sembilan

1935 (2 Dec)–**41**. Wmk Mult Script CA. Ordinary paper (6c. grey, 15c.) or chalk-surfaced paper (others). P 14.

21	**6**	1c. black (1.1.36)	1·00	20
22		2c. green (1.1.36)	1·00	20
23		2c. orange (*Thin striated paper*) (11.12.41)	4·25	75·00
24		3c. green (*ordinary paper*) (21.8.41)	48·00	8·00
		a. Thin striated paper (12.41)	8·00	25·00
25		4c. orange	2·00	10
26		5c. brown (5.12.35)	2·00	10
27		6c. scarlet (1.1.37)	18·00	4·25
		a. Stop omitted at right (R. 10/4)	£900	£275
28		6c. grey (18.12.41)	4·75	£130
		a. Stop omitted at right (R. 10/4)	£350	
29		8c. grey	2·00	10
30		10c. dull purple (1.1.36)	1·25	10
31		12c. bright ultramarine (1.1.36)	3·25	50
32		15c. ultramarine (1.10.41)	11·00	60·00
33		25c. dull purple and scarlet (1.4.36)	1·50	70
		a. Thin striated paper (1941)	—	£110
34		30c. dull purple and orange (1.1.36)	3·50	3·25
		a. Thin striated paper	£110	
35		40c. scarlet and dull purple	3·75	2·00
36		50c. black/*emerald* (1.2.36)	6·50	2·25
37		$1 black and red/*blue* (1.4.36)	5·00	7·50
38		$2 green and scarlet (16.5.36)	60·00	22·00
39		$5 green and red/*emerald* (16.5.36)	45·00	£130
21/39 *Set of 19*			£160	£375
21s/39s Perf 'SPECIMEN' *Set of 19*			£475	

The stamps issued in 1941 were printed by Harrison and Sons following bomb damage to the De La Rue works on 29 December 1940. The used prices quoted for Nos. 23, 28 and 32 are for examples with clearly identifiable 1941 cancellations. These stamps, and No. 39, are commonly found with forged cancellations.

An 8c. scarlet on both ordinary and thin striated paper was printed but only issued with opt during Japanese Occupation of Malaya. Unoverprinted specimens result from leakages.

During shortages in 1941 stamps of STRAITS SETTLEMENTS (2c. green, 25c., 30c.), SELANGOR (2c. green, 2c. orange (both perfs), 8c. grey, 25c.), PERAK (2c. orange, 25c., 50c.) and PAHANG (8c. scarlet) were issued in Negri Sembilan.

1948 (1 Dec). Royal Silver Wedding. As Nos. 112/113 of Antigua.

40		10c. violet	40	50
41		$5 green	23·00	32·00

1949 (1 Apr)–**55**. Chalk-surfaced paper. Wmk Mult Script CA. P 17½×18.

42	**7**	1c. black	1·25	10
43		2c. orange	1·25	10
44		3c. green	60	30
45		4c. brown	30	10
46		5c. bright purple (1.9.52)	5·00	1·25
		a. Bright mauve (25.8.53)	5·00	45
47		6c. grey	2·75	10
		a. Pale grey (25.8.53)	12·00	2·50
48		8c. scarlet	1·00	75
49		8c. green (1.9.52)	8·00	1·60
50		10c. purple	40	10
51		12c. scarlet (1.9.52)	8·00	3·25
52		15c. ultramarine	5·00	10
53		20c. black and green	3·75	4·25
54		20c. bright blue (1.9.52)	4·00	10
55		25c. purple and orange	1·25	10
56		30c. scarlet and purple (4.9.55)	1·25	2·50
57		35c. scarlet and purple (1.9.52)	7·00	1·00
58		40c. red and purple	7·00	4·75
59		50c. black and blue	7·00	20
60		$1 blue and purple	7·50	2·50
61		$2 green and scarlet	25·00	48·00
62		$5 green and brown	55·00	£120
42/62 *Set of 21*			£130	£160

1949 (10 Oct). 75th Anniversary of UPU. As Nos. 114/117 of Antigua.

63		10c. purple	20	20
64		15c. deep blue	1·40	3·50
		a. 'A' of 'CA' missing from wmk	£900	
65		25c. orange	30	3·00
66		50c. blue-black	60	3·25
63/66 *Set of 4*			2·25	9·00

1953 (2 June). Coronation. As No. 120 of Antigua.

67		10c. black and reddish purple	1·50	50

1957 (26 June)–**63**. As Nos. 92/102 of Kedah but with inset Arms of Negri Sembilan.

68	**9**	1c. black (21.8.57)	10	10
69	**10**	2c. orange-red (25.7.57)	10	10
70	**11**	4c. sepia (21.8.57)	10	10
71	**12**	5c. carmine-lake (21.8.57)	10	10
72	**13**	8c. myrtle-green (21.8.57)	3·00	1·40
73	**14**	10c. deep brown (4.8.57)	2·00	10
74		10c. deep maroon (10.1.61)	14·00	10
75	**15**	20c. blue	1·00	10
76	**16**	50c. black and blue (P 12½) (25.7.57)	30	1·40
		a. Perf 12½×13 (19.7.60)	75	10
77	**17**	$1 ultramarine and reddish purple (25.7.57)	10·00	2·00
78	**18**	$2 bronze-green and scarlet (P 12½) (21.8.57)	18·00	20·00
		a. Perf 13×12½ (15.1.63)	25·00	55·00
79	**19**	$5 brown and bronze-green (P 12½)	20·00	32·00
		a. Perf 13×12½ (6.3.62)	35·00	45·00
		ab. Perf 13×12½. *Brown and yellow-olive* (13.11.62)	£350	£110
68/79 *Set of 12*			60·00	50·00

The 6, 12, 25 and 30c. values used with this issue were Nos. 1/4 of Malayan Federation.

8 Tuanku Munawir

9 *Vanda hookeriana*

(Photo Enschedé)

1961 (17 Apr). Installation of Tuanku Munawir as Yang di-Pertuan Besar of Negri Sembilan. No wmk. P 14×13.

80	**8**	10c. multicoloured	30	70

A 10c. stamp similar to T **8** but in red and inscribed '25th ANNIVERSARY of ACCESSION' was intended for release on 26 November 1959 to mark Tuanku Abdul Rahman's silver jubilee, but was cancelled due to his ill health and subsequent death. (*Price £750 unused*).

1965 (15 Nov)–**69**. As Nos. 166/172 of Johore but with Arms of Negri Sembilan inset and inscr 'NEGERI SEMBILAN' as in T **9**. W w **13** (upright).

81		1c. multicoloured	10	1·60
82		2c. multicoloured	10	1·60
		w. Wmk inverted	6·00	
83		5c. multicoloured	2·00	10
		b. Yellow omitted	£100	
		c. Red (leaves, etc) omitted	£100	
84		6c. multicoloured	40	60
85		10c. multicoloured	1·00	10
86		15c. multicoloured	80	10
87		20c. jet-black and multicoloured	2·25	1·00
		a. Blackish brown and mult (19.12.69)	9·50	3·25
81/87 *Set of 7*			6·00	4·50

The 2c., 6c., 15c. and 20c. exist with PVA gum as well as gum arabic.

The higher values used with this issue were Nos. 20/27 of Malaysia (National Issues).

See also No. 90.

10 Negri Sembilan Crest and Tuanku Ja'afar

(Des Z. Noor. Photo Japanese Govt Ptg Wks)

1968 (8 Apr). Installation of Tuanku Ja'afar as Yang di-Pertuan Besar of Negri Sembilan. P 13.

88 **10** 15c. multicoloured ... 20 1·40
89 50c. multicoloured ... 40 1·40

1970 (27 May). As No. 81 but with W w **13** (sideways).

90 **9** 1c. multicoloured ... 2·75 9·50

STAMP BOOKLETS

1935. Stapled.

SB1 $1 booklet containing 205c. (No. 26) in blocks of 10 ... £3750
SB2 $1.30 booklet containing 5c. and 8c. (Nos. 26, 29), each in block of 10 ... £4250

PAHANG

The first British Resident was appointed in 1888. Pahang joined the Federated Malay States in 1896.

> Until 1 January 1899, when the Federated Malay States joined the UPU, mail for addresses outside Malaya was franked with stamps of the STRAITS SETTLEMENTS.

PRICES FOR STAMPS ON COVER TO 1945

No. 1	*from* × 50
Nos. 2/3	—
No. 4	*from* × 100
No. 5	—
No. 6	*from* × 100
Nos. 7/10	*from* × 8
Nos. 11/13	*from* × 25
Nos. 14/16	*from* × 20
Nos. 17/17*a*	—
Nos. 18/18*d*	*from* × 6
Nos. 19/24	*from* × 8
No. 25	*from* × 20
Nos. 26/27	—
No. 28	*from* × 15
Nos. 29/46	*from* × 6

Overprints and surcharges were applied by the Government Printer, Singapore.

PAHANG (**1**) PAHANG (**2**) PAHANG (**2a**) (Antique letters)

1889 (Jan). Nos. 52/53 and 63 of Straits Settlements optd with T **1**.

1 2c. pale rose ... £170 50·00
2 8c. orange ... £1800 £1800
3 10c. slate ... £225 £275

All three values were overprinted from a triplet setting, but the 2c. also exists from a similar setting of 30 or 60.

1889. No. 63 of Straits Settlements optd with T **2**.

4 2c. pale rose ... 28·00 35·00
a. Bright rose ... 19·00 18·00
ab. Opt Type **2a**. Antique letters ... £1000

No. 4 was overprinted from a setting of 60. No. 4ab usually occurs on R. 10/1, but has also been found on R. 8/1 as the result of revision of the setting.

PAHANG (**3**) PAHANG (**4**)

1890 (Feb–Dec). No. 63*a* of Straits Settlements optd.

5 **3** 2c. bright rose ... £13000 £3500
6 **4** 2c. bright rose (12.90) ... £140 14·00
w. Wmk inverted ... £750 £550

No. 5 may have been overprinted from a triplet setting. No. 6 was from a setting of 60.

PAHANG Two CENTS (**5**) PAHANG Two CENTS (**6**)

PAHANG Two CENTS (**7**) PAHANG Two CENTS (**8**)

1891 (May). No. 68 of Straits Settlements surch with Types **5/8**.

7 **5** 2c. on 24c. green ... £275 £300
8 **6** 2c. on 24c. green ... £1200 £1300
9 **7** 2c. on 24c. green ... £450 £475
10 **8** 2c. on 24c. green ... £1200 £1300

Nos. 7/10 come from one setting used to surcharge the panes of sixty. No. 7 occurs in rows 1 to 5, No. 8 on row 6, No. 9 on rows 7 to 9 and No. 10 on row 10.

9

10

1891 (Nov)–**95**. Wmk Crown CA. P 14.

11 **9** 1c. green (3.95) ... 4·25 3·25
12 2c. rose ... 4·50 3·75
13 5c. blue (6.93) ... 11·00 48·00
11/13 *Set of 3* ... 18·00 50·00
11s/13s Optd 'SPECIMEN' *Set of 3* ... 90·00

> Following an increase of postage rates on 1 March 1894 1 cent stamps of STRAITS SETTLEMENTS were used in Pahang until the spring of the following year.

1895 (Nov)–**99**. Wmk Crown CA. P 14.

14 **10** 3c. dull purple and carmine ... 14·00 4·50
15 4c. dull purple and carmine (8.99) ... 17·00 22·00
16 5c. dull purple and olive-yellow (10.97) ... 55·00 25·00
14/16 *Set of 3* ... 75·00 48·00
14s/16s Optd 'SPECIMEN' *Set of 3* ... 85·00

1897 (2 Aug). No. 13 bisected, surch in red manuscript at Kuala Lipis and initialled 'JFO'.

(a) Bisected horizontally

17 2c. on half of 5c. blue (surch '2' and bar across '5') ... — £2750
17*a* 3c. on half of 5c. blue (surch '3') ... £7000 £2750

(b) Bisected diagonally

18 2c. on half of 5c. blue (surch '2' and bar across '5') ... £1500 £400
a. Unsevered pair. Nos. 18 and 18*d* ... £15000 £4250
b. Se-tenant pair. Nos. 18 and 18*d* ... £4500 £1100
c. Surch in black manuscript ... £11000 £3500
18*d* 3c. on half of 5c. blue (surch '3') ... £1500 £400
dc. Surch in black manuscript ... £11000 £3500

The initials are those of John Fortescue Owen, the Superintendent at Kuala Lipis.

Nos. 17 and 18 only occur on the bottom half of the 5c. and Nos. 17*a* and 18*d* on the top half. No. 18a is a complete example of No. 13 showing the two surcharges. No. 18*b* is a *se-tenant* pair of bisects from adjoining stamps.

Three types of these manuscript surcharges may be distinguished. an initial group, including the black surcharges Nos. 18c and 18dc, showed the value as '2cts' or '3cts'. A second group, including the horizontal bisects Nos. 17 and 17*a*, had figures of value only ('2' or '3'). A third group, in which the values (but not the initials) were written by Owen's clerk, Mr. Mitchell, showed the values as '2c' and '3c', with a vertical stroke through the 'c'. Examples of diagonal bisects from the first and third groups, with 'cts' or 'c' after the figure of value, are worth a premium over the prices quoted above.

Pahang. (**11**) Pahang. (**12**)

1898 (18 Mar–Sept).

(a) Nos. 72/75 of Perak optd with T **11**

19 10c. dull purple and orange ... 29·00 32·00
20 25c. green and carmine ... 85·00 £170
21 50c. dull purple and greenish black (9.98) ... £475 £550
22 50c. green and black ... £300 £425

(b) Nos. 76 and 79 of Perak optd with T **12**

23 $1 green and pale green ... £425 £700
24 $5 green and ultramarine ... £1700 £3500

Pahang Four cents (**13**) Four cents. (**14**)

1899.

(a) No. 71 of Perak surch with T **13**

25 4c. on 8c. dull purple and ultramarine (1.99) ... 15·00 15·00
a. Surch inverted ... £5000 £1800
b. Surch double ... £950

(b) T **13** *on plain paper (no stamp), but issued for postage. Imperf*

26 4c. black (4.99) ... — £5000
27 5c. black ... £3000

No. 26 also exists pin-perforated.

1899 (May). No. 16 surch with T **14**.

28 **10** 4c. on 5c. dull purple and olive-yellow ... 27·00 75·00
a. Surch double, one albino inverted ... — †

> Pending the arrival of the permanent Federated Malay States issue the stamps of SELANGOR, FEDERATED MALAY STATES provisional overprints and PERAK were used at various times between November 1899 and July 1902.
> The general issues for the FEDERATED MALAY STATES were used in Pahang from July 1902 until 1935.

15 Sultan Sir Abu Bakar

16 Sultan Sir Abu Bakar

1935 (2 Dec)–**41**. Chalk-surfaced paper. Wmk Mult Script CA. P 14.

29 **15** 1c. black (1.1.36) ... 30 40
30 2c. green (1.1.36) ... 4·25 50
31 3c. green (*ordinary paper*) (21.8.41) ... 65·00 8·50
a. Thin striated paper ... 32·00 32·00
32 4c. orange ... 70 50
33 5c. brown (5.12.35) ... 70 10
34 6c. scarlet (1.1.37) ... 32·00 1·75
35 8c. grey ... 60 10
36 8c. scarlet (*Thin striated paper*) (11.12.41) ... 13·00 80·00
37 10c. dull purple (1.1.36) ... 3·50 10
a. Thin striated paper (1941) ... £300 £120
38 12c. bright ultramarine (1.1.36) ... 7·00 1·25
39 15c. ultram (*ordinary paper*) (*shades*) (1.10.41) ... 45·00 70·00
40 25c. dull purple and scarlet (1.4.36) ... 4·00 1·50
41 30c. dull purple and orange (1.1.36) ... 2·50 1·10
a. Thin striated paper (1941) ... 25·00
42 40c. scarlet and dull purple ... 1·75 2·00
43 50c. black/*emerald* (1.2.36) ... 8·50 1·50
44 $1 black and red/*blue* (1.4.36) ... 8·50 9·00
45 $2 green and scarlet (16.5.36) ... 48·00 50·00
46 $5 green and red/*emerald* (16.5.36) ... 17·00 90·00
29/46 *Set of 18* ... £200 £275
29s/46s Perf 'SPECIMEN' *Set of 18* ... £500

The stamps issued during 1941 were printed by Harrison and Sons following bomb damage to the De La Rue works on 29 December 1940. The used prices quoted for Nos. 36 and 39 are for examples with clearly identifiable 1941 cancellations.

Examples of the 1c. on thin striated paper exist from a sheet with misplaced T **16** Japanese Occupation opt. See No. J239a in the Japanese Occupation listing.

A 2c. orange and a 6c. grey, both on thin striated paper, were prepared but not officially issued. (*Price mint £4 each*).

> During shortages in 1941 stamps of STRAITS SETTLEMENTS (2c., 25c.), SELANGOR (2c. orange, 3c., 8c.), NEGRI SEMBILAN (6c.) and PERAK (2c. orange) were issued in Pahang.

1948 (1 Dec). Royal Silver Wedding. As Nos. 112/113 of Antigua.

47 10c. violet ... 15 60
48 $5 green ... 25·00 50·00

1949 (10 Oct). 75th Anniversary of UPU. As Nos. 114/117 of Antigua.

49 10c. purple ... 30 25
50 15c. deep blue ... 1·10 1·50
51 25c. orange ... 35 2·75
52 50c. blue-black ... 70 5·00
49/52 *Set of 4* ... 2·25 8·50

1950 (1 June)–**56**. Wmk Mult Script CA. Chalk-surfaced paper. P 17½×18.

53 **16** 1c. black ... 20 10
54 2c. orange ... 30 10
55 3c. green ... 55 80
56 4c. brown ... 2·75 10
a. Chocolate (24.3.54) ... 23·00 3·75
57 5c. bright purple (1.9.52) ... 1·50 70
a. Bright mauve (10.9.53) ... 1·00 15
58 6c. grey ... 1·50 30
59 8c. scarlet ... 65 1·50
60 8c. green (1.9.52) ... 1·50 75
61 10c. magenta ... 35 10
62 12c. scarlet (1.9.52) ... 3·50 1·25
63 15c. ultramarine ... 1·25 10
64 20c. black and green ... 2·50 3·00
65 20c. bright blue (1.9.52) ... 4·50 10
a. Ultramarine (8.3.56) ... 13·00 3·25
66 25c. purple and orange ... 1·00 10
67 30c. scarlet and brown-purple (4.9.55) ... 5·00 35
a. Scarlet and purple (8.3.56) ... 42·00 10·00
68 35c. scarlet and purple (1.9.52) ... 1·50 25
69 40c. red and purple ... 6·00 12·00
70 50c. black and blue ... 1·75 10
71 $1 blue and purple ... 6·50 3·50
72 $2 green and scarlet ... 18·00 32·00
73 $5 green and brown ... 85·00 £110
a. Green and sepia (24.3.54) ... £150 £160
53/73 *Set of 21* ... £120 £140

1953 (2 June). Coronation. As No. 120 of Antigua.

74 10c. black and reddish purple ... 2·75 10

1957 (26 June)–**62**. As Nos. 92/102 of Kedah but with inset portrait of Sultan Sir Abu Bakar.

75 **9** 1c. black (21.8.57) ... 10 10
76 **10** 2c. orange-red (25.7.57) ... 15 10
77 **11** 4c. sepia (21.8.57) ... 15 10
78 **12** 5c. carmine-lake (21.8.57) ... 15 10
79 **13** 8c. myrtle-green (21.8.57) ... 5·50 2·25
80 **14** 10c. deep brown (4.8.57) ... 1·25 10
81 10c. deep maroon (21.2.61) ... 8·50 30
82 **15** 20c. blue ... 2·25 20
83 **16** 50c. black and blue (P 12½) (25.7.57) ... 45 75
a. Perf 12½×13 (17.5.60) ... 1·00 20
84 **17** $1 ultramarine and reddish purple (25.7.57) ... 18·00 2·25
85 **18** $2 bronze-green and scarlet (P 12½) (21.8.57) ... 15·00 9·00
a. Perf 13×12½ (13.11.62) ... 17·00 38·00
86 **19** $5 brown and bronze-green (P 12½) ... 12·00 15·00
a. Perf 13×12½ (17.5.60) ... 13·00 40·00
b. Perf 13×12½. *Brown and yellow olive* (23.10.62) ... 60·00 70·00
75/86 *Set of 12* ... 55·00 26·00

The 6, 12, 25 and 30c. values used with this issue were Nos. 1/4 of Malayan Federation.

17 *Vanda hookeriana*

1965 (15 Nov). As Nos. 166/172 of Johore but with inset portrait of Sultan Sir Abu Bakar as in T **17**. W w **13** (upright).

87		1c. multicoloured	10	1·25
		c. Grey (flower name, etc) omitted	£150	
		w. Wmk inverted	12·00	
88		2c. multicoloured	10	1·25
89		5c. multicoloured	15	10
		c. Red (leaves, etc) omitted	£150	
		d. Blue (background and value) omitted		
90		6c. multicoloured	30	1·25
91		10c. multicoloured	20	10
		a. Red omitted	£150	
92		15c. multicoloured	1·00	10
93		20c. multicoloured	1·60	40
87/93 *Set of 7*			3·00	3·75

The 2c., 5c. and 6c. exist with PVA gum as well as gum arabic.

The higher values used with this issue were Nos. 20/27 of Malaysia (National Issues).

1970 (27 May). As Nos. 87 and 91 but W w **13** (sideways).

94	**17**	1c. multicoloured	2·50	9·00
95	–	10c. multicoloured	1·00	3·75

STAMP BOOKLETS

1935. Black on buff covers. Stapled.

SB1	$1 booklet containing 20×5c. (No. 33) in blocks of 10	£3750
SB2	$1.30 booklet containing 5c. and 8c. (Nos. 33, 35) each in block of 10 and pane of airmail labels	£4000

PENANG

One of the Straits Settlements which joined the Federation of Malaya on 1 February 1948.

1948 (1 Dec). Royal Silver Wedding. As Nos. 112/113 of Antigua.

1	10c. violet	30	20
2	$5 brown	38·00	38·00

1949 (21 Feb)–**52**. As T **58** of Straits Settlements, but inscr 'PENANG' at foot. Wmk Mult Script CA. Chalk-surfaced paper. P 17½×18.

3	1c. black	1·75	20
4	2c. orange	1·75	20
5	3c. green	60	1·00
6	4c. brown	50	10
7	5c. bright purple (1.9.52)	9·00	5·00
8	6c. grey	2·00	20
9	8c. scarlet	1·25	8·00
10	8c. green (1.9.52)	9·00	4·50
11	10c. purple	50	10
12	12c. scarlet (1.9.52)	9·00	17·00
13	15c. ultramarine	3·75	30
14	20c. black and green	3·75	1·50
15	20c. bright blue (1.9.52)	9·00	1·50
16	25c. purple and orange	3·75	1·50
17	35c. scarlet and purple (1.9.52)	9·00	1·25
18	40c. red and purple	8·50	19·00
19	50c. black and blue	8·00	20
20	$1 blue and purple	20·00	3·50
21	$2 green and scarlet	23·00	2·00
22	$5 green and brown	48·00	3·00
3/22 *Set of 20*		£140	55·00

1949 (10 Oct). 75th Anniversary of UPU. As Nos. 114/117 of Antigua.

23	10c. purple	20	10
24	15c. deep blue	2·50	3·75
25	25c. orange	45	5·50
26	50c. blue-black	1·50	3·25
23/26 *Set of 4*		4·25	11·50

1953 (2 June). Coronation. As No. 120 of Antigua.

27	10c. black and reddish purple	2·75	10

1954 (9 June)–**57**. As T **1** of Malacca (Queen Elizabeth II) but inscr 'PENANG' at foot. Chalk-surfaced paper. Wmk Mult Script CA. P 17½×18.

28	1c. black (5.1.55)	10	70
29	2c. yellow-orange (8.9.54)	1·25	30
30	4c. brown (1.9.54)	2·00	10
	a. Yellow-brown (17.7.57)	15·00	11·00
31	5c. bright purple (1.10.54)	2·00	5·00
	a. Bright mauve (17.7.57)	15·00	11·00
32	6c. grey	20	80
33	8c. green (5.1.55)	40	3·50
34	10c. brown-purple (1.9.54)	20	10
35	12c. rose-red (5.1.55)	40	3·50
36	20c. bright blue (1.9.54)	50	10
37	25c. brown-purple and yellow-orange (1.12.54)	40	10
38	30c. rose-red and brown-purple (5.9.55)	40	10
39	35c. rose-red and brown-purple (8.9.54)	70	60
40	50c. black and bright blue (1.12.54)	1·50	10
41	$1 bright blue and brown-purple (1.10.54)	3·00	30
42	$2 emerald and scarlet (1.10.54)	21·00	3·75
43	$5 emerald and brown (5.1.55)	48·00	3·75
28/43 *Set of 16*		70·00	20·00

1957. As Nos. 92/102 of Kedah, but with inset portrait of Queen Elizabeth II.

44	**9**	1c. black (21.8)	10	1·50
45	**10**	2c. orange-red (25.7)	10	1·00
46	**11**	4c. sepia (21.8)	10	10
47	**12**	5c. carmine-lake (21.8)	10	30
48	**13**	8c. myrtle-green (21.8)	3·00	2·25
49	**14**	10c. deep brown (4.8)	30	10
50	**15**	20c. blue (26.6)	1·50	40
51	**16**	50c. black and blue (25.7)	2·00	70
52	**17**	$1 ultramarine and reddish purple (25.7)	15·00	1·00
53	**18**	$2 bronze-green and scarlet (21.8)	24·00	22·00
54	**19**	$5 brown and bronze-green (26.6)	29·00	14·00
44/54 *Set of 11*			65·00	38·00

The note after No. 86 of Pahang also applies here.

1 Copra

2 *Vanda hookeriana*

(Recess D.L.R.)

1960 (15 Mar). As Nos. 44/54, but with inset Arms of Penang as in T **1**. W w **12**. P 13×12½ (1c. to 8c., $2, $5), 12½×13 (10c. to 50c.) or 13½ ($1).

55	1c. black	10	1·60
56	2c. orange-red	10	1·60
57	4c. sepia	10	10
58	5c. carmine-lake	10	10
59	8c. myrtle-green	2·75	4·50
60	10c. deep maroon	30	10
61	20c. blue	55	10
62	50c. black and blue	30	30
	a. Imperf (pair)	£650	
63	$1 ultramarine and reddish purple	7·50	1·75
64	$2 bronze-green and scarlet	13·00	9·00
65	$5 brown and bronze-green	15·00	9·00
55/65 *Set of 11*		35·00	25·00

No. 62a comes from four panes which had the upper five horizontal rows imperforate.

1965 (15 Nov)–**68**. As Nos. 166/172 of Johore but with Arms of Penang inset and inscr 'PULAU PINANG' as in T **2**. W w **13** (upright).

66	1c. multicoloured	10	1·25
67	2c. multicoloured	10	1·50
68	5c. multicoloured	2·00	10
	b. Yellow (flower) omitted	85·00	
	c. Red omitted	£150	
	d. Blue (background and inscr) omitted	£950	
	da. Blue and yellow omitted	£900	
	w. Wmk inverted	4·25	
69	6c. multicoloured	30	1·25
	b. Yellow omitted	85·00	
70	10c. grey and multicoloured	20	10
	a. *Jet-black and multicoloured* (12.11.68)	2·50	75
71	15c. multicoloured	1·00	10
	b. Green (value and leaves) omitted	£700	
	c. Black (country name and Arms) omitted (horizontal pair with normal)	£1600	
72	20c. multicoloured	1·60	30
	a. Bright purple (blooms) omitted	£1000	
	b. Yellow (leaves) omitted	£1000	
66/72 *Set of 7*		4·50	4·00

The 2c., 5c., 6c., 10c. and 20c. exist with PVA gum as well as gum arabic.

The higher values used with this issue were Nos. 20/27 of Malaysia (National Issues).

1970. As Nos. 66 and 70 but W w **13** (sideways).

73	**2**	1c. multicoloured (27.5.70)	1·60	7·00
74	–	10c. multicoloured (20.11.70)	7·00	4·50

PERAK

Perak accepted a British Resident in 1874, although he was later murdered.

The state joined the Federated Malay States in 1896.

The stamps of the STRAITS SETTLEMENTS were used in Perak during 1877/1878.

Until 1 January 1899, when the Federated Malay States joined the UPU, mail for addresses outside Malaya was franked with stamps of the STRAITS SETTLEMENTS.

PRICES FOR STAMPS ON COVER TO 1945

No.	1	—
Nos.	2/9	*from* × 60
Nos.	10/13	*from* × 30
Nos.	14/16	*from* × 8
Nos.	17/22	*from* × 20
No.	23	—
Nos.	24/25	—
Nos.	26/28	*from* × 15
No.	29	*from* × 75
No.	30	*from* × 20
Nos.	31/32	—
Nos.	33/40	*from* × 15
Nos.	43/60	*from* × 6
Nos.	61/65	*from* × 20
Nos.	66/79	*from* × 12
No.	80	—
Nos.	81/87	*from* × 8
Nos.	88/102	*from* × 4
Nos.	103/121	*from* × 3

The Official stamps of Perak are rare used on cover.

Overprints and surcharges were applied by the Government Printer, Singapore, *unless otherwise stated.*

(1)

1878. No. 11 of Straits Settlements handstamped with T **1**.

1	2c. brown	£2000	£2500

PERAK (**2**) (14½ *mm* long) PERAK (**3**) (11 *mm* long) PERAK (**4**) (10¼ *mm* long)

PERAK (**5**) (17 *mm* long) PERAK (**6**) ('RA' narrow) PERAK (**7**) ('R' narrow)

PERAK (**8**) ('P' and 'K' wide) PERAK (**9**) (12 to 13½ *mm* long)

1880–81. No. 11 (wmk Crown CC) of Straits Settlements optd with T **2**/**9**.

2	**2**	2c. brown	£4750	£1400
3	**3**	2c. brown	£4000	£850
4	**4**	2c. brown	£2500	£900
5	**5**	2c. brown (1881)	50·00	85·00
		w. Wmk inverted	†	£750
6	**6**	2c. brown (1881)	£350	£350
7	**7**	2c. brown (1881)	£200	£225
8	**8**	2c. brown (1881)	£1300	£1100
		a. Opt double	†	£3250
9	**9**	2c. brown (1881)	£200	£200

Of the above No. 2 is from a single unit overprint, No. 5 from a setting of 60 and the remainder from settings applied as horizontal strips of three. Nos. 6/8 come from mixed triplets, either 6+7+7 or 7+7+8. No. 4 is believed to come from a single unit overprint in addition to a triplet.

PERAK (**10**) ('A' wide) PERAK (**11**) ('E' wide)

1882–83. Nos. 50 (wmk Crown CA) and 63 of Straits Settlements optd with T **9**/**11**.

10	**9**	2c. brown	28·00	85·00
		a. Opt double	£700	
11		2c. pale rose (1883)	50·00	65·00
		a. Opt double	£700	
12	**10**	2c. pale rose (1883)	55·00	£120
13	**11**	2c. pale rose (1883)	50·00	80·00
		a. Opt double	£700	

The above were all overprinted as triplet settings. Those for the 2c. rose were 11+12+13, 13+11+11 and 13+11+12.

(12) (13)

1883 (July). No. 51 (wmk Crown CA) of Straits Settlements surch.

(a) Surch with T **12**

14		2c. on 4c. rose	£4500	
		a. On Straits Settlements No. 12 (wmk Crown CC)	£8000	

(b) Optd as Types **9** *or* **11** *and surch with T* **13**

15	**11**	2c. on 4c. rose	£1200	£500
16	**9**	2c. on 4c. rose	£750	£325

It is believed that No. 14 occurred on the top row of the sheet with the remaining nine rows surcharged with a triplet containing 15+16+16.

Only one unused example, with defects, of No. 14a is recorded.

PERAK (**14**) ('E' wide) PERAK (**15**) ('E' narrow) PERAK (**16**) (12½–13 *mm* long)

PERAK (**17**) (12–12½ *mm* long) PERAK (**18**) (10½ *mm* long) PERAK (**19**) (10 *mm* long)

PERAK (**20**) (13 *mm* long)

1884–91. Nos. 63/63*a* of Straits Settlements optd with Types **14**/**20**.

17	**14**	2c. pale rose	11·00	3·75
		a. Opt double	£650	£650
		b. Opt inverted	£450	£600
		c. Bright rose (1889)	14·00	2·75
18	**15**	2c. pale rose	70·00	70·00
		a. Opt double	£1100	
		b. Opt inverted	£1600	£1700
		c. Opt triple	£1500	
		d. Bright rose	£150	
19	**16**	2c. pale rose (1886)	£150	42·00
		a. Bright rose (1891)	2·25	7·50
		ab. Optd 'FERAK'*	£425	£600
20	**17**	2c. pale rose (1886)	18·00	55·00
		a. Opt double	£1600	
21	**18**	2c. pale rose (1886)	£200	£225
		a. Bright rose		
22	**19**	2c. bright rose (1890)	30·00	60·00
23	**20**	2c. bright rose (1891)	£3750	

Settings:

Nos. 17/18	– triplets (either 17 + 17 + 17 or 18 + 17 + 17) 30 (3×10) (containing 28 as No. 17 and two as No. 18) 60 (6×10) (containing either 57 as No. 17 and three as No. 18 or all as No. 17)
No. 19	– 60 (6×10) (*No. 19ab occurs on one position of the setting, it is often found amended in manuscript)
No. 20	– triplet
No. 21	– triplet
No. 22	– 60 (6×10)
No. 23	– not known

1 CENT
(**21**)

1886. No. 17 surch with T **21**.

24	**14**	1c. on 2c. pale rose	£5000	£4000

ONE CENT PERAK (22) **ONE CENT PERAK.** (23) **ONE CFNT PERAK.** (24) ('N' wide in 'ONE' and 'CENT')

1886. No. 63 of Straits Settlements surch with Types **22/24**.

25	**22**	1c. on 2c. pale rose	£850	£850
26	**23**	1c. on 2c. pale rose	75·00	90·00
		a. Surch double	£1200	
27	**24**	1c. on 2c. pale rose	£130	£140

Nos. 26/27 are from a triplet setting, Types **23-24-23**, in which the two T **23**'s can be differentiated by the height of the right upright of the 'N' of 'CENT', which is short on one. This triplet was used for the top nine rows of the sheet. T **22** may have been used on the bottom row.

1 CENT PERAK (25) *One CENT PERAK* (26) ONE CENT PERAK (27)

1886. No. 63 of Straits Settlements surch with T **25**.

28	1c. on 2c. pale rose	£200	£200
	a. Surch double	£1800	£1800

No. 28 comes from a triplet setting.

1886. No. 63 of Straits Settlements surch with T **26**.

29	1c. on 2c. pale rose	4·00	21·00
	a. 'One' inverted	£3750	
	b. Surch double	£1200	

No. 29 comes from a triplet setting. It is believed that No. 29a occurred when the type was dropped and 'One' replaced upside down.

1887. No. 63 of Straits Settlements surch with T **27** in blue.

30	1c. on 2c. pale rose	75·00	75·00
	a. Optd in black	£2000	£1500

No. 30 was printed from a setting of 60.

1 CENT PERAK (28) 1 CENT PERAK (29)

1887. No. 63 of Straits Settlements surch with T **28**.

31	1c. on 2c. pale rose	£1900	£1100

No. 31 comes from a triplet setting.

1887. No. 63 of Straits Settlements surch with T **29**.

32	1c. on 2c. pale rose	£3500	£3500

The size of setting used for No. 32 is not known.

One CENT PERAK (30) *One CENT* PERAK (31) *One* CENT PERAK (32) One CENT PERAK (33)

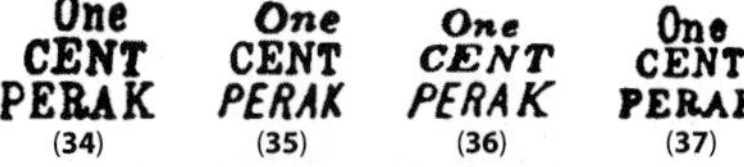

One CENT PERAK (34) One CENT *PERAK* (35) *One CENT PERAK* (36) One CENT PERAK (37)

Short 'R' (different positions in different settings of No. 37, but R. 8/2 on Nos. 46 and 51)

1887–89. No. 63 of Straits Settlements surch with Types **30/37**.

33	**30**	1c. on 2c. pale rose	4·75	13·00
		a. Surch double	£1300	
		b. Bright rose	2·75	4·50
34	**31**	1c. on 2c. pale rose (1889)	£130	£160
		b. Bright rose	£180	
35	**32**	1c. on 2c. pale rose (1889)	32·00	55·00
		a. 'PREAK' (R. 6/1)	£900	£1100
		b. Bright rose	29·00	50·00
		ba. 'PREAK' (R. 6/1)	£950	£1200
		w. Wmk inverted	£450	
36	**33**	1c. on 2c. pale rose (1889)	21·00	29·00
		b. Bright rose	8·50	29·00
37	**34**	1c. on 2c. pale rose (1889)	21·00	32·00
		b. Bright rose	5·00	28·00
		c. Short 'R'	85·00	£180
38	**35**	1c. on 2c. bright rose (1889)	£700	£1000
39	**36**	1c. on 2c. bright rose (1889)	£400	£500
40	**37**	1c. on 2c. pale rose (1889)	45·00	55·00
		b. Bright rose	18·00	50·00

Settings. No. 33 originally appeared as a triplet, then as a block of 30 (3×10) and, finally, as part of a series of composite settings of 60. Specialists recognise four such composite settings:

Setting I contained No. 33 in Rows 1 to 4, R. 5/1 to 5/5 and Row 7; No. 34 on R. 5/6, 6/1 and 6/2; No. 35 on R. 6/3–6; No. 36 on Row 8; No. 37 on Rows 9 and 10.

Setting II was similar, but had the example of No. 33 on R. 3/5 replaced by No. 38 and those on R. 7/4 and R. 7/6 by No. 39.

Setting III contained No. 33 in Rows 1 to 5; No. 35 in Row 6 with the 'PREAK' error on the first position; No. 36 in Row 7; No. 37 in Rows 8 and 9; No. 40 in Row 10.

Setting IV was similar, but showed the 'PREAK' error on R. 6/1 corrected.

ONE CENT. (38) ONE CENT (39)

1889 (Nov)–**90**. No. 17 surch with Types **38/39**.

41	**38**	1c. on 2c. bright rose	£350	£130
42	**39**	1c. on 2c. bright rose (1890)	—	£250

PERAK Two CENTS (40) PERAK *One* CENT (41)

1891. Nos. 63*a*, 66 and 68 of Straits Settlements surch.

(a) As Types **30**, **32/34** *and* **37**, *but with 'PERAK' at top and a bar through the original value (May 1891)*

43	**30**	1c. on 6c. lilac	60·00	35·00
		a. 'Slug' flaw	£850	£375
44	**32**	1c. on 6c. lilac	£190	£160
45	**33**	1c. on 6c. lilac	£190	£160
46	**34**	1c. on 6c. lilac	£110	80·00
		a. Short 'R'	£325	£275
47	**37**	1c. on 6c. lilac	£190	£160

(b) With T **40** *and as Types* **32/34** *and* **37** *but with 'PERAK' at top, all with a bar through the original value (May 1891)*

48	**40**	2c. on 24c. green	35·00	16·00
		w. Wmk inverted	£450	
49	**32**	2c. on 24c. green	£120	65·00
		w. Wmk inverted	£1000	
50	**33**	2c. on 24c. green	£120	65·00
		w. Wmk inverted	£1000	
51	**34**	2c. on 24c. green	75·00	35·00
		a. Short 'R'	£250	£140
52	**37**	2c. on 24c. green	£120	65·00

(c) With T **41** *and as Types* **30**, **34** *and* **37**, *but with 'PERAK' at top (July 1891)*

(i) Without bar over original value

53	**30**	1c. on 2c. bright rose	£200	
		a. Narrow 'O' in 'One' (R. 3/3)	£3000	
54	**41**	1c. on 2c. bright rose	£1000	
55	**34**	1c. on 2c. bright rose	£450	
56	**37**	1c. on 2c. bright rose	£1000	

(ii) With bar through original value

57	**30**	1c. on 2c. bright rose	2·25	17·00
		a. Narrow 'O' in 'One' (R. 3/3)	38·00	£110
58	**41**	1c. on 2c. bright rose	8·50	55·00
59	**34**	1c. on 2c. bright rose	2·25	24·00
60	**37**	1c. on 2c. bright rose	8·50	55·00

Settings. Nos. 43/47 were arranged as Setting IV described under Nos. 33/40.

Nos. 48/52 were similar except that T **40** replaced T **30** on the first five rows.

The first printing of the 1c. on 2c. was without a bar through the original face value. Both printings, Nos. 53/60, were from the same setting with T **30** on Rows 1 to 5, T **41** on Row 6, T **34** on Rows 7 to 9 and T **37** on Row 10.

42

3 CENTS (43)

1892 (1 Jan)–**95**. Wmk Crown CA. P 14.

61	**42**	1c. green	2·25	15
62		2c. rose	1·75	30
63		2c. orange (9.9.95)	1·00	12·00
64		5c. blue	3·25	7·50
61/64 *Set of 4*			7·50	18·00
61s/64s Optd 'SPECIMEN' *Set of 4*			£120	

1895 (26 Apr). Surch with T **43** by De La Rue. Wmk Crown CA. P 14.

65	**42**	3c. on 5c. rose	3·75	7·00
		s. Optd 'SPECIMEN'	35·00	

44

45

Malformed 'C' in left value tablet (R. 9/3, both panes)

1895 (2 Sept)–**99**. P 14.

(a) Wmk Crown CA

66	**44**	1c. dull purple and green	2·75	50
		a. Malformed 'C'	£140	65·00
67		2c. dull purple and brown	3·25	50
68		3c. dull purple and carmine	6·00	50
69		4c. dull purple and carmine (1899)	23·00	8·50
70		5c. dull purple and olive-yellow	14·00	1·00
71		8c. dull purple and ultramarine	45·00	65
72		10c. dull purple and orange	20·00	50
73		25c. green and carmine (1897)	£225	13·00
74		50c. dull purple and greenish black	48·00	50·00
75		50c. green and black (12.98)	£225	£170

(b) Wmk Crown CC

76	**45**	$1 green and pale green (1896)	£300	£225
77		$2 green and carmine (1896)	£450	£375
78		$3 green and ochre (1898)	£650	£550
79		$5 green and ultramarine (1896)	£650	£600
80		$25 green and orange (1899?)	£12000	£4500
		s. Optd 'SPECIMEN'	£425	
66/76 *Set of 11*			£800	£425
66s/79s Optd 'SPECIMEN' *Set of 14*			£550	

Pending the arrival of the permanent Federated Malay States issue the stamps of FEDERATED MALAY STATES provisional overprints, SELANGOR and STRAITS SETTLEMENTS were used at various times between June 1900 and 31 December 1901.

The general issues for the FEDERATED MALAY STATES were used in Perak from 1901 until 1935.

One Cent. (46) ONE CENT. (47)

Three Cent. (48) Three Cent. (49)

Three Cent. Thinner 't' in 'Cent'

1900. Stamps of 1895–1899 surch.

81	**46**	1c. on 2c. dull purple and brown (13.7*)	1·00	2·50
		a. Antique 'e' in 'One' (R. 5/2)	60·00	£130
		b. Antique 'e' in 'Cent' (R. 9/4)	60·00	£130
82	**47**	1c. on 4c. dull purple and carmine (25.7*)	1·00	17·00
		a. Surch double	£1300	
83	**46**	1c. on 5c. dull purple and olive-yellow (30.6*)	3·00	23·00
		a. Antique 'e' in 'One' (R. 5/2)	£100	£325
		b. Antique 'e' in 'Cent' (R. 9/4)	£100	£325
84	**48**	3c. on 8c. dull purple and ultramarine (22.9*)	16·00	21·00
		a. Antique 'e' in 'Cent' (R. 9/4)	£225	£325
		b. No stop after 'Cent' (R. 9/5)	£225	£325
		c. Surch double	£550	£600
85		3c. on 50c. green and black (31.8*)	7·00	15·00
		a. Antique 'e' in 'Cent' (R. 9/4)	£150	£225
		b. No stop after 'Cent' (R. 9/5)	£150	£225
86	**49**	3c. on $1 green and pale green (20.10*)	55·00	£150
		a. Thinner 't' in 'Cent'	£300	£550
		b. Surch double	£1600	
		w. Wmk inverted	£400	£600
87		3c. on $2 green and carmine (23.10*)	50·00	85·00
		a. Surch double, one albino		
		w. Wmk inverted		
81/87 *Set of 7*			£110	£275

* Earliest known postmark date.

With exception of No. 86a, whose sheet position is not known, the remaining surcharge varieties all occur in the left-hand pane.

No. 86b is also known showing the thinner 't' in 'Cent' variety. (*Price £4500 unused*).

During a shortage of low values, on 22 October 1900 the Government of Perak announced that articles on which postage was less than 4 cents should be handed in at the post office and the postage paid in cash. The stamp vendor gave the sender a perforated and postmarked receipt inscribed 'Postal/Receipt for/1 cent', some of which are known attached to envelopes, although this is not what the authorities intended. Collectors know these as the 'Tanjong Malim provisionals', although they were also used in other offices.

The $5, No. 79, surcharged 'Three cents/Revenue/only' is also known used postally during the shortage.

50 Sultan Iskandar

51 Sultan Iskandar

Malformed '2c.' (R. 10/10)

1935 (2 Dec)–**37**. Chalk-surfaced paper. Wmk Mult Script CA. P 14.

88	**50**	1c. black (1.1.36)	3·50	10
89		2c. green (1.1.36)	3·50	10
90		4c. orange	3·75	10
91		5c. brown (5.12.35)	75	10
92		6c. scarlet (1.1.37)	15·00	7·50
93		8c. grey	1·00	10
94		10c. dull purple (1.1.36)	80	15
95		12c. bright ultramarine (1.1.36)	5·50	1·00
96		25c. dull purple and scarlet (1.4.36)	3·50	1·00
97		30c. dull purple and orange (1.1.36)	5·50	1·50
98		40c. scarlet and dull purple	9·00	8·00
99		50c. black/*emerald* (1.2.36)	10·00	1·50
100		$1 black and red/*blue* (1.4.36)	3·00	1·25
101		$2 green and scarlet (16.5.36)	48·00	7·00
102		$5 green and red/*emerald* (16.5.36)	£170	35·00
88/102 *Set of 15*			£250	55·00
88s/102s Perf 'SPECIMEN' *Set of 15*			£500	

No. 91 exists in coils constructed from normal sheets in 1936.

1938 (2 May)–**41**. Wmk Mult Script CA. Chalk-surfaced paper. P 14.

103	**51**	1c. black (4.39)	21·00	10
104		2c. green (13.1.39)	17·00	10
105		2c. orange (*Thin striated paper*) (30.10.41)	3·50	11·00
		a. Malformed '2c'	£110	£250

b. Ordinary paper 9·50 †
ba. Malformed '2c' £180 †
106 3c. green (*ordinary paper*) (21.8.41) 50·00 22·00
a. Thin striated paper (10.41) 2·75 17·00
107 4c. orange (5.39) 42·00 10
108 5c. brown (1.2.39) 6·50 10
109 6c. scarlet (12.39) 27·00 10
110 8c. grey (1.12.38) 40·00 10
111 8c. scarlet (*Thin striated paper*) (18.12.41) 1·00 90·00
a. Ordinary paper 2·50
112 10c. dull purple (17.10.38) 40·00 10
113 12c. bright ultramarine (17.10.38) 30·00 1·25
114 15c. bright ultramarine (*ordinary paper*) (*shades*) (8.41) 4·25 13·00
115 25c. dull purple and scarlet (12.39) 50·00 3·50
116 30c. dull purple and orange (17.10.38) 12·00 2·25
a. Thin striated paper (1941) 15·00 35·00
117 40c. scarlet and dull purple 50·00 3·25
118 50c. black/*emerald* (17.10.38) 32·00 1·00
119 $1 black and red/*blue* (7.40) £150 40·00
120 $2 green and scarlet (9.40) £250 80·00
121 $5 green and red/*emerald* (1.41) £450 £500
103/121 *Set of* 19 £1100 £700
103s/121s perf 'SPECIMEN' *Set of* 19 £650

No. 108 exists in coils constructed from normal sheets.

The stamps issued during 1941 were printed by Harrison and Sons following bomb damage to the De La Rue works on 29 December 1940. The used price quoted for No. 111 is for an example with clearly identifiable 1941 cancellation.

During shortages in 1941 stamps of STRAITS SETTLEMENTS (2c. green) and SELANGOR (2c. orange (both perfs), 3c.) were issued in Perak.

1948 (1 Dec). Royal Silver Wedding. As Nos. 112/113 of Antigua.
122 10c. violet 15 10
123 $5 green 23·00 50·00

1949 (10 Oct). 75th Anniversary of UPU. As Nos. 114/117 of Antigua.
124 10c. purple 15 10
125 15c. deep blue 1·50 2·00
126 25c. orange 30 6·00
127 50c. blue-black 1·25 3·00
a. 'C' of 'CA' missing from Wmk £800
124/127 *Set of* 4 2·75 10·00

52 Sultan Yussuf 'Izzuddin Shah

53 Sultan Idris Shah

1950 (17 Aug)–**56**. Chalk-surfaced paper. Wmk Mult Script CA. P 17½×18.
128 **52** 1c. black 10 10
129 2c. orange 20 10
130 3c. green 7·00 10
a. Yellowish green (15.11.51) 24·00 9·00
131 4c. brown 80 10
a. Yellow-brown (20.6.56) 22·00 1·00
132 5c. bright purple (1.9.52) 75 2·75
a. Bright mauve (10.11.54) 1·50 2·75
133 6c. grey 50 10
134 8c. scarlet 4·50 4·25
135 8c. green (1.9.52) 1·50 1·00
136 10c. purple 30 10
a. Brown-purple (20.6.56) 21·00 65
137 12c. scarlet (1.9.52) 1·50 9·50
138 15c. ultramarine 1·25 10
139 20c. black and green 2·25 65
140 20c. bright blue (1.9.52) 1·50 10
141 25c. purple and orange 1·50 10
142 30c. scarlet and purple (4.9.55) 4·25 20
143 35c. scarlet and purple (1.9.52) 1·75 25
144 40c. red and purple 11·00 8·00
145 50c. black and blue 10·00 10
146 $1 blue and purple 10·00 1·00
147 $2 green and scarlet 25·00 7·00
148 $5 green and brown 45·00 32·00
128/148 *Set of* 21 £110 55·00

1953 (2 June). Coronation. As No. 120 of Antigua.
149 10c. black and reddish purple 2·50 10

1957 (26 June)–**61**. As Nos. 92/102 of Kedah but with inset portrait of Sultan Yussuf 'Izzuddin Shah.
150 **9** 1c. black (21.8.57) 10 20
151 **10** 2c. orange-red (25.7.57) 30 1·00
a. Red-orange (15.12.59) 1·75 3·50
152 **11** 4c. sepia (21.8.57) 20 10
153 **12** 5c. carmine-lake (21.8.57) 20 10
154 **13** 8c. myrtle-green (21.8.57) 2·00 3·50
155 **14** 10c. deep brown (4.8.57) 2·75 10
156 10c. deep maroon (21.2.61) 11·00 10
157 **15** 20c. blue 2·25 10
158 **16** 50c. black and blue (P 12½) (25.7.57) 1·00 1·00
a. Perf 12½×13 (24.5.60) 40 10
159 **17** $1 ultramarine and reddish purple (25.7.57) 6·50 40
160 **18** $2 bronze-green and scarlet (P 12½) (21.8.57) 4·00 8·50
a. Perf 13×12½ (21.2.61) 10·00 8·00
161 **19** $5 brown and bronze-green (P 12½) 19·00 10·00
a. Perf 13×12½ (24.5.60) 18·00 9·00
150/161 *Set of* 12 42·00 20·00

The 6, 12, 25 and 30c. values used with this issue were Nos. 1/4 of Malayan Federation.

(Photo Harrison)

1963 (26 Oct). Installation of the Sultan of Perak. W w **13**. P 14½.
162 **53** 10c. red, black, blue and yellow 15 10

54 *Vanda hookeriana*

1965 (15 Nov)–**68**. As Nos. 166/172 of Johore but with inset portrait of Sultan Idris as in T **54**. W w **13** (upright).
163 1c. multicoloured 10 50
w. Wmk inverted 8·00
164 2c. multicoloured 10 70
a. Dark green omitted £140
w. Wmk inverted 19·00
165 5c. pale black and multicoloured 10 10
a. Grey-black and multicoloured (2.4.68) 3·50 30
b. Yellow (flower) omitted 90·00
166 6c. multicoloured 15 40
167 10c. multicoloured 15 10
a. Red omitted £140
168 15c. multicoloured 80 10
a. Black (country name and head) omitted (horizontal pair with normal) £1600
c. Magenta (background) omitted £1400
169 20c. multicoloured 1·25 10
a. Bright purple (blooms) omitted £190
163/169 *Set of* 7 2·40 1·60

No. 168a comes from a horizontal strip of three, the centre stamp having the black completely omitted. The two outer stamps show the colour partly omitted.

The 2c. to 15c. exist with PVA gum as well as gum arabic.

The higher values used with this issue were Nos. 20/27 of Malaysia (National Issues).

1970. As Nos. 163 and 167, but W w **13** (sideways).
170 **54** 1c. multicoloured (27.5.70) 2·50 8·50
171 – 10c. multicoloured (20.11.70) 10·00 4·25

STAMP BOOKLETS

1935.
SB1 $1 booklet containing 20×5c. (No. 91) in blocks of 10
SB2 $1.30 booklet containing 5c. and 8c. (Nos. 91, 93), each in block of 10

1938.
SB3 $1 booklet containing 20×5c. (No. 108) in blocks of 10 £3750
SB4 $1.30 booklet containing 5c. and 8c. (Nos. 108, 110), each in block of 10 £4000

OFFICIAL STAMPS

P.G.S. (O 1) Service. (O 2)

1889 (1 Nov). Stamps of Straits Settlements optd T O **1**. Wmk Crown CC (Nos. O6 and O8) or Crown CA (others).
O1 2c. bright rose 9·50 12·00
a. Opt double £900 £900
b. Wide space between 'G' and 'S' 90·00 £110
c. No stop after 'S' 95·00 £120
O2 4c. brown 38·00 40·00
a. Wide space between 'G' and 'S' £160 £180
b. No stop after 'S' £200 £250
c. Broken oval £650
w. Wmk inverted £170
O3 6c. lilac 48·00 55·00
a. Wide space between 'G' and 'S' £200 £225
O4 8c. orange 50·00 65·00
a. Wide space between 'G' and 'S' £225 £275
O5 10c. slate 75·00 75·00
a. Wide space between 'G' and 'S' £325 £325
O6 12c. blue (CC) £325 £400
a. Wide space between 'G' and 'S' £1200
O7 12c. brown-purple (CA) £250 £325
a. Wide space between 'G' and 'S' £850
O8 24c. green (CC) £750 £850
a. Wide space between 'G' and 'S' £2500
O9 24c. green (CA) £200 £225
a. Wide space between 'G' and 'S' £750

Nos. O1/O9 were overprinted from a setting of 30 (3×10). The variety 'wide space between G and S' occurs on R. 10/3 and R. 10/6 of the original printing. A later printing of the 2c. and 4c. values had this variety corrected, but was without a stop after 'S' on R. 10/1 and R. 10/4.

The broken oval flaw occurs on R. 10/5 (lower right pane) of the basic stamp. For illustration see Straits Settlements.

1894 (1 June). No. 64 optd with T O **2**.
O10 5c. blue £130 1·00
a. Overprint inverted £1700 £500

1897. No. 70 optd with T O **2**.
O11 5c. dull purple and olive-yellow 3·25 50
a. Overprint double £700 £400

PERLIS

The Thai monarchy exercised suzerainty over Perlis and the other northern states of the Malay peninsula from the 16th-century onwards.

The Siamese post office at Kangar is recorded as opening during 1894. It is believed that the initial cancellation showed Thai characters only, but no complete example has so far been discovered.

Stamps of SIAM cancelled as Type B inscr 'PERLIS' (from July 1904).

1887–91. (Nos. 11/18).
Z401 **9** 12a. purple and carmine £550
Z402 24a. purple and blue £650

1897. Surch as T **39** (Siamese) and T **41** (English) (No. 52).
Z403 **9** 4a. on 12a. purple and carmine £700

1899–1904. (Nos. 67/81).
Z404 **49** 1a. olive-green (wide Siamese characters in face value) £400
Z405 2a. grass-green £400
Z406 2a. scarlet and pale blue £400
Z407 3a. red and blue £550
Z408 4a. carmine £375
Z409 4a. chocolate and pink £400
Z410 8a. deep green and orange £400
Z411 10a. ultramarine £400
Z412 12a. brown-purple and carmine £375
Z413 24a. brown-purple and blue £650

1905–09. (Nos. 92/105).
Z416 **53** 1a. green and orange £375
Z417 2a. grey and deep violet £375
Z418 3a. green £400
Z419 4a. pale red and sepia £350
Z420 5a. carmine £400
Z421 8a. olive-bistre and dull black £375
Z422 12a. blue £425
Z423 24a. red-brown £550

Stamps of SIAM cancelled as Type C inscr 'Perlis' at foot(from Sept. 1907).

1887–91. (Nos. 11/18).
Z425 **9** 12a. purple and carmine £550

1899–1904. (Nos. 67/81).
Z426 **49** 1a. olive-green (narrow Siamese characters in face value) £425
Z427 8a. deep green and orange £400
Z428 10a. ultramarine £425

1905–09. (Nos. 92/105).
Z429 **53** 1a. green and orange £400
Z430 2a. grey and deep violet £375
Z431 3a. green £400
Z432 4a. pale red and sepia £350
Z433 4a. scarlet £400
Z434 5a. carmine £400
Z435 8a. olive-bistre and dull black £400
Z436 9a. blue £375
Z437 24a. red-brown £650

1907. Surch with T **56** (No. 109).
Z438 **9** 1a. on 24a. purple and blue £400

Suzerainty over Perlis was transferred by Thailand to Great Britain on 15 July 1909, although the use of Siamese stamps appears to have extended into early August. Stamps of the Federated Malay States were used there until 1912.

Stamps of the Federated Malay States used in Perlis

Cancelled as Type C inscribed 'Perlis' at foot.

1909–12. (Nos. 29/34).
Z441 **3** 1c. green (Die II) £190
Z442 3c. carmine £190

Cancelled as Type B inscribed 'PERLIS'.

1909–12. (Nos. 29/36*d*).
Z443 **3** 1c. green (Die II) £190
Z444 3c. carmine £110
Z445 4c. black and rose £190

Federated Malay States stamps were withdrawn on 15 June 1912.

The stamps of Kedah were in use in Perlis between 1912 and 1941, as were contemporary 1c. and 4c. stamps of Straits Settlements for a period following March 1919.

A Treaty of Friendship between Great Britain and Perlis was signed on 28 April 1930 and the state joined the Federation of Malaya on 1 February 1948.

1948 (1 Dec). Royal Silver Wedding. As Nos. 112/113 of Antigua.
1 10c. violet 30 2·75
2 $5 brown 32·00 55·00

1949 (10 Oct). 75th Anniversary of UPU. As Nos. 114/117 of Antigua.
3 10c. purple 30 2·25
4 15c. deep blue 1·25 5·00
5 25c. orange 45 7·00
6 50c. blue-black 1·00 3·75
a. 'A' of 'CA' missing from wmk £1600
3/6 *Set of* 4 2·75 16·00

Due to the exhaustion of certain B.M.A. values, KEDAH 2c., 3c., 6c., 15c. and 25c. stamps were used in Perlis from 1st June 1950 until the issue of Nos. 7/27.

1 Raja Syed Putra

1951 (26 Mar)–**55**. Chalk-surfaced paper. Wmk Mult Script CA. P 17½×18.
7 **1** 1c. black 20 1·00
8 2c. orange 1·00 2·00
9 3c. green 3·25 7·50
10 4c. brown 3·25 1·75
11 5c. bright purple (1.9.52) 1·00 5·50
12 6c. grey 1·50 2·75
13 8c. scarlet 8·00 14·00
14 8c. green (1.9.52) 3·25 3·50
15 10c. purple 2·50 75
a. Error. St Edward's Crown W **9b**. £16000
16 12c. scarlet (1.9.52) 4·50 9·50
17 15c. ultramarine 9·00 12·00
18 20c. black and green 9·00 19·00
19 20c. bright blue (1.9.52) 2·00 2·00
20 25c. purple and orange 3·75 5·50
21 30c. scarlet and purple (4.9.55) 3·75 19·00
22 35c. scarlet and purple (1.9.52) 5·00 9·50
23 40c. red and purple 9·00 45·00
24 50c. black and blue 6·50 8·00
25 $1 blue and purple 13·00 40·00
26 $2 green and scarlet 28·00 70·00
27 $5 green and brown 80·00 £140
7/27 *Set of* 21 £160 £350

1953 (2 June). Coronation. As No. 120 of Antigua.

28		10c. black and reddish purple	2·50	3·75

1957 (26 June)–**62**. As Nos. 92/102 of Kedah but with inset portrait of Raja Syed Putra.

29	**9**	1c. black (21.8.57)	10	50
30	**10**	2c. orange-red (25.7.57)	15	50
31	**11**	4c. sepia (21.8.57)	15	40
32	**12**	5c. carmine-lake (21.8.57)	15	15
33	**13**	8c. myrtle-green (21.8.57)	2·00	1·75
34	**14**	10c. deep brown (4.8.57)	1·50	2·25
35		10c. deep maroon (14.3.61)	19·00	5·50
36	**15**	20c. blue	4·00	6·00
37	**16**	50c. black and blue (P 12½) (25.7.57)	1·50	4·50
		a. Perf 12½×13 (8.5.62)	3·50	6·00
38	**17**	$1 ultramarine and reddish purple (25.7.57)	18·00	24·00
39	**18**	$2 bronze-green and scarlet (25.7.57)	17·00	13·00
40	**19**	$5 brown and bronze-green (21.8.57)	18·00	18·00
29/40 *Set of* 12			70·00	65·00

The 6, 12, 25 and 30c. values used with this issue were Nos. 1/4 of Malayan Federation.

1965 (15 Nov). As Nos. 166/172 of Johore but with inset portrait of Raja Syed Putra.

41		1c. multicoloured	10	1·00
		w. Wmk inverted	20·00	
42		2c. multicoloured	10	1·50
43		5c. multicoloured	25	40
44		6c. multicoloured	1·00	1·50
45		10c. multicoloured	1·00	40
46		15c. multicoloured	1·00	40
		a. Green (value and leaves) omitted		
47		20c. multicoloured	1·00	1·75
41/47 *Set of* 7			3·75	6·25

The 6c. exists with PVA gum as well as gum arabic.

The higher values used with this issue were Nos. 20/27 of Malaysia (National Issues).

SABAH

SABAH (**136**) SABAH (**137**)

1964 (1 July)–**65**. Nos. 391/406 of North Borneo (D.L.R. printings), optd with T **136** (Nos. 408/419) or T **137** (Nos. 420/423).

408		1c. emerald and brown-red	10	10
409		4c. bronze-green and orange	15	50
410		5c. sepia and violet	30	10
		a. Light sepia and deep violet (17.8.65)	6·00	4·00
411		6c. black and blue-green	1·25	10
412		10c. green and red	2·25	10
413		12c. brown and grey-green	20	10
414		20c. blue-green and ultramarine	6·00	10
415		25c. grey-black and scarlet	1·25	90
416		30c. sepia and olive	30	10
417		35c. slate-blue and red-brown	30	20
418		50c. emerald and yellow-brown	1·00	10
419		75c. grey-blue and bright purple	5·50	1·00
420		$1. brown and yellow-green	16·00	2·25
421		$2. brown and slate	17·00	3·25
422		$5. emerald and maroon	17·00	17·00
423		$10. carmine and blue	20·00	42·00
408/423 *Set of* 16			75·00	60·00

Old stocks bearing Waterlow imprints of the 4c., 5c., 20c. and 35c. to $10 were used for overprinting, but in addition new printings of all values by De La Rue using the original plates with the De La Rue imprint replacing the Waterlow imprint were specially made for overprinting.

138 *Vanda hookeriana*

1965 (15 Nov)–**68**. As Nos. 166/172 of Johore, but with Arms of Sabah inset as in T **138**. W w **13** (upright).

424		1c. multicoloured	10	1·25
425		2c. multicoloured	10	2·00
		a. Dark green omitted	£180	
426		5c. multicoloured	10	10
427		6c. multicoloured	30	1·50
428		10c. multicoloured	30	10
429		15c. multicoloured (pale black panel)	3·50	10
		a. Brown-black panel (20.2.68)	5·50	55
430		20c. multicoloured	3·50	75
424/340 *Set of* 7			7·00	5·00

The 5c. to 15c. exist with PVA gum as well as gum arabic.

The higher values used with this issue were Nos. 20/27 of Malaysia (National Issues).

1970 (20 Nov). As No. 428, but W w **13** (sideways).

431		10c. multicoloured	5·00	7·00

SARAWAK

Sarawak joined the Federation of Malaysia at its formation on 16 September 1963. For the convenience of collectors, stamps issued after this date continue to be listed with earlier issues of Sarawak.

SELANGOR

The first British Resident was appointed in 1874. Selangor joined the Federated Malay States in 1896.

> The stamps of the STRAITS SETTLEMENTS were used in Selangor from 1879 until 1881.
>
> Until 1 January 1899, when the Federated Malay States joined the UPU, mail for addresses outside Malaya was franked with stamps of the STRAITS SETTLEMENTS.

PRICES FOR STAMPS ON COVER TO 1945

Nos. 1/8	—
Nos. 9/19	*from* × 10
Nos. 20/30	*from* × 12
Nos. 31/33	*from* × 25
Nos. 34/36	*from* × 20
Nos. 37/38	*from* × 15
Nos. 38*a*/40	—
Nos. 41/42	*from* × 8
Nos. 43	—
Nos. 44/48	*from* × 8
Nos. 49/53	*from* × 30
Nos. 54/66	*from* × 10
Nos. 66*a*/67	*from* × 4
Nos. 68/85	*from* × 3
Nos. 86/87	*from* × 4

Overprints and surcharges were applied by the Government Printer, Singapore, *unless otherwise stated.*

The Straits Settlements 1867 2c. brown with Crown CC watermark (No. 11) has been known since 1881 overprinted in black with a crescent and star over a capital S, all within an oval, similar in style to the overprints listed for Perak and Sungei Ujong.

The status of this item remains unclear, but it may well represent the first issue of distinctive stamps for Selangor. A similar overprint in red on the Straits Settlements 2c. brown with Crown CA watermark also exists and may have been produced for sale to collectors (*Price £425, unused*).

This overprint should not be confused with a somewhat similar cancellation used on Selangor stamps of the same period. This cancellation differs in having a circular frame with the capital S shown above the crescent and star. It is usually struck in red.

SELANGOR (**1**) ('S' inverted and narrow letters) SELANCOR (**2**) ('S' wide) SELANCOR (**3**) (narrow letters)

SELANCOR (**4**) ('N' wide) SELANCOR (**5**) ('SE' and 'AN' wide) SELANCOR (**6**) ('SEL' and 'N' wide)

SELANCOR (**7**) ('SELAN' wide)

1881 (Oct)–**82**. No. 11 (wmk Crown CC) of Straits Settlements optd with Types **1/7**.

1	**1**	2c. brown	£950	£1200
2	**2**	2c. brown	£275	£375
3	**3**	2c. brown	£170	£190
4	**4**	2c. brown	£9000	£3500
5	**5**	2c. brown (1882)	£275	£400
6	**6**	2c. brown (1882)	£275	£400
7	**7**	2c. brown (1882)	£275	£400

Nos. 1/3 and 5/7 have been identified as coming from triplet settings, either Nos. 1+2+3, 2+3+3 or 5+6+7. The setting for No. 4 is unknown.

(**8**)

1882 (June). No. 50 (wmk Crown CA) of Straits Settlements optd with T **8**.

8	**8**	2c. brown	—	£5000

SELANGOR (**9**) ('SEL' and 'NG' wide) SELANGOR (**10**) ('E' and 'ANG' wide) SELANGOR (**11**) ('ELANG' wide)

SELANCOR (**12**) ('S' and 'L' wide) SELANCOR (**13**) ('S' and 'A' wide) SELANCOR (**14**) ('E' wide)

SELANCOR (**15**) ('EL' wide) SELANCOR (**16**) ('SE' and 'N' wide) SELANCOR (**17**) ('S' and 'N' wide)

1882 (Oct)–**83**. No. 50 (wmk Crown CA) of Straits Settlements optd with Types **2/3** and **9/17**.

9	**9**	2c. brown	£400	£500
10	**10**	2c. brown	£400	£500
11	**11**	2c. brown	£400	£500
12	**2**	2c. brown (1883)	£200	£160
13	**3**	2c. brown (1883)	£350	£170
14	**12**	2c. brown (1883)	—	£3750
15	**13**	2c. brown (1883)	£950	£750
16	**14**	2c. brown (1883)	£650	£475
17	**15**	2c. brown (1883)	£650	£475
18	**16**	2c. brown (1883)	£225	£225
		a. Opt double	£1100	
19	**17**	2c. brown (1883)	£225	£225

The above were all printed from triplet settings. Those so far identified are Nos. 9+10+11, 12 (with defective 'G') +13+13, 15+16+17 and 18+12+19. No. 14 occurs as the first position of a triplet, but the second and third units are not yet known.

SELANCOR (**18**) ('E' and 'A' wide) SELANCOR (**19**) ('A' wide) SELANCOR (**20**) ('L' wide)

SELANGOR (**21**) ('L' narrow) SELANGOR (**22**) ('A' narrow) SELANGOR (**23**) (wide letters)

1883 (Sept)–**85**. No. 63 of Straits Settlements optd with Types **2**, **4**, **12**, **14/15** and **18/23**.

20	**12**	2c. pale rose	£300	£190
21	**14**	2c. pale rose	£200	£130
		a. Opt double		
22	**4**	2c. pale rose (1884)	£225	£180
23	**15**	2c. pale rose (1884)	£170	£120
		a. Opt double	£1000	
		b. Opt triple		
24	**2**	2c. pale rose (1884)	£200	£150
25	**18**	2c. pale rose (1884)	£190	£140
26	**19**	2c. pale rose (1884)	£500	£190
27	**20**	2c. pale rose (1884)	£950	£300
28	**21**	2c. pale rose (1885)	£170	£100
29	**22**	2c. pale rose (1885)	£225	£170
30	**23**	2c. pale rose (1885)	£1000	£300
		a. Opt double	†	£1500

The above come from triplet settings with Nos. 20+21+21, 22+22+23, 23+26 (with defective 'A') +26, 24+25+23 and 28+29+28 so far identified. The triplets for Nos. 27 and 30 are not known.

SELANGOR (**24**) *Selangor* (**25**) SELANGOR (**26**)

SELANGOR (**27**) SELANGOR (**28**) SELANGOR (**29**) SELANGOR (**30**)

SELANGOR (**31**) SELANGOR (**32**) SELANGOR (**33**) *SELANGOR* (**34**)

1885–91. Nos. 63/63*a* of Straits Settlements optd with Types **24/34**.

31	**24**	2c. pale rose	24·00	45·00
		a. Opt double	£1100	£950
		w. Wmk inverted	—	£700
32	**25**	2c. pale rose	£3000	£3000
33	**26**	2c. pale rose	50·00	55·00
34	**27**	2c. pale rose (1886)	75·00	65·00
		a. Opt double	†	£800
35	**28**	2c. pale rose (horiz opt without stop) (1887)	26·00	2·75
		a. Opt double	£800	
		b. Bright rose	26·00	2·25
36		2c. pale rose (horiz opt with stop) (1887)	£170	90·00
		a. Bright rose		
37	**29**	2c. pale rose (1889)	£400	90·00
38	**30**	2c. pale rose (vert opt) (1889)	95·00	6·00
		a. Bright rose		
38*b*		2c. bright rose (horiz opt) (1889)	£4750	
39	**31**	2c. pale rose (diagonal opt) (1889)	£5000	
40	**32**	2c. pale rose (1889)	£750	50·00
41	**28**	2c. bright rose (vert opt without stop) (1890)	32·00	50·00
42	**33**	2c. bright rose (1890)	£120	3·00
		a. Opt double	†	£600
43	**34**	2c. bright rose (1891)	£375	£150

Settings:

Nos. 31/34	– each in triplet containing three examples of the same stamp
No. 35	– triplet or 60 (6×10)
No. 36	– 60 (6×10)
Nos. 37/38	– 60 (6×10) containing both overprints in an unknown combination, but with No. 38 predominating
Nos. 38*b*/39	– not known
Nos. 40/43	– each in 60 (6×10)

SELANGOR *Two* CENTS (**35**) SELANGOR *Two* CENTS (**36**) SELANGOR Two CENTS (**37**)

SELANGOR Two CENTS (**38**) SELANGOR Two CENTS (**39**)

1891 (May). No. 68 of Straits Settlements, surch with Types **35/39**, each with bar obliterating old value.

44	**35**	2c. on 24c. green	55·00	80·00
45	**36**	2c. on 24c. green	£300	£350
46	**37**	2c. on 24c. green	£300	£350
47	**38**	2c. on 24c. green	£150	£170
		a. 'SELANGCR'		
48	**39**	2c. on 24c. green	£300	£350

Nos. 44/48 come from the one setting used to surcharge the panes of 60. No. 44 occurs in rows 1 to 5, No. 45 on row 6, No. 46 on row 7, No. 47 on rows 8 and 9, and No. 48 on row 10.

The error, No. 47a, occurs in the first printing only and is No. 45 (R. 8/3) on the pane.

40

3 CENTS (**41**)

1891 (1 Nov)–**95**. Wmk Crown CA. P 14.

49	**40**	1c. green (5.93)	1·50	25
50		2c. rose	3·50	2·25
51		2c. orange (27.5.95)	3·00	2·75
52		5c. blue (8.92)	24·00	8·50
49/52 *Set of* 4			29·00	12·50
49s/52s Optd 'SPECIMEN' *Set of* 4			£120	

1894 (Dec). Surch with T **41** by De La Rue. Wmk Crown CA. P 14.

53 **40** 3c. on 5c. rose ... 6·00 50
s. Optd 'SPECIMEN' ... 35·00

42

43

50c. Dented frame above 'A' of 'SELANGOR' (left pane R. 4/5)

1895 (Sept)–**99**. Wmk Crown CA or Crown CC (dollar values). P 14.

54 **42** 3c. dull purple and carmine ... 6·50 30
55 5c. dull purple and olive-yellow ... 16·00 1·25
56 8c. dull purple and ultramarine (1898) ... 50·00 11·00
57 10c. dull purple and orange ... 15·00 4·00
58 25c. green and carmine (1896) ... 80·00 65·00
59 50c. dull purple and greenish black (1896) ... £100 40·00
a. Dented frame ... £1000
60 50c. green and black (1898) ... £450 £130
a. Dented frame ...
61 **43** $1 green and yellow-green ... 75·00 £170
62 $2 green and carmine (1897) ... £300 £350
63 $3 green and ochre (1896) ... £700 £700
64 $5 green and blue ... £350 £450
65 $10 green and purple (1899) (F.C. £100) ... £900 £1500
s. Optd 'SPECIMEN' ... £180
66 $25 green and orange (1897) (F.C. £225) ... £5000 £5000
s. Optd 'SPECIMEN' ... £400
54/62 *Set of* 9 ... £1000 £700
54s/64s Optd 'SPECIMEN' *Set of* 11 ... £500

Pending the arrival of the permanent Federated Malay States issue the stamps of STRAITS SETTLEMENTS and PERAK were used at various times between July 1900 and 31 December 1901.

The general issues for the FEDERATED MALAY STATES were used in Selangor from 1901 until 1935.

One cent. (**44**)

Three cents. (**45**)

Antique 't' (R. 3/4 and 8/4)

1900 (Oct). Nos. 55 and 59 surch with Types **44** or **45**.

66*a* **42** 1c. on 5c. dull purple and olive-yellow (31.10*) ... 70·00 £130
66*b* 1c. on 50c. green and black (22.10*) ... 7·00 45·00
bc. 'cent' repeated at left ... £4250
bd. Dented frame ... £275
67 3c. on 50c. green and black (24.10*) ... 6·50 35·00
a. Antique 't' in 'cents' ... £375 £650
b. Dented frame ... £400

* Earliest known postmark date.

It is believed that these stamps were surcharged from settings of 30, repeated four times to complete the sheet of 120.

No. 66bc occurred on two separate vertical strips of five stamps where two impressions of the setting overlapped.

46 Mosque at Palace, Klang

47 Sultan Suleiman

2c. Joined script (R. 2/1)

(Des E. J. McNaughton)

1935 (2 Dec)–**41**. Wmk Mult Script CA (sideways on T **46**). Chalk-surfaced paper. P 14 or 14×14½ (No. 70).

68 **46** 1c. black (1.1.36) ... 30 10
69 2c. green (1.1.36) ... 1·00 10
a. Joined script ... 75·00 30·00
70 2c. orange (*ordinary paper*) (P 14×14½) (21.8.41) ... 8·50 75
aa. Joined script ... £190 55·00
a. Perf 14. Ordinary paper (9.41) ... 20·00 1·00
ab. Joined script ... £425 75·00
b. Perf 14. Thin striated paper ... £160
ba. Joined script ...
71 3c. green (*ordinary paper*) (21.8.41) ... 7·00 11·00
a. Thin striated paper (10.41) ... 50·00 2·75
72 4c. orange ... 50 10
73 5c. brown (5.12.35) ... 70 10
74 6c. scarlet (1.1.37) ... 15·00 10
75 8c. grey ... 60 10
76 10c. dull purple (1.1.36) ... 60 10
77 12c. bright ultramarine (1.1.36) ... 2·25 10
78 15c. bright ultramarine (*ordinary paper*) (*shades*) (1.10.41) ... 12·00 32·00
79 25c. dull purple and scarlet (1.4.36) ... 1·00 60
a. Thin striated paper (1941) ... 4·00 £100
80 30c. dull purple and orange (1.4.36) ... 1·00 85
a. Thin striated paper (1941) ... 4·00 £100
81 40c. scarlet and dull purple ... 1·50 1·00
82 50c. black/*emerald* (1.2.36) ... 1·00 15
83 **47** $1 black and rose/*blue* (1.4.36) ... 18·00 90
84 $2 green and scarlet (16.5.36) ... 40·00 6·00
85 $5 green and red/*emerald* (16.5.36) ... £110 18·00
68/85 *Set of* 18 ... £180 55·00
68s/85s Perf 'SPECIMEN' *Set of* 18 ... £500

The stamps issued during 1941 were printed by Harrison and Sons following bomb damage to the De La Rue works on 29 December 1940. The used prices quoted for Nos. 79a and 80a are for examples with clearly indentifiable 1941 cancellations.

No. 69 exists in coils constructed from normal sheets.

Supplies of an unissued 8c. scarlet on thin striated paper were diverted to Australia in 1941. Examples circulating result from leakages of this supply (*Price* £1200).

48 Sultan Hisamud-din Alam Shah

49 Sultan Hisamud-din Alam Shah

1941. Wmk Mult Script CA. Chalk-surfaced paper. P 14.

86 **48** $1 black and red/*blue* (15.4.41) ... 24·00 7·50
87 $2 green and scarlet (7.7.41) ... 50·00 50·00
s. Perf 'SPECIMEN' ... 75·00

A $5 green and red on emerald, T **48**, was issued overprinted during the Japanese occupation of Malaya. Unoverprinted examples are known, but were not issued (*Price* £180).

During shortages in 1941 stamps of STRAITS SETTLEMENTS (2c. and 30c.) and PERAK (2c., 25c. and 50c.) were issued in Selangor.

1948 (1 Dec). Royal Silver Wedding. As Nos. 112/113 of Antigua.

88 10c. violet ... 20 30
89 $5 green ... 27·00 22·00

1949 (12 Sept)–**55**. Wmk Mult Script CA. Chalk-surfaced paper. P 17½×18.

90 **49** 1c. black ... 10 60
91 2c. orange ... 30 1·50
92 3c. green ... 4·75 1·00
93 4c. brown ... 60 10
94 5c. bright purple (1.9.52) ... 2·00 3·25
a. Bright mauve (17.9.53) ... 50 2·00
95 6c. grey ... 30 40
96 8c. scarlet ... 4·25 1·00
97 8c. green (1.9.52) ... 1·25 1·75
98 10c. purple ... 20 10
99 12c. scarlet (1.9.52) ... 2·75 4·75
w. Wmk inverted ... £1200
100 15c. ultramarine ... 10·00 10
101 20c. black and green ... 10·00 35
102 20c. bright blue (1.9.52) ... 1·00 10
103 25c. purple and orange ... 2·00 20
104 30c. scarlet and purple (4.9.55) ... 3·50 2·25
105 35c. scarlet and purple (1.9.52) ... 1·25 1·50
106 40c. scarlet and purple ... 17·00 10·00
107 50c. black and blue ... 3·50 10
108 $1 blue and purple ... 3·50 60
109 $2 green and scarlet ... 15·00 60
110 $5 green and brown ... 48·00 3·75
90/110 *Set of* 21 ... £110 27·00

1949 (10 Oct). 75th Anniversary of UPU. As Nos. 114/117 of Antigua.

111 10c. purple ... 30 10
112 15c. deep blue ... 2·50 2·50
113 25c. orange ... 35 4·50
114 50c. blue-black ... 1·00 7·00
111/114 *Set of* 4 ... 3·75 12·50

1953 (2 June). Coronation. As No. 120 of Antigua.

115 10c. black and reddish purple ... 2·00 10

1957 (26 June)–**61**. As Nos. 92/102 of Kedah but with inset portrait of Sultan Hisamud-din Alum Shah.

116 **9** 1c. black (21.8.57) ... 10 2·25
117 **10** 2c. orange-red (25.7.57) ... 30 1·00
a. *Red-orange* (10.11.59) ... 13·00 7·50
118 **11** 4c. sepia (21.8.57) ... 10 10
119 **12** 5c. carmine-lake (21.8.57) ... 10 10
120 **13** 8c. myrtle-green (21.8.57) ... 4·25 3·00
121 **14** 10c. deep brown (4.8.57) ... 2·50 10
122 10c. deep maroon (9.5.61) ... 17·00 10
123 **15** 20c. blue ... 2·75 20
124 **16** 50c. black and blue (P 12½) (25.7.57) ... 75 10
a. Perf 12½×13 (10.5.60) ... 2·00 30
125 **17** $1 ultramarine and reddish purple (25.7.57) ... 10·00 10
126 **18** $2 bronze-green and scarlet (P 12½) (21.8.57) ... 9·50 3·00
a. Perf 13×12½ (6.12.60) ... 11·00 3·00
127 **19** $5 brown and bronze-green (P 12½) ... 16·00 3·25
a. Perf 13×12½ (10.5.60) ... 16·00 2·50
116/127 *Set of* 12 ... 55·00 10·50

The 6, 12, 25 and 30c. values used with this issue were Nos. 1/4 of Malayan Federation.

50 Sultan Salahuddin Abdul Aziz Shah

51 Sultan Salahuddin Abdul Aziz Shah

(Photo Harrison)

1961 (28 June). Coronation of the Sultan. W w **12**. P 15×14.

128 **50** 10c. multicoloured ... 20 10

A sheet existed showing the black printing so misplaced as to produce an effect of a 'Double-headed' Sultan (*Price* £180 *un*.).

1961–62. As Nos. 92/98 of Kedah but with inset portrait of Sultan Salahuddin Abdul Aziz as in T **51**. W w **13**. P 12½×13 (vert) or 13×12½ (horiz).

129 1c. black (1.3.62) ... 1·75 3·75
130 2c. orange-red (1.3.62) ... 2·50 3·75
131 4c. sepia (1.3.62) ... 2·75 10
132 5c. carmine-lake (1.3.62) ... 2·75 10
133 8c. myrtle-green (1.3.62) ... 9·50 8·50
134 10c. deep maroon (1.11.61) ... 1·50 10
135 20c. blue (1.3.62) ... 11·00 2·25
129/135 *Set of* 7 ... 29·00 16·00

52 *Vanda hookeriana*

1965 (15 Nov). As Nos. 166/172 of Johore but with inset portrait of Sultan Salahuddin Abdul Aziz Shah as in T **52**.

136 1c. multicoloured ... 10 20
a. Grey (flower stems and shading) omitted ...
b. Magenta omitted ... £180
w. Wmk inverted ... 1·00
137 2c. multicoloured ... 10 1·75
a. Red (blooms and value) omitted ...
b. Yellow (flower) omitted ... 75·00
138 5c. multicoloured ... 2·25 10
b. Yellow (flower) omitted ... 80·00
c. Red (leaves, etc) omitted ... £375
139 6c. multicoloured ... 20 10
140 10c. multicoloured ... 20 10
a. Red omitted ... £150
141 15c. multicoloured ... 1·25 10
b. Green (value and leaves) omitted ... £800
142 20c. multicoloured ... 1·90 70
a. Bright purple (blooms) omitted ... £200
b. Yellow (leaves) omitted ... 85·00
c. Green (leaves) omitted ...
136/142 *Set of* 7 ... 5·50 2·50

The 2c. to 20c. values exist with PVA gum as well as gum arabic.

The higher values used with this issue were Nos. 20/27 of Malaysia (National Issues).

1970 (20 Nov). As Nos. 136 etc. but W w **13** (sideways).

143 **52** 1c. multicoloured ... 1·75 9·50
144 – 10c. multicoloured ... 5·00 2·25
145 – 20c. multicoloured ... 9·00 15·00
143/145 *Set of* 3 ... 14·00 24·00

STAMP BOOKLETS

1935. Stapled.

SB1 $1 booklet containing 20×5c. (No. 73) in blocks of 10 ... £4000
SB2 $1.30 booklet containing 5c. and 8c. (Nos. 73, 75), each in block of 10 ... £4000

TRENGGANU

A Thai post office operated at Kuala Trengganu between 1892 and 1895. A single example of the 1887–1891 8a. green and yellow has been seen with a type B circular postmark inscribed 'TRINGANU'.

Suzerainty over Trengganu was transferred by Thailand to Great Britain in 1909. A British adviser was appointed in 1919.

The state joined the Federation of Malaya on 1 February 1948.

PRICES FOR STAMPS ON COVER TO 1945	
Nos. 1/15	*from* × 12
No. 16/18	—
Nos. 19/22	*from* × 10
Nos. 23/33	*from* × 12
Nos. 34/36	—
Nos. 37/47	*from* × 15
Nos. 48/60	*from* × 6
Nos. D1/D4	—

1 Sultan Zain ul ab din

2 Sultan Zain ul ab din

RED CROSS

2c.

(**3**)

1910 (14 Dec)–**19**. Wmk Mult Crown CA. Ordinary paper (1c. to 10c.) or chalk-surfaced paper (20c. to $25). P 14.

No.	Type	Description	Unused	Used
1	**1**	1c. blue-green	1·75	1·00
		a. Green	2·75	1·50
2		2c. brown and purple (1915)	1·00	1·00
3		3c. carmine-red	2·25	2·25
4		4c. orange	3·50	8·00
5		4c. red-brown and green (1915)	2·00	5·00
5*a*		4c. carmine-red (1919)	1·25	3·00
6		5c. grey	1·25	8·00
7		5c. grey and brown (1915)	2·25	2·00
8		8c. ultramarine	1·25	17·00
9		10c. purple/*yellow*	6·50	23·00
		a. On pale yellow	3·50	18·00
10		10c. green and red/*yellow* (1915)	1·25	2·25
11		20c. dull and bright purple	4·00	10·00
12		25c. green and dull purple (1915)	15·00	50·00
13		30c. dull purple and black (1915)	15·00	70·00
14		50c. black/*green*	4·50	18·00
15		$1 black and carmine/*blue*	17·00	29·00
16		$3 green and red/*green* (1915)	£250	£650
17	**2**	$5 green and dull purple (1912)	£275	£900
18		$25 rose-carmine and green (1912) (F.C. £200)	£1700	£4000
		s. Optd 'SPECIMEN'	£400	
1/17 *Set of* 18			£500	£1600
1s/17s Optd 'SPECIMEN' *Set of* 18			£750	

The 8c. is known used bisected at Kretai in December 1918. Such use was not officially authorised.

1917 (June)–**18**. Surch with T **3**.

No.	Type	Description	Unused	Used
19	**1**	3c. + 2c. carmine-red	50	11·00
		a. Comma after '2c.'	10·00	48·00
		b. 'SS' in 'CROSS' inverted	£425	£500
		c. 'CSOSS' for 'CROSS'	95·00	£225
		d. '2' in thick block type	22·00	75·00
		e. Surch inverted	£1200	£1300
		f. Pair, one without surch	£5000	£5000
		g. 'RED CROSS' omitted	£450	
		h. 'RED CROSS' twice	£550	
		i. '2c.' omitted	£450	
		j. '2c.' twice	£550	
20		4c. + 2c. orange	1·50	20·00
		a. Comma after '2c.'	18·00	70·00
		b. 'SS' in 'CROSS' inverted	£2000	£1600
		c. 'CSOSS' for 'CROSS'	£180	£425
		d. Surch double	£1300	
		e. 'RED CROSS' omitted	£500	
		f. 'RED CROSS' twice	£750	
		g. '2c.' omitted	£500	
		h. '2c.' twice	£700	
21		4c. + 2c. red-brown and green (1918)	3·75	50·00
		a. Pair, one without surch	£4750	
		b. 'RED CROSS' omitted	£1000	
		c. 'RED CROSS' twice	£1000	
		d. 'SS' in 'CROSS' inverted	—	£4000
22		8c. + 2c. ultramarine (1917)	1·25	38·00
		a. Comma after '2c.'	9·00	85·00
		b. 'SS' in 'CROSS' inverted	£1000	£1100
		c. 'CSOSS' for 'CROSS'	£150	£425
		d. 'RED CROSS' omitted	£500	
		e. 'RED CROSS' twice	£650	
		f. '2c.' omitted	£500	
		g. '2c.' twice	£600	

Nos. 19/22 were sold at face, plus 2c. on each stamp for Red Cross funds.

The surcharges on Nos. 19/22 were arranged in settings of 18 (6×3) applied three times to cover the top nine rows of the sheet with the tenth row completed by a further impression so that 'RED CROSS' from the centre row of the setting appears on the bottom sheet margin. Specialists recognise six different settings:

Setting I – Shows comma after '2' on both R. 1/3 and 1/5, 'SS' inverted on R. 1/6 and 'CSOSS' for 'CROSS' on R. 2/1. Used for 4c. orange and 8c.

Setting Ia – Inverted 'SS' on R. 1/6 corrected. Other varieties as Setting I. Used for 3c., 4c. orange and 8c.

Setting II – 'CSOSS' on R. 2/1 corrected. Comma varieties as Setting I. Used for 3c., 4c. orange and 8c.

Setting III – Both comma varieties now corrected. Used for 3c., both 4c. and 8c.

Setting IIIa – 'SS' inverted on R. 2/5. Used for 3c. only

Setting IV – Thick block '2' on R. 2/2. Inverted 'SS' on R. 2/5 corrected. Used for 3c. only.

Nos. 19g/19j, 20e/20h, 21b/21c and 22d/22g result from the misplacement of the surcharge.

> During a temporary shortage between March and August 1921 2c., 4c. and 6c. stamps of the STRAITS SETTLEMENTS were authorised for use in Trengganu.

4 Sultan Suleiman

5 Sultan Suleiman

2 CENTS
(**6**)

1921–41. Chalk-surfaced paper. P 14.

(a) Wmk Mult Crown CA

No.	Type	Description	Unused	Used
23	**4**	$1 purple and blue/*blue*	12·00	23·00
24		$3 green and red/*emerald*	£130	£275
25	**5**	$5 green and red/*pale yellow*	£170	£450
23/25 *Set of* 3			£275	£700
23s/25s Optd 'SPECIMEN' *Set of* 3			£200	

(b) Wmk Mult Script CA

No.	Type	Description	Unused	Used
26	**4**	1c. black (1926)	1·75	1·50
		a. Ordinary paper (1941)	—	£110
27		2c. green	2·50	2·00
		a. Ordinary paper (1941)	£425	£110
28		3c. green (1926)	2·00	1·00
29		3c. reddish brown (1938)	48·00	14·00
		a. Ordinary paper. *Chestnut* (1941)	—	35·00
30		4c. rose-red	4·75	1·25
		a. Ordinary paper. *Scarlet-vermilion* (1941)	£425	50·00
31		5c. grey and deep brown	2·00	5·00
32		5c. purple/*yellow* (1926)	1·75	1·25
		a. Deep reddish purple/bright yellow (1939)	£250	5·00
33		6c. orange (1924)	8·50	1·00
		a. Ordinary paper (1941)	—	£300
34		8c. grey (1938)	50·00	9·50
		a. Ordinary paper (1941)	—	50·00
35		10c. bright blue	3·75	1·25
36		12c. bright ultramarine (1926)	4·25	1·75
37		20c. dull purple and orange	4·50	1·50
38		25c. green and deep purple	5·50	2·50
39		30c. dull purple and black	4·25	3·75
40		35c. carmine/*yellow* (1926)	4·75	3·25
41		50c. green and bright carmine	12·00	2·75
42		$1 purple and blue/*blue* (1929)	9·00	3·25
43		$3 green and lake/*green* (1926)	65·00	£190
		a. Green and brown-red/green (1938)	£170	
44	**5**	$5 green and red/*yellow* (1938)	£500	£3750
45		$25 purple and blue (F.C. £200)	£1300	£3000
		s. Optd 'SPECIMEN'	£325	
46		$50 green and yellow (F.C. £600)	£3250	£5000
		s. Optd 'SPECIMEN'	£600	
47		$100 green and scarlet (F.C. £600)	£9500	£11000
		s. Optd 'SPECIMEN'	£1100	
26/43 *Set of* 18			£200	£225
26s/44s Optd or Perf (3c. reddish brown, 8c., $1, $5) 'SPECIMEN' *Set of* 19			£1000	

The used price quoted for No. 44 is for an example with an identifiable cancellation from 1938–1941.

Printings of the 2c. yellow-orange, 3c. blue-green, 4c. purple/*yellow*, 6c. slate-grey, 8c. rose, 15c. ultramarine and $1 black and red/*blue* on ordinary paper were despatched to Malaya in late 1941, but did not arrive before the Japanese occupation. Unused examples are known of the 2, 3, 6, 8 and 15c. (*Prices*, 3c. £1400, *others* £325 *each, unused*).

The 12c. bright ultramarine was also printed on ordinary paper, and exists overprinted during the Japanese occupation. See No. J107b.

OVERPRINT SETTINGS FOR NOS. 48/58. The low values in Types **1** and **4** were overprinted using Setting II as detailed under Straits Settlements. The three listed constant varieties from the original typeset block of 12 occur in the same positions for these Trengganu stamps as does the No stop variety from R. 1/5 of the left pane.

A separate setting, believed to be of 30 (6×5), was required for the $5 in the larger design. This was constructed by duplicating the second horizontal row of the original typeset block five times so that the raised stop after 'EXHIBITION' variety occurs on all stamps in the second vertical row and the small second 'A' in 'MALAYA' on all stamps in the sixth.

1922 (Apr). Malaya-Borneo Exhibition, Singapore. Optd as T **56** of Straits Settlements at Singapore.

No.	Type	Description	Unused	Used
48	**4**	2c. green	8·50	45·00
		b. Oval last 'O' in 'BORNEO'	17·00	80·00
		c. Raised stop after 'EXHIBITION'	17·00	80·00
		d. Small second 'A' in 'MALAYA'	17·00	80·00
		f. No stop	95·00	
49		4c. rose-red	6·50	50·00
		b. Oval last 'O' in 'BORNEO'	14·00	85·00
		c. Raised stop after 'EXHIBITION'	14·00	85·00
		d. Small second 'A' in 'MALAYA'	14·00	85·00
		f. No stop	90·00	
50	**1**	5c. grey and brown	3·50	50·00
		b. Oval last 'O' in 'BORNEO'	8·00	85·00
		c. Raised stop after 'EXHIBITION'	8·00	85·00
		d. Small second 'A' in 'MALAYA'	8·00	85·00
		f. No stop	90·00	
51		10c. green and red/*yellow*	5·50	50·00
		b. Oval last 'O' in 'BORNEO'	12·00	85·00
		c. Raised stop after 'EXHIBITION'	12·00	85·00
		d. Small second 'A' in 'MALAYA'	12·00	85·00
		f. No stop	£100	
52		20c. dull and bright purple	9·00	50·00
		b. Oval last 'O' in 'BORNEO'	19·00	85·00
		c. Raised stop after 'EXHIBITION'	19·00	85·00
		d. Small second 'A' in 'MALAYA'	19·00	85·00
		f. No stop	£130	
53		25c. green and dull purple	5·00	50·00
		b. Oval last 'O' in 'BORNEO'	11·00	85·00
		c. Raised stop after 'EXHIBITION'	11·00	85·00
		d. Small second 'A' in 'MALAYA'	11·00	85·00
		f. No stop	90·00	
54		30c. dull purple and black	5·50	50·00
		b. Oval last 'O' in 'BORNEO'	12·00	85·00
		c. Raised stop after 'EXHIBITION'	12·00	85·00
		d. Small second 'A' in 'MALAYA'	12·00	85·00
		f. No stop	£100	
55		50c. black/*green*	11·00	50·00
		b. Oval last 'O' in 'BORNEO'	22·00	95·00
		c. Raised stop after 'EXHIBITION'	22·00	95·00
		d. Small second 'A' in 'MALAYA'	22·00	95·00
		f. No stop	£140	
56		$1 black and carmine/*blue*	14·00	75·00
		b. Oval last 'O' in 'BORNEO'	27·00	£160
		c. Raised stop after 'EXHIBITION'	27·00	£160
		d. Small second 'A' in 'MALAYA'	27·00	£160
		f. No stop	£190	
57		$3 green and red/*green*	£225	£475
		b. Oval last 'O' in 'BORNEO'	£425	£900
		c. Raised stop after 'EXHIBITION'	£425	£900
		d. Small second 'A' in 'MALAYA'	£425	£900
		f. No stop	£2750	
58	**2**	$5 green and dull purple	£375	£700
		c. Raised stop after 'EXHIBITION'	£600	£1200
		d. Small second 'A' in 'MALAYA'	£600	£1200
48/58 *Set of* 11			£600	£1400

1941 (1 May). Nos. 32*a* and 35 surch as T **6**.

No.	Type	Description	Unused	Used
59	**4**	2c. on 5c. deep reddish purple/*bright yellow*	6·50	3·50
60		8c. on 10c. bright blue	7·00	9·00

1948 (2 Dec). Royal Silver Wedding. As Nos. 112/113 of Antigua.

No.	Description	Unused	Used
61	10c. violet	15	1·75
62	$5 carmine	26·00	42·00

1949 (10 Oct). 75th Anniversary of UPU. As Nos. 114/117 of Antigua.

No.	Description	Unused	Used
63	10c. purple	30	75
64	15c. deep blue	1·90	4·25
65	25c. orange	40	4·00
66	50c. blue-black	1·00	3·50
	a. 'C' of 'CA' missing from wmk	£900	
63/66 *Set of* 4		3·25	11·00

7 Sultan Ismail

8 *Vanda hookeriana*

1949 (27 Dec)–**55**. Wmk Mult Script CA. Chalk-surfaced paper. P 17½×18.

No.	Type	Description	Unused	Used
67	**7**	1c. black	1·00	75
68		2c. orange	1·25	75
69		3c. green	7·50	7·50
70		4c. brown	30	60
71		5c. bright purple (1.9.52)	50	1·75
72		6c. grey	2·25	60
73		8c. scarlet	1·25	5·00
74		8c. green (1.9.52)	1·25	1·75
		a. Deep green (11.8.53)	20·00	20·00
75		10c. purple	30	30
76		12c. scarlet (1.9.52)	1·25	4·25
77		15c. ultramarine	11·00	30
78		20c. black and green	11·00	3·75
79		20c. bright blue (1.9.52)	1·50	40
80		25c. purple and orange	3·00	2·00
81		30c. scarlet and purple (4.9.55)	1·25	2·25
82		35c. scarlet and purple (1.9.52)	2·75	2·25
83		40c. red and purple	16·00	29·00
84		50c. black and blue	2·25	2·25
85		$1 blue and purple	7·00	18·00
86		$2 green and scarlet	45·00	50·00
87		$5 green and brown	75·00	70·00
67/87 *Set of* 21			£160	£180

1953 (2 June). Coronation. As No. 120 of Antigua.

No.	Description	Unused	Used
88	10c. black and reddish purple	2·50	1·25

1957 (26 June)–**63**. As Nos. 92/102 of Kedah, but with inset portrait of Sultan Ismail.

No.	Type	Description	Unused	Used
89	**9**	1c. black (21.8.57)	10	20
90	**10**	2c. orange-red (25.7.57)	1·50	30
		a. *Red-orange* (21.2.61)	45·00	15·00
91	**11**	4c. sepia (21.8.57)	15	10
92	**12**	5c. carmine-lake (21.8.57)	15	10
93	**13**	8c. myrtle-green (21.8.57)	4·00	60
94	**14**	10c. deep brown (4.8.57)	2·75	10
94*a*		10c. deep maroon (21.2.61)	15·00	30
95	**15**	20c. blue	2·75	1·60
96	**16**	50c. black and blue (P 12½) (25.7.57)	55	2·50
		a. Perf 12½×13 (17.5.60)	55	2·75
		ab. Black and ultramarine (20.3.62)	2·00	1·75
97	**17**	$1 ultramarine and reddish purple (25.7.57)	17·00	10·00
98	**18**	$2 bronze-green and scarlet (21.8.57)	20·00	9·50
99	**19**	$5 brown and bronze-green	35·00	22·00
		a. Perf 13×12½ (13.8.63)	25·00	48·00
89/99 *Set of* 12			75·00	42·00

The 6, 12, 25 and 30c. values used with this issue were Nos. 1/4 of Malayan Federation.

1965 (15 Nov). As Nos. 166/172 of Johore but with inset portrait of Sultan Ismail Nasiruddin Shah as in T **8**.

No.	Description	Unused	Used
100	1c. multicoloured	10	2·00
101	2c. multicoloured	10	2·00
102	5c. multicoloured	15	1·00
	w. Wmk inverted		
103	6c. multicoloured	15	2·00
104	10c. multicoloured	20	25
105	15c. multicoloured	1·50	10
	a. Black (country name and portrait) omitted (horizontal pair with normal)	£1700	
106	20c. multicoloured	1·50	1·50
	a. Bright purple (blooms) omitted	£250	
	b. Purple-brown (value and background) omitted		
100/106 *Set of* 7		3·25	8·00

The 5c. value exists with PVA gum as well as gum arabic.

No. 101a, formerly listed here, is now listed as Sarawak No. 213a.

The higher values used with this issue were Nos. 20/27 of Malaysia (National Issues).

9 Sultan of Trengganu

(Des Enche Nik Zainal Abidin. Photo Harrison)

1970 (16 Dec). 25th Anniversary of Installation of HRH Tuanku Ismail Nasiruddin Shah as Sultan of Trengganu. P 14½×13½.

No.	Type	Description	Unused	Used
107	**9**	10c. multicoloured	1·00	3·25
108		15c. multicoloured	75	1·25
109		50c. multicoloured	1·25	3·25
107/109 *Set of* 3			2·75	7·00

POSTAGE DUE STAMPS

D 1

1937 (10 Aug). Wmk Mult Script CA (sideways). P 14.

D1	**D 1**	1c. scarlet	8·50	55·00
D2		4c. green	9·50	60·00
D3		8c. yellow	55·00	£375
D4		10c. brown	£120	£110
D1/D4 *Set of 4*			£170	£550
D1s/D4s Perf 'SPECIMEN' *Set of 4*			£160	

VIII. JAPANESE OCCUPATION OF MALAYA

PRICES FOR STAMPS ON COVER

Nos. J1/J55	*from* × 10
Nos. J56/J76	*from* × 12
Nos. J77/J89	*from* × 20
Nos. J90/J91	*from* × 15
Nos. J92/J115	*from* × 6
Nos. J116/J118	—
Nos. J119/J132	*from* × 12
Nos. J133/J145	*from* × 10
Nos. J146/J223	*from* × 6
Nos. J224/J258	*from* × 12
No. J259	*from* × 15
Nos. J260/J296	*from* × 12
Nos. J297/J310	*from* × 20
Nos. J311/J317	—
Nos. JD1/JD10	*from* × 30
Nos. JD11/JD16	*from* × 12
Nos. JD17/JD20	*from* × 30
Nos. JD21/JD27	*from* × 20
Nos. JD28/JD33	*from* × 30
Nos. JD34/JD41	*from* × 60

Japanese forces invaded Malaya on 8 December 1941 with the initial landings taking place at Kota Bharu on the east coast. Penang fell, to a force which crossed the border from Thailand, on 19 December, Kuala Lumpur on 11 January 1942 and the conquest of the Malay peninsula was completed by the capture of Singapore on 15 February.

During the Japanese Occupation various small Dutch East Indies islands near Singapore were administered as part of Malaya. Stamps of the Japanese Occupation of Malaya were issued to the post offices of Dabo Singkep, Puloe Samboe, Tanjong Balei, Tanjong Batu, Tanjong Pinang and Terempa between 1942 and 1945. The overprinted issues were also used by a number of districts in Atjeh (Northern Sumatra) whose postal services were administered from Singapore until the end of March 1943.

Malayan post offices were also opened in October 1943 to serve camps of civilians working on railway construction and maintenance in Thailand. Overprinted stamps of the Japanese Occupation of Malaya were used at these offices between October 1943 and the end of the year after which mail from the camps was carried free. Their postmarks were inscribed in Japanese Katakana characters, and, uniquely, showed the Japanese postal symbol.

JOHORE

The postal service in Johore was reconstituted in mid-April 1942 using Nos. J146/J160 and subsequently other general issues. Stamps of Johore overprinted 'DAI NIPPON 2602' were, however, only used for fiscal purposes. Overprinted Johore postage due stamps were not issued for use elsewhere in Malaya.

POSTAGE DUE STAMPS

(**1**) (Upright)

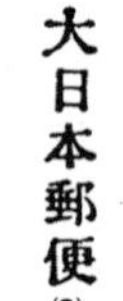

(**2**)

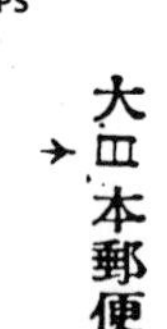

Second character sideways (R. 6/3)

1942 (1 Apr). Nos. D1/D5 of Johore optd as T **1** in brown.

JD1	**D 1**	1c. carmine	50·00	85·00
		a. Black opt	20·00	70·00
JD2		4c. green	80·00	£100
		a. Black opt	65·00	80·00
JD3		8c. orange	£140	£160
		a. Black opt	80·00	95·00
JD4		10c. brown	50·00	70·00
		a. Black opt	16·00	50·00
JD5		12c. purple	£100	£110
		a. Black opt	48·00	55·00

1943. Nos. D1/D5 of Johore optd with T **2**.

JD6	**D 1**	1c. carmine	10·00	35·00
		a. Second character sideways	£375	£800
JD7		4c. green	8·00	40·00
		a. Second character sideways	£400	£800
JD8		8c. orange	10·00	40·00
		a. Second character sideways	£450	£850
JD9		10c. brown	9·50	50·00
		a. Second character sideways	£450	£950
JD10		12c. purple	11·00	65·00
		a. Second character sideways	£500	£1100
JD6/JD10 *Set of 5*			45·00	£200

KEDAH

Postal services resumed by 31 January 1942 using unoverprinted Kedah values from 1c. to 8c. which were accepted for postage until 13 May 1942.

During the Japanese occupation Perlis was administered as part of Kedah.

DAI NIPPON
2602
(**3**)

DAI NIPPON
2602
(**4**)

1942 (13 May)–**43**. Stamps of Kedah (Script wmk) optd with T **3** (1c. to 8c.) or T **4** (10c. to $5), both in red.

J1	**1**	1c. black (No. 68*a*)	11·00	17·00
J2		2c. bright green (No. 69)	27·00	30·00
J3		4c. violet	13·00	4·00
		a. Short sheaf	£300	£180
J4		5c. yellow	5·50	6·50
		a. Black opt (1943)	£200	£225
J5		6c. carmine (No. 56) (Blk.)	8·00	26·00
		a. Carmine-red (No. 56*a*)	50·00	75·00
J6		8c. grey-black	9·00	5·00
J7	**6**	10c. ultramarine and sepia	18·00	20·00
J8		12c. black and violet	42·00	60·00
J9		25c. ultramarine and purple	16·00	29·00
		a. Black opt (1943)	£475	£375
J10		30c. green and scarlet	70·00	80·00
J11		40c. black and purple	42·00	50·00
J12		50c. brown and blue	42·00	50·00
J13		$1 black and green	£140	£150
		a. Opt inverted	£900	£1000
J14		$2 green and brown	£170	£170
		a. Opt double	—	£1400
J15		$5 black and scarlet	80·00	£110
		a. Black opt (1943)	£1600	£1300
J1/J15 *Set of 15*			£600	£700

Nos. J1/J15 were gradually replaced by issues intended for use throughout Malaya. Kedah and Perlis were ceded to Thailand by the Japanese on 19 October 1943.

KELANTAN

Postal services resumed on 1 June 1942. Stamps used in Kelantan were overprinted with the personal seals of Sunagawa, the Japanese Governor, and of Handa, the Assistant Governor.

(**5**) Sunagawa Seal

(**6**) Handa Seal

40 CENTS
(**7**)

$1.00
(**8**)

1 Cents
(**9**)

1942 (June). Stamps of Kelantan surch.

		*(a) As Types **7** or **8** (dollar values). Optd with T **5** in red*		
J16	**4**	1c. on 50c. grey-olive and orange	£550	£250
J17		2c. on 40c. orange and blue-green	£1500	£400
J18		4c. on 30c. violet and scarlet	£4000	£2750
J19		5c. on 12c. blue (R.)	£475	£250
J20		6c. on 25c. vermilion and violet	£475	£250
J21		8c. on 5c. red-brown (R.)	£750	£170
J22		10c. on 6c. lake	£100	£140
		a. 'CENST' for 'CENTS'	£15000	
J23		12c. on 8c. grey-olive (R.)	65·00	£130
J24		25c. on 10c. purple (R.)	£2500	£2250
J25		30c. on 4c. scarlet	£3250	£3000
J26		40c. on 2c. green (R.)	80·00	£100
		a. Surch double (B.+R.)	£7000	
J27		50c. on 1c. grey-olive and yellow	£2500	£2000
J28	**1**	$1 on 4c. black and red (R., bars Blk.)	50·00	95·00
J29		$2 on 5c. green and red/*yellow*	50·00	95·00
J30		$5 on 6c. scarlet	50·00	95·00
		a. Surch double	£600	
		*(b) As T **7**. Optd with T **6** in red*		
J31	**4**	12c. on 8c. grey-olive	£275	£450
		a. Type **6** omitted (in horiz pair with normal)	£5500	
		*(c) As T **9**. Optd with T **5** in red*		
J32	**4**	1c. on 50c. grey-olive and orange	£300	£130
		a. 'Cente' for 'Cents' (R. 5/1)	£4000	£1700
J33		2c. on 40c. orange and blue-green	£400	£190
		a. 'Cente' for 'Cents' (R. 5/1)	£4500	£2250
J34		5c. on 12c. blue (R.)	£225	£250
		a. 'Cente' for 'Cents' (R. 5/1)	£3500	
J35		8c. on 5c. red-brown (R.)	£190	95·00
		a. 'Cente' for 'Cents' (R. 5/1)	£2750	£1500
J36		10c. on 6c. lake	£700	£750
		a. 'Cente' for 'Cents' (R. 5/1)	£6000	
		*(d) As T **9**. Optd with T **6** in red*		
J41	**4**	1c. on 50c. grey-olive and orange	£200	£250
		a. 'Cente' for 'Cents' (R. 5/1)	£2750	
J42		2c. on 40c. orange and blue-green	£225	£250
		a. 'Cente' for 'Cents' (R. 5/1)	£3000	
J43		8c. on 5c. red-brown (R.)	95·00	£170
		a. 'Cente' for 'Cents' (R. 5/1)	£1900	
J44		10c. on 6c. lake	£150	£250
		a. 'Cente' for 'Cents' (R. 5/1)	£2500	

As stamps of the above series became exhausted the equivalent values from the series intended for use throughout Malaya were introduced. Stamps as Nos. J28/J30, J32/J33 and J35/J36, but without Types **5** or **6**, are from remainders sent to Singapore or Kuala Lumpur after the state had been ceded to Thailand (*Price from £16 each unused*). Nos. J19, J21, J23 and J25/J26 have also been seen without T **5** (*Price from £90 each unused*).

The 12c. on 8c., 30c. on 4c., 40c. on 2c. and 50c. on 1c. surcharged with T **9**, formerly listed as Nos. J37/J40, are now believed to exist only as remainders without the T **5** red handstamp (*Price from £20 each, unused*).

Kelantan was ceded to Thailand by the Japanese on 19 October 1943.

MALACCA

Postal services from Malacca resumed on 21 April 1942, but there were no stamps available for two days.

PRICES. Those quoted are for single stamps. Blocks of four showing complete handstamp are worth from five times the price of a single stamp.

(**10**) 'Military Administration Malacca State Government Seal'

1942 (23 Apr). Stamps of Straits Settlements handstamped as T **10**, in red, each impression covering four stamps.

J45	**58**	1c. black	£130	95·00
J46		2c. orange	70·00	75·00
J47		3c. green	75·00	85·00
J48		5c. brown	£180	£180
J49		8c. grey	£350	£140
J50		10c. dull purple	£150	£150
J51		12c. ultramarine	£140	£150
J52		15c. ultramarine	£100	£120
J53		40c. scarlet and dull purple	£650	£800
J54		50c. black/*emerald*	£1300	£1300
J55		$1 black and red/*blue*	£1500	£1500

The 30c., $2 and $5 also exist with this overprint, but these values were not available to the public. (*Price for set of 3 £11000 unused*).

POSTAGE DUE STAMPS

1942 (23 Apr). Postage Due stamps of Malayan Postal Union handstamped as T **10**, in red, each impression covering four stamps.

JD11	**D 1**	1c. slate-purple	£300	£250
JD12		4c. green	£250	£250
JD13		8c. scarlet	£4500	£3250
JD14		10c. yellow-orange	£600	£500
JD15		12c. ultramarine	£1000	£800
JD16		50c. black	£3750	£2750

Nos. J45/J55 and JD11/JD16 were replaced during May 1942 by the overprinted issues intended for use throughout Malaya.

PENANG

Postal services on Penang Island resumed on 30 March 1942 using Straits Settlements stamps overprinted by Japanese seals of the Government Accountant, Mr. A. Okugawa, and his assistant, Mr. Itchiburi.

(**11**) Okugawa Seal

(**12**) Itchiburi Seal

DAI NIPPON
2602
PENANG
(**13**)

1942 (30 Mar). Straits Settlements stamps optd.

		*(a) As T **11** (three forms of the seal)*		
J56	**58**	1c. black	15·00	19·00
J57		2c. orange	24·00	30·00
		a. Pair, one without handstamp	£1600	
J58		3c. green	20·00	30·00
J59		5c. brown	24·00	45·00
J60		8c. grey	40·00	50·00
J61		10c. dull purple	55·00	55·00
J62		12c. ultramarine	50·00	55·00
J63		15c. ultramarine	60·00	60·00
J64		40c. scarlet and dull purple	£110	£120
J65		50c. black/*emerald*	£225	£225
J66		$1 black and red/*blue*	£300	£350
J67		$2 green and scarlet	£950	£800
J68		$5 green and red/*emerald*	£3250	£1700
		*(b) With T **12***		
J69	**58**	1c. black	£200	£170
J70		2c. orange	£200	£140
J71		3c. green	£120	£120
J72		5c. brown	£3500	£3500
J73		8c. grey	£120	£120
J74		10c. dull purple	£200	£225
J75		12c. ultramarine	£140	£150
J76		15c. ultramarine	£160	£160

Straits Settlements 1, 2, 3, 4 and 5c. values exist with a similar but circular seal containing four characters, but these were not available to the public.

1942 (15 Apr). Straits Settlements stamps optd with T **13** by Penang Premier Press.

J77	**58**	1c. black (R.)	10·00	3·75
		a. Opt inverted	£700	£700
		b. Opt double	£325	£325
J78		2c. orange	12·00	5·00
		a. 'PE' for 'PENANG'	£140	£100
		b. Opt inverted	£170	
		c. Opt double	£650	
J79		3c. green (R.)	10·00	9·00
		a. Opt double, one inverted	£450	
J80		5c. brown (R.)	4·75	9·00
		a. 'N PPON'	£200	
		b. Opt double	£650	£500
J81		8c. grey (R.)	3·00	1·40
		a. 'N PPON'	70·00	65·00
		b. Opt double, one inverted	£600	

J82 10c. dull purple (R.) 1·50 2·25
a. Opt double £475 £475
b. Opt double, one inverted £425 £425
J83 12c. ultramarine (R.) 6·50 26·00
a. 'N PPON' £550
b. Opt double £475
c. Opt double, one inverted £700 £700
J84 15c. ultramarine (R.) 1·75 4·75
a. 'N PPON' £110 £140
b. Opt inverted £425 £425
c. Opt double £650 £650
J85 40c. scarlet and dull purple 8·50 26·00
J86 50c. black/*emerald* (R.) 3·75 40·00
J87 $1 black and red/*blue* 6·00 50·00
a. Opt inverted £1300
J88 $2 green and scarlet 65·00 £110
J89 $5 green and red/*emerald* £900 £950
J77/J89 *Set of* 13 £950 £1100

Nos. J77/J89 were replaced by the overprinted issues intended for use throughout Malaya.

SELANGOR

Postal services resumed in the Kuala Lumpur area on 3 April 1942 and gradually extended to the remainder of the state. Stamps of the general overprinted issue were used, but the following commemorative set was only available in Selangor.

SELANGOR EXHIBITION DAI NIPPON 2602 MALAYA
(**14**)

1942 (3 Nov). Selangor Agri-horticultural Exhibition. Nos. 294 and 283 of Straits Settlements optd with T **14**.
J90 **58** 2c. orange 12·00 24·00
a. 'C' for 'G' in 'SELANGOR' (R. 1/9). £400 £450
b. Opt inverted £300 £400
J91 8c. grey 13·00 24·00
a. 'C' for 'G' in 'SELANGOR' (R. 1/9). £400 £450
b. Opt inverted £300 £400

SINGAPORE

The first post offices re-opened in Singapore on 16 March 1942.

(**15**) 'Malaya Military Government Division Postal Services Bureau Seal'

(Handstamped at Singapore)

1942 (16 Mar). Stamps of Straits Settlements optd with T **15** in red.
J92 **58** 1c. black 22·00 22·00
J93 2c. orange 16·00 13·00
a. Pair, one without handstamp £2500
J94 3c. green 55·00 70·00
J95 8c. grey 28·00 18·00
J96 15c. ultramarine 21·00 15·00
J92/J96 *Set of* 5 £130 £120

The overprint T **15** has a double-lined frame, although the two lines are not always apparent, as in the illustration. Three chops were used, differing slightly in the shape of the characters, but forgeries also exist. It is distinguishable from T **1**, used for the general issues, by its extra width, measuring approximately 14 mm against 12½ mm.

The 6, 10, 30, 40, 50c., $2 and $5 also exist with this overprint, but were not sold to the public.

Nos. J92/J96 were replaced on the 3 May 1942 by the stamps overprinted with T **1** which were intended for use throughout Malaya.

TRENGGANU

Postal services resumed in Trengganu on 5 March 1942 using unoverprinted stamps up to the 35c. value. These remained in use until September 1942.

1942 (Sept). Stamps of Trengganu (Script wmk) optd as T **1** at Kuala Lumpur.
J97 **4** 1c. black (No. 26*a*) 90·00 £100
a. Chalk-surfaced paper (No. 26) — £325
b. Red opt £225 £225
c. Brown opt (chalk-surfaced paper) £750 £400
J98 2c. green (No. 27*a*) £140 £140
a. Chalk-surfaced paper (No. 27) — £450
b. Red opt £275 £300
c. Brown opt £750 £425
J99 2c. on 5c. deep reddish purple/*bright yellow* (No. 59) 42·00 42·00
a. Red opt 65·00 80·00
J100 3c. chestnut (No. 29*a*) £100 90·00
a. Brown opt £1000 £650
J101 4c. scarlet-vermilion (No. 30*a*) £200 £150
J102 5c. deep reddish purple/*bright yellow* (No. 32*a*) 11·00 19·00
a. Purple/yellow (No. 32) £250 £250
b. Red opt 42·00
J103 6c. orange (No. 33*a*) 14·00 28·00
a. Red opt £475
b. Brown opt £1100 £1100
J104 8c. grey (No. 34*a*) 9·00 13·00
a. Chalk-surfaced paper (No. 34) £350
b. Brown to red opt 70·00 75·00
J105 8c. on 10c. bright blue (No. 60) 13·00 50·00
a. Red opt 26·00
J106 10c. bright blue 42·00 50·00
a. Red opt £425
b. Brown opt £1200 £1100
J107 12c. bright ultramarine (No. 36) 8·00 50·00
a. Red opt 38·00 65·00
b. Ordinary paper 50·00
J108 20c. dull purple and orange 16·00 55·00
a. Red opt 35·00
J109 25c. green and deep purple 11·00 55·00
a. Red opt 38·00
b. Brown opt £1200 £1200
J110 30c. dull purple and black 18·00 50·00
a. Red opt 50·00 80·00
J111 35c. carmine/*yellow* 40·00 65·00
a. Red opt 42·00
J112 50c. green and bright carmine 90·00 £100
J113 $1 purple and blue/*blue* £5500 £5500
J114 $3 green and brown-red/*green* (No. 43*a*) 80·00 £130
a. Green and lake/green (No. 43) £500
b. Red opt 85·00
J115 **5** $5 green and red/*yellow* £350 £425
J116 $25 purple and blue £2250
a. Red opt £10000
J117 $50 green and yellow £20000
J118 $100 green and scarlet £2500

DAI NIPPON 2602 MALAYA
(**16**)

1942 (Sept). Stamps of Trengganu (Script wmk) optd with T **16**.
J119 **4** 1c. black (No. 26*a*) 17·00 13·00
J120 2c. green (No. 27*a*) £325 £325
J121 2c. on 5c. deep reddish purple/*bright yellow* (No. 59) 6·50 8·00
J122 3c. chestnut (No. 29*a*) 24·00 29·00
J123 4c. scarlet-vermilion (No. 30*a*) 24·00 11·00
J124 5c. deep reddish purple/*bright yellow* (No. 32*a*) 6·00 13·00
J125 6c. orange (No. 33*a*) 9·50 14·00
J126 8c. grey (No. 34*a*) 95·00 30·00
J127 8c. on 10c. bright blue (No. 60) 9·50 10·00
J128 12c. bright ultramarine (No. 36) 11·00 50·00
J129 20c. dull purple and orange 21·00 20·00
J130 25c. green and deep purple 9·00 50·00
J131 30c. dull purple and black 16·00 50·00
J132 $3 green and brown-red/*green* (No. 43*a*) £100 £190
J119/J132 *Set of* 14 £600 £700

1943. Stamps of Trengganu (Script wmk) optd with T **2**.
J133 **4** 1c. black (No. 26*a*) 28·00 30·00
a. Chalk-surfaced paper 85·00
J134 2c. green (No. 27*a*) 19·00 50·00
J135 2c. on 5c. bright reddish purple/*bright yellow* (No. 59) 12·00 35·00
J136 5c. bright reddish purple/*bright yellow* (No. 32*a*) 17·00 50·00
J137 6c. orange (No. 33*a*) 18·00 50·00
J138 8c. grey (No. 34*a*) 90·00 £120
J139 8c. on 10c. bright blue (No. 60) 35·00 55·00
J140 10c. bright blue £110 £250
J141 12c. bright ultramarine (No. 36) 21·00 50·00
J142 20c. dull purple and orange 28·00 50·00
J143 25c. green and deep purple 29·00 55·00
J144 30c. dull purple and black 40·00 55·00
J145 35c. carmine/*yellow* 30·00 75·00
J133/J145 *Set of* 13 £400 £800

POSTAGE DUE STAMPS

1942 (Sept). Nos. D1/D4 of Trengganu optd with T **1** sideways.
JD17 **D 1** 1c. scarlet 55·00 90·00
JD18 4c. green 90·00 £130
a. Brown opt 50·00 90·00
JD19 8c. yellow 14·00 50·00
JD20 10c. brown 14·00 50·00

The Trengganu 8c. postage due also exists overprinted with T **16**, but this was not issued (*Price £600 unused*).

Trengganu was ceded to Thailand by the Japanese on 19 October 1943.

GENERAL ISSUES

The following stamps were produced for use throughout Malaya, except for Trengganu.

1942 (3 Apr). Stamps optd as T **1**.

(a) On Straits Settlements

J146 **58** 1c. black (R.) 4·25 3·25
a. Black opt £400 £400
b. Violet opt £1600 £750
J147 2c. green (V.) £4000 £3000
J148 2c. orange (R.) 4·00 2·25
a. Black opt £140 £150
b. Violet opt £250 £225
c. Brown opt £1200 £750
J149 3c. green (R.) 4·50 2·25
a. Black opt £425 £450
b. Violet opt £1600 £800
J150 5c. brown (R.) 27·00 30·00
a. Black opt £600 £600
J151 8c. grey (R.) 9·00 2·25
a. Pair, one without handstamp † £3000
b. Black opt £275 £275
J152 10c. dull purple (R.) 75·00 50·00
a. Brown opt £1500 £850
J153 12c. ultramarine (R.) £120 £160
J154 15c. ultramarine (R.) 3·75 3·75
a. Violet opt £1000 £750
J155 30c. dull purple and orange (R.) £4250 £4250
J156 40c. scarlet and dull purple (R.) £160 £100
a. Brown opt £1200 £550
J157 50c. black/*emerald* (R.) 75·00 50·00
J158 $1 black and red/*blue* (R.) £100 75·00
J159 $2 green and scarlet (R.) £180 £225
J160 $5 green and red/*emerald* (R.) £275 £300

The 2c. green is known with the overprint in red, but this was not available to the public (*Price, £375 unused*).

(b) On Negri Sembilan

J161 **6** 1c. black (R.) 19·00 13·00
a. Violet opt 23·00 20·00
b. Brown opt 13·00 21·00
c. Black opt 70·00 40·00
d. Pair. Nos. J161/J161a £300
e. Pair. Nos. J161 and J161b £350
J162 2c. orange (R.) 40·00 26·00
a. Violet opt 55·00 30·00
b. Black opt 38·00 32·00
c. Brown opt 70·00 55·00
J163 3c. green (R.) 55·00 26·00
a. Violet opt 26·00 29·00
c. Brown opt £250 75·00
d. Black opt 80·00 55·00
J164 5c. brown 50·00 24·00
a. Pair, one without opt £2500
b. Brown opt 17·00 15·00
c. Red opt 24·00 11·00
d. Violet opt 65·00 42·00
e. Pair. Nos. J164c/J164d £375
J165 6c. grey £200 £170
a. Brown opt £325 £350
J166 8c. scarlet (*ordinary paper*) £325 £250
J167 10c. dull purple £350 £275
a. Red opt £750 £550
b. Brown opt £950 £650
J168 12c. bright ultramarine (Br.) £2750 £2750
J169 15c. ultramarine (R.) 42·00 8·00
a. Violet opt £160 30·00
b. Brown opt 50·00 12·00
J170 25c. dull purple and scarlet 28·00 38·00
a. Red opt 70·00 80·00
b. Brown opt £950 £700
J171 30c. dull purple and orange £350 £300
a. Brown opt £2250 £1500
J172 40c. scarlet and dull purple £3000 £1600
a. Brown opt £1700 £1300
J173 50c. black/*emerald* £2500 £2250
J174 $1 black and red/*blue* £275 £300
a. Red opt £180 £200
b. Brown opt £475 £475
J175 $5 green and red/*emerald* £800 £1000
a. Red opt £1800 £1800

Nos. J161a and J163a exist with the handstamped overprint sideways.

(c) On Pahang

J176 **15** 1c. black 55·00 50·00
a. Red opt 80·00 75·00
b. Violet opt £425 £275
c. Brown opt £325 £250
J177 3c. green £600 £325
a. Red opt £225 £275
b. Violet opt £650 £475
J178 5c. brown 20·00 13·00
a. Red opt £375 £130
b. Brown opt £300 £120
c. Violet opt £500 £275
d. Pair. Nos. J178/J178b £850
J179 8c. grey £1600 £1000
J180 8c. scarlet 32·00 8·00
a. Red opt £120 50·00
b. Violet opt £110 60·00
c. Brown opt £110 65·00
d. Pair. Nos. J180a/J180c £475
J181 10c. dull purple £550 £200
a. Red opt £375 £250
b. Brown opt £425 £275
J182 12c. bright ultramarine £2750 £2750
a. Brown *to* red opt £1200 £1200
J183 15c. ultramarine £180 £120
a. Red opt £550 £275
b. Violet opt £800 £500
c. Brown opt £700 £350
J184 25c. dull purple and scarlet 28·00 30·00
J185 30c. dull purple and orange 20·00 32·00
a. Red opt £150 £170
J186 40c. scarlet and dull purple 30·00 38·00
a. Brown opt £650 £400
b. Red opt £100 £100
J187 50c. black/*emerald* £1900 £1900
a. Red opt £2250 £2250
J188 $1 black and red/*blue* (R.) £170 £180
a. Black opt £325 £325
b. Brown opt £750 £750
J189 $5 green and red/*emerald* £850 £950
a. Red opt £1400 £1500

(d) On Perak

J190 **51** 1c. black 75·00 50·00
a. Violet opt £425 £180
b. Brown opt £130 £110
J191 2c. orange 38·00 20·00
a. Violet opt 90·00 70·00
b. Red opt 85·00 40·00
c. Brown opt 80·00 60·00
J192 3c. green 35·00 32·00
a. Violet opt £550 £350
b. Brown opt £225 £160
c. Red opt £400 £275
J193 5c. brown 13·00 6·00
a. Pair, one without opt £1500
b. Brown opt 55·00 38·00
c. Violet opt £375 £200
d. Red opt £225 £200
J194 8c. grey £110 65·00
a. Red opt £650 £250
b. Brown opt £475 £250
J195 8c. scarlet 55·00 48·00
a. Violet opt £700 £350
J196 10c. dull purple 26·00 24·00
a. Red opt £550 £325
J197 12c. bright ultramarine £300 £250
J198 15c. ultramarine 24·00 32·00
a. Red opt £250 £250

b. Violet opt £750 £375
c. Brown opt £450 £300
J199 25c. dull purple and scarlet .... 14·00 28·00
a. Red opt £450
J200 30c. dull purple and orange (No. 116a) 17·00 32·00
a. Pair, one without opt £2000
b. Brown opt £1200 £650
c. Red opt .... 45·00 60·00
ca. Pair, one without opt £2750
J201 40c. scarlet and dull purple £850 £400
a. Brown opt £650 £450
J202 50c. black/*emerald* .... 55·00 60·00
a. Red opt .... 60·00 65·00
b. Brown opt £700 £400
J203 $1 black and red/*blue* £650 £425
a. Brown opt £450 £400
J204 $2 green and scarlet £5500 £5500
J205 $5 green and red/*emerald* £600
a. Brown opt £3750

(e) On Selangor

J206 **46** 1c. black, S .... 15·00 28·00
a. Red opt, SU .... 55·00 42·00
b. Violet opt, SU .... 65·00 50·00
J207 2c. green, SU £2750 £1500
a. Violet opt, SU £3250 £1500
J208 2c. orange (P 14×14½), S .... £100 60·00
a. Red opt, U £200 £170
b. Violet opt, U £225 £160
c. Brown opt, S .... 85·00 80·00
J209 2c. orange (P 14), S £180 £100
a. Red opt, U £250 £170
b. Violet opt, U £500 £170
c. Brown opt, S .... — £180
J210 3c. green, SU .... 23·00 15·00
a. Red opt, SU .... 28·00 16·00
b. Violet opt, SU .... 80·00 50·00
c. Brown opt, SU .... 19·00 15·00
d. Pair. Nos. J210a/J210c £350
J211 5c. brown, SU .... 7·50 5·50
a. Red opt, SU .... 24·00 19·00
b. Violet opt, SU .... 21·00 22·00
c. Brown opt, SU .... 60·00 50·00
J212 6c. scarlet, SU £450 £450
a. Red opt, S £225 £275
b. Brown opt, S £1300 £1300
J213 8c. grey, S .... 35·00 17·00
a. Red opt, SU .... 70·00 40·00
b. Violet opt, U .... 50·00 35·00
c. Brown opt, S .... £225 80·00
J214 10c. dull purple, S .... 23·00 21·00
a. Red opt, S .... £120 90·00
b. Brown opt, S £275 £120
J215 12c. bright ultramarine, S .... 70·00 80·00
a. Red opt, S £180 £180
b. Brown opt, S £170 £170
J216 15c. ultramarine, S .... 19·00 27·00
a. Red opt, SU £100 £100
b. Violet opt, U £225 £110
c. Brown opt, S £170 £110
J217 25c. dull purple and scarlet, S £130 £160
a. Red opt, S .... 65·00 90·00
J218 30c. dull purple and orange, S (No. 80a) .... 11·00 24·00
a. Brown opt, S £650 £300
J219 40c. scarlet and dull purple, S £200 £150
a. Brown opt, S £600 £250
b. Red opt, S £500
J220 50c. black/*emerald*, S £225 £225
a. Red opt, S £250 £300
b. Brown opt, S £900 £500
J221 **48** $1 black and red/*blue* .... 40·00 55·00
a. Red opt £160 £180
J222 $2 green and scarlet .... 42·00 70·00
a. Pair, one without opt £2500
b. Red opt £1100 £1100
J223 $5 green and red/*emerald* .... 90·00 £120

On T **46** the overprint is normally sideways (with 'top' to either right or left), but on T **48** it is always upright.

S = Sideways.
U = Upright.
SU = Sideways or upright (our prices being for the cheaper).

Specialists recognise nine slightly different chops as T **1**. Initial supplies with the overprint in red were produced at Singapore. Later overprintings took place at Kuala Lumpur in violet, red or brown and finally, black. No. J155 was from the Kuala Lumpur printing only. Except where noted, these overprints were used widely in Malaya and, in some instances, Sumatra.

The following stamps also exist with this overprint, but were not available to the public:

Straits Settlements (in red) 6, 25c.
Kelantan (in black) 10c.
Negri Sembilan 2c. green (Blk. or Brn.), 4c. (Blk.), 6c. scarlet (Blk.), 8c. grey (Blk.), 12c. (Blk.), $2 (Blk. or Brn.).
Pahang (in black, 2c. also in brown) 2, 4, 6c., $2.
Perak 2c. green (R.), 6c. (Blk.).
Selangor 4c. (Blk.).

1942 (May). Optd with T **16**.

(a) On Straits Settlements

J224 **58** 2c. orange .... 3·50 60
a. Opt inverted .... 16·00 28·00
b. Opt double, one inverted .... 55·00 65·00
J225 3c. green .... 50·00 65·00
J226 8c. grey .... 12·00 4·50
a. Opt inverted .... 21·00 48·00
J227 15c. blue .... 26·00 16·00
J224/J227 *Set of 4* .... 80·00 80·00

(b) On Negri Sembilan

J228 **6** 1c. black (*Thin striated paper*) .... 3·00 60
a. Opt inverted .... 9·00 30·00
b. Opt double, one inverted .... 35·00 55·00
c. Chalk-surfaced paper .... 4·00 1·00
J229 2c. orange .... 13·00 50
J230 3c. green (No. 24a) .... 9·00 50
J231 5c. brown .... 1·75 7·00
J232 6c. grey .... 7·50 7·50
a. Opt inverted .... † £1900
b. Stop omitted at right (R. 10/4) £250 £275
J233 8c. scarlet (*Ordinary paper*) .... 9·00 1·25
a. Thin striated paper .... 11·00 3·25
J234 10c. dull purple .... 3·25 2·50
J235 15c. ultramarine .... 25·00 2·50
J236 25c. dull purple and scarlet (*Ordinary paper*) .... 7·00 24·00
J237 30c. dull purple and orange (*Thin striated paper*) .... 13·00 6·50
J238 $1 black and red/*blue* .... 85·00 £110
J228/J238 *Set of 11* £150 £140

(c) On Pahang

J239 **15** 1c. black (*Thin striated paper*) .... 3·50 5·00
a. Opt omitted (in pair with normal) £600
J240 5c. brown .... 1·25 70
J241 8c. scarlet .... 42·00 3·50
a. Opt omitted (in pair with normal) £1700
J242 10c. dull purple .... 17·00 10·00
J243 12c. bright ultramarine .... 4·50 25·00
J244 25c. dull purple and scarlet (*Thin striated paper*) .... 9·00 42·00
J245 30c. dull purple and orange (No. 41a) .... 3·75 19·00
J239/J245 *Set of 7* .... 70·00 95·00

(d) On Perak

J246 **51** 2c. orange (No. 105) .... 4·50 4·00
a. Opt inverted .... 75·00 75·00
b. Malformed '2c' £150 £160
J247 3c. green (No. 106a) .... 1·50 1·50
a. Opt inverted .... 18·00 28·00
b. Opt omitted (in pair with normal) £800
J248 8c. scarlet (No. 111) .... 1·50 50
a. Opt inverted .... 4·50 7·00
b. Opt double, one inverted £225 £250
c. Opt omitted (in horiz pair with normal) £400
J249 10c. dull purple (*Thin striated paper*) .... 22·00 9·50
a. Chalk-surfaced paper .... — 17·00
J250 15c. ultramarine .... 18·00 2·00
J251 50c. black/*emerald* .... 4·00 7·50
J252 $1 black and red/*blue* £600 £650
J253 $5 green and red/*emerald* .... 70·00 95·00
a. Opt inverted £325 £425
J246/J253 *Set of 8* £650 £700

(e) On Selangor

J254 **46** 3c. green (No. 71a) .... 2·25 6·00
a. Ordinary paper
J255 12c. bright ultramarine .... 3·00 26·00
J256 15c. ultramarine .... 9·00 1·50
J257 40c. scarlet and dull purple .... 2·25 7·50
J258 **48** $2 green and scarlet .... 11·00 55·00
J254/J258 *Set of 5* .... 24·00 85·00

On T **46** the overprint is sideways, with 'top' to left or right.

The following stamps also exist with this overprint, but were not available to the public.

Perak 1, 5, 30c. (*Price for set of 3 £400 unused*).
Selangor 1, 5, 10, 30c., $1, $5 (*Price for set of 6 £850 unused*).

DAI NIPPON
2602
MALAYA
2 Cents
(**17**)

DAI NIPPON
YUBIN
2 Cents
(**18**) *'Japanese Postal Service'*

1942 (Nov). No. 108 of Perak surch with T **17**.

J259 **51** 2c. on 5c. brown .... 1·75 5·50
a. Inverted 's' in 'Cents' (R. 3/5) .... 70·00 £100

1942 (Nov). Perak stamps surch or opt only, as in T **18**.

J260 **51** 1c. black (*Thin striated paper*) .... 7·00 11·00
a. Opt inverted .... 19·00 48·00
J261 2c. on 5c. brown .... 2·75 6·50
a. 'DAI NIPPON YUBIN' inverted .... 17·00 48·00
b. Ditto and '2 Cents' omitted .... 50·00 70·00
c. Inverted 's' in 'Cents' (R. 3/5) .... 75·00 £140
J262 8c. scarlet (No. 111) .... 14·00 3·50
a. Opt inverted .... 13·00 28·00
J260/J262 *Set of 3* .... 21·00 19·00

A similar overprint exists on the Selangor 3c. but this was not available to the public (*Price £350 unused*).

On 8 December 1942 contemporary Japanese 3, 5, 8 and 25s. stamps were issued without overprint in Malaya and the 1, 2, 4, 6, 7, 10, 30 and 50s. and 1y. values followed on 15 February 1943.

大日本郵便 (**19**) 6cts. (**20**) 6 cts. (**21**)

2 Cents (**22**) 6 cts. (**23**) $1.00 (**24**)

1942 (4 Dec)–**44**. Stamps of various Malayan territories optd 'Japanese Postal Service' in Kanji characters as Types **2** or **19**, some additionally surch as Types **20** to **24**.

(a) Stamps of Straits Settlements optd with T **2**

J263 **58** 8c. grey (Blk.) (1943) .... 1·40 50
a. Opt inverted .... 60·00 75·00
b. Opt omitted (in pair with normal) £850
c. Red opt .... 2·50 3·50
J264 12c. ultramarine (1943) .... 1·75 18·00
J265 40c. scarlet and dull purple (1943) .... 4·00 7·50
J263/J265 *Set of 3* .... 6·50 22·00

(b) Stamps of Negri Sembilan optd with T **2** *or surch also*

J266 **6** 1c. black (*Thin striated paper*) .... 75 5·00
a. Opt inverted .... 13·00 35·00
b. Sideways second character .... 35·00 45·00
ba. Opt inverted with sideways second character £800
c. Chalk-surfaced paper .... 1·25 5·00
J267 2c. on 5c. brown (surch as Type **20**) .... 1·00 2·75
J268 6c. on 5c. brown (surch Type **21**) (1943) .... 40 3·50
a. Opt Type **2** and surch as Type **21** both inverted £275 £275
b. Opt Type **2** and surch as Type **21** both double £150
J269 25c. dull purple and scarlet (*Ordinary paper*) (1943) .... 2·75 28·00
J266/J269 *Set of 4* .... 4·50 35·00

(c) Stamp of Pahang optd with T **2** *and surch also*

J270 **15** 6c. on 5c. brown (surch Type **20**) (1943) 50 75
J271 6c. on 5c. brown (surch Type **21**) (1943) .... 1·00 2·50

(d) Stamps of Perak optd with T **2** *or surch also*

J272 **51** 1c. black (*Thin striated paper*) .... 1·25 1·75
a. Sideways second character £225 £250
J273 2c. on 5c. brown (surch as Type **20**) .... 1·00 50
a. Opt Type **2** and surch Type **20** both inverted .... 25·00 40·00
b. Opt Type **2** inverted .... 25·00 40·00
c. Sideways second character .... 65·00 70·00
J274 2c. on 5c. brown (surch Type **22**) 60 50
a. Surch Type **22** inverted .... 20·00 38·00
b. Opt Type **2** and surch Type **22** both inverted .... 40·00 48·00
c. Sideways second character .... 30·00 42·00
ca. Surch Type **22** inverted £1500
cb. Opt Type **2** with sideways second character and surch Type **22** both inverted £1500
J275 5c. brown 55 65
a. Opt inverted .... 50·00 60·00
b. Sideways second character £550 £425
J276 8c. scarlet (No. 111) .... 1·25 3·25
a. Opt inverted .... 17·00 35·00
b. Sideways second character .... 50·00 70·00
ba. Opt inverted with sideways second character £750
c. Opt omitted (in pair with normal) £1400
J277 10c. dull purple (No. 112) (1943) .... 75 1·50
a. Thin striated paper .... 75 1·50
J278 30c. dull purple and orange (No. 116a) (1943) .... 5·50 9·50
J279 50c. black/*emerald* (1943) .... 4·50 35·00
J280 $5 green and red/emerald (1943) .... 90·00 £150
J272/J280 *Set of 9* .... 95·00 £170

(e) Stamps of Selangor optd with T **2** *(sideways on T* **46***)*

J281 **46** 1c. black (No. 68) (1943) .... 1·50 5·00
a. Thin striated paper .... 1·25 5·00
J282 3c. green (No. 71a) .... 40 1·50
a. Sideways second character .... 17·00 28·00
J283 12c. bright ultramarine .... 45 2·75
a. Sideways second character £110 £140
J284 15c. ultramarine .... 4·50 3·75
a. Sideways second character .... 50·00 55·00
J285 **48** $1 black and red/*blue* .... 3·00 30·00
a. Opt inverted £250 £250
b. Sideways second character £375 £500
J286 $2 green and scarlet (1943) .... 10·00 55·00
J287 $5 green and red/*emerald* (1943) .... 22·00 85·00
a. Opt inverted £325 £375
J281/J287 *Set of 7* .... 38·00 £160

(f) Stamps of Selangor optd with T **19** *or surch also*

J288 **46** 1c. black (No. 68) (R.) (1943) 50 60
a. Thin striated paper 35 50
J289 2c. on 5c. brown (surch as Type **21**) (R.) (1943) .... 2·00 50
J290 3c. on 5c. brown (surch as Type **21**) (1943) .... 30 5·00
a. 's' in 'cts.' inverted (R. 4/3) .... 35·00 80·00
b. Comma after 'cts' (R. 9/3) .... 35·00 80·00
J291 5c. brown (R.) (1944) .... 2·50 10·00
J292 6c. on 5c. brown (surch Type **21**) (1944) .... 1·25 1·75
J293 6c. on 5c. brown (surch Type **23**) (1944) 50 70
a. '6' inverted (R. 7/8) £1200
b. Full stop between '6' and 'cts' (R. 8/6)
c. Surch and opt double £650
J294 15c. ultramarine .... 4·00 4·00
J295 $1 on 10c. dull purple (surch Type **24**) (18.12.1944) .... 40 1·25
J296 $1.50 on 30c. dull purple and orange (No. 80a) (surch Type **24**) (18.12.1944) .... 40 1·25
J288/J296 *Set of 9* .... 10·50 22·00

The error showing the second character in T **2** sideways occurred on R. 6/3 in the first of four settings only.

The 2c. orange, 3c. and 8c. grey of Perak also exist overprinted with T **2**, but these stamps were not available to the public (*Price for set of 3 £100 unused*).

Examples of No. J275 are known postally used from the Shan States (part of pre-war Burma).

In 1943 the use of Japanese stamps was approved in occupied Malaya.

25 Tapping Rubber

26 Fruit

27 Tin dredger

28 War Memorial, Bukit Bartok, Singapore

29 Fishing village

30 Japanese shrine, Singapore

31 Sago Palms **32** Straits of Johore **33** Malay Mosque, Kuala

(Litho Kolff & Co, Batavia)

1943 (29 Apr–1 Oct). P 12½.

J297	**25**	1c. grey-green (1.10)	1·75	55
J298	**26**	2c. pale emerald (1.6)	1·00	20
J299	**25**	3c. drab (1.10)	1·00	20
J300	**27**	4c. carmine-rose	3·00	20
J301	**28**	8c. dull blue	50	20
J302	**29**	10c. brown-purple (1.10)	1·25	20
J303	**30**	15c. violet (1.10)	1·75	5·00
J304	**31**	30c. olive-green (1.10)	1·50	35
J305	**32**	50c. blue (1.10)	5·00	5·00
J306	**33**	70c. blue (1.10)	32·00	14·00
J297/J306 *Set of* 10			45·00	23·00

The 2c. and 4c. values exist, printed by letterpress, in paler shades either imperforate or rouletted. It is suggested that these may have been available in Singapore at the very end of the Japanese Occupation.

34 Ploughman **35** Rice-Planting

1943 (1 Sept). Savings Campaign. Litho. P 12½.

J307	**34**	8c. violet	9·50	2·75
J308		15c. scarlet	6·50	2·75

(Des Hon Chin. Litho)

1944 (15 Feb). 'Re-birth' of Malaya. P 12½.

J309	**35**	8c. rose-red	17·00	3·25
J310		15c. magenta	4·00	3·25

大日本 マライ郵便 50セント **(36)**

大日本 マライ郵便 1ドル **(37)**

大日本 マライ郵便 1½ドル **(38)**

1944 (16 Dec). Stamps intended for use on Red Cross letters. Surch with Types **36/38** in red.

(a) On Straits Settlements

J311	**58**	50c. on 50c. black/*emerald*	10·00	24·00
J312		$1 on $1 black and red/*blue*	22·00	35·00
J313		$1.50 on $2 green and scarlet	48·00	70·00

(b) On Johore

J314	**34**	50c. on 50c. dull purple and red (No. 119a)	9·50	20·00
J315	**35**	$1.50 on $2 green and carmine (No. 121a)	4·25	12·00

(c) On Selangor

J316	**48**	$1 on $1 black and red/*blue*	3·50	14·00
J317		$1.50 on $2 green and scarlet	12·00	20·00
J311/J317 *Set of* 7			95·00	£180

Nos. J311/J317 were issued in Singapore but were withdrawn after one day, probably because supplies of Nos. J295/J296 were received and issued on the 18 December.

A similar 6c. surcharge exists on the Straits Settlements 5c. but this was not available to the public (*Price* £700 *unused*).

STAMP BOOKLETS

1942. Nos. SB3/SB4 of Perak and SB2 of Selangor with covers optd with T **1**.

SBJ1	$1 booklet containing 20×5c. (No. J193) in blocks of 10	£4000
SBJ2	$1.30 booklet containing 5c. and 8c. (Nos. J193/J194), each in block of 10	£4000
SBJ3	$1.30 booklet containing 5c. and 8c. (Nos. J211 and J213), each in block of 10	£4000

POSTAGE DUE STAMPS

Postage Due stamps of the Malayan Postal Union overprinted.

1942 (3 Apr). Handstamped as T **1** in black.

JD21	**D 1**	1c. slate-purple	12·00	35·00
		a. Red opt	£225	£250
		b. Brown opt	£200	£225
JD22		3c. green	90·00	£100
		a. Red opt	£500	£500
JD23		4c. green	£100	60·00
		a. Red opt	70·00	60·00
		b. Brown opt	£200	£250
JD24		8c. scarlet	£200	£150
		a. Red opt	£275	£180
		b. Brown opt	£425	£425
JD25		10c. yellow-orange	45·00	65·00
		a. Red opt	£550	£550
		b. Brown opt	£120	£150
JD26		12c. ultramarine	25·00	60·00
		a. Red opt	£500	£475
JD27		50c. black	80·00	£120
		a. Red opt	£850	£900

1942. Optd with T **16**.

JD28	**D 1**	1c. slate-purple	3·50	10·00
JD29		3c. green	26·00	32·00
JD30		4c. green	26·00	11·00
JD31		8c. scarlet	40·00	27·00
JD32		10c. yellow-orange	2·00	17·00
JD33		12c. ultramarine	1·75	50·00
JD28/JD33 *Set of* 6			90·00	£130

The 9c. and 15c. also exist with this overprint, but these were not issued (*Price* £800 *each unused*).

1943–45. Optd with T **2**.

JD34	**D 1**	1c. slate-purple	2·25	6·00
JD35		3c. green	2·25	4·50
		a. Opt omitted (in pair with normal)	£850	
JD36		4c. green	65·00	50·00
JD37		5c. scarlet	1·50	5·00
JD38		9c. yellow-orange	80	8·50
		a. Opt inverted	22·00	28·00
JD39		10c. yellow-orange	2·25	9·00
		a. Opt inverted	90·00	90·00
JD40		12c. ultramarine	2·25	26·00
JD41		15c. ultramarine	2·25	9·00
JD34/JD41 *Set of* 8			70·00	£100

IX. THAI OCCUPATION OF MALAYA

Stamps issued for use in the Malay States of Kedah (renamed Syburi), Kelantan, Perlis and Trengganu, ceded by Japan to Thailand on 19 October 1943. British rule was restored on 9 (Kelantan), 18 (Perlis), 22 (Kedah) and 24 September 1945 (Trengganu). Nos. TM1/TM6 continued to be used for postage until replaced by the overprinted B.M.A. Malaya issues on 10 October 1945.

PRICES FOR STAMPS ON COVER	
Nos. TK1/TK5	*from* × 30
Nos. TM1/TM6	*from* × 25
Nos. TT1/TT35	—

KELANTAN

TK **1**

(Typo Kelantan Ptg Dept, Khota Baru)

1943 (15 Nov). Handstamped with State Arms in violet. No gum. P 11.

TK1	**TK 1**	1c. black	£275	£450
TK2		2c. black	£450	£300
		a. Handstamp omitted	£750	
TK3		4c. black	£450	£450
		a. Handstamp omitted	£950	
TK4		8c. black	£450	£300
		a. Handstamp omitted	£650	
TK5		10c. black	£550	£700
TK1/TK5 *Set of* 5			£2000	£2000

Nos. TK1/TK5 were printed in sheets of 84 (12×7) and have sheet watermarks in the form of 'STANDARD' in block capitals with curved 'CROWN' above and 'AGENTS' below in double-lined capitals. This watermark occurs four times in the sheet.

Sheets were imperforate at top and left so that stamps exist imperforate at top, left or at top and left.

Genuine examples have a solid star at the top centre of the Arms, as shown in T TK **1**. Examples with a hollow outline star in this position are forgeries.

Similar stamps, but with red handstamps, were for fiscal use.

GENERAL ISSUE

TM **1** War Memorial

(Litho Defence Ministry, Bangkok)

1944 (15 Jan–4 Mar). Thick opaque, or thin semi-transparent paper. Gummed or ungummed. P 12½.

TM1	**TM 1**	1c. yellow (4.3)	30·00	32·00
TM2		2c. red-brown	12·00	20·00
		a. Imperf (pair)	£1000	
		b. Perf 12½×11	20·00	20·00
TM3		3c. green (4.3)	20·00	38·00
		a. Perf 12½×11	30·00	42·00
TM4		4c. purple (4.3)	14·00	28·00
		a. Perf 12½×11	20·00	35·00
TM5		8c. carmine (4.3)	14·00	20·00
		a. Perf 12½×11	20·00	20·00
TM6		15c. blue (4.3)	38·00	60·00
		a. Perf 12½×11	42·00	60·00
TM1/TM6 *Set of* 6			£110	£180

5c. and 10c. stamps in this design were prepared, but never issued.

TRENGGANU

TRENGGANU

(TT **1**)

(Overprinted at Trengganu Survey Office)

1944 (1 Oct). Various stamps optd with Type TT **1**.

(a) On Trengganu without Japanese opt

TT1	**4**	1c. black (No. 26a)		
TT2		30c. dull purple and black (No. 39)		

(b) On Trengganu stamps optd as T **1** *of Japanese Occupation*

TT2*a*	**4**	1c. black (No. J97)	—	£4000
TT3		8c. grey (No. J104)	£1300	£800

(c) On stamps optd with T **16** *of Japanese Occupation*

(i) Pahang

TT4	**15**	12c. bright ultramarine (No. J243)	£900	£250

(ii) Trengganu

TT5	**4**	2c. on 5c. deep reddish purple/*bright yellow* (No. J121)*	£1000	£1000
TT6		8c. on 10c. bright blue (No. J127) (inverted)	£900	£900
TT7		12c. bright ultramarine (No. J128) (inverted)	£950	£950

* This is spelt 'TRENGANU' with one 'G'.

(d) On stamps optd with T **2** *of Japanese Occupation*

(i) Straits Settlements

TT8	**58**	12c. ultramarine (No. J264)	£950	£950
TT9		40c. scarlet and dull purple (No. J265)	£950	£950

(ii) Negri Sembilan

TT9*a*	**6**	25c. dull purple and scarlet (No. J269)	—	£4000

(iii) Pahang

TT10	**15**	6c. on 5c. brown (No. J271)		

(iv) Perak

TT11	**51**	1c. black (No. J272)		
TT12		10c. dull purple (No. J277)		
TT13		30c. dull purple and orange (No. J278)	£1800	£950
TT13*a*		50c. black/*emerald* (No. J279)	—	£4000

(v) Selangor

TT14	**46**	3c. green (J282)	£650	£650
TT15		12c. bright ultramarine (No. J283) (L. to R.)	£250	£140
TT16		12c. bright ultramarine (No. J283) (R. to L.)	£225	£140
		a. Sideways second character	£3750	£3750

(e) On Selangor stamps optd with T **19** *of Japanese Occupation*

TT16*b*	**46**	1c. black (No. J288)	—	£4000
TT17		2c. on 5c. brown (No. J289)	£900	£900
		a. Opt inverted	—	£4000
TT18		3c. on 5c. brown (No. J290)	£900	£900

(f) On pictorials of 1943 (Nos. J297/J306)

TT19	**25**	1c. grey-green	£650	£475
TT20	**26**	2c. pale emerald	£650	£275
TT21	**25**	3c. drab	£375	£180
TT22	**27**	4c. carmine-rose	£600	£275
TT23	**28**	8c. dull blue	£900	£850
TT24	**29**	10c. brown-purple	£2000	£1100
TT25	**30**	15c. violet	£600	£275
TT26	**31**	30c. olive-green	£850	£225
TT27	**32**	50c. blue	£850	£425
TT28	**33**	70c. blue	£2250	£1400

(g) On Savings Campaign stamps (Nos. J307/J308)

TT29	**34**	8c. violet	£1000	£900
TT30		15c. scarlet	£700	£275

(h) On stamps of Japan

TT31	–	3s. green (No. 319)		
TT32	–	5s. claret (No. 396)	£850	£650
TT33	–	25c. brown and chocolate (No. 326)	£600	£180
TT34	–	30c. blue-green (No. 327)	£850	£275

(i) On Trengganu Postage Due stamp optd with T **1** *of Japanese Occupation*

TT35	**D 1**	1c. scarlet (No. JD17)	£5000	£5000

Maldive Islands

PRICES FOR STAMPS ON COVER TO 1945	
Nos. 1/6	*from* × 10
Nos. 7/10	*from* × 50
Nos. 11/20	*from* × 20

BRITISH PROTECTORATE

(Currency. 100 cents = 1 Ceylon rupee)

MALDIVES
(1)

2 Minaret, Juma Mosque, Malé

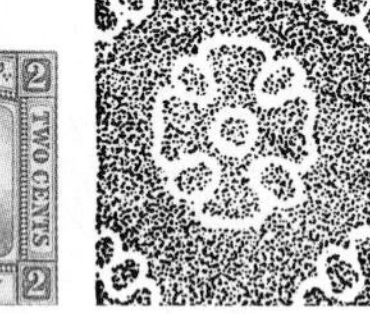
3

1906 (9 Sept). Nos. 277/279, 280a and 283/284 of Ceylon optd with T **1**. Wmk Mult Crown CA. P 14.

1	**44**	2c. red-brown	26·00	50·00
2	**45**	3c. green	42·00	55·00
3		4c. orange and ultramarine	55·00	90·00
4	**46**	5c. dull purple	4·25	6·50
5	**48**	15c. blue	£110	£180
6		25c. bistre	£120	£225
1/6 *Set of 6*			£300	£550

The T **1** opt has been extensively forged.

Supplies of Nos. 1/6 were exhausted by March 1907 and the stamps of CEYLON were used until 1909.

(Recess D.L.R.)

1909 (May). T **2** (18½×22½ *mm*). W **3**. P 14×13½ (2c., 5c.) or 13½×14 (3c., 10c.).

7	**2**	2c. orange-brown	2·25	4·50
		a. Perf 13½×14	2·50	90
8		3c. deep myrtle	75	70
9		5c. purple	75	35
10		10c. carmine	7·50	80
7/10 *Set of 4*			10·00	2·50

These stamps perforated 14×13½ (14×13.7) are from a line machine and those perforated 13½×14 (13.7×13.9) from a comb machine.

4

(Photo Harrison)

1933. T **2** redrawn (reduced to 18×21½ *mm*). W **4**. P 15×14.

A. Wmk upright

11A	**2**	2c. grey	2·75	2·00
12A		3c. red-brown	70	2·75
14A		5c. mauve	55·00	10·00
15A		6c. scarlet	1·50	5·50
16A		10c. green	85	55
17A		15c. black	10·00	32·00
18A		25c. brown	10·00	30·00
19A		50c. purple	11·00	35·00
20A		1r. deep blue	18·00	28·00
11A/20A *Set of 9*			95·00	£130

B. Wmk sideways

11B	**2**	2c. grey	12·00	5·50
12B		3c. red-brown	5·00	1·75
13B		5c. claret	40·00	32·00
15B		6c. scarlet	10·00	11·00
16B		10c. green	3·75	13·00
17B		15c. black	15·00	32·00
18B		25c. brown	11·00	25·00
19B		50c. purple	16·00	28·00
20B		1r. deep blue	16·00	6·50
11B/20B *Set of 9*			£110	£140

(New Currency. 100 larees = 1 rupee)

5 Palm Tree and Dhow

(Recess B.W.)

1950 (24 Dec)–**52**. P 13.

21	**5**	2l. olive-green	5·50	6·50
		a. *Olive-brown* (1952)	14·00	14·00
22		3l. blue	18·00	3·75
23		5l. emerald-green	18·00	3·75
24		6l. red-brown	1·25	2·00
25		10l. scarlet	1·25	1·00
26		15l. orange	1·25	1·00
27		25l. purple	1·25	4·00
28		50l. violet	1·50	6·00
29		1r. chocolate	14·00	42·00
21/29 *Set of 9*			55·00	65·00

7 Fish

8 Native Products

1952. P 13.

30	**7**	3l. blue	2·25	60
31	**8**	5l. emerald	1·00	2·00

SULTANATE

Sultan Mohamed Farid Didi
20 November 1953–10 November 1968

The Maldive Islands became a republic on 1 January 1953, but reverted to a sultanate on 29 November 1953.

9 Malé Harbour

10 Fort and Building

(Recess B.W.)

1956 (1 Feb). P 13½ (T **9**) or 11½×11 (T **10**).

32	**9**	2l. purple	10	10
33		3l. slate	10	10
34		5l. red-brown	10	10
35		6l. blackish violet	10	10
36		10l. emerald	10	10
37		15l. chocolate	10	85
38		25l. rose-red	10	10
39		50l. orange	10	10
40	**10**	1r. bluish green	15	10
41		5r. blue	2·75	30
42		10r. magenta	2·75	1·25
32/42 *Set of 11*			5·50	2·75

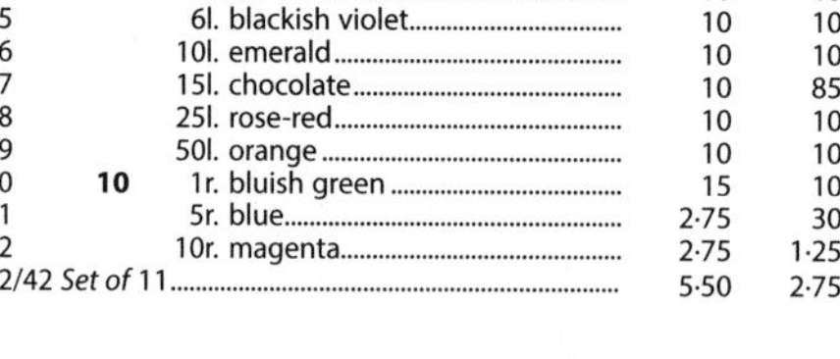

11 Cycling

12 Basketball

(Des C. Bottiau. Recess and typo B.W.)

1960 (20 Aug). Olympic Games. P 11½×11 (T **11**) or 11×11½ (T **12**).

43	**11**	2l. purple and green	15	1·00
44		3l. greenish slate and purple	15	1·00
45		5l. red-brown and ultramarine	15	30
46		10l. emerald-green and brown	15	30
47		15l. sepia and blue	15	30
48	**12**	25l. rose-red and olive	15	30
49		50l. orange and violet	20	45
50		1r. emerald and purple	40	1·25
43/50 *Set of 8*			1·40	4·50

13 Tomb of Sultan

14 Custom House

15 Cowrie Shells

16 Old Royal Palace

17 Road to Junin Mosque, Malé

18 Council House

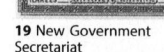

19 New Government Secretariat

20 Prime Minister's Office

21 Old Ruler's Tomb

22 Old Ruler's Tomb (distant view)

23 Maldivian Port

24 'Care of Refugees'

(Recess B.W.)

1960 (15 Oct). Types **13/23**. P 11½×11.

51	**13**	2l. purple	10	10
52	**14**	3l. emerald-green	10	10
53	**15**	5l. orange-brown	3·75	4·00
54	**16**	6l. bright blue	10	10
55	**17**	10l. carmine	10	10
56	**18**	15l. sepia	10	10
57	**19**	25l. deep violet	10	10
58	**20**	50l. slate-grey	10	10
59	**21**	1r. orange	15	10
60	**22**	5r. deep ultramarine	11·00	60
61	**23**	10r. grey-green	15·00	1·25
51/61 *Set of 11*			27·00	6·00

25r, 50r and 100r values in similar designs were also issued, intended mainly for fiscal use (*Price* £150 *for set of* 3, *unused*).

(Recess B.W.)

1960 (15 Oct). World Refugee Year. P 11½×11.

62	**24**	2l. deep violet, orange and green	10	15
63		3l. brown, green and red	10	15
64		5l. deep green, sepia and red	10	10
65		10l. bluish green, reddish violet and red	10	10
66		15l. reddish violet, grey-green and red	10	10
67		25l. blue, red-brown and bronze-green	10	10
68		50l. yellow-olive, rose-red and blue	10	10
69		1r. carmine, slate and violet	15	35
62/69 *Set of 8*			60	1·00

25 Coconuts

26 Map of Malé

(Photo Harrison)

1961 (20 Apr). P 14×14½ (Nos. 70/74) or 14½×14 (others).

70	**25**	2l. yellow-brown and deep green	10	1·25
71		3l. yellow-brown and bright blue	10	1·25
72		5l. yellow-brown and magenta	10	15
73		10l. yellow-brown and red-orange	15	15
74		15l. yellow-brown and black	20	15
75	**26**	25l. multicoloured	55	20
76		50l. multicoloured	55	40
77		1r. multicoloured	60	70
70/77 *Set of 8*			2·00	3·75

27 5c. Stamp of 1906

30 Malaria Eradication Emblem

(Des M. Shamir. Photo Harrison)

1961 (9 Sept). 55th Anniversary of First Maldivian Stamp. T **27** and similar horiz designs. P 14½×14.

78	2l. brown-purple, ultramarine and light green	10	1·25
79	3l. brown-purple, ultramarine and light green	10	1·25
80	5l. brown-purple, ultramarine and light green	10	15
81	6l. brown-purple, ultramarine and light green	10	1·60
82	10l. green, claret and maroon	10	15
83	15l. green, claret and maroon	15	15
84	20l. green, claret and maroon	15	20
85	25l. claret, green and black	20	20
86	50l. claret, green and black	35	80
87	1r. claret, green and black	50	2·00
78/87 *Set of 10*		1·60	7·00
MS87*a* 114×88 mm. No. 87 (block of four). Imperf.		1·50	7·50

Designs: 2 to 6l. T **27**; 10 to 20l. 1906 3c. and posthorn; 25l. to 1r. 1906 2c. and olive sprig.

(Recess B.W.)

1962 (7 Apr). Malaria Eradication. P 13½×13.

88	**30**	2l. chestnut	10	1·50
89		3l. emerald	10	1·50
90		5l. turquoise-blue	10	15
91		10l. red	10	15
92	–	15l. deep purple-brown	15	15
93	–	25l. deep blue	20	20
94	–	50l. deep green	25	55
95	–	1r. purple	55	80
88/95 *Set of* 8			1·40	4·50

Nos. 92/95 are as T **30**, but have English inscriptions at the side.

31 Children of Europe and America

33 Sultan Mohamed Farid Didi

(Des C. Bottiau. Photo Harrison)

1962 (9 Sept). 15th Anniversary of UNICEF T **31** and similar horiz design. Multicoloured. P 14½×14.

96		2l. Type **31**	10	1·50
97		6l. Type **31**	10	1·50
98		10l. Type **31**	10	15
99		15l. Type **31**	10	15
100		25l. Children of Middle East and Far East	15	15
101		50l. As 25l.	20	15
102		1r. As 25l.	25	20
103		5r. As 25l.	1·25	5·00
96/103 *Set of* 8			2·00	8·00

(Photo Harrison)

1962 (29 Nov). Ninth Anniversary of Enthronement of Sultan. P 14×14½.

104	**33**	3l. orange-brown and bluish green	10	1·50
105		5l. orange-brown and indigo	15	20
106		10l. orange-brown and blue	20	20
107		20l. orange-brown and olive-green	30	25
108		50l. orange-brown and deep magenta	35	45
109		1r. orange-brown and slate-lilac	45	65
104/109 *Set of* 6			1·40	3·00

34 Royal Angelfish

(Des R. Hegeman. Photo Enschedé)

1963 (2 Feb). Tropical Fish. T **34** and similar triangular designs. Multicoloured. P 13½.

110		2l. Type **34**	15	1·50
111		3l. Type **34**	15	1·50
112		5l. Type **34**	20	55
113		10l. Moorish Idol	35	55
114		25l. As 10l.	1·00	55
115		50l. Diadem Soldierfish	1·50	70
116		1r. Powder-blue Surgeonfish	1·75	75
117		5r. Racoon Butterflyfish	6·25	12·00
110/117 *Set of* 8			10·00	16·00

39 Fish in Net

40 Handful of Grain

(Photo State Ptg Wks, Vienna)

1963 (21 Mar). Freedom from Hunger. P 12.

118	**39**	2l. brown and deep bluish green	40	3·50
119	**40**	5l. brown and orange-red	75	2·00
120	**39**	7l. brown and turquoise	95	2·00
121	**40**	10l. brown and blue	1·25	2·00
122	**39**	25l. brown and brown-red	3·25	4·00
123	**40**	50l. brown and violet	4·75	8·00
124	**39**	1r. brown and deep magenta	7·00	12·00
118/124 *Set of* 7			16·00	30·00

41 Centenary Emblem

42 Maldivian Scout Badge

(Photo Harrison)

1963 (1 Oct). Centenary of Red Cross. P 14×14½.

125	**41**	2l. red and deep purple	30	2·00
126		15l. red and deep bluish green	1·00	1·00
127		50l. red and deep brown	1·75	1·75
128		1r. red and indigo	2·50	2·00
129		4r. red and deep brown-olive	5·00	21·00
125/129 *Set of* 5			9·50	25·00

(Photo Enschedé)

1964. World Scout Jamboree, Marathon (1963). P 13½.

130	**42**	2l. green and violet	10	65
131		3l. green and bistre-brown	10	65
132		25l. green and blue	15	15
133		1r. green and crimson	55	1·50
130/133 *Set of* 4			80	2·50

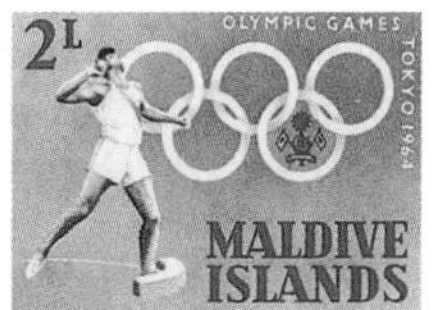

43 Mosque, Malé

44 Putting the Shot

(Recess B.W.)

1964 (10 Aug). 'Maldives Embrace Islam'. W w **12**. P 11½.

134	**43**	2l. purple	10	60
135		3l. emerald-green	10	60
136		10l. carmine	10	10
137		40l. deep dull purple	30	25
138		60l. blue	50	40
139		85l. orange-brown	60	60
134/139 *Set of* 6			1·50	2·25

(Litho Enschedé)

1964 (1 Oct). Olympic Games, Tokyo. T **44** and similar horiz design. W w **12**. P 14×13½.

140		2l. deep maroon and turquoise-blue	10	2·00
141		3l. crimson and chestnut	10	2·00
142		5l. bronze-green and deep green	15	35
143		10l. slate-violet and reddish purple	20	35
144		15l. sepia and yellow-brown	30	35
145		25l. indigo and deep blue	40	35
146		50l. deep olive-green and yellow-olive	60	40
147		1r. deep maroon and olive-grey	1·00	75
140/147 *Set of* 8			2·50	6·00
MS147*a* 126×140 mm. Nos. 145/147. Imperf			1·75	4·50

Designs: 2 to 10l. T **44**; 15l. to 1r. Running.

46 Telecommunications Satellite

(Des M. Shamir. Photo Harrison)

1965 (1 July). International Quiet Sun Years. P 14½.

148	**46**	5l. blue	20	75
149		10l. brown	25	75
150		25l. green	50	75
151		1r. deep magenta	1·00	1·25
148/151 *Set of* 4			1·75	3·25

On 26 July 1965, Maldive Islands became independent and left the Commonwealth, rejoining the organisation on 9 July 1982.

47 Isis (wall carving, Abu Simbel)

48 President Kennedy and Doves

(Des M. and G. Shamir. Litho Harrison)

1965 (1 Sept). Nubian Monuments Preservation. T **47** and similar vert design. W w **12**. P 14½.

152	**47**	2l. bluish green and brown-purple	15	1·25
153	–	3l. lake and deep green	15	1·25
154	**47**	5l. dull green and brown-purple	20	15
155	–	10l. steel-blue and orange	35	15
156	**47**	15l. red-brown and deep violet	60	15
		w. Wmk inverted	£100	
157	–	25l. reddish purple and deep blue	90	15
158	**47**	50l. yellow-green and sepia	1·10	45
159	–	1r. ochre and myrtle-green	1·50	55
152/159 *Set of* 8			4·50	3·50

Design: 3, 10, 25l., 1r. Rameses II on throne (wall carving, Abu Simbel).

(Photo State Ptg Wks, Vienna)

1965 (10 Oct). Second Death Anniversary of President Kennedy. T **48** and similar horiz design. P 12.

160	**48**	2l. black and mauve	10	1·00
161		5l. bistre-brown and mauve	10	10
162		25l. indigo and mauve	20	10
163	–	1r. bright reddish purple, yellow and blue-green	35	25
164	–	2r. bronze-green, yellow and blue-green	50	1·10
160/164 *Set of* 5			1·00	2·25
MS164*a* 150×130 mm. No. 164 in block of four. Imperf			2·25	3·25

Design: 1r., 2r. President Kennedy and hands holding olive-branch.

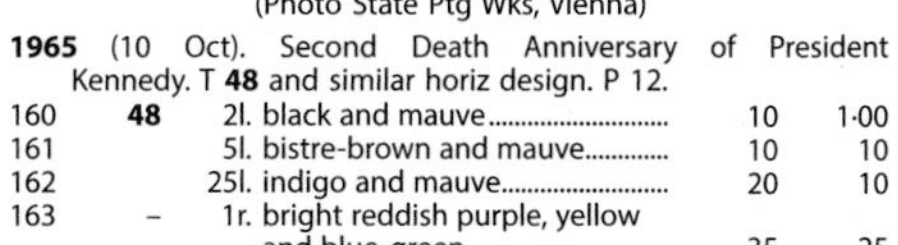

49 'XX' and UN Flag

50 ICY Emblem

(Des O. Adler. Photo State Ptg Wks, Vienna)

1965 (24 Nov). 20th Anniversary of UN. P 12.

165	**49**	3l. turquoise-blue and red-brown	15	70
166		10l. turquoise-blue and violet	40	10
167		1r. turquoise-blue and bronze-green	1·25	35
165/167 *Set of* 3			1·60	1·00

(Des M. and G. Shamir. Photo State Ptg Wks, Vienna)

1965 (20 Dec). International Co-operation Year. P 12.

168	**50**	5l. brown and yellow-bistre	40	20
169		15l. brown and slate-lilac	60	20
170		50l. brown and yellow-olive	1·25	30
171		1r. brown and orange-red	1·75	1·50
172		2r. brown and new blue	2·00	5·00
168/172 *Set of* 5			5·50	6·50
MS173 101×126 mm. Nos. 170/172. Imperf			7·00	10·00

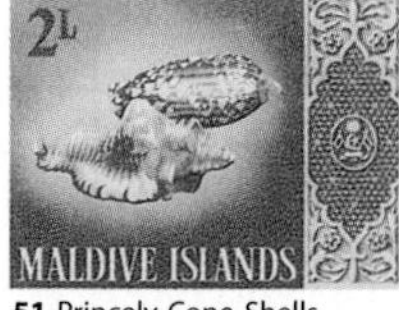

51 Princely Cone Shells

(Des M. and G. Shamir. Photo State Ptg Wks, Vienna)

1966 (1 June). T **51** and similar multicoloured designs. P 12.

174		2l. Type **51**	20	1·75
175		3l. Yellow flowers	20	1·75
176		5l. Reticulate Distorsio and Leopard Cone shells	30	15
177		7l. Camellias	30	15
178		10l. Type **51**	1·00	15
179		15l. Crab Plover and Seagull	3·75	30
180		20l. As 3l.	80	30
181		30l. Type **51**	2·75	35
182		50l. As 15l.	6·00	55
183		1r. Type **51**	4·00	70
184		1r. As 7l.	3·50	70
185		1r.50 As 3l.	3·75	3·75
186		2r. As 7l.	5·00	4·25
187		5r. As 15l.	23·00	17·00
188		10r. As 5l.	23·00	25·00
174/188 *Set of* 15			70·00	50·00

The 3l., 7l., 20l., 1r. (No. 184), 1r.50 and 2r. are diamond-shaped (43½×43½ *mm*); the others are horizontal designs as T **51**.

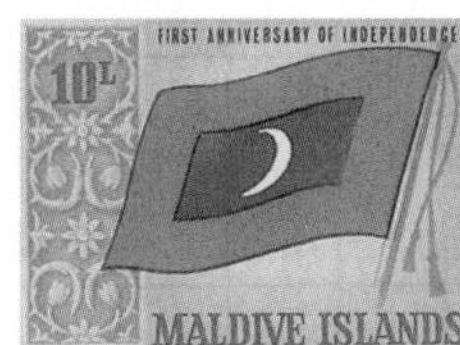

52 Maldivian Flag

(Des M. and G. Shamir. Litho Harrison)

1966 (26 July). First Anniversary of Independence. P 14×14½.

189	**52**	10l. green, red and turquoise	4·00	75
190		1r. green, red, brown orange-yellow	10·00	1·25

53 *Luna 9* on Moon

(Des M. and G. Shamir. Litho Harrison)

1966 (1 Nov). Space Rendezvous and Moon Landing. T **53** and similar horiz designs. W w **12**. P 15×14.

191		10l. light brown, grey-blue and bright blue	40	10
192		25l. green and carmine	60	10
193		50l. orange-brown and green	90	15
194		1r. turquoise-blue and chestnut	1·50	35
195		2r. green and violet	2·00	65
196		5r. rose-pink and deep turquoise-blue	3·00	1·60
191/196 *Set of* 6			7·50	2·50
MS197 108×126 mm. Nos. 194/196. Imperf			3·75	7·00

Designs: 10l., 50l. T **53**; 25l., 1r., 5r. *Gemini 6* and *7* rendezvous in space; 2r. Gemini spaceship as seen from the other spaceship.

54 UNESCO Emblem, and Owl on Book **55** Sir Winston Churchill and Cortège

(Litho Harrison)

1966 (15 Nov). 20th Anniversary of UNESCO T **54** and similar vert designs. W w **12**. Multicoloured. P 15×14.

198	1l. Type **54**	40	2·50
199	3l. UNESCO emblem, and globe and microscope	40	2·50
200	5l. UNESCO emblem, and mask, violin and palette	80	50
201	50l. Type **54**	8·00	75
202	1r. Design as 3l.	9·00	1·00
203	5r. Design as 5l.	26·00	28·00
198/203 *Set of 6*		40·00	32·00

(Des M. and G. Shamir. Litho Harrison)

1967 (1 Jan). Churchill Commemoration. T **55** and similar horiz design. Flag in red and blue. P 14½×13½.

204	**55**	2l. olive-brown	40	3·50
205	–	10l. turquoise-blue	3·25	60
206	**55**	15l. green	4·00	60
207	–	25l. violet	6·00	70
208	–	1r. brown	16·00	1·50
209	**55**	2r.50 crimson	26·00	23·00
204/209 *Set of 6*			50·00	27·00

Design: 10l., 25l.,1r. Churchill and catafalque.

IMPERFORATE STAMPS. From No. 210 onwards some sets and perforated miniature sheets exist imperforate from limited printings.

56 Footballers and Jules Rimet Cup

(Des M. and G. Shamir. Photo Govt Printer, Israel)

1967 (22 Mar). England's Victory in World Cup Football Championship. T **56** and similar horiz designs. Multicoloured. P 14×13½.

210	2l. Type **56**	30	2·00
211	3l. Player in red shirt kicking ball	30	2·00
212	5l. Scoring goal	30	50
213	25l. As 3l.	2·25	50
	a. Emerald (face value and inscr) omitted	£475	
214	50l. Making a tackle	3·00	50
215	1r. Type **56**	4·75	80
216	2r. Emblem on Union Jack	7·00	7·00
210/216 *Set of 7*		16·00	12·00
MS217	100×121 mm. Nos. 214/216. Imperf	16·00	12·00

57 Ornate Butterflyfish

(Des M. and G. Shamir. Photo Govt Printer, Israel)

1967 (1 May). Tropical Fish. T **57** and similar horiz designs. Multicoloured. P 14.

218	2l. Type **57**	15	1·50
219	3l. Black-saddled Pufferfish	20	1·50
220	5l. Blue Boxfish	50	30
221	6l. Picasso Triggerfish	50	40
222	50l. Semicircle Angelfish	4·50	50
223	1r. As 3l.	6·50	1·00
224	2r. As 50l.	10·00	9·50
218/224 *Set of 7*		20·00	13·00

58 Hawker Siddeley HS.748 over Hulule Airport Building

(Des M. and G. Shamir. Photo Govt Printer, Israel)

1967 (26 July). Inauguration of Hulule Airport. T **58** and similar horiz design. P 14×13½.

225	2l. reddish violet and yellow-olive	25	75
226	5l. deep green and lavender	50	10
227	10l. reddish violet and light turquoise-green	65	10
228	15l. deep green and yellow-ochre	1·00	10
229	30l. deep ultramarine and light blue	1·75	10
230	50l. deep brown and magenta	2·50	20
231	5r. deep ultramarine and yellow-orange	6·00	5·50
232	10r. deep brown and blue	8·00	9·00
225/232 *Set of 8*		18·00	14·00

Designs: 2l., 10l., 30l., 5r., T **58**; 5l., 15l., 50l., 10r. Airport building and Hawker Siddeley HS.748. Higher values were also issued, intended mainly for fiscal use.

International Tourist Year 1967

59 'Man and Music' Pavilion (**60**)

(Des M. and G. Shamir. Photo Govt Printer, Israel)

1967 (1 Sept). World Fair Montréal. T **59** and similar horiz design. Multicoloured. P 14×13½.

233	2l. Type **59**	10	1·00
234	5l. 'Man and His Community' Pavilion	10	10
235	10l. Type **59**	15	10
236	50l. As 5l.	60	30
237	1r. Type **59**	1·00	50
238	2r. As 5l.	2·00	2·25
233/238 *Set of 6*		3·50	3·75
MS239	102×137 mm. Nos. 237/238. Imperf	2·50	4·75

1967 (1 Dec). International Tourist Year. Nos. 225/232 optd as T **60** (in one or three lines), in gold.

240	2l. reddish violet and yellow-olive	20	1·25
241	5l. deep green and lavender	40	25
242	10l. reddish violet and light turquoise-green	55	25
243	15l. deep green and yellow-ochre	60	25
244	30l. deep ultramarine and light blue	80	30
245	50l. deep brown and magenta	1·00	35
246	5r. deep ultramarine and yellow-orange	4·50	5·50
247	10r. deep brown and blue	5·50	8·00
240/247 *Set of 8*		12·00	14·50

61 Cub signalling and Lord Baden-Powell **62** French Satellite *A 1*

(Litho Harrison)

1968 (1 Jan). Maldivian Scouts and Cubs. T **61** and similar vert design. P 14×14½.

248	**61**	2l. brown, green and yellow	10	1·25
249	–	3l. carmine, bright blue and light blue	10	1·25
250	**61**	25l. bluish violet, lake and orange-red	1·50	40
251	–	1r. blackish green, chestnut and apple-green	3·00	1·60
248/251 *Set of 4*			4·00	4·00

Design: 3l., 1r. Scouts and Lord Baden-Powell.

(Des M. and G. Shamir. Photo Govt Printer, Israel)

1968 (27 Jan). Space Martyrs. Triangular designs as T **62**. P 14.

252	2l. magenta and ultramarine	20	1·00
253	3l. violet and yellow-brown	20	1·00
254	7l. olive-brown and lake	50	1·00
255	10l. deep blue, pale drab and black	55	20
256	25l. bright emerald and reddish violet	1·25	20
257	50l. blue and orange-brown	1·60	30
258	1r. purple-brown and deep bluish green	2·25	50
259	2r. deep brown, pale blue and black	2·75	2·50
260	5r. magenta, light drab and black	3·50	4·00
252/260 *Set of 9*		11·50	9·50
MS261	110×155 mm. Nos. 258/259. Imperf	7·00	7·50

Designs: 2l., 50l. T **62**; 3l., 25l. *Luna 10*; 7l.,1r. Orbiter and Mariner; 10l., 2r. Astronauts White, Grissom and Chaffee; 5r. Cosmonaut V. M. Komarov.

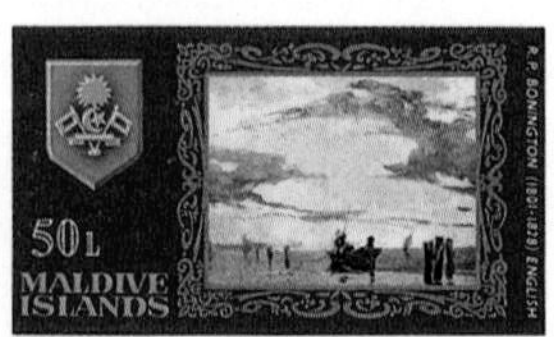

63 Putting the Shot **64** *Adriatic Seascape* (Bonington)

(Des M. Shamir. Litho Harrison)

1968 (1 Feb). Olympic Games, Mexico (1st issue). T **63** and similar vert design. Multicoloured. P 14½.

262	2l. Type **63**	10	1·00
263	6l. Throwing the discus	25	1·00
264	10l. Type **63**	40	15
265	15l. As 6l.	55	15
266	1r. Type **63**	1·00	35
267	2r.50 As 6l.	2·25	2·75
262/267 *Set of 6*		4·00	4·75

See also Nos. 294/297.

(Des M. Shamir. Litho Govt Printer, Israel)

1968 (1 Apr). Paintings. T **64** and similar horiz designs. Multicoloured. P 14.

268	50l. Type **64**	2·25	30
269	1r. *Ulysses deriding Polyphemus* (Turner)	2·75	45
270	2r. *Sailing Boat at Argenteuil* (Monet)	3·50	2·75
271	5r. *Fishing Boats at Les Saintes-Maries* (Van Gogh)	6·00	7·00
268/271 *Set of 4*		13·00	9·50

65 LZ-130 *Graf Zeppelin II* and Montgolfier's Balloon

(Des M. Shamir. Photo Govt Printer, Israel)

1968 (1 June). Development of Civil Aviation. T **65** and similar horiz designs. P 14×13½.

272	2l. orange-brown, yellow-green and ultramarine	20	1·25
273	3l. turquoise-blue, violet and orange-brown	20	1·25
274	5l. slate-green, crimson and turquoise-blue	20	20
275	7l. bright blue, purple and red-orange	4·00	1·75
276	10l. brown, turquoise-blue and bright purple	45	20
277	50l. crimson, slate-green and yellow-olive	1·50	30
278	1r. emerald, blue and vermilion	3·25	60
279	2r. maroon, bistre and bright blue	22·00	12·00
272/279 *Set of 8*		28·00	16·00

Designs: 3l., 10l. T **65**; 3l., 1r. Boeing 707-420 and Douglas DC-3; 5l., 50l. Wright Type A and Lilienthal's glider; 7l., 2r. Projected Boeing 733 and Concorde.

International Boy Scout Jamboree, Farragut Park, Idaho, U.S.A. August 1-9, 1967

66 WHO Building, Geneva (**67**)

(Litho Harrison)

1968 (15 July). 20th Anniversary of World Health Organisation. P 14½×13½.

280	**66**	10l. violet, turquoise-blue and light greenish blue	1·50	30
281		25l. bronze-green, yellow-brown and orange-yellow	2·00	30
282		1r. deep brown, emerald and bright green	4·50	1·00
283		2r. bluish violet, magenta and mauve	6·50	8·00
280/283 *Set of 4*			13·00	8·75

1968 (1 Aug). First Anniversary of Scout Jamboree, Idaho. Nos. 248/251 optd with T **67**.

284	2l. brown, green and yellow	10	1·00
285	3l. carmine, bright blue and light blue	10	1·00
286	25l. bluish violet, lake and orange-red	1·50	55
287	1r. blackish green, chestnut and apple-green	4·00	2·10
284/287 *Set of 4*		5·00	4·25

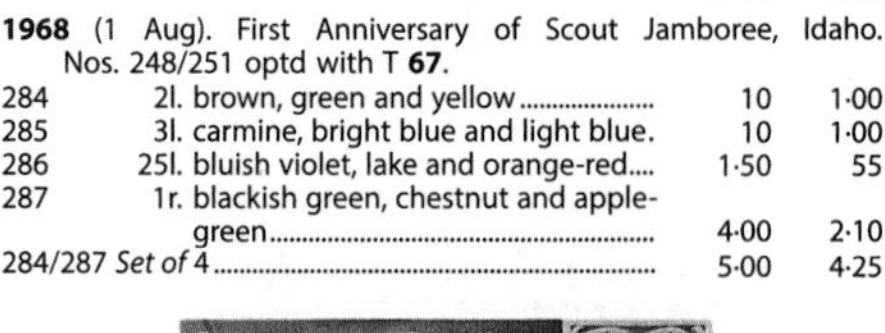

68 Curlew and Redshank

1968 (24 Sept). T **68** and similar horiz designs. Photo. Multicoloured. P 14×13½.

288	2l. Type **68**	50	1·25
289	10l. Pacific Grinning Tun and Papal Mitre shells	1·25	20
290	25l. Oriental Angel Wing and Tapestry Turban shells	1·75	25
291	50l. Type **68**	9·50	1·10
292	1r. As 25l.	4·50	1·10
293	2r. As 10l.	5·50	5·00
288/293 *Set of 6*		21·00	8·00

69 Throwing the Discus

(Des M. Shamir. Photo Govt Printer, Israel)

1968 (12 Oct). Olympic Games, Mexico (2nd issue). T **69** and similar multicoloured designs. P 14.

294	10l. Type **69**	10	10
295	50l. Running	20	20
296	1r. Cycling	6·00	1·25
297	2r. Basketball	8·00	4·00
294/297 *Set of 4*		13·00	5·00

INDEPENDENT REPUBLIC

11 November 1968

70 Fishing Dhow

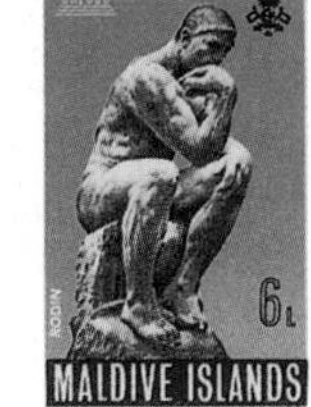

71 *The Thinker* (Rodin)

(Photo Harrison)

1968 (11 Nov). Republic Day. T **70** and similar horiz design. P 14×14½.

298	10l. brown, ultramarine and light yellow-green	1·50	50
299	1r. green, red and bright blue	11·00	2·00

Designs: 10l. T **70**; 1r. National Flag, Crest and map.

(Des M. Shamir. Litho Rosenbaum Brothers, Vienna)

1969 (10 Apr). UNESCO 'Human Rights'. T **71** and similar vert designs, showing sculptures by Rodin. Multicoloured. P 13½.

300	6l. Type **71**	75	60
301	10l. *Hands*	75	20
302	1r.50 *Eve*	3·75	3·75
303	2r.50 *Adam*	4·00	4·00
300/303 *Set of 4*		8·25	7·75
MS304 112×130 mm. Nos. 302/303. Imperf		13·00	13·00

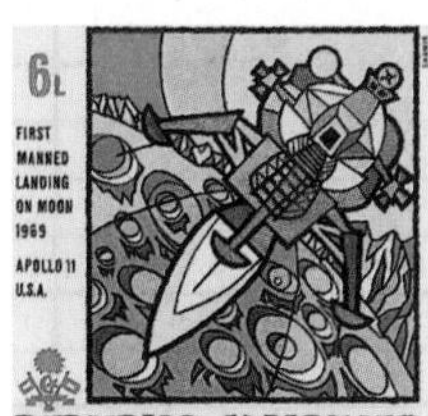

72 Module nearing Moon's Surface

(Des M. Shamir. Litho Govt Printer, Israel)

1969 (25 Sept). First Man on the Moon. T **72** and similar square designs. Multicoloured. P 14.

305	6l. Type **72**	50	35
306	10l. Astronaut with hatchet	50	20
307	1r.50 Astronaut and module	3·25	2·25
308	2r.50 Astronaut using camera	3·50	2·75
305/308 *Set of 4*		7·00	5·00
MS309 101×130 mm. Nos. 305/308. Imperf		6·50	7·50

Gold Medal Winner
Mohamed Gammoudi
5000m. run
Tunisia
REPUBLIC OF MALDIVES

(73)

1969 (1 Dec). Gold-medal Winners, Olympic Games, Mexico (1968). Nos. 295/296 optd with T **73**, or similar inscr honouring P. Trentin (cycling) of France.

310	50l. multicoloured	60	60
311	1r. multicoloured	1·40	90

74 Racoon Butterflyfish

(Des M. Shamir. Litho)

1970 (1 Jan). Tropical Fish. T **74** and similar diamond-shaped designs. Multicoloured. P 10½.

312	2l. Type **74**	40	1·25
313	5l. Clown Triggerfish	65	60
314	25l. Broad-barred Lionfish	1·25	60
315	50l. Long-nosed Butterflyfish	1·50	1·00
316	1r. Emperor Angelfish	1·75	1·25
317	2r. Royal Angelfish	2·25	7·50
312/317 *Set of 6*		7·00	11·00

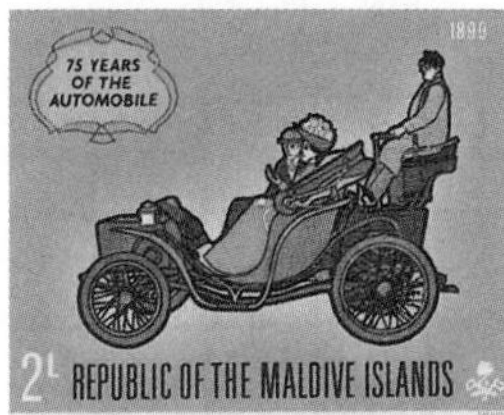

75 Columbia Dauman Victoria, 1899

(Des M. Shamir. Litho)

1970 (1 Feb). 75 Years of the Automobile. T **75** and similar horiz designs. Multicoloured. P 12.

318	2l. Type **75**	30	1·00
319	5l. Duryea Phaeton, 1902	45	50
320	7l. Packard S-24, 1906	60	50
321	10l. Autocar Runabout, 1907	60	50
322	25l. Type **75**	1·40	50
323	50l. As 5l.	1·60	70
324	1r. As 7l.	1·75	1·00
325	2r. As 10l.	1·90	7·00
318/325 *Set of 8*		7·75	10·00
MS326 95×143 mm. Nos. 324/325. P 11½		3·25	8·00

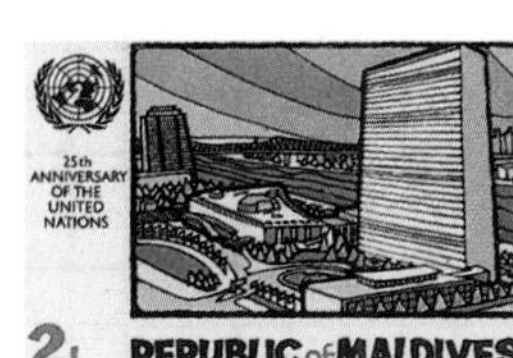

76 UN Headquarters, New York

77 Ship and Light Buoy

(Des M. Shamir. Litho Rosenbaum Brothers, Vienna)

1970 (26 June). 25th Anniversary of United Nations. T **76** and similar horiz designs. Multicoloured. P 13½.

327	2l. Type **76**	10	1·00
328	10l. Surgical operation (WHO)	2·25	40
329	25l. Student, actress and musician (UNESCO)	3·75	50
330	50l. Children at work and play (UNICEF)	2·00	70
331	1r. Fish, corn and farm animals (FAO)	2·00	1·00
332	2r. Miner hewing coal (ILO)	7·50	7·50
327/332 *Set of 6*		16·00	10·00

(Des M. Shamir. Litho)

1970 (26 July). Tenth Anniversary of Inter-governmental Maritime Consultative Organisation. T **77** and similar vert design. Multicoloured. P 13½.

333	50l. Type **77**	1·25	50
334	1r. Ship and lighthouse	7·00	1·50

78 *Guitar-player and Masqueraders* (A. Watteau)

79 Australian Pavilion

(Des M. Shamir. Litho Govt Printer, Israel)

1970 (1 Aug). Famous Paintings showing the Guitar. T **78** and similar vert designs. Multicoloured. P 14.

335	3l. Type **78**	15	80
336	7l. *Spanish Guitarist* (E. Manet)	25	80
337	50l. *Costumed Player* (Watteau)	1·25	40
338	1r. *Mandolins-player* (Roberti)	2·00	55
339	2r.50 *Guitar-player and Lady* (Watteau)	3·50	4·00
340	5r. *Mandolins-player* (Frans Hals)	6·50	7·50
335/340 *Set of 6*		12·00	12·50
MS341 132×80 mm. Nos. 339/340. Roul		9·50	12·00

(Des M. Shamir. Litho Rosenbaum Brothers, Vienna)

1970 (1 Aug). EXPO 70 World Fair, Osaka, Japan. T **79** and similar vert designs. Multicoloured. P 13½.

342	2l. Type **79**	15	1·00
343	3l. West German Pavilion	15	1·00
344	10l. USA Pavilion	65	10
345	25l. British Pavilion	2·00	15
346	50l. Soviet Pavilion	2·50	45
347	1r. Japanese Pavilion	2·75	65
342/347 *Set of 6*		7·25	3·00

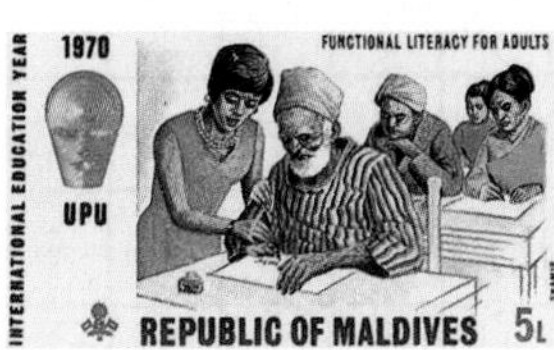

80 Learning the Alphabet

(Des M. Shamir. Litho Govt Printer, Israel)

1970 (7 Sept). International Education Year. T **80** and similar horiz designs. Multicoloured. P 14.

348	5l. Type **80**	50	60
349	10l. Training teachers	60	40
350	25l. Geography lesson	2·75	60
351	50l. School inspector	2·75	80
352	1r. Education by television	3·00	1·00
348/352 *Set of 5*		8·75	3·00

Philympia
London 1970

(81)

82 Footballers

1970 (18 Sep). Philympia 1970 Stamp Exhibition, London. Nos. 306/**MS**309 optd with T **81**, in silver.

353	10l. multicoloured	20	10
354	1r.50 multicoloured	1·25	1·00
355	2r.50 multicoloured	1·25	1·50
353/355 *Set of 3*		2·40	2·25
MS356 101×130 mm. Nos. 305/308 optd. Imperf		6·50	8·50

(Des M. Shamir. Litho Rosenbaum Brothers, Vienna)

1970 (1 Dec). World Cup Football Championship, Mexico. T **82** and similar vert designs, each showing football scenes and outline of the Jules Rimet Trophy. P 13½.

357	3l. multicoloured	20	1·50
358	6l. multicoloured	35	1·00
359	7l. multicoloured	35	60
360	25l. multicoloured	1·25	30
361	1r. multicoloured	2·75	1·00
357/361 *Set of 5*		4·25	4·00

Malta

Early records of the postal services under the British Occupation are fragmentary, but it is known that an Island Postmaster was appointed in 1802. A British Packet Agency was established in 1806 and it later became customary for the same individual to hold the two appointments together. The inland posts continued to be the responsibility of the local administration, but the overseas mails formed part of the British GPO system.

The stamps of Great Britain were used on overseas mails from September 1857. Previously during the period of the Crimean War letters franked with Great Britain stamps from the Crimea were cancelled at Malta with a wavy line obliterator. Such postmarks are known between April 1855 and September 1856.

The British GPO relinquished control of the overseas posts on 31 December 1884 when Great Britain stamps were replaced by those of Malta.

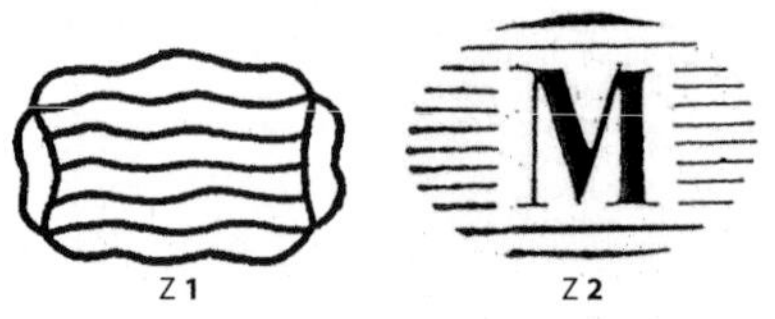

Z 1 Z 2

1855–56. Stamps of GREAT BRITAIN cancelled with wavy lines obliteration, T Z **1**.

Z1 1d. red-brown (1854), Die I, wmk Small Crown, perf 16 ... £1000
Z2 1d. red-brown (1855), Die II, wmk Small Crown, perf 14 ... £1000
a. Very blued paper ...
Z3 1d. red-brown (1855), Die II, wmk Large Crown, perf 16 ... £1000
Z3*a* 1d. red-brown (1855), Die II, wmk Large Crown, perf 14 ... £1000
Z4 2d. blue (1855), wmk Large Crown, perf 14 ...
Plate No. 5 ...
Z5 6d. (1854) embossed ... £4500
Z6 1s. (1847) embossed ... £5000

It is now established that this obliterator was sent to Malta and used on mail in transit emanating from the Crimea.

1857 (18 Aug)–**59**. Stamps of GREAT BRITAIN cancelled 'M', T Z **2**.

Z7 1d. red-brown (1841), imperf ... £2500
Z8 1d. red-brown, Die I, wmk Small Crown, perf 16 ... £160
Z9 1d. red-brown, Die II, wmk Small Crown, perf 16 ... £950
Z10 1d. red-brown, Die II (1855), wmk Small Crown, perf 14 ... £250
Z11 1d. red-brown, Die II (1855), wmk Large Crown, perf 14 ... 80·00
Z11*a* 1d. rose-red (1857) wmk Large Crown, perf 16 ...
Z12 1d. rose-red (1857), wmk Large Crown, perf 14 ... 22·00
Z13 2d. blue (1841), imperf ... £3750
Z14 2d. blue (1854) wmk Small Crown, perf 16 ... £850
Plate No. 4 ...
Z15 2d. blue (1855), wmk Large Crown, perf 14 *From* 65·00
Plate Nos. 5, 6 ...
Z16 2d. blue (1858), wmk Large Crown, perf 16 ... £350
Plate No. 6 ...
Z17 2d. blue (1858) (Plate Nos. 7, 8, 9) ... *From* 45·00
Z18 4d. rose (1857) ... 40·00
a. Thick glazed paper ... £225
Z19 6d. violet (1854), embossed ... £5000
Z20 6d. lilac (1856) ... 42·00
a. Thick paper ... £250
Z21 6d. lilac (1856) (*blued paper*) ... £900
Z22 1s. green (1856) ... £130
a. Thick paper ... £200

Z 3 Z 6

Z 4

Z 5

Z 7

It should be noted that prices given here are for stamps bearing a portion of the 'A25' obliterator. Stamps in fine condition bearing only the datestamp are worth a premium.

1859–84. Stamps of GREAT BRITAIN cancelled 'A25' as in Types Z **3/7**.

Z23 ½d. rose-red (1870–1879) ... *From* 32·00
Plate Nos. 4, 5, 6, 8, 9, 10, 11, 12, 13, 14, 15, 19, 20 ...
Z24 1d. red-brown (1841), *imperf* ... £3250
Z25 1d. red-brown (1854), wmk Small Crown, perf 16 ... £375
Z26 1d. red-brown (1855), wmk Large Crown, perf 14 ... 85·00
Z27 1d. rose-red (1857), wmk Large Crown, perf 14 ... 9·00
Z28 1d. rose-red (1861), Alphabet IV ... £475
Z30 1d. rose-red (1864–1879) ... *From* 19·00
Plate Nos, 71, 72, 73, 74, 76, 78, 79, 80, 81, 82, 83, 84, 85, 86, 87, 88, 89, 90, 91, 92, 93, 94, 95, 96, 97, 98, 99, 100, 101, 102, 103, 104, 105, 106, 107, 108, 109, 110, 111, 112, 113, 114, 115, 116, 117, 118, 119, 120, 121, 122, 123, 124, 125, 127, 129, 130, 131, 132, 133, 134, 135, 136, 137, 138, 139, 140, 141, 142, 143, 144, 145, 146, 147, 148, 149, 150, 151, 152, 153, 154, 155, 156, 157, 158, 159, 160, 161, 162, 163, 164, 165, 166, 167, 168, 169, 170, 171, 172, 173, 174, 175, 176, 177, 178, 179, 180, 181, 182, 183, 184, 185, 186, 187, 188, 189, 190, 191, 192, 193, 194, 195, 196, 197, 198, 199, 200, 201, 202, 203, 204, 205, 206, 207, 208, 209, 210, 211, 212, 213, 214, 215, 216, 217, 218, 219, 220, 221, 222, 223, 224 ...
Z31 1½d. lake-red (1870–1879) (Plate Nos. 1, 3) ... *From* £600
Z32 2d. blue (1841), *imperf* ... £4500
Z33 2d. blue (1855) wmk Large Crown perf 14 ... 80·00
Z34 2d. blue (1858–1869) ... *From* 19·00
Plate Nos. 7, 8, 9, 12, 13, 14, 15 ...
Z35 2½d. rosy mauve (1875) (*blued paper*) ... *From* 80·00
Plate Nos. 1, 2 ...
Z36 2½d. rosy mauve (1875–1876) ... *From* 35·00
Plate Nos. 1, 2, 3 ...
Z37 2½d. rosy mauve (Error of Lettering) ... £3500
Z38 2½d. rosy mauve (1876–1879) ... *From* 17·00
Plate Nos. 3, 4, 5, 6, 7, 8, 9, 10, 11, 12, 13, 14, 15, 16, 17 ...
Z39 2½d. blue (1880–1881) ... *From* 11·00
Plate Nos. 17, 18, 19, 20 ...
Z40 2½d. blue (1881) (Plate Nos. 21, 22, 23) ... *From* 8·00
Z41 3d. carmine-rose (1862) ... £130
Z42 3d. rose (1865) (Plate No. 4) ... 80·00
Z43 3d. rose (1867–1873) ... *From* 32·00
Plate Nos. 4, 5, 6, 7, 8, 9, 10 ...
Z44 3d. rose (1873–1876) ... *From* 38·00
Plate Nos. 11, 12, 14, 15, 16, 17, 18, 19, 20 ...
Z45 3d. rose (1881) (Plate Nos. 20, 21) ... *From* £1000
Z46 3d. on 3d. lilac (1883) ... £550
Z47 4d. rose (or rose-carmine) (1857) ... 40·00
a. Thick glazed paper ... £150
Z48 4d. red (1862) (Plate Nos. 3, 4) ... *From* 35·00
Z49 4d. vermilion (1865–1873) ... *From* 18·00
Plate Nos. 7, 8, 9, 10, 11, 12, 13, 14 ...
Z50 4d. vermilion (1876) (Plate No. 15) ... £225
Z51 4d. sage-green (1877) (Plate Nos. 15, 16) ... *From* £110
Z52 4d. grey-brown (1880) wmk Large Garter ... £180
Plate No. 17 ...
Z53 4d. grey-brown (1880) wmk Crown ... *From* 55·00
Plate Nos. 17, 18 ...
Z54 6d. violet (1854), embossed ... £3750
Z55 6d. lilac (1856) ... 48·00
a. Thick paper ...
Z56 6d. lilac (1862) (Plate Nos. 3, 4) ... *From* 40·00
Z57 6d. lilac (1865–1867) (Plate Nos. 5, 6) ... *From* 30·00
Z58 6d. lilac (1865–1867) (Wmk error) ... £1300
Z59 6d. lilac (1867) (Plate No. 6) ... 38·00
Z60 6d. violet (1867–1870) (Plate Nos. 6, 8, 9) ... *From* 26·00
Z61 6d. buff (1872–1873) (Plate Nos. 11, 12) ... *From* £100
Z62 6d. chestnut (1872) (Plate No. 11) ... 35·00
Z63 6d. grey (1873) (Plate No. 12) ... 75·00
Z64 6d. grey (1873–1880) ... *From* 35·00
Plate Nos. 13, 14, 15, 16, 17 ...
Z65 6d. grey (1881–1882) (Plate Nos. 17, 18) ... *From* 80·00
Z66 6d. on 6d. lilac (1883) ... £150
Z67 8d. orange (1876) ... £475
Z68 9d. straw (1862) ... £700
Z69 9d. bistre (1862) ... £650
Z70 9d. straw (1865) ... £650
Z71 9d. straw (1867) ... £800
Z72 10d. red-brown (1867) ... £130
Z73 1s. (1847), embossed ... £4000
Z74 1s. green (1856) ... 80·00
Z75 1s. green (1856) (*thick paper*) ... £275
Z76 1s. green (1862) ... 70·00
Z77 1s. green ('K' *variety*) ... £2250
Z78 1s. green (1865) (Plate No. 4) ... 48·00
Z79 1s. green (1867–1873) (Plate Nos. 4, 5, 6, 7) *From* 32·00
Z80 1s. green (1873–1877) ... *From* 45·00
Plate Nos. 8, 9, 10, 11, 12, 13 ...
Z81 1s. orange-brown (1880) (Plate No. 13) ... £300
Z82 1s. orange-brown (1881) ... *From* 90·00
Plate Nos. 13, 14 ...
Z83 2s. blue (*shades*) (1867) ... *From* £160
Z84 2s. brown (1880) ... £3250
Z85 5s. rose (1867–1874) (Plate Nos. 1, 2) ... *From* £425
Z86 5s. rose (1882) (Plate No. 4), *blued paper* ... £2500
Z87 5s. rose (1882) (Plate No. 4), *white paper* ... £1800
Z88 10s. grey-green (1878) ... £3500

1880.

Z89 ½d. deep green ... 16·00
Z90 ½d. pale green ... 16·00
Z91 1d. Venetian red ... 16·00
Z92 1½d. Venetian red ... £500
Z93 2d. pale rose ... 40·00
Z94 2d. deep rose ... 42·00
Z95 5d. indigo ... 75·00

1881.

Z96 1d. lilac (*14 dots*) ... 35·00
Z97 1d. lilac (*16 dots*) ... 9·00

1883–84.

Z98 ½d. slate-blue ... 20·00
Z99 1½d. lilac ...
Z100 2d. lilac ... £110
Z101 2½d. lilac ... 13·00
Z102 3d. lilac ...
Z103 4d. dull green ... £180
Z104 5d. dull green ... £150
Z105 6d. dull green ... £400
Z106 9d. dull green ...
Z107 1s. dull green ... £400
Z108 5s. rose (*blued paper*) ... £2000
Z109 5s. rose (*white paper*) ... £1100

POSTAL FISCALS

Z109*a* 1d. reddish lilac (Type F **8**) (1867) wmk Anchor ...
Z110 1d. purple (Type F **12**) (1871) wmk Anchor ... £850
Z111 1d. purple (Type F **12**) (1881) wmk Orb ... £650

PRICES FOR STAMPS ON COVER TO 1945

Nos. 1/3	*from* × 5
Nos. 4/17	*from* × 6
Nos. 18/19	*from* × 12
Nos. 20/29	*from* × 6
No. 30	—
Nos. 31/33	*from* × 4
Nos. 34/37	*from* × 10
Nos. 38/88	*from* × 4
Nos. 92/93	*from* × 5
Nos. 97/103	*from* × 3
Nos. 104/105	—
Nos. 106/120	*from* × 3
No. 121	—
Nos. 122/138	*from* × 3
Nos. 139/140	—
Nos. 141/172	*from* × 4
Nos. 173/209	*from* × 3
Nos. 210/231	*from* × 2
Nos. D1/D10	*from* × 30
Nos. D11/D20	*from* × 15

CROWN COLONY

PRINTERS. Nos. 1/156. Printed by De La Rue; typographed *except where otherwise stated.*

1

Type **1**

The first Government local post was established on 10 June 1853 and, as an experiment, mail was carried free of charge. During 1859 the Council of Government decided that a rate of ½d. per ½ ounce should be charged for this service and stamps in T **1** were ordered for this purpose. Both the new rate and the stamps were introduced on 1 December 1860. Until 1 January 1885 the ½d stamps were intended for the local service only; mail for abroad being handled by the British Post Office on Malta, using GB stamps.

Specialists now recognise 29 printings in shades of yellow and one in green during the period to 1884. These printings can be linked to the changes in watermark and perforation as follows:

Ptg 1—Blued paper without wmk. P 14.
Ptgs 2 and 3—White paper without wmk. P 14.
Ptgs 4 to 9, 11, 13 to 19, 22 to 24—Crown CC wmk. P 14.
Ptg 10—Crown CC wmk. P 12½ (rough).
Ptg 12—Crown CC wmk. P 12½ (clean-cut).
Ptgs 20 and 21—Crown CC wmk. P 14×12½.
Ptgs 25 to 28, 30—Crown CA wmk. P 14.
Ptg 29—In green (No. 20).

PRICES. The prices quoted for Nos. 1/19 are for examples in very fine condition, with fresh colour. Unused examples should have original gum, used examples should have neat clear cancels. The many surviving stamps which do not meet these criteria are usually worth only a fraction of the prices quoted, with stamps of poor colour being virtually worthless.

(Des E. Fuchs)

1860 (1 Dec)–**63**. No wmk. P 14.

(a) Blued paper

1 ½d. buff (1.12.60) ... £1300 £650

(b) Thin, hard white paper

2 ½d. brown-orange (11.61) ... £1300 £500
3 ½d. buff (1.63) ... £850 £400
a. Pale buff ... £850 £400

No. 1 is printed in fugitive ink. It is known imperforate but was not issued in that state (*Price* £12000 *unused*).

The printing on No. 2 gives a very blurred and muddy impression; on Nos. 3/3*a* the impression is clear.

Specks of carmine can often be detected with a magnifying glass on Nos. 2/3*a*, and also on No. 4. Examples also exist on which parts of the design are in pure rose, due to defective mixing of the ink.

1863–81. Wmk Crown CC.

		(a) P 14		
4		½d. buff (6.63) (*shades*)	£120	75·00
		w. Wmk inverted	£500	£450
		x. Wmk reversed	£1700	
5		½d. bright orange (11.64)	£900	£250
		w. Wmk inverted	£1700	£1200
6		½d. orange-brown (4.67)	£425	£110
7		½d. dull orange (4.70)	£300	90·00
		w. Wmk inverted	†	£700
		x. Wmk reversed	£2000	
8		½d. orange-buff (5.72)	£190	80·00
9		½d. golden yellow (aniline) (10.74)	£350	£400
10		½d. yellow-buff (9.75) (*shades*)	85·00	60·00
11		½d. pale buff (3.77)	£190	75·00
		w. Wmk inverted	£1200	£600
12		½d. bright orange-yellow (4.80)	£275	£120
13		½d. yellow (4.81)	£150	75·00
		w. Wmk inverted	†	£600
		(b) P 12½ rough (No. 14) or clean-cut (No. 15)		
14		½d. buff-brown (11.68)	£160	£110
15		½d. yellow-orange (5.71)	£400	£180
		(c) P 14×12½		
16		½d. yellow-buff (7.78)	£200	£100
		w. Wmk inverted	†	£1700
17		½d. yellow (2.79)	£275	£110

Examples of No. 4 from the 1863 printing are on thin, surfaced paper; later printings in the same shade were on unsurfaced paper.

The ink used for No. 5 is mineral and, unlike that on No. 9, does not stain the paper.

Some variations of shade on No. 6 may be described as chestnut. The ink of No. 6 is clear and never muddy, although some examples are over-inked. Deeper shades of No. 4, with which examples of No. 6 might be confused, have muddy ink.

Nos. 7/8 and 11 are distinctive shades which should not be confused with variants of No. 10.

It is believed that there are no surviving pairs of the buff-brown imperforate between variety previously listed.

The Royal Collection contains an unused horizontal pair of the yellow-buff perforated 12½×14.

1882 (Mar)–**84.** Wmk Crown CA. P 14.

18		½d. orange-yellow	40·00	35·00
19		½d. red-orange (9.84)	18·00	50·00

2

3

4

5

1885 (1 Jan)–**90.** Wmk Crown CA. P 14.

20	1	½d. green	5·50	50
		w. Wmk inverted	£170	£110
21	2	1d. rose	85·00	26·00
		w. Wmk inverted	£2250	
22		1d. carmine (*shades*) (1890)	13·00	35
		w. Wmk inverted	†	£1400
23	3	2d. grey	13·00	2·50
24	4	2½d. dull blue	65·00	3·00
25		2½d. bright blue	50·00	1·00
26		2½d. ultramarine	50·00	1·00
27	3	4d. brown	11·00	3·00
		a. Imperf (pair)	£5500	£6500
		w. Wmk inverted	£2500	
28		1s. violet	50·00	12·00
29		1s. pale violet (1890)	60·00	21·00
		w. Wmk inverted	£1100	£350
20/28 *Set of 6*			£120	17·00
20s/28s Optd 'SPECIMEN' *Set of 6*			£4750	

Although not valid for postage until 1 January 1885 these stamps were available at the GPO, Valletta from 27 December 1884.

Three unused examples of the ½d. green, No. 20, are known line perforated 12. These originated from proof books, the stamp not being issued for use with this perforation.

The Royal Philatelic Collection includes an example of the 1d. carmine printed on the gummed side.

1886 (1 Jan). Wmk Crown CC. P 14.

30	5	5s. rose	£110	80·00
		s. Optd 'SPECIMEN'	£1000	
		w. Wmk inverted	£160	£130

6 Harbour of Valletta

7 Gozo Fishing Boat

8 Galley of Knights of St John

9 Emblematic figure of Malta

10 Shipwreck of St Paul

(Types **6**/**10** recess)

1899 (4 Feb)–**1901.** P 14.

		(a) Wmk Crown CA (sideways on ¼d.)*		
31	6	¼d. brown (4.1.01)	9·00	2·75
		a. Red-brown	1·50	40
		b. Wmk upright	£3000	
		bx. Wmk upright (reversed)	†	£3000
		w. Wmk Crown to left of CA	2·50	75
		ws. Optd 'SPECIMEN'	80·00	
		x. Wmk sideways reversed	48·00	25·00
		y. Wmk Crown to left of CA and reversed	80·00	32·00
		ys. Optd 'SPECIMEN'	£275	
32	7	4½d. sepia	27·00	16·00
		x. Wmk reversed	£1000	
33	8	5d. vermilion	48·00	19·00
		x. Wmk reversed	£225	£225
		(b) Wmk Crown CC		
34	9	2s.6d. olive-grey	45·00	17·00
		x. Wmk reversed	£1500	
35	10	10s. blue-black	£100	65·00
		x. Wmk reversed	—	£1200
		y. Wmk inverted and reversed	£900	£700
31/35 *Set of 5*			£190	£100
31s/35s Optd 'SPECIMEN' *Set of 5*			£300	

* The normal sideways watermark shows Crown to right of CA, *as seen from the back of the stamp.*

One Penny
(11)

12

1902 (4 July). Nos. 24 and 25 surch locally at Govt Ptg Office with T **11**.

36		1d. on 2½d. dull blue	2·00	2·50
		a. Surch double	£16000	£3750
		b. 'One Pnney' (R. 9/2)	32·00	55·00
		ba. Surch double, with 'One Pnney'	£42000	
		s. Optd 'SPECIMEN'	70·00	
		w. Wmk inverted	—	£2000
37		1d. on 2½d. bright blue	1·50	2·50
		a. 'One Pnney' (R. 9/2)	32·00	55·00

(Des E. Fuchs)

1903 (12 Mar)–**04.** Wmk Crown CA. P 14.

38	12	½d. green	11·00	85
39		1d. blackish brown and red (7.5.03)	15·00	40
40		2d. purple and grey	29·00	6·00
41		2½d. maroon and blue (1903)	32·00	4·50
42		3d. grey and purple (26.3.03)	2·00	50
43		4d. blackish brown and brown (19.5.04)	26·00	19·00
44		1s. grey and violet (6.4.03)	35·00	9·00
38/44 *Set of 7*			£130	35·00
38s/44s Optd 'SPECIMEN' *Set of 7*			£190	

Broken Crown (Lower right pane. R. 7/3)

1904–14. Wmk Mult Crown CA (sideways* on ¼d.). P 14.

45	6	¼d. red-brown (10.10.05)	9·00	2·50
		a. Deep brown (1910)	9·50	10
		w. Wmk Crown to left of CA	29·00	1·50
		x. Wmk reversed	£350	
		y. Wmk Crown to left of CA and reversed	£250	
47	12	½d. green (6.11.04)	5·50	30
		aw. Wmk inverted		
		b. Deep green (1909)	6·00	10
		bw. Wmk inverted		
48		1d. black and red (24.4.05)	26·00	20
		c. Broken Crown	£550	50·00
49		1d. red (2.4.07)	3·50	10
50		2d. purple and grey (22.2.05)	18·00	3·75
51		2d. grey (4.10.11)	6·50	7·00
		c. Broken Crown	£250	£250
52		2½d. maroon and blue (8.10.04)	40·00	60
		c. Broken Crown	£750	70·00
53		2½d. bright blue (15.1.11)	5·50	4·25
		c. Broken Crown	£200	£150
54		4d. black and brown (1.4.06)	11·00	8·50
		c. Broken Crown	£325	
		w. Wmk inverted		
55		4d. black and red/*yellow* (21.11.11)	4·75	5·50
		c. Broken Crown	£180	£200
57	7	4½d. brown (27.2.05)	40·00	8·50
		w. Wmk inverted	£550	£375
58		4½d. orange (6.3.12†)	4·75	4·50
59	8	5d. vermilion (20.2.05)	48·00	8·00
60		5d. pale sage-green (1910)	4·75	4·25
		a. Deep sage-green (1914)	11·00	14·00
		y. Wmk inverted and reversed	†	£1100
61	12	1s. grey and violet (14.12.04)	50·00	2·00
		c. Broken Crown	—	£100
62		1s. black/*green* (15.3.11)	7·50	4·25
		c. Broken Crown	£275	£160
63		5s. green and red/*yellow* (22.3.11)	65·00	75·00
		c. Broken Crown	£1100	
45/63 *Set of 17*			£300	£110
45as, 47bs, 49s, 51s, 53s, 55s, 58s, 60s, 62s/3s Optd 'SPECIMEN' *Set of 10*			£500	

* The normal sideways watermark shows Crown to right of CA, *as seen from the back of the stamp.*

† This is the earliest known date of use.

13

14

15

1914–21. Ordinary paper (¼d. to 2½d., 2s.6d.) or chalk-surfaced paper (others). Wmk Mult Crown CA. P 14.

69	13	¼d. brown (2.1.14)	2·00	10
		a. Deep brown (1919)	3·25	1·75
		x. Wmk reversed	†	£1600
71		½d. green (20.1.14)	3·75	30
		aa. Wmk sideways	†	£11000
		a. Deep green (1919)	7·50	1·50
		aw. Wmk inverted	†	£450
73		1d. carmine-red (15.4.14)	1·50	10
		a. Scarlet (1915)	3·25	40
		w. Wmk inverted	†	£500
		y. Wmk inverted and reversed	†	£1600
75		2d. grey (12.8.14)	15·00	8·50
		aw. Wmk inverted	†	£1400
		b. Deep slate (1919)	15·00	19·00
77		2½d. bright blue (11.3.14)	3·00	65
		w. Wmk inverted	†	£225
78	14	3d. purple/*yellow* (1.5.20)	2·50	22·00
		a. On orange-buff	75·00	50·00
		bs. On yellow, white back (opt. 'SPECIMEN')	£375	
79	6	4d. black (21.8.15)	15·00	7·00
		a. Grey-black (28.10.16)	45·00	10·00
80	13	6d. dull and bright purple (10.3.14)	11·00	21·00
		a. Dull purple and magenta (1918)	16·00	21·00
		w. Wmk inverted		
81	14	1s. black/*green* (*white back*) (2.1.14)	17·00	48·00
		a. On green, green back (1915)	13·00	27·00
		ab. Wmk sideways	†	£2500
		as. Optd 'SPECIMEN'	70·00	
		b. On blue-green, olive back (1918)	19·00	38·00
		c. On emerald surface (1920)	9·00	48·00
		d. On emerald back (1921)	42·00	90·00
86	15	2s. purple and bright blue/*blue* (15.4.14)	50·00	38·00
		a. Break in scroll	£375	
		b. Broken crown and scroll	£400	£400
		c. Nick in top right scroll	£375	£375
		f. Damaged leaf at bottom right	£500	£500
		g. Dull purple and blue/grey-blue (1921)	90·00	65·00
		ga. Break in scroll	£650	
		gb. Broken crown and scroll	£700	
		ge. Break in lines below left scroll	£700	
		gf. Damaged leaf at bottom right	£700	£700
87	9	2s.6d. olive-green (1919)	75·00	80·00
		a. Olive-grey (1920)	80·00	£110
88	15	5s. green and red/*yellow* (21.3.17)	£100	£110
		a. Break in scroll	£550	
		b. Broken crown and scroll	£600	£650
		c. Nick in top right scroll	£600	£650
		e. Break in lines below left scroll	£800	£800
		f. Damaged leaf at bottom right	£750	
69/88 *Set of 12*			£250	£275
69s/88s (*ex* 2s.6d.) Optd 'SPECIMEN' *Set of 11*			£550	

The design of Nos. 79/79*a* differs in various details from that of T **6**.

We have only seen one example of No. 71aa; it is in used condition.

No. 78*bs*, the 3d. purple on yellow on white back, was prepared for use in 1914, and 'SPECIMEN' examples were distributed to UPU members, but the stamp was never issued.

An example of the 2s.6d. olive-grey with bottom margin attached exists with the 'A' omitted from 'CA' in the watermark on the margin.

For illustrations of the varieties on Nos. 86 and 88 see above No. 51*b* of Bermuda.

WAR TAX
(16)

17

18

1917–18. Optd with T **16** by De La Rue.

92	13	½d. deep green (14.12.17*)	2·25	15
		w. Wmk inverted	£650	
		y. Wmk inverted and reversed	£950	
93	12	3d. grey and purple (15.2.18*)	3·50	16·00
92s/93s Optd 'SPECIMEN' *Set of 2*			£150	

* These are the earliest known dates of use.

(T **17** recess)

1919 (6 Mar). Wmk Mult Crown CA. P 14.

96	17	10s. black	£3250	£4750
		s. Optd 'SPECIMEN'	£1000	

Dark flaw on scroll (R. 2/4 1st state)

Lines omitted from scroll (R. 2/4 later state)

1921 (16 Feb)–**22**. Chalk-surfaced paper (6d., 2s.) or ordinary paper (others). Wmk Mult Script CA. P 14.

97 **13** ¼d. brown (12.1.22) 6·00 40·00
98 ½d. green (19.1.22) 6·50 35·00
99 1d. scarlet (24.12.21) 7·00 2·75
w. Wmk inverted £1200 £500
100 **18** 2d. grey 12·00 1·75
101 **13** 2½d. bright blue (15.1.22) 7·00 48·00
102 6d. dull purple and bright purple (19.1.22) 35·00 85·00
sa. Opt 'SPECIMEN' double £750
103 **15** 2s. purple and blue/*blue* (shades) (19.1.22) 70·00 £225
a. Break in scroll £350 £750
b. Broken crown and scroll £375
c. Dark flaw on scroll £3500
d. Lines omitted from scroll £550
e. Break in lines below left scroll £400
f. Damaged leaf at bottom right £400
g. Nick in top right scroll £375
104 **17** 10s. black (19.1.22) £350 £800
97/104 *Set of 8* £450 £1100
97s/104s Optd 'SPECIMEN' *Set of 8* £475

For illustrations of other varieties on No. 103 see above No. 51*b* of Bermuda.

Examples of all values are known showing a forged GPO Malta postmark dated 'MY 10 22'.

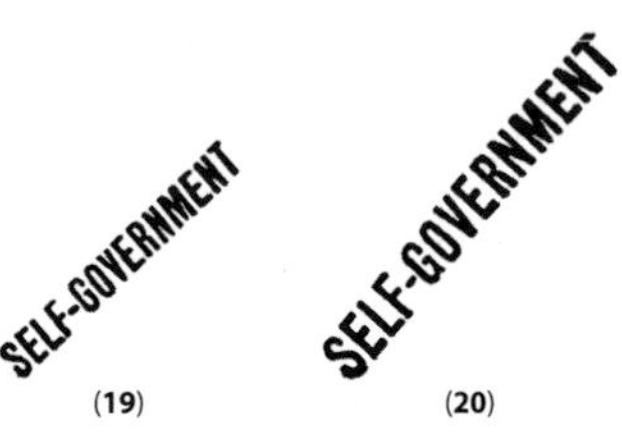

(**19**) (**20**)

1922 (12 Jan–Apr). Optd with Types **19** or **20** (large stamps), at Govt Printing Office, Valletta.

(a) On No. 35. Wmk Crown CC

105 **10** 10s. blue-black (R.) £250 £400
x. Wmk reversed £1800

(b) On Nos. 71, 77, 78a, 80, 81d, 86c, 87a and 88. Wmk Mult Crown CA

106 **13** ½d. green 2·25 4·25
w. Wmk inverted £200
107 2½d. bright blue 19·00 50·00
108 **14** 3d. purple/*orange-buff* 5·00 27·00
109 **13** 6d. dull and bright purple 7·00 42·00
x. Wmk reversed £1500 £1500
110 **14** 1s. black/*emerald* 7·00 30·00
111 **15** 2s. purple and blue/*blue* (R.) £250 £500
a. Break in scroll £1100
b. Broken crown and scroll £1100
c. Nick in top right scroll £1300
e. Break in lines below left scroll £1300
f. Damaged leaf at bottom right £1300
112 **9** 2s.6d. olive-grey 32·00 55·00
a. 'C' of 'CA' missing from wmk £1400
113 **15** 5s. green and red/*yellow* 60·00 £100
a. Break in scroll £375
b. Broken crown and scroll £375
c. Lines omitted from scroll £375
e. Break in lines below left scroll £475
f. Damaged leaf at bottom right £475
106/113 *Set of 8* £350 £700

(c) On Nos. 97/104. Wmk Mult Script CA

114 **13** ¼d. brown 30 1·25
w. Wmk inverted
115 ½d. green (29.4) 5·50 16·00
116 1d. scarlet 1·00 20
117 **18** 2d. grey 6·50 45
118 **13** 2½d. bright blue (15.1) 1·10 2·50
119 6d. dull and bright purple (19.4) 26·00 55·00
120 **15** 2s. purple and blue/*blue* (R.) (25.1) 50·00 95·00
a. Break in scroll £300
b. Broken crown and scroll £300
c. Lines omitted from scroll £425
e. Break in lines below left scroll £375
f. Damaged leaf at bottom right £375 £600
121 **17** 10s. black (R.) (9.3) £140 £250
x. Wmk reversed £3250
114/121 *Set of 8* £200 £375

Examples of all values are known showing a forged GPO Malta postmark dated 'MY 10 22'.

One Farthing
(**21**)

22

23

1922 (15 Apr.). No. 100 surch with T **21**, at Govt Printing Office, Valletta.

122 **18** ¼d. on 2d. grey 85 30
a. Dot to 'i' of 'Farthing' omitted £425

No. 122a occurred on R. 4/4 of the lower left pane during part of the printing only. Small or faint dots are found on other positions.

(Des E. C. Dingli (T **22**) and G. Vella (**23**))

1922 (1 Aug)–**26**. Wmk Mult Script CA (sideways* on T **22**, except No. 140). P 14.

(a) Typo. Chalk-surfaced paper

123 **22** ¼d. brown (22.8.22) 3·00 60
a. Chocolate-brown 7·50 80
w. Wmk Crown to right of CA — £160
124 ½d. green 2·50 15
w. Wmk Crown to right of CA — £160
125 1d. orange and purple 7·50 20
w. Wmk Crown to right of CA — £120
126 1d. bright violet (25.4.24) 4·25 80
127 1½d. brown-red (1.10.23) 5·50 15
128 2d. bistre-brown and turquoise (28.8.22) 3·75 1·25
w. Wmk Crown to right of CA — £190
129 2½d. ultramarine (16.2.26) 6·50 20·00
130 3d. cobalt (28.8.22) 9·50 3·25
a. Bright ultramarine 7·50 3·00
131 3d. black/*yellow* (16.2.26) 5·50 26·00
132 4d. yellow and bright blue (28.8.22) 3·00 6·50
w. Wmk Crown to right of CA £375
133 6d. olive-green and reddish violet 7·50 4·75
134 **23** 1s. indigo and sepia 17·00 4·50
135 2s. brown and blue 14·00 25·00
136 2s.6d. bright magenta and black (28.8.22) 13·00 15·00
137 5s. orange-yellow and bright ultramarine (28.8.22) 21·00 50·00
138 10s. slate-grey and brown (28.8.22) 65·00 £160

(b) Recess

139 **22** £1 black and carmine-red (wmk sideways) (28.8.22) £150 £350
140 £1 black and bright carmine (wmk upright) (14.5.25) £110 £325
123/140 *Set of 17* £250 £550
123s/139s Optd 'SPECIMEN' *Set of 17* £550

* The normal sideways watermark shows Crown to left of CA, *as seen from the back of the stamp.*

Two pence halfpenny
(**24**)

POSTAGE
(**25**)

1925. Surch with T **24**, at Govt Printing Office, Valletta.

141 **22** 2½d. on 3d. cobalt (3.12) 3·00 9·50
142 2½d. on 3d. bright ultramarine (9.12) 1·75 7·50

1926 (1 Apr). Optd with T **25** at Govt Printing Office, Valletta.

143 **22** ¼d. brown 1·75 9·00
144 ½d. green 70 15
w. Wmk Crown to right of CA £170
145 1d. bright violet 1·00 25
146 1½d. brown-red 1·25 60
147 2d. bistre-brown and turquoise 75 2·50
148 2½d. ultramarine 1·25 2·25
149 3d. black/*yellow* 75 1·00
a. Opt inverted £170 £500
150 4d. yellow and bright blue 27·00 45·00
w. Wmk Crown to right of CA £350
151 6d. olive-green and violet 2·75 8·00
152 **23** 1s. indigo and sepia 5·50 26·00
153 2s. brown and blue 55·00 £150
154 2s.6d. bright magenta and black 18·00 50·00
155 5s. orange-yellow and bright ultramarine 10·00 50·00
156 10s. slate-grey and brown 7·00 22·00
143/156 *Set of 14* £110 £325

26

27 Valletta Harbour

28 St Publius

29 Mdina (Notabile)

30 Gozo fishing boat

31 Neptune

32 Neolithic temple, Mnajdra

33 St Paul

(T **26** typo, others recess Waterlow)

1926 (6 Apr)–**27**. Types **26**/**33**. Inscr 'POSTAGE'. Wmk Mult Script CA. P 15×14 (T **26**) or 12½ (others).

157 **26** ¼d. brown 80 15
158 ½d. yellow-green (5.8.26) 60 15
a. Printed on the gummed side £1700
w. Wmk inverted † £1600
159 1d. rose-red (1.4.27) 3·00 2·00
160 1½d. chestnut (7.10.26) 2·00 10
161 2d. greenish grey (1.4.27) 4·50 16·00
162 2½d. blue (1.4.27) 4·00 3·00
162*a* 3d. violet (1.4.27) 4·25 6·50
163 4d. black and red 3·75 18·00
164 4½d. lavender and ochre 3·50 7·50
165 6d. violet and scarlet (5.5.26) 4·25 10·00
166 **27** 1s. black 7·00 13·00
167 **28** 1s.6d. black and green 8·00 23·00
168 **29** 2s. black and purple 8·50 28·00
169 **30** 2s.6d. black and vermilion 21·00 55·00
170 **31** 3s. black and blue 21·00 48·00
171 **32** 5s. black and green (5.5.26) 24·00 75·00
172 **33** 10s. black and carmine (9.2.27) 65·00 £110
157/172 *Set of 17* £160 £350
157s/172s Optd 'SPECIMEN' *Set of 17* £400

AIR MAIL
(**34**)

POSTAGE AND REVENUE
(**35**)

POSTAGE AND REVENUE.
(**36**)

1928 (1 Apr). Air. Optd with T **34**.

173 **26** 6d. violet and scarlet 1·75 2·25

1928 (1 Oct–5 Dec). As Nos. 157/172, optd.

174 **35** ¼d. brown 1·50 10
175 ½d. yellow-green 1·50 10
176 1d. rose-red 1·75 3·25
177 1d. chestnut (5.12.28) 4·50 10
178 1½d. chestnut 3·00 85
179 1½d. rose-red (5.12.28) 4·25 10
180 2d. greenish grey 4·25 9·00
181 2½d. blue 2·00 10
182 3d. violet 2·00 80
183 4d. black and red 2·00 1·75
184 4½d. lavender and ochre 2·25 1·00
185 6d. violet and scarlet 2·25 1·75
186 **36** 1s. black (R.) 5·50 2·50
187 1s.6d. black and green (R.) 15·00 12·00
188 2s. black and purple (R.) 27·00 70·00
189 2s.6d. black and vermilion (R.) 17·00 21·00
190 3s. black and blue (R.) 23·00 24·00
191 5s. black and green (R.) 38·00 70·00
192 10s. black and carmine (R.) 70·00 £100
174/192 *Set of 19* £200 £275
174s/192s Optd 'SPECIMEN' *Set of 19* £425

1930 (20 Oct). As Nos. 157/172, but inscr 'POSTAGE (&) REVENUE'.

193 ¼d. brown 60 10
194 ½d. yellow-green 60 10
195 1d. chestnut 60 10
196 1½d. rose-red 70 10
197 2d. greenish grey 1·25 50
198 2½d. blue 2·00 10
199 3d. violet 1·50 20
200 4d. black and red 1·25 8·00
201 4½d. lavender and ochre 3·25 1·25
202 6d. violet and scarlet 3·00 2·75
203 1s. black 10·00 25·00
204 1s.6d. black and green 8·50 35·00
205 2s. black and purple 15·00 27·00
206 2s.6d. black and vermilion 17·00 60·00
207 3s. black and blue 50·00 60·00
208 5s. black and green 55·00 75·00
209 10s. black and carmine £110 £180
193/209 *Set of 17* £225 £425
193s/209s Perf 'SPECIMEN' *Set of 17* £400

1935 (6 May). Silver Jubilee. As Nos. 91/94 of Antigua, but printed by B.W. P 11×12.

210 ½d. black and green 50 70
a. Extra flagstaff 26·00 50·00
b. Short extra flagstaff 65·00 £150
c. Lightning conductor 40·00 65·00
211 2½d. brown and deep blue 2·50 4·50
a. Extra flagstaff £140 £190
b. Short extra flagstaff £180 £250
c. Lightning conductor £160 £225
212 6d. light blue and olive-green 7·00 14·00
a. Extra flagstaff £180 £275
b. Short extra flagstaff £325 £375
c. Lightning conductor £200 £275
213 1s. slate and purple 19·00 30·00
a. Extra flagstaff £425 £550
b. Short extra flagstaff £450 £600
c. Lightning conductor £400 £550
210/213 *Set of 4* 26·00 45·00
210s/213s Perf 'SPECIMEN' *Set of 4* £180

For illustrations of plate varieties see Omnibus section following Zanzibar.

Sheets from the second printing of the ½d., 6d. and 1s. in November 1935 had the extra flagstaff partially erased from the stamp with a sharp point.

1937 (12 May). Coronation. As Nos. 95/97 of Antigua, but printed by D.L.R. P 14.

214 ½d. green 10 20
215 1½d. scarlet 1·50 65
a. Brown-lake £650 £650
216 2½d. bright blue 1·50 80
214/216 *Set of 3* 2·75 1·50
214s/216s Perf 'SPECIMEN' *Set of 3* £160

37 Grand Harbour, Valletta

38 HMS *St Angelo*

39 Verdala Palace

40 Hypogeum, Hal Saflieni

41 Victoria and Citadel, Gozo

42 De L'Isle Adam entering Mdina

43 St John's Co-Cathedral

44 Ruins at Mnajdra

45 Statue of Manoel de Vilhena

46 Maltese girl wearing faldetta

47 St Publius

48 Mdina Cathedral

49 Statue of Neptune

50 Palace Square, Valletta

51 St Paul

1½d. Broken cross (Right pane R. 5/7)

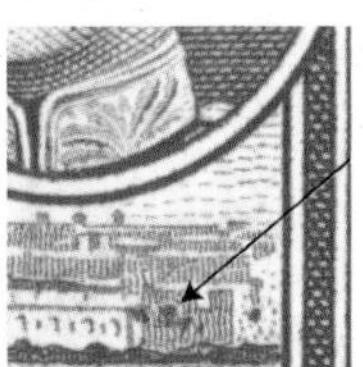
2d. Extra windows (R. 2/7) (corrected in 1945)

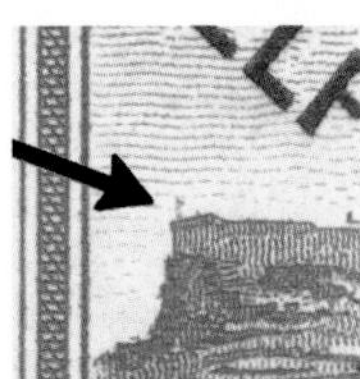
2d. Flag on citadel (R. 5/8)

Damaged value tablet (R. 4/9)

5s. Semaphore flaw (R. 2/7)

(Recess Waterlow)

1938 (17 Feb*)–**43**. Types **37**/**51**. Wmk Mult Script CA (sideways on No. 217). P 12½.

217	**37**	¼d. brown	10	10
218	**38**	½d. green	4·50	30
218*a*		½d. red-brown (8.3.43)	55	30
219	**39**	1d. red-brown	7·00	40
219*a*		1d. green (8.3.43)	60	10
220	**40**	1½d. scarlet	3·75	30
		a. Broken cross	£400	90·00
220*b*		1½d. slate-black (8.3.43)	30	30
		ba. Broken cross	80·00	70·00
221	**41**	2d. slate-black	3·75	2·00
		a. Extra windows	£190	
221*b*		2d. scarlet (8.3.43)	40	30
		ba. Extra windows	85·00	60·00
		bb. Flag on citadel	£130	£100
222	**42**	2½d. greyish blue	9·00	1·25
222*a*		2½d. dull violet (8.3.43)	60	10
223	**43**	3d. dull violet	6·50	80
223*a*		3d. blue (8.3.43)	30	20
224	**44**	4½d. olive-green and yellow-brown	50	30
225	**45**	6d. olive-green and scarlet	3·00	30
226	**46**	1s. black	3·00	30
227	**47**	1s.6d. black and olive-green	8·50	4·00
228	**48**	2s. green and deep blue	5·50	7·50
229	**49**	2s.6d. black and scarlet	9·00	6·00
		a. Damaged value tablet	£400	£250
230	**50**	5s. black and green	5·50	9·00
		a. Semaphore flaw	85·00	£170
231	**51**	10s. black and carmine	19·00	19·00
217/231 *Set of 21*			75·00	45·00
217s/231s Perf 'SPECIMEN' *Set of 21*			£700	

* This is the local date of issue but the stamps were released in London on 15 February.

1946 (3 Dec). Victory. As Nos. 110/111 of Antigua, but inscr 'MALTA' between Maltese Cross and George Cross.

232		1d. green	15	10
		w. Wmk inverted	£1800	
233		3d. blue	75	2·00
232s/233s Perf 'SPECIMEN' *Set of 2*			£120	

SELF-GOVERNMENT

(**52**)

½d. and **5s.** 'NT' joined (R. 4/10)

1½d. 'NT' joined (R. 4/6)

2d. Halation flaw (Pl 2 R. 2/5) (ptg of 8 Jan 1953)

2d. Cracked plate (Pl 2 R. 5/1) (ptg of 8 Jan 1953)

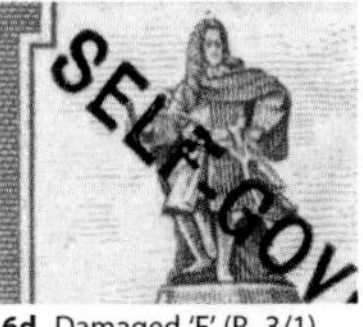
6d. Damaged 'F' (R. 3/1)

'F' repaired

(Optd by Waterlow)

1948 (25 Nov)–**53**. New Constitution. As Nos. 217/231 but optd as T **52**; reading up on ½d. and 5s., down on other values, and smaller on ¼d. value.

234	**37**	¼d. brown	30	20
235	**38**	½d. red-brown	30	10
		a. 'NT' joined	19·00	25·00
236	**39**	1d. green	30	10
236*a*		1d. grey (R.) (8.1.53)	75	10
237	**40**	1½d. blue-black (R.)	1·25	10
		aa. Broken cross	£170	75·00
		a. 'NT' joined (R. 4/6)		
237*b*		1½d. green (8.1.53)	30	10
		ba. Albino opt	†	£18000
238	**41**	2d. scarlet	1·25	10
		a. Extra windows	£200	£120
		b. Flag on citadel	£160	£110
238*c*		2d. yellow-ochre (8.1.53)	30	10
		ca. Halation flaw	£200	£225
		cc. Cracked plate	£190	£200
239	**42**	2½d. dull violet (R.)	80	10
239*a*		2½d. scarlet-vermilion (8.1.53)	75	1·50
240	**43**	3d. blue (R.)	3·25	15
		aa. 'NT' joined (R.4/6)		
240*a*		3d. dull violet (R.) (8.1.53)	50	15
241	**44**	4½d. olive-green and yellow-brown	2·75	1·00
241*a*		4½d. olive-green and deep ultramarine (R.) (8.1.53)	50	90
242	**45**	6d. olive-green and scarlet	3·25	15
		a. Damaged 'F'	£110	70·00
		b. 'F' repaired	95·00	70·00
243	**46**	1s. black	3·75	40
244	**47**	1s.6d. black and olive-green	2·50	50
245	**48**	2s. green and deep blue (R.)	9·50	2·50
246	**49**	2s.6d. black and scarlet	12·00	2·50
		a. Damaged value tablet	£2000	
247	**50**	5s. black and green (R.)	30·00	3·50
		a. 'NT' joined	£300	£150
		b. Semaphore flaw	—	£3750
248	**51**	10s. black and carmine	30·00	27·00
234/248 *Set of 21*			90·00	35·00

1949 (4 Jan). Royal Silver Wedding. As Nos. 112/113 of Antigua, but inscr 'MALTA' between Maltese Cross and George Cross and with £1 ptd in recess.

249		1d. green	50	10
250		£1 indigo	38·00	48·00

1949 (10 Oct). 75th Anniversary of UPU As Nos. 114/117 of Antigua, but inscr 'MALTA' in recess.

251		2½d. violet	30	10
		a. 'A' of 'CA' omitted from wmk	£1200	£1200
252		3d. deep blue	3·00	1·00
		a. 'C' of 'CA' omitted from wmk	£1200	
		b. 'A' of 'CA' omitted from wmk	£1200	
253		6d. carmine-red	60	1·00
254		1s. blue-black	60	2·50
251/254 *Set of 4*			4·00	4·25

53 Queen Elizabeth II when Princess

54 *Our Lady of Mount Carmel* (attrib Palladino)

(T **53**/**4**. Recess B.W.)

1950 (1 Dec). Visit of Princess Elizabeth to Malta. Wmk Mult Script CA. P 12×11½.

255	**53**	1d. green	15	15
256		3d. blue	25	20
257		1s. black	1·00	3·00
255/257 *Set of 3*			1·25	3·00

1951 (12 July). Seventh Centenary of the Scapular. Wmk Mult Script CA. P 12×11½.

258	**54**	1d. green	20	30
259		3d. violet	50	10
260		1s. black	2·10	2·50
258/260 *Set of 3*			2·50	2·50

1953 (3 June). Coronation. As No. 120 of Antigua.

261		1½d. black and deep yellow-green	70	10

55 St John's Co-Cathedral

56 *Immaculate Conception* (Caruana) (altar-piece, Cospicua)

(Recess Waterlow)

1954 (3 May). Royal Visit. Wmk Mult Script CA. P 12½.

262	**55**	3d. violet	45	10

(Photo Harrison)

1954 (8 Sept). Centenary of Dogma of the Immaculate Conception. Wmk Mult Script CA. Chalk-surfaced paper. P 14×14.

263	**56**	1½d. emerald	15	10
264		3d. bright blue	15	10
265		1s. grey-black	35	20
263/265 *Set of 3*			60	35

57 Monument of the Great Siege, 1565

58 Wignacourt aqueduct horse trough

59 Victory Church

60 Second World War Memorial

61 Mosta Church

62 Auberge de Castile

63 The King's Scroll

64 Roosevelt's Scroll

65 Neolithic temples Tarxien

66 Vedette (tower)

67 Mdina gate

68 *Les Gavroches* (statue)

69 Monument of Christ the King

70 Grand Master Cottener's monument

71 Grand Master Perello's monument

72 St Paul

73 Baptism of Christ

(Recess Waterlow (2s.6d. to £1). B.W. (others))

1956 (23 Jan)–**58**. Types **57/73**. Wmk Mult Script CA. P 14×13½ (2s.6d. to £1) or 11½ (others).

266	**57**	¼d. violet	20	10
267	**58**	½d. orange	50	10
268	**59**	1d. black (9.2.56)	3·25	10
269	**60**	1½d. bluish green (9.2.56)	30	10
270	**61**	2d. brown (9.2.56)	3·50	10
		a. Deep brown (26.2.58)	9·00	40
271	**62**	2½d. orange-brown	2·25	30
272	**63**	3d. rose-red (22.3.56)	1·50	10
		w. Wmk inverted	†	£1500
273	**64**	4½d. deep blue	2·50	1·00
274	**65**	6d. indigo (9.2.56)	1·50	10
		w. Wmk inverted	£325	
275	**66**	8d. bistre-brown	4·50	1·00
276	**67**	1s. deep reddish violet	1·75	10
277	**68**	1s.6d. deep turquoise-green	18·00	35
278	**69**	2s. olive-green	13·00	5·00
279	**70**	2s.6d. chestnut (22.3.56)	11·00	2·50
280	**71**	5s. green (11.10.56)	17·00	3·25
281	**72**	10s. carmine-red (19.11.56)	38·00	16·00
282	**73**	£1 yellow-brown (5.1.57)	38·00	35·00
266/282 *Set of 17*			£130	55·00

See also Nos. 314/315.

74 'Defence of Malta'

75 Searchlights over Malta

(Des E. Cremona. Photo Harrison)

1957 (15 Apr). George Cross Commemoration. Cross in silver. Types **74/75** and similar design. Wmk Mult Script CA. P 14½×14 (3d.) or P 14×14½ (others).

283	1½d. deep dull green	20	10
284	3d. vermilion	20	10
285	1s. reddish brown	20	10
283/285 *Set of 3*		55	25

Designs: Vert—1½d. T **74**; 1s. Bombed buildings. Horiz—3d. T **75**.

77 'Design'

(Des E. Cremona. Photo Harrison)

1958 (15 Feb). Technical Education in Malta. T **77** and similar designs. W w **12**. P 14×14½ (3d.) or 14½×14 (others).

286	1½d. black and deep green	25	10
287	3d. black, scarlet and grey	25	10
288	1s. grey, bright purple and black	30	10
286/288 *Set of 3*		70	25

Designs: Vert—3d. 'Construction'. Horiz—1½d. T **77**; 1s. Technical School, Paola.

80 Bombed-out Family

81 Sea Raid on Grand Harbour, Valletta

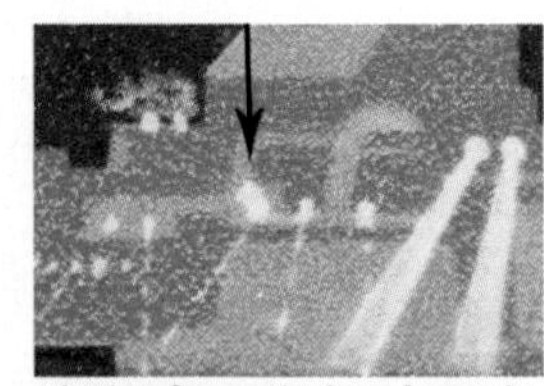

3d. White flaw on third gun from right appearing as larger gunflash (Pl. 1A R. 5/7)

(Des E. Cremona. Photo Harrison)

1958 (15 Apr). George Cross Commemoration. Cross in first colour, outlined in silver. Types **80/81** and similar design. W w **12**. P 14×14½ (3d.) or 14½×14 (others).

289	1½d. blue-green and black	25	10
290	3d. red and black	25	10
	a. 'Gunflash' flaw	4·75	
291	1s. reddish violet and black	35	10
	a. Silver (outline) omitted	£800	
289/291 *Set of 3*		75	25

Designs: Horiz—1½d. T **80**; 1s. Searchlight crew. Vert—3d. T **81**.

83 Air Raid Casualties

84 'For Gallantry'

(Des E. Cremona. Photo Harrison)

1959 (15 Apr). George Cross Commemoration. Types **83/84** and similar design. W w **12**. P 14½×14 (3d.) or 14×14½ (others).

292	1½d. grey-green, black and gold	30	10
293	3d. reddish violet, black and gold	30	10
294	1s. blue-grey, black and gold	1·40	1·75
292/294 *Set of 3*		1·75	1·75

Designs: Vert—1½d. T **83**; 1s. Maltese under bombardment. Horiz—3d. T **84**.

86 Shipwreck of St Paul (after Palombi)

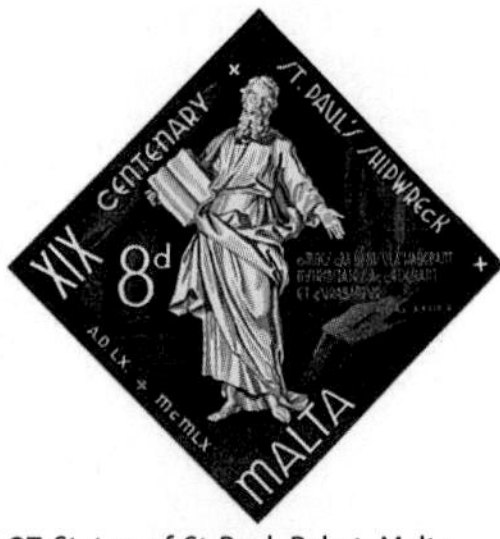

87 Statue of St Paul, Rabat, Malta

8d. Two white flaws in 'PAUL' one giving the 'P' the appearance of 'R' and other a blob over the 'L' (Pl. 1A-1A R.5/2).

(Des E. Cremona. Photo Harrison)

1960 (9 Feb). 19th Centenary of the Shipwreck of St Paul. Types **86/87** and similar designs. W w **12**.

295	1½d. blue, gold and yellow-brown	15	10
	a. Gold (dates and crosses) omitted	75·00	£110
296	3d. bright purple, gold and blue	15	10
	a. Printed on the gummed side		
297	6d. carmine, gold and pale grey	25	10
298	8d. black and gold	40	60
	a. 'RAUL' flaw	7·00	
299	1s. maroon and gold	30	10
300	2s.6d. blue, deep bluish green and gold	1·00	2·75
	a. Gold omitted	£1900	£750
295/300 *Set of 6*		2·00	3·25

Designs: Vert as T **86**—1½d. T **86**; 3d. Consecration of St Publius (first Bishop of Malta) (after Palombi); 6d. Departure of St Paul (after Palombi). Diamond shaped as T **87**—8d. T **87**; 1s. Angel with *Acts of the Apostles*; 2s.6d. St Paul with *Second Epistle to the Corinthians*.

92 Stamp of 1860

(Centre litho; frame recess. Waterlow)

1960 (1 Dec). Stamp Centenary. W w **12**. P 13½.

301	**92**	1½d. buff, pale blue and green	30	10
		a. *Buff, pale blue and myrtle* (white paper)	9·50	3·75
302		3d. buff pale blue and deep carmine	35	10
		a. Blank corner	£650	
303		6d. buff, pale blue and ultramarine	1·00	1·00
301/303 *Set of 3*			1·50	1·10

Examples of the 1½d. apparently with the blue omitted are from sheets with a very weak printing of this colour.

No. 302a shows the right-hand bottom corner of the 1860 stamp blank. It occurs on R. 4/7 from early trial plates and sheets containing the error should have been destroyed, but some were sorted into good stock and issued at a post office.

93 George Cross

(Photo Harrison)

1961 (15 Apr). George Cross Commemoration. T **93** and similar designs showing medal. W w **12**. P 15×14.

304	1½d. black, cream and bistre	30	10
305	3d. olive-brown and greenish blue	30	10
306	1s. olive-green, lilac and deep reddish violet	1·40	2·50
304/306 *Set of 3*		1·75	2·50

96 *Madonna Damascena*

(Photo Harrison)

1962 (7 Sept). Great Siege Commemoration. T **96** and similar vert designs. W w **12** P 13×12.

307	2d. bright blue	10	10
308	3d. red	10	10
309	6d. bronze-green	30	10
310	1s. brown-purple	30	40
307/310 *Set of 4*		70	60

Designs: 2d. T **96**; 3d. Great Siege Monument; 6d. Grand Master La Valette; 1s. Assault on Fort St Elmo.

1963 (4 June). Freedom from Hunger. As No. 146 of Antigua.

311 1s.6d. sepia .... 1·50 2·50

1963 (2 Sept). Red Cross Centenary. As Nos. 147/148 of Antigua.

312 2d. red and black 25 15
313 1s. 6d. red and blue .... 1·50 4·50

1963 (15 Oct)–**64**. As Nos. 268 and 270, but wmk. w **12**.

314 **59** 1d. black 50 30
315 **61** 2d. deep brown (11.7.64*) .... 1·50 4·25

* This is the earliest known date recorded in Malta.

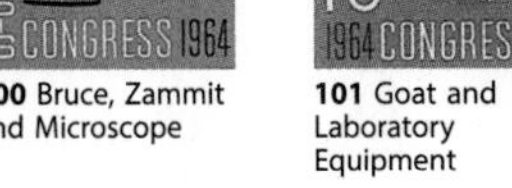

100 Bruce, Zammit and Microscope

101 Goat and Laboratory Equipment

(Des E. Cremona. Photo Harrison)

1964 (14 Apr). Anti-Brucellosis Congress. W w **12**. P 14.

316 **100** 2d. light brown, black and bluish green 10 10
a. Black (microscope, etc) omitted £450
317 **101** 1s.6d. black and maroon .... 1·25 2·00

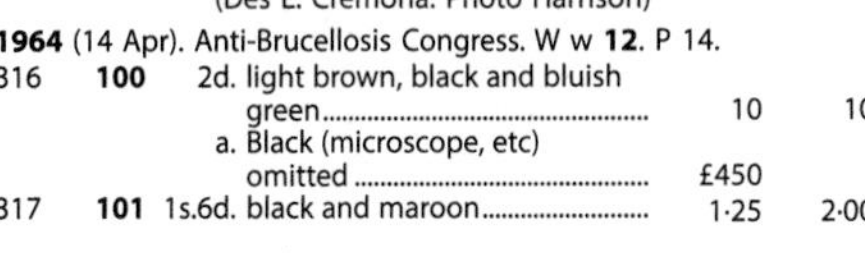

102 *Nicole Cotoner tending Sick Man* (M. Preti)

105 Maltese Cross (Upright)

In this illustration the points of the crosses meet in a vertical line. When the watermark is sideways they meet in a horizontal line.

(Des E. Cremona. Photo Harrison)

1964 (5 Sept). First European Catholic Doctors' Congress, Vienna. T **102** and similar horiz designs. (sideways). W **105**. P 13½×11½.

318 2d. red, black, gold and grey-blue 20 10
319 6d. red, black, gold and bistre 50 15
320 1s.6d. red, black, gold and reddish violet .... 1·10 1·90
318/320 *Set of 3* .... 1·60 1·90

Designs: 2d. T **102**; 6d. St Luke and Hospital; 1s.6d. Sacra Infermeria, Valletta.

INDEPENDENT

106 Dove and British Crown

109 The Nativity

(Des E. Cremona. Photo Harrison)

1964 (21 Sept). Independence. T **106** and similar vert designs. W w **105**. P 14½×13½.

321 2d. olive-brown, red and gold 30 10
a. Gold omitted .... 75·00
322 3d. brown-purple, red and gold 30 10
a. Gold omitted .... 75·00
323 6d. slate, red and gold 60 15
324 1s. blue, red and gold 60 15
325 1s.6d. indigo, red and gold .... 1·25 1·00
326 2s.6d. deep violet-blue, red and gold .... 1·50 3·75
321/326 *Set of 6* .... 4·00 4·75

Designs: 2d, 1s. T **106**; 3d., 1s.6d. Dove and Pope's Tiara; 6d., 2s.6d. Dove and UN emblem.

4d. White flaw on Virgin's head-shawl appearing as earring (Pl. 1B-2B. R. 6/1)

(Des E. Cremona. Photo D.L.R.)

1964 (3 Nov). Christmas. W **105** (sideways). P 13×13½.

327 **109** 2d. bright purple and gold 10 10
328 4d. bright blue and gold 20 15
a. 'Earring' flaw .... 3·00
329 8d. deep bluish green and gold 45 45
327/329 *Set of 3* 65 60

110 Neolithic era **111** Punic era **112** Roman era

113 Proto Christian era **114** Saracenic era **115** Siculo Norman era

116 Knights of Malta **117** Galleys of Knights of St John **117a** Fortifications

118 French occupation **119** British rule

119a Naval arsenal **120** Maltese corps of the British army

121 International Eucharistic congress **122** Self-government

123 Gozo civic council **124** State of Malta

125 Independence **126** HAFMED (Allied forces, Mediterranean)

127 The Maltese Islands (map) **128** Patron saints

(Des E. Cremona. Photo Harrison)

1965 (7 Jan)–**70**. Types **110/128**. W **105**. Chalk-surfaced paper. P 14×14½ (vert) or 14½ (horiz).

330 **110** ½d. multicoloured 10 10
a. '½d.' (white) printed twice† .... 10·00
ab. ditto, once inverted .... † £2250
b. Rose-pink ('MALTA') printed twice .... 10·00
c. White (face value) omitted .... 85·00
331 **111** 1d. multicoloured 10 10
a. Gold (ancient lettering) omitted £150
b. White (Greek lettering and 'PUNIC') omitted £110
c. White ptg double .... 30·00
d. 'PUNIC' omitted £160
332 **112** 1½d. multicoloured 30 10
333 **113** 2d. multicoloured 10 10
a. Gold omitted .... 26·00
b. Imperf (pair) £275
334 **114** 2½d. multicoloured .... 1·00 10
a. Orange omitted* £110
b. Gold ('SARACENIC') omitted .... 55·00
c. Salmon printed twice† £110
335 **115** 3d. multicoloured 10 10
a. Gold (windows) omitted £100
b. 'MALTA' (silver) omitted .... 26·00
c. 'MALTA' (silver) printed twice £400
d. Bright lilac ('SICULO NORMAN') omitted £425
e. Imperf (pair) £300
f. Value omitted (vert pair with normal) £1100
336 **116** 4d. multicoloured .... 1·00 10
a. 'KNIGHTS OF MALTA' (silver) omitted .... 45·00
b. 'MALTA' (silver) omitted £120
c. Black (shield surround) omitted .... 70·00
d. Imperf (pair) £170
e. Gold omitted £150
337 **117** 4½d. multicoloured .... 1·00 75
a. Silver ('MALTA', etc) omitted £1900
337*b* **117a** 5d. multicoloured (1.8.70) 30 20
ba. 'FORTIFICATIONS' (gold) omitted £140
338 **118** 6d. multicoloured 30 10
a. 'MALTA' (silver) omitted .... 45·00
b. Black omitted £110
339 **119** 8d. multicoloured 50 10
a. Gold (centre) omitted .... 42·00
b. Gold (frame) omitted .... 65·00
339*c* **119a** 10d. multicoloured (1.8.70) .... 50 1·50
ca. 'NAVAL ARSENAL' (gold) omitted £325
340 **120** 1s. multicoloured 30 10
a. Gold (centre) omitted £250
b. Gold (framework) omitted .... 48·00
c. Gold (framework) doubled ....
341 **121** 1s.3d. multicoloured .... 2·00 1·40
a. Gold (centre) omitted .... 65·00
b. Gold (framework) omitted £250
c. Imperf (pair) £400
342 **122** 1s.6d. multicoloured 60 20
a. Head (black) omitted £375
b. Gold (centre) omitted .... 55·00
c. Gold (frame) omitted £150
343 **123** 2s. multicoloured 70 10
a. Gold (centre) omitted £170
b. Gold (framework) omitted .... 70·00
344 **124** 2s.6d. multicoloured 70 50
345 **125** 3s. multicoloured .... 1·00 75
a. Gold (framework) omitted .... 45·00
b. Gold ('1964') omitted £200
346 **126** 5s. multicoloured .... 4·00 1·00
a. Gold (HAFMED emblem) omitted £180
b. Gold (framework) omitted £180
347 **127** 10s. multicoloured .... 2·00 5·00
a. Gold (centre) omitted £425
348 **128** £1 multicoloured .... 2·25 5·50
a. Pink omitted .... 32·00
330/348 *Set of 21* .... 16·00 15·00

* The effect of this is to leave the Saracenic pattern as a pink colour.

† On the ½d. the second impression is 6½ mm lower or 3 mm to the left, and on the 2½d. 1 mm lower so that it falls partly across 'MALTA' and '2½d.' Stamps with almost coincidental double impression are common. The ½d. and 1d. had white printing plates. Two silver plates were used on the 4d., one for 'KNIGHTS OF MALTA' and the other for 'MALTA'. Two gold plates were used for the 8d. to 10s., one for the framework and the other for the gold in the central part of the designs.

No. 335f comes from a sheet showing a major shift of the grey-black colour, so that stamps in the top horizontal row are without the face value.

No. 337a comes from a sheet on which the silver printing was so misplaced that it missed the top horizontal row entirely.

The ½d. to 4d., 1s. and 1s.6d. to 5s. values exist with PVA gum as well as gum arabic and the 5d. and 10d. have PVA gum only.

129 *Dante* (Raphael)

(Des E. Cremona. Photo Govt Ptg Works, Rome)

1965 (7 July). 700th Birth Anniversary of Dante. P 14.

349	**129**	2d. indigo	10	10
350		6d. bronze-green	25	10
351		2s. chocolate	1·10	1·50
349/351 *Set of 3*			1·25	1·50

130 Turkish Camp **131** Turkish Fleet

(Des E. Cremona. Photo Harrison)

1965 (1 Sept). 400th Anniversary of Great Siege. Types **130/131** and similar designs. W **105** (sideways). P 13 (6d., 1s.) or 14½×14 (others).

352		2d. olive-green, red and black	25	10
		a. Red (flag) omitted	£425	
353		3d. olive-green, red, black and light drab	25	10
354		6d. multicoloured	35	10
		a. Gold (framework and dates) omitted	£375	
		b. Black (on hulls) omitted	£375	
355		8d. red, gold, indigo and blue	70	90
		a. Gold (flag and dates) omitted	£180	
356		1s. red, gold and deep grey-blue	35	10
357		1s.6d. ochre, red and black	70	30
358		2s.6d. sepia, black, red and yellow-olive	1·10	3·00
352/358 *Set of 7*			3·25	4·00

Designs: Square (as T **130**)—2d. T **130**; 3d. Battle scene; 8d. Arrival of relief force; 1s.6d. 'Allegory of Victory' (from mural by M. Preti); 2s.8d. Victory medal. Vert (as T **131**)—6d. T **131**; 1s. Grand Master J. de La Valette's Arms.

137 The Three Kings **138** Sir Winston Churchill

(Des E. Cremona. Photo Enschedé)

1965 (7 Oct). Christmas. W **105** (sideways). P 11×11½.

359	**137**	1d. slate-purple and red	10	10
360		4d. slate-purple and blue	30	30
361		1s.3d. slate-purple and bright purple	30	30
359/361 *Set of 3*			65	60

(Des E. Cremona. Photo Harrison)

1966 (24 Jan). Churchill Commemoration. T **138** and similar square design. W **105** (sideways). P 14½×14.

362	**138**	2d. black, red and gold	30	10
363	–	3d. bronze-green, yellow-olive and gold	30	10
		a. Gold omitted	£375	
364	**138**	1s. maroon, red and gold	45	10
		a. Gold (shading) omitted	£170	
365	–	1s.6d. chalky blue, violet-blue and gold	65	1·10
362/365 *Set of 4*			1·50	1·25

Design: 3d., 1s.6d. Sir Winston Churchill and George Cross.

140 Grand Master La Valette **145** President Kennedy and Memorial

(Des E. Cremona. Photo State Ptg Works, Vienna)

1966 (28 Mar). 400th Anniversary of Valletta. T **140** and similar square designs. Multicoloured. W **105** (sideways). P 12.

366		2d. Type **140**	10	10
367		3d. Pope Pius V	15	10
		a. Gold omitted	£850	
368		6d. Map of Valletta	20	10
369		1s. Francesco Laparelli (architect)	20	10
370		2s.6d. Girolamo Cassar (architect)	45	60
366/370 *Set of 5*			1·00	80

(Des E. Cremona. Photo Harrison)

1966 (28 May). President Kennedy Commemoration. W **105** (sideways). P 15×14.

371	**145**	3d. olive, gold and black	10	10
		a. Gold inscr omitted	£300	
372		1s.6d. Prussian blue, gold and black	10	10

146 'Trade'

(Des E. Cremona. Photo D.L.R.)

1966 (16 June). Tenth Malta Trade Fair. W **105** (sideways). P 13½.

373	**146**	2d. multicoloured	10	10
		a. Gold omitted	80·00	
374		8d. multicoloured	50	1·10
375		2s.6d. multicoloured	55	1·10
		a. Gold omitted	85·00	
373/375 *Set of 3*			1·00	2·00

147 The Child in the Manger **148** George Cross

(Des E. Cremona. Photo D.L.R.)

1966 (7 Oct). Christmas. W **105**. P 13½.

376	**147**	1d. black, gold, turquoise-blue and slate-purple	10	10
377		4d. black, gold, ultramarine and slate-purple	10	10
378		1s.3d. black, gold, bright purple and slate purple	10	10
		a. Gold omitted	70·00	
376/378 *Set of 3*			25	25

(Des E. Cremona. Photo Harrison)

1967 (1 Mar). 25th Anniversary of George Cross Award to Malta. W **105** (sideways). P 14½×14.

379	**148**	2d. multicoloured	10	10
380		4d. multicoloured	10	10
381		3s. multicoloured	20	40
379/381 *Set of 3*			30	45

149 Crucifixion of St Peter

150 Open Bible and Episcopal Emblems

(Des E. Cremona. Photo Harrison)

1967 (28 June). 1900th Anniversary of Martyrdom of Saints Peter and Paul. Types **149/150** and similar design. W **105** (sideways). P 13½×14½ (8d.) or 14½ (others).

382		2d. chestnut, orange and black	10	10
383		8d. yellow-olive, gold and black	15	10
384		3s. blue, light blue and black	20	20
382/384 *Set of 3*			40	30

Designs: Square as T **149**—2d. T **149**; 3s. Beheading of St Paul. Horiz—8d. T **150**.

152 *St Catherine of Siena* **156** Temple Ruins, Tarxien

(Des E. Cremona. Photo Enschedé)

1967 (1 Aug). 300th Death Anniversary of Melchior Gafà (sculptor). T **152** and similar horiz designs. Multicoloured. W **105** (sideways). P 13½×13.

385		2d. Type **152**	10	10
386		4d. *Thomas of Villanova*	10	10
387		1s.6d. *Baptism of Christ* (detail)	15	10
388		2s.6d. St John the Baptist (from *Baptism of Christ*)	25	20
385/388 *Set of 4*			40	35

(Des E. Cremona. Photo Harrison)

1967 (12 Sept). 15th International Historical Architecture Congress, Valletta. T **156** and similar square designs. Multicoloured. W **105**. P 15×14½.

389		2d. Type **156**	10	10
390		6d. Facade of Palazzo Falzon, Notabile	10	10
391		1s. Parish Church, Birkirkara	10	10
392		3s. Portal, Auberge de Castille	25	25
389/392 *Set of 4*			40	40

160 Angels **161** Crib **162** Angels

(Des E. Cremona. Photo D.L.R.)

1967 (20 Oct). Christmas. W **105** (sideways). P 14.

393	**160**	1d. multicoloured	10	10
		a. Horiz strip of 3. Nos. 393/395	45	25
		b. White stars (red omitted)	£120	
394	**161**	8d. multicoloured	20	10
395	**162**	1s.4d. multicoloured	20	10
393/395 *Set of 3*			45	25

Nos. 393/395 were issued in sheets of 60 of each value (arranged *tête-bêche*), and also in sheets containing the three values *se-tenant*, thus forming a triptych of the Nativity.

163 Queen Elizabeth II and Arms of Malta

(Des E. Cremona. Photo Harrison)

1967 (13 Nov). Royal Visit. T **163** and similar designs. W **105** (sideways on 2d., 3s.). P 14×15 (4d.) or 15×14 (others).

396		2d. multicoloured	10	10
		a. Grey-brown omitted*	£150	
397		4d. black, brown-purple and gold	10	10
398		3s. multicoloured	20	30
396/398 *Set of 3*			35	40

Designs: Vert—4d. Queen in Robes of Order of St Michael and St George. Horiz—2d. T **163**; 3s. Queen and outline of Malta.

* This affects the Queen's face.

166 Human Rights Emblem and People **167**

(Des E. Cremona. Photo Harrison)

1968 (2 May). Human Rights Year. W **105**. P 12½ (6d.) or 14½ (others).

399	**166**	2d. multicoloured	10	10
400	**167**	6d. multicoloured	10	10
401	–	2s. multicoloured	10	15
399/401 *Set of 3*			25	25

The design of the 2s. value is a reverse of T **166**.

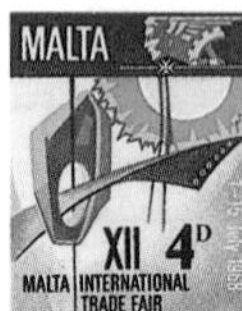

169 Fair 'Products'

(Des E. Cremona. Photo Harrison)

1968 (1 June). Malta International Trade Fair. W **105** (sideways). P 14½×14.

402	**169**	4d. multicoloured	10	10
403		8d. multicoloured	10	10
404		3s. multicoloured	20	15
402/404 *Set of 3*			30	25

170 Arms of the Order of St John and La Valette **171** *La Valette* (A. de Favray)

172 La Valette's Tomb

173 Angels and Scroll bearing Date of Death

(Des E. Cremona. Photo Govt Printer, Israel)

1968 (1 Aug). Fourth Death Centenary of Grand Master La Valette. W **105** (upright, 1s.6d.; sideways, others). P 13×14 (1d., 1s.6d.) or 14×13 (others).

405	**170**	1d. multicoloured	10	10
406	**171**	8d. multicoloured	15	10
407	**172**	1s.6d. multicoloured	15	10
408	**173**	2s.6d. multicoloured	20	25
405/408 *Set of 4*			55	45

174 Star of Bethlehem and Angel waking Shepherds

177 'Agriculture'

(Des E. Cremona. Photo Harrison)

1968 (3 Oct). Christmas. T **174** and similar shaped designs. Multicoloured. W **105** (sideways). P 14½×14.

409	1d. Type **174**	10	10
410	8d. Mary and Joseph with shepherd watching over cradle	15	10
411	1s.4d. Three Wise Men and Star of Bethlehem	15	20
409/411 *Set of 3*		35	35

The shortest side at top and the long side at the bottom both gauge 14½, the other three sides are 14. Nos. 409/411 were issued in sheets of 60 arranged in ten strips of six, alternately upright and inverted.

2s.6d. Large white flaw on chest (left pane, R. 1/10)

(Des E. Cremona. Photo Enschedé)

1968 (21 Oct). Sixth Food and Agricultural Organisation Regional Conference for Europe. T **177** and similar vert designs. Multicoloured. W **105** (sideways). P 12½×12.

412	4d. Type **177**	10	10
413	1s. FAO emblem and coin	10	10
414	2s.6d. 'Agriculture' sowing seeds	20	15
	a. White chest	5·00	
412/414 *Set of 3*		30	30

180 Mahatma Gandhi

181 ILO Emblem

(Des E. Cremona. Photo Enschedé)

1969 (24 Mar). Birth Centenary of Mahatma Gandhi. W **105**. P 12×12½.

415	**180**	1s.6d. blackish brown, black and gold	65	10

(Des E. Cremona. Photo Harrison)

1969 (26 May). 50th Anniversary of International Labour Organisation. W **105** (sideways). P 13½×14½.

416	**181**	2d. indigo, gold and turquoise	10	10
417		6d. sepia gold and chestnut	10	10

182 Robert Samut (birth centenary)

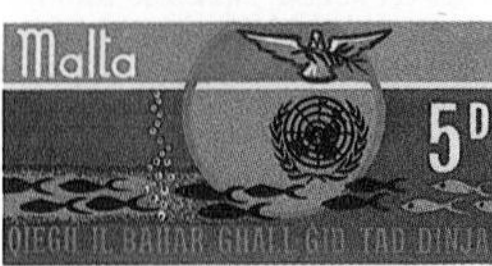

183 Dove of Peace, UN Emblem and Sea-Bed (UN Resolution on Oceanic Resources)

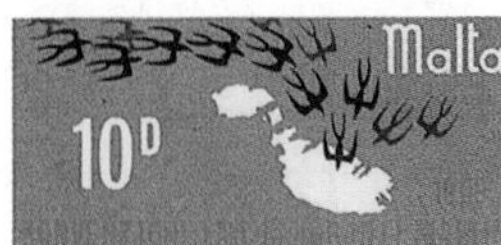

184 'Swallows' returning to Malta (Maltese Migrants' Convention)

185 University Arms and Grand Master de Fonseca (founder) (Bicentenary of University)

(Des E. Cremona. Photo D.L.R.)

1969 (26 July). Anniversaries. W **105** (sideways). P 13.

418	**182**	2d. multicoloured	10	10
419	**183**	5d. multicoloured	10	10
420	**184**	10d. black, gold and yellow-olive	10	10
421	**185**	2s. multicoloured	15	20
418/421 *Set of 4*			25	25

186 1919 Monument **187** Flag of Malta and Birds

(Des E. Cremona. Photo Enschedé)

1969 (20 Sept). Fifth Anniversary of Independence. Types **186/187** and similar designs. W **105** (upright on 5d., sideways others). P 13½×12½ (2d.), 12×12½ (5d.), or 12½×12 (others).

422	2d. multicoloured	10	10
423	5d. black, red and gold	10	10
424	10d. black, turquoise-blue and gold	10	10
425	1s.6d. multicoloured	20	40
426	2s.6d. black, olive-brown and gold	25	50
422/426 *Set of 5*		50	1·00

Designs: 2d. T **186**; 5d. T **187**. Vert as T **187**—10d. 'Tourism'; 1s.6d. UN and Council of Europe emblems; 2s.6d. 'Trade and Industry'.

191 Peasants playing Tambourine and Bagpipes

(Des E. Cremona. Litho D.L.R.)

1969 (8 Nov). Christmas. Children's Welfare Fund. T **191** and similar horiz designs. Multicoloured. W **105** (sideways). P 12½.

427	1d. +1d. Type **191**	10	20
	a. Gold omitted	£180	
	b. Horiz strip of 3. Nos. 427/429	35	75
428	5d. +1d. Angels playing trumpet and harp	15	20
429	1s.6d. +3d. Choirboys singing	15	45
427/429 *Set of 3*		35	75

Nos. 427/429 were issued in sheets of 60 of each value, and also in sheets containing the three values *se-tenant*, thus forming the triptych No. 427b.

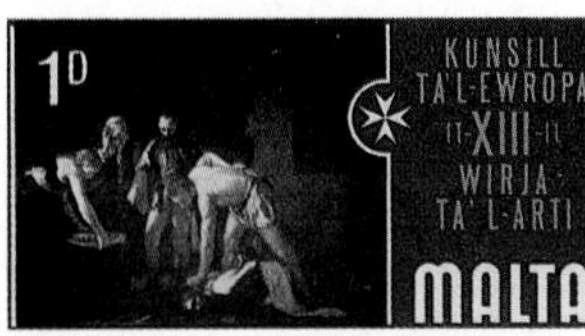

194 *The Beheading of St John* (Caravaggio)

(Des E. Cremona. Photo Enschedé)

1970 (21 Mar). 13th Council of Europe Art Exhibition. T **194** and similar multicoloured designs. W **105** (upright, 10d., 2s.; sideways, others). P 14×13 (1d., 8d.), 12 (10d., 2s.) or 13×13½ (others).

430	1d. Type **194**	10	10
431	2d. *St John the Baptist* (M. Preti) (45×32 *mm*)	10	10
432	5d. Interior of St John's Co-Cathedral, Valletta (39×39 *mm*)	10	10
433	6d. *Allegory of the Order* (Neapolitan School) (45×32 *mm*)	15	10
434	8d. *St Jerome* (Caravaggio)	15	50
435	10d. Articles from the Order of St John in Malta (63×21 *mm*)	15	10
436	1s.6d. *The Blessed Gerard receiving Godfrey de Bouillon* (A. de Favray) (45×35 *mm*)	25	40
437	2s. Cape and Stolone (16th-century) (63×21 *mm*)	25	55
	a. Blue omitted	£300	
430/437 *Set of 8*		1·00	1·50

202 Artist's Impression of Fujiyama

(Des E. Cremona. Photo D.L.R.)

1970 (29 May). World Fair, Osaka. W **105** (sideways). P 15.

438	**202**	2d. multicoloured	10	10
439		5d. multicoloured	10	10
440		3s. multicoloured	15	15
438/440 *Set of 3*			30	30

203 'Peace and Justice'

204 Carol-Singers, Church and Star

(Des J. Casha. Litho Harrison)

1970 (30 Sept). 25th Anniversary of United Nations. W **105**. P 14×14½.

441	**203**	2d. multicoloured	10	10
442		5d. multicoloured	10	10
443		2s.6d. multicoloured	15	15
441/443 *Set of 3*			30	30

(Des E. Cremona. Photo Govt Printer, Israel)

1970 (7 Nov). Christmas. T **204** and similar vert designs. Multicoloured. W **105** (sideways). P 14×13.

444	1d. +½d. Type **204**	10	10
445	10d. +2d. Church, star and Angels with Infant	15	20
446	1s.6d. +3d. Church, star and nativity scene	20	40
444/446 *Set of 3*		40	60

STAMP BOOKLETS

B 1

1970 (16 May). Brownish black on brownish grey cover as T B **1** depicting GPO Palazzo Parisio, Valletta. Stitched.

SB1	2s.6d. booklet containing 6×1d. and 12×2d. (Nos. 331, 333) in blocks of 6	5·50

1970 (18 May). Black on pink cover as T B **1** depicting Magisterial Palace, Valletta. Stitched.

SB2	2s.6d. booklets containing 6×1d. and 12×2d. (Nos. 331, 333) in blocks of 6	4·00

POSTAGE DUE STAMPS

D 1

D 2

1925 (16 Apr). Typeset by Govt Printing Office, Valletta. Imperf.

D1	D **1**	½d. black	1·25	11·00
		a. *Tête-bêche* (horiz pair)	5·00	24·00
D2		1d. black	3·25	4·75
		a. *Tête-bêche* (horiz pair)	10·00	13·00
D3		1½d. black	3·00	3·75
		a. *Tête-bêche* (horiz pair)	10·00	15·00
D4		2d. black	15·00	26·00
		a. *Tête-bêche* (horiz pair)	32·00	65·00

D5 2½d. black 2·75 2·75
a. '2' of '½' omitted £900 £1300
b. *Tête-bêche* (horiz pair) 12·00 15·00
D6 3d. black/*grey* 9·00 15·00
a. *Tête-bêche* (horiz pair) 30·00 48·00
D7 4d. black/*buff* 5·00 9·50
a. *Tête-bêche* (horiz pair) 17·00 38·00
D8 6d. black/*buff* 5·00 32·00
a. *Tête-bêche* (horiz pair) 17·00 70·00
D9 1s. black/*buff* 6·50 35·00
a. *Tête-bêche* (horiz pair) 25·00 70·00
D10 1s.6d. black/*buff* 20·00 75·00
a. *Tête-bêche* (horiz pair) 42·00 £150
D1/D10 *Set of* 10 60·00 £190

Nos. D1/D10 were each issued in sheets containing four panes (6×7) printed separately, the impressions in the two left-hand panes being inverted. 14 horizontal *tête-bêche* pairs occur from the junction of the left and right-hand panes.

No. D5a occurred on R. 4/4 of the last 2½d. pane position to be printed. Forgeries exist, but can be detected by comparison with a normal example under ultra-violet light. They are often found in pair with normal, showing forged cancellations of 'VALLETTA AP 20 25' or 'G.P.O. MY 7 25'.

(Typo B.W.)

1925 (20 July). Wmk Mult Script CA (sideways). P 12.
D11 D **2** ½d. green 1·25 60
D12 1d. violet 1·25 45
D13 1½d. brown 1·50 80
D14 2d. grey 6·50 1·00
D15 2½d. orange 2·00 1·25
x. Wmk reversed £160
D16 3d. blue 4·00 1·25
D17 4d. olive-green 8·00 16·00
D18 6d. purple 3·50 8·00
D19 1s. black 5·00 18·00
D20 1s.6d. carmine 7·50 50·00
D11/D20 *Set of* 10 35·00 85·00
D11s/D20s Optd 'SPECIMEN.' *Set of* 10 £275

1953–63. Chalk-surfaced paper. Wmk Mult Script CA (sideways). P 12.
D21 D **2** ½d. emerald 70 4·00
D22 1d. purple 70 1·25
a. Deep purple (17.9.63) 75 3·75
D23 1½d. yellow-brown 2·50 18·00
D24 2d. grey-brown (20.3.57) 6·00 9·50
a. Blackish brown (3.4.62) 29·00 13·00
D25 3d. deep slate-blue 1·00 2·00
D26 4d. yellow-olive 2·50 4·25
D21/D26 *Set of* 6 12·00 35·00

1966 (1 Oct). As No. D24, but wmk w **12** (sideways).
D27 D **2** 2d. grey-brown 10·00 20·00

1967–70. Ordinary paper. W **105** (sideways).

(a) P 12, line (9.11.67)
D28 D **2** ½d. emerald 4·00 9·00
D29 1d. purple 4·00 9·00
D30 2d. blackish brown 6·50 9·00
D31 4d. yellow-olive 45·00 £110
D28/D31 *Set of* 4 55·00 £120

(b) P 12½, comb (30.5.68–70)
D32 D **2** ½d. emerald 35 2·00
D33 1d. purple 30 1·50
D34 1½d. yellow-brown 35 3·25
a. Orange-brown (23.10.70) 1·25 3·00
D35 2d. blackish brown 85 70
a. Brownish black (23.10.70) 3·25 3·00
D36 2½d. yellow-orange 60 70
D37 3d. deep slate-blue 60 60
D38 4d. yellow-olive 1·00 80
D39 6d. purple 75 1·75
D40 1s. black 90 1·50
D41 1s.6d. carmine 2·75 7·50
D32/D41 *Set of* 10 7·00 18·00

The above are the local release dates. In the 12½ perforation the London release dates were 21 May for the ½d. to 4d. and 4 June for the 6d. to 1s.6d.

Nos. D34*a* and D35*a* are on glazed paper.

Mauritius

GREAT BRITAIN STAMPS USED IN MAURITIUS. We no longer list the Great Britain stamps with obliteration 'B 53' as there is no evidence that British stamps were available from the Mauritius Post Office.

See under SEYCHELLES for stamps of Mauritius used at Victoria with 'B 64' cancellations between 1861 and 1890.

A similar 'B 65' cancellation was used on the island of Rodrigues, a dependency of Mauritius, from 11 December 1861 onwards.

PRICES FOR STAMPS ON COVER TO 1945	
Nos. 1/5	*from* × 2
Nos. 6/9	*from* × 3
Nos. 10/15	*from* × 4
Nos. 16/25	*from* × 5
Nos. 26/29	*from* × 3
Nos. 30/31	†
Nos. 32/35	*from* × 4
Nos. 36/44	*from* × 5
Nos. 46/72	*from* × 3
Nos. 76/82	*from* × 5
Nos. 83/91	*from* × 6
Nos. 92/100	*from* × 4
Nos. 101/111	*from* × 5
Nos. 112/114	*from* × 3
No. 115	*from* × 10
Nos. 116/117	*from* × 5
Nos. 118/124	*from* × 8
Nos. 127/132	*from* × 7
No. 133	*from* × 4
Nos. 134/135	*from* × 10
No. 136	*from* × 8
Nos. 137/156	*from* × 6
Nos. 157/163	*from* × 5
Nos. 164/221	*from* × 3
No. 222	—
Nos. 223/241	*from* × 3
Nos. 242/244	*from* × 10
Nos. 245/248	*from* × 3
Nos. 249/263	*from* × 2
Nos. E1/E2	*from* × 10
No. E3	*from* × 30
No. E4	—
No. E5	*from* × 10
No. E6	*from* × 25
Nos. D1/D5	*from* × 40
Nos. R1/R3	*from* × 15

CROWN COLONY

Nos. 1/25 and 36/44 were printed in Mauritius.

1 ('POST OFFICE')

2 ('POST PAID')

(Engraved on copper by J. O. Barnard)

1847 (21 Sept). Head of Queen on groundwork of diagonal and perpendicular lines. Imperf.
1 **1** 1d. orange-red — £1300000
2 2d. deep blue — £1500000

A single plate contained one example of each value.

It is generally agreed that 15 examples of No. 1 have survived (including two unused) and 12 of No. 2 (including four unused). Most are now in permanent museum collections.

NOTE. Our prices for early Mauritius are for stamps in very fine condition. Exceptional copies are worth more, poorer copies considerably less.

(Engraved on copper by J. O. Barnard)

1848 (June)–**59**. Imperf.

A. Earliest impressions. Design deep, sharp and clear. Diagonal lines predominate. Thick paper (Period of use: 1d. 1852–1854, 2d. 1848–1849)
3 **2** 1d. orange-vermilion/*yellowish* £70000 £18000
4 2d. indigo-blue/*grey to bluish* £65000 £26000
a. 'PENOE' for 'PENCE' (R. 3/1) £130000 £45000
5 2d. deep blue/*grey to bluish* £65000 £26000
a. 'PENOE' for 'PENCE' (R. 3/1) £130000 £45000

B. Early impressions. Design sharp and clear but some lines slightly weakened. Paper not so thick, grey to yellowish white or bluish (Period of use: 1d. 1853–1855, 2d. 1849–1854)
6 **2** 1d. vermilion £35000 £7500
7 1d. orange-vermilion £35000 £7000
8 2d. blue £38000 £9000
a. 'PENOE' for 'PENCE' (R. 3/1) £70000 £17000
9 2d. deep blue £45000 £9500

C. Intermediate impressions. White patches appear where design has worn. Paper yellowish white, grey or bluish, of poorish quality (Period of use: 1d and 2d. 1854–1857)
10 **2** 1d. bright vermilion £23000 £3000
11 1d. dull vermilion £23000 £3000
12 1d. red £23000 £3000
13 2d. deep blue £30000 £4250
14 2d. blue £24000 £3500
a. 'PENOE' for 'PENCE' (R. 3/1) *from* £42000 £8000
15 2d. light blue £24000 £3500

D. Worn impressions. Much of design worn away but some diagonal lines distinct. Paper yellowish, grey or bluish, of poorish quality (Period of use: 1d. 1857–1859, 2d. 1855–1858)
16 **2** 1d. red/*yellowish or grey* £8000 £950
17 1d. red-brown/*yellowish or grey* £8000 £950
18 1d. red/*bluish* £7500 £900
a. Doubly printed
19 1d. red-brown/*bluish* £7500 £900
20 2d. blue (*shades*)/*yellowish or grey* £10000 £1700
a. 'PENOE' for 'PENCE' (R. 3/1) *from* — £3500
21 2d. grey-blue/*yellowish or grey* £11000 £1600
22 2d. blue (*shades*)/*bluish* £10000 £1600
a. Doubly printed

E. Latest impressions. Almost none of design showing except part of Queens's head and frame. Paper yellowish, grey or bluish, of poorish quality (Period of use: 1d. 1859, 2d. 1856–1858)
23 **2** 1d. red £6500 £800
24 1d. red-brown £6500 £800
25 2d. grey-blue/*bluish* £8000 £1200
a. 'PENOE' for 'PENCE' (R. 3/1) £15000 £2250

Earliest known use of the 2d. value is on 19 June 1848, but the 1d. value is not known used before 16 May 1852.

There were separate plates for the 1d. and 2d. values, each of 12 (3×4).

3

(4)

5

(Eng G. Fairman. Recess P.B.)

1858*. Surch with T **4**. Imperf.
26 **3** 4d. green £1800 £450

* Although originally gazetted for use from 8 April 1854, research into the archives indicates that No. 26 was not actually issued until 1858, when the stamps were mentioned in an ordinance of 30 April. The earliest dated postmark known is 27 March 1858.

PERKINS BACON 'CANCELLED'. For notes on these handstamps, showing 'CANCELLED' between horizontal bars forming an oval, see Catalogue Introduction.

1858–62. No value expressed. Imperf.
27 **3** (4d.) green £450 £200
28 (6d.) vermilion 65·00 £120
29 (9d.) dull magenta (1859) £900 £225
a. Reissued as (1d.) value (11.62) † £170

Prepared for use but not issued
30 **3** (No value), red-brown 27·00
31 (No value), blue (H/S 'CANCELLED' in oval £13000) 13·00

Use of the dull magenta as a 1d. value can be confirmed by the presence of the 'B 53' cancellation which was first introduced in 1861.

Remainders of Nos. 30/31, overprinted 'L.P.E. 1890' in red, were perforated at the London Philatelic Exhibition and sold as souvenirs.

(Recess P.B.)

1859–61. Imperf.
32 **5** 6d. blue (H/S 'CANCELLED' in oval £13000) £800 55·00
33 6d. dull purple-slate (1861) 45·00 65·00
34 1s. vermilion (H/S 'CANCELLED' in oval £11000) £3250 70·00
35 1s. yellow-green (1861) £650 £150

The 1859 printings had the colours transposed by mistake.

6

7

8

(Engraved on copper by J. Lapirot)

1859 (Mar–Nov). Imperf.

(a) Early impressions
36 **6** 2d. deep blue £20000 £3750
37 2d. blue £18000 £3250

(b) Intermediate prints. Lines of background, etc, partly worn away (July)
38 **6** 2d. blue £9500 £1400
a. Doubly printed † —

(c) Worn impressions, bluish paper (Oct)
39 **6** 2d. blue £4750 £900

(d) Retouched impression (Nov)
39*a* **6** 2d. blue † —
ab. 'MAURITUIS' (R. 2/4) † £130000
ac. 'MAURITUS' (R. 3/1) † £130000

Nos. 36/39*a* were printed from a plate of 12 (4×3).

Research by Mr A. Rudge has established the existence of an initial state of the plate, before the lines were deepened to produce the 'Early impression'. Only one stamp from this state has so far been identified.

The plate became worn through use, and was eventually extensively re-engraved. Only two pairs (one on cover) have been recorded from this re-touched impression. The errors made in the re-engraving of the inscriptions probably resulted in it being withdrawn from use.

(1848 plate re-engraved by R. Sherwin)

1859 (Oct). Bluish paper. Imperf.
40 **7** 2d. deep blue £225000 £8000

The 1d. plate was also re-engraved, but was not put into use. Reprints in black were made in 1877 from both 1d. and 2d. re-engraved plates. Coloured autotype illustrations were prepared from these reprints and 600 were included in the R.P.S.L. handbook on *British Africa* in 1900. Further reprints in black were made in 1911 after the plates had been presented to the R.P.S.L. and defaced.

(Lithographed by L. A. Dardenne)

1859 (12 Dec). White laid paper. Imperf.
41 **8** 1d. deep red £16000 £2500
41*a* 1d. red £12000 £1700
42 1d. dull vermilion £10000 £1400

43 2d. slate-blue £11000 £1300
43*a* 2d. blue £6500 £950
44 2d. pale blue £6000 £850
a. Heavy retouch on neck .... — £2000
b. Retouched below 'TWO' .... — £1200

The neck retouch shows a prominent curved white line running from the base of the chignon to the nape of the neck. No. 44b shows several diagonal lines in the margin below 'TWO'.

9

10

(Typo D.L.R.)

1860 (7 Apr)–**63**. No wmk. P 14.

No.	Type	Description	Unused	Used
46	9	1d. purple-brown	£425	48·00
47		2d. blue	£450	55·00
48		4d. rose	£450	42·00
49		6d. green (1862)	£1100	£170
50		6d. slate (1863)	£425	£110
51		9d. dull purple	£225	42·00
52		1s. buff (1862)	£425	95·00
53		1s. green (1863)	£950	£200

Collectors should beware of faked unused examples of Nos. 49 and 52, made from imperforate plate proofs.

(Recess P.B.)

1862. Intermediate perf 14 to 16.

No.	Type	Description	Unused	Used
54	5	6d. slate	42·00	£110
		a. Imperf between (horiz pair)	£8000	
55		1s. deep green	£2750	£325

(Typo D.L.R.)

1863–72. Wmk Crown CC. P 14.

No.	Type	Description	Unused	Used
56	9	1d. purple-brown	80·00	17·00
		w. Wmk inverted	95·00	40·00
		y. Wmk inverted and reversed	—	£150
57		1d. brown	£100	13·00
58		1d. bistre (1872)	£140	17·00
		w. Wmk inverted		
59		2d. pale blue	75·00	13·00
		a. Imperf (pair)	£1800	£2000
		w. Wmk inverted	£190	38·00
		x. Wmk reversed	—	£170
		y. Wmk inverted and reversed		
60		2d. bright blue	95·00	13·00
61		3d. deep red	£170	45·00
61*a*		3d. dull red	90·00	21·00
		aw. Wmk inverted	£225	55·00
62		4d. rose	95·00	3·75
		w. Wmk inverted	£275	30·00
63		6d. dull violet	£425	50·00
		w. Wmk inverted		
		x. Wmk reversed		
		y. Wmk inverted and reversed	†	£225
64		6d. yellow-green (1865)	£325	16·00
65		6d. blue-green	£250	6·50
		w. Wmk inverted	£400	55·00
		y. Wmk inverted and reversed		
66		9d. yellow-green (1872)	£190	£400
		w. Wmk inverted		
67	10	10d. maroon (1872)	£375	60·00
		w. Wmk inverted		
68	9	1s. yellow	£375	32·00
		w. Wmk inverted	£550	75·00
69		1s. blue (1866)	£130	30·00
		w. Wmk inverted	—	90·00
		x. Wmk reversed	—	£300
70		1s. orange (1872)	£300	12·00
		w. Wmk inverted	£425	70·00
		x. Wmk reversed	—	£225
		y. Wmk inverted and reversed	†	£250
71		5s. rosy mauve	£275	55·00
		w. Wmk inverted	£500	£150
72		5s. bright mauve (1865)	£325	55·00
		w. Wmk inverted	£500	£140

Most values of the above set, including the 2d. bright blue, exist imperforate, but these are from proof sheets. The 2d. pale blue imperforate (No. 59a) was issued in error.

HALF PENNY (11)   ½ d HALF PENNY (12)

1876.

(a) Nos. 51 and 67 surch with T **11** *locally*

No.	Type	Description	Unused	Used
76	9	½d. on 9d. dull purple (2.79)	27·00	25·00
		a. Surch inverted	£750	
		b. Surch double	—	£2250
77	10	½d. on 10d. maroon (10.79)	5·50	30·00
		y. Wmk inverted and reversed		

(b) Prepared for use, but not issued. No. 51 surch with T **12**

No.	Type	Description	Unused	Used
78	9	½d. on 9d. dull purple (R.)	£3250	
		a. 'PRNNY'		
		b. Black surch	£5000	

HALF PENNY (13)   One Penny (14)   One Shilling (15)

1877 (Apr–Dec). Nos. 62, 67 (colour changed) and 71/72 surch T **13** by D.L.R. or Types **14/15** locally.

No.	Type	Description	Unused	Used
79	10	½d. on 10d. rose	13·00	50·00
		w. Wmk inverted	£120	
80	9	1d. on 4d. rose-carmine (6.12)	28·00	30·00
		w. Wmk inverted	£150	£110
81		1s. on 5s. rosy mauve (6.12)	£350	£120
		w. Wmk inverted	£550	£200
82		1s. on 5s. bright mauve (6.12)	£350	£150
		w. Wmk inverted	—	£250

(New Currency. 100 cents = 1 rupee)

'CANCELLED' OVERPRINTS. Following the change of currency in 1878 various issues with face values in sterling were overprinted 'CANCELLED' in serifed type and sold as remainders. The stamps involved were Nos. 51, 56/62, 65, 67/68, 71/72, 76, 78/78b, 79 and 81/82. Examples of such overprints on stamps between Nos. 51 and 72 are worth about the same as the prices quoted for used, on No. 78 they are worth 5% of the unused price, on No. 78b 20%, No. 79 65% and on Nos. 81/82 20%.

2 CENTS (16)   2 Rs.50C. (17)

1878 (3 Jan). Surch as Types **16** or **17** (No. 91) by De La Rue. Wmk Crown CC. P 14.

No.	Type	Description	Unused	Used
83	10	2c. dull rose (lower label blank)	20·00	15·00
		w. Wmk inverted	£140	90·00
84	9	4c. on 1d. bistre	28·00	13·00
85		8c. on 2d. blue	85·00	4·25
		w. Wmk inverted	—	£400
86		13c. on 3d. orange-red	28·00	55·00
87		17c. on 4d. rose	£190	4·50
88		25c. on 6d. slate-blue	£275	8·00
89		38c. on 9d. pale violet	50·00	£100
90		50c. on 1s. green	90·00	7·00
		w. Wmk inverted		
91		2r.50 on 5s. bright mauve	24·00	29·00
83/91 *Set of 9*			£700	£200

18 19 20
21 22 23
24 25 26

(Typo D.L.R.)

1879 (Mar)–**80**. Wmk Crown CC. P 14.

No.	Type	Description	Unused	Used
92	18	2c. Venetian red (1.80)	55·00	28·00
93	19	4c. orange	65·00	3·50
		w. Wmk inverted		
94	20	8c. blue (1.80)	48·00	4·00
		w. Wmk inverted	—	£160
95	21	13c. slate (1.80)	£180	£325
96	22	17c. rose (1.80)	95·00	10·00
		w. Wmk inverted	—	£200
97	23	25c. olive-yellow	£475	19·00
98	24	38c. bright purple (1.80)	£200	£375
99	25	50c. green (1.80)	8·00	7·00
		w. Wmk inverted	£160	
100	26	2r.50 brown-purple (1.80)	55·00	80·00
92/100 *Set of 9*			£1000	£750

27

(Typo D.L.R.)

1883–94. Wmk Crown CA. P 14.

No.	Type	Description	Unused	Used
101	18	1c. pale violet (1893)	3·25	45
102		2c. Venetian red	40·00	8·50
103		2c. green (1885)	6·00	60
104	19	4c. orange	95·00	8·50
		w. Wmk inverted		
105		4c. carmine (1885)	7·00	1·00
		w. Wmk inverted	—	£130
		x. Wmk reversed	†	£275
106	20	8c. blue (1891)	6·50	1·50
		w. Wmk inverted		
		x. Wmk reversed	†	£275
107	27	15c. chestnut (1893)	9·50	1·25
		w. Wmk inverted	—	£160
108		15c. blue (1894)	14·00	1·75
109		16c. chestnut (1885)	13·00	2·75
110	23	25c. olive-yellow	16·00	4·00
		w. Wmk inverted	£400	£200
111	25	50c. orange (1887)	45·00	23·00
		w. Wmk inverted		
101/111 *Set of 11*			£225	48·00
101s, 103s, 105s, 107s/109s, 111s Optd 'SPECIMEN' *Set of 7*			£750	

16 CENTS (28)   16 CENTS (28a)

1883 (26 Feb). No. 96 surch with Types **28/28a** locally.

No.	Type	Description	Unused	Used
112	22	16c. on 17c. rose (surch Type **28**– 14½ *mm* long)	£170	55·00
		a. Surch double	†	£2750
		b. Horiz pair. Nos. 112/113	£850	£750
113		16c. on 17c. rose (surch Type **28**– 15½ *mm* long)	£180	55·00
		a. Surch double	—	£3000
114		16c. on 17c. rose (surch Type **28a**)	£375	£140

These stamps were surcharged using two different settings, each of which produced three horizontal rows at a time.

The length of the surcharge in the first setting (T **28**) is either 14½ mm or 15½ mm and these exist in horizontal *se-tenant* pairs. In T **28** the height of the surcharge is 3.25 mm. On the second setting (T **28a**) the type differs, especially the numerals and 'S', with the surcharge measuring 15-15½ mm long and 3 mm high.

SIXTEEN CENTS (29)   2 CENTS (30)   2 CENTS (31)

1883 (14 July). Surch with T **29** by D.L.R. Wmk Crown CA. P 14.

No.	Type	Description	Unused	Used
115	22	16c. on 17c. rose	£110	2·50
		w. Wmk inverted		

1886 (11 May). No. 98 surch with T **30** locally.

No.	Type	Description	Unused	Used
116	24	2c. on 38c. bright purple	£160	45·00
		a. Without bar	—	£250
		b. Surch inverted	£1200	£950
		c. Surch double	£1300	

1887 (6 July). No. 95 surch with T **31** locally.

No.	Type	Description	Unused	Used
117	21	2c. on 13c. slate (R.)	75·00	£120
		a. Surch inverted	£275	£300
		b. Surch double	£850	£750
		c. Surch double, one on back of stamp	£950	
		d. Surch double, both inverted	†	£1600

TWO CENTS (32)   TWO CENTS (33)

1891 (10–16 Sept). Nos. 88, 96, 98 and 105 surch locally as T **32** (Nos. 118/119, 121) or T **33** (No. 120).

No.	Type	Description	Unused	Used
118	19	2c. on 4c. carmine (No. 105) (12.9)	3·00	1·00
		a. Surch inverted	85·00	
		b. Surch double	90·00	85·00
		c. Surch double, one inverted	90·00	85·00
119	22	2c. on 17c. rose (No. 96) (16.9)	£140	£150
		a. Surch inverted	£550	£600
		b. Surch double	£900	£900
120	9	2c. on 38c. on 9d. pale violet (No. 89) (16.9)	17·00	8·50
		a. Surch inverted	£600	
		b. Surch double	£800	£800
		c. Surch double, one inverted	£190	£200
		w. Wmk inverted	£400	£400
121	24	2c. on 38c. bright purple (No. 98)	12·00	19·00
		a. Surch inverted	£1300	
		b. Surch double	£250	£275
		c. Surch double, one inverted	£275	£300

Minor varieties are also known with portions of the surcharge missing, due to defective printing.

ONE CENT (34)   ONE CENT (35)

1893 (1–7 Jan). Surch with T **34** by D.L.R. or T **35** locally. Wmk Crown CA. P 14.

No.	Type	Description	Unused	Used
123	18	1c. on 2c. pale violet	2·50	2·25
		s. Optd 'SPECIMEN'	35·00	
124	27	1c. on 16c. chestnut (7.1)	3·75	5·50
		w. Wmk inverted	90·00	

36

37

(Typo D.L.R.)

1895–99. Wmk Crown CA. P 14.

No.	Type	Description	Unused	Used
127	36	1c. dull purple and ultramarine (8.7.97)	1·00	1·50
128		2c. dull purple and orange (8.7.97)	8·50	50
129		3c. dull purple and deep purple	70	50
130		4c. dull purple and emerald (8.7.97)	6·00	50
131		6c. green and rose-red (1899)	7·50	4·00
132		18c. green and ultramarine (8.7.97)	24·00	3·50
127/132 *Set of 6*			42·00	9·50
127s/132s Optd 'SPECIMEN' *Set of 6*			£150	

(Des L. Duvergé. Typo D.L.R.)

1898 (15 Apr). Diamond Jubilee. Wmk CA over Crown (sideways). P 14.

No.	Type	Description	Unused	Used
133	37	36c. orange and ultramarine	14·00	29·00
		s. Optd 'SPECIMEN'	55·00	

6 CENTS (38)   15 CENTS (39)

1899 (23–28 May). Nos. 132/133 surcharged with Types **38/39** locally.

No.	Type	Description	Unused	Used
134	36	6c. on 18c. green and ultramarine (R.)	2·00	1·00
		a. Surch inverted	£700	£300
135	37	15c. on 36c. orange and ultramarine (B) (28.5)	4·25	1·75
		a. Bar of surch omitted	£500	

The space between '6' and 'CENTS' varies from 2½ to 4½ mm.

40 Admiral Mahé de La Bourdonnais, Governor of Mauritius, 1735–1746

4
Cents

(**41**)

(Recess D.L.R.)

1899 (13 Dec). Birth Bicentenary of La Bourdonnais. Wmk Crown CC. P 14.

136	**40**	15c. ultramarine	35·00	4·75
		s. Optd 'SPECIMEN'	80·00	
		w. Wmk inverted	£200	£160

1900. No. 109 surch with T **41** locally.

137	**27**	4c. on 16c. chestnut	17·00	28·00

42

12
CENTS

(**43**)

(Typo D.L.R.)

1900–05. Ordinary paper. Wmk Crown CC (1r.) or Crown CA (others) (sideways on 2r.50, 5r.). P 14.

138	**36**	1c. grey and black (1901)	50	10
139		2c. dull purple and bright purple (4.01)	1·00	20
140		3c. green and carmine/*yellow* (1902)	4·25	1·25
141		4c. purple and carmine/*yellow*	3·50	40
		w. Wmk inverted	—	£150
142		4c. grey-green and violet (1903)	3·50	2·00
		w. Wmk inverted		
143		4c. black and carmine/*blue* (14.10.04)	18·00	60
		w. Wmk inverted	28·00	17·00
144		5c. dull purple and bright purple/*buff* (8.10.02)	12·00	£120
145		5c. dull purple and black/*buff* (2.03)	2·50	2·50
146		6c. purple and carmine/*red* (1902)	5·00	80
		a. Wmk sideways	£2500	£2500
		w. Wmk inverted	32·00	20·00
147		8c. green and black/*buff* (16.7.02)	5·50	18·00
148		12c. grey-black and carmine (16.7.02)	3·00	2·25
149		15c. green and orange	35·00	10·00
		w. Wmk inverted		
150		15c. black and blue/*blue* (1905)	65·00	1·25
151		25c. green and carmine/*green* (1902)	35·00	55·00
		a. Chalk-surfaced paper	6·00	30·00
152		50c. dull green and deep green/*yellow* (1902)	17·00	75·00
153	**42**	1r. grey-black and carmine (1902)	65·00	55·00
		w. Wmk inverted	£140	£150
154		2r.50 green and black/*blue* (1902)	40·00	£160
155		5r. purple and carmine/*red* (1902)	£110	£180
138/155 *Set of 18*			£350	£550
138s/155s Optd 'SPECIMEN' *Set of 18*			£425	

Examples of Nos. 144 and 151/155 are known showing a forged Port Louis postmark dated 'SP 29 10'.

1902. No. 132 surch with T **43**.

156	**36**	12c. on 18c. green and ultramarine	4·00	13·00

The bar cancelling the original value seems in some cases to be one thick bar and in others two thin ones.

Postage & Revenue.

(**44**)

1902 (7 July). Various stamps optd with T **44** locally.

157	**36**	4c. purple and carmine/*yellow* (No. 141)	2·50	20
158		6c. green and rose-red (No. 131)	3·50	3·25
159		15c. green and orange (No. 149)	9·00	1·25
160	**23**	25c. olive-yellow (No. 110)	9·00	3·50
161	**25**	50c. green (No. 99)	28·00	8·00
162	**26**	2r.50 brown-purple (No. 100)	£130	£225
157/162 *Set of 6*			£160	£225

Nos. 157/162 were overprinted to make surplus stocks of postage stamps available for revenue (fiscal) purposes also.

1902 (22 Sept). No. 133 surch as T **43**, but with longer bar.

163	**37**	12c. on 36c. orange and ultramarine	3·00	1·25
		a. Surch inverted	£800	£475

The note below No. 156 also applies to No. 163.

Forged double surcharge errors show a straight, instead of a curved, serif to the '1' of '12'.

(Typo D.L.R.)

1904–07. Ordinary paper (2c., 4c., 6c.) or chalk-surfaced paper (others). Wmk Mult Crown CA. P 14.

164	**36**	1c. grey and black (1907)	8·00	4·50
165		2c. dull and bright purple (1905)	35·00	3·00
		a. Chalk-surfaced paper	32·00	1·75
166		3c. green and carmine/*yellow*	21·00	15·00
167		4c. black and carmine/*blue*	40·00	1·50
		a. Chalk-surfaced paper	16·00	10
		aw. Wmk inverted	†	£350
168		6c. purple and carmine/*red*	25·00	30
		a. Chalk-surfaced paper	14·00	10
		aw. Wmk inverted	†	£350
171		15c. black and blue/*blue* (1907)	4·00	35
174		50c. green and deep green/*yellow*	3·25	9·00
175	**42**	1r. grey-black and carmine (1907)	50·00	60·00
164/175 *Set of 8*			£130	80·00

Nos. 176 to 180 are vacant.

46 **47**

(Typo D.L.R.)

1910 (17 Jan). Ordinary paper (1c. to 15c.) or chalk-surfaced paper (25c. to 10r.). Wmk Mult Crown CA. P 14.

181	**46**	1c. black	3·00	30
		w. Wmk inverted	†	
182		2c. brown	2·75	10
		w. Wmk inverted	†	£150
183		3c. green	3·00	10
		a. 'A' of 'CA' missing from wmk	†	—
		w. Wmk inverted	50·00	
184		4c. pale yellow-green and carmine	4·00	10
		w. Wmk inverted	—	75·00
		y. Wmk inverted and reversed	†	£170
185	**47**	5c. grey and carmine	4·25	3·00
186	**46**	6c. carmine-red	7·50	20
		a. Pale red	14·00	2·50
		ab. 'A' of 'CA' missing from wmk	†	—
187		8c. orange	3·50	2·75
188	**47**	12c. greyish slate	4·50	2·75
189	**46**	15c. blue	19·00	20
190	**47**	25c. black and red/*yellow*	2·00	12·00
191		50c. dull purple and black	5·00	23·00
192		1r. black/*green*	22·00	17·00
193		2r.50 black and red/*blue*	30·00	75·00
194		5r. green and red/*yellow*	48·00	95·00
195		10r. green and red/*green*	£170	£325
181/195 *Set of 15*			£300	£500
181s/195s Optd 'SPECIMEN' *Set of 15*			£375	

On Nos. 185, 191, 192, 193 and 194 the value labels are as in T **48**.

48 **49**

(Typo D.L.R.)

1913–22. Die I. Ordinary paper (5c., 12c.) or chalk-surfaced paper (others). Wmk Mult Crown CA. P 14.

196	**48**	5c. grey and carmine (1913)	4·75	4·25
		a. Slate-grey and carmine	13·00	12·00
198	**49**	12c. greyish slate (1914)	9·50	1·00
199		25c. black and red/*yellow* (1913)	50	1·40
		a. White back (1914)	3·25	22·00
		aw. Wmk inverted and reversed	65·00	
		b. On orange-buff (1920)	35·00	60·00
		c. On pale yellow (1921)	35·00	40·00
		cs. Optd 'SPECIMEN'	55·00	
		cw. Wmk inverted	£180	
		d. Die II. *On pale yellow* (1921)	1·25	26·00
		ds. Optd 'SPECIMEN'	50·00	
200	**48**	50c. dull purple and black (1920)	50·00	£130
201		1r. black/*blue-green (olive back)* (1917)	11·00	26·00
		a. On emerald (olive back) (1921)	16·00	55·00
		b. Die II. *On emerald (emerald back)* (1921)	2·25	7·50
		bs. Optd 'SPECIMEN'	50·00	
202		2r.50 black and red/*blue* (1916)	45·00	75·00
203		5r. green and red/*orange-buff* (1921)	£150	£250
		a. On pale yellow (1921)	£130	£180
		b. Die II. *On pale yellow* (1922)	90·00	£200
204	**49**	10r. green and red/*green (blue-green back)* (1913)	£110	£250
		a. On blue-green (olive back) (1919)	£1100	
		b. On emerald (olive back) (1921)	£160	£250
		c. On emerald (emerald back) (1921)	90·00	£225
		d. Die II. *On emerald (emerald back)* (1922)	55·00	£200
		ds. Optd 'SPECIMEN'	70·00	
196/204*d Set of 8*			£225	£550
196s/202s, 203as, 204s Optd 'SPECIMEN' *Set of 8*			£300	

Examples of Nos. 200/204*d* are known showing part strikes of the forged Port Louis postmark mentioned after Nos. 138/155.

49a

(Typo D.L.R.)

1921–26. Chalk-surfaced paper (50r). Wmk Mult Script CA. P 14.

205	**46**	1c. black	1·00	1·00
		w. Wmk inverted	45·00	55·00
206		2c. brown	1·00	10
		w. Wmk inverted		
207		2c. purple/*yellow* (1926)	4·00	3·25
		w. Wmk inverted	28·00	38·00
208		3c. green (1926)	5·50	5·00
209		4c. pale olive-green and carmine	1·50	1·75
		x. Wmk reversed	£130	
210		4c. green (1922)	1·00	10
		w. Wmk inverted	£100	
		x. Wmk reversed		
211		4c. brown (1926)	7·50	4·00
212		6c. carmine	12·00	6·50
		x. Wmk reversed	95·00	95·00
213		6c. bright mauve (1922)	1·25	10
214		8c. orange (1925)	2·25	28·00
215		10c. grey (1922)	2·00	3·25
216		10c. carmine-red (1926)	15·00	9·00
217		12c. carmine-red (1922)	1·50	40
218		12c. grey (1926)	1·75	7·50
219		15c. blue	5·50	7·50
		ax. Wmk reversed	£120	£120
		b. Cobalt (1926)	1·00	25
220		20c. blue (1922)	2·00	80
221		20c. purple (1926)	8·50	17·00
222	**49a**	50r. dull purple and green (1924)	£950	£2750
		s. Optd 'SPECIMEN'	£400	
205/221 *Set of 17*			60·00	80·00
205s/221s Optd 'SPECIMEN' *Set of 17*			£475	

4c 4c

Normal — Open 'C' (R. 9/6 of right pane)

MAURITIUS
12c

A

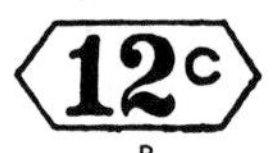

B

Two types of duty plate in the 12c. In Type B the letters of 'MAURITIUS' are larger; the extremities of the downstroke and the tail of the '2' are pointed, instead of square, and the 'c' is larger.

(Typo D.L.R.)

1921–34. Die II. Chalk-surfaced paper (25c. to 10r.). Wmk Mult Script CA. P 14.

223	**49**	1c. black (1926)	2·25	3·25
224		2c. brown (1926)	1·25	10
225		3c. green (1926)	3·00	40
226		4c. sage-green and carmine (1926)	3·75	30
		a. Open 'C'	80·00	25·00
		b. Die I (1932)	19·00	60·00
		ba. Open 'C'	£190	
226*c*		4c. green (Die I) (1932)	16·00	45
		ca. Open 'C'	£180	35·00
227	**48**	5c. grey and carmine (1922)	1·00	10
		a. Die I (1932)	14·00	6·00
228	**49**	6c. sepia (1927)	5·50	60
229		8c. orange (1926)	3·75	20·00
230		10c. carmine-red (1926)	4·75	20
		a. Die I (1932)	17·00	19·00
231		12c. grey (Type A) (1922)	2·25	26·00
232		12c. carmine-red (Type A) (1922)	65	3·75
232*a*		12c. pale grey (Type A) (1926)	7·00	26·00
		as. Optd 'SPECIMEN'	50·00	
232*b*		12c. grey (Type B) (1934)	22·00	20
233		15c. Prussian blue (1926)	4·75	20
234		20c. purple (1926)	6·00	40
235		20c. Prussian blue (Die I) (1932)	10·00	2·75
		a. Die II (1934)	29·00	40
236		25c. black and red/*pale yellow* (1922)	1·50	15
		a. Die I (1932)	13·00	70·00
237	**48**	50c. dull purple and black (1921)	7·50	4·50
238		1r. black/*emerald* (1924)	7·50	2·00
		a. Die I (1932)	30·00	65·00
239		2r.50 black and red/*blue* (1922)	20·00	18·00
240		5r. green and red/*yellow* (1924)	50·00	£110
241	**49**	10r. green and red/*emerald* (1924)	£160	£375
223/241 *Set of 20*			£275	£475
223s/241s Optd or Perf (Nos. 226cs, 235s) 'SPECIMEN' *Set of 20*			£600	

3
Cents

(**50**)

51

1925 (25 Nov). Nos. 210, 217 and 220 surch locally as T **50**.

242	**46**	3c. on 4c. green	9·50	7·00
243		10c. on 12c. carmine-red	45	1·75
244		15c. on 20c. blue	60	1·75
242/244 *Set of 3*			9·50	9·50
242s/244s Optd 'SPECIMEN' *Set of 3*			£100	

1935 (6 May). Silver Jubilee. As Nos. 91/94 of Antigua. P 13½×14.

245	5c. ultramarine and grey	50	10
	f. Diagonal line by turret	85·00	30·00
	g. Dot to left of chapel	£140	65·00
	h. Dot by flagstaff	£160	75·00
246	12c. green and indigo	4·50	10
	f. Diagonal line by turret	£150	50·00
	g. Dot to left of chapel	£350	80·00
247	20c. brown and deep blue	5·50	20
	f. Diagonal line by turret	£225	70·00
	g. Dot to left of chapel	£325	90·00
248	1r. slate and purple	29·00	50·00
	h. Dot by flagstaff	£400	£550
245/248 *Set of 4*		35·00	50·00
245s/248s Perf 'SPECIMEN' *Set of 4*		£130	

For illustrations of plate varieties see Omnibus section following Zanzibar.

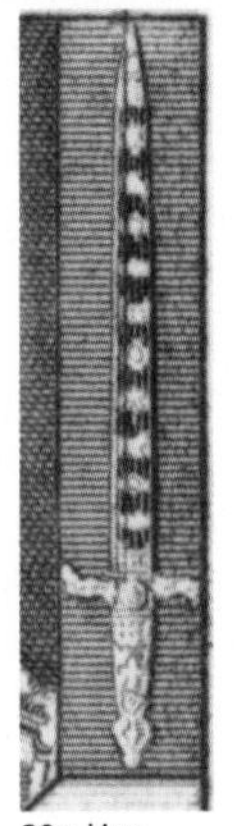
20c. Line through sword (R. 2/2)

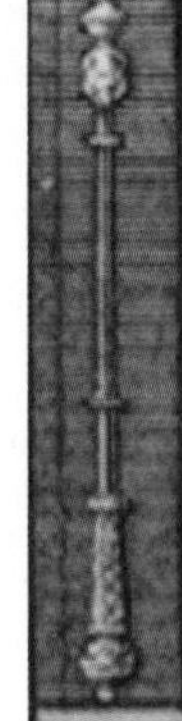
20c. Line by sceptre (R. 5/3)

1937 (12 May). Coronation. As Nos. 95/97 of Antigua but printed by D.L.R. Perf 14.

No.	Description	Unused	Used
249	5c. violet	40	20
250	12c. scarlet	75	2·25
251	20c. bright blue	1·75	1·00
	a. Line through sword	90·00	50·00
	b. Line by sceptre	90·00	50·00
249/251	*Set of 3*	2·50	3·00
249s/251s	Perf 'SPECIMEN' *Set of 3*	£110	

Similar but less pronounced examples of the 'Line by sceptre' occur on R. 5/2 and R. 5/6.

3c. Sliced 'S' at right (R. 2/2, 3/2, right pane)

3c. Split frame (R. 7/6, right pane, Key Plate 1)

4c. Damaged 'S' (R. 4/4, right pane).

10c. Sliced 'S' at top (R. 4/1, left pane and R. 8/4, right pane)

20c., 2r.50 Broken frame under 'A' of 'MAURITIUS' (R. 9/3 left pane, Key Plate 2)

25c. 'IJ' flaw (R. 3/6 of right pane)

1r. Battered 'A' (R. 6/1 of right pane)

(Typo D.L.R.)

1938–49. T **51** and similar types. Chalk-surfaced paper (25c. to 10r.). Wmk Mult Script CA. P 14.

No.	Description	Unused	Used
252	2c. olive-grey (9.3.38)	30	10
	a. Perf 15×14 (1942)	1·00	10
253	3c. reddish purple and scarlet (27.10.38)	2·00	2·00
	a. Sliced 'S' at right	85·00	85·00
	b. Split frame	£225	
	c. Reddish lilac and red (4.43)	5·50	4·00
	ca. Sliced 'S' at right	£225	£200
254	4c. dull green (26.2.38)	7·50	2·00
	a. Open 'C'	£225	£120
	b. Deep dull green (4.43)	2·50	2·25
	ba. Open 'C'	£150	£130
	bb. Damaged 'S'	£275	
255	5c. slate-lilac (23.2.38)	18·00	85
	a. Pale lilac (shades) (4.43)	3·25	20
	b. Perf 15×14 (1942)	60·00	10
256	10c. rose-red (9.3.38)	2·75	30
	a. Sliced 'S' at top	£170	48·00
	b. Deep reddish rose (shades) (4.43)	2·50	20
	ba. Sliced 'S' at top	£160	38·00
	c. Perf 15×14. *Pale reddish rose* (1942).	42·00	3·00
	ca. Sliced 'S' at top (RP 8/4 only)	£700	£150
257	12c. salmon (*shades*) (26.2.38)	1·00	20
	a. Perf 15×14 (1942)	55·00	1·25
258	20c. blue (26.2.38)	1·00	10
	a. Broken frame	£1500	£400
259	25c. brown-purple (2.3.38)	23·00	20
	b. Ordinary paper (1942)	9·00	10
	ba. 'IJ' flaw	£300	48·00
260	1r. grey-brown (2.3.38)	45·00	3·00
	a. Battered 'A'	£900	£250
	b. Ordinary paper (1942)	20·00	1·75
	ba. Battered 'A'	£650	£170
	c. Drab (4.49)	55·00	21·00
	ca. Battered 'A'	£1000	£475
261	2r.50 pale violet (2.3.38)	60·00	32·00
	a. Ordinary paper (8.4.43)	42·00	30·00
	ab. Broken frame	£1500	£850
	b. Slate-violet (4.48)	70·00	50·00
262	5r. olive-green (2.3.38)	55·00	45·00
	a. Ordinary paper. *Sage-green* (8.4.43)	38·00	45·00
263	10r. reddish purple (*shades*) (2.3.38)	80·00	55·00
	a. Ordinary paper (8.4.43)	17·00	48·00
252/263a	*Set of 12*	£120	£110
252s/263s	Perf 'SPECIMEN' *Set of 12*	£425	

Less pronounced examples of the 'Sliced 'S'' variety on the 3c. occur in other positions the slice on the 10c. at R.4/1 also varies considerably. The prices for the listed varieties being for pronounced examples, as illustrated. The illustration of the 'Battered 'A'' on the 1r. value shows the variety as it appears on issues between 1942 and 1949. On early printings of No. 260a the top of the 'A' is normal.

The broken frame on the 2r.50 (No. 261ab) differs slightly from that on the 20c. but the distorted frame above 'AU' is the same.

The stamps perf 15×14 were printed by Bradbury Wilkinson from De La Rue plates and issued only in the colony in 1942. De La Rue printings of the 2c. to 20c. in 1943–1945 were on thin, whiter paper. 1942–1945 printings of the 25c. to 10r. were on ordinary paper.

1946 (20 Nov). Victory. As. Nos. 110/111 of Antigua.

No.	Description	Unused	Used
264	5c. lilac	10	75
265	20c. blue	20	25
264s/265s	Perf 'SPECIMEN' *Set of 2*	95·00	

52 1d. 'Post Office' Mauritius and King George VI

(Recess B.W.)

1948 (22 Mar). Centenary of First British Colonial Postage Stamp. Wmk Mult Script CA. P 11½×11.

No.	Type	Description	Unused	Used
266	**52**	5c. orange and magenta	10	50
267		12c. orange and green	15	50
268	–	20c. blue and light blue	20	10
269	–	1r. blue and red-brown	1·25	30
266/269		*Set of 4*	1·50	1·25
266s/269s		Perf 'SPECIMEN' *Set of 4*	£180	

Design: 20c., 1r. As T **52** but showing 2d. 'Post Office' Mauritius.

1948 (25 Oct). Royal Silver Wedding. As Nos. 112/113 of Antigua.

No.	Description	Unused	Used
270	5c. violet	10	10
271	10r. magenta	17·00	42·00

1949 (10 Oct). 75th Anniversary of UPU. As Nos. 114/117 of Antigua.

No.	Description	Unused	Used
272	12c. carmine	50	4·00
273	20c. deep blue	2·25	2·50
274	35c. purple	60	1·50
275	1r. sepia	50	20
272/275	*Set of 4*	3·50	7·50

53 Labourdonnais Sugar Factory

54 Grand Port

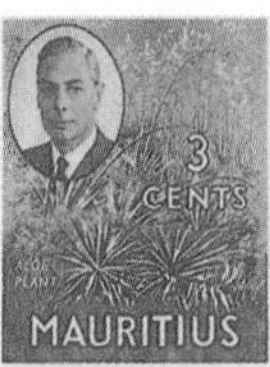

55 Aloe Plant

56 Tamarind Falls

57 Rempart Mountain

58 Transporting cane

59 Mauritius Dodo and map

60 Legend of Paul and Virginie

61 La Bourdonnais Statue

62 Government House, Reduit

63 Pieter Both Mountain

64 Timor Deer

65 Port Louis

66 Beach scene

67 Arms of Mauritius

(Photo Harrison)

1950 (1 July). Types **53**/**67**. Chalk-surfaced paper. Wmk Mult Script CA. P 13½×14½ (horiz), 14½×13½ (vert).

No.	Type	Description	Unused	Used
276	**53**	1c. bright purple	10	50
277	**54**	2c. rose-carmine	15	10
278	**55**	3c. yellow-green	60	4·50
279	**56**	4c. green	20	3·25
280	**57**	5c. blue	15	10
281	**58**	10c. scarlet	30	75
282	**59**	12c. olive-green	1·50	3·00
283	**60**	20c. ultramarine	1·00	15
284	**61**	25c. brown-purple	2·50	40
285	**62**	35c. violet	40	10
		w. Wmk inverted	†	£3250
286	**63**	50c. emerald-green	2·75	50
287	**64**	1r. sepia	9·50	10
288	**65**	2r.50 orange	23·00	21·00
289	**66**	5r. red-brown	25·00	21·00
		w. Wmk inverted	†	£3250
290	**67**	10r. dull blue	17·00	48·00
276/290		*Set of 15*	75·00	90·00

The latitude is incorrectly shown on No. 282.

1953 (2 June). Coronation. As No. 120 of Antigua.

No.	Description	Unused	Used
291	10c. black and emerald	1·50	15

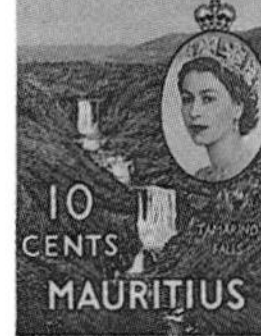

68 Tamarind Falls

69 Historical Museum, Mahebourg

(Photo Harrison)

1953 (3 Nov)–**58**. Designs previously used for King George VI issue but with portrait of Queen Elizabeth II as in Types **68**/**69**. Chalk-surfaced paper. Wmk Mult Script CA. P 13½×14½ (horiz) or 14½×13½ (vert).

No.	Type	Description	Unused	Used
293	**54**	2c. bright carmine (1.6.54)	10	10
294	**55**	3c. yellow-green (1.6.54)	30	40
295	**53**	4c. bright purple	10	1·00
		w. Wmk inverted	£110	
296	**57**	5c. Prussian blue (1.6.54)	10	10
297	**68**	10c. bluish green	20	10
		a. Yellowish green (9.2.55)	1·00	10
298	**69**	15c. scarlet	10	10
299	**61**	20c. brown-purple	15	20
		w. Wmk inverted	6·00	10·00
300	**60**	25c. bright ultramarine	1·50	10
		a. Bright blue (19.6 57)	7·50	75
301	**62**	35c. reddish violet (1.6.54)	20	10
		w. Wmk inverted	£375	£250
302	**63**	50c. bright green	55	85
302*a*	**59**	60c. deep green (2.8.54)	10·00	10
		ab. Bronze-green (27.8.58)	14·00	10
303	**64**	1r. sepia	30	10
		a. Deep grey-brown (19.6.57)	5·00	65
		w. Wmk inverted	£400	
304	**65**	2r.50 orange (1.6.54)	14·00	9·00
305	**66**	5r. red-brown (1.6.54)	28·00	10·00
		a. Orange-brown (19.6.57)	60·00	16·00
306	**67**	10r. deep grey-blue (1.6.54)	17·00	2·00
293/306		*Set of 15*	65·00	21·00

Nos. 296 and 300 exist in coils, constructed from normal sheets.

See also Nos. 314/316.

70 Queen Elizabeth II and King George III (after Lawrence)

(Litho Enschedé)

1961 (11 Jan). 150th Anniversary of British Post Office in Mauritius. W w **12**. P 13½×14.

No.	Type	Description	Unused	Used
307	**70**	10c. black and brown-red	10	10
		w. Wmk inverted	40·00	20·00
308		20c. ultramarine and light blue	30	50
		w. Wmk inverted	70·00	35·00
309		35c. black and yellow	40	50
310		1r. deep maroon and green	60	30
		w. Wmk inverted	£170	
307/310 *Set of 4*			1·25	1·25

1963 (4 June). Freedom from Hunger. As No. 146 of Antigua.

No.	Type	Description	Unused	Used
311		60c. reddish violet	40	10

1963 (2 Sept). Red Cross Centenary. As No. 147/148 of Antigua.

No.	Type	Description	Unused	Used
312		10c. red and black	15	10
313		60c. red and blue	60	20

1963 (12 Nov)–**65**. As Nos. 297, 302*ab* and 304 but wmk w **12**.

No.	Type	Description	Unused	Used
314	**68**	10c. bluish green (1964)	15	10
		a. Yellowish green (21.1.65)	25	10
315	**59**	60c. bronze-green (28.5.64)	4·00	10
316	**65**	2r.50 orange	13·00	8·50
314/316 *Set of 3*			15·00	8·50

71 Bourbon White Eye

72 Rodriquez Fody

73 Mauritius Olive White-eye

74 Mascarene Paradise Flycatcher

75 Mauritius Fody

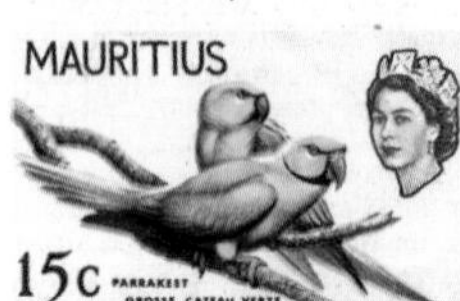

76 Mauritius Parakeet

77 Mauritius Greybird

78 Mauritius Kestrel

79 Pink Pigeon

80 Réunion Bulbul

81 Mauritius Blue Pigeon (extinct)

82 Mauritius Dodo (extinct)

83 Rodriquez Solitaire (extinct)

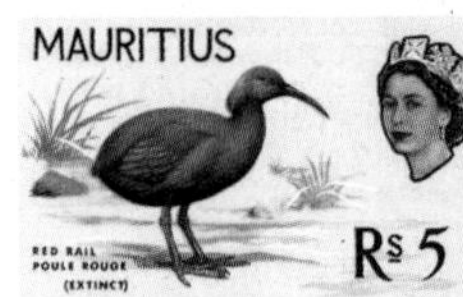

84 Mauritius Red Rail (extinct)

85 Broad-billed Parrot (extinct)

(Des D. M. Reid-Henry. Photo Harrison)

1965 (16 Mar). Horiz designs as Types **71/85**. W w **12** (upright). Multicoloured; background colours given. P 14½×14.

No.	Type	Description	Unused	Used
317	**71**	2c. lemon	40	15
		a. Grey (leg) omitted	£375	
		w. Wmk inverted	20·00	
318	**72**	3c. brown	1·00	15
		a. Black (eye and beak) omitted	£450	
		w. Wmk inverted	70·00	
319	**73**	4c. light reddish purple	30	15
		a. Mauve-pink omitted*	80·00	
		b. Pale grey omitted	£350	
		c. Orange omitted	£450	
		w. Wmk inverted	9·00	8·00
320	**74**	5c. grey-brown	3·75	10
		w. Wmk inverted	£110	
321	**75**	10c. light grey-green	30	10
		w. Wmk inverted	17·00	
322	**76**	15c. pale grey	2·00	40
		a. Red (beak) omitted	£900	
		w. Wmk inverted	80·00	
323	**77**	20c. light yellow-bistre	2·00	10
		w. Wmk inverted	28·00	
324	**78**	25c. bluish grey	2·00	30
		w. Wmk inverted	11·00	
325	**79**	35c. greyish blue	3·75	10
		w. Wmk inverted	£130	
326	**80**	50c. light yellow-buff	50	65
		w. Wmk inverted	95·00	
327	**81**	60c. light greenish yellow	60	10
		w. Wmk inverted	1·50	75
328	**82**	1r. light yellow-olive	12·00	10
		a. Pale orange omitted	£325	
		b. Light grey (ground) omitted	£475	£475
329	**83**	2r.50 pale stone	5·00	10·00
330	**71**	5r. pale grey-blue	15·00	17·00
		a. Brown-red omitted	£450	£450
331	**85**	10r. pale bluish green	35·00	38·00
317/331 *Set of 15*			70·00	60·00

* On the 4c. the background is printed in two colours so that in No. 319a the background colour is similar to that of the 5c.

On No. 317a it is the deep grey which is missing, affecting the leg, beak and part of the branch. On No. 319c the missing orange affects the under breast of the bird, which appears much paler. On No. 328a the omission affects the legs and part of the body and on No. 330a the whole of the bird appears in the same colour as the legs.

The 50c. and 2r.50 exist with PVA gum as well as gum arabic.

Nos. 320 and 324 exist in coils, constructed from normal sheets.

See also Nos. 340/341 and 370/375.

1965 (17 May). ITU Centenary. As No. 166/167 of Antigua.

No.	Type	Description	Unused	Used
332		10c. red-orange and apple-green	20	10
333		60c. yellow and bluish violet	70	20

1965 (25 Oct). International Co-operation Year. As No. 168/169 of Antigua.

No.	Type	Description	Unused	Used
334		10c. reddish purple and turquoise-green	15	10
335		60c. deep bluish green and lavender	30	20

1966 (24 Jan). Churchill Commemoration. As No. 170/173 of Antigua.

No.	Type	Description	Unused	Used
336		2c. new blue	10	4·00
		w. Wmk inverted	60·00	
337		10c. deep green	50	10
		w. Wmk inverted	45·00	
338		60c. brown	1·75	20
		w. Wmk inverted	19·00	
339		1r. bluish violet	1·75	20
336/339 *Set of 4*			3·50	4·00

1966–67. As Nos. 320, 325 but wmk w **12** sideways*.

No.	Type	Description	Unused	Used
340		5c. grey-brown (1966)	70	15
		w. Wmk Crown to right of CA	50·00	
341		35c. greyish blue (27.6.67)	30	15

* The normal sideways watermark shows Crown to left of CA, *as seen from the back of the stamp.*

No. 340 exists in coils, constructed from normal sheets.

1966 (1 Dec). 20th Anniversary of UNESCO. As No. 196/198 of Antigua.

No.	Type	Description	Unused	Used
342		5c. slate-violet, red, yellow and orange	25	30
343		10c. orange-yellow, violet and deep olive	30	10
344		60c. black, bright purple and orange	1·40	15
342/344 *Set of 3*			1·75	50

86 Red-tailed Tropicbird

(Des D. M. Reid-Henry. Photo Harrison)

1967 (1 Sept). Self-Government. T **86** and similar horiz designs. Multicoloured. W w **12**. P 14½.

No.	Type	Description	Unused	Used
345		2c. Type **86**	25	3·00
		w. Wmk inverted	20·00	
346		10c. Rodriguez Brush Warbler	80	10
347		60c. Rose-ringed Parakeet (extinct)	85	10
348		1r. Grey-rumped Swiftlet	90	10
345/348 *Set of 4*			2·50	3·00

SELF GOVERNMENT 1967
(**90**)

1967 (1 Dec). Self-Government. As Nos. 317/331 but wmk sideways* on Nos. 352/353 and 357. Optd with T **90**. P 14×14½.

No.	Type	Description	Unused	Used
349		2c. lemon	10	50
		w. Wmk inverted	17·00	
350		3c. brown	10	50
		w. Wmk inverted	23·00	
351		4c. light reddish purple	10	50
		a. Orange omitted	£325	
352		5c. grey-brown	10	10
353		10c. light grey-green	10	10
		w. Wmk Crown to right of CA	23·00	
354		15c. pale grey	10	30
355		20c. light yellow-bistre	15	10
		w. Wmk inverted	17·00	
356		25c. bluish grey	15	10
357		35c. greyish blue	20	10
		w. Wmk Crown to right of CA	£100	
358		50c. light yellow-buff	30	15
359		60c. light greenish yellow	30	10
		w. Wmk inverted	13·00	
360		1r. light yellow-olive	1·50	10
361		2r.50 pale stone	1·00	2·25
362		5r. pale grey-blue	6·00	3·25
363		10r. pale bluish green	10·00	15·00
349/363 *Set of 15*			18·00	21·00

* The normal sideways watermark shows Crown to the left of CA, *as seen from the back of the stamp.*

91 Flag of Mauritius

92 Arms and Mauritius Dodo Emblem

(Litho D.L.R.)

1968 (12 Mar). Independence. Types **91/92**. P 13½×13.

No.	Type	Description	Unused	Used
364	**91**	2c. multicoloured	10	2·50
365	**92**	3c. multicoloured	20	2·50
366	**91**	15c. multicoloured	60	10
367	**92**	20c. multicoloured	60	10
368	**91**	60c. multicoloured	1·10	10
369	**92**	1r. multicoloured	1·10	10
364/369 *Set of 6*			3·25	4·75

1968 (12 July). As Nos. 317/318, 322/323 and 327/328 but background colours changed as below.

No.	Type	Description	Unused	Used
370	**71**	2c. olive-yellow	20	4·50
		a. Black printed double	£150	
		b. Grey printed double	£110	
371	**72**	3c. cobalt	1·75	9·00
		w. Wmk inverted	85·00	
372	**76**	15c. cinnamon	55	20
		a. Greenish blue omitted	£500	
373	**77**	20c. buff	3·50	4·00
374	**81**	60c. rose	1·50	1·25
		w. Wmk inverted	50·00	
375	**82**	1r. reddish purple	3·25	1·50
370/375 *Set of 6*			9·50	18·00

93 Dominique rescues Paul and Virginie

(Des V. Whiteley, from prints. Litho Format)

1968 (2 Dec). Bicentenary of Bernardin de St Pierre's Visit to Mauritius. Multicoloured designs as T **93**. P 13½.

No.	Description	Unused	Used
376	2c. Type **93**	10	1·25
377	15c. Paul and Virginie crossing the river	65	10
378	50c. Visit of La Bourdonnais to Madame de la Tour (*horiz*)	1·25	10
379	60c. Meeting of Paul and Virginie in Confidence (*vert*)	1·25	10
380	1r. Departure of Virginie for Europe (*horiz*)	1·25	20
381	2r.50 Bernardin de St Pierre (*vert*)	1·75	3·75
376/381 *Set of 6*		5·50	5·00

99 Black-spotted Emperor

(Des J. Vinson (3c., 20c., 1r.) R. Granger Barrett (others). Photo Harrison)

1969 (12 Mar)–**73**. W w **12** (sideways* on 2, 3, 4, 5, 10, 15, 60 and 75c). Chalk-surfaced paper. P 14.

No.	Description	Unused	Used
382	2c. multicoloured	10	2·75
	a. Pale green printed double**	£120	
383	3c. multicoloured	10	3·50
	w. Wmk Crown to right of CA	£150	
384	4c. multicoloured	2·50	4·50
	w. Wmk Crown to right of CA	26·00	
385	5c. multicoloured	30	10
386	10c. scarlet, black and flesh	2·00	10
	w. Wmk Crown to right of CA	40·00	
387	15c. ochre, black and cobalt	30	10
	w. Wmk Crown to right of CA	2·75	
388	20c. multicoloured	65	70
	a. Glazed ordinary paper (20.2.73)	45	13·00
389	25c. red, black and pale apple-green	30	3·75
	a. Glazed ordinary paper (22.1.71)	3·75	6·50
	aw. Wmk inverted	4·00	8·00
390	30c. multicoloured	1·50	1·75
	a. Glazed, ordinary paper (20.3.73)	8·00	18·00
391	35c. multicoloured	1·75	1·25
	a. Glazed ordinary paper (3.2.71)	1·00	3·50
	aw. Wmk inverted	2·50	
392	40c. multicoloured	35	1·25
	a. Glazed ordinary paper (20.2.73)	8·00	18·00
	aw. Wmk inverted	25·00	
393	50c. multicoloured	1·00	10
	a. Red omitted	£190	
	b. Glazed ordinary paper (22.1.71)	1·50	1·25
	ba. Red printed double		
	bw. Wmk inverted	1·50	20
394	60c. black, rose and ultramarine	1·50	10
395	75c. multicoloured	1·50	2·75
	w. Wmk Crown to right of CA	32·00	
396	1r. multicoloured	60	10
	a. Glazed ordinary paper (22.1.71)	2·25	15
	aw. Wmk inverted	95·00	
397	2r. 50 multicoloured	3·00	8·50
	a. Glazed ordinary paper (20.2.73)	2·00	20·00
398	5r. multicoloured	12·00	12·00
	a. Glazed ordinary paper (22.1.71)	12·00	3·50
	aw. Wmk inverted	55·00	
399	10r. multicoloured	2·50	4·75
	w. Wmk inverted (26.1.72)	1·50	1·50
382/399 *Set of 18*		27·00	40·00
388a/398a *Set of 9*		35·00	75·00

Designs: 2c. T **99**; 3c. Red Reef Crab; 4c. Episcopal Mitre (*Mitra mitra*); 5c. Black-saddled Pufferfish ('Bourse'); 10c. Starfish; 15c. Sea Urchin; 20c. Fiddler Crab 25c. Spiny Shrimp; 30c. Single Harp Shells and Double Harp Shell; 35c. Common Paper Nautilus (*Argonauta argo*); 40c. Spanish Dancer (*Hexabranchus sanguineus*); 50c. Orange Spider Conch (*Lambis crocata*) and Violet Spider Conch (*Lambis violacea*); 60c. Blue Marlin; 75c. *Conus clytospira*; 1r. Dolphinfish; 2r.50, Spiny Lobster; 5r. Ruby Snapper ('Sacre Chien Rouge'); 10r. Yellowedged Lyretail ('Croissant Queue Jaune').

* The normal sideways watermark shows Crown to left of CA, *as seen from the back of the stamp.*

** No. 382a occurs from a sheet on which a second printing of the pale green appears above the normal.

Nos. 385/386 and 389 exist in coils constructed from normal sheets.

This set was re-issued between 1972 and 1974 with watermark w **12** upright on 2c. to 15c., 60c. and 75c. and sideways on other values. Between 1974 and 1977 it was issued on Multiple Crown CA Diagonal watermark paper.

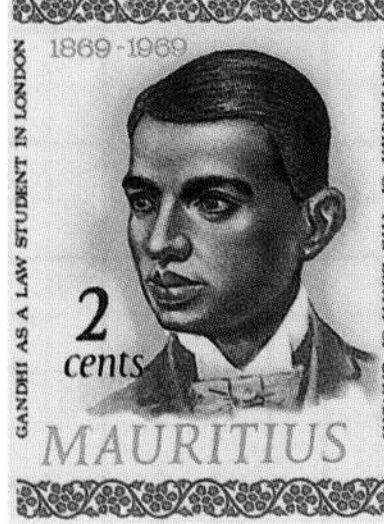

117 Gandhi as Law Student

124 Frangourinier Cane-crusher (18th-century)

(Des J. W. Litho Format)

1969 (1 July). Birth Centenary of Mahatma Gandhi. T **117** and similar vert designs. Multicoloured. W w **12**. P 13½.

No.	Description	Unused	Used
400	2c. Type **117**	30	20
401	15c. Gandhi as stretcher-bearer during Zulu Revolt	65	10
402	50c. Gandhi as Satyagrahi in South Africa	80	50
403	60c. Gandhi at No. 10 Downing Street, London	80	10
404	1r. Gandhi in Mauritius, 1901	90	10
405	2r. 50 Gandhi, the 'Apostle of Truth and Non-Violence'	2·00	2·00
400/405 *Set of 6*		5·00	2·75
MS406 153×153 mm. Nos. 400/405		13·00	8·00

(Des V. Whiteley. Photo Enschedé)

1969 (22 Dec*). 150th Anniversary of Telfair's Improvements to the Sugar Industry. T **124** and similar multicoloured designs. W w **12** (sideways on 2c. to 1r.), P 11½×11 (2r.50) or 11×11½ (others).

No.	Description	Unused	Used
407	2c. Three-roller Vertical Mill	10	20
408	15c. Type **124**	10	10
409	60c. Beau Rivage Factory, 1867	10	10
410	1r. Mon Desert-Alma Factory, 1969	10	10
411	2r.50 Dr. Charles Telfair (*vert*)	25	1·25
407/411 *Set of 5*		60	1·60
MS412 159×88 mm. Nos. 407/411†. Wmk sideways. P 11×11½		1·75	2·50

* This was the local release date but the Crown Agents issued the stamps on 15 December.

† In the miniature sheet the 2r.50 is perf 11 at the top and imperf on the other three sides.

EXPO '70'
OSAKA
(**128**)

129 Morne Plage, Mountain and Boeing 707

1970 (7 Apr). World Fair, Osaka. Nos. 394 and 396 optd with T **128** by Harrison & Sons.

No.	Description	Unused	Used
413	60c. black, rose and ultramarine	10	10
	w. Wmk Crown to right of CA	70·00	
414	1r. multicoloured	20	20

(Des H. Rose. Litho G. Gehringer, Kaiserslautern, Germany)

1970 (2 May). Inauguration of Lufthansa Flight, Mauritius–Frankfurt. T **129** and similar multicoloured design. P 14.

No.	Description	Unused	Used
415	25c. Type **129**	30	20
416	50c. Boeing 707 and Map (*vert*)	30	20

131 Lenin as a Student

133 2d. 'Post Office' Mauritius and original Post Office

(Photo State Ptg Works, Moscow)

1970 (15 May). Birth Centenary of Lenin. T **131** and similar vert design. P 12×11½.

No.	Description	Unused	Used
417	15c. blackish green and silver	10	10
418	75c. blackish brown and gold	20	20

Design: 15c. T **131**; 75c. Lenin as Founder of USSR.

(Des and litho D.L.R.)

1970 (15 Oct). Port Louis, Old and New. T **133** and similar horiz designs. Multicoloured. W w **12** (sideways). P 14.

No.	Description	Unused	Used
419	5c. Type **133**	20	10
420	15c. GPO Building (built 1870)	20	10
421	50c. Mail Coach (*c.* 1870)	80	15
422	75c. Port Louis Harbour (1970)	95	25
423	2r.50 Arrival of Pierre A. de Suffren (1783)	1·00	3·00
419/423 *Set of 5*		2·75	3·25
MS424 165×95 mm. Nos. 419/423		5·25	8·50

138 UN Emblem and Symbols

(Des Jennifer Toombs. Litho Format)

1970 (24 Oct). 25th Anniversary of United Nations. W w **12** (sideways). P 14½.

No.	Type	Description	Unused	Used
425	**138**	10c. multicoloured	10	10
426		60c. multicoloured	40	10

STAMP BOOKLETS

1953 (10 Oct). Black on white cover. Stapled.

No.	Description	Price
SB1	5r. booklet containing 4×5c., 8×10c. and 8×50c. (Nos. 280, 286, 291) in blocks of 4 and one pane of 4 air mail labels	£225

1954 (23 Sept). Black on white or grey cover. Stapled.

No.	Description	Price
SB2	5r. booklet containing 4×5c., 8×10c. and 8×50c. (Nos. 296/297, 302) in blocks of 4 and one pane of 4 air mail labels	40·00

1955. Black on grey cover. Stapled.

No.	Description	Price
SB3	5r. booklet containing 4×5c., 8×10c. and 8×50c. (Nos. 296, 297*a*, 302) in block of 4 and one pane of 4 air mail labels	50·00

EXPRESS DELIVERY STAMPS

EXPRESS
DELIVERY
15c.
(E **1**)

EXPRESS
DELIVERY
(INLAND)
15c.
(E **2**)

EXPRESS
DELIVERY
(INLAND)
15c.
(E **3**)

EXPRESS
DELIVERY
(INLAND)
15 c
(E **4**)

Type E **2**. '(INLAND)' was inserted at a second printing on stamps already surcharged with T E **1** (No. E1).

Type E **3**. New setting made at one printing. More space above and below '(INLAND)'.

Type E **4**. New setting with smaller '15c' and no stop.

1903 (10 Aug)–**04**. No. 136 surch locally in red.

No.	Type	Description	Unused	Used
E1	E **1**	15c. on 15c. ultramarine	20·00	50·00
E2	E **2**	15c. on 15c. ultramarine (28.3.04)	65·00	£100
		a. 'A' inverted	£1700	£1300
		b. '(INLAND)' inverted	†	£3500
E3	E **3**	15c. on 15c. ultramarine (4.04)	14·00	4·50
		a. Surch inverted	£1300	£850
		aw. Surch and wmk inverted	—	£1200
		b. Surch double, both inverted	£1900	£1900
		c. Imperf between (vert pair)	£8000	
		w. Wmk inverted		
		x. Wmk reversed		
E4	E **4**	15c. on 15c. ultramarine (1904)	£850	£800
		a. Surch inverted	—	£1900
		b. Surch double	—	£3500
		c. Surch double, both inverted	—	£5000
		d. 'c' omitted	—	£2500

(FOREIGN)
EXPRESS
DELIVERY
18 CENTS
(E **5**)

1904. T **42** (without value in label), surch with T E **5** locally. Wmk Crown CC. P 14.

No.	Description	Unused	Used
E5	18c. green	5·00	45·00
	a. Exclamation mark for 'I' in 'FOREIGN'	£750	

1904. T **42** (without value in label) surch with T E **3** locally.

No.	Description	Unused	Used
E6	15c. grey-green (R.)	26·00	8·50
	a. Surch inverted	£1000	£900
	b. Surch double	£750	£750
	c. Surch double, one 'LNIAND'	£850	£800

POSTAGE DUE STAMPS

D 1

(Typo Waterlow)

1933–54. Wmk Mult Script CA. P 15×14.

No.	Type	Description	Unused	Used
D1	**D 1**	2c. black	1·25	50
D2		4c. violet	50	65
D3		6c. scarlet	60	80
D4		10c. green	70	3·00
D5		20c. bright blue	70	3·50
D6		50c. deep magenta (1.3.54)	55	20·00
D7		1r. orange (1.3.54)	70	17·00
D1/D7 *Set of 7*			4·50	40·00
D1s/D5s Perf 'SPECIMEN' *Set of 5*			£120	

(Typo D.L.R.)

1966–72. Chalk-surfaced paper. Wmk w **12**. P 13½×14 (2c.) or 15×14 (others).

No.	Type	Description	Unused	Used
D8	**D 1**	2c. black (11.7.67)	3·00	6·00
D9		4c. slate-lilac (7.1.69)	1·75	8·00
D10		6c. red-orange (7.1.69)	6·50	35·00
		a. Perf 13½×14	23·00	65·00
D11		10c. yellow-green (16.2.67)	30	2·00
D12		20c. blue (3.1.66)	2·25	7·50
		a. Deep blue (7.1.69)	2·25	17·00
D13		50c. deep magenta (7.1.69)	1·00	15·00
		a. Magenta (10.1.72)	2·00	16·00
D8/D13 *Set of 6*			13·00	65·00

FISCALS USED FOR POSTAGE

INLAND
REVENUE
(F **1**)

INLAND REVENUE
(F **2**)

F **3**

1889. T **19**, wmk Crown CA, optd. P 14.

No.	Type	Description	Unused	Used
R1	**F 1**	4c. carmine	38·00	9·00
R2	**F 2**	4c. lilac	13·00	13·00

(Typo D.L.R.)

1896. Wmk Crown CA. P 14.

No.	Type	Description	Unused	Used
R3	**F 3**	4c. dull purple	50·00	70·00

Montserrat

A local post office operated on Montserrat from 1702, although the first recorded postal marking does not occur until 1791. A branch of the British GPO was established at Plymouth, the island capital, in 1852.

The stamps of Great Britain were used from 1858 until the overseas postal service reverted to local control on 1 April 1860.

In the interim period between 1860 and the introduction of Montserrat stamps in 1876 No. CC1 and a similar 'uncrowned' handstamp were again used.

PLYMOUTH

CROWNED-CIRCLE HANDSTAMPS

C **1**

CC1 C **1** MONTSERRAT (R.) (15.7.1852) *Price on cover* £4750

No. CC1 was used as an emergency measure, struck in red or black, between 1883 and 1886.

Stamps of GREAT BRITAIN cancelled 'A 08' as T Z **1** of Jamaica.

1858 (8 May)–**60.**

No.	Description	Price
Z1	1d. rose-red (1857), *perf* 14	£1300
Z2	4d. rose (1857)	
Z3	6d. lilac (1856)	£550
Z4	1s. green (1856)	£2750

PRICES FOR STAMPS ON COVER TO 1945

Nos. 1/2	*from* × 50
No. 3	†
Nos. 4/5	*from* × 10
Nos. 6/13	*from* × 12
Nos. 14/22	*from* × 4
No. 23	—
Nos. 24/33	*from* × 4
Nos. 35/47	*from* × 3
No. 48	—
Nos. 49/59	*from* × 3
Nos. 60/62	*from* × 15
Nos. 63/83	*from* × 3
Nos. 84/93	*from* × 4
Nos. 94/97	*from* × 3
Nos. 98/100	*from* × 8
Nos. 101/112	*from* × 5

1

(**2**)

3 (Die I)

(T **1** recess D.L.R.)

1876 (Aug)–**83**. Stamps of Antigua optd with T **2**. Wmk Crown CC. P 14.

No.	Type	Description	Unused	Used
1	**1**	1d. red	32·00	17·00
		a. Bisected (½d.) (1883) (*on cover*)	†	£1400
		b. Inverted 'S'	£1000	£750
		w. Wmk inverted	50·00	45·00
		x. Wmk reversed	35·00	22·00
		y. Wmk inverted and reversed	50·00	60·00
2		6d. green	70·00	40·00
		a. Trisected (used as 2d.) (12.83) (*on cover*)	†	£6500
		b. Inverted 'S'	£1900	£1200
		x. Wmk reversed	—	£110
3		6d. blue-green	£1300	
		a. Inverted 'S'	£13000	

Nos. 1/3 were overprinted either from a setting of 120 (12×10) or from a setting of 60 (6×10) applied twice to each sheet. This setting of 60 had an inverted 'S' on R. 2/3. The same setting was subsequently used for some sheets of Nos. 6 and 8.

No. 1 was bisected and used for a ½d. in 1883. This bisected stamp is found surcharged with a small '½' in *black* and also in *red*; both were unofficial and they did not emanate from the Montserrat PO (*Price on cover, from £500*).

The 6d. in blue-green is only known unused.

(T **3** typo D.L.R.)

1880 (Jan). Wmk Crown CC. P 14.

No.	Type	Description	Unused	Used
4	**3**	2½d. red-brown	£250	£180
5		4d. blue	£150	30·00
		w. Wmk inverted	—	£250
		x. Wmk reversed	£600	

1883 (Mar). Wmk Crown CA. P 12.

No.	Type	Description	Unused	Used
6	**1**	1d. red	80·00	65·00
		a. Inverted 'S'	£2000	£1300
		b. Bisected (½d.) (*on cover*)	†	£1600
		x. Wmk reversed	—	60·00

Top left triangle detached
(Pl 2 R. 3/3 of right pane)

1884–85. Wmk Crown CA. P 14.

No.	Type	Description	Unused	Used
7	**3**	½d. dull green	1·00	11·00
		a. Top left triangle detached	£200	
8	**1**	1d. red	28·00	16·00
		a. Inverted 'S'	£1000	£1000
		bx. Wmk reversed	—	26·00
		c. Rose-red (1885)	32·00	13·00
		ca. Bisected vert (½d.) (*on cover*)	†	£1300
		cb. Inverted 'S'	£1100	£1000
		cx. Wmk reversed	35·00	21·00
9	**3**	2½d. red-brown	£275	65·00
10		2½d. ultramarine (1885)	30·00	21·00
		a. Top left triangle detached	£600	£450
		w. Wmk inverted	£140	£160
11		4d. blue	£1800	£250
12		4d. mauve (1885)	5·50	3·00
		a. Top left triangle detached	£375	£375
10s, 12s Optd 'SPECIMEN' *Set of 2*			£475	

The stamps for Montserrat were superseded by the general issue for Leeward Islands in November 1890, but the following issues were in concurrent use with the stamps inscribed 'LEEWARD ISLANDS' until 1 July 1956, when Leeward Islands stamps were withdrawn and invalidated.

4 Device of the Colony

5

(Typo D.L.R.)

1903 (Aug).

(a) Wmk Crown CA. P 14

No.	Type	Description	Unused	Used
14	**4**	½d. grey-green and green	75	19·00
15		1d. grey-black and red	75	40
		w. Wmk inverted	£275	
16		2d. grey and brown	5·50	50·00
17		2½d. grey and blue	1·50	1·75
18		3d. dull orange and deep purple	9·00	50·00
19		6d. dull purple and olive	16·00	65·00
20		1s. green and bright purple	10·00	26·00
21		2s. green and brown-orange	42·00	27·00
22		2s.6d. green and black	28·00	60·00

(b) Wmk Crown CC. P 14

No.	Type	Description	Unused	Used
23	**5**	5s. black and scarlet	£160	£225
14/23 *Set of 10*			£225	£450
14s/23s Optd 'SPECIMEN' *Set of 10*			£225	

1904–08. Ordinary paper (½d., 2d., 3d., 6d.) or chalk-surfaced paper (others). Wmk Mult Crown CA. P 14.

No.	Type	Description	Unused	Used
24	**4**	½d. grey-green and green	14·00	4·25
		a. Chalk-surfaced paper (3.06)	1·00	1·25
25		1d. grey-black and red (11.07)	18·00	24·00
26		2d. grey and brown	3·75	14·00
		a. Chalk-surfaced paper (5.06)	2·25	1·25
27		2½d. grey and blue (12.05)	2·50	7·00
28		3d. dull orange and deep purple	14·00	8·00
		a. Chalk-surfaced paper (5.08)	12·00	2·50
29		6d. dull purple and olive	14·00	42·00
		a. Chalk-surfaced paper (5.08)	16·00	6·50
30		1s. green and bright purple (5.08)	12·00	7·00
31		2s. green and orange (5.08)	60·00	55·00
32		2s.6d. green and black (5.08)	65·00	60·00
33	**5**	5s. black and red (9.07)	£160	£190
24/33 *Set of 10*			£300	£325

1908 (June)–**14**. Ordinary paper (½d. to 2½d.) or chalk-surfaced paper (3d. to 5s.). Wmk Mult Crown CA. P 14.

No.	Type	Description	Unused	Used
35	**4**	½d. deep green (4.10)	13·00	1·00
36		1d. rose-red	1·40	30
38		2d. greyish slate (9.09)	1·75	21·00
39		2½d. blue	2·25	3·50
40		3d. purple/*yellow* (9.09)	1·00	18·00
		a. White back (1.14)	4·00	40·00
		as. Optd 'SPECIMEN'	32·00	
43		6d. dull and deep purple (9.09)	12·00	55·00
		a. Dull and bright purple (1914)	20·00	55·00
44		1s. black/*green* (9.09)	9·00	45·00
45		2s. purple and bright blue/*blue* (9.09)	50·00	60·00
46		2s.6d. black and red/*blue* (9.09)	48·00	80·00
47	**5**	5s. red and green/*yellow* (9.09)	65·00	85·00
35/47 *Set of 10*			£170	£325
35s/47s Optd 'SPECIMEN' *Set of 10*			£275	

Examples of most values are known showing forged Montserrat postmarks dated 'OC 16 1909' or 'NO 26 1910'.

7

8

WAR STAMP
(**9**)

(Typo D.L.R.)

1914. Chalk-surfaced paper. Wmk Mult Crown CA. P 14.
48 **7** 5s. red and green/*yellow* 90·00 £160
s. Optd 'SPECIMEN' 85·00

(Typo D.L.R.)

1916 (10 Oct)–**22.** Ordinary paper (½d. to 2½d.) or chalk-surfaced paper (3d. to 5s.). Wmk Mult Crown CA. P 14.
49 **8** ½d. green 30 2·50
50 1d. scarlet 3·25 75
a. Carmine-red 40·00 9·00
51 2d. grey 3·50 5·00
52 2½d. bright blue 2·00 26·00
53 3d. purple/*yellow* 1·25 23·00
a. On pale yellow (13.7.22) 1·00 20·00
as. Optd 'SPECIMEN' 30·00
54 4d. grey-black and red/*pale yellow* (13.7.22) 9·00 45·00
55 6d. dull and deep purple 4·00 40·00
56 1s. black/*blue-green (olive back)* 3·25 45·00
57 2s. purple and blue/*blue* 24·00 60·00
58 2s.6d. black and red/*blue* 40·00 90·00
59 5s. green and red/*yellow* 55·00 95·00
49/59 *Set of* 11 £130 £375
49s/59s Optd 'SPECIMEN' *Set of* 11 £250

1917 (8 Oct)–**18.** No. 49 optd with T **9**.
60 **8** ½d. green (R.) 10 1·50
a. Short opt (right pane R. 10/1) 11·00
y. Wmk inverted and reversed 70·00
61 ½d. green (Blk.) (5.18) 4·50 8·00
a. Short opt (right pane R. 10/1) 50·00
b. Deep green (10.18) 15 1·75
ba. 'C' and 'A' missing from wmk £1200
bb. Short opt (right pane R. 10/1) 11·00
w. Wmk inverted £140

Nos. 60a, 61a, and 61bb show the overprint 2 mm high instead of 2½ mm.

No. 61ba shows the 'C' omitted from one impression and the 'A' missing from the next. The price quoted is for a horizontal pair.

1919 (4 Mar). T **8**. Special printing in orange. Value and 'WAR STAMP' as T **9** inserted in black at one printing.
62 1½d. black and orange 20 30
60s/62s Optd 'SPECIMEN' *Set of* 3 £110

1922 (13 July)–**29.** Ordinary paper (¼d. to 3d.) (No. 73) or chalk-surfaced paper (others). Wmk Mult Script CA. P 14.
63 **8** ¼d. brown 15 5·50
64 ½d. green (5.4.23) 30 30
65 1d. bright violet (5.4.23) 30 60
66 1d. carmine (1929) 75 1·50
67 1½d. orange-yellow 1·75 9·50
68 1½d. carmine (5.4.23) 45 6·00
69 1½d. red-brown (1929) 3·50 50
70 2d. grey 50 2·00
71 2½d. deep bright blue 8·50 17·00
a. Pale bright blue (17.8.26) 70 90
as. Optd 'SPECIMEN' 42·00
72 2½d. orange-yellow (5.4.23) 1·25 19·00
73 3d. dull blue (5.4.23) 75 16·00
74 3d. purple/*yellow* (2.1.27) 1·10 8·50
75 4d. black and red/*pale yellow* (5.4.23) 75 13·00
76 5d. dull purple and olive 6·50 10·00
77 6d. pale and bright purple (5.4.23) 3·00 7·50
78 1s. black/*emerald* (5.4.23) 3·00 7·00
79 2s. purple and blue/*blue* 7·00 24·00
80 2s.6d. black and red/*blue* (5.4.23) 12·00 65·00
81 3s. green and violet 12·00 24·00
82 4s. black and scarlet 15·00 50·00
83 5s. green and red/*pale yellow* (6.23) 38·00 65·00
63/83 *Set of* 21 95·00 £300
63s/83s Optd or Perf (Nos. 66s, 69s) 'SPECIMEN' *Set of* 21 £375

10 Plymouth

(Recess D.L.R.)

1932 (18 Apr). 300th Anniversary of Settlement of Montserrat. Wmk Mult Script CA. P 14.
84 **10** ½d. green 1·75 16·00
85 1d. scarlet 1·75 5·50
86 1½d. red-brown 1·75 3·75
87 2d. grey 2·00 23·00
88 2½d. ultramarine 2·00 21·00
89 3d. orange 1·75 21·00
90 6d. violet 2·25 38·00
91 1s. olive-brown 12·00 50·00
92 2s.6d. purple 48·00 85·00
93 5s. chocolate £110 £190
84/93 *Set of* 10 £160 £400
84s/93s Perf 'SPECIMEN' *Set of* 10 £250

Examples of all values are known showing a forged GPO Plymouth postmark dated 'MY 13 32'.

1935 (6 May). Silver Jubilee. As Nos. 91/94 of Antigua, but ptd by Waterlow & Sons. P 11×12.
94 1d. deep blue and scarlet 1·00 3·25
95 1½d. ultramarine and grey 2·25 3·50
96 2½d. brown and deep blue 2·25 4·50
97 1s. slate and purple 6·50 19·00
94/97 *Set of* 4 11·00 27·00
94s/97s Perf 'SPECIMEN' *Set of* 4 £110

1937 (12 May). Coronation. As Nos. 95/97 of Antigua, but printed by D.L.R. P 14.
98 1d. scarlet 35 1·75
99 1½d. yellow-brown 1·00 40
100 2½d. bright blue 60 1·75
98/100 *Set of* 3 1·75 3·50
98s/100s Perf 'SPECIMEN' *Set of* 3 80·00

11 Carr's Bay

12 Sea Island cotton

13 Botanic Station

3d. 'Tower' on hill (R. 2/2, later printings)

1s. Plate scratch (R. 10/5)

(Recess D.L.R.)

1938 (2 Aug)–**48.** Wmk Mult Script CA. P 12 (10s., £1) or 13 (others).
101 **11** ½d. blue-green 6·50 2·00
a. Perf 14 (1942) 15 20
102 **12** 1d. carmine 6·50 40
a. Perf 14 (1943) 1·75 30
103 1½d. purple 25·00 1·25
a. Perf 14 (1942) 1·75 50
ab. 'A' of 'CA' missing from wmk £1400
104 **13** 2d. orange 25·00 1·00
a. Perf 14 (1942) 2·00 70
105 **12** 2½d. ultramarine 6·50 1·50
a. Perf 14 (1943) 50 30
106 **11** 3d. brown 11·00 2·00
a. Perf 14. Red-brown (1942) 3·50 40
ab. Deep brown (1943) 1·75 7·50
ac. 'Tower' on hill £300 £400
107 **13** 6d. violet 25·00 1·50
a. Perf 14 (1943) 4·25 60
108 **11** 1s. lake 29·00 1·50
aa. Plate scratch £300 70·00
a. Perf 14 (1942) 2·50 30
109 **13** 2s.6d. slate-blue 45·00 1·25
a. Perf 14 (1943) 27·00 4·00
110 **11** 5s. rose-carmine 50·00 12·00
a. Perf 14 (1942) 30·00 4·25
111 **13** 10s. pale blue (1.4.48) 23·00 24·00
112 **11** £1 black (1.4.48) 30·00 45·00
101a/112 *Set of* 12 £110 70·00
101s/112s Perf 'SPECIMEN' *Set of* 12 £325

Nos. 101/102 exist in coils constructed from normal sheets.

1946 (1 Nov). Victory. As Nos. 110/111 of Antigua.
113 1½d. purple 15 15
114 3d. chocolate 15 15
113s/114s Perf 'SPECIMEN' *Set of* 2 85·00

1949 (3 Jan). Royal Silver Wedding. As Nos. 112/113 of Antigua.
115 2½d. ultramarine 10 10
116 5s. carmine 7·00 16·00

1949 (10 Oct). 75th Anniversary of UPU. As Nos. 114/117 of Antigua.
117 2½d. ultramarine 15 1·25
118 3d. brown 2·25 2·00
119 6d. purple 30 3·00
120 1s. purple 30 2·50
117/120 *Set of* 4 2·75 8·00

(New Currency. 100 cents = 1 West Indies, later Eastern Caribbean dollar)

1951 (16 Feb). Inauguration of BWI University College. As Nos. 118/119 of Antigua.
121 3c. black and purple 20 1·25
122 12c. black and violet 20 1·25

14 Government House

15 Sea Island cotton: cultivation

16 Map of colony

17 Picking tomatoes

17a St Anthony's Church

18 Badge of Presidency

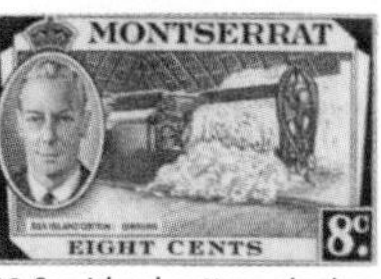

19 Sea Island cotton: ginning

19a Government House

(Recess B.W.)

1951 (17 Sept). Types **14/19a**. Wmk Mult Script CA. P 11½×11.
123 **14** 1c. black 10 2·75
124 **15** 2c. green 15 1·25
125 **16** 3c. orange-brown 40 70
126 **17** 4c. carmine 30 2·75
a. 'A' of 'CA' missing from wmk £850
127 **17a** 5c. reddish violet 30 1·50
128 **18** 6c. olive-brown 30 30
a. 'A' of 'CA' missing from wmk £850
129 **19** 8c. deep blue 2·75 20
130 **17a** 12c. blue and chocolate 1·00 30
131 **17** 24c. carmine and yellow-green 1·25 1·00
132 **19** 60c. black and carmine 11·00 6·00
133 **15** $1.20 yellow-green and blue 9·00 8·50
134 **19a** $2.40 black and green 18·00 23·00
135 **18** $4.80 black and purple 30·00 32·00
123/135 *Set of* 13 65·00 70·00

In the 4c. and 5c. the portrait is on the left and on the 12c. and 24c. it is on the right.

1953 (2 June). Coronation. As No. 120 of Antigua.
136 2c. black and deep green 60 40

20 Government House

Two Types of ½c., 3c., 6c. and $4.80: I. Inscr 'PRESIDENCY'. II. Inscr 'COLONY'.

1953 (15 Oct)–**62.** As King George VI issue, but with portrait of Queen Elizabeth II as in T **20**. Wmk Mult Script CA. P 11½×11.
136*a* **16** ½c. deep violet (I) (3.7.56) 50 10
136*b* ½c. deep violet (II) (1.9.58) 80 10
137 **20** 1c. black 10 10
138 **15** 2c. green 15 10
139 **16** 3c. orange-brown (I) 50 10
139*a* 3c. orange-brown (II) (1.9.58) 1·00 2·00
140 **17** 4c. carmine-red (1.6.55) 30 20
141 **17a** 5c. reddish lilac (1.6.55) 30 1·00
142 **18** 6c. deep bistre-brown (I) (1.6.55) 30 10
142*a* 6c. deep bistre-brown (II) (1.9.58) 55 15
ab. Deep sepia-brown (30.7.62) 14·00 6·50
143 **19** 8c. deep bright blue (1.6.55) 1·00 10
144 **17a** 12c. blue and red-brown (1.6.55) 1·50 10
145 **17** 24c. carmine-red and green (1.6.55) 1·50 20
145*a* **15** 48c. yellow-olive and purple (15.10.57) 17·00 7·50
146 **19** 60c. black and carmine (1.6.55) 10·00 2·25
147 **15** $1.20 green and greenish blue (1.6.55) 19·00 13·00
148 **19a** $2.40 black and bluish green (1.6.55) 27·00 27·00
149 **18** $4.80 black and deep purple (I) (1.6.55) 6·50 10·00
149*a* $4.80 black and deep purple (II) (1.9.58) 30·00 15·00
136*a*/149 *Set of* 15 75·00 50·00

See also No. 157.

1958 (22 Apr). Inauguration of British Caribbean Federation. As Nos. 135/137 of Antigua.
150 3c. deep green 1·00 20
151 6c. blue 1·00 75
152 12c. scarlet 1·10 15
150/152 *Set of* 3 2·75 1·00

1963 (8 July). Freedom from Hunger. As No. 146 of Antigua.
153 12c. reddish violet 30 15

1963 (2 Sept). Red Cross Centenary. As Nos. 147/148 of Antigua.
154 4c. red and black 25 20
155 12c. red and blue 45 50

1964 (23 Apr). 400th Birth Anniversary of William Shakespeare. As No. 164 of Antigua.
156 12c. indigo 35 10

1964 (29 Oct). As No. 138 but wmk w **12**.
157 2c. green 1·00 20

1965 (17 May). ITU Centenary. As Nos. 166/167 of Antigua.
158 4c. vermilion and violet 15 10
159 48c. light emerald and carmine 40 20

21 Pineapple

22 Avocado

(Des Sylvia Goaman. Photo Harrison)

1965 (16 Aug). Types **21/22** and similar vert designs showing vegetables, fruit or plants. Multicoloured. W w **12** (upright). P 15×14.

160 1c. Type **21** 10 10
w. Wmk inverted .... 1·00 1·50
161 2c. Type **22** 10 10
162 3c. Soursop 10 10
163 4c. Pepper 10 10
164 5c. Mango 10 10
165 6c. Tomato 10 10
166 8c. Guava 10 10
167 10c. Ochro 10 10
168 12c. Lime 50 75
w. Wmk inverted .... — 50·00
169 20c. Orange 30 10
170 24c. Banana 20 10
171 42c. Onion 75 60
172 48c. Cabbage .... 2·00 75
173 60c. Pawpaw .... 3·00 1·10
174 $1.20 Pumpkin .... 2·00 6·00
175 $2.40 Sweet Potato .... 8·00 8·50
176 $4.80 Egg Plant .... 8·00 12·00
160/176 *Set of 17* .... 23·00 26·00

See also Nos. 213/222.

1965 (25 Oct). International Co-operation Year. As Nos. 168/169 of Antigua.

177 2c. reddish purple and turquoise-green 10 20
178 12c. deep bluish green and lavender 25 10

1966 (26 Jan). Churchill Commemoration. As Nos. 170/173 of Antigua.

179 1c. new blue .... 10 2·50
a. Cerise (sky) omitted £750
180 2c. deep green 30 20
181 24c. brown .... 1·00 10
182 42c. bluish violet .... 1·10 1·25
179/182 *Set of 4* .... 2·25 3·75

1966 (4 Feb). Royal Visit. As No. 174 of Antigua.

183 14c. black and ultramarine .... 1·00 15
184 24c. black and magenta .... 1·50 15

1966 (20 Sept). Inauguration of WHO Headquarters, Geneva. As Nos. 178/179 of Antigua.

185 12c. black, yellow-green and light blue 20 25
186 60c. black, light purple and yellow-brown 55 75

1966 (1 Dec). 20th Anniversary of UNESCO. As Nos. 196/198 of Antigua.

187 4c. slate-violet, red, yellow and orange. 10 10
a. Orange omitted £140
188 60c. orange-yellow, violet and deep olive 70 20
189 $1.80 black, bright purple and orange .... 2·25 85
187/189 *Set of 3* .... 2·75 1·00

On No. 187a the omission of the orange only affects the squares of the lower case letters so that they appear yellow, the same as the capital squares.

25 Yachting

$1.00

(**26**)

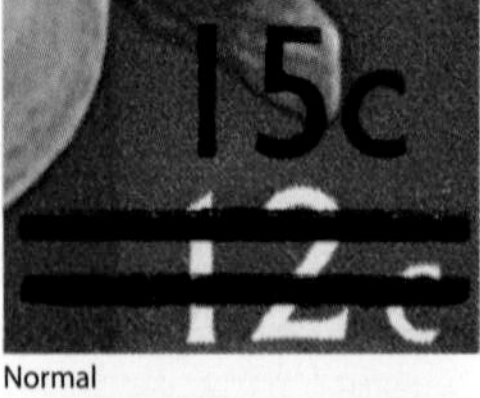

Normal

Narrow bars

The gap between the obliterating bars is normally ¾ mm. On Nos. 194a and 195a it is ¼ mm (R. 5/10).

(Des and photo Harrison)

1967 (29 Dec). International Tourist Year. T **25** and similar multicoloured designs. W w **12** (sideways on 15c.). P 14.

190 5c. Type **25** 10 10
191 15c. Waterfall near Chance Mountain (*vert*) 15 10
192 16c. Fishing, skin-diving and swimming. 20 70
193 24c. Playing golf .... 1·00 45
190/193 *Set of 4* .... 1·25 1·25

1968 (6 May). Nos. 168, 170, 172 and 174/176 surch as T **26**. W w **12** (upright).

194 15c. on 12c. Lime 20 15
a. Narrow bars .... 6·00
195 25c. on 24c. Banana 25 15
a. Narrow bars .... 6·00
196 50c. on 48c. Cabbage 45 15
197 $1 on $1.20 Pumpkin .... 1·10 40
198 $2.50 on $2.40 Sweet Potato .... 1·10 4·25
199 $5 on $4.80 Egg Plant .... 1·10 4·25
194/199 *Set of 6* .... 3·75 8·50

See also Nos. 219 etc.

27 Sprinting

28 Sprinting, and Aztec Pillars

(Des G. Vasarhelyi. Photo Harrison)

1968 (31 July). Olympic Games, Mexico. Types **27/28** and similar designs. W w **12** (sideways on $1). P 14.

200 **27** 15c. deep claret, emerald and gold. 10 10
201 – 25c. blue, orange and gold 15 10
202 – 50c. green, red and gold 25 15
203 **28** $1 multicoloured 35 30
200/203 *Set of 4* 75 55

Designs: Horiz as T **27**—25c. Weightlifting; 50c. Gymnastics.

31 Alexander Hamilton

(Des and photo Harrison)

1968 (6 Dec*). Human Rights Year. T **31** and similar horiz designs. Multicoloured. W w **12**. P 14×14½.

204 5c. Type **31** 10 10
205 15c. Albert T. Marryshow 10 10
206 25c. William Wilberforce 10 10
207 50c. Dag Hammarskjöld 10 15
208 $1 Dr. Martin Luther King 25 30
204/208 *Set of 5* 60 65

* Although first day covers were postmarked 2 December, these stamps were not put on sale in Montserrat until 6 December.

32 *The Two Trinities* (Murillo)

33 *The Adoration of the Kings* (detail, Botticelli)

(Des and photo Harrison)

1968 (16 Dec). Christmas. W w **12** (sideways). P 14½×14.

209 **32** 5c. multicoloured 10 10
210 **33** 15c. multicoloured 10 10
211 **32** 25c. multicoloured 10 10
212 **33** 50c. multicoloured 25 25
209/212 *Set of 4* 50 45

1969–70. As Nos. 160/164, 167, 167 and 194/196 but wmk w **12** sideways*.

213 1c. Type **21** (24.6.69) 10 10
214 2c. Type **22** (23.4.70) .... 1·25 85
215 3c. Soursop (24.6.69) 30 15
w. Wmk Crown to right of CA .... 25·00
216 4c. Pepper (24.6.69) 60 15
217 5c. Mango (23.4.70) .... 2·50 85
218 10c. Ochro (24.6.69) 50 15
w. Wmk Crown to right of CA .... 90·00
219 15c. on 12c. Lime (24.6.69) 60 20
220 20c. Orange (17.3.69) 75 20
221 25c. on 24c. Banana (24.6.69) .... 1·00 25
222 50c. on 48c. Cabbage (24.6.69) .... 7·00 14·00
213/222 *Set of 10* .... 13·00 15·00

* The normal sideways watermark shows Crown to left of CA, *as seen from the back of the stamp*.

The 1c., 3c., 4c., 10c., 15c. and 20c. exist with PVA gum as well as gum arabic, but the 2c. and 5c. exist with PVA gum only.

34 Map showing 'CARIFTA' Countries

35 'Strength in Unity'

(Des J. Cooter. Photo Harrison)

1969 (27 May). First Anniversary of CARIFTA (Caribbean Free Trade Area). W w **12** (sideways* on T **34**). P 14.

223 **34** 15c. multicoloured 10 10
224 20c. multicoloured 10 10
w. Wmk Crown to right of CA .... 1·00
225 **35** 35c. multicoloured 10 20
226 30c. multicoloured 15 20
223/226 *Set of 4* 40 55

* The normal sideways watermark shows Crown to left of CA, *as seen from the back of the stamp*.

36 Telephone Receiver and Map of Montserrat

40 Dolphinfish

(Des R. Reid, adapted by V. Whiteley. Litho P.B.)

1969 (29 July). Development Projects. T **36** and similar vert designs. Multicoloured. W w **12**. P 13½.

227 15c. Type **36** 10 10
228 25c. School symbols and map 10 10
229 50c. Hawker Siddeley H.S.748 aircraft and map 15 20
230 $1 Electricity pylon and map 25 75
227/230 *Set of 4* .... 55 1·00

(Des Harrison. Photo Enschedé)

1969 (1 Nov). Game Fish. T **40** and similar horiz designs. Multicoloured. P 13×13½.

231 5c. Type **40** 25 10
232 15c. Atlantic Sailfish 30 10
233 25c. Black-finned Tuna 35 10
234 40c. Spanish Mackerel 45 55
231/234 *Set of 4* .... 1·25 75

41 King Caspar before the Virgin and Child (detail) (Norman 16th-cent stained glass window)

42 *Nativity* (Leonard Limosin)

(Des J. Cooter. Litho D.L.R.)

1969 (10 Dec). Christmas. Paintings multicoloured; frame colours given. W w **12** (sideways on 50c.). P 13.

235 **41** 15c. black, gold and violet 10 10
236 25c. black and vermilion 10 10
237 **42** 50c. black, ultramarine and yellow-orange 15 15
235/237 *Set of 3* 30 30

43 'Red Cross Sale'

(Des and litho J. W.)

1970 (13 Apr). Centenary of British Red Cross. T **43** and similar horiz designs. Multicoloured. W w **12** (sideways). P 14½×14.

238 3c. Type **43** 15 25
239 4c. School for deaf children 15 25
240 15c. Transport services for disabled 20 20
241 20c. Workshop 20 60
238/241 *Set of 4* .... 65 1·10

44 Red-footed Booby

45 *Madonna and Child with Animals* (Brueghel the Elder, after Dürer)

(Des V. Whiteley. Photo Harrison)

1970 (2 July)–**74.** Birds. T **44** and similar multicoloured designs. W w **12** (sideways* on vert designs and upright on horiz designs). Glazed ordinary paper ($10) or chalk-surfaced paper (others). P 14×14½ (horiz) or 14½×14 (vert).

242 1c. Type **44** 10 10
w. Wmk inverted .... 24·00
243 2c. American Kestrel (*vert*) 15 15
a. Glazed, ordinary paper (22.1.71) .... 1·25 3·00

244	3c. Magnificent Frigatebird (*vert*)	15	15
	w. Wmk Crown to right of CA		
245	4c. Great Egret (*vert*)	2·00	15
246	5c. Brown Pelican (*vert*)	2·50	10
	aw. Wmk Crown to right of CA	2·50	
	b. Glazed, ordinary paper (22.1.71)	1·50	2·00
	bw. Wmk Crown to right of CA		
247	10c. Bananaquit (*vert*)	40	60
	a. Glazed, ordinary paper (22.1.71)	1·50	2·00
248	15c. Smooth-billed Ani	30	15
	a. Glazed, ordinary paper (22.1.71)	4·50	5·00
	aw. Wmk inverted	4·50	
249	20c. Red-billed Tropicbird	35	15
	a. Glazed, ordinary paper (22.1.71)	1·50	2·00
250	25c. Montserrat Oriole	50	50
	a. Glazed, ordinary paper (22.1.71)	5·00	6·00
251	50c. Green-throated Carib (*vert*)	11·00	1·50
	a. Glazed, ordinary paper (22.1.71)	4·00	4·50
252	$1 Antillean Crested Hummingbird	13·00	1·00
	aw. Wmk inverted	32·00	
	b. Glazed, ordinary paper (22.1.71)	4·25	5·00
253	$2.50 Little Blue Heron (*vert*)	5·50	12·00
	a. Glazed, ordinary paper (22.1.71)	8·00	10·00
254	$5 Purple-throated Carib	7·50	20·00
	a. Glazed, ordinary paper (22.1.71)	13·00	18·00
254*c*	$10 Forest Thrush (30.10.74)	18·00	24·00
242/254c	*Set of* 14	40·00	50·00

* The normal sideways watermark shows Crown to left of CA, *as seen from the back of the stamp.*

Eight values in this set were subsequently reissued with the watermark sideways on horizontal designs and upright on vertical designs.

(Des G. Drummond. Litho D.L.R.)

1970 (1 Oct*). Christmas. T **45** and similar multicoloured design. W w **12**. P 13½×14.

255	5c. Type **45**	10	10
	w. Wmk inverted	29·00	
256	15c. *The Adoration of the Shepherds* (Domenichino)	10	10
257	20c. Type **45**	10	10
	w. Wmk inverted	3·25	
258	$1 As 15c.	35	1·50
255/258	*Set of* 4	60	1·60

* This was the local date of issue but the stamps were released by the Crown Agents on 21 September.

46 War Memorial

47 Girl Guide and Badge

(Des V. Whiteley. Litho J.W.)

1970 (30 Nov). Tourism. T **46** and similar horiz designs. Multicoloured. W w **12** (sideways*). P 14½×14.

259	5c. Type **46**	10	10
260	15c. Plymouth from Fort St George	10	10
261	25c. Carr's Bay	15	15
262	50c. Golf Fairway	1·00	2·25
	w. Wmk Crown to right of CA	7·00	
259/262	*Set of* 4	1·25	2·40
MS263	135×109 mm. Nos. 259/262	3·25	2·25

* The normal sideways watermark shows Crown to left of CA, *as seen from the back of the stamp.*

(Des V. Whiteley. Litho Questa)

1970 (31 Dec). Diamond Jubilee of Montserrat Girl Guides. T **47** and similar vert design. Multicoloured. W w **12**. P 14.

264	10c. Type **47**	10	10
265	15c. Brownie and Badge	10	10
266	25c. As 15c.	15	15
267	40c. Type **47**	20	80
264/267	*Set of* 4	50	1·00

Morocco Agencies (British Post Offices)

With the growth of trade and commerce during the 19th-century European powers opened post offices or postal agencies in various ports along the Moroccan coast from the early 1850's onwards. French and, in the north, Spanish influence eventually became predominant, leading to the protectorates of 1912. The British, who had inaugurated a regular postal service between Gibraltar and Tangier or Tetuan in May 1778, established their first postal agency in 1857. German offices followed around the turn of the century.

Before 1892 there was no indigenous postal service and those towns where there was no foreign agency were served by a number of private local posts which continued to flourish until 1900. In November 1892 the Sultan of Morocco established the Cherifian postal service, but this was little used until after its reorganisation at the end of 1911. The Sultan's post was absorbed by the French postal service on 1 October 1913. Issues of the local posts and of the Sultan's post can occasionally be found used on cover in combination with stamps of Gibraltar or the Morocco Agencies.

On 1 April 1857 the first British postal agency was established at Tangier within the precincts of the Legation and was run by the official interpreter. From 1 March 1858 all letters for Great Britain sent via the British mail packets from Gibraltar required franking with Great Britain stamps.

In 1872 the Tangier office was relocated away from the Legation and the interpreter was appointed British Postal Agent and supplied with a stock of British postage stamps which would be cancelled on arrival in Gibraltar with the 'A26' obliterator. Such stamps used in Morocco can therefore only be identified when on cover or large piece, also showing the Tangier datestamp. British stamps known to have been used in Morocco are the ½d. of 1870, 1880 and 1884; 1d. of 1864 and 1881; 2d. of 1858; 2½d. of 1876, 1880, 1881 and 1884; 4d. of 1865 and 6d. stamps of 1856, 1865 and 1872. At the same time the agency was placed under the control of the Gibraltar postmaster.

When the colonial posts became independent of the British GPO on 1 January 1886 Gibraltar retained responsibility for the Morocco Agencies. Further offices, each under the control of the local Vice-Consul, were opened from 1886 onwards.

I. GIBRALTAR USED IN MOROCCO

Details of the various agencies are given below. Type C, the 'A26' killer, is very similar to postmarks used at Gibraltar during this period. In addition to the town name, postmarks as Types A, B and D from Fez, Mazagan, Saffi and Tetuan were also inscribed 'MOROCCO'.

Postmark Types used on Gibraltar issues.

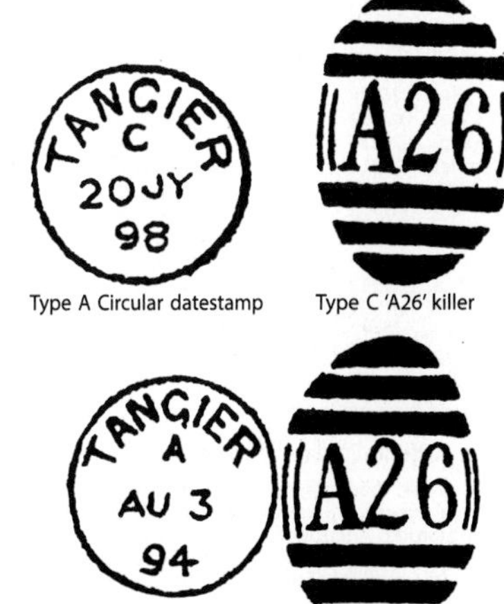

Type A Circular datestamp

Type C 'A26' killer

Type B Duplex cancellation

Type D Registered oval

BISECTS. The 1886-1887 1d. and the 10c., 40c. and 50c. values of the 1889 surcharges and the 1889–1896 issue are known bisected and used for half their value from various of the Morocco Agencies (price on cover from £500). These bisects were never authorised by the Gibraltar Post Office.

CASABLANCA

The British postal agency opened on 1 January 1887 and was initially supplied with ½d., 4d. and 6d. stamps from the Gibraltar 1886 overprinted on Bermuda issue and 1d., 2d. and 2½d. values from the 1886–1887 set.

Stamps of GIBRALTAR cancelled with Types A (without code or code 'C'), B (without code or code 'A') or D.

1886. Optd on Bermuda (Nos. 1/7).

Z1	½d. dull green	£150
Z2	4d. orange-brown	£550
Z3	6d. deep lilac	£550

1886–87. Queen Victoria £sd issue (Nos. 8/14).

Z4	½d. dull green	80·00
Z5	1d. rose	65·00
Z6	2d. brown-purple	£150
Z7	2½d. blue	80·00
Z8	4d. orange-brown	£225
Z10	1s. bistre	£600

1889. Surch in Spanish currency (Nos. 15/21).

Z11	5c. on ½d. green	£100
Z12	10c. on 1d. rose	90·00
Z13	25c. on 2d. brown-purple	£130
Z14	25c. on 2½d. bright blue	80·00
Z15	40c. on 4d. orange-brown	£275
Z16	50c. on 6d. bright lilac	£225
Z17	75c. on 1s. bistre	£300

1889–96. Queen Victoria Spanish currency issue (Nos. 22/33).

Z18	5c. green	25·00
Z19	10c. carmine	22·00
Z20	20c. olive-green and brown	70·00
Z21	20c. olive-green	£225
Z22	25c. ultramarine	22·00
Z23	40c. orange-brown	70·00
Z24	50c. bright lilac	55·00
Z25	75c. olive-green	£190
Z26	1p. bistre	£160
Z28	1p. bistre and ultramarine	80·00
Z29	2p. black and carmine	£110

FEZ

The British postal agency in this inland town opened on 13 February 1892 and was initially supplied with stamps up to the 50c. value from the Gibraltar 1889–1896 issue.

Stamps of GIBRALTAR cancelled with Types A (without code) or D.

1889–96. Queen Victoria Spanish currency issue (Nos. 22/33).

Z31	5c. green	55·00
Z32	10c. carmine	45·00
Z33	20c. olive-green and brown	£150
Z35	25c. ultramarine	70·00
Z36	40c. orange-brown	£170
Z37	50c. bright lilac	£150

LARAICHE

The British postal agency at Laraiche opened on 3 April 1886, although the first postmark, an 'A26' killer, was not supplied until May.

Stamps of GIBRALTAR cancelled with Types B (without code) or D.

1886. Optd on Bermuda (Nos. 1/7).

Z39	½d. dull green	
Z40	1d. rose-red	
Z41	2½d. ultramarine	

1886–87. Queen Victoria £sd issue (Nos. 8/14).

Z42	½d. dull green	£200
Z43	1d. rose	£190
Z45	2½d. blue	£200

1889. Surch in Spanish currency (Nos. 15/21).

Z47	5c. on ½d. green	£170
Z48	10c. on 1d. rose	
Z49	25c. on 2½d. bright blue	

It is believed that the other surcharges in this series were not supplied to Laraiche.

1889–96. Queen Victoria Spanish currency issue (Nos. 22/33).

Z50	5c. green	70·00
Z51	10c. carmine	75·00
Z52	20c. olive-green and brown	£180
Z54	25c. ultramarine	75·00
Z55	40c. orange-brown	£180
Z56	50c. bright-lilac	£180
Z57	1p. bistre and ultramarine	

MAZAGAN

This was the main port for the inland city of Marrakesh. The British postal agency opened on 1 March 1888 and was initially supplied with stamps from the Gibraltar 1886–1887 series.

Stamps of GIBRALTAR cancelled with Types A (codes 'A' or 'C') or D (without code, code 'A' or code 'C').

1886–87. Queen Victoria £sd issue (Nos. 8/14).

Z58	½d. dull green	65·00
Z59	1d. rose	75·00
Z60	2d. brown-purple	
Z61	2½d. blue	80·00
Z62	4d. orange-brown	£275
Z63	6d. lilac	£325

1889. Surch in Spanish currency (Nos. 15/21).

Z64	5c. on ½d. green	£120
Z65	10c. on 1d. rose	
Z66	25c. on 2½d. bright blue	

It is believed that the other surcharges in this series were not supplied to Mazagan.

1889–96. Queen Victoria Spanish currency issue (Nos. 22/33).

Z67	5c. green	30·00
Z68	10c. carmine	26·00
Z69	20c. olive-green and brown	£120
Z70	25c. ultramarine	60·00
Z71	40c. orange-brown	£140
Z72	50c. bright lilac	£170
Z74	1p. bistre and ultramarine	£190
Z75	2p. black and carmine	£190

MOGADOR

The British postal agency at this port opened on 1 June 1887 and was initially supplied with stamps from the Gibraltar 1886–1887 series.

Stamps of GIBRALTAR cancelled with Types A (code 'C'), B (code 'C') or D.

1886. Optd on Bermuda (Nos. 1/7).

Z75*d*	4d. orange-brown	£550

1886–87. Queen Victoria £sd issue (Nos. 8/14).

Z76	½d. dull green	60·00
Z77	1d. rose	85·00
Z78	2d. brown-purple	£170
Z79	2½d. blue	70·00
Z79*b*	6d. lilac	£300

1889. Surch in Spanish currency (Nos. 15/21).

Z80 5c. on ½d. green £100
Z81 10c. on 1d. rose 95·00
Z82 25c. on 2½d. bright blue 85·00

It is believed that the other surcharges in this series were not supplied to Mogador.

1889–96. Queen Victoria Spanish currency issue (Nos. 22/33).

Z83 5c. green 25·00
Z84 10c. carmine 25·00
Z85 20c. olive-green and brown £110
Z87 25c. ultramarine 29·00
Z88 40c. orange-brown £120
Z89 50c. bright lilac 90·00
Z89*a* 1p. bistre £180
Z90 1p. bistre and ultramarine £120
Z91 2p. black and carmine £150

RABAT

The British postal agency at this port on the north-west coast of Morocco opened on 6 April 1886, although the first cancellation, an 'A26' killer, was not supplied until May. The initial stock of stamps was from the Gibraltar 1886 overprinted on Bermuda issue.

Stamps of GIBRALTAR cancelled with Types B (code 'O') or D.

1886. Optd on Bermuda (Nos. 1/7).

Z92 ½d. dull green
Z93 1d. rose-red
Z94 2½d. ultramarine £325

1886–87. Queen Victoria £sd issue (Nos. 8/14).

Z95 ½d. dull green 75·00
Z96 1d. rose 70·00
Z97 2d. brown-purple £150
Z98 2½d. blue 80·00
Z101 1s. bistre £700

1889. Surch in Spanish currency (Nos. 15/21).

Z102 5c. on ½d. green £110
Z103 10c. on 1d. rose 90·00
Z104 25c. on 2½d. bright blue 95·00

It is believed that the other surcharges in this series were not supplied to Rabat.

1889–96. Queen Victoria Spanish currency issue (Nos. 22/33).

Z105 5c. green 30·00
Z106 10c. carmine 27·00
Z107 20c. olive-green and brown £130
Z108 25c. ultramarine 29·00
Z109 40c. orange-brown £130
Z110 50c. bright lilac 95·00
Z110*a* 1p. bistre and ultramarine £150

SAFFI

The British postal agency at this port opened on 1 July 1891 and was supplied with stamps from the Gibraltar 1889–1896 series.

Stamps of GIBRALTAR cancelled with Types B (code 'C')or D (code 'C').*

1889–96. Queen Victoria Spanish currency issue (Nos. 22/33).

Z111 5c. green 45·00
Z112 10c. carmine 40·00
Z113 20c. olive-green and brown £110
Z115 25c. ultramarine 48·00
Z116 40c. orange-brown £150
Z117 50c. bright lilac £110
Z118 1p. bistre and ultramarine £140
Z119 2p. black and carmine £160

* Stamps of this issue can also be found with double-circle datestamps of the French Post Office at Saffi. These are worth less than prices quoted.

TANGIER

The British postal agency in Tangier opened on 1 April 1857 and from 1 March of the following year letters from it sent via the packet service to Great Britain required franking with Great Britain stamps.

No identifiable postmark was supplied to Tangier until 1872 and all earlier mail was cancelled with one of the Gibraltar marks. In April 1872 a postmark as Type A was supplied on which the 'N' of 'TANGIER' was reversed. A corrected version, with code letter 'A', followed in 1878, but both were used as origin or arrival marks and the Great Britain stamps continued to be cancelled with Gibraltar obliterators. The Type A postmarks generally fell into disuse after 1880 and very few identifiable marks occur on mail from Tangier until the introduction of Gibraltar stamps on 1 January 1886.

Type E Horizontal
'A26' killer

New cancellers were not ready on 1 January and, as a temporary measure, the old horizontal 'A26' killer, which was very worn by this time, was sent from Gibraltar. Strikes of this handstamp on the overprinted Bermuda stamps tend to be blurred but are indicative of use in Tangier. Use of Type E lasted until 4 May, when it was replaced by Type C.

Stamps of GIBRALTAR cancelled with Types A (codes 'A' or 'C'), B (code 'A'), D or E.

1886. Optd on Bermuda (Nos. 1/7).

Z120 ½d. dull green 75·00
Z121 1d. rose-red £100
Z122 2d. purple-brown £225
Z123 2½d. ultramarine 95·00
Z124 4d. orange-brown £300
Z125 6d. deep lilac £300
Z126 1s. yellow-brown £650

1886–87. Queen Victoria £sd issue (Nos. 8/14).

Z127 ½d. dull green 25·00
Z128 1d. rose 25·00
Z129 2d. brown-purple 80·00
Z130 2½d. blue 32·00
Z131 4d. orange-brown £130
Z132 6d. lilac £200
Z133 1s. bistre £400

1889. Surch in Spanish currency (Nos. 15/21).

Z134 5c. on ½d. green 50·00
Z135 10c. on 1d. rose 32·00
Z136 25c. on 2d. brown-purple 65·00
Z137 25c. on 2½d. bright blue 48·00
Z138 40c. on 4d. orange-brown £180
Z139 50c. on 6d. bright lilac £170
Z140 75c. on 1s. bistre £225

1889–96. Queen Victoria Spanish currency issue (Nos. 22/33).

Z141 5c. green 7·00
Z142 10c. carmine 6·00
Z143 20c. olive-green and brown 26·00
Z144 20c. olive-green £140
Z145 25c. ultramarine 9·00
Z146 40c. orange-brown 14·00
Z147 50c. bright lilac 13·00
Z148 75c. olive-green 95·00
Z149 1p. bistre 85·00
Z150 1p. bistre and ultramarine 32·00
Z151 2p. black and carmine 60·00
Z152 5p. slate-grey £130

TETUAN

The British postal agency in this northern town opened on 4 May 1890 and was supplied with stamps from the Gibraltar 1889–1896 series.

Stamps of GIBRALTAR cancelled with Types A (code 'C'), B (code 'C' often inverted) or D (code 'C').

1889–96. Queen Victoria Spanish currency issue (Nos. 22/33).

Z153 5c. green 45·00
Z154 10c. carmine 45·00
Z155 20c. olive-green and brown £100
Z157 25c. ultramarine 48·00
Z158 40c. orange-brown £120
Z159 50c. bright lilac £120
Z161 1p. bistre and ultramarine £160
Z162 2p. black and carmine £170
Z163 5p. slate-grey £200

PRICES FOR STAMPS ON COVER TO 1945

Nos. 1/16	*from* × 7
Nos. 17/30	*from* × 3
Nos. 31/74	*from* × 3
Nos. 75/76	*from* × 4
Nos. 112/124	*from* × 4
No. 125	—
Nos. 126/135	*from* × 5
Nos. 136/142	*from* × 2
Nos. 143/159	*from* × 3
Nos. 160/175	*from* × 8
Nos. 191/199	*from* × 5
Nos. 200/201	*from* × 3
Nos. 202/211	*from* × 4
Nos. 212/215	*from* × 5
Nos. 216/224	*from* × 8
Nos. 225/226	*from* × 2
Nos. 227/230	*from* × 8
Nos. 231/252	*from* × 6

The above prices apply to stamps used on cover from Morocco. Examples of Nos. 31/76 & 231/252 used on cover in GB after 1950 have little value.

II. GIBRALTAR ISSUES OVERPRINTED

Following a decision to identify the exact revenue derived from the Morocco postal service, it became necessary to provide separate issues for the Morocco Agencies. The need was reinforced when the Revision of Fees Ordinance in Gibraltar required all fees there to be collected in sterling, while the Morocco Agencies continued to use Spanish currency.

The following were used in all the British postal agencies. Unoverprinted stamps of Gibraltar remained valid for postage until 15 June 1898.

Morocco Agencies (1) Morocco Agencies (2)

Agencies — Inverted 'V' for 'A' (Right-hand pane R. 6/6)
Agencies — Long tail to 'S' (Right-hand pane R. 8/2)
Morocco — Deformed 'M' (Second setting, left-hand pane R. 1/1)

Broken 'M' (Pl 2 R. 4/5)

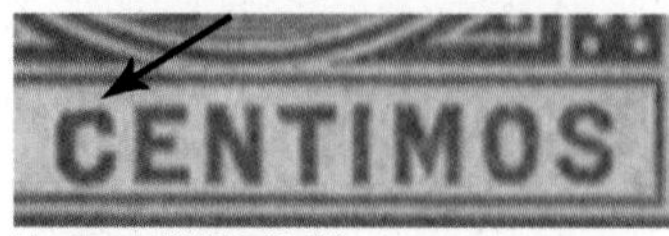

Flat top to 'C' (Pl 2 R. 4/4)

Exclamation mark for 'I' (Pl 2 R. 8/4)

1898 (1 June)–**1900**. Nos. 22/28 and 31/32 (Queen Victoria) of Gibraltar optd typographically (No. 2e) or by lithography (others) with T **1** (wide 'M' and ear of 'g' projecting upwards), in black at *Gibraltar Chronicle* office.

1 5c. green 6·00 6·50
a. Inverted 'V' for 'A' 60·00 75·00
b. Long tail to 'S' 70·00 85·00
c. Deformed 'M' 95·00
d. Broken 'M' in 'CENTIMOS' 90·00
2 10c. carmine 11·00 3·00
a. Inverted 'V' for 'A' £225 £275
b. Long tail to 'S' £225
c. Deformed 'M' £120 80·00
e. Lines of opt 5 mm apart (6.00) 17·00 8·50
ea. Opt double £750 £650
g. Bisected (5c.) (*on cover*) † £1100
3 20c. olive-green and brown 23·00 4·25
a. Inverted 'V' for 'A' £120 £120
b. Long tail to 'S' £130 £130
3*c* 20c. olive-green 20·00 12·00
ca. Opt double £500 £650
cb. Inverted 'V' for 'A' £150 £170
cc. Long tail to 'S' £160 £180
cd. Flat top to 'C' in 'CENTIMOS' £200 £225
4 25c. ultramarine 10·00 2·50
a. Inverted 'V' for 'A' £150 £130
b. Long tail to 'S' £160 £140
c. Deformed 'M' — £160
5 40c. orange-brown (2.6.98) 6·50 3·50
a. Inverted 'V' for 'A' £180 £200
b. Long tail to 'S' £190 £225
c. Deformed 'M' £250 £275
d. Exclamation mark for 'I' £150 £150
f. Blue-black opt (7.98) 50·00 32·00
fa. 'Morocco' omitted (R. 1/1) £1000
fc. Deformed 'M' £400
fd. Exclamation mark for 'I' £275
6 50c. bright lilac (2.6.98) 17·00 23·00
a. Inverted 'V' for 'A' £275 £350
b. Long tail to 'S' £325 £375
f. Blue-black opt (7.98) 24·00 19·00
fc. Deformed 'M' £275
7 1p. bistre and ultramarine (2.6.98) 21·00 32·00
a. Inverted 'V' for 'A' £275 £375
b. Long tail to 'S' £325 £425
c. Deformed 'M' £300
f. Blue-black opt (7.98) £180 £325
fc. Deformed 'M'
8 2p. black and carmine (4.6.98) 35·00 38·00
a. Inverted 'V' for 'A' £375 £425
b. Long tail to 'S' £425 £475
c. Deformed 'M' £375
1/8 *Set of* 8 £110 95·00

The blue-black overprint can be easily distinguished by looking through the stamp in front of a strong light. The overprint on the 50c. value shows more blue than on the 40c. and 1p. values.

The Inverted 'V' for 'A' and Long tail to 'S' varieties occur from the first 12×10 litho setting. They were not present on the second 12×10 setting of July 1898, which produced further supplies of Nos. 5/8, and included the blue-black overprints, listed as Nos. 5f, 6f, 7f. The same setting was subsequently used to produce additional stocks of Nos. 1/2 and is also recorded on No. 4. This second setting includes the Deformed 'M' variety. Numerous more minor varieties exist from both settings.

No. 2e comes from two further printings in 1900 using a third setting (6×10) on which the two lines of the overprint were 5 mm apart instead of the 4 mm space used previously and applied typographically.

Early release of No. 1 is known at Saffi (from 26 May).

Agencies — 'CD' sideways flaw (Left-hand pane R. 1/5)
Morocco — Broad top to 'M' (Left-hand pane R. 7/3)
Agencies — Hyphen between 'nc' (Right-hand pane R. 3/5)

1899 (Feb–Mar). Nos. 22/23, 25/28 and 31/32 (Queen Victoria) of Gibraltar optd typographically with T **2** (narrow 'M' and ear of 'g' horizontal), in black by D.L.R., London.

9 5c. green 4·00 3·25
a. 'CD' sideways 42·00 48·00
b. Broad top to 'M' 12·00 20·00
c. Hyphen between 'nc' 12·00 20·00
d. Broken 'M' in 'CENTIMOS' 80·00
10 10c. carmine 6·00 3·25
a. 'CD' sideways 65·00 50·00
b. Broad top to 'M' 15·00 20·00
c. Hyphen between 'nc' 15·00 20·00
d. Opt double £850 £800
e. Bisected (5c.) (*on cover*) † £1100
11 20c. olive-green (3.99) 15·00 2·75
b. Broad top to 'M' 65·00 60·00
c. Hyphen between 'nc' 65·00 60·00
d. Flat top to 'C' in 'CENTIMOS' £150 £110
12 25c. ultramarine (3.99) 11·00 1·00
a. 'CD' sideways £100 80·00
b. Broad top to 'M' 55·00 60·00
c. Hyphen between 'nc' 55·00 60·00
13 40c. orange-brown (3.99) 50·00 50·00
b. Broad top to 'M' £275 £325
c. Hyphen between 'nc' £275 £325
d. Exclamation mark for 'I' £225
14 50c. bright lilac (3.99) 16·00 6·50
b. Broad top to 'M' £130 £140
c. Hyphen between 'nc' £130 £140
15 1p. bistre and ultramarine (3.99) 29·00 48·00
b. Broad top to 'M' £180 £300
c. Hyphen between 'nc' £180 £300
16 2p. black and carmine (3.99) 60·00 48·00
b. Broad top to 'M' £350 £375
c. Hyphen between 'nc' £350 £375
9/16 *Set of* 8 £170 £140
9s/16s Optd 'SPECIMEN' *Set of* 8 £225

1903–05. As Nos. 46/51 (King Edward VII) of Gibraltar, but with value in Spanish currency, optd with T **2**. Wmk Crown CA. P 14.

17 5c. grey-green and green (1.04) 10·00 3·00
a. 'CD' sideways 80·00 70·00
b. Broad top to 'M' 60·00 65·00
c. Hyphen between 'nc' 60·00 65·00

18	10c. dull purple/*red* (8.03)	9·00	40
	a. 'CD' sideways	75·00	45·00
	b. Broad top to 'M'	60·00	45·00
	c. Hyphen between 'nc'	60·00	45·00
	w. Wmk inverted	70·00	
19	20c. grey-green and carmine (9.04)	22·00	50·00
	a. 'CD' sideways	£170	£275
	b. Broad top to 'M'	£150	£275
	c. Hyphen between 'nc'	£150	£275
	d. Flat top to 'C' in 'CENTIMOS'	£225	
20	25c. purple and black/*blue* (1.7.03)	8·00	30
	a. 'CD' sideways	80·00	48·00
	b. Broad top to 'M'	60·00	48·00
	c. Hyphen between 'nc'	70·00	48·00
21	50c. purple and violet (3.7.05)	80·00	£325
	a. 'CD' sideways	£425	
	b. Broad top to 'M'	£375	
	c. Hyphen between 'nc'	£375	
22	1p. black and carmine (19.11.05)	35·00	£275
	a. 'CD' sideways	£300	
	b. Broad top to 'M'	£225	
	c. Hyphen between 'nc'	£225	
23	2p. black and blue (19.11.05)	50·00	£250
	a. 'CD' sideways	£350	
	b. Broad top to 'M'	£275	
	c. Hyphen between 'nc'	£275	
17/23 *Set of 7*		£190	£800
17s/23s Optd 'SPECIMEN' *Set of 7*		£225	

Examples of Nos. 19 and 21/23 are known showing a forged Registered Mazagan postmark dated '15 SP 10'.

1905 (Jan)–**06**. As Nos. 17/23 but wmk Mult Crown CA. Ordinary paper (5, 10, 20c.) or chalk-surfaced paper (others).

24	5c. grey-green and green (4.05)	22·00	13·00
	a. 'CD' sideways	£130	90·00
	b. Broad top to 'M'	£120	90·00
	c. Hyphen between 'nc'	£900	£1200
	d. Chalk-surfaced paper (1.06)	9·00	15·00
	da. 'CD' sideways	70·00	£110
	db. Broad top to 'M'	70·00	£110
25	10c. dull purple/*red*	24·00	2·00
	a. 'CD' sideways	£110	42·00
	b. Broad top to 'M'	£100	42·00
	cw. Wmk inverted	35·00	23·00
	d. Chalk-surfaced paper (12.05)	9·00	3·50
	da. 'CD' sideways	65·00	45·00
	db. Broad top to 'M'	65·00	45·00
26	20c. grey-green and carmine (1.06)	9·50	35·00
	a. 'CD' sideways	80·00	£200
	b. Broad top to 'M'	80·00	£200
	d. Flat top to 'C' in 'CENTIMOS'	£110	
27	25c. purple and black/*blue* (6.06)	70·00	8·50
	a. 'CD' sideways	£475	£170
	b. Broad top to 'M'	£475	£170
28	50c. purple and violet (7.05)	11·00	65·00
	a. 'CD' sideways	£180	£425
	b. Broad top to 'M'	£160	£400
29	1p. black and carmine (11.05)	50·00	90·00
	a. 'CD' sideways	£300	£500
	b. Broad top to 'M'	£275	£500
30	2p. black and blue (11.05)	28·00	38·00
	a. 'CD' sideways	£225	£300
	b. Broad top to 'M'	£200	£300
24/30 *Set of 7*		£160	£225

Examples of Nos. 26 and 28/30 are known showing a forged Registered Mazagan postmark dated '15 SP 10'.

Control of the British postal agencies in Morocco returned to the GPO, London, from 1 January 1907. The Gibraltar overprints remained vaild until 28 February of that year.

All the following issues are overprinted on Great Britain

III. BRITISH CURRENCY

Stamps overprinted 'MOROCCO AGENCIES' only were primarily intended for use on parcels (and later, air-mail correspondence), and were on sale at British POs throughout Morocco including Tangier, until 1937.

> **PRICES.** Our prices for used stamps with these overprints are for specimens used in Morocco. These stamps were valid for postal purposes in Great Britain from the summer of 1950 onwards. Examples with GB postmarks are worth 50 per cent of the used prices quoted.

MOROCCO AGENCIES (4) MOROCCO AGENCIES (5) MOROCCO AGENCIES (6)

1907 (30 Apr)–**13**. King Edward VII optd as Types **4** or **5** (2s.6d.).

(a) De La Rue printings. Ordinary paper (½d., 1d., 4d. (Nos. 35/35a) or chalk-surfaced paper (others)

31	½d. pale yellowish green (29.5.07)	2·25	15·00
32	1d. scarlet (5.5.07)	9·50	9·50
33	2d. pale grey-green and carmine-red	10·00	6·00
34	4d. green and chocolate-brown (29.5.07)	3·75	4·25
35	4d. pale orange (3.12)	19·00	25·00
	a. Orange-red	10·00	22·00
36	6d. pale dull purple (5.5.07)	15·00	35·00
	a. Dull purple	22·00	42·00
37	1s. dull green and carmine (5.5.07)	26·00	17·00
38	2s.6d. pale dull purple (5.5.07)	95·00	£170
	a. Dull purple	95·00	£170
31/38 *Set of 8*		£150	£250
37s/38s Optd 'SPECIMEN' *Set of 2*		£140	

(b) Harrison printing. Ordinary paper

40	4d. bright orange (No. 286) (1913)	48·00	32·00

Note that No. 40 is perf 15×14, whereas Nos. 35/35*a* are perf 14.

(c) Somerset House printing. Ordinary paper

41	2s.6d. dull reddish purple (No. 316) (1913)	£150	£250

1914–31. King George V.

(a) W **100** *(Simple Cypher). Optd with T* **4**

42	½d. green	8·50	50
43	1d. scarlet	2·25	20
44	1½d. red-brown (1921)	8·50	19·00
45	2d. orange (Die I)	6·00	60
46	3d. bluish violet (1921)	1·75	35
47	4d. grey-green (1921)	9·50	1·50
48	6d. reddish purple (*chalk-surfaced paper*) (1921)	10·00	15·00
49	1s. bistre-brown (1917)	16·00	2·50
	a. Opt triple, two albino	£120	

(b) W **110** *(Single Cypher). Optd with T* **6**

50	2s.6d. sepia-brown (*Waterlow ptg*) (No. 400) (1914)	55·00	65·00
	a. Re-entry (R. 2/1)	£800	£1000
	b. Opt double, one albino	£200	
51	2s.6d. yellow-brown (*D.L.R. ptg*) (No. 406) (1917)	55·00	35·00
	a. Opt double	£1600	£1400
	b. Opt triple, two albino	£275	
	c. Pale brown (No. 407)	50·00	55·00
53	2s.6d. chocolate-brown (*B.W. ptg*) (No. 414)	50·00	27·00
	a. Opt double, one albino*	£200	
54	5s. rose-red (*B.W. ptg*) (No. 416) (30.6.31)	55·00	£110
	a. Opt triple, two albino	£300	
42/54 *Set of 10*		£140	£150
49s/50s, 54s Optd *'SPECIMEN'* or 'SPECIMEN' (No. 54s) *Set of 3*		£225	

* The albino overprint is quite clear, with 'MOROCCO' appearing just below 'AGENCIES' on the normal overprint and a little to the right *as seen from the back*. There is also a second faint albino impression just below the normal overprint.

MOROCCO AGENCIES S (7) MOROCCO AGENCIES S (8)

T **7**: Opt 14 mm long; ends of 's' cut off diagonally.
T **8**: Opt 15½ mm long; ends of 's' cut off horizontally

1925–36. King George V (W **111** (Block Cypher)) optd with T **8** (4d.) or T **7** (others).

55	½d. green	3·50	50
	aw. Wmk inverted	75·00	
	b. Optd with Type **8**	22·00	65·00
56	1½d. chestnut (20.5.31)	12·00	19·00
57	2d. orange	2·25	1·00
58	2½d. blue	9·50	1·50
	a. Optd with Type **8**	£100	13·00
59	4d. grey-green (1.36)	16·00	50·00
60	6d. purple (1931)	3·75	8·50
	a. Opt double, one albino	£140	
	b. Optd with Type **8**	2·00	60
61	1s. bistre-brown	18·00	6·00
	as. Optd *'SPECIMEN'*	75·00	
	b. Optd with Type **8**	55·00	50·00
55/61 *Set of 7*		55·00	65·00

1935 (8 May). Silver Jubilee (Nos. 453/456) optd 'MOROCCO AGENCIES' only, as in T **17**.

62	½d. green (B.)	1·50	6·50
63	1d. scarlet (B.)	1·50	13·00
64	1½d. red-brown (B.)	7·00	24·00
65	2½d. blue (R.)	8·00	2·50
62/65 *Set of 4*		16·00	42·00

1935–37. King George V.

(a) Harrison photo ptgs (Nos. 440/445 and 449). W **111** *(Block Cypher). Optd with T* **8**

66	1d. scarlet (11.35)	3·25	23·00
67	1½d. red-brown (14.10.35)	6·50	27·00
68	2d. orange (1.5.36)	1·25	16·00
69	2½d. ultramarine (11.2.36)	1·75	4·25
70	3d. violet (2.3.36)	50	30
71	4d. deep grey-green (14.5.36)	50	30
72	1s. bistre-brown (31.8.36)	1·00	9·50
	s. Optd 'SPECIMEN'	75·00	

(b) Waterlow re-engraved ptgs. W **110** *(Single Cypher) optd with T* **6**

73	2s.6d. chocolate-brown (No. 450) (14.10.35)	55·00	75·00
	s. Optd *'SPECIMEN'*	85·00	
74	5s. bright rose-red (No. 451) (23.2.37)	28·00	£140
66/74 *Set of 9*		85·00	£250

1936 (26 Oct)–**37**. King Edward VIII, optd 'MOROCCO AGENCIES' only, as in T **18** with 'MOROCCO' 14¼ mm long.

75	1d. scarlet	10	40
	a. 'MOROCCO' 15¼ mm long (5.1.37)	7·00	28·00
76	2½d. bright blue	10	15
	a. 'MOROCCO' 15¼ mm long (5.1.37)	1·00	6·50

The first two printings of both values showed all the stamps with the short overprint, Nos. 75/76.

On 5 January 1937 a further printing of both values was placed on sale in London which had the 24 stamps from the bottom two horizontal rows (Rows 19 and 20) with the long overprint, Nos. 75a/76a. Subsequent printings increased the number of long overprints in the sheet to 25 by the addition of R. 8/9, and, finally, to 31 (R. 1/7, R. 7/1, R. 8/1, R. 13/3, 4 and 10, R. 14/6, but without R. 8/9).

For the 1d. value all sheets from cylinder 2 show the first setting. Sheets from cylinder 6 were also used for the first, and for all subsequent settings. The 2½d. value was overprinted on sheets from cylinder 2 throughout.

From 3 June 1937 unoverprinted stamps of Great Britain were supplied to the post offices at Tangier and Tetuan (Spanish Zone) as local stocks of issues overprinted 'MOROCCO AGENCIES' were exhausted.

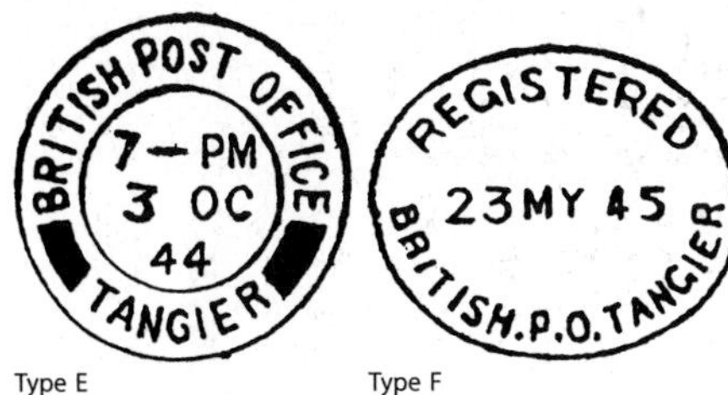

Type E Type F

Stamps of GREAT BRITAIN cancelled as Types E or F at Tangier.

1937. King George V.

Z170	1½d. red-brown (No. 441)	
Z171	2d. orange (No. 442)	18·00
Z172	3d. violet (No. 444)	18·00
Z173	4d. deep grey-green (No. 445)	11·00
Z174	6d. purple (No. 426*a*)	10·00
Z175	1s. bistre-brown (No. 449)	35·00
Z176	2s.6d. chocolate-brown (No. 450)	£110
Z177	5s. bright rose-red (No. 451)	£150

1937–39. King George VI (Nos. 462/475).

Z178	½d. green	15·00
Z179	1d. scarlet	15·00
Z180	1½d. red-brown	13·00
Z181	2d. orange	13·00
Z182	2½d. ultramarine	9·50
Z183	3d. violet	9·50
Z184	4d. grey-green	9·50
Z185	5d. brown	13·00
Z186	6d. purple	6·50
Z187	7d. emerald-green	11·00
Z188	8d. bright carmine	20·00
Z189	9d. deep olive-green	14·00
Z190	10d. turquoise-blue	20·00
Z191	1s. bistre-brown	6·50

1939–42. King George VI (Nos. 476/478*b*).

Z192	2s.6d. brown	70·00
Z193	2s.6d. yellow-green	16·00
Z194	5s. red	23·00
Z195	10s. dark blue	£140
Z196	10s. ultramarine	50·00

1941–42. King George VI pale colours (Nos. 485/490).

Z197	½d. pale green	9·50
Z198	1d. pale scarlet	9·50
Z199	1½d. pale red-brown	10·00
Z200	2d. pale orange	10·00
Z201	2½d. light ultramarine	9·00
Z202	3d. pale violet	6·50

1946. Victory (Nos. 491/492).

Z203	2½d. ultramarine	9·00
Z204	3d. violet	9·00

Type G

Stamps of GREAT BRITAIN cancelled as Type G or registered oval as Type F at Tetuan.

1937. King George V.

Z208	4d. deep grey-green (No. 445)	25·00
Z209	6d. purple (No. 426*a*)	23·00
Z210	1s. bistre-brown (No. 449)	

1937–39. King George VI (Nos. 465/475).

Z211	2d. orange	22·00
Z212	2½d. ultramarine	
Z213	3d. violet	
Z214	4d. grey-green	22·00
Z215	6d. purple	13·00
Z216	9d. deep olive-green	28·00
Z216*a*	10d. turquoise-blue	42·00
Z217	1s. bistre-brown	13·00

1939–42. King George VI (Nos. 476/477).

Z218	2s.6d. brown	
Z219	2s.6d. yellow-green	45·00
Z220	5s. red	60·00

1941. King George VI pale colours (Nos. 485/490).

Z221	½d. pale green	21·00
Z221*a*	1d. pale scarlet	21·00
Z222	2d. pale orange	
Z223	2½d. light ultramarine	
Z224	3d. pale violet	13·00

Other unoverprinted stamps of Great Britain are known with Morocco Agencies postmarks during this period, but it is believed that only Nos. Z170/Z224 were sold by the local post offices.

The use of unoverprinted stamps in Tangier ceased with the issue of Nos. 261/275 on 1 January 1949. Stamps overprinted 'MOROCCO AGENCIES' replaced the unoverprinted values at Tetuan on 16 August 1949.

MOROCCO AGENCIES (9) MOROCCO AGENCIES (10)

1949 (16 Aug). King George VI, optd with Types **9** or **10** (2s.6d., 5s.).

77	½d. pale green	1·75	8·50
78	1d. pale scarlet	2·75	11·00
79	1½d. pale red-brown	2·75	9·50
80	2d. pale orange	3·00	14·00
81	2½d. light ultramarine	3·25	14·00
82	3d. pale violet	1·50	3·00
83	4d. grey-green	50	1·25
84	5d. brown	3·00	15·00
85	6d. purple	1·50	2·50
86	7d. emerald-green	50	17·00
87	8d. bright carmine	3·00	7·50
88	9d. deep olive-green	50	13·00
89	10d. turquoise-blue	50	11·00
90	11d. plum	70	12·00
91	1s. bistre-brown	3·00	7·00
92	2s.6d. yellow-green	22·00	48·00
93	5s. red	42·00	75·00
77/93 *Set of 17*		80·00	£225

1951 (3 May). King George VI (Nos. 503/507, 509/510), optd with Types **9** or **10** (2s.6d., 5s.).

94	½d. pale orange	2·00	1·00
95	1d. light ultramarine	2·00	1·40
96	1½d. pale green	2·00	11·00
97	2d. pale red-brown	2·25	7·00
98	2½d. pale scarlet	2·00	6·50

99	2s.6d. yellow-green (HMS *Victory*)	13·00	21·00
100	5s. red (Dover)	13·00	23·00
94/100 *Set of 7*		32·00	60·00

1952–55. Queen Elizabeth II. W **153** (Tudor Crown). Optd with T **9**.

101	½d. orange-red (31.8.53)	10	10
102	1d. ultramarine (31.8.53)	15	1·75
103	1½d. green (5.12.52)	15	20
104	2d. red-brown (31.8.53)	20	2·50
105	2½d. carmine-red (5.12.52)	15	1·25
106	4d. ultramarine (1.3.55)	4·50	5·00
107	5d. brown (6.7.53)	60	1·00
108	6d. reddish purple (1.3.55)	1·25	4·50
109	8d. magenta (6.7.53)	60	1·00
110	1s. bistre-brown (6.7.53)	60	1·50
101/110 *Set of 10*		7·50	17·00

1956 (10 Sept). Queen Elizabeth II. W **165** (St Edward's Crown). Optd with T **9**.

111	2½d. carmine-red (No. 544)	2·00	4·50

Stamps overprinted 'MOROCCO AGENCIES' were withdrawn from sale on 31 December 1956.

IV. SPANISH CURRENCY

Stamps surcharged in Spanish currency were sold at British POs throughout Morocco until the establishment of the French Zone and the Tangier International Zone, when their use was confined to the Spanish Zone.

During this period further British postal agencies were opened at Alcazar (1907–1916), Fez–Mellah (Jewish quarter) (1909), Marrakesh (1909), Marrakesh–Mellah (Jewish quarter) (1909–1917) and Mequinez (1907–1916).

MOROCCO AGENCIES 5 CENTIMOS (11)

MOROCCO AGENCIES 6 PESETAS (12)

1907 (1 Jan)–**12**. King Edward VII surch as T **11** (5c. to 1p.) or T **12** (3p. to 12p.).

(a) De La Rue printings. Ordinary paper (Nos. 112/113, 116, 118, 122/123) or chalk-surfaced paper (others)

112	5c. on ½d. pale yellowish green	14·00	20
	a. Yellowish green	14·00	20
113	10c. on 1d. scarlet	22·00	10
	a. Bright scarlet	22·00	10
114	15c. on 1½d. pale dull purple and green	16·00	1·75
	a. Slate-purple and bluish green	9·00	20
	b. '1' of '15' omitted	£7000	
115	20c. on 2d. pale grey-green and carmine-red	7·00	3·00
	a. Pale grey-green and scarlet	9·50	3·25
116	25c. on 2½d. ultramarine	3·50	20
	a. Pale ultramarine	3·00	20
117	40c. on 4d. green and chocolate-brown (29.10.07)	3·25	6·50
	a. Deep green and chocolate-brown	6·00	4·50
118	40c. on 4d. pale orange (12.5.10)	4·25	2·75
	a. Orange-red	1·50	2·00
119	50c. on 5d. dull purple and ultramarine	13·00	9·00
	a. Slate-purple and ultramarine	12·00	9·00
120	1p. on 10d. dull purple and carmine	50·00	26·00
	a. Slate-purple and carmine	23·00	24·00
	b. No cross on crown		
121	3p. on 2s.6d. pale dull purple	25·00	40·00
	a. Dull purple	25·00	40·00
122	6p. on 5s. bright carmine	35·00	45·00
	a. Deep bright carmine	35·00	45·00
123	12p. on 10s. ultramarine (30.4.07)	80·00	80·00
112/123 *Set of 12*		£200	£180
117s, 123s Optd 'SPECIMEN' *Set of 2*		£150	

(b) Harrison printing Ordinary paper

124	25c. on 2½d. bright blue (No. 283) (1912)	60·00	50·00
	a. Dull blue	45·00	50·00

(c) Somerset House printing. Ordinary paper

125	12p. on 10s. blue (No. 319) (1912)	£200	£250

No. 114b occurred on stamps from the first vertical row of one sheet.

1912. King George V (W **49** (Imperial Crown)) surch as T **11**.

126	5c. on ½d. green (No. 339)	4·75	20
127	10c. on 1d. scarlet (No. 342)	1·25	10
	a. No cross on crown	£120	55·00

MOROCCO AGENCIES 3 CENTIMOS (13)

MOROCCO AGENCIES 10 CENTIMOS (14)

MOROCCO AGENCIES 15CENTIMOS (15)

MOROCCO AGENCIES 6 PESETAS (16)

1914–26. King George V.

*(a) W **100** (Simple Cypher). Surch as T **11** (5c.), T **13** (3c. and 40c.)*, T **15** (15c.) and T **14** (remainder)*

128	3c. on ½d. green (1917)	4·00	14·00
129	5c. on ½d. green	3·00	10
130	10c. on 1d. scarlet	4·75	10
	y. Wmk inverted and reversed	—	£250
131	15c. on 1½d. red-brown (1915)	1·50	10
	a. Surch double, one albino	80·00	
132	20c. on 2d. orange (Die I)	1·50	25
	a. Surch double, one albino	80·00	
133	25c. on 2½d. blue (*shades*)	3·50	25
	a. Surch double, one albino	80·00	
	w. Wmk inverted	£100	
134	40c. on 4d. grey-green (1917)	10·00	4·00
	a. Surch double, one albino		
135	1p. on 10d. turquoise-blue	9·00	18·00
	a. Surch double, one albino	90·00	

* The surcharge on Nos. 134, 148 and 158 is as T **13** for the value and T **15** for 'MOROCCO AGENCIES'.

*(b) W **110** (Single Cypher). Surch as T **16***

(i) Waterlow printings

136	6p. on 5s. rose-carmine	38·00	50·00
	a. Surch double, one albino	£160	
	b. Surch triple, two albino	£180	
137	6p. on 5s. pale rose-carmine	£150	£200
	a. Surch double, one albino	£225	
	b. Surch triple, two albino	£275	
138	12p. on 10s. indigo-blue (R.)	£110	£200
	a. Surch double, one albino	£250	
	b. Surch triple, two albino		
136s, 138s Optd '*SPECIMEN*' or 'SPECIMEN' (No. 138s) *Set of 2*		£190	

(ii) De La Rue printings

139	3p. on 2s.6d. grey-brown (1918)	50·00	£140
	a. Surch double, one albino	£180	
140	3p. on 2s.6d. yellow-brown	50·00	£170
	a. Surch double, one albino	£170	
141	12p. on 10s. blue (R.)	95·00	£170
	a. Surch double, one albino	£275	

(iii) Bradbury Wilkinson printings

142	3p. on 2s.6d. chocolate-brown (27.4.26)	28·00	75·00
128/142 *Set of 11*		£170	£275

1925 (12 Oct)–**31**. King George V (W **111** (Block Cypher)), surch as Types **11**, **13**, **14** or **15**.

143	5c. on ½d. green (3.1.31)	9·00	32·00
144	10c. on 1d. scarlet (4.11.29)	38·00	38·00
145	15c. on 1½d. red-brown	7·50	23·00
146	20c. on 2d. orange (1931)	3·00	14·00
	a. Surch double, one albino	85·00	
147	25c. on 2½d. blue	7·50	2·50
	a. Surch double, one albino	80·00	
	w. Wmk inverted	65·00	
148	40c. on 4d. grey-green (1930)	8·00	2·50
	a. Surch double, one albino	90·00	
143/148 *Set of 6*		65·00	£100

MOROCCO AGENCIES 10 CENTIMOS (17)

MOROCCO AGENCIES 10 CENTIMOS (18)

1935 (8 May). Silver Jubilee (Nos. 453/456). Surch as T **17**.

149	5c. on ½d. green (B.)	1·00	1·25
150	10c. on 1d. scarlet (B.)	2·75	2·75
	a. Pair, one with 'CENTIMES'	£1700	£2500
151	15c. on 1½d. red-brown (B.)	7·50	24·00
152	25c. on 2½d. blue (R.)	3·50	2·25
149/152 *Set of 4*		13·00	27·00

No. 150a occurred on R. 5/4 of a small second printing made in June 1935. The error can only be identified when *se-tenant* with a normal No. 150. Beware of forgeries.

1935–37. King George V (Harrison photo ptgs) (Nos. 439/443, 445 and 448). Surch as Types **11**, **13**, **14** or **15**. W **111** (Block Cypher).

153	5c. on ½d. green (9.6.36)	1·50	23·00
154	10c. on 1d. scarlet (24.11.35)	5·00	23·00
155	15c. on 1½d. red-brown (11.4.35)	13·00	3·25
156	20c. on 2d. orange (26.10.36)	50	35
157	25c. on 2½d. ultramarine (8.9.36)	1·25	12·00
158	40c. on 4d. deep grey-green (18.5.37)	50	8·50
159	1p. on 10d. turquoise-blue (14.4.37)	6·00	4·00
153/159 *Set of 7*		25·00	65·00

1936 (26 Oct)–**37**. King Edward VIII surch as T **18** with 'MOROCCO' 14¼ mm long.

160	5c. on ½d. green	10	10
161	10c. on 1d. scarlet	50	2·00
	a. 'MOROCCO' 15¼ mm long (5.1.37)	2·75	20·00
162	15c. on 1½d. red-brown	10	15
163	25c. on 2½d. bright blue	10	10
160/163 *Set of 4*		65	2·00

The first three printings of the 10c. on 1d. (from cyls 4, 5 and 6) showed all stamps with the short surcharge (No. 161).

On 5 January 1937 a further printing was placed on sale in London which had 49 stamps in the sheet (R. 1/2 to 11, R. 2/1, 5 and 6, 8 and 9, R. 3/5, R. 4/5, R. 5/4 and 5, 10, R. 6/6 and 7, R. 7/8, R. 8/8, R. 9/8, R. 11/7, 9, R. 13/2 to 5, 7 and 8, R. 14/1, 7, R. 15/7, 11, R. 16/5, 10, R. 17/4, 10 and 11, R. 18/1, R. 19/2, R. 20/1 and 2, 3, 7, 9) with long surcharge (No. 161a). The next printing increased the number of long surcharges in the sheet to 50 (R. 10/2), but the final version, although retaining 50 long surcharges, showed them on R. 1/2 to 11, R. 17/5 to 8 and the entire rows 18, 19 and 20. The first two printings with long surcharges were from cylinder 6 and the last from cylinder 13.

MOROCCO 15 CENTIMOS AGENCIES (19)

1937 (13 May). Coronation (No. 461), surch as T **19**.

164	15c. on 1½d. maroon (B.)	1·00	70

MOROCCO AGENCIES 10 CENTIMOS (20)

MOROCCO AGENCIES 10 CENTIMOS (21)

1937 (11 June)–**52**. King George VI (Nos. 462/464, 466, 468, 471 and 474), surch as T **20**.

165	5c. on ½d. green (B.)	1·25	30
166	10c. on 1d. scarlet	1·00	10
167	15c. on 1½d. red-brown (B.) (4.8.37)	3·50	25
168	25c. on 2½d. ultramarine	2·00	1·25
169	40c. on 4d. grey-green (9.40)	40·00	17·00
170	70c. on 7d. emerald-green (9.40)	3·50	24·00
171	1p. on 10d. turquoise-blue (16.6.52)	2·25	11·00
165/171 *Set of 7*		48·00	48·00

1940 (6 May). Centenary of First Adhesive Postage Stamps (Nos. 479/481 and 483), surch as T **21**.

172	5c. on ½d. green (B.)	30	2·75
173	10c. on 1d. scarlet	3·75	5·50
174	15c. on 1½d. red-brown (B.)	70	6·50
175	25c. on 2½d. ultramarine	80	5·50
172/175 *Set of 4*		5·00	18·00

25 CENTIMOS MOROCCO AGENCIES (22)

45 PESETAS MOROCCO AGENCIES (23)

1948 (26 Apr). Silver Wedding (Nos. 493/494), surch with Types **22** or **23**.

176	25c. on 2½d. ultramarine	1·25	1·00
177	45p. on £1 blue	17·00	23·00

1948 (29 July). Olympic Games (Nos. 495/498), variously surch as T **22**.

178	25c. on 2½d. ultramarine	50	1·50
179	30c. on 3d. violet	50	1·50
	a. Crown flaw	90·00	£140
180	60c. on 6d. bright purple	50	1·50
181	1p.20c. on 1s. brown	60	1·50
	a. Surch double	£1500	
178/181 *Set of 4*		1·90	5·50

1951 (3 May)–**52**. King George VI (Nos. 503/505 and 507/508), surch as T **20**.

182	5c. on ½d. pale orange	2·00	7·00
183	10c. on 1d. light ultramarine	3·25	10·00
184	15c. on 1½d. pale green	1·75	26·00
185	25c. on 2½d. pale scarlet	1·75	25·00
186	40c. on 4d. light ultramarine (26.5.52)	1·00	13·00
182/186 *Set of 5*		8·75	70·00

1954–55. Queen Elizabeth II. W **153** (Tudor Crown). Surch as T **20**.

187	5c. on ½d. orange-red (1.9.54)	30	4·00
188	10c. on 1d. ultramarine (1.3.55)	70	2·75

1956. Queen Elizabeth II. W **165** (St Edward's Crown). Surch as T **20**.

189	5c. on ½d. orange-red (6.56)	15	4·50
190	40c. on 4d. ultramarine (15.8)	70	4·00

The British postal agency at Laraiche closed on 30 June 1938. Stamps surcharged in Spanish currency were withdrawn from sale when the Tetuan agency closed on 31 December 1956.

V. FRENCH CURRENCY

For use in the British postal agencies at Casablanca (closed 14.8.37), Fez (closed 8.1.38), Fez–Mellah (closed after 1930), Marrakesh (closed 14.8.37), Mazagan (closed 14.8.37), Mogador (closed 31.10.33), Rabat (closed 8.1.38) and Saffi (closed 14.8.37).

MOROCCO AGENCIES 25 CENTIMES (24)

MOROCCO AGENCIES 1 FRANC (25)

1917 (Dec)–**24**. King George V (W **100** (Simple Cypher)), surch as Types **24** or **25** (1f.).

191	3c. on ½d. green (R.)	3·25	3·00
192	5c. on ½d. green	75	20
193	10c. on 1d. scarlet	4·75	40
194	15c. on 1½d. red-brown	4·50	20
195	25c. on 2½d. blue	1·50	20
196	40c. on 4d. slate-green	2·00	1·50
	a. Surch double, one albino		
197	50c. on 5d. yellow-brown (24.10.23)	1·00	2·75
198	75c. on 9d. olive-green (1924)	1·00	75
	a. Surch double, one albino	£110	
199	1f. on 10d. turquoise-blue	13·00	4·25
	a. Surch double, one albino	85·00	
191/199 *Set of 9*		28·00	12·00

1924–32. King George V (B.W. ptg). W **110** (Single Cypher), surch as T **25**, but closer vertical spacing.

200	3f. on 2s.6d. chocolate-brown	5·00	1·50
	a. Major re-entry (R. 1/2)	£500	£500
	b. Surch double, one albino		
	c. Reddish brown	8·00	10·00
201	6f. on 5s. rose-red (23.9.32)	32·00	40·00
200s/201s Optd '*SPECIMEN*' or 'SPECIMEN' (No. 201s) *Set of 2*		£160	

1925–34. King George V (W **111** (Block Cypher)), surch as Types **24** or **25** (1f.).

202	5c. on ½d. green	30	6·50
203	10c. on 1d. scarlet	30	2·00
	a. Surch double, one albino	95·00	
204	15c. on 1½d. red-brown	2·50	1·40
205	25c. on 2½d. blue	3·75	50
206	40c. on 4d. grey-green	75	80
	a. Surch double, one albino	80·00	
207	50c. on 5d. yellow-brown	1·50	10
	w. Wmk inverted	75·00	
208	75c. on 9d. olive-green	15·00	20
	a. Surch double, one albino	£130	
	w. Wmk inverted	—	£200
209	90c. on 9d. olive-green (8.5.34)	23·00	15·00
210	1f. on 10d. turquoise-blue	1·50	10
	a. Surch double, one albino	£110	
211	1f.50 on 1s. bistre-brown (8.5.34)	21·00	2·25
	s. Optd 'SPECIMEN'	65·00	
202/211 *Set of* 10		60·00	26·00

1935 (8 May). Silver Jubilee (Nos. 453/456), surch as T **17**, but in French currency.

212	5c. on ½d. green (B.)	20	20
213	10c. on 1d. scarlet (B.)	4·50	70
214	15c. on 1½d. red-brown (B.)	1·75	2·50
215	25c. on 2½d. blue (R.)	45	25
212/215 *Set of* 4		6·25	3·25

1935–37. King George V (Harrison photo ptgs. W **111** (Block Cypher)), surch as Types **24** or **25** (1f.).

216	5c. on ½d. green (21.10.35)	75	8·50
217	10c. on 1d. scarlet (2.3.36)	35	30
218	15c. on 1½d. red-brown	13·00	6·00
219	25c. on 2½d. ultramarine (25.9.36)	30	15
220	40c. on 4d. deep grey-green (2.12.36)	30	15
221	50c. on 5d. yellow-brown (15.9.36)	30	15
222	90c. on 9d. deep olive-green (15.2.37)	75	2·00
223	1f. on 10d. turquoise-blue (10.2.37)	30	30
224	1f.50 on 1s. bistre-brown (20.7.37)	75	3·50
	s. Optd 'SPECIMEN'	70·00	

1935–36. King George V (Waterlow re-engraved ptgs. W **100** (Single Cypher)), surch as T **25**, but closer vertical spacing.

225	3f. on 2s.6d. chocolate-brown (No. 450)	4·75	12·00
226	6f. on 5s. bright rose-red (No. 451) (9.6.36)	9·50	24·00
216/226 *Set of* 11		28·00	50·00
225s/226s Optd '*SPECIMEN*' or 'SPECIMEN' (No. 226s) *Set of* 2		£150	

1936 (26 Oct). King Edward VIII, surch as T **18**, but in French currency.

227	5c. in ½d. green	10	15
	a. Bar through 'POSTAGE'	£750	
228	15c. on 1½d. red-brown	10	15

No. 227a involved R. 18/10 to 12 on a total of eight sheets. The bar, probably a printers rule, became progressively longer so that on four of the sheets it extends over all three stamps. Price quoted is for an example with the bar through the entire word.

1937 (13 May). Coronation (No. 461), surch as T **19**, but in French currency.

229	15c. on 1½d. maroon (B.)	50	20

1937 (11 June). King George VI, surch as T **20**, but in French currency.

230	5c. on ½d. green (B.)	4·50	4·25

Stamps surcharged in French currency were withdrawn from sale on 8 January 1938.

VI. TANGIER INTERNATIONAL ZONE

By an agreement between Great Britain, France and Spain, Tangier was declared an international zone in 1924. Stamps overprinted 'Morocco Agencies' or surcharged in Spanish currency were used there until replaced by Nos. 231/234.

PRICES. Our note re UK usage (at beginning of Section III) also applies to 'TANGIER' optd stamps.

TANGIER (26) TANGIER TANGIER (27)

1927 (29 Apr). King George V (W **111** (Block Cypher)), optd with T **26**.

231	½d. green	7·50	20
	a. Opt double, one albino		
232	1d. scarlet	10·00	25
	a. Inverted 'Q' for 'O' (R. 20/3)	£800	
233	1½d. chestnut	8·50	9·00
234	2d. orange	3·25	20
	a. Opt double, one albino	80·00	
231/234 *Set of* 4		26·00	9·00

1934 (13 Dec)–**35.** King George V (Harrison photo ptgs. W **111** (Block Cypher)), optd with T **26**.

235	½d. green (16.2.35)	1·25	3·00
236	1d. scarlet	13·00	4·00
237	1½d. red-brown	75	20
235/237 *Set of* 3		13·50	6·50

1935 (8 May). Silver Jubilee (Nos. 453/455), optd with T **27** in blue.

238	½d. green	2·75	9·00
239	1d. scarlet	25·00	22·00
240	1½d. red-brown	1·25	2·25
238/240 *Set of* 3		26·00	30·00

1936 (26 Oct). King Edward VIII, optd with T **26**.

241	½d. green	10	20
242	1d. scarlet	10	10
243	1½d. red-brown	15	10
241/243 *Set of* 3		30	30

TANGIER (28) TANGIER TANGIER (29)

1937 (13 May). Coronation (No. 461), optd with T **28**.

244	1½d. maroon (B.)	1·50	50

1937. King George VI (Nos. 462/464), optd with T **29**.

245	½d. green (B.) (6.37)	9·00	1·75
246	1d. scarlet (6.37)	27·00	1·75
247	1½d. red-brown (B.) (4.8)	2·75	40
245/247 *Set of* 3		35·00	3·50

TANGIER (30) TANGIER (31)

1940 (6 May). Centenary of First Adhesive Postage Stamps (Nos. 479/481), optd with T **30**.

248	½d. green (B.)	30	9·00
249	1d. scarlet	55	1·00
250	1½d. red-brown (B.)	2·00	13·00
248/250 *Set of* 3		2·50	21·00

1944. King George VI pale colours (Nos. 485/486), optd with T **29**.

251	½d. pale green (B.)	12·00	5·00
252	1d. pale scarlet	12·00	5·00

1946 (11 June). Victory (Nos. 491/492), optd as T **31**.

253	2½d. ultramarine	1·00	65
254	3d. violet	1·00	2·00

The opt on No. 254 is smaller (23×2½ *mm*).

1948 (26 Apr). Royal Silver Wedding (Nos. 493/494), optd with T **30**.

255	2½d. ultramarine	50	15
	a. Opt omitted (in vert pair with stamp optd at top)	£9000	
256	£1 blue	20·00	25·00

No. 255a comes from a sheet on which the overprint is misplaced downwards resulting in the complete absence of the opt from the six stamps of the top row. On the rest of the sheet the opt falls at the top of each stamp instead of at the foot (*Price £250, unused, £350 used*).

1948 (29 July). Olympic Games (Nos. 495/498), optd with T **30**.

257	2½d. ultramarine	1·00	2·00
258	3d. violet	1·00	2·25
	a. Crown flaw	£110	
259	6d. bright purple	1·00	2·25
260	1s. brown	1·00	2·25
257/260 *Set of* 4		3·50	8·00

1949 (1 Jan). King George VI, optd with T **29**.

261	2d. pale orange	8·50	11·00
262	2½d. light ultramarine	6·50	11·00
263	3d. pale violet	70	1·25
264	4d. grey-green	11·00	17·00
265	5d. brown	5·50	35·00
266	6d. purple	1·50	30
267	7d. emerald-green	2·50	19·00
268	8d. bright carmine	5·00	17·00
269	9d. deep olive-green	2·50	17·00
270	10d. turquoise-blue	2·75	16·00
271	11d. plum	4·50	25·00
272	1s. bistre-brown	1·50	2·75
273	2s.6d. yellow-green	9·50	28·00
274	5s. red	21·00	48·00
275	10s. ultramarine	55·00	£140
261/275 *Set of* 15		£120	£325

1949 (10 Oct). 75th Anniversary of UPU (Nos. 499/502), optd with T **30**.

276	2½d. ultramarine	75	4·50
	a. Lake in India	90·00	
277	3d. violet	75	7·50
278	6d. bright purple	75	1·25
279	1s. brown	75	3·25
276/279 *Set of* 4		2·75	15·00

1950 (2 Oct)–**51.** King George VI, optd with Types **29** or **30** (shilling values).

280	½d. pale orange (3.5.51)	1·00	1·50
281	1d. light ultramarine (3.5.51)	1·25	3·00
282	1½d. pale green (3.5.51)	1·25	24·00
283	2d. pale red-brown (3.5.51)	1·25	5·00
284	2½d. pale scarlet (3.5.51)	1·25	11·00
285	4d. light ultramarine	4·50	3·00
286	2s.6d. yellow-green (HMS *Victory*) (3.5.51)	10·00	5·00
287	5s. red (Dover) (3.5.51)	17·00	15·00
288	10s. ultramarine (St George) (3.5.51)	32·00	15·00
280/288 *Set of* 9		60·00	75·00

1952–54. Queen Elizabeth II (W **153** (Tudor Crown)), optd with T **29**.

289	½d. orange-red (31.8.53)	10	50
290	1d. ultramarine (31.8.53)	15	50
291	1½d. green (5.12.52)	10	30
292	2d. red-brown (31.8.53)	20	1·25
293	2½d. carmine-red (5.12.52)	10	1·00
294	3d. deep lilac (B.) (18.1.54)	20	1·25
295	4d. ultramarine (2.11.53)	60	4·25
296	5d. brown (6.7.53)	60	1·00
297	6d. reddish purple (18.1.54)	60	15
298	7d. bright green (18.1.54)	1·00	4·25
299	8d. magenta (6.7.53)	60	1·50
300	9d. bronze-green (8.2.54)	1·40	1·75
301	10d. Prussian blue (8.2.54)	1·40	2·75
302	11d. brown-purple (8.2.54)	1·40	3·25
303	1s. bistre-brown (6.7.53)	60	70
304	1s.3d. green (2.11.53)	1·00	7·50
305	1s.6d. grey-blue (2.11.53)	1·50	2·25
289/305 *Set of* 17		10·00	30·00

1953 (3 June). Coronation (Nos. 532/535), optd with T **30**.

306	2½d. carmine-red	75	50
307	4d. ultramarine	2·25	50
308	1s.3d. deep yellow-green	2·00	1·50
309	1s.6d. deep grey-blue	2·00	2·00
306/309 *Set of* 4		6·25	4·00

1955 (23 Sept). Queen Elizabeth II, Castle high values (W **165** (St Edward's Crown)), optd with T **30**.

310	2s.6d. black-brown	3·50	10·00
311	5s. rose-red	4·50	24·00
312	10s. ultramarine	18·00	29·00
310/312 *Set of* 3		23·00	55·00

1956. Queen Elizabeth II (W **165** (St Edward's Crown)), optd with T **29**.

313	½d. orange-red (21.3)	10	1·00
314	1d. ultramarine (13.4)	20	50
315	1½d. green (22.10)	40	3·00
316	2d. red-brown (25.7)	1·25	1·75
317	2d. light red-brown (10.12)	70	40
318	2½d. carmine-red (19.12)	40	40
319	3d. deep lilac (B) (22.10)	40	7·50
320	4d. ultramarine (25.6)	65	2·00
321	6d. reddish purple (22.10)	50	7·50
322	1s.3d. green (26.11)	1·75	13·00
313/322 *Set of* 10		5·75	32·00

1857·1957

TANGIER (32) 1857·1957 TANGIER (33)

1957 (1 Apr). Centenary of British Post Office in Tangier.

*(a) Nos. 540/542 and 543b/566 (W **165** (St Edward's Crown)), optd as Types **32** or **33** (7d)*

323	½d. orange-red	10	15
324	1d. ultramarine	10	15
325	1½d. green	10	15
326	2d. light red-brown	10	15
327	2½d. carmine-red	15	1·25
328	3d. deep lilac (B.)	15	40
329	4d. ultramarine	30	30
330	5d. brown	30	35
331	6d. reddish purple	30	35
332	7d. bright green	30	35
333	8d. magenta	30	1·00
334	9d. bronze-green	30	30
	a. 'TANGIER' omitted	£7500	
335	10d. Prussian blue	30	30
336	11d. brown-purple	30	30
337	1s. bistre-brown	30	30
338	1s.3d. green	45	5·00
339	1s.6d. grey-blue	50	1·60

*(b) Nos. 536/538 (W **165** (St Edward's Crown)), optd as T **32***

340	2s.6d. black-brown	2·00	7·00
	a. Hyphen omitted	£100	£180
	b. Hyphen inserted	32·00	
341	5s. rose-red	2·75	13·00
	a. Hyphen omitted	£130	£200
	b. Hyphen inserted	19·00	
342	10s. ultramarine	3·75	13·00
	a. Hyphen omitted	£130	£225
	b. Hyphen inserted	26·00	
323/342 *Set of* 20		11·50	40·00

Nos. 340a/340b, 341a/341b and 342a/342b occur on R.9/2 in the sheet of 40 (4×10). They are best collected in marginal blocks of four from the bottom left corner of the sheet. Specialists recognise two forms of No. 340b; one where the hyphen on R.9/2 was inserted separately to correct the error, No. 340a; the other from a later printing where a new and corrected overprinting plate was used. (*Price £12 un.*).

All stamps overprinted 'TANGIER' were withdrawn from sale on 30 April 1957.

Muscat

An independent Arab Sultanate in Eastern Arabia with an Indian postal administration.

The Indian post office at Muscat town is officially recorded as having opened on 1 May 1864. Stamps of India were provided for its use.

The office was initially included in the Bombay Postal Circle and the first postmark, so far only recorded on stampless covers, was a single circle, 21½ mm in diameter, broken at the top by 'MUSCAT' and with the date in two lines across the centre. This was followed by a cancellation showing the post office number, '309', within a diamond of 13, later 16, bars. It is believed that this was used in conjunction with a single-ring date stamp inscribed 'MUSCAT'.

1864 Diamond

In 1869 the office was transferred to the Sind Circle, assigned a new number, '23', and issued with a duplex cancellation. Major reorganisation of the postal service in 1873 resulted in Muscat becoming office 'K-4'. For ten years from 1873 the cancellations do not, very confusingly, carry any indication of the year of use.

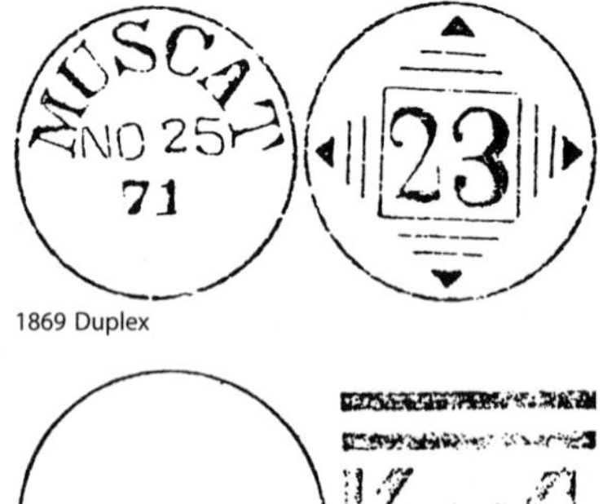

1869 Duplex

MUSCAT.
NOV 10
K-4

1873 Duplex

Muscat rejoined the Bombay Circle in 1879 and was issued with a cancellation showing a 'B' within a square of horizontal bars. The date stamp used at this time was unique in that it carried the inscription 'MASKAT', although the spelling reverted to the more usual form by 1882. The square cancellation had been replaced by a similar circular mark by 1884.

Subsequent postmarks were of various circular types, all inscribed 'MUSCAT'.

There was only one Indian post office in Muscat, but a further office did exist, from 12 April 1868, at the Muscat dependency of Guadur, a port on the Mekran coast of Baluchistan.

Stamps of INDIA cancelled by numeral, duplex or circular types inscribed 'MUSCAT' or 'MASKAT'.

1856–64. (Nos. 37/49).
Z1 ½a. blue 85·00
Z1a 1a. brown £250
Z3 2a. yellow £140
Z4 4a. grey-black £140
Z5 8a. carmine £275

1865. (Nos. 54/63).
Z7 ½a. blue (Die I) 22·00
Z9 1a. pale brown 28·00
Z10 2a. yellow 48·00
Z11 2a. brown-orange 42·00

1866. (Nos. 69/71).
Z13 4a. green (Die I) 65·00
Z14 4a. blue-green (Die II) 70·00

1868. (Nos. 73/74).
Z15 8a. pale rose (Die II) 90·00

1873. (Nos. 75/76).
Z16 ½a. blue (Die II) 13·00

1874. (Nos. 77/79).
Z17 9p. bright mauve £120
Z18 1r. slate £300

1876. (Nos. 80/82).
Z19 6a. pale brown 42·00
Z20 12a. Venetian red £180

1882–90. (Nos. 84/101).
Z21 ½a. blue green 11·00
Z23 1a. brown-purple 11·00
Z24 1a.6p. sepia 23·00
Z25 2a. blue 14·00
Z26 3a. orange 26·00
Z27 3a. brown-orange 17·00
Z28 4a. olive-green 25·00
Z29 4a.6p. yellow-green 35·00
Z30 8a. dull mauve 35·00
Z31 12a. purple/*red* 75·00
Z32 1r. slate 90·00

1891. (No. 102).
Z33 2½a. on 4½a. yellow-green 30·00

1892–97. (Nos. 103/106).
Z34 2a.6p. yellow-green 11·00
Z35 1r. green and aniline carmine 90·00

1898. (No. 110).
Z37 ¼ on ½a. blue-green 35·00

1899. (No. 111).
Z38 3p. carmine 23·00

1900–02. (Nos. 112/118).
Z39 3p. grey 90·00
Z40 ½a. pale yellow-green 13·00
Z41 1a. carmine 13·00
Z42 2a. pale violet 30·00
Z43 2a.6p. ultramarine 16·00

1902–11. (Nos. 119/136).
Z44 3p. grey 13·00
Z45 ½a. green 7·50
Z46 1a. carmine 8·50
Z47 2a. mauve 12·00
Z48 2a.6p. ultramarine 7·50
Z50 4a. olive 14·00
Z52 8a. purple 29·00
Z54 1r. green and carmine 60·00

1905. (No. 148).
Z57 ¼ on ½a. green 29·00

1906–07. (Nos. 149/150).
Z58 ½a. green 7·50
Z59 1a. carmine 7·50

1911–22. (Nos. 151/186).
Z60 3p. grey 13·00
Z61 ½a. light green 7·50
Z62 1a. carmine 7·50
Z63 1½a. chocolate (No. 163) 29·00
Z64 1½a. chocolate (No. 165) 35·00
Z65 2a. purple 11·00
Z66 2a.6p. ultramarine (No. 170) 19·00
Z67 2a.6p. ultramarine (No. 171) 11·00
Z69 4a. olive-green 22·00
Z70 6a. brown-ochre 29·00
Z71 8a. deep mauve 35·00
Z73 1r. brown and green 45·00

1921. (Nos. 192/194).
Z76 9p. on 1a. rose-carmine 35·00

1922. (Nos. 195/196).
Z77 ¼ on ½a. bright green 35·00

1922–26. (Nos. 197/200).
Z78 1a. chocolate 11·00
Z80 2a.6p. orange 23·00
Z81 3a. ultramarine 28·00

1926–33. (Nos. 201/217).
Z82 3p. slate 5·50
Z83 ½a. green 5·50
Z84 1a. chocolate 5·50
Z87 2a.6p. orange 18·00
Z88 3a. blue 12·00
Z89 4a. sage-green (No. 211) 13·00
Z90 8a. reddish purple 18·00
Z91 12a. claret 30·00
Z92 1r. chocolate and green 29·00
Z93 2r. carmine and orange 42·00
Z95 10r. green and scarlet £140

1929. (Nos. 221/224).
Z97 3a. blue 19·00
Z99 6a. bistre 24·00
Z100 8a. purple 29·00

1931. (Nos. 227/228).
Z103 ½a. violet and green 29·00
Z104 1a. mauve and chocolate 29·00

1932–36. (Nos. 232/239).
Z107 ½a. green 7·50
Z109 1a. chocolate 7·50
Z110 1a.3p. mauve 7·50
Z112 3a. carmine 18·00
Z114 6a. bistre 40·00

1935. (Nos. 240/246).
Z115 ½a. black and yellow-green 14·00
Z116 9p. black and grey-green 18·00
Z117 1a. black and brown 14·00
Z118 1¼a. black and bright violet 18·00
Z119 2½a. black and orange 25·00
Z121 8a. black and purple 48·00

1937–40. (Nos. 247/260).
Z122 3p. slate 5·50
Z123 ½a. red-brown 5·50
Z124 9p. green 8·00
Z125 1a. carmine 5·50
Z126 2a. vermilion 11·00
Z127 2a.6p. bright violet 13·00
Z130 4a. brown 14·00
Z131 6a. turquoise-green 29·00
Z132 8a. slate-violet 29·00
Z133 12a. lake 35·00
Z134 1r. grey and red-brown 22·00
Z135 2r. purple and brown 28·00

1940. (Nos. 265/277).
Z138 3p. slate 5·50
Z139 ½a. purple 5·50
Z140 9p. green 7·00
Z141 1a. carmine 5·50
Z142 1a.3p. yellow-brown 7·00
Z143 1½a. dull violet 6·50
Z144 2a. vermilion 6·50
Z145 3a. bright violet 6·50
Z146 3½a. bright blue 8·00
Z147 4a. brown 5·50
Z148 6a. turquoise-green 8·50
Z149 8a. slate-violet 6·50
Z150 12a. lake 15·00
Z151 14a. purple 22·00

1946. (Nos. 278/281).
Z152 9p. yellow-green 30·00
Z153 1½a. dull violet 30·00
Z154 3½a. bright blue 42·00
Z155 12a. claret 60·00

1946. (No. 282).
Z156 3p. on 1a.3p. yellow-brown 15·00

OFFICIAL STAMPS

1866–72. (No. O12).
Z158 2a. yellow £400

1867–73. (Nos. O23/O29).
Z160 1a. brown 85·00
Z161 2a. yellow £120
Z162 4a. green (Die I) £130

1874. (No. O31).
Z163 ½a. blue (Die II) 70·00

1883–99. (Nos. O39/O42).
Z165 ½a. blue-green 32·00
Z166 1a. brown-purple 32·00
Z167 2a. blue 32·00

1902–09. (No. O59).
Z171 2a. mauve 32·00

1909. (No. O68).
Z174 2r. carmine and yellow-brown £140

1912–13. (Nos. O76/O83*a*).
Z178 ½a. light green 16·00
Z179 1a. carmine 16·00
Z180 2a. reddish purple 22·00

1921. (No. O97).
Z183 9p. on 1a. rose-carmine 60·00

1922. (No. O98).
Z184 1a. chocolate 22·00

1926–31. (Nos. O109/O116).
Z185 3p. slate 17·00
Z188 2a. purple 22·00
Z189 4a. sage-green 28·00
Z190 8a. reddish purple 28·00
Z191 12a. claret 48·00

1932–36. (Nos. O127/O133).
Z195 9p. deep green 22·00
Z197 1a.3p. mauve 27·00
Z199 6a. bistre 60·00

1937–39. (Nos. O137/O140).
Z202 1a. carmine 16·00
Z203 1r. grey and red-brown 32·00
Z204 2r. purple and brown 42·00
Z205 5r. green and blue 80·00

1939–42. (Nos. O144/O150).
Z207 ½a. red-brown 18·00
Z208 1a. carmine 18·00
Z209 1½a. dull violet 18·00
Z210 2a. vermilion 23·00
Z211 4a. brown 29·00
Z212 8a. slate-violet 40·00

GUADUR

No cancellations have been reported from Guadur before its transfer to the Sind Circle in 1869. Cancellations are all similar in style to those for Muscat, Guadur being initially assigned number '24', although an office in Southern India is also known to have used this numeral. The 1869 duplex is interesting in that it is inscribed 'GWADUR'. Under the 1873 reorganisation the office became '4/K-1', this postmark using the 'GUADUR' spelling.

1869 Duplex

Stamps of INDIA cancelled by duplex or circular types inscribed 'GWADUR' or 'GUADUR'.

1865. (Nos. 54/65)
Z301 ½a. blue 22·00
Z303 1a. brown 28·00
Z304 2a. orange 42·00

1866. (Nos. 69/72)
Z305 4a. green (Die I) 65·00

1873. (Nos. 75/76)
Z309 ½a. blue (Die II) 13·00

1882-90. (Nos. 84/101)
Z312 ½a. blue-green 12·00
Z313 9p. rose
Z314 1a. brown-purple 12·00
Z316 2a. blue 16·00
Z319 4a.6p. yellow-green 40·00

1891. (No. 102)
Z323 2½a. on 4½a. yellow-green 35·00

1892-97. (Nos. 103/106)
Z324 2a.6p. yellow-green 12·00
Z325 1r. green and carmine 95·00

1898. (No. 110)
Z327 ¼ on ½a. blue-green 35·00

1899. (No. 111)
Z328 3p. carmine 25·00

1900-02. (Nos. 112/118)
Z329 3p. grey
Z330 ½a. yellow-green 15·00
Z331 1a. carmine 15·00

1902-11. (Nos. 119/147)
Z334 3p. grey 14·00
Z335 ½a. yellow-green 8·00
Z336 1a. carmine 9·00
Z339 3a. orange-brown 20·00
Z345 3r. brown and green £100

1906-07. (Nos. 149/150)
Z347 ½a. yellow-green 8·50
Z348 1a. carmine 8·50

1911-22. (Nos. 151/191)
Z349 3p. grey 15·00
Z350 ½a. green 8·50
Z351 1a. carmine 8·50
Z353 1½a. chocolate (No. 165) 35·00
Z354 2a. purple 12·00
Z357 4a. olive-green 24·00

1921. (Nos. 192/194)
Z363 9p. on 1a. carmine 35·00

1922-26. (Nos. 197/200)
Z364 1a. chocolate 15·00

1926-33. (Nos. 201/219)
Z367 3p. slate 6·00
Z369 1a. chocolate 7·00
Z371 2a. purple 15·00
Z373 4a. sage-green (No. 211) 15·00
Z374 8a. reddish purple 20·00
Z375 12a. claret 35·00
Z376 1r. chocolate and green 32·00
Z377 2r. carmine and orange 45·00

1929. (Nos. 220/225)
Z379 2a. deep blue-green 20·00
Z380 3a. blue 20·00
Z381 4a. olive-green 20·00
Z382 6a. bistre 20·00
Z384 12a. rose red 75·00

1931. (Nos. 226/231)
Z385 ¼a. olive-green and orange-brown 20·00
Z386 ½a. violet and green 20·00
Z387 1a. mauve and chocolate 20·00
Z388 2a. green and blue 20·00
Z389 3a. chocolate and carmine 20·00

1932-36. (Nos. 232/239)
Z392 9p. deep green 12·00
Z393 1a. chocolate 8·00
Z395 1a.3p. mauve 8·50
Z396 2a. vermilion (*large die*) (No. 236*b*) 15·00
Z397 2a. vermilion (*small die*) (No. 236*c*) 15·00

1935. (Nos. 240/246)
Z401 9p. black and grey-green 25·00
Z402 1a. black and brown 20·00
Z403 1¼a. black and bright violet 25·00
Z404 2½a. black and orange 30·00
Z405 3½a. black and dull ultramarine 40·00

1937-40. (Nos. 247/264)
Z406 3p. slate 8·00
Z407 ½a. red-brown 6·00
Z409 1a. carmine 6·00
Z412 3a. yellow-green 15·00
Z414 4a. brown 15·00

1940-43. (Nos. 265/277)
Z423 1a.3p. yellow-brown 9·00

OFFICIAL STAMPS

1874-82. (Nos. O31/O37)
Z430 ½a. blue 75·00

1883-99. (Nos. O37*a*/O48)
Z433 3p. carmine 45·00
Z434 ½a. blue-green 35·00
Z435 1a. brown-purple 35·00
Z436 2a. blue 35·00

1900. (Nos. O49/O52)
Z440 1a. carmine 38·00

1902-09. (Nos. O54/O65)
Z443 3p. grey 35·00
Z444 ½a. green 25·00
Z445 1a. carmine 25·00
Z446 2a. mauve 30·00

1906. (Nos. O66/O67)
Z450 ½a. yellow-green 25·00
Z451 1a. carmine 25·00

1909. (Nos. O68/O72)
Z453 5r. ultramarine and violet

1912-13. (Nos. O73/O96)
Z456 1a. carmine 20·00

1921. (Nos. O97)
Z472 9p. on 1a. rose carmine

PRICES FOR STAMPS ON COVER TO 1945
Nos. 1/15 *from* × 75
Nos. O1/O10 *from* × 100

(Currency 12 pies = 1 anna; 16 annas = 1 Indian rupee)

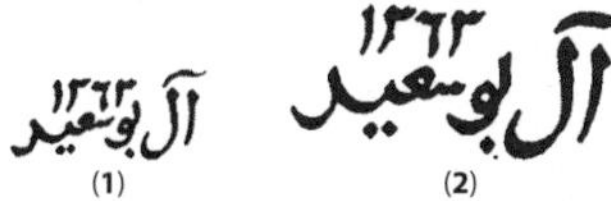

(1) (2)

1944 (20 Nov). Bicentenary of Al-Busaid Dynasty. Nos. 259/260, 265/268 and 269*c*/277 (King George VI) of India optd ('AL BUSAID 1363' in Arabic script) as Types **1** or **2** (rupee values).

1 3p. slate 50 8·50
w. Wmk inverted 9·00
2 ½a. purple 50 8·50
3 9p. green 50 8·50
4 1a. carmine 50 8·50
5 1½a. dull violet 50 8·50
6 2a. vermilion 50 8·50
w. Wmk inverted 27·00
7 3a. bright violet 1·00 8·50
w. Wmk inverted 10·00 20·00
8 3½a. bright blue 1·00 8·50
9 4a. brown 1·25 8·50
10 6a. turquoise-green 1·25 8·50
11 8a. slate-violet 1·50 8·50
12 12a. lake 2·00 8·50
13 14a. purple 4·00 14·00
14 1r. grey and red-brown 5·00 13·00
15 2r. purple and brown 12·00 22·00
1/15 *Set of* 15 29·00 £140

OFFICIAL STAMPS

1944 (20 Nov). Bicentenary of Al-Busaid Dynasty. Nos. O138, O143, O144*ba*/O146 and O146*b*/O150 of India optd as Types **1** or **2** (1r.).

O1 3p. slate 60 16·00
O2 ½a. purple 1·50 16·00
O3 9p. green 1·00 16·00
O4 1a. carmine 1·00 16·00
O5 1½a. dull violet 1·50 16·00
O6 2a. vermilion 1·50 16·00
O7 2½a. bright violet 7·50 16·00
O8 4a. brown 2·75 16·00
O9 8a. slate-violet 5·00 18·00
O10 1r. grey and red-brown 10·00 30·00
O1/O10 *Set of* 10 29·00 £160

Used prices quoted for Nos. 1/15 and O1/O10 are for stamps cancelled with contemporary postmarks of the Indian postal administration. Those with cancellations of the subsequent British post office are worth considerably less. Collectors are warned against forged overprints and cancellations.

From December 1947 there was a Pakistani postal administration and stamps of Pakistan were used until 31 March 1948. The subsequent British administration operated from 1 April 1948 to 29 April 1966 when the stamps of the BRITISH POSTAL AGENCIES IN EASTERN ARABIA were used. Guadur, however, continued to use the stamps of Pakistan until the dependency was finally ceded to that country in 1953.

Natal *see* South Africa

Nauru

Stamps of MARSHALL ISLANDS were used in Nauru from the opening of the German Colonial Post Office on 14 July 1908 until 8 September 1914.

Following the occupation by Australian forces on 6 November 1914 the 'N.W. PACIFIC ISLANDS' overprints on Australia (see NEW GUINEA) were used from 2 January 1915.

PRICES FOR STAMPS ON COVER TO 1945
Nos. 1/12 *from* × 10
Nos. 13/16 *from* × 4
Nos. 17/25 —
Nos. 26/39 *from* × 6
Nos. 40/43 *from* × 10
Nos. 44/47 *from* × 15

BRITISH MANDATE

NAURU (1) NAURU (2) NAURU (3)

1916 (2 Sept)–**23**. Stamps of Great Britain (1912–1922) overprinted at Somerset House.

(a) With T **1** *(12½ mm long) at foot*
1 ½d. yellow-green 2·25 11·00
a. 'NAUP.U' £450
b. Double opt, one albino 60·00
c. Triple opt, two albino £400
2 1d. bright scarlet 2·50 14·00
a. 'NAUP.U' £700 £1300
b. Double opt, one albino £325
2*c* 1d. carmine-red 21·00
cb. Double opt, one albino £225
3 1½d. red-brown (1923) 55·00 85·00
4 2d. orange (Die I) 2·00 13·00
a. 'NAUP.U' £425 £950
b. Double opt, one albino £110
c. Triple opt, two albino £425
y. Wmk inverted and reversed £120 £275
5 2d. orange (Die II) (1923) 70·00 £100
6 2½d. blue 2·75 7·00
a. 'NAUP.U' £475 £1000
b. Double opt, one albino £225
7 3d. bluish violet 2·00 6·00
a. 'NAUP.U' £475 £1100
b. Double opt, one albino £350
8 4d. slate-green 2·00 8·50
a. 'NAUP.U' £700 £1600
b. Double opt, one albino £225
9 5d. yellow-brown 2·25 14·00
a. 'NAUP.U' £2250
b. Double opt, one albino £180
10 6d. purple (*chalk-surfaced paper*) 7·50 10·00
a. 'NAUP.U' £1600
b. Double opt, one albino £375
11 9d. agate 8·50 23·00
a. Double opt, one albino £350
12 1s. bistre-brown 7·00 19·00
a. Double opt, one albino £400
s. Optd '*SPECIMEN*' £140
1/12 *Set of* 11 85·00 £190

(b) With T **2** *(13½ mm long) at centre (1923)*
13 ½d. green 4·00 55·00
14 1d. scarlet 19·00 45·00
15 1½d. red-brown 28·00 55·00
a. Double opt, one albino £225
16 2d. orange (Die II) 30·00 80·00
13/16 *Set of* 4 70·00 £200

The 'NAUP.U' errors occur on R. 6/2 from Control I 16 only. The ink used on this batch of overprints was shiny jet-black.

There is a constant variety consisting of short left stroke to 'N' which occurs at R. 1/8 on Nos. 1, 2, 4 (£30 *each*); 2*c* (£75); 3 (£175); 5 (£200); 6, 7 (£40 *each*); 8, 9, 10 (£60 *each*); 11, 12 (£85 *each*). *All unused prices.*

(c) With T **3**
(i) Waterlow printing
17 5s. rose-carmine £2500 £2250
s. Optd '*SPECIMEN*' £1800
18 10s. indigo-blue (R.) £11000 £5000
a. Double opt, one albino £13000 £7000
s. Optd '*SPECIMEN*' £1000
sa. Ditto 'NAURU' double, one albino £2500
(ii) De La Rue printing
19 2s.6d. sepia-brown (*shades*) £600 £1600
a. Double opt, one albino £1700
b. Treble opt, two albino £1800
s. Optd '*SPECIMEN*' £350
20 2s.6d. yellow-brown (*shades*) 70·00 £120
21 2s.6d. brown (*shades*) 70·00 £120
a. Re-entry (R. 2/1) £6000
22 5s. bright carmine (*shades*) £100 £150
a. Treble opt, two albino £1500
s. Optd '*SPECIMEN*' £325
sa. Ditto 'NAURU' double, one albino £1500
23 10s. pale blue (R.) £250 £350
a. Treble opt (Blk.+R.+albino) £3750
b. Double opt, one albino £1600
c. Treble opt, two albino £1700
23*d* 10s. deep bright blue (R.) £500 £700
(iii) Bradbury Wilkinson printing (1919)
24 2s.6d. chocolate-brown 90·00 £200
b. Double opt, one albino £500
25 2s.6d. pale brown 80·00 £190
a. Double opt, one albino £500

The initial printing of the 2s.6d. to 10s. values, made in Sept 1915 but not known to have been issued before 2 Sept 1916, comprised one and a half sheets each of the 2s.6d. (No. 19) and 10s. (No. 18) and three sheets of the 5s. (No. 17), as well as the supply of 'Specimens', where the 5s. value was mostly from the De La Rue printing (No. 22).

The original supply of the 2s.6d. value (No. 19) included distinct shade variants, covered by 'sepia-brown (*shades*)'. The 'Specimens' are mostly in a deeper shade than the issued stamp. One half-sheet of 20 was quite deep, and only appears to exist cancelled 'SE 2 16', apart from a mint block of four in the Royal Collection. The full sheet of 40 was in a slightly paler shade and included 12 double, one albino and eight treble, two albino varieties. A few sheets in sepia-brown shades were also included in later supplies of the 2s.6d. value, but these were mostly in shades of yellow-brown (No. 20) and brown (No. 21).

Examples of most values between Nos. 1 and 25 are known showing a forged PO. Pleasant Island postmark dated 'NO 2 21'.

AUSTRALIAN MANDATE

4 *Century* (freighter)

(Des R. A. Harrison. Eng T. S. Harrison. Recess Note Printing Branch of the Treasury, Melbourne and from 1926 by the Commonwealth Bank of Australia)

1924–48. No wmk. P 11.

A. Rough surfaced, greyish paper (1924–1934)

No.	Type	Description	Unused	Used
26A	**4**	½d. chestnut	3·00	2·75
27A		1d. green	3·50	2·75
28A		1½d. scarlet	4·00	4·00
29A		2d. orange	4·00	19·00
30A		2½d. slate-blue	6·00	25·00
		c. Greenish blue (1934)	19·00	32·00
31A		3d. pale blue	4·00	13·00
32A		4d. olive-green	7·50	27·00
33A		5d. brown	4·25	7·00
34A		6d. dull violet	4·75	20·00
35A		9d. olive-brown	9·50	19·00
36A		1s. brown-lake	6·50	13·00
37A		2s.6d. grey-green	32·00	55·00
38A		5s. claret	50·00	£110
39A		10s. yellow	£130	£190
26A/39A *Set of* 14			£225	£450

B. Shiny surfaced, white paper (1937–1948)

No.	Type	Description	Unused	Used
26B	**4**	½d. chestnut	4·00	13·00
		c. Perf 14 (1947)	1·60	10·00
27B		1d. green	2·50	3·00
28B		1½d. scarlet	1·00	1·50
29B		2d. orange	6·50	8·00
30B		2½d. dull blue (1948)	5·00	4·00
		a. Imperf between (vert pair)	£17000	£18000
		b. Imperf between (horiz pair)	£17000	£18000
31B		3d. greenish grey (1947)	7·50	22·00
32B		4d. olive-green	7·50	13·00
33B		5d. brown	14·00	4·00
34B		6d. dull violet	11·00	5·00
35B		9d. olive-brown	13·00	22·00
36B		1s. brown-lake	14·00	2·75
37B		2s.6d. grey-green	32·00	35·00
38B		5s. claret	38·00	50·00
39B		10s. yellow	85·00	£100
26B/39B *Set of* 14			£200	£225

HIS MAJESTY'S JUBILEE.

1910 - 1935

(**5**)

6

1935 (12 July). Silver Jubilee. T **4** (shiny surfaced, white paper) optd with T **5**.

No.	Description	Unused	Used
40	1½d. scarlet	75	80
41	2d. orange	1·50	4·25
42	2½d. dull blue	1·50	1·50
43	1s. brown-lake	7·25	3·50
40/43 *Set of* 4		10·00	9·00

2½d. Re-entry (R. 4/4)

(Recess John Ash, Melbourne)

1937 (10 May). Coronation. P 11.

No.	Type	Description	Unused	Used
44	**6**	1½d. scarlet	45	1·75
45		2d. orange	45	2·75
46		2½d. blue	45	1·75
		a. Re-entry	35·00	55·00
47		1s. purple	65	2·00
44/47 *Set of* 4			1·75	7·50

Japanese forces invaded Nauru on 26 August 1942 and virtually all the inhabitants were removed to Truk in the Caroline Islands.

The Australian army liberated Nauru on 13 September 1945. After an initial period without stamps, Australian issues were supplied during October 1945 and were used from Nauru until further supplies of Nos. 26/39B became available. The deportees did not return until early in 1946

7 Nauruan Netting Fish

8 Anibare Bay

9 Loading phosphate from cantilever

10 Great Frigatebird

11 Nauruan canoe

12 Domaneab (meeting-house)

13 Palm trees

14 Buada lagoon

15 Map of Nauru

(Recess Note Printing Branch, Commonwealth Bank, Melbourne, and from 1960 by Note Ptg Branch, Reserve Bank of Australia, Melbourne)

1954 (6 Feb)–**65.** Types **7/15**. Toned paper. P 13½×14½ (horiz) or 14½×13½ (vert).

No.	Type	Description	Unused	Used
48	**7**	½d. deep violet	20	2·00
		a. Violet (8.5.61)	30	80
49	**8**	1d. bluish green	30	2·00
		a. Emerald-green (8.5.61)	1·25	55
		b. Deep green (1965)	4·50	3·25
50	**9**	3½d. scarlet	1·75	1·00
		a. Vermilion (1958)	9·00	75
51	**10**	4d. grey-blue	3·00	2·00
		a. Deep blue (1958)	20·00	4·25
52	**11**	6d. orange	70	20
53	**12**	9d. claret	60	20
54	**13**	1s. deep purple	30	30
55	**14**	2s.6d. deep green	2·75	1·00
56	**15**	5s. magenta	8·00	2·25
48*a*/56 *Set of* 9			15·00	7·00

Nos. 48*a*, 49*a*/49*b*, 50*a* and 51*a* are on white paper.

16 Micronesian Pigeon

17 Poison Nut

18 'Iyo' (*calophyllum*)

19 Black Lizard

20 Capparis

21 White Tern

21a Coral pinnacles

21b Finsch's Reed Warbler

(Recess (10d., 2s.3d.) or photo (others) Note Ptg Branch, Reserve Bank of Australia, Melbourne)

1963–65. Types **16/21b**. P 13½×13 (5d.), 13×13½ (8d.), 14×13½ (10d.), 15×14½ (1s.3d.) or 13½ (others).

No.	Type	Description	Unused	Used
57	**16**	2d. black, blue, red-brown and orange-yellow (3.5.65)	75	2·25
58	**17**	3d. multicoloured (16.4.64)	40	35
59	**18**	5d. multicoloured (22.4.63)	40	75
60	**19**	8d. black and green (1.7.63)	1·75	80
61	**20**	10d. black (16.4.64)	40	30
62	**21**	1s.3d. blue, black and yellow-green (3.5.65)	1·00	4·75
63	**21a**	2s.3d. ultramarine (16.4.64)	2·00	55
64	**21b**	3s.3d. multicoloured (3.5.65)	1·00	4·25
57/64 *Set of* 8			7·00	12·50

22 *Simpson and his Donkey*

(Des C. Andrew (after statue, Shrine of Remembrance, Melbourne. Photo Note Ptg Branch, Reserve Bank of Australia, Melbourne))

1965 (14 Apr). 50th Anniversary of Gallipoli Landing. P 13½.

No.	Type	Description	Unused	Used
65	**22**	5d. sepia, black and emerald	15	10

(New Currency. 100 cents = 1 Australian dollar)

24 Anibare Bay

25 'Iyo' (*calophyllum*)

(Recess (1, 2, 3, 5, 8, 19, 25c. and $1) or photo (others))

1966 (14 Feb–25 May). Decimal Currency. Various stamps with values in cents and dollars as Types **24/25** and some colours changed. Recess printed stamps on Helecon paper.

No.	Type	Description	Unused	Used
66	**24**	1c. deep blue	15	10
67	**7**	2c. brown-purple (25.5)	15	50
68	**9**	3c. bluish green (25.5)	30	2·25
69	**25**	4c. multicoloured	20	10
70	**13**	5c. deep ultramarine (25.5)	25	60
71	**19**	7c. black and chestnut	30	10
72	**20**	8c. olive-green	20	10
73	**10**	10c. red (as 4d.)	40	10
74	**21**	15c. blue, black and yellow-green (25.5)	60	3·25
75	**21a**	25c. deep brown (25.5)	30	1·25
76	**17**	30c. multicoloured	45	30
77	**21b**	35c. multicoloured (25.5)	75	35
78	**16**	50c. multicoloured	1·50	80
79	**15**	$1 magenta	75	1·00
66/79 *Set of* 14			5·50	9·50

The 25c. is as No. 63, but larger, 27½×24½ mm.

REPUBLIC

Nauru became independent on 31 January 1968 and was later admitted into special membership of the Commonwealth.

REPUBLIC OF NAURU

(**26**)

1968 (31 Jan–15 May). Nos. 66/79 optd with T **26**.

No.	Type	Description	Unused	Used
80	**24**	1c. deep blue (R.)	10	30
81	**7**	2c. brown-purple	10	10
82	**9**	3c. bluish green	15	10
83	**25**	4c. multicoloured (15.5.68)	10	10
84	**13**	5c. deep ultramarine (R.)	10	10
85	**19**	7c. black and chestnut (R.) (15.5.68)	25	10
86	**20**	8c. olive-green (R.)	10	10
87	**10**	10c. red	50	15
88	**21**	15c. blue, black and yellow-green	1·00	2·75
89	**21a**	25c. deep brown (R.)	15	15
90	**17**	30c. multicoloured (15.5.68)	40	15
91	**21b**	35c. multicoloured (15.5.68)	1·25	30
92	**16**	50c. multicoloured	1·00	35
93	**15**	$1 magenta	75	50
80/93 *Set of* 14			5·00	4·25

27 'Towards the Sunrise'

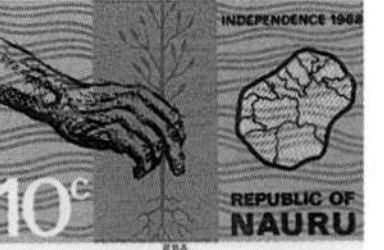

28 Planting Seedling, and Map

(Des H. Fallu (5c.), Note Ptg Branch (10c.). Photo Note Ptg Branch, Reserve Bank of Australia, Melbourne)

1968 (11 Sept). Independence. P 13½.

94	**27**	5c. black, slate-lilac, orange-yellow and yellow-green	10	10
95	**28**	10c. black, yellow-green and new blue	10	10

29 Flag of Independent Nauru

(Des J. Mason. Photo Note Ptg Branch, Reserve Bank of Australia, Melbourne)

1969 (31 Jan). P 13½.

96	**29**	15c. yellow, orange and royal blue	65	15

This is a definitive issue which was put on sale on the first anniversary of Independence.

Nevis *see* **St. Kitts-Nevis**

New Brunswick *see* **Canada**

Newfoundland *see* **Canada**

New Guinea *see after* **Australia**

New Hebrides

Stamps of NEW SOUTH WALES were used by various Postal Agencies in the New Hebrides from August 1891 onwards. From late 1892 the N.S.W. agency at Port Vila was run by the Australian New Hebrides Company who, from 1897, issued local 1d. and 2d. stamps for the carriage of mail on the Company's ships. These can be found used in combination with N.S.W. issues. Similar Postal Agencies supplying the stamps of NEW CALEDONIA were opened from 1903 onwards. The use of New South Wales and New Caledonia stamps was prohibited after 1 December 1908.

PRICES FOR STAMPS ON COVER TO 1945

Nos. 1/8 (F1/F5)	*from* × 10
No. 9	*from* × 2
Nos. 10/16 (F6/F10)	*from* × 8
Nos. 18/28 (F11/F32)	*from* × 6
Nos. 30/34 (F33/F37)	*from* × 4
No. 35 (F32*a*)	—
Nos. 36/39	*from* × 3
Nos. 40/42 (F38/F41)	*from* × 4
Nos. 43/51 (F42/F52)	*from* × 5
Nos. 52/63 (F53/F64)	*from* × 3
Nos. D1/D5 (FD53/FD57)	*from* × 100
Nos. D6/D10 (FD65/FD69)	*from* × 8

ANGLO-FRENCH CONDOMINIUM

The New Hebrides, an island group in the south-west Pacific, were recognised as an area of joint Anglo-French influence in 1878. The position was regularised by the Convention of 20 October 1906 which created a Condominium, the two nations having equal rights and shares in the administration of the islands.

Stamps inscribed in English or French were issued concurrently and had equal validity throughout the islands. A common currency was reflected in the face values from 1938.

Where common designs were used, the main differences between stamps inscribed in English and those in French are as follows:

(a) Inscriptions in English or French.

(b) Position of cyphers. French issues normally have 'RF' to the right or above the British royal cypher.

(c) French issues are without watermark, *unless otherwise stated.*

Inscriptions in English

Inscriptions in French

I. STAMPS INSCRIBED IN ENGLISH

NEW HEBRIDES. CONDOMINIUM. (1)

NEW HEBRIDES CONDOMINIUM (2)

1908 (29 Oct). Types **23** and **24** of Fiji optd with T **1** by Govt Printing Establishment, Suva. On the bicoloured stamps the word 'FIJI' obliterated by a bar in the colour of the word. P 14.

(a) Wmk Mult Crown CA. Ordinary paper (½d., 1d.) or chalk-surfaced paper (1s.)

1		½d. green and pale green (No. 115)	18·00	27·00
1*a*		½d. green (No. 118)	40	7·00
2		1d. red	50	40
		a. Opt omitted (in vert pair with normal)	£10000	
3		1s. green and carmine	29·00	3·75

(b) Wmk Crown CA

4		½d. green and grey-green	60·00	85·00
5		2d. dull purple and orange	60	70
6		2½d. dull purple and blue/*blue*	60	70
7		5d. dull purple and green	80	2·00
8		6d. dull purple and carmine	70	1·25
9		1s. green and carmine	£140	£300
1*a*/9 *Set of 9*			£200	£350

1910 (15 Dec). Types as last optd with T **2** by D.L.R. Ordinary paper (½d. to 2½d.) or chalk-surfaced paper (5d., 6d., 1s.). Wmk Mult Crown CA. P 14.

10		½d. green	3·50	32·00
11		1d. red	11·00	8·50
12		2d. grey	70	3·00
13		2½d. bright blue	75	8·00
14		5d. dull purple and olive-green	2·25	5·50
15		6d. dull and deep purple	1·50	8·50
16		1s. black/*green* (R.)	1·50	7·50
10/16 *Set of 7*			19·00	65·00
10s/16s Optd 'SPECIMEN' *Set of 7*			£275	

3 Weapons and Idols

1d. **(4)**

(Des J. Giraud. Recess D.L.R.)

1911 (25 July). Wmk Mult Crown CA. P 14.

18	**3**	½d. green	85	1·75
19		1d. red	5·50	2·00
20		2d. grey	9·00	3·00
21		2½d. ultramarine	5·00	5·50
24		5d. sage-green	4·50	7·00
25		6d. purple	3·00	5·00
26		1s. black/*green*	2·75	13·00
27		2s. purple/*blue*	48·00	22·00
28		5s. green/*yellow*	48·00	55·00
18/28 *Set of 9*			£110	£100
18s/28s Optd 'SPECIMEN' *Set of 9*			£250	

1920 (June)–**21**. Surch with T **4** at Govt Printing Establishment, Suva.

(a) On Nos. 24 and 26/28

30	**3**	1d. on 5d. sage-green (10.3.21)	11·00	65·00
		a. Surch inverted	£4500	
31		1d. on 1s. black/*green*	4·25	13·00
32		1d. on 2s. purple/*blue*	2·00	10·00
33		1d. on 5s. green/*yellow*	1·00	10·00

(b) On No. F16

34	**3**	2d. on 40c. red/*yellow*	1·00	23·00

(c) On No. F27

35	**3**	2d. on 40c. red/*yellow*	£130	£700

1921 (Sept–Oct). Wmk Mult Script CA. P 14.

36	**3**	1d. scarlet	2·50	14·00
37		2d. slate-grey	4·25	45·00
39		6d. purple	14·00	80·00
36/39 *Set of 3*			19·00	£130
36s/39s Optd 'SPECIMEN' *Set of 3*			85·00	

1924 (1 May). Surch as T **4**, at Suva.

40	**3**	1d. on ½d. green (No. 18)	4·00	24·00
41		3d. on 1d. scarlet (No. 36)	4·00	11·00
42		5d. on 2½d. ultramarine (No. 21)	7·50	29·00
		a. Surch inverted	£3500	
40/42 *Set of 3*			14·00	55·00

5

(Recess D.L.R.)

1925 (June). Wmk Mult Script CA. P 14.

43	**5**	½d. (5c.) black	1·25	21·00
44		1d. (10c.) green	1·00	19·00
45		2d. (20c.) slate-grey	1·75	2·50
46		2½d. (25c.) brown	1·00	13·00
47		5d. (50c.) ultramarine	3·00	2·75
48		6d. (60c.) purple	4·00	18·00
49		1s. (1.25fr.) black/*emerald*	3·25	19·00
50		2s. (2.50fr.) purple/*blue*	6·00	22·00
51		5s. (6.25fr.) green/*yellow*	6·00	25·00
43/51 *Set of 9*			23·00	£120
43s/51s Optd 'SPECIMEN' *Set of 9*			£225	

(New Currency. 100 gold centimes = 1 gold franc)

The currency used for the face values of issues to 1977 was an artificial, rather than an actual, monetary unit. The actual currencies in use were Australian dollars and the local franc.

6 Lopevi Island and Outrigger Canoe

(Des J. Kerhor. Eng J. G. Hall. Recess B.W.)

1938 (1 June). Gold Currency. Wmk Mult Script CA. P 12.

52	**6**	5c. blue-green	2·50	4·50
53		10c. orange	3·50	2·25
54		15c. bright violet	3·50	4·50
55		20c. scarlet	4·25	6·50
56		25c. reddish brown	1·60	3·00
57		30c. blue	4·50	2·75
58		40c. grey-olive	4·50	6·50
59		50c. purple	1·60	2·75
60		1f. red/*green*	11·00	9·00
61		2f. blue/*green*	30·00	25·00
62		5f. red/*yellow*	75·00	55·00
63		10f. violet/*blue*	£225	80·00
52/63 *Set of 12*			£325	£170
52s/63s Perf 'SPECIMEN' *Set of 12*			£275	

(Recess Waterlow)

1949 (10 Oct). 75th Anniversary of UPU. As No. 117 of Antigua. Wmk Mult Script CA. P 13½×14.

64		10c. red-orange	30	1·25
65		15c. violet	30	1·25
66		30c. ultramarine	30	1·25
67		50c. purple	40	1·25
64/67 *Set of 4*			1·10	4·50

7 Outrigger Sailing Canoes

8 Native carving

9 Two natives outside hut

(Des C. Hertenberger (1f. to 5f.), R. Serres (others). Recess Waterlow)

1953 (30 Apr). Types **7/9**. Wmk Mult Script CA. P 12½.

No.	Type	Description	Unused	Used
68	**7**	5c. green	1·00	2·25
69		10c. scarlet	1·50	1·25
70		15c. yellow-ochre	1·50	20
71		20c. ultramarine	1·50	20
72	**8**	25c. olive	60	20
73		30c. brown	60	20
74		40c. blackish brown	60	20
75		50c. violet	1·00	20
76	**9**	1f. orange	7·00	3·25
77		2f. reddish purple	7·00	8·50
78		5f. scarlet	8·50	22·00
68/78 *Set of* 11			27·00	32·00

1953 (2 June). Coronation. As No. 120 of Antigua.

No.	Description	Unused	Used
79	10c. black and carmine	1·00	50

10 *San Pedro y San Paulo* (Quiros)

11 'Marianne', 'Talking Drum' and 'Britannia'

(Photo Harrison)

1956 (20 Oct). 50th Anniversary of Condominium. Types **10/11**. Wmk Mult Script CA. P 14½×14.

No.	Type	Description	Unused	Used
80	**10**	5c. emerald	15	10
81		10c. scarlet	40	10
82	**11**	20c. deep bright blue	10	10
83		50c. deep lilac	15	15
80/83 *Set of* 4			70	40

12 Port Vila: Iririki Islet

13 River scene and spear fisherman

14 Woman drinking from coconut

(Des H. Cheffér (T **12**), P. Gandon (others). Recess Waterlow)

1957 (3 Sept). Wmk Mult Script CA. Types **12/14**. P 13½.

No.	Type	Description	Unused	Used
84	**12**	5c. green	40	1·50
85		10c. scarlet	30	10
86		15c. yellow-ochre	50	1·50
87		20c. ultramarine	40	10
88	**13**	25c. olive	45	10
89		30c. brown	45	10
90		40c. sepia	45	10
91		50c. violet	45	10
92	**14**	1f. orange	1·00	1·00
93		2f. mauve	4·00	2·50
94		5f. black	9·00	3·25
84/94 *Set of* 11			15·00	9·00

1963 (2 Sept). Freedom from Hunger. As No. 146 of Antigua.

No.	Description	Unused	Used
95	60c. green	50	15

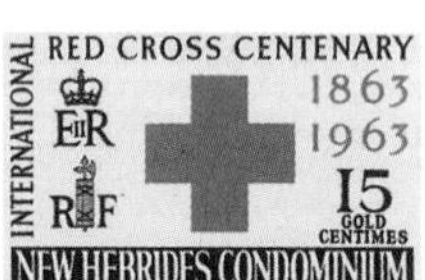

15 Red Cross Emblem

(Des V. Whiteley. Litho B.W.)

1963 (2 Sept). Red Cross Centenary. W w **12**. P 13½.

No.	Type	Description	Unused	Used
96	**15**	15c. red and black	40	10
97		45c. red and blue	60	20

16 Exporting Manganese, Forari

17 Cocoa Beans

18 Copra

19 Fishing from Palikulo Point

20 Painted Triggerfish

21 New Caledonian Nautilus Shell

22 Lionfish

23 Clown Surgeonfish

24 Cardinal Honeyeater

25 Buff-bellied Flycatcher

26 Thicket Warbler

27 White-collared Kingfisher

(Des V. Whiteley, from drawings by J. White (10c., 20c.), K. Penny (40c.), C. Robin (3f.). Photo Harrison. Des C. Robin (5c., 1f.), J. White (15c.), G. Vasarhelyi (25c., 5f.), A. Larkins, Turrell and Thomas (30c., 50c., 2f.). Recess Govt Printing Works, Paris)

1963 (25 Nov)–**72**. Types **16/27**. W w **12** (10c., 20c., 40c., 3f.) or no wmk (others). P 14 (3f.), 12½ (10c., 20c., 40c.) or 13 (others).

No.	Type	Description	Unused	Used
98	**16**	5c. lake, purple-brown and greenish blue (15.8.66)	2·00	50
		*a. Lake and greenish blue** (29.2.72)	42·00	8·00
99	**17**	10c. light brown, buff and emerald (16.8.65)	15	10
100	**18**	15c. yellow-bistre, red-brown and deep violet	15	10
101	**19**	20c. black, olive-green and greenish blue (16.8.65)	55	10
102	**20**	25c. reddish violet, orange-brown and crimson (15.8.66)	50	70
103	**21**	30c. chestnut, bistre and violet	75	10
104	**22**	40c. vermilion and deep blue (16.8.65)	80	1·40
105	**23**	50c. green, yellow and greenish blue	60	10
106	**24**	1f. red, black and deep bluish green (15.8.66)	2·00	3·00
107	**25**	2f. black, brown-purple and yellow-olive	2·00	1·25
108	**26**	3f. deep violet, orange-brown, emerald and black (16.8.65)	6·00	3·50
		w. Wmk inverted	7·00	
109	**27**	5f. blue, deep blue and black (24.1.67)	6·00	19·00
98/109 *Set of* 12			19·00	26·00

* In No. 98*a* the globe is printed in the same colour as the centre, instead of in purple-brown.

See also No. 129.

28 ITU Emblem

(Des M. Goaman. Litho Enschedé)

1965 (17 May). ITU Centenary. W w **12**. P 11×11½.

No.	Type	Description	Unused	Used
110	**28**	15c. scarlet and drab	20	10
111		60c. blue and light red	35	20

29 ICY Emblem

(Des V. Whiteley. Litho Harrison)

1965 (24 Oct). International Co-operation Year. W w **12**. P 14½.

No.	Type	Description	Unused	Used
112	**29**	5c. reddish purple and turquoise-green	15	10
113		55c. deep bluish green and lavender	20	20

30 Sir Winston Churchill and St Paul's Cathedral in Wartime

(Des Jennifer Toombs. Photo Harrison)

1966 (24 Jan). Churchill Commemoration. W w **12**. P 14.

No.	Type	Description	Unused	Used
114	**30**	5c. black, cerise, gold and new blue	20	15
115		15c. black, cerise, gold and deep green	70	10
116		25c. black, cerise, gold and brown	80	10
117		30c. black, cerise, gold and bluish violet	80	15
114/117 *Set of* 4			2·25	45

31 Footballer's Legs, Ball and Jules Rimet Cup

(Des V. Whiteley. Litho Harrison)

1966 (1 July). World Cup Football Championship. W w **12** (sideways). P 14.

No.	Type	Description	Unused	Used
118	**31**	20c. violet, yellow-green, lake and yellow-brown	30	15
119		40c. chocolate, blue-green, lake and yellow-brown	70	15

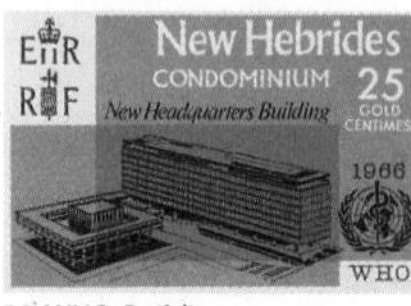

32 WHO Building

(Des M. Goaman. Litho Harrison)

1966 (20 Sept). Inauguration of WHO Headquarters, Geneva. W w **12** (sideways). P 14.

No.	Type	Description	Unused	Used
120	**32**	25c. black, yellow-green and light blue	15	10
121		60c. black, light purple and yellow-brown	40	20

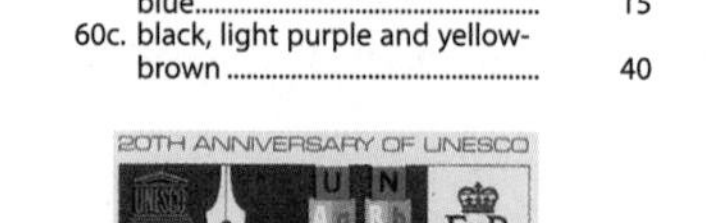

33 'Education'

(Des Jennifer Toombs. Litho Harrison)

1966 (1 Dec). 20th Anniversary of UNESCO. W w **12** (sideways). T **33** and similar horiz designs. P 14.

No.	Description	Unused	Used
122	15c. slate-violet, red, yellow and orange	25	10
123	30c. orange-yellow, violet and deep olive	65	10
124	45c. black, bright purple and orange	75	15
122/124 *Set of* 3		1·50	30

Designs: 15c. T **33**; 30c. 'Science'; 45c. 'Culture'.

36 The Coast Watchers

(Des R. Granger Barrett. Photo Enschedé)

1967 (26 Sept). 25th Anniversary of the Pacific War. T **36** and similar horiz designs. Multicoloured. W w **12**. P 14×13.

No.	Description	Unused	Used
125	15c. Type **36**	40	15
126	25c. Map of war zone, US marine and Australian soldier	70	25
127	60c. HMAS *Canberra* (cruiser)	70	40
128	1f. Boeing B-17 Flying Fortress	70	1·25
125/128 *Set of* 4		2·25	1·90

1967 (5 Dec). New value with W w **12** (sideways).

No.	Description	Unused	Used
129	60c. vermilion and deep blue (as No. 104)	40	15

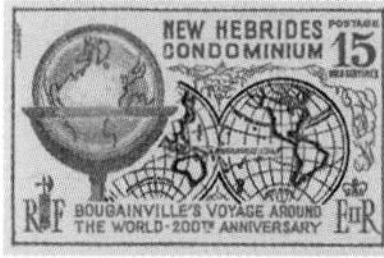

40 Globe and Hemispheres

(Des and eng J. Combet. Recess Govt Printing Works, Paris)

1968 (23 May). Bicentenary of Bougainville's World Voyage. T **40** and similar horiz designs. P 13.

No.	Description	Unused	Used
130	15c. emerald, slate-violet and red	20	10
131	25c. deep olive, maroon and ultramarine	45	15
132	60c. bistre-brown, brown-purple and myrtle-green	45	20
130/132 *Set of* 3		1·00	40

Designs: 15c. T **40**; 25c. Ships *La Boudeuse* and *L'Etoile*, and map; 60c. Bougainville, ship's figure-head and bougainvillea flowers.

43 Concorde and Vapour Trails

45 Kauri Pine

(Des S. W. Moss (25c.), R. Granger Barrett (60c.). Litho D.L.R.)

1968 (9 Oct). Anglo-French Concorde Project. T **43** and similar horiz design. W w **12** (sideways). P 14.

133 25c. light blue, orange-red and deep violet-blue 35 30
134 60c. red, black and bright blue 40 45

Design: 25c. T **43**; 60c. Concorde in flight.

(Des V. Whiteley. Litho Format)

1969 (30 June). Timber Industry. W w **12**. P 14½.

135 **45** 20c. multicoloured (*shades*) 10 10

No. 135 was issued in small sheets of nine (3×3) printed on a simulated wood-grain background and with a decorative border showing various stages of the local timber industry. There is a wide range of shades on the printing.

46 Cyphers, Flags and Relay Runner receiving Baton

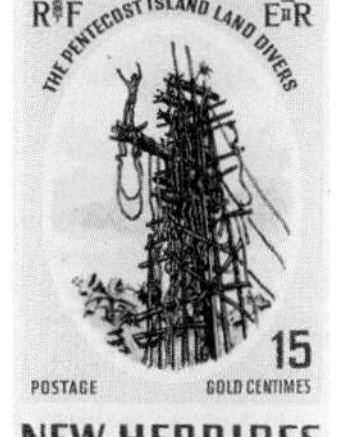

48 Diver on Platform

(Des C. Haley. Photo Delrieu)

1969 (13 Aug). Third South Pacific Games, Port Moresby. T **46** and similar horiz design. Multicoloured. P 12½.

136 25c. Type **46** 10 10
137 1f. Cyphers, flags and relay runner passing baton 20 20

(Des V. Whiteley. Litho P.B.)

1969 (15 Oct). Pentecost Island Land Divers. T **48** and similar vert designs. Multicoloured. W w **12** (sideways). P 12½.

138 15c. Type **48** 10 10
139 25c. Diver jumping 10 10
140 1f. Diver at end of fall 20 20
138/140 *Set of* 3 35 35

51 UPU Emblem and New Headquarters Building

52 General Charles de Gaulle

(Des and eng J. Gauthier. Recess Govt Ptg Wks, Paris)

1970 (20 May). Inauguration of New UPU Headquarters Building. P 13.

141 **51** 1f.05 slate, red-orange and bright purple 20 20

(Des V. Whiteley. Photo Govt Ptg Wks, Paris)

1970 (20 July). 30th Anniversary of New Hebrides' Declaration for the Free French Government. P 13.

142 **52** 65c. multicoloured 35 70
143 1f.10 multicoloured 45 70

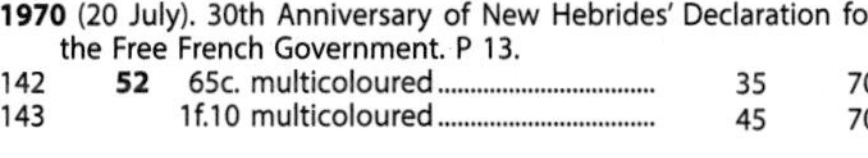

(53)

54 *The Virgin and Child* (Bellini)

1970 (15 Oct). As No. 101, but W w **12** (sideways) and surch with T **53**.

144 35c. on 20c. black, olive-green and greenish blue 30 30

(Des V. Whiteley. Litho Harrison)

1970 (30 Nov). Christmas. T **54** and similar vert design. Multicoloured. W w **12** (sideways). P 14½×14.

145 15c. Type **54** 10 10
146 50c. *The Virgin and Child* (Cima) 20 20

POSTAGE DUE STAMPS

POSTAGE DUE (D 1) **POSTAGE DUE** (D 2) **POSTAGE DUE** (D 3)

1925 (June). Optd with T D **1**, by D.L.R.

D1 **5** 1d. (10c.) green 30·00 1·00
D2 2d. (20c.) slate-grey 32·00 1·50
D3 3d. (30c.) red 32·00 2·75
D4 5d. (50c.) ultramarine 35·00 4·75
D5 10d. (1f.) carmine/*blue* 40·00 6·00
D1/D5 *Set of* 5 £150 14·00
D1s/D5s Optd 'SPECIMEN' *Set of* 5 £180

1938 (1 June). Optd with T D **2**, by B.W.

D6 **6** 5c. blue-green 35·00 50·00
D7 10c. orange 35·00 50·00
D8 20c. scarlet 42·00 75·00
D9 40c. grey-olive 48·00 85·00
D10 1f. red/*green* 48·00 90·00
D6/D10 *Set of* 5 £190 £325
D6s/D10s Perf 'SPECIMEN' *Set of* 5 £160

1953 (30 Apr). Nos. 68/69, 71, 74 and 76 optd with T D **3**, by Waterlow.

D11 5c. green 5·00 19·00
D12 10c. scarlet 1·75 16·00
D13 20c. ultramarine 5·00 25·00
D14 40c. blackish brown 17·00 45·00
D15 1f. orange 4·50 45·00
D11/D15 *Set of* 5 30·00 £130

1957 (3 Sept). Nos. 84/85, 87, 90 and 92 optd with T D **3**, by Waterlow.

D16 **12** 5c. green 30 1·50
D17 10c. scarlet 30 1·50
D18 20c. ultramarine 75 1·75
D19 **13** 40c. sepia 1·00 2·50
D20 **14** 1f. orange 1·25 3·25
D16/D20 *Set of* 5 3·25 9·50

II. STAMPS INSCRIBED IN FRENCH

(Currency. 100 centimes = 1 French franc)

NOUVELLES HÉBRIDES (F 1) **NOUVELLES-HÉBRIDES** (F 2)

1908 (21 Nov). Types **15/17** of New Caledonia. optd with Types F **1** or F **2** (1f.), by Govt Ptg Wks, Paris.

F1 5c. green 13·00 4·75
F2 10c. carmine 13·00 3·50
F3 25c. blue/*greenish* (R.) 9·50 2·25
F4 50c. red/*orange* 8·50 4·75
F5 1f. blue/*green* (R.) 30·00 20·00
F1/F5 *Set of* 5 65·00 30·00

CONDOMINIUM (F 3) **10c.** (F 6)

1910 (Aug)–**11**. Nos. F1/F5 further optd with T F **3**, or larger (1f.), by Govt Ptg Wks, Paris.

F6 5c. green 10·00 3·00
F7 10c. carmine 10·00 1·25
F8 25c. blue/*greenish* (R.) (1911) 3·25 4·50
F9 50c. red/*orange* (1911) 14·00 38·00
F10 1f. blue/*green* (R.) 32·00 22·00
F6/F10 *Set of* 5 60·00 60·00

All the above were released in Paris on 16 March 1910. The 5c., 10c. and 1f. were issued in New Hebrides in August but the 25c. and 50c. were not received until 1911 after the issue of the definitive stamps and they were placed in reserve, although some may have been issued on request.

1911 (12 July). Wmk Mult Crown CA. P 14.

F11 **3** 5c. green 1·00 3·00
F12 10c. carmine 50 1·00
F13 20c. greyish slate 1·00 2·25
F14 25c. ultramarine 2·75 7·00
F15 30c. brown/*yellow* 6·50 5·25
F16 40c. red/*yellow* 1·40 6·00
F17 50c. sage-green 2·00 6·50
F18 75c. orange 7·00 32·00
F19 1f. red/*blue* 7·50 4·50
F20 2f. violet 12·00 22·00
F21 5f. red/*green* 12·00 48·00
F11/F21 *Set of* 11 45·00 £120

1913. As last but wmk 'R F' in sheet or without wmk.

F22 **3** 5c. green 1·25 5·50
F23 10c. carmine 1·00 6·00
F24 20c. greyish slate 1·00 2·40
F25 25c. ultramarine 1·25 7·50
F26 30c. brown/*yellow* 2·50 19·00
F27 40c. red/*yellow* 24·00 80·00
F28 50c. sage-green 20·00 40·00
F29 75c. orange 9·00 42·00
F30 1f. red/*blue* 9·00 10·00
F31 2f. violet 9·00 50·00
F32 5f. red/*green* 35·00 60·00
F22/F32 *Set of* 11 £100 £275

The above were placed on sale in Paris on 29 April 1912.

1920–21. Surch as T F **6**, at Govt Printing Establishment, Suva, Fiji.

(a) On stamps of 1908–1911 (June 1920)

F32*a* 5c. on 50c. red/*orange* (No. F4) £550 £650
F33 5c. on 50c. red/*orange* (No. F9) 2·40 22·00
F33*a* 10c. on 25c. blue/*greenish* (No. F8) 50 1·50

(b) On stamps of 1911–1913 (10.3.21)

F34 **3** 5c. on 40c. red/*yellow* (No. F27) 27·00 £100
F35 20c. on 30c. brown/*yellow* (No. F15) 15·00 70·00
F36 20c. on 30c. brown/*yellow* (No. F26) 11·00 80·00

(c) On Inscr in English (10.3.21)

F37 **3** 10c. on 5d. sage-green (No. 24) 16·00 60·00

1924 (1 May). Stamps of 1911–1913 surch as T F **6**, at Suva.

F38 **3** 10c. on 5c. green (No. F22) 1·00 11·00
F39 30c. on 10c. carmine (No. F23) 1·00 3·00
F40 50c. on 25c. ultramarine (No. F14) 50·00 £110
F41 50c. on 25c. ultramarine (No. F25) 2·50 29·00
F38/F41 *Set of* 4 50·00 £140

F 7

France Libre (F 9)

(Recess D.L.R.)

1925 (June). Wmk 'R F' in sheet or without wmk. P 14.

F42 **F 7** 5c. (½d.) black 75 13·00
F43 10c. (1d.) green 1·00 9·00
F44 20c. (2d.) greyish slate 4·00 3·00
F45 25c. (2½d.) brown 1·50 9·00
F46 30c. (3d.) red 1·75 18·00
F47 40c. (4d.) red/*yellow* 3·25 16·00
F48 50c. (5d.) ultramarine 2·00 1·75
F49 75c. (7½d.) yellow-brown 1·50 23·00
F50 1f. (10d.) carmine/*blue* 1·50 2·50
F51 2f. (1/8) violet 2·50 38·00
F52 5f. (4s.) carmine/*green* 3·50 38·00
F42/F52 *Set of* 11 20·00 £150
F42s/F52s Optd 'SPECIMEN' *Set of* 11 £250

In July 1929 a batch of mail was carried by aircraft from Port Vila to the French cruiser *Tourville* for sorting and forwarding at Nouméa, New Caledonia. Stamps of the above issue (including those with English inscriptions) were affixed to covers and handstamped 'PAR AVION' before cancellation.

(New Currency. 100 gold centimes = 1 gold franc)

1938 (1 June). Gold Currency. Wmk 'R F' in sheet or without wmk. P 12.

F53 **6** 5c. blue-green 6·00 14·00
F54 10c. orange 6·50 4·00
F55 15c. bright violet 6·50 10·00
F56 20c. scarlet 6·50 7·50
F57 25c. reddish brown 13·00 9·50
F58 30c. blue 13·00 10·00
F59 40c. grey-olive 7·00 18·00
F60 50c. purple 7·00 7·00
F61 1f. lake/*pale green* (*shades*) 8·00 11·00
F62 2f. blue/*pale green* (*shades*) 50·00 50·00
F63 5f. red/*yellow* 75·00 80·00
F64 10f. violet/*blue* £160 £170
F53/F64 *Set of* 12 £300 £350
F53s/F64s Perf 'SPECIMEN' *Set of* 12 £350

1941 (15 Apr). Adherence to General de Gaulle. Optd with T **F 9**, at Nouméa, New Caledonia.

F65 **6** 5c. blue-green 2·00 25·00
F66 10c. orange 6·00 24·00
F67 15c. bright violet 9·50 40·00
F68 20c. scarlet 27·00 32·00
F69 25c. reddish brown 29·00 42·00
F70 30c. blue 30·00 38·00
F71 40c. grey-olive 30·00 40·00
F72 50c. purple 25·00 38·00
F73 1f. lake/*pale green* 25·00 38·00
F74 2f. blue/*pale green* 24·00 38·00
F75 5f. red/*yellow* 19·00 38·00
F76 10f. violet/*blue* 18·00 38·00
F65/F76 *Set of* 12 £200 £375

1949 (10 Oct). 75th Anniversary of UPU. As Nos. 64/67. Wmk 'R F' in sheet or without wmk. P 13½.

F77 10c. red-orange 3·50 7·50
F78 15c. violet 4·75 12·00
F79 30c. ultramarine 7·50 16·00
F80 50c. purple 8·50 19·00
F77/F80 *Set of* 4 22·00 50·00

1953 (30 Apr). As Nos. 68/78. Wmk 'R F' in sheet or without wmk. P 12½.

F81 **7** 5c. green 3·25 8·00
F82 10c. scarlet 6·50 8·00
F83 15c. yellow-ochre 6·50 8·50
F84 20c. ultramarine 6·50 6·50
F85 **8** 25c. olive 3·50 6·50
F86 30c. brown 1·75 6·50
F87 40c. blackish brown 2·00 6·50
F88 50c. violet 2·00 4·50
F89 **9** 1f. orange 15·00 13·00
F90 2f. reddish purple 19·00 50·00
F91 5f. scarlet 19·00 85·00
F81/F91 *Set of* 11 75·00 £170

1956 (20 Oct). 50th Anniversary of Condominium. As Nos. 80/83. Wmk 'R F' in sheet or without wmk. P 14½×14.

F92 **10** 5c. emerald 2·00 2·25
F93 10c. scarlet 2·25 2·25
F94 **11** 20c. deep bright blue 1·50 2·75
F95 50c. deep lilac 1·50 2·75
F92/F95 *Set of* 4 6·50 9·25

1957 (3 Sept). As Nos. 84/94. Wmk 'R F' in sheet or without wmk. P 13½.

F96 **12** 5c. green 1·75 3·00
F97 10c. scarlet 2·25 3·50
F98 15c. orange-yellow 2·50 3·50
F99 20c. ultramarine 2·75 3·50
F100 **13** 25c. yellow-olive 2·50 3·00
F101 30c. brown 2·50 1·75
F102 40c. sepia 2·25 2·00
F103 50c. reddish violet 2·75 1·60

F104	14	1f. red-orange	9·00	4·00
F105		2f. mauve	12·00	21·00
F106		5f. black	32·00	35·00
F96/F106 *Set of* 11			60·00	75·00

F **14** Emblem and Globe

(Des and eng J. Derrey. Recess Govt Ptg Wks, Paris)

1963 (2 Sept). Freedom from Hunger. P 13.

F107	F **14**	60c. deep bluish green and chestnut	19·00	18·00

F **15** Centenary Emblem

(Des and eng J. Combet. Recess Govt Ptg Wks, Paris)

1963 (2 Sept). Red Cross Centenary. P 13.

F108	F **15**	15c. red, grey and orange	11·00	11·00
F109		45c. red, grey and yellow-bistre	14·00	29·00

1963 (25 Nov)–**72**. As Nos. 98/109 and 129. No wmk. P 12½ (10, 20, 40, 60c.), 14 (3f.) or 13 (others).

F110	**16**	5c. lake, purple-brown and greenish blue (15.8.66)	55	2·00
		a. Lake and greenish blue (29.2.72)	65·00	65·00
F111	**17**	10c. light brown, buff and emerald* (16.8.65)	2·00	4·50
F112		10c. light brown, buff and emerald (5.8.68)	1·00	2·25
F113	**18**	15c. Yellow-bistre, red-brown and deep violet	6·00	1·25
F114	**19**	20c. black, olive-green and greenish blue* (16.8.65)	2·25	5·50
F115		20c. black, olive-green and greenish blue (5.8.68)	2·00	2·50
F116	**20**	25c. reddish violet, orange-brown and crimson (15.8.6)	70	2·00
F117	**21**	30c. chestnut, bistre and violet	7·50	1·25
F118	**22**	40c. vermilion and deep blue* (16.8.65)	3·25	9·00
F119	**23**	50c. green, yellow and greenish blue	8·50	2·50
F120	**22**	60c. vermilion and deep blue (5.12.67)	1·75	3·50
F121	**24**	1f. red, black and deep bluish green (15.8.66)	2·00	5·00
F122	**25**	2f. black, brown purple and yellow-olive	17·00	7·00
F123	**26**	3f. multicoloured* (16.8.65)	8·50	23·00
F124		3f. multicoloured (5.8.68)	8·50	12·00
F125	**27**	5f. blue, deep blue and black (24.1.67)	30·00	23·00
F110/F125 *Set of* 16			90·00	95·00

* Normally all French New Hebrides issues have the 'RF' inscription on the right to distinguish them from the British New Hebrides stamps which have it on the left. The stamps indicated by an asterisk have 'RF' wrongly placed on the left.

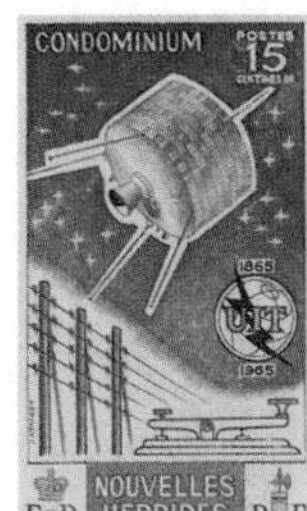

F **16a** *Syncom* Communications Satellite, Telegraph Poles and Morse Key

(Des and eng J. Combet. Recess Govt Ptg Wks, Paris)

1965 (17 May). ITU Centenary. P 13.

F126	F **16a**	15c. blue, chocolate and emerald	10·00	9·00
F127		60c. carmine, deep bluish green and slate	28·00	35·00

1965 (24 Oct). International Co-operation Year. As Nos. 112/113. P 14½.

F128	**29**	5c. deep reddish purple and turquoise-green	3·00	7·00
F129		55c. deep bluish green and lavender	11·00	12·00

1966 (24 Jan). Churchill Commemoration. As Nos. 114/117. P 14.

F130	**30**	5c. black, cerise, gold and new blue	2·10	8·00
F131		15c. black, cerise, gold and deep green	3·00	3·00
F132		25c. black, cerise, gold and brown	4·00	9·00
F133		30c. black, cerise, gold and bluish violet	4·25	10·00
F130/F133 *Set of* 4			12·00	27·00

1966 (1 July). World Cup Football Championship. As Nos. 118/119. P 14.

F134	**31**	20c. violet, yellow-green lake and yellow-brown	2·25	5·50
F135		40c. chocolate, blue-green, lake and yellow-brown	4·00	5·50

1966 (20 Sept). Inauguration of WHO Headquarters, Geneva. As Nos. 120/121. P 14.

F136	**32**	25c. black, yellow-green and light blue	4·00	4·50
F137		60c. black, mauve and yellow-ochre	6·00	10·00

1966 (1 Dec). 20th Anniversary of UNESCO. As Nos. 122/124. P 14.

F138	**33**	15c. slate-violet, red, yellow and orange	2·50	3·25
F139	–	30c. orange-yellow, violet and deep olive	3·50	4·75
F140	–	45c. black, bright purple and orange	4·00	6·50
F138/F140 *Set of* 3			9·00	13·00

1967 (26 Sept). 25th Anniversary of the Pacific War. As Nos. 125/128. P 14×13.

F141		15c. Type **36**	1·40	1·50
F142		25c. Map of war zone, US marine and Australian soldier	2·00	3·00
F143		60c. HMAS *Canberra* (cruiser)	2·00	2·50
F144		1f. Boeing B-17 Flying Fortress	2·25	2·75
F141/F144 *Set of* 4			7·00	8·75

1968 (23 May). Bicentenary of Bougainville's World Voyage. As Nos. 130/132. P 13.

F145	**40**	15c. emerald, slate-violet and red	55	1·10
F146	–	25c. deep olive, maroon and ultramarine	65	1·25
F147	–	60c. bistre-brown, brown-purple and myrtle-green	1·10	1·50
F145/F147 *Set of* 3			2·10	3·50

1968 (9 Oct). Anglo-French Concorde Project. As Nos. 133/134. P 14.

F148	**43**	25c. light blue, orange-red and deep violet-blue	1·90	2·40
F149	–	60c. red, black and bright blue	2·25	4·25

1969 (30 June). Timber Industry. As No. 135. P 14½.

F150	**45**	20c. multicoloured (*shades*)	45	1·00

1969 (13 Aug). Third South Pacific Games, Port Moresby, Papua New Guinea. As Nos. 136/137. Multicoloured. P 12½.

F151		25c. Type **46**	50	1·40
F152		1f. Runner passing baton, and flags	1·50	2·00

1969 (15 Oct). Pentecost Island Land Divers. As Nos, 138/140. Multicoloured. P 12½.

F153		15c. Type **48**	55	1·25
F154		25c. Diver jumping	45	1·25
F155		1f. Diver at end of fall	1·10	2·00
F153/F155 *Set of* 3			1·90	4·00

1970 (20 May). Inauguration of New UPU Headquarters Building, Berne. As No. 141. P 13.

F156	**51**	1f.05 slate, red-orange and bright purple	1·00	2·75

1970 (20 July). 30th Anniversary of New Hebrides' Declaration for the Free French Government. As Nos. 142/143. P 13.

F157	**52**	65c. multicoloured	2·75	2·00
F158		1f.10 multicoloured	3·00	2·25

1970 (15 Oct). No. F115 surch with T **53**.

F159		35c. on 20c. black, olive-green and greenish blue	65	1·75

1970 (30 Nov). Christmas. As Nos. 145/146. Multicoloured. P 14½×14.

F160		15c. Type **54**	25	1·00
F161		50c. *The Virgin and Child* (G. Cima)	45	1·25

POSTAGE DUE STAMPS

CHIFFRE TAXE	CHIFFRE TAXE	TIMBRE-TAXE
(FD **1**)	(FD **2**)	(FD **3**)

1925 (June). Optd with T FD **1**, by D.L.R.

FD53	F **7**	10c. (1d.) green	55·00	4·25
FD54		20c. (2d.) greyish slate	55·00	4·25
FD55		30c. (3d.) red	55·00	4·25
FD56		50c. (5d.) ultramarine	55·00	4·25
FD57		1f. (10d.) carmine/*blue*	55·00	4·25
FD53/FD57 *Set of* 5			£250	19·00
FD53s/FD57s Optd 'SPECIMEN' *Set of* 5			£250	

Although on sale in Paris, the Postmaster would not issue any in unused condition for about a year and most copies are cancelled-to-order.

1938 (1 June). Optd with T FD **2**, by Bradbury Wilkinson.

FD65	**6**	5c. blue-green	20·00	75·00
FD66		10c. orange	23·00	75·00
FD67		20c. scarlet	29·00	80·00
FD68		40c. grey-olive	65·00	£160
FD69		1f. lake/*pale green*	65·00	£160
FD65/FD69 *Set of* 5			£180	£500
FD65s/FD69s Perf 'SPECIMEN' *Set of* 5			£200	

1941 (15 Apr). Nos. FD65/FD69 optd with T F **9** at Nouméa, New Caledonia.

FD77	**6**	5c. blue-green	19·00	48·00
FD78		10c. orange	19·00	48·00
FD79		20c. scarlet	19·00	48·00
FD80		40c. grey-olive	24·00	48·00
FD81		1f. lake/*pale green*	22·00	48·00
FD77/FD81 *Set of* 5			95·00	£200

1953 (30 Apr). Optd with T FD **3**, by Waterlow.

FD92	**7**	5c. green	11·00	25·00
FD93		10c. scarlet	10·00	24·00
FD94		20c. ultramarine	25·00	40·00
FD95	**8**	40c. blackish brown	18·00	38·00
FD96	**9**	1f. orange	20·00	60·00
FD92/FD96 *Set of* 5			75·00	£170

1957 (3 Sept). Optd with T FD **3**, by Waterlow.

FD107	**12**	5c. green	1·50	9·50
FD108		10c. scarlet	2·00	9·50
FD109		20c. ultramarine	3·50	14·00
FD110	**13**	40c. sepia	8·00	27·00
FD111	**14**	1f. red-orange	7·00	35·00
FD107/FD111 *Set of* 5			20·00	85·00

New Republic *see* South Africa

New South Wales *see* Australia

New Zealand

From 1831 mail from New Zealand was sent to Sydney, New South Wales, routed through an unofficial postmaster at Kororareka.

The first official post office opened at Kororareka in January 1840 to be followed by others at Auckland, Britannia, Coromandel Harbour, Hokianga, Port Nicholson, Russell and Waimate during the same year. New South Wales relinquished control of the postal service when New Zealand became a separate colony on 3 May 1841.

The British GPO was responsible for the operation of the overseas mails from 11 October 1841 until the postal service once again passed under colonial control on 18 November 1848.

CC **1**

CC **2**

AUCKLAND

CROWNED-CIRCLE HANDSTAMPS

CC1	CC **1**	AUCKLAND NEW ZEALAND (R.) (31.10.1846) .... *Price on cover*	£300

NELSON

CROWNED-CIRCLE HANDSTAMPS

CC2	CC **1**	NELSON NEW ZEALAND (R.) (31.10.1846) .... *Price on cover*	£1100

NEW PLYMOUTH

CROWNED-CIRCLE HANDSTAMPS

CC3	CC **1**	NEW PLYMOUTH NEW ZEALAND (R. or Black) (31.10.1846)........ *Price on cover*	£2750
CC3*a*	CC **2**	NEW PLYMOUTH NEW ZEALAND (R. or Black) (1854)........ *Price on cover*	£3250

OTAGO

CROWNED-CIRCLE HANDSTAMPS

CC4	CC **2**	OTAGO NEW ZEALAND (R.) (1851) .... *Price on cover*	£1900

PETRE

CROWNED-CIRCLE HANDSTAMPS

CC5	CC **1**	PETRE NEW ZEALAND (R.) (31.10.1846) .... *Price on cover*	£1400

PORT VICTORIA

CROWNED-CIRCLE HANDSTAMPS

CC6	CC **2**	PORT VICTORIA NEW ZEALAND (R.) (1851) .... *Price on cover*	£1200

RUSSELL

CROWNED-CIRCLE HANDSTAMPS

CC7	CC **1**	RUSSELL NEW ZEALAND (R.) (31.10.1846) .... *Price on cover*	£8000

WELLINGTON

CROWNED-CIRCLE HANDSTAMPS

CC8	CC **1**	WELLINGTON NEW ZEALAND (R.) (31.10.1846)........ *Price on cover*	£350

A similar mark for Christchurch as CC **2** is only known struck, in black, as a cancellation after the introduction of adhesive stamps.

No. CC3*a* is a locally-cut replacement with the office name around the circumference, but a straight 'PAID AT' in the centre.

PRICES FOR STAMPS ON COVER TO 1945

Nos. 1/125	*from* × 2
Nos. 126/136	*from* × 3
Nos. 137/139	*from* × 2
No. 140	—
No. 141	*from* × 2
No. 142	—
Nos. 143/148	*from* × 2
Nos. 149/151	*from* × 10
Nos. 152/184	*from* × 2
Nos. 185/186	—
Nos. 187/203	*from* × 3
Nos. 205/207*e*	—
Nos. 208/213	*from* × 2
Nos. 214/216*j*	—
Nos. 217/258	*from* × 3
No. 259	—
Nos. 260/269	*from* × 3
No. 270	—
Nos. 271/276	*from* × 3
Nos. 277/307	*from* × 2
Nos. 308/316	*from* × 3
No. 317	—
Nos. 318/328	*from* × 3
Nos. 329/348	—
No. 349	*from* × 5
Nos. 350/351	—
No. 352	*from* × 5
Nos. 353/369	—
Nos. 370/386	*from* × 2
No. 387	*from* × 4
Nos. 388/399	*from* × 3
Nos. 400/666	*from* × 2
Nos. E1/E5	*from* × 5

PRICES FOR STAMPS ON COVER TO 1945

No. E6	*from* × 10
Nos. D1/D8	*from* × 3
Nos. D9/D16	*from* × 5
Nos. D17/D20	*from* × 3
Nos. D21/D47	*from* × 6
Nos. O1/O34	*from* × 5
Nos. O59/O66	*from* × 4
Nos. O67/O68	—
Nos. O69/O81	*from* × 5
Nos. O82/O87	—
Nos. O88/O93	*from* × 20
Nos. O94/O99	*from* × 12
Nos. O100/O111	*from* × 5
Nos. O112/O113	—
Nos. O115/O119	*from* × 15
Nos. O120/O133	*from* × 10
Nos. O134/O151	*from* × 4
Nos. P1/P7	*from* × 8
Nos. L1/L9	*from* × 10
Nos. L9a/L12	—
Nos. L13/L20	*from* × 15
Nos. L21/L23	—
Nos. L24/L41	*from* × 12
No. F1	—
No. F2	*from* × 5
Nos. F3/F144	—
Nos. F145/F158	*from* × 3
Nos. F159/F168	—
Nos. F169/F179	*from* × 3
Nos. F180/F186	—
Nos. F187/F190	*from* × 2
Nos. F191/F203	*from* × 3
Nos. F204/F211	—
Nos. F212/F218	*from* × 2
Nos. A1/A3	*from* × 2

CROWN COLONY

PERKINS BACON 'CANCELLED'. For notes on these handstamps, showing 'CANCELLED' between horizontal bars forming an oval, see Catalogue Introduction.

1

2

(Eng by Humphreys. Recess P.B.)

1855 (20 July)–**57**. Wmk Large Star, W w **1**. Imperf.

1	**1**	1d. dull carmine *(white paper)* (H/S 'CANCELLED' in oval £32000).....	£70000	£20000
2		2d. dull blue *(blued paper)* (H/S 'CANCELLED' in oval £32000).....	£35000	£650
3		1s. pale yellow-green *(blued paper)* (H/S 'CANCELLED' in oval £26000)........	£45000	£5500
		a. Bisected (6d.) *(on cover)* (1857)	†	£42000

The 2d. and 1s. on white paper formerly listed are now known to be stamps printed on blued paper which have had the bluing washed out. Nos. 3a and 6a were used at Port Chalmers between March 1857, when the rate for ½ oz. letters to Great Britain was reduced to 6d., and August 1859. All known examples are bisected vertically.

(Printed by J. Richardson, Auckland, N.Z.)

1855 (Dec). First printing. White paper. Wmk Large Star. Imperf.

3*b*	**1**	1d. orange........	£32000	

1855 (Nov)–**58**. Blue paper. No wmk. Imperf.

4	**1**	1d. red........	£13000	£2000
5		2d. blue (3.56)........	£3000	£300
6		1s. green (9.57)........	£40000	£3750
		a. Bisected (6d.) *(on cover)* (1858).	†	£26000

These stamps on blue paper may occasionally be found watermarked with the names of the manufacturers. Four such watermarks are known: 'SANDS & McDOUGALL MELBOURNE', 'CHARLES SKIPPER & EAST LONDON' and 'SANDS & KENNY' all in uppercase double-lined letters, or 'IPM Co 1852' in upper case script lettering.

1857 (Jan). White paper similar to the issue of July 1855. Wmk Large Star.

7	**1**	1d. dull orange........	†	£30000

This stamp is in the precise shade of the 1d. of the 1858 printing by Richardson on *no wmk* white paper. An unsevered pair is known with Dunedin cancellation on a cover front showing an Auckland arrival postmark of 19.1.1857.

The paper employed for the local printings was often too small to cover the full printing plate, a problem which was overcome by overlapping two sheets on the press. Depending on how accurately the sheets were overlapped, stamps may be found with portions of the design missing (including a unique example of the 2d. value in the Royal Philatelic Collection with the value tablet missing, formerly listed as No. 5a), or may resemble marginal copies, in spite of coming from the middle of the plate.

1857–63. Hard or soft white paper. No wmk.

(a) Imperf

8	**1**	1d. dull orange (1858)........	£3750	£750
8*a*		2d. deep ultramarine (1858)........	£3000	£1000
9		2d. pale blue........	£1400	£180
10		2d. blue (12.57)........	£1400	£180
11		2d. dull deep blue........	£2000	£275
12		6d. bistre-brown (8.59)........	£4250	£500
13		6d. brown........	£3250	£300
14		6d. pale brown........	£3250	£300
15		6d. chestnut........	£5000	£600
16		1s. dull emerald-green (1858)........	£20000	£1800
17		1s. blue-green........	£17000	£1800

(b) Pin-roulette, about 10 at Nelson (1860)

18	**1**	1d. dull orange........	†	£5500
19		2d. blue........	†	£3500
20		6d. brown........	†	£4250
20*a*		1s. dull emerald-green........	†	£7000
21		1s. blue-green........	†	£8000

(c) Serrated perf about 16 or 18 at Nelson (1862)

22	**1**	1d. dull orange........	†	£5000
23		2d. blue........	†	£3750
24		6d. brown........	†	£3500
25		6d. chestnut........	†	£7000
26		1s. blue-green........	†	£6500

(d) Rouletted 7 at Auckland (April 1859)

27	**1**	1d. dull orange........	£10000	£5500
		a. Imperf between (horiz pair).......		
28		2d. blue........	£7500	£3250
29		6d. brown........	£7500	£2750
		a. Imperf between (pair)........	£27000	£13000
30		1s. dull emerald-green........	†	£4750
31		1s. blue-green........	†	£5500

(e) P 13 at Dunedin (1863)

31*a*	**1**	1d. dull orange........	†	£7500
31*b*		2d. pale blue........	£7500	£3500
32		6d. pale brown........	†	£6500

(f) 'H' roulette 16 at Nelson

32*a*	**1**	2d. blue........	†	£4750
32*b*		6d. brown........	†	£5000

(g) 'Y' roulette 18 at Nelson

32*c*	**1**	1d. dull orange........	†	£6000
32*d*		2d. blue........	†	£4000
32*e*		6d. brown........	†	£4750
32*f*		6d. chestnut........	†	£5500
32*g*		1s. blue-green........	†	£8000

(h) Oblique roulette 13 at Wellington

32*h*	**1**	1d. dull orange........	†	£6500

The various separations detailed above were all applied by hand to imperforate sheets. The results were often poorly cut and badly aligned and examples showing separations on all sides are rare. Nos. 32*a*/32*b* and 32*c*/32*g* were produced using roulette wheels fitted with cutting edges in the shape of 'H' or 'Y', and cannot readily be distinguished from Nos. 22/26 unless the separations are well-preserved.

The separation type described as 'Serrated perf' in these listings is technically a form of roulette.

(Printed by John Davies at the GPO, Auckland, N.Z.)

1862 (Feb)–**64**. Wmk Large Star.

(a) Imperf

33	**1**	1d. orange-vermilion........	£1000	£275
34		1d. vermilion (9.62)........	£750	£275
35		1d. carmine-vermilion (10.63)........	£450	£300
36		2d. deep blue (Plate I)........	£850	95·00
		a. Double print........	—	£4000
37		2d. slate-blue (Plate I)........	£2000	£200
37*a*		2d. milky blue (Plate I, worn) (1863)..	—	£225
38		2d. pale blue (Plate I, worn)........	£750	90·00
39		2d. blue *(to deep)* (Plate I, very worn) (1864)........	£750	90·00
40		3d. brown-lilac (01.63)........	£600	£160
41		6d. black-brown........	£2000	£130
42		6d. brown........	£2250	£130
43		6d. red-brown (1863)........	£1700	£110
44		1s. green........	£2500	£325
45		1s. yellow-green........	£2250	£350
46		1s. deep green........	£2500	£375

The 2d. in a distinctive deep bright blue on white paper wmkd. Large Star is believed by experts to have been printed by Richardson in 1861 or 1862. This also exists doubly printed and with serrated perf.

No. 37 shows traces of plate wear to the right of the Queen's head. This is more pronounced on Nos. 37*a*/38 and quite extensive on No. 39.

(b) Rouletted 7 at Auckland (5.62)

47	**1**	1d. orange-vermilion........	£4750	£850
48		1d. vermilion........	£3500	£800
48*a*		1d. carmine-vermilion........	£5000	£1000
49		2d. deep blue........	£3750	£475
50		2d. slate-blue........	£4500	£850
51		2d. pale blue........	£3000	£600
52		3d. brown-lilac........	£3750	£800
53		6d. black-brown........	£3750	£475
54		6d. brown........	£3750	£600
55		6d. red-brown........	£3500	£475
56		1s. green........	£4000	£900
57		1s. yellow-green........	£4000	£900
58		1s. deep green........	£5000	£1100

(c) Serrated perf 16 or 18 at Nelson (7.62)

59	**1**	1d. orange-vermilion........	£10000	£2250
60		2d. deep blue........	†	£1300
61		2d. slate-blue........		
62		3d. brown-lilac........	£6000	£1800
63		6d. black-brown........	†	£1800
64		6d. brown........	†	£2250
65		1s. yellow-green........	†	£4500

(d) Pin-perf 10 at Nelson (8.62)

66	**1**	2d. deep blue........	†	£3000
67		6d. black-brown........	†	£4000

(e) 'H' roulette 16 at Nelson

67*a*	**1**	2d. deep blue (Plate I)........	†	£2000
67*b*		6d. black-brown........	†	£2250
67*c*		1s. green........	†	£4250

(f) 'Y' roulette 18 at Nelson (6.62)

67*d*	**1**	1d. orange-vermilion........	†	£2500
67*e*		2d. deep blue (Plate I)........	†	£2000
		a. Imperf between (horiz pair)........	†	£7000
67*f*		2d. slate-blue (Plate I)........	†	£2000
67*g*		3d. brown-lilac........	†	£2500
67*h*		6d. black-brown........	†	£2000
67*i*		6d. brown........	†	£2000
67*j*		1s. yellow-green........	†	£4250

(g) Oblique roulette 13 at Wellington

67*k*	**1**	2d. deep blue (Plate I)........	†	£2500
67*l*		2d. slate-blue (Plate I)........		
67*m*		3d. brown-lilac........	†	£3000
67*n*		6d. brown........	†	£2500

(h) Square roulette 14 at Auckland

67*o*	**1**	1d. orange-vermilion........	†	£2500
67*p*		2d. deep blue (Plate I)........	†	£2000
67*q*		3d. brown-lilac........	†	£3000
67*r*		6d. red-brown........	†	£2500

(i) Serrated perf 13 at Dunedin

No.	Type	Description	Unused	Used
67*s*	1	1d. orange-vermilion	†	£3000
67*t*		2d. deep blue (Plate I)	†	£2000
67*u*		3d. brown-lilac	£4250	£1800
67*v*		6d. brown	†	£2000
67*w*		1s. yellow-green	†	£4250

The dates put to the above varieties are the earliest recorded.

1862 (Dec)–**64**. Wmk Large Star. P 13 (at Dunedin by Ferguson & Mitchell).

No.	Type	Description	Unused	Used
68	1	1d. orange-vermilion	£3250	£350
		a. Imperf between (horiz pair)	†	£11000
69		1d. carmine-vermilion	£3250	£350
70		2d. deep blue (Plate I)	£1200	£110
71		2d. slate-blue (Plate I)	†	£750
72		2d. blue (Plate I)	£750	80·00
72*a*		2d. milky blue (Plate I)	—	£500
73		2d. pale blue (Plate I)	£750	80·00
74		3d. brown-lilac	£3250	£500
75		6d. black-brown	£2250	£225
		a. Imperf between (horiz pair)		
76		6d. brown	£2000	£160
77		6d. red-brown	£1600	£120
78		1s. dull green	£3250	£425
79		1s. deep green	£3500	£400
80		1s. yellow-green	£3250	£375

See also Nos. 110/125 and the note that follows these.

1862 (Aug)–**63**. Pelure paper. No wmk.

(a) Imperf

No.	Type	Description	Unused	Used
81	1	1d. orange-vermilion (1863)	£12000	£2500
82		2d. ultramarine (10.62)	£6500	£850
83		2d. pale ultramarine	£5500	£800
84		3d. lilac (1863)	£50000	†
85		6d. black-brown	£3500	£250
86		1s. deep green	£14000	£1100

The 3d. is known only unused.

(b) Rouletted 7 at Auckland

No.	Type	Description	Unused	Used
87	1	1d. orange-vermilion	†	£6500
88		6d. black-brown	£4000	£475
89		1s. deep green	£15000	£1800

(c) P 13 at Dunedin

No.	Type	Description	Unused	Used
90	1	1d. orange-vermilion	£15000	£3500
91		2d. ultramarine	£8500	£800
92		2d. pale ultramarine	£7500	£700
93		6d. black-brown	£7500	£400
94		1s. deep green	£14000	£2000

(d) Serrated perf 16 at Nelson

No.	Type	Description	Unused	Used
95	1	6d. black-brown	—	£5500

(e) Serrated perf 13 at Dunedin

No.	Type	Description	Unused	Used
95*a*	1	1d. orange-vermilion	†	£10000

1863 (early). Thick soft white paper. No wmk.

(a) Imperf

No.	Type	Description	Unused	Used
96	1	2d. dull deep blue *(shades)*	£3750	£800

(b) P 13

No.	Type	Description	Unused	Used
96*a*	1	2d. dull deep blue *(shades)*	£2000	£475

These stamps show slight beginnings of wear of the printing plate in the background to right of the Queen's ear, as one looks at the stamps. By the early part of 1864, the wear of the plate had spread, more or less, all over the background of the circle containing the head. The major portion of the stamps of this printing appears to have been consigned to Dunedin and to have been there perforated 13.

1864. Wmk 'N Z', W **2**.

(a) Imperf

No.	Type	Description	Unused	Used
97	1	1d. carmine-vermilion	£950	£350
98		2d. pale blue (Plate I worn)	£1700	£275
99		6d. red-brown	£6000	£700
100		1s. green	£2250	£275

(b) Rouletted 7 at Auckland

No.	Type	Description	Unused	Used
101	1	1d. carmine-vermilion	£6000	£3000
102		2d. pale blue (Plate I worn)	£2500	£750
103		6d. red-brown	£7000	£3000
104		1s. green	£4500	£1100

(c) P 13 (line) at Dunedin

No.	Type	Description	Unused	Used
104*a*	1	1d. carmine-vermilion	£11000	£5500
105		2d. pale blue (Plate I worn)	£1200	£190
106		1s. green	£2750	£500
		a. Imperf between (horiz pair)	†	£40000
		aa. Perf 6½×13	†	£4250

(d) 'Y' roulette 18 at Nelson

No.	Type	Description	Unused	Used
106*b*	1	1d. carmine-vermilion	†	£6500

(e) P 12½ (comb) at Auckland

No.	Type	Description	Unused	Used
106*c*	1	1d. carmine-vermilion	£11000	£4750
107		2d. pale blue (Plate I worn)	£475	75·00
108		6d. red-brown	£700	60·00
109		1s. yellow-green	£7500	£2750

The 'NZ' watermark is frequently found inverted.

1864–71. Wmk Large Star. P 12½ (comb or line)* (at Auckland).

No.	Type	Description	Unused	Used
110	1	1d. carmine-vermilion (1865)	£250	45·00
111		1d. pale orange-vermilion (1866)	£300	45·00
		a. Imperf (pair)	£4500	£2750
		b. Imperf between (vert pair)	†	—
112		1d. orange (1871)	£650	90·00
113		2d. pale blue (Plate I worn)	£350	30·00
114		2d. deep blue (Plate II) (7.65)	£250	22·00
		a. Imperf vert (horiz pair)	†	£5500
115		2d. blue (Plate II)	£250	22·00
		a. Retouched (Plate II) (1867)	£375	50·00
		c. Imperf (pair) (Plate II)	£3000	£2500
		d. Retouched. Imperf (pair)	£4000	£4250
116		3d. brown-lilac	£2750	£650
117		3d. lilac (1867)	£170	35·00
		a. Imperf (pair)	£4500	£2000
		b. Imperf between (horiz pair)	†	—
118		3d. deep mauve (1867)	£850	75·00
		a. Imperf (pair)	£5000	£2000
119		4d. deep rose (1.6.65)	£3250	£250
120		4d. yellow (1866)	£275	£120
121		4d. orange (1869)	£2500	£1000
122		6d. red-brown	£350	28·00
122*a*		6d. brown (1867)	£375	42·00
		b. Imperf (pair)	£3000	£3000
123		1s. deep green	£1400	£350
124		1s. green	£800	£140
125		1s. yellow-green	£350	£120

The above issue is sometimes difficult to distinguish from Nos. 68/80 because the vertical perforations usually gauge 12¾ and sometimes a full 13. However, stamps of this issue invariably gauge 12½ horizontally, whereas the 1862 stamps measure a full 13.

* Until late1866 two comb perforating heads were in use. These were then converted to single-line heads, and all subsequent printings were line perforated. Some stamps (such as Nos. 110, 113, 116 and 119) only exist with the early comb perforation, while others (such as Nos. 112, 117/118, 121 and 122*a*) are always line perforated.

Nos. 111a, 115c/115d, 117a, 118a and 122b were issued during problems with the perforation machine which occurred in 1866–1867, 1869–1870 and 1871–1873. Imperforate sheets of the 1s. were also released, but these stamps are very similar to Nos. 44/46.

The new plate of the 2d. showed signs of deterioration during 1866 and 30 positions in rows 13 and 16 to 20 were retouched by a local engraver.

The 1d., 2d. and 6d. were officially reprinted imperforate, without gum, in 1884 for presentation purposes. They can be distinguished from the errors listed by their shades which are pale orange, dull blue and dull chocolate-brown respectively, and by the worn state of the plates from which they were printed *(Prices £95 each unused)*.

1871 (1 Oct)–**73**. Wmk Large Star. New colours (except No. 129/129a).

(a) P 10

No.	Type	Description	Unused	Used
126	1	1d. brown	£1100	£130

(b) P 12½×10

No.	Type	Description	Unused	Used
127	1	1d. deep brown	†	£4750

(c) P 10×12½

No.	Type	Description	Unused	Used
128	1	1d. brown	£375	55·00
		a. Perf 12½ comp 10 (1 side)	£750	£200
129		2d. deep blue (Plate II)	†	£14000
		a. Perf 10*	†	£32000
130		2d. vermilion	£325	42·00
		a. Retouched	£475	60·00
		b. Perf 12½ comp 10 (1 side)	£2000	£475
		c. Perf 10*	†	£25000
131		6d. deep blue	£3500	£900
		a. Blue	£2000	£550
		b. Imperf between (vert pair)		
		c. Perf 12½ comp 10 (1 side)	£1800	£450
		ca. Imperf vert (horiz pair)	†	—

(d) P 12½ (1872–1873)

No.	Type	Description	Unused	Used
132	1	1d. red-brown	£275	48·00
		a. Brown (shades, worn plate) (1873)	£250	42·00
		b. Imperf horiz (vert pair)	—	£6500
133		2d. orange	£180	29·00
		a. Retouched	£300	50·00
134		2d. vermilion	£225	32·00
		a. Retouched	£325	60·00
135		6d. blue	£350	65·00
136		6d. pale blue	£250	55·00

* Only one used copy of No. 129a and two of No. 130c have been reported.

1873 (Aug–Sept). No wmk. P 12½.

No.	Type	Description	Unused	Used
137	1	1d. brown	£1300	£275
		a. Watermarked (script letters)*	£4250	£2250
		b. Watermarked (double-lined capitals)*	£2000	£600
138		2d. vermilion	£180	55·00
		a. Retouched	£300	85·00
		b. Watermarked (script letters)*	£4000	£1400
		c. Watermarked (double-lined capitals)*	£1900	£800
139		4d. orange-yellow	£225	£850
		a. Watermarked (double-lined capitals)*	£450	£2000

* 1d., 2d. and 4d. stamps were printed on paper showing sheet watermarks of either 'W. T. & Co.' (Wiggins Teape & Co.) in script letters or 'T. H. Saunders' in double-lined capitals (the former appearing once, at the top or bottom of the sheet, and the latter occurring twice in the sheet); portions of these letters are occasionally found on stamps. A third, as yet unidentified script watermark has also been identified on the 1d. and 2d. values.

It seems likely that Nos. 137/139 were printed and issued after Nos. 140/142.

1873 (July?). Wmk 'N Z', W **2**. P 12½.

No.	Type	Description	Unused	Used
140	1	1d. brown	†	£9000
141		2d. vermilion	£1500	£350
		a. Retouched	£1900	£425

The 'NZ' watermark may be found inverted or inverted and reversed.

1873 (Aug). Wmk Lozenges, with 'INVICTA' reading upwards in double-lined capitals four times in the sheet. P 12½.

No.	Type	Description	Unused	Used
142	1	2d. vermilion	£3250	£500
		a. Retouched	£4750	£750

3 4

(Des John Davies. Die eng on wood in Melbourne. Printed from electrotypes at Govt Ptg Office, Wellington)

1873 (1 Jan).

*(a) Wmk 'NZ', W F **5***

No.	Type	Description	Unused	Used
143	3	½d. pale dull rose (P 10)	£110	60·00
144		½d. pale dull rose (P 12½)	£180	85·00
145		½d. pale dull rose (P 12½×10)	£200	85·00
		a. Perf 10×12½	£350	£150

(b) No wmk

No.	Type	Description	Unused	Used
146	3	½d. pale dull rose (P 10)	£200	75·00
147		½d. pale dull rose (P 12½)	£250	£100
148		½d. pale dull rose (P 12½×10)	£275	£110
		a. Perf 10×12½	£550	£190

As the paper used for Nos. 143/145 was originally intended for fiscal stamps which were more than twice as large, about one-third of the impressions fall on portions of the sheet showing no watermark, giving rise to varieties Nos. 146/148. In later printings of No. 151 a few stamps in each sheet are without watermark. These can be distinguished from No. 147 by the shade.

1875 (Jan). Wmk Star, W **4**.

No.	Type	Description	Unused	Used
149	3	½d. pale dull rose (P 12½)	30·00	3·00
		a. Imperf horiz (vert pair)	£850	£750
		b. Imperf between (horiz pair)	†	£850
		c. Perf compound of 12½ and 10	†	—
150		½d. dull pale rose (P *nearly* 12)	70·00	13·00

1892 (May). Wmk 'NZ and Star'. W **12b**. P 12½.

No.	Type	Description	Unused	Used
151	3	½d. bright rose *(shades)*	14·00	2·00
		a. No wmk	25·00	16·00
		w. Wmk inverted	75·00	50·00
		x. Wmk reversed	—	£180

5 6 7

8 9 10

11 12 **12a** 6 mm

12b 7 mm **12c** 4 mm

(Types **5/10** eng De La Rue. T **11** and T **12** des, eng and plates by W. R. Bock. Typo Govt Ptg Office, Wellington)

1874 (2 Jan)–**78.**

*A. White paper. W **12a***

(a) P 12½

No.	Type	Description	Unused	Used
152	5	1d. lilac	£120	18·00
		a. Imperf (pair)	—	£2000
		w. Wmk inverted	†	£110
		x. Wmk reversed	†	£450
		y. Wmk inverted and reversed	†	£1000
153	6	2d. rose	£130	8·00
154	7	3d. brown	£170	80·00
155	8	4d. maroon	£300	70·00
		w. Wmk inverted	£800	£250
156	9	6d. blue	£250	12·00
		w. Wmk inverted	—	£100
		x. Wmk reversed	†	£425
157	10	1s. green	£600	38·00
		w. Wmk inverted	£1500	£350

(b) Perf nearly 12 (line)

No.	Type	Description	Unused	Used
158	6	2d. rose (1878)	£1200	£190

(c) Perf compound of 12½ and 10

No.	Type	Description	Unused	Used
159	5	1d. lilac	£170	45·00
		w. Wmk inverted	—	£130
160	6	2d. rose	£225	85·00
		w. Wmk inverted	—	£170
161	7	3d. brown	£200	85·00
		w. Wmk inverted	†	—
162	8	4d. maroon	£800	£160
163	9	6d. blue	£300	50·00
		w. Wmk inverted	—	£130
164	10	1s. green	£650	£140
		a. Imperf between (vert pair)	†	£7000
		bw. Wmk inverted	†	£475

(d) Perf nearly 12×12½

No.	Type	Description	Unused	Used
164*c*	5	1d. lilac (1875)	£1500	£375
165	6	2d. rose (1878)	£1200	£325

B. Blued paper

(a) P 12½

No.	Type	Description	Unused	Used
166	5	1d. lilac	£225	40·00
167	6	2d. rose	£225	40·00
		w. Wmk inverted	—	£130
		x. Wmk reversed	†	£250
168	7	3d. brown	£375	£110
169	8	4d. maroon	£600	£120
170	9	6d. blue	£425	55·00
171	10	1s. green	£1100	£190

(b) Perf compound of 12½ and 10

No.	Type	Description	Unused	Used
172	5	1d. lilac	£250	60·00
173	6	2d. rose	£550	£100
174	7	3d. brown	£400	£110
175	8	4d. maroon	£800	£160
176	9	6d. blue	£450	£100
177	10	1s. green	£1100	£250

1875. Wmk Large Star, W w **1**. P 12½.

No.	Type	Description	Unused	Used
178	5	1d. deep lilac	£2250	£300
179	6	2d. rose	£850	38·00

1878. W **12a**. P 12×11½ (comb).

No.	Type	Description	Unused	Used
180	5	1d. mauve-lilac	65·00	8·00
181	6	2d. rose	70·00	7·00

182	**8**	4d. maroon	£190	55·00
183	**9**	6d. blue	£130	12·00
184	**10**	1s. green	£200	50·00
		w. Wmk inverted	†	£450
185	**11**	2s. deep rose (1.7)	£375	£300
186	**12**	5s. grey (1.7)	£375	£300

This perforation is made by a horizontal 'comb' machine, giving a gauge of 12 horizontally and about 11¾ vertically. Single examples can be found apparently gauging 11½ all round or 12 all round, but these are all from the same machine. The perforation described above as 'nearly 12' was from a single-line machine.

13 14 15 16 17 18 19 20 21 22

Description of Watermarks

W **12a**. 6 mm between 'NZ' and star; broad irregular star; comparatively wide 'N'; 'N Z' 11½ mm wide.

W **12b**. 7 mm between 'N Z' and star; narrower star; narrow 'N'; 'N Z' 10 mm wide.

W **12c**. 4 mm between 'N Z' and star; narrow star; wide 'N'; 'N Z' 11½ mm wide.

Description of Papers

1882–1888. Smooth paper with horizontal mesh. W **12a**.
1888–1898. Smooth paper with vertical mesh. W **12b**.
1890–1891. Smooth paper with vertical mesh. W **12c**.
1898. Thin yellowish toned, coarse paper with clear vertical mesh. W **12b**. Perf 11 only.

In 1899–1900 stamps appeared on medium to thick white coarse paper but we do not differentiate these (except where identifiable by shade) as they are more difficult to distinguish.

PAPER MESH. This shows on the back of the stamp as a series of parallel grooves, either vertical or horizontal. It is caused by the use of a wire gauze conveyor-belt during paper-making.

Description of Dies

1d.

Die 1

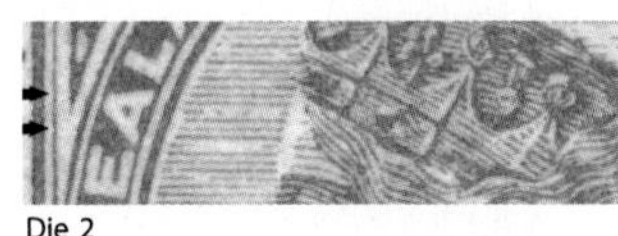

Die 2

Die 3

1882. Die 1. Background shading complete and heavy.
1886. Die 2. Background lines thinner. Two lines of shading weak or missing left of Queen's forehead.
1889. Die 3. Shading on head reduced; ornament in crown left of chignon clearer, with unshaded 'arrow' more prominent.

2d.

Die 1

Die 2

Die 3

1882. Die 1. Background shading complete and heavy.
1886. Die 2. Weak line of shading left of forehead and missing shading lines below 'TA'.
1889. Die 3. As Die 2 but with comma-like white notch in hair below '&'.

6d.

Die 1

Die 2

1882. Die 1. Shading heavy. Top of head merges into shading. Second ornament from the right on the crown shows a line in its left portion.
1892. Die 2. Background lines thinner. Shading on head more regular with clear line of demarcation between head and background shading. Second ornament from the right in the crown has small dots in its left portion. Most examples also show a break in the back line of the neck immediately above its base.

1d. 'Ellipse' flaw (Die 3, lower left pane, R. 9/2)

1d. 'Chisel' flaw (Die 3 upper left pane, R. 4/6) (a smaller break occurs in the lower right frame of this stamp)

'2' and '1' joined (Upper right pane, R. 9/1)

1s. 'Bulbous nose' (Lower right pane, R. 1/1)

HIGH VALUES. From 1882 to 1931 postal requirements for higher value stamps were met by the Queen Victoria 'Stamp Duty' adhesives (F5/F144).

Truebridge Miller

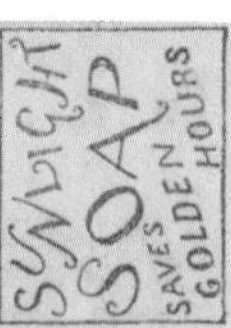

Sunlight Soap

STAMPS WITH ADVERTISEMENTS. During November 1891 the New Zealand Post Office invited tenders for the printing of advertisements on the reverse of the current 1d. to 1s. stamps. The contract was awarded to Messrs Miller, Truebridge & Reich and the first sheets with advertisements on the reverse appeared in February 1893. Different advertisements were applied to the backs of the individual stamps within the sheets of 240 (four panes of 60).

On the first setting those in a vertical format were inverted in relation to the stamps and each of the horizontal advertisements had its base at the left-hand side of the stamp *when seen from the back.* For the second and third settings the vertical advertisements were the same way up as the stamps and the bases of those in the horizontal format were at the right *as seen from the back.* The third setting only differs from the second in the order of the individual advertisements.

Examples of the advertisements being printed double are known, but we do not list them.

The experiment was not, however, a success and the contract was cancelled at the end of 1893.

(Des F. W. Sears (½d.), A. E. Cousins (2½d.), A. W. Jones (5d.); others adapted from 1874 issue by W. H. Norris. Dies eng A. E. Cousins (½d., 2½d., 5d.), W. R. Bock (others). Typo Govt Ptg Office)

1882–1900. Inscr 'POSTAGE & REVENUE'.

A. Paper with horiz mesh (1.4.1882–1886). W **12a**

(a) P 12×11½

187	**14**	1d. rose *to* rose-red (Die 1)	50·00	7·00
		a. Imperf (pair)	£1200	
		b. Imperf between (vert pair)	£1300	
		cw. Wmk inverted		
		d. Die 2. *Pale rose to carmine-rose* (1886)	65·00	8·00
		dw. Wmk inverted	†	£110
		dx. Wmk reversed	£180	85·00
188	**15**	2d. lilac *to* lilac-purple (Die 1)	60·00	4·00
		a. Imperf (pair)	£1200	
		b. Imperf between (vert pair)	£1300	
		cw. Wmk inverted	£170	80·00
		d. Die 2. *Lilac* (1886)	70·00	15·00
189	**17**	3d. yellow	80·00	20·00
190	**18**	4d. blue-green	85·00	11·00
191	**20**	6d. brown (Die 1)	£120	3·75
		w. Wmk inverted	£425	85·00
192	**21**	8d. blue (1885)	£100	65·00
193	**22**	1s. red-brown	£150	16·00
		(b) P 12½ (1884?)		
193*a*	**14**	1d. rose *to* rose-red (Die 1)	£500	£300

B. Paper with vert mesh (1888–1895). W **12b**

(a) P 12×11½ (1888–1895)

194	**13**	½d. black (1.4.95)	42·00	90·00
195	**14**	1d. rose *to* rosine (Die 2)	50·00	5·00
		aw. Wmk inverted	£250	40·00
		b. Die 3. *Rose to carmine* (1889)	50·00	4·50
		bb. Red-brown advert (1st setting) (2.93)	£250	70·00
		bc. Red advert (1st setting) (3.93)	£250	70·00
		bd. Blue advert (2nd setting) (4.93)	£500	£180
		be. Mauve advert (2nd setting) (5.93)	£250	60·00
		bf. Green advert (2nd setting) (6.93)	†	—
		bg. Brown-red advert (3rd setting) (9.93)	£250	55·00
		bh. 'Ellipse' flaw	£140	30·00
		bi. 'Chisel' flaw	£140	30·00
		bw. Wmk inverted	£150	40·00
		bx. Wmk reversed	£180	75·00
196	**15**	2d. lilac (Die 2)	60·00	5·50
		a. Die 3. *Lilac to purple* (1889)	60·00	6·50
		ab. Red advert (1st setting) (3.93)	£350	60·00
		ac. Mauve advert (2nd setting) (5.93)	£350	60·00
		ad. Sepia advert (2nd setting) (5.93)	£350	60·00
		ae. Green advert (2nd setting) (6.93)	—	£170
		af. Brown-red advert (3rd setting) (9.93)	£350	60·00
		aw. Wmk inverted	£180	40·00
197	**16**	2½d. pale blue (1891)	80·00	5·50
		a. Brown-red advert (2nd setting) (4.93)	£650	£200
		ax. Wmk reversed	£650	£250
		b. Ultramarine (green advert. 2nd setting) (6.93)	£650	£200
198	**17**	3d. yellow	70·00	23·00
		a. Brown-red advert (2nd setting) (4.93)	£650	£225
		b. Sepia advert (2nd setting) (5.93)	—	£350
199	**18**	4d. green *to* bluish green	75·00	4·00
		a. Sepia advert (2nd setting) (5.93)	£375	£200
		aw. Wmk inverted	†	£300
200	**19**	5d. olive-black (1.2.91)	80·00	18·00
		a. Imperf (pair)	£1100	
		b. Brown-purple advert (3rd setting) (9.93)	£750	£180
201	**20**	6d. brown (Die 1)	£100	6·50
		a. Die 2 (1892)	£200	£150
		ab. Sepia advert (2nd setting) (5.93)	—	£750
		ac. Brown-red advert (3rd setting) (9.93)	—	£450
		ax. Wmk reversed	†	—
202	**21**	8d. blue	85·00	60·00
203	**22**	1s. red-brown	£130	6·00
		a. Black advert (2nd setting) (5.93)	—	£500
		b. Brown-purple advert (3rd setting) (9.93)	£475	75·00
		w. Wmk inverted	£600	£130

(b) P 12×12½ (1888–1891)

No.	Type	Description	Unused	Used
204	**14**	1d. rose (Die 2)	£375	£500
		a. Die 3 (1889)	†	—

(c) P 12½ (1888–1889)

No.	Type	Description	Unused	Used
205	**14**	1d. rose (Die 3) (1889)	£450	£300
		a. Mauve advert (3rd setting) (5.93)	†	£650
		x. Wmk reversed	†	£750
206	**15**	2d. lilac (Die 2)	£475	£475
		a. Die 3. *Deep lilac* (1889)	£475	£550
		ab. Brown-red advert (3rd setting) (9.93)	£650	£350
207	**16**	2½d. blue (1891)	£550	£350

(d) Mixed perfs 12×11½ and 12½ (1891–1893)

No.	Type	Description	Unused	Used
207*a*	**14**	1d. rose (Die 3) (brown-red advert. 3rd setting)	£375	£225
207*b*	**15**	2d. lilac (Die 3)	†	£450
		ba. Brown-red advert (3rd setting) (9.93)	†	—
207*c*	**18**	4d. green	†	£325
207*d*	**19**	5d. olive-black	†	£350
207*e*	**20**	6d. brown (Die 1)	†	£225
		ea. Die 2	†	£250

C. Paper with vert mesh (1890). W **12c**

(a) P 12×11½

No.	Type	Description	Unused	Used
208	**14**	1d. rose (Die 3)	£275	32·00
		a. 'Ellipse' flaw	£700	£100
		b. 'Chisel' flaw	£700	£100
209	**15**	2d. purple (Die 3)	95·00	20·00
		x. Wmk reversed		
210	**16**	2½d. ultramarine (27.12)	60·00	14·00
		x. Wmk reversed	†	£225
211	**17**	3d. yellow	£110	50·00
		a. Lemon-yellow	£110	55·00
212	**20**	6d. brown (Die 1)	£170	50·00
213	**22**	1s. deep red-brown	£275	£275

(b) P 12½

No.	Type	Description	Unused	Used
214	**14**	1d. rose (Die 3)	£450	£375
215	**15**	2d. purple (Die 3)	£550	£650
216	**16**	2½d. ultramarine	£550	£450

(c) P 12×12½

No.	Type	Description	Unused	Used
216*a*	**20**	6d. brown (Die 1)	£475	£375

D. Paper with vert mesh (1891–1900). Continuation of W **12b**

(a) P 10×12½ (1891–1894)

No.	Type	Description	Unused	Used
216*b*	**14**	1d. rose (Die 3)	£225	£250
		ba. Perf 12½×10	£300	£250
		bb. Red-brown advert (1st setting) (2.93)	£750	£400
		bc. Brown-red advert (2nd setting) (4.93)	£750	£400
		bd. Mauve advert (2nd setting) (5.93)	£750	£400
		be. Green advert (2nd setting) (6.93)	£750	£400
		bf. 'Ellipse' flaw	£650	
		bg. 'Chisel' flaw	£650	
216*c*	**15**	2d. lilac (Die 3)	£450	£300
216*d*	**16**	2½d. blue (1893)	£350	£275
		da. Perf 12½×10	£650	£450
		dab. Mauve advert (2nd setting)	†	£400
216*e*	**17**	3d. yellow	£500	£600
		ea. Perf 12½×10		
216*f*	**18**	4d. green	£500	£450
		fa. Perf 12½×10, brown-purple advert (3rd setting)	†	£1200
216*g*	**19**	5d. olive-black (1894)	£300	£275
		ga. Perf 12½×10	£375	£300
216*h*	**20**	6d. brown (Die 1)	£550	£600
		i. Die 2 (1892)	£475	£475
		ia. Brown-purple advert (3rd setting) (9.93)		
216*j*	**22**	1s. red-brown	£250	£275
		ja. Perf 12½×10	£425	£350

(b) P 10 (1891–1895)

No.	Type	Description	Unused	Used
217	**13**	½d. black (1895)	10·00	2·25
		x. Wmk reversed	†	—
218	**14**	1d. rose (Die 3)	15·00	1·00
		a. Carmine	15·00	1·50
		b. Imperf (pair)	£1100	£1100
		c. Imperf between (pair)	£1200	
		d. Imperf horiz (vert pair)	£1100	
		e. Mixed perfs 10 and 12½	£300	£250
		f. Red-brown advert (1st setting) (2.93)	50·00	7·00
		g. Red advert (1st setting) (3.93)	50·00	9·00
		h. Brown-red advert (2nd and 3rd settings) (4.93)	42·00	4·00
		i. Blue advert (2nd setting) (4.93)	£130	48·00
		j. Mauve advert (2nd setting) (5.93)	42·00	4·00
		k. Green advert (2nd setting) (6.93)	£100	30·00
		l. Brown-purple advert (3rd setting) (9.93)	42·00	5·50
		m. 'Ellipse' flaw	48·00	11·00
		n. 'Chisel' flaw	48·00	11·00
		w. Wmk inverted	£180	90·00
		x. Wmk reversed	£300	£180
219	**15**	2d. lilac (Die 3)	22·00	1·75
		a. Purple	22·00	1·75
		b. Imperf between (pair)	£1200	
		c. Mixed perfs 10 and 12½	£750	£500
		d. Red-brown advert (1st setting) (2.93)	55·00	12·00
		e. Red advert (1st setting) (3.93)	55·00	9·00
		f. Brown-red advert (2nd and 3rd settings) (4.93)	55·00	4·50
		g. Sepia advert (2nd setting) (5.93)	55·00	6·00
		h. Green advert (2nd setting) (6.93)	80·00	15·00
		i. Brown-purple advert (3rd setting) (9.93)	55·00	4·50
		x. Wmk reversed	£180	75·00
220	**16**	2½d. blue (1892)	65·00	3·50
		a. Ultramarine	65·00	4·00
		b. Mixed perfs 10 and 12½	£425	£225
		c. Mauve advert (2nd setting) (5.93)	£200	16·00
		d. Green advert (2nd setting) (6.93)	£225	23·00
		e. Brown-purple advert (3rd setting) (9.93)	£200	16·00
		ex. Wmk reversed	£300	£120
221	**17**	3d. pale orange-yellow	65·00	19·00
		a. Orange	65·00	25·00
		b. Lemon-yellow	65·00	25·00
		c. Mixed perfs 10 and 12½	£750	£650
		d. Brown-red advert (2nd and 3rd settings) (4.93)	£160	30·00
		e. Sepia advert (2nd setting) (5.93)	£170	50·00
		f. Brown-purple advert (3rd setting) (9.93)	£160	28·00
222	**18**	4d. green (1892)	65·00	8·50
		a. Blue-green	65·00	8·50
		b. Mixed perfs 10 and 12½	£300	£200
		c. Brown-red advert (2nd setting) (4.93)	£180	13·00
		d. Brown-purple advert (3rd setting) (9.93)	£180	13·00
223	**19**	5d. olive-black (1893)	65·00	30·00
		a. Brown-purple advert (3rd setting) (9.93)	£190	50·00
		ab. Mixed perfs 10 and 12½	£450	£325
224	**20**	6d. brown (Die 1)	£160	48·00
		a. Mixed perfs 10 and 12½		
		b. Die 2 (1892)	80·00	9·00
		ba. Black-brown	80·00	9·00
		bb. Imperf (pair)	£1200	
		bc. Mixed perfs 10 and 12½	£375	£200
		bd. Sepia advert (2nd setting) (4.93)	£400	20·00
		be. Brown-red advert (3rd setting) (9.93)	£400	20·00
		bf. Brown-purple advert (3rd setting) (9.93)	£400	20·00
		bx. Wmk reversed (with brown-purple advert)	†	£140
225	**21**	8d. blue (brown-purple advert. 3rd setting) (9.93)	90·00	70·00
226	**22**	1s. red-brown	£120	16·00
		a. Imperf between (pair)	£2000	
		b. Mixed perfs 10 and 12½	£425	£275
		c. Sepia advert (2nd setting) (5.93)	£375	55·00
		d. Black advert (2nd setting) (5.93)	£400	£150
		e. Brown-red advert (3rd setting) (9.93)	£375	55·00
		f. Brown-purple advert (3rd setting) (9.93)	£375	55·00
		g. 'Bulbous nose'	£650	£110

(c) P 10×11 (1895–1897)

No.	Type	Description	Unused	Used
227	**13**	½d. black (1896)	5·50	60
		a. Mixed perfs 10 and 11	£170	£120
		b. Perf 11×10 (11.95)	42·00	18·00
228	**14**	1d. rose (Die 3)	14·00	15
		a. Mixed perfs 10 and 11	£180	£100
		b. Perf 11×10 (10.95)	75·00	13·00
		c. 'Ellipse' flaw	45·00	12·00
		d. 'Chisel' flaw	45·00	12·00
		x. Wmk reversed	£120	85·00
229	**15**	2d. purple (Die 3)	25·00	30
		a. Mixed perfs 10 and 11	£100	75·00
230	**16**	2½d. blue (1896)	65·00	3·75
		a. Ultramarine	65·00	4·50
		b. Mixed perfs 10 and 11	—	£150
		c. '2' and '1' joined	£275	30·00
231	**17**	3d. lemon-yellow (1896)	75·00	23·00
232	**18**	4d. pale green (1896)	95·00	12·00
		a. Mixed perfs 10 and 11	—	£180
233	**19**	5d. olive-black (1897)	70·00	15·00
234	**20**	6d. deep brown (Die 2) (1896)	90·00	20·00
		a. Mixed perfs 10 and 11	†	£325
		b. Perf 11×10	†	—
235	**22**	1s. red-brown (1896)	£100	10·00
		a. Mixed perfs 10 and 11	£300	£150
		b. 'Bulbous nose'	£500	90·00

(d) P 11 (1895–1900)

No.	Type	Description	Unused	Used
236	**13**	½d. black (1896)	9·50	15
		aw. Wmk inverted	80·00	35·00
		ax. Wmk reversed	£180	90·00
		b. Thin coarse toned paper (1898)	38·00	6·50
		ba. Wmk sideways	†	£2000
237	**14**	1d. rose (Die 3) (6.95)	6·00	10
		a. Deep carmine	6·00	1·50
		b. Imperf between (pair)	£1100	
		c. Deep carmine/thin coarse toned (1898)	15·00	3·25
		ca. Wmk sideways	†	£2000
		d. 'Ellipse' flaw	35·00	10·00
		e. 'Chisel' flaw	35·00	10·00
		w. Wmk inverted	80·00	48·00
		x. Wmk reversed	90·00	60·00
		y. Wmk inverted and reversed	£160	90·00
238	**15**	2d. mauve (Die 3)	18·00	1·00
		a. Purple	18·00	1·00
		b. Deep purple/thin coarse toned (1898)	25·00	6·00
		ba. Wmk sideways	†	£2000
		w. Wmk inverted	90·00	40·00
		x. Wmk reversed	£190	65·00
239	**16**	2½d. blue (1897)	55·00	4·00
		a. Thin coarse toned paper (1898)	£110	27·00
		b. '2' and '1' joined	£225	30·00
240	**17**	3d. pale yellow (1897)	55·00	8·50
		a. Pale dull yellow/thin coarse toned (1898)	£110	27·00
		b. Orange (1899)	55·00	15·00
		c. Dull orange-yellow (1900)	50·00	29·00
241	**18**	4d. yellowish green (7.96)	60·00	5·00
		a. Bluish green (1897)	55·00	4·50
		w. Wmk inverted	£225	£110
242	**19**	5d. olive-black/*thin coarse toned* (1899)	70·00	40·00
243	**20**	6d. brown (Die 2) (1897)	70·00	6·00
		a. Black-brown	80·00	5·00
		b. Brown/thin coarse toned (1898)	£150	17·00
		x. Wmk reversed	†	£120
244	**21**	8d. blue (1898)	80·00	60·00
245	**22**	1s. red-brown (1897)	£100	7·00
		a. Imperf between (vert pair)	£2000	
		b. 'Bulbous nose'	£500	90·00

Only the more prominent shades have been included.
Stamps perf compound of 10×11 and 12½ and 11 and 12½ exist.
For the ½d. and 2d. with double-lined watermark, see Nos. 271/272.

23 Mount Cook or Aorangi
24 Lake Taupo and Mount Ruapehu
25 Pembroke Peak, Milford Sound

26 Lake Wakatipu and Mount Earnslaw, inscribed 'WAKITIPU'
27 Lake Wakatipu and Mount Earnslaw, inscribed 'WAKATIPU'

28 Huia
29 White Terrace, Rotomahana
30 Otira Gorge and Mount Ruapehu

31 Brown Kiwi
32 Maori War Canoe

33 Pink Terrace, Rotomahana
34 Kea and Kaka

35 Milford Sound
36 Mount Cook

(Des H. Young (½d.), J. Gaut (1d.), W. Bock (2d., 3d., 9d., 1s.), E. Howard (4d., 6d., 8d.), E. Luke (others). Eng A. Hill (2½d., 1s.), J. A. C. Harrison (5d.), Rapkin (others). Recess Waterlow)

1898 (5 Apr). No wmk. P 12 to 16.

No.	Type	Description	Unused	Used
246	**23**	½d. purple-brown	8·50	1·50
		a. Imperf between (pair)	£1700	£1400
		b. Purple-slate	8·50	1·50
		c. Purple-black	8·50	2·75
247	**24**	1d. blue and yellow-brown	6·00	60
		a. Imperf between (horiz pair)	£1300	£1300
		b. Imperf vert (horiz pair)	£900	£1000
		c. Imperf horiz (vert pair)	£900	£1000
		d. Blue and brown	6·50	80
		da. Imperf between (vert pair)	£1300	£1300
248	**25**	2d. lake	38·00	25
		a. Imperf vert (horiz pair)	£600	£1000
		b. Rosy lake	38·00	25
		ba. Imperf between (vert pair)	£1400	
		bb. Imperf vert (horiz pair)	£600	
249	**26**	2½d. sky-blue (inscr 'WAKITIPU')	11·00	50·00
		a. Blue	11·00	50·00
250	**27**	2½d. blue (inscr 'WAKATIPU')	50·00	8·50
		a. Deep blue	50·00	8·50
251	**28**	3d. yellow-brown	27·00	7·50
252	**29**	4d. bright rose	18·00	19·00
		a. Lake-rose	18·00	23·00
		b. Dull rose	16·00	19·00
253	**30**	5d. sepia	85·00	£200
		a. Purple-brown	55·00	22·00
254	**31**	6d. green (*to deep green*)	65·00	45·00
		a. Grass-green	£200	£225
255	**32**	8d. indigo	75·00	50·00
		a. Prussian blue	75·00	50·00
256	**33**	9d. purple	75·00	45·00
257	**34**	1s. vermilion	80·00	30·00
		a. Dull red	80·00	30·00
		ab. Imperf between (pair)	£5500	
258	**35**	2s. grey-green	£160	£140
		a. Imperf between (vert pair)	£5500	£5500
259	**36**	5s. vermilion	£300	£475
246/259 *Set of 13*			£850	£800

Collectors are warned against faked examples of the imperforate between errors, made from imperforate plate proofs.

37 Lake Taupo and Mount Ruapehu

(Recess Govt Printer, Wellington)

1899 (May)–**03**. Thick, soft Pirie paper. No wmk. P 11.

260	**27**	2½d. blue (6.99)	25·00	5·00
		a. Imperf between (horiz pair)	£1500	
		b. Imperf horiz (vert pair)	£600	
		c. Deep blue	25·00	5·00
261	**28**	3d. yellow-brown (5.00)	25·00	2·25
		a. Imperf between (pair)	£1500	
		b. Imperf vert (horiz pair)	£600	
		c. Deep brown	25·00	2·25
		ca. Imperf between (horiz pair)	£1500	
262	**37**	4d. indigo and brown (8.99)	6·00	3·50
		a. Bright blue and chestnut	6·00	3·50
		b. Deep blue and bistre-brown	6·00	3·50
263	**30**	5d. purple-brown (6.99)	50·00	6·50
		a. Deep purple-brown	50·00	6·50
		ab. Imperf between (pair)	£3250	
264	**31**	6d. deep green	70·00	75·00
		a. Yellow-green	£100	£130
265		6d. pale rose (5.5.00)	50·00	9·00
		a. Imperf vert (horiz pair)	£550	
		b. Imperf between (horiz pair)	£1200	
		c. Rose-red	50·00	9·00
		ca. Printed double	£800	£850
		cb. Imperf between (vert pair)	£1600	
		cc. Imperf vert (horiz pair)	£450	
		cd. Showing part of sheet wmk (7.02)*	£100	£110
		d. Scarlet	80·00	26·00
		da. Imperf vert (horiz pair)	£750	
266	**32**	8d. indigo	55·00	22·00
		a. Prussian blue	55·00	22·00
267	**33**	9d. deep purple (8.99)	60·00	40·00
		a. Rosy purple	50·00	19·00
268	**34**	1s. red (5.00)	70·00	14·00
		a. Dull orange-red	70·00	8·00
		b. Dull brown-red	70·00	19·00
		c. Bright red	75·00	42·00
269	**35**	2s. blue-green (7.99)	£150	55·00
		a. Laid paper (1.03)	£225	£250
		b. Grey-green	£150	65·00
270	**36**	5s. vermilion (7.99)	£275	£375
		a. Carmine-red	£325	£450
260/270 *Set of 11*			£700	£500

* No. 265cd is on paper without general watermark, but showing the words 'LISBON SUPERFINE' wmkd once in the sheet; the paper was obtained from Parsons Bros, an American firm with a branch at Auckland.

38

1900. Thick, soft Pirie paper. Wmk double-lined 'NZ' and Star, W **38** (sideways*). P 11.

271	**13**	½d. black	7·50	20·00
		x. Wmk sideways reversed	£300	£250
272	**15**	2d. bright purple	32·00	21·00
		w. Wmk sideways inverted	£100	50·00
		y. Wmk sideways inverted and reversed	—	£250

* The normal sideways wmk on Nos. 271/272 shows the top of the star pointing to the left, *as seen from the back of the stamp.*

39 White Terrace, Rotomahana

40 Commemorative of the New Zealand Contingent in the South African War

41

1½d. Major re-entry (R. 2/12)

(Des J. Nairn (1½d.). Recess Govt Printer, Wellington)

1900 (Mar–Dec). Thick, soft Pirie paper. W **38**. P 11.

273	**23**	½d. pale yellow-green (7.3.00)	19·00	7·00
		a. Yellow-green	10·00	2·25
		b. Green	10·00	2·00
		ba. Imperf between (pair)	£600	
		c. Deep green	10·00	2·00
		w. Wmk inverted	55·00	28·00
		y. Wmk inverted and reversed	£110	50·00
274	**39**	1d. crimson (7.3.00)	14·00	20
		a. Rose-red	14·00	20
		ab. Imperf between (pair)	£1600	£1800
		ac. Imperf vert (horiz pair)	£650	
		b. Lake	50·00	5·00
		w. Wmk inverted	†	£300
		x. Wmk reversed	†	£225
		y. Wmk inverted and reversed	†	£400
275	**40**	1½d. khaki (7.12.00)	£1200	£750
		a. Brown	60·00	50·00
		ab. Imperf vert (horiz pair)	£1200	
		ac. Imperf (pair)	£1300	
		b. Chestnut	10·00	4·00
		ba. Imperf vert (horiz pair)	£1200	
		bb. Imperf horiz (vert pair)	£1800	
		c. Pale chestnut	10·00	4·00
		ca. Imperf (pair)	£1300	
		d. Major re-entry	£200	£130
276	**41**	2d. dull violet (3.00)	20·00	65
		a. Imperf between (pair)	£1500	
		b. Mauve	25·00	1·50
		c. Purple	16·00	75
		ca. Imperf between (pair)	£1400	

The above ½d. stamps are slightly smaller than those of the previous printing. A new plate was made to print 240 stamps instead of 120 as previously, and to make these fit the watermarked paper, the border design was redrawn and contracted, the centre vignette remaining as before. The 2d. stamp is also from a new plate providing smaller designs.

42

(Des G. Bach and G. Drummond. Eng J. A. C. Harrison. Recess Waterlow)

1901 (1 Jan). Universal Penny Postage. No wmk. P 12 to 16.

277	**42**	1d. carmine	3·50	4·50

All examples of No. 277 show a minute dot above the upper left corner of the value tablet which is not present on later printings.

(Recess Govt Printer, Wellington)

1901 (Feb–Dec). Thick, soft Pirie paper with vertical mesh. W **38**.

(a) P 11

278	**42**	1d. carmine	6·00	25
		a. Imperf vert (horiz pair)	£400	
		b. Deep carmine	6·00	25
		ba. Imperf vert (horiz pair)	£400	
		c. Carmine-lake	24·00	11·00
		x. Wmk reversed	†	80·00
		y. Wmk inverted and reversed	—	£120

(b) P 14

279	**23**	½d. green (11.01)	24·00	7·50
280	**42**	1d. carmine	65·00	25·00
		a. Imperf vert (horiz pair)	£325	
		y. Wmk inverted and reversed	£170	80·00

(c) P 14×11

281	**23**	½d. green	13·00	17·00
		a. Deep green	13·00	17·00
		b. Perf 11×14	14·00	27·00
282	**42**	1d. carmine	£275	£110
		a. Perf 11×14	£2250	£850

*(d) P 11 and 14 mixed**

283	**23**	½d. green	55·00	85·00
284	**42**	1d. carmine	£275	£110

* The term 'mixed' is applied to stamps from sheets which were at first perforated 14, or 14×11, and either incompletely or defectively perforated. These sheets were patched on the back with strips of paper, and re-perforated 11 in those parts where the original perforation was defective.

Nos. 278/284 were printed from new plates supplied by Waterlow. These were subsequently used for Nos. 285/307 with later printings on Cowan paper showing considerable plate wear.

WATERMARK VARIETIES. The watermark on the Basted Mills version of the W **38** paper used for Nos. 285/292 occurs indiscriminately normal, reversed, inverted etc.

(Recess Govt Printer, Wellington)

1901 (Dec). Thin, hard Basted Mills paper with vertical mesh. W **38**.

(a) P 11

285	**23**	½d. green	90·00	£130
286	**42**	1d. carmine	£150	£130

(b) P 14

287	**23**	½d. green	45·00	45·00
		a. Imperf vert (horiz pair)	£425	
288	**42**	1d. carmine	21·00	10·00
		a. Imperf vert (horiz pair)	£300	
		b. Imperf horiz (vert pair)	£300	

(c) P 14×11

289	**23**	½d. green	50·00	70·00
		a. Deep green	50·00	70·00
		b. Perf 11×14	28·00	50·00
290	**42**	1d. carmine	38·00	20·00
		a. Perf 11×14	10·00	4·50

(d) Mixed perfs

291	**23**	½d. green	70·00	£130
292	**42**	1d. carmine	75·00	80·00

(Recess Govt Printer, Wellington)

1902 (Jan). Thin, hard Cowan paper with horizontal mesh. No wmk.

(a) P 11

293	**23**	½d. green	£200	£225

(b) P 14

294	**23**	½d. green	35·00	9·00
295	**42**	1d. carmine	13·00	4·50

(c) P 14×11

296	**23**	½d. green	£140	£225
		a. Perf 11×14	£200	£350
297	**42**	1d. carmine	£110	£130
		a. Perf 11×14	£130	£180

(d) Mixed perfs

298	**23**	½d. green	£180	£250
299	**42**	1d. carmine	£120	£160

43 'Single' Wmk

SIDEWAYS WATERMARKS. In its sideways format the single NZ and Star watermark W **43**, exists indiscriminately sideways, sideways inverted, sideways reversed and sideways inverted plus reversed.

(Recess Govt Printer, Wellington)

1902 (Apr). Thin, hard Cowan paper. W **43**.

(a) P 11

300	**23**	½d. green	85·00	£130
301	**42**	1d. carmine	£800	£750

(b) P 14

302	**23**	½d. green	10·00	1·50
		a. Imperf vert (horiz pair)	£300	
		b. Deep green	10·00	1·50
		ba. Imperf vert (horiz pair)	£300	
		c. Yellow green	12·00	1·50
		d. Pale yellow-green	22·00	4·25
		w. Wmk inverted	55·00	23·00
		x. Wmk reversed	55·00	32·00
		y. Wmk inverted and reversed	90·00	45·00
303	**42**	1d. carmine	3·00	10
		a. Imperf horiz (vert pair)	£200	
		b. Booklet pane of 6 (21.8.02)	£275	
		c. Pale carmine	3·00	10
		ca. Imperf horiz (vert pair)	£200	
		cb. Booklet pane of 6	£275	
		*d. Deep carmine**	32·00	4·00
		w. Wmk inverted	90·00	42·00
		x. Wmk reversed	90·00	42·00
		y. Wmk inverted and reversed	95·00	42·00

(c) P 14×11

304	**23**	½d. green	32·00	£140
		a. Deep green	35·00	£140
		b. Perf 11×14	32·00	£100
305	**42**	1d. carmine	£100	£120
		a. Perf 11×14	£150	£140
		*ab. Deep carmine**	£550	£550

(d) Mixed perfs

306	**23**	½d. green	42·00	75·00
		a. Deep green	50·00	75·00
307	**42**	1d. carmine	38·00	50·00
		a. Pale carmine	38·00	50·00
		*b. Deep carmine**	£275	£300
		y. Wmk inverted and reversed		

* Nos. 303*d*, 305*ab* and 307*b* were printed from a plate made by Waterlow & Sons, known as the 'Reserve' plate. The stamps do not show evidence of wearing and the area surrounding the upper part of the figure is more deeply shaded. This plate was subsequently used to produce Nos. 362, 364 and 366/369.

A special plate, made by W. R. Royle & Sons, showing a minute dot between the horizontal rows, was introduced in 1902 to print the booklet pane, No. 303b. A special characteristic of the booklet pane was that the pearl in the top left-hand corner was large. Some panes exist with the outer edges imperforate.

(Recess Govt Printer, Wellington)

1902 (28 Aug)–**07**. Thin, hard Cowan paper. W **43** (sideways on 3d., 5d., 6d., 8d., 1s. and 5s.).

(a) P 11

308	**27**	2½d. blue (5.03)	38·00	12·00
		a. Deep blue	38·00	12·00
		w. Wmk inverted	£200	95·00
		x. Wmk reversed	£225	55·00
		y. Wmk inverted and reversed	£350	90·00
309	**28**	3d. yellow-brown	42·00	3·50
		a. Bistre-brown	48·00	3·50
		b. Pale bistre	55·00	6·00
310	**37**	4d. deep blue and deep brown/bluish (27.11.02)	6·00	75·00
		a. Imperf vert (horiz pair)	£650	
311	**30**	5d. red-brown (4.03)	55·00	10·00
		a. Deep brown	50·00	8·00
		b. Sepia	60·00	21·00
312	**31**	6d. rose (9.02)	40·00	7·50
		a. Rose-red	40·00	7·50
		ab. Wmk upright (?1.03)	£2750	£2000
		b. Rose-carmine	50·00	7·50
		ba. Imperf vert (horiz pair)	£850	
		bb. Imperf horiz (vert pair)		
		c. Bright carmine-pink	60·00	8·00
		d. Scarlet	75·00	18·00
313	**32**	8d. blue (2.03)	55·00	11·00
		a. Steel-blue	55·00	11·00
		ab. Imperf vert (horiz pair)	£2000	
		ac. Imperf horiz (vert pair)	£2000	
314	**33**	9d. purple (5.03)	70·00	12·00
		w. Wmk inverted	£250	£140
		x. Wmk reversed	£275	£225
		y. Wmk inverted and reversed	£325	£275
315	**34**	1s. brown-red (11.02)	75·00	16·00
		a. Bright red	75·00	16·00
		b. Orange-red	75·00	9·00
		ba. Error. Wmk W **12b** (inverted)	—	£2000
		c. Orange-brown	70·00	23·00
316	**35**	2s. green (4.03)	£160	65·00
		a. Blue-green	£150	45·00

No.	Type	Description	Unused	Used
		x. Wmk reversed	£750	
		w. Wmk inverted	£450	£180
317	**36**	5s. deep red (6.03)	£300	£400
		a. Wmk upright	£325	£425
		b. Vermilion	£275	£375
		ba. Wmk upright	£325	£425
		w. Wmk inverted	£1500	£850
		(b) P 14		
318	**40**	1½d. chestnut (2.07)	27·00	60·00
		a. Major re-entry	£300	
319	**41**	2d. grey-purple (12.02)	5·50	3·00
		a. Purple	5·50	3·00
		ab. Imperf vert (horiz pair)	£550	£850
		ac. Imperf horiz (vert pair)	£800	
		b. Bright reddish purple	6·50	4·00
320	**27**	2½d. blue (1906)	27·00	5·00
		a. Deep blue	27·00	5·00
		w. Wmk inverted	£170	£130
		x. Wmk reversed	†	£300
		y. Wmk inverted and reversed	£375	£200
321	**28**	3d. bistre-brown (1906)	30·00	8·00
		a. Imperf vert (horiz pair)	£950	
		b. Bistre	30·00	8·00
		c. Pale yellow-bistre	65·00	20·00
322	**37**	4d. deep blue and deep brown/*bluish* (1903)	7·50	4·00
		a. Imperf vert (horiz pair)	£650	
		b. Imperf horiz (vert pair)	£650	
		c. Centre inverted	†	*
		d. Blue and chestnut/bluish	4·00	3·25
		e. Blue and ochre-brown/bluish	4·00	3·25
		w. Wmk inverted	60·00	35·00
		x. Wmk reversed	£140	£100
		y. Wmk inverted and reversed	£225	£180
323	**30**	5d. black-brown (1906)	60·00	38·00
		a. Red-brown	40·00	16·00
324	**31**	6d. bright carmine-pink (1906)	60·00	9·50
		a. Imperf vert (horiz pair)	£850	
		b. Rose-carmine	60·00	9·50
325	**32**	8d. steel-blue (1907)	50·00	11·00
326	**33**	9d. purple (1906)	50·00	9·00
		w. Wmk inverted	£375	£275
327	**34**	1s. orange-brown (1906)	80·00	9·50
		a. Orange-red	75·00	9·50
		b. Pale red	£170	65·00
328	**35**	2s. green (1.06)	£130	32·00
		a. Blue-green	£150	42·00
		aw. Wmk inverted	£800	£250
		ax. Wmk reversed	†	—
		ay. Wmk inverted and reversed	£800	£250
329	**36**	5s. deep red (1906)	£225	£300
		a. Wmk upright	£225	£375
		b. Dull red	£225	£300
		ba. Wmk upright	£225	£375
		(c) Perf compound of 11 and 14		
330	**40**	1½d. chestnut (1907)	£1600	
331	**41**	2d. purple (1903)	£500	£425
332	**28**	3d. bistre-brown (1906)	£950	£750
333	**37**	4d. blue and yellow-brown (1903)	£450	£500
		x. Wmk reversed	—	£850
334	**30**	5d. red-brown (1906)	£1700	£1400
335	**31**	6d. rose-carmine (1907)	£450	£450
336	**32**	8d. steel-blue (1907)	£1400	£1500
337	**33**	9d. purple (1906)	£1700	£1600
338	**36**	5s. deep red (wmk sideways)(1906)	£3250	£3250
		(d) Mixed perfs		
339	**40**	1½d. chestnut (1907)	£1600	
340	**41**	2d. purple (1903)	£450	£325
341	**28**	3d. bistre-brown (1906)	£900	£700
342	**37**	4d. blue and chestnut/*bluish* (1904)	£400	£450
		a. Blue and yellow-brown/bluish	£400	£450
		w. Wmk inverted	£950	£850
		x. Wmk reversed	£950	£900
343	**30**	5d. red-brown (1906)	£1300	£110
344	**31**	6d. rose-carmine (1907)	£425	£425
		a. Bright carmine-pink	£450	£450
345	**32**	8d. steel-blue (1907)	£1400	£1400
346	**33**	9d. purple (1906)	£1500	£1600
347	**35**	2s. blue-green (1906)	£1700	£1800
348	**36**	5s. vermilion (Wmk upright) (1906)	£2500	£3000
		w. Wmk inverted		

Two sizes of paper were used for the above stamps:

(1) A sheet containing 240 wmks, with a space of 9 mm between each.

(2) A sheet containing 120 wmks, with a space of 24 mm between each vertical row.

Size (1) was used for the ½d., 1d., 2d. and 4d., and size (2) for 2½d., 5d., 9d. and 2s. The paper in each case exactly fitted the plates, and had the watermark in register, though in the case of the 4d., the plate of which contained only 80 stamps, the paper was cut up to print it. The 3d., 6d., 8d. and 1s. were printed on variety (1), but with watermark sideways: by reason of this, examples from the margins of the sheets show parts of the words 'NEW ZEALAND POSTAGE' in large letters, and some have no watermark at all. For the 1½d. and 5s. stamps variety (1) was also used, but two watermarks appear on each stamp.

* The only known example of No. 322c, postmarked at Picton on 21 March 1904, was purchased for the New Zealand Post archive collection in 1998.

(Recess Govt Printer, Wellington)

1904 (Feb). Printed from new 'dot' plates made by W. R. Royle & Sons. Thin, hard Cowan paper. W **43**.

No.	Type	Description	Unused	Used
		(a) P 14		
349	**42**	1d. rose-carmine	11·00	50
		a. Pale carmine	11·00	50
		w. Wmk inverted	£120	38·00
		y. Wmk inverted and reversed	£120	45·00
		(b) P 11×14		
350	**42**	1d. rose-carmine	£180	£130
		(c) Mixed perfs		
351	**42**	1d. rose-carmine	42·00	55·00
		a. Pale carmine	42·00	55·00

These plates have a dot in the margins between stamps, level with the small pearls at the side of the design, but it is frequently cut out by the perforations. However, they can be further distinguished by the notes below.

In 1906 fresh printings were made from four new plates, two of which, marked in the margin 'W1' and 'W2', were supplied by Waterlow Bros and Layton, and the other two, marked 'R1' and 'R2', by W. R. Royle & Son. The intention was to note which pair of plates wore the best and produced the best results. They can be distinguished as follows:

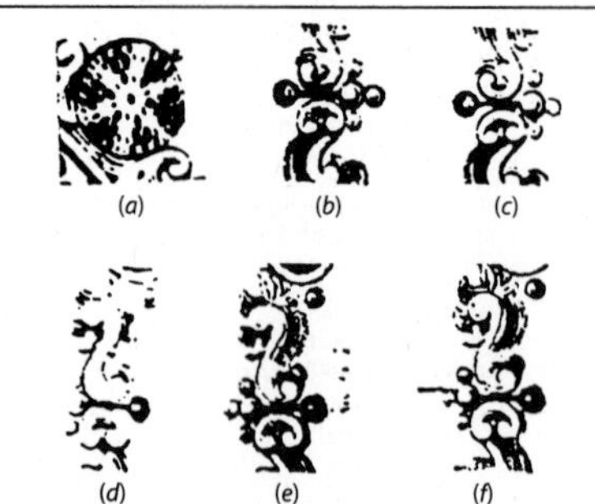

(*a*) Four o'clock flaw in rosette at top right corner. Occurs in all these plates but not in the original Waterlow plates.
(*b*) Pearl at right strong.
(*c*) Pearl at right weak.
(*d*) Dot at left and S-shaped ornament unshaded.
(*e*) S-shaped ornament with one line of shading within.
(*f*) As (*e*) but with line from left pearl to edge of stamp.

'Dot' plates comprise (*a*) and (*d*).
Waterlow plates comprise (*a*), (*b*) and (*e*).
Royle plates comprise (*a*), (*c*) and (*e*) and the line in (*f*) on many stamps but not all.

(Recess Govt Printer, Wellington)

1906. Thin, hard Cowan paper. W **43**.

No.	Type	Description	Unused	Used
		(a) Printed from new Waterlow plates		
		(i) P 14		
352	**42**	1d. deep rose-carmine	55·00	3·75
		a. Imperf horiz (vert pair)	£300	
		b. Aniline carmine	50·00	3·75
		ba. Imperf vert (horiz pair)	£300	
		c. Rose-carmine	50·00	3·75
		y. Wmk inverted and reversed	—	£400
		(ii) P 11		
353	**42**	1d. aniline carmine	£700	£850
		(iii) P 11×14		
354	**42**	1d. rose-carmine	£475	£900
		a. Perf 14×11	£500	£850
		(iv) Mixed perfs		
355	**42**	1d. deep rose-carmine	£425	£650
		(b) Printed from new Royle plates		
		(i) P 14		
356	**42**	1d. rose-carmine	12·00	1·25
		a. Imperf horiz (vert pair)	£250	£325
		b. Bright rose-carmine	13·00	1·40
		w. Wmk inverted	†	£500
		y. Wmk inverted and reversed	—	£250
		(ii) P 11		
357	**42**	1d. bright rose-carmine	£110	£225
		(iii) P 11×14		
358	**42**	1d. rose-carmine	£100	£200
		a. Perf 14×11	£150	£200
		(iv) Mixed perfs		
359	**42**	1d. rose-carmine	£160	£275
		(v) P 14×14½ (comb)		
360	**42**	1d. bright rose-carmine	85·00	60·00
		a. Rose-carmine	85·00	60·00

Nos. 360/360*a* are known both with and without the small dot. See also No. 386.

1905 (15 June)–**06**. Stamps supplied to penny-in-the-slot machines.

(i) 'Dot' plates of 1904
(ii) Waterlow 'reserve' plate of 1902

No.	Type	Description	Unused	Used
		(a) Imperf top and bottom; zigzag roulette 9½ on one or both sides, two large holes at sides		
361	**42**	1d. rose-carmine (*i*)	£200	£300
362		1d. deep carmine (*ii*)	£225	
		(b) As last but rouletted 14½ (8.7.05)		
363	**42**	1d. rose-carmine (*i*)	£200	£300
364		1d. deep carmine (*ii*)	£425	
		(c) Imperf all round, two large holes each side (6.3.06)		
365	**42**	1d. rose-carmine (*i*)	£160	
366		1d. deep carmine (*ii*)	£170	£300
		(d) Imperf all round (21.6.06)		
367	**42**	1d. deep carmine (*ii*)	£180	£300
		(e) Imperf all round. Two small indentations on back of stamp (1.06)		
368	**42**	1d. deep carmine (*ii*)	£225	£300
		(f) Imperf all round; two small pin-holes in stamp (21.6.06)		
369	**42**	1d. deep carmine (*ii*)	£200	£300

No. 365 *only* exists from strips of Nos. 361 or 363 (resulting from the use of successive coins) which have been separated by scissors. Similarly strips of Nos. 362 and 364 can produce single copies of No. 366 but this also exists in singles from a different machine.

Most used copies of Nos. 361/367 are forgeries and they should only be collected on cover.

44 Maori Canoe, *Te Arawa*

45 Maori art

46 Landing of Cook

46a Annexation of New Zealand

3d. White flaw behind Chieftain (Left pane, R. 4/2)

(Des L. J. Steele. Eng W. R. Bock. Typo Govt Printer, Wellington)

1906 (1–17 Nov). New Zealand Exhibition, Christchurch. W **43** (sideways). P 14.

No.	Type	Description	Unused	Used
370	**44**	½d. emerald-green	40·00	40·00
371	**45**	1d. vermilion	16·00	16·00
		a. Claret	£8000	£11000
372	**46**	3d. brown and blue	55·00	85·00
		a. Flaw behind Chieftain	£350	£450
373	**46a**	6d. pink and olive-green (17.11)	£200	£275
370/373 *Set of 4*			£275	£375

The 1d. in claret was the original printing, which was considered unsatisfactory.

47 (T **28** reduced)

48 (T **31** reduced)

49 (T **34** reduced)

(New plates (except 4d.), supplied by Perkins Bacon. Recess Govt Printer, Wellington).

1907–08. Thin, hard Cowan paper. W **43**.

No.	Type	Description	Unused	Used
		(a) P 14 (line)		
374	**23**	½d. green (1907)	42·00	16·00
		a. Imperf (pair)	£375	
		b. Yellow-green	35·00	7·50
		c. Deep yellow-green	35·00	7·50
375	**47**	3d. brown (6.07)	95·00	28·00
376	**48**	6d. carmine-pink (3.07)	48·00	14·00
		a. Red	55·00	40·00
		(b) P 14×13, 13½ (comb)		
377	**23**	½d. green (1907)	17·00	17·00
		a. Yellow-green	10·00	8·50
		b. Imperf three sides (top stamp of vert pair)	£500	
378	**47**	3d. brown (2.08)	55·00	50·00
		a. Yellow-brown	55·00	50·00
379	**37**	4d. blue and yellow-brown/*bluish* (6.08)	42·00	60·00
380	**48**	6d. pink (2.08)	£425	£170
381	**49**	1s. orange-red (12.07)	£140	65·00
		(c) P 14×15 (comb)		
382	**23**	½d. yellow-green (1907)	8·50	1·00
		a. Imperf three sides (top stamp of vert pair)	£450	
		y. Wmk inverted and reversed	—	£325
383	**47**	3d. brown (8.08)	50·00	15·00
		a. Yellow-brown	50·00	15·00
384	**48**	6d. carmine-pink (8.08)	50·00	11·00
385	**49**	1s. orange-red (8.08)	£110	24·00
		a. Deep orange-brown	£325	£900

The ½d. stamps of this 1907–1908 issue have a minute dot in the margin between the stamps, where not removed by the perforation. (See note after No. 351*a*). Those perforated 14 can be distinguished from the earlier stamps, Nos. 302/302*d*, by the absence of plate wear. This is most noticeable on the 1902 printings as a white patch at far left, level with the bottom of the 'P' in 'POSTAGE'. Such damage is not present on the new plates used for Nos. 374/374*c*.

Stamps of Types **47**, **48** and **49** also have a small dot as described in note after No. 351*a*.

TYPOGRAPHY PAPERS.

1908–30. De La Rue paper is chalk-surfaced and has a smooth finish. The watermark is as illustrated. The gum is toned and strongly resistant to soaking.

Jones paper is chalk-surfaced and has a coarser texture, is poorly surfaced and the ink tends to peel. The outline of the watermark commonly shows on the surface of the stamp. The gum is colourless or only slightly toned and washes off readily.

Cowan paper is chalk-surfaced and is white and opaque. The watermark is usually smaller than in the 'Jones' paper and is often barely visible.

Wiggins Teape paper is chalk-surfaced and is thin and hard. It has a vertical mesh with a narrow watermark, whereas the other papers have a horizontal mesh and a wider watermark.

50

(Typo Govt Printer, Wellington, from Perkins Bacon plate).

1908 (1 Dec). De La Rue chalk-surfaced paper. W **43**. P 14×15 (comb).

No.	Type	Description	Unused	Used
386	**50**	1d. carmine	23·00	3·25
		w. Wmk inverted	—	£120

The design of T **50** differs from T **42** by alterations in the corner rosettes and by the lines on the globe which are diagonal instead of vertical.

51

52

53

(Eng. P.B. Typo Govt Printer, Wellington)

1909 (8 Nov)–**12**. De La Rue chalk-surfaced paper with toned gum. W **43**. P 14×15 (comb).

387 **51** ½d. yellow-green ... 5·00 50
aa. Deep green ... 5·00 50
a. Imperf (pair) ... £275
b. Booklet pane. 5 stamps plus label in position 1 (4.10) ... £800
c. Ditto, but label in position 6 (4.10) ... £800
d. Booklet pane of 6 (4.10) ... £250
e. Ditto, but with coloured bars on selvedge (5.12) ... £225
w. Wmk inverted ... † £750

Stamps with blurred and heavy appearance are from booklets.

(Eng W. R. Royle & Son, London. Recess Govt Printer, Wellington)

1909 (8 Nov)–**16**. T **52** and similar portraits.

*(a) W **43**. P 14×14½ (comb)*

388 2d. mauve ... 9·50 6·50
a. Deep mauve ... 18·00 6·50
w. Wmk inverted ... † £900
389 3d. chestnut ... 23·00 1·25
390 4d. orange-red ... 27·00 27·00
390*a* 4d. yellow (1912) ... 7·00 10·00
aw. Wmk inverted ... £550 £225
391 5d. brown (1910) ... 17·00 5·00
a. Red-brown ... 17·00 5·00
w. Wmk inverted ... — —
392 6d. carmine (1910) ... 40·00 2·00
a. Deep carmine (29.10.13) ... 50·00 3·50
393 8d. indigo-blue ... 13·00 3·50
a. Deep bright blue ... 13·00 3·50
w. Wmk inverted ... 90·00 55·00
394 1s. vermilion (1910) ... 50·00 5·00
w. Wmk inverted ... £400 £170
388/394 *Set of 8* ... £160 55·00

*(b) W **43**. P 14 (line)**

395 3d. chestnut (1910) ... 50·00 20·00
396 4d. orange (1910) ... 22·00 15·00
397 5d. brown ... 26·00 4·50
a. Red-brown (15.9.11) ... 26·00 5·00
w. Wmk inverted
398 6d. carmine ... 42·00 10·00
399 1s. vermilion ... 65·00 14·00
395/399 *Set of 5* ... £180 55·00

*(c) W **43** (sideways) (paper with widely spaced wmk as used for Nos. 308 and 320 – see note below No. 348). P 14 (line)**

400 8d. indigo-blue (8.16) ... 55·00 95·00
a. No wmk ... £120 £200

*(d) W **43**. P 14×13½ (comb)†*

401 3d. chestnut (1915) ... 75·00 £130
a. Vert pair. P 14×13½ and 14×14½ ... £250 £475
w. Wmk inverted ... £450 £450
402 5d. red-brown (1916) ... 19·00 3·00
a. Vert pair. P 14×13½ and 14×14½ ... 60·00 £170
403 6d. carmine (1915) ... 75·00 £130
a. Vert pair. P 14×13½ and 14×14½ ... £250 £600
404 8d. indigo-blue (3.16) ... 50·00 3·25
a. Vert pair. P 14×13½ and 14×14½ ... 70·00 £160
b. Deep bright blue ... 55·00 3·25
ba. Vert pair. P 14×13½ and 14×14½ ... 80·00 £170
w. Wmk inverted ... £180 55·00
401/404 *Set of 4* ... £190 £225

* In addition to showing the usual characteristics of a line perforation, these stamps may be distinguished by their vertical perforation which measures 13.8. Nos. 388/394 generally measure vertically 14 to 14.3. An exception is 13.8 one vertical side but 14 the other.

† The 3d. and 6d. come in full sheets perf 14×13½. The 3d., 5d. and 6d. values also exist in two combinations: (*a*) five top rows perf 14×13½ with five bottom rows perf 14×14½ and (*b*) four top rows perf 14×13½ with six bottom rows perf 14×14½. The 8d. perf 14×13½ only exists from combination (*b*).

1d. 'Feather' flaw (Plate 12, R. 3/1)

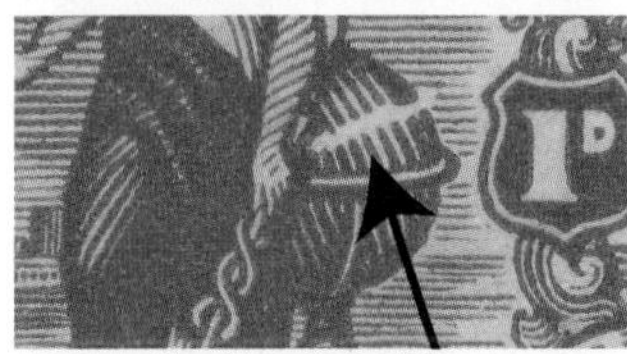

1d. 'Globe' flaw (Plate 12, R. 5/24)

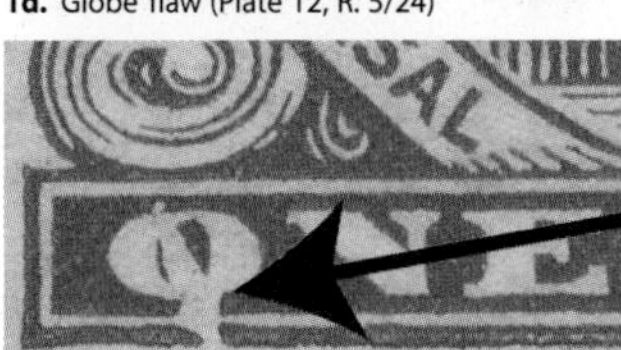

1d. 'Q' flaw (Plate 13, R. 10/19)

1d. 'N' flaw (Plate 12, R. 9/23, *printings from 1925*)

(Eng P.B. Typo Govt Printer, Wellington)

1909 (8 Nov)–**27**. P 14×15 (comb).

*(a) W **43**. De La Rue chalk-surfaced paper with toned gum*

405 **53** 1d. carmine ... 1·75 10
a. Imperf (pair) ... £400
b. Booklet pane of 6 (4.10) ... £200
c. Ditto, but with coloured bars on selvedge (5.12) ... £160
d. 'Feather' flaw ... 32·00 10·00
e. 'Globe' flaw ... 32·00 10·00
f. 'Q' flaw ... 70·00 30·00
w. Wmk inverted ... £120 £110
y. Wmk inverted and reversed

*(b) W **43**. Jones chalk-surfaced paper with white gum*

406 **53** 1d. deep carmine (6.24) ... 21·00 9·00
a. On unsurfaced paper. Pale carmine ... £400
b. Booklet pane of 6 with bars on selvedge (1.12.24) ... £160
c. 'Feather' flaw ... £100 60·00
d. 'Globe' flaw ... £100 55·00
w. Wmk inverted ... £140 70·00

*(c) W **43**. De La Rue unsurfaced medium paper with toned gum*

407 **53** 1d. rose-carmine (4.25) ... 45·00 £140
a. 'Feather' flaw ... £325
b. 'Globe' flaw ... £325

*(d) W **43** (sideways). De La Rue chalk-surfaced paper with toned gum*

408 **53** 1d. bright carmine (4.25) ... 12·00 50·00
a. No wmk ... 24·00 80·00
b. Imperf (pair) ... £250
c. 'Feather' flaw ... £100
d. 'Globe' flaw ... £100

(e) No wmk, but bluish 'NZ' and Star lithographed on back. Art paper

409 **53** 1d. rose-carmine (7.25) ... 2·00 8·00
a. 'NZ' and Star in black ... 24·00
b. 'NZ' and Star colourless ... 24·00
c. 'Feather' flaw ... 70·00 95·00
d. 'Globe' flaw ... 70·00 95·00

*(f) W **43**. Cowan thick, opaque, chalk-surfaced paper with white gum*

410 **53** 1d. deep carmine (8.25) ... 12·00 1·00
a. Imperf (pair) ... £200 £225
b. Booklet pane of 6 with bars and adverts on selvedge ... £190
c. 'Feather' flaw ... 75·00 45·00
d. 'Globe' flaw ... 75·00 45·00
e. 'N' flaw ... £130 £130
w. Wmk inverted ... £120 60·00
x. Wmk reversed (1926) ... 14·00 4·00
xa. Booklet pane of 6 with bars and adverts on selvedge (1927) ... £180
xc. 'Feather' flaw ... £140 70·00
xd. 'Globe' flaw ... £140 70·00
xe. 'N' flaw ... £180 £110
y. Wmk inverted and reversed (1926) ... £150 £120

*(g) W **43**. Wiggins Teape thin, hard, chalk-surfaced paper with white gum*

411 **53** 1d. rose-carmine (6.26) ... 40·00 28·00
a. 'Feather' flaw ... £180 75·00
b. 'Globe' flaw ... £180 75·00
c. 'N' flaw ... £200 £100
w. Wmk inverted ... £110 60·00

Examples of No. 405 with a blurred and heavy appearance are from booklets.

No. 406*a* comes from a sheet on which the paper coating was missing from the right-hand half.

Many stamps from the sheets of No. 408 were without watermark or showed portions of 'NEW ZEALAND POSTAGE' in double-lined capitals.

AUCKLAND EXHIBITION, 1913.
(**59**) **60**

1913 (1 Dec). Auckland Industrial Exhibition. Nos. 387*aa*, 389, 392 and 405 optd with T **59** by Govt Printer, Wellington.

412 **51** ½d. deep green ... 22·00 55·00
413 **53** 1d. carmine ... 28·00 50·00
a. 'Feather' flaw ... £325 £425
b. 'Globe' flaw ... £325 £425
414 **52** 3d. chestnut ... £130 £250
415 6d. carmine ... £160 £300
412/415 *Set of 4* ... £300 £600

These overprinted stamps were only available for letters in New Zealand and to Australia.

(Des H. L. Richardson. Recess Govt Printer, Wellington, from plates made in London by P.B.)

1915 (30 July)–**30**. W **43**. P 14×13½ (comb) (see notes below).

(a) Cowan unsurfaced paper

416 **60** 1½d. grey-slate ... 3·25 2·50
a. Perf 14×14½ (1915) ... 5·00 1·75
aw. Wmk inverted ... £500 £500
b. Vert pair. Nos. 416/416a ... 35·00 £100
417 2d. bright violet ... 12·00 65·00
a. Perf 14×14½ ... 6·00 50·00
b. Vert pair. Nos. 417/417a ... 28·00 £160
418 2d. yellow (15.1.16) ... 7·50 32·00
a. Perf 14×14½ ... 7·50 32·00
b. Vert pair. Nos. 418/418a ... 21·00 £250
419 2½d. blue ... 3·25 7·00
a. Perf 14×14½ (1916) ... 8·00 32·00
b. Vert pair. Nos. 419/419a ... 40·00 £180
420 3d. chocolate ... 22·00 1·25
aw. Wmk inverted ... £225 £150
ax. Wmk reversed
b. Perf 14×14½ ... 13·00 2·00
bw. Wmk inverted ... £450 £170
bx. Wmk reversed ... £650
c. Vert pair. Nos. 420 and 420b ... 50·00 £140
cw. Wmk inverted
cx. Wmk reversed
421 4d. yellow ... 4·25 60·00
a. Re-entry (Pl 20 R. 1/6) ... 50·00
b. Re-entry (Pl 20 R. 4/10) ... 60·00
c. Perf 14×14½ ... 4·25 60·00
d. Vert pair. Nos. 421 and 421c ... 27·00 £250
422 4d. bright violet (7.4.16) ... 11·00 50
a. Imperf three sides (top stamp of vertical pair) ... £1500
b. Re-entry (Pl 20 R. 1/6) ... 55·00 35·00
c. Re-entry (Pl 20 R. 4/10) ... 65·00 40·00
dx. Wmk reversed ... — £350
e. Perf 14×14½ ... 7·00 50
ex. Wmk reversed ... — £350
f. Vert pair. Nos. 422 and 422e ... 60·00 £150
fx. Wmk reversed
g. Deep purple (7.26) ... 50·00 15·00
h. Ditto. Perf 14×14½ ... 7·00 50
ha. Imperf three sides (top stamp of vertical pair) ... £1500
hb. Vert pair. Nos. 422*g*/422*h* ... £2500
hw. Wmk inverted ... † £1900
423 4½d. deep green ... 18·00 28·00
a. Perf 14×14½ (1915) ... 12·00 55·00
b. Vert pair. Nos. 423/423a ... 55·00 £170
424 5d. light blue (4.22) ... 7·00 1·00
a. Imperf (pair) ... £140 £180
aa. Imperf (top stamp of vertical pair) ... £850
bw. Wmk inverted ... — £300
c. Perf 14×14½ ... 12·00 38·00
d. Pale ultramarine (5.30) ... 17·00 13·00
da. Perf 14×14½ ... 32·00 25·00
db. Vert pair. Nos. 424*d*/424da ... 80·00 £250
425 6d. carmine ... 9·00 50
a. Imperf three sides (top stamp of vert pair) ... £1500
bw. Wmk inverted ... £200 £160
bx. Wmk reversed ... — £250
by. Wmk inverted and reversed ... † £1900
c. Carmine-lake (11.27) ... £500 £400
d. Perf 14×14½ (1915) ... 10·00 60
dw. Wmk inverted ... £190 65·00
e. Vert pair. Nos. 425 and 425d ... 65·00 £140
426 7½d. red-brown ... 14·00 32·00
a. Perf 14×14½ (10.20) ... 11·00 80·00
b. Vert pair. Nos. 426/426a ... 50·00 £225
427 8d. indigo-blue (19.4.21) ... 15·00 60·00
a. Perf 14×14½ ... 8·50 55·00
b. Vert pair. Nos. 427/427a ... 38·00 £180
428 8d. red-brown (3.22) ... 32·00 1·50
429 9d. sage-green ... 17·00 2·75
a. Imperf (pair) ... £1500
b. Imperf three sides (top stamp of vert pair) ... £1500
c. Yellowish olive (12.25) ... 20·00 24·00
dw. Wmk inverted ... † £1900
e. Perf 14×14½ ... 15·00 32·00
f. Vert pair. Nos. 429 and 429e ... 75·00 £225
430 1s. vermilion ... 21·00 2·25
a. Imperf (pair) ... £2250
aa. Imperf (top stamp of vertical pair) ... £2000
bw. Wmk inverted ... £375 £350
c. Perf 14×14½ (1915) ... 14·00 50
ca. Pale orange-red (4.24) ... 30·00 25·00
cb. Imperf (pair) ... £325
cba. Imperf (top stamp of vertical pair) ... £750
cc. Orange-brown (20.1.28) ... £600 £450
cw. Wmk inverted ... £300
d. Vert pair. Nos. 430 and 430c ... 75·00 £275
dw. Wmk inverted
416/430c *Set of 15* ... £130 £225

*(b) W **43** (sideways on 2d., 3d. and 6d.). Thin paper with widely spaced watermark as used for Nos. 308 and 320 (see note below No. 348). P 14×13½ (comb) (see notes below) (1½d.) or 14 (line) (others)*

431 **60** 1½d. grey-slate (3.16) ... 3·00 11·00
a. No wmk ... 5·50 23·00
b. Perf 14×14½ ... 3·00 11·00
ba. No wmk ... 5·50 23·00
by. Wmk inverted and reversed ... £500 £500
c. Vert pair. Nos. 431 and 431b ... 26·00 £120
ca. Vert pair. Nos. 431a and 431ba ... 60·00 £190
432 2d. yellow (6.16) ... 6·00 60·00
a. No wmk ... 75·00 £160
433 3d. chocolate (6.16) ... 7·00 50·00
a. No wmk ... 75·00 £160
434 6d. carmine (6.16) ... 11·00 £110
a. No wmk ... £100 £225
431/434 *Set of 4* ... 25·00 £200

The 1½d., 2½d., 4½d. and 7½d. have value tablets as shown in T **60**. For the other values the tablets are shortened and the ornamental border each side of the crown correspondingly extended.

With the exception of Nos. 432/434 stamps in this issue were comb-perforated 14×13½, 14×14½ or a combination of the two.

The 1½d. (No. 416), 2½d., 4d. (both), 4½d., 5d., 6d., 7½d., 8d. red-brown, 9d. and 1s. are known to have been produced in sheets perforated 14×13½ throughout with the 4d. bright violet, 5d., 6d. and 1s. known perforated 14×14½ throughout.

On the sheets showing the two perforations combined, the top four rows are usually perforated 14×13½ and the bottom six 14×14½. Combination sheets are known to have been produced in this form for the 1½d. (Nos. 416 and 431), 2d. (both), 2½d., 3d., 4d. (both), 4½d., 6d., 7½d., 8d. indigo-blue, 9d. and 1s. On a late printing of the 4d. deep purple and 5d. pale ultramarine the arrangement is different with the top five rows perforated 14×14½ and the bottom five 14×13½.

With the exception of Nos. 432/4 any with perforations measuring 14×14 or nearly must be classed as 14×14½, this being an irregularity of the comb machine, and not a product of the 14-line machine.

4d Re-entry (Plate 20, R. 1/6)

4d Re-entry (Plate 20, R. 4/10)

During the laying-down of plate 20 for the 4d., from the roller-die which also contained dies of other values, an impression of the 4½d. value was placed on R. 1/6 and of the 2½d. on R. 4/10. These errors were subsequently corrected by re-entries of the 4d. impression, but on R. 1/6 traces of the original impression can be found in the right-hand value tablet and above the top frame line, while on R. 4/10 the foot of the '2' is visible in the left-hand value tablet with traces of '½' to its right.

61

62

WAR STAMP
(63)

T **62** (from local plates) can be identified from T **61** (prepared by Perkins Bacon) by the shading on the portrait. This is diagonal on T **62** and horizontal on T **61**.

(Die eng W. R. Bock. Typo Govt Printer, Wellington, from plates made by P.B. (T **61**) or locally (T **62**))

1915 (30 July)–**33**. W **43**. P 14×15.

No.	Type	Description	Unused	Used
		(a) De La Rue chalk-surfaced paper with toned gum		
435	**61**	½d. green	1·50	20
		a. Booklet pane of 6 with bars on selvedge	£170	
		b. Yellow-green	4·00	1·75
		ba. Booklet pane of 6 with bars on selvedge	£150	
		c. Very thick, hard, highly surfaced paper with white gum (12.15)	12·00	55·00
		w. Wmk inverted	£100	£140
		x. Wmk reversed	—	£180
		y. Wmk inverted and reversed	—	£225
436	**62**	1½d. grey-black (4.16)	13·00	1·75
		a. Black	13·00	2·00
		y. Wmk inverted and reversed	—	£350
437	**61**	1½d. slate (5.9.16)	9·00	20
		w. Wmk inverted	—	£400
438		1½d. orange-brown (9.18)	2·25	20
		w. Wmk inverted	£200	£170
		x. Wmk reversed	†	—
		y. Wmk inverted and reversed	£350	£300
439		2d. yellow (9.16)	2·25	20
		a. Pale yellow	6·00	1·25
		w. Wmk inverted	£150	
440		3d. chocolate (5.19)	7·00	1·50
435/440 *Set of 6*			32·00	3·50
		(b) W **43**. *Jones chalk-surfaced paper with white gum*		
441	**61**	½d. green (10.24)	10·00	15·00
		a. Booklet pane of 6 with bars on selvedge (1.12.24)	£160	
		w. Wmk inverted	£110	£110
442		2d. dull yellow (7.24)	10·00	60·00
		w. Wmk inverted	£150	
443		3d. deep chocolate (3.25)	22·00	35·00
441/443 *Set of 3*			38·00	£100
		(c) No wmk, but bluish 'NZ' and Star lithographed on back. Art paper		
444	**61**	½d. apple-green (4.25)	2·75	9·50
		a. 'NZ' and Star almost colourless	5·00	
445		2d. yellow (7.25)	13·00	75·00
		(d) W **43**. *Cowan thick, opaque, chalk-surfaced paper with white gum*		
446	**61**	½d. green (8.25)	1·75	20
		a. Booklet pane of 6 with bars and adverts on selvedge	£180	
		aa. Imperf 3 sides (top stamp of vertical pair)	£1200	
		ab. Booklet pane of 6 with bars on selvedge (1928)	£425	
		bw. Wmk inverted	£110	£110
		bx. Wmk reversed (1926)	13·00	3·75
		bxa. Booklet pane of 6 with bars and adverts on selvedge (1927)	£150	
		by. Wmk inverted and reversed (1926)	£140	£110
		c. Perf 14 (1927)	3·00	35
		ca. Booklet pane of 6 with bars on selvedge (1928)	£140	
		cb. Booklet pane of 6 with bars and adverts on selvedge (1928)	£140	
		cw. Wmk inverted	£200	£110
447		1½d. orange-brown (P 14) (8.29)	8·50	45·00
		a. Perf 14×15 (7.33)	38·00	90·00
448		2d. yellow (8.25)	11·00	1·50
		ax. Wmk reversed (1927)	35·00	£130
		ay. Wmk inverted and reversed (1927)	£300	£650
		b. Perf 14 (1929)	2·75	20
		bw. Wmk inverted	£140	50·00
449		3d. chocolate (8.25)	8·00	2·00
		aw. Wmk inverted	£110	
		b. Perf 14 (1929)	7·50	4·25
446/449 *Set of 4*			18·00	45·00
		(e) W **43**. *Wiggins Teape thin, hard, chalk-surfaced paper*		
450	**61**	1½d. orange-brown (P 14) (1930)	55·00	£130
451		2d. yellow (5.26)	14·00	25·00
		aw. Wmk inverted	90·00	60·00
		b. Perf 14 (10.27)	15·00	24·00
		bw. Wmk inverted	£110	55·00

The designs of these stamps also differ as described beneath No. 434.

Stamps from booklet panes often have blurred, heavy impressions. Different advertisements can be found on the listed booklet panes.

Examples of No. 446aa, which occur in booklet panes, show the stamps perforated at top.

The ½d. and 2d. (Nos. 446c and 448b) are known showing ½d. and 1d. local surcharges from 1932 applied diagonally in blue to stamps previously stuck on to envelopes or cards at Christchurch (½d.) or Wellington (1d.).

1915 (24 Sept). No. 435 optd with T **63**.

No.	Type	Description	Unused	Used
452	**61**	½d. green	2·25	50

64 'Peace' and Lion

65 'Peace' and Lion

66

67

66a

67a

(Des and typo D.L.R. from plates by P.B., Waterlow and D.L.R.)

1920 (27 Jan). Victory. De La Rue chalk-surfaced paper. W **43** (sideways on ½d., 1½d., 3d. and 1s.). P 14.

No.	Type	Description	Unused	Used
453	**64**	½d. green	3·00	2·50
		a. Pale yellow-green	27·00	28·00
454	**65**	1d. carmine-red	4·50	60
		a. Bright carmine	7·50	70
		w. Wmk inverted	35·00	22·00
		x. Wmk reversed	£120	60·00
455	**66**	1½d. brown-orange	3·00	50
456	**66a**	3d. chocolate	12·00	14·00
457	**67**	6d. violet	14·00	17·00
		a. Wmk sideways	†	£1000
		w. Wmk inverted	£650	£450
458	**67a**	1s. orange-red	24·00	50·00
453/458 *Set of 6*			55·00	75·00

The above stamps were placed on sale in London in November, 1919.

2d. 2d.

TWOPENCE
(68)

69

1922 (Mar). No. 453 surch with T **68**.

No.	Type	Description	Unused	Used
459	**64**	2d. on ½d. green (R.)	6·50	1·40

(Des and eng W. R. Bock, Typo Govt Printer, Wellington)

1923 (1 Oct)–**25**. Restoration of Penny Postage. W **43**. P 14×15.

No.	Type	Description	Unused	Used
		(a) De La Rue chalk-surfaced paper with toned gum		
460	**69**	1d. carmine	4·75	60
		(b) Jones chalk-surfaced paper with white gum		
461	**69**	1d. carmine (3.24)	14·00	11·00
		a. Wmk sideways	†	£700
		w. Wmk inverted	80·00	60·00
		(c) Cowan unsurfaced paper with very shiny gum		
462	**69**	1d. carmine-pink (4.25)	48·00	27·00

The paper used for No. 462 is similar to that of Nos. 416/430.

70 Exhibition Buildings

(Des H. L. Richardson. Eng and typo Govt Printer, Wellington)

1925 (17 Nov). Dunedin Exhibition. Cowan chalk-surfaced paper. W **43**. P 14×15.

No.	Type	Description	Unused	Used
463	**70**	½d. yellow-green/*green*	3·00	16·00
		w. Wmk inverted	£225	£180
464		1d. carmine/*rose*	4·25	7·50
		w. Wmk inverted	£325	£200
465		4d. mauve/*pale mauve*	30·00	75·00
		a. 'POSTAGF' at right (R. 10/1)	£100	£180
463/465 *Set of 3*			32·00	90·00

71 King George V as Field-Marshal

72 King George V as Admiral

(Des H. L. Richardson; plates by B.W. (1d. from sheets), P.B. (1d. from booklets), Royal Mint, London (others). Typo Govt Printer, Wellington)

1926 (12 July)–**34**. W **43**. P 14.

No.	Type	Description	Unused	Used
		(a) Jones chalk-surfaced paper with white gum		
466	**72**	2s. deep blue	80·00	70·00
		w. Wmk inverted	65·00	80·00
467		3s. mauve	£110	£200
		w. Wmk inverted	£130	£250
		(b) Cowan thick, opaque, chalk-surfaced paper with white gum		
468	**71**	1d. rose-carmine (15.11.26)	75	20
		a. Imperf (pair)	£250	
		ab. Imperf three sides (horiz pair)	£400	£500
		b. Booklet pane of 6 with bars on selvedge (1928)	£150	
		c. Booklet pane of 6 with bars and adverts on selvedge (1928)	£130	
		dw. Wmk inverted	£100	55·00
		e. Perf 14×15 (3.27)	65	50
		ea. Booklet pane of 6 with bars and adverts on selvedge (1934)	£140	
		ew. Wmk inverted	£120	55·00
		ex. Wmk reversed	15·00	
469	**72**	2s. light blue (5.27)	75·00	29·00
470		3s. pale mauve (9.27)	£130	£190
468/470 *Set of 3*			£180	£200
		(c) Wiggins Teape thin, hard, chalk-surfaced paper with white gum		
471	**71**	1d. rose-carmine (6.30)	45·00	16·00
		w. Wmk inverted	£225	£110

No. 468ex exists in a range of colours including scarlet and deep carmine to magenta but we have insufficient evidence to show that these were issued.

Following the reduction of the postage rate to ½d. on 1 June 1932 the firm of R. H. White & Co. Ltd. of Stratford returned a quantity of envelopes stamped with 1d. stamps (No. 468) to the New Plymouth post office who surcharged the stamps 'HALFPENNY' in purple using a handstamp. The covers were then returned to the firm for normal use. Similar local surcharges were applied diagonally to 1d. stamps stuck onto postcards or lettercards at Dunedin, Greymouth and Invercargill in blue or at Palmerston North in purple. With the exception of the Greymouth provisional, where 40 mint examples were acquired by a stamp dealer, these local surcharges are only found unused, no gum, or used.

Nos. 472 to 543 are vacant.

73 Nurse

74 Smiling Boy

(Typo Govt Printing Office, Wellington)

1929–30. Anti-Tuberculosis Fund. T **73** and similar design. W **43**. P 14.

No.	Type	Description	Unused	Used
		(a) Inscribed 'HELP STAMP OUT TUBERCULOSIS'		
544		1d. +1d. scarlet (11.12.29)	11·00	19·00
		w. Wmk inverted	£375	£275
		(b) Inscribed 'HELP PROMOTE HEALTH'		
545		1d. +1d. scarlet (29.10.30)	20·00	45·00

HIGH VALUES. From 1931 postal requirements for higher values were met by the 'Arms' 'Stamp Duty' adhesives (F145 etc).

(Des L. C. Mitchell. Dies eng and plates made Royal Mint, London (1d.), Govt Ptg Office, Wellington from W. R. Bock die (2d.). Typo Govt Ptg Office, Wellington)

1931 (31 Oct). Health Stamps. W **43** (sideways). P 14½×14.

No.	Type	Description	Unused	Used
546	**74**	1d. +1d. scarlet	75·00	75·00
547		2d. +1d. blue	75·00	60·00

75 New Zealand Lake Scenery

FIVE PENCE
(76)

(Des L. C. Mitchell. Plates, Royal Mint, London. Typo Govt Ptg Office)

1931 (10 Nov)–**35**. Air. W **43**. P 14×14½.

No.	Type	Description	Unused	Used
548	**75**	3d. chocolate	20·00	16·00
		a. Perf 14×15 (4.35)	£130	£425
549		4d. blackish purple	20·00	22·00
550		7d. brown-orange	20·00	9·00
548/550 *Set of 3*			55·00	42·00

1931 (18 Dec). Air. Surch with T **76**. W **43**. P 14×14½.

No.	Type	Description	Unused	Used
551	**75**	5d. on 3d. green (R.)	10·00	10·00

77 Hygeia, Goddess of Health

78 The Path to Health

(Des R. E. Tripe and W. J. Cooch. Eng H. T. Peat. Recess Govt Printing Office, Wellington)

1932 (18 Nov). Health Stamp. W **43**. P 14.

No.	Type	Description	Unused	Used
552	**77**	1d. +1d. carmine	25·00	32·00
		w. Wmk inverted	£450	£250
		x. Wmk reversed	†	£600

(Des J. Berry. Eng H. T. Peat. Recess Govt Printing Office, Wellington)

1933 (8 Nov). Health Stamp. W **43**. P 14.

No.	Type	Description	Unused	Used
553	**78**	1d. +1d. carmine	17·00	22·00
		w. Wmk inverted	£325	£200

TRANS-TASMAN
AIR MAIL
"FAITH IN AUSTRALIA."
(79)

80 Crusader

1934 (17 Jan). Air. T **75** in new colour optd with T **79**. W **43**. P 14×14½.

554	**75**	7d. light blue (B.)	35·00	50·00

(Des J. Berry. Recess D.L.R.)

1934 (25 Oct). Health Stamp. W **43** (sideways). P 14×13½.

555	**80**	1d. +1d. carmine	11·00	17·00

81 Collared Grey Fantail

82 Brown Kiwi

83 Maori Woman

84 Maori Carved House

85 Mt. Cook

86 Maori Girl

87 Mitre Peak

88 Striped Marlin

89 Harvesting

90 Tuatara Lizard

91 Maori Panel

92 Parson Bird

93 Captain Cook at Poverty Bay

94 Mt. Egmont

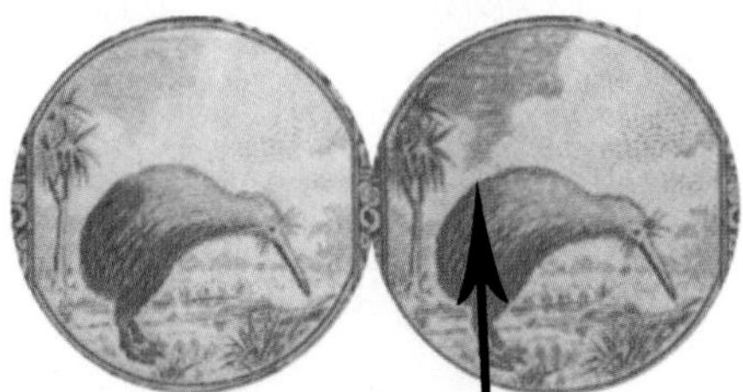
Die I Die II

2s. 'CAPTAIN COQK' (R. 1/4)

(Des J. Fitzgerald (½d., 4d.), C. H. and R. J. G. Collins (1d.) M. Matthews (1½d.), H. W. Young (2d.), L. C. Mitchell (2½d., 3d., 8d., 1s., 3s.), W. J. Cooch and R. E. Tripe (5d.), T. I. Archer (6d.), I. F. Calder (9d.) and I. H. Jenkins (2s.). Litho Waterlow (9d.). Recess D.L.R. (remainder))

1935 (1 May)–**36**. W **43** (sideways on. 8d.).

556	**81**	½d. bright green, P 14×13½	3·25	1·50
		w. Wmk inverted (12.35)	6·50	8·00
557	**82**	1d. scarlet (Die I), P 14×13½	3·50	1·50
		aw. Wmk inverted (2.36)	8·50	14·00
		b. Perf 13½×14 (1936)	75·00	65·00
		c. Die II. Perf 14×13½ (18.11.35)	13·00	4·75
		ca. Booklet pane of 6 with adverts on selvedge	60·00	
		cw. Wmk inverted	17·00	7·50
558	**83**	1½d. red-brown, P 14×13½	15·00	21·00
		a. Perf 13½×14 (11.35)	6·50	14·00
		ay. Wmk inverted and reversed (2.36)	20·00	45·00
559	**84**	2d. orange, P 14×13½	3·75	3·50
		w. Wmk inverted	£1200	£600
560	**85**	2½d. chocolate and slate, P 13–14×13½	14·00	40·00
		aw. Wmk inverted	40·00	95·00
		b. Perf 13½×14 (11.35)	11·00	30·00
		bx. Wmk reversed	†	£2750
561	**86**	3d. brown, P 14×13½	12·00	4·25
		w. Wmk inverted	£1100	£500
562	**87**	4d. black and sepia, P 14	4·75	3·75
		w. Wmk inverted	£850	£550
563	**88**	5d. ultramarine, P 13–14×13½	23·00	40·00
		a. Double print, one albino	†	—
		bw. Wmk inverted	†	£750
		c. Perf 13½×14	28·00	50·00
564	**89**	6d. scarlet, P 13½×14	9·00	12·00
		w. Wmk inverted	£650	£475
565	**90**	8d. chocolate, P 14×13½	13·00	20·00
		w. Wmk sideways inverted	£600	£375
566	**91**	9d. scarlet and black, P 14×14½	16·00	7·00
567	**92**	1s. deep green, P 14×13½	24·00	20·00
		w. Wmk inverted	—	£650
568	**93**	2s. olive-green, P 13–14×13½	50·00	50·00
		a. 'CAPTAIN COQK'	£190	£160
		bw. Wmk inverted	£170	95·00
		c. Perf 13½×14 (1935)	65·00	60·00
		ca. 'CAPTAIN COQK'	£200	£170
569	**94**	3s. chocolate and yellow-brown, P 13–14×13½	19·00	55·00
		a. Perf 13½×14 (11.35)	20·00	60·00
		aw. Wmk inverted	†	£1500
		ay. Wmk inverted and reversed (1936)	£450	£475
556/569 *Set of* 14			£170	£225

Some stamps from sheets perforated 14×13½ by De La Rue sometimes show the horizontal perforations nearer 13½.

In the 2½d., 5d., 2s. and 3s. perf 13–14×13½ the horizontal perforations of each stamp are in two sizes, one half of each horizontal side measuring 13 and the other 14.

See also Nos. 577/590 and 630/631.

95 Bell Block Aerodrome

96 King George V and Queen Mary

(Des J. Berry. Eng Stamp Printing Office, Melbourne. Recess Govt Printing Office, Wellington)

1935 (4 May). Air. W **43**. P 14.

570	**95**	1d. carmine	1·00	70
		w. Wmk inverted	£200	£110
571		3d. violet	4·50	3·00
		w. Wmk inverted	£250	£120
572		6d. blue	8·00	3·00
		w. Wmk inverted	£300	£130
570/572 *Set of* 3			12·00	6·00

(Frame by J. Berry. Recess B.W.)

1935 (7 May). Silver Jubilee. W **43**. P 11×11½.

573	**96**	½d. green	75	1·00
574		1d. carmine	1·00	80
575		6d. red-orange	20·00	35·00
573/575 *Set of* 3			20·00	35·00

97 The Key to Health

98 'Multiple Wmk'

(Des S. Hall. Recess John Ash, Melbourne)

1935 (30 Sept). Health Stamp. W **43**. P 11.

576	**97**	1d. +1d. scarlet	2·50	3·75

WATERMARKS. In W 43 the wmk units are in vertical columns widely spaced and the sheet margins are unwatermarked or wmkd 'NEW ZEALAND POSTAGE' in large letters.

In W **98** the wmk units are arranged alternately in horizontal rows closely spaced and are continued into the sheet margins.

Stamps with W **98** sideways show the top of the star pointing to the right, *as seen from the back*. Sideways inverted varieties have the top of the star to left *as seen from the back*.

(Litho Govt Ptg Office, Wellington (9d). Recess Waterlow or D.L.R. (others))

1936–42. W **98**.

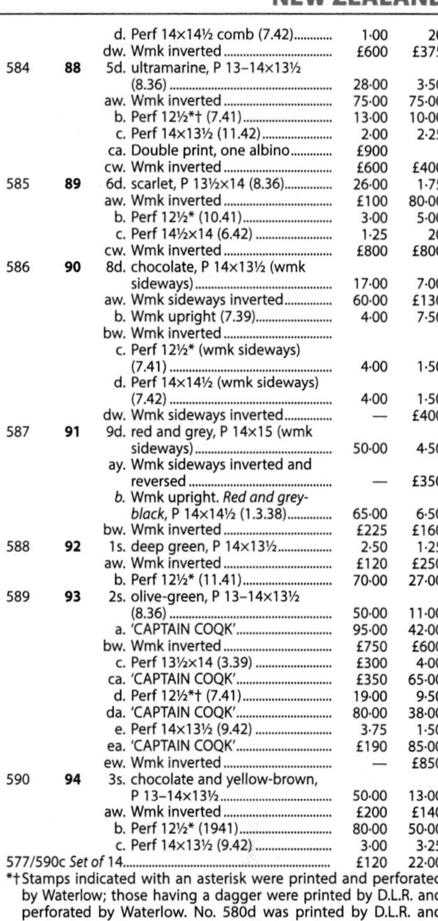

577	**81**	½d. bright green, P 14×13½	3·50	10
		w. Wmk inverted	5·50	11·00
578	**82**	1d. scarlet (Die II), P 14×13½ (4.36)	4·50	10
		w. Wmk inverted	10·00	8·50
579	**83**	1½d. red-brown, P 14×13½ (6.36)	20·00	7·50
580	**84**	2d. orange, P 14×13½ (3.36)	30	10
		aw. Wmk inverted	£600	£400
		b. Perf 12½† (6.41)	7·00	20
		bw. Wmk inverted		
		c. Perf 14 (6.41)	38·00	1·25
		d. Perf 14×15 (6.41)	38·00	26·00
581	**85**	2½d. chocolate and slate, P 13–14×13½	11·00	26·00
		aw. Wmk inverted	80·00	£150
		b. Perf 14 (11.36)	10·00	1·50
		bw. Wmk inverted	60·00	95·00
		c. Perf 14×13½ (11.42)	1·00	5·50
582	**86**	3d. brown, P 14×13½	35·00	1·50
		w. Wmk inverted	75·00	75·00
583	**87**	4d. black and sepia, P 14×13½	9·00	1·00
		aw. Wmk inverted	32·00	42·00
		b. Perf 12½* (8.41)	48·00	20·00
		bw. Wmk inverted	†	—
		c. Perf 14, line (11.41)	65·00	£130
		d. Perf 14×14½ comb (7.42)	1·00	20
		dw. Wmk inverted	£600	£375
584	**88**	5d. ultramarine, P 13–14×13½ (8.36)	28·00	3·50
		aw. Wmk inverted	75·00	75·00
		b. Perf 12½*† (7.41)	13·00	10·00
		c. Perf 14×13½ (11.42)	2·00	2·25
		ca. Double print, one albino	£900	
		cw. Wmk inverted	£600	£400
585	**89**	6d. scarlet, P 13½×14 (8.36)	26·00	1·75
		aw. Wmk inverted	£100	80·00
		b. Perf 12½* (10.41)	3·00	5·00
		c. Perf 14½×14 (6.42)	1·25	20
		cw. Wmk inverted	£800	£800
586	**90**	8d. chocolate, P 14×13½ (wmk sideways)	17·00	7·00
		aw. Wmk sideways inverted	60·00	£130
		b. Wmk upright (7.39)	4·00	7·50
		bw. Wmk inverted		
		c. Perf 12½* (wmk sideways) (7.41)	4·00	1·50
		d. Perf 14×14½ (wmk sideways) (7.42)	4·00	1·50
		dw. Wmk sideways inverted	—	£400
587	**91**	9d. red and grey, P 14×15 (wmk sideways)	50·00	4·50
		ay. Wmk sideways inverted and reversed	—	£350
		b. Wmk upright. *Red and grey-black*, P 14×14½ (1.3.38)	65·00	6·50
		bw. Wmk inverted	£225	£160
588	**92**	1s. deep green, P 14×13½	2·50	1·25
		aw. Wmk inverted	£120	£250
		b. Perf 12½* (11.41)	70·00	27·00
589	**93**	2s. olive-green, P 13–14×13½ (8.36)	50·00	11·00
		a. 'CAPTAIN COQK'	95·00	42·00
		bw. Wmk inverted	£750	£600
		c. Perf 13½×14 (3.39)	£300	4·00
		ca. 'CAPTAIN COQK'	£350	65·00
		d. Perf 12½*† (7.41)	19·00	9·50
		da. 'CAPTAIN COQK'	80·00	38·00
		e. Perf 14×13½ (9.42)	3·75	1·50
		ea. 'CAPTAIN COQK'	£190	85·00
		ew. Wmk inverted	—	£850
590	**94**	3s. chocolate and yellow-brown, P 13–14×13½	50·00	13·00
		aw. Wmk inverted	£200	£140
		b. Perf 12½* (1941)	80·00	50·00
		c. Perf 14×13½ (9.42)	3·00	3·25
577/590c *Set of* 14			£120	22·00

*†Stamps indicated with an asterisk were printed and perforated by Waterlow; those having a dagger were printed by D.L.R. and perforated by Waterlow. No. 580d was printed by D.L.R. and perforated by Harrison and No. 583c was printed by Waterlow and perforated by D.L.R. These are all known as 'Blitz perfs' because De La Rue were unable to maintain supplies after their works were damaged by enemy action. All the rest, except the 9d., were printed and perforated by D.L.R.

On stamps printed and perforated by De La Rue the perf 14×13½ varies in the sheet and is sometimes nearer 13½. 2d. perf 14×15 is sometimes nearer 14×14½.

2½d., 5d., 2s. and 3s. In perf 13–14×13½ one half the length of each horizontal perforation measures 13 and the other 14. In perf 14×13½ the horizontal perforation is regular.

4d. No. 583c. is line-perf measuring 14 exactly and has a blackish sepia frame. No. 583d is a comb-perf measuring 14×14.3 or 14×14.2 and the frame is a warmer shade.

2s. No. 589c is comb-perf and measures 13.5×13.75.

For 9d. typographed, see Nos. 630/631.

99 NZ Soldier at Anzac Cove

100 Wool

101 Butter

102 Sheep

103 Apples

104 Exports

(Des L. C. Mitchell. Recess John Ash, Melbourne)

1936 (27 Apr). Charity. 21st Anniversary of 'Anzac' Landing at Gallipoli. W **43**. P 11.

591	**99**	½d. +½d. green	75	1·40
592		1d. +1d. scarlet	1·25	1·10

(Des L. C. Mitchell. Recess John Ash, Melbourne)

1936 (1 Oct). Congress of British Empire Chambers of Commerce, Wellington. Industries Issue. Types **100**/**104**. W **43** (sideways). P 11½.

593		½d. emerald-green	30	30
594		1d. scarlet	30	20
595		2½d. blue	1·50	8·00
596		4d. violet	1·25	5·50
597		6d. red-brown	4·00	6·50
593/597 *Set of* 5			6·50	18·00

105 Health Camp

106 King George VI and Queen Elizabeth

(Des J. Berry. Recess John Ash, Melbourne)

1936 (2 Nov). Health Stamp. W **43** (sideways). P 11.

598	**105**	1d. +1d. scarlet	2·75	3·75

(Recess B.W.)

1937 (13 May). Coronation. W **98**. P 14×13½.

599	**106**	1d. carmine	30	10
600		2½d. Prussian blue	60	2·00
601		6d. red-orange	80	1·75
599/601 *Set of* 3			1·50	3·50

107 Rock climbing

108 King George VI **108a**

(Des G. Bull and J. Berry. Recess John Ash, Melbourne)

1937 (1 Oct). Health Stamp. W **43**. P 11.

602	**107**	1d. +1d. scarlet	4·25	3·75

Broken ribbon flaw (R. 6/6 of Pl 8)

(Des W. J. Cooch. Recess B.W.)

1938–44. W **98**. P 14×13½.

603	**108**	½d. green (1.3.38)	7·00	10
		w. Wmk inverted (from booklets)	30·00	7·00
604		½d. orange-brown (10.7.41)	20	40
		w. Wmk inverted		
605		1d. scarlet (1.7.38)	5·00	10
		a. Broken ribbon	£110	
		w. Wmk inverted (from booklets)	24·00	4·75
606		1d. green (21.7.41)	20	10
		w. Wmk inverted	£110	75·00
607	**108a**	1½d. purple-brown (26.7.38)	26·00	3·25
		w. Wmk inverted (from booklets)	42·00	13·00
608		1½d. scarlet (1.2.44)	20	80
		w. Wmk inverted	—	£225
609		3d. blue (26.9.41)	20	10
		w. Wmk inverted	—	£275
603/609 *Set of* 7			38·00	4·00

For other values see Nos. 680/689.

109 Children playing

110 Beach Ball

(Des J. Berry. Recess B.W.)

1938 (1 Oct). Health Stamp. W **98**. P 14×13½.

610	**109**	1d. +1d. scarlet	5·50	3·25

(Des S. Hall. Recess Note Printing Branch, Commonwealth Bank of Australia, Melbourne)

1939 (16 Oct). Health Stamps. Surcharged with new value. W **43**. P 11.

611	**110**	1d. on ½d. +½d. green	4·75	6·00
612		2d. on 1d. +1d. scarlet	5·50	6·00

111 Arrival of the Maoris, 1350

112 *Endeavour*, Chart of NZ and Captain Cook

113 British Monarchs

114 Tasman with his ship and chart

115 Signing Treaty of Waitangi, 1840

116 Landing of immigrants, 1840

117 Road, rail, sea and air transport

118 HMS *Britomart* at Akaroa, 1840

119 *Dunedin* and 'frozen mutton route' to London

120 Maori council

121 Gold mining in 1861 and 1940

122 Giant Kauri tree

(Des L. C. Mitchell (½d., 3d., 4d.); J. Berry (others). Recess B.W.)

1940 (2 Jan–8 Mar). Centenary of Proclamation of British Sovereignty. Types **111**/**122**. W **98**. P 14×13½ (2½d.), 13½×14 (5d.) or 13½ (others).

613	**111**	½d. blue-green	60	10
614	**112**	1d. chocolate and scarlet	4·00	10
615	**113**	1½d. light blue and mauve	30	60
616	**114**	2d. blue-green and chocolate	1·50	10
617	**115**	2½d. blue-green and blue	2·00	1·00
618	**116**	3d. purple and carmine	4·00	1·25
619	**117**	4d. chocolate and lake	14·00	1·50
620	**118**	5d. pale blue and brown	10·00	3·75
621	**119**	6d. emerald-green and violet	11·00	1·25
622	**120**	7d. black and red	2·25	4·00
623		8d. black and red (8.3)	11·00	6·00
624	**121**	9d. olive-green and orange	8·00	2·00
625	**122**	1s. sage-green and deep green	13·00	4·25
613/625 *Set of* 13			70·00	23·00

1940 (1 Oct). Health Stamps. As T **110**, but without extra surcharge. W **43**. P 11.

626	**110**	1d. +½d. blue-green	11·00	11·00
627		2d. +1d. brown-orange	11·00	11·00

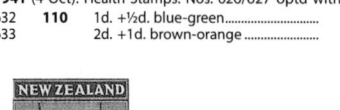

(123) **(123a)** Inserted '2' **(124)**

1941. Nos. 603 and 607 surch as Types **123**/**123a**.

628	**108**	1d. on ½d. green (1.5.41)	1·75	10
629	**108a**	2d. on 1½d. purple-brown (4.41)	1·75	10
		a. Inserted '2'	£650	£450

The variety 'Inserted 2' occurs on the 10th stamp, 10th row. It is identified by the presence of remnants of the damaged '2', and by the spacing of '2' and 'D' which is variable and different from the normal.

(Typo Govt Printing Office, Wellington)

1941. As T **91**, but smaller (17½×20½ *mm*). Chalk-surfaced paper. P 14×15.

(a) W **43**

630	**91**	9d. scarlet and black (5.41)	95·00	32·00
		w. Wmk inverted	†	£450

(b) W **98**

631	**91**	9d. scarlet and black (29.9.41)	3·00	5·00
		w. Wmk inverted	£500	£375

1941 (4 Oct). Health Stamps. Nos. 626/627 optd with T **124**.

632	**110**	1d. +½d. blue-green	50	2·25
633		2d. +1d. brown-orange	50	2·25

125 Boy and Girl on Swing

126 Princess Margaret

127 Queen Elizabeth II as Princess

(Des S. Hall. Recess Note Printing Branch, Commonwealth Bank of Australia, Melbourne)

1942 (1 Oct). Health Stamps. W **43**. P 11.

634	**125**	1d. +½d. blue-green	30	1·25
635		2d. +1d. orange-red	30	1·25

(Des J. Berry. Recess B.W.)

1943 (1 Oct). Health Stamps. Types **126**/**127**. W **98**. P 12.

636		1d. +½d. green	30	1·50
		a. Imperf between (vert pair)	£15000	
637		2d. +1d. red-brown	30	25
		a. Imperf between (vert pair)	£18000	£18000

The watermark is at an angle in relation to the design on single stamps.

TENPENCE

(128)

1944 (1 May). No. 615 surch with T **128**.

662		10d. on 1½d. light blue and mauve	15	30

129 Queen Elizabeth II as Princess and Princess Margaret

130 Statue of Peter Pan, Kensington Gardens

(Recess B.W.)

1944 (9 Oct). Health Stamps. W **98**. P 13½.

663	**129**	1d. +½d. green	30	40
664		2d. +1d. blue	30	30

(Des J. Berry. Recess B.W.)

1945 (1 Oct). Health Stamps. W **98**. P 13½.

665	**130**	1d. +½d. green and buff	15	20
		w. Wmk inverted	£110	£140
666		2d. +1d. carmine and buff	15	20
		w. Wmk inverted	£350	£225

131 Lake Matheson

132 King George VI and Parliament House, Wellington

133 St Paul's Cathedral

134 The Royal Family

135 RNZAF badge and aircraft

136 Army badge, tank and plough

137 Navy badge, HMNZS *Achilles* (cruiser) and *Dominion Monarch* (liner)

138 NZ Coat of Arms, foundry and farm

139 'St George' (Wellington College War Memorial Window)

140 Southern Alps and Franz Joseph Glacier

141 National Memorial Campanile

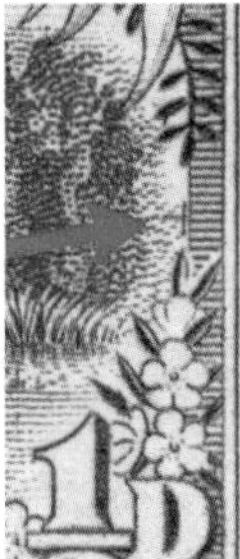

½d. Printer's guide mark (R. 12/3)

3d. Completed rudder (R. 3/2 of Pl 42796 and R. 2/4 of Pl 42883, the latter also showing retouching in the sky around the wing-tip at left, as illustrated)

5d. Trailing aerial (R. 8/1 of Pl 42794)

9d. Guide mark (R. 3/3 of Pl 42723)

(Des J. Berry. Photo Harrison (1½d. and 1s.). Recess B.W. (1d. and 2d.) and Waterlow (others))

1946 (1 Apr). Peace issue. Types **131/141**. W **98** (sideways on 1½d.). P 13 (1d., 2d.), 14×14½ (1½d., 1s.), 13½ (others).

No.	Type	Description	Unused	Used
667	**131**	½d. green and brown	20	65
		a. Printer's guide mark	23·00	38·00
		w. Wmk inverted	£120	80·00
668	**132**	1d. green	10	10
		w. Wmk inverted	85·00	50·00
669	**133**	1½d. scarlet	10	50
		w. Wmk sideways inverted	10	50
670	**134**	2d. purple	15	10
671	**135**	3d. ultramarine and grey	45	15
		a. Completed rudder	19·00	22·00
		b. Ultramarine omitted	£15000	
672	**136**	4d. bronze-green and orange	50	20
		w. Wmk inverted	£200	90·00
673	**137**	5d. green and ultramarine	1·25	1·75
		a. Trailing aerial	40·00	50·00
674	**138**	6d. chocolate and vermilion	20	30
675	**139**	8d. black and carmine	20	30
676	**140**	9d. blue and black	20	30
		a. Guide mark	30·00	42·00
677	**141**	1s. grey-black	1·00	40
667/677 *Set of 11*			3·50	4·00

Only one example of No. 671b is known. It was caused by a paper fold.

142 Soldier helping Child over Stile

2d. +1d. Feathers in hat (R. 8/8 of Pl 43010)

(Des J. Berry. Recess Waterlow)

1946 (24 Oct). Health Stamps. W **98**. P 13½.

No.	Type	Description	Unused	Used
678	**142**	1d. +½d. green and orange-brown	15	15
		a. *Yellow-green and orange-brown*	6·00	12·00
		w. Wmk inverted	80·00	85·00
679		2d. +1d. chocolate and orange-brown	15	15
		a. Feathers in hat	35·00	35·00

144 King George VI

145 Statue of Eros

Plate 1

Plate 2

(Des W. J. Cooch. Recess T **108a**, B.W.; T **144**, D.L.R.)

1947 (1 May)–**52**. W **98** (sideways on 'shilling' values).

No.	Type	Description	Unused	Used
		(a) P 14×13½		
680	**108a**	2d. orange	30	10
		w. Wmk inverted	£250	£350
681		4d. bright purple	80	1·00
682		5d. slate	1·00	1·00
683		6d. carmine	1·00	10
		w. Wmk inverted	£325	£225
684		8d. violet	1·25	1·25
685		9d. purple-brown	2·00	60
		w. Wmk inverted	£110	75·00
		(b) P 14		
686	**144**	1s. red-brown and carmine (Plate 1)	2·00	1·50
		aw. Wmk sideways inverted	25·00	45·00
		b. Wmk upright (Plate 1)	60	80
		c. Wmk upright (Plate 2) (1950)	2·25	1·25
		cw. Wmk inverted	£180	£100
687		1s.3d. red-brown and blue (Plate 2)	2·75	1·25
		aw. Wmk sideways inverted	22·00	45·00
		b. Wmk upright (14.1.52)	2·25	4·50
		bw. Wmk inverted	†	—
688		2s. brown-orange and green (Plate 1)	9·00	2·50
		aw. Wmk sideways inverted	38·00	75·00
		b. Wmk upright (Plate 1)	13·00	20·00
689		3s. red-brown and grey (Plate 2)	4·50	3·50
		w. Wmk sideways inverted	55·00	55·00
680/689 *Set of 10*			20·00	11·00

In head-plate 2 the diagonal lines of the background have been strengthened and result in the upper corners and sides appearing more deeply shaded.

For details of the sideways watermarks, see above No. 577.

(Des J. Berry. Recess Waterlow)

1947 (1 Oct). Health Stamps. W **98** (sideways). P 13½.

No.	Type	Description	Unused	Used
690	**145**	1d. +½d. green	15	15
		w. Wmk sideways inverted	£120	£120
691		2d. +1d. carmine	15	15
		w. Wmk sideways inverted	£150	£170

146 Port Chalmers, 1848

147 Cromwell, Otago

148 First Church, Dunedin

149 University of Otago

(Des J. Berry. Recess B.W.)

1948 (23 Feb). Centennial of Otago. Types **146/149**. W **98** (sideways inverted on 3d.). P 13½.

No.	Type	Description	Unused	Used
692	**146**	1d. blue and green	25	35
		w. Wmk inverted	95·00	85·00
693	**147**	2d. green and brown	25	35
694	**148**	3d. purple	30	60
695	**149**	6d. black and rose	30	60
		w. Wmk inverted	—	£400
692/695 *Set of 4*			1·00	1·75

150 Boy Sunbathing and Children Playing

151 Nurse and Child

(Des E. Linzell. Recess B.W.)

1948 (1 Oct). Health Stamps. W **98**. P 13½.

No.	Type	Description	Unused	Used
696	**150**	1d. +½d. blue and green	15	20
		w. Wmk inverted	£130	£100
697		2d. +1d. purple and scarlet	15	20

1949 ROYAL VISIT ISSUE. Four stamps were prepared to commemorate this event: 2d. Treaty House, Waitangi; 3d. HMS *Vanguard*; 5d. Royal portraits; 6d. Crown and sceptre. The visit did not take place and the stamps were destroyed, although a few examples of the 3d. later appeared on the market. A similar set was prepared in 1952, but was, likewise, not issued.

(Des J. Berry. Photo Harrison)

1949 (3 Oct). Health Stamps. W **98**. P 14×14½.

No.	Type	Description	Unused	Used
698	**151**	1d. +½d. green	25	20
699		2d. +1d. ultramarine	25	20
		a. No stop below 'D' of '1D.' (R. 1/2)	7·00	21·00

POSTAGE

(152)

153 Queen Elizabeth II as Princess and Prince Charles

1950 (28 July). As T F **6**, but without value, surch with T **152**. Chalk-surfaced paper. W **98** (inverted). P 14.

No.	Type	Description	Unused	Used
700	F **6**	1½d. carmine	40	30
		w. Wmk upright	7·50	8·50

(Des J. Berry and R. S. Phillips. Photo Harrison)

1950 (2 Oct). Health Stamps. W **98**. P 14×14½.

No.	Type	Description	Unused	Used
701	**153**	1d. +½d. green	25	20
		w. Wmk inverted	9·00	13·00
702		2d. +1d. plum	25	20
		w. Wmk inverted	£110	£110

154 Christchurch Cathedral

155 Cairn on Lyttelton Hills

156 John Robert Godley

157 Canterbury University College

158 Aerial view of Timaru

(Des L. C. Mitchell (2d.), J. A. Johnstone (3d.) and J. Berry (others). Recess B.W.)

1950 (20 Nov). Centennial of Canterbury, NZ Types **154/158**. W **98** (sideways inverted on 1d. and 3d.). P 13½.

703	**154**	1d. green and blue	40	85
704	**155**	2d. carmine and orange	40	1·00
705	**156**	3d. dark blue and blue	45	1·25
706	**157**	6d. brown and blue	50	1·00
707	**158**	1s. reddish purple and blue	50	1·60
703/707 *Set of 5*			2·00	5·00

159 Takapuna class Yachts

(Des J. Berry and R. S. Phillips. Recess B.W.)

1951 (1 Nov). Health Stamps. W **98**. P 13½.

708	**159**	1½d. +½d. scarlet and yellow	50	1·00
709		2d. +1d. deep green and yellow	50	25
		w. Wmk inverted	£110	£120

160 Princess Anne

161 Prince Charles

3D

(162)

(From photographs by Marcus Adams. Photo Harrison)

1952 (1 Oct). Health Stamps. W **98**. P 14×14½.

710	**160**	1½d. +½d. carmine-red	15	30
711	**161**	2d. +1d. brown	15	20

1952–53. Nos. 604 and 606 surch as T **162**.

712	**108**	1d. on ½d. brown-orange (11.9.53)	50	1·00
		a. 'D' omitted	†	£4500
713		3d. on 1d. green (12.12.52)	10	10

163 Buckingham Palace

164 Queen Elizabeth II

165 Coronation State Coach

166 Westminster Abbey

167 St Edward's Crown and Royal Sceptre

(Des L. C. Mitchell (1s.6d.), J. Berry (others). Recess D.L.R. (2d., 4d.), Waterlow (1s.6d.) Photo Harrison (3d., 8d.))

1953 (25 May). Coronation. Types **163/167**. W **98**. P 13 (2d., 4d.), 13½ (1s.6d.) or 14×14½ (3d., 8d.).

714	**163**	2d. deep bright blue	40	30
715	**164**	3d. brown	30	10
716	**165**	4d. carmine	1·40	2·50
717	**166**	8d. slate-grey	1·00	1·60
718	**167**	1s.6d. purple and ultramarine	2·75	3·25
714/718 *Set of 5*			5·00	7·00

168 Girl Guides

169 Boy Scouts

(Des J. Berry. Photo Harrison)

1953 (7 Oct). Health Stamps. W **98**. P 14×14½.

719	**168**	1½d. +½d. blue	15	10
720	**169**	2d. +1d. deep yellow-green	15	40
		a. Imperf 3 sides (block of 4)	£3500	

No. 720a shows the left-hand vertical pair imperforate at right and the right-hand pair imperforate at left, top and bottom.

170 Queen Elizabeth II

171 Queen Elizabeth II and Duke of Edinburgh

(Des L. C. Mitchell. Recess Waterlow)

1953 (9 Dec). Royal Visit. W **98**. P 13×14 (3d.) or 13½ (4d.).

721	**170**	3d. dull purple	15	10
		w. Wmk inverted	—	£225
722	**171**	4d. deep ultramarine	15	60

172

173 Queen Elizabeth II

174

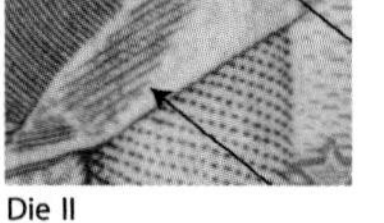

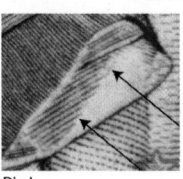

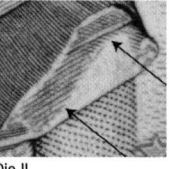

Die I Die II

(Des L. C Mitchell (Types **172/173**), J. Berry (T **174**). Recess D.L.R. (T **173**), B.W. (others))

1953 (15 Dec)–**59**. W **98**. P 14×13½ (T **172**), 14 (T **173**) or 13½ (T **174**).

723	**172**	½d. slate-black (1.3.54)	15	30
724		1d. orange (1.3.54)	15	10
		w. Wmk inverted	40	2·25
725		1½d. brown-lake	20	10
		w. Wmk inverted	†	£500
726		2d. bluish green (1.3.54)	20	10
		w. Wmk inverted	†	£500
727		3d. vermilion (1.3.54)	20	10
		w. Wmk inverted (from booklets)	40	2·50
728		4d. blue (1.3.54)	40	50
		w. Wmk inverted	†	£750
729		6d. purple (1.3.54)	70	2·00
		w. Wmk inverted	£550	£350
730		8d. carmine (1.3.54)	60	60
		w. Wmk inverted	£950	£700
731	**173**	9d. brown and bright green (1.3.54)	60	60
		w. Wmk inverted	£500	£375
732		1s. black and carmine-red (Die I) (1.3.54)	65	10
		aw. Wmk inverted	£550	£425
		b. Die II (1958)	£180	20·00
733		1s.6d. black and bright blue (1.3.54)	1·75	60
		aw. Wmk inverted	£475	£375
733*b*		1s.9d. black and red-orange (1.7.57)	5·50	1·50
		bw. Wmk inverted	£750	£450
		c. White opaque paper (2.2.59)	3·50	1·50
733*d*	**174**	2s.6d. brown (1.7.57)	13·00	4·00
734		3s. bluish green (1.3.54)	15·00	50
		w. Wmk inverted	£800	£500
735		5s. carmine (1.3.54)	30·00	3·25
736		10s. deep ultramarine (1.3.54)	50·00	18·00
723/736 *Set of 16*			£100	28·00

1s. Dies I and II. The two dies of the Queen's portrait differ in the shading on the sleeve at right. The long lines running upwards from left to right are strong in Die I and weaker in Die II. In the upper part of the shading the fine cross-hatching is visible in Die I only between the middle two of the four long lines, but in Die II it extends clearly across all four lines.

In the lower part of the shading the strength of the long lines in Die I makes the cross-hatching appear subdued, whereas in Die II the weaker long lines make the cross-hatching more prominent.

Centre plates 1A, 1B and 2B are Die I; 3A and 3B are Die II.

For stamps as T **172** but with larger figures of value see Nos. 745/751.

WHITE OPAQUE PAPER. A new white opaque paper first came into use in August 1958. It is slightly thicker than the paper previously used, but obviously different in colour (white, against cream) and opacity (the previous paper being relatively transparent).

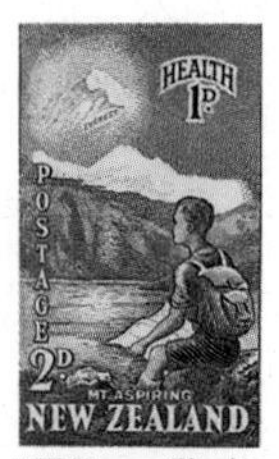

175 Young Climber and Mts Aspiring and Everest

(Des J. Berry. Recess; vignette litho B.W.)

1954 (4 Oct). Health Stamps. W **98**. P 13½.

737	**175**	1½d. +½d. sepia and deep violet	15	30
738		2d. + 1d. sepia and blue-black	15	30

176 Maori Mail Carrier

177 Queen Elizabeth II

178 Douglas DC-3 Airliner

(Des R. M. Conly (2d.), J. Berry (3d.), A. G. Mitchell (4d.). Recess D.L.R.)

1955 (18 July). Centenary of First New Zealand Postage Stamps. W **98**. P 14 (2d.) 14×14½ (3d.) or 13 (4d.)

739	**176**	2d. sepia and deep green	10	10
		w. Wmk inverted	—	£325
740	**177**	3d. brown-red	10	10
741	**178**	4d. black and bright blue	70	1·00
739/741 *Set of 3*			80	1·00

179 Children's Health Camps Federation Emblem

180

(Des E. M. Taylor. Recess B.W.)

1955 (3 Oct). Health Stamps. W **98** (sideways). P 13½×13.

742	**179**	1½d. +½d. sepia and orange-brown	10	60
743		2d. +1d. red-brown and green	10	35
744		3d. +1d. sepia and deep rose-red	15	15
		a. Centre omitted	£15000	
742/744 *Set of 3*			30	1·00

Only one example of No. 744a is known. It was caused by a paper fold.

1955–59. As Nos. 724/730 but larger figures of value with stars omitted from lower right corner and new colour (8d.).

745	**180**	1d. orange (12.7.56)	50	10
		aw. Wmk inverted	1·50	3·50
		b. White opaque paper (2.6.59)	50	75
		bw. Wmk inverted	1·50	4·25
746		1½d. brown-lake (1.12.55)	60	60
747		2d. bluish green (19.3.56)	40	10
		a. White opaque paper (10.11.59)	55	10
748		3d. vermilion (1.5.56)	50	50
		aw. Wmk inverted	1·50	2·50
		b. White opaque paper (20.6.59)	30	10
		bw. Wmk inverted	2·00	4·25
749		4d. blue (3.2.58)	1·00	80
		a. White opaque paper (9.9.59)	1·00	2·50
750		6d. purple (20.10.55)	5·00	20
751		8d. chestnut (*white opaque paper*) (1.12.59)	2·75	4·25
745/751 *Set of 7*			9·50	5·50

See note *re* white opaque paper after No. 736.

181 'The Whalers of Foveaux Strait'

182 Farming

183 Takahe

(Des E. R. Leeming (2d.), L. C. Mitchell (3d.), M. R. Smith (8d.). Recess D.L.R.)

1956 (16 Jan). Southland Centennial. Types **181/183**. W **98**. P 13½×13 (8d.) or 13×12½ (others).

752	**181**	2d. deep blue-green	30	15
753	**182**	3d. sepia	10	10
		w. Wmk inverted	—	£300
754	**183**	8d. slate-violet and rose-red	1·25	1·50
752/754 *Set of 3*			1·50	1·50

184 Children picking Apples

(Des L. C. Mitchell, after photo by J. F. Louden. Recess B.W.)

1956 (24 Sept). Health Stamps. W **98**. P 13×13½.

755	**184**	1½d. +½d. purple-brown	15	70
		a. Blackish brown	2·00	7·00
756		2d. +1d. blue-green	15	55
757		3d. +1d. claret	15	15
755/757 *Set of 3*			40	1·25

185 New Zealand Lamb and Map
186 Lamb, *Dunedin* and *Port Brisbane* (refrigerated freighter)

(Des M. Goaman. Photo Harrison)

1957 (15 Feb). 75th Anniversary of First Export of NZ Lamb. W **98** (sideways inverted on 4d.). P 14×14½ (4d.) or 14½×14 (8d.).

758	**185**	4d. blue	50	1·00
		w. Wmk sideways	14·00	22·00
759	**186**	8d. deep orange-red	75	1·00

187 Sir Truby King

(Des M. R. Smith. Recess B.W.)

1957 (14 May). 50th Anniversary of Plunket Society. W **98**. P 13.

760	**187**	3d. bright carmine-red	10	10
		w. Wmk inverted	£180	

188 Life-savers in Action
189 Children on Seashore

(Des L. Cutten (2d.), L. C. Mitchell (3d.). Recess Waterlow)

1957 (25 Sept). Health Stamps. W **98** (sideways). P 13½.

761	**188**	2d. +1d. black and emerald	15	70
762	**189**	3d. +1d. ultramarine and rose-red	15	10

MS762*b* Two sheets each 112×96 mm with Nos. 761 and 762 in blocks of 6 (2×3) *Per pair* 6·00 23·00
MS762*c* As last but with wmk upright *Per pair* 9·00 45·00

(190)

1958 (6 Jan–Mar). No. 746 surch as T **190**.

763	**180**	2d. on 1½d. brown-lake	70	10
		a. Smaller dot in surch	15	10
		b. Error. Surch on No. 725 (3.58)	£130	£170

Diameter of dot on No. 763 is 4¼ mm; on No. 763a 3¾ mm.
Forgeries of No. 763b are known.
Almost all examples of No. 763b have the 4¼ mm dot, but examples with the smaller dot are known.

191 Girls' Life Brigade Cadet
192 Boys' Brigade Bugler

(Des J. Berry. Photo Harrison)

1958 (20 Aug). Health Stamps. W **98**. P 14×14½.

764	**191**	2d. +1d. green	20	40
765	**192**	3d. +1d. blue	20	40

MS765*a* Two sheets each 104×124 mm with Nos. 764/765 in blocks of 6 (3×2) *Per pair* 7·00 20·00

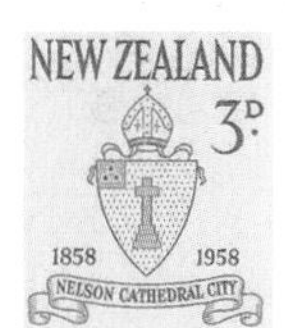
193 Sir Charles Kingsford-Smith and Fokker F.VIIa/3m *Southern Cross*
194 Seal of Nelson

(Des J. E. Lyle. Eng F. D. Manley. Recess Commonwealth Bank of Australia Note Ptg Branch)

1958 (27 Aug). 30th Anniversary of First Air Crossing of the Tasman Sea. W **98** (sideways). P 14×14½.

766	**193**	6d. deep ultramarine	50	75

(Des M. J. Macdonald. Recess B.W.)

1958 (29 Sept). Centenary of City of Nelson. W **98**. P 13½×13.

767	**194**	3d. carmine	10	10

195 *Pania* Statue, Napier
196 Australian Gannets on Cape Kidnappers

(Des M. R. Smith (2d.), J. Berry (3d.), L. C. Mitchell (8d.). Photo Harrison)

1958 (3 Nov). Centenary of Hawke's Bay Province. Types **195/196** and similar design. W **98** (sideways on 3d.). P 14½×14 (3d.) or 13½×14½ (others).

768	**195**	2d. yellow-green	10	10
769	**196**	3d. blue	30	10
770	–	8d. red-brown	70	1·00
768/770 *Set of 3*			1·00	1·00

Design: Vert—8d. Maori sheep-shearer.

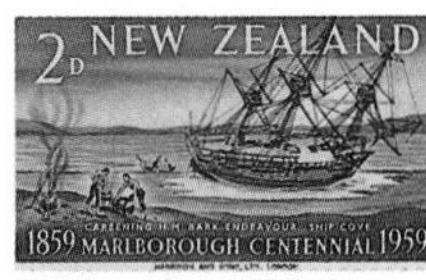
197 'Kiwi' Jamboree Badge
198 Careening HMS *Endeavour* at Ship Cove

(Des Mrs. S. M. Collins. Recess B.W.)

1959 (5 Jan). Pan-Pacific Scout Jamboree, Auckland. W **98**. P 13½×13.

771	**197**	3d. sepia and carmine	30	10

(Des G. R. Bull and G. R. Smith. Photo Harrison)

1959 (2 Mar). Centenary of Marlborough Province. T **198** and similar horiz designs. W **98** (sideways). P 14½×14.

772	**198**	2d. green	30	10
773	–	3d. deep blue	30	10
774	–	8d. light brown	1·10	1·00
772/774 *Set of 3*			1·40	1·00

Designs: 3d. Shipping wool, Wairau Bar, 1857; 8d. Salt industry, Grassmere.

201 Red Cross Flag

(Photo Harrison)

1959 (3 June). Red Cross Commemoration. W **98** (sideways). P 14½×14.

775	**201**	3d. +1d. red and ultramarine	20	10
		a. Red Cross omitted	£3250	

202 Grey Teal
203 New Zealand Stilt

(Des Display Section, GPO. Photo Harrison)

1959 (16 Sept). Health Stamps. W **98** (sideways). P 14×14½.

776	**202**	2d. +1d. greenish yellow, olive and rose-red	50	65
777	**203**	3d. +1d. black, pink and light blue	50	65
		a. Pink omitted	£180	£120
		bw. Wmk sideways inverted	20·00	32·00

MS777*c* Two sheets, each 95×109 mm with Nos. 776/777 in blocks of 6 (3×2) *Per pair* 8·00 24·00

204 'The Explorer'
205 'The Gold Digger'
206 'The Pioneer Woman'

(Des G. R. Bull and G. R. Smith. Photo Harrison)

1960 (16 May). Centenary of Westland Province. Types **204/206** and similar vert design. W **98**. P 14×14½.

778	**204**	2d. deep dull green	20	10
779	**205**	3d. orange-red	30	10
780	**206**	8d. grey-black	90	2·00
778/80 *Set of 3*			1·25	2·00

207 Manuka (Tea Tree)
208 Karaka
209 Kowhai Ngutu-kaka (Kaka-Beak)
209a Titoki

210 Kowhai
211 Puarangi (Hibiscus)
211a Matua Tikumu (Mountain Daisy)
212 Pikiarero

212a Koromiko
213 Rata
214 National Flag

215 Timber Industry
216 Rainbow Trout
217 Tiki

218 Aerial Top Dressing
218a Aerial Top Dressing
219 Taniwha (Maori Rock Drawing)

220 Butter Making
221 Tongariro National Park and Château

221a Tongariro National Park and Château

222 Sutherland Falls

223 Tasman Glacier

224 Pohutu Geyser

2d. 'F' for 'E' in 'ZEALAND'. (R. 3/1, black Pl. 2)

(Des Harrison (½d.), G. F. Fuller (1d., 3d., 6d.), A. G. Mitchell (2d., 4d., 5d., 8d., 3s., 10s., £1), PO Public Relations Division (7d.), PO Publicity Section (9d.), J. Berry (1s., 1s.6d.), R. E. Barwick (1s.3d.), J. C. Boyd (1s.9d.), D. F. Kee (2s.), L. C. Mitchell (2s.6d., 5s.). Photo D.L.R. (½d., 1d., 2d., 3d., 4d., 6d., 8d.) or Harrison (others))

1960 (11 July)–**66**. Types **207/224**. Chalk-surfaced paper (2½d., 5d., 7d., 1s.9d. (No. 795), 3s. (No. 799). W **98** (sideways on 5d., 1s.3d., 1s.6d., 2s.6d., 3s. and 10s. or sideways inverted (2½d.)). P 14×14½ (1s.3d., 1s.6d., 2s., 5s., £1) or 14½×14 (others).

No.	Type	Description	Unused	Used
781	**207**	½d. pale blue, green and cerise (1.9.60)	10	10
		a. Pale blue omitted	£325	£250
		b. Green omitted	£450	
782	**208**	1d. orange, green, lake and brown (1.9.60)	10	10
		a. Orange omitted	£650	£375
		b. Coil. Perf 14½×13. Wmk sideways (11.63)	1·40	2·75
		ba. Orange omitted	£2000	£1000
		c. Chalk-surfaced paper (1965?)	10	2·00
783	**209**	2d. carmine, black, yellow and green	10	10
		a. Black omitted	£550	£400
		b. Yellow omitted	£600	
		c. 'ZFALAND'	85·00	
784	**209a**	2½d. red, yellow, black and green (1.11.61)	1·00	10
		a. Red omitted	£850	£600
		b. Yellow omitted	£325	
		c. Green omitted	£400	£225
		d. Red and green omitted	£1100	
		w. Wmk sideways	£150	£120
785	**210**	3d. yellow, green, yellow-brown and deep greenish blue (1.9.60)	30	10
		a. Yellow omitted	£200	£170
		b. Green omitted	£325	£225
		c. Yellow-brown omitted	£225	
		e. Coil. Perf 14½×13. Wmk sideways (3.10.63)	1·40	2·75
		f. Chalk-surfaced paper (1965?)	30	2·25
		fa. Yellow-brown omitted	£650	
786	**211**	4d. purple, buff, yellow-green and light blue	40	10
		a. Purple omitted	£650	£500
		b. Buff omitted	£900	
		d. Chalk-surfaced paper (6.65)	£950	18·00
787	**211a**	5d. yellow, deep green, black and violet (14.5.62)	1·00	10
		a. Yellow omitted	£425	£425
		w. Wmk sideways inverted	£170	£100
788	**212**	6d. lilac, green and deep bluish green (1.9.60)	50	10
		a. No wmk	55·00	
		b. Lilac omitted	£425	
		c. Green omitted	£425	£425
		d. Chalk-surfaced paper (1966?)	65	4·50
788*e*	**212a**	7d. red, green, yellow and pale red (16.3.66)	1·00	1·10
		ew. Wmk inverted	4·50	12·00
789	**213**	8d. rose-red, yellow, green and grey (1.9.60)	40	10
790	**214**	9d. red and ultramarine (1.9.60)	40	10
		a. Red omitted	£550	
791	**215**	1s. brown and deep green	30	10
792	**216**	1s.3d. carmine, sepia and bright blue	2·50	70
		a. Carmine omitted	£850	
		b. Carmine, sepia and greyish blue	1·50	25
		w. Wmk sideways inverted	£325	£200
793	**217**	1s.6d. olive-green and orange-brown	75	10
794	**218**	1s.9d. bistre-brown	12·00	15
795	**218a**	1s.9d. orange-red, blue, green and yellow (4.11.63)	2·50	1·00
		a. Wmk sideways	£950	
		w. Wmk inverted	£750	£750
796	**219**	2s. black and orange-buff	2·00	10
		a. Chalk-surfaced paper (1966)	1·00	2·75
797	**220**	2s.6d. yellow and light brown	1·00	1·00
		a. Yellow omitted	£1400	£850
798	**221**	3s. blackish brown	15·00	1·00
799	**221a**	3s. bistre, blue and green (1.4.64)	1·50	2·00
		w. Wmk sideways inverted	90·00	90·00
800	**222**	5s. blackish green	1·50	60
		a. Chalk-surfaced paper (1966)	1·25	5·50
801	**223**	10s. steel-blue	3·50	2·50
		a. Chalk-surfaced paper (1966)	2·50	10·00
802	**224**	£1 deep magenta	10·00	7·00
781/802 *Set of 23*			48·00	15·00

Nos. 782b and 785e were replaced by coils with upright watermark perf 14½×14 in 1966.

Examples of the 3d., perf 14×14½ with watermark sideways inverted (top of star pointing to the left, *as seen from the back of the stamp*) are known. They are believed to come from a trial printing.

CHALKY PAPER. The chalk-surfaced paper is not only whiter but also thicker, making the watermark difficult to see. Examples of the 4d. value can be found on a thick surfaced paper. These should not be confused with the rare chalk-surfaced printing, No. 786d, which can be identified by its positive reaction to the silver test and fluoresces brightly, both front and back, under ultraviolet light.

225 Sacred Kingfisher

226 New Zealand Pigeon

(Des Display Section, GPO. Recess B.W.)

1960 (10 Aug). Health Stamps. W **98**. P 13½.

No.	Type	Description	Unused	Used
803	**225**	2d. +1d. sepia and turquoise-blue	50	75
804	**226**	3d. +1d. deep purple-brown and orange	50	75
MS804*b* Two sheets each 95×107 mm with Nos. 803 and 804 in blocks of 6. P 11½×11 *Per pair*			20·00	38·00

227 *The Adoration of the Shepherds* (Rembrandt)

(Photo Harrison)

1960 (1 Nov). Christmas. W **98**. P 12.

No.	Type	Description	Unused	Used
805	**227**	2d. red and deep brown/*cream*	15	10
		a. Red omitted	£425	£425

228 Great Egret

229 New Zealand Falcon

(Des Display Section, GPO. Recess B.W.)

1961 (2 Aug). Health Stamps. W **98**. P 13½.

No.	Type	Description	Unused	Used
806	**228**	2d. +1d. black and purple	50	70
807	**229**	3d. +1d. deep sepia and yellow-green	50	70
MS807*a* Two sheets each 97×121 mm with Nos. 806/807 in blocks of 6 (3×2) *Per pair*			24·00	35·00

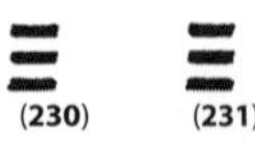

(230) **(231)**

232 *Adoration of the Magi* (Dürer)

1961 (1 Sept). No. 748 surch with T **230** (wide setting).

No.	Type	Description	Unused	Used
808	**180**	2½d. on 3d. vermilion	25	30
		a. Narrow setting (Type **231**)	15	30
		b. Pair, wide and narrow	16·00	35·00

The difference in the settings is in the overall width of the new value, caused by two different spacings between the '2', '½' and 'd'.

(Photo Harrison)

1961 (16 Oct). Christmas. W **98** (sideways). P 14½×14.

No.	Type	Description	Unused	Used
809	**232**	2½d. multicoloured	10	10
		w. Wmk sideways inverted	80·00	48·00

233 Morse Key and Port Hills, Lyttelton

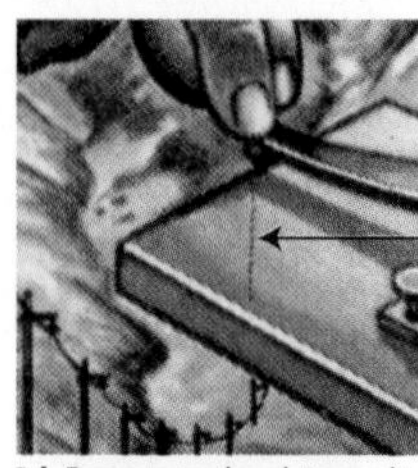
3d. Damage to the plate resulted in a vertical green dotted line below the fingers (R. 14/1)

(Des A. G. Mitchell (3d.) and L. C. Mitchell (8d.). Photo Harrison)

1962 (1 June). Telegraph Centenary. T **233** and similar horiz design. W **98** (sideways). P 14½×14.

No.	Type	Description	Unused	Used
810		3d. sepia and bluish green	10	10
		a. Bluish green omitted	£3000	
		b. Dotted line flaw	15·00	
811		8d. black and brown-red	90	90
		a. Imperf (pair)	£2500	
		b. Black omitted	£2750	

Design: 3d. T **233**; 8d. Modern teleprinter.

No. 811a comes from a sheet with the two top rows imperforate and the third row imperforate on three sides.

235 Red-fronted Parakeet

236 Tieke Saddleback

(Des Display Section, GPO. Photo D.L.R.)

1962 (3 Oct). Health Stamps. W **98**. P 15×14.

No.	Type	Description	Unused	Used
812	**235**	2½d. +1d. multicoloured	50	70
		a. Orange omitted	£2250	£1200
		b. Printed on the gummed side	£1500	
		w. Wmk inverted	£160	£150
813	**236**	3d. +1d.multicoloured	50	70
		a. Orange omitted	£2750	
MS813*b* Two sheets each 96×101 mm with Nos. 812/813 in blocks of 6 (3×2) *Per pair*			32·00	50·00

No. 812b comes from a miniature sheet.

237 *Madonna in Prayer* (Sassoferrato)

(Photo Harrison)

1962 (15 Oct). Christmas. W **98**. P 14½×14.

No.	Type	Description	Unused	Used
814	**237**	2½d. multicoloured	10	10

238 Prince Andrew

239

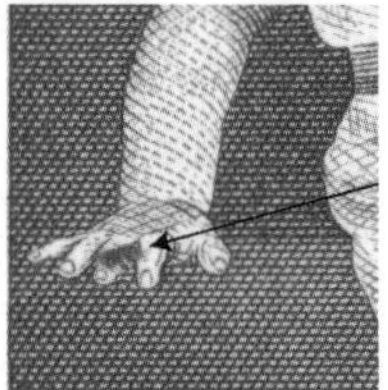
3d.+1d. A prominent flaw on the middle finger of the Prince's right hand appears as a bloodstain. Later attempts to remove the flaw met with only partial success (Pl. 1B, R. 3/5)

(Design after photographs by Studio Lisa, London. Recess D.L.R.)

1963 (7 Aug). Health Stamps. W **98**. P 14.
815 **238** 2½d. +1d. dull ultramarine 30 70
a. Ultramarine 40 80
b. Deep blue 30 40
816 **239** 3d. +1d. carmine 30 10
a. Bloodstained finger .... 90·00 50·00
MS816b Two sheets each 93×100 mm with Nos. 815/816 in blocks of 6 (3×2) .... *Per pair* 17·00 35·00

The price for No. 816a is for the flaw in its original state, as illustrated. Examples with the flaw partially removed are worth less.

240 *The Holy Family* (Titian)

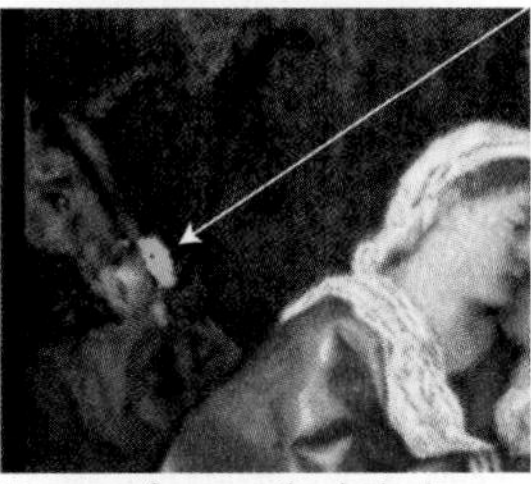
An orange flaw over the donkey's nose appears as a nosebag (Pl. 1B, R. 3/8)

(Photo Harrison)

1963 (14 Oct). Christmas. W **98** (sideways). P 12½.
817 **240** 2½d. multicoloured 10 10
a. Imperf (pair) £275
b. Yellow omitted £300
c. Nosebag flaw .... 5·00 2·00
w. Wmk sideways inverted 40 40

241 Steam Locomotive *Pilgrim* (1863) and Class DG Diesel Locomotive

242 Diesel Express and Mt Ruapehu

(Des Commercial Art Section, NZ Railways. Photo D.L.R.)

1963 (25 Nov). Railway Centenary. W **98** (sideways on 3d., sideways inverted on 1s.9d). P 14.
818 **241** 3d. multicoloured 40 10
a. Blue (sky) omitted £750
819 **242** 1s.9d. multicoloured .... 1·75 1·25
a. Red (value) omitted £2750

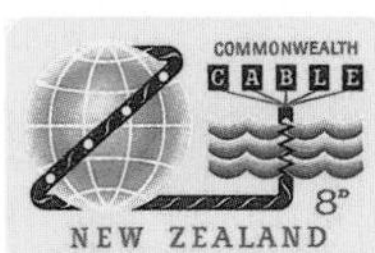

243 'Commonwealth Cable'

(Des P. Morriss. Photo Note Printing Branch, Reserve Bank of Australia)

1963 (3 Dec). Opening of COMPAC (Trans-Pacific Telephone Cable). No wmk. P 13½.
820 **243** 8d. red, blue and yellow .... 50 1·00

244 Road Map and Car Steering-wheel

245 Silver Gulls

3d. Flaw between 'W' and 'Z' of 'NEW ZEALAND' resembling an apostrophe (R. 3/2)

(Des L. C. Mitchell. Photo Harrison)

1964 (1 May). Road Safety Campaign. W **98**. P 15×14.
821 **244** 3d. black, ochre-yellow and blue 30 10
a. 'Apostrophe' flaw .... 13·00 14·00

(Des Display Section GPO, after Miss T. Kelly. Photo Harrison)

1964 (5 Aug). Health Stamps. T **245** and similar horiz design. Multicoloured. W **98**. P 14½.
822 2½d. +1d. Type **245** 40 50
a. Red (beak and legs) omitted £350 £250
w. Wmk inverted .... † £475
823 3d. +1d. Little Penguin 40 50
aw. Wmk inverted £225
MS823*b* Two sheets each 171×84 mm with Nos. 822/823 in blocks of 8 (4×2) .... *Per pair* 35·00 65·00
bw. Wmk inverted (No. 823 only) ....

246 Rev. S. Marsden taking first Christian service at Rangihoua Bay, 1814

7D
POSTAGE
(247)

(Des L. C. Mitchell. Photo Harrison)

1964 (12 Oct). Christmas. W **98** (sideways). P 14×13½.
824 **246** 2½d. multicoloured 10 10

1964 (14 Dec). As T F **6**, but without value, surch with T **247**. W **98**. Unsurfaced paper. P 14×13½.
825 F **6** 7d. carmine-red .... 50 1·00

248 Anzac Cove

(Des R. M. Conly. Photo Harrison)

1965 (14 Apr). 50th Anniversary of Gallipoli Landing. T **248** and similar horiz design. W **98**. P 12½.
826 **248** 4d. yellow-brown 10 10
827 – 5d. green and red 10 60
Design: 5d. Anzac Cove and poppy.

249 ITU Emblem and Symbols

250 Sir Winston Churchill

(Photo Harrison)

1965 (17 May). ITU Centenary. W **98**. P 14½×14.
828 **249** 9d. blue and pale chocolate 55 35

(Des P. Morriss from photograph by Karsh. Photo Note Ptg Branch, Reserve Bank of Australia)

1965 (24 May). Churchill Commemoration. P 13½.
829 **250** 7d. black, pale grey and light blue 30 50

251 Wellington Provincial Council Building

(Des from painting by L. B. Temple (1867). Photo Harrison)

1965 (26 July). Centenary of Government in Wellington. W **98** (sideways). P 14½×14.
830 **251** 4d. multicoloured 10 10

252 Kaka

253 Collared Grey Fantail (after Miss T. Kelly)

(Des Display Section, GPO. Photo Harrison)

1965 (4 Aug). Health Stamps. W **98**. P 14×14½.
831 **252** 3d. +1d. multicoloured 40 65
w. Wmk inverted .... † £110
832 **253** 4d. +1d. multicoloured 40 65
a. Green ('POSTAGE HEALTH' and on leaves) omitted £2250 £1200
bw. Wmk inverted .... 90·00 £140
MS832*c* Two sheets each 100×109 mm with Nos. 831/832 in blocks of 6 (3×2) .... *Per pair* 29·00 48·00
cw. Wmk inverted (No. 831 only) ..... † —

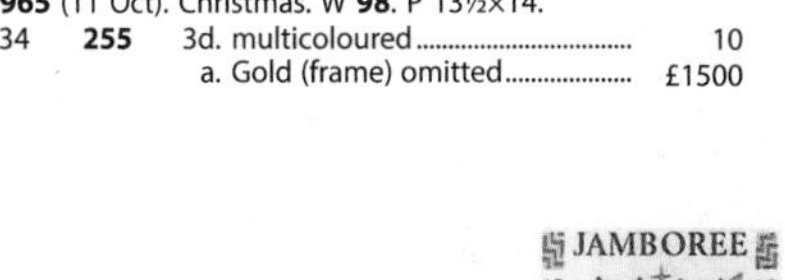

254 ICY Emblem

255 *The Two Trinities* (Murillo)

(Litho D.L.R.)

1965 (28 Sept). International Co-operation Year. W **98** (sideways inverted). P 14.
833 **254** 4d. carmine-red and light yellow-olive 20 10
w. Wmk sideways .... 4·25 4·50

(Photo Harrison)

1965 (11 Oct). Christmas. W **98**. P 13½×14.
834 **255** 3d. multicoloured 10 10
a. Gold (frame) omitted £1500

256 Arms of New Zealand

259 'Progress' Arrowhead

(Des Display Section, GPO. Photo D.L.R.)

1965 (30 Nov). 11th Commonwealth Parliamentary Conference. T **256** and similar horiz designs. Multicoloured. P 14.
835 4d. Type **256** 15 10
a. Blue (incl value) omitted £1300
b. Printed on the gummed side £1300
836 9d. Parliament House, Wellington and Badge 30 35
837 2s. Wellington from Mt. Victoria .... 1·40 2·50
a. Carmine omitted £1400
835/837 *Set of 3* .... 1·60 2·50

There is invariably a faint impression of the crossed regalia at upper left on No. 837a.

(Des Display Section, GPO. Photo Harrison)

1966 (5 Jan). Fourth National Scout Jamboree, Trentham. W **98**. P 14×15.
838 **259** 4d. gold and myrtle-green 15 10
a. Gold (arrowhead) omitted £1200 £1100

260 New Zealand Bell Bird

262 *The Virgin with Child* (Maratta)

(Des Display Section, GPO. Photo Harrison)

1966 (3 Aug). Health Stamps. T **260** and similar vert design. Multicoloured. W **98** (sideways). P 14×14½.
839 3d. +1d. Type **260** 40 65
w. Wmk sideways inverted £120
840 4d. +1d. Weka Rail 40 65
a. Deep brown (values and date) omitted £2750
w. Wmk sideways inverted £120
MS841 Two sheets each 107×91 mm. Nos. 839/840 in blocks of 6 (3×2) .... *Per pair* 13·00 50·00

In No. 840a besides the value, '1966' and 'Weka' are also omitted and the bird, etc. appears as light brown.

(Photo Harrison)

1966 (3 Oct). Christmas. W **98** (sideways). P 14½.
842 **262** 3d. multicoloured 10 10
a. Red omitted £350

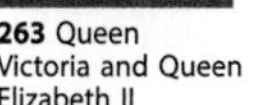

263 Queen Victoria and Queen Elizabeth II

264 Half-sovereign of 1867 and Commemorative Dollar Coin

(Des Display Section, GPO. Photo Harrison)

1967 (3 Feb). Centenary of New Zealand Post Office Savings Bank. W **98** (sideways on 4d.). P 14×14½.

843 **263** 4d. black, gold and maroon 10 10
w. Wmk sideways inverted .... £100 32·00
844 **264** 9d. gold, silver, black, light blue and deep green 10 20
w. Wmk inverted £600

(New Currency. 100 cents = 1 New Zealand Dollar)

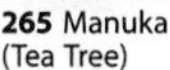

265 Manuka (Tea Tree)

266 Pohutu Geyser

(Photo D.L.R. (½c. to 3c., 5c. and 7c.) or Harrison (others))

1967 (10 July). Decimal Currency. Designs as 1960–1966 issue, but with values inscr in decimal currency as Types **265/266**. Chalky paper. W **98** (sideways on 8c., 10c., 20c., 50c. and $2). P 13½×14 (½c. to 3c., 5c. and 7c.), 14½×14 (4c., 6c., 8c., 10c., 25c. and $1) or 14×14½ (15c., 20c., 50c. and $2).

845 **265** ½c. pale blue, yellow-green and cerise 10 10
846 **208** 1c. yellow, carmine, green and light brown (as 1d.) 10 10
a. Booklet pane. Five stamps plus one printed label .... 2·25
847 **209** 2c. carmine, black, yellow and green (as 2d.) 10 10
848 **210** 2½c. yellow, green, yellow-brown and deep bluish green (as 3d.) 10 10
a. Deep bluish green omitted* £3750
b. Imperf (pair)† £150
849 **211** 3c. purple, buff, yellow-green and light greenish blue (as 4d.) 10 10
850 **211a** 4c. yellow, deep green, black and violet (as 5d.) 30 10
851 **212** 5c. lilac, yellow-olive and bluish green (as 6d.) .... 50 1·00
852 **212a** 6c. red, green, yellow and light pink (as 7d.) .... 50 1·00
853 **213** 7c. rose-red, yellow, green and grey (as 8d.) .... 60 1·50
w. Wmk inverted ....
854 **214** 8c. red and ultramarine 60 60
a. Red omitted £1200
855 **215** 10c. brown and deep green (as 1s.) .... 60 1·00
w. Wmk sideways inverted £750 £550
856 **217** 15c. olive-green and orange-brown (as 1s.6d.) .... 2·50 2·25
w. Wmk inverted .... 2·75 10·00
857 **219** 20c. black and buff .... 1·00 20
858 **220** 25c. yellow and light brown .... 1·00 2·00
859 **221a** 30c. olive-yellow, green and greenish blue .... 1·25 25
w. Wmk inverted .... £130 85·00
860 **222** 50c. blackish green (as 5s.) .... 1·75 50
861 **223** $1 Prussian blue (as 10s.) .... 9·00 1·00
w. Wmk inverted £375 £200
862 **266** $2 deep magenta .... 4·25 6·00
845/862 *Set of* 18 .... 21·00 15·00

* This occurred on one horizontal row of ten, affecting the background colour so that the value is also missing. In the row above and the row below, the colour was partially omitted. The price is for a vertical strip.

The 2½c. value has been seen with the yellow omitted, but only on a used example.

† This comes from a sheet of which the six right-hand vertical rows were completely imperforate and the top, bottom and left-hand margins had been removed.

The 4c., 30c. and 50c. exist with PVA gum as well as gum arabic. For $4 to $10 in the 'Arms' type, see under Postal Fiscal stamps. For other versions of 15c., 30c. and $2 see Nos. 870/879.

268 Running with Ball

(Des L. C. Mitchell. Photo Harrison)

1967 (2 Aug). Health Stamps. Rugby Football. T **268** and similar multicoloured design. W **98** (sideways on 2½c.). P 14½×14 (2½c.) or 14×14½ (3c.)

867 2½c. +1c. Type **268** 15 15
868 3c. +1c. Positioning for a place-kick (*horiz*) 15 15
MS869 Two sheets; (a) 76×130 mm (No. 867); (b) 130×76 mm (No. 868). Containing blocks of 6 .... *Per pair* 12·00 32·00

270 *Kaita* (trawler) and Catch

271 Brown Trout

272 Apples and Orchard

273 Forest and Timber

274 Sheep and the 'Woolmark'

275 Consignments of Beef and Herd of Cattle

276 Dairy Farm, Mt. Egmont and Butter Consignment

277 Fox Glacier, Westland National Park

(Des Display Section, GPO (7, 8, 10, 18, 20, 25c. and 28c. from photo), R. M. Conly (7½c.). Litho B.W. (7, 8, 18, 20c.) or photo D.L.R. (7½c.) and Harrison (10, 25, 28c.). Others (15, 30c., $2) as before)

1967–70. Types **270/277**. Chalky paper (except 7, 8, 18, 20c.). No wmk (7, 8, 20, 30c.) or W **98** (sideways inverted on 7½c., sideways on 10, 15, 25c., upright on 18, 28c., $2). P 13½ (7, 7½c.), 13×13½ (8, 18, 20c.), 14½×14 (10, 25, 30c.) or 14×14½ (15, 28c., $2).

870 **270** 7c. multicoloured (3.12.69) .... 1·00 1·00
871 **271** 7½c. multicoloured* (29.8.67) 50 70
a. Wmk upright (10.68) .... 50 1·00
872 **272** 8c. multicoloured (8.7.69) 75 70
873 **273** 10c. multicoloured (2.4.68) 50 10
a. Green (background) omitted £1000
w. Wmk sideways inverted .... † £1100
874 **217** 15c. apple-green, myrtle-green and carmine (as No. 856†) (19.3.68) .... 1·00 1·00
w. Wmk sideways inverted .... † £180
875 **274** 18c. multicoloured (8.7.69) .... 1·00 55
a. Printed on the gummed side £1000
876 **275** 20c. multicoloured (8.7.69) .... 1·00 20
877 **276** 25c. multicoloured (10.12.68) .... 1·00 1·50
878 **277** 28c. multicoloured (30.7.68) 60 10
a. Yellow omitted £2000
bw. Wmk inverted .... † £1200
878c **221a** 30c. olive-green, green and greenish blue (as No. 859) (2.6.70) .... 4·00 5·00
879 **266** $2 black, ochre and pale blue (as No. 862) (10.12.68) .... 13·00 13·00
870/879 *Set of* 11 .... 22·00 22·00

* No. 871 was originally issued to commemorate the introduction of the brown trout into New Zealand.

† No. 874 is slightly larger than No. 856, measuring 21×25 mm and the inscriptions and numerals differ in size.

278 *The Adoration of the Shepherds* (Poussin)

279 Mount Aspiring, Aurora Australis and Southern Cross

280 Sir James Hector (founder)

(Photo Harrison)

1967 (3 Oct). Christmas. W **98** (sideways). P 13½×14.

880 **278** 2½c. multicoloured 10 10

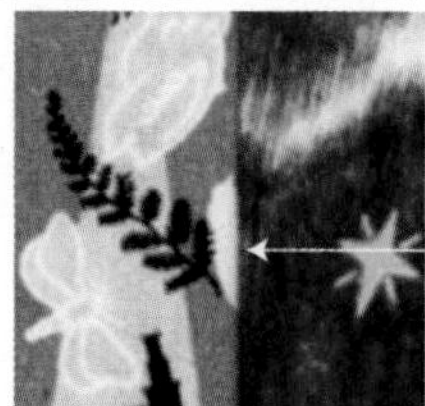

4c. A large white flaw to the right of the fern (a multipositive flaw affecting all plates, R. 1/10)

(Des J. Berry. Litho D.L.R.)

1967 (10 Oct). Centenary of the Royal Society of New Zealand. W **98** (sideways on 4c.). P 14 (4c.) or 13×14 (8c.)

881 **279** 4c. multicoloured 25 20
a. Fern flaw .... 6·00
w. Wmk sideways inverted .... 8·00 9·00
882 **280** 8c. multicoloured 25 80

281 Open Bible

282 Soldiers and Tank

(Des Display Section, GPO. Litho D.L.R.)

1968 (23 Apr). Centenary of Maori Bible. W **98**. P 13½.

883 **281** 3c. multicoloured 10 10
a. Gold (inscr etc.) omitted £160 £130
w. Wmk inverted .... 45·00 38·00

(Des L. C. Mitchell. Litho D.L.R.)

1968 (7 May). New Zealand Armed Forces. T **282** and similar horiz designs. Multicoloured. W **98** (sideways). P 14×13½.

884 4c. Type **282** 25 10
w. Wmk sideways inverted .... 9·50 14·00
885 10c. Airmen, Fairey Firefly and English Electric Canberra aircraft 40 50
886 28c. Sailors and HMNZS *Achilles*, 1939, and HMNZS *Waikato*, 1968 .... 70 1·60
w. Wmk sideways inverted .... 1·50 5·00
884/886 *Set of* 3 .... 1·25 2·00

285 Boy breasting Tape, and Olympic Rings

287 Placing Votes in Ballot Box

(Des L. C. Mitchell. Photo Harrison)

1968 (7 Aug). Health Stamps. T **285** and similar horiz design. Multicoloured. P 14½×14.

887 2½c. +1c. Type **285** 20 15
888 3c. +1c. Girl swimming and Olympic rings 20 15
a. Red (ring) omitted £3500
b. Blue (ring) omitted £2250
MS889 Two sheets each 145×95 mm. Nos. 887/888 in blocks of six .... *Per pair* 11·00 40·00

No. 888a occurred in one miniature sheet. Six examples are known, one being used. No. 888b occurred from a second miniature sheet.

(Des J. Berry. Photo Japanese Govt Ptg Bureau, Tokyo)

1968 (19 Sept). 75th Anniversary of Universal Suffrage in New Zealand. P 13.

890 **287** 3c. ochre, olive-green and light blue 10 10

288 Human Rights Emblem

289 *Adoration of the Holy Child* (G. van Honthorst)

(Photo Japanese Govt Ptg Bureau, Tokyo)

1968 (19 Sept). Human Rights Year. P 13.

891 **288** 10c. scarlet, yellow and deep green 10 30

(Photo Harrison)

1968 (1 Oct). Christmas. W **98** (sideways). P 14×14½.

892 **289** 2½c. multicoloured 10 10

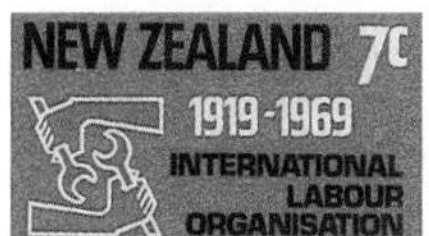

290 ILO Emblem

(Photo Harrison)

1969 (11 Feb). 50th Anniversary of International Labour Organisation. W **98** (sideways inverted). P 14½×14.

893 **290** 7c. black and carmine-red 15 30

291 Supreme Court Building, Auckland

292 Law Society's Coat of Arms

(Des R. M. Conly. Litho B.W.)

1969 (8 Apr). Centenary of New Zealand Law Society. Types **291/292** and similar design. P 13½×13 (3c.) or 13×13½ (others).

894	**291**	3c. multicoloured (*shades*)	10	10
895	**292**	10c. multicoloured	20	35
896	–	18c. multicoloured (*shades*)	30	95
894/6 *Set of 3*			55	1·25

Design: Vert—18c. 'Justice' (from Memorial Window in University of Canterbury, Christchurch).

295 Student being conferred with Degree

(Des R. M. Conly. Litho B.W.)

1969 (3 June). Centenary of Otago University. T **295** and similar multicoloured design. P 13×13½ (3c.) or 13½×13 (10c.)

897		3c. Otago University (*vert*)	15	10
898		10c. Type **295**	30	25

296 Boys playing Cricket

298 Dr. Elizabeth Gunn (founder of First Children's Health Camp)

(Des R. M. Conly (4c.); L. C. Mitchell (others). Litho B.W.)

1969 (6 Aug). Health Stamps. T **296** and similar horiz design and T **298**. P 12½×13 (No. 901) or 13×12½ (others).

899	**296**	2½c. +1c. multicoloured	40	65
900	—	3c. +1c. multicoloured	40	65
901	**298**	4c. +1c. brown and ultramarine	40	1·50
899/901 *Set of 3*			1·10	2·50
MS902 Two sheets each 144×84 mm. Nos. 899/900 in blocks of six		*Per pair*	13·00	50·00

Design: 3c. Girls playing cricket.

299 Oldest existing House in New Zealand, and Old Stone Mission Store, Kerikeri

(Litho D.L.R.)

1969 (18 Aug). Early European Settlement in New Zealand, and 150th Anniversary of Kerikeri. T **299** and similar horiz design. Multicoloured. W **98** (sideways inverted). P 13×13½.

903		4c. Type **299**	20	25
904		6c. View of Bay of Islands	30	1·75

301 *The Nativity* (Federico Fiori (Barocci))

302 Captain Cook, Transit of Venus and 'Octant'

(Photo Harrison)

1969 (1 Oct). Christmas. W **98**. P 13×14.

905	**301**	2½c. multicoloured	10	10
		a. No wmk	10	15

(Des Eileen Mayo. Photo; portraits embossed Harrison)

1969 (9 Oct). Bicentenary of Captain Cook's Landing in New Zealand. T **302** and similar horiz designs. P 14½×14.

906		4c. black, cerise and blue	30	15
		a. Imperf (pair)	£425	
907		6c. slate-green, purple-brown and black	40	1·00
908		18c. purple-brown, slate-green and black	60	40
909		28c. cerise, black and blue	1·00	1·25
906/909 *Set of 4*			2·10	2·50
MS910 109×90 mm. Nos. 906/909			14·00	25·00

Designs: 4c. T **302**; 6c. Sir Joseph Banks (naturalist) and outline of HMS *Endeavour*; 18c. Dr. Daniel Solander (botanist) and his plant; 28c. Queen Elizabeth II and Cook's chart 1769.

The miniature sheet exists additionally inscribed on the selvedge at bottom. 'A SOUVENIR FROM NEW ZEALAND STAMP EXHIBITION, NEW PLYMOUTH 6TH–11TH OCTOBER. 1969'. These were not sold from Post Offices.

306 Girl, Wheat Field and CORSO Emblem

307 Mother feeding her Child, Dairy Herd and CORSO Emblem

(Des L. C. Mitchell. Photo Japanese Govt Printing Bureau, Tokyo)

1969 (18 Nov). 25th Anniversary of CORSO (Council of Organisations for Relief Services Overseas). P 13.

911	**306**	7c. multicoloured	35	85
912	**307**	8c. multicoloured	35	90

308 Cardigan Bay (champion trotter)

(Des L. C. Mitchell. Photo Courvoisier)

1970 (28 Jan). Return of Cardigan Bay to New Zealand. P 11½.

913	**308**	10c. multicoloured	30	30

309 *Vanessa gonerilla* (Red Admiral)

310 Queen Elizabeth II and New Zealand Coat of Arms

(Des Enid Hunter (½c., 1c., 2c., 18c., 20c.), Eileen Mayo (2½c. to 7c.), D. B. Stevenson (7½c., 8c.), M. Cleverley (10, 15, 25, 30c., $1, $2), M. V. Askew (23, 50c.). Photo Harrison (½c. to 20c.), Enschedé (23, 50c.), Courvoisier ($1, $2) or Litho B.W. (25, 30c.))

1970 (12 Mar)–**76**. Various designs as Types **309/310**. W **98** (sideways on 10c., or sideways inverted on 15, 20c.) or No wmk (23c. to $2).

*(a) Size as T **309**. P 13½×13*

914	½c. multicoloured (2.9.70)	10	20
	w. Wmk inverted	—	£200
915	1c. multicoloured (2.9.70)	10	10
	aw. Wmk inverted	50·00	35·00
	b. Wmk sideways inverted (booklets) (6.7.71)	80	2·50
	ba. Booklet pane. No. 915b×3 with three *se-tenant* printed labels	2·25	
	bb. Red omitted	£275	
	bc. Blue omitted (booklets)	£250	£200
	bw. Wmk sideways	£120	
916	2c. multicoloured (2.9.70)	10	10
	a. Black (inscr, etc) omitted	£400	
	w. Wmk inverted	4·00	1·50
917	2½c. multicoloured (2.9.70)	30	20
918	3c. black, brown and orange (2.9.70)	15	10
	aw. Wmk inverted	2·50	2·75
	b. Wmk sideways inverted (booklets) (6.7.71)	55	1·50
	bw. Wmk sideways	32·00	32·00
919	4c. multicoloured (2.9.70)	15	10
	aw. Wmk inverted	3·00	1·75
	b. Wmk sideways inverted (booklets) (6.7.71)	55	1·75
	ba. Bright green (wing veins) omitted	£250	£110
	bw. Wmk sideways	85·00	75·00
	c. Bright green (wing veins) omitted	†	£250
920	5c. multicoloured (4.11.70)	30	10
	w. Wmk inverted	†	—
921	6c. blackish green, yellow-green and carmine (4.11.70)	30	1·00
	w. Wmk inverted	†	£250
922	7c. multicoloured (4.11.70)	50	1·00
	w. Wmk inverted	—	£300
923	7½c. multicoloured (4.11.70)	75	2·00
	w. Wmk inverted	†	—
924	8c. multicoloured (4.11.70)	50	1·00
	w. Wmk inverted	†	£250

*(b) Size as T **310**. Various perfs*

925	10c. multicoloured (P 14½×14)	50	10
	w. Wmk sideways inverted	8·00	3·75
926	15c. black, flesh and pale brown (P 13½×13) (20.1.71)	75	30
	a. Pale brown omitted	£700	
	w. Wmk sideways	50·00	45·00
927	18c. chestnut, black and apple-green (P 13×13½) (20.1.71)	75	30
	w. Wmk inverted	55·00	45·00
928	20c. black and yellow-brown (P 13½×13) (20.1.71)	75	10
929	23c. multicoloured (P 13½×12½) (1.12.71)	60	15
930	25c. multicoloured (P 13×13½) (1.9.71)	1·00	35
	a. Printed on the gummed side	£750	
	b. Perf 14 (11.76?)	50	75
931	30c. multicoloured (P 13×13½) (1.9.71)	50	15
	a. Perf 14 (9.76?)	1·00	1·75
932	50c. multicoloured (P 13½×12½) (1.9.71)	50	20
	a. Apple green (hill on right) omitted	28·00	24·00
	b. Buff (shore) omitted	55·00	
	c. Dark green (hill on left) omitted	£350	
933	$1 multicoloured (P 11½) (14.4.71)	1·00	1·00
934	$2 multicoloured (P 11½) (14.4.71)	2·50	1·00
914/934 *Set of 21*		10·00	8·00

Designs: Vert—½c. *Lycaena salustius* (Glade Copper Butterfly); 1c. T **309**; 2c. *Argyrophenga antipodum* (Tussock Butterfly); 2½c. *Nyctemera annulata* (Magpie Moth); 3c. *Detunda egregia* (Lichen Moth); 4c. *Charagia virescens* (Puriri Moth); 5c. Scarlet Wrasse ('Scarlet Parrot Fish'); 6c. Big-bellied Sea Horses; 7c. Leather jacket (fish); 7½c. Intermediate Halfbeak ('Garfish'); 8c. John Dory (fish); 18c. Maori club; 25c. Hauraki Gulf Maritime Park; 30c. Mt. Cook National Park. Horiz—10c. T **310**: 15c. Maori fish hook; 20c. Maori tattoo Pattern, 23c. Egmont National Park; 50c. Abel Tasman National Park; $1 Geothermal Power; $2 Agricultural Technology.

Although issued as a definitive No. 925 was put on sale on the occasion of the Royal Visit to New Zealand.

Used examples of No. 931 are known showing the sky in light blue instead of the normal stone colour. It was suggested by the printer involved that this was caused by a residue of ink used for another stamp remaining in the ink ducts when a printing of the 30c. commenced. Most authorities, however, agree that the 'blue sky' stamps are colour changelings.

The 1c., 2c., 3c. to 7c. and 8c. to 20c. values were re-issued between 1973 and 1976 on unwatermarked paper.

311 Geyser Restaurant

312 UN HQ Building

(Des M. Cleverley. Photo Japanese Govt Printing Bureau, Tokyo)

1970 (8 Apr). World Fair, Osaka. T **311** and similar horiz designs. Multicoloured. P 13.

935	7c. Type **311**	20	55
936	8c. New Zealand Pavilion	20	55
937	18c. Bush Walk	40	55
935/937 *Set of 3*		70	1·50

(Des R. M. Conly (3c.), L. C. Mitchell (10c.). Litho D.L.R.)

1970 (24 June). 25th Anniversary of United Nations. T **312** and similar vert design. P 13½.

938	3c. multicoloured	10	10
939	10c. scarlet and yellow	20	20

Design: 3c. T **312**; 10c. Tractor on horizon.

313 Soccer

(Des L. C. Mitchell. Litho D.L.R.)

1970 (5 Aug). Health Stamps. T **313** and similar multicoloured design. P 13½.

940	2½c. +1c. Netball (*vert*)	25	70
941	3c. +1c. Type **313**	25	70
MS942 Two sheets: (a) 102×125 mm (No. 940); (b) 125×102 mm (No. 941), containing blocks of 6 *Per pair*		13·00	50·00

314 *The Virgin adoring the Child* (Correggio)

315 *The Holy Family* (stained glass window, Invercargill Presbyterian Church)

(Litho D.L.R.)

1970 (1 Oct). Christmas. Types **314/315** and similar design. P 12½.

943	2½c. multicoloured	10	10
944	3c. multicoloured	10	10
	a. Green (inscr and value) omitted	£300	£200
945	10c. black, orange and silver	30	75
943/945 *Set of 3*		35	75

Design: Vert—2½c. T **314**; 3c. T **315**. Horiz—10c. Tower of Roman Catholic Church, Sockburn.

No. 943 exists as an imperforate proof with the country inscription and face value omitted.

316 Chatham Islands Lily

(Des Eileen Mayo. Photo Japanese Govt Printing Bureau, Tokyo)

1970 (2 Dec). Chatham Islands. T **316** and similar horiz design. Multicoloured. P 13.

946 1c. Type **316** ... 10 35
947 2c. Shy Albatross ... 30 40

STAMP BOOKLETS

Nos. SB1 to SB24 are stapled.

Nos. SB1/SB5 were sold at ½d. above the face value of the stamps to cover the cost of manufacture.

1901 (1 Apr). White card covers with postage rates.

SB1 1s.½d. booklet containing 12×1d. (No. 278) in blocks of 6 ... £2250
SB2 2s. 6½d. booklet containing 30×1d. (No. 278) in blocks of 6 ... £3000

Original printings of Nos. SB1/SB2 showed the face value on the cover in small figures. Subsequent printings show large figures of value on the covers and the prices quoted are for this type.

1902 (21 Aug)–**05**. White card covers with postage rates.

SB3 1s.½d. booklet containing 12×1d. in panes of 6 (Nos. 303b or 303cb) ... £1800
SB4 2s.½d. booklet containing 24×1d. in panes of 6 (Nos. 303b or 303cb) (21.3.05) ... £2250
SB5 2s. 6½d. booklet containing 30×1d. in panes of 6 (Nos. 303b or 303cb) ... £2750

1910 (Apr). White card cover with postage rates.

SB6 2s. booklet containing 11×½d. in pane of 5 with 1 label (Nos. 387b or 387c) and pane of 6 (No. 387d), and 18×1d. in three panes of 6 (No. 405b) ... £5000

1912 (May). White card cover.

SB7 2s. booklet containing 12×½d. and 18×1d. in panes of 6 with bars on the selvedge (Nos. 387e, 405c) ... £3000

1915 (Feb). Red card cover.

SB8 2s. booklet containing 12×½d. and 18×1d. in panes of 6 with bars on the selvedge (Nos. 435a or 435ba, 405c) ... £1800
a. Grey cover ...
b. Blue cover ...
c. Yellow-buff cover ...
d. Purple-buff cover ...

1924 (1 Dec)–**25**. Cover inscription within frame.

SB9 2s. booklet containing 12×½d. and 18×1d. in panes of 6 with bars on the selvedge (Nos. 441a, 406b) (lilac cover) ... £2000
a. Grey cover ...
b. Pale blue cover ... £2250
SB10 2s. booklet containing 12×½d. and 18×1d. in panes of 6 with bars and advertisements on the selvedge (Nos. 446a, 410b) (yellow-buff cover) (1925) ... £2500
a. Grey-green cover ... £2500
b. Grey-buff cover ...
c. Grey-pink cover ... £2500

1928–34.

SB11 2s. booklet containing 12×½d. (P 14×15) and 18×1d. in panes of 6 with bars on the selvedge (Nos. 446ab, 468b) ... £3000
a. As No. SB11, but ½d. (P 14) (Nos. 446ca, 468b) ... £1800
b. As No. SB11 but panes with bars and advertisements on the selvedge (Nos. 446cb, 468c) ... £2000
SB12 2s. booklet containing 24×1d. (P 14) in panes of 6 with bars and advertisements on the selvedge (No. 468c) (1930) ... £1800
a. As No. SB12, but 1d. (P 14×15) (No. 468ea) (1934) ... £1700

1935 (18 Nov).

SB15 2s. booklet containing 24×1d., in panes of 6 with advertisements on the selvedge (No. 557ca) ... £375

1936 (Nov).

SB16 2s. booklet containing 24×1d. (No. 578) in blocks of 6 ... £300

NEW ZEALAND
Post and Telegraph Department
EIGHTEEN PRICE
1d. STAMPS 2s.3d

B 1

1938 (1 July). Cream cover as T B 1.

SB17 2s. booklet containing 24×1d. (No. 605) in blocks of 6 ... £375

1938 (Nov). Cream (No. SB18) or blue (No. SB19) covers as T B 1.

SB18 2s. booklet containing 12×½d. and 18×1d. (Nos. 603, 605) in blocks of 6 ... £500
SB19 2s.3d. booklet containing 18×1½d. (No. 607) in blocks of 6 ... £400

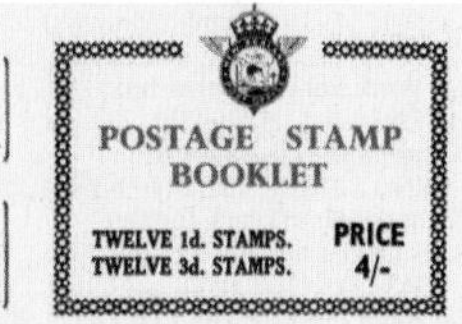

POSTAGE STAMP
BOOKLET
TWELVE 1d. STAMPS.
TWELVE 3d. STAMPS.
PRICE
4/-

B 2

1954 (1 Apr)–**55**. Black and green on cream cover as T B **2**.

SB20 4s. booklet containing 12×1d. and 12×3d. (Nos. 724, 727), each in blocks of 6 ... 4·00
a. Contents as SB20 but with one pane of air mail labels (9.55) ... 21·00

1956 (1 May). Black and green on cream cover as T B **2**.

SB21 4s. booklet containing 12×1d. and 12×3d. (Nos. 724, 748), each in blocks of 6, and one pane of air mail labels ... 10·00

1957 (5 Sept). Black and green on cream cover as T B **2**.

SB22 4s. booklet containing 12×1d. and 12×3d. (Nos. 745, 748), each in blocks of 6, and one pane of air mail labels ... 9·00

B **3**

1960 (1 Sept). Black and red on cream cover as T B **3**.

SB23 4s. booklet containing 12×1d. and 12×3d. (Nos. 782, 785), each in blocks of 6, and one pane of air mail labels ... 14·00

1962 (21 May). Black and red on cream cover as T B **3**.

SB24 4s.6d. booklet containing 12×½d., 12×1d. and 12×3d. (Nos. 781, 782, 785), each in blocks of 6, and one pane of air mail labels ... 50·00

1964. Black and carmine on cream cover as T B **3**. Stitched.

SB25 4s.3d. booklet containing 6×½d. and 12×1d. and 12×3d. (Nos. 781/782, 785), each in blocks of 6, and one pane of air mail labels ... 16·00

POSTAGE STAMPS
SIX ½c
ELEVEN 1c
TWELVE 3c
PRICE 50c

B **4** Maori Art

1967 (10 July). Black and carmine on pale lemon cover as T B **4**. Stitched.

SB26 50c. booklet containing ½c. (No. 845) in block of 6, 11×1c. in block of 6 (No. 846) and pane of 5 stamps and 1 label (No. 846a), and 12×3c. (No. 849) in blocks of 6 ... 6·50

EXPRESS DELIVERY STAMPS

SECURES IMMEDIATE DELIVERY
AT A SPECIAL DELIVERY OFFICE.

E **1**

(Typo Govt Printing Office, Wellington)

1903 (9 Feb). Value in first colour. W **43** (sideways). P 11.

E1 E **1** 6d. red and violet ... 38·00 23·00

1926–36. Thick, white, opaque chalk-surfaced Cowan paper. W **43**.

(a) P 14×14½

E2 E **1** 6d. vermilion and bright violet ... 50·00 26·00
w. Wmk inverted ... £300

(b) P 14×15 (1936)

E3 E **1** 6d. carmine and bright violet ... 70·00 60·00

1937–39. Thin, hard, chalk-surfaced Wiggins Teape paper.

(a) P 14×14½

E4 E **1** 6d. carmine and bright violet ... £110 50·00

(b) P 14×15 (4.39)

E5 E **1** 6d. vermilion and bright violet ... £180 £350

E **2** Express Mail Delivery Van

(Des J. Berry. Eng Stamp Ptg Office, Melbourne. Recess Govt Ptg Office, Wellington)

1939 (16 Aug). W **43**. P 14.

E6 E **2** 6d. violet ... 1·50 1·75
w. Wmk inverted ... 90·00

No. E6 was withdrawn on 30 June 1948, when the Express Delivery Service ceased.

POSTAGE DUE STAMPS

D **1**

(I)

(II)

3D. *(a)* Large 'D' **5D.** *(b)* Small 'D'

(Typo Govt Printing Office, Wellington)

1899 (1 Dec)–**1900**. Coarse paper. W **12b**. P 11.

I. Type I. Circle of 14 ornaments 17 dots over 'N.Z.', 'N.Z.' large

(a) Large 'D'

D1 D **1** ½d. carmine and green ... 45·00 45·00
a. No stop after 'D' (Right pane R. 2/3) ... £225 £250
D2 8d. carmine and green ... 75·00 £100
a. Carmine '8D.' printed double ...
D3 1s. carmine and green ... £100 £120
D4 2s. carmine and green ... £130 £170
D1/D4 *Set of 4* ... £300 £400

To avoid further subdivision the 1s. and 2s. are placed with the *pence* values, although the two types of 'D' do not apply to the higher values.

(b) Small 'D'

D6 D **1** 5d. carmine and green ... 40·00 50·00
D7 6d. carmine and green ... 48·00 55·00
D8 10d. carmine and green ... 85·00 £130
D6/D8 *Set of 3* ... £150 £200

II. Type II. Circle of 13 ornaments, 15 dots over 'N.Z.', 'N.Z.' small

(a) Large 'D'

D9 D **1** ½d. vermilion and green (5.00) ... 4·25 17·00
a. No stop after 'D' (Right pane R. 2/3) ... 65·00 £120
D10 1d. vermilion and green ... 26·00 3·75
D11 2d. vermilion and green ... 55·00 9·00
D12 3d. vermilion and green ... 19·00 7·00
D9/D12 *Set of 4* ... 85·00 32·00

(b) Small 'D'

D14 D **1** 1d. vermilion and green ... 26·00 3·75
D15 2d. vermilion and green ... 55·00 9·50
D16 4d. vermilion and green ... 40·00 21·00
D14/D16 *Set of 3* ... £100 30·00

Nos. D9/D16 were printed from a common frame plate of 240 (4 panes of 60) used in conjunction with centre plates of 120 (2 panes of 60) for the ½d. and 4d. or 240 for the other values. Sheets of the 1d. and 2d. each contained two panes with large 'D' and two panes with small 'D'.

D **2**

D **3**

(Des W. R. Bock. Typo Govt Printing Office)

1902 (28 Feb). No wmk. P 11.

D17 D **2** ½d. red and deep green ... 3·75 9·00

1904–08. Cowan unsurfaced paper. W **43** (sideways).

(a) P 11

D18 D **2** ½d. red and green (4.04) ... 3·75 3·00
a. Imperf between (horiz pair) ... £1400
D19 1d. red and green (5.12.05) ... 24·00 3·50
D20 2d. red and green (5.4.06) ... £120 £130
D18/D20 *Set of 3* ... £130 £130

(b) P 14

D21 D **2** 1d. carmine and green (12.06) ... 27·00 1·50
a. Rose-pink and green (9.07) ... 15·00 1·50
D22 2d. carmine and green (10.06) ... 15·00 11·00
a. Rose-pink and green (6.08) ... 10·00 3·00

The note regarding sideways watermark varieties below No. 299 applies here also.

1919 (Jan)–**20**. De La Rue chalky paper. Toned gum. W **43**. P 14×15.

D23 D **2** ½d. carmine and green (6.19) ... 3·75 6·00
D24 1d. carmine and green ... 10·00 50
w. Wmk inverted ... † £500
D25 2d. carmine and green (8.20) ... 28·00 4·50
D23/D25 *Set of 3* ... 38·00 9·50

1925 (May). Jones chalky paper. White gum. W **43**. P 14×15.

D26 D **2** ½d. carmine and green ... 48·00 65·00

1925 (July). No wmk, but bluish 'N Z' and Star lithographed on back. P 14×15.

D27 D **2** ½d. carmine and green ... 2·00 25·00
D28 2d. carmine and green ... 4·00 38·00

1925 (Nov)–**35**. Cowan thick, opaque chalky paper. W **43**.

(a) P 14×15

D29 D **2** ½d. carmine and green (12.26) ... 2·25 14·00
D30 1d. carmine and green ... 4·25 80
D31 2d. carmine and green (6.26) ... 30·00 4·25
x. Wmk reversed ... 65·00 35·00
D32 3d. carmine and green (6.35) ... 55·00 55·00
D29/D32 *Set of 4* ... 80·00 65·00

(b) P 14

D33 D **2** ½d. carmine and green (10.28) ... 65·00 55·00
D34 1d. rose and pale yellow-green (6.28) ... 4·00 1·25
D35 2d. carmine and green (10.29) ... 7·50 3·00
D36 3d. carmine and green (5.28) ... 17·00 50·00
D33/D36 *Set of 4* ... 85·00 £100

1937–38. Wiggins Teape thin, hard chalky paper. W **43**. P 14×15.

D37 D **2** ½d. carmine and yellow-green (2.38) ... 25·00 45·00
D38 1d. carmine and yellow-green (1.37) ... 18·00 4·25

D39 2d. carmine and yellow-green (6.37) 30·00 15·00
D40 3d. carmine and yellow-green (11.37) £100 75·00
D37/D40 *Set of 4* £160 £120

(Des J. Berry. Typo Govt Printing Office, Wellington)

1939–49. P 15×14.

(a) W **43** *(sideways inverted) (16.8.39)*

D41 D **3** ½d. turquoise-green 5·00 5·00
D42 1d. carmine 4·00 4·25
w. Wmk sideways £225 14·00
D43 2d. bright blue 6·00 2·75
w. Wmk sideways £275
D44 3d. orange-brown 38·00 25·00
w. Wmk sideways £225
D41/D44 *Set of 4* 48·00 32·00

(b) W **98** *(sideways (1d.), sideways inverted (2d.) or upright (3d.)*

D45 D **3** 1d. carmine (4.49) 20·00 7·50
D46 2d. bright blue (12.46) 11·00 5·00
w. Wmk sideways (4.49) 2·75 13·00
D47 3d. orange-brown (1943) 60·00 50·00
a. Wmk sideways inverted (6.45) 32·00 17·00
aw. Wmk sideways (28.11.49) 9·00 22·00
D45/D47aw *Set of 3* 29·00 26·00*

* The use of Postage Due stamps ceased on 30 September 1951, our used price for No. D45 being for stamps postmarked after this date (*price for examples clearly cancelled 1949–1951, £35*).

OFFICIAL STAMPS

1891 (Dec)–**1906**. Contemporary issues handstamped 'O.P.S.O.' in 3½mm capital letters.

(a) Stamps of 1873 type optd in violet. P 12½

O1 **3** ½d. pale dull rose (W **4**) (No. 149) — £1400
O2 ½d. bright rose (W **12b**) (No. 151) — £900

(b) Stamps of 1882–1897 optd in rose/magenta. W **12b**

O3 **13** ½d. black (P 10) (No. 217) — £800
a. Violet opt — £950
O4 ½d. black (P 10×11) (No. 227) — £800
O5 1d. rose (P 12×11½) (No. 195*b*) — £800
a. Violet opt —
O6 1d. rose (P 10) (violet opt) (No. 218) —
O7 1d. rose (P 11) (No. 237) — £800
a. Violet opt —
O8 2d. purple (P 11) (No. 238) — £850
a. Violet opt —
O9 2d. mauve-lilac (P 10) (No. 219) — £850
a. Advert on back (3rd setting) —
b. Violet opt — £1200
ba. Advert on back —
O10 2½d. blue (P 12×11½) (violet opt) (No. 197) —
O11 2½d. blue (P 11) (violet opt) (No. 239) — £850
O12 2½d. ultramarine (P 10) (No. 220) — £850
a. Advert on back —
b. Violet opt —
ba. Green advert (2nd setting) —
bb. Mauve advert (3rd setting) —
O13 2½d. ultramarine (P 10×11) (No. 230) — £850
a. Violet opt —
O14 5d. olive-black (P 12×11½) (No. 200) — £1100
a. violet opt —
O15 6d. brown (P 12½×11½) (No. 201) — £1300

(c) Stamps of 1898–1903 optd in violet. P 11

(i) No wmk

O16 ½d. green (P 14) (No. 294) — £800
a. Rose or magenta opt —
O17 2½d. blue (P 12-16) (No. 249) — £1200
O18 2½d. blue (No. 260) — £950
a. Rose/magenta opt —
O19 4d. indigo and brown (No. 262) — £1100
O20 5d. purple-brown (No. 263) — £1100
a. Rose/magenta opt —
b. Greenish blue opt —
O21 8d. Indigo (No. 266) — £1300
O22 1s. red (No. 268) — £2500

(ii) W **38**

O23 ½d. green (No. 273*b*) —
O24 1d. carmine (No. 278) — £850
a. Blue opt —

(iii) W **43** *(sideways on 3d. 5d., 1s.)*

O25 ½d. green (P 14) (No. 302) —
a. Rose or magenta opt —
O26 1d. carmine (P 14) (No. 303) — £850
a. Green opt — £850
O27 1d. carmine (P 14) (No. 349) —
O28 1d. carmine (P 14) (No. 356) — £850
O29 1d. carmine (No. 357) (black opt) —
O30 2½d. blue (No. 308) — £900
O31 3d. yellow-brown (No. 309) — £1100
O32 5d. red-brown (No. 311) —
O33 1s. orange-red (No. 315*b*) — £2500
O34 2s. green (No. 316) — £3750

The letters signify 'On Public Service Only' and stamps so overprinted were used exclusively at the General Post Office, Wellington, on official correspondence to foreign countries between December 1891 and 31 December 1906.

Four different handstamps were used, differing slightly in the length of the overprint. The handstamp was normally applied diagonally reading upwards but other positions are known.

The stamps were not available unused and such examples with the 'O.P.S.O.' handstamp are generally considered to be reprints.

OFFICIAL.

(O 3)

1907–11. Stamps of 1902–1906 optd with T O **3** (vertically, upwards). W **43** (sideways on 3d., 6d., 1s. and 5s.). P 14.

O59 **23** ½d. yellow-green 18·00 75
a. Perf 11×14 £350
b. Mixed perfs £350 £350
O60 **42** 1d. carmine (No. 303) (1.7.07*) 14·00 22·00
a. Booklet pane of 6 55·00
ab. Imperf horiz (booklet pane of 6) £2750
O60*b* 1d. rose-carmine (Waterlow) (No. 352) 32·00 70
ba. Perf 11×14 — £550
bb. Mixed perfs — £550
bc. Perf 14×11 — £1000
O60*c* 1d. carmine (Royle) 60·00 70
ca. Perf 11×14 £375 £600
cb. Mixed perfs £375 £475
O61 **41** 2d. purple 19·00 1·75
a. Bright reddish purple 8·50 1·60
ab. Mixed perfs £550 £425
O63 **28** 3d. bistre-brown 50·00 1·75
a. Mixed perfs — £1600
O64 **31** 6d. bright carmine-pink £250 25·00
a. Imperf vert (horiz pair) £1500
b. Mixed perfs £1000 £750
c. Opt inverted (reading downwards) † £4250
O65 **34** 1s. orange-red £110 22·00
O66 **35** 2s. blue-green 85·00 £140
a. Imperf between (pair) £4000
b. Imperf vert (horiz pair) £2750
w. Wmk inverted £750 £550
O67 **36** 5s. deep red £170 £190
a. Wmk upright (1911) £1200 £1200

* Though issued in 1907 a large quantity of booklets was mislaid and not utilised until they were found in 1930.

1908–09. Optd as T O **3**. W **43**.

O69 **23** ½d. green (P 14×15) 20·00 6·00
O70 **50** 1d. carmine (P 14×15) 70·00 6·00
O71 **48** 6d. pink (P 14×13, 13½) £200 48·00
O72 6d. pink (P 14×15) (1909) £225 35·00
O72*a* F **4** £1 rose-pink (P 14) (No. F89) £650 £450

1910. No. 387 optd with T O **3**.

O73 **51** ½d. yellow-green 18·00 40
a. Opt inverted (reading downwards) † £3000

1910–16. Nos. 389 and 392/394 optd with T O **3**. P 14×14½.

O74 **52** 3d. chestnut 14·00 80
a. Perf 14×13½ (1915) 75·00 £130
ab. Vert pair. Nos. O74/O74a £350 £750
O75 — 6d. carmine 19·00 5·50
a. Perf 14 (line) (No. 398) † £5000
b. Deep carmine 25·00 6·00
w. Wmk inverted
O76 – 8d. indigo-blue (R.) (5.16) 12·00 29·00
aw. Wmk inverted 75·00 85·00
b. Perf 14×13½ 12·00 29·00
bw. Wmk inverted 75·00 85·00
c. Vert pair, Nos. O76 and O76b 70·00 £140
cw. Wmk inverted £275 £325
O77 1s. vermilion 55·00 20·00
O74/O77 *Set of 4* 90·00 50·00

1910–26. Optd with T O **3**.

(a) W **43**. *De La Rue chalk-surfaced paper with toned gum*

O78 **53** 1d. carmine (No. 405) 5·50 10
a. 'Feather' flaw 75·00 15·00
b. 'Globe' flaw 75·00 15·00
c. 'Q' flaw 80·00 50·00
y. Wmk inverted and reversed

(b) W **43**. *Jones chalk-surfaced paper with white gum*

O79 **53** 1d. deep carmine (No. 406) (1925) 17·00 11·00
a. 'Feather' flaw £170 85·00
b. 'Globe' flaw £170 85·00

(c) No wmk, but bluish 'NZ' and Star lithographed on back. Art paper

O80 **53** 1d. rose-carmine (No. 409) (1925) 7·00 22·00
a. 'Feather' flaw 75·00
b. 'Globe' flaw 75·00

(d) W **43**. *Cowan thick, opaque, chalk-surfaced paper with white gum*

O81 **53** 1d. deep carmine (No. 410) (1925) 8·00 1·25
a. 'Feather' flaw 80·00 35·00
b. 'Globe' flaw 80·00 35·00
c. 'N' flaw £200 £110
x. Wmk reversed (1926) 60·00 40·00
xa. 'Feather' flaw £350 £250
xb. 'Globe' flaw £350 £250
xc. 'N' flaw £350 £250

1913–25. Postal Fiscal stamps optd with T O **3**.

(i) Chalk-surfaced De La Rue paper

(a) P 14 (1913–1914)

O82 F **4** 2s. blue (30.9.14) 65·00 50·00
O83 5s. yellow-green (13.6.13) 90·00 £130
O84 £1 rose-carmine (1913) £650 £550
O82/O84 *Set of 3* £750 £650

(b) P 14½×14, comb (1915)

O85 F **4** 2s. deep blue (8.15) 65·00 50·00
a. No stop after 'OFFICIAL' (R. 2/5) £180 £160
O86 5s. yellow-green (1.15) 90·00 £130
a. No stop after 'OFFICIAL' (R. 2/5) £275 £350

(ii) Thick, white, opaque chalk-surfaced Cowan paper. P 14½×14 (1925)

O87 F **4** 2s. blue 85·00 £100
a. No stop after 'OFFICIAL' (R. 2/5) £250 £300

The overprint on these last, and on Nos. O69 and O72*a* is from a new set of type, giving a rather sharper impression than T O **3**, but otherwise resembling it closely.

1915 (12 Oct)–**34.** Optd with T O **3**. P 14×15.

(a) On Nos. 435/440 (De La Rue chalk-surfaced paper with toned gum)

O88 **61** ½d. green 1·25 20
O89 **62** 1½d. grey-black (6.16) 8·50 2·75
O90 **61** 1½d. slate (12.16) 5·50 1·00
O91 1½d. orange-brown (4.19) 5·00 30
O92 2d. yellow (4.17) 13·00 20
O93 3d. chocolate (11.19) 12·00 1·00
O88/O93 *Set of 6* 40·00 5·00

(b) On Nos. 441 and 443 (Jones chalk-surfaced paper with white gum)

O94 **61** ½d. green (1924) 4·50 3·50
O95 3d. deep chocolate (1924) 50·00 9·50

(c) On Nos. 446/447 and 448a/449 (Cowan thick, opaque, chalk surfaced paper with white gum)

O96 **61** ½d. green (1925) 6·00 10
ax. Wmk reversed (1927) 85·00 27·00
ay. Wmk inverted and reversed (1927) £325 65·00
b. Perf 14 (1929) 3·75 70
ba. No stop after 'OFFICIAL' 35·00 40·00
O97 1½d. orange-brown (P 14) (1929) 16·00 17·00
a. No stop after 'OFFICIAL' £110 £110
b. Perf 14×15 (1934) 50·00 48·00
O98 2d. yellow (P 14) (1931) 2·50 50
a. No stop after 'OFFICIAL' 75·00 80·00
O99 3d. chocolate (1925) 7·00 70
a. No stop after 'OFFICIAL' 75·00 55·00
b. Perf 14 (1930) 70·00 16·00
ba. No stop after 'OFFICIAL' £275 £200
O96/O99 *Set of 4* 26·00 17·00

1915 (Dec)–**27.** Optd with T O **3**. P 14×13½.

(a) Nos. 420, 422, 425, 428 and 429/430 (Cowan unsurfaced paper)

O100 **60** 3d. chocolate 4·50 1·50
aw. Wmk inverted 32·00 7·00
b. Perf 14×14½ 4·50 1·75
bw. Wmk inverted 50·00 12·00
c. Vert pair, Nos. O100 and O100b 40·00 £120
cw. Wmk inverted £140 £225
d. Opt double † £1400
O101 4d. bright violet (4.25) 14·00 7·50
a. Re-entry (Pl 20 R. 1/6) 85·00 60·00
b. Re-entry (Pl 20 R. 4/10) 90·00 70·00
c. Perf 14×14½ (Deep purple) (4.27) 40·00 1·25
O102 6d. carmine (6.16) 5·00 75
aw. Wmk inverted £140
b. Perf 14×14½ 5·00 2·00
c. Vert pair, Nos. O102 and O102b 55·00 £140
O103 8d. red-brown (8.22) 65·00 £190
O104 9d. sage-green (4.25) 42·00 38·00
O105 1s. vermilion (9.16) 25·00 14·00
aw. Wmk inverted £275 £170
ax. Wmk reversed † —
b. Perf 14×14½ 7·00 2·00
ba. Pale orange-red 15·00 20·00
bw. Wmk inverted £250 £275
c. Vert pair. Nos. O105 and O105b. 65·00 £190
cw. Wmk inverted £650
O100/O105 *Set of 6* £120 £200

(b) No. 433 (Thin paper with widely spaced sideways wmk)

O106 **60** 3d. chocolate (P 14) (7.16) 3·00 15·00
a. No wmk 50·00 80·00

1927–33. Optd with T O **3**. W **43**. P 14.

O111 **71** 1d. rose-carmine (No. 468) 2·00 20
a. No stop after 'OFFICIAL' (R. 1/2, 5/24) 42·00 £110
bw. Wmk inverted † 50·00
c. Perf 14×15 9·00 20
O112 **72** 2s. light blue (No. 469) (2.28) 85·00 £130
O113 F **6** 5s. green (1933) £325 £375
O111/O113 *Set of 3* £375 £475

Unused examples of No. O111 are known printed on Cowan unsurfaced paper.

Official (O 4) *Official* (O 5)

1936–61. Pictorial issue optd horiz or vert (2s.) with T O **4**.

(a) W **43** *(Single 'N Z' and Star)*

O115 **82** 1d. scarlet (Die I) (P 14×13½) (21.3.36) 10·00 1·25
a. Perf 13½×14 £140 85·00
O116 **83** 1½d. red-brown (P 13½×14) (3.36) 45·00 35·00
a. Perf 14×13½ £20000
O118 **92** 1s. deep green (P 14×13½) (3.36) 50·00 65·00
w. Wmk inverted † £650
O119 F **6** 5s. green (P 14) (12.38) £160 65·00
O115/O119 *Set of 4* £225 £160

The watermark of No. O119 is almost invisible.

Only four examples of No. O116a exist. The error occurred when a sheet of No. 558a was found to have a block of four missing. This was replaced by a block of No. 558 and the sheet was then sent for overprinting.

(b) W **98** *(Mult 'N Z' and Star)*

O120 **81** ½d. bright green, P 14×13½ (7.37) 7·50 4·50
O121 **82** 1d. scarlet (Die II), P 14×13½ (11.36) 12·00 50
w. Wmk inverted (2.37) 48·00 55·00
O122 **83** 1½d. red-brown, P 14×13½ (7.36) 35·00 5·00
O123 **84** 2d. orange, P 14×13½ (1.38) 13·00 10
aw. Wmk inverted — £400
b. Perf 12½ (1941) £200 60·00
c. Perf 14 (1941) 65·00 16·00
O124 **85** 2½d. chocolate and slate, P 13-14×13½ (26.7.38) 70·00 £110
a. Perf 14 (1938) 14·00 21·00
O125 **86** 3d. brown, P 14×13½ (1.3.38) 48·00 3·50
w. Wmk inverted — £400
O126 **87** 4d. black and sepia, P 14×13½ (8.36) 23·00 1·10
a. Perf 14 (8.41) 24·00 4·50
b. Perf 12½ (12.41) 24·00 10·00
c. Perf 14×14½ (10.42) 10·00 1·00
cw. Wmk inverted — £800
O127 **89** 6d. scarlet, P 13½×14 (12.37) 40·00 80
aw. Wmk inverted † £750
b. Perf 12½ (1941) 15·00 10·00
c. Perf 14½×14 (7.42) 17·00 40
O128 **90** 8d. chocolate, P 12½ (wmk sideways) (17.8.42) 23·00 17·00
a. Perf 14×14½ (wmk sideways) (8.45) 8·50 16·00
aw. Wmk sideways inverted † —
b. Perf 14×13½ (1942) † £3750
O129 **91** 9d. red and grey-black (G.) (No. 587*b*), P 13½×14 (1.3.38) 90·00 40·00
O130 9d. scarlet and black (*chalk-surfaced paper*) (Blk.) (No. 631), P 14×15 (10.43) 20·00 22·00
O131 **92** 1s. deep green, P 14×13½ (2.37) 50·00 1·50
aw. Wmk inverted — £750
b. Perf 12½ (4.42) 40·00 3·00

O132	**93**	2s. olive-green, P 13–14×13½ (5.37)	80·00	45·00
		a. 'CAPTAIN COQK'	£225	£130
		b. Perf 13½×14 (5.39)	£250	11·00
		ba. 'CAPTAIN COQK'	£350	85·00
		c. Perf 12½ (3.42)	80·00	22·00
		ca. 'CAPTAIN COQK'	£225	85·00
		d. Perf 14×13½ (1944)	50·00	11·00
		da. 'CAPTAIN COQK'	£500	£225
O133	**F 6**	5s. green (*chalk-surfaced paper*), P 14 (3.43)	50·00	6·00
		aw. Wmk inverted	40·00	6·00
		b. Perf 14×13½. Yellow-green (ordinary paper) (10.61)	14·00	30·00
O120/O133 *Set of 14*			£350	£120

The opt on No. O127b was sometimes applied at the top of the stamp, instead of always at the bottom as on No. O127.

All examples of No. O128b were used by a government office in Whangarei.

The 5s. value on ordinary paper perforated 14×13½ does not exist without the 'Official' overprint.

See notes on perforations after No. 590c.

1938–51. Nos. 603 etc., optd with T O **4**.

O134	**108**	½d. green (1.3.38)	20·00	2·25
O135		½d. brown-orange (1946)	2·75	4·25
O136		1d. scarlet (1.7.38)	30·00	15
O137		1d. green (10.7.41)	7·00	10
O138	**108a**	1½d. purple-brown (26.7.38)	75·00	20·00
O139		1½d. scarlet (2.4.51)	12·00	5·00
O140		3d. blue (16.10.41)	7·50	10
O134/O140 *Set of 7*			£140	28·00

1940 (2 Jan–8 Mar). Centennial. Nos. 613, etc., optd with T O **5**.

O141	½d. blue-green (R.)	3·00	35
	a. 'ff' joined, as Type O **4**	55·00	65·00
O142	1d. chocolate and scarlet	7·50	10
	a. 'ff' joined, as Type O **4**	50·00	60·00
O143	1½d. light blue and mauve	6·50	2·00
O144	2d. blue-green and chocolate	9·50	10
	a. 'ff' joined, as Type O **4**	65·00	65·00
O145	2½d. blue-green and ultramarine	5·00	2·25
	a. 'ff' joined, as Type O **4**	50·00	75·00
O146	3d. purple and carmine (R.)	8·00	1·00
	a. 'ff' joined, as Type O **4**	45·00	55·00
O147	4d. chocolate and lake	42·00	1·50
	a. 'ff' joined, as Type O **4**	£120	£100
O148	6d. emerald-green and violet	35·00	1·50
	a. 'ff' joined, as Type O **4**	80·00	75·00
O149	8d. black and red (8.3)	35·00	15·00
	a. 'ff' joined, as Type O **4**	80·00	£120
O150	9d. olive-green and vermilion	14·00	3·00
O151	1s. sage-green and deep green	50·00	2·50
O141/O151 *Set of 11*		£190	26·00

For this issue the T O **4** overprint occurs on R. 4/3 of the 2½d. and on R. 1/10 of the other values.

1947 (1 May)–**51**. Nos. 680, etc., optd with T O **4**.

O152	**108a**	2d. orange	3·00	10
O153		4d. bright purple	4·75	4·50
O154		6d. carmine	15·00	50
O155		8d. violet	9·00	7·50
O156		9d. purple-brown	10·00	6·50
O157	**144**	1s. red-brown and carmine (wmk upright) (Plate 1)	17·00	1·00
		a. Wmk sideways (Plate 1) (6.49)	8·50	12·00
		aw. Wmk sideways inverted	55·00	45·00
		b. Wmk upright (Plate 2) (4.51)	24·00	7·50
		bw. Wmk inverted	£225	75·00
O158		2s. brown-orange and green (wmk sideways) (Plate 1)	42·00	16·00
		a. Wmk upright (Plate 1)	35·00	48·00
O152/O158 *Set of 7*			75·00	32·00

O **6** Queen Elizabeth II

6d (O **7**)

(Des J. Berry. Recess B.W.)

1954 (1 Mar)–**63**. W **98**. P 14×13½.

O159	**O6**	1d. orange	75	1·00
		a. White opaque paper (8.7.59)	50	1·00
O160		1½d. brown-lake	2·75	3·50
O161		2d. bluish green	50	50
		a. White opaque paper (11.12.58)	40	60
O162		2½d. olive (*white opaque paper*) (1.3.63)	3·00	1·50
O163		3d. vermilion	70	10
		a. White opaque paper (1960)	40	10
		aw. Wmk inverted	40·00	30·00
O164		4d. blue	1·50	75
		a. Printed on the gummed side	£200	
		b. White opaque paper (1.9.61)	1·00	50
O165		9d. carmine	7·50	3·25
O166		1s. purple	1·75	30
		a. White opaque paper (2.10.61)	2·50	1·00
O167		3s. slate (*white opaque paper*) (1.3.63)	24·00	40·00
O159/O167 *Set of 9*			38·00	48·00

See note *re* white opaque paper after No. 736.

No. O164a shows the watermark inverted and reversed.

1959 (1 Oct). No. O160 surch with T O **7**.

O168	O **6**	6d. on 1½d. brown-lake	50	1·10

1961 (1 Sept). No. O161 surch as T O **7**.

O169	O **6**	2½d. on 2d. bluish green	1·25	2·50

Owing to the greater use of franking machines by Government Departments, the use of official stamps was discontinued on 31 March 1965, but they remained on sale at the GPO until 31 December 1965.

STAMP BOOKLET

1907 (1 July). White card cover.

OB1	10s. booklet containing 120×1d. in panes of 6 (No. O60a)	£1200

PROVISIONALS ISSUED AT REEFTON AND USED BY THE POLICE DEPARTMENT

1907 (Jan). Current stamps of 1906, optd 'Official', in red manuscript and handstamped with a circular 'Greymouth—PAID—3'. P 14.

P1	**23**	½d. green	£1300	£1600
P2	**40**	1d. carmine	£1300	£1500
P3	**38**	2d. purple	£1500	£2000
P4	**28**	3d. bistre	£2250	
P5	**31**	6d. pink	£2250	
P6	**34**	1s. orange-red	£3000	
P7	**35**	2s. green	£8500	

Only the ½d., 1d. and 2d. are known postally used, cancelled with the Reefton squared circle postmark. The 3d. and 6d. were later cancelled by favour at Wanganui.

LIFE INSURANCE DEPARTMENT

L **1** Lighthouse

L **2** Lighthouse

2d. 'Z' flaw (R. 1/6, upper right pane)

(Des W. B. Hudson and J. F. Rogers; Eng. A. E. Cousins. Typo Govt Printing Office, Wellington)

1891 (2 Jan)–**98**.

A. W **12c**. *P 12×11½*

L1	L **1**	½d. bright purple	£110	6·00
		a. Mixed perf 12×11 and 12½	†	—
		x. Wmk reversed	†	£190
L2		1d. blue	90·00	4·00
		ax. Wmk reversed	†	£190
		ay. Wmk inverted and reversed	†	£110
		b. Wmk **12b**	£180	28·00
		bx. Wmk reversed	†	£500
L3		2d. brown-red	£170	15·00
		ax. Wmk reversed	†	£160
		b. Wmk **12b**	£190	22·00
L4		3d. deep brown	£325	38·00
L5		6d. green	£400	80·00
L6		1s. rose	£600	£150
L1/L6 *Set of 6*			£1500	£250

B. W **12b** *(1893–1898)*

(a) P 10 (1893)

L7	L **1**	½d. bright purple	£110	23·00
L8		1d. blue	90·00	1·75
L9		2d. brown-red	£150	3·75
		a. 'Z' flaw	—	£110
L7/L9 *Set of 3*			£300	26·00

(b) P 11×10

L10	L **1**	½d. bright purple (1896)	£120	28·00
		a. Perf 10×11	£300	£110
L11		1d. blue (1897)	†	90·00
		a. Perf 10×11	£110	14·00

(c) Mixed perfs 10 and 11 (1897)

L12	L **1**	2d. brown-red	£1400	£1000

(d) P 11 (1897–1898)

L13	L **1**	½d. bright purple	95·00	4·00
		a. Thin coarse toned paper (1898)	£180	15·00
L14		1d. blue	90·00	75
		a. Thin coarse toned paper (1898)	£190	6·50
		x. Wmk reversed	£275	55·00
		y. Wmk inverted and reversed	£275	60·00
L15		2d. brown-red	£170	3·50
		a. Chocolate	£190	25·00
		b. Thin coarse toned paper (1898)	£300	6·00
		c. 'Z' flaw	—	£110
L13/L15 *Set of 3*			£300	7·50

1902–04. W **43** (sideways).

(a) P 11

L16	L **1**	½d. bright purple (1903)	£110	15·00
L17		1d. blue (1902)	90·00	3·25
L18		2d. brown-red (1904)	£225	22·00
L16/L18 *Set of 3*			£375	35·00

(b) P 14×11

L19	L **1**	½d. bright purple (1903)	£2500	£1500
L20		1d. blue (1904)	£160	15·00

Nos. L16/L17 and L20 are known without watermark from the margins of the sheet. Note that the W **43** watermark may be found both sideways and sideways inverted.

1905–06. Redrawn, with 'V.R.' omitted. W **43** (sideways).

(a) P 11

L21	L **2**	2d. brown-red (12.05)	£1500	£130

(b) P 14

L22	L **2**	1d. blue (7.06)	£275	30·00

(c) P 14×11

L23	L **2**	1d. blue (7.06)	£850	£225
		a. Mixed perfs	†	£750

Between January 1907 and the end of 1912 the Life Insurance Department used ordinary Official stamps.

1913 (2 Jan)–**37**. New values and colours. W **43**.

(a) De La Rue paper. P 14×15

L24	L **2**	½d. green	22·00	2·50
		a. Yellow-green	22·00	2·50
L25		1d. carmine	21·00	1·25
		a. Carmine-pink	24·00	1·75
L26		1½d. black (1917)	50·00	8·50
L27		1½d. chestnut-brown (1919)	1·50	3·00
L28		2d. bright purple	60·00	35·00
		w. Wmk inverted	†	£350
L29		2d. yellow (1920)	12·00	4·00
L30		3d. yellow-brown	55·00	38·00
L31		6d. carmine-pink	50·00	35·00
L24/L31 *Set of 8*			£225	£110

(b) Cowan paper

(i) P 14×15

L31*a*	L **2**	½d. yellow-green (1925)	45·00	4·50
		aw. Wmk inverted	†	—
L31*b*		1d. carmine-pink (1925)	42·00	3·50
		bw. Wmk inverted	£200	75·00

(ii) P 14

L32	L **2**	½d. yellow-green (1926)	24·00	4·00
		w. Wmk inverted	†	90·00
L33		1d. scarlet (1931)	8·50	2·00
		w. Wmk inverted	£100	50·00
L34		2d. yellow (1937)	7·00	13·00
		w. Wmk inverted	£100	£130
L35		3d. brown-lake (1931)	14·00	24·00
		a. 'HREE' for 'THREE' (R. 7/11)	£375	
L36		6d. pink (1925)	55·00	60·00
L32/L36 *Set of 5*			95·00	90·00

(c) Wiggins Teape paper. P 14×15

L36*a*	L **2**	½d. yellow-green (3.37)	8·00	12·00
L36*b*		1d. scarlet (3.37)	22·00	3·25
L36*c*		6d. pink (7.37)	35·00	40·00
L36*a*/L36*c* *Set of 3*			60·00	50·00

For descriptions of the various types of paper, see after No. 385. In the 1½d. the word 'POSTAGE' is in both the side-labels instead of at left only.

1944–47. W **98**. P 14×15.

L37	L **2**	½d. yellow-green (7.47)	8·50	9·00
L38		1d. scarlet (6.44)	3·25	2·00
L39		2d. yellow (1946)	17·00	40·00
L40		3d. brown-lake (10.46)	32·00	42·00
		a. 'HREE' for 'THREE' (R. 7/11)	£400	
L41		6d. pink (7.47)	20·00	55·00
L37/L41 *Set of 5*			70·00	£130

L **3** Castlepoint lighthouse

L **4** Taiaroa lighthouse

L **5** Cape Palliser lighthouse

L **6** Cape Campbell lighthouse

L **7** Eddystone lighthouse

L **8** Stephens Island lighthouse

L **9** The Brothers lighthouse

L **10** Cape Brett lighthouse

(Des J. Berry. Recess B.W.).

1947 (1 Aug)–**65**. Types L **3**/L **10**. W **98** (sideways inverted on 1d., 2d., sideways on 2½d.). P 13½.

L42	L **3**	½d. grey-green and orange-red	1·75	70
L43	L **4**	1d. olive-green and pale blue	1·75	1·25
L44	L **5**	2d. deep blue and grey-black	3·75	1·00
L45	L **6**	2½d. black and bright blue (*white opaque paper*) (4.11.63)	9·50	13·00
L46	L **7**	3d. mauve and pale blue	4·50	1·25
L47	L **8**	4d. brown and yellow-orange	4·25	1·75
		a. Wmk sideways (*white opaque paper*) (13.10.65)	3·00	14·00
L48	L **9**	6d. chocolate and blue	4·50	2·75
L49	L **10**	1s. red-brown and blue	5·00	4·00
L42/L49 *Set of 8*			30·00	23·00

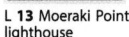

(L 11) (L 12)

1967 (10 July)–**68**. Decimal currency. Stamps of 1947–1965, surch as Types L **12** or L **11** (2c.).

No.	Description	Unused	Used
L50	1c. on 1d. (No. L43)	1·75	4·25
	a. Wmk upright (*white opaque paper*) (10.5.68)	1·00	7·00
L51	2c. on 2½d. (No. L45)	6·00	14·00
L52	2½c. on 3d. (No. L46)	1·25	4·00
	a. Horiz pair, one without surcharge	£4250	
	b. Wmk sideways (*white opaque paper*) (4.68?)	1·90	4·75
L53	3c. on 4d. (No. L47a)	2·25	5·00
	w. Wmk sideways inverted	£1600	£750
L54	5c. on 6d. (No. L48)	75	6·50
	a. White opaque paper	1·00	6·50
L55	10c. on 1s. (No. L49)	1·00	10·00
	a. Wmk sideways (*white opaque paper*)	75	4·00
	aw. Wmk sideways inverted	†	£475
L50/L55a	*Set of 6*	11·00	32·00

See note *re* white paper below No. 736.

L **13** Moeraki Point lighthouse

L **14** Puysegur Point lighthouse

L **14a** Baring Head lighthouse

L **14b** Cape Egmont lighthouse

L **14c** East Cape

L **14d** Farewell Spit

L **15** Dog Island lighthouse

(Des J. Berry. Litho B.W.)

1969 (27 Mar)–**76**. Types L **13**/L **15**. No wmk. Chalk-surfaced paper (8, 10c.), ordinary paper (others). P 14 (8, 10c.) or 13½ (others).

No.	Type	Description	Unused	Used
L56	L **13**	½c. greenish yellow, red and deep blue	55	1·50
L57	L **14**	2½c. ultramarine, green and pale buff	40	1·00
L58	L **14a**	3c. reddish brown and yellow	40	60
		a. Chalk-surfaced paper (1974)	40	2·75
L59	L **14b**	4c. light new blue, yellowish green and apple-green	40	75
		a. Chalk-surfaced paper (1975)	40	2·25
L60	L **14c**	8c. multicoloured (17.11.76)	30	2·00
L61	L **14d**	10c. multicoloured (17.11.76)	30	2·00
L62	L **15**	15c. black, light yellow and ultramarine	30	1·25
		a. Chalk-surfaced paper (3.75)	20·00	22·00
		ab. Perf 14 (24.12.76)	90	3·50
L56/L62		*Set of 7*	2·40	8·00

The ordinary paper stamps have shiny gum and fluoresce brightly under UV light. The chalk-surfaced paper stamps have matt, PVA gum and the front of the stamps give a dull reaction under UV light.

POSTAL FISCAL STAMPS

As from 1 April 1882 fiscal stamps were authorised for postal use and conversely postage stamps became valid for fiscal use. Stamps in the designs of 1867 with 'STAMP DUTY' above the Queen's head were withdrawn and although some passed through the mail quite legitimately they were mainly 'philatelic' and we no longer list them. The issue which was specifically authorised in 1882 was the one which had originally been put on sale for fiscal use in 1880.

There is strong evidence that the authorities used up existing low value revenue stamps for postage, delaying the general release of the new 'Postage and Revenue' low values (Types **14**, **15** and **18-22**) to achieve this. Used prices for such stamps are for examples with 1882–1883 postal cancellations.

Although all fiscal stamps were legally valid for postage, only values between 2s. and £1 were stocked at ordinary post offices. Other values could only be obtained by request from the GPO, Wellington or from offices of the Stamp Duties Department. From 1884 these stamps were also supplied to major telegraph offices in values between £1 and £10, where they were cancelled with postal datestamps until specific 'Telegraph office' cancellers were provided in the late 1890s. Later the Arms types above £1 could also be obtained from the head post offices in Auckland, Christchurch, Dunedin and also a branch post office at Christchurch North where there was a local demand for them.

It seems sensible to list under Postal Fiscals the Queen Victoria stamps up to the £1 value and the Arms types up to the £5 because by 1931 the higher values were genuinely needed for postal purposes. The £10 was occasionally used on insured airmail parcels and is therefore also listed.

Although 2s. and 5s. values were included in the 1898 pictorial issue, it was the general practice for the Postal Department to limit the postage issues to 1s. until 1926 when the 2s. and 3s. appeared. These were then dropped from the fiscal issues and when in turn the 5s. and 10s. were introduced in 1953 and the £1 in 1960 no further printings of these values occurred in the fiscal series.

FORGED POSTMARKS. Our prices are for stamps with genuine postal cancellations. Beware of forged postmarks on stamps from which fiscal cancellations have been cleaned off.

Many small post offices acted as agents for government departments and it was the practice to use ordinary postal date-stamps on stamps used fiscally, so that when they are removed from documents they are indistinguishable from postally used specimens unless impressed with the embossed seal of the Stamp Duties Department.

Date-stamps very similar to postal date-stamps were sometimes supplied to offices of the Stamp Duties Department and it is not clear when this practice ceased. Prior to the Arms types the only sure proof of the postal use of off-cover fiscal stamps is when they bear a distinctive duplex, registered or parcel post cancellation, but beware of forgeries of the first two.

F **1**

F **2**

F **3**

(Die eng W. R. Bock. Typo Govt Ptg Office)

1882 (Feb). W **12a**. P 12×11½.

No.	Type	Description	Unused	Used
F1	F **1**	1d. lilac	£1200	£600
F2		1d. blue	£275	45·00
		w. Wmk inverted	—	£250

The 1d. fiscal was specifically authorised for postal use in February 1882 owing to a shortage of the 1d. T **5** and pending the introduction of the 1d. T **14** on 1 April.

The 1d. lilac fiscal had been replaced by the 1d. blue in 1878 but postally used copies with 1882 duplex postmarks are known although most postally used examples are dated from 1890 and these must have been philatelic.

1882 (early). W **12a**. P 12×11½.

No.	Type	Description	Unused	Used
F3	F **2**	1s. grey-green		
F4	F **3**	1s. grey-green and red		
F4*a*		2s. rose and blue		

Examples of these are known postally used in 1882 and although not specifically authorised for postal use it is believed that their use was permitted where there was a shortage of the appropriate postage value.

WMK TYPE F 5. The balance of the paper employed for the 1867 issue was used for early printings of T F **4** introduced in 1880 before changing over to the 'N Z' and Star watermark. The values we list with this watermark are known with 1882–1883 postal date stamps. Others have later dates and are considered to be philatelic but should they be found with 1882–1883 postal dates we would be prepared to add them to the list.

F **4**

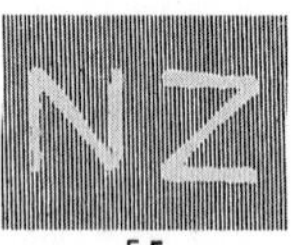

F **5**

The 12s.6d. value has the head in an oval (as T **10**), and the 15s. and £1 values have it in a broken circle (as T **7**).

(Dies eng W.R. Bock. Typo Govt Ptg Office)

1882 (1 Apr)–**1930**. T F **4** and similar types. De La Rue paper.

A. W **12a** *(6 mm)*

(a) P 12 (1882)

No.	Description	Unused	Used
F5	4d. orange-red (Wmk F **5**)	—	£425
F6	6d. lake-brown	—	£325
	a. Wmk F **5**	—	£850
F7	8d. green (Wmk F **5**)	—	£850
F8	1s. pink	—	£400
	a. Wmk F **5**		
F9	2s. blue	£150	10·00
F10	2s.6d. grey-brown	£200	10·00
	a. Wmk F **5**		
F11	3s. mauve	£275	15·00
F12	4s. brown-rose	£325	22·00
	a. Wmk F **5**		
F13	5s. green	£375	20·00
	a. Yellow-green	£375	20·00
F14	6s. rose	£400	55·00
	a. Wmk F **5**		
F15	7s. ultramarine	£425	95·00
	a. Wmk F **5**		
F16	7s.6d. bronze-grey	£1600	£325
F17	8s. deep blue	£500	£120
	a. Wmk F **5**		
F18	9s. orange	£600	£130
F19	10s. brown-red	£375	32·00
	a. Wmk F **5**		
F20	15s. green	£1200	£275
F21	£1 rose-pink	£600	£100

(b) P 12½ (1886)

No.	Description	Unused	Used
F22	2s. blue	£150	10·00
F23	2s.6d. grey-brown	£200	10·00
F24	3s. mauve	£300	15·00
F25	4s. purple-claret	£325	22·00
	a. Brown-rose	£325	22·00
F26	5s. green	£375	20·00
	a. Yellow-green	£375	20·00
F27	6s. rose	£450	55·00
F28	7s. ultramarine	£450	95·00
F29	8s. deep blue	£500	£120
F30	9s. orange	£600	£130
F31	10s. brown-red	£375	32·00
F32	15s. green	£1200	£275
F33	£1 rose-pink	£600	£100

B. W **12b** *(7 mm). P 12½ (1888)*

No.	Description	Unused	Used
F34	2s. blue	£150	10·00
F35	2s.6d. grey-brown	£200	10·00
F36	3s. mauve	£275	15·00
F37	4s. brown-rose	£300	22·00
	a. Brown-red	£300	22·00
F38	5s. green	£350	20·00
	a. Yellow-green	£350	20·00
F39	6s. rose	£450	55·00
F40	7s. ultramarine	£475	95·00
F41	7s.6d. bronze-grey	£1600	£325
F42	8s. deep blue	£500	£120
F43	9s. orange	£600	£130
F44	10s. brown-red	£375	30·00
	a. Maroon	£375	30·00
F45	£1 pink	£600	£100

C. W **12c** *(4 mm). P 12½ (1890)*

No.	Description	Unused	Used
F46	2s. blue	£225	24·00
F46*a*	2s.6d. grey-brown	£325	26·00
F47	3s. mauve	£425	60·00
F48	4s. brown-red	£375	40·00
F49	5s. green	£400	26·00
F50	6s. rose	£500	65·00
F51	7s. ultramarine	£600	£120
F52	8s. deep blue	£600	£140
F53	9s. orange	£650	£160
F54	10s. brown-red	£475	42·00
F55	15s. green	£1500	£325

D. Continuation of W **12b**. *P 11 (1895–1901)*

No.	Description	Unused	Used
F56	2s. blue	95·00	10·00
F57	2s.6d. grey-brown	£190	9·50
	a. Inscr 'COUNTERPART' (1901)*	£200	£300
F58	3s. mauve	£250	14·00
F59	4s. brown-red	£300	20·00
F60	5s. yellow-green	£350	20·00
F61	6s. rose	£400	55·00
F62	7s. pale blue	£450	95·00
F63	7s.6d. bronze-grey	£1600	£325
F64	8s. deep blue	£500	£110
F65	9s. orange	£600	£150
	a. Imperf between (horiz pair)	£3500	
F66	10s. brown-red	£375	30·00
	a. Maroon	£375	30·00
F67	15s. green	£1200	£275
F68	£1 rose-pink	£600	£100

* The plate normally printed in yellow and inscribed 'COUNTERPART' just above the bottom value panel, was for use on the counterparts of documents but was issued in error in the colour of the normal fiscal stamp and accepted for use.

E. W **43** *(sideways)*

(i) Unsurfaced Cowan paper

(a) P 11 (1903)

No.	Description	Unused	Used
F69	2s.6d. grey-brown	£250	9·50
F70	3s. mauve	£300	15·00
F71	4s. orange-red	£300	20·00
F72	6s. rose	£375	55·00
F73	7s. pale blue	£475	£100
F74	8s. deep blue	£500	£110
F75	10s. brown-red	£375	32·00
	a. Maroon	£375	32·00
F76	15s. green	£1300	£275
F77	£1 rose-pink	£550	£100

(b) P 14 (1906)

No.	Description	Unused	Used
F78	2s.6d. grey-brown	£160	9·50
F79	3s. mauve	£225	14·00
F80	4s. orange-red	£225	18·00
F81	5s. yellow-green	£250	18·00
F82	6s. rose	£350	55·00
F83	7s. pale blue	£400	95·00
F84	7s.6d. bronze-grey	£1500	£300
F85	8s. deep blue	£475	£110
F86	9s. orange	£500	£120
F87	10s. maroon	£350	30·00
F88	15s. green	£1300	£275
F89	£1 rose-pink	£500	£100

(c) P 14½×14, comb (clean-cut) (1907)

No.	Description	Unused	Used
F90	2s. blue	95·00	9·00
F91	2s.6d. grey-brown	£190	9·50
F92	3s. mauve	£250	15·00
F93	4s. orange-red	£250	19·00
F94	6s. rose	£375	55·00
F95	10s. maroon	£350	30·00
F96	15s. green	£1300	£275
F97	£1 rose-pink	£500	£100

(ii) Chalk-surfaced De la Rue paper

(a) P 14 (1913)

No.	Description	Unused	Used
F98	2s. blue	75·00	8·50
	a. Imperf horiz (vert pair)	£2000	
F99	2s.6d. grey-brown	90·00	9·50
F100	3s. purple	£180	13·00
F101	4s. orange-red	£180	15·00
F102	5s. yellow-green	£190	16·00
F103	6s. rose	£325	35·00
F104	7s. pale blue	£350	60·00
F105	7s.6d. bronze-grey	£1600	£325
F106	8s. deep blue	£450	70·00
F107	9s. orange	£550	£120
F108	10s. maroon	£350	29·00
F109	15s. green	£1300	£275
F110	£1 rose-carmine	£475	95·00

(b) P 14½×14, comb (1913–1921)

No.	Description	Unused	Used
F111	2s. deep blue	75·00	8·50
F112	2s.6d. grey-brown	90·00	9·50
F113	3s. purple	£180	12·00

F114	4s. orange-red	£180	15·00
F115	5s. yellow-green	£190	16·00
F116	6s. rose	£325	35·00
F117	7s. pale blue	£350	60·00
F118	8s. deep blue	£450	70·00
F119	9s. orange	£500	£120
F120	10s. maroon	£350	29·00
F121	12s.6d. deep plum (1921)	£18000	£7500
F122	15s. green	£1300	£275
F123	£1 rose-carmine	£450	95·00

The De La Rue paper has a smooth finish and has toned gum which is strongly resistant to soaking.

(iii) Chalk-surfaced Jones paper. P 14½×14, comb (1924)

F124	2s. deep blue	£110	12·00
F125	2s.6d. deep grey-brown	£120	13·00
F126	3s. purple	£250	17·00
F127	5s. yellow-green	£250	20·00
F128	10s. brown-red	£400	32·00
F129	12s.6d. deep purple	£18000	£7500
F130	15s. green	£1100	£300

The Jones paper has a coarser texture, is poorly surfaced and the ink tends to peel. The outline of the watermark commonly shows on the surface of the stamp. The gum is colourless or only slightly toned and washes off readily.

(iv) Thick, opaque, chalk-surfaced Cowan paper. P 14½×14, comb (1925–1930)

F131	2s. blue	80·00	10·00
F132	2s.6d. deep grey-brown	95·00	11·00
F133	3s. mauve	£250	21·00
F134	4s. orange-red	£180	21·00
F135	5s. yellow-green	£190	22·00
	x. Wmk reversed (1927)	£300	45·00
F136	6s. rose	£325	40·00
F137	7s. pale blue	£350	65·00
F138	8s. deep blue	£550	75·00
	a. *Blue* (1930)	£550	
F139	10s. brown-red	£350	35·00
	x. Wmk reversed (1927)	£425	£300
F140	12s.6d. blackish purple	£18000	£7500
F141	15s. green	£1200	£300
F142	£1 rose-pink	£450	£100

The Cowan paper is white and opaque and the watermark, which is usually smaller than in the Jones paper, is often barely visible.

(v) Thin, hard, chalk-surfaced Wiggins Teape paper. P 14½×14, comb (1926)

F143	4s. orange-red	£200	28·00
F144	£1 rose-pink	£500	£180

The Wiggins Teape paper has a horizontal mesh, in relation to the design, with narrow watermark, whereas other chalk-surfaced papers with this perforation have a vertical mesh and wider watermark.

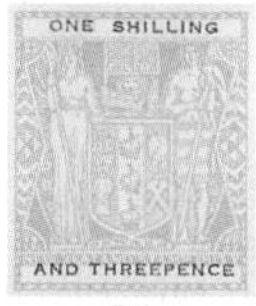

F **6**

35/-

(F **7**)

PRICES. Collectors should note that in the T **F6** 'Arms' design, prices quoted for unused examples refer to hinged mint for Nos. F145/F168a. Unused prices for Nos. F169/F185 and all subsequent issues are for unmounted examples.

(Des H. L. Richardson. Typo Govt Ptg Office)

1931–40. As T F **6** (various frames). W **43**. P 14.

(i) Thick, opaque, chalk-surfaced Cowan paper, with horizontal mesh (1931–1935)

F145	1s.3d. lemon (4.31)	6·50	50·00
F146	1s.3d. orange-yellow	18·00	22·00
F147	2s.6d. deep brown	16·00	4·50
F148	4s. red	15·00	13·00
F149	5s. green	45·00	16·00
F150	6s. carmine-rose	32·00	16·00
F151	7s. blue	28·00	27·00
F152	7s.6d. olive-grey	85·00	£110
F153	8s. slate-violet	32·00	35·00
F154	9s. brown-orange	32·00	29·00
F155	10s. carmine-lake	24·00	10·00
F156	12s.6d. deep plum (9.35)	£170	£170
F157	15s. sage-green	95·00	42·00
F158	£1 pink	85·00	19·00
F159	25s. greenish blue	£700	£950
F160	30s. brown (1935)	£425	£250
F161	35s. orange-yellow	£5500	£6500
F162	£2 bright purple	£425	85·00
F163	£2 10s. red	£500	£650
F164	£3 green	£700	£350
F165	£3 10s. rose (1935)	£2250	£3000
F166	£4 light blue (1935)	£600	£250
F167	£4 10s. deep olive-grey (1935)	£2000	£2500
F168	£5 indigo-blue	£500	£150
F168*a*	£10 deep blue	£1700	£500

(ii) Thin, hard Wiggins Teape paper with vertical mesh (1936–1940)

(a) Chalk-surfaced (1936–1939)

F169	1s.3d. pale orange-yellow	50·00	6·00
F170	2s.6d. dull brown	£130	4·00
F171	4s. pale red-brown	£170	23·00
F172	5s. green	£170	7·00
	w. Wmk inverted	—	£800
F173	6s. carmine-rose	£180	55·00
F174	7s. pale blue	£300	60·00
F175	8s. slate-violet	£325	85·00
F176	9s. brown-orange	£375	£120
F177	10s. pale carmine-lake	£300	7·00
F178	15s. sage-green	£475	90·00
F179	£1 pink	£300	45·00
F180	30s. brown (1.39)	£850	£275
F181	35s. orange-yellow	£8000	£7500
F182	£2 bright purple (1937)	£1300	£170
	w. Wmk inverted	£3500	
F183	£3 green (1937)	£1700	£500
F184	£5 indigo-blue (1937)	£2500	£425

(b) Unsurfaced (1940)

F185	7s.6d. olive-grey	£250	90·00

Not all values listed above were stocked at ordinary post offices as some of them were primarily required for fiscal purposes but all were valid for postage.

1939. No. F161 and F168*a* surch as T F **7**.

F186	35/- on 35s. orange-yellow	£900	£400
F186*a*	£10 on £10 deep blue	£2500	£500
	aw. Wmk inverted		

Because the 35s. orange-yellow could so easily be confused with the 1s.3d. and the £10 with the £5 in similar colours, they were surcharged.

1940 (June). New values surch as T F **7**. Wiggins Teape chalk-surfaced paper. W **43**. P 14.

F187	3/6 on 3s.6d. grey-green	80·00	42·00
F188	5/6 on 5s.6d. lilac	£140	75·00
F189	11/- on 11s. yellow	£275	£225
F190	22/- on 22s. scarlet	£700	£500
F187/F190 *Set of 4*		£1100	£750

These values were primarily needed for fiscal use.

1940–58. As T F **6** (various frames). W **98**. P 14.

(i) Wiggins Teape chalk-surfaced paper with vertical mesh (1940–1956)

F191	1s.3d. orange-yellow	21·00	4·25
	w. Wmk inverted	—	£375
F192	1s.3d. yellow and black (wmk inverted) (14.6.55)	9·00	4·50
	aw. Wmk upright (9.9.55)	35·00	35·00
	b. Error. Yellow and blue (wmk inverted) (7.56)	4·75	4·50
F193	2s.6d. deep brown	17·00	1·40
	w. Wmk inverted (3.49)	20·00	1·50
F194	4s. red-brown	40·00	2·00
	w. Wmk inverted (3.49)	50·00	2·75
F195	5s. green	24·00	1·25
	w. Wmk inverted (1.5.50)	32·00	1·25
F196	6s. carmine-rose	55·00	3·75
	w. Wmk inverted (1948)	65·00	3·75
F197	7s. pale blue	55·00	6·00
F198	7s.6d. olive-grey (wmk inverted) (21.12.50)	90·00	£100
F199	8s. slate-violet	95·00	17·00
	w. Wmk inverted (6.12.50)	£110	23·00
F200	9s. brown-orange (1.46)	50·00	60·00
	w. Wmk inverted (9.1.51)	£100	50·00
F201	10s. carmine-lake	60·00	2·50
	w. Wmk inverted (4.50)	70·00	2·50
F202	15s. sage-green	90·00	26·00
	w. Wmk inverted (8.12.50)	£110	26·00
F203	£1 pink	32·00	3·75
	w. Wmk inverted (1.2.50)	65·00	5·50
F204	25s. greenish blue (1946)	£800	£800
	w. Wmk inverted (7.53)	£1000	£1000
F205	30s. brown (1946)	£475	£190
	w. Wmk inverted (9.49)	£400	£170
F206	£2 bright purple (1946)	£225	32·00
	w. Wmk inverted (17.6.52)	£200	22·00
F207	£2 10s. red (wmk inverted) (9.8.51)	£475	£500
F208	£3 green (1946)	£300	60·00
	w. Wmk inverted (17.6.52)	£250	65·00
F209	£3 10s. rose (11.48)	£3500	£2250
	w. Wmk inverted (5.52)	£3500	£2250
F210	£4 light blue (wmk inverted) (12.2.52)	£350	£200
	w. Wmk upright	†	£1800
F211	£5 indigo-blue	£700	£100
	w. Wmk inverted (11.9.50)	£400	70·00
F191/F211 *Set of 21*		£6250	£3750

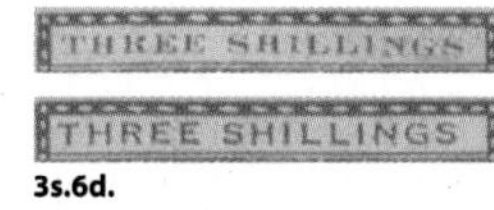

3s.6d.

Type I. Broad serifed capitals

Type II. Taller capitals, without serifs

Surcharged as T F 7.

F212	3/6 on 3s.6d. grey-green (I) (1942)	21·00	8·50
	w. Wmk inverted (12.10.50)	50·00	24·00
F213	3/6 on 3s.6d. grey-green (II) (6.53)	17·00	50·00
	w. Wmk inverted (6.53)	55·00	55·00
F214	5/6 on 5s.6d. lilac (1944)	70·00	29·00
	w. Wmk inverted (13.9.50)	80·00	20·00
F215	11/- on 11s. yellow (1942)	£100	48·00
F216	22/- on 22s. scarlet (1945)	£450	£200
	aw. Wmk inverted (1.3.50)	£475	£225
F216*b*	£10 on £10 deep blue	£1700	£450
	bw. Wmk inverted	£1700	£450
F212/F216 *Set of 5*		£600	£275

(ii) P 14×13½. Wiggins Teape unsurfaced paper with horizontal mesh (1956–1958)

F217	1s.3d. yellow and black (11.56)	4·75	5·00
	w. Wmk inverted	48·00	48·00
F218	£1 pink (20.10.58)	40·00	12·00

No. F192b had the inscription printed in blue in error but as many as 378,000 were printed.

From 1949–1953 inferior paper had to be used and for technical reasons it was necessary to feed the paper into the machine in a certain way which resulted in whole printings with the watermark inverted for most values.

F **8**

1967 (10 July)–**84**. Decimal currency. W **98** (sideways inverted). Unsurfaced paper. P 14 (line).

F219	F **8**	$4 deep reddish violet	7·00	7·00
		a. Perf 14 (comb) (wmk sideways) (17.9.68)	2·00	1·50
		aw. Wmk sideways inverted (6.7.84)	2·50	9·00
F220		$6 emerald	10·00	21·00
		a. Perf 14 (comb) (wmk sideways) (17.9.68)	2·50	3·50
		aw. Wmk sideways inverted (6.7.84)	3·25	11·00
F221		$8 light greenish blue	26·00	38·00
		a. Perf 14 (comb) (wmk sideways) (20.6.68)	3·00	4·50
		aw. Wmk sideways inverted (6.7.84)		
F222		$10 deep ultramarine	24·00	20·00
		a. Perf 14 (comb) (wmk sideways) (20.6.68)	3·00	3·50
		aw. Wmk sideways inverted (6.7.84)	25·00	30·00
F219/F222 *Set of 4*			60·00	75·00
F219a/F222a *Set of 4*			9·50	11·50

The original printings were line perforated on paper with the watermark sideways inverted (top of star pointing to left, *when viewed from the back*). In 1968 the stamps appeared comb perforated with the watermark sideways (top of star to right). A further comb perforated printing in July 1984 showed the sideways inverted watermark.

ANTARCTIC EXPEDITIONS

VICTORIA LAND

These issues were made under authority of the New Zealand Postal Department and, while not strictly necessary, they actually franked correspondence to New Zealand. They were sold to the public at a premium.

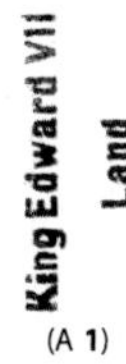

(A **1**)

1908 (15 Jan). Shackleton Expedition. T **42** of New Zealand (P 14), optd with T A **1**, by Coulls, Culling and Co., Wellington.

A1	1d. rose-carmine (No. 356 Royle) (G.)	£475	42·00
	a. Opt double	†	£1600
A1*b*	1d. rose-carmine (No. 352*c* Waterlow) (G.)	£1600	£850

Nos. A1/A1*b* were used on board the expedition ship, *Nimrod*, and at the Cape Royds base in McMurdo Sound. Due to adverse conditions Shackleton landed in Victoria Land rather than King Edward VII Land, the intended destination.

VICTORIA LAND. (A **2**) VICTORIA LAND. (A **3**)

1911 (9 Feb)–**13**. Scott Expedition. Stamps of New Zealand optd with Types A **2** (½d.) or A **3** (1d.) by Govt Printer, Wellington.

A2	**51**	½d. deep green (No. 387*aa*) (18.1.13)	£750	£850
A3	**53**	1d. carmine (No. 405)	55·00	£120
		a. No stop after 'LAND' (R. 7/5)	£425	£850
		b. 'Q' flaw	£650	

Nos. A2/A3 were used at the Cape Evans base on McMurdo Sound or on the *Terra Nova*.

ROSS DEPENDENCY

This comprises a sector of the Antarctic continent and a number of islands. It was claimed by Great Britain on 30 July 1923 and soon afterward put under the jurisdiction of New Zealand.

1 HMS *Erebus*

2 Shackleton and Scott

3 Map of Ross Dependency and New Zealand

4 Queen Elizabeth II

(Des E. M. Taylor (3d.), L. C. Mitchell (4d.), R. Smith (8d.), J. Berry (1s.6d.). Recess D.L.R.)

1957 (11 Jan). W **98** of New Zealand (Mult N Z and Star). P 13 (1s.6d.) or 14 (others).

1	**1**	3d. indigo	1·00	60
2	**2**	4d. carmine-red	1·00	60
3	**3**	8d. bright carmine-red and ultramarine	1·00	60
		a. Bright carmine-red and blue	4·25	3·75
4	**4**	1s.6d. slate-purple	1·00	60
1/4 Set of 4			3·50	2·25

(New Currency. 100 cents = 1 New Zealand dollar)

5 HMS *Erebus*

1967 (10 July). Decimal currency. As Nos. 1/4 but with values inscr in decimal currency as T **5**. Chalky paper (except 15c.). W **98** of New Zealand (sideways on 7c.). P 13 (15c.) or 14 (others).

5	**5**	2c. indigo	9·00	8·00
		a. Deep blue	18·00	9·50
6	**2**	3c. carmine-red	2·50	4·25
		w. Wmk inverted	75·00	
7	**3**	7c. bright carmine-red and ultramarine	3·00	5·00
8	**4**	15c. slate-purple	1·75	10·00
		w. Wmk inverted	£100	
5/8 Set of 4			14·50	25·00

TOKELAU ISLANDS

Formerly known as the Union Islands, and administered as part of the Gilbert & Ellice Islands Colony, Tokelau was transferred to New Zealand on 4 November 1925 and administered with Western Samoa. The Islands were finally incorporated in New Zealand on 1 January 1949 and became a dependency. The name Tokelau was officially adopted on 7 May 1946.

> Stamps of GILBERT AND ELLICE ISLANDS were used in Tokelau from Febuary 1911 until June 1926 when they were replaced by those of SAMOA. These were current until 1948.
>
> The post office on Atafu opened in 1911, but the cancellations for the other two islands, Fakaofo and Nukunono, did not appear until 1926.

NEW ZEALAND ADMINISTRATION

1 Atafu Village and Map **2** Nukunono hut and map

3 Fakaofo village and map

(Des J. Berry from photographs by T. T. C. Humphrey. Recess B.W.)

1948 (22 June). Types **1/3**. Wmk T **98** of New Zealand (Mult N Z and Star). P 13½.

1	**1**	½d. red-brown and purple	15	75
2	**2**	1d. chestnut and green	15	50
		w. Wmk inverted	£275	
3	**3**	2d. green and ultramarine	15	50
1/3 Set of 3			40	1·60

Covers are known postmarked 16 June 1948, but this was in error for 16 July.

1953 (16 June*). Coronation. As No. 715 of New Zealand, but inscr 'TOKELAU ISLANDS'.

4	**164**	3d. brown	2·00	1·75

* This is the date of issue in Tokelau. The stamps were released in New Zealand on 25 May.

ONE SHILLING

(4)

6D TOKELAU ISLANDS

(5)

1956 (27 Mar). No. 1 surch with T **4** by Govt Printer, Wellington.

5	**1**	1s. on ½d. red-brown and purple	75	1·25

1966 (8 Nov). Postal fiscal stamps of New Zealand (T F **6**), but without value, surch as T **5** by Govt Printer, Wellington. W **98** of New Zealand. P 14.

6	6d. light blue	25	80
7	8d. light emerald	25	80
8	2s. light pink	30	80
6/8 Set of 3		70	2·25

(New Currency. 100 cents = 1 New Zealand dollar)

 1c 

(6)

5c TOKELAU ISLANDS

(7)

R. 7/1

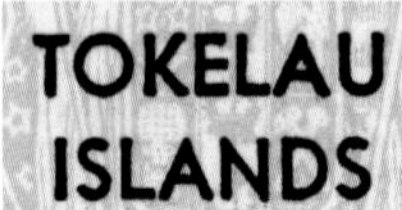

Normal

On R. 7/1 of Nos. 12/15 the words 'TOKELAU' and 'ISLANDS' are ½ mm apart instead of 1½ mm.

1967 (4 Sept*)–**68**. Decimal currency.

(a) Nos. 1/3 surch in decimal currency as T **6** *by Govt Printer, Wellington*

9		1c. on 1d.	20	1·00
10		2c. on 2d.	40	1·50
11		10c. on ½d.	70	2·00

(b) Postal Fiscal stamps of New Zealand (T F **6***), but without value, surch as T* **7** *by Govt Printer, Wellington. W* **98** *of New Zealand (sideways). P 14 (line or comb)*

12	**F 6**	3c. reddish lilac	30	20
		a. Narrow setting	10·00	10·00
13		5c. light blue	30	20
		a. Narrow setting	10·00	10·00
		b. *Pale blue* (second setting) (18.9.68)	2·00	2·50
14		7c. light emerald	30	20
		a. Narrow setting	10·00	10·00
15		20c. light pink	30	30
		a. Narrow setting	10·00	10·00
9/15 Set of 7			2·25	4·75

* This is the date of issue in Tokelau. The stamps were released in New Zealand on 10 July.

In the second setting of the 5c. the words 'TOKELAU' and 'ISLANDS' are in thinner letters and almost 2 mm apart.

8 British Protectorate (1877)

(Des New Zealand PO artists from suggestions by Tokelau Administration. Litho B.W.)

1969 (8 Aug). History of Tokelau. T **8** and similar horiz designs. W **98** of New Zealand. P 13×12½.

16	5c. ultramarine, yellow and black	15	10
17	10c. vermilion, yellow and black	15	10
18	15c. green, yellow and black	20	15
19	20c. yellow-brown, yellow and black	25	15
16/19 Set of 4		65	45

Designs: 5c. T **8**; 10c. Annexed to Gilbert and Ellice Islands, 1916; 15c. New Zealand Administration, 1925; 20c. New Zealand Territory, 1948.

1969 (14 Nov*). Christmas. As T **301** of New Zealand, but inscr 'TOKELAU ISLANDS'. W **98** of New Zealand. P 13½×14½.

20	2c. multicoloured	10	15

* This is the date of issue in Tokelau. The stamps were released in New Zealand on 1 October.

1970 (15 Nov*). Christmas. As T **314** of New Zealand, but inscr 'TOKELAU ISLANDS'. P 12½.

21	2c. multicoloured	10	20

* This is the date of issue in Tokelau. The stamps were released in New Zealand on 1 October.

NIUE

Niue became a British Protectorate on 20 April 1900 and was transferred to New Zealand control on 11 June 1901. There was considerable local resentment at attempts to incorporate Niue into the Cook Islands and, in consequence, the island was recognised as a separate New Zealand dependency from 1902.

PRICES FOR STAMPS ON COVER TO 1945

No. 1	*from* × 3
Nos. 2/5	*from* × 8
Nos. 6/7	—
Nos. 8/9	*from* × 30
Nos. 10/12	—
Nos. 13/31	*from* × 3
Nos. 32/37c	—
Nos. 38/47	*from* × 5
Nos. 48/49	—
No. 50	*from* × 15
Nos. 51/54	—
Nos. 55/61	*from* × 8

PRICES FOR STAMPS ON COVER TO 1945

Nos. 62/68	*from* × 12
Nos. 69/71	*from* × 3
Nos. 72/74	*from* × 10
Nos. 75/78	*from* × 8
Nos. 79/88	—
Nos. 89/97	*from* × 2

NEW ZEALAND DEPENDENCY

Stamps of New Zealand overprinted

NIUE

(1)

1902 (4 Jan). Handstamped with T **1** in green or bluish green. Pirie paper. Wmk double-lined 'N Z' and Star, W **38** of New Zealand. P 11.

1	**42**	1d. carmine	£300	£300

A few overprints were made with a *greenish violet* ink. These occurred only in the first vertical row and part of the second row of the first sheet overprinted owing to violet ink having been applied to the pad (*Price* £1500 *un*).

NIUE. ½ PENI. (2) NIUE. TAHA PENI. (3) 1d. NIUE. 2½ PENI. (4)

1902 (4 Apr). Type-set surcharges. Types **2**, **3**, and **4**.

(i) Pirie paper. No wmk. P 11

2	**27**	2½d. blue (R.)	1·50	4·50
		a. No stop after 'PENI'	28·00	55·00
		b. Surch double	£2500	

(ii) Basted Mills paper. Wmk double-lined 'N Z' and Star, W **38** *of New Zealand*

(a) P 14

3	**23**	½d. green (R.)	6·00	7·50
		a. Spaced 'U' and 'E' (R. 3/3, 3/6, 8/3, 8/6)	23·00	35·00
		b. Surch inverted	£325	£600
		c. Surch double	£1200	
4	**42**	1d. carmine (B.)	50·00	55·00
		a. Spaced 'U' and 'E' (R. 3/3, 3/6, 8/6)	£190	£225
		b. No stop after 'PENI' (R. 9/3)	£500	£600
		c. Varieties a. and b. on same stamp (R. 8/3)	£500	£600

(b) P 11×14

5	**42**	1d. carmine (B.)	1·75	4·25
		b. Spaced 'U' and 'E' (R. 3/3, 3/6, 8/6)	14·00	28·00
		c. No stop after 'PENI' (R. 9/3)	50·00	70·00
		d. Varieties b. and c. on same stamp (R. 8/3)	50·00	70·00

(c) Mixed perfs

6	**23**	½d. green (R.)	£1900	
7	**42**	1d. carmine (B.)	£1000	

1902 (2 May). Type-set surcharges, Types **2**, **3**. Cowan paper. Wmk single-lined 'N Z' and Star, W **43** of New Zealand.

(a) P 14

8	**23**	½d. green (R.)	1·50	1·50
		a. Spaced 'U' and 'E' (R. 3/3, 3/6, 8/3, 8/6)	9·00	13·00
9	**42**	1d. carmine (B.)	60	1·00
		a. Surch double	£1800	£2000
		b. Spaced 'U' and 'E' (R. 3/3, 3/6, 8/6)	11·00	20·00
		c. No stop after 'PENI' (R. 5/3, 7/3, 9/3, 10/3, 10/6)	9·00	17·00
		d. Varieties b. and c. on same stamp (R. 8/3)	45·00	70·00
		e. 'I' of 'NIUE' omitted (R. 6/5 from end of last ptg)	£1000	

(b) P 14×11

10	**23**	½d. green (R.)		

(c) Mixed perfs

11	**23**	½d. green (R.)	£1800	
12	**42**	1d. carmine (B.)	£200	£250
		a. Spaced 'U' and 'E' (R. 3/3, 3/6, 8/3, 8/6)	£600	
		b. No stop after 'PENI' (R. 5/3, 7/3, 9/3, 10/3, 10/6)	£550	

NIUE. (5) Tolu e Pene. (6) 3d.

Ono e Pene. (7) 6d. Taha e Sileni. (8) 1s.

1903 (2 July). Optd with name at top, T **5**, and values at foot, Types **6/8**, in blue. W **43** of New Zealand (sideways). P 11.

13	**28**	3d. yellow-brown	9·50	5·00
14	**31**	6d. rose-red	15·00	11·00
15	**34**	1s. brown-red ('Tahae' joined)	£650	†
		a. Surch double, one albino	£850	†
16		1s. bright red	40·00	48·00
		a. Orange-red	45·00	48·00
13/16 Set of 3			55·00	60·00

No. 15/15a with 'Tahae' joined as one word comes from the small first printing, which was withdrawn when it was discovered that the absence of a space between 'Taha' and 'e' gave the meaning 'thief' rather than 'one'. One sheet had been sold in Auckland, but no supplies were ever sent to Niue. Other examples emanate from record sheets retained in New Zealand, later distributed in presentation sets.

NIUE. ½ PENI. (9) NIUE. 2½ PENI. (9a) NIUE. (10)

1911 (30 Nov). ½d. surch with T **9**, others optd at top as T **5** and values at foot as Types **7**, **8**. W **43** of New Zealand. P 14×15 (½d.) or 14×14½ (others).

17 **51** ½d. green (C.) 50 50
18 **52** 6d. carmine (B.) 2·00 7·00
19 1s. vermilion (B.) 6·50 48·00
17/19 *Set of 3* 8·00 50·00

1915 (Sept). Surch with T **9a**. W **43** of New Zealand. P 14.

20 **27** 2½d. deep blue (C.) 26·00 55·00

1917 (Aug). 1d. surch as T **3**, 3d. optd as T **5** with value as T **6**. W **43** of New Zealand.

21 **53** 1d. carmine (P 14×15) (Br.) 24·00 5·50
a. No stop after 'PENI' (R. 10/16) £850
22 **60** 3d. chocolate (P 14×14½) (B.) 50·00 £110
a. No stop after 'Pene' (R. 10/4) £850
b. Perf 14×13½ 65·00 £130
c. Vert pair, Nos. 22/22b £180

1917–21. Optd with T **10**. W **43** of New Zealand.

(a) P 14×15

23 **61** ½d. green (R.) (2.20) 70 3·25
24 **53** 1d. carmine (B.) (10.17) 10·00 16·00
f. 'Q' flaw £250
25 **61** 1½d. slate (R.) (11.17) 1·00 2·75
26 1½d. orange-brown (R.) (2.19) 70 8·50
27 3d. chocolate (B.) (6.19) 1·60 38·00

(b) P 14×13½

28 **60** 2½d. blue (R.) (10.20) 4·75 19·00
a. Perf 14×14½ 1·25 16·00
ab. Opt double, one albino £500
b. Vert pair, Nos. 28/28a 18·00 70·00
29 3d. chocolate (B.) (10.17) 3·50 2·00
a. Perf 14×14½ 1·25 1·75
b. Vert pair, Nos. 29/29a 22·00 50·00
30 6d. carmine (B.) (8.21) 11·00 24·00
a. Perf 14×14½ 4·75 24·00
b. Vert pair, Nos. 30/30a 32·00 £120
31 1s. vermilion (B.) (10.18) 17·00 40·00
a. Perf 14×14½ 5·50 28·00
b. Vert pair, Nos. 31/31a 45·00 £130
23/31a *Set of 9* 24·00 £120

For illustration of No. 24f see above New Zealand No. 405.

1918–29. Postal Fiscal stamps as T F **4** of New Zealand optd with T **10**. W **43** of New Zealand (sideways).

(i) Chalk-surfaced De La Rue paper

(a) P 14

32 5s. yellow-green (R.) (7.18) £110 £120

(b) P 14½×14, comb

33 2s. deep blue (R.) (9.18) 17·00 32·00
34 2s.6d. grey-brown (B.) (2.23) 25·00 50·00
35 5s. yellow-green (R.) (10.18) 25·00 55·00
36 10s. maroon (B.) (2.23) £140 £180
37 £1 rose-carmine (B.) (2.23) £180 £275
33/37 *Set of 5* £350 £550

(ii) Thick, opaque, white chalk-surfaced Cowan paper. P 14½×14

37*a* 5s. yellow-green (R.) (10.29) 27·00 65·00
37*b* 10s. brown-red (B.) (2.27) 95·00 £160
37*c* £1 rose-pink (B.) (2.28) £160 £275
37*a*/37*c* *Set of 3* £250 £450

11 Landing of Captain Cook

12 Landing of Captain Cook

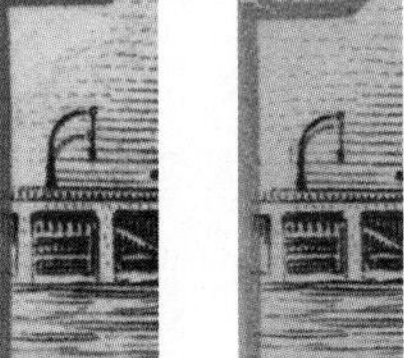
1d. R. 2/8 R. 3/6 R. 5/2

Double derrick flaws

(Des, eng and recess P.B.)

1920 (23 Aug). T **11** and similar designs. No wmk. P 14.

38 ½d. black and green 3·75 4·50
39 1d. black and dull carmine 2·00 1·25
a. Double derrick flaw (R. 2/8, 3/6 or 5/2) 7·00 7·00
40 1½d. black and red 2·75 18·00
41 3d. black and blue 1·75 17·00
42 6d. red-brown and green 5·00 18·00
43 1s. black and sepia 7·00 18·00
38/43 *Set of 6* 20·00 70·00

Designs: ½d. T **11**. As Cook Islands Types **10/14**: Vert—1d. Wharf at Avarua; 1½d. 'Captain Cook (Dance)'; 3d. Palm tree. Horiz—6d. Huts at Arorangi; 1s. Avarua Harbour.

Examples of the 6d. with inverted centre were not supplied to the Post Office (*Price*, £850, *unused*).

1925–27. As Nos. 38/39 and new values. W **43** of New Zealand (sideways on 4d.) P 14.

44 ½d. black and green (1927) 3·50 13·00
45 1d. black and deep carmine (1925) 1·75 1·00
a. Double derrick flaw (R. 2/8, 3/6 or 5/2) 5·50 4·75
46 2½d. black and blue (10.27) 4·25 16·00
47 4d. black and violet (10.27) 8·00 20·00
44/47 *Set of 4* 16·00 45·00

Designs: ½d. T **11**. As Cook Islands Types **16/17**: Vert—2½d. Te Po, Rarotongan chief. Horiz—4d. Harbour, Rarotonga, and Mount Ikurangi.

1927–28. Admiral type of New Zealand optd as T **10**. W **43** of New Zealand. P 14.

(a) Jones paper (wmk inverted)

48 **72** 2s. deep blue (2.27) (R.) 15·00 48·00

(b) Cowan paper

49 **72** 2s. light blue (R.) (2.28) 18·00 32·00

1931 (1 Apr). No. 40 surch as T **18** of Cook Is.

50 2d. on 1½d. black and red 5·50 1·00

1931 (12 Nov). Postal Fiscal stamps as T F **6** of New Zealand optd as T **10**. W **43** of New Zealand. Thick, opaque, chalk-surfaced Cowan paper. P 14.

51 2s.6d. deep brown (B.) 4·00 11·00
52 5s. green (R.) 35·00 70·00
53 10s. carmine-lake (B.) 35·00 £110
54 £1 pink (B.) 75·00 £160
51/54 *Set of 4* £140 £325

See also Nos. 79/82 for different type of overprint.

(Des L. C. Mitchell. Recess P.B.)

1932 (16 Mar). T **12** and similar designs inscr 'NIUE' and 'COOK ISLANDS'. No wmk. P 13.

55 ½d. black and emerald 14·00 26·00
a. Perf 13×14×13×13 £250
56 1d. black and deep lake 1·00 70
57 2d. black and red-brown 8·00 4·50
a. Perf 14×13×13×13 £140 £180
58 2½d. black and slate-blue 8·00 85·00
59 4d. black and greenish blue 14·00 70·00
a. Perf 14 16·00 65·00
60 6d. black and orange-vermilion 2·50 2·00
61 1s. black and purple (P 14) 4·00 6·00
55/61 *Set of 7* 45·00 £170

Designs: ½d. T **12**. As Cook Islands Types **21/26**: Vert—1d. Captain Cook; 1s. King George V. Horiz—2d. Double Maori canoe; 2½d. Islanders working cargo; 4d. Port of Avarua; 6d. RMS *Monowai*.

Examples of the 2½d. with inverted centre were not supplied to the Post Office. (*Price*, £300, *unused*).

Nos. 55a and 57a are mixed perforations, each having one side perforated 14 where the original perforation, 13, was inadequate.

(Recess from Perkins Bacon's plates at Govt Ptg Office, Wellington, N.Z.)

1932 (May)–**36.** As Nos. 55/61, but W **43** of New Zealand. P 14.

62 ½d. black and emerald (10.8.32) 50 3·50
63 1d. black and deep lake (10.8.32) 50 2·25
w. Wmk inverted 50·00
64 2d. black and yellow-brown (1.4.36) 50 1·75
w. Wmk inverted 32·00 55·00
65 2½d. black and slate-blue 50 4·25
w. Wmk inverted 50·00
66 4d. black and greenish blue 1·75 4·25
w. Wmk inverted £160
67 6d. black and red-orange (1.4.36) 70 75
68 1s. black and purple (1.4.36) 10·00 27·00
62/68 *Set of 7* 13·00 40·00

Imperforate proofs of No. 65 are known used on registered mail from Niue postmarked 30 August 1945 or 29 October 1945.

See also Nos. 89/97.

SILVER JUBILEE OF KING GEORGE V 1910-1935. (13)

Normal Letters B K E N
B K E N Narrow Letters

1935 (7 May). Silver Jubilee. Designs as Nos. 63, 65 and 67 (colours changed) optd with T **13** (wider vertical spacing on 6d.). W **43** of New Zealand. P 14.

69 1d. red-brown and lake 60 3·50
a. Narrow 'K' in 'KING' 2·75 9·00
b. Narrow 'B' in 'JUBILEE' 9·50 22·00
70 2½d. dull and deep blue (R.) 4·25 13·00
a. Narrow first 'E' in 'GEORGE' 4·25 13·00
71 6d. green and orange 7·50 10·00
a. Narrow 'N' in 'KING' 15·00 35·00
69/71 *Set of 3* 11·00 24·00

Examples of No. 70 imperforate horizontally are from proof sheets not issued through the Post and Telegraph Department (*Price* £250 *for vert pair*).

NIUE (14) NIUE Short opt (R. 9/4)

1937 (13 May). Coronation. Nos. 599/601 of New Zealand optd with T **14**.

72 1d. carmine 30 10
a. Short opt 15·00
73 2½d. Prussian blue 40 1·50
a. Short opt 17·00
74 6d. red-orange 40 20
a. Short opt 17·00
72/74 *Set of 3* 1·00 1·60

15 King George VI

16 Tropical Landscape

1938 (2 May). T **15** and similar designs inscr 'NIUE COOK ISLANDS'. W **43** of New Zealand. P 14.

75 1s. black and violet 18·00 8·00
76 2s. black and red-brown 12·00 18·00
w. Wmk inverted £225 £350
77 3s. blue and yellowish green 35·00 17·00
75/77 *Set of 3* 60·00 38·00

Designs: 1s. T **15**. As Cook Islands Types **30/31**: Vert—2s. Island village. Horiz—3s. Cook Islands canoe.

1940 (2 Sept). Unissued stamp surch as in T **16**. W **98** of New Zealand. P 13½×14.

78 3d. on 1½d. black and purple 75 60

T **16** was not issued without surcharge but archival examples exist. (*Price*, £250, *unused*).

NIUE. (17)

1941–67. Postal Fiscal stamps as T F **6** of New Zealand with thin opt, T **17**. P 14.

(i) Thin, hard, chalk-surfaced Wiggins Teape paper with vertical mesh (1941–1943)

(a) W 43 of New Zealand

79 2s.6d. deep brown (B.) (4.41) £110 £120
80 5s. green (R.) (4.41) £400 £400
81 10s. pale carmine-lake (B.) (6.42) £140 £325
82 £1 pink (B.) (2.43?) £200 £500
79/82 *Set of 4* £750 £1200

(b) W 98 of New Zealand (1942–1954)

83 2s.6d. deep brown (B.) (3.45) 4·75 10·00
w. Wmk inverted (11.51) 25·00 42·00
84 5s. green (R.) (11.44) 16·00 17·00
w. Wmk inverted (19.5.54) 10·00 25·00
85 10s. carmine-lake (B.) (11.45) 60·00 £130
w. Wmk inverted 75·00 £140
86 £1 pink (B.) (6.42) 65·00 75·00
83/86 *Set of 4* £120 £200

(ii) Unsurfaced Wiggins Teape paper with horizontal mesh. W 98 of New Zealand (1957–1967)

87 2s.6d. deep brown (P 14×13½) (1.11.57) 18·00 12·00
88 5s. pale yellowish green (wmk sideways) (6.67) 16·00 75·00

No. 88 came from a late printing made to fill demands from Wellington, but no supplies were sent to Niue. It exists in both line and comb perf.

1944–46. As Nos. 62/67 and 75/77, but W **98** of New Zealand (sideways on ½d., 1d., 1s. and 2s.).

89 **12** ½d. black and emerald 50 5·00
90 – 1d. black and deep lake 1·00 4·50
91 – 2d. black and red-brown 12·00 14·00
92 – 2½d. black and slate-blue (1946) 60 3·50
93 – 4d. black and greenish blue 4·25 1·00
y. Wmk inverted and reversed 23·00
94 – 6d. black and red-orange 2·25 1·40
95 **15** 1s. black and violet 1·50 1·25
96 – 2s. black and red-brown (1945) 8·50 5·00
97 – 3s. blue and yellowish green (1945) 15·00 10·00
89/97 *Set of 9* 40·00 40·00

1946 (4 June). Peace. Nos. 668, 670, 674/675 of New Zealand optd as T **17** without stop (twice, reading up and down on 2d.).

98 1d. green (Blk.) 40 10
99 2d. purple (B.) 40 10
100 6d. chocolate and vermilion (Blk.) 40 80
a. Opt double, one albino £550
101 8d. black and carmine (B.) 50 80
98/101 *Set of 4* 1·50 1·60

Nos. 102/112 are vacant.

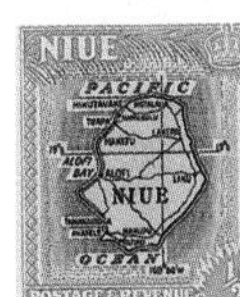

18 Map of Niue

19 HMS *Resolution*

20 Alofi landing

20a Native hut

21 Arch at Hikutavake

21a Alofi Bay

22 Spearing fish

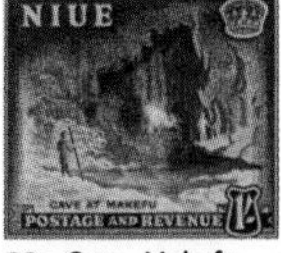
22a Cave, Makefu

23 Bananas

24 Matapa Chasm

(Des J. Berry. Recess B.W.)

1950 (3 July). W **98** of New Zealand (sideways inverted on 1d., 2d., 3d., 4d., 6d. and 1s.). P 13½×14 (horiz) or 14×13½ (vert).

113	**18**	½d. orange and blue	20	1·75
114	**19**	1d. brown and blue-green	2·25	3·00
115	**20**	2d. black and carmine	1·25	3·00
116	**20a**	3d. blue and violet-blue	10	20
117	**21**	4d. olive-green and purple-brown	10	20
118	**21a**	6d. green and brown-orange	1·00	1·25
119	**22**	9d. orange and brown	15	1·40
120	**22a**	1s. purple and black	15	20
121	**23**	2s. brown-orange and dull green	6·50	6·00
122	**24**	3s. blue and black	5·50	5·50
113/122 *Set of* 10			15·00	20·00

1953 (25 May). Coronation. As Nos. 715 and 717 of New Zealand, but inscr 'NIUE'.

123	3d. brown	80	40
124	6d. slate-grey	95	40

(New Currency. 100 cents = 1 New Zealand dollar)

(25)

26

1967 (10 July). Decimal currency.

(a) No. 113/122 surch as T **25**

125		½c. on ½d.	10	10
126		1c. on 1d.	1·10	15
127		2c. on 2d.	10	10
128		2½c. on 3d.	10	10
129		3c. on 4d.	10	10
130		5c. on 6d.	10	10
131		8c. on 9d.	10	10
132		10c. on 1s.	10	10
133		20c. on 2s.	35	2·00
134		30c. on 3s.	65	1·50
125/134 *Set of* 10			2·00	3·50

(b) Arms type of New Zealand without value, surch as in T **26**. *W* **98** *of New Zealand (sideways). P 14*

135	**26**	25c. deep yellow-brown	30	55
		a. Rough perf 11	6·00	18·00
136		50c. pale yellowish green	70	80
		a. Rough perf 11	6·00	19·00
137		$1 magenta	45	1·25
		a. Rough perf 11	7·50	13·00
138		$2 light pink	50	2·00
		a. Rough perf 11	8·50	14·00
135/138 *Set of* 4			1·75	4·25
135a/138a *Set of* 4			25·00	55·00

The 25c., $1 and $2 perf 14 exist both line and comb perforated. The 50c. is comb perforated only. The perf 11 stamps resulted from an emergency measure in the course of printing.

1967 (3 Oct). Christmas. As T **278** of New Zealand, but inscr 'NIUE'. W **98** (sideways) of New Zealand. P 13½×14.

139	2½c. multicoloured	10	10
	w. Wmk sideways inverted	15	30

1969 (1 Oct). Christmas. As T **301** of New Zealand, but inscr 'NIUE'. W **98** of New Zealand. P 13½×14½.

140	2½c. multicoloured	10	10

27 'Pua'

37 Kalahimu

(Des Mrs. K. W. Billings. Litho Enschedé)

1969 (27 Nov). T **27** and similar vert designs. Multicoloured. P 12½×13½.

141	½c. Type **27**	10	10
142	1c. 'Golden Shower'	10	10
143	2c. Flamboyant	10	10
144	2½c. Frangipani	10	10
145	3c. Niue Crocus	10	10
146	5c. Hibiscus	10	10
147	8c. 'Passion Fruit'	10	10
148	10c. 'Kampui'	10	10
149	20c. Queen Elizabeth II (after Anthony Buckley)	35	1·75
150	30c. Tapeu Orchid	1·10	2·25
141/150 *Set of* 10		1·60	4·00

(Des G. F. Fuller. Photo Enschedé)

1970 (19 Aug). Indigenous Edible Crabs. T **37** and similar horiz designs. Multicoloured. P 13½×12½.

151	3c. Type **37**	10	10
152	5c. Kalavi	10	10
153	30c. Unga	30	25
151/153 *Set of* 3		45	40

1970 (1 Oct). Christmas. As T **314** of New Zealand, but inscr 'NIUE'.

154	2½c. multicoloured	10	10

38 Outrigger Canoe and Fokker F.27 Friendship Aircraft over Jungle

(Des L. C. Mitchell. Litho B.W.)

1970 (9 Dec). Opening of Niue Airport. T **38** and similar horiz designs. Multicoloured. P 13½.

155	3c. Type **38**	10	20
156	5c. *Tofua II* (cargo liner) and Fokker F.27 Friendship over harbour	15	20
157	8c. Fokker F.27 Friendship over Airport	15	30
155/157 *Set of* 3		35	65

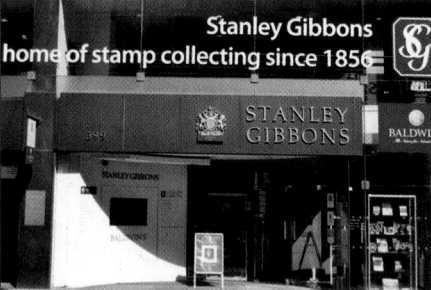

Nigeria

LAGOS

A British Consul was established at Lagos during 1853 as part of the anti-slavery policy, but the territory was not placed under British administration until occupied by the Royal Navy in August 1861. From 19 February 1866 Lagos was administered with Sierra Leone and from July 1874 as part of Gold Coast. It became a separate colony on 13 January 1886.

Although a postal service had been established by the British G...in April 1852 no postal markings were supplied to Lagos until 1859. The British GPO retained control of the postal service until June 1863, when it became the responsibility of the colonial authorities.

CROWNED-CIRCLE HANDSTAMPS

CC **1**

CC1 CC **1** LAGOS (19.12.1859)........................*Price on cover* £4000

First recorded use of No. CC **1** is 12 December 1871. It is later known used as a cancellation.

PRICES FOR STAMPS ON COVER 1945	
Nos. 1/9	*from* × 15
Nos. 10/26	*from* × 12
Nos. 27/29	—
Nos. 30/38	*from* × 12
Nos. 39/41	—
No. 42	*from* × 40
Nos. 44/50	*from* × 10
Nos. 51/53	—
Nos. 54/60	*from* × 10
Nos. 61/63	—

PRINTERS. All the stamps of Lagos were typographed by D.L.R.

1

1874 (10 June)–**75**. Wmk Crown CC. P 12½.

No.	Type	Description	Unused	Used
1	**1**	1d. lilac-mauve	80·00	50·00
2		2d. blue	80·00	45·00
3		3d. red-brown (2.75)	£130	42·00
5		4d. carmine	£150	50·00
6		6d. blue-green	£150	20·00
8		1s. orange (value 15½ *mm*) (2.75)	£700	£150
		a. Value 16½ mm long (7.75)	£425	70·00
1/8a *Set of* 6			£900	£225

1876–79. Wmk Crown CC. P 14.

No.	Type	Description	Unused	Used
10	**1**	1d. lilac-mauve	50·00	20·00
11		2d. blue	80·00	15·00
12		3d. red-brown	£120	18·00
		w. Wmk inverted	†	£350
13		3d. chestnut	£130	42·00
14		4d. carmine	£225	12·00
		a. Wmk sideways	£1700	£130
15		6d. green	£130	6·50
16		1s. orange (value 16½ *mm* long) (1879)	£950	85·00
10/16 *Set of* 6			£1400	£130

1882 (June). Wmk Crown CA. P 14.

No.	Type	Description	Unused	Used
17	**1**	1d. lilac-mauve	42·00	30·00
18		2d. blue	£200	8·50
19		3d. chestnut	30·00	9·00
		w. Wmk inverted	†	£350
20		4d. carmine	£225	12·00
17/20 *Set of* 4			£450	55·00

1884 (Dec)–**86**. New values and colours. Wmk Crown CA. P 14.

No.	Type	Description	Unused	Used
21	**1**	½d. dull green (1885)	2·00	80
		w. Wmk inverted	†	£350
22		1d. rose-carmine	2·00	80
		w. Wmk inverted	£180	£120
23		2d. grey	£100	9·50
24		4d. pale violet	£160	13·00
		w. Wmk inverted	—	£300
		y. Wmk inverted and reversed	†	£400
25		6d. olive-green	8·00	55·00
26		1s. orange (3.85)	22·00	25·00
27		2s.6d. olive-black (1886)	£350	£275
28		5s. blue (1886)	£700	£500
29		10s. purple-brown (1886)	£1600	£1100
21/29 *Set of* 9			£2500	£1800
27s/29s Optd 'SPECIMEN' *Set of* 3			£425	

We would warn collectors against clever forgeries of Nos. 27 to 29 on genuinely watermarked paper.

2½ PENNY

A

2½ PENNY

B

1887 (Mar)–**1902**. Wmk Crown CA. P 14.

No.	Type	Description	Unused	Used
30	**1**	2d. dull mauve and blue	8·50	2·00
31		2½d. ultramarine (A) (1891)	8·00	1·75
		a. Larger letters of value (B)	22·00	17·00
		b. Blue (A)	80·00	50·00
32		3d. dull mauve and chestnut (4.91)	2·50	3·25
33		4d. dull mauve and black	2·25	1·75
34		5d. dull mauve and green (2.94)	2·25	11·00
35		6d. dull mauve and mauve	4·75	3·00
		a. Dull mauve and carmine (10.02)	5·00	10·00
36		7½d. dull mauve and carmine (2.94)	4·50	38·00
37		10d. dull mauve and yellow (2.94)	4·50	13·00
38		1s. yellow-green and black	5·50	29·00
		a. Blue-green and black	7·50	40·00
39		2s.6d. green and carmine	23·00	80·00
40		5s. green and blue	48·00	£150
41		10s. green and brown	£120	£250
30/41 *Set of* 12			£200	£500
30s/41s Optd 'SPECIMEN' *Set of* 12			£325	

HALF PENNY

(2)

3

1893 (2 Aug). No. 33 surch with T **2** locally.

No.	Type	Description	Unused	Used
42	**1**	½d. on 4d. dull mauve and black	11·00	4·00
		a. Surch double	70·00	55·00
		b. Surch treble	£170	
		c. Error. ½d. on 2d. (No. 30)	—	£25000

There were two separate settings of No. 42. The most common, of which there were five separate printings, shows 'HALF PENNY' 16 mm long and was applied as a horizontal pair or triplet. The scarcer setting, also applied as a triplet, shows 'HALF PENNY' 16½ mm long.

Three examples of No. 42c are known, two unused and one used. Only the latter is in private hands.

1904 (22 Jan–Nov). Wmk Crown CA. P 14.

No.	Type	Description	Unused	Used
44	**3**	½d. dull green and green	3·25	5·50
45		1d. purple and black/*red*	1·25	15
46		2d. dull purple and blue	6·00	3·50
47		2½d. dull purple and blue/*blue* (B)	1·50	1·50
		aw. Wmk inverted	—	£130
		b. Smaller letters of value as A	4·50	8·50
		bw. Wmk inverted	£200	£180
48		3d. dull purple and brown	3·50	1·75
49		6d. dull purple and mauve	35·00	9·00
50		1s. green and black	35·00	42·00
51		2s.6d. green and carmine	£160	£325
52		5s. green and blue	£130	£325
53		10s. green and brown (11.04)	£350	£950
44/53 *Set of* 10			£650	£1500
44s/53s Optd 'SPECIMEN' *Set of* 10			£225	

1904–06. Ordinary paper. Wmk Mult Crown CA. P 14.

No.	Type	Description	Unused	Used
54	**3**	½d. dull green and green (12.10.04)	19·00	3·25
		a. Chalk-surfaced paper (12.3.06)	13·00	1·75
		w. Wmk inverted		
55		1d. purple and black/*red* (22.10.04)	10·00	10
		a. Chalk-surfaced paper (21.9.05)	1·50	10
		aw. Wmk inverted	—	£120
56		2d. dull purple and blue (2.05)	6·50	3·25
		a. Chalk-surfaced paper (25.9.06)	22·00	11·00
		aw. Wmk inverted	£180	
57		2½d. dull purple and blue/*blue* (B) (*chalk-surfaced paper*) (13.10.05)	1·75	16·00
		a. Smaller letters of value as A	55·00	£120
58		3d. dull purple and brown (27.4.05)	3·50	1·25
		a. Chalk-surfaced paper (2.8.06)	15·00	1·75
		w. Wmk inverted		
59		6d. dull purple and mauve (31.10.04)	6·50	7·50
		a. Chalk-surfaced paper (1.3.06)	4·25	1·50
60		1s. green and black (15.10.04)	24·00	35·00
		a. Chalk-surfaced paper (4.06)	28·00	2·25
		w. Wmk inverted		
61		2s.6d. green and carmine (3.12.04)	28·00	75·00
		a. Chalk-surfaced paper (21.10.06)	50·00	70·00
62		5s. green and blue (1.05)	26·00	£110
		a. Chalk-surfaced paper (21.10.06)	80·00	£180
63		10s. green and brown (3.12.04)	£100	£275
		a. Chalk-surfaced paper (12.3.06)	90·00	£250
54/63 *Set of* 10			£170	£400

Lagos was incorporated into the Colony and Protectorate of Southern Nigeria, previously formed from Niger Coast Protectorate and part of the Niger Company territories, on 16 February 1906. Stamps of Lagos were then authorised for use throughout Southern Nigeria.

NIGER COAST PROTECTORATE

OIL RIVERS PROTECTORATE

A British consulate for the Bights of Benin and Biafra was established in 1849 on the off-shore Spanish island of Fernando Po. In 1853 the appointment was divided with a consul for the Bight of Benin at Lagos. The consulate for the Bight of Biafra was transferred to Old Calabar in 1882.

A British protectorate was proclaimed over the coastal area, with the exceptions of the colony of Lagos and the centre of the Niger delta, on 5 June 1885. It was not, however, until July 1891 that steps were taken to set up an administration with a consul-general at Old Calabar and vice-consuls at some of the river ports.

The consulate-general at Old Calabar and the vice-consulates at Benin, Bonny, Brass, Forcados and Opobo acted as collection and distribution centres for mail from November 1891, but were not recognised as post offices until 20 July 1892.

For a few months from July 1892 local administrative handstamps, as T Z **1**, were in use either as obliterators or in conjunction with the c.d.s.

Z 1

These oval handstamps are usually found on the 1892–1894 overprinted issue, but the following are known on unoverprinted stamps of Great Britain:

1892.

BENIN

Stamps of GREAT BRITAIN cancelled with oval postmark, T Z **1**, inscribed 'BENIN'.

No.	Description	Price
Z1	2½d. purple/*blue* (V.)	£1500

BONNY

Stamps of GREAT BRITAIN cancelled with oval postmark, T Z **1**, inscribed 'BONNY'.

No.	Description	Price
Z2	2½d. purple/*blue* (V.)	£1100

BRASS RIVER

Stamps of GREAT BRITAIN cancelled with oval postmark, T Z **1**, inscribed 'BRASS'.

No.	Description	Price
Z3	2½d. purple/*blue* (Blk.)	£1000

OLD CALABAR RIVER

Stamps of GREAT BRITAIN cancelled with oval postmark, T Z **1**, inscribed 'OLD CALABAR'.

No.	Description	Price
Z4	2½d. purple/*blue* (Blk.)	£1000

Stamps of GREAT BRITAIN cancelled 'BRITISH VICE-CONSULATE OLD CALABAR' within double-lined circle.

No.	Description	Price
Z5	2½d. purple/*blue* (V.)	£750
Z6	5d. dull purple and blue (V.)	

For later use of T Z **1** and the circular Vice-Consulate marks see note beneath No. 6.

Z 2

Unoverprinted stamps of Great Britain remained officially valid for postage in the Protectorate until 30 September 1892, but were available from post offices in the Niger Company Territories up to the end of 1899. The two areas were so closely linked geographically that offices in the Protectorate continued to accept letters franked with Great Britain stamps until the reorganisation of 1900. The listing below covers confirmed examples, known on cover or piece, the prices quoted being for the latter.

1892–99.

Stamps of GREAT BRITAIN cancelled with circular postmarks as T Z **2**.

BENIN RIVER

No.	Description	Price
Z7	2d. green and carmine	
Z8	2½d. purple/*blue*	£1000
Z9	3d. purple/*yellow*	£1500
Z10	5d. dull purple and blue	
Z11	1s. green	

BONNY RIVER

No.	Description	Price
Z12	½d. vermilion	£500
Z12*a*	1d. lilac	£450
Z13	2½d. purple/*blue*	£400
Z14	5d. dull purple and blue	£500
Z15	6d. deep purple/*red*	£850

BRASS RIVER

No.	Description	Price
Z16	1½d. dull purple and green	£1000
Z17	2½d. purple/*blue*	£850
Z17*a*	2½d. purple/*blue* (squared-circle cancellation)	£1000
Z18	6d. purple/*red*	£900

FORCADOS RIVER

No.	Description	Price
Z19	1d. lilac	£750
Z20	2½d. purple/*blue*	
Z21	5d. dull purple and blue (m/s cancellation)	£1000
Z22	10d. dull purple and carmine	

OLD CALABAR RIVER

No.	Description	Price
Z23	½d. vermilion	£400
Z24	1d. lilac	£375
Z25	1½d. dull purple and green	£500
Z26	2d. green and vermilion	£500
Z27	2½d. purple/*blue*	£375
Z28	5d. dull purple and blue	£475
Z29	6d. purple/*red*	£475
Z30	1s. green	£700

OPOBO RIVER

No.	Description	Price
Z31	2½d. purple/*blue*	£450
Z32	10d. dull purple and carmine	£750

Some later covers are known franked with GB stamps, but the origin of the stamps involved is uncertain.

PRICES FOR STAMPS ON COVER TO 1945

Nos. 1/6	*from* × 15
Nos. 7/37	*from* × 6
Nos. 38/44	—
Nos. 45/50	*from* × 15
Nos. 51/56	*from* × 20
Nos. 57/65	*from* × 5
Nos. 66/72	*from* × 15
Nos. 73/74	—

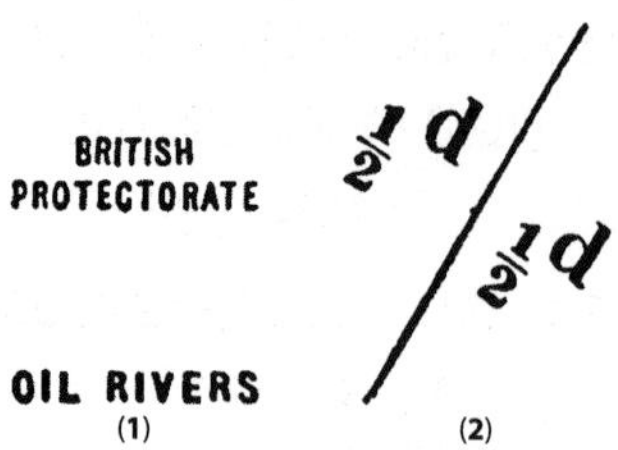

(1) (2)

1892 (20 July)–**94**. Nos. 172, 197, 200/201, 207*a* and 211 of Great Britain optd by D.L.R. with T **1**.

1	½d. vermilion	21·00	13·00
2	1d. lilac	13·00	11·00
	a. Opt reversed 'OIL RIVERS' at top	£9000	
	b. Bisected (½d.) (*on cover*)	†	£2000
3	2d. grey-green and carmine	35·00	9·00
	a. Bisected (1d.) (*on cover*)	†	£2000
4	2½d. purple/*blue*	11·00	2·50
5	5d. dull purple and blue (Die II) (No. 207*a*)	19·00	6·50
6	1s. dull green	70·00	90·00
1/6 *Set of 6*		£150	£120
1s/6s H/S 'SPECIMEN' *Set of 6*		£300	

Nos. 2b and 3a were used at Bonny River during August and September 1894.

OVAL HANDSTAMPS. In addition to Nos. Z1/Z4 postmarks as T Z **1** are also known used on the 1892–1894 overprinted issue from the following offices:

Bakana (Nos. 2, 4/6)
Benin (Nos. 1/6)
Bonny (No. 2)
Brass (Nos. 3/5)
Buguma (Nos. 4 and 6)
Old Calabar (No. 4)
Opobo (Nos. 1/3)
Sombreiro River (Nos. 1/6)

The Vice-Consulate marks, as Nos. Z5/Z6, are also known struck on examples of No. 4 from Bonny, Forcados or Old Calabar.

Nos. 2 to 6 surcharged locally

1893 (3 Sept). Issued at Old Calabar. Surch with T **2** and then bisected.

7	½d. on half of 1d. (R.)	£160	£140
	a. Unsevered pair	£500	£450
	ab. Surch inverted and dividing line reversed (unsevered pair)	—	£25000
	b. Surch reversed (dividing line running from left to right) (unsevered pair)	—	£17000
	c. Straight top to '1' in '½'	£350	£350
	d. '½' omitted	†	—
	e. Surch double (unsevered pair with normal)	—	£1800
	f. Vert *se-tenant* pair. Nos. 7a/8a	—	£23000
8	½d. on half of 1d. (V.)	£7000	£5000
	a. Unsevered pair	£18000	£16000
	b. Surch double (pair)	£25000	

The surcharge was applied in a setting covering one horizontal row at a time. Violet ink was used for the top row in the first sheet, but was then replaced with red.

HALF PENNY. (3) HALF PENNY. (4)

In T **3** 'HALF' measures 9½ mm and 'PENNY' 12½ mm with space 1½ mm between the words. Bar 14½ mm ending below the stop. The 'F' is nearly always defective.

In T **4** 'HALF' is 8½ mm, 'PENNY' 12½ mm, spacing 2½ mm, and bar 16 mm, extending beyond the stop.

HALF PENN.Y **5** (Stop after 'N') HALF PENNY **6** (No stop after 'N')

In T **5** the 'P' and 'Y' are raised, and the space between the words is about 4 mm. Bar is short, approx 13½ mm. T **6** is similar but without the stop after 'N'.

Half Penny (7) Half Penny (8)

In T **7** the 'a' and 'e' are narrow and have a short upward terminal hook. The '1' has a very small hook. The letters 'nny' have curved serifs, and the distance between the words is 5½ mm.

In T **8** the 'a' and 'e' are wider. The '1' has a wider hook. The letters 'nny' have straight serifs, and the distance between the words is 4¼ mm.

HALF PENNY. (9) HALF PENNY (10)

1893 (Dec). Issue at Old Calabar. Nos. 3/4 handstamped.

	(a) With T **3**		
9	½d. on 2d. (V.)	£500	£350
	a. Surch inverted	£17000	
	b. Surch diagonal (up or down)	£7000	
	c. Surch vertical (up or down)	£9000	
10	½d. on 2½d. (Verm.)	£14000	
10*a*	½d. on 2½d. (C.)	£35000	
	(b) With T **4**		
11	½d. on 2½d. (G.)	£300	£250
	a. Surch double	£2750	£2750
	b. Surch diagonally inverted		
12	½d. on 2½d. (Verm.)	£1200	£300
13	½d. on 2½d. (C.)	£425	£450
	a. Surch omitted (in pair)		
14	½d. on 2½d. (B.)	£425	£475
15	½d. on 2½d. (Blk.)	£4250	
	a. Surch inverted	£15000	
	b. Surch diagonal inverted (up or down)	£13000	
16	½d. on 2½d. (B.-Blk.)	£4750	
	(c) With T **5**		
17	½d. on 2½d. (Verm.)	£1300	£200
	a. Surch double	†	£2250
	b. Surch vertical (up)	†	£10000
	(d) With T **6**		
18	½d. on 2d. (V.)	£1100	£500
19	½d. on 2½d. (Verm.)	£600	£325
	a. Surch inverted	£10000	
	b. Surch double	—	£2500
	c. Surch diagonal (up or down)	£4500	
	d. Surch omitted (in vert strip of 3)	£35000	
	e. Surch vertical (up or down)	£13000	
	f. Surch diagonal, inverted (up or down)	£7500	
	(e) With T **7**		
20	½d. on 2d. (V.)	£475	£250
	a. Surch double	†	£6500
	b. Surch vertical (up or down)	£7500	
	c. Surch diagonal (up or down)	£7500	
	d. Surch diagonal (inverted)	£17000	
	e. Surch inverted	£17000	
21	½d. on 2½d. (Verm.)	£375	£180
	a. Surch double	†	£7500
	b. Surch vertical (up or down)	£8000	
	c. Surch inverted	£12000	
	d. Surch diagonal (up or down)	£5500	
	e. Surch diagonal, inverted (up)	£14000	
22	½d. on 2½d. (B.)	£35000	
23	½d. on 2½d. (C.)		
24	½d. on 2½d. (V.)	£12000	
	(f) With T **8**		
25	½d. on 2½d. (Verm.)	£550	£650
	a. Surch diagonal (up)	£7500	
26	½d. on 2½d. (B.)	£35000	
27	½d. on 2½d. (G.)	£500	
	a. Surch double	£6000	
28	½d. on 2½d. (C.)	£22000	£22000
	(g) With T **9**		
29	½d. on 2d. (V.)	£500	£375
30	½d. on 2d. (B.)	£2000	£750
	a. Surch double		
31	½d. on 2½d. (Verm.)	£600	£700
	a. Surch double		
32	½d. on 2½d. (B.)	£425	£400
33	½d. on 2½d. (G.)	£450	£500
	a. Surch double (G.)	£2000	
	b. Surch double (G.+Verm.)		
34	½d. on 2½d. (V.)	£7000	
	(h) With T **10**		
35	½d. on 2½d. (G.)	£500	£450
36	½d. on 2½d. (Verm.)	£9000	

Various types of surcharges on Nos. 9 to 36 were printed on the same sheet, and different types in different colours may be found *se-tenant (Prices, from £5000 per pair, unused)*.

Unused examples of Nos. 11, 12 and 31 with surcharge omitted in pair with normal (No. 11) or as the first and third stamps in a strip of three (Nos. 12 and 31) exist in the Royal collection.

One Shilling (11) 5/- (12)

1893 (Dec). Issued at Old Calabar. Nos. 3 and 5/6 handstamped.

	(a) With T **11**		
37	1s. on 2d. (V.)	£450	£375
	a. Surch inverted	£12000	
	b. Surch vertical (up or down)	£7000	
	c. Surch diagonal (up or down)	£9000	
	d. Surch diagonal, inverted (up or down)	£12000	
	e. Pair, Nos. 37 and 38	£6000	
38	1s. on 2d. (Verm.)	£750	£4000
	a. Surch inverted	£18000	
	b. Surch diagonal (up or down)	£10000	
	c. Surch vertical (up or down)	£15000	
39	1s. on 2d. (Blk.)	£6000	
	a. Surch inverted	£20000	
	b. Surch vertical (up or down)	£15000	
	c. Surch diagonal (up)	£15000	
	(b) As T **12**		
40	5s. on 2d. (V.)	£9000	£11000
	a. Surch inverted	£50000	
	b. Surch vertical (up or down)	£45000	£45000
	c. Surch diagonal (down)	£35000	
41	10s. on 5d. (Verm.)	£6500	£10000
	a. Surch inverted	£50000	
	b. Surch vertical (up or down)	£45000	
	c. Surch diagonal (down)	£35000	
42	20s. on 1s. (V.)	£140000	
	a. Surch inverted	£180000	
43	20s. on 1s. (Verm.)	£120000	
44	20s. on 1s. (Blk.)	£120000	

There are two main settings of the 'One Shilling' surcharge: Type A. The 'O' is over the 'hi' of 'Shilling' and the downstrokes on the 'n' in 'One', if extended, would meet the 'll' of 'Shilling'. The 'g' is always raised. Type A is known in all three colours from one sheet of 120.

Type B. The 'O' is over the first 'i' of 'Shilling' and the downstrokes of the 'n' would meet the 'li' of 'Shilling'. Type B is known in violet (two sheets) and vermilion (one sheet).

An example of No. 38 with surcharge diagonal, inverted exists in the Royal collection.

NIGER COAST PROTECTORATE

The protectorate was extended into the interior and the name changed to Niger Coast Protectorate on 12 May 1893.

PERFORATION. There are a number of small variations in the perforation of the Waterlow issues of 1893 to 1898 which were due to irregularity of the pins rather than different perforators.

In the following lists, stamps perf 12, 12½, 13 or compound are described as perf 12–13, stamps perf 13½, 14 or compound are described as perf 13½–14 and those perf 14½, 15 or compound are listed as perf 14½–15. In addition the 13½–14 perforation exists compound with 14½–15 and with 12–13, whilst perf 15½–16 comes from a separate perforator.

13 14

(Des G. D. Drummond. Recess Waterlow)

1894 (1 Jan). T **13** (with 'OIL RIVERS' obliterated and 'NIGER COAST' in top margin). Various frames. Thick and thin papers. No wmk. P 14½–15.

45	½d. vermilion	11·00	11·00
	a. Perf 13½–14	8·00	12·00
46	1d. pale blue	6·00	5·00
	a. Bisected (½d.) (*on cover*)	†	£750
	b. Dull blue	8·50	4·50
	ba. Bisected (½d.) (*on cover*)	†	£650
	c. Perf 13½–14	5·50	4·75
	d. Perf 13½–14, comp 12–13	30·00	25·00
	e. Perf 12–13	£150	£120
47	2d. green	50·00	50·00
	a. Imperf between (horiz pair)	†	£17000
	b. Bisected (1d.) (*on cover*)	†	£900
	c. Perf 14½–15, comp 12–13		
	d. Perf 13½–14	19·00	19·00
	e. Perf 13½–14, comp 12–13	50·00	45·00
	f. Perf 12–13	£300	£190
48	2½d. carmine-lake	20·00	4·25
	a. Perf 13½–14	28·00	12·00
	b. Perf 13½–14, comp 12–13	40·00	38·00
	c. Perf 12–13	£275	£250
49	5d. grey-lilac	23·00	17·00
	a. Lilac (1894)	17·00	23·00
	b. Perf 13½–14	23·00	13·00
	c. Perf 13½–14, comp 12–13	70·00	
50	1s. black	14·00	15·00
	a. Perf 14½–15, comp 12–13	£110	90·00
	b. Perf 13½–14	35·00	22·00
	c. Perf 13½–14, comp 12–13	50·00	40·00
	d. Perf 14½–15, comp 13½–14	55·00	38·00
45/50 *Set of 6*		75·00	60·00

There were three printings of each value, in November 1893, January 1894 and March 1894.

Nos. 46a, 46ba and 47b were used at Bonny River during August and September 1894.

(Recess Waterlow)

1894 (May). T **14** (various frames). No wmk. P 14½–15.

51	½d. yellow-green	5·00	5·00
	a. Deep green	5·50	6·00
	b. Perf 14½–15, comp 13½–14		
	c. Perf 13½–14	17·00	17·00
	d. Perf 13½–14, comp 12–13	42·00	38·00
52	1d. orange-vermilion	23·00	17·00
	a. Vermilion	14·00	8·50
	b. Bisected diagonally (½d.) (*on cover*)	†	£800
	c. Perf 15½–16	—	85·00
	d. Perf 13½–14	40·00	
	e. Perf 13½–14, comp 12–13	70·00	23·00
53	2d. lake	35·00	6·50
	a. Bisected diagonally (1d.) (*on cover*)	†	—
	b. Perf 13½–14	45·00	9·50
	c. Perf 13½–14, comp 12–13	85·00	22·00
54	2½d. blue	20·00	4·50
	a. Pale blue	8·50	7·50
	b. Perf 13½–14	45·00	15·00
55	5d. purple	16·00	5·50
	a. Deep violet	13·00	5·50
56	1s. black	80·00	27·00
	a. Perf 13½–14	60·00	7·00
	b. Perf 13½–14, comp 12–13	80·00	50·00
51/56 *Set of 6*		£120	32·00

Nos. 52b and 53a were used at Bonny River during August and September 1894.

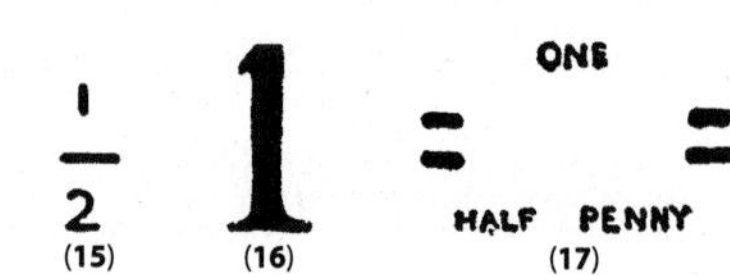

(15) (16) (17)

1894. Provisionals. Issued at Opobo.

(a) Nos. 46b and 46 bisected vertically and surch with T **15** *(May–June)*

57 '½' on half of 1d. dull blue (R.) (5.94) £2250 £650
a. Surch inverted (in strip of 3 with normals) £20000
58 '½' on half of 1d. pale blue (R.) (6.94) £1200 £375
a. Surch *tête-bêche* (pair)
b. Surcharge inverted £14000
c. Perf 13½–14 — £350
d. Perf 13½–14, comp 12–13 — £400

(b) No. 3 bisected vertically and surch

(i) With T **16** *(12 mm high) (June–Oct)*

59 '1' on half of 2d. (Verm.) £1700 £375
a. Surch double £6500 £1200
b. Surch inverted † £2000
c. Unsevered pair † £4000

(ii) Smaller '1' (4¾ mm high)

60 '1' on half of 2d. (C.) † £10000

(iii) Smaller '1' (3¾ mm high)

61 '1' on half of 2d. (C.) † —

Nos. 60 and 61 exist *se-tenant*. *(Price £40,000 used).*

(c) No. 52a (Perf 14½–15) bisected, surch with T **15** *(Aug–Sept)*

62 '½' on half of 1d. vermilion (Blk.) £5500 £1000
63 '½' on half of 1d. vermilion (V.) £4000 £700
64 '½' on half of 1d. vermilion (B.) £3500 £500
a. '½' double
b. Perf 13½–14 £3500 £500
c. Perf 13½–14, comp 12–13 — £600

The stamp is found divided down the middle and also diagonally.

1894 (10 Aug). Issued at Old Calabar. No. 54 surch with T **17** and two bars through value at foot.

65 ½d. on 2½d. blue £425 £250
a. Surch double £8000 £2000
b. 'OIE' for 'ONE' £2000 £1200
c. Ditto. Surch double † £10000

There are eight types in the setting of T **17**, arranged as a horizontal row. No. 65b occurred on No. 8 in the setting at some point during surcharging.

(Recess Waterlow)

1897 (Mar)–**98.** As T **14** (various frames). Wmk Crown CA. P 14½–15.

66 ½d. green (7.97) 9·00 1·50
a. Sage-green 9·00 2·75
b. Perf 13½–14 3·25 3·00
by. Wmk inverted and reversed — £275
c. Perf 15½–16 20·00 6·50
d. Perf 13½–14, comp 12–13 45·00 27·00
x. Wmk reversed £170
67 1d. orange-vermilion 4·50 1·50
a. Vermilion 9·00 1·50
b. Imperf vert (horiz pair) £16000
c. Perf 15½–16 12·00 7·50
d. Perf 13½–14 2·50 2·75
e. Perf 13½–14, comp 12–13 24·00 17·00
f. Perf 13½–14, comp 14½–15 — 22·00
x. Wmk reversed † —
68 2d. lake (7.97) 5·50 2·00
a. Perf 15½–16 5·50 3·00
b. Perf 13½–14 4·75 3·75
c. Perf 13½–14, comp 12–13 55·00 38·00
x. Wmk reversed £130 £120
69 2½d. slate-blue (8.97) 7·50 2·75
a. Deep bright blue 18·00 3·00
b. Perf 13½–14 7·00 4·00
c. Perf 15½–16 — 60·00
w. Wmk inverted — £300
x. Wmk reversed £750 £350
70 5d. red-violet (P 13½–14) (1898) 24·00 90·00
a. Purple 14·00 95·00
b. Perf 13½–14, comp 12–13 45·00 £200
c. Perf 14½–15 — £225
71 6d. yellow-brown (6.98) 7·00 11·00
a. Perf 13½–14 8·50 14·00
b. Perf 15½–16 70·00 45·00
x. Wmk reversed £275
72 1s. black (1898) 15·00 29·00
a. Perf 13½–14 14·00 30·00
b. Perf 13½–14, comp 12–13 75·00
73 2s.6d. olive-bistre (6.98) 95·00 £170
a. Perf 15½–16 80·00 £180
b. Perf 13½–14 24·00 90·00
74 10s. deep violet (6.98) £180 £300
a. Bright violet £225 £375
b. Perf 13½–14 £130 £225
ba. Bright violet £120 £200
bx. Wmk reversed £600
c. Perf 13½–14, comp 12–13 £275 £425

66/74 *Set of 9* £170 £375
71s, 73s/74s Optd 'SPECIMEN' *Set of 3* £275

Owing to temporary shortages in Southern Nigeria, the above issue was again in use at various times from 1902 until 1907.

On 1 January 1900 the Niger Coast Protectorate together with the southern portion of the Niger Company Territories became the protectorate of Southern Nigeria.

NIGER COMPANY TERRITORIES

Following the development of trade along the Niger, British commercial interests formed the United African Company in 1879 which became the National African Company in 1882 and the Royal Niger Company in 1886. A charter was granted to the Company in the same year to administer territory along the Rivers Niger and Benue over which a British protectorate had been proclaimed in June 1885. The Company's territories extended to the Niger delta to provide access to the interior.

Post Offices were opened at Akassa (1887), Burutu (1896), Lokoja (1899) and Abutshi (1899). The stamps of Great Britain were used from 1888.

On the establishment of postal services in 1887 the Company arranged with the British GPO that unstamped mail marked with their handstamps would be delivered in Great Britain, the recipients only being charged the normal rate of postage from West Africa. This system was difficult to administer, however, so the British authorities agreed in 1888 to the supply of GB stamps for use at the Company post offices.

Initially the stamps on such covers were left uncancelled until the mail arrived in the United Kingdom, the Company handstamp being struck elsewhere on the address side. This method continued to be used until early 1896, although a number of covers from the 12 months prior to that date do show the Company handstamp cancelling the stamps. Some of these covers were later recancelled on arrival in Great Britain. From May 1896 the postage stamps were cancelled in the Niger Territories.

In the following listings no attempt has been made to cover the use of the Company marks on the reverse of envelopes.

Dates given are those of earliest known postmarks. Colour of postmarks in brackets. Where two or more colours are given, price is for cheapest.

Stamps of GREAT BRITAIN cancelled as indicated below.

ABUTSHI

1899. Cancelled as T **8**, but inscribed 'THE ROYAL NIGER CO. C. & L. ABUTSHI' with 'CUSTOMS (date) OFFICE' in central oval.

Z1 ½d. vermilion (V.) £1000
Z2 1d. lilac (V.) £700
Z3 2½d. purple/*blue* (V.) £1000
Z4 5d. dull purple and blue (V.) £1100
Z5 10d. dull purple and carmine (V.) £1300
Z6 2s.6d. deep lilac (V.) £1700

AKASSA

The listings for Nos. Z7/Z15*a* are for covers on which the Akassa handstamp appears on the front, but is not used as a cancellation for the GB stamps. Examples of Nos. Z16/Z26 occur, from 1895–1896, with the handstamp struck on the front of the cover away from the stamps, or, from 1896, used as a cancellation. The prices quoted are for single stamps showing the cancellation; covers from either period being worth considerably more. On Nos. Z29/Z42*b* the handstamp was used as a cancellation and the prices quoted are for single stamps.

1

2

1888–90. Cancelled as T **3**, but with Maltese cross each side of 'AKASSA'. Size 36×22 mm.

Z7 6d. deep purple/*red* (V.) £2500

1889–94. Size 39×24 mm.

Z8 **1** 2½d. purple/*blue* (V.) £900
Z9 3d. purple/*yellow* (V.) £1000
Z10 5d. dull purple and blue (V.) £1000
Z11 6d. deep purple/*red* (V.) £700
Z12 10d. dull purple and carmine (V.) £1000
Z12*a* 1s. green (V.) £1800
Z13 2s.6d. lilac (V.) £1300

1894–95.

Z14 **2** 1d. lilac (V.) £1200
Z15 2½d. purple/*blue* (V.) £1200
Z15*a* 2s.6d. lilac (V.)

3

THE ROYAL NIGER COMPANY
CHARTERED & LIMITED.
7 - AUG. 98
POST OFFICE
AKASSA.

4

1895. Size 39×25 mm.

Z16 **3** 2½d. purple/*blue* (V.) £3000

1895–99.

Z17 **4** ½d. vermilion (V.) £130
Z18 1d. lilac (V.) £120
Z19 2d. green and carmine (V.) £600
Z20 2½d. purple/*blue* (V.) 70·00
Z21 3d. purple/*yellow* (V.) £425
Z22 5d. dull purple and blue (V.) £100
Z23 6d. deep purple/*red* (V.) £475
Z24 9d. dull purple and blue (V.) £900
Z25 10d. dull purple and carmine (V.) £160
Z26 2s.6d. deep lilac (V.) £375

THE ROYAL NIGER COMPANY,
CHARTERED & LIMITED.
4 NOV. 1889
POST OFFICE,
AKASSA.

5

1897–99.

Z29 **5** ½d. vermilion (V.) £100
Z30 1d. lilac (V.) 70·00
a. 'RECD' for year in postmark £1000
Z31 2d. green and carmine (V.) £400
Z32 2½d. purple/*blue* (V.) 80·00
a. 'RECD' for year in postmark (1898) £1200
Z33 3d. purple/*yellow* (V.) £350
Z34 4d. green and brown (V.) £550
Z35 4½d. green and carmine (V.) £1700
Z36 5d. dull purple and blue (V.) 95·00
Z37 6d. deep purple/*red* (V.) £425
Z38 9d. dull purple and blue (V.) £900
Z39 10d. dull purple and carmine (V.) £250
Z40 1s. green (V.) £1700
Z41 2s.6d. deep lilac (V.) £500

1899. Cancelled as T **7** but inscribed 'AKASSA'.

Z42 5d. dull purple and blue (V.) £1500

1899. Cancelled as T **4**, but 'CUSTOMS DEPT' in place of 'POST OFFICE'.

Z42*a* 1d. lilac (V.) £1000
Z42*b* 2½d. purple/*blue* (V.) £1000

BURUTU

THE ROYAL NIGER COMPANY
CHARTERED & LIMITED.
31 MAR 1898
POST OFFICE.
BURUTU.

6

1896–99. Cancelled as T **6**, 'BURUTU' in sans-serif caps. Size 44×24 mm.

Z43 **6** ½d. vermilion (V., Blk.) £150
Z44 1d. lilac (V.) £100
Z45 1½d. dull purple and green (V.) £800
Z46 2d. green and carmine (V., Blk.) £325
Z47 2½d. purple/*blue* (V., Blk.) 50·00
Z48 3d. purple/*yellow* (V., Blk.) £350
Z49 4d. green and brown (V., Blk.) £450
Z50 5d. dull purple and blue (V., Blk.) £120
Z51 6d. deep purple/*red* (V.) £450
Z52 9d. dull purple and blue (V.) £900
Z53 10d. dull purple and carmine (V., Blk.) £180
Z54 1s. green (V.) £1400
Z55 2s.6d. lilac (V.) £425

1898–99. Cancelled as T **4**, but inscribed 'BURUTU' in serifed caps. Size 44×27 mm.

Z56 ½d. vermilion (V., Blk.) 85·00
Z57 1d. lilac (V., Blk.) 55·00
Z58 2d. green and carmine (V.) £450
Z59 2½d. purple/*blue* (V., Blk.) 65·00
Z60 3d. purple/*yellow* (V.) £425
Z61 4d. green and brown (V.) £550
Z62 4½d. green and carmine (V.) £1700
Z63 5d. dull purple and blue (V.) £120
Z64 6d. deep purple/*red* (V.) £450
Z65 9d. dull purple and blue (V.) £900
Z66 10d. dull purple and carmine (V., Blk.) £160
Z67 2s.6d. lilac (V., Blk.) £425

THE ROYAL NIGER COMPANY
Chartered & Limited.
9 JUL 1898
BURUTU

7

1898–99.

Z68 **7** 1d. lilac (V.)
Z69 2½d. purple/*blue* (V.) £350

1899. Cancelled as T **4**, but inscribed 'CUSTOM DEPT. BURUTU'.

Z70 1d. lilac (V.)

LOKOJA

8

1899.

Z71	8	½d. vermilion (V.)	£170
Z72		1d. lilac (V.)	£110
Z73		2½d. purple/*blue* (V.)	£350
Z74		5d. dull purple and blue (V.)	£650
Z75		10d. dull purple and carmine (V.)	£800
Z76		2s.6d. deep lilac (V.)	£1200

AGENT GENERAL NIGER TERRITORIES

The listings for Nos. Z78/Z81 are for covers showing a handstamp struck on the address side, but not used as a cancellation for the GB stamp.

1894–99. Cancelled as T **8**, but inscribed 'AGENT GENERAL NIGER TERRITORIES'.

Z77	1d. lilac (V.)	
Z78	2½d. purple/*blue* (V.)	£2500

1895–96. Cancelled as T **7**, but inscribed as Nos. Z77/Z78.

Z79	2½d. purple/*blue* (V.)	£2500
Z80	5d. dull purple and blue (V.)	£2500
Z81	10d. dull purple and carmine (V.)	£2500
Z82	2s.6d. deep lilac (V.)	

It is now believed that these cancellations may have been used at Asaba. They all occur on covers with Akassa handstamps, often of different dates.

The British Government purchased the Royal Niger Company territories and from 1 January 1900 they were incorporated into the protectorates of Northern and Southern Nigeria. Of the post offices listed above, only Lokoja was then situated in Northern Nigeria, the remainder joining Niger Coast in forming Southern Nigeria.

Issues for Northern Nigeria did not reach Lokoja until sometime in March 1900 and the post office there continued to use unoverprinted stamps of Great Britain until these supplies arrived.

NORTHERN NIGERIA

The protectorate of Northern Nigeria was formed on 1 January 1900 from the northern part of the Niger Company Territories. Only one post office existed in this area, at Lokoja, and this continued to use unoverprinted stamps of GREAT BRITAIN until the arrival of Nos. 1/9 during April 1900.

PRICES FOR STAMPS ON COVER TO 1945

Nos. 1/7	*from* × 6
Nos. 8/9	—
Nos. 10/16	*from* × 5
Nos. 17/19	—
Nos. 20/26	*from* × 5
No. 27	—
Nos. 28/37	*from* × 5
Nos. 38/39	—
Nos. 40/49	*from* × 5
Nos. 50/52	—

PRINTERS. All issues were typographed by De La Rue & Co.

1

2

1900 (Apr). Wmk Crown CA. P 14.

1	1	½d. dull mauve and green	9·00	22·00
2		1d. dull mauve and carmine	6·00	5·50
3		2d. dull mauve and yellow	16·00	60·00
4		2½d. dull mauve and ultramarine	13·00	48·00
5	2	5d. dull mauve and chestnut	32·00	70·00
6		6d. dull mauve and violet	32·00	50·00
7	1	1s. green and black	32·00	85·00
8		2s.6d. green and ultramarine	£180	£850
9		10s. green and brown	£325	£950
1/9 *Set of 9*			£550	£1900
1s/9s Optd 'SPECIMEN' *Set of 9*			£225	

Examples of all values are known showing a forged Northern Nigeria postmark dated 'AU 14 1900'.

3

4

1902 (1 July). Wmk Crown CA. P 14.

10	3	½d. dull purple and green	2·00	2·00
		w. Wmk inverted	—	£375
11		1d. dull purple and carmine	4·75	1·00
12		2d. dull purple and yellow	2·00	3·00
13		2½d. dull purple and ultramarine	1·75	13·00
14	4	5d. dull purple and chestnut	7·00	9·00
15		6d. dull purple and violet	20·00	8·50
16	3	1s. green and black	9·00	9·00
17		2s.6d. green and ultramarine	20·00	75·00
18		10s. green and brown	50·00	55·00
10/18 *Set of 9*			£100	£150
10s/18s Optd 'SPECIMEN' *Set of 9*			£170	

1904 (Apr). Wmk Mult Crown CA. P 14.

19	4	£25 green and carmine	£60000

No. 19, although utilising the 'POSTAGE & REVENUE' Key type, was intended to pay the fiscal fee for liquor licences.

1905 (Aug)–**07**. Ordinary paper. Wmk Mult Crown CA. P 14.

20	3	½d. dull purple and green (10.05)	30·00	8·00
		a. Chalk-surfaced paper (1906)	5·50	5·00
21		1d. dull purple and carmine	21·00	1·50
		a. Chalk-surfaced paper (1906)	5·50	1·25
22		2d. dull purple and yellow (10.05)	26·00	32·00
		a. Chalk-surfaced paper (1907)	19·00	32·00
23		2½d. dull purple and ultramarine (10.05)	6·50	13·00
24	4	5d. dull purple and chestnut (10.05)	42·00	85·00
		a. Chalk-surfaced paper (1907)	38·00	80·00
25		6d. dull purple and violet (10.05)	27·00	65·00
		a. Chalk-surfaced paper (1906)	55·00	55·00
26	3	1s. green and black (10.05)	70·00	£110
		a. Chalk-surfaced paper (1906)	22·00	55·00
27		2s.6d. green and ultramarine (10.05)	60·00	70·00
		a. Chalk-surfaced paper (1906)	45·00	60·00
20a/27a *Set of 8*			£150	£275

1910 (30 Jan)–**11**. Ordinary paper (½d. to 2½d.) or chalk-surfaced paper (others). Wmk Mult Crown. CA. P 14.

28	3	½d. green (15.4.10)	2·00	1·25
29		1d. carmine	6·00	1·25
30		2d. grey (26.10.11)	9·50	6·50
31		2½d. blue (10.10)	4·50	11·00
32	4	3d. purple/*yellow* (10.9.11)	4·00	1·25
34		5d. dull purple and olive-green (26.2.11)	6·00	19·00
35		6d. dull purple and purple (10.11.10)	6·00	28·00
		a. Dull and bright purple (1911)	5·00	6·00
36	3	1s. black/*green* (10.11.10)	6·00	75
37		2s.6d. black and red/*blue* (15.3.11)	19·00	48·00
38	4	5s. green and red/*yellow* (10.9.11)	28·00	75·00
39	3	10s. green and red/*green* (15.3.11)	55·00	48·00
28/39 *Set of 11*			£120	£190
28s/39s Optd 'SPECIMEN' *Set of 11*			£350	

5

6

1912 (Sept). Ordinary paper (½d., 1d., 2d.) or chalk-surfaced paper (others). Wmk Mult Crown CA. P 14.

40	5	½d. deep green	4·25	1·50
41		1d. red	4·50	60
42		2d. grey	6·50	18·00
43	6	3d. purple/*yellow*	3·00	1·25
44		4d. black and red/*yellow*	1·25	2·50
45		5d. dull purple and olive-green	4·00	20·00
46		6d. dull and bright purple	4·00	4·25
47		9d. dull purple and carmine	2·25	12·00
48	5	1s. black/*green*	4·75	2·25
49		2s.6d. black and red/*blue*	11·00	55·00
50	6	5s. green and red/*yellow*	26·00	85·00
51	5	10s. green and red/*green*	45·00	48·00
52	6	£1 purple and black/*red*	£180	£110
40/52 *Set of 13*			£250	£325
40s/52s Optd 'SPECIMEN' *Set of 13*			£225	

Examples of most values are known showing forged postmarks of Lokoja dated 'MR 22 12' or Minna dated 'JN 16 1913'. These forged postmarks have also been seen on examples of earlier issues.

On 1 January 1914 Northern Nigeria became part of Nigeria.

SOUTHERN NIGERIA

The Colony and Protectorate of Southern Nigeria was formed on 1 January 1900 by the amalgamation of Niger Coast Protectorate with the southern part of the Niger Territories. Lagos was incorporated into the territory on 1 May 1906.

The stamps of NIGER COAST PROTECTORATE were used in Southern Nigeria until the introduction of Nos. 1/9, and also during a shortage of these values in mid-1902. The issues of LAGOS were utilised throughout Southern Nigeria after 1 May 1906 until supplies were exhausted.

PRICES FOR STAMPS ON COVER TO 1945

Nos. 1/7	*from* × 8
Nos. 8/9	—
Nos. 10/18	*from* × 4
Nos. 19/20	—
Nos. 21/30	*from* × 4
Nos. 31/32	—
Nos. 33/42	*from* × 4
Nos. 43/44	—
Nos. 45/53	*from* × 4
Nos. 55/56	—

PRINTERS. All issues of Southern Nigeria were typographed by De La Rue & Co, Ltd, London.

1

2

3

1901 (Mar)–**02**. Wmk Crown CA. P 14.

1	1	½d. black and pale green	1·75	3·00
		a. Sepia and green (1902)	2·50	2·75
2		1d. black and carmine	3·50	2·75
		a. Sepia and carmine (1902)	4·50	1·75
3		2d. black and red-brown	3·50	7·00
4		4d. black and sage-green	3·50	30·00
5		6d. black and purple	5·00	13·00
6		1s. green and black	11·00	35·00
7		2s.6d. black and brown	48·00	95·00
8		5s. black and orange-yellow	65·00	£130
9		10s. black and purple/*yellow*	£150	£300
1/9 *Set of 9*			£250	£550
1s/9s Optd 'SPECIMEN' *Set of 9*			£225	

1903 (Mar)–**04**. Wmk Crown CA. P 14.

10	2	½d. grey-black and pale green	1·00	30
		w. Wmk inverted		
11		1d. grey-black and carmine	1·25	70
12		2d. grey-black and chestnut	18·00	1·50
13		2½d. grey-black and blue (1904)	2·00	2·50
14		4d. grey-black and olive-green	6·00	5·50
15		6d. grey-black and purple	9·50	8·00
16		1s. green and black	42·00	19·00
17		2s.6d. grey-black and brown	42·00	75·00
18		5s. grey-black and yellow	90·00	£225
19		10s. grey-black and purple/*yellow*	45·00	£150
20		£1 green and violet	£475	£1000
10/20 *Set of 11*			£650	£1300
10s/20s Optd 'SPECIMEN' *Set of 11*			£325	

Two Dies of Head Plate:

A

B

In Head A the fifth line of shading on the king's cheek shows as a line of dots and the lines of shading up to the king's hair are broken in places. In Head B the lines of shading are more regular, especially the fifth line.

1904 (June)–**09**. Head Die A. Ordinary paper. Wmk Mult Crown CA. P 14.

21	2	½d. grey-black and pale green	60	10
		a. Chalk-surfaced paper (1905)	2·25	90
22		1d. grey-black and carmine	18·00	20
		a. Chalk-surfaced paper (1905)	12·00	10
23		2d. grey-black and chestnut (1905)	2·75	45
		a. Pale grey and chestnut (Head Die B) (1907)	4·50	40
24		2½d. grey-black and bright blue (9.09)	1·00	1·00
25		3d. orange-brown and bright purple (chalk-surfaced paper) (Head Die B) (18.8.07)	9·50	1·25
		s. Optd 'SPECIMEN'	27·00	
26		4d. grey-black and olive-green (12.05)	14·00	25·00
		a. Chalk-surfaced paper (1906)	26·00	30·00
		ab. Grey-black and pale olive-green (Head Die B) (1907)	50·00	50·00
27		6d. grey-black and bright purple (9.05)	13·00	9·50
		a. Chalk-surfaced paper (1906)	13·00	15·00
		ab. Head Die B (1907)	18·00	2·25
28		1s. grey-green and black (19.9.07)	3·25	3·50
		a. Chalk-surfaced paper (Head Die B) (1907)	42·00	3·25
29		2s.6d. grey-black and brown (30.4.06)	24·00	29·00
		a. Chalk-surfaced paper (1906)	55·00	20·00
		ab. Head Die B (1907)	65·00	29·00
30		5s. grey-black and yellow (10.12.07)	60·00	90·00
		a. Chalk-surfaced paper (Head Die B) (1908)	85·00	£100
31		10s. grey-black and purple/*yellow* (*chalk-surfaced paper*) (Head Die B) (9.08)	£170	£225
32		£1 green and violet (19.3.06)	£350	£425
		a. Chalk-surfaced paper (1906)	£325	£425
		ab. Head Die B (1907)	£325	£400
21/32ab *Set of 12*			£550	£700

I

II

Die I. Thick '1', small 'd'. (double working plate).
Die II. Thinner '1', larger 'd' (single working plate).

1907–11. Colours changed. Head Die B. Ordinary paper (½d. to 2½d.) or chalk-surfaced paper (others). Wmk Mult Crown CA. P 14.

33	2	½d. grey-green (1907)	7·50	20
		a. Head Die A	17·00	3·25
		b. Blue-green (1910)	2·25	20
34		1d. carmine (I) (12.8.07)	4·00	60
		a. Head Die A	28·00	3·25
		ab. Die II. *Carmine-red* (1910)	1·00	10
35		2d. greyish slate (9.09)	2·75	70
36		2½d. blue (9.09)	8·50	3·75
37		3d. purple/*yellow* (7.09)	2·00	30
38		4d. black and red/*yellow* (9.09)	2·25	80
39		6d. dull purple and purple (9.09)	50·00	3·25
		a. Dull purple and bright purple (1911)	28·00	3·25
		aw. Wmk inverted	†	£275

40		1s. black/*green* (7.09)	7·00	40
41		2s.6d. black and red/*blue* (9.09)	18·00	3·25
42		5s. green and red/*yellow* (9.09)	40·00	48·00
43		10s. green and red/*green* (9.09)	£100	£140
44		£1 purple and black/*red* (9.09)	£250	£300
33/44 *Set of* 12			£400	£450
33s/44s Optd 'SPECIMEN' *Set of* 12			£400	

1912. Wmk Mult Crown CA. P 14.

45	3	½d. green	2·25	10
46		1d. red	2·50	10
		w. Wmk inverted	£225	£170
		y. Wmk inverted and reversed	†	£300
47		2d. grey	1·00	85
48		2½d. bright blue	6·00	2·75
49		3d. purple/*yellow*	1·00	30
50		4d. black and red/*yellow*	1·25	2·00
51		6d. dull and bright purple	3·00	1·25
52		1s. black/*green*	2·75	75
53		2s.6d. black and red/*blue*	9·00	50·00
54		5s. green and red/*yellow*	20·00	80·00
55		10s. green and red/*green*	48·00	£100
56		£1 purple and black/*red*	£200	£275
45/56 *Set of* 12			£250	£450
45s/56s Optd 'SPECIMEN' *Set of* 12			£275	

STAMP BOOKLETS

1904. Black on red cover. Stapled.

SB1	2s.1d. booklet containing 24×1d (No. 11) in blocks of 6	

1905 (1 June)–**06.** Black on red cover. Stapled.

SB2	2s.1d. booklet containing 24×1d. (No. 22) in blocks of 6	£2000
	a. As No. SB2 but containing No. 22a (1906)	£1800

1907 (7 Oct). Black on red cover. Stapled.

SB3	2s.1d. booklet containing 24×1d (No. 34) in blocks of 6	£2250

1910 (19 Sept). Black on red cover. Stapled.

SB4	2s. booklet containing 11×½d. and 18×1d. (Nos. 33*b*, 34*ab*) in blocks of 6 or 5	

1912 (Oct). Black on red cover. Stapled.

SB5	2s. booklet containing 12×½d. and 18×1d. (Nos. 45/46) in blocks of 6	£2000

On 1 January 1914 Southern Nigeria became part of Nigeria.

NIGERIA

Nigeria was formed on 1 January 1914 from the former protectorates of Northern and Southern Nigeria.

PRICES FOR STAMPS ON COVER TO 1945	
Nos. 1/10	*from* × 3
Nos. 11/12	—
Nos. 15/28	*from* × 3
Nos. 29/29a	—
Nos. 30/33	*from* × 3
Nos. 34/59	*from* × 2

CROWN COLONY

1

2

(Typo D.L.R.)

1914 (1 June)–**29.** Die I. Ordinary paper (½d. to 2½d.) or chalk-surfaced paper (others). Wmk Mult Crown CA. P 14.

1	1	½d. green	5·50	70
2		1d. carmine-red	4·75	10
		a. Scarlet (1916)	15·00	20
		w. Wmk inverted	£160	£120
3		2d. grey	8·00	1·75
		a. Slate-grey (1918)	9·00	75
4		2½d. bright blue	10·00	8·50
		a. Dull blue (1915)	28·00	12·00
5	2	3d. purple/*yellow* (white back)	2·75	12·00
		a. Lemon back (19.8.15)	1·50	2·75
		b. On deep yellow (yellow back) (thick paper) (1915)	50·00	7·50
		bs. Optd 'SPECIMEN'	40·00	
		c. On orange-buff (1920)	9·00	22·00
		d. On buff (1920)	12·00	
		e. On pale yellow (1921)	14·00	15·00
6		4d. black and red/*yellow* (white back)	1·40	10·00
		a. Lemon back (19.8.15)	1·00	5·50
		b. On deep yellow (yellow back) (thick paper) (1915)	50·00	8·50
		bs. Optd 'SPECIMEN'	40·00	
		c. On orange-buff (1920)	14·00	10·00
		d. On buff (1920)	14·00	
		e. On pale yellow (1921)	10·00	18·00
7		6d. dull purple and bright purple	9·00	10·00
		y. Wmk inverted and reversed	†	£350
8	1	1s. black/*blue-green* (white back)	1·50	23·00
		a. On yellow-green (white back) (1915)	£225	
		b. Yellow-green back (19.8.15)	60·00	60·00
		c. Blue-green back (1915)	3·50	9·50
		cs. Optd 'SPECIMEN'	40·00	
		d. Pale olive back (1917)	40·00	50·00
		dw. Wmk inverted		
		e. On emerald (pale olive back) (1920)	8·00	50·00
		f. On emerald (emerald back) (1920)	1·25	15·00
9		2s.6d. black and red/*blue*	17·00	6·50
10	2	5s. green and red/*yellow* (white back)	25·00	65·00
		a. Lemon back (19.8.15)	21·00	60·00
		b. On deep yellow (yellow back) (thick paper) (1915)	60·00	75·00
		bs. Optd 'SPECIMEN'	45·00	
		c. On orange-buff (1920)	70·00	£110
		d. On buff (1920)	80·00	
		e. On pale yellow (1921)	£130	£180
11	1	10s. green and red/*blue-green* (white back)	50·00	£180
		a. Blue-green back (19.8.15)	70·00	£100
		as. Optd 'SPECIMEN'	55·00	
		b. Pale olive back (1917)	£1100	£1800
		c. On emerald (pale olive back) (1920)	£160	£250
		d. On emerald (emerald back) (1921)	35·00	£120
12	2	£1 deep purple and black/*red*	£190	£275
		a. Purple and black/red (1917)	£225	£250
		b. Die II. Deep purple and black/red (19.1.27)	£275	£350
		ba. Purple and black/red (1929)	£225	£325
1/12 *Set of* 12			£275	£400
1s/12s Optd 'SPECIMEN' *Set of* 12			£325	

The ½d. and 1d. were printed in sheets of 240 using two plates one above the other.

1921–32. Ordinary paper (½d. to 3d.) or chalk-surfaced paper (others). Wmk Mult Script CA. P 14.

15	1	½d. green (Die I) (1921)	1·25	75
		aw. Wmk inverted	£160	£120
		b. Die II (1925)	6·50	85
		c. Vert gutter pair. Die I and Die II. Nos. 15/15b (1925)	£475	
16		1d. rose-carmine (Die I) (1921)	3·25	30
		aw. Wmk inverted	£140	£100
		b. Die II (1925)	1·75	35
		c. Vert gutter pair. Die I and Die II. Nos. 16/16b (1925)	£425	
17	2	1½d. orange (Die II) (1.4.31)	9·50	15
18	1	2d. grey (Die I) (1921)	1·50	8·00
		a. Die II (1924)	10·00	40
19		2d. chestnut (Die II) (1.10.27)	4·50	1·00
20		2d. chocolate (Die II) (1.7.28)	5·00	15
		a. Die I (1932)	5·50	75
21		2½d. bright blue (Die I) (1921)	1·25	15·00
22	2	3d. bright violet (Die I) (1924)	6·00	4·75
		a. Die II (1925)	10·00	1·00
23		3d. bright blue (Die II) (1.4.31)	11·00	1·00
24		4d. black and red/*pale yellow* (Die II) (1923)	65	55
		a. Die I (1932)	4·00	4·75
25		6d. dull purple and bright purple (Die I) (1921)	13·00	42·00
		a. Die II (1923)	7·00	8·00
		aw. Wmk inverted	£180	
26	1	1s. black/*emerald* (Die II) (1924)	7·00	2·00
27		2s.6d. black and red/*blue* (Die II) (1925)	6·50	50·00
		a. Die I (1932)	50·00	85·00
28	2	5s. green and red/*pale yellow* (Die II) (1926)	15·00	80·00
		a. Die I (1932)	75·00	£250
29	1	10s. green and red/*green* (Die II) (1925)	65·00	£225
		a. Die I (1932)	£130	£500
15/29 *Set of* 15			£120	£350
15s/29s (ex 2d. chocolate) Optd or Perf (1½d., 3d. blue) 'SPECIMEN' *Set of* 14			£450	

The ½d. and 1d., together with the 1½d. from 1932, were printed in sheets of 240 using two plates one above the other. Nos. 15c and 16c come from printings in November 1924 which combined Key Plate No. 7 (Die I) above Key Plate No. 12 (Die II).

1935 (6 May). Silver Jubilee. As Nos. 91/94 of Antigua, but ptd by Waterlow. P 11×12.

30	1½d. ultramarine and grey	1·00	1·50
31	2d. green and indigo	2·00	2·00
	k. Kite and vertical log	£130	£110
32	3d. brown and deep blue	3·25	19·00
33	1s. slate and purple	10·00	45·00
30/33 *Set of* 4		14·50	60·00
30s/33s Perf 'SPECIMEN' *Set of* 4		£120	

For illustration of plate variety see Omnibus section following Zanzibar.

3 Apapa Wharf **4** Cocoa **5** Tin dredger

6 Timber industry **7** Fishing Village **8** Cotton ginnery

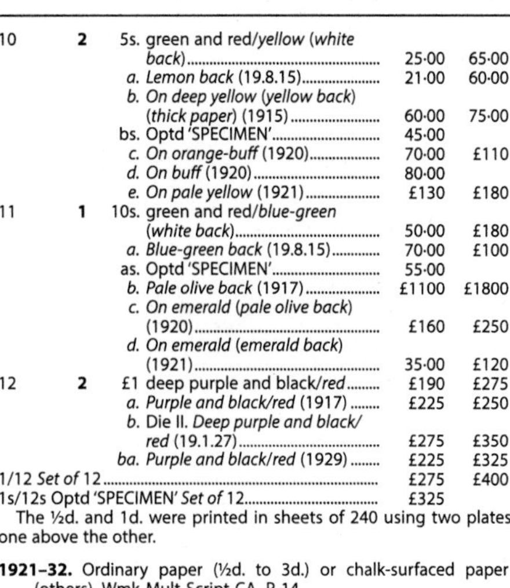

9 Habe Minaret **10** Fulani cattle

11 Victoria-Buea Road

12 Oil Palms

13 River Niger at Jebba

14 Canoe Pulling

(Recess D.L.R.)

1936 (1 Feb). Types **3/14**. Wmk Mult Script CA.

(a) P 11½×13

34	3	½d. green	1·50	1·40
35	4	1d. carmine	50	40
36	5	1½d. brown	2·00	40
		a. Perf 12½×13½	85·00	4·00
37	6	2d. black	50	80
38	7	3d. blue	2·00	1·50
		a. Perf 12½×13½	£150	24·00
39	8	4d. red-brown	2·25	2·00
40	9	6d. dull violet	50	60
41	10	1s. sage-green	1·75	4·75

(b) P 14

42	11	2s.6d. black and ultramarine	9·00	45·00
43	12	5s. black and olive-green	22·00	60·00
44	13	10s. black and grey	90·00	£140
45	14	£1 black and orange	£130	£200
34/45 *Set of* 12			£225	£400
34s/45s Perf 'SPECIMEN' *Set of* 12			£300	

1937 (12 May). Coronation. As Nos. 95/97 of Antigua. P 11×11½.

46	1d. carmine	1·00	2·50
47	1½d. brown	3·00	3·00
48	3d. blue	3·00	6·00
46/48 *Set of* 3		6·25	10·50
46s/48s Perf 'SPECIMEN' *Set of* 3		£110	

15 King George VI

16 Victoria-Buea Road

(Recess B.W. (T **15**), D.L.R. (others))

1938 (1 May)–**51.** Designs as Types **15/16.** Wmk Mult Script CA. P 12 (T **15**) or 13×11½ (others).

49	15	½d. green	10	10
		a. Perf 11½ (15.2.50)	2·25	1·75
50		1d. carmine	19·00	2·50
		a. Rose-red (shades) (1940)	75	30
		ab. 'A' of 'CA' missing from wmk	£2250	
50*b*		1d. bright purple (1.12.44)	10	20
		ba. Perf 11½ (15.2.50)	1·00	60
		bw. Wmk inverted (P 12)	†	£5500
51		1½d. brown	20	10
		a. Perf 11½ (15.11.50)	30	10
52		2d. black	10	3·25
52*a*		2d. rose-red (1.12.44)	10	3·50
		ab. Perf 11½ (15.2.50)	1·50	70
		aba. Wmk sideways	†	—
52*b*		2½d. orange (4.41)	10	3·00
53		3d. blue	10	10
		a. Wmk sideways	†	£6000
53*b*		3d. black (1.12.44)	15	3·25
54		4d. orange	50·00	3·75
54*a*		4d. blue (1.12.44)	15	4·50
55		6d. blackish purple	40	10
		a. Perf 11½ (17.4.51)	3·00	60
56		1s. sage-green	60	10
		a. Perf 11½ (15.2.50)	1·75	10
57		1s.3d. light blue (1940)	1·00	30
		a. Perf 11½ (14.6.50)	4·50	70
		ab. Wmk sideways	†	£5500
58	16	2s.6d. black and blue	60·00	26·00
		a. Perf 13½ (6.42)	4·75	9·00
		ab. Black and deep blue (1947)	55·00	55·00
		b. Perf 14 (1942)	3·75	3·50
		bw. Wmk inverted	£3250	£4500
		c. Perf 12 (15.8.51)	2·75	5·00
59	13	5s. black and orange	£110	23·00
		a. Perf 13½ (8.42)	7·50	4·50
		b. Perf 14 (1948)	11·00	3·00
		c. Perf 12 (19.5.49)	10·00	4·00
49/59a *Set of* 16			55·00	23·00
49s/59s (ex 2½d.) Perf 'SPECIMEN' *Set of* 15			£450	

The ½d., No. 49a, and 1d., No. 50ba, exist in coils constructed from normal sheets.

1946 (21 Oct). Victory. As Nos. 110/111 of Antigua.

60	1½d. chocolate	50	10
61	4d. blue	50	2·50
60s/61s Perf 'SPECIMEN' *Set of* 2		85·00	

1948 (20 Dec). Royal Silver Wedding. As Nos. 112/113 of Antigua.

62	1d. bright purple	35	40
63	5s. brown-orange	17·00	26·00

1949 (10 Oct). 75th Anniversary of UPU. As Nos. 114/117 of Antigua.

64	1d. bright reddish purple	15	30
65	3d. deep blue	1·25	3·75
66	6d. purple	30	3·75
67	1s. olive	50	2·00
64/67 *Set of* 4		2·00	9·00

1953 (2 June). Coronation. As No. 120 of Antigua but ptd by B.W.

68		1½d. black and emerald	50	10
		w. Wmk inverted	†	—

18 Old Manilla Currency

19 Bornu horsemen

1d. Die I Flat-bed **1d.** Die Ia Rotary

Two types of 1d.:

The Belgian rotary printings have thicker lines of shading giving blotches of black colour instead of fine lines, particularly in the stirrups.

20 Groundnuts

21 Tin

2d. Major re-entry showing duplication of steps of the terraces (Pl 3, R. 1/5)

2d. Type A Gap in row of dots

2d. Type B Unbroken row of dots

Two types of 2d. slate-violet:

Nos. 72c/72f. The original cylinder used was Type A (July 1956); later Type B (Sept 1957). The above illustrations will help classification, but two stamps per sheet of 60 of Type A show faint dots. Shades are distinctive.

'2d' re-entry. Partial doubling of the '2d' and dot (Type A, R. 5/2 and 3). Also known on booklet panes

2d. A flaw resembles an extra figure (Type A, R. 5/4)

22 Jebba Bridge and River Niger

23 Cocoa

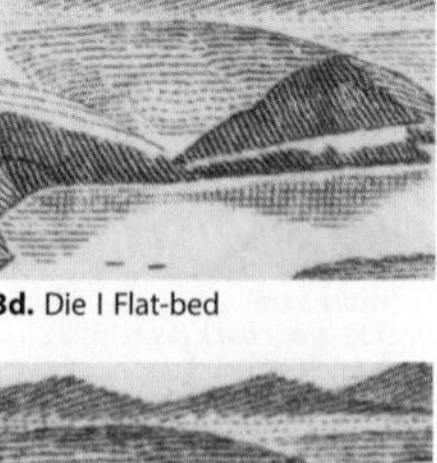

3d. Die I Flat-bed

3d. Die Ia Rotary

Two types of 3d.:

As in the 1d. the Belgian rotary printings have thicker lines of shading and this is particularly noticeable in the dark hills in the background.

24 Ife Bronze

25 Timber

26 Victoria Harbour

27 Palm-oil

28 Hides and skins

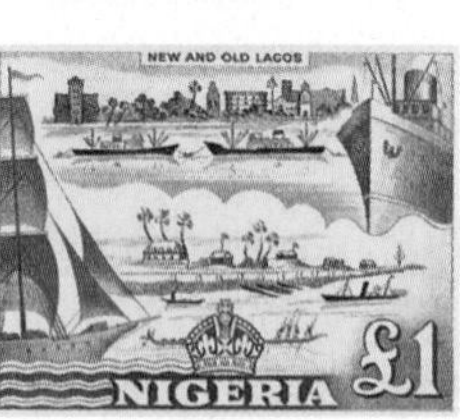

29 New and Old Lagos

(Des M. Fievet. Recess Waterlow)

1953 (1 Sept)–**58**. Types **18/29**. Wmk Mult Script CA. P 14.

69	**18**	½d. black and orange	15	30
70	**19**	1d. black and bronze-green (Die I)	20	10
		a. Die Ia (1.9.58)	20	20
71	**20**	1½d. blue-green	50	40
72	**21**	2d. black and yellow-ochre	4·00	30
		a. Black and ochre (18.8.54)	5·00	30
		b. Re-entry	£150	
72*c*		2d. slate-violet (Type A) (23.7.56)	3·00	2·00
		ca. '2d.' re-entry	40·00	
		cb. Extra figure	40·00	
		d. Slate-blue (shades) (Type A)	9·00	40
		da. '2d.' re-entry	80·00	
		db. Extra figure	85·00	
		e. Bluish grey (Type B) (25.9.57)	4·75	40
		f. Grey (shades) (Type B)	6·50	30
73	**22**	3d. black and purple (Die I)	55	10
		a. Die Ia. *Black and reddish purple* (1.9.58)	55	10
		b. Imperf (pair)	£400	
74	**23**	4d. black and blue	2·50	20
75	**24**	6d. orange-brown and black	30	10
		a. Chestnut and black (18.8.54)	2·75	10
76	**25**	1s. black and maroon	50	10
77	**26**	2s.6d. black and green	19·00	1·25
		a. Black and deep green (18.8.54)	35·00	1·25
78	**27**	5s. black and red-orange	7·50	1·40
79	**28**	10s. black and red-brown	24·00	3·25
80	**29**	£1 black and violet	35·00	20·00
69/80 *Set of* 13			80·00	24·00

Nos. 70a, 72c/72db and 73*a* were printed on rotary machines by a subsidiary company, Imprimerie Belge de Securité, in Belgium.

Nos. 72*d* and 72*f* were only available in Nigeria.

The ½d. and 1d. (Die I) exist in coils constructed from sheets. Coils containing the 1d. (Die Ia) and 2d. (Type A) appeared in 1958 from continuously printed reels.

ROYAL VISIT
1956
(**30**)

1956 (28 Jan). Royal Visit. No. 72*a* optd with T **30**.

81	**21**	2d. black and ochre	40	30
		a. Opt inverted	£350	

31 Victoria Harbour

(Recess Waterlow)

1958 (1 Dec). Centenary of Victoria. W w **12**. P 13½×14.

82	**31**	3d. black and purple	40	30

32 Lugard Hall

33 Kano Mosque

(Recess Waterlow)

1959 (14 Mar). Attainment of Self-Government, Northern Region of Nigeria. Types **32/33**. W w **12**. P 13½ (3d.) or 13½×14 (1s.).

83	**32**	3d. black and purple	30	10
84	**33**	1s. black and green	95	60

INDEPENDENT FEDERATION

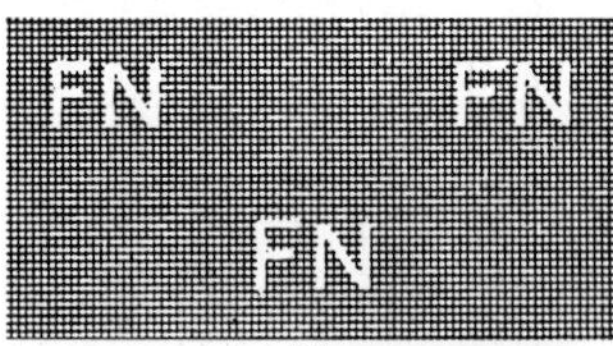

34

35 Legislative Building

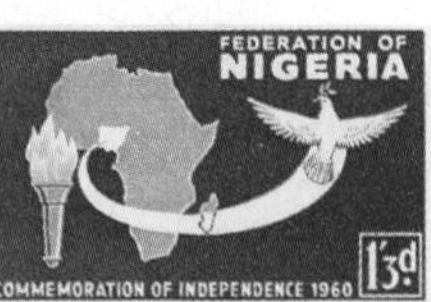

38 Dove, Torch and Map

(Des L. J. Wittington (1d.), R. Crawford (3d.), R. D. Baxter (6d.), J. White (1s.3d.), Photo Waterlow)

1960 (1 Oct). Independence. Types **35**, **38** and similar horiz designs. W **34**. P 13½ (1s.3d.) or 14 (others).

85	1d. black and scarlet	10	10
86	3d. black and greenish blue	15	10
87	6d. green and red-brown	20	20
88	1s.3d. bright blue and yellow	40	20
85/88 *Set of* 4		70	50

Designs: 1d. T **35**; (As T **35**)—3d. African paddling canoe; 6d. Federal Supreme Court; 1s. 3d T **38**.

39 Groundnuts **40** Coal mining

41 Adult education

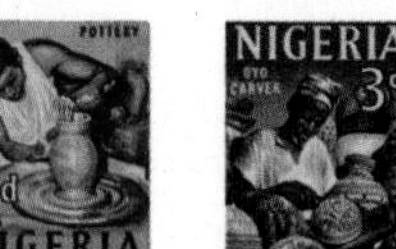

42 Pottery **43** Oyo carver

44 Weaving

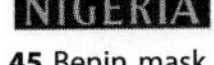

45 Benin mask

46 Yellow-casqued Hornbill

47 Camel train

48 Central Bank

49 Nigeria Museum

50 Kano Airport

51 Lagos railway station

1961 (1 Jan). Types **39/51**. W **34**. P 15×14 (½d. to 1s.3d.) or 14½ (others).

89	**39**	½d. emerald	10	60
90	**40**	1d. reddish violet	80	10
91	**41**	1½d. carmine-red	80	2·25
92	**42**	2d. deep blue	30	10
		w. Wmk inverted	†	—
93	**43**	3d. deep green	40	10
94	**44**	4d. blue	40	2·00
95	**45**	6d. yellow and black	80	10
		a. Yellow omitted	£3250	£1500
96	**46**	1s. yellow-green	4·50	10
97	**47**	1s.3d. orange	1·50	10
98	**48**	2s.6d. black and yellow	2·75	15
99	**49**	5s. black and emerald	65	1·25
		w. Wmk inverted	†	—
100	**50**	10s. black and ultramarine	3·75	4·25
101	**51**	£1 black and carmine-red	14·00	18·00
		w. Wmk inverted		
89/101 *Set of 13*			27·00	26·00

Nos. 90 and 92 were produced in continuous coils.

PRINTERS. The above and all following issues to No. 206 were printed in photogravure by Harrison & Sons, except where otherwise stated.

52 Globe and Diesel-electric Locomotive

56 Coat of Arms

(Des M. Goaman)

1961 (25 July). Admission of Nigeria into UPU. T **52** and similar horiz designs. W **34**. P 14½.

102	1d. red-orange and blue	30	10
103	3d. olive-yellow and black	30	10
104	1s.3d. blue and carmine-red	80	20
105	2s.6d. deep green and blue	85	2·00
102/105 *Set of 4*		2·00	2·00

Designs: 1d. T **52**; 3d. Globe and mail-van; 1s.3d. Globe and Bristol 175 Britannia aircraft; 2s.6d. Globe and liner.

(Des S. Bodo (3d.), R. Hopeman (4d.), C. Adesina (6d.), M. Shamir (1s.6d), B. Endwonwu (2s.6d.))

1961 (1 Oct). First Anniversary of Independence. T **56** and similar designs. W **34**. P 14½.

106	3d. multicoloured	10	10
107	4d. yellow-green, yellow-orange and dull vermilion	30	1·00
108	6d. emerald-green	40	10
109	1s.3d. grey, emerald and blue	45	10
110	2s.6d. green, grey-blue and blackish brown	55	1·75
106/110 *Set of 5*		1·60	2·75

Designs: Vert—3d. T **56**. Horiz—4d. Natural resources and map; 6d. Nigerian Eagle; 1s.3d. Eagles in flight; 2s.6d. Nigerians and flag.

A used copy of No. 106 has been seen with both the silver (large 'Y' appearing grey) and the yellow (appearing white) omitted.

61 'Health'

66 Malaria Eradication Emblem and Parasites

(Des M. Shamir)

1962 (25 Jan). Lagos Conference of African and Malagasy States. T **61** and similar vert designs. W **34**. P 14×14½.

111	1d. yellow-bistre	10	10
112	3d. deep reddish purple	10	10
113	6d. deep green	15	10
114	1s. brown	20	10
115	1s.3d. blue	25	20
111/115 *Set of 5*		65	40

Designs: 1d. T **61**; 3d. 'Culture'; 6d. 'Commerce'; 1s. 'Communications'; 1s.3d. 'Co-operation'.

1962 (7 Apr). Malaria Eradication. T **66** and similar horiz designs. W **34**. P 14½.

116	3d. green and orange-red	15	10
	w. Wmk inverted	†	—
117	6d. blue and bright purple	20	10
118	1s.3d. magenta and violet-blue	30	10
119	2s.6d. blue and yellow-brown	45	90
116/119 *Set of 4*		1·00	1·00

Designs: 3d T **66**; 6d. Insecticide spraying; 1s.3d. Aerial spraying; 2s.6d. Mother, child and microscope.

70 National Monument

71 Benin Bronze

(Des S. Bodo (3d.), B. Endwonwu (5s.))

1962 (1 Oct). Second Anniversary of Independence. W **34**. P 14½×14 (3d.) or 14×14½ (5s.).

120	**70**	3d. emerald and blue	10	10
		a. Emerald omitted	£800	£475
121	**71**	5s. red, emerald and violet	1·00	1·00

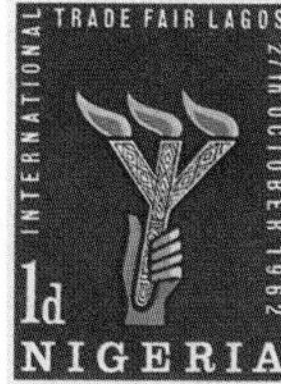

72 Fair Emblem

73 Cogwheels of Industry

(Des M. Goaman (1d., 2s.6d), J. O. Gbagbeolu and M. Goaman (6d), R. Hegeman (1s.))

1962 (27 Oct). International Trade Fair, Lagos. W **34**. Types **72/73** and similar designs. P 14½.

122	**72**	1d. olive-brown and orange-red	10	10
123	**73**	6d. carmine-red and black	15	10
124	–	1s. orange-brown and black	15	10
125	–	2s.6d. ultramarine and yellow	60	20
122/125 *Set of 4*			85	30

Designs: Horiz as T **73**—1s. Cornucopia of Industry; 2s.6d. Oilwells and tanker.

76 Arrival of Delegates

77 Mace as Palm Tree

(Des S. Akosile (2½d.), M. Goaman (others))

1962 (5 Nov). Eighth Commonwealth Parliamentary Conference, Lagos. Types **76/77** and similar design. W **34**. P 14½.

126	**76**	2½d. greenish blue	15	1·10
127	–	4d. indigo and rose-red	15	30
		a. Wmk inverted		
128	**77**	1s.3d. sepia and lemon	20	20
126/128 *Set of 3*			45	1·50

Design: Horiz—4d. National Hall.

80 Tractor and Maize

81 Mercury Capsule and Kano Tracking Station

(Des M. Goaman)

1963 (21 Mar). Freedom from Hunger. T **80** and similar design. W **34**. P 14.

129	**80**	3d. olive-green	2·00	20
130	–	6d. magenta	2·25	20

Design: Vert—3d. Herdsman.

(Des R. Hegeman)

1963 (21 June). 'Peaceful Use of Outer Space'. T **81** and similar vert design. W **34**. P 14½×14.

131	**81**	6d. blue and yellow-green	25	10
132	–	1s.3d. black and blue-green	35	20

Design: 1s.3d. Satellite and Lagos Harbour.

83 Scouts shaking Hands

(Des S. Apostolou (3d), G. Okiki (1s.))

1963 (1 Aug). 11th World Scout Jamboree, Marathon. T **83** and similar triangular-shaped design. W **34**. P 14.

133	**83**	3d. red and bronze-green	30	20
134	–	1s. black and red	95	80
MS134*a* 93×95 mm. Nos. 133/134			1·75	1·75
		ab. Red omitted (on 3d. value)	£1400	

Design: 1s. Campfire.

85 Emblem and First Aid Team

88 President Azikiwe and State House

(Des M. Goaman)

1963 (1 Sept). Red Cross Centenary. T **85** and similar horiz designs. W **34**. P 14½.

135	3d. red and deep ultramarine	60	10
136	6d. red and deep green	80	10
137	1s.3d. red and deep sepia	1·00	70
135/137 *Set of 3*		2·25	80
MS137*a* 102×102 mm. No. 137 (block of 4)		8·50	11·00

Designs: 3d. T **85**; 6d. Emblem and 'Hospital Services'; 1s.3d. Patient and emblem.

(Des M. Shamir. Photo Govt Printer, Israel)

1963 (1 Oct). Republic Day. T **88** and similar vert designs showing administrative buildings and President Azikiwe. P 14×13.

138	3d. yellow-olive and grey-green	10	10
139	1s.3d. yellow-brown and sepia	10	10
	a. Yellow-brown (portrait) omitted		
140	2s.6d. turquoise-blue and deep violet-blue	15	15
138/140 *Set of 3*		30	30

Designs: 3d. T **88**; 1s.3d. Federal Supreme Court Building; 2s.6d. Parliament Building.

89 Charter and Broken Whip

90 Freedom of Worship

(Des S. Apostolou (3d.), Mrs. F. P. Effiong (others). Photo D.L.R.)

1963 (10 Dec). 15th Anniversary of Declaration of Human Rights. Types **89/90** and similar designs. W **34**. P 13.

141	**89**	3d. vermilion	10	10
142	**90**	6d. blue-green	15	10
143	–	1s.3d. ultramarine	30	10
144	–	2s.6d. bright purple	45	30
141/4 *Set of 4*			85	35

Designs: Vert as T **90**—1s.3d. Freedom from want; 2s.6d. Freedom of speech.

93 Queen Nefertari **94** Rameses II

(Des M. Shamir)

1964 (8 Mar). Nubian Monuments Preservation. W **34**. P 14½.

145 **93** 6d. yellow-olive and emerald 50 10
146 **94** 2s.6d. brown, deep olive and emerald .... 1·75 2·25

95 President Kennedy

(Des M. Shamir (1s.3d), M. Goaman (2s.6d), Mr. Bottiau (5s.). Photo Govt Printer, Israel (1s.3d.); litho Lewin-Epstein, Bat Yam, Israel (others))

1964 (27 Aug). President Kennedy Memorial Issue. T **95** and similar horiz designs. P 13×14 (1s.3d.) or 14 (others).

147 1s.3d. light violet and black 30 15
148 2s.6d. black, red, blue and green 40 65
149 5s. black, deep blue, red and green .... 70 1·75
147/149 *Set of 3* .... 1·25 2·25
MS149*a* 154×135 mm. No. 149 (block of 4). Imperf .... 6·00 12·00

Designs: 1s.6d. T **95**; 2s.6d. President Kennedy and flags; 5s. President Kennedy (US coin head) and flags.

98 President Azikiwe **99** Herbert Macaulay

(Des S. Apostolou (3d), W. H. Irvine (others). Photo Govt Printer, Israel (3d); Harrison (others))

1964 (1 Oct). First Anniversary of Republic. Types **98** or **99** and similar vert design. P 14×13 (3d) or 14½ (others).

150 **98** 3d. red-brown 10 10
151 **99** 1s.3d. green 35 10
152 – 2s.6d. deep grey-green .... 70 1·50
150/152 *Set of 3* .... 1·00 1·50

Design: 2s.6d. King Jaja of Opobo.

101 Boxing Gloves

102 Hurdling

(Des A. Adalade (3d), S. Medahunsi (6d.), M. Shamir (1s.3d.), M. Goaman (2s.6d.))

1964 (10 Oct). Olympic Games, Tokyo. T **101** and similar designs, and T **102**. W **34**. P 14 (2s. 6d) or 14½ (others).

153 **101** 3d. sepia and olive green 45 10
154 – 6d. emerald and indigo 60 10
155 – 1s.3d. sepia and yellow-olive .... 1·00 15
156 **102** 2s.6d. sepia and chestnut .... 1·75 3·75
153/156 *Set of 4* .... 3·50 3·75
MS156a 102×102 mm. No. 156 (block of 4). Imperf .... 3·00 4·25

Designs: Horiz—6d. High jumping. Vert—1s.3d. Running.

105 Scouts on Hill-top

(Des S. Apostolou (1d., 1s.3d), H. N. G. Cowham and Eagle Scout N. A. Lasisi (3d.), W. H. Irvine (6d.))

1965 (1 Jan). 50th Anniversary of Nigerian Scout Movement. T **105** and similar vert designs. P 14×14½.

157 1d. brown .... 10 1·25
158 3d. red, black and emerald 20 10
159 6d. red, sepia and yellow-green 30 20
160 1s.3d. bistre-brown, greenish yellow and black-green 55 55
157/160 *Set of 4* .... 1·00 1·75
MS160*a* 76×104 mm. No. 160 (block of 4). Imperf. .... 5·00 8·50

Designs: 1d. T **105**; 3d. Scout badge on shield; 6d. Scout badges; 1s.3d. Chief Scout and Nigerian scout.

109 *Telstar* **110** Solar Satellite

(Des M. Shamir. Photo Govt Printer, Israel)

1965 (1 Apr). International Quiet Sun Years. P 14×13.

161 **109** 6d. reddish violet and turquoise-blue 15 15
162 **110** 1s.3d. green and reddish lilac 15 15

111 Native Tom-tom and Modern Telephone

(Des C. Botham (5s.), H. N. G. Cowham (others). Photo Enschedé)

1965 (2 Aug). ITU Centenary. T **111** and similar designs. P 11½×11 (1s.3d.) or 11×11½ (others).

163 3d. black, carmine and yellow-brown 30 10
164 1s.3d. black, blue-green and chalky blue .... 2·75 1·00
165 5s. black, carmine, blue and bright greenish blue .... 7·00 7·00
163/165 *Set of 3* .... 9·00 7·25

Designs: Vert—1s.3d. Microwave aerial. Horiz—3d. T **111**; 5s. Telecommunications satellite and part of globe.

114 ICY Emblem and Diesel-hydraulic Locomotive **117** Carved Frieze

(Des W. H. Irvine. Photo D.L.R.)

1965 (1 Sept). International Co-operation Year. T **114** and similar horiz designs. W **34**. P 14×15.

166 3d. green, red and orange .... 4·00 20
167 1s. black, bright blue and lemon .... 3·00 40
168 2s.6d. green, bright blue and yellow .... 9·50 7·00
166/168 *Set of 3* .... 15·00 7·00

Designs: 3d. T **114**; 1s. Students and Lagos Teaching Hospital; 2s.6d. Kainji (Niger) Dam.

(Des S. Apostolou (3d.), W. H. Irvine (others). Photo D.L.R.)

1965 (1 Oct). Second Anniversary of Republic. T **117** and similar designs. P 14×15 (3d.) or 15×14 (others).

169 3d. black, red and orange-yellow 10 10
170 1s.3d. red-brown, deep green and light ultramarine 25 10
171 5s. brown, blackish brown and light green .... 60 1·25
169/171 *Set of 3* .... 85 1·25

Designs: Horiz—3d. T **117**. Vert—1s.3d. Stone images at Ikom; 5s. Tada bronze.

120 Lion and Cubs **121** African Elephants

122 Splendid Sunbird **123** Village Weaver and Red-headed Malimbe

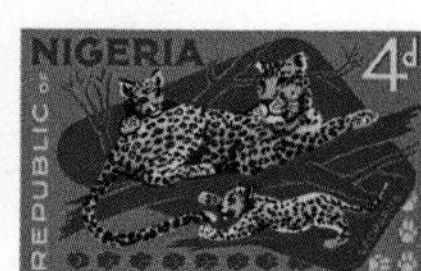

124 Cheetah **125** Leopards

126 Saddle-bill Stork **127** Grey Parrots

128 Blue-breasted Kingfishers

129 Crowned Cranes

130 Kobs

131 Giraffes

132 Hippopotamus **133** African Buffalo

(Des M. Fievet. Photo Harrison (1d., 2d., 3d., 4d. (No. 177a), 9d.) or Delrieu (others))

1965 (1 Nov)–**66**. Types **120/133**. Without printer's imprint. Chalk-surfaced paper (1d., 2d., 3d., 4d., 9d.). P 12×12½ (½d., 6d.), 12½×12 (1½d., 4d.), 14×13½ (1d., 2d., 3d., 9d.) or 12½ (others).

172 **120** ½d. multicoloured (1.11.65) .... 1·00 2·75
173 **121** 1d. multicoloured (1.11.65) 50 15
174 **122** 1½d. multicoloured (2.5.66) .... 7·00 10·00
175 **123** 2d. multicoloured (1.4.66) .... 3·75 15
176 **124** 3d. multicoloured (17.10.66) .... 1·25 30
177 **125** 4d. multicoloured (2.5.66) .... 2·00 4·25
a. Perf 14×13½ (1966) 30 10
178 **126** 6d. multicoloured (2.5.66) .... 1·50 40
179 **127** 9d. Prussian blue and orange-red (17.10.66) .... 2·50 60
180 **128** 1s. multicoloured (2.5.66) .... 5·00 2·00
181 **129** 1s.3d. multicoloured (2.5.66) .... 8·50 2·00

182 **130** 2s.6d. orange-brown, buff and brown (2.5.66) .... 1·00 2·50
183 **131** 5s. chestnut, light yellow and brown (2.5.66) .... 2·50 3·50
a. *Pale chestnut, yellow and brown-purple* (1966) .... 5·50 3·50
184 **132** 10s. multicoloured (2.5.66) .... 7·50 4·00
185 **133** £1 multicoloured (2.5.66) .... 22·00 9·00
172/185 *Set of* 14 .... 60·00 35·00

The 2d. and 3d. exist with PVA gum as well as gum arabic.
See also Nos. 220, etc.

The 1d., 2d., 3d., 4d. (No. 177a), 1s., 1s.3d., 2s.6d., 5s. and £1 values exist overprinted 'F.G.N.' (Federal Government of Nigeria) twice in black. They were prepared during 1968 at the request of one of the State Governments for use as official stamps, but the scheme was abandoned and meter machines were used instead. Some stamps held at Lagos Post Office were sold over the counter in error and passed through the post in October 1968. The Director of Posts made limited stocks of all values, except the 1s., available from the Philatelic Bureau from 11 April 1969 'in order not to create an artificial scarcity', but they had no postal validity. Covers do, however, exist showing the 4d. value used by Lagos Federal Income Tax Office in April 1969, the 1s.3d. on commercial mail to Britain in May 1969 and others from the Office of the Secretary to the Military Government in 1973 carry the 3d., 4d. and 2s.6d. values.

COMMONWEALTH
P. M. MEETING
11. JAN. 1966
(**134**)

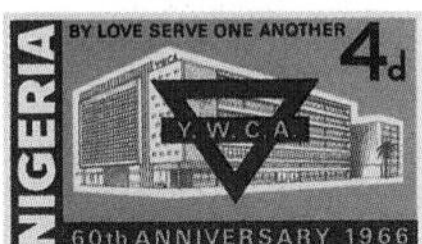

135 YWCA Emblem and HQ, Lagos

1966 (11 Jan). Commonwealth Prime Ministers Meeting, Lagos. No. 98 optd with T **134** by the Nigerian Security Printing and Minting Co, Lagos, in red.
186 **48** 2s.6d. black and yellow 30 30

(Des S. B. Ajayi. Litho Nigerian Security Printing & Minting Co Ltd)

1966 (1 Sept). Nigerian YWCA's Diamond Jubilee. P 14.
187 **135** 4d. yellow-orange, ultramarine, orange brown and yellow-green 15 10
188 9d. yellow-orange, ultramarine, brown and turquoise-green 15 60

137 Telephone Handset and Linesman

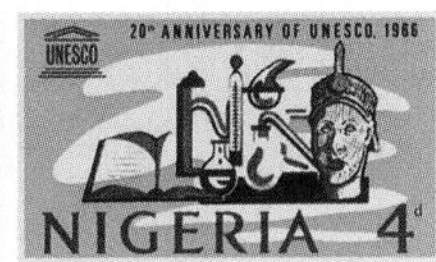

139 Education, Science and Culture

(Des S. B. Ajayi (4d.), N. Lasisi (1s.6d.), B. Endwonwu (2s.6d)

1966 (1 Oct). Third Anniversary of Republic. T **137** and similar designs. W **34**. P 14½×14.
189 4d. green 10 10
190 1s.6d. black, brown and reddish violet 30 50
191 2s.6d. blue, yellow and slate .... 1·00 2·25
189/191 *Set of* 3 .... 1·25 2·50
Designs: Vert—4d. Dove and flag. Horiz—1s.6d. T **137**; 2s.6d. North Channel Bridge over Niger, Jebba.

(Des V. Whiteley from sketch by B. Salisu)

1966 (4 Nov). 20th Anniversary of UNESCO. W **34** (sideways). P 14½×14.
192 **139** 4d. black, lake and orange-yellow .. 65 20
193 1s.6d. black, lake and turquoise-green .... 3·00 3·50
194 2s.6d. black, lake and rose-pink .... 4·00 9·50
192/194 *Set of* 3 .... 7·00 12·00

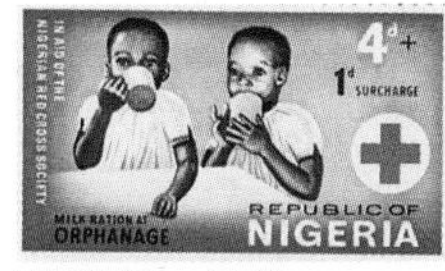

140 Children drinking

(Des V. Whiteley, after M. O. Afamefuna (4d.), I. U. Anawanti (1s.6d.) and S. Adeyemi (2s.6d.))

1966 (1 Dec). Nigerian Red Cross. T **140** and similar designs. W **34**. P 14×14½ (1s.6d.) or 14½×14 (others).
195 4d. +1d. black, reddish violet and red 30 30
196 1s.6d. +3d. multicoloured .... 55 3·75
197 2s.6d. +3d. multicoloured .... 65 4·25
195/197 *Set of* 3 .... 1·25 7·50
Designs: Vert—1s.6d. Tending patient. Horiz—4d. T **140**; 2s.6d. Tending casualties, and badge.

143 Surveying

(Des M. Goaman)

1967 (1 Feb). International Hydrological Decade. T **143** and similar multicoloured design. W **34**. P 14½×14 (4d.) or 14×14½ (2s.6d.).
198 4d. Type **143** 10 10
199 2s.6d. Water gauge on dam (*vert*) .... 40 2·50

145 Globe and Weather Satellite

147 Eyo Masqueraders

(Des M. Shamir (4d.), S. Bodo (1s.6d.))

1967 (23 Mar). World Meteorological Day. T **145** and similar horiz design. W **34**. P 14½×14.
200 4d. magenta and blue 15 10
201 1s.6d. black, yellow and blue 65 90
Design: 4d. T **145**; 1s.6d. Passing storm and sun.

(Des G. A. Okiki (4d.), A. B. Saka Lawal (1s.6d.), S. Bodo (2s.6d.). Photo Enschedé)

1967 (1 Oct). Fourth Anniversary of Republic. T **147** and similar multicoloured designs. P 11½×11 (2s.6d.) or 11×11½ (others).
202 4d. Type **147** 15 10
203 1s.6d. Crowd watching acrobat .... 50 1·50
204 2s.6d. Stilt dancer (*vert*) .... 75 3·50
202/204 *Set of* 3 .... 1·25 4·50

150 Tending Sick Animal

151 Smallpox Vaccination

(Des G. Drummond)

1967 (1 Dec). Rinderpest Eradication Campaign. P 14½×14.
205 **150** 4d. multicoloured 15 10
206 1s.6d. multicoloured .... 55 1·50

PRINTERS AND PROCESS. Nos. 207/255 were printed in photogravure by the Nigerian Security Printing and Minting Co Ltd, *unless otherwise stated*.

(Des J. Owei. Litho)

1968 (7 Apr). 20th Anniversary of World Health Organisation. T **151** and similar horiz design. P 14.
207 4d. magenta and black 15 10
208 1s.6d. orange, lemon and black .... 55 1·00
Design: 4d. T **151**; 1s.6d. African and mosquito.

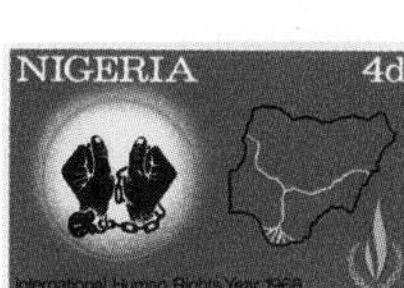

153 Chained Hands and Outline of Nigeria

155 Hand grasping at Doves of Freedom

(Des Jennifer Toombs)

1968 (1 July). Human Rights Year. T **153** and similar design. P 14.
209 4d. greenish blue, black and yellow 15 10
210 1s.6d. myrtle-green, orange-red and black .... 85 1·00
Design: Horiz—4d. T **153**; Vert—1s.6d. Nigerian flag and Human Rights emblem.

(Des G. Vasarhelyi)

1968 (1 Oct). Fifth Anniversary of Federal Republic. P 13½×14.
211 **155** 4d. multicoloured 10 10
212 1s.6d. multicoloured 20 75

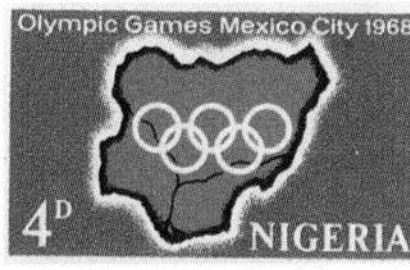

156 Map of Nigeria and Olympic Rings

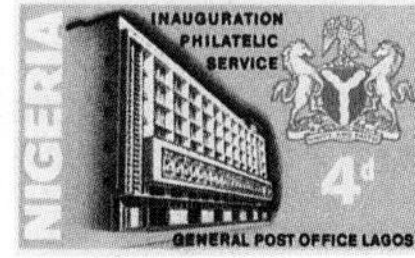

158 GPO, Lagos

(Des J. Owei)

1968 (14 Oct). Olympic Games, Mexico. T **156** and similar horiz design. P 14.
213 4d. black, green and scarlet 20 10
214 1s.6d. multicoloured 80 30
Design: 4d. T **156**; 1s.6d. Nigerian athletes, flag and Olympic rings.

(Des D.L.R.)

1969 (11 Apr). Inauguration of Philatelic Service. P 14.
215 **158** 4d. black and green 10 10
216 1s.6d. black and blue 20 50

159 Yakubu Gowon and Victoria Zakari

(Des adapted from photo by Jackie Phillips. Litho)

1969 (20 Sept). Wedding of General Gowon. P 13×13½.
217 **159** 4d. chocolate and emerald 10 10
218 1s.6d. black and emerald 90 30

1969–72.
(a) As No. 173 etc, but printed by Nigerian Security Printing and Minting Co Ltd. With printer's imprint 'N.S.P. & M. CO. LTD.' P 13½ (6d.) or P 13×13½ (others)
220 **121** 1d. multicoloured .... 3·00 2·25
222 **123** 2d. multicoloured .... 4·50 2·75
a. Smaller imprint* (13.1.71) .... 1·00 1·75
223 **124** 3d. multicoloured (7.71) .... 65 2·00
a. Larger imprint* (22.10.71) .... 1·00 1·50
224 **125** 4d. multicoloured .... 8·50 10
a. Smaller imprint† .... 90·00 20·00
225 **126** 6d. multicoloured (1971) .... 2·25 20
226 **127** 9d. Prussian blue and orange-red (1970) .... 5·00 50
a. 'TD' of 'LTD' omitted from imprint (Pl. 1B, R. 10/2) .... 70·00
227 **128** 1s. multicoloured (8.71) .... 2·50 20
228 **129** 1s.3d. multicoloured (1971) .... 11·00 4·75
229 **130** 2s.6d. multicoloured (1972) .... 22·00 7·00
230 **131** 5s. multicoloured (1972) .... 3·25 27·00
220/230 *Set of* 10 .... 55·00 40·00

* On No. 222a the designer's name measures 4¾ mm. On No. 223a the imprints measure 9 and 8½ mm respectively. The normal imprints on Nos. 222/223 both measure 5½ mm.

The date given for Nos. 222a and 223a are for the earliest known used copies.

† No. 224 has the left-hand imprint 6 mm long and the right-hand 5½ mm. On No. 224a the imprints are 5½ mm and 4½ mm respectively. The width of the design is also ½ mm smaller.

Postal forgeries of the 2s.6d. exist printed by lithography and roughly perforated 11–12.

Imperforate proofs of similar 10s. and £1 values are known.

(b) As Nos. 222 and 224, but redrawn, and printed by Enschedé. No printer's imprint; designer's name at right. P 14½×13
231 **123** 2d. multicoloured (9.70) .... 50·00 2·00
232 **125** 4d. multicoloured (3.71) .... 2·00 30
In the 2d. the face value is white instead of yellow, and in the 4d. the white lettering and value are larger.

160 Bank Emblem and '5th Anniversary'

161 Bank Emblem and Rays

(Des J. Owei (4d.), B. Salisu (1s.6d.). Litho)

1969 (18 Oct). Fifth Anniversary of African Development Bank. P 14.
233 **160** 4d. orange, black and blue 10 10
234 **161** 1s.6d. lemon, black and plum .... 20 1·25

162 ILO Emblem

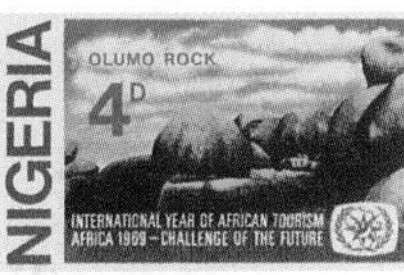

164 Olumo Rock

(Des D. West)

1969 (15 Nov). 50th Anniversary of International Labour Organisation. T **162** and similar horiz design. P 14.
235 4d. black and bright reddish violet 10 10
236 1s.6d. emerald and black .... 75 1·50
Design: 4d. T **162**; 1s.6d. World map and ILO emblem.

(Des A. Onwudimegwu)

1969 (30 Dec). International Year of African Tourism. T **164** and similar designs. P 14.
237 4d. multicoloured 15 10
238 1s. black and bright emerald 20 10
239 1s.6d. multicoloured .... 1·25 95
237/239 *Set of* 3 .... 1·40 1·00
Designs: Horiz—4d. T **164**. Vert—1s. Traditional musicians; 1s.6d. Assob Falls.

167 Symbolic Tree

168 UPU HQ Building

(Des E. Emokpae (4d., 1s., 2s.), B. Onobrakpeya (1s.6d.). Photo Enschedé)

1970 (28 May). Stamp of Destiny; End of Civil War. T **167** and similar designs. P 11×11½ (2s.) or 11½×11 (others).
240 4d. gold, new blue and black 10 10
241 1s. multicoloured 10 10
242 1s.6d. yellow-green and black 15 10
243 2s. multicoloured 20 20
240/243 *Set of* 4 .... 40 30
Designs: Vert—4d. T **167**; 1s. Symbolic Wheel 1s.6d. United Nigerians supporting Map. Horiz—2s. Symbolic Torch.

(Des A. Onwudimegwu)

1970 (29 June). New UPU Headquarters Building. P 14.
244 **168** 4d. reddish violet and greenish yellow 10 10
245 1s.6d. light greenish blue and deep blue 40 20

169 Scroll **170** Oil Rig

(Des A. Onwudimegwu)

1970 (1 Sept). 25th Anniversary of United Nations. T **169** and similar vert design. P 14.

246		4d. orange-brown, buff and black	10	10
247		1s.6d. steel-blue, cinnamon and gold	30	20

Design: 4d. T **169**; 1s.6d. UN Building.

(Des E. Emokpae. Litho Enschedé)

1970 (30 Sept). Tenth Anniversary of Independence. T **170** and similar vert designs. Multicoloured. P 13½×13.

248		2d. Type **170**	25	25
249		4d. University Graduate	15	10
250		6d. Durbar Horsemen	30	10
251		9d. Servicemen raising Flag	40	10
252		1s. Footballer	40	10
253		1s.6d. Parliament Building	40	40
254		2s. Kainji Dam	70	1·60
255		2s.6d. Agricultural Produce	70	2·25
248/255 *Set of 8*			3·00	4·25

STAMP BOOKLETS

1915. Black on crimson cover, inscribed 'NIGERIA'.

SB1 2s. booklet containing 12×½d. and 18×1d. (Nos. 1/2) in blocks of 6 £2750

1921–26. Black on scarlet cover, inscribed 'NIGERIA'.

SB2 4s. booklet containing 12×1d. and 18×2d. grey (both Die I) (Nos. 16, 18) in blocks of 6 £2750
a. Containing Nos. 16 and 18a (1924) £2500
b. Containing Nos. 16b and 18a (1926) £2500

1926(?). Black on scarlet cover, inscribed 'STAMPS BOOKLET/ NIGERIA'.

SB3 4s. booklet containing 12×1d. and 18×2d. grey (both Die II) (Nos. 16b, 18a) in blocks of 6 £2750

1928. Black on scarlet cover, inscribed 'STAMPS BOOKLET/NIGERIA'.

SB5 4s. booklet containing 12×1d. (Die II) and 18×2d. chestnut (Nos. 16b, 19) in blocks of 6 £2750

1929. Black on scarlet cover, inscribed 'STAMPS BOOKLET/NIGERIA'.

SB6 4s. booklet containing 12×1d. (Die II) and 18×2d. chocolate (Nos. 16b, 20) in blocks of 6 £2250

1931 (Jan). Black on scarlet cover, inscribed 'STAMPS BOOKLET/ NIGERIA'.

SB7 4s. booklet containing 12×1d. and 24×1½d. (Nos. 16b, 17) in blocks of 6 £2750

1957 (Aug). Black on green cover. Stitched.

SB8 2s. booklet containing 4×1d. and 8×½d. and 8×2d. (Nos. 69/70, 72c) in blocks of 4 24·00
a. Contents as No. SB8, but containing No. 72*d*. 60·00

1957 (Oct). Black on buff cover. Stitched.

SB9 10s. booklet containing 8×3d. and 8×1s. (Nos. 73, 76) in blocks of 4 and a pane of air mail labels 32·00

1963. Black on green (No. SB10) or buff (No. SB11) covers. Stitched.

SB10 2s. booklet containing 1d. and 3d. (Nos. 90, 93) in blocks of 6 5·50
SB11 10s.6d. booklet containing 6×1s.3d. and 12×3d. (Nos. 93, 97) in blocks of 6 and two panes of air mail labels 16·00

1966. Black on green cover. Stitched.

SB12 3s. booklet containing 4×1d. and 4×4d. and 8×2d. (Nos. 173, 175, 177a) in blocks of 4 50·00

POSTAGE DUE STAMPS

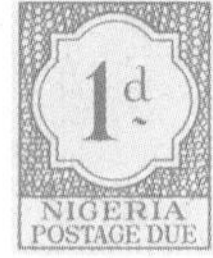

D **1**

(Litho BW.)

1959 (4 Jan). Wmk Mult Script CA. P 14½×14.

D1	D **1**	1d. red-orange	15	1·00
D2		2d. red-orange	20	1·00
D3		3d. red-orange	25	1·50
D4		6d. red-orange	25	5·50
D5		1s. grey-black	50	7·50
D1/D5 *Set of 5*			1·25	15·00

1961 (1 Aug). W **34**. P 14½×14.

D6	D **1**	1d. red	15	40
D7		2d. light blue	20	45
D8		3d. emerald	25	60
D9		6d. yellow	30	1·40
D10		1s. blue (*shades*)	50	2·25
D6/D10 *Set of 5*			1·25	4·50

BIAFRA

The Eastern Region of Nigeria declared its independence on 30 May 1967 as the Republic of Biafra. Nigerian military operations against the breakaway republic commenced in July 1967.

The Biafran postal service continued to use Nigerian stamps and when supplies of these became low in July 1967 'Postage Paid' cachets were used pending the issue of Nos. 1/3.

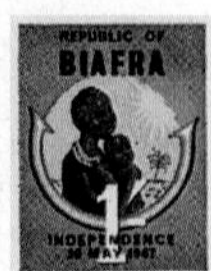

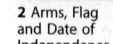

1 Map of Republic **2** Arms, Flag and Date of Independence **3** Mother and Child

(Typo and litho Mint, Lisbon)

1968 (5 Feb). Independence. P 12½.

1	**1**	2d. multicoloured	25	70
2	**2**	4d. multicoloured	25	70
3	**3**	1s. multicoloured	25	2·00
1/3 *Set of 3*			65	3·00

(**4**)

1968 (1 Apr). Nos. 172/175 and 177/185 of Nigeria optd as T **4** (without 'SOVEREIGN' on 10s.) by Govt Printer at Enugu.

4		½d. multicoloured (No. 172)	2·25	7·00
5		1d. multicoloured (No. 173)	3·50	10·00
		a. Opt double	£200	
		b. Opt omitted (in pair with normal)	£550	
6		1½d. multicoloured (No. 174)	12·00	20·00
7		2d. multicoloured (No. 175)	38·00	55·00
8		4d. multicoloured (No. 177a)	19·00	55·00
9		6d. multicoloured (No. 178)	9·00	18·00
10		9d. Prussian blue and orange-red (No. 179)	3·75	4·50
11		1s. multicoloured (Blk.+R.) (No. 180)	65·00	£130
12		1s.3d. multicoloured (Blk.+R.) (No. 181)	35·00	60·00
		a. Black opt omitted	£400	
		b. Red opt omitted	£375	
13		2s.6d. orange-brown, buff and brown (Blk.+R.) (No. 182)	4·75	20·00
		a. Red opt omitted	£300	
14		5s. chestnut, light yellow and brown (Blk.+R.) (No. 183)	3·75	19·00
		a. Red opt omitted	£300	
		b. Black opt omitted	£300	
		c. Red opt double	£350	
		d. Pale chestnut, yellow and brown-purple (No. 183*a*)	4·50	13·00
15		10s. multicoloured (No. 184)	10·00	42·00
16		£1 multicoloured (Blk.+R.) (No. 185)	10·00	42·00
		a. Black ('SOVEREIGN BIAFRA') opt omitted	£300	
		b. Red (Coat of Arms) opt omitted	£300	
4/16 *Set of 13*			£190	£425

Nos. 172/173 of Nigeria also exist surcharged 'BIAFRA– FRANCE FRIENDSHIP 1968 SOVEREIGN BIAFRA', clasped hands and '+5/-' (½d.) or '+£1' (1d.). There is no evidence that these two surcharges were used for postage within Biafra (*Price for set of 2 £20 mint*).

5 Flag and Scientist **8** Biafran Arms and Banknote **9** Orphaned Child

(Des S. Okeke. Litho Mint, Lisbon)

1968 (30 May). First Anniversary of Independence. Types **5**, **8/9** and similar vert designs. P 12½.

17	**5**	4d. multicoloured	25	20
18	–	1s. multicoloured	25	30
19	–	2s.6d. multicoloured	70	5·50
20	**8**	5s. multicoloured	80	6·00
		a. Indigo (banknote) omitted	£110	
		b. Red (from flag) omitted	£100	
21	**9**	10s. multicoloured	1·10	6·50
		a. Bright green (from flag) omitted	60·00	
17/21 *Set of 5*			2·75	16·00

Designs: 1s. Victim of atrocity; 2s.6d. Nurse and refugees.

Nos. 17/21 also exist surcharged 'HELP BIAFRAN CHILDREN' and different charity premium ranging from 2d. on the 4d. to 2s.6d. on the 10s. There is no evidence that these surcharges were used for postage within Biafra (*Price for set of 5 £2 mint*).

In September 1968 a set of four values, showing butterflies and plants, was offered for sale outside Biafra. The same stamps also exist overprinted 'MEXICO OLYMPICS 1968' and Olympic symbol. There is no evidence that either of these issues were used for postage within Biafra (*Price for set of 4 £4* (*Butterflies and Plants*) *or £5* (*Olympic overprints*), *both mint*).

CANCELLED-TO-ORDER. Many issues of Biafra, including the three unissued sets mentioned above, were available cancelled-to-order with a special 'UMUAHIA' handstamp. This was the same diameter as postal cancellations, but differed from them by having larger letters, 3 mm. high, and the year date in full. Where such cancellations exist on issued stamps the used prices quoted are for c-t-o examples. Postally used stamps are worth considerably more.

16 Child in Chains and Globe **17** Pope Paul VI, Map of Africa and Papal Arms

1969 (30 May). Second Anniversary of Independence. Multicoloured; frame colours given. Litho (in Italy). P 13×13½.

35	**16**	2d. yellow-orange	1·25	4·25
36		4d. red-orange	1·25	4·25
		a. Green (wreath) and orange (Sun) omitted	£375	
37		1s. new blue	1·75	7·50
38		2s.6d. emerald	2·00	15·00
35/38 *Set of 4*			5·75	28·00

A miniature sheet with a face value of 10s. was also released.

1969 (1 Aug). Visit of Pope Paul to Africa. T **17** and similar vert designs. Multicoloured. Litho (in Italy). P 13×13½.

39		4d. Type **17**	1·25	3·00
40		6d. Pope Paul VI, map of Africa and Arms of the Vatican	1·50	7·50
41		9d. Pope Paul VI, map of Africa and St Peter's Basilica, Vatican	1·75	8·50
42		3s. Pope Paul VI, map of Africa and Statue of St Peter	3·25	16·00
39/42 *Set of 4*			7·00	32·00

A miniature sheet with a face value of 10s. was also released.

No. 42 has a magenta background. This value is also known with the background in brown-red or brown.

On 17 December the French Agency released a Christmas issue consisting of Nos. 39/42 overprinted 'CHRISTMAS 1969 PEACE ON EARTH AND GOODWILL TO ALL MEN' together with the miniature sheet overprinted 'CHRISTMAS 1969' and surcharged £1. Later Nos. 35/38 were released overprinted in red 'SAVE BIAFRA 9TH JAN 1970' with a premium of 8d., 1s.4d., 4s., and 10s. respectively together with the miniature sheet with a premium of £1. We have no evidence that these issues were actually put on sale in Biafra before the collapse, but it has been reported that the 4d. Christmas issue and 2d.+8d. Save Biafra exist genuinely used before capitulation.

Nos. 40/41 have been seen surcharged '+ 10/-HUMAN RIGHTS' and the United Nations emblem but it is doubtful if they were issued.

No. 81 of Nigeria has also been reported with the original 'ROYAL VISIT 1956' overprint, together with 'NIGERIA' from the basic stamp, obliterated and a 'SERVICE' overprint added. Such stamps were not used for official mail in Biafra, although an example is known with the 'UMUAHIA' c-t-o mark.

Biafra was overrun by Federal troops in January 1970 and surrender took place on 15 January.

Niue *see after* **New Zealand**

Norfolk Island *see after* **Australia**

North Borneo

PRICES FOR STAMPS ON COVER TO 1945

No. 1	*from* × 100
Nos. 2/3	*from* × 10
Nos. 4/5	—
Nos. 6/19	*from* × 10
No. 21*b*	—
Nos. 22/28	*from* × 50
Nos. 29/35	—
Nos. 36/44	*from* × 100
Nos. 45/50	—
Nos. 51/52	*from* × 10
No. 54	—
Nos. 55/65	*from* × 10
Nos. 66/79	*from* × 4
Nos. 81/86	—
Nos. 87/91	*from* × 12
Nos. 92/111	*from* × 4
Nos. 112/126	*from* × 10
Nos. 127/140	*from* × 6
Nos. 141/145	—
Nos. 146/157	*from* × 5
Nos. 158/179	*from* × 8
Nos. 181/185	—
Nos. 186/188	*from* × 10
Nos. 189/230	*from* × 4
Nos. 231/234	—
Nos. 235/249	*from* × 3
Nos. 250/252	—
Nos. 253/275	*from* × 12
Nos. 276/292	*from* × 7
Nos. 293/294	—
Nos. 295/300	*from* × 6
Nos. 301/302	—
Nos. 303/317	*from* × 3
Nos. 318/319	*from* × 20
Nos. 320/334	*from* × 3
Nos. F1/F3	—
Nos. D1/D30	*from* × 25
Nos. D31/D36	*from* × 12
No. D37	—
Nos. D38/D84	*from* × 40
Nos. D85/D89	*from* × 8

BRITISH NORTH BORNEO COMPANY ADMINISTRATION

PRINTERS. The stamps of this country up to 1894 were designed by T. Macdonald and printed in lithography by Blades, East and Blades, London.

1

8 Cents.
(2)

EIGHT CENTS
(3)

1883 (Mar). P 12.

No.	Type	Description	Unused	Used
1	**1**	2c. red-brown	50·00	75·00
		a. Imperf between (horiz pair)	£15000	

The figure '2' varies in size.

1883 (June). No. 1 surch as Types **2** or **3**.

No.	Type	Description	Unused	Used
2	**2**	8c. on 2c. red-brown	£1400	£850
3	**3**	8c. on 2c. red-brown	£500	£190
		a. Surch double	†	£6000

T **2** was handstamped and stamps without stop are generally forgeries. T **3** was a setting of 50 (10×5) providing ten varieties; it normally has a stop which sometimes failed to print.

CANCELLED-TO-ORDER. Prices are separately indicated in a third price column, for stamps showing the recognisable black bars remainder cancellation. The issues since 1916 have not been thus cancelled.

It should be noted, however, that a postmark of this form was in use for postal purposes up to this period, and was used at one or two of the smaller post-offices until 1949. A small oval with five bars was used to mark railway mail during 1945/1955 and also as a paquebot mark at Jesselton *c.* 1950.

4

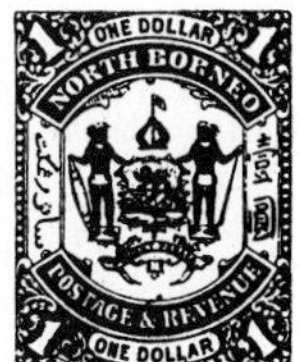
5

and Revenue
(6)

1883. P 14.

No.	Type	Description	Unused	Used	CTO
4	**4**	50c. violet	£225	£300	40·00
		a. Inverted 'L' for first 'F' in 'FIFTY' (R. 5/2)	£2000	—	£350
5	**5**	$1 scarlet	£180	£250	18·00

1883 (July). P 12.

No.	Type	Description	Unused	Used
6	**1**	4c. pink	65·00	70·00
		a. Imperf between (horiz pair)	£5500	
7		8c. green	85·00	60·00

1886. P 14.

No.	Type	Description	Unused	Used
8	**1**	½c. magenta	£120	£200
9		1c. orange	£200	£325
		a. Imperf (pair)	£275	£275
		b. Imperf horiz (vert pair)	£1500	
10		2c. brown	50·00	42·00
		a. Imperf between (horiz pair)	£700	
11		4c. pink	19·00	55·00
		a. Imperf between (horiz pair)	†	£1700
12		8c. green	22·00	50·00
		a. Imperf between (horiz pair)	£850	
13		10c. blue	55·00	65·00
		a. Imperf (pair)	£350	
8/13 *Set of* 6			£400	£650

1886 (Sept). Nos. 8 and 13 optd with T **6**.

No.	Description	Unused	Used
14	½c. magenta	£250	£325
15	10c. blue	£300	£375

3 CENTS
(7)

5 CENTS
(8)

3 CENTS
Small '3' variety (R. 3/1, 3/4, 3/7)

(Surch by *North Borneo Herald*, Sandakan)

1886 (Sept). T **1** surch as Types **7/8**.

(a) P 12

No.	Type	Description	Unused	Used
16	**7**	3c. on 4c. pink	£325	£375
		a. Small '3'	—	£16000
17	**8**	5c. on 8c. green	£325	£375

(b) P 14

No.	Type	Description	Unused	Used
18	**7**	3c. on 4c. pink	£130	£150
		a. Small '3'	£1500	
19	**8**	5c. on 8c. green	£140	£150
		a. Surch inverted	£2750	

No. 16 is known fiscally used with error surcharge double.

9

10

11

12

13

1886–87.

(a) P 14

No.	Type	Description	Unused	Used
21*b*	**9**	½c. magenta	21·00	50·00
22		½c. rose	4·75	21·00
		a. Imperf (pair)	65·00	
23		1c. orange-yellow	19·00	42·00
		a. Imperf between (vert pair)	£425	
		b. Imperf (pair)	75·00	
24		1c. orange	2·00	16·00
		a. Imperf (pair)	50·00	
25		2c. brown	2·00	14·00
		a. Imperf (pair)	50·00	
26		4c. pink	7·00	20·00
		a. Imperf (pair)	60·00	
		b. Imperf between (horiz or vert pair)	£400	
		c. Imperf vert (horiz pair)	£325	
		d. Error. 1c. pink (R. 2/3) (centre stamp of strip of 3)	£350	£1300
		da. Imperf vert (strip of 3)	£7500	
		db. Imperf (strip of 3)	£6500	
27		8c. green	30·00	28·00
		a. Imperf (pair)	55·00	
28		10c. blue	16·00	45·00
		a. Imperf between (vert pair)	£425	
		b. Imperf (pair)	55·00	
29	**10**	25c. indigo	£475	26·00
		a. Imperf between (vert pair)		
		b. Imperf (pair)	£425	50·00
30	**11**	50c. violet	£475	27·00
		a. Imperf (pair)	£550	50·00
31	**12**	$1 scarlet	£400	26·00
		a. Imperf (pair)	£600	50·00
32	**13**	$2 sage-green	£700	32·00
		a. Imperf (pair)	£600	55·00
22/32 *Set of* 10			£1900	£200

(b) P 12

No.	Type	Description	Unused	Used
34	**9**	½c. magenta	£400	£700
35		1c. orange	£250	£400

Nos. 21*b*/32 are known to have been sold as cancelled remainders, but these are difficult to distinguish from postally used. Values above 10c. are infrequently found postally used so that the used prices quoted are for the remainders.

14

15

16

17

18

1888–92. T **14** (as T **9** but inscr 'POSTAGE & REVENUE') and Types **15/18** (Types **10/13** redrawn). P 14.

No.	Type	Description	Unused	Used	CTO
36	**14**	½c. magenta (1889)	4·00	30·00	2·50
		a. Imperf vert (horiz pair)	†	†	£250
		b. Rose	1·50	9·00	60
		ba. Imperf between (horiz pair)	£400		
		c. Imperf (pair)	50·00	—	11·00
37		1c. orange (1892)	8·00	8·00	50
		a. Imperf vert (horiz pair)	£375		
		b. Imperf (pair)	50·00	—	10·00
38		2c. brown (1889)	20·00	27·00	90
		a. Imperf between (horiz pair)	†	†	£400
		b. Lake-brown	9·00	27·00	50
		c. Imperf (pair)	50·00	—	9·50
39		3c. violet (1889)	2·50	13·00	50
		b. Imperf (pair)	35·00	—	9·50
40		4c. rose-pink (1889)	15·00	50·00	50
		a. Imperf vert (horiz pair)	†	†	£250
		b. Imperf (pair)	55·00	—	10·00
41		5c. slate (1889)	2·75	30·00	50
		a. Imperf between (pair)			
		b. Imperf (pair)	55·00	—	10·00
42		6c. lake (1892)	19·00	32·00	50
		a. Imperf (pair)	55·00	—	14·00
43		8c. blue-green (1891)	45·00	50·00	1·00
		a. Yellow-green	30·00	40·00	50
		c. Imperf (pair)	55·00	—	13·00
44		10c. blue (1891)	9·50	40·00	1·00
		a. Imperf between (vert pair)	†	†	£300
		b. Dull blue	7·50	23·00	50
		ba. Imperf between (horiz pair)			
		d. Imperf (pair)	50·00	—	11·00
45	**15**	25c. indigo	£110	£110	75
		a. Imperf (pair)	£500	†	22·00
		b. Imperf vert (horiz pair)	†	†	£300
46	**16**	50c. violet	£130	£150	75
		a. Imperf (pair)	£600	†	22·00
		b. Chalky blue	£140	£150	†
47	**17**	$1 scarlet	70·00	£110	75
		a. Imperf (pair)	£475	†	22·00
48	**18**	$2 dull green	£250	£250	1·50
		a. Imperf (pair)	£750	†	25·00
36*b*/48 *Set of* 13			£600	£750	7·50

Nos. 39, 43 and 44 showing stamps printed double or triple, one inverted, are from waste sheets subsequently sold by the British North Borneo Company to collectors.

These stamps to the 10c. value were forged on several occasions. Most forgeries of the ½c. value can be identified by the presence of a diagonal line joining the top two horizontal strokes of the uppermost Chinese character.

The new 25c. has the inscription 'BRITISH NORTH BORNEO' in taller capitals. In the 50c. the '0' of the numerals '50' in the two upper corners is square-shaped at the top and bottom instead of being oval. The 1 dollar has 14 pearls instead of 13 at each side, and on the 2 dollars the word 'BRITISH' measures 10½ to 11 mm in length in place of 12 mm.

19

20

1889. P 14.

No.	Type	Description	Unused	Used	CTO
49	**19**	$5 bright purple	£375	£400	8·50
		a. Imperf (pair)	£1000	†	75·00
50	**20**	$10 brown	£375	£400	12·00
		a. Imperf (pair)	£1200	†	85·00

b. 'DOLLAPS' for 'DOLLARS' at foot (R. 2/1) £1500 £2000 £375
ba. Ditto. Imperf (pair) .... £4750 † £750

Two Cents. (21) **6 cents.** (22) **1 cent.** (23)

1890 (Dec). Surch as T **21**, in red.

51 **15** 2c. on 25c. indigo .... 85·00 95·00
a. Surch inverted £450 £450
52 8c. on 25c. indigo £130 £140

The first printing of Nos. 51/52 had the two lines of the surcharge 3.5 mm apart. On a second printing of both values this gap widened to 5 mm.

1891–92. Surch with T **22**.

54 **9** 6c. on 8c. green (1892) £9000 £5000
a. Large 's' in 'cents' £16000
55 **14** 6c. on 8c. yellow-green .... 29·00 10·00
a. Surch inverted £475 £500
b. Inverted 'c' in 'cents' (R. 5/4) £700 £750
c. 'cetns.' for 'cents' (R. 3/7) £700 £750
d. Large 's' in 'cents' (R. 2/9 or 3/7) £250 £200
56 **9** 6c. on 10c. blue .... 60·00 23·00
a. Surch inverted £300 £350
b. Surch double £1400
c. Surch treble £550
d. Large 's' in 'cents' £325 £180
57 **14** 6c. on 10c. blue .... £200 26·00
a. Large 's' in 'cents' £850 £225

Unused examples of Nos. 55 and 57 are normally without gum.

There were three settings of the surcharge for No. 55. On the first two the large 's' in 'cents' occurred on R. 2/9 with the other two listed varieties also included. Nos. 55b/55c were corrected on the third setting and the large 's' in cents occurred on R. 3/7.

1892 (Mar–Nov). Surch as T **23** ('Cents.' with capital 'C' as in T **21** on No. 65), in red.

63 **14** 1c. on 4c. rose-pink .... 27·00 14·00
a. Surch double £1600
b. Surch on back and on front .... † £600
64 1c. on 5c. slate (11.92) .... 7·00 6·00
65 **15** 8c. on 25c. indigo (date?) £180 £190

Unused examples of Nos. 63/65 are normally without gum.

24 Dyak Chief

25 Sambar Stag (*Cervus unicolor*)

26 Sago Palm

27 Great Argus Pheasant

28 Arms of the Company

29 Malay Dhow

30 Estuarine Crocodile

31 Mount Kinabalu

32 Arms of the Company with Supporters

PERFORATION. There are a number of small variations in the perforation of the Waterlow issues of 1894 to 1922 which we believe were due to irregularity of the pins rather than different perforators.

In the following lists, stamps perf 12, 12½, 13 or compound are described as perf 12–13, stamps perf 13½, 14 or compound are described as perf 13½–14 and those perf 14½, 15 or compound are listed as perf 14½–15. In addition the 13½–14 perforation exists compound with 14½–15 and with 12–13, whilst perf 15½–16 comes from a separate perforator.

(Recess Waterlow)

1894 (Feb). P 14½–15.

66 **24** 1c. black and olive-bistre .... 1·25 9·50 50
a. Imperf between (horiz or vert pair) £950
b. Perf 13½–14 .... 1·75 15·00 50
c. Perf 13½–14, comp 14½–15 .... 50·00 60·00 —
d. Perf 13½–14, comp 12–13 .... 29·00 60·00 —
e. Perf 12–13 ....
67 1c. black and bistre-brown .... 4·25 23·00 50
a. Perf 13½–14 .... 5·50 23·00 1·00
b. Perf 13½–14, comp 12–13 .... 38·00 70·00 —
c. Perf 12–13 ....
sa. Opt 'SPECIMEN' double £200
68 **25** 2c. black and rose-lake .... 5·50 1·50 50
a. Imperf between (horiz or vert pair) .... £1500 £1500 †
b. Perf 13½–14 .... 55·00 55·00 75
c. Perf 13½–14, comp 14½–15 ....
69 2c. black and lake .... 5·50 2·50 50
a. Perf 13½–14 .... 50·00 50·00 2·25
b. Perf 13½–14, comp 12–13 .... 42·00 45·00 —
c. Imperf between (horiz pair) ....
70 **26** 3c. olive-green and dull purple .... 2·75 8·50 50
a. Imperf between (horiz pair) .... £1200 £1100 †
ab. Imperf between (vert pair) £1400
b. Perf 13½–14, comp 14½–15 ....
c. Bronze-green and dull purple .... 5·50 — 50
d. Perf 13½–14 ....
71 3c. olive-green and violet (P 13½–14) .... 45·00 60·00 2·25
a. Imperf between (horiz pair) .... † £1500 †
72 **27** 5c. black and vermilion .... 14·00 11·00 60
a. Imperf between (horiz or vert pair) £900
b. Perf 13½–14 .... 50·00 60·00 1·25
c. Perf 13½–14, comp 12–13 .... — 65·00 5·50
d. Perf 13½–14, comp 14½–15 ....
e. Perf 12–13 ....
73 **28** 6c. black and bistre-brown .... 65·00 85·00 60
a. Perf 13½–14 .... 4·50 18·00 60
b. Perf 13½–14, comp 12–13 .... — 65·00 5·50
c. Perf 13½–14, comp 14½–15 .... 65·00
d. Imperf between (horiz pair) ....
74 **29** 8c. black and dull purple .... 6·50 11·00 60
a. Imperf between (vert pair) £800
b. Perf 13½–14 .... 10·00 42·00 1·00
ba. Imperf between (vert pair) .... £550 † £300
d. Perf 13½–14, comp 12–13 ....
75 **30** 12c. black and blue .... 40·00 85·00 2·50
a. Perf 13½–14 .... 29·00 80·00 2·50
b. Imperf between (horiz pair) .... £1800 † £700
c. Perf 13½–14, comp 14½–15 .... — — 5·00
76 12c. black and ultramarine .... 50·00 85·00 3·00
a. Perf 13½–14 .... 50·00 85·00 3·00
b. Imperf between (pair) ....
78 **31** 18c. black and deep green .... 28·00 50·00 2·00
a. Perf 13½–14 .... 48·00 50·00 2·00
b. Perf 13½–14, comp 14½–15 .... — — 5·00
c. Perf 13½–14 comp 12–13 .... — — 5·00
79 **32** 24c. blue and rose-lake .... 23·00 85·00 2·00
a. Imperf between (vert pair) .... — — £500
b. Imperf between (vert strip of 3) .... † † £650
c. Perf 13½–14 .... 23·00 70·00 2·00
d. Perf 13½–14, comp 14½–15 ....
66/79 *Set of 9* .... £100 £225 9·00

32a

32b

32c

32d

32e

32f

(Litho Blades, East & Blades, London)

1894 (Jan). Types **32a** to **32f**. P 14.

81 **32a** 25c. indigo .... 9·50 30·00 1·00
a. Imperf (pair) .... 70·00 † 12·00
b. Imperf between (horiz or vert pair) .... £900 — £110
82 **32b** 50c. deep slate-purple .... 50·00 65·00 2·00
a. Imperf (pair) .... — † 12·00
b. Imperf between (horiz pair) ....
d. Chalky blue .... — 65·00 —
83 **32c** $1 scarlet .... 15·00 32·00 1·25
a. Perf 14×11 .... £300
b. Imperf (pair) .... 50·00 † 13·00
84 **32d** $2 dull green .... 28·00 80·00 2·50
a. Imperf (pair) .... — † 18·00
85 **32e** $5 bright purple .... £275 £375 17·00
a. Imperf (pair) .... £900 † 65·00
b. Dull purple .... £325 £400 11·00
86 **32f** $10 brown .... £325 £425 16·00
a. Imperf (pair) .... £950 † 65·00
81/86 *Set of 6* .... £650 £900 30·00
81s/86s Optd 'SPECIMEN' *Set of 6* £170

For Nos. 81 to 83 in other colours, see Labuan 80a, 81a and 82a.

Nos. 81/84 showing stamps printed double, double, one inverted, or on both sides, are from waste sheets subsequently sold by the British North Borneo Company to collectors.

No. 83a comes from a sheet (10×5) in which columns 3 to 10 were perf 14×11, column 2 perf compound of 14 and 11 (at right only) and column 1 perf 14 all round.

4 CENTS
(33) (3½ *mm* between lines of surcharge)

(Surcharged by Waterlow)

1895 (June). No. 83 surch as T **33**.

87 **32c** 4c. on $1 scarlet .... 7·00 1·50 50
a. Surch double, one diagonal £950
88 10c. on $1 scarlet .... 28·00 1·50 50
89 20c. on $1 scarlet .... 55·00 17·00 50
90 30c. on $1 scarlet .... 50·00 40·00 1·75
91 40c. on $1 scarlet .... 60·00 65·00 1·75
87/91 *Set of 5* .... £180 £110 4·50
87s/91s Optd 'SPECIMEN' *Set of 5* .... 90·00

For 4c. on $1 with wider spacing see No. 121.

No. 88 exists with the figures of the surcharge 2½ mm away from 'CENTS'. The normal setting has a space of 3½ mm. Examples of the narrow setting have, so far, only been seen on cancelled-to-order stamps.

34

35

36

37 Orangutan

38

39

40

41 Sun Bear

42

43 Borneo Railway Train

44

45

(Recess Waterlow)

1897 (Mar)–**1902**. Types **34** to **45**. New frames. P 13½–14.

92 **34** 1c. black and bistre-brown .... 40·00 5·50 40
aa. Perf 16 ....
a. Perf 14½–15 .... 11·00 2·75 40
b. Perf 13½–14, comp 12–13 .... 70·00 50·00 —
c. Imperf between (horiz pair) .... † † £650
d. Perf 12–13 .... £250
93 1c. black and ochre .... 65·00 15·00 50
a. Perf 14½–15 .... 50·00 15·00 50
ab. Imperf between (horiz pair) .... † † £650
b. Perf 13½–14 comp 12–13 ....
c. Perf 16 .... £250
94 **35** 2c. black and lake .... 65·00 3·50 40
a. Perf 14½–15 .... 25·00 1·50 40
ab. Imperf between (horiz pair) .... † † £650
b. Perf 13½–14, comp 12–13 .... — 21·00 2·25
c. Perf 12–13 ....
d. Imperf between (vert pair) .... † † £850
e. Perf 13½–14, comp 14½–15 .... — — 3·75

95 2c. black and green (1900) 70·00 2·00 60
a. Perf 14½–15 £150 23·00 3·00
b. Perf 13½–14, comp 12–13 £180 40·00 —
c. Perf 12–13
d. Imperf between (horiz pair) — £1200 †
96 **36** 3c. green and rosy mauve 75·00 22·00 40
a. Perf 14½–15 75·00 55·00 1·00
b. Perf 13½–14, comp 12–13 £120 75·00 —
97 3c. green and dull mauve (P 14½–15) 40·00 3·00 50
98 **37** 4c. black and green (1900) 13·00 — 1·50
a. Perf 13½–14, comp 12–13
99 4c. black and carmine (1900) 42·00 12·00 50
a. Perf 16 £140 50·00 50
b. Perf 14½–15 90·00 1·50 50
c. Perf 13½–14, comp 12–13 60·00 50·00 3·25
d. Perf 12–13
100 **38** 5c. black and orange-vermilion £120 3·00 70
a. Perf 14½–15 £120 1·50 70
ab. Imperf between (horiz pair) † £1700 †
b. Perf 13½–14, comp 12–13 £160 14·00 80
c. Perf 12–13
101 **39** 6c. black and bistre-brown 95·00 40·00 50
a. Perf 14½–15 55·00 4·50 50
b. Perf 13½–14, comp 12–13 — — 3·75
102 **40** 8c. black and brown-purple 90·00 50·00 1·00
a. Perf 16 £110 25·00 70
ab. Imperf between (vert pair) £475 £600 £350
b. Perf 14½–15 55·00 2·75 60
103 8c. black and brown 16·00 50·00 1·00
a. Perf 14½–15 65·00 80·00 1·00
b. Perf 16
104 **41** 10c. brown and slate-lilac (1902) £150 55·00 4·75
a. Imperf between (vert pair) † † £1100
105 10c. brown and slate-blue (1902) £425 £110 1·50
106 **42** 12c. black and dull blue £225 50·00 2·00
a. Imperf between (vert pair) † † £750
b. Perf 14½–15 £150 35·00 1·50
c. Perf 13½–14, comp 12–13 £250 55·00 —
d. Perf 12–13
107 **43** 16c. green and chestnut (1902) £140 90·00 3·25
a. Perf 14½–15 £275 £150 10·00
108 **44** 18c. black and green (P 16) 38·00 80·00 4·25
a. Imperf vert (horiz pair) † † 85·00
b. Imperf between (vert pair) † † £350
c. Imperf (pair) † † £180
d. Perf 14½–15 — — 10·00
109 **45** 24c. blue and lake 50·00 95·00 4·25
a. Perf 13½–14, comp 12–13 55·00 £100 4·25
b. Perf 12–13 £325
92/109 (*one of each value*) *Set of* 12 £700 £325 16·00
92s/109s (*excl* 93, 97, 103, 105) Optd 'SPECIMEN' *Set of* 14 £325

No. 98 was printed in an incorrect frame colour and it is doubtful if it was issued for postal purposes in North Borneo. Used examples come from dealers' stock sent to the territory for cancellation.

In the above the 18c. has 'POSTAL REVENUE' instead of 'POSTAGE & REVENUE' and the 24c. has those words omitted. These stamps were replaced by others with corrected inscriptions; see Nos. 110 and 111.

46

47

1897. Corrected inscriptions. P 13½–14.
110 **46** 18c. black and green £225 48·00 4·50
a. Imperf between (horiz pair) † † £700
b. Perf 14½–15 £130 12·00 1·50
c. Perf 13½–14, comp 12–13 — — 3·50
111 **47** 24c. blue and lake £130 50·00 2·25
a. Perf 16 £225 £120 2·00
b. Perf 14½–15 60·00 55·00 3·75
c. Perf 13½–14, comp 12–13 — — 5·50
d. Perf 12–13
110s/111s Optd 'SPECIMEN' *Set of* 2 55·00

BRITISH

4 CENTS (**48**) (4½ *mm between lines of surcharge*)

PROTECTORATE. (**49**)

4 cents (**50**)

1899 (22 July–Oct). Surch with T **48**. P 14½–15 (Nos. 112/117) or 14 (Nos. 118/126).

(a) 4½ mm between lines of surch

112 4c. on 5c. (No. 100a) 60·00 50·00
a. Perf 13½–14 50·00 10·00
asa. Surch inverted, optd 'SPECIMEN' £800
b. Perf 13½–14, comp 12–13 60·00 32·00
113 4c. on 6c. (No. 101a) (date?) 19·00 24·00
a. Perf 13½–14 27·00 50·00
b. Perf 13½–14 comp 14½–15
114 4c. on 8c. (No. 102b) (10.99) 17·00 10·00
115 4c. on 12c. (No. 106b) (10.99) 48·00 13·00
a. Imperf between (horiz pair) £850
b. Imperf between (vert pair) £950 £950
c. Perf 13½–14 60·00 65·00
d. Perf 12–13
e. Perf 13½–14, comp 12–13 55·00 45·00
116 4c. on 18c. (No. 110b) (10.99) 22·00 14·00
a. Perf 13½–14 50·00 50·00
117 4c. on 24c. (No. 111b) (10.99) 48·00 23·00
a. Perf 16 60·00 60·00
b. Perf 13½–14 32·00 38·00
c. Perf 13½–14, comp 12–13 50·00 50·00
d. Perf 12–13 £160 £170
118 4c. on 25c. indigo (No. 81) 5·50 8·50
a. Imperf between (horiz strip of 3) £1400
119 4c. on 50c. deep slate-purple (No. 82) 28·00 16·00
a. Chalky blue 30·00 38·00
121 4c. on $1 scarlet (No. 83) 5·50 12·00
122 4c. on $2 dull green (No. 84) 5·50 13·00
123 4c. on $5 bright purple (No. 85) £180 £250
a. Dull purple £325 £350
124 4c. on $10 brown (No. 86) £130 £250
112/124 *Set of* 12 £450 £550
112s/124s Optd 'SPECIMEN' *Set of* 12 £225

(b) 8½ mm between lines of surch. P 14

125 4c. on $5 (No. 85) 8·00 19·00
126 4c. on $10 (No. 86) 8·00 19·00

No. 121 differs only from No. 87 in having the '4' and 'cents' wider apart.

Examples of the Kudat postmark dated 'AU 15 1899' struck on Nos. 112/126 are generally considered to be faked.

A new setting of the surcharge, with 2½ mm between '4' and 'CENTS' for values to $2 and 3½ mm on the $5 and $10, was used for the SPECIMEN overprints, including unissued surcharges on the 1c., 2c. and 3c. values (*price* £130 *the set of three*).

(Optd by Waterlow)

1901 (8 Oct)–**05**. Optd as T **49**.

(a) P 13½–14

127 1c. (No. 92) (R.) 3·50 1·50 30
a. Perf 14½–15 2·50 1·75 30
128 2c. (No. 95) (R.) 11·00 1·00 30
a. Perf 16 3·50 21·00 40
b. Perf 14½–15 18·00 12·00 30
129 3c. (No. 96) 1·75 5·50 30
a. Imperf between (vert pair) † † £1500
b. Perf 14½–15 16·00 2·75 30
c. Perf 13½–14, comp 14½–15 60·00 — 2·00
130 4c. (No. 99) (G.) 9·00 1·00 30
a. Perf 14½–15 40·00 1·00 50
131 5c. (No. 100) (G.) 70·00 4·75 30
a. Perf 14½–15 14·00 3·25 30
132 6c. (No. 101) (R.) 65·00 70·00 1·25
a. No stop after 'Protectorate' 90·00 90·00 1·25
b. Perf 16 4·00 15·00 70
133 8c. (No. 103) (B.) 6·50 3·75 50
a. No stop after 'Protectorate' 3·00 27·00 1·50
b. Perf 13½–14, comp 12–13 80·00 35·00 —
c. Imperf horiz (vert pair) † † £350
134 10c. (No. 104) (R.) (7.02) £100 5·00 2·00
a. Perf 14½–15 £180 32·00 2·75
c. Perf 13½–14. No stop after 'Protectorate' £325 — 14·00
d. Opt double £1000 † £325
e. (No. 105) £375 £225 1·00
f. Imperf vert (horiz pair) † † £850
135 12c. (No. 106) (R.) 70·00 12·00 1·50
136 16c. (No. 107) (7.02) £225 38·00 2·25
a. Perf 14½–15 £190 55·00 2·25
b. Perf 13½–14 comp 12–13 £425 90·00 —
137 18c. (No. 110) (R.) 21·00 26·00 1·25
a. No stop after 'Protectorate'
b. Perf 13½–14, comp 12–13 85·00 — 1·50
138 24c. (No. 111) 19·00 40·00 1·50
a. Perf 14½–15 70·00 95·00 1·75
ab. Imperf between (horiz pair) † † £1700

(b) P 14

139 25c. (No. 81) (R.) 2·00 10·00 50
a. No stop after 'Protectorate' £250 £300 27·00
b. Overprints *tête-bêche* (horiz pair)
c. Overprint inverted £750
140 50c. (No. 82) (R.) 2·75 11·00 55
a. No stop after 'Protectorate' £130 £180 —
b. Chalky blue
141 $1 (No. 83) (R.) (1.04) 5·00 65·00 —
142 $1 (No. 83) 4·00 38·00 2·00
a. Imperf horiz (vert pair) £800
b. Opt double † † £375
c. Opt treble
143 $2 (No. 84) (R.) (1903) 50·00 £100 2·75
a. Opt double £1700 † £550
144 $5 (No. 85*b*) (R.) (2.05) £425 £550 9·00
145 $10 (No. 86) (R.) (2.05) £750 £1100 11·00
a. Opt inverted £3250 † £550
127/145 *Set of* 18 £1400 £1800 30·00
127s/140s Optd 'SPECIMEN' *Set of* 14 £350

There was more than one setting of the overprint for some of the values. Full sheets of the 6c. and 8c. are known, without stop throughout.

See also Nos. 184/185.

1904–05. Surch locally with T **50**.

(a) P 14½–15

146 4c. on 5c. (No. 100a) 50·00 55·00 12·00
147 4c. on 6c. (No. 101a) 7·00 21·00 12·00
a. Surch inverted £225
148 4c. on 8c. (No. 102b) 21·00 26·00 12·00
a. Surch inverted £325
149 4c. on 12c. (No. 106b) 55·00 40·00 12·00
a. Perf 13½–14 65·00 65·00 12·00
b. Perf 13½–14 comp 12–13 55·00 65·00 —
150 4c. on 18c. (No. 110b) 14·00 38·00 12·00
a. Perf 13½–14
151 4c. on 24c. (No. 111b) 45·00 50·00 12·00
a. Perf 16 26·00 50·00 12·00
b. Perf 13½–14 48·00 55·00 12·00
c. Perf 12–13

(b) P 14

152 4c. on 25c. (No. 81) 6·00 26·00 12·00
153 4c. on 50c. (No. 82) 6·00 38·00 12·00
154 4c. on $1 (No. 83) 6·00 48·00 12·00
155 4c. on $2 (No. 84) 6·00 48·00 12·00
156 4c. on $5 (No. 85) 16·00 48·00 12·00
a. Surch on No. 85*b* 35·00 50·00 —
157 4c. on $10 (No. 86) 13·00 48·00 12·00
a. Surch inverted £3000
146/157 *Set of* 12 £200 £425 £130

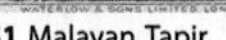
51 Malayan Tapir

52 Travellers' Tree

53 Jesselton Railway Station

54 The Sultan of Sulu, his staff and W. C. Cowie, Managing Director of the Company

55 Indian Elephant

56 Sumatran Rhinoceros

57 Ploughing with Buffalo

58 Wild Boar

59 Palm Cockatoo

60 Rhinoceros Hornbill

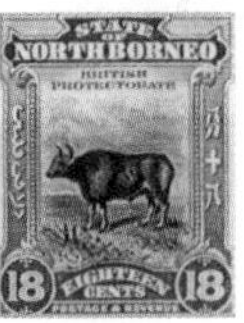
61 Banteng

62 Dwarf Cassowary

(Recess Waterlow)

1909 (1 July)–**23**. Centres in black. P 13½–14.

158 **51** 1c. chocolate-brown 7·00 2·75 30
a. Perf 14½–15 60·00 18·00 40
159 1c. brown 30·00 1·25 30
a. Perf 14½–15 55·00 4·50 30
b. Imperf between (vert pair) £2750
160 **52** 2c. green 1·00 70 30
a. Imperf between (pair)
b. Perf 14½–15 4·75 70 30
161 **53** 3c. lake 5·00 2·75 30
162 3c. rose-lake 6·00 2·75 50
a. Perf 14½–15 50·00 — 55
163 3c. green (1923) 55·00 1·25 †
164 **54** 4c. scarlet 3·75 30 30
a. Imperf between (vert pair)
b. Perf 14½–15 27·00 2·00 35
165 **55** 5c. yellow-brown 18·00 3·50 40
a. Perf 14½–15
166 5c. dark brown 48·00 5·50 —
167 **56** 6c. olive-green 13·00 1·25 30
a. Perf 14½–15 80·00 6·50 60
168 6c. apple-green 45·00 1·50 60
169 **57** 8c. lake 4·00 1·00 60
a. Perf 14½–15 — — 13·00
170 **58** 10c. greyish blue 48·00 8·00 1·25
a. Perf 14½–15 £100 50·00 —
171 10c. blue 55·00 2·25 —
172 10c. turquoise-blue 50·00 1·50 1·50
a. Perf 14½–15 70·00 3·50 —
173 **59** 12c. deep blue 55·00 1·50 1·00
a. Perf 14½–15 — — 12·00
b. Imperf vert (horiz pair) † † £800
173*c* 12c. deep bright blue
174 **60** 16c. brown-lake 26·00 2·50 1·00
175 **61** 18c. blue-green £160 38·00 1·00
176 **62** 24c. deep rose-lilac 28·00 1·50 1·75
a. Deep lilac 55·00 6·50 —
158/176 *Set of* 13 £375 50·00 —
158s/176s Optd 'SPECIMEN' *Set of* 13 £350

For this issue perf 12½ see Nos. 277, etc.

20

CENTS
(63)

64

65

1909 (7 Sept). No. 175 surch with T **63** by Waterlow. P 13½–14.

No.	Type	Description	Unused	Used	
177		20c. on 18c. blue-green (R.)	7·00	1·00	30
		a. Perf 14½–15	£250	70·00	—
		s. Optd 'SPECIMEN.'	50·00		

Re-entry. Doubled oars and dots behind lion (R. 4/9).

(Recess Waterlow)

1911 (7 Mar). P 13½–14.

No.	Type	Description	Unused	Used	
178	**64**	25c. black and yellow-green	25·00	5·50	2·00
		a. Perf 14½–15	28·00	48·00	—
		b. Imperf (pair) (*no gum*)	55·00		
		c. Re-entry	90·00	32·00	
178*d*		25c. black and blue-green	60·00		
		e. Re-entry	£180		
179		50c. black and steel-blue	22·00	6·00	2·25
		a. Perf 14½–15	32·00	38·00	—
		ab. Imperf between (horiz pair)	£4000	£5000	
		c. Imperf (pair) (*no gum*)	90·00		
		d. Re-entry	85·00	35·00	
180		$1 black and chestnut	20·00	4·75	4·50
		a. Perf 14½–15	65·00	16·00	9·50
		b. Imperf (pair) (*no gum*)	£190		
		c. Re-entry	85·00	30·00	
181		$2 black and lilac	85·00	20·00	8·00
		a. Re-entry	£275	80·00	
182	**65**	$5 black and lake	£200	£140	35·00
		a. Imperf (pair) (*no gum*)	£225		
183		$10 black and brick-red	£750	£850	£100
		a. Imperf (pair) (*no gum*)	£550		
178/183 *Set of 6*			£1000	£950	£140
178s/183s Optd 'SPECIMEN.' *Set of 6*			£375		

BRITISH

PROTECTORATE
(66)

2

cents
(67)

(68)

1912 (July). Nos. 85*b* and 86 optd with T **66**.

No.	Type	Description	Unused	Used	
184		$5 dull purple (R.)	£2000	£2250	12·00
185		$10 brown (R.)	£2250	—	12·00
		a. Opt inverted	†	†	—

1916 (Feb). Nos. 162, 167 and 173 surch as T **67** by Govt Printing Office, Sandakan. P 13½–14.

No.	Type	Description	Unused	Used
186	**53**	2c. on 3c. black and rose-lake	30·00	15·00
		a. 's' inverted (R. 2/5)	£110	£100
		b. Surch double	£2500	
187	**56**	4c. on 6c. black and olive-green (R.)	32·00	25·00
		a. 's' inverted (R. 2/5)	£110	£110
		b. 's' inserted by hand	—	£1800
		c. Perf 14½–15	£200	£200
		ca. 's' inverted		
188	**59**	10c. on 12c. black and deep blue (R.)	60·00	70·00
		a. 's' inverted (R. 2/5)	£180	£200
		b. 's' inserted by hand	£1700	
186/188 *Set of 3*			£110	£100
186s/188s Optd 'SPECIMEN' *Set of 3*			£120	

Nos. 186/188 were surcharged from a setting of 25 (5×5) on which the required face values were inserted.

1916 (May). Stamps of 1909–1911 optd with T **68** by Waterlow. Centres in black. P 13½–14.

No.	Type	Description	Unused	Used
		(a) Cross in vermilion (thick shiny ink)		
189	**51**	1c. brown	11·00	35·00
190	**52**	2c. green	70·00	85·00
		a. Perf 14½–15	32·00	85·00
		ab. Opt double, one albino	£425	
191	**53**	3c. rose-lake	27·00	50·00
		a. Nos. 191 and 204 *se-tenant* (vert pair)	£5000	
192	**54**	4c. scarlet	5·50	32·00
		a. Perf 14½–15	£300	£200
193	**55**	5c. yellow-brown	60·00	60·00
		a. Perf 14½–15		
194	**56**	6c. apple-green	75·00	75·00
		a. Perf 14½–15	£250	£250
195	**57**	8c. lake	25·00	60·00
196	**58**	10c. blue	65·00	75·00
197	**59**	12c. deep blue	£110	£110
198	**60**	16c. brown-lake	£120	£120
199	**61**	20c. on 18c. blue-green	70·00	£110
200	**62**	24c. dull mauve	£150	£150
201	**64**	25c. green (P 14½–15)	£400	£500
		a. Re-entry	£1600	
189/201 *Set of 13*			£1000	£1300
		(b) Cross in shades of carmine (matt ink)		
202	**51**	1c. brown	26·00	65·00
		a. Perf 14½–15	£300	
203	**52**	2c. green	32·00	50·00
		b. Perf 14½–15	£225	
		ba. Opt double	†	£2500
204	**53**	3c. rose-lake	55·00	70·00
204*a*	**54**	4c. scarlet	£850	£950
		ab. Perf 14½–15	†	—
205	**55**	5c. yellow-brown	70·00	80·00
206	**56**	6c. apple-green	65·00	80·00
		a. Perf 14½–15	£225	£250
207	**57**	8c. lake	29·00	55·00
208	**58**	10c. blue	70·00	80·00
209	**59**	12c. deep blue	£110	£120
210	**60**	16c. brown-lake	£110	£120
211	**61**	20c. on 18c. blue-green	£110	£120
212	**62**	24c. dull mauve	£130	£140
		a. Imperf between (vert pair)	£4250	
213	**64**	25c. green	£950	
		a. Perf 14½–15	£450	£475
		ab. Re-entry	£1800	
202/213a (*ex* 4c.) *Set of 12*			£1100	£1300

The British North Borneo Company donated a proportion of the above issue to be sold by the National Philatelic War Fund for the benefit of the Red Cross and St John's Ambulance Brigade.

RED CROSS +

TWO CENTS
(69)

FOUR CENTS
(70)

1918 (Aug). Stamps of 1909–1911 surch as T **69**. P 13½–14.

No.	Type	Description	Unused	Used
		(a) Lines of surcharge 9 mm apart		
214	**51**	1c. +2c. brown	3·50	18·00
		a. Imperf between (horiz pair)	£3250	
		b. Imperf between (vert pair)	£3250	
215	**52**	2c. +2c. green	1·00	8·50
		a. Imperf between (horiz or vert pair)	£4250	
		b. Imperf (pair)		
		c. Perf 14½–15		
216	**53**	3c. +2c. rose-red	14·00	19·00
		a. Imperf between (horiz pair)	£5000	
		b. Perf 14½–15	42·00	70·00
217		3c. +2c. dull rose-carmine	£150	
		a. Perf 14½–15	£190	
218	**54**	4c. +2c. scarlet	70	5·50
		a. Surch inverted	£450	
		b. 'TWO CENTS' omitted	£1100	
219	**55**	5c. +2c. deep brown	8·00	38·00
220		5c. +2c. pale brown	16·00	28·00
221	**56**	6c. +2c. olive-green	5·00	38·00
		a. Perf 14½–15	£225	£250
221*b*		6c. +2c. apple-green	5·00	29·00
		c. Perf 14½–15	£275	£300
222	**57**	8c. +2c. lake	5·50	11·00
		a. Inverted figure '3' for 'C' in 'CENTS'		
223	**58**	10c. +2c. blue	8·00	32·00
224	**59**	12c. +2c. deep bright blue	21·00	55·00
		a. Surch inverted	£600	
225	**60**	16c. +2c. brown-lake	22·00	45·00
226	**62**	24c. +2c. mauve	22·00	45·00
		(b) Lines of surch 13–14 mm apart		
227	**52**	2c. +2c. green	55·00	£120
228	**56**	6c. +2c. olive-green	£475	£900
229	**64**	25c. +2c. green	10·00	45·00
		a. Re-entry	60·00	£180
230		50c. +2c. steel-blue	12·00	45·00
		a. Re-entry	70·00	
231		$1 +2c. chestnut	50·00	55·00
		a. Surcharge double, one albino	£400	
		b. Re-entry	£180	£200
232		$2 +2c. lilac	75·00	95·00
		a. Re-entry	£275	£325
233	**65**	$5 +2c. lake	£500	£800
234		$10 +2c. brick-red	£600	£850
214/234 *Set of 17*			£1200	£2000

The above stamps were dispatched from London in three consignments, of which two were lost through enemy action at sea.

No. 218a normally shows a second inverted albino surcharge.

No. 218b occurs from the top row of a sheet on which the surcharge was misplaced downwards. Stamps from the other rows show the lines of the surcharge transposed (with 'TWO CENTS' above 'RED CROSS').

Only one sheet was found of No. 228.

These stamps were sold at a premium of 2c. per stamp, which went to the Red Cross Society.

1918 (Oct). Stamps of 1909–1911 surch with T **70**, in red. P 13½–14.

No.	Type	Description	Unused	Used
235	**51**	1c. +4c. chocolate	60	5·00
		a. Imperf between (horiz pair)	£3000	
236	**52**	2c. +4c. green	65	8·00
237	**53**	3c. +4c. rose-lake	1·00	3·75
238	**54**	4c. +4c. scarlet	40	5·00
239	**55**	5c. +4c. brown	2·00	25·00
240	**56**	6c. +4c. apple-green	1·90	12·00
		a. Imperf between (vert pair)	£2750	
241	**57**	8c. +4c. lake	1·25	9·50
242	**58**	10c. +4c. turquoise-blue	2·25	12·00
242*a*		10c. +4c. greenish blue	9·00	45·00
243	**59**	12c. +4c. deep blue	12·00	14·00
		a. Surch double	£2000	
244	**60**	16c. +4c. brown-lake	7·00	16·00
245	**62**	24c. +4c. mauve	9·00	20·00
246	**64**	25c. +4c. yellow-green	12·00	50·00
		a. Re-entry	60·00	
247		25c. +4c. blue-green	25·00	75·00
		a. Re-entry	90·00	
248		50c. +4c. steel-blue	15·00	45·00
		a. Perf 14½–15	60·00	
		b. Re-entry	75·00	
249		$1 +4c. chestnut	30·00	65·00
		a. Perf 14½–15	£200	
		b. Re-entry	95·00	
250		$2 +4c. lilac	60·00	85·00
		a. Re-entry	£190	
251	**65**	$5 +4c. lake	£300	£400
252		$10 +4c. brick-red	£400	£475
235/252 *Set of 17*			£750	£1100

Nos. 235/252 were sold at face, plus 4c. on each stamp for Red Cross Funds.

Examples of a double-ring 'SANDAKAN N. BORNEO' postmark dated '1 NOV 1918' on these stamps are generally considered to be faked.

MALAYA-BORNEO

EXHIBITION

1922.
(71)

THREE

CENTS
(72)

1922 (31 Mar). Malaya–Borneo Exhibition, Singapore. Stamps of 1909–1922 some in different shades, optd as T **71** by Govt Printing Office, Sandakan. P 13½–14.

No.	Type	Description	Unused	Used
253	**51**	1c. brown (R.)	26·00	90·00
		a. 'BORHEO'	£325	£900
		b. 'BORNEQ'	£500	£1000
		c. Stop after 'EXHIBITION.'	£120	
		d. Raised stop after '1922'	£950	£1400
		e. 'EXHIBITICN.' with stop	£950	
		f. Perf 14½–15	50·00	75·00
		fa. 'BORHEO'	£550	£1000
		fb. 'BORNEQ'	£850	£1400
		fc. Raised stop after '1922'	£800	
		fd. 'EXHIBITICN.' with stop	£800	
		fe. 'MHLAYA' and 'EXHIBITICN.' with stop	£8000	
		ff. Stop after 'EXHIBITION.'	£250	
253*g*		1c. brown (B.) (P 14½–15)	£1700	
		ga. Vert pair, with and without opt	£8500	
		gb. Raised stop after '1922'	£9500	
		gc. 'BORHEO'	£6500	
		gd. 'BORNEQ'	£9500	
		gg. 'MHLAYA' and 'EXHIBITICN.' with stop	£9500	
		gh. 'EXHIBITIOH'	£9500	
254		1c. orange-brown (R.)	65·00	95·00
255	**52**	2c. green (R.)	3·75	30·00
		a. Stop after 'EXHIBITION.'	42·00	£170
		b. No hyphen	£110	
256	**53**	3c. rose-lake (B.)	16·00	65·00
		a. Stop after 'EXHIBITION.'	80·00	£275
		b. 'EXHIBITICN.' with stop	£5000	
		c. Raised stop after '1922'	£5000	
257	**54**	4c. scarlet (B.)	3·75	50·00
		a. Stop after 'EXHIBITION.'	55·00	£250
		b. Perf 14½–15	£130	
		ba. Stop after 'EXHIBITION.'	£800	
258	**55**	5c. orange-brown (B.)	10·00	70·00
		a. Imperf between (vert pair)	£2000	£2500
		b. Stop after 'EXHIBITION.'	85·00	£275
		c. Opt double	£2500	
		d. Opt double (with stop)	£8500	
259		5c. chestnut (B.)	23·00	75·00
		a. Stop after 'EXHIBITION.'	£110	
260	**56**	6c. apple-green (R.)	10·00	70·00
		a. Stop after 'EXHIBITION.'	65·00	£250
		b. Opt double	£2500	
		c. Opt double (with stop)	£8500	
261	**57**	8c. dull rose (B.)	12·00	50·00
		a. Stop after 'EXHIBITION.'	£100	
262		8c. deep rose-lake (B.)	9·50	50·00
		a. Stop after 'EXHIBITION.'	£100	
263	**58**	10c. turquoise-blue (R.)	21·00	70·00
		a. Stop after 'EXHIBITION.'	£130	£300
		b. Perf 14½–15	50·00	£140
		ba. Stop after 'EXHIBITION.'	£425	
264		10c. greenish blue (R.)	30·00	85·00
		a. Stop after 'EXHIBITION.'	£150	
265	**59**	12c. deep blue (R.)	13·00	21·00
		a. Stop after 'EXHIBITION.'	95·00	£170
266		12c. deep bright blue (R.)	50·00	
		a. Stop after 'EXHIBITION.'	£300	
267	**60**	16c. brown-lake (B.)	29·00	75·00
		a. Stop after 'EXHIBITION.'	£140	£350
		b. Opt in red	£11000	
268	**61**	20c. on 18c. blue-green (B.)	29·00	95·00
		a. Stop after 'EXHIBITION.'	£225	
269		20c. on 18c. blue-green (R.)	29·00	£170
		a. Stop after 'EXHIBITION.'	£375	£1200
270	**62**	24c. mauve (R.)	55·00	80·00
		a. Stop after 'EXHIBITION.'	£250	£350
271		24c. lilac (R.)	55·00	80·00
		a. Stop after 'EXHIBITION.'	£250	£350
272		24c. reddish lilac (R.)	70·00	£110
		a. Stop after 'EXHIBITION.'	£375	
273	**64**	25c. blue-green (R.)	48·00	95·00
		a. Stop after 'EXHIBITION.'	£425	
		b. Re-entry	£325	
274		25c. yellow-green (R.)	14·00	75·00
		a. Stop after 'EXHIBITION.'	£275	
		b. Re-entry	£140	
		c. Opt double	£4500	
		d. Perf 14½–15	19·00	80·00
		da. Stop after 'EXHIBITION.'	£250	£475
		db. Re-entry	£200	
275		50c. steel-blue (R.)	19·00	75·00
		a. Stop after 'EXHIBITION.'	£250	£550
		b. Re-entry	£200	£550

		c. Perf 14½–15	30·00	90·00
		ca. Stop after 'EXHIBITION.'	£250	
		cb. Re-entry	£225	
253/275 *Set of* 14			£225	£800
253s/275s Optd 'SPECIMEN' *Set of* 14			£475	

These overprints were applied from a number of settings covering 10, 20, 25 or 30 stamps at a time.

Of the ten settings known for the horizontal stamps the earliest were only used for the 1c. on which most of the varieties occur. Of the others the vast majority come from settings of 20 (10×2) with the stop after 'EXHIBITION' variety on R. 2/7 or R. 2/9, or 25 (5×5) on which the same variety can be found on R. 5/4. In addition the 3c. comes from a different setting of 20 (10×2) on which there is a raised stop after '1922' on R. 2/8 and 'EXHIBITICN.' on R. 2/9.

The 1c. sequence is complicated, but additionally includes a setting of 10 with 'BORHEO' on stamps 3 and 10, 'BORNEQ' on stamp 4, raised stop on stamp 8 and 'EXHIBITICN.' on stamp 9. A setting of 20 repeats this sequence on its bottom line as does one of 30, although in this instance 'MHLAYA' joins 'EXHIBITICN' as the variety on stamp 9.

For the vertical stamps (2, 6, 10, 12, 16 and 20c. on 18c.) the settings were of 20 (10×2) or 25 (5×5). The stop after 'EXHIBITION' occurs on R. 2/7 or R. 2/9 of the former and R. 5/4 of the latter.

The 25c. and 50c. high values were overprinted from a setting of 10×1 or 25 (5×5), with the stop after 'EXHIBITION' on R. 5/4 of the latter.

1923 (Oct). T **54** surch with T **72**.

276		3c. on 4c. black and scarlet	4·50	6·00
		a. Surch double	£1300	
		s. Optd 'SPECIMEN'	55·00	

1925–28. Designs as 1909–1922 issue with centres in black and some frame colours changed. P 12½.

277	**51**	1c. chocolate-brown	1·00	70
		a. Imperf between (horiz pair)	£1700	
278	**52**	2c. claret	85	60
		a. Imperf between (vert pair)	—	£1900
		b. Imperf between (horiz pair)		
279	**53**	3c. green	3·00	50
		a. Imperf between (horiz pair)	†	£2750
280	**54**	4c. scarlet	50	10
		a. Imperf between (vert pair)	£275	£450
		b. Imperf between (horiz pair)	£750	
		c. Imperf between (vert strip of 3)	£1200	
281	**55**	5c. yellow-brown	6·50	1·75
		a. Imperf between (vert pair)	£1200	
282	**56**	6c. olive-green	15·00	65
283	**57**	8c. carmine	7·50	50
		a. Imperf between (vert pair)	£600	
		b. Imperf between (horiz pair)		
		c. Imperf between (vert strip of 4)	£2000	
284	**58**	10c. turquoise-blue	4·25	70
		a. Imperf between (horiz pair)	£1700	£2500
		b. Imperf between (vert pair)	£2000	
285	**59**	12c. deep blue	30·00	70
286	**60**	16c. red-brown	50·00	£250
287	**61**	20c. on 18c. blue-green (R.)	20·00	3·00
288	**62**	24c. violet	80·00	£250
289	**64**	25c. green	22·00	4·25
		a. Re-entry	£100	32·00
290		50c. steel-blue	32·00	14·00
		a. Re-entry	£130	70·00
291		$1 chestnut	38·00	£900
		a. Re-entry	£150	
292		$2 mauve	95·00	£1100
		a. Re-entry	£300	
293	**65**	$5 lake (1928)	£225	£1800
294		$10 orange-red (1928)	£650	£2000
277/294 *Set of* 18			£1100	£5500

Examples of No. 278 were supplied for UPU distribution punched with a 3½ mm diameter hole.

Examples of the 24c., $1, $2, $5 and $10 in this perforation were not supplied to the territory for postal purposes. Used examples exist from covers prepared by stamp dealers and the prices quoted above are for stamps with verified contemporary cancels.

73 Head of a Murut

74 Orangutan

75 Dyak warrior

76 Mount Kinabalu

77 Clouded Leopard

78 Badge of the Company

79 Arms of the Company

80 Arms of the Company

(Eng J. A. C. Harrison. Recess Waterlow)

1931 (1 Jan). 50th Anniversary of British North Borneo Company. Types **73/80**. P 12½.

295	**73**	3c. black and blue-green	1·50	80
296	**74**	6c. black and orange	20·00	2·75
297	**75**	10c. black and scarlet	5·50	13·00
298	**76**	12c. black and ultramarine	5·50	8·00
299	**77**	25c. black and violet	48·00	35·00
300	**78**	$1 black and yellow-green	27·00	£110
301	**79**	$2 black and chestnut	50·00	£110
302	**80**	$5 black and purple	£180	£750
295/302 *Set of* 8			£300	£950
295s/302s Optd 'SPECIMEN' *Set of* 8			£350	

Examples of all values are known showing a forged Jesselton postmark dated '22 AUG 1931'.

81 Buffalo Transport

82 Palm Cockatoo

83 Native

84 Proboscis Monkey

85 Mounted Bajaus

86 Eastern Archipelago

87 Orangutan

88 Murut with blowpipe

89 Dyak

90 River scene

91 Native boat

92 Mt. Kinabalu

93 Badge of the Company

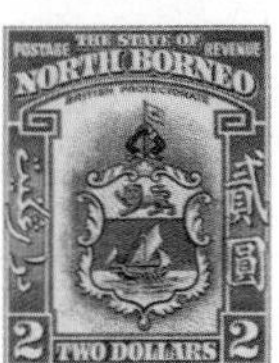
94 Arms of the Company

95 Arms of the Company

1c. 'Ant trail' (R. 8/8)

(Eng J. A. C. Harrison. Recess Waterlow)

1939 (1 Jan). Types **81/95**. P 12½.

303	**81**	1c. green and red-brown	5·00	3·00
		a. Ant trail	£110	65·00
304	**82**	2c. purple and greenish blue	5·00	4·00
305	**83**	3c. slate-blue and green	6·00	4·00
306	**84**	4c. bronze-green and violet	20·00	1·00
307	**85**	6c. deep blue and claret	15·00	21·00
308	**86**	8c. scarlet	26·00	2·50
309	**87**	10c. violet and bronze-green	42·00	9·00
310	**88**	12c. green and royal blue	50·00	13·00
		a. Green and blue	70·00	19·00
311	**89**	15c. blue-green and brown	35·00	18·00
312	**90**	20c. violet and slate-blue	29·00	11·00
313	**91**	25c. green and chocolate	45·00	21·00
		a. Vignette printed double, one albino	£350	£350
314	**92**	50c. chocolate and violet	48·00	19·00
315	**93**	$1 brown and carmine	£150	23·00
316	**94**	$2 violet and olive-green	£300	£180
317	**95**	$5 indigo and pale blue	£850	£425
303/317 *Set of* 15			£1400	£600
303s/317s Perf 'SPECIMEN' *Set of* 15			£650	

Examples of most values are known showing forged Jesselton postmarks dated '22 AUG 1941' or '15 JA 48'.

No. 313a has the albino impression sideways.

WAR TAX
(96)

WAR
TAX
(97)

1941 (24 Feb). Nos. 303/304 optd at the offices of the *North Borneo Herald*, Sandakan with Types **96/97**.

318		1c. green and red-brown	2·75	7·50
		a. Optd front and back	£850	
		b. Ant trail	75·00	£130
319		2c. purple and greenish blue	12·00	8·00

The 1c. was for compulsory use on internal mail and the 2c. on overseas mail, both in addition to normal postage.

BRITISH MILITARY ADMINISTRATION

North Borneo, including Labuan, was occupied by the Japanese in January 1942. Australian forces landed on Labuan on 10 June 1945 and by the end of the war against Japan on 14 August had liberated much of western North Borneo. Prior to the issue of Nos. 320/334 Australian stamps were made available for civilian use. The territory was placed under British Military Administration on 5 January 1946.

BMA
(98)

(99)

1945 (17 Dec). Nos. 303/317 optd with T **98**.

320	**81**	1c. green and red-brown	24·00	3·00
		a. Ant trail	£225	65·00
321	**82**	2c. purple and greenish blue	14·00	2·00
		a. Opt double	£9500	
322	**83**	3c. slate-blue and green	1·25	1·25
323	**84**	4c. bronze-green and violet	26·00	16·00
324	**85**	6c. deep blue and claret	1·25	1·25
325	**86**	8c. scarlet	3·00	75
326	**87**	10c. violet and bronze-green	3·00	40
327	**88**	12c. green and blue	6·00	6·50
		a. Green and royal blue	22·00	7·50
328	**89**	15c. blue-green and brown	3·75	1·00
329	**90**	20c. violet and slate-blue	9·50	3·25
330	**91**	25c. green and chocolate	9·00	2·00
		a. Vignette printed double, one albino	£400	
331	**92**	50c. chocolate and violet	9·00	3·75
332	**93**	$1 brown and carmine	65·00	45·00
333	**94**	$2 violet and olive-green	75·00	50·00
		a. Opt double	£4250	
334	**95**	$5 indigo and pale blue	40·00	22·00
320/334 *Set of* 15			£250	£130

These stamps and the similarly overprinted stamps of Sarawak were obtainable at all post offices throughout British Borneo (Brunei, Labuan, North Borneo and Sarawak), for use on local and overseas mail.

CROWN COLONY

North Borneo became a Crown Colony on 15 July 1946.

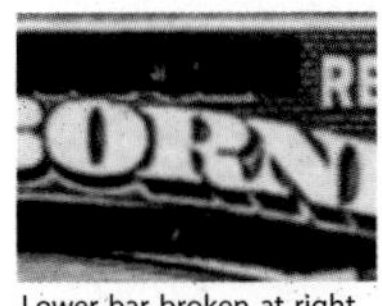
Lower bar broken at right (R. 8/3)

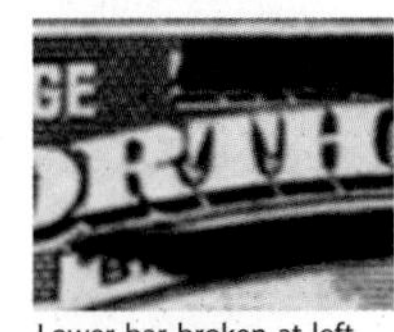
Lower bar broken at left (R. 8/4 and R. 8/8)

1947 (1 Sept–22 Dec). Nos. 303 to 317 optd with T **99** and bars obliterating words 'THE STATE OF' and 'BRITISH PROTECTORATE'.

335	**81**	1c. green and red-brown (15.12)	30	1·00
		b. Lower bar broken at right	22·00	40·00
		c. Lower bar broken at left (R. 8/4)	22·00	40·00
		d. Ant trail and lower bar broken at left (R. 8/8)	27·00	48·00
336	**82**	2c. purple and greenish blue (22.12)	2·25	1·00

337	**83**	3c. slate-blue and green (R.) (22.12)	30	1·00
338	**84**	4c. bronze-green and violet	1·00	1·00
339	**85**	6c. deep blue and claret (R.) (22.12)	40	20
340	**86**	8c. scarlet	1·00	20
		b. Lower bar broken at right	28·00	22·00
341	**87**	10c. violet and bronze-green (15.12)	1·50	40
342	**88**	12c. green and royal blue (22.12)	5·50	2·75
		a. Green and blue	21·00	16·00
343	**89**	15c. blue-green and brown (22.12)	2·25	30
344	**90**	20c. violet and slate-blue (22.12)	4·75	85
		b. Lower bar broken at right	80·00	35·00
345	**91**	25c. green and chocolate (22.12)	3·00	50
		a. Vignette printed double, one albino		
		b. Lower bar broken at right	80·00	35·00
346	**92**	50c. chocolate and violet (22.12)	4·25	85
		b. Lower bar broken at right	90·00	38·00
		c. Lower bar broken at left	80·00	35·00
347	**93**	$1 brown and carmine (22.12)	17·00	1·75
348	**94**	$2 violet and olive-green (22.12)	22·00	18·00
349	**95**	$5 indigo and pale blue (R.) (22.12)	42·00	32·00
		b. Lower bar broken at right	£350	£300
335/349 *Set of* 15			95·00	55·00
335s/349s Perf 'SPECIMEN' *Set of* 15			£325	

1948 (1 Nov). Royal Silver Wedding. As Nos. 112/113 of Antigua.

350	8c. scarlet	30	80
351	$10 mauve	32·00	40·00

1949 (10 Oct). 75th Anniversary of UPU. As Nos. 114/117 of Antigua.

352	8c. carmine	60	30
353	10c. brown	3·25	2·25
354	30c. orange-brown	1·50	2·25
355	55c. blue	1·50	3·00
352/355 *Set of* 4		6·00	7·00

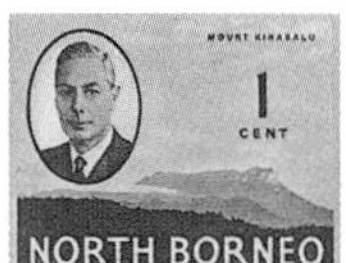

100 Mount Kinabalu

101 Native musical instrument

102 Coconut Grove

103 Hemp drying

104 Cattle at Kota Belud

105 Map

106 Log pond

107 Malay prau, Sandakan

108 Bajau Chief

109 Suluk river canoe, Lahad Datu

110 Clock Tower Jesselton

111 Bajau horsemen

112 Murut with blowpipe

113 Net-fishing

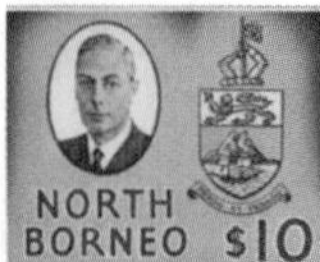

114 Arms of North Borneo

(Photo Harrison)

1950 (1 July)–**52**. Types **100/114**. Chalk-surfaced paper. Wmk Mult Script CA. P 13½×14½ (horiz), 14½×13½ (vert).

356	**100**	1c. red-brown	15	1·25
357	**101**	2c. blue	15	50
358	**102**	3c. green	30	15
359	**103**	4c. bright purple	1·00	10
360	**104**	5c. violet	1·00	10
361	**105**	8c. scarlet	2·75	85
362	**106**	10c. maroon	2·25	15
363	**107**	15c. ultramarine	2·25	65
364	**108**	20c. brown	3·75	10
365	**109**	30c. olive-brown	5·50	30
366	**110**	50c. rose-carmine ('JESSLETON')	2·75	8·00
366*a*		50c. rose-carmine ('JESSELTON') (1.5.52)	17·00	2·75
		aw. Wmk inverted	£1000	
367	**111**	$1 red-orange	10·00	2·25
368	**112**	$2 grey-green	17·00	23·00
369	**113**	$5 emerald-green	28·00	38·00
370	**114**	$10 dull blue	70·00	95·00
356/370 *Set of* 16			£140	£150

1953 (3 June). Coronation. As No. 120 of Antigua.

371	10c. black and bright scarlet	2·50	1·00

115 Log Pond

10c. Vertical line appears as an extra chimney (R. 1/10)

(Photo Harrison)

1954 (1 Mar)–**59**. Designs previously used for King George VI issue, but with portrait of Queen Elizabeth II as in T **115**. Chalk-surfaced paper. Wmk Mult Script CA. P 14½×13½ (vert) or 13½×14½ (horiz).

372	**100**	1c. red-brown (1.10.54)	10	30
373	**101**	2c. blue (1.6.56)	2·00	15
374	**102**	3c. green (1.2.57)	4·75	2·00
		a. Deep green (14.1.59)	11·00	4·50
375	**103**	4c. bright purple (16.5.55)	2·00	20
376	**104**	5c. reddish violet (1.7.54)	1·00	10
377	**105**	8c. scarlet (1.10.54)	1·25	30
378	**115**	10c. maroon	30	10
		a. Extra chimney	40·00	12·00
379	**107**	15c. bright blue (16.5.55)	1·00	10
380	**108**	20c. brown (3.8.54)	50	15
381	**109**	30c. olive-brown (3.8.54)	3·25	20
382	**110**	50c. rose-carmine ('JESSELTON') (10.2.56)	6·00	20
		a. Rose (9.12.59)	25·00	1·75
		aw. Wmk inverted	£1000	£475
383	**111**	$1 red-orange (1.4.55)	6·50	20
384	**112**	$2 deep green (1.10.55)	18·00	1·50
		a. Grey-green (22.1.58)	48·00	7·00
385	**113**	$5 emerald-green (1.2.57)	15·00	38·00
386	**114**	$10 deep blue (1.2.57)	30·00	45·00
372/386 *Set of* 15			75·00	75·00

Plate 2 of the 30c., released 10 August 1960, had a finer, 250 screen, instead of the previous 200 (*price £5 mint*).

116 Borneo Railway, 1902

117 Malay prau

118 Mount Kinabalu

119 Arms of Chartered Company

(Recess Waterlow)

1956 (1 Nov). 75th Anniversary of British North Borneo Co. Types **116/119**. Wmk Mult Script CA. P 13×13½ (horiz) or 13½×13 (vert).

387	**116**	10c. black and rose-carmine	1·25	40
388	**117**	15c. black and red-brown	1·75	30
389	**118**	35c. black and bluish green	1·00	2·25
390	**119**	$1 black and slate	1·50	3·00
387/390 *Set of* 4			5·00	5·50

120 Sambar Stag

121 Sun Bear

122 Clouded Leopard

123 Dusun woman with gong

124 Map of Borneo

125 Banteng

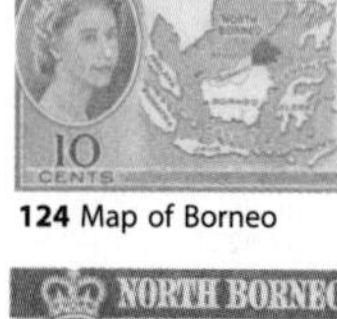

126 Butterfly orchid

127 Sumatran Rhinoceros

128 Murut with blow-pipe

129 Mount Kinabalu

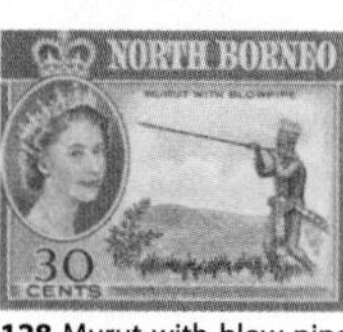

130 Dusun and buffalo transport

131 Bajau horsemen

132 Orangutan

133 Rhinoceros Hornbill

134 Crested Wood Partridge

135 Arms of North Borneo

(Des Chong Yun Fatt. Recess Waterlow (until 1962), then D.L.R.)

1961 (1 Feb). Types **120/135**. W w **12**. P 13.

391	**120**	1c. emerald and brown-red	20	10
392	**121**	4c. bronze-green and orange	1·50	90
393	**122**	5c. sepia and violet	1·50	10
394	**123**	6c. black and blue-green	1·25	40
395	**124**	10c. green and red	2·00	10
396	**125**	12c. brown and grey-green	1·00	10
397	**126**	20c. blue-green and ultramarine	4·00	10
398	**127**	25c. grey-black and scarlet	1·75	1·50
399	**128**	30c. sepia and olive	2·00	20
400	**129**	35c. slate-blue and red-brown	2·75	2·50
401	**130**	50c. emerald and yellow-brown	2·75	20
402	**131**	75c. grey-blue and bright purple	19·00	90
403	**132**	$1 brown and yellow-green	18·00	2·00
404	**133**	$2 brown and slate	35·00	4·00
405	**134**	$5 emerald and maroon	38·00	24·00
406	**135**	$10 carmine and blue	55·00	50·00
391/406 *Set of* 16			£160	75·00

(Des M. Goaman. Photo Harrison)

1963 (4 June). Freedom from Hunger. As No. 146 of Antigua.

407	12c. ultramarine	1·75	75

POSTAL FISCALS

Three Cents. Revenue (F 1) (Raised stop)

Ten Cents. Revenue (F 2)

1886. Regular issues surch as Types F **1** or F **2**.

F1 **1** 3c. on 4c. pink (No. 6) £140 £190
a. Raised stop after 'Cents' £120 £180
F2 5c. on 8c. green (No. 7) £140 £190
a. Raised stop after 'Cents' £120 £180
F3 **4** 10c. on 50c. violet (No. 4) £225 £250
a. Surch double — £1700
b. No stop after 'Cents' and stop after 'Revenue.' £600 £650
c. Inverted 'L' for first 'F' in 'FIFTY' (R. 5/2) £1500 £1500

It is believed that Nos. F1/F2 were each surcharged from a horizontal setting of five so that the raised stop variety occurs on every stamp in the first, second, third, sixth, seventh and eighth vertical columns in the sheets of 50 (10×5).

No. F1 is known fiscally used with error surcharge inverted.

POSTAGE DUE STAMPS

POSTAGE DUE (D 1)

1895 (1 Aug)–**97**. Nos. 68/79 optd with T D **1** horizontally (8, 12, 18 and 24c.) or vertically, reading upwards (others). P 14½–15.

D1 **25** 2c. black and rose-lake 42·00 50·00 4·25
a. Opt double* † † £350
b. Opt vertical, reading downwards* † † £550
D2 2c. black and lake 28·00 24·00 3·75
a. Perf 13½–14
b. Perf 13½–14, comp 12–13* † † 14·00
c. Opt omitted (in vert pair with normal)* † † £2000
D3 **26** 3c. olive-green and dull purple 6·00 16·00 1·25
a. Bronze-green and dull purple 10·00 20·00
b. Opt vertical, reading downwards* † † £600
D4 3c. olive-green and violet
a. Perf 13½–14
b. Opt double* † † £425
D5 **27** 5c. black and vermilion 70·00 40·00 4·00
a. Printed double † — —
b. With stop after 'DUE' in opt (1897) £400
c. Opt double £800 £900 †
d. Perf 13½–14 — 80·00 2·50
da. Opt double † † £600
e. Perf 13½–14, comp 12–13 — £100 10·00
D6 **28** 6c. black and bistre-brown 90·00 75·00 3·75
a. Perf 13½–14 25·00 50·00 3·75
b. Perf 12–13* † † —
c. Perf 13½–14, comp 12–13 † † 14·00
d. Opt vertical, reading downwards* † † £550
D7 **29** 8c. black and dull purple 65·00 50·00 4·00
a. Opt double* † † £375
b. Perf 13½–14 † † 5·00
ba. Opt inverted* † † £200
c. Perf 13½–14, comp 12–13 £130 † 15·00
D8 **30** 12c. black and blue — 60·00 4·25
a. Opt double* † † £400
b. Perf 13½–14 70·00 50·00 4·25
c. Perf 13½–14, comp 14½–15 £100
D9 12c. black and ultramarine (P 13½–14) 95·00 75·00 —
D10 **31** 18c. black and deep green 75·00 65·00 6·00
a. Opt inverted £375 £400 †
b. Perf 13½–14 £150 £120 6·00
ba. Opt double* † † £325
c. Opt vertical, reading upwards (1897) 80·00 95·00 †
ca. Opt vertical, reading downwards £600 £375 †
D11 **32** 24c. blue and rose-lake £130 £110 4·25
a. Opt double* † † £350
b. Perf 13½–14 32·00 55·00 4·25
c. Perf 13½–14, comp 14½–15 55·00 — —
D3s, D5s, D8s, D10cs, D11s Optd 'SPECIMEN' *Set of 5* £160

There were two local overprintings of these stamps which show variations in the distance between the two words. Further overprints were produced in London for sale to dealers by the British North Borneo Company. Those listings marked with an * only exist from the London overprinting and are usually only known cancelled-to-order.

No. D5b comes from at least one sheet which was included in a later overprinting.

The 18c. with vertical opt (No. D10c) is P 14½-15. It also exists P 13½-14 and P 13½-14, comp 12-13, but only with 'SPECIMEN' opt (*Prices from £100 each*).

1897–99. Nos. 94/97, 99/103, 106, 108/111 optd with T D **1** horizontally (8c.) or vertically reading upwards (others). P 14½–15.

D12 **35** 2c. black and lake (1898) 14·00 9·00 1·50
a. Perf 13½–14 90·00
b. Opt horizontal* £325
s. Optd 'SPECIMEN' 35·00
D13 2c. black and green (P 13½–14)* £110 † 70
a. Perf 13½–14, comp 12–13* £160 † 1·00
b. Perf 16*
c. Perf 12–13* £375
d. Opt vertical, reading downwards*
e. Opt horizontal* £350
D14 **36** 3c. green and rosy mauve* 55·00 † 50
a. Perf 13½–14* 75·00 † 2·75
b. Perf 13½–14, comp 14½–15*
c. Opt double*
D15 3c. green and dull mauve 48·00 55·00 †
D16 **37** 4c. black and carmine* — † 2·25
a. Perf 13½–14 95·00 † 50
b. Perf 13½–14, comp 12-13 † † 5·00
D17 **38** 5c. black and orange-vermilion (1899) 90·00 65·00 1·00
a. Perf 13½–14 29·00 65·00 1·75
b. Perf 13½–14, comp 12-13 60·00
D18 **39** 6c. black and bistre-brown 10·00 50·00 70
a. Perf 13½–14 — 75·00 50
b. Perf 13½–14, comp 12–13* — † 3·25
s. Optd 'SPECIMEN' 35·00
D19 **40** 8c. black and brown-purple (1898) 65·00 90·00 †
a. Opt vertical, reading upwards (P 16)* † † £500
s. Optd 'SPECIMEN' 35·00
D20 8c. black and brown (opt vert, reading upwards)* 15·00 † 50
a. Opt vertical, reading downwards* † † £700
b. Perf 13½–14*
c. Perf 16 £500 † †
D21 **42** 12c. black and dull blue* — † 7·50
a. Perf 13½–14* £170 † 4·25
D22 **44** 18c. black and green (P 16)* † † £1200
D23 **46** 18c. black and green (P 13½–14)* £110 † 4·75
a. Perf 13½–14, comp 12–13* £180 † 4·75
D24 **45** 24c. blue and lake (P 13½–14)* — † £900
D25 **47** 24c. blue and lake* 75·00 † 2·50
a. Perf 13½–14*

In addition to local overprints, stamps from the 1897–1902 series were also overprinted by Waterlow on two occasions for sale by the British North Borneo Company to dealers from London. These Waterlow overprints were not supplied to North Borneo for postal purposes and are indicated by an * in the above listing.

1901–02. Nos. 96/97, 100 and 102/103 optd locally as T D **1**, but with stop after 'DUE', horizontally (8c.) or vertically reading upwards (others). P 13½–14.

D26 **36** 3c. green and rosy mauve (1902) 80·00 75·00
a. Opt double £325
D27 3c. green and dull mauve (P 14½–15) (1902) 50·00 55·00
a. Opt double £275 £325
b. Stop after 'DUE' omitted (in pair with normal) £250
D28 **38** 5c. black and orange-vermilion £150
a. Perf 14½–15 £110 £190
D29 **40** 8c. black and brown-purple (P 14½–15) 23·00 75·00
D30 8c. black and brown (P 14½–15) £325 £350

The 'stop omitted' variety on the 3c. occurs on R. 6/10, but has also been recorded on other positions.

1902 (10 Oct)–**12**. Stamps of 1901–1905 (optd 'BRITISH PROTECTORATE') further optd with T D **1** locally (No. D31) or by Waterlow (others). P 13½–14.

(a) Optd horizontally showing stop after 'DUE'

D31 **34** 1c. black and bistre-brown 8·00 65·00
a. With raised stop after 'DUE' 9·00 70·00

(b) Optd vertically reading upwards

D32 **35** 2c. black and green (P 16) £700 £350
D33 **36** 3c. green and rosy mauve £200 £170
D34 **38** 5c. black and orange-vermilion (P 14½–15) £350 £190
D35 **40** 8c. black and brown £275 £110
D36 **47** 24c. blue and lake £450 £190

(c) Optd horizontally at centre of stamp

D37 **34** 1c. black and bistre-brown* — † 38·00
a. Perf 14½–15* £325 † 38·00
D38 **35** 2c. black and green (1909) 40·00 4·50 30
a. Perf 14½–15 (1903) 85·00 35·00 †
D39 **36** 3c. green and rosy mauve (1912) 9·00 5·00 30
a. Perf 14½–15 (1904) 50·00 48·00 †
ab. Type D **1** opt double £475
D40 **37** 4c. black and carmine (1912) 32·00 8·00 30
a. Type D **1** opt double* £600 † £225
b. Perf 14½–15 (1.3.03) 12·00 20·00 3·00
D41 **38** 5c. black and orange-vermilion (1905) 60·00 5·50 30
a. No stop after 'PROTECTORATE' † £250 †
b. Perf 14½–15 (1905) £110 48·00 4·00
D42 **39** 6c. black and bistre-brown (1912) 30·00 11·00 40
a. Type D **1** opt inverted* £550 † £140
b. Type D **1** opt double £850 — —
c. No stop after 'PROTECTORATE' (1912)
d. Perf 16 (1906) £100 40·00 †
D43 **40** 8c. black and brown (1912) 40·00 5·00 40
a. No stop after 'PROTECTORATE' (1903) 48·00 25·00 †
D44 **41** 10c. brown and slate-lilac (1906) £425 £130 9·00
a. No stop after 'PROTECTORATE' (1906) — — †
D45 10c. brown and slate-blue (1912) £110 26·00 1·60
D46 **42** 12c. black and dull blue (2.12.10) 55·00 26·00 4·25
D47 **43** 16c. green and chestnut (2.12.10) £110 40·00 4·25
D48 **46** 18c. black and green (2.12.10) 23·00 27·00 1·50
a. Type D **1** opt double* £550 † 85·00
b. Imperf between (vert pair) — † £1100
D49 **47** 24c. blue and lake (1905) 27·00 48·00 4·25
a. Perf 14½–15 (1909) 60·00 85·00 †
b. Type D **1** opt double* £375 † £110

(d) Optd horizontally at top of stamp

D50 **35** 2c. black and green (P 16) (1906) £110 55·00
a. Perf 14½–15 (1908) 80·00 50·00
D51 **37** 4c. black and carmine (1906) 65·00 30·00

Items marked * only occur in stocks obtained from the British North Borneo Company in London.

POSTAGE DUE (D 2) POSTAGE DUE (D 3)

Type D **2**. Thick letters. Ends of 'S' and top of 'G' straight. Pointed beard to 'G'.

Type D **3**. Thinner letters. Ends of 'S' and top of 'G' slanted. Square beard to 'G'.

1918–30. Opt with T D **2** locally.

(a) On stamps of 1909–1923. P 13½–14

D52 **52** 2c. black and green (opt at foot) (1.24) 12·00 80·00
a. Perf 14½–15 35·00 £100
s. Optd 'SPECIMEN' 38·00
D53 **53** 3c. black and green (opt at foot) (1.9.23) 4·75 50·00
D54 **54** 4c. black and scarlet (opt at top) (10.18) £150 17·00
D55 4c. black and scarlet (opt at foot) (1.22) 1·00 1·25
D56 4c. black and scarlet (opt in centre) (5.23) £190 30·00
D57 **55** 5c. black and yellow-brown (opt at foot) (1.22) 10·00 42·00
D58 5c. black and yellow-brown (opt in centre) (1.23) 50·00 45·00
D59 **56** 6c. black and olive-green (opt at foot) (1.9.23) 26·00 26·00
D60 6c. black and olive-green (opt in centre) (6.23) 50·00 7·50
D61 – 6c. black and apple-green (opt at foot) (1.9.23) 15·00 16·00
D62 **57** 8c. black and rose-lake (opt at foot) (1.9.23) 1·50 1·50
a. Opt double £1400
D63 **58** 10c. black and turquoise-blue (opt at foot) (1.8.24) 23·00 19·00
a. Perf 14½–15 £150 £250
D64 **59** 12c. black and deep blue (1.8.24) 80·00 55·00
a. Horiz pair, one without opt £14000
D65 **60** 16c. black and brown-lake (2.29)
a. Black and red-brown 38·00 60·00

(b) On stamps of 1925–1928 with opt at foot. P 12½ (1926–1930)

D66 **52** 2c. black and claret (3.30) 1·50 2·00
D67 **53** 3c. black and green (1926) 12·00 48·00
D68 **54** 4c. black and scarlet (1926) 1·50 2·75
D69 **55** 5c. black and yellow-brown (1926) 8·50 £100
D70 **56** 6c. black and olive-green (3.28) 35·00 2·75
D71 **57** 8c. black and carmine (2.28) 42·00 48·00
D72 **58** 10c. black and turquoise-blue (1926) 19·00 90·00
D73 **59** 12c. black and deep blue (1926) 35·00 £180

Dates given as month and year only indicate first known postmark where recorded.

1930–38. Optd with T D **3**, locally, at foot of stamp.

(a) On stamps of 1909–1923. P 13½–14

D74 **57** 8c. black and carmine (1931) 20·00 2·00
D75 **60** 16c. black and brown-lake (11.31) 17·00 75·00
a. Black and red-brown 6·50
s. Optd 'SPECIMEN' 45·00

(b) On stamps of 1925–1928. P 12½

D76 **52** 2c. black and claret (5.31) 50 2·00
D77 **53** 3c. black and green (11.38) 20·00 42·00
D78 **54** 4c. black and scarlet (6.36) 60·00 5·00
D79 **55** 5c. black and yellow-brown 24·00
D80 **56** 6c. black and olive-green (12.30) 9·50 2·50
D81 **57** 8c. black and carmine (9.31) 3·75 32·00
D82 **58** 10c. black and turquoise-blue (12.32) 38·00 £130
D83 **59** 12c. black and deep blue 75·00
D84 **60** 16c. black and red-brown 65·00 £225

Dates given are those of earliest postmark where recorded.

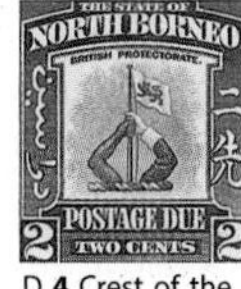

D **4** Crest of the Company

(Recess Waterlow)

1939 (1 Jan). P 12½.

D85 D **4** 2c. brown 7·00 80·00
D86 4c. scarlet 12·00 £110
D87 6c. violet 40·00 £160
D88 8c. green 48·00 £300
D89 10c. blue 80·00 £475
D85/D89 *Set of 5* £160 £1000
D85s/D89s Perf 'SPECIMEN' *Set of 5* £200

The used prices quoted for Nos. D85/D89 are for stamps with identifiable authentic cancellations. Forged postmarks are frequently met with.

The stamps of North Borneo were withdrawn on 30 June 1964. For later issues see Malaysia/Sabah.

LABUAN

CROWN COLONY

The island of Labuan, off the northern coast of Borneo, was ceded to Great Britain by the Sultan of Brunei in December 1846.

Stamps of STRAITS SETTLEMENTS were used from 1867 until 1879. Covers of 1864 and 1865 are known from Labuan franked with stamps of INDIA or HONG KONG.

PRICES FOR STAMPS ON COVER TO 1945

Nos. 1/4	—
Nos. 5/10	*from* × 40
Nos. 11/13	—
Nos. 14/21	*from* × 40
Nos. 22/25	—
Nos. 26/35	*from* × 50
Nos. 36/38	—
Nos. 39/47	*from* × 100
Nos. 49/50	*from* × 15
Nos. 51/57	*from* × 60
Nos. 62/74	*from* × 15
Nos. 75/79	*from* × 40
Nos. 80/88	*from* × 20
Nos. 89/97	*from* × 15
Nos. 98/116	*from* × 10
Nos. 117/128	*from* × 30
Nos. 129/137	*from* × 10
Nos. 138/142	—
Nos. D1/D9	*from* × 30

1

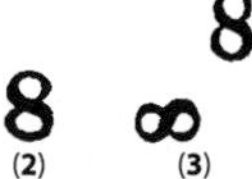
(2) (3)

Normal

6c. No dot at upper left (R. 2/4)

Normal

12c. No right foot to second Chinese character (R. 2/3)

(Recess D.L.R.)

1879 (May). Wmk CA over Crown W w **7**, sideways. P 14.

1	1	2c. blue-green	£1600	£900
2		6c. orange-brown	£225	£250
		a. No dot at upper left	£600	£600
3		12c. carmine	£1900	£800
		a. No right foot to second Chinese character	£4000	£1600
4		16c. blue	70·00	£200

This watermark is always found sideways and may be sideways inverted or reversed. It extends over two stamps, a single specimen showing only a portion of the Crown or the letters CA, these being tall and far apart. This paper was chiefly used for long fiscal stamps.

Normal

8c. No dot at lower left (R. 2/5)

1880 (Jan)–**82**. Wmk Crown CC (reversed on 8c.). P 14.

5	1	2c. yellow-green	32·00	55·00
		w. Wmk inverted	£170	
		x. Wmk reversed	60·00	80·00
		y. Wmk inverted and reversed	£130	£140
6		6c. orange-brown	£140	£150
		a. No dot at upper left	£325	£350
		w. Wmk inverted	£325	£350
7		8c. carmine (4.82)	£130	£130
		a. No dot at lower left	£325	£325
		x. Wmk normal (not reversed)	£375	£375
		y. Wmk inverted and reversed	†	£450
8		10c. brown	£200	£100
		w. Wmk inverted	£160	£130
		x. Wmk reversed		
9		12c. carmine	£300	£400
		a. No right foot to second Chinese character	£600	£750
		w. Wmk inverted	£550	
		x. Wmk reversed	£375	£400
		y. Wmk inverted and reversed	£600	
10		16c. blue (1881)	£100	£130
		w. Wmk inverted	£225	£275
		x. Wmk reversed	£170	£200
		y. Wmk inverted and reversed	£325	£375
5/10 *Set of 6*			£750	£850

1880 (Aug).

(a) No. 9 surch with T **2** *in black and with the original value obliterated by manuscript bar in red or black*

11		8c. on 12c. carmine	£1800	£850
		a. Type **2** inverted	£2000	£1000
		b. '12' not obliterated	£3500	£1800
		c. As b. with Type **2** inverted	£4000	
		d. No right foot to second Chinese character	£3750	£1700
		x. Wmk reversed	£2000	£850

(b) No. 4 surch with two upright figures and No. 9 surch with two at right angles as T **3**

12		6c. on 16c. blue (R.)	£4000	£1300
		a. With one '6' only		
13		8c. on 12c. carmine	£2250	£1200
		a. Both '8's' upright	—	£1500
		b. Upright '8' inverted	£2250	£1300
		c. No right foot to second Chinese character	£4000	£2000
		w. Wmk inverted	†	£2000
		x. Wmk reversed	£2250	£1200
		y. Wmk inverted and reversed		

EIGHT CENTS (4) Eight Cents (5) (6)

1881 (Mar). No. 9 handstamped with T **4**.

14		8c. on 12c. carmine	£475	£500
		a. No right foot to second Chinese character	£1100	£1100
		w. Wmk inverted	£700	
		x. Wmk reversed	£425	£450

1881 (June). No. 9 surch with T **5**.

15		8c. on 12c. carmine	£150	£160
		a. Surch double	£2750	£2250
		b. Surch inverted	£12000	
		c. 'Eighr'	£20000	
		d. No right foot to second Chinese character	£325	£375
		w. Wmk inverted	£400	£400
		x. Wmk reversed	£150	£160

The error 'Eighr' occurred on R. 2/1 of the first printing, but was soon corrected.

Only one sheet of ten existed of No. 15b, which also shows wmk inverted and reversed.

1883. Wmk Crown CA (reversed on 8c.). P 14.

17	1	2c. yellow-green	30·00	55·00
		a. Imperf between (horiz pair)	£18000	
		w. Wmk inverted	90·00	
		x. Wmk reversed	32·00	60·00
		y. Wmk inverted and reversed	£130	
18		8c. carmine	£325	£110
		a. No dot at lower left	£650	£250
		x. Wmk normal (not reversed)	—	£300
19		10c. yellow-brown	60·00	55·00
		w. Wmk inverted	£110	£110
		x. Wmk reversed	£110	£110
20		16c. blue	£100	£200
21		40c. amber	30·00	£140
		x. Wmk reversed	35·00	£120
17/21 *Set of 5*			£475	£475

1883 (May). No. 10 surch 'One Dollar A.S.H.' by hand as T **6**.

22	1	$1 on 16c. blue (R.)	£4500	

The initials are those of the postmaster, Mr. A. S. Hamilton.

2 CENTS (7) 2 Cents (8) 2 Cents (9)

1885 (June). Nos. 18 and 10 handstamped as T **7**.

23	1	2c. on 8c. carmine	£225	£550
		a. No dot at lower left	£450	
		x. Wmk normal (not reversed)	£400	
24		2c. on 16c. blue	£950	£900
		w. Wmk inverted	£1100	
		x. Wmk reversed	£1200	£900
		y. Wmk inverted and reversed	£1100	

No. 23 is known with handstamped surcharge applied diagonally rather than horizontally, and also with surcharge double.

1885 (July). No. 20 surch as T **8**.

25	1	2c. on 16c. blue	£110	£160
		a. Surch double	†	£7000
		b. '2' inserted	£1800	
		w. Wmk inverted		

No. 25b shows a second '2' applied by a separate handstamp to correct indistinct impressions of T **8**.

1885 (Sept). No. 18 handstamped diag as T **9**.

26	1	2c. on 8c. carmine	80·00	£130
		a. No dot at lower left	£180	£325
		x. Wmk normal (not reversed)	£225	

1885 (Sept)–**86**. Wmk Crown CA. P 14.

30	1	2c. rose-red	4·00	19·00
		a. Pale rose-red (1886)	4·50	17·00
		w. Wmk inverted	95·00	
		x. Wmk reversed	17·00	
		xs. Ditto, optd 'SPECIMEN'	£200	
31		8c. deep violet	50·00	9·00
		a. No dot at lower left	£110	24·00
		bxs. Wmk reversed, optd 'SPECIMEN'	£200	
		c. Mauve (1886)	48·00	13·00
		ca. No dot at lower left	£100	28·00
		cw. Wmk inverted	£130	
		cx. Wmk reversed	90·00	
32		10c. sepia (1886)	40·00	70·00
		w. Wmk inverted	80·00	
		x. Wmk reversed	45·00	
33		16c. grey (1886)	£170	
		x. Wmk reversed	£120	£180
30/33x *Set of 4*			£180	£250
30s/33s Optd 'SPECIMEN' *Set of 4*			£550	

ISSUES OF BRITISH NORTH BORNEO COMPANY

From 1 January 1890 while remaining a Crown Colony, the administration of Labuan was transferred to the British North Borneo Co, which issued the following stamps.

6 Cents (10) Two CENTS (11) Six CENTS (12)

1891 (July)–**92**. Handstamped with T **10**.

34	1	6c. on 8c. deep violet (No. 31)	£225	£200
		a. Surch inverted	£300	£275
		b. Surch double	£600	
		c. Surch double, one inverted	£1000	
		d. 'Cents' omitted	£475	£500
		da. Surch inverted with 'Cents' omitted	£600	
		f. Pair, one without surch, one surch inverted	£2000	
		g. No dot at lower left	£450	£425
35		6c. on 8c. mauve (No. 31c)	16·00	16·00
		a. Surch inverted	80·00	75·00
		b. Surch double, one inverted	£900	
		c. Surch double, both inverted	£900	
		d. '6' omitted	£600	
		e. Pair, one without surcharge	£2000	£2000
		f. 'Cents' omitted	—	£550
		fa. Surch inverted with 'Cents' omitted	£550	
		g. Pair, one without surch, one surch inverted	£2250	£2250
		h. Surch double	£350	
		i. No dot at lower left	38·00	35·00
		j. Imperf between (horiz pair)	£18000	
		w. Wmk inverted	90·00	90·00
		x. Wmk reversed	45·00	
36		6c. on 8c. mauve (R.) (No. 31c) (2.92)	£1500	£850
		a. Surch inverted	£1800	£1000
		b. No dot at lower left	£3000	
37		6c. on 16c. blue (No. 4) (3.92)	£2750	£2500
		a. Surch inverted	£15000	£8000
38		6c. on 40c. amber (No. 21)	£14000	£5000
		a. Surch inverted	£12000	£8000

There are two different versions of T **10** with the lines of the surcharge either 1 mm or 2 mm apart.

Normal

10c. Missing stroke at left of third Chinese character (R. 2/3)

Normal

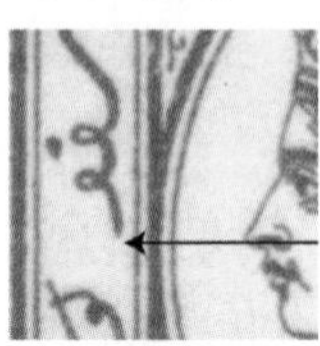
10c. Short tail to upper Jawi character (R. 4/4)

Normal

10c. 'Stolen jewel' (R. 1/1)

2c. Scar over eyebrow (R. 4/1)

(Recess D.L.R.)

1892–93. No wmk. P 14.

39 **1** 2c. rose-lake 6·50 3·50
a. Scar over eyebrow 30·00 20·00
40 6c. bright green 14·00 4·50
a. No dot at upper left 30·00 15·00
41 8c. violet 13·00 19·00
a. Pale violet (1893) 9·00 19·00
43 10c. brown 32·00 8·00
a. Sepia-brown (1893) 26·00 19·00
b. Missing stroke to Chinese character £110 35·00
c. Short tail to Jawi character £110 35·00
d. 'Stolen jewel' £110 35·00
45 12c. bright blue 15·00 6·50
a. No right foot to second Chinese character 30·00 18·00
46 16c. grey 15·00 18·00
47 40c. ochre 23·00 45·00
a. Brown-buff (1893) 50·00 25·00
39/47 *Set of 7* £100 75·00

The 6c., 12c., 16c. and 40c. are in sheets of ten, as are all the earlier issues. The other values are in sheets of 30.

1892 (Dec). Nos. 47 and 46 surch locally as Types **11** or **12**.

49 **1** 2c. on 40c. ochre (13.12) £170 £100
a. Surch inverted £450 £600
50 6c. on 16c. grey (20.12) £375 £150
a. Surch inverted £550 £300
b. Surch sideways £550 £300
c. Surch 'Six Cents' £1900

There are ten slightly different versions of each of these surcharges which were applied in settings of 5×2, although instances of single handstamps are known.

A 'SIX CENTS' handstamp with Roman 'I' in 'SIX' (without dot) is a clandestine surcharge, although it can be found with genuine postmarks. It also exists sideways or inverted.

The 'Six Cents' surcharge of No. 50c was handstamped onto examples where the T **12** surcharge had failed to print or where it was partially or completely albino.

CANCELLED-TO-ORDER. Prices are separately indicated, in a third price column, for stamps showing the recognisable black bars remainder cancellation. Earlier issues of the Company administration were also so treated, but, as similar postal cancellations were used, these cannot be identified.

(Litho D.L.R.)

1894 (Apr). No wmk. P 14.

51 **1** 2c. carmine-pink 2·00 18·00 50
52 6c. bright green 28·00 65·00 50
a. Imperf between (horiz pair) £11000
b. No dot at upper left 55·00 £140 1·25
53 8c. bright mauve 29·00 70·00 50
54 10c. brown 55·00 90·00 50
a. Missing stroke to Chinese character £200 — 4·00
b. Short tail to Jawi character £200 — 4·00
c. 'Stolen jewel' £200 — 4·00
55 12c. pale blue 38·00 £110 70
a. No right foot to second Chinese character 70·00 £250 2·00
56 16c. grey 40·00 £190 50
57 40c. orange-buff 60·00 £225 50
51/57 *Set of 7* £225 £700 3·25
51s/57s H/S 'SPECIMEN' *Set of 7* £130

Collectors are warned against forgeries of this issue.

PERFORATION. There are a number of small variations in the perforation of the Waterlow issues of 1894 to 1905 which we believe to be due to irregularity of the pins rather than different perforators.

In the following lists, stamps perf 12, 12½, 13 or compound are described as perf 12–13, stamps perf 13½, 14 or compound are described as perf 13½–14 and those perf 14½, 15 or compound are listed as perf 14½–15. In addition the 13½–14 perforation exists compound with 14½–15 and with 12–13, whilst perf 16 comes from a separate perforator.

13

LABUAN
40
CENTS
(14)

1894 (May)–**96**. Types **24/32** of North Borneo (colours changed), with 'LABUAN' engraved on vignette plate as T **13** (8, 12, 24c.) or horizontally (others). P 14½–15.

(a) Name and central part of design in black

62 **24** 1c. grey-mauve 1·50 14·00 50
a. Imperf between (vert pair) † † £650
b. Perf 13½–14 17·00 10·00 —
ba. Imperf between (vert pair) £1200 — £500
c. Perf 13½–14, comp 14½–15 40·00
d. Perf 13½–14, comp 12–13 42·00 17·00 1·00
e. Perf 12–13
63 **25** 2c. blue 2·50 15·00 50
a. Imperf (pair) £600
b. Perf 13½–14 9·00 15·00 —
c. Perf 13½–14, comp 14½–15 42·00
d. Perf 13½–14, comp 12–13
e. Perf 12–13 £190
64 **26** 3c. ochre 3·75 25·00 50
a. Perf 13½–14 18·00 9·00 —
b. Perf 13½–14, comp 14½–15
c. Perf 13½–14, comp 12–13 50·00
d. Perf 12–13
65 **27** 5c. green 32·00 45·00 1·25
a. Perf 13½–14 50·00 25·00 —
ab. Imperf between (horiz pair) £1500
b. Perf 13½–14, comp 12–13 65·00
c. Perf 12–13 £225
67 **28** 6c. brown-lake 2·50 24·00 50
a. Imperf (pair) £600 † £300
b. Perf 13½–14 — — 3·00
c. Perf 13½–14, comp 14½–15 — — 2·50
d. Perf 13½–14, comp 12–13
e. Perf 12–13
68 **29** 8c. rose-red 35·00 45·00 2·25
a. Perf 13½–14 45·00 55·00 —
69 8c. pink (1896) 12·00 35·00 50
a. Perf 13½–14 48·00 32·00 1·00
70 **30** 12c. orange-vermilion 23·00 55·00 50
a. Imperf between (vert pair) † † £3250
b. Perf 13½–14 65·00 90·00 3·00
c. Perf 12–13 £250
d. Perf 13½–14, comp 12–13 80·00 £110 —
71 **31** 18c. olive-brown 28·00 60·00 50
a. Perf 13½–14 70·00
72 18c. olive-bistre (1896) 55·00 75·00 50
a. Perf 13½–14 27·00 70·00 —
b. Perf 13½–14, comp 12–13
c. Imperf between (vert pair) † † £2000
d. Perf 13½–14, comp 14½–15 † † 2·25

(b) Name and central part in blue

73 **32** 24c. pale mauve 42·00 65·00 50
a. Perf 13½–14 42·00 65·00 —
b. Perf 13½–14 comp 14½–15
74 24c. dull lilac (1896) 23·00 55·00 1·25
a. Perf 13½–14 22·00 55·00 1·25
62/74 *Set of 9* £110 £250 4·50
62s/74s Optd 'SPECIMEN' *Set of 9* £160

1895 (June). No. 83 of North Borneo ($1 inscr 'STATE OF NORTH BORNEO') surch as T **14**.

75 **32c** 4c. on $1 scarlet 5·00 5·50 40
76 10c. on $1 scarlet 11·00 1·40 40
77 20c. on $1 scarlet 50·00 14·00 50
78 30c. on $1 scarlet 55·00 65·00 1·50
79 40c. on $1 scarlet 55·00 55·00 1·50
75/79 *Set of 5* £160 £120 3·75
75s/79s Optd 'SPECIMEN' *Set of 5* 80·00

No. 76 exists with the figures of the surcharge 2½ mm away from 'CENTS'. The normal setting has a space of 4 mm. Examples of the narrow setting have, so far, only been seen on cancelled-to-order stamps (*Price £20 c.t.o.*).

LABUAN
(15)

1846
JUBILEE
1896
(16)

4
CENTS
(17)

1896. Types **32a** to **32c** of North Borneo (as Nos. 81 to 83, but colours changed) optd with T **15**.

80 25c. green 42·00 50·00 60
a. Opt omitted 35·00 — 2·00
b. Imperf (pair) — — 60·00
ba. Opt omitted 50·00
81 50c. maroon 42·00 50·00 60
a. Opt omitted 32·00 — 2·00
b. Imperf (pair) — — 60·00
ba. Opt omitted 50·00
82 $1 blue 80·00 75·00 1·25
a. Opt omitted 48·00 — 2·75
b. Imperf (pair) — — 60·00
ba. Opt omitted 55·00
80s/82s Optd 'SPECIMEN' *Set of 3* 70·00

Nos. 80/81 showing stamps either printed double or double, one inverted, are from waste sheets subsequently sold by the British North Borneo Company to collectors.

1896 (24 Sept). Jubilee of Cession of Labuan to Gt Britain. Nos. 62 to 68 optd with T **16**. P 14½–15.

83 1c. black and grey-mauve 25·00 25·00 1·75
b. Opt in orange £200 £200 20·00
c. 'JEBILEE' (R. 8/7) £1200 £650 £300
d. 'JUBILE' (R. 3/10) £2750
e. Perf 13½–14 35·00 26·00 —
ea. Opt double £375 £375 —
eb. Opt in orange £325 £200 †
f. Perf 13½–14, comp 12–13 48·00 23·00 —
fa. Opt in orange — £200 †
fb. Opt double £475 £475
g. Perf 12–13
84 2c. black and blue 50·00 35·00 1·75
a. Imperf horiz (vert pair) £1500 £1600 †
b. 'JEBILEE' (R. 8/7) £1800 £1200 —
c. 'JUBILE' (R. 3/10) £3000 £3000
d. Perf 13½–14 50·00 24·00 —
e. Perf 13½–14, comp 14½–15 — 45·00 —
f. Perf 13½–14 comp 12–13 60·00
85 3c. black and ochre 50·00 22·00 1·50
a. 'JEBILEE' (R. 8/7) £2000 £1700 £700
b. 'JUBILE' (R. 3/10)
d. Perf 13½–14 55·00 35·00 1·50
da. Opt double — — £150
db. Opt treble £650
e. Perf 13½–14, comp 14½–15
f. Perf 13½–14, comp 12–13
fa. Opt double £375 £375 £160
fb. Opt treble £650
86 5c. black and green 70·00 16·00 1·50
a. Opt double £950 £700 —
b. Perf 13½–14 70·00 22·00 1·50
c. Perf 13½–14, comp 12–13 95·00
d. Perf 13½–14, comp 14½–15 — — 3·50
87 6c. black and brown-lake 48·00 35·00 80
a. Opt double £850 £650 †
b. 'JEBILEE' (R.8/7) † † £2750
c. 'JUBILE' (R. 3/10) £3500 — £2750
d. Perf 13½–14, comp 14½–15
e. Perf 13½–14 — £100 —
88 8c. black and pink 55·00 18·00 80
a. Opt double † £3500 †
b. Perf 13½–14 55·00 15·00 1·00
c. Perf 13½–14, comp 14½–15 55·00 22·00 —
83/88 *Set of 6* £250 £110 7·25
83s/88s Optd 'SPECIMEN' *Set of 6* £150

The normal overprint on the 1c. varies in appearance from pure black to brownish black due to a mixing of the inks. The orange overprint on this value is in a clear, bright, unadulterated ink.

No. 84b is known in a vertical strip of three imperf horizontally except at the base of the bottom stamp (*Price £7500 unused*).

Nos. 87b and 87c are known with additional 'SPECIMEN' overprint. (*Price £2000 each*).

1897 (Apr)–**1901**. Types **34/45** of North Borneo (colours changed), with 'LABUAN' engraved on vignette plate as T **13** (8, 12, 24c.) or horizontally (others). Name and central part in black (24c. in blue). P 13½–14.

89 **34** 1c. dull claret (P 14½–15) 8·00 4·75 50
a. Perf 13½–14, comp 14½–15
ab. Perf 16 — — 2·00
b. Brown (1901) 26·00 29·00 65
ba. Perf 14½–15 3·00
bb. Perf 16 24·00 21·00 —
90 **35** 2c. blue 28·00 6·00 65
a. Imperf between (vert pair) † † £1100
b. Imperf between (horiz pair) † † £1500
c. Perf 14½–15 38·00 — 1·00
d. Perf 13½–14, comp 12–13 60·00 25·00 —
e. Perf 16 — — 7·00
91 **36** 3c. ochre 9·00 32·00 50
a. Imperf between (vert pair) £1300 † £650
b. Perf 14½–15 9·00 7·00 50
c. Perf 13½–14, comp 12–13 22·00 50·00 2·50
d. Perf 12–13 £100
92 **38** 5c. green 70·00 60·00 70
a. Perf 14½–15 65·00 60·00 70
b. Perf 13½–14, comp 12–13
93 **39** 6c. brown-lake 6·50 50·00 1·50
b. Perf 14½–15 15·00 21·00 50
ba. Imperf between (vert pair) † † £750
c. Perf 13½–14, comp 12–13 — — 8·00
94 **40** 8c. rose-red 55·00 — 1·00
a. Perf 14½–15 28·00 12·00 —
b. Perf 13½–14, comp 12–13 55·00 — 3·00
c. Vermilion 12·00 — 75
ca. Perf 16 — — 7·00
95 **42** 12c. vermilion £150 £170 3·00
a. Perf 14½–15 32·00 55·00 2·50
96 **44** 18c. olive-bistre £140 £140 2·25
a. Perf 16 12·00 45·00 50
ab. Imperf between (vert pair) † † £3250
97 **45** 24c. grey-lilac 60·00 £120 2·25
a. Perf 14½–15 12·00 55·00 50
89/97a *Set of 9* £160 £225 6·50
89s/97s Optd 'SPECIMEN' *Set of 9* £180

The 12, 18 and 24c. above were errors; in the 12c., 'LABUAN' is over the value at the top; the 18c. has 'POSTAL REVENUE' instead of 'POSTAGE & REVENUE', and the 24c. is without 'POSTAGE & REVENUE'.

1897 (Nov)–**98**.

(a) Types of North Borneo (colours changed), with 'LABUAN' engraved on the vignette plate as in T **13**. *P 13½–14*

98 **42** 12c. black and vermilion (3.98) † — 3·75
a. Perf 14½–15 55·00 55·00 —
b. Perf 13½–14, comp 14½–15
c. Perf 16 85·00 85·00 —
99 **46** 18c. black and olive-bistre
a. Perf 14½–15 95·00 60·00 2·00
b. Perf 13½–14, comp 12–13 £150
c. Perf 16 † — 10·00
100 **47** 24c. blue and lilac-brown 60·00 70·00 2·00
a. Perf 14½–15 50·00 60·00 —
b. Perf 13½–14, comp 12–13 — 70·00 —
c. Perf 16 60·00 60·00
d. Blue and ochre (P 14½–15) — — 5·00

In the 12c. 'LABUAN' is now correctly placed at foot of stamp. The 18c. and 24c. have the inscriptions on the stamps corrected, but the 18c. still has 'LABUAN' *over* the value at foot, and was further corrected as follows.

(b) As No. 99, but 'LABUAN' at top

101 **46** 18c. black and olive-bistre (3.98) 70·00 60·00 —
a. Perf 14½–15 42·00 75·00 3·50
b. Perf 13½–14, comp 12–13 55·00 60·00 —
c. Perf 12–13
98s, 100s/101as Optd 'SPECIMEN' *Set of 3* 70·00

1899 (July). Surch with T **17**.

(a) P 14½–15

102 **38** 4c. on 5c. (No. 92a) 60·00 26·00

103	39	4c. on 6c. (No. 93b)	32·00	19·00	
		a. Perf 13½–14	45·00	40·00	
		b. Perf 13½–14 comp 12–13	55·00	65·00	
104	40	4c. on 8c. (No. 94a)	65·00	50·00	
		a. Perf 13½–14	50·00	38·00	
		b. Perf 13½–14, comp 12–13	40·00	50·00	
		c. Perf 12–13			
105	42	4c. on 12c. (No. 98a)	65·00	35·00	
		a. Perf 13½–14	65·00	45·00	
		b. Perf 16	65·00	42·00	
		c. Perf 13½–14, comp 12–13	75·00	80·00	
106	46	4c. on 18c. (No. 101a)	40·00	18·00	
		a. Surch double	£550	£650	
107	47	4c. on 24c. (No. 100a)	42·00	38·00	
		a. Perf 13½–14	27·00	25·00	
		b. Perf 13½–14, comp 12–13	50·00	30·00	
		c. Perf 16	55·00	55·00	
		(b) P 14			
108	32a	4c. on 25c. (No. 80)	6·00	7·50	
109	32b	4c. on 50c. (No. 81)	8·50	7·50	
110	32c	4c. on $1 (No. 82)	8·50	7·50	
102/110 *Set of 9*			£250	£160	
102s/110s Optd 'SPECIMEN' *Set of 9*			£170		

A new setting of the surcharge with closer spacing (2½ *mm*) between '4' and 'CENTS' was used for the Specimen overprints, including unissued surcharges on the 1c., 2c. and 3c. values (*Price £140 for the set of 3*).

1900–02. Types of North Borneo with 'LABUAN' engraved on the vignette plate as in T **13** (10, 16c,) or horizontally (others), in brown on 10c. and in green on 16c. P 13½–14.

111	35	2c. black and green	3·75	2·50	30
		a. Imperf between (horiz pair)	£3000	†	£1500
		b. Perf 13½–14, comp 12–13			
112	37	4c. black and yellow-brown	8·50	75·00	60
		a. Imperf between (vert pair)	£1400		
		b. Perf 13½–14, comp 12–13	55·00		
113		4c. black and carmine (8.1900)	26·00	3·50	75
		a. Perf 14½–15	5·00	18·00	50
		b. Perf 13½–14, comp 12–13	50·00	13·00	1·50
		c. Perf 16			
114	38	5c. black and pale blue	20·00	23·00	65
		a. Perf 13½–14, comp 12–13	—	95·00	—
		b. Perf 12–13	£250		
115	41	10c. brown and slate-lilac (P 14½–15) (1902)	60·00	£100	60
116	43	16c. green and chestnut (1902)	50·00	£140	2·50
		a. Perf 13½–14, comp 12–13	£110	£170	—
		b. Perf 12–13	£475		
		c. Perf 14½–15	£200		
		sa. Opt 'SPECIMEN', double, one albino	£250		
111/116 *Set of 6*			£130	£300	4·75
111s/116s Optd 'SPECIMEN' *Set of 6*			£180		

No. 112 was printed in an incorrect frame colour and was not issued for postal purposes in Labuan. Used examples come from dealers' stock sent to the island for cancellation.

18

Line through 'B' (R. 5/10)

(Recess Waterlow)

1902 (Sept)–**03.** P 13½–14.

117	18	1c. black and purple (10.03)	7·50	7·00	50
		a. Perf 14½–15	£100	9·00	—
		b. Perf 13½–14 comp 12–13	90·00	50·00	
		c. Line through 'B'	£120	£130	12·00
118		2c. black and green	4·50	6·50	30
		a. Perf 14½–15	£120	5·50	—
		b. Perf 13½–14, comp 12–13	£120	55·00	
		c. Line through 'B'	95·00	£120	12·00
119		3c. black and sepia (10.03)	3·25	23·00	30
		a. Line through 'B'	90·00	£200	12·00
120		4c. black and carmine	3·25	4·00	30
		a. Perf 14½–15	12·00	19·00	—
		b. Perf 13½–14 comp 12–13	80·00	50·00	—
		c. Line through 'B'	90·00	£100	12·00
121		8c. black and vermilion	14·00	9·00	75
		a. Perf 14½–15	8·00		
		b. Line through 'B'	£130	£140	13·00
122		10c. brown and slate-blue	3·25	19·00	30
		b. Perf 14½–15	12·00	19·00	50
		ba. Imperf between (vert pair)	†	†	£1000
		c. Line through 'B'	£100	£190	12·00
123		12c. black and yellow	16·00	26·00	30
		a. Imperf between (vert strip of 3)	†	†	£3500
		b. Perf 16	17·00	26·00	50
		c. Line through 'B'	£160	£250	12·00
124		16c. green and brown	4·75	38·00	30
		a. Imperf between (vert pair)	†	†	£2000
		b. Line through 'B'	£120	£350	12·00
125		18c. black and pale brown	3·25	38·00	30
		a. Line through 'B'	95·00	£350	12·00
126		25c. green and greenish blue	7·50	29·00	50
		a. Perf 14½–15	15·00	50·00	1·00
		b. Error. Black and greenish blue	—	†	£600
		c. Line through 'B'	£150	£300	13·00
127		50c. dull purple and lilac	11·00	50·00	2·75
		a. Perf 13½–14 comp 12–13	16·00	60·00	—
		b. Line through 'B'	£200	£550	27·00
128		$1 claret and orange	10·00	50·00	2·50
		a. Perf 14½–15	10·00	—	2·25
		b. Line through 'B'	£200	£550	27·00
117/128 *Set of 12*			65·00	£275	8·00
117s/128s Optd 'SPECIMEN' *Set of 12*			£200		

4
cents
(19)

1904 (Dec). Issues of 1896, 1897–1898 and 1897/1901 surch with T **19**.

		(a) P 14½–15			
129	38	4c. on 5c. (No. 92a)	55·00	50·00	14·00
130	39	4c. on 6c. (No. 93b)	12·00	50·00	14·00
131	40	4c. on 8c. (No. 94a)	25·00	55·00	14·00
132	42	4c. on 12c. (No. 98a)	50·00	50·00	14·00
		a. Perf 16	50·00	50·00	—
133	46	4c. on 18c. (No. 101) (P 13½–14)	23·00	50·00	14·00
		a. Perf 13½–14, comp 12–13	45·00	50·00	—
		b. Perf 12–13			
134	47	4c. on 24c. (No. 100a)	16·00	50·00	14·00
		a. Perf 13½–14	42·00	42·00	—
		b. Perf 13½–14, comp 12–13	50·00	50·00	—
		c. Perf 16	38·00	50·00	14·00
		(b) P 14			
135	32a	4c. on 25c . (No. 80)	8·50	40·00	14·00
136	32b	4c. on 50c. (No. 81)	8·50	40·00	14·00
		a. Surch double	£375		
137	32c	4c. on $1 (No. 82)	13·00	40·00	14·00
129/137 *Set of 9*			£170	£350	£110

No. 136a usually shows one complete surcharge and parts of two further surcharges due to the position of the misplaced second impression.

The barred cancels can be found used on 'philatelic' covers of this issue.

LABUAN (20) **LABUAN** (21)

1901 (?)–**05.** Nos. 81, 83 (in Labuan colour), and 84/86 of North Borneo optd locally with T **20** (25c. $2) or T **21** (others).

138	32a	25c. indigo (2.05)	£1200	†	£900
		a. Opt double	—	†	†
139	32c	$1 blue (2.05)	†	†	£1000
140	32d	$2 dull green	£3500	£3750	—
141	32e	$5 bright purple	£6000	†	£1800
		a. Dull purple	£6000	£7500	—
142	32f	$10 brown	£60000	†	£15000

Dangerous forgeries exist.

The overprint on No. 140 is 12 mm long.

POSTAGE DUE STAMPS

POSTAGE DUE
(D 1)

1901. Optd with T D **1**, reading vertically upwards. P 13½–14.

D1	35	2c. black and green (111)	28·00	45·00	50
		a. Opt double	£275		
		b. Perf 13½–14, comp 12–13	£130	£150	11·00
D2	36	3c. black and ochre (91)	38·00	£130	1·00
		a. Perf 13½–14, comp 12–13	£120	—	4·00
D3	37	4c. black and carmine (113)	60·00	—	3·00
		a. Opt double	†	†	£850
		b. Perf 14½–15	50·00	£110	50
D4	38	5c. black and pale blue (114)	55·00	£170	1·75
		a. Perf 14½–15	—	—	2·25
		b. Perf 13½–14, comp 12–13	£130	£325	—
D5	39	6c. black and brown-lake (93)	45·00	£120	1·00
		a. Perf 14½–15	60·00	£140	—
		b. Perf 16	95·00	—	1·75
D6	40	8c. black and vermilion (94c)	£120	£130	2·75
		b. Perf 14½–15	£100	£160	85
		ba. Frame inverted	†	†	£8500
		c. Perf 16	£110	£120	—
		d. Black and rose-red (94)	95·00	£140	—
		da. Perf 14½–15	£150	—	9·00
		db. Perf 13½–14, comp 12–13	£160		
D7	42	12c. black and vermilion (98)	£170	—	6·50
		a. Opt reading downwards	†	†	£1300
		b. Perf 14½–15	£120	£170	14·00
D8	46	18c. black and olive-bistre (101) (P 14½–15)	42·00	£140	1·75
D9	47	24c. blue and lilac-brown (100)	80·00	£180	7·50
		a. Perf 13½–14, comp 12–13	£110		
		b. Perf 14½–15	65·00		
		ba. Blue and ochre	£100	—	2·25
		c. Perf 16	65·00	£130	—
		d. Opt double, one albino	£225		
D1/D9 *Set of 9*			£450	£1000	14·00

No. D6ba only exists cancelled-to-order.

The administration of Labuan reverted to Colonial Office control, as part of an agreement with Brunei on 1 January 1906. By Letters Patent dated 30 October 1906 Labuan was incorporated with Straits Settlements and ceased issuing its own stamps. In 1946 it became part of the Colony of North Borneo.

JAPANESE OCCUPATION OF NORTH BORNEO

Japanese forces landed in Northern Borneo on 15 December 1941 and the whole of North Borneo had been occupied by 19 January 1942.

Brunei, North Borneo, Sarawak and, after a short period, Labuan, were administered as a single territory by the Japanese. Until 12 December 1942, previous stamp issues, without overprint, continued to be used in conjunction with existing postmarks. From November 1942 onwards unoverprinted stamps of Japan were made available and examples can be found used from the area for much of the remainder of the War. Japanese Occupation issues for Brunei, North Borneo and Sarawak were equally valid throughout the combined territory but not, in practice, equally available.

PRICES FOR STAMPS ON COVER TO 1945	
Nos. J1/J17	*from* × 5
Nos. J18/J19	*from* × 6
Nos. J20/J32	*from* × 25
Nos. J33/J34	*from* × 2
Nos. J35/J48	*from* × 12

府政國本日大
(1)

2 Mt. Kinabalu

3 Borneo Scene

1942 (30 Sept). Stamps of North Borneo handstamped with T **1**.

	(a) In violet on Nos. 303/317		
J1	1c. green and red-brown	£180	£250
	a. Black opt	£400	£200
	ab. Pair, one without opt	£6000	
J2	2c. purple and greenish blue	£200	£275
	a. Black opt	£650	£300
J3	3c. slate-blue and green	£170	£300
	a. Black opt	£700	£375
J4	4c. bronze-green and violet	£300	£375
	a. Black opt	65·00	£140
J5	6c. deep blue and claret	£190	£350
	a. Black opt	£700	£450
J6	8c. scarlet	£250	£200
	a. Pair, one without opt	£6000	
	b. Black opt	£325	£200
J7	10c. violet and bronze-green	£225	£350
	a. Black opt	£650	£400
J8	12c. green and bright blue	£250	£500
	a. Black opt	£1000	£550
J9	15c. blue-green and brown	£225	£500
	a. Pair, one without opt	£6000	
	b. Black opt	£1100	£550
J10	20c. violet and slate-blue	£325	£650
	a. Black opt	£1300	£800
J11	25c. green and chocolate	£300	£650
	a. Black opt	£1300	£800
J12	50c. chocolate and violet	£350	£700
	a. Black opt	£1500	£900
J13	$1 brown and carmine	£425	£900
	a. Black opt	£1700	£1300
J14	$2 violet and olive-green	£600	£1100
	a. Pair, one without opt	£8000	
	b. Black opt	£2750	£1500
J15	$5 indigo and pale blue	£700	£1200
	a. Black opt	£3500	£2250
	(b) In black on Nos. 318/319 ('WAR TAX')		
J16	1c. green and red-brown	£700	£325
	a. Pair, one without opt	†	£6000
	b. Violet opt	—	£1200
J17	2c. purple and greenish blue	£2000	£650
	a. Pair, one without opt	†	£9000
	b. Violet opt	—	£1500

(Litho Kolff & Co., Batavia)

1943 (29 Apr). P 12½.

J18	2	4c. red	32·00	60·00
J19	3	8c. blue	28·00	55·00

本日大
便郵國帝
オネルボ北
(4)

本日大
便郵國帝
貳
弗
(5)

('Imperial Japanese Postal Service North Borneo')

1944 (30 Sept). Nos. 303/315 of North Borneo optd with T **4** at Chinese Press, Kuching.

J20	1c. green and red-brown	8·00	12·00
	a. Ant trail		
J21	2c. purple and greenish blue	8·00	9·00
	a. Optd on No. J2	£450	
J22	3c. slate-blue and green	8·00	10·00
	a. Optd on No. J3	£450	

J23 4c. bronze-green and violet 17·00 25·00
J24 6c. deep blue and claret 11·00 6·50
J25 8c. scarlet 10·00 17·00
a. Optd on No. J6 £450
J26 10c. violet and bronze-green 8·50 13·00
a. Optd on No. J7 £450
b. Optd on No. J7a £250 £475
J27 12c. green and bright blue 17·00 13·00
a. Optd on No. J8 £450
J28 15c. blue-green and brown 17·00 16·00
a. Optd on No. J9 £450
J29 20c. violet and slate-blue 40·00 50·00
a. Optd on No. J10 £3750
J30 25c. green and chocolate 40·00 50·00
a. Optd on No. J11 £3750
J31 50c. chocolate and violet 90·00 £130
a. Optd on No. J12 £4500
J32 $1 brown and carmine £100 £150
J20/J32 *Set of* 13 £325 £450

The spacing between the second and third lines of the overprint is 12 mm on the horizontal stamps, and 15 mm on the upright.

1944 (11 May). No. J1 surch with T **5**.
J33 **81** $2 on 1c green and red-brown £6000 £5000

本 日 大

便 郵 国 帝

(**6**)

7 Girl War-worker

オネルボ北

(**8**) ('North Borneo')

1944 (11 May). North Borneo No. 315 surch with T **6**.
J34 $5 on $1 brown and carmine £5000 £4000
a. Surch on No. J13 £10000 £6000

1944 (2 Oct)–**45**. Contemporary stamps of Japan as T **7** (various subjects) optd with T **8** at Chinese Press, Kuching.
J35 1s. red-brown (No. 391) (1.45) 9·00 42·00
J36 2s. scarlet (No. 392b) (10.44) 7·50 35·00
J37 3s. emerald-green (No. 316) (8.45) 9·00 42·00
J38 4s. yellow-green (No. 395) (10.44) 18·00 28·00
J39 5s. claret (No. 396) (1.45) 15·00 38·00
J40 6s. orange (No. 319) (8.45) 24·00 40·00
a. Opt double, one inverted £650 £650
J41 8s. violet (No. 321) (11.44) 6·50 40·00
a. Opt double £350
J42 10s. carmine and pink (No. 399) (1.45) 15·00 42·00
J43 15s. blue (No. 401) (11.44) 14·00 42·00
J44 20s. blue-slate (No. 325) (11.44) 85·00 90·00
J45 25s. brown and chocolate (No. 326) (2.45) 70·00 90·00
J46 30s. turquoise-blue (No. 327) £180 95·00
J47 50s. olive and bistre (No. 328) (8.45) 80·00 85·00
J48 1y. red-brown and chocolate (No. 329) (5.45) 95·00 £120
J35/J48 *Set of* 14 £550 £700

Designs: 1s. T **7**; 2s. General Nogi; 3s. Hydro-electric Works; 4s. Hyuga Monument and Mt Fuji; 5s. Admiral Togo; 6s. Garambi Lighthouse, Formosa; 8s. Meiji Shrine; 10s. Palms and map of S.E. Asia; 15s. Airman; 20s. Mt Fuji and cherry blossoms; 25s. Horyu Temple; 30s. Torii, Itsukushima Shrine at Miyajima; 50s. Kinkaku Temple; 1y. Great Buddha, Kamakura.

Examples of some values have been found with hand-painted forged overprints.

POSTAGE DUE STAMPS

1942 (30 Sept). Nos. D85/D89 of North Borneo handstamped with T **1** in black.
JD1 **D 2** 2c. brown — £6000
JD2 4c. scarlet — £6000
JD3 6c. violet — £6000
JD4 8c. green — £6000
JD5 10c. blue — £6000

Northern Nigeria *see* Nigeria

Northern Rhodesia

The north-eastern and north-western provinces of Rhodesia, previously administered by the British South Africa Company, became a Crown Colony on 1 April 1924.

The current stamps of Rhodesia (the 'Admiral' design first issued in 1913) remained in use until 31 March 1925 and continued to be valid for postal purposes until 30 September of that year.

PRICES FOR STAMPS ON COVER TO 1945	
Nos. 1/21	*from* × 3
Nos. 22/24	*from* × 6
Nos. 25/45	*from* × 3
Nos. D1/D2	*from* × 30
Nos. D3/D4	*from* × 15

1

2

(Des W. Fairweather. Eng J. A. C. Harrison. Recess Waterlow)

1925 (1 Apr)–**29**. Wmk Mult Script CA. P 12½.
1 **1** ½d. green 1·75 80
2 1d. brown 1·75 10
3 1½d. carmine-red 4·25 30
4 2d. yellow-brown 4·50 10
5 3d. ultramarine 4·50 1·25
6 4d. violet 7·50 50
7 6d. slate-grey 9·00 40
8 8d. rose-purple 9·50 55·00
9 10d. olive-green 9·50 50·00
10 **2** 1s. yellow-brown and black 4·50 1·75
11 2s. brown and ultramarine 30·00 48·00
12 2s.6d. black and green 25·00 15·00
13 3s. violet and blue (1929) 48·00 27·00
14 5s. slate-grey and violet 55·00 19·00
15 7s.6d. rose-purple and black £190 £300
16 10s. green and black £120 £100
17 20s. carmine-red and rose-purple £350 £375
1/17 *Set of* 17 £800 £900
1s/17s Optd or Perf (3s.) 'SPECIMEN' *Set of* 17 £1200

A used example of the 4d. exists imperforate between the stamp and a fragment of another below it.

1935 (6 May). Silver Jubilee. As Nos. 91/94 of Antigua. P 13½×14.
18 1d. light blue and olive-green 1·50 1·50
f. Diagonal line by turret £120 £130
g. Dot to left of chapel £375 £400
h. Dot by flagstaff £275 £300
i. Dash by turret £300 £325
19 2d. green and indigo 3·75 2·75
f. Diagonal line by turret £180 £180
g. Dot to left of chapel £325 £350
20 3d. brown and deep blue 4·75 12·00
f. Diagonal line by turret £275 £375
g. Dot to left of chapel £425 £550
21 6d. slate and purple 12·00 1·75
a. Frame printed double, one albino £3000 £3250
h. Dot by flagstaff £650 £375
18/21 *Set of* 4 20·00 16·00
18s/21s Perf 'SPECIMEN' *Set of* 4 £225

For illustrations of plate varieties see Omnibus section following Zanzibar.

THERN–RHODE

Hyphen between 'NORTHERN' and 'RHODESIA' (R. 9/6)

1937 (12 May). Coronation. As Nos. 95/97 of Antigua. P 11×11½.
22 1½d. carmine 30 50
23 2d. buff 40 1·75
24 3d. blue 60 1·25
a. Hyphen flaw £400
22/24 *Set of* 3 1·10 3·25
22s/24s Perf 'SPECIMEN' *Set of* 3 £180

Fakes of No. 24a exist.

3

4

½d. Re-entry to giraffe (Plate 2, R. 12/2)

1d. 'Extra boatman' (Pl 4 R. 3/2)

1½d. 'Tick bird' flaw (Pl 1 R. 7/1 of ptgs from Sept 1938 onwards)

(Recess Waterlow)

1938 (1 Mar)–**52**. Wmk Mult Script CA. P 12½.
25 **3** ½d. green 10 10
a. 'C' of 'CA' missing from wmk £2250
b. Re-entry to giraffe 85·00 60·00
26 ½d. chocolate (15.11.51) 2·25 1·50
a. Perf 12½×14 (22.10.52) 1·40 6·00
27 1d. brown 20 20
a. Chocolate (1948) 2·00 1·00
ab. 'Extra boatman' £375 £300
28 1d. green (15.11.51) 1·50 2·25
a. 'Extra boatman' £375 £450
29 1½d. carmine-red 50·00 75
a. Imperf between (horiz pair) £30000
b. 'Tick bird' flaw £6500 £450
30 1½d. yellow-brown (10.1.41) 75 10
b. 'Tick bird' flaw £200 70·00
31 2d. yellow-brown 50·00 1·75
32 2d. carmine-red (10.1.41) 1·75 50
33 2d. purple (1.12.51) 60 1·50
34 3d. ultramarine 70 30
35 3d. scarlet (1.12.51) 60 3·00
36 4d. dull violet 40 40
37 4½d. blue (5.5.52) 3·25 12·00
38 6d. grey 40 10
39 9d. violet (5.5.52) 3·25 14·00
40 **4** 1s. yellow-brown and black 4·00 60
41 2s.6d. black and green 16·00 8·00
42 3s. violet and blue 29·00 19·00
43 5s. grey and dull violet 29·00 18·00
44 10s. green and black 30·00 35·00
45 20s. carmine-red and rose-purple 70·00 80·00
25/45 *Set of* 21 £250 £170
25s/45s Perf 'SPECIMEN' *Set of* 15 £750

Nos. 26a and 28 exist in coils, constructed from normal sheets.

1946 (26 Nov). Victory. As Nos. 110/111 of Antigua. P 13½×14.
46 1½d. red-orange 1·00 1·75
a. Perf 13½ 10·00 9·00
47 2d. carmine 10 50
46s/47s Perf 'SPECIMEN' *Set of* 2 £150

The decimal perforation gauge for Nos. 46/47 is 13.7×14.1 and for No. 46a 13.7×13.4.

1948 (1 Dec). Royal Silver Wedding. As Nos. 112/113 of Antigua, but 20s. ptd entirely in recess.
48 1½d. orange 30 10
49 20s. brown-lake £110 £100

1949 (10 Oct). 75th Anniversary of UPU. As Nos. 114/117 of Antigua.
50 2d. carmine 20 1·50
51 3d. deep blue 2·00 3·00
52 6d. grey 2·25 4·25
53 1s. red-orange 75 2·75
50/53 *Set of* 4 4·75 10·50

5 Cecil Rhodes and Victoria Falls

(Recess D.L.R.)

1953 (30 May). Birth Centenary of Cecil Rhodes. Wmk Mult Script CA. P 12×11½.
54 **5** ½d. brown 55 2·25
55 1d. green 45 2·25
56 2d. mauve 1·00 30
57 4½d. blue 45 5·00
58 1s. orange and black 1·50 5·00
54/58 *Set of* 5 3·50 13·00

1953 (30 May). Rhodes Centenary Exhibition. As No. 171 of Nyasaland.
59 **6** 6d. violet 70 1·50

1953 (2 June). Coronation. As No. 120 of Antigua but des and eng B.W. Recess D.L.R.
60 1½d. black and yellow-orange 1·00 20

7

8

(Recess Waterlow)

1953 (15 Sept). Wmk Mult Script CA. P 12½×14 (pence values) or 12½×13½ (shilling values).
61 **7** ½d. deep brown 65 10
62 1d. bluish green 65 10
63 1½d. orange-brown 1·25 10
64 2d. reddish purple 1·25 10
65 3d. scarlet 1·00 10
66 4d. slate-lilac 1·25 2·00
67 4½d. deep blue 1·50 5·50
68 6d. grey-black 1·25 10
w. Wmk inverted £5000 £7000
69 9d. violet 1·25 4·25
70 **8** 1s. orange-brown and black 1·25 10
71 2s.6d. black and green 16·00 8·50
72 5s. grey and dull purple 18·00 15·00
73 10s. green and black 16·00 40·00
74 20s. rose-red and rose-purple 35·00 42·00
61/74 *Set of* 14 85·00 £100

No. 62 is known bisected vertically and endorsed '½d' in red at Mkushi between 17 and 20 November 1953.

For issues from 1954 to 1963, see RHODESIA AND NYASALAND.

9 Arms

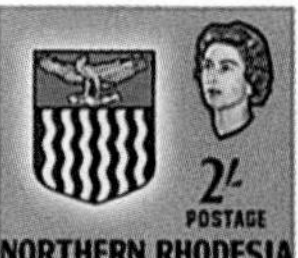

10 Arms

Parting in hair (Right pane, R. 4/11)

(Photo Harrison)

1963 (10 Dec). Arms black, orange and blue; portrait and inscriptions black; background colours below. P 14½ (T **9**) or 13½×13 (T **10**).

No.	Type	Description	Unused	Used
75	**9**	½d. bright violet	70	1·25
		a. Value omitted	£1200	
		b. Orange (eagle) omitted	£1400	
		c. Parting in hair		
76		1d. light blue	1·50	10
		a. Value omitted	6·00	£100
77		2d. brown	70	10
		c. Parting in hair	50·00	
78		3d. yellow	1·25	10
		a. Value omitted	£120	
		b. Value and orange (eagle) omitted	£250	£1000
		c. Eagle printed double	£4500	
		d. Orange (eagle) omitted	£1200	
79		4d. green	1·00	30
		a. Value omitted	£130	£500
		c. Parting in hair	55·00	
80		6d. light olive-green	1·25	10
		a. Value omitted	£850	
		c. Parting in hair	55·00	
81		9d. yellow-brown	70	1·60
		a. Value omitted	£600	
		b. Value and orange (eagle) omitted	£600	
		c. Parting in hair	70·00	
82		1s. slate-purple	50	10
		c. Parting in hair	70·00	
83		1s.3d. bright purple	2·50	10
		c. Parting in hair	85·00	
84	**10**	2s. orange	2·50	8·50
85		2s.6d. lake-brown	3·75	3·00
86		5s. magenta	12·00	9·00
		a. Value omitted	£3000	
87		10s. bright magenta	21·00	25·00
88		20s. blue	22·00	48·00
		a. Value omitted	£1200	
75/88 *Set of 14*			60·00	85·00

Nos. 75/76 exist in coils, constructed from normal sheets.

STAMP BOOKLET

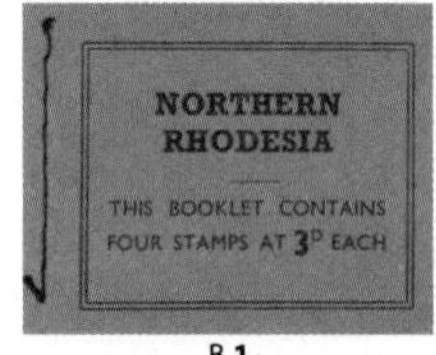

B **1**

1964. Black on blue cover as T B **1**. Stitched.

SB1 1s. booklet containing 3d. (No. 78) in block of 4. 16·00

POSTAGE DUE STAMPS

D **1**

D **2**

(Typo D.L.R.)

1929 (June)–**52**. Wmk Mult Script CA. Ordinary paper. P 14.

No.	Type	Description	Unused	Used
D1	D **1**	1d. grey-black	3·00	2·50
		a. Chalk-surfaced paper. Black (22.1.52)	30·00	85·00
		ab. Error. St Edward's Crown, W **9b**	£7500	
D2		2d. grey-black	9·50	3·00
		a Bisected (1d.) (*on cover*)	†	£900
D3		3d. grey-black	3·00	26·00
		a. Chalk-surfaced paper. *Black* (22.1.52)	8·00	75·00
		ab. Error. Crown missing, W **9a**	£700	
		ac. Error. St Edward's Crown, W **9b**	£425	
D4		4d. grey-black	14·00	45·00
D1/D4 *Set of 4*			26·00	70·00
D1s/D4s Perf 'SPECIMEN' *Set of 4*			£190	

The 2d. is known bisected and used as a 1d. at Luanshya, Ndola or Nkana on various dates between 1937 and 1951 and on understamped letters from South Africa at Chingola in May 1950. One example of the 1d. bisected as a ½d. is known at Kitwe in 1944. Various offices are known to have used definitive stamps in lieu of postage dues between 1932 and 1963.

Following an increase in the internal letter rate from 1½d. to 2d. on 1 July 1953 stocks of postage due stamps at Mkushi became exhausted. As an emergency measure the sub-postmaster was authorised to surcharge examples of No. 28 'POSTAGE DUE (or Postage Due, or 'postage due') 1d.' in red by typewriter. No. 55, the 1d. Rhodes Centenary stamp was also surcharged. Examples properly used on cover between 23 July and 15 September 1953 are of considerable scarcity (*Price on cover from* £4750). No unused examples exist.

(Des D. Smith. Litho Govt Ptr, Lusaka)

1963 (10 Dec). P 12½.

No.	Type	Description	Unused	Used
D5	D **2**	1d. orange	3·25	7·00
D6		2d. deep blue	3·25	5·50
D7		3d. lake	3·25	9·00
D8		4d. ultramarine	3·25	16·00
D9		6d. purple	10·00	12·00
D10		1s. light emerald	12·00	38·00
		a. Imperf (vert pair)	£350	
		b. Block of four imperf horiz and imperf between vert	£1600	
D5/D10 *Set of 6*			32·00	75·00

In all values the stamps in the right-hand vertical row of the sheet are imperforate on the right.

The stamps of Northern Rhodesia were withdrawn on 23 October 1964 when the territory attained independence as the Republic of Zambia.

North-West Pacific Islands
see **New Guinea** *after* **Australia**

Nova Scotia *see* **Canada**

Nyasaland

PRICES FOR STAMPS ON COVER TO 1945	
Nos. 1/9*a*	*from* × 15
Nos. 10/19	—
No. 20	*from* × 10
Nos. 21/26	*from* × 5
Nos. 27/31	—
Nos. 32/37	*from* × 6
Nos. 38/42	—
Nos. 43/47	*from* × 12
Nos. 48/52	—
No. 53	*from* × 15
No. 54	*from* × 2
No. 55	*from* × 4
Nos. 55*b*/57*a*	*from* × 7
Nos. 57*d*/63	*from* × 6
Nos. 64/71	—
Nos. 72/79	*from* × 5
Nos. 80/82	—
Nos. 83/95	*from* × 4
Nos. 96/99	—
Nos. 100/157	*from* × 2

By 1891 the territory west of Lake Nyasa was recognised as being under British protection and the southern, eastern and northern borders had been delineated with the Portuguese and German governments.

BRITISH CENTRAL AFRICA

A protectorate under the name 'Nyassaland Districts' was declared on 14 May 1891, the title being changed to the 'British Central Africa Protectorate' on 22 February 1893. Such a description had been in use for some time previously and the handwritten notice of 20 July 1891, announcing the introduction of postal services, described the area as 'British Central Africa'.

Until 1895 the British South Africa Company contributed to the revenues of the protectorate administration which, in return governed North-eastern Rhodesia. Stamps of the British South Africa Company overprinted 'B.C.A.', in addition to use in British Central Africa, were issued to post offices at Fife, Fort Rosebery, Katwe, Johnston Falls, Rhodesia (later Kalungwisi) and Tanganyika (later Abercorn) in North-eastern Rhodesia from 1893 until 1899.

B.C.A. (1) B.C.A. FOUR SHILLINGS. (2) ONE PENNY. (3)

1891 (20 July)–**95**. Stamps of Rhodesia optd as T **1**. P 14, 14½.

No.	Type	Description	Unused	Used
1	**1**	1d. black	12·00	13·00
2	**4**	2d. sea-green and vermilion	13·00	5·00
		a. Bisected (1d.) (*on cover*) (1895).	†	£7500
3		4d. reddish chestnut and black	17·00	7·50
4	**1**	6d. ultramarine	60·00	20·00
5		6d. deep blue	21·00	11·00
6	**4**	8d. rose-lake and ultramarine	20·00	35·00
6*a*		8d. red and ultramarine	42·00	50·00
7	**1**	1s. grey-brown	32·00	19·00
8		2s. vermilion	50·00	60·00
9		2s.6d. grey-purple	90·00	£100
9*a*		2s.6d. lilac	95·00	£100
10	**4**	3s. brown and green (1895)	90·00	90·00
11		4s. grey-black and vermilion (2.93)	£100	£110
12	**1**	5s. orange-yellow	£110	£120
13		10s. deep green	£200	£225
14	**2**	£1 deep blue	£1300	£700
15		£2 rose-red	£1400	£1600
16		£5 sage-green	£2000	
17		£10 brown	£4500	£6500
1/13 *Set of 12*			£650	£700

Sheet watermarks 1 to 4, as listed under Rhodesia No. 13 are known on this issue.

The overprint varies on values up to 10s. Sets may be made with *thin* or *thick* letters.

Specialists have identified four separate settings; either of 30 (10×3) or 60 (10×6) impressions.

The bisected 2d, No. 2a, was authorised for use at Blantyre, Chiromo and Zomba in July and October 1895.

1892 (Aug)–**93**. Stamps of Rhodesia surch as T **2**.

No.	Type	Description	Unused	Used
18	**4**	3s. on 4s. grey-black and vermilion (10.93)	£375	£375
19	**1**	4s. on 5s. orange-yellow	£100	£100

1895. No. 2 surch at Cape Town with T **3**.

No.	Type	Description	Unused	Used
20	**4**	1d. on 2d. sea-green and vermilion	42·00	65·00
		a. Surch double	£11000	£8000

Examples are known with double surcharge, without stop after 'PENNY'. These are from a trial printing made at Blantyre, but it is believed that they were not issued to the public (*Price* £650 *un.*).

5 Arms of the Protectorate

6 Arms of the Protectorate

(Des Sir Harry Johnston. Litho D.L.R.)

1895. No wmk. P 14.

No.	Type	Description	Unused	Used
21	**5**	1d. black	23·00	18·00
22		2d. black and green	55·00	12·00

23		4d. black and reddish buff	90·00	50·00
24		6d. black and blue	95·00	8·00
25		1s. black and rose	£120	35·00
26	**6**	2s.6d. black and bright magenta	£375	£375
27		3s. black and yellow	£225	65·00
28		5s. black and olive	£300	£275
29		£1 black and yellow-orange	£1400	£600
30		£10 black and orange-vermilion	£8000	£5500
31		£25 black and blue-green	£16000	£16000
21/28 *Set of* 8			£1200	£750
21s/29s Optd 'SPECIMEN' *Set of* 9			£450	

Cancellations inscribed 'BRITISH CENTRAL AFRICA' within a double-circle and with the name of a town across the centre or at foot were intended for use on stamps presented for the payment of the hut tax. Such marks can be found in black, violet or blue and are without date. Stamps with such fiscal obliterations are of little value. Prices quoted are for postally used.

1896 (Feb). Wmk Crown CA (T **5**) or CC (sideways) (T **6**). P 14.

32	**5**	1d. black	3·25	13·00
		x. Wmk reversed	£950	£950
		y. Wmk inverted and reversed	†	£750
33		2d. black and green	24·00	6·50
34		4d. black and orange-brown	42·00	17·00
35		6d. black and blue	50·00	18·00
36		1s. black and rose	50·00	28·00
37	**6**	2s.6d. black and magenta	£200	£150
38		3s. black and yellow	£200	75·00
39		5s. black and olive	£275	£275
40		£1 black and blue	£1200	£650
41		£10 black and orange	£11000	£6000
		s. Optd 'SPECIMEN'	£300	
42		£25 black and green	£26000	
		s. Optd 'SPECIMEN'	£450	
32/39 *Set of* 8			£750	£500
32s/40s Optd 'SPECIMEN' *Set of* 9			£450	

7

8

(Typo D.L.R.)

1897 (Aug)–**1900**. T **7** (wmk Crown CA) and T **8** (wmk Crown CC). P 14.

43	**7**	1d. black and ultramarine	3·25	1·25
		w. Wmk inverted	£170	£350
44		2d. black and yellow	4·25	2·00
45		4d. black and carmine	6·50	1·50
46		6d. black and green	60·00	4·25
47		1s. black and dull purple	11·00	7·00
48	**8**	2s.6d. black and ultramarine	£110	50·00
49		3s. black and sea-green	£350	£375
50		4s. black and carmine	£130	£100
50*a*		10s. black and olive-green (1900)	£325	£350
51		£1 black and dull purple	£500	£275
		w. Wmk inverted	£3250	£3000
52		£10 black and yellow	£8500	£2750
		s. Optd 'SPECIMEN'	£300	
43/51 *Set of* 10			£1300	£1100
43s/51s Optd 'SPECIMEN' *Set of* 10			£425	

ONE

PENNY

(9)

10

1897 (31 Dec). No. 49 surch with T **9**, in red.

53	**8**	1d. on 3s. black and sea-green	14·00	22·00
		a. 'PNNEY' (R. 4/2)	£10000	£7500
		b. 'PENN'	£5500	£4500
		c. Surch double	£750	£1300

No. 53b shows an albino impression of the 'Y'.

1898 (11 Mar). Imperf.

(a) Setting I. The vertical frame lines of the stamps cross the space between the two rows of the sheet

(i) With the initials 'J.G.' or 'J.T.G.' on the back in black ink

54	**10**	1d. vermilion and grey-blue	£16000	£1100
		a. Without the initials	£8000	
		b. Without the initials and centre inverted	£32000	

(ii) With a control number and letter or letters, printed in plain relief at the back

55	**10**	1d. vermilion and grey-blue	—	£750

(b) Setting II. The vertical frame lines do not cross the space between the rows except at the extreme ends of the sheet. Control as No. 55.

55*b*	**10**	1d. vermilion and pale ultramarine	—	£140
		c. Control on face	—	£3500
		d. Centre omitted (pair with normal)	£32000	
56		1d. vermilion and deep ultramarine	—	£150
		a. Without Control at back	£7000	£200
		b. Control doubly impressed	—	£450

1898 (June). Setting II. Control as No. 55. P 12.

57	**10**	1d. vermilion and pale ultramarine	£6500	35·00
57*a*		1d. vermilion and deep ultramarine	—	45·00
		ab. Without Control at back	£6000	£110
		ac. Two different Controls on back	—	£750
		ad. Control printed in black	£9000	

The two different settings of these stamps are each in 30 types, issued without gum.

1901. Wmk Crown CA. P 14.

57*d*	**7**	1d. dull purple and carmine-rose	3·00	50
57*e*		4d. dull purple and olive-green	16·00	11·00
58		6d. dull purple and brown	14·00	6·50
57d/58 *Set of* 3			30·00	16·00
57ds/58s Optd 'SPECIMEN' *Set of* 3			90·00	

11

12

(Typo D.L.R.)

1903–04. T **11** (Wmk Crown CA) and T **12** (Wmk Crown CC). P 14.

59	**11**	1d. grey and carmine	8·00	1·75
60		2d. dull and bright purple	3·50	1·00
61		4d. grey-green and black	2·50	9·00
62		6d. grey and reddish buff	3·75	2·00
		aw. Wmk inverted	£225	
62*b*		1s. grey and blue	4·75	17·00
63	**12**	2s.6d. grey-green and green	70·00	£110
64		4s. dull and bright purple	90·00	90·00
		w. Wmk inverted	£1500	
65		10s. grey-green and black	£200	£300
66		£1 grey and carmine	£325	£225
67		£10 grey and blue	£8000	£4750
		s. Optd 'SPECIMEN'	£500	
59/66 *Set of* 9			£650	£650
59s/66s Optd 'SPECIMEN' *Set of* 9			£425	

1907. Chalk-surfaced paper. Wmk Mult Crown CA. P 14.

68	**11**	1d. grey and carmine	12·00	2·75
69		2d. dull and bright purple	£19000	
70		4d. grey-green and black	£19000	
71		6d. grey and reddish buff	50·00	55·00

Nos. 69/70 were prepared, but not issued in Nyasaland due to the Protectorate's name being changed. It is estimated that no more than a dozen examples of each remain in collectors' hands. Dangerous fakes, made from Nos. 60/61, are in circulation, but note that genuine examples are on chalk-surfaced paper, whereas the previous issue was on ordinary paper.

NYASALAND PROTECTORATE

The title of the Protectorate was changed again from 6 July 1907.

13

14

POSTAGE

£1 Serif on 'G' (R. 4/5. All ptgs of £1 Duty plate)

(Typo D.L.R.)

1908 (22 July)–**11**. P 14.

(a) Wmk Crown CA. Chalk-surfaced paper

72	**13**	1s. black/*green*	6·50	18·00

(b) Wmk Mult Crown CA. Ordinary paper (½d., 1d.) or chalk-surfaced paper (others)

73	**13**	½d. green	2·00	2·25
74		1d. carmine	9·50	1·00
75		3d. purple/*yellow*	2·00	4·25
		w. Wmk inverted	£400	£425
76		4d. black and red/*yellow*	2·25	1·50
		w. Wmk inverted	£150	£180
77		6d. dull purple and bright purple	6·50	11·00
78	**14**	2s.6d. brownish black and carmine-red/*blue*	75·00	£110
		a. Brownish black and deep rose-red/pale blue (1911)	£300	£375
79		4s. carmine and black	£110	£180
80		10s. green and red/*green*	£200	£325
81		£1 purple and black/*red*	£650	£750
		c. Serif on 'G'	£3000	£3250
82		£10 purple and ultramarine	£12000	£8000
		s. Optd 'SPECIMEN'	£1100	
72/81 *Set of* 10			£950	£1250
72s/81s Optd 'SPECIMEN' *Set of* 10			£600	

15

16

'Bullet holes' flaw (R. 5/2. March 1919 ptgs)

Triangle flaw (R. 3/5. March 1919 ptg of 4s.)

1913 (1 Apr)–**21**. Wmk Mult Crown CA. Ordinary paper (½d. to 2½d.) or chalk-surfaced paper (others). P 14.

83	**15**	½d. green	2·25	2·25
84		½d. blue-green (1918)	4·25	2·75
		w. Wmk inverted	†	£600
85		1d. carmine-red	4·25	2·00
86		1d. scarlet (1916)	8·50	1·00
87		2d. grey (1916)	11·00	1·00
88		2d. slate	23·00	6·50
89		2½d. bright blue	2·75	8·50
90		3d. purple/*yellow* (1914)	8·50	4·50
		a. On pale yellow	6·50	10·00
		w. Wmk inverted		
91		4d. black and red/*yellow* (*shades*)	2·00	2·50
		a. On pale yellow	6·50	8·50
92		6d. dull and bright purple	6·00	10·00
92*a*		6d. dull purple and bright violet	17·00	13·00
93		1s. black/*green*	2·00	8·50
		a. On blue-green, olive back	5·50	1·50
		aw. Wmk inverted	£200	£225
		b. On emerald back (1921)	5·00	6·50
		bs. Optd 'SPECIMEN'	75·00	
94	**16**	2s.6d. black and red/*blue*	12·00	30·00
		a. Break in scroll	£200	
		b. Broken crown and scroll	£300	
		c. Nick in top right scroll	£225	£325
		f. Damaged leaf at bottom right	£275	
		h. 'Bullet-holes' flaw	£550	£650
		x. Wmk reversed	—	£3500
95		4s. carmine and black	50·00	£100
		a. Break in scroll	£350	
		b. Broken crown and scroll	£375	
		d. Nick in top right scroll	£350	£500
		f. Damaged leaf at bottom right	£375	
		h. 'Bullet-holes' flaw	£550	£850
		i. Triangle flaw	£500	
96		10s. pale green and deep scarlet/*green*	£130	£160
		d. Nick in top right scroll	£500	
		e. Green and deep scarlet/green (1919)	£150	£190
		ea. Break in scroll	£600	
		eb. Broken crown and scroll	£650	
		ef. Damaged leaf at bottom right	£700	
		eh. 'Bullet holes' flaw	£1000	
98		£1 purple and black/*red*	£200	£170
		a. Break in scroll	£900	£750
		b. Broken crown and scroll	£900	£750
		c. Nick in top right scroll	£900	
		e. Break in lines below left scroll	£1000	
		f. Damaged leaf at bottom right	£900	
		h. 'Bullet-holes' flaw	£1700	
		i. Serif on 'G'	£1100	£850
		w. Wmk inverted		
99		£10 purple and dull ultramarine	£8000	
		c. Nick in top right scroll	£10000	
		e. Purple and royal blue (1919) (f.c. £150)	£4000	£2000
		ea. Break in scroll	£8000	£4000
		eb. Broken crown and scroll	£8000	£4000
		ef. Damaged leaf at bottom right	£8500	
		eh. 'Bullet holes' flaw	£9500	
		s. Optd 'SPECIMEN'	£800	
83/98 *Set of* 12			£375	£425
83s/98s Optd 'SPECIMEN' *Set of* 12			£600	

For illustrations of the other varieties on Nos. 94/99 see above Bermuda No. 51*b*.

For stamps overprinted 'N.F.' see TANGANYIKA.

Damaged crown (R. 4/1. 2s.6d. ptg of June 1924)

Lines omitted from scroll (R. 2/4)

1921–33. Wmk Mult Script CA. Ordinary paper (½d. to 2d.) or chalk-surfaced paper (others). P 14.

100 **15** ½d. green ... 3·50 50
w. Wmk inverted ... — £450
y. Wmk inverted and reversed ... — £550
101 1d. carmine ... 4·00 50
102 1½d. orange ... 3·25 17·00
103 2d. grey ... 4·00 50
105 3d. purple/*pale yellow* ... 22·00 3·25
106 4d. black and red/*yellow* ... 7·00 11·00
107 6d. dull and bright purple ... 7·00 3·25
108 1s. black/*emerald* (1930) ... 14·00 4·50
109 **16** 2s. purple and blue/*pale blue* (1926) ... 22·00 12·00
a. Break in scroll ... £180 £160
b. Broken crown and scroll ... £180 £160
c. Nick in top right scroll ... £180 £160
e. Break in lines below left scroll ... £180 £160
f. Damaged leaf at bottom right ... £180 £160
g. Purple and blue/grey-blue (10.33) ... 55·00 26·00
ga. Break in scroll ... £450 £300
gb. Broken crown and scroll ... £450 £300
gd. Break through scroll ... £450 £300
ge. Break in lines below left scroll ... £450 £300
gf. Damaged leaf at bottom right ... £450 £300
gg. Gash in fruit and leaf ... £450 £300
gh. Breaks in scrolls at right ... £450 £300
110 2s.6d. black and carmine-red/*pale blue* (30.9.24) ... 28·00 42·00
a. Break in scroll ... £200 £250
b. Broken crown and scroll ... £200 £250
c. Nick in top right scroll ... £200 £250
e. Break in lines below left scroll ... £200 £250
f. Damaged leaf at bottom right ... £200 £250
i. Damaged crown ... £400 £425
j. Grey-black and scarlet-vermilion/pale blue (10.26) ... 48·00 19·00
ja. Break in scroll ... £375 £180
jb. Broken crown and scroll ... £375 £180
je. Break in lines below left scroll ... £375 £180
jf. Damaged leaf at bottom right ... £375 £180
k. Black and scarlet-vermilion/grey-blue (10.33) ... 60·00 38·00
ka. Break in scroll ... £450 £325
kb. Broken crown and scroll ... £450 £325
kd. Break through scroll ... £450 £350
ke. Break in lines below left scroll ... £450 £325
kf. Damaged leaf at bottom right ... £450 £325
kg. Gash in fruit and leaf ... £450 £350
kh. Breaks in scrolls at right ... £450 £350
ki. 'C' of 'CA' omitted from watermark ...
111 4s. carmine and black (1927) ... 28·00 48·00
a. Break in scroll ... £225 £325
b. Broken crown and scroll ... £225
c. Nick in top right scroll ... £225
e. Break in lines below left scroll ... £225 £325
f. Damaged leaf at bottom right ... £225 £325
112 5s. green and red/*yellow* (1929) ... 55·00 85·00
a. Break in scroll ... £375
b. Broken crown and scroll ... £375
c. Nick in top right scroll ... £375
e. Break in lines below left scroll ... £375
f. Damaged leaf at bottom right ... £375
113 10s. green and red/*pale emerald* (1926) ... £120 £120
a. Break in scroll ... £550 £600
b. Broken crown and scroll ... £550 £600
c. Nick in top right scroll ... £550 £600
e. Break in lines below left scroll ... £550 £600
f. Damaged leaf at bottom right ... £750
g. Lines omitted from scroll ... £550 £600
h. Green and scarlet/emerald (1927) ... £750 £850
ha. Break in scroll ... £2250
hb. Broken crown and scroll ... £2250
he. Break in lines below left scroll ... £2250 £3750
hf. Damaged leaf at bottom right ... £2250
100/113 *Set of* 13 ... £275 £275
100s/113s Optd or Perf (1s., 5s.) 'SPECIMEN' *Set of* 13 ... £600

For illustrations of the other varieties on Nos. 109/113 see above Bermuda No. 51*b*.

17 King George V and Symbol of the Protectorate

(Des Major H. E. Green. Recess Waterlow)

1934 (June)–**35.** Wmk Mult Script CA. P 12½.

114 **17** ½d. green ... 75 1·25
115 1d. brown ... 75 75
116 1½d. carmine ... 75 3·00
117 2d. pale grey ... 1·00 1·25
118 3d. blue ... 3·00 1·75
119 4d. bright magenta (20.5.35) ... 9·00 3·50
120 6d. violet ... 2·75 50
121 9d. olive-bistre (20.5.35) ... 9·50 17·00
122 1s. black and orange ... 23·00 14·00
114/122 *Set of* 9 ... 45·00 38·00
114s/122s Perf 'SPECIMEN' *Set of* 9 ... £350

1935 (6 May). Silver Jubilee. As Nos. 91/94 of Antigua, but ptd by Waterlow. P 11×12.

123 1d. ultramarine and grey ... 1·00 2·00
k. Kite and vertical log ... £170 £250
m. 'Bird' by turret ... £250 £300
124 2d. green and indigo ... 1·00 2·25
m. 'Bird' by turret ... £225 £275
125 3d. brown and deep blue ... 12·00 22·00
k. Kite and vertical log ... £400 £550
126 1s. slate and purple ... 29·00 55·00
k. Kite and vertical log ... £450 £700
123/126 *Set of* 4 ... 38·00 70·00
123s/126s Perf 'SPECIMEN' *Set of* 4 ... £140

For illustrations of plate varieties see Omnibus section following Zanzibar.

1937 (12 May). Coronation. As Nos. 95/97 of Antigua. P 11×11½.

127 ½d. green ... 30 2·25
128 1d. brown ... 50 1·50
129 2d. grey-black ... 50 3·25
127/129 *Set of* 3 ... 1·10 6·25
127s/129s Perf 'SPECIMEN' *Set of* 3 ... £150

18 Symbol of the Protectorate

19

(T **18** recess Waterlow; T **19** typo D.L.R.)

1938 (1 Jan)–**44.** Chalk-surfaced paper (2s. to £1). P 12½ (T **18**) or 14 (T **19**).

(a) Wmk Mult Script CA

130 **18** ½d. green ... 1·50 2·50
130*a* ½d. brown (12.12.42) ... 10 2·50
131 1d. brown ... 4·25 30
a. 'A' of 'CA' omitted from watermark ... † £1300
131*b* 1d. green (12.12.42) ... 30 2·25
132 1½d. carmine ... 11·00 8·50
132*a* 1½d. grey (12.12.42) ... 30 8·50
ab. 'A' of 'CA' missing from wmk ... £1600
133 2d. grey ... 8·00 1·25
aa. 'A' of 'CA' missing from wmk ... † £1300
133*a* 2d. carmine (12.12.42) ... 30 1·75
b. 'A' of 'CA' missing from wmk ... £1600
134 3d. blue ... 1·25 1·50
135 4d. bright magenta ... 3·00 2·00
136 6d. violet ... 2·75 2·00
137 9d. olive-bistre ... 3·00 5·00
138 1s. black and orange ... 3·50 3·25
139 **19** 2s. purple and blue/*blue* ... 10·00 17·00
140 2s.6d. black and red/*blue* ... 17·00 22·00
141 5s. pale green and red/*yellow* ... 55·00 35·00
a. Ordinary paper. *Green and red/pale yellow* (3.44) ... 80·00 £150
142 10s. emerald and deep red/*pale green* ... 55·00 80·00
a. Ordinary paper. *Bluish green and brown-red/pale green* (1.38) ... £425 £500

(b) Wmk Mult Crown CA

143 **19** £1 purple and black/*red* ... 50·00 50·00
c. Serif on 'G' ... £1100 £1200
130/143 *Set of* 18 ... £200 £200
130s/143s Perf 'SPECIMEN' *Set of* 18 ... £1000

No. 141*a* has a yellow surfacing often applied in horizontal lines giving the appearance of laid paper.

The printer's archives record the despatch of No. 142*a* to Nyasaland in January 1938, but no examples have been reported used before 1945. The paper coating on this printing varied considerably across the sheet. It is reported that some examples show a faint reaction to the silver test.

20 Lake Nyasa

21 King's African Rifles

22 Tea estate

23 Map of Nyasaland

24 Fishing village

25 Tobacco

25a Badge of Nyasaland

(Recess B.W.)

1945 (1 Sept). Types **20**/**25a**. Wmk Mult Script CA (sideways on horiz designs). P 12.

144 **20** ½d. black and chocolate ... 50 10
145 **21** 1d. black and emerald ... 20 70
146 **22** 1½d. black and grey-green ... 30 50
147 **23** 2d. black and scarlet ... 1·50 85
148 **24** 3d. black and light blue ... 60 30
149 **25** 4d. black and claret ... 2·25 80
150 **22** 6d. black and violet ... 4·00 90
151 **20** 9d. black and olive ... 4·25 3·00
152 **23** 1s. indigo and deep green ... 3·75 20
153 **24** 2s. emerald and maroon ... 10·00 6·00
154 **25** 2s.6d. emerald and blue ... 10·00 7·50
155 **25a** 5s. purple and blue ... 7·00 9·00
156 **23** 10s. claret and emerald ... 26·00 19·00
157 **25a** 20s. scarlet and black ... 29·00 42·00
144/157 *Set of* 14 ... 85·00 80·00
144s/157s Perf 'SPECIMEN' *Set of* 14 ... £550

1946 (16 Dec). Victory. As Nos. 110/111 of Antigua.

158 1d. green ... 20 30
159 2d. red-orange ... 30 30
158s/159s Perf 'SPECIMEN' *Set of* 2 ... £140

26 Symbol of the Protectorate

27 Arms in 1891 and 1951

(Des A. E. Wilson. Recess B.W.)

1947 (20 Oct). Wmk Mult Script CA. P 12.

160 **26** 1d. red-brown and yellow-green ... 50 30
s. Perf 'SPECIMEN' ... 90·00

1948 (15 Dec). Royal Silver Wedding. As Nos. 112/113 of Antigua.

161 1d. green ... 15 10
162 10s. mauve ... 18·00 35·00

1949 (21 Nov). 75th Anniversary of UPU. As Nos. 114/117 of Antigua.

163 1d. blue-green ... 30 30
a. 'A' of 'CA' missing from wmk ... £900
164 3d. greenish blue ... 2·25 4·50
165 6d. purple ... 50 1·25
166 1s. ultramarine ... 30 1·00
163/166 *Set of* 4 ... 3·00 6·25

(Des C. Twynam. Recess B.W.)

1951 (15 May). Diamond Jubilee of Protectorate. Wmk Mult Script CA. P 11×12.

167 **27** 2d. black and scarlet ... 1·25 1·50
168 3d. black and turquoise-blue ... 1·25 1·50
169 6d. black and violet ... 1·50 2·50
170 5s. black and indigo ... 9·00 11·00
167/170 *Set of* 4 ... 11·50 15·00

28 Arms of Rhodesia and Nyasaland

29 Grading Cotton

(Recess Waterlow)

1953 (30 May). Rhodes Centenary Exhibition. Wmk Mult Script CA. P 14×13½.

171 **28** 6d. violet ... 50 50

1953 (2 June). Coronation. As No. 120 of Antigua but des and recess B.W.

172 2d. black and brown-orange ... 70 80

(Recess B.W.)

1953 (1 Sept)–**54**. Designs previously used for King George VI issue, but with portrait of Queen Elizabeth II. Wmk Mult Script CA. P 12.

173	**20**	½d. black and chocolate	10	1·75
		a. Perf 12×12½ (8.3.54)	10	1·75
174	**26**	1d. brown and bright green	65	65
175	**22**	1½d. black and deep grey-green	30	1·90
176	**23**	2d. black and yellow-orange	85	40
		a. Perf 12×12½ (8.3.54)	70	30
177	**29**	2½d. green and black	30	50
178	**25**	3d. black and scarlet	30	20
179	**24**	4½d. black and light blue	1·00	60
180	**22**	6d. black and violet	1·00	1·50
		a. Perf 12×12½ (8.3.54)	2·00	1·00
181	**20**	9d. black and deep olive	1·25	3·75
182	**23**	1s. deep blue and slate-green	3·75	50
183	**24**	2s. deep green and brown-red	3·50	5·00
184	**25**	2s.6d. deep emerald and deep blue	4·25	9·50
185	**25a**	5s. purple and Prussian blue	13·00	9·50
186	**23**	10s. carmine and deep emerald	17·00	27·00
187	**25a**	20s. red and black	28·00	48·00
173/187 *Set of* 15			65·00	95·00

Stamps perf 12×12½ come from sheets comb-perforated 11.8×12.25. They were also issued in coils of 480 stamps made up from sheets.

For issues between 1954 and 1963, see RHODESIA AND NYASALAND.

30

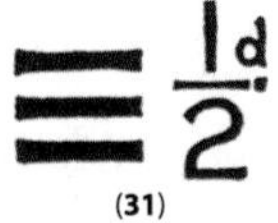

(31)

(Recess B.W.)

1963 (1 Nov). Revenue stamps optd 'POSTAGE', as in T **30**, or additionally surch as T **31**. P 12.

188	½d. on 1d. greenish blue	30	30
189	1d. green	30	10
190	2d. scarlet	30	30
191	3d. blue	30	10
192	6d. brown-purple	30	10
193	9d. on 1s. cerise	40	25
194	1s. purple	45	10
195	2s.6d. black	1·25	2·75
196	5s. chocolate	3·25	3·75
197	10s. yellow-olive	5·50	8·50
	a. Greenish olive	21·00	18·00
198	£1 deep violet	5·50	11·00
188/198 *Set of* 11		16·00	24·00

32 Mother and Child

33 Chambo (fish)

34 Tea Industry

35 Nyala

(Des V. Whiteley. Photo Harrison)

1964 (1 Jan). Designs as Types **32/35**. P 14½.

199	**32**	½d. reddish violet	10	30
200	**33**	1d. black and green	10	10
201		2d. light red-brown	10	10
202		3d. red-brown, yellow-green and bistre-brown	10	10
203		4d. indigo and orange-yellow	20	30
204	**34**	6d. purple, yellow-green and light blue	85	70
205		1s. brown, turquoise-blue and pale yellow	15	10
206		1s.3d. bronze-green and chestnut	3·75	10
207		2s.6d. brown and blue	3·25	50
208		5s. blue, green, yellow and black	1·50	1·75
209		10s. green, orange-brown and black	2·50	3·25
210	**35**	£1 deep reddish purple and yellow	11·00	14·00
199/210 *Set of* 12			21·00	19·00

Designs: ½d. T **32**; 1d. T **33**. As Types **32/33**—2d. Zebu Bull; 3d. Groundnuts; 4d. Fishing. 6d. T **34**. As T **34**—1s. Timber; 1s.3d. Turkish tobacco industry; 2s.6d. Cotton industry; 5s. Monkey Bay, Lake Nyasa; 10s. Forestry, Afzelia. £1. T **35**.

Nos. 199 and 200 exist in coils constructed from normal sheets.

STAMP BOOKLETS

1954 (1 Jan). Black on green cover, stitched (No. SB1) or buff cover, stapled (No. SB2). R. W. Gunson (Seeds) Ltd. advertisement on front.

SB1	2s.6d. booklet containing 4×½d., 4×1d., and 12×2d. (Nos. 173/174, 176), each in blocks of 4	29·00
SB2	5s. booklet containing 8×½d., 8×1d., 8×6d. and 12×2d. (Nos. 173/174, 176, 180), each in blocks of 4	35·00

POSTAGE DUE STAMPS

D 1

(Typo D.L.R.)

1950 (1 July). Wmk Mult Script CA. P 14.

D1	D **1**	1d. scarlet	4·25	32·00
D2		2d. ultramarine	21·00	32·00
D3		3d. green	17·00	6·00
D4		4d. purple	30·00	60·00
D5		6d. yellow-orange	42·00	£160
D1/D5 *Set of* 5			£100	£250

Nyasaland attained independence on 5 July 1964 when the country was renamed Malawi.

Orange Free State *see* South Africa

Pakistan

On 14 August 1947 the predominately Muslim areas of India became West and East Pakistan. Until 1 October Indian stamps remained on sale in the new Dominion and such use can only be identified by cancellation. A commemorative postmark inscribed 'Pakistan Zindabad' (Long live Pakistan) was in use on Independence Day.

(Currency. 12 pies = 1 anna; 16 annas = 1 rupee)

DOMINION

PAKISTAN (1) PAKISTAN (2)

1947 (1 Oct). Nos. 259/268 and 269b/277 (King George VI) of India optd by litho at Nasik, as T **1** (3p. to 12a.) or T **2** (14a. and rupee values).

1	3p. slate	30	10
2	½a. purple	30	10
	w. Wmk inverted	—	55·00
3	9p. green	30	10
4	1a. carmine	30	10
5	1½a. dull violet	2·25	10
	w. Wmk inverted	—	30·00
6	2a. vermilion	30	20
7	3a. bright violet	35	20
8	3½a. bright blue	1·25	2·25
9	4a. brown	35	20
10	6a. turquoise-green	1·25	1·25
11	8a. slate-violet	45	60
12	12a. lake	1·25	20
13	14a. purple	3·25	4·75
14	1r. grey and red-brown	9·00	1·25
	w. Wmk inverted	80·00	55·00
15	2r. purple and brown	3·50	6·00
16	5r. green and blue	10·00	9·50
17	10r. purple and claret	10·00	15·00
18	15r. brown and green	90·00	£160
19	25r. slate-violet and purple	95·00	£110
1/19 *Set of* 19		£200	£275

Numerous provisional 'PAKISTAN' overprints, both handstamped and machine-printed, in various sizes and colours, on Postage and Official stamps, also exist.

These were made under authority of Provincial Governments, District Head Postmasters or Local Postmasters and are of considerable philatelic interest.

The 1a.3p. (India No. 269) exists only as a local issue (*Price*, Karachi opt £3 *unused*; £4 *used*).

The 12a., as No. 12 but overprinted at Karachi, exists with overprint inverted (*Price £70 unused*).

The 1r. value with Karachi local overprint exists with overprint inverted (*Price* £250 *unused*) or as a vertical pair with one stamp without overprint (*Price* £1000 *unused*).

3 Constituent Assembly Building, Karachi

4 Karachi Airport entrance

5 Gateway to Lahore Fort

6 Crescent and Stars

(Des A. Chughtai (1r.). Recess D.L.R.)

1948 (9 July). Independence. Types **3/6** . P 13½×14 or 11½ (1r.).

20	1½a. ultramarine	1·25	2·25
21	2½a. green	1·25	20
22	3a. purple-brown	1·25	35
23	1r. scarlet	1·25	70
	a. Perf 14×13½	4·75	27·00
20/23 *Set of* 4		4·50	3·25

7 Scales of Justice

8 Star and Crescent

9 Lloyds Barrage

10 Karachi Airport

11 Karachi Port Trust

12 Salimullah Hostel, Dacca **13** Khyber Pass

(Des M. Suharwardi (T **8**). Recess Pakistan Security Ptg Corp Ltd, Karachi (P 13 and 13½), D.L.R. (others))

1948 (14 Aug)–**57**. Types **7/13**.

24	**7**	3p. red (P 12½)	10	10
		a. Perf 13½ (5.54)	3·75	1·00
25		6p. violet (P 12½)	1·25	10
		a. Perf 13½ (1954)	8·50	6·00
26		9p. green (P 12½)	50	10
		a. Perf 13½ (1954)	11·00	1·75
27	**8**	1a. blue (P 12½)	30	50
28		1½a. grey-green (P 12½)	30	10
29		2a. red (P 12½)	7·50	70
30	**9**	2½a. green (P 14×13½)	9·50	14·00
31	**10**	3a. green (P 14)	7·50	1·00
32	**9**	3½a. bright blue (P 14×13½)	9·50	5·50
33		4a. reddish brown (P 12½)	1·25	10
34	**11**	6a. blue (P 14×13½)	2·00	50
35		8a. black (P 12)	1·50	1·50
36	**10**	10a. scarlet (P 14)	9·00	12·00
37	**11**	12a. scarlet (P 14×13½)	11·00	1·00
38	**12**	1r. ultramarine (P 14)	26·00	10
		a. Perf 13½ (1954)	23·00	12·00
39		2r. chocolate (P 14)	20·00	75
		a. Perf 13½ (5.54)	26·00	11·00
40		5r. carmine (P 14)	26·00	2·75
		a. Perf 13½ (7.53)	18·00	25
41	**13**	10r. magenta (P 14)	22·00	48·00
		a. Perf 12	£140	12·00
		b. Perf 13 (1951)	19·00	3·50
42		15r. blue-green (P 12)	18·00	32·00
		a. Perf 14	25·00	£110
		b. Perf 13 (27.7.57)	27·00	38·00
43		25r. violet (P 14)	55·00	£140
		a. Perf 12	42·00	42·00
		b. Perf 13 (1.11.54)	50·00	48·00
24/43a *Set of 20*			£160	£100

For 25r. with W **98**, see No. 210.

The 6p. (No. 25) exists from coils made up from normal sheets.

14 Star and Crescent **15** Karachi Airport

15a Karachi Port Trust

(Recess Pakistan Security Ptg Corp (P 13½), D.L.R. (others).

1949 (Feb)–**53**. Redrawn. Crescent moon with points to left as Types **14/15a**.

44	**14**	1a. blue (P 12½)	4·00	85
		a. Perf 13½ (1952)	13·00	10
45		1½a. grey-green (P 12½)	3·75	85
		a. Perf 13½ (1953)	3·50	10
		ab. Printed on the gummed side	65·00	
46		2a. red (P 12½)	4·50	10
		a. Perf 13½ (1952)	7·00	10
47	**15**	3a. green (P 14)	16·00	1·00
48	**15a**	6a. blue (as No. 34) (P 14×13½)	24·00	2·50
49		8a. black (as No. 35) (P 12½)	24·00	2·50
50	**15**	10a. scarlet (P 14)	28·00	4·00
51	**15a**	12a. scarlet (as No. 37) (P 14×13½)	30·00	60
44/51 *Set of 8*			£110	9·50

The 1a. (No. 44) exists from coils made up from normal sheets.

16 **16a**

(Recess D.L.R.)

1949 (11 Sept). First Death Anniversary of Mohammed Ali Jinnah. T **16/16a**. P 14.

52	**16**	1½a. brown	3·25	2·00
53		3a. green	3·25	1·50
54	**16a**	10a. black	10·00	8·00
52/54 *Set of 3*			15·00	10·50

17 Pottery **18** Stylised aeroplane and Hourglass

Two Types of 3½a.:

I II

19 Saracenic Leaf Pattern **20** Archway and Lamp

(Des A. Chughtai. Recess D.L.R., later printings, Pakistan Security Ptg Corp)

1951 (14 Aug)–**56**. Fourth Anniversary of Independence. P 13.

55	**17**	2½a. carmine	1·75	1·25
56	**18**	3a. purple	1·00	10
57	**17**	3½a. blue (I)	1·50	9·00
57*a*		3½a. blue (II) (12.56)	5·00	6·00
58	**19**	4a. green	2·25	10
59		6a. brown-orange	2·25	10
60	**20**	8a. sepia	4·50	25
61		10a. violet	2·00	2·25
62	**18**	12a. slate	3·00	10
55/62 *Set of 9*			21·00	17·00

The above and the stamps issued on the 14 August 1954, 1955 and 1956, are basically definitive issues, although issued on the Anniversary date of Independence.

21 Scinde Dawk stamp and Ancient and Modern Transport

(Recess D.L.R.)

1952 (14 Aug). Centenary of Scinde Dawk Issue of India. P 13.

63	**21**	3a. deep olive/*yellow-olive*	1·00	85
64		12a. deep brown/*salmon*	1·25	15

PRINTERS. All issues up to No. 219 were recess-printed by the Pakistan Security Printing Corporation, *unless otherwise stated.*

22 Kaghan Valley **23** Mountains, Gilgit

24 Bahshahi Mosque, Lahore **25** Mausoleum of Emperor Jehangir, Lahore

26 Tea Plantation, East Pakistan **27** Cotton plants, West Pakistan

28 Jute fields and River, East Pakistan

1954 (14 Aug). Seventh Anniversary of Independence. Types **22/28**. P 13½ (14a., 1r., 2r.) or 13 (others).

65	**22**	6p. reddish violet	25	10
66	**23**	9p. blue	3·75	3·00
67	**24**	1a. carmine	30	10
68	**25**	1½a. red	30	10
69	**26**	14a. deep green	6·00	10
70	**27**	1r. green	11·00	10
71	**28**	2r. red-orange	3·00	10
65/71 *Set of 7*			22·00	3·00

29 View of K 2

1954 (25 Dec). Conquest of K 2 (Mount Godwin-Austen). P 13.

72	**29**	2a. deep violet	40	40

30 Karnaphuli Paper Mill, Type I (Arabic fraction on left) **31** Textile Mill, West Pakistan

32 Jute Mill, East Pakistan **33** Main Sui gas plant

Type II (Arabic fraction on right)

1955 (14 Aug)–**56**. Eighth Anniversary of Independence. Types **30/33**. P 13.

73	**30**	2½a. scarlet (I)	1·25	1·40
73*a*		2½a. scarlet (II) (12.56)	3·25	1·40
74	**31**	6a. deep ultramarine	2·00	10
75	**32**	8a. deep reddish violet	3·75	10
76	**33**	12a. carmine and orange	4·00	10
73/76 *Set of 5*			13·00	2·75

TENTH ANNIVERSARY UNITED NATIONS

24. 10. 55.

(**34**)

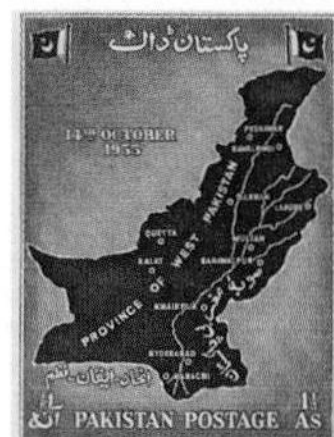

35 Map of West Pakistan

TENTH ANNIVERSARY UNITED NATIONS

24. 10. 55.

'UNITED NATIONS' shifted 1 mm to left (1½a. R. 7/10; 12a. R. 1/8, 3/8, 5/8, 7/8, 9/8)

1955 (24 Oct). Tenth Anniversary of United Nations. Nos. 68 and 76 optd as T **34**.

77		1½a. red (B.)	1·50	5·00
		a. 'UNITED NATIONS' 1 mm to left	30·00	45·00
78		12a. carmine and orange (B.)	50	3·50
		a. 'UNITED NATIONS' 1 mm to left	7·00	16·00

Forgeries exist of the overprint on No. 77. These are in very uneven thin type and measure 20×18 mm instead of the genuine 19½×19 mm.

1955 (7 Dec). West Pakistan Unity. P 13½.

79	**35**	1½a. myrtle-green	1·25	2·50
80		2a. sepia	1·00	45
81		12a. deep rose-red	1·50	50
79/81 *Set of 3*			3·25	3·00

REPUBLIC

36 Constituent Assembly Building, Karachi

(Litho D.L.R.)

1956 (23 Mar). Republic Day. P 13.
82 **36** 2a. myrtle-green 80 10

37 **38** Map of East Pakistan

1956 (14 Aug). Ninth Anniversary of Independence. P 13½.
83 **37** 2a. scarlet 65 10
a. Printed on the gummed side .... 8·00

1956 (15 Oct). First Session of National Assembly of Pakistan at Dacca. P 13½.
84 **38** 1½a. myrtle-green .... 50 1·75
85 2a. sepia 50 10
86 12a. deep rose-red .... 55 1·25
84/86 *Set of 3* .... 1·40 2·75

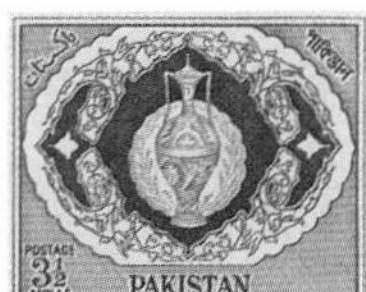

39 Karnaphuli Paper Mill, East Bengal **40** Pottery

41 Orange Tree

1957 (23 Mar). First Anniversary of Republic. P 13.
87 **39** 2½a. scarlet 25 10
88 **40** 3½a. blue 30 10
89 **41** 10r. myrtle-green and yellow-orange .... 1·00 25
87/89 *Set of 3* .... 1·40 35

The above and No. 95 are primarily definitive issues, although issued on the Anniversary of Republic Day.
For 10r. with W **98**, see No. 208.

42 Pakistani Flag **43** Pakistani Industries

(Des Ahsan. Litho D.L.R.)

1957 (10 May). Centenary of Struggle for Independence (Indian Mutiny). P 13.
90 **42** 1½a. bronze-green 50 50
91 12a. light blue .... 1·25 10

(Litho D.L.R.)

1957 (14 Aug). Tenth Anniversary of Independence. P 14.
92 **43** 1½a. ultramarine 20 45
93 4a. orange-red .... 45 1·75
94 12a. mauve 45 50
92/94 *Set of 3* .... 1·00 2·40

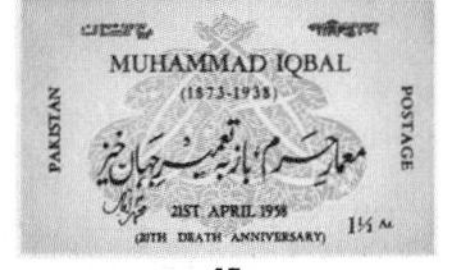

44 Coconut Tree **45**

1958 (23 Mar). Second Anniversary of Republic. P 13.
95 **44** 15r. red and deep reddish purple .... 2·50 1·50
This is a definitive issue, see note below No. 89.
See No. 209 for this stamp with W **98**.

(Photo Harrison)

1958 (21 Apr). 20th Death Anniversary of Mohammed Iqbal (poet). P 14½×14.
96 **45** 1½a. yellow-olive and black .... 55 1·00
97 2a. orange-brown and black 55 25
98 14a. turquoise-blue and black 90 10
96/98 *Set of 3* .... 1·75 1·25

46 UN Charter and Globe

PAKISTAN
BOY SCOUT
2nd NATIONAL
JAMBOREE

CHITTAGONG
Dec. 58—Jan. 59
(**47**)

1958 (10 Dec). Tenth Anniversary of Declaration of Human Rights. P 13.
99 **46** 1½a. turquoise-blue 10 10
100 14a. sepia 45 10

1958 (28 Dec). Second Pakistan Boy Scouts National Jamboree, Chittagong. Nos. 65 and 75 optd with T **47**.
101 6p. reddish violet 20 10
102 8a. deep reddish violet 40 10

REVOLUTION
DAY
Oct. 27, 1959
(**48**)

49 'Centenary of An Idea'

1959 (27 Oct). Revolution Day. No. 74 optd with T **48** in red.
103 6a. deep ultramarine 80 10

1959 (19 Nov). Red Cross Commemoration. Recess; cross typo. P 13.
104 **49** 2a. red and green 30 10
105 10a. red and deep blue 55 10

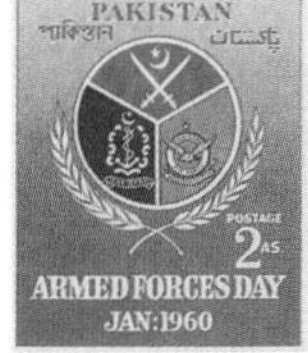

50 Armed Forces Badge **51** Map of Pakistan

(Litho D.L.R.)

1960 (10 Jan). Armed Forces Day. P 13½×13.
106 **50** 2a. red, ultramarine and blue-green 50 10
107 14a. red and bright blue .... 1·00 10

1960 (23 Mar). P 13×13½.
108 **51** 6p. deep purple 40 10
109 2a. brown-red 60 10
110 8a. deep green .... 1·25 10
111 1r. blue .... 2·00 10
a. Printed on the gummed side ....
108/111 *Set of 4* .... 3·75 20

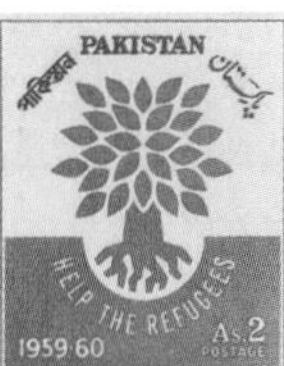

52 Uprooted Tree **53** Punjab Agricultural College

1960 (7 Apr). World Refugee Year. P 13.
112 **52** 2a. rose-carmine 20 10
113 10a. green 30 10

1960 (10 Oct). Golden Jubilee of Punjab Agricultural College, Lyallpur. T **53** and similar horiz design. P 12½×14.
114 2a. slate-blue and carmine-red 15 10
115 8a. bluish green and reddish violet 40 10
Design: 2a. T **53**; 8a. College Arms.

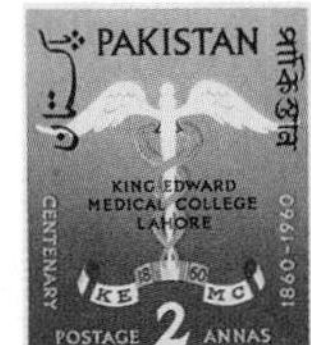

55 Land Reforms, Rehabilitation and Reconstruction **56** Caduceus

(Des M. Hanjra. Photo D.L.R.)

1960 (27 Oct). Revolution Day. P 13×13½.
116 **55** 2a. green, pink and brown 10 10
a. Green and pink omitted .... 27·00
b. Pink omitted .... 7·50
117 14a. green, yellow and ultramarine... 50 75

(Photo D.L.R.)

1960 (16 Nov). Centenary of King Edward Medical College, Lahore. P 13.
118 **56** 2a. yellow, black and blue 50 10
119 14a. emerald, black and carmine....... 1·75 1·00

57 'Economic Co-operation' **58** Zam-Zama Gun, Lahore (*Kim's Gun*, after Rudyard Kipling)

1960 (5 Dec). International Chamber of Commerce CAFEA Meeting, Karachi. P 13.
120 **57** 14a. orange-red 75 20

(Centre typo, background recess Pakistan Security Ptg Corp)

1960 (24 Dec). Third Pakistan Boy Scouts National Jamboree, Lahore. P 12½×14.
121 **58** 2a. carmine, yellow and deep bluish green 80 30

(New Currency. 100 paisa = 1 rupee)

1 PAISA
(**59**)

1961 (1 Jan–14 Feb). Nos. 24a, 67/68, 83 and 108/109, surch as T **59**. Nos. 123/124 and 126 surch by Pakistan Security Ptg Corp and others by the *Times Press*, Karachi.
122 1p. on 1½a. red (10.1) 40 10
a. Printed and surch on the gummed side .... 60·00
123 2p. on 3p. red 10 10
124 3p. on 6p. deep purple 15 10
a. 'PASIA' for 'PAISA' .... 11·00
125 7p. on 1a. carmine (14.2) 40 10
126 13p. on 2a. brown-red (14.2) 40 10
a. 'PAIS' for 'PAISA' .... 11·00
127 13p. on 2a. scarlet (14.2) 30 10
122/127 *Set of 6* .... 1·60 30

No. 122. Two settings were used, the first with figure '1' 2½ mm tall and the second 3 mm.

On the 1p. with tall '1' and the 13p. (No. 127), the space between the figures of value and 'P' of 'PAISA' varies between 1½ mm and 3 mm.

See also Nos. 262/4.

ERRORS. In the above issue and the corresponding official stamps we have listed errors in the stamps surcharged by the Pakistan Security Printing Corp but have not included the very large number of errors which occurred in the stamps surcharged by the less experienced Times Press. This was a very hurried job and there was no time to carry out the usual checks. It is also known that some errors were not issued to the public but came on the market by other means.

NOTE. Stamps in the old currency were also handstamped with new currency equivalents and issued in various districts but these local issues are outside the scope of this catalogue.

60 Khyber Pass **61** Shalimar Gardens, Lahore

62 Chota Sona Masjid (gateway)

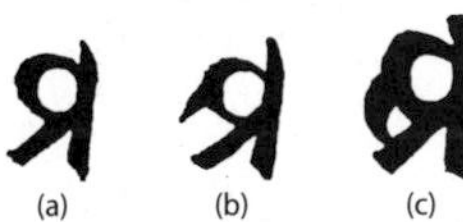

(a) (b) (c)

Types (a) and (b) show the first letter in the top right-hand inscription; (a) wrongly engraved, 'SH' (b) corrected to 'P'.

On Nos. 131/132 and 134 the corrections were made individually on the plate, so that each stamp in the sheet may be slightly different.

Type (c) refers to No. 133a only.

1961–63. No wmk. P 13 (T **62**) or 14 (others).
(a) Inscribed 'SHAKISTAN' in Bengali
128 **60** 1p. violet (1.6.61) .... 1·50 30
129 2p. rose-red (12.1.61) .... 1·50 10
130 5p. ultramarine (23.3.61) .... 3·00 10

(b) Inscribed 'PAKISTAN' in Bengali

131 **60** 1p. violet ... 1·00 10
a. Printed on the gummed side ....
132 2p. rose-red ... 1·00 10
133 3p. reddish purple (27.10.61) ... 75 10
a. Re-engraved. First letter of Bengali inscription as Type (c) (1963) ... 9·00 4·00
134 5p. ultramarine ... 8·00 10
a. Printed on the gummed side ....
135 7p. emerald (23.3.61) ... 2·00 10
136 **61** 10p. brown (14.8.61) ... 30 10
137 13p. slate-violet (14.8.61) ... 30 10
138 25p. deep blue (1.1.62) ... 5·50 10
139 40p. deep purple (1.1.62) ... 1·50 10
140 50p. deep bluish green (1.1.62) ... 50 10
141 75p. carmine-red (23.3.62) ... 1·00 70
142 90p. yellow-green (1.1.62) ... 1·25 70
143 **62** 1r. vermilion (7.1.63) ... 11·00 10
a. Imperf (pair) ...
144 1r.25 reddish violet (27.10.61) ... 1·25 2·00
144*a* 2r. orange (7.1.63) ... 5·50 15
144*b* 5r. green (7.1.63) ... 6·00 3·00
128/144*b* *Set of* 19 ... 45·00 6·25

See also Nos. 170/181 and 204/207.

(**63**)

64 Warsak Dam and Power Station

1961 (12 Feb). Lahore Stamp Exhibition. No. 110 optd with T **63**.
145 **51** 8a. deep green (R.) ... 1·00 1·75

(Des A. Ghani)

1961 (1 July). Completion of Warsak Hydro-Electric Project. P 12½×14.
146 **64** 40p. black and blue ... 60 10

65 Narcissus

66 Ten Roses

(Des A. Ghani)

1961 (2 Oct). Child Welfare Week. P 14.
147 **65** 13p. turquoise-blue ... 50 10
148 90p. bright purple ... 1·25 20

(Des A. Ghani)

1961 (4 Nov). Co-operative Day. P 13.
149 **66** 13p. rose-red and deep green ... 40 10
150 90p. rose-red and blue ... 85 90

67 Police Crest and 'Traffic Control'

68 Locomotive *Eagle*, 1861

(Photo D.L.R.)

1961 (30 Nov). Police Centenary. P 13.
151 **67** 13p. silver, black and blue ... 50 10
152 40p. silver, black and red ... 1·00 20

(Des M. Thoma. Photo D.L.R.)

1961 (31 Dec). Railway Centenary. T **68** and similar horiz design. P 14.
153 13p. green, black and yellow ... 75 80
154 50p. yellow, black and green ... 1·00 1·50

Design: 13p. T **68**; 50p. Diesel locomotive No. 20 and tracks forming '1961'.

(**70**)

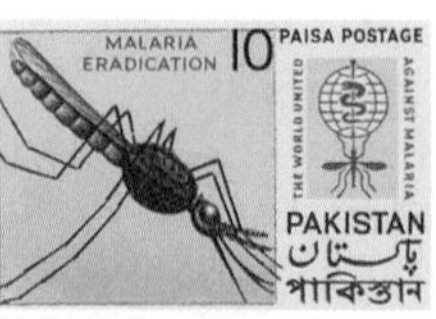

71 *Anopheles* sp (mosquito)

1962 (6 Feb). First Karachi–Dacca Jet Flight. No. 87 surch with T **70**.
155 **39** 13p. on 2½a. scarlet (R.) ... 1·75 1·25

(Photo D.L.R.)

1962 (7 Apr). Malaria Eradication. T **71** and similar horiz design. P 14.
156 10p. black, yellow and red ... 35 10
157 13p. black, greenish yellow and red ... 35 10

Design: 10p. T **71**; 13p. Mosquito pierced by blade.

73 Pakistan Map and Jasmine

(Photo Courvoisier)

1962 (8 June). New Constitution. P 12.
158 **73** 40p. yellow-green, bluish green and grey ... 1·00 10

74 Football

78 Marble Fruit Dish and Bahawalpuri Clay Flask

(Des A. Ghani and M. Bhatti)

1962 (14 Aug). Sports. T **74** and similar horiz designs. P 12½×14.
159 7p. black and blue ... 10 10
160 13p. black and green ... 60 2·25
161 25p. black and purple ... 20 10
162 40p. black and orange-brown ... 2·00 2·25
159/162 *Set of* 4 ... 2·50 4·00

Designs: 7p. T **74**; 13p. Hockey; 25p. Squash; 40p. Cricket.

(Des A. Ghani and M. Bhatti)

1962 (10 Nov). Small Industries. T **78** and similar vert designs. P 13.
163 7p. brown-lake ... 10 10
164 13p. deep green ... 2·50 3·00
165 25p. reddish violet ... 10 10
166 40p. yellow-green ... 10 10
167 50p. deep red ... 10 10
163/167 *Set of* 5 ... 2·50 3·00

Designs: 7p. T **78**; 13p. Sports equipment; 25p. Camel-skin lamp and brassware; 40p. Wooden powderbowl and basket-work; 50p. Inlaid cigarette-box and brassware.

83 Child Welfare

(Des M. Thoma. Photo D.L.R.)

1962 (11 Dec). 16th Anniversary of UNICEF. P 14.
168 **83** 13p. black, light blue and maroon ... 35 10
169 40p. black, yellow and turquoise-blue ... 35 10

Nos. 170, etc.

Nos. 131/142

1962–70. As Types **60/61** but with redrawn Bengali inscription at top right. No wmk.
170 **60** 1p. violet (1963) ... 10 10
171 2p. rose-red (1964) ... 2·75 10
a. Imperf (pair) ... 3·00
172 3p. reddish purple (1970) ... 16·00 7·50
173 5p. ultramarine (1963) ... 10 10
a. Printed on the gummed side ... 13·00
174 7p. emerald (1964) ... 7·00 3·50
175 **61** 10p. brown (1963) ... 20 10
a. Printed on the gummed side ... 13·00
176 13p. slate-violet ... 20 10
176*a* 15p. bright purple (31.12.64) ... 30 10
ab. Imperf (pair) ... 4·50
ac. Printed on the gummed side ... 15·00
176*b* **61** 20p. myrtle-green (26.1.70) ... 40 10
ba. Imperf (pair) ... 3·50
bb. Printed on the gummed side ... 15·00
177 25p. deep blue (1963) ... 11·00 10
a. Imperf (pair) ... 10·00
178 40p. deep purple (1964) ... 30 30
a. Imperf (pair) ... 6·50
179 50p. deep bluish green (1964) ... 30 10
a. Printed on the gummed side ...
180 75p. carmine-red (1964) ... 70 70
a. Printed on the gummed side ... 13·00
181 90p. yellow-green (1964) ... 70 1·00
170/181 *Set of* 14 ... 35·00 12·00

Other values in this series and the high values (Nos. 204/210) are known imperforate but we are not satisfied as to their status.

U.N.FORCE W. IRIAN
(**84**)

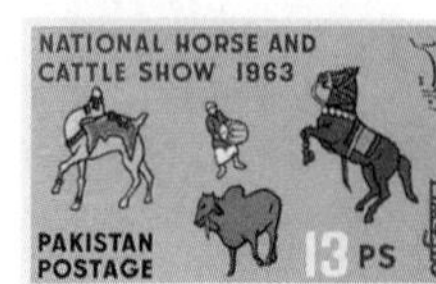

85 'Dancing' Horse, Camel and Bull

1963 (15 Feb). Pakistan UN Force in West Irian. No. 176 optd with T **84**.
182 **61** 13p. slate-violet (R.) ... 10 2·00

(Des S. Jahangir. Photo Courvoisier)

1963 (13 Mar). National Horse and Cattle Show. P 11½.
183 **85** 13p. blue, sepia and cerise ... 10 10

86 Wheat and Tractor

(Des B. Mirza)

1963 (21 Mar). Freedom from Hunger. T **86** and similar horiz design. P 12½×14.
184 13p. orange-brown ... 3·00 10
185 50p. bistre-brown ... 4·50 55

Design: 13p. T **86**; 50p. Rice.

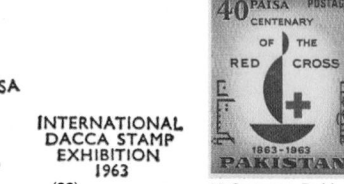

13 PAISA
INTERNATIONAL
DACCA STAMP
EXHIBITION
1963
(**88**)

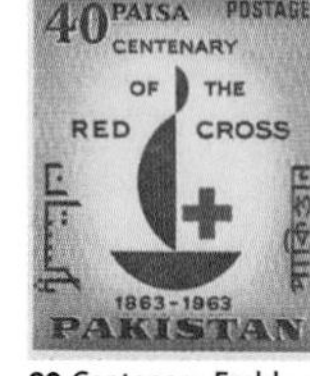

89 Centenary Emblem

1963 (23 Mar). Second International Stamp Exhibition, Dacca. No. 109 surch with T **88**.
186 **51** 13p. on 2a. brown-red ... 50 50

1963 (25 June). Centenary of Red Cross. Recess; cross typo. P 13.
187 **89** 40p. red and deep olive ... 2·25 15

90 Paharpur

100 YEARS OF P.W.D.
OCTOBER, 1963
13
(**94**)

(Des A. Ghani)

1963 (16 Sept). Archaeological Series. T **90** and similar designs. P 14×12½ (13p.) or 12½×15 (others).
188 7p. ultramarine ... 55 10
189 13p. sepia ... 55 10
190 40p. carmine ... 90 10
191 50p. deep reddish violet ... 95 10
188/191 *Set of* 4 ... 2·75 35

Designs: Vert—13p. Moenjodaro; Horiz—7p. T **90**; 40p. Taxila; 50p. Mainamati.

1963 (7 Oct). Centenary of Public Works Department. No. 133 surch with T **94** by typography.
192 **60** 13p. on 3p. reddish purple ... 10 10

Forged surcharges applied in lithography exist.

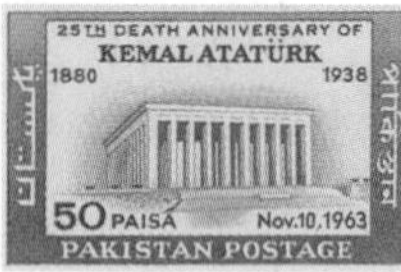

95 Atatürk's Mausoleum

(Des A. Ghani)

1963 (10 Nov). 25th Death Anniversary of Kemal Atatürk. P 13½.
193 **95** 50p. red ... 50 10

96 Globe and UNESCO Emblem

(Photo D.L.R.)

1963 (10 Dec). 15th Anniversary of Declaration of Human Rights. P 14.
194 **96** 50p. brown, red and ultramarine ... 40 10

97 Thermal Power Installations

(Des A. Ghani)

1963 (25 Dec). Completion of Multan Thermal Power Station. P 12½×14.
195 **97** 13p. ultramarine ... 10 10

98 Multiple Star and Crescent

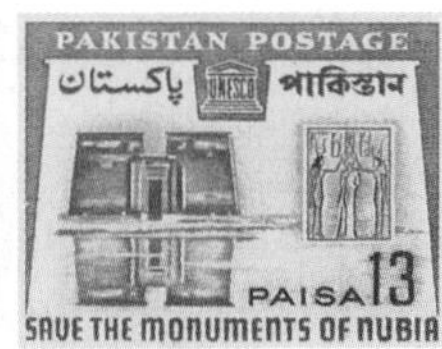

99 Temple of Thot, Queen Nefertari and Maids

1963–79. As Nos. 43b, 89, 95 and 143/144*b*, but W **98** (sideways* on 15r.).

204	**62**	1r. vermilion	1·75	10
		a. Printed on the gummed side	13·00	
		b. Imperf (pair)	7·50	
		w. Wmk inverted	2·25	
205		1r.25 reddish violet (1964)	3·25	2·50
		aw. Wmk inverted	3·75	
		b. Purple (1975?)	7·00	2·75
		ba. Imperf (pair)	6·00	
206		2r. orange (1964)	1·50	15
		a. Imperf (pair)	8·00	
		w. Wmk inverted	2·25	
207		5r. green (1964)	8·00	1·00
		a. Imperf (pair)	11·00	
		w. Wmk inverted	8·00	
208	**41**	10r. myrtle-green and yellow-orange (1968)	8·50	7·00
		a. Imperf (pair)		
		bw. Wmk inverted		
		c. Wmk sideways	5·00	5·50
209	**44**	15r. red and deep reddish purple (20.3.79)	2·50	4·75
		a. Imperf (pair)	13·00	
		w. Wmk tips of crescent pointing downwards		
210	**13**	25r. violet (1968)	18·00	24·00
		aw. Wmk inverted	20·00	
		b. Wmk sideways	8·50	13·00
		ba. Imperf (pair)	15·00	
204/210b *Set of 7*			27·00	24·00

MULTIPLE STAR AND CRESCENT WATERMARKED PAPER. When viewed from the back with the stamp upright, upright and sideways reversed watermarks show the tips of the crescents pointing upwards and to the right; reversed and sideways watermarks show the tips pointing upwards to the left; inverted and sideways inverted and reversed watermarks show the tips pointing downwards and to the left, while sideways inverted and upright inverted and reversed watermarks show them pointing downwards and to the left. Upright and sideways reversed watermarks may be differentiated by the angle of the row of stars which is approximately 60° for the upright and 30° for the sideways reversed.

(Des A. Ghani)

1964 (30 Mar). Nubian Monuments Preservation. T **99** and similar horiz design. P 13×13½.

211		13p. turquoise-blue and red	30	10
212		50p. bright purple and black	70	10

Design: 13p. T **99**; 50p. Temple of Abu Simbel.

101 'Unisphere' and Pakistan Pavilion

103 Shah Abdul Latif's Mausoleum

(Des A. Ghani)

1964 (22 Apr). New York World's Fair. T **101** and similar design. P 12½×14 (13p.) or 14×12½ (1r.25).

213		13p. ultramarine	10	10
214		1r.25 ultramarine and red-orange	40	20

Design: Horiz—13p. T **101**; Vert—1r.25 Pakistan Pavilion on 'Unisphere'.

(Des A. Ghani)

1964 (25 June). Death Bicentenary of Shah Abdul Latif of Bhit. P 13½×13.

215	**103**	50p. bright blue and carmine-lake	1·00	10

104 Mausoleum of Quaid-i-Azam

105 Mausoleum

(Des A. Ghani)

1964 (11 Sept). 16th Death Anniversary of Mohammed Ali Jinnah (Quaid-i-Azam). P 13½ (15p.) or 13 (50p.)

216	**104**	15p. emerald-green	1·00	10
217	**105**	50p. bronze-green	2·25	10

106 Bengali and Urdu Alphabets

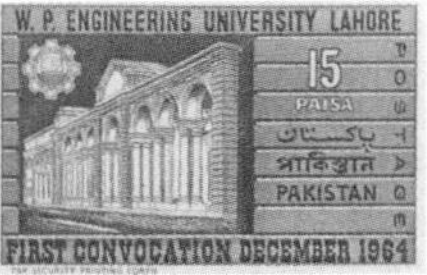

107 University Building

(Des N. Rizvi)

1964 (5 Oct). Universal Children's Day. P 13.

218	**106**	15p. brown	10	10

(Des N. Rizvi)

1964 (21 Dec). First Convocation of the West Pakistan University of Engineering and Technology, Lahore. P 12½×14.

219	**107**	15p. chestnut	10	10

PROCESS. All the following issues were lithographed by the Pakistan Security Printing Corporation, *unless otherwise stated.*

108 'Help the Blind'

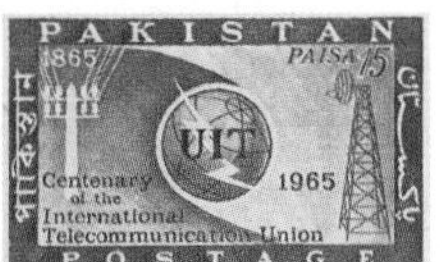

109 ITU Emblem and Symbols

(Des A. Chughtai)

1965 (28 Feb). Blind Welfare. P 13.

220	**108**	15p. ultramarine and yellow	20	10

(Des N. Rizvi. Recess)

1965 (17 May). ITU Centenary. P 12½×14.

221	**109**	15p. reddish purple	1·50	30

110 ICY Emblem

1965 (26 June). International Co-operation Year. P 13×13½.

222	**110**	15p. black and light blue	1·00	15
223		50p. green and yellow	1·75	40

111 'Co-operation'

112 Globe and Flags of Turkey, Iran and Pakistan

1965 (21 July). First Anniversary of Regional Development Co-operation Pact. P 13½×13 (15p.) or 13 (50p.)

224	**111**	15p. multicoloured	20	10
225	**112**	50p. multicoloured	1·10	10

113 Soldier and Tanks

(Des S. Ghori (7p.), N. Rizvi (15p.), A. Ghani (50p.))

1965 (25 Dec). Pakistan Armed Forces. T **113** and similar horiz designs. Multicoloured. P 13½×13.

226		7p. Type **113**	75	70
227		15p. Naval officer and *Tughril* (destroyer)	1·50	10
228		50p. Pilot and Lockheed F-104C Star fighters	2·50	30
226/228 *Set of 3*			4·25	1·00

116 Army, Navy and Air Force Crests

117 Atomic Reactor, Islamabad

(Des A. Ghani)

1966 (13 Feb). Armed Forces Day. P 13½×13.

229	**116**	15p. royal blue, dull green, bright blue and buff	1·00	10

(Des A. Ghani. Recess)

1966 (30 Apr). Inauguration of Pakistan's First Atomic Reactor. P 13.

230	**117**	15p. black	10	10

118 Bank Crest

119 Children

(Des A. Ghani)

1966 (25 Aug). Silver Jubilee of Habib Bank. P 12½×14.

231	**118**	15p. blue-green, yellow-orange and sepia	10	10

(Des S. Nagi)

1966 (3 Oct). Universal Children's Day. P 13½.

232	**119**	15p. light brown, black, red and pale yellow	10	10

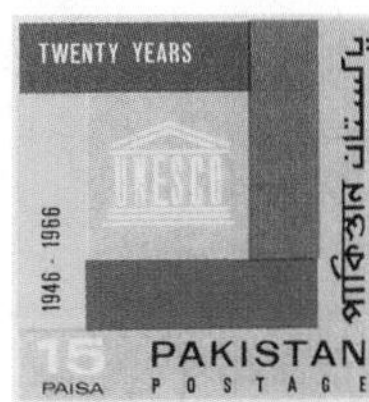

120 UNESCO Emblem

1966 (24 Nov). 20th Anniversary of UNESCO. P 14.

233	**120**	15p. multicoloured	3·75	30

121 Flag, Secretariat Building and President Ayub

(Des A. Ghani)

1966 (29 Nov). Islamabad (new capital). P 13.

234	**121**	15p. deep bluish green, chestnut, light blue and bistre-brown	35	10
235		50p. deep bluish green, chestnut, light blue and black	65	10

122 Avicenna

123 Mohammed Ali Jinnah

(Des A. Ghani)

1966 (3 Dec). Foundation of Health and Tibbi Research Institute. P 13×13½.

236	**122**	15p. dull green and salmon	40	10
		a. Imperf (pair)	75·00	

(Des A. Ghani. Recess and litho)

1966 (25 Dec). 90th Birth Anniversary of Mohammed Ali Jinnah. T **123** and similar design bearing same portrait, but in different frame. P 13.

237	**123**	15p. black, orange and greenish blue	15	10
238	–	50p. black, purple and ultramarine	35	10

124 Tourist Year Emblem

125 Emblem of Pakistan TB Association

(Des A. Ghani)

1967 (1 Jan). International Tourist Year. P 13½×13.
239 **124** 15p. black, light blue and yellow-brown 10 10

1967 (10 Jan). Tuberculosis Eradication Campaign. P 13½×13.
240 **125** 15p. red, sepia and chestnut 10 10

126 Scout Salute and Badge

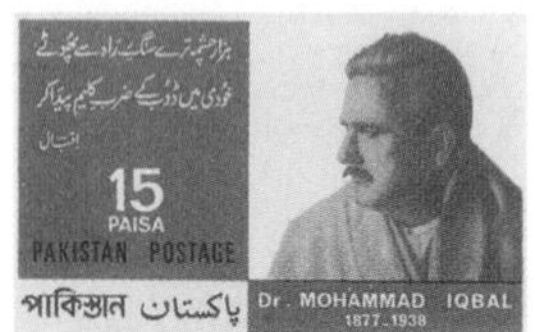

127 'Justice'

(Des A. Rauf. Photo)

1967 (29 Jan). Fourth National Scout Jamboree. P 12½×14.
241 **126** 15p. light orange-brown and maroon 15 10

(Des A. Rauf)

1967 (17 Feb). Centenary of West Pakistan High Court. P 13.
242 **127** 15p. black, slate, light red and slate-blue 10 10

128 Dr. Mohammed Iqbal (philosopher)

(Des A. Rauf)

1967 (21 Apr). Iqbal Commemoration. P 13.
243 **128** 15p. sepia and light red 15 10
244 1r. sepia and deep green 35 10

129 Hilal-i-Isteqlal Flag

(Des A. Rahman)

1967 (15 May). Award of Hilal-i-Isteqlal (for Valour) to Lahore, Sialkot, and Sargodha. P 13.
245 **129** 15p. multicoloured 10 10

130 '20th Anniversary'

(Des F. Karim. Photo)

1967 (14 Aug). 20th Anniversary of Independence. P 13.
246 **130** 15p. red and deep bluish green 10 10

131 'Rice Exports'

132 Cotton Plant, Yarn and Textiles

(Des S. Nagi (10p.), F. Karim (others). Photo)

1967 (26 Sept). Pakistan Exports. T **131/2** and similar design. P 13×13½.
247 **131** 10p. yellow, deep bluish green and deep blue 10 15
248 **132** 15p. multicoloured 10 10
a. Pale orange (top panel) omitted .... 27·00
249 – 50p. multicoloured 20 15
247/249 *Set of 3* 35 35
Design: Vert as T **132**—50p. Raw jute, bale and bags.

134 Clay Toys

(Des F. Karim)

1967 (2 Oct). Universal Children's Day. P 13.
250 **134** 15p. multicoloured 10 10

135 Shah and Empress of Iran and Gulistan Palace, Teheran

(Des S. Ghori. Recess and litho)

1967 (26 Oct). Coronation of Shah Mohammed Riza Pahlavi and Empress Farah of Iran. P 13.
251 **135** 50p. purple, blue and light yellow-ochre .... 1·25 10

136 'Each For All—All For Each'

(Des A. Rauf)

1967 (4 Nov). Co-operative Day. P 13.
252 **136** 15p. multicoloured 10 10

137 Mangla Dam

(Des S. Nagi)

1967 (23 Nov). Indus Basin Project. P 13.
253 **137** 15p. multicoloured 10 10

138 Crab pierced by Sword

139 Human Rights Emblem

(Des F. Karim)

1967 (26 Dec). The Fight against Cancer. P 13.
254 **138** 15p. red and black 70 10

1968 (31 Jan). Human Rights Year. Photo. P 14×13.
255 **139** 15p. red and deep turquoise-blue 10 15
256 50p. red, yellow and silver-grey 10 15

140 Agricultural University, Mymensingh

141 WHO Emblem

(Des S. Ghori. Photo)

1968 (28 Mar). First Convocation of East Pakistan Agricultural University. P 13½×13.
257 **140** 15p. multicoloured 10 10

(Des A. Salahuddin. Photo)

1968 (7 Apr). 20th Anniversary of World Health Organisation. P 14×13.
258 **141** 15p. green and orange-red 10 15
a. 'PAIS' for 'PAISA' (R. 4/5) .... 4·00
259 50p. red-orange and indigo 10 15

142 Kazi Nazrul Islam (poet, composer and patriot)

(Des F. Karim. Recess and litho)

1968 (25 June). Nazrul Islam Commemoration. P 13.
260 **142** 15p. sepia and pale yellow 35 15
261 50p. sepia and pale rose-red 65 15
Nos. 260/261 with a two-line inscription giving the wrong date of birth ('1889') were prepared but not issued. Some are known to have been released in error.

4 PAISA
(**143**)

1968 (18 July–Aug). Nos. 56, 74 and 61 surch as T **143**.
262 4p. on 3a. purple .... 1·00 1·75
263 4p. on 6a. deep ultramarine (R.) (8.68) .... 1·25 1·75
264 60p. on 10a. violet (R.) .... 1·00 35
a. Surch in black .... 40 2·50
b. Surch triple .... 50·00
262/264 *Set of 3* .... 3·00 3·50

144 Children running with Hoops

(Des A. Rauf)

1968 (7 Oct). Universal Children's Day. P 13.
265 **144** 15p. multicoloured 10 10

145 National Assembly

(Des M. Khatoon)

1968 (27 Oct). A Decade of Development. T **145** and similar horiz designs. P 13.
266 10p. multicoloured 10 45
267 15p. multicoloured 10 10
268 50p. multicoloured .... 2·00 30
269 60p. light blue, dull purple and vermilion .... 50 1·40
266/269 *Set of 4* .... 2·40 2·00
Designs: 10p. T **145**; 15p. Industry and agriculture; 50p. Army, Navy and Air Force; 60p. Minaret and atomic reactor plant.

149 Chittagong Steel Mill

(Des M. Khatoon)

1969 (7 Jan). Pakistan's First Steel Mill, Chittagong. P 13.
270 **149** 15p. grey, light blue and pale yellow-olive 10 10

150 'Family'

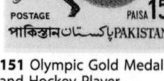

151 Olympic Gold Medal and Hockey Player

(Des M. Khatoon)

1969 (14 Jan). Family Planning. P 13½×13.

271	**150**	15p. bright purple and pale greenish blue	10	10

(Des S. Ghori. Photo)

1969 (30 Jan). Olympic Hockey Champions. P 13½.

272	**151**	15p. black, gold, deep green and pale blue	75	50
273		1r. black, gold, deep green and flesh-pink	2·25	1·00

152 Mirza Ghalib and Lines of Verse

(Des A. Rauf)

1969 (15 Feb). Death Centenary of Mirza Ghalib (poet). P 13.

274	**152**	15p. multicoloured	20	15
275		50p. multicoloured	50	15

The lines of verse on No. 275 are different from those in T **152**.

153 Dacca Railway Station

(Des F. Karim)

1969 (27 Apr). First Anniversary of New Dacca Railway Station. P 13.

276	**153**	15p. multicoloured	65	10

154 ILO Emblem and '1919–1969'

155 *Lady on Balcony* (18th-century Mogul)

(Des R-ud Din)

1969 (15 May). 50th Anniversary of International Labour Organisation. P 13½.

277	**154**	15p. buff and bluish green	10	10
278		50p. cinnamon and cerise	40	10

(Des S. Ghori, A. Rauf, F. Karim, A. Salahuddin, N. Mohammad and M. Khatoon)

1969 (21 July). Fifth Anniversary of Regional Co-operation for Development. T **155** and similar vert designs showing miniatures. Multicoloured. P 13.

279	20p. Type **155**	15	10
280	50p. *Kneeling Servant* (17th-cent Persian)	15	10
281	1r. *Suleiman the Magnificent holding Audience* (16th-cent Turkish)	20	10
279/281 *Set of 3*		45	25

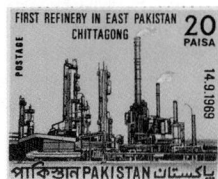

158 Eastern Refinery, Chittagong

(Des M. Khatoon. Photo)

1969 (14 Sept). First Oil Refinery in East Pakistan. P 13½×13.

282	**158**	20p. multicoloured	10	10

159 Children playing outside 'School'

(Des M. Khatoon. Photo)

1969 (6 Oct). Universal Children's Day. P 13.

283	**159**	20p. multicoloured	10	10

160 Japanese Doll and PIA Air Routes

(Des N. Mohammad)

1969 (1 Nov). Inauguration of PIA Pearl Route, Dacca–Tokyo. P 13½×13.

284	**160**	20p. multicoloured	40	10
		a. Yellow and pink omitted	11·00	
285		50p. multicoloured	60	40
		a. Yellow and pink omitted	11·00	

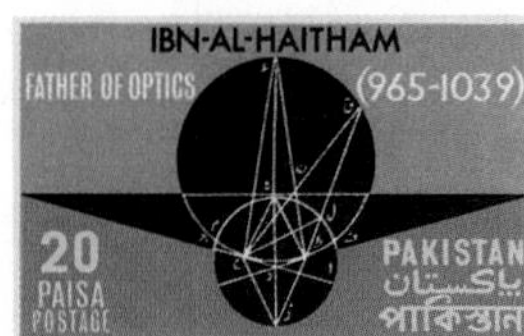

161 Reflection of Light Diagram

(Des A. Rauf. Photo)

1969 (4 Nov). Millenary Commemorative of Ibn-al-Haitham (physicist). P 13.

286	**161**	20p. black, lemon and light blue	10	10

162 Vickers Vimy and Karachi Airport

163 Flags, Sun Tower and Expo Site Plan

(Des N. Mohammad. Photo)

1969 (2 Dec). 50th Anniversary of First England–Australia Flight. P 13½×13.

287	**162**	50p. multicoloured	1·50	35

(Des R-ud Din)

1970 (15 Mar). World Fair, Osaka. P 13.

288	**163**	50p. multicoloured	20	30

164 New UPU HQ Building

(Des R-ud Din)

1970 (20 May). New UPU Headquarters Building. P 13½×13.

289	**164**	20p. multicoloured	15	10
290		50p. multicoloured	25	25

The above, in a miniature sheet, additionally inscr 'UPU Day 9th Oct, 1971', were put on sale on that date in very limited numbers.

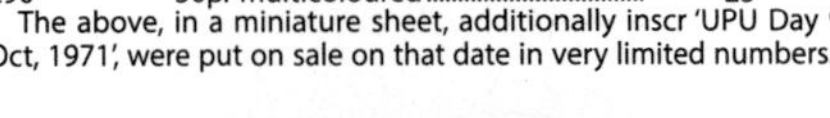

165 UN HQ Building

(Des A. Rauf)

1970 (26 June). 25th Anniversary of United Nations. T **165** and similar horiz design. Multicoloured. P 13×13½.

291	20p. Type **165**	10	10
292	50p. UN emblem	15	20

167 IEY Emblem, Book and Pen

(Des M. Khatoon)

1970 (6 July). International Education Year. P 13.

293	**167**	20p. multicoloured	10	10
294		50p. multicoloured	20	20

168 Saiful Malook Lake (Pakistan)

1970 (21 July). Sixth Anniversary of Regional Co-operation for Development. T **168** and similar square designs. Multicoloured. P 13.

295	20p. Type **168**	25	10
296	50p. Seeyo-Se-Pol Bridge, Esfahan (Iran)	35	10
297	1r. View from Fethiye (Turkey)	50	15
295/297 *Set of 3*		1·00	30

171 Asian Productivity Symbol

172 Dr. Maria Montessori

1970 (18 Aug). Asian Productivity Year. Photo. P 12½×14.

298	**171**	50p. multicoloured	20	20

(Des M. Khatoon)

1970 (31 Aug). Birth Centenary of Dr. Maria Montessori (educationist). P 13.

299	**172**	20p. multicoloured	15	10
300		50p. multicoloured	15	30

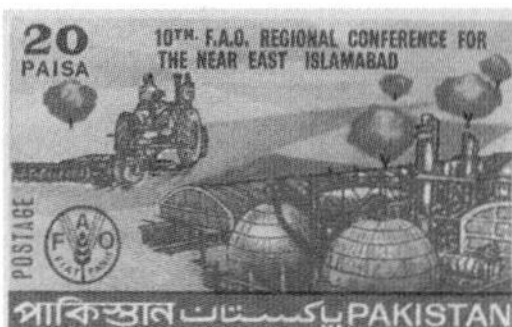

173 Tractor and Fertiliser Factory

1970 (12 Sept). Tenth Near East FAO Regional Conference, Islamabad. P 13.

301	**173**	20p. bright green and orange-brown	15	50

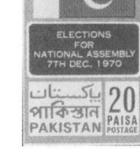

174 Children and Open Book

175 Pakistan Flag and Text

(Des F. Karim. Photo)

1970 (5 Oct). Universal Children's Day. P 13.

302	**174**	20p. multicoloured	15	10

(Des A. Salahuddin)

1970 (7 Dec). General Elections for National Assembly. P 13½×13.

303	**175**	20p. green and bluish violet	15	10

(Des A. Salahuddin)

1970 (17 Dec). General Elections for Provincial Assemblies. As No. 303, but inscr 'PROVINCIAL ASSEMBLIES 17TH DEC., 1970'.

304	**175**	20p. green and pale magenta	15	10

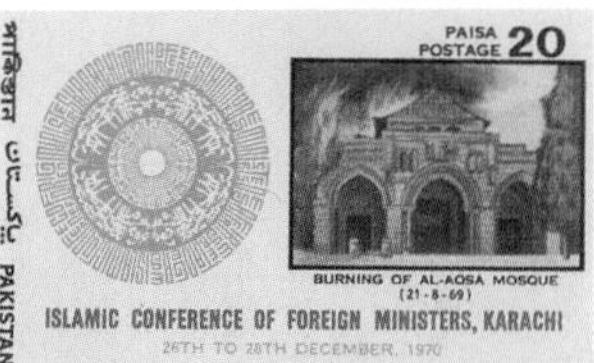

176 Conference Crest and burning Al-Aqsa Mosque

(Des R-ud Din)

1970 (26 Dec). Conference of Islamic Foreign Ministers, Karachi. P 13.

305	**176**	20p. multicoloured	1·00	15

STAMP BOOKLETS

1956 (23 Mar). Black on green cover. Stapled.

SB1	1r. 08 booklet containing 12×6p. and 12×1½a. (Nos. 65, 68) in blocks of 4	9·00	

OFFICIAL STAMPS

PAKISTAN

PAKISTAN (O 1) SERVICE (O 1a)

1947. Nos. O143, O144*b*, O145/O146, O146*b*/O150 and 259/262 (King George VI) of India, optd as T O **1** (Nos. O1/O9) or as T O **1a** (Nos. O10/O13), both in litho by Nasik.

No.	Description	Unused	Used
O1	3p. slate	3·50	2·75
O2	½a. purple	60	10
O3	9p. green	5·50	4·50
O4	1a. carmine	60	10
	w. Wmk inverted	—	28·00
O5	1½a. dull violet	60	10
	w. Wmk inverted	30·00	17·00
O6	2a. vermilion	60	1·00
O7	2½a. bright violet	7·50	17·00
O8	4a. brown	1·50	1·75
O9	8a. slate-violet	2·25	3·25
O10	1r. grey and red-brown	1·25	4·50
O11	2r. purple and brown	14·00	14·00
O12	5r. green and blue	35·00	65·00
O13	10r. purple and claret	90·00	£180
O1/O13 *Set of* 13		£140	£250

See note after No. 19. The 1a.3p. (India No. O146*a*) exists as a local issue (*Price*, Karachi opt, £16 *mint*, £42 *used*).

Whereas the Nasik overprints on the Rupee values were applied to the Indian postage stamps (Nos. 259/262). Those applied at Karachi were on the official stamps (O138/O141). The two overprints may be identified by the relative positions of the two words and the shape of the 'R' of 'SERVICE'.

SERVICE (O 2) SERVICE (O 3) SERVICE (O 4)

NOTE. Apart from a slight difference in size, Types O **2** and O **3** can easily be distinguished by the difference in the shape of the 'c'. T O **4** is taller and thinner in appearance.

PRINTERS. T O 2 was overprinted by De La Rue and T O 3 by the Pakistan Security Ptg Corp.

1948 (14 Aug)–**54?** Optd with T O **2**.

No.	Type	Description	Unused	Used
O14	**7**	3p. red (No. 24)	10	10
O15		6p. violet (No. 25) (R.)	10	10
O16		9p. green (No. 26) (R.)	30	10
O17	**8**	1a. blue (No. 27) (R.)	3·75	10
O18		1½a. grey-green (No. 28) (R.)	3·50	10
O19		2a. red (No. 29)	2·00	10
O20	**10**	3a. green (No. 31)	26·00	20·00
O21	**9**	4a. reddish brown (No. 33)	3·00	10
O22	**11**	8a. black (No. 35) (R.)	3·00	10·00
O23	**12**	1r. ultramarine (No. 38)	1·50	10
O24		2r. chocolate (No. 39)	14·00	11·00
O25		5r. carmine (No. 40)	65·00	30·00
O26	**13**	10r. magenta (No. 41)	26·00	80·00
		a. Perf 12 (10.10.51)	38·00	85·00
		b. Perf 13 (1954?)	26·00	90·00
O14/O26 *Set of* 13			£130	£130

1949. Optd with T O **2**.

No.	Description	Unused	Used
O27	1a. blue (No. 44) (R.)	7·00	10
O28	1½a. grey-green (No. 45) (R.)	5·00	10
	a. Opt inverted	£375	60·00
O29	2a. red (No. 46)	11·00	10
	a. Opt omitted (in pair with normal)	—	£180
O30	3a. green (No. 47)	42·00	9·00
O31	8a. black (No. 49) (R.)	65·00	25·00
O27/O31 *Set of* 5		£110	30·00

1951 (14 Aug). Fourth Anniversary of Independence. As Nos. 56, 58 and 60, but inscr 'SERVICE' instead of 'PAKISTAN POSTAGE'.

No.	Type	Description	Unused	Used
O32	**18**	3a. purple	10·00	10·00
O33	**19**	4a. green	2·50	20
O34	**20**	8a. sepia	11·00	12·00
O32/O34 *Set of* 3			21·00	20·00

1953. Optd with T O **3**.

No.	Description	Unused	Used
O35	3p. red (No. 24a)	10	10
O36	6p. violet (No. 25a) (R.)	10	10
O37	9p. green (No. 26a) (R.)	15	10
O38	1a. blue (No. 44a) (R.)	20	10
O39	1½a. grey-green (No. 45a) (R.)	20	10
O40	2a. red (No. 46a) (1953?)	35	10
O41	1r. ultramarine (No. 38a)	10·00	7·50
O42	2r. chocolate (No. 39a)	8·50	1·25
O43	5r. carmine (No. 40a)	95·00	35·00
O44	10r. magenta (No. 41b) (date?)	28·00	90·00
O35/O44 *Set of* 10		£120	£120

1954 (14 Aug). Seventh Anniversary of Independence. Nos. 65/71 optd with T O **3**.

No.	Description	Unused	Used
O45	6p. reddish violet (R.)	15	4·00
O46	9p. blue (R.)	3·75	15·00
O47	1a. carmine	20	2·50
O48	1½a. red	20	2·50
O49	14a. deep green (R.)	2·50	15·00
O50	1r. green (R.)	1·00	10
O51	2r. red-orange	8·00	15
O45/O51 *Set of* 7		14·00	35·00

1955 (14 Aug). Eighth Anniversary of Independence. No. 75 optd with T O **3**.

No.	Description	Unused	Used
O52	8a. deep reddish violet (R.)	1·50	10

1957 (Jan)–**59.** Nos. 65/71 optd with T O **4**.

No.	Description	Unused	Used
O53	6p. reddish violet (R.)	10	10
	a. Opt inverted	†	—
O54	9p. blue (R.) (1.59)	15	10
	a. Opt inverted	26·00	
O55	1a. carmine	15	10
	a. Opt inverted	—	60·00
	b. Printed on the gummed side		
O56	1½a. red	15	10
	a. Opt double		
	b. Printed on the gummed side		
O57	14a. deep green (R.) (2.59)	75	6·50
O58	1r. green (R.) (4.58)	75	10
O59	2r. red-orange (4.58)	6·00	10
O53/O59 *Set of* 7		7·25	6·50

1958 (Jan)–**61.** Optd with O **4**.

No.	Type	Description	Unused	Used
O60	**7**	3p. red (No. 24a)	10	10
O61	–	5r. carmine (No. 40a) (7.59)	8·00	15
O62	**41**	10r. myrtle-green and yellow-orange (No. 89) (R.) (1961)	7·00	12·00
		a. Opt inverted	17·00	
O60/O62 *Set of* 3			14·00	12·00

1958 (Jan)–**61.** Nos. 74/75 optd with T O **4**.

No.	Description	Unused	Used
O63	6a. deep ultramarine (R.) (4.61)	50	10
O64	8a. deep reddish violet (R.)	1·25	10

1959 (Aug). No. 83 optd with T O **4**.

No.	Type	Description	Unused	Used
O65	**37**	2a. scarlet	30	10

1961 (Apr). Nos. 110/111 optd with T O **4**.

No.	Type	Description	Unused	Used
O66	**51**	8a. deep green	50	10
O67		1r. blue	50	10
		a. Opt inverted	13·00	

NEW CURRENCY. In addition to the local handstamped surcharges mentioned in the note above No. 122, the following typographed surcharges were made at the Treasury at Mastung and issued in the Baluchi province of Kalat: 6p. on 1a. (No. O55), 9p. on 1½a. (No. O56) and 13p. on 2a. (No. O65). They differ in that the surcharges are smaller and 'PAISA' is expressed as 'Paisa'. Being locals they are outside the scope of this catalogue.

1961. Optd with T O **4**.

No.	Description	Unused	Used
O68	1p. on 1½a. (No. 122)	10	10
	a. Optd with Type O **3**	9·50	2·00
O69	2p. on 3p. (No. 123) (1.1.61)	10	10
	a. Surch double		
	b. Optd with Type O **3**	27·00	6·50
O70	3p. on 6p. (No. 124)	10	10
O71	7p. on 1a. (No. 125)	10	10
	a. Optd with Type O **3**	27·00	22·00
O72	13p. on 2a. (No. 126)	10	10
O73	13p. on 2a. (No. 127)	10	10
O68/O73 *Set of* 6		55	30

No. O68 exists with small and large '1' (see note below Nos. 122/127, etc.).

ERRORS. See note after No. 127.

SERVICE (O **5**)

1961–63. Nos. 128/144*b* optd with T O **4** (rupee values) or T O **5** (others).

No.	Description	Unused	Used
	(a) Inscribed 'SHAKISTAN'		
O74	1p. violet (R.) (1.1.61)	10	10
O75	2p. rose-red (R.) (12.1.61)	10	10
O76	5p. ultramarine (R.) (23.3.61)	15	10
	a. Opt inverted		
	(b) Inscribed 'PAKISTAN'		
O77	1p. violet (R.)	9·00	10
	a. Printed on the gummed side		
	b. Opt inverted		
O78	2p. rose-red (R.)	1·00	10
	a. Printed on the gummed side		
O79	3p. reddish purple (R.) (27.10.61)	10	10
O80	5p. ultramarine (R.)	8·00	10
O81	7p. emerald (R.) (23.3.61)	15	10
O82	10p. brown (R.)	15	10
	a. Opt inverted		
O83	13p. slate-violet (R.) (14.2.61)	15	10
O85	40p. deep purple (R.) (1.1.62)	25	10
O86	50p. deep bluish green (R.) (1.1.62)	25	10
	a. Opt double		
O87	75p. carmine-red (R.) (23.3.62)	35	10
	a. Opt double		
O88	1r. vermilion (7.1.63)	45	10
	a. Opt double	27·00	
	b. Opt as Type O **3**	55·00	38·00
	c. Opt inverted	17·00	
O89	2r. orange (7.1.63)	1·50	20
O90	5r. green (R.) (7.1.63)	4·25	9·50
O74/O90 *Set of* 16		23·00	9·50

1963–78?. Nos. 170, etc., optd with T O **5**, in red.

No.	Description	Unused	Used
O91	1p. violet	10	10
O92	2p. rose-red (1965)	10	10
	a. Opt inverted	3·25	
	b. Albino opt		
	c. Opt double, one albino		
O93	3p. reddish purple (1967)	3·75	1·50
	a. Opt double	20·00	
	b. Opt inverted	3·75	
	c. Printed on the gummed side		
O94	5p. ultramarine	10	10
	a. Opt inverted	2·00	
	ab. Vert pair, top stamp without opt, lower with opt inverted		
O95	7p. emerald (date?)	50·00	17·00
O96	10p. brown (1965)	10	10
	a. Opt inverted	3·75	
O97	13p. slate-violet	10	10
O98	15p. bright purple (31.12.64)	10	2·50
O99	20p. myrtle-green (26.1.70)	10	40
	a. Opt double	26·00	
O100	25p. deep blue (1977)	22·00	5·50
O101	40p. deep purple (1972?)	28·00	13·00
O102	50p. deep bluish green (1965)	15	15
O103	75p. carmine-red (date?)	42·00	35·00
O104	90p. yellow-green (5.78?)	18·00	13·00
O91/O104 *Set of* 14		£130	75·00

1968?. Nos. 204, 206 and 207 optd with T O **4**.

No.	Type	Description	Unused	Used
O105	**62**	1r. vermilion	4·75	1·25
		a. Opt inverted	13·00	
		b. Printed and overprinted on the gummed side	17·00	
		w. Wmk inverted	13·00	
O107		2r. orange (date?)	23·00	2·25
		a. Opt inverted	13·00	
O108		5r. green (R.) (date?)	50·00	14·00
		a. Opt inverted	18·00	
O105/O108 *Set of* 3			65·00	16·00

BAHAWALPUR

Bahawalpur, a former feudatory state situated to the west of the Punjab, was briefly independent following the partition of India on 15 August 1947 before acceding to Pakistan on 3 October of the same year.

East India Company and later Indian Empire post offices operated in Bahawalpur from 1854. By a postal agreement of 1879 internal mail from the state administration was carried unstamped, but this arrangement was superseded by the issue of Official stamps in 1945.

These had been preceded by a series of pictorial stamps prepared in 1933–1934 on unwatermarked paper. It was intended that these would be used as state postage stamps, but permission for such use was withheld by the Indian Government so they were used for revenue purposes. The same designs were utilised for the 1945 Official series, Nos. O1/O6, on paper watermarked Star and Crescent. Residual stocks of the unwatermarked 1a., 8a., 1r. and 2r. were used for the provisional Officials, Nos. O7 and O11/O13.

A commemorative 1a. Receipt stamp showing the State Arms was recess-printed by D.L.R. in black on unwatermarked green paper perf 14 (*Price* £10 *unused*). It was produced to mark the centenary of the alliance with Great Britain and was used in a series of postal trials, but was not available to the public. An example of this stamp is known used on cover from Deh Rawal to Sadiq Garh and postmarked 14 August 1933. Both this 1a. and the same value from the unwatermarked set also exist with Official Arabic overprint in black. These were not issued for postal purposes although one used example of the latter has been recorded postmarked 22 February 1933 also from Deh Rawal.

Stamps of India were overprinted in the interim period between 15 August and 3 October 1947. After the state joined Pakistan postage stamps were issued for internal use until 1953.

PRICES FOR STAMPS ON COVER TO 1945
The postage and Official stamps of Bahawalpur are rare used on cover.

Nawab (from 1947 Amir) Sadiq Mohammad Khan Abbasi V, 1907–1966

(**1**)

1947 (15 Aug). Nos. 265/268, 269*b*/277 and 259/262 (King George VI) of India optd locally with T **1**.

No.	Description	Unused
1	3p. slate (R.)	45·00
2	½a. purple	45·00
3	9p. green (R.)	45·00
4	1a. carmine	45·00
5	1½a. dull violet (R.)	45·00
6	2a. vermilion	45·00
	a. Opt double	£4750
7	3a. bright violet (R.)	45·00
8	3½a. bright blue (R.)	45·00
9	4a. brown	45·00
10	6a. turquoise-green (R.)	45·00
	a. Opt double	£4750
11	8a. slate-violet (R.)	45·00
12	12a. lake	45·00
13	14a. purple	90·00
14	1r. grey and red-brown	60·00
	a. Opt double, one albino	£550
15	2r. purple and brown (R.)	£4750
16	5r. green and blue (R.)	£4750
17	10r. purple and claret	£4750
1/17 *Set of* 17		£14000

Nos. 1/17 were issued during the interim period, following the implementation of the Indian Independence Act, during which time Bahawalpur was part of neither of the two Dominions created. The Amir acceded to the Dominion of Pakistan on 3 October 1947 and these overprinted stamps of India were then withdrawn.

The stamps of Bahawalpur only had validity for use within the state. For external mail Pakistan stamps were used.

PRINTERS. All the following issues were recess-printed by De La Rue & Co, Ltd, London.

2 Amir Muhammad Bahawal Khan I Abbasi

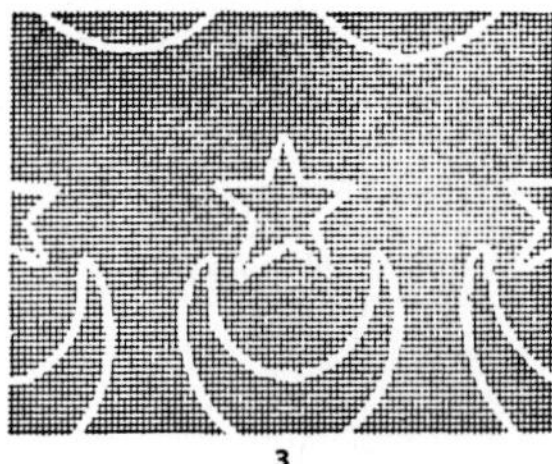
3

1947 (1 Dec). Bicentenary Commemoration. W **3** (sideways). P 12½×11½.
18 **2** ½a. black and carmine 3·75 11·00

4 HH the Amir of Bahawalpur

5 The Tombs of the Amirs

6 Mosque in Sadiq-Garh

7 Fort Derawar from the Lake

8 Nur-Mahal Palace

9 The Palace, Sadiq-Garh

10 HH the Amir of Bahawalpur

11 Three Generations of Rulers; HH the Amir in centre

1948 (1 Apr). W **3** (sideways on vert designs). P 12½ (T **4**), 11½×12½ (Types **5**, **7**, **8** and **9**), 12½×11½ (Types **6** and **10**) or 13½×14 (T **11**).
19 **4** 3p. black and blue 3·00 20·00
20 ½a. black and claret 2·75 20·00
21 9p. black and green 2·75 20·00
22 1a. black and carmine 2·75 20·00
23 1½a. black and violet 4·00 16·00
24 **5** 2a. green and carmine 4·00 20·00
25 **6** 4a. orange and brown 4·00 20·00
26 **7** 6a. violet and blue 4·00 20·00
27 **8** 8a. carmine and violet 5·50 20·00
28 **9** 12a. green and carmine 7·00 30·00
29 **10** 1r. violet and brown 7·00 45·00
30 2r. green and claret 3·00 80·00
31 5r. black and violet 3·00 £100
32 **11** 10r. scarlet and black 32·00 £130
19/32 *Set of* 14 75·00 £500

12 H. H. The Amir of Bahawalpur and Mohammed Ali Jinnah

13 Soldiers of 1848 and 1948

1948 (3 Oct). First Anniversary of Union of Bahawalpur with Pakistan. W **3**. P 13.
33 **12** 1½a. carmine and blue-green 1·75 7·50

1948 (15 Oct). Multan Campaign Centenary. W **3**. P 11½.
34 **13** 1½a. black and lake 1·25 16·00

1948. As Nos. 29/32, but colours changed.
35 **10** 1r. deep green and orange 1·00 20·00
36 2r. black and carmine 1·00 24·00
37 5r. chocolate and ultramarine 1·00 42·00
38 **11** 10r. red-brown and green 1·00 55·00
35/38 *Set of* 4 3·50 £130

14 Irrigation

15 Wheat

16 Cotton

17 Sahiwal bull

1949 (3 Mar). Silver Jubilee of Accession of HH the Amir of Bahawalpur. Types **14/17**. W **3**. P 14.
39 3p. black and ultramarine 10 8·00
40 ½a. black and brown-orange 10 8·00
41 9p. black and green 10 8·00
42 1a. black and carmine 10 8·00
39/42 *Set of* 4 35 29·00
Nos. 39/42 exist imperforate (*Prices, £28 per pair, unused*).

18 UPU Monument, Berne

1949 (10 Oct). 75th Anniversary of Universal Postal Union. W **3**. P 13.
43 **18** 9p. black and green 20 2·75
a. Perf 17½×17 3·00 24·00
44 1a. black and magenta 20 2·75
a. Perf 17½×17 3·00 24·00
45 1½a. black and orange 20 2·75
a. Perf 17½×17 3·00 24·00
46 2½a. black and blue 20 2·75
a. Perf 17½×17 3·00 24·00
43/46 *Set of* 4 70 10·00
43a/46a *Set of* 4 11·00 85·00
Nos. 43/46 exist imperforate (*Prices, £5 per pair, unused*).

OFFICIAL STAMPS

O **1** Panjnad Weir

O **2** Dromedary and Calf

O **3** Blackbuck

O **4** Eastern White Pelicans

O **5** Friday Mosque, Fort Derawar

O **6** Temple at Pattan Munara

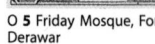

Normal

'Sarkark': Part of the overprint at left is missing, altering the word from 'Sarkari' (Official) to 'Sarkark' (R. 6/3)

1945 (1 Jan). Various horizontal pictorial designs, with red Arabic opt. W **3**. P 14.
O1 O **1** ½a. black and green 15·00 15·00
O2 O **2** 1a. black and carmine 3·75 18·00
a. Opt omitted † £1400
b. 'Sarkark' £180 £300
O3 O **3** 2a. black and violet 3·25 18·00
a. 'Sarkark' £130
O4 O **4** 4a. black and olive-green 18·00 35·00
O5 O **5** 8a. black and brown 40·00 22·00
a. 'Sarkark' £450 £850
O6 O **6** 1r. black and orange 42·00 22·00
O1/O6 *Set of* 6 £110 £120
Examples of No. O2a come from a sheet used at Rahimya Khan.
It is believed that examples of Nos. O1/O2 in different shades and with white gum appeared in 1949 and were included in the Silver Jubilee Presentation Booklet.
The 4a. is known with an earlier state of the 'Sarkark' variety.

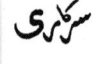

O **7** Baggage Camels

(O **8**)

1945 (10 Mar). Revenue stamp opt in red as T O **7** at Nasik. No wmk. P 14.
O7 O **7** 1a. black and brown £130 85·00

1945 (Mar–May). Surch as T O **8** (at Security Printing Press, Nasik) instead of red Arabic opt. No wmk. P 14.
O11 O **5** ½a. on 8a. black and purple 12·00 7·00
O12 O **6** 1½a. on 1r. black and orange 45·00 11·00
O13 O **1** 1½a. on 2r. black and blue (1.5) £140 8·50
O11/O13 *Set of* 3 £170 24·00
The stamps used as a basis for Nos. O7 and O11/O13 were part of the Revenue series issued in 1933–1934.

SERVICE

(O **9**)

O **10** HH the Amir of Bahawalpur

1945 (June). Optd with T O **9** (by D.L.R.) instead of red Arabic opt. No wmk. P 14.
O14 O **1** ½a. black and carmine 1·25 11·00
O15 O **2** 1a. black and carmine 2·00 13·00
O16 O **3** 2a. black and orange 4·00 55·00
O14/O16 *Set of* 3 6·50 70·00

1945 (Sept). P 14.
O17 O **10** 3p. black and blue 8·00 19·00
O18 1½a. black and violet 27·00 8·50

O **11** Allied Banners

(Des E. Meronti. Recess, background litho)

1946 (1 May). Victory. P 14.
O19 O **11** 1½a. green and grey 6·00 7·00

1948. Nos. 19, 22, 24/25 and 35/38 optd as Nos. O1/O6.
O20 **4** 3p. black and blue (R.) 65 13·00
O21 1a. black and carmine (Blk.) 65 12·00
O22 **5** 2a. green and carmine (Blk.) 65 13·00
O23 **6** 4a. orange and brown (Blk.) 65 18·00
O24 **10** 1r. deep green and orange (R.) 65 20·00
O25 2r. black and carmine (R.) 65 26·00
O26 5r. chocolate and ultramarine (R.) 65 42·00
O27 **11** 10r. red-brown and green (R.) 65 42·00
O20/O27 *Set of* 8 4·50 £170

1949 (10 Oct). 75th Anniversary of Universal Postal Union. Nos. 43/46 optd as Nos. O1/O6.
O28 **18** 9p. black and green 15 4·50
aw. Wmk inverted † £500
b. Perf 17½×17 2·50 32·00
O29 1a. black and magenta 15 4·50
b. Perf 17½×17 2·50 32·00
O30 1½a. black and orange 15 4·50
b. Perf 17½×17 2·50 32·00
O31 2½a. black and blue 15 4·50
b. Perf 17½×17 2·50 32·00
O28/O31 *Set of* 4 55 16·00
O28b/O31b *Set of* 4 9·00 £110
Nos. O28/O31 exist imperforate (*Prices, £5 per pair, unused*).

From 1947 stamps of Pakistan were used on all external mail. Bahawalpur issues continued to be used on internal mail until 1953.

Palestine

The stamps of TURKEY were used in Palestine from 1865.

In addition various European Powers, and Egypt, maintained post offices at Jerusalem (Austria, France, Germany, Italy, Russia), Jaffa (Austria, Egypt, France, Germany, Russia) and Haifa (Austria, France) using their own stamps or issues specially prepared for Levant post offices. All foreign post offices had closed by the time of the British Occupation.

PRICES FOR STAMPS ON COVER TO 1945

No. 1/1*b*	*from* × 6
No. 2	*from* × 4
Nos. 3/4	*from* × 5
Nos. 5/15	*from* × 4
Nos. 16/29	*from* × 3
Nos. 30/42	*from* × 4
No. 43	—
No. 44	*from* × 10
No. 44*a*	—
Nos. 45/46	*from* × 10
Nos. 47/57	*from* × 3
Nos. 58/59	—
Nos. 60/68	*from* × 3
Nos. 69/70	—
Nos. 71/89	*from* × 3
Nos. 90/100	*from* × 4
No. 101	*from* × 15
Nos. 102/103	*from* × 10
Nos. 104/109	*from* × 10
Nos. 110/111	*from* × 100
Nos. D1/D5	*from* × 40
Nos. D6/D11	*from* × 100
Nos. D12/D20	*from* × 20

BRITISH MILITARY OCCUPATION

British and allied forces invaded Palestine in November 1917 capturing Gaza (7 November), Jaffa (16 November) and Jerusalem (9 December). The front line then stabilised until the second British offensive of September 1918.

Nos. 1/15 were issued by the British military authorities for use by the civilian population in areas they controlled previously, part of the Ottoman Empire. Before the issue of Nos. 1/2 in February 1918, civilian mail was carried free. In addition to Palestine the stamps were available from E.E.F. post offices in Syria (including what subsequently became Transjordan) from 23 September 1918 to 23 February 1922, Lebanon from 21 October 1918 to September 1920 and Cilicia from 2 September 1919 to 16 July 1920. Use in the following post offices outside Palestine is recorded in *British Empire Campaigns and Occupations in the Near East, 1914–1924* by John Firebrace:

Adana, Cilicia
Akkari ('Akkar'), Syria
Aleih ('Alie'), Lebanon
Aleppo ('Alep, Halep'), Syria
Alexandretta, Syria
Antakie, Syria
Baalbek, Lebanon
Bab, Syria
Babitoma, Syria
Ba'abda, Lebanon
Behamdoun, Lebanon
Beit Mery, Beyrouth Lebanon
Beit ed Dine, Lebanon
Bekaa, Lebanon
Beyrouth, Lebanon
Bouzanti, Syria
Broumana, Lebanon
Damascus ('Damas'), Syria
Damour ('Damor'), Lebanon
Der'a ('Deraa'), Syria
Deurt-Yol, Syria
Djey Han, Syria
Djezzin ('Djezzine'), Lebanon
Djon, Lebanon
Djounie, Lebanon
Djubeil, Lebanon
Douma, Syria
Edleb, Syria
Feke, Turkey
Habib Souk, Syria
Hajjin ('Hadjin'), Cilicia Hama, Syria
Hasbaya, Lebanon
Hasine, Cilicia
Hommana, Lebanon
Homs, Syria
Kozan, Cilicia
Lattakia ('Laskie, Lattaquie'), Syria
Massel el Chouf ('Moussalc'), Lebanon
Merdjajoun Lebanon
Mersina ('Mersine'), Cilicia
Mounboudje, Syria
Nabatti, Lebanon
Nebk ('Nebik'), Syria
Payass, Syria
Racheya, Lebanon
Safita, Syria
Savour, Tyre, Lebanon
Selimie, Syria
Sidan ('Saida (Echelle)'), Lebanon
Suweidiya ('Suvedie'), Syria
Talia, Syria
Tarsous, Cilicia
Tartous, Syria
Tibnin, Lebanon
Tripoli, Syria
Zahle, Lebanon
Zebdani, Syria

This information is reproduced here by permission of the publishers, Robson Lowe Publications.

(Currency. 10 milliemes = 1 piastre)

1

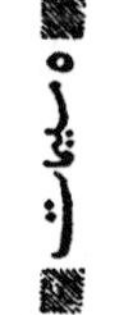
(2)

3

'E.E.F.' = Egyptian Expeditionary Force

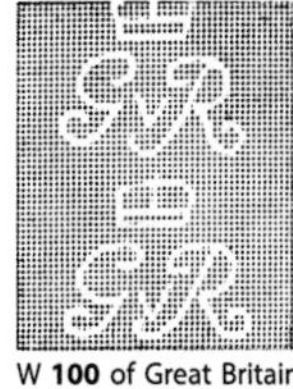
W **100** of Great Britain

(Des G. Rowntree. Litho Typographical Dept, Survey of Egypt, Giza, Cairo)

1918 (10 Feb). Wmk Simple Cypher (W **100** of Great Britain). Ungummed. Roul 20.

1	**1**	1p. indigo	£200	£110
		a. Deep blue	£160	£100
		b. Blue	£160	£100
		s. Optd 'SPECIMEN'	£300	

Control: A 18 (*Prices, corner block of 4*; No. 1 £900. No. 1a, £800. No. 1b, £850).

1918 (16 Feb). As last (ungummed) surch with T **2**.

2	**1**	5m. on 1p. cobalt-blue	£110	£500
		a. 'MILLILMES' (R. 1/10)	£3750	£9500
		s. Optd 'SPECIMEN'	£300	

Control: B 18 A (*Corner block*, £1200).

1918 (5 Mar). As No. 1 but colour changed. With gum.

3	**1**	1p. ultramarine (*shades*)	2·00	2·00
		a. Crown missing from wmk	60·00	65·00
		b. Printed on the gummed side		
		w. Wmk inverted	£250	£300

Control: C 18. (*Corner block*, £85).

1918 (5 Mar–13 May). No. 3 surch with T **2**.

4	**1**	5m. on 1p. ultramarine	8·00	2·75
		a. Arabic surch wholly or partly missing (R. 1/11)	£375	£425
		b. Crown missing from wmk	95·00	
		w. Wmk inverted	£325	

Controls: C 18 B (3.18). (*Corner block*, £1000).
D 18 C (5.18). (*Corner block*, £225).

4m. Arabic '40' (R. 10/3 and 18/3)

(Typo Stamping Dept, Board of Inland Revenue, Somerset House, London)

1918 (16 July–27 Dec). Wmk Simple Cypher (W **100** of Great Britain). P 15×14.

5	**3**	1m. sepia	30	40
		a. Deep brown	60	40
6		2m. blue-green	30	45
		a. Deep green	2·00	1·00
7		3m. yellow-brown (17.12)	50	35
		a. Chestnut	15·00	6·00
8		4m. scarlet	35	40
		a. Arabic '40'	12·00	13·00
9		5m. yellow-orange (25.9)	4·50	50
		a. Orange	65	30
		b. Crown missing from wmk	£180	
		w. Wmk inverted	†	£1600
10		1p. deep indigo (9.11)	50	25
		a. Crown missing from wmk	£150	£170
		w. Wmk inverted	£225	£250
11		2p. pale olive	3·50	60
		a. Olive	3·50	1·10
12		5p. purple	3·75	2·50
13		9p. ochre (17.12)	12·00	7·50
14		10p. ultramarine (17.12)	12·00	4·50
		w. Wmk inverted	£600	
15		20p. pale grey (27.12)	18·00	20·00
		a. Slate-grey	24·00	27·00
5/15 *Set of* 11			45·00	32·00

Nos. 5/15 exist imperforate, from imprimatur sheets sold by the National Postal Museum in 2013.

There are two sizes of the design of this issue:
19×23 mm. 1, 2, and 4m., and 2 and 5p.
18×21½ mm. 3 and 5m., and 1, 9, 10 and 20p.

There are numerous minor plate varieties in this issue, such as stops omitted in 'E.E.F.', malformed Arabic characters, etc.

CIVIL ADMINISTRATION UNDER BRITISH HIGH COMMISSIONER

Palestine was placed under civil administration by a British High Commissioner on 1 July 1920.

PALESTINE PALESTINE PALESTINE

(4) (5) (6)

Differences:—

T **5**. 20 mm vert and 7 mm between English and Hebrew.
T **6**. 19 mm and 6 mm respectively.

Two settings of T **4**:

Setting I (used for Nos. 16/26). This consisted of two horizontal rows of 12 of which the first setting row appeared on Rows 1, 3/7, 15, 17/18 and 20 of the sheet and the second on Rows 2, 8/14, 16 and 19.

On the first position in the top setting row the Arabic 't' (third character from the left) is incorrectly shown as an Arabic 'z' by the addition of a dot to its right. On the eleventh position in the same row the first two letters in the Hebrew overprint were transposed so that ' character appears first. On row 12 stamp 1 the final 'E' of 'PALESTINE' appears as a 'B' on certain values. Once the errors were noticed vertical columns one and eleven were removed from the remaining sheets.

PALESTINB

'PALESTINB' (Setting I)

PALESTINB

'PALESTINB' (Setting II)

Setting II (used for Nos. 16/29). This consisted of a single horizontal row of 12 reproduced to overprint the complete sheet of 240. The order in which the horizontal rows were used was changed several times during overprinting. During one such re-arrangement a damaged impression was replaced by one from Setting I showing the Arabic 'z' error. (R. 14/8 for 1, 2, 3, 4, 5m (P 14), 20p.). The 'B' error also occurs in the second setting, once in each sheet on either R. 17/8, 18/8 or 19/8.

TRIAL OVERPRINT. Before the issue of Nos. 16/26 (from Setting I), a trial overprint was prepared, resembling T **4** but with the two Hebrew words in the bottom line transposed, the short word appearing on the right. This overprint was rejected for political reasons, but one sheet of each value existed, with the opt in *gold* on the 1p.
Price from £250, per stamp.

(Optd at Greek Orthodox Convent, Jerusalem)

1920 (1 Sept). Optd with T **4** (Arabic 8 *mm* long).

(a) P 15×14

16	**3**	1m. sepia	9·50	1·90
		b. Arabic 'z' (Settings I and II)	£2750	
		c. Hebrew characters transposed (I)	£1400	
		d. 'PALESTINB' (II)	£130	
17		2m. blue-green	14·00	6·00
		b. 'Arabic 'z' (Settings I and II)	£1000	
		c. Hebrew characters transposed (I)	£1000	
		d. 'PALESTINB' (II)	£150	
18		3m. chestnut	18·00	8·50
		a. Opt inverted	£550	£700
		b. Arabic 'z' (Settings I and II)	£2250	
		c. Hebrew characters transposed (I)	£2250	
		d. 'PALESTINB' (II)	£100	
19		4m. scarlet	5·00	1·75
		b. Arabic 'z' (Settings I and II)	£2500	
		c. Hebrew characters transposed (I)	£2500	
		d. PALESTINB' (II)	80·00	
		e. Arabic '40'	48·00	38·00
20		5m. yellow-orange	25·00	4·25
		c. Hebrew characters transposed (I)	†	£5500
		d. 'PALESTINB' (II)	£160	
21		1p. deep indigo (Sil.)	5·50	1·00
		d. 'PALESTINB' (II)	60·00	
		w. Wmk inverted	£160	£170
22		2p. deep olive	7·00	2·50
		a. Crown missing from wmk	£600	
		b. Arabic 'z' (I)	£250	
		c. Hebrew characters transposed (I)	£250	£250
		d. 'PALESTINB' (Settings I and II)	£140	
23		5p. deep purple	27·00	30·00
		b. Arabic 'z' (I)	£1100	
		c. Hebrew characters transposed (I)	£650	
		d. 'PALESTINB' (Setting I and II)	£250	
24		9p. ochre	15·00	20·00
		b. Arabic 'z' (I)	£500	
		c. Hebrew characters transposed (I)	£600	
		d. 'PALESTINB' (Settings I and II)	£250	
25		10p. ultramarine	13·00	17·00
		b. Arabic 'z' (I)	£400	

		c. Hebrew characters transposed (I)	£500	
		d. 'PALESTINB' (Settings I and II)	£300	
26		20p. pale grey	35·00	50·00
		b. Arabic 'z' (Settings I and II)	£1000	
		c. Hebrew characters transposed (I)	£1000	
		d. 'PALESTINB' (Settings I and II)	£1900	
16/26 *Set of* 11			£150	£130
		(b) P 14		
27	**3**	2m. blue-green	4·50	1·75
		d. 'PALESTINB' (II)	60·00	
28		3m. chestnut	£130	65·00
29		5m. orange	8·00	75
		b. Arabic 'z' (II)	£300	£250
		d. 'PALESTINB' (II)	£150	

Faulty registration of the overprint in this issue has resulted in numerous misplaced overprints, either vertically or horizontally. All values exist with the overprint out of sequence, i.e. Hebrew/Arabic/English or English/Arabic/Hebrew. Also all values are known with Arabic/English or English/Hebrew only.

1920 (Dec)–**21**. Optd with T **5*** (Arabic 10 *mm* long).

		(a) P 15×14		
30	**3**	1m. sepia (27.12.20)	2·50	1·00
		a. Opt inverted	£450	†
31		2m. blue-green (27.12.20)	11·00	4·00
		a. Opt double		
32		3m. yellow-brown (27.12.20)	4·00	1·00
33		4m. scarlet (27.12.20)	6·00	1·50
		a. Arabic '40'	65·00	40·00
34		5m. yellow-orange	4·25	75
35		1p. deep indigo (Silver) (21.6.21)	£550	38·00
36		2p. olive (21.6.21)	85·00	40·00
37		5p. deep purple (21.6.21)	50·00	10·00
		(b) P 14		
38	**3**	1m. sepia	£850	£950
39		2m. blue-green	5·50	5·50
40		4m. scarlet	90·00	£120
		a. Arabic '40'	£375	£425
41		5m. orange	85·00	9·00
		a. *Yellow-orange*	11·00	1·25
42		1p. deep indigo (Silver)	65·00	1·75
43		5p. purple	£225	£500

* In this setting the Arabic and Hebrew characters are badly worn and blunted, the Arabic 'S' and 'T' are joined (i.e. there is no break in the position indicated by the arrow in our illustration); the letters of 'PALESTINE' are often irregular or broken; and the space between the two groups of Hebrew characters varies from 1 mm to over 1¾ mm. The ' character in the left-hand Hebrew word extends above the remainder of the line (*For clear, sharp overprint, see Nos.* 47/59.).

The dates of issue given are irrespective of the perforations, i.e. one or both perfs could have been issued on the dates shown.

Nos. 31 and 39 exist with any one line of the overprint partly missing.

1920 (6 Dec). Optd with T **6**.

		(a) P 15×14		
44	**3**	3m. yellow-brown	60·00	32·00
44*a*		5m. yellow-orange	£15000	£12000
		(b) P 14		
45	**3**	1m. sepia	60·00	35·00
46		5m. orange	£450	30·00

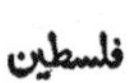

فلسطين فلسطين فلسطين

PALESTINB PALESTINE PALESTINE

פלשתינה א״י פלשתינה א״י פלשתינה א״י

(6a) **(7)** **(8)**

1921 (29 May–4 Aug). Optd as T **6a**.

		(a) P 15×14		
47	**3**	1m. sepia (23.6)	20·00	4·00
48		2m. blue-green (18.6)	35·00	6·00
49		3m. yellow-brown (23.6)	48·00	3·00
50		4m. scarlet (23.6)	50·00	3·50
		a. Arabic '40'	£250	65·00
51		5m. yellow-orange	80·00	1·00
52		1p. deep indigo (Silver) (1.7)	32·00	1·50
53		2p. olive (4.8)	25·00	6·50
54		5p. purple (4.8)	25·00	8·00
55		9p. ochre (4.8)	75·00	£120
56		10p. ultramarine (4.8)	90·00	15·00
57		20p. pale grey (4.8)	£140	70·00
47/57 *Set of* 11			£550	£200
		(b) P 14		
58	**3**	1m. sepia	†	£2250
59		20p. pale grey	£12000	£2500

In this setting the Arabic and Hebrew characters are sharp and pointed and there is usually a break between the Arabic 'S' and 'T', though this is sometimes filled with ink. The space between the two groups of Hebrew characters is always 1¾ mm. The top of the ' character in the Hebrew aligns with the remainder of the word.

The 3m. with 'PALESTINE' omitted is an essay (*Price* £2500 *unused*).

1921 (26 Sept)–**22**. Optd with T **7** ('PALESTINE' in sans-serif letters) by Stamping Dept, Board of Inland Revenue, Somerset House, London. Wmk Simple Cypher (W **100** of Great Britain). P 15×14.

60	**3**	1m. sepia (5.10.21)	2·00	30
61		2m. blue-green (11.10.21)	3·00	30
62		3m. yellow-brown (17.10.21)	3·25	30
63		4m. scarlet (15.10.21)	3·75	60
		a. Arabic '40'	50·00	14·00
64		5m. yellow-orange	3·50	20
65		1p. bright turquoise-blue (14.11.21)	2·75	35
		w. Wmk inverted	†	—
66		2p. olive (7.12.21)	4·75	50
67		5p. deep purple (11.12.21)	12·00	6·00
		a. Opt double, one albino	£1000	
68		9p. ochre (10.3.22)	25·00	14·00
69		10p. ultramarine (10.3.22)	28·00	£650
		w. Wmk inverted	†	—
70		20p. pale grey (10.3.22)	80·00	£1500
60/70 *Set of* 11			£150	

Dates quoted are of earliest known postmarks.

(Printed and optd by Waterlow & Sons from new plates)

1922 (Sept–Nov). T **3** (redrawn), optd with T **8**. Wmk Mult Script CA.

		(a) P 14		
71	**3**	1m. sepia	2·25	30
		a. *Deep brown*	2·75	30
		b. Opt inverted	†	£12000
		c. Opt double	£250	£450
		w. Wmk inverted	55·00	42·00
72		2m. yellow	3·00	30
		a. *Orange-yellow*	5·00	50
		b. Wmk sideways	†	£2000
		w. Wmk inverted	45·00	40·00
73		3m. greenish blue	3·25	15
		w. Wmk inverted	48·00	40·00
74		4m. carmine-pink	3·25	20
		w. Wmk inverted	70·00	55·00
75		5m. orange	3·50	20
		w. Wmk inverted	90·00	60·00
76		6m. blue-green	2·75	30
		w. Wmk inverted	65·00	70·00
77		7m. yellow-brown	2·75	30
		w. Wmk inverted	£325	£325
78		8m. scarlet	2·75	30
		w. Wmk inverted	75·00	80·00
79		1p. grey	3·25	30
		w. Wmk inverted	90·00	80·00
80		13m. ultramarine	4·00	15
		w. Wmk inverted	45·00	35·00
		x. Wmk reversed	†	£750
81		2p. olive	4·00	35
		a. Opt inverted	£325	£550
		b. *Ochre*	£130	6·50
		w. Wmk inverted	£325	£325
82		5p. deep purple	6·00	1·25
		aw. Wmk inverted	†	£750
82*b*		9p. ochre	£1100	£250
83		10p. light blue	90·00	17·00
		a. 'E.F.F.' for 'E.E.F.' in bottom panel (R. 10/3)	£2000	£550
84		20p. bright violet	£200	£120
		(b) P 15×14		
86	**3**	5p. deep purple	65·00	7·00
87		9p. ochre	10·00	9·00
88		10p. light blue	8·50	4·00
		a. 'E.F.F.' for 'E.E.F.' in bottom panel (R. 10/3)	£450	£300
		w. Wmk inverted	£550	£325
89		20p. bright violet	12·00	5·50
71s/89s Optd 'SPECIMEN' *Set of* 15			£450	

Most values can be found on thin paper.

All known examples of the 1m. with inverted opt (No. 71b) also have inverted wmk.

In this issue the design of all denominations is the same size, 18×21½ mm. Varieties may be found with one or other of the stops between 'E.E.F.' missing.

BRITISH MANDATE TO THE LEAGUE OF NATIONS

The League of Nations granted a mandate to Great Britain for the administration of Palestine on 29 September 1923.

(New Currency. 1,000 mils = 1 Palestine pound)

9 Rachel's Tomb

10 Dome of the Rock

11 Citadel, Jerusalem

12 Sea of Galilee

(Des F. Taylor. Typo Harrison)

1927 (1 June)–**45**. Wmk Mult Script CA. P 13½×14½ (2m. to 20m.) or 14.

90	**9**	2m. greenish blue (14.8.27) *(a) (b) (c) (d)*	2·75	10
		w. Wmk inverted	†	£550
91		3m. yellow-green *(a) (b) (c) (d)*	1·75	10
		w. Wmk inverted	†	£325
92	**10**	4m. rose-pink (14.8.27) *(a) (b)*	9·00	1·50
93	**11**	5m. orange (14.8.27) *(a) (b) (c) (d)*	4·25	10
		a. From coils. Perf 14½×14 (1936)	16·00	20·00
		ac. *Yellow*. From coils. Perf 14½×14 (1945)	45·00	35·00
		aw. Wmk inverted	22·00	26·00
		b. *Yellow* (12.44)	3·00	15
		w. Wmk inverted	40·00	40·00
94	**10**	6m. pale green (14.8.27) *(a) (b)*	6·00	1·75
		a. *Deep green*	1·50	20
95	**11**	7m. scarlet (14.8.27) *(a) (b)*	11·00	60
96	**10**	8m. yellow-brown (14.8.27) *(a) (b)*	18·00	6·50
97	**9**	10m. slate (14.8.27) *(a) (b) (c) (d)*	2·00	10
		a. *Grey*. From coils. Perf 14½×14 (11.38)	20·00	27·00
		aw. Wmk inverted		
		b. *Grey* (1944)	2·25	10
98	**10**	13m. ultramarine *(a) (b)*	17·00	30
99	**11**	20m. dull olive-green (14.8.27) *(a) (b) (d)*	3·50	15
		a. *Bright olive-green* (12.44)	2·25	15
		w. Wmk inverted	†	£550
100	**12**	50m. deep dull purple (14.8.27) *(a) (b) (d)*	3·25	30
		a. *Bright purple* (12.44)	6·00	30
		x. Wmk reversed	†	£650
101		90m. bistre (14.8.27) *(a) (b)*	85·00	60·00
102		100m. turquoise-blue (14.8.27) *(a) (b) (d)*	2·25	70
103		200m. deep violet (14.8.27) *(a) (b) (d)*	8·00	5·00
		a. *Bright violet* (1928)	38·00	17·00
		b. *Blackish violet* (12.44)	13·00	3·75
90/103 *Set of* 14			£150	65·00
90s/103s Handstamped 'SPECIMEN' *Set of* 14			£450	

Nos 90/103 were printed on four distinct papers. The original issue in 1927 was on thin semi-transparent paper ('*a*'). In 1928 a special thick paper with vertical ribbing ('*b*') was introduced, the purpose of the ribbing being to prevent curling of the sheets. A similar paper with horizontal ribbing ('*c*') was used for an experimental printing C.1937.

From 1936 paper '*b*' was replaced by ordinary opaque white wove paper ('*d*'). The papers known for each value are indicated in the above listing by letters in brackets.

2m. stamps in the grey colour of the 10m., including an example postmarked in 1935, exist as do 50m. stamps in blue, but it has not been established whether they were issued.

Nos. 90/91 and 93 exist in coils, constructed from normal sheets.

1932 (1 June)–**44**. New values and colours. Wmk Mult Script CA. P 13½×14½ (4m. to 15m.) or 14.

104	**10**	4m. purple (1.11.32) *(b) (d)*	3·00	10
		w. Wmk inverted	†	£650
105	**11**	7m. deep violet *(b) (c) (d)*	1·50	10
106	**10**	8m. scarlet *(b) (c) (d)*	1·75	20
		w. Wmk inverted	†	£800
107		13m. bistre (1.8.32) *(b) (d)*	3·75	10
108		15m. ultramarine (1.8.32) *(b) (c) (d)*	6·50	10
		a. *Grey-blue* (12.44)	5·50	40
		b. *Greenish blue*	5·50	40
		w. Wmk inverted	†	£800
109	**12**	250m. brown (15.1.42) *(d)*	7·50	3·50
110		500m. scarlet (15.1.42) *(d)*	8·50	3·50
111		£P1 black (15.1.42) *(d)*	12·00	3·50
104/111 *Set of* 8			40·00	10·00
104s/111s Perf 'SPECIMEN' *Set of* 8			£475	

No. 108 exists in coils, constructed from normal sheets.

Nos 104/111 were printed on papers '*b*', '*c*' and '*d*', as defined in the note after Nos 90/103.

STAMP BOOKLETS

1929. Blue cover inscr 'PALESTINE POSTAGE STAMP BOOKLET' and contents in English. Without advertisements on front. Stitched.

SB1	150m. booklet containing 12×2m., 12×3m. and 18×5m. (Nos. 90/91, 93) in blocks of 6	£2500
	a. As No. SB1, but stapled	£2500

1933. Blue cover inscr 'PALESTINE POSTS & TELEGRAPHS POSTAGE STAMP BOOKLET' and contents all in English, Arabic and Hebrew. Without advertisements on front. Stapled.

SB2	150m. booklet. Contents as No. SB1	£3000

1937–38. Red cover inscr 'POSTAGE STAMP BOOKLET' and contents in English, Hebrew and Arabic. With advertisements on front. Stapled.

SB3	150m. booklet containing 2m., 3m., 5m. and 15m. (Nos. 90/91, 93, 108) in blocks of 6	£2750
	a. Blue cover (1938)	£2500

1939. Pink cover inscr 'POSTAGE STAMP BOOKLET' and contents in English, Hebrew and Arabic. With advertisements on front. Stapled.

SB4	120m. booklet containing 6×10m. and 12×5m. (Nos. 93, 97) in blocks of 6	£2500

POSTAL FISCALS

Type-set stamps inscribed 'O.P.D.A.' (= Ottoman Public Debt Administration) or 'H.J.Z.' (Hejaz Railway); British 1d. stamps of 1912–1924 and Palestine stamps overprinted with one or other of the above groups of letters, or with the word 'Devair', with or without surcharge of new value, are fiscal stamps. They are known used as postage stamps, alone, or with other stamps to make up the correct rates, and were passed by the postal authorities, although they were not definitely authorised for postal use.

POSTAGE DUE STAMPS

D 1

D 2 (MILLIEME)

D 3 (MIL)

(Typo Greek Orthodox Convent Press, Jerusalem)

1923 (1 Apr). P 11.

D1	**D 1**	1m. yellow-brown	26·00	38·00
		a. Imperf (pair)	£325	
		b. Imperf between (horiz pair)	£1300	
D2		2m. blue-green	21·00	10·00
		a. Imperf (pair)	£450	
D3		4m. scarlet	10·00	13·00
D4		8m. mauve	7·50	7·00
		a. Imperf (pair)	£140	
		b. Imperf between (horiz pair)	†	£2250
D5		13m. steel blue	7·50	8·00
		a. Imperf between (horiz pair)	£1100	
D1/D5 *Set of* 5			65·00	70·00

Perfectly centred and perforated stamps of this issue are worth considerably more than the above prices, which are for average examples.

(Types D **2**/D **3**. Typo D.L.R.)

1924 (3 Oct). Wmk Mult Script CA. P 14.

D6	**D 2**	1m. deep brown	1·00	2·00
D7		2m. yellow	4·00	1·75
		w. Wmk inverted	†	£500
D8		4m. green	2·00	1·25
D9		8m. scarlet	3·00	90
D10		13m. ultramarine	3·25	2·50
D11		5p. violet	14·00	1·75
D6/D11 *Set of* 6			24·00	9·00
D6s/D11s Optd 'SPECIMEN' *Set of* 6			£300	

1928 (1 Feb)–**44**. Wmk Mult Script CA. P 14.

D12	D **3**	1m. brown	2·50	85
		a. Perf 15×14 (1944)	42·00	80·00
D13		2m. yellow	3·50	60
		w. Wmk inverted	†	£550
D14		4m. green	4·00	1·60
		a. Perf 15×14 (1942)	75·00	£110
D15		6m. orange-brown (10.33)	18·00	5·00
D16		8m. carmine	2·75	1·75
D17		10m. pale grey	1·75	60
D18		13m. ultramarine	4·50	2·75
D19		20m. pale olive-green	4·50	1·25
D20		50m. violet	4·75	2·25
D12/D20 *Set of 9*			42·00	15·00
D12s/D20s Optd or Perf (6m.) 'SPECIMEN' *Set of 9*			£350	

Nos. D12a and D14a were printed and perforated by Harrison and Sons following bomb damage to the De La Rue works on 29 December 1940.

The British Mandate terminated on 14 May 1948. Later issues of stamps and occupation issues will be found listed under Gaza, Israel and Jordan in the Stanley Gibbons *Middle East Catalogue*.

Papua *see after* Australia

Penrhyn Island *see after* Cook Islands

Pitcairn Islands

CROWN COLONY

The settlement of Pitcairn Island by the *Bounty* mutineers in 1790 was not discovered until the American whaler *Topaz*, Capt. Mayhew Folger, called there in 1808. A visit by two Royal Navy frigates followed in 1814 and reports from their captains resulted in considerable interest being taken in the inhabitants' welfare by religious and philanthropic circles in Great Britain.

Due to overcrowding the population was resettled on Tahiti in 1831, but many soon returned to Pitcairn which was taken under British protection in 1838. The island was again evacuated in 1856, when the inhabitants were moved to Norfolk Island, but a number of families sailed back to their original home in 1859 and 1864.

The earliest surviving letter from the island is dated 1849. Before 1921 the mail service was irregular, as it depended on passing ships, and mail for the island was often sent via Tahiti. Some covers, purportedly sent from Pitcairn between 1883 and 1890 are known handstamped 'Pitcairn Island' or 'PITCAIRN ISLAND', but these are now believed to be forgeries.

In 1920 a regular mail service was introduced. As there were no stamps available, letters were allowed free postage as long as they carried a cachet, or manuscript endorsement, indicating their origin. Illustrations of Cachets I/VI, VIII, VIIIa, X and XIII are taken from *Pitcairn Islands Postal Markings 1883–1991*, published by the Pitcairn Islands Study Group, and are reproduced by permission of the author, Mr. Cy Kitching. Cachets I to XIII are shown three-quarter size.

POSTED IN PITCAIRN
NO STAMPS AVAILABLE

Cachet I

Cat No.		Value on cover
C1	**1920–25.** Cachet I (62×8 *mm*) (*violet or black*)	£3250

POSTED AT PITCAIRN ISLAND
NO STAMPS AVAILABLE.

Cachet II

C2 **1921–25.** Cachet II (*violet or red*) £2750

POSTED AT PITCAIRN ISLAND
NO STAMPS AVAILABLE.

Cachet III

C3 **1922–28.** Cachet III (49×8½ *mm*) (*violet, purple or black*) £2000

POSTED IN PITCAIRN ISLAND
1923 NO STAMPS AVAILABLE

Cachet IV

C4 **1923.** Cachet IV (*black*) £2750

Posted at Pitcairn
Island no Stamps
Available

Cachet IVa

C4*a* **1923.** Cachet IVa (73½×22 *mm*) (*red*) £2750

POSTED AT PITCAIRN ISLAND
NO STAMPS AVAILABLE

Cachet V

C5 **1923–28.** (Aug). Cachet V (47×9 *mm*) (*red, violet or black*) £2500

C5a **1925–26.** As Cachet V, but second line shown as 'No Stamps Available' (*black*) £3250

POSTED AT PITCAIRN ISLAND.
NO STAMPS AVAILABLE.
NOT TO BE SURCHARGED.

Cachet VI

C6 **1923.** Cachet VI (*blue-green or red*) £3000

C7 **1923.** As Cachet V, but in three lines (*red*) ....

POSTED.IN.PITCAIRN.
NO'STAMPS.AVAILABLE

Cachet VIa

C7a **1923–24.** Cachet VIa (66×10 *mm*) (*blue-black or violet*) £2250

POSTED AT PITCAIRN ISLAND
NO STAMPS AVAILABLE.

Cachet VII

C8 **1923–27.** Cachet VII (*violet or black*) £1900

C9 **1924.** As Cachet IV, but dated '1924' (*black*) £2500

POSTED AT PITCAIRN ISLAND.
NO STAMPS AVAILABLE.

Cachet VIII

C10 **1924–26.** Cachet VIII (36×8 *mm*) (*violet, black or red*) £2500

POSTED AT PITCAIRN
NO STAMPS AVAILABLE

Cachet VIIIa

C10*a* **1924–26.** Cachet VIIIa (36×8¾ *mm*) (*violet or black*) £2250

POSTED AT PITCAIRN ISLAND
NO STAMPS AVAILABLE.

Cachet IX

C11 **1923–26.** Cachet IX (63×7 *mm*) (*violet or black*) £2750

C12 **1925.** (Sept). As Cachet IV, but dated '1925' (*black*) £2750

POSTED IN PITCAIRN
NO STAMPS AVAILABLE.

Cachet X

C13 **1925.** Cachet X (48×5 *mm*) ....

POSTED AT PITCAIRN ISLAND,
NO STAMPS AVAILABLE.

Cachet XI

C14 **1925–26.** Cachet XI (50×10 *mm*) (*violet or black*) £2500

Posted at PITCAIRN ISLAND
No Stamps Available

Cachet XII

C15 **1925.** Cachet XII (55×7½ *mm*) (*violet*) ....

C15*a* As Cachet XII but 'POSTED AT' in capital letters ....

POSTED IN PITCAIRN
NO STAMPS AVAILABLE.

Cachet XIII

C16 **1926.** (Jan). Cachet XIII (64×8 *mm*) (*purple or black*) £3000

The New Zealand Government withdrew the free postage concession on 12 May 1926, but after representations from the islanders, opened a postal agency on Pitcairn using New Zealand stamps cancelled with T Z **1**. Some impressions of this postmark appear to show a double ring, but this is the result of heavy or uneven use of the handstamp. The postal agency operated from 7 June 1927 until 14 October 1940.

The Earlier New Zealand stamps are known cancelled with T Z **1**, but these were not supplied to the postal agency and their use is considered to be contrived.

PRICES. Those quoted for Nos. Z1/Z72 and ZF1 are for examples showing a virtually complete strike of T Z **1**. Due to the size of the cancellation such examples will usually be on piece.

Z 1

Stamps of New Zealand cancelled with T Z **1**.

1915–29. King George V (Nos. 419, 422/426, 428/431 and 446/449).

Z1	½d. green	30·00
Z2	1½d. grey-slate	65·00
Z3	1½d. orange-brown	50·00
Z4	2d. yellow	48·00
Z5	2½d. blue	85·00
Z6	3d. chocolate	90·00
Z7	4d. bright violet	85·00
Z8	4½d. deep green	£120
Z9	5d. light blue	90·00
Z10	6d. carmine	£100
Z11	7½d. red-brown	£130
Z12	8d. red-brown	£170
Z13	9d. yellowish olive	£170
Z14	1s. vermilion	£160

1923. Map of New Zealand (No. 460).

Z14*a*	1d. carmine	£100

1925. Dunedin Exhibition (No. 464).
Z14b ½d. yellow-green/*green* £150
Z14c 1d. carmine/*rose* £120

1926–27. King George V in Field-Marshal's or Admiral's uniform (Nos. 468/469).
Z15 1d. rose-carmine .... 30·00
Z16 2s. light blue £350

1929. Anti-Tuberculosis Fund (No. 544).
Z17 1d. +1d. scarlet £160

1931. Air (Nos. 548/549).
Z18 3d. chocolate £300
Z19 4d. blackish purple £350

1932. Health (No. 552).
Z21 1d. +1d. carmine £170

1935. Pictorials (Nos. 556/558 and 560/569). W **43**.
Z22 ½d. bright green .... 65·00
Z23 1d. scarlet .... 40·00
Z24 1½d. red-brown £100
Z26 2½d. chocolate and slate .... 85·00
Z27 3d. brown £100
Z28 4d. black and sepia £130
Z29 5d. ultramarine £150
Z30 6d. scarlet £130
Z31 8d. chocolate £150
Z32 9d. scarlet and black £150
Z33 1s. deep green £130
Z34 2s. olive-green £350
Z35 3s. chocolate and yellow-brown £400

1935. Silver Jubilee (Nos. 573/575).
Z36 ½d. green .... 50·00
Z37 1d. carmine .... 50·00
Z38 6d. red-orange £100

1935. Health (No. 576).
Z39 1d. +1d. scarlet .... 75·00

1936. Pictorials (Nos. 577/582). W **98**.
Z40 ½d. bright green .... 50·00
Z41 1d. scarlet .... 17·00
Z42 1½d. red-brown .... 85·00
Z43 2d. orange .... 70·00
Z44 2½d. chocolate and slate .... 75·00
Z45 3d. brown .... 80·00

1936. 21st Anniversary of 'Anzac' Landing at Gallipoli (Nos. 591/592).
Z46 ½d. +½d. green .... 50·00
Z47 1d. +1d. scarlet .... 50·00

1936. Congress of British Empire Chambers of Commerce (Nos. 593/597).
Z48 ½d. emerald-green .... 48·00
Z49 1d. scarlet .... 48·00
Z50 2½d. blue .... 65·00
Z51 4d. violet .... 95·00
Z52 6d. red-brown .... 95·00

1936. Health (No. 598).
Z53 1d. +1d. scarlet .... 75·00

1937. Coronation (Nos. 599/601).
Z54 1d. carmine .... 40·00
Z55 2½d. Prussian blue .... 45·00
Z56 6d. red-orange .... 45·00

1937. Health (No. 602).
Z57 1d. +1d. scarlet .... 75·00

1938. King George VI (Nos. 603, 605, 607).
Z58 ½d. green .... 75·00
Z59 1d. scarlet .... 75·00
Z60 1½d. purple-brown .... 85·00

1939. Health (Nos. 611/612).
Z60a 1d. on ½d.+½d. green .... 75·00
Z60b 2d. on 1d.+1d. scarlet .... 75·00

1940. Centenary of British Sovereignty (Nos. 613/622, 624/625).
Z61 ½d. blue-green .... 38·00
Z62 1d. chocolate and scarlet .... 42·00
Z63 1½d. light blue and mauve .... 50·00
Z64 2d. blue-green and chocolate .... 45·00
Z65 2½d. blue-green and blue .... 50·00
Z66 3d. purple and carmine .... 50·00
Z67 4d. chocolate and lake .... 85·00
Z68 5d. pale blue and brown .... 95·00
Z69 6d. emerald-green and violet .... 95·00
Z70 7d. black and red £130
Z71 9d. olive-green and orange £130
Z72 1s. sage-green and deep green £130

POSTAL FISCAL STAMPS

1932. Arms (No. F147).
ZF1 2s.6d. deep brown £400

PRICES FOR STAMPS ON COVER TO 1945
Nos. 1/8 *from* × 10

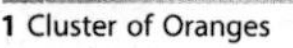
1 Cluster of Oranges

2 Christian on *Bounty* and Pitcairn Island

3 John Adams and his house

4 Lt. Bligh and HMS *Bounty*

5 Pitcairn Islands and the Pacific Ocean

5a *Bounty* Bible

6 HMS *Bounty*

6a School, 1949

7 Fletcher Christian and Pitcairn Island

8 Christian on HMS *Bounty* and Pitcairn Coast

(Recess B.W. (1d., 3d., 4d., 8d. and 2s.6d.), and Waterlow (others))

1940 (15 Oct)–**51**. Types **1/8**. Wmk Mult Script CA. P 11½×11 (1d., 3d., 4d., 8d. and 2s.6d.) or 12½ (others).
1 **1** ½d. orange and green .... 1·25 1·25
2 **2** 1d. mauve and magenta .... 1·50 80
3 **3** 1½d. grey and carmine .... 1·50 50
4 **4** 2d. green and brown .... 2·50 1·40
5 **5** 3d. yellow-green and blue .... 1·25 1·40
aw. Wmk inverted £5000
5b **5a** 4d. black and emerald-green (1.9.51) .... 23·00 12·00
6 **6** 6d. brown and deep greenish grey .... 7·00 1·50
6a **6a** 8d. olive-green and magenta (1.9.51) .... 24·00 8·00
7 **7** 1s. violet and grey .... 6·50 3·50
8 **8** 2s.6d. green and brown .... 17·00 4·00
1/8 *Set of* 10 .... 75·00 30·00
1s/8s (ex 4d., 8d.) Perf 'SPECIMEN' *Set of* 8 .... £1400

2d. Flaw by launch (R. 6/3, subsequently retouched)

3d. Flagstaff flaw (R. 8/2)

1946 (2 Dec). Victory. As Nos. 110/111 of Antigua.
9 2d. brown 70 30
a. Flaw by launch .... 75·00
10 3d. blue .... 1·00 30
a. Flagstaff flaw .... 60·00 60·00
9s/10s Perf 'SPECIMEN' *Set of* 2 .... £425

1949 (1 Aug). Royal Silver Wedding. As Nos. 112/113 of Antigua.
11 1½d. scarlet .... 1·50 1·50
12 10s. mauve .... 40·00 50·00

1949 (10 Oct). 75th Anniversary of UPU. As Nos. 114/117 of Antigua.
13 2½d. red-brown .... 2·25 3·50
14 3d. deep blue .... 7·00 4·25
15 6d. deep blue-green .... 3·50 4·25
16 1s. purple .... 3·50 3·75
13/16 *Set of* 4 .... 14·50 14·00

1953 (2 June). Coronation. As No. of 120 Antigua, but ptd by B.W.
17 4d. black and deep bluish green .... 2·00 3·75

9 *Cordyline terminalis*

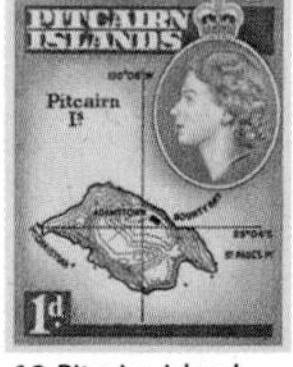

10 Pitcairn Island Map

11 John Adams and *Bounty* bible

12 Handicrafts: Bird model

13 Bounty Bay

14 Pitcairn School

15 Pacific Ocean map

16 Island scene

17 Handicrafts: Ship model

18 Island wheelbarrow

19 Lauching new whaleboat

(Recess D.L.R.)

1957 (2 July)–**63**. Types **9/19**. Wmk Mult Script CA. P 13×12½ (horiz) or 12½×13 (vert).
18 **9** ½d. green and reddish lilac .... 1·00 1·50
a. Green and reddish purple (9.3.63) .... 1·25 3·25
19 **10** 1d. black and olive-green .... 4·50 2·25
a. Black and yellow-olive (19.2.59) .... 21·00 22·00
b. Black and light olive-green (24.2.60) .... 65·00 27·00
20 **11** 2d. brown and greenish blue .... 2·25 60
21 **12** 2½d. deep brown and red-orange 75 40
22 **13** 3d. emerald and deep ultramarine 80 40
23 **14** 4d. scarlet and deep ultramarine (I) 90 40
23a 4d. carmine-red and deep ultramarine (II) (5.11.58) .... 4·00 1·50
24 **15** 6d. pale buff and indigo .... 3·50 55
25 **16** 8d. deep olive-green and carmine-lake 75 40
26 **17** 1s. black and yellowish brown .... 2·25 40
27 **18** 2s. green and red-orange .... 11·00 10·00
28 **19** 2s.6d. ultramarine and lake .... 26·00 13·00
a. Blue and deep lake (10.2.59) .... 48·00 15·00
18/28 *Set of* 12 .... 50·00 28·00

Nos. 23/23*a*. Type I is inscribed 'PITCAIRN SCHOOL'; Type II 'SCHOOL TEACHER'S HOUSE'.

See also No. 33.

20 Pitcairn Island and Simon Young

21 Norfolk Island and Pitcairn Islands

22 Migrant brigantine *Mary Ann*

6d. Right-angle over crown (R. 4/2)

(Des H. E. Maud. Photo Harrison)

1961 (15 Nov). Centenary of Return of Pitcairn Islanders from Norfolk Island. Types **20/22**. W w **12**. P 14½×13½.

29	**20**	3d. black and yellow	50	45
30	**21**	6d. red-brown and blue	1·00	75
		a. Right-angle over crown	23·00	
31	**22**	1s. red-orange and blue-green	1·00	75
29/31 *Set of 3*			2·25	1·75

1963 (4 June). Freedom from Hunger. As No. 146 of Antigua.

32		2s.6d. ultramarine	3·00	1·50

1963 (4 Dec). As No. 18*a*, but wmk w **12**.

33	**9**	½d. green and reddish purple	65	60

1963 (9 Dec). Red Cross Centenary. As Nos. 147/148 of Antigua.

34		2d. red and black	1·00	1·00
35		2s.6d. red and blue	1·50	3·00

23 Pitcairn Is. Longboat

24 Queen Elizabeth II (after Anthony Buckley)

(Des M. Farrar Bell. Photo Harrison)

1964 (5 Aug)–**65**. Types **23/24** and similar horiz designs. Multicoloured. W w **12**. P 14×14½.

36		½d. Type **23**	10	30
		a. Blue omitted	£750	
37		1d. HMS *Bounty*	30	30
38		2d. 'Out from Bounty Bay'	30	30
39		3d. Great Frigatebird	75	30
40		4d. White Tern	75	30
41		6d. Pitcairn Warbler	75	30
42		8d. Red-footed Booby	75	30
		a. Pale blue (beak) omitted	£600	
		b. Pale blue (beak) printed double		
43		10d. Red-tailed Tropicbirds	60	30
44		1s. Henderson Island Crake	60	30
45		1s.6d. Stephen's Lory	1·50	1·25
46		2s.6d. Murphy's Petrel	1·50	1·50
47		4s. Henderson Island Fruit Dove	2·00	1·50
48		8s. Type **24** (5.4.65)	1·25	2·00
36/48 *Set of 13*			10·00	8·00

1965 (17 May). ITU Centenary. As Nos. 166/167 of Antigua.

49		1d. mauve and orange-brown	40	40
50		2s.6d. turquoise-green and bright blue	1·25	1·50
		w. Wmk inverted	£200	

1965 (25 Oct). International Co-operation Year. As Nos. 168/169 of Antigua.

51		1d. reddish purple and turquoise-green	40	40
		a. 'TRISTAN DA CUNHA' offset on back in reddish purple	£800	
52		1s.6d. deep bluish green and lavender	1·25	1·50

No. 51a was caused by the back of one sheet of stamps coming into contact with the blanket plate used for applying the Tristan da Cunha inscription to the same basic design.

1966 (24 Jan). Churchill Commemoration. As Nos. 170/173 of Antigua.

53		2d. new blue	70	85
54		3d. deep green	1·25	1·00
55		6d. brown	1·25	1·75
56		1s. bluish violet	1·25	2·50
53/56 *Set of 4*			4·00	5·50

1966 (1 Aug). World Cup Football Championship. As Nos. 176/177 of Antigua.

57		4d. violet, yellow-green, lake and yellow-brown	75	1·00
58		2s.6d. chocolate, blue-green, lake and yellow-brown	1·25	1·25

1966 (20 Sept). Inauguration of WHO Headquarters, Geneva. As Nos. 178/179 of Antigua.

59		8d. black, yellow-green and light blue	2·00	3·25
60		1s.6d. black, light purple and yellow-brown	3·50	3·75

1966 (1 Dec). 20th Anniversary of UNESCO. As Nos. 196/198 of Antigua.

61		½d. slate-violet, red, yellow and orange	20	1·00
62		10d. orange-yellow, violet and deep olive	1·25	75
63		2s. black, bright purple and orange	2·50	2·25
61/63 *Set of 3*			3·50	3·50

36 Mangarevan Canoe, *circa* 1325

(Des V. Whiteley. Photo Harrison)

1967 (1 Mar). Bicentenary of Discovery of Pitcairn Islands. T **36** and similar horiz designs. Multicoloured. W w **12**. P 14½.

64	½d. Type **36**	10	20
65	1d. P. F. de Quiros and *San Pedro y San Pablo*, 1606	20	20
66	8d. *San Pedro y San Pablo* and *Los Tres Reyes*, 1606	25	20
67	1s. Carteret and HMS *Swallow*, 1767	25	25
68	1s.6d. *Hercules*, 1819	25	25
64/68 *Set of 5*		1·00	1·00

(New Currency. 100 cents = 1 New Zealand dollar)

½c

(**41** *Bounty* Anchor)

1967 (10 July). Decimal currency. Nos. 36/48 surch in decimal currency by die-stamping in gold as T **41**.

69	½c. on ½d. multicoloured	10	10
	a. Deep brown omitted	£1500	
	b. Surch double, one albino	£200	
70	1c. on 1d. multicoloured	30	1·25
71	2c. on 2d. multicoloured	25	1·25
72	2½c. on 3d. multicoloured	25	1·25
73	3c. on 4d. multicoloured	25	20
74	5c. on 6d. multicoloured	30	1·25
75	10c. on 8d. multicoloured	50	30
	a. '10c.' omitted	£2000	
	b. Pale blue (beak) omitted	£900	
76	15c. on 10d. multicoloured	1·50	40
77	20c. on 1s. multicoloured	1·50	55
78	25c. on 1s.6d. multicoloured	1·50	1·25
79	30c. on 2s.6d. multicoloured	1·75	1·25
80	40c. on 4s. multicoloured	1·75	1·25
81	45c. on 8s. multicoloured	1·50	1·50
69/81 *Set of 13*		10·00	10·50

On No. 75a the anchor emblem is still present. Several examples of this variety have been identified as coming from R9/1.

The ½c. and 1c. exist with PVA gum as well as gum arabic.

42 Bligh and *Bounty's* Launch

(Des Jennifer Toombs. Litho D.L.R.)

1967 (7 Dec). 150th Death Anniversary of Admiral Bligh. T **42** and similar horiz designs. P 13½×13.

82	1c. turquoise-blue, black and royal blue (*shades*)	10	10
83	8c. black, yellow and magenta	50	50
84	20c. black, brown and pale buff	55	55
82/84 *Set of 3*		1·00	1·00

Designs: 1c. T **42**; 8c. Bligh and followers cast adrift; 20c. Bligh's tomb.

45 Human Rights Emblem

(Des G. Hamori. Litho D.L.R.)

1968 (4 Mar). Human Rights Year. P 13½×13.

85	**45**	1c. multicoloured	10	10
86		2c. multicoloured	10	10
87		25c. multicoloured	35	35
85/87 *Set of 3*			50	50

46 Miro Wood and Flower

(Des Jennifer Toombs. Photo Harrison)

1968 (19 Aug). Handicrafts. T **46** and similar designs. W w **12** (sideways* on vert designs). P 14×13½ (5, 10c.) or 13½×14 (others).

88	5c. multicoloured	20	30
89	10c. bronze-green, brown and orange	20	40
90	15c. deep bluish violet, chocolate and salmon	25	40
91	20c. multicoloured	25	45
	w. Wmk Crown to right of CA	£225	
88/91 *Set of 4*		80	1·40

Designs: Horiz—5c. T **46**; 10c. Flying Fish model. Vert—15c. 'Hand' vases; 20c. Woven baskets.

* The normal sideways watermark shows Crown to left of CA, *as seen from the back of the stamp.*

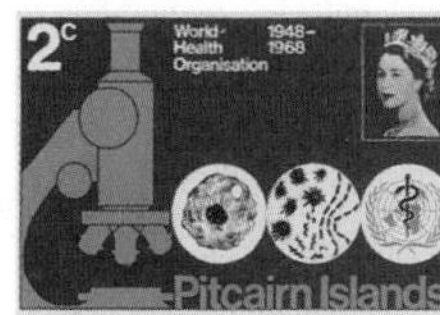

50 Microscope and Slides

(Des Jennifer Toombs. Litho D.L.R.)

1968 (25 Nov). 20th Anniversary of World Health Organisation. T **50** and similar horiz design. W w **12** (sideways). P 14.

92	2c. black, turquoise-blue and ultramarine	10	20
93	20c. black, orange and bright purple	40	50

Design: 2c. T **50**; 20c. Hypodermic syringe and jars of tablets.

52 Pitcairn Island

62 Flying Fox Cable System

(Des Jennifer Toombs. Litho Questa (50c., $1), D.L.R. (others))

1969 (17 Sept)–**75**. Types **52**, **62** and similar designs. Chalk-surfaced paper. W w **12** (upright on 3c., 25c. sideways* on $1 and horiz designs). P 14½×14 (50c.), 14 ($1) or 13 (others).

94	1c. multicoloured	2·25	2·00
	a. Glazed, ordinary paper (9.8.71)	1·25	2·00
	aw. Wmk Crown to right of CA	2·25	2·75
95	2c. multicoloured	25	15
96	3c. multicoloured	25	15
97	4c. multicoloured	2·50	15
98	5c. multicoloured	70	15
	a. Gold (Queens head) omitted	£2000	
99	6c. multicoloured	30	20
100	8c. multicoloured	2·00	20
101	10c. multicoloured	2·00	85
	a. Glazed, ordinary paper (9.8.71)	2·00	3·50
	aw. Wmk Crown to right of CA	6·00	6·50
102	15c. multicoloured	2·25	1·75
	a. Queen's head omitted	£1000	
103	20c. multicoloured	60	40
104	25c. multicoloured	70	40
	w. Wmk inverted		
105	30c. multicoloured	55	45
106	40c. multicoloured	75	60
106*a*	50c. multicoloured (*glazed, ordinary paper*) (2.1.73)	2·00	12·00
106*b*	$1 multicoloured (*glazed, ordinary paper*) (21.4.75)	5·50	17·00
94/106b *Set of 15*		20·00	32·00

Designs: Horiz—1c. T **52**; 2c. Captain Bligh and *Bounty* chronometer; 4c. Plans and drawing of *Bounty*; 5c. Breadfruit containers and plant; 6c. Bounty Bay; 8c. Pitcairn longboat; 10c. Ship landing point; 15c. Fletcher Christian's Cave; 20c. Thursday October Christian's House; 30c. Radio Station, Taro Ground; 40c. *Bounty* Bible; 50c. Pitcairn Coat of Arms. Vert—3c. *Bounty* anchor; 25c. T **62**; $1 Queen Elizabeth II.

* The normal sideways watermark shows Crown to left of CA, *as seen from the back of the stamp.*

The 1c. was reissued in 1974, W w **12** upright.

65 Lantana

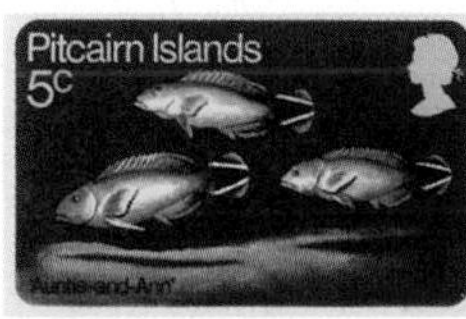

69 Band-tailed Hind

(Des Jennifer Toombs. Litho D.L.R.)

1970 (23 Mar). Flowers. T **65** and similar vert designs. Multicoloured. W w **12**. P 14.

107	1c. Type **65**	15	50
108	2c. 'Indian Shot'	20	60
109	5c. Pulau	25	70
110	25c. Wild Gladiolus	60	1·00
107/110 *Set of 4*		1·10	2·50

(Des Jennifer Toombs. Photo Harrison)

1970 (12 Oct). Fish. T **69** and similar horiz designs. Multicoloured. W w **12**. P 14.

111	5c. Type **69**	1·25	1·25
	w. Wmk inverted	8·00	3·00
112	10c. High-finned Rudderfish	1·25	1·25
	w. Wmk inverted	16·00	3·50

113	15c. Elwyn's Wrasse	1·25	1·50
	w. Wmk inverted	9·00	3·50
114	20c. Yellow Wrasse ('Whistling Daughter')	1·75	1·50
	w. Wmk inverted	25·00	8·50
111/114 *Set of 4*		5·00	5·00

STAMP BOOKLET

1940 (15 Oct). Black on deep green cover. Stapled.

SB1 4s.8d. booklet containing one each ½d., 1d., 1½d., 2d., 3d., 6d., 1s. and 2s.6d. (Nos. 1/5, 6, 7/8) ... £3250

Genuine examples of No. SB1 are interleaved with ordinary kitchen wax-paper, which frequently tones the stamps, and are secured with staples 17 mm long.

The status of other booklets using different size staples or paper fasteners is uncertain although it is believed that some empty booklet covers were available on the island.

Prince Edward Island *see* Canada

Qatar

1957. 100 Naye Paise = 1 Rupee 1966. 100 Dirhams = 1 Riyal

The Arab Sheikhdom of Qatar consists of a large peninsula jutting into the Persian Gulf. In 1868, after Qatar had been invaded by Bahrain, a member of the leading Al Thani family was installed as Sheikh and an agreement was made by which he referred to the British Resident all disputes in which the sheikhdom was involved. Qatar was under nominal Turkish suzerainty, and Turkish troops were stationed there from 1871 until August 1915, when the Royal Navy forced them to abandon Doha, the capital, to the sheikh. On 3 November 1916 the sheikhdom entered into special treaty relations with the United Kingdom giving it British naval and military protection from attack. Oil was discovered on the peninsula in January 1940 and was first shipped to Europe at the end of 1949. On the withdrawal of British forces from the Gulf, Qatar declined to join the United Arab Emirates, terminated the Treaty with Great Britain and became fully independent on 3 September 1971.

There was no postal service from Qatar until 18 May 1950. Prior to this date the few foreign residents made their own arrangements for their mail to be carried to Bahrain for onward transmission through the postal service.

The first organised post from the capital, Doha, was an extension of the work in the state by the British Political Officer. From 18 May 1950 British residents were able to send mail via his office. The first three sendings had the Bahrain or British Postal Agencies in Eastern Arabia stamps cancelled by a circular office stamp, but later batches, up to the introduction of the first Doha postmark in July 1950, had the stamps cancelled on arrival at Bahrain.

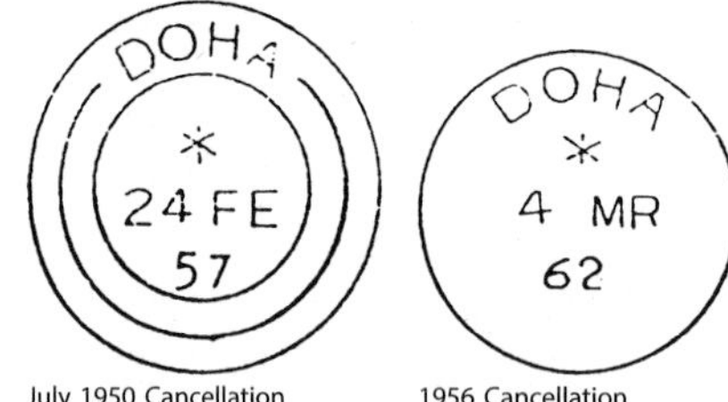

July 1950 Cancellation — 1956 Cancellation

The Post Office became a seperate entity in August 1950 when its services were made available to the general public. After initially using the Bahrain surcharges on Great Britain the supply of stamps for the Qatar office was switched to the British Postal Agencies in Eastern Arabia surcharges.

The circular cancellation, dating from July 1950, continued to be used until replaced by a slightly smaller version in early 1956.

A further post office was opened on 1 February 1956 at the Umm Said oil terminal, using its own cancellation.

Both offices were issued with standard oval Registered handstamps, Doha in 1950 and Umm Said in 1956.

1956. Umm Said Cancellation

All stamps to 1960 surcharged on Queen Elizabeth II issues of Great Britain.

QATAR NP 1 NP (1) — QATAR 3 NP NP (2) — QATAR 75 NP (3)

1957 (1 Apr)–**59**.

(a) Nos. 540/542, 543b/548, 551 and 555/556 (St Edward's Crown wmk), surch as Types **1** *to* **3**

1	**1**	1n.p. on 5d. brown	20	20
2	**2**	3n.p. on ½d. orange-red	40	50
3		6n.p. on 1d. ultramarine	40	30
4		9n.p. on 1½d. green	1·00	25
5		12n.p. on 2d. light red-brown	55	4·00
6	**1**	15n.p. on 2½d. carmine-red (I)	15	10
7	**2**	20n.p. on 3d. deep lilac (B.)	15	10
8	**1**	25n.p. on 4d. ultramarine	2·75	4·25
9		40n.p. on 6d. reddish purple	15	30
		a. Deep claret (21.7.59)	2·00	10
10		50n.p. on 9d. bronze-green	80	4·25
11	**3**	75n.p. on 1s.3d. green	1·00	7·00
12		1r. on 1s.6d. grey-blue	19·00	10
1/12 *Set of 12*			23·00	19·00

Designs: Nos. 1/12, Various portraits of Queen Elizabeth II.

QATAR 2 RUPEES
I
QATAR 2 RUPEES
(4) II

QATAR 5 RUPEES
I
QATAR 5 RUPEES
(5) II

QATAR 10 RUPEES
I
QATAR 10 RUPEES
(6) II

Type I (Types **4/6**). Type-set overprints. Bold thick letters with sharp corners and straight edges. Bars close together and usually slightly longer than in Type II.

Type II (Types **4/6**). Plate-printed overprints by Harrison. Thinner letters, rounded corners and rough edges. Bars wider apart.

(b) Nos. 536/538 (St Edward's Crown wmk) surcharged with Types **4/6**

13	2r. on 2s.6d. black-brown (I) (1.4.57)	7·00	7·00
	a. Type II (18.9.57)	15·00	8·00
14	5r. on 5s. rose-red (1) (1.4.57)	7·00	10·00
	a. Type II (18.9.57)	16·00	28·00
15	10r. on 10s. ultramarine (I) (1.4.57)	7·00	16·00
	a. Type II (18.9.57)	55·00	£150
13/15 *Set of 3*		19·00	30·00
13a/15a *Set of 3*		75·00	£160

Designs: No. 13, Carrickfergus Castle; 14, Caernarvon Castle; 15, Edinburgh Castle.

QATAR
15 NP

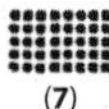

(7)

1957 (1 Aug). World Scout Jubilee Jamboree. Nos. 557/559 surch in two lines as T **7** (15n.p.) or in three lines (others).

16	15n.p. on 2½d. carmine-red	35	80
17	25n.p. on 4d. ultramarine	35	55
18	75n.p. on 1s.3d. green	40	60
16/18 *Set of 3*		1·00	1·75

Designs: No. 16, Scout badge and 'Rolling Hitch'; 17, 'Scouts coming to Britain'; 18, Globe within a Compass.

1960 (26 Apr–28 Sept). Nos. 570/575 and 579 (Mult Crown wmk) surcharged as Types **1** or **2**.

20	**2**	3n.p. on ½d. orange-red (28.9)	1·00	1·75
21		6n.p. on 1d. ultramarine (21.6)	4·50	2·75
22		9n.p. on 1½d. green (28.9)	1·00	1·50
23		12n.p. on 2d. light red-brown (28.9)	7·00	6·50
24	**1**	15n.p. on 2½d. carmine-red (11)	3·50	10
25	**2**	20n.p. on 3d. deep lilac (B.) (28.9)	75	10
26	**1**	40n.p. on 6d. deep claret (21.6)	4·50	2·50
20/26 *Set of 7*			20·00	13·50

Designs: Various portraits of Queen Elizabeth II.

Sheikh Ahmad bin Ali al-Thani
24 October 1960–22 February 1972

8 Sheikh Ahmad bin Ali al-Thani

9 Peregrine Falcon

10 Dhow

11 Oil Derrick

12 Mosque

(Des O. C. Meronti (T **8**), M. Goaman (T **9**), M. Farrar Bell (T **10**), J. Constable and O. C. Meronti (Types **11/12**). Photo Harrison, (Types **8/10**). Recess D.L.R. (Types **11/12**))

1961 (2 Sept). P 14½ (5n.p. to 75n.p.) or 13 (1r. to 10r.).

27	**8**	5n.p. carmine	30	15
28		15n.p. black	30	25

29		20n.p. reddish purple	30	15
30		30n.p. deep green	35	30
31	9	40n.p. red	4·50	30
32		50n.p. sepia	4·50	40
33	10	75n.p. ultramarine	1·60	4·50
34	11	1r. scarlet	5·50	35
35		2r. ultramarine	5·50	3·25
36	12	5r. bronze-green	38·00	14·00
37		10r. black	75·00	22·00
27/37 *Set of* 11			£120	40·00

The Qatar Post Department took over the postal services on 23 May 1963.

Queensland *see* Australia

Rarotonga *see* Cook Islands

Rhodesia

Stamps of BECHUANALAND were used in Matabeleland on the runner post between Gubulawayo and Mafeking (Bechuanaland) from 9 August 1888 until 5 May 1894. Such stamps were cancelled 'GUBULAWAYO' or by the barred oval '678' obliteration.

Between 27 June 1890 and 13 May 1892 external mail from Mashonaland sent via Bechuanaland was franked with that territory's stamps. A similar arrangement, using the stamps of MOZAMBIQUE existed for the route via Beira inaugurated on 29 August 1891. In both instances the stamps were cancelled by the post offices receiving the mail from Mashonaland. From 14 May until 31 July 1892 letters via Bechuanaland were franked with a combination of B.S.A Company and Bechuanaland issues.

Rhodesia joined the South African Postal Union on 1 August 1892 when its stamps became valid for international mail. Combination frankings with Mozambique stamps continued to be required until April 1894.

For the use of British Central Africa overprints in North-eastern Rhodesia from 1893 to 1899 see NYASALAND.

PRICES FOR STAMPS ON COVER TO 1945

Nos. 1/7	*from* × 6
Nos. 8/13	—
Nos. 14/17	*from* × 2
Nos. 18/24	*from* × 10
Nos. 25/26	—
Nos. 27/28	*from* × 7
Nos. 29/35	*from* × 10
Nos. 36/37	—
Nos. 41/46	*from* × 6
Nos. 47/50	—
Nos. 51/53	*from* × 2
Nos. 58/64	*from* × 3
Nos. 66/72	*from* × 8
Nos. 73/74	—
Nos. 75/87	*from* × 6
Nos. 88/93*a*	—
Nos. 94/99	*from* × 3
Nos. 100/110	*from* × 5
Nos. 111/113*e*	—
Nos. 114/118	*from* × 7
Nos. 119/121	*from* × 15
No. 122	*from* × 3
Nos. 123/125	*from* × 10
No. 126	*from* × 20
No. 127	—
Nos. 128/130	*from* × 15
Nos. 131/133	*from* × 6
Nos. 134/154	*from* × 10
Nos. 154*a*/156b	—
Nos. 167/178	*from* × 6
Nos. 179/181*a*	—
Nos. 182/185*a*	*from* × 4
Nos. 186/208	*from* × 8
Nos. 209/241	*from* × 8
Nos. 242/254*a*	—
Nos. 255/277	*from* × 8
Nos. 278/279*c*	—
Nos. 280/281	*from* × 15
Nos. 282/310	*from* × 8
Nos. 311/322	—

A. ISSUES FOR THE BRITISH SOUTH AFRICA COMPANY TERRITORY

1

2

½d.
(3)

(Recess B.W.)

1892 (2 Jan*)–**93**. Thin wove paper. P 14, 14½.

1	1	1d. black	19·00	4·25
2		6d. ultramarine	80·00	26·00
3		6d. deep blue (1893)	50·00	4·25
4		1s. grey-brown	50·00	16·00
5		2s. vermilion	75·00	45·00
6		2s.6d. grey-purple	50·00	55·00
7		2s.6d. lilac (1893)	65·00	55·00
8		5s. orange-yellow	90·00	60·00
9		10s. deep green	£130	£100
10	2	£1 deep blue	£325	£170
11		£2 rose-red** (f.c. £20)	£550	£170
12		£5 sage-green (f.c. £50)	£1600	£450
13		£10 brown (f.c. £70)	£2750	£700
1/10 *Set of* 8			£700	£400

Great caution is needed in buying the high values in either used or unused condition, many stamps offered being revenue stamps cleaned and re-gummed or with forged postmarks.

* Printing of stamps in Types **1**, **2** and **4** commenced in 1890, although none were used for postal purposes before 2 January 1892 when the route to the East Coast was inaugurated.

** For later printings of the £2 see No. 74.

The following sheet watermarks are known on Nos. 1/26: (1) William Collins, Sons & Co's paper watermarked with the firm's monogram, and PURE LINEN WOVE BANK in double-lined capitals (1890 and 1891 ptgs). (2) As (1) with EXTRA STRONG and 139 added (1892 ptgs). (3) Paper by Wiggins Teape & Co, watermarked W T & Co in script letters in double-lined wavy border (1893 ptgs). (4) The same firm's paper, watermarked 1011 in double-lined figures (1894 ptgs except ½d.). (5) WIGGINS TEAPE & CO LONDON in double-lined block capitals (1894 ptg of No. 18). Many values can also be found on a slightly thicker paper without wmk, but single specimens are not easily distinguishable.

1892 (2 Jan). Nos. 2 and 4 surch as T **3**.

14	1	½d. on 6d. ultramarine	£140	£500
15		2d. on 6d. ultramarine	£190	£700
16		4d. on 6d. ultramarine	£200	£800
17		8d. on 1s. grey-brown	£225	£850
14/17 *Set of* 4			£650	£2500

Caution is needed in buying these surcharges as both forged surcharges and forged postmarks exist.

4

5 (Ends of scrolls behind legs of springboks)

(T **4**. Centre recess; value B.W.)

1892 (2 Jan)–**94**. Thin wove paper (wmks as note after No. 13). P 14, 14½.

18	4	½d. dull blue and vermilion	4·75	4·75
19		½d. deep blue and vermilion (1893)	5·50	7·00
20		2d. deep dull green and vermilion	28·00	8·50
21		3d. grey-black and green (8.92)	26·00	5·00
22		4d. chestnut and black	48·00	7·00
23		8d. rose-lake and ultramarine	22·00	25·00
24		8d. red and ultramarine (1892)	17·00	25·00
25		3s. brown and green (1894)	£190	90·00
26		4s. grey-black and vermilion (1893)	48·00	55·00
18/26 *Set of* 7			£325	£170

(Recess P.B. from the Bradbury Wilkinson plates)

1895. Thick soft wove paper. P 12½.

27	4	2d. green and red	35·00	20·00
28		4d. yellow-brown and black	35·00	20·00
		a. Imperf (pair)	£2000	

(T **5**. Centre recess; value typo P.B.)

1896–97. Wove paper. P 14.

(a) Die I. Plates 1 and 2. Small dot to the right of the tail of the right-hand supporter in the Coat of Arms. Body of Lion only partly shaded

29	5	1d. scarlet and emerald	42·00	6·00
		a. Carmine-red and emerald		
30		2d. brown and mauve	42·00	3·00
		a. Yellow-brown and mauve	42·00	3·75
31		3d. chocolate and ultramarine	11·00	2·50
32		4d. ultramarine and mauve	55·00	
		a. Imperf between (pair)		
		b. Blue and mauve	48·00	27·00
33		6d. mauve and pink	85·00	28·00
34		8d. green and mauve/*buff*	21·00	75
		a. Imperf between (pair)		
		b. Imperf (pair)	£4250	
35		1s. green and blue	29·00	3·75
36		3s. green and mauve/*blue*	90·00	42·00
		a. Imperf (pair)	£13000	
37		4s. orange-red and blue/*green*	75·00	3·00
29/37 *Set of* 9			£375	£100

(b) Die II. Plates 3 and 4. No dot. Body of Lion heavily shaded all over

41	5	½d. slate and violet	4·75	4·25
42		1d. scarlet and emerald	15·00	5·50
43		2d. brown and mauve	32·00	13·00
		a. Yellow-brown and mauve	38·00	15·00
44		4d. ultramarine and mauve	75·00	13·00
		a. Blue and mauve	25·00	70
46		6d. mauve and rose	19·00	1·50
47		2s. indigo and green/*buff*	55·00	15·00
48		2s.6d. brown and purple/*yellow*	90·00	65·00
49		5s. chestnut and emerald	65·00	16·00
50		10s. slate and vermilion/*rose*	£150	75·00
41/50 *Set of* 9			£400	£160

One Penny
(6)

THREE
PENCE.
(7)

(Surch by Bulawayo Chronicle)

1896 (Apr–May). Matabele Rebellion provisionals. Surch with T **6** and **7**.

51	6	1d. on 3d. (No. 21)	£600	£750
		a. 'P' in 'Penny' inverted	£48000	
		b. 'y' in 'Penny' inverted		
52		1d. on 4s. (No. 26)	£300	£350
		a. 'P' in 'Penny' inverted	£35000	
		b. 'y' in 'Penny' inverted	£35000	
		c. Single bar through original value	£1100	£1200
53	7	3d. on 5s. (No. 8) (5.96)	£190	£250
		a. 'R' in 'THREE' inverted	£35000	
		b. 'T' in 'THREE' inverted	£48000	

Nos. 51 and 52 occur in two settings, one with 9¾ mm between value and upper bar, the other with 11 mm between value and upper bar.

Nos. 54 to 57 are vacant.

BRITISH
SOUTH AFRICA
COMPANY.
(8)

9 (Ends of scrolls between legs of Springboks)

1896 (22 May–Aug). Cape of Good Hope stamps optd by Argus Printing Co, Cape Town, with T **8**. Wmk Anchor (3d. wmk Crown CA). P 14.

58 **6** ½d. grey-black (No. 48*a*) 20·00 25·00
59 **17** 1d. rose-red (No. 58) 23·00 29·00
60 **6** 2d. deep bistre (No. 50*a*) 30·00 15·00
61 3d. pale claret (No. 40) 55·00 75·00
62 4d. blue (No. 51) 38·00 28·00
a. 'COMPANY.' omitted £9500
63 **4** 6d. deep purple (No. 52*a*) 70·00 80·00
64 **6** 1s. yellow-ochre (No. 65) (8.96) £150 £150
58/64 *Set of 7* £325 £350

No. 62 also exists with 'COMPANY' partially omitted. Examples with the word completely omitted, as No. 62a, are known from positions 1 to 6 of the setting.

Forgeries of this overprint show a narrow final 'A' in 'AFRICA' and have a rectangular full stop. On the genuine overprint both 'As' are the same and the stop is oval.

(T **9**. Eng J. A. C. Harrison (vignette), Bain or Rapkin (£1) (frames). Recess Waterlow)

1897. P 13½–16.

66 **9** ½d. grey-black and purple 8·00 9·50
67 1d. scarlet and emerald 13·00 12·00
68 2d. brown and mauve 28·00 4·50
69 3d. brown-red and slate-blue 11·00 50
a. Imperf between (vert pair) £4750
70 4d. ultramarine and claret 35·00 4·00
a. Imperf between (horiz pair) £18000 £18000
71 6d. dull purple and pink 23·00 3·50
72 8d. green and mauve/*buff* 35·00 50
a. Imperf between (vert pair) † £3750
73 £1 black and red-brown/*green* £450 £225
66/73 *Set of 8* £500 £225

(T **2**. Recess Waterlow)

1897 (Jan). P 15.

74 **2** £2 rosy red £1900 £475

10

11

12

£2. Re-entry (R. 6/5)

(Recess Waterlow)

1898–1908. P 13½–15½.

75 **10** ½d. dull bluish green 18·00 3·75
a. Yellow green (1904) 7·00 3·75
aa. Imperf vert (horiz pair) £850
ab. Imperf (pair) £900
ac. Imperf between (vert pair) £1600
76 ½d. deep green (*shades*) (1908) 40·00 4·00
77 1d. rose (*shades*) 16·00 1·00
a. Imperf (pair) £700 £750
b. Imperf between (vert pair) £550
c. Imperf between (horiz pair) — £950
78 1d. red (*shades*) (1905) 12·00 1·00
a. Imperf vert (horiz pair) £400 £450
ab. Imperf horiz (vert pair) £1000
b. Imperf (pair) £600 £600
c. Imperf between (horiz pair) £800 £500
d. Imperf between (vert strip of 4) £2750
79 2d. brown 15·00 3·00
80 2½d. dull blue (*shades*) 27·00 2·00
a. Imperf vert (horiz pair) £950 £1100
b. Grey-blue (*shades*) (1903) 27·00 1·75
81 3d. claret 24·00 80
a. Imperf between (vert pair) £700
82 4d. olive 22·00 1·00
a. Imperf between (vert pair) £700
83 6d. reddish purple 29·00 3·50
a. Reddish mauve (1902) 35·00 7·50
84 **11** 1s. bistre 42·00 6·00
a. Imperf between (vert pair) £3250
ab. Imperf between (horiz pair) £3750
b. Deep olive-bistre (1907) £350
bc. Imperf (pair) £3250
bd. Imperf between (horiz pair) £4500
c. Bistre-brown (1908) 75·00 19·00
d. Brownish yellow (1908) 42·00 16·00
85 2s.6d. bluish grey (11.06) 75·00 2·50
a. Imperf between (vert pair) £1100 £500
86 3s. deep violet (1902) 42·00 4·50
a. Deep bluish violet (1908) 85·00 17·00
87 5s. brown-orange 70·00 29·00
88 7s.6d. black (11.01) £110 38·00
89 10s. grey-green 65·00 2·75
90 **12** £1 greyish red-purple (P 15½) (7.01) £375 £170
a. Perf 14. *Blackish purple* (1902) £650 £160
91 £2 brown (5.08) £130 6·50
a. Re-entry £650 £100
92 £5 deep blue (7.01) (f.c. £25) £3250 £2500
93 £10 lilac (7.01) (f.c. £50) £3500 £2250
93*a* £20 yellow-bistre (1901?) (f.c. £100) £16000
75/90 *Set of 14* £750 £200
80s/81s, 85s/86s, 88s/93s Perf 'SPECIMEN' *Set of 10* £900

A £100 cherry-red, perf 13½, was ordered in June 1901, a number of mint, together with several examples showing fiscal cancellations being known (*Price, £1500 with fiscal cancellation*).

13 Victoria Falls

5d. Bird in tree (R. 2/5)

RHODESIA.

(**14**)

(Recess Waterlow)

1905 (13 July). Visit of British Association and Opening of Victoria Falls Bridge. P 14½–15 (5d.), 14 (others).

94 **13** 1d. red 9·00 11·00
a. Perf 14½ to 15 22·00 22·00
95 2½d. deep blue 19·00 12·00
a. Perf 14½ to 15 32·00 20·00
96 5d. claret 42·00 60·00
a. Bird in tree £225
b. Perf 14 80·00 £100
ba. Bird in tree £350
sa. Optd 'SPECIMEN' £170
97 1s. blue-green 45·00 50·00
a. Imperf (pair) £28000
b. Imperf between (horiz pair) £35000
c. Imperf between (vert pair) £38000
d. Imperf vert (horiz pair) £29000
e. Perf 14½ to 15 £550 £475
98 2s.6d. black £140 £170
99 5s. violet £140 48·00
a. Perf 14½ to 15 £550
94/99 *Set of 6* £350 £325
94s/99s Optd or Perf (5d.) 'SPECIMEN' *Set of 6* £425

Nos. 96a and 96ba are as illustrated. Lesser variations in a similar position exist on all stamps in row 3.

1909 (15 Apr)–**12**. Optd as T **14**. P 13½–15.

100 **10** ½d. green to deep green 6·50 3·50
a. No stop 75·00 48·00
b. Yellow-green (1911) 45·00 32·00
101 1d. carmine-rose 12·00 1·50
a. No stop 90·00 35·00
b. Imperf between (horiz pair) £450
c. Deep carmine-rose 13·00 1·50
cd. Imperf between (horiz pair) £450
102 2d. brown 7·50 10·00
a. No stop £140 £110
103 2½d. pale dull blue 5·00 80
a. No stop 65·00 30·00
104 3d. claret 5·00 2·75
a. No stop £170 75·00
b. Opt inverted † 18·00
c. Opt double † £1100
105 4d. olive 18·00 4·25
a. No stop £100 65·00
b. Opt inverted † 15·00
106 6d. reddish purple 12·00 12·00
a. No stop 90·00 90·00
b. Reddish mauve
c. Dull purple 27·00 12·00
ca. No stop £140 75·00
107 **11** 1s. bistre 40·00
a. No stop £170
b. Bistre-brown
ba. No stop
c. Deep brownish bistre 20·00 12·00
ca. No stop £110 60·00
108 2s.6d. bluish grey 42·00 14·00
a. No stop £140 75·00
b. Opt inverted † 24·00
109 3s. deep violet 30·00 14·00
110 5s. orange 55·00 85·00
a. No stop £180 £275
111 7s.6d. black £110 40·00
112 10s. dull green 75·00 24·00
a. No stop £400 £250
113 **12** £1 grey-purple £200 £110
a. Vert pair, lower stamp without opt £38000
b. Opt in violet £375 £190
113*c* £2 brown (f.c. £50) £5000 £325
ca. Re-entry — £1200
113*d* £2 rosy brown (*bluish paper*) (P 14½×15) (1912) (f.c. £50) £4000 £300
da. Re-entry £10000 £1200
113*e* £5 deep blue (*bluish paper*) (f.c. £100) £9000 £5000
100/113 *Set of 14* £500 £275
100s/113s Perf 'SPECIMEN' *Set of 14* £425

In some values the no stop variety occurs on every stamp in a vertical row of a sheet, in other values only once in a sheet. Other varieties, such as no serif to the right of apex of 'A', no serif to top of 'E', etc., exist in some values.

No. 113a comes from a sheet with the overprint omitted from the bottom row.

RHODESIA.
5d

(**15**)

RHODESIA.
TWO SHILLINGS.

(**16**)

1909 (Apr)–**11**. Surch as Types **15** and **16** (2s.) in black.

114 **10** 5d. on 6d. reddish purple 16·00 23·00
a. Surcharge in violet 90·00
b. Reddish mauve
c. Dull purple 27·00 23·00
116 **11** 7½d. on 2s.6d. bluish grey 7·00 3·75
a. Surcharge in violet 26·00 10·00
ab. Surch double † £6500
117 10d. on 3s. deep violet 18·00 19·00
a. Surcharge in violet 9·00 4·50
118 2s. on 5s. orange 17·00 8·50
114/118 *Set of 4* 45·00 35·00
114s/118s Perf 'SPECIMEN' *Set of 4* £180

In the 7½d. and 10d. surcharges the bars are spaced as in T **16**.

17

18

(Recess Waterlow)

1910 (11 Nov)–**13**.

(a) P 14

119 **17** ½d. yellow-green 16·00 2·25
a. Imperf between (horiz pair) £28000
120 ½d. bluish green 40·00 4·75
a. Imperf (pair) £15000 £7500
121 ½d. olive-green 48·00 5·50
122 ½d. dull green 70·00 80·00
123 1d. bright carmine 38·00 6·00
a. Imperf between (vert pair) £22000 £14000
b. Imperf between (horiz pair)
124 1d. carmine-lake 80·00 4·00
125 1d. rose-red 50·00 3·75
126 2d. black and grey 65·00 12·00
127 2d. black-purple and slate-grey £160 £750
128 2d. black and slate-grey 65·00 7·50
129 2d. black and slate 80·00 10·00
130 2d. black and grey-black 95·00 24·00
131 2½d. ultramarine 38·00 12·00
131*a* 2½d. bright ultramarine 28·00 12·00
132 2½d. dull blue 38·00 16·00
133 2½d. chalky blue 29·00 24·00
134 3d. purple and ochre 50·00 55·00
135 3d. purple and yellow-ochre 65·00 22·00
136 3d. magenta and yellow-ochre £200 17·00
137 3d. violet and ochre £150 £100
138 4d. greenish black and orange £120 £120
139 4d. brown-purple and orange 90·00 70·00
140 4d. black and orange 50·00 29·00
141 5d. purple-brown and olive-green 65·00 75·00
141*a* 5d. purple-brown and olive-yellow 50·00 65·00
ab. Error. Purple-brown and ochre £650 £150
143 5d. lake-brown and olive £325 65·00
143*a* 5d. lake-brown and green (9.12) £24000 £1600
144 6d. red-brown and mauve 50·00 50·00
145 6d. brown and purple 65·00 26·00
145*a* 6d. bright chestnut and mauve £700 70·00
146 8d. black and purple £6500
147 8d. dull purple and purple £180 £120
148 8d. greenish black and purple £180 £100
149 10d. scarlet and reddish mauve 50·00 50·00
150 10d. carmine and deep purple £650 60·00
151 1s. grey-black and deep blue-green 65·00 40·00
151*a* 1s. black and deep blue-green £250 55·00
152 1s. black and pale blue-green 70·00 24·00
152*a* 1s. purple-black and blue-green £250 80·00
153 2s. black and ultramarine £120 75·00
154 2s. black and dull blue £1200 85·00
154*a* 2s. purple-black and ultramarine £3000 £225
155 2s.6d. black and lake £400 £450
155*a* 2s.6d. black and crimson £350 £300
156 2s.6d. sepia and deep crimson £425 £375
156*a* 2s.6d. bistre-brown and crimson £1100 £700
157 2s.6d. black and rose-carmine £350 £425
158 3s. green and violet (*shades*) £250 £200
158*a* 3s. bright green and magenta £1300 £850
159 5s. vermilion and deep green £325 £425
160 5s. scarlet and pale yellow-green £350 £200
160*a* 5s. crimson and yellow-green £300 £200
160*b* 7s.6d. carmine and pale blue £650 £425
161 7s.6d. carmine and light blue £900 £1200
sa. Opt 'SPECIMEN.' double £3500
162 7s.6d. carmine and bright blue £4500 £1400
163 10s. deep myrtle and orange £650 £300
164 10s. blue-green and orange £425 £500
165 £1 carmine-red and bluish black £1700 £700
166 £1 rose-scarlet and bluish black £1600 £375
166*a* £1 crimson and slate-black £2000 £2000
b. Scarlet and reddish mauve (prepared for use but not issued) £10000

(b) P 15

167 **17** ½d. blue-green £300 13·00
168 ½d. yellow-green £350 11·00
169 ½d. apple-green £600 30·00
170 1d. carmine £300 8·50
170*a* 1d. carmine-lake £450 20·00
170*b* 1d. rose-carmine £350 12·00
171 2d. black and grey-black £900 50·00
171*a* 2d. black and grey £900 50·00
171*b* 2d. black and slate £1000 50·00
172 2½d. ultramarine (*shades*) 75·00 42·00
173 3d. purple and yellow-ochre £9000 90·00
173*a* 3d. claret and pale yellow-ochre £4000 75·00
174 4d. black and orange (*shades*) 60·00 75·00
175 5d. lake-brown and olive £800 80·00
176 6d. brown and mauve £900 60·00
177 1s. black and blue-green (*shades*) £1300 60·00
178 2s. black and dull blue £2500 £350
179 £1 red and black £18000 £3250

(c) P 14×15 (½d., 3d., 1s.) or 15×14 (1d., 4d.)

179*a* **17** ½d. yellow-green † £3500
179*b* 1d. carmine † £7000
180 3d. purple and ochre £7500 £300
181 4d. black and orange £450
181*a* 1s. black and blue-green £30000 £2750

(d) P 13½

182 **17** ½d. yellow-green £300 55·00
182*a* ½d. green £350 60·00
183 1d. bright carmine £2000 50·00
184 2½d. ultramarine (*shades*) 38·00 70·00
185 8d. black and purple (*shades*) 60·00 £250
185*a* 8d. grey-purple and dull purple £375 £450
119s/185s Optd 'SPECIMEN.' (all perf 14 except 2½d. and 8d. perf 13½) *Set of 18* £3500

Plate varieties in T **17** are: ½d., double dot below 'D' in right-hand value tablet (R. 3/9) (*from £550 un. £375 used*); 2d. to £1 excluding 2½d., straight stroke in Queen's right ear known as the 'gash in ear' variety (R. 1/2) (*from 3 to 5 times normal*).

Stamps from the above and the next issue are known compound perf with 14 or 15 on one side only or on adjoining sides but we no longer list them.

Examples of some values are known with a forged registered Bulawayo postmark dated 'JA 10 11'.

(Recess Waterlow)

1913 (1 Sept)–**19**. No wmk.

(i) From single working plates

(a) P 14

No.	Type	Description	Unused	Used
186	**18**	½d. blue-green	13·00	2·25
187		½d. deep green	11·00	2·25
		a. Imperf horiz (vert pair)	£950	
		b. Imperf between (vert strip of 5)	£4000	
		c. Imperf between (vert strip of 6)	£4750	
188		½d. yellow-green	23·00	2·25
		a. Imperf between (horiz pair)	£1100	
188*b*		½d. dull green	14·00	2·25
		ba. Imperf vert (horiz pair)	£1000	£1000
		bb. Imperf between (horiz pair)	£1300	
189		½d. bright green	30·00	2·25
		a. Imperf between (vert pair)	£1800	
190		1d. rose-carmine	9·00	2·25
		a. Imperf between (horiz pair)	£1200	£950
191		1d. carmine-red (*shades*)	14·00	2·75
		a. Imperf between (pair)	£1700	
192		1d. brown-red	5·00	4·00
193		1d. red	9·50	2·25
		a. Imperf between (horiz pair)	£1100	
194		1d. scarlet	25·00	2·50
		a. Imperf between (horiz pair)	£1400	
195		1d. rose-red	13·00	2·25
		a. Imperf between (horiz pair)	£1000	£1000
		b. Imperf between (vert pair)	£3000	
196		1d. rosine	£500	20·00
197		1½d. brown-ochre (1919)	5·50	2·25
		a. Imperf between (horiz pair)	£850	£850
198		1½d. bistre-brown (18.5.17)	7·00	2·25
		a. Imperf between (horiz pair)	£850	£850
199		1½d. drab-brown (1917)	8·00	2·25
		a. Imperf between (horiz pair)	£850	
		b. Imperf between (vert pair)	£2500	
200		2½d. deep blue	11·00	48·00
201		2½d. bright blue	11·00	42·00

(b) P 15

No.	Type	Description	Unused	Used
202	**18**	½d. blue-green	10·00	32·00
203		½d. green	14·00	25·00
204		1d. rose-red	£600	22·00
		a. Imperf between (horiz pair)	£18000	
205		1d. brown-red	7·50	11·00
206		1½d. bistre-brown (1919)	50·00	7·00
		a. Imperf between (horiz pair)	£24000	
206*b*		1½d. brown-ochre (1917)	50·00	14·00
207		2½d. deep blue	24·00	70·00
208		2½d. bright blue	16·00	65·00

(c) P 14×15

No.	Type	Description	Unused	Used
208*a*	**18**	½d. green	£7500	£200

(d) P 15×14

No.	Type	Description	Unused	Used
208*b*	**18**	½d. green	£8000	£350
208*c*		1½d. drab-brown		

(e) P 13½

No.	Type	Description	Unused	Used
208*d*	**18**	1d. red (1914)	†	£550

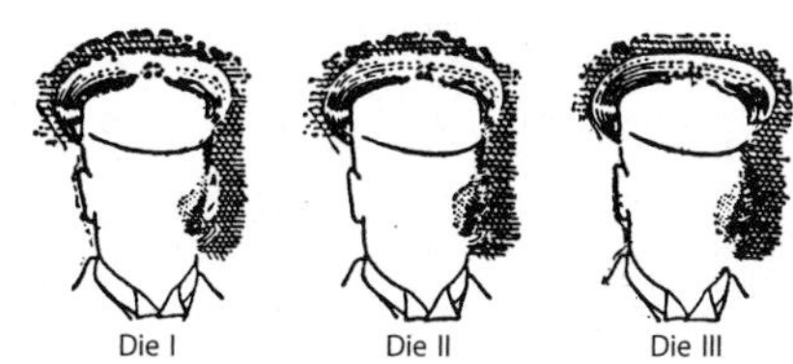

Die I Die II Die III

The remaining values were printed from double, i.e. head and duty, plates. There are at least four different head plates made from three different dies, which may be distinguished as follows: Die I. The King's left ear is neither shaded nor outlined; no outline to top of cap. Shank of anchor in cap badge is complete.

Die II. The ear is shaded all over, but has no outline. The top of the cap has a faint outline. Anchor as Die I.

Die III. The ear is shaded and outlined; a heavy continuous outline round the cap. Shank of anchor is broken just below the lowest line which crosses it.

(ii) Printed from double plates. Head Die I

(a) P 14

No.	Type	Description	Unused	Used
209	**18**	2d. black and grey	25·00	13·00
210		3d. black and yellow	85·00	25·00
211		4d. black and orange-red	16·00	45·00
212		5d. black and green	8·50	26·00
213		6d. black and mauve	£250	32·00
213*a*		8d. violet and green	£5500	
214		2s. black and brown	£160	£120

(b) P 15

No.	Type	Description	Unused	Used
215	**18**	3d. black and yellow	11·00	30·00
216		4d. black and orange-red	£170	30·00
217		6d. black and mauve	13·00	15·00
217*a*		8d. violet and green	£22000	£22000
218		2s. black and brown	22·00	65·00

(iii) Head Die II

(a) P 14

No.	Type	Description	Unused	Used
219	**18**	2d. black and grey	26·00	9·50
220		2d. black and brownish grey	75·00	16·00
221		3d. black and deep yellow	60·00	15·00
222		3d. black and yellow	85·00	15·00
223		3d. black and buff	18·00	13·00
224		4d. black and orange-red	42·00	17·00
225		4d. black and deep orange-red	26·00	17·00
226		5d. black and grey-green	29·00	55·00
227		5d. black and bright green	27·00	55·00
228		6d. black and mauve	50·00	7·50
229		6d. black and purple	85·00	8·50
230		8d. violet and green	23·00	75·00
231		10d. blue and carmine-red	35·00	55·00
232		1s. black and greenish blue	60·00	55·00
233		1s. black and turquoise-blue	22·00	22·00
234		2s. black and brown	£100	20·00
235		2s. black and yellow-brown	£375	50·00
236		2s.6d. indigo and grey-brown	85·00	60·00
236*a*		2s.6d. pale blue and brown	£1500	80·00
236*b*		3s. brown and blue	£120	£140
237		3s. chestnut and bright blue	£130	£170
238		5s. blue and yellow-green	£170	£120
239		5s. blue and blue-green	95·00	£100
240		7s.6d. blackish purple and slate-black	£350	£400
241		10s. crimson and yellow-green	£200	£350
242		£1 black and purple	£425	£650
243		£1 black and violet	£450	£600

(b) P 15

No.	Type	Description	Unused	Used
244	**18**	2d. black and grey	17·00	32·00
245		4d. black and deep orange-vermilion	£1600	£300
246		8d. violet and green	£200	£170
247		10d. blue and red	18·00	50·00
248		1s. black and greenish blue	75·00	26·00
249		2s.6d. indigo and grey-brown	55·00	£100
250		3s. chocolate and blue	£750	£300
251		5s. blue and yellow-green	£225	£250
251*a*		5s. blue and blue-green	£2250	
252		7s.6d. blackish purple and slate-black	£160	£275
253		10s. red and green	£225	£375
		a. Frame double, one albino	£650	
254		£1 black and purple	£1800	£1600
254*a*		£1 black and deep purple	£3000	£2500

186s, 190s, 198s, 208s, 209s, 211s/212s, 215s, 217s/218s, 230s, 232s, 237s/238s, 240s/242s, 247s, 249s Optd 'SPECIMEN' *Set of* 19 £2750

(iv) Head Die III (1919). Toned paper, yellowish gum

(a) P 14

No.	Type	Description	Unused	Used
255	**18**	2d. black and brownish grey	23·00	6·50
256		2d. black and grey-black	16·00	3·50
		a. Imperf between (horiz pair)	£7000	
		b. Imperf between (horiz strip of 3)	£16000	£16000
		c. Imperf vert (horiz pair)	£6500	£6500
257		2d. black and grey	22·00	15·00
258		2d. black and sepia	70·00	18·00
259		3d. black and yellow	22·00	4·50
260		3d. black and ochre	25·00	5·50
261		4d. black and orange-red	28·00	14·00
262		4d. black and dull red	26·00	19·00
263		5d. black and pale green	14·00	50·00
		a. Imperf between (horiz strip of 3)	£38000	
264		5d. black and green	14·00	50·00
265		6d. black and reddish mauve	23·00	8·50
		a. Imperf between (horiz pair)	£30000	
266		6d. black and dull mauve	23·00	8·50
267		8d. mauve and dull blue-green	32·00	70·00
268		8d. mauve and greenish blue	28·00	70·00
		a. Imperf vert (horiz pair)	£16000	
269		10d. indigo and carmine	26·00	55·00
270		10d. blue and red	24·00	60·00
271		1s. black and greenish blue	22·00	24·00
272		1s. black and pale blue-green	16·00	18·00
272*a*		1s. black and light blue	22·00	28·00
272*b*		1s. black and green	85·00	60·00
273		2s. black and brown	27·00	23·00
		aa. Imperf between (vert pair)	†	£42000
273*a*		2s. black and yellow-brown	£4250	£180
274		2s.6d. dp ultramarine and grey-brn	55·00	80·00
274*a*		2s.6d. pale blue and pale bistre-brown (*shades*)	£130	80·00
274*b*		3s. chestnut and light blue	£275	£180
275		5s. deep blue and blue-green (*shades*)	£150	85·00
276		5s. blue and pale yell-grn (*shades*).	£150	85·00
276*a*		7s.6d. maroon and slate-black	£900	£1400
277		10s. carmine-lake and yellow-green	£400	£275
278		£1 black and bright purple	£550	£700
279		£1 black and deep purple	£600	£700
279*a*		£1 black and violet-indigo	£700	£800
279*b*		£1 black and deep violet	£650	£700

(b) P 15

No.	Type	Description	Unused	Used
279*c*	**18**	2d. black and brownish grey	£5500	£400

Half Penny (**19**) **Half- Penny.** (**20**)

1917 (15 Aug). No. 190 surch at the Northern Rhodesian Administrative Press, Livingstone, with T **19**, in violet or violet-black.

No.	Type	Description	Unused	Used
280	**18**	½d. on 1d. rose-carmine (*shades*)	2·50	11·00
		a. Surch inverted	£1200	£1500
		b. Letters 'n n' spaced wider	11·00	40·00
		c. Letters 'n y' spaced wider	7·50	30·00

The setting was in two rows of ten repeated three times in the sheet. The two colours of the surcharge occur on the same sheet.

1917 (22 Sept). No. 190 surch as T **20** (new setting with hyphen, and full stop after 'Penny'), in deep violet.

No.	Type	Description	Unused	Used
281	**18**	½d. on 1d. rose-carmine (*shades*)	3·00	9·50

1922–24. New printings on white paper with clear white gum.

(i) Single working plates

(a) P 14

No.	Type	Description	Unused	Used
282	**18**	½d. dull green (1922)	5·50	12·00
		a. Imperf between (vert pair)	£3000	£2000
283		½d. deep blue-green (1922)	5·50	13·00
284		1d. bright rose (1922)	13·00	10·00
285		1d. bright rose-scarlet (1923)	13·00	10·00
		a. Imperf between (horiz pair)	£2000	
		b. Imperf between (vert pair)	£3000	
286		1d. aniline red (8.24) (*toned paper*)	20·00	25·00
287		1½d. brown-ochre (1923)	13·00	7·50
		a. Imperf between (vert pair)	£3000	£1900

(b) P 15

No.	Type	Description	Unused	Used
288	**18**	½d. dull green (1923)	50·00	
289		1d. bright rose-scarlet (1923)	50·00	
290		1½d. brown-ochre (1923)	50·00	

(ii) Double plates. Head Die III

(a) P 14

No.	Type	Description	Unused	Used
291	**18**	2d. black and grey-purple (1922)	19·00	11·00
292		2d. black and slate-purple (1923)	14·00	16·00
293		3d. black and yellow (1922)	21·00	48·00
294		4d. black and orange-vermilion (1922–1923)	30·00	50·00
295		6d. jet-black and lilac (1922–1923).	12·00	12·00
296		8d. mauve and pale blue-green (1922)	45·00	90·00
297		8d. violet and grey-green (1923)	55·00	90·00
298		10d. bright ultramarine and red (1922)	25·00	70·00
299		10d. bright ultramarine and carmine-red (1923)	35·00	70·00
300		1s. black and dull blue (1922–1923).	19·00	25·00
		a. Imperf between (horiz pair)	£30000	
		b. Imperf between (vert pair)	£25000	
301		2s. black and brown (1922–1923)	28·00	60·00
302		2s.6d. ultramarine and sepia (1922)	65·00	£100
303		2s.6d. violet-blue and grey-brown (1923)	80·00	£110
304		3s. red-brown and turquoise-blue (1922)	£130	£170
305		3s. red-brown and grey-blue (1923)	£140	£190
306		5s. bright ultramarine and emerald (1922)	£160	£190
307		5s. deep blue and bright green (1923)	£170	£190
308		7s.6d. brown-purple and slate (1922).	£250	£425
309		10s. crimson and bright yellow-green (1922)	£275	£325
310		10s. carmine and yellow-green (1923)	£300	£375
311		£1 black and magenta (1922)	£700	£900
311*a*		£1 black and deep magenta (1923)	£1000	£1300

(b) P 15 (1923)

No.	Type	Description	Unused	Used
312	**18**	2d. black and slate-purple	55·00	
313		4d. black and orange-vermilion	55·00	
314		6d. jet-black and lilac	70·00	
315		8d. violet and grey-green	75·00	
316		10d. bright ultramarine and carmine-red	85·00	
317		1s. black and dull blue	95·00	
318		2s. black and brown	£140	
319		2s.6d. violet-blue and grey-brown	£150	
320		3s. red-brown and grey-blue	£190	
321		5s. deep blue and bright green	£325	
322		£1 black and deep magenta	£1100	

The 1922 printing shows the mesh of the paper very clearly through the gum. In the 1923 printing the gum is very smooth and the mesh of the paper is not so clearly seen. Where date is given as '(1922–1923)' two printings were made, which do not differ sufficiently in colour to be listed separately.

Nos. 288/290 and 312/322 were never sent out to Rhodesia, but only issued in London. Any used copies could, therefore, only have been obtained by favour.

Southern Rhodesia, that part of the Company's territory south of the River Zambesi, became a self-governing colony on 1 October 1923. British South Africa Company rule continued in Northern Rhodesia until the administration was transferred to the Colonial Office on 1 April 1924.

The current stamps of Rhodesia, the Admiral series first issued in 1913, continued to be used in Southern Rhodesia until 1 April 1924 (invalidated 1 May 1924) and in Northern Rhodesia until 1 April 1925 (invalidated 30 September 1925).

TELEGRAPH STAMPS

Stamps were prepared by the Reuters agent in Bulawayo, Captain C. L. Norris-Newman to cover the cost of sending messages to the northern end of the telegraph line, then under construction from Tati towards Bulawayo.

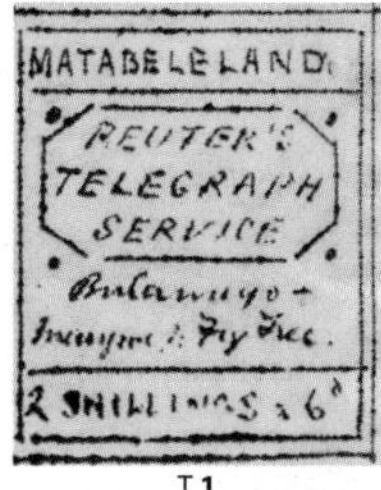

T1

T2

T3

1894 (28 Mar). Cyclostyled. Imperf.

No.	Type	Description	Unused	Used
T1	**T 1**	2s.6d. black	£600	£950
		a. Vert *se-tenant* strip of 3	£3000	†
T2	**T 2**	5s. black	£600	£1100
T3	**T 3**	10s. black	£550	£1200

These stamps were produced from a hand-drawn stencil in sheets of 18 (6×3) with the three values *se-tenant*. The 10s. value (top row, inscribed 'Bulawayo-Ramaguabane') was issued first, while the distance to the construction point was 96 miles. The 5s. value (middle row, inscribed 'Bulawayo-Mangwe') came into use when the distance was reduced to 60 miles. The 2s.6d. value (bottom row, inscribed 'Bulawayo-Fig Tree') was used only in the last phase, as the line neared Bulawayo, Fig Tree being 29 miles from Bulawayo. In June 1894 the Post Office took over the service and the stamps were withdrawn.

Used stamps were cancelled in blue crayon or ink with Captain Norris-Newman's initials and the date.

For issues from 1924 to 1964 see SOUTHERN RHODESIA.

In October 1964 Southern Rhodesia was renamed Rhodesia.

RHODESIA

59 'Telecommunications'

60 Bangala Dam

(Des V. Whiteley. Photo Harrison)

1965 (17 May). ITU Centenary. P 14½.

351 **59** 6d. violet and light yellow-olive ...... 1·75 45
352 1s.3d. violet and lilac ...... 1·75 45
353 2s.6d. violet and light brown ...... 6·00 6·50
351/353 *Set of 3* ...... 8·50 6·75

(Des V. Whiteley. Photo Harrison)

1965 (19 July). Water Conservation. T **60** and similar vert designs. Multicoloured. P 14.

354 3d. Type **60** 30 10
355 4d. Irrigation canal ...... 1·50 2·25
356 2s.6d. Cutting sugar cane ...... 2·25 5·00
354/356 *Set of 3* ...... 3·50 6·50

63 Sir Winston Churchill, Quill, Sword and Houses of Parliament

(Des H. Baxter. Photo Harrison)

1965 (16 Aug). Churchill Commemoration. P 14½.

357 **63** 1s.3d. black and bright blue 70 35

UNILATERAL DECLARATION OF INDEPENDENCE

Independence was declared by Rhodesia on 11 November 1965 but this was not recognised by the British Government. Following a conference in London during 1979 it was agreed that the British Government should resume control, pending elections to he held in February 1980.

After the elections Rhodesia became an independent republic within the Commonwealth on 18 April 1980, as ZIMBABWE.

64 Coat of Arms

(Des C. Hartley. Litho Mardon Printers, Salisbury)

1965 (8 Dec). 'Independence'. P 11.

358 **64** 2s.6d. multicoloured 15 15
a. Imperf (pair) £900

INDEPENDENCE
11th November
1965

INDEPENDENCE
11th November 1965 (**65**)

5/- (**66**)

1966 (17 Jan).

*(a) Nos. 92/105 of Southern Rhodesia optd with T **65** or larger (5s. to £1) by Mardon Printers, Salisbury*

359 ½d. yellow, yellow-green and light blue 10 10
a. Pair, one stamp without opt £7500
360 1d. reddish violet and yellow-ochre 10 10
361 2d. yellow and deep violet 10 10
362 3d. chocolate and pale blue 10 10
363 4d. yellow-orange and deep green 15 10
364 6d. carmine-red, yellow and deep dull green 15 10
a. Vertical strip of 6, bottom 3 stamps without opt £4500
365 9d. red-brown, yellow and olive-green 30 10
a. Opt double £800
b. Vertical strip of 6, bottom 2 stamps without opt £4500
366 1s. blue-green and ochre 40 10
a. Opt double £800
b. Vertical strip of 6, bottom 4 stamps without opt £4500
367 1s.3d. red, violet and yellow-green 50 50
368 2s. blue and ochre ...... 60 3·25
a. Dot over 'IA' ...... 12·00
369 2s.6d. ultramarine and vermilion ...... 60 1·00
370 5s. light brown, bistre-yellow and light blue ...... 1·50 5·50
a. Opt double £850
371 10s. black, yellow-ochre, light blue and carmine-red ...... 3·50 2·25
a. Extra 'feather' ...... 40·00
372 £1 brown, yellow-green, buff and salmon-pink ...... 1·25 2·25

*(b) No. 357 surch with T **66***

373 5s. on 1s.3d. black and bright blue (R.) ...... 6·50 14·00
a. '5/-' omitted ......
359/373 *Set of 15* ...... 14·00 26·00

Owing to the existence of forgeries, the errors should only be purchased when accompanied by a certificate of genuineness. Unique pairs of the 1d and 3d exist with the overprint omitted from one stamp, but both are defective. Other overprint errors exist from the clandestine use of the original settings.

67 Emeralds

68 Zeederberg Coach, *circa* 1895

(Des V. Whiteley. Photo Harrison)

1966 (9 Feb). As Nos. 92/105, but inscr 'RHODESIA' as T **67**. Some designs and colours changed. P 14½ (1d. to 4d.), 13½×13 (6d. to 2s.6d) or 14½×14 (5s. to £1).

374 – 1d. reddish violet and yellow-ochre 10 10
375 – 2d. yellow-orange and deep green (as No. 96) 10 10
a. Yellow-orange omitted £3250
376 – 3d. chocolate and pale blue 10 10
a. Chocolate omitted £7000
b. Pale blue omitted £5000
377 **67** 4d. emerald and sepia ...... 1·75 10
378 **50** 6d. carmine-red, yellow and deep dull green 15 10
379 – 9d. yellow and deep violet (as No. 94) 60 20
380 **45** 1s. yellow, yellow-green and light blue 15 10
381 – 1s.3d. blue and ochre (as No. 101) 25 15
a. Ochre omitted £4000
382 – 1s.6d. red-brown, yellow and olive-green (as No. 98) ...... 1·75 25
383 – 2s. red, violet and yellow-green (as No. 100) ...... 60 2·50
384 – 2s.6d. blue, vermilion and turquoise-blue ...... 1·00 20
385 **56** 5s. light brown, bistre-yellow and light blue ...... 1·00 90
386 – 10s. black, yellow-ochre, light blue and carmine-red ...... 4·25 4·00
387 **58** £1 brown, yellow-green, buff and salmon-pink ...... 3·25 8·00
374/387 *Set of 14* ...... 13·00 15·00

Nos. 379/380 are in larger format, as T **50**.

No. 374 exists in coils constructed from normal sheets. Coil-vending machines were withdrawn from service in 1967.

No. 375a occurred on single rows from two separate sheets, No. 376a in the bottom row of a sheet, No. 376b in the top two rows of a sheet and No. 381a in the third vertical row on two sheets.

For stamps printed by lithography, see Nos. 397/407.

PRINTERS. All the following stamps were printed by lithography by Mardon Printers, Salisbury.

(Des V. Whiteley (Nos. 388/390))

1966 (2 May). 28th Congress of Southern Africa Philatelic Federation (Rhopex). T **68** and similar horiz designs. P 14½.

388 3d. multicoloured 20 10
389 9d. grey-buff, sepia and grey-green 20 25
390 1s.6d. pale blue and black 30 35
391 2s.6d. salmon-pink, pale dull green and black ...... 40 1·00
388/391 *Set of 4* ...... 1·00 1·50
MS392 126×84 mm. Nos. 388/391 (*toned paper*) ...... 4·00 11·00
a. White paper ...... 6·50 13·00

Designs: 3d. T **68**; 9d. Sir Rowland Hill; 1s.6d. The Penny Black; 2s.6d. Rhodesian stamp of 1892 (No. 12).

The 3d., 2s.6d. and minature sheet exist imperforate from sheets prepared for presentation purposes.

69 de Havilland DH.89 Dragon Rapide (1946)

70 Kudu

1966 (1 June). 20th Anniversary of Central African Airways. T **69** and similar horiz designs. P 14½×14.

393 6d. black, blue, yellow and green ...... 1·00 35
394 1s.3d. blue, yellow-orange, black and green ...... 1·00 40
395 2s.6d. black, blue, yellow and green ...... 1·25 1·50
396 5s. black and blue ...... 1·75 4·50
393/396 *Set of 4* ...... 4·50 6·00

Aircraft: 6d. T **69**; 1s.3d. Douglas DC-3 (1953); 2s.6d. Vickers Viscount 748 *Matopos* (1956); 5s. BAC One Eleven 200.

The 6d., 2s.6d. and 5s. values exist imperforate from sheets prepared for presentation purposes.

1966–68. As Nos. 374/387 but litho. P 14½ (1d. to 2s.) or 14½×14 (others).

397 1d. reddish violet and yellow-ochre (*shades*) (2.6.66) 15 10
398 2d. orange and green (1.11.67) ...... 1·00 65
399 3d. chocolate-brown and pale greenish blue (29.1.68) ...... 2·50 10
400 4d. emerald, bistre-brown and drab (21.9.66) 65 10
401 6d. carmine-red, yellow and olive-grey (1.11.66) 60 50
402 9d. yellow and light violet (20.11.67) ...... 2·50 10
403 1s.3d. blue and ochre (9.11.66) ...... 1·00 30
404 2s. dull red, violet and sage-green (18.7.66) ...... 1·00 3·50
405 5s. yellow-brown, deep bistre-yellow and light blue (25.6.66) ...... 1·50 4·00
406 10s. black, buff, light blue and carmine-red (10.8.66) ...... 6·00 13·00
407 £1 pale brown, yellow-green, brown-ochre and salmon (10.8.66) ...... 6·00 19·00
397/407 *Set of 11* ...... 20·00 35·00

In addition to the change in printing process from photogravure to lithography and the difference in perforation in the 6d. to 2s. values (14½ instead of 13½×13) and shade variations, the oval portrait frame is larger (and in some values thicker) in the 1d. to 2s., and in the 1s.3d. the Queen's head is also larger.

Trial printings, made in June 1966, exist of the 5s., 10s. and £1 values on a slightly thinner paper. These are rare.

The 1d., 3d. and 5s. values exist imperforate from sheets prepared for presentation purposes.

1967–68. Dual Currency Issue. As Nos. 376, 380 and 382/384 but value in decimal currency in addition as in T **70**. P 14½. White gum (No. 408) or cream gum (others).

408 3d./2½c. chocolate-brown and pale greenish blue (14.3.67) 50 15
409 1s./10c. yellow, green and greenish blue (1.11.67) 50 25
410 1s.6d./15c. red-brown, yellow and yellow-green (11.3.68) ...... 4·75 40
411 2s./20c. dull red, violet and sage-green (11.3.68) ...... 4·50 4·50
412 2s.6d./25c. ultramarine-blue, vermilion and bright turquoise-blue (9.12.68) ...... 20·00 26·00
408/412 *Set of 5* ...... 27·00 28·00

71 Dr. Jameson (administrator)

(Des from painting by F. M. Bennett)

1967 (17 May). Famous Rhodesians (1st issue) and 50th Death Anniversary of Dr. Jameson. P 14½.

413 **71** 1s.6d. multicoloured 20 35

See also Nos. 426, 430 and 457. Further stamps in this series appeared after 1970.

72 Soapstone Sculpture (Joram Mariga)

1967 (12 July). Tenth Anniversary of Opening of Rhodes National Gallery. T **72** and similar vert designs. P 14½×14 (3d., 9d.) or 14 (others).

414 3d. reddish chestnut, yellow-olive and black 10 10
415 9d. light greenish blue, deep olive-brown and black 20 20
a. Perf 13½ ...... 4·75 12·00
416 1s.3d. multicoloured 20 25
417 2s.6d. multicoloured 25 60
414/417 *Set of 4* ...... 65 1·00

Designs: 3d. T **72**; 9d. *The Burgher of Calais* (detail, Rodin); 1s.3d. *The Knight* (stamp design wrongly inscr) (Roberto Crippa); 2s.6d. *John the Baptist* (M. Tossini).

73 Baobab Tree

1967 (6 Sept). Nature Conservation. T **73** and similar designs. P 14½.

418 4d. light brown and black 10 20
419 4d. yellow-olive and black 25 20
420 4d. deep grey and black 25 20
421 4d. yellow-orange and black 10 20
418/421 *Set of 4* 60 70

Designs: Horiz—No. 418, Type **73**; No. 419, White Rhinoceros; No. 420, African Elephants. Vert—No. 421, Wild Gladiolus.

74 Wooden Hand Plough

(Des Rose Martin)

1968 (26 Apr). 15th World Ploughing Contest, Norton, Rhodesia. T **74** and similar horiz designs. P 14½.

422 3d. pale orange, orange-vermilion and lake-brown 10 10
423 9d. multicoloured 15 20
424 1s.6d. multicoloured 20 55
425 2s.6d. multicoloured 20 75
422/425 *Set of 4* ...... 60 1·40

Designs: 3d. T **74**; 9d. Early wheel plough; 1s.6d. Steam powered tractor, and ploughs; 2s.6d. Modern tractor, and plough.

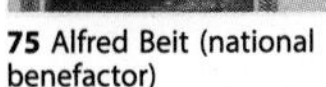

75 Alfred Beit (national benefactor)

76 Raising the Flag, Bulawayo, 1893

(Des from painting by A. Haywood)

1968 (15 July). Famous Rhodesians (2nd issue). P 14½.

426	**75**	1s.6d. pale orange, black and brown	20	30

(Des Rose Martin)

1968 (4 Nov). 75th Anniversary of Matabeleland. T **76** and similar vert designs. P 14½.

427	3d. pale orange, red-orange and black	15	10
428	9d. multicoloured	15	20
429	1s.6d. pale turquoise-green, deep emerald and blackish green	20	60
427/429 *Set of 3*		45	80

Designs: 3d. T **76**; 9d. View and Coat of Arms of Bulawayo; 1s.6d. Allan Wilson (combatant in the Matabele War).

77 Sir William Henry Milton (administrator)

(Des from painting by S. Kendrick)

1969 (15 Jan). Famous Rhodesians (3rd issue). P 14½.

430	**77**	1s.6d. multicoloured	30	40

78 2ft Gauge Steam Locomotive No. 15, 1897

(Des Rose Martin)

1969 (22 May). 70th Anniversary of Opening of Beira–Salisbury Railway. T **78** and similar horiz designs showing locomotives. Multicoloured. P 14½.

431	3d. Type **78**	30	10
432	9d. 7th Class steam locomotive No. 43, 1903	60	25
433	1s.6d. Beyer Peacock 15th Class steam locomotive No. 413, 1951	75	45
434	2s.6d. Class DE2 diesel-electric locomotive No. 1203, 1955	1·10	2·50
431/434 *Set of 4*		2·50	3·00

79 Low Level Bridge

(Des Rose Martin)

1969 (18 Sept). Bridges of Rhodesia. T **79** and similar horiz designs. Multicoloured. P 14½.

435	3d. Type **79**	20	10
436	9d. Mpudzi bridge	40	20
437	1s.6d. Umniati bridge	60	60
438	2s.6d. Birchenough bridge	80	1·25
435/438 *Set of 4*		1·75	1·90

(New Currency. 100 cents = 1 dollar)

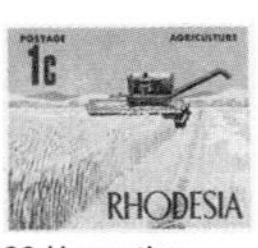

80 Harvesting Wheat

81 Devil's Cataract, Victoria Falls

(Des from colour-transparencies (3, 6c.), Rose Martin (others))

1970 (17 Feb)–**73**. Decimal Currency. Types **80/81** and similar horiz designs. P 14½.

439	1c. multicoloured	10	10
	a. Booklet pane of 4	30	
440	2c. multicoloured	10	10
441	2½c. multicoloured	10	10
	a. Booklet pane of 4	35	
441*c*	3c. multicoloured (1.1.73)	1·25	10
	ca. Booklet pane of 4	4·50	
442	3½c. multicoloured	10	10
	a. Booklet pane of 4	65	
442*b*	4c. multicoloured (1.1.73)	2·75	1·25
	ba. Booklet pane of 4	10·00	
443	5c. multicoloured	15	10
443*b*	6c. multicoloured (1.1.73)	4·25	6·50
443*c*	7½c. multicoloured (1.1.73)	9·00	60
444	8c. multicoloured	75	20
445	10c. multicoloured	60	10
446	12½c. multicoloured	1·75	10
446*a*	14c. multicoloured (1.1.73)	12·00	70
447	15c. multicoloured	1·25	15
448	20c. multicoloured	1·00	15
449	25c. multicoloured	4·00	60
450	50c. turquoise and ultramarine	1·25	55
451	$1 multicoloured	6·00	3·00
452	$2 multicoloured	8·50	15·00
439/452 *Set of 19*		48·00	26·00

Designs: Size as T **80**—1c. T **80**; 2c. Pouring molten metal; 2½c. Zimbabwe Ruins; 3c. Articulated lorry; 3½c. and 4c. Statute of Cecil Rhodes; 5c. Mine headgear. Size as T **81**—6c. Hydrofoil *Seaflight*; 7½c. As 8c.; 8c. T **81**; 10c. Yachting on Lake McIlwaine; 12½c. Hippopotamus in river; 14c. and 15c. Kariba Dam; 20c. Irrigation canal. As Types **80/81** *but larger* (31×26 *mm*)—25c. Bateleurs; 50c. Radar antenna and Vickers Viscount 810; $1 'Air Rescue'; $2 Rhodesian flag.

Booklet panes Nos. 439a, 441a, 441ca, 442a and 442ba have margins all round.

82 Despatch Rider, *circa* 1890

(Des Rose Martin)

1970 (1 July). Inauguration of Posts and Telecommunications Corporation. T **82** and similar horiz designs. Multicoloured. P 14½.

453	2½c. Type **82**	40	10
454	3½c. Loading mail at Salisbury airport	45	50
455	15c. Constructing telegraph line, *circa* 1890	50	90
456	25c. Telephone and modern telecommunications equipment	55	1·75
453/456 *Set of 4*		1·75	2·75

83 Mother Patrick (Dominican nurse and teacher)

(Des Rose Martin from photograph)

1970 (16 Nov). Famous Rhodesians (4th issue). P 14½.

457	**83**	15c. multicoloured	45	50

STAMP BOOKLETS

1967 (Feb). Black on orange cover, size 57×45 mm. Stitched.

SB7	1s. booklet containing 3d. (No. 376) in block of 4	3·75

Although not issued in Rhodesia until February 1967, No. SB7 was released in London in June 1966.

1968 (21 Dec). Black on yellow cover, size 51×94 mm. Stapled.

SB8	5s. booklet containing 12×1d. and 12×3d., and 6×2d. (Nos. 397/399) in blocks of 6	18·00

1970 (17 Feb). Red on yellow cover. Stapled.

SB9	46c. booklet containing 12×1c., 8×2½c. and 4×3½c. in panes of 4 (Nos. 439a, 441a, 442a)	5·00

POSTAGE DUE STAMPS

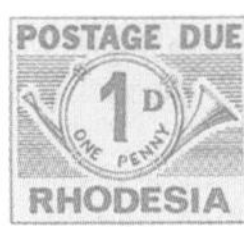

D 2

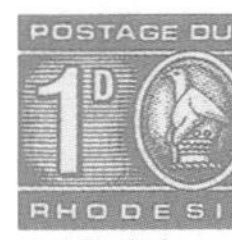

D 3 Zimbabwe Bird (soapstone sculpture)

(Des E.W. Jones Typo Printing and Stationery Dept, Salisbury)

1965 (17 June). Roul 9.

D8	D **2**	1d. orange-red (roul 5)	50	12·00
		a. Roul 9	6·00	12·00
D9		2d. deep blue	40	8·00
D10		4d. green	50	8·00
D11		6d. plum	50	6·00
D8/D11 *Set of 4*			1·75	30·00

The 2d. has a stop below the 'D'.

(Litho Mardon Printers, Salisbury)

1966 (15 Dec). P 14½.

D12	D **3**	1d. red	60	4·50
D13		2d. bluish violet	75	2·50
D14		4d. pale green	75	4·75
D15		6d. reddish violet	75	1·50
D16		1s. red-brown	75	1·50
D17		2s. black	1·00	6·50
D12/D17 *Set of 6*			4·25	19·00

1970 (17 Feb)–**73**. Decimal Currency. As T D **3**, but larger (26×22½ *mm*). P 14½.

D18	D **3**	1c. bright green	60	1·25
D19		2c. ultramarine	60	60
		a. Printed on the gummed side	50·00	
D20		5c. bright reddish violet	1·00	1·75
D21		6c. pale lemon (7.5.73)	5·50	4·00
D22		10c. cerise	1·00	4·00
D18/D22 *Set of 5*			8·00	10·50

Rhodesia & Nyasaland

Stamps for the Central Africa Federation of Northern and Southern Rhodesia and Nyasaland Protectorate.

1

2

3 Queen Elizabeth II

(Recess Waterlow)

1954 (1 July)–**56**. P 13½×14 (T **1**), 13½×13 (T **2**) or 14½×13½ (T **3**).

1	**1**	½d. orange-red	15	10
		a. Coil stamp. Perf 12½×14. *Reddish orange* (6.2.56)	30	3·00
2		1d. ultramarine	15	10
		a. Coil stamp. Perf 12½×14. *Deep blue* (9.55)	1·50	22·00
		ab. *Ultramarine* (1.10.55)	4·75	20·00
3		2d. bright green	15	10
3*a*		2½d. ochre (15.2.56)	6·50	10
4		3d. carmine-red	20	10
5		4d. red-brown	60	20
6		4½d. blue-green	30	1·75
7		6d. bright reddish purple	2·25	10
		a. *Bright purple* (5.5.56)	6·00	10
8		9d. violet	2·50	1·00
9		1s. grey-black	2·50	10
10	**2**	1s.3d. red-orange and ultramarine	8·00	40
11		2s. deep blue and yellow-brown	9·00	6·50
12		2s.6d. black and rose-red	9·00	2·25
13		5s. violet and olive-green	26·00	8·50
14	**3**	10s. dull blue-green and orange	26·00	11·00
15		£1 olive-green and lake	45·00	32·00
1/15 *Set of 16*			£120	55·00

Nos. 1*a* and 2*a* printed on rotary machines by subsidiary company, Imprimerie Belge de Securité, in Belgium.

4 de Havilland DH.106 Comet 1 over Victoria Falls

5 Livingstone and Victoria Falls

3d. Wing flaw (R. 3/3)

(Des J. E. Hughes (3d.), V. E. Horne (1s.). Recess Waterlow)

1955 (15 June). Centenary of Discovery of Victoria Falls. P 13½ (3d.) or 13 (1s.).

16	**4**	3d. ultramarine and deep turquoise-green	1·00	30
		a. Wing flaw	24·00	13·00
17	**5**	1s. purple and deep blue	55	70

6 Tea Picking

7 VHF mast

8 Copper mining

9 Fairbridge Memorial

10 Rhodes's Grave

11 Lake Bangweulu

12 Eastern Cataract, Victoria Falls

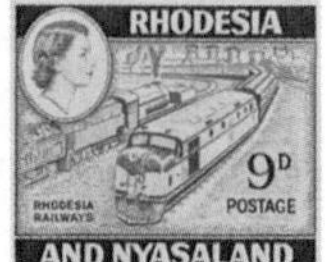

12a Rhodesian Railway Trains

13 Tobacco

14 Lake Nyasa

15 Chirondu Bridge

16 Salisbury Airport

17 Rhodes Statue

18 Mlanje

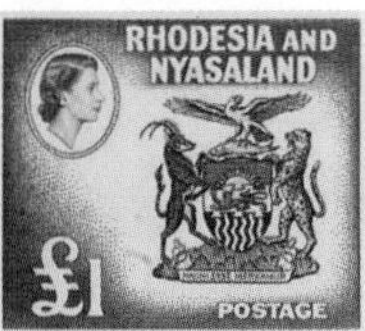

19 Federal Coat of Arms

1d. Pylon re-entry. The diagonal lines representing the pylon arms are doubled (R. 3/6)

(Des M. Kinsella (9d.). Recess Waterlow (½d., 1d., 2d., 1s.) until 1962, then D.L.R.; D.L.R. (2½d., 4d., 6d., 9d., 2s., 2s.6d.) and B.W. (others))

1959 (12 Aug)–**62**. Types **6/19**. P 13½×14 (½d., 1d., 2d.), 14½ (2½d., 4d., 6d., 9d., 2s., 2s.6d.), 14×13½ (3d.), 13½×13 (1s.), 14 (1s.3d.) or 11 (others).

No.	Type	Description	Unused	Used
18	**6**	½d. black and light emerald	1·25	2·25
		a. Coil stamp. Perf 12½×14 *black and light green*	3·50	7·00
19	**7**	1d. carmine-red and black	30	10
		aa. Pylon re-entry	15·00	
		a. Coil stamp. Perf 12½×14	3·50	14·00
		ab. Carmine-red and grey-black	8·50	20·00
		ac. Carmine-red (centre) omitted	£200	
20	**8**	2d. violet and yellow-brown	2·50	50
21	**9**	2½d. purple and grey-blue	2·00	2·25
22	**10**	3d. black and blue	1·00	10
		a. Black (centre) omitted	£30000	
		b. Printed on the gummed side	£450	
23	**11**	4d. maroon and olive	1·50	10
24	**12**	6d. ultramarine and deep myrtle-green	2·75	10
24*a*	**12a**	9d. orange-brown and reddish violet (15.5.62)	9·00	3·75
25	**13**	1s. light green and ultramarine	1·25	10
26	**14**	1s.3d. emerald and deep chocolate	6·00	10
27	**15**	2s. grey-green and carmine	4·25	60
28	**16**	2s.6d. light blue and yellow-brown	13·00	1·00
29	**17**	5s. deep chocolate and yellow-green	16·00	2·75
30	**18**	10s. olive-brown and rose-red	28·00	26·00
31	**19**	£1 black and deep violet	48·00	65·00
18/31 *Set of 15*			£110	90·00

Only three examples from two different sheets, all unused, are believed to exist of No. 22a, although further stamps from the same sheets can be found with the centre partially omitted.

20 Kariba Gorge, 1955

Gorge flaw (R. 4/6)

1s.3d. Earring flaw (R. 1/4)

(Photo Harrison (3d., 6d.), D.L.R. (others))

1960 (17 May). Opening of Kariba Hydro-Electric Scheme. T **20** and similar horiz designs. P 14½×14 (3d., 6d.) or 13 (others).

No.	Description	Unused	Used
32	3d. blackish green and red-orange	70	10
	a. Red-orange omitted	£6000	
	b. Gorge flaw	32·00	8·50
33	6d. brown and yellow-brown	1·00	20
34	1s. slate-blue and green	2·50	4·00
35	1s.3d. light blue and orange-brown	2·75	3·50
	aa. Earring flaw	55·00	
	a. Blue and deep orange-brown	15·00	11·00
36	2s.6d. deep slate-purple and orange-red	4·00	8·50
37	5s. reddish violet and turquoise-blue	11·00	12·00
32/37 *Set of 6*		20·00	25·00

Designs: 3d. T **20**; 6d. 330 kV power lines; 1s. Barrage wall; 1s.3d. Barrage and lake; 2s.6d. Interior of power station; 5s. Barrage wall and Queen Mother (top left).

No. 35aa comes on the first shade only.

26 Miner Drilling

(Des V. Whiteley. Photo Harrison)

1961 (8 May). Seventh Commonwealth Mining and Metallurgical Congress. T **26** and similar horiz design. P 15×14.

No.	Description	Unused	Used
38	6d. olive-green and orange-brown	1·00	20
39	1s.3d. black and light blue	1·25	80

Design: 6d. T **26**; 1s.3d. Surface installations, Nchanga Mine.

Imperforate examples of the 6d. are believed to be printer's waste.

28 de Havilland DH.66 Hercules *City of Basra* on Rhodesian Airstrip

31 Tobacco Plant

2s.6d. Extra landing light (Cyl. B, R. 9/2)

1962 (6 Feb). 30th Anniversary of First London-Rhodesia Airmail Service. T **28** and similar horiz designs. P 14½×14.

No.	Description	Unused	Used
40	6d. bronze-green and vermilion	2·50	75
41	1s.3d. light blue, black and yellow	1·50	50
42	2s.6d. rose-red and deep violet	2·00	6·50
	a. Extra landing light	45·00	
40/42 *Set of 3*		5·50	7·00

Designs: 6d. T **28**; 1s.3d. Short S.23 flying boat *Canopus* taking off from Zambesi; 2s.6d. Hawker Siddeley Comet 4 at Salisbury airport.

(Des V. Whiteley. Photo Harrison)

1963 (18 Feb). World Tobacco Congress, Salisbury. T **31** and similar vert designs. P 14×14½.

No.	Description	Unused	Used
43	3d. green and olive-brown	30	10
44	6d. green, brown and blue	40	35
45	1s.3d. chestnut and indigo	1·50	45
46	2s.6d. yellow and brown	1·75	3·25
43/46 *Set of 4*		3·50	3·75

Designs: 3d. T **31**; 6d. Tobacco field; 1s.3d. Auction floor; 2s.6d. Cured tobacco.

35 Red Cross Emblem

(Photo Harrison)

1963 (6 Aug). Red Cross Centenary. P 14½×14.

No.	Type	Description	Unused	Used
47	**35**	3d. red	1·50	10

36 African Round Table Emblem

(Des V. Whiteley. Photo Harrison)

1963 (11 Sept). World Council of Young Men's Service Clubs, Salisbury. P 14½×14.

No.	Type	Description	Unused	Used
48	**36**	6d. black, gold and yellow-green	75	1·50
49		1s.3d. black, gold, yellow-green and lilac	1·00	1·25

STAMP BOOKLETS

1955 (1 Jan). Black on yellow cover. Stitched.

SB1	5s. booklet containing 12×½d. and 18×1d. and 18×2d. (Nos. 1/3) in blocks of 6	35·00

1963 (4 Apr). Black on yellow cover. Stitched.

SB2	1s. booklet containing 3d. (No. 22) in block of 4.	2·00

POSTAGE DUE STAMPS

After Federation in 1954 existing stocks of Postage Due Stamps from Northern Rhodesia, Nyasaland and Southern Rhodesia continued to be used and were sometimes distributed throughout the federation.

Increased postal rates in July 1956 and in 1959 led to the exhaustion of certain values, in particular the 1d., and various offices then used Rhodesia and Nyasaland postage issues for postage due purposes. There were isolated instances of such stamps being cancelled 'POSTAGE DUE' from December 1956 onwards.

Some of these handstamps may have been applied at Bulawayo while others, in violet or black, originate from the Salisbury Delivery Room at Kingsway Post Office. Only the 1d. and 2d. (Nos. 2/3) are known with such handstamps. After mint examples began to appear the Postmaster General suppressed the use of the handstamps in August 1959.

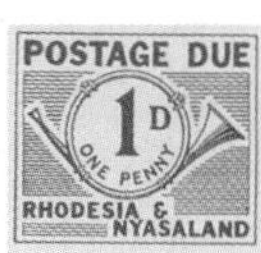

D **1**

(Des E.W. Jones. Typo Federal Printing and Stationery Dept, Salisbury)

1961 (19 Apr). P 12½.

No.	Type	Description	Unused	Used
D1	D **1**	1d. vermilion	3·75	5·50
		a. Imperf between (horiz pair)	£800	£900
D2		2d. deep violet-blue	3·00	3·00
D3		4d. green	3·50	9·50
D4		6d. purple	4·50	7·50
		a. Imperf between (horiz pair)	£1900	
D1/D4 *Set of 4*			13·00	23·00

The 2d. has a stop below the 'D'.

The stamps of the Federation were withdrawn on 19 February 1964 when all three constituent territories had resumed issuing their own stamps.

St Helena

CROWN COLONY

PRICES FOR STAMPS ON COVER TO 1945	
Nos. 1/5	*from* × 12
Nos. 6/30	*from* × 10
Nos. 34/45	*from* × 15
Nos. 46/52	*from* × 6
Nos. 53/67	*from* × 5
No. 71	—
Nos. 72/86	*from* × 5
Nos. 87/88	*from* × 12
Nos. 89/95	*from* × 5
No. 96	—
Nos. 97/110	*from* × 5
Nos. 111/113	—
Nos. 114/140	*from* × 4

PERKINS BACON 'CANCELLED'. For notes on these handstamps, showing 'CANCELLED' between horizontal bars forming an oval, see Catalogue Introduction.

1

ONE PENNY (2) FOUR PENCE (3)

(Recess P.B.)

1856 (1 Jan). Wmk Large Star, W w **1**. Imperf.

1	1	6d. blue (H/S 'CANCELLED' in oval £10000)	£500	£200

1861 (Apr?). Wmk Large Star, W w **1**.

(a) Clean-cut perf 14 to 16

2	1	6d. blue	£1700	£275

(b) Rough perf 14 to 16

2*a*	1	6d. blue	£425	£140

NOTE: The issues which follow consist of 6d. stamps, T **1**, printed in various colours and (except in the case of the 6d. values) surcharged with a new value, as Types **2** to **10**, *e.g.* stamps described as '1d.' are, in fact, 1d. on 6d stamps, and so on.

The numbers in the Type column below refer to the *types of the lettering* of the surcharged value.

(Printed by D.L.R. from P.B. plate)

Two Types of Bar on 1d. value:

A. Bar 16–17 mm long.

B. Bar 18½–19 mm long.

1863 (July). Surch as Types **2/3** with thin bar approximately the same length as the words. Wmk Crown CC. Imperf.

3	2	1d. lake (Type A)	£150	£250
		a. Surch double	£6500	£4250
		b. Surch omitted	£21000	
		w. Wmk inverted	£750	
4		1d. lake (Type B)	£160	£275
		a. Vert pair. Nos. 3/4	£11000	
5	3	4d. carmine (*bar 15½–16½ mm*)	£500	£250
		a. Surch double	£15000	£7500

ONE PENNY (4 (A)) ONE PENNY (4 (B)) ONE PENNY (4 (C))

TWO PENCE (5) THREE PENCE (6) FOUR PENCE (7)

ONE SHILLING (8) FIVE SHILLINGS (9)

Three Types of Bar:

A. Thin bar (16½ to 17 *mm*) nearly the same length as the words.

B. Thick bar (14 to 14½ *mm*) much shorter than the words, except on the 2d. (Nos. 9, 22, 28) where it is nearly the same length.

C. Long bar (17 to 18 *mm*) same length as the words.

1864–80. 6d. as T **1**, without surcharge. Wmk Crown CC.

(a) P 12½ (1864–1873)

6	4	1d. lake (Type A) (1864)	70·00	29·00
		a. Surch double	£12000	
7		1d. lake (Type B) (1868)	£225	60·00
		a. Surch double		
		b. Imperf	£3000	
		w. Wmk inverted	—	£225
		x. Wmk reversed	—	£160
8	4	1d. lake (Type C) (1871)	£140	17·00
		a. Surch in blue-black	£1000	£550
		x. Wmk reversed	£300	55·00
		y. Wmk inverted and reversed	£400	
9	5	2d. yellow (Type B) (1868)	£180	60·00
		a. Imperf	£10000	
		x. Wmk reversed	£475	
10		2d. yellow (Type C) (1873)	£160	45·00
		a. Surch in blue-black	£4000	£2250
		b. Surch double, one albino	£2000	
		x. Wmk reversed	£225	80·00
11	6	3d. deep dull purple (Type B) (1868)	£120	50·00
		a. Surch double	—	£7500
		b. Imperf	£850	
		c. Light purple	£3000	£750
		x. Wmk reversed	£300	
12		3d. deep dull purple (Type A) (1873)	£150	65·00
13	7	4d. carmine (Type A) (*words 17 mm long*) (1864)	£170	50·00
		a. Surch double	†	£6000
14		4d. carmine (Type B) (*words 18 mm long*) (1868)	£150	60·00
		a. Surch double	†	£6000
		b. Surch double (18+19 *mm widths*)	£26000	£12000
		c. Imperf	£12000	
		x. Wmk reversed	£350	£150
15		4d. carmine-rose (Type B) (*words 19 mm long*) (1868)	£325	£120
		a. Surch omitted	†	£6000
		x. Wmk reversed	—	£225
16	–	6d. dull blue (1871)	£850	£120
		a. Ultramarine (1873)	£550	85·00
		x. Wmk reversed	£1600	£250
17	8	1s. deep yellow-green (Type A) (1864)	£450	28·00
		a. Surch double	†	£24000
		w. Wmk inverted	—	£100
18		1s. deep yellow-green (Type B) (1868)	£750	£130
		a. Surch double	£21000	
		b. Imperf	£18000	
		c. Surch omitted*	£21000	
19		1s. deep green (Type C) (1871)	£750	16·00
		a. Surch in blue-black		
		x. Wmk reversed	£1000	75·00
20	9	5s. orange (Type B) (1868)	60·00	70·00
		a. Yellow	£450	£450
		w. Wmk inverted	£550	£600
		x. Wmk reversed	£170	£190
		y. Wmk inverted and reversed		

(b) P 14×12½ (1876)

21	4	1d. lake (Type B)	85·00	15·00
		w. Wmk inverted	£325	
22	5	2d. yellow (Type B)	£140	50·00
23		3d. purple (Type B)	£350	70·00
24		4d. carmine (Type B) (*words 16½ mm long*)	£170	60·00
		y. Wmk inverted and reversed	£170	75·00
25	–	6d. milky blue	£550	50·00
26	8	1s. deep green (Type C)	£900	24·00

(c) P 14 (1880)

27	4	1d. lake (Type B)	£120	20·00
		w. Wmk inverted	£400	
28	5	2d. yellow (Type B)	£150	45·00
29	–	6d. milky blue	£550	50·00
		x. Wmk reversed	†	£180
30	8	1s. yellow-green (Type B)	21·00	12·00
		y. Wmk inverted and reversed	—	£160

Two used examples of No. 15a are known, one being in the Royal Collection and the other damaged at bottom right. The price is for the latter.

* No. 18c is from a sheet of the 1s. with surcharge misplaced, the fifth row of 12 stamps being thus doubly surcharged and the tenth row without surcharge.

2½d (10)

11

12

FOUR PENCE

Additional thin bar in surch (R. 7/2)

1884–94. T **1** surch. Bars similar to Type B above (except 2½d., T **10**, and the 1s., in which the bar is nearly the same length as the words). The 6d. as before without surcharge. Wmk Crown CA. P 14.

34	–	½d. emerald (*words 17 mm*) (1884)	20·00	26·00
		a. 'N' and 'Y' spaced	£1100	£1200
		b. Surch double	£1300	£1400
		ba. Ditto. 'N' and 'Y' spaced	£11000	
		w. Wmk inverted	—	75·00
		y. Wmk inverted and reversed	—	75·00
35	–	½d. green (*words 17 mm*) (1885)	13·00	22·00
		a. 'N' and 'Y' spaced	£475	£700
		x. Wmk reversed	12·00	24·00
36	–	½d. green (*words 14½ mm*) (1893)	2·50	2·75
		a. 'N' and 'Y' spaced	£1600	
37	4	1d. red (1887)	4·75	3·25
		x. Wmk reversed	5·50	4·50
38		1d. pale red (1890)	8·50	3·25
		x. Wmk reversed	16·00	7·00
39	5	2d. yellow (1894)	3·00	8·00
40	10	2½d. ultramarine (1893)	3·75	5·50
		a. Surch double	£25000	
		b. Stamp doubly printed	£10000	
		w. Wmk inverted	32·00	
		x. Wmk reversed	40·00	
41	6	3d. deep mauve (1887)	7·50	11·00
		a. Surch double	—	£10000
42		3d. deep reddish lilac (1887)	9·00	5·00
		a. Surch double	£10000	£6000
		w. Wmk reversed	10·00	6·00
43	7	4d. pale brown (*words 16½ mm*) (1890)	45·00	40·00
		by. Wmk inverted and reversed	65·00	
43*c*		4d. sepia (*words 17 mm*) (1894)	27·00	17·00
		ca. Additional thin bar in surch (R. 7/2)	£850	£850
		cx. Wmk reversed	40·00	29·00
44	–	6d. grey (1887)	45·00	5·00
		x. Wmk reversed	55·00	5·00
		y. Wmk inverted and reversed	—	£110
45	8	1s. yellow-green (1894)	65·00	30·00
		a. Surch double	£4750	
36/45 *Set of 8*			£140	70·00
40s/1s, 43bys, 44s Optd 'SPECIMEN' *Set of 4*			£200	

Examples of the above are sometimes found showing no watermark; these are from the bottom row of the sheet, which had escaped the watermark, the paper being intended for stamps of a different size to T **1**.

Some are found without bar and others with bar at top of stamp, due to careless overprinting.

Nos. 34a and 35a occur on R. 18/12 and show a minimum space between the letters of 0.8 mm. Normal examples are spaced 0.5 mm, but some stamps show intermediate measurements due to loose type. On No. 34ba only one impression of the surcharge shows 'N' and 'Y' spaced. On the reset surcharge, No. 36, a similar variety occurs on R. 5/9.

Of the 2½d. with double surcharge only six copies exist, and of the 2½d. doubly printed, one row of 12 stamps existed on one sheet only.

CANCELLATIONS. Nos. 40/45 and No. 20 were sold as remainders in 1904 defaced with a violet diamond-shaped grill with four interior bars extending over two stamps. These cannot be considered as used stamps, and they are consequently not priced in the list.

This violet obliteration is easily removed and many of these remainders have been cleaned and offered as unused; some are repostmarked with a date and name in thin type rather larger than the original, a usual date being 'Ap.4.01.'

(Typo D.L.R.)

1890–97. Die I for the 1½d. Die II for the other values (for differences see Seychelles). Wmk Crown CA. P 14.

46	11	½d. green (1897)	2·75	7·50
47		1d. carmine (1896)	19·00	3·00
48		1½d. red-brown and green (1890)	4·50	15·00
49		2d. orange-yellow (1896)	5·00	14·00
50		2½d. ultramarine (1896)	18·00	12·00
51		5d. mauve (1896)	11·00	35·00
52		10d. brown (1896)	27·00	70·00
46/52 *Set of 7*			75·00	£140
46s/52s Optd 'SPECIMEN' *Set of 7*			£350	

The note below No. 45a *re* violet diamond-shaped grill cancellation also applies to Nos. 48/52.

1902. Wmk Crown CA. P 14.

53	12	½d. green (3.02)	2·00	2·75
54		1d. carmine (24.02.02)	13·00	70
53s/54s Optd 'SPECIMEN' *Set of 2*			£100	

13 Government House

14 The Wharf

(Typo D.L.R.)

1903 (May). Wmk Crown CC. P 14.

55	13	½d. brown and grey-green	2·00	3·50
		w. Wmk inverted	£200	£275
56	14	1d. black and carmine	1·50	35
		w. Wmk inverted	—	£700
		x. Wmk reversed	£700	
57	13	2d. black and sage-green	13·00	1·25
58	14	8d. black and brown	23·00	32·00
59	13	1s. brown and brown-orange	26·00	40·00
60	14	2s. black and violet	65·00	95·00
55/60 *Set of 6*			£110	£150
55s/60s Optd 'SPECIMEN' *Set of 6*			£275	

15

(Typo D.L.R.)

1908 (May)–**11**. Ordinary paper (2½d.) or chalk-surfaced paper (4d., 6d.). P 14.

(a) Wmk Mult Crown CA

64	15	2½d. blue	2·00	1·50
66		4d. black and red/*yellow*	17·00	38·00
		a. Ordinary paper (1911)	8·00	19·00
67		6d. dull and deep purple	48·00	55·00
		a. Ordinary paper (1911)	14·00	14·00

(b) Wmk Crown CA. Chalk-surfaced paper

70	15	10s. green and red/*green*	£275	£325
64/70 *Set of 4*			£275	£325
64s/70s Optd 'SPECIMEN' *Set of 4*			£300	

Examples of Nos. 58/60 and 66/70 are known showing a forged St Helena postmark dated 'JY 28 1'.

1911. Wmk Mult Crown CA. P 14. Prepared for use but not issued.

71s	14	1d. red (optd 'SPECIMEN')	£425	

This stamp was printed in error, as a result of a misunderstanding between the Postmaster and De La Rue. The supply was sent to St Helena, but withdrawn and destroyed. Specimen examples were sent to UPU member countries.

16

17

(Typo D.L.R.)

1912–16. Wmk Mult Crown CA. P 14.

72	16	½d. black and green	2·25	10·00
73	17	1d. black and carmine-red	4·75	1·75
		a. Black and scarlet (1916)	10·00	17·00

No.	Type	Description	Unused	Used
74		1½d. black and dull orange (1913)	3·50	9·00
75	16	2d. black and greyish slate	7·50	1·75
76	17	2½d. black and bright blue	3·50	7·00
77	16	3d. black and purple/*yellow* (1913)	3·50	5·00
78	17	8d. black and dull purple	13·00	65·00
79	16	1s. black/*green*	9·00	35·00
80	17	2s. black and blue/*blue*	55·00	£110
81		3s. black and violet (1913)	75·00	£160
72/81 *Set of* 10			£150	£350
72s/81s Optd 'SPECIMEN' *Set of* 10			£375	

No. 73*a* is on thicker paper than 73.

18

19

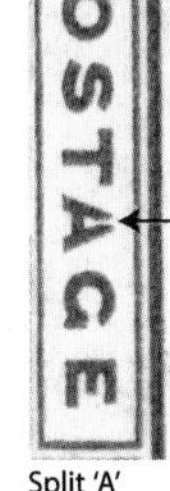

Split 'A' (R. 8/3 of left pane)

(Typo D.L.R.)

1912. Chalk-surfaced paper. Wmk Mult Crown CA. P 14.

No.	Type	Description	Unused	Used
83	18	4d. black and red/*yellow*	15·00	30·00
84		6d. dull and deep purple	4·25	5·50
83s/84s Optd 'SPECIMEN' *Set of* 2			£140	

1913. Wmk Mult Crown CA. P 14.

No.	Type	Description	Unused	Used
85	19	4d. black and red/*yellow*	8·00	2·75
		a. Split 'A'	£400	£300
86		6d. dull and deep purple	14·00	28·00
		a. Split 'A'	£650	£1000
85s/86s Optd 'SPECIMEN' *Set of* 2			£140	

WAR TAX

ONE PENNY

(20)

WAR TAX

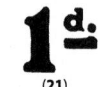

1d.

(21)

1916 (Sept). As No. 73*a*, on thin paper, surch with T **20**.

No.	Type	Description	Unused	Used
87	17	1d.+1d. black and scarlet	3·50	3·25
		a. Surch double	†	£18000
		s. Optd 'SPECIMEN'	70·00	

1919. No. 73 on thicker paper, surch with T **21**.

No.	Type	Description	Unused	Used
88	17	1d.+1d. black and carmine-red (*shades*)	2·00	4·50
		s. Optd 'SPECIMEN'	70·00	

1922 (Jan). Printed in one colour. Wmk Mult Script CA. P 14.

No.	Type	Description	Unused	Used
89	17	1d. green	3·25	60·00
		w. Wmk inverted	£700	
		y. Wmk inverted and reversed	£350	
90		1½d. rose-scarlet	12·00	55·00
91	16	3d. bright blue	25·00	£100
		y. Wmk inverted and reversed	£325	£650
89/91 *Set of* 3			35·00	£200
89s/91s Optd 'SPECIMEN' *Set of* 3			£200	

22 Badge of St Helena

PLATE FLAWS ON THE 1922–1937 ISSUE. Many constant plate varieties exist on both the vignette and duty plates of this issue. The major varieties are illustrated and listed below.

a. Broken mainmast. Occurs on R. 2/1 of all sheets from the second printing onwards. It does not appear on Nos. 93/96 and 111/113 as these stamps only exist from the initial printing invoiced in May 1922.

1936 and subsequent printings show additional minor varieties to the vignette of this stamp; a dent in the lower left frame and breaks in the bottom frame.

b. Torn flag. Occurs on R. 4/6 of all sheets from printings up to and including that invoiced in December 1922. The flaw was retouched for the printing invoiced in December 1926 and so does not occur on Nos. 97*h*, 99*f*, 103/103*d*, 107/110 and 111*d*.

c. Cleft rock. Occurs on R. 5/1 of all sheets from the second printing onwards. It does not appear on Nos. 93/96 and 111/113 as these stamps only exist from the initial printing invoiced in May 1922.

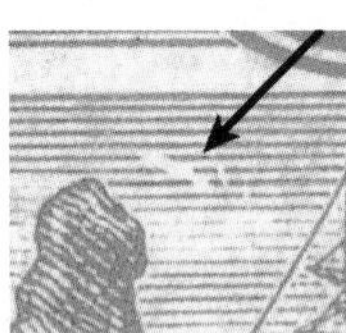

'Storm over rock' (R. 3/5, December 1922 printings only)

Damaged value tablet (R. 1/4 of first printing and part of second (1932) printing)

(Des T. Bruce. Typo D.L.R.)

1922 (June)–**37.** P 14

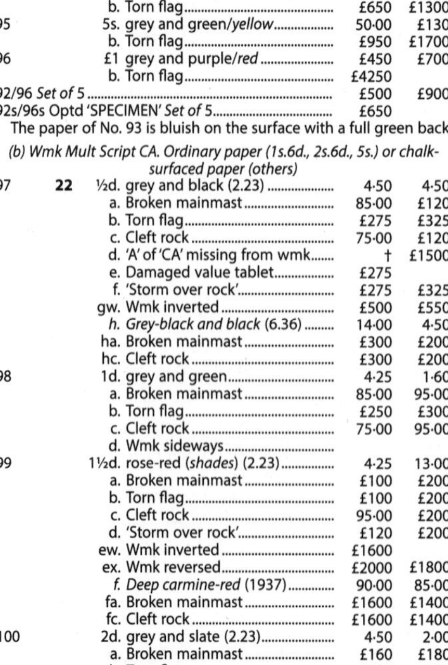

(a) Wmk Mult Crown CA. Chalk-surfaced paper

No.	Type	Description	Unused	Used
92	22	4d. grey and black/*yellow* (2.23)	15·00	6·00
		a. Broken mainmast	£275	£300
		b. Torn flag	£275	£300
		c. Cleft rock	£250	£275
		d. 'Storm over rock'	£275	£300
93		1s.6d. grey and green/*blue-green*	22·00	70·00
		b. Torn flag	£550	£1200
94		2s.6d. grey and red/*yellow*	28·00	75·00
		b. Torn flag	£650	£1300
95		5s. grey and green/*yellow*	50·00	£130
		b. Torn flag	£950	£1700
96		£1 grey and purple/*red*	£450	£700
		b. Torn flag	£4250	
92/96 *Set of* 5			£500	£900
92s/96s Optd 'SPECIMEN' *Set of* 5			£650	

The paper of No. 93 is bluish on the surface with a full green back.

(b) Wmk Mult Script CA. Ordinary paper (1s.6d., 2s.6d., 5s.) or chalk-surfaced paper (others)

No.	Type	Description	Unused	Used
97	22	½d. grey and black (2.23)	4·50	4·50
		a. Broken mainmast	85·00	£120
		b. Torn flag	£275	£325
		c. Cleft rock	75·00	£120
		d. 'A' of 'CA' missing from wmk	†	£1500
		e. Damaged value tablet	£275	
		f. 'Storm over rock'	£275	£325
		gw. Wmk inverted	£500	£550
		h. Grey-black and black (6.36)	14·00	4·50
		ha. Broken mainmast	£300	£200
		hc. Cleft rock	£300	£200
98		1d. grey and green	4·25	1·60
		a. Broken mainmast	85·00	95·00
		b. Torn flag	£250	£300
		c. Cleft rock	75·00	95·00
		d. Wmk sideways		
99		1½d. rose-red (*shades*) (2.23)	4·25	13·00
		a. Broken mainmast	£100	£200
		b. Torn flag	£100	£200
		c. Cleft rock	95·00	£200
		d. 'Storm over rock'	£120	£200
		ew. Wmk inverted	£1600	
		ex. Wmk reversed	£2000	£1800
		f. Deep carmine-red (1937)	90·00	85·00
		fa. Broken mainmast	£1600	£1400
		fc. Cleft rock	£1600	£1400
100		2d. grey and slate (2.23)	4·50	2·00
		a. Broken mainmast	£160	£180
		b. Torn flag	£325	£375
		c. Cleft rock	£150	£180
		d. 'Storm over rock'	£325	£375
101		3d. bright blue (2.23)	2·25	4·00
		a. Broken mainmast	£130	£200
		b. Torn flag	£130	£200
		c. Cleft rock	£110	£190
		d. 'Storm over rock'	£130	£200
		x. Wmk reversed	£800	
103		5d. green and deep carmine/*green* (1927)	6·50	5·50
		a. Broken mainmast	£275	£350
		c. Cleft rock	£250	£350
		d. Green and carmine-red/green (1936)	13·00	7·50
		da. Broken mainmast	£425	£450
		dc. Cleft rock	£400	£450
104		6d. grey and bright purple	7·50	9·50
		a. Broken mainmast	£300	£425
		b. Torn flag	£300	£425
		c. Cleft rock	£275	£400
105		8d. grey and bright violet (2.23)	4·75	8·00
		a. Broken mainmast	£200	£375
		b. Torn flag	£200	£375
		c. Cleft rock	£180	£375
		d. 'Storm over rock'	£200	£375
		w. Wmk inverted	†	£2750
106		1s. grey and brown	7·00	9·00
		a. Broken mainmast	£375	£500
		b. Torn flag	£500	£650
		c. Cleft rock	£350	£475
107		1s.6d. grey and green/*green* (1927)	16·00	65·00
		a. Broken mainmast	£475	£950
		c. Cleft rock	£450	£950
108		2s. purple and blue/*blue* (1927)	26·00	60·00
		a. Broken mainmast	£550	£900
		c. Cleft rock	£500	
109		2s.6d. grey and red/*yellow* (1927)	21·00	80·00
		a. Broken mainmast	£450	£1400
		c. Cleft rock	£425	£1400
110		5s. grey and green/*yellow* (1927)	45·00	95·00
		a. Broken mainmast	£750	£1500
		c. Cleft rock	£700	£1500
111		7s.6d. grey-brown and yellow-orange	£150	£225
		b. Torn flag	£1300	£2750
		d. Brownish grey and orange (1937)	£1300	£2000
		da. Broken mainmast	£27000	
		dc. Cleft rock	£27000	
112		10s. grey and olive-green	£170	£250
		b. Torn flag	£1800	£3250
113		15s. grey and purple/*blue*	£1100	£2750
		b. Torn flag	£8500	£15000
97/112 *Set of* 15			£425	£750
97s/113s Optd 'SPECIMEN' *Set of* 16			£1600	

Examples of all values are known showing forged St Helena postmarks dated 'JU 20 24', 'OC 2 25', '4 DE 27', '11 DE 27' and 'DE 18 27'.

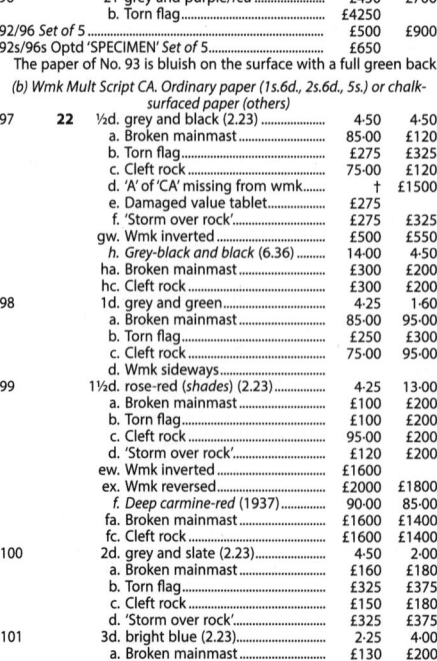

23 Lot and Lot's Wife

24 The 'Plantation'

25 Map of St Helena

26 Quay at Jamestown

27 James Valley

28 Jamestown

29 Munden's Promontory

30 St Helena

31 High Knoll

32 Badge of St Helena

(Recess B.W.)

1934 (23 Apr). Centenary of British Colonisation. T **23/32.** Wmk Mult Script CA. P 12.

No.	Type	Description	Unused	Used
114	23	½d. black and purple	1·25	80
115	24	1d. black and green	75	85
116	25	1½d. black and scarlet	2·50	3·25
117	26	2d. black and orange	4·25	1·25
118	27	3d. black and blue	1·40	4·50
119	28	6d. black and light blue	3·25	3·00
120	29	1s. black and chocolate	6·50	18·00
121	30	2s.6d. black and lake	50·00	60·00
122	31	5s. black and chocolate	£100	£100
123	32	10s. black and purple	£300	£350
114/123 *Set of* 10			£425	£475
114s/123s Perf 'SPECIMEN' *Set of* 10			£475	

Examples of all values are known showing a forged St Helena postmark dated 'MY 12 34'.

1935 (6 May). Silver Jubilee. As Nos. 91/94 of Antigua. P 13½×14.
124 1½d. deep blue and carmine ... 1·50 5·50
f. Diagonal line by turret ... £100 £200
125 2d. ultramarine and grey ... 3·75 90
f. Diagonal line by turret ... £180 £225
g. Dot to left of chapel ... £350
126 6d. green and indigo ... 9·50 3·25
a. Frame printed double, one albino ... £3500
f. Diagonal line by turret ... £500 £550
g. Dot to left of chapel ... £800
h. Dot by flagstaff ... £750
127 1s. slate and purple ... 26·00 32·00
h. Dot by flagstaff ... £950 £1000
i. Dash by turret ... £1200
124/127 *Set of 4* ... 35·00 38·00
124s/127s Perf 'SPECIMEN' *Set of 4* ... £190

For illustrations of plate varieties see Omnibus section following Zanzibar.

1937 (19 May). Coronation. As Nos. 95/97 of Antigua, but ptd by D.L.R. P 14.
128 1d. green ... 40 75
129 2d. orange ... 55 45
130 3d. bright blue ... 80 50
128/130 *Set of 3* ... 1·60 1·50
128s/130s Perf 'SPECIMEN' *Set of 3* ... £160

33 Badge of St Helena

(Recess Waterlow)

1938 (12 May)–**44**. Wmk Mult Script CA. P 12½.
131 **33** ½d. violet ... 15 65
132 1d. green ... 14·00 3·75
132*a* 1d. yellow-orange (8.7.40) ... 30 30
133 1½d. scarlet ... 30 40
134 2d. red-orange ... 30 15
135 3d. ultramarine ... 80·00 18·00
135*a* 3d. grey (8.7.40) ... 30 30
135*b* 4d. ultramarine (8.7.40) ... 2·50 2·50
136 6d. light blue ... 2·50 2·75
136*a* 8d. sage-green (8.7.40) ... 4·50 2·25
b. Olive-green (24.5.44) ... 7·00 4·25
137 1s. sepia ... 1·25 1·75
138 2s.6d. maroon ... 20·00 7·50
139 5s. chocolate ... 20·00 17·00
140 10s. purple ... 20·00 20·00
131/140 *Set of 14* ... £140 65·00
131s/140s Perf 'SPECIMEN' *Set of 14* ... £600

See also Nos. 149/151.

1946 (21 Oct). Victory. As Nos. 110/111 of Antigua.
141 2d. red-orange ... 40 50
142 4d. blue ... 60 30
141s/142s Perf 'SPECIMEN' *Set of 2* ... £150

1948 (20 Oct). Royal Silver Wedding. As Nos. 112/113 of Antigua.
143 3d. black ... 30 30
144 10s. violet-blue ... 28·00 45·00

1949 (10 Oct). 75th Anniversary of UPU. As Nos. 114/117 of Antigua.
145 3d. carmine ... 25 1·25
146 4d. deep blue ... 3·00 3·50
147 6d. olive ... 1·50 4·25
148 1s. blue-black ... 35 1·10
145/148 *Set of 4* ... 4·50 9·00

1949 (1 Nov). Wmk Mult Script CA. P 12½.
149 **33** 1d. black and green ... 1·50 1·50
150 1½d. black and carmine ... 1·50 1·50
151 2d. black and scarlet ... 1·50 1·50
149/151 *Set of 3* ... 4·00 4·00

1953 (2 June). Coronation. As No. 120 of Antigua.
152 3d. black and deep reddish violet ... 1·75 1·50

34 Badge of St Helena

34a Flax plantation

35 Heart-shaped Waterfall

35a Lace-making

36 Drying flax

37 St Helena Sand Plover

38 Flagstaff and The Barn

39 Donkeys carrying flax

40 Island map

41 The Castle

42 Cutting flax

43 Jamestown

44 Longwood House

(Recess D.L.R.)

1953 (4 Aug)–**59**. Types **34/44**. Wmk Mult Script CA. P 14.
153 **34** ½d. black and bright green ... 30 30
154 **34a** 1d. black and deep green ... 15 20
155 **35** 1½d. black and reddish purple ... 4·75 1·50
a. Black and deep reddish purple (14.1.59) ... 12·00 4·25
156 **35a** 2d. black and claret ... 1·00 60
157 **36** 2½d. black and red ... 40 30
158 **37** 3d. black and brown ... 3·25 30
159 **38** 4d. black and deep blue ... 40 1·00
160 **39** 6d. black and deep lilac ... 40 30
161 **40** 7d. black and grey-black ... 2·00 1·75
162 **41** 1s. black and carmine ... 40 70
163 **42** 2s.6d. black and violet ... 20·00 9·00
164 **43** 5s. black and deep brown ... 25·00 12·00
165 **44** 10s. black and yellow-orange ... 40·00 14·00
153/165 *Set of 13* ... 85·00 38·00

45 Stamp of 1856

46 Arms of East India Company

47 East Indiaman *London* off James Bay

48 Commemoration Stone

(Recess D.L.R.)

1956 (3 Jan). St Helena Stamp Centenary. Wmk Mult Script CA. P 11½.
166 **45** 3d. Prussian blue and carmine ... 15 10
167 4d. Prussian blue and reddish brown ... 15 20
168 6d. Prussian blue and deep reddish purple ... 15 25
166/168 *Set of 3* ... 40 50

(Recess Waterlow)

1959 (5 May). Tercentenary of Settlement. Types **46/48**. W w **12**. P 12½×13.
169 **46** 3d. black and scarlet ... 15 15
170 **47** 6d. light emerald and slate-blue ... 65 75
171 **48** 1s. black and orange ... 30 75
169/171 *Set of 3* ... 1·00 1·50

ST. HELENA
Tristan Relief
9d +
(**49**)

1961 (12 Oct). Tristan Relief Fund. Nos. 46 and 49/51 of Tristan da Cunha surch as T **49** by Govt Printer, Jamestown.
172 2½c. +3d. black and brown-red ... £1500 £650
173 5c. +6d. black and blue ... £1800 £700
174 7½c. +9d. black and rose-carmine ... £3000 £1300
175 10c. +1s. black and light brown ... £2250 £1300
172/175 *Set of 4* ... £8000 £3500

The above stamps were withdrawn from sale on 19 October, 434 complete sets having been sold.

50 St Helena Butterflyfish

51 Yellow Canary

53 Queen Elizabeth II

63 Queen Elizabeth II with Prince Andrew (after Cecil Beaton)

(Des V. Whiteley. Photo Harrison)

1961 (12 Dec)–**65**. Types **50/51**, **53**, **63** and similar designs. W w **12**. P 11½×12 (horiz), 12×11½ (vert) or 14½×14 (£1).
176 **50** 1d. bright blue, dull violet, yellow and carmine ... 40 20
a. Chalk-surfaced paper (4.5.65) ... 1·40 30
177 **51** 1½d. yellow, green, black and light drab ... 50 20
178 2d. scarlet and grey ... 15 20
179 **53** 3d. light blue, black, pink and deep blue ... 1·50 20
a. Chalk-surfaced paper (30.11.65) ... 9·00 1·75
180 4½d. yellow-green, green, brown and grey ... 60 60
181 6d. red, sepia and light yellow-olive ... 5·50 70
a. Chalk-surfaced paper (30.11.65) ... 10·00 1·00
182 7d. red-brown, black and violet ... 35 70
183 10d. brown-purple and light blue ... 35 70
184 1s. greenish yellow, bluish green and brown ... 55 1·25
185 1s.6d. grey, black and slate-blue ... 11·00 4·75
186 2s.6d. red, pale yellow and turquoise (*chalk-surfaced paper*) ... 2·50 2·50
187 5s. yellow, brown and green ... 14·00 5·50
188 10s. orange-red, black and blue ... 13·00 10·00
189 **63** £1 chocolate and light blue ... 22·00 24·00
a. Chalk-surfaced paper (30.11.65) ... 50·00 50·00
176/189 *Set of 14* ... 60·00 45·00

Designs: Horiz (as T **50**)—1d. T **50**; 2d. Brittle Starfish; 7d. Trumpetfish; 10d. Feather Starfish; 2s.6d. Orange Starfish; 10s. Deep-water Bullseye. Vert (as T **51**)—1½d. T **51**; 4½d. Red-wood Flower; 6d. Madagascar Red Fody; 1s. Gum-wood Flower; 1s.6d. White Tern; 5s. Night-blooming Cereus. £1 T **63**.

1963 (4 June). Freedom from Hunger. As No. 146 of Antigua.
190 1s. 6d. ultramarine ... 75 40

1963 (2 Sept). Red Cross Centenary. As Nos. 147/148 of Antigua.
191 3d. red and black ... 30 50
192 1s.6d. red and blue ... 70 2·00

FIRST LOCAL POST
4th JANUARY 1965
(**64**)

65 Badge of St Helena

1965 (4 Jan). First Local Post. Nos. 176, 179, 181 and 185 optd with T **64**.
193 1d. bright blue, dull violet, yellow and carmine ... 10 25
194 3d. light blue, black, pink and deep blue ... 10 25
195 6d. red, sepia and light yellow-olive ... 40 30
196 1s.6d. grey, black and slate-blue ... 60 35
193/196 *Set of 4* ... 1·10 1·00

1965 (17 May). ITU Centenary. As Nos. 166/167 of Antigua.
197 3d. blue and grey-brown ... 25 25
198 6d. bright purple and bluish green ... 35 25

1965 (15 Oct). International Co-operation. Year. As Nos. 168/169 of Antigua.
199 1d. reddish purple and turquoise-green ... 30 15
200 6d. deep bluish green and lavender ... 30 15
w. Wmk inverted ...

1966 (24 Jan). Churchill Commemoration. As Nos. 170/173 of Antigua.
201 1d. new blue ... 15 25
202 3d. deep green ... 25 25
203 6d. brown ... 40 30
204 1s.6d. bluish violet ... 45 85
201/204 *Set of 4* ... 1·10 1·50

1966 (1 July). World Cup Football Championships. As Nos. 176/177 of Antigua.
205 3d. violet, yellow-green, lake and yellow-brown ... 45 35
206 6d. chocolate, blue-green, lake and yellow-brown ... 55 35

1966 (20 Sept). Inauguration of WHO Headquarters, Geneva. As Nos. 178/179 of Antigua.
207 3d. black, yellow-green and light blue ... 75 20
208 1s.6d. black, light purple and yellow-brown ... 2·25 1·00

1966 (1 Dec). 20th Anniversary of UNESCO. As Nos. 196/198 of Antigua.
209 3d. slate-violet, red, yellow and orange ... 1·00 30
210 6d. orange-yellow, violet and deep olive ... 1·25 1·00
211 1s.6d. black, bright purple and orange ... 2·50 2·50
209/211 *Set of 3* ... 4·25 3·50

(Des W. H. Brown. Photo Harrison)

1967 (5 May). New Constitution. W w **12** (sideways). P 14½×14.
212 **65** 1s. multicoloured ... 10 10
213 2s.6d. multicoloured ... 20 20
a. Red (ribbon, etc.) omitted ... £1500

66 Fire of London

(Des M. Goaman. Recess D.L.R.)

1967 (4 Sept). 300th Anniversary of Arrival of Settlers after Great Fire of London. T **66** and similar horiz designs. W w **12**. P 13.
214 1d. carmine-red and black ... 15 10
a. Carmine and black ... 1·75 2·50
215 3d. ultramarine and black ... 20 10
216 6d. slate-violet and black ... 20 15
217 1s.6d. olive-green and black ... 20 20
214/217 *Set of 4* ... 65 50

Designs: 1d. T **66**; 3d. East Indiaman *Charles*; 6d. Settlers landing at Jamestown; 1s.6d. Settlers clearing scrub.

70 Interlocking Maps of Tristan and St Helena

(Des Jennifer Toombs. Photo Harrison)

1968 (4 June). 30th Anniversary of Tristan da Cunha as a Dependency of St Helena. T **70** and similar horiz design. W w **12**. P 14×14½.
218 **70** 4d. purple and chocolate ... 10 10
219 – 8d. olive and brown ... 10 30
220 **70** 1s.9d. ultramarine and chocolate ... 15 40
221 – 2s.3d. greenish blue and brown ... 20 40
218/221 *Set of 4* ... 50 1·10

Design: 8d., 2s.3d. Interlocking maps of St Helena and Tristan.

72 Queen Elizabeth and Sir Hudson Lowe

(Des M. Farrar Bell. Litho D.L.R.)

1968 (4 Sept). 150th Anniversary of the Abolition of Slavery in St Helena. T **72** and similar horiz design. Multicoloured. W w **12** (sideways). P 13×12½.
222 3d. Type **72** ... 10 15
223 9d. Type **72** ... 10 20
224 1s.6d. Queen Elizabeth and Sir George Bingham ... 15 30
225 2s.6d. As 1s. 6d ... 25 45
222/225 *Set of 4* ... 55 1·00

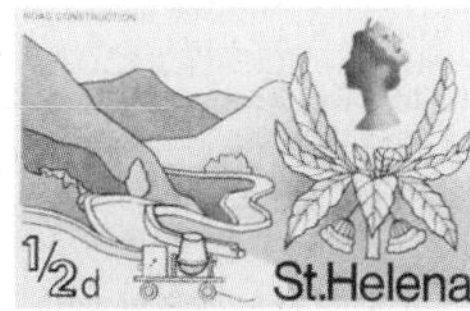

74 Blue Gum Eucalyptus and Road Construction

(Des Sylvia Goaman. Litho P.B.)

1968 (4 Nov). Horiz designs as T **74**. Multicoloured. W w **12** (sideways*). P 13½.
226 ½d. Type **74** ... 10 20
227 1d. Cabbage-tree and electricity development ... 10 20
w. Wmk Crown to right of CA ... 9·50
228 1½d. St Helena Redwood and dental unit ... 15 20
229 2d. Scrubweed and pest control ... 15 20
230 3d. Tree-fern and flats in Jamestown ... 30 20
231 4d. Blue gum Eucalyptus, pasture and livestock improvement ... 20 20
232 6d. Cabbage-tree and schools broadcasting ... 50 20
233 8d. St Helena Redwood and country cottages ... 30 20
234 10d. Scrubweed and new school buildings ... 30 20
235 1s. Tree-fern and reafforestation ... 30 20
236 1s.6d. Blue gum Eucalyptus and heavy lift crane ... 70 3·00
237 2s.6d. Cabbage-tree and Lady Field Children's Home ... 70 3·50
238 5s. St Helena Redwood and agricultural training ... 70 3·50
239 10s. Scrubweed and New General Hospital ... 2·00 4·50
240 £1 Tree-fern and lifeboat *John Dutton* ... 10·00 15·00
226/240 *Set of 15* ... 15·00 28·00

* The normal sideways watermark shows Crown to left of CA, *as seen from the back of the stamp.*

A distinct shade of the £1 value was issued in 1971, with the decimal currency definitives.

89 Brig *Perseverance*

93 WO and Drummer of the 53rd Foot, 1815

(Des J.W. Litho P.B.)

1969 (19 Apr). Mail Communications. T **89** and similar horiz designs. Multicoloured. W w **12** (sideways). P 13½.
241 4d. Type **89** ... 20 20
242 8d. *Phoebe* (screw steamer) ... 25 40
243 1s.9d. *Llandovery Castle* (liner) ... 25 60
244 2s.3d. *Good Hope Castle* (cargo liner) ... 25 75
241/244 *Set of 4* ... 85 1·75

No. 242 is inscribed 'DANE' in error.

(Des R. North. Litho Format)

1969 (3 Sept). Military Uniforms. T **93** and similar vert designs. Multicoloured. W w **12**. P 14.
245 6d. Type **93** ... 15 25
w. Wmk inverted ... £180
246 8d. Officer and Surgeon, 20th Foot, 1816 ... 15 25
247 1s.8d. Drum Major, 66th Foot, 1816, and Royal Artillery Officer, 1820 ... 20 45
248 2s.6d. Private, 91st Foot, and 2nd Corporal, Royal Sappers and Miners, 1832 ... 20 55
245/248 *Set of 4* ... 65 1·40

97 Dickens, Mr. Pickwick and Job Trotter (*Pickwick Papers*)

(Des Jennifer Toombs. Litho P.B.)

1970 (9 June). Death Centenary of Charles Dickens. T **97** and similar horiz designs each incorporating a portrait of Dickens. Multicoloured. Chalk-surfaced paper. W w **12** (sideways*). P 13½×13.
249 4d. Type **97** ... 80 15
a. Shiny unsurfaced paper ... 30 1·40
b. Yellow omitted ... £600
w. Wmk Crown to right of CA ... 60·00
250 8d. Mr. Bumble and Oliver (*Oliver Twist*) ... 90 15
a. Shiny unsurfaced paper ... 30 1·60
251 1s.6d. Sairey Gamp and Mark Tapley (*Martin Chuzzlewit*) ... 1·00 20
a. Shiny unsurfaced paper ... 40 2·25
252 2s.6d. Jo and Mr. Turveydrop (*Bleak House*) ... 1·00 25
a. Shiny unsurfaced paper ... 40 2·50
249/252 *Set of 4* ... 3·25 65
249a/252a *Set of 4* ... 1·25 7·00

* The normal sideways watermark shows Crown to left of CA, *as seen from the back of the stamp.*

Supplies sent to St Helena were on paper with a dull surface which reacts to the chalky test and with PVA gum. Crown Agents supplies were from a later printing on shiny paper which does not respond to the chalky test and with gum arabic.

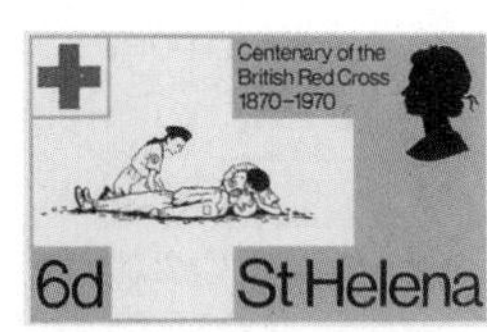

98 'Kiss of Life'

99 Officer's Shako Plate (20th Foot)

(Des Jennifer Toombs. Litho J.W.)

1970 (15 Sept). Centenary of British Red Cross. T **98** and similar horiz designs. W w **12** (sideways). P 14.
253 6d. bistre, vermilion and black ... 15 15
254 9d. turquoise-green, vermilion and black ... 15 20
255 1s.9d. pale grey, vermilion and black ... 20 30
256 2s.3d. pale lavender, vermilion and black ... 20 45
253/256 *Set of 4* ... 65 1·00

Designs: 6d. T **98**; 9d. Nurse with girl in wheelchair; 1s.9d. Nurse bandaging child's knee; 2s.3d. Red Cross emblem.

(Des J.W. Litho Questa)

1970 (2 Nov). Military Equipment (1st issue). T **99** and similar vert designs. Multicoloured. W w **12**. P 12.
257 4d. Type **99** ... 20 20
258 9d. Officer's Breast-plate (66th Foot) ... 25 30
259 1s.3d. Officer's Full Dress Shako (91st Foot) ... 25 40
260 2s.11d. Ensign's Shako (53rd Foot) ... 40 60
257/260 *Set of 4* ... 1·00 1·40

Further stamps in this series appeared after 1970.

STAMP BOOKLETS

1962 (2 Mar). Black on green cover. Stitched.
SB1 4s.6d. booklet containing 1d., 1½d., 2d., 3d. and 6d. (Nos. 176/179, 181), each in block of 4 ... 55·00

1969. Black on grey-green cover. Stapled.
SB2 5s.4d. booklet containing 1d., 2d., 3d., 4d. and 6d. (Nos. 227, 229/232), each in block of 4 ... 30·00

St Kitts-Nevis

ST CHRISTOPHER

From 1760 the postal service for St Christopher was organised by the Deputy Postmaster General on Antigua. It was not until May 1779 that the first postmaster was appointed to the island and the use of postmarks on outgoing mail commenced.

Stamps of Great Britain were used between May 1858 and the end of March 1860 when control of the postal services passed to the local authorities. In the years which followed, prior to the introduction of St Christopher stamps in April 1870, a circular 'PAID' handstamp was used on overseas mail.

BASSETERRE

Stamps of GREAT BRITAIN cancelled 'A12' as T Z **1** of Jamaica.

1858–60.

Z1	1d. rose-red (1857), perf 14	£750
Z2	2d. blue (1858) (Plate No. 7)	£1600
Z3	4d. rose (1857)	£500
Z4	6d. lilac (1856)	£250
Z5	1s. green (1856)	£2250

PRICES FOR STAMPS ON COVER TO 1945

Nos. 1/9	*from* × 25
Nos. 11/18	*from* × 30
Nos. 19/21	*from* × 10
Nos. 22/26	*from* × 25
No. 27	—
No. 28	*from* × 25
Nos. R1/R6	—

1

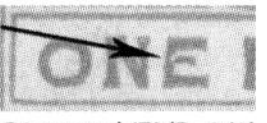
Distorted 'E' (R. 2/1)

1870 (1 Apr)–**82**. Wmk Crown CC.

(a) P 12½

1	1	1d. dull rose	90·00	50·00
		a. Wmk sideways	£225	£160
		w. Wmk inverted	£300	£250
2		1d. magenta (*shades*) (1871)	80·00	32·00
		a. Wmk sideways	†	£950
		w. Wmk inverted	£170	80·00
		x. Wmk reversed		
4		6d. yellow-green	£130	19·00
		w. Wmk inverted		
5		6d. green (1871)	£130	6·50
		w. Wmk inverted	—	£180
		x. Wmk reversed	£500	£325

(b) P 14

6	1	1d. magenta (*shades*) (1875)	80·00	7·00
		a. Bisected diag or vert (½d.) (*on cover*) (3.82)	†	£2500
		w. Wmk inverted	£275	£120
7		2½d. red-brown (11.79)	£190	£250
8		4d. blue (11.79)	£200	15·00
		a. Wmk sideways	£1700	£275
		w. Wmk inverted	£425	65·00
9		6d. green (1876)	60·00	5·00
		a. Imperf between (pair)		
		b. Wmk sideways	£1000	£300
		w. Wmk inverted	—	£150
		x. Wmk reversed	£425	

The magenta used for the 1d. was a fugitive colour which reacts to both light and water.

No. 1a is known with both Crown to left of CC and Crown to right of CC, *as seen from the back of the stamp.*

No. 6a was authorised for use between March and June 1882 to make up the 2½d. letter rate and for ½d. book post.

1882 (June)–**90**. Wmk Crown CA. P 14.

11	1	½d. dull green	7·00	4·50
		a. Wmk sideways	£300	
		x. Wmk reversed	£300	
12		1d. dull magenta	£550	70·00
		a. Bisected diagonally (½d.) (*on cover*) (2.83)	†	£1500
		w. Wmk inverted	£1000	£200
13		1d. carmine-rose (2.84)	3·75	2·25
		a. Bisected (½d.) (*on cover*)	†	—
		b. Distorted 'E'	35·00	
		c. Wmk sideways	†	£1500
		w. Wmk inverted	£200	
		x. Wmk reversed	£250	
14		2½d. pale red-brown	£180	60·00
15		2½d. deep red-brown	£190	65·00
16		2½d. ultramarine (2.84)	6·00	1·50
		x. Wmk reversed	£325	
17		4d. blue	£650	16·00
		w. Wmk inverted		
18		4d. grey (10.84)	1·75	1·00
		w. Wmk inverted	£225	
		x. Wmk reversed	£400	
19		6d. olive-brown (3.90)	90·00	£400
		w. Wmk inverted		
20		1s. mauve (6.86)	£100	65·00
		w. Wmk inverted	—	£190
21		1s. bright mauve (1890)	90·00	£180
19s/20s Optd 'SPECIMEN' *Set of 2*			£120	

FOUR PENCE (2) Halfpenny (3)

1884 (Dec). No. 9 surch with T **2** by The Advertiser Press.

22	1	4d. on 6d. green	70·00	50·00
		a. Full stop after 'PENCE'	70·00	50·00
		b. Surch double	—	£2750
		w. Wmk inverted	—	£300

No. 22a occurred on alternate stamps.

1885 (Mar). No. 13 bisected and each half diagonally surch with T **3**.

23	1	½d. on half of 1d. carmine-rose	30·00	45·00
		a. Unsevered pair	£120	£120
		ab. Ditto, one surch inverted	£425	£300
		b. Surch inverted	£225	£110
		ba. Ditto, unsevered pair	£1000	
		c. Surch double		

ONE PENNY. (4) 4d. (5)

1886 (June). No. 9 surch with Types **4** or **5** each showing a manuscript line through the original value.

24	1	1d. on 6d. green	20·00	50·00
		a. Surch inverted	£9000	
		b. Surch double	—	£2500
25		4d. on 6d. green	60·00	95·00
		a. No stop after 'd'	£225	£325
		b. Surch double	£2500	£2750

No. 24b is only known penmarked with dates between 21 July and 3 August 1886, or with violet handstamp.

1887 (May). No. 11 surch with T **4** showing a manuscript line through the original value.

26	1	1d. on ½d. dull green	50·00	60·00

The genuine surcharge on No. 26 is from worn type and always shows a stop after 'PENNY'. A similar surcharge from fresh type and without stop is of clandestine origin.

ONE PENNY. (7)

1888 (May). No. 16 surch.

*(a) With T **4**. Original value unobliterated.*

27	1	1d. on 2½d. ultramarine	£25000	£20000

*(b) With T **7** showing a manuscript line through the original value*

28	1	1d. on 2½d. ultramarine	70·00	70·00
		a. Surch inverted	£27000	£11000

The 1d. of Antigua was used provisionally in St Christopher between January and March 1890 during a shortage of 1d. stamps. Such use can be distinguished by the postmark, which is 'A12' in place of 'A02' (*price from £130 used*).

REVENUE STAMPS USED FOR POSTAGE

Saint Christopher (R **1**) SAINT KITTS NEVIS REVENUE (R **2**)

1883. Nos. F6 and F8 of Nevis optd with T R **1**, in violet. Wmk Crown CA. P 14.

R1	1d. lilac-mauve	£375	
R2	6d. green	£130	£170

1885. Optd with T R **2**. Wmk Crown CA. P 14.

R3	1	1d. rose	3·00	18·00
		a. Distorted 'E'	30·00	
R4		3d. mauve	17·00	65·00
R5		6d. orange-brown	22·00	50·00
R6		1s. olive	4·25	42·00

Other fiscal stamps with overprints as above also exist, but none of these were ever available for postal purposes.

The stamps for St Christopher were superseded by the general issue for Leeward Islands on 31 October 1890.

NEVIS

Little is known concerning the early postal affairs of Nevis, although several covers exist from the island in the 1660s. It is recorded that the British GPO was to establish a branch office on the island under an Act of Parliament of 1710, although arrangements may not have been finalised for a number of years afterwards. Nevis appears as 'a new office' in the PO Accounts of 1787.

Stamps of Great Britain were used on the island from May 1858 until the colonial authorities assumed control of the postal service on 1 May 1860. Between this date and the introduction of Nevis stamps in 1862 No. CC1 was again used on overseas mail.

CHARLESTOWN

CROWNED-CIRCLE HANDSTAMPS

CC **1**

CC1 CC **1** NEVIS (R.) (9.1852) *Price on cover* £4500

No. CC1, struck in red, was in use between 1854 and 1858, and again between 1860 and 1862, prior to the introduction of Nevis stamps. Later examples, struck in black (Nov 1870 and Jan 1871) or red (Jan 1882), date from periods of stamp shortage.

Stamps of GREAT BRITAIN cancelled 'A09' as T Z **1** of Jamaica.

1858 (May)–**60.**

Z1	1d. rose-red (1857), perf 14	£650
Z2	2d. blue (1858) (Plate No. 8)	£2000
Z3	4d. rose (1857)	£550
Z4	6d. lilac (1856)	£300
Z5	1s. green (1856)	

PRICES FOR STAMPS ON COVER TO 1945

No. 1	—
Nos. 2/3	*from* × 30
No. 4	—
Nos. 9/10	—
Nos. 11/14	*from* × 30
Nos. 15/17	*from* × 100
No. 18	*from* × 20
Nos. 19/21	—
No. 22	*from* × 40
No. 23	*from* × 20
Nos. 24	—
Nos. 25/27	*from* × 20
Nos. 28/29	—
No. 30	*from* × 40
No. 31	*from* × 60
Nos. 32/33	—
No. 34	*from* × 15
Nos. 35/36	*from* × 10
Nos. F1/F8	*from* × 30

1 2

3 4

The design on the stamps refers to a medicinal spring on the island, and is taken from the Great Seal of the colony.

(Recess Nissen & Parker, London)

1862 (19 July). Greyish paper. P 13.

1	1	1d. dull lake	£110	55·00
2	2	4d. rose	£160	75·00
3	3	6d. grey-lilac	£170	60·00
4	4	1s. green	£350	90·00

Types **1/4** were printed in sheets of 12 (3×4). Each position on the original engraved plates was individually engraved by hand.

The greyish paper used for Nos. 1/4 sometimes shows a degree of blueing, but there was only one printing of each value.

Crossed lines on hill

1867 (Jan)–**76.** White paper. P 15.

9	1	1d. pale red	65·00	50·00
10		1d. deep red	65·00	50·00
11	2	4d. orange	£150	23·00
12		4d. deep orange	£150	23·00
13	4	1s. blue-green	£300	40·00
14		1s. yellow-green (1876)	£850	£110
		a. Vertically laid paper	—	£5000
		b. No. 9 on sheet with crossed lines on hill	£3500	£500
		c. Ditto. On laid paper	†	£16000

Examples of the 4d. exist showing part of a papermakers watermark reading 'A. COWAN & SONS EXTRA SUPERFINE'.

(Lithographed by transfer from the engraved plates Nissen and Parker, London)

1871–78.

(a) P 15

15	1	1d. pale rose-red	32·00	25·00
		a. Imperf (pair)	£1800	
16		1d. deep rose-red	45·00	29·00
17		1d. vermilion-red (1877)	42·00	42·00
		a. Bisected (½d.) (*on cover*)	†	—
18	2	4d. orange-yellow (1878)	£170	38·00
		a. Imperf between (vert pair)	£11000	
19	3	6d. grey (1878)	£225	£200
20	4	1s. pale green (1878)	90·00	£110
		a. Imperf		
		b. Imperf between (horiz strip of 3)	£16000	
		c. No. 9 on sheet with crossed lines on hill	£250	
21		1s. deep green	£120	£160
		c. No. 9 on sheet with crossed lines on hill	£1000	

(b) P 11½

22	1	1d. vermilion-red (1878)	60·00	55·00
		a. Bisected (½d.) (*on cover*)	†	—
		b. Imperf (pair)	£1100	
		c. Imperf between (horiz pair)		
		d. Perf compound of 11½ and 15		

A total of 24 different transfers were used for the 1d. value, in a sequence of seven printings between June 1871 and Feb 1878. The retouches listed below occurred in the group of four transfers used for the 31 Dec 1876 printing.

Four different transfers were used for the 4d. value, but only one for the 6d. The two printings of the 1s. value, in Feb 1878 (pale green) and Nov 1878 (deep green) were from different transfers. The 'crossed lines on hill' variety was retouched early in the second printing, so that No. 21c is only found on a small number of sheets.

RETOUCHES. 1d. Vermilion-red Lithograph (No. 17).

i. No. 1 on sheet (Pane 'A'). Top of hill over kneeling figure redrawn by five thick lines and eight small slanting lines ... £150 £160
ii. No. 1 on sheet (Pane 'C'). Another retouch. Three series of short vertical strokes behind the kneeling figure ... £150 £160
iii. No. 3 on sheet (Pane 'A'). Right upper corner star and border below star retouched ... £150 £160
iv. No. 9 on sheet (Pane 'B'). Retouch in same position as on No. 3 but differing in detail ... £170 £180
v. No. 12 on sheet (Pane 'C'). Dress of standing figure retouched by a number of horizontal and vertical lines ... £150 £160

5 (Die I)

(6)

(Typo D.L.R.)

1879–80. Wmk Crown CC. P 14.

23 **5** 1d. lilac-mauve (1880) ... 80·00 50·00
a. Bisected (½d.) (*on cover*) ... † £1000
w. Wmk inverted ...
24 2½d. red-brown ... £160 90·00

1882–90. Wmk Crown CA. P 14.

25 **5** ½d. dull green (11.83) ... 14·00 27·00
a. Top left triangle detached ... £425
26 1d. lilac-mauve ... £110 48·00
a. Bisected (½d.) *on cover* (1883) ... † £700
27 1d. dull rose (11.83) ... 42·00 35·00
a. Carmine (1884) ... 20·00 20·00
ab. Top left triangle detached ... £600
28 2½d. red-brown ... £120 50·00
29 2½d. ultramarine (11.83) ... 23·00 27·00
a. Top left triangle detached ... £800
30 4d. blue ... £350 50·00
31 4d. grey (1884) ... 24·00 9·00
a. Top left triangle detached ... £800 £450
32 6d. green (11.83) ... £450 £350
33 6d. chestnut (10.88) ... 24·00 75·00
a. Top left triangle detached ... £850
34 1s. pale violet (3.90) ... £110 £200
a. Top left triangle detached ... £1600
33s/34s Optd 'SPECIMEN' *Set of 2* ... £110

For illustration of the 'top left triangle detached' variety, which occurs on Plate 2 R. 3/3 of the right pane, see above No. 21 of Antigua.

1883 (4 Sept). No. 26 bisected vertically and surch with T **6**, reading upwards or downwards.

35 ½d. on half 1d. lilac-mauve (V.) ... £1100 55·00
a. Surch double ... — £350
b. Surch on half 'REVENUE' stamp No. F6 ... — £550
36 ½d. on half 1d. lilac-mauve ... £1100 50·00
a. Surch double ... — £325
b. Unsevered pair ... £6500 £750
c. Surch on half 'REVENUE' stamp No. F6 ... — £550

FISCALS USED FOR POSTAGE

Revenue (F 1)   REVENUE (F 2)

1882.

(a) Stamps of 1876–1878 optd with T F **1** *by Nissen & Parker, London*

F1 **1** 1d. bright red ... £150 £100
F2 1d. rose ... 85·00 40·00
F3 **2** 4d. orange ... £170
F4 **3** 6d. grey ... £325
F5 **4** 1s. green ... £350
a. No. 9 on sheet with crossed lines on hill ...

(b) Nos. 26, 30 and 32 optd with T F **2** *by D.L.R.*

F6 **5** 1d. lilac-mauve ... 80·00 55·00
a. Bisected (½d.) (*on cover*) ... † —
F7 4d. blue ... 55·00 60·00
F8 6d. green ... 29·00 65·00

Nos. F1/F5 were produced from fresh transfers. Similar 'Revenue.' handstamps, with stop, were also applied to postage issues.

The stamps of Nevis were superseded by the general issue for Leeward Islands on 31 October 1890.

ST KITTS-NEVIS

CROWN COLONY

Stamps for the combined colony were introduced in 1903, and were used concurrently with the general issues of Leeward Islands until the latter were withdrawn on 1 July 1956.

PRICES FOR STAMPS ON COVER TO 1945	
Nos. 1/9	*from* × 3
No. 10	—
Nos. 11/20	*from* × 3
No. 21	—
Nos. 22/23	*from* × 15
Nos. 24/34	*from* × 3
Nos. 35/36	—
Nos. 37/47	*from* × 2
Nos. 47a/47b	—

PRICES FOR STAMPS ON COVER TO 1945	
Nos. 48/57	*from* × 2
Nos. 58/60	—
Nos. 61/64	*from* × 2
Nos. 65/67	*from* × 5
Nos. 68/77	*from* × 2

1 Christopher Columbus

2 Medicinal Spring

(Typo D.L.R.)

1903. Wmk Crown CA. P 14.

1 **1** ½d. dull purple and deep green ... 1·75 70
2 **2** 1d. grey-black and carmine ... 4·75 20
3 **1** 2d. dull purple and brown ... 4·75 11·00
4 2½d. grey-black and blue ... 19·00 5·50
5 **2** 3d. deep green and orange ... 25·00 30·00
6 **1** 6d. grey-black and bright purple ... 10·00 48·00
7 1s. grey-green and orange ... 7·50 11·00
8 **2** 2s. deep green and grey-black ... 10·00 20·00
9 **1** 2s.6d. grey-black and violet ... 16·00 50·00
10 **2** 5s. dull purple and sage-green ... 70·00 60·00
1/10 *Set of 10* ... £150 £200
1s/10s Optd 'SPECIMEN' *Set of 10* ... £160

1905–18. Chalk-surfaced paper (1d. (No. 13), 5s.) or ordinary paper (others). Wmk Mult Crown CA. P 14.

11 **1** ½d. dull purple and deep green ... 17·00 8·00
12 ½d. grey-green (1907) ... 1·00 1·00
a. Dull blue-green (1916) ... 1·00 3·75
13 **2** 1d. grey-black and carmine (1906) ... 10·00 25
14 1d. carmine (1907) ... 2·25 15
a. Scarlet (1916) ... 1·50 20
15 **1** 2d. dull purple and brown ... 11·00 8·00
a. Chalk-surfaced paper (1906) ... 6·50 8·00
16 2½d. grey-black and blue (1907) ... 42·00 6·50
17 2½d. bright blue (1907) ... 2·50 50
18 **2** 3d. deep green and orange ... 40·00 21·00
a. Chalk-surfaced paper (1906) ... 3·75 2·75
19 **1** 6d. grey-black and deep violet ... 45·00 55·00
a. Chalk-surfaced paper. *Grey-black and deep purple* (1908) ... 27·00 25·00
ab. Grey-black and bright purple (1916) ... 13·00 35·00
20 1s. grey-green and orange (1909) ... 50·00 65·00
a. Chalk-surfaced paper ... 3·50 35·00
21 **2** 5s. dull purple and sage-green (11.18) ... 45·00 £120
11/21 *Set of 11* ... £130 £180
12s, 14s, 17s Optd 'SPECIMEN' *Set of 3* ... 70·00

WAR TAX (3)   **WAR STAMP** (3a)

1916 (Oct). Optd with T **3**. Wmk Mult Crown CA. P 14.

22 **1** ½d. dull blue-green (No. 12*a*) ... 2·50 50
a. Deep green ... 1·00 50
s. Optd 'SPECIMEN' ... 50·00
x. Wmk reversed ... 55·00

No. 22*a* was a special printing produced for this overprint.

1918 (26 July). Optd with T **3a**. Wmk Mult Crown CA. P 14.

23 **1** 1½d. orange ... 1·75 1·00
a. Short opt (right pane R. 10/1) ... 26·00
s. Optd 'SPECIMEN' ... 55·00

No. 23 was a special printing produced for this overprint.
No. 23a shows the overprint 2 mm high instead of 2½ mm.

4

5

(Typo D.L.R.)

1920–22. Ordinary paper (½d. to 2½d.) or chalk-surfaced paper (others). Wmk Mult Crown CA (sideways*). P 14.

24 **4** ½d. blue-green ... 3·75 5·50
a. 'C' of 'CA' missing from wmk ... £500
25 **5** 1d. scarlet ... 4·00 6·00
26 **4** 1½d. orange-yellow ... 1·25 1·75
x. Wmk sideways reversed ... £160
y. Wmk sideways inverted and reversed ... £225
27 **5** 2d. slate-grey ... 3·25 8·00
28 **4** 2½d. ultramarine ... 8·00 9·00
a. 'A' of 'CA' missing from wmk ... £600
29 **5** 3d. purple/*yellow* ... 1·75 11·00
30 **4** 6d. dull purple and bright mauve ... 3·50 11·00
31 **5** 1s. grey and black/*green* ... 3·50 4·00
32 **4** 2s. dull purple and blue/*blue* ... 29·00 60·00
x. Wmk sideways reversed ... £325
33 **5** 2s.6d. grey and red/*blue* ... 5·00 42·00
x. Wmk sideways reversed ... £325
y. Wmk sideways inverted and reversed ... £350
34 **4** 5s. green and red/*pale yellow* ... 5·00 42·00
x. Wmk sideways reversed ... £250
35 **5** 10s. green and red/*green* ... 12·00 48·00
36 **4** £1 purple and black/*red* (1922) ... £300 £375
24/36 *Set of 13* ... £350 £550
24s/36s Optd 'SPECIMEN' *Set of 13* ... £350

* The normal sideways watermark shows Crown to left of CA, *as seen from the back of the stamp.*

Examples of most values are known showing a forged St Kitts postmark dated '8 DE 23'.

1921–29. Chalk-surfaced paper (2½d. (No. 44), 3d. (No. 45*a*) and 6d. to 5s.) or ordinary paper (others). Wmk Mult Script CA (sideways*).

37 **4** ½d. blue-green ... 2·50 1·50
a. Yellow-green (1922) ... 3·75 1·00
38 **5** 1d. rose-carmine ... 1·25 15
sa. Perf 'SPECIMEN' (1929) ... 70·00
39 1d. deep violet (1922) ... 7·50 1·00
a. Pale violet (1929) ... 12·00 1·75
sa. Opt 'SPECIMEN' double ... £650
40 **4** 1½d. red (1925) ... 7·50 1·00
40*a* 1½d. red-brown (1929) ... 2·50 30
41 **5** 2d. slate-grey (1922) ... 1·00 60
42 **4** 2½d. pale bright blue (1922) ... 4·50 2·00
43 2½d. brown (1922) ... 4·75 13·00
44 2½d. ultramarine (1927) ... 1·50 1·00
45 **5** 3d. dull ultramarine (1922) ... 1·50 3·00
45*a* 3d. purple/*yellow* (1927) ... 2·50 2·00
46 **4** 6d. dull and bright purple (1924) ... 9·00 6·00
aw. Wmk Crown to right of CA ... 9·00 6·50
46*b* **5** 1s. black/*green* (1929) ... 7·00 3·25
47 **4** 2s. purple and blue/*blue* (1922) ... 16·00 38·00
asa. Opt 'SPECIMEN' double ... £600
47*b* **5** 2s.6d. black and red/*blue* (1927) ... 25·00 29·00
47*c* **4** 5s. green and red/*yellow* (1929) ... 55·00 £100
37/47c *Set of 16* ... £130 £170
37s/47cs Optd or Perf (1½d. red-brown, 1s., 5s.) 'SPECIMEN' *Set of 16* ... £400

* The normal watermark shows Crown to left of CA, *as seen from the back of the stamp.*

6 Old Road Bay and Mount Misery

1d. Damaged second 'E' of 'REVENUE' (R. 8/1)

(Typo D.L.R.)

1923 (1 Jan). Tercentenary of Colony. Chalk-surfaced paper. P 14.

(a) Wmk Mult Script CA (sideways)

48 **6** ½d. black and green ... 2·25 9·00
49 1d. black and bright violet ... 4·50 3·25
a. Damaged second 'E' of 'REVENUE' ... £170 £225
50 1½d. black and scarlet ... 4·50 10·00
51 2d. black and slate-grey ... 3·75 1·75
52 2½d. black and brown ... 6·00 38·00
53 3d. black and ultramarine ... 7·00 15·00
54 6d. black and bright purple ... 9·50 32·00
55 1s. black and sage-green ... 14·00 35·00
56 2s. black and blue/*blue* ... 50·00 85·00
57 2s.6d. black and red/*blue* ... 50·00 £100
58 10s. black and red/*emerald* ... £325 £600

(b) Wmk Mult Crown CA (sideways)

59 **6** 5s. black and red/*pale yellow* ... 90·00 £250
60 £1 black and purple/*red* ... £800 £1600
48/60 *Set of 13* ... £1200 £2250
48s/60s Optd 'SPECIMEN' *Set of 13* ... £800

Examples of all values are known showing a forged St Kitts postmark dated '8 DE 23'.

1935 (6 May). Silver Jubilee. As Nos. 91/94 of Antigua, but ptd by Waterlow. P 11×12.

61 1d. deep blue and scarlet ... 1·00 70
k. Kite and vertical log ... £160 £170
l. Kite and horizontal log ... £250 £250
62 1½d. ultramarine and grey ... 75 1·00
k. Kite and vertical log ... £130 £140
63 2½d. brown and deep blue ... 1·00 1·00
64 1s. slate and purple ... 17·00 18·00
k. Kite and vertical log ... £500
l. Kite and horizontal log ... £475 £550
61/64 *Set of 4* ... 18·00 19·00
61s/64s Perf 'SPECIMEN' *Set of 4* ... £100

For illustrations of plate varieties see Omnibus section following Zanzibar.

1937 (12 May). Coronation. As Nos. 95/97 of Antigua, but ptd by D.L.R. P 14.

65 1d. scarlet ... 30 25
66 1½d. buff ... 40 10
67 2½d. bright blue ... 60 1·60
65/67 *Set of 3* ... 1·10 1·75
65s/67s Perf 'SPECIMEN' *Set of 3* ... 90·00

Nos. 61/67 are inscribed 'ST CHRISTOPHER AND NEVIS'.

7 King George VI

8 King George VI and Medicinal Spring

9 King George VI and Christopher Columbus

10 King George VI and Anguilla Island

Break in value tablet (R. 12/5) (1947 ptg only)

6d. Break in oval (R. 12/1) (1938 ptg only)

Break in value tablet frame (R. 3/2)

Break in value tablet frame (R. 12/3) (ptgs between 1941 and 1945)

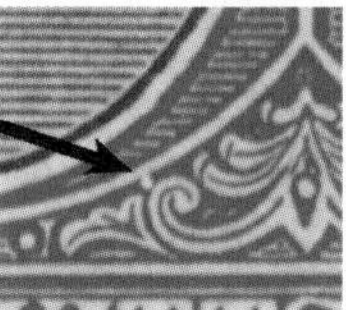
5s. Break in frame above ornament (R. 2/4) (ptgs between 1941 and 1950)

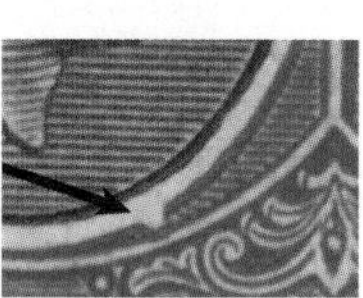
5s. Break in oval at foot (R. 12/5) (ptgs between 1941 and 1945 only). Sometimes touched-in by hand painting

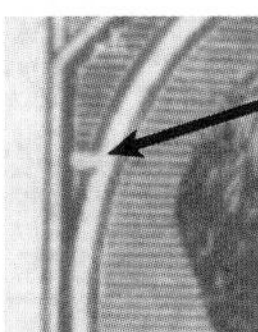
5s. Break in oval at left (R. 7/1) (ptgs between 1941 and 1945 only)

(Typo; centre litho (T **10**). D.L.R.)

1938 (15 Aug)–**50**. Chalk-surfaced paper (10s., £1). Wmk Mult Script CA (sideways on Types **8** and **9**). P 14 (Types **7** and **10**) or 13×12 (Types **8/9**).

68 **7** ½d. green ... 4·50 20
 a. Blue-green (5.4.43) ... 10 10
69 1d. scarlet ... 8·00 70
 a. Carmine (5.43) ... 2·75 50
 b. Carmine-pink (4.47) ... 65·00 16·00
 c. Rose-red (7.47) ... 4·25 80
70 1½d. orange ... 20 30
71 **8** 2d. scarlet and grey ... 32·00 2·75
 a. Chalk-surfaced paper. *Carmine and deep grey* (18.2.41*) ... 55·00 12·00
 b. Perf 14. *Scarlet and pale grey* (6.43*) ... 1·50 1·25
 ba. Scarlet and deep grey (6.42*) ... 28·00 2·25
 c. Perf 14. Chalk-surfaced paper. *Scarlet and pale grey* (2.50*) ... 9·00 5·50
72 **7** 2½d. ultramarine ... 10·00 30
 a. Bright ultramarine (5.4.43) ... 70 30
73 **8** 3d. dull reddish purple and scarlet ... 28·00 8·00
 a. Chalk-surfaced paper. *Brown-purple and carmine-red* (1940) ... 42·00 11·00
 b. Perf 14. Chalk-surfaced paper. *Dull reddish purple and carmine-red* (6.43*) ... 50·00 5·50
 c. Perf 14. Ordinary paper. *Reddish lilac and scarlet* (8.46*) ... 5·00 45·00
 d. Perf 14. Ordinary paper. *Purple and bright scarlet* (1.46*) ... 38·00 19·00
 da. Break in value tablet ... £350 £400
 e. Perf 14. Chalk-surfaced paper. *Deep purple and scarlet* (12.47*) ... £100 45·00
 f. Perf 14. Ordinary paper. *Rose-lilac and bright scarlet* (1.49*) ... 25·00 17·00
 g. Perf 14. Chalk-surfaced paper. *Deep reddish purple and bright scarlet* (8.50*) ... 15·00 15·00
74 **9** 6d. green and bright purple ... 13·00 3·00
 a. Break in oval ... £200 £120
 b. Perf 14. Chalk-surfaced paper. *Green and deep claret* (17.5.43*) ... 55·00 14·00
 c. Perf 14. Ordinary paper. *Green and purple* (10.44*) ... 10·00 1·75
 d. Perf 14. Chalk-surfaced paper. *Green and purple* (11.48*) ... 10·00 6·00
75 **8** 1s. black and green ... 12·00 2·25
 a. Break in value tablet frame ... £250 £110
 b. Perf 14 (8.43*) ... 4·75 85
 ba. Break in value tablet frame ... £140 90·00
 c. Perf 14. Chalk-surfaced paper (7.50*) ... 17·00 12·00
 ca. Break in value tablet frame ... £275 £400
76 2s.6d. black and scarlet ... 32·00 9·00
 a. Perf 14. Chalk-surfaced paper (12.43*) ... 30·00 6·00
 ab. Ordinary paper (5.45*) ... 12·00 4·50
77 **9** 5s. grey-green and scarlet ... 65·00 25·00
 a. Perf 14. Chalk-surfaced paper (25.10.43*) ... £140 50·00
 ab. Break in value tablet frame ... £800 £500
 ac. Break in frame above ornament ... £800 £500
 ad. Break in oval at foot ... £800 £500
 ae. Break in oval at left ... £800 £500
 b. Perf 14. Ordinary paper. *Bluish green and scarlet* (7.11.45*) ... 28·00 12·00
 ba. Break in value tablet frame ... £350 £250
 bb. Break in frame above ornament ... £350 £250
 bc. Break in oval at foot ... £350 £250
 bd. Break in oval at left ... £350 £250
 c. Perf 14. Chalk-surfaced paper. *Green and scarlet-vermilion* (10.50*) ... 55·00 70·00
 cb. Break in frame above ornament ... £500
77*e* **10** 10s. black and ultramarine (1.9.48) ... 15·00 19·00
77*f* £1 black and brown (1.9.48) ... 19·00 24·00
68*a*/77*f* *Set of* 12 ... 85·00 60·00
68s/77s Perf 'SPECIMEN' *Set of* 10 ... £325

* Earliest postmark date. Many printings were supplied to St Kitts-Nevis considerably earlier. Details of many of the dates are taken, with permission, from *A Study of the King George VI Stamps of St. Kitts-Nevis* by P. L. Baldwin (2nd edition 1997).

1946 (1 Nov). Victory. As Nos. 110/111 of Antigua.

78 1½d. red-orange ... 10 10
79 3d. carmine ... 10 10
78s/79s Perf 'SPECIMEN' *Set of* 2 ... 90·00

1949 (3 Jan). Royal Silver Wedding. As Nos. 112/113 of Antigua.

80 2½d. ultramarine ... 10 50
81 5s. carmine ... 9·50 11·00

1949 (10 Oct). 75th Anniversary of UPU. As Nos. 114/117 of Antigua.

82 2½d. ultramarine ... 15 30
83 3d. carmine-red ... 2·10 2·75
84 6d. magenta ... 20 2·00
85 1s. blue-green ... 20 40
 a. 'A' of 'CA' missing from wmk ... — £800
82/85 *Set of* 4 ... 2·40 5·00

ANGUILLA ANGUILLA

TERCENTENARY 1650-1950 (**11**) TERCENTENARY 1650—1950 (**12**)

1950 (10 Nov). Tercentenary of British Settlement in Anguilla. Nos. 69*c*, 70 and 72*a* (perf 14) optd as T **11** and new ptgs of Types **8/9** on chalk-surfaced paper perf 13×12½ optd as T **12**.

86 **7** 1d. rose-red ... 10 20
87 1½d. orange ... 10 50
 a. Error. Crown missing, W **9a** ... £3250
 b. Error. St Edward's Crown, W **9b** ... £1400
88 2½d. bright ultramarine ... 25 20
89 **8** 3d. dull purple and scarlet ... 80 75
90 **9** 6d. green and bright purple ... 45 20
91 **8** 1s. black and green (R.) ... 1·40 25
 a. Break in value tablet frame ... 20·00 20·00
86/91 *Set of* 6 ... 2·75 1·90

Nos. 87a/b occur on a row in the watermark, in which the crowns and letters 'CA' alternate.

(New Currency. 100 cents = 1 West Indian dollar)

1951 (16 Feb). Inauguration of BWI University College. As Nos. 118/119 of Antigua.

92 3c. black and yellow-orange ... 30 15
93 12c. turquoise-green and magenta ... 30 2·00

ST CHRISTOPHER, NEVIS AND ANGUILLA

LEGISLATIVE COUNCIL

13 Bath House and Spa, Nevis

14 Warner Park

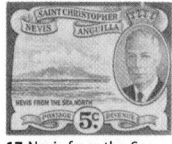

15 Map of the Islands

16 Brimstone Hill

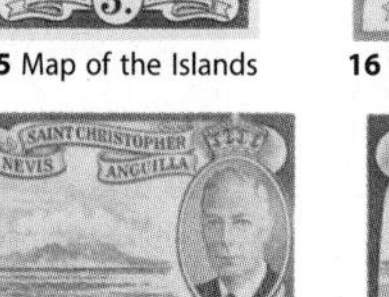
17 Nevis from the Sea, North

18 Pinney's Beach

19 Sir Thomas Warner's Tomb

20 Old Road Bay

21 Sea Island Cotton

22 The Treasury

23 Salt Pond, Anguilla

24 Sugar Factory

(Recess Waterlow)

1952 (14 June). Types **13/24**. Wmk Mult Script CA. P 12½.

94 **13** 1c. deep green and ochre ... 15 3·00
95 **14** 2c. green ... 1·00 1·00
96 **15** 3c. carmine-red and violet ... 30 1·25
97 **16** 4c. scarlet ... 20 20
98 **17** 5c. bright blue and grey ... 30 10
99 **18** 6c. ultramarine ... 30 15
100 **19** 12c. deep blue and reddish brown ... 1·50 10
101 **20** 24c. black and carmine-red ... 1·50 10
102 **21** 48c. olive and chocolate ... 3·75 6·00
103 **22** 60c. ochre and deep green ... 2·75 4·50
104 **23** $1.20 deep green and ultramarine ... 8·00 7·00
105 **24** $4.80 green and carmine ... 17·00 21·00
94/105 *Set of* 12 ... 32·00 40·00

1953 (2 June). Coronation. As No. 120 of Antigua.

106 2c. black and bright green ... 30 30

25 Sombrero Lighthouse

26 Map of Anguilla and Dependencies

(Recess Waterlow (until 1961), then D.L.R.)

1954 (1 Mar)–**63**. Designs previously used for King George VI issue, but with portrait of Queen Elizabeth II as in Types **25/26** or new values and designs (½c., 8c., $2.40). Wmk Mult Script CA. P 12½.

106*a* **23** ½c. deep olive (3.7.56) ... 70 10
107 **13** 1c. deep green and ochre ... 20 10
 a. Deep green and orange-ochre (13.2.62) ... 1·25 3·75
 b. Imperf vert (horiz strip of 3) ... † £9000
108 **14** 2c. green ... 1·00 10
 a. Yellow-green (31.7.63) ... 5·00 9·00
109 **15** 3c. carmine-red and violet ... 65 10
 a. Carmine and deep violet (31.7.63) ... 5·00 9·50
110 **16** 4c. scarlet ... 15 10
111 **17** 5c. bright blue and grey ... 15 10
112 **18** 6c. ultramarine ... 70 10
 a. Blue (19.2.63) ... 2·25 1·00
112*b* **25** 8c. grey-black (1.2.57) ... 3·00 25
113 **19** 12c. deep blue and red-brown ... 30 10
114 **20** 24c. black and carmine-red (1.12.54) ... 30 10
115 **21** 48c. olive-bistre and chocolate (1.12.54) ... 2·50 1·50
116 **22** 60c. ochre and deep green (1.12.54) ... 7·00 7·50
117 **23** $1.20 deep green and ultramarine (1.12.54) ... 27·00 4·25
 a. Deep green and violet-blue (19.2.63) ... 55·00 20·00
117*b* **26** $2.40 black and red-orange (1.2.57) ... 27·00 19·00
118 **24** $4.80 green and carmine (1.12.54) ... 27·00 11·00
106*a*/118 *Set of* 15 ... 85·00 40·00

27 Alexander Hamilton and View of Nevis

(Des Eva Wilkin. Recess Waterlow)

1957 (11 Jan). Birth Bicentenary of Alexander Hamilton. Wmk Mult Script CA. P 12½.

119 **27** 24c. green and deep blue ... 60 25

1958 (22 Apr). Inauguration of British Caribbean Federation. As Nos. 135/137 of Antigua.

120 3c. deep green ... 1·25 15
121 6c. blue ... 1·25 2·50
122 12c. scarlet ... 1·25 35
120/122 *Set of* 3 ... 3·25 2·75

MINISTERIAL GOVERNMENT

28 One Penny Stamp of 1862

(Recess Waterlow)

1961 (15 July). Nevis Stamp Centenary. T **28** and similar horiz designs. W w **12**. P 14.

123 2c. red-brown and green 30 1·00
124 8c. red-brown and deep blue 35 15
125 12c. black and carmine-red 40 20
126 24c. deep bluish green and red-orange 60 30
123/126 *Set of 4* 1·50 1·50

It is now accepted that the first stamps of Nevis were issued in 1862.

Designs: 2c. T **28**; 8c. 4d. stamp of 1862; 12c. 6d. stamp of 1862; 24c. 1s. stamp of 1862.

1963 (2 Sept). Red Cross Centenary. As Nos. 147/148 of Antigua.

127 3c. red and black 20 20
128 12c. red and blue 40 60

32 New Lighthouse, Sombrero

33 Loading Sugar Cane, St Kitts

34 Pall Mall Square, Basseterre

35 Gateway, Brimstone Hill Fort, St Kitts

36 Nelson's Spring, Nevis

37 Grammar School, St Kitts

38 Crater, Mt. Misery, St Kitts

39 Hibiscus

40 Sea Island cotton, Nevis

41 Boat building, Anguilla

42 White-crowned Pigeon

43 St George's Church Tower, Basseterre

44 Alexander Hamilton

45 Map of St Kitts-Nevis

46 Map of Anguilla

47 Arms of St Christopher, Nevis and Anguilla

(Des V. Whiteley. Photo Harrison)

1963 (20 Nov)–**69**. Types **32/47**. W w **12** (upright). P 14.

129 **32** ½c. sepia and light blue 10 10
w. Wmk inverted £225
130 **33** 1c. multicoloured 10 10
131 **34** 2c. multicoloured 10 10
a. Yellow omitted (White fountain and church) £300
w. Wmk inverted † £110
132 **35** 3c. multicoloured 10 10
w. Wmk inverted † £100
133 **36** 4c. multicoloured 10 10
w. Wmk inverted
134 **37** 5c. multicoloured 3·75 10
135 **38** 6c. multicoloured 10 10
w. Wmk inverted (19.12.69) 30 30
136 **39** 10c. multicoloured 15 10
137 **40** 15c. multicoloured 70 10
w. Wmk inverted — £100
138 **41** 20c. multicoloured 30 10
139 **42** 25c. multicoloured 2·25 10
a. Turquoise-green background (13.4.65) 14·00 1·75
w. Wmk inverted — 80·00
140 **43** 50c. multicoloured 75 25
141 **44** 60c. multicoloured 1·00 30
142 **45** $1 greenish yellow and blue 2·50 40
143 **46** $2.50 multicoloured 3·75 4·25
144 **47** $5 multicoloured 13·00 14·00
129/144 *Set of 16* 25·00 18·00

The 1, 4, 5, 6, 10 and 20c. values exist with PVA gum as well as gum arabic.

See also Nos. 166/171.

ARTS FESTIVAL ST KITTS 1964
(**48**)

49 Festival Emblem

1964 (14 Sept). Arts Festival. Nos. 132 and 139 optd as T **48**.

145 3c. Gateway, Brimstone Hill Fort, St Kitts 10 15
a. Opt double £400
146 25c. White-crowned Pigeon 20 15
a. 'FESTIVAl' (R. 1/10) 75·00
w. Wmk inverted — 8·50

1965 (17 May). ITU Centenary. As Nos. 166/167 of Antigua.

147 2c. bistre-yellow and rose-carmine 10 10
148 50c. turquoise-blue and yellow-olive 40 50

1965 (15 Oct). International Co-operation Year. As Nos. 168/169 of Antigua.

149 2c. reddish purple and turquoise-green 10 20
150 25c. deep bluish green and lavender 65 10

1966 (24 Jan). Churchill Commemoration. As Nos. 170/173 of Antigua.

151 ½c. new blue 10 3·00
a. Value omitted £500
b. Value at left instead of right £140
152 3c. deep green 35 10
153 15c. brown 80 20
154 25c. bluish violet 85 20
151/154 *Set of 4* 1·75 3·25

1966 (4 Feb). Royal Visit. As Nos. 174/175 of Antigua.

155 3c. black and ultramarine 25 30
156 25c. black and magenta 55 30

1966 (1 July). World Cup Football Championship. As Nos. 176/177 of Antigua.

157 6c. violet, yellow-green, lake and yellow-brown 40 20
158 25c. chocolate, blue-green, lake and yellow-brown 60 10

(Photo Harrison)

1966 (15 Aug). Arts Festival. P 14×14½.

159 **49** 3c. black, buff, emerald-green and gold 10 10
160 25c. black, buff, emerald-green and silver 20 10

1966 (20 Sept). Inauguration of WHO Headquarters, Geneva. As Nos. 178/179 of Antigua.

161 3c. black, yellow-green and light blue 10 10
162 40c. black, light purple and yellow-brown 30 20

1966 (1 Dec). 20th Anniversary of UNESCO. As Nos. 196/198 of Antigua.

163 3c. slate-violet, red, yellow and orange 10 10
164 6c. orange-yellow, violet and deep olive 10 10
165 40c. black, bright purple and orange 30 35
163/165 *Set of 3* 45 50

ASSOCIATED STATEHOOD

1967–69. As Nos. 129, 131/132, 137, 139 and 142 but wmk sideways.

166 **32** ½c. sepia and light blue (9.1.69) 20 2·75
167 **34** 2c. multicoloured (27.6.67) 1·75 10
168 **35** 3c. multicoloured (16.7.68) 20 10
169 **40** 15c. multicoloured (16.7.68) 70 30
170 **42** 25c. multicoloured (16.7.68) 2·50 20
171 **45** $1 greenish yellow and blue (16.7.68) 5·00 4·00
a. Greenish yellow and ultramarine-blue (19.12.69) 13·00 6·50
166/171 *Set of 6* 9·25 6·50

The 2c. and $1 values exist with PVA gum as well as gum arabic.

Nos. 172/181 are vacant.

50 Government Headquarters, Basseterre

53 John Wesley and Cross

(Des V. Whiteley. Photo Harrison)

1967 (1 July). Statehood. T **50** and similar horiz designs. Multicoloured. W w **12**. P 14½×14.

182 3c. Type **50** 10 10
183 10c. National Flag 10 10
w. Wmk inverted 28·00
184 25c. Coat of Arms 15 15
182/184 *Set of 3* 30 30

(Litho D.L.R.)

1967 (1 Dec). West Indies Methodist Conference. T **53** and similar vert designs. P 13×13½.

185 3c. black, cerise and reddish violet 10 10
186 25c. black, light greenish blue and blue 15 10
187 40c. black, yellow and orange 15 15
185/187 *Set of 3* 35 30

Designs: 3c. T **53**; 25c. Charles Wesley and Cross; 40c. Thomas Coke and Cross.

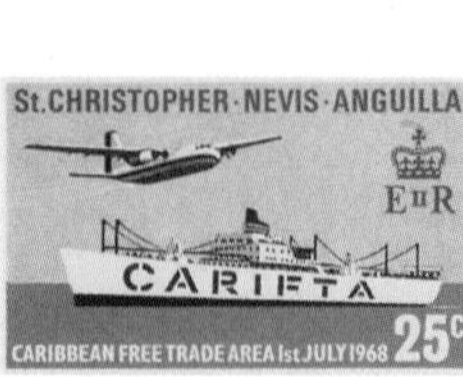

56 Handley Page HPR.7 Dart Herald Aircraft over *Jamaica Producer* (freighter)

57 Dr. Martin Luther King

(Des and litho D.L.R.)

1968 (30 July). Caribbean Free Trade Area. W w **12** (sideways). P 13.

188 **56** 25c. multicoloured 40 10
189 50c. multicoloured 40 20

(Des G. Vasarhelyi. Litho Enschedé)

1968 (30 Sept). Martin Luther King Commemoration. W w **12**. P 12×12½.

190 **57** 50c. multicoloured 15 10

58 *Mystic Nativity* (Botticelli)

60 Tarpon Snook

(Des and photo Harrison)

1968 (27 Nov). Christmas. Paintings. T **58** and similar vert design. Multicoloured. W w **12** (sideways). P 14½×14.

191	12c. Type **58**	10	10
192	25c. *The Adoration of the Magi* (Rubens)..	10	10
193	40c. Type **58**	15	10
194	50c. As 25c.	15	10
191/194	*Set of 4*	45	35

(Des G. Drummond. Photo Harrison)

1969 (25 Feb). Fish. T **60** and similar horiz designs. W w **12**. P 14×14½.

195	6c. multicoloured	10	10
196	12c. black, turquoise-green and greenish blue	15	10
197	40c. multicoloured	25	10
198	50c. multicoloured	30	15
195/198	*Set of 4*	70	40

Designs: 6c. T **60**; 12c. Needlefish; 40c. Horse-eyed Jack; 50c. Blackfinned Snapper.

64 The Warner Badge and Islands

67 *The Adoration of the Kings* (Mostaert)

(Des V. Whiteley. Litho Format)

1969 (1 Sept). Sir Thomas Warner Commemoration. T **64** and similar horiz designs. Multicoloured. W w **12** (sideways). P 13½×14.

199	20c. Type **64**	10	10
200	25c. Sir Thomas Warner's tomb	10	10
201	40c. Charles I's commission	15	15
199/201	*Set of 3*	30	30

(Des Enschedé. Litho B.W.)

1969 (17 Nov). Christmas. Paintings. T **67** and similar vert design. Multicoloured. W w **12** (sideways). P 13½.

202	10c. Type **67**	10	10
203	25c. Type **67**	10	10
204	40c. *The Adoration of the Kings* (Geertgen)	10	10
205	50c. As 40c.	10	10
202/205	*Set of 4*	35	35

73 Portuguese Caravels (16th-century)

(Des and litho J.W.)

1970 (2 Feb)–**74**. Designs as T **73** in black, pale orange and emerald (½c.) or multicoloured (others). W w **12** (upright on vert designs, sideways* on horiz designs). P 14.

206	½c. Pirates and treasure at Frigate Bay (*vert*)	10	10
	w. Wmk inverted (15.3.71)	20	20
207	1c. English two-decker warship, 1650 (*vert*)	30	10
208	2c. Naval flags of colonising nations (*vert*)	15	10
209	3c. Rapier hilt (17th-century) (*vert*)	15	10
210	4c. Type **73**	20	10
	w. Wmk Crown to right of CA (24.7.74)	70	50
211	5c. Sir Henry Morgan and fireships, 1669	60	60
	w. Wmk Crown to right of CA (24.7.74)	40	60
212	6c. L'Ollonois and pirate carrack (16th-century)	30	10
	w. Wmk Crown to right of CA (24.7.74)	40	50
213	10c. 17th-century smugglers' ship	30	10
	w. Wmk Crown to right of CA (24.7.74)	40	15
214	15c. 'Piece-of-eight' (*vert*) (I)	2·50	40
214*a*	15c. 'Piece-of-eight' (*vert*) (II) (8.9.70)	5·50	10
215	20c. Cannon (17th-century)	35	10
	w. Crown to right of CA (24.7.74)	50	20
216	25c. Humphrey Cole's *Astrolabe*, 1574 (*vert*)	40	10
217	50c. Flintlock pistol (17th-century)	85	80
	w. Wmk Crown to right of CA (24.7.74)	1·25	80
218	60c. Dutch flute (17th-century) (*vert*)	1·50	70
219	$1 Captain Bartholomew Roberts and his crew's death warrant (*vert*)	1·50	75
220	$2.50 Railing piece (16th-century)	1·25	5·50
	w. Wmk Crown to right of CA (24.7.74)	2·00	5·50
221	$5 Drake, Hawkins and sea battle	1·50	4·50
	w. Wmk Crown to right of CA (24.7.74)	3·25	5·00
206/221	*Set of 17*	15·00	12·00

Nos. 214/214*a*. Type I, coin inscribed 'HISPANIANUM'; Type II corrected to 'HISPANIARUM'. No. 214*a* also differs considerably in shade from No. 214.

* The normal sideways watermark shows Crown to left of CA, *as seen from the back of the stamp.*

Values from this set were subsequently reissued with W w **12** sideways on vertical designs and upright on horizontal designs. Later values were issued on paper watermarked W w **14**.

85 Graveyard Scene (*Great Expectations*)

(Des Jennifer Toombs. Litho B. W.)

1970 (1 May). Death Centenary of Charles Dickens. T **85** and similar designs. W w **12** (sideways on horiz designs). P 13.

222	4c. bistre-brown, gold and deep blue-green	10	90
223	20c. bistre-brown, gold and reddish purple	15	20
224	25c. bistre-brown, gold and olive-green.	15	20
225	40c. bistre-brown, gold and ultramarine	25	35
222/225	*Set of 4*	55	1·50

Designs: Horiz—4c. T **85**; 20c. Miss Havisham and Pip (*Great Expectations*). Vert—25c. Dickens's Birthplace; 40c. Charles Dickens.

86 Local Steel Band

(Des V. Whiteley. Litho Enschedé)

1970 (1 Aug). Festival of Arts. T **86** and similar horiz designs. Multicoloured. W w **12** (sideways). P 13½.

226	20c. Type **86**	10	10
227	25c. Local String Band	10	10
228	40c. Scene from *A Midsummer Night's Dream*	15	15
226/228	*Set of 3*	30	30

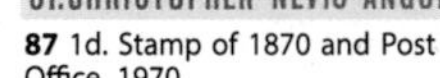

87 1d. Stamp of 1870 and Post Office, 1970

88 *Adoration of the Shepherds* (detail) (Frans van Floris)

(Des J. Cooter. Litho J.W.)

1970 (14 Sept). Stamp Centenary. T **87** and similar horiz designs. W w **12** (sideways). P 14½.

229	½c. green and rose	10	10
230	20c. deep blue, green and rose	10	10
231	25c. brown-purple, green and rose	10	10
232	50c. scarlet, green and black	30	45
229/232	*Set of 4*	55	65

Designs: ½c. T **87**; 20c., 25c., 1d. and 6d. Stamps of 1870; 50c., 6d. Stamp of 1870 and early postmark.

(Des Enschedé. Litho Format)

1970 (16 Nov). Christmas. T **88** and similar vert design. Multicoloured. W w **12**. P 14.

233	3c. Type **88**	10	10
234	20c. *The Holy Family* (Van Dyck)	10	10
235	25c. As 20c.	10	10
236	40c. Type **88**	15	50
235/236	*Set of 4*	40	70

St Lucia

Although a branch office of the British GPO was not opened at Castries, the island capital, until 1844 some form of postal arrangements for overseas mails existed from at least 1841 when the issue of a Ship Letter handstamp is recorded.

The stamps of Great Britain were used on the island from May 1858 until the end of April 1860 when the local authorities assumed responsibility for the postal service. No. CC1 was again used on overseas mail between 1 May and the introduction of St. Lucia stamps in December 1860.

CASTRIES

CROWN-CIRCLE HANDSTAMPS

CC 1

CC1	CC **1** ST. LUCIA (R.) (1.5.1844)	*Price on cover*	£900

No. CC1 was utilised, struck in black, during a shortage of 1d. stamps in late April and early May 1904. *Price on cover* £325.

Stamps of GREAT BRITAIN cancelled 'A11' as T Z **1** of Jamaica.

1858–60.

Z1	1d. rose-red (1857), perf 14	£1300
Z2	2d. blue (1855)	
Z3	4d. rose (1857)	£475
Z4	6d. lilac (1856)	£275
Z5	1s. green (1856)	£2250

PRICES FOR STAMPS ON COVER TO 1945

Nos. 1/3	*from* × 60
Nos. 5/8	*from* × 30
Nos. 9/10	†
Nos. 11/24	*from* × 15
Nos. 25/30	*from* × 10
Nos. 31/36	*from* × 6
Nos. 39/42	*from* × 10
Nos. 43/50	*from* × 15
Nos. 51/52	—
Nos. 53/62	*from* × 6
No. 63	*from* × 15
Nos. 64/75	*from* × 4
Nos. 76/77	—
Nos. 78/88	*from* × 3
No. 89	*from* × 4
No. 90	*from* × 20
Nos. 91/112	*from* × 3
Nos. 113/124	*from* × 2
Nos. 125/127	*from* × 10
Nos. 128/141	*from* × 2
Nos. D1/D6	*from* × 10
Nos. F1/F28	—

CROWN COLONY

PERKINS BACON 'CANCELLED'. For notes on these handstamps, showing 'CANCELLED' between horizontal bars forming an oval, see Catalogue Introduction.

1

Half penny

(**2**)

(Recess P.B.)

1860 (18 Dec). Wmk Small Star, W w **2**. P 14 to 16.

1	**1**	(1d.) rose-red (H/S 'CANCELLED' in oval £8500)	£100	65·00
		a. Imperf vert (horiz pair)		
		b. Double impression	£2500	
2		(4d.) blue (H/S 'CANCELLED' in oval £9000)	£225	£150
		a. Deep blue		
		b. Imperf vert (horiz pair)		
3		(6d.) green (H/S 'CANCELLED' in oval £12000)	£300	£200
		a. Imperf vert (horiz pair)		
		b. Deep green	£350	£225

(Recess D.L.R.)

1863. Wmk Crown CC. P 12½.

5	**1**	(1d.) lake	95·00	£110
		ax. Wmk reversed	70·00	90·00
		b. Brownish lake	£110	£110
		bx. Wmk reversed	85·00	90·00
7		(4d.) indigo	£140	£140
		x. Wmk reversed		
8		(6d.) emerald-green	£225	£225
		w. Wmk inverted		
		x. Wmk reversed	£190	£180

All three values exist imperforate from proof sheets.

Prepared for use, but not issued. Surch as T **2**

9	**1**	½d. on (6d.) emerald-green	70·00	
		x. Wmk reversed	£110	

10 6d. on (4d.) indigo £1100
a. Surch 'Sex pence' £3500

Nos. 9/10 were first recorded in 1885. They may have been prepared in 1876.

1864 (19 Nov)–**76**. Wmk Crown CC.

(a) P 12½

11 1 (1d.) black 35·00 13·00
a. Intense black 35·00 13·00
x. Wmk reversed 40·00 16·00
y. Wmk inverted and reversed £120
12 (4d.) yellow £200 50·00
b. Lemon-yellow £1500
c. Chrome-yellow £200 42·00
d. Olive-yellow £375 90·00
w. Wmk inverted
x. Wmk reversed £170 50·00
y. Wmk inverted and reversed
13 (6d.) violet £140 42·00
a. Mauve £200 32·00
b. Deep lilac £170 42·00
w. Wmk inverted — £120
x. Wmk reversed £160 60·00
14 (1s.) brown-orange £325 30·00
b. Orange £250 30·00
c. Pale orange £225 30·00
ca. Imperf between (horiz pair)
x. Wmk reversed £275 60·00

(b) P 14

15 1 (1d.) black (6.76) 50·00 22·00
a. Imperf between (horiz pair)
x. Wmk reversed 50·00 22·00
16 (4d.) yellow (6.76) £130 24·00
a. Olive-yellow £325 £100
w. Wmk inverted
x. Wmk reversed £130 24·00
17 (6d.) mauve (6.76) £120 42·00
a. Pale lilac £120 22·00
b. Violet £250 70·00
x. Wmk reversed — 55·00
18 (1s.) orange (10.76) £250 24·00
a. Deep orange £170 16·00
w. Wmk inverted — £110
x. Wmk reversed £190 25·00

All four values exist imperforate from proof sheets.

HALFPENNY (3) 2½ PENCE (4) 5

1881 (Sept). Surch with Types **3** or **4**. Wmk Crown CC. P 14.

23 1 ½d. green 85·00 £120
x. Wmk reversed — £190
24 2½d. brown-red 60·00 28·00

The (1d.) black is known surcharged '1d.' in violet ink by hand, but there is no evidence that this was done officially.

1882–84. Surch as T **3**. Wmk Crown CA.

(a) P 14

25 1 ½d. green (1882) 35·00 50·00
26 1d. black (C.) 50·00 17·00
a. Bisected (*on cover*) † —
27 4d. yellow £300 24·00
28 6d. violet 50·00 50·00
29 1s. orange £275 £170

(b) P 12

30 1 4d. yellow £275 28·00

Deep blue stamps, wmk Crown CA, perf 14 or 12 are fiscals from which the overprint 'THREE PENCE—REVENUE', or 'REVENUE', has been fraudulently removed.

(Typo D.L.R.)

1883 (6 July)–**86**. Die I. Wmk Crown CA. P 14.

31 5 ½d. dull green 18·00 12·00
a. Top left triangle detached £450
32 1d. carmine-rose 55·00 19·00
33 2½d. blue 75·00 3·00
a. Top left triangle detached £1000 £200
34 4d. brown (1885) 50·00 1·25
a. Top left triangle detached £850 £150
35 6d. lilac (1885) £300 £200
36 1s. orange-brown (1886) £400 £160
31/36 *Set of 6* £800 £350

The 4d. and 6d. exist imperforate from proof sheets.

For illustration of 'top left triangle detached' variety on this and the following issue see above No. 21 of Antigua.

1886–87. Die I. Wmk Crown CA. P 14.

39 5 1d. dull mauve 18·00 6·00
a. Top left triangle detached £400 £225
40 3d. dull mauve and green £120 22·00
a. Top left triangle detached £1200 £475
41 6d. dull mauve and blue (1887) 9·00 21·00
a. Top left triangle detached £275 £400
42 1s. dull mauve and red (1887) £120 50·00
a. Top left triangle detached £1300 £750
39/42 *Set of 4* £225 85·00
39s/42s Optd 'SPECIMEN' *Set of 4* £225

The 1d. exists imperforate from proof sheets.

1891–98. Die II. Wmk Crown CA. P 14.

43 5 ½d. dull green 4·00 1·00
w. Wmk inverted £500
44 1d. dull mauve 7·00 30
45 2d. ultramarine and orange (1898) 6·50 2·00
46 2½d. ultramarine 13·00 1·00
47 3d. dull mauve and green 10·00 5·50
48 4d. brown 9·00 3·75
49 6d. dull mauve and blue 45·00 26·00
50 1s. dull mauve and red 15·00 6·00
51 5s. dull mauve and orange 55·00 £160
52 10s. dull mauve and black 95·00 £160
43/52 *Set of 10* £200 £325
45s, 51s/52s Optd 'SPECIMEN' *Set of 3* £120

For description and illustration of differences between Die I and Die II see Introduction.

ONE HALF PENNY (6) ½d (7) ONE PENNY (8)

N Normal 'N' N Thick 'N'

Three types of T **8**

I. All letters 'N' normal.
II. Thick diagonal stroke in first 'N' of 'PENNY'.
III. Thick diagonal stroke in second 'N' of 'PENNY'.

1891–92.

(a) Stamps of Die I surch

53 6 ½d. on 3d. dull mauve and green £150 70·00
a. Small 'A' in 'HALF' £375 £150
b. Small 'O' in 'ONE' £375 £150
c. Top left triangle detached £1400
54 7 ½d. on half 6d. dull mauve and blue 35·00 3·25
a. No fraction bar £300 £130
b. Surch sideways £1700
c. Surch double £650 £650
d. '2' in fraction omitted £500 £500
e. Thick '1' with sloping serif £200 £130
f. Surch triple £1300
g. Figure '1' used as fraction bar £475 £275
h. Top left triangle detached — £375
55 8 1d. on 4d. brown (I) (12.91) 9·00 4·50
a. Surch double £250
b. Surch inverted £950 £850
c. Type II 30·00 25·00
ca. Surch double £475
cb. Surch inverted — £1500
d. Type III 30·00 25·00
e. Top left triangle detached £275 £190

(b) Stamp of Die II surch

56 6 ½d. on 3d. dull mauve and green 85·00 29·00
a. Surch double £900 £700
b. Surch inverted £1900 £650
c. Surch both sides £1100 £750
d. Small 'O' in 'ONE' (R. 2/6) £225 90·00
e. Small 'A' in 'HALF' £225 90·00
f. 'ONE' misplaced ('O' over 'H') (R. 4/6) £225 90·00

Nos. 53 and 56 were surcharged with a setting of 30 (6×5). No. 55 was surcharged by a vertical setting of ten, repeated six times across each pane, with Type II (thick first 'N') at pos. 1 and Type III (thick second 'N') at pos. 9.

9

10

(Typo D.L.R.)

1902–03. Wmk Crown CA. P 14.

58 9 ½d. dull purple and green 4·00 1·50
59 1d. dull purple and carmine 6·50 50
60 2½d. dull purple and ultramarine 40·00 8·50
61 10 3d. dull purple and yellow 11·00 8·50
62 1s. green and black 17·00 50·00
58/62 *Set of 5* 70·00 60·00
58s/62s Optd 'SPECIMEN' *Set of 5* £120

11 The Pitons

(Recess D.L.R.)

1902 (15 Dec). 400th Anniversary of Discovery by Columbus. Wmk Crown CC (sideways). P 14.

63 11 2d. green and brown 18·00 1·75
s. Optd 'SPECIMEN' 65·00

This stamp was formerly thought to have been issued on 16 December but it has been seen on a postcard clearly postmarked 15 December.

1904–10. Chalk-surfaced paper (Nos. 71, 73/75 and 77) or ordinary paper (others). Wmk Mult Crown CA. P 14.

64 9 ½d. dull purple and green 12·00 60
a. Chalk-surfaced paper 12·00 1·25
65 ½d. green (1907) 1·75 1·00
66 1d. dull purple and carmine 8·50 1·25
a. Chalk-surfaced paper 11·00 1·25
aw. Wmk inverted £225
67 1d. carmine (1907) 4·25 30
68 2½d. dull purple and ultramarine 35·00 3·00
a. Chalk-surfaced paper 17·00 4·50
69 2½d. blue (1907) 3·75 2·25
70 10 3d. dull purple and yellow 13·00 3·00
71 3d. purple/*yellow* (1909) 4·75 21·00
72 6d. dull purple and violet (1905) 27·00 40·00
a. Chalk-surfaced paper 20·00 50·00
ab. Dull purple and bright purple (1907) 8·50 50·00
73 6d. dull purple (1910) 75·00 95·00
74 1s. green and black (1905) 50·00 38·00
75 1s. black/*green* (1909) 5·00 8·00
76 5s. green and carmine (1905) 85·00 £200
77 5s. green and red/*yellow* (1907) 60·00 70·00
64/77 *Set of 14* £300 £425
65s, 67s, 69s, 71s/72s, 72abs and 75s/77s Optd 'SPECIMEN' *Set of 9* £325

Examples of Nos. 71/77 are known with a forged Castries postmark dated 'JA 21 09'.

12

13

14

15

16

(Typo D.L.R.)

1912–21. Die I. Chalk-surfaced paper (3d. to 5s.). Wmk Mult Crown CA. P 14.

78 12 ½d. deep green 70 50
a. Yellow-green (1916) 3·50 30
79 1d. carmine-red 1·90 10
a. Scarlet (1916) 8·50 10
b. Rose-red 9·00 1·00
80 13 2d. grey 1·50 4·25
a. Slate-grey (1916) 23·00 17·00
81 12 2½d. ultramarine 3·75 2·75
a. Bright blue 4·25 2·75
b. Deep bright blue (1916) 17·00 10·00
82 15 3d. purple/*yellow* 1·25 2·25
b. Die II. *On pale yellow* (1921) 30·00 60·00
bw. Wmk inverted
83 14 4d. black and red/*yellow* 1·00 2·75
a. White back 70 1·50
as. Optd 'SPECIMEN' 30·00
84 15 6d. dull and bright purple 2·00 21·00
a. Grey-purple and purple (1918) 16·00 29·00
85 1s. black/*green* 8·00 6·00
a. On blue-green (olive back) (1918) 17·00 24·00
86 1s. orange-brown (1920) 20·00 48·00
87 16 2s.6d. black and red/blue 27·00 55·00
88 15 5s. green and red/yellow 25·00 85·00
78/88 *Set of 11* 80·00 £200
78s/88s Optd 'SPECIMEN' *Set of 11* £225

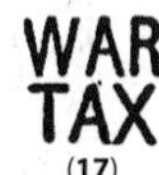
WAR TAX (17) WAR TAX (18)

1916 (1 June). No. 79*a* optd locally with T **17**.

89 12 1d. scarlet 15·00 25·00
a. Opt double £550 £650
b. Carmine-red 65·00 55·00

For overprinting with T **17** the sheets were vertically divided to the left of the centre margin and the top margin of the sheet was folded beneath the top row of stamps so that the marginal examples from this row show an inverted albino impression of the overprint in the top margin.

Examples are also recorded of similar albino overprints in the right-hand and bottom margins but it is unclear if some sheets had all margins folded under before overprinting.

1916 (Sept). No. 79*a* optd in London with T **18**.

90 12 1d. scarlet 1·75 30
s. Optd 'SPECIMEN' 55·00

1921–30. Die II. Chalk-surfaced paper (3d. (No. 100) to 5s.). Wmk Mult Script CA. P 14.

91 12 ½d. green 1·50 50
92 1d. rose-carmine 16·00 22·00
93 1d. deep brown (1922) 1·40 15
94 14 1½d. dull carmine (1922) 75 2·50
95 13 2d. slate-grey 75 15
96 12 2½d. bright blue 9·00 2·75
97 2½d. orange (1925) 16·00 65·00
98 2½d. dull blue (1926) 11·00 2·75
99 15 3d. bright blue (1922) 8·50 22·00
a. Dull blue (1924) 9·00 11·00
100 3d. purple/*pale yellow* (1926) 3·75 12·00
a. Deep purple/pale yellow (1930) 40·00 12·00
101 14 4d. black and red/*yellow* (1924) 1·25 3·50
102 15 6d. grey-purple and purple 2·00 4·75
103 1s. orange-brown 7·00 3·25
104 16 2s.6d. black and red/*blue* (1924) 18·00 40·00
105 15 5s. green and red/*pale yellow* (1923) 60·00 95·00
91/105 *Set of 15* £140 £225
91s/105s Optd 'SPECIMEN' *Set of 15* £325

1935 (6 May). Silver Jubilee. As Nos. 91/94 of Antigua. P 13½×14.

109 ½d. black and green 30 2·50
f. Diagonal line by turret 55·00 £100
g. Dot to left of chapel £110
110 2d. ultramarine and grey 1·50 1·75
f. Diagonal line by turret £110 £130
111 2½d. brown and deep blue 1·75 1·75
a. Frame printed double, one albino † —
f. Diagonal line by turret £130
g. Dot to left of chapel £180 £190
112 1s. slate and purple 18·00 23·00
h. Dot by flagstaff £500
109/112 *Set of 4* 19·00 26·00
109s/112s Perf 'SPECIMEN' *Set of 4* 95·00

For illustrations of plate varieties see Omnibus section following Zanzibar.

19 Port Castries

20 Columbus Square, Castries (inscr 'COLOMBUS SQUARE' in error)

21 Ventine Falls

22 Fort Rodney, Pigeon Island

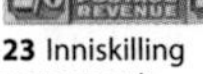

23 Inniskilling monument

24 Government House

25 The Badge of the Colony

(Recess D.L.R.)

1936 (1 Mar–Apr). T **19**/**25**. Wmk Mult Script CA. P 14 or 13×12 (1s. and 10s.).

113	**19**	½d. black and bright green	30	50
		a. Perf 13×12 (8.4.36)	6·50	28·00
114	**20**	1d. black and brown	40	10
		a. Perf 13×12 (8.4.36)	11·00	4·50
115	**21**	1½d. black and scarlet	70	30
		a. Perf 12×13	18·00	2·25
116	**19**	2d. black and grey	60	20
117	**20**	2½d. black and blue	60	15
118	**21**	3d. black and dull green	1·50	70
119	**19**	4d. black and red-brown	3·00	1·25
120	**20**	6d. black and orange	3·00	1·25
121	**22**	1s. black and light blue	4·50	2·50
122	**23**	2s.6d. black and ultramarine	17·00	14·00
123	**24**	5s. black and violet	21·00	20·00
124	**25**	10s. black and carmine	65·00	£100
113/124 *Set of 12*			£100	£130
113s/124s Perf 'SPECIMEN' *Set of 12*			£300	

Examples of most values are known with a forged Castries postmark dated '1 MR 36'.

1937 (12 May). Coronation. As Nos. 95/97 of Antigua. P 11×11½.

125	1d. violet	30	35
126	1½d. carmine	55	20
127	2½d. blue	55	1·25
125/127 *Set of 3*		1·25	1·60
125s/127s Perf 'SPECIMEN' *Set of 3*		90·00	

26 King George VI

27 Columbus Square

28 Government House

29 The Pitons

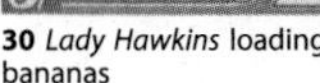

30 *Lady Hawkins* loading bananas

31 Device of St Lucia

(Des Miss M. Byer and E. Crafer (T **26**), H. Fleury (5s.). Recess Waterlow (½d. to 3½d., 8d., 3s., 5s., £1), D.L.R. (6d., 1s.) and B.W. (2s., 10s.))

1938 (22 Sept)–**48**. Types **26**/**31**. Wmk Mult Script CA (sideways on 2s.).

128	**26**	½d. green (P 14½×14)	2·00	10
		a. Perf 12½ (22.5.43)	10	10
129		1d. violet (P 14½×14)	8·00	75
		a. Perf 12½	30	15
129*b*		1d. scarlet (P 12½) (8.4.47)	1·50	10
		c. Perf 14½×14 (20.9.48)	10	10
130		1½d. scarlet (P 14½×14)	4·00	40
		a. Perf 12½ (22.5.43)	1·50	2·75
131		2d. grey (P 14½×14)	5·50	2·00
		a. Perf 12½ (22.5.43)	15	10
132		2½d. ultramarine (P 14½×14)	8·50	15
		a. Perf 12½ (22.5.43)	40	10
132*b*		2½d. violet (P 12½) (8.4.47)	1·00	10
133		3d. orange (P 14½×14)	4·50	10
		a. Perf 12½ (22.5.43)	30	10
133*b*		3½d. ultramarine (P 12½) (1.4.47)	1·00	15
134	**27**	6d. claret (P 13½)	16·00	1·50
		a. Carmine-lake (P 13½) (30.7.45)	7·00	35
		b. Perf 12. *Claret* (23.2.48)	4·00	2·50
134*c*	**26**	8d. brown (P 12½) (4.2.46)	3·50	30
135	**28**	1s. brown (P 13½)	3·50	30
		a. Perf 12 (23.2.48)	2·25	30
136	**29**	2s. blue and purple (P 12)	14·00	1·25
136*a*	**26**	3s. bright purple (P 12½) (4.2.46)	8·00	1·75
137	**30**	5s. black and mauve (P 12½)	24·00	16·00
138	**31**	10s. black/*yellow* (P 12)	18·00	9·00
141	**26**	£1 sepia (P 12½) (4.2.46)	16·00	14·00
128a/141 *Set of 17*			80·00	40·00
128s/141s Perf 'SPECIMEN' *Set of 17*			£475	

1946 (8 Oct). Victory. As Nos. 110/111 of Antigua.

142	1d. lilac	10	30
143	3½d. blue	10	30
142s/143s Perf 'SPECIMEN' *Set of 2*		80·00	

1948 (26 Nov). Royal Silver Wedding. As Nos. 112/113 of Antigua.

144	1d. scarlet	15	10
145	£1 purple-brown	17·00	35·00

(New Currency. 100 cents = 1 West Indian dollar)

32 King George VI

33 Device of St Lucia

(Recess Waterlow (**32**), B.W. (**33**))

1949 (1 Oct)–**50**. Value in cents or dollars. Wmk Mult Script CA. P 12½ (1c. to 16c.), 11×11½ (others).

146	**32**	1c. green	25	10
		a. Perf 14 (1949)	3·75	40
147		2c. magenta	1·00	10
		a. Perf 14½×14 (1949)	6·50	1·50
148		3c. scarlet	1·75	3·25
149		4c. grey	2·00	65
		a. Perf 14½×14 (1950)	†	£17000
150		5c. violet	1·75	10
151		6c. orange	1·50	4·00
152		7c. ultramarine	4·00	3·50
153		12c. claret	5·50	4·75
		a. Perf 14½×14 (1950)	£800	£550
154		16c. brown	5·00	50
155	**33**	24c. light blue	50	10
156		48c. olive-green	2·00	1·25
157		$1.20 purple	5·50	14·00
158		$2.40 blue-green	9·50	22·00
159		$4.80 rose-carmine	14·00	18·00
146/159 *Set of 14*			48·00	60·00

Most examples of Nos. 146a and 147a were produced as coils, but a few sheets in these perforations were distributed and blocks of four are scarce.

No genuine mint example of No. 149a is known. Photographic forgeries do, however, exist.

1949 (10 Oct). 75th Anniversary of UPU. As Nos. 114/117 of Antigua.

160	5c. violet	15	1·00
161	6c. orange	1·60	3·00
	a. 'A' of 'CA' missing from wmk	£650	
162	12c. magenta	20	30
163	24c. blue-green	30	30
160/163 *Set of 4*		2·00	4·25

1951 (16 Feb). Inauguration of BWI University College. As Nos. 118/119 of Antigua.

164	3c. black and scarlet	45	1·50
165	12c. black and deep carmine	65	1·50

34 Phoenix rising from Burning Buildings

N 1
E 9
W 5
1
CONSTITUTION

(35)

(Flames typo, rest recess B.W.)

1951 (19 June). Reconstruction of Castries. Wmk Mult Script CA. P 13½×13.

166	**34**	12c. red and blue	35	1·00

1951 (25 Sept). New Constitution. Nos. 147, 149/150 and 153 optd with T **35** by Waterlow. P 12½.

167	**32**	2c. magenta	20	80
168		4c. grey	20	60
169		5c. violet	25	80
170		12c. claret	1·00	60
167/170 *Set of 4*			1·50	2·50

1953 (2 June). Coronation. As No. 120 of Antigua.

171	3c. black and scarlet	70	10

36 Queen Elizabeth II

37 Device of St Lucia

(Recess Waterlow (T **36**), until 1960, then D.L.R. B.W. (T **37**))

1953 (28 Oct)–**63**. Wmk Mult Script CA. P 14½×14 (T **36**) or 11×11½ (T **37**).

172	**36**	1c. green (1.4.54)	10	10
173		2c. magenta	10	10
174		3c. red (2.9.54)	10	10
175		4c. slate (7.1.54)	10	10
176		5c. violet (1.4.54)	10	10
		a. Slate-violet (19.2.63)	26·00	4·75
177		6c. orange (2.9.54)	15	1·00
		a. Brown-orange (26.9.61)	22·00	3·00
178		8c. lake (2.9.54)	30	10
179		10c. ultramarine (2.9.54)	10	10
		a. Blue (14.8.62)	50	10
180		15c. red-brown (2.9.54)	30	10
		a. Brown (30.10.57)	2·50	10
181	**37**	25c. deep turquoise-blue (2.9.54)	30	10
182		50c. deep olive-green (2.9.54)	4·50	3·75
183		$1 bluish green (2.9.54)	4·00	7·00
184		$2.50 carmine (2.9.54)	7·00	6·50
172/184 *Set of 13*			15·00	16·00

1958 (22 Apr). Inauguration of British Caribbean Federation. As Nos. 135/137 of Antigua.

185	3c. deep green	1·10	20
186	6c. blue	1·10	1·75
187	12c. scarlet	1·10	80
185/187 *Set of 3*		3·00	2·50

MINISTERIAL GOVERNMENT

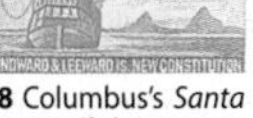

38 Columbus's *Santa Maria* off the Pitons

39 Stamp of 1860

(Recess Waterlow)

1960 (1 Jan). New Constitution for the Windward and Leeward Islands. W w **12**. P 13.

188	**38**	8c. carmine-red	40	45
189		10c. red-orange	40	45
190		25c. deep blue	60	50
188/190 *Set of 3*			1·25	1·25

(Eng H. Bard. Recess Waterlow)

1960 (18 Dec). Stamp Centenary. W w **12**. P 13½.

191	**39**	5c. rose-red and ultramarine	25	10
192		16c. deep blue and yellow-green	45	90
193		25c. green and carmine-red	45	15
191/193 *Set of 3*			1·00	1·00

1963 (4 June). Freedom from Hunger. As No. 146 of Antigua.

194	25c. bluish green	40	10

1963 (2 Sept). Red Cross Centenary. As Nos. 147/148 of Antigua.

195	4c. red and black	20	1·50
196	25c. red and blue	50	1·50

40

41

Queen Elizabeth II (after A.C. Davidson-Houston)

42 Fishing Boats

43 Pigeon Island

44 Reduit Beach

45 Castries Harbour

46 The Pitons

47 Vigie Beach

48 Queen Elizabeth II

(Des V. Whiteley. Photo Harrison)

1964 (1 Mar)–**69**. Designs as Types **40/48**, W w **12**. P 14½ (T **40**), others 14½×14 (vert) or 14×14½ (horiz).

No.	Type	Description	Unused	Used
197	**40**	1c. crimson	10	10
		w. Wmk inverted	75	1·50
198		2c. bluish violet	30	1·00
		w. Wmk inverted	—	6·50
199		4c. turquoise-green	1·00	30
		a. Deep turquoise (5.8.69)	9·00	3·25
		w. Wmk inverted	—	7·50
200		5c. Prussian blue	30	10
		w. Wmk inverted		
201		6c. yellow-brown	1·00	2·50
202	**41**	8c. multicoloured	10	10
203		10c. multicoloured	1·00	10
204	**42**	12c. multicoloured	50	1·75
205	**43**	15c. multicoloured	20	10
206	**44**	25c. multicoloured	20	10
207	**45**	35c. blue and buff	3·00	10
208	**46**	50c. multicoloured	2·50	10
209	**47**	$1 multicoloured	1·25	2·50
210	**48**	$2.50 multicoloured	3·00	2·25
197/210 *Set of 14*			13·00	9·50

See also No. 249.

1964 (23 Apr). 400th Birth Anniversary of William Shakespeare. As No. 164 of Antigua.

No.	Type	Description	Unused	Used
211		10c. blue-green	30	10

1965 (17 May). ITU Centenary. As Nos. 166/167 of Antigua.

No.	Type	Description	Unused	Used
212		2c. mauve and magenta	10	10
213		50c. lilac and light olive-green	70	90

1965 (25 Oct). International Co-operation Year. As Nos. 168/169 of Antigua.

No.	Type	Description	Unused	Used
214		1c. reddish purple and turquoise-green	10	80
215		25c. deep bluish green and lavender	20	20

1966 (24 Jan). Churchill Commemoration. As Nos. 170/173 of Antigua.

No.	Type	Description	Unused	Used
216		4c. new blue	15	10
217		6c. deep green	70	4·00
218		25c. brown	80	15
219		35c. bluish violet	85	20
216/219 *Set of 4*			2·25	4·00

1966 (4 Feb). Royal Visit. As Nos. 174/175 of Antigua.

No.	Type	Description	Unused	Used
220		4c. black and ultramarine	65	25
221		25c. black and magenta	1·25	75

1966 (1 July). World Cup Football Championship, England. As Nos. 176/177 of Antigua.

No.	Type	Description	Unused	Used
222		4c. violet, yellow-green, lake and yellow-brown	25	10
223		25c. chocolate, blue-green, lake and yellow-brown	75	30

1966 (20 Sept). Inauguration of WHO Headquarters, Geneva. As Nos. 178/179 of Antigua.

No.	Type	Description	Unused	Used
224		4c. black, yellow-green and light blue	25	30
225		25c. black, light purple and yellow-brown	75	40

1966 (1 Dec). 20th Anniversary of UNESCO. As Nos. 196/198 of Antigua.

No.	Type	Description	Unused	Used
226		4c. slate-violet, red, yellow and orange	20	10
227		12c. orange-yellow, violet and deep olive	40	65
228		25c. black, bright purple and orange	75	35
226/228 *Set of 3*			1·25	1·00

ASSOCIATED STATEHOOD

STATEHOOD
1st MARCH 1967
(**49**)

STATEHOOD
1st MARCH 1967
(**50**)

51 Map of St Lucia

(Optd by Art Printery, Castries from dies supplied by Harrison. Photo Harrison (No. 240))

1967 (7 Mar). Statehood.

(a) Postage. Nos. 198 and 200/209 optd with T **49** *(2, 5, 6c.) or T* **50** *(others) in red*

No.	Type	Description	Unused	Used
229		2c. bluish violet	20	20
		a. Horiz pair, one without opt		
230		5c. Prussian blue	20	10
		a. Opt inverted	50·00	
231		6c. yellow-brown	20	20
232		8c. multicoloured	1·00	10
		a. Opt double	£1500	
233		10c. multicoloured	40	30
234		12c. multicoloured	40	10
235		15c. multicoloured	75	1·25
236		25c. multicoloured	40	2·00
237		35c. blue and buff	2·00	1·00
238		50c. multicoloured	1·50	2·25
239		$1 multicoloured	65	1·25
229/239 *Set of 11*			7·00	7·75

Overprinted 1c. and $2.50 stamps were prepared for issue but were not put on sale over the post office counter. Later, however, they were accepted for franking (*Price for set of 2 £2 mint, £8 used*).

The 1c., 6c. and $2.50 also exist with overprint in black, instead of red, and the 25c. UNESCO value is also known with a similar overprint in blue or black.

(b) Air. P 14½×14

No.	Type	Description	Unused	Used
240	**51**	15c. new blue	10	10

52 *Madonna and Child with the Infant Baptist* (Raphael)

53 Batsman and Sir Frederick Clarke (Governor)

(Des and photo Harrison)

1967 (16 Oct). Christmas. W w **12** (sideways). P 14½.

No.	Type	Description	Unused	Used
241	**52**	4c. multicoloured	10	10
242		25c. multicoloured	30	10

(Des V. Whiteley. Photo Harrison)

1968 (8 Mar). MCC's West Indies Tour. W w **12** (sideways). P 14½×14.

No.	Type	Description	Unused	Used
243	**53**	10c. multicoloured	20	30
244		35c. multicoloured	45	55

54 *The Crucified Christ with the Virgin Mary, Saints and Angels* (Raphael)

55 *Noli me tangere* (detail by Titian)

(Des and photo Harrison)

1968 (25 Mar). Easter. W w **12** (sideways). P 14×14½.

No.	Type	Description	Unused	Used
245	**54**	10c. multicoloured	10	10
246	**55**	15c. multicoloured	10	10
247	**54**	25c. multicoloured	15	10
248	**55**	35c. multicoloured	15	10
		a. Yellow (sunset) omitted	£200	
245/248 *Set of 4*			45	35

1968 (14 May*). As No. 205 but W w **12** (sideways).

No.	Type	Description	Unused	Used
249	**43**	15c. multicoloured	40	30

* This is the London release date. Stamps from this printing were available some months earlier on St Lucia.

56 Dr. Martin Luther King

57 *Virgin and Child in Glory* (Murillo)

(Des V. Whiteley. Litho D.L.R.)

1968 (4 July). Martin Luther King Commemoration. W w **12**. P 13½×14.

No.	Type	Description	Unused	Used
250	**56**	25c. blue, black and flesh	15	15
251		35c. violet-black, black and flesh	15	15

(Des and photo Harrison)

1968 (17 Oct). Christmas. Paintings. T **57** and similar vert design. Multicoloured. W w **12** (sideways). P 14½×14.

No.	Type	Description	Unused	Used
252		5c. Type **57**	10	10
253		10c. *Madonna with Child* (Murillo)	10	10
254		25c. Type **57**	15	10
255		35c. As 10c	15	10
252/255 *Set of 4*			45	35

59 Purple-throated Carib

(Des V. Whiteley. Litho Format)

1969 (10 Jan). Birds. T **59** and similar horiz design. Multicoloured. W w **12** (sideways). P 14.

No.	Type	Description	Unused	Used
256		10c. Type **59**	30	35
257		15c. St Lucia Amazon	35	40
258		25c. Type **59**	40	45
259		35c. As 15c.	60	50
256/259 *Set of 4*			1·50	1·50

61 *Head of Christ Crowned with Thorns* (Reni)

62 *Resurrection of Christ* (Sodoma)

(Des and photo Harrison)

1969 (20 Mar). Easter. W w **12** (sideways). P 14½×14.

No.	Type	Description	Unused	Used
260	**61**	10c. multicoloured	10	10
261	**62**	15c. multicoloured	10	10
262	**61**	25c. multicoloured	15	15
263	**62**	35c. multicoloured	15	15
260/263 *Set of 4*			45	45

63 Map showing CARIFTA Countries

(Des J. Cooter. Photo Harrison)

1969 (29 May). First Anniversary of CARIFTA (Caribbean Free Trade Area). T **63** and similar horiz design. Multicoloured. W w **12**. P 14.

No.	Type	Description	Unused	Used
264		5c. Type **63**	10	15
265		10c. Type **63**	10	15
266		25c. Handclasp and names of CARIFTA countries	15	15
267		35c. As 25c.	15	15
264/267 *Set of 4*			45	55

65 Emperor Napoléon and Empress Josephine

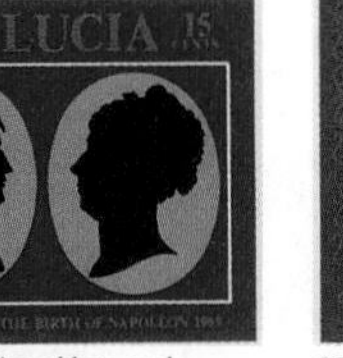

66 *Virgin and Child* (P. Delaroche)

(Des and litho Enschedé)

1969 (22 Sept). Birth Bicentenary of Napoléon Bonaparte. P 14×13.

No.	Type	Description	Unused	Used
268	**65**	15c. multicoloured	10	10
269		25c. multicoloured	10	10
270		35c. multicoloured	10	10
271		50c. multicoloured	15	55
268/271 *Set of 4*			40	75

(Des J. W. Photo Harrison)

1969 (27 Oct). Christmas. Paintings. T **66** and similar vert design. Multicoloured. W w **12** (sideways). P 14½×14.

No.	Type	Description	Unused	Used
272		5c. Type **66**	10	10
273		10c. *Holy Family* (Rubens)	10	10
274		25c. Type **66**	20	10
275		35c. As 10c.	20	10
272/275 *Set of 4*			55	35

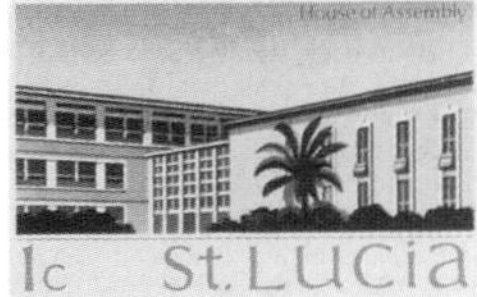

68 House of Assembly

(Des J. Cooter ($10), Sylvia and M. Goaman (others). Litho Questa ($10), Format (others))

1970 (2 Feb)–**73**. T **68** and similar designs. Multicoloured. W w **12** (sideways* on 1c. to 35c. and $10). P 14.

276		1c. Type **68**	10	10
277		2c. Roman Catholic Cathedral	15	10
278		4c. The Boulevard, Castries	1·00	10
		w. Wmk Crown to right of CA	6·50	
279		5c. Castries Harbour	1·50	10
280		6c. Sulphur springs	15	10
281		10c. Vigie Airport	2·00	10
282		12c. Reduit Beach	20	10
283		15c. Pigeon Island	30	10
284		25c. The Pitons and yacht	80	10
		w. Wmk Crown to right of CA	20·00	
285		35c. Marigot Bay	40	10
		w. Wmk Crown to right of CA	20·00	
286		50c. Diamond Waterfall (*vert*)	70	80
287		$1 Flag of St Lucia (*vert*)	40	70
288		$2.50 St Lucia Coat of Arms (*vert*)	55	1·75
289		$5 Queen Elizabeth II (*vert*)	1·00	4·00
289a		$10 Map of St Lucia (*vert*) (3.12.73)	6·00	9·00
276/289a *Set of* 15			13·50	15·00

* The normal sideways watermark shows Crown to left of CA, *as seen from the back of the stamp.*

The 2c. and 4c. were subsequently reissued with W w **12** upright and the 4c., 5c., 10c. and 13c. on W w **14**.

69 *The Sealing of the Tomb* (Hogarth)

(Des V. Whiteley. Litho Enschedé)

1970 (7 Mar). Easter. Triptych by Hogarth. T **69** and similar multicoloured designs. W w **12** (sideways). Roul. 9×P 12½.

290		25c. Type **69**	15	20
		a. Strip of 3. Nos. 290/292	55	70
291		35c. *The Three Marys at the Tomb*	15	20
292		$1 *The Ascension* (39×55 *mm*)	30	40
290/292 *Set of* 3			55	70

Nos. 290/292 were issued in sheets of 30 (6×5) containing the Hogarth Triptych spread over all three values of the set. This necessitated a peculiar arrangement with the $1 value (which depicts the centre portion of the triptych) 10 mm higher than the other values in the *se-tenant* strip.

72 Charles Dickens and Dickensian Characters

(Des V. Whiteley. Litho B.W.)

1970 (8 June). Death Centenary of Charles Dickens. W w **12** (sideways). P 14.

293	**72**	1c. multicoloured	10	10
294		25c. multicoloured	20	10
295		35c. multicoloured	25	10
296		50c. multicoloured	35	1·25
293/296 *Set of* 4			80	1·40

73 Nurse and Emblem

(Des R. Granger Barrett. Litho J.W.)

1970 (18 Aug). Centenary of British Red Cross. T **73** and similar horiz designs. Multicoloured. W w **12** (sideways*). P 14.

297		10c. Type **73**	15	15
298		15c. Flags of Great Britain, Red Cross and St Lucia	25	25
299		25c. Type **73**	35	40
300		35c. As 15c.	40	40
		w. Wmk Crown to right of CA	28·00	
297/300 *Set of* 4			1·00	1·10

* The normal sideways watermark shows Crown to left of CA, *as seen from the back of the stamp.*

74 *Madonna with the Lilies* (Luca della Robbie)

(Des P. B. Litho and embossed Walsall)

1970 (16 Nov). Christmas. P 11.

301	**74**	5c. multicoloured	10	10
302		10c. multicoloured	15	10
303		35c. multicoloured	30	10
304		40c. multicoloured	30	30
301/304 *Set of* 4			75	55

POSTAGE DUE STAMPS

D 1

No. **No.**

Normal Wide fount

(Type-set Government Printing Office)

1930. Each stamp individually handstamped with different number. No gum. Rough perf 12.

(a) Horizontally laid paper

D1	D **1**	1d. black/*blue*	11·00	23·00
		b. Wide, wrong fount 'No.'	25·00	50·00
		c. Missing stop after 'ST'	£325	£475
		d. Missing stop after 'LUCIA'	£275	£475
		e. Handstamped number double	£900	£1100
		f. Handstamped number triple	£2000	
		g. Incorrect number with correction above		
		h. Two different numbers on same stamp	£2000	
		i. Number omitted	£4000	

(b) Wove paper

D2	D **1**	2d. black/*yellow*	23·00	50·00
		a. Imperf between (vert pair)	£8000	
		b. Wide, wrong fount 'No.'	48·00	£100
		c. Missing stop after 'ST'	£650	£950
		d. Missing stop after 'LUCIA'	£900	
		e. Handstamped number double	†	£1900
		g. Incorrect number with correction above	£2000	£2250
		h. Two different numbers on same stamp	£2250	

Nos. D1/D2 were produced in sheets of 60 (6×10) usually with imperforate outer edges at the top, at right and at foot. It would appear that the sheets were bound into books from which they could be detached using the line of perforations along the left-hand side.

There were three printings of each value, utilising the same basic type. The paper for the first two printings of the 1d. and the first printing of the 2d. showed papermaker's watermarks, that for the 1d. being KINGSCLERE in double-lined capitals below a crown with parts occurring on between ten and fourteen stamps in *some sheets.*

Details of the printings are as follows:

1d.

First printing. On paper with sheet watermark. Shows wide fount 'No.' on R. 10/3–6 and missing stop after 'ST' on R. 5/3

Second printing. On paper with sheet watermark. Shows wide fount 'No.' on R. 10/2–6 and missing stop after 'ST' on R. 5/3. The first two printings of the 1d. were numbered together as 1 to 12000.

Third printing. On paper without watermark. Shows wide fount 'No.' on all stamps in Row 10. Missing stop after 'ST' on R. 5/3 corrected, but missing stop after 'LUCIA' occurs on R. 9/2. Numbered 12001 to 24000.

2d.

First printing. On paper with sheet watermark. Shows wide fount 'No.' on R. 10/2–6 and missing stop after 'ST' on R. 5/3 (as 1d. second printing). Numbered 1 to 4800.

Second printing. On paper without watermark. Shows wide fount 'No.' on all stamps in Row 10. Missing stop after 'ST' corrected (printed *before* 1d. third printing). Numbered 4801 to 14400.

Third printing. On paper without watermark. Shows wide fount 'No.' on all stamps in Row 10. Missing stop after 'ST' corrected, but missing stop after 'LUCIA' occurs on R. 4/4 and 9/2 (printed *after* 1d. third printing). Numbered 14401 to 16800.

The handstamped numbers were applied at the Post Office using a numbering machine. Mistakes in the numbering on the 1d. were sometimes partially erased and then corrected with a second strike, either of the complete number or of incorrect digits, using a machine with a smaller fount.

D **2**

D **3**

(Typo D.L.R.)

1933–47. Wmk Mult Script CA. P 14.

D3	D **2**	1d. black	6·00	8·50
D4		2d. black	24·00	11·00
D5		4d. black (28.6.47)	13·00	55·00
D6		8d. black (28.6.47)	15·00	65·00
D3/D6 *Set of* 4			50·00	£120
D3s/D6s Perf 'SPECIMEN' *Set of* 4			£150	

1949 (1 Oct)–**52**. Value in cents. Typo. Wmk Mult Script CA. P 14.

D7	D **3**	2c. black	3·00	30·00
		a. Chalk-surfaced paper (27.11.52)	10	9·50
		ab. Error. Crown missing, W **9a**	£200	
		ac. Error. St Edward's Crown, W **9b**	38·00	
D8		4c. black	3·50	24·00
		a. Chalk-surfaced paper (27.11.52)	50	14·00
		ab. Error. Crown missing, W **9a**	£275	
		ac. Error. St Edward's Crown, W **9b**	55·00	
D9		8c. black	3·25	30·00
		a. Chalk-surfaced paper (27.11.52)	2·25	50·00
		ac. Error. St Edward's Crown, W **9b**	£350	
D10		16c. black	15·00	70·00
		a. Chalk-surfaced paper (27.11.52)	3·75	65·00
		ac. Error. St Edward's Crown, W **9b**	£475	
D7/D10 *Set of* 4			22·00	£140
D7a/D10a *Set of* 4			6·00	£120

1965 (9 Mar). As Nos. D7/D8, but wmk w **12**. Ordinary paper. P 14.

D11	D **3**	2c. black	50	14·00
D12		4c. black	1·00	15·00

Nos. D9a, D10a and D11/D12 exist with a similar overprint to T **49** in red (*Price for set of* 4 £100 *mint*).

POSTAL FISCAL STAMPS

Nos. F1/F28 were authorised for postal use from 14 April 1885.

CANCELLATIONS. Many used examples of the Postal Fiscal stamps have had previous pen cancellations removed before being used postally.

SHILLING STAMP (F **1**) — One Penny Stamp (F **2**) — Stamp (F **3**)

1881. Wmk Crown CC. P 14.

(a) Surch as T F **1**

F1	**1**	ONE PENNY STAMP, black (C.)	80·00	50·00
		a. Surch inverted	£750	£750
		b. Surch double	£650	£700
F2		FOUR PENNY STAMP, yellow	£130	80·00
		a. Bisected (2d.) (*on cover*)	†	—
F3		SIX PENCE STAMP, mauve	£200	£150
F4		SHILLING STAMP, orange	£150	85·00
		a. 'SHILEING'	£1100	£750
		b. 'SHILDING'	£700	£650

(b) Surch as T F **2**

F7	**1**	One Penny Stamp, black (R.)	80·00	55·00
		a. Surch double	£750	
		w. Wmk inverted		
F8		Four Pence Stamp, yellow	£120	65·00
		x. Wmk reversed		
F9		Six Pence Stamp, mauve	£150	65·00
F10		Shilling Stamp, orange	£160	85·00

(c) Nos. 23 and 29 Surch as T F **3**

F11	**1**	HALFPENNY Stamp, green	75·00	55·00
		a. 'Stamp' double	£450	£450
F12		ONE SHILLING Stamp, orange (wmk Crown CA)	£150	75·00
		a. 'Stamp' double	£450	£500

Fiscally used examples are known of No. F1b showing one red and one black surcharge and No. F9 with surcharge double.

FOUR PENCE REVENUE (F **4**) — Revenue (F **5**) — REVENUE (F **6**)

1882. Surch as T F **4** by D.L.R. Wmk Crown CA.

(a) P 14

F13	**1**	1d. black (C.)	55·00	25·00
F14		2d. pale blue	50·00	12·00
F15		3d. deep blue (C.)	£100	50·00
F16		4d. yellow	50·00	4·00
F17		6d. mauve	75·00	40·00
		x. Wmk reversed		

(b) P 12

F18	**1**	1d. black (C.)	55·00	30·00
F19		3d. deep blue (C.)	80·00	20·00
F20		1s. orange	80·00	13·00

The 1d. and 2d. exist as imperforate proofs.

1883. Nos. 25, 26, 30 and 32 optd locally as T F **5**.

(a) Word 11 mm long

F21		1d. black (C.)	50·00	50·00
		a. Opt inverted		
		b. Opt double	£375	£350

(b) Word 13 mm

F22		1d. black (C.)	—	65·00

(c) Word 15½ mm

F23		½d. green	—	60·00
		a. 'Revenue' double	—	£275
F24		1d. black (C.)	50·00	10·00
		a. 'Revenue' double	£170	
		b. 'Revenue' triple	£325	
		c. 'Revenue' double, one inverted	£300	£300
F25		1d. rose (No. 32)	—	70·00
F26		4d. yellow	—	£100

1884–85. Optd with T F **6**. Wmk Crown CA. P 14.

F27	**5**	1d. slate (C.)	48·00	25·00
F28		1d. dull mauve (Die I) (1885)	48·00	14·00

No. F27 exists as an imperforate proof.

St Vincent

Although postal markings for St Vincent are recorded as early as 1793 it was not until 1852 that the British GPO opened a branch office at Kingstown, the island's capital.

The stamps of Great Britain were used between May 1858 and the end of April 1860. From 1 May in that year the local authorities assumed responsibility for the postal services and fell back on the use of No. CC 1 until the introduction of St Vincent stamps in 1861.

KINGSTOWN

CROWNED-CIRCLE HANDSTAMPS

CC **1**

CC1	CC **1** ST. VINCENT (R.) (30.1.1852)	*Price on cover*	£950

Stamps of GREAT BRITAIN cancelled 'A10' as T Z **1** of Jamaica.

1858–60.

Z1	1d. rose-red (1857), perf 14	£700
Z2	2d. blue (1855)	
Z3	4d. rose (1857)	£425
Z4	6d. lilac (1856)	£325
Z5	1s. green (1856)	£2000

PRICES FOR STAMPS ON COVER TO 1945

No. 1	*from* × 50
No. 2	*from* × 15
Nos. 4/5	*from* × 40
Nos. 6/7	*from* × 20
No. 8	—
No. 9	*from* × 12
No. 10	—
No. 11	*from* × 15
Nos. 12/13	*from* × 20
No. 14	*from* × 10
No. 15	*from* × 50
No. 16	*from* × 15
No. 17	*from* × 10
No. 18	*from* × 100
No. 19	*from* × 20
Nos. 20/21	*from* × 7
No. 22	*from* × 100
No. 23	*from* × 25
No. 24	*from* × 15
No. 25	*from* × 25
No. 26	—
No. 26a	*from* × 50
Nos. 27/28	—
No. 29	*from* × 100
Nos. 30/31	*from* × 30
Nos. 32/34	—
No. 35	*from* × 30
Nos. 36/37	*from* × 50
No. 38	*from* × 10
Nos. 39/40	*from* × 100
No. 41	*from* × 25
Nos. 42/45	*from* × 8
No. 46	*from* × 15
Nos. 47/54	*from* × 4
Nos. 55/58	*from* × 8
No. 59	*from* × 10
No. 60	*from* × 6
Nos. 61/63	*from* × 8
Nos. 67/75	*from* × 3
Nos. 76/84	*from* × 2
Nos. 85/92	*from* × 3
No. 93	—
Nos. 94/98	*from* × 3
Nos. 99/107	*from* × 2
Nos. 108/119	*from* × 3
No. 120	—
No. 121	*from* × 3
No. 122	*from* × 5
No. 123	—
No. 124	*from* × 5
Nos. 126/129	*from* × 10
Nos. 131/145	*from* × 3
Nos. 146/148	*from* × 6
Nos. 149/159	*from* × 2

CROWN COLONY

1

(2)

3

(Types **1**, **3** and **7** recess P.B.)

1861 (8 May). No Wmk. Rough to intermediate perf 14 to 16.

1	1	1d. rose-red	50·00	14·00
		a. Imperf vert (horiz pair)	£350	
		b. Imperf (pair)	£275	
2		6d. deep yellow-green	£7500	£200

The perforations on the 1d. are usually rough, but individual examples can be found on which some, or all, of the holes have the appearance of the intermediate perforations. All examples of the 6d. show intermediate perforations.

Imperforate examples, possibly proofs, exist of the 1d. rose-red and 6d. deep green handstamped 'CANCELLED' in oval of bars (see note on Perkins Bacon 'CANCELLED' in Catalogue Introduction). (*Price* 1d. £8500, 6d. £9500).

1862 (Sept). No wmk. Rough perf 14 to 16.

4	1	6d. deep green	60·00	19·00
		a. Imperf between (horiz pair)	£13000	£14000
		b. Imperf (pair)	£1100	

1862 (Dec)–**68**. No wmk.

(a) P 11 to 12½

5	1	1d. rose-red	42·00	20·00
6		4d. deep blue (*shades*) (1866)	£275	£110
		a. Imperf between (horiz pair)	†	—
7		6d. deep green (7.68)	£225	75·00
8		1s. slate-grey (8.66)	£2500	£900

(b) P 14 to 16

9	1	1s. slate-grey (*shades*) (8.66)	£375	£140

(c) P 11 to 12½×14 to 16

10	1	1d. rose-red (1866)	£6000	£1100
11		1s. slate-grey (*shades*) (8.66)	£275	£120

1869 (Apr–Sept). Colours changed. No wmk. P 11 to 12½.

12	1	4d. yellow (9.69)	£350	£160
13		1s. indigo	£375	90·00
14		1s. brown (9.69)	£500	£160

1871 (Apr). Wmk Small Star, W w **2**. Rough perf 14 to 16.

15	1	1d. black	60·00	15·00
		a. Imperf between (vert pair)	£17000	
16		6d. deep green	£325	70·00
		a. Wmk sideways	—	90·00

1872 (June). Colour changed. W w **2** (sideways). P 11 to 12½.

17	1	1s. deep rose-red	£750	£140

1872–75. W w **2** (sideways).

(a) Perf about 15

18	1	1d. black (*shades*) (11.72)	60·00	15·00
		a. Wmk upright	70·00	16·00
19		6d. dull blue-green (*shades*) (1873)	£2000	50·00
		b. Deep blue-green (1875)	£1500	50·00
		c. Wmk upright	£2250	

(b) P 11 to 12½×15

20	1	1s. lilac-rose (1873)	£5500	£350

1875. Colour changed. W w **2** (sideways). P 11 to 12½.

21		1s. claret	£600	£250

1875–78. W w **2** (sideways).

(a) P 11 to 12½×15

22	1	1d. black (*shades*) (4.75)	85·00	16·00
		a. Imperf between (horiz pair)	†	£23000
		b. Wmk upright	£150	50·00
23		6d. pale green (1877)	£650	50·00
24		1s. vermilion (2.77)	£1000	85·00
		a. Imperf vert (horiz pair)		

(b) P 11 to 12½

25	1	4d. deep blue (7.77)	£550	90·00

(c) Perf about 15

26	1	6d. pale green (3.77)	£1600	£450
		a. Wmk upright. *Lt yellow-green* (1878)	£700	29·00
27		1s. vermilion (1878?)	†	£40000

Only two examples of No. 27 have been recorded. The 1s vermilion is also known apparently imperforate and used.

1880 (May). No. 19*b* divided vertically by a line of perforation gauging 12, and surch locally with T **2** in red.

28	1	1d. on half 6d. deep blue-green	£550	£375
		a. Unsevered pair	£2000	£1200

1880 (June). W w **2** (sideways on 1d., 6d. and 1s.). P 11 to 12½.

29	1	1d. olive-green	£180	5·50
30		6d. bright green	£475	70·00
31		1s. bright vermilion	£800	60·00
		a. Imperf between (horiz pair)	£25000	
32	3	5s. rose-red	£1100	£1500
		a. Imperf	£7500	

d 1/2

(4)

ONE PENNY

(5)

4d

(6)

1881. Nos. 30/31 surch locally. No. 33 is divided vertically as No. 28.

33	4	½d. on half 6d. bright green (R.) (1.9)	£160	£170
		a. Unsevered pair	£475	£500
		b. Fraction bar omitted (pair with and without bar)	£4250	£5000
34	5	1d. on 6d. bright green (30.11)	£475	£350
35	6	4d. on 1s. bright vermilion (28.11)	£1600	£800
		a. 3mm space between '4d.' and bar	£3000	£2250

No. 33 exists showing the '1' of '½' with a straight serif. Some examples come from a constant variety on R. 6/20, but others are the result of faulty type.

It is believed that T **4** was applied as a setting of 36 (6×6) surcharges repeated three times on each sheet across rows 1 to 9. The missing fraction bar occurs on R. 6/3 of the setting.

The tenth vertical row of stamps appears to have been surcharged from a separate setting of 12 (2×6) on which a constant 'straight serif' flaw occurs on the bottom right half-stamp.

Three unused single copies of No. 33 are known with the surcharge omitted.

It is believed that Nos. 34 and 35 were surcharged in settings of 30 (10×3).

No. 34 was only on sale between the 30 November and 3 December when supplies of No. 37 became available.

7

2½ PENCE

(8)

1d
2½ PENCE

(9)

1881 (3 Dec). W w **2**. P 11 to 12½.

36	7	½d. orange (*shades*)	8·50	12·00
37	1	1d. drab (*shades*)	£700	16·00
38		4d. bright blue	£1200	£120
		a. Imperf between (horiz pair)		

(Recess D.L.R. from Perkins Bacon plates)

1882 (Nov)–**83**. No. 40 is surch with T **8**. Wmk Crown CA. P 14.

39	1	1d. drab	75·00	3·00
		x. Wmk reversed	95·00	10·00
40		2½d. on 1d. lake (1883)	30·00	1·50
		w. Wmk inverted	85·00	12·00
		x. Wmk reversed	42·00	5·00
		y. Wmk inverted and reversed		
41		4d. ultramarine	£650	75·00
		a. Dull ultramarine (wmk reversed)	£1000	£350
		w. Wmk inverted		
		x. Wmk reversed	£450	40·00
		y. Wmk inverted and reversed		

1883–84. Wmk Crown CA. P 12.

42	7	½d. green (1884)	£110	38·00
		x. Wmk reversed	—	£160
43	1	4d. ultramarine-blue	£750	50·00
		a. Grey-blue	£2250	£250
		w. Wmk inverted		
		x. Wmk reversed	£450	24·00
		y. Wmk inverted and reversed	†	£200
44		6d. bright green	£150	£300
		x. Wmk reversed	£400	
45		1s. orange-vermilion	£150	60·00
		x. Wmk reversed	£400	£130

The ½d. orange, 1d. rose-red, 1d. milky blue (without surcharge) and 5s. carmine-lake which were formerly listed are now considered to be colour trials. They are, however, of great interest (*Prices un.* ½d. £950, 1d. red £1000, 1d. blue £1300, 5s. £2500).

1885 (Mar). No. 40 further surch locally as in T **9**.

46	1	1d. on 2½d. on 1d. lake	42·00	35·00
		w. Wmk inverted	£100	
		x. Wmk reversed	42·00	35·00

Stamps with three cancelling bars instead of two are considered to be proofs.

1885–93. No. 49 is surch with T **8**. Wmk Crown CA. P 14.

47	7	½d. green	1·00	60
		a. Deep green	2·50	60
		w. Wmk inverted	50·00	17·00
		x. Wmk reversed	17·00	20·00
48	1	1d. rose-red	4·25	1·00
		a. Rose (1886)	6·00	1·75
		b. Red (1887)	4·25	85
		c. Carmine-red (1889)	24·00	3·75
		w. Wmk inverted		
		x. Wmk reversed	7·00	1·50
49		2½d. on 1d. milky blue (1889)	32·00	11·00
		x. Wmk reversed		
50		4d. red-brown	£950	22·00
		x. Wmk reversed	—	£110
51		4d. purple-brown (1886)	£100	75
		a. Chocolate (1887)	£100	1·40
		w. Wmk inverted	—	65·00
		x. Wmk reversed	£190	12·00
		y. Wmk inverted and reversed		
52		6d. violet (1888)	£180	£225
		w. Wmk inverted	£225	£275
		ws. Optd 'SPECIMEN'	85·00	
		x. Wmk reversed	£650	
53	3	5s. lake (1888)	30·00	55·00
		a. Printed both sides	£7500	
		b. Brown-lake (1893)	35·00	55·00
		w. Wmk inverted	£500	
		49s, 51s/52s Optd 'SPECIMEN' *Set of 3*	£200	

2½d.

(10)

5 PENCE

(11)

1890 (Aug). No. 51*a* surch locally with T **10**.

54	1	2½d. on 4d. chocolate	80·00	£120
		a. No fraction bar (R. 1/7, 2/4)	£400	£500

1890–93. No. 55 is surch with T **8**. Colours changed. Wmk Crown CA. P 14.

55	1	2½d. on 1d. grey-blue (1890)	25·00	55
		a. Blue (1893)	1·75	35
		b. Surch double	†	£3250
		w. Wmk inverted	†	£100
		x. Wmk reversed	45·00	35·00

56 4d. yellow (1893) 1·75 15·00
s. Optd 'SPECIMEN' 35·00
57 6d. dull purple (1891) 3·75 25·00
58 1s. orange (1891) 5·50 18·00
a. Red-orange (1892) 14·00 23·00
ax. Wmk reversed £100

Apart from the shades, Nos. 49 and 55/55*a* can be differentiated by the perforations, which are always comb on No. 49 and line on Nos. 55/55*a*.

1892 (Nov). No. 51*a* surch locally with T **11**, in purple.

59 **1** 5d. on 4d. chocolate 45·00 60·00
s. Optd '*specimen*' 50·00
sa. Error. '*spicemen*' (R.3/3) £1300

The overprint also included two ornaments in the upper corners of the stamp.

Some letters are known double due to loose type, the best known being the first 'E', but they are not constant.

FIVE PENCE (12) 13 14

Short 'F' (R. 5/1)

1893–94. Surch with T **12**. Wmk Crown CA. P 14.

60 **1** 5d. on 6d. carmine-lake 21·00 30·00
a. Deep lake (1893) 3·25 2·00
b. Lake (1894) 3·75 4·25
c. Surch double £6000 £3000
d. Short 'F' 42·00 45·00
s. Optd 'SPECIMEN' 50·00

(Recess D.L.R.)

1897 (13 July). New values. Wmk Crown CA. P 14.

61 **1** 2½d. blue 13·00 2·25
62 5d. sepia 11·00 32·00
61s/62s Optd 'SPECIMEN' *Set of 2* 70·00

1897 (6 Oct). Surch as T **12**. Wmk Crown CA. P 14.

63 **1** 3d. on 1d. mauve 5·00 26·00
a. Red-mauve 16·00 50·00
s. Optd 'SPECIMEN' 45·00

The 3d. on 6d. in lilac is a fiscal stamp from which the 'REVENUE' overprint was omitted. This stamp is also known with reversed watermark.

(Typo D.L.R.)

1899 (1 Jan). Wmk Crown CA. P 14.

67 **13** ½d. dull mauve and green 2·75 2·50
68 1d. dull mauve and carmine 4·50 1·50
w. Wmk inverted £300 £250
69 2½d. dull mauve and blue 9·00 3·00
70 3d. dull mauve and olive 4·00 23·00
71 4d. dull mauve and orange 7·00 27·00
72 5d. dull mauve and black 8·00 23·00
73 6d. dull mauve and brown 13·00 50·00
74 **14** 1s. green and carmine 17·00 60·00
75 5s. green and blue £100 £170
67/75 *Set of 9* £150 £325
67s/75s Optd 'SPECIMEN' *Set of 9* £170

15 16

(Typo D.L.R.)

1902. Wmk Crown CA. P 14.

76 **15** ½d. dull purple and green 4·25 70
77 1d. dull purple and carmine 4·25 30
78 **16** 2d. dull purple and black 6·50 7·50
79 **15** 2½d. dull purple and blue 5·00 4·00
80 3d. dull purple and olive 5·00 8·50
81 6d. dull purple and brown 11·00 50·00
82 **16** 1s. green and carmine 35·00 70·00
83 **15** 2s. green and violet 25·00 60·00
84 **16** 5s. green and blue 80·00 £140
76/84 *Set of 9* £150 £300
76s/84s Optd 'SPECIMEN' *Set of 9* £170

1904–11. Ordinary paper (½d., 1d., 1s.) or chalk-surfaced paper (others). Wmk Mult Crown CA. P 14.

85 **15** ½d. dull purple and green (1905) 7·50 9·00
a. Chalk-surfaced paper 1·25 1·25
86 1d. dull purple and carmine 28·00 1·50
a. Chalk-surfaced paper 28·00 1·50
88 2½d. dull purple and blue (1906) 17·00 50·00
89 6d. dull purple and brown (1905) 16·00 50·00
90 **16** 1s. green and carmine (1906) 38·00 60·00
a. Chalk-surfaced paper 15·00 70·00
91 **15** 2s. purple and bright blue/*blue* (3.09?) 23·00 50·00
92 **16** 5s. green and red/*yellow* (3.09?) 17·00 55·00
93 £1 purple and black/*red* (22.7.11) £275 £350
85/93 *Set of 8* £350 £500
91s/93s Optd 'SPECIMEN' *Set of 3* £190

Examples of most values are known showing a forged Kingstown postmark code letter 'O', dated 'JA 7 10' or a forged Calliaqua postmark dated 'SP 20 09'. Both have also been seen on some values of the 1899 and 1902 issues.

17 18

(Recess D.L.R.)

1907–08. Wmk Mult Crown CA. P 14.

94 **17** ½d. green (2.7.07) 3·50 2·50
95 1d. carmine (26.4.07) 4·00 15
96 2d. orange (5.08) 1·50 6·50
97 2½d. blue (8.07) 42·00 8·50
98 3d. violet (1.6.07) 8·00 17·00
94/98 *Set of 5* 55·00 30·00
94s/98s Optd 'SPECIMEN' *Set of 5* £130

1909. No dot below 'd'. Wmk Mult Crown CA. P 14.

99 **18** 1d. carmine (3.09) 1·50 30
100 6d. dull purple (16.1.09) 9·00 48·00
101 1s. black/*green* (16.1.09) 4·25 10·00
99/101 *Set of 3* 13·00 50·00
99s/101s Optd 'SPECIMEN' *Set of 3* 80·00

1909 (Nov)–**11.** T **18**, redrawn (dot below 'd', as in T **17**). Wmk Mult Crown CA. P 14.

102 ½d. green (31.10.10) 4·50 60
w. Wmk inverted £150
103 1d. carmine 5·50 20
104 2d. grey (3.8.11) 6·50 15·00
105 2½d. ultramarine (25.7.10) 8·00 3·75
106 3d. purple/*yellow* 2·50 15·00
107 6d. dull purple 22·00 16·00
102/107 *Set of 6* 45·00 45·00
102s, 104s/106s Optd 'SPECIMEN' *Set of 4* 90·00

19 ONE PENNY. (20)

(Recess D.L.R.)

1913 (1 Jan)–**17.** Wmk Mult Crown CA. P 14.

108 **19** ½d. green 75 20
109 1d. red 80 30
a. Rose-red 1·00 55
b. Scarlet (1.17) 19·00 5·00
w. Wmk inverted £120
y. Wmk inverted and reversed £120
110 2d. grey 8·00 38·00
a. Slate 3·00 38·00
111 2½d. ultramarine 75 75
x. Wmk reversed £250
112 3d. purple/*yellow* 80 5·00
a. On lemon 2·75 12·00
aw. Wmk inverted £160
ax. Wmk reversed £160
b. On pale yellow 2·50 9·50
ba. 'A' of 'CA' missing from wmk £500
113 4d. red/*yellow* 80 2·00
114 5d. olive-green (7.11.13) 2·25 16·00
x. Wmk reversed £170
115 6d. claret 2·00 4·50
116 1s. black/*green* 1·50 3·75
117 1s. bistre (1.5.14) 4·00 32·00
118 **18** 2s. blue and purple 4·75 40·00
119 5s. carmine and myrtle 13·00 60·00
x. Wmk reversed £250
120 £1 mauve and black £120 £180
108/120 *Set of 13* £140 £350
108s/120s Optd 'SPECIMEN' *Set of 13* £250

Nos. 118/120 are from new centre and frame dies, the motto 'PAX ET JUSTITIA' being slightly over 7 mm long, as against just over 8 mm in Nos. 99 to 107.

Nos. 139/141 are also from the new dies.

Examples of several values are known showing part strikes of the forged postmarks mentioned below Nos. 85/93.

1915 (30 Jan). No. 116 surch locally with T **20**.

121 **19** 1d. on 1s. black/*green* (R.) 10·00 40·00
a. 'ONE' omitted £1400 £1200
b. 'ONE' double £650
c. 'PENNY' and bar double £650 £650
d. 'PENNY' and bar omitted £1300

The two lines of the surcharge were applied in separate operations, so that the spacing between them varies considerably.

WAR STAMP. (21) WAR STAMP. (22) WAR STAMP (24)

1916 (June). No. 109 optd locally with T **21**.

(a) First and second settings; words 2 to 2½ mm apart

122 **19** 1d. red 13·00 24·00
a. Opt double £180 £180
b. Comma for stop 13·00 30·00
w. Wmk inverted

In the first printing every second stamp has the comma for stop. The second printing of this setting has full stops only. These two printings can therefore only be distinguished in blocks or pairs.

(b) Third setting; words only 1½ mm apart

123 **19** 1d. red £130
a. Opt double £1300

Stamps of the first setting are offered as this rare one. Care must be taken to see that the distance between the lines is not over 1½ mm.

*(c) Fourth setting; optd with T **22**. Words 3½ mm apart*

124 **19** 1d. carmine-red 3·00 26·00
a. Opt double £250
w. Wmk inverted
y. Wmk inverted and reversed

1916 (Aug)–**18.** T **19**, from new printings, optd with T **24** by De La Rue.

126 1d. carmine-red 1·50 2·25
s. Optd 'SPECIMEN' 60·00
w. Wmk inverted
x. Wmk reversed
y. Wmk inverted and reversed £150
127 1d. pale rose-red 1·50 2·25
w. Wmk inverted £100
x. Wmk reversed — £200
128 1d. deep rose-red 1·75 2·25
129 1d. pale scarlet (1918) 3·50 4·75
y. Wmk inverted and reversed — £200

1921–32. Wmk Mult Script CA. P 14.

131 **19** ½d. green (3.21) 1·75 30
x. Wmk reversed † £275
132 1d. carmine (6.21) 1·00 80
a. Red 2·50 15
x. Wmk reversed — £250
132*b* 1½d. brown (1.12.32) 6·50 15
133 2d. grey (3.22) 2·50 1·00
133*a* 2½d. bright blue (12.25) 1·25 1·50
134 3d. bright blue (3.22) 1·00 6·00
x. Wmk reversed † £250
135 3d. purple/*yellow* (1.12.26) 1·00 1·50
135*a* 4d. red/*yellow* (9.30) 1·75 6·00
136 5d. sage-green (8.3.24) 1·00 12·00
137 6d. claret (1.11.27) 1·50 3·50
138 1s. bistre-brown (9.21) 6·00 30·00
a. Ochre (1927) 9·00 17·00
139 **18** 2s. blue and purple (8.3.24) 7·50 13·00
140 5s. carmine and myrtle (8.3.24) 18·00 45·00
141 £1 mauve and black (9.28) £120 £140
131/141 *Set of 14* £150 £200
131s/141s Optd or Perf (1½d., 4d., £1) 'SPECIMEN' *Set of 14* £350

Examples of Nos. 140/141 are known with forged postmarks, including part strikes of those mentioned above, and others from Kingstown dated '6 MY 35' and '16 MY 41'.

1935 (6 May). Silver Jubilee. As Nos. 91/94 of Antigua, but ptd by Waterlow. P 11×12.

142 1d. deep blue and scarlet 50 2·50
143 1½d. ultramarine and grey 1·00 4·75
144 2½d. brown and deep blue 2·00 6·00
145 1s. slate and purple 8·50 15·00
l. Kite and horizontal log £500 £650
142/145 *Set of 4* 11·00 25·00
142s/145s Perf 'SPECIMEN' *Set of 4* £100

For illustration of plate variety see Omnibus section following Zanzibar.

1937 (12 May). Coronation. As Nos. 95/7 of Antigua. P 11×11½.

146 1d. violet 35 1·25
147 1½d. carmine 40 1·25
148 2½d. blue 45 2·25
146/148 *Set of 3* 1·10 4·25
146s/148s Perf 'SPECIMEN' *Set of 3* 80·00

25

26 Young's Island and Fort Duvernette

27 Kingstown and Fort Charlotte

28 Bathing Beach at Villa

29 Victoria Park, Kingstown

NEW CONSTITUTION 1951 (29a)

(Recess B.W.)

1938 (11 Mar)–**47.** Wmk Mult Script CA. P 12.

149 **25** ½d. blue and green 20 10
150 **26** 1d. blue and lake-brown 20 10
151 **27** 1½d. green and scarlet 20 10
152 **25** 2d. green and black 40 35
153 **28** 2½d. blue-black and blue-green 20 40
153*a* **29** 2½d. green and purple-brown (14.1.47) 40 20
154 **25** 3d. orange and purple 20 10
154*a* **28** 3½d. blue-black and blue-green (1.4.47) 75 2·50
155 **25** 6d. black and lake 1·50 40
156 **29** 1s. purple and green 1·50 80
157 **25** 2s. blue and purple 8·00 75
157*a* 2s.6d. red-brown and blue (14.1.47) 1·25 3·50
158 5s. scarlet and deep green 20·00 2·50
158*a* 10s. violet and brown (14.1.47) 7·50 9·00
aw. Wmk inverted £12000 £4250
159 £1 purple and black 28·00 15·00
149/159 *Set of 15* 60·00 32·00
149s/159s Perf 'SPECIMEN' *Set of 15* £325

1946 (15 Oct). Victory. As Nos. 110/111 of Antigua.

160 1½d. carmine 10 10
161 3½d. blue 10 10
sa. 'SPECIMEN' double £500
160s/161s Perf 'SPECIMEN' *Set of 2* 75·00

1948 (30 Nov). Royal Silver Wedding. As Nos. 112/113 of Antigua.

162		1½d. scarlet	10	10
163		£1 bright purple	28·00	40·00

No. 163 was originally printed in black, but later changed to bright purple. The only surviving examples in the original colour are in the Royal Philatelic Collection.

(New Currency. 100 cents = 1 West Indian dollar)

1949 (26 Mar)–**52**. Value in cents and dollars. Wmk Mult Script CA. P 12.

164	**25**	1c. blue and green	20	1·75
164*a*		1c. green and black (10.6.52)	50	2·50
165	**26**	2c. blue and lake-brown	15	50
166	**27**	3c. green and scarlet	50	1·00
166*a*	**25**	3c. orange and purple (10.6.52)	1·00	2·50
167		4c. green and black	35	20
167*a*		4c. blue and green (10.6.52)	1·00	20
168	**29**	5c. green and purple-brown	15	10
169	**25**	6c. orange and purple	50	1·25
169*a*	**27**	6c. green and scarlet (10.6.52)	60	2·25
170	**28**	7c. blue-black and blue-green	6·50	1·50
170*a*		10c. blue-black and blue-green (10.6.52)	1·00	20
171	**25**	12c. black and lake	35	15
172	**29**	24c. purple and green	35	55
173	**25**	48c. blue and purple	7·50	9·00
174		60c. red-brown and blue	6·00	8·50
175		$1.20 scarlet and deep green	6·50	4·50
176		$2.40 violet and brown	6·50	10·00
177		$4.80 purple and black	15·00	20·00
164/177 *Set of* 19			45·00	55·00

1949 (10 Oct). 75th Anniversary of UPU. As Nos. 114/117 of Antigua.

178		5c. blue	20	20
179		6c. purple	1·50	2·25
180		12c. magenta	20	2·25
181		24c. blue-green	20	1·00
		a. 'C' of 'CA' missing from wmk	—	£750
178/181 *Set of* 4			1·90	5·25

1951 (16 Feb). Inauguration of BWI University College. As Nos. 118/119 of Antigua.

182		3c. deep green and scarlet	30	65
183		12c. black and purple	30	1·75

1951 (21 Sept). New Constitution. Optd with T **29a** by B.W.

184	**27**	3c. green and scarlet	20	1·75
185	**25**	4c. green and black	20	60
186	**29**	5c. green and purple-brown	20	60
187	**25**	12c. black and lake	1·25	1·25
184/187 *Set of* 4			1·60	3·75

1953 (2 June). Coronation. As No. 120 of Antigua.

188		4c. black and green	30	20

30 31

(Recess Waterlow (until 1961), then D.L.R.)

1955 (16 Sept)–**63**. Wmk Mult Script CA. P 13½×14 (T **30**) or 14 (T **31**).

189	**30**	1c. orange	10	10
		a. Deep orange (11.12.62)	11·00	7·00
190		2c. ultramarine	10	10
		a. Blue (26.9.61)	4·50	2·25
191		3c. slate	30	10
192		4c. brown	20	10
193		5c. scarlet	60	10
194		10c. reddish violet	20	65
		a. Deep lilac (12.2.58)	2·50	10
195		15c. deep blue	2·50	1·00
196		20c. green	60	10
197		25c. black-brown	50	10
198	**31**	50c. red-brown	5·00	3·75
		a. Chocolate (11.6.58)	6·00	1·50
		aw. Wmk inverted	†	£1000
199		$1 myrtle-green	10·00	1·00
		a. Deep myrtle-green (11.6.58)	22·00	4·25
		b. Deep yellowish green (15.1.63)	55·00	20·00
200		$2.50 deep blue	11·00	13·00
		a. Indigo-blue (30.7.62)	60·00	22·00
189/200 *Set of* 12			28·00	15·00

See also Nos. 207/220.

1958 (22 Apr). Inauguration of British Caribbean Federation. As Nos. 135/137 of Antigua.

201		3c. deep green	75	20
202		6c. blue	80	1·25
203		12c. scarlet	90	50
201/203 *Set of* 3			2·25	1·75

MINISTERIAL GOVERNMENT

1963 (4 June). Freedom from Hunger. As No. 146 of Antigua.

204		8c. reddish violet	45	50

1963 (2 Sept). Red Cross Centenary. As Nos. 147/148 of Antigua.

205		4c. red and black	15	20
206		8c. red and blue	35	50

(Recess D.L.R.)

1964–65. As 1955–1963 but wmk w **12**.

(a) P 12½ (14 Jan–Feb 1964)

207	**30**	10c. deep lilac	30	20
208		15c. deep blue	30	50
209		20c. green (24.2.64*)	1·75	25
210		25c. black-brown	30	3·00
211	**31**	50c. chocolate	2·50	5·00
207/211 *Set of* 5			4·75	8·00

*(b) P 13×14 (T **30**) or 14 (T **31**)*

212	**30**	1c. orange (15.12.64)	15	10
213		2c. blue (15.12.64)	15	10
214		3c. slate (15.12.64)	50	10
215		5c. scarlet (15.12.64)	15	10
216		10c. deep lilac (15.12.64)	1·00	10
217		15c. deep blue (9.11.64)	1·00	30
218		20c. green (1964)	45	10
		w. Wmk inverted		
219		25c. black-brown (20.10.64)	1·00	15
220	**31**	50c. chocolate (18.1.65)	9·00	7·00
212/220 *Set of* 9			12·00	7·00

* This is the earliest known date recorded in St Vincent although it may have been put on sale on 14.1.64.

32 Scout Badge and Proficiency Badges

33 Tropical Fruits

(Des V. Whiteley. Litho Harrison)

1964 (23 Nov). 50th Anniversary of St Vincent Boy Scouts Association. W w **12**. P 14½.

221	**32**	1c. yellow-green and chocolate	10	10
222		4c. blue and brown-purple	10	10
223		20c. yellow and black-violet	30	10
224		50c. red and bronze-green	45	70
221/224 *Set of* 4			85	90

(Des V. Whiteley. Photo Harrison)

1965 (23 Mar). Botanic Gardens Bicentenary. T **33** and similar multicoloured designs. W w **12**. P 14½×13½ (horiz) or 13½×14½ (vert).

225		1c. Type **33**	10	10
226		4c. Breadfruit and HMS *Providence* (sloop), 1793	10	10
227		25c. Doric Temple and pond (*vert*)	15	10
228		40c. Talipot Palm and Doric Temple (*vert*)	30	1·25
225/228 *Set of* 4			60	1·40

1965 (17 May). ITU Centenary. As Nos. 166/167 of Antigua.

229		4c. light blue and light olive-green	15	10
230		48c. ochre-yellow and orange	35	45

37 Boat-building, Bequia (inscr 'BEOUIA')

(Des M. Goaman. Photo Harrison)

1965 (16 Aug)–**67**. T **37** and similar multicoloured designs. W w **12**. P 14½×13½ (horiz designs) or 13½×14½ (vert).

231		1c. Type **37** ('BEOUIA')	10	1·00
231*a*		1c. Type **37** ('BEQUIA') (27.6.67)	65	40
232		2c. Friendship Beach, Bequia	10	10
233		3c. Terminal Building, Amos Vale Airport	1·00	10
		w. Wmk inverted	6·00	
234		4c. Woman with bananas (*vert*)	1·00	30
		w. Wmk inverted		
235		5c. Crater Lake	15	10
236		6c. Carib Stone (*vert*)	15	40
237		8c. Arrowroot (*vert*)	30	10
238		10c. Owia Salt Pond	30	10
239		12c. Deep water wharf	70	10
		w. Wmk inverted	†	£100
240		20c. Sea Island cotton (*vert*)	30	10
		w. Wmk inverted	—	50·00
241		25c. Map of St Vincent and islands (*vert*)	35	10
		w. Wmk inverted	50·00	
242		50c. Breadfruit (*vert*)	50	30
243		$1 Baleine Falls (*vert*)	3·00	30
244		$2.50 St Vincent Amazon (*vert*)	20·00	11·00
245		$5 Arms of St Vincent (*vert*)	3·00	14·00
231/245 *Set of* 16			27·00	25·00

The 1c. (No. 231*a*), 2c., 3c., 5c. and 10c. exist with PVA gum as well as gum arabic.

See also No. 261.

1966 (24 Jan). Churchill Commemoration. As Nos. 170/173 of Antigua.

246		1c. new blue	10	10
247		4c. deep green	25	10
248		20c. brown	45	30
249		40c. bluish violet	55	1·00
246/249 *Set of* 4			1·25	1·25

1966 (4 Feb). Royal Visit. As Nos. 174/175 of Antigua.

250		4c. black and ultramarine	50	25
251		25c. black and magenta	1·50	1·00

1966 (20 Sept). Inauguration of WHO Headquarters, Geneva. As Nos. 178/179 of Antigua.

252		4c. black, yellow-green and light blue	45	10
253		25c. black, light purple and yellow-brown	80	80

1966 (1 Dec). 20th Anniversary of UNESCO. As Nos. 196/198 of Antigua.

254		4c. slate-violet, red, yellow and orange	25	25
255		8c. orange-yellow, violet and deep olive	50	45
256		25c. black, bright purple and orange	1·50	1·10
254/256 *Set of* 3			2·00	1·60

38 Coastal View of Mount Coke Area

(Des and photo Harrison)

1967 (1 Dec). Autonomous Methodist Church. T **38** and similar horiz designs. Multicoloured. W w **12**. P 14×14½.

257		2c. Type **38**	10	1·10
258		8c. Kingstown Methodist Church	10	10
259		25c. First Licence to perform marriages	25	10
260		35c. Conference Arms	25	10
257/260 *Set of* 4			60	1·25

1968 (20 Feb). As No. 234, but W w **12** sideways.

261		4c. Woman with bananas	30	30

The above exists with PVA gum as well as gum arabic.

39 Meteorological Institute

(Des G. Vasarhelyi. Photo Harrison)

1968 (28 May). World Meteorological Day. W w **12**. P 14×14½.

262	**39**	4c. multicoloured	10	10
263		25c. multicoloured	10	10
264		35c. multicoloured	15	15
262/264 *Set of* 3			30	30

40 Dr. Martin Luther King and Cotton Pickers

(Des V. Whiteley. Litho D.L.R.)

1968 (28 Aug). Martin Luther King Commemoration. W w **12** (sideways). P 13.

265	**40**	5c. multicoloured	10	10
266		25c. multicoloured	10	10
267		35c. multicoloured	15	15
265/267 *Set of* 3			30	30

41 Speaker addressing Demonstrators

42 Scales of Justice and Human Rights Emblem

(Des V. Whiteley. Photo Enschedé)

1968 (1 Nov). Human Rights Year. P 13×14 (3c.) or 14×13 (35c.).

268	**41**	3c. multicoloured	10	10
269	**42**	35c. royal blue and turquoise-blue	20	10

43 Male Masquerader

44 Steel Bandsman

(Des V. Whiteley. Litho Format)

1969 (17 Feb). St Vincent Carnival. Types **43/44** and similar designs. P 14.

270		1c. multicoloured	10	20
271		5c. red and deep chocolate	10	10
272		8c. multicoloured	10	10
273		25c. multicoloured	15	10
270/273 *Set of* 4			40	45

Designs: Horiz—8c. Carnival Revellers. Vert—1c. T **43**; 5c. T **44**; 25c. Queen of Bands.

METHODIST CONFERENCE MAY 1969
(47)

1969 (14 May). Methodist Conference. Nos. 257/258, 241 and 260 optd with T **47**.

274		2c. multicoloured	10	15
275		8c. multicoloured	15	25
276		25c. multicoloured	15	25
277		35c. multicoloured	75	2·00
274/277 *Set of 4*			1·00	2·40

48 'Strength in Unity'

49 Map of CARIFTA Countries

(Des J. Cooter. Litho D.L.R.)

1969 (1 July). First Anniversary of CARIFTA (Caribbean Free Trade Area). W w **12** (sideways on T **48**). P 13.

278	**48**	2c. black, pale buff and red	10	10
279	**49**	5c. multicoloured	15	10
280	**48**	8c. black, pale buff and pale green	10	10
281	**49**	25c. multicoloured	35	15
278/281 *Set of 4*			60	40

ASSOCIATED STATEHOOD

50 Flag of St Vincent

(Des V. Whiteley, based on local designs. Photo Harrison)

1969 (27 Oct). Statehood. T **50** and similar horiz designs. W w **12**. P 14×14½.

282		4c. multicoloured	10	10
283		10c. multicoloured	10	10
284		50c. grey, black and orange	35	20
282/284 *Set of 3*			50	35

Designs: 4c. T **50**; 10c. Battle scene with insets of Petreglyph and Carib chief Chatoyer; 50c. Carib House with maces and scales.

51 Green Heron

(Des J.W. Photo Harrison)

1970 (12 Jan)–**71**. T **51** and similar multicoloured designs. Chalk-surfaced paper. W w **12** (sideways* on 1, 2, 3, 6, 8, 20, 25c., $1, 2.50 and upright on others). P 14.

285		½c. House Wren (*vert*)	10	1·75
286		1c. Type **51**	35	3·25
		a. Glazed, ordinary paper (9.8.71)	30	1·50
		aw. Wmk Crown to right of CA	1·00	1·75
287		2c. Lesser Antillean Bullfinches	15	40
		w. Wmk Crown to right of CA	23·00	
288		3c. St Vincent Amazons	15	30
289		4c. Rufous-throated Solitaire (*vert*)	20	30
290		5c. Red-necked Pigeon (*vert*)	2·50	30
		a. Glazed, ordinary paper (9.8.71)	1·00	30
291		6c. Bananaquits	30	40
292		8c. Purple-throated Carib	40	30
		w. Wmk Crown to right of CA	48·00	
293		10c. Mangrove Cuckoo (*vert*)	30	10
294		12c. Common Black Hawk (*vert*)	40	10
295		20c. Bare-eyed Thrush	40	15
296		25c. Hooded Tanager	50	20
297		50c. Blue Hooded Euphonia	2·00	75
		w. Wmk inverted	75·00	
298		$1 Barn Owl (*vert*)	8·00	1·50
299		$2.50 Yellow-bellied Elaenia (*vert*)	3·50	6·00
300		$5 Ruddy Quail Dove	2·50	6·50
285/300 *Set of 16*			17·00	18·00

* The normal sideways watermark shows Crown to left of CA, *as seen from the back of the stamp.*

Values in this set (and three additional values) were subsequently issued W w **12** upright on 2c., 3c., 6c., 20c. and 30c. and sideways on others.

52 de Havilland DHC-6 Twin Otter 100

(Des R. Granger Barrett. Litho Enschedé)

1970 (13 Mar). 20th Anniversary of Regular Air Services. T **52** and similar horiz designs. Multicoloured. W w **12** (sideways). P 14×13.

301		5c. Type **52**	10	10
302		8c. Grumman G.21 Goose	15	10
303		10c. Hawker Siddeley HS.748	20	10
304		25c. Douglas DC-3	65	30
301/304 *Set of 4*			1·00	55

53 'Children's Nursery'

54 Angel and the Two Marys at the Tomb (stained-glass window)

(Des R. Granger Barrett. Photo Harrison)

1970 (1 June). Centenary of British Red Cross. T **53** and similar horiz designs. Multicoloured. W w **12**. P 14.

305		3c. Type **53**	10	10
306		5c. 'First Aid'	15	10
		w. Wmk inverted	75·00	
307		12c. 'Voluntary Aid Detachment'	35	1·00
		w. Wmk inverted	2·25	
308		25c. 'Blood Transfusion'	55	50
305/308 *Set of 4*			1·00	1·50

(Des L. Curtis. Litho J.W.)

1970 (7 Sept). 150th Anniversary of St George's Cathedral, Kingstown. T **54** and similar multicoloured designs. W w **12** (sideways* on horiz designs). P 14.

309		½c. Type **54**	10	10
310		5c. St George's Cathedral (*horiz*)	10	10
		w. Wmk Crown to right of CA	60·00	
311		25c. Tower, St George's Cathedral	10	10
312		35c. Interior, St George's Cathedral (*horiz*)	15	10
313		50c. Type **54**	20	30
309/313 *Set of 5*			45	60

* The normal sideways watermark shows Crown to left of CA, *as seen from the back of the stamp.*

55 *The Adoration of the Shepherds* (Le Nain)

(Des J. Cooter. Litho Questa)

1970 (23 Nov). Christmas. T **55** and similar vert design. Multicoloured. W w **12** (sideways* on 25c., 50c.). P 14.

314		8c. *The Virgin and Child* (Bellini)	10	10
315		25c. Type **55**	10	10
		w. Wmk Crown to right of CA	1·00	
316		35c. As 8c.	10	10
317		50c. Type **55**	15	20
		w. Wmk Crown to right of CA	1·50	
314/317 *Set of 4*			40	45

* The normal sideways watermark shows Crown to left of CA, *as seen from the back of the stamp.*

Samoa

PRICES FOR STAMPS ON COVER TO 1945

Nos. 1/20 are very rare used on cover.

Nos. 21/40	*from* × 20
Nos. 41/48	*from* × 100
Nos. 49/51	—
No. 52	*from* × 20
Nos. 53/56	—
Nos. 57/64	*from* × 12
Nos. 65/70	*from* × 3
Nos. 71/97	*from* × 20
Nos. 101/109	*from* × 4
Nos. 110/114	—
Nos. 115/121	*from* × 4
Nos. 122/132	—
Nos. 134/164	*from* × 4
Nos. 165/176	—
Nos. 177/214	*from* × 2

INDEPENDENT KINGDOM OF SAMOA

The first postal service in Samoa was organised by C. L. Griffiths, who had earlier run the *Fiji Times* Express post in Suva. In both instances the principal purpose of the service was the distribution of newspapers of which Griffiths was the proprietor. The first issue of the *Samoa Times* (later the *Samoa Times and South Sea Gazette*) appeared on 6 October 1877 and the newspaper continued in weekly publication until 27 August 1881.

Mail from the Samoa Express post to addresses overseas was routed via New South Wales, New Zealand or USA and received additional franking with stamps of the receiving country on landing.

Cancellations, inscribed 'APIA SAMOA', did not arrive until March 1878 so that examples of Nos. 1/9 used before that date were cancelled in manuscript. The Samoa Express stamps may also be found cancelled at Fiji, Auckland and Sydney.

1

A 2nd State (Nos. 4/9)

B 3rd State (Nos. 10/19)

(Des H. H. Glover. Litho S. T. Leigh & Co, Sydney, N.S.W.)

1877 (1 Oct)–**80**.

A. 1st state: white line above 'X' in 'EXPRESS' not broken. P 12½

1	**1**	1d. ultramarine	£375	£275
2		3d. deep scarlet	£450	£250
3		6d. bright violet	£475	£250
		a. Pale lilac	£500	£250

B. 2nd state: white line above 'X' usually broken by a spot of colour, and dot between top of 'M' and 'O' of 'SAMOA'. P 12½ (1878–1879)

4	**1**	1d. ultramarine	£160	£250
5		3d. bright scarlet	£550	£650
6		6d. bright violet	£700	£700
7		1s. dull yellow	£325	£120
		b. Perf 12 (1879)	£100	£275
		c. Orange-yellow	£325	£130
8		2s. red-brown	£375	£600
		a. Chocolate	£400	£600
9		5s. green	£4000	£1300

C. 3rd state: line above 'X' repaired, dot merged with upper right serif of 'M' (1879)

(a) P 12½

10	**1**	1d. ultramarine	£300	£120
11		3d. vermilion	£450	£200
12		6d. lilac	£550	£140

13		2s. brown	£400	£425
		a. Chocolate	£400	£425
14		5s. green	£2250	£800
		a. Line above 'X' not repaired (R. 2/3)	£3250	
		(b) P 12		
15	1	1d. blue	40·00	£700
		a. Deep blue	45·00	
		b. Ultramarine	40·00	£700
16		3d. vermilion	70·00	£750
		a. Carmine-vermilion	70·00	
17		6d. bright violet	65·00	£500
		a. Deep violet	60·00	
18		2s. deep brown	£275	
19		5s. yellow-green	£600	
		a. Deep green	£800	
		b. Line above 'X' not repaired (R. 2/3)	£900	
		D. 4th state: spot of colour under middle stroke of 'M'. P 12 (1880)		
20	1	9d. orange-brown	80·00	£400

Originals exist imperf, but are not known used in this state.

On sheets of the 1d., 1st state, at least eight stamps have a stop after 'PENNY'. In the 2nd state, three stamps have the stop, and in the 3rd state, only one.

In the 1st state, all the stamps, 1d., 3d. and 6d., were in sheets of 20 (5×4) and also the 1d. in the 3rd state.

All values in the 2nd state, all values except the 1d. in the 3rd state and No. 20 were in sheets of ten (5×2).

As all sheets of all printings of the originals were imperf at the outer edges, the only stamps which can have perforations on all four sides are Nos. 1 to 3*a*, 10 and 15 to 15*b*, all other originals being imperf on one or two sides.

The perf 12 stamps, which gauge 11.8, are generally very rough but later the machine was repaired and the 1d., 3d. and 6d. are known with clean-cut perforations.

Remainders of the 1d., unissued 2d. rose, 6d. (in sheets of 21 (7×3), 3d., 9d., 5s. (in sheets of 12 (4×3)) and of the 1s. and 2s. (sheet format unknown) were found in the Samoan post office when the service closed down in 1881. The remainders are rare in complete sheets.

Reprints of all values, in sheets of 40 (8×5), were made after the originals had been withdrawn from sale. These are practically worthless.

The majority of both reprints and remainders are in the 4th state as the 9d. with the spot of colour under the middle stroke of the 'M', but a few stamps (both remainders and reprints) do not show this, while on some it is very faint.

There are six known types of forgery, one of which is rather dangerous, the others being crude.

The last mail despatch organised by the proprietors of the *Samoa Express* took place on 31 August 1881, although one cover is recorded postmarked 24 September 1881.

After the withdrawal of the *Samoa Express* service it would appear that the Apia municipality appointed a postmaster to continue the overseas post. Covers are known franked with USA or New Zealand stamps in Samoa, or routed via Fiji.

In December 1886 the municipal postmaster, John Davis, was appointed Postmaster of the Kingdom of Samoa by King Malietoa. Overseas mail sent via New Zealand was subsequently accepted without the addition of New Zealand stamps, although letters to the USA continued to require such franking until August 1891.

2 Palm Trees

3 King Malietoa Laupepa

4a 6 mm

4b 7 mm

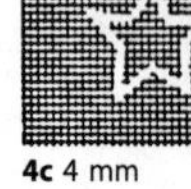

4c 4 mm

Description of Watermarks

(These are the same as W **12a**/**12c** of New Zealand)

W **4a**. 6 mm between 'N Z' and star; broad irregular star; comparatively wide 'N'; 'N Z' 11½ mm wide, with horizontal mesh.

W **4b**. 7 mm between 'N Z' and star; narrower star; narrow 'N'; 'N Z' 10 mm wide, with vertical mesh.

W **4c**. 4 mm between 'N Z' and star; narrow star; wide 'N'; 'N Z' 11 mm wide, with vertical mesh.

(Des A. E. Cousins (T **3**). Dies eng W. R. Bock and A. E. Cousins (T **2**) or A. E. Cousins (T **3**). Typo Govt Ptg Office, Wellington)

1886–1900.

		(i) W 4a		
		(a) P 12½ (15 Oct–Nov 1886)		
21	2	½d. purple-brown	35·00	55·00
22		1d. yellow-green	21·00	16·00
23		2d. dull orange	45·00	17·00
24		4d. blue	50·00	13·00
25		1s. rose-carmine	65·00	13·00
		a. Bisected (2½d.) (*on cover*)*	†	£350
26		2s.6d. reddish lilac	65·00	75·00
		(b) P 12×11½ (6 July–Nov 1887)		
27	2	½d. purple-brown	70·00	85·00
28		1d. yellow-green	£110	35·00
29		2d. yellow	95·00	£140
30		4d. blue	£275	£225
31		6d. brown-lake	50·00	20·00
32		1s. rose-carmine	—	£200
33		2s.6d. reddish lilac	£1500	
		(ii) W 4c. P 12×11½ (9 May 1890)		
34	2	½d. purple-brown	80·00	42·00
35		1d. green	55·00	50·00
36		2d. brown-orange	80·00	50·00
37		4d. blue	£140	5·00
38		6d. brown-lake	£300	11·00
39		1s. rose-carmine	£350	15·00
		x. Wmk reversed	£600	£180
40		2s.6d. reddish lilac	£450	8·50
		(iii) W 4b		
		(a) P 12×11½ (9 May 1890–1892)		
41	2	½d. pale purple-brown	8·00	7·00
		a. Blackish purple	8·50	7·00
42		1d. myrtle-green	38·00	2·50
		a. Green	38·00	2·50
		b. Yellow-green	38·00	2·50
43		2d. dull orange	45·00	1·75
		x. Wmk reversed	£190	£190
44	3	2½d. rose (22.11.92)	75·00	6·00
		a. Pale rose	75·00	6·00
45	2	4d. blue	£225	28·00
46		6d. brown-lake	£110	12·00
47		1s. rose-carmine	£250	6·00
48		2s.6d. slate-lilac	£325	12·00
		(b) P 12½ (Mar 1891–1892)		
49	2	½d. purple-brown		
50		1d. green		
51		2d. orange-yellow	—	£1500
52	3	2½d. rose (7.1.92)	40·00	4·50
53	2	4d. blue	£4500	£1500
54		6d. brown-purple	£4500	£2500
55		1s. rose-carmine	£1200	£1500
56		2s.6d. slate-lilac	£5000	
		(c) P 11 (May 1895–1900)		
57	2	½d. purple-brown	8·00	2·75
		a. Deep purple-brown	5·50	1·75
		b. Blackish purple (1900)	3·75	35·00
58		1d. green	14·00	2·25
		a. Bluish green (1897)	12·00	2·50
		b. Deep green (1900)	4·25	26·00
		w. Wmk inverted	£750	£300
59		2d. pale yellow	45·00	45·00
		a. Orange (1896)	25·00	25·00
		b. Bright yellow (1.97)	18·00	12·00
		c. Pale ochre (10.97)	7·00	12·00
		d. Dull orange (1900)	9·00	
60	3	2½d. rose	7·00	10·00
		a. Deep rose-carmine (1900)	3·00	42·00
61	2	4d. blue	19·00	11·00
		a. Deep blue (1900)	2·75	50·00
62		6d. brown-lake	20·00	3·00
		a. Brown-purple (1900)	1·75	60·00
63		1s. rose	18·00	3·75
		a. Dull rose-carmine/toned (5.98)	5·00	38·00
		b. Carmine (1900)	1·50	
64		2s.6d. purple	55·00	10·00
		a. Reddish lilac (wmk inverted) (1897)	19·00	14·00
		b. Deep purple/toned (wmk reversed) (17.5.98)	4·75	10·00
		ba. Imperf between (vert pair)	£450	
		c. Slate-violet	£120	

* Following a fire on 1 April 1895 which destroyed stocks of all stamps except the 1s. value perf 12½, this was bisected diagonally and used as a 2½d. stamp for overseas letters between 24 April and May 1895, and was cancelled in blue. Fresh supplies of the 2½d. did not arrive until July 1895, although other values were available from 23 May.

Examples of the 1s. rose perforated 11, No. 63, were subsequently bisected and supplied cancelled-to-order by the post office to collectors, often with backdated cancellations. Most of these examples were bisected vertically and all were cancelled in black (*Price £7*).

The dates given relate to the earliest dates of printing in the various watermarks and perforations and not to issue dates.

The perf 11 issues (including those later surcharged or overprinted), are very unevenly perforated owing to the large size of the pins. Evenly perforated copies are extremely hard to find.

For the 2½d. black, see Nos. 81/82 and for the ½d. green and 1d. red-brown, see Nos. 88/89.

FIVE PENCE (5) FIVE PENCE (6) 5d (7)

1893 (Nov–Dec). Handstamped singly, at Apia.

		(a) In two operations		
65	5	5d. on 4d. blue (No. 37)	75·00	50·00
66		5d. on 4d. blue (No. 45)	65·00	£100
67	6	5d. on 4d. blue (No. 37)	£100	£110
68		5d. on 4d. blue (No. 45)	80·00	
		(b) In three operations (Dec)		
69	7	5d. on 4d. blue (No. 37) (R.)	45·00	38·00
70		5d. on 4d. blue (No. 45) (R.)	50·00	50·00

In Types **5** and **6** the bars obliterating the original value vary in length from 13½ to 16½ mm and can occur with either the thick bar over the thin one or vice versa. Examples can be found with the bars omitted.

Double handstamps exist but we do not list them.

A surcharge as T **7** but with stop after 'd' is now considered to be a trial. It exists in black and in red. Where the 'd' was applied separately its position in relation to the '5' naturally varies.

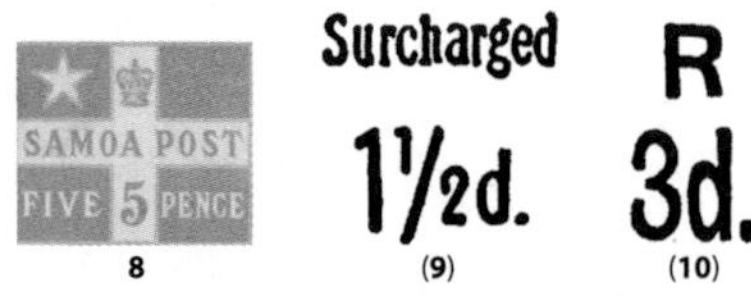

8 (9) (10)

The 'R' in T **10** indicates use for registration fee.

(Des and die eng A. E. Cousins. Typo New Zealand Govt Ptg Office)

1894 (26 Feb)–**1900**. W **4b** (sideways).

		(a) P 11½×12		
71	8	5d. dull vermilion	38·00	3·50
		a. Dull red	38·00	3·75
		ab. Mixed perfs 11½×12 and 12½		
		(b) P 11		
72	8	5d. dull red (1895)	48·00	14·00
		a. Deep red (1900)	6·00	23·00

No. 72 (like Nos. 71/71*a*) shows wmk sideways to left (*as seen from the back of the stamp*), whereas No. 72*a* shows wmk sideways to right.

1895–1900. W **4b**.

		(i) Handstamped with Types 9 or 10		
		(a) P 12×11½ (28.1.95)		
73	2	1½d. on 2d. dull orange (B.)	27·00	18·00
74		3d. on 2d. dull orange	55·00	23·00
		(b) P 11 (6.95)		
75	2	1½d. on 2d. orange (B.)	8·00	7·50
		a. Pair, one without handstamp	£650	
		b. On 2d. yellow	9·00	7·50
76		3d. on 2d. orange	9·50	15·00
		a. On 2d. yellow	11·00	15·00
		(ii) Handstamped as Types 9 or 10. P 11 (1896)		
78	2	1½d. on 2d. orange-yellow (B.)	4·50	28·00
79		3d. on 2d. orange-yellow	6·00	50·00
		a. Imperf between (vert pair)	£700	
		b. Pair, one without handstamp		
		(iv) Surch typo as Types 10. P 11 (7 Feb 1900)		
80	2	3d. on 2d. deep red-orange (G.)	2·25	£130

In No. 78 the '2' has a serif and the handstamp is in pale greenish blue instead of deep blue. In No. 79 the 'R' is slightly narrower. In both instances the stamp is in a different shade.

A special printing in a distinctly different colour was made for No. 80 and the surcharge is in green.

Most of the handstamps exist double.

1896 (Aug). Printed in the wrong colour. W **4b**.

		(a) P 10×11		
81	3	2½d. black	3·00	3·50
		(b) P 11		
82	3	2½d. black	80·00	70·00
		a. Mixed perfs 10 and 11	£425	

Surcharged 2½d. (11) PROVISIONAL GOVT. (12)

1898–99. W **4b**. P 11.

		(a) Handstamped as T 11 (10.98)		
83	2	2½d. on 1s. dull rose-carmine/toned	50·00	50·00
		(b) Surch as T 11 (1899)		
84	2	2½d. on 1d. bluish green (R.)	75	3·00
		a. Surch inverted	£850	£425
85		2½d. on 1s. dull rose-carmine/toned (R.)	9·00	17·00
		a. Surch double	£400	
86		2½d. on 1s. dull rose-carmine/toned (Blk.)	14·00	13·00
		a. Surch double	£500	
87		2½d. on 2s.6d. deep purple/toned (wmk reversed)	14·00	26·00

Nos. 83/87 were produced to replace the 2½d. T **3**, showing King Malietou Laupepa, who died on 23 August 1898.

The typographed surcharge was applied in a setting of nine, giving seven types differing in the angle and length of the fractional line, the type of stop, etc.

1899 (18 July). Colours changed. W **4b**. P 11.

88		½d. dull blue-green	3·75	6·00
		a. Deep green	3·75	6·00
89		1d. deep red-brown	4·75	5·50

1899 (20 Sept)–**1900**. Provisional Government. New printings optd with T **12** (longer words and shorter letters on 5d.). W **4b**. P 11.

90	2	½d. dull blue-green (R.)	3·75	5·50
		a. Yellowish green (1900)	4·75	11·00
91		1d. chestnut (B.)	4·50	18·00
92		2d. dull orange (R.)	2·50	12·00
		a. Orange-yellow (1900)	4·75	14·00
93		4d. deep dull blue (R.)	70	16·00
94	8	5d. dull vermilion (B.)	3·75	15·00
		a. Red (1900)	5·50	15·00
95	2	6d. brown-lake (B.)	1·50	14·00
96		1s. rose-carmine (B.)	1·50	48·00
97		2s.6d. reddish purple (R.)	4·75	30·00
90/97 *Set of 8*			21·00	£150

The Samoan group of islands was partitioned on 1 March 1900: Western Samoa (Upolu, Savaii, Apolima and Manono) to Germany and Eastern Samoa (Tutuila, the Manu'a Is and Rose Is) to the United States. German issues of 1900–1914 will be found listed in the Stanley Gibbons *Germany Catalogue*, there were no US issues.

The Samoan Kingdom post office run by John Davis was suspended in March 1900.

NEW ZEALAND OCCUPATION

The German Islands of Samoa surrendered to the New Zealand Expeditionary Force on 30 August 1914 and were administered by New Zealand until 1962.

G.R.I. 1d. (13) G.R.I. 1 Shillings. (14)

SETTINGS. Nos. 101/109 were surcharged by a vertical setting of ten, repeated ten times across the sheet. Nos. 110/114 were from a horizontal setting of four repeated five times in the sheet.

Nos. 101b, 102a and 104a occurred on position 6. The error was corrected during the printing of No. 102.
Nos. 101c, 102c, 104d and 105b are from position 10.
Nos. 101d, 102e and 104b are from position 1.
No. 108b is from position 9.

(Surch by *Samoanische Zeitung*, Apia)

1914 (3 Sept). German Colonial issue (ship) (no wmk) inscr 'SAMOA' surch as Types **13** or **14** (mark values).

No.	Description	Unused	Used
101	½d. on 3pf. brown	60·00	17·00
	a. Surch double	£750	£600
	b. No fraction bar	90·00	45·00
	c. Comma after 'I'	£700	£425
	d. '1' to left of '2' in '½'	85·00	42·00
102	½d. on 5pf. green	65·00	21·00
	a. No fraction bar	£140	60·00
	c. Comma after 'I'	£425	£180
	d. Surch double	£750	£600
	e. '1' to left of '2' in '½'	£110	45·00
103	1d. on 10pf. carmine	£100	40·00
	a. Surch double	£800	£650
104	2½d. on 20pf. ultramarine	60·00	14·00
	a. No fraction bar	95·00	42·00
	b. '1' to left of '2' in '½'	90·00	42·00
	c. Surch inverted	£1100	£1000
	d. Comma after 'I'	£550	£350
	e. Surch double	£750	£650
105	3d. on 25pf. black and red/*yellow*	80·00	40·00
	a. Surch double	£1100	£800
	b. Comma after 'I'	£5000	£1100
106	4d. on 30pf. black and orange/*buff*	£130	60·00
107	5d. on 40pf. black and carmine	£130	70·00
108	6d. on 50pf. black and purple/*buff*	65·00	35·00
	a. Surch double	£1100	£1000
	b. Inverted '9' for '6'	£180	£100
109	9d. on 80pf. black and carmine/*rose*	£200	£100
110	'1 shillings' on 1m. carmine	£3250	£3500
111	'1 shilling' on 1m. carmine	£11000	£7000
112	2s. on 2m. blue	£3500	£3000
113	3s. on 3m. violet-black	£1400	£1200
	a. Surch double	£10000	£11000
114	5s. on 5m. carmine and black	£1200	£1000
	a. Surch double	£13000	£14000

No. 108b is distinguishable from 108, as the 'd' and the '9' are not in a line, and the upper loop of the '9' turns downwards to the left.

UNAUTHORISED SURCHARGES. Examples of the 2d. on 20pf., 3d. on 30pf., 3d. on 40pf., 4d. on 40pf., 6d. on 80pf., 2s. on 3m. and 2s. on Marshall Islands 2m., together with a number of errors not listed above, were produced by the printer on stamps supplied by local collectors. These were not authorised by the New Zealand Military Administration.

SAMOA.
(15)

1914 (29 Sept)–**15**. Stamps of New Zealand. Types **53**, **51**, **52** and **27**, optd as T **15**, but opt only 14 mm long on all except 2½d. Wmk 'N Z' and Star, W **43** of New Zealand.

No.	Description	Unused	Used
115	½d. yellow-green (R.) (P 14×15)	1·75	30
116	1d. carmine (B.) (P 14×15)	1·25	10
	a. 'Q' flaw	50·00	15·00
117	2d. mauve (R.) (P 14×14½) (10.14)	1·25	1·00
118	2½d. deep blue (R.) (P 14) (10.14)	2·00	1·75
	w. Wmk inverted		
119	6d. carmine (B.) (P 14×14½) (10.14)	2·00	1·75
	a. Perf 14×13½	17·00	23·00
	b. Vert pair. Nos. 119/119a (1915)	55·00	£100
	c. Pale carmine (P 14×14½)	11·00	10·00
121	1s. vermilion (B.) (P 14×14½) (10.14)	15·00	24·00
115/121 *Set of 6*		21·00	26·00

1914–24. Postal Fiscal stamps as T F **4** of New Zealand optd with T **15**. W **43** of New Zealand (sideways). Chalk-surfaced 'De La Rue' paper.

(a) P 14 (Nov 1914–1917)

No.	Description	Unused	Used
122	2s. blue (R.) (9.17)	£100	£100
123	2s.6d. grey-brown (B.) (9.17)	6·50	19·00
124	5s. yellow-green (R.)	26·00	11·00
125	10s. maroon (B.)	40·00	28·00
126	£1 rose-carmine (B.)	90·00	45·00

(b) P 14½×14, comb (1917–1924)

No.	Description	Unused	Used
127	2s. deep blue (R.) (3.18)	8·50	5·50
128	2s.6d. grey-brown (B.) (10.24)	£425	£170
129	3s. purple (R.) (6.23)	16·00	65·00
130	5s. yellow-green (R.) (9.17)	30·00	17·00
131	10s. maroon (B.) (11.17)	85·00	48·00
132	£1 rose-carmine (B.) (3.18)	£110	70·00

We no longer list the £2 value as it is doubtful this was used for postal purposes.
See also Nos. 165/166*e*.

1916–19. King George V stamps of New Zealand optd as T **15**, but 14 mm long.

(a) Typo. P 14×15

No.	Type	Description	Unused	Used
134	**61**	½d. yellow-green (R.)	1·25	1·25
135		1½d. slate (R.) (1917)	50	25
136		1½d. orange-brown (R.) (1919)	30	50
137		2d. yellow (R.) (14.2.18)	2·00	25
138		3d. chocolate (B.) (1919)	4·75	23·00

(b) Recess. P 14×13½

No.	Type	Description	Unused	Used
139	**60**	2½d. blue (R.)	2·50	75
		a. Perf 14×14½	1·25	75
		b. Vert pair. Nos. 139/139a	17·00	27·00
140		3d. chocolate (B.) (1917)	65	1·50
		a. Perf 14×14½	65	1·00
		b. Vert pair. Nos. 140/140a	17·00	30·00
141		6d. carmine (B.) (5.5.17)	4·00	3·25
		a. Perf 14×14½	1·50	1·50
		b. Vert pair. Nos. 141/141a	19·00	40·00
142		1s. vermilion (B.)	7·00	1·50
		a. Perf 14×14½	7·00	9·00
		b. Vert pair. Nos. 142/142a	29·00	55·00
134/142 *Set of 9*			17·00	28·00

LEAGUE OF NATIONS MANDATE

Administered by New Zealand.

1920 (July). Victory. Nos. 453/458 of New Zealand optd as T **15**, but 14 mm long.

No.	Description	Unused	Used
143	½d. green (R.)	6·50	18·00
144	1d. carmine (B.)	3·75	24·00
145	1½d. brown-orange (R.)	2·00	13·00
146	3d. chocolate (B.)	8·00	12·00
147	6d. violet (R.)	4·50	7·50
148	1s. orange-red (B.)	11·00	11·00
143/148 *Set of 6*		32·00	75·00

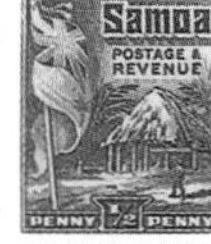

16 Native Hut

SILVER JUBILEE
OF
KING GEORGE V
1910-1935.
(17)

(Eng B.W. Recess-printed at Wellington, NZ)

1921 (23 Dec). W **43** of New Zealand.

(a) P 14×14½

No.	Type	Description	Unused	Used
149	**16**	½d. green	6·50	16·00
150		1d. lake	11·00	2·00
151		1½d. chestnut	1·75	22·00
152		2d. yellow	3·00	3·25
149/152 *Set of 4*			20·00	40·00

(b) P 14×13½

No.	Type	Description	Unused	Used
153	**16**	½d. green	4·00	1·75
154		1d. lake	7·00	20
155		1½d. chestnut	24·00	14·00
156		2d. yellow	14·00	80
157		2½d. grey-blue	1·75	10·00
158		3d. sepia	1·75	6·50
159		4d. violet	1·75	3·75
160		5d. light blue	1·75	9·50
161		6d. bright carmine	1·75	8·50
162		8d. red-brown	1·75	16·00
163		9d. olive-green	2·00	30·00
164		1s. vermilion	1·75	24·00
153/164 *Set of 12*			55·00	£110

1925–28. Postal Fiscal stamps as T F **4** of New Zealand optd with T **15**. W **43** of New Zealand (sideways). P 14½×14.

(a) Thick, opaque, white chalk-surfaced Cowan paper

No.	Description	Unused	Used
165	2s. blue (R.) (12.25)	£200	£225
166	2s.6d. deep grey-brown (B.) (10.28)	50·00	£110
166*a*	3s. mauve (R.) (9.25)	70·00	£120
166*b*	5s. yellow-green (R.) (11.26)	42·00	55·00
	ba. Opt at top of stamp	£2000	£2250
166*c*	10s. brown-red (B.) (12.25)	£200	£150
166*d*	£1 rose-pink (B.) (11.26)	£110	£120
165/166*d Set of 6*		£600	£700

(b) Thin, hard, chalk-surfaced Wiggins Teape paper

No.	Description	Unused	Used
166*e*	£1 rose-pink (B.) (1928)	£2750	£1200

1926–27. T **72** of New Zealand, optd with T **15**, in red.

(a) Jones paper

No.	Description	Unused	Used
167	2s. deep blue (11.26)	5·00	18·00
	w. Wmk inverted	—	27·00
168	3s. mauve (10.26)	28·00	50·00
	w. Wmk inverted	35·00	55·00

(b) Cowan paper.

No.	Description	Unused	Used
169	2s. light blue (10.11.27)	6·00	45·00
170	3s. pale mauve (10.11.27)	60·00	£110

1932 (Aug). Postal Fiscal stamps as T F **6** of New Zealand optd with T **15**. W **43** of New Zealand. Thick, opaque, white chalk-surfaced Cowan paper. P 14.

No.	Description	Unused	Used
171	2s.6d. deep brown (B.)	16·00	50·00
172	5s. green (R.)	26·00	55·00
173	10s. carmine-lake (B.)	50·00	£100
174	£1 pink (B.)	75·00	£150
175	£2 bright purple (R.)	£1000	
176	£5 indigo-blue (R.)	£2500	

The £2 and £5 values were primarily for fiscal use.

1935 (7 May). Silver Jubilee. Optd with T **17**. P 14×13½.

No.	Type	Description	Unused	Used
177	**16**	1d. lake	30	30
		a. Perf 14×14½	95·00	£170
178		2½d. grey-blue	60	65
179		6d. bright carmine	2·75	5·75
177/179 *Set of 3*			3·25	6·00

18 Samoan Girl

19 Apia

20 River scene

21 Chief and Wife

22 Canoe and house

23 R. L. Stevenson's home *Vailima*

24 Stevenson's tomb

25 Lake Lanuto'o

26 Falefa Falls

(Recess D.L.R.)

1935 (7 Aug). Types **18/26**. W **43** of New Zealand ('N Z' and Star). P 14×13½ (½d., 2½d., 2s., 3s.), 14 (2d.) or 13½×14 (others).

No.	Description	Unused	Used
180	½d. green	10	35
	w. Wmk inverted		
181	1d. black and carmine	10	10
	w. Wmk inverted	£100	
182	2d. black and orange	3·50	4·75
	aw. Wmk inverted	£250	
	b. Perf 13½×14	4·00	4·25
	bw. Wmk inverted		
183	2½d. black and blue	10	10
184	4d. slate and sepia	70	15
185	6d. bright magenta	50	10
186	1s. violet and brown	30	10
187	2s. green and purple-brown	1·00	50
188	3s. blue and brown-orange	4·00	3·50
180/188 *Set of 9*		9·00	8·00

See also Nos. 200/203.

WESTERN
SAMOA.
(27)

1935–42. Postal Fiscal stamps as T F **6** of New Zealand optd with T **27**. W **43** of New Zealand. P 14.

(a) Thick, opaque chalk-surfaced Cowan paper (7.8.35)

No.	Description	Unused	Used
189	2s.6d. deep brown (B.)	6·00	16·00
190	5s. green (B.)	26·00	40·00
191	10s. carmine-lake (B.)	70·00	90·00
192	£1 pink (B.)	60·00	£110
193	£2 bright purple (R.)	£160	£400
194	£5 indigo-blue (R.)	£225	£475

(b) Thin, hard chalk-surfaced Wiggins Teape paper (1941–1942)

No.	Description	Unused	Used
194*a*	5s. green (B.) (6.42)	£180	£225
194*b*	10s. pale carmine-lake (B.) (6.41)	£150	£200
194*c*	£2 bright purple (R.) (2.42)	£550	£1000
194*d*	£5 indigo-blue (R.) (2.42)	£3000	£3750

The £2 and £5 values were primarily for fiscal use. A £10 deep blue (on Cowan paper) was also issued, and exists with postal cancellations.
See also Nos. 207/214.

28 Coastal Scene

29 Map of Western Samoa

30 Samoan dancing party

31 Robert Louis Stevenson

(Des J. Berry (1d. and 1½d.). L. C. Mitchell (2½d. and 7d.). Recess B.W.)

1939 (29 Aug). 25th Anniversary of New Zealand Control. Types **28/31**. W **98** of New Zealand. P 13½×14 or 14×13½ (7d.).

No.	Type	Description	Unused	Used
195	**28**	1d. olive-green and scarlet	1·00	25
196	**29**	1½d. light blue and red-brown	1·75	75
197	**30**	2½d. red-brown and blue	3·00	1·00
198	**31**	7d. violet and slate-green	8·00	4·00
195/198 *Set of 4*			12·00	5·50

32 Samoan Chief

33 Apia Post Office

(Recess B.W.)

1940 (2 Sept). W **98** of New Zealand (Mult 'N Z' and Star). P 14×13½.

No.	Type	Description	Unused	Used
199	**32**	3d. on 1½d. brown	75	20

T **32** was not issued without surcharge but archival examples exist (*Price*, £200 *unused*).

(T **33**. Des L. C. Mitchell. Recess B.W.)

1944–49. As Nos. 180, 182/183 and T **33**. W **98** of New Zealand (Mult 'N Z' and Star) (sideways on 2½d.). P 14 or 13½×14 (5d.)

200	½d. green	30	21·00
202	2d. black and orange	3·50	7·50
203	2½d. black and blue (1948)	8·50	45·00
205	5d. sepia and blue (8.6.49)	2·75	1·50
200/205 *Set of 4*		13·50	65·00

1945–53. Postal Fiscal stamps as T F **6** of New Zealand optd with T **27**. W **98** of New Zealand. Thin hard, chalk-surfaced Wiggins Teape paper. P 14.

207	2s.6d. deep brown (B.) (6.45)	24·00	40·00
	w. Wmk inverted	40·00	55·00
208	5s. green (B.) (5.45)	21·00	13·00
	w. Wmk inverted	40·00	50·00
209	10s. carmine-lake (B.) (4.46)	20·00	15·00
	w. Wmk inverted	60·00	60·00
210	£1 pink (B.) (6.48)	£140	£200
211	30s. brown (8.48)	£200	£300
212	£2 bright purple (R.) (11.47)	£200	£275
	w. Wmk inverted	£600	£750
213	£3 green (8.48)	£300	£375
214	£5 indigo-blue (R) (1946)	£425	£500
	w. Wmk inverted (5.53)	£425	£500
207/210 *Set of 4*		£180	£225

Values over £1 were mainly used for fiscal purposes.

WESTERN SAMOA
(34)

1946 (4 June). Peace Issue. Nos. 668, 670 and 674/675 of New Zealand optd with T **34** (reading up and down at sides on 2d.).

215	1d. green	40	15
	w. Wmk inverted	£180	
216	2d. purple (B.)	40	15
217	6d. chocolate and vermilion	80	15
218	8d. black and carmine (B.)	40	15
215/218 *Set of 4*		1·75	55

UNITED NATIONS TRUST TERRITORY

Administered by New Zealand.

35 Making Siapo Cloth

36 Native Houses and flags

37 Seal of Samoa

38 Malifa Falls (wrongly inscribed 'Aleisa Falls')

39 Tooth-billed Pigeon

40 Bonito fishing canoe

41 Cacao harvesting

42 Thatching a Native Hut

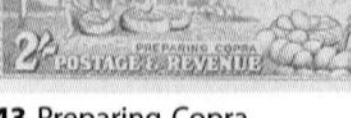
43 Preparing Copra

44 Samoan Chieftainess

1952 (10 Mar). Types **35/44**. W **98** of New Zealand (sideways on 1s. and 3s.). P 13 (½d., 2d. and 1s.) or 13½ (others).

219	**35**	½d. claret and orange-brown	10	2·25
220	**36**	1d. olive-green and green	30	50
221	**37**	2d. carmine-red	30	10
222	**38**	3d. pale ultramarine and indigo	50	20
223	**39**	5d. brown and deep green	10·00	1·50
224	**40**	6d. pale ultramarine and rose-magenta	1·00	10
225	**41**	8d. carmine	30	30
226	**42**	1s. sepia and blue	20	10
227	**43**	2s. yellow-brown	1·00	25
228	**44**	3s. chocolate and brown-olive	3·50	2·75
219/228 *Set of 10*			15·00	7·00

1953 (25 May). Coronation. Designs as Nos. 715 and 717 of New Zealand, but inscr 'WESTERN SAMOA'.

229	2d. brown	1·25	15
230	6d. slate-grey	1·25	35

WESTERN

SAMOA
(45)

1955 (14 Nov). Postal Fiscal stamps as T F **6** of New Zealand optd with T **45**. W **98** (inverted). Chalk-surfaced Wiggins, Teape paper. P 14.

232	5s. green (B.)	8·00	29·00
233	10s. carmine-lake (B.)	8·00	50·00
234	£1 pink (B.)	15·00	60·00
235	£2 bright purple (R.)	70·00	£160
232/235 *Set of 4*		90·00	£275

The £2 value was mainly used for fiscal purposes.

46 Native Houses and Flags

47 Seal of Samoa

48 Map of Samoa and the Mace

(Recess B.W.)

1958 (21 Mar). Inauguration of Samoan Parliament. Types **46/48**. W **98** of New Zealand (sideways). P 13½×13 (6d.) or 13½ (others).

236	**46**	4d. cerise	35	30
237	**47**	6d. deep reddish violet	35	30
238	**48**	1s. deep ultramarine	85	50
236/238 *Set of 3*			1·40	1·00

INDEPENDENT

Samoa became independent on 1 January 1962.

49 Samoan Fine Mat

50 Samoa College

(Litho B.W.)

1962 (2 July). Independence. Types **49/50** and similar designs. W **98** of New Zealand (sideways on horiz stamps). P 13½.

239	1d. brown and rose-carmine	10	10
240	2d. brown, green, yellow and red	10	10
241	3d. brown, blue-green and blue	10	10
242	4d. magenta, yellow, blue and black	15	80
243	6d. yellow and blue	80	80
244	8d. bluish green, yellow-green and blue	80	10
245	1s. brown and bluish green	20	10
246	1s.3d. yellow-green and blue	1·00	70
247	2s.6d. red and ultramarine	2·25	2·00
248	5s. ultramarine, yellow, red and drab	2·50	3·00
239/248 *Set of 10*		7·00	6·50

Designs: Horiz—2d. T **50**; 3d. Public library; 4d. Fono House; 6d. Map of Samoa; 8d. Airport; 1s.3d. *Vailima*; 2s.6d. Samoan flag; 5s. Samoan Seal. Vert—1d. T **49**; 1s. Samoan orator.

See Nos. 257/262.

59 Seal and Joint Heads of State

60 Signing the Treaty

(Des L. C. Mitchell. Photo Harrison)

1963 (1 Oct). First Anniversary of Independence. W **98** of New Zealand. P 14.

249	**59**	1d. deep sepia and green	10	10
250		4d. deep sepia and blue	10	10
251		8d. deep sepia and rose-pink	15	10
252		2s. deep sepia and orange	20	15
249/252 *Set of 4*			45	40

(Des L. C. Mitchell. Photo Enschedé)

1964 (1 Sept). Second Anniversary of New Zealand-Samoa Treaty of Friendship. P 13½.

253	**60**	1d. multicoloured	10	10
254		8d. multicoloured	10	10
255		2s. multicoloured	20	10
256		3s. multicoloured	25	30
253/256 *Set of 4*			55	55

61 Kava Bowl

1965 (4 Oct)–**66?**. As Nos. 239, 241/245, but W **61** (sideways on horiz designs).

257	1d. brown and rose-carmine	20	1·25
258	3d. brown, blue-green and blue (1966?)	28·00	3·50
259	4d. magenta, yellow, blue and black	25	60
260	6d. yellow and blue	75	50
261	8d. bluish green, yellow-green and blue	30	10
262	1s. brown and bluish green	25	60
257/262 *Set of 6*		28·00	6·00

62 Red-tailed Tropicbird

63 Flyingfish

(Des L. C. Mitchell. Photo Harrison)

1965 (29 Dec). Air. W **61** (sideways). P 14½.

263	**62**	8d. black, red-orange and blue	50	10
264	**63**	2s. black and blue	75	20

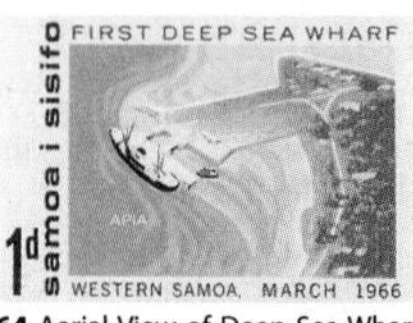
64 Aerial View of Deep Sea Wharf

(Des Tecon Co (USA). Photo Enschedé)

1966 (3 Mar). Opening of First Deep Sea Wharf Apia. T **64** and similar horiz design. Multicoloured. W **61** (sideways). P 13½.

265	1d. Type **64**	10	10
266	8d. Aerial view of wharf and bay	15	10
267	2s. As 8d.	25	25
268	3s. Type **64**	30	35
265/268 *Set of 4*		70	70

66 WHO Building

(Des M. Goaman. Photo D.L.R.)

1966 (4 July). Inauguration of WHO Headquarters. Geneva. T **66** and similar horiz design. W **61** (sideways*). P 14.

269	3d. yellow-ochre, blue and light slate-lilac	40	10
270	4d. blue, yellow, green and light orange-brown	55	1·00
271	6d. reddish lilac, emerald and yellow-olive	55	70
	w. Wmk legs to left	1·75	
272	1s. blue, yellow, green and turquoise-green	1·50	75
269/272 *Set of 4*		2·75	2·25

Designs: 3d., 6d. T **66**; 4d., 1s. WHO Building on flag.

* The normal sideways watermark has the legs of the bowl pointing to the right, *as seen from the back of the stamp.*

HURRICANE RELIEF
6d
(68)

1966 (1 Sept). Hurricane Relief Fund. No. 261 surch with T **68** by Bradbury Wilkinson.

273	8d. +6d. bluish green, yellow-green and blue	10	10

69 Hon. Tuatagaloa L. S. (Minister of Justice)

(Des and photo Harrison)

1967 (16 Jan). Fifth Anniversary of Independence. T **69** and similar horiz designs. W **61** (sideways). P 14½×14.

274	3d. sepia and bluish violet	10	10
275	8d. sepia and light new blue	10	10
276	2s. sepia and olive	10	10
277	3s. sepia and magenta	15	15
274/277 *Set of 4*		40	40

Designs: 3d. T **69**; 8d. Hon F. C. F. Nelson (minister of Works, Marine and Civil Aviation); 2s. Hon To'omata T. L. (minister of Lands); 3s. Hon Fa'alava'au G. (minister of Post Office, Radio and Broadcasting).

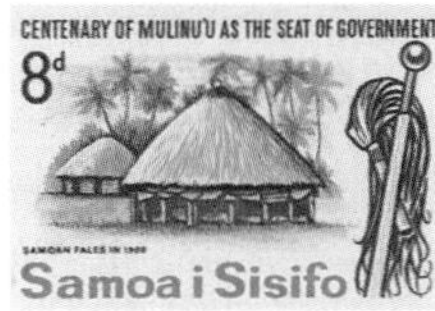

73 Samoan Fales (houses), 1890

(Des V. Whiteley. Photo Harrison)

1967 (16 May). Centenary of Mulinu'u as Seat of Government. T **73** and similar horiz design. Multicoloured. W **61**. P 14½×14.

278	8d. Type **73**	15	10
279	1s. Fono (Parliament) House, 1967	15	10

(New Currency. 100 sene or cents=1 tala or dollar)

75 Caruncluated Honeyeater

76 Black-breasted Honeyeater

(Des V. Whiteley. Litho Format ($2, $4). Photo Harrison (others))

1967 (10 July)–**69**. Decimal currency Multicoloured designs as T **75** (1s. to $1) or T **76** ($2, $4). W **61** (sideways). P 13½ ($2, $4) or 14×14½ (others).

280	1s. Type **75**	10	10
281	2s. Pacific Pigeon	10	10
282	3s. Samoan Starling	10	10
283	5s. White-vented Flycatcher	10	10
284	7s. Red-headed Parrot Finch	10	10
285	10s. Purple Swamphen	15	10
286	20s. Barn Owl	1·25	40
287	25s. Tooth-billed Pigeon	50	15
288	50s. Island Thrush	50	30
289	$1 Samoan Fantail	75	1·75
289*a*	$2 Type **76** (14.7.69)	2·00	4·00
289*b*	$4 Savaii White Eye (6.10.69)	25·00	13·00
280/289*b*	*Set of* 12	27·00	18·00

85 Nurse and Child

(Des G. Vasarhelyi. Photo D.L.R.)

1967 (1 Dec). South Pacific Health Service. T **85** and similar horiz designs. Multicoloured. P 14.

290	3s. Type **85**	15	15
291	7s. Leprosartum	20	15
292	20s. Mobile X-ray Unit	35	30
293	25s. Apia Hospital	40	35
290/293	*Set of* 4	1·00	85

89 Thomas Trood

93 Cocoa

(Des M. Farrar-Bell. Litho B.W.)

1968 (15 Jan). Sixth Anniversary of Independence. T **89** and similar horiz designs. Multicoloured. P 13½.

294	2s. Type **89**	10	10
295	7s. Dr Wilhelm Solf	10	10
296	20s. J. C. Williams	10	10
297	25s. Fritz Marquardt	15	10
294/297	*Set of* 4	40	35

(Des Jennifer Toombs. Photo Enschedé)

1968 (15 Feb). Agricultural Development. T **93** and similar vert designs. W **61**. P 13×12½.

298	3s. deep red-brown, yellow-green and black	10	10
299	5s. myrtle-green, greenish yellow and light brown	10	10
300	10s. scarlet, blackish brown and olive-yellow	10	10
301	20s. yellow-bistre, yellow and blackish olive	15	15
298/301	*Set of* 4	40	40

Designs: 3s. T **93**; 5s. Breadfruit; 10s. Copra; 20s. Bananas.

97 Women weaving Mats

(Des G. Vasarhelyi. Photo Harrison)

1968 (22 Apr). 21st Anniversary of the South Pacific Commission. T **97** and similar horiz designs. Multicoloured. W **61**. P 14½×14.

302	7s. Type **97**	10	10
303	20s. Palm trees and bay	15	10
304	25s. Sheltered cove	15	15
302/304	*Set of* 3	35	30

1928-1968
KINGSFORD-SMITH
TRANSPACIFIC FLIGHT
20
SENE 

(**100**)

1968 (13 June). 40th Anniversary of Kingsford Smith's Trans-Pacific Flight. No. 285 surch with T **100**.

305	20s. on 10s. Purple Swamphen	10	30

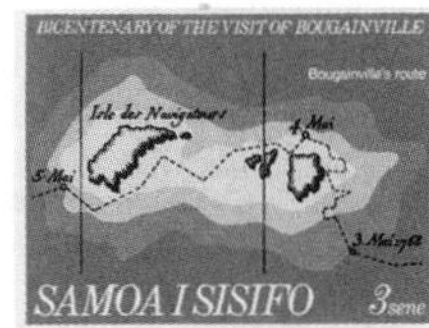

101 Bougainville's Route

(Des Jennifer Toombs. Litho B.W.)

1968 (17 June). Bicentenary of Bougainville's Visit to Samoa. T **101** and similar horiz designs. W **61** (sideways). P 14.

306	3s. new blue and black	10	20
307	7s. light ochre and black	15	20
308	20s. multicoloured	45	30
309	25s. multicoloured	60	40
306/309	*Set of* 4	1·10	1·00

Designs: 3s. T **101**; 7s. Louis de Bougainville; 20s. Bougainvillea flower; 25s. Ships *La Boudeuse* and *L'Etoile*.

105 Globe and Human Rights Emblem

106 Dr. Martin Luther King

(Des G. Vasarhelyi. Photo Harrison)

1968 (26 Aug). Human Rights Year. W **61**. P 14.

310	**105**	7s. greenish blue, brown and gold	10	10
311		20s. orange, green and gold	10	15
312		25s. violet, green and gold	15	15
310/312		*Set of* 3	30	35

(Des and litho D.L.R.)

1968 (23 Sept). Martin Luther King Commemoration. W **61**. P 14½×14.

313	**106**	7s. black and olive-green	15	10
314		20s. black and bright purple	15	10

107 Polynesian Version of Madonna and Child

108 Frangipani-*Plumeria acuminata*

(Des and litho D.L.R.)

1968 (14 Oct). Christmas. W **61**. P 14.

315	**107**	1s. multicoloured	10	10
316		3s. multicoloured	10	10
317		20s. multicoloured	10	10
318		30s. multicoloured	15	15
315/318		*Set of* 4	30	30

(Des J.W. Litho Format)

1969 (20 Jan). Seventh Anniversary of Independence. T **108** and similar multicoloured designs. P 14½.

319	2s. Type **108**	10	10
320	7s. Hibiscus (*vert*)	10	10
321	20s. Red-Ginger (*vert*)	15	10
322	30s. 'Moso'oi'	20	80
319/322	*Set of* 4	50	1·00

109 R. L. Stevenson and *Treasure Island*

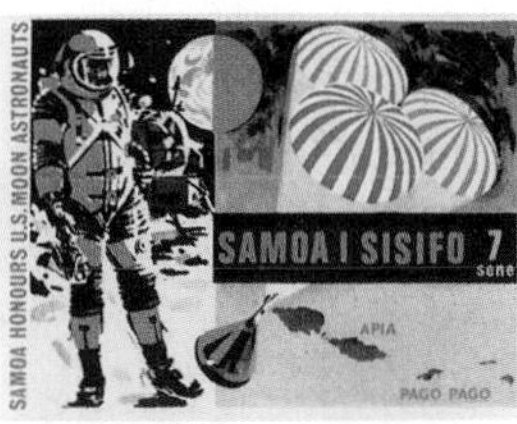

110 Weightlifting

(Des Jennifer Toombs. Litho D.L.R.)

1969 (21 Apr). 75th Death Anniversary of Robert Louis Stevenson. Horiz designs, each showing portrait as in T **109**. Multicoloured. W **61** (sideways). P 14.

323	3s. Type **109**	15	10
324	7s. *Kidnapped*	20	10
325	20s. *Dr. Jekyll and Mr. Hyde*	20	50
326	22s. *Weir of Hermiston*	20	50
323/326	*Set of* 4	65	1·10

(Des J. Mason. Photo Note Ptg Branch, Reserve Bank of Australia)

1969 (21 July). Third South Pacifc Games, Port Moresby. T **110** and similar vert designs. P 13½.

327	3s. black and sage-green	10	10
328	20s. black and light blue	15	15
329	22s. black and dull orange	15	15
327/329	*Set of* 3	30	30

Designs: 3s. T **110**; 20s. Yachting; 22s. Boxing.

113 US Astronaut on the Moon and the Splashdown near Samoan Islands

(Des J. Mason. Photo Note Ptg Branch, Reserve Bank of Australia)

1969 (24 July). First Man on the Moon. P 13½.

330	**113**	7s. multicoloured	15	15
331		20s. multicoloured	15	15

114 *Virgin with Child* (Murillo)

(Des and photo Heraclio Fournier)

1969 (13 Oct). Christmas. T **114** and similar vert designs. Multicoloured. P 14.

332	1s. Type **114**	10	10
333	3s. *The Holy Family* (El Greco)	10	10
334	20s. *The Nativity* (El Greco)	20	10
335	30s. *The Adoration of the Magi* (detail, Velazquez)	25	15
332/335	*Set of* 4	45	40
MS336	116×126 mm. Nos. 332/335	75	1·25

115 Seventh Day Adventists' Sanatorium, Apia

(Des V. Whiteley. Litho Format)

1970 (19 Jan). Eighth Anniversary of Independence. T **115** and similar designs. W **61** (sideways on 2, 7 and 22s.). P 14.

337	2s. yellow-brown, pale slate and black	10	15
338	7s. violet, buff and black	10	10
339	20s. rose, lilac and black	15	10
340	22s. olive-green, cinnamon and black	15	15
337/340	*Set of* 4	45	40

Designs: Horiz—2s. T **115**; 7s. Rev. Father Violette and Roman Catholic Cathedral, Apia; 22s. John Williams, 1797–1839 and London Missionary Society Church, Sapapali'I. Vert—20s. Mormon Church of Latter Day Saints, Tuasivi-on-Safotulafai.

119 Wreck of *Adler* (German steam gunboat)

(Des J.W. Litho Questa)

1970 (27 Apr). Great Apia Hurricane of 1889. T **119** and similar horiz designs. Multicoloured. W **61** (sideways). P 13½.

341	5s. Type **119**	30	10
342	7s. USS *Nipsic* (steam sloop)	30	10
343	10s. HMS *Calliope* (screw corvette)	30	25
344	20s. Apia after the hurricane	50	75
341/344 *Set of 4*		1·25	1·10

120 Sir Gordon Taylor's Short 825 Sandringham 7 Flying Boat *Frigate Bird III*

(Des R. Honisett. Photo Note Ptg Branch, Reserve Bank of Australia)

1970 (27 July). Air. Aircraft. T **120** and similar horiz designs. Multicoloured. P 13½×13.

345	3s. Type **120**	45	45
346	7s. Polynesian Airlines Douglas DC-3	55	20
347	20s. Pan-American Sikorsky S-42A flying boat *Samoan Clipper*	75	60
348	30s. Air Samoa Britten Norman Islander	75	2·25
	a. Pale purple omitted	£400	
345/348 *Set of 4*		2·25	3·25

121 Kendal's Chronometer and Cook's Sextant

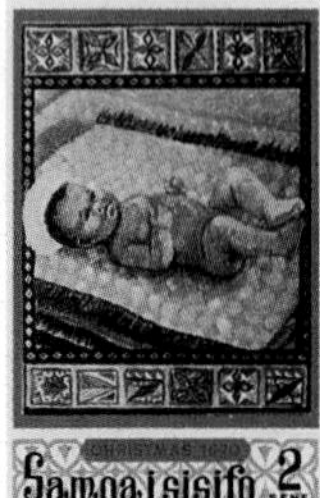

122 *Peace for the World* (F. B. Eccles)

(Des J. Berry, adapted J. Cooler. Litho Questa)

1970 (14 Sept). Cook's Exploration of the Pacific. T **121** and similar designs. W **61** (sideways on 30s.). P 14.

349	1s. carmine, silver and black	10	15
350	2s. multicoloured	10	15
351	20s. black, bright blue and gold	25	25
352	30s. multicoloured	75	80
349/352 *Set of 4*		1·00	1·25

Designs: Vert—1s. T **121**; 2s. Cook's statue, Whitby; 20s. Cook's head. Horiz (83×25 *mm*)—30s. Cook, HMS *Endeavour* and island.

(Des from paintings. Photo Heraclio Fournier)

1970 (26 Oct). Christmas. T **122** and similar vert designs. Multicoloured. P 13.

353	2s. Type **122**	10	10
354	3s. *The Holy Family* (W. E. Jahnke)	10	10
355	20s. *Mother and Child* (F. B. Eccles)	15	10
356	30s. *Prince of Peace* (Meleane Fe'ao)	20	15
353/356 *Set of 4*		35	40
MS357 111×158 mm. Nos. 353/356		60	1·25

123 Pope Paul VI

(Des J. Cooter. Litho Format)

1970 (20 Nov). Visit of Pope Paul to Samoa. W **61**. P 14×14½.

358	**123**	8s. black and grey-blue	15	15
359		20s. black and plum	35	15

STAMP BOOKLETS

1958. Blue on yellow (No. SB1) and blue (No. SB3) or black on pink (No. SB2). Stapled.

SB1	2s.7d. booklet containing ½d. and 2d. (Nos. 219, 221), each in block of 6, 1d. and 3d. (Nos. 220, 222), each in block of 4	
SB2	6s. booklet containing 1d., 3d., 6d. and 8d. (Nos. 220, 222, 224/225), each in block of 4	
SB3	9s.9d. booklet containing ½d., 2d., 5d. and 1s. (Nos. 219, 221, 223, 226), each in block of 6	
	Set of 3	£500

1960 (1 Apr). Contents as Nos. SB1/SB3, but Arms and inscription in black, and colour of covers changed. Stapled.

SB4	2s.7d. Green cover	
	a. Buff cover	
SB5	6s. Grey cover	
	a. Blue cover	
SB6	9s.9d. Yellow cover	
	a. White cover	
Set of 3 (Nos. SB4, SB5, SB6)		£200
Set of 3 (Nos. SB4a, SB5a, SB6a)		£200

1962 (1 Sept). Black on buff (No. SB7) or green (No. SB8) covers. Inscr 'POSTAGE STAMP BOOKLET NO. 1' (1s.9d.) or 'NO. 2' (6s.9d.). Stapled.

SB7	6s.9d. booklet containing one each of 1d., 2d., 3d., 4d., 6d., 8d., 1s., 1s.3d. and 2s.6d. (Nos. 239/247) (loose in cellophane bag)	48·00
SB8	11s.9d. booklet containing one each of 1d., 2d., 3d., 4d., 6d., 8d., 1s., 1s.3d., 2s.6d. and 5s. (Nos. 239/248) (loose in cellophane bag)	48·00

1962 (1 Sept)–**64**. Black on pink (No. SB9) or blue (No. SB10) covers. Inscr 'POSTAGE STAMP BOOKLET NO. 3' (12s.) or 'NO. 4' (6s.). Stapled.

SB9	6s. booklet containing 1d., 3d., 6d. and 8d. (Nos. 239 241, 243/244), each in block of 4	42·00
SB10	12s. booklet containing 1d., 2d., 3d., 4d., 6d., 8d. and 1s. (Nos. 239/245), each in block of 4	42·00

1964 (1 Sept)–**67**. As Nos. SB9/SB10 but containing stamps with mixed wmks (W **98** of New Zealand or W **61** of Samoa). Stapled.

SB11	6s. As No. SB9 *From*	45·00
	a. Including block of 3d. W **61** (No. 258)	£130
SB12	12s. As No. SB10 *From*	50·00
	a. Including block of 3d. W **61** (No. 258)	£130

The composition of Nos. SB11/SB12 can vary as to the watermark and we do not attempt to list them in detail.

1965 (1 Feb)–**67**. As Nos. SB7/SB8, but containing stamps with mixed wmks (W **98** of New Zealand or W **61** of Samoa). Stapled.

SB13	6s.9d. As No. SB7 *From*	42·00
SB14	11s.9d. As No. SB8 *From*	50·00

The composition of Nos. SB13/SB14 can vary as to the watermark. Since the precise contents can only be established by dismantling the booklets, it is not possible to give a more detailed listing.

Sarawak

Sarawak was placed under British protection in 1888. It was ceded to Great Britain on 1 July 1946 and was administered as a Crown Colony until 16 September 1963 when it became a state of the Federation of Malaysia.

From 1859 letters from Sarawak to overseas addresses, other than to other British possessions in Borneo and Singapore, were franked by stamps of INDIA and, after 1867, STRAITS SETTLEMENTS, a stock of which was kept by the Sarawak Post Office. The stamps of Sarawak continued to have this limited validity until 1 July 1897 when the country joined the UPU.

PRICES FOR STAMPS ON COVER TO 1945

No. 1	—
Nos. 2/7	*from* × 50
Nos. 8/21	*from* × 8
Nos. 22/26	*from* × 6
No. 27	*from* × 40
Nos. 28/35	*from* × 6
Nos. 36/47	*from* × 8
No. 48	†
No. 49	*from* × 10
Nos. 50/61	*from* × 6
No. 62	†
Nos. 63/71	*from* × 4
Nos. 72/73	*from* × 8
Nos. 74/75	—
Nos. 76/90	*from* × 7
Nos. 91/105	*from* × 5
Nos. 106/125	*from* × 3
Nos. 126/145	*from* × 2

BROOKE FAMILY ADMINISTRATION

Sir James Brooke. 1842–11 June 1868

Sir Charles Brooke. 11 June 1868–17 May 1917

UNUSED PRICES. Nos. 1/7, 27 and 32/35 in unused condition are normally found without gum. Prices in the unused column are for stamps in this state. Examples of these issues with original gum are worth considerably more.

1 Sir James Brooke

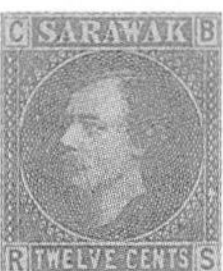

2 Sir Charles Brooke

The initials in the corners of Types **1** and **2** stand for 'James (Charles) Brooke, Rajah (of) Sarawak'.

(Types **1** and **2**. Die eng Wm. Ridgeway. Litho Maclure, Macdonald & Co, Glasgow)

1869 (1 Mar). P 11.

1	**1**	3c. brown/*yellow*	55·00	£225

Similar stamps are known printed from the engraved die in orange-brown on orange surface-coloured paper, and perf 12. These are specimens submitted to the Sarawak authorities and exist both with and without obliterations.

1871 (1 Jan). P 11 (irregular).

2	**2**	3c. brown/*yellow*	3·50	4·00
		a. Stop after 'THREE'	70·00	85·00
		b. Imperf between (vert pair)	£550	
		c. Imperf between (horiz pair)	£950	

The 'stop' variety, No. 2a, which occurs on R. 10/7 of one printing stone is of no more philatelic importance than any of the numerous other variations, such as narrow first 'A' in 'SARAWAK' (R. 2/7) and 'R' with long tail in left lower corner (R. 9/10), but it has been accepted by collectors for many years, and we therefore retain it. The papermaker's wmk 'L N L' appears once or twice in sheets of No. 2.

Examples are known, recess-printed, similar to those mentioned in the note after No. 1.

TWO CENTS

Examples of No. 2 surcharged as above were first reported in 1876 but following the discovery of dies for forgeries and faked postmarks in 1891 it was concluded that the issue was bogus, especially as the availability of the 2c. of 1875 made it unnecessary to issue a provisional. It has now been established that a 2c. postal rate was introduced from 1 August 1874 for the carriage of newspapers. Moreover four examples are known with a stop after 'CENTS.' and showing other minor differences from the forgery illustrated. This version could be genuine and if others come to light we will reconsider listing it.

1875 (1 Jan). P 11½–12.

3	**2**	2c. mauve/*lilac* (*shades*)	27·00	17·00
4		4c. red-brown/*yellow*	7·00	3·00
		a. Imperf between (vert pair)	£800	£900
5		6c. green/*green*	5·50	5·50
6		8c. bright blue/*blue*	6·00	8·00
7		12c. red/*pale rose*	13·00	6·50
3/7 *Set of 5*			50·00	35·00

Nos. 3, 4, 6 and 7 have the watermark 'L N L' in the sheet, as No. 2. No. 5 is watermarked 'L N T'.

All values exist imperf and can be distinguished from the proofs by shade and impression. Stamps rouletted, pin-perf, or roughly perf 6½ to 7 are proofs clandestinely perforated.

The 12c. 'laid' paper, formerly listed, is not on a true laid paper, the 'laid' effect being accidental and not consistent.

The lithographic stones for Nos. 3 to 7 were made up from strips of five distinct impressions hence there are five types of each value differing mainly in the lettering of the tablets of value. There are flaws on nearly every individual stamp, from which they can be plated.

4 Sir Charles Brooke

(Typo D.L.R.)

1888 (10 Nov)–**97**. No wmk. P 14.

8	**4**	1c. purple and black (6.6.92)	7·00	1·50
9		2c. purple and carmine (11.11.88)	7·00	3·25
		a. Purple and rosine (1897)	17·00	6·50
10		3c. purple and blue (11.11.88)	13·00	5·50
11		4c. purple and yellow	48·00	65·00
12		5c. purple and green (12.6.91)	45·00	5·00
13		6c. purple and brown (11.11.88)	32·00	65·00
14		8c. green and carmine (11.11.88)	24·00	5·50
		a. Green and rosine (1897)	40·00	18·00
15		10c. green and purple (12.6.91)	60·00	15·00
16		12c. green and blue (11.11.88)	19·00	15·00
17		16c. green and orange (28.12.97)	70·00	90·00
18		25c. green and brown (19.11 88)	80·00	50·00
19		32c. green and black (28.12.97)	60·00	75·00
20		50c. green (26.7.97)	85·00	£130
21		$1 green and black (2.11.97)	£120	£130
8/21 *Set of 14*			£600	£600
		Prepared for use but not issued		
21*a*		$2 green and blue	£1200	
21*b*		$5 green and violet	£1300	
21*c*		$10 green and carmine	£1300	

On No. 21*c* the value is on an uncoloured ground.

The tablet of value in this and later similar issues is in the second colour given.

One Cent. (5) **one cent.** (6)

2c. (7) **5c** (8) **5c.** (9)

1889 (3 Aug)–**92**. T **4** surch by Government Printing Office, Kuching. P 14.

22	**5**	1c. on 3c. purple and blue (12.1.92)	80·00	50·00
		a. Surch double	£750	£650
23	**6**	1c. on 3c. purple and blue (2.92)	3·50	2·75
		a. No stop after 'cent' (R. 2/6, 7/6)	£250	£275
24	**7**	2c. on 8c. green and carmine (3.8.89)	4·25	13·00
		a. Surch double	£475	
		b. Surch inverted	£4250	
		c. Surch omitted (in pair with normal)	£8000	
25	**8**	5c. on 12c. green and blue (with stop after 'C') (17.2.91)	40·00	60·00
		a. No stop after 'C'	50·00	75·00
		b. 'C' omitted (in pair with normal)	£900	£1000
		c. Surch double	£1400	
		d. Surch double, one vertical	£4000	
		e. Surch omitted (in pair with normal)	£12000	
26	**9**	5c. on 12c. green and blue (17.2.91)	£325	£350
		a. No stop after 'C'	£190	£200
		b. 'C' omitted (in pair with normal)	£1300	£1400
		c. Surch double	£1500	

Nos. 22/23 were surcharged with settings of 60 (6×10). Nos. 24/26/26a were produced with handstamps.

ONE
CENT

(10)

1892 (23 May). No. 2 surch with T **10**.

27	**2**	1c. on 3c. brown/*yellow*	1·40	2·00
		a. Stop after 'THREE.'	55·00	65·00
		b. Imperf between (vert pair)	£750	
		c. Imperf horiz (vert pair)	£750	
		d. Bar omitted (1st ptg)	£225	£250
		e. Bar at top and bottom (1st ptg)	£375	
		f. Surch double (2nd ptg)	£450	£500

No. 27 was surcharged with a setting of 100 (10×10). It was originally intended that there should be no bar at foot, but this was then added at a second operation before the stamps were issued. Subsequent supplies were surcharged with 'ONE CENT' and bar at one operation.

Varieties with part of the surcharge missing are due to gum on the face of the unsurcharged stamps receiving part of the surcharge, which was afterwards washed off.

11 12 13 14

Sir Charles Brooke

(Die eng Wm. Ridgeway. Recess P.B.)

1895 (12 Feb–Sept). No wmk. P 11½–12.

28	**11**	2c. brown-red	18·00	9·00
		a. Imperf between (vert pair)	£600	
		b. Imperf between (horiz pair)	£450	£500
		c. Second ptg. Perf 12½ (9.95)	26·00	5·50
		ca. Perf 12½. Imperf between (horiz pair)	£700	
29	**12**	4c. black	18·00	3·50
		a. Imperf between (horiz pair)	£850	
30	**13**	6c. violet	21·00	9·00
31	**14**	8c. green	48·00	6·00
28/31 *Set of 4*			95·00	22·00

Stamps of these types, printed in wrong colours, are trials and these, when surcharged with values in 'pence', are from waste sheets that were used by Perkins Bacon & Co as trial paper when preparing the 1896–1897 issue of stamps for British South Africa Company (Rhodesia).

4
CENTS.
(15)

16

1899 (29 June–16 Nov). Surch as T **15**.

32	**2**	2c. on 3c. brown/*yellow* (19.9)	4·00	1·75
		a. Stop after 'THREE'	90·00	90·00
		b. Imperf between (vert pair)	£900	
33		2c. on 12c. red/*pale rose*	3·75	6·00
		a. Surch inverted	£900	£1400
34		4c. on 6c. green/*green* (R.) (16.11)	60·00	£120
35		4c. on 8c. bright blue/*blue* (R.)	9·50	17·00
32/35 *Set of 4*			70·00	£120

A variety of surcharge with small 'S' in 'CENTS' may be found in the 2c. on 12c. and 4c. on 8c. (R. 1/2, 1/8 and 3/1, first setting) and a raised stop after 'CENTS' on the 4c. on 6c. (R. 1/5).

The omission of parts of the surcharge is due to gum on the surface of the stamps (see note after No. 27).

No. 35 is known with compound perforation, perf 12.7 on one or two sides, from the margins of sheets. Examples are rare. (*Price, £225 unused*)

(Typo D.L.R.)

1899 (10 Nov)–**1908**. Inscribed 'POSTAGE POSTAGE'. No wmk. P 14.

36	**4**	1c. grey-blue and rosine (1.1.01)	1·50	1·25
		a. Grey-blue and red	6·50	2·75
		b. Ultramarine and rosine	12·00	3·75
		c. Dull blue and carmine	19·00	6·00
37		2c. green (16.12.99)	2·00	90
38		3c. dull purple (1.2.08)	28·00	65
39		4c. rose-carmine (10.11.99)	17·00	2·50
		a. Aniline carmine	3·00	15
40		8c. yellow and black (6.12.99)	2·75	80
41		10c. ultramarine (10.11.99)	8·50	1·00
42		12c. mauve (16.12.99)	7·00	4·50
		a. Bright mauve (1905)	50·00	14·00
43		16c. chestnut and green (16.12.99)	8·50	1·75
44		20c. bistre and bright mauve (4.00)	9·00	7·50
45		25c. brown and blue (16.12.99)	11·00	7·00
46		50c. sage-green and carmine (16.12.99)	38·00	40·00
47		$1 rose-carmine and green (16.12.99)	£100	£130
		a. Rosine and pale green	£120	£140
36/47 *Set of 12*			£180	£170
		Prepared for use but not issued		
48	**4**	5c. olive-grey and green	15·00	

The figures of value in the $1 are in colour on an uncoloured ground.

1902. Inscribed 'POSTAGE POSTAGE'. W **16**. P 14.

49	**4**	2c. green	60·00	22·00

Sir Charles Vyner Brooke. 17 May 1917–1 June 1946

17 Sir Charles Vyner Brooke

ONE
cent
(18)

(Typo D.L.R.)

1918 (24 Mar–Apr). Chalk-surfaced paper. No wmk. P 14.

50	**17**	1c. slate-blue and red	2·25	3·25
		a. Dull blue and carmine	2·25	3·50
51		2c. green	2·50	1·50
52		3c. brown-purple (4.18)	3·25	2·75
53		4c. rose-carmine (4.18)	9·50	4·25
		a. Rose-red	14·00	3·00
54		8c. yellow and black (4.18)	19·00	75·00
55		10c. blue (*shades*) (4.18)	7·00	6·50
56		12c. purple (4.18)	25·00	55·00
57		16c. chestnut and green (4.18)	5·50	7·50
58		20c. olive and violet (*shades*) (4.18)	9·50	6·50
59		25c. brown and bright blue (4.18)	4·00	25·00
60		50c. olive-green and carmine (4.18)	10·00	15·00
61		$1 bright rose and green (4.18)	45·00	30·00
50/61 *Set of 12*			£120	£200
50s/61s Optd 'SPECIMEN' *Set of 12*			£400	
		Prepared for use but not issued		
62	**17**	1c. slate-blue and slate	22·00	

On the $1 the figures of value are in colour on an uncoloured ground.

Most values are known with part strikes of a forged Kuching postmark dated '12 MAR 90'.

1922 (Jan)–**23**. New colours and values. Chalk-surfaced paper. No wmk. P 14.

63	**17**	2c. purple (5.3.23)	2·00	2·75
64		3c. dull green (23.3.22)	5·50	1·25
65		4c. brown-purple (10.4.23)	2·50	2·50
66		5c. yellow-orange	3·00	2·75
67		6c. claret	2·25	1·40
68		8c. bright rose-red (1922)	4·50	32·00
69		10c. black (1923)	4·75	5·00
70		12c. bright blue (12.22)	15·00	18·00
		a. Pale dull blue	12·00	27·00
71		30c. ochre-brown and slate	3·75	4·25
63/71 *Set of 9*			35·00	60·00

1923 (Jan). Surch as T **18**.

		(a) First printing. Bars 1¼ mm apart		
72	**17**	1c. on 10c. dull blue	10·00	65·00
		a. 'cnet' for 'cent' (R. 9/5)	£425	£900
73		2c. on 12c. purple	7·00	55·00
		a. Thick, narrower 'W' in 'TWO'	23·00	£120
		(b) Second printing. Bars ¾ mm apart		
74	**17**	1c. on 10c. dull blue	£600	
		b. 'cnet' for 'cent' (R. 9/5)	£24000	
		c. Bright blue	£180	£500
		ca. 'en' of 'cent' scratched out and 'ne' overprinted (R. 9/5)	£9000	
75		2c. on 12c. purple	90·00	£350
		a. Thick, narrower 'W' in 'TWO'	£160	

In the 2c. on 12c. the words of the surcharge are about 7½ mm from the bars.

The 'cnet' error occurred on R. 9/5 of all sheets from the first printing of the 1c. on 10c. A single example of the error, No. 74b, is known from the second printing, but the error was then corrected, as shown by the evidence of a surviving plate block, only to have the correct spelling scratched out by a local employee, and 'ne' substituted (No. 74ca).

The thick 'W' variety occurs on all stamps of the last two horizontal rows of the first printing (12 stamps per sheet), and in the last two vertical rows of the second (20 stamps per sheet).

1928 (7 Apr)–**29**. Chalk-surfaced paper. W **16** (Multiple). P 14.

76	**17**	1c. slate-blue and carmine	1·50	1·25
77		2c. bright purple	2·25	2·00
78		3c. green	4·50	5·50
79		4c. brown-purple	1·75	10
80		5c. yellow-orange (7.8.29)	12·00	5·00
81		6c. claret	1·25	30
82		8c. bright rose-red	3·25	38·00
83		10c. black	1·75	2·75
84		12c. bright blue	3·25	45·00
85		16c. chestnut and green	3·75	4·25
86		20c. olive-bistre and violet	3·75	11·00
87		25c. brown and bright blue	7·00	8·50
88		30c. bistre-brown and slate	4·50	10·00
89		50c. olive-green and carmine	17·00	25·00
90		$1 bright rose and green	21·00	25·00
76/90 *Set of 15*			75·00	£160
76s/90s Optd or Perf (5c.) 'SPECIMEN' *Set of 15*			£425	

In the $1 the value is as before.

19 Sir Charles Vyner Brooke

20

(Recess Waterlow)

1932 (1 Jan). W **20**. P 12½.

91	**19**	1c. indigo	80	1·00
92		2c. green	1·00	2·25
		w. Wmk inverted	—	£500
93		3c. violet	4·00	1·00
94		4c. red-orange	13·00	75
95		5c. deep lake	6·50	1·25
96		6c. scarlet	7·00	11·00
97		8c. orange-yellow	11·00	8·50
98		10c. black	2·25	3·25
99		12c. deep ultramarine	4·00	9·50
100		15c. chestnut	6·50	14·00
101		20c. red-orange and violet	6·50	8·00
102		25c. orange-yellow and chestnut	10·00	28·00
103		30c. sepia and vermilion	9·50	45·00
104		50c. carmine-red and olive-green	14·00	13·00
105		$1 green and carmine	22·00	35·00
91/105 *Set of 15*			£100	£160
91s/105s Perf 'SPECIMEN' *Set of 15*			£425	

21 Sir Charles Vyner Brooke

BMA
(22)

(Recess B.W.)

1934 (1 May)–**41**. No wmk. P 12.

106	**21**	1c. purple	1·25	10
107		2c. green	1·50	10
107*a*		2c. black (1.3.41)	4·75	1·60
108		3c. black	1·25	10
108*a*		3c. green (1.3.41)	7·50	4·50
109		4c. bright purple	2·00	15
110		5c. violet	2·00	10
111		6c. carmine	2·75	60
111*a*		6c. lake-brown (1.3.41)	8·50	8·00
112		8c. red-brown	2·25	10
112*a*		8c. carmine (1.3.41)	9·00	10
113		10c. scarlet	5·00	40
114		12c. blue	3·00	25

114*a*		12c. orange (1.3.41)	7·50	4·75
115		15c. orange	8·00	10·00
115*a*		15c. blue (1.3.41)	9·00	15·00
116		20c. olive-green and carmine	8·00	1·25
117		25c. violet and orange	8·00	1·25
118		30c. red-brown and violet	8·00	2·00
119		50c. violet and scarlet	12·00	75
120		$1 scarlet and sepia	7·00	75
121		$2 bright purple and violet	30·00	38·00
122		$3 carmine and green	50·00	55·00
123		$4 blue and scarlet	50·00	80·00
124		$5 scarlet and red-brown	75·00	85·00
125		$10 black and yellow	35·00	85·00
106/125 *Set of* 26			£325	£350
106s/125s Perf 'SPECIMEN' *Set of* 26			£850	

The original set of 20 (excluding Nos. 107*a*, 108*a*, 111*a*, 112*a*, 114*a*, 115*a*) exist imperforate from proof sheets. (*Price for set of 20 imperforate pairs, £1300 unused)*

For the 3c. green, wmkd Mult Script CA, see No. 152a.

BRITISH MILITARY ADMINISTRATION

Following the Japanese surrender, elements of the British Military Administration reached Kuching on 11 September 1945. From 5 November 1945 current Australian 1d., 3d., 6d. and 1s. stamps were made available for civilian use until replaced by Nos. 126/145. Other Australian stamps were also accepted as valid for postage during this period.

1945 (17 Dec). Optd with T **22**.

126	**21**	1c. purple	1·25	60
127		2c. black (R.)	5·50	1·50
		a. Opt double	£8500	£5500
128		3c. green	1·25	2·00
129		4c. bright purple	5·00	2·00
		a. Opt double, one albino	£2250	
130		5c. violet (R.)	6·50	2·50
131		6c. lake-brown	6·00	75
132		8c. carmine	19·00	28·00
133		10c. scarlet	2·75	70
134		12c. orange	7·00	3·75
135		15c. blue	11·00	40
136		20c. olive-green and carmine	7·00	7·50
137		25c. violet and orange (R.)	7·50	4·50
138		30c. red-brown and violet	12·00	5·50
139		50c. violet and scarlet	2·50	50
140		$1 scarlet and sepia	3·50	7·00
141		$2 bright purple and violet	16·00	28·00
142		$3 carmine and green	50·00	£100
143		$4 blue and scarlet	45·00	70·00
144		$5 scarlet and red-brown	£200	£300
145		$10 black and yellow (R.)	£225	£275
126/145 *Set of* 20			£550	£750

These stamps, and the similarly overprinted stamps of North Borneo, were obtainable at all post offices throughout British Borneo (Brunei, Labuan, North Borneo and Sarawak), for use on local and overseas mail.

The administration of Sarawak was returned to the Brooke family on 15 April 1946, but the Rajah, after consulting the inhabitants, ceded the territory to Great Britain on 1 June 1946. Values from the 1934–1941 issue were used until replaced by Nos. 150/164.

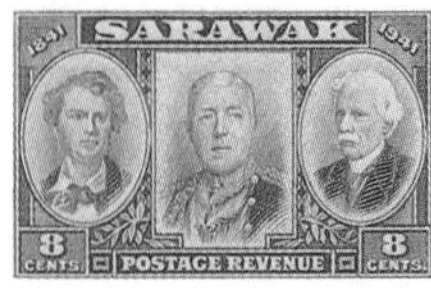

23 Sir James Brooke, Sir Charles Vyner Brooke and Sir Charles Brooke

(**24**)

(Recess B.W.)

1946 (18 May). Centenary Issue. P 12.

146	**23**	8c. lake	4·75	1·75
147		15c. blue	5·00	2·25
148		50c. black and scarlet	5·00	2·50
149		$1 black and sepia	5·00	42·00
146/149 *Set of* 4			18·00	45·00
146s/149s Perf 'SPECIMEN' *Set of* 4			£225	

Nos. 146/149 exist imperforate from proof sheets. (*Price for set of 4 imperforate pairs, £300 unused)*

CROWN COLONY

1947 (16 Apr). Optd with T **24**, typo by B.W. in blue-black or red. Wmk Mult Script CA. P 12.

150	**21**	1c. purple	20	30
151		2c. black (R.)	25	15
152		3c. green (R.)	25	15
		a. Albino opt	£9500	
153		4c. bright purple	30	15
154		6c. lake-brown	50	90
155		8c. carmine	1·00	10
156		10c. scarlet	50	20
157		12c. orange	70	1·00
158		15c. blue (R.)	50	40
159		20c. olive-green and carmine (R.)	2·25	50
160		25c. violet and orange (R.)	65	30
161		50c. violet and scarlet (R.)	1·25	40
162		$1 scarlet and sepia	1·50	90
163		$2 bright purple and violet	4·00	8·00
164		$5 scarlet and red-brown	13·00	3·25
150/164 *Set of* 15			24·00	15·00
150s/164s Perf 'SPECIMEN' *Set of* 15			£400	

No. 152a shows an uninked impression of T **24**.

1948 (25 Oct). Royal Silver Wedding. As Nos. 112/113 of Antigua.

165	8c. scarlet	30	30
166	$5 brown	48·00	60·00

1949 (10 Oct). 75th Anniversary of UPU. As Nos. 114/117 of Antigua.

167	8c. carmine	1·25	60
168	15c. deep blue	3·50	2·50
169	25c. deep blue-green	2·00	2·00
170	50c. violet	2·00	7·00
167/170 *Set of* 4		8·00	11·00

25 *Trogonoptera brookiana*

26 Western Tarsier

27 Kayan tomb

28 Kayan girl and boy

29 Bead work

30 Dyak dancer

31 Malayan Pangolin

32 Kenyan boys

33 Fire making

34 Kelemantan rice barn

35 Pepper vines

36 Iban woman

37 Kelabit Smithy

38 Map of Sarawak

39 Arms of Sarawak

(Recess; $5 Arms typo B.W.)

1950 (3 Jan). Types **25/39**. Wmk Mult Script CA. P 11½×11 (horiz) or 11×11½ (vert).

171	**25**	1c. black	75	30
172	**26**	2c. red-orange	45	40
173	**27**	3c. green	60	1·25
174	**28**	4c. chocolate	1·25	20
175	**29**	6c. turquoise-blue	75	20
176	**30**	8c. scarlet	1·00	30
177	**31**	10c. orange	3·25	6·00
178	**32**	12c. violet	3·50	1·50
179	**33**	15c. blue	4·50	15
180	**34**	20c. purple-brown and red-orange	3·00	30
181	**35**	25c. green and scarlet	3·75	30
182	**36**	50c. brown and violet	8·50	45
183	**37**	$1 green and chocolate	27·00	4·50
184	**38**	$2 blue and carmine	45·00	17·00
185	**39**	$5 black, yellow, red and purple	35·00	20·00
171/185 *Set of* 15			£120	48·00

40 Map of Sarawak

(Recess B.W.)

1952 (1 Feb). Wmk Mult Script CA. P 11½×11.

186	**40**	10c. orange	1·75	50

1953 (3 June). Coronation. As No. 120 of Antigua.

187	10c. black and deep violet-blue	2·25	1·75

41 Logging

42 Young Orangutan

43 Kayan dancing

44 Malabar Pied Hornbill

45 Shield with spears

46 Kenyah ceremonial carving

47 Barong panau (sailing prau)

48 Turtles

49 Melanau basket-making

50 Astana, Kuching

51 Queen Elizabeth II

52 Queen Elizabeth II (after Annigoni)

(Des M. Thoma (1, 2c.), R. Turrell (4c.), J. D. Hughes (6, 12c.) A. Hakim bin Moliti (8c.), J. Woodcock (10c.), J. Browning (15c.), G. Gundersen (20c.), K. Munich (25c.), Recess, Arms typo ($5). B.W.)

1955 (1 June)–**59**. Types **41/52**. Wmk Mult Script CA. P 11×11½ (1c., 2c., 4c.), 12×13 (30c., 50c., $1, $2) or 11½×11 (others).

188	**41**	1c. green (1.10.57)	10	30
189	**42**	2c. red-orange (1.10.57)	30	55
190	**43**	4c. lake-brown (1.10.57)	1·50	60
		a. Brown-purple (18.3.59)	12·00	7·00
191	**44**	6c. greenish blue (1.10.57)	3·75	3·25
192	**45**	8c. rose-red (1.10.57)	40	30
193	**46**	10c. deep green (1.10.57)	30	10
194	**47**	12c. plum (1.10.57)	3·75	55
195	**48**	15c. ultramarine (1.10.57)	2·25	30
196	**49**	20c. olive and brown (1.10.57)	1·00	10
197	**50**	25c. sepia and green (1.10.57)	6·50	20
198	**51**	30c. red-brown and deep lilac	9·00	30
199		50c. black and carmine (1.10.57)	2·50	30
200	**52**	$1 myrtle-green and orange-brown (1.10.57)	16·00	1·75
201		$2 violet and bronze-green (1.10.57)	27·00	2·50
202	–	$5 multicoloured (1.10.57)	42·00	17·00
188/202 *Set of* 15			£100	25·00

1963 (4 June). Freedom from Hunger. As No. 146 of Antigua.

203	12c. sepia	1·75	1·25

STATE OF MALAYSIA

1964–65. As 1955–1957 but wmk w **12**. Perfs as before.

No.	Type	Description	Unused	Used
204	**41**	1c. green (8.9.64)	15	75
205	**42**	2c. red-orange (11.10.65)	1·25	16·00
206	**44**	6c. greenish blue (8.9.64)	6·50	5·00
207	**46**	10c. deep green (8.9.64)	2·25	1·00
208	**47**	12c. plum (8.9.64)	5·00	15·00
209	**48**	15c. ultramarine (17.8.65)	1·25	14·00
210	**49**	20c. olive and brown (9.6.64)	1·25	1·00
211	**50**	25c. deep sepia and bluish green (8.9.64)	5·50	5·50
204/211 *Set of 8*			21·00	50·00

53 *Vanda hookeriana*

1965 (15 Nov). As Nos. 166/172 of Johore but with Arms of Sarawak inset as in T **53**.

No.	Description	Unused	Used
212	1c. multicoloured	10	1·10
	c. Grey omitted	£150	
213	2c. multicoloured	1·25	2·00
	a. Black (country name and shield) omitted	£300	
	c. Yellow-olive (stems) omitted	£200	
214	5c. multicoloured	1·75	10
215	6c. multicoloured	1·25	1·50
	a. Black (country name and shield) omitted	£400	
216	10c. multicoloured	1·25	10
	a. Red omitted	£180	
	b. Intense black	2·00	20
217	15c. multicoloured	1·50	10
218	20c. multicoloured	2·00	50
212/218 *Set of 7*		8·00	4·75

The 1c., 6c., 10c. and 15c. exist with PVA gum as well as gum arabic.

No. 213a was formerly listed with Trengganu No. 101 but there is evidence that it was issued in Sarawak.

A used example of No. 218 is known with the bright purple (blooms) omitted.

The higher values used with this issue were Nos. 20/27 of Malaysia (National Issues).

TELEGRAPH STAMPS

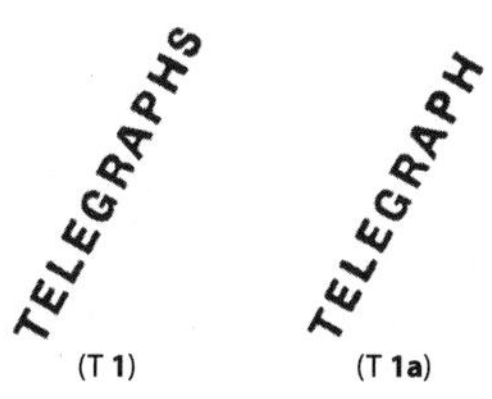

(T **1**) (T **1a**)

1933 (1 Jan). Revenue stamps of 1927 opt at Government Printing Office, Kuching as Types T **1**/**1 a**. No wmk. Chalk-surfaced paper. Perf 14.

*(a) Opt Type T **1**, inscr 'TELEGRAPHS'*

No.	Description	Unused	Used
T1	3c. purple and carmine	†	£800
T2	5c. purple and green	†	£425
T3	10c. purple and violet	†	£425
T4	25c. purple and blue	†	£325
T5	50c. purple and black	†	£600

*(b) Opt Type T **1a**, inscr 'TELEGRAPH'*

No.	Description	Unused	Used
T9	5c. purple and green	†	£400
T10	$1 yellow-green and green	†	£900

Higher values up to $10 are believed to have been issued, but no examples have been seen. The values listed above are only known in used condition, with circular datestamps of Trusan or Sarikei.

Telegraph
(T **2**)

Telegraph
50 Cts.
(T **3**)

Telegraph
$2.
(T **4**)

1934(?). Postage stamps of 1932 (Nos. 91, 93/100, 102, 105) optd or surch as Types T **2**/**4**.

No.	Type	Description	Unused
T12	T **2**	1c. indigo	17·00
T13		3c. violet	8·50
T14		5c. deep lake	8·50
T15		10c. black	9·50
T16		25c. orange-yellow and chestnut	9·50
T17	T **3**	50c. on 4c. red-orange	12·00
		a. '5' with straight top and 'Cts' sans-serif	£100
T18	T **2**	$1 green and carmine	14·00
T19	T **4**	$2 on 6c. scarlet	14·00
T20		$3 on 12c. deep ultramarine	17·00
T21		$4 on 15c. chestnut	17·00
T22		$5 on 8c. orange-yellow	17·00
T12/T22 *Set of 11*			£130

No. T17a occurs at R. 1/5–8 in the setting of 100 (10×10).

No used examples of Nos. T12/T22 have been seen.

JAPANESE OCCUPATION OF SARAWAK

Japanese forces landed in North Borneo on 16 December 1941 and Sarawak was attacked on 23 December 1941.

Brunei, North Borneo, Sarawak and after a short period, Labuan, were administered as a single territory by the Japanese. Until September–October 1942, previous stamp issues, without overprint, continued to be used in conjunction with existing postmarks. From 1 October 1942 onwards unoverprinted stamps of Japan were made available and examples can be found used from the area for much of the remainder of the War. Japanese Occupation issues for Brunei, North Borneo and Sarawak were equally valid throughout the combined territory but not, in practice, equally available.

PRICES FOR STAMPS ON COVER TO 1945

Nos. J1/J21	*from* × 8
Nos. J22/J26	—

府政國帝本日大

(**1**) ('Imperial Japanese Government')

1942 (Oct). Stamps of Sarawak handstamped with T **1** in violet.

No.	Type	Description	Unused	Used
J1	**21**	1c. purple	48·00	95·00
		a. Pair, one without opt	£5500	
J2		2c. green	£190	£250
		a. Black opt	£130	
J3		2c. black	£180	£200
		a. Black opt	£350	£400
J4		3c. black	£650	£650
J5		3c. green	£100	£130
		a. Black opt	£300	
J6		4c. bright purple	£140	£160
		a. Black opt	£300	
J7		5c. violet	£170	£180
		a. Black opt	£275	
J8		6c. carmine	£225	£225
J9		6c. lake-brown	£170	£180
		a. Black opt	£300	£325
J10		8c. red-brown	£600	£600
		a. Black opt	£1000	
J11		8c. carmine	75·00	£130
		a. Black opt	£475	£600
J12		10c. scarlet	£140	£160
		a. Black opt	£300	
J13		12c. blue	£250	£250
		a. Black opt	£500	
J14		12c. orange	£200	£200
J15		15c. orange	£600	£650
		a. Black opt	£950	
J16		15c. blue	£200	£225
J17		20c. olive-green and carmine	95·00	£140
		a. Black opt	£300	
J18		25c. violet and orange	£140	£180
		a. Black opt	£325	
J19		30c. red-brown and violet	£100	£150
		a. Black opt	£325	
J20		50c. violet and scarlet	95·00	£140
		a. Black opt	£600	
		b. Blue opt	£1000	
J21		$1 scarlet and sepia	£190	£225
		a. Blue opt	£550	
J22		$2 bright purple and violet	£350	£550
		a. Blue opt	£600	
J23		$3 carmine and green	£4500	£4500
		a. Black opt	£6500	
J24		$4 blue and scarlet	£350	£650
J25		$5 scarlet and red-brown	£350	£650
J26		$10 black and yellow	£350	£650

The overprint, being handstamped, exists inverted or double on some values. Those on Nos. J20b, J21a and J22a are diagonal. The remainder are horizontal.

Stamps of T **21** optd with Japanese symbols within an oval frame are revenue stamps, while the same stamps overprinted with three Japanese characters between two vertical double rules, were used as seals.

Nos. J1/J26 have been extensively forged. Recent research indicates that complete or part sets *on cover* cancelled by Japanese circular postmarks in violet dated '17 11 21' (21 Nov 1942) or '18 3 1' (1 Mar 1943) have forged overprints.

Seychelles

Seychelles was administered as a dependency of Mauritius from 1810 until 1903, although separate stamp issues were provided from April 1890 onwards.

The first post office was opened, at Victoria on Mahé, on 11 December 1861 and the stamps of Mauritius were used there until 1890. No further post offices were opened until 1901.

Z **1**

Stamps of MAURITIUS cancelled with T Z **1**.

1859–61.

No.	Description	Used
Z2	6d. blue (No. 32)	£900
Z3	6d. dull purple-slate (No. 33)	£2250
Z4	1s. vermilion (No. 34)	£1400

1860–63. (Nos. 46/53).

No.	Description	Used
Z5	1d. purple-brown	£225
Z6	2d. blue	£275
Z7	4d. rose	£250
Z8	6d. green	£1000
Z9	6d. slate	£650
Z10	9d. dull purple	£120
Z11	1s. buff	£325
Z12	1s. green	£800

1862.

No.	Description	Used
Z13	6d. slate (No. 54)	£800

1863–72. (Nos. 56/72).

No.	Description	Used
Z14	1d. purple-brown	£130
Z14*a*	1d. brown	£110
Z15	1d. bistre	£120
Z16	2d. pale blue	£130
Z17	2d. bright blue	£130
Z18	3d. deep red	£160
Z19	3d. dull red	95·00
Z20	4d. rose	48·00
Z21	6d. dull violet	£250
Z22	6d. yellow-green	£110
Z23	6d. blue-green	80·00
Z24	9d. yellow-green	£2250
Z25	10d. maroon	£325
Z26	1s. yellow	£110
Z27	1s. blue	£325
Z28	1s. orange	£110
Z29	5s. rosy mauve	£950
Z30	5s. bright mauve	£950

1876. (Nos. 76/77).

No.	Description	Used
Z31	½d. on 9d. dull purple	£325
Z32	½d. on 10d. maroon	£300

1877. (Nos. 79/82).

No.	Description	Used
Z33	½d. on 10d. rose	£650
Z34	1d. on 4d. rose-carmine	
Z35	1s. on 5s. rosy mauve	
Z36	1s. on 5s. bright mauve	

1878. (Nos. 83/91).

No.	Description	Used
Z37	2c. dull rose (lower label blank)	£100
Z38	4c. on 1d. bistre	£375
Z39	8c. on 2d. blue	40·00
Z40	13c. on 3d. orange-red	£120
Z41	17c. on 4d. rose	40·00
Z42	25c. on 6d. slate-blue	£120
Z43	38c. on 9d. pale violet	£600
Z44	50c. on 1s. green	£120
Z45	2r.50 on 5s. bright mauve	£500

1879–80. (Nos. 92/100).

No.	Description	Used
Z46	2c. Venetian red	£130
Z47	4c. orange	£130
Z48	8c. blue	40·00
Z49	13c. slate	£1500
Z50	17c. rose	95·00
Z51	25c. olive-yellow	£200
Z52	38c. bright purple	£2250
Z53	50c. green	£850
Z54	2r.50 brown-purple	£850

1883–90.

No.	Description	Used
Z55	2c. Venetian red (No. 102)	£100
Z56	2c. green (No. 103)	£200
Z57	4c. orange (No. 104)	70·00
Z58	4c. carmine (No. 105)	95·00
Z59	16c. chestnut (No. 109)	55·00
Z60	25c. olive-yellow (No. 110)	£110
Z61	50c. orange (No. 111)	£950

1883.

No.	Description	Used
Z62	16c. on 17c. rose (No. 112)	£120

1883.

No.	Description	Used
Z63	16c. on 17c. rose (No. 115)	48·00

1885.

No.	Description	Used
Z64	2c. on 38c. bright purple (No. 116)	

1887.

No.	Description	Used
Z65	2c. on 13c. slate (No. 117)	

POSTAL FISCAL

1889.

ZR1 4c. lilac (No. R2) ... £2250

Mauritius stamps are occasionally found cancelled with the 'SEYCHELLES' cds. Examples are known dated between 25 and 29 February 1884 when it seems that T Z **1** may have been mislaid (*Price from* £500).

We no longer list the GB 1862 6d. lilac with this obliteration as there is no evidence that the stamps of Great Britain were sold by the Victoria post office.

PRICES FOR STAMPS ON COVER TO 1945

Nos. 1/8	*from* × 20
Nos. 9/24	*from* × 30
No. 25	*from* × 10
No. 26	*from* × 20
No. 27	*from* × 10
Nos. 28/32	*from* × 20
No. 33	*from* × 5
No. 34	*from* × 30
Nos. 35/36	—
Nos. 37/40	*from* × 40
Nos. 41/42	*from* × 25
Nos. 43/45	*from* × 10
Nos. 46/50	*from* × 30
Nos. 51/54	*from* × 10
Nos. 55/56	—
Nos. 57/59	*from* × 10
Nos. 60/67	*from* × 20
Nos. 68/70	—
Nos. 71/81	*from* × 10
Nos. 82/131	*from* × 5
Nos. 132/134	*from* × 10
Nos. 135/149	*from* × 3

(Currency: 100 cents = 1 Mauritius, later Seychelles rupee)

DEPENDENCY OF MAURITIUS

PRINTERS. Nos. 1 to 123 were typographed by De La Rue & Co.

1

Die I

Die II

In Die I there are lines of shading in the middle compartment of the diadem which are absent from Die II.

Normal

Malformed 'S'

Repaired 'S'

The malformed 'S' occurs on R. 7/3 of the left pane from Key Plate 2. It is believed that the repair to it took place in mid-1898. Both states may occur on other stamps in Types **1** and **4**. Stamps subsequently printed from Key Plate 3 showed the 'S' normal.

1890 (5 Apr)–**92**. Wmk Crown CA. P 14.

(i) Die I

1	1	2c. green and carmine	10·00	21·00
2		4c. carmine and green	48·00	21·00
3		8c. brown-purple and blue	19·00	3·50
4		10c. ultramarine and brown	18·00	42·00
5		13c. grey and black	6·00	20·00
6		16c. chestnut and blue	16·00	4·25
7		48c. ochre and green	28·00	10·00
8		96c. mauve and carmine	70·00	48·00
1/8 *Set of 8*			£190	£150
1s/8s Optd 'SPECIMEN' *Set of 8*			£225	

(ii) Die II (1892)

9	1	2c. green and rosine	2·50	1·00
10		4c. carmine and green	2·50	1·75
11		8c. brown-purple and ultramarine	16·00	1·75
12		10c. bright ultramarine and brown	16·00	3·25
13		13c. grey and black	8·00	2·50
14		16c. chestnut and ultramarine	45·00	11·00
		a. Malformed 'S'	£750	£950
9/14 *Set of 6*			80·00	19·00

The 10c. Die I also exists in ultramarine and chestnut, but has so far only been found with 'SPECIMEN' overprint (*Price* £800).

3 cents (2)

18 CENTS (3)

4

1893 (1 Jan). Surch locally as T **2**.

15	3c. on 4c. (No. 10)	1·10	1·50
	a. Surch inverted	£300	£375
	b. Surch double	£475	
	c. Surch omitted (in horiz pair with normal)	£14000	
16	12c. on 16c. (No. 6)	9·50	10·00
	a. Surch inverted	£500	
	b. Surch double	£15000	£9000
17	12c. on 16c. (No. 14)	22·00	2·50
	a. Surch double	£4500	£4500
	b. Surch omitted (in pair with normal)		
18	15c. on 16c. (No. 6)	18·00	13·00
	a. Surch inverted	£325	£300
	b. Surch double	£1300	£1300
19	15c. on 16c. (No. 14)	28·00	3·00
	a. Surch inverted	£900	£1000
	b. Surch double	£700	£750
	c. Surch triple	£4500	
20	45c. on 48c. (No. 7)	35·00	9·00
21	90c. on 96c. (No. 8)	70·00	50·00
	a. Wide 'O' (3½ *mm* wide instead of 3 *mm*) (R. 1/1, 2/1 of setting)	£400	£375
15/21 *Set of 7*		£160	80·00

Nos. 15/21 were each produced from settings of 30.

Nos. 15, 16, 18, 19 and 20 exist with 'cents' omitted and with 'cents' above value due to misplacement of the surcharge.

Some examples of No. 15b occur in the same sheet as No. 15c with the double surcharge on stamps from the last vertical row of the left pane and the surcharge omitted on stamps from the last vertical row of the right pane.

Most examples of the inverted surcharge error No. 16a were officially defaced with a red vertical ink line (*Price* £200, *unused*). Similarly examples of No. 19a exist defaced with a horizontal ink line (*Price* £400, *unused*).

1893 (Nov). New values. Die II. Wmk Crown CA. P 14.

22	1	3c. dull purple and orange	1·50	50
23		12c. sepia and green	2·50	1·75
24		15c. sage-green and lilac	10·00	2·00
25		45c. brown and carmine	25·00	35·00
22/25 *Set of 4*			35·00	35·00
22s/25s Optd 'SPECIMEN' *Set of 4*			£100	

1896 (1 Aug). No. 25 surch locally as T **3**.

26	1	18c. on 45c. brown and carmine	12·00	4·00
		a. Surch double	£1500	£1500
		b. Surch triple	£2250	
27		36c. on 45c. brown and carmine	12·00	60·00
		a. Surch double	£1800	
26s/27s Optd 'SPECIMEN' *Set of 2*			70·00	

1897–1900. Colours changed and new values. Die II. Wmk Crown CA. P 14.

28	1	2c. orange-brown and green (1900)	2·00	3·50
		a. Repaired 'S'	£350	£375
29		6c. carmine (1900)	5·00	50
		a. Repaired 'S'	£450	£300
30		15c. ultramarine (1900)	12·00	10·00
		a. Repaired 'S'	£550	£400
31		18c. ultramarine	16·00	1·50
32		36c. brown and carmine	48·00	8·00
33	4	75c. yellow and violet (1900)	55·00	70·00
		a. Repaired 'S'	£650	£850
34		1r. bright mauve and deep red	18·00	9·00
35		1r.50 grey and carmine (1900)	85·00	95·00
		a. Repaired 'S'	£800	£1000
36		2r.25 bright mauve and green (1900)	£110	85·00
		a. Repaired 'S'	£1000	
28/36 *Set of 9*			£300	£250
28s/36s Optd 'SPECIMEN' *Set of 9*			£275	

3 cents

(5)

6 cents (5a)

1901 (21 June–Sept). Surch locally with Types **5** or **5a**.

37	3c. on 10c. bright ultramarine and brown (No. 12) (9.01)	3·50	75
	a. Surch double	£900	
	b. Surch triple	£3250	
38	3c. on 16c. chestnut and ultramarine (No. 14) (8.01)	8·00	12·00
	a. Surch inverted	£700	£700
	b. Surch double	£500	£550
	c. '3 cents' omitted	£550	£550
	d. Malformed 'S'	£275	£425
39	3c. on 36c. brown and carmine (No. 32)	2·50	80
	a. Surch double	£750	£850
	b. '3 cents' omitted	£650	£700
40	6c. on 8c. brown-purple and ultramarine (No. 11) (7.01)	8·00	4·00
	a. Surch inverted	£650	£750
37/40 *Set of 4*		20·00	16·00
37s/40s H/S 'Specimen' (No. 37) or 'SPECIMEN' *Set of 4*		£110	

1902 (June). Surch locally as T **5**.

41	1	2c. on 4c. carmine and green (No. 10)	5·00	3·00
42	4	30c. on 75c. yellow and violet (No. 33)	3·00	8·00
		a. Narrow 'O' in '30' (R. 3/6, 5/2-4)	10·00	48·00
		b. Repaired 'S'	£350	£550
43		30c. on 1r. bright mauve and deep red (No. 34)	19·00	50·00
		a. Narrow 'O' in '30' (R. 3/6, 5/2-4)	40·00	£120
		b. Surch double	£1500	
44		45c. on 1r. bright mauve and deep red (No. 34)	10·00	50·00
45		45c. on 2r.25 bright mauve and green (No. 36)	50·00	£110
		a. Narrow '5' in '45' (R. 4/1)	£200	£375
		b. Repaired 'S'	£750	£1200
41/45 *Set of 5*			75·00	£200
41s/45s Optd 'Specimen' *Set of 5*			£140	

6

7

3 cents (8)

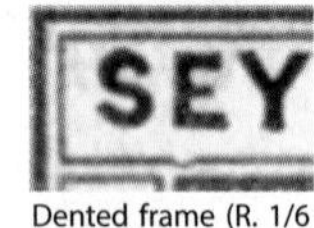
Dented frame (R. 1/6 of left pane)

1903 (26 May). Wmk Crown CA. P 14.

46	6	2c. chestnut and green	1·75	2·00
		a. Dented frame	£160	£190
47		3c. dull green	1·00	1·25
		a. Dented frame	£140	£170
48		6c. carmine	4·00	1·25
		a. Dented frame	£275	£170
49		12c. olive-sepia and dull green	6·50	2·50
		a. Dented frame	£325	£250
50		15c. ultramarine	8·00	3·50
		a. Dented frame	£375	£275
51		18c. sage-green and carmine	5·50	5·50
		a. Dented frame	£325	£400
52		30c. violet and dull green	11·00	20·00
		a. Dented frame	£425	£650
53		45c. brown and carmine	7·00	20·00
		a. Dented frame	£425	£650
		w. Wmk inverted	£500	£650
54	7	75c. yellow and violet	10·00	40·00
		a. Dented frame	£550	
55		1r.50 black and carmine	55·00	70·00
		a. Dented frame	£950	£1100
56		2r.25 purple and green	50·00	90·00
		a. Dented frame	£1000	£1400
46/56 *Set of 11*			£130	£225
46s/56s Optd 'SPECIMEN' *Set of 11*			£225	

1903. Surch locally with T **8**.

57	6	3c. on 15c. ultramarine (3.7)	1·00	3·75
		a. Dented frame	£275	£325
58		3c. on 18c. sage-green and carmine (2.9)	2·75	48·00
		a. Dented frame	£400	£1000
59		3c. on 45c. brown and carmine (21.7)	3·00	4·50
		a. Dented frame	£350	£350
57/59 *Set of 3*			6·00	50·00
57s/59s H/S 'Specimen' *Set of 3*			90·00	

CROWN COLONY

The Seychelles became a Separate Crown Colony by Letters Patent dated 31 August 1903.

1906. Wmk Mult Crown CA. P 14.

60	6	2c. chestnut and green	1·50	4·25
		a. Dented frame	£130	£225
61		3c. dull green	1·50	1·50
		a. Dented frame	£150	£170
62		6c. carmine	2·50	80
		a. Dented frame	£180	£130
63		12c. olive-sepia and dull green	3·00	3·25
		a. Dented frame	£275	£300
64		15c. ultramarine	3·00	2·00
		a. Dented frame	£275	£200
65		18c. sage-green and carmine	3·00	6·50
		a. Dented frame	£300	£400
66		30c. violet and dull green	6·00	8·00
		a. Dented frame	£350	£450
67		45c. brown and carmine	4·25	15·00
		a. Dented frame	£425	£550
68	7	75c. yellow and violet	8·50	55·00
		a. Dented frame	£550	£1300
69		1r.50 black and carmine	60·00	65·00
		a. Dented frame	£950	£950
70		2r.25 purple and green	55·00	65·00
		a. Dented frame	£950	£1000
60/70 *Set of 11*			£130	£200

9

10

Split 'A' (R. 8/3 of left pane)

1912 (Apr)–**16**. Wmk Mult Crown CA. P 14.

71	**9**	2c. chestnut and green	1·00	8·50
		a. Split 'A'	£130	£300
72		3c. green	7·00	60
		a. Split 'A'	£275	£130
73		6c. Carmine-red (6.13)	4·25	3·00
		a. Aniline-carmine (1916)	13·00	4·50
		b. Split 'A'	£325	£170
74		12c. olive-sepia and dull green (1.13)	1·50	8·00
		a. Split 'A'	£180	£325
75		15c. ultramarine	5·00	2·50
		a. Split 'A'	£325	£200
76		18c. sage-green and carmine (1.13)	3·25	15·00
		a. Split 'A'	£225	£425
77		30c. violet and green (1.13)	16·00	3·50
		a. Split 'A'	£375	£190
78		45c. brown and carmine (1.13)	2·75	50·00
		a. Split 'A'	£275	
79	**10**	75c. yellow and violet (1.13)	2·75	7·50
		a. Split 'A'	£300	£400
80		1r.50 black and carmine (1.13)	14·00	1·50
		a. Split 'A'	£475	£150
81		2r.25 deep magenta and green (*shades*) (1.13)	75·00	3·50
		a. Split 'A'	£1100	£250
71/81 *Set of* 11			£110	90·00
71s/81s Optd 'SPECIMEN' *Set of* 11			£250	

11

12

13

1917–22. Die I. Chalk-surfaced paper (18c. to 5r.). Wmk Mult Crown CA. P 14.

82	**11**	2c. chestnut and green	50	2·75
83		3c. green	2·00	1·25
84	**12**	5c. deep brown (1920)	5·00	16·00
85	**11**	6c. carmine	5·00	1·00
		a. Rose (1919)	13·00	2·50
86		12c. grey (1919)	2·50	2·50
87		15c. ultramarine	2·50	1·50
88		18c. purple/*yellow* (1919)	5·50	48·00
		a. On orange-buff (1920)	17·00	60·00
		b. On buff (1920)		
		c. Die II. *On pale yellow* (1922)	4·50	28·00
89	**13**	25c. black and red/*buff* (1920)	4·25	50·00
		a. On orange buff (1920)	40·00	75·00
		b. Die II. *On pale yellow* (1922)	6·00	20·00
90	**11**	30c. dull purple and olive (1918)	1·50	17·00
91		45c. dull purple and orange (1919)	4·50	48·00
92	**13**	50c. dull purple and black (1920)	15·00	60·00
93		75c. black/*blue-green* (*olive back*) (1918)	2·00	32·00
		a. Die II. *On emerald back* (1922)	1·40	26·00
94		1r. dull purple and red (1920)	23·00	70·00
95		1r.50 reddish purple and blue/*blue* (1918)	9·00	55·00
		a. Die II. *Blue-purple and blue/blue* (1922)	22·00	32·00
96		2r.25 yellow-green and violet (1918)	50·00	£160
97		5r. green and blue (1920)	£140	£300
82/97 *Set of* 16			£225	£700
82s/97s Optd 'SPECIMEN' *Set of* 16			£325	

Examples of most values are known showing forged postmarks. These include part strikes of Seychelles postmarks dated '24 AP 93' and 'AU 6 1903', and Victoria postmarks dated 'NO 27' or 'MY 6 35'.

1921–32. Die II. Chalk-surfaced paper (18c. and 25c. to 5r.). Wmk Mult Script CA. P 14.

98	**11**	2c. chestnut and green	25	15
99		3c. green	1·75	15
100		3c. black (1922)	1·25	30
101		4c. green (1922)	1·00	2·50
102		4c. sage-green and carmine (1928)	6·50	22·00
103	**12**	5c. deep brown	75	5·50
104	**11**	6c. carmine	6·00	9·00
		w. Wmk inverted	£250	£300
105		6c. deep mauve (1922)	1·50	10
106	**13**	9c. red (1927)	5·00	4·25
107	**11**	12c. grey	2·75	20
		a. Die I (1932)	30·00	65
108		12c. carmine-red (1922)	2·50	30
110		15c. bright blue	2·00	65·00
111		15c. yellow (1922)	1·00	2·75
112		18c. purple/*pale yellow* (1925)	2·50	22·00
113	**13**	20c. bright blue (1922)	1·50	35
		a. Dull blue (1924)	8·50	55
114		25c. black and red/*pale yellow* (1925)	2·75	27·00
115	**11**	30c. dull purple and olive	1·25	15·00
		w. Wmk inverted		
116		45c. dull purple and orange	1·25	7·50
117	**13**	50c. dull purple and black	2·50	2·25
118		75c. black/*emerald* (1924)	8·00	22·00
119		1r. dull purple and red	28·00	18·00
		a. Die I (1932)	12·00	35·00
121		1r.50 purple and blue/*blue* (1924)	17·00	22·00
122		2r.25 yellow-green and violet	21·00	15·00
123		5r. yellow-green and blue	£120	£170
98/123 *Set of* 24			£190	£375
98s/123s Optd 'SPECIMEN' *Set of* 24			£400	

The 3c. green and 12c. grey (Die II) were reissued in 1927. 'SPECIMEN' overprints on these printings are 15.5×1.75 mm instead of the 14.5×2.5 mm of the original issue. (*Price*, 3c. £650, 12c. £100).

Examples of most values are known showing the forged postmarks mentioned above.

1935 (6 May). Silver Jubilee. As Nos. 91/94 of Antigua, but ptd by B.W. P 11×12.

128	6c. ultramarine and grey-black	1·25	2·50
	a. Extra flagstaff	£250	£425
	b. Short extra flagstaff	£275	£400
	c. Lightning conductor	£375	
	d. Flagstaff on right-hand turret	£425	£450
	e. Double flagstaff	£475	£500
129	12c. green and indigo	5·50	1·50
	a. Extra flagstaff	£3500	£3750
	b. Short extra flagstaff	£450	£300
	c. Lightning conductor	£2500	
	d. Flagstaff on right-hand turret	£700	£700
	e. Double flagstaff	£700	£700
130	20c. brown and deep blue	4·00	5·50
	a. Extra flagstaff	£400	£500
	b. Short extra flagstaff	£325	
	c. Lightning conductor	£500	£550
	d. Flagstaff on right-hand turret	£750	£650
	e. Double flagstaff	£800	
131	1r. slate and purple	7·50	38·00
	a. Extra flagstaff	£225	£450
	b. Short extra flagstaff	£425	£700
	c. Lightning conductor	£325	£550
	d. Flagstaff on right-hand turret	£750	£850
	e. Double flagstaff	£650	
128/131 *Set of* 4		16·00	42·00
128s/131s Perf 'SPECIMEN' *Set of* 4		£170	

For illustrations of plate varieties see Omnibus section following Zanzibar.

Examples are known showing forged Victoria 'B MY 6 35' postmarks.

1937 (12 May). Coronation. As Nos. 95/97 of Antigua. P 11×11½

132	6c. sage-green	1·00	15
133	12c. orange	1·00	50
134	20c. blue	1·00	1·00
132/134 *Set of* 3		2·75	1·50
132s/134s Perf 'SPECIMEN' *Set of* 3		£110	

14 Coco-de-mer Palm

15 Giant Tortoise

16 Fishing Pirogue

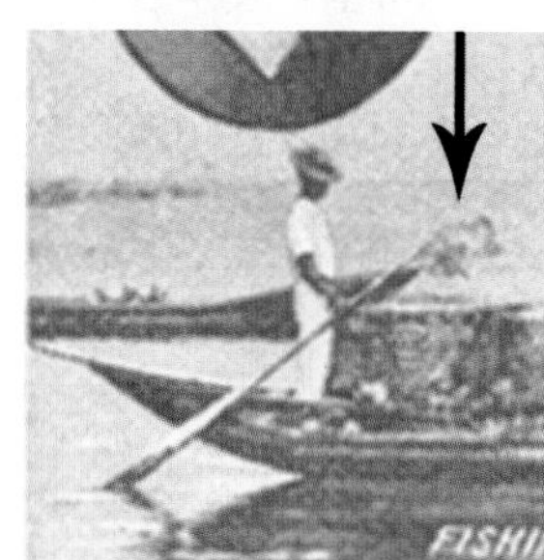
'Handkerchief' on oar flaw (R. 6/2)

(Photo Harrison)

1938 (1 Jan)–**49**. Wmk Mult Script CA. Chalk-surfaced paper. P 14½×13½ (vert) or 13½×14½ (horiz).

135	**14**	2c. purple-brown (10.2.38)	1·50	40
		a. Ordinary paper (18.11.42)	30	1·75
136	**15**	3c. green	12·00	3·00
136*a*		3c. orange (8.8.41)	1·25	1·00
		ab. Ordinary paper (18.11.42)	55	1·50
137	**16**	6c. orange	17·00	3·50
137*a*		6c. greyish green (8.8.41)	6·00	1·25
		aw. Wmk inverted	£1500	
		b. Ordinary paper. *Green* (18.11.42)	3·25	2·25
		c. Green (5.4.49)	22·00	1·50
138	**14**	9c. scarlet (10.2.38)	18·00	4·25
138*a*		9c. grey-blue (8.8.41)	38·00	40
		ab. Ordinary paper (18.11.42)	25·00	1·50
		ac. Ordinary paper. *Dull blue* (19.11.45)	8·50	3·25
		ad. Dull blue (5.4.49)	32·00	6·50
		aw. Wmk inverted	£5000	
139	**15**	12c. reddish violet	50·00	1·25
139*a*		15c. brown-carmine (8.8.41)	28·00	40
		ab. Ordinary paper. *Brown-red* (18.11.42)	10·00	4·75
139*c*	**14**	18c. carmine-lake (8.8.41)	14·00	60
		ca. Ordinary paper (18.11.42)	9·00	3·50
		cb. Rose-carmine (5.4.49)	42·00	18·00
140	**16**	20c. blue	45·00	6·00
140*a*		20c. brown-ochre (8.8.41)	29·00	65
		ab. 'Handkerchief' flaw	£600	£180
		b. Ordinary paper (18.11.42)	3·25	3·00
		ba. 'Handkerchief' flaw	£275	£180
141	**14**	25c. brown-ochre	50·00	14·00
142	**15**	30c. carmine (10.2.38)	50·00	11·00
142*a*		30c. blue (8.8.41)	50·00	50
		ab. Ordinary paper (18.11.42)	2·50	6·50
143	**16**	45c. chocolate (10.2.38)	45·00	4·50
		a. Ordinary paper. *Purple-brown* (18.11.42)	6·50	3·50
		b. Purple-brown (5.4.49)	48·00	23·00
144	**14**	50c. deep reddish violet (10.2.38)	20·00	60
		a. Ordinary paper (18.11.42)	1·75	3·25
144*b*		50c. bright lilac (13.6.49)	5·50	4·50
145	**15**	75c. slate-blue (10.2.38)	85·00	50·00
145*a*		75c. deep slate-lilac (8.8.41)	32·00	10·00
		ab. Ordinary paper (18.11.42)	4·75	10·00
146	**16**	1r. yellow-green (10.2.38)	£160	90·00
146*a*		1r. grey-black (8.8.41)	75·00	6·50
		ab. Ordinary paper (18.11.42)	6·00	8·00
147	**14**	1r.50 ultramarine (10.2.38)	48·00	8·50
		a. Ordinary paper (18.11.42)	9·00	18·00
		aw. Wmk inverted	£5000	
148	**15**	2r.25 olive (10.2.38)	75·00	19·00
		a. Ordinary paper (18.11.42)	32·00	45·00
149	**16**	5r. red (10.2.38)	32·00	17·00
		a. Ordinary paper (18.11.42)	35·00	48·00
135/149 *Set of* 25			£550	£225
135s/149s (*ex* 50c. bright lilac) Perf 'SPECIMEN' *Set of* 24			£850	

Examples of most values are known showing forged Victoria postmarks dated 'NO 27', 'SP 17 41', 'DE 12 41', 'SP 14 42', 'DE 21 42' or 'NO 16 43'.

Lamp on mast flaw (R. 1/5)

1946 (23 Sept). Victory. As Nos. 110/111 of Antigua.

150	9c. light blue	10	10
151	30c. deep blue	30	20
	a. Lamp on mast flaw	50·00	42·00
150s/151s Perf 'SPECIMEN' *Set of* 2		95·00	

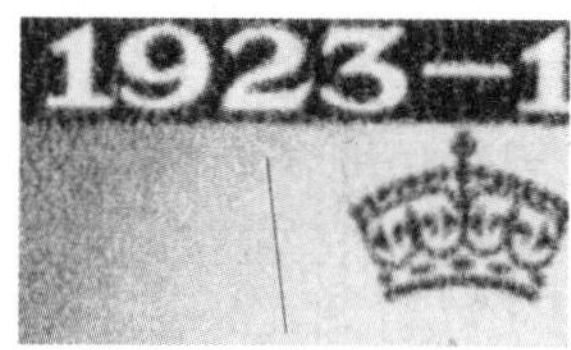

Line by crown (R. 1/3)

1948 (5 Nov). Royal Silver Wedding. As Nos 112/113 of Antigua.

152	9c. ultramarine	15	60
	a. Line by crown	48·00	65·00
153	5r. carmine	15·00	48·00

Examples are known showing forged Victoria 'C 11 NOV 48' postmarks.

1949 (10 Oct). 75th Anniversary of UPU. As Nos 114/117 of Antigua, but inscribed 'SEYCHELLES' in recess.

154	18c. bright reddish purple	20	25
155	50c. purple	1·75	4·00
156	1r. grey	50	60
157	2r.25 olive	35	1·50
154/157 *Set of* 4		2·50	5·75

17 Sailfish

18 Map of Indian Ocean

(Photo Harrison)

1952 (3 Mar). Various designs as Types **14/16** but with new portrait and crown as in Types **17/18**. Chalk-surfaced paper. Wmk Mult Script CA. P 14½×13½ (vert) or 13½×14½ (horiz).

158	**17**	2c. lilac	75	70
		a. Error. Crown missing, W **9a**	£850	
		b. Error. St Edward's Crown, W **9b**.	£140	£190
159	**15**	3c. orange	1·25	30
		a. Error. Crown missing, W **9a**	£650	£700
		b. Error. St Edward's Crown, W **9b**.	£180	£180
160	**14**	9c. chalky blue	60	1·75
		a. Error. Crown missing, W **9a**	£1400	
		b. Error. St Edward's Crown, W **9b**.	£375	£500
161	**16**	15c. deep yellow-green	50	1·00
		a. Error. Crown missing, W **9a**	£900	
		b. Error. St Edward's Crown, W **9b**.	£325	£400
162	**18**	18c. carmine-lake	1·75	20
		a. Error. Crown missing, W **9a**	£1300	
		b. Error. St Edward's Crown, W **9b**.	£375	£425
163	**16**	20c. orange-yellow	3·00	1·75
		a. Error. Crown missing, W **9a**	£1400	£1200
		b. Error. St Edward's Crown, W **9b**.	£450	£600
164	**15**	25c. vermilion	70	4·00
		a. Error. Crown missing, W **9a**	£1800	
		b. Error. St Edward's Crown, W **9b**.	£450	
165	**17**	40c. ultramarine	1·25	3·00
		a. Error. Crown missing, W **9a**	£1900	
		b. Error. St Edward's Crown, W **9b**.	£850	
166	**16**	45c. purple-brown	2·00	30
		a. Error. Crown missing, W **9a**	£2250	
		b. Error. St Edward's Crown, W **9b**.	£475	£475
167	**14**	50c. reddish violet	1·50	1·75
		a. Error. Crown missing, W **9a**	£1700	£1700
		b. Error. St Edward's Crown, W **9b**.	£600	£700
168	**18**	1r. grey-black	6·50	4·50
		a. Error. Crown missing, W**9a**	£4250	

		b. Error. St Edward's Crown, W **9b**.	£1400	
169	**14**	1r.50 blue	14·00	18·00
		b. Error. St Edward's Crown, W **9b**.	£3500	
170	**15**	2r.25 brown-olive	19·00	21·00
		b. Error. St Edward's Crown, W **9b**.	£1600	
171	**18**	5r. red	21·00	22·00
		b. Error. St Edward's Crown, W **9b**.	£1100	£1100
172	**17**	10r. green	28·00	50·00
158/172 *Set of* 15			90·00	£110

See *Introduction* re the watermark errors.

1953 (2 June). Coronation. As No. 120 of Antigua.

173	9c. black and deep bright blue	60	70

19 Sailfish

20 Seychelles Flying Fox

(Photo Harrison)

1954 (1 Feb)–**61**. Designs previously used for King George VI issue, but with portrait of Queen Elizabeth II, as in T **19** and T **20**. Chalk-surfaced paper. Wmk Mult Script CA. P 14½×13½ (vert) or 13½×14½ (horiz).

174	**19**	2c. lilac	10	10
175	**15**	3c. orange	10	10
175*a*	**20**	5c. violet (25.10.57)	2·75	30
176	**14**	9c. chalky blue	10	10
176*a*		10c. chalky blue (15.9.56)	1·50	2·25
		ab. Blue (11.7.61)	13·00	5·50
177	**16**	15c. deep yellow-green	2·50	30
178	**18**	18c. crimson	30	10
179	**16**	20c. orange-yellow	1·50	20
180	**15**	25c. vermilion	2·25	1·00
180*a*	**18**	35c. crimson (15.9.56)	6·50	1·75
181	**19**	40c. ultramarine	1·00	25
182	**16**	45c. purple-brown	20	15
183	**14**	50c. reddish violet	30	80
183*a*	**16**	70c. purple-brown (15.9.56)	6·50	2·25
184	**18**	1r. grey-black	1·75	40
185	**14**	1r.50 blue	11·00	17·00
186	**15**	2r.25 brown-olive	11·00	12·00
187	**18**	5r. red	18·00	9·00
188	**19**	10r. green	28·00	18·00
174/188 *Set of* 19			80·00	55·00

21 'La Pierre de Possession'

5
cents
(**22**)

(Photo Harrison)

1956 (15 Nov). Bicentenary of 'La Pierre de Possession'. Wmk Mult Script CA. P 14½×13½.

189	**21**	40c. ultramarine	20	20
190		1r. black	35	50

e e s s c c
191 191a 191 191b 191 191c

1957 (16 Sept). No. 182 surch with T **22**.

191	5c. on 45c. purple-brown	15	10
	a. Italic 'e'	15·00	15·00
	b. Italic 's'	6·00	6·50
	c. Italic 'c'	3·75	3·75
	d. Thick bars omitted	£1100	
	e. Surch double	£550	

There were two settings of this surcharge. The first setting contained No. 191a on R. 3/1, No. 191b on R. 5/3, No. 191c on R. 6/1 and 9/2, and No. 191d on R. 5/2. Nos. 191a and 191d did not occur on the second setting which shows No. 191b on R. 1/4, and No. 191c on R. 5/1 and R. 10/4.

23 Mauritius 6d. Stamp with Seychelles 'B 64' Cancellation

(Recess: cancellation typo B.W.)

1961 (11 Dec). Centenary of First Seychelles Post Office. W w **12**. P 11½.

193	**23**	10c. blue, black and purple	25	10
194		35c. blue, black and myrtle-green	40	10
195		2r.25 blue, black and orange-brown	70	70
193/195 *Set of* 3			1·25	75

24 Black Parrot

25 Vanilla vine

26 Fisherman

27 Denis Island Lighthouse

28 Clock Tower, Victoria

29 Anse Royale Bay

30 Government House

31 Fishing pirogue

32 Cascade church

33 Sailfish

34 Coco-de-Mer palm

35 Cinnamon

36 Copra

37 Map

38 Land Settlement

39 Regina Mundi Convent

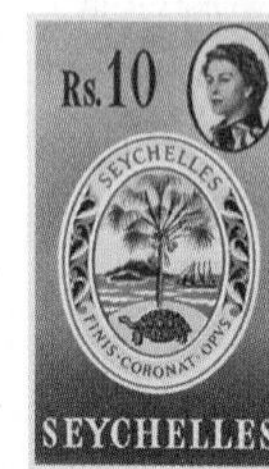

40 Colony's Badge

(Des V. Whiteley. Photo Harrison)

1962 (21 Feb)–**68**. Types **24/40**. W w **12** (upright). P 13½×14½ (horiz designs and 10r.) or 14½×13½ (others).

196	**24**	5c. multicoloured	3·25	10
197	**25**	10c. multicoloured	1·50	10
198	**26**	15c. multicoloured	30	10
199	**27**	20c. multicoloured	2·00	10
200	**28**	25c. multicoloured	50	10
200*a*		30c. multicoloured (15.7.68)	8·50	7·00
201	**29**	35c. multicoloured	1·75	1·50
202	**30**	40c. multicoloured	20	1·50
203	**31**	45c. multicoloured (1.8.66)	3·50	5·00
204	**32**	50c. multicoloured	40	25
205	**33**	70c. ultramarine and light blue	7·00	2·00
206	**34**	75c. multicoloured (1.8.66)	2·75	4·25
207	**35**	1r. multicoloured	1·00	10
208	**36**	1r.50 multicoloured	5·50	6·50
209	**37**	2r.25 multicoloured	5·50	12·00
210	**38**	3r.50 multicoloured	2·25	6·50
211	**39**	5r. multicoloured	9·00	2·50
212	**40**	10r. multicoloured	16·00	4·00
196/212 *Set of* 18			60·00	45·00

The 1r. exists with PVA gum as well as gum arabic, but the 30c. exists with PVA gum only.

See also Nos. 233/237.

For stamps of the above issue overprinted 'B.I.O.T.' see under British Indian Ocean Territory.

1963 (4 June). Freedom from Hunger. As No. 146 of Antigua.

213	70c. reddish violet	60	25

1963 (16 Sept). Red Cross Centenary. As Nos. 147/148 of Antigua.

214	10c. red and black	25	10
215	75c. red and blue	75	2·00

(**41**)

42 Seychelles Flying Fox

1965 (15 Apr). Nos. 201 and 205 surch as T **41**.

216	45c. on 35c. multicoloured	15	15
217	75c. on 70c. ultramarine and light blue	35	15

No. 216 was surcharged in photogravure; for No. 217 the surcharge was applied typographically.

1965 (1 June). ITU Centenary. As Nos. 166/167 of Antigua.

218	5c. orange and ultramarine	10	10
219	1r.50 mauve and apple-green	50	25

1965 (25 Oct). International Co-operation Year. As Nos. 168/169 of Antigua.

220	5c. reddish purple and turquoise-green	15	10
221	40c. deep bluish green and lavender	35	30

1966 (24 Jan). Churchill Commemoration. As Nos. 170/173 of Antigua.

222	5c. new blue	15	75
223	15c. deep green	45	10
224	75c. brown	1·25	65
225	1r.50 bluish violet	1·40	4·50
222/225 *Set of* 4		3·00	5·50

1966 (1 July). World Cup Football Championship. As Nos. 176/177 of Antigua.

226	15c. violet, yellow-green, lake and yellow-brown	20	35
	a. '50 c GRENADA' on front of stamp	£375	
227	1r. chocolate, blue-green, lake and yellow-brown	35	65

No. 226a shows a positive offset of the Grenada duty plate from the blanket on the front and a negative offset on the reverse.

1966 (20 Sept). Inauguration of WHO Headquarters, Geneva. As Nos. 178/179 of Antigua.

228	20c. black, yellow-green and light blue	35	10
229	50c. black, light purple and yellow-brown	65	20

1966 (1 Dec). 20th Anniversary of UNESCO. As Nos. 196/198 of Antigua.

230	15c. slate-violet, red, yellow and orange	20	10
231	1r. orange-yellow, violet and deep olive	35	10
232	5r. black, bright purple and orange	80	1·00
230/232 *Set of* 3		1·25	1·00

1967–69. As Nos. 196/197, 204 and new values as T **42** but wmk w **12** (sideways).

233	**24**	5c. multicoloured (7.2.67)	35	2·75
234	**25**	10c. multicoloured (4.6.68)	30	40
235	**32**	50c. multicoloured (13.5.69)	2·25	3·75
236	**42**	60c. red, blue and blackish brown (15.7.68)	2·00	45
237	**33**	85c. ultramarine and light blue (15.7.68)	1·00	40
233/237 *Set of* 5			5·50	7·00

The 10c. exists with PVA gum as well as gum arabic, but the 50c. to 85c. exist with PVA gum only.

UNIVERSAL
ADULT
SUFFRAGE
1967
(**43**)

44 Money Cowrie, Mole Cowrie and Tiger Cowrie

1967 (18 Sept). Universal Adult Suffrage. As Nos. 198 and 206, but W w **12** (sideways), and Nos. 203 and 210 (wmk upright), optd with T **43**.

No.	Description	Unused	Used
238	15c. multicoloured	10	10
	a. Opt double	£750	
239	45c. multicoloured	10	10
240	75c. multicoloured	10	10
241	3r.50 multicoloured	20	50
238/241	*Set of* 4	30	65

(Des V. Whiteley. Photo Harrison)

1967 (4 Dec). International Tourist Year. T **44** and similar horiz designs. Multicoloured. W w **12**. P 14×13.

No.	Description	Unused	Used
242	15c. Type **44**	20	10
243	40c. Beech Cone, Textile or Cloth of Gold Cone and Virgin Cone	25	10
244	1r. Arthritic Spider Conch	35	10
245	2r.25 Subulate Auger and Trumpet Triton Shells	60	1·25
242/245	*Set of* 4	1·25	1·25

= 30
(**48**)

49 Farmer with Wife and Children at Sunset

1968 (16 Apr). Nos. 202/203 and as No. 206 surch as T **48** (30c.) or with 'CENTS' added, and three bars (others). W w **12** (sideways on No. 248)

No.	Description	Unused	Used
246	30c. on 40c. multicoloured	15	50
247	60c. on 45c. multicoloured	20	30
248	85c. on 75c. multicoloured	20	30
246/248	*Set of* 3	50	1·00

(Des Mary Hayward. Litho Harrison)

1968 (2 Sept). Human Rights Year. W w **12**. P 14½×13½.

No.	Description	Unused	Used
249	**49** 20c. multicoloured	10	10
250	50c. multicoloured	10	10
251	85c. multicoloured	10	10
252	2r.25 multicoloured	25	1·60
249/252	*Set of* 4	40	1·60

50 Expedition landing at Anse Possession

54 Apollo Launch

(Des Mary Hayward. Litho and die-stamped Harrison)

1968 (30 Dec). Bicentenary of First Landing on Praslin. T **50** and similar multicoloured designs. W w **12** (sideways on 50c., 85c.). P 14.

No.	Description	Unused	Used
253	20c. Type **50**	35	10
254	50c. French warships at anchor (*vert*)	40	15
255	85c. Coco-de-Mer and Black Parrot (*vert*)	90	25
256	2r.25 French warships under sail	90	3·50
253/256	*Set of* 4	2·25	3·50

(Des V. Whiteley. Litho Format)

1969 (9 Sept). First Man on the Moon. T **54** and similar horiz designs. Multicoloured. W w **12** (sideways on horiz designs). P 13½.

No.	Description	Unused	Used
257	5c. Type **54**	10	50
258	20c. Module leaving Mother-ship for Moon	15	10
259	50c. Astronauts and Space Module on Moon	20	15
260	85c. Tracking station	25	25
261	2r.25 Moon craters with Earth on the 'Horizon'	45	1·75
257/261	*Set of* 5	1·00	2·50

59 Picault's Landing, 1742

60 Badge of Seychelles

(Des Mary Hayward. Litho Enschedé)

1969 (3 Nov)–**75**. Horiz designs as Types **59/60**. Multicoloured. W w **12** (sideways*). Slightly toned paper. P 13×12½.

No.	Description	Unused	Used
262	5c. Type **59**	10	10
	w. Wmk Crown to right of CA	2·75	
263	10c. US satellite-tracking station	10	10
	a. Whiter paper (8.3.73)	70	75
264	15c. *Königsberg* (German cruiser) at Aldabra, 1914	3·00	2·00
	a. Whiter paper (8.3.73)	5·50	9·00
265	20c. Fleet re-fuelling off St Anne, 1939–1945	1·75	10
	a. Whiter paper (13.6.74)	1·25	2·00
266	25c. Exiled Ashanti King Prempeh	20	10
	a. Whiter paper (8.3.73)	65	2·75
267	30c. Laying Stone of Possession, 1756	1·00	4·00
268	40c. As 30c. (11.12.72)	3·25	1·25
	a. Whiter paper (13.6.74)	1·60	1·60
269	50c. Pirates and treasure	30	15
	a. Whiter paper (13.6.74)	1·50	1·75
270	60c. Corsairs attacking merchantman	1·00	1·50
271	65c. As 60c. (11.12.72)	6·00	8·00
	aw. Wmk Crown to left of CA	6·00	
	b. Whiter paper (13.8.75)	6·50	9·50
272	85c. Impression of proposed airport	3·50	1·75
273	95c. As 85c. (11.12.72)	6·50	4·25
	a. Whiter paper (13.6.74)	6·50	3·25
	aw. Wmk Crown to left of CA		
274	1r. French Governor capitulating to British naval officer, 1794	35	15
	a. Whiter paper (8.3.73)	1·00	1·75
275	1r.50 HMS *Sybille* (frigate) and *Chiffone* (French frigate) in battle, 1801	1·75	2·00
	a. Whiter paper (8.3.73)	3·50	11·00
276	3r.50 Visit of the Duke of Edinburgh, 1956	1·00	2·25
	a. Whiter paper (13.8.75)	5·50	17·00
277	5r. Chevalier Queau de Quincy	1·00	2·75
278	10r. Indian Ocean chart, 1574	2·75	8·00
279	15r. Type **60**	4·00	14·00
262/279	*Set of* 18	28·00	48·00
263a/276a	*Set of* 11	30·00	50·00

* The normal sideways watermark shows Crown to right of CA on the 40, 65 and 95c. and to left of CA on the others, *as seen from the back of the stamp.*

The stamps on the whiter paper are highly glazed, producing shade variations and are easily distinguishable from the original printings on toned paper.

74 White Terns, French Warship and Island

(Des A. Smith; adapted V. Whiteley. Litho D.L.R.)

1970 (27 Apr). Bicentenary of First Settlement, St Anne Island. T **74** and similar horiz designs. Multicoloured. W w **12** (sideways). P 14.

No.	Description	Unused	Used
280	20c. Type **74**	1·40	10
281	50c. Spot-finned Flyingfish, ship and island	45	10
282	85c. Compass and chart	45	10
283	3r.50 Anchor on sea-bed	70	1·50
280/283	*Set of* 4	2·75	1·60

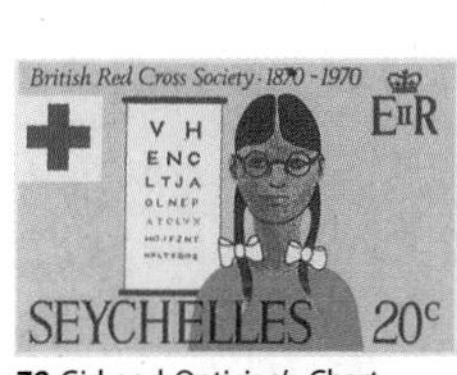

78 Girl and Optician's Chart

79 Pitcher Plant

(Des A. Smith. Litho Questa)

1970 (4 Aug). Centenary of British Red Cross. T **78** and similar multicoloured designs. W w **12** (sideways on horiz designs). P 14.

No.	Description	Unused	Used
284	20c. Type **78**	30	10
285	50c. Baby, scales and milk bottles	30	10
286	85c. Woman with child and umbrella (*vert*)	30	10
287	3r.50 Red Cross local HQ building	1·25	2·75
284/287	*Set of* 4	2·00	2·75

(Des G. Drummond. Litho J.W.)

1970 (29 Dec). Flowers. T **79** and similar vert designs. Multicoloured. W w **12**. P 14.

No.	Description	Unused	Used
288	20c. Type **79**	25	15
289	50c. Wild Vanilla	30	15
290	85c. Tropicbird Orchid	80	30
291	3r.50 Vare Hibiscus	1·00	2·25
288/291	*Set of* 4	2·10	2·50
MS292	81×133 mm. Nos. 288/291. Wmk inverted	2·75	13·00

POSTAGE DUE STAMPS

D **1**

(Frame recess, value typo B.W.)

1951 (1 Mar). Wmk Mult Script CA. P 11½.

No.	Description	Unused	Used
D1	D **1** 2c. scarlet and carmine	80	1·50
D2	3c. scarlet and green	3·50	1·50
D3	6c. scarlet and bistre	2·25	1·25
D4	9c. scarlet and orange	2·50	1·25
D5	15c. scarlet and violet	2·25	12·00
D6	18c. scarlet and blue	2·25	13·00
D7	20c. scarlet and brown	2·25	13·00
D8	30c. scarlet and claret	2·25	8·50
D1/D8	*Set of* 8	16·00	48·00

1964 (7 July)–**65**. As 1951 but W w **12**.

No.	Description	Unused	Used
D9	D **1** 2c. scarlet and carmine	2·50	15·00
D10	3c. scarlet and green (14.9.65)	1·25	17·00

Sierra Leone

PRICES FOR STAMPS ON COVER TO 1945

Nos. 1/15	*from* × 10
Nos. 16/26	*from* × 15
Nos. 27/34	*from* × 20
Nos. 35/37	*from* × 10
No. 38	—
No. 39	*from* × 15
Nos. 41/52	*from* × 8
No. 53	—
No. 54	*from* × 40
Nos. 55/63	*from* × 5
Nos. 64/71	—
Nos. 73/84	*from* × 4
No. 85	—
Nos. 86/97	*from* × 4
No. 98	—
Nos. 99/110	*from* × 4
No. 111	—
Nos. 112/126	*from* × 2
Nos. 127/130	—
Nos. 131/145	*from* × 2
Nos. 146/148	—
Nos. 155/166	*from* × 2
No. 167	—
Nos. 168/178	*from* × 2
Nos. 179/180	—
Nos. 181/184	*from* × 6
Nos. 185/187	*from* × 5
Nos. 188/200	*from* × 2

CROWN COLONY AND PROTECTORATE

The first settlement in Sierra Leone intended as a home for repatriated Africans, and subsequently those released by the Royal Navy from slave ships, was established in 1787. The Sierra Leone Company was created by Act of Parliment in 1791, but its charter was surrendered in 1808 and the coastal settlements then became a Crown Colony. The inland region was proclaimed a British protectorate on 21 August 1896.

A post office was established in 1843 but, until the inclusion of Freetown in the British Post Office packet system in 1850, overseas mail was carried at irregular intervals by passing merchant or naval vessels.

The stamps of GREAT BRITAIN were not sold at Sierra Leone post offices, although examples from ships of the West African Squadron do exist with local cancellations.

PRINTERS. All issues of Sierra Leone until 1932 were typographed by De La Rue & Co. Ltd, London.

1

2

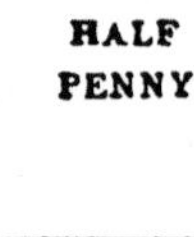

(3)

Dot after 'SIX' and break in octagonal frame (R. 19/11)

1859 (21 Sept)–**74**. No wmk. P 14 (comb).

1	1	6d. dull purple	£250	50·00
		a. Dot after 'SIX'	£1800	£550
2		6d. grey-lilac (1865)	£300	42·00
		a. Dot after 'SIX'	£2500	£475
3		6d. reddish violet (P 12½, line) (1872)	£425	60·00
		a. Dot after 'SIX	—	£650
4		6d. reddish lilac (1874)	70·00	27·00
		a. Dot after 'SIX'	£650	£300

Imperforate proofs exist.

The paper used for the 6d. value often shows varying degrees of blueing, caused by a chemical reaction.

The 6d. plate contained 240 stamps arranged in panes of 20 (4×5) with the sheets containing 12 such panes in four horizontal rows of three.

A second plate flaw, consisting of a dot after the 'E' of 'PENCE' occurs at R. 11/8. It may be found on all printings of the 6d. from 1872 onwards.

1872–73. Wmk Crown CC. P 12½.

(a) Wmk sideways (Apr 1872)*

7	2	1d. rose-red	85·00	50·00
		w. Wmk Crown to left of CC	—	£130
8		3d. buff	£160	48·00
9		4d. blue	£200	40·00
10		1s. green	£500	60·00

* The normal sideways watermark shows Crown to right of CC, *as seen from the back of the stamp.*

(b) Wmk upright (Sept 1873)

11	2	1d. rose-red	£130	30·00
		w. Wmk inverted	£300	£120
12		2d. magenta	£140	50·00
13		3d. saffron-yellow	£500	85·00
14		4d. blue	£350	50·00
15		1s. green	£650	90·00

1876. Wmk Crown CC. P 14.

16	2	½d. brown	7·50	18·00
		w. Wmk inverted	£250	
17		1d. rose-red	60·00	15·00
18		1½d. lilac (11.76)	50·00	10·00
19		2d. magenta	75·00	4·50
20		3d. buff	65·00	8·50
		w. Wmk inverted		
21		4d. blue	£225	6·50
		w. Wmk inverted		
22		1s. green	90·00	6·50
16/22 *Set of 7*			£500	60·00

1883 (May–13 Sept). Wmk Crown CA. P 14.

23	2	½d. brown	50·00	65·00
24		1d. rose-red (13.9.83*)	£200	35·00
25		2d. magenta	75·00	8·50
26		4d. blue	£1100	28·00
		x. Wmk reversed	†	£500

* Earliest known postmark date.

1884 SIERRA 5s. LEONE SURCHARGE. From 2 June 1884 the administration decided that, as a temporary measure, revenue and fiscal duties were to be paid with ordinary postage stamps. At that time there was no postage value higher than 1s., so a local surcharge, reading 'SIERRA 5s. LEONE', was applied to No. 22 (Price £225 unused). Until withdrawal on 1 March 1885 this surcharge was valid for both fiscal and postal purposes, although no genuine postal cover or piece has yet been found. One mint example is known with overprint inverted (*Price* £1200).

Remainders of the surcharge were cancelled by a horizontal red brush stroke (*Price £32 with upright surcharge, £160 with inverted surcharge*).

1884 (July)–**91**. Wmk Crown CA. P 14.

27	2	½d. dull green	3·00	3·25
		w. Wmk inverted	£250	£180
28		1d. carmine	17·00	1·75
		a. Rose-carmine (1885?)	30·00	8·50
		aw. Wmk inverted	†	£200
29		1½d. pale violet (1889)	3·50	9·50
30		2d. grey	60·00	4·50
31		2½d. ultramarine (1891)	19·00	2·00
		w. Wmk inverted	†	£250
32		3d. yellow (1889)	3·50	16·00
33		4d. brown	2·50	4·00
		w. Wmk inverted	£425	
		ws. Ditto, optd 'SPECIMEN'	£400	
34		1s. red-brown (1888)	27·00	22·00
27/34 *Set of 8*			£120	55·00
27s/34s (*ex* 1½d., 3d.) Optd 'SPECIMEN' *Set of 6*			£950	
27sa/28sa, 30sa, 33sa Optd 'SPECIMEN' (perf 12) *Set of 4*			£2500	

1885–96. Wmk Crown CC. P 14.

35	1	6d. dull violet (1885)	70·00	26·00
		a. Dot after 'SIX'	—	£275
36		6d. brown-purple (1890)	28·00	14·00
		a. Dot after 'SIX'	£375	£180
		s. Optd 'SPECIMEN'	85·00	
		w. Wmk inverted		
37		6d. purple-lake (1896)	2·75	10·00
		a. Dot after 'SIX'	£110	£170

Proofs of the 6d. brown-purple exist from 1889 on Crown CA watermark and perforated 12 (*Price £1800, unused*).

1893 (8 Jan). Surch with T **3** by Govt Printer, Freetown.

(a) On No. 18. Wmk Crown CC

38	2	½d. on 1½d. lilac	£550	£750
		a. 'PFNNY'(R.3/1)	£3750	£4500

(b) On No. 29. Wmk Crown CA

39	2	½d. on 1½d. pale violet	9·50	4·75
		a. Surch inverted	£120	£120
		b. 'PFNNY' (R. 3/1)	85·00	75·00
		ba. Ditto. Surch inverted	£3750	£5000

On Nos. 38/39 the surcharge and the cancelling bars were often applied separately using a separate forme. When the bar missed its intended position across the value tablet, second, or even third bars were added, sometimes by pen or brush. No. 39a exists with the bars either normal or inverted with the rest of the surcharge.

Forged surcharges with 'HALF PENNY' shown on one line were prepared by employees of the printer. It is believed that only two examples of this forgery still exist.

The 6d. fiscal, inscribed 'STAMP DUTY' as T **6** surcharged 'ONE-PENNY' is known used for postage between May and August 1894, but no official sanction for such usage has been found.

4

5

1896–97. Wmk Crown CA. P 14.

41	4	½d. dull mauve and green (1897)	2·50	3·00
42		1d. dull mauve and carmine	5·00	1·75
43		1½d. dull mauve and black (1897)	4·00	22·00
44		2d. dull mauve and orange	2·50	5·00
45		2½d. dull mauve and ultramarine	2·50	1·25
46	5	3d. dull mauve and slate	8·50	7·00
47		4d. dull mauve and carmine (1897)	9·50	13·00
48		5d. dull mauve and black (1897)	13·00	15·00
49		6d. dull mauve (1897)	8·00	28·00
		w. Wmk inverted	—	£350
50		1s. green and black	6·00	28·00
51		2s. green and ultramarine	32·00	80·00
52		5s. green and carmine	90·00	£250
53		£1 purple/*red*	£325	£600
41/53 *Set of 13*			£450	£900
41s/53s Optd 'SPECIMEN' *Set of 13*			£300	

Examples of most values are known showing forged oval registered postmarks dated '16 JUL 11' or '4 SP 11'.

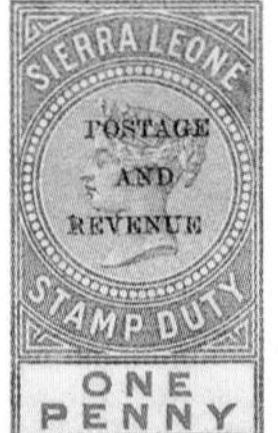

6

POSTAGE
AND
REVENUE
(7)

2½d. (8) 2½d. (9) 2½d. (10)

2½d. (11) 2½d. (12) 2½d. (13)

POSTAGE AND REVENUE
(14)

REVENUE
Italic 'N' (R. 3/4 of the setting)

1897. Fiscal stamps as T **6**. Wmk CA over Crown, w **7**. P 14.

(a) Optd with T 7 (26 Feb)*

54		1d. dull purple and green	9·50	3·75
		a. Opt double	£2000	£2000

*(b) Optd with T **7** and surch Types **8**, **10**, **11** (with square stop) or T **12** with six thin bars across the original face value (27 Feb*)*

55	8	2½d. on 3d. dull purple and green	11·00	21·00
		a. Surch double	£40000	
		b. Surch double (Types **8+10**)	£32000	
		c. Surch double (Types **8+11**)	£55000	
		d. Bars omitted	£2250	
56	10	2½d. on 3d. dull purple and green	70·00	95·00
57	11	2½d. on 3d. dull purple and green	£200	£250
58	12	2½d. on 3d. dull purple and green	£400	£500
59	8	2½d. on 6d. dull purple and green	8·50	22·00
60	10	2½d. on 6d. dull purple and green	55·00	85·00
61	11	2½d. on 6d. dull purple and green	£150	£190
62	12	2½d. on 6d. dull purple and green	£325	£400

* Earliest known postmark date.

Nos. 55/58 and 59/62 were surcharged from a setting of 30 (10×3) which contained 22 examples of T **8** (including three with square stops), five of T **10**, two of T **11** and one of T **12**.

Two examples are known of No. 55a, five of No. 55b (of which two are in the Royal Collection) and two of No. 55c (one in the Royal Collection). A unique example of a double surcharge on No. 55 showing Types **8+12** is also in the Royal Collection.

No. 55d comes from the top row of a setting and was caused by the downward displacement of the overprint. Stamps in the lower rows show the overprint transposed with the obliterating bars at the top of the stamp.

*(c) Optd with T **14** and surch Types **8**, **9**, **10**, **11** (with round stop) or T **13** with five thin bars across the original face value (1 Mar)*

63	8	2½d. on 1s. dull lilac	£110	70·00
64	9	2½d. on 1s. dull lilac	£1800	£1300
65	10	2½d. on 1s. dull lilac	£950	£750
66	11	2½d. on 1s. dull lilac	£550	£425
		a. Italic 'N'	£1800	£1400
66*b*	13	2½d. on 1s. dull lilac	£1800	£1300
67	8	2½d. on 2s. dull lilac	£2000	£3000
68	9	2½d. on 2s. dull lilac	£50000	£55000
69	10	2½d. on 2s. dull lilac	£20000	£25000
70	11	2½d. on 2s. dull lilac	£12000	£17000
		a. Italic 'N'	£50000	£55000
71	13	2½d. on 2s. dull lilac	£45000	†

The setting of 30 (10×3) used for both Nos. 63/66*b* and 67/71 contained 22 examples of T **8** (including one with square stop), one of T **9**, two of T **10**, four of T **11** (including one with italic 'N') and one of T **13**.

Most examples of Nos. 63/66*b* are water-stained. Stamps in this condition are worth about 25% of the price quoted.

15

16

1903. Wmk Crown CA. P 14.

73	15	½d. dull purple and green	3·00	6·50
74		1d. dull purple and rosine	2·00	1·00
75		1½d. dull purple and black	1·50	23·00
76		2d. dull purple and brown-orange	3·75	16·00
77		2½d. dull purple and ultramarine	4·50	8·00
78	16	3d. dull purple and grey	18·00	24·00
79		4d. dull purple and rosine	7·00	21·00
80		5d. dull purple and black	16·00	50·00
81		6d. dull purple	12·00	45·00
82		1s. green and black	27·00	80·00
83		2s. green and ultramarine	55·00	80·00
84		5s. green and carmine	80·00	£140
85		£1 purple/*red*	£275	£400
73/85 *Set of 13*			£450	£800
73s/85s Optd 'SPECIMEN' *Set of 13*			£250	

1904–05. Ordinary paper (1d.) or chalk-surfaced paper (others). Wmk Mult Crown CA. P 14.

86	15	½d. dull purple and green (1905)	5·00	4·50
87		1d. dull purple and rosine	1·50	1·75
		a. Chalk-surfaced paper (1905)	7·50	1·50
88		1½d. dull purple and black (1905)	3·00	19·00
89		2d. dull purple and brown-orange (1905)	4·25	4·00
90		2½d. dull purple and ultramarine (1905)	9·00	3·00
91	16	3d. dull purple and grey (1905)	55·00	4·75
		w. Wmk inverted	40·00	45·00

No.	Type	Description	Un	Used
92		4d. dull purple and rosine (1905)	15·00	8·00
		w. Wmk inverted	£140	
93		5d. dull purple and black (1905)	17·00	38·00
94		6d. dull purple (1905)	10·00	3·75
95		1s. green and black (1905)	7·50	9·00
96		2s. green and ultramarine (1905)	40·00	42·00
97		5s. green and carmine (1905)	50·00	65·00
98		£1 purple/*red* (1905)	£300	£350
86/98 *Set of* 13			£425	£475

1907–12. Ordinary paper (½d. to 2½d.) or chalk-surfaced paper (others). Wmk Mult Crown CA. P 14.

No.	Type	Description	Un	Used
99	15	½d. green	1·25	50
100		1d. carmine	21·00	75
		a. Red	18·00	60
101		1½d. orange (1910)	4·00	2·00
102		2d. greyish slate (1909)	3·25	1·50
103		2½d. blue	3·75	3·00
104	16	3d. purple/*yellow* (1909)	17·00	2·75
		a. Ordinary paper (1912)	30·00	12·00
105		4d. black and red/*yellow* (1908)	2·25	1·60
106		5d. purple and olive-green (1908)	26·00	8·50
107		6d. dull and bright purple (1908)	24·00	8·00
108		1s. black/*green* (1908)	6·00	5·00
109		2s. purple and bright blue/*blue* (1908)	26·00	19·00
110		5s. green and red/*yellow* (1908)	50·00	70·00
111		£1 purple and black/*red* (1911)	£300	£250
99/111 *Set of* 13			£425	£325
99s/111s Optd 'SPECIMEN' *Set of* 13			£400	

Most values from the 1903, 1904–1905 and 1907–1912 issues are known with forged postmarks. These include oval registered examples dated '16 JUL 11' or '4 SP 11'.

USED HIGH VALUES. The £2 and £5 values of the King George V series were intended for fiscal use only. Before the introduction of the airmail service at the end of 1926 there was no postal rate for which they could be used. Under the airmail rates used between 1926 and 1932 it is just possible that a very heavy letter may have required a £2 value. Postmarks on the £5 and on the £2 before December 1926 can only have been applied 'by favour' or, in the case of the cds type, are on stamps removed from telegraph forms. Used prices quoted for Nos. 129/130 and 147/148 are for 'by favour' cancellations.

17

18

19

20

1912–21. Die I. Chalk-surfaced paper (3d. and 6d. to £5). Wmk Mult Crown CA. P 14.

No.	Type	Description	Un	Used
112	17	½d. blue-green	4·75	3·50
		a. Yellow-green (1914)	7·00	2·50
		aw. Wmk inverted	†	£275
		b. Deep green (1919)	8·50	4·50
113		1d. carmine-red	2·25	30
		a. Scarlet (1916)	10·00	1·00
		b. Rose-red (1918)	10·00	80
		bw. Wmk inverted	†	£250
		bx. Wmk reversed	£225	£200
114		1½d. orange (1913)	2·00	2·50
		a. Orange-yellow (1919)	8·00	1·00
115		2d. greyish slate	1·25	20
		a. 'A' of 'CA' missing from wmk		
		w. Wmk inverted	40·00	40·00
116		2½d. deep blue	20·00	4·00
		a. Ultramarine (1917)	1·25	1·00
116*b*	20	3d. purple/*yellow*	6·50	3·25
		ba. On pale yellow (1921)	6·50	3·25
117	18	4d. black and red/*yellow*	2·75	17·00
		a. On lemon (1915)	5·00	14·00
		b. Die II. *On pale yellow* (1921)	7·50	5·50
118		5d. purple and olive-green	2·00	7·00
		sa. Opt 'SPECIMEN' double	£325	
119		6d. dull and bright purple	5·50	6·00
120	19	7d. purple and orange	3·00	14·00
121		9d. purple and black	5·00	12·00
122	18	10d. purple and red	3·00	21·00
124	20	1s. black/*green*	13·00	4·75
		a. On blue-green, green back	12·00	3·50
		w. Wmk inverted	70·00	60·00
125		2s. blue and purple/*blue*	30·00	7·50
126		5s. red and green/*yellow*	28·00	45·00
127		10s. red and green/*green*	£120	£170
		a. Carmine and blue-green/green	£150	£200
		b. Carmine and yellow-green/green	£160	£225
128		£1 black and purple/*red*	£250	£350
129		£2 blue and dull purple	£950	£1400
		s. Optd 'SPECIMEN'	£200	
130		£5 orange and green (f.c. £225)	£3750	£5000
		s. Optd 'SPECIMEN'	£500	
112/128 *Set of* 17			£400	£600
112s/128s Optd 'SPECIMEN' *Set of* 17			£450	

Examples of Nos. 127/128 are known with part strikes of the forged postmarks mentioned after Nos. 99/111.

1921–27. Die II. Chalk-surfaced paper (6d. to £5). Wmk Mult Script CA. P 14.

No.	Type	Description	Un	Used
131	17	½d. dull green	2·75	1·00
		a. Bright green	7·00	2·00
132		1d. bright violet (Die I) (1924)	8·00	2·25
		a. Die II (1925)	9·50	20
133		1½d. scarlet (1925)	2·25	1·25
134		2d. grey (1922)	2·00	20
135		2½d. ultramarine	3·75	21·00
136	18	3d. bright blue (1922)	2·75	1·25
137		4d. black and red/*pale yellow* (1925)	7·50	3·25
138		5d. purple and olive-green	1·75	1·25
139		6d. grey-purple and bright purple	1·75	2·75
		y. Wmk inverted and reversed		
140	19	7d. purple and orange (1927)	6·00	30·00
141		9d. purple and black (1922)	7·00	26·00
142	18	10d. purple and red (1925)	7·00	38·00
143	20	1s. black/*emerald* (1925)	17·00	5·00
144		2s. blue and dull purple/*blue*	12·00	10·00
		w. Wmk inverted	£200	£225
145		5s. red and green/*yellow* (1927)	12·00	60·00
146		10s. red and green/*green* (1927)	£170	£350
147		£2 blue and dull purple (1923)	£900	£1300
		s. Optd 'SPECIMEN'	£200	
148		£5 orange and green (1923) (f.c. £180)	£3500	£4750
		s. Optd 'SPECIMEN'	£500	
131/146 *Set of* 16			£225	£475
131s/146s Optd 'SPECIMEN' *Set of* 16			£500	

21 Rice Field

22 Palms and Cola Tree

(Eng J. A. C. Harrison (T **21**))

1932 (1 Mar). Wmk Mult Script CA.

(a) Recess Waterlow. P 12½

No.	Type	Description	Un	Used
155	21	½d. green	25	1·00
156		1d. violet	40	30
157		1½d. carmine	1·00	3·00
		a. Imperf between (horiz pair)		
158		2d. brown	60	30
159		3d. blue	2·50	3·25
160		4d. orange	2·00	16·00
161		5d. bronze-green	3·25	10·00
162		6d. light blue	2·50	6·00
163		1s. lake	8·50	17·00

(b) Recess B.W. P 12

No.	Type	Description	Un	Used
164	22	2s. chocolate	8·00	10·00
165		5s. deep blue	22·00	29·00
166		10s. green	90·00	£150
167		£1 purple	£180	£300
155/167 *Set of* 13			£275	£475
155s/167s Perf 'SPECIMEN' *Set of* 13			£325	

23 Arms of Sierra Leone

23a 'Freedom'

23b Map of Sierra Leone

24 Old Slave Market, Freetown

25 Native fruit seller

25a Government sanatorium

25b Bullom canoe

26 Punting near Banana Islands

26a Government buildings, Freetown

26b Bunce Island

27 African Elephant

28 King George V

29 Freetown harbour

(Des Father F. Welch. Recess B.W.)

1933 (2 Oct). Centenary of Abolition of Slavery and of Death of William Wilberforce. Types **23/29**. Wmk Mult Script CA (sideways on horiz designs). P 12.

No.	Type	Description	Un	Used
168	23	½d. green	1·00	1·25
169	23a	1d. black and brown	65	10
170	23b	1½d. chestnut	8·50	4·50
171	24	2d. purple	3·25	20
172	25	3d. blue	6·50	1·75
173	25a	4d. brown	6·50	8·00
174	25b	5d. green and chestnut	7·00	8·00
175	26	6d. black and brown-orange	13·00	5·00
176	26a	1s. violet	7·00	19·00
177	26b	2s. brown and light blue	42·00	50·00
178	27	5s. black and purple	£160	£190
179	28	10s. black and sage-green	£300	£500
180	29	£1 violet and orange	£650	£850
168/180 *Set of* 13			£1100	£1500
168s/180s Perf 'SPECIMEN' *Set of* 13			£850	

1935 (6 May). Silver Jubilee. As Nos. 91/94 of Antigua, but ptd by B.W. P 11×12.

No.	Description	Un	Used
181	1d. ultramarine and grey-black	2·25	2·50
	a. Extra flagstaff	80·00	£120
	b. Short extra flagstaff	£250	£325
	c. Lightning conductor	£100	£130
182	3d. brown and deep blue	3·50	8·50
	a. Extra flagstaff	£110	£170
	b. Short extra flagstaff	£500	
	c. Lightning conductor	£150	£225
183	5d. green and indigo	5·00	25·00
	a. Extra flagstaff	£180	£375
	b. Short extra flagstaff	£600	
	c. Lightning conductor	£225	£375
184	1s. slate and purple	25·00	25·00
	a. Extra flagstaff	£475	£475
	b. Short extra flagstaff	£550	£600
	c. Lightning conductor	£475	£475
181/184 *Set of* 4		32·00	55·00
181s/184s Perf 'SPECIMEN' *Set of* 4		£140	

For illustrations of plate varieties see Omnibus section following Zanzibar.

1937 (12 May). Coronation. As Nos. 95/97 of Antigua. P 11×11½.

No.	Description	Un	Used
185	1d. orange	70	1·00
186	2d. purple	1·00	1·25
187	3d. blue	2·00	5·50
185/187 *Set of* 3		3·25	7·00
185s/187s Perf 'SPECIMEN' *Set of* 3		£130	

30 Freetown from the Harbour

31 Rice Harvesting

(Des Father F. Welch. Recess Waterlow)

1938 (1 May)–**44**. Wmk Mult Script CA (sideways). P 12½.

No.	Type	Description	Un	Used
188	30	½d. black and blue-green	15	40
189		1d. black and lake	40	60
		a. Imperf between (vert pair)	†	—
190	31	1½d. scarlet	20·00	1·00
190*a*		1½d. mauve (1.2.41)	30	60
191		2d. mauve	50·00	3·00
191*a*		2d. scarlet (1.2.41)	30	2·00
192	30	3d. black and ultramarine	65	50
193		4d. black and red-brown (20.6.38)	2·50	4·00
194	31	5d. olive-green (20.6.38)	2·75	4·25
195		6d. grey (20.6.38)	1·50	50
196	30	1s. black and olive-green (20.6.38)	3·75	70
196*a*	31	1s.3d. yellow-orange (1.7.44)	75	60
197	30	2s. black and sepia (20.6.38)	4·75	2·75
198	31	5s. red-brown (20.6.38)	15·00	17·00
199		10s. emerald-green (20.6.38)	38·00	19·00
200	30	£1 deep blue (20.6.38)	21·00	35·00
188/200 *Set of* 16			£140	80·00
188s/200s Perf 'SPECIMEN' *Set of* 16			£475	

1946 (1 Oct). Victory. As Nos. 110/111 of Antigua.

No.	Description	Un	Used
201	1½d. lilac	20	10
202	3d. ultramarine	20	30
201s/202s Perf 'SPECIMEN' *Set of* 2		£110	

1948 (1 Dec). Royal Silver Wedding. As Nos. 112/113 of Antigua.

No.	Description	Un	Used
203	1½d. bright purple	15	15
204	£1 indigo	20·00	35·00

1949 (10 Oct). 75th Anniversary of UPU As Nos. 114/117 of Antigua.

No.	Description	Un	Used
205	1½d. purple	20	50
206	3d. deep blue	2·00	6·00
207	6d. grey	75	8·00
208	1s. olive	35	1·00
205/208 *Set of* 4		3·00	14·00

1953 (2 June). Coronation. As No. 120 of Antigua, but ptd by B.W.

209		1½d. black and purple	75	30

32 Cape Lighthouse

33 Queen Elizabeth II Quay

34 Piassava workers

35 Cotton Tree, Freetown

36 Rice harvesting

37 Iron ore production

38 Whale Bay, York Village

39 Bullom canoe

40 Bristol 170 freighter Mk 31 aircraft and map

41 Orugu Railway Bridge

42 Kuranco Chief

43 Law Courts, Freetown

44 Government House

(Recess Waterlow)

1956 (2 Jan)–**61**. Types **32/44**. Wmk Mult Script CA. P 13½×13 (horiz) or 14 (vert).

210	**32**	½d. black and deep lilac	1·00	2·75
211	**33**	1d. black and olive	90	40
212	**34**	1½d. black and ultramarine	1·60	6·50
213	**35**	2d. black and brown	70	40
214	**36**	3d. black and bright blue	1·25	10
		a. Perf 13×13½	2·50	18·00
215	**37**	4d. black and slate-blue	2·50	2·25
216	**38**	6d. black and violet	1·00	30
217	**39**	1s. black and scarlet	1·25	50
218	**40**	1s.3d. black and sepia	11·00	30
219	**41**	2s.6d. black and chestnut	19·00	13·00
220	**42**	5s. black and deep green	9·00	3·75
221	**43**	10s. black and bright reddish purple	4·50	3·00
		a. Black and purple (19.4.61)	14·00	38·00
222	**44**	£1 black and orange	30·00	45·00
210/222 *Set of* 13			75·00	70·00

Nos. 210/211 and 214 exist in coils, constructed from normal sheets.

INDEPENDENT

45 Palm Fruit Gathering

46 Licensed Diamond Miner

47 Bunda Mask

48 Bishop Crowther and Old Fourah Bay College

49 Sir Milton Margai

50 Lumley Beach, Freetown

51 Forces bugler

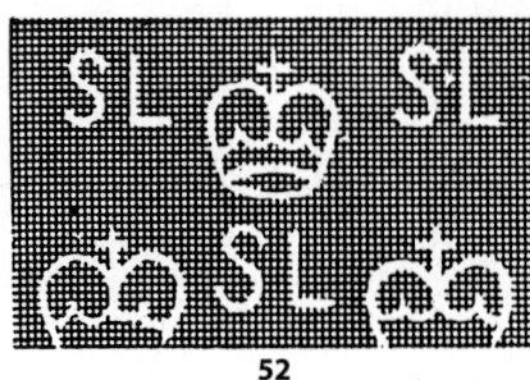

52

(Des K. Penny (½d., 1s.), Messrs Thorns, Turrell and Larkins (1d., 3d., 6d., 2s.6d.), W. G. Burnley (1½d., 5s.), J. H. Vandi (2d., 10s.), R. A. Sweet (4d., 1s 3d.), J. White (£1). Recess B. W.)

1961 (27 Apr). Independence. Types **45/51**. W **52**. P 13½.

223	**45**	½d. chocolate and deep bluish green	20	30
224	**46**	1d. orange-brown and myrtle-green	1·50	10
225	**47**	1½d. black and emerald	20	30
226	**48**	2d. black and ultramarine	20	10
227	**49**	3d. orange-brown and blue	20	10
228	**50**	4d. turquoise-blue and scarlet	20	10
229	**49**	6d. black and purple	20	10
230	**45**	1s. chocolate and yellow-orange	20	10
231	**50**	1s.3d. turquoise-blue and violet	20	10
232	**46**	2s.6d. deep green and black	2·75	50
233	**47**	5s. black and red	1·00	1·25
234	**48**	10s. black and green	1·00	1·25
235	**51**	£1 carmine-red and yellow	9·00	24·00
223/235 *Set of* 13			15·00	25·00

53 Royal Charter, 1799

54 King's Yard Gate, Freetown

55 Old House of Representatives, Freetown, 1924

56 Royal Yacht *Britannia* at Freetown

(Des C. P. Rang (3d., 4d.), F. H. Burgess (1s.3d.). Recess B.W.)

1961 (25 Nov). Royal Visit. Types **53/56**. W **52**. P 13½.

236	**53**	3d. black and rose-red	20	10
237	**54**	4d. black and violet	50	2·00
238	**55**	6d. black and yellow-orange	25	15
239	**56**	1s.3d. black and blue	3·50	2·00
236/239 *Set of* 4			4·00	3·75

57 Campaign Emblem

(Recess B.W.)

1962 (7 Apr). Malaria Eradication. W **52**. P 11×11½.

240	**57**	3d. carmine-red	10	10
241		1s.3d. deep green	20	10

58 Fireball Lily

59 Jina-gbo

(Des M. Goaman. Photo Harrison)

1963 (1 Jan). Flowers. Vert designs as T **58** (½d., 1½d., 3d., 4d., 1s., 2s.6d., 5s., 10s.) or horiz as T **59** (others). Multicoloured. W **52** (sideways on vert designs). P 14.

242		½d. Type **58**	10	50
243		1d. Type **59**	10	10
244		1½d. *Stereospermum*	20	40
245		2d. Black-eyed Susan	20	10
246		3d. Beniseed	20	10
247		4d. Blushing Hibiscus	20	30
248		6d. Climbing Lily	30	10
249		1s. Beautiful Crinum	40	10
250		1s.3d. Blue Bells	1·50	20
251		2s.6d. Broken Hearts	1·25	50
252		5s. Ra-ponthi	1·25	80
253		10s. Blue Plumbago	4·00	1·50
254		£1 African Tulip Tree	6·00	15·00
242/254 *Set of* 13			14·00	17·00

71 Threshing Machine and Corn Bins

72 Girl with onion crop

(Des V. Whiteley. Recess B.W.)

1963 (21 Mar). Freedom from Hunger. Types **71/72**. W **52**. P 11½×11.

255	**71**	3d. black and yellow-ochre	30	10
256	**72**	1s.3d. sepia and emerald-green	35	10

2ND YEAR OF INDEPENDENCE
19 PROGRESS 63
DEVELOPMENT
3d.
(73)

2nd Year Independence Progress Development 1963
10d.
(74)

(Optd by Govt Printer, Freetown)

1963 (27 Apr). Second Anniversary of Independence. Surch or optd as Types **73/74**.

(a) Postage

257		3d. on ½d. black and deep lilac (No. 210) (R.)	40	10
		a. Small 'c' in 'INDEPENDENCE' (R. 4/5)	7·00	7·00
258		4d. on 1½d. black and ultramarine (No. 212) (Br.)	15	10
259		6d. on ½d. black and deep lilac (No. 210) (O.)	30	10
		a. Small 'c' in 'INDEPENDENCE' (R. 4/5)	7·50	7·50
260		10d. on 3d. black and bright blue (No. 214) (R.)	50	10
261		1s.6d. on 3d. black and bright blue (No. 214) (V.)	30	20
262		3s.6d. on 3d black and bright blue . (No. 214) (Ult.)	40	20

(b) Air. Additionally optd 'AIR MAIL'

263		7d. on 1½d. black and ultramarine (No. 212) (C.)	20	10
264		1s.3d. on 1½d. black and ultramarine (No. 212) (R.)	20	10
265		2s.6d. black and chestnut (No. 219) (V.)	2·50	40
266		3s. on 3d black and bright blue (No. 214) (B.)	40	20

267 6s. on 3d. black and bright blue (No. 214) (R.) 1·00 20
268 11s. on 10s. black and bright reddish purple (No. 221) (C.) 2·75 4·50
a. Black and purple 6·50 7·50
269 11s. on £1 black and orange (No. 222) (C.) £750 £250
257/268 *Set of 12* 8·25 5·50

75 Centenary Emblem **76** Red Cross Emblem **77** Centenary Emblem

(Des M. Goaman. Recess B.W.)

1963 (1 Nov). Centenary of Red Cross. Types **75/77**. W **52**. P 11×11½.

270 **75** 3d. red and violet 50 10
271 **76** 6d. red and black 50 15
272 **77** 1s.3d. red and deep bluish green 65 20
270/272 *Set of 3* 1·50 40

1853–1859–1963
Oldest Postal Service
Newest G.P.O.
in West Africa
1s.
(**78**)

1853–1859–1963
Oldest Postage Stamp
Newest G.P.O.
in West Africa
AIRMAIL
(**79**)

1963 (4 Nov). Postal Commemorations. Optd or surch by Govt Printer, Freetown.

(a) Postage. As T **78**

273 3d. black and bright blue (No. 214) 10 10
a. '1895' for '1859' (R. 3/3) 3·00
b. '1853/1859/1963' (R. 2/3) 3·00
ba. As No. 273b, but showing 'S vice' also (R. 2/3)
274 4d. on 1½d. black and ultramarine (No. 212) (C.) 10 10
a. '1895' for '1859' (R. 1/2) 4·00
b. '1853*1859*1963' (R. 3/2, 11/4) 3·25 3·75
c. '1853 1859*1963' (R. 11/4) 4·25 4·75
d. No stop after 'O', but stop after 'Africa' (R. 10/1) 3·50 4·00
275 9d. on 1½d. black and ultramarine (No. 212) (V.) 10 10
a. '1853*1859*1963' (R. 3/2,11/4) 3·50
b. No stop after 'O' (R. 7/5) 60·00
c. No stop after 'O', but stop after 'Africa' (R. 10/1) 3·50
276 1s. on 1s.3d. turquoise-blue and violet (No. 231) (C.) 10 10
a. '1853*1859*1963' (R. 3/4, 10/2) 3·50 4·00
277 1s.6d. on ½d. black and deep lilac (No. 210) (Mag.) 15 10
a. '1853*1859*1963'(R. 11/1.) 5·50 5·50
b. '1853*1859 1963' (R. 4/5) 18·00
278 2s. on 3d. black and bright blue (No. 214) (Br.) 15 10
a. '1895' for '1859' (R. 4/10) 18·00 19·00
b. '1853/1859/1963' (R. 2/3) 14·00

(b) Air. As T **79**

279 7d. on 3d. black and rose-red (No. 236) (Br.) 20 1·50
a. '1895' for '1859'(R.3/6, 4/4) 3·25 5·50
b. '1853-1859-1963' (R.2/3, 4/10) 2·50 4·75
c. No stop after 'O' (R.1/2) 4·00
280 1s.3d. black and blue (No. 239) (C.) 2·00 1·50
a. '1895' for '1859' (R.7/3) 32·00
b. '1853*1859*1963' (R.3/2,10/4) 10·00
c. No stop after 'O' (R.8/3) 24·00
281 2s.6d. on 4d. turquoise-blue and scarlet (No. 228) 1·25 1·75
a. '1895' for '1859' (R.7/3) 65·00
b. '1853*1859*1963' (R.3/2, 10/4) 6·50 8·00
c. No stop after 'O' (R.8/3) 28·00
282 3s. on 3d. black and rose-red (No. 236) (V.) 2·50 4·00
a. '1895' for '1859' (R.3/3) £500
b. '1853-1859-1963' (R.2/3, 4/10) 14·00
c. No stop after 'O' (R.1/2) 27·00
283 6s. on 6d. black and yellow-orange (No. 238) (Ult.) 1·00 2·75
a. '1895' for '1859' (R.1/1) 65·00
b. '1853*1859*1963' (R.3/2, 10/4) 8·00 11·00
c. No stop after 'O' (R.8/3) 14·00 18·00
284 £1 black and orange (No. 222) (R.) 38·00 45·00
a. '1895' for '1859' (R.11/4) £500
b. '1853*1859*1963'(R.4/5, 11/1) £100
273/284 *Set of 12* 40·00 50·00

The events commemorated are: 1853, 'First Post Office'; 1859, 'First Postage Stamps'; and 1963 'Newest G.P.O.' in West Africa. Nos. 273, 278 have the overprint in five lines; Nos. 279, 282 in six lines (incl 'AIRMAIL').

Some of the overprint varieties were corrected during printing.

80 Lion Emblem and Map **81** Globe and Map

Extended 'A' in 'SIERRA' (R. 3/3, later corrected on the 4d. value)

(Thermography and litho Walsall Lithographic Co. Ltd)

1964 (10 Feb). World's Fair, New York. Imperf. Self-adhesive.

(a) Postage

285 **80** 1d. multicoloured 10 10
286 3d. multicoloured 10 10
a. Lion omitted £500
287 4d. multicoloured 10 10
b. Extended 'A' 2·75
288 6d. multicoloured 10 10
b. Extended 'A' 2·75
289 1s. multicoloured 15 10
a. 'POSTAGE 1/-' omitted 55·00
b. Extended 'A' 2·75
290 2s. multicoloured 40 30
b. Extended 'A' 4·50
291 5s. multicoloured 60 85
a. 'POSTAGE 5/-' omitted 60·00
b. Extended 'A' 7·00

(b) Air

292 **81** 7d. multicoloured 10 10
293 9d. multicoloured 10 10
a. 'AIR MAIL 9d.' omitted
294 1s.3d. multicoloured 30 10
a. 'AIR MAIL 1/3' omitted 60·00
295 2s.6d. multicoloured 40 15
a. 'AIR MAIL 2/6' omitted
296 3s.6d. multicoloured 40 25
a. 'AIR MAIL 3/6' omitted
297 6s. multicoloured 65 85
a. 'AIR MAIL 6/-' omitted 85·00
298 11s. multicoloured 80 1·75
a. 'AIR MAIL 11/-' omitted 95·00
285/298 *Set of 14* 3·75 4·25

Nos. 285/298 were issued in sheets of 30 (6×5) on green (postage) or yellow (airmail) backing paper with the emblems of Samuel Jones & Co. Ltd, self-adhesive paper-makers, on the back.

WARNING. These and later self-adhesive stamps should be kept on their backing paper except commercially used, which should be retained *on cover or piece.*

'POSTAGE' or 'AIR MAIL' and value omitted: We only list examples where these are completely missing. This error also exists on other values but the only examples we have seen have the missing wording on the back of the backing paper due to a paper fold before printing.

82 Inscription and Map **83** President Kennedy and Map

(Thermography and litho Walsall)

1964 (11 May). President Kennedy Memorial Issue. Imperf. Self-adhesive.

(a) Postage. Green backing paper

299 **82** 1d. multicoloured 10 10
300 3d. multicoloured 10 10
301 4d. multicoloured 10 10
302 6d. multicoloured 10 10
b. Extended 'A' 2·75
303 1s. multicoloured 15 10
b. Extended 'A' 2·75
304 2s. multicoloured 50 1·75
b. Extended 'A' 5·00
305 5s. multicoloured 75 2·75
b. Extended 'A' 8·00

(b) Air. Yellow backing paper

306 **83** 7d. multicoloured 15 10
307 9d. multicoloured 15 10
308 1s.3d. multicoloured 35 10
309 2s.6d. multicoloured 50 50
310 3s.6d. multicoloured 50 65
311 6s. multicoloured 75 2·00
312 11s. multicoloured 1·00 3·25
299/312 *Set of 14* 4·50 10·00

(New Currency. 100 cents = 1 leone)

3c (**84**) AIRMAIL 7c (**85**) LE 1·00 (**86**)

1964–66. Decimal currency. Various stamps surch locally.

(i) First issue (4.8.64)

(a) Postage. Surch as T **84**

313 – 1c. on 6d. multicoloured (No. 248) (R.) 10 10
a. Surch inverted
314 **53** 2c. on 3d. black and rose-red 10 10
315 – 3c. on 3d. multicoloured (No. 246) 10 10
a. Surch inverted £160
316 **45** 5c. on ½d. chocolate and deep bluish green (B.) 10 10
317 **71** 8c. on 3d. black and yellow-ochre (R.) 15 10
318 – 10c. on 1s.3d. mult (No. 250) (R.) 15 10
319 – 15c. on 1s. multicoloured (No. 249) 1·00 10
320 **55** 25c. on 6d. black and yellow-orange (V.) 30 35
321 – 50c. on 2s.6d. deep green and black (No. 232) (O.) 2·75 2·00

(b) Air. As Types **85** *or* **86** *(Nos. 326/327)*

322 – 7c. on 1s.3d. sepia and emerald-green (No. 256) (B.) 15 10
a. Surch omitted (in horiz pair with normal) £425
b. Surch double 85·00
323 – 20c. on 4d. turquoise-blue and scarlet (No. 228) 25 20
324 – 30c. on 10s. black and green (No. 234) (R.) 30 50
325 – 40c. on 5s. black and red (No. 233) (B.) 35 65
326 **83** 1l. on 1s.3d. multicoloured (R.) 50 2·25
327 2l. on 11s. multicoloured 75 4·25
313/327 *Set of 15* 6·00 9·50

TWO LEONES 1c (**87**) Le 2·00 (**88**)

(ii) Second issue (20.1.65). Surch as Types **87** *or* **88** *(Nos. 332/333)*

(a) Postage

328 – 1c. on 3d. orange-brown and blue (No. 227) 10 30
329 **82** 2c. on 1d. multicoloured 10 30
330 4c. on 3d. multicoloured 10 30
a. Error. 4c. on 1d £170 £250
b. Stamp omitted (in pair with normal)
331 – 5c. on 2d. multicoloured (No. 245) 10 10
332 – 1l. on 5s. multicoloured (No. 252) (Gold) 1·75 4·00
333 – 2l. on £1 carmine-red and yellow (No. 235) (B.) 4·00 6·50
a. Surch double (B.+Blk.) £200 £110

(b) Air

334 **83** 7c. on 7d. multicoloured (R.) 15 10
335 60c. on 9d. multicoloured 1·00 2·00
328/335 *Set of 8* 6·50 12·00

On No. 330b the stamp became detached before the surcharge was applied so that '4c' appears on the backing paper.

1c Normal 1c Small 'c' (R. 3/3)

(iii) Third issue (4.65). Surch in figures (various sizes)

(a) Postage

336 – 1c. on 1½d. black and emerald (No. 225) (R.) 10 20
a. Small 'c' 4·00
337 **82** 2c. on 3d. multicoloured 10 25
338 **80** 2c. on 4d. multicoloured 10 25
b. Extended 'A' 2·75
339 **59** 3c. on 1d. multicoloured 10 25
340 – 3c. on 2d. black and ultramarine (No. 226) (R.) 10 25
a. Small 'c' (R. 3/3) 4·00
341 – 5c. on 1s.3d. turquoise-blue and violet (No. 231) (R.) 10 10
a. Surch inverted
342 **82** 15c. on 6d. multicoloured 1·00 50
b. Extended 'A' 10·00
343 15c. on 1s. multicoloured (R.) 1·50 90
b. Extended 'A' 13·00
344 – 20c. on 6d. black and purple (No. 229) (R.) 40 15
345 – 25c. on 6d. multicoloured (No. 248) (R.) 45 20
346 – 50c. on 3d. orange-brown and blue (No. 227) (R.) 1·25 70
347 **80** 60c. on 5s. multicoloured (V.) 4·25 2·50
b. Extended 'A' 45·00
348 **82** 1l. on 4d. multicoloured (R.) 4·50 5·50
349 – 2l. on £1 carmine-red and yellow (No. 235) (B.) 14·00 14·00

(b) Air

350 **81** 7c. on 9d. multicoloured 25 10
336/350 *Set of 15* 25·00 23·00

2c (**89**) TWO Leones (**90**)

(iv) Fourth issue (9.11.65). Surch as T **89**

(a) Postage

351 **80** 1c. on 6d. multicoloured (V.) 3·50 9·00
a. Stamp omitted (in pair with normal)
b. Extended 'A' 35·00
352 1c. on 2s. multicoloured (V.) 3·50 9·00
b. Extended 'A' 35·00

353	**82**	1c. on 2s. multicoloured (V.)	3·50	9·00
		b. Extended 'A'	35·00	
354		1c. on 5s. multicoloured (V.)	3·50	9·00
		b. Extended 'A'	35·00	
		(b) Air		
355	**81**	2c. on 1s.3d. multicoloured	3·50	9·00
356	**83**	2c. on 1s.3d. multicoloured	3·50	9·00
		a. Stamp omitted (in pair with normal)		
357		2c. on 3s.6d. multicoloured	3·50	9·00
358	**81**	3c. on 7d. multicoloured	3·50	9·00
359	**83**	3c. on 9d. multicoloured	3·50	9·00
360	**81**	5c. on 2s.6d. multicoloured	3·50	9·00
361	**83**	5c. on 2s.6d. multicoloured	3·50	9·00
362	**81**	5c. on 3s.6d. multicoloured	3·50	9·00
363		5c. on 6s. multicoloured	3·50	9·00
364	**83**	5c. on 6s. multicoloured	3·50	9·00
351/364 *Set of 14*			42·00	£110
		(v) Fifth issue (28.1.66). Air. No. 374 further surch with T **90**		
365	–	2l. on 30c. on 6d. multicoloured	1·50	2·50

On Nos. 351a and 356a the stamps became detached before the surcharge was applied so the new values appear on the backing paper.

91 Margai and Churchill

1965 (19 May). Sir Milton Margai and Sir Winston Churchill Commemoration. Nos. 242/243, 245/250 and 252/254 surch as T **91** on horiz designs or with individual portraits on vert designs as indicated.

	(a) Postage		
366	2c. on 1d. Type **59**	75	30
	a. Horiz pair, one with '2 c' omitted	£500	
	b. Surch and portraits omitted (in horiz pair with normal)	£500	
367	3c. on 3d. Beniseed (Margai)	10	20
	a. Portrait and '3 c' double	£190	
	b. Portrait and '3 c' double, one inverted	£150	
	c. '3 c' omitted	£500	
368	10c. on 1s. Beautiful Crinum (Churchill)	1·90	20
	a. '10 c' omitted	£375	
369	20c. on 1s.3d. Blue Bells	2·00	20
	a. Portraits and '20 c' double, one inverted	£190	
	b. '20 c' omitted	£500	
	c. '20 c' double, one inverted	£150	
370	50c. on 4d. Blushing Hibiscus (Margai)	90	45
	a. Portrait inverted	£140	
	ab. Portrait inverted and '50 c' omitted	£225	
371	75c. on 5s. Ra-ponthi (Churchill)	4·75	1·25
	a. Surch value inverted	£225	
	(b) Air. Additionally optd 'AIRMAIL'		
372	7c. on 2d. Black-eyed Susan	1·50	20
	a. 'AIRMAIL' and '7c.' omitted	£150	
	b. 'AIRMAIL' and '7 c' double, one inverted	£150	
373	15c. on ½d. Type **58** (Margai)	45	20
	a. 'AIRMAIL' and '15 c' double, one inverted	£160	
	b. Portrait double, one inverted	£150	
374	30c. on 6d. Climbing Lily (O. and W.)	2·75	35
	a. 'AIRMAIL' and '30 c' double, one inverted	£140	
	b. 'AIRMAIL' and '30 c' omitted	£130	
375	1l. on £1 African Tulip Tree	6·50	1·50
	a. 'AIRMAIL' and '1 l' double, one inverted	£140	
	b. 'AIRMAIL' and '1 l' omitted	£500	
376	2l. on 10s. Blue Plumbago (Churchill)	13·00	5·50
	a. Surch value omitted	£200	
366/376 *Set of 11*		30·00	9·00

On Nos. 366/376 the portraits and commemorative inscription were applied in a separate operation from the surcharge and, on Nos. 372/376, the word 'AIRMAIL'.

92 Cola Plant and Nut

93 Arms of Sierra Leone

94 Inscription and Necklace

(Des M. Meers. Manufactured by Walsall Lithographic Co, Ltd)

1965 (17 Dec*). Imperf. Self-adhesive.

		A. Embossed on silver foil, backed with paper bearing advertisements. Emerald, olive-yellow and carmine; denominations in colours given. Postage		
377	**92**	1c. emerald	25	10
378		2c. carmine	25	10
379		3c. olive-yellow	25	10
380		4c. silver/*emerald*	30	10
381		5c. silver/*carmine*	30	10
		B. Typo and embossed on cream paper backed with advertisements		
		(a) Postage		
382	**93**	20c. multicoloured	2·25	60
383		50c. multicoloured	4·00	4·00
		(b) Air		
384	**93**	40c. multicoloured	4·00	4·00
		C. Die-stamped and litho, with advertisements on white paper backing (see footnote). Air		
385	**94**	7c. multicoloured	80	15
		a. Bright green and gold (inscr and face value) omitted	£120	
386		15c. multicoloured	1·50	90
377/386 *Set of 10*			12·00	9·00

* It is believed that some values may have been released as early as 22 November.

The above stamps were issued in single form with attached tabs to remove the backing paper, with the exception of No. 385 which was in sheets of 25 bearing a single large advertisement on the back.

No. 385a shows the die-stamping omitted.

For other stamps in T **92** see Nos. 421/431 and 435/442*a*.

For 10c. stamps in T **93** see Nos. 433/433*b*.

2c — FIVE YEARS INDEPENDENCE 1961-1966 (**95**)

15c AIRMAIL — FIVE YEARS INDEPENDENCE 1961-1966 (**96**)

1966 (27 Apr). Fifth Anniversary of Independence. Various stamps surch.

	(a) Postage. As T **95**		
387	1c. on 6d. multicoloured (No. 248)	10	40
388	2c. on 4d. multicoloured (No. 247)	10	40
389	3c. on 1½d. black and ultramarine (No. 212) (B.)	10	40
390	8c. on 1s. multicoloured (No. 249) (B.)	1·50	40
391	10c. on 2s.6d. multicoloured (No. 251) (B.)	25	10
392	20c. on 2d. black and brown (No. 213) (B.)	40	10
	(b) Air. As T **96**		
393	7c. on 3d. red and violet (No. 270)	25	10
394	15c. on 1s. multicoloured (No. 249)	1·75	30
395	25c. on 2s.6d. multicoloured (No. 251)	75	70
396	50c. on 1½d. multicoloured (No. 244)	1·75	1·75
397	1l. on 4d. multicoloured (No. 247)	2·00	3·25
387/397 *Set of 11*		7·75	7·00

The inscription on No. 387 is in larger type.

97 Lion's Head **98** Map of Sierra Leone

(Des and embossed Walsall)

1966 (12 Nov). First Sierra Leone Gold Coinage Commemoration. Circular designs, embossed on gold foil, backed with paper bearing advertisements. Imperf.

		(a) Postage		
		(i) ¼ golde coin. Diameter 1½ in		
398	**97**	2c. magenta and yellow-orange	10	10
399	**98**	3c. emerald and bright purple	10	10
		(ii) ½ golde coin. Diameter 2⅛ in		
400	**97**	5c. vermilion and ultramarine	10	10
401	**98**	8c. turquoise-blue and black	20	20
		(iii) 1 golde coin. Diameter 3¼ in		
402	**97**	25c. violet and emerald	40	35
403	**98**	1l. orange and cerise	2·75	3·25
		(b) Air. (i) ¼ golde coin. Diameter 1½ in		
404	**98**	7c. red-orange and cerise	15	10
405	**97**	10c. cerise and greenish blue	20	25
		(ii) ½ golde coin. Diameter 2⅛ in		
406	**98**	15c. orange and cerise	35	35
407	**97**	30c. bright purple and black	50	60
		(iii) 1 golde coin. Diameter 3¼ in		
408	**98**	50c. bright green and purple	1·00	1·00
409	**97**	2l. black and emerald	4·00	4·50
398/409 *Set of 12*			8·75	9·75

12½ (**99**) 17½ (**100**) =17½ (**101**)

1967 (2 Dec). Decimal Currency Provisionals. Surch as T **99** (Nos. 410/413), T **100** (Nos. 415/417) or T **101** (others).

		(a) Postage		
410	–	6½c. on 75c. on 5s. multicoloured (No. 371) (R.)	50	25
411	–	7½c. on 75c. on 5s. multicoloured (No. 371) (S.)	50	25
412	–	9½c. on 50c. on 4d. multicoloured (No. 370) (G.)	35	25
413	–	12½c. on 20c. on 1s.3d. multicoloured (No. 369) (V.)	65	35
414	**93**	17½c. on 50c. multicoloured	2·50	3·50
415	**82**	17½c. on 1l. on 4d. multicoloured (No. 348) (B.)	2·50	3·50
416		18½c. on 1l. on 4d. multicoloured (No. 348)	2·50	3·50
417	**80**	18½c. on 60c. on 5s. multicoloured (No. 347)	6·50	9·50
		b. Extended 'A'	60·00	
418	**93**	25c. on 50c. multicoloured	1·00	1·50
		(b) Air		
419	**93**	11½c. on 40c. multicoloured	45	40
420		25c. on 40c. multicoloured	1·00	1·50
410/420 *Set of 11*			17·00	22·00

102 Eagle

(Manufactured by Walsall)

1967 (2 Dec)–**69**. Decimal Currency. Imperf. Self-adhesive.

		(a) Postage. As T **92**, *but embossed on white paper, backed with paper bearing advertisements. Background colours given first, and value tablet colours in brackets*		
421	**92**	½c. carmine-red (carmine/*white*)	10	75
422		1c. carmine (carmine/*white*)	15	25
423		1½c. orange-yellow (green/*white*)	25	40
424		2c. carmine-red (green/*white*)	45	10
425		2½c. apple-green (yellow/*white*)	75	75
426		3c. carmine-red (white/*carmine*)	50	10
427		3½c. reddish purple (white/*green*)	70	75
428		4c. carmine-red (white/*green*)	70	15
429		4½c. dull green (green/*white*)	70	75
430		5c. carmine (yellow/*white*)	70	15
431		5½c. brown-red (green/*white*)	70	1·00
		(b) Air. T **102** *embossed on black paper, backed with paper bearing advertisements; or, (No. 433), as T* **93**, *typo and embossed on cream paper, also with advertisements*		
432	**102**	9½c. red and gold/*black*	90	1·00
432*a*		9½c. blue and gold/*black* (10.9.69)	11·00	11·00
433	**93**	10c. multicoloured (red frame)	90	80
		a. Face value omitted		
433*b*		10c. mult (black frame) (10.9.69)	12·00	12·00
434	**102**	15c. green and gold/*black*	1·50	1·25
434*a*		15c. red and gold/*black* (10.9.69)	13·00	13·00
421/434*a* *Set of 17*			40·00	40·00

The ½, 1½, 2, 2½, 3, 3½ and 5c. also exist without advertisements.

The footnote below Nos. 377/386 also applies here.

Although only released for collectors on 2 December, the 5c. was known to be in use locally in February and the 3c. in March. The 1c. and 2c. were also released locally some months earlier.

See also Nos. 538/544.

1968. No advertisements on back, and colours in value tablet reversed. Background colours given first, and value tablet colours in brackets.

435	**92**	½c. carmine-red (white/*green*)	10	1·00
436		1c. carmine (white/*carmine*)	20	1·00
437		2c. carmine (white/*green*)	6·50	9·00
438		2½c. apple-green (white/*yellow*)	7·00	9·50
439		3c. carmine-red (carmine/*white*)	3·25	1·00

On Nos. 435 and 438, the figure '½' is larger than in Nos. 421 and 425.

It is believed that the ½c. was released in February, the 2½c. in April and the others in March.

The 1c. also exists with advertisements on the backing paper.

The footnote below Nos. 377/386 also applies here.

1968–69. No advertisements on back, colours changed and new value (7c.). Background colours given first, and value tablet colours in brackets.

		(a) Postage		
440	**92**	2c. pink (white/*brown-lake*)	3·00	3·50
441		2½c. deep bluish green (white/*orange*)	3·00	3·50
442		3½c. olive-yellow (blue/*white*)	3·25	4·50
		(b) Air		
442*a*	**92**	7c. yellow (carmine/*white*) (10.9.69)	9·50	4·50
435/442*a* *Set of 9*			32·00	32·00

On Nos. 441/442 the fraction '½' is larger than in Nos. 425 and 427.

It is believed that the 3½c. was released in March 1968 and the 2 and 2½c. in May 1968.

The 2c. also exists with advertisements on the backing paper.

The footnote below Nos. 377/386 also applies here.

103 Outline Map of Africa

(Litho Walsall)

1968 (25 Sept). Human Rights Year. Each value comes in six types, showing different territories in yellow, as below. Imperf. self-adhesive.

A. Portuguese Guinea. D. Rhodesia.
B. South Africa. E. South West Africa.
C. Mozambique. F. Angola.

To indicate yellow territory use above letters as suffix to the following catalogue numbers.

(a) Postage

No.	Type	Description	Unused	Used
443	**103**	½c. multicoloured	10	10
444		2c. multicoloured	10	10
445		2½c. multicoloured	10	10
446		3½c. multicoloured	10	10
447		10c. multicoloured	25	15
448		11½c. multicoloured	30	20
449		15c. multicoloured	40	25
		(b) Air		
450	**103**	7½c. multicoloured	25	15
451		9½c. multicoloured	30	20
452		14½c. multicoloured	40	25
453		18½c. multicoloured	50	30
454		25c. multicoloured	60	40
455		1l. multicoloured	3·25	5·50
456		2l. multicoloured	9·00	12·00
443/456 Each territory *Set of* 14			14·00	18·00
443/456 Six territories *Set of* 84			70·00	90·00

Nos. 443/456 were issued in sheets of 30 (6×5) on backing paper depicting diamonds or the Coat of Arms on the reverse. The six types occur once in each horizontal row.

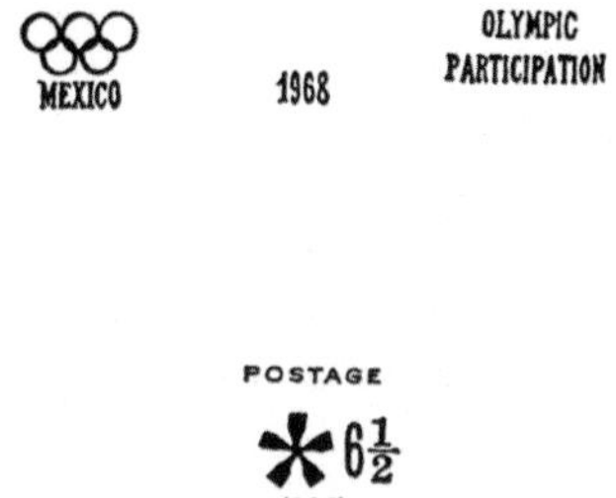

MEXICO 1968 OLYMPIC PARTICIPATION

POSTAGE
*6½
(104)

1968 (30 Nov). Mexico Olympics Participation.

(a) Postage. No. 383 surch or optd (No. 461) as T **104**

No.	Type	Description	Unused	Used
457	**93**	6½c. on 50c. multicoloured	40	30
458		17½c. on 50c. multicoloured	45	35
459		22½c. on 50c. multicoloured	65	50
		a. Surch double	£225	
460		28½c. on 50c. multicoloured	85	1·50
461		50c. multicoloured	1·25	2·50
		(b) Air. No. 384 surch or optd (No. 466) as T **104** *in red*		
462	**93**	6½c. on 40c. multicoloured	45	30
		a. Surch double	£225	
463		17½c. on 40c. multicoloured	55	35
464		22½c. on 40c. multicoloured	70	50
465		28½c. on 40c. multicoloured	85	1·50
466		40c. multicoloured	1·25	2·50
457/466 *Set of* 10			6·50	9·00

105 1859 6d.

111 1965 15c. Self-adhesive

(Litho Walsall)

1969 (1 Mar). Fifth Anniversary of World's First Self-adhesive Postage Stamps. Reproductions of earlier issues. Multicoloured. Imperf. Self-adhesive.

(a) Postage. Vert designs

No.	Description	Unused	Used
467	1c. Type **105**	10	10
468	2c. 1965 2c. self-adhesive	10	10
469	3½c. 1961 Independence £1	10	10
470	5c. 1965 20c. self-adhesive	10	10
471	12½c. 1948 Royal Silver Wedding £1	30	15
472	1l. 1923 £2	2·50	1·50
	(b) Air. Horiz designs		
473	7½c. Type **111**	20	10
474	9½c. 1967 9½c. self-adhesive	20	10
475	20c. 1964 1s.3d. self-adhesive	40	25
476	30c. 1964 President Kennedy Memorial 6s. commemorative self-adhesive	55	35
477	50c. 1933 Centenary of Abolition of Slavery £1 commemorative	1·50	75
478	2l. 1963 2nd Anniversary of Independence 11s. commemorative	9·00	8·00
467/478 *Set of* 12		13·00	10·00

Nos. 467 and 473 were issued with tabs as note under Nos. 377/386 and No. 474 exists with tabs and also in the normal version on backing paper.

All values are on white backing paper with advertisements printed on the reverse.

117 Ore Carrier, Globe and Flags of Sierra Leone and Japan

118 Ore Carrier, Map of Europe and Africa and Flags of Sierra Leone and Netherlands

The 3½c., 9½c., 2l. and 10c., 50c., 1l. are as T **118** but show respectively the flags of Great Britain and West Germany instead of the Netherlands.

(Litho Walsall)

1969 (10 July). Pepel Port Improvements. Imperf. Self-adhesive, backed with paper bearing advertisements.

(a) Postage

No.	Type	Description	Unused	Used
479	**117**	1c. multicoloured	25	10
480	**118**	2c. multicoloured	35	10
481	–	3½c. multicoloured	45	10
482	–	10c. multicoloured	70	10
483	**118**	18½c. multicoloured	1·00	25
484	–	50c. multicoloured	1·75	1·00
		(b) Air		
485	**117**	7½c. multicoloured	80	10
486	–	9½c. multicoloured	80	10
487	**117**	15c. multicoloured	1·00	25
488	**118**	25c. multicoloured	1·50	35
489	–	1l. multicoloured	2·25	2·00
490	–	2l. multicoloured	2·75	4·50
479/490 *Set of* 12			12·00	8·00

119 African Development Bank Emblem

(Litho and embossed Walsall)

1969 (10 Sept). Fifth Anniversary of African Development Bank. Self adhesive, backed with paper bearing advertisements. Imperf.

(a) Postage

No.	Type	Description	Unused	Used
491	**119**	3½c. deep green, gold and blue	25	1·00
		(b) Air		
492	**119**	9½c. bluish violet, gold and apple green	35	70

120 Boy Scouts Emblem in 'Diamond'

(Litho Walsall)

1969 (6 Dec). Boy Scouts Diamond Jubilee. T **120** and similar design. Imperf. Self-adhesive, backed with paper bearing advertisements.

(a) Postage

No.	Type	Description	Unused	Used
493	**120**	1c. multicoloured	10	10
494		2c. multicoloured	10	10
495		3½c. multicoloured	15	10
496		4½c. multicoloured	15	15
497		5c. multicoloured	15	15
498		75c. multicoloured	5·50	2·75
		(b) Air		
499	–	7½c. multicoloured	35	20
500	–	9½c. multicoloured	45	25
501	–	15c. multicoloured	70	50
502	–	22c. multicoloured	90	70
503	–	55c. multicoloured	4·00	2·00
504		3l. multicoloured	50·00	38·00
493/504 *Set of* 12			55·00	40·00

Design: *Octagonal Shape* (65×51 *mm*)—Nos. 499/504 Scout saluting, Baden-Powell and badge.

(121)

1970 (28 Mar). Air. No. 443 surch as T **121**.

No.	Type	Description	Unused	Used
505	**103**	7½c. on ½c. multicoloured (G.)	60	20
506		9½c. on ½c. multicoloured (P.)	60	20
507		15c. on ½c. multicoloured (B.)	1·00	40
508		28c. on ½c. multicoloured (G.)	1·50	75
509		40c. on ½c. multicoloured (B.)	2·00	2·00
510		2l. on ½c. multicoloured (Sil.)	7·50	19·00
505/510 Each Territory *Set of* 6			12·00	20·00
505/510 Six Territories *Set of* 36			65·00	£110

122 Expo Symbol and Maps of Sierra Leone and Japan

(Litho Walsall)

1970 (22 June). World Fair, Osaka. T **122** and similar design. Imperf. Self-adhesive, backed with paper bearing advertisements.

(a) Postage

No.	Type	Description	Unused	Used
511	**122**	2c. multicoloured	10	10
512		3½c. multicoloured	15	10
513		10c. multicoloured	25	10
514		12½c. multicoloured	25	10
515		20c. multicoloured	30	10
516		45c. multicoloured	60	45
		(b) Air		
517	–	7½c. multicoloured	20	10
518	–	9½c. multicoloured	25	10
519	–	15c. multicoloured	30	10
520	–	25c. multicoloured	55	20
521	–	50c. multicoloured	65	50
522		3l. multicoloured	1·50	5·50
511/522 *Set of* 12			4·50	6·50

Design: *Chrysanthemum shape* (43×42 *mm*)—Nos. 517/522 Maps of Sierra Leone and Japan.

123 Diamond **124** Palm Nut

(Litho and embossed Walsall)

1970 (3 Oct). Imperf. Self-adhesive, backed with paper bearing advertisements.

No.	Type	Description	Unused	Used
523	**123**	1c. multicoloured	55	40
524		1½c. multicoloured	55	40
525		2c. multicoloured	55	10
526		2½c. multicoloured	55	10
527		3c. multicoloured	65	10
528		3½c. multicoloured	65	10
529		4c. multicoloured	70	10
530		5c. multicoloured	80	20
531	**124**	6c. multicoloured	50	20
532		7c. multicoloured	55	20
533		8½c. multicoloured	70	25
534		9c. multicoloured	70	25
535		10c. multicoloured	75	25
536		11½c. multicoloured	1·25	30
537		18½c. multicoloured	2·25	85

1970 (3 Oct). Air. As T **102**, but embossed on white paper. Backed with paper bearing advertisements.

538	**102**	7½c. gold and red	60	10
539		9½c. rose and bright green	70	10
540		15c. pink and greenish blue	2·00	20
541		25c. gold and purple	3·00	50
542		50c. bright green and orange	6·50	3·50
543		1l. royal blue and silver	13·00	16·00
544		2l. ultramarine and gold	20·00	32·00
523/544 *Set of* 22			50·00	50·00

126 'Jewellery Box' and Sewa Diadem

(Litho and embossed Walsall)

1970 (30 Dec). Diamond Industry. T **126** and similar design. Imperf (backing paper roul 20). Self-adhesive, backed with paper bearing advertisements.

(a) Postage

545	**126**	2c. multicoloured	45	20
546		3½c. multicoloured	45	20
547		10c. multicoloured	70	20
548		12½c. multicoloured	1·00	30
549		40c. multicoloured	2·50	1·25
550		1l. multicoloured	12·00	11·00

(b) Air

551	–	7½c. multicoloured	75	20
552	–	9½c. multicoloured	85	20
553	–	15c. multicoloured	1·50	35
554	–	25c. multicoloured	2·00	60
555	–	75c. multicoloured	7·00	6·00
556		2l. multicoloured	27·00	27·00
545/556 *Set of* 12			50·00	42·00

Design: Horiz (63×61 *mm*)—Nos. 551/556, Diamond and curtain.

STAMP BOOKLETS

1929 (22 Jan).

SB1	1s. booklet containing 12×1d. (No. 132a)
SB2	2s. booklet containing 12×2d. (No. 134)

Singapore

A Crown Colony until the end of 1957. From 1 August 1958, an internally self-governing territory designated the State of Singapore. From 16 September 1963, part of the Malaysian Federation until 9 August 1965, when it became an independent republic within the Commonwealth.

Stamps in the Crown Colony Victory design with face values of 8c. and 15c. were prepared for Singapore in 1946, but were not issued.

(Currency. 100 cents = 1 Malayan, dollar)

CROWN COLONY

(Typo D.L.R.)

1948 (1 Sept)–**52**. As T **58** of Malaysia (Straits Settlements), but inscribed 'SINGAPORE' at foot. Chalk-surfaced paper. Wmk Mult Script CA.

(a) P 14

1	1c. black	30	1·50
2	2c. orange	20	1·00
3	3c. green	50	2·25
4	4c. brown	20	2·25
5	6c. grey	1·00	1·00
6	8c. scarlet (1.10.48)	50	1·00
7	10c. purple	30	10
8	15c. ultramarine (1.10.48)	11·00	10
9	20c. black and green (1.10 48)	5·50	1·25
10	25c. purple and orange (1.10.48)	7·00	60
11	40c. red and purple (1.10.48)	9·50	7·50
12	50c. black and blue (1.10.48)	3·25	10
13	$1 blue and purple (1.10.48)	14·00	4·25
14	$2 green and scarlet (25.10.48)	48·00	7·50
15	$5 green and brown (1.10.48)	£110	9·00
1/15 *Set of* 15		£180	35·00

(b) P 17½×18

16	1c. black (21.5.52)	2·00	4·75
17	2c. orange (31.10.49)	2·00	2·75
19	4c. brown (1.7.49)	2·25	10
19*a*	5c. bright purple (1.9.52)	6·50	2·75
21	6c. grey (10.12.52)	3·25	4·50
21*a*	8c. green (1.9.52)	11·00	6·00
22	10c. purple (9.2.50)	1·25	10
22*a*	12c. scarlet (1.9.52)	14·00	20·00
23	15c. ultramarine (9.2.50)	27·00	1·00
24	20c. black and green (31.10.49)	13·00	4·50
24*a*	20c. bright blue (1.9.52)	13·00	10
25	25c. purple and orange (9.2.50)	5·50	10
25*a*	35c. scarlet and purple (1.9.52)	12·00	1·00
26	40c. red and purple (30.4.51*)	50·00	22·00
27	50c. black and blue (9.2.50)	8·50	10
28	$1 blue and purple (31.10.49)	17·00	20
	a. Error. St Edward's Crown, W **9b**	£16000	£6000
29	$2 green and scarlet (24.5.51)	90·00	1·25
	a. Error. St Edward's Crown. W **9b**	£20000	
	w. Wmk inverted	†	£7500
30	$5 green and brown (19.12.51)	£190	1·50
	w. Wmk inverted	†	£5000
16/30 *Set of* 18		£400	60·00

* Earliest known postmark date.

Single-colour values were from single plate printings (Die II) and all bi-colour, except the 25c., from separate head and duty plates (Die I). For differences between the Dies see after Nos. 278/298 of Malaysia (Straits Settlements). The 25c. is unique in this series in that it combines a Die II frame with a separate head plate.

Nos. 28a and 29a occur on rows in the watermark in which the crowns and letters 'CA' alternate. The only unused examples seen show the wmk error in the top sheet margin.

Postal forgeries of the 50c., $1 and $2 exist on unwatermarked paper and perforated 14×14½.

1948 (25 Oct). Royal Silver Wedding. As Nos. 112/113 of Antigua.

31	10c. violet	75	1·00
32	$5. brown	£100	50·00

1949 (10 Oct). 75th Anniversary of UPU As Nos. 114/117 of Antigua.

33	10c. purple	75	70
34	15c. deep blue	3·50	5·50
	a. 'A' of 'CA' missing from wmk	—	£1000
35	25c. orange	3·50	3·00
36	50c. blue-black	3·50	3·25
33/36 *Set of* 4		10·00	11·00

1953 (2 June). Coronation. As No. 120 of Antigua.

37	10c. black and reddish purple	3·00	30

1 Chinese Sampan

2 Malay kolek

3 Twa-kow lighter

4 Lombok sloop

5 Trengganu pinas

6 Palari schooner

7 Timber tongkong

8 Hainan junk

9 Cocos-Keeling schooner

10 Douglas DC-4M2 Argonaut aircraft

11 Oil tanker

12 *Chusan III* (liner)

13 Raffles Statue

14 Singapore River

15 Arms of Singapore

1c. A flaw between the two Sampans resembles a reflection in the water of one of the figures (Pl. 1B, R. 9/1)

(Des Dr. C. A. Gibson-Hill, except 25c., 30c., 50c. and $5 (from photographs, etc.). Photo Harrison (1c. to 50c.). Recess (centre typo on $5) B.W. (others)

1955 (4 Sept)–**59**. Types **1/15**. Wmk Mult Script CA. P 13½×14½ (1c. to 50c.) or 14 (others).

38	**1**	1c. black	10	1·00
		a. Reflection in water	5·00	
39	**2**	2c. yellow-orange	2·50	1·50
40	**3**	4c. brown	2·25	15
		w. Wmk inverted	£375	£375
41	**4**	5c. bright purple	65	50
42	**5**	6c. deep grey-blue	65	70
43	**6**	8c. turquoise-blue	1·25	2·00
44	**7**	10c. deep lilac	3·00	10
45	**8**	12c. rose-carmine	5·00	3·00
46	**9**	20c. ultramarine	2·25	10
		a. Blue (13.3.58)	8·50	30
47	**10**	25c. orange-red and bluish violet	7·00	1·50
		a. Orange-red and purple (21.1.59)	32·00	4·25
48	**11**	30c. violet and brown-purple	3·75	10
49	**12**	50c. blue and black	2·25	10
50	**13**	$1 blue and deep purple	40·00	30
		a. Deep purple (Queen's head) omitted	£32000	
51	**14**	$2 blue-green and scarlet	42·00	1·75
52	**15**	$5 yellow, red, brown and slate-black	42·00	5·00
38/52 *Set of* 15			£130	15·00

Plate 2A and 2B of the 10c. (12 April 1960) and the blue '3A' and '3B' plates of the 50c. '3A-2A' '3B-2B' (part of the 24 January 1961 issue and later printings) were printed with a finer screen (250 dots per inch, instead of the normal 200) (*Price* 10c. £3.75 *un*, 20p *us*. 50c. £3.50 *un*, 10p *us*).

No. 50a was caused by a paper fold.

INTERNAL SELF-GOVERNMENT

16 The Singapore Lion

17 State Flag

(Photo Harrison)

1959 (1 June). New Constitution. W w **12.** P 11½×12.

No.	Type	Description	Unused	Used
53	**16**	4c. yellow, sepia and rose-red	65	75
54		10c. yellow, sepia and reddish purple	1·00	40
55		20c. yellow, sepia and bright blue	2·25	3·00
56		25c. yellow, sepia and green	2·50	2·25
57		30c. yellow, sepia and violet	2·50	3·25
58		50c. yellow, sepia and deep slate	3·25	3·25
53/58 *Set of 6*			11·00	11·50

(Litho Enschedé)

1960 (3 June). National Day. W w **12** (sideways*). P 13½.

No.	Type	Description	Unused	Used
59	**17**	4c. red, yellow and blue	1·50	2·25
		w. Wmk Crown to right of CA	£110	
60		10c. red, yellow and grey	2·75	30
		w. Wmk Crown to right of CA	£100	£100

* The normal sideways watermark shows Crown to left of CA, *as seen from the back of the stamp.*

18 Clasped Hands

(Photo Enschedé)

1961 (3 June). National Day. W w **12** P 13½.

No.	Type	Description	Unused	Used
61	**18**	4c. black, brown and pale yellow	1·00	2·00
62		10c. black, deep green and pale yellow	1·25	10

19 *Arachnis* 'Maggie Oei' (orchid)

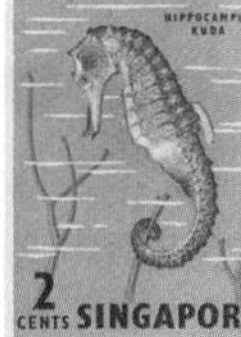

20 Yellow Seahorse

21 Tiger Barb

22 Orange Clownfish

23 Archerfish

24 *Vanda* 'Tan Chay Yan' (orchid)

25 Harlequinfish

26 *Grammatophyllum speciosum* (orchid)

26a Black-naped Tern

27 Copper-banded Butterflyfish

28 Three-spotted Gorami

29 *Vanda* 'Miss Joaquim' (orchid)

30 White-rumped Shama

31 White-breasted Kingfisher

32 Yellow-bellied Sunbird

33 White-bellied Sea Eagle

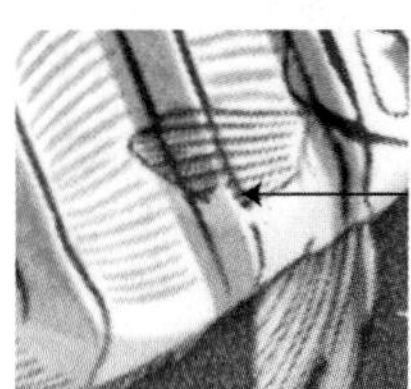
20c. Nick in fin (R. 1/1)

(Photo Harrison orchids, fish and 15c. bird) D.L.R. (birds, except 15c.)

1962 (31 Mar)–**66.** Types **19/33.** W w **12.** P 12½ (i), 14½×13½ (ii), 13½×14½ (iii), 13½×13 (iv) or 13×13½ (v).

No.	Type	Description	Unused	Used
63	**19**	1c. multicoloured (i)	30	1·00
64	**20**	2c. brown and green (ii)	30	2·00
65	**21**	4c. black and orange-red (iii)	30	1·25
		a. Black omitted	£1500	
66	**22**	5c. red and black (iii)	20	10
		a. Red omitted	£1200	
67	**23**	6c. black and greenish yellow (ii)	75	1·25
68	**24**	8c. multicoloured (i) (10.3.63)	1·25	3·50
69	**25**	10c. red-orange and black (iii)	40	10
		a. Red-orange omitted	£475	£425
		b. Black omitted	£8000	
70	**26**	12c. multicoloured (i) (10.3.63)	1·25	3·50
70*a*	**26a**	15c. multicoloured (i) (9.11.66)	4·50	10
		ab. Orange (eye) omitted	75·00	
		ac. Stone (shading in wings) omitted	£325	
		aw. Wmk inverted	38·00	
71	**27**	20c. orange and blue (ii)	1·25	10
		a. Orange omitted	£1300	
		b. Nick in fin	18·00	4·00
72	**28**	25c. black and orange (iii)	75	10
		a. Black omitted	£1500	
73	**29**	30c. multicoloured (i) (10.3.63)	1·25	40
		a. Yellow (flowers) omitted	£130	
		w. Wmk inverted	£110	
74	**30**	50c. multicoloured (iv) (10.3.63)	1·25	10
75	**31**	$1 multicoloured (iv) (10.3.63)	20·00	60
76	**32**	$2 multicoloured (iv) (10.3.63)	12·00	1·00
77	**33**	$5 multicoloured (v) (10.3.63)	20·00	9·00
		w. Wmk inverted	£300	
63/77 *Set of 16*			60·00	21·00

The 10c. exists in coils, constructed from normal sheets.

The 15c., 30c., $2 and $5 exist with PVA gum as well as gum arabic.

The errors, Nos. 70ab, 70ac and 73a, also exist with both gums.

See also Nos. 83/88.

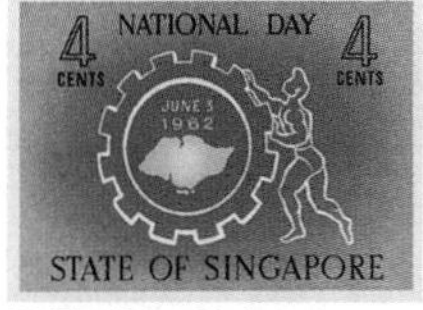

34 'The Role of Labour in Nation-Building'

35 Blocks of Flats, Singapore

(Photo Courvoisier)

1962 (3 June). National Day. P 11½×12.

No.	Type	Description	Unused	Used
78	**34**	4c. yellow, rose-carmine and black	1·25	2·25
79		10c. yellow, blue and black	1·50	75

(Photo Harrison)

1963 (3 June). National Day. W w **12.** P 12½.

No.	Type	Description	Unused	Used
80	**35**	4c. orange-red, black, blue and turquoise-blue	50	1·75
81		10c. orange-red, black, yellow-olive and turquoise-blue	1·75	20
		w. Wmk inverted	75·00	

36 Dancers in National Costume

37 Workers

(Photo Harrison)

1963 (8 Aug). South East Asia. Cultural Festival. W w **12.** P 14×14½.

No.	Type	Description	Unused	Used
82	**36**	5c. multicoloured	50	50

INDEPENDENT REPUBLIC

1966 (1 Mar)–**67.** As Nos. 63, 66, 69, 72, 74/75, but W w **12** (sideways*).

No.	Type	Description	Unused	Used
83		1c. multicoloured (16.6.67)	10	2·00
84		5c. red and black (30.5.67)	4·75	3·25
85		10c. red-orange and black (19.5.67†)	3·00	3·25
86		25c. black and orange (9.66†)	70	2·00
		w. Wmk Crown to right of CA	3·75	5·50
87		50c. multicoloured (11.1.66†)	4·50	2·00
		a. Imperf (pair)	£650	
88		$1 multicoloured (18.5.67)	16·00	15·00
83/88 *Set of 6*			26·00	25·00

* The normal sideways watermark show Crown to left of CA, *as seen from the back of the stamp.*

† The 25 and 50c. values were not released in London until 30.5.67 and 9.6.66. The 25c. value, however, is known used in September 1966 and the 50c. on 11.1.66. The 10c., released in London on 30 May 1967, is known used locally on 19 May.

The 1c. and 25c. exist with PVA gum as well as gum arabic.

(Photo D.L.R.)

1966 (9 Aug). First Anniversary of Republic. (30c.) or no wmk (others). W w **12.** P 12½×13.

No.	Type	Description	Unused	Used
89	**37**	15c. multicoloured	75	30
90		20c. multicoloured	1·00	1·25
91		30c. multicoloured	1·25	2·00
89/91 *Set of 3*			2·75	3·25

38 Flag Procession

(Photo D.L.R.)

1967 (9 Aug). National Day. P 14×14½.

No.	Type	Description	Unused	Used
92	**38**	6c. rosine, brown and slate	50	90
93		15c. reddish purple, brown and slate	80	10
94		50c. bright blue, brown and slate	1·50	1·60
92/94 *Set of 3*			2·50	2·25

Nos. 92/94 are respectively inscribed 'Build a Vigorous Singapore' in Chinese, Malay and Tamil in addition to the English inscription.

39 Skyscrapers and Afro-Asian Map

40 Symbolical Figure wielding Hammer, and Industrial Outline of Singapore

(Photo D.L.R.)

1967 (7 Oct). Second Afro-Asian Housing Congress. P 14×13.

95	**39**	10c. multicoloured	30	10
		a. Opt omitted	£1600	£1600
96		25c. multicoloured	75	1·00
97		50c. multicoloured	1·40	1·60
95/97 *Set of 3*			2·25	2·40

The above were originally scheduled for release in 1966, and when finally issued were overprinted with the new date and a black oblong obliterating the old date.

(Photo Harrison)

1968 (9 Aug). National Day. Inscription at top in Chinese (6c.), Malay (15c.) or Tamil (50c.). P 13½×14.

98	**40**	6c. orange-red, black and gold	35	1·75
99		15c. apple-green, black and gold	45	15
100		50c. greenish blue, black and gold	1·00	1·25
98/100 *Set of 3*			1·60	2·75

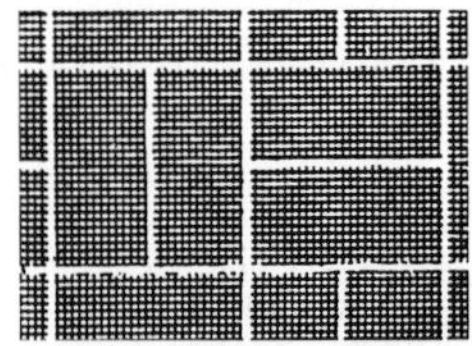

41 Half check Pattern

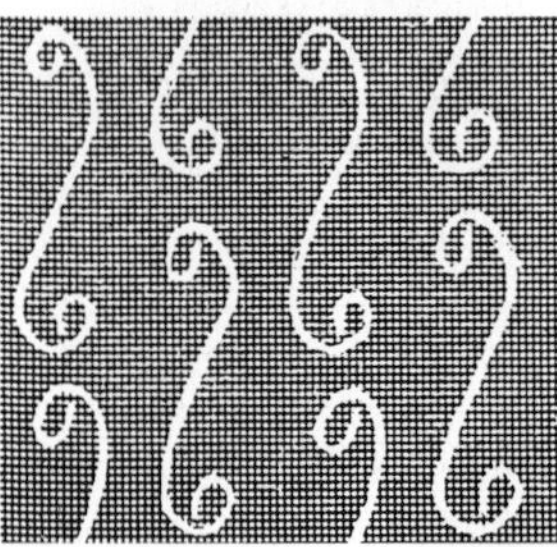

42 Scrolled 'S' multiple

43 Mirudhangam

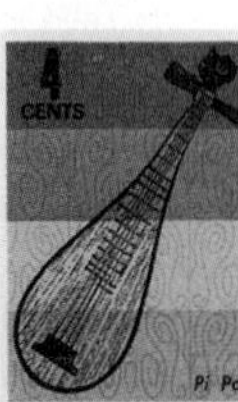

44 Pi Pa

45 Sword Dance

51 Dragon Dance

(Photo D.L.R. (5c. to $1), Japanese Govt Printing Bureau, Tokyo

1968 (1 Dec)–**73**. Types **43/45**, **51** and similar designs. (5c. to $1) or W **42** (upright on 1c., $5; sideways on 4c., $2, $10). Chalk-surfaced paper (5c. to $1). W **41**. P 14 (5c. to $1) or 13½ (others).

101	1c. multicoloured (10.11.69)	15	2·25
102	4c. multicoloured (10.11.69)	60	4·25
103	5c. multicoloured (29.12.68)	60	1·75
	a. Glazed unsurfaced paper (16.12.70)	14·00	24·00
	b. Perf 13 (27.6.73)	7·50	10·00
104	6c. black, lemon and orange	1·75	2·25
105	10c. multicoloured (29.12.68)	20	10
	a. Glazed unsurfaced paper (16.12.70)	15·00	14·00
	b. Perf 13 (14.7.73*)	24·00	9·50
106	15c. multicoloured (29.12.68)	60	10
107	20c. multicoloured	1·00	1·75
	a. Perf 13 (12.9.73)	13·00	24·00
108	25c. multicoloured (29.12.68)	1·25	1·75
	a. Perf 13 (27.6.73)	8·00	13·00
109	30c. multicoloured	40	1·50
	a. Perf 13 (12.9.73)	13·00	22·00
110	50c. black, orange-red and light yellow-brown	50	1·00
	a. Perf 13 (12.9.73)	14·00	40·00
111	75c. multicoloured	3·00	2·00
112	$1 multicoloured (29.12.68)	4·50	1·25
	a. Perf 13 (12.9.73)	25·00	30·00
113	$2 multicoloured (10.11.69)	3·50	1·00
114	$5 multicoloured (10.11.69)	14·00	1·50
115	$10 multicoloured (6.12.69)	38·00	15·00
101/115 *Set of 15*		60·00	35·00
103b/112a *Set of 7*		90·00	£130

Designs: Vert (as T **45**)—5c. T **45**; 6c. Lion dance; 10c. Bharatha Natyam; 15c. Tari Payong; 20c. Kathak Kali; 25c. Lu Chih Shen and Lin Chung; 50c. Tari Lilin; 75c. Tarian Kuda Kepang; $1 Yao Chi. (As T **44**—4c. T **44**; $2, Rebab; $10 Ta Ku. Horiz (as T **43**)—1c. T **43**; $5 Vina; 30c. T **51**.

* Earliest known date of use.

58 ECAFE Emblem

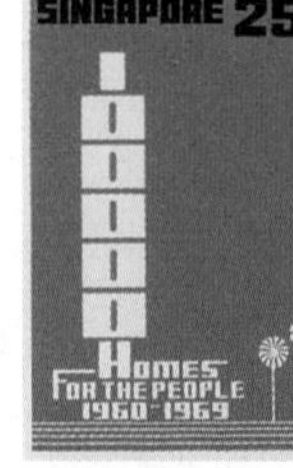

59 '100000' and Slogan as Block of Flats

(Des Eng Sisk Loy. Photo Japanese Govt Ptg Bureau, Tokyo)

1969 (15 Apr). 25th Plenary Session of the UN Economic Commission for Asia and the Far East. P 13.

116	**58**	15c. black, silver and pale blue	35	20
117		30c. black, silver and red	65	1·25
118		75c. black, silver and violet-blue	1·00	2·50
116/118 *Set of 3*			1·75	3·50

(Des Tay Siew Chiah. Litho B. W.)

1969 (20 July). Completion of '100,000 Homes for the People' Project. P 13½.

119	**59**	25c. black and emerald	1·00	50
120		50c. black and deep blue	1·25	1·25

60 Aircraft over Silhouette of Singapore Docks

61 Sea Shells

(Des Eng Siak Loy and Han Kuan Cheng. Litho B.W.)

1969 (9 Aug). 150th Anniversary of Founding of Singapore. T **60** and similar vert designs. P 14×14½.

121	15c. black, vermilion and yellow	2·50	70
122	30c. black, blue and new blue	2·50	1·00
123	75c. multicoloured	4·00	1·00
124	$1 black and vermilion	8·00	10·00
125	$5 vermilion and black	15·00	45·00
126	$10 black and bright green	23·00	45·00
121/126 *Set of 6*		50·00	90·00
MS127 120×120 mm. Nos. 121/126. P 13½		£375	£400

Designs: 15c. T **60**; 30c. UN emblem and outline of Singapore; 75c. Flags and outline of Malaysian Federation; $1 Uplifted hands holding crescent and stars; $5 Tail of Japanese aircraft and searchlight beams; $10 Bust from statue of Sir Stamford Raffles.

(Des Tay Siew Chiah (15c.), Eng Siak Loy (others). Litho Rosenbaum Bros, Vienna)

1970 (15 Mar). World Fair, Osaka. T **61** and similar vert designs. Multicoloured. P 13½.

128	15c. Type **61**	1·00	15
129	30c. Veil-tailed Guppys	1·50	70
130	75c. Greater Flamingo and Helmeted Hornbill	4·00	2·75
131	$1 Orchid	4·50	6·50
128/131 *Set of 4*		10·00	9·00
MS132 94×154 mm. Nos. 128/131		24·00	24·00

62 'Kindergarten'

63 Soldier charging

(Des Choy Weng Yang. Litho B.W.)

1970 (1 July). Tenth Anniversary of People's Association. T **62** and similar square designs. P 13½.

133	15c. agate and bright orange	60	20
134	50c. ultramarine and yellow-orange	1·40	2·00
135	75c. bright, purple and black	2·25	3·50
133/135 *Set of 3*		3·75	5·25

Designs: 15c. T **62**; 50c. 'Sport'; 75c. 'Culture'.

(Des Choy Weng Yang. Litho Rosenbaum Bros, Vienna)

1970 (9 Aug). National Day. T **63** and similar vert designs. Multicoloured. P 13½.

136	15c. Type **63**	1·25	20
137	50c. Soldier on assault course	3·00	2·75
138	$1 Soldier jumping	4·00	9·50
136/138 *Set of 3*		7·50	11·00

64 Sprinters

(Des Choy Weng Yang. Photo Japanese Govt Ptg Bureau, Tokyo)

1970 (23 Aug). Festival of Sports. T **64** and similar horiz designs. P 13×13½.

139	10c. magenta, black and ultramarine	1·50	3·25
	a. Horiz strip of 4. Nos. 139/142	6·75	13·00
140	15c. black, ultramarine and red-orange	1·75	3·50
141	25c. black, red-orange and bright green	2·00	3·75
142	50c. black, bright green and magenta	2·25	3·75
139/142 *Set of 4*		6·75	13·00

Designs: 10c. T **64**; 15c. Swimmers; 25c. Tennis-players; 50c. Racing cars.

Nos. 139/142 were issued together *se-tenant* in horizontal strips of four within the sheet.

65 *Neptune Aquamarine* (freighter)

(Des W. Lee. Litho Rosenbaum Bros, Vienna)

1970 (1 Nov). Singapore Shipping. T **65** and similar horiz designs. P 12.

143	15c. multicoloured	2·50	65
144	30c. yellow-ochre and ultramarine	4·50	4·25
145	75c. yellow-ochre and vermilion	8·00	10·00
143/145 *Set of 3*		13·50	13·50

Designs: 15c. T **65**; 30c. Container berth; 75c. Shipbuilding.

STAMP BOOKLET

1969 (1 Nov). Black on green cover. Stapled.

SB1	$1.80 booklet containing 12×15c. (No. 106) in blocks of 4	55·00

POSTAGE DUE STAMPS

The postage due stamps of Malayan Postal Union were in use in Singapore until replaced by the following issues.

D **1**

(Litho B.W.)

1968 (1 Feb)–**69**. Toned paper. W w **12**. P 9.

D1	D **1**	1c. green	60	2·00
D2		2c. red	1·60	2·50
D3		4c. yellow-orange	2·00	5·50
D4		8c. chocolate	1·00	2·00
D5		10c. magenta	1·00	90
		a. White paper (16.12.69)	2·25	8·00
D6		12c. slate-violet	2·75	3·25
		a. White paper (16.12.69)	7·00	20·00
D7		20c. new blue	2·00	3·50
		a. White paper (16.12.69)	10·00	15·00
D8		50c. drab	11·00	5·50
D1/D8 *Set of 8*			20·00	22·00

In 1973 the 10c. and 50c. were reissued on whiter paper, perf 13×13½. In 1977–1978 the 1c., 4c., 10c., 20c. and 50c. were issued on unwatermarked paper, perf 13×13½.

Somaliland Protectorate

Egyptian post offices were opened in Somaliland during 1876 and the stamps of Egypt were used there until the garrisons were withdrawn in 1884.

Cancellations for these offices have been identified as follows (for illustrations of postmark types see SUDAN).

BARBARA (Berbera). Open 1876 to 1 November 1884. Circular datestamp as Sudan Type I.

ZEILA. Open 1876 to 1 November 1884. Circular datestamp as Sudan Types G and I, sometimes inscr ZEJLA. One example with seal type cancellation as Sudan Type B is also known.

Stamps of India were used at the two post offices from 1 January 1887 until 1903 usually cancelled with circular datestamps or the 'B' obliterator used by all offices controlled from Bombay.

The Protectorate Post Office was established on 1 June 1903, when control of British Somaliland was transferred from the Indian Government to the British Foreign Office.

PRICES FOR STAMPS ON COVER TO 1945	
Nos. 1/11	from × 25
Nos. 12/13	—
Nos. 18/22	from × 12
Nos. 23/24	—
Nos. 25/30	from × 30
Nos. 32/59	from × 12
Nos. 60/92	from × 6
Nos. 93/104	from × 3
Nos. 105/116	from × 4
Nos. O1/O13	from × 20
Nos. O4/O9f	—
Nos. O10/O13	from × 20
Nos. O14/O15	—

(Currency. 12 pies = 1 anna; 16 annas = 1 rupee)

BRITISH SOMALILAND
(1)

2

3

SETTINGS OF TYPE 1

In all printings the ½, 1, 2, 2½, 3, 4, 8, 12a. and 1r. values were overprinted from a setting of 240 (2 panes 12×10, one above the other), covering the entire sheet at one operation.

The 6a., which was in sheets of 320 (4 panes, each 8×10), had a modified setting of 160, applied twice to each sheet.

The high values were overprinted in sheets of 96 (8 panes, each 4×3).

The settings for the low value stamps contained two slightly different styles of overprint, identified by the position of 'B' of 'BRITISH'. Type A shows this letter over the 'M' of 'SOMALILAND' and Type B over the 'OM'.

For the first printing with the overprint at the top of the design the 240 position setting showed all the stamps in the upper pane and 63 in the lower as Type A, with the remaining 57 as Type B. When the setting was used for the printing with overprint at foot it was amended slightly so that one of the Type A examples in the upper pane became a Type B.

The 6a. value with overprint at top shows 250 examples of Type A and 70 as Type B in each sheet. This proportion altered in the printing with overprint at foot to 256 as Type A and 64 as Type B.

OVERPRINT VARIETIES

Missing second 'I' in 'BRITISH'—Occurs on the stamps with overprint at top from R. 2/6 of the upper pane and R. 5/1 of the lower, although it is believed that the example on the 2½a. (No. 4a) only occurs from the second position. On the later printing with overprint at foot a similar error can be found on R. 7/12 of the upper pane. Some examples of both these errors show traces of the letter remaining, but the prices quoted are for stamps with it completely omitted.

BR1TISH SOMALILAND
i

Figure '1' for first 'I' in 'BRITISH' (i)—Occurs on R. 6/4 of the upper pane for all printings of the 240 impression setting. In addition it has been reported from R. 7/12 of the Queen Victoria 2½, 12a. and 1r. with overprint at foot. Both versions of the 6a. show the variety on R. 6/4 of the upper left and upper right panes.

BRITISH SOMALILAND
ii

Curved overprint (ii)—Occurs on R. 3/4 of the top right-hand pane of the high values.

SUMALILAND iii   **SOMAL.LAND** iv

'SUMALILAND'—Occurs on R. 2/9 of the upper pane for all low values with the overprint at foot, except the 6a (iii). A similar variety occurs on the high values from the same series on R. 1/3 of the top left pane (iv).

'SOMAL.LAND'—Occurs on R. 7/5 of the lower pane from the 240 impression setting with the overprint at foot. In addition the Edwardian values of this series also have an example on R. 6/7. The 6a. has examples of the flaw on R. 6/9 and R. 7/5 of both the lower right and left panes. A similar variety occurs on the high values from the same series at R. 3/4 of the third pane in the right-hand column.

1903 (1 June). Nos. 80, 94, 96, 98, 100, 106/109, 114/116 and 118 of India (Queen Victoria) optd with T **1**, at top of stamp, in Calcutta. Wmk Elephant Head (6a.) or Star (others).

1		½a. yellow-green	2·75	4·25
		a. 'BRIT SH'	£170	£275
		b. 'BR1TISH'	£200	£275
2		1a. carmine	3·00	3·75
		a. 'BRIT SH'	£200	£275
		b. 'BR1TISH'	£200	
3		2a. pale violet	2·25	1·50
		a. 'BRIT SH'	£400	£500
		b. 'BR1TISH'	£375	
		c. Opt double	£800	
4		2½a. ultramarine	2·00	1·75
		a. 'BRIT SH'	£725	
		b. 'BR1TISH'	£500	
5		3a. brown-orange	3·25	3·00
		a. 'BRIT SH'	£850	
		b. 'BR1TISH'	£450	£450
6		4a. slate-green	3·50	2·75
		a. 'BR1TISH'	£525	£475
7		6a. olive-bistre	8·00	4·50
		a. 'BR1TISH'	£300	£350
8		8a. dull mauve	4·50	5·00
		a. 'BR1TISH'	£425	£550
9		12a. purple/*red*	7·50	7·00
		a. 'BR1TISH'	£500	£600
10		1r. green and aniline carmine	7·50	10·00
		a. 'BR1TISH'	£500	£650
11		2r. carmine and yellow-brown	35·00	45·00
		a. Curved opt	£750	
12		3r. brown and green	32·00	55·00
		a. Curved opt	£750	
13		5r. ultramarine and violet	48·00	65·00
		a. Curved opt	£750	
1/13 *Set of 13*			£130	£190

1903 (1 Sept–2 Nov). Stamps of India optd with T 1, at bottom of stamp, in Calcutta.

(a) On Nos. 80, 100, 106/109 and 118 (Queen Victoria)

18		2½a. ultramarine (2.11)	8·00	8·50
		a. 'BR1TISH'	£200	
		b. 'SUMALILAND'	£250	
		c. 'SOMAL.LAND'	£275	
		d. 'BRIT SH'	£1500	
19		6a. olive-bistre (2.11)	9·50	7·00
		a. 'BR1TISH'	£350	
		b. 'SOMAL.LAND'	£225	
20		12a. purple/*red* (2.11)	11·00	14·00
		a. 'BR1TISH'	£425	
		b. 'SUMALILAND'	£350	£500
		c. 'SOMAL.LAND'	£450	
21		1r. green and aniline carmine (2.11)	11·00	11·00
		a. 'BR1TISH'	£475	
		b. 'SUMALILAND'	£475	
		c. 'SOMAL.LAND'	£500	
22		2r. carmine and yellow-brown (2.11)	£130	£200
		a. Curved opt	£850	£1300
		b. 'SUMALILAND'	£850	
		c. 'SOMAL.LAND'	£850	
23		3r. brown and green (2.11)	£140	£200
		a. Opt double, both inverted with one albino	£950	
		b. Curved opt	£950	
		c. 'SUMALILAND'	£950	
		d. 'SOMAL.LAND'	£950	
		e. Opt. double, one albino	£1200	
24		5r. ultramarine and violet (2.11)	£130	£200
		a. Curved opt	£950	
		b. 'SUMALILAND'	£950	
		c. 'SOMAL.LAND'	£950	

(b) On Nos. 122/124, 127/128 and 133 (King Edward VII)

25		½a. green	2·25	55
		a. 'BRIT SH'	£550	
		b. 'BR1TISH'	£130	
		c. 'SUMALILAND'	£130	£140
		d. 'SOMAL.LAND'	80·00	95·00
26		1a. carmine (8.10)	1·25	30
		a. 'BRIT SH'	£350	
		b. 'BR1TISH'	£130	£140
		c. 'SUMALILAND'	£130	£140
		d. 'SOMAL.LAND'	60·00	70·00
27		2a. violet (2.11)	2·75	1·75
		a. 'BRIT SH'	£1300	
		b. 'BR1TISH'	£250	
		c. 'SUMALILAND'	£225	
		d. 'SOMAL.LAND'	£120	
28		3a. orange-brown (2.11)	2·50	1·75
		a. 'BR1TISH'	£275	£350
		b. 'SUMALILAND'	£225	
		c. 'SOMAL.LAND'	£140	£170
29		4a. olive (2.11)	1·50	1·75
		a. 'BR1TISH'	£225	
		b. 'SUMALILAND'	£200	
		c. 'SOMAL.LAND'	£150	
30		8a. purple (2.11)	3·75	1·75
		a. 'BR1TISH'	£375	
		b. 'SUMALILAND'	£375	
		c. 'SOMAL.LAND'	£225	
18/30 *Set of 13*			£400	£600

(Typo D.L.R.)

1904 (15 Feb–3 Sept).

(a) Wmk Crown CA. P 14

32	**2**	½a. dull green and green	3·00	4·25
33		1a. grey-black and red (3.9)	19·00	3·25
34		2a. dull and bright purple (3.9)	2·25	2·75
35		2½a. bright blue (3.9)	10·00	3·75
36		3a. chocolate and grey-green (3.9)	2·50	7·00
37		4a. green and black (3.9)	4·00	9·50
38		6a. green and violet (3.9)	11·00	17·00
39		8a. grey-black and pale blue (3.9)	10·00	9·50
40		12a. grey-black and orange-buff (3.9)	14·00	11·00

(b) Wmk Crown CC. P 14

41	**3**	1r. green (3.9)	22·00	40·00
42		2r. dull and bright purple (3.9)	60·00	90·00
43		3r. green and black (3.9)	70·00	£130
44		5r. grey-black and red (3.9)	70·00	£140
32/44 *Set of 13*			£250	£425
32s/44s Optd 'SPECIMEN' *Set of 13*			£250	

1905 (July)–**11**. Ordinary paper. Wmk Mult Crown CA. P 14.

45	**2**	½a. dull green and green	1·25	7·50
46		1a. grey-black and red (10.7.05)	28·00	10·00
		a. Chalk-surfaced paper (1906)	24·00	1·60
47		2a. dull and bright purple	9·00	22·00
		a. Chalk-surfaced paper (1909)	23·00	18·00
48		2½a. bright blue	3·00	11·00
49		3a. chocolate and grey-green	2·00	17·00
		a. Chalk-surfaced paper (1911)	22·00	50·00
50		4a. green and black	4·50	26·00
		a. Chalk-surfaced paper (1911)	25·00	55·00
51		6a. green and violet	3·00	26·00
		a. Chalk-surfaced paper (1911)	40·00	80·00
52		8a. grey-black and pale blue	8·00	11·00
		a. Chalk-surfaced paper. *Black and blue* (27.1.11)	27·00	70·00
53		12a. grey-black and orange-buff	6·50	10·00
		a. Chalk-surfaced paper. *Black and orange-brown* (9.11.11)	17·00	70·00

1909 (30 Apr–May). Wmk Mult Crown CA. P 14.

58	**2**	½a. bluish green (5.09)	45·00	42·00
59		1a. red	2·50	2·00
		s. Optd 'SPECIMEN'	40·00	
45/59 *Set of 11*			95·00	£150

4

5

(Typo D.L.R.)

1912 (Sept)–**19**. Chalk-surfaced paper (2a. and 3a. to 5r.). Wmk Mult Crown CA. P 14.

60	**4**	½a. green (11.13)	65	13·00
		w. Wmk inverted	15·00	65·00
61		1a. red	2·75	50
		a. Scarlet (1917)	3·00	1·25
62		2a. dull and bright purple (12.13)	3·50	16·00
		a. Dull purple and violet-purple (4.19)	28·00	50·00
63		2½a. bright blue (10.13)	1·00	8·50
64		3a. chocolate and grey-green (10.13)	2·50	14·00
		w. Wmk inverted	£120	
65		4a. green and black (12.12)	2·50	10·00
66		6a. green and violet (4.13)	2·50	11·00
67		8a. grey-black and pale blue (10.13)	3·50	15·00
68		12a. grey-black and orange-buff (10.13)	3·50	21·00
69	**5**	1r. green (11.12)	24·00	28·00
70		2r. dull purple and purple (4.19)	29·00	80·00
71		3r. green and black (4.19)	85·00	£170
72		5r. black and scarlet (4.19)	95·00	£250
60/72 *Set of 13*			£225	£550
60s/72s Optd 'SPECIMEN' *Set of 13*			£325	

1921. Chalk-surfaced paper (2a. and 3a. to 5r.). Wmk Mult Script CA. P 14.

73	**4**	½a. blue-green	2·75	17·00
74		1a. carmine-red	3·50	70
75		2a. dull and bright purple	4·25	1·00
76		2½a. bright blue	1·00	10·00
77		3a. chocolate and green	2·50	7·50
78		4a. green and black	2·50	17·00
79		6a. green and violet	1·50	14·00
80		8a. grey-black and pale blue	2·00	14·00
81		12a. grey-black and orange-buff	8·50	15·00
82	**5**	1r. dull green	8·50	50·00
83		2r. dull purple and purple	28·00	55·00
84		3r. dull green and black	42·00	£120
85		5r. black and scarlet	95·00	£200
73/85 *Set of 13*			£180	£450
73s/85s Optd 'SPECIMEN' *Set of 13*			£300	

Examples of most values are known showing a forged Berbera postmark dated '21 OC 1932'.

1935 (6 May). Silver Jubilee. As Nos. 91/94 of Antigua, but ptd by Waterlow. P 11×12.

86		1a. deep blue and scarlet	2·50	4·25
		m. 'Bird' by turret	£160	£200
87		2a. ultramarine and grey	2·75	4·25
		k. Kite and vertical log	£150	£200
88		3a. brown and deep blue	2·50	22·00
		k. Kite and vertical log	£180	£325
		l. Kite and horizontal log	£180	£325
89		1r. slate and purple	10·00	26·00
		k. Kite and vertical log	£225	£375
		l. Kite and horizontal log	£190	£350
86/89 *Set of 4*			16·00	50·00
86s/89s Perf 'SPECIMEN' *Set of 4*			£110	

For illustrations of plate varieties see Omnibus section following Zanzibar.

1937 (13 May). Coronation. As Nos. 95/97 of Antigua, but ptd by D.L.R. P 14.

90		1a. scarlet	15	50
91		2a. grey-black	55	2·00
92		3a. bright blue	1·10	1·25
90/92 *Set of 3*			1·60	3·25
90s/92s Perf 'SPECIMEN' *Set of 3*			£100	

6 Berbera Blackhead Sheep

7 Greater Kudu

8 Somaliland Protectorate

(Des H. W. Claxton. Recess Waterlow)

1938 (10 May). Portrait to left. Wmk Mult Script CA. P 12½.

93	**6**	½a. green	2·75	9·00
94		1a. scarlet	1·75	3·25
95		2a. maroon	4·00	5·00
96		3a. bright blue	18·00	22·00
97	**7**	4a. sepia	6·50	16·00
98		6a. violet	16·00	13·00
99		8a. grey	8·50	16·00
100		12a. red-orange	20·00	45·00
101	**8**	1r. green	16·00	90·00
102		2r. purple	26·00	90·00
103		3r. bright blue	25·00	55·00
104		5r. black	32·00	55·00
		a. Imperf between (horiz pair)	£34000	
93/104 *Set of* 12			£150	£350
93s/104s Perf 'SPECIMEN' *Set of* 12			£350	

Examples of most values are known showing a forged Berbera postmark dated '15 AU 38'.

Italian forces occupied the Protectorate between 19 August 1940 and 16 March 1941. From 1 July of that year until 26 April 1942 contemporary Aden stamps and datestamps were in use.

9 Berbera Blackhead Sheep

5 Cents (**10**)

1 Shilling (**11**)

(Recess Waterlow)

1942 (27 Apr). As Types **6/8** but with full-face portrait of King George VI, as in T **9**. Wmk Mult Script CA. P 12½.

105	**9**	½a. green	25	55
106		1a. scarlet	25	10
107		2a. maroon	70	20
108		3a. bright blue	2·25	20
109	**7**	4a. sepia	3·00	30
110		6a. violet	3·00	20
111		8a. grey	4·00	20
112		12a. red-orange	3·25	3·00
113	**8**	1r. green	4·25	3·50
114		2r. purple	7·00	12·00
115		3r. bright blue	12·00	21·00
116		5r. black	18·00	13·00
105/116 *Set of* 12			50·00	48·00
105s/116s Perf 'SPECIMEN' *Set of* 12			£300	

1946 (15 Oct). Victory. As Nos. 110/111, of Antigua.

117	1a. carmine	10	10
	a. Perf 13½	11·00	50·00
118	3a. blue	10	10
117s/118s Perf 'SPECIMEN' *Set of* 2		85·00	

1949 (28 Jan). Royal Silver Wedding. As Nos. 112/113 of Antigua.

119	1a. scarlet	10	10
120	5r. black	4·75	7·00

1949 (24 Oct*). 75th Anniversary of UPU. As Nos. 114/117 of Antigua. Surch with face values in annas.

121	1a. on 10c. carmine	20	50
122	3a. on 30c. deep blue (R.)	1·25	5·50
123	6a. on 50c. purple	35	4·50
124	12a. on 1s. red-orange	90	1·75
121/124 *Set of* 4		2·40	11·00

* This is the local date of issue. The Crown Agents released these stamps in London on 10 October.

(New Currency. 100 cents = 1 shilling)

1951 (1 Apr). 1942 issue surch as Types **10/11**.

125	5c. on ½a. green	40	3·25
126	10c. on 2a. maroon	40	2·00
127	15c. on 3a. bright blue	1·75	3·25
128	20c. on 4a. sepia	2·00	30
129	30c. on 6a. violet	2·00	3·00
130	50c. on 8a. grey	2·50	30
131	70c. on 12a. red-orange	4·25	13·00
132	1s. on 1r. green	2·50	2·25
133	2s. on 2r. purple (21.4.51)*	5·50	25·00
134	2s. on 3r. bright blue	18·00	13·00
135	5s. on 5r. black (R.)	26·00	16·00
125/135 *Set of* 11		55·00	70·00

* Earliest reported date.

1953 (2 June). Coronation. As No. 120 of Antigua.

136	15c. black and green	30	35

12 Camel and Gurgi

13 Sentry, Somaliland Scouts

14 Somali Stock Dove

15 Martial Eagle

16 Berbera Blackhead Sheep

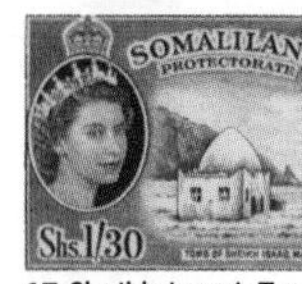

17 Sheikh Isaaq's Tomb, Mait

18 Taleh Fort

(Recess B.W.)

1953 (15 Sept)–**58**. Types **12/18**. Wmk Mult Script CA. P 12½.

137	**12**	5c. slate-black	15	60
138	**13**	10c. red-orange	2·25	1·50
		a. Salmon (20.3.58)	17·00	3·50
139	**12**	15c. blue-green	60	70
140		20c. scarlet	60	40
141	**13**	30c. reddish brown	2·25	40
142	**14**	35c. blue	5·50	1·75
143	**15**	50c. brown and rose-carmine	6·50	55
144	**16**	1s. light blue	1·25	30
145	**17**	1s.30 ultramarine and black (1.9.58)	27·00	4·50
146	**14**	2s. brown and bluish violet	28·00	7·50
147	**15**	5s. red-brown and emerald	35·00	11·00
148	**18**	10s. brown and reddish violet	32·00	45·00
137/148 *Set of* 12			£120	65·00

OPENING OF THE LEGISLATIVE COUNCIL 1957 (**19**)

LEGISLATIVE COUNCIL UNOFFICIAL MAJORITY, 1960 (**20**)

1957 (21 May). Opening of Legislative Council. Nos. 140 and 144 optd with T **19**.

149	20c. scarlet	10	15
150	1s. light blue	30	15

1960 (5 Apr). Legislative Council's Unofficial Majority. Nos, 140 arid 145 optd as T **20**.

151	20c. scarlet	75	15
152	1s.30 ultramarine and black	1·50	15

OFFICIAL STAMPS

BRITISH SOMALILAND (**O 1**)

SERVICE BRITISH SOMALILAND (**O 2**)

SETTING OF TYPE O 1

The 240 impression setting used for the Official stamps differs considerably from that on the contemporary postage issue with overprint at foot, although the 'BR1TISH' error can still be found on R. 6/4 of the upper pane. The Official setting is recorded as consisting of 217 overprints as Type A and 23 as Type B.

OVERPRINT VARIETIES

Figure '1' for first 'I' in 'BRITISH'—Occurs on R. 6/4 of the upper pane as for the postage issue.

'BRITIS H'—Occurs on R. 8/4 of the lower pane.

1903 (1 June). Nos. O45, O48, O49a and O50/O51 of India (Queen Victoria optd 'On H.M.S.') additionally optd with T O **1** in Calcutta.

O1	½a. yellow-green	7·00	55·00
	a. 'BR1TISH'	£475	
	b. 'BRITIS H'	£350	£850
O2	1a. carmine	15·00	18·00
	a. 'BR1TISH'	£475	£550
	b. 'BRITIS H'	£350	£450
O3	2a. pale violet	15·00	55·00
	a. 'BR1TISH'	£650	
	b. 'BRITIS H'	£500	
O4	8a. dull mauve	12·00	£475
	a. 'BR1TISH'	£1700	
	b. 'BRITIS H'	£1400	
	c. Stop omitted after 'M' of 'On H.M.S.' (lower pane R. 10/12)	£4250	
O5	1r. green and carmine	12·00	£750
	a. 'BR1TISH'	£1900	
	b. 'BRITIS H'	£1600	
O1/O5 *Set of* 5		55·00	£1200

No. O4c was caused by an attempt to correct a minor spacing error of the 'On H.M.S.' overprint which is known on the equivalent India Official stamp.

SETTING OF TYPE O 2

This 240 impression setting of 'BRITISH SOMALILAND' also differs from that used to prepare the postage issue with overprint at foot, although many of the errors from the latter still occur in the same positions for the Official stamps. The setting used for Nos. O6/9f contained 180 overprints as Type A and 60 as Type B.

OVERPRINT VARIETIES

Missing second 'I' in 'BRITSH'—Occurs R. 7/12 of upper pane as for the postage issue.

Figure '1' for first 'I' in 'BRITISH'—Occurs R. 6/4 of upper pane as for the postage issue.

'SUMALILAND'—Occurs R. 2/9 of the upper pane as for the postage issue.

'SOMAL.LAND'—Occurs R. 6/7 of the lower pane as for the postage issue.

SERVICE (**O 2a**)

'SERVICE' in wrong fount (T O **2a**)—Occurs R. 1/7 of lower pane.

1903. Prepared for use but not issued. Nos. 106, 122/124 and 133 of India (1r. Queen Victoria, rest King Edward VII), optd with T O **2** in Calcutta.

O6	½a. green	40	
	a. 'BRIT SH'	95·00	
	b. 'BR1TISH'	85·00	
	c. 'SUMALILAND'	85·00	
	d. 'SOMAL.LAND'	85·00	
	e. 'SERVICE' as Type O **2a**	85·00	
O7	1a. carmine	40	
	a. 'BRIT SH'	95·00	
	b. 'BR1TISH'	85·00	
	c. 'SUMALILAND'	85·00	
	d. 'SOMAL.LAND'	85·00	
	e. 'SERVICE' as Type O **2a**	85·00	
O8	2a. violet	70	
	a. 'BRIT SH'	£130	
	b. 'BR1TISH'	£120	
	c. 'SUMALILAND'	£120	
	d. 'SERVICE' as Type O **2a**	£120	
O9	8a. purple	9·00	
	a. 'BRIT SH'	£3000	
	b. 'BR1TISH'	£2500	
	c. 'SUMALILAND'	£2500	
	d. 'SERVICE' as Type O **2a**	£2500	
O9*f*	1r. green and aniline carmine	18·00	
	fa. 'BRIT SH'	£3000	
	fb. 'BR1TISH'	£2500	
	fc. 'SUMALILAND'	£2500	
	fd. 'SOMAL.LAND'	£2500	
	fe. 'SERVICE' as Type O **2a**	£2500	
O6/O9*f Set of* 5		26·00	

Used examples of Nos. O6/9f are known, but there is no evidence that such stamps did postal duty.

O.H.M.S. (**O 3**)

O.H.M.S. (**O 4**)

1904 (1 Sept)–**05**. Stamps of Somaliland Protectorate optd with Types O **3** or O **4** (No. O15).

(a) Wmk Crown CA. P 14

O10	**2**	½a. dull green and green	12·00	48·00
		a. No stop after 'M'	£300	
O11		1a. grey-black and carmine	5·50	6·00
		a. No stop after 'M'	£200	£300
O12		2a. dull and bright purple	£300	70·00
		a. No stop after 'M'	£3250	£900
O13		8a. grey-black and pale blue	60·00	£140
		a. No stop after 'M'	£600	£950
		(b) Wmk Mult Crown CA		
O14	**2**	2a. dull and bright purple, (7.05?)	£120	£1100
		a. No stop after 'M'	£2500	
		(c) Wmk Crown CC		
O15	**3**	1r. green	£275	£1100
O10s/O13s, O15s Optd 'SPECIMEN' *Set of* 5			£160	

SETTING OF TYPE O 3

The anna values were overprinted in sheets of 120 (2 panes 6×10) from a setting matching the pane size. The full stop after the 'M' on the fifth vertical column was either very faint or completely omitted. The prices quoted are for stamps with the stop missing; examples with a partial stop are worth much less.

The 1r. value was overprinted with T O **4** from a setting of 60.

All Somaliland Protectorate stamps were withdrawn from sale on 25 June 1960 and until the unification on 1 July, issues of Italian Somalia together with Nos. 353/355 of Republic of Somalia were used. Later issues will be found listed in the Stanley Gibbons *North East Africa Catalogue*.

South Africa

South Africa as a nation, rather than a geographical term, came into being with the creation of the Union of South Africa on 31 May 1910.

The development, both political and philatelic, of the area is very complex and the method adopted by the catalogue is to first list, in alphabetical order, the various colonies and republics which formed this federation, followed by stamps for the Union of South Africa.

The section is divided as follows:

I. CAPE OF GOOD HOPE.
British Kaffraria. Mafeking Siege Stamps. Vryburg
II. GRIQUALAND WEST
III. NATAL
IV. NEW REPUBLIC
V. ORANGE FREE STATE.
Orange River Colony
VI. TRANSVAAL.
Pietersburg. Local British Occupation Issues
VII. ZULULAND
VIII. BRITISH ARMY FIELD OFFICES
DURING SOUTH AFRICAN WAR
IX. UNION OF SOUTH AFRICA
X. REPUBLIC OF SOUTH AFRICA

I. CAPE OF GOOD HOPE

PRICES FOR STAMPS ON COVER

Nos. 1/4	*from* × 4
Nos. 5/14	*from* × 3
Nos. 18/21	*from* × 5
No. 22	—
Nos. 23/26	*from* × 5
Nos. 27/31	*from* × 8
Nos. 32/33	*from* × 10
No. 34	*from* × 25
No. 35	*from* × 20
No. 36	*from* × 10
Nos. 37/38	*from* × 25
Nos. 39/45	*from* × 10
Nos. 46/47	*from* × 12
Nos. 48/54	*from* × 10
Nos. 55/56	*from* × 25
No. 57	*from* × 50
Nos. 58/69	*from* × 10
Nos. 70/78	*from* × 6

PRICES. Our prices for early Cape of Good Hope are for stamps in very fine condition. Exceptional copies are worth more, poorer copies considerably less.

1 Hope

2

(Des Charles Bell, Surveyor-General. Eng W. Humphrys. Recess P.B.)

1853 (1 Sept). W **2**. Imperf.

(a) Paper deeply blued

No.	Type	Description	Unused	Used
1	1	1d. pale brick-red	£4500	£450
		a. Deep brick-red	£6000	£475
		b. Wmk sideways	†	£500
2		4d. deep blue	£3500	£275
		a. Wmk sideways	£5000	£375

Plate proofs of the 4d. in a shade similar to the issued stamp exist on ungummed watermarked paper. (*Price* £550) The blueing on the reverse of these proofs is uneven giving a blotchy appearance.

(b) Paper slightly blued (blueing not pronounced at back)

No.	Type	Description	Unused	Used
3	1	1d. brick-red	£3500	£350
		a. Brown-red	£3750	£375
		b. Wmk sideways	†	£425
4		4d. deep blue	£1900	£170
		a. Blue	£2000	£200
		b. Wmk sideways	†	£375

PERKINS BACON 'CANCELLED'. For notes on these handstamps showing 'CANCELLED' between horizontal bars forming an oval, see Catalogue Introduction.

1855–63. W **2**.

(a) Imperf

No.	Type	Description	Unused	Used
5	1	1d. brick-red/*cream toned paper* (1857)	£5000	£900
		a. Rose (1858) (H/S 'CANCELLED' in oval £20000)	£800	£300
		ab. Wmk sideways	—	£650
		b. Deep rose-red	£1200	£375
		ba. Wmk sideways	—	£650
6		4d. deep blue/*white paper* (1855)	£1400	95·00
		a. Blue (H/S 'CANCELLED' in oval £20000)	£1100	90·00
		b. Bisected (*on cover*)	†	£35000
		c. Wmk sideways	£3000	£325
7		6d. pale rose-lilac (*shades*)/*white paper* (18.2.58) (H/S 'CANCELLED' in oval £16000)	£1200	£325
		a. Wmk sideways	†	£1500
		b. Deep rose-lilac/white paper	£2250	£400
		c. Slate-lilac/blued paper (1862)	£4500	£500
		d. Slate-purple/blued paper (1863)	£4000	£1000
		e. Bisected (*on cover*)	†	—
8		1s. bright yellow-green/*white paper* (18.2.58) (H/S 'CANCELLED' in oval £20000)	£3500	£300
		a. Wmk sideways	†	£3000
		b. Deep dark green (1859)	£450	£550

The method adopted for producing the plate of the 4d., 6d and 1s. stamps involved the use of two dies, so that there are two types of each of these values differing slightly in detail, but produced in equal numbers.

The 1d. value in dull rose on ungummed watermarked paper with the watermark sideways is a plate proof. (*Price* £425).

The 4d. is known bisected in 1858 and used with two other 4d. values to pay the inland registered fee. The 6d. is known bisected and used with 1d. for 4d. rate.

The paper of No. 5 is similar to that of Nos. 1/4, but is without the blueing. It is much thicker than the white paper used for later printings of the 1d. The evolution of the paper on these Cape of Good Hope stamps is similar to that of the line-engraved issues of Great Britain. Examples of the 6d. slate-lilac apparently on white paper have had the blueing washed out.

The 4d. value is known printed in black on white watermarked paper. 12 authenticated copies have been recorded, the majority of which show cancellations or, at least, some indication that they have been used.

It was, at one time, believed that these stamps came from a small supply printed in black to mark the death of the Prince Consort, but references to examples can be found in the philatelic press before news of this event reached Cape Town.

It is now thought that these stamps represent proof sheets, possibly pressed into service during a shortage of stamps in 1861.

There is, however, no official confirmation of this theory. (*Price* £45000 *un*, £35000 *with obliteration*).

(b) Unofficially rouletted

No.	Type	Description	Unused	Used
9	1	1d. brick-red	†	£3000
10		4d. blue	†	£2250
11		6d. rose-lilac	†	£1500
12		1s. bright yellow-green	†	£3250
		a. Deep dark green	†	£3500

These rouletted stamps are best collected on cover.

3 Hope

(Local provisional (so-called 'wood-block') issue. Engraved on steel by C. J. Roberts. Printed from stereotyped plates by Saul Solomon & Co, Cape Town)

1861 (Feb–Apr). Laid paper. Imperf.

No.	Type	Description	Unused	Used
13	3	1d. vermilion (27.2)	£17000	£2750
		a. Carmine (7.3)	£30000	£3500
		b. Brick-red (10.4)	£50000	£5000
		c. Error. Pale milky blue	£200000	£30000
		ca. Pale bright blue	—	£32000
14		4d. pale milky blue (23.2)	£25000	£2000
		aa. Retouch or repair to right-hand corner	—	£9000
		a. Pale grey-blue (3.61?)	£26000	£2000
		b. Pale bright blue (3.61)	£26000	£2250
		ba. Retouch or repair to right-hand corner	—	£9000
		c. Deep bright blue (12.4)	£120000	£5000
		d. Blue	£32000	£3250
		e. Error. Vermilion	£200000	£40000
		ea. Carmine	—	£95000
		f. Sideways *tête-bêche* (pair)	†	£200000

Nos. 13/14 were each issued in *tête-bêche* pairs normally joined at edges bearing the same inscription ('POSTAGE' against 'POSTAGE', etc). No. 14f, of which only one used example is known, comes from the first printing and shows the right-hand stamp misplaced so that 'FOUR PENCE' adjoins 'POSTAGE'.

Nos. 13c/13*ca* and 14e/14*ea* were caused by the inclusion of incorrect clichés in the plates of the 1d. or 4d. values.

Both values were officially reprinted in March 1883, on wove paper. The 1d. is in deep red, and the 4d. in a deeper blue than that of the deepest shade of the issued stamp.

Examples of the reprints have done postal duty, but their use thus was not intended. There are no reprints of the errors or of the retouched 4d.

Further reprints were made privately but with official permission, in 1940/1941, in colours much deeper than those of any of the original printings, and on thick carton paper.

Examples of the 4d. are known unofficially rouletted.

Early in 1863, Perkins Bacon Ltd handed over the four plates used for printing the triangular Cape of Good Hope stamps to De La Rue & Co, Ltd, who made all the subsequent printings.

(Printed from the P.B. plates by D.L.R.)

1863–64. Imperf.

(a) W **2**

No.	Type	Description	Unused	Used
18	1	1d. deep carmine-red (1864)	£325	£325
		a. Wmk sideways	£700	£600
		b. Deep brown-red	£650	£350
		ba. Wmk sideways	£750	£400
		c. Brownish red	£650	£325
		ca. Wmk sideways	£750	£375
19		4d. deep blue (1864)	£300	£130
		a. Blue	£325	£140
		b. Slate-blue	£2500	£500
		c. Steel-blue	£2250	£275
		d. Wmk sideways	£1100	£375
20		6d. bright mauve (1864)	£425	£500
		a. Wmk sideways	†	£2500
21		1s. bright emerald-green	£650	£700
		a. Pale emerald-green	£1400	

(b) Wmk Crown CC (sideways)

No.	Type	Description	Unused	Used
22	1	1d. deep carmine-red	£25000	

No. 22 was a trial printing, and is only known unused.

Our prices for the 4d. blue are for stamps which are blue by comparison with the other listed shades. An exceptionally pale shade is recognised by specialists and is rare.

With the exception of the 4d., these stamps may be easily distinguished from those printed by Perkins Bacon by their colours, which are quite distinct.

The De La Rue stamps of all values are less clearly printed, the figure of Hope and the lettering of the inscriptions standing out less boldly, while the fine lines of the background appear blurred and broken when examined under a glass. The background as a whole often shows irregularity in the apparent depth of colour, due to wear of the plates.

For note regarding the two dies of the 4d., 6d., and 1s. values, see after No. 8.

All the triangular stamps were demonetised as from 1 October 1900.

4 'Hope' seated, with vine and ram. (With outer frame-line)

Four Pence.

(5)

(Des Charles Bell. Die engraved on steel and stamps typo by D.L.R.)

1864–77. With outer frame-line surrounding the design. Wmk Crown CC. P 14.

No.	Type	Description	Unused	Used
23	4	1d. carmine-red (5.65)	£130	45·00
		a. Rose-red	£130	42·00
		w. Wmk inverted	£500	£225
24		4d. pale blue (8.65)	£225	4·50
		a. Blue	£225	4·50
		b. Ultramarine	£375	55·00
		c. Deep blue (1872)	£300	4·50
		w. Wmk inverted	£750	£250
25		6d. pale lilac (before 21.3.64)	£225	28·00
		a. Deep lilac	£400	8·00
		b. Violet (to bright) (1877)	£250	1·50
		w. Wmk inverted	†	£475
		x. Wmk reversed	†	£700
26		1s. deep green (1.64)	£850	22·00
		a. Green	£250	4·75
		ax. Wmk reversed	†	£750
		b. Blue-green	£275	6·00
		w. Wmk inverted	£1000	£275

The 1d. rose-red, 6d. lilac, and 1s. blue-green are known imperf, probably from proof sheets.

The 1d. and 4d. stamps of this issue may be found with side and/or top outer frame-lines missing, due to wear of the plates.

See also Nos. 44 and 52/53.

(Surch by Saul Solomon & Co, Cape Town)

1868 (17 Nov). No. 25a surch with T **5**.

No.	Type	Description	Unused	Used
27	4	4d. on 6d. deep lilac (R.)	£600	18·00
		a. 'Peuce' for 'Pence'	£2500	£700
		b. 'Fonr' for 'Four'	—	£700
		w. Wmk inverted	—	£600

Examples may also be found with bars omitted or at the top of the stamp, due to misplacement of the sheet.

The space between the words and bars varies from 12½ to 16 mm, stamps with spacing 15½ and 16 mm being rare. There were two printings, one of 120,000 in November 1868 and another of 1,000,000 in December. Stamps showing widest spacings are probably from the earlier printing.

6 (No outer frame-line)

(Die re-engraved. Typo D.L.R.)

1871–76. Outer frame-line removed. Wmk Crown CC. P 14.

No.	Type	Description	Unused	Used
28	6	½d. grey-black (*shades*) (12.75)	40·00	18·00
		w. Wmk inverted	£500	£200
29		1d. carmine-red (*shades*) (2.72)	60·00	1·25
		w. Wmk inverted	£500	£200
30		4d. dull blue (*shades*) (12.76)	£225	75
		b. Ultramarine	£375	55·00
		w. Wmk inverted	£650	£160
31		5s. yellow-orange (25.8.71)	£700	26·00
		w. Wmk inverted	†	£550

The ½d., 1d. and 5s. are known imperf, probably from proof sheets.

See also Nos. 36, 39, 40/43, 48/51, 54, 61/62 and 64/68.

ONE PENNY **THREE PENCE**

(7) **(8)**

(Surch by Saul Solomon & Co, Cape Town)

1874–76. Nos. 25a and 26a surch with T **7**.

No.	Type	Description	Unused	Used
32	4	1d. on 6d. deep lilac (R.) (1.9.74)	£900	£140
		a. 'E' of 'PENNY' omitted	†	£1800
33		1d. on 1s. green (11.76)	£150	80·00

These provisionals are found with the bar only, either across the centre of the stamp or at top, with value only; or with value and bar close together, either at top or foot. Such varieties are due to misplacement of sheets during surcharging.

(Surch by Saul Solomon & Co, Cape Town)

1879 (1 Nov). No. 30 surch with T **8**.

34	**6**	3d. on 4d. blue (R.)	£190	2·25
		a. 'PENCB' for 'PENCE'	£3500	£225
		b. 'THE.EE' for 'THREE'	£4000	£275
		c. Surch double	£13000	£4500
		d. Variety b. double		

The double surcharge must also have existed showing variety a. but only variety b. is known.

There are numerous minor varieties, including letters broken or out of alignment, due to defective printing and use of poor type.

The spacing between the bar and the words varies from 16½ to 18 mm.

THREEPENCE (9) 3 (10) 3 (11)

(Surch by D.L.R.)

1880 (Feb). Special printing of the 4d. in new colour, surch, with T **9**. Wmk Crown CC.

35	**6**	3d. on 4d. pale dull rose	£150	3·25
		w. Wmk inverted	—	£425

A minor constant variety exists with foot of 'P' in 'PENCE' broken off, making the letter appear shorter.

1880 (1 July). Wmk Crown CC. P 14.

36	**6**	3d. pale dull rose	£375	42·00
		w. Wmk inverted	—	£475

(Surch by Saul Solomon & Co, Cape Town)

1880 (Aug). No. 36 surch.

37	**10**	'3' on 3d. pale dull rose	£140	2·25
		a. Surch inverted	£1700	45·00
		b. Vert pair. Nos. 37/8	£2500	£700
		w. Wmk inverted	—	£300
38	**11**	'3' on 3d. pale dull rose	£425	12·00
		a. Surch inverted	£13000	£1600
		w. Wmk inverted	—	£750

The '3' (T **10**) is sometimes found broken. Vert pairs are known showing the two types of surcharge *se-tenant*, and vertical strips of three exist, the top stamp having surcharge T **10**, the middle stamp being without surcharge, and the lower stamp having surcharge T **11** (*Price for strip of 3 £5500 un.*).

1881 (Jan). Wmk Crown CC. P 14.

39	**6**	3d. pale claret	£250	5·00
		a. Deep claret	£190	4·50
		w. Wmk inverted		

This was a definite colour change made at the request of the Postmaster-General owing to the similarity between the colours of the 1d. stamp and the 3d. in pale dull rose. Imperf copies are probably from proof sheets.

Proofs of this value were printed in brown, on unwatermarked wove paper and imperf, but the colour was rejected as unsuitable.

1882 (July)–**83**. Wmk Crown CA. P 14.

40	**6**	½d. black (1.9.82)	48·00	3·00
		a. Grey-black	45·00	3·00
		w. Wmk inverted	—	£250
41		1d. rose-red	90·00	2·50
		a. Deep rose-red	90·00	2·50
		w. Wmk inverted	—	£275
42		2d. pale bistre (1.9.82)	£150	1·75
		a. Deep bistre	£160	1·75
		w. Wmk inverted	—	£300
43		3d. pale claret	13·00	1·75
		a. Deep claret	21·00	75
		aw. Wmk inverted	—	£200
		ax. Wmk reversed		
44	**4**	6d. mauve (*to bright*) (8.82)	£170	80
45	**6**	5s. orange (8.83)	£1000	£300

Imperf pairs of the ½d., 1d. and 2d. are known, probably from proof sheets.

One Half-penny.

(12)

13 'Cabled Anchor'

(Surch by Saul Solomon & Co, Cape Town)

1882 (July). Nos. 39*a* and 43*a* surch with T **12**.

46	**6**	½d. on 3d. deep claret (Wmk CC)	£5000	£180
		a. Hyphen omitted	—	£4000
47		½d. on 3d. deep claret (Wmk CA)	60·00	8·00
		a. 'p' in 'penny' omitted	£2500	£800
		b. 'y' in 'penny' omitted	£2000	£800
		c. Hyphen omitted	£900	£375
		w. Wmk inverted	—	£500

Varieties also exist with broken and defective letters, and with the obliterating bar omitted or at the top of the stamp. The surcharge particularly on No. 46. is also frequently found misplaced.

1884–90. W **13**. P 14.

48	**6**	½d. black (1.86)	12·00	10
		a. Grey-black	12·00	10
		w. Wmk inverted	—	£600
49		1d. rose-red (12.85)	16·00	10
		a. Carmine-red	16·00	10
		w. Wmk inverted	—	£300
50		2d. pale bistre (12.84)	45·00	1·75
		a. Deep bistre	16·00	10
		w. Wmk inverted	—	£250
51		4d. blue (6.90)	26·00	50
		a. Deep blue	26·00	50
52	**4**	6d. reddish purple (12.84)	65·00	1·75
		a. Purple (shades)	23·00	20
		b. Bright mauve	17·00	50
		w. Wmk inverted	—	£500
53		1s. green (12.85)	£250	8·50
		a. Blue-green (1889)	£180	1·25
		w. Wmk inverted	—	£600
54	**6**	5s. orange (7.87)	£180	9·50
48/54 *Set of 7*			£375	10·50

All the above stamps are known in imperf pairs, probably from proof sheets.

For later shade and colour changes, etc., see Nos. 61, etc.

2½d (14) 15 ONE PENNY. (16)

(Surch by D.L.R.)

1891 (Mar). Special printing of the 3d. in new colour, surch with T **14**.

55	**6**	2½d. on 3d. pale magenta	18·00	2·25
		a. Deep magenta	9·00	20
		b. '1' with horiz serif	95·00	35·00

No. 55b occurs on two stamps (Nos. 8 and 49) of the pane of 60.

Two types of 'd' are found in the surcharge, one with square end to serif at top, and the other with pointed serif.

1892 (June). W **13**. P 14.

56	**15**	2½d. sage-green	28·00	10
		a. Olive-green	28·00	55

See also No. 63.

(Surch by W. A. Richards & Sons, Cape Town)

1893 (Mar). Nos. 50/*a* surch with T **16**.

57	**6**	1d. on 2d. pale bistre	18·00	3·00
		a. Deep bistre	6·00	50
		b. No stop after 'PENNY'	£100	28·00
		c. Surch double	—	£600

No. 57b occurs on R. 7/6 of the upper left-hand pane, and on R. 1/6 of the lower right-hand pane.

Minor varieties exist showing broken letters and letters out of alignment or widely spaced. Also with obliterating bar omitted, due to misplacement of the sheet during surcharging.

17 'Hope' standing. Table Bay in background

18 Table Mountain and Bay with Arms of the Colony

(Des Mr. Mountford. Typo D.L.R.)

1893 (Oct)–**1902**. W **13**. P 14.

58	**17**	½d. green (9.98)	11·00	20
59		1d. rose-red	15·00	3·00
		a. Carmine	4·50	10
		aw. Wmk inverted	†	£225
60		3d. magenta (3.02)	8·50	4·00

The 1d. is known in imperf pairs, probably from proof sheets.

1893–98. New colours, etc. W **13**. P 14.

61	**6**	½d. yellow-green (12.96)	1·50	1·00
		a. Green	2·75	1·00
62		2d. chocolate-brown (3.97)	5·00	4·00
63	**15**	2½d. pale ultramarine (3.96)	15·00	15
		a. Ultramarine	15·00	10
64	**6**	3d. bright magenta (9.98)	21·00	1·50
65		4d. sage-green (3.97)	13·00	4·25
66		1s. blue-green (12.93)	£110	9·50
		a. Deep blue-green	£150	15·00
67		1s. yellow-ochre (5.96)	21·00	3·25
		w. Wmk inverted	†	£600
68		5s. brown-orange (6.96)	£150	5·50
61/68 *Set of 8*			£300	26·00

(Des E. Sturman. Typo D.L.R.)

1900 (Jan). W **13**. P 14.

69	**18**	1d. carmine	9·50	10
		w. Wmk inverted	—	£250

19 20 21

22 23 24

25 26 27

(Typo D.L.R.)

1902 (Dec)–**04**. W **13**. P 14.

70	**19**	½d. green	3·75	10
71	**20**	1d. carmine	3·25	10
		w. Wmk inverted		
		y. Wmk inverted and reversed		
72	**21**	2d. brown (10.04)	25·00	80
		w. Wmk inverted		
73	**22**	2½d. ultramarine (3.04)	5·50	14·00
74	**23**	3d. magenta (4.03)	18·00	1·25
75	**24**	4d. olive-green (2.03)	21·00	65
76	**25**	6d. bright mauve (3.03)	32·00	30
77	**26**	1s. yellow-ochre	18·00	1·25
78	**27**	5s. brown-orange (2.03)	£160	28·00
70/78 *Set of 9*			£250	42·00

All values exist in imperf pairs, from proof sheets.

The ½d. exists from coils constructed from normal sheets for use in stamp machines introduced in 1911.

STAMP BOOKLET

1905 (Dec). Black on red cover. Stapled.

SB1	2s.7d. booklet containing 30×1d. (No. 71) in blocks of 6	£3000

OFFICIAL STAMPS

The following stamps, punctured with a double triangle device, were used by the Stationery and Printed Forms Branch of the Cape of Good Hope Colonial Secretary's Department between 1904 and 1906. Later South Africa issues may have been similarly treated, but this has not been confirmed.

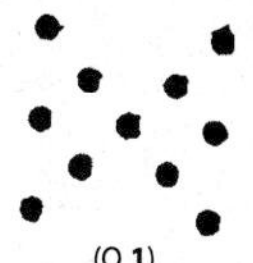

(O 1)

1904. Various issues punctured as T O **1**.

		(a) Nos. 50 and 52a	
O1	**6**	2d. pale bistre	32·00
O2	**4**	6d. purple	40·00
		(b) Nos. 58 and 60	
O3	**17**	½d. green	42·00
O4		3d. magenta	35·00
		(c) Nos. 62 and 64/65	
O5	**6**	2d. chocolate-brown	32·00
O6		3d. bright magenta	42·00
O7		4d. sage-green	42·00
		(d) No. 69	
O8	**18**	1d. carmine	30·00
		(e) Nos. 70/72 and 74/78	
O9	**19**	½d. green	42·00
O10	**20**	1d. carmine	24·00
O11	**21**	2d. brown	40·00
O12	**23**	3d. magenta	32·00
O13	**24**	4d. olive-green	35·00
O14	**25**	6d. bright mauve	38·00
O15	**26**	1s. yellow-ochre	50·00
O16	**27**	5s. brown-orange	£110

Nos. O1/O16 are only known used. They are best collected on piece.

Cape of Good Hope became a province of the Union of South Africa on 31 May 1910. Stamps used during the Interprovincial Period (1 June 1910–1931 August 1913) will be found listed under South Africa.

BRITISH KAFFRARIA

The history of the Cape eastern frontier was punctuated by a series of armed conflicts with the native population, known as the Kaffir Wars. After a particularly violent outbreak in 1846 the Governor, Sir Harry Smith, advanced the line of the Cape frontier to the Keikama and Tyumie Rivers. In the area between the new frontier and the Kei River a buffer state, British Kaffraria, was established on 17 December 1847. This area was not annexed to the Cape, but was administered as a separate Crown dependency by the Governor of Cape Colony in his capacity as High Commissioner for South Africa.

The territory, with its administration based on King William's Town, used the stamps of the Cape of Good Hope from 1853 onwards, the mail being sent via Port Elizabeth or overland from the Cape. Covers from British Kaffraria franked with the triangular issues are rare.

The first postal marking known from British Kaffraria is the 1849 type octagonal numeral No 47 from Port Beaufort. Oval post-marks of the 1853 type were used at Alice, Aliwal North, Bedford, Fort Beaufort, King William's Town and Queenstown. In 1864 numeral cancellations were issued to all post offices within the Cape system and it is known that the following numbers were initially assigned to post towns in Kaffraria: 4 (King William's Town), 7 (Bedford), 11 (Queenstown), 29 (East London), 32 (Fort Beaufort), 38 (Aliwal North) and 104 (Cathcart).

It is believed that post offices may have also existed at Adelaide, Barkly East, Sterkstoom and Stutterheim, but, to date, no examples of handstamps or cancellations are known from them during the British Kaffraria period.

Following the decimation by famine of the Xhosa tribes in 1857 British Kaffraria was annexed to Cape Colony in 1865.

MAFEKING SIEGE STAMPS

PRICES FOR STAMPS ON COVER	
Nos. 1/16	*from* × 12
Nos. 17/18	*from* × 25
Nos. 19/20	*from* × 15
Nos. 21/22	*from* × 12

23 MARCH to 17 MAY 1900

There are numerous forgeries of the Mafeking overprints, many of which were brought home by soldiers returning from the Boer War.

MAFEKING, 3d. BESIEGED. (1)

MAFEKING 3d. BESIEGED. (2)

(Surcharged by Townsend & Co, Mafeking)

1900 (23 Mar–28 Apr). Various stamps surch as Types **1** and **2**.

(a) Cape of Good Hope stamps surch as T **1** *(23 Mar)*

1 **6** 1d. on ½d. green .... £325 85·00
2 **17** 1d. on ½d. green (24.3) £375 £120
3 3d. on 1d. carmine .... £325 65·00
4 **6** 6d. on 3d. magenta (24.3) £45000 £350
5 1s. on 4d. sage-green (24.3) £8000 £425

A variety in the setting of each value exists without comma after 'MAFEKING'.

(b) Nos. 59 and 61/63 of Bechuanaland Protectorate (previously optd on Great Britain) surch as T **1**

6 1d. on ½d. vermilion (28.3) .... £325 80·00
a. Surch inverted .... † £8000
b. Vert pair, surch *tête-bêche* .... † £40000
7 3d. on 1d. lilac (4.4) £1000 £150
a. Surch double .... † £38000
8 6d. on 2d. green and carmine (6.4) £3000 £120
9 6d. on 3d. purple/*yellow* (30.3) £7500 £425
a. Surch inverted .... † £42000
b. Surch double ....

(c) Nos. 12, 35 and 37 of British Bechuanaland (4d. and 1s. previously optd on Great Britain) surch as T **1**

10 6d. on 3d. lilac and black (27.3) .... £550 95·00
11 1s. on 4d. green and purple-brown (29.3) £1600 £110
a. Surch double (both Type **1**) .... † £30000
ab. Surch double (Type **1** and Type **2**) ... £14000 £8000
b. Surch treble .... † £30000
c. Surch double, one inverted .... † £30000
11*d* 2s. on 1s. green .... † £38000

(d) Nos. 61/62 and 65 of Bechuanaland Protectorate (previously optd on Great Britain) surch as T **2**

12 3d. on 1d. lilac (1.4) £1100 £100
a. Surch double .... † £11000
13 6d. on 2d. green and carmine (1.4) £1600 £100
14 1s. on 6d. purple/*rose-red* (12.4) £7500 £130

(e) Nos. 36/37 of British Bechuanaland (previously optd on Great Britain) surch as T **2**

15 1s. on 6d. purple/*rose-red* (28.4) £35000 £850
16 2s. on 1s. green (13.4) £15000 £650

On the stamps overprinted 'BECHUANALAND PROTECTORATE' and 'BRITISH BECHUANALAND' the local surcharge is so adjusted as not to overlap the original overprint.

3 Cadet Sergt.-Major Goodyear

4 General Baden-Powell

(Des Dr. W. A. Hayes (T **3**), Capt. H. Greener (T **4**))

1900 (6–10 Apr). Produced photographically by Dr. D. Taylor. Horiz laid paper with sheet wmk 'OCEANA FINE'. P 12.

(a) 18½ mm wide. (b) 21 mm wide

17 **3** 1d. pale blue/*blue* (7.4) £1200 £325
18 1d. deep blue/*blue* £1200 £325
19 **4** 3d. pale blue/*blue* (*a*) £1700 £475
a. Reversed design £100000 £55000
20 3d. deep blue/*blue* (*a*) £1700 £425
a. Imperf between (horiz pair) ... † £100000
b. Double print .... † £25000
21 3d. pale blue/*blue* (*b*) (10.4) £12000 £1200
a. Vert laid paper £20000 £6000
22 3d. deep blue/*blue* (*b*) (10.4) £14000 £1400

These stamps vary a great deal in colour from deep blue to pale grey.

No. 18 imperforate and without gum is believed to be a proof (*Price for unused pair £25000*).

No. 19a comes from a sheet of 12 printed in reverse of which ten, three mint and seven used, are known to have survived.

VRYBURG

PRICES FOR STAMPS ON COVER

Nos. 1/4	*from* × 5
Nos. 11/12	*from* × 2

BOER OCCUPATION

Vryburg was occupied by Boer forces on 15 October 1899. Unoverprinted stamps of Transvaal were used initially. Nos. 1/4 were only available from 25 to 29 November. The Boers evacuated the town on 7 May 1900.

½ PENCE

Z.A.R.
(1)

1899 (25 Nov). Cape stamps surch as T **1** at the offices of *De Stellalander*. Surch 12.5 mm high on No. 3 and 10.5 mm on all other values.

1 **6** ½ PENCE green .... £225 80·00
a. Italic 'Z' £2250 £800
b. Surch 12.5 mm high £2250 £800
2 **17** 1 PENCE rose £250 £100
a. Italic 'Z' £2500 £900
b. Surch 12.5 mm high £2500 £900
c. 'I' for '1' £1600 £550
3 **4** 2 PENCE on 6d. mauve £2000 £500
a. Italic 'Z' £15000 £4500
4 **15** 2½ PENCE on 2½d. blue £1700 £425
a. Italic 'Z' £15000 £4500
b. Surch 12.5 mm high £15000 £4500

On the '2 PENCE' on 6d. the space between the lines of the surcharge is 7.3 mm. It is possible that this was the first value surcharged, as the remaining three show the space reduced to 5.3 mm, with the exception of R. 4/2 which remained at 7.3 mm. The 'Italic 'Z'' variety occurs on R. 3/6 of the setting of 60.

Nos. 1-4 were subsequently declared valid for postage within Transvaal.

BRITISH REOCCUPATION

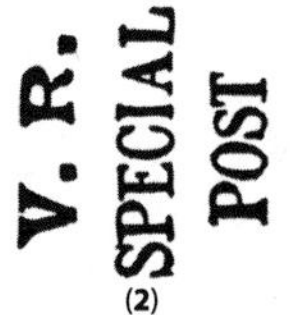

(2)

1900 (16 May). Provisionals issued by the Military Authorities. Stamps of Transvaal handstamped with T **2**.

11 **30** ½d. green .... — £3500
11*a* 1d. rose-red (No. 206) ....
12 1d. rose-red and green (No. 217) £14000 £6000
13 2d. brown and green .... † £48000
14 2½d. dull blue and green .... † £48000

No. 11 is known used with double handstamp and Nos. 11/12 with the overprint reading downwards.

II. GRIQUALAND WEST

Griqualand West was situated to the North of Cape Colony, bounded on the north by what became British Bechuanaland and on the east by the Orange Free State.

The area was settled in the early 19th-century by the Griqua tribal group, although many members of the tribe, including the paramount chief, migrated to Griqualand East (between Basutoland and the east coast of South Africa) in 1861–1863. There was little European involvement in Griqualand West before 1866, but in that year the diamond fields along the Vaal River were discovered. Sovereignty was subsequently claimed by the Griqua Chief, the Orange Free State and the South African Republic (Transvaal). In 1871 the British authorities arbitrated in favour of the Griqua Chief who promptly ceded his territory to Great Britain. Griqualand West became a separate Crown Colony in January 1873.

During the initial stages of the prospecting boom, mail was passed via the Orange Free State, but a post office connected to the Cape Colony postal system was opened at Klip Drift (subsequently Barkly) in late 1870. Further offices at De Beer's New Rush (subsequently Kimberley), Douglas and Du Toit's Pan (subsequently Beaconsfield) were open by September 1873.

Cape of Good Hope stamps to the 5s. value were in use from October 1871, but those originating in Griqualand West can only be identified after the introduction of Barred Oval Diamond Numeral cancellations in 1873. Numbers known to have been issued in the territory are:

1 De Beers N.R. (New Rush) (subsequently Kimberley)
3 Junction R. & M. (Riet and Modder Rivers)
4 Barkly
6 or 9 Du Toit's Pan (subsequently Beaconsfield)
8 Langford (transferred to Douglas)
10 Thornhill

PRICES FOR STAMPS ON COVER. The stamps of Griqualand West are worth from ×10 the price quoted for used stamps, when on cover from the territory.

FORGED OVERPRINTS. Many stamps show forged overprints. Great care should be taken when purchasing the scarcer items.

Stamps of the Cape of Good Hope,* Crown CC, *perf 14, overprinted.

(1)

1874 (Sept). No. 24*a* of Cape of Good Hope surch '1d.' in red manuscript as T **1** by the Kimberley postmaster.

1 1d. on 4d. blue £1800 £2500

G. W.
(1aa)

1877 (1 Mar). Nos. 29/30 of Cape of Good Hope optd with T **1aa**.

2 1d. carmine-red £750 £110
a. Opt double .... † £3000
3 4d. dull blue (R.) .... £400 80·00
w. Wmk inverted £1300 £275

G (1a) G (2) G (3) G (4) G (5) G (6)

G (7) G (8) G (9) G (10) G (11)

G (12) G (13) G (14)

1877 (Mar)–**78**. Nos. 24*a*, 25*a*, 26*a* and 28/31 Cape of Good Hope optd with capital 'G'.

(a) First printing. Optd with Types **1a/6** *and* **8** *in black (1d.) or red (others)*

4 ½d. grey-black
a. Opt Type **1a** .... 42·00 45·00
b. Opt Type **2** £100 £120
c. Opt Type **3** .... 60·00 70·00
d. Opt Type **4** £100 £120
e. Opt Type **5** £110 £130
f. Opt Type **6** .... 55·00 65·00
g. Opt Type **8** £750 £800

5 1d. carmine-red
a. Opt Type **1a** .... 42·00 28·00
b. Opt Type **2** .... £110 65·00
c. Opt Type **3** .... 60·00 40·00
d. Opt Type **4** .... £110 65·00
e. Opt Type **5** .... £120 80·00
f. Opt Type **6** .... 42·00 28·00
g. Opt Type **8** .... *

6 4d. blue (with frame-line) (No. 24*a*)
a. Opt Type **1a** .... £450 70·00
b. Opt Type **2** £1100 £180
c. Opt Type **3** £750 £100
d. Opt Type **4** £1100 £180
e. Opt Type **5** £1200 £225
f. Opt Type **6** .... £550 90·00
g. Opt Type **8** £3500 £950

7 4d. dull blue (without frame-line) (No. 30)
a. Opt Type **1a** .... £400 48·00
b. Opt Type **2** £850 £140
c. Opt Type **3** .... £550 70·00
d. Opt Type **4** £850 £140
e. Opt Type **5** £900 £160
f. Opt Type **6** .... £500 60·00
g. Opt Type **8** £3250 £750

8 6d. deep lilac
a. Opt Type **1a** .... £300 55·00
b. Opt Type **2** £600 £150
c. Opt Type **3** .... £400 75·00
cw. Wmk inverted .... † £550
d. Opt Type **4** £600 £150
e. Opt Type **5** £700 £170
f. Opt Type **6** .... £375 75·00
g. Opt Type **8** £3000 £900

9 1s. green
a. Opt Type **1a** .... £350 45·00
ab. Opt inverted .... — £950
b. Opt Type **2** £750 £110
ba. Opt inverted .... — £1500
c. Opt Type **3** .... £550 60·00
d. Opt Type **4** £750 £110
da. Opt inverted .... — £1500
e. Opt Type **5** £850 £140
f. Opt Type **6** .... £500 55·00
fa. Opt inverted .... — £1100
g. Opt Type **8** £4500 £900

10 5s. yellow-orange
a. Opt Type **1a** .... £1100 55·00
b. Opt Type **2** £1800 £130
c. Opt Type **3** .... £1500 75·00
cw. Wmk inverted .... † £1200
d. Opt Type **4** £1800 £130
dw. Wmk inverted .... † £1700
e. Opt Type **5** £2750 £160
f. Opt Type **6** .... £1400 65·00
fw. Wmk inverted .... † £1300
g. Opt Type **8** £4500 £1000

* The 1d. with overprint T **8** from this setting can only be distinguished from that of the second printing when *se-tenant* with overprint T **3**.

Nos. 4/10 were overprinted by a setting of 120 covering two panes of 60 (6×10). This setting contained 41 examples of T **1a**, ten of T **2**, 23 of T **3**, ten of T **4**, eight of T **5**, 27 of T **6** and one of T **8**. Sub-types of Types **1a** and **2** exist. The single example of T **8** occurs on R. 7/4 of the right-hand pane.

It is believed that there may have been an additional setting used for the 5s. which was in considerable demand to cover the postage and registration on diamond consignments. It is also possible that single panes of this value and of the 1s. were overprinted using the right-hand half of the normal 120 setting.

(b) Second printing. Optd with Types **6/14** *in black (1878)*

11 1d. carmine-red
a. Opt Type **6** .... *
b. Opt Type **7** .... 48·00 30·00
c. Opt Type **8** .... £110 50·00
d. Opt Type **9** .... 55·00 32·00
e. Opt Type **10** .... £140 90·00
f. Opt Type **11** .... £120 70·00
g. Opt Type **12** .... £120 80·00
h. Opt Type **13** £190 £130
i. Opt Type **14** £600 £400

12 4d. dull blue (without frame-line) (No. 30)
a. Opt Type **6** .... £600 95·00
b. Opt Type **7** .... £275 45·00
c. Opt Type **8** .... £550 85·00
d. Opt Type **9** .... £300 45·00
e. Opt Type **10** £700 £110
f. Opt Type **11** £600 £100
g. Opt Type **12** £600 £100
h. Opt Type **13** £950 £180
i. Opt Type **14** £2750 £600

13 6d. deep lilac
a. Opt Type **6** £850 £140
b. Opt Type **7** .... £450 80·00
ba. Opt double ....
c. Opt Type **8** £800 £130
d. Opt Type **9** .... £500 90·00
da. Opt double .... — £1500
e. Opt Type **10** £950 £180
ea. Opt double .... — £1600
f. Opt Type **11** £850 £150
g. Opt Type **12** £850 £150
h. Opt Type **13** £1300 £275
i. Opt Type **14** £3500 £850

* The 1d. with overprint T **6** from this setting can only be distinguished from that of the first printing when *se-tenant* with Types **11**, **12** or **13**.

Nos. 11/13 were overprinted by another double-pane setting of 120 in which only Types **6** and **8** were repeated from that used for the first printing. The second printing setting contained 12 examples of T **6**, 30 of T **7**, 13 of T **8**, 27 of T **9**, nine of T **10**, 11 of T **11**, 11 of T **12**, six of T **13** and one of T **14**. Sub-types of Types **7** and **12** exist.

G (15) G (16) G (17)

1878 (June). Nos. 24*a*, 25*a* and 28/30 of Cape of Good Hope optd with small capital 'G', Types **15/16**.

14 **15** ½d. grey-black (R.) .... 27·00 27·00
a. Opt inverted .... 29·00 29·00
b. Opt double .... 80·00 95·00
c. Opt double, both inverted £160 £180

d. Black opt £350 £180
da. Opt inverted £375
db. Opt double, one inverted in red £600
dc. Opt double, one inverted (Type **16**) in red £325
15 **16** ½d. grey-black (R.) .... 28·00 28·00
a. Opt inverted .... 28·00 29·00
b. Opt double £130 £130
c. Opt double, both inverted £100 £120
d. Black opt .... 80·00 80·00
da. Opt inverted £170 £120
db. Opt double, one inverted (Type **15**) in red £325
16 **15** 1d. carmine-red .... 28·00 19·00
a. Opt inverted .... 28·00 28·00
b. Opt double .... £350 85·00
c. Opt double, both inverted £350 £110
d. Opt double, both inverted with one in red £100 £100
e. Opt double, both inverted with one (Type **16**) in red ....
17 **16** 1d. carmine-red .... 28·00 20·00
a. Opt inverted .... £140 48·00
b. Opt double .... — £150
c. Opt double, both inverted .... — £180
d. Opt double, both inverted with one in red £180 £180
18 **15** 4d. blue (with frame-line) (No. 24*a*) .... — £275
19 **16** 4d. blue (with frame-line) (No. 24*a*) .... — £275
20 **15** 4d. dull blue (without frame-line) (No. 30) .... £250 48·00
a. Opt inverted £400 £140
b. Opt double .... — £375
c. Opt double, both inverted .... — £450
d. Red opt £600 £160
da. Opt inverted £650 £130
21 **16** 4d. dull blue (without frame-line) (No. 30) .... £275 26·00
a. Opt inverted .... £425 48·00
b. Opt double .... — £350
c. Opt double, both inverted .... — £425
d. Red opt .... — £140
da. Opt inverted £600 £140
22 **15** 6d. deep lilac .... £275 48·00
23 **16** 6d. deep lilac .... — 48·00

Nos. 14/23 were also overprinted using a double-pane setting of 120. Based on evidence from surviving ½d. and 1d. sheets all overprints in the left-hand pane were roman, T **15**, and all those in the right-hand pane italic, T **16**, except for R. 1/6, 4/5, 6/6, 7/6, 8/6, 9/6 and 10/6 which were T **15**. There is considerable evidence to suggest that after the ½d. value had been overprinted the setting was amended to show a T **15**, instead of a T **16**, on R. 10/5 of the right-hand pane. Two strikes of the setting were required to overprint the sheets of 240 and it would appear that on many sheets the bottom two panes had the overprints inverted.

1879. Nos. 25*b*, 26*b* and 28/31 of Cape of Good Hope optd with small capital 'G', T **17**.

24 ½d. grey-black .... 32·00 11·00
a. Opt double £500 £325
25 1d. carmine-red .... 35·00 8·50
a. Opt inverted .... — £110
b. Opt double .... — £160
c. Opt treble .... — £300
w. Wmk inverted .... † £450
26 4d. dull blue .... 65·00 8·50
a. Opt double .... — £140
27 6d. violet .... £275 14·00
a. Opt inverted .... — 60·00
b. Opt double £1100 £200
28 1s. green .... £250 9·00
a. Opt double £600 £130
29 5s. yellow-orange .... £800 26·00
a. Opt double £1000 £130
b. Opt treble .... — £400

Nos. 24/29 were also overprinted using a setting of 120 which contained a number of minor type varieties.

Griqualand West was merged with Cape Colony in October 1880. The remaining stock of the overprinted stamps was returned from Kimberley to Cape Town and redistributed among various post offices in Cape Colony where they were used as ordinary Cape stamps.

III. NATAL

PRICES FOR STAMPS ON COVER

No. 1	*from* × 2
Nos. 2/3	*from* × 3
Nos. 4/7	*from* × 2
Nos. 9/25	*from* × 3
Nos. 26/49	*from* × 5
Nos. 50/56	*from* × 4
No. 57	—
No. 58	*from* × 10
Nos. 59/60	*from* × 5
Nos. 61/63	*from* × 8
No. 65	*from* × 10
Nos. 66/70	*from* × 8
Nos. 71/73	—
Nos. 76/82	*from* × 6
Nos. 83/84	*from* × 5
Nos. 85/90	*from* × 5
Nos. 96/103	*from* × 6
Nos. 104/105	*from* × 10
Nos. 106/107	*from* × 6
No. 108	*from* × 50
Nos. 109/125	*from* × 6
Nos. 127/142	*from* × 4
Nos. 143/145*b*	—
Nos. 146/157	*from* × 4
No. 162	—
Nos. 165/171	*from* × 3
No. F1	—
Nos. O1/O6	*from* × 10

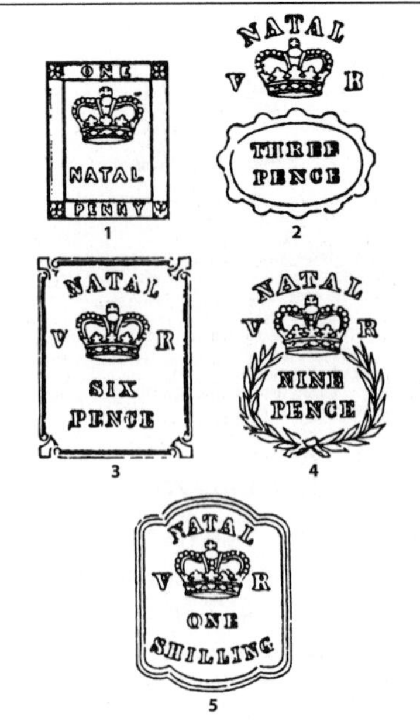

1 2 3 4 5

(Embossed in plain relief on coloured wove paper by May and Davis, Pietermaritzburg)

1857 (26 May)–**61**. Imperf.

1 **1** 1d. blue (9.59) .... — £1200
2 1d. rose (1861) .... — £1900
3 1d. buff (1861) .... — £1400
4 **2** 3d. rose .... — £400
a. *Tête-bêche* (pair) .... — £50000
5 **3** 6d. green .... — £1100
a. Bisected (3d.) (*on cover*) .... † £15000
6 **4** 9d. blue .... — £7500
7 **5** 1s. buff .... — £5500

All the above have been reprinted more than once, and the early reprints of some values cannot always be distinguished with certainty from originals.

For the 1d. stamp on yellow surfaced paper, perf 12½, see No. F1.

Stamps on surface-coloured paper with higher face values and perforated 12½ are fiscals.

NOTE. The value of the above stamps depends on their dimensions, and the clearness of the embossing, but our prices are for fine used.
It should be noted that, at the time they were current, only Pietermaritzburg, Ladysmith and Durban were supplied with handstamps. Stamps used in other offices were usually cancelled in manuscript.

PERKINS BACON 'CANCELLED'. For notes on these handstamps showing 'CANCELLED' between horizontal bars forming an oval, see Catalogue Introduction.

6

7

(Eng C. H. Jeens. Recess P.B.)

1859–60. No wmk. P 14.

9 **6** 1d. rose-red (1860) (H/S 'CANCELLED' in oval £13000) .... £180 85·00
10 3d. blue .... £225 55·00
a. Imperf between (vert pair) .... † £13000

No. 10a is only known from a cover of 1867 franked with two such pairs.

The 3d. also exists with 'CANCELLED' in oval, but no examples are believed to be in private hands.

1861. No wmk. Intermediate perf 14 to 16.

11 **6** 3d. blue .... £350 65·00

1861–62. No wmk. Rough perf 14 to 16.

12 **6** 3d. blue .... £170 40·00
a. Imperf between (horiz pair) £6000
13 6d. grey (3.62) .... £275 70·00

1862. Wmk Small Star. Rough perf 14 to 16.

15 **6** 1d. rose-red .... £170 65·00

The 1d. without watermark and the 3d. watermark Small Star, both imperforate, are proofs.

(Recess D.L.R.)

1863. Thick paper. No wmk. P 13.

18 **6** 1d. lake .... £130 29·00
19 1d. carmine-red .... £130 29·00

Nos. 18/19 were printed on paper showing a papermakers watermark of 'TH SAUNDERS 1862', parts of which can be found on individual stamps. Examples are rare and command a premium.

1863–65. Wmk Crown CC. P 12½.

20 **6** 1d. brown-red .... £190 48·00
y. Wmk inverted and reversed .... — £160
21 1d. rose .... £130 38·00
w. Wmk inverted .... † £170
x. Wmk reversed .... £130 38·00
y. Wmk inverted and reversed .... † £160
22 1d. bright red .... £140 45·00
x. Wmk reversed .... £140 45·00
y. Wmk inverted and reversed £600
23 6d. lilac .... £120 17·00
w. Wmk inverted £600

y. Wmk inverted and reversed ....
24 6d. violet .... 90·00 35·00
w. Wmk inverted £400
x. Wmk reversed .... 90·00 35·00

The 1d. stamp in yellow and the 6d. in rose are both fiscals.

(Typo D.L.R.)

1867 (Apr). Wmk Crown CC. P 14.

25 **7** 1s. green .... £250 50·00
w. Wmk inverted .... † £400

Stamps as T **7** in purple-brown or deep blue are fiscals.

POSTAGE (**7a**) Postage. (**7b**) Postage. (**7c**)

Postage. (**7d**) POSTAGE. (**7e**)

1869 (23 Aug). Optd horiz by Keith and Co. No wmk (3d.), wmk Crown CC (others). P 14 or 14–16 (3d.), 12½ (1d., 6d) or 14 (1s.).

(a) With T **7a** *(tall capitals without stop)*

26 **6** 1d. rose £650 £120
x. Wmk reversed £600 £110
27 1d. bright red £550 £110
x. Wmk reversed .... — £100
28 3d. blue (No. 10) £4000 £900
28*a* 3d. blue (No. 11) £1200 £375
28*b* 3d. blue (No. 12) £800 £140
29 6d. lilac £850 £100
30 6d. violet £800 £120
x. Wmk reversed £800 £120
31 **7** 1s. green £35000 £1800

(b) With T **7b** *(12¾ mm long)*

32 **6** 1d. rose £550 £110
w. Wmk inverted .... † £400
x. Wmk reversed .... — £100
33 1d. bright red .... £500 95·00
x. Wmk reversed .... £475 90·00
34 3d. blue (No. 10) .... — £700
34*a* 3d. blue (No. 11) £1000 £325
34*b* 3d. blue (No. 12) £700 £110
35 6d. lilac .... £750 85·00
36 6d. violet £650 £110
x. Wmk reversed £650 £100
37 **7** 1s. green £29000 £1900

(c) With T **7c** *(13¾ mm long)*

38 **6** 1d. rose £1200 £300
39 1d. bright red £1200 £275
x. Wmk reversed .... — £250
40 3d. blue (No. 10) ....
40*a* 3d. blue (No. 11) .... — £1000
40*b* 3d. blue (No. 12) £2750 £500
41 6d. lilac £2750 £225
42 6d. violet £2500 £225
x. Wmk reversed .... — £225
43 **7** 1s. green .... — £3000

(d) With T **7d** *(14½ to 15½ mm long)*

44 **6** 1d. rose £1000 £225
x. Wmk reversed £1000
45 1d. bright red £1000 £190
x. Wmk reversed £1000 £190
46 3d. blue (No. 10) .... † —
46*a* 3d. blue (No. 11) .... — £750
46*b* 3d. blue (No. 12) .... — £425
47 6d. lilac .... — £150
48 6d. violet £2000 £140
x. Wmk reversed £2000 £140
49 **7** 1s. green £29000 £2500

(e) With T **7e** *(small capitals with stop)*

50 **6** 1d. rose .... £150 50·00
x. Wmk reversed .... £150 50·00
y. Wmk inverted and reversed .... † £250
51 1d. bright red .... £200 50·00
x. Wmk reversed .... £200 50·00
52 3d. blue (No. 10) .... £400 85·00
53 3d. blue (No. 11) .... £225 50·00
54 3d. blue (No. 12) .... £250 50·00
a. Opt double .... † £1600
54*b* 6d. lilac .... £275 85·00
by. Wmk inverted and reversed .... † £450
55 6d. violet .... £200 70·00
x. Wmk reversed .... £200 70·00
56 **7** 1s. green .... £350 80·00

There were two settings of these overprints. The first setting, probably of 240, contained 60 examples of T **7a**, 72 of T **7b**, 20 of T **7c**, 28 of T **7d** and 60 of T **7e**. The second, probably of 60 (6×10), contained T **7e** only.

In the first setting the overprint is in the bottom half of the stamp on the 1d. and 1s. and in the top half on the 3d. and 6d. In the second setting the overprints were at the top of the 1d. and 1s. and at the bottom of the 3d. and 6d. Prices for Nos. 50/56 are for stamps from the second setting.

A single used example of No. 33 with overprint double is in the Royal Philatelic Collection.

(**8**)

1870. No. 25 optd with T **8** by De La Rue.

57 **7** 1s. green (C.) .... † £8500
58 1s. green (Blk.) .... † £1600
a. Opt double .... † £3500
59 1s. green (G.) .... £150 10·00

For 1s. orange, see No. 108.

POSTAGE POSTAGE (**9**) POSTAGE (**10**) POSTAGE POSTAGE (**11**)

1870–73. Optd with T **9** by De La Rue. Wmk Crown CC. P 12½.

60 **6** 1d. bright red .... £120 13·00
w. Wmk inverted .... † £250

x. Wmk reversed £120 13·00
y. Wmk inverted and reversed † £250
61 3d. bright blue (R.) (1872) £130 13·00
w. Wmk inverted † £250
x. Wmk reversed £130 13·00
62 6d. mauve (1873) £250 48·00
x. Wmk reversed £300

1873 (July). Fiscal stamp optd locally with T **10**. Wmk Crown CC. P 14.
63 **7** 1s. purple-brown £425 35·00
w. Wmk inverted — £450

1874 (Apr). No. 21 optd locally with T **11**.
65 **6** 1d. rose £375 85·00
w. Wmk inverted
x. Wmk reversed — 85·00

Two examples of No. 65 with overprint double are known. Both are in permanent museum collections.

12

13

14

15

16

(Typo D.L.R.)

1874 (Jan)–**99**. Wmk Crown CC (sideways on 5s.). P 14.
66 **12** 1d. dull rose 65·00 9·00
67 1d. bright rose 65·00 9·00
68 **13** 3d. blue £190 45·00
a. Perf 14×12½ £2500 £1100
69 **14** 4d. brown (1878) £200 20·00
aw. Wmk inverted £550 £180
b. Perf 12½ £375 70·00
70 **15** 6d. bright reddish violet £110 7·50
w. Wmk inverted † £250
71 **16** 5s. maroon (1882) £400 £110
a. Perf 15½×15 (1874) £475 £110
72 5s. rose £150 45·00
73 5s. carmine (1899) £110 38·00
s. Handstamped '*SPECIMEN*' £225

POSTAGE (17) POSTAGE (18) ½ HALF (19)

1875–76. Wmk Crown CC. P 14 (1s.) or 12½ (others).

(a) Optd locally with T **17**
76 **6** 1d. rose £170 65·00
a. Opt double £1800 £600
x. Wmk reversed £170 65·00
77 1d. bright red £160 75·00
x. Wmk reversed £160 75·00

(b) Optd by Davis and Sons with T **18** *(14½ mm long, without stop)*
81 **6** 1d. rose (1876) £130 80·00
a. Opt inverted £2000 £500
w. Wmk inverted
x. Wmk reversed £130 80·00
y. Wmk inverted and reversed
82 1d. yellow (1876) 90·00 90·00
a. Opt double, one albino £250
x. Wmk reversed 95·00 95·00
83 6d. violet (1876) 85·00 8·00
a. Opt double † £950
b. Opt inverted £750 £150
w. Wmk inverted — £160
x. Wmk reversed 85·00 8·00
y. Wmk inverted and reversed † £190
84 **7** 1s. green (1876) £140 7·50
a. Opt double † £325

TYPE 19. There are several varieties of this surcharge, of which T **19** is an example. They may be divided as follows:
(*a*) '½' 4½ mm high, '2' has straight foot.
(*b*) As last but '½' is 4 mm high.
(*c*) As last but '2' has curled foot.
(*d*) '½' 3½ mm. high, '2' has straight foot.
(*e*) As last but '2' has curled foot.
(*f*) As last but '2' smaller.

As the '½' and 'HALF' were overprinted separately, they vary in relative position, and are frequently overlapping.

1877 (13 Feb). No. 66 surch locally as T **19**.
85 **12** ½d. on 1d. rose (*a*) 48·00 75·00
86 ½d. on 1d. rose (*b*) £170
87 ½d. on 1d. rose (*c*) £150
88 ½d. on 1d. rose (*d*) 85·00 £120
89 ½d. on 1d. rose (*e*) 90·00
90 ½d. on 1d. rose (*f*) £100

The Royal Philatelic Collection contains a single example of No. 85 with '½' double.

POSTAGE Half-penny (21)

23

ONE HALF-PENNY. (24)

1877 (7 Oct)–**79**. T **6** (wmk Crown CC. P 12½) surch locally as T **21**.
91 ½d. on 1d. yellow 13·00 25·00
a. Surch inverted £375 £225
b. Surch double £375 £200
c. Surch omitted (lower stamp, vertical pair) £4250 £2750
d. 'POSTAGE' omitted (in pair with normal) £2250
e. 'S' of 'POSTAGE' omitted (R. 8/3) £325 £225
f. 'T' of 'POSTAGE' omitted £325 £300
x. Wmk reversed 13·00 25·00
y. Wmk inverted and reversed £110
92 1d. on 6d. violet (10.10.77) 75·00 11·00
a. 'S' of 'POSTAGE' omitted (R. 8/3) £600 £150
x. Wmk reversed — 11·00
93 1d. on 6d. rose (12.2.79) £140 55·00
a. Surch inverted £1700 £600
b. Surch double † £325
c. Surch double, one inverted £375 £200
d. Surch four times £500 £275
e. 'S' of 'POSTAGE' omitted (R. 8/3) £950 £375
w. Wmk inverted † £150
x. Wmk reversed — 55·00

No. 93c. is known with one surcharge showing variety 'S' of 'POSTAGE' omitted.

Other minor varieties exist in these surcharges.

Nos. 94 and 95 are vacant.

(Typo D.L.R.)

1880 (13 Oct). Wmk Crown CC. P 14.
96 **23** ½d. blue-green 30·00 40·00
a. Imperf between (vert pair)

1882 (20 Apr)–**89**. Wmk Crown CA. P 14.
97 **23** ½d. blue-green (23.4.84) £100 21·00
a. Dull green (10.4.85) 6·50 1·25
aw. Wmk inverted £350 £225
99 **12** 1d. rose (*shades*) (17.12.83*) 8·00 25
a. Carmine 8·00 35
w. Wmk inverted † £200
100 **13** 3d. blue (23.4.84) £160 17·00
101 3d. grey (11.89) 12·00 5·50
w. Wmk inverted † £300
102 **14** 4d. brown 17·00 1·75
103 **15** 6d. mauve 14·00 2·50
w. Wmk inverted † £180
97*a*/103 *Set of 6* £190 25·00
97*as*, 99*as*, 101s/103s H/S '*SPECIMEN*' *Set of 5* £350
* Earliest recorded date.

1885 (26 Jan). No. 99 surch locally with T **24**.
104 **12** ½d. on 1d. rose 25·00 15·00
a. No hyphen after 'HALF' £120 55·00

TWO PENCE (25)

26

TWOPENCE HALFPENNY (27)

1886 (7 Jan). No. 101 surch with T **25** by D.L.R.
105 **13** 2d. on 3d. grey 42·00 5·50

(Typo D.L.R.)

1887 (Sept)–**89**. Wmk Crown CA. P 14.
106 **26** 2d. olive-green (Die I) 55·00 2·25
a. Top left triangle detached £650 £250
s. Optd 'SPECIMEN' £100
x. Wmk reversed † £350
107 2d. olive-green (Die II) (1889) 5·50 1·40
s. Handstamped '*SPECIMEN*' 80·00

The differences between Dies I and II are shown in the introduction. For illustration of 'top left triangle detached' variety see above No. 21 of Antigua.

1888 (16 Mar). As No. 25, but colour changed and wmk Crown CA, optd with T **8** by D.L.R.
108 **7** 1s. orange (C.) 13·00 1·75
a. Opt double † £2750
s. Handstamped '*SPECIMEN*' £120

1891 (22 Apr). Surch locally with T **27**.
109 **14** 2½d. on 4d. brown 16·00 18·00
a. 'TWOPENGE' 70·00
b. 'HALFPENN' £300 £275
c. Surch double £375 £325
d. Surch inverted £550 £450
e. Vert pair, one normal, one surch double £650 £650
f. Surch *tête-bêche* (vert pair) £2000 £2000
s. Handstamped '*SPECIMEN*' 75·00

The overprint setting comprised two rows of six stamps and was applied five times to each pane of 60. The 'TWOPENGE' variety occurred on stamp ten of the setting. The 'HALFPENN' variety was not present on all sheets, its exact position is unknown, but it occurred in the upper row of the setting.

(28)

POSTAGE. Half-Penny (29)

POSTAGE. Varieties of long-tailed letters

(Typo D.L.R.)

1891 (June). Wmk Crown CA. P 14.
113 **28** 2½d. bright blue 10·00 1·50
s. Handstamped '*SPECIMEN*' 75·00

1895 (12 Mar). No. 24 surch locally with T **29** in carmine.
114 ½d. on 6d. violet 3·00 10·00
a. 'Ealf-Penny' 26·00 75·00
b. 'Half-Penny' and long 'P' 26·00 75·00
ba. 'Half Penny' and long 'T' and 'A' 26·00 75·00
c. No stop after 'POSTAGE' and long 'P', 'T' and 'A' 26·00 75·00
d. Long 'P' 3·25 13·00
e. Long 'T' 3·25 13·00
f. Long 'A' 4·00 15·00
g. Long 'P' and 'T' 3·25 13·00
h. Long 'P' and 'A' 3·25 13·00
i. Long 'T' and 'A' 3·75 14·00
k. Long 'P', 'T' and 'A' 3·75 16·00
ka. Long 'P', 'T' and 'A' with comma after 'POSTAGE' 16·00 42·00
l. Surch double £325
la. Surch double, one vertical £325
m. 'POSTAGE' omitted (in pair with normal) £2000
s. Handstamped '*SPECIMEN*' 60·00
x. Wmk reversed 3·00 10·00

The surcharge was applied as a setting of 60 (12×5) which contained 17 normals, one each of Nos. 114a, 114b, 114ba, 114c, six of No. 114d, six of No. 114e, three of No. 114f, six of No. 114g, seven of No. 114h, five of No. 114i, four of No. 114k and two of No. 114ka.

Following the rapid sell-out of No. 114, due to speculation, and pending the arrival of No. 125, postal items requiring a ½d. franking were marked 'One halfpenny received in money' and signed by the postmaster.

(30)

31

32

1895 (18 Mar). No. 99 surch locally with T **30**.
125 HALF on 1d. rose (*shades*) 3·00 2·25
a. Surch double £475 £500
b. 'H' with longer left limb 40·00
c. Pair, one without surcharge
s. Handstamped '*SPECIMEN*' 65·00

No. 125b, in which the 'A' also has a short right leg, occurs on the second, fourth, sixth etc., stamps of the first vertical column of the right-hand pane of the first printing only.

In the second printing what appears to be a broken 'E' (with the top limb removed) was used instead of 'L' in 'HALF' on the last stamp in the sheet (*Price* £40), No. 125c also comes from this second printing.

(Typo D.L.R)

1902–03. Inscr 'POSTAGE REVENUE'. Wmk Crown CA. P 14.
127 **31** ½d. blue-green 7·50 50
128 1d. carmine 13·00 15
129 1½d. green and black 4·00 7·00
130 2d. red and olive-green 6·50 40
131 2½d. bright blue 2·00 5·50
132 3d. purple and grey 1·50 2·50
133 4d. carmine and cinnamon 13·00 27·00
134 5d. black and orange 4·75 3·75
w. Wmk inverted £300 £150
135 6d. green and brown-purple 4·75 4·50
136 1s. carmine and pale blue 6·00 4·75
w. Wmk inverted † £550
137 2s. green and bright violet 55·00 9·00
138 2s.6d. purple 50·00 12·00
139 4s. deep rose and maize 95·00 95·00
127/139 *Set of* 13 £225 £150
127s/139s Optd 'SPECIMEN' *Set of* 13 £275

No. 139 exists imperforate and partly perforated, from a proof sheet.

(Typo D.L.R.)

1902. Wmk Crown CC. P 14.
140 **32** 5s. dull blue and rose 65·00 12·00
141 10s. deep rose and chocolate £130 50·00
142 £1 black and bright blue £350 80·00
143 £1.10s. green and violet £600 £130
s. Optd 'SPECIMEN' £130
144 £5 mauve and black £5500 £1500
s. Optd 'SPECIMEN' £275
145 £10 green and orange £14000 £6500
as. Optd 'SPECIMEN' £450
145*b* £20 red and green £28000 £19000
bs. Optd 'SPECIMEN' £650
140s/142s Optd 'SPECIMEN' *Set of* 3 £190

USED HIGH VALUES. Collectors are warned against fiscally used high value Natal stamps with penmarks cleaned off and forged postmarks added.

1904–08. Chalk-surfaced paper (£1. 10s.). Wmk Mult Crown CA. P 14.
146 **31** ½d. blue-green 12·00 15
147 1d. rose-carmine 12·00 15
a. Booklet pane of 6, one stamp optd 'NOT FOR USE' (1907) £475
ay. Ditto. Wmk inverted and reversed £3500
b. deep carmine 16·00 30
w. Wmk inverted † £150
y. Wmk inverted and reversed
149 2d. red and olive-green 18·00 3·25
152 4d. carmine and cinnamon 3·00 1·25
153 5d. black and orange (1908) 6·50 4·00
155 1s. carmine and pale blue 85·00 7·00
156 2s. dull green and bright violet 70·00 50·00
157 2s.6d. purple 65·00 50·00
162 **32** £1. 10s. brown-orange and deep purple (1908) £1800 £4750
s. Optd 'SPECIMEN' £375
146/157 *Set of* 8 £250 £100

1908–09. Inscr 'POSTAGE POSTAGE'. Wmk Mult Crown CA. P 14.
165 **31** 6d. dull and bright purple 5·00 3·00
166 1s. black/*green* 6·00 3·00
167 2s. purple and bright blue/*blue* 15·00 3·00
w. Wmk inverted † £550
168 2s.6d. black and red/*blue* 25·00 3·00

169 **32** 5s. green and red/*yellow* 30·00 50·00
170 10s. green and red/*green* £130 £130
171 £1 purple and black/*red* £425 £375
165/171 *Set of 7* £550 £500
165s/171s Optd 'SPECIMEN' *Set of 7* £425

STAMP BOOKLETS

1906. Black on red cover. Stapled.
SB1 2s.7d. booklet containing 30×1d. (No. 147) in blocks of 6 £3750

1907. Black on red cover. Stapled.
SB2 2s.6d. booklet containing 30×1d. (No. 147) in blocks of 6 £3750

The first or third stamp of the first pane in No. SB2 was overprinted 'NOT FOR USE' (No. 147a), the additional penny being used to defray the cost of production.

FISCALS USED FOR POSTAGE

1869. Embossed on coloured wove, surfaced paper. P 12½.
F1 **1** 1d. yellow 55·00 85·00

Examples of 1d. yellow and 6d. rose values as T **6**, 1s. purple-brown as T **7** and various values between 5s, and £10 in the design illustrated above are believed to exist postally used, but, as such use was not authorised, they are not now listed.

OFFICIAL STAMPS

OFFICIAL
(O **1**)

1904. T **31**, wmk Mult Crown CA, optd with T O **1** by De La Rue. P 14.
O1 ½d. blue-green 3·50 1·00
O2 1d. carmine 15·00 1·25
O3 2d. red and olive-green 48·00 22·00
O4 3d. purple and grey 27·00 7·00
O5 6d. green and brown-purple 85·00 80·00
O6 1s. carmine and pale blue £250 £275
O1/O6 *Set of 6* £375 £350

Nos. O4 and O5 were from special printings of the 3d. and 6d. stamps, which were not issued on wmk Mult Crown CA paper without opt.

The use of stamps overprinted as above was discontinued after 30 May 1907, although later use has been reported. Stamps perforated with the letters 'N.G.R.' were for use on Government Railways.

TELEGRAPH STAMPS

T **1**

(Typo D.L.R.)

1881. Wmk Crown CA (sideways). P 14.
T1 **T 1** 1d. red-brown 16·00 19·00
T2 3d. rose-carmine 22·00 24·00
T3 6d. brown-olive 22·00 19·00
T4 1s. deep blue-green 27·00 25·00
T5 2s. purple 55·00 48·00
T6 5s. blue 85·00 90·00
T7 10s. slate £160 £180
T8 £1 chocolate £450 £250
T9 £5 orange £5500 £3250

Nos. T4 and T7 are known imperforate, from proof sheets.

TELEGRAPH
T **2**

1888. No. 24 optd locally with Type T **2**.
T10 6d. violet
a. Opt double £2500

TELEGRAPH TELEGRAPH

THREE PENCE. THREE PENCE
(T **3**) (T **4**)

TELEGRAPH

Three Pence
(T **5**)

1902. Fiscal stamps of 1886–1890 (as £10 stamp illustrated below No. F1) surch as Types T **3/5** by Davis & Son. Wmk Crown CA. P 14.
T11 3d. on 4d. dull mauve (surch Type T **3**) 40·00 45·00
a. Narrow spacing 30·00 35·00
ab. Small 'P' in 'PENCE' (R. 2/4) £180 £200
T12 3d. on 4d. dull mauve (surch Type T **4**, narrow spacing) 35·00 40·00
T13 3d. on 4d. dull mauve (surch Type T **5**, narrow spacing) 45·00 55·00
a. Antique 'e' in 'Three' (R. 5/6) £180 £200
T14 6d. on 9d. dull mauve (surch as Type T **3**) 85·00 95·00
a. Narrow spacing 38·00 45·00
b. Surcharged both sides (inverted on reverse) £475
T15 1s. on 9s. dull mauve and carmine (surch as Type T **3**) 65·00 80·00
a. Narrow spacing 35·00 40·00
b. Large 'SHILLING' (narrow spacing) 70·00 80·00
T16 1s. on 9s. dull mauve and carmine (surch as Type T **4**, narrow spacing) (R. 5/6) £200 £225
T17 1s. on £1 dull blue-green (surch as Type T **3**) 70·00 80·00
a. Narrow spacing 38·00 45·00
b. Large 'SHILLING' (narrow spacing) 80·00 95·00
T18 1s. on £1 dull blue-green (surch as Type T **4**, narrow spacing) (R. 5/6) £250 £275
T19 1s. on £1.10s. dull mauve and blue (surch as Type T **3**) 85·00 95·00
a. Narrow spacing 45·00 50·00
b. Large 'SHILLING' (narrow spacing) 95·00 £110
T20 1s. on £1.10s. dull mauve and blue (surch as Type T **4**, narrow spacing) (R. 5/6) £275 £300

For Type T **3** the space between the bar obliterating 'REVENUE' and the overprinted 'TELEGRAPH' is 1.8 mm, for the narrow spacing varieties the space measures 1.2 mm. For the 1s. the word 'SHILLING' is 9.3 mm long, but on Nos. T15b, T17b and T19b it measures 9.7 mm.

All values were surcharged in settings of 30 (6×5), eight of which made up the sheet of 240. For the 3d. the top row of the setting comprised Type T **3**, the second and third row (1-4), Type T **3** (narrow), the third row (5 and 6) and the fourth row, Type T **4** and the fifth row Type T **5**.

For the 1s. the top row was as Type T **3**, the second, third and fourth rows as Type T **3** (narrow) and the fifth row as Type T **3** (large 'SHILLING'), apart from R. 5/6, which was as Type T **4**.

Natal became a province of the Union of South Africa on 31 May 1910. Stamps used during the Interprovincial Period (1 June 1910–1931 August 1913) are listed under South Africa.

IV. NEW REPUBLIC

During the unrest following the death of Cetshwayo, the Zulu king, in 1884, a group of Boers from the Transvaal offered their support to his son, Dinizulu. The price for this support was the cession of a sizeable portion of Zulu territory to an independent Boer republic. The New Republic, centred on Vryheid, was proclaimed on 16 August 1884 with the remaining Zulu territory becoming a protectorate of the new administration. The first reference to an organised postal service occurs in December 1884.

Alarmed by these developments the British authorities annexed the southernmost part of the land grant, around St Lucia Bay, to prevent access to the Indian Ocean. The remainder of the New Republic was, however, recognised as independent on 22 October 1886. Zululand was annexed by the British on 22 May 1887.

Difficulties beset the New Republic, however, and its Volksraad voted for union with the South African Republic (Transvaal). The two republics united on 21 July 1888. In 1903 the territory of the former New Republic was transferred to Natal.

Mail from Vryheid in 1884–1885 was franked with issues of Transvaal (for dispatches made via Utrecht) or Natal (for those sent via Dundee from August 1885 onwards). Issues of the New Republic were never accepted as internationally valid by these administrations so that all external mail continued to show Transvaal or Natal stamps used in combination with those of the Republic.

PRICES FOR STAMPS ON COVER TO 1945

No. 1	—
Nos. 2/5	*from* × 50
Nos. 6/25	—
Nos. 26/29	*from* × 50
Nos. 30/47	—
Nos. 48/50	*from* × 50
No. 51	—
Nos. 52/53	*from* × 50
Nos. 72/75	*from* × 50
Nos. 76/77b	—
Nos. 78/80	*from* × 50
Nos. 81/95	—

1

Printed with a rubber handstamp on paper bought in Europe and sent out ready gummed and perforated.

1886 (7 Jan)–**87.** Various dates indicating date of printing. P 11½.

A. Without Arms

(i) Yellow paper

1 **1** 1d. black (9.1.86) — £3000
2 1d. violet (9.1.86) 20·00 22·00
a. '1d.' omitted (in pair with normal) (24.4.86) £2500
3 2d. violet (9.1.86) 22·00 26·00
a. 'd' omitted (13.10.86) £4250
b. '2d.' omitted (in pair with normal) (30.8.86) £3000
4 3d. violet (13.1.86) 48·00 60·00
a. 'd' omitted (13.10.86) £4250
b. *Tête-bêche* (pair) (13.10.86)
5 4d. violet (30.8.86) 85·00
a. '4' omitted (in pair with normal) (13.10.86) £2500
6 6d. violet (20.2.86) 65·00 70·00
a. '6d.' omitted (in pair with normal) (2.7.86)
7 9d. violet (13.1.86) £120
8 1s. violet (30.8.86) £120
a. '1s.' omitted (in pair with normal) (6.9.86)
9 1/s. violet (13.10.86) £750
10 1/6 violet (30.8.86) £120
11 1s.6d. violet (13.1.86) £550
a. *Tête-bêche* (pair) (6.9.86)
b. 'd' omitted (13.10.86) £140
12 2s. violet (30.8.86) 75·00
a. *Tête-bêche* (pair) (6.9.86) £800
13 2/6 violet (13.1.86) £170
14 2s.6d. violet (1.86) £170
15 4/s. violet (17.1.87) £750
15*a* 4s. violet (17.1.87)
16 5s. violet (1.86) 55·00 65·00
a. 's' omitted (in pair with normal) (7.3.86) £3250
17 5/6 violet (20.2.86) £275
18 5s.6d. violet (13.1.86) £500
19 7/6 violet (13.1.86) £225
20 7s.6d. violet (24.5.86) £160
21 10s. violet (13.1.86) £225 £275
a. *Tête-bêche* (pair) (2.7.86)
22 10s.6d. violet (1.86) £225
a. 'd' omitted (1.86) £200
23 13s. violet (24.11.86) £550
24 £1 violet (13.1.86) £140
a. *Tête-bêche* (pair) (13.10.86) £600
25 30s. violet (13.1.86) £130
a. *Tête-bêche* (pair) (24.11.86) £600

(ii) Blue granite paper

26 **1** 1d. violet (20.1.86) 28·00 30·00
a. 'd' omitted (24.11.86) £650
b. '1' omitted (in pair with normal) (24.11.86)
27 2d. violet (24.1.86) 21·00 23·00
a. 'd' omitted (24.4.86) £1200
b. '2d.' omitted (in pair with normal) (24.4.86)
28 3d. violet (30.8.86) 38·00 38·00
a. *Tête-bêche* (pair) (13.10.86) £350
29 4d. violet (24.5.86) 55·00 60·00
30 6d. violet (20.2.86) 90·00 90·00
a. '6' omitted in pair with normal (24.5.86) £2500
31 9d. violet (6.9.86) £150
32 1s. violet (1.86) 42·00 48·00
a. *Tête-bêche* (pair) (21.5.86) £375
b. '1s.' omitted (in pair with normal) (29.4.86) £2500
32*c* 1-s. violet (2.7.86) (f.c. £250) † —
33 1s.6d. violet (2.7.86) £120
a. *Tête-bêche* (pair) (6.9.86) £650
b. 'd' omitted (13.10.86)
34 1/6 violet (6.9.86) £180
35 2s. violet (21.5.86) £150
a. '2s.' omitted (in pair with normal) (24.5.86) £3000
36 2s.6d. violet (19.8.86) £225
37 2/6 violet (19.8.86) £225
38 4/s. violet (17.1.87) £500
39 5/6 violet (13.1.86) £300
a. '/' omitted (13.1.87)
b. '6' omitted £4000
40 5s.6d. violet (13.1.86) £375
41 7/6 violet (13.1.86) £300
41*a* 7s.6d. violet (13.1.86) £400
42 10s. violet (1.86) £200 £200
a. *Tête-bêche* (pair) (2.7.86) £475
b. 's' omitted (13.1.86)
43 10s.6d. violet (1.86) £250
a. *Tête-bêche* (pair) (13.1.86)
b. 'd' omitted (1.86) £550
44 12s. violet (13.1.86) £400
45 13s. violet (17.1.87) £500
46 £1 violet (13.1.86) £350
47 30s. violet (13.1.86) £300

B. With embossed Arms of New Republic

(i) Yellow paper

48 **1** 1d. violet (20.1.86) 22·00 24·00
a. Arms inverted (20.1.86) 28·00 32·00
b. Arms *tête-bêche* (pair) (14.4.86) £100 £120
c. *Tête-bêche* (pair) (3.11.86) £800
49 2d. violet (30.8.86) 26·00 28·00
a. Arms inverted (24.11.86) 30·00 35·00
50 4d. violet (2.12.86) 80·00 80·00
a. Arms inverted (12.86) £110 85·00
b. Arms *tête-bêche* (pair) (12.86) £275
51 6d. violet (2.12.86) £350

(ii) Blue granite paper

52 **1** 1d. violet (20.1.86) 28·00 28·00
a. Arms inverted (10.2.86) 40·00 42·00
b. Arms *tête-bêche* (pair) (3.11.86) £500
53 2d. violet (24.5.86) 29·00 29·00
a. Arms inverted (30.8.86) 50·00 60·00
b. Arms *tête-bêche* (pair) (2.12.86) £500 £500
c. Arms reversed (20.1.87) £400

Stamps as T **1** were produced as and when stocks were required, each printing including in its design the date on which it was prepared. The dates quoted above for Nos. 1/53 are those on which the various stamps first appeared. Details of the various printing dates are given below. From these dates it can be seen that some values share common printing dates, and, it is believed, that the different values were produced *se-tenant* within the same sheet, at least in some instances. A reported proof sheet of Nos. 79/95 in the Pretoria Postal Museum, on yellow paper and embossed, contains four examples of the 6d. value and three each of the 3d., 4d., 9d., 1s., 1/6, 2/-, 2/6, 3s., 4s., 5s., 5/6, 7/6, 10s., 10/6, £1 and 30s.

The date on No. 1 measures 17 mm; on all others it is 15 mm.

The significance, if any, of the two coloured papers and the use of the embossing machine have never been satisfactorily explained. Both the different papers and the embossing machine were introduced in January 1886, and occur throughout the period that the stamps with dates were used.

PRINTINGS

Date	Paper	Face value	Cat No.	Unused	Used
Jan 86	*Yellow*	5s.	16	55·00	65·00
		10s.6d.	22	£250	
		10s.6	22a	£250	
	Blue	1s.	32		
		10s.	42	£200	£200
		10s.6d.	43		
		10s.6	43b	£600	
7 Jan 86	*Yellow*	10s.6d.	22	£200	
	Blue	10s.	42		
		10s.6d.	43	£475	
9 Jan 86	*Yellow*	1d. blk	1	—	£3000
		1d. vio	2	20·00	22·00
		2d.	3	45·00	55·00
13 Jan 86	*Yellow*	1d.	2	42·00	
		2d.	3	38·00	42·00
		3d.	4	85·00	
		9d	7	£200	
		1s.6d.	11	£600	
		2/6	13	£200	
		2s.6d.	14	£350	
		5s.6d.	18		
		7/6	19	£225	
		10s.	21		
		£1	24	£225	
		30s.	25	£225	
	Blue	5/6	39	£300	
		5s.6d.	40	£375	
		7/6	41	£300	
		7s.6d.	41*a*	£400	
		10s.	42	£400	
		10s.	42b		
		10s.6d.	43	£250	
		10s.6d.	43a		
		12s.	44	£400	
		£1	46	£350	
		30s.	47	£300	
20 Jan 86	*Yellow*	1d.	2		
	Blue	1d.	26	£275	
	Yellow, embossed	1d.	48	80·00	
		1d.	48a	£100	
	Blue, embossed	1d.	52	£140	
Jan 20 86	*Blue*	1d.	26	75·00	
	Yellow, embossed	1d.	48a	£275	
	Blue, embossed	1d.	52	£130	
24 Jan 86	*Blue*	1d.	26	38·00	
		2d.	27	60·00	
10 Feb 86	*Yellow*	1d.	2		
	Yellow, embossed	1d.	48	£100	
		1d.	48a	80·00	
	Blue, embossed	1d.	52	£130	
		1d.	52a	50·00	
20 Feb 86	*Yellow*	6d.	6		
		1s.6d.	11		
		2s.6d.	14	£200	
		5/6	17	£275	
		5s.6d.	18		
	Blue	6d.	30		
7 Mar 86	*Yellow*	1d.	2	£120	
		2/6	13		
		2s.6d.	14	£190	
		5s.	16	£225	£120
		5s.	16a	£3250	
		5/6	17	£300	
		5s.6d.	18	£500	
	Blue	2d.	27	£100	
		6d.	30		
		1s.	32		
17 Mar 86	*Yellow*	1d.	2	£110	
	Yellow, embossed	1d.	48	50·00	
	Blue, embossed	1d.	52	£150	
		1d.	52a	£130	
26 Mar 86	*Blue, embossed*	1d.	52a	£150	
14 Apr 86	*Yellow*	1d.	2		
	Yellow, embossed	1d.	48	35·00	
		1d.	48a	60·00	
		1d.	48b	£100	£120
	Blue, embossed	1d.	52	55·00	
		1d.	52a		
24 Apr 86	*Yellow*	1d.	2	£110	
		1d.	2a	£2500	
		5s.	16		
	Blue	2d.	27	85·00	
		2d.	27a	£1200	
		2d.	27b		
29 Apr 86	*Blue*	1s.	32	£120	
		1s.	32b		
21 May 86	*Yellow*	6d.	6	£130	
	Blue	1d.	26	90·00	
		1s.	32	42·00	48·00
		1s.	32a	£375	
		1s.	32b	£2500	
		2s.	35	£300	
23 May 86	*Blue, embossed*	1d.	52a	£120	
24 May 86	*Yellow*	1d.	2	£130	£140
		2d.	3	£120	
		5s.	16	£225	
		7/6	19	£225	
		7s.6d.	20	£160	
	Blue	1d.	26	45·00	48·00
		2d.	27	£300	£300
		4d.	29	£120	
		6d.	30	£120	
		6d.	30a	£2500	
		1s.	32	£200	
		1s.	32b	£2500	
		2s.	35	£170	
		2s.	35a	£3000	
	Blue, embossed	2d.	53	£110	
26 May 86	*Yellow*	1d.	2		
	Blue	1d.	26	£120	
	Yellow, embossed	1d.	48	£250	
		1d.	48a	£100	
	Blue, embossed	1d.	52	£130	
		1d.	52a	50·00	55·00
28 May 86	*Yellow, embossed*	1d.	48	£200	
30 Jun 86	*Blue*	1d.	26	28·00	30·00
	Yellow, embossed	1d.	48	24·00	26·00
		1d.	48a	28·00	32·00
		1d.	48b	£200	£225
	Blue, embossed	1d.	52	48·00	42·00
2 July 86	*Yellow*	6d.	6	£200	
		6d.	6a		
		9d	7	£275	£275
		10s.	21		
		10s.	21a		
	Blue	1–s	32c (f.c. £250)		
		1s.6d.	33	£130	
		10s.	42	£200	
		10s.	42a	£475	
		10s.6d.	43		
		10s.6	43b	£550	
3 July 86	*Blue*	10s.	42		
7 July 86	*Yellow*	1d.	2		
	Blue	1d.	26		
	Yellow, embossed	1d.	48	90·00	
		1d.	48a	£110	£110
	Blue, embossed	1d.	52	30·00	32·00
		1d.	52a	60·00	45·00
4 Aug 86	*Yellow*	1d.	2		
	Yellow, embossed	1d.	48	65·00	
	Blue, embossed	1d.	52	75·00	
		1d.	52a		
19 Aug 86	*Yellow*	2/6	13		
		2s.6d.	14	£170	
	Blue	2s.6d.	36	£225	
		2/6	37	£225	
30 Aug 86	*Yellow*	1d.	2	20·00	22·00
		2d.	3	80·00	
		2d.	3b	£3000	
		3d.	4	90·00	
		4d.	5	85·00	
		6d.	6	£120	
		9d.	7	£120	
		1s.	8	£120	
		1/6	10	£120	
		2s.	12	£130	
		2/6	13	£190	
	Blue	2d.	27	22·00	23·00
		3d.	28		
	Yellow, embossed	2d.	49	£110	
	Blue, embossed	2d.	53	50·00	
		2d.	53a	£110	
6 Sept 86	*Yellow*	1d.	2	£100	
		2d.	3	38·00	42·00
		3d.	4	55·00	
		4d.	5	85·00	
		6d.	6	£100	
		9d.	7	£120	
		1s.	8	£130	
		1s.	8a		
		1/6	10	£200	
		1s.6d.	11	£550	
		1s.6d.	11a		
		2s.	12	£160	
		2s.	12a	£800	
		2/6	13	£170	
		2s.6d.	14		
		5s.	16	£200	
		7s.6d.	20	£275	
		10s.	21	£225	
		£1	24	£180	
	Blue	6d.	30	90·00	90·00
		9d.	31	£150	
		1s.	32	85·00	
		1s.6d.	33	£120	
		1s.6d.	33a	£650	
		1/6	34		
		2s.6d.	36		
		2/6	37	£425	
		7s.6d.	41*a*	£400	
		10s.6d.	43 (f.c. £200)	†	—
13 Sept 86	*Yellow*	1d.	2		
	Yellow, embossed	1d.	48	85·00	
		1d.	48a	85·00	
	Blue, embossed	1d.	52	£110	
6 Oct 86	*Yellow*	1d.	2		
	Blue	1d.	26	£100	
	Yellow, embossed	1d.	48	85·00	70·00
		1d.	48a		
	Blue, embossed	1d.	52	48·00	28·00
		1d.	52a	90·00	
13 Oct 86	*Yellow*	1d.	2	30·00	30·00
		2d.	3	28·00	35·00
		2d.	3a	£4250	
		3d.	4	48·00	60·00
		3d.	4a	£4250	
		3d.	4b		
		4d.	5	90·00	
		4d.	5a	£2500	
		6d.	6	65·00	70·00
		9d.	7	£130	
		1s.	8	£250	
		1/s	9	£750	
		1/6	10	£170	
		1s6	11b	£140	
		2s.	12	75·00	
		2/6	13	£200	
		5s.	16	£100	£130
		10s.	21	£250	£275
		10s.6	22a	£200	
		£1	24	£140	
		£1	24a	£600	
	Blue	2d.	27	21·00	23·00
		3d.	28	38·00	38·00
		3d.	28a	£350	
		4d.	29	55·00	60·00
		1s.	32	60·00	
		1s6	33b		
		1/6	34	£180	
		2s.	35	£150	
3 Nov 86	*Yellow*	1d.	2	50·00	
	Blue	1d.	26		
	Yellow, embossed	1d.	48	22·00	24·00
		1d.	48a	28·00	32·00
		1d.	48b	£100	£120
		1d.	48c	£800	
	Blue, embossed	1d.	52	28·00	
		1d.	52a	40·00	42·00
		1d.	52b	£500	
13 Nov 86	*Yellow*	1d.	2	£180	
24 Nov 86	*Yellow*	1d.	2	£130	£140
		2d.	3	22·00	26·00
		3d.	4	60·00	65·00
		1/6	10	£200	
		10s.	21	£250	
		13s.	23	£550	
		30s.	25	£130	
		30s.	25a	£600	
	Blue	1d.	26	48·00	35·00
		1d.	26a	£650	
		1d.	26b		
		2d.	27	55·00	
		2d.	27a		
		4d.	29	55·00	60·00
		6d.	30	£110	£110
		9d.	31	£190	
		1s.	32	£120	£130
		1/6	34	£300	
		2s.	35	£180	
		2s.	35a	£3250	
	Yellow, embossed	2d.	49	£160	
		2d.	49a		
26 Nov 86	*Yellow*	1/6	10	£200	
2 Dec 86	*Yellow*	1d.	2		
		2d.	3		
	Blue	2d.	27		
	Yellow, embossed	1d.	48	32·00	35·00
		1d.	48a	£160	
		2d.	49	26·00	28·00
		2d.	49a	30·00	35·00
		4d.	50	£275	
		6d.	51	£400	
	Blue, embossed	1d.	52	40·00	
		1d.	52a	£160	
		2d.	53	29·00	29·00
		2d.	53a	50·00	60·00
		2d.	53b	£500	£500
3 Dec 86	*Yellow, embossed*	6d.	51		
Dec 86	*Yellow*	6d.	6		
	Blue	4d.	29		
	Yellow, embossed	4d.	50	80·00	80·00
		4d.	50a	£110	85·00
		4d.	50b	£275	
		6d.	51	£350	
4 Jan 87	*Yellow*	1d.	2	£110	
		2d.	3	45·00	
		13s.	23	£550	
	Blue	1d.	26	28·00	30·00
		2d.	27	28·00	28·00
	Blue, embossed	2d.	53	45·00	
13 Jan 87	*Yellow*	7/6	19		
	Blue	5/6	39	£450	
		5/6	39a		
		7/6	41	£500	
17 Jan 87	*Yellow*	1d.	2	75·00	
		2d.	3	80·00	
		3d.	4	85·00	
		4/s.	15	£750	
		4s.	15*a*		
	Blue	1d.	26	85·00	
		4/s.	38	£500	
		13s.	45	£500	
		30s.	47	£350	
20 Jan 87	*Blue*	2d.	27	40·00	
	Yellow, embossed	2d.	49	75·00	
		2d.	49a	£140	
	Blue, embossed	2d.	53	55·00	
		2d.	53a	£100	
		2d.	53c	£400	
20 Jan 87	*Yellow, embossed*	1d.	48a	£400	

1887 (Jan–Mar). As T **1**, but without date. With embossed Arms.

(a) Blue granite paper

No.	Description	Unused	Used
72	1d. violet	32·00	18·00
	b. Stamps *tête-bêche* (pair)	£550	
	c. Arms *tête-bêche* (pair)		
	d. Arms inverted	27·00	25·00
	e. Arms omitted	£140	£140
	f. Arms sideways		
73	2d. violet	18·00	18·00
	a. Stamps *tête-bêche* (pair)	£375	
	b. Arms inverted	50·00	50·00
	c. Arms omitted	£120	£110
	d. Arms *tête-bêche* (pair)		
74	3d. violet	32·00	32·00
	a. Stamps *tête-bêche* (pair)	£400	
	b. Arms *tête-bêche* (pair)		
	c. Arms inverted	65·00	65·00
75	4d. violet	27·00	27·00
	a. Stamps *tête-bêche* (pair)	£350	
	b. Arms *tête-bêche* (pair)	£275	
	c. Arms inverted	£100	
76	6d. violet	35·00	35·00
	a. Arms inverted	95·00	
	ab. Arms inverted and reversed	£400	
77	1/6 violet	50·00	42·00
	a. Arms inverted	£150	
	b. Arms *tête-bêche* (pair)	£425	
77*c*	2/6 violet	†	£1000

(b) Yellow paper (March 1887)

No.	Description	Unused	Used
78	2d. violet (*arms omitted*)	40·00	50·00
79	3d. violet	26·00	26·00
	b. Stamps *tête-bêche* (pair)	£350	£400
	c. Arms *tête-bêche* (pair)	£200	
	d. Arms inverted	28·00	29·00
	e. Arms sideways	£350	
80	4d. violet	17·00	17·00
	a. Arms inverted	24·00	24·00
81	6d. violet	17·00	17·00
	a. Arms *tête-bêche* (pair)	£350	
	b. Arms inverted	45·00	45·00
	c. Arms omitted	90·00	
82	9d. violet	16·00	19·00
	a. Arms inverted	£225	
	b. Arms *tête-bêche* (pair)	£375	
83	1s. violet	20·00	20·00
	a. Arms inverted	70·00	
84	1/6 violet	55·00	45·00
85	2s. violet	40·00	42·00
	a. Arms inverted	60·00	55·00
	b. Arms omitted	£140	

86 2/6 violet 38·00 38·00
a. Arms inverted 42·00 42·00
87 3s. violet 65·00 65·00
a. Arms inverted 75·00 75·00
b. Stamps *tête-bêche* (pair) £550
88 4s. violet £650
a. Arms omitted
88*b* 4/s violet 65·00 65·00
ba. Arms omitted £250
89 5s. violet 60·00 60·00
b. Arms inverted — £150
90 5/6 violet 28·00 32·00
91 7/6 violet 35·00 38·00
a. Arms *tête-bêche* (pair)
b. Arms inverted £110
92 10s. violet 32·00 35·00
b. Arms *tête-bêche* (pair) £130
c. Arms inverted 40·00
d. Arms omitted £120 80·00
93 10/6 violet 28·00 32·00
b. Arms inverted 55·00
94 £1 violet 75·00 80·00
a. Stamps *tête-bêche* (pair) £500 £600
b. Arms inverted 80·00 £100
95 30s. violet £190

A £15 value as Nos. 78/95 exists, but is only known fiscally used (*Price* £9000).

Many values exist with double impressions of the handstamp.

New Republic united with the South African Republic (Transvaal) on 21 July 1888. In 1903 the territory of the former New Republic was transferred to Natal.

V. ORANGE FREE STATE

PRICES FOR STAMPS ON COVER TO 1945

Nos. 1/9	*from* × 20
Nos. 10/13	*from* × 30
Nos. 18/19	*from* × 20
No. 20	—
Nos. 21/42	*from* × 40
Nos. 48/51	*from* × 25
Nos. 52/138	*from* × 10
Nos. 139/151	*from* × 7
Nos. RO1/RO17	—
Nos. PF1/PF3	*from* × 20
No. M1	*from* × 25
Nos. F1/F17	—

Supplies of Cape of Good Hope stamps were available at Bloemfontein and probably elsewhere in the Orange Free State, from mid-1856 onwards for use on mail to Cape Colony and beyond. Such arrangements continued after the introduction of Orange Free State stamps in 1868. It is not known if the dumb cancellations used on the few surviving covers were applied in the Free State or at Cape Town.

1

(Typo D.L.R.)

1868 (1 Jan)–**94**. P 14.
1 1 1d. pale brown 32·00 2·50
2 1d. red-brown 21·00 45
3 1d. deep brown 32·00 55
4 6d. pale rose (1868) 65·00 8·00
5 6d. rose (1871) 35·00 5·50
6 6d. rose-carmine (1891) 28·00 12·00
7 6d. bright carmine (1894) 17·00 2·00
8 1s. orange-buff £100 7·00
9 1s. orange-yellow 60·00 1·50
a. Double print — £3000

4 (2) (*a*) 4 (*b*) 4 (*c*) 4 (*d*)

1877. No. 5 surcharged T **2** (*a*) to (*d*).
10 1 4d. on 6d. rose (*a*) £400 65·00
a. Surch inverted — £550
b. Surch double (*a* + *c*)
c. Surch double, one inverted (*a* + *c* inverted) † £3750
d. Surch double, one inverted (*a* inverted + *c*) † £5000
11 4d. on 6d. rose (*b*) £1300 £180
a. Surch inverted — £1100
b. Surch double (*b* + *d*)
12 4d. on 6d. rose (*c*) £200 40·00
a. Surch inverted — £350
b. Surch double
13 4d. on 6d. rose (*d*) £250 42·00
a. Surch inverted £1200 £375
b. Surch double, one inverted (*d* + *c* inverted) † £3750

The setting of 60 comprised nine stamps as No. 10, four as No. 11, 27 as No. 12 and 20 as No. 13.

1878 (July). P 14.
18 1 4d. pale blue 25·00 5·00
19 4d. ultramarine 6·50 4·25
20 5s. green 13·00 22·00

1d. (3) (*a*) 1d. (*b*) 1d. (*c*) 1d. (*d*) 1d. (*e*) 1d. (*f*)

Type **3**: (*a*) Small '1' and 'd.' (*b*) Sloping serif. (*c*) Same size as (*b*), but '1' with straighter horizontal serif. (*d*) Taller '1' with horizontal serif and antique 'd'. (*e*) Same size as (*d*) but with sloping serif and thin line at foot. (*f*) as (*d*) but with Roman 'd'.

1881 (19 May). No. 20 surch T **3** (*a*) to (*f*) with heavy black bar cancelling the old value.
21 1 1d. on 5s. green (*a*) £110 30·00
22 1d. on 5s. green (*b*) 60·00 30·00
a. Surch inverted — £900
b. Surch double — £1200
23 1d. on 5s. green (*c*) £275 85·00
a. Surch inverted — £1300
b. Surch double — £1500
24 1d. on 5s. green (*d*) 90·00 30·00
a. Surch inverted £1800 £900
b. Surch double — £1200
25 1d. on 5s. green (*e*) £550 £250
a. Surch inverted † £2250
b. Surch double † £2250
26 1d. on 5s. green (*f*) 85·00 30·00
a. Surch inverted — £800
b. Surch double — £800

No. 21 was the first printing in one type only. Nos. 22 to 25 constitute the second printing about a year later, and are all found on the same sheet; and No. 26 the third printing of which about half have the stop raised.

Owing to defective printing, examples of Nos. 22 and 24/25 may be found with the obliterating bar at the top of the stamps or, from the top row, without the bar.

½d (4)

1882 (Aug). No. 20 surch with T **4** and with a thin black line cancelling old value.
36 1 ½d. on 5s. green 25·00 7·00
a. Surch double £475 £350
b. Surch inverted £1300 £800

3d (5) (*a*) 3d (*b*) 3d (*c*) 3d (*d*) 3d (*e*)

1882. No. 19 surch with T **5** (*a*) to (*e*) with thin black line cancelling value.
38 1 3d. on 4d. ultramarine (*a*) 90·00 35·00
a. Surch double † £1200
39 3d. on 4d. ultramarine (*b*) 90·00 18·00
a. Surch double † £1200
40 3d. on 4d. ultramarine (*c*) 50·00 25·00
a. Surch double † £1200
41 3d. on 4d. ultramarine (*d*) 90·00 24·00
a. Surch double † £1200
42 3d. on 4d. ultramarine (*e*) £250 70·00
a. Surch double † £2750

Examples of Nos. 39 and 41/42 exist without the cancelling bar due to the misplacement of the surcharge.

1883–84. P 14.
48 1 ½d. chestnut 8·00 50
49 2d. pale mauve 19·00 1·75
50 2d. bright mauve 22·00 30
51 3d. ultramarine 8·00 2·00

For 1d. purple, see No. 68.

2d (6) (*a*) 2d (*b*) 2d (*c*)

1888 (Sept–Oct). No. 51 surch with T **6** (*a*), (*b*) or (*c*).

(a) Wide '2'. (b) Narrow '2'

52 1 2d. on 3d. ultramarine (*a*) (9.88) 70·00 9·00
a. Surch inverted — £750
53 2d. on 3d. ultramarine (*b*) 55·00 2·00
a. Surch inverted — £300
b. '2' with curved foot (*c*) £1300 £500

1d (7) (*a*) 1d (*b*) Id (*c*)

1890 (Dec)–**91.** Nos. 51 and 19 surch with T **7** (*a*) to (*c*).
54 1 1d. on 3d. ultramarine (*a*) 8·50 1·00
a. Surch double 90·00 70·00
c. '1' and 'd' wide apart £150 £110
d. Dropped 'd' (Right pane R. 5/6) £160 £120
55 1d. on 3d. ultramarine (*b*) 24·00 2·75
a. Surch double £300 £275
57 1d. on 4d. ultramarine (*a*) 45·00 15·00
a. Surch double £150 £120
b. Surch double (*a* + *b*) £400
c. Surch triple — £2750
d. Raised '1' (Left pane R. 3/1) £150 60·00
58 1d. on 4d. ultramarine (*b*) 85·00 55·00
a. Surch double £425 £325
59 1d. on 4d. ultramarine (*c*) £2000 £600
a. Surch double

The settings of the 1d. on 3d. and on 4d. are not identical. The variety (*c*) does not exist on the 3d.

2½d. (8) 2½d.▪ Printer's quad after surcharge (Lower right pane No. 43)

1892 (Oct). No. 51 surch with T **8**.
67 1 2½d. on 3d. ultramarine 21·00 70
a. No stop after 'd' 90·00 50·00
b. Printer's quad after surcharge 90·00 50·00

1894 (Sept). Colour changed. P 14.
68 1 1d. purple 5·00 30

½d (9) (*a*) ½d (*b*) ½d (*c*) ½d (*d*) ½d (*e*) ½d (*f*) ½d (*g*)

Types (*a*) and (*e*) differ from types (*b*) and (*f*) respectively, in the serifs of the '1', but owing to faulty overprinting this distinction is not always clearly to be seen.

1896 (Sept). No. 51 surch with T **9** (*a*) to (*g*).
69 1 ½d. on 3d. ultramarine (*a*) 7·50 11·00
70 ½d. on 3d. ultramarine (*b*) 14·00 14·00
71 ½d. on 3d. ultramarine (*c*) 13·00 2·75
72 ½d. on 3d. ultramarine (*d*) 13·00 2·25
73 ½d. on 3d. ultramarine (*e*) 13·00 2·25
74 ½d. on 3d. ultramarine (*f*) 14·00 15·00
75 ½d. on 3d. ultramarine (*g*) 8·00 5·00
a. Surch double 13·00 10·00
b. Surch triple 70·00 70·00

The double and triple surcharges are often different types, but are always type (*g*), or in combination with type (*g*).

Double surcharges in the same type, but without the 'd' and bar, also exist, probably from a trial sheet prepared by the printer. Both unused and used examples are known.

Halve Penny.

(10) 2½ (11) ½ (12)

1896. No. 51 surch with T **10**.
77 1 ½d. on 3d. ultramarine 1·00 50

(i) Errors in setting

78 1 ½d. on 3d. (no stop) 22·00 35·00
79 ½d. on 3d. ('Peuny') 22·00 35·00

(ii) Surch inverted

81 1 ½d. on 3d. 60·00 65·00
81*a* ½d. on 3d. (no stop) £2000
81*b* ½d. on 3d. ('Peuny') £1500

(iii) Surch double, one inverted

81*c* 1 ½d. on 3d. (Nos. 77 and 81) £180 £200
81*d* ½d. on 3d. (Nos. 77 and 81*a*) £800 £800
81*e* ½d. on 3d. (Nos. 77 and 81*b*) £900 £900
81*f* ½d. on 3d. (Nos. 81 and 78) £1500 £900
82 ½d. on 3d. (Nos. 81 and 79) — £900

Examples from the top horizontal row can be found without the bar due to the surcharge being misplaced.

Nos. 69 to 75 also exist surcharged as last but they are considered not to have been issued with authority (*Prices from £30 each, unused*).

1897 (1 Jan). No. 51 surch with T **11**. (a) or T **12** (b) With Roman '1' and antique '2' in fraction.
83 1 2½d. on 3d. ultramarine (*a*) 10·00 1·50
83*a* 2½d. on 3d. ultramarine (*b*) £170 90·00

1897. P 14.
84 1 ½d. yellow (3.97) 2·75 35
85 ½d. orange 2·75 50
87 1s. brown (8.97) 32·00 1·50

The 6d. blue was prepared for use in the Orange Free State, but had not been brought into use when the stamps were seized in Bloemfontein. A few have been seen without the 'V.R.I.' overprint but they were not authorized or available for postage (*Price* £65).

BRITISH OCCUPATION

V. R. I. V. R. I. V. R. I.

4d **31** (Level stops) ½d (**32**) Thin 'V' (Raised stops) ½d (**33**) Thick 'V'

V. R I. Inserted 'R'

(Surch by Curling & Co, Bloemfontein)

1900. T **1** surch as Types **31/33** (2½d. on 3d. optd 'V.R.I.' only).

*(a) First printings surch as T **31** with stops level (March)*

101 ½d. on ½d. orange 4·75 7·00
a. No stop after 'V' (R.10/3) 23·00 29·00
b. No stop after 'I' (R.1/3) £160 £160
c. '½' omitted (R.7/5) £190 £190
d. 'I' and stops after 'I' and 'R' omitted (R. 2/3) £275 £250
e. 'V.R.I.' omitted £180
f. Value omitted £120
g. Small '½' (R. 1/1, 1/3 or R. 5/1, 8/1) 60·00 60·00
h. Surch double £180
102 1d. on 1d. purple 2·75 1·75
a. Surch on 1d. deep brown (No. 3) £600 £400
b. No stop after 'V' (R. 10/3) 19·00 18·00
c. No stop after 'R' £180 £190
d. No stop after 'I' £1000
e. '1' omitted (R. 7/5) £200 £200
f. 'I' omitted (with stops present) £350 £350
g. 'I' and stop after 'R' omitted (R. 2/3) £275 £275
ga. 'I' omitted, with raised stop after 'R' (R. 2/3) £250 £250
h. 'V.R.I.' omitted £160 £180
i. 'd' omitted £400 £400
j. Value omitted 90·00 £100
k. Inverted stop after 'R' £250 £275

l. Wider space between '1' and 'd' £100 £100
m. 'V' and 'R' close £160 £160
n. Pair, one without surch £550
o. 'V' omitted £850

103 2d. on 2d. bright mauve .... 4·25 2·75
a. No stop after 'V' (R. 10/3) .... 22·00 25·00
b. No stop after 'R' £325 £325
c. No stop after 'I' £325 £325
d. 'V.R.I.' omitted £300 £300
e. Value omitted £300

104 2½d. on 3d. ultramarine (*a*) .... 23·00 22·00
a. No stop after 'V' (R. 10/3) .... 95·00 95·00

105 2½d. on 3d. ultramarine (*b*) £250 £250

106 3d. on 3d. ultramarine .... 3·25 4·75
a. No stop after 'V' (R. 10/3) .... 25·00 30·00
b. Pair, one without surch £650
c. 'V.R.I.' omitted £250 £250
d. Value omitted £250 £250

107 4d. on 4d. ultramarine .... 11·00 17·00
a. No stop after 'V' (R.10/3) .... 65·00 75·00

108 6d. on 6d. bright carmine .... 45·00 40·00
a. No stop after 'V' (R. 10/3) £250 £275
b. '6' omitted (R. 7/5) £300 £300

109 6d. on 6d. blue .... 15·00 7·50
a. No stop after 'V' (R. 10/3) .... 55·00 50·00
b. '6' omitted (R. 7/5) .... 85·00 90·00
c. 'V.R.I.' omitted £500 £375

110 1s. on 1s. brown .... 7·00 2·75
a. Surch on 1s. orange-yellow (No. 9) £3500 £2500
b. No stop after 'V' (R. 10/3) .... 55·00 32·00
c. '1' omitted (R. 4/6) £150 £140
ca. '1' inserted by hand .... † £1000
d. '1' omitted and spaced stop after 's' (R. 4/6) £160 £160
e. 'V.R.I.' omitted £200 £200
f. Value omitted £200 £200
g. Raised stop after 's' (R. 1/5, 6/6, 7/2) 28·00 12·00
h. Wider space between '1' and 's' (R. 4/6) £150 £150

111 5s. on 5s. green .... 32·00 55·00
a. No stop after 'V' (R. 10/3) £275 £325
b. '5' omitted £950 £1000
c. Inverted stop after 'R' (R. 2/2) £800 £850
d. Wider space between '5' and 's' (R. 3/6) £130 £140
e. Value omitted £425 £450

All values are found with a rectangular, instead of an oval, stop after 'R'. Misplaced surcharges (upwards or sideways) occur.

No. 110ca shows the missing '1' replaced by a handstamp in a different type face.

On No. 111c the stop is near the top of the 'R'. On 111d there is a 2mm space between '5' and 's'; lesser displacements exist on other positions.

(b) Subsequent printings

(i) Surch as T **32**

112 ½d. on ½d. orange 30 20
a. Raised and level stops mixed .... 3·25 2·00
b. Pair, one with level stops .... 15·00 19·00
c. No stop after 'V' (R. 6/1) .... 4·00 4·25
d. No stop after 'I' (R. 4/6) .... 42·00 42·00
e. 'V' omitted (R. 4/6) £600
f. Small '½' (R. 7/3 or 10/6) .... 19·00 21·00
g. As a, and small '½' ....
i. Space between 'V' and 'R' .... 75·00 80·00
j. Value omitted £120 £120

113 1d. on 1d. purple 30 20
a. Raised and level stops mixed .... 2·50 3·00
b. Pair, one with level stops .... 25·00 27·00
c. No stop after 'V' (R. 6/1) .... 4·25 8·50
d. No stop after 'R' (R. 1/2, 1/6, 5/5 or 7/6) .... 18·00 18·00
e. No stop after 'I' (R. 1/4, 1/5, 6/6, 7/6 or 9/1) .... 18·00 18·00
f. No stops after 'V' and 'I' (R. 9/1) £350
g. Surch inverted £400
h. Surch double £120 £110
i. Pair, one without surch £300
j. Short figure '1' (R. 1/5) £110 £110
k. Space between 'V' and 'R' (R. 7/5 or 7/6) .... 50·00 55·00
l. Space between 'R' and 'I' (R. 7/6) £120 £130
m. Space between '1' and 'd' (R. 10/5) £190 £190
n. Inserted 'R' £450 £450
o. Inserted 'V' £750
p. Stamp doubly printed, one impression inverted £2500

114 2d. on 2d. bright mauve .... 3·50 30
a. Raised and level stops mixed .... 8·50 5·00
b. Pair, one with level stops .... 14·00 15·00
c. Surch inverted £350 £350
d. 'I' and stop raised .... 75·00 75·00
e. Pair, one without surch £300 £350
f. No stop after 'V' (R. 6/6) £1000
g. No stop after 'I' ....

115 2½d. on 3d. ultramarine (*a*) £225 £200
a. Level stop after 'V' (R.10/6) £800

116 2½d. on 3d. ultramarine (*b*) £1200

117 3d. on 3d. ultramarine .... 2·50 30
a. Raised and level stops mixed .... 10·00 10·00
b. Pair, one with level stops .... 24·00 25·00
c. No stop after 'V' £140 £140
d. No stop after 'R' £400 £475
e. 'I' and stop omitted (R. 6/6) £425 £450
ea. 'I' and stop inserted ....
f. Surch double £400
g. Surch double, one diagonal £375
h. Ditto, diagonal surch with mixed stops £6500
n. Inserted 'R' ....
o. Space between '3' and 'd' £150

118 4d. on 4d. ultramarine .... 3·00 4·75
a. Raised and level stops mixed .... 10·00 15·00
b. Pair, one with level stops .... 22·00 35·00

119 6d. on 6d. bright carmine .... 40·00 50·00
a. Raised and level stops mixed £140 £160
b. Pair, one with level stops £225 £300

120 6d. on 6d. blue .... 1·00 40
a. Raised and level stops mixed .... 11·00 12·00
b. Pair, one with level stops .... 25·00 29·00
c. No stop after 'V' £550 £550
d. No stop after 'R' £375
e. Value omitted £450

121 1s. on 1s. brown .... 11·00 45
a. Surch on 1s. orange-yellow (No. 9) £1300 £1300
b. Raised and level stops mixed .... 27·00 23·00
c. Pair, one with level stops .... 50·00 50·00
f. 's' omitted £250
g. 'V.R.I.' omitted £400

122 5s. on 5s. green .... 10·00 19·00
a. Raised and level stops mixed £350 £350
b. Pair, one with level stops £1000
c. Short top to '5' (R. 1/2) .... 60·00 70·00
s. Handstamped 'SPECIMEN' .... 55·00

In the initial ('second') setting with raised stops (T **32**), there were still level stops at R. 7/4, and three positions showed raised and level stops mixed: R. 9/4 (level stops after 'V' and 'I'), R. 9/5 (level stop after 'V') and R. 10/4 (level stops after 'R' and 'I'). No. 115a comes from a later setting, as do examples of a level stop after 'V' at R. 1/6 and a level stop after 'I' at R. 3/2, both on the 1d. value.

(ii) Surch as T **33**

123 ½d. on ½d. orange .... 8·50 5·00

124 1d. on 1d. purple .... 8·50 35
a. Inverted '1' for 'I' (R. 7/1) .... 27·00 27·00
b. No stops after 'R' and 'I' (R. 10/4) £160 £160
c. No stop after 'R' (R. 10/4) .... 65·00 70·00
d. Surch double £375 £375
n. Inserted 'R' £400 £400
p. Stamp doubly printed, one impression inverted £6500

125 2d. on 2d. bright mauve .... 20·00 18·00
a. Inverted '1' for 'I' (R. 7/1) .... 42·00 45·00

126 2½d. on 3d. ultramarine (*a*) £750 £850

127 2½d. on 3d. ultramarine (*b*) £3750

128 3d. on 3d. ultramarine .... 10·00 18·00
a. Inverted '1' for 'I' (R. 7/1) .... 65·00 75·00
b. Surch double £550
ba. Surch double, one diagonal £550

129 6d. on 6d. bright carmine £425 £450

130 6d. on 6d. blue .... 23·00 32·00

131 1s. on 1s. brown .... 40·00 13·00

132 5s. on 5s. green .... 65·00 55·00
s. Handstamped 'SPECIMEN' £170

Stamps with thick 'V' occur in seven or later six positions in *later* settings of the type with stops above the line (T **32**). *Earlier* settings with stops above the line have all stamps with thin 'V'.

Some confusion has previously been caused by the listing of certain varieties as though they occurred on stamps with thick 'V' in fact they occur on stamps showing the normal thin 'V', included in the settings which also contained the thick 'V'.

For a short period small blocks of unsurcharged Free State stamps could be handed in for surcharging so that varieties occur which are not found in the complete settings. Nos. 102a, 110a and 121a also occur from such stocks.

The inserted 'R' variety occurs on positions 6 (T **32**) and 12 (T **33**) of the forme. The 'R' of the original surcharge failed to print and the 'R', but not the full stop, was added by the use of a handstamp. Traces of the original letter are often visible. The broken 'V' flaw, also shown in the illustration, does not appear on No. 124n.

ORANGE RIVER COLONY

CROWN COLONY

E. R. I.

ORANGE RIVER COLONY. **(34)**

4d **(35)**

6d **(36)**

1900 (10 Aug)–**02**. Nos. 58, 59*a* and 63*a* of Cape of Good Hope (wmk Cabled Anchor. P 14) optd with T **34** by W. A. Richards and Sons, Cape Town.

133 ½d. green (13.10.00) 65 10
a. No stop .... 12·00 25·00
b. Opt double £650 £700

134 1d. carmine (5.1902) .... 2·25 10
a. No stop .... 25·00 32·00

135 2½d. ultramarine .... 5·50 1·50
a. No stop .... 75·00 75·00

133/135 *Set of 3* .... 7·75 1·50

In the ½d. and 2½d., the 'no stop' after 'COLONY' variety was the first stamp in the left lower pane. In the 1d. it is the 12th stamp in the right lower pane on which the stop was present at the beginning of the printing but became damaged and soon failed to print.

1902 (14 Feb). Surch with T **35** by 'Bloemfontein Express'.

136 4d. on 6d. on 6d. blue (No. 120) (R.) .... 1·50 3·25
a. No stop after 'R' (R. 5/5) .... 38·00 55·00
b. No stop after 'I' £1200
c. Surch on No. 130 (Thick 'V') .... 2·50 9·50
ca. Inverted '1' for 'I' (R. 7/1) .... 7·50 26·00

1902 (Aug). Surch with T **36**.

137 **1** 6d. on 6d. blue .... 7·00 20·00
a. Surch double, one inverted ....
b. Wide space between '6' and 'd' (R. 4/2) .... 60·00 £100

One Shilling * **(37)**

38 King Edward VII, Springbok and Gnu

1902 (Sept). Surch with T **37**.

138 **1** 1s. on 5s. green (O.) .... 10·00 25·00
a. Thick 'V' .... 17·00 50·00
b. Short top to '5' .... 70·00 85·00
c. Surch double £1000

(Typo D.L.R.)

1903 (3 Feb)–**04**. Wmk Crown CA. P 14.

139 **38** ½d. yellow-green (6.7.03) .... 9·00 2·25
w. Wmk inverted £250 £100

140 1d. scarlet .... 12·00 10
w. Wmk inverted .... £250 80·00

141 2d. brown (6.7.03) .... 10·00 1·75

142 2½d. bright blue (6.7.03) .... 8·00 2·25

143 3d. mauve (6.7.03) .... 9·50 1·25

144 4d. scarlet and sage-green (6.7.03) 38·00 7·50
a. 'IOSTAGE' for 'POSTAGE' £1200 £450

145 6d. scarlet and mauve (6.7.03) .... 8·50 2·00

146 1s. scarlet and bistre (6.7.03) .... 50·00 4·00

147 5s. blue and brown (31.10.04) .... £160 30·00

139/147 *Set of 9* .... £275 45·00

139s/147s Optd 'SPECIMEN' *Set of 9* £275

No. 144a occurs on R. 10/2 of the upper left pane.

The 2d. exists from coils constructed from normal sheets for use in stamp machines introduced in 1911.

1905 (Nov)–**09**. Wmk Mult Crown CA. P 14.

148 **38** ½d. yellow-green (28.7.07) .... 18·00 1·50

149 1d. scarlet .... 11·00 30

150 4d. scarlet and sage-green (8.11.07) .... 4·50 7·00
a. 'IOSTAGE' for 'POSTAGE' £200 £250

151 1s. scarlet and bistre (2.09) .... 80·00 27·00

148/151 *Set of 4* .... £100 32·00

POSTCARD STAMPS

From 1889 onwards the Orange Free State Post Office sold postcards franked with adhesives as T **1**, some subsequently surcharged, over which the State Arms had been overprinted by Curling and Co., Bloemfontein. Examples are known of adhesives being affixed to cards upside-down, resulting in the overprint being inverted on loose stamps.

There are five known dies of the Arms overprint which can be identified as follows:

(a) Shield without flags. Single 15 mm diameter circle. Three cows (two lying down, one standing) at left. Point of shield complete.
(b) Shield with flags. Single 13 mm diameter circle. Four cows (two lying down, two standing) at left (*illustrated*).
(c) Shield with flags. Double 13 mm diameter circle. Three cows (one lying down, two standing) at left.
(d) Shield without flags. Single 14.5 mm diameter circle. Three cows (one lying down, two standing) at left.
(e) Shield without flags. Double 15 mm diameter circle. Three cows (two lying down, one standing) at left. Point of shield broken.

There are also other differences between the dies.

PRICES. Those in the left-hand column are for unused examples on complete postcard; those on the right for used examples off card. Examples used on postcard are worth more.

1889 (Feb). No. 2 (placed sideways on card) optd Shield Type (a).

P1 **1** 1d. red-brown .... £250 42·00
a. Optd Shield Type (b) .... 40·00 8·00

1891 (Aug)–**94**. No. 48 optd Shield Type (b).

P2 **1** ½d. chestnut .... 7·00 2·00
a. Optd Shield Type (c) .... 16·00 4·50
b. Optd Shield Type (d) .... 7·50 2·50
ba. Error. Optd with *Bloemfontein Express* die (1894) £200
c. Optd Shield Type (e) .... 17·00 5·50

No. P2ba was caused when the trademark of the *Bloemfontein Express* newspaper was substituted for Type d in error.

1892 (June). No. 54 optd Shield Type (c).

P3 **1** 1d. on 3d. ultramarine .... 18·00 3·50

1½d. **(P 1)** 1½d. **(P 2)** 1½d. **(P 3)**

1892 (Sept)–**95**. Nos. 50/51 optd Shield Type (b) or (d) (No. P6) and surch with Types P **1**/P **3**.

P4 **1** 1½d. on 2d. bright mauve (Type P **1**) (11.92) .... 9·50 4·00

P5 1½d. on 2d. bright mauve (Type P **2**) (9.93) .... 7·50 2·00
a. Surch inverted £150

P6 1½d. on 2d. bright mauve (Type P **3**) (R.) (6.95) .... 16·00 4·75

P7 1½d. on 3d. ultramarine (Type P **1**) .... 9·00 2·50

No. P5a shows the stamp affixed to the card upside down with the surcharge correctly positioned in relation to the card.

½d. **(P 4)**

1895 (Aug). No. 48 optd Shield Type (e) and surch with T P **4**.

P8 **1** ½d. on ½d. chestnut .... 16·00 3·00

1½d. **(P 5)** 1½d. **(P 6)**

1895 (Dec)–**97**. No. 50 optd Shield Type (e) and surch with Types P **5**/P **6**.

P9 **1** 1½d. on 2d. bright mauve (Type P **5**) 8·00 3·00

P10 1½d. on 2d. bright mauve (Type P **6**) (12.97) .... 9·00 3·50

P11 1½d. on 2d. bright mauve (as Type P **6**, but without stop) (12.97) .... 9·00 3·50

1897 (Mar). No. 85 optd Shield Type (d).

P12 **1** ½d. orange .... 16·00 2·00
a. Optd Shield Type (e) .... 17·00 3·00

V.R.I.
(P 7)

1900. Nos. P10/11 optd as Types **31/32** or with T P **7**.
P13 **1** 1½d. on 2d. bright mauve (No. P10) (Type **31**) 32·00 6·50
P14 1½d. on 2d. bright mauve (No. P11) (Type **31**) 32·00 6·50
P15 1½d. on 2d. bright mauve (No. P10) (Type **32**) 32·00 6·50
P16 1½d. on 2d. bright mauve (No. P11) (Type **32**) 32·00 6·50
P17 1½d. on 2d. bright mauve (No. P10) (Type P **7**) 45·00 12·00
P18 1½d. on 2d. bright mauve (No. P11) (Type P **7**) 45·00 12·00

RAILWAY OFFICIAL STAMPS

The following stamps were provided for use on official correspondence of the Central Southern Africa Railways.

C.S.A.R.
RO **1**

1905 (Feb). Nos. 139/141 and 143/146 optd with T RO **1** at CSAR's Departmental Printing Office, Germiston.
RO1 ½d. yellow-green £100 25·00
RO2 1d. scarlet £100 20·00
RO3 2d. brown £200 75·00
RO4 3d. mauve £375 £150
RO5 4d. scarlet and sage-green £375 £150
RO6 6d. scarlet and mauve £425 £200
RO7 1s. scarlet and bistre — £300

The overprint on Nos. RO1/RO7 was applied in a setting of 120 and was normally placed either at the top or bottom of the stamps, although central placings are known. The stamps were withdrawn on 13 October 1905, but examples of genuine late use have been recorded. Dangerous forgeries exist.

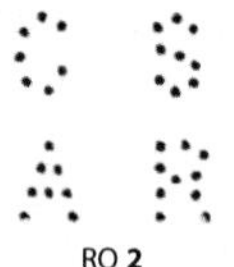
RO **2**

1907. Nos. 139/141 and 143/146 punctured with T RO **2**.
RO8 ½d. yellow-green £100 50·00
RO9 1d. scarlet £150 75·00
RO10 2d. brown £200 £100
RO11 3d. mauve — £150
RO12 4d. scarlet and sage-green £250 £200
RO13 6d. scarlet and mauve
RO14 1s. scarlet and bistre

1907. Nos. 148/150 punctured with T RO **2**.
RO15 ½d. yellow-green £100 50·00
RO16 1d. scarlet £100 50·00
RO17 4d. scarlet and sage-green — £200

Nos. RO8/RO17 were replaced by Transvaal stamps punctured 'S/AR' and finally withdrawn on 1 April 1912, although later usages are known.

POLICE FRANK STAMPS

The following frank stamps were issued to members of the Orange Free State Mounted Police ('Rijdende Dienst Macht') for use on official correspondence.

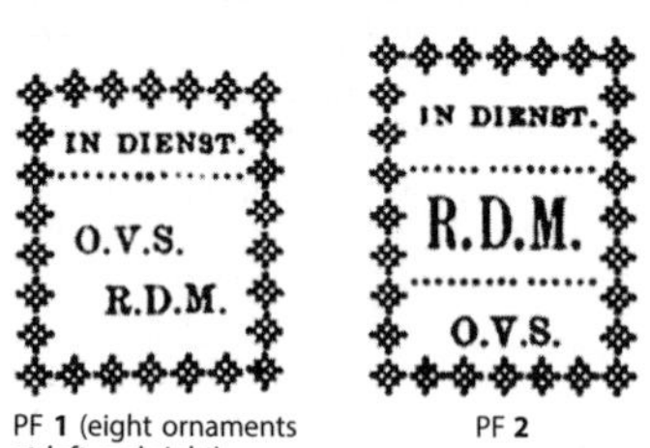

PF **1** (eight ornaments at left and right) PF **2**

1896. P 12.
PF1 PF **1** (–) Black £400 £500

No. PF1 was printed in horizontal strips of five surrounded by wide margins.

1898. As T PF **1**, but with nine ornaments at left and right. P 12.
PF2 (–) Black £250 £300
a. No stop after 'V' £500 £600

No. PF2 was printed in blocks of four (2×2) surrounded by wide margins. No. PF2a occurs on R1/1 of the setting.

1899. P 12.
PF3 PF **2** (–) Black/*yellow* £225 £300
a. No stop after 'V' £650 £850

No. PF3 was printed in sheets of 24 (6×4) with the edges of the sheet imperforate. It is believed that they were produced from a setting of eight (2×4) repeated three times. No. PF3a occurs on R. 1/2 of the setting.

Examples of No. PF3 are known postmarked as late as 28 April 1900. The O.F.S. Mounted Police were disbanded by the British authorities at the end of the following month.

MILITARY FRANK STAMP

M **1**

(Typeset Curling & Co, Bloemfontein)

1899 (15 Oct). P 12.
M1 M **1** (–) Black/*bistre-yellow* 35·00 70·00

Supplies of No. M1 were issued to members of the Orange Free State army on active service during the Second Boer War. To pass free through the O.F.S. fieldpost system, letters had to be franked with No. M1 or initialled by the appropriate unit commander. The franks were in use between October 1899 and February 1900.

No. M1 was printed in sheets of 20 (5×4) using a setting of five different types in a horizontal row. The colour in the paper runs in water.

Typeset forgeries can be identified by the appearance of 17 pearls, instead of the 16 of the originals, in the top and bottom frames. Forgeries produced by lithography omit the stops after 'BRIEF' and 'FRANKO'.

FISCAL STAMPS USED FOR POSTAGE

The following were issued in December 1877 (Nos. F1 and F3 in 1882) and were authorised for postal use between 1882 and 1886.

F **1**

F **2**

F **3**

(Typo D.L.R.)

1882–86. P 14.
F1 F **1** 6d. pearl-grey 21·00 23·00
F2 6d. purple-brown £110 48·00
F3 F **2** 1s. purple-brown 27·00 29·00
F4 1s. pearl-grey £150 £130
F5 1s.6d. blue 48·00 38·00
F6 2s. magenta 42·00 35·00
F7 3s. chestnut 50·00 90·00
F8 4s. grey £400
F9 5s. rose 48·00 42·00
F10 6s. green £400 £150
F11 7s. violet £400
F11*a* 8s. yellow £150
F11*b* 9s. olive-bistre £400
F12 10s. orange £100 55·00
F13 F **3** £1 purple £130 60·00
a. 'VRY-STAAT' (R. 1/5)
F14 £2 red-brown £160 £130
a. 'VRY-STAAT' (R. 1/5)
F14*b* £4 carmine
ba. 'VRY-STAAT' (R. 1/5)
F15 £5 green £250 85·00
a. 'VRY-STAAT' (R. 1/5) £2500

Die proofs of T F **3** showed a hyphen in error between 'VRY' and 'STAAT'. This was removed from each impression on the plate before printing, but was missed on R. 1/5.

A fiscally used example of No. F2 exists showing 'ZES PENCE' double, one inverted.

The 8s. yellow and 9s. olive-bistre have not been reported with postal cancels, but were later surcharged for telegraphic use (Nos. T11/T14), while the 8s. yellow also exists with T F **4** surcharge (No. F17).

ZES PENCE.
(F **4**)

1886. Surch with T F **4**.
F16 F **2** 6d. on 4s. grey
F17 6d. on 8s. yellow £600

TELEGRAPH STAMPS

(T **1**)

1885 (Sept). Postage stamps as T **1** handstamped as Type T **1**.
T1 1d. red-brown (No. 2) (V.) 24·00 7·00
T2 3d. ultramarine (No. 51) (V.) 35·00 8·00
T3 3d. ultramarine (No. 51) (C.) 80·00 21·00
T4 6d. rose (No. 5) (V.) 35·00 9·00
T5 6d. rose (No. 5) (Blk.) 80·00 27·00
T6 1s. orange-yellow (No. 9) (V.) £225 40·00

The handstamp is known reading vertically up or down or diagonally; double handstamps also exist. The 5s. (No. 20) has also been reported with Type T **1** handstamp but it is believed not to have been issued.

1886 (Feb). Fiscal stamps as T F **2** handstamped as Type T **1**.
T7 1s. purple-brown (No. F3) (V.) 60·00 15·00
T8 1s. purple-brown (No. F3) (Blk.) 75·00 24·00
T9 1s. pearl-grey (No. F4) (V.) 55·00 14·00

The handstamp is known reading horizontally, diagonally and inverted.

T F (T **2**) **Een Shilling.** (T **3**)

1888 (Apr). Fiscal stamps as T F **2** optd and surch Type T **2** and Type T **3** by C. Borckenhagen, Bloemfontein.
T10 1s. on 7s. violet (No. F11) 80·00 15·00
T11 1s. on 8s. yellow (small 'TF') 90·00 24·00
a. Large 'T' in 'TF' £180 45·00
T12 1s. on 8s. yellow (large 'TF') 80·00 15·00
T13 1s. on 9s. olive-bistre (small 'TF') £130 38·00
a. Large 'T' in 'TF' £275 75·00
T14 1s. on 9s. olive-bistre (large 'TF') 90·00 25·00

The 'TF' overprint measures 8.2×2.9 mm on No. T10, 6.6×3.4 mm on Nos. T12 and T14 and 6.6×2.9 mm on T11 and T13.

No. T10 exists with an additional manuscript line through the original value, to correct misplacement of the Type T **3** surcharge. The type used for Type T **3** was in poor condition and numerous broken letter varieties exist, including 'Ecn', 'E-n' and damage to the first or second 'l' or 'n' of 'Shilling'.

T F (T **4**) **T F** (T **5**) **T F** (T **6**) **T F** (T **7**)

1888 (May). Postage stamps as T **1** optd as Type T **4** by C. Borckenhagen, Bloemfontein.
T15 1d. red-brown (No. 2) 35·00 11·00
T16 3d. ultramarine (No. 51) 6·00 2·00
T17 6d. rose (No. 5) 7·00 2·00
a. Opt double 70·00 28·00
T18 1s. orange-yellow (No. 9) 8·00 2·00

Opt Type T **4** measures 6.5×2.8 mm.

1890 (July). Postage stamps as T **1** optd as Types T **5**/T **6** by C. Borckenhagen, Bloemfontein.
T19 6d. rose (No. 5) (Optd Type **5**) £100 29·00
T20 1s. orange-yellow (No. 9) (Optd Type **6**) £130 40·00

In T19/T20 the letters are smaller than other issues, the overprint measuring 5.5×2.1 mm on No. T19 and 6.0×2.25 mm on T20.

1891 (Jan). Postage stamps as T **1** optd as Type T **7** by C. Borckenhagen, Bloemfontein.
T21 3d. ultramarine (No. 51) 7·00 2·00
a. 'FT' for 'TF' 70·00 30·00
T22 6d. rose-carmine (No. 6) 7·00 2·00
a. 'FT' for 'TF' 70·00 30·00
b. Wide 'TF' 29·00 8·50
c. Opt double £110 80·00
d. Opt inverted
T23 1s. orange-yellow (No. 9) 8·00 2·00
a. 'FT' for 'TF' 80·00 35·00
b. Wide 'TF' 29·00 8·50

Type T **7** is similar to Type T **4** but the letters are thicker, the lower stroke of the 'F' forms a triangle touching the upright, without the horizontal line found in Type T **4**. In the 'wide 'TF' varieties there is a 4 mm space between the letters.

T F (T **8**) **T F** (T **9**) **T F.** (T **10**)

1891 (Jan?). Postage stamps as T **1** optd as Types T **8**/T **9** by C. Borckenhagen, Bloemfontein.
T24 1d. red-brown (No. 2) (optd Type T **8**) 7·50 1·50
a. Opt inverted
b. Optd Type T **9** 7·50 1·50
ba. Ditto, opt inverted
c. Vert pair Nos. T24/T24b
T25 6d. rose (No. 5) (optd Type T **8**) 8·50 1·50
a. Opt double
b. Optd Type T **9** 8·50 1·50
ba. Ditto, opt double
c. Vert pair Nos. T25/T25b
T26 1s. orange-yellow (No. 9) 15·00 1·50
a. Optd Type T **9** 15·00 1·50
c. Vert pair Nos. T26/T26a

Opts Type T **8** (*9.3×3.9 mm*) and Type T **9** (*8.5×3.3 mm*) appeared in the same sheet, Type T **8** in the upper part and Type T **9** in the lower.

1892 (Oct). No. 6 optd Type T **10** by C. Borckenhagen, Bloemfontein.
T27 6d. rose-carmine 32·00 11·00
a. Stop omitted 65·00 22·00
b. 'TE.' For 'TF.' £100 40·00
c. Inverted 'L' for 'T'

Type T **10** measures 5.4×2.5 mm, excluding the stop.

T.F. (T **11**) **TF** (T **12**)

1892 (Nov). No 9 optd with Type T **11** by C. Borckenhagen, Bloemfontein.
T28 1s. orange-yellow 26·00 5·00
a. Stop omitted after 'T' 55·00 14·00
b. Stop omitted after 'F' 55·00 14·00
c. Stops omitted after 'T' and 'F' 65·00 17·00
d. Comma for stop after 'F' 55·00 14·00

1893. Postage stamps as T **1** opt with Type T **12** by C. Borckenhagen, Bloemfontein.
T29 1d. red-brown (No. 2) 5·00 1·00
a. Opt inverted 75·00 35·00
T30 3d. ultramarine (No. 51) 5·00 1·00
T31 6d. rose-carmine (No. 6) 6·00 1·25
T32 1s. orange-yellow (No. 9) 8·00 1·25

Type T **12** measures 4.7×2.6 mm.

1898 (June)–**99**. As Nos. T29 and T31/T32 but colours changed.
T33 1d. purple (No. 68) (5.99) 2·00 1·00
T34 6d. blue (8.98) 2·00 1·25
T35 1s. brown (No. 87) 2·00 1·25

The 6d. blue was not issued without the Type T **12** opt.

British Occupation

The Army controlled the telegraph system from the start of the British occupation in 1900. Initially existing telegraph stamps were overprinted 'V.R.I.', they were later supplemented by stamps overprinted 'V.R.I./AT'.

1900 (Apr). Nos. T30 and T33/T35 optd 'V.R.I.' (as T **32**, thin 'V', raised stops).
T36 1d. purple 3·00 2·00
a. Raised and level stops mixed 12·00 8·50
b. Horiz gutter pair, right stamp 'V.R.I.' omitted £750
T37 3d. ultramarine 12·00 9·00
a. Raised and level stops mixed 40·00 28·00
b. 'V.R.I.' double £325 £250

T38 6d. blue .... 24·00 12·00
a. Raised and level stops mixed .... 70·00 35·00
T39 1s. brown .... 6·00 4·00
a. Raised and level stops mixed .... 17·00 13·00

The 'V.R.I.' overprint is usually positioned at the top of the stamp but lower positions are not uncommon.

Mixed stop varieties occur as follows: level stop after 'V' at R. 1/6, R. 5/6, R. 9/5 and R. 10/1, level stops after 'V' and 'I' at R. 9/4, level stops after 'R' and 'I' at R. 7/4 and R. 10/4, level stop after 'R' at R. 8/4, level stop after 'I' at R. 2/5 and R. 6/6.

V. R. I. V. R. I.

T F (T **13**) A T (T **14**) A T (T **15**)

T Six Pence (T **16**)

1900 (Apr). As No. T38 but optd as Type T **13** and 'V.R.I.' (as T **32**).

T40 6d. blue .... 55·00 30·00
a. Raised and level stops mixed .... £150 85·00

Type T **13** measures 7.1×3.0 mm.

1900 (Apr). No. T33 surcharged as T **32**.

T41 1d. on 1d. purple ....

It is believed that No. T41 was the result of a sheet of telegraph stamps receiving the overprint due for the postage stamp in error. Forgeries exist.

1900 (Apr?). Postage stamps as T **1** and fiscal stamps as T F **2** optd with Type T **14** (Nos. T42/T45) or Type T **15** (others).

T42 1d. purple .... 2·75 1·00
a. Thick 'V' (as Type **33**) .... 8·50 3·50
T43 3d. ultramarine .... 5·50 3·00
a. Thick 'V' (as Type **33**) .... 16·00 9·00
b. Opt inverted £350 £300
T44 6d. blue .... 6·50 4·00
a. Thick 'V' (as Type **33**) .... 19·00 12·00
T45 1s. brown .... 5·50 3·00
a. Thick 'V' (as Type **33**) .... 16·00 9·00
b. Opt double £300
T46 5s. green .... 19·00 10·00
a. Thick 'V' (as Type **33**) .... 55·00 28·00
b. No stop after 'V' (R. 6/1) .... £110 55·00
c. Low stop after 'V' (R. 10/6) .... £110 55·00
d. Broad short 'A' in 'AT' (R. 6/5) .... £110 55·00
e. 'V.R.I.' omitted (lower stamp of vertical pair) ....
T47 10s. orange .... 35·00 25·00
a. Thick 'V' (as Type **33**) .... 85·00 60·00
b. No stop after 'V' (R. 6/1) £200 £130
c. Low stop after 'V' (R. 10/6) £200 £130
d. Broad short 'A' in 'AT' (R. 6/5) £200 £130
e. Opt inverted £900
T48 £1 purple .... 48·00 32·00
a. Thick 'V' (As Type **33**) .... £120 80·00
b. No stop after 'V' (R. 6/1) £275 £160
c. Low stop after 'V' (R. 10/6) £275 £160
d. Broad short 'A' in 'AT' (R. 6/5) £275 £160
e. 'VRY-STAAT' £325
T49 £4 carmine .... £110 80·00
a. Thick 'V' (as Type **33**) £275 £180
b. No stop after 'V' (R. 6/1) £600 £400
c. Low stop after 'V' (R. 10/6) £600 £400
d. Broad short 'A' in 'AT' (R. 6/5) £600 £400
e. 'VRY-STAAT' £750

In Type T **14** 'AT' measures 6.5 mm, in Type T **15** it measures 7.5 mm. The thick 'V' occurs at R. 1/5, R. 3/5, R. 4/5, R. 7/3, R. 8/3 and R. 8/6 in the case of Nos. T42a/T45a and at R. 1/2, R. 3/2, R. 4/2, R. 7/4, R. 8/1 and R. 8/4 in the case of Nos. T46a/T49a.

1903 (Mar). Postage stamps Nos. 114 and 117 additionally surch as Type T **16**.

T50 6d. on 2d. on 2d. bright mauve .... 90·00 90·00
a. Thick 'V' (as Type **33**) £180 £180
ab. Inverted '1' for 'I' (R. 7/1) £325 £325
T51 1s. on 3d. on 3d. ultramarine .... 75·00 75·00
a. Thick 'V' (as Type **33**) £150 £150
ab. Inverted '1' for 'I' (R. 7/1) £300 £300

The 'One Shilling' surcharge of No. T51 includes numerous wrong fount letters.

Orange Free State became a province of the Union of South Africa on 31 May 1910. Stamps used during the Interprovincial Period (1 June 1910–1931 August 1913) are listed under South Africa.

VI. TRANSVAAL

(*formerly* South African Republic)

From 1852 mail from the Transvaal was forwarded to the Cape of Good Hope, via the Orange Free State, by a post office at Potchefstroom. In 1859 the Volksraad voted to set up a regular postal service and arrangements were made for letters sent to the Cape and for overseas to be franked with Cape of Good Hope stamps.

The Potchefstroom postmaster placed his first order for these on 23 August 1859 and examples of all four triangular values are known postmarked there. From 1868 mail via the Orange Free State required franking with their issues also.

A similar arrangement covering mail sent overseas via Natal was in operation from 9 July 1873 until the first British Occupation. Such letters carried combinations of Transvaal stamps, paying the rate to Natal, and Natal issues for the overseas postage. Such Natal stamps were sold, but not postmarked, by Transvaal post offices.

PRICES FOR STAMPS ON COVER TO 1945

Nos. 1/6 are rare used on cover.

Nos. 7/80	*from* × 20
Nos. 86/155	*from* × 3
Nos. 156/162	*from* × 6
Nos. 163/169	*from* × 5
Nos. 170/225	*from* × 10
Nos. 226/234	*from* × 20
Nos. 235/237	—
Nos. 238/243	*from* × 12
Nos. 244/255	*from* × 4
Nos. 256/257	*from* × 6
Nos. 258/259	—
Nos. 260/276	*from* × 20
Nos. F1/F5	*from* × 5
Nos. D1/D7	*from* × 20
Nos. RO1/RO27	—

The issues for Pietersburg, Lydenburg, Rustenburg, Schweizer Renecke and Wolmaransstad are very rare when on cover.

1 (Eagle with spread wings)

2

3

(Typo Adolph Otto, Gustrow, Mecklenburg-Schwerin)

1870 (1 May). Thin paper, clear and distinct impressions.

(a) Imperf

1 **1** 1d. brown-lake £550
a. Orange-red £700 £700
2 6d. bright ultramarine £300 £300
a. Pale ultramarine £325 £325
3 1s. deep green £850 £850
a. *Tête-bêche* (pair) ....

(b) Fine roulette, 15½ to 16

4 **1** 1d. brown-lake £200
a. Brick-red £180
b. Orange-red £180
c. Vermilion £180
5 6d. bright ultramarine £160 £160
a. Pale ultramarine £170 £170
6 1s. deep green £325 £350
a. Yellow-green £275 £250
b. Emerald-green £200 £200

Examples of Nos. 1/6 may have been sold to dealers at some stage between their arrival in Transvaal during August 1869 and the sale of stamps to the public for postal purposes on 1 May 1870.

PLATES. The German printings of the 1d., 6d. and 1s. in T **1** were from two pairs of plates, each pair printing sheets of 80 in two panes of five horizontal rows of eight.

One pair of plates, used for Nos. 4*a*, 4*c*, 5*a* and 6/6*a*, produced stamps spaced 1¼ to 1½ mm apart with the rouletting close to the design on all four sides. The 1d. from these 'narrow' plates shows a gap in the outer frame line at the bottom right-hand corner. The second pair, used for Nos. 1/3, 4, 4*b*, 5/5*a* and 6*b*, had 2½ to 3½ mm between the stamps. These 'wide' plates were sent to the Transvaal in 1869 and were used there to produce either single or double pane printings until 1883.

The 6d. and 1s. 'wide' plates each had an inverted *cliché*. When printed these occurred on right-hand pane R. 4/1 of the 6d. and right-hand pane R. 1/1 of the 1s. These were never corrected and resulted in *tête-bêche* pairs of these values as late as 1883.

REPRINTS AND IMITATIONS. A number of unauthorised printings were made of these stamps by the German printer. Many of these can be identified by differences in the central arms, unusual colours or, in the case of the 1d., by an extra frame around the numeral tablets at top.

Genuine stamps always show the 'D' of 'EENDRAGT' higher than the remainder of the word, have no break in the border above 'DR' and depict the flagstaff at bottom right, behind 'MAGT', stopping short of the central shield. They also show the eagle's eye as a clear white circle. On the forgeries the eye is often blurred.

The most difficult of the reprints to detect is the 1s. yellow-green which was once regarded as genuine, but was subsequently identified, by J. N. Luff in *The Philatelic Record* 1911–12, as coming from an unauthorised plate of four. Stamps from this plate show either a white dot between 'EEN' and 'SHILLING' or a white flaw below the wagon pole.

(Typo M. J. Viljoen, Pretoria)

1870 (1 May–4 July).

I. Thin gummed paper from Germany. Impressions coarse and defective

(a) Imperf

8 **1** 1d. dull rose-red £130
a. Reddish pink £120
b. Carmine-red £100 £120
9 6d. dull ultramarine £425 £100
a. *Tête-bêche* (pair) ....

(b) Fine roulette, 15½ to 16

10 **1** 1d. carmine-red £850 £350
11 6d. dull ultramarine £300 £130
a. Imperf between (vert pair) £1300

(c) Wide roulette, 6½

12 **1** 1d. carmine-red .... — £1100

II. Thick, hard paper with thin yellow smooth gum (No. 15) or yellow streaky gum (others)

(a) Imperf

13 **1** 1d. pale rose-red £110
a. Carmine-red £110 £120
14 1s. yellow-green £200 £170
a. *Tête-bêche* (pair) £28000
b. Bisected (6d.) (*on cover*) .... † £2750

(b) Fine roulette, 15½ to 16

15 **1** 1d. carmine-red (24.5) £130
16 6d. ultramarine (10.5) £150 £150
a. *Tête-bêche* (pair) £35000 £25000
17 1s. yellow-green £850 £850

III. Medium paper, blotchy heavy printing and whitish gum. Fine roulette 15½ to 16 (4 July)

18 **1** 1d. rose-red £110 £130
a. Carmine-red .... 85·00 90·00
b. Crimson. From over-inked plate £190 £160
19 6d. ultramarine .... £140 95·00
a. *Tête-bêche* (pair) ....
b. Deep ultramarine. From over-inked plate £550 £200
20 1s. deep green £250 £120
a. From over-inked plate £650 £225

The rouletting machine producing the wide 6½ gauge was not introduced until 1875.

Nos. 18*b*, 19*b* and 20a were printed from badly over-inked plates giving heavy blobby impressions.

(Typo J. P. Borrius, Potchefstroom)

1870 (Sept)–**71**. Stout paper, but with colour often showing through, whitish gum.

(a) Imperf

21 **1** 1d. black £190 £170

(b) Fine roulette, 15½ to 16

22 **1** 1d. black .... 30·00 40·00
a. Grey-black .... 30·00 40·00
23 6d. blackish blue (7.71) .... £200 85·00
a. Dull blue £140 £110

(Typo Adolph Otto, Gustrow, Mecklenburg-Schwerin)

1871 (July). Thin paper, clear and distinct impressions. Fine roulette, 15½ to 16.

24 **2** 3d. pale reddish lilac .... 90·00 £100
a. Deep lilac £110 £120
b. Vert laid paper ....

No. 24 and later printings in the Transvaal were produced from a pair of plates in the same format as the 1869 issue. All genuine stamps have a small dot on the left leg of the eagle.

Imperforate examples in the issued shade, without the dot on eagle's leg, had been previously supplied by the printer, probably as essays, but were not issued for postal purposes. (*Price* £550 *unused*). They also exist *tête-bêche* (*Price for un pair* £3250).

Imperforate and rouletted stamps in other colours are reprints.

(Typo J. P. Borrius, Potchefstroom)

1872–74. Fine roulette, 15½ to 16.

(a) Thin transparent paper

25 **1** 1d. black £300 £750
26 1d. bright carmine .... £250 85·00
27 6d. ultramarine .... £190 65·00
28 1s. green .... £225 90·00

(b) Thinnish opaque paper, clear printing (Dec 1872)

29 **1** 1d. reddish pink .... £100 60·00
a. Carmine-red .... £100 60·00
30 **2** 3d. grey-lilac .... £150 70·00
31 **1** 6d. ultramarine .... £100 40·00
a. Pale ultramarine .... £110 45·00
32 1s. yellow-green .... £130 70·00
a. Green .... £130 70·00
aa. Bisected (6d.) (*on cover*) .... † £2750

(c) Thickish wove paper (1873–1874)

33 **1** 1d. dull rose £500 £110
a. Brownish rose £650 £150
b. Printed on both sides ....
34 6d. milky blue .... £225 70·00
a. Deep dull blue .... £130 55·00
aa. Imperf (pair) £900
ab. Imperf between (horiz pair) £950
ac. Wide roulette 6½ ....

(d) Very thick dense paper (1873–1874)

35 1d. dull rose £800 £190
a. Brownish rose £600 £170
36 6d. dull ultramarine .... £275 85·00
a. Bright ultramarine .... £300 85·00
37 1s. yellow-green £1300 £850

(Typo P. Davis & Son, Pietermaritzburg)

1874 (Sept). P 12½.

(a) Thin transparent paper

38 **1** 1d. pale brick-red .... £180 60·00
a. Brownish red .... £180 60·00
39 6d. deep blue .... £250 85·00

(b) Thicker opaque paper

40 **1** 1d. pale red .... £225 95·00
41 6d. blue .... £225 75·00
a. Imperf between (pair) ....
b. Deep blue .... £225 75·00

(Typo Adolph Otto, Gustrow, Mecklenburg-Schwerin)

1874 (Oct). Thin smooth paper, clearly printed. Fine roulette 15½ to 16.

42 **3** 6d. bright ultramarine .... 85·00 32·00
a. Bisected (3d.) (*on cover*) .... † £1800

Stamps in other shades of blue, brown or red, often on other types of paper, are reprints.

(Typo J. F. Celliers on behalf of Stamp Commission, Pretoria)

1875 (29 Apr)–**77**.

I. Very thin, soft opaque (semi-pelure) paper

(a) Imperf

43 **1** 1d. orange-red .... £180 70·00
a. Pin-perf £950 £450
44 **2** 3d. lilac .... £130 70·00
45 **1** 6d. blue .... £120 55·00
a. Milky blue .... £180 60·00
aa. *Tête-bêche* (pair) £21000
ab. Pin-perf .... — £450

(b) Fine roulette, 15½ to 16

46 **1** 1d. orange-red £650 £180
47 **2** 3d. lilac £700 £200
48 **1** 6d. blue £650 £190

(c) Wide roulette, 6½

49 **1** 1d. orange-red .... — £300
50 **2** 3d. lilac £850 £400
51 **1** 6d. blue .... — £200
a. Bright blue .... — £200
b. Milky blue .... — £200

II. Very thin, hard transparent (pelure) paper (1875–1876)

(a) Imperf

52 1 1d. brownish red 80·00 42·00
a. Orange-red 70·00 35·00
b. Dull red 75·00 65·00
ba. Pin-perf £750 £450
53 2 3d. lilac 80·00 55·00
a. Pin-perf — £475
b. Deep lilac 90·00 55·00
54 1 6d. pale blue 80·00 70·00
a. Blue 80·00 55·00
ab. *Tête-bêche* (pair)
ac. Pin-perf — £425
b. Deep blue 85·00 60·00

(b) Fine roulette 15½ to 16

55 1 1d. orange-red £450 £170
a. Brown-red £450 £170
56 2 3d. lilac £500 £180
57 1 6d. blue £225 £130
a. Deep blue £225 £150

(c) Wide roulette, 6½

58 1 1d. orange-red £1200 £250
a. Bright red — £250
59 2 3d. lilac £1100 £325
60 1 6d. deep blue £1200 £140

III. Stout hard-surfaced paper with smooth, nearly white, gum (1876)

(a) Imperf

61 1 1d. bright red 38·00 29·00
62 2 3d. lilac £475 £160
63 1 6d. bright blue £140 32·00
a. *Tête-bêche* (pair)
b. Pale blue £140 32·00
c. Deep blue (deep brown gum) 85·00 28·00
ca. *Tête-bêche* (pair) — £22000

(b) Fine roulette, 15½ to 16

64 1 1d. bright red £550 £200
65 2 3d. lilac £500
66 1 6d. bright blue £900 £130
a. Deep blue (deep brown gum) £750 £350

(c) Wide roulette, 6½

67 1 1d. bright red £750 £200
68 6d. pale blue — £300
a. Deep blue (deep brown gum) £800 £350

IV. Coarse, soft white paper (1876–1877)

(a) Imperf

69 1 1d. brick-red £250 75·00
70 6d. deep blue £300 £650
a. Milky blue £450 £140
71 1s. yellow-green £600 £180
a. Bisected (6d.) (*on cover*) † £2250

(b) Fine roulette, 15½ to 16

72 1 1d. brick-red — £500
73 6d. deep blue — £250
74 1s. yellow-green £1000 £450

(c) Wide roulette, 6½

75 1 1d. brick-red — £550
76 6d. deep blue — £1300
77 1s. yellow-green — £1400

(d) Fine × wide roulette

78 1 1d. brick-red £850 £425

V. Hard, thick, coarse yellowish paper (1876–1877)

79 1 1d. brick-red (imperf) — £450
80 1d. brick-red (*wide roulette*) — £600

The pin-perforated stamps have various gauges and were probably produced privately or by one or more post offices other than Pretoria.

On Nos. 63c/63ca, 66*a* and 68*a* the brown gum used was so intense that it caused staining of the paper which is still visible on used examples.

See also Nos. 171/174.

FIRST BRITISH OCCUPATION

By 1876 conditions in the Transvaal had deteriorated and the country was faced by economic collapse, native wars and internal dissension. In early 1877 Sir Theophilus Shepstone, appointed Special Commissioner to the South African Republic by the British Government, arrived in Pretoria and on 12 April annexed the Transvaal with the acquiesence of at least part of the European population.

V. R. V. R.

TRANSVAAL. TRANSVAAL.
(4) (5)

T **4** is the normal overprint, but Setting I No. 11 (R. 2/3) has a wider-spaced overprint as T **5**.

1877 (Apr). Optd with T **4** in red.

(a) Imperf

86 2 3d. lilac (*semi-pelure*) (No. 44) £1700 £400
a. Opt Type **5**
87 3d. lilac (*pelure*) (No. 53) £1700 £275
a. Opt Type **5** £8500 £2750
b. Opt on back £4000 £3750
c. Opt double, in red and in black £7500
88 1 6d. milky blue (No. 70) £2250 £275
a. Opt inverted — £5500
b. Opt double £5000 £1200
c. Opt Type **5** £9000 £3250
d. Deep blue — £350
89 1s. yellow-green (No. 71) £850 £275
a. Bisected (6d.) (*on cover*) † £2750
b. Opt inverted — £4750
c. Opt Type **5** £6000 £1700
d. *Tête-bêche* (pair)

(b) Fine roulette, 15½ to 16

90 2 3d. lilac (*pelure*) (No. 56) — £1700
91 1 6d. deep blue (No. 73) — £1800
92 1s. yellow-green (No. 74) £19000 £850
a. Opt Type **5**

(c) Wide roulette, 6½

93 2 3d. lilac (*pelure*) (No. 59) — £2500
a. Opt Type **5**
94 1 6d. deep blue (No. 76) — £2500
a. Opt Type **5**
95 1s. yellow-green (No. 77) £4500 £2250
a. Opt inverted — £6500

Nos. 88a, 89b and 95a occurred on the inverted *cliché* of the basic stamps.

1877 (June). Optd with T **4** in black.

I. Very thin, hard transparent (pelure) paper

96 1 1d. orange-red (imperf) (No. 52*a*) £375 £180
97 1d. orange-red (*fine roulette*) (No. 55) — £1100

II. Stout hard-surfaced paper with smooth, nearly white, gum

98 1 1d. bright red (imperf) (No. 61) 40·00 30·00
a. Opt inverted £650 £600
b. Opt Type **5** £850 £900
99 1d. bright red (*fine roulette*) (No. 64) £250 70·00
a. Opt inverted
b. Opt double — £1300
c. Imperf between (horiz pair) £1200
d. Imperf vert (horiz pair) £1200
100 1d. bright red (*wide roulette*) (No. 67) £800 £250
100*a* 1d. bright red (*fine×wide roulette*) (No. 78)

III. New ptgs on coarse, soft white paper

(a) Imperf

101 1 1d. brick-red (5.77) 40·00 32·00
a. Opt double — £1400
b. Opt Type **5** £900
102 2 3d. lilac £140 70·00
a. Opt inverted
b. Deep lilac £250 £120
103 1 6d. dull blue £160 42·00
a. Opt double £3750 £2250
b. Opt inverted £1600 £200
d. Opt Type **5** — £1300
da. Opt Type **5** inverted
e. Blue (bright to deep) £250 42·00
ea. Bright blue, opt inverted — £550
f. Pin-perf — £700
104 1s. yellow-green £200 80·00
a. Opt inverted £1500 £300
b. *Tête-bêche* (pair) £27000 £27000
c. Opt Type **5** £5500 £1700
d. Bisected (6d.) (*on cover*) † £2000

(b) Fine roulette, 15½ to 16

105 1 1d. brick-red £120 £110
a. Imperf horiz (vert strip of 3)
b. Imperf between (horiz pair) † £750
c. Imperf vert (horiz pair) £1500
106 2 3d. lilac £325 90·00
107 1 6d. dull blue £375 80·00
a. Opt inverted — £850
b. Opt Type **5** £6000
108 1s. yellow-green £400 £130
a. Opt inverted £1600 £600
b. Opt Type **5** — £3000

(c) Wide roulette, 6½

109 1 1d. brick-red £800 £180
a. Opt Type **5** — £1300
110 2 3d. lilac — £900
111 1 6d. dull blue — £1500
a. Opt inverted — £4750
112 1s. yellow-green £700 £180
a. Opt inverted £2250 £750

1877 (31 Aug). Optd with T **4** in black.

113 1 6d. blue/*rose* (imperf) £140 65·00
a. Bisected (3d.) (*on cover*) † —
b. Opt inverted £160 65·00
c. *Tête-bêche* (pair)
d. Opt omitted £3750 £2500
114 6d. blue/*rose* (*fine roulette*) £400 85·00
a. Opt inverted £700 85·00
b. *Tête-bêche* (pair)
c. Opt omitted
d. Bisected (3d.) (*on cover*) † —
115 6d. blue/*rose* (*wide roulette*)
a. Opt inverted — £800
b. Opt omitted

Nos. 113/115 were overprinted from a setting of 40 which was applied upright to one pane in each sheet and inverted on the other.

V. R. *V. R.*

Transvaal Transvaal
(6) (7)

1877 (28 Sept)–**79**. Optd with T **6** in black.

(a) Imperf

116 1 1d. red/*blue* 80·00 40·00
a. 'Transvral' (Right pane R. 2/3) £5500 £2500
b. Opt double £4250
c. Opt inverted £950 £475
d. Opt omitted
117 1d. red/*orange* (6.12.77) 38·00 28·00
a. Pin-perf
b. Printed both sides
c. Opt double £3750
d. Optd with Type **7** (15.4.78) 90·00 60·00
e. Pair. Nos. 117 and 117d £275
118 2 3d. mauve/*buff* (24.10.77) 85·00 38·00
a. Opt inverted — £850
b. Pin-perf
c. Bisected (1½d) (*on cover*) † —
d. Optd with Type **7** (15.4.78) £100 48·00
da. Pin-perf £850 £850
e. Pair. Nos. 118 and 118d £400
119 3d. mauve/*green* (18.4.79) £275 55·00
a. Pin-perf
b. Opt inverted — £2500
c. Opt double
d. Printed both sides † —
e. Optd with Type **7** £225 48·00
ea. Opt inverted — £2500
eb. Printed both sides — £1200
f. Opt omitted — £4000
g. Pair. Nos. 119 and 119e £850
120 1 6d. blue/*green* (27.11.77) £150 48·00
a. Deep blue/green £160 50·00
c. Small 'v' in 'Transvaal' (Left pane R. 5/2) — £850
d. 'V..R.' (Right pane R. 3/4) — £850
e. *Tête-bêche* (pair) — £22000
f. Opt inverted — £1400
g. Pin-perf
h. Bisected (3d.) (*on cover*) † —
121 6d. blue/*blue* (20.3.78) £110 38·00
a. *Tête-bêche* (pair)
b. Opt inverted — £1400
c. Opt omitted — £2500
d. Opt double — £3750
e. Pin-perf
f. Bisected (3d.) (*on cover*) † £1100
g. Optd with Type **7** £225 40·00
ga. *Tête-bêche* (pair) £19000
gb. Opt inverted — £850
gc. Bisected (3d.) (*on cover*) † —
h. Pair. Nos. 121 and 121g £650

(b) Fine roulette, 15½ to 16

122 1 1d. red/*blue* £150 48·00
a. 'Transvral' (Right pane R. 2/3) — £3000
123 1d. red/*orange* (6.12.77) 50·00 38·00
a. Imperf between (pair) £700
b. Optd with Type **7** (15.4.78) £225 £160
c. Pair. Nos. 123 and 123b £600
124 2 3d. mauve/*buff* (24.10.77) £150 38·00
a. Imperf horiz (vert pair) £950
b. Opt inverted — £3500
c. Optd with Type **7** (15.4.78) £275 £150
ca. Imperf between (pair)
d. Pair. Nos. 124 and 124c £900
125 3d. mauve/*green* (18.4.79) £850 £225
a. Optd with Type **7** £850 £225
b. Pair. Nos. 125 and 125a
126 1 6d. blue/*green* (27.11.77) £130 38·00
a. 'V..R' (Right pane R. 3/4) — £1400
b. *Tête-bêche* (pair)
c. Opt inverted — £800
d. Opt omitted — £4250
e. Bisected (3d.) (*on cover*) † £950
127 6d. blue/*blue* (20.3.78) £375 75·00
a. Opt inverted — £1100
b. Opt omitted — £3750
c. Imperf between (pair)
d. Bisected (3d.) (*on cover*) † £1000
e. Optd with Type **7** £600 £150
ea. Opt inverted — £1400

(c) Wide roulette, 6¼

128 1 1d. red/*orange* (15.4.78) £350 £130
a. Optd with Type **7** — £375
129 2 3d. mauve/*buff* (24.10.77) — £130
a. Optd with Type **7** (15.4.78) — £425
130 3d. mauve/*green* (18.4.79) £850 £375
a. Optd with Type **7** — £400
131 1 6d. blue/*green* (27.11.77) — £1400
132 6d. blue/*blue* (20.3.78) — £375
a. Opt inverted
b. Opt with Type **7** — £425
ba. Opt inverted

(d) Fine×wide roulette

132c 1 1d. red/*orange* £850

Nos. 116/132c were overprinted from various settings covering sheets of 80 or panes of 40 (8×5). Initially these settings contained T **6** only, but from March 1878 settings also contained examples of T **7**. Details of these mixed settings are as follows:

1d. red/*orange* (sheets of 80): all T **6** except for 16 T **7**.
3d. mauve/*buff* (panes of 40): 16 T **7**.
3d. mauve/*green* (panes of 40): uncertain, some panes at least contained 27 T **7**.
6d. blue/*blue* (sheets of 80): either 24 or 27 T **7**.

9

(Recess B.W.)

1878 (26 Aug)–**80**. P 14, 14½.

133 9 ½d. vermilion (1.9.80) 32·00 95·00
134 1d. pale red-brown 23·00 7·50
a. Brown-red 23·00 7·00
135 3d. dull rose (25.11.78) 38·00 10·00
a. Claret 42·00 12·00
136 4d. sage-green 48·00 12·00
137 6d. olive-black (25.11.78) 21·00 10·00
a. Black-brown 23·00 7·50
138 1s. green (25.11.78) £180 55·00
139 2s. blue (25.11.78) £325 £100
133/139 *Set of 7* £600 £250

The ½d. is printed on paper bearing the sheet watermark 'R TURNER/ CHAFFORD MILLS' in double-lined block capitals. Other values are generally on unwatermarked paper, but examples of the 1s. are known with the same watermark as the ½d.

The above prices are for examples perforated on all four sides. Stamps from margins of sheets, with perforations absent on one or two sides, can be supplied for about 30% less.

The used price quoted for No. 139 is for an example with telegraphic cancel, a 23.5 mm circular datestamp of Pretoria (or more rarely Heidelberg or Standerton). Postally used examples are worth much more.

1 Penny (10) 1 Penny (11) 1 Penny (12)

1 Penny (13) 1 Penny (14)

1 PENNY (15) *1 Penny* (16)

1879 (22 Apr). No. 137*a* surch with Types **10** to **16** in black.

No.	Type	Description	Unused	Used
140	**10**	1d. on 6d.	£110	48·00
		a. Surch in red	£350	£180
141	**11**	1d. on 6d.	£300	90·00
		a. Surch in red	£800	£400
142	**12**	1d. on 6d.	£300	90·00
		a. Surch in red	£800	£400
143	**13**	1d. on 6d.	£130	60·00
		a. Surch double		
		b. Surch in red	£400	£200
144	**14**	1d. on 6d.	£750	£180
		a. Surch in red	£6500	£1700
145	**15**	1d. on 6d.	65·00	27·00
		a. Surch in red	£200	90·00
146	**16**	1d. on 6d.	£275	85·00
		a. Surch in red	£750	£375

Nos. 140/146 were surcharged from a setting of 60 containing 11 examples of T **10**, four of T **11**, four of T **12**, nine of T **13**, two of T **14** (although there may have been only one in the first two ptgs), 25 of T **15** and five of T **16**.

The red surcharges may have been produced first.

V. R. V. R.

Transvaal (**16a**) Transvaal Small 'T' (R. 2/8, 3/8, 4/8, 5/8 on right pane of 1d. and left pane of 3d.)

1879 (Aug–Sept). Optd with T **16a** in black.

No.	Type	Description	Unused	Used
		(a) Imperf		
147	**1**	1d. red/*yellow*	70·00	45·00
		a. Small 'T'	£375	£250
		b. Red/orange	70·00	38·00
		ba. Small 'T'	£350	£200
148	**2**	3d. mauve/*green* (9.79)	60·00	32·00
		a. Small 'T'	£300	£130
149		3d. mauve/*blue* (9.79)	70·00	38·00
		a. Small 'T'	£350	£130
		(b) Fine roulette 15½ to 16		
150	**1**	1d. red/*yellow*	£425	£275
		a. Small 'T'	£1300	£800
		b. Red/orange	£950	£450
		ba. Small 'T'	£2500	
151	**2**	3d. mauve/*green*	£900	£325
		a. Small 'T'	—	£1000
152		3d. mauve/*blue*	—	£250
		a. Small 'T'	—	£800
		(c) Wide roulette 6½		
153	**1**	1d. red/*yellow*	£850	£750
		a. Small 'T'		
		b. Red/orange	£1800	£1400
154	**2**	3d. mauve/*green*	£1300	£750
		a. Small 'T'		
155		3d. mauve/*blue*	—	£850
		(d) Pin-perf about 17		
156	**1**	1d. red/*yellow*	—	£850
		a. Small 'T'		
157	**2**	3d. mauve/*blue*	—	£1400

SECOND REPUBLIC

Following the first Boer War the independence of the South African Republic was recognised by the Convention of Pretoria from 8 August 1881.

Nos. 133/139 remained valid and some values were available for postage until 1885.

EEN PENNY (**17**)

1882 (11 Aug). No. 136 surch with T **17**.

No.	Type	Description	Unused	Used
170	**9**	1d. on 4d. sage-green	25·00	8·50
		a. Surch inverted	£350	£200

Used examples of a similar, but larger, surcharge (width 20 *mm*) are known. These were previously considered to be forgeries, but it is now believed that some, at least, may represent a trial printing of the 'EEN PENNY' surcharge.

(Typo J. F. Celliers)

1883 (20 Feb–3 Aug). Re-issue of Types **1** and **2**. P 12.

No.	Type	Description	Unused	Used
171	**1**	1d. grey (*to black*) (5.4)	9·00	3·50
		a. Imperf vert (horiz pair)	£350	
		b. Imperf horiz (vert pair)	£650	£475
172	**2**	3d. grey-black (*to black*)/*rose*	38·00	8·50
		a. Bisected (1d.) (*on cover*)	†	£800
173		3d. pale red (7.5)	18·00	3·75
		a. Bisected (1d.) (*on cover*)	†	£800
		b. Imperf horiz (vert pair)	†	£1200
		c. Chestnut	38·00	7·50
		ca. Imperf between (horiz pair)	†	—
		d. Vermilion	38·00	8·00
174	**1**	1s. green (*to deep*) (3.8)	90·00	8·50
		a. Bisected (6d.) (*on cover*)	†	£600
		b. *Tête-bêche* (pair)	£1300	£180

Reprints are known of Nos. 172, 173, 173b and 173c. The paper of the first is *bright rose* in place of *dull rose*, and the impression is brownish black in place of grey-black to deep black. The reprints on white paper have the paper thinner than the originals, and the gum yellowish instead of white. The colour is a dull deep orange-red.

The used price quoted for No. 174b is for an example with telegraphic cancel. Postally used examples are worth much more. (See note below No. 139).

18

PERFORATIONS. Stamps perforated 11½×12 come from the first vertical row of sheets of the initial printing otherwise perforated 12½×12.

REPRINTS. Reprints of the general issues 1885–1893, 1894–1895, 1895–1896 and 1896–1897 exist in large quantities produced using the original plates from 1911 onwards. They cannot readily be distinguished from genuine originals except by comparison with used stamps, but the following general characteristics may be noted. The reprints are all perf 12½, large holes; the paper is whiter and thinner than that usually employed for the originals and their colours lack the lustre of those of the genuine stamps.

Forged surcharges have been made on these reprints.

(Des J. Vurtheim. Typo Enschedé)

1885 (13 Mar)–**93**. P 12½.

No.	Type	Description	Unused	Used
175	**18**	½d. grey (30.3.85)	2·50	10
		a. Perf 13½	9·50	1·75
		b. Perf 12½×12	4·00	10
		ba. Perf 11½×12	35·00	9·00
176		1d. carmine	2·25	10
		a. Perf 12½×12	2·25	10
		aa. Perf 11½×12	22·00	3·75
		b. Rose	2·00	10
		ba. Perf 12½×12	2·00	10
177		2d. brown-purple (P 12½×12) (9.85)	3·50	4·75
178		2d. olive-bistre (14.4.87)	3·50	10
		a. Perf 12½×12	5·50	10
179		2½d. mauve (*to bright*) (8.93)	4·50	55
180		3d. mauve (*to bright*)	5·00	3·25
		a. Perf 12½×12	10·00	2·75
		aa. Perf 11½×12	40·00	20·00
181		4d. bronze-green	7·00	2·25
		a. Perf 13½	14·00	2·75
		b. Perf 12½×12	20·00	2·25
		ba. Perf 11½×12	£200	80·00
182		6d. pale dull blue	5·00	4·50
		a. Perf 13½	8·00	2·50
		b. Perf 12½×12	10·00	1·00
		ba. Perf 11½×12		
183		1s. yellow-green	4·75	2·50
		a. Perf 13½	40·00	7·50
		b. Perf 12½×12	16·00	1·50
184		2s.6d. orange-buff (*to buff*) (2.12.85)	17·00	4·25
		a. Perf 12½×12	27·00	10·00
185		5s. slate (2.12.85)	10·00	7·50
		a. Perf 12½×12	50·00	12·00
186		10s. dull chestnut (2.12.85)	45·00	17·00
		a. Yellow-brown (1891)		
187		£5 deep green (3.92)*	£3250	£190
		s. Optd 'Monster'	£170	

Singles of the 6d. pale dull blue imperforate have been reported used in 1893.

* Most examples of No. 187 on the market are either forgeries or reprints.

HALVE PENNY (**19**)

1885 (22 May–Aug). Surch with T **19**. Reading up or down.

No.	Type	Description	Unused	Used
188	**2**	½d. on 3d. (No. 173)	15·00	15·00
189	**1**	½d. on 1s. (No. 174) (8.85)	45·00	70·00
		a. *Tête-bêche* (pair)	£1000	£450

Nos. 188/189 were surcharged by a setting of 40. After the left pane had been surcharged reading down, the sheets were turned so that the right pane had the surcharges reading up.

HALVE PENNY Z.A.R (**20**) TWEE PENCE Z. A. R. (**21**) HALVE PENNY (**22**)

1885 (1 Sept). No. 137*a* surch with Types **20/21** in red.

No.	Type	Description	Unused	Used
190	**9**	½d. on 6d. black-brown	85·00	£120
191		2d. on 6d. black-brown	20·00	25·00

1885 (28 Sept). No. 180a surch with T **22**.

No.	Type	Description	Unused	Used
192	**18**	½d. on 3d. mauve	10·00	10·00
		a. 'PRNNY' (R. 6/6)	65·00	85·00
		b. 2nd 'N' inverted (R. 3/8)	£110	£130
		c. Perf 11½×12	20·00	20·00

2d (**23**) 2d (**24**)

1887 (15 Jan). No. 180a surch with Types **23/24**.

No.	Type	Description	Unused	Used
193	**18**	2d. on 3d. mauve (Type **23**)	16·00	13·00
		a. Surch double	—	£400
		b. Perf 11½×12	40·00	28·00
194		2d. on 3d. mauve (Type **24**)	3·00	6·00
		a. Surch double	£225	£225
		b. Perf 11½×12	10·00	16·00

Nos. 193/194 were surcharged from the same setting of 60 (10×6) which showed T **24** on the top five horizontal rows and T **23** on the sixth horizontal row.

Halve Penny (**25**) 1 Penny (**26**)

2½ Pence (**27**) 2½ Pence (**28**)

Two types of surcharge:
A. Vertical distance between bars 12½ mm.
B. Distance 13½ mm.

1893. T **18** surch. P 12½.

No.	Type	Description	Unused	Used
		(a) In red		
195	**25**	½d. on 2d. olive-bistre (A) (27.5)	1·50	3·50
		a. Surch inverted	3·25	4·00
		b. Surch Type B	2·25	4·25
		ba. Surch inverted	6·50	13·00
		(b) In black		
196	**25**	½d. on 2d. olive-bistre (A) (2.7)	1·75	3·50
		a. Surch inverted	5·00	6·00
		b. Extra surch on back inverted	£170	
		c. Surch Type B	2·50	4·50
		ca. Surch inverted	22·00	19·00
		cb. Extra surch on back inverted	£300	
197	**26**	1d. on 6d. blue (A) (26.1)	2·75	2·50
		a. Surch double	60·00	48·00
		b. Surch inverted	3·25	3·50
		c. Surch treble		
		d. Surch Type B	3·50	3·50
		da. Surch inverted	7·00	5·50
		db. Surch double	—	90·00
		e. Pair, one without surch	£300	
198	**27**	2½d. on 1s. green (A) (2.1)	3·25	8·00
		a. '2/½d' for '2½' (R. 1/10)	50·00	90·00
		b. Surch inverted	8·50	9·00
		ba. Surch inverted and '2/½d' for '2½'	£375	£325
		c. Extra surch on back inverted	£475	£475
		d. Surch double, one inverted	£750	
		e. Surch Type B	4·00	10·00
		ea. Surch inverted	11·00	20·00
199	**28**	2½d. on 1s. green (A) (24.6)	12·00	9·50
		a. Surch double	55·00	50·00
		b. Surch inverted	12·00	12·00
		c. Surch Type B	15·00	15·00
		ca. Surch double	90·00	£100
		cb. Surch inverted	24·00	24·00

Surcharge Types **25/28** all show a similar setting of the horizontal bars at top and bottom. On horizontal rows 1 to 4 and 6, the bars are 12½ mm apart and on row 5 the distance is 13½ mm.

29 (Wagon with shafts) **30** (Wagon with pole)

1894 (July). P 12½.

No.	Type	Description	Unused	Used
200	**29**	½d. grey	2·50	1·50
201		1d. carmine	4·00	20
202		2d. olive-bistre	4·00	30
203		6d. pale dull blue	4·50	1·00
204		1s. yellow-green	24·00	32·00

For note *re* reprints, see below T **18**.

1895 (16 Mar)–**96**. P 12½.

No.	Type	Description	Unused	Used
205	**30**	½d. pearl-grey (1895)	2·25	10
		a. Lilac-grey	2·25	10
206		1d. rose-red	2·25	10
207		2d. olive-bistre (1895)	2·75	30
208		3d. mauve (1895)	3·75	1·25
209		4d. olive-black (1895)	4·00	1·00
210		6d. pale dull blue (1895)	4·00	1·00
211		1s. yellow-green (18.3.95)	5·00	1·50
212		5s. slate (1896)	24·00	45·00
212*a*		10s. pale chestnut (1896)	24·00	9·00
		205s/208s, 211s Optd 'Monster' *Set of 5*	£170	

For note *re* reprints, see below T **18**.

Halve Penny (**31**)

1d. (**32**—Round dot) 1d. (**32a**—Square dot)

1895 (July–Aug). Nos. 211 and 179 surch with Types **31/32**.
213 **30** ½d. on 1s. green (R.) 2·50 60
a. Surch spaced 4·00 2·50
b. 'Pennij' for 'Penny' (R. 6/6) 70·00 80·00
c. Surch inverted 5·50 5·00
d. Surch double 75·00 £100
214 **18** 1d. on 2½d. bright mauve (G.) 50 30
a. Surch inverted 23·00 15·00
b. Surch double 75·00 75·00
c. Surch on back only 85·00
d. Surch Type **32a** 1·75 1·75
da. Surch inverted 75·00
e. Surch treble £600

The normal space between 'Penny' and the bars is 3 mm. On No. 213a, which comes from the fifth horizontal row of the setting, this is increased to 4 mm. Copies may be found in which one or both of the bars have failed to print.

T **32a** with square stop occurred on R. 3/3-4, 3/6-8, 4/4-5, 4/7-8, 4/10, 6/3, 6/7-8 and 6/10 of the setting of 60.

33

34

1895 (July). Fiscal stamp optd 'POSTZEGEL'. P 11½.
215 **33** 6d. bright rose (G.) 3·25 3·00
a. Imperf between (pair)
b. Opt inverted

(Litho The Press Printing and Publishing Works, Pretoria)

1895 (6 Sept). Introduction of Penny Postage. P 11.
215*c* **34** 1d. red (pale to deep) 2·75 3·25
ca. Imperf between (pair) £225 £250
cb. Imperf vert (horiz pair)
cc. Imperf (pair)

1896–97. P 12½.
216 **30** ½d. green (1896) 1·75 10
217 1d. rose-red and green (1896) 1·75 10
218 2d. brown and green (2.97) 2·00 20
219 2½d. dull blue and green (6.96) 3·00 30
220 3d. purple and green (3.97) 3·25 3·00
221 4d. sage-green and green (3.97) 3·25 4·00
222 6d. lilac and green (11.96) 3·00 2·75
223 1s. ochre and green (3.96) 2·50 1·50
224 2s.6d. dull violet and green (6.96) 3·75 4·50

For note *re* reprints, see below T **18**.

SECOND BRITISH OCCUPATION

The Second Boer War began on 11 October 1899 and was concluded by the Peace of Vereeniging on 31 May 1902. Pretoria was occupied by the British on 5 June 1900 and a civilian postal service began operating 13 days later.

FORGERIES. The forgeries of the 'V.R.I.' and 'E.R.I.' overprints most often met with can be recognised by the fact that the type used is perfect and the three stops are always in alignment with the bottom of the letters. In the genuine overprints, which were made from old type, it is impossible to find all three letters perfect and all three stops perfect and in exact alignment with the bottom of the letters.

V. R. I. (35)　　**E. R. I.** (36)　　**E. R. I. Half Penny** (37)

1900 (18 June). Optd with T **35**.
226 **30** ½d. green 40 1·75
a. No stop after 'V' 14·00 18·00
b. No stop after 'R' 11·00 14·00
c. No stop after 'I' 9·50 13·00
d. Opt inverted 13·00 19·00
e. Opt double
f. 'V.I.R.' (R. 4/4) £850
227 1d. rose-red and green 75 1·75
a. No stop after 'V' 15·00 19·00
b. No stop after 'R' 12·00 15·00
c. No stop after 'I' 9·00 12·00
d. Opt inverted 14·00 24·00
e. Opt double 90·00 £120
f. No stops after 'R' and 'I' 90·00 90·00
g. Opt omitted (in pair with normal) £325
228 2d. brown and green 4·50 4·25
a. No stop after 'V' 40·00 48·00
c. No stop after 'I' 48·00 50·00
d. Opt inverted 26·00 30·00
e. Opt double
f. 'V.I.R.' (R. 4/4) £900 £950
g. Opt albino
229 2½d. dull blue and green 1·25 3·50
a. No stop after 'V' 22·00 30·00
b. No stop after 'R' 50·00 70·00
c. No stop after 'I' 18·00 24·00
d. Opt inverted 16·00 18·00
230 3d. purple and green 1·75 3·75
a. No stop after 'V' 27·00 40·00
b. No stop after 'R' 55·00 70·00
c. No stop after 'I' 38·00 50·00
d. Opt inverted 90·00 £100
231 4d. sage-green and green 4·00 4·50
a. No stop after 'V' 50·00 50·00
b. No stop after 'R' 70·00 70·00
c. No stop after 'I' 45·00 45·00
d. Opt inverted 35·00 40·00
f. 'V.I.R.' (R. 4/4) £900
232 6d. lilac and green 4·25 3·50
a. No stop after 'V' 28·00 28·00
b. No stop after 'R' 38·00 38·00
c. No stop after 'I' 38·00 38·00
d. Opt inverted 40·00 48·00
233 1s. ochre and green 4·25 5·50
a. No stop after 'V' 30·00 38·00
b. No stop after 'R' 30·00 38·00
c. No stop after 'I' 55·00 60·00
d. Opt inverted 55·00 60·00
e. Opt double 95·00 £100
234 2s.6d. dull violet and green 5·00 18·00
a. No stop after 'V' 60·00
b. No stop after 'R' £100
c. No stop after 'I' — £500
235 5s. slate 11·00 27·00
a. No stop after 'V' £170
236 10s. pale chestnut 14·00 29·00
a. No stop after 'V' £170
c. No stop after 'I' £170
237 **18** £5 deep green* £2000 £800
a. No stop after 'V'
234s/237s Handstamped 'SPECIMEN' *Set of 4* £225

* Many examples of No. 237 on the market are forgeries and the stamps should only be purchased if accompanied by a recent expert committee certificate.

The error 'V.I.R.' occurred on R. 4/4 in the first batch of stamps to be overprinted—a few sheets of the ½d., 2d. and 4d. The error was then corrected and stamps showing it are very rare. The corrected overprint shows the 'I' dropped by 0.75mm. This variety is known on all values apart from the £5, but was later corrected.

A number of different settings were used to apply the overprint to Nos. 226/237. The missing stop varieties listed above developed during overprinting and occur on different positions in the various settings.

1901 (Jan)–**02**. Optd with T **36**.
238 **30** ½d. green 50 2·75
a. Opt double
239 1d. rose-red and green (20.3.01) 50 10
a. 'E.' of opt omitted 80·00
240 3d. purple and green (6.02) 2·25 4·75
241 4d. sage-green and green (6.02) 2·75 11·00
242 2s.6d. dull violet and green (10.02) 15·00 42·00

1901 (July). Surch with T **37**.
243 **30** ½d. on 2d. brown and green 65 2·00
a. No stop after 'E' (R. 4/6) 50·00 65·00

38 (POSTAGE REVENUE)

39 (POSTAGE POSTAGE)

(Typo D.L.R.)

1902 (1 Apr–17 Dec). Wmk Crown CA. P 14.
244 **38** ½d. black and bluish green 2·75 20
w. Wmk inverted £170 £100
245 1d. black and carmine 1·50 15
w. Wmk inverted £130 85·00
246 2d. black and purple 8·50 1·50
w. Wmk inverted † £250
247 2½d. black and blue 15·00 2·50
w. Wmk inverted £100 60·00
248 3d. black and sage-green (17.12.02) 19·00 2·25
249 4d. black and brown (17.12.02) 19·00 3·50
250 6d. black and orange-brown 4·50 1·50
251 1s. black and sage-green 20·00 27·00
252 2s. black and brown 75·00 85·00
253 **39** 2s.6d. magenta and black 20·00 19·00
254 5s. black and purple/*yellow* 45·00 50·00
255 10s. black and purple/*red* 85·00 50·00
244/255 *Set of 12* £275 £200
244s/255s (*inc* 247ws) Optd 'SPECIMEN' *Set of 12* £200

The colour of the 'black' centres varies from brownish grey or grey to black.

1903 (1 Feb). Wmk Crown CA. P 14.
256 **39** 1s. grey-black and red-brown 20·00 6·50
257 2s. grey-black and yellow 22·00 26·00
258 £1 green and violet £375 £225
259 £5 orange-brown and violet £2250 £950
256s/259s Optd 'SPECIMEN' *Set of 4* £275

1904–09. Ordinary paper. Wmk Mult Crown CA. P 14.
260 **38** ½d. black and bluish green 14·00 3·00
w. Wmk inverted £250 £110
y. Wmk inverted and reversed £190 80·00
261 1d. black and carmine 13·00 2·00
262 2d. black and purple (*chalk-surfaced paper*) (1906) 30·00 2·00
263 2½d. black and blue (1905) 30·00 15·00
aw. Wmk inverted £190 £130
b. Chalk-surfaced paper 30·00 9·00
264 3d. black and sage-green (*chalk-surfaced paper*) (1906) 4·25 50
265 4d. black and brown (*chalk-surfaced paper*) (1906) 7·00 70
w. Wmk inverted £190 £110
266 6d. black and orange (1905) 20·00 2·00
a. Chalk-surfaced paper. *Black and brown-orange* (1906) 6·50 50
w. Wmk inverted £225 £120
267 **39** 1s. black and red-brown (1905) 16·00 50
268 2s. black and yellow (1906) 35·00 17·00
269 2s.6d. magenta and black (1909) 60·00 12·00
270 5s. black and purple/*yellow* 35·00 1·75
271 10s. black and purple/*red* (1907) 90·00 5·00
272 £1 green and violet (1908) £425 50·00
a. Chalk-surfaced paper £300 25·00
260/272a *Set of 13* £550 70·00

There is considerable variation in the 'black' centres as in the previous issue.

1905–09. Wmk Mult Crown CA. P 14.
273 **38** ½d. yellow-green 4·00 10
a. Deep green (1908) 4·00 20
w. Wmk inverted £250 £130
274 1d. scarlet 1·25 10
aw. Wmk inverted — £325
b. Error. Wmk Cabled Anchor, Type **13** of Cape of Good Hope (3.3.06*) — £325
275 2d. purple (1909) 5·00 1·50
276 2½d. bright blue (1909) 25·00 15·00
273/276 *Set of 4* 35·00 15·00
273s/276s Optd 'SPECIMEN' *Set of 4* £110

* Earliest known date of use.

The monocoloured ½d. and 1d. are printed from new combined plates. These show a slight alteration in that the frame does not touch the crown.

1909. Prepared for use but not issued. Wmk Mult Crown CA. P 14.
277s **38** 2d. grey (optd 'SPECIMEN') £300

Although this stamp was distributed in 'SPECIMEN' form by the UPU, the entire supply sent to Transvaal was destroyed.

The ½d., 1d. and 2d. exist from coils constructed from normal sheets for use in stamp machines introduced in 1911. These coils were originally joined horizontally but the 1d. was subsequently issued joined vertically.

STAMP BOOKLETS

1905 (July). Black on red cover showing arms. Stapled.
SB1 2s.7d. booklet containing 30×1d. (No. 261) in blocks of 6 £3250

1905. Black on red cover. Stapled.
SB2 2s.7d. booklet containing 30×1d. (No. 274) in blocks of 6 £3500

1909. Black on red cover. Stapled.
SB3 2s.6d. booklet containing 10×½d. (No. 273) in block of 6 and block of 4, and 24×1d. (No. 274) in blocks of 6 £4000

Stocks of No. SB3 were supplied containing 12 examples of the ½d., it being intended that the postal clerks would remove two stamps before the booklets were sold. In some instances this did not occur.

POSTAL FISCAL STAMPS

1900–02. Fiscal stamps as in T **33**, but optd with T **35**. P 11½.
F1 1d. pale blue — 45·00
F2 6d. dull carmine — 75·00
F3 1s. olive-bistre — 90·00
F4 1s.6d. brown — £120
F5 2s.6d. dull purple — £150

Nos. F1/F5, previously listed as Nos. 1/5 of Volksrust, are fiscal issues which are known postally used from various Transvaal post offices between June 1900 and June 1902.

Nos. F1/F5, and higher values to £5, were also used on telegrams.

POSTAGE DUE STAMPS

D 1

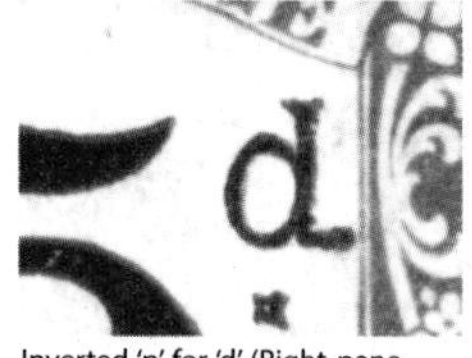
Inverted 'p' for 'd' (Right pane R. 10/6)

(Typo D.L.R.)

1907. Wmk Mult Crown CA. P 14.
D1 **D 1** ½d. black and blue-green 3·50 1·25
D2 1d. black and scarlet 4·00 85
D3 2d. brown-orange 7·50 1·25
D4 3d. black and blue 7·50 7·00
D5 5d. black and violet 4·00 12·00
a. Inverted 'p' for 'd' 60·00
D6 6d. black and red-brown 4·25 12·00
D7 1s. scarlet and black 18·00 13·00
D1/D7 *Set of 7* 42·00 42·00

RAILWAY OFFICIAL STAMPS

The following stamps were provided for use on official correspondence of the Central Southern Africa Railways.

RO **1**

1904. Nos, 244/245 stencil-cut as T RO **1** at CSAR's Departmental Printing Office, Germiston.
RO1 ½d. grey-black and bluish green † £750
RO2 1d. grey-black and carmine † £750

Contemporary reports exist of these stamps with 'CSAR' stencil-cut in a single line, but no examples are known. The stencil-cut exists sideways on No. RO1 and inverted on No. RO2. They were probably trials, only used at CSAR's head office in Johannesburg.

1905 (Feb). Nos. 244/246, 228/250 and 256 optd with T RO **1** of Orange River Colony at CSAR's Departmental Printing Office, Germiston.
RO3 ½d. grey-black and bluish green 50·00 15·00
RO4 1d. grey-black and carmine 50·00 10·00
a. Opt double £150 —
RO5 2d. grey-black and purple £100 50·00
RO6 3d. grey-black and sage-green £150 75·00
RO7 4d. grey-black and brown £150 75·00
RO8 6d. black and orange brown £200 £100
RO9 1s. bluish grey and red-brown £350 £250

1905. As Nos. RO3/RO04 but Wmk Multiple Crown CA.

RO10	½d. grey-black and bluish green	75·00	45·00
RO11	1d. grey-black and carmine	75·00	45·00

The overprint on Nos. RO3/RO11 was applied in a setting of 120 and was normally placed either at the top or the bottom of the stamp, although central placings are known. The stamps were withdrawn on 13 October 1905, but examples of genuine late usage have been recorded. Dangerous forgeries, including a 2½d. duty, exist.

1907. No. 246 punctured with T RO **2** of Orange River Colony.

RO12	2d. black and purple	—	£100

1907. Nos, 262, 264/267, and 273/275 punctured with T RO **2** of Orange River Colony.

RO13	2d. black and purple	—	50·00
RO14	3d. black and sage-green	—	£100
RO15	4d. black and brown	—	£120
RO16	6d. black and orange	—	£120
RO17	1s. black and red-brown		

1907. No. 273/275 punctured with T RO **2** of Orange River Colony.

RO18	½d. yellow-green	—	20·00
RO19	1d. scarlet	—	15·00
RO20	2d. purple	—	75·00

RO **2**

1910 (Sept). Nos, 262, 264/267, and 273/275 punctured with T RO **2**.

RO21	½d. yellow-green	—	25·00
RO22	1d. scarlet	—	25·00
RO23	2d. black and purple		
RO24	2d. purple		
RO25	3d. black and sage-green		
RO26	4d. black and brown		
RO27	6d. black and brown-orange		
RO28	1s. black and red-brown		

Nos. RO21/RO27 were produced by removing the 'C' from the perforating heads used to prepare Nos. RO12/RO20.

Forgeries of the punctured initials stamps are known but the height of the 'CS/AR' or 'S/AR' is 17-17.5 mm, compared with 13.5 mm of genuine examples.

Nos. RO12/RO27 were withdrawn on 1 April 1912.

TELEGRAPH STAMPS

In the 1880s Queen's Head postage stamps (T **9**) and fiscal stamps were used for the prepayment of telegraph communication. Once these were used up it would seem that just postage stamps were used until the British occupation in 1900. In the early period of the occupation, postage stamps overprinted 'V.R.I.' up to the value of 2s.6d. and high value fiscal stamps similarly overprinted were used for telegraph purposes (Cape of Good Hope 'Hope standing' 6d. and 1s. fiscal stamps overprinted 'TRANSVAAL' were also used). The following stamps were overprinted or surcharged specifically for telegraphic use.

Transvaal
Telegraphs.
(T **1**)

Transvaal
Telegraphs
ONE
Shilling.
(T **2**)

Transvaal
Telegraphs.
FIVE
Shillings.
(T **3**)

Transvaal
Telegraphs
(T **4**)

1901 (Sept–Oct). Nos. 217, 222 and 224 optd as Type T **1** or optd and surch as Type T **2**.

T1	1d. rose-red and green (10.01)	45·00	30·00
T2	6d. lilac and green (10.01)	70·00	40·00
T3	1s. on 2s.6d. dull violet and green	45·00	30·00
T4	2s.6d. dull violet and green (10.01)	70·00	40·00

Forgeries of T14 exist, used examples should have a clear 'Army Telegraphs' cancellation.

1902. Fiscal stamp (as T **33**) optd T **35** and surch as Type T **3**. Perf 11, 11×11½ or 11½.

T5	5s. on £2 red-brown (*shades*)	—	£275

1902 (June?). No 222 optd T **36** and handstamped as Type T **4**.

T6	6d. lilac and green	£400	£250

1902 (June?). Nos. 217 and 222 handstamped as Type T **4**.

T7	1d. rose-red and green		
T8	6d. lilac and green		

Only unused examples of Nos. T7/T8 are known, and it is possible that they were not issued.

1902 (June). King Edward VII fiscal stamps handstamped as Type T **4**.

T9	10s. grey-black and bright blue	£450	£225
T10	£1 grey-black and sage-green	£850	£375
T11	£5 grey-black and purple	£4000	

Forgeries of the Type T **4** handstamp are known on cleaned fiscally used stamps.

There are two versions of the Type T **4** handstamp, one as illustrated and the other with 'T' of 'Transvaal' above the 'T' of 'Telegraphs'.

From 1903 postage stamps were once again used to pay telegraph charges.

Transvaal became a province of the Union of South Africa on 31 May 1910.

Stamps used during the Interprovincial Period (1 June 1910–1931 August 1913) are listed under South Africa.

PIETERSBURG

After the fall of Pretoria to the British in June 1900 the Transvaal government withdrew to the north of the country. Those post offices in areas not occupied by the British continued to function. The following stamps were then authorised by the State Secretary. Pietersburg itself was taken by British forces on 9 April 1901.

PRICES. Genuinely used examples are very rare. Stamps cancelled by favour exist and are worth the same as the unused prices quoted.
The issued stamps are initialled by the Controller, J. T. de V. Smit. All values exist without his signature and these come from clandestine printings in excess of the official government print order. Unsigned stamps were not issued by the Post Office.

P **1**

P **2**

P **3**

TYPES P **1/3.** Each value was printed in sheets of 24 (6×4) of which the first two horizontal rows were as T P **1** (Large 'P' in 'POSTZEGEL' and large date), the third row as T P **2** (Large 'P' in 'POSTZEGEL' and small date) and the fourth as T P **3** (Small 'P' in 'POSTZEGEL' and small date).

(Type-set *De Zoutpansberg Wachter* Press, Pietersburg)

1901 (20 Mar (1d.)–3 Apr (others)).

A. Imperf

(a) Controller's initials in black

1	P **1**	½d. black/*green*	15·00
		e. Controller's initials omitted	95·00
2	P **2**	½d. black/*green*	45·00
		d. Controller's initials omitted	95·00
3	P **3**	½d. black/*green*	45·00
		d. Controller's initials omitted	95·00
4	P **1**	1d. black/*red*	3·50
5	P **2**	1d. black/*red*	5·50
6	P **3**	1d. black/*red*	7·00
7	P **1**	2d. black/*orange*	6·00
8	P **2**	2d. black/*orange*	14·00
9	P **3**	2d. black/*orange*	22·00
10	P **1**	4d. black/*blue*	5·50
11	P **2**	4d. black/*blue*	9·50
12	P **3**	4d. black/*blue*	32·00
13	P **1**	6d. black/*green*	9·50
14	P **2**	6d. black/*green*	15·00
15	P **3**	6d. black/*green*	40·00
16	P **1**	1s. black/*yellow*	8·00
17	P **2**	1s. black/*yellow*	14·00
18	P **3**	1s. black/*yellow*	25·00

(b) Controller's initials in red

19	P **1**	½d. black/*green*	15·00
20	P **2**	½d. black/*green*	35·00
21	P **3**	½d. black/*green*	40·00

B. P 11½

(a) Controller's initials in red

22	P **1**	½d. black/*green*	5·50
		c. Imperf vert (horiz pair)	95·00
23	P **2**	½d. black/*green*	17·00
		f. Imperf vert (horiz pair)	£120
24	P **3**	½d. black/*green*	12·00
		b. Imperf vert (horiz pair)	£120

(b) Controller's initials in black

25	P **1**	1d. black/*red*	2·00
		m. Imperf vert (horiz pair)	55·00
		n. Imperf between (vert pair: No. 25+No. 26)	75·00
		o. Imperf horiz (vert pair)	55·00
26	P **2**	1d. black/*red*	2·75
		f. Imperf vert (horiz pair)	80·00
		g. Imperf horiz (vert pair: No. 26+No. 27)	60·00
27	P **3**	1d. black/*red*	4·00
		f. Imperf vert (horiz pair)	80·00
28	P **1**	2d. black/*orange*	5·50
29	P **2**	2d. black/*orange*	8·00
30	P **3**	2d. black/*orange*	14·00

For the ½d. the First printing had initials in red, those of the Second printing had them in black or red, and all of the Third were in red.

CONSTANT VARIETIES

½d. value

First printing

R.3/5	Centre figures '½' level	Imperf	(No. 20a)	70·00
		Perf	(No. 23d)	40·00
R.3/6	No stop after right 'AFR'	Imperf	(No. 20b)	70·00
		Perf	(No. 23e)	40·00
R.4/6	Hyphen between right 'AFR' and 'REP'	Imperf	(No. 21a)	70·00
		Perf	(No. 24a)	40·00

Second printing—Imperf

R.1/1 & 4	Top left '½' inverted, no stop after right 'AFR'	(No. 19c)	70·00
R.1/2	Top right '½' inverted	(No. 19d)	90·00
R.1/3	'½' at lower right	(No. 19e)	90·00
R.1/5	'POSTZFGEL'	(No. 19f)	90·00
R.1/6	Left spray inverted, 'AFB' at right	(No. 19g)	90·00
R.2/1	'REB' at left, left side of inner frame 3 mm too high	(No. 19h)	90·00
R.2/2	'BEP' at left	(No. 19i)	90·00
R.2/3	'POSTZEOEL'	(No. 19j)	90·00
R.2/4	'AER' at right, left side of inner frame 2 mm too high	(No. 19k)	90·00
R.2/5	No stop after date	(No. 19l)	90·00
R.2/6	No stop after 'PENNY'	(No. 19m)	
R.3/1	'½' at top left, 'PE' of 'PENNY' spaced	(No. 20c)	90·00
R.3/2	Right spray inverted	(No. 20d)	90·00
R.3/3	Top left '½' inverted	(No. 20e)	90·00
R.3/4	No stop after 'Z' at left	(No. 20f)	
R.3/5	Centre figures '½' level	(No. 20g)	
R.3/6	'POSTZEGFL', no stop after right 'AFR'	(No. 20h)	
R.4/3	'½' at top right	(No. 21b)	90·00
R.4/4	Lower left '½' inverted	(No. 21c)	90·00
R.4/5	'¼' at top left	(No. 21d)	90·00
R.4/6	Left spray inverted, '901' for '1901'	(No. 21e)	

Third printing

R.1/2	No stop after left 'AFR'	Imperf	(No. 1a)	60·00
R.1/3	'½' at top left, no bar over lower right '½'	Imperf	(No. 1b)	60·00
R.1/6	No stop after date	Imperf	(No. 1c)	60·00
R.2/5	'BEP' at left, no stop after date	Imperf	(No. 1d)	60·00
R.3/3	'AFB' at left	Imperf	(No. 2a)	60·00
		Perf	(No. 23a)	
R.3/4	'POSTZEGEI'	Imperf	(No. 2b)	60·00
		Perf	(No. 23b)	
R.3/6	No bar over lower right '½'	Imperf	(No. 2c)	60·00
R.4/1	No stop after right 'AFR'	Imperf	(No. 3a)	60·00
R.4/4	No stop after left 'Z', no bar under top right '½'	Imperf	(No. 3b)	60·00
		Perf	(No. 23c)	
R.4/5	'POSTZECEL, AER' at left	Imperf	(No. 3c)	60·00

1d. value

First printing

R.1/2	First '1' in date dropped	Imperf	(No. 4l)	35·00
		Perf	(No. 25l)	22·00
R.3/6	No stop after right 'AFR'	Imperf	(No. 5e)	35·00
		Perf	(No. 26e)	22·00
R.4/5	Dropped 'P' in 'PENNY'	Imperf	(No. 6e)	35·00
		Perf	(No. 27e)	22·00

Second printing

R.1/2	Inverted '1' at lower left, first '1' of date dropped	Imperf	(No. 4a)	35·00
		Perf	(No. 25a)	22·00
R.1/3	No bar under top left '1'	Imperf	(No. 4b)	35·00
		Perf	(No. 25b)	22·00
R.1/4	No bar over lower right '1'	Imperf	(No. 4c)	35·00
		Perf	(No. 25c)	22·00
R.1/5	'POSTZFGEL'	Imperf	(No. 4d)	35·00
		Perf	(No. 25d)	22·00
R.1/6	'AFB' at right	Imperf	(No. 4e)	35·00
		Perf	(No. 25e)	22·00
R.2/1	'REB' at left	Imperf	(No. 4f)	35·00
		Perf	(No. 25f)	22·00
R.2/2	'BEP' at left	Imperf	(No. 4g)	35·00
		Perf	(No. 25g)	22·00
R.2/3	'POSTZEOEL'	Imperf	(No. 4h)	35·00
		Perf	(No. 25h)	22·00
R.2/4	'AER' at right	Imperf	(No. 4i)	35·00
		Perf	(No. 25i)	22·00
R.2/5	No stop after date	Imperf	(No. 4j)	35·00
		Perf	(No. 25j)	22·00
R.2/6	No stop after 'PENNY'	Imperf	(No. 4k)	35·00
		Perf	(No. 25k)	22·00
R.3/2	Right spray inverted	Imperf	(No. 5a)	35·00
		Perf	(No. 26a)	22·00
R.3/3	No bar over lower left '1'	Imperf	(No. 5b)	35·00
		Perf	(No. 26b)	22·00
R.3/4	No stop after left 'Z'	Imperf	(No. 5c)	35·00
		Perf	(No. 26c)	22·00
R.3/6	'POSTZEGFL', no stop after right 'AFR'	Imperf	(No. 5d)	35·00
		Perf	(No. 26d)	22·00
R.4/1	No stop after right 'AFR'	Imperf	(No. 6a)	35·00
		Perf	(No. 27a)	22·00
R.4/2 & 6	Left spray inverted	Imperf	(No. 6b)	22·00
		Perf	(No. 27b)	13·00
R.4/3	'POSTZEGEI'	Imperf	(No. 6c)	35·00
		Perf	(No. 27c)	22·00
R.4/4	No bar under top right '1'	Imperf	(No. 6d)	35·00
		Perf	(No. 27d)	22·00

2d. value

First printing

R.1/2	First '1' in date dropped	Imperf	(No. 7m)	45·00
		Perf	(No. 28a)	30·00
R.2/1	No stop after left 'REP'	Imperf	(No. 7n)	45·00
		Perf	(No. 28b)	30·00
R.3/6	No stop after right 'AFR'	Imperf	(No. 8f)	45·00
		Perf	(No. 29a)	30·00
R.4/1	Centre 2 wider, no stop after right 'AFR'	Imperf	(No. 9a)	38·00
		Perf	(No. 30a)	30·00
R.4/2	Centre '2' wider	Imperf	(No. 9g)	45·00
		Perf	(No. 30b)	30·00
R.4/5	'P' in 'PENCE' dropped	Imperf	(No. 9h)	45·00
		Perf	(No. 30c)	30·00

The variety at R. 4/1 is also found in the second and third printings, while the varieties at R. 2/1 and R. 4/2 recur in the third printing.

Second printing—Imperf

R.1/1	'1' at lower right	(No. 7a)	45·00
R.1/3	'PENNY' for 'PENCE'	(No. 7d)	45·00
R.1/5	'POSTZFGEL'	(No. 7e)	45·00
R.1/6	'AFB' at right	(No. 7f)	45·00
R.2/1	'REB' at left	(No. 7g)	45·00
R.2/2	'AFB' at left	(No. 7h)	45·00

R.2/3 'POSTZEOEL'.......... (No. 7i) 45·00
R.2/4 'AER' at right.......... (No. 7j) 45·00
R.2/5 No stop after date.......... (No. 7k) 45·00
R.2/6 No stop after date (part printing only) and vertical line after 'POSTZEGEL'.......... (No. 7l) 45·00
R.3/2 Right spray inverted.......... (No. 8a) 45·00
R.3/3 No bar over lower left '2'.......... (No. 8b) 45·00
R.3/4 Centre '2' inverted, no stop after left 'Z'.......... (No. 8c) 45·00
R.3/6 'POSTZEGFL', no stop after right 'AFR'.......... (No. 8d) 45·00
R.4/2 Centre '2' wider, left spray inverted... (No. 9b) 45·00
R.4/3 'POSTZEGEI'.......... (No. 9c) 45·00
R.4/4 No bar under top right '2'.......... (No. 9d) 45·00
R.4/5 '1' at lower left, 'P' in 'PENCE' dropped.......... (No. 9e) 45·00
R.4/6 Left spray inverted.......... (No. 9f) 45·00

The varieties at R. 2/5 and R. 4/4 recur in the third printing.

Third Printing — Imperf

R. 1/2 No stop after left 'AFR'.......... (No. 7o) 60·00
R. 1/3 No bar over lower right '2'.......... (No. 7p) 60·00
R. 1/5 'POSTZEGEI'.......... (No. 7q) 60·00
R. 3/4 No stop after left 'Z'.......... (No. 8g) 60·00
R. 3/5 '4' at lower right.......... (No. 8h) 60·00
R. 4/5 '4' at upper left and 'AER' at left.......... (No. 9i) 60·00

4d. value

First printing

R.2/1 Left inner frame too high.......... (No. 10k) 45·00
R.4/1–2 Centre '4' wider.......... (No. 12g) 35·00
R.4/5 'P' in 'PENCE' dropped.......... (No. 12h) 45·00

The variety at R. 4/1 recurs in the third printing.

Second printing

R.1/3 'PENNY' for 'PENCE' (*on small part of printing*).......... (No. 10c) 90·00
R.1/5 'POSTZFGEL'.......... (No. 10d) 45·00
R.1/6 'AFB' at right.......... (No. 10e) 45·00
R.2/1 'REB' at left.......... (No. 10f) 45·00
R.2/2 'AFB' at left.......... (No. 10g) 45·00
R.2/3 'POSTZEOEL'.......... (No. 10h) 45·00
R.2/4 'AER' at right.......... (No. 10i) 45·00
R.2/5 No stop after date.......... (No. 10j) 45·00
R.3/2 Right spray inverted.......... (No. 11a) 45·00
R.3/3 No bar over lower left '4' (*on small part of printing*).......... (No. 11b) 90·00
R.3/4 No stop after left 'Z'.......... (No. 11c) 45·00
R.3/6 'POSTZEGFL'.......... (No. 11d) 45·00
R.4/1 Centre '4' wider, no stop after right 'AFR'.......... (No. 12a) 45·00
R.4/2 Centre '4' wider, left spray inverted... (No. 12b) 45·00
R.4/3 'POSTZEGEI'.......... (No. 12c) 45·00
R.4/4 No bar under top right '4'.......... (No. 12d) 45·00
R.4/5 'P' in 'PENCE' dropped.......... (No. 12e) 45·00
R.4/6 Left spray inverted.......... (No. 12f) 45·00

Varieties at R. 1/5, R. 2/1, R. 2/2, R. 2/3, R. 2/4, R. 2/5, R. 3/2, R. 3/4, R. 3/6, R. 4/2, R. 4/4 and R. 4/6 also occur on the third printing.

Third printing

R. 1/2 No stop after left 'AFR'.......... (No. 10l) 60·00
R. 1/3 No bar over lower right '4'.......... (No. 10m) 60·00
R. 3/5 '4' at lower right.......... (No. 11e) 60·00
R. 4/5 'AER' at left and 'P' in 'PENCE' dropped.......... (No. 12i) 60·00

6d. value

First printing

R.2/1 Left inner frame too high, no stop after left 'REP'.......... (No. 13k) 55·00
R.4/1–2 Centre '6' wider.......... (No. 15g) 40·00
R.4/5 'P' in 'PENCE' dropped.......... (No. 15h) 55·00

Second printing

R.1/3 'PENNY' for 'PENCE' (*on small part of printing*).......... (No. 13c) £110
R.1/5 'POSTZFGEL'.......... (No. 13d) 55·00
R.1/6 'AFB' at right.......... (No. 13e) 55·00
R.2/1 'REB' at left.......... (No. 13f) 55·00
R.2/2 'AFB' at left.......... (No. 13g) 55·00
R.2/3 'POSTZEOEL'.......... (No. 13h) 55·00
R.2/4 'AER' at right.......... (No. 13i) 55·00
R.2/5 No stop after date.......... (No. 13j) 55·00
R.3/2 Right spray inverted.......... (No. 14a) 55·00
R.3/4 Centre '6' inverted, no stop after left 'Z' (*on small part of printing*).......... (No. 14b) £150
R.3/4 No stop after left 'Z'.......... (No. 14c) 55·00
R.3/6 'POSTZEGFL'.......... (No. 14d) 55·00
R.4/1 Centre '6' wider, no stop after right 'AFR'.......... (No. 15a) 55·00
R.4/2 Centre '6' wider, left spray inverted.. (No. 15b) 55·00
R.4/3 'POSTZEGEI'.......... (No. 15c) 55·00
R.4/4 No bar under top right '6'.......... (No. 15d) 55·00
R.4/5 'P' in 'PENCE' dropped.......... (No. 15e) 55·00
R.4/6 Left spray inverted.......... (No. 15f) 55·00

Varieties at R. 1/5, R. 1/6, R. 2/1, R. 2/2, R. 2/3, R. 2/4, R. 2/5, R. 3/2, R. 3/4, R. 3/6, R. 4/1, R. 4/2, R. 4/3, R. 4/4 and R. 4/6 also occur on the third printing.

Third printing

R. 1/2 No stop after left 'AFR'.......... (No. 13l) 75·00
R. 1/3 No bar over lower right '6'.......... (No. 13m) 75·00
R. 4/5 'AER' at left, 'P' in 'PENCE' dropped.... (No. 15i) 75·00

1s. value

R.1/2 No stop after left 'AFR'.......... (No. 16a) 40·00
R.1/3 No bar over lower right '1'.......... (No. 16b) 40·00
R.2/5 No stop after date.......... (No. 16c) 40·00
R.3/3 Centre '1' inverted (*on small part of printing*).......... (No. 17a)
R.3/4 'POSTZEGEI', no stop after left 'Z'....... (No. 17b) 40·00
R.4/1 No stop after right 'AFR'.......... (No. 18a) 40·00
R.4/4 No bar under top right '1'.......... (No. 18b) 40·00
R.4/5 'AER' at left.......... (No. 18c) 40·00

LOCAL BRITISH OCCUPATION ISSUES DURING THE SOUTH AFRICAN WAR 1900–1902

Stamps of the Transvaal Republic, unless otherwise stated, variously overprinted or surcharged.

LYDENBURG

Lydenburg was occupied by the British on 6 September 1900.

V.R.I.
3d.
(L 1)

1900 (Sept). Nos. 215*c* and 217 surch as T L **1**, others optd 'V.R.I' only.

1 **30** ½d. green.......... £190 £190
2 1d. rose-red and green.......... £180 £170
3 **30** 2d. brown and green.......... £1500 £1000
4 2½d. blue and green.......... £2500 £1100
5 3d. on 1d. rose-red and green.......... £160 £140
7 4d. sage-green and green.......... £3750 £1100
8 6d. lilac and green.......... £3750 £1000
9 1s. ochre and green.......... £5500 £3750

The above were cancelled by British Army postal service postmarks. These overprints with Transvaal cancellations are believed to be forgeries.

RUSTENBURG

British forces in Rustenburg, west of Pretoria, utilised Transvaal stamps, handstamped 'V.R' on the command of Colonel Baden-Powell.

V.R.
(R 1)

1900 (22 June). Handstamped with T R **1** in violet.

1 **30** ½d. green.......... £200 £150
2 1d. rose-red and green.......... £150 £110
3 2d. brown and green.......... £425 £180
4 2½d. blue and green.......... £275 £150
5 3d. purple and green.......... £350 £200
6 6d. lilac and green.......... £1500 £600
7 1s. ochre and green.......... £2250 £1400
8 2s.6d. dull violet and green.......... £9000 £4500
a. Handstamp in black.......... † £8000

Nos. 2 and 5 exist with the handstamp inverted.

SCHWEIZER RENECKE

BESIEGED
(SR 1)

1900 (Sept). Handstamped with T SR **1** in black, reading vert up or down.

(a) On stamps of Transvaal

1 **30** ½d. green.......... † £350
2 1d. rose-red and green.......... † £350
3 2d. brown and green.......... † £475
4 6d. lilac and green.......... † £1300

(b) On stamps of Cape of Good Hope

5 **17** ½d. green.......... † £600
6 1d. carmine.......... † £600

Schweizer Renecke, near the Bechuanaland border, was occupied by a British garrison, beseiged by a large Boer force, from July 1900 to 9 January 1901. The British commander authorised the above stamps shortly after 19 August. All stamps were cancelled with the dated circular town postmark ('Schweizer Renecke, Z.A.R.'), usually after having been stuck on paper before use. Unused, without the postmark, do not exist.

No. 4 exists with double handstamp.

WOLMARANSSTAD

A British party occupied this town in the south-west of the Transvaal from 15 June to 27 July 1900. Transvaal stamps, to a face value of £5. 2s.6d., were found at the local firm of Thos. Leask and Co. and surcharged as below. The first mail left on 24 June and the last on 21 July.

Cancelled V-R-I.
(L 3)

Cancelled V-R-I.
(L 4)

1900 (24 June). Optd with T L **3**.

1 **30** ½d. green (B.).......... £375 £500
a. Opt inverted.......... £1500
b. Opt in black..........
1*c* ½d. on 1s. green (B.).......... £5000
2 1d. rose-red and green (B.).......... £250 £400
a. Opt in green.......... £2000
b. Opt in black.......... £3000
3 2d. brown and green (B.).......... £2250 £2250
a. Opt in black.......... £3500
4 2½d. blue and green (R.).......... £2250
a. Opt in blue.......... £2750 £2750
b. Opt in black..........
5 3d. purple and green (B.).......... £3500 £3500
6 4d. sage-green and green (B.).......... £5000 £5000
7 6d. lilac and green (B.).......... £6000 £6500
8 1s. ochre and green (B.).......... — £13000

The two lines of the overprint were handstamped separately. The ½d. exists with two impressions of the 'Cancelled' handstamp, the 2½d. with two impressions of 'V-R-I', one in red and one in blue and the 3d. with 'Cancelled' in green and 'V.R.I.' in blue.

1900 (24 June). Optd with T L **4**.

9 **34** 1d. red (B.).......... £250 £450

The ½d., 1d. and 3d. in T **30** are also known with this overprint.

VII. ZULULAND

Zululand remained an independent kingdom until annexed by Great Britain on 19 May 1887 when it was declared a Crown Colony.

The first European postal service was operated by a Natal postal agency at Eshowe opened in 1876 which cancelled Natal stamps with a 'No. 56 P.O. Natal' postmark. The agency closed during the Zulu War of 1879 and did not re-open until 1885 when an Eshowe postmark was provided. 'ZULULAND' was added to the cancellation in 1887 and stamps of Natal continued to be used until replaced by the overprinted series on 1 May 1888.

PRICES FOR STAMPS ON COVER TO 1945	
Nos. 1/2	*from* × 100
Nos. 3/10	*from* × 20
No. 11	—
Nos. 12/16	*from* × 20
Nos. 20/23	*from* × 30
No. 24	*from* × 20
Nos. 25/26	*from* × 12
Nos. 27/29	—
No. F1	*from* × 100

ZULULAND
(1)

ZULULAND.
(2)

1888 (1 May)–**93**.

(a) Nos. 173, 180, 197, 200/202, 205a, 207a/208, 209 and 211 of Great Britain (Queen Victoria) optd with T **1** *by D.L.R.*

1 ½d. vermilion (11.88).......... 8·50 3·00
2 1d. deep purple.......... 28·00 6·50
3 2d. grey-green and carmine.......... 29·00 50·00
4 2½d. purple/*blue* (9.91).......... 42·00 23·00
5 3d. purple/*yellow*.......... 32·00 22·00
6 4d. green and deep brown.......... 60·00 75·00
7 5d. dull purple and blue (3.93).......... £100 £120
w. Wmk inverted.......... † £1800
8 6d. purple/*rose-red*.......... 24·00 15·00
9 9d. dull purple and blue (4.92).......... £120 £130
10 1s. dull green (4.92).......... £150 £170
11 5s. rose (4.92).......... £700 £800
1/11 *Set of* 11.......... £1100 £1300
1s/11s (ex 1d.) H/S '*SPECIMEN*' *Set of* 10.......... £650

(b) No. 97a of Natal optd with T **2** *at Pietermaritzburg*

12 ½d. dull green (with stop) (7.88).......... 55·00 95·00
a. Opt double.......... £1100 £1200
d. Opt omitted (vert pair with normal) £7000
13 ½d. dull green (without stop).......... 29·00 50·00

The T **2** opt has been extensively forged. Examples of No. 12 with opt inverted and No. 13 with opt double are now considered to be forgeries.

1893 (29 Nov*). T **15** of Natal optd with T **1** by D.L.R. (Wmk Crown CA. P 14).

16 6d. dull purple.......... 65·00 55·00

* Earliest known date of use. No. 16 was, apparently, originally supplied in 1889 for fiscal purposes.

3

4

1d. Shaved 'Z' (R. 4/3 and R. 6/3)

(Typo D.L.R.)

1894 (18 Apr)–**96**. Wmk Crown CA. P 14.

20 **3** ½d. dull mauve and green.......... 8·00 7·00
w. Wmk inverted.......... £325 £400
21 1d. dull mauve and carmine.......... 6·50 2·75
a. Shaved 'Z'.......... £120 70·00
22 2½d. dull mauve and ultramarine.......... 14·00 12·00
23 3d. dull mauve and olive-brown.......... 8·00 3·25
24 **4** 6d. dull mauve and black.......... 20·00 16·00
25 1s. green.......... 50·00 38·00
26 2s.6d. green and black (2.96).......... 90·00 £110
27 4s. green and carmine.......... £150 £225
28 £1 purple/*red*.......... £600 £650
29 £5 purple and black/*red*.......... £5500 £1600
s. Optd 'SPECIMEN'.......... £475
20/28 *Set of* 9.......... £850 £950
20s/28s Optd 'SPECIMEN' *Set of* 9.......... £500

Dangerous forgeries exist of the £1 and £5.

FISCAL STAMP USED FOR POSTAGE

ZULULAND
F 1

1891 (5 May*). F **1**, Fiscal stamp of Natal optd with T **1**. Wmk Crown CA. P 14.

F1 1d. dull mauve.......... 4·50 3·00
a. Top left triangle detached.......... £250 £190
s. Handstamped '*SPECIMEN*'.......... 65·00

* Earliest known date of postal use. A proclamation published in the *Natal Government Gazette* on 27 June 1891 authorised the use of this stamp for postal purposes, but it is clear from the wording that such use had already commenced.

For illustration of 'top left triangle detached' variety see above No. 21 of Antigua.

Other values, 1s. to £20 as No. F1 exist apparently with postmarks, but, as these were never authorised for postal use, they are no longer listed.

Zululand was annexed to Natal on 31 December 1897 and its stamps were withdrawn from sale on 30 June 1898.

VIII. BRITISH ARMY FIELD OFFICES DURING SOUTH AFRICAN WAR, 1899–1902

Z 1

Z 2

Stamps of GREAT BRITAIN used by British Army Field Offices in South Africa cancelled as Types Z **1**, Z **2** or similar postmarks.

1881. Stamp of Queen Victoria.

Z1	1d. lilac (16 *dots*)	6·00

1883–84. Stamps of Queen Victoria.

Z1*a*	2s.6d lilac	£350
Z2	5s. rose	£475
Z2*a*	10s. ultramarine	£950

1887–92. Stamps of Queen Victoria.

Z3	½d. vermilion	7·00
Z4	1½d. dull purple and green	45·00
Z5	2d. grey-green and carmine	20·00
Z6	2½d. purple/*blue*	7·00
Z7	3d. purple/*yellow*	18·00
Z8	4d. green and brown	30·00
Z9	4½d. green and carmine	£120
Z10	5d. dull purple and blue (Die II)	20·00
Z11	6d. purple/*rose-red*	16·00
Z12	9d. dull purple and blue	£110
Z13	10d. dull purple and carmine	£100
Z14	1s. dull green	£160
Z15	£1 green	£1800

1900. Stamps of Queen Victoria.

Z16	½d. blue-green	7·00
Z17	1s. green and carmine	£225

1902. Stamps of King Edward VII.

Z18	½d. blue-green	16·00
Z19	1d. scarlet	11·00
Z20	1½d. purple and green	90·00
Z21	2d. yellowish green and carmine-red	65·00
Z22	2½d. ultramarine	25·00
Z23	3d. purple/*orange-yellow*	80·00
Z24	4d. green and grey-brown	90·00
Z25	5d. dull purple and ultramarine	90·00
Z26	6d. pale dull purple	40·00
Z27	9d. dull purple and ultramarine	£160
Z28	10d. dull purple and carmine	£170
Z29	1s. dull green and carmine	£110

ARMY OFFICIAL STAMPS

1896–1901. Stamps of Queen Victoria optd 'ARMY OFFICIAL'.

ZO1	½d. vermilion	£120
ZO2	½d. blue-green	£120
ZO3	1d. lilac (16 *dots*)	95·00
ZO4	6d. purple/*rose-red*	

ARMY TELEGRAPH STAMPS

Army Telegraph stamps were used between November 1899 and August 1900, during the second Anglo-Boer War in South Africa.

(T **1**)

(T **2**)

(T **3**)

(T **4**)

1899–1900. Nos. 197 and 213 of Great Britain opt with Type T **1** by D.L.R. or as Types T **2**/T **4**.

AT1	T **1** ½d. vermilion	40·00	45·00
AT2	½d. blue-green (1900)	£140	
AT3	T **2** 1d. lilac and black	30·00	5·00
AT4	2d. lilac and blue	30·00	6·00
	a. Bisected (1d.) *on piece* (1900)	†	£425
AT5	3d. lilac and brown	55·00	10·00
AT6	6d. lilac and green	25·00	12·00
	a. Bisected (3d.) *on piece* (1900)	†	£275
AT7	8d. lilac and carmine	£140	£140
AT8	T **3** 1s. green and black	55·00	15·00
	a. Bisected (6d.) *on piece* (1900)	†	£750
AT9	2s.6d. green and brown	55·00	50·00
AT10	5s. green and mauve	80·00	45·00
AT11	10s. green and red	£120	45·00
AT12	T **4** £1 lilac and black	£225	55·00
AT13	£5 lilac and green	£500	

Nos. AT3/AT4, AT6 and AT8/AT12 had originally been issued in 1895, and were used in small quantities during the Ashanti expedition. Nos. AT1, AT5 and AT7 followed in 1896, and were used with other values to 2s.6d. during Autumn manoeuvres in England, but the main usage of these stamps was in South Africa.

TWO
PENCE
(T **5**)

1900 (Feb). Nos. AT9 and AT10 surch as Type T **5**.

AT14	'TWO PENCE' on 2s.6d.green and brown (Verm.)	£3200	£140
	a. Bisected (1d.) *on piece*	†	£475
AT15	'ONE SHILLING' on 5s. green and mauve (B.)	£3200	£125
	a. Bisected (6d.) *on piece*	†	£600

Used stamps usually bear a metal 'ARMY TELEGRAPHS' datestamp with code letters either side of the date.

As the Anglo-Boer War progressed the 'Army Telegraphs' stamps were replaced by overprinted Telegraph stamps in the occupied Orange Free State and by Fiscal and postage stamps in the Transvaal.

IX. UNION OF SOUTH AFRICA

The Interprovincial Period (1 June 1910 – 31 August 1913)

With the establishment of the Union on 31 May 1910, the only definitive stamps available were those of the four provinces; Cape of Good Hope, Natal, Orange River Colony and Transvaal. These became available for use throughout the Union from 1 June, although the public was not officially informed of the fact until it was published in the *Government Gazette* on 19 August.

The collecting of 'Interprovincials' is best thought of as the study of the period from 1 June 1910 until the issue of the first Union definitives on 1 September 1913, although in the case of the postage dues of Transvaal, the period can be extended until the issue of the relevant Union values in 1914–1915. The only provincial stamps reprinted and issued during this period were those of Transvaal. As collectors generally include the use of provincial stamps in their 'home' province during the period, these are included in the listings below.

Usage of provincial stamps continued after 1 September 1913, until demonetisation on 1 January 1938, although during this period usage became increasingly philatelic and included stocks of earlier stamps, such as the Orange Free State 'V.R.I.' overprints. Our listings comprise only those stamps which were generally available at the time of Union. The 2½d. values are relatively scarce used in the true Interprovincial period, but there were considerable stocks left in September 1913 and their use outside the period is more common.

Our prices are for fine used stamps clearly dated within the period and showing the place they were used. Stamps on piece or cover showing full cancellations, and stamps used in smaller offices are worth more. Collectors are warned against the Natal high values with faked interprovincial cancels.

Cape of Good Hope

(i) Used in Cape of Good Hope

Z1	½d. green (No. 70)	50
Z2	1d. carmine (No. 71)	50
Z3	2d. brown (No. 72)	1·50
Z4	2½d. ultramarine (No. 73)	15·00
Z5	3d. magenta (No. 74)	2·00
Z6	4d. olive-green (No. 75)	3·00
Z7	6d. bright mauve (No. 76)	3·00
Z8	1s. yellow-ochre (No. 77)	6·00
Z9	5s. brown-orange (No. 78)	40·00

(ii) Used in Natal

Z10	½d. green (No. 70)	2·00
Z11	1d. carmine (No. 71)	1·50
Z12	2d. brown (No. 72)	3·00
Z13	2½d. ultramarine (No. 73)	25·00
Z14	3d. magenta (No. 74)	4·00
Z15	4d. olive-green (No. 75)	6·00
Z16	6d. bright mauve (No. 76)	7·00
Z17	1s. yellow-ochre (No. 77)	12·00
Z18	5s. brown-orange (No. 78)	65·00

(iii) Used in Orange River Colony

Z19	½d. green (No. 70)	5·00
Z20	1d. carmine (No. 71)	3·00
Z21	2d. brown (No. 72)	4·00
Z22	2½d. ultramarine (No. 73)	30·00
Z23	3d. magenta (No. 74)	6·00
Z24	4d. olive-green (No. 75)	9·00
Z25	6d. bright mauve (No. 76)	10·00
Z26	1s. yellow-olive (No. 77)	20·00
Z27	5s. brown-orange (No. 78)	90·00

(iv) Used in Transvaal

Z28	½d. green (No. 70)	2·00
Z29	1d. carmine (No. 71)	1·50
Z30	2d. brown (No. 72)	2·50
Z31	2½d. ultramarine (No. 73)	22·00
Z32	3d. magenta (No. 74)	3·00
Z33	4d. olive-green (No. 75)	6·00
Z34	6d. bright mauve (No. 76)	6·00
Z35	1s. yellow-ochre (No. 77)	12·00
Z36	5s. brown-orange (No. 78)	60·00

Natal

(i) Used in Natal

Z37	½a. blue-green (No. 146)	50
Z38	1d. carmine (No. 147)	50
Z39	1d. deep carmine (No. 148)	1·00
Z40	1½d. green and black (No. 129)	12·00
Z41	2d. red and olive-green (No. 149)	4·00
Z42	2½d. bright blue (No. 131)	8·00
Z43	3d. purple and grey (No. 132)	3·50
Z44	4d. carmine and cinnamon (No. 152)	8·00
Z45	5d. black and orange (No. 153)	10·00
Z46	6d. dull and bright purple (No. 165)	5·00
Z47	1s. black/*green* (No. 166)	25·00
Z48	2s. purple and bright blue/*blue* (No. 167)	15·00
Z49	2s.6d. black and green/*blue* (No. 168)	15·00
Z50	5s. green and red/*yellow* (No. 169)	75·00
Z51	10s. green and red/*green* (No. 170)	£200
Z52	£1 purple and black/*red* (No. 171)	£500

(ii) Used in Cape of Good Hope

Z53	½d. blue-green (No. 146)	1·00
Z54	1d. carmine (No. 147)	1·00
Z55	1d. deep carmine (No. 148)	2·00
Z56	1½d. green and black (No. 129)	40·00
Z57	2d. red and olive-green (No. 149)	5·00
Z58	2½d. bright blue (No. 131)	12·00
Z59	3d. purple and grey (No. 132)	5·00
Z60	4d. carmine and cinnamon (No. 152)	12·00
Z61	5d. black and orange (No. 153)	20·00
Z62	6d. dull and bright purple (No. 165)	10·00
Z63	1s. black/*green* (No. 166)	£100
Z64	2s. purple and bright blue/*blue* (No. 167)	25·00
Z65	2s.6d. black and green/*blue* (No. 168)	25·00
Z66	5s. green and red/*yellow* (No. 169)	£150
Z67	10s. green and red/*green* (No. 170)	£350
Z68	£1 purple and black/*red* (No. 171)	£900

(iii) Used in Orange River Colony

Z69	½d. blue-green (No. 146)	5·00
Z70	1d. carmine (No. 147)	5·00
Z71	1d. deep carmine (No. 148)	8·00
Z72	1½d. green and black (No. 129)	80·00
Z73	2d. red and olive-green (No. 149)	12·00
Z74	2½d. bright blue (No. 131)	40·00
Z75	3d. purple and grey (No. 132)	18·00
Z76	4d. carmine and cinnamon (No. 152)	30·00
Z77	5d. black and orange (No. 153)	38·00
Z78	6d. dull and bright purple (No. 165)	28·00
Z79	1s. black/*green* (No. 166)	£350
Z80	2s. purple and bright blue/*blue* (No. 167)	£350
Z81	2s.6d. black and red/*blue* (No. 168)	£350
Z82	5s. green and red/*yellow* (No. 169)	£250
Z83	10s. green and red/*green* (No. 170)	£800
Z84	£1 purple and black/*red* (No. 171)	—

(iv) Used in Transvaal

Z85	½d. blue-green (No. 146)	1·00
Z86	1d. carmine (No. 147)	1·00
Z87	1d. bright carmine (No. 148)	2·00
Z88	1½d. green and black (No. 129)	45·00
Z89	2d. red and olive-green (No. 149)	5·00
Z90	2½d. bright blue (No. 131)	15·00
Z91	3d. purple and grey (No. 132)	5·00
Z92	4d. carmine and cinnamon (No. 152)	12·00
Z93	5d. black and orange (No. 153)	20·00
Z94	6d. dull and bright purple (No. 165)	12·00
Z95	1s. black/*green* (No. 166)	£100
Z96	2s. purple and bright blue/*blue* (No. 167)	30·00
Z97	2s.6d. black and red/*blue* (No. 168)	40·00
Z98	5s. green and red/*yellow* (No. 169)	80·00
Z99	10s. green and red/*green* (No. 170)	£350
Z100	£1 purple and black/*red* (No. 171)	£900

Orange River Colony

(i) Used in Orange River Colony

Z101	½d. yellow-green (No. 148)	2·00
Z102	1d. scarlet (No. 149)	1·00
Z103	2d. brown (No. 141)	2·50
Z104	2½d. bright blue (No. 142)	3·00
Z105	3d. mauve (No. 143)	3·00
Z106	4d. scarlet and sage-green (No. 150)	7·00
Z107	6d. scarlet and mauve (No. 145)	3·00
Z108	1s. scarlet and bistre (No. 146)	12·00
Z109	1s. scarlet and bistre (No. 151)	28·00
Z110	5s. blue and brown (No. 147)	40·00

(ii) Used in Cape of Good Hope

Z111	½d. yellow-green (No. 148)	3·00
Z112	1d. scarlet (No. 149)	1·50
Z113	2d. brown (No. 141)	3·50
Z114	2½d. bright blue (No. 142)	4·00
Z115	3d. mauve (No. 143)	4·00
Z116	4d. scarlet and sage-green (No. 150)	9·00
Z117	6d. scarlet and mauve (No. 145)	5·00
Z118	1s. scarlet and bistre (No. 146)	24·00
Z119	1s. scarlet and bistre (No. 151)	50·00
Z120	5s. blue and brown (No. 147)	50·00

(iii) Used in Natal

Z121	½d. yellow-green (No. 148)	4·00
Z122	1d. scarlet (No. 149)	2·00
Z123	2d. brown (No. 141)	4·50
Z124	2½d. bright blue (No. 142)	6·00
Z125	3d. mauve (No. 143)	5·00
Z126	4d. scarlet and sage-green (No. 150)	11·00
Z127	6d. scarlet and mauve (No. 145)	7·00
Z128	1s. scarlet and bistre (No. 146)	30·00
Z129	1s. scarlet and bistre (No. 151)	65·00
Z130	5s. scarlet blue and brown (No. 147)	70·00

(iv) Used in Transvaal

Z131	½d. yellow-green (No. 148)	3·00
Z132	1d. scarlet (No. 149)	1·50
Z133	2d. brown (No. 141)	3·50
Z134	2½d. bright blue (No. 142)	4·50
Z135	3d. mauve (No. 143)	4·50
Z136	4d. scarlet and sage-green (No. 150)	10·00
Z137	6d. scarlet and mauve (No. 145)	5·00
Z138	1s. scarlet and bistre (No. 146)	26·00
Z139	1s. scarlet and bistre (No. 151)	55·00
Z140	5s. blue and brown (No. 147)	60·00

Transvaal

(i) Used in Transvaal

Z141	½d. yellow-green (No. 273)	50
Z142	1d. scarlet (No. 274)	50
Z143	2d. purple (No. 275)	70
Z144	2½d. bright blue (No. 276)	15·00
Z145	3d. black and sage-green (No. 264)	1·00
Z146	4d. black and brown (No. 265)	1·50
Z147	6d. black and orange (No. 266a)	1·50
Z148	1s. black and red-brown (No. 267)	2·00
Z149	2s. black and yellow (No. 268)	16·00
Z150	2s.6d. magenta and black (No. 269)	14·00
Z151	5s. black and purple/*yellow* (No. 270)	4·00
Z152	10s. black and purple/*red* (No. 271)	6·00
Z153	£1 green and violet (No. 272a)	28·00

(ii) Used in Cape of Good Hope

Z154	½d. yellow-green (No. 273)	50
Z155	1d. scarlet (No. 274)	50
Z156	2d. purple (No. 275)	1·00
Z157	2½d. bright blue (No. 276)	15·00

Z158	3d.	black and sage-green (No. 264)	2·00
Z159	4d.	black and brown (No. 265)	2·50
Z160	6d.	black and orange (No. 266a)	2·00
Z161	1s.	black and red-brown (No. 267)	3·00
Z162	2s.	black and yellow (No. 268)	20·00
Z163	2s.6d.	magenta and black (No. 269)	16·00
Z164	5s.	black and purple/*yellow* (No. 270)	6·00
Z165	10s.	black and purple/*red* (No. 271)	8·00
Z166	£1	green and violet (No. 272a)	30·00
		(iii) Used in Natal	
Z167	½d.	yellow-green (No. 273)	50
Z168	1d.	scarlet (No. 274)	50
Z168	2d.	brown (No. 275)	1·50
Z170	2½d.	bright blue (No. 276)	18·00
Z171	3d.	black and sage-green (No. 264)	3·00
Z172	4d.	black and brown (No. 265)	3·00
Z173	6d.	black and orange (No. 266a)	3·00
Z174	1s.	black and red-brown (No. 267)	4·00
Z175	2s.	black and yellow (No. 268)	22·00
Z176	2s.6d.	magenta and black (No. 269)	20·00
Z177	5s.	black and purple/*yellow* (No. 270)	7·00
Z178	10s.	black and purple/*red* (No. 271)	10·00
Z179	£1	green and violet (No. 272a)	35·00
		(iv) Used in Orange River Colony	
Z180	½d.	yellow-green (No. 273)	1·00
Z181	1d.	scarlet (No. 274)	1·00
Z182	2d.	brown (No. 275)	2·00
Z183	2½d.	bright blue (No. 276)	20·00
Z184	3d.	black and sage-green (No. 264)	4·00
Z185	4d.	black and brown (No. 265)	4·00
Z186	6d.	black and orange (No. 266a)	4·00
Z187	1s.	black and red-brown (No. 267)	5·00
Z188	2s.	black and yellow (No. 268)	28·00
Z189	2s.6d.	magenta and black (No. 269)	24·00
Z190	5s.	black and purple/*yellow* (No. 270)	10·00
Z191	10s.	black and purple/*red* (No. 271)	12·00
Z192	£1	green and violet (No. 272a)	£130

PRICES FOR STAMPS ON COVER TO 1945

Nos. 1/15	*from* × 4
Nos. 16/17	—
Nos. 18/21	*from* × 6
Nos. 26/32	*from* × 2
No. 33	*from* × 4
Nos. 34/110	*from* × 1
Nos. D1/D7	*from* × 4
Nos. D8/D33	*from* × 6
Nos. O1/O33	*from* × 4

1

(Des H. S. Wilkinson. Recess D.L.R.)

1910 (4 Nov). Opening of Union Parliament. Inscribed bilingually. Wmk Multiple Rosettes. P 14.

1	**1**	2½d. deep blue	3·75	1·75
		s. Handstamped *'Specimen.'*	£550	
2		2½d. blue	2·75	1·00

The deep blue shade is generally accompanied by a blueing of the paper.

2

3

4 Springbok's Head

(Typo D.L.R.)

1913 (1 Sept)–**24**. Inscribed bilingually. W **4**.

		(a) P 14		
3	**2**	½d. green	1·75	30
		a. Stamp doubly printed	£10000	
		b. Blue-green	2·00	20
		c. Yellow-green	2·75	1·00
		d. Printed on the gummed side	£1500	
		w. Wmk inverted	2·00	1·00
4		1d. rose-red (*shades*)	1·75	10
		a. Carmine-red	2·25	10
		b. Scarlet (*shades*)	4·50	1·00
		w. Wmk inverted	2·50	1·00
5		1½d. chestnut (*shades*) (23.8.20)	80	10
		a. *Tête-bêche* (pair)	1·75	18·00
		c. Wmk sideways	†	£1800
		w. Wmk inverted	80	10
6	**3**	2d. dull purple	1·75	10
		a. Deep purple	2·50	10
		w. Wmk inverted	2·25	2·25
7		2½d. bright blue	4·50	1·00
		a. Deep blue	4·00	3·00
		w. Wmk inverted	£140	£170
8		3d. black and orange-red	13·00	30
		a. Black and dull orange-red	10·00	70
		w. Wmk inverted	25·00	9·50
9		3d. ultramarine (*shades*) (4.10.22)	4·75	1·00
		w. Wmk inverted	13·00	5·50
10		4d. orange-yellow and olive-green	10·00	75
		a. Orange-yellow and sage-green	6·50	55
		w. Wmk inverted	8·00	1·50
11		6d. black and violet	7·00	60
		a. Black and bright violet	10·00	1·50
		aw. Wmk inverted	18·00	10·00
12		1s. orange	8·50	60
		a. Orange-yellow	15·00	1·00
		w. Wmk inverted	24·00	2·25
13		1s.3d. violet (*shades*) (1.9.20)	9·00	6·00
		w. Wmk inverted	£160	£225
14		2s.6d. purple and green	55·00	1·50
15		5s. purple and blue	£120	9·50
		a. Reddish purple and light blue	£120	9·50
		w. Wmk inverted	£9000	£3500
16		10s. deep blue and olive-green	£180	7·50
		w. Wmk inverted	£7000	£2000
17		£1 green and red (7.16)	£650	£350
		a. Pale olive-green and red (1924)	£850	£1200
3/17 *Set of 15*			£950	£350
3s/8s, 10s/17s Optd or H/S (1½d. and 1s.3d. in violet, £1 in green) 'SPECIMEN' *Set of 14*			£1600	
		(b) Coil stamps. P 14×imperf		
18	**2**	½d. green	6·00	1·00
		w. Wmk inverted	—	£600
19		1d. rose-red (13.2.14)	24·00	3·00
		a. Scarlet	28·00	8·50
		w. Wmk inverted	£1000	£400
20		1½d. chestnut (15.11.20)	11·00	15·00
		w. Wmk inverted	†	£3500
21	**3**	2d. dull purple (7.10.21)	16·00	4·75
18/21 *Set of 4*			50·00	21·00

The 6d. exists with 'Z' of 'ZUID' wholly or partly missing at R. 8/3, lower right pane, due to wear of plate (*Price wholly missing, £95 un, £55 us*).

5 de Havilland DH.9 Biplane

(Eng A. J. Cooper. Litho *Cape Times* Ltd)

1925 (26 Feb). Air. Inscr bilingually. P 12.

26	**5**	1d. carmine	5·50	16·00
27		3d. ultramarine	8·00	12·00
28		6d. magenta	12·00	14·00
29		9d. green	25·00	75·00
26/29 *Set of 4*			45·00	£100

Beware of forgeries of all values perforated 11, 11½ or 13.

INSCRIPTIONS. From 1926 until 1951 most issues were inscribed in English and Afrikaans alternately throughout the sheets.

PRICES for Nos. 30/135 are for unused horizontal pairs, used horizontal pairs and used singles (either inscription), unless otherwise indicated. Vertical pairs are worth between 20% and 35% of the prices quoted for horizontal pairs.

6 Springbok

7 *Dromedaris* (Van Riebeeck's ship)

8 Orange Tree

9

(Typo Waterlow until 1927, thereafter Govt Printer, Pretoria)

1926 (2 Jan)–**27**. W **9**. P 14½×14.

			Un pair	*Used pair*	*Used single*
30	**6**	½d. black and green	2·75	3·25	10
		a. Missing '1' in '½'	£2750		
		b. Centre omitted (in pair with normal)	£3500		
		cw. Wmk inverted	5·00	8·50	20
		d. Frame printed double (horiz pair)	£22000		
		e. Perf 13½×14 (1927)	90·00	90·00	4·00
		ea. *Tête-bêche* (pair)	£1500		
		ew. Wmk inverted	90·00	90·00	4·00
		f. Wmk sideways**	—	£3250	
31	**7**	1d. black and carmine	1·50	50	10
		a. Imperf (vert pair)*	£1100		
		b. Imperf 3 sides (vert pair)*	£1100	£1200	
		c. Centre omitted (in pair with normal) (R. 19/9)	£5000		
		dw. Wmk inverted	6·00	2·75	20
		e. Perf 13½×14 (1927)	£120	85·00	4·00
		ea. *Tête-bêche* (pair)	£1500		
		ew. Wmk inverted	£120	85·00	4·00
		f. Wmk sideways**	£2750	£2500	
32	**8**	6d. green and orange (1.5.26)	42·00	48·00	1·50
		w. Wmk inverted	70·00	75·00	
30/32 *Set of 3*			42·00	48·00	1·50

No. 30a exists in Afrikaans only. Nos. 30e and 31e were only issued in booklets.

No. 30d occurred on the bottom left-hand corner of one sheet and included the bottom four stamps in the first vertical row and the bottom two in the second. As listed No. 30d shows the left-hand stamp with the frame completely double and the right-hand stamp with two-thirds of the frame double.

* Both Nos. 31a and 31b occur in blocks of four with the other vertical pair imperforate at left.

** Nos. 30f and 31f are known with the top of the Springbok's head to the left or to the right, *as seen from the back of the stamp.*

No 31c. developed from a plate crack during the second Pretoria printing, affecting R. 18/9, 19/9 and 20/9. On 19/9 the vignette failed to print altogether for a few sheets, but was soon repaired.

For ½d. with pale grey centre, see No. 126.

For rotogravure printing see Nos. 42, etc.

10 'Hope'

(Recess B.W.)

1926 (2 Jan). T **10**. Inscribed in English or Afrikaans. W **9** (upright or inverted in equal quantities).

			Single stamps	
33		4d. grey-blue (English inscr) (*shades*)	1·75	1·25
		a. Inscr in Afrikaans	1·75	1·25

In this value the English and Afrikaans inscriptions are on separate sheets.

This stamp is known with private perforations or roulettes.

11 Union Buildings, Pretoria

12 Groot Schuur

12a A Native Kraal

13 Black and Blue Wildebeest

14 Ox-wagon inspanned

15 Ox-wagon outspanned

16 Cape Town and Table Bay

2d. 'Split 'd'' (Right pane, R. 8/2)

(Recess B.W.)

1927 (1 Mar)–**30**. 'SUIDAFRIKA' in one word on Afrikaans stamps. W **9**. P 14.

			Un pair	*Used pair*	*Used single*
34	**11**	2d. grey and maroon	16·00	35·00	60
		aa. Split 'd'	£300		
		aw. Wmk inverted	£900	£1000	60·00
		b. Perf 14×13½ (2.30)	50·00	55·00	1·00
		ba. Split 'd'	£160	£200	
35	**12**	3d. black and red	17·00	35·00	60
		a. Perf 14×13½ (1930)	80·00	80·00	1·25
35*b*	**12a**	4d. brown (23.3.28)	32·00	50·00	1·00
		c. Perf 14×13½ (1930)	60·00	70·00	1·25
		cw. Wmk inverted	£1000	£1000	55·00
36	**13**	1s. brown and deep blue	30·00	55·00	1·00
		a. Perf 14×13½ (1930)	75·00	90·00	2·00
37	**14**	2s.6d. green and brown	£150	£500	17·00
		a. Perf 14×13½ (1930)	£400	£700	24·00
38	**15**	5s. black and green	£300	£900	35·00
		a. Perf 14×13½ (1930)	£500	£1100	42·00
39	**16**	10s. bright blue and brown	£200	£160	10·00
		a. Centre inverted (*single stamp*)	£22000		
		b. Perf 14×13½ (1930)	£250	£200	12·00
34/39 *Set of 7*			£650	£1400	55·00
34s/39s H/S 'SPECIMEN' *Set of 7*			£1100		

Two vertical pairs and a few single unused examples of No. 39a are known.

17 de Havilland DH.60 Cirrus Moth

(Typo Govt Ptg Wks, Pretoria)

1929 (16 Aug). Air. Inscribed bilingually. No wmk. P 14×13½.

			Un single	*Us single*
40	**17**	4d. green	5·00	1·75
41		1s. orange	8·00	14·00

PRINTER. All the following issues to 1961, except where stated otherwise, are printed by rotogravure (the design having either plain lines or a dotted screen) by the Government Printer, Pretoria.

I II

I

II

The two types of the 1d. differ in the spacing of the horizontal lines in the side panels:—Type I close; Type II wide. The Afrikaans had the spacing of the words POSSEEL-INKOMSTE close in Type I and more widely spaced in Type II.

½d. 'Cobweb' variety (retouch between horns) (Cyl. 1 R. 9/5)

½d. 'Dollar' variety (Cyl. 2 R. 10/9)

2d. Airship flaw (Cyl 34 R. 9/4)

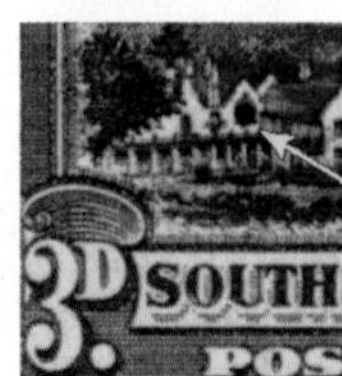

3d. Window flaw (R. 20/4 on all ptgs before 1937)

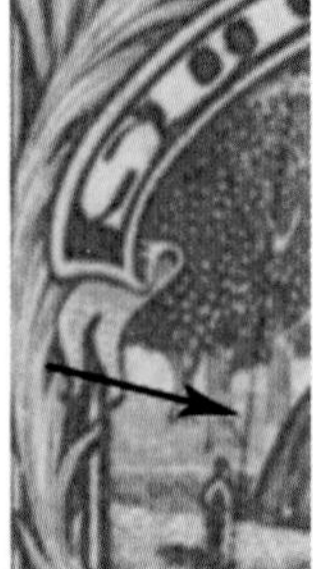

4d. Spear flaw (R. 9/2)

4d. 'Monkey' in tree (R. 2/2)

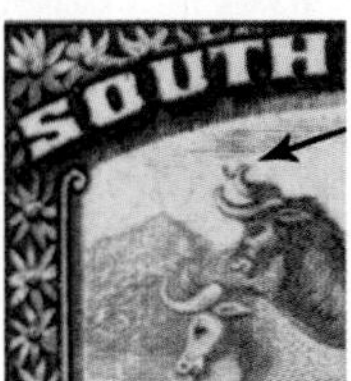

1s. Twisted horn (Cyl 7020 R. 1/5)

1s. Dart in Gnu's back (Cyl 6926 R. 20/1)

1930–44. Types **6** to **8** and Types **11** to **14** redrawn, 'SUIDAFRIKA' (in one word) on Afrikaans stamps. W **9**. P 15×14 (½d., 1d., and 6d.) or 14.

		Un pair	*Used pair*	*Used single*
42	½d. black and green (5.30)	6·50	3·75	10
	a. Two English or two Afrikaans stamps *se-tenant* (vert strip of 4)	40·00		
	b. *Tête-bêche*	£1400		
	c. 'Cobweb' variety	50·00		
	d. 'Dollar' variety	50·00		
	w. Wmk inverted	6·50	3·75	10
43	1d. black and carmine (I) (4.30)	7·00	3·00	10
	a. *Tête-bêche*	£1400		
	b. Frame omitted (*single stamp*)	£600		
	cw. Wmk inverted	7·00	3·00	10
	cwa. Vignette omitted	£1800		
43*d*	1d. black and carmine (II) (8.32)	60·00	4·00	10
	dw. Wmk inverted	50·00	4·00	10
44	2d. slate-grey and lilac (4.31)	28·00	28·00	50
	a. *Tête-bêche*	£8000		
	bw. Wmk inverted	22·00	12·00	20
	c. Frame omitted (*single stamp*)	£6000		
	cwa. Frame omitted (*single stamp*)	£6000	£6500	
	d. Airship flaw	£140	£150	
44*e*	2d. blue and violet (3.38)	£350	75·00	2·50
	ea. Airship flaw	£950	£350	
45	3d. black and red (11.31)	£130	£100	2·25
	aw. Wmk inverted	38·00	60·00	1·25
	b. Window flaw	£200		
	bw. Ditto. Wmk inverted	£150		
45*c*	3d. blue (10.33)	25·00	7·00	20
	cw. Wmk inverted	6·00	6·00	10
	d. Window flaw	£110		
	dw. Ditto. Wmk inverted	60·00		
	e. Centre omitted	£32000		
	f. Frame omitted (*single stamp*)	£16000		
46	4d. brown (19.11.32)	£325	£150	6·50
	aw. Wmk inverted	35·00	32·00	40
	b. Spear flaw	£400	£325	
	bw. Ditto. Wmk inverted	£170	£170	
46*c*	4d. brown (*shades*) (*again redrawn*) (1936)	3·25	2·75	10
	ca 'Monkey' in tree	50·00		
	cw. Wmk inverted	13·00	12·00	30
47	6d. green and orange (*wmk inverted*) (13.5.31)	13·00	5·50	10
	w. Wmk upright (8.32)	75·00	22·00	30
48	1s. brown and deep blue (14.9.32)	£120	60·00	55
	a. Dart in gnu's back	£375	£400	
	bw. Wmk inverted	35·00	26·00	35
	c. Twisted horn flaw	£350	£425	
	cw. Ditto. Wmk inverted	£225	£325	
49	2s.6d. green and brown (*shades*) (24.12.32)	£100	£120	3·25
	aw. Wmk inverted	£225	£250	3·25
49*b*	2s.6d. blue and brown (11.44)	26·00	15·00	20
42/49*b* *Set of* 13		£500	£275	6·50

For similar designs with 'SUID-AFRIKA' hyphenated, see Nos. 54 etc. and Nos. 114 etc.

Nos. 42/43, 43*d*/44 exist in coils.

The unused prices quoted for Nos. 44*e* and 49*b* are for unmounted examples.

No. 42a comes from the coil printing on the cylinder for which two horizontal rows were incorrectly etched so that two Afrikaans-inscribed stamps were followed by two English. This variety is normally without a coil join, although some examples do occur showing a repair join.

The 1d. (Type I) exists without watwermark from a trial printing (*Price £30 un*).

No. 44 exists in sepia and mauve with smaller vignettes. Believed to be an early or trial printing replaced due to the vignette being too narrow for the frames. (*Price £900 unused, £700 used*).

Although it appears to be printed in one colour No. 45*c* was produced from vignette and frame cylinders in the same way as the bicoloured version. The clouds in the background, which are present on No. 45e, were printed from the frame cylinder.

The Rotogravure printings may be distinguished from the preceding Typographed and Recess printed issues by the following tests:—

Typo

Roto

2d. Recess

2d. Roto

3d. Recess

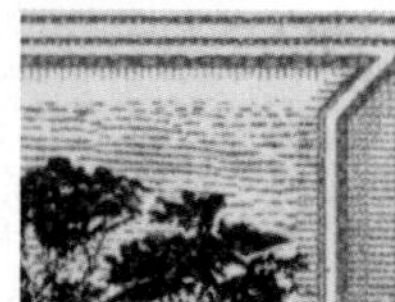

3d. Roto

4d. No. 35*b* Recess

4d. No. 46 Roto

4d. No. 46*c* Roto

1s. Recess

1s. Roto

2s.6d. Recess

2s.6d. Roto

5s. Recess

5s. Roto

ROTOGRAVURE:

½d. 1d. and 6d. Leg of 'R' in 'AFR' ends squarely on the bottom line.

2d. The newly built War Memorial appears to the left of the value.

3d. Two fine lines have been removed from the top part of the frame.

4d. No. 46. The scroll is in solid colour.
No. 46*c*. The scroll is white with a crooked line running through it. (No. 35*b*. The scroll is shaded by the diagonal lines.)

1s. The shading of the last 'A' partly covers the flower beneath.

2s.6d. The top line of the centre frame is thick and leaves only one white line between it and the name.

5s. (Nos. 64/*b*). The leg of the 'R' is straight.

Rotogravure impressions are generally coarser.

18 Church of the Vow

19 *The Great Trek* (C. Michell)

20 A Voortrekker

21 Voortrekker Woman

1d. Blurred 'SOUTH AFRICA' and red 'comet' flaw (Cyls 6917/6922 R. 2/7)

(Des J. Prentice (½d., 2d., 3d.))

1933 (3 May)–**36**. Voortrekker Memorial Fund. W **9** (sideways). P 14.

50	**18**	½d. +½d. black and green (16.1.36)	4·50	13·00	1·00
51	**19**	1d. +½d. grey-black and pink	3·25	2·50	25
		a. Blurred 'SOUTH AFRICA' and red 'comet' flaw	75·00	80·00	
		w. Wmk horns pointing to left	3·25	2·50	25
52	**20**	2d. +1d. grey-green and purple	4·50	4·50	55
53	**21**	3d. +1½d. grey-green and blue	7·00	5·00	70
50/53 *Set of* 4			17·00	22·00	2·25

The normal sideways watermark shows the horns of the springbok pointing to the right, *as seen from the back of the stamp.*

22 Gold Mine

22a Groot Schuur

Dies of 6d.

I

II

III

23 Groot Constantia

1½d. Broken chimney and fainter headgear (Cyl 62 R. 11/6)

1½d. Flag on chimney at right (Cyl 62 R. 20/2)

6d. 'Falling ladder' flaw (R. 5/10)

6d. 'Molehill' flaw (R. 20/11)

Normal

5s. Broken yoke-pin (R. 18/5)

1933–48. 'SUID-AFRIKA' (hyphenated) on Afrikaans stamps. W **9**. P 15×14 (½d., 1d. and 6d.) or 14 (others).

54	**6**	½d. grey and green (*wmk inverted*) (9.35)	7·50	3·00	10
		aw. Wmk upright (1936)	18·00	10·00	20
		b. Coil stamp. Perf 13½×14 (1935)	40·00	70·00	1·00
		bw. Wmk upright	40·00	70·00	1·00
		c. Booklet pane of 6 (with adverts on margins) (*wmk inverted*)	32·00		
56	**7**	1d. grey and carmine (*shades*) (19.4.34)	1·75	2·25	10
		a. Imperf (pair) (*wmk inverted*)	£180		
		b. Frame omitted (*single stamp*)	£350		
		cw. Wmk inverted	1·75	2·25	10
		d. Coil stamp. Perf 13½×14 (1935)	45·00	70·00	1·40
		dw. Wmk inverted	45·00	70·00	1·40
		e. Booklet pane of 6 (with adverts on margins) (wmk inverted) (1935)	38·00		
		f. Booklet pane of 6 (with blank margins) (1937)	38·00		
		h. Booklet pane of 6 (with postal slogans on margins) (1948)	4·00		
		i. Grey and bright rose-carmine (7.48)	70	2·75	10
57	**22**	1½d. green and bright gold (12.11.36)	8·00	3·75	10
		a. Shading omitted from mine dump (in pair with normal)	£275	£180	
		b. Broken chimney and faint headgear	29·00		
		c. Flag on chimney at right	29·00		
		dw. Wmk inverted	1·75	3·25	10
		dwa. Gold omitted	£25000		
		e. Blue-green and dull gold (8.40)	8·50	3·75	10
58	**11**	2d. blue and violet (11.38)	75·00	50·00	1·00
58*a*		2d. grey and dull purple (5.41)	65·00	£120	2·25
59	**22a**	3d. ultramarine (2.40)	15·00	4·25	10
61	**8**	6d. green and vermilion (I) (10.37)	70·00	50·00	1·00
		a. 'Falling ladder' flaw	£300	£350	
		b. 'Molehill' flaw	£250	£275	
61*c*		6d. green and vermilion (II) (6.38)	42·00	1·00	10
61*d*		6d. green and red-orange (III) (11.46)	20·00	75	10
62	**13**	1s. brown and chalky blue (2.39) (*shades*)	55·00	18·00	20
		a. Frame omitted (vert pair with normal)	£13000		
		b. Frame omitted (*single stamp*)	£9000		
64	**15**	5s. black and green (10.33)	60·00	75·00	1·75
		aw. Wmk inverted	£120	£150	3·00
		b. Black and blue-green (9.44)	42·00	21·00	35
		ba. Broken yoke-pin	£120	90·00	
64*c*	**23**	10s. blue and sepia (*shades*) (8.39)	65·00	10·00	70
		ca. Blue and charcoal (1944)	45·00	5·50	30
54/59, 61*d*/64*ca* *Set of* 10			£300	£190	3·25

The ½d. and 1d. coil stamps may be found in blocks emanating from the residue of the large rolls which were cut into sheets and distributed to Post Offices.

Nos. 54 and 56 also exist in coils.

1d. Is printed from Type II. Frames of different sizes exist due to reductions made from time to time for the purpose of providing more space for the perforations.

3d. In No. 59 the frame is unscreened and composed of solid lines. Centre is diagonally screened. Scrolls above '3d.' are clear lined, light in the middle and dark at sides.

6d. Die I. Green background lines faint. 'SUID-AFRIKA' 16¼ mm long.
Die II. Green background lines heavy. 'SUID-AFRIKA' 17 mm long. 'S' near end of tablet. Scroll open.
Die III. Scroll closed up and design smaller (18×22 *mm*).

Single specimens of the 1933–1948 issue inscribed in English may be distinguished from those of 1930–1945 as follows:—

½d. and 1d. Centres in grey instead of varying intensities of black.
2d. The letters of 'SOUTH AFRICA' are narrower and thinner.
3d. The trees are taller and the sky is without lines.
6d. The frame is vermilion.
1s. The frame is chalky blue.

For similar designs, but printed in screened rotogravure, see Nos. 114 to 122a.

BOOKLET PANES. Booklets issued in 1935 contained ½d. and 1d. stamps in panes with advertisements in the top and bottom margins and no margin at right (Nos. 54c and 56e). These were replaced in 1937 by editions showing blank margins on all four sides (Nos. 56f and 75ca). Following a period when the booklet panes were without margins a further 3s. booklet was issued in 1948 which had four margins on the panes and postal slogans at top and bottom (Nos. 56h, 87c and 114a).

24

JIPEX

1936

(24a)

'Cleft skull' flaw (R. 14/2)

Spots above head and behind neck (R. 12/5)

(Des J. Booysen)

1935 (1 May). Silver Jubilee. Inscr bilingually. W **9**. P 15×14.

65	**24**	½d. black and blue-green	3·00	16·00	20
		a. 'Cleft skull' flaw	8·50	32·00	
		b. Spots above head and behind neck	9·50	40·00	
66		1d. black and carmine	3·00	8·50	10
		a. 'Cleft skull' flaw	8·50	21·00	
		b. Spots above head and behind neck	11·00	29·00	
67		3d. blue	15·00	60·00	2·25
		a. 'Cleft skull' flaw	50·00	£130	
		b. Spots above head and behind neck	55·00	£140	
68		6d. green and orange	30·00	80·00	3·25
		a. 'Cleft skull' flaw	80·00	£190	
		b. Spots above head and behind neck	85·00	£200	
65/68 *Set of* 4			45·00	£140	5·00

In stamps with English at top the ½d., 3d. and 6d. have 'SILWER JUBILEUM' to left of portrait, and 'POSTAGE REVENUE' or 'POSTAGE' (3d. and 6d.) in left value tablet. In the 1d., 'SILVER JUBILEE' is to the left of portrait. In alternate stamps the positions of English and Afrikaans inscriptions are reversed.

1936 (2 Nov). Johannesburg International Philatelic Exhibition. Optd with T **24a**. W **9** (inverted).

	Un sheet	*Us sheet*
MS69 **6** ½d. grey and green (No. 54)	4·75	13·00
MS70 **7** 1d. grey and carmine (No. 56)	3·50	8·50

Issued each in miniature sheet of six stamps with marginal advertisements. Ten different arrangements of advertisements exist on the ½d. sheets, 21 different on the 1d.

25

1½d. 'Mouse' flaw (R. 4/1)

(Des J. Prentice)

1937 (12 May). Coronation. W **9** (sideways*). P 14.

			Un pair	*Used pair*	*Used single*
71	**25**	½d. grey-black and blue-green	1·00	1·25	10
		w. Wmk horns pointing to left	1·00	1·25	10
72		1d. grey-black and carmine	1·00	1·00	10
		w. Wmk horns pointing to left	1·00	1·00	10

73		1½d. orange and greenish blue	1·00	80	10
		a. 'Mouse' flaw	12·00		
		w. Wmk horns pointing to left	1·00	80	10
74		3d. ultramarine	1·25	3·00	10
		w. Wmk horns pointing to left	1·25	3·00	10
75		1s. red-brown and turquoise-blue	2·75	5·00	15
		a. Hyphen on Afrikaans stamp omitted (R. 2/13)	80·00	90·00	
		bw. Wmk horns pointing to left	2·75	5·00	15
71/75 *Set of 5*			6·25	10·00	40

* The normal sideways watermark shows the horns of the springbok pointing to the right, *as seen from the back of the stamp*.

No. 75a shows the hyphen completely omitted and the top of the 'K' damaged. A less distinct flaw, on which part of the hyphen is still visible and with no damage to the 'K', occurs on R. 4/17.

25a

½d. 'Tick' flaw on ear and spot on nose (multipositive flaw (occurring in 1947) (R. 3/4 or 3/1 on some ptgs of No. 114))

1937–40. W **9**. P 15×14.

75*c*	**25a**	½d. grey and green	14·00	2·50	10
		ca. Booklet pane of 6 (with blank margins) (1937)	65·00		
		cd. Grey and blue green (1940)	11·00	1·25	10
		ce. 'Tick' flaw and spot on nose	75·00		

The lines of shading in T **25a** are all horizontal and thicker than in T **6**. In Nos. 75*c* and 75*cd* the design is composed of solid lines. For stamps with designs composed of dotted lines, see No. 114. Later printings of No. 75*cd* have a smaller design.

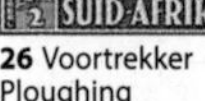

26 Voortrekker Ploughing

27 Wagon crossing Drakensberg

28 Signing of Dingaan–Retief Treaty

29 Voortrekker Monument

(Des W. Coetzer and J. Prentice)

1938 (14 Dec). Voortrekker Centenary Memorial Fund. W **9**. P 14 (Nos. 76/77) or 15×14 (others).

76	**26**	½d. +½d. blue and green	18·00	8·00	50
77	**27**	1d. +1d. blue and carmine	22·00	5·50	40
78	**28**	1½d. +1½d. chocolate and blue-green	26·00	10·00	1·00
79	**29**	3d. +3d.bright blue	26·00	10·00	1·00
76/79 *Set of 4*			80·00	29·00	2·50

30 Wagon Wheel

31 Voortrekker Family

1d. Three bolts in wheel rim (R. 15/5)

(Des W. Coetzer and J. Prentice)

1938 (14 Dec). Voortrekker Commemoration. W **9**. P 15×14.

80	**30**	1d. blue and carmine	9·50	3·50	30
		a. Three bolts in wheel rim	65·00	40·00	
81	**31**	1½d. greenish blue and brown	12·00	3·50	30

32 Old Vicarage, Paarl, now a museum

33 Symbol of the Reformation

34 Huguenot Dwelling, Drakenstein Mountain Valley

(Des J. Prentice)

1939 (17 July). 250th Anniversary of Huguenot Landing in South Africa and Huguenot Commemoration Fund. W **9**. P 14 (Nos. 82/83) or 15×14 (No. 84).

82	**32**	½d. +½d. brown and green	9·00	8·00	40
83	**33**	1d. +1d. green and carmine	15·00	8·00	40
84	**34**	1½d. +1½d. blue-green and purple	32·00	22·00	1·25
82/84 *Set of 3*			50·00	35·00	1·90

34a Gold Mine

Large gold blob on headgear (Cyl 31, R. 3/4)

1941 (Aug)–**48.** W **9** (sideways). P 14×15.

87	**34a**	1½d. blue-green and yellow-buff (*shades*)	3·50	1·50	10
		a. Yellow-buff (centre) omitted	£5000	£2500	
		ab. Ditto (one stamp in pair)	£3000		
		b. Gold blob on headgear	42·00		
		c. Booklet pane of 6 (with postal slogans on margins) (1948)	9·00		

Due to changes in the frame-plate make-up, the 'Gold blob on headgear' variety may be found on stamps with both Afrikaans and English inscriptions.

35 Infantry

36 Nurse and Ambulance

37 Airman

38 Sailor, Destroyer and Lifebelts

39 Women's Auxiliary Services

40 Artillery

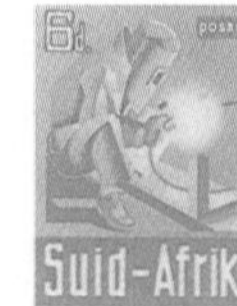

41 Electric Welding

42 Tank Corps

42a Signaller

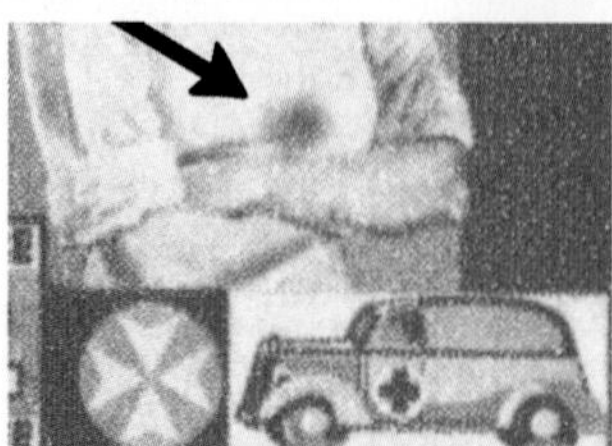

1d. 'Stain' on uniform (R. 14/11)

3d. 'Cigarette' flaw (R. 18/2)

1941–46. War Effort. W **9** (sideways on 2d., 4d., 6d.). P 14 (2d., 4d., 6d.) or 15×14 (others).

(a) Inscr alternately

88	**35**	½d. green (19.11.41)	1·50	4·00	15
		a. Blue-green (7.42)	3·75	5·50	15
89	**36**	1d. carmine (3.10.41)	2·00	4·00	15
		a. 'Stain' on uniform flaw	38·00	55·00	
90	**37**	1½d. myrtle-green (12.1.42)	1·50	4·00	15
91	**39**	3d. blue (1.8.41)	20·00	50·00	80
		a. 'Cigarette' flaw	£120	£225	
92	**40**	4d. orange-brown (20.8.41)	22·00	35·00	25
		a. Red-brown (6.42)	38·00	42·00	1·25
93	**41**	6d. red-orange (3.9.41)	9·00	19·00	20
94	**42a**	1s.3d. olive-brown (2.1.43)	20·00	16·00	30
		a. Blackish brown (5.46)	6·00	10·00	20

(b) Inscr bilingually

			Un single	*Us single*
95	**38**	2d. violet (15.9.41)	1·00	75
96	**42**	1s. brown (27.10.41)	2·75	1·00
88/96 *Set of 7 pairs and 2 singles*			60·00	£110

43 Infantry

44 Nurse

45 Airman

46 Sailor

47 Women's Auxiliary Services

48 Electric Welding

49 Heavy Gun in Concrete Turret

50 Tank Corps

Unit (*pair*)

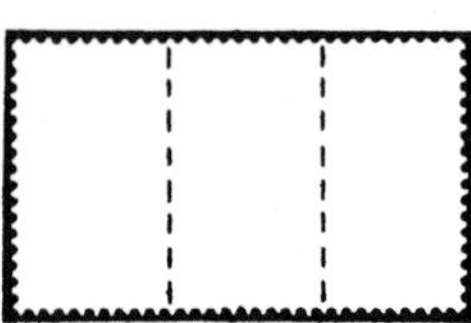

Unit (*triplet*)

Ear Flap flaw (Cyl 43 R. 13/3)

Apostrophe flaw (Cyl 6931 R. 19/1) (later corrected)

Line on Cap (Cyl 39 R. 12/11)

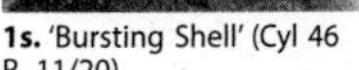

1s. 'Bursting Shell' (Cyl 46 R. 11/20)

1½d. Smoking 'L' (Cyl 46 R. 8/2)

1942–44. War Effort. Reduced sizes. In pairs perf 14 (P) or strips of three, perf 15×14 (T), subdivided by roulette 6½. W **9** (sideways* on 3d., 4d. and 1s.).

		(a) Inscr alternately	*Un unit*	*Us unit*	*Us single*
97	**43**	½d. blue-green (T) (10.42)	2·00	1·50	10
		a. Green (3.43)	3·00	2·50	10
		b. Greenish blue (7.44)	2·00	2·25	10
		c. Roulette omitted	£1400	£1300	
98	**44**	1d. carmine-red (T) (5.1.43)	1·50	1·50	10
		a. Bright carmine (3.44)	1·00	1·25	10
		b. Both roulettes omitted	£1200	£1200	
		ba. Left-hand roulette omitted	£1500		
99	**45**	1½d. red-brown (P) (9.42)	65	2·25	10
		aa. Nos. 99 and 99a *se-tenant* (strip of 4)	15·00	22·00	
		a. Roulette 13 (8.42)	1·50	5·00	30
		b. Roulette omitted	£375	£400	
		c. Ear flap flaw	20·00		
100	**46**	2d. violet (P) (2.43)	1·00	2·00	10
		a. Reddish violet (6.43)	1·50	1·00	10
		b. Roulette omitted	£1300	£1300	
		c. Apostrophe flaw	75·00	80·00	
		d. Line on cap	75·00	80·00	
101	**47**	3d. blue (T) (10.42)	10·00	18·00	10
102	**48**	6d. red-orange (P) (10.42)	2·00	2·25	10
		(b) Inscr bilingually			
103	**49**	4d. slate-green (T) (10.42)	20·00	11·00	10
104	**50**	1s. brown (P) (11.42)	20·00	4·25	10
		a. 'Bursting shell'	95·00	95·00	
		b. Smoking 'L'	95·00	95·00	
97/104 *Set of 8*			50·00	38·00	65

* The sideways watermark shows springbok horns pointing to left on the 3d. and 1s., and to right on the 4d., *all as seen from the back of the stamp.*

52

53

1943. Coil stamps. Redrawn. In single colours with plain background. W **9**. P 15×14.

			Un pair	*Used pair*	*Used single*
105	**52**	½d. blue-green (6.8.43*)	3·75	7·50	25
106	**53**	1d. carmine (4.11.43*)	4·50	7·00	20

Quoted prices are for *vertical* pairs.

* Earliest recorded dates.

54 Union Buildings, Pretoria

1945–47. Redrawn. W **9**. P 14.

107	**54**	2d. slate and deep reddish violet (3.45)	25·00	2·50	10
		a. Slate and deep lilac (10.46)	25·00	6·00	20
		b. Slate and bright violet (1947)	4·50	10·00	20

In Nos. 107 to 107*b* the Union Buildings are shown at a different angle from Nos. 58 and 58*a*. Only the centre is screened i.e., composed of very small square dots of colour arranged in straight diagonal lines. For whole design screened and colours changed, see No. 116. No. 107*a*/107*b* also show '2' of '2d.' clear of white circle at top.

55 'Victory'

56 'Peace'

57 'Hope'

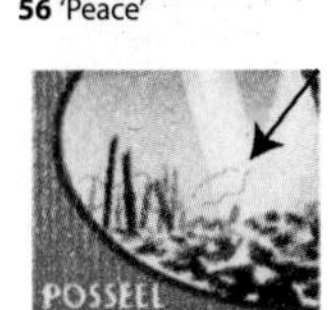

1d. 'Barbed wire' (R. 9/6)

1945 (3 Dec). Victory. W **9**. P 14.

108	**55**	1d. brown and carmine	20	1·25	10
		a. barbed wire flaw	15·00		
109	**56**	2d. slate-blue and violet	20	1·25	10
110	**57**	3d. deep blue and blue	20	1·50	10
108/110 *Set of 3*			55	3·50	25

58 King George VI

59 King George VI and Queen Elizabeth

60 Queen Elizabeth II as Princess, and Princess Margaret

'Bird' on '2' (Cyl 6912 R. 10/6)

3d. 'Black-eyed Princess' (R. 19/2)

(Des J. Prentice)

1947 (17 Feb). Royal Visit. W **9**. P 15×14.

111	**58**	1d. black and carmine	10	35	10
112	**59**	2d. violet	15	60	10
		a. 'Bird' on '2' flaw	6·00	9·00	
113	**60**	3d. blue	15	60	10
		a. 'Black-eyed Princess'	7·50	12·00	
111/113 *Set of 3*			35	1·40	20

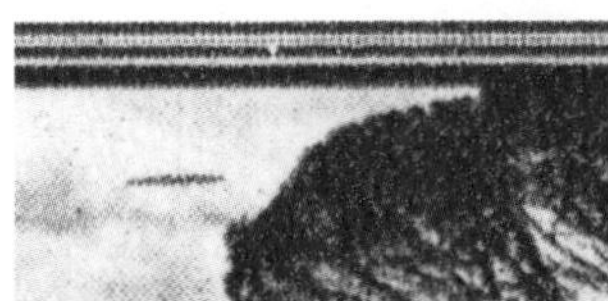

3d. 'Flying saucer' flaw (Cyl 17 R. 17/2)

I

II **5s.**

5s. 'Rain' flaw (R. 20/6)

1947–54. 'SUID-AFRIKA' hyphenated on Afrikaans stamps. Printed from new cylinders with design in screened rotogravure. W **9**. P 15×14 (½d., 1d. and 6d.) or 14 (others).

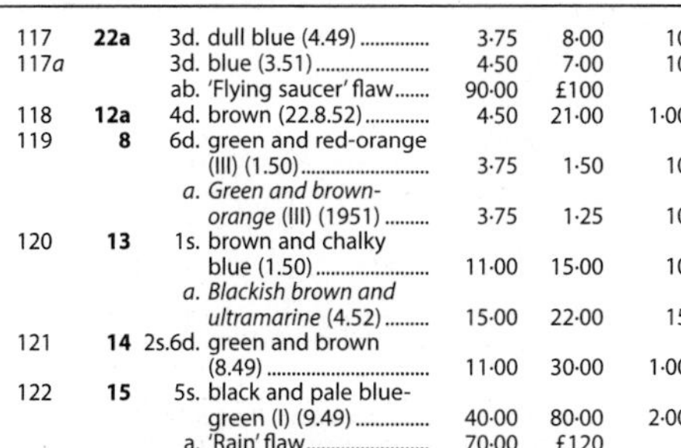

114	**25a**	½d. grey and green (frame only screened) (9.47)	3·00	7·50	10
		a. Booklet pane of 6 (with postal slogans on margins) (1948)	6·00		
		b. 'Tick' flaw and spot on nose	45·00		
		c. Entire design screened (7.1.49)	2·75	7·50	10
		ca. Booklet pane of 6 (with margin at right) (1951)	6·00		
		cb. 'Tick' flaw and spot on nose	45·00		
115	**7**	1d. grey and carmine (1.9.50)	2·25	5·50	10
		a. Booklet pane of 6 (with margin at right) (1951)	6·00		
116	**54**	2d. slate-blue and purple (3.50)	5·50	25·00	1·25
117	**22a**	3d. dull blue (4.49)	3·75	8·00	10
117*a*		3d. blue (3.51)	4·50	7·00	10
		ab. 'Flying saucer' flaw	90·00	£100	
118	**12a**	4d. brown (22.8.52)	4·50	21·00	1·00
119	**8**	6d. green and red-orange (III) (1.50)	3·75	1·50	10
		a. Green and brown-orange (III) (1951)	3·75	1·25	10
120	**13**	1s. brown and chalky blue (1.50)	11·00	15·00	10
		a. Blackish brown and ultramarine (4.52)	15·00	22·00	15
121	**14**	2s.6d. green and brown (8.49)	11·00	30·00	1·00
122	**15**	5s. black and pale blue-green (I) (9.49)	40·00	80·00	2·00
		a. 'Rain' flaw	70·00	£120	
122*b*		5s. black and deep yellow-green (II) (1.54)	50·00	£100	4·25
114/122 *Set of 9*			75·00	£170	5·00

In screened rotogravure the design is composed of very small squares of colour arranged in straight diagonal lines.

½d. Size 17¾×21¾ mm. Early printings have only the frame screened.

Due to changes in the frame-plate make-up, the 'Tick' flaw and spot on nose may be found on stamps with both Afrikaans and English inscriptions.

For the final printing of 114c, issued December 1951, the 'Tick' flaw was removed, leaving a white 'tick', but the spot on nose remained on R. 2/4.

1d. Size 18×22 mm. For smaller, redrawn design, see No. 135.

2d. For earlier issue with centre only screened, and in different colours, see Nos. 107/107*a*.

3d. No. 117. Whole stamp screened with irregular grain. Scrolls above '3d.' solid and toneless. Printed from two cylinders.

No. 117*a*. Whole stamp diagonally screened. Printed from one cylinder. Clouds more pronounced. Late printings were often in deep shades.

4d. Two groups of white leaves below name tablet and a clear white line down left and right sides of stamp.

61 Gold Mine

62 King George VI and Queen Elizabeth

1948 (1 Apr). Unit of four, perf 14, sub-divided by roulette 6½. W **9** (sideways).

			Un unit of 4	*Us unit*	*Used single*
124	**61**	1½d. blue-green and yellow-buff	2·50	7·00	10

(Des J. Booysen and J. Prentice)

1948 (26 Apr). Silver Wedding. W **9**. P 14.

			Un pair	*Used pair*	*Used single*
125	**62**	3d. blue and silver	1·50	1·25	10

(Typo Government Printer, Pretoria)

1948 (July). W **9**. P 14½×14.

126	**6**	½d. pale grey and blue-green	2·25	14·00	1·60

This was an economy printing made from the old plates of the 1926 issue for the purpose of using up a stock of cut paper. For the original printing in black and green, see No. 30.

63 *Wanderer* (emigrant ship) entering Durban

Extended rigging on mainmast (R. 14/2)

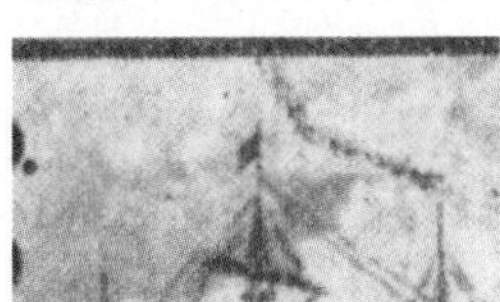

'Pennant' flaw (R. 17/5)

(Des J. Prentice)

1949 (2 May). Centenary of Arrival of British Settlers in Natal. W **9**. P 15×14.

127	**63**	1½d. claret	1·00	80	10
		a. Extended rigging	16·00	18·00	
		b. 'Pennant' flaw	16·00	18·00	

64 Hermes **3d.** Serif on 'C' (R. 1/1)

3d. 'Lake' in East Africa (R. 2/19)

(Des J. Booysen and J. Prentice)

1949 (1 Oct). 75th Anniversary of Universal Postal Union. As T **64** inscr 'UNIVERSAL POSTAL UNION' and 'WERELDPOSUNIE' alternately. W **9** (sideways). P 14×15.

128	**64**	½d. blue-green	50	1·00	10
129		1½d. brown-red	50	1·00	10
130		3d. bright blue	60	1·00	10
		a. Serif on 'C'	55·00		
		b. 'Lake' in East Africa	55·00		
128/130 *Set of 3*			1·40	2·75	25

65 Wagons approaching Bingham's Berg **67** Bible, candle and Voortrekkers

66 Voortrekker Monument, Pretoria

(Des W. Coetzer and J. Prentice)

1949 (1 Dec). Inauguration of Voortrekker Monument, Pretoria. Types **65/67**. W **9**. P 15×14.

			Un single	*Us single*
131	**65**	1d. magenta	10	10
132	**66**	1½d. blue-green	10	10
133	**67**	3d. blue	15	15
131/3 *Set of 3*			30	30

68 Union Buildings, Pretoria

1950 (Apr)–**51**. W **9** (sideways). P 14×15.

			Un pair	*Used pair*	*Used single*
134	**68**	2d. blue and violet	1·00	1·00	10
		a. Booklet pane of 6 (with margin at right) (1951).	4·00		

1951 (22 Feb). As No. 115, but redrawn with the horizon clearly defined. Size reduced to 17¼×21¼ mm.

135	**7**	1d. grey and carmine	1·75	2·50	10

69 Seal and monogram **70** *Maria de la Quellerie* (D. Craey)

2d. 'Full Moon' flaw under 'R' of 'AFRICA' (R. 6/3)

2d. Line through sails consists of a vertical line from near the top of the upper stamp, extending through the sails to the stamp below (pair comprising R. 11/2 and R. 12/12)

(Des Miss R. Reeves and J. Prentice (1d., 4½d.), Mrs. T. Campbell and J. Prentice (others))

1952 (14 Mar). Tercentenary of Landing of Van Riebeeck. Types **69/70** and similar designs. W **9** (sideways on 1d. and 4½d.) P 14×15 (1d. and 4½d.) or 14×15 (others).

136	½d. brown-purple and olive-grey	10	10
137	1d. deep blue-green	10	10
138	2d. deep violet	50	10
	a. 'Full Moon'	12·00	
	b. 'Line through sails' (vert pair)	17·00	
139	4½d. blue	15	15
140	1s. brown	1·00	10
136/140 *Set of 5*		1·50	45

Designs: Horiz—1½d. T **69**; 2d. Arrival of Van Riebeeck's ships; 1s. *Landing at the Cape* (C. Davidson Bell). Vert—1d. T **70**; 4½d. *Jan van Riebeeck* (D. Craey).

SATISE (74) **SADIPU** (75)

1952 (26 Mar). South African Tercentenary International Stamp Exhibition, Cape Town. No. 137 optd with T **74** and No. 138 with T **75**.

141	1d. deep blue-green	40	1·25
142	2d. deep violet	60	1·00
	a. 'Full Moon'	14·00	
	b. 'Line through sails' (vert pair)	19·00	

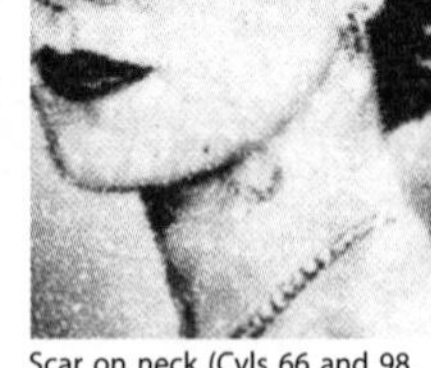

76 Queen Elizabeth II Scar on neck (Cyls 66 and 98, R. 4/7)

(Des H. Kumst)

1953 (3 June). Coronation. W **9** (sideways). P 14×15.

143	**76**	2d. deep violet-blue	50	10
		a. *Ultramarine*	60	10
		b. Scar on neck	10·00	

77 1d. 'Cape Triangular' Stamp **4d.** Broken knee (lower pane, R. 10/4)

(Des H. Kumst)

1953 (1 Sept). Centenary of First Cape of Good Hope Stamp. T **77** and similar horiz design. W **9**. P 15×14.

144	1d. sepia and vermilion	10	10
145	4d. deep blue and light blue	50	20
	a. Broken knee	10·00	

Designs: 1d. T **77**; 4d. Four pence 'Cape Triangular' stamp.

79 Merino Ram  **80** Springbok

81 Aloes

(Des A. Hendriksz and J. Prentice (4½d.))

1953 (1 Oct). W **9**. P 14.

146	**79**	4½d. slate-purple and yellow	20	10
		a. Yellow omitted	†	£3000
147	**80**	1s.3d. chocolate	1·25	10
148	**81**	1s.6d. vermilion and deep blue-green	50	35
146/148 *Set of 3*			1·75	45

82 Arms of Orange Free State and Scroll

(Des H. Kumst)

1954 (23 Feb). Centenary of Orange Free State. W **9**. P 15×14.

149	**82**	2d. sepia and pale vermilion	10	10
150		4½d. purple and slate	20	50

83 Warthog **84** Black Wildebeest **85** Leopard

86 Mountain Zebra **87** White Rhinoceros **88** African Elephant

89 Hippopotamus **90** Lion **91** Greater Kudu

92 Springbok **93** Gemsbok **94** Nyala

95 Giraffe **96** Sable Antelope

(Des H. Kumst)

1954 (14 Oct). Types **83/96**. W **9** (sideways on large vert designs). P 15×14 (½d. to 2d.), 14 (others).

151	**83**	½d. deep blue-green	10	10
152	**84**	1d. brown-lake	10	10
153	**85**	1½d. sepia	10	10
154	**86**	2d. plum	10	10
155	**87**	3d. chocolate and turquoise-blue	1·00	10
156	**88**	4d. indigo and emerald	1·00	30

157	**89**	4½d. blue-black and grey-blue	60	1·00
158	**90**	6d. sepia and orange	50	10
159	**91**	1s. deep brown and pale chocolate	1·25	10
160	**92**	1s.3d. brown and bluish green	3·25	10
161	**93**	1s.6d. brown and rose	1·75	60
162	**94**	2s.6d. brown-black and apple-green	3·50	20
163	**95**	5s. black-brown and yellow-orange	12·00	1·60
164	**96**	10s. black and cobalt	12·00	3·50
151/164 *Set of* 14			32·00	6·50

No. 152 exists in coils.
See also Nos. 170/177 and 185/197.

97 President Kruger

98 President M. Pretorius

6d. 'Scar' on chin (R. 1/7)

(Des H. Kumst)

1955 (21 Oct). Centenary of Pretoria. W **9** (sideways). P 14×15.

165	**97**	3d. slate-green	10	10
166	**98**	6d. maroon	10	30
		a. 'Scar' on chin	8·00	

99 A. Pretorius, Church of the Vow and Flag

100 Settlers' Block-wagon and House

(Des H. Kumst)

1955 (1 Dec). Voortrekker Covenant Celebrations, Pietermaritzburg. W **9**. P 14.

			Un pair	*Us pair*	*Us single*
167	**99**	2d. blue and magenta	45	2·75	10

(Des H. Kumst)

1958 (1 July). Centenary of Arrival of German Settlers in South Africa. W **9**. P 14.

168	**100**	2d. chocolate and pale purple	10	10

101 Arms of the Academy

(Des H. Kumst)

1959 (1 May). 50th Anniversary of the South African Academy of Science and Art, Pretoria. W **9**. P 15×14.

169	**101**	3d. deep blue and turquoise-blue	10	10
		a. Deep blue printing omitted	£6500	

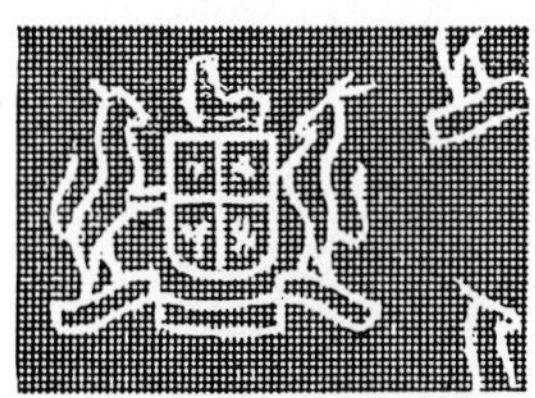
102 Union Coat of Arms

1 1
S S
I II

1959–60. As Nos. 151/152, 155/156, 158/159 and 162/163, but W **102** (sideways on Nos. 172/173 and 175/177).

170	**83**	½d. deep greenish blue (12.60)	15	7·00
171	**84**	1d. brown-lake (I) (11.59)	10	10
		a. Redrawn. Type II (10.60)	20	10
172	**87**	3d. chocolate and turquoise-blue (9.59)	25	10
173	**88**	4d. indigo and emerald (1.60)	50	20
174	**90**	6d. sepia and orange (2.60)	70	2·75
175	**91**	1s. deep brown and pale chocolate (11.59)	7·00	1·75
176	**94**	2s.6d. brown-black and apple-green (12.59)	2·75	4·00
177	**95**	5s. black-brown and yellow-orange (10.60)	9·00	35·00
170/177 *Set of* 8			18·00	45·00

Nos. 171/171a. In Type II '1d. Posgeld Postage' is more to the left in relation to 'South Africa', with '1' almost central over 'S' instead of to right as in Type I.
No. 171 exists in coils.

103 Globe and Antarctic Scene

(Des H. Kumst)

1959 (16 Nov). South African National Antarctic Expedition. W **102**. P 14×15.

178	**103**	3d. blue-green and orange	20	10

104 Union Flag

105 Union Arms

106 'Wheel of Progress'

107 Union Festival emblem

(Des V. Ivanoff and H. Kumst (1s.), H. Kumst (others))

1960 (2 May). 50th Anniversary of Union of South Africa. Types **104/107**. W **102** (sideways on 4d. and 6d.). P 14×15 (4d., 6d.) or 15×14 (others).

179	**104**	4d. orange-red and blue	30	10
180	**105**	6d. red, brown and light green	30	10
181	**106**	1s. deep blue and light yellow	30	10
182	**107**	1s. 6d. black and light blue	70	1·00
179/182 *Set of* 4			1·40	1·00

See also No. 190, 192/193.

108 Steam Locomotives *Natal* (1860) and Class 25 (1950s)

(Des V. Ivanoff)

1960 (2 May). Centenary of South African Railways. W **102**. P 15×14.

183	**108**	1s.3d. deep blue	1·10	30

109 Prime Ministers Botha, Smuts, Hertzog, Malan, Strijdom and Verwoerd

1960 (31 May). Union Day. W **102**. P 15×14.

184	**109**	3d. brown and pale brown	15	10
		a. Pale brown omitted*	£9000	

* This is due to a rectangular piece of paper adhering to the background cylinder, resulting in R.2/1 missing the colour completely and six adjoining stamps having it partially omitted. The item in block of eight is probably unique.

(New Currency. 100 cents = 1 rand)

1961 (14 Feb). As previous issues but with values in cents and rand. W **102** (sideways on 3½c., 7½c., 20c., 50c., 1r.). P 15×14 (½c., to 2½c., 10c.), 14×15 (3½c., 7½c.) or 14 (others).

185	**83**	½c. deep bluish green (as No. 151)	10	10
186	**84**	1c. brown-lake (as No. 152)	10	10
187	**85**	1½c. sepia (as No. 153)	10	10
188	**86**	2c. plum (as No. 154)	10	1·00
189	**109**	2½c. brown (as No. 184)	20	10
190	**104**	3½c. orange-red and blue (as No. 179)	20	2·75
191	**90**	5c. sepia and orange (as No. 158)	20	10
192	**105**	7½c. red, brown and light green (as No. 180)	20	3·50
193	**106**	10c. deep blue and light yellow (as No. 181)	40	60
194	**92**	12½c. brown and bluish green (as No. 160)	1·00	1·25
195	**93**	20c. brown and rose (as No. 161)	3·00	3·75
196	**95**	50c. black-brown and orange-yellow (as No. 163)	4·75	11·00
197	**96**	1r. black and cobalt (as No. 164)	15·00	25·00
185/197 *Set of* 13			22·00	42·00

X. REPUBLIC OF SOUTH AFRICA

OUTSIDE THE COMMONWEALTH

110 African Pygmy Kingfisher

111 Kafferboom Flower

112 Afrikander Bull

113 Pouring Gold

114 Groot Constantia

115 Burchell's Gonolek

116 Baobab Tree

117 Maize

118 Cape Town Castle Entrance

119 Protea

120 Secretary Bird

121 Cape Town Harbour

122 Strelitzia

Two types of ½c.:

I

II

Type I from sheets. Reeds indistinct.
Type II from coils. Reeds strengthened.

Three types of 1c.:

I

II

III

Type I. Lowest point of flower between 'OS' of 'POSTAGE'. Right-hand petal over 'E'.
Type II. Flower has moved fractionally to the right so that lowest point is over 'S' of 'POSTAGE'. Right-hand petal over 'E'.
Type III. Lowest point directly over 'O'. Right-hand petal over 'G'.

Two types of 2½c.

I

II

In Type I the lines of the building are quite faint.
In Type II all lines of the building have been strengthened by re-engraving.

(Des Mrs. T. Campbell (½c., 3c., 1r.); Miss N. Desmond (1c.); De La Rue (2½c., 5c., 12½c.); H. L. Prager (50c.); Govt. Ptg Dept artist (others))

1961 (31 May)–**63**. Unsurfaced paper. W **102** (sideways* on ½c., 1½c., 2½c., 5c. to 20c.). P 14×15 (½c., 1½c.), 15×14 (1c.). or 14 (others).

No.	Type	Description	Unused	Used
198	**110**	½c. bright blue, carmine and brown (I)	10	10
		a. Perf 14 (3.63)	10	15
		b. Type II (coils) (18.5.63)	1·25	3·00
199	**111**	1c. red and olive-grey (I)	10	10
		a. Type II (1.62)	10	10
		b. Type III (coils) (5.63)	2·00	3·75
200	**112**	1½c. brown-lake and light purple	10	10
201	**113**	2c. ultramarine and yellow	2·00	10
202	**114**	2½c. violet and green (I)	15	10
		aw. Wmk top of Arms to right	1·75	10
		b. Type II. *Deep violet and green* (9.61)	20	10
203	**115**	3c. red and deep blue	2·75	1·25
204	**116**	5c. yellow and greenish blue	30	10
205	**117**	7½c. yellow-brown and light green	60	10
206	**118**	10c. sepia and green	75	10
207	**119**	12½c. red, yellow and black-green	2·00	30
		a. Yellow omitted	£1600	
		b. Red omitted	£2750	
208	**120**	20c. turquoise-blue, carmine and brown-orange	3·00	30
209	**121**	50c. black and bright blue	14·00	2·00
210	**122**	1r. orange, olive-green and light blue	7·00	2·00
198/210 *Set of 13*			29·00	5·00

* The normal sideways watermark shows the top of the Arms to left, *as seen from the back of the stamp.*

1961–1974 Definitives

Key to designs, perfs, watermarks, papers and phosphors

Value		*Type*	*Perf*	*W* **102** *Ordinary*	*No wmk Ordinary*	*W* **127** *Chalky*
½c.	**110**	(I)	14×15	198	—	—
		(I)	14	198a	—	—
		(II)	14×15	198b	—	—
1c.	**111**	(I)	15×14	199	211	—
		(II)		199a	211a	227
		(III)		199b	—	—
1½c.	**112**		14×15	200	—	228
2c.	**113**		14	201	212	229
2½c.	**114**	(I)	14	202	—	—
		(II)		202b	213/*a*	230/*a*
3c.		**115**	14	203	214	—
5c.		**116**	14	204	215	231
7½c.		**117**	14	205	216	232
10c.		**118**	14	206	217/*b*	233/*a*
12½c.		**119**	14	207	—	—
20c.		**120**	14	208	218	234/*a*
50c.		**121**	14	209	219	235
1r.		**122**	14	210	—	236

Redrawn Designs

Value	*Type*	*Perf*	*W* **127**	*W* **127a** *plain or phos*	*W* **127** *Phos frame*	*W* **127a** *Phos frame*	*No wmk. Phosphorised Glossy*	*No wmk. Phosphorised Chalky*
½c.	**130a**	14	A238	B238	—	—	—	—
		14×15	A238b	—	—	—	—	—
		14	—	B238c/d	—	—	—	—
1c.	**131**	15×14	A239	B239	—	—	—	—
		13½×14	A239a	B239a	—	—	—	—
1½c.	**132**	14×15	—	B240/b	—	284	—	—
		14×13½	—	B240c	—	—	—	—
2c.	**133**	14	A241	B241/b	—	285/*a*	315a	—
		12½	—	—	—	—	315	315b
2½c.	**134**	14	A242	B242*a*	286aa	286/*a*	—	—
3c.	**135**	14	A243	B243/a	—	287	—	—
		12½	—	—	—	—	316	316a
4c.	**134**	14	—	B243*b*	—	288	—	—
5c.	**136**	14	—	B244/a	—	289	318a	—
		12½	—	—	—	—	318	318b
6c.	**137**	14	—	—	—	290	—	—
		12½	—	—	—	—	—	319
7½c.	**137**	14	—	B245	—	291	—	—
9c.	**139**	14	—	B245*a*	—	292	—	—
		12½	—	—	—	—	320/a	—
10c.	**138**	14	—	B246/a	—	293	321a	—
		12½	—	—	—	—	321	321b
12½c.	**139**	14	A247/a	—	—	294	—	—
15c.	**140**	14	A248	B248	—	295	—	—
20c.	**141**	14	—	B249/a	—	296/*a*	—	—
		12½	—	—	—	—	323	323a
50c.	**142**	14	—	B250	—	—	—	—
		12½	—	—	—	—	324	324a
1r.	**143**	14	A251	B251	—	—	—	—
		12½	—	—	—	—	325	—

New Designs

			W **127a**. *Plain or phos*	*W* **127a** *Phos frame*	*No wmk. Phosphorised Glossy*	*No wmk. Phosphorised Chalky*
½c.	**168**	14×13½	276	282	—	—
		14×14½	276a	—	313	—
		14×15	—	282a	—	—
1c.	**169**	13½×14	277	283	—	—
		14	—	—	314	—
4c.	**182**	14	310/a	—	—	—
		12½	—	—	317/b	317c
15c.	**182a**	14	311	—	—	—
		12½	—	—	—	322

Although several of the stamps included in this table were issued after 1970 and are therefore not listed in this catalogue, the table has been shown here in full for the convenience of collectors

1961 (1 Aug)–**63**. As Nos. 199, 201/206 and 208/209 but without wmk.

No.	Type	Description	Unused	Used
211	**111**	1c. red and olive-grey (I)	10	50
		a. Type II (9.62)	1·00	1·25
212	**113**	2c. ultramarine and yellow (8.63)	9·00	3·75
213	**114**	2½c. deep violet and green (II)	20	30
		a. Violet and green (12.61)	20	10
214	**115**	3c. red and deep blue (10.61)	45	10
		a. Deep blue (face value, etc) omitted	£3250	
215	**116**	5c. yellow and greenish blue (12.61)	35	10
216	**117**	7½c. yellow-brown and light green (3.62)	60	15
217	**118**	10c. sepia and green (11.61)	2·25	1·00
		a. Sepia and emerald	50·00	18·00
		b. Sepia-brown and light green (7.63)	2·50	1·75
218	**120**	20c. turquoise-blue carmine and brown-orange (4.63)	8·00	2·75
219	**121**	50c. black and bright blue (8.62)	8·00	3·00
211/219 *Set of 9*			25·00	10·00

123 Blériot XI Monoplane and Boeing 707 Airliner over Table Mountain

124 Folk-dancers

1961 (1 Dec). 50th Anniversary of First South African Aerial Post. W **102** (sideways). P 14×15.

220	**123**	3c. blue and red	50	10

(Des K. Esterhuysen)

1962 (1 Mar). 50th Anniversary of Volkspele (folk-dancing) in South Africa. W **102** (sideways). P 14×15.

221	**124**	2½c. orange-red and brown	15	10

125 *The Chapman* (emigrant ship)

1962 (20 Aug). Unveiling of Precinct Stone, British Settlers Monument Grahamstown. W **102**. P 15×14.

222	**125**	2½c. turquoise-green and purple	40	10
223		12½c. blue and deep chocolate	1·50	1·00

126 Red Disa (orchid), Castle Rock and Gardens

(Des M. F. Stern)

1963 (14 Mar). 50th Anniversary of Kirstenbosch Botanic Gardens, Cape Town. P 13½×14.

224	**126**	2½c. multicoloured	20	10
		a. Red (orchid, etc) omitted	£3750	£2250

127 RSA (upright)

127a RSA (*tête-bêche*)

128 Centenary Emblem and Nurse

129 Centenary Emblem and Globe

1963 (30 Aug). Centenary of Red Cross. Chalk-surfaced paper. Wmk **127** (sideways on 2½c.). P 14×13½ (2½c.) or 15×14 (12½c.)

No.	Type	Description	Mint	Used
225	**128**	2½c. red, black and reddish purple	20	10
		w. Wmk reversed	3·25	1·75
226	**129**	12½c. red and indigo	1·75	1·00
		a. Red cross omitted	£5000	£3000

1963–67. As 1961–1963 but chalk-surfaced paper and W **127** (sideways on 1½c., 2½c., (Nos. 230, 230aw) and 5c.), (sideways inverted on 2½c. (No. 230*a*), 7½c., 10c. and 20c.). P 15×14 (1c.) 14×15 (1½c.), or 14 (others).

No.	Type	Description	Mint	Used
227	**111**	1c. red and olive-grey (II) (9.63)	10	10
		w. Wmk reversed	65	65
228	**112**	1½c. brown-lake and light purple (1.67)	1·75	3·25
229	**113**	2c. ultramarine and yellow (11.64)	15	20
230	**114**	2½c. violet and green (II) (10.63)	10	10
		a. Bright reddish violet and emerald (II) (wmk sideways inverted) (3.66)	20	20
		aw. Wmk sideways (top of triangle to right)	2·50	1·00
231	**116**	5c. yellow and greenish blue (9.66)	1·00	75
232	**117**	7½c. yellow-brown and bright green (23.2.66)	3·00	6·50
		w. Wmk sideways (top of triangle to right)	15·00	7·50
233	**118**	10c. sepia-brown and light emerald (9.64)	40	10
		a. Sepia-brown and green (1.67)	45	20
234	**120**	20c. turquoise-blue, carmine and brown orange (7.64)	1·00	2·25
		a. Deep turquoise-blue, carmine and flesh (20.7.65)	1·75	1·25
235	**121**	50c. black and ultramarine (4.66)	30·00	10·00
236	**122**	1r. orange, light green and pale blue (7.64)	48·00	48·00
227/236 *Set of 10*			80·00	60·00

In the 2½c. (No. 230*a*), 5c., 7½c., 10c. (Jan 1967 printing only) and 50c. the watermark is indistinct but they can easily be distinguished from the stamps without watermark by their shades and the chalk-surfaced paper which is appreciably thicker and whiter.

The sideways watermark shows the top of the triangle pointing to the left on Nos. 228, 230*a*, 232, 233 and 234 and to the right on Nos. 230, 230aw, 231 and 232w *as seen from the back of the stamp.*

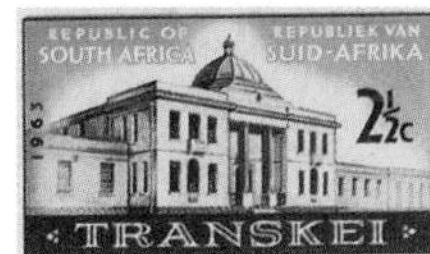

130 Assembly Building, Umtata

1963 (11 Dec). First Meeting of Transkei Legislative Assembly. Chalk-surfaced paper. W **127**. P 15×14.

No.	Type	Description	Mint	Used
237	**130**	2½c. sepia and light green	10	10
		a. Light green omitted	£3250	

130a African Pygmy Kingfisher

131 Kafferboom Flower

132 Afrikander Bull

133 Pouring Gold

134 Groot Constantia

135 Burchell's Gonolek

136 Baobab Tree

137 Maize

138 Cape Town Castle Entrance

139 Protea

140 Industry

141 Secretary Bird

142 Cape Town Harbour

143 Strelitzia

(15c. des C. E. F. Skotnes)

Redrawn types.

½c. '½C' larger and REPUBLIEK VAN REPUBLIC OF' smaller.
3c. and 12½c. Inscriptions and figures of value larger.
Others. 'SOUTH AFRICA' and SUID-AFRIKA larger and bolder. The differences vary in each design but are easy to see by comparing the position of the letters of the country name with 'REPUBLIC OF' and 'REPUBLIEK VAN'.

1964–72. As 1961–1963 but redrawn and new values (4c, 9c and 15c). Chalk-surfaced paper.

(a) wmk **127** *(sideways on ½, 1½, 2½, 4, 5, 7½, 9, 10, 15, 20c.). P 14×15 (1½c.), 15×14 (1c.) or 14 (others)*

No.	Description	Mint	Used
A238	½c. bright blue, carmine and brown (21.5.64)	10	10
	a. Imperf (pair)	£375	
	b. Perf 14×15	20	20
A239	1c. red and olive-grey (9.3.67)	10	10
	a. Perf 13½×14 (7.68)	30	10
A241	2c. ultramarine and yellow (8.1.68)	20	10
	a. Yellow omitted	£1400	
A242	2½c. violet and green (19.4.67)	20	10
	w. Wmk top of RSA to left	£450	75·00
A243	3c. red and deep blue (11.64)	30	10
A247	12½c. red, yellow and black-green (3.64)	1·00	40
	a. Red, pale yellow and blue-green (2.2.66)	2·75	40
A248	15c. black, light olive-yellow and red-orange (1.3.67)	1·25	25
A251	1r. orange, light green and light blue (6.65)	2·00	1·00
	w. Wmk inverted		
A238/A251 *Set of 8*		4·50	2·00

(b) wmk **127a**. *P 14×15 (1½c.), 15×14 (1c.) or 14 (others)*

No.	Description	Mint	Used
B238	½c. bright blue, carmine and yellow-brown (1.68)	10	10
	c. Perf 14. *Bright blue, lake and yellow-brown* (3.68)	60	70
	d. Perf 14. *Bright blue, carmine-lake and yellow-brown* (3.98)	30	10
B239	1c. red and olive-grey (7.67)	10	10
	a. Perf 13½×14 (9.68)	30	10
B240	1½c. dull red-brown and light purple (21.9.67)	15	10
	a. Purple-brown and light purple (1968)	15	10
	b. Bright red-brown and light purple (5.68)	15	10
	c. Perf 14×13½. *Red-brown and light purple* (14.8.69)	2·25	2·50
B241	2c. Ultramarine and yellow	1·50	20
	b. Blue and yellow	80	10
B242*a*	2½c. reddish violet and green (7.67)	30	10
B243	3c. red and deep blue (19.12.67)	30	10
	a. Brown-red and deep blue (3.72)	4·50	30
B243*b*	4c. violet and green (10.71)	1·00	30
B244	5c. orange-yellow and greenish blue (14.2.68)	40	10
	a. Lemon and deep greenish blue	8·50	1·00
B245	7½c. yellow-brown and bright green (26.7.67)	60	10
B245*a*	9c. red, yellow and slate-green (2.72)	7·50	7·50
B246	10c. sepia and green (10.6.68)	1·75	1·25
	a. Brown and pale green (7.68)	4·50	4·50
B248	15c. black, light olive-yellow and red-orange (4.3.69)	3·00	50
B249	20c. turquoise-blue, carmine and brown-orange (2.68)	6·50	15
	a. Turquoise-blue, carmine and orange-buff (12.71)	8·50	2·00
B250	50c. black and bright blue (17.6.68)	2·00	40
B251	1r. orange, light green and light blue (6.68)	2·00	1·00
B238/B251 *Set of 14*		30·00	10·00

* The normal sideways watermark shows the top of RSA to right on No. A242 and to the left on Nos. A238/A238b, A247/A247*a* and A248 *as seen from the back of the stamp.*

WATERMARK. The first stamps on T **127** showed a reasonably clear watermark, but a new paper introduced in late 1966 had a much fainter watermark. T **127a** was introduced in mid-1967 and is invariably quite difficult to see, so care should be exercised in correctly identifying single stamps from this issue.

GUM. The 2, 3, 5, 20, 50c. and 1r. on W **127a** exist with PVA gum as well as gum arabic.

PHOSPHORISED PAPER. From October 1971 onwards phosphor bands (see Nos. 282/296) gave way to phosphorised paper which cannot be distinguished from non-phosphor stamps without the aid of a lamp. For this reason we do not distinguish these printings in the above issue, but some are slightly different shades and all have PVA gum. The 4c. and 9c. are on phosphorised paper only and differ from Nos. 288 and 292 by the lack of phosphor bands.

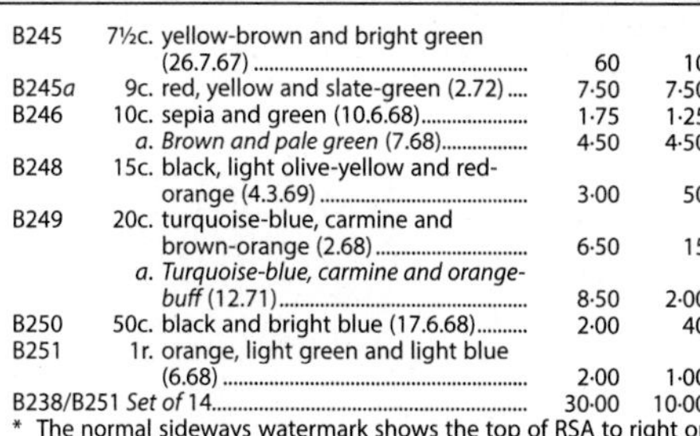

145 Springbok Badge of Rugby Board

147 Calvin

1964 (8 May). 75th Anniversary of South African Rugby Board. Chalk-surfaced paper. T **145** and similar horiz design. W **127** (sideways on 2½c.). P 14×15 (2½c.) or 15×14 (12½c.)

No.	Description	Mint	Used
252	2½c. yellow-brown and deep green	15	10
253	12½c. black and light yellow-green	1·25	1·25

Designs: 2½c. T **145**; 12½c. Rugby footballer.

1964 (10 July). 400th Death Anniversary of Calvin (Protestant reformer). Chalk-surfaced paper. W **127** (sideways). P 14×13½.

No.	Type	Description	Mint	Used
254	**147**	2½c. cerise, violet and brown	10	10

148 Nurse's Lamp

149 Nurse holding Lamp

I. Screened base to lamp

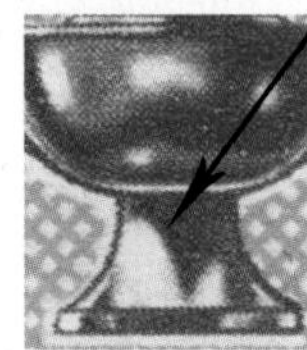
II. Clear base to lamp

1964 (12 Oct). 50th Anniversary of South African Nursing Association. Chalk-surfaced paper. W **127** (sideways on 2½c.). P 14×15 (2½ c.) or 15×14 (12½c.)

No.	Type	Description	Mint	Used
255	**148**	2½c. ultramarine and dull gold (Type I)	10	10
256		2½c. bright blue and yellow-gold (Type II)	30	10
		a. Ultramarine and dull gold	15	10
257	**149**	12½c. bright blue and gold	1·50	1·25
		a. Gold omitted	£3750	
255/257 *Set of 3*			1·50	1·25

150 ITU Emblem and Satellites

1965 (17 May). ITU Centenary. T **150** and similar horiz design. Chalk-surfaced paper. W **127**. P 15×14.

No.	Description	Mint	Used
258	2½c. orange and blue	25	10
259	12½c. brown-purple and green	1·25	1·00

Designs: 2½c. T **150**; 12½c. ITU emblem and symbols.

152 Pulpit in Groote Kerk, Cape Town

153 Church Emblem

1965 (21 Oct). Tercentenary of Nederduites Gereformeerde Kerk (Dutch Reformed Church) in South Africa. Chalk-surfaced paper. W **127** (sideways on 2½c., inverted on 12½c.). P 14×15 (2½c.) or 15×14 (12½c.).

260	**152**	2½c. brown and light yellow	15	10
261	**153**	12½c. black, light orange and blue	70	70

154 Diamond

155 Bird in flight

(Des C.E.F. Skotnes)

1966 (31 May). Fifth Anniversary of Republic. Types **154/155** and similar designs. Chalk-surfaced paper. W **127** (sideways on 1c., 3c.). P 14×13½ (1c.), 13½×14 (2½c.), 14×15 (3c.) or 15×14 (7½c.).

		Un pair	*Us pair*	*Us single*
262	1c. black, bluish green and olive-yellow	45	60	10
263	2½c. blue, deep blue and yellow-green	50	1·00	10
264	3c. red, greenish yellow and red-brown	1·25	1·75	10
265	7½c. blue, ultramarine and yellow	1·25	1·75	10
262/265	*Set of 4*	3·00	4·50	35

Designs: Vert—1c. T **154**; 3c. Maize plants. Horiz—2½c. T **155**; 7½c. Mountain landscape.

Nos. 262/265 exist on Swiss made paper with *tête bêche* watermark from a special printing made for use in presentation albums for delegates to the UPU Congress in Tokyo in 1969 as supplies of the original Harrison paper were by then exhausted (*Set of 4 pairs price £140 mint*).

158 Verwoerd and Union Buildings, Pretoria

(Des from portrait by Dr. Henkel)

1966 (6 Dec). Verwoerd Commemoration. T **158** and similar designs. Chalk-surfaced paper. W **127** (sideways on 3c.). P 14×15 (3c.) or 15×14 (others).

266	2½c. blackish brown and turquoise	10	10
267	3c. blackish brown and yellow-green	10	10
	a. Blackish brown (portrait) omitted	£8000	
268	12½c. blackish brown and greenish blue	60	60
266/268	*Set of 3*	70	60

Designs: Vert—3c. *Dr. H. F. Verwoerd* (I. Henkel). Horiz—2½c. T **158**; 12½c. Verwoerd and map of South Africa.

161 *Martin Luther* (Cranach the Elder)

162 Wittenberg Church Door

1967 (31 Oct). 450th Anniversary of Reformation. W **127** ((sideways), on 2½c., W **127a** on 12½c.). P 14×15.

269	**161**	2½c. black and rose-red	10	10
270	**162**	12½c. black and yellow-orange	1·00	1·50

163 'Profile of President Fouche' (I. Henkel)

164 Portrait of President Fouche

1968 (10 Apr). Inauguration of President Fouche. W **127** (sideways). P 14×15.

271	**163**	2½c. chocolate and pale chocolate	10	10
272	**164**	12½c. deep blue and light blue	60	1·00
		a. Wmk **127a**	1·00	1·50

165 Hertzog in 1902

1968 (21 Sept). Inauguration of General Hertzog Monument, Bloemfontein. T **165** and similar designs. W **127**, (inverted on 3c., sideways on 12½c. or **127a** (2½c.)). P 14×13½ (12½c.) or 13½×14 (others).

273	2½c. black, brown and olive-yellow	10	10
274	3c. black, red-brown, red-orange and yellow	15	10
275	12½c. red and yellow-orange	1·00	1·00
273/275	*Set of 3*	1·00	1·00

Designs: Horiz—2½c. T **165**; 3c. Hertzog in 1924. Vert—12½c. Hertzog Monument.

168 African Pygmy Kingfisher

169 Kafferboom Flower

1969. W **127a** (sideways on ½c.). P 14×13½ (½c.) or 13½×14 (1c.)

276	**168**	½c. new blue, carmine-red and yellow-ochre (1.69)	10	60
		a. Coil. Perf 14×14½ (5.69)	1·75	4·25
277	**169**	1c. rose-red and olive-brown (1.69)	10	10

See also Nos. 282/283.

170 Springbok and Olympic Torch

171 Professor Barnard and Groote Schuur Hospital

1969 (15 Mar). South African Games, Bloemfontein. W **127a** (sideways). P 14×13½.

278	**170**	2½c. black, blue-black, red and sage-green	15	10
279		12½c. black, blue-black, red and cinnamon	70	1·00

1969 (7 July). World's First Heart Transplant and 47th South African Medical Association Congress. T **171** and similar horiz design. W **127a**. P 13½×14 (2½c.) or 15×14 (12½c.).

280	2½c. plum and rose-red	15	10
281	12½c. carmine-red and royal blue	1·00	1·40

Designs: 2½c. T **171**; 12½c. Hands holding heart.

1969–72. As 1964–1972 issue, Nos. 276/277, and new value (6c.), but with phosphor bands printed horizontally and vertically between the stamp designs, over the perforations, producing a frame effect. W **127a** (upright on 1, 2 and 3c., sideways on others). P 14×13½ (½, 1½c.), 13½×14 (1c.), or 14 (others).

282	**168**	½c. new blue, carmine-red and yellow-ochre (1.70)	15	70
		a. Coil. Perf 14×15 (2.71)	3·50	7·50
		w. Wmk reversed	65	2·50
283	**169**	1c. rose-red and olive-brown (12.69)	15	10
		w. Wmk reversed	60	1·00
284	**132**	1½c. red-brown and light purple (12.69)	20	1·00
285	**133**	2c. ultramarine and yellow (11.69)	1·00	10
		aa. Yellow omitted	£1500	
		a. Deep ultramarine and yellow (8.70)	1·00	1·00
286	**134**	2½c. violet and green (1.70)	15	10
		aa. Wmk **127**	1·00	1·00
		a. Purple and green (24.7.70)	1·75	10
		w. Wmk reversed	20·00	17·00
287	**135**	3c. red and deep blue (30.9.69)	1·00	1·50
288	**134**	4c. violet and green (1.3.71)	40	2·25
289	**136**	5c. yellow and greenish blue (17.11.69)	60	10
290	**137**	6c. yellow-brown and bright green (3.5.71)	70	2·25
291		7½c. yellow-brown and bright green (17.11.69)	2·00	30
292	**139**	9c. red, yellow and black-green (17.5.71)	4·50	3·25
293	**138**	10c. brown and pale green (1.70)	1·00	10
294	**139**	12½c. red, yellow and black-green (2.5.70)	4·00	7·50
295	**140**	15c. black, light olive-yellow and red-orange (1.70)	1·00	2·50
296	**141**	20c. turquoise-blue, carmine and brown-orange 18.2.70)	8·00	4·75
		a. Turquoise-blue, carmine and orange-buff (9.72)	11·00	4·75
282/296		*Set of 15*	22·00	23·00

The 1, 2, 2½, 3, 10, 15 and 20c. exist with PVA gum as well as gum arabic, but the 4, 6 and 9c. exist with PVA gum only. Stamps without watermark in these designs were issued between 1972 and 1974.

173 Mail Coach

174 Transvaal Stamp of 1869

1969 (6 Oct). Centenary of First Stamps of South African Republic (Transvaal). Phosphor bands on all four sides (2½c.). W **127a** (sideways on 12½c.). P 13½×14 (2½c.) or 14×13½ (12½c.)

297	**173**	2½c. yellow, indigo and yellow-brown	15	10
298	**174**	12½c. emerald, gold and yellow-brown	2·25	3·00

PHOSPHOR FRAME. Nos. 299/302 have phosphor applied on all four sides as a frame.

175 'Water 70' Emblem

177 'The Sower'

1970 (14 Feb). Water 70 Campaign. T **175** and similar design. W **127a** (sideways on 2½c.). P 14×13½ (2½c.) or 13½×14 (3c.)

299	2½c. green, bright blue and chocolate	30	10
300	3c. Prussian blue, royal blue and buff	30	20

Designs: Vert—2½c. T **175**. Horiz—3c. Symbolic waves.

1970 (24 Aug). 150th Anniversary of Bible Society of South Africa. T **177** and similar horiz design (gold die-stamped on 12½c.). W **127a** (sideways on 2½c.). P 14×13½ (2½c.) or 13½×14 (12½c.)

301	2½c. multicoloured	15	10
302	12½c. gold, black and blue	1·00	1·40

Designs: 2½c. T **177**; 12½c. 'Biblia' and open book.

STAMP BOOKLETS

1913. Black on red cover. With 'UNION OF SOUTH AFRICA' at top and 'UNIE VAN ZUID AFRIKA' at foot. Stapled.

SB1	2s.6d. booklet containing 12×½d. and 24×1d. (Nos. 3/4) in blocks of 6	£10000

B **1**

1913–20. Black on red cover with 'UNION OF SOUTH AFRICA' and 'UNIE VAN ZUID AFRIKA' both at top. as T B **1** Stapled.

SB2	2s.6d. booklet containing 12×½d. and 24×1d. (Nos. 3/4) in blocks of 6	£10000
	a. Black on pink cover (1920)	£10000

B **1a**

1921. Black on salmon-pink cover with 'UNION OF SOUTH AFRICA' and 'UNIE VAN ZUID AFRIKA' either side of Arms and telegraph rates beneath as T B **1a**. Stapled.

SB3	3s. booklet containing 12×½d., 12×1d. and 12×1½d. (Nos. 3/5) in blocks of 6	£500

1922. Black on salmon-pink cover as T B **1a** surch. Stapled.

SB4 3s.6d. on 3s. booklet containing 12×½d., 12×1d. and 12×2d. (Nos. 3/4, 6) in blocks of 6 .... £1400

1926. Black on salmon-pink cover as T B **1a**. Stitched.

SB5 2s.6d. booklet containing 12×½d. and 24×1d. (Nos. 30/31) £4000

B **1b**

1927. Black on salmon-pink cover as No. SB3, but inscr 'Union of South Africa' and 'Unie van Suidafrika' as T B **1b**. Stitched.

SB6 2s.6d. booklet containing 12×½d. and 24×1d. (Nos. 30e, 31e) £8500

B **1c**

1930. Black on pink cover as No. SB6, but with advertisement at foot instead of telegraph rates as T B **1c**. Stitched.

SB7 2s.6d. booklet containing 12×½d. and 24×1d. (Nos. 42/43) in blocks of 6 .... £3500

1931. Black on pink cover. As T B **1c** but with smaller inscr and advertisement on front cover. Stitched.

SB8 3s. booklet containing 12×1d. (No. 43) in blocks of 6 and 12×2d. (No. 44) in blocks of 4 .... £3750

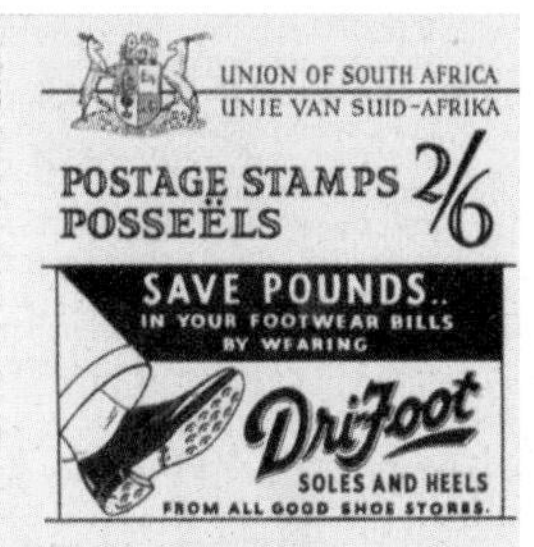

B **1d**

1935. Black on lemon cover. Advertisement on front cover as T B **1d**. Stitched.

SB9 2s.6d. booklet containing two panes of 6×½d. (No. 54c) and four panes of 6×1d. (No. 56e), all with adverts on margins £350

1937. Black on lemon cover. Advertisement on front cover as T B **1d**. Stitched.

SB10 2s.6d. booklet containing two panes of 6×½d. (No. 75ca) and four panes of 6×1d. (No. 56f), all with blank margins £750

B **1e**

1937. Machine vended booklets. Red cover as T B **1e**. Stitched.

SB11 6d. booklet containing 4×½d. and 4×1d. (Nos. 75c, 56) in pairs .... 7·00

1938. Machine vended booklets. As T B **1e** but blue cover. Stitched.

SB12 3d. booklet containing ½d. and 1d. (Nos. 75c, 56), each in pair .... 42·00

B **1f**

1938. Black on buff cover. Union Arms at top left with advertisement at foot as T B **1f**. Stitched.

SB13 2s.6d. booklet containing 12×½d. and 24×1d. (Nos. 75c, 56) in blocks of 6 .... £1200

1939. Black on buff cover. As T B **1f** but Union Arms centred at top with advertisement at foot. Stitched.

SB14 2s.6d. booklet containing 12×½d. and 24×1d. (Nos. 75c, 56) in blocks of 6 .... £1200

B **1g**

1939–40. Green on buff cover. Union Arms centred at top with large advertisement at bottom left as T B **1g**. Stitched.

SB15 2s.6d. booklet containing 12×½d. and 24×1d. (Nos. 75c, 56) in blocks of 6 .... £3500
a. Blue on buff cover (1940) £180

1941. As T B **1g** but blue on buff cover as No. SB15. Stitched.

SB17 2s.6d. booklet containing 12×½d. and 12×1d. (Nos. 75c, 56) in blocks of 6 and 12×1½d. (No. 57) in blocks of 4 .... £180

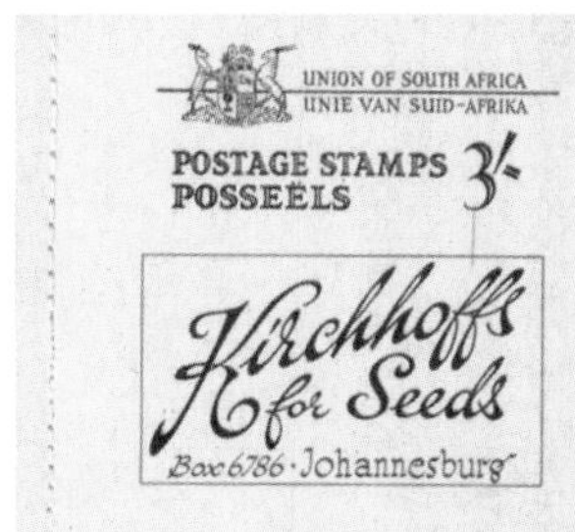

B **1h**

1948. Black on buff cover. With advertisement as T B **1h**. Stitched.

SB18 3s. booklet containing two panes of 6×½d., 6×1d. and 6×1½d. (Nos. 114a, 56h, 87c), all with postal slogans on margins, and pane of air mail labels .... 32·00

B **1i**

1951. Black on buff cover as Type B **1i**. Stitched.

SB19 3s.6d. booklet containing two panes of 6×½d., 6×1d. and 6×2d. (Nos. 114ca, 115a, 134a), each with margins at right .... 13·00

POSTAGE DUE STAMPS

The Interprovincial Period (1 June 1912–1914-1915)

For postage due stamps the Interprovincial period is extended until the replacement of the relevant Transvaal stamps by the first Union issues on 12 December 1914 (2d.), 2 February 1915 (3d.) or 19 March 1915 (all other values).

Postage due stamps of Transvaal

(i) Used in Transvaal

ZD1	½d. black and green (No. D1)	2·00
ZD2	1d. black and scarlet (No. D2)	1·50
ZD3	2d. brown-orange (No. D3)	1·50
ZD4	3d. black and blue (No. D4)	7·50
ZD5	5d. black and violet (No. D5)	15·00
ZD6	6d. black and red-brown (No. D6)	18·00
ZD7	1s. scarlet and black (No. D7)	14·00

(ii) Used in Cape of Good Hope

ZD8	½d. black and green (No. D1)	3·00
ZD9	1d. black and scarlet (No. D2)	2·00
ZD10	2d. brown-orange (No. D3)	1·50
ZD11	3d. black and blue (No. D4)	8·00
ZD12	5d. black and violet (No. D5)	18·00
ZD13	6d. black and red-brown (No. D6)	18·00
ZD14	1s. scarlet and black (No. D7)	21·00

(iii) Used in Natal

ZD15	½d. black and green (No. D1)	4·00
ZD16	1d. black and scarlet (No. D2)	3·00
ZD17	2d. brown-orange (No. D3)	2·00
ZD18	3d. black and blue (No. D4)	9·50
ZD19	5d. black and violet (No. D5)	25·00
ZD20	6d. black and red brown (No. D6)	25·00
ZD21	1s. scarlet and black (No. D7)	27·00

(iv) Used in Orange River Colony

ZD22	½d. black and green (No. D1)	8·00
ZD23	1d. black and scarlet (No. D2)	5·00
ZD24	2d. brown-orange (No. D3)	5·00
ZD25	3d. black and blue (No. D4)	18·00
ZD26	5d. black and violet (No. D5)	£100
ZD27	6d. black and red-brown (No. D6)	45·00
ZD28	1s. scarlet and black (No. D7)	£100

D 1

UNION OF SOUTH AFRICA (A)

UNION OF SOUTH AFRICA (B)

(Typo D.L.R.)

1914–22. Inscribed bilingually. Lettering as A. W **4**. P 14.

			Un single	Used single
D1	D **1**	½d. black and green (19.3.15)	2·25	3·75
D2		1d. black and scarlet (19.3.15)	2·25	15
		a. Black ptd double	£3250	
		w. Wmk inverted	£150	£150
D3		2d. black and reddish violet (12.12.14)	6·50	50
		a. Black and bright violet (1922)	7·00	60
		w. Wmk inverted	£190	
D4		3d. black and bright blue (2.2.15)	2·25	60
		w. Wmk inverted	48·00	75·00
D5		5d. black and sepia (19.3.15)	4·00	40·00
D6		6d. black and slate (19.3.15)	7·00	45·00
D7		1s. red and black (19.3.15)	60·00	£170
D1/D7 *Set of 7*			75·00	£225

There are interesting minor varieties in some of the above values, e.g. ½d. to 3d., thick downstroke to 'd'; 1d., short serif to '1'; raised 'd'; 2d., forward point of '2' blunted; 3d., raised 'd'; very thick 'd'.

(Litho Govt Printer, Pretoria)

1922. Lettering as A. No wmk. Rouletted 7-8.

D8	D **1**	½d. black and bright green (6.6.22)	2·00	17·00
D9		1d. black and rose-red (3.10.22)	1·00	1·25
D10		1½d. black and yellow-brown (3.6.22)	1·25	1·75
D8/D10 *Set of 3*			3·75	18·00

(Litho Govt Printer, Pretoria)

1922–26. T D **1** redrawn. Lettering as B. P 14.

D11	½d. black and green (1.8.22)	80	1·25
D12	1d. black and rose (16.5.23)	90	15
D13	1½d. black and yellow-brown (12.1.24)	1·00	1·00
D14	2d. black and pale violet (16.5.23)	1·00	70
	a. Imperf (pair)	£400	£500
	b. Black and deep violet	16·00	1·00
D15	3d. black and blue (3.7.26)	7·00	20·00
D16	6d. black and slate (9.23)	10·00	1·50
D11/D16 *Set of 6*		19·00	22·00

The locally printed stamps, perf 14, differ both in border design and in figures of value from the rouletted stamps. All values except the 3d. and 6d. are known with closed 'G' in 'POSTAGE' usually referred to as the 'POSTADE' variety. This was corrected in later printings.

D **2**

D **3**

D **4**

Blunt '2' (R. 3/6, 8/6)

(Typo Pretoria)

1927–28. Inscribed bilingually. No wmk. P 13½×14.

D17	D **2**	½d. black and green	1·00	1·75
		a. Blunt '2'	11·00	
D18		1d. black and carmine	1·25	30
D19		2d. black and mauve	1·25	30
		a. Black and purple	20·00	80
D20		3d. black and blue	7·00	22·00
D21		6d. black and slate	18·00	2·00
D17/D21 *Set of 5*			26·00	24·00

On Nos. D20 and D21 there is no dot below 'd'.

1932–42. T D **2** redrawn. W **9**. P 15×14.

(a) Frame roto, value typo

D22	½d. black and blue-green (1934)	2·75	1·00
	w. Wmk inverted	2·50	1·00
D23	2d. black and deep purple (10.4.33)	22·00	1·25
	w. Wmk inverted	22·00	1·25

(b) Whole stamp roto

D25	1d. black and carmine (wmk inverted) (3.34)	2·50	10
D26	2d. black and deep purple (10.39)	50·00	10
	a. Thick (double) '2d.' (R. 5/6, R. 18/2)	£500	50·00
	w. Wmk inverted	50·00	50
D27	3d. black and Prussian blue (3.8.32)	25·00	6·00
D28	3d. deep blue and blue (wmk inverted) (1935)	6·00	30
	a. Indigo and milky blue (wmk inverted) (1942)	75·00	3·25
	w. Wmk upright	50·00	3·00
D29	6d. green and brown-ochre (wmk inverted) (7.6.33)	22·00	1·75
	a. Green and bright orange (wmk inverted) (1938)	16·00	1·50
D22/D29a *Set of 7*		£110	9·00

In No. D26 the value is screened, whereas in No. D23 the black of the value is solid.

1943–44. Inscr bilingually. Roto. W **9**. In units of three, perf 15×14 subdivided by roulette 6½.

			Un unit	Us unit	Us single
D30	D **3**	½d. blue-green (1944)	13·00	65·00	60
D31		1d. carmine	9·00	5·50	10

D32 2d. dull violet 6·50 11·00 15
a. Bright violet 16·00 50·00 65
D33 3d. indigo 55·00 60·00 1·25
D30/D33 *Set of 4* 75·00 £130 1·90

Split 'D' (R. 7/5 on every fourth sheet)

1948–49. New figure of value and capital 'D'. Whole stamp roto. W **9**. P 15×14.

D34 D **4** ½d. black and blue-green 6·00 20·00
D35 1d. black and carmine 19·00 5·50
D36 2d. black and violet (1949) 23·00 11·00
a. Thick (double) '2D.' (R. 15/5-6, R. 16/5-6) £100 50·00
D37 3d. deep blue and blue 15·00 17·00
a. Split 'D' £450 £450
D38 6d. green and bright orange (1949) 25·00 6·00
D34/D38 *Set of 5* 80·00 55·00

3d. 'Swallow in flight' (R. 16/8)

4d. Crude retouch to flaw on '4' (R. 1/1)

1950–58. As T D **4**, but 'SUID-AFRIKA' hyphenated. Whole stamp roto. W **9**. P 15×14.

D39 1d. black and carmine (5.50) 1·00 30
D40 2d. black and violet (4.51) 50 20
a. Thick (double) '2D.' (R. 15/5-6, R. 16/5-6) 8·00 11·00
b. Black and reddish violet (12.52) 1·00 1·00
ba. Thick (double) '2D.' 13·00 16·00
bb. Black (value) omitted £5500
D41 3d. deep blue and blue (5.50) 3·50 2·50
a. Split 'D' £140 90·00
b. 'Swallow' variety 90·00 75·00
D42 4d. deep myrtle-green and emerald (2.58) 12·00 15·00
a. Retouch 70·00 70·00
D43 6d. green and bright orange (3.50) 7·00 7·00
D44 1s. black-brown and purple-brown (2.58) 12·00 13·00
D39/D44 *Set of 6* 32·00 35·00

No. D40bb occurs in horizontal pair with a normal.

D **5** D **6** Afrikaans at top D **7** English at top

1961 (14 Feb). Values in cents as T D **5**. Whole stamp roto. W **102**. P 15×14.

D45 1c. black and carmine 20 3·75
D46 2c. black and violet 35 3·75
D47 4c. deep myrtle-green and emerald 80 8·50
D48 5c. deep blue and blue 1·75 8·50
D49 6c. green and orange-red 5·00 8·50
D50 10c. sepia and brown-lake 6·00 10·00
D45/D50 *Set of 6* 13·00 38·00

1961 (31 May)–**69**. Roto. W **102**. P 15×14.

D51 D **6** 1c. black and carmine 40 60
D52 D **7** 1c. black and carmine (6.62) 40 3·75
D53 2c. black and deep reddish violet 40 55
D54 D **6** 4c. deep myrtle-green and light emerald* 2·25 2·25
D54*a* D **7** 4c. deep myrtle-green and light emerald (6.69)* 12·00 27·00
D55 5c. deep blue and grey-blue 2·00 4·25
D56 5c. black and grey-blue (6.62) 1·25 4·00
D57 D **6** 6c. deep green and red-orange 6·50 4·75
D58 D **7** 10c. sepia and purple-brown 2·00 1·40
D51/D58 *Set of 9* 24·00 45·00

1967 (1 Dec)–**71**. Roto. W **127** (Nos. D62*b*/D62*c*) or **127a** (others)*. P 15×14.

D59 D **6** 1c. black and carmine 20 55
D60 D **7** 1c. black and carmine 20 30
D61 D **6** 2c. black and deep reddish violet 30 2·00
D62 D **7** 2c. black and deep reddish violet 30 2·00
D62*b* 4c. deep myrtle-green and emerald (6.69)* 35·00 42·00
D62*c* D **6** 4c. deep myrtle-green and emerald (6.69)* £375 £375
D63 4c. dark green and pale green (4.71) 32·00 42·00
D64 D **7** 4c. dark green and pale green (4.71) 32·00 42·00
D65 D **6** 5c. black and deep blue 50 1·50
D66 D **7** 5c. black and deep blue 50 50
D67 D **6** 6c. green and orange-red (1968) 3·50 11·00
D68 D **7** 6c. green and orange-red (1968) 3·50 11·00
D69 D **6** 10c. black and purple-brown 1·00 4·50
a. Black and brown-lake (12.69) 1·00 3·00
D70 D **7** 10c. black and purple-brown 1·00 4·50
a. Black and brown-lake (12.69) 1·00 3·00
D59/D70a *except* D62*b/c* *Set of 12* 70·00 £110

Nos. D59/D70 were printed in two panes, one with inscriptions as T D **6** and the other as T D **7**.

* Nos. D54*a*, D62*b*/D62*c* and further supplies of D54 were part of a printing released in June 1969. Most sheets were printed on paper with the Arms watermark, but some were printed on RSA paper with the watermark upright and faint (W **127**). Of these many were spoilt, but a few sheets were issued in Types D **7** and D **6**, the latter being very scarce.

The 2c. (Types D **6** and D **7**) and 4c. (T D **7** only) were reissued in 1971, perf 14.

OFFICIAL STAMPS

OFFICIAL. OFFISIEEL. OFFISIEEL OFFICIAL

(O **1**) (O **2**)

(Approximate measurements of the space between the two lines of overprint are quoted in millimetres, either in the set headings or after individual listings)

1926 (1 Dec). Optd with T O **1** (reading upwards with stops and 12½ *mm* between lines of opt).

(a) On 1913 issue (No. 6)

O1 3 2d. purple 25·00 1·75

(b) On 1926 issue (Nos. 30/32)

			Un pair	*Us pair*	*Us single*
O2	6	½d. black and green	9·00	27·00	2·00
O3	7	1d. black and carmine	4·00	8·00	50
O4	8	6d. green and orange	£650	75·00	10·00
		w. Wmk inverted	£1700	£475	32·00

The overprint occurs on both the London and Pretoria printings of Nos. 30/32. For the lower two values the overprinted London printings are scarcer than the Pretoria, but for the 6d. the ratio is reversed.

1928–30. Nos. 32 and 34 optd as T O **1** (reading upwards without stops).

O5 11 2d. grey and maroon (P 14) (17½ *mm*) 6·00 23·00 2·00
a. Lines of opt 19 mm apart (1929) 7·00 35·00 2·50
ab. Split 'd' £170
ac. On No. 34b (P 14×13½) (1930) 95·00 £100 6·50
aca. Split 'd' £500
O6 8 6d. green and orange (11½–12 *mm*) 24·00 55·00 3·00

1929–31. Optd with T O **2**.

(a) On 1926 (Typo) issue (Nos. 30/32) (13½–15 mm between lines of opt)

O7 6 ½d. black and green 2·75 4·50 35
a. Stop after 'OFFISIEEL' on English inscr stamp (1930) 50·00 55·00 3·25
b. Ditto, but on Afrikaans inscr stamp (1930) 70·00 75·00 3·25
O8 7 1d. black and carmine 3·00 7·00 45
O9 8 6d. green and orange 7·00 45·00 3·25
a. Stop after 'OFFISIEEL' on English inscr stamp (1930) 95·00 £170 10·00
b. Ditto, but on Afrikaans inscr stamp (1930) £100 £180 12·00

(b) On 1927 (Recess) issue (Nos. 36a/37) (17½–19 mm between lines of opt)

O10 13 1s. brown and deep blue (1931) 45·00 £100 9·50
a. Stop after 'OFFICIAL' on Afrikaans inscr stamp (R. 10/1, 10/7) £160 £300
b. Lines of opt 20½–21 mm apart £1600
ba. Stop after 'OFFICIAL' on Afrikaans inscr stamp £4000
O11 14 2s.6d. green and brown (1931) 70·00 £190 19·00
a. Stop after 'OFFICIAL' on Afrikaans inscr stamp (R. 10/1) £375 £700
O7/O11 *Set of 5* £110 £300 29·00

The 'stop' varieties for the ½d., and 6d. occur on R. 5/3, 5/11, 8/12, 15/3, 15/11, 18/12 with English inscriptions and R. 9/10, 9/12, 19/10, 19/12 with Afrikaans on the 1930 overprinting only.

The 1932 printing of the 2s.6d. did not include No. O11a.

1930–47. Nos. 42/44 and 47/49 ('SUIDAFRIKA' in one word) optd with T O **2**.

O12 6 ½d. black and green (9½–12½ mm) (1931) 2·25 5·00 40
a. Stop after 'OFFISIEEL' on English inscr stamp 50·00 75·00 4·00
b. Ditto, but on Afrikaans inscr stamp 28·00 60·00 3·50
c. 'Cobweb' variety 65·00
d. 'Dollar' variety 65·00
e. Opt double £500
f. Opt double, one inverted £600
w. Wmk inverted (1934) 6·50 11·00 60
O13 7 1d. black and carmine (I) (12½–14 *mm*) 4·50 7·00 55
a. Stop after 'OFFISIEEL' on English inscr stamp 65·00 90·00 4·00
b. Ditto, but on Afrikaans inscr stamp 40·00 65·00 3·50
cw. Wmk inverted (1931) 4·50 7·00 55
d. On Type II (No. 43d) (12½–13½ *mm*) (1933) 17·00 9·00 90
da. Opt double £300 £400
O14 11 2d. slate-grey and lilac (20½–22½ *mm*) (1931) 6·50 11·00 1·50
a. Airship flaw £200
w. Wmk inverted (1934) £120 £130 8·00
O15 2d. blue and violet (20½–22½ *mm*) (1938) £160 £100 9·00
a. Airship flaw £1000
O16 8 6d. green and orange (12½–13½ *mm*) (*wmk inverted*) (1931) 6·50 8·50 85
a. Stop after 'OFFISIEEL' on English inscr stamp £130 £150 6·50
b. Ditto, but on Afrikaans inscr stamp £100 £120 5·50
c. 'OFFISIEEL' reading upwards (R. 17/12, 18/12, 19/12, 20/12) (1933) £2250
w. Wmk upright (1935) £110 £130 7·00
O17 13 1s. brown and deep blue (19 *mm*) (*wmk inverted*) (1932) 65·00 95·00 8·50
a. Twisted horn flaw £500
b. Lines of opt 21 mm apart (*wmk inverted*) (1933) 70·00 £110 7·50
ba. Twisted horn flaw £500
bw. Wmk upright (1936) £100 £180 10·00
O18 14 2s.6d. green and brown (17½–18½ *mm*) (1933) 85·00 £170 15·00
a. Lines of opt 21 mm apart (1934) 60·00 75·00 8·50
aw. Wmk inverted (1937) £850 £900
O19 2s.6d. blue and brown (19–20.5 *mm*) (1946) 55·00 £110 6·50
a. Diaeresis over second 'E' of 'OFFISIEEL' on Afrikaans and English inscr stamps (1946) £2750 £3000
b. Ditto, but on Afrikaans inscr stamp only £1500 £1600
c. Ditto, but on English inscr stamp only £1500 £1600

The stop varieties for the ½d., 1d. and 6d. occur on R. 9/10, 9/12, 19/10, 19/12 with English inscriptions and R. 5/3, 5/11, 8/12, 15/3, 15/11, 18/12 with Afrikaans on the 1930 and 1931 overprintings only.

OFFICIAL OFFISIEEL OFFISIEEL OFFICIAL

(O **3**) (O **4**)

1935–49. Nos. 54, 56/58, 61/62 and 64*b*/64*c* ('SUID-AFRIKA' hyphenated) optd.

*(a) With T O **2** (reading downwards with 'OFFICIAL' at right)*

O20 6 ½d. grey and green (12½ *mm*) (*wmk inverted*) (1936) 75·00 85·00 2·75
w. Wmk upright (1937) 11·00 45·00 2·00
O21 7 1d. grey and carmine (11½–13 *mm*) (*wmk inverted*) 7·50 9·00 35
aa. Pair, one stamp 'OFFICIAL OFFICIAL' † £4500 —
aw. Wmk upright (1937) 5·50 3·00 20
b. Grey and bright rose-carmine (No. 56*i*) (1949) 4·00 7·00 40
O22 22 1½d. green and bright gold (20 *mm*) (*wmk inverted*) (1937) 50·00 35·00 1·75
ab. Broken chimney and faint headgear £160
ac. Flag on chimney at right £160
aw. Wmk upright (1939) 32·00 24·00 1·00
b. Blue-green and dull gold (No. 57*e*) (1941) 50·00 11·00 1·10
O23 11 2d. blue and violet (20 *mm*) (1939) £150 50·00 2·25
O24 8 6d. green and vermilion (I) (11½–13 *mm*) (1937) 85·00 55·00 3·75
a. 'Falling ladder' flaw £1400 £1100
b. 'Molehill' flaw £1200 £950
c. Die II (No. 61*c*) (1938) 14·00 10·00 1·25
d. Die III *Green and red-orange* (No. 61*d*) (11.47) 4·00 8·50 85
O25 1s. brown and chalky blue (18.5–20 *mm*) (*shades*) (1939) 80·00 50·00 2·25
a. Diaeresis over second 'E' of 'OFFISIEEL' on Afrikaans and English inscr stamps (1946) £3750 £2750
b. Ditto, but on Afrikaans inscr stamp only £2000 £1500
c. Ditto, but on English inscr stamp only £2000 £1500

O26 **15** 5s. black and blue-green (20 *mm*) (6.48) ... 65·00 £160 13·00
a. Broken yoke-pin ... £225
O27 **23** 10s. blue and blackish brown (No. 64*c*) (20 *mm*) (6.48) ... £110 £275 23·00

(b) With T O **3** *(reading downwards with 'OFFICIAL' at left and 18–19 mm between lines of opt)*

O28 **15** 5s. black and blue-green (1940) ... £120 £140 12·00
a. Broken yoke-pin ... £375
O29 **23** 10s. blue and sepia (1940). £500 £500 38·00

(c) With T O **4** *(reading upwards with 'OFFICIAL' at right and 18½ mm between lines of opt*

O30 **11** 2d. grey and dull purple (No. 58*a*) (1941) ... 11·00 40·00 2·25

Nos. O19a/O19c and O25a/O25c first appeared in a 1946 overprinting where the variety occurs on R. 1/5 (Afrikaans) and R. 1/6 (English). A setting of 60 (6×10) was applied to the top halves of the sheets only. The same setting was used for a printing of the 2d. value, applied twice to each sheet of 120, resulting in O36a. The diaeresis variety reappeared in the November 1947 printing of the 1s. and 2s.6d. values in position R. 6/2 on the Afrikaans stamp and R. 6/3 on the English stamp.

Horizontal rows of six of the 1s. exist with 'OFFICIAL' twice on the first stamp and 'OFFISIEEL' twice on the last stamp. Such rows are believed to come from two half sheets which were overprinted in 1947, but not placed into normal stock (*Price for row of 6, £4000, unused*).

OFFICIAL OFFISIEEL (O **5**)   OFFICIAL OFFISIEEL (O **6**)

1937–44. No. 75c (redrawn design) optd.

(a) With T O **2** *(reading downwards with 'OFFICIAL' at right and 11–12½ mm between lines of opt)*

O31 **25a** ½d. grey and green ... 35·00 35·00 1·75
a. Grey and blue-green (No. 75cd) (1944) ... 4·75 11·00 60

(b) With T O **5** *(reading up and down with 'OFFICIAL' at left and diaeresis over the second 'E' of 'OFFISIEEL'. 10 mm between lines of opt)*

O32 **25a** ½d. grey and blue-green (No. 75*cd*) (1944) ... 50·00 30·00 2·00

1944–50. Nos. 87 and 134 optd.

(a) With T O **2** *(reading downwards with 'OFFICIAL' at right)*

O33 **34a** 1½d. blue-green and yellow-buff (14½ *mm*) 2·50 10·00 80
a. With diaeresis over second 'E' of 'OFFISIEEL' ... £800 £475 30·00
b. Gold blob on headgear ... 55·00
c. Lines of opt 16½ mm apart (6.48) ... 2·25 12·00 60

(b) With T O **6** *(reading upwards with 'OFFICIAL' at left and 16 mm between lines of opt)*

O34 **34a** 1½d. blue-green and yellow-buff (1949) ... 85·00 £100 5·00
O35 **68** 2d. blue and violet (1950) £4250 £4750 £275

Two different formes were used to overprint T **34a** between 1944 and 1946. The first, applied to the left halves of sheets only, had a diaeresis over the second 'E' of 'OFFISIEEL' on all positions of the setting, except for R. 1/2, 2/2, 3/2 and 8/1. The second form, from which the majority of the stamps came, was applied twice to overprint complete sheets, had no diaeresis.

Examples of T **34a** overprinted with T O **2** *horizontally* exist, but their status is unclear. (*Price* £1000, *unused pair*).

1947 (Nov)–**49**. No. 107*a* optd with T O **2** (reading downwards with 'OFFICIAL' at right and 20 *mm* between lines of opt).

O36 **54** 2d. slate and deep lilac ... 5·50 30·00 2·00
a. With diaeresis over second 'E' of 'OFFISIEEL' (R. 1/5-6, 11/5-6) ... £700 £1000
b. Slate and bright violet (No. 107b) (1949) ... 13·00 16·00 1·60

1949–50. Nos. 114 and 120 optd with T O **2** (reading downwards with 'OFFICIAL' at right).

O37 **25a** ½d. grey and green (11 *mm*) ... 5·00 18·00 1·25
a. 'Tick' flaw and spot on nose ... 75·00
b. Entire design screened (No. 114c) ... 5·50 13·00 1·00
ba. 'Tick' flaw and spot on nose ... 75·00
O38 **13** 1s. brown and chalky blue (17½–18½ *mm*) (1950) ... 17·00 28·00 2·50

OFFISIEEL OFFICIAL (O **7**)

1950 (June)–**54**. Optd as T O **7** using stereo blocks measuring either 10 (½d., 1d., 6d.), 14½ (1½d., 2d.) or 19 mm (others) between the lines of opt.

O39 **25a** ½d. grey and green (No. 54aw) (6.51) ... 70 1·50 15
O40 ½d. grey and green (No. 114c) ... 3·00 3·00
a. 'Tick' flaw and spot on nose ... 65·00
O41 **7** 1d. grey and bright rose-carmine (No. 56*i*) ... 1·00 6·00 50
O42 1d. grey and carmine (No. 115) (3.51) ... 1·00 3·25 20
O43 1d. grey and carmine (No. 135) (6.52) ... 1·25 2·00 20
O44 **34a** 1½d. blue-green and yellow-buff (No. 87) (3.51) ... 4·50 4·50 30
O45 **68** 2d. blue and violet (No. 134) ... 1·00 2·00 20
a. Opt inverted ... £1100 †
O46 **8** 6d. green and red-orange (No. 119) ... 2·75 4·00 35
a. Green and brown-orange (No. 119a) (6.51) ... 1·75 3·50 35
O47 **13** 1s. brown and chalky blue (No. 120) ... 5·50 18·00 2·00
a. Blackish brown and ultramarine (No. 120a) (2.53) ... £170 £190 18·00
O48 **14** 2s.6d. green and brown (No. 121) ... 8·50 35·00 3·50
O49 **15** 5s. black and blue-green (No. 64b) (3.51) ... £180 £140 9·00
O50 5s. black and pale blue-green (I) (No. 122) (2.53) ... 70·00 95·00 6·50
aa. 'Rain' flaw ... £150 £200
a. Black and deep yellow-green (II) (No. 122b) (1.54) ... 75·00 £100 9·00
O51 **23** 10s. blue and charcoal (No. 64*ca*) ... 80·00 £250 22·00

No. O39ab is from the final printing (see note below No. 114/122) with a white 'tick' (R. 2/4).

The use of the official stamps ceased in January 1955 although isolated examples of later use are known.

South Arabian Federation

Comprising Aden and most of the territories of the former Western Aden Protectorate plus one from the Eastern Aden Protectorate.

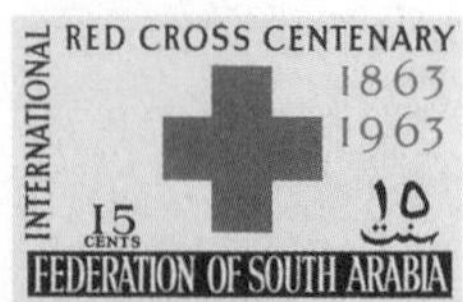

1 Red Cross Emblem

1963 (25 Nov). Red Cross Centenary. W w **12**. P 13½.

No.	Type	Description	Unused	Used
1	**1**	15c. red and black	30	30
2		1s.25 red and blue	70	1·25

(New Currency. 1000 fils = 1 dinar)

2 Federal Crest **3** Federal Flag

(Des V. Whiteley. Photo Harrison)

1965 (1 Apr). P 14½×14 (T **2**) or 14½ (T **3**).

No.	Type	Description	Unused	Used
3	**2**	5f. blue	20	10
4		10f. violet-blue	20	10
5		15f. turquoise-green	20	10
6		20f. green	20	10
7		25f. yellow-brown	20	10
8		30f. yellow-bistre	20	10
9		35f. chestnut	20	10
10		50f. red	20	10
11		65f. yellow-green	30	30
12		75f. crimson	30	10
13	**3**	100f. multicoloured	50	10
14		250f. multicoloured	5·00	1·50
15		500f. multicoloured	9·00	1·50
16		1d. multicoloured	16·00	19·00
3/16 *Set of 14*			29·00	21·00

4 ICY Emblem

(Des V. Whiteley. Litho Harrison)

1965 (24 Oct). International Co-operation Year. W w **12**. P 14½.

No.	Type	Description	Unused	Used
17	**4**	5f. reddish purple and turquoise-green	25	10
18		65f. deep bluish green and lavender	1·00	30

5 Sir Winston Churchill and St Paul's Cathedral in Wartime

(Des Jennifer Toombs. Photo Harrison)

1966 (24 Jan). Churchill Commemoration. No wmk. P 14.

No.	Type	Description	Unused	Used
19	**5**	5f. black, cerise, gold and new blue	15	10
20		10f. black, cerise, gold and deep green	55	10
21		65f. black, cerise, gold and brown	1·25	20
22		125f. black, cerise, gold and bluish violet	1·75	1·75
19/22 *Set of 4*			3·25	1·90

6 Footballer's Legs, Ball and Jules Rimet Cup

(Des V. Whiteley. Litho Harrison)

1966 (1 July). World Cup Football Championship, England. No wmk. P 14.

No.	Type	Description	Unused	Used
23	**6**	10f. violet, yellow-green, lake and yellow brown	40	10
24		50f. chocolate, blue-green, lake and yellow-brown	1·00	30

7 WHO Building

(Des M. Goaman. Litho Harrison)

1966 (20 Sept). Inauguration of WHO Headquarters, Geneva. No wmk. P 14.

No.	Type	Description	Unused	Used
25	**7**	10f. black, yellow-green and light blue	50	10
26		75f. black, light purple and yellow-brown	1·25	55

8 'Education'

9 'Science'

10 'Culture'

(Des Jennifer Toombs. Litho Harrison)

1966 (15 Dec). 20th Anniversary of UNESCO. No wmk. P 14.

No.	Type	Description	Unused	Used
27	**8**	10f. slate-violet, red, yellow and orange	30	20
28	**9**	65f. orange-yellow, violet and deep olive	1·25	1·40
29	**10**	125f. black, bright purple and orange	3·25	4·75
27/29 *Set of 3*			4·25	5·75

The South Arabian Federation became fully independent on 30 November 1967. Later issues for this area will be found listed in the Stanley Gibbons *Arabia catalogue* under Yemen People's Democratic Republic.

KATHIRI STATE OF SEIYUN

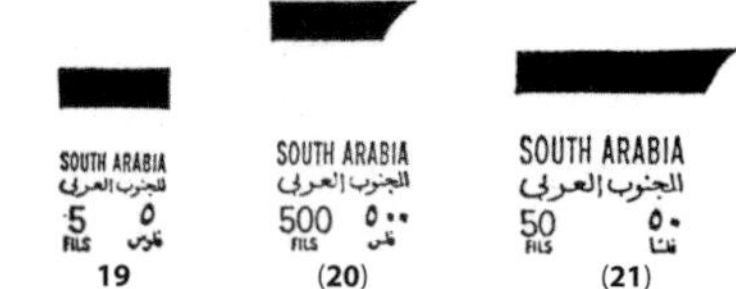

(19) (20) (21)

1966 (1 Apr). New Currency. Nos. 29/41 of Aden-Kathiri State of Seiyun surch as Types **19/21**.

No.	Description	Unused	Used
42	5f. on 5c. (Type **19**)	30	60
	a. Surch quadruple, one inverted	75·00	
43	5f. on 10c. (Type **19**) (R.)	30	1·75
44	10f. on 15c. (Type **21**) (R.)	30	2·25
	a. Surch inverted	£140	
45	15f. on 25c. (Type **20**)	1·25	1·25
	w. Wmk inverted	65·00	
46	20f. on 35c. (Type **20**) (R.)	40	1·50
47	25f. on 50c. (Type **21**) (R.)	1·25	1·50
48	35f. on 70c. (Type **20**) (R.)	1·50	2·50
49	50f. on 1s. (Type **21**)	50	1·00
50	65f. on 1s.25 (Type **21**)	50	35
51	75f. on 1s.50 (Type **21**)	2·00	1·00
52	100f. on 2s. (Type **20**) (R.)	40·00	55·00
53	250f. on 5s. (Type **21**) (R.)	2·50	4·00
54	500f. on 10s. (Type **20**)	2·50	4·00
42/54 *Set of 13*		48·00	65·00

(22) (23) (24)

1966 (13 Aug). Nos. 29/41 surch with Types **22/24**.

No.	Description	Unused	Used
55	5f. on 5c. (Type **22**) (B.)	1·75	40
	a. Surch inverted	85·00	
56	5f. on 10c. (Type **22**) (R.)	2·25	40
57	10f. on 15c. (Type **23**) (Y.)	2·25	1·75
	a. Surch inverted	65·00	
58	15f. on 25c. (Type **24**) (B.)	2·25	50
	a. Surch inverted	75·00	
59	20f. on 35c. (Type **24**) (Y.)	2·25	50
60	25f. on 50c. (Type **23**) (B.)	2·25	50
61	35f. on 70c. (Type **24**) (Br.)	2·50	75
62	50f. on 1s. (Type **23**) (G.)	2·75	1·75
	a. Stop after FILS' (R. 1/3)	32·00	
63	65f. on 1s.25 (Type **23**) (Y.)	4·50	1·50
64	75f. on 1s.50 (Type **23**) (G.)	5·50	2·75
	a. Surch inverted	75·00	
65	100f. on 2s. (Type **24**) (Y.)	6·50	2·50
	a. Surch inverted	75·00	
66	250f. on 5s. (Type **23**) (Y.)	6·00	4·00
	a. Surch inverted	60·00	
67	500f. on 10s. (Type **24**) (G.)	6·00	8·50
55/67 *Set of 13*		42·00	23·00

HELSINKI 1952 (25) INTERNATIONAL COOPERATION THROUGH OLYMPICS (26)

1966 (13 Aug). History of Olympic Games. Nos. 57, 59 and 61/67 optd as Types **25/26** in red.

No.	Description	Unused	Used
68	10f. on 15c. deep bluish green (Type **25** ('LOS ANGELES 1932'))	30	70
	a. Optd as Type **25** inverted		
69	20f. on 35c. deep blue (Type **25** ('BERLIN 1936'))	40	75
70	35f. on 70c. black (Type **26**)	40	75
	a. Opt Type **26** inverted	50·00	
71	50f. on 1s. brown-orange (Type **25** ('LONDON 1948'))	40	1·00
	a. Stop after 'FILS' (R. 1/3)	19·00	
72	65f. on 1s.25, blue-green (Type **25**)	40	1·00
73	75f. on 1s.50, deep reddish violet (Type **25** ('MELBOURNE 1956'))	50	1·50
74	100f. on 2s. deep yellow-green (Type **25** ('ROME 1960'))	60	1·75
75	250f. on 5s. deep blue and violet (Type **25** ('TOKYO 1964'))	80	3·75
	a. Surch inverted	75·00	
76	500f. on 10s. yellow-brown and violet (Type **25** ('MEXICO CITY 1968'))	1·00	4·50
68/76 *Set of 9*		4·25	14·00

CHAMPION: ENGLAND (27) **FOOTBALL 1966** (28)

1966 (19 Sept). World Cup Football Championships. Nos. 57, 59, 61/62, 65/67 optd with Types **27/28**.

No.	Description	Unused	Used
77	10f. on 15c. deep bluish green (Type **27**)	60	1·00
78	20f. on 35c. deep blue (Type **28**)	80	1·00
79	35f. on 70c. black (Type **28**)	1·00	1·00
80	50f. on 1s. brown-orange (Type **27**)	1·10	1·00
	a. Stop after 'FILS' (R. 1/3)	30·00	
81	100f. on 2s. deep yellow-green (Type **28**)	2·00	2·75
82	250f. on 5s. deep blue and violet (Type **27**)	4·50	9·50
83	500f. on 10s. yellow-brown and violet (Type **28**)	5·50	13·00
77/83 *Set of 7*		14·00	26·00

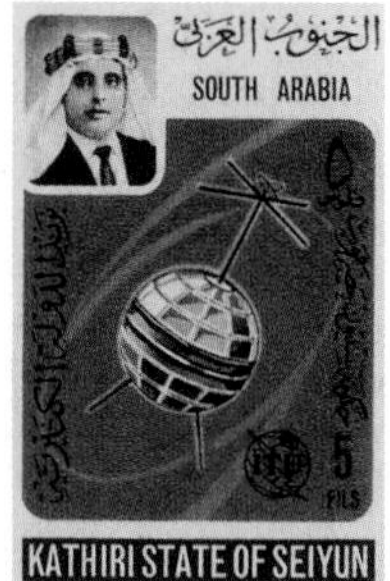

29 *Telstar*

(Photo State Ptg Wks, Vienna)

1966 (25 Oct). ITU Centenary (1965). T **29** and similar vert designs. P 13½.

No.	Description	Unused	Used
84	5f. blackish green, black and reddish violet	2·50	15
85	10f. maroon, black and bright green	2·75	20
86	15f. Prussian blue, black and orange	3·25	20
87	25f. blackish green, black and orange-red	3·75	20
88	35f. maroon, black and deep olive-yellow	3·75	20
89	50f. Prussian blue, black and orange-brown	3·75	25
90	65f. blackish green, black and orange-yellow	4·00	30
84/90 *Set of 7*		21·00	1·25

Designs: 10, 35f. *Relay*; 15, 50f. *Ranger*; others, T **29**.

32 Churchill at Easel

(Photo State Ptg Wks, Vienna)

1966 (1 Dec). Sir Winston Churchill's Paintings. T **32** and similar designs in black and gold (5f.) or multicoloured (others). P 13½.

No.	Description	Unused	Used
91	5f. Type **32**	1·75	15
92	10f. *Antibes*	2·00	15
93	15f. *Flowers (vert)*	2·00	20
94	20f. *Tapestries*	2·00	35
95	25f. *Village, Lake Lugano*	2·00	35
96	35f. *Church, Lake Como (vert)*	2·00	40
97	50f. *Flowers at Chartwell (vert)*	2·25	65
98	65f. Type **32**	2·75	90
91/98 *Set of 8*		15·00	2·75

WORLD PEACE
PANDIT NEHRU
(39)

40 *Master Crewe as Henry VIII* (Sir Joshua Reynolds)

1967 (1 Jan). 'World Peace'. Nos. 57, 59 and 61/67 optd as T **39** in various sizes of type.

99	10f. on 15c. deep bluish green (Type **39**) (R.)	5·00	2·00
100	20f. on 35c. deep blue ('WINSTON CHURCHILL') (R.)	7·00	2·75
101	35f. on 70c. black ('DAG HAMMAR SKJOLD') (B.)	50	80
102	50f. on 1s. brown-orange ('JOHN F. KENNEDY') (R.)	60	90
	a. Stop after 'FILS'	22·00	
103	65f. on 1s.25 blue-green ('LUDWIG ERHARD') (Pk.)	70	1·10
104	75f. on 1s.50 deep reddish violet ('LYNDON JOHNSON') (B.)	80	1·25
105	100f. on 2s. deep yellow-green ('ELEANOR ROOSEVELT') (B.)	1·00	2·25
106	250f. on 5s. deep blue and violet ('WINSTON CHURCHILL') (R.)	18·00	12·00
107	500f. on 10s. yellow-brown and violet ('JOHN F. KENNEDY') (R.)	5·00	13·00
99/107 *Set of* 9		35·00	32·00

(Photo State Ptg Wks, Vienna)

1967 (1 Feb). Paintings. T **40** and similar multicoloured designs. P 13½.

108	5f. Type **40**	40	25
109	10f. *The Dancer* (Degas)	45	30
110	15f. *The Filet* (Manet)	50	35
111	20f. *Stag at Sharkey's* (boxing match, G. Bellows)	55	40
112	25f. *Don Manuel Osorio* (Goya)	60	45
113	35f. *St Martin distributing his Cloak* (A. van Dyck)	60	65
114	50f. *The Blue Boy* (Gainsborough)	70	75
115	65f. *The White Horse* (Gauguin)	80	1·00
116	75f. *Mona Lisa* (Da Vinci) (45×62 *mm*)	90	1·25
108/116 *Set of* 9		5·00	4·75

SCOTT CARPENTER
(49)

50 Churchill Crown

1967. American Astronauts. Nos. 57, 59, 61/62 and 65/66 optd as T **49** in various sizes of type, in red.

117	10f. on 15c. deep bluish green ('ALAN SHEPARD, JR.')	55	1·25
118	20f. on 35c. deep blue ('VIRGIL GRISSOM')	70	1·25
119	35f. on 70c. black ('JOHN GLENN, JR.')	95	1·50
120	50f. on 1s. brown-orange (Type **49**)	95	1·50
	a. Stop after 'FILS'	26·00	
121	100f. on 2s. deep yellow-green ('WALTER SCHIRRA, JR.')	1·75	3·50
122	250f. on 5s. deep blue and violet ('GORDON COOPER, JR.')	2·50	8·00
	a. Opt (as Type **49**) double	£120	
117/122 *Set of* 6		6·50	15·00

1967 (1 Mar). Churchill Commemoration Photo. P 13½.

123	**50**	75f. multicoloured	8·00	7·50

Appendix

The following stamps have either been issued in excess of postal needs, or have not been made available to the public in reasonable quantities at face value. Miniature sheets, imperforate stamps etc., are excluded from this section.

1967

Hunting. 20f.
Olympic Games, Grenoble. Postage 10, 25, 35, 50, 75f. Air 100, 200f.
Scout Jamboree, Idaho. Air 150f.
Paintings by Renoir. Postage 10, 35, 50, 65, 75f. Air 100, 200, 250f.
Paintings by Toulouse-Lautrec. Postage 10, 35, 50, 65, 75f. Air 100, 200, 250f.

The National Liberation Front is said to have taken control of Kathiri State of Seiyun on 1 October 1967.

QU'AITI STATE IN HADHRAMAUT

(New Currency. 1000 fils = 1 dinar)

1966 (1 Apr). New currency. Nos. 41/52 of Aden-Qu'aiti State in Hadhramaut surch as Type **20/21** of Kathiri State of Seiyun.

53	5f. on 5c. greenish blue (Type **20**) (R.)	10	1·25
54	5f. on 10c. grey-black (Type **20**) (R.)	2·00	2·00
55	10f. on 15c. bronze-green (Type **20**) (R.)	10	1·00
56	15f. on 25c. carmine-red (Type **20**)	15	2·00
57	20f. on 35c. blue (Type **20**) (R.)	20	3·25
58	25f. on 50c. red-orange (Type **20**)	20	2·50
59	35f. on 70c. deep brown (Type **20**) (R.)	25	2·00
60	50f. on 1s. black and deep lilac (Type **21**) (R.)	65	30
61	65f. on 1s.25 black and red-orange (Type **21**) (R.)	1·50	40
62	100f. on 2s. black and indigo-blue (Type **21**) (R.)	4·25	1·25
63	250f. on 5s. black and bluish green (Type **21**) (R.)	2·25	1·50
64	500f. on 10s. black and lake (Type **21**) (R.)	28·00	3·00
53/64 *Set of* 12		35·00	18·00

1874–1965
WINSTON CHURCHILL
(23)

1917-1963
JOHN F. KENNEDY
(24)

1966 (1 Apr). Churchill Commemoration. Nos. 54/56 optd with T **23**.

65	5f. on 10c. grey-black (R.)	9·00	17·00
66	10f. on 15c. bronze-green (R.)	10·00	18·00
	a. Opt Type **23** inverted	90·00	
67	15f. on 25c. carmine-red (B.)	11·00	18·00
65/67 *Set of* 3		27·00	48·00

1966 (1 Apr). President Kennedy Commemoration. Nos. 57/59 optd with T **24**.

68	20f. on 35c. blue (R.)	1·25	6·00
69	25f. on 50c. red-orange (B.)	1·25	6·50
70	35f. on 70c. deep brown (B.)	1·25	7·50
68/70 *Set of* 3		3·25	18·00

25 World Cup Emblem

(Photo State Ptg Wks, Vienna)

1966 (11 Aug). World Cup Football Championship, England. T **25** and similar diamond-shaped designs. P 13½.

71	5f. maroon and yellow-orange	2·25	25
72	10f. slate-violet and light green	2·50	25
73	15f. maroon and yellow-orange	2·75	30
74	20f. slate-violet and light green	3·00	30
75	25f. blackish green and orange-red	3·25	30
76	35f. blue and yellow	3·75	35
77	50f. blackish green and orange-red	4·25	40
78	65f. blue and yellow	5·00	40
71/78 *Set of* 8		24·00	2·25
MS78*a* 110×110 mm. Nos. 77/78		55·00	7·50

Designs: 10, 35f. Wembley Stadium; 15, 50f. Footballers; 20f. Jules Rimet Cup and football; 5, 25, 65f. T **25**.

29 Mexican Hat and Blanket

(Photo State Ptg Wks, Vienna)

1966 (25 Oct). Pre-Olympic Games, Mexico (1968). P 13½.

79	**29**	75f. sepia and light yellow-green	2·00	75

30 Telecommunications Satellite

(Photo State Ptg Wks, Vienna)

1966 (1 Dec). International Co-operation Year (1965). T **30** and similar horiz designs. P 13½.

80	5f. maroon, bright purple and emerald	2·75	30
81	10f. violet, orange, blue-green and new blue	3·00	30
82	15f. maroon, new blue and red	3·25	35
83	20f. Prussian blue, purple and red	3·50	40
84	25f. violet, olive-yellow, red and emerald	3·50	40
85	35f. maroon, rose-red and new blue	4·00	40
	a. New blue (face value) omitted	£450	
86	50f. maroon, green and red	4·75	45
87	65f. chocolate, bluish violet and red	5·50	45
80/87 *Set of* 8		27·00	2·75

Designs: 10f. Olympic runner (inscribed 'ROME 1960'); 15f. Fish; 25f. Olympic runner (inscribed 'TOKIO 1964'); 50f. Tobacco plant; others, T **30**.

Appendix

The following stamps have either been issued in excess of postal needs, or have not been made available to the public in reasonable quantities at face value. Miniature sheets, imperforate stamps etc. are excluded from this section.

1967

Stampex Stamp Exhibition, London. Postage 5, 10, 15, 20, 25f. Air 50, 65f.
Amphilex International Stamp Exhibition, Amsterdam. Air 75f.
Olympic Games, Mexico (*1968*). 75f.
Paintings. Postage 5, 10, 15, 20, 25f. Air 50, 65f.
Scout Jamboree, Idaho. Air 35f.
Space Research. Postage 10, 25, 35, 50, 75f. Air 100, 250f.

The National Liberation Front is said to have taken control of Qu'aiti State in Hadhramaut on 17 September 1967.

MAHRA SULTANATE OF QISHN AND SOCOTRA

1 Mahra Flag

(Des and litho Harrison)

1967 (12 Mar). Flag in green, black and vermilion; inscriptions in black; background colours given. P 14×14½.

1	**1**	5f. mauve	4·00	55
2		10f. buff	4·00	55
3		15f. sage-green	4·00	55
4		20f. red-orange	4·00	55
5		25f. yellow-brown	4·00	55
6		35f. turquoise-green	4·00	55
7		50f. new blue	4·00	55
8		65f. blackish brown	4·00	55
9		100f. violet	4·00	55
10		250f. rose-red	4·00	55
11		500f. grey-green	4·00	55
1/11 *Set of* 11			40·00	5·50

Appendix

The following stamps have either been issued in excess of postal needs, or have not been made available to the public in reasonable quantities at face value. Miniature sheets, imperforate stamps etc., are excluded from this section.

1967

Scout Jamboree, Idaho. 15, 75, 100, 150f.
President Kennedy Commemoration. Postage 10, 15, 25, 50, 75, 100, 150f. Air 250, 500f.
Olympic Games, Mexico (1968). Postage 10, 25, 50f. Air 250, 500f.

The National Liberation Front is said to have taken control of Mahra Sultanate of Qishn and Socotra on 1 October 1967.

South Australia *see* **Australia**

Southern Cameroons *see* **Cameroon**

Southern Nigeria *see* **Nigeria**

Southern Rhodesia

PRICES FOR STAMPS ON COVER TO 1945
Nos. 1/61 *from* × 2

SELF-GOVERNMENT

The southern part of Rhodesia, previously administered by the British South Africa Company, was annexed by the British Government and granted the status of a self-governing colony from 1 October 1923.

The existing stamps of Rhodesia (the "Admiral" design first issued in 1913) remained in use until 31 March 1924 and continued to be valid for postal purposes until 30 April of that year.

1

2 King George V

3 Victoria Falls

(Recess Waterlow)

1924 (1 Apr)–**29**. P 14.

No.	Type	Description	Unused	Used
1	**1**	½d. blue-green	4·50	1·25
		a. Imperf between (horiz pair)	£1200	£1300
		b. Imperf between (vert pair)	£1200	£1300
		c. Imperf vert (horiz pair)	£1300	
2		1d. bright rose	4·00	10
		a. Imperf between (horiz pair)	£950	£1100
		b. Imperf between (vert pair)	£1700	
		c. Perf 12½ (coil) (1929)	4·50	80·00
3		1½d. bistre-brown	4·50	80
		a. Imperf between (horiz pair)	£15000	
		b. Imperf between (vert pair)	£8000	
		c. Printed double, one albino	£400	
4		2d. black and purple-grey	7·50	2·75
		a. Imperf between (horiz pair)	£17000	
5		3d. blue	6·50	7·00
6		4d. black and orange-red	6·50	2·75
7		6d. black and mauve	6·50	8·50
		a. Imperf between (horiz pair)	£45000	
8		8d. purple and pale green	16·00	50·00
		a. Frame double, one albino	£550	
9		10d. blue and rose	20·00	55·00
10		1s. black and light blue	9·00	13·00
11		1s.6d. black and yellow	23·00	45·00
12		2s. black and brown	17·00	20·00
13		2s.6d. blue and sepia	35·00	65·00
14		5s. blue and blue-green	90·00	£170
1/14 *Set of* 14			£225	£375

Prices for 'imperf between' varieties are for adjacent stamps from the same pane and not for those separated by wide gutter margins between vertical or horizontal pairs, which come from the junction of two panes.

(T **2** recess by B.W.; T **3** typo by Waterlow)

1931 (1 Apr)–**37**. T **2** (line perf 12 unless otherwise stated) and T **3** (comb perf 15×14). (The 11½ perf is comb.).

No.	Type	Description	Unused	Used
15	**2**	½d. green	3·50	1·00
		a. Perf 11½ (1933)	3·00	20
		b. Perf 14 (1935)	2·75	1·00
16		1d. scarlet	4·00	1·00
		a. Perf 11½ (1933)	4·25	20
		b. Perf 14 (1935)	1·25	20
16*c*		1½d. chocolate (3.3.33)	55·00	38·00
		d. Perf 11½ (1.4.32)	2·50	60
17	**3**	2d. black and sepia	13·00	1·40
18		3d. deep ultramarine	10·00	11·00
19	**2**	4d. black and vermilion	1·50	1·50
		a. Perf 11½ (1935)	19·00	7·00
		b. Perf 14 (10.37)	38·00	70·00
20		6d. black and magenta	2·25	3·00
		a. Perf 11½ (1933)	15·00	2·00
		b. Perf 14 (1936)	7·00	2·00
21		8d. violet and olive-green	1·75	4·50
		a. Perf 11½ (1934)	18·00	35·00
21*b*		9d. vermilion and olive-green (1.9.34)	12·00	14·00
22		10d. blue and scarlet	7·00	2·25
		a. Perf 11½ (1933)	6·00	13·00
23		1s. black and greenish blue	2·00	2·50
		a. Perf 11½ (1935)	£140	50·00
		b. Perf 14 (10.37)	£225	£160
24		1s.6d. black and orange-yellow	16·00	28·00
		a. Perf 11½ (1936)	75·00	£140
25		2s. black and brown	38·00	8·00
		a. Perf 11½ (1933)	35·00	32·00
26		2s.6d. blue and drab	50·00	35·00
		a. Perf 11½ (1933)	32·00	50·00
27		5s. blue and blue-green	50·00	50·00
		a. Printed on gummed side	£8500	
15/27 *Set of* 15			£160	£140

No. 16*c* was only issued in booklets.

PRINTERS. All stamps from Types **4** to **29** were recess-printed by Waterlow and Sons, Ltd, London, *except where otherwise stated.*

4

1932 (1 May). P 12½.

No.	Type	Description	Unused	Used
29	**4**	2d. green and chocolate	15·00	2·25
30		3d. deep ultramarine	15·00	3·25
		a. Imperf horiz (vert pair)	£17000	£18000
		b. Imperf between (vert pair)	£38000	

5 Victoria Falls

1935 (6 May). Silver Jubilee. P 11×12.

No.	Type	Description	Unused	Used
31	**5**	1d. olive and rose-carmine	5·00	3·25
32		2d. emerald and sepia	8·50	8·50
33		3d. violet and deep blue	6·50	11·00
34		6d. black and purple	11·00	24·00
31/34 *Set of* 4			28·00	42·00

1935–41. Inscr 'POSTAGE AND REVENUE'

No.	Type	Description	Unused	Used
35	**4**	2d. green and chocolate (P 12½)	6·00	20·00
		a. Perf 14 (1941)	3·25	10
35*b*		3d. deep blue (P 14) (1938)	6·00	1·25

6 Victoria Falls and Railway Bridge

7 King George VI

1937 (12 May). Coronation. P 12½.

No.	Type	Description	Unused	Used
36	**6**	1d. olive and rose-carmine	60	1·25
37		2d. emerald and sepia	60	1·75
38		3d. violet and blue	3·50	9·50
39		6d. black and purple	1·50	4·00
36/39 *Set of* 4			5·50	15·00

1937 (25 Nov). P 14.

No.	Type	Description	Unused	Used
40	**7**	½d. green	70	10
41		1d. scarlet	50	10
42		1½d. red-brown	1·00	30
43		4d. red-orange	2·25	10
44		6d. grey-black	1·50	50
45		8d. emerald-green	2·25	4·25
46		9d. pale blue	1·50	1·00
47		10d. purple	3·00	3·50
48		1s. black and blue-green	3·75	10
		a. Frame double, one albino	£3750	
49		1s.6d. black and orange-yellow	18·00	3·25
50		2s. black and brown	30·00	75
51		2s.6d. ultramarine and purple	17·00	8·50
52		5s. blue and blue-green	18·00	3·75
40/52 *Set of* 13			85·00	23·00

Nos. 40/41 exist in coils, constructed from normal sheets.

On No. 48a the frame appears blurred and over-inked.

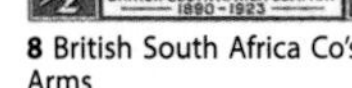

8 British South Africa Co's Arms

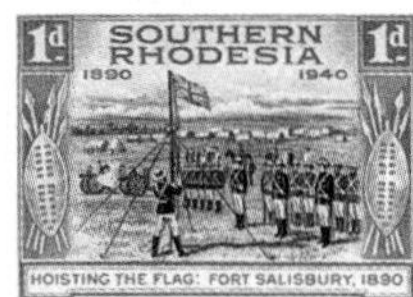

9 Fort Salisbury, 1890

10 Cecil John Rhodes (after S. P. Kendrick)

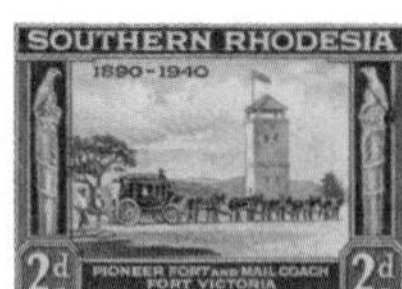

11 Fort Victoria

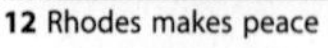

12 Rhodes makes peace

13 Victoria Falls Bridge

14 Statue of Sir Charles Coghlan

15 Lobengula's Kraal and Govt House, Salisbury

Recut shirt collar (R. 6/1)

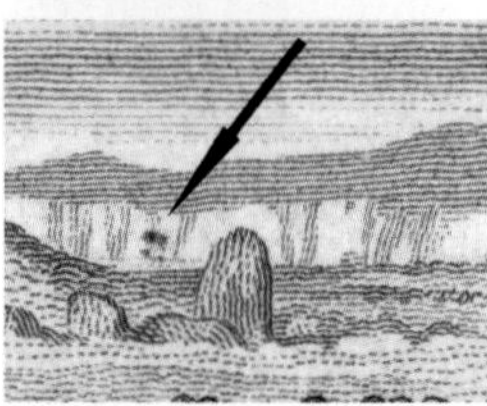
"Cave" flaw (R. 6/6)

(Des Mrs. L. E. Curtis (½d., 1d., 1½d., 3d.), Mrs I. Mount (others))

1940 (3 June). British South Africa Company's Golden Jubilee. P 14.

No.	Type	Description	Unused	Used
53	**8**	½d. slate-violet and green	10	65
54	**9**	1d. violet-blue and scarlet	80	10
55	**10**	1½d. black and red-brown	15	80
		a. Recut shirt collar	28·00	55·00
56	**11**	2d. green and bright violet	30	70
57	**12**	3d. black and blue	1·50	1·50
		a. Cave flaw	£110	£140
58	**13**	4d. green and brown	2·50	3·75
59	**14**	6d. chocolate and green	2·50	4·50
60	**15**	1s. blue and green	3·75	4·50
53/60 *Set of* 8			10·00	15·00

16 Mounted Pioneer

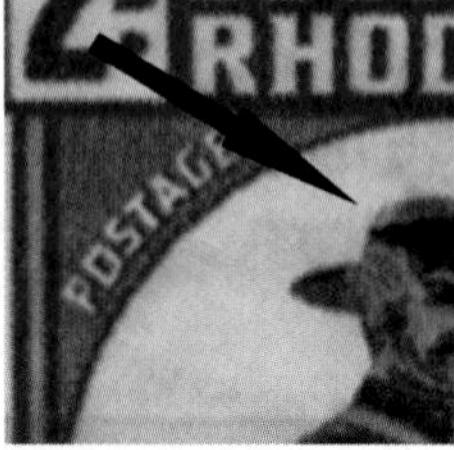

Hat brim retouch (Pl 1B R. 1/8)

Line under saddlebag (Pl 1A R. 6/10)

(Roto South African Govt Printer, Pretoria)

1943 (1 Nov). 50th Anniversary of Occupation of Matabeleland. W **9** of South Africa (Mult Springbok) sideways. P 14.

No.	Type	Description	Unused	Used
61	**16**	2d. brown and green	25	2·00
		a. Hat brim retouch	27·00	45·00
		b. Line under saddlebag	27·00	45·00

17 Queen Elizabeth II when Princess and Princess Margaret

18 King George VI and Queen Elizabeth

1947 (1 Apr). Royal Visit. Types **17**/**18**. P 14.

No.	Type	Description	Unused	Used
62	**17**	½d. black and green	30	60
63	**18**	1d. black and scarlet	30	60

19 Queen Elizabeth

20 King George VI

21 Queen Elizabeth II when Princess

22 Princess Margaret

Damage to right-hand frame (R. 1/10)

1947 (8 May). Victory. P 14.

No.	Type	Description	Unused	Used
64	**19**	1d. carmine	10	15
65	**20**	2d. slate	15	15
		a. Double print	£3500	
		b. Damaged frame	£375	
66	**21**	3d. blue	1·00	2·25
67	**22**	6d. orange	40	1·40
64/67 *Set of 4*			1·50	3·50

(Recess B.W.)

1949 (10 Oct). 75th Anniv of UPU. As Nos. 115/116 of Antigua.

No.	Description	Unused	Used
68	2d. slate-green	80	25
69	3d. blue	80	4·50

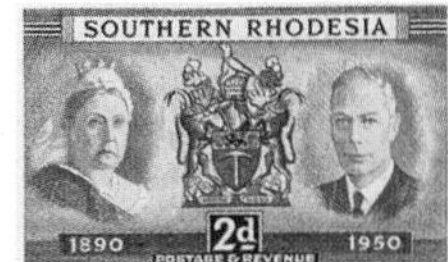

23 Queen Victoria, Arms and King George VI

1950 (12 Sept). Diamond Jubilee of Southern Rhodesia. P 14.

No.	Type	Description	Unused	Used
70	**23**	2d. green and brown	1·25	2·00

24 'Medical Services'

25 'Agriculture'

26 'Building'

27 'Water Supplies'

28 'Transport'

(Des A. R. Winter (2d.), Mrs. J. M. Enalim (others))

1953 (15 Apr). Birth Centenary of Cecil Rhodes. P 14.

No.	Type	Description	Unused	Used
71	**24**	½d. pale blue and sepia	15	2·50
72	**25**	1d. chestnut and blue-green	1·75	10
73	**26**	2d. grey-green and violet	20	10
74	**27**	4½d. deep blue-green and deep ultramarine	80	3·50
75	**28**	1s. black and red-brown	3·00	2·25
71/75 *Set of 5*			5·50	7·50

No. 74 also commemorates the Diamond Jubilee of Matabeleland.

1953 (30 May). Rhodes Centenary Exhibition, Bulawayo. As No. 171 of Nyasaland, but without watermark.

No.	Description	Unused	Used
76	6d. violet	1·00	1·00

30 Queen Elizabeth II

(Recess D.L.R.)

1953 (1 June). Coronation. P 12×12½.

No.	Type	Description	Unused	Used
77	**30**	2s.6d. carmine	7·00	7·50

31 Sable Antelope

32 Tobacco planter

33 Rhodes's Grave

34 Farm Worker

35 Flame Lily

36 Victoria Falls

37 Baobab tree

38 Lion

39 Zimbabwe Ruins

40 Birchenough Bridge

41 Kariba Gorge

42 Basket Maker

43 Balancing Rocks

44 Coat of Arms

(Recess, centre typo (4d.), B.W.)

1953 (31 Aug). P 13½×14 (2d., 6d., 5s.), 14 (10s., £1) or 14×13½ (others).

No.	Type	Description	Unused	Used
78	**31**	½d. grey-green and claret	30	50
79	**32**	1d. green and brown	30	10
80	**33**	2d. deep chestnut and reddish violet	30	10
81	**34**	3d. chocolate and rose-red	55	2·75
82	**35**	4d. red, green and indigo	3·50	50
83	**36**	4½d. black and deep bright blue	2·50	4·50
84	**37**	6d. brown-olive and deep turquoise-green	4·50	1·75
85	**38**	9d. deep blue and reddish brown	4·50	5·00
86	**39**	1s. reddish violet and light blue	2·25	10
87	**40**	2s. purple and scarlet	16·00	10·00
88	**41**	2s.6d. yellow-olive and orange-brown	8·50	9·50
89	**42**	5s. yellow-brown and deep green	12·00	12·00
90	**43**	10s. red-brown and olive	22·00	40·00
91	**44**	£1 rose-red and black	25·00	48·00
78/91 *Set of 14*			90·00	£110

For issues from 1954 to 1963 see under RHODESIA AND NYASALAND.

45 Maize

46 African Buffalo

47 Tobacco

48 Greater Kudu

49 Citrus

50 Flame Lily

51 Ansellia Orchid

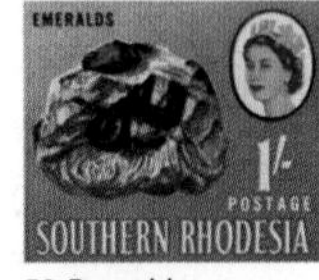

52 Emeralds

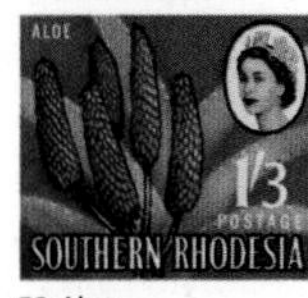

53 Aloe

54 Lake Kyle

55 Tigerfish

56 Cattle

57 Helmet Guineafowl

58 Coat of Arms

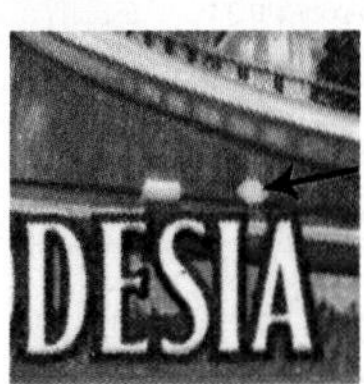

2s. Large white dot over 'IA' of 'RHODESIA' (R. 5/8)

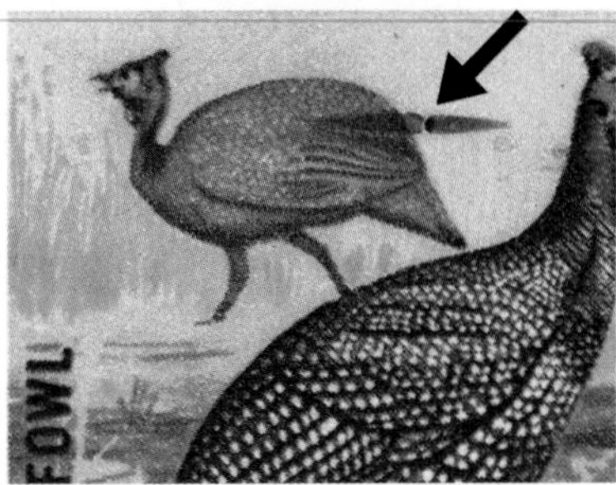

10s. A large coloured flaw on the small guinea fowl gives the appearance of an extra feather (R. 2/2)

(Des V. Whiteley. Photo Harrison)

1964 (19 Feb). Types **45/58**. P 14½ (½d. to 4d.), 13½×13 (6d. to 2s.6d.) or 14½×14 (others).

No.	Type	Description	Unused	Used
92	**45**	½d. yellow, yellow-green and light blue	20	2·75
93	**46**	1d. reddish violet and yellow-ochre	15	10
		a. Reddish violet omitted	£4500	
94	**47**	2d. yellow and deep violet	60	10
95	**48**	3d. chocolate and pale blue	20	10
96	**49**	4d. yellow-orange and deep green	30	10
97	**50**	6d. carmine-red, yellow and deep dull green	40	10
98	**51**	9d. red-brown, yellow and olive-green	2·75	1·50

No.	Type	Description	Un	Us
99	**52**	1s. blue-green and ochre	3·75	30
		a. Blue-green (Queen and emeralds) omitted	£6000	
100	**53**	1s.3d. red, violet and yellow-green	3·00	10
101	**54**	2s. blue and ochre	2·50	3·50
		a. Dot over 'IA'	22·00	
102	**55**	2s.6d. ultramarine and vermilion	4·00	1·00
		a. Vermilion omitted	£8500	
		b. Ultramarine omitted	£22000	
103	**56**	5s. light brown, bistre-yellow and light blue	3·50	2·75
104	**57**	10s. black, yellow-ochre, light blue and carmine-red	11·00	11·00
		a. Extra 'feather'	26·00	45·00
105	**58**	£1 brown, yellow-green, buff and salmon-pink	9·00	24·00
92/105 *Set of* 14			38·00	42·00

Nos. 92 and 93 exist in coils constructed from normal sheets.

Nos. 102a and 102b occur on different sheets and involve one or two vertical rows of stamps in each instance. They were caused by the printing press being stopped and then restarted. Three such sheets showing No. 102a have been reported.

See also Nos. 359/372 of Rhodesia.

In October 1964 Southern Rhodesia was renamed Rhodesia.

STAMP BOOKLETS

1928 (1 Jan). Black on blue cover. Stitched.

SB1 2s.6d. booklet containing 12×½d. and 24×1d. (Nos. 1/2) in blocks of 6 ..... £6500

1931 (1 Apr). Black on blue cover. Stitched.

SB2 2s.6d. booklet containing 12×½d. and 24×1d. (Nos. 15/16) in blocks of 6 ..... £7500

1933 (3 Mar). Black on red cover, size 69×53 mm. Stitched.

SB3 3s. booklet containing 12×½d., 12×1d. and 12×1½d. (Nos. 15, 16, 16c) in blocks of 6 ..... £4500

The 1½d. postage rate was reduced to 1d. eight weeks after No. SB3 was issued. Postal officials were instructed to detach the 1½d. panes and use them for other purposes. The remaining stocks of the booklet were then sold for 1s.6d.

1938 (Oct)–**45**. Black on yellow cover. Stitched.

SB4 2s.6d. booklet containing 24×½d. and 18×1d. (Nos. 40/41) in blocks of 6 with postage rates on inside front cover £325

a. Label with new rates affixed to inside front cover (1945) £375

b. Inside front cover blank £350

No. SB4b was issued sometime between 1945 and 1949.

1954 (Jan). Black on yellow cover, size 71×54 mm. Stitched.

SB5 2s.6d. booklet containing 12×½d. and 24×1d. (Nos. 78/79) in blocks of 6 ..... 75·00

1964 (19 Feb). Black on orange cover, size 57×45 mm. Stitched.

SB6 1s. booklet containing 3d. (No. 95) in block of 4. ..... 3·25

POSTAGE DUE STAMPS

SOUTHERN

RHODESIA

(D 1)

1951 (1 Oct). Postage Due stamps of Great Britain optd with T D **1**.

No.	Type	Description	Un	Us
D1	D **1**	½d. emerald (No. D27)	3·25	19·00
D2		1d. violet-blue (No. D36)	3·00	2·00
D3		2d. agate (No. D29)	2·50	1·75
D4		3d. violet (No. D30)	2·75	3·25
D5		4d. blue (No. D38)	1·75	4·00
D6		4d. dull grey-green (No. D31)	£300	£700
D7		1s. deep blue (No. D33)	2·50	6·50
D1/D5, 7 *Set of* 6			14·00	32·00

No. D6 is reported to have been issued to Fort Victoria and Gwelo main post offices only.

South West Africa

Walvis (or Walfish) Bay, the major anchorage on the South West Africa coast, was claimed by Great Britain as early as 1796. In 1878 the 430 sq. mile area around the port, together with a number of offshore islands, was annexed to Cape Province, passing to the Union in 1910. Stamps of Cape of Good Hope and, later, South Africa, were used at Walvis Bay, often cancelled with the numeral obliterator '300', until the enclave was transferred to the South West African administration on 1 October 1922.

Germany declared a protectorate over the southern part of the territory, around Luderitzbucht, in 1884, extending its reach and establishing borders with surrounding administrations by 1890, establishing authority over the entire country, apart from the Walvis Bay enclave.

German post offices were opened from 1888, selling current German stamps which may be identified by their cancellations. In 1897 the German stamps overprinted 'Deutsch-/Sudwest-Afrika' and, later 'Deutsch-/Sudwestafrica' were introduced, to be followed by the colonial 'Yacht' series in 1901.

After a rebellion in South Africa, aided by arms supplied from German South West Africa, had been defeated in December 1914, South African troops invaded the protectorate, with the German forces finally capitulating on 9 July 1915.

As civil post offices were opened by the occupying forces, they sold South African stamps, generally postmarked by altered German colonial cancellers.

On 17 December 1920 the League of Nations conferred a mandate of administration of the territory on His Britannic Majesty, to be exercised by the government in South Africa. The Mandate came into force on 1 January 1923, on which date the first South African stamps overprinted for use in the territory were issued.

The following listing covers South African stamps used in South West Africa up to 31 January 1923 when they ceased to be valid. The cancellations during this period are of great interest with many provisional and altered German types; the prices given are for the more common markings.

Stamps of SOUTH AFRICA cancelled by South West Africa postmarks (various types).

1910 (Nos. 1/2).

No.	Description	Price
Z1	2½d. blue	75·00

1913-24 (Nos. 3/17).

No.	Description	Price
Z2	½d. green	1·00
Z3	1d. red	1·00
Z4	1½d. chesnut	1·50
Z5	2d. purple	1·50
Z6	2½d. blue	3·00
Z7	3d. black and orange-red	6·00
Z8	3d. ultramarine	£100
Z9	4d. orange-yellow and sage-green	4·00
Z10	6d. black and violet	8·00
Z11	1s. orange	12·00
Z12	1s. 3d. violet	£130
Z13	2s. 6d. purple and green	70·00
Z14	5s. purple and blue	80·00
Z15	10s. deep blue and olive-green	90·00
Z16	£1 green and red	£750

1913-21 Coil stamps (Nos. 18/21).

No.	Description	Price
Z17	½d. green	35·00
Z18	1d. red	50·00
Z19	1½d. chesnut	£160
Z20	2d. purple	£250

Interprovincial stamps (see South Africa Nos. Z1/Z192) were also valid for use in South West Africa, but their use was almost entirely philatelic and they are not listed.

PRICES FOR STAMPS ON COVER TO 1945

Nos. 1/40*a*	*from* × 6
Nos. 41/133	*from* × 2
Nos. D1/D5	*from* × 10
Nos. D6/D51	*from* × 20
Nos. O1/O4	*from* × 3
Nos. O5/O20	*from* × 15
No. O21	*from* × 2
No. O22	*from* × 15

INSCRIPTIONS. Most of the postage stamps up to No. 140 are inscribed alternately in English and Afrikaans throughout the sheets and the same applies to all the Official stamps and to Nos. D30/D33.

PRICES for Nos. 1/140 are for unused horizontal pairs, used horizontal pairs or used singles (either inscr), *unless otherwise indicated*. Vertical pairs are worth between 20% and 35% of the prices quoted for horizontal pairs.

OVERPRINT SETTINGS. Between 1923 and 1928 the King George V definitives of South Africa, Types **2** and **3**, and the various postage due stamps were issued overprinted for use in South West Africa. A number of overprint settings were used:

Setting I – Overprint Types **1** and **2** ('Zuid-West Afrika'). 14 mm between lines of overprint. See Nos. 1/12 and D1/D9

Setting II – As Setting I, but 10 mm between lines of overprint. See Nos. 13/15 and D10/D13

Setting III – Overprint Types **3** ('Zuidwest Afrika') and **4**. 'South West' 14 mm long. 'Zuidwest' 11 mm long. 14 mm between lines of overprint. See Nos. 16/27 and D14/D17

Setting IV – As Setting III, but 'South West' 16 mm long, 'Zuidwest' 12 mm long and 14 mm between lines of overprint. See Nos. 28 and D17*a*/D20

Setting V – As Setting IV, but 12 mm between lines of overprint. See Nos. D21/D24

Setting VI – As Setting IV, but 9½ mm between lines of overprint. See Nos. 29/40 and D25/D32.

South West   **Zuid-West**

Africa. (**1**)   **Afrika.** (**2**)

1923 (1 Jan–17 June). Nos. 3/4, 6 and 9/17 of South Africa optd alternately with Types **1** and **2** by typography.

(a) Setting I (14 mm between lines of opt)

No.	Description	*Un pair*	*Us pair*	*Us single*
1	½d. green	4·75	9·00	1·00
	a. 'Wes' for 'West' (R. 20/8)	£120	£160	
	b. 'Afr ica' (R. 20/2)	£130		
	c. 'Afrika' without stop (R. 17/8)			
	d. Litho opt in shiny ink (17.6)	12·00	65·00	5·00
2	1d. rose-red	8·50	9·50	1·00
	a. Opt inverted	£500		
	b. 'Wes' for 'West' (R. 12/2)	£190		
	c. 'Af.rica' for 'Africa' (R. 20/6)	£180	£300	
	d. Opt double	£1000		
	e. 'Afr ica' (R. 20/2)	£130		
	f. 'Afrika' without stop (R. 17/8)	£350		
3	2d. dull purple	11·00	17·00	1·50
	a. Opt inverted	£700	£800	
	b. 'Wes' for 'West' (R. 20/8)	£325		
	c. Litho opt in shiny ink (30.3)	75·00	£150	10·00
4	3d. ultramarine	13·00	20·00	2·75
5	4d. orange-yellow and sage-green	20·00	50·00	4·50
	a. Litho opt in shiny ink (19.4)	48·00	70·00	8·00
6	6d. black and violet	8·50	50·00	4·50
	a. Litho opt in shiny ink (19.4)	38·00	85·00	7·50
7	1s. orange-yellow	19·00	50·00	5·00
	a. Litho opt in shiny ink (19.4)	65·00	£130	11·00
	b. 'Afrika' without stop (R. 17/8)	£6000		
8	1s.3d. pale violet	45·00	60·00	5·50
	a. Opt inverted	£400		
	b. Litho opt in shiny ink (19.4)	85·00	£160	14·00
9	2s.6d. purple and green	70·00	£140	18·00
	a. Litho opt in shiny ink (19.4)	£150	£300	35·00
10	5s. purple and blue	£225	£375	50·00
11	10s. blue and olive-green	£1400	£3250	£400
12	£1 green and red	£750	£1900	£250
1/12 *Set of* 12		£2250	£5250	£650
1s/12s Optd 'SPECIMEN' *Set of* 12 *singles*		£1700		

Nos. 1/12 were overprinted in complete sheets of 240 (4 panes 6×10).

No. 3b shows traces of a type spacer to the right of where the 't' should have been. This spacer is not visible on Nos. 1a and 2b.

Minor varieties, such as broken 't' in 'West', were caused by worn type. Stamps showing one line of overprint only or with the lower line above the upper line due to overprint misplacement may also be found. All values exist showing a faint stop after 'Afrika' on R. 17/8, but only examples of the 1d. and 1s. have been seen with it completely omitted.

(b) Setting II (10 mm between lines of opt) (31 Mar)

No.	Description	*Un pair*	*Us pair*	*Us single*
13	5s. purple and blue	£160	£275	45·00
	a. 'Afrika' without stop (R. 6/1)	£1200	£1400	£225
14	10s. blue and olive-green	£500	£850	£140
	a. 'Afrika' without stop (R. 6/1)	£2500	£3000	£550
15	£1 green and red	£1000	£1400	£200
	a. 'Afrika' without stop (R. 6/1)	£4500	£5500	£1000
13/15 *Set of* 3		£1500	£2250	£350

Nos. 13/15 were overprinted in separate panes of 60 (6×10).

Examples of most values are known showing a forged Windhoek postmark dated '30 SEP 24'.

Zuidwest   **South West**

Afrika. (**3**)   **Africa.** (**4**)

1923 (15 July)–**26**. Nos. 3/4, 6 and 9/17 of South Africa optd as Types **3** ('Zuidwest' in one word, without hyphen) and **4** alternately.

(a) Setting III ('South West' 14 mm long, 'Zuidwest' 11 mm long, 14 mm between lines of opt)

No.	Description	*Un pair*	*Us pair*	*Us single*
16	½d. green (5.9.24)	12·00	40·00	4·25
	a. 'outh' for 'South' (R. 1/1)	£2250		
17	1d. rose-red (28.9.23)	6·50	9·00	1·40
	a. 'outh' for 'South' (R. 1/1)	£2000		
18	2d. dull purple (28.9.23)	12·00	17·00	1·50
	a. Opt double	£1000		
19	3d. ultramarine	5·50	15·00	1·40
20	4d. orange-yellow and sage-green	7·50	22·00	2·75

w. Wmk inverted £2500 — —
21 6d. black and violet (28.9.23) 12·00 45·00 5·00
22 1s. orange-yellow 12·00 45·00 5·00
23 1s.3d. pale violet 28·00 50·00 5·50
24 2s.6d. purple and green 50·00 90·00 10·00
25 5s. purple and blue 75·00 £140 18·00
26 10s. blue and olive-green £170 £275 40·00
27 £1 green and red (28.9.23) £325 £475 60·00
16/27 *Set of 12* £650 £1100 £140

Nos. 16/27 were overprinted in complete sheets of 240 (4 panes 6×10).

Two sets may be made with this overprint, one with bold lettering, and the other from September 1924, with thinner lettering and smaller stops.

(b) Setting IV ('South West' 16 mm long, 'Zuidwest' 12 mm long, 14 mm between lines of opt)

28 2s.6d. purple and green (29.6.24) 90·00 £170 28·00

No. 28 was overprinted on two panes of 60 horizontally side by side.

(c) Setting VI ('South West' 16 mm long, 'Zuidwest' 12 mm long, 9½ mm between lines of opt)

29 ½d. green (16.12.25) 7·00 48·00 5·50
30 1d. rose-red (9.12.24) 5·50 10·00 1·40
a. Opt omitted (in pair with normal) £2000
31 2d. dull purple (9.12.24) 4·00 22·00 1·75
32 3d. ultramarine (31.1.26) 6·00 40·00 3·00
a. Deep bright blue (20.4.26) 42·00 £100 12·00
33 4d. orange-yellow and sage-green (9.12.24) 7·00 48·00 4·00
34 6d. black and violet (9.12.24) 10·00 48·00 5·00
35 1s. orange-yellow (9.12.24) 8·50 48·00 5·00
36 1s.3d. pale violet (9.12.24) 11·00 48·00 5·00
37 2s.6d. purple and green (9.12.24) 45·00 75·00 10·00
38 5s. purple and blue (31.1.26) 60·00 £120 14·00
39 10s. blue and olive-green (9.12.24) 95·00 £180 20·00
40 £1 green and red (9.1.26) £300 £450 55·00
a. Pale olive-green and red (8.11.26) £300 £475 65·00
as. Ditto. H/S 'SPECIMEN' £250
29/40 *Set of 12* £500 £1000 £120
35s, 39s/40 H/S 'SPECIMEN' *Set of 3** £500

Nos. 29/40 were overprinted in complete sheets of 240 (4 panes of 6×10) with, initially, 'South West Africa' 16½ mm long on the upper two panes and 16 mm long on the lower two. This order was subsequently reversed. For printings from 8 November 1926 all four panes showed the 16½ mm measurement. No. 40*a* only comes from this printing.

* The UPU distribution of Nos. 35s, 39s, 40s in 1928 included mixed stock of the £1 value (in both shades).

Examples of most values are known showing a forged Windhoek postmark dated '30 SEP 24'.

Suidwes Afrika. (5) South West Africa. (6)

1926 (1 Jan–1 May). Nos. 30/32 of South Africa (Waterlow printings) optd with Types **5** (on stamps inscr in Afrikaans) and **6** (on stamps inscr in English) sideways, alternately in black.

41 ½d. black and green 4·75 14·00 1·50
42 1d. black and carmine 4·00 8·00 90
43 6d. green and orange (1.5) 27·00 55·00 7·00
41/43 *Set of 3* 32·00 70·00 8·50

SOUTH WEST AFRICA (7) SUIDWES-AFRIKA (8)

1926. No. 33 of South Africa, imperf optd.

(a) With T 7 (English)

Single Stamps
44A 4d. grey-blue 75 3·00

(b) With T 8 (Afrikaans)

44B 4d. grey-blue 75 3·00

1927. As Nos. 41/43, but Afrikaans opt on stamp inscr in English and vice versa.

45 ½d. black and green 2·00 14·00 1·50
a. 'Africa' without stop (R. 13/8) £160
46 1d. black and carmine 5·00 2·50 50
a. 'Africa' without stop (R. 13/8) £300
47 6d. green and orange 8·00 35·00 3·00
a. 'Africa' without stop (R. 13/8) £180
45/47 *Set of 3* 13·50 45·00 4·50

The overprints on Nos. 45/47 were applied to both the Waterlow and Pretoria printings of South Africa Nos. 30/32.

SOUTH WEST AFRICA (9) S.W.A. (10) S.W.A. (11)

1927. As No. 44A, but overprint T **9**.

Single Stamps
48 4d. grey-blue 6·50 17·00
s. Handstamped 'SPECIMEN' 70·00

1927 (Apr). Nos. 34/39 of South Africa optd alternately as Types **5** and **6**, in blue, but with lines of overprint spaced 16 mm.

49 2d. grey and purple 7·00 16·00 1·75
50 3d. black and red 4·75 32·00 2·50
51 1s. brown and blue 16·00 32·00 4·00
52 2s.6d. green and brown 40·00 95·00 13·00
53 5s. black and green 75·00 £190 20·00
54 10s. blue and bistre-brown 65·00 £160 20·00
49/54 *Set of 6* £180 £475 50·00
49s/51s, 54s H/S 'SPECIMEN' *Set of 4* £400

A variety of Nos. 49, 50, 51 and 54 with spacing 16½ mm between lines of overprint, occurs in the third vertical row of each sheet.

1927. As No. 44, but perf 11½ by John Meinert Ltd, Windhoek.

(a) Optd with T 7 (English)

Single Stamps
55A 4d. grey-blue 1·25 6·00
a. Imperf between (pair) 50·00 90·00
s. Handstamped 'SPECIMEN' 70·00

(b) Optd with T 8 (Afrikaans)

55B 4d. grey-blue 1·25 6·00
a. Imperf between (pair) 50·00 90·00
s. Handstamped 'SPECIMEN' 70·00

1927 (Aug)–**30**. Optd with T **10**.

(a) On Nos. 13 and 17a of South Africa

56 1s.3d. pale violet 1·25 6·50
a. Without stop after 'A' (R. 3/4) £100
s. Handstamped 'SPECIMEN' 75·00
57 £1 pale olive-green and red 95·00 £170
a. Without stop after 'A' (R. 3/4) £1600 £2500

(b) On Nos. 30/32 and 34/39 of South Africa

Un pair Us pair Us single
58 ½d. black and green 2·50 8·50 80
a. Without stop after 'A' 42·00 75·00
b. 'S.W.A.' opt above value 2·75 16·00 2·25
c. As b, in vert pair, top stamp without opt £650
59 1d. black and carmine 1·25 4·25 55
a. Without stop after 'A' 40·00 75·00
b. 'S.W.A.' opt at top (30.4.30) 1·75 14·00 1·60
c. As b, in vert pair, top stamp without opt £700
60 2d. grey and maroon 9·00 45·00 2·75
c. Perf 14×13½ 32·00 55·00
ca. Without stop after 'A' 85·00 £150
cb. Opt double, one inverted £750 £1000
cc. Split 'd' £160
61 3d. black and red 5·00 32·00 3·25
a. Without stop after 'A' 75·00 £130
b. Perf 14×13½ 18·00 50·00
ba. Without stop after 'A' 95·00 £170
bb. Without stop after 'W' £190
62 4d. brown (4.28) 12·00 50·00 7·00
a. Without stop after 'A' 90·00 £140
b. Perf 14×13½ 50·00 70·00
63 6d. green and orange 6·00 30·00 2·75
a. Without stop after 'A' £120
64 1s. brown and deep blue 10·00 50·00 5·00
b. Perf 14×13½ 60·00 90·00
ba. Without stop after 'A' £1700 £1900 £350
65 2s.6d. green and brown 42·00 85·00 12·00
a. Without stop after 'A' £160 £275
b. Perf 14×13½ 80·00 £140
ba. Without stop after 'A' £225 £350
66 5s. black and green 65·00 £120 18·00
a. Without stop after 'A' £250 £375
b. Perf 14×13½ £110 £180
ba. Without stop after 'A' £300 £450
67 10s. bright blue and brown £110 £200 28·00
a. Without stop after 'A' £375 £600
58/67 *Set of 10* £225 £550 70·00
58s/61s, 63s/67s H/S 'SPECIMEN' *Set of 9* £600

On the ½d., 1d. and 6d. the missing stop variety occurs three times on each sheet, R. 1/7, 13/4 and one position not yet identified. For the other values it comes on R. 2/3 of the right pane and, for the 2s.6d., 5s. and 10s., on R. 8/1 of the left pane.

The missing stop after 'W' on the 3d. occurs on R. 10/5 of the right pane.

The overprint is normally found at the base of the ½d., 1d., 6d., 1s.3d. and £1 values and at the top of the remainder.

Examples of all values are known showing a forged Windhoek postmark dated '20 MAR 31'.

1930–31. Nos. 42 and 43 of South Africa (rotogravure printing) optd with T **10**.

68 ½d. black and green (1931) 24·00 50·00 5·00
69 1d. black and carmine 16·00 27·00 2·75

1930 (27 Nov–Dec). Air. Nos. 40/41 of South Africa optd.

(a) As T 10

Un single Us single
70 4d. green (*first printing*) 7·00 28·00
a. No stop after 'A' of 'S.W.A.' 70·00 £140
b. Later printings 3·00 28·00
71 1s. orange (*first printing*) 70·00 £120
a. No stop after 'A' of 'S.W.A.' £450 £650
b. Later printings 4·50 55·00

First printing: Thick letters, blurred impression. Stops with rounded corners.

Later printings: Thinner letters, clear impression. Clean cut, square stops.

(b) As T 11 (12.30)

72 4d. green 1·25 5·00
a. Opt double £200
b. Opt inverted £200
73 1s. orange 2·00 15·00
a. Opt double £550

12 Kori Bustard

13 Cape Cross

14 Bogenfels

15 Windhoek

16 Waterberg

17 Luderitz Bay

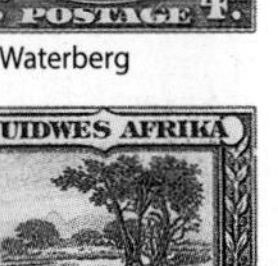

18 Bush Scene

19 Elands

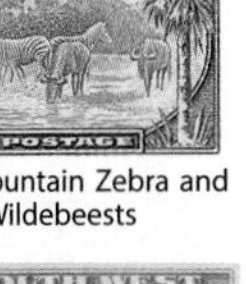

20 Mountain Zebra and Blue Wildebeests

21 Herero Huts

22 Welwitschia Plant

23 Okuwahaken Falls

24 Monoplane over Windhoek

25 Biplane over Windhoek

(Recess B.W.)

1931 (5 Mar). Types **12** to **25** (inscr alternately in English and Afrikaans). W **9** of South Africa. P 14×13½.

(a) Postage

74 **12** ½d. black and emerald 3·00 2·50 10
75 **13** 1d. indigo and scarlet 3·00 2·50 10
76 **14** 2d. blue and brown 2·50 10·00 20
w. Wmk inverted £900
77 **15** 3d. grey-blue and blue 1·50 4·50 15
78 **16** 4d. green and purple 2·00 7·00 20
79 **17** 6d. blue and brown 1·50 11·00 20
80 **18** 1s. chocolate and blue 3·50 18·00 25
81 **19** 1s.3d. violet and yellow 6·00 11·00 50
82 **20** 2s.6d. carmine and grey 29·00 24·00 1·75
83 **21** 5s. sage-green and red-brown 16·00 35·00 2·75
84 **22** 10s. red-brown and emerald 50·00 50·00 6·00
85 **23** 20s. lake and blue-green 75·00 80·00 10·00

(b) Air

86 **24** 3d. brown and blue 29·00 35·00 2·50
87 **25** 10d. black and purple-brown 55·00 85·00 7·00
74/87 *Set of 14* £225 £300 28·00

Examples of most values are known showing a forged Windhoek postmark dated '20 MAR 31'.

26

(Recess B.W.)

1935 (1 May). Silver Jubilee. Inscr bilingually. W **9** of South Africa. P 14×13½.

Un single Us single
88 **26** 1d. black and scarlet 1·00 25
89 2d. black and sepia 1·50 25
90 3d. black and blue 7·50 25·00
91 6d. black and purple 3·00 15·00
88/91 *Set of 4* 11·50 35·00

1935–36. Voortrekker Memorial Fund. Nos. 50/53 of South Africa optd with T **10**.

92 ½d. +½d. black and green 1·75 5·50 75
a. Opt inverted £275
93 1d. +½d. grey-black and pink 2·25 3·25 40
a. Blurred 'SOUTH AFRICA' and red 'comet' flaw 80·00
94 2d. +1d. grey-green and purple 7·00 6·00 80
a. Without stop after 'A' £200 £225
b. Opt double £250
95 3d. +1½d. grey-green and blue 21·00 50·00 4·25
a. Without stop after 'A' £275 £375
92/95 *Set of 4* 29·00 60·00 5·50

27 Mail Train

28

Re-entry (R. 6/3)

(Recess B.W.)

1937 (1 Mar). W **9** of South Africa. P 14×13½.

96	**27**	1½d. purple-brown	29·00	4·50	35

(Recess B.W.)

1937 (12 May). Coronation. W **9** of South Africa (sideways). P 13½×14.

97	**28**	½d. black and emerald	40	15	10
98		1d. black and scarlet	40	15	10
99		1½d. black and orange	40	15	10
100		2d. black and brown	40	15	10
101		3d. black and blue	50	15	10
102		4d. black and purple	50	20	10
		a. Re-entry	22·00	20·00	
103		6d. black and yellow	50	3·25	20
104		1s. black and grey-black	55	3·50	25
97/104 *Set of* 8			3·25	7·00	65

On. No. 102a the frame and leaves at lower left are doubled. The stamp is inscribed in Afrikaans.

1938 (14 Dec). Voortrekker Centenary Memorial. Nos. 76/79 of South Africa optd as T **11**.

105	½d. +½d. blue and green	12·00	32·00	2·25
106	1d. +1d. blue and carmine	30·00	22·00	1·50
107	1½d. +1½d. chocolate and blue-green	32·00	38·00	3·25
108	3d. +3d. bright blue	55·00	95·00	8·50
105/108 *Set of* 4		£110	£160	14·00

1938 (14 Dec). Voortrekker Commemoration. Nos. 80/81 of South Africa optd as T **11**.

109	1d. blue and carmine	16·00	26·00	1·75
	a. Three bolts in wheel rim	85·00		
110	1½d. greenish blue and brown	22·00	32·00	2·25

1939 (17 July). 250th Anniversary of Landing of Huguenots in South Africa and Huguenot Commemoration Fund. Nos. 82/84 of South Africa optd as T **11**.

111	½d. +½d. brown and green	14·00	18·00	1·40
112	1d. +1d. green and carmine	23·00	18·00	1·40
113	1½d. +1½d. blue-green and purple	38·00	17·00	1·25
111/113 *Set of* 3		65·00	48·00	3·50

SWA	SWA	SWA	S W A
(29)	(30)	(31)	(32)

1941 (1 Oct)–**43**. War Effort. Nos. 88/96 of South Africa optd with Types **29** or **30** (3d. and 1s.).

(a) Inscr alternately

114	½d. green (1.12.41)	1·50	6·00	40
	a. Blue-green (1942)	2·50	2·50	15
115	1d. carmine (1.11.41)	2·50	3·75	20
	a. 'Stain' on uniform	27·00		
116	1½d. myrtle-green (21.1.42)	2·75	4·00	20
117	3d. blue	24·00	32·00	1·25
	a. Cigarette flaw	£130		
118	4d. orange-brown	10·00	21·00	1·00
	a. Red-brown	21·00	38·00	3·25
119	6d. red-orange	7·50	9·00	50
120	1s.3d. olive-brown (15.1.43)	13·00	23·00	1·25

(b) Inscr bilingually

		Un single	*Us single*
121	2d. violet	50	1·75
122	1s. brown (17.11.41)	1·60	2·00
114/122 *Set of 7 pairs and 2 singles*		50·00	85·00

1943–44. War Effort (reduced sizes). Nos. 97/104 of South Africa, optd with T **29** (1½d. and 1s., No. 130), or T **31** (others).

(a) Inscr alternately

		Un unit	*Us unit*	*Us single*
123	½d. blue-green (T)	50	9·50	55
	a. Green	7·00	13·00	70
	b. Greenish blue	4·25	10·00	55
124	1d. carmine-red (T)	4·50	8·50	30
	a. Bright carmine	2·50	8·50	30
125	1½d. red-brown (P)	50	1·75	15
	a. Ear flap flaw	16·00		
126	2d. violet (P)	7·00	5·50	20
	a. Reddish violet	14·00	8·50	30
	b. Apostrophe flaw	65·00		
127	3d. blue (T)	3·25	28·00	1·00
128	6d. red-orange (P)	4·00	3·00	30
	a. Opt inverted	£650		

(b) Inscr bilingually

129	4d. slate-green (T)	2·00	23·00	75
	a. Opt inverted	£900	£650	70·00
130	1s. brown (opt Type **29**) (P)	19·00	40·00	2·00
	a. Opt inverted	£800	£450	
	b. Opt Type **31** (1944)	4·00	6·00	30
	c. Opt Type **31** inverted	£650	£425	48·00
	d. 'Bursting shell'	50·00		
	e. Smoking 'L'	50·00		
123/130*b Set of* 8		21·00	75·00	3·25

The 'units' referred to above consist of pairs (P) or triplets (T).

No. 128 exists with another type of opt as T **31**, but with broader 's', narrower 'w' and more space between the letters.

1945. Victory. Nos. 108/110 of South Africa optd with T **30**.

131	1d. brown and carmine	25	75	10
	a. Opt inverted	£400	£425	
	b. Barbed wire flaw	15·00		
132	2d. slate-blue and violet	30	75	10
133	3d. deep blue and blue	1·50	1·75	10
131/133 *Set of* 3		1·75	3·00	20

1947 (17 Feb). Royal Visit. Nos. 111/113 of South Africa optd as T **31**, but 8½×2 mm.

134	1d. black and carmine	10	10	10
135	2d. violet	10	60	10
	a. 'Bird' on '2'	8·50		
136	3d. blue	15	40	10
	a. 'Black-eyed Princess'	10·00		
134/136 *Set of* 3		30	1·00	15

1948 (26 Apr). Royal Silver Wedding. No. 125 of South Africa, optd as T **31**, but 4×2 mm.

137	3d. blue and silver	1·00	35	10

1949 (1 Oct). 75th Anniversary of UPU. Nos. 128/130 of South Africa optd as T **30**, but 13×4 mm.

138	½d. blue-green	75	2·25	25
139	1½d. brown-red	75	1·75	15
140	3d. bright blue	1·25	1·00	25
	a. Serif on 'C'	65·00		
	b. 'Lake' in East Africa	65·00		
138/140 *Set of* 3		2·50	4·50	60

1949 (1 Dec). Inauguration of Voortrekker Monument, Pretoria. Nos. 131/133 of South Africa optd with T **32**.

		Un single	*Us single*
141	1d. magenta	10	10
142	1½d. blue-green	10	10
143	3d. blue	15	60
141/143 *Set of* 3		30	70

1952 (14 Mar). Tercentenary of Landing of Van Riebeeck. Nos. 136/140 of South Africa optd as T **30**, but 8×3½ mm (1d., 4½d.) or 11×4 mm (others).

144	½d. brown-purple and olive-grey	10	50
145	1d. deep blue-green	10	10
146	2d. deep violet	50	10
	a. 'Full Moon'	12·00	
	b. 'Line through sails' (vert pair)	17·00	
147	4½d. blue	30	1·75
148	1s. brown	75	20
144/148 *Set of* 5		1·50	2·25

33 Queen Elizabeth II and *Catophracies alexandri*

1953 (2 June). Coronation. T **33** and similar horiz designs. W **9** of South Africa. P 14.

149	1d. bright carmine	40	10
150	2d. deep bluish green	40	10
151	4d. magenta	65	35
152	6d. dull ultramarine	65	85
153	1s. deep orange-brown	70	30
149/153 *Set of* 5		2·50	1·50

Designs: 1d. T **33**; 2d. *Bauhinia macrantha*, 4d. *Caralluma nebrownii*, 6d. *Gloriosa virescens*, 1s. *Rhigozum trieholotum*.

34 Two Bucks (rock painting)

35 White Lady (rock painting)

36 Rhinoceros Hunt (rock painting)

37 White Elephant and Giraffe (rock painting)

38 Karakul Lamb

39 Ovambo Woman blowing Horn

40 Ovambo woman

41 Herero woman

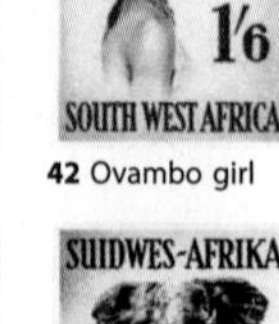

42 Ovambo girl

43 Lioness

44 Gemsbok

45 African Elephant

(Des O. Schroeder (1d. to 4d.), M. Vandenschen (4½d. to 10s.))

1954 (15 Nov). Types **34/45**. W **9** of South Africa (sideways* on vert designs). P 14.

154	**34**	1d. brown-red	30	10
		w. Wmk horns of springbok to right	18·00	13·00
155	**35**	2d. deep brown	35	10
156	**36**	3d. dull purple	1·25	10
157	**37**	4d. blackish olive	1·50	10
158	**38**	4½d. deep blue	70	40
159	**39**	6d. myrtle-green	70	70
		w. Wmk horns of springbok to right	80·00	40·00
160	**40**	1s. deep mauve	70	50
161	**41**	1s.3d. cerise	2·00	1·25
162	**42**	1s.6d. purple	2·00	50
163	**43**	2s.6d. bistre-brown	3·50	70
164	**44**	5s. deep bright blue	5·00	2·75
165	**45**	10s. deep myrtle-green	38·00	16·00
154/165 *Set of* 12			50·00	21·00

* The normal sideways watermark shows the horns of the springbok pointing left, *as seen from the back of the stamp.*

1960. As Nos. 154/157, 159, 162, but W **102** of South Africa (sideways on vert designs). P 14.

166	**34**	1d. brown-red	55	2·25
167	**35**	2d. deep brown	70	2·25
168	**36**	3d. dull purple	1·40	4·50
169	**37**	4d. blackish olive	2·75	3·50
169*a*	**39**	6d. myrtle-green	£1700	£550
170	**42**	1s.6d. purple	20·00	9·00
166/170 (ex 169*a*) *Set of* 5			23·00	19·00

(New Currency. 100 cents = 1 South African rand)

46 GPO Windhoek

47 Finger Rock

48 Mounted Soldier Monument

49 Quivertree

50 SWA House, Windhoek

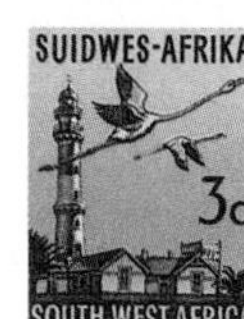

50a Greater Flamingoes and Swakopmund Lighthouse

51 Fishing Industry

52 Greater Flamingo

53 German Lutheran Church, Windhoek

54 Diamond

55 Fort Namutoni

55a Hardap Dam

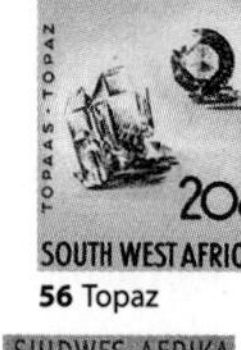

56 Topaz

57 Tourmaline

58 Heliodor

1961 (14 Feb)–**63**. Unsurfaced paper. W **102** of South Africa (sideways on vert designs). P 14.

171	**46**	½c. brown and pale blue	60	10
172	**47**	1c. sepia and reddish lilac	15	10

173	**48**	1½c. slate-violet and salmon	20	10
174	**49**	2c. deep green and yellow	75	1·40
175	**50**	2½c. red-brown and light blue	35	10
176	**50a**	3c. ultramarine and rose-red (1.10.62)	6·00	40
177	**51**	3½c. indigo and blue-green	1·00	15
178	**52**	5c. scarlet and grey-blue	8·00	10
179	**53**	7½c. sepia and pale lemon	70	15
180	**54**	10c. blue and greenish yellow	1·75	60
181	**55**	12½c. indigo and lemon	60	40
182	**55a**	15c. chocolate and light blue (16.3.63)	18·00	3·25
183	**56**	20c. brown and red-orange	4·00	30
184	**57**	50c. deep bluish green and yellow-orange	4·50	1·50
185	**58**	1r. yellow, maroon and blue	7·50	12·00
171/185 *Set of 15*			48·00	18·00

See also Nos. 186/191, 202/216 and 224/226.

1962–66. As No. 171, etc., but without watermark.

186	**46**	½c. brown and pale blue (8.62)	50	1·50
187	**48**	1½c. slate-violet and salmon (9.62)	4·00	45
188	**49**	2c. deep green and yellow (5.62)	2·50	3·50
189	**50**	2½c. red-brown and light blue (1964)	13·00	6·50
190	**51**	3½c. indigo and blue-green (1966)	6·00	3·75
191	**52**	5c. scarlet and grey-blue (9.62)	5·50	1·50
186/191 *Set of 6*			28·00	15·00

59 'Agricultural Development'

60 Centenary Emblem and Map

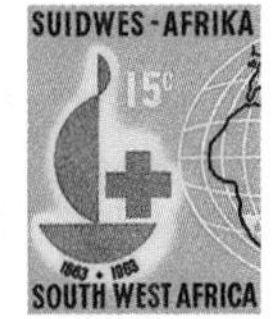

61 Centenary Emblem and part of Globe

1963 (16 Mar). Opening of Hardap Dam. W **102** of South Africa (sideways). P 14.

192	**59**	3c. chocolate and light green	30	15

1963 (30 Aug). Centenary of Red Cross. P 14.

193	**60**	7½c. red, black and light blue	4·50	5·00
194	**61**	15c. red, black and orange-brown	6·50	8·00

62 Interior of Assembly Hall

63 Calvin

1964 (14 May). Opening of Legislative Assembly Hall, Windhoek. W **102** of South Africa. P 14.

195	**62**	3c. ultramarine and salmon	50	30

1964 (1 Oct). 400th Death Anniversary of Calvin (Protestant reformer). P 14.

196	**63**	2½c. brown-purple and gold	50	15
197		15c. deep bluish green and gold	2·25	3·75

64 Mail Runner of 1890

65 Kurt von Francois (founder)

66 Dr. H. Vedder

(Des D. Aschenborn)

1965 (18 Oct). 75th Anniversary of Windhoek. Chalk-surfaced paper. W **127** of South Africa (sideways). P 14.

198	**64**	3c. sepia and scarlet	50	15
199	**65**	15c. red-brown and blue-green	90	1·75

1966 (4 July). 90th Birth Anniversary, of Dr. H. Vedder (philosopher and writer). Chalk-surfaced paper. W **127** of South Africa (sideways). P 14.

200	**66**	3c. blackish green and salmon	30	15
201		15c. deep sepia and light blue	70	40

No. 200 exists on Swiss-made paper with *tête-bêche* watermark from a special printing made for use in presentation albums for delegates to the UPU Congress in Tokyo in 1969, as supplies of the original Harrison paper were by then exhausted (*Price* £30 *mint*).

1966–72. As 1961–1966 but W **127** (inverted on No. A202) or W **127a** of South Africa and new values (4c., 6c., 9c.).

(a) wmk **127** *(sideways on vertical designs)*

A202	½c. brown and pale blue (1967)	10·00	2·50
A203	1c. sepia and light reddish lilac (1967)	1·50	10
A205	2c. deep bluish green and yellow	5·50	10
A206	2½c. deep red-brown and light turquoise-blue	2·50	3·00
A208	3½c. indigo and blue-green (1967)	5·00	9·00
A212	7½c. sepia and pale lemon (1967)	3·50	30
	w. Wmk top of triangle to right	5·50	75
A202/A212 *Set of 6*		25·00	13·00

(b) wmk **127a**

B202	½c. brown and pale blue (1968)	1·25	10
B203*a*	1c. sepia and light reddish lilac (1972)	4·25	10
B204	1½c. slate-violet and salmon (1968)	8·00	1·25
B206*a*	2½c. deep red-brown and pale blue (1967)	70	10
B207	3c. ultramarine and rose-red (1970)	8·50	3·50
B209	4c. deep red-brown and light turquoise-blue (1.4.71)	1·50	2·50
B210	5c. scarlet and grey-blue (1968)	3·50	10
B211	6c. sepia and greenish yellow (31.8.71)	11·00	12·00
B213	9c. indigo and greenish yellow (1.7.71)	13·00	13·00
B214	10c. bright blue and greenish yellow (6.70)	18·00	3·00
	a. Whiter background (9.72)**	18·00	4·00
B215	15c. chocolate and light blue (1.72)	25·00	7·00
B216	20c. brown and red-orange (1968)	16·00	1·75
B202/B216 *Set of 12*		£100	38·00

* The watermarks in this issue are indistinct but the stamps can be distinguished from each other and the stamps without watermark by their shades and the chalk-surfaced paper which is appreciably thicker and whiter.

† The normal sideways watermark shows top of triangle pointing to left, *as seen from the back of the stamp.*

** No. B214a, printed from sheets, has a much whiter background around the value and behind 'SOUTH WEST AFRICA' compared with No. B214, which was issued in coils only.

See also Nos. 224/226.

67 Camelthorn Tree

(Des D. Aschenborn (2½c., 3c.), Govt Printer, Pretoria (15c.))

1967 (6 Jan). Verwoerd Commemoration. Chalk-surfaced paper. T **67** and similar designs. W **127** of South Africa (sideways on vert designs). P 14.

217	2½c. black and emerald-green	15	10
218	3c. brown and new blue	15	10
219	15c. blackish brown and reddish purple	55	45
217/219 *Set of 3*		75	60

Designs: Horiz—2½c. T **67**. Vert—3c. Waves breaking against rock; 15c. Dr. H. F. Verwoerd.

70 President Swart

71 President and Mrs. Swart

1968 (2 Jan). Swart Commemoration. Chalk-surfaced paper. W **127** of South Africa (*tête-bêche*, sideways). P 14×15.

220	**70**	3c. orange-red, black and turquoise-blue		
		G. Inscribed in German	35	20
		A. Inscribed in Afrikaans	35	20
		E. Inscribed in English	35	20
221	**71**	15c. red, blackish olive and dull green		
		G. Inscribed in German	1·10	1·75
		A. Inscribed in Afrikaans	1·10	1·75
		E. Inscribed in English	1·10	1·75
		a. Red, brownish olive and bronze-green		
		G. Inscribed in German	3·00	3·25
		A. Inscribed in Afrikaans	3·00	3·25
		E. Inscribed in English	3·00	3·25
220/221 *Set of 2 values in strips of three*			4·00	5·50
Set of 6 singles			1·50	2·50

The three languages appear, *se-tenant*, both horizontally and vertically, throughout the sheet.

The 15c. also exists on Harrison paper, wmk w **102** of South Africa, from a special printing made for use in presentation albums for delegates to the UPU Congress in Tokyo in 1965. (*Price* £30 *mint*).

1970 (14 Feb). Water 70 Campaign. As Nos. 299/300 of South Africa, but with phosphor band and inscr 'SWA'.

222	2½c. green, bright blue and chocolate	50	30
223	3c. Prussian blue, royal blue and buff	50	30

72 GPO, Windhoek

1970–71. As Nos. 202 and 204/205 but 'POSGELD INKOMSTE' omitted and larger figure of value as in T **72**. W **127a** of South Africa (sideways on 1½ and 2c.).

224	**72**	½c. brown and pale blue (6.70)	1·00	30
225	–	1½c. slate-violet and salmon (1.6.71)	17·00	22·00
226	–	2c. deep bluish green and lemon (11.70)	3·50	40
224/226 *Set of 3*			19·00	22·00

1970 (24 Aug). 150th Anniversary of Bible Society of South Africa. As Nos. 301/302 of South Africa, but inscr 'SWA'.

228	2½c. multicoloured	75	10
229	12½c. gold, black and blue	3·50	4·50

No. 228 has a phosphor frame, probably added in error.

A mint example of No. 229 exists with a second, blind, impression of the die-stamped features.

POSTAGE DUE STAMPS

At the outset of the campaign in South West Africa, Transvaal postage due stamps were in general use in South Africa, before being replaced by South Africa Nos. D1/D7.

Postage Due stamps of TRANSVAAL cancelled with South West Africa postmarks (various types).

1907 (Nos. D1/D7).

ZD1	½d. black and blue green	22·00
ZD3	2d. brown orange	4·00
ZD5	5d. black and violet	40·00
ZD6	6d. black and red-brown	50·00
ZD7	1s. scarlet and black	70·00

Postage due stamps of SOUTH AFRICA cancelled with South West Africa postmarks (various types).

1914–22 (Nos. D1/D7).

ZD8	½d. black and green	22·00
ZD9	1d. black and scarlet	4·00
ZD10	2d. black and violet	5·00
ZD11	3d. black and bright blue	28·00
ZD12	5d. black and sepia	£125
ZD14	1s. red and black	£400

PRICES for Nos. D1/D39 are for unused horizontal pairs, used horizontal pairs and used singles.

1923 (1 Jan–July). Optd with Types **1** and **2** alternately.

(a) Setting I (14 mm between lines of overprint)

(i) On Nos. D5/D6 of Transvaal

		Un pair	Us pair	Us single
D1	5d. black and violet	4·00	55·00	11·00
	a. 'Wes' for 'West' (R. 8/6, 10/2 left pane)	£200		
	b. 'Afrika' without stop (R. 6/1)	£140		
	c. Inverted 'p' for 'd'			
D2	6d. black and red-brown	17·00	50·00	11·00
	a. 'Wes' for 'West' (R. 10/2)	£500		
	b. 'Afrika' without stop (R. 6/1, 7/2)	£275		
	c. 12 mm between lines of opt (R. 1/1)	£325		

(ii) On Nos. D3/D4 and D6 of South Africa (De La Rue printing)

		Un pair	Us pair	Us single
D3	2d. black and violet	50·00	55·00	10·00
	a. 'Wes' for 'West' (R. 10/2)	£350	£450	
	b. 'Afrika' without stop (R. 6/1, 7/2)	£300		
D4	3d. black and blue	21·00	55·00	10·00
	a. 'Wes' for 'West' (R. 8/6, 10/2)	£200		
	b. 'Africa' without stop (R. 9/1)	£350		
D5	6d. black and slate (20.4)	50·00	70·00	13·00
	a. 'Wes' for 'West' (R. 8/6)	£350		

(iii) On Nos. D9/D10, D11 and D14 of South Africa (Pretoria printings)

		Un pair	Us pair	Us single
D6	½d. black and green (P 14)	6·00	32·00	6·00
	a. Opt inverted	£600		
	b. Opt double	£1500	£1700	
	c. 'Wes' for 'West' (R. 10/2)	£160		
	d. 'Afrika' without stop (R. 6/1, 7/2)	£130		
D7	1d. black and rose (*roul*)	7·00	32·00	6·00
	a. 'Wes' for 'West' (R. 10/2)	£150	£350	
	b. 'Afrika' without stop (R. 6/1)	£150		
	c. Imperf between (horiz pair)	£1800		
D8	1½d. black and yellow-brown (*roul*)	1·25	14·00	2·75
	a. 'Wes' for 'West' (R. 8/6, 10/2)	£130		
	b. 'Afrika' without stop (R. 6/1)	£110		
D9	2d. black and violet (P 14) (21.6)	4·75	28·00	5·00
	a. 'Wes' for 'West' (R. 8/6)	£150		
	b. 'Afrika' without stop (R. 6/1)	£180		

Nos. D1/D9 were initially overprinted as separate panes of 60, but some values were later done as double panes of 120.

A variety of Nos. D1, D4/D5 and D9 with 15 mm between the lines of overprint occurs on four positions in each pane from some printings.

(b) Setting II (10 mm between lines of overprint)

(i) On No. D5 of Transvaal

		Un pair	Us pair	Us single
D10	5d. black and violet (20.4)	55·00	£200	

(ii) On Nos. D3/D4 of South Africa (De La Rue printing)

		Un pair	Us pair	Us single
D11	2d. black and violet (20.4)	19·00	55·00	9·50
	a. 'Afrika' without stop (R. 6/1)	£300		
D12	3d. black and blue (20.4)	7·50	29·00	5·50
	a. 'Afrika' without stop (R. 6/1)	£130		

(iii) On No. D9 of South Africa (Pretoria printing). Roul.

		Un pair	Us pair	Us single
D13	1d. black and rose (7.23)	£22000	—	£1800

1923 (30 July)–**26.** Optd as Types **3** ('Zuidwest' in one word without hyphen) and **4**.

(a) Setting III ('South West' 14 mm long, 'Zuidwest' 11 mm long and 14 mm between lines of overprint)

(i) On No. D6 of Transvaal

		Un pair	Us pair	Us single
D14	6d. black and red-brown	21·00	90·00	20·00

(ii) On Nos. D9 and D11/D12 of South Africa (Pretoria printing).

		Un pair	Us pair	Us single
D15	½d. black and green (P 14)	20·00	45·00	6·50
D16	1d. black and rose (*roul*)	14·00	45·00	6·50
D17	1d. black and rose (P 14) (2.8.23)	45·00	45·00	6·50

(b) Setting IV ('South West' 16 mm long, 'Zuidwest' 12 mm long and 14 mm between lines of overprint)

(i) On No. D5 of Transvaal

		Un pair	Us pair	Us single
D17*a*	5d. black and violet (1.7.24)	£950	£1500	

(ii) On Nos. D11/D12 and D16 of South Africa (Pretoria printing). P 14

		Un pair	Us pair	Us single
D18	½d. black and green (1.7.24)	7·50	38·00	5·50
D19	1d. black and rose (1.7.24)	10·00	30·00	5·50
D20	6d. black and slate (1.7.24)	2·25	42·00	9·00
	a. 'Africa' without stop (R. 9/5)	£130	£325	

(c) Setting V (12 mm. between lines of overprint)

(i) On No. D5 of Transvaal

		Un pair	Us pair	Us single
D21	5d. black and violet (6.8.24)	12·00	70·00	10·00

(ii) On No. D4 of South Africa (De La Rue printing)

D22 3d. black and blue (6.8.24) 16·00 55·00 11·00

(iii) On Nos. D11 and D13 of South Africa (Pretoria printing). P 14

D23 ½d. black and green (6.8.24) 3·00 30·00 6·50
D24 1½d. black and yellow-brown (6.8.24) 6·00 50·00 8·00

(d) Setting VI (9½ mm between lines of overprint)

(i) On No. D5 of Transvaal

D25 5d. black and violet (7.9.24) 2·75 22·00 3·50
a. 'Africa' without stop (R. 9/5) 85·00

(ii) On No. D4 of South Africa (De La Rue printing)

D26 3d. black and blue (3.2.26) 12·00 65·00 11·00

(iii) On Nos. D11/D16 of South Africa (Pretoria printing). P 14

D27 ½d. black and green (1.3.26) 15·00 35·00 7·50
D28 1d. black and rose (16.3.25) 2·00 12·00 1·60
a. 'Africa' without stop (R. 9/5 right pane) 85·00
D29 1½d. black and yellow-brown (1.10.26) 4·50 40·00 8·00
a. 'Africa' without stop (R. 9/5 right pane) 95·00
D30 2d. black and violet (7.9.24) 2·50 18·00 3·50
a. 'Africa' without stop (R. 9/5) right pane) 80·00
D31 3d. black and blue (6.5.26) 4·50 19·00 3·75
a. 'Africa' without stop (R. 9/5) right pane) 90·00
D32 6d. black and slate (1.10.26) 17·00 55·00 14·00
a. 'Africa' without stop (R. 9/5 right pane) £180
D27/D32 *Set of 6* 40·00 £160 35·00

For Setting VI the overprint was applied to sheets of 120 (2 panes of 60) of the 1d., 3d. and 6d., and to individual panes of 60 for the other values. The two measurements of 'South West', as detailed under No. 40, also occur on the postage dues. Nos. D25 and D31/D32 show it 16 mm long, No. 27 16½ mm long and the other stamps can be found with either measurement. In addition to the complete panes the 16½ mm long 'South West' also occurs on R. 2/4 in the 16 mm left pane for Nos. D28 and D30/D32.

Suidwes **South West**

Afrika. **Africa.**
(D 1) (D 2)

1927 (14 May–27 Sept). Optd as Types D **1** and D **2**, alternately, 12 mm between lines of overprint.

(a) On No. D5 of Transvaal

D33 5d. black and violet (27.9) 24·00 £100 23·00

(b) On Nos. D13/D16 of South Africa (Pretoria printing). P 14

D34 1½d. black and yellow-brown 1·00 21·00 3·50
D35 2d. black and pale violet (27.9) 4·75 18·00 3·25
a. Black and deep violet 9·00 18·00 3·50
D37 3d. black and blue (27.9) 16·00 50·00 11·00
D38 6d. black and slate (27.9) 14·00 40·00 8·50

(c) On No. D18 of South Africa (Pretoria printing). P 14

D39 1d. black and carmine 1·00 12·00 2·25
D33/D39 *Set of 6* 55·00 £225 45·00

No. D33 was overprinted in panes of 60 and the remainder as complete sheets of 120.

Examples of all values can be found with very small or very faint stops from various positions in the sheet.

1928–29. Optd with T **10**.

(a) On Nos. D15/D16 of South Africa

		Un single	*Us single*
D40	3d. black and blue	1·50	18·00
	a. Without stop after 'A' (R. 3/6)	45·00	
D41	6d. black and slate	6·00	35·00
	a. Without stop after 'A' (R. 3/6)	£150	
	(b) On Nos. D17/D21 of South Africa		
D42	½d. black and green	50	10·00
D43	1d. black and carmine	50	3·25
	a. Without stop after 'A' (R. 3/6)	40·00	
D44	2d. black and mauve	50	4·50
	a. Without stop after 'A' (R. 3/6)	55·00	
D45	3d. black and blue	2·25	26·00
D46	6d. black and slate	1·50	26·00
	a. Without stop after 'A' (R. 3/6)	60·00	£225
D42/D46	*Set of 5*	4·75	60·00

D 3 D 4

(Litho B.W.)

1931 (23 Feb). Inscribed bilingually. W **9** of South Africa. P 12.

D47 D **3** ½d. black and green 1·00 7·50
D48 1d. black and scarlet 1·00 1·25
D49 2d. black and violet 1·00 2·25
D50 3d. black and blue 4·25 13·00
D51 6d. black and slate 13·00 25·00
D47/D51 *Set of 5* 18·00 45·00

PRINTER. The following issues have been printed by the South African Government Printer, Pretoria.

1959 (18 May). Centre typo; frame roto. W **9** of South Africa. P 15×14.

D52 D **4** 1d. black and scarlet 1·50 15·00
D53 2d. black and reddish violet 1·50 15·00
D54 3d. black and blue 1·50 15·00
D52/D54 Set of 3 4·00 40·00

1960 (1 Dec). As Nos. D52 and D54 but W **102** of South Africa.

D55 1d. black and scarlet 1·50 2·50
D56 3d. black and blue 1·50 3·00

1961 (14 Feb). As Nos. D52 etc, but whole stamp roto, and value in cents. W **102** of South Africa.

D57 1c. black and blue-green 70 3·25
D58 2c. black and scarlet 70 3·25
D59 4c. black and reddish violet 70 4·50
D60 5c. black and light blue 80 3·25
D61 6c. black and green 1·00 5·00
D62 10c. black and yellow 3·00 6·50
D57/D62 *Set of 6* 6·00 23·00

OFFICIAL STAMPS

OFFICIAL **South West** **Africa.** (O 1)

OFFISIEEL **Suidwes** **Afrika.** (O 2)

1927 (16 Mar). Nos. 30, 31, 6 and 32 of South Africa optd with T O **1** on English stamp and T O **2** on Afrikaans stamp alternately.

		Un pair	*Us pair*	*Us single*
O1	½d. black and green	£100	£225	30·00
O2	1d. black and carmine	£110	£225	30·00
O3	2d. dull purple	£275	£400	45·00
O4	6d. green and orange	£140	£250	30·00
O1/O4	*Set of 4*	£550	£1000	£120

Overprints O1 and O2 were applied to the London printing of the ½d. and the Pretoria printings of the 1d. and 6d.

OFFICIAL **OFFISIEEL**

S.W.A. **S.W.A.**
(O 3) (O 4)

1929 (May). Nos. 30, 31, 32 and 34 of South Africa optd with T O **3** on English stamp and T O **4** on Afrikaans stamp.

O5 ½d. black and green 1·00 17·00 2·75
O6 1d. black and carmine 1·00 17·00 2·75
w. Wmk inverted £500
O7 2d. grey and purple 1·50 24·00 3·50
a. Pair, one stamp without stop after 'OFFICIAL' 9·00 60·00
b. Pair, one stamp without stop after 'OFFISIEEL' 9·00 60·00
c. Pair, comprising a and b 15·00 90·00
d. Split 'd' 65·00
O8 6d. green and orange 2·00 20·00 3·75
O5/O8 *Set of 4* 5·00 70·00 11·50

Types O **3** and O **4** are normally spaced 17 mm between lines on all except the 2d. value, which is spaced 13 mm.

Except on No. O7, the words 'OFFICIAL' or 'OFFISIEEL' normally have no stops after them.

The setting of 60 (5×10) used for No. O7 (and subsequently, after re-arrangement, for No. O11) showed no stop after 'OFFICIAL' at R. 1/1, 2/6, 6/6, 7/5, 8/6 and 9/5, and no stop after 'OFFISIEEL' at R. 5/6, 7/6, 8/5, 9/6 and 10/5. No. O7c therefore occurs only at R. 7/5-6, 8/5-6 and 9/5-6.

OFFICIAL **S.W.A.** (O 5) **OFFISIEEL** **S.W.A.** (O 6)

OFFICIAL. **S.W.A.** (O 7) **OFFISIEEL.** **S.W.A.** (O 8)

1929 (Aug). Nos. 30, 31 and 32 of South Africa optd with Types O **5** and O **6**, and No. 34 with Types O **7** and O **8**, languages to correspond.

O9 ½d. black and green 75 16·00 2·75
O10 1d. black and carmine 1·00 17·00 2·75
O11 2d. grey and purple 1·00 18·00 3·25
a. Pair, one stamp without stop after 'OFFICIAL' 6·00 50·00
b. Pair, one stamp without stop after 'OFFISIEEL' 6·00 50·00
c. Pair, comprising a and b 10·00 85·00
d. Split 'd' 65·00
O12 6d. green and orange 2·50 27·00 6·50
O9/O12 *Set of 4* 4·75 70·00 13·50

Examples of Nos. O1/O12 are known showing forged Windhoek postmarks dated '30 SEP 24' or '20 MAR 31'.

OFFICIAL **OFFISIEEL**
(O 9) (O 10)

1931. English stamp optd with T O **9** and Afrikaans stamp with T O **10** in red.

O13 **12** ½d. black and emerald 8·00 24·00 3·75
O14 **13** 1d. indigo and scarlet 1·00 19·00 3·50
O15 **14** 2d. blue and brown 2·25 10·00 2·25
O16 **17** 6d. blue and brown 4·00 14·00 3·25
O13/O16 *Set of 4* 13·50 60·00 11·50

OFFICIAL **OFFISIEEL**
(O 11) (O 12)

1938 (1 July). English stamp optd with T O **11** and Afrikaans with T O **12** in red.

O17 **27** 1½d. purple-brown 32·00 50·00 6·00
a. 'OFFICIAI' for 'OFFICIAL' (R. 10/2) £250

OFFICIAL **OFFISIEEL**
(O 13) (O 14)

1945–50. English stamp optd with T O **13**, and Afrikaans stamp with T O **14** in red.

O18 **12** ½d. black and emerald 13·00 38·00 5·00
O19 **13** 1d. indigo and scarlet (1950) 17·00 23·00 3·25
a. Opt double £700
O20 **27** 1½d. purple-brown 35·00 55·00 7·00
O21 **14** 2d. blue and brown (1947?) £700 £850 £100
O22 **17** 6d. blue and brown 25·00 70·00 8·00
O18/O20, O22 *Set of 4* 80·00 £170 21·00

OFFICIAL **OFFISIEEL**
(O 15) (O 16)

1951 (16 Nov)–**52**. English stamp optd with T O **15** and Afrikaans stamp with T O **16**, in red.

O23 **12** ½d. black and emerald (1952) 18·00 25·00 4·50
O24 **13** 1d. indigo and scarlet 5·50 27·00 3·50
a. Opts transposed £100 £250
O25 **27** 1½d. purple-brown 32·00 32·00 5·00
a. Opts transposed 75·00 95·00
O26 **14** 2d. blue and brown 5·00 32·00 4·00
a. Opts transposed 75·00 £250
O27 **17** 6d. blue and brown 2·75 55·00 7·50
a. Opts transposed 29·00 £170
O23/O27 *Set of 5* 55·00 £150 22·00

The above errors refer to stamps with the English overprint on Afrikaans stamp and *vice versa*.

The transposed overprint varieties occur on the lower five rows of the right pane from the first printing of Nos. O24/O27 and on alternate horizontal rows of both panes from the second printing (Nos. O25 and O27 only).

The use of official stamps ceased in January 1955.

Sudan

ANGLO-EGYPTIAN CONDOMINIUM

An Egyptian post office was opened at Suakin in 1867 and the stamps of Egypt, including postage dues and the official (No. O64). were used in the Sudan until replaced by the overprinted 'SOUDAN' issue of 1897.

Cancellations have been identified from eleven post offices, using the following postmark types:

BERBER (*spelt* BARBAR). *Open* 1 October 1873 *to* 20 May 1884. *Postmark type* G.

DABROUSSA. *Open* 1891 *onwards. Postmark as type* J *but with* 11 *bars in arcs.*

DONGOLA. *Open* 1 October 1873 *to* 13 June 1885 *and* 1896 *onwards. Postmark types* F, G, K, L.

GEDAREF. *Open* August 1878 *to* April 1884. *Postmark type* H.

KASSALA. *Open* 15 May 1875 *to* 30 July 1885. *Postmark type* G.

KHARTOUM. *Open* 1 October 1873 *to* 14 December 1885. *Postmark types* E (*spelt* KARTUM), G (*spelt* HARTUM), I (*with or without line of Arabic above date*).

KORTI. *Open* January *to* March 1885 *and* 1897. *Postmark type* K.

SUAKIN. *Open* November 1867 *onwards. Postmark types* A, B, C (*spelt* SUAKIM), D (*spelt* SUAKIM *and also with year replaced by concentric arcs*), I (*spelt* SOUAKIN), J (*spelt* SAWAKIN, *number of bars differs*).

TANI. *Open* 1885. *Postmark type* K.

TOKAR. *Open* 1891 *onwards. Postmark type* J (*7 bars in arcs*).

WADI HALFA. *Open* 1 October 1873 *onwards. Postmark types* F (*spelt* WADI HALFE), G (*spelt* WADI HALFE), I, J (*number of bars differs*).

WADI HALFA CAMP. *Open* 1896 *onwards. Postmark type* I.

Official records also list post offices at the following locations, but no genuine postal markings from them have yet been reported: Chaka, Dara, Debeira, El Abiad, El Fasher, El Kalabat, Faras, Fashoda, Fazogl, Ishkeit, Kalkal, Karkok, Mesellemia, Sara, Sennar and Taoufikia (not to be confused with the town of the same name in Egypt).

M

The post office at Kassala was operated by Italy from 1894 until 1896, using stamps of Eritrea cancelled with postmark type M.

From the last years of the 19th-century that part of Sudan lying south of the 5 degree North latitude line was administered by Uganda (the area to the east of the Nile) (until 1912) or by Belgium (the area to the west of the Nile, known as the Lado Enclave) (until 1910).

Stamps of Uganda or East Africa and Uganda were used at Gondokoro and Nimuli between 1901 and 1911, usually cancelled with circular date stamps or, probably in transit at Khartoum, by a lozenge-shaped grid of 18×17 dots.

Stamps of Belgian Congo were used from the Lado Enclave between 1897 and 1910, as were those of Uganda (1901–1910) and Sudan (1902–1910), although no local postmarks were supplied, examples being initially cancelled in manuscript.

Stamps of Sudan were used at Gambeila (Ethiopia) between 1910 and 10 June 1940 and from 22 March 1941 until 15 October 1956. Sudan stamps were also used at Sabderat (Eritrea) between March 1910 and 1940.

PRICES FOR STAMPS ON COVER TO 1945	
Nos. 1/9	*from* × 20
Nos. 10/17	*from* × 6
Nos. 18/29	*from* × 5
Nos. 30/95	*from* × 2
Nos. D1/D11	*from* × 30
Nos. O1/O3	*from* × 10
No. O4	*from* × 15
Nos. O5/O10	*from* × 50
No. O11	*from* × 10
Nos. O12/O31	*from* × 15
Nos. O32/O42	*from* × 10
No. A1	*from* × 20
Nos. A2/A5	—
Nos. A6/A10	*from* × 50
Nos. A11	*from* × 15
Nos. A12/A13	—
Nos. A14	*from* × 15
Nos. A15/A16	—
Nos. A17/A22	*from* × 20
Nos. A23/A26	—
Nos. A27/A28	*from* × 10

السودان
SOUDAN
(**1**)

1897 (1 Mar). Nos. 54*b*, 55, 56*a*, 58/58*a*, 59*a*, 61*a*, 63 and 64 of Egypt optd as T **1** by Govt Ptg Wks, Bûlaq, Cairo.

1	1m. pale brown	4·50	2·00
	a. Opt inverted	£225	
	b. Opt omitted (in vert pair with normal)	£1500	
	c. Deep brown	4·25	2·50
	w. Wmk inverted		
3	2m. green	1·25	1·75
4	3m. orange-yellow	1·40	1·50
5	5m. rose-carmine	2·00	70
	a. Opt inverted	£250	£300
	b. Opt omitted (in vert pair with normal)	£1600	
6	1p. ultramarine	7·50	2·00
7	2p. orange-brown	80·00	16·00
8	5p. slate	80·00	24·00
	a. Opt double	£6000	
	b. Opt omitted (in vert pair with normal)	£6000	
9	10p. mauve	50·00	60·00
1/9 *Set of* 8		£200	£100

Numerous forgeries exist including some which show the characteristics of the varieties mentioned below.

There are six varieties of the overprint on each value. Vertical strips of six showing them are worth a premium.

Four settings of the overprint were previously recognised by specialists, but one of these is now regarded as an unauthorised reprint from the original type. Here reprints can only be detected when in multiples. The 2pi. with inverted watermark only exists with this unauthorised overprint so it is not listed.

In some printings the large dot is omitted from the left-hand Arabic character on one stamp in the pane of 60.

Only two examples, one unused and the other used (in the Royal Collection), are known of No. 8a. In both instances one impression is partially albino.

PRINTERS. All stamps of Sudan were printed by De La Rue & Co, Ltd, London, *except where otherwise stated.*

(Currency. 10 milliemes = 1 piastre. 100 piastres = £1 Sudanese)

2 Arab Postman

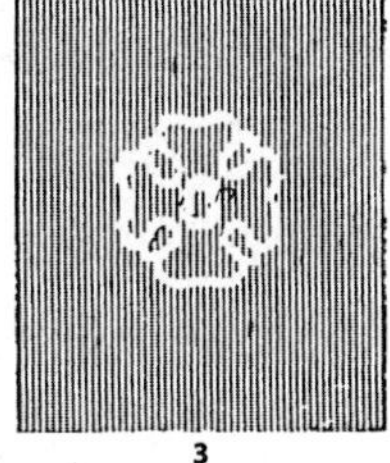

3

(Des E. A. Stanton. Typo)

1898 (1 Mar). W **3**. P 14.

10	**2**	1m. brown and pink	1·00	3·00
11		2m. green and brown	2·25	2·75
12		3m. mauve and green	2·25	2·25
13		5m. carmine and black	2·25	1·50
14		1p. blue and brown	21·00	2·75
15		2p. black and blue	50·00	3·50
16		5p. brown and green	50·00	17·00
17		10p. black and mauve	42·00	2·25
10/17 *Set of* 8			£150	32·00

4

5 Milliemes
(**5**)

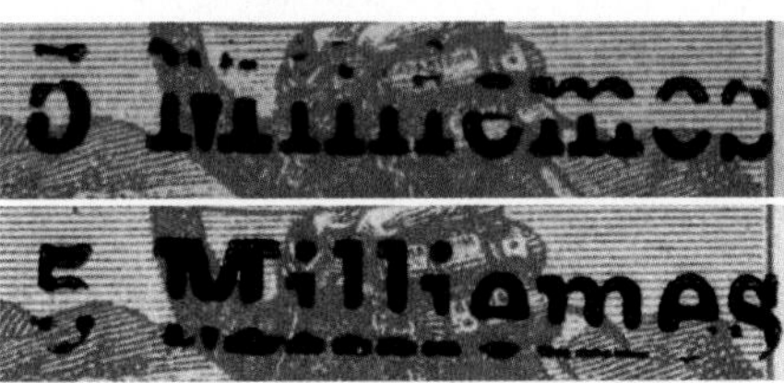

Damaged stereos (R. 2/5 and 2/6)

1902–21. Ordinary paper. W **4**. P 14.

18	**2**	1m. brown and carmine (5.05)	1·25	65
19		2m. green and brown (11.02)	1·75	10
20		3m. mauve and green (3.03)	2·25	25
21		4m. blue and bistre (20.1.07)	1·50	2·50
22		4m. vermilion and brown (10.07)	1·50	75
23		5m. scarlet and black (12.03)	2·00	10
		w. Wmk inverted	—	£200
24		1p. blue and brown (12.03)	3·00	30
25		2p. black and blue (2.08)	50·00	1·25
26		2p. purple and orange-yellow (*chalk-surfaced paper*) (22.12.21)	13·00	14·00
27		5p. brown and green (2.08)	38·00	30
		a. Chalk-surfaced paper	50·00	4·00
28		10p. black and mauve (2.11)	30·00	4·25
		a. Chalk-surfaced paper	50·00	15·00
18/28 *Set of* 11			£120	22·00

1903 (Sept). No. 16 surch at Khartoum with T **5**, in blocks of 30.

29	**2**	5m. on 5 pi. brown and green	6·50	9·50
		a. Surch inverted	£325	£275
		b. Damaged stereos horiz (pair)	£180	

The stereos on R. 2/5 and 2/6 were damaged towards the end of production of No. 29. They were replaced by new stereos showing a gap between the 'm' and second 'e' of 'Milliemes' (R. 2/5) and a narrower than usual gap between '5' and 'M' (R. 2/6).

6

7

1921–23. Chalk-surfaced paper. Typo. W **4**. P 14.

30	**6**	1m. black and orange (4.2.22)	80	5·50
31		2m. yellow-orange and chocolate (1922)	9·00	11·00
		a. Yellow and chocolate (1923)	13·00	16·00
32		3m. mauve and green (25.1.22)	2·50	13·00
33		4m. green and chocolate (21.3.22)	11·00	16·00
34		5m. olive-brown and black (4.2.22)	2·25	10
35		10m. carmine and black (1922)	9·00	10
36		15m. bright blue and chestnut (14.12.21)	6·00	1·00
30/36 *Set of* 7			35·00	42·00

1927–41. Chalk-surfaced paper. W **7**. P 14.

No.	Type	Description	Unused	Used
37	**6**	1m. black and orange	70	40
		a. Ordinary paper (1941)	70	2·00
38		2m. orange and chocolate	75	10
		aw. Wmk inverted	†	£300
		b. Ordinary paper (1941)	1·50	10
39		3m. mauve and green	70	10
		a. Ordinary paper (1941)	2·75	30
40		4m. green and chocolate	60	10
		a. Ordinary paper (1941)	4·50	1·25
		aw. Wmk inverted	80·00	90·00
41		5m. olive-brown and black	60	10
		a. Ordinary paper (1941)	4·50	10
42		10m. carmine and black	1·50	10
		a. Ordinary paper (1941)	9·50	10
43		15m. bright blue and chestnut	4·00	10
		aw. Wmk inverted	†	£300
		b. Ordinary paper (1941)	7·00	10
44	**2**	2p. purple and orange-yellow	4·50	10
		a. Ordinary paper (1941)	12·00	10
44*b*		3p. red-brown and blue (1.1.40)	11·00	10
		ba. Ordinary paper (1941)	22·00	10
44*c*		4p. ultramarine and black (2.11.36)	4·25	10
45		5p. chestnut and green	1·25	10
		a. Ordinary paper (1941)	17·00	3·75
45*b*		6p. greenish blue and black (2.11.36)	20·00	3·00
		ba. Ordinary paper (1941)	65·00	7·00
45*c*		8p. emerald and black (2.11.36)	20·00	8·50
		ca. Ordinary paper (1941)	75·00	12·00
46		10p. black and reddish purple	9·50	50
		a. Ordinary paper. Black and bright mauve (1941)	18·00	70
46*b*		20p. pale blue and blue (17.10.35)	15·00	60
		ba. Ordinary paper (1941)	15·00	20
37/46*b*		*Set of* 15	80·00	11·50

The ordinary paper of this issue is thick, smooth and opaque and was a wartime substitute for chalk-surfaced paper.

For similar stamps, but with different Arabic inscriptions, see Nos. 96/111.

AIR MAIL (8) AIR MAIL (9) AIR Extended foot to 'R' (R. 5/12)

1931 (15 Feb–Mar). Air. Nos. 41/42 and 44 optd with Type **8** or Type **9** (2p.).

No.	Type	Description	Unused	Used
47	**6**	5m. olive-brown and black (3.31)	35	70
48		10m. carmine and black	1·00	17·00
49	**2**	2p. purple and orange-yellow	85	7·50
		a. Extended foot to 'R'	30·00	
47/49		*Set of* 3	2·00	23·00

2½ 2½

10 Statue of Gen. Gordon

AIR MAIL ٢½ ٢½ (11)

1931 (1 Sept)–**37**. Air. Recess. W **7** (sideways*). P 14.

No.	Type	Description	Unused	Used
49*b*	**10**	3m. green and sepia (1.1.33)	4·00	6·50
50		5m. black and green	1·00	10
51		10m. black and carmine	1·25	20
52		15m. red-brown and sepia	40	10
		aw. Wmk sideways inverted (top of G to right)	£275	£250
		b. Perf 11½×12½ (1937)	4·50	10
		bx. Wmk reversed	†	£375
		by. Wmk sideways inverted (top of G to right) and reversed	£425	
53		2p. black and orange	50	10
		ab. Frame printed double, one albino	£850	
		ax. Wmk reversed	£300	
		ay. Wmk sideways inverted (top of G to right) and reversed	£300	
		b. Perf 11½×12½ (1937)	4·50	23·00
53*c*		2½p. magenta and blue (1.1.33)	4·75	10
		cw. Wmk sideways inverted (top of G to right)	—	£375
		cy. Wmk sideways inverted (top of G to right) and reversed	£375	
		d. Perf 11½×12½ (1936)	5·00	10
		da. Aniline magenta and blue	13·00	3·50
		dx. Wmk reversed	£275	
		dy. Wmk sideways inverted (top of G to right) and reversed	£300	£325
54		3p. black and grey	60	15
		a. Perf 11½×12½ (1937)	1·00	35
55		3½p. black and violet	1·50	80
		a. Perf 11½×12½ (1937)	2·50	21·00
		ay. Wmk sideways inverted (top of G to right) and reversed	£325	£350
56		4½p. red-brown and grey	14·00	15·00
57		5p. black and ultramarine	1·00	30
		a. Perf 11½×12½ (1937)	3·75	35
57*b*		7½p. green and emerald (17.10.35)	9·50	8·00
		bx. Wmk reversed	£275	
		by. Wmk sideways inverted (top of G to right) and reversed	£275	£275
		c. Perf 11½×12½ (1937)	4·00	11·00
57*d*		10p. brown and greenish blue (17.10.35)	10·00	1·75
		e. Perf 11½×12½ (1937)	8·00	28·00
		ey. Wmk sideways inverted (top of G to right) and reversed	£325	
49*b*/57*d*		*Set of* 12 (P 14)	42·00	29·00
52*b*/57*e*		*Set of* 8 (P 11½×12½)	30·00	75·00

* The normal sideways watermark shows the top of the G pointing left *as seen from the back of the stamp.*

1932 (18 July). Air. No. 44 surch with T **11**.

No.	Type	Description	Unused	Used
58	**2**	2½p. on 2p. purple and orange-yellow	1·40	5·00

12 Gen. Gordon (after C. Ouless)

13 Gordon Memorial College, Khartoum

14 Gordon Memorial Service, Khartoum (after R. C. Woodville)

1935 (1 Jan). 50th Death Anniversary of General Gordon. Recess. W **7**. P 14.

No.	Type	Description	Unused	Used
59	**12**	5m. green	35	10
60		10m. yellow-brown	85	25
61		13m. ultramarine	85	14·00
62		15m. scarlet	1·75	25
63	**13**	2p. blue	2·75	20
64		5p. orange-vermilion	2·75	1·25
65		10p. purple	10·00	10·00
66	**14**	20p. black	32·00	65·00
67		50p. red-brown	£100	£150
59/67		*Set of* 9	£130	£200

7½ PIASTRES ٧ ١/٢ قروش (15)

5 MILLIEMES ٥ مليمات (16)

1935. Air. Nos. 49*b*/51 and 56 surch as T **15** at Khartoum.

No.	Type	Description	Unused	Used
68	**10**	15m. on 10m. black and carmine (4.35)	40	10
		a. Surch double	£1000	£1400
69		2½p. on 3m. green and sepia (4.35)	85	2·75
		a. Second arabic letter from left missing	50·00	£110
		b. Small '½'	2·25	21·00
70		2½p. on 5m. black and green (4.35)	50	1·00
		a. Second Arabic letter from left missing	20·00	60·00
		b. Small '½'	1·25	2·50
		c. Surch inverted	£1000	£1400
		d. Ditto with variety a	£30000	
		e. Ditto with variety b.	£4500	£6000
71		3p. on 4½p. red-brown and grey (4.35)	1·75	22·00
72		7½p. on 4½p. red-brown and grey (3.35)	6·50	55·00
73		10p. on 4½p. red-brown and grey (3.35)	6·50	55·00
68/73		*Set of* 6	15·00	£120

Nos. 69a and 70a occur on R. 10/4 of the sheet of 50; the small '½' variety occurs on R. 4/2, R. 6/2, R. 7/2, R. 8/1, R. 9/1, R. 9/2 and R. 10/1.

The 15m. on 10m. surcharged in red (*Price,* £*275*) and the 2½p. on 3m. and 2½p. on 5m. in green are from proof sheets; the latter two items being known cancelled (*Price,* £*225 each, unused*).

There were four proof sheets of the 7½p. on 4½p., two in red and two in black. The setting on these proof sheets showed three errors subsequently corrected before No. 72 was surcharged. 12 positions showed an Arabic '⅓' instead of '½', one an English '¼' for '½' and another one of the Arabic letters inverted. (*Price for red surcharge,* £*375*).

1938 (1 July). Air. Nos. 53d, 55, 57*b* and 57*d* surch as T **16** by De La Rue.

No.	Type	Description	Unused	Used
74	**10**	5m. on 2½p. magenta and blue (P 11½×12½)	3·50	10
		w. Wmk sideways inverted (top of G to right)	£250	£225
		x. Wmk reversed		
75		3p. on 3½p. black and violet (P 14)	48·00	60·00
		a. Perf 11½×12½	£750	£850
76		3p. on 7½p. green and emerald (P 14)	6·00	6·50
		ax. Wmk reversed		
		ay. Wmk sideways inverted (top of G to right) and reversed	£120	£140
		b. Perf 11½×12½	£750	£850
77		5p. on 10p. brown and greenish blue (P 14)	1·75	4·00
		ax. Wmk reversed	£225	
		b. Perf 11½×12½	£750	£850
74/77		*Set of* 4	55·00	65·00

A 5p. on 2½p., perf 11½×12½ exists either mint or cancelled from a trial printing (*Price £400 unused*).

5 Mills. ٥ مليم (17)

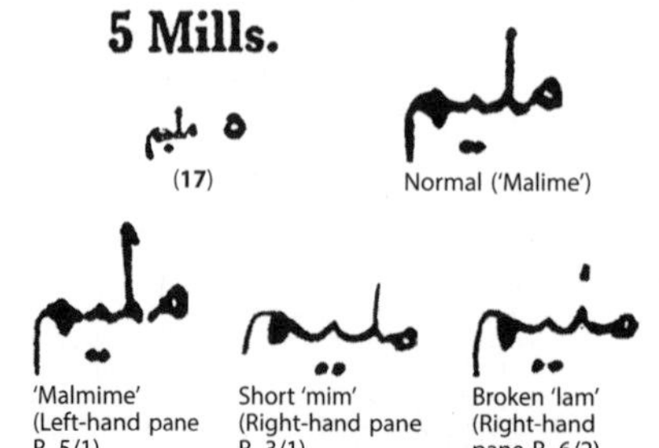
Normal ('Malime')

'Malmime' (Left-hand pane R. 5/1)

Short 'mim' (Right-hand pane R. 3/1)

Broken 'lam' (Right-hand pane R. 6/2)

5 M

Inserted '5' (Bottom right-hand pane R. 4/5)

1940 (25 Feb). No. 42 surch with T **17** by McCorquodale (Sudan) Ltd, Khartoum.

No.	Type	Description	Unused	Used
78	**6**	5m. on 10m. carmine and black	2·00	2·00
		a. 'Malmime'	65·00	85·00
		b. Two dots omitted (Right-hand pane R. 8/6)	65·00	85·00
		c. Short 'mim'	65·00	85·00
		d. Broken 'lam'	65·00	85·00
		e. Inserted '5'	£190	

4½ PIASTRES (18)

4½ Piastres

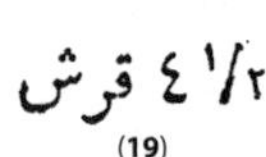
(19)

1940–41. Nos. 41 and 45c surch as Type **18** or Type **19** at Khartoum.

No.	Type	Description	Unused	Used
79	**6**	4½p. on 5m. olive-brown and black (9.2.41)	48·00	15·00
80	**2**	4½p. on 8p. emerald and black (12.12.40)	42·00	9·00

20 Tuti Island, R. Nile, near Khartoum

21 Tuti Island, R. Nile near Khartoum

(Des Miss H. M. Hebbert. Litho Security Printing Press, Nasik, India)

1941 (25 Mar–10 Aug). P 14×13½ (T **20**) or P 13½×14 (T **21**).

No.	Type	Description	Unused	Used
81	**20**	1m. slate and orange (10.8)	5·00	4·00
82		2m. orange and chocolate (10.8)	5·00	6·50
83		3m. mauve and green (10.8)	5·50	20
84		4m. green and chocolate (10.8)	1·00	1·75
85		5m. olive-brown and black (10.8)	50	10
86		10m. carmine and black (10.8)	30·00	7·50
87		15m. bright blue and chestnut	1·50	10
88	**21**	2p. purple and orange-yellow (10.8)	7·50	60
89		3p. red-brown and blue	1·25	10
90		4p. ultramarine and black	6·50	10
91		5p. chestnut and green (10.8)	11·00	17·00
92		6p. greenish blue and black (10.8)	27·00	2·25
93		8p. emerald and black (10.8)	30·00	2·25
94		10p. slate and purple (10.8)	£120	2·00
95		20p. pale blue and blue (10.8)	£100	50·00
81/95		*Set of* 15	£325	80·00

22

23

1m.–15m. 'nun' flaw (R. 2/3)

1948 (1 Jan–June). Arabic inscriptions below camel altered. Typo. Ordinary paper (8, 10, 20p.) or chalk-surfaced paper (others). W **7**. P 14.

No.	Type	Description	Unused	Used
96	**22**	1m. black and orange	35	7·00
		a. 'nun' flaw	9·00	
97		2m. orange and chocolate	80	6·00
		a. 'nun' flaw	17·00	
98		3m. mauve and green	30	9·50
		a. 'nun' flaw	9·00	35·00
99		4m. deep green and chocolate	50	4·25
		a. 'nun' flaw	22·00	
100		5m. olive-brown and black	12·00	3·00
		a. 'nun' flaw	30·00	15·00
		w. Wmk inverted	80·00	
101		10m. rose-red and black	5·50	10
		a. Centre inverted	†	£40000
		b. 'nun' flaw	21·00	5·50
102		15m. ultramarine and chestnut	5·00	20
		a. 'nun' flaw	21·00	6·50
103	**23**	2p. purple and orange-yellow	12·00	5·00
104		3p. red-brown and deep blue	7·50	30
105		4p. ultramarine and black	4·00	1·75
106		5p. brown-orange and deep green	4·00	7·00
107		6p. greenish blue and black	4·50	3·50
108		8p. bluish green and black	4·50	6·00
109		10p. black and mauve	16·00	10·00
		a. Chalk-surfaced paper (6.48)	55·00	6·00
110		20p. pale blue and deep blue	4·50	50
		a. Perf 13. Chalk-surfaced paper (6.48)	40·00	£250
111		50p. carmine and ultramarine	9·00	3·00
96/111		*Set of* 16	75·00	55·00

A single used example is known of No. 101a.

The 2m. and 4m. are known without the 'nun' flaw on R. 2/3.

For similar stamps, but with different Arabic inscriptions, see Nos. 37/46*b*.

24

25

1948 (1 Oct). Golden Jubilee of 'Camel Postman' design. Chalk-surfaced paper. Typo. W **7**. P 13.

112	**24**	2p. black and light blue	50	10

1948 (23 Dec). Opening of Legislative Assembly, Chalk-surfaced paper. Typo. W **7**. P 13.

113	**25**	10m. rose-red and black	1·25	10
114		5p. brown-orange and deep green	1·75	3·25

26 Blue Nile Bridge, Khartoum **27** Kassala Jebel

28 Sagia (water wheel) **29** Port Sudan

30 Gordon Memorial College **31** *Gordon Pasha* (Nile mail boat)

32 Suakin

33 GPO, Khartoum

(Des Col. W. L. Atkinson (2½p., 6p.), G. R. Wilson (3p.), others from photographs. Recess)

1950 (1 July). Air. Types **26/33**. W **7**. P 12.

115	**26**	2p. black and blue-green	6·50	1·50
116	**27**	2½p. light blue and red-orange	1·25	2·25
117	**28**	3p. reddish purple and blue	4·50	1·25
118	**29**	3½p. purple-brown and yellow-brown	6·50	6·50
119	**30**	4p. brown and light blue	2·00	3·50
120	**31**	4½p. black and ultramarine	3·50	7·00
		a. Black and steel-blue	24·00	11·00
121	**32**	6p. black and carmine	4·75	4·00
122	**33**	20p. black and purple	3·50	8·00
115/122 *Set of* 8			28·00	30·00

34 Ibex

35 Whale-headed stork

36 Giraffe

37 Baggara girl **38** Shilluk warrior

39 Hadendowa

40 Policeman

41 Cotton Picking

42 Ambatch reed canoe **43** Nuba wrestlers

44 Weaving **45** Saluka farming

46 Gum tapping

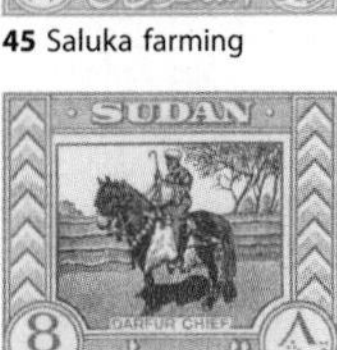
47 Darfur chief

48 Stack Laboratory

49 Nile Lechwe

50 Camel postman

(Des Col. W. L. Atkinson (1m., 2m., 4m., 5m., 10m., 3p., 3½p., 20p.), Col. E. A. Stanton (50p.) others from photographs. Typo)

1951 (1 Sept)–**61**. Designs as Types **34/50**. Chalk-surfaced paper. W **7**. P 14 (millieme values) or 13 (piastre values).

123	**34**	1m. black and orange	4·00	1·50
124	**35**	2m. black and bright blue	4·00	1·50
125	**36**	3m. black and green	13·00	8·00
126	**37**	4m. black and yellow-green	3·50	8·00
127	**38**	5m. black and purple	2·25	10
		a. Black and reddish purple (8.6.59)	7·00	70
128	**39**	10m. black and pale blue	30	10
129	**40**	15m. black and chestnut	12·00	10
		a. Black and brown-orange (1961*)	7·00	10
130	**41**	2p. deep blue and pale blue	30	10
		a. Deep blue and very pale blue (9.58*)	7·00	1·25
131	**42**	3p. brown and dull ultramarine	25·00	10
		a. Brown and deep blue (11.58*)	14·00	2·75
132	**43**	3½p. bright green and red-brown	3·25	10
		a. Light emerald and red-brown (11.61*)	6·00	10
133	**44**	4p. ultramarine and black	8·00	25
		a. Deep blue and black (7.59*)	9·00	10
134	**45**	5p. orange-brown and yellow-green	4·50	10
135	**46**	6p. blue and black	9·00	3·75
		a. Deep blue and black (8.61*)	16·00	7·00
136	**47**	8p. blue and brown	14·00	5·00
		a. Deep blue and brown (5.60*)	17·00	9·50
137	**48**	10p. black and green	1·50	1·50
138	**49**	20p. blue-green and black	12·00	3·75
139	**50**	50p. carmine and black	20·00	5·50
123/139 *Set of* 17			£100	35·00

* Earliest known postmark date.

SELF-GOVERNMENT

51 Camel Postman

1954 (9 Jan). Self-Government. Chalk-surfaced paper. Typo. W **7**. P 13.

140	**51**	15m. orange-brown and bright green	50	1·25
141		3p. blue and indigo	75	5·00
142		5p. black and reddish purple	50	2·50
140/142 *Set of* 3			1·60	8·00

Stamps as T **51**, but dated 1953 were released in error at the Sudan Agency in London. They had no postal validity (*Price per set* £18 *un*).

Sudan became an independent republic on 1 January 1956. Later issues will be found in the Stanley Gibbons *North East Africa catalogue*.

STAMP BOOKLETS

Nos. SB1/SB3 have one cover inscribed in English and one in Arabic. Listings are provided for booklets believed to have been issued, with prices quoted for those known to still exist.

1912 (Dec). Black on pink cover, size 74×29 mm. Stapled.
SB1 100m. booklet containing 20×5m. (No. 23) in pairs. £900

1924. Black on pink cover, size 45×50 mm. Stapled.
SB2 105m. booklet containing 20×5m. (No. 34) in blocks of 4

1930. Black on pink cover, size 45×50 mm. Stapled.
SB3 100m. booklet containing 20×5m. (No. 41) in blocks of 4 £1800

Some supplies of No. SB3 included a page of air mail labels.

POSTAGE DUE STAMPS

1897 (1 Mar). T D **24** of Egypt, optd with T **1** at Bûlaq.

D1	2m. green	1·75	5·00
	a. Opt omitted (in horiz pair with normal)	£3250	
D2	4m. maroon	1·75	5·00
	a. Bisected (2m.) (*on cover*)	†	—
D3	1p. ultramarine	10·00	3·50
D4	2p. orange	10·00	7·00
	a. Bisected (1p.) (*on cover*)	†	£1400
D1/D4 *Set of* 4		21·00	18·00

In some printings the large dot is omitted from the left-hand Arabic character on one stamp in the pane.

No. D1 has been recorded used as a bisect.

D **1** Gunboat *Zafir* D **2**

1901 (1 Jan)–**26**. Typo. Ordinary paper. W **4** (sideways). P 14.

D5	D **1**	2m. black and brown	55	60
		a. Wmk upright (1912)	£225	75·00
		b. Chalk-surfaced paper (6.24*)	3·00	15·00
D6		4m. brown and green	2·00	90
		a. Chalk-surfaced paper (9.26*)	12·00	15·00
D7		10m. green and mauve	9·00	4·00
		a. Wmk upright (1912)	£130	60·00
		b. Chalk-surfaced paper (6.24*)	18·00	17·00
D8		20m. ultramarine and carmine	3·25	3·50
D5/D8 *Set of* 4			13·50	8·00

* Dates quoted for the chalk-surfaced paper printings are those of the earliest recorded postal use. These printings were despatched to the Sudan in March 1922 (10m.) or September 1922 (others).

The 4m. is known bisected at Khartoum or Omdurman in November/December 1901 and the 20m. at El Obeid in 1904–1905.

1927–30. Chalk-surfaced paper. W **7**. P 14.

D9	D **1**	2m. black and brown (1930)	2·50	2·50
D10		4m. brown and green	1·00	80
D11		10m. green and mauve	1·75	1·25
		a. Ordinary paper	22·00	8·00
D9/D11 *Set of* 3			4·75	4·00

1948 (1 Jan). Arabic inscriptions altered. Chalk-surfaced paper. Typo. W **7**. P 14.

D12	D **2**	2m. black and brown-orange	4·75	50·00
D13		4m. brown and green	11·00	55·00
D14		10m. green and mauve	21·00	21·00
D15		20m. ultramarine and carmine	21·00	40·00
D12/D15 *Set of* 4			50·00	£150

The 10 and 20m. were reissued in 1979 on Sudan Arms watermarked paper.

OFFICIAL STAMPS

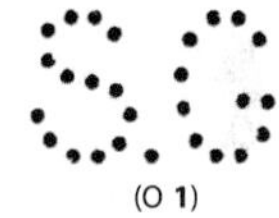
(O **1**)

1900 (8 Feb). 5 mils of 1897 punctured as T O **1** by hand.

O1	5m. rose-carmine	60·00	16·00

1901 (Jan). 1m. wmk Quatrefoil, punctured as T O **1**.

O2	1m. brown and pink	55·00	30·00

Due to the method of production, Nos. O1/O2 are found with the punctured 'SG' upright, inverted, reversed or inverted and reversed.

O.S.G.S. O.S.G.S.
(O **1a**) ('On Sudan Government Service') (O **2**) ('On Sudan Government Service')

O.S.G.S.
Malformed 'O' (lower pane, R. 1/7)

O.S.G.S.
Accent over 'G' (upper pane, R. 4/12)

1902. No. 10 optd at Khartoum as T O **1a** in blocks of 30 stamps.

O3	**2**	1m. brown and pink	3·50	15·00
		a. Oval 'O' (No. 19)	40·00	£110
		b. Round stops. (Nos. 25 to 30)	7·50	45·00
		c. Opt inverted	£350	£475
		d. Ditto and oval 'O'	£4250	£5000
		e. Ditto and round stops	£900	£1200
		f. Opt double	£500	
		g. Ditto and round stops	£1500	
		h. Ditto and oval 'O'	£5000	

1903–12. T **2** optd as T O **2**, by D.L.R. in sheets of 120 stamps.

(i) W **3** *(Quatrefoil)*

O4	10p. black and mauve (3.06)	24·00	26·00
	a. Malformed 'O'	£150	

(ii) W **4** *(Mult Star and Crescent)*

O5	1m. brown and carmine (9.04)	50	10
	a. Opt double		
	b. Malformed 'O'	20·00	10·00

O6		3m. mauve and green (2.04)	2·50	15
		a. Opt double	£850	£850
		b. Malformed 'O'	45·00	12·00
		c. Accent over 'G'		
O7		5m. scarlet and black (1.1.03)	2·50	10
		a. Malformed 'O'	45·00	10·00
		b. Accent over 'G'		
O8		1p. blue and brown (1.1.03)	13·00	10
		a. Malformed 'O'	£100	10·00
		b. Accent over 'G'		
O9		2p. black and blue (1.1.03)	45·00	20
		a. Malformed 'O'	£250	14·00
		b. Accent over 'G'		
O10		5p. brown and green (1.1.03)	3·00	30
		a. Malformed 'O'	60·00	15·00
		b. Accent over 'G'		
O11		10p. black and mauve (9.12)	4·00	70·00
		a. Malformed 'O'	70·00	
O4/O11 *Set of 8*			85·00	85·00

(O **2a**) (O **2b**)

1913 (1 Jan)–**22**. Nos. 18/20 and 23/28 punctured as T O **2a** by machine.

O12	**2**	1m. brown and carmine	22·00	25
O13		2m. green and brown (1915)	18·00	7·50
O14		3m. mauve and green	32·00	70
O15		5m. scarlet and black	13·00	15
O16		1p. blue and brown	18·00	35
O17		2p. black and blue	45·00	65
O18		2p. purple and orange-yellow (*chalk-surfaced paper*) (1922)	16·00	15·00
O19		5p. brown and green	60·00	3·25
		a. Chalk-surfaced paper	70·00	9·00
O20		10p. black and mauve (1914)	80·00	50·00
		a. Chalk-surfaced paper	90·00	50·00
O12/O20 *Set of 9*			£250	65·00

1922. Nos. 32/35 punctured as T O **2b** by machine.

O21	**6**	3m. mauve and green	25·00	14·00
O22		4m. green and chocolate	40·00	9·00
O23		5m. olive-brown and black	10·00	3·00
O24		10m. carmine and black	12·00	3·00
O21/O24 *Set of 4*			80·00	26·00

1927–30. Nos. 39/42 punctured as T O **2b** and Nos. 44, 45 and 46 as T O **2a**.

O25	**6**	3m. mauve and green (1928)	32·00	5·50
O26		4m. green and chocolate (1930)	90·00	50·00
O27		5m. olive-brown and black	13·00	10
O28		10m. carmine and black	35·00	35
O29	**2**	2p. purple and orange-yellow	42·00	1·00
O30		5p. chestnut and green	32·00	3·50
O31		10p. black and reddish purple	65·00	10·00
O25/O31 *Set of 7*			£275	60·00

The use of Nos. O25/O31 on internal official mail ceased in 1932, but they continued to be required for official mail to foreign destinations until replaced by Nos. O32/O46 in 1936.

S.G. (O **3**) **S.G.** (O **4**) **S.G.** (O **4a**)

1936 (19 Sept)–**46**. Nos. 37a, 38b, 39/43 optd with T O **3**, and 44, 44ba, 44c, 45, 45ba, 45ca, 46 and 46ba with T O **4**. W **7**. P 14.

O32	**6**	1m. black and orange (22.11.46)	2·50	17·00
		a. Opt double	†	£225
O33		2m. orange and chocolate (*ordinary paper*) (4.45)	6·00	9·00
		a. Chalk-surfaced paper	£120	70·00
O34		3m. mauve and green (*chalk-surfaced paper*) (1.37)	6·00	10
O35		4m. green and chocolate (*chalk-surfaced paper*)	11·00	5·00
		a. Ordinary paper		
O36		5m. olive-brown and black (*chalk-surfaced paper*) (3.40)	8·50	10
		a. Ordinary paper	32·00	40
O37		10m. carmine and black (*chalk-surfaced paper*) (6.46)	1·75	10
O38		15m. bright blue and chestnut (*chalk-surfaced paper*) (21.6.37)	16·00	30
		a. Ordinary paper	85·00	4·50
O39	**2**	2p. purple and orange-yellow (*chalk-surfaced paper*) (4.37)	20·00	10
		a. Ordinary paper	50·00	1·00
O39*b*		3p. red-brown and blue (4.46)	7·50	2·75
O39*c*		4p. ultramarine and black (*chalk-surfaced paper*) (4.46)	55·00	9·00
		ca. Ordinary paper	85·00	4·50
O40		5p. chestnut and green (*chalk-surfaced paper*)	17·00	10
		a. Ordinary paper	£100	6·50
O40*b*		6p. greenish blue and black (4.46)	15·00	13·00
O40*c*		8p. emerald and black (4.46)	7·00	45·00
O41		10p. black and reddish purple (*chalk-surfaced paper*) (10.37)	65·00	24·00
		a. Ordinary paper. *Black and bright mauve* (1941)	65·00	10·00
O42		20p. pale blue and blue (6.46)	38·00	35·00
O32/O42 *Set of 15*			£250	£130

1948 (1 Jan). Nos. 96/102 optd with T O **3**, and 103/111 with T O **4**.

O43	**22**	1m. black and orange	30	7·00
		a. 'nun' flaw	9·00	5·00
O44		2m. orange and chocolate	2·50	1·75
		a. 'nun' flaw	20·00	15·00
O45		3m. mauve and green	5·00	13·00
		a. 'nun' flaw	25·00	20·00
O46		4m. deep green and chocolate	4·25	8·00
		a. 'nun' flaw	50·00	35·00
O47		5m. olive-brown and black	4·00	10
		a. 'nun' flaw	22·00	20·00
O48		10m. rose-red and black	4·25	3·00
		a. 'nun' flaw	22·00	20·00
O49		15m. ultramarine and chestnut	4·50	10
		a. 'nun' flaw	22·00	
O50	**23**	2p. purple and orange-yellow	4·75	10
O51		3p. red-brown and deep blue	4·75	10
O52		4p. ultramarine and black	6·00	40
		a. Perf 13 (optd Type O **4a**)	13·00	25·00
O53		5p. brown-orange and deep green	6·50	10
O54		6p. greenish blue and black	3·50	10
O55		8p. bluish green and black	3·50	9·00
O56		10p. black and mauve	8·00	30
O57		20p. pale blue and deep blue	7·00	1·75
O58		50p. carmine and ultramarine	70·00	60·00
O43/O58 *Set of 16*			£120	90·00

1950 (1 July). Air. Nos. 115/122 optd with T O **4a**.

O59	**26**	2p. black and blue-green (R.)	16·00	4·50
O60	**27**	2½p. light blue and red-orange	1·50	1·75
O61	**28**	3p. reddish purple and blue	1·00	1·00
O62	**29**	3½p. purple-brown and yellow-brown	1·25	13·00
O63	**30**	4p. brown and light blue	1·00	11·00
O64	**31**	4½p. black and ultramarine (R.)	4·75	24·00
		a. Black and steel-blue	22·00	29·00
O65	**32**	6p. black and carmine (R.)	1·00	6·00
O66	**33**	20p. black and purple (R.)	4·50	12·00
O59/O66 *Set of 8*			28·00	65·00

1951 (1 Sept)–**62?**. Nos. 123/129 optd with T O **3**, and 130/139 with T O **4a**.

O67	**34**	1m. black and orange (R.)	50	7·50
O68	**35**	2m. black and bright blue (R.)	50	3·75
O69	**36**	3m. black and green (R.)	14·00	24·00
O70	**37**	4m. black and yellow-green (R.)	10	5·50
O71	**38**	5m. black and purple (R.)	10	10
		a. Black and reddish purple		
O72	**39**	10m. black and pale blue (R.)	10	10
O73	**40**	15m. black and chestnut (R.)	1·00	10
		a. Black and brown-orange		
O74	**41**	2p. deep blue and pale blue	10	10
		a. Opt inverted	£1200	
		b. Deep blue and very pale blue (9.61*)	2·25	10
O75	**42**	3p. brown and dull ultramarine	38·00	10
		a. Brown and deep blue (8.60*)	35·00	3·25
O76	**43**	3½p. bright green and red-brown	30	10
		a. Light emerald and red-brown (1962?)	9·00	6·00
O77	**44**	4p. ultramarine and black	8·00	10
		a. Deep blue and black (1961)	8·50	10
O78	**45**	5p. orange-brown and yellow-green	40	10
O79	**46**	6p. blue and black	70	4·50
		a. Deep blue and black (1962?)	16·00	11·00
O80	**47**	8p. blue and brown	1·00	30
		a. Deep blue and brown (1962?)	12·00	6·00
O81	**48**	10p. black and green (R.)	70	10
O81*a*		10p. black and green (Blk.) (1958)	22·00	4·00
O82	**49**	20p. blue-green and black	1·50	30
		a. Opt inverted	†	£4500
O83	**50**	50p. carmine and black	6·00	1·75
O67/O83 *Set of 18*			75·00	45·00

The 5, 10 and 15m. values were reissued between 1957 and 1960 with a thinner overprint with smaller stops.

* Earliest known postmark date.

ARMY SERVICE STAMPS

ARMY OFFICIAL (A **1**) ARMY OFFICIAL (A **2**) Army Service (A **3**)

1905 (1 Jan). T **2** optd at Khartoum as Types A **1** or A **2**. W **4** (Mult Star and Crescent).

(i) 'ARMY' reading up

A1		1m. brown and carmine (Type A **1**)	11·00	4·00
		a. 'I' for '1'	85·00	50·00
		b. Opt Type A **2**	65·00	32·00
		c. Pair. Types A **1** and A **2** *se-tenant*	£130	£180

(ii) Overprint horizontal

A2		1m. brown and carmine (Type A **1**)	£600	†
		a. 'I' for '1'	£6500	†
		b. Opt Type A **2**	£4250	†

The horizontal overprint exists with either 'ARMY' or 'OFFICIAL' reading the right way up. It did not fit the stamps, resulting in misplacements where more than one whole overprint appears, or when the two words are transposed.

(iii) 'ARMY' reading down

A3		1m. brown and carmine (Type A **1**)	£200	£100
		a. 'I' for '1'	£1500	£1500
		b. Opt Type A **2**	£1300	£800

1905 (Nov). As No. A1, W **3** (Quatrefoil).

A4		1m. brown and pink (Type A **1**)	£225	£250
		a. 'I' for '1'	£6000	£4000
		b. Opt Type A **2**	£3500	£3500
		c. Pair. Types A **1** and A **2** *se-tenant*	£5000	

The setting used for overprinting Nos. A1/A4 was 30 (6×5). The 'I' for first 'I' variety occurs on R. 5/4 and overprint T A **2** on R. 1/6 and 2/6 of the setting.

Two varieties of the 1 millieme.

A. 1st Ptg. 14 mm between lines of opt.

B. Later Ptgs. 12 mm between lines.

All other values are Type B.

1906 (Jan)–**11**. T **2** optd as T A **3**.

(i) W 4 (Mult Star and Crescent)

A5		1m. brown and carmine (Type A)	£700	£450
		a. Opt double, one albino	£800	
A6		1m. brown and carmine (Type B)	4·50	20
		a. Opt double, one diagonal	†	£1600
		b. Opt inverted	£800	£800
		c. Pair, one without opt	†	£7500
		d. 'Service' omitted	†	£4750
A7		2m. green and brown	30·00	1·00
		a. Pair, one without opt	£5000	
		b. 'Army' omitted	£4500	£4500
A8		3m. mauve and green	26·00	40
		a. Opt inverted	£2000	
A9		5m. scarlet and black	5·00	10
		a. Opt. double	£400	£250
		ab. Opt double, one diagonal	£350	
		b. Opt inverted	†	£450
		c. 'Amry'	†	£2750
		e. Opt double, one inverted	£1800	£700
		f. 'Armv' for 'Army' (R. 4/9)		
A10		1p. blue and brown	30·00	15
		a. 'Army' omitted	—	£3500
		b. Opt double	†	£3000
A11		2p. black and blue (1.09)	£100	13·00
		a. Opt double	—	£3000
A12		5p. brown and green (5.08)	£190	70·00
A13		10p. black and mauve (5.11)	£600	£750
A6s/A10s Optd 'SPECIMEN' *Set of 5*			£130	

There were a number of printings of these Army Service stamps; the earlier are as T A **3**; the 1908 printing has a narrower 'A' in 'Army' and the 1910–1911 printings have the tail of the 'y' in 'Army' much shorter.

The two overprints on No. A11a are almost coincident. The error comes from the 'short 'y'' printing.

A variety with no cross-bar to 'A' of 'Army' is known on some values, but does not appear to be constant.

No. A13 has been extensively forged, and should only be purchased with a reliable gurantee.

(ii) W 3 (Quatrefoil)

A14		2p. black and blue	95·00	10·00
A15		5p. brown and green	£130	£275
A16		10p. black and mauve	£160	£425
A14/A16 *Set of 3*			£350	£650
A14s/A16s Optd 'SPECIMEN' *Set of 3*			£120	

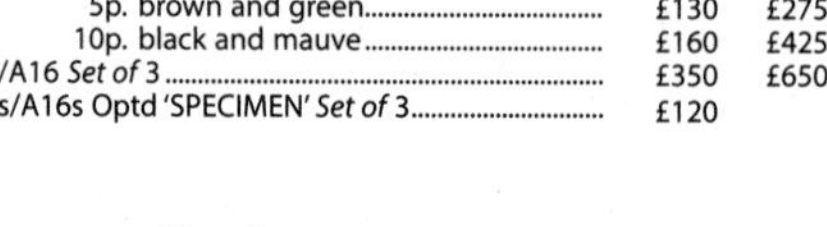

(A **4**) (A **5**)

1913 (1 Jan)–**22**. Nos. 18/20 and 23/28 punctured as T A **4**.

A17	**2**	1m. brown and carmine	60·00	7·50
A18		2m. green and brown	17·00	70
A19		3m. mauve and green	75·00	6·50
A20		5m. scarlet and black	23·00	50
		a. On No. 13		
A21		1p. blue and brown	50·00	1·50
A22		2p. black and blue	90·00	8·00
A23		2p. purple and orange-yellow (*chalk-surfaced paper*) (1922)	£130	60·00
A24		5p. brown and green	£110	50·00
		a. Chalk-surfaced paper	£140	50·00
A25		10p. black and mauve (1914)	£500	£275
A17/A25 *Set of 9*			£950	£375

1922–24. Nos. 31*a* and 34/35 punctured as T A **5**.

A26	**6**	2m. yellow and chocolate (1924)	£110	55·00
A27		5m. olive-brown and black (4.2.22)	27·00	8·00
A28		10m. carmine and black	38·00	12·00
A26/A28 *Set of 3*			£160	65·00

The use of Nos. A17/A28 on internal Army mail ceased when the Egyptian units were withdrawn at the end of 1924, but existing stocks continued to be used on Army mail to foreign destinations until supplies were exhausted.

MILITARY TELEGRAPH STAMPS

From March to May 1885 the Military Telegraph stamps of Great Britain (Bechuanaland Nos. MT1/MT8) were in use in Sudan. Identifying postmark codes are 'SK' (Suakin), 'QI' (Quarantine Island), 'HQ' (Headquarters), 'WR' (Western Redoubt) and 'ZA' (No.1 Post and, later, 2nd Brigade HQ).

1885. Nos. MT1/MT8 of Bechuanaland.

(a) Wmk Orb. P 14

MT1	1d. lilac and black		£200
MT2	3d. lilac and brown		£200
MT3	6d. lilac and green		£200

(b) Wmk script 'VR' (sideways). P 13½

MT4	1s. green and black		£300
MT5	2s. green and blue		£500
MT6	5s. green and mauve		£600
MT7	10s. green and red		£750

(c) Wmk Two Orbs (sideways). P 14×13½

MT8	£1 lilac and black		

Used prices for Nos. MT1/MT8 are for stamps with identifiable Sudan cancellations. For mint prices see Bechuanaland Nos. T1/T8.

Telegraph stamps were reintroduced during the Sudan campaign of 1896–1898.

(T **1**)

T **2**

1897 (July?). Nos. 5/9 handstamped as Type T **1**.

T1	5m. rose-carmine	7·00	2·00
	a. Opt in blue	21·00	6·00
T2	1p. ultramarine	14·00	4·00
	a. Opt in blue	22·00	10·00
T3	2p. orange-brown	25·00	5·00
T4	5p. slate	30·00	8·00
	a. Opt in blue	50·00	20·00
T5	10p. mauve	25·00	10·00
	a. Opt in blue	80·00	40·00

Handstamp Type T **1** is known sideways, diagonal and inverted.

Nos. 1, 3 and 4 are also known handstamped Type T **1**, but their authenticity is in doubt.

(Typo D.L.R.)

1898 (1 March). W **3**. P 14.

			Un whole stamp	*Used whole stamp*	*Used half*
T6	**T 2**	5m. brown-purple and violet	5·00	6·00	75
T7		1p. black and bright carmine	5·00	6·00	75
T8		2p. green and lilac-brown	5·00	6·00	75
T9		5p. violet and black	5·00	6·00	75

PRICES for Nos. T6/T17 are for unused whole stamps, used whole stamps or used half stamps. Each stamp has an extra central vertical line of perforations to allow 'bisection' in use.

1898 (June). W **8a** of Egypt (sideways). P 14.

T10	**T 2**	10p. bright rose and bluish green	75·00	95·00	21·00

1898–99. W **4**. P 14.

T11	**T 2**	5m. brown-purple and violet	1·50	3·00	50
T12		5m. brown and blue (1899)	3·00	5·00	75
T13		1p. black and bright carmine	1·50	3·00	50
T14		2p. green and lilac-brown (1899)	15·00	20·00	2·00
T15		5p. violet and black (1899)	2·00	3·00	50
T16		10p. bright rose and bluish green	2·50	3·50	50
T17		25p. blue and brown (1899)	3·00	5·00	75

The use of telegraph stamps was discontinued in 1902. Postage stamps which had been used for telegraph purposes in parallel with telegraph stamps throughout, were exclusively used thereafter.

Swaziland

PRICES FOR STAMPS ON COVER TO 1945

Nos. 1/10	*from* × 40
Nos. 11/20	*from* × 4
Nos. 21/24	*from* × 5
Nos. 25/27	*from* × 10
Nos. 28/38	*from* × 4
Nos. 39/41	*from* × 5
Nos. D1/D2	*from* × 30

TRIPARTITE GOVERNMENT

Following internal unrest and problems caused by the multitude of commercial concessions granted by the Swazi king the British and Transvaal governments intervened during 1889 to establish a tripartite administration under which the country was controlled by their representatives, acting with the agent of the Swazi king.

The Pretoria government had previously purchased the concession to run the postal service and, on the establishment of the tripartite administration, provided overprinted Transvaal stamps for use from a post office at Embekelweni and later at Bremersdorp and Darkton.

Swazieland
(**1**)

1889 (18 Oct)–**90**. Stamps of Transvaal (South African Republic) optd with T **1**, in black.

(a) P 12½×12

1	**18**	1d. carmine	25·00	25·00
		a. Opt inverted	£700	£650
2		2d. olive-bistre	85·00	38·00
		a. Opt inverted	—	£1700
		b. 'Swazielan'	£1100	£650
		c. 'Swazielan' inverted		
3		1s. green	20·00	15·00
		a. Opt inverted	£800	£475

(b) P 12½

4	**18**	½d. grey	9·00	26·00
		a. Opt inverted	£1200	£850
		b. 'Swazielan'	£2000	£1100
		c. 'Swazielan' inverted	—	£8000
5		2d. olive-bistre	32·00	18·00
		a. Opt inverted	£950	£450
		b. 'Swazielan'	£475	£400
		c. 'Swazielan' inverted	£7500	£5000
6		6d. blue	45·00	60·00
7		2s.6d. buff (20.10.90)	£325	£475
8		5s. slate-blue (20.10.90)	£170	£325
		a. Opt inverted	£1900	£3000
		b. 'Swazielan'	£4500	
		c. 'Swazielan' inverted		
9		10s. dull chestnut (20.10.90)	£7000	£4750

The 'Swazielan' variety occurs on R. 6/1 in each sheet of certain printings.

A printing of the ½d, 1d., 2d. and 10s. yellow-brown with stop after 'Swazieland' was made in July 1894, but such stamps were not issued.

It is possible that the dates quoted above were those on which the overprinting took place in Pretoria and that the stamps were issued slightly later in Swaziland itself.

1892 (Aug). Optd in carmine. P 12½.

10	**18**	½d. grey	7·50	16·00
		a. Opt inverted	£500	
		b. Opt double	£500	£500
		c. Pair, one without opt	†	£2000

No. 10 was overprinted in Pretoria during August 1892 when Swaziland was under quarantine due to smallpox. It is unlikely that it saw much postal use before all the overprints were withdrawn, although cancelled-to-order examples are plentiful.

It appears likely that no further supplies of stamps overprinted 'Swazieland' were provided by Pretoria after December 1892, although stocks held at post offices were used up. The overprinted stamps were declared to be invalid from 7 November 1894. They were replaced by unoverprinted issues of the Transvaal (South African Republic).

Stamps of TRANSVAAL (SOUTH AFRICAN REPUBLIC) used in Swaziland between December 1892 and January 1900.

1885–93. (Nos. 175/187).

Z1	½d. grey	45·00
Z2	1d. carmine	45·00
Z3	2d. olive-bistre	25·00
Z4	2½d. mauve	65·00
Z5	3d. mauve	65·00
Z6	4d. bronze-green	60·00
Z9	2s.6d. orange-buff	

1893. (Nos. 195/199).

Z10	½d. on 2d. olive-bistre (Type A surch in red)	70·00
	a. Surch Type B	
Z11	½d. on 2d. olive-bistre (Type A surch in black)	
Z12	1d. on 6d. blue (Type A surch)	60·00
	a. Surch Type B	70·00
Z13	2½d. on 1s. green ('2½ Pence' in one line) (Type A surch)	60·00
	a. Surch Type B	70·00

1894. (Nos. 200/204).

Z16	1d. carmine	45·00
Z17	2d. olive-bistre	45·00

1895–96. (Nos. 205/212*a*).

Z20	½d. pearl-grey	45·00
Z21	1d. rose-red	25·00
Z22	2d. olive-bistre	25·00
Z24	4d. olive-black	55·00
Z25	6d. pale dull blue	50·00

1895. (Nos. 213/214).

Z27	½d. on 1s. green	

1895. Introduction of Penny Postage (No. 215b).

Z29	1d. red	90·00

1896–97. (Nos. 216/224).

Z30	½d. green	45·00
Z31	1d. rose-red and green	25·00
Z32	2d. brown and green	55·00
Z33	2½d. dull blue and green	50·00
Z34	3d. purple and green	55·00
Z35	4d. sage-green and green	45·00
Z36	6d. lilac and green	45·00
Z37	1s. ochre and green	90·00
Z38	2s.6d. dull violet and green	£160

Prices are for clear and fairly complete postmarks. Examples dated in 1892 and 1893 are worth a premium. For list of post offices open during this period see boxed note below. Most known examples are from Bremersdorp (squared circle inscr 'SWAZIEL' later replaced by 'Z.A.R.' or c.d.s.) or Darkton (c.d.s.).

Shortly after the outbreak of the Boer War in 1899 the Transvaal administration withdrew from Swaziland, although the post office at Darkton, which was on the border, was still operating in early 1900. There was, however, no further organised postal service in Swaziland until the country became a British Protectorate in March 1902.

The following post offices or postal agencies existed in Swaziland before 1933. Dates given are those on which it is generally accepted that the offices were first opened. Some were subsequently closed before the end of the period. This revised listing is based on that in *Swaziland Philately to 1968*, edited by Peter van der Molen.

Bremersdorp (1890)	Mbabane (*previously* Embabaan) (1904)
Darkton (1889)	M'dimba (1889?)
Dwaleni (1917)	Mhlotsheni (1908)
Embabaan (1895)	Mooihoek (1919)
Embekelweni (1889)	Motshane (1929)
Ezulweni (1909)	Nomahasha (1903)
Forbes Reef (1906)	Nsoko (1927)
Goedgegun (1925)	Piggs Peak (1899)
Hlatikulu (1903)	Sandhlan (1906)
Hluti (1911)	Sicunusa (1913)
Ivy (1912)	Singceni (1929)
Kubuta (1924)	Stegi (1907)
Mahamba (1899)	Talwane (1928)
Malkerns (1914)	Umkwakweni (1899)
Maloma (1926)	White Umbuluzi (1922)
Mankaiana (1913)	

BRITISH PROTECTORATE

Stamps of Transvaal used in Swaziland from 1902.

1900. (Nos. 226/236).

Z41	1d. rose-red and green	£100
Z44	3d. purple and green	£150
Z45	4d. sage-green and green	£150

1902. (Nos. 244/255).

Z51	½d. black and bluish green	12·00
Z52	1d. black and carmine	10·00
Z54	2½d. black and blue	27·00
Z57	6d. black and orange-brown	30·00
Z60	2s.6d. magenta and black	50·00

1903. (Nos. 256/258).

Z63	1s. grey-black and red-brown	38·00
Z64	2s. grey-black and yellow	70·00

1904–09. (Nos. 260/272).

Z67	1d. black and carmine	10·00
Z68	2d. black and purple	16·00
Z70	3d. black and sage-green	20·00
Z71	4d. black and brown	16·00
Z72	6d. black and orange	16·00
Z73	1s. black and red-brown	20·00
Z74	2s. black and yellow	55·00
Z75	2s.6d. magenta and black	50·00
Z76	5s. black and purple/*yellow*	55·00
Z77	10s. black and purple/*red*	55·00
Z78	£1 green and violet	£190

1905–09. (Nos. 273/276).

Z79	½d. yellow-green	12·00
Z80	1d. scarlet	10·00
Z81	2d. purple	16·00
Z82	2½d. bright blue	38·00

The stamps of South Africa replaced those of Transvaal from 1913. Stamps of the other provinces were also valid for postal use.

2 King George V

3 King George VI

(Des Rev. C. C. Tugman. Recess D.L.R.)

1933 (3 Jan). Wmk Mult Script CA. P 14.

11	**2**	½d. green	30	30
12		1d. carmine	30	20
13		2d. brown	30	45
14		3d. blue	45	4·00
15		4d. orange	3·50	4·00
16		6d. bright purple	1·25	1·25
17		1s. olive	1·50	3·25
18		2s.6d. bright violet	15·00	22·00
19		5s. grey	38·00	55·00
20		10s. sepia	£140	£180
11/20 *Set of* 10			£180	£225
11s/20s Perf 'SPECIMEN' *Set of* 10			£325	

The ½d, 1d., 2d. and 6d. values exist overprinted 'OFFICIAL', but authority for their use was withdrawn before any were actually used. However, some stamps had already been issued to the Secretariat staff before instructions were received to invalidate their use (*Price* £50000 *per set un*).

1935 (4 May). Silver Jubilee. As Nos. 91/94 of Antigua, but ptd by B.W. P 11×12.

21 1d. deep blue and scarlet .... 50 1·50
a. Extra flagstaff £300 £400
b. Short extra flagstaff £550
c. Lightning conductor £550
d. Flagstaff on right-hand turret £130 £250
e. Double flagstaff £130 £275
22 2d. ultramarine and grey-black .... 2·75 5·00
a. Extra flagstaff £140 £250
b. Short extra flagstaff £170 £275
c. Lightning conductor £160 £250
23 3d. brown and deep blue .... 1·25 8·50
a. Extra flagstaff £110 £300
b. Short extra flagstaff £150 £325
c. Lightning conductor £130 £325
24 6d. slate and purple .... 4·50 7·50
a. Extra flagstaff £140 £250
b. Short extra flagstaff £170 £300
c. Lightning conductor £170 £300
21/24 *Set of 4* .... 8·00 20·00
21s/24s Perf 'SPECIMEN' *Set of 4* £140

For illustrations of plate varieties see Omnibus section following Zanzibar.

1937 (12 May). Coronation. As Nos. 95/97 of Antigua. P 11×11½.

25 1d. carmine .... 50 2·50
26 2d. yellow-brown 50 50
27 3d. blue .... 50 1·50
25/27 *Set of 3* .... 1·40 4·00
25s/27s Perf 'SPECIMEN' *Set of 3* £120

(Recess D.L.R.)

1938 (1 Apr)–**54**. Wmk Mult Script CA. P 13½×13.

28 **3** ½d. green .... 2·50 1·25
a. Perf 13½×14 (1.43) .... 30 2·75
b. Perf 13½×14. Bronze-green (2.50) .... 3·25 12·00
29 1d. rose-red .... 2·75 1·25
a. Perf 13½×14 (1.43) .... 1·00 1·75
30 1½d. light blue .... 7·00 75
a. Perf 14 (1941) .... 2·75 1·00
b. Perf 13½×14 (1.43) .... 40 1·00
ba. Printed on the gummed side £6000
31 2d. yellow-brown .... 2·50 1·25
a. Perf 13½×14 (1.43) 40 50
32 3d. ultramarine .... 11·00 1·75
a. Deep blue (10.38) .... 17·00 1·75
b. Perf 13½×14. Ultramarine (1.43) .. 9·50 10·00
c. Perf 13½×14. Light ultramarine (10.46) .... 26·00 32·00
d. Perf 13½×14. Deep blue (10.47) .... 20·00 12·00
33 4d. orange .... 14·00 3·50
a. Perf 13½×14 (1.43) .... 1·25 1·40
34 6d. deep magenta .... 26·00 2·75
a. Perf 13½×14 (1.43) .... 6·00 4·50
b. Perf 13½×14. Reddish purple (shades) (7.44) .... 4·50 1·50
c. Perf 13½×14. Claret (13.10.54) ... 10·00 8·50
35 1s. brown-olive .... 28·00 2·00
a. Perf 13½×14 (1.43) .... 1·25 65
36 2s.6d. bright violet .... 35·00 6·00
a. Perf 13½×14. Violet (1.43) .... 32·00 7·00
b. Perf 13½×14. Reddish violet (10.47) .... 25·00 18·00
37 5s. grey .... 70·00 25·00
a. Perf 13½×14. Slate (1.43) .... 60·00 55·00
b. Perf 13½×14. Grey (5.44) .... 50·00 20·00
38 10s. sepia .... 75·00 9·00
a. Perf 13½×14 (1.43) .... 10·00 7·00
28/38a *Set of 11* .... 95·00 35·00
28s/38s Perf 'SPECIMEN' *Set of 11* £325

The above perforations vary slightly from stamp to stamp, but the average measurements are respectively: 13.3×13.2 comb (13½×13), 14.2 line (14) and 13.3×13.8 comb (13½×14).

Swaziland
(4)

1945 (3 Dec). Victory. Nos. 108/110 of South Africa optd with T **4**.

		Un pair	*Us pair*	*Us single*
39	1d. brown and carmine	65	80	10
	a. Barbed wire flaw	15·00		
40	2d. slate-blue and violet	65	80	10
41	3d. deep blue and blue	65	2·50	20
39/41 *Set of 3*		1·75	3·75	35

1947 (17 Feb). Royal Visit. As Nos. 32/35 of Basutoland.

		Un	*Us*
42	1d. scarlet	10	10
43	2d. green	10	10
44	3d. ultramarine	10	10
45	1s. mauve	10	10
42/45 *Set of 4*		35	35
42s/45s Perf 'SPECIMEN' *Set of 4*		£150	

1948 (1 Dec). Royal Silver Wedding. As Nos. 112/113 of Antigua.

46 1½d. ultramarine .... 50 1·00
47 10s. purple-brown .... 40·00 45·00

1949 (10 Oct). 75th Anniversary of UPU. As Nos. 114/117 of Antigua.

48 1½d. blue 15 30
a. 'A' of 'CA' missing from wmk £750
49 3d. deep blue .... 2·00 4·50
50 6d. magenta .... 30 1·00
51 1s. olive .... 30 4·75
a. 'A' of 'CA' missing from wmk £1000
48/51 *Set of 4* .... 2·25 9·50

1953 (3 June). Coronation. As No. 120 of Antigua.

52 2d. black and yellow-brown 45 20

5 Havelock Asbestos Mine

6 A Highveld view

7 Swazi Married Woman

8 Swazi courting couple

9 Swazi warrior in ceremonial dress

10 Greater Kudu

(Recess B.W.)

1956 (2 July). Types **5/10**. Wmk Mult Script CA. P 13×13½ (horiz) or 13½×13 (vert).

53 **5** ½d. black and orange 50 10
54 **6** 1d. black and emerald 30 10
55 **7** 2d. black and brown .... 1·00 10
56 **8** 3d. black and rose-red 75 10
57 **9** 4½d. black and deep bright blue .... 1·50 1·00
58 **10** 6d. black and magenta .... 3·00 10
59 **5** 1s. black and deep olive .... 1·75 10
60 **8** 1s.3d. black and sepia .... 7·00 7·50
61 **6** 2s.6d. emerald and carmine-red .... 4·75 4·25
62 **9** 5s. deep lilac and slate-black .... 16·00 9·50
63 **7** 10s. black and deep lilac .... 27·00 22·00
64 **10** £1 black and turquoise-blue .... 60·00 48·00
53/64 *Set of 12* .... £110 80·00

(New Currency. 100 cents = 1 rand)

½c (11) 1c (12) 2c (13) 3½c (14)

2½c (I) 2½c (II) 4c (I) 4c (II)

5c (I) 5c (II) 25c (I) 25c (II)

50c (I) 50c (II) 50c (III)

R1 (I) R1 (II) R1 (III) R2 (I) R2 (II)

1961 (14 Feb–May). Nos. 53/64 surch as Types **11** to **14** by the South African Govt Printer, Pretoria.

65 ½c. on ½d. .... 4·50 9·00
a. Surch inverted £1900
66 1c. on 1d. .... 10 2·25
a. Surch double* £2250
67 2c. on 2d. .... 10 3·00
68 2½c. on 2d. .... 10 1·25
69 2½c. on 3d. (Type I) 10 50
a. Type II .... 10 2·25
70 3½c. on 2d. (5.61) .... 10 1·25
71 4c. on 4½d. (Type I) 10 30
a. Type II .... 60 2·00
72 5c. on 6d. (Type I) 50 10
a. Type II .... 20 1·75
73 10c. on 1s. .... 42·00 11·00
a. Surch double* £2500
74 25c. on 2s.6d. (Type I) .... 50 1·75
a. Type II (central) .... 2·25 2·50
ab. Surch double, one albino £850
b. Type II (bottom left) £800 £850
75 50c. on 5s. (Type I) .... 1·00 2·00
a. Type II .... 16·00 4·75
b. Type III £950 £1100
76 1r. on 10s. (Type I) .... 2·00 1·75
a. Type II .... 6·00 11·00
b. Type III £120 £160
77 2r. on £1 (Type I) .... 27·00 23·00
a. Type II (middle left) .... 17·00 26·00
b. Type II (bottom) £150 £275
65/77a *Set of 13* .... 60·00 50·00

* On both Nos. 66a and 73a the second surcharge falls across the horizontal perforations.

No. 74b has the thin Type II surcharge at bottom left, in similar position to the thicker Type I, No. 74, with which it should not be confused.

No. 77b has the surcharge centrally placed at bottom. No. 77a has it at middle left, above 'KUDU'.

No. 66 with surcharge central (instead of bottom left) and No. 75a bottom left (instead of middle left) are believed to be from trial sheets released with the normal stocks. They do not represent separate printings. (No. 66 *price* £180 *un*, No. 75a *price* £325 *un*.).

(Recess B.W.)

1961. As 1956 issue, but with values in cents and rands. Wmk Mult Script CA. P 13×13½ (horiz) or 13½×13 (vert).

78 ½c. black and orange (as ½d.) (14.2) .... 10 1·25
79 1c. black and emerald (as 1d.) (14.2) 10 10
80 2c. black and brown (as 2d.) (10.9) .... 10 2·50
81 2½c. black and rose-red (as 3d.) (14.2) 15 10
82 4c. black and deep bright blue (as 4½d.) (10.9) .... 20 1·50
83 5c. black and magenta (as 6d.) (10.9) .... 1·25 15
84 10c. black and deep olive (as 1s.) (14.2) 20 10
85 12½c. black and sepia (as 1s 3d.) (14.2) .... 1·25 70
86 25c. emerald and carmine-red (as 2s 6d.) (1.8) .... 4·50 8·50
87 50c. deep lilac and slate-black (as 5s.) (10.9) .... 6·00 3·75
88 1r. black and deep lilac (as 10s.) (10.9) .... 14·00 18·00
89 2r. black and turquoise-blue (as £1) (1.8) .... 22·00 15·00
78/89 *Set of 12* .... 45·00 45·00

15 Swazi Shields

16 Battle Axe

(Des Mrs. C. Hughes. Photo Enschedé)

1962 (24 Apr)–**66**. Various designs as Types **15/16**. W w **12**. P 14×13 (horiz) or 13×14 (vert).

90 ½c. black, brown and yellow-brown 10 10
w. Wmk inverted .... 45·00 23·00
91 1c. yellow-orange and black 10 10
w. Wmk inverted .... 1·75 2·25
92 2c. deep bluish green, black and yellow-olive .... 10 1·75
w. Wmk inverted .... 50·00 42·00
93 2½c. black and vermilion 10 10
a. Black and dull red (5.66) .... 3·00 80
w. Wmk inverted .... 2·50 2·00
94 3½c. yellow-green and deep grey 10 40
w. Wmk inverted .... 10·00 7·50
95 4c. black and turquoise-green 10 50
a. Black and deep turquoise-green (5.66) .... 3·00 1·00
w. Wmk inverted .... 11·00 8·00
96 5c. black, red and orange-red .... 1·50 10
w. Wmk inverted .... 13·00 8·00
97 7½c. deep brown and buff .... 2·00 1·50
a. Blackish brown and yellowish buff (5.66) .... 9·50 6·00
w. Wmk inverted .... 13·00 12·00
98 10c. black and light blue .... 5·50 35
w. Wmk inverted .... 80·00 42·00
99 12½c. carmine and grey-olive .... 3·00 3·50
w. Wmk inverted .... 80·00
100 15c. black and bright purple .... 1·50 1·75
101 20c. black and green .... 40 1·00
w. Wmk inverted .... — £225
102 25c. black and bright blue .... 50 1·00
w. Wmk inverted .... 55·00 40·00
103 50c. black and rose-red .... 20·00 7·00
w. Wmk inverted .... — £200
104 1r. emerald and ochre .... 3·50 2·50
105 2r. carmine-red and ultramarine .... 24·00 15·00
90/105 *Set of 16* .... 50·00 30·00

Designs: Vert—½c. T **15**; 1c. T **16**; 2c. Forestry; 2½c. Ceremonial headdress; 3½c. Musical instrument; 4c. Irrigation; 5c. Long-tailed Whydah; 7½c. Rock paintings; 10c. Secretary Bird; 12½c. Pink Arum; 15c. Swazi married woman; 20c. Malaria control; 25c. Swazi warrior; 1r. Aloes. Horiz—50c. Southern Ground Hornbill; 2r. Msinsi in flower.

1963 (4 June). Freedom from Hunger. As No. 146 of Antigua.

106 15c. reddish violet 50 15

1963 (2 Sept). Red Cross Centenary. As Nos. 147/148 of Antigua.

107 2½c. red and black 30 10
108 15c. red and blue 70 90

31 Goods Train and Map of Swaziland Railway

(Des R. A. H. Street. Recess B.W.)

1964 (5 Nov). Opening of Swaziland Railway. W w **12**. P 11½.

109 **31** 2½c. emerald-green and purple 65 10
110 3½c. turquoise-blue and deep yellow-olive .... 65 1·00
111 15c. red-orange and deep chocolate .... 1·00 70
112 25c. olive-yellow and deep ultramarine .... 1·10 80
109/112 *Set of 4* .... 3·00 2·25

1965 (17 May). ITU Centenary. As Nos. 166/167 of Antigua.

113 2½c. light blue and bistre 15 10
114 15c. bright purple and rose 35 20

1965 (25 Oct). International Co-operation Year. As Nos. 168/169 of Antigua.

115 ½c. reddish purple and turquoise-green . 10 30
116 15c. deep bluish green and lavender 40 20

1966 (24 Jan). Churchill Commemoration. As Nos. 170/173 of Antigua.

117 ½c. new blue .... 10 3·00
118 2½c. deep green 45 10
119 15c. brown 85 25
w. Wmk inverted .... 75·00 55·00
120 25c. bluish violet .... 90 1·10
117/120 *Set of 4* .... 2·00 4·00

1966 (1 Dec). 20th Anniversary of UNESCO. As Nos. 196/198 of Antigua.

121	2½c. slate-violet, red, yellow and orange	30	10
122	7½c. orange-yellow, violet and deep olive	85	85
123	15c. black, bright purple and orange	1·40	1·60
121/123 *Set of 3*		2·25	2·25

PROTECTED STATE

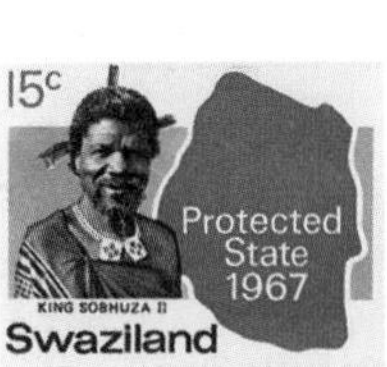

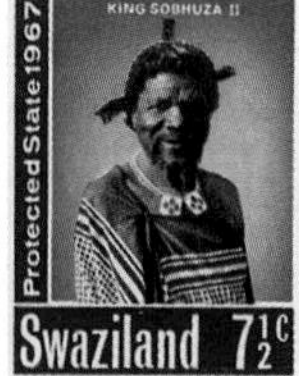

32 King Sobhuza II and Map **33** King Sobhuza II

(Des and photo Harrison)

1967 (25 Apr). Protected State. W w **12** (sideways on horiz designs). P 14½.

124	**32**	2½c. multicoloured	10	10
125	**33**	7½c. multicoloured	15	20
126	**32**	15c. multicoloured	20	30
127	**33**	25c. multicoloured	25	55
124/127 *Set of 4*			65	1·00

34 Students and University

(Des V. Whiteley. Photo Harrison)

1967 (7 Sept). First Conferment of University Degrees. P 14×14½.

128	**34**	2½c. sepia, ultramarine and light yellow-orange	10	10
129		7½c. sepia, ultramarine and light greenish blue	15	15
130		15c. sepia, ultramarine and rose	25	30
131		25c. sepia, ultramarine and light violet	30	35
128/131 *Set of 4*			65	75

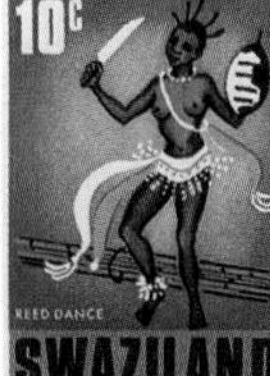

35 Incwala Ceremony **36** Reed Dance

(Des Mrs. G. Ellison. Photo Harrison)

1968 (5 Jan). Traditional Customs. P 14.

132	**35**	3c. silver, vermilion and black	10	10
133	**36**	10c. silver, light brown, orange and black	10	10
134	**35**	15c. gold, vermilion and black	15	20
135	**36**	25c. gold, light brown, orange and black	15	20
132/135 *Set of 4*			40	50

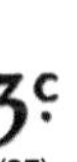

(**37**) **38** Cattle Ploughing

1968 (1 May). No. 96 surch with T **37**.

136	3c. on 5c. black, red and orange-red	1·50	10
	w. Wmk inverted	8·50	2·00

INDEPENDENT

(Des Mrs. G. Ellison. Photo Enschedé)

1968 (6 Sept). Independence. T **38** and similar horiz designs. W w **12** (sideways). P 14×12½.

137	3c. multicoloured	10	10
	a. Imperf (pair)	£250	
138	4½c. multicoloured	10	45
	a. Imperf (pair)	£250	
139	17½c. yellow, green, black and gold	15	70
140	25c. slate, black and gold	45	90
137/140 *Set of 4*		65	1·75
MS141	180×162 mm. Nos. 137/140 each×5	14·00	23·00
	a. Error Imperf	£2250	

Designs: 3c. T **38**; 4½c. Overhead cable carrying asbestos; 17½c. Cutting sugar cane; 25c. Iron ore mining and railway map.

Nos. 137/140 were printed in sheets of 50, but also in miniature sheets of 20 (4×5) containing *se-tenant* strips of each value.

INDEPENDENCE
1968

(**42**) **43** Cape Porcupine

1968 (6 Sept). Nos. 90/105 optd as T **42**, and No. 93 additionally surch 3c., by Enschedé.

(a) Wmk upright

142	½c. black, brown and yellow-brown	10	10
	a. Brown omitted	£425	
	b. Albino opt	50·00	
143	1c. yellow-orange and black	10	10
	w. Wmk inverted	50·00	40·00
144	2c. deep bluish green, black and yellow-olive	10	10
	w. Wmk inverted	—	40·00
145	2½c. black and vermilion	1·25	1·40
	a. Black and dull red	3·75	10
	w. Wmk inverted	42·00	32·00
146	3c. on 2½c. black and vermilion	10	10
	a. Black and dull red	10	10
	w. Wmk inverted	40·00	32·00
147	3½c. yellow-green and deep grey	15	10
	w. Wmk inverted	50·00	40·00
148	4c. black and turquoise-green	10	10
	a. Black and deep turquoise-green	25	15
	b. Black and pale turquoise-green	20	1·50
149	5c. black, red and orange-red	4·25	10
	w. Wmk inverted	65·00	40·00
150	7½c. deep brown and buff	60	10
151	10c. black and light blue	4·50	10
152	12½c. carmine and grey-olive	25	1·00
	w. Wmk inverted	2·00	3·00
153	15c. black and bright purple	25	1·25
154	20c. black and green	75	2·00
155	25c. black and bright blue	35	1·25
156	50c. black and rose-red	6·00	4·00
157	1r. emerald and ochre	2·00	4·50
158	2r. carmine-red and ultramarine	4·00	9·00

(b) Wmk sideways

159	50c. black and rose-red	3·50	12·00
160	2r. carmine-red and ultramarine	8·50	5·50
142/160 *Set of 19*		32·00	35·00

The 2½c., 3½c., 5c., 12½c., 50c. (No. 156) and 2r. (No. 158) exist with gum arabic only, the 1c., 2c., 3c., 4c., and 15c. with both gum arabic and PVA gum and the remainder with PVA gum only.

(Des and litho D.L.R.)

1969 (1 Aug)–**75**. T **43** and similar designs showing animals. Multicoloured. W w **12** (sideways on 3c., 3½c., 1r., 2r.). P 13×13½ (3, 3½c.), 12½×13 (1, 2r.) or 13×12½ (others).

161	½c. Caracal	10	10
162	1c. Type **43**	10	10
163	2c. Crocodile	20	10
	aw. Wmk inverted	4·25	
	b. Perf 12½×12 (29.9.75)	3·25	5·50
164	3c. Lion	1·00	10
165	3½c. African Elephant	1·00	10
166	5c. Bush Pig	30	10
167	7½c. Impala	35	10
168	10c. Charmer Baboon	45	10
169	12½c. Ratel	70	4·00
170	15c. Leopard	1·25	70
171	20c. Blue Wildebeest	1·00	60
172	25c. White Rhinoceros	1·75	1·75
	w. Wmk inverted	3·75	
173	50c. Common Zebra	1·50	3·25
174	1r. Waterbuck (*vert*)	3·00	6·50
175	2r. Giraffe (*vert*)	11·00	11·00
161/175 *Set of 15*		21·00	25·00

Nos. 161/173 are horizontal as T **43** but the 3c. and 3½c. are larger, 35×24½ mm.

No. 163b and a 1975 printing of No. 166 were printed by the D.L.R. works in Bogota, Colombia, these are on white paper.

Nos. 174 and 175 were reissued in new currency and No. 164 with Ww **12** upright in 1975.

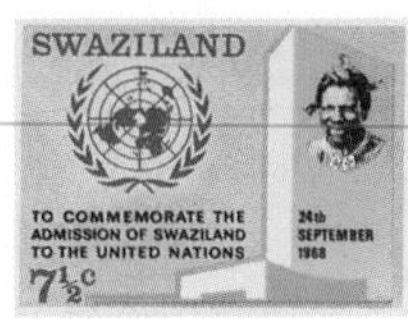

44 King Sobhuza II and Flags **45** King Sobhuza II, UN Building and Emblem

(Des D.L.R. Litho P.B.)

1969 (24 Sept). Admission of Swaziland to the United Nations. W w **12** (sideways). P 13½.

176	**44**	3c. multicoloured	10	10
177	**45**	7½c. multicoloured	15	10
178	**44**	12½c. multicoloured	25	10
179	**45**	25c. multicoloured	40	40
176/179 *Set of 4*			75	55

46 Athlete, Shield and Spears

(Des L. Curtis. Litho Format)

1970 (16 July). Ninth Commonwealth Games, Edinburgh. T **46** and similar vert designs. Multicoloured. W w **12**. P 14.

180	3c. Type **46**	10	10
181	7½c. Runner	20	10
182	12½c. Hurdler	25	10
183	25c. Procession of Swaziland competitors	35	40
180/183 *Set of 4*		75	55

POSTAGE DUE STAMPS

Postage Due stamps of Transvaal used in Swaziland.

1907. (Nos. D1/D7).

ZD1	½d. black and blue-green	28·00
ZD2	1d. black and scarlet	23·00
ZD3	2d. brown-orange	21·00
ZD4	3d. black and blue	35·00
ZD5	5d. black and violet	35·00
ZD6	6d. black and red-brown	60·00

These stamps were replaced by those of South Africa from 1914.

D 1

Postage Due
2d
(D 2)

D 3

(Typo D.L.R.)

1933 (23 Jan)–**57**. Wmk Mult Script CA. P 14.

D1	D **1**	1d. carmine	2·25	18·00
		a. Chalk-surfaced paper. Deep carmine (24.10.51)	1·25	22·00
		ac. Error. St Edward's Crown, W **9b**	£425	
D2		2d. pale violet	5·00	38·00
		a. Chalk-surfaced paper (22.2.57)	6·50	55·00
		ab. Large 'd'	55·00	
D1s/D2s Perf 'SPECIMEN' *Set of 2*			75·00	

For illustration of No. D2ab see above No. D1 of Basutoland.

1961 (8 Feb). No. 55 surch with T D **2**.

D3	**7**	2d. on 2d.	1·25	2·75

Another 2d. on 2d. Postage Due, with small surcharge as T D **5**, was produced *after the currency change*, to meet the philatelic demand (*Price* 30p *unused*, £1·00 *used*).

(Typo D.L.R.)

1961 (14 Feb). Chalk-surfaced paper. Wmk Mult Script CA. P 14.

D4	D **3**	1c. carmine	15	1·10
D5		2c. violet	15	1·10
D6		5c. green	20	1·10
D4/D6 *Set of 3*			45	3·00

Postage Due
1c
(D **4**)

Postage Due
1c
(D **5**)

2c
Narrow '2'
(R. 8/4)

1961. No. 55 surcharged.

a. As T D **4**. *(14 Feb)*

D7	**7**	1c. on 2d.	1·25	2·50
D8		2c. on 2d.	1·25	2·50
		a. Narrow '2'	25·00	
D9		5c. on 2d.	2·25	2·50
D7/D9 *Set of 3*			4·25	6·75

b. As T D **5**. *(Date?)*

D10	**7**	1c. on 2d.	70	4·25
D11		2c. on 2d.	50	2·75
D12		5c. on 2d.	90	2·25
D10/D12 *Set of 3*			1·90	8·25

Tanganyika

The stamps of GERMANY were used in the colony between October 1890 and July 1893 when issues for GERMAN EAST AFRICA were provided.

PRICES FOR STAMPS ON COVER TO 1945

The Mafia Island provisionals (Nos. M1/M52) are very rare used on cover.

Nos. N1/N5	*from* × 8
Nos. 45/59	*from* × 6
Nos. 60/62	—
Nos. 63/73	*from* × 6
Nos. 74/86	*from* × 8
Nos. 87/88	—
Nos. 89/92	*from* × 6
Nos. 93/106	*from* × 3
No. 107	—

MAFIA ISLAND

BRITISH OCCUPATION

Mafia Island was captured by the British from the Germans in January 1915. Letters were first sent out unstamped, then with stamps handstamped with T M **1**. Later the military were supplied with handstamps by the post office in Zanzibar. These were used to produce Nos. M11/M52

There is continuing debate about the status of the Mafia provisional issues, but we are satisfied that they were produced with proper authorisation, under wartime conditions.

(Currency. 100 heller = 1 rupee)

G.R.
MAFIA
(M **1**)

(M **3**)

1915 (Jan). German East Africa Yacht types, handstamped with T M **1**. Wmk Lozenges, or no wmk (1r., 2r.). A. In black (2½h. in blackish lilac). B. In deep purple. C. In reddish violet.

			A	B	C
M1	2½h. brown		£1100	†	£225
		a. Pair, one without handstamp	†	†	£4000
M2	4h. green		£1000	£1100	£325
		a. Pair, one without handstamp	†	†	£4000
M3	7½h. carmine		£650	£700	£100
		a. Pair, one without handstamp	£8500	†	£2750
M4	15h. ultramarine		£650	£900	£170
		a. Pair, one without handstamp	†	†	£3750
M5	20h. black and red/*yellow*		£950	£950	£350
		a. Pair, one without handstamp	†	£7500	£4000
M6	30h. black and carmine		£1100	£1300	£425
		a. Pair, one without handstamp	£9000	†	£3750
M7	45h. black and mauve		£1100	£1300	£500
		a. Pair, one without handstamp	£9000	†	£4750
M8	1r. carmine		£14000	†	£12000
M9	2r. green		£15000	†	£13000
M10	3r. blue-black and red		£16000	†	£14000

Prices are for unused examples.

A few contemporary Zanzibar stamps (1, 3, 6 and 15c.) and India – I.E.F. ½a and 1a are known with the above handstamp.

(Currency. 100 cents = 1 rupee)

1915 (May). German East Africa Yacht types with handstamped four-line surcharge 'G.R.—POST—6 CENTS—MAFIA' in black, green or violet. Wmk Lozenges or no wmk (1r., 2r.).

M11	6c. on 2½h. brown	£3000	£2500
	a. Pair, one without handstamp	†	£7500
M12	6c. on 4h. green	£2750	£2750
	a. Pair, one without handstamp	£8000	
M13	6c. on 7½h. carmine	£2750	£2750
	a. Pair, one without handstamp	£8000	
M14	6c. on 15h. ultramarine	£2500	£2750
M15	6c. on 20h. black and red/*yellow*	£4000	£4000
M16	6c. on 30h. black and carmine	£5000	£5500
M17	6c. on 45h. black and mauve	£4000	£4250
	a. Pair, one without handstamp	£9000	
M18	6c. on 1r. carmine	£40000	
M19	6c. on 2r. green	£55000	
M20	6c. on 3r. blue-black and red	£55000	

The 5, 20 and 40 pesa values of the 1901 Yacht issue are also known with the above surcharge as are the contemporary 1c. and 6c. Zanzibar stamps.

1915 (Sept).

(a) German East African fiscal stamps. 'Statistik des Waaren-Verkehrs' (Trade Statistical Charge) handstamped in bluish green or violet, 'O.H.B.M.S. Mafia' in a circle, as T M **3**

M21	24 pesa, vermilion/*buff*	£900	£1400
M22	12½ heller, drab	£1100	£1500
	a. Pair, one without handstamp	£12000	
M23	25 heller, dull green	£1100	£1500
M24	50 heller, slate	£1100	£1500
	a. Pair, one without handstamp	£12000	
M25	1 rupee, lilac	£1100	£1500

(b) German East African 'Ubersetzungs- Gebühren' (Fee) stamp, overprinted as before

M26	25 heller, grey	£1100	£1500

G. R
POST
MAFIA
(M **4**)

G. R.
Post
MAFIA.
(M **5**)

(c) Stamps as above, but with further opt as T M **4**, *in bluish green or violet*

M27	24 pesa, vermilion/*buff*	£1400
M28	12½ heller, drab	£1500
M29	25 heller, dull green	£1500
M30	50 heller, slate	£1500
M31	1 rupee, lilac	£1500
M32	25 heller, grey (No. M26)	£1500
	a. Pair, one without handstamp Type M **4**	£8000

T M **3** is also known handstamped on the 7½h., 20h. and 30h. values of German East Africa 1905 Yacht issue and also on contemporary 1, 3, 6 and 25c. Zanzibar stamps.

(Currency. 12 pies = 1 anna. 16 annas = 1 rupee)

1915 (Nov)–**16**. Nos. E1/E2, E4/E9, E11 and E13 of Indian Expeditionary Forces (India King George V optd 'I.E.F.') with a further opt T M **4** handstruck in green, greenish black or dull blue.

M33	3p. grey	42·00	£110
	a. Pair, one stamp without handstamp	—	£1900
M34	½a. light green	65·00	£110
	a. Pair, one stamp without handstamp	£2500	£1900
M35	1a. aniline carmine	65·00	90·00
M36	2a. purple	£110	£190
M37	2½a. ultramarine	£120	£200
M38	3a. orange	£130	£200
	a. Pair, one stamp without handstamp	†	£3500
M39	4a. olive-green	£200	£300
M40	8a. deep magenta	£375	£475
	a. Pair, one stamp without handstamp	†	£3750
M41	12a. carmine-lake	£475	£650
M42	1r. red-brown and deep blue-green	£500	£750
	a. 'I.E.F.' opt double, one albino	£1000	
M33/M42 *Set of* 10		£1900	£2750

All values exist with the overprint inverted, and several are known with overprint double or sideways.

T M **4** (a handstamp made up from metal type) was originally applied as a combined overprint and postmark, between November 1915 and July 1916, and can be found tying the 3p., ½a. and 1a. values to *piece* or *cover*. A 'MAFIA' circular datestamp was supplied from Zanzibar in early July 1916, and from July to September 1916 T M **4** was used as an overprint only, mainly for philatelic purposes.

Until early April 1917 India 'I.E.F.' stamps were in use on Mafia without additional overprint, but the new overprint T M **5** (a rubber handstamp) was then introduced, producing Nos. M43/M52.

1917 (Apr). Nos. E1/E2, E4/E9, E11 and E13 of Indian Expeditionary Forces (India King George V optd 'I.E.F.') with further opt T M **5** handstruck in green, greenish black, dull blue or violet.

M43	3p. grey	£150	£160
M44	½a. light green	£160	£160
M45	1a. aniline carmine	£120	£130
M46	2a. purple	£190	£190
M47	2½a. ultramarine	£200	£200
M48	3a. orange	£225	£225
M49	4a. olive-green	£300	£300
M50	8a. deep magenta	£475	£475
M51	12a. carmine-lake	£475	£600
M52	1r. red-brown and deep blue-green	£650	£750
M43/M52 *Set of* 10		£2500	£2750

Stamps with handstamp inverted are known.

Used examples of Nos. M43/M52 with black double-ring backdated postmarks of 'JA 23 1915' and other dates prior to April 1917 are worth about 50% of the prices quoted.

Nos. M43/M52 were in use until August 1918, when they were replaced by the Tanganyika 'G.E.A.' issue (Nos. 45/61). India 'I.E.F.' stamps without additional overprint also remained in use during the period.

NYASALAND-RHODESIAN FORCE

This issue was sanctioned for use by the Nyasaland-Rhodesian Force during operations in German East Africa, Mozambique and Nyasaland. Unoverprinted Nyasaland stamps were used by the Force prior to the introduction of Nos. N1/N5 and, again, in 1918.

N. F.
(N **1**)

1916 (7 Aug–18 Sept*). Nos. 83, 86, 90/91 and 93 of Nyasaland optd with T N **1** by Govt Printer, Zomba.

N1	½d. green	1·50	8·00
N2	1d. scarlet	1·50	3·25
N3	3d. purple/*yellow* (15.9*)	27·00	17·00
	a. Opt double	†	£22000
N4	4d. black and red/*yellow* (13.9*)	50·00	40·00
N5	1s. black/*green* (18.9*)	70·00	70·00
N1/N5 *Set of* 5		£130	£120
N1s/N5s Optd 'SPECIMEN' *Set of* 5		£250	

* Earliest known dates of use.

Of No. N3a only six examples were printed, these being the bottom row on one pane issued at M'bamba Bay FPO, German East Africa in March 1918.

This overprint was applied in a setting of 60 (10 rows of 6) and the following minor varieties occur on all values: small stop after 'N' (R. 1/1); broken 'F' (R. 4/3); very small stop after 'F' (R. 6/5); no serifs at top left and bottom of 'N' (R. 10/1).

TANGANYIKA

BRITISH OCCUPATION OF GERMAN EAST AFRICA

Following the invasion of German East Africa by Allied forces civilian mail was accepted by the Indian Army postal service, using Indian stamps overprinted 'I.E.F.'. Some offices reverted to civilian control on 1 June 1917 and these used stamps of East Africa and Uganda until the 'G.E.A.' overprints were ready. The last field post offices, in the southern part of the country, did not come under civilian control until 15 March 1919.

(Currency. 100 cents = 1 rupee)

G.E.A. (**1**) **G.E.A.** (**2**) **G.E.A.** (**3**)

1917 (Oct)–**21**. Nos. 44/45, 46*a*/51, 52*b*, 53/59 and 61 of East Africa and Uganda optd with Types **1** and **2** by De La Rue. Ordinary paper (1c. to 15c.) or chalk-surfaced paper (others). Wmk Mult Crown CA.

45	1c. black (R.)	15	80
	aw. Wmk inverted	£375	
	ay. Wmk inverted and reversed	£200	
	b. Vermilion opt	20·00	16·00
47	3c. green	20	15
48	6c. scarlet	20	10
	a. Wmk sideways	£2250	£2500
	w. Wmk inverted	£375	£250
49	10c. yellow-orange	50	60
	y. Wmk inverted and reversed	£325	
50	12c. slate-grey	75	4·00
	y. Wmk inverted and reversed	£325	
51	15c. bright blue	2·25	6·50
	w. Wmk inverted	£400	
	y. Wmk inverted and reversed	£375	
52	25c. black and red/*yellow*	80	7·00
	a. On pale yellow (1921)	2·00	18·00
	as. Optd 'SPECIMEN'	40·00	
53	50c. black and lilac	2·75	6·50
54	75c. black/*blue-green, olive back* (R.)	1·00	5·00
	a. On emerald back (1921)	3·50	50·00
	as. Optd 'SPECIMEN'	50·00	
55	1r. black/*green* (R.)	6·50	8·00
	a. On emerald back (1919)	14·00	65·00
56	2r. red and black/*blue*	15·00	60·00
	x. Wmk reversed	£650	£650
57	3r. violet and green	17·00	80·00
58	4r. red and green/*yellow*	26·00	£120
59	5r. blue and dull purple	50·00	£140
60	10r. red and green/*green*	£150	£450
	a. On emerald back	£200	£750
61	20r. black and purple/*red*	£325	£700
62	50r. carmine and green	£750	£1300
	s. Optd 'SPECIMEN'	£300	
45/61 *Set of* 16		£550	£1400
45s/61s Optd 'SPECIMEN' *Set of* 16		£600	

Early printings of the rupee values exist with very large stop after the 'E' in 'G.E.A.' (R. 5/3). There are round stops after 'E' varieties, which in one position of later printings became a small stop.

Examples of Nos. 45/55 can also be found handstamped with T M **5**, but these were not issued.

1921. Nos. 69/74 of East Africa and Uganda optd with Types **1** or **2** by De La Rue. Chalk-surfaced paper (50c. to 5r.). Wmk Mult Script CA.

63	12c. slate-grey	11·00	£130
	a. Raised stop after 'A'	£100	
64	15c. bright blue	9·50	19·00
	a. Raised stop after 'A'	£100	
65	50c. black and dull purple	18·00	£120
	a. Raised stop after 'A'	£160	
66	2r. red and black/*blue*	55·00	£170
67	3r. violet and green	£130	£425
68	5r. blue and dull purple	£180	£550
63/68 *Set of* 6		£350	£1300
63s/68s Optd 'SPECIMEN' *Set of* 6		£300	

The raised stop after 'A' occurs on R. 1/6, right pane.

1922. Nos. 65 and 68 of East Africa and Uganda optd by the Government Printer at Dar-es-Salaam with T **3**. Wmk Mult Script CA.

72	1c. black (R.)	2·00	25·00
73	10c. orange	4·25	14·00
	y. Wmk inverted and reversed	£250	

No. 73 is known with the overprint inverted, but this is of clandestine origin.

BRITISH MANDATED TERRITORY

(New Currency. 100 cents = 1 shilling)

4 Giraffe

5 Giraffe

(Recess B.W.)

1922–24. Head in black.

(a) Wmk Mult Script CA. P 15×14

74	**4**	5c. slate-purple	3·25	20
75		10c. green	4·50	85
76		15c. carmine-red	4·50	10
77		20c. orange	7·00	10
78		25c. black	10·00	6·50
79		30c. blue	6·50	5·00
80		40c. yellow-brown	7·50	4·50
81		50c. slate-grey	8·50	1·50
82		75c. yellow-bistre	7·50	26·00

(b) Wmk Mult Script CA (sideways). P 14

83	**5**	1s. green	15·00	35·00
		a. Wmk upright (1923)	9·50	12·00
84		2s. purple	13·00	35·00
		a. Wmk upright (1924)	10·00	50·00
85		3s. black	65·00	70·00
86		5s. scarlet	95·00	£150
		a. Wmk upright (1923)	48·00	£120
87		10s. deep blue	£275	£500
		a. Wmk upright (1923)	£140	£250
88		£1 yellow-orange	£500	£800
		a. Wmk upright (1923)	£450	£750
74/88a *Set of* 15			£700	£1200
74s/88s Optd 'SPECIMEN' (Nos. 74/82) or 'SPECIMEN.' *Set of* 15			£900	

On the £1 stamp the words of value are on a curved scroll running across the stamp above the words 'POSTAGE AND REVENUE'.

Nos. 83/88 are known showing a forged Dodoma postmark, dated '16 JA 22'. This issue was extensively used for fiscal purposes, and collectors are warned against examples which have been cleaned and regummed, or provided with forged postmarks.

1925. As 1922. Frame colours changed.

No.	Type	Description	Unused	Used
89	4	5c. green	15·00	1·50
90		10c. orange-yellow	15·00	1·50
91		25c. blue	4·75	19·00
92		30c. purple	10·00	35·00
89/92 *Set of 4*			40·00	50·00
89s/92s Optd 'SPECIMEN.' *Set of 4*			£150	

6

7

(Typo D.L.R.)

1927–31. Head in black. Chalk-surfaced paper (5s., 10s., £1). Wmk Mult Script CA. P 14.

No.	Type	Description	Unused	Used
93	6	5c. green	1·75	10
94		10c. yellow	2·00	10
95		15c. carmine-red	1·75	10
96		20c. orange-buff	2·75	10
97		25c. bright blue	3·75	2·00
98		30c. dull purple	2·75	4·00
98*a*		30c. bright blue (1931)	26·00	30
99		40c. yellow-brown	2·00	10·00
100		50c. grey	2·50	1·00
101		75c. olive-green	2·00	27·00
102	7	1s. green	4·25	2·75
103		2s. deep purple	30·00	9·50
104		3s. black	50·00	£110
105		5s. carmine-red	48·00	30·00
		a. Ordinary paper		
106		10s. deep blue	£100	£160
		a. Ordinary paper. *Deep dark blue*		
107		£1 brown-orange	£275	£425
93/107 *Set of 16*			£500	£700
93s/107s Optd or Perf (No. 98as) 'SPECIMEN' *Set of 16*			£375	

Examples of Nos. 104/107 are known showing a forged Dar-es-Salaam postmark dated '20 NO 1928'.

Tanganyika became part of the joint East African postal administration on 1 January 1933 and subsequently used the stamps of KENYA, UGANDA AND TANGANYIKA.

INDEPENDENT REPUBLIC

8 Teacher and Pupils

9 District Nurse and Child

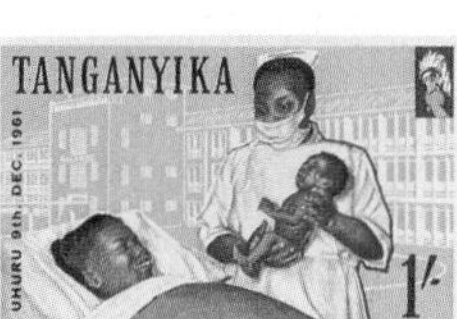

14 'Maternity'

15 Freedom Torch over Mt Kilimanjaro

UHURU 196

30c. 'UHURU 196' (Pl. 1C. R. 10/10, later corrected)

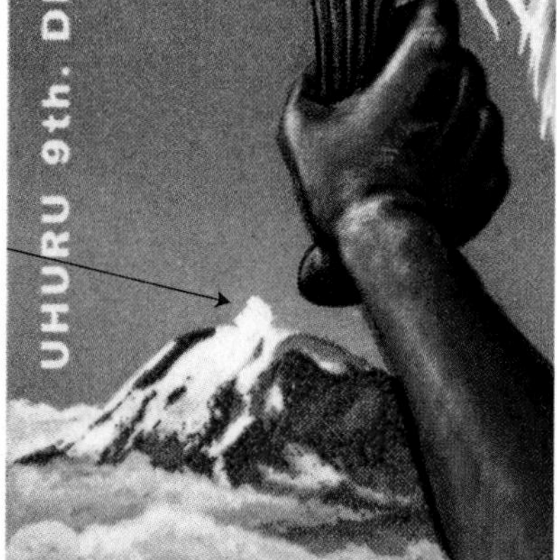

20s. Mountain flaw (R. 8/8)

(Des V. Whiteley. Photo Harrison)

1961 (9 Dec)–**64**. Independence. Types **8/9**, **14/15** and similar designs. P 14×15 (5c., 30c.), 15×14 (10c.,15c., 20c., 50c.) or 14½ (others).

No.	Description	Unused	Used
108	5c. sepia and light apple-green	10	10
109	10c. deep bluish green	10	10
110	15c. sepia and blue	10	10
	a. Blue omitted	£1700	
111	20c. orange-brown	10	10
112	30c. black, emerald and yellow	10	10
	a. Inscr 'UHURU 196'	£950	£425
	b. '1' inserted after '196'	30·00	
113	50c. black and yellow	10	10
114	1s. brown, blue and olive-yellow	15	10
115	1s.30 red, yellow, black, brown and blue	4·50	10
	a. Red, yellow, black, brown and deep blue (10.3.64)	9·50	1·00
116	2s. blue, yellow, green and brown	1·00	10
117	5s. deep bluish green and orange-red	1·00	50
118	10s. black, reddish purple and light blue	15·00	4·75
	a. Reddish purple (diamond) omitted	£275	£190
119	20s. red, yellow, black, brown and green	4·00	9·00
	a. Mountain flaw	45·00	60·00
108/119 *Set of 12*		23·00	13·50

Designs: Vert 10c. T **9**. As T **9**—15c. Coffee-picking; 20c. Harvesting maize; 50c. Serengeti lions. Horiz 5c. T **8.** As T **8**—30c. Tanganyikan flag. 1s. T **14.** As T **14**—2s. Dar-es-Salaam waterfront; 5s. Land tillage; 10s. Diamond and mine. Vert—1s.30, 20s. T **15**.

On the corrected version of No. 112a the number '1' is very slightly shorter and the figure is more solid than normal.

19 President Nyerere inaugurating Self-help Project

20 Hoisting Flag on Mt Kilimanjaro

(Photo Harrison)

1962 (9 Dec). Inauguration of Republic. Vert designs as Types **19/20**. P 14½.

No.	Description	Unused	Used
120	30c. emerald	10	10
121	50c. yellow, black, green, red and blue	10	10
122	1s.30 multicoloured	10	10
123	2s.50 black, red and blue	30	50
120/123 *Set of 4*		55	70

Designs: 30c. T **19**; 50c. T **20**; 1s.30, Presidential emblem; 2s.50, Independence Monument.

23 Map of Republic

24 Torch and Spear Emblem

(Des M. Goaman. Photo Harrison)

1964 (7 July). United Republic of Tanganyika and Zanzibar Commemoration. P 14×14½.

No.	Type	Description	Unused	Used
124	23	20c. yellow-green and light blue	30	10
125	24	30c. blue and sepia	10	10
126		1s.30 orange-brown and ultramarine	10	10
127	23	2s.50 purple and ultramarine	2·25	2·25
124/127 *Set of 4*			2·50	2·25

Despite the inscription on the stamps the above issue was only on sale in Tanganyika and had no validity in Zanzibar.

STAMP BOOKLETS

1922–25. Black on red cover.

No.	Description	Price
SB1	3s. booklet containing 5c., 10c., 15c. and 20c. (Nos. 74/77), each in block of 6	£3500
	a. As No. SB1, but contents changed (Nos. 89/90, 76/77) (1925)	

1922–26. Black on red cover. Stapled.

No.	Description	Price
SB2	3s. booklet containing 6×10c., and 12×5c. and 12×15c. (Nos. 74/76) in blocks of 6	
	a. As No. SB2, but contents changed (Nos. 74, 90, 76) (1925)	
	b. As No. SB2, but contents changed (Nos. 89/90, 76) (1926)	£3000

1927. Black on red covers. Stapled.

No.	Description	Price
SB3	3s. booklet containing 6×10c., and 12×5c. and 12×15c. (Nos. 93/95) in blocks of 6	£1500
SB4	3s. booklet containing 5c., 10c. and 15c. (Nos. 93/95), each in block of 10	£1900

1961 (9 Dec). Black on blue-green cover, size 48×46 mm. Stitched.

No.	Description	Price
SB5	5s. booklet containing 10c., 15c., 20c., 30c. and 50c. (Nos. 109/113), each in block of 4	5·00

OFFICIAL STAMPS

OFFICIAL
(O 1)

OFFICIAL
(O **2**) (3½ *mm* tall)

1961 (9 Dec). Nos. 108/114 and 117 optd with T O **1** (10, 15, 20, 50c. or larger (17 *mm*) 5, 30c.) or with T O **2** (1s. or larger (22 *mm*) 5s.).

No.	Description	Unused	Used
O1	5c. sepia and light apple-green	10	10
O2	10c. deep bluish green	10	10
O3	15c. sepia and blue	10	10
O4	20c. orange-brown	10	10
O5	30c. black, emerald and yellow	10	10
O6	50c. black and yellow	10	10
O7	1s. brown, blue and olive-yellow	10	10
O8	5s. deep bluish green and orange-red	75	85
O1/O8 *Set of 8*		1·00	1·00

Tanzania

The United Republic of Tanganyika and Zanzibar, formed 26 April 1964, was renamed the United Republic of Tanzania on 29 October 1964.

Issues to No. 176, except Nos. Z142/Z145, were also valid in Kenya and Uganda.

(Currency. 100 cents = 1 shilling)

25 Hale Hydro Electric Scheme

26 Tanzanian Flag

27 National Servicemen

33 Dar-es-Salaam Harbour

38 Arms of Tanzania

(Des V. Whiteley. Photo Harrison)

1965 (9 Dec). Types **25/27**, **33**, **38** and similar designs. P 14×14½ (5c., 10c., 20c., 50c., 65c.), 14½×14 (15c., 30c., 40c.), or 14 (others).

128	5c. ultramarine and yellow-orange	10	10
129	10c. black, greenish yellow, green and blue	10	10
130	15c. multicoloured	10	10
131	20c. sepia, grey-green and greenish blue	10	10
132	30c. black and red-brown	10	10
133	40c. multicoloured	1·00	20
134	50c. multicoloured	1·00	10
135	65c. green, red-brown and blue	2·75	2·50
136	1s. multicoloured	1·50	10
137	1s.30 multicoloured	6·50	1·50
138	2s.50 blue and orange-brown	6·50	1·25
139	5s. lake-brown, yellow-green and blue	80	20
140	10s. olive-yellow, olive-green and blue	1·00	4·00
141	20s. multicoloured	7·00	19·00
128/141 *Set of 14*		25·00	26·00

Designs: Horiz 5c. T **25**. As T **25**—20c. Road-building; 50c. Common Zebras, Manyara National Park; 65c. Mt. Kilimanjaro. 10c. T **26**. Vert 15c. T **27**. As T **27**—30c. Drum, spear, shield and stool; 40c. Giraffes, Mikumi National Park. Horiz 1s. T **33**; As T **33**—1s.30, Skull of *Zinjanthropus* and excavations, Olduvai Gorge, 2s.50, Fishing; 5s. Sisal industry; 10s. State House, Dar-es-Salaam. 20s. T **38**.

Z 39 President Nyerere and First Vice-President Karume within Bowl of Flame

Z 40 Hands supporting Bowl of Flame

(Des J. Ahmed (T Z **39**), G. Vasarhelyi (T Z **40**). Photo Enschedé)

1966 (26 Apr). Second Anniversary of United Republic. P 14×13.

Z142	Z **39**	30c. multicoloured	25	50
Z143	Z **40**	50c. multicoloured	25	50
Z144		1s.30, multicoloured	40	50
Z145	Z **39**	2s.50, multicoloured	55	1·75
Z142/Z145 *Set of 4*			1·25	3·00

Nos. Z142/Z145 were on sale in Zanzibar only.

39 Black-footed Cardinalfish

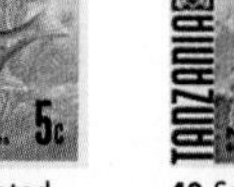

40 Sobrinus Mudskipper

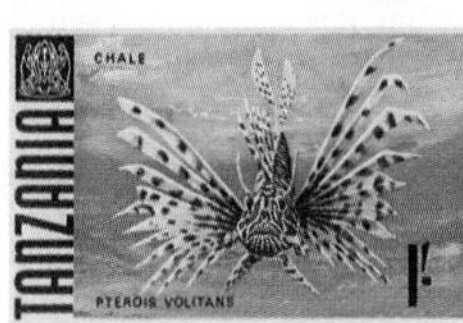

41 Lionfish

(Des Rena Fennesy. Photo Harrison)

1967 (9 Dec)–**73**. Designs as Types **39/41**. Chalk-surfaced paper. P 14×15 (5c. to 70c.) or 14½ (others).

142	5c. magenta, yellow-olive and black	10	2·75
	a. Glazed, ordinary paper (22.1.71)	30	3·75
143	10c. brown and bistre	10	10
	a. Glazed, ordinary paper (27.9.72)	50	2·25
144	15c. grey, turquoise-blue and black	10	2·00
	a. Glazed, ordinary paper (22.1.71)	45	6·50
145	20c. brown and turquoise-green	10	10
	a. Glazed, ordinary paper (16.7.73)	50	9·50
146	30c. sage-green and black	20	10
	a. Glazed, ordinary paper (3.5.71)	17·00	4·75
147	40c. yellow, chocolate and bright green	1·00	10
	a. Glazed, ordinary paper (10.2.71)	1·00	60
148	50c. multicoloured	20	10
	a. Glazed, ordinary paper (10.2.71)	50	3·00
149	65c. orange-yellow, bronze-green and black	1·25	4·50
150	70c. multicoloured (15.9.69)	1·00	3·50
	a. Glazed, ordinary paper (22.1.71)	4·50	13·00
151	1s. orange-brown, slate-blue and maroon	30	10
	a. Glazed ordinary paper (3.2.71)	1·00	10
152	1s.30 multicoloured	2·50	10
153	1s.50 multicoloured (15.9.69)	1·50	50
	a. Glazed, ordinary paper (27.9.72)	2·50	10
154	2s.50 multicoloured	2·25	3·25
	a. Glazed, ordinary paper (27.9.72)	17·00	10
155	5s. greenish yellow, black and turquoise-green	4·00	2·75
	a. Glazed, ordinary paper (12.12.70*)	3·50	10
156	10s. multicoloured	1·00	3·75
	a. Glazed, ordinary paper (*dull blue-green background*) (12.12.70*)	1·00	10
	ab. Deep dull green background (12.9.73)	1·75	50
157	20s. multicoloured	1·25	7·00
	a. Glazed, ordinary paper (12.12.70*)	6·00	15
142/157 *Set of 16*		15·00	27·00
142a/157a *Set of 14*		50·00	38·00

* Earliest known postmark date.

Designs: Horiz 5c. T **39**; 10c. T **40**. As T **39/40**—15c. White-spotted Puffer; 20c. Thorny Seahorse; 30c. Dusky Batfish; 40c. Black-spotted Sweetlips 50c. Blue Birdwrasse; 65c. Bennett's Butterflyfish; 70c. Black-tipped Grouper. Horiz 1s. T **41**. As T **41**:—1s.30, Powder-blue Surgeonfish; 1s.50, Yellow-finned Fusilier; 2s.50, Emperor Snapper; 5s. Moorish Idol; 10s. Painted Triggerfish; 20s. Horned Squirrelfish.

On chalk-surfaced paper all values except the 30c. exist with PVA gum as well as gum arabic, but the 70c. and 1s.50 exist with PVA gum only. Stamps on glazed, ordinary paper come only with PVA gum.

STAMP BOOKLETS

1965 (9 Dec). Black on blue (No. SB6) or buff (No. SB7) covers, size 48×46 mm. Stitched.

SB6	3s. booklet containing 4×15c. and 8×30c. (Nos. 130, 132) in blocks of 4	5·50
SB7	5s. booklet containing 4×15c. and 4×50c. and 8×30c. (Nos. 130, 132, 134) in blocks of 4	6·00

1967 (9 Dec). Black on blue (No. SB8) or buff (No. SB9) covers, size 48×45 mm. Stitched.

SB8	3s. booklet containing 4×15c. and 8×30c. (Nos. 144, 146) in blocks of 4	3·00
SB9	5s. booklet containing 4×10c., 4×15c., 4×20c., 4×30c. and 4×50c. and 8×30c. (Nos. 143/146, 148), each in blocks of 4	3·50

OFFICIAL STAMPS

(Opt photo Harrison)

1965 (9 Dec). Nos. 128/132, 134, 136, 139 optd as T O **1** (15c., 30c. or larger (17 *mm*) 5c., 10c., 20c., 50c.), or with T O **2** of Tanganyika (1s., 5s.).

O9	5c. ultramarine and yellow-orange	10	2·50
O10	10c. black, greenish yellow, green and blue	10	1·50
O11	15c. multicoloured	10	1·50
O12	20c. sepia, grey-green and greenish blue	10	2·75
O13	30c. black and red-brown	10	1·75
O14	50c. multicoloured	15	1·50
O15	1s. multicoloured	30	1·50
O16	5s. lake-brown, yellow-green and blue	1·75	10·00
O9/O16 *Set of 8*		2·25	21·00

OFFICIAL
(O **3**)

(Opt litho Govt Printer, Dar-es-Salaam)

1967 (10–18 Nov). Nos. 134, 136 and 139 optd as No. O14 (50c.) or with T O **3** (others).

O17	50c. multicoloured (18.11)	—	17·00
O18	1s. multicoloured (18.11)	22·00	9·50
O19	5s. lake-brown, yellow-green and blue	10·00	18·00

The issue dates given are for the earliest known postmarked examples.

Nos. O9/O16 were overprinted by Harrison in photogravure and Nos. O17/O19 have litho overprints by the Government Printer, Dar-es-Salaam. On No. O17 the overprint is the same size (17 *mm* long) as on No. O14.

1967 (9 Dec)–**71**. Nos. 142/146, 148, 151 and 155 optd as T O **1**, but larger (measuring 17 *mm*) (5c. to 50c.) or as T O **2** of Tanganyika (1s. and 5s.). Chalk-surfaced paper.

O20	5c. magenta, yellow-olive and black	10	5·00
	a. Glazed, ordinary paper (22.1.71)	3·50	4·75
O21	10c. brown and bistre	10	1·00
	a. Glazed, ordinary paper (1971)	17·00	4·25
O22	15c. grey turquoise-blue and black	10	7·50
	a. Glazed, ordinary paper (22.1.71)	3·50	5·50
O23	20c. brown and turquoise-green	15	1·00
O24	30c. sage-green and black	10	30
O25	50c. multicoloured	15	1·60
	a. Glazed, ordinary paper (22.1.71)	3·50	5·50
O26	1s. orange-brown, slate-blue and maroon	30	3·00
	a. Glazed, ordinary paper (3.2.71)	17·00	5·50
O27	5s. greenish yellow, black and turquoise-green	2·50	17·00
	a. Glazed, ordinary paper (3.2.71)	20·00	22·00
O20/O27 *Set of 8*		3·00	32·00
O20a/O27a *Set of 6*		55·00	42·00

The chalk-surfaced paper exists with both PVA gum and gum arabic, but the glazed, ordinary paper exists PVA gum only.

OFFICIAL
(O **4**)

1970 (10 Dec)–**73**. Nos. 142/148, 151 and 155 optd locally by letterpress as T O **4** (5 to 50c.) or as T O **2** of Tanganyika, but measuring 28 mm (1s. and 5s.).

(a) Chalk-surfaced paper

O28	5c. magenta, yellow-olive and black	75	11·00
	a. 'OFFCIAL' (R.7/6)	—	£150
O29	10c. brown and bistre	1·25	4·00
	a. 'OFFCIAL' (R.7/6)		
O30	20c. brown and turquoise-green	1·60	4·50
O31	30c. sage-green and black	1·90	4·50
O28/O31 *Set of 4*		5·00	22·00

(b) Glazed, ordinary paper (1973)

O32	5c. magenta, yellow-olive and black	20·00	8·00
	a. 'OFFCIAL' (R.7/6)	£500	90·00
	b. 'OFFICIA' (R.10/9)	—	£110
O33	10c. brown and bistre	85·00	8·00
	a. 'OFFCIAL' (R.7/6)	—	£120
O34	15c. grey, turquoise-blue and black	85·00	8·00
	a. 'OFFCIAL' (R.7/6)	—	£110
O35	20c. brown and turquoise-green	—	5·00
O36	40c. yellow, chocolate and bright green	45·00	4·25
	a. Opt double	—	£200
	b. 'OFFICIA' (R.10/9)	£500	£110
O37	50c. multicoloured	—	4·25
	a. 'OFFCIAL' (R.7/6)	—	£100
O38	1s. orange-brown, slate-blue and maroon	65·00	13·00
	a. Opt double	—	£400
O39	5s. greenish yellow, black and turquoise green	75·00	70·00

The letterpress overprint can be distinguished from the photogravure by its absence of screening dots and the overprint showing through to the reverse, apart from the difference in length.

The 'OFFICIA' error (Nos. O32b, O36b) occurred initially only on R10/9 of the setting of 100. Subsequently the 'L' of 'OFFICIAL' deteriorated on R10/10 also, and examples of the 40c. value have been seen with complete omission from this second position.

No. O36a comes from a sheet used at Kasulu in 1973–1974. A second overprint was deliberately applied to part of the sheet to correct a weak first impression.

No. O38a comes from a sheet used at Masasi in 1973.

POSTAGE DUE STAMPS

Postage Due stamps of Kenya and Uganda wre issued for provisional use as such in Tanganyika on 1 July 1933. The postmark is the only means of identification.

The Postage Due stamps of Kenya, Uganda and Tanganyika were used in Tanganyika/Tanzania until 2 January 1967.

D **1**

(Litho D.L.R.)

1967 (3 Jan). P 14×13½.

D1	D **1**	5c. scarlet	35	10·00
D2		10c. green	45	10·00
D3		20c. deep blue	50	13·00
D4		30c. red-brown	50	15·00
D5		40c. bright purple	50	18·00
D6		1s. orange	80	12·00
D1/D6 *Set of 6*			2·75	70·00

1969 (12 Dec)–**71**. Chalk-surfaced paper. P 14×15.

D7	D **1**	5c. scarlet	30	14·00
		a. Glazed, ordinary paper (13.7.71)	4·00	8·00
D8		10c. green	65	6·00
		a. Glazed, ordinary paper (13.7.71)	75	5·50
D9		20c. deep blue	70	13·00
		a. Glazed, ordinary paper (13.7.71)	2·50	9·00
D10		30c. red-brown	65	23·00
		a. Glazed, ordinary paper (13.7.71)	85	6·50
D11		40c. bright purple	2·00	23·00
		a. Glazed, ordinary paper (13.7.71)	6·50	48·00
D12		1s. orange (*glazed, ordinary paper*) (13.7.71)	4·75	40·00
D7/D11 *Set of 5*			3·75	70·00
D7a/D12 *Set of 6*			17·00	£100

The stamps on chalk-surfaced paper exist only with gum arabic, but the stamps on glazed paper exist only with PVA gum.

Tasmania *see* Australia

Tobago *see* Trinidad and Tobago

Togo

The stamps of GERMANY were used in the colony from March 1888 until June 1897 when issues for TOGO were provided.

PRICES FOR STAMPS ON COVER TO 1945

Nos. H1/H7	from × 6
No. H8	—
No. H9	from × 6
No. H10	from × 2
No. H11	—
Nos. H12/H13	from × 6
Nos. H14/H16	—
Nos. H17/H19	from × 12
Nos. H20/H26	—
Nos. H27/H28	from × 20
No. H29	—
Nos. H30/H31	from × 6
Nos. H32/H33	—
Nos. H34/H58	from × 6

ANGLO-FRENCH OCCUPATION

French forces invaded southern Togo on 8 August 1914 and the British had entered Lomé by the same date, examples of Gold Coast stamps being known cancelled there on the 8th. The German administration surrendered on 26 August 1914.

The territory was jointly administered under martial law, but was formally divided between Great Britain and France, effective 1 October 1920. League of Nations mandates were issued for both areas from 20 July 1922.

(Currency. 100 pfennig = 1 mark)

Stamps of German Colonial issue Yacht Types 1900 and 1909–1914 (5pf. and 10pf.)

TOGO
Anglo-French
Occupation
(1)

Half penny
(2)

SETTINGS. Nos. H1/H33 were all overprinted or surcharged by the Catholic Mission, Lomé.

The initial setting for the 3pf. to 80pf. was of 50 (10×5), repeated twice on each sheet of 100. Overprints from this setting, used for Nos. H1/H9, had the lines of type 3 mm apart.

Nos. H1/H2 were subsequently surcharged, also from a setting of 50, to form Nos. H12/H13. The surcharge setting showed a thin dropped 'y' with small serifs on R. 1/1–2, 2/1, 3/1, 4/1 and 5/1–2.

The type from the overprint and surcharge was then amalgamated in a new setting of 50 on which the lines of the overprint were only 2 mm apart. On this amalgamated setting, used for Nos. H27/H28, the thin 'y' varieties were still present and R. 4/7 showed the second 'O' of 'TOGO' omitted.

The surcharge was subsequently removed from this '2 mm' setting which was then used to produce Nos. H17/H19. The missing 'O' was spotted and corrected before any of the 30pf. stamps were overprinted.

The remaining low values of the second issue, Nos. H14/H16 and H20/H22, were overprinted from settings of 25 (5×5), either taken from the last setting of 50 or from an amended version on which there was no space either side of the hyphen. This slightly narrower overprint was subsequently used for Nos. H29/H33. It shows the top of the second 'O' broken so that it resembles a 'U' on R. 1/5.

The mark values were overprinted from settings of 20 (5×4), showing the same differences in the spacing of the lines as on the low values.

It is believed that odd examples of some German colonial values were overprinted from individual settings in either spacing.

1914 (17 Sept*). Optd with T **1** by Catholic Mission, Lomé. Wide setting. Lines 3 mm apart.

H1	3pf. brown	£130	£100
H2	5pf. green	£130	£100
H3	10pf. carmine (Wmk Lozenges)	£130	£100
	a. Opt inverted	£10000	£3000
	b. Opt *tête-bêche* in vert pair	†	£8500
	c. No wmk	†	£5500
H4	20pf. ultramarine	42·00	50·00
H5	25pf. black and red/*yellow*	40·00	50·00
H6	30pf. black and orange/*buff*	50·00	60·00
H7	40pf. black and carmine	£225	£250
H8	50pf. black and purple/*buff*	£13000	£11000
H9	80pf. black and carmine/*rose*	£275	£275
H10	1m. carmine	£5000	£2750
H11	2m. blue	£13000	£15000
	a. 'Occupation' double	£24000	£16000
	b. Opt inverted	£16000	

* The post office at Lomé was open for four hours on 17 September, before closing again on instructions from Accra. It finally reopened on 24 September.

The *tête-bêche* overprint on the 10pf. is due to the sheet being turned round after the upper 50 stamps had been overprinted so that vertical pairs from the two middle rows have the overprint *tête-bêche*.

1914 (1 Oct). Nos. H1 and H2 surch as T **2**.

H12	½d. on 3pf. brown	£160	£140
	a. Thin 'y' in 'penny'	£400	£350
H13	1d. on 5pf. green	£160	£140
	a. Thin 'y' in 'penny'	£400	£350

TOGO
Anglo-French
Occupation
(3)

TOGO
Anglo-French
Occupation
Half penny
(4)

1914 (Oct).

*(a) Optd with T **3**. Narrow Setting. Lines 2 mm apart. 'Anglo-French' measures 16 mm*

H14	3pf. brown	£6500	£1100
H15	5pf. green	£1500	£750
H16	10pf. carmine	†	£3000
	a. No wmk	†	£7000
H17	20pf. ultramarine	35·00	12·00
	a. 'TOG'	£3500	£2500
	b. Nos. H4 and H17 *se-tenant* (vert pair)	£9000	
H18	25pf. black and red/*yellow*	45·00	38·00
	a. 'TOG'	£12000	
H19	30pf. black and orange/*buff*	20·00	29·00
H20	40pf. black and carmine	£6000	£1600
H21	50pf. black and purple/*buff*	†	£9000
H22	80pf. black and carmine/*rose*	£3250	2500
H23	1m. carmine	£8000	£4250
H24	2m. blue	†	£14000
H25	3m. violet-black	†	£100000
H26	5m. lake and black	†	£100000
	*(b) Narrow setting, but including value, as T **4***		
H27	½d. on 3pf. brown	48·00	26·00
	a. 'TOG'	£425	£300
	b. Thin y' in 'penny'	75·00	60·00
H28	1d. on 5pf. green	7·00	4·25
	a. 'TOG'	£130	£110
	b. Thin 'y' in 'penny'	12·00	15·00

In the 20pf. one half of a sheet was overprinted with the wide setting (3 mm), and the other half with the narrow setting (2 *mm*), so that vertical pairs from the middle of the sheet show the two varieties of the overprint.

TOGO
Anglo-French
Occupation
(6)

1915 (7 Jan). Optd as T **6**. The words 'Anglo-French' measure 15 mm instead of 16 mm as in T **3**.

H29	3pf. brown	£9000	£2500
H30	5pf. green	£225	£130
	a. 'Occupation' omitted	£12000	
H31	10pf. carmine	£200	£130
	a. No wmk	†	£7000
H32	20pf. ultramarine	£1400	£400
H32*a*	40pf. black and carmine	†	£9000
H33	50pf. black and purple/*buff*	£16000	£11000

This printing was made on another batch of German Togo stamps, found at Sansane-Mangu.

TOGO
ANGLO-FRENCH
OCCUPATION
(7)

OCCU
Accra opt

OCCU
London opt

Stamps of Gold Coast overprinted

1915 (May). Nos. 70/81, 82*b* and 83/84 of Gold Coast (King George V) optd at Govt Press, Accra, with T **7** ('OCCUPATION' 14½ *mm* long).

H34	½d. green (*shades*)	1·00	5·00
	a. Small 'F' in 'FRENCH'	2·50	13·00
	b. Thin 'G' in 'TOGO'	4·75	23·00
	c. No hyphen after 'ANGLO'	4·75	23·00
	e. 'CUPATION' for 'OCCUPATION'	£140	
	f. 'CCUPATION' for 'OCCUPATION'	80·00	
	g. Opt double		
H35	1d. red	1·50	75
	a. Small 'F' in 'FRENCH'	2·75	3·75
	b. Thin 'G' in 'TOGO'	9·00	15·00
	c. No hyphen after 'ANGLO'	9·00	15·00
	f. 'CCUPATION' for 'OCCUPATION'	£225	
	g. Opt double	£350	£475
	h. Opt inverted	£170	£250
	ha. Ditto. 'TOGO' omitted	£8000	
H36	2d. grey	1·50	2·50
	a. Small 'F' in 'FRENCH'	3·00	8·00
	b. Thin 'G' in 'TOGO'	6·50	19·00
	c. No hyphen after 'ANGLO'	£250	
	d. Two hyphens after 'ANGLO'	55·00	
	f. 'CCUPATION' for 'OCCUPATION'	£275	
H37	2½d. bright blue	5·00	9·00
	a. Small 'F' in 'FRENCH'	9·00	15·00
	b. Thin 'G' in 'TOGO'	17·00	38·00
	c. No hyphen after 'ANGLO'	£170	
	d. Two hyphens after 'ANGLO'	60·00	
	f. 'CCUPATION' for 'OCCUPATION'	£170	
H38	3d. purple/*yellow*	4·50	8·00
	a. Small 'F' in 'FRENCH'	8·00	15·00
	b. Thin 'G' in 'TOGO'	22·00	40·00
	c. No hyphen after 'ANGLO'	55·00	
	f. 'CCUPATION' for 'OCCUPATION'	£250	
	g. White back	5·00	28·00
	ga. Small 'F' in 'FRENCH'	27·00	80·00
	gb. Thin 'G' in 'TOGO'	65·00	£160
H40	6d. dull and bright purple	3·75	3·50
	a. Small 'F' in 'FRENCH'	9·00	15·00
	b. Thin 'G' in 'TOGO'	22·00	32·00
	f. 'CCUPATION' for 'OCCUPATION'	£325	
H41	1s. black/*green*	3·50	15·00
	a. Small F' in 'FRENCH'	5·00	26·00
	b. Thin 'G' in 'TOGO'	21·00	65·00
	f. 'CCUPATION' for 'OCCUPATION'	£180	
	g. Opt double	£1500	
H42	2s. purple and blue/*blue*	19·00	27·00
	a. Small 'F' in 'FRENCH'	50·00	80·00
	b. Thin 'G' in 'TOGO'	£100	£160
	c. No hyphen after 'ANGLO'	£325	
	f. 'CCUPATION' for 'OCCUPATION'	£475	
H43	2s.6d. black and red/*blue*	6·00	35·00
	a. Small 'F' in 'FRENCH'	23·00	£100
	b. Thin 'G' in 'TOGO'	55·00	£200
	c. No hyphen after 'ANGLO'	£325	
	f. 'CCUPATION' for 'OCCUPATION'	£350	
H44	5s. green and red/*yellow* (*white back*)	13·00	15·00
	a. Small 'F' in 'FRENCH'	65·00	£100
	b. Thin 'G' in 'TOGO'	90·00	£200
	c. No hyphen after 'ANGLO'	£325	
	f. 'CCUPATION' for 'OCCUPATION'	£550	
H45	10s. green and red/*green*	50·00	60·00
	a. Small 'F' in 'FRENCH'	£120	
	b. Thin 'G' in 'TOGO'	£225	
	f. 'CCUPATION' for 'OCCUPATION'	£700	
H46	20s. purple and black/*red*	£150	£160
	a. Small 'F' in 'FRENCH'	£350	
	b. Thin 'G' in 'TOGO'	£650	
	f. 'CCUPATION' for 'OCCUPATION'	£850	
H34/H46 *Set of 12*		£200	£275

Nos. H34/H46 were overprinted in panes of 60 (6×10), using a setting of movable type. There were three printings:

1st printing (all values, 3d. No. H38 only).
2nd printing (all values, 3d. No. H38*g* only).
3rd printing (recorded on 1d., 3d. (H38), 2s., 2s.6d., 5s. only.)

Varieties occur as follows (Nos. indicate position in setting)

a. Small 'F' in 'FRENCH' (25, 58, 59). Present in all three printings on pos. 25, and on pos. 58 and 59 in first and second printings.
b. Thin 'G' in 'TOGO' (24) Constant in all three printings. The letter is from a slightly smaller fount.
c. No hyphen after 'ANGLO' (5, 28). Occurs on pos. 5 during the first printing (½d., 1d., 2d., 2½d., 3d. (No. H38), rare on the 2d. and 2½d.), and again on the third printing (1d., 3d., (No. H38), 2s., 2s.6d., 5s.). It is also found on pos. 28 in the first printing (½d. and 1d. only).
d. Two hyphens after 'ANGLO' (5). Occurs on pos. 5 during the first printing (2d., 2½d. only). The two hyphens vary in character. The same two values are also found with misplaced hyphen from this position.
e. 'CUPATION' for 'OCCUPATION' (33) ½d. value only, first printing.
f. 'CCUPATION' for 'OCCUPATION' (57). All values, first printing.

CHARACTERISTICS OF THE ACCRA OVERPRINT

Being set up from movable type, no two positions are exactly the same and there are many minor varieties of broken type. The two 'C's in 'OCCUPATION' often differ slightly in shape and one or both usually have closed jaws. The word 'OCCUPATION' is generally fractionally shorter (at 14½ to 14¾ *mm*) than in the subsequent London overprint, where the length is consistently 15 mm. The impression is variable, but usually appears weaker than the London overprint, which is normally bold and well-inked.

The position of the overprint on the stamp varies greatly, with the word 'TOGO' often encroaching on the crown above the King's head (high position) or the word 'OCCUPATION' encroaching on the value tablet (low position). The subsequent London overprint is invariably well-centred, leaving both crown and value tablet clear.

Note that the 3d. (No. H38*g*) and 5s. (No. H44) with white back do not occur with the London overprint.

The 1d. opt inverted (No. H35h) exists with small 'F' (*Price* £1700 *unused*), thin 'G' (*Price* £4500 *unused*) and 'No hyphen' (*Price* £4500 *unused*).

Examples of all values, and especially the varieties, are known showing a forged Lomé postmark dated '22 1 15'.

TOGO
ANGLO-FRENCH
OCCUPATION
8

1916 (Apr)–**20**. Nos. 70/84 of Gold Coast (King George V) optd in London with T **8** ('OCCUPATION' 15 *mm* long). Heavy type and thicker letters showing through on back.

H47	½d. green	30	2·75
H48	1d. red	30	85
H49	2d. grey	1·00	4·00
H50	2½d. bright blue	1·50	1·50
H51	3d. purple/*yellow*	8·00	1·25
	a. On buff-yellow (1919)	10·00	3·00
H52	6d. dull and bright purple	2·75	2·25
	w. Wmk inverted	£160	£275
H53	1s. black/*green*	11·00	17·00
	a. On blue-green (olive back) (1918)	16·00	18·00
	b. On emerald-green (olive back) (1920)	£1100	
	c. On emerald-green (emerald-green back) (1920)	£425	£900
H54	2s. purple and blue/*blue*	6·50	8·50
	a. Wmk sideways	£3250	£3250
H55	2s.6d. black and red/*blue*	4·50	7·00
H56	5s. green and red/*yellow*	45·00	27·00
	a. On buff-yellow (1919)	40·00	50·00
H57	10s. green and red/*green*	28·00	65·00
	a. On blue-green (olive back) (1920)	22·00	75·00
H58	20s. purple and black/*red*	£160	£190
H47/H58 *Set of 12*		£200	£275
H47s/H58s Optd 'SPECIMEN' *Set of 12*		£350	

Nos. H47/H58 were overprinted by De La Rue using a stereotyped plate, probably of 120 (two panes, each 6×10). The overprint is much more consistent than the Accra printings and is usually bold and well-inked, with letters that appear thicker, particularly in the word 'TOGO'. 'OCCUPATION' measures 15 mm in length. The two 'C's in 'OCCUPATION' are identical in size and style, with open jaws.

The overprint is invariably well-centred, with the top of the word 'TOGO' placed just below the top of the King's head on the 1d. and just below the base of the crown on the other values, leaving the value tablet completely clear.

Nos. H51*a*, H53*a*/H53*c*, H56/H56*a* and H57*a* are all shades which were overprinted only in London and do not exist with the Accra overprint. Nos. H51*a* and H56*a*, described as on 'buff-yellow' paper, include second printings made in 1920, which are not easy to distinguish. Viewed from the back, the paper appears rather pale and dull, in comparison with the bright (almost lemon) yellow of Nos. H51 and H56.

Nos. H47/H58 were withdrawn in October 1920 when Gold Coast stamps were introduced.

The mandates were transferred to the United Nations in January 1946. The inhabitants of the British mandate voted to join Ghana in 1957.

Tokelau *see after* **New Zealand**

Tonga

The Tongan Post Office was established in 1885 and FIJI 2d. and 6d. stamps are recorded in use until the arrival of Nos. 1/4.

PRICES FOR STAMPS ON COVER TO 1945

Nos. 1/4	*from* × 60
Nos. 5/9	*from* × 20
Nos. 10/28	*from* × 8
Nos. 29/31	*from* × 7
Nos. 32/37	*from* × 6
Nos. 38/54	*from* × 5
Nos. 55/63	*from* × 6
Nos. 64/70	*from* × 3
Nos. 71/87	*from* × 2
Nos. O1/O10	*from* × 25

PROTECTORATE KINGDOM

King George I, 1845–93

1 King George I

2

(Eng Bock and Cousins. Plates made and typo Govt Ptg Office, Wellington)

1886–88. W **2**. P 12½ (line) or 12×11½ (comb)*.

1	1	1d. carmine (P 12½) (27.8.86)	£475	6·00
		a. Perf 12½×10		
		b. Perf 12×11½ (15.7.87)	10·00	3·25
		ba. Pale carmine (P 12×11½)	16·00	9·00
2		2d. pale violet (P 12½) (27.8.86)	50·00	10·00
		a. Bright violet	70·00	3·50
		b. Perf 12×11½ (15.7.87)	45·00	2·75
		ba. Bright violet (P 12×11½)	50·00	3·00
3		6d. blue (P 12½) (9.10.86)	60·00	2·25
		a. Perf 12×11½ (15.10.88)	50·00	2·25
		ab. Dull blue (P 12×11½)	35·00	2·25
4		1s. pale green (P 12½) (9.10.86)	95·00	4·50
		a. Deep green (P 12½)	£100	2·25
		b. Perf 12×11½ (15.10.88)	55·00	6·00
		ba. Deep green (P 12×11½)	55·00	3·25

* See note after New Zealand, No. 186.

FOUR PENCE. (3)   EIGHT PENCE. (4)

(Surch Messrs Wilson & Horton, Auckland, NZ)

1891 (10 Nov). Nos. 1b and 2b surch.

5	3	4d. on 1d. carmine	3·00	14·00
		a. No stop after 'PENCE'	50·00	£130
6	4	8d. on 2d. violet	45·00	£110
		a. Short 'T' in 'EIGHT'	£170	£325

No. 5a occurred on R. 6/8 and 9, R. 10/11, all from the right-hand pane.

1891 (23 Nov). Optd with stars in upper right and lower left corners by lithography. P 12½.

7	1	1d. carmine	50·00	70·00
		a. Three stars	£400	
		b. Four stars	£550	
		c. Five stars	£800	
		d. Perf 12×11½	£300	
		da. Three stars	£550	
		db. Four stars	£700	
		dc. Five stars	£950	
8		2d. violet	80·00	38·00
		a. Perf 12×11½	£400	

Stamps with forged stars are known, but the stars are invariably applied by typography (letterpress) and indent the paper.

The varieties with three, four or five stars emanate from sheets which received a double overprint, one impression being sideways.

1892 (15 Aug). W **2**. P 12×11½.

9	1	6d. yellow-orange	16·00	38·00

5 Arms of Tonga

6 King George I

Damaged 'O' in 'TONGA' (R. 1/1, later corrected)

(Dies eng A. E. Cousins. Typo at Govt Printing Office, Wellington, NZ)

1892 (10 Nov). W **2**. P 12×11½.

10	5	1d. pale rose	24·00	38·00
		a. Bright rose	18·00	38·00
		b. Bisected diag (½d.) (1893) (*on cover*)	†	£850
		c. Damaged 'O'	£110	£170
11	6	2d. olive	40·00	16·00
12	5	4d. chestnut	50·00	75·00
13	6	8d. bright mauve	70·00	£180
14		1s. brown	85·00	£140
10/14 *Set of 5*			£225	£400

No. 10b was used from 31 May 1893 to provide a 2½d. rate before the arrival of No. 15, and on subsequent occasions up to 1895.

½d. (7)   2½d. (8)   FIVE PENCE. (9)   7½d. (10)

1893. Printed in new colours and surch with Types **7/10** by Govt Printing Office, Wellington.

(a) In carmine. P 12½ (21 Aug)

15	5	½d. on 1d. bright ultramarine	23·00	27·00
		a. Surch omitted		
16	6	2½d. on 2d. green	26·00	12·00
17	5	5d. on 4d. orange	4·50	8·50
18	6	7½d. on 8d. carmine	35·00	80·00

(b) In black. P 12×11½ (Nov)

19	5	½d. on 1d. dull blue	42·00	50·00
20	6	2½d. on 2d. green	17·00	18·00
		a. Surch double	£2000	£2000
		b. Fraction bar completely omitted (R. 3/3)		

King George II, 1893–1918

SURCHARGE. HALF-PENNY (11)   SURCHARGE, 2½d. (12)   HALF-PEI Small 'F' in 'HALF'

(Surch at the *Star* Office, Auckland, NZ)

1894 (June–Nov). Surch with Types **11** or **12**.

21	5	½d. on 4d. chestnut (B.) (11.94)	2·00	7·00
		a. 'SURCHARCE'	9·00	22·00
		b. Small 'F'	9·00	22·00
22	6	½d. on 1s. brown	2·50	11·00
		a. 'SURCHARCE'	11·00	42·00
		b. Small 'F'	11·00	42·00
		c. Surch double	£275	
		d. Surch double with 'SURCHARCE'	£900	
		e. Surch double with small 'F'	£750	
23		2½d. on 8d. mauve	13·00	8·00
		a. No stop after 'SURCHARGE'	48·00	55·00
		b. Mixed perfs 12×11½ and 12½		
24	1	2½d. on 1s. deep green (No. 4*a*) (11.94)	65·00	28·00
		a. No stop after 'SURCHARGE'	£200	
		b. Perf 12×11½	15·00	48·00
		ba. No stop after 'SURCHARGE'	55·00	

Nos. 21/24 were surcharged in panes of 60 (6×10) with No. 21a occurring on R. 2/6, 4/6, 5/6, 8/6 and 10/6, No. 21b on R. 1/4, 3/4, 6/4, 7/4 and 9/4, No. 22a on R. 1/6, 3/6, 5/6, 8/6 and 10/6, No. 22b on R. 2/4, 4/4, 6/4, 7/4 and 9/4 (both after the setting had been rearranged), No. 23a on R. 3/1–3 and Nos. 24a and 24ba on R. 6/3 and R. 7/3 or R. 7/1–2.

Sheets used for these provisionals were surcharged with the remains of the tissue interleaving still in place. This sometimes subsequently fell away taking parts of the surcharge with it.

Deformed 'E' in 'PENI' (R. 2/2)

(Design resembling No. 11 litho and surch at *Star* Office Auckland, NZ)

1895 (22 May*). As T **6** surch as Types **11** and **12**. No wmk. P 12.

25	11	1d. on 2d. pale blue (C.)	50·00	42·00
		a. Deformed 'E'	£130	£100
26	12	1½d. on 2d. pale blue (C.)	65·00	50·00
		a. Deformed 'E'	£170	£120
		b. Perf 12×11	50·00	50·00
		ba. Deformed 'E'	£130	£120
27		2½d. on 2d. pale blue (C.)†	42·00	50·00
		a. No stop after 'SURCHARGE'	£225	£225
		b. Deformed 'E'	£110	£130
28		7½d. on 2d. pale blue (C.)	£500	
		a. Deformed 'E'		
		b. Perf 12×11	65·00	50·00
		ba. Deformed 'E'	£170	£140

* Earliest known date of use.

† The 2½d. on 2d. is the only value which normally has a stop after the word 'SURCHARGE'.

No. 27a occurs on R. 1/3 of the right-hand pane.

12a King George II

13 King George II

(14)

'BU' joined (R. 1/1)

Missing eyebrow (R. 2/4)

'7' for '1' in '½d.' (R. 2/1)

1895 (20 June*). Unissued stamp surch as in T **12a**. No wmk. P 12.

29	11	½d. on 2½d. vermilion	50·00	32·00
		a. 'BU' joined	£100	75·00
		b. 'SURCHARCE'	90·00	70·00
		c. Missing eyebrow	£100	75·00
		d. Stop after 'POSTAGE' (R. 2/5)	£100	75·00
		e. '7' for '1' in '½d.'	£100	75·00
30		1d. on 2½d. vermilion	£100	50·00
		a. 'BU' joined	£170	£110
		c. Missing eyebrow	£170	£110
		d. Stop after 'POSTAGE' (R. 2/5)	£170	£110
		e. '7' for '1' in '½d.'	£170	£110
31	12	7½d. on 2½d. vermilion	60·00	75·00
		a. 'BU' joined	£110	£120
		c. Missing eyebrow	£110	£120
		d. Stop after 'POSTAGE' (R. 2/5)	£110	£120
		e. '7' for '1' in '½d.'	£110	£120

* Earliest known date of use.

No. 29b occurs on R. 1/6 and 3/6 of both the right and the left pane.

In the ½d. surcharge there is a stop after 'SURCHARGE' and not after 'PENNY'. In the 1d. and 7½d. the stop is after the value only.

'Black Eye' flaw (Rt pane R. 2/4)

(Litho *Star* Office, Auckland, N.Z.)

1895 (9 July–Sept). No wmk. P 12.

32	13	1d. olive-green	32·00	32·00
		a. Bisected diagonally (½d.) (*on cover*) (9.95)	†	£750
		b. Imperf between (horiz pair)	—	£7500
33		2½d. rose	30·00	9·00
		a. Stop (flaw) after 'POSTAGE' (R. 4/5)	85·00	50·00
34		5d. blue	42·00	70·00
		a. 'Black eye' flaw	£110	
		b. Perf 12×11	24·00	65·00
		ba. 'Black eye' flaw	70·00	
		c. Perf 11	£400	
		ca. 'Black eye' flaw		
35		7½d. orange-yellow	45·00	55·00
		a. Yellow	45·00	55·00

1896 (May). Nos. 26b and 28b with typewritten surcharge 'Half-Penny-', in violet, and Tongan surcharge, in black, as T **14**.

a. Tongan surch reading downwards (right panes)

36A	6	½d. on 1½d. on 2d.	£450	
		a. Perf 12	£425	£425
		e. 'Halef'	£7000	
		f. 'H' over 'G'		
		g. 'Pen?y'	£6000	
37A		½d. on 7½d. on 2d.	85·00	£120
		a. 'Hafl' for 'Half'	£2250	£2500
		b. 'Hafl' ('Penny' omitted)	£5500	
		c. 'PPenny'	£750	
		d. Stops instead of hyphens	£1100	
		e. 'Halyf'		
		f. 'Half-Penny-' inverted	£3250	
		g. No hyphen after 'Penny'		
		i. No hyphen after 'Half'	£1000	
		l. Capital 'P' over small 'p'		
		m. Hyphen after 'Penny' over capital 'Y'	£2250	
		p. Perf 12	£800	
		pa. No hyphen after 'Half'		

b. Tongan surch reading upwards (left panes)

36B	6	½d. on 1½d. on 2d.	£450	£450
		a. Perf 12	£475	£475
		ab. 'Haalf'	£3500	
		c. 'H' double		
		e. 'Penyny'	£3500	
37B		½d. on 7½d. on 2d.	85·00	£120
		c. 'PPenny'	£950	
		d. Stops instead of hyphens	£1100	
		f. 'Half-Penny-' inverted	£4500	
		g. Comma instead of hyphen after 'Penny'	£750	
		h. 'Hwlf'		
		i. No hyphen after 'Half'	£1500	
		j. 'Penny' double		
		k. 'Penny' twice, with 'Half' on top of upper 'Penny'	£4750	
		m. 'Half H'	£1000	
		n. Tongan surch double	£1600	
		o. Two hyphens between 'Half' and 'Penny'		
		p. Perf 12	£800	

Nos. 26b and 28b were in sheets of 48 (2 panes 6×4). The panes were separated before the surcharges were applied.

There are variations in the relative positions of the words 'Half' and 'Penny', both vertically and horizontally.

Dangerous forgeries of the above issue are known to exist, particularly of the ½d. on 1½d. on 2d. (Nos. 36A/36B), and no rarity should be acquired without a reliable guarantee. But note that whereas the violet typewritten part of the surcharge has been cleverly imitated, using a machine of the same model as was used for the original issue, such fakes also have a forged version of the black typeset Tongan surcharge.

Genuine typewritten surcharges show the letters 'Hal' or 'Half' spaced as in T **14**, with the 'a' much closer to the 'H'. Examples with 'Hal' evenly spaced are forged.

15 Arms

16 Ovava Tree, Kana-Kubolu

17 King George II

18 Prehistoric Trilith at Haamonga

19 Bread Fruit

20 Coral

21 View of Haapai

22 Red Shining Parrot

23 View of Vavau Harbour

24 Tortoises (*upright*)

Types of Type **17**:

Type I. Top of hilt showing

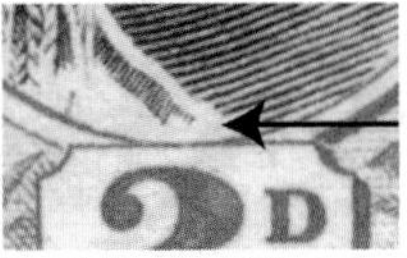

Type II. No sword hilt

1d. Normal

1d. Lopped branch (R. 8/5) (ptgs from 1934 onwards)

Normal

Smaller '2' (R. 1/2, 1/4–5, 2/8, 4/4, 5/4 and 6/1)

HOGOFULU

10d. Normal

10d. Both 'O's small in 'HOGOFULU' (R. 1/7)

10d. Small second 'O' in 'HOGOFULU' (R. 2/7)

WATERMARKS. Stamps with W **24** upright show all the tortoise heads pointing upwards, or downwards if inverted. On stamps with sideways watermark the heads point upwards or downwards alternately. Stamps with inverted or sideways inverted watermarks are not separately listed and should be assumed to have the same value as the upright (or sideways) versions.

(Recess D.L.R.)

1897 (1 June). W **24**. P 14.

38	15	½d. indigo	7·50	3·50
		a. Wmk sideways	70	3·00
39	16	1d. black and scarlet	80	80
		a. Wmk sideways	10·00	3·50
		b. Lopped branch	£150	
40	17	2d. sepia and bistre (I)	32·00	9·50
		a. Wmk sideways	20·00	3·50
		b. Smaller '2'	60·00	15·00
41		2d. sepia and bistre (II)	50·00	11·00
		a. Wmk sideways	45·00	11·00
		b. Smaller '2'	85·00	27·00
42		2d. grey and bistre (II)	50·00	3·50
		a. Wmk sideways	30·00	3·75
		b. Smaller '2'	70·00	10·00
43		2½d. black and blue	13·00	1·40
		a. No fraction bar in '½' (R. 2/10)	£130	60·00
		b. Wmk sideways	13·00	1·60
		ba. No fraction bar in '½' (R. 2/10)	£120	60·00
44	18	3d. black and yellow-green	3·50	17·00
		a. Wmk sideways	2·50	6·50
45	19	4d. green and purple	5·00	4·00
		a. Wmk sideways	4·00	4·50
46	17	5d. black and orange (II)	32·00	12·00
		a. Wmk sideways		
47	20	6d. red	13·00	8·50
		a. Wmk sideways	8·50	14·00
48	17	7½d. black and green (II)	20·00	21·00
		a. Centre inverted	£9000	
49		10d. black and lake (II)	48·00	45·00
		a. Wmk sideways		
		b. Both 'O's small	£225	£225
		c. Small second 'O'	£225	£225
50		1s. black and red-brown (II)	14·00	12·00
		a. No hyphen before 'TAHA' (R. 3/5)	£160	£140
		b. Wmk sideways		
51	21	2s. black and ultramarine	£140	£150
		a. Wmk sideways	32·00	32·00
52	22	2s.6d. deep purple	50·00	30·00
		a. Wmk sideways	65·00	50·00
53	23	5s. black and brown-red	48·00	50·00
		a. Wmk sideways	26·00	32·00
38a/53a *Set of* 14			£225	£180

The 1d., 3d. and 4d. are known bisected and used for half their value.

T - L

1 June, 1899.

(25)

26 Queen Salote

1899 (1 June). Royal Wedding. No. 39a optd with T **25** at *Star Office*, Auckland, NZ

54	16	1d. black and scarlet (hyphen *2 mm* long)	42·00	70·00
		a. '1889' for '1899' (R. 8/1, 8/4)	£250	£400
		b. Hyphen 3 mm long	60·00	85·00
		c. Wmk upright	65·00	95·00
		ca. '1889' for '1899' (R. 8/1, 8/4)	£450	£700
		cb. Hyphen 3 mm long	90·00	£150

The letters 'T L' stand for Taufa'ahau, the King's family name, and Lavinia, the bride.

No. 54 was overprinted from a setting of 30 (3×10) applied twice to the sheets of 60. The setting contains twenty-one examples of the 2 mm hyphen and nine of the 3 mm.

Queen Salote, 1918–1965

Dies of the 2d.:

Die I (As used for 1897 issue)

Die II

Normal

'2½' recut (note lines on '2' and different '½') (R. 1/1)

Retouched (small) hyphen (R. 3/5)

(Recess D.L.R.)

1920 (Apr)–**35**. W **24** (sideways). P 14.

55	15	½d. yellow-green (1934)	1·00	1·25
		a. Wmk upright	55·00	75·00
56	26	1½d. grey-black (1935)	50	2·00
57		2d. agate and aniline violet (Die I)	18·00	13·00
		a. Wmk upright	48·00	50·00
		b. Smaller '2'	70·00	85·00
		c. *Black and slate-violet* (1924)	23·00	2·25
		ca. Wmk upright		
		cb. Smaller '2'	75·00	20·00
		d. *Black and deep purple* (1925)	22·00	3·00
		db. Smaller '2'	75·00	25·00
57*e*		2d. black and blackish lilac (Die II) (1932)	10·00	10·00
58		2½d. black and blue (3.21)	9·00	48·00
59		2½d. bright ultramarine (1934)	11·00	1·00
		a. Recut '2½'	50·00	9·50
60		5d. black and orange-vermilion (1921)	3·25	8·50
61		7½d. black and yellow-green (1921)	1·75	2·00
62		10d. black and lake (1921)	2·50	4·75
		a. Both 'O's small	28·00	45·00
		b. Small second 'O'	28·00	45·00
		c. *Black and aniline carmine* (9.25)	7·00	20·00
		ca. Both 'O's small	75·00	£140
		cb. Small second 'O'	75·00	£140
63		1s. black and red-brown (1921)	1·25	2·50
		a. Retouched (small) hyphen	16·00	26·00
		b. Wmk upright	55·00	55·00
		ba. Retouched (small) hyphen	£200	£200
55/63 *Set of* 10			50·00	75·00
55s/63s Optd or Perf (Nos. 55s/56s and 59s) 'SPECIMEN' *Set of* 9			£275	

In Die II the ball of the '2' is larger and the word 'PENI-E-UA' is re-engraved and slightly shorter; the 'U' has a spur on the left side.

For illustrations of Nos. 62a/62b see above No. 38.

TWO PENCE

PENI-E-UA

(27)

TWO PENCE

PENI-E-UA

(28)

1923 (20 Oct)–**24**. Nos. 46, 48/49, 50, 51/52 and 53a surch as T **27** (vert stamps) or T **28** (horiz stamps).

64	17	2d. on 5d. black and orange (II) (B.)	1·00	85
		a. Wmk sideways	35·00	24·00
65		2d. on 7½d. black and green (II) (B.)	38·00	48·00
		a. Wmk sideways	£150	£160
66		2d. on 10d. black and lake (II) (B.)	24·00	70·00
		a. Wmk sideways	£110	£140
		b. Both 'O's small	£120	
		c. Small second 'O'	£120	
67		2d. on 1s. black and red-brown (II) (B.)	75·00	22·00
		a. No hyphen before 'TAHA' (R. 3/5)	£375	£200
		b. Wmk sideways	£160	£130
68	21	2d. on 2s. black and ultramarine (R)	65·00	48·00
		a. Wmk sideways	12·00	14·00
69	22	2d. on 2s.6d. deep purple (R.)	32·00	6·50
		a. Wmk sideways	£170	90·00
70	23	2d. on 5s. black and brown-red (R.)	42·00	42·00
		a. Wmk sideways	3·25	2·50
64/70a *Set of* 7			£160	£140

29 Queen Salote

(Recess D.L.R.)

1938 (12 Oct). 20th Anniversary of Queen Salote's Accession. Tablet at foot dated '1918–1938'. W **24** (sideways). P 13½.

71	**29**	1d. black and scarlet	1·25	9·00
72		2d. black and purple	16·00	9·00
73		2½d. black and ultramarine	16·00	11·00
71/73 *Set of 3*			30·00	26·00
71s/73s Perf 'SPECIMEN' *Set of 3*			£100	

For Silver Jubilee issue in a similar design, see Nos. 83/87.

Further die of 2d.:

Die III

(Recess D.L.R.)

1942–49. Wmk Mult Script CA (sideways on 5s.). P 14.

74	**15**	½d. yellow-green	30	3·50
		a. 'A' of 'CA' missing from wmk	£650	
75	**16**	1d. black and scarlet	2·50	3·00
		a. Lopped branch	£140	£160
76	**26**	2d. black and purple (Die II)	5·50	2·75
		a. Die III (4.49)	13·00	15·00
77		2½d. bright ultramarine	1·75	2·75
		a. Recut '2½'	35·00	
78	**18**	3d. black and yellow-green	65	6·00
79	**20**	6d. red	3·50	2·50
80	**26**	1s. black and red-brown	5·00	3·50
		a. Retouched (small) hyphen	55·00	40·00
81	**22**	2s.6d. deep purple (1943)	38·00	42·00
82	**23**	5s. black and brown-red (1943)	16·00	60·00
74/82 *Set of 9*			65·00	£110
74s/82s Perf 'SPECIMEN' *Set of 9*			£250	

In Die III the foot of the '2' is longer than in Die II and extends towards the right beyond the curve of the loop; the letters of 'PENI-E-UA are taller and differently shaped.

Damage to the '2' on R. 4/9 of No. 77 was frequently corrected by hand-painting.

For illustration of No. 75a see above No. 38 and of No. 77a see above No. 55.

The ½d. 1d., 3d. and 1s. exist perforated from either line or comb machines. The other values only come line perforated.

30

(Recess D.L.R.)

1944 (25 Jan). Silver Jubilee of Queen Salote's Accession. As T **29**, but inscr '1918–1943' at foot, as T **30**. Wmk Mult Script CA. P 14.

83		1d. black and carmine	15	1·25
84		2d. black and purple	15	1·25
85		3d. black and green	15	1·25
86		6d. black and orange	1·00	2·00
87		1s. black and brown	75	2·00
83/87 *Set of 5*			2·00	7·00
83s/87s Perf 'SPECIMEN' *Set of 5*			£140	

1949 (10 Oct). 75th Anniversary of UPU. As Nos. 114/117 of Antigua.

88		2½d. ultramarine	20	1·00
89		3d. olive	2·00	4·50
90		6d. carmine-red	20	1·00
91		1s. red-brown	25	1·00
88/91 *Set of 4*			2·40	6·75

31 Queen Salote

33 Queen Salote

32 Queen Salote

(Photo Waterlow)

1950 (1 Nov). Queen Salote's 50th Birthday. Wmk Mult Script CA. P 12½.

92	**31**	1d. carmine	1·40	5·00
93	**32**	5d. green	1·40	4·25
94	**33**	1s. violet	1·40	4·25
92/94 *Set of 3*			3·75	12·00

34 Map

35 Palace, Nuku'alofa

37 HMNZS *Bellona*

36 Beach scene

38 Flag

39 Arms of Tonga and Great Britain

(Recess Waterlow)

1951 (2 July). 50th Anniversary of Treaty of Friendship between Great Britain and Tonga. Types **34/39**. Wmk Mult Script CA. P 12½ (3d.), 13×13½ (½d.), 13½×13 (others).

95	**34**	½d. green	30	4·25
96	**35**	1d. black and carmine	30	5·00
97	**36**	2½d. green and brown	30	4·25
98	**37**	3d. yellow and bright blue	2·75	3·00
99	**38**	5d. carmine and green	5·50	2·00
100	**39**	1s. yellow-orange and violet	4·50	2·00
95/100 *Set of 6*			12·00	18·00

40 Royal Palace, Nuku'alofa

41 Shore fishing with throw-net

42 *Hifofua* and *Aoniu* (ketches)

43 Swallows' Cave, Vava'u

44 Map of Tongatapu

45 Vava'u harbour

46 Post Office, Nuku'alofa

47 Aerodrome, Fua'amotu

48 *Matua* (inter-island freighter)

49 Map of Tonga Islands

50 Lifuka, Ha'apai

51 Mutiny on the *Bounty*

52 Queen Salote

53 Arms of Tonga

(Des J. Berry. Centre litho, frame recess (£1), recess (others) B.W.)

1953 (1 July). Types **40/53**. W **24** (sideways). P 11×11½ (vert) or 11½×11 (horiz).

101	**40**	1d. black and red-brown	10	10
102	**41**	1½d. blue and emerald	20	10
103	**42**	2d. deep turquoise-green and black	1·25	20
104	**43**	3d. blue and deep bluish green	2·50	20
105	**44**	3½d. yellow and carmine-red	1·75	70
106	**45**	4d. yellow and deep rose-carmine	2·50	10
107	**46**	5d. blue and red-brown	1·00	10
108	**47**	6d. black and deep blue	1·50	30
109	**48**	8d. emerald and deep reddish violet	1·50	2·25
110	**49**	1s. blue and black	2·00	10
111	**50**	2s. sage-green and brown	10·00	1·25
112	**51**	5s. orange-yellow and slate-lilac	25·00	9·50
113	**52**	10s. yellow and black	14·00	9·50
114	**53**	£1 yellow, scarlet, ultramarine and deep bright blue	14·00	6·50
101/114 *Set of 14*			70·00	26·00

54 Stamp of 1886

55 Whaling Ship and Whaleboat

(Des D. Bakeley. Photo Harrison)

1961 (1 Dec). 75th Anniversary of Tongan Postal Service. Types **54/55** and similar horiz designs. W **24** (sideways). P 14½×13½.

115		1d. carmine and brown-orange	10	10
116		2d. ultramarine	1·25	45
117		4d. blue-green	20	45
118		5d. violet	1·25	45
119		1s. red-brown	1·25	45
115/119 *Set of 5*			3·50	1·60

Designs: 1d. T **54**; 2d. T **55**; 4d. Queen Salote and Post Office, Nuku'alofa; 5d. *Aoniu II* (inter-island freighter); 1s. Douglas DC-4 mailplane over Tongatapu.

1862
TAU'ATĀINA
EMANCIPATION
1962
(59)

60 Protein Foods

1962 (7 Feb). Centenary of Emancipation. Nos. 101, 104, 107/110, 112, 117 optd with T **59** (No. 126 surch also), in red, by R. S. Wallbank Govt Printer.

120		1d. black and red-brown	10	2·25
121		4d. blue-green	10	90
122		5d. blue and red-brown	15	90
123		6d. black and deep blue	20	1·25
124		8d. emerald and deep reddish violet	40	3·25
125		1s. blue and black	20	1·00
		a. Opt inverted	£650	£200
126		2s. on 3d. blue and deep bluish green	40	8·00
		a. Missing fraction-bar in surch	12·00	50·00
127		5s. orange-yellow and slate-lilac	6·50	8·00
		a. Opt inverted	£225	£300
120/127 *Set of 8*			7·00	23·00

Nos. 120/124 and 127 were overprinted in sheets of 60 (5×12), using a 5×6 setting which was applied first to the lower half sheets, then to the upper. One full sheet of the 5s. (No. 127) received inverted opts on both halves.

Nos. 125/126 were overprinted or surcharged in half-sheets of 30 (6×5), using adjusted settings. The missing fraction bar variety (No. 126a) occurred at R. 3/1 on both upper and lower half sheets. One upper half sheet of the 1s (No. 125) inadvertently received an inverted opt (intended for a lower half sheet), from which only two unused examples survived, with the remainder used on first day covers at Vava'u.

(Des M. Goaman. Photo Harrison)

1963 (4 June). Freedom from Hunger. W **24**. P 14×14½.

128	**60**	11d. ultramarine	50	1·00

61 Coat of Arms

62 Queen Salote

63 Queen Salote

(Des Ida West. Die-cut Walsall)

1963 (17 June). First Polynesian Gold Coinage Commemoration. Circular designs. Embossed on gold foil backed with paper, inscr overall 'TONGA THE FRIENDLY ISLANDS'. Imperf.

(a) Postage. ¼ koula coin. Diameter 1⅝ in

No.	Type	Description	Unused	Used
129	**61**	1d. carmine	10	10
130	**62**	2d. deep blue	10	10
131	**61**	6d. blue-green	20	15
132	**62**	9d. bright purple	20	15
133	**61**	1s.6d. violet	30	30
134	**62**	2s. light emerald	40	40
		(b) Air. (i) ½ koula coin. Diam 2⅛ in		
135	**63**	10d. carmine	20	20
136	**61**	11d. blue-green	30	30
137	**63**	1s.1d. deep blue	30	30
		(ii) 1 koula coin. Diam 3⅛ in		
138	**63**	2s.1d. bright purple	45	50
139	**61**	2s.4d. light emerald	50	60
140	**63**	2s.9d. violet	50	60
129/140 and O17 *Set of* 13			14·00	15·00

Examples of a 9d. Postage value in the design of the 1s.6d. exists, but these have been identified as proofs.

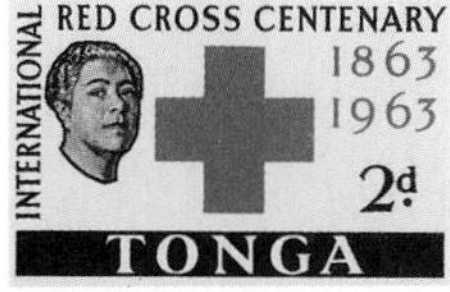

64 Red Cross Emblem

(Des V. Whiteley. Litho B.W.)

1963 (7 Oct). Red Cross Centenary. W **24** (sideways). P 13½.

No.	Type	Description	Unused	Used
141	**64**	2d. red and black	30	10
142		11d. red and blue	1·00	1·50

65 Queen Salote

66 Map of Tongatapu

(Des M. Meers. Die-cut Walsall)

1964 (19 Oct). Pan-Pacific South-East Asia Women's Association Meeting, Nuku'alofa. Embossed on gold foil, backed with paper inscr overall 'TONGA THE FRIENDLY ISLANDS'. Imperf.

No.	Type	Description	Unused	Used
		(a) Postage		
143	**65**	3d. pink	25	40
144		9d. light blue	35	40
145		2s. yellow-green	55	65
146		5s. lilac	90	1·50
		(b) Air		
147	**66**	10d. blue-green	35	30
148		1s.2d. black	45	45
149		3s.6d. cerise	75	1·50
150		6s.6d. violet	1·10	2·75
143/150 *Set of* 8			4·25	7·00

(67)

1965 (18 Mar). 'Gold Coin' stamps of 1963 surch as T **67** by Walsall Lithographic Co. New figures of value in gold; obliterating colours shown in brackets.

No.	Type	Description	Unused	Used
		(a) Postage		
151	**61**	1s.3d. on 1s.6d. violet (R.)	25	25
152	**62**	1s.9d. on 9d. bright purple (W.)	25	25
153	**61**	2s.6d. on 6d. blue-green (R.)	30	55
154		5s. on 1d. carmine	17·00	28·00
155	**62**	5s. on 2d. deep blue	2·75	4·00
156		5s. on 2s. light emerald	70	1·25
		(b) Air		
157	**63**	2s.3d. on 10d. carmine	25	40
158	**61**	2s.9d. on 11d. blue-green (W.)	30	55
159	**63**	4s.6d. on 2s.1d. bright purple (R.)	13·00	17·00
		a. Opt double		
160	**61**	4s.6d. on 2s.4d. light emerald (R.)	13·00	17·00
161	**63**	4s.6d. on 2s.9d. violet (R.)	7·50	17·00
151/161 and O18 *Set of* 12			50·00	75·00

Examples of No. 160 are known with a larger surcharge panel. These may have come from a trial printing which was subsequently released to the stamp trade.

King Taufa'ahau IV, 16 December 1965

1866-1966
TUPOU COLLEGE
& SECONDARY
EDUCATION
(68)

AIRMAIL
1866 CENTENARY 1966
TUPOU COLLEGE
&
SECONDARY EDUCATION
10d XX
(69)

OU COLLE
&
ARY EDUC
Misplaced '&'
(R. 5/5)

1966 (18 June). Centenary of Tupou College and Secondary Education. Nos. 115/116 and 118/119 optd or surch.

No.	Type	Description	Unused	Used
		(a) Postage. As T **68**		
162		1d. carmine and brown-orange (P.)	10	10
163		3d. on 1d. carmine and brown-orange (P.)	10	10
		a. Misplaced '3d' (R. 2/5)	2·75	
		b. Surch inverted	†	£900
164		6d. on 2d ultramarine (R.)	10	10
165		1s.2d. on 2d. ultramarine (R.)	20	10
166		2s.. on 2d. ultramarine (R.)	25	10
167		3s. on 2d. ultramarine (R.)	25	15
		(b) Air. As T **69**		
168		5d. violet	10	10
		b. Misplaced '&'	2·75	
169		10d. on 1d. carmine and brown-orange	10	10
		b. Misplaced '&'	2·75	
170		1s. red-brown	20	10
		b. Misplaced '&'	2·75	
171		2s.9d. on 2d. ultramarine	25	15
		a. Sideways second 'X' (R. 3/4)	9·00	
		b. Misplaced '&'	8·00	
172		3s.6d. on 5d. violet	25	15
		a. Sideways second 'X' (R. 3/4)	9·00	
		b. Misplaced '&'	8·00	
173		4s.6d. on 1s. red-brown	35	15
		a. Sideways second 'X' (R. 3/4)	9·00	
		b. Misplaced '&'	8·00	
162/173 and O19/O20 *Set of* 14			2·75	1·75

On No. 163a the 'd' is 20 mm from the 'X' instead of the normal 22 mm.

(70)

(71)

1966 (16 Dec). Queen Salote Commemoration. Nos. 143/144 and 147/148 optd as Types **70**/**71**, or surch also, by Walsall Lithographic Co. Inscriptions and new figures of value in first colour and obliterating shapes in second colour given.

No.	Type	Description	Unused	Used
		(a) Postage. Optd as T **70**		
174	**65**	3d. (silver and ultramarine)	35	20
175		5d. on 9d. (silver and black)	40	20
176		9d. (silver and black)	40	20
177		1s.7d. on 3d. (silver and ultramarine)	1·40	1·00
178		3s.6d. on 9d. (silver and black)	2·00	1·25
179		6s.6d. on 3d. (silver and ultramarine)	2·50	3·50
		(b) Air. Optd as T **71**		
180	**66**	10d. (silver and black)	70	20
181		1s.2d. (black and gold)	80	35
182		4s. on 10d. (silver and black)	2·25	1·25
183		5s.6d. on 1s.2d. (black and gold)	2·50	2·50
184		10s.6d. on 1s.2d. (gold and black)	3·00	4·00
174/184 *Set of* 11			14·50	13·00

(New Currency. 100 seniti = 1 pa'anga)

1 SENITI 1
(72)

10
Seniti
10
(73)

1967 (25 Mar). Decimal currency. Various stamps surch as Types **72**/**73**.

No.	Description	Unused	Used
185	1s. on 1d. (No. 101)	10	20
186	2s. on 4d. (No. 106)	20	20
187	3s. on 5d. (No. 107)	10	20
188	4s. on 5d. (No. 107)	30	50
189	5s. on 3½d. (No. 105)	10	20
190	6s. on 8d. (No. 109)	30	20
191	7s. on 1½d. (No. 102)	10	20
192	8s. on 6d. (No. 108)	30	20
193	9s. on 3d. (No. 104)	15	20
194	10s. on 1s. (No. 110)	25	20
195	11s. on 3d. on 1d. (No. 163)	30	30
	a. Misplaced '3d' (R. 2/5)	14·00	
196	21s. on 3s. on 2d. (No. 167)	25	35
197	23s. on 1d. (No. 101)	25	35
198	30s. on 2s. (No. 111)* (R.)	2·25	4·25
199	30s. on 2s. (No. 111)* (R.)	2·25	4·25
200	50s. on 6d. (No. 108) (R.)	1·00	2·25
201	60s. on 2d. (No. 103) (R.)	1·25	2·50
185/201 and O21 *Set of* 18		14·00	18·00

The above surcharges come in a variety of types and sizes.

* No. 198 has the surcharged value expressed horizontally; No. 199 has the figures '30' above and below 'SENITI'.

74 Coat of Arms (reverse)

75 King Taufa'ahau IV (obverse)

(Die-cut Walsall)

1967 (4 July). Coronation of King Taufa'ahau IV. Circular designs. Embossed on palladium foil, backed with paper inscr overall 'The Friendly Islands Tonga', etc. Imperf.

Sizes

(a) Diameter 1½ in.	*(d) Diameter 2³⁄₁₀ in.*
(b) Diameter 1⁷⁄₁₀ in.	*(e) Diameter 2⁷⁄₁₀ in.*
(c) Diameter 2 in.	*(f) Diameter 2⁹⁄₁₀ in.*

No.	Type	Description	Unused	Used
		(a) Postage		
202	**74**	1s. orange and greenish blue (*b*)	10	30
203	**75**	2s. greenish blue and deep magenta (*c*)	10	30
204	**74**	4s. emerald and bright purple (*d*)	15	25
205	**75**	15s. turquoise and violet (*e*)	55	25
206	**74**	28s. black and bright purple (*a*)	1·25	60
207	**75**	50s. carmine-red and ultramarine (*c*)	2·00	2·00
208	**74**	1p. blue and carmine (*f*)	2·75	3·25
		(b) Air		
209	**75**	7s. carmine-red and black (*b*)	25	10
210	**74**	9s. brown-purple and emerald (*c*)	35	10
211	**75**	11s. greenish blue and orange (*d*)	40	15
212	**74**	21s. black and emerald (*e*)	75	30
213	**75**	23s. bright purple and light emerald (*a*)	85	45
214	**74**	29s. ultramarine and emerald (*c*)	1·10	60
215	**75**	2p. bright purple and orange (*f*)	3·75	4·50
202/215 *Set of* 14			13·00	11·50

The commemorative coins depicted in reverse (T **74**) are inscribed in various denominations as follows: 1s.—'20 SENITI'; 4s.—'PA' ANGA'; 9s.—'50 SENITI'; 21s.—'TWO PA' ANGA'; 28s.—'QUARTER HAU'; 29s.—'HALF HAU'; 1p. 'HAU'.

The Friendly Islands welcome the United States Peace Corps

S

(76)

1967 (15 Dec). Arrival of US Peace Corps in Tonga. As Nos. 101/114, but imperf in different colours and surch as T **76**.

(a) Postage

216	1s. on 1d. black and orange-yellow	10	20
217	2s. on 2d. ultramarine and carmine-red	10	20
218	3s. on 3d. chestnut and yellow	10	20
219	4s. on 4d. reddish violet and yellow	10	20
220	5s. on 5d. green and yellow	10	10
221	10s. on 1s. carmine-red and yellow	10	10
222	20s. on 2s. claret and new blue	20	15
223	50s. on 5s. sepia and orange-yellow	2·50	1·75
224	1p. on 10s. orange-yellow	50	2·00

(b) Air

225	11s. on 3½d. ultramarine (R.)	10	10
226	21s. on 1½d. emerald	20	20
227	23s. on 3½d. ultramarine	20	20
216/227 and O26/O28 *Set of* 15		5·00	9·00

On Nos. 219 and 224 the opt is smaller, and in four lines instead of five. On Nos. 216/220 the surcharge takes the form of an alteration to the currency name as in T **76**.

2 SENITI 2 (77)

10 SENITI 10 (78)

1968 (6 Apr). Various stamps surch as Types **77/78**.

(a) Postage

228	1s. on 1d. (No. 101) (R.)	10	10
229	2s. on 4d. (No. 106)	10	20
230	3s. on 3d. (No. 104) (B.)	10	20
231	4s. on 5d. (No. 107) (R.)	10	20
232	5s. on 2d. (No. 103) (R.)	10	20
233	6s. on 6d. (No. 108) (R.)	10	20
234	7s. on 1½d.(No. 102) (R.)	10	15
235	8s. on 8d. (No. 109) (R.)	10	25
236	9s. on 3½d. (No. 105)	20	30
237	10s. on 1s. (No. 110) (R.)	20	20
238	20s. on 5s. (No. 112) (R.)	1·75	70
239	2p. on 2s. (No. 111) (R.)	1·50	2·75

(b) Air. Surch as T **78** *with 'AIRMAIL' added*

240	11s. on 10s. (No. 113) (R.)	20	30
241	21s. on 10s. (No. 113) (R.)	30	50
242	23s. on 10s. (No. 113) (R.)	30	50
228/242 and O22/O25 *Set of* 19		7·00	12·50

(79)

Friendly Islands Field & Track Trials South Pacific Games Port Moresby 1969

S

(80)

1968 (4 July). 50th Birthday of King Taufa'ahua IV. Nos. 202/215 optd as T **79**.

(a) Postage

243	**74**	1s. orange and greenish blue (*b*) (R.)	10	60
244	**75**	2s. greenish blue and deep magenta (*b*) (B.)	20	60
245	**74**	4s. emerald and bright purple (*d*) (R.)	40	60
246	**75**	15s. turquoise and violet (*e*) (R.)	1·75	35
247	**74**	28s. black and bright purple (*a*) (R.)	2·50	45
248	**75**	50s. carmine-red and ultramarine (*c*) (B.)	3·25	2·25
249	**74**	1p. blue and carmine (*f*) (R.)	6·50	8·50

(b) Air

250	**75**	7s. carmine-red and black (*b*) (B.)	80	20
251	**74**	9s. brown-purple and emerald (*c*) (R.)	85	20
252	**75**	11s. greenish blue and orange (*d*) (B.)	1·00	25
253	**74**	21s. black and emerald (*e*) (R.)	2·25	30
		a. Opt (gold only) double	£275	
254	**75**	23s. bright purple and light emerald (*a*) (B.)	2·25	30
255	**74**	29s. ultramarine and emerald (*c*) (R.)	2·50	40
256	**75**	2p. bright purple and orange (*f*) (B.)	10·00	15·00
243/256 and O29/O32 *Set of* 18			50·00	45·00

The overprints vary in size, but are all crescent-shaped as T **79** and inscribed 'H.M'S BIRTHDAY 4 JULY 1968' (T **79**) or 'HIS MAJESTY'S 50th BIRTHDAY' (others).

1968 (19 Dec). South Pacific Games Field and Track Trials, Port Moresby, Papua New Guinea. Nos. 101/113, but imperf, in different colours and surch as T **80**.

(a) Postage

257	5s. on 5d green and yellow (R.)	10	15
258	10s. on 1s. carmine-red and yellow	20	15
259	15s. on 2s. claret and new blue	30	20
260	25s. on 2d. ultramarine and carmine-red	30	25
261	50s. on 1d. black and orange-yellow	35	65
262	75s. on 10s. orange-yellow (G.)	60	1·50

(b) Air

263	6s. on 6d. black and yellow*	10	15
264	7s. on 4d. reddish violet and yellow	10	15
265	8s. on 8d. black and greenish yellow	25	15
	a. Surch 11½ mm as on 6d	£140	£100
266	9s. on 1½d. emerald	10	15
267	11s. on 3d. chestnut and yellow	15	15
268	21s. on 3½d. ultramarine	20	20
269	38s. on 5s. sepia and orange-yellow	3·00	1·25
270	1p. on 10s. orange-yellow	70	2·00
257/270 and O33/O34 *Set of* 16		6·25	8·25

* On No. 263 the surcharge is smaller (11½ *mm* wide).

1•s (81)

1s (82)

1969. Emergency Provisionals. Various stamps (Nos. 273/276 are imperf and in different colours) surch as Types **81** or **82**.

(a) Postage

271	1s. on 1s.2d. on 2d. ultramarine (No. 165)	2·75	5·00
272	1s. on 2s. on 2d. ultramarine (No. 166)	2·75	5·00
273	1s. on 6d. black and yellow (as No. 108)	70	2·00
274	2s. on 3½d. ultramarine (as No. 105)	75	2·00
275	3s. on 1½d. emerald (as No. 102)	75	2·00
276	4s. on 8d. black and greenish yellow (as No. 109)	1·00	2·00

(b) Air. Nos. 171/173 surch with T **82**

277	1s. on 2s.9d. on 2d. ultramarine	3·00	5·00
	a. Sideways second 'X' (R. 3/4)	42·00	
	b. Misplaced '&'	40·00	
278	1s. on 3s.6d. on 5d. violet	3·00	5·00
	a. Sideways second 'X' (R. 3/4)	42·00	
	b. Misplaced '&'	40·00	
279	1s. on 4s.6d. on 1s. red-brown	3·00	5·00
	a. Sideways second 'X' (R. 3/4)	42·00	
	b. Misplaced '&'	40·00	
271/279 *Set of* 9		16·00	30·00

SELF-ADHESIVE ISSUES. From No. 280 until No. 344 all stamps were manufactured by Walsall Security Printers Ltd and are self-adhesive. This also applies to the Official stamps.

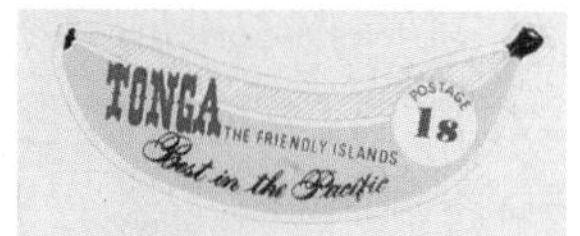

83 Banana

1969 (21 Apr). Coil stamps.

280	**83**	1s. scarlet, black and greenish yellow	1·10	2·50
281		2s. bright green, black and greenish yellow	1·25	2·50
282		3s. violet, black and greenish yellow	1·25	2·50
283		4s. ultramarine, black and greenish yellow	1·25	2·50
284		5s. bronze-green, black and greenish yellow	1·50	2·50
280/284 *Set of* 5			5·75	11·00

Nos. 280/284 were produced in rolls of 200, each even stamp having a number applied to the front of the backing paper, with the usual inscription on the reverse.

See also Nos. 325/329.

84 Putting the Shot

86 Oil Derrick and Map

1969 (13 Aug). Third South Pacific Games, Port Moresby. T **84** and similar design.

(a) Postage

285	**84**	1s. black, red and buff	10	15
286		3s. bright green, red and buff	10	15
287		6s. blue, red and buff	10	15
288		10s. bluish violet, red and buff	15	15
289		30s. blue, red and buff	30	30

(b) Air

290	–	9s. black, violet and orange	15	15
291	–	11s. black, ultramarine and orange	15	15
292	–	20s. black, bright green and orange	25	25
293	–	60s. black, cerise and orange	75	1·25
294	–	1p. black, blue-green and orange	1·10	2·00
285/294 and O35/O36 *Set of* 12			4·25	7·00

Design: 9, 11, 20, 60s., 1p. Boxing.

1969 (23 Dec). First Oil Search in Tonga. T **86** and similar vert design.

(a) Postage

295	**86**	3s. multicoloured	65	25
296		7s. multicoloured	85	25
297		20s. multicoloured	1·50	50
298		25s. multicoloured	1·50	50
299		35s. multicoloured	1·75	80

(b) Air

300	–	9s. multicoloured	85	25
301	–	10s. multicoloured	85	25
302	–	24s. multicoloured	1·50	50
303	–	29s. multicoloured	1·75	70
304	–	38s. multicoloured	2·00	80
295/304 and O37/O38 *Set of* 12			19·00	16·00

Design: Nos. 300/304, Oil derrick and island of Tongatapu.

87 Members of the British and Tongan Royal Families

1970 (7 Mar). Royal Visit. T **87** and similar design. Multicoloured.

(a) Postage

305	**87**	3s. multicoloured	60	40
306		5s. multicoloured	70	40
307		10s. multicoloured	1·00	45
308		25s. multicoloured	2·50	75
309		50s. multicoloured	4·25	4·25

(b) Air

310	–	7s. multicoloured	90	25
311	–	9s. multicoloured	1·00	30
312	–	24s. multicoloured	2·50	75
313	–	29s. multicoloured	2·75	80
314	–	38s. multicoloured	3·75	1·50
305/314 and O39/O41 *Set of* 13			45·00	32·00

Design: Nos. 310/314, Queen Elizabeth II and King Taufu'ahau Tupou IV.

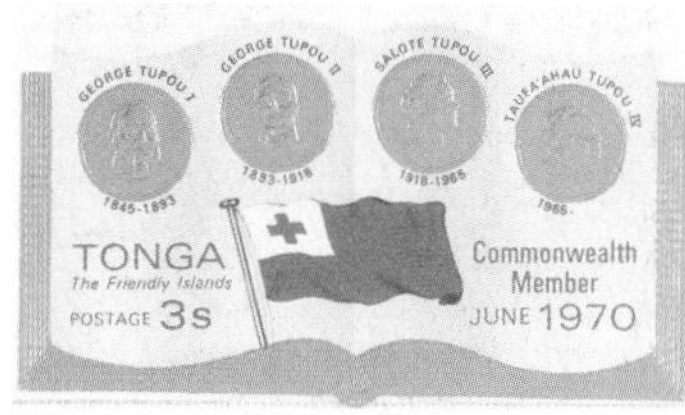

89 Book, Tongan Rulers and Flag

1970 (4 June). Entry into British Commonwealth. T **89** and similar design.

(a) Postage

315	**89**	3s. multicoloured	65	25
316		7s. multicoloured	90	30
317		15s. multicoloured	1·40	40
318		25s. multicoloured	1·75	50
319		50s. multicoloured	2·75	2·50

(b) Air

320	–	9s. turquoise-blue, gold and scarlet	20	20
321	–	10s. bright purple, gold and greenish blue	20	20
322	–	24s. olive-yellow, gold and green	50	30
323	–	29s. new blue, gold and orange-red	55	30
324	–	38s. deep orange-yellow, gold and bright emerald	70	55
315/324 and O42/O44 *Set of* 13			35·00	19·00

Design: 'Star' shaped (44×51 *mm*)—Nos. 320/324, King Taufa'ahau Tupou IV.

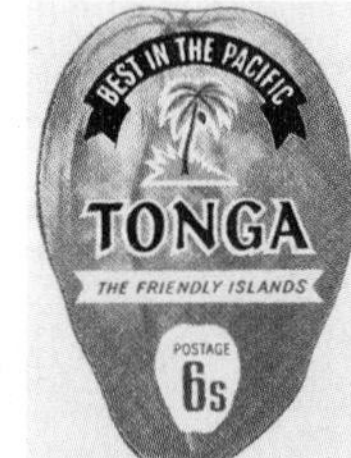

90 Coconut

1970 (9 June). Coil stamps.

(a) As T **83** *but colours changed*

325	**83**	1s. greenish yellow, bright purple and black	1·00	1·75
326		2s. greenish yellow, ultramarine and black	1·00	1·75
327		3s. greenish yellow, chocolate and black	1·00	1·75
328		4s. greenish yellow, emerald and black	1·00	1·75
329		5s. greenish yellow, orange-red and blue	1·00	1·75

(b) T **90**. *Multicoloured; colour of face value given*

330	**90**	6s. rose-carmine	1·00	1·75
331		7s. bright purple	1·10	1·75
332		8s. bluish violet	1·25	1·75
333		9s. turquoise	1·40	1·75
334		10s. pale orange	1·40	1·75
325/334 *Set of 10*			10·00	16·00

Nos. 325/334 and O45/O54 were produced in rolls of 200, each even stamp having a number applied to the front of the backing paper, with the usual inscription on the reverse.

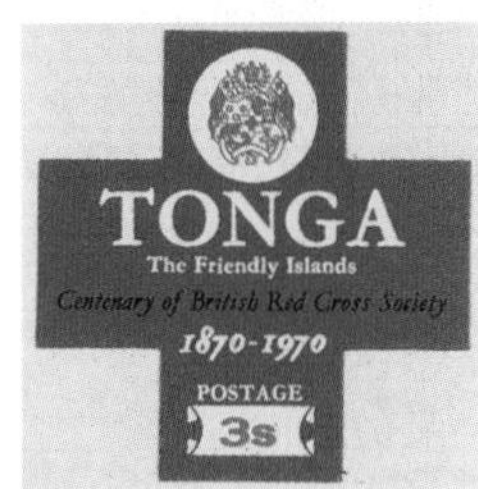

91 Red Cross

(Litho (postage) or litho and die-stamped (air))

1970 (17 Oct). Centenary of British Red Cross. T **91** and similar cross shaped design.

(a) Postage

335	**91**	3s. vermilion, black and light green	40	30
336		7s. vermilion, black and ultramarine	55	20
337		15s. vermilion and bright purple	1·25	60
338		25s. vermilion, black and turquoise-blue	1·60	90
339		75s. vermilion and deep red-brown	7·50	9·50

(b) Air

340	–	9s. vermilion and silver	60	20
341	–	10s. vermilion and bright purple	60	20
342	–	18s. vermilion and green	1·25	60
343	–	38s. vermilion and ultramarine	3·25	2·25
344	–	1p. vermilion and turquoise-blue	8·50	13·00
335/344 and O55/O57 *Set of 13*			48·00	42·00

Design: As T **91**—Nos. 340/344 as Nos. 335/339 but with inscription rearranged and Coat of Arms omitted.

On Nos. 335/336 and 338 the black colour is produced as a composite of the other two colours used.

OFFICIAL STAMPS

G.F.B.

(O 1)

(O 2)

(G.F.B. = Gaue Faka Buleaga = On Government Service)

1893 (13 Feb). Optd with T O **1** by Govt Printing Office, Wellington, NZ W **2**. P 12×11½.

O1	**5**	1d. ultramarine (C.)	24·00	50·00
		a. Bisected diagonally (½d.) (*on cover*)	†	—
O2	**6**	2d. ultramarine (C.)	40·00	55·00
O3	**5**	4d. ultramarine (C.)	50·00	£100
O4	**6**	8d. ultramarine (C.)	95·00	£180
O5		1s. ultramarine (C.)	£110	£200
O1/O5 *Set of 5*			£275	£500

Above prices are for stamps in good condition and colour. Faded and stained stamps from the remainders are worth much less.

1893 (16 Oct*). Nos. O1 to O5 variously surch with new value, sideways as T O **2**.

O6	**5**	½d. on 1d. ultramarine	26·00	50·00
O7	**6**	2½d. on 2d. ultramarine	32·00	50·00
O8	**5**	5d. on 4d. ultramarine	35·00	50·00
O9	**6**	7½d. on 8d. ultramarine	35·00	80·00
		a. 'D' of '7½D.' omitted	£1300	
		b. Surch double	£2250	
O10		10d. on 1s. ultramarine	42·00	85·00
O6/O10 *Set of 5*			£150	£275

* Earliest known date of use.

The surcharges on Nos. O6/O10 were applied by two-unit handstamps to each vertical pair. The two types of each value show slight differences.

OFFICIAL AIR MAIL
1862
TAU'ATAINA
EMANCIPATION
1962

(O 3)

OFFICIAL
AIRMAIL
40
SENITI

(O 4)

1962 (7 Feb). Air. Centenary of Emancipation. Nos. 112/114, 116 and 118/119 optd with T O **3** in red by R. S. Wallbank, Govt Printer.

O11	–	2d. ultramarine	23·00	7·50
		a. 'OFFICIAI'	65·00	25·00
		b. 'MAII'	90·00	40·00
O12	–	5d. violet	23·00	7·50
		a. 'OFFICIAI'	65·00	25·00
		b. 'MAII'	90·00	40·00
O13	–	1s. red-brown	20·00	4·50
		a. 'OFFICIAI'	65·00	15·00
		b. 'MAII'	90·00	25·00
		c. Opt double	£350	
		ca. 'OFFICIAI'	£900	
		cb. 'MAII'	£900	
O14	–	5s. orange-yellow and slate-lilac	£150	80·00
		a. 'MAII'	£425	£150
		b. 'OFFICIAI'		
O15	**52**	10s. yellow and black	60·00	30·00
		a. 'MAII'	£200	
O16	**53**	£1 yellow, scarlet, ultramarine and deep bright blue	85·00	50·00
		a. 'MAII'	£300	
		b. 'OFFICIAI'		
O11/O16 *Set of 6*			£325	£160

Nos. O11/O14 were overprinted in sheets of 60 (5×12), using a 5×6 setting which was applied first to the lower half sheets, then to the upper. The variety 'OFFICIAI' occurred at R. 4/2 on both the upper and lower halves, whereas 'MAII' occurred at R. 2/5 on the upper halves only. One sheet of the 1s. value (No. O13) received a double overprint on the upper half only, making Nos. O13ca and O13cb both unique.

Nos O15/O16 were overprinted in sheets of 60 (6×10), using adjusted 5×6 settings, with a smaller space between 'OFFICIAL' and 'AIR MAIL' at top. The variety 'MAII' occurred at R. 2/5, probably on both halves of each sheet, but the position of No. O16b has not been established.

The listed 'I' for 'L' must show no trace of horizontal bar. Varieties with a short horizontal bar occur on other positions in the settings, but are worth much less.

> **SET PRICES.** Official stamps from here onwards are included in the complete commemorative set prices given for any corresponding Postage issues

1963 (15 July). Air. First Polynesian Gold Coinage Commemoration. As T **63** but inscr 'OFFICIAL AIRMAIL'. 1 koula coin (diam 3⅛ in.). Imperf.

O17	**63**	15s. black	12·00	13·00

1965 (18 Mar). No. O17 surch as T **67**.

O18	**63**	30s. on 15s. black	3·75	5·00

1966 (18 June). Air. Centenary of Tupou College and Secondary Education. No. 117 surch with 'OFFICIAL AIRMAIL' and new value, with commemorative inscription as in T **69** but in italic capital letters.

O19		10s. on 4d. blue-green	40	35
		a. Surch inverted	£275	£120
O20		20s. on 4d. blue-green	60	50

1967 (25 Mar). Air. Decimal currency. No. 112 surch 'OFFICIAL AIRMAIL ONE PA' ANGA' in three lines, in red.

O21		1p. on 5s. yellow and lilac	7·00	3·50
		a. 'AIRMAIL' above 'OFFICIAL'	£180	

No. O21a occurred at R.8/3 in a number of sheets until it was corrected.

1967 (4 July). Air. No. 114 surch in various denominations as T O **4**.

O22	**53**	40s. on £1 yellow, red and blue	50	75
O23		60s. on £1 yellow, red and blue	60	1·25
O24		1p. on £1 yellow, red and blue	80	2·25
O25		2p. on £1 yellow, red and blue	1·25	3·00

Nos. O22/O25 were first used on 4 July 1967, but supplies of unused stamps were not made available until April 1968.

The Friendly Islands
welcome the
United States
Peace Corps Official Airmail
30s

(O 5)

Friendly Islands
Trials
Field & Track
South Pacific
Games
Port Moresby
1969
T$1·00
OFFICIAL
AIRMAIL

(O 6)

1967 (15 Dec). Air. Arrival of US Peace Corps in Tonga. As No. 114, but imperf, and background colour changed, and surch as T O **5**.

O26	**53**	30s. on £1 yellow, scarlet, ultramarine and emerald-green	40	30
O27		70s. on £1 yellow, scarlet, ultramarine and emerald-green	60	1·50
O28		1p.50 on £1 yellow, scarlet, ultramarine and emerald-green	75	2·75

1968 (4 July). Air. 50th Birthday of King Taufa'ahua IV. No. 207 surch 'HIS MAJESTY'S 50th BIRTHDAY' (as T **79**), 'OFFICIAL AIRMAIL' and new value.

O29	**75**	40s. on 50s. (Turq.)	3·25	80
O30		60s. on 50s. (G.)	3·75	2·00
O31		1p. on 50s. (V.)	5·00	5·50
O32		2p. on 50s. (P.)	9·00	13·00

1968 (19 Dec). Air. South Pacific Games Field and Track Trials, Port Moresby, New Guinea. As No. 114, but imperf, background colour changed and surch as T O **6**.

O33	**53**	20s. on £1 yellow, scarlet, ultramarine and emerald-green	20	30
O34		1p. on £1 yellow, scarlet, ultramarine and emerald-green	70	1·75

1969 (13 Aug). Air. Third South Pacific Games, Port Moresby. Design as Nos. 290/294.

O35		70s. carmine-red, bright green and turquoise	75	1·60
O36		80s. carmine-red, orange and turquoise	85	1·60

OFFICIAL AIRMAIL
1969 OIL SEARCH
90s

(O 7)

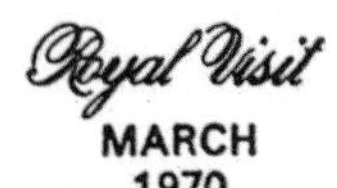

MARCH
1970
OFFICIAL
AIRMAIL
T$1·25

(O 8)

1969 (23 Dec). Air. First Oil Search in Tonga. As No. 114 but imperf, background colour changed to emerald-green, and surch as Type O **7**.

O37	**53**	90s. on £1 multicoloured	4·25	6·50
		a. '1966' for '1969' (R. 3/5)	£160	
O38		1p.10 on £1 multicoloured (R.)	4·25	6·50
		a. '1966' for '1969' (R. 3/5)	£160	

The '1966' error was later corrected.

No. O38 is surch as T O **7**, but without 'OFFICIAL AIRMAIL'.

1970 (7 Mar). Royal Visit. As No. 110 but imperf colours changed, and surch as T O **8**.

O39		75s. on 1s. carmine-red and yellow	9·50	7·00
O40		1p. on 1s. carmine-red and yellow (B.)	10·00	8·50
O41		1p.25 on 1s. carmine-red and yellow (G.)	11·00	10·00

OFFICIAL
Commonwealth
Member
JUNE 1970
50s
AIRMAIL

(O 9)

1970 (4 June). Air. Entry into British Commonwealth. As No. 112 but imperf, background colour changed, and surch as T O **9**.

O42		50s. on 5s. orange-yellow and sepia	9·00	2·25
O43		90s. on 5s. orange-yellow and sepia (R.)	10·00	4·25
O44		1p.50 on 5s. orange-yellow and sepia (G.)	12·00	9·50

1970 (4 June). As Nos. 325/334, but inscr 'OFFICIAL POST'. Colour of 'TONGA' given for 6 to 10s.

O45	**83**	1s. greenish yellow, bright purple and black	90	1·75
O46		2s. greenish yellow, ultramarine and black	1·00	1·75
O47		3s. greenish yellow, chocolate and black	1·00	1·75
O48		4s. greenish yellow, emerald and black	1·00	1·75
O49		5s. greenish yellow, orange-red and black	1·00	1·75
O50	**90**	6s. ultramarine	1·10	1·75
O51		7s. deep mauve	1·25	1·75
O52		8s. gold	1·25	1·75
O53		9s. bright carmine	1·40	1·75
O54		10s. silver	1·40	1·75
O45/O54 *Set of 10*			10·00	16·00

The note after No. 334 also applies here.

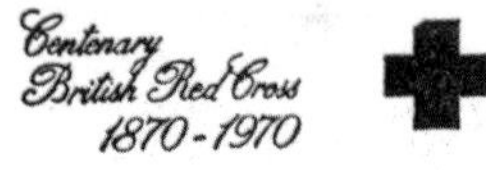

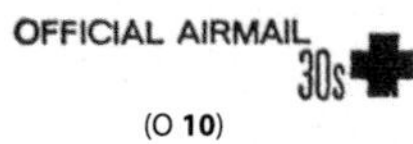

(O 10)

1970 (17 Oct). Centenary of British Red Cross. As Nos. 102 and 112 but imperf, colours changed and surch as T O **10**.

O55		30s. on 1½d. emerald (Blk. and R.)	2·00	2·25
O56		80s. on 5s. orange-yellow and sepia (B. and R.)	13·00	8·50
O57		90s. on 5s. orange-yellow and sepia (B. and R.)	13·00	8·50

Transjordan

PRICES FOR STAMPS ON COVER

Nos. 1/88*a*	*from* × 10
Nos. 89/142	*from* × 5
Nos. 143/243	*from* × 3
Nos. D112/D124	*from* × 6
Nos. D159/D248	*from* × 4
No. O117	—

Transjordan was part of the Turkish Empire from 1516 to 1918.

Turkish post offices are known to have existed at Ajlun ('Adjiloun'), Amman ('Omman'), Amman Station, Kerak ('Kerek'), Ma'an ('Mohan' or 'Maan'), Qatrana, Salt and Tafila ('Tafile'). Stamps cancelled 'Ibin' may have been used at Ibbin.

The area was overrun by British and Arab forces, organised by Colonel T. E. Lawrence, in September 1918, and as Occupied Enemy Territory (East), became part of the Syrian state under the Emir Faisal, who was king of Syria from 11 March to 24 July 1920. During 1920 the stamps of the Arab Kingdom of Syria were in use. On 25 April 1920 the Supreme Council of the Allies assigned to the United Kingdom a mandate to administer both Palestine and Transjordan, as the area to the east of the Jordan was called. The mandate came into operation on 29 September 1923.

E.E.F. post offices, using the stamps of Palestine, operated in the area from September 1918.

FORGERIES. Collectors are warned that the early provisional overprints and surcharges on T **3** or Palestine have been extensively forged. This particularly concerns Nos. 1/8, 20/88a and 98A/109A. Nos. 9/19 and 106A/106B and 107A/107B must, however, always be genuine, as the underlying stamps of Palestine T **3** were never issued perf 14 without opt.

BRITISH MANDATED TERRITORY

(Currency. 1000 milliemes = 100 piastres = £1 Egyptian)

'EAST'. Where the word 'East' appears in Arabic overprints it is not used in its widest sense but as implying the land or government 'East of Jordan'.

(**1**) ('East of Jordan') (**1a**)

(Optd at Greek Orthodox Convent, Jerusalem)

1920 (Nov). T **3** of Palestine optd with T **1**.

(a) P 15×14

No.	Type	Description	Unused	Used
1	1	1m. sepia	3·75	6·50
		a. Opt inverted	£140	£275
2		2m. blue-green	23·00	27·00
		a. Silver opt		
3		3m. yellow-brown	4·00	4·75
		a. Opt Type **1a**	£1100	
4		4m. scarlet	4·25	4·50
		a. Arabic '40'	75·00	
5		5m. yellow-orange	11·00	3·75
5*a*		1p. deep indigo (Silver)	£2000	
6		2p. olive	15·00	17·00
		a. Opt Type **1a**	£850	
7		5p. deep purple	50·00	80·00
		a. Opt Type **1a**	£1400	
8		9p. ochre	£850	£1400
1/7 (*ex 5a*) *Set of 7*			95·00	£120

(b) P 14

No.	Type	Description	Unused	Used
9	1	1m. sepia	1·40	6·50
		a. Opt inverted	£170	
10		2m. blue-green	3·50	6·00
		a. Silver opt	£550	£600
11		3m. yellow-brown	23·00	35·00
12		4m. scarlet	17·00	48·00
		a. Arabic '40'	£150	
13		5m. orange	2·75	3·75
14		1p. deep indigo (Silver)	3·75	4·75
15		2p. deep olive	15·00	15·00
16		5p. purple	7·50	18·00
17		9p. ochre	7·50	55·00
18		10p. ultramarine	18·00	55·00
19		20p. pale grey	20·00	90·00
9/19 *Set of 11*			£100	£300

Nos. 1/19 were surcharged from five different settings of 120 (12×10) which produced eight sub-types of T **1**. T **1a** occurred on R. 8/12 from one setting. The 9p. also exists with this overprint, but no example appears to have survived without further overprint or surcharge.

Nos. 9/19 (P 14) were never issued without opt, and the T **1** opt on this perforation must always be genuine.

The T **1** opt ('Sharqi Al-urdun') comprises seven Arabic characters, reading (from right to left) Sh-R-Qi-Al-R-D-N. The key features of the rare T **1a** are a) the absence of the dots above 'Qi' and b) the short left stroke of the 'Al'. Other variants exist with the missing dots, but only T **1a** also has the short left stroke. T **1a** is often misidentified, and forgeries exist.

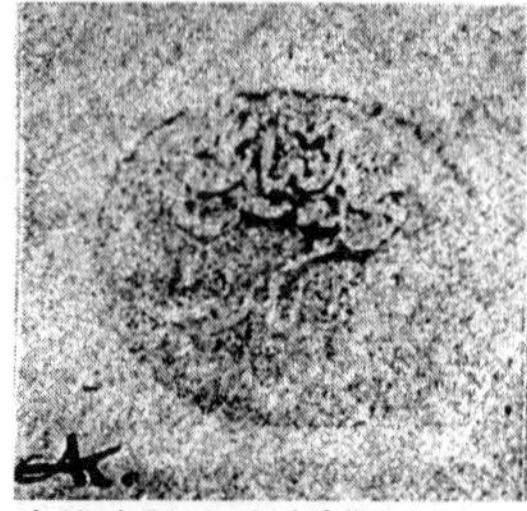

1b Moab District Seal (*full size*)

1920 (Nov). Issued at Kerak. Handstamped. Manuscript initials 'AK' in violet. Imperf.

No.	Type	Description	Unused	Used
19*a*	**1b**	(1p.) pale blue	£3500	£4000

No. 19*a* was issued in November 1920 by the political officer for Moab District, Captain (later Sir) Alex Kirkbride, and was used until supplies of Nos. 1/19 reached the area in March 1921. The local Turkish canceller was used as a postmark.

Emir Abdullah, 1 April 1921–22 May 1946

Abdullah, a son of the King of the Hejaz, was made Emir of Transjordan in 1921. On 26 May 1923 Transjordan was recognised as an autonomous state and on 20 February 1928 it was accorded a degree of independence.

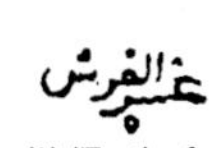

(**2**) ('Tenth of a piastre') (**3**) ('Piastre') (**4**) ('Arab Government of the East, April 1921')

1922 (Nov). Nos. 1/19 additionally handstamped with steel dies at Amman as Types **2** or **3**.

(a) P 15×14

No.	Type	Description	Unused	Used
20	2	1/10p. on 1m. sepia	29·00	50·00
		a. Red surch	70·00	70·00
		b. Violet surch	70·00	70·00
21		2/10p. on 2m. blue-green	35·00	35·00
		a. Error. Surch '3/10' for '2/10'	£120	£110
		b. Red surch	80·00	80·00
		c. Violet surch	£100	£100
		ca. Error. '3/10' for '2/10'		
22		3/10p. on 3m. yellow-brown	15·00	15·00
		a. Pair, one without surch	£800	
		b. Opt Type **1a**	£1200	£1200
		c. Error. '2/10' for '3/10'		
		d. Violet surch	£150	£150
		da. Opt Type **1a**	£2750	
23		4/10p. on 4m. scarlet	60·00	65·00
		a. Violet surch		
24		5/10p. on 5m. yellow-orange	£180	£100
		a. Pair, one without surch		
		b. Violet surch	£250	£225
25	3	2p. on 2p. olive	£250	75·00
		a. Opt Type **1a**	£1300	
		b. Red surch	£325	80·00
		ba. Opt Type **1a**		
		c. Violet surch	£300	90·00
26		5p. on 5p. deep purple	65·00	80·00
		a. Opt Type **1a**	£1600	
		b. Violet surch		
27		9p. on 9p. ochre	£300	£350
		a. Red surch	£130	£140
		b. Violet surch		

(b) P 14

No.	Type	Description	Unused	Used
28	2	1/10p. on 1m. sepia	25·00	30·00
		a. Pair, one without surch	£1500	
		b. Red surch	60·00	60·00
		c. Violet surch	£250	£300
29		2/10p. on 2m. blue-green	29·00	29·00
		a. Pair, one without surch	£1500	
		b. Error. Surch '3/10' for '2/10'	£110	£110
		c. Red surch	80·00	80·00
		ca. Error. Surch '3/10' for '2/10'		
		d. Violet surch	80·00	80·00
30		5/10p. on 5m. orange	£225	£100
		a. Pair, one without surch	†	£2000
		b. Violet surch	£275	
31	3	1p. on 1p. deep indigo (R.)	£200	60·00
		a. Pair, one without surch	£1800	
		b. Violet surch	£400	
32		9p. on 9p. ochre (R.)	£550	£550
		a. Violet surch		
33		10p. on 10p. ultramarine	£850	£1000
		a. Violet surch inverted		
34		20p. on 20p. pale grey	£650	£850
		a. Violet surch	£900	£950

*T **3** of Palestine (perf 15×14) similarly surch*

No.	Type	Description	Unused	Used
35	3	10p. on 10p. ultramarine	£1800	£2500
36		20p. on 20p. pale grey	£2500	£3000
		a. Violet surch		

T **2** reads 'tenths of a piastre' and T **3** 'the piastre', both with Arabic figures below. These surcharges were applied in order to translate the Egyptian face values of the stamps into the currency of the Arab Kingdom of Syria, but the actual face value of the stamps remained unchanged.

Being handstamped the surcharge may be found either at the top or bottom of the stamp, and exists double on most values.

The Types **2/3** handstamped surcharges have been extensively forged. Forged examples of Nos. 20/27 also often have a forged T **1** opt.

1922 (Dec). Stamps of 1920 handstamped with a steel die as T **4** in red-purple, violet or black*.

(a) P 15×14

No.	Type	Description	Unused	Used
37	4	1m. sepia (R.P.)	29·00	30·00
		a. Violet opt	30·00	35·00
		b. Black opt	26·00	26·00
38		2m. blue-green (R.P.)	27·00	27·00
		a. Violet opt	24·00	24·00
		b. Black opt	23·00	23·00
39		3m. yellow-brown (R.P.)	48·00	48·00
		a. Opt Type **1a**	£1600	
		b. Violet opt	9·00	9·00
		ba. Pair, one without opt	£1300	
		bb. Opt Type **1a**	£1500	£2000
		c. Black opt	10·00	10·00
		ca. Opt Type **1a**		
40		4m. scarlet (R.P.)	60·00	65·00
		b. Violet opt	60·00	65·00
		c. Black opt	60·00	65·00
41		5m. yellow-orange (R.P.)	45·00	12·00
		a. Violet opt	19·00	12·00
42		2p. olive (R.P.)	60·00	45·00
		a. Opt Type **1a**	£1500	
		b. Violet opt	26·00	18·00
		ba. Opt Type **1a**	£1500	£1300
		c. Black opt	17·00	12·00
43		5p. deep purple (R.P.)	£100	£120
		a. Pair, one without opt	£1600	
		b. Violet opt	65·00	85·00
		c. Black opt		
44		9p. ochre (R.P.)	£400	£450
		a. Violet opt	£200	£250
		ab. Opt Type **1a**	£2250	
		b. Black opt	70·00	85·00

(b) P 14

No.	Type	Description	Unused	Used
45	4	1m. sepia (R.P.)	16·00	20·00
		a. Pair, one without opt	£1300	
		b. Violet opt	27·00	24·00
		c. Black opt	23·00	23·00
46		2m. blue-green (R.P.)	32·00	32·00
		a. Violet opt	10·00	10·00
		b. Black opt	15·00	15·00
46*c*		3m. yellow-brown (V.)	£800	£350
47		5m. orange (R.P.)	£300	75·00
		a. Violet opt	32·00	22·00
48		1p. deep indigo (R.P.)	38·00	17·00
		a. Violet opt	22·00	11·00
49		2p. deep olive (V.)	80·00	85·00
50		5p. purple (R.P.)	£100	£110
		a. Violet opt	£110	£120
		b. Black opt		
51		9p. ochre (V.)	£900	£1000
52		10p. ultramarine (R.P.)	£1800	£1900
		a. Violet opt	£1100	£1600
		b. Black opt		
53		20p. pale grey (R.P.)	£1600	£2000
		a. Violet opt	£1100	£1800
		b. Black opt		

* The ink of the 'black' overprint is not a true black, but is caused by a mixture of inks from different ink-pads. The colour is, however, very distinct from either of the others.

Most values are known with inverted and/or double overprints.

The T **4** handstamp has been extensively forged, often in conjunction with a forged T **1** opt on stamps perf 15×14.

حكومة الشرق

العربية

نيسان سنة ٩٢.١

(**5**) ('Arab Government of the East, April 1921')

1923 (1 Mar). Stamps of 1920, with typographed overprint, T **5** applied by Govt Printing Press, Amman.

(a) P 15×14

No.	Type	Description	Unused	Used
54	5	1m. sepia (Gold)	£1500	£1800
55		2m. blue-green (Gold)	24·00	26·00
56		3m. yellow-brown (Gold)	18·00	19·00
		a. Opt double	£500	
		b. Opt inverted	£550	
		c. Black opt	75·00	85·00
57		4m. scarlet	20·00	19·00
58		5m. yellow-orange	60·00	50·00
		a. Opt Type **1** albino	£1200	£1400
59		2p. olive (Gold)	23·00	21·00
		a. Opt Type **1a**	£1200	£1000
		b. Black opt	£250	£250
		ba. Opt Type **1a**		
60		5p. deep purple (Gold)	75·00	£100
		a. Opt inverted	£225	
		b. Opt Type **1a**	£2000	
		ba. Opt inverted	£2500	
		c. Black opt inverted	£1500	

(b) P 14

No.	Type	Description	Unused	Used
62	5	1m. sepia (Gold)	19·00	32·00
		a. Opt inverted	£750	
63		2m. blue-green (Gold)	18·00	21·00
		a. Opt inverted	£350	£350
		b. Opt double	£300	
		c. Black opt	£300	
		ca. Opt double	£1500	
64		5m. orange	14·00	14·00
65		1p. deep indigo (Gold)	14·00	18·00
		a. Opt double	£500	£550
		b. Black opt	£800	£850
66		9p. ochre	90·00	£130
		a. Gold opt	£3000	
67		10p. ultramarine (Gold)	85·00	£130
		a. Black opt		
68		20p. pale grey (Gold)	85·00	£130
		a. Opt inverted	£375	
		b. Opt double	£450	
		c. Opt double, one inverted	£450	
		e. Opt double, one gold, one black, latter inverted	£750	
		f. Opt treble, one inverted	£1100	
		g. Black opt	£850	
		ga. Opt inverted	£1100	
		gb. Opt double, one inverted	£1300	

The gold overprints were created by sprinkling gold dust on wet black ink.

There are numerous constant minor varieties in this overprint in all values.

The 9p. perforated 15×14 was also prepared with this overprint, but the entire stock was used for No. 85.

The 20p. exists with top line of overprint only or with the lines transposed, both due to misplacement.

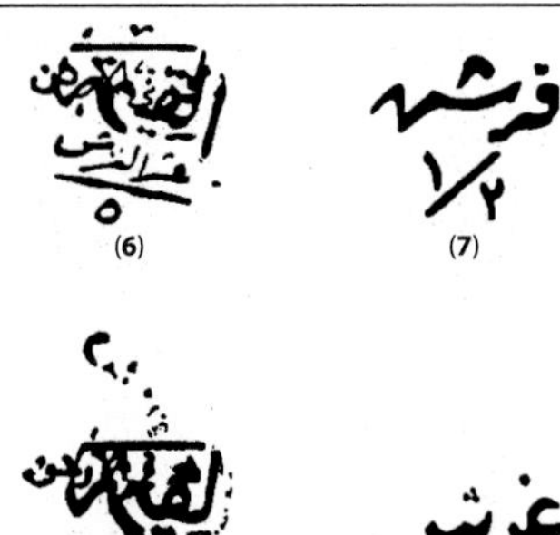

(6) (7) (8) (9)

1923 (Apr–Oct). Stamps of the preceding issues further surch by means of handstamps.

No.	Type	Description	Unused	Used
		(a) Issue of Nov 1920		
70	–	2½ /10ths p. on 5m. (13) (B.–Blk.)	£170	£170
		a. Black surch	£170	£170
		b. Violet surch	£170	£170
70*c*	6	5/10p. on 3m. (No. 3)	†	£5000
70*d*		5/10p. on 5m. (No. 13)	£2500	
70*e*	9	2p. on 20p. (No. 19)		
		(b) Stamp of Palestine		
71	6	5/10p. on 3m. (P 15×14)	£3000	
		(c) Issue of Nov 1922		
72	6	5/10p. on 3m. (No. 22)	£7000	
		a. Pair, one without surch	£7500	
73		5/10p. on 5p. (No. 26) (V.)	75·00	85·00
		a. Black surch		
		ab. Opt Type **3** omitted	£1200	
73*b*		5/10p. on 9p. (No. 27a)	£1300	
74	7	½p. on 5p. (No. 26)	75·00	85·00
		a. Pair, one without surch	£750	
75		½p. on 9p. (No. 27)	£3500	
		a. On No. 27a	£350	£400
		ab. Opt Type **1a**	£3500	
76		½p. on 9p. (No. 32)	—	£8000
77	8	1p. on 5p. (No. 26)	85·00	£110
		(d) Issue of Dec 1922		
78	6	5/10p. on 3m. (No. 39) (V.)	85·00	£100
		a. Black surch	£750	
		ab. Opt Type **1a**		
		b. On No. 39b	50·00	60·00
		ba. Pair, one without surch	£1400	
		bb. Without numeral of value		
		bc. Black surch	£750	
79		5/10p. on 5p. (No. 43b) (Blk.)	10·00	19·00
		a. Opt Type **1a**	£2000	
		b. Pair, one without surch	£500	
		c. Violet surch		
79*d*		5/10p. on 9p. (No. 44b)	—	£1200
		da. On No. 44a. Violet surch	—	£1300
80	7	½p. on 2p. (No. 42)	£100	£120
		a. Opt Type **1a**	£2000	
		b. On No. 42b	80·00	£110
		c. On No. 42c	60·00	£110
		ca. Pair, one without surch	£1000	
		w. Wmk inverted		
81		½p. on 5p. (No. 43)	£3000	
		a. On No. 43b	£1000	
82		½p. on 5p. (No. 50)	£2000	
		a. On No. 50a	£2500	
83	8	1p. on 5p. (No. 43)	£3750	
		b. On No. 43b	£2000	£2250
83*c*		1p. on 5p. (No. 50)	£2500	
		(e) Issue of 1 March 1923		
84	6	5/10p. on 3m. (No. 56)	29·00	45·00
		a. On No. 56c	£750	
85	7	½p. on 9p. (P 15×14)	95·00	£160
		a. Pair, one without surch	£5000	
86		½p. on 9p. (No. 66)	£170	
87	9	1p. on 10p. (No. 67)	£2250	£2500
		a. Violet surch	£2750	
88		2p. on 20p. (No. 68)	65·00	85·00
88*a*		2p. on 20p. (No. 68g)	£2000	

The handstamp on Nos. 70*c*, 88 and 88*a* has an Arabic '2' in place of the '1' shown in the illustration of T **9**.

Being handstamped many of the above exist inverted or double.

The Types **6/9** provisional surcharges have been extensively forged and should only be acquired from reliable sources.

Types of Saudi Arabia overprinted

11

20

21

22

(**10**) ('Arab Government of the East, 9 Sha'ban 1341')

(**11**) ('Arab Government of the East. Commemoration of Independence, 25 May 1923')

It should be noted that as Arabic is read from right to left, the overprint described as reading downwards appears to the English reader as though reading upwards. Our illustration of T **11** shows the overprint reading downwards

1923 (Apr). Stamps of Saudi Arabia. T **11**, with typographed opt, T **10**.

No.	Type	Description	Unused	Used
89	10	⅛p. chestnut	5·50	4·25
		a. Opt double	£200	
		b. Opt inverted	£110	
90		½p. scarlet	5·50	4·25
		a. Opt inverted		
91		1p. blue	4·25	1·25
		a. Opt inverted	£120	£140
92		1½p. lilac	4·50	2·50
		a. Opt double	£150	
		b. Top line omitted	—	£250
		c. Pair, one without opt	£250	
		d. Imperf between (horiz pair)	£170	
93		2p. orange	5·50	8·00
94		3p. brown	14·00	20·00
		a. Opt inverted	£225	
		b. Opt double	£225	£250
		c. Pair, one without opt	£375	
95		5p. olive	32·00	45·00
89/95 *Set of 7*			65·00	75·00
		On same stamps, surcharged with new values (Saudi Arabia, Nos. 47 and 49)		
96	10	¼p. on ⅛p. chestnut	16·00	8·00
		a. Opt and surch inverted	£150	
		b. Ditto but 2nd and 3rd lines of opt omitted	£200	
		c. Opt double	†	£200
97		10p. on 5p. olive	35·00	40·00
		a. Top line omitted	£350	

In this setting the third line of the overprint measures 19–21 mm. On 35 stamps out of the setting of 36 the Arabic '9' (right-hand character in bottom line) is widely spaced from the rest of the inscription. Minor varieties of this setting exist on all values.

For later setting, varying from the above, see Nos. 121/124.

Normal. '923' Error. '933'

An error reading '933' instead of '923' occurs as No. 3 in the setting of 24 on all values. Only 24 stamps are believed to have been overprinted for each of Nos. 103A, 108A, 105B and 107B so that for these stamps only one example of the error can exist. No example has yet been confirmed for Nos. 103A or 105B.

1923 (25 May). T **3** of Palestine optd with T **11**, reading up or down, in black or gold by Govt Press, Amman, in a setting of 24 (12×2). P 14 (9p., 10p.) or 15×14 (other values).

No.	Description	Unused	Used
	A. Reading downwards		
98A	1m. (Blk.)	23·00	23·00
	a. Opt double, one inverted (Blk.)	£650	£650
	b. Arabic '933'	£100	
	c. Gold opt	£150	£160
	ca. Opt double, one inverted (Gold)	£900	
	cb. Opt double (Blk.+Gold)	£900	£900
	cc. Arabic '933'	£550	
99A	2m. (Blk.)	42·00	50·00
	a. Arabic '933'	£180	
100A	3m. (Blk.)	14·00	18·00
	a. Arabic '933'	80·00	
101A	4m. (Blk.)	15·00	18·00
	a. Arabic '933'	85·00	
102A	5m. (Blk.)	70·00	80·00
	a. Arabic '933'	£375	
103A	1p. (Blk.)	£750	£850
	a. Opt double	£800	£900
104A	2p. (Blk.)	70·00	90·00
	a. Arabic '933'	£375	
105A	5p. (Gold)	80·00	90·00
	a. Opt double (Gold)	£650	
	b. Arabic '933'	£400	
	c. Opt double (Blk.)	£1500	
106A	9p. (Blk.)	90·00	£130
	a. Arabic '933'	£425	
107A	10p. (Blk.)	80·00	£100
	a. Arabic '933'	£400	
108A	20p. (Blk.)	£800	£800
	a. Arabic '933'	£3000	
	B. Reading upwards		
98B	1m. (Blk.)	95·00	£120
	b. Arabic '933'	£400	
	c. Gold opt	£150	£160
	cc. Arabic '933'	£550	
99B	2m. (Blk.)	60·00	70·00
	a. Arabic '933'	£300	
100B	3m. (Blk.)	£100	£130
	a. Arabic '933'	£400	
101B	4m. (Blk.)	32·00	45·00
	a. Arabic '933'	£150	
103B	1p. (Gold)	70·00	85·00
	a. Opt double	£600	
	b. Black opt		
	c. Arabic '933'	£375	
105B	5p. (Gold)	£800	£650
	a. Opt double		
106B	9p. (Blk.)	70·00	85·00
	a. Arabic '933'	£375	
107B	10p. (Blk.)	£700	
	a. Arabic '933'	£3000	
108B	20p. (Blk.)	85·00	£110
	a. Arabic '933'	£425	

The T **11** opt has been extensively forged on all values, but note that the 9p. and 10p. (Nos. 106A/106B and 107A/107B) will always be genuine, if correctly perf 14. The genuine T **11** opt shows numerous breaks in the Arabic lettering, which tend to be absent from the more heavily printed forged opts.

No. 107A surch with T **9**.

No.	Description	Unused	Used
109	1p. on 10p. ultramarine	£6000	

(**12**)

1923 (Sept). No. 92 surch with T **12**.

No.	Type	Description	Unused	Used
		(a) Handstamped		
110	12	½p. on 1½p. lilac	12·00	14·00
		a. Surch and opt inverted	55·00	
		b. Opt double	75·00	
		c. Opt double, one inverted	90·00	£100
		d. Pair, one without opt	£150	

This handstamp is known inverted, double and double, one inverted.

No.	Type	Description	Unused	Used
		(b) Typographed		
111	12	½p. on 1½p. lilac	55·00	55·00
		a. Surch inverted	£150	
		b. Surch double	£180	
		c. Pair, one without surch	£500	

(**13a**) (**13b**)

('Arab Government of the East, 9 Sha'ban, 1341')

These two types differ in the spacing of the characters and in the position of the bottom line which is to the left of the middle line in T **13a** and centrally placed in T **13b**.

1923 (Oct). T **11** of Saudi Arabia handstamped as Types **13a** or **13b**.

No.	Type	Description	Unused	Used
112	13a	½p. scarlet	15·00	16·00
113	13b	½p. scarlet	15·00	16·00

No. 112 exists with handstamp inverted.

15 ('Arab Government of the East')

(**16**) ('Commemorating the coming of His Majesty the King of the Arabs' and date)

1924 (Jan). T **11** of Saudi Arabia with typographed opt T **15**.

No.	Type	Description	Unused	Used
114	15	½p. scarlet	22·00	16·00
		a. Opt inverted	£180	
115		1p. blue	£300	£200
116		1½p. lilac	£350	
		a. Pair, one without opt	£1500	

The ½p. exists with thick, brown gum, which tints the paper, and with white gum and paper.

The 2p. in the same design was also overprinted, but was not issued without the subsequent T **16** overprint.

1924 (18 Jan). Visit of King Hussein of Hejaz. Nos. 114/116 and unissued 2p. with further typographed opt T **16** in black.

No.	Type	Description	Unused	Used
117	16	½p. scarlet	3·25	3·25
		a. Type **15** omitted	£150	
		b. Type **16** inverted	£150	
		c. Imperf between (pair)	£110	
		d. Type **16** in gold	3·25	3·25
		dc. Imperf between (pair)	£250	
118		1p. blue	4·00	3·50
		a. Type **15** omitted	£150	
		b. Both opts inverted	£200	
		c. Imperf between (pair)		
		d. Type **16** in gold	4·00	3·50
		db. Both opts inverted	£300	
		dc. Imperf between (pair)	£225	
119		1½p. lilac	4·25	4·50
		a. Type **15** omitted		
		b. Type **15** inverted	£130	
		d. Type **16** in gold	4·25	4·50
		da. Type **15** inverted	£150	
120		2p. orange	13·00	13·00
		d. Type **16** in gold	12·00	12·00

The spacing of the lines of the overprint varies considerably, and a variety dated '432' for '342' occurs on the twelfth stamp in each sheet (*Price* £75 *un*).

حكومة

الشرق العربية
٩ شعبان ١٣٤١
(**16a**)

شعبان	شعبال	شعبن
'Shaban' (normal)	'Shabal' (R. 4/6)	'Shabn' (R. 5/3)

1924 (Mar–May). T **11** of Saudi Arabia optd with T **16a** (new setting of T **10**).

No.	Type	Description	Unused	Used
121		⅛p. chestnut	45·00	22·00
		a. Opt inverted	£100	
122		½p. scarlet	14·00	4·50
		a. 'Shabal'	55·00	
		b. 'Shabn'	55·00	
		c. Opt inverted	£120	
123		1p. blue	24·00	2·25
		a. 'Shabal'	80·00	
		b. 'Shabn'	80·00	
		c. Opt double	£120	
		d. Imperf between (horiz pair) with opt double	£500	
124		1½p. lilac	28·00	28·00
		a. 'Shabal'	95·00	
		b. 'Shabn'	95·00	

This setting is from fresh type with the third line measuring 18¼ mm.

On all stamps in this setting (except Nos. 1, 9, 32 and 33) the Arabic '9' is close to the rest of the inscription.

The dots on the character 'Y' (the second character from the left in the second line) are on many stamps vertical (:) instead of horizontal (..).

On some sheets of the ⅛p. and ½p. the right-hand character, 'H', in the first line, was omitted from the second stamp in the first row of the sheet.

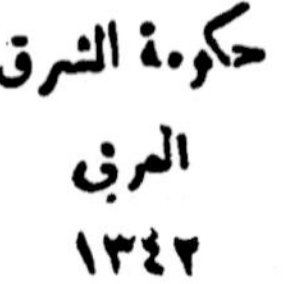

(**17**) ('Government of the Arab East, 1342')

(**18**) ('Government of the Arab East, 1343')

'Hukumat' (normal)

'Jakramat' (R. 2/1)

١٣٤٢	١٣٤٣	١٢٤٢
'1342' (normal)	'1343' (R. 4/2)	'1242' (R. 6/1)

1924 (Sept–Nov). T **11** of Saudi Arabia with type-set opt as T **17** by Govt Press, Amman.

No.	Type	Description	Unused	Used
125	**17**	⅛p. chestnut	1·50	1·25
		a. Opt inverted	£130	
		b. 'Jakramat'	30·00	
		c. '1242'	30·00	
126		¼p. green	1·50	70
		a. *Tête-bêche* (pair, both opts normal)	9·00	12·00
		b. Opt inverted	85·00	
		c. *Tête-bêche* (pair, one with opt inverted)	£300	
		d. 'Jakramat'	30·00	
		e. '1242'	30·00	
127		½p. bright scarlet	1·50	70
		a. Deep rose-red		
		b. '1343'	30·00	
129		1p. blue	10·00	1·50
		a. Imperf between (horiz pair)	£130	
		b. Opt inverted		
		c. 'Jakramat'	50·00	
		d. '1242'	50·00	
130		1½p. lilac	6·50	6·50
		a. '1343'	55·00	
131		2p. orange	4·75	3·50
		a. Opt double		
		b. '1343'	55·00	
132		3p. brown-red	4·75	4·75
		a. Opt inverted	£100	
		b. Opt double	£100	
		c. '1343'	75·00	
133		5p. olive	6·50	6·50
		a. 'Jakramat'	60·00	
		b. '1242'	60·00	
134		10p. brown-purple and mauve (R.)	15·00	16·00
		a. Centre inverted	£2500	
		b. Black opt	£250	
		c. 'Jakramat'	£100	
		d. '1242'	£100	
125/134 *Set of* 9			45·00	38·00

T **11** of Saudi Arabia was printed in sheets of 36 (6×6). The ¼p. value had the bottom three rows inverted, giving six vertical *tête-bêche* pairs. A few sheets were overprinted with the normal setting of T **17**, with the result that the overprints on the bottom rows were inverted in relation to the stamp, including on one of the stamps in the *tête-bêche* pair (No. 126c). A corrected setting with the overprint inverted on the lower rows was used for the majority of the printing giving *tête-bêche* pairs with the overprints both normal in relation to the stamps (No. 126a).

1925 (2 Aug). Types **20/22** of Saudi Arabia with lithographed opt T **18** applied in Cairo.

No.	Type	Description	Unused	Used
135	**18**	⅛p. chocolate	1·00	1·50
		a. Imperf vert (horiz pair)	£130	£150
		b. Opt inverted	70·00	
136		¼p. ultramarine	2·00	3·00
		a. Opt inverted	70·00	
137		½p. carmine	1·50	60
		a. Opt inverted	70·00	
138		1p. green	1·50	1·50
139		1½p. orange	3·50	4·00
		a. Opt inverted	70·00	
140		2p. blue	4·50	6·00
		a. Opt treble	£160	£225
141		3p. sage-green (R.)	5·00	8·00
		a. Imperf vert (horiz pair)	£130	£170
		b. Opt inverted	90·00	
		c. Black opt	£130	£160
142		5p. chestnut	7·50	15·00
		a. Opt inverted	85·00	
135/142 *Set of* 8			24·00	35·00

All values exist imperforate.

No. 141 imperforate with gold overprint comes from a presentation sheet for the Emir.

(**19**) ('East of the Jordan')

22 Emir Abdullah

23 Emir Abdullah

(Opt typo by Waterlow)

1925 (1 Nov)–**26**. Stamps of Palestine, 1922 (without the three-line Palestine opt), optd with T **19**. Wmk Mult Script CA. P 14.

No.	Type	Description	Unused	Used
143	**19**	1m. deep brown	55	3·50
144		2m. yellow	1·00	75
145		3m. greenish blue	2·75	2·00
146		4m. carmine-pink	2·75	4·25
147		5m. orange	3·25	50
		a. Yellow-orange	42·00	22·00
148		6m. blue-green	2·75	2·50
149		7m. yellow-brown	2·75	2·50
150		8m. scarlet	2·75	1·25
151		1p. grey	2·75	70
152		13m. ultramarine	3·25	3·00
153		2p. olive	4·25	4·75
		a. Olive-green	£120	35·00
154		5p. deep purple	9·50	11·00
155		9p. ochre	14·00	28·00
		a. Perf 15×14 (1926)	£900	£1400
156		10p. light blue	29·00	42·00
		a. Error. 'E.F.F.' in bottom panel (R.10/3)	£800	£1000
		b. Perf 15×14 (1926)	80·00	£100
157		20p. light violet	48·00	85·00
		a. Perf 15×14 (1926)	£850	£1000
143/157 *Set of* 15			£110	£160
143s/157s Optd 'SPECIMEN' *Set of* 15			£350	

(New Currency. 1000 milliemes = £1 Palestinian)

(Recess Perkins Bacon & Co)

1927 (1 Nov)–**29**. New Currency. Wmk Mult Script CA. P 14.

No.	Type	Description	Unused	Used
159	**22**	2m. greenish blue	3·50	1·75
160		3m. carmine-pink	4·75	4·25
161		4m. green	6·50	8·50
162		5m. orange	3·25	30
163		10m. scarlet	5·50	8·50
164		15m. ultramarine	4·50	1·00
165		20m. olive-green	4·50	4·75
166	**23**	50m. purple	4·50	15·00
167		90m. bistre	7·50	38·00
168		100m. blue	8·50	27·00
169		200m. violet	17·00	50·00
170		500m. brown (5.29)	60·00	85·00
171		1000m. slate-grey (5.29)	£100	£150
159/171 *Set of* 13			£200	£350
159s/171s Optd or Perf (500, 1000m.) 'SPECIMEN' *Set of* 13			£375	

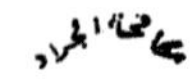

(**24**) ('Constitution')

(**27**)

1928 (1 Sept). New Constitution of 20 February 1928. Optd with T **24** by lithography by Atwood, Morris & Co., Cairo.

No.	Type	Description	Unused	Used
172	**22**	2m. greenish blue	7·00	7·50
173		3m. carmine-pink	8·00	13·00
174		4m. green	8·00	16·00
175		5m. orange	8·00	4·50
176		10m. scarlet	8·00	17·00
177		15m. ultramarine	8·00	5·00
178		20m. olive-green	16·00	27·00
179	**23**	50m. purple	21·00	30·00
180		90m. bistre	25·00	£100
181		100m. blue	25·00	£100
182		200m. violet	90·00	£180
172/182 *Set of* 11			£200	£450

1930 (1 Apr). Locust Campaign. Optd as T **27** by lithography by Whitehead, Morris & Co, Alexandria.

No.	Type	Description	Unused	Used
183	**22**	2m. greenish blue	3·25	7·50
		a. Opt inverted	£300	£600
184		3m. carmine-pink	2·50	6·50
185		4m. green	3·75	19·00
186		5m. orange	23·00	14·00
		a. Opt double	£425	£700
		b. Vert pair, top stamp opt double. Lower stamp without bottom line of opt	£1800	
187		10m. scarlet	2·25	4·25
188		15m. ultramarine	2·25	4·00
		a. Opt inverted	£225	£450
189		20m. olive-green	4·00	4·00
190	**23**	50m. purple	5·00	11·00
191		90m. bistre	10·00	48·00
192		100m. blue	12·00	50·00
193		200m. violet	32·00	85·00
194		500m. brown	75·00	£200
		a. 'C' of 'LOCUST' omitted (R. 5/3)	£800	£1200
183/194 *Set of* 12			£150	£400

No. 186a was sold at Kerak.

28

29

(Re-engraved with figures of value at left only. Recess Perkins, Bacon)

1930 (1 June)–**39**. Wmk Mult Script CA. P 14.

No.	Type	Description	Unused	Used
194*b*	**28**	1m. red-brown (6.2.34)	10·00	1·00
		c. Perf 13½×13 (1939)	20·00	7·00
195		2m. greenish blue	2·25	50
		a. Perf 13½×13. *Bluish green* (1939)	26·00	4·50
196		3m. carmine-pink	6·00	70
196*a*		3m. green (6.2.34)	11·00	85
		b. Perf 13½×13 (1939)	38·00	9·00
197		4m. green	6·00	9·00
197*a*		4m. carmine-pink (6.2.34)	11·00	1·00
		b. Perf 13½×13 (1939)	£140	48·00
198		5m. orange	3·75	40
		a. Coil stamp. Perf 13½×14 (29.2.36)	32·00	24·00
		b. Perf 13½×13 (1939)	70·00	3·00
199		10m. scarlet	4·75	15
		a. Perf 13½×13 (1939)	£190	4·25
200		15m. ultramarine	4·75	20
		a. Coil stamp. Perf 13½×14 (29.2.36)	29·00	23·00
		b. Perf 13½×13 (1939)	42·00	5·50
201		20m. olive-green	5·00	35
		a. Perf 13½×13 (1939)	65·00	12·00
202	**29**	50m. purple	6·50	1·25
203		90m. bistre	3·75	4·25
204		100m. blue	5·00	4·25
205		200m. violet	23·00	14·00
206		500m. brown	32·00	55·00
207		£P1 slate-grey	70·00	£110
194*b*/207 *Set of* 16			£170	£180
194*b*s/207s Perf 'SPECIMEN' *Set of* 16			£375	

For stamps perf 12 see Nos. 230/243, and for T **28** lithographed, perf 13½, see Nos. 222/229.

30 Mushetta

30a Nymphaeum, Jerash

30b Kasr Kharana

30c Kerak Castles

30d Temple of Artemis, Jerash

31 Ajlun Castle

31a The Khazneh at Petra

31b Allenby Bridge over the Jordan

31c Threshing scene

31d Kasr Kharana

32 Temple of Artemis, Jerash

32a Ajlun Castle

32b The Khazneh at Petra

33 Emir Abdullah

(Vignettes from photographs; frames des Yacoub Sukker. Recess Bradbury, Wilkinson)

1933 (1 Feb). As Types **30/33**. Wmk Mult Script CA. P 12.

208	**30**	1m. black and maroon	1·75	1·60
209	**30a**	2m. black and claret	6·50	1·40
210	**30b**	3m. blue-green	6·50	1·75
211	**30c**	4m. black and brown	13·00	8·00
212	**30d**	5m. black and orange	7·50	1·40
213	**31**	10m. carmine	16·00	5·00
214	**31a**	15m. blue	9·00	1·40
215	**31b**	20m. black and sage-green	9·00	5·50
216	**31c**	50m. black and purple	38·00	22·00
217	**31d**	90m. black and yellow	38·00	65·00
218	**32**	100m. black and blue	38·00	65·00
219	**32a**	200m. black and violet	65·00	£150
220	**32b**	500m. scarlet and red-brown	£250	£550
221	**33**	£P1 black and yellow-green	£550	£1350
208/221 *Set of 14*			£900	£2000
208s/221s Perf 'SPECIMEN' *Set of 14*			£950	

34

(Litho Survey Dept, Cairo)

1942 (18 May). T **28**, but with Arabic characters above portrait and in top left circle modified as in T **34**. No wmk. P 13½.

222	**34**	1m. red-brown	1·25	9·00
223		2m. green	3·75	3·25
224		3m. yellow-green	4·00	8·50
225		4m. carmine-pink	4·00	8·50
226		5m. yellow-orange	7·50	2·00
227		10m. scarlet	14·00	3·75
228		15m. blue	27·00	9·50
229		20m. olive-green	48·00	50·00
222/229 *Set of 8*			95·00	85·00

Forgeries of the above exist on whiter paper with rough perforations.

(Recess Bradbury Wilkinson)

1943 (1 Jan)–**46**. Wmk Mult Script CA. P 12.

230	**28**	1m. red-brown	30	75
231		2m. bluish green	4·25	3·00
232		3m. green	2·00	3·75
233		4m. carmine-pink	1·75	3·75
234		5m. orange	1·75	20
235		10m. red	3·00	1·25
236		15m. blue	3·00	3·00
237		20m. olive-green (26.8.46)	3·00	1·00
238	**29**	50m. purple (26.8.46)	3·00	1·50
239		90m. bistre (26.8.46)	6·00	9·50
240		100m. blue (26.8.46)	5·50	1·75
241		200m. violet (26.8.46)	13·00	16·00
242		500m. brown (26.8.46)	15·00	12·00
243		£P1 slate-grey (26.8.46)	27·00	22·00
230/243 *Set of 14*			80·00	70·00

Nos. 237/243 were released in London by the Crown Agents in May 1944, but were not put on sale in Transjordan until 26 August 1946.

Printings of the 3, 4, 10, 15 and 20m. in changed colours, together with a new 12m. value, were released on 12 May 1947.

POSTAGE DUE STAMPS

حكومة

مستحق

الشرق العربية

مستحق ٩ شعبان ١٣٤١

(D **12** 'Due') (D **13**)

1923 (Sept). Issue of April 1923, with opt T **10** with further typographed opt T D **12** (the 3p. with handstamped surch as T **12** at top).

D112	½p. on 3p. brown	42·00	45·00
	a. 'Due' inverted	50·00	55·00
	b. 'Due' double	50·00	60·00
	ba. 'Due' double, one inverted	£150	
	c. Arabic 't' & 'h' transposed (R. 1/2)	£110	
	ca. As c, inverted	£350	
	d. Surch at foot of stamp	50·00	
	da. Ditto, but with var. c	£130	
	e. Surch omitted	£200	
D113	1p. blue	25·00	27·00
	a. Type **10** inverted	80·00	
	b. 'Due' inverted	50·00	45·00
	c. 'Due' double	50·00	
	d. 'Due' double, one inverted	£150	
	e. Arabic 't' & 'h' transposed (R. 1/2)	75·00	
	f. 'Due' omitted (in vertical pair with normal)	£200	
D114	1½p. lilac	38·00	40·00
	a. 'Due' inverted	50·00	50·00
	b. 'Due' double	50·00	
	ba. 'Due' double, one diagonal	75·00	
	c. Arabic 't' & 'h' transposed (R. 1/2)	75·00	
	ca. As c, inverted	£275	
	d. 'Due' omitted (in pair with normal)	£200	
D115	2p. orange	40·00	42·00
	a. 'Due' inverted	60·00	60·00
	b. 'Due' double	65·00	
	ba. 'Due' double, one diagonal	£100	
	c. 'Due' treble	£150	
	d. Arabic 't' & 'h' transposed (R. 1/2)	80·00	
	e. Arabic 'h' omitted	£100	

The variety, Arabic 't' and 'h' transposed, occurred on R. 1/2 of all values in the first batch of sheets printed. The variety, Arabic 'h' omitted, occurred on every stamp in the first three rows of at least three sheets of the 2p.

Genuine examples of Nos. D113/D115 are known with additional forged T D **12** opts, in imitation of the 'double' and 'double, one inverted' errors. Most such forged opts show the left-hand Arabic character dropped out of alignment with the other characters.

Handstamped in four lines as T D **13** and surch as on No. D112

D116	½p. on 3p. brown	55·00	60·00
	a. Opt and surch inverted	£200	
	b. Opt double	£200	
	c. Surch omitted	£225	
	d. Opt inverted. Surch normal, but at foot of stamp	£150	
	e. Opt omitted and opt inverted (pair)	£300	
	f. 'Due' double, one inverted	£160	
	h. Surch double	£250	

حكومة

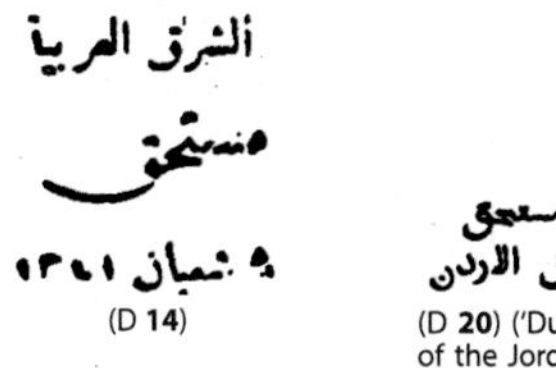

(D **14**) (D **20**) ('Due. East of the Jordan')

1923 (Oct). T **11** of Saudi Arabia handstamped with T D **14**.

D117	½p. scarlet	4·50	10·00
D118	1p. blue	9·00	9·00
	a. Pair, one without handstamp		
D119	1½p. lilac	6·50	10·00
D120	2p. orange	9·00	11·00
D121	3p. brown	22·00	28·00
	a. Pair, one without handstamp	£600	
D122	5p. olive	24·00	45·00
D117/D122 *Set of 6*		65·00	£100

There are three types of this handstamp, differing in some of the Arabic characters. They occur inverted, double etc.

1923 (Nov). T **11** of Saudi Arabia with opt similar to T D **14** but first three lines typo and fourth handstruck.

D123	1p. blue	80·00	
D124	5p. olive	30·00	
	a. Imperf between (vert pair)	£750	

(Opt typo by Waterlow)

1925 (Nov). Stamps of Palestine 1922 (without the three-line Palestine opt), optd with T D **20**. P 14.

D159	1m. deep brown	2·75	16·00
D160	2m. yellow	5·00	10·00
D161	4m. carmine-pink	5·00	23·00
D162	8m. scarlet	7·50	24·00
D163	13m. ultramarine	12·00	25·00
D164	5p. deep purple	14·00	42·00
	a. Perf 15×14	65·00	£100
D159/D164 *Set of 6*		42·00	£130
D159s/D164s Optd 'SPECIMEN' *Set of 6*		£140	

Stamps as No. D164, but with a different top line to overprint T D **20**, were for revenue purposes.

مستحق

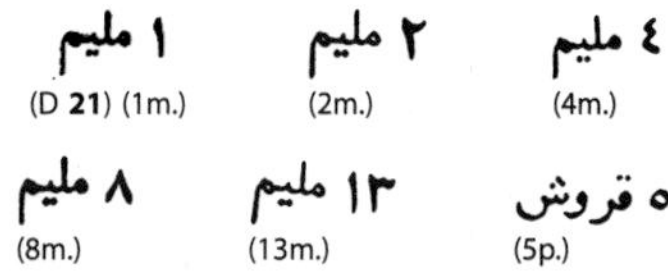

(D **21**) (1m.) (2m.) (4m.) (8m.) (13m.) (5p.)

(Surch typo at Jerusalem)

1926 (Feb–May). Postage stamps of 1 November 1925, surch 'Due' and new value as T D **21** by Greek Orthodox Printing Press, Jerusalem. Bottom line of surcharge differs for each value as illustrated.

D165	1m. on 1m. deep brown	14·00	40·00
	a. Red opt	£160	
D166	2m. on 1m. deep brown	13·00	40·00
D167	4m. on 3m. greenish blue	14·00	42·00
D168	8m. on 3m. greenish blue	14·00	42·00
D169	13m. on 13m. ultramarine	19·00	48·00
D170	5p. on 13m. ultramarine	23·00	70·00
D165/D170 *Set of 6*		85·00	£250

١ مستحق ١

1 1 مستحق

(D **25** 'Due') Extra Arabic character in opt (R. 4/10)

1929 (1 Jan). Nos. 159 etc. optd only or surch in addition as T D **25** by lithography by Whitehead, Morris & Co, Alexandria.

D183	**22**	1m. on 3m. carmine-pink	1·75	8·00
		a. Extra Arabic character	40·00	
D184		2m. greenish blue	4·50	7·50
		a. Pair, one without opt	£475	
D185		4m. on 15m. ultramarine	5·00	20·00
		a. Surch inverted	£190	£325
D186		10m. scarlet	9·50	9·50
D187	**23**	20m. on 100m. blue	8·00	32·00
		a. Horiz pair, one without surch	£800	
D188		50m. purple	6·00	27·00
		a. Horiz pair, one without opt	£800	
D183/D188 *Set of 6*			32·00	95·00

D **26**

D **35**

(Recess Perkins, Bacon)

1929 (1 Apr)–**39**. Wmk Mult Script CA. P 14.

D189	D **26**	1m. red-brown	2·50	16·00
		a. Perf 13½×13 (1939)	£160	£130
D190		2m. orange-yellow	5·00	8·50
D191		4m. green	6·50	20·00
D192		10m. scarlet	13·00	15·00
D193		20m. olive-green	17·00	28·00
D194		50m. blue	20·00	38·00
D189/D194 *Set of 6*			55·00	£110
D189s/D194s Perf 'SPECIMEN' *Set of 6*			£150	

(Litho Survey Dept, Cairo)

1942 (22 Dec). Redrawn. Top line of Arabic in taller lettering. No wmk. P 13½.

D230	D **35**	1m. red-brown	4·50	25·00
D231		2m. orange-yellow	12·00	13·00
D232		10m. scarlet	19·00	7·00
D230/D232 *Set of 3*			32·00	40·00

Forgeries of the above exist on whiter paper with rough perforations.

(Recess Bradbury Wilkinson)

1944–49. Wmk Mult Script CA. P 12.

D244	D **26**	1m. red-brown	1·50	9·00
D245		2m. orange-yellow	2·75	9·00
D246		4m. green	2·75	15·00
D247		10m. carmine	8·00	17·00
D248		20m. olive-green (1949)	80·00	£100
D244/D248 *Set of 5*			85·00	£130

OFFICIAL STAMP

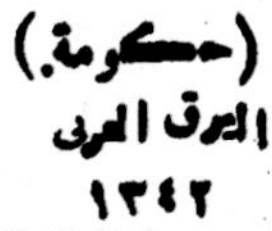

(O **16**) ('Arab Government of the East, 1342' = 1924)

1924. T **11** of Saudi Arabia with typographed opt, T O **16**.

O117	½p. scarlet	35·00	£110
	a. Arabic '1242' (R. 2/2, 3/6, 4/5, 4/6)	£160	
	b. Imperf between (vert pair)		

By treaty of 22 March 1946 with the United Kingdom, Transjordan was proclaimed an independent kingdom on 25 May 1946.

Later issues are listed under JORDAN in the Stanley Gibbons *Middle East catalogue*.

Transvaal *see* South Africa

Trinidad and Tobago

TRINIDAD

CROWN COLONY

The first post office was established at Port of Spain in 1800 to deal with overseas mail. Before 1851 there was no post office inland service, although a privately-operated one along the coast did exist, for which rates were officially fixed (see No. 1). During 1851 the colonial authorities established an inland postal system which commenced operation on 14 August. Responsibility for the overseas mails passed to the local post authorities in 1858.

No. CC1 is recorded in the GPO Record Book on 21 March 1852, but no examples have been recorded used on cover before February 1858. The prepayment of postage on mail to Great Britain was made compulsory from 9 October 1858. From March 1859 it was used with the early Britannia 1d. stamps to indicate prepayment of the additional overseas rate in cash or, later, to show that letters were fully franked with adhesive stamps. This is the normal usage of the handstamp and commands little, if any premium over the cover price quoted below for the stamps involved. The use of the handstamp without an adhesive is rare.

PORT OF SPAIN

CROWNED-CIRCLE HANDSTAMPS

CC 1

CC1 CC **1** TRINIDAD (R.) (*without additional adhesive stamp*) (21.3.52) .... *Price on cover* £3000

PRICES FOR STAMPS ON COVER TO 1945	
No. 1	*from* × 2
Nos. 2/12	*from* × 10
Nos. 13/20	*from* × 4
Nos. 25/29	*from* × 10
No. 30	—
Nos. 31/44	*from* × 4
No. 45	—
Nos. 46/59	*from* × 4
Nos. 60/63	*from* × 5
Nos. 64/68	*from* × 4
Nos. 69/74	*from* × 20
Nos. 75/78	*from* × 50
No. 79	—
No. 87	*from* × 20
Nos. 98/102	*from* × 6
No. 103	—
Nos. 104/105	*from* × 20
Nos. 106/112	*from* × 12
No. 113	—
Nos. 114/121	*from* × 4
Nos. 122/124	—
No. 125	*from* × 10
Nos. 126/130	*from* × 5
No. 131	—
Nos. 132/143	*from* × 3
Nos. 144/145	—
Nos. 146/148	*from* × 3
Nos. D1/D17	*from* × 15

1

2 Britannia

1847 (16 Apr). Litho. Imperf.

1	**1**	(5c.) blue	£30000	£10000

The 'LADY McLEOD' stamps were issued in April 1847, by David Bryce, owner of the SS *Lady McLeod*, and sold at five cents each for the prepayment of the carriage of letters by his vessel between Port of Spain and San Fernando.

The price quoted for used examples of No. 1 is for pen-cancelled. Stamps cancelled by having a corner skimmed-off are worth less.

(Recess P.B.)

1851 (14 Aug)–**55**. No value expressed. Imperf. Blued paper.

2	**2**	(1d.) purple-brown (1851)	21·00	80·00
3		(1d.) blue *to* deep blue (12.51)	23·00	65·00
4		(1d.) deep blue (1852)*	£150	85·00
5		(1d.) grey (12.51)	80·00	70·00
6		(1d.) brownish grey (2.53)	55·00	80·00
7		(1d.) brownish red (1853)	£300	70·00
8		(1d.) brick-red (8.55)	£180	75·00

No. 2 is known on paper bearing the sheet watermark 'STACEY WISE/RUSH MILLS'.

* No. 4 shows the paper deeply and evenly blued, especially on the back. It has more the appearance of having been printed on blue paper rather than on white paper that has become blued.

1854 (Aug)–**57**. Imperf. White paper.

9	**2**	(1d.) deep purple	32·00	95·00
10		(1d.) dark grey	55·00	90·00
12		(1d.) rose-red (1857)	£2500	70·00

PRICES. Prices quoted for the unused of most of the above issues and Nos. 25 and 29 are for 'remainders' with original gum, found in London. Old colours that have been out to Trinidad are of much greater value.

3 Britannia

4 Britannia

The following provisional issues were lithographed in the Colony (from die engraved by Charles Petit), and brought into use to meet shortages of the Perkins Bacon stamps during the following periods: (1) Sept 1852–May 1853; (2) March 1855–June 1855; (3) Dec 1856–Jan 1857; (4) Oct 1858–Jan 1859; (5) March 1860–June 1860.

1852–60. No value expressed. Imperf.

A. First Issue (September 1852). Fine impression; lines of background clear and distinct

(i) Yellowish paper

13	**3**	(1d.) blue	£9000	£1700
		(ii) Bluish cartridge paper (February 1853)		
14	**3**	(1d.) blue	—	£1900
		B. Second issue (March 1855). Thinner paper. Impression less distinct than before.		
15	**3**	(1d.) pale blue *to* greenish blue	—	£1000
		C. Third issue (August 1856). Background often of solid colour, but with clear lines in places		
16	**3**	(1d.) bright blue *to* deep blue	£4500	£1000
		D. Fourth issue (October 1858). Impression less distinct, and rarely showing more than traces of background lines		
17	**3**	(1d.) very deep greenish blue	—	£750
18		(1d.) slate-blue	£4000	£650
		E. Fifth issue (March 1860). Impression shows no (or hardly any) background lines		
19	**3**	(1d.) grey to bluish grey	£4000	£400
20		(1d.) red (*shades*)	16·00	£600

In the worn impression of the fourth and fifth issues, the impression varies according to the position on the stone. Generally speaking, stamps of the fifth issue have a flatter appearance and cancellations are often less well defined. The paper of both these issues is thin or very thin. In all issues except 1853 (Feb) the gum tends to give the paper a toned appearance.

Stamps in the slate-blue shade (No. 18) also occur in the fifth issue, but are not readily distinguishable.

PERKINS BACON 'CANCELLED'. For notes on these handstamps, showing 'CANCELLED' between horizontal bars forming an oval, see Catalogue Introduction.

(Recess P.B.)

1859 (9 May). Imperf.

25	**4**	4d. grey-lilac (H/S 'CANCELLED' in oval £9000)	£120	£325
28		6d. deep green (H/S 'CANCELLED' in oval £9000)	£12000	£425
29		1s. indigo	£100	£350
30		1s. purple-slate	£7000	

'CANCELLED' examples of No. 25 are in lilac rather than grey-lilac. No. 30 may be of unissued status.

1859 (Sept). Pin-perf with a spiked wheel.

(a) Pin-perf 12½

31	**2**	(1d.) rose-red	£1600	55·00
32		(1d.) carmine-lake	£1800	50·00
33	**4**	4d. dull lilac	—	£900
34		4d. dull purple	£6500	£900
35		6d. yellow-green	£2750	£200
36		6d. deep green	£2750	£200
37		1s. purple-slate	£7000	£1300
		(b) Pin-perf 13½–14		
38	**2**	(1d.) rose-red	£250	42·00
39		(1d.) carmine-lake	£325	40·00
40	**4**	4d. dull lilac	£1200	80·00
40*a*		4d. brownish purple	£225	£110
41		4d. dull purple	£500	£110
42		6d. yellow-green	£600	80·00
43		6d. deep green	£600	75·00
43*a*		6d. bright yellow-green	£160	£110
		b. Imperf between (vert pair)	£7500	
44		1s. purple-slate	£7500	£800
		(c) Compound pin-perf 13½–14×12½		
45	**2**	(1d.) carmine-lake	†	£3750
45*a*	**4**	4d. dull purple	†	—

PRICES. The Pin-perf stamps are very scarce with perforations on all sides and the prices quoted above are for good average specimens.

The note after No. 12 also applies to Nos. 38, 40*a*, 43*a*, 46, 47 and 50.

1860 (Aug). Clean-cut perf 14–16½.

46	**2**	(1d.) rose-red	£190	55·00
		a. Imperf vert (horiz pair)	£1100	
47	**4**	4d. brownish lilac	£200	80·00
48		4d. lilac	—	£350
49		6d. bright yellow-green	£550	£110
50		6d. deep green	£275	£160

1861 (June). Rough perf 14–16½.

52	**2**	(1d.) rose-red (H/S 'CANCELLED' in oval £9000)	£170	42·00
53		(1d.) rose	£180	38·00
54	**4**	4d. brownish lilac	£275	70·00
55		4d. lilac	£600	95·00
		a. Imperf		
56		6d. yellow-green	£325	80·00
57		6d. deep green	£400	70·00
58		1s. indigo	£850	£275
59		1s. deep bluish purple (H/S 'CANCELLED' in oval £9000)	£1500	£425

(Recess D.L.R.)

1862–63. Thick paper.

(a) P 11½, 12

60	**2**	(1d.) crimson-lake	£150	28·00
61	**4**	4d. deep purple	£225	60·00
62		6d. deep green	£1300	85·00
63		1s. bluish slate	£2250	£110
		(b) P 11½, 12, compound with 11		
63*a*	**2**	(1d.) crimson-lake	£1600	£500
63*b*	**4**	6d. deep green	†	£6500
		(c) P 13 (1863)		
64	**2**	(1d.) lake	50·00	28·00
65	**4**	6d. emerald-green	£500	60·00
67		1s. bright mauve	£4500	£300
		(d) P 12½ (1863)		
68	**2**	(1d.) lake	60·00	28·00

1863–80.

(a) Wmk Crown CC. P 12½

69	**2**	(1d.) lake	65·00	8·00
		a. Wmk sideways	£120	21·00
		b. Rose	65·00	3·00
		ba. Imperf (pair)		
		c. Scarlet	70·00	3·50
		d. Carmine	70·00	3·75
		w. Wmk inverted	†	65·00
		x. Wmk reversed	70·00	4·00
		y. Wmk inverted and reversed	—	75·00
70	**4**	4d. bright violet	£130	20·00
		a. Pale mauve	£200	23·00
		b. Dull lilac	£160	23·00
		w. Wmk inverted	£275	75·00
		x. Wmk reversed	£140	21·00
71		4d. grey (1872)	£130	8·00
		a. Bluish grey	£120	8·50
		ax. Wmk reversed	£120	10·00
		w. Wmk inverted	—	75·00
72		6d. emerald-green	£120	18·00
		a. Deep green	£400	9·50
		b. Yellow-green	£110	6·00
		c. Apple-green	£110	7·50
		d. Blue-green	£180	9·00
		w. Wmk inverted	—	75·00
		x. Wmk reversed	£130	7·50
73		1s. bright deep mauve	£190	11·00
		a. Lilac-rose	£160	11·00
		b. Mauve (aniline)	£140	7·00
		bw. Wmk inverted		
		bx. Wmk reversed	—	8·50
74		1s. chrome-yellow (1872)	£170	2·25
		w. Wmk inverted	—	85·00
		x. Wmk reversed	£200	7·50
		(b) P 14 (1876)		
75	**2**	(1d.) lake	50·00	2·75
		a. Bisected (½d.) (*on cover*)	†	£600
		b. Rose-carmine	50·00	2·75
		c. Scarlet	60·00	2·75
		w. Wmk inverted	—	60·00
		x. Wmk reversed	55·00	2·75
76	**4**	4d. bluish grey	£130	2·00
		w. Wmk inverted	†	90·00
		y. Wmk inverted and reversed	†	90·00
77		6d. bright yellow-green	£120	3·00
		a. Deep yellow-green	£150	3·00
		w. Wmk inverted	†	80·00
		x. Wmk reversed	£130	4·00
78		1s. chrome-yellow	£160	4·50
		w. Wmk inverted		
		x. Wmk reversed		
		(c) P 14×12½ (1880)		
79	**4**	6d. yellow-green	†	£6500

The 1s. perforated 12½ in purple-slate is a colour changeling.

5

(Typo D.L.R.)

1869. Wmk Crown CC. P 12½.

87	**5**	5s. rose-lake	£170	75·00

HALFPENNY (6) **ONE PENNY** (7)

1879–82. Surch with Types **6** or **7**. P 14.

(a) Wmk Crown CC (June 1879)

98	**2**	½d. lilac	20·00	13·00
		w. Wmk inverted	£110	38·00
		x. Wmk reversed	20·00	13·00
99		½d. mauve	20·00	13·00
		a. Wmk sideways	50·00	50·00
		w. Wmk inverted	†	£300
		(b) Wmk Crown CA (1882)		
100	**2**	½d. lilac (wmk reversed)	£180	75·00
101		1d. rosy carmine	80·00	2·50
		a. Bisected (½d.) (*on cover*)	†	£550
		x. Wmk reversed	80·00	2·75

1882. Wmk Crown CA. P 14.

102	**4**	4d. bluish grey	£200	17·00
		x. Wmk reversed		

(**8**) Various styles

1882 (9 May). Surch by hand in various styles as T **8** in red or black ink and the original value obliterated by a thick or thin bar or bars, of the same colour.

103		1d. on 6d. (No. 77) (Bk.)	—	£1600
104		1d. on 6d. (No. 77) (R.)	15·00	9·00
		x. Wmk reversed	20·00	14·00
105		1d. on 6d. (No. 77*a*) (R.)	15·00	9·00
		a. Bisected (½d.) (*on cover*)	†	£300

10

11 Britannia

12 Britannia

(Typo D.L.R.)

1883–94. P 14.

		(a) Wmk Crown CA		
106	**10**	½d. dull green	12·00	1·50
107		1d. carmine	25·00	50
		a. Bisected (½d.) (*on cover*)	†	£950
		w. Wmk inverted	†	£200
108		2½d. bright blue	28·00	60
110		4d. grey	5·50	60
		w. Wmk inverted	†	£250
111		6d. olive-black (1884)	8·50	6·50
112		1s. orange-brown (1884)	16·00	6·50
		(b) Wmk Crown CC		
113	**5**	5s. maroon (1894)	55·00	£110
106/113 *Set of 7*			£130	£110
106s/112s Optd 'SPECIMEN' *Set of 6*			£750	

Two types of 1d. value:

ONE PENNY (I) (round 'o')   **ONE PENNY** (II) (oval 'o')

(Typo D.L.R.)

1896 (17 Aug)–**1906.** P 14.

		(a) Wmk Crown CA		
114	**11**	½d. dull purple and green	3·25	30
115		1d. dull purple and rose (I)	3·50	10
		w. Wmk inverted		
116		1d. dull purple and rose (II) (1900)	£325	4·00
117		2½d. dull purple and blue	6·00	20
118		4d. dull purple and orange	10·00	27·00
119		5d. dull purple and mauve	11·00	15·00
120		6d. dull purple and black	7·50	5·50
121		1s. green and brown	7·50	6·50
		(b) Wmk CA over Crown. Ordinary paper		
122	**12**	5s. green and brown	60·00	£100
123		10s. green and ultramarine	£325	£550
124		£1 green and carmine	£200	£325
		a. Chalk-surfaced paper (1906)	£350	
114/124 *Set of 10*			£550	£950
114s/124s Optd 'SPECIMEN' *Set of 10*			£200	

Collectors are warned against apparently postally used examples of this issue which bear 'REGISTRAR-GENERAL' obliterations and are of very little value.

13 Landing of Columbus

(Recess D.L.R.)

1898 (31 July). 400th Anniversary of Discovery of Trinidad. Wmk Crown CC. P 14.

125	**13**	2d. brown and dull violet	3·25	1·25
		s. Optd 'SPECIMEN'	65·00	

3d

(**13a**)

1899 (Oct). No. 119 surch T **13a** by D.L.R. Prepared for use but not issued.

126	**11**	3d. on 5d. dull purple and mauve	£3250
		s. Optd 'SPECIMEN'	75·00

1901–06. Colours changed. Ordinary paper. Wmk Crown CA or CA over Crown (5s.). P 14.

127	**11**	½d. grey-green (1902)	1·00	2·00
128		1d. black/*red* (II)	5·50	10
		a. Value omitted	£35000	
		w. Wmk inverted	†	£200
129		2½d. purple and blue/*blue* (1902)	27·00	30
130		4d. green and blue/*buff* (1902)	4·25	22·00
		a. Chalk-surfaced paper	3·50	14·00
131		1s. black and blue/*yellow* (1903)	19·00	5·50
132	**12**	5s. lilac and mauve	75·00	90·00
		a. Chalk-surfaced paper. Deep purple and mauve (1906)	85·00	£100
127/132 *Set of 6*			£110	£100
127s/132s Optd 'SPECIMEN' *Set of 6*			£150	

A pane of 60 of No. 128a was found at the San Fernando post office of which 51 were subsequently returned to London and destroyed. Only three unused examples, one of which is in the Royal Collection, are now thought to survive; all show traces of the value still present.

1904–09. Ordinary paper (½d., 1d., 2½d. (No. 137)) or chalk-surfaced paper (others). Wmk Mult Crown CA. P 14.

133	**11**	½d. grey-green	10·00	1·00
		a. Chalk-surfaced paper	13·00	2·25
		b. blue-green (1906)	15·00	3·00
134		1d. black/*red* (II)	15·00	10
		a. Chalk-surfaced paper	15·00	10
135		1d. rose-red (1906)	3·50	10
		w. Wmk inverted	†	£225
136		2½d. purple and blue/*blue*	27·00	90
137		2½d. blue (1906)	12·00	15
138		4d. grey and red/*yellow* (1906)	7·00	16·00
		a. Black and red/yellow	13·00	25·00
139		6d. dull purple and black (1905)	24·00	16·00
140		6d. dull and bright purple (1909)	12·00	17·00
141		1s. black and blue/*yellow*	26·00	12·00
142		1s. purple and blue/*golden yellow* (1906)	18·00	29·00
143		1s. black/*green* (1909)	3·00	1·25
144	**12**	5s. deep purple and mauve (1907)	80·00	£110
145		£1 green and carmine (1907)	£300	£375
133/145 *Set of 13*			£475	£500
135s/143s (*ex* Nos. 136, 139, 141) Optd 'SPECIMEN' *Set of 6*			£150	

No. 135 is from a new die, the letters of 'ONE PENNY' being short and thick, while the point of Britannia's spear breaks the uppermost horizontal line of shading in the background.

14

15

16

(Typo D.L.R.)

1909 (Dec). Wmk Mult Crown CA. P 14.

146	**14**	½d. green	10·00	10
		y. Wmk inverted and reversed	—	£200
147	**15**	1d. rose-red	14·00	10
148	**16**	2½d. blue	27·00	4·50
146/148 *Set of 3*			45·00	4·50
146s/148s Optd 'SPECIMEN' *Set of 3*			85·00	

TOBAGO

Although a Colonial Postmaster was appointed in January 1765 it was not until 1841 that the British GPO established a branch office at Scarborough, the island capital, to handle the overseas mail.

The stamps of Great Britain were in use from May 1858 to the end of April 1860 when the control of the postal service passed to the local authorities.

From April 1860 Nos. CC1/CC2 were again used on overseas mail, pending the introduction of Tobago stamps in 1879.

SCARBOROUGH

CROWNED-CIRCLE HANDSTAMPS

CC **1**

CC **2**

CC1	CC **1** TOBAGO (R.) (31.10.1851)	*Price on cover*	£1300
CC2	CC **2** TOBAGO (R.) (1875)	*Price on cover*	£5000

Stamps of GREAT BRITAIN cancelled 'A14' as T Z **1** of Jamaica.

1858–60.

Z1	1d. rose-red (1857), perf 14	£900
Z2	4d. rose (1857)	£425
Z3	6d. lilac (1856)	£275
Z4	1s. green (1856)	£2250

PRICES FOR STAMPS ON COVER TO 1945

Nos. 1/2	—
Nos. 3/4	*from* × 30
Nos. 5/7	—
Nos. 8/12	*from* × 10
Nos. 13/19	*from* × 6
Nos. 20/24	*from* × 40
Nos. 26/33	*from* × 25

CANCELLATIONS. Beware of early stamps of Tobago with fiscal endorsements removed and forged wide 'A14' postmarks added.

1

2

2½ PENCE

(**3**)

(Typo D.L.R.)

1879 (1 Aug). Fiscal stamps issued provisionally pending the arrival of stamps inscr 'POSTAGE'. Wmk Crown CC. P 14.

1	**1**	1d. rose	£140	£100
2		3d. blue	£140	85·00
3		6d. orange	65·00	80·00
		w. Wmk inverted	£140	£180
4		1s. green	£400	80·00
		a. Bisected (6d.) (*on cover*)	†	—
5		5s. slate	£900	£800
6		£1 mauve	£4250	

The stamps were introduced for fiscal purposes on 1 July 1879.

Stamps of T **1**, watermark Crown CA, are fiscals which were never admitted to postal use.

1880 (Nov). No. 3 bisected vertically and surch with pen and ink.

7	**1**	1d. on half of 6d. orange	£6000	£850
		w. Wmk inverted	£7000	£1200

(Typo D.L.R.)

1880 (20 Dec). Wmk Crown CC. P 14.

8	**2**	½d. purple-brown	75·00	£110
9		1d. Venetian red	£140	70·00
		a. Bisected (½d.) (*on cover*)	†	£2000
10		4d. yellow-green	£300	38·00
		a. Bisected (2d.) (*on cover*)	†	£2000
		b. Malformed 'CE' in 'PENCE'	£1900	£400
		w. Wmk inverted	—	£250
11		6d. stone	£400	£120
12		1s. yellow-ochre	£110	£140
		w. Wmk inverted	£325	

For illustration of Nos. 10b, 18a, 22b, 30b, 31a and 33b see above No. 4 of Dominica.

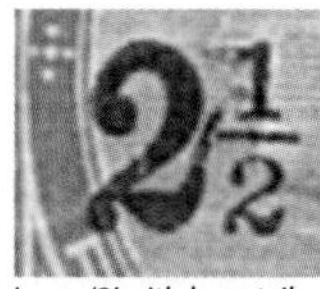

Large '2' with long tail (R. 2/6, 4/6, 6/6, 8/6 and 10/6)

1883 (Apr). No. 11 surch with T **3** by the Government Printing Office, Scarborough.

13	**2**	2½d. on 6d. stone	£100	£100
		a. Surch double	£4000	£2250
		b. Large '2' with long tail	£190	£200

Slash flaw

Slash flaw repaired

'SLASH' FLAW. Stamps as T **2** were produced from Key and Duty plates. On the Key plate used for consignments between 2 October 1892 and 16 December 1896, damage in the form of a large cut or 'slash' shows after the 'E' of 'POSTAGE' on R. 1/4.

After 1896 an attempt was made to repair the 'slash'. This resulted in its disappearance, but left an incomplete edge to the circular frame at right.

1882–84. Wmk Crown CA. P 14.

14	**2**	½d. purple-brown (1882)	3·50	21·00
15		1d. Venetian red (1882)	15·00	3·75
		a. Bisected diag (½d.) (*on cover*)		
16		2½d. dull blue (1883)	65·00	3·50
		a. Bright blue	16·00	1·50
		b. Ultramarine	17·00	1·50
		c. 'Slash' flaw	£140	60·00
		ca. 'Slash' flaw repaired	£225	
18		4d. yellow-green (1882)	£225	95·00
		a. Malformed 'CE' in 'PENCE'	£1400	£500
19		6d. stone (1884)	£550	£500

1885–96. Colours changed and new value. Wmk Crown CA. P 14.

20	**2**	½d. dull green (1886)	6·00	2·50
		a. 'Slash' flaw	80·00	70·00
		ab. 'Slash' flaw repaired	£140	
		w. Wmk inverted		
21		1d. carmine (1889)	9·50	2·00
		a. 'Slash' flaw	£110	60·00
		ab. 'Slash' flaw repaired	£170	
22		4d. grey (1885)	9·50	4·00
		a. Imperf (pair)	£2000	
		b. Malformed 'CE' in 'PENCE'	90·00	£100
		c. 'Slash' flaw	£190	£200
		ca. 'Slash' flaw repaired	£250	
23		6d. orange-brown (1886)	2·50	9·50
		a. 'Slash' flaw	£190	£275
		ab. 'Slash' flaw repaired	£275	
24		1s. olive-yellow (1894)	4·75	32·00
		a. Pale olive-yellow	7·00	
		b. 'Slash' flaw	£250	£550
		ba. 'Slash' flaw repaired	£375	
24c		1s. orange-brown (1896)	28·00	£140
		ca. 'Slash' flaw	£425	
20s/23s (*ex* 4d.) Optd 'SPECIMEN' *Set of 3*			£170	

No. 24c was printed in the colour of the 6d. by mistake.

½d

½ PENNY (**4**)   **2½ PENCE** (**5**)   **POSTAGE** (**6**)

1886–89. Nos. 16, 19 and 23 surch as T **4** by the Government Printing Office, Scarborough.

26 ½d. on 2½d. dull blue (4.86) 11·00 28·00
a. Figure further from word 40·00 80·00
b. Surch double £2750 £2500
c. Surch omitted. Vert pair with No. 26 £15000
d. Ditto with No. 26a £25000
27 ½d. on 6d. stone (1.86) 4·00 28·00
a. Figure further from word 26·00 £110
b. Surch inverted £3250
c. Surch double £3750
28 ½d. on 6d. orange-brown (8.87) £150 £200
a. Figure further from word £375 £450
b. Surch double — £2750
29 1d. on 2½d. dull blue (7.89) £110 24·00
a. Figure further from word £300 90·00

The surcharge is in a setting of 12 (two rows of six), repeated five times in a pane.

The measurements given below (and below Nos. 31 and 33) are to the nearest ¼ mm and are for the space between the upright of '1' of '½' or '1' and the upright of the 'P'.

On Nos. 26/29 the normal spacing is 3¼ mm, but there are slightly narrower spacings on stamps 1 (*3 mm*) and 7 (*2¾ mm*) of most settings. The listed wider spacing (*4¼ mm*) occurs on stamp 10 of Nos. 26, 28, one of the four settings of No. 27 and one of the two settings of No. 29. It occurs on stamps 3 and 10 of a second setting of No. 27 and on stamp 7 in a second setting of No. 29. The 'P' may be found raised in various positions in some settings.

1891–92. No. 22 surch with Types **4** or **5** by the Government Printing Office, Scarborough.

30 ½d. on 4d. grey (3.92) 30·00 85·00
a. Figure further from word 75·00
b. Malformed 'CE' in 'PENCE' £325 £750
c. Surch double £3500
31 2½d. on 4d. grey (8.91) 25·00 10·00
a. Malformed 'CE' in 'PENCE' £200 £200
b. Surch double £3500

On Nos. 30/31 the normal spacing is 2¾ mm, but there is a slightly wider space (*3 mm*) on stamps 3 and 7 of No. 30 and stamp 12 of No. 31. There is a slightly narrower space (*2½ mm*) on stamp 9 of No. 30. A new setting of No. 30 gave rise to the listed wider space (*3¼ mm*) on stamp 7.

1896. Fiscal stamp (T **1**, value in second colour, wmk Crown CA, P 14), surch with T **6** by the Government Printing Office, Scarborough.

33 ½d. on 4d. lilac and carmine £100 55·00
a. Space between '½' and 'd' £140 80·00
b. Malformed 'CE' in 'PENCE' £1300 £800
c. Surch double

On No. 33 there are two settings, a scarcer one with a normal space of 3½ mm between the '1' of '½' and the upright of the 'd' and a more common one with wide spacings on stamp 5 (*5 mm*), stamps 6 and 8 (*4½ mm*) and stamps 9 and 11 (*4¼ mm*).

Tobago became a ward of Trinidad on 1 January 1899. Stamps of Trinidad were used until issues inscribed 'TRINIDAD AND TOBAGO' appeared in 1913.

TRINIDAD AND TOBAGO

PRICES FOR STAMPS ON COVER TO 1945

Nos. 149/155	*from* × 3
Nos. 156/157	—
Nos. 174/189	*from* × 10
Nos. 206/256	*from* × 2
Nos. D18/D25	*from* × 12

17

18

(Typo D.L.R.)

1913–23. Ordinary paper (½d. to 2½d.) or chalk-surfaced paper (others). Wmk Mult Crown CA. P 14.

149 **17** ½d. green 3·00 10
a. Yellow-green (1915) 6·00 20
b. Blue-green (thick paper) (1917) 7·00 1·00
ba. Wmk sideways † £2000
c. Blue-green/bluish (3.18) 15·00 12·00
w. Wmk inverted
150 1d. bright red 1·50 10
a. Red (thick paper) (1916) 3·25 30
b. Pink (1918) 50·00 4·50
c. Carmine-red (5.18) 2·50 10
w. Wmk inverted
151 2½d. ultramarine 13·00 50
a. Bright blue (thick paper) (1916) 6·50 50
b. Bright blue (thin paper) (1918) 8·00 50
152 4d. black and red/*yellow* 70 6·00
a. Ordinary paper
b. White back (12.13) 1·75 11·00
bs. Optd 'SPECIMEN' 25·00
c. On lemon (1917) 10·00
d. On pale yellow (1923) 6·50 12·00
ds. Optd 'SPECIMEN' 40·00
153 6d. dull and reddish purple 10·00 11·00
a. Dull and deep purple (1918) 21·00 15·00
b. Dull purple and mauve (2.18) 10·00 8·00
154 1s. black/*green* 2·00 4·50
a. White back 1·50 16·00
as. Optd 'SPECIMEN' 25·00
b. On blue-green, olive back 18·00 9·00
c. On emerald back 1·50 3·00
cs. Optd 'SPECIMEN' 40·00
155 **18** 5s. dull purple and mauve (1914) 75·00 £110
a. Deep purple and mauve (1918) 80·00 £110
b. Lilac and violet £120 £170
c. Dull purple and violet £130 £180
d. Brown-purple and violet £110 £140
156 £1 grey-green and carmine (1914) £250 £325
a. Deep yellow-green and carmine (1918) £250 £300
149/156 *Set of* 8 £325 £400
149s/156s Optd 'SPECIMEN' *Set of* 8 £275

No. 156*a* is from a plate showing background lines very worn.

18a

1914 (18 Sept). Red Cross Label authorised for use as ½d. stamp. Typo. P 11–12.

157 **18a** (½d.) red 28·00 £225

The above was authorised for internal postal use on one day only, to frank circular letters appealing for funds for the Red Cross. It had gone on sale the previous day (advertised price 24c. per 100) but has long been accepted as a ½d. value as this was the rate it covered during its one day of postal validity. The used price is for stamp on cover cancelled on 18 Sept 1914. Labels affixed to earlier or later items of mail had no postal validity.

21. 10. 15.
(19)

19. 10. 16.
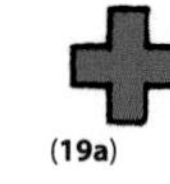
(19a)

1915 (21 Oct). Optd with T **19**. Cross in red with outline and date in black.

174 **17** 1d. red 3·25 6·00
a. Cross 2 mm to right 40·00 75·00
b. '1' of '15' forked foot 19·00 38·00
c. Broken '0' in '10' 19·00 38·00

The varieties occur in the following positions on the pane of 60: a. No. 11. b. No. 42. c. No. 45. Variety a. is only found on the right-hand pane.

1916 (19 Oct). Optd with T **19a**. Cross in red with outline and date in black.

175 **17** 1d. scarlet 50 2·00
a. No stop after '16' 20·00 60·00
b. '19.10.16' omitted
c. Red shading on cross omitted

No. 175a appears on stamp No. 36 on the right-hand pane only.

PRINTING METHOD. The 'War Tax' overprints, Types **19a** to **26a**, were lithographed locally by the Govt Printer, using settings of 120.

FORGERIES. Beware of forgeries of the 'War Tax' errors listed below. There are also other unlisted errors which are purely fakes.

WAR TAX (19b) | WAR TAX (20) | WAR TAX (21) | WAR TAX (22)

1917 (29 Mar). Optd with T **19b**.

176 **17** 1d. red 4·75 3·25
a. Opt inverted £225 £300
b. Scarlet 4·75 3·25
w. Wmk inverted

1917 (May). Optd with T **20**.

177 **17** ½d. green (10.5.17) 1·50 40
a. Pair, one without opt £900 £1400
178 1d. red (7.5.17) 4·75 2·25
a. Pair, one without opt £900 £1400
b. Scarlet 6·50 1·00
ba. Opt double £160

The varieties without overprint were caused by the overprint being shifted over towards the left so that some stamps in the right-hand column of each pane escaped.

1917 (June). Optd with T **21**.

179 **17** ½d. yellow-green (21.6.17) 8·00 28·00
a. Pale green 1·00 17·00
b. Deep green 4·00 17·00
180 1d. red (25.6.17) 15 75
a. Pair, one without opt

No. 180a was caused by a shifting of the overprint to the left-hand side, but only a few stamps on the right-hand vertical row escaped the overprint and such pairs are very rare.

1917 (21 July–Sept). Optd with T **22**.

181 **17** ½d. yellow-green 7·50 15·00
a. Deep green 10 5·00
aw. Wmk inverted £150
182 1d. red (6.9.17) 7·50 1·00

WAR TAX (23) | WAR TAX (24) | WAR TAX (25)

1917 (1 Sept). Optd with T **23** (closer spacing between lines of opt).

183 **17** ½d. deep green 10 3·00
a. Pale yellow-green
184 1d. red 70·00 60·00

1917 (31 Oct). Optd with T **24**.

185 **17** 1d. scarlet 60 1·00
a. Opt inverted £170

1918 (7 Jan). Optd with T **25**.

186 **17** 1d. scarlet 2·25 15
a. Opt double £225 £225
b. Opt inverted £150 £160

War Tax (26) | War Tax (26a)

27

1918 (13 Feb–Dec). Optd with T **26**.

187 **17** ½d. bluish green 10 3·75
a. Pair, one without opt £1500
y. Wmk inverted and reversed £150
188 1d. scarlet 2·25 1·25
a. Opt double £160
b. Rose-red (12.18) 10 60

Both values exist with 'Tax' omitted, the ½d. due to a paper fold and the 1d. due to misplacement.

1918 (14 Sept). New printing as T **26**, but 19 stamps on each sheet have the letters of the word 'Tax' wider spaced, the 'x' being to the right of 'r' of 'War' as T **26a**. Thick bluish paper.

189 **17** 1d. scarlet ('Tax' spaced) 8·00 25·00
a. Opt double £300
b. Pair, one without opt £1600
c. Opt inverted on back £1600

The sheet positions of No. 189 are as follows: Left pane; R. 3/2, 3/4, 5/2, 5/6, 6/3, 7/6, 8/1, 8/5 and 10/3. Right pane; R. 1/3, 2/2, 5/3, 5/5, 6/6, 7/3, 8/6, 9/3 and 9/4.

The varieties 189b and 189c are caused by a paper fold.

1921–22. Chalk-surfaced paper (6d. to £1). Wmk Mult Script CA. P 14.

206 **17** ½d. green 3·50 2·25
207 1d. scarlet 60 30
208 1d. brown (17.2.22) 60 1·50
209 2d. grey (17.2.22) 1·00 1·25
210 2½d. bright blue 80 24·00
211 3d. bright blue (17.2.22) 8·50 3·00
212 6d. dull and bright purple 5·00 16·00
213 **18** 5s. dull purple and purple (1921) 75·00 £170
a. deep purple and purple (1922) £100 £180
215 £1 green and carmine £180 £375
206/215 *Set of* 9 £225 £550
206s/215s Optd 'SPECIMEN' *Set of* 9 £300

(Typo D.L.R.)

1922–28. Chalk-surfaced paper (4d. to £1). P 14.

(a) Wmk Mult Crown CA

216 **27** 4d. black and red/*pale yellow* 5·00 21·00
217 1s. black/*emerald* 6·50 9·50

(b) Wmk Mult Script CA

218 **27** ½d. green 50 10
219 1d. brown 50 10
w. Wmk inverted 35·00 38·00
220 1½d. bright rose 3·75 20
aw. Wmk inverted 70·00 70·00
b. Scarlet 2·25 30
bw. Wmk inverted
222 2d. grey 60 1·25
w. Wmk inverted — £170
223 3d. blue 60 1·25
224 4d. black and red/*pale yellow* (1928) 3·50 3·25
w. Wmk inverted — £325
225 6d. dull purple and bright magenta 2·50 27·00
226 6d. green and red/*emerald* (1924) 1·25 60
227 1s. black/*emerald* 5·50 1·75
228 5s. dull purple and mauve 32·00 38·00
229 £1 green and bright rose £150 £275
216/229 *Set of* 13 £180 £325
216s/229s Optd 'SPECIMEN' *Set of* 13 £400

(New Currency. 100 cents = 1 West Indian dollar)

28 First Boca

29 Imperial College of Tropical Agriculture

30 Mt. Irvine Bay, Tobago

31 Discovery of Lake Asphalt

32 Queen's Park, Savannah

33 Town Hall, San Fernando

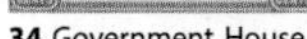

34 Government House

35 Memorial Park

36 Blue Basin

(Des and Recess B.W.)

1935 (1 Feb)–**37**. Types **28/36**. Wmk Mult Script CA (sideways). P 12.

230	**28**	1c. blue and green	40	85
		a. Perf 12½ (1936)	30	10
231	**29**	2c. ultramarine and yellow-brown	3·00	1·00
		a. Perf 12½ (1936)	3·00	10
232	**30**	3c. black and scarlet	2·00	30
		a. Perf 12½ (1936)	3·50	30
233	**31**	6c. sepia and blue	4·25	2·50
		a. Perf 12½ (1937)	18·00	12·00
234	**32**	8c. sage-green and vermilion	3·75	3·50
235	**33**	12c. black and violet	4·50	1·75
		a. Perf 12½ (1937)	20·00	14·00
236	**34**	24c. black and olive-green	10·00	2·75
		a. Perf 12½ (1937)	30·00	23·00
237	**35**	48c. deep green	11·00	15·00
238	**36**	72c. myrtle-green and carmine	45·00	30·00
230/238 *Set of* 9			75·00	50·00
230s/238s Perf 'SPECIMEN' *Set of* 9			£180	

The original printings of Nos. 230/238 were P 12 (line). Later printings (Nos. 230a/236a) were comb perforated (exact gauge P 12·7×12·6).

1935 (6 May). Silver Jubilee. As Nos. 91/94 of Antigua, but ptd by B.W. P 11×12.

239	2c. ultramarine and grey-black	30	75
	a. Extra flagstaff	35·00	55·00
	b. Short extra flagstaff	95·00	
	c. Lightning conductor	50·00	75·00
	d. Flagstaff on right-hand turret	£130	£160
	e. Double flagstaff	£140	
240	3c. deep blue and scarlet	30	2·50
	a. Extra flagstaff	60·00	£120
	c. Lightning conductor	80·00	
241	6c. brown and deep blue	3·00	2·50
	a. Extra flagstaff	90·00	£150
	b. Short extra flagstaff	£200	
	c. Lightning conductor	£120	£180
242	24c. slate and purple	14·00	27·00
	a. Extra flagstaff	£180	£325
	c. Lightning conductor	£200	
	d. Flagstaff on right-hand turret	£325	
	e. Double flagstaff	£350	
239/242 *Set of* 4		16·00	29·00
239s/242s Perf 'SPECIMEN' *Set of* 4		£110	

For illustrations of plate varieties see Omnibus section following Zanzibar.

1937 (12 May). Coronation. As Nos. 95/97 of Antigua, but ptd by D.L.R. P 14.

243	1c. green	15	60
244	2c. yellow-brown	40	15
245	8c. orange	1·10	2·25
243/245 *Set of* 3		1·50	2·75
243s/245s Perf 'SPECIMEN' *Set of* 3		95·00	

37 First Boca

38 Imperial College of Tropical Agriculture

39 Mt. Irvine Bay, Tobago

40 Memorial Park

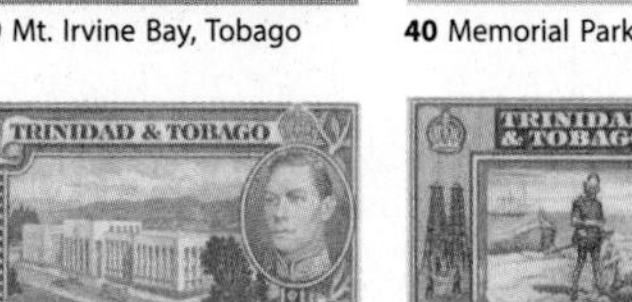

41 GPO and Treasury

42 Discovery of Lake Asphalt

43 Queen's Park, Savannah

44 Town Hall, San Fernando

45 Government House

46 Blue Basin

47 King George VI

(Recess B.W.)

1938 (2 May)–**44**. Types **37/47**. Wmk Mult Script CA (sideways on 1c. to 60c.).

		(a) P 11½×11		
246	**37**	1c. blue and green	1·00	30
247	**38**	2c. blue and yellow-brown	1·25	20
248	**39**	3c. black and scarlet	11·00	1·00
248*a*		3c. green and purple-brown (1941)	30	20
		ab. 'A' of 'CA' missing from wmk		
249	**40**	4c. chocolate	30·00	3·00
249*a*		4c. scarlet (1941)	50	1·00
249*b*	**41**	5c. magenta (1.5.41)	50	15
250	**42**	6c. sepia and blue	2·75	80
251	**43**	8c. sage-green and vermilion	2·75	1·00
		a. 'A' of 'CA' missing from wmk	£950	
252	**44**	12c. black and purple	35·00	2·50
		a. Black and slate-purple (1944)	6·00	10
253	**45**	24c. black and olive-green	9·00	10
254	**46**	60c. myrtle-green and carmine	17·00	1·00
		(b) T **47**. *P 12*		
255	**47**	$1.20 blue-green (1.40)	13·00	1·75
256		$4.80 rose-carmine (1.40)	40·00	55·00
246/256 *Set of* 14			£110	60·00
246s/256s (*ex* 5c.) Perf 'SPECIMEN' *Set of* 13			£400	

1946 (1 Oct). Victory. As Nos. 110/111 of Antigua.

257	3c. chocolate	10	10
258	6c. blue	55	1·50
257s/258s Perf 'SPECIMEN' *Set of* 2		85·00	

1948 (22 Nov). Royal Silver Wedding. As Nos. 112/113 of Antigua, but $4.80 in recess.

259	3c. red-brown	10	10
260	$4.80 carmine	30·00	48·00

1949 (10 Oct). 75th Anniversary of UPU. As Nos. 114/117 of Antigua.

261	5c. bright reddish purple	35	1·00
262	6c. deep blue	2·00	2·50
263	12c. violet	55	1·75
264	24c. olive	55	1·25
261/264 *Set of* 4		3·00	6·00

1951 (16 Feb). Inauguration of BWI University College. As Nos. 118/119 of Antigua.

265	3c. green and red-brown	20	1·25
266	12c. black and reddish violet	30	1·25

Nos. 265/266 are inscribed 'TRINIDAD'.

48 First Boca

49 Mt. Irvine Bay, Tobago

(Recess B.W.)

1953 (20 Apr)–**59**. Designs previously used for King George VI issue, but with portrait of Queen Elizabeth II as is T **48** (1c., 2c., 12c.) or T **49** (other values). Wmk Mult Script CA. P 12 (dollar values) or 11½×11 (others).

267	**48**	1c. blue and green	20	40
		a. Blue and bluish green (10.6.59)	6·00	7·00
268	**38**	2c. indigo and orange-brown	20	40
269	**49**	3c. deep emerald and purple-brown	20	10
270	**40**	4c. scarlet	30	40
271	**41**	5c. magenta	40	30
272	**42**	6c. brown and greenish blue	60	30
273	**43**	8c. deep yellow-green and orange-red	2·50	30
274	**44**	12c. black and purple	40	10
275	**45**	24c. black and yellow-olive	2·75	30
		a. Black and olive (16.11.55)	6·50	1·50
		b. Black and greenish olive (12.12.56)	11·00	1·25
276	**46**	60c. blackish green and carmine	27·00	1·75
277	**47**	$1.20 bluish green	1·00	2·25
		a. Perf 11½ (19.1.55)	2·00	30
278		$4.80 cerise	9·00	27·00
		a. Perf 11½ (16.12.55)	12·00	20·00
267/278a *Set of* 12			40·00	22·00

1953 (3 June). Coronation. As No. 120 of Antigua.

279	3c. black and green	30	10

ONE CENT

(**50**)

1956 (20 Dec). No. 268 surch with T **50**.

280	1c. on 2c. indigo and orange-brown	1·25	2·25

1958 (22 Apr). Inauguration of British Caribbean Federation. As Nos. 135/137 of Antigua.

281	5c. deep green	60	10
282	6c. blue	65	1·50
283	12c. scarlet	70	10
281/283 *Set of* 3		1·75	1·50

PRINTERS. Nos. 284 to 354 were printed in photogravure by Harrison & Sons, unless otherwise stated.

51 Cipriani Memorial

52 Queen's Hall

53 Whitehall

54 Treasury Building

55 Governor General's House

56 General Hospital, San Fernando

57 Oil refinery

58 Crest

58a Coat of Arms

59 Scarlet Ibis

60 Pitch Lake

61 Mohammed Jinnah Mosque

62 Anthurium Lilies

63 Copper-rumped Hummingbird

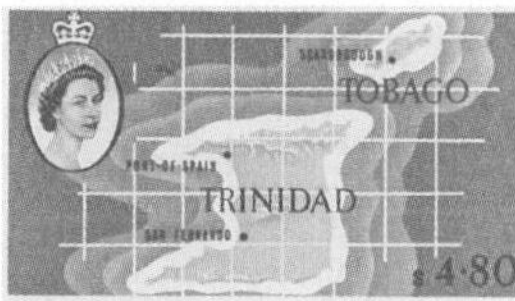

64 Map of Trinidad and Tobago

(Des V. Whiteley (1, 2, 12, 35, 60c., $4.80), J. Matthews (5c.), H. Baxter (6, 8, 10, 15c.), M. Goaman (25c., 50c., $1.20))

1960 (24 Sept)–**67**. Designs as Types **51/64**. W w **12** (upright). P 13½×14½ (1c., 60c., $1.20, $4.80) or 14½×13½ (others).

284	**51**	1c. stone and black	1·25	20
285	**52**	2c. bright blue	65	20
		a. Blue (23.6.64)	6·00	1·00
		b. New blue (18.4.67)	6·00	1·00
		w. Wmk inverted	7·50	
286	**53**	5c. chalky blue	10	10
		w. Wmk inverted	9·50	2·25
287	**54**	6c. red-brown	1·00	1·00
		a. Pale chestnut (13.4.67)	9·00	3·25
		w. Wmk inverted	70·00	70·00
288	**55**	8c. yellow-green	10	1·50
289	**56**	10c. deep lilac	10	10
290	**57**	12c. vermilion	10	1·25
291	**58**	15c. orange	3·50	1·00
291*a*	**58a**	15c. orange (15.9.64)	15·00	10
292	**59**	25c. rose-carmine and deep blue	80	10
		w. Wmk inverted	3·50	1·75

293 **60** 35c. emerald and black .... 3·75 10
w. Wmk inverted .... — £225
294 **61** 50c. yellow, grey and blue .... 35 1·50
295 **62** 60c. vermilion, yellow-green and indigo 55 30
a. Perf 14½ (17.7.65*) .... £140 50·00
296 **63** $1.20 multicoloured .... 15·00 4·00
297 **64** $4.80 apple-green and pale blue .... 22·00 21·00
284/297 *Set of* 15 .... 50·00 29·00

* This is the earliest date reported to us. It comes from an unannounced printing which was despatched to Trinidad on 3 December 1964.

The 2, 5, 6, 12 and 25c. exist with PVA gum as well as gum arabic. See also No. 317.

65 Scouts and Gold Wolf Badge

1961 (4 Apr). Second Caribbean. Scout Jamboree. Design multicoloured; background colours below. W w **12**. P 13½×14½.

298 **65** 8c. light green 15 10
299 25c. light blue 15 10
w. Wmk inverted .... £170 85·00

INDEPENDENT

66 *Buccoo Reef* (painting by Carlisle Chang) **71** Protein Foods

1962 (31 Aug). Independence. T **66** and similar horiz designs. W w **12**. P 14½.

300 5c. bluish green 10 10
301 8c. grey .... 40 1·00
302 25c. reddish violet 15 10
303 35c. brown, yellow, green and black .... 2·25 15
304 60c. red, black and blue .... 2·75 3·75
300/304 *Set of* 5 .... 5·00 4·50

Designs: 5c. T **66**; 8c. Piarco Air Terminal; 25c. Hilton Hotel, Port-of-Spain; 35c. Greater Bird of Paradise and map; 60c. Scarlet Ibis and map.

(Des M. Goaman)

1963 (4 June). Freedom from Hunger. W w **12**. P 14×13½.

305 **71** 5c. brown-red 40 10
306 8c. yellow-bistre 65 85
307 25c. violet-blue 90 20
305/307 *Set of* 3 .... 1·75 1·00

72 Jubilee Emblem

1964 (15 Sept). Golden Jubilee of Trinidad and Tobago Girl Guides' Association. W w **12**. P 14½×14.

308 **72** 6c. yellow, ultramarine and rose-red 10 70
309 25c. yellow, ultramarine and bright blue 15 20
310 35c. yellow, ultramarine and emerald-green 20 20
308/310 *Set of* 3 .... 40 1·00

73 ICY Emblem

(Litho State Ptg Wks, Vienna)

1965 (15 Nov). International Co-operation Year. P 12.

311 **73** 35c. red-brown, deep green and ochre-yellow 65 20

74 Eleanor Roosevelt, Flag and UN Emblem

1965 (10 Dec). Eleanor Roosevelt Memorial Foundation. W w **12**. P 13½×14.

312 **74** 25c. black, red and ultramarine 15 10

FIFTH YEAR OF
INDEPENDENCE
31st AUGUST 1967

75 Parliament Building (**79**)

1966 (8 Feb). Royal Visit. T **75** and similar horiz designs. Multicoloured. W w **12** (sideways). P 13½×14½.

313 5c. Type **75** .... 1·10 10
314 8c. Map, Royal Yacht *Britannia* and Arms .... 1·90 1·00
315 25c. Map and flag .... 1·90 55
316 35c. Flag and panorama .... 1·90 70
313/316 *Set of* 4 .... 6·00 2·00

1966 (15 Nov). As No. 284 but W w **12** (sideways*).

317 1c. stone and black 10 70
w. Wmk Crown to right of CA ....

* The normal sideways watermark shows Crown to left of CA, *as seen from the back of the stamp.*

No. 317 exists with PVA gum as well as gum arabic.

1967 (31 Aug). Fifth Year of Independence. Nos. 288/289, 291*a* and 295 optd as T **79**.

318 8c. yellow-green 10 10
319 10c. deep lilac 10 10
320 15c. orange 10 10
321 60c. vermilion, yellow-green and indigo. 25 15
318/321 *Set of* 4 .... 30 30

On No. 321 the overprint is in five lines.

80 Musical Instruments **81** Calypso King

1968 (17 Feb). Trinidad Carnival. Horiz designs as T **80** (15 and 25c.), or vert designs as T **81** (35 and 60c.). Multicoloured. P 12.

322 5c. Type **80** 10 10
323 10c. Type **81** 10 10
324 15c. Steel band 15 10
325 25c. Carnival procession 20 10
326 35c. Carnival King 20 10
327 60c. Carnival Queen .... 40 1·00
322/327 *Set of* 6 .... 1·00 1·10

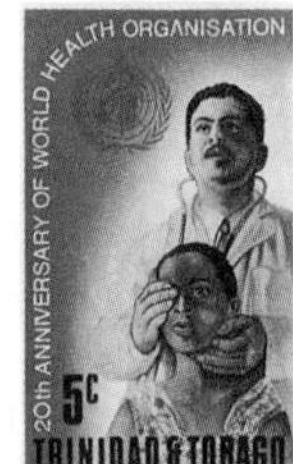

86 Doctor giving Eye-Test **87** Peoples of the World and Emblem

1968 (7 May). 20th Anniversary of World Health Organisation. W w **12** (sideways). P 14.

328 **86** 5c. red, blackish brown and gold 15 10
329 25c. orange, blackish brown and gold 35 15
330 35c. bright blue, black and gold 40 25
328/330 *Set of* 3 .... 80 45

1968 (5 Aug). Human Rights Year. W w **12** (sideways). P 13½×14.

331 **87** 5c. cerise, black and greenish yellow 10 10
332 10c. new blue, black and greenish yellow 15 10
333 25c. apple-green, black and greenish yellow 30 15
331/333 *Set of* 3 .... 45 30

88 Cycling

(Des G. Vasarhelyi. Islands additionally die-stamped in gold (5c. to 35c.))

1968 (14 Oct). Olympic Games, Mexico. T **88** and similar horiz designs. Multicoloured. W w **12**. P 14.

334 5c. Type **88** 80 10
w. Wmk inverted .... † £200
335 15c. Weightlifting 20 10
w. Wmk inverted .... 9·00
336 25c. Relay-racing 20 10
337 35c. Sprinting 20 10
338 $1.20 Maps of Mexico and Trinidad .... 1·60 1·50
334/338 *Set of* 5 .... 2·75 1·60

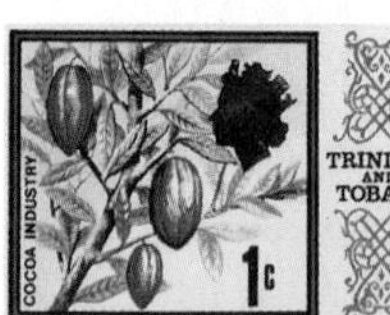

93 Cocoa Beans **94** Green Hermit

(Des G. Vasarhelyi. Queen's profile die-stamped in gold (G.) or silver (S.), also the Islands on 20, 25c.)

1969 (1 Apr)–**72**. Designs as Types **93**/**94**. W w **12** (sideways* on 1 to 8c., 40c., 50c.). Chalk-surfaced paper. P 14×14½ ($2.50, $5) or 14 (others).

339 1c. multicoloured (S.) .... 20 1·25
a. Queen's head omitted £170
bw. Wmk Crown to right of CA ....
c. Glazed, ordinary paper (24.3.72) 10 45
cw. Wmk Crown to right of CA ....
340 3c. multicoloured (G.) 10 10
aw. Wmk Crown to right of CA ....
b. Glazed, ordinary paper (24.3.72) 10 10
bw. Wmk Crown to right of CA ....
341 5c. multicoloured (G.) .... 3·50 10
a. Glazed, ordinary paper (24.3.72) .... 2·00 10
ab. Queen's head omitted £250
ac. Imperf (pair) £275
ad. Ditto and Queen's head omitted £400
aw. Wmk Crown to right of CA .... 7·50
342 6c. multicoloured (G.) 10 10
a. Queen's head omitted £300
b. Imperf (pair) £350
c. Glazed, ordinary paper (24.3.72) .... 2·75 10·00
cw. Wmk Crown to right of CA .... 4·75
343 8c. multicoloured (S.) .... 5·00 3·25
344 10c. multicoloured (G.) .... 4·50 20
a. Glazed, ordinary paper (24.3.72) .... 2·00 20
aw. Wmk inverted .... 11·00
345 12c. multicoloured (blue-green leaves) (S.) .... 15 3·75
a. Myrtle-green leaves .... 4·75 8·50
b. Glazed, ordinary paper (24.3.72) .... 50 6·50
346 15c. multicoloured (S.) 10 10
a. Queen's head omitted £475
b. Glazed, ordinary paper (24.3.72) 20 10
347 20c. scarlet, black and grey (G.) 30 10
a. Glazed, ordinary paper (24.3.72) .... 50 3·75
348 25c. scarlet, black and new blue (S.) .... 30 1·00
a. Glazed, ordinary paper (24.3.72) .... 4·75 4·00
ab. Silver (Queen's head and island) omitted £325
349 30c. multicoloured (S.) 30 10
a. Glazed, ordinary paper (24.3.72) .... 50 2·25
aw. Wmk inverted .... 18·00
350 40c. multicoloured (G.) .... 5·50 10
a. Glazed, ordinary paper (24.3.72) .... 6·50 60
351 50c. multicoloured (S.) .... 30 4·25
a. Glazed, ordinary paper (24.3.72) .... 1·50 8·50
aw. Wmk Crown to right of CA .... 7·00
352 $1 multicoloured (G.) 60 15
a. Gold (Queen's head) omitted £275
b. Glazed, ordinary paper (24.3.72) .... 1·50 7·00
ba. Gold (Queen's head) omitted ....
353 $2.50 multicoloured (G.) .... 1·00 5·50
a. Perf 14 (1972) .... 4·00 12·00
aw. Wmk inverted .... 40·00
354 $5 multicoloured (G.) .... 1·00 5·50
a. Gold (Queen's head) omitted £450
b. Perf 14 (1972) .... 5·00 25·00
bw. Wmk inverted .... 38·00 50·00
339/354 *Set of* 16 .... 20·00 22·00
339c/352b *Set of* 13 .... 21·00 38·00

Designs: Horiz 1c. T **93**. As T **93**—3c. Sugar refinery; 5c. Rufous vented Chachalaca; 6c. Oil refinery; 8c. Fertilizer plant 40c. Scarlet Ibis; 50c. Maracas Bay; $2.50, Fishing; $5 Red House. Vert 10c. T **94**. As T **94**—12c. Citrus fruit; 15c. Arms of Trinidad and Tobago; 20c, 25c. Flag and outline of Trinidad and Tobago; 30c. Chaconia plant; $1, Poui tree.

* The normal sideways watermark shows the Crown to the left of CA, *as seen from the back of the stamp.*

The date quoted for the glazed, ordinary paper printings is that of receipt at the GPO; the dates of issue are not known.

The listed missing die-stamped heads have the heads completely omitted and, except for No. 352a which results from a shift, show a blind impression of the die. They should not be confused with stamps from sheets containing a row of partly missing heads progressing down to mere specks of foil. The 20c. value also exists with the gold omitted from the map only. We have also seen stamps with an additional 'blind' profile cutting into the rear of the head but without a second die-stamped impression. Varieties of this nature are outside the scope of this catalogue.

Nos. 340/342 were later reissued with W w **12** upright and No. 344a with W w **14**.

108 Captain A. A. Cipriani (labour leader) and Entrance to Woodford Square

(Photo State Ptg Works, Vienna)

1969 (1 May). 50th Anniversary of International Labour Organisation. T **108** and similar horiz design. P 12.

355 6c. black, gold and carmine-red 15 25
356 15c. black, gold and new blue 15 25

Design: 6c. T **108**; 15c. Arms of Industrial Court and entrance to Wood-ford Square.

110 Cornucopia and Fruit

111 CARIFTA Countries

(Des and photo State Ptg Works, Vienna)

1969 (1 Aug). First Anniversary of CARIFTA (Caribbean Free Trade Area). Types **110/111** and similar multicoloured designs. P 13½.

357	6c. Type **110**	10	10
358	10c. British and member Nations' Flags (*horiz*)	10	10
359	30c. Type **111**	20	20
360	40c. Boeing 727-100 Sunjet in flight (*horiz*)	40	90
357/360 *Set of 4*		65	1·10

114 Space Module landing on Moon

(Des G. Vasarhelyi. Litho D.L.R.)

1969 (2 Sept). First Man on the Moon. T **114** and similar multicoloured designs. P 14.

361	6c. Type **114**	20	10
362	40c. Space module and astronauts on Moon (*vert*)	30	10
363	$1 Astronauts seen from inside space module	60	35
361/363 *Set of 3*		1·00	50

The above were released by the Philatelic Agency in the USA on 1 September, but not sold locally until 2 September.

117 Parliamentary Chamber, Flags and Emblems

(Photo Harrison)

1969 (23 Oct*). 15th Commonwealth Parliamentary Association Conference, Port-of-Spain. T **117** and similar horiz designs. Multicoloured. W w **12**. P 14½×13½.

364	10c. Type **117**	10	10
365	15c. J. F. Kennedy College	10	10
366	30c. Parliamentary maces	25	50
367	40c. Cannon and emblem	25	50
364/367 *Set of 4*		60	1·00

* This was the local release date; the Philatelic Agency in New York released the stamps ten days earlier.

121 Congress Emblem

122 Emblem and Islands at Daybreak

(Photo Rosenbaum Bros, Vienna)

1969 (3 Nov). International Congress of the Junior Chamber of Commerce. Types **121/122** and similar vert design. P 13½.

368	6c. black, red and gold	10	10
369	30c. gold, lake and light blue	25	40
370	40c. black, gold and ultramarine	25	40
368/370 *Set of 3*		50	75

Design: 6c. T **121**; 30c. T **122**; 40c. Emblem palm-trees and ruin.

The above were released by the Philatelic Agency in the USA on 2 November, but not sold locally until 3 November.

124 'Man in the Moon'

129 Statue of Gandhi

(Des V. Whiteley. Litho Questa)

1970 (6 Feb). Carnival Winners. T **124** and similar multicoloured designs. W w **12** (sideways on 40c.). P 14.

371	5c. Type **124**	10	10
372	6c. 'City beneath the Sea'	10	10
373	15c. 'Antelope' God Bamibara	15	10
	w. Wmk inverted	—	16·00
374	30c. 'Chanticleer' Pheasant Queen of Malaya	25	10
375	40c. Steel Band of the Year (*horiz*)	25	30
371/375 *Set of 5*		70	50

The above were released by the Philatelic Agency in the USA on 2 February, but not sold locally until 6 February.

(Photo State Printing Works, Vienna)

1970 (2 Mar). Gandhi Centenary Year (1969). T **129** and similar multicoloured design. P 12.

376	10c. Type **129**	40	10
377	30c. Head of Gandhi and Indian flag (*horiz*)	85	20

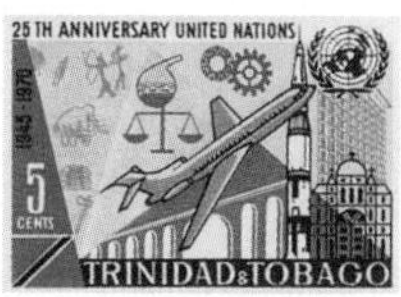

131 Symbols of Culture, Science, Arts and Technology

132 New UPU HQ Building

(Des G. Lee. Photo State Printing Works, Vienna)

1970 (26 June). 25th Anniversary of United Nations. Types **131/132** and similar designs. Multicoloured. P 12 (30c.) 13½×14 (10c.) or 13½ (others).

378	5c. Type **131**	10	10
379	10c. Children of different races, map and flag (34×25 *mm*)	20	10
380	20c. Noah's Ark, rainbow and dove (35×24 *mm*)	20	45
381	30c. Type **132**	25	30
378/381 *Set of 4*		65	75

NATIONAL
COMMERCIAL
BANK
ESTABLISHED
1.7.70
(**133**)

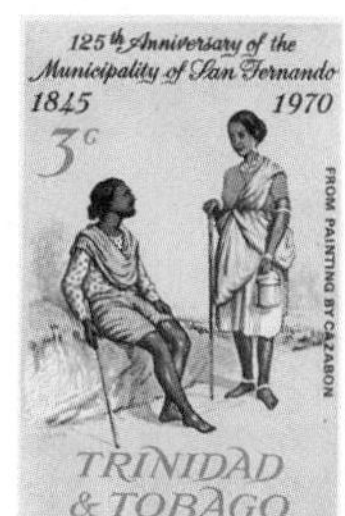

134 *East Indian Immigrants* (J. Cazabon)

1970 (1 July). Inauguration of National Commercial Bank. No. 341 optd with T **133**.

382	5c. multicoloured	30	10

(Des from paintings by Cazabon. Litho Questa)

1970 (1 Oct). 125th Anniversary of San Fernando. T **134** and similar designs. W w **12** (sideways on 5c. and 40c.). P 13½.

383	3c. multicoloured	10	90
	w. Wmk inverted	—	40·00
384	5c. black, blue and yellow-ochre	10	10
385	40c. black, blue and yellow-ochre	95	20
383/385 *Set of 3*		1·00	1·10

Designs: Vert—3c. T **134**. Horiz—5c. *San Fernando Town Hall*; 40c. *San Fernando Harbour, 1860*

135 *The Adoration of the Shepherds* (detail, School of Seville)

(Des G. Drummond. Litho Format)

1970 (8 Dec). Christmas. Paintings. T **135** and similar vert designs. Multicoloured. P 13½.

386	3c. Type **135**	10	10
387	5c. *Madonna and Child with Saints* (detail, Titian)	10	10
388	30c. *The Adoration of the Shepherds* (detail, Le Nain)	15	20
389	40c. *The Virgin and Child, St John and an Angel* (Morando)	15	10
390	$1 *The Adoration of the Kings* (detail, Veronese)	35	2·50
386/390 *Set of 5*		75	2·75
MS391	114×153 mm. Nos. 386/389	1·00	1·25

STAMP BOOKLETS

1925.

SB1	2s. booklet containing 8×½d., 8×1d. and 8×1½d. (Nos. 218/220) in blocks of 4	

1931–32. Black on pink covers.

SB2	1s.8d. booklet containing 8×½d. and 16×1d. (Nos. 218/219) in blocks of 8	
SB3	2s. booklet containing 8×½d., 8×1d. and 8×1½d. (Nos. 218/220) in blocks of 8 (1932)	

1936.

SB4	48c. booklet containing 8×1c., 8×2c. and 8×3c. (Nos. 230a/232a) in blocks of 4	

1970 (8 Dec). Christmas. Olive-green printed cover inscr 'CHRISTMAS GREETINGS'.

SB5	$1.78 booklet containing 6×3c., 4×5c. and 2×30c. and 2×40c. (Nos. 386/389) in pairs	4·50

POSTAGE DUE STAMPS

D **1**

D **2**

1/- 1/- 1/-

Column 4 Column 5 Short upright stroke (R. 4/5)

The degree of inclination of the stroke on the 1s. value varies for each vertical column of the sheet: Columns 1, 2 and 6 104°, Column 3 108°, Column 4 107° and Column 5 (Nos. D9a, D17a, D25a) 100°.

(Typo D.L.R.)

1885 (1 Jan). Wmk Crown CA. P 14.

D1	D **1**	½d. slate-black	19·00	50·00
D2		1d. slate-black	18·00	20
D3		2d. slate-black	50·00	20
		w. Wmk inverted	†	£450
D4		3d. slate-black	60·00	40
D5		4d. slate-black	50·00	7·00
D6		5d. slate-black	24·00	60
D7		6d. slate-black	50·00	15·00
D8		8d. slate-black	60·00	5·50
D9		1s. slate-black	80·00	5·00
		a. Upright stroke	£150	15·00
		ab. Short upright stroke	£275	35·00
D1/D9 *Set of 9*			£350	70·00

1905–06. Wmk Mult Crown CA. P 14.

D10	D **1**	1d. slate-black	9·00	20
D11		2d. slate-black	40·00	20
		w. Wmk inverted	†	£350
D12		3d. slate-black	14·00	3·75
		w. Wmk inverted	—	£180
D13		4d. slate-black	14·00	22·00
		w. Wmk inverted		
D14		5d. slate-black	22·00	23·00
D15		6d. slate-black	6·50	17·00
D16		8d. slate-black	22·00	23·00
D17		1s. slate-black	29·00	45·00
		a. Upright stroke	45·00	75·00
		ab. Short upright stroke	£110	£180
D10/D17 *Set of 8*			£140	£120

1923–45. Wmk Mult Script CA. P 14.

D18	D **1**	1d. black	4·00	4·00
D19		2d. black	8·50	1·50
D20		3d. black (1925)	13·00	6·50
D21		4d. black (1929)	8·50	30·00
D22		5d. black (1944)	40·00	£140
D23		6d. black (1945)	75·00	55·00
D24		8d. black (1945)	45·00	£200
D25		1s. black (1945)	85·00	£160
		a. Upright stroke	£140	£275
		ab. Short upright stroke	£325	
D18/D25 *Set of 8*			£250	£550
D18s/D25s Optd or Perf (5d. to 1s.) 'SPECIMEN' *Set of 8*			£200	

1947 (1 Sept)–**61.** Values in cents. Ordinary paper. Wmk Mult Script CA. P 14.

D26	D **1**	2c. black	5·50	10·00
		a. Chalk-surfaced paper (20.1.53)	20	6·50
		ab. Error. Crown missing. W **9a**	£150	
		ac. Error. St Edward's Crown. W **9b**	38·00	
D27		4c. black	2·75	3·00
		a. Chalk-surfaced paper (10.8.55)	11·00	4·50
D28		6c. black	5·00	7·00
		a. Chalk-surfaced paper (20.1.53)	30	7·50
		ab. Error. Crown missing. W **9a**	£450	
		ac. Error. St Edward's Crown. W **9b**	95·00	
D29		8c. black	1·25	42·00
		a. Chalk-surfaced paper (10.9.58)	35	32·00

D30		10c. black	3·25	10·00
		a. Chalk-surfaced paper (10.8.55)	9·50	24·00
D31		12c. black	4·25	30·00
		a. Chalk-surfaced paper (20.1.53)	40	25·00
		ab. Error. Crown missing. W **9a**	£650	
		ac. Error. St Edward's Crown. W **9b**	£170	
D32		16c. black	2·00	55·00
		a. Chalk-surfaced paper (22.8.61)	16·00	70·00
D33		24c. black	13·00	16·00
		a. Chalk-surfaced paper (10.8.55)	14·00	55·00
D26/D33 *Set of* 8			32·00	£150
D26a/D33a *Set of* 8			45·00	£200
D26s/D33s Perf 'SPECIMEN' *Set of* 8			£140	

(Litho B.W.)

1969 (25 Nov)–**70**. Size 19×24 mm. P 14×13½.

D34	D **2**	2c. pale blue-green	15	2·50
D35		4c. magenta (1970)	25	8·50
D36		6c. brown (1970)	50	4·50
D37		8c. slate-lilac (1970)	65	4·75
D38		10c. dull red (1970)	1·00	8·50
D39		12c. pale orange (1970)	80	6·50
D40		16c. bright apple-green (1970)	1·00	6·50
D41		24c. grey (1970)	1·00	11·00
D42		50c. grey-blue (1970)	1·00	4·50
D43		60c. sage-green (1970)	1·00	4·00
D34/D43 *Set of* 10			6·50	55·00

Postage due stamps as T D **2** but smaller (17×21 *mm*) were issued in 1976 and 1977.

'TOO LATE' STAMPS

A handstamp with the words 'TOO LATE' was used upon letters on which a too-late fee had been paid, and was sometimes used for cancelling the stamps on such letters.

OFFICIAL STAMPS

O S (O **1**) **OFFICIAL** (O **2**) **OFFICIAL** (O **3**)

1894. Optd with T O **1**.

(a) On Nos. 106/112. Wmk Crown CA. P 14

O1	**10**	½d. dull green	48·00	65·00
O2		1d. carmine	50·00	70·00
O3		2½d. bright blue	55·00	£100
O4		4d. grey	60·00	£130
O5		6d. olive-black	60·00	£140
O6		1s. orange-brown	80·00	£190

(b) On No. 87. Wmk Crown CC. P 12½

O7	**5**	5s. rose-lake	£180	£900

1909. Nos. 133 and 135 optd with T O **2**. Wmk Mult Crown CA. P 14.

O8	**11**	½d. blue-green	4·00	12·00
O9		1d. rose-red	3·50	13·00
		a. Opt double	—	£325
		b. Opt vertical	£130	£150
		c. Opt inverted	£750	£225

1910. No. 146 optd with T O **2**. Wmk Mult Crown CA. P 14.

O10	**14**	½d. green	13·00	17·00
		w. Wmk inverted	£170	

1913. No. 149 optd with T O **3** by lithography.

O11	**17**	½d. green	2·75	18·00
		a. Opt vertical		

OFFICIAL (O **4**) **OFFICIAL** (O **5**) **OFFICIAL** (O **6**)

1914. No. 149 optd with T O **4**.

O12	**17**	½d. green	4·25	25·00

1914–17. No. 149 optd with T O **5** (without stop).

O13	**17**	½d. green	7·00	28·00
		a. Blue-green (thick paper) (1917)	65	10·00

1916. No. 149*a* optd with T O **5** (with stop).

O14	**17**	½d. yellow-green	6·00	10·00
		a. Opt double	55·00	

1917 (22 Aug). No. 149 optd with T O **6**.

O15	**17**	½d. green	6·50	30·00
		a. Yellow-green	6·50	32·00
		b. Blue-green (thick paper)	3·25	32·00

Tristan da Cunha

Although first settled in 1817 no surviving mail is known from Tristan da Cunha until two whaler's letters written in 1836 and 1843, these being carried home in other whaling ships. Then there is a long gap until the late 1800's when other letters are known—surprisingly only some seven in number, up to 1908 when the first of the island cachet handstamps came into use.

The collecting of postal history material from 1908 to 1952, when Tristan's first stamps were issued, revolves around the numerous cachets of origin which were struck on mail from the island during these 44 years. The handstamps producing these cachets were supplied over the years by various people particularly interested in the island and the islanders, and were mostly used by the clergymen who volunteered to go and serve as the community's ministers.

The postal cachets are illustrated below. The use of the different cachets on mail frequently overlapped, at one period in 1930 there were five different types of handstamp in use. As there was no official source for providing them they appeared on the island from various donors; then disappeared without trace once they became worn out. Only one of these early rubber handstamps has apparently survived, Cachet Va.

Covers bearing the cachets are recognised collector's items, but are difficult to value in general terms. As elsewhere the value is discounted by poor condition of the cover, and may be increased by use on a scarce date or with additional postal markings. Some cachets are known in more than one colour, but we do not list these variations.

Cachet Types V and VII on cover are the commonest, Type Va, used only for three months, and Type IVa are the scarcest, equalling the scarcest use of Type I examples. All cacheted covers, particularly if non-philatelic, are desirable forerunner items. Even a philatelic cover of Type V is, at present, worth in the region of £35.

Dates given are of the first recorded use.

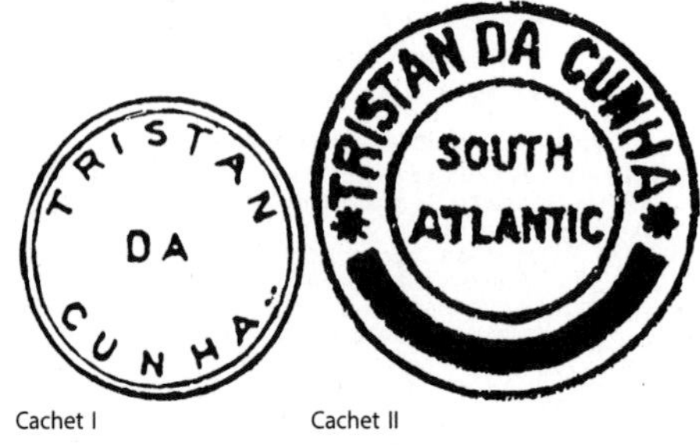

Cachet I Cachet II

Cat. No.			Value on cover
C1	**1908** (May). Cachet I	*from*	£4000
C2	**1919** (31 July). Cachet II	*from*	£425

Cachet III

C3	**1921** (8 Feb). Cachet III	*from*	£300

Cachet IVa

C4	**1927** (1 Oct). Cachet IV (*as* IVa, *but without centre label*)	*from*	£850
C5	**1928** (28 Oct). Cachet IVa	*from*	£5500

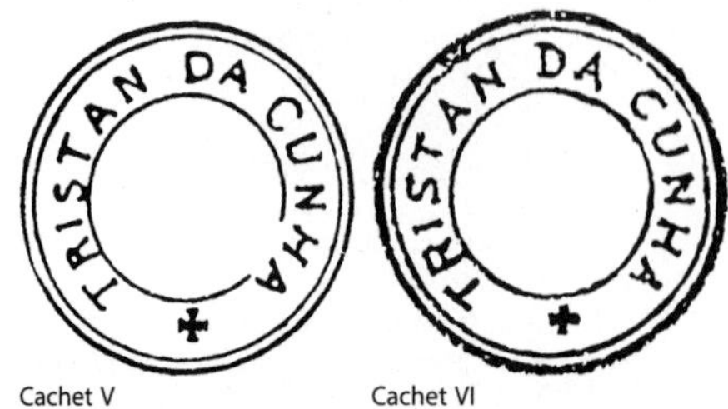

Cachet V Cachet VI

C6	**1929** (24 Feb). Cachet V	*from*	35·00
C7	**1929** (15 May). Cachet Va (*as* V, *but without break in inner ring. Shows 'T' 'C' and 'N' damaged*)	*from*	£6500
C8	**1936** (Aug). Cachet VI	*from*	60·00

Cachet VII

C9	**1936** (1 Feb). Cachet VII	*from*	22·00

During World War II there was little mail from the island as its function as a meteorological station was cloaked by security. Such covers as are known are generally struck with the 'tombstone' naval censor mark and postmarked 'maritime mail' or have South African postal markings. A few philatelic items from early in the war bearing cachets exist, but this usage was soon stopped by the military commander and the handstamps were put away until peace returned. Covers from the period would be worth from £75 to at least £350.

Cachet VIII

C10	**1946** (8 May). Cachet VIII	*from*	90·00

Cachet IX

C11	**1948** (29 Feb). Cachet IX	*from*	55·00

Cachet X

C12	**1948** (2 Feb). Cachet X	*from*	45·00

This cachet with 'A.B.C.' below the date was in private use between 1942 and 1946.

Although an earlier example of Cachet X is now known, we have retained the traditional sequence insofar as Cachets IX and X are concerned, for the convenience of collectors.

Cachet XI

Cachet XII

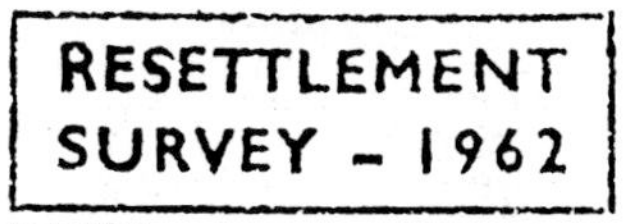

RESETTLEMENT SURVEY – 1962

Cachet XIII

Cachets XI to XIII from the 1961/63 'volcano eruption' and 'return to the island' period vary in value from £30 to £120, due to philatelic usage on the one hand and scarce mailings from the small survey parties on shore during this period on the other.

TRISTAN DA CUNHA
(1)

1952 (1 Jan). Nos. 131, 135*a*/140 and 149/151 of St Helena optd with T **1**.

No.	Description	Unused	Used
1	½d. violet	15	3·50
2	1d. black and green	1·00	1·50
3	1½d. black and carmine	1·00	1·50
4	2d. black and scarlet	1·00	1·50
5	3d. grey	1·00	1·50
6	4d. ultramarine	7·00	2·50
7	6d. light blue	7·00	2·50
8	8d. olive-green	7·00	8·50
9	1s. sepia	5·50	2·00
10	2s.6d. maroon	24·00	19·00
11	5s. chocolate	38·00	25·00
12	10s. purple	60·00	42·00
1/12 *Set of* 12		£140	£100

1953 (2 June). Coronation. As No. 120 of Antigua.

No.	Description	Unused	Used
13	3d. black and grey-green	1·00	2·00

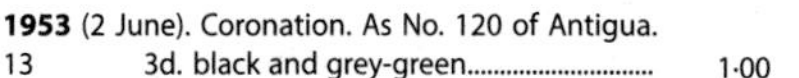

2 Tristan Crawfish

3 Carting Flax for Thatching

4 Rockhopper Penguin

5 Big Beach factory

6 Yellow-nosed Albatross

7 Island longboat

8 Tristan from the south-west

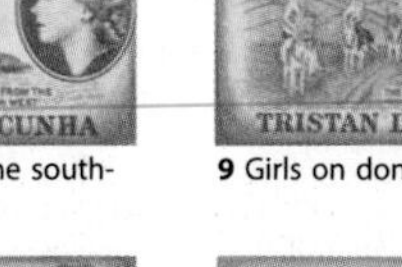

9 Girls on donkeys

10 Inaccessible Island from Tristan

11 Nightingale Island

12 St Mary's Church

13 Southern Elephant seal at Gough Island

14 Inaccessible Island Rail

15 Island spinning wheel

(Des D.L.R. (5d. and 10s.), H. Elliott (others). Recess D.L.R.)

1954 (2 Jan). Types **2/15**. Wmk Mult Script CA. P 12½×13 (horiz) or 13×12½ (vert).

No.	Type	Description	Unused	Used
14	**2**	½d. red and deep brown	10	10
15	**3**	1d. sepia and bluish green	10	50
16	**4**	1½d. black and reddish purple	2·00	1·75
17	**5**	2d. grey-violet and brown-orange	30	20
18	**6**	2½d. black and carmine-red	1·75	60
19	**7**	3d. ultramarine and olive-green	2·50	1·75
20	**8**	4d. turquoise-blue and deep blue	60	70
21	**9**	5d. emerald and black	60	70
22	**10**	6d. deep green and violet	60	75
23	**11**	9d. reddish violet and Venetian red	60	45
24	**12**	1s. deep yellow-green and sepia	60	45
25	**13**	2s.6d. deep brown and light blue	17·00	11·00
26	**14**	5s. black and red-orange	50·00	15·00
27	**15**	10s. brown-orange and purple	24·00	14·00
14/27 *Set of* 14			90·00	42·00

16 Starfish

17 Concha Wrasse

18 Two-spined Thornfish

19 Atlantic Saury

20 Bristle Snipefish

21 Tristan Crawfish

22 False Jacopever

23 Five-fingered Morwong

24 Long-finned Scad

25 Christophersen's Medusafish

26 Blue Medusafish

27 Snoek

28 Blue Shark

29 Black Right Whale

(Des Mr. and Mrs. G. F. Harris. Recess Waterlow)

1960 (1 Feb). Marine Life. Types **16/29**. W w **12**. P 13.

No.	Type	Description	Unused	Used
28	**16**	½d. black and orange	15	40
29	**17**	1d. black and bright purple	15	20
30	**18**	1½d. black and light turquoise-blue	20	1·00
31	**19**	2d. black and bluish green	30	1·25
32	**20**	2½d. black and sepia	55	60
33	**21**	3d. black and brown-red	1·25	2·00
34	**22**	4d. black and yellow-olive	1·25	1·25
35	**23**	5d. black and orange-yellow	1·50	1·00
36	**24**	6d. black and blue	1·75	1·00
37	**25**	9d. black and rose-carmine	1·75	1·50
38	**26**	1s. black and light brown	3·50	1·00
39	**27**	2s.6d. black and ultramarine	11·00	11·00
40	**28**	5s. black and light emerald	12·00	12·00
41	**29**	10s. black and violet	48·00	35·00
28/41 *Set of* 14			75·00	60·00

1961 (15 Apr). As Nos. 28/30 and 32/41 but values in South African decimal currency.

No.	Description	Unused	Used
42	½c. black and orange (as ½d.)	20	1·25
43	1c. black and bright purple (as 1d.)	20	1·25
44	1½c. black and light turquoise-blue (as 1½d.)	35	1·25
45	2c. black and sepia (as 2½d.)	65	1·25
46	2½c. black and brown-red (as 3d.)	1·00	1·25
47	3c. black and yellow-olive (as 4d.)	1·00	1·25
48	4c. black and orange-yellow (as 5d.)	1·25	1·25
49	5c. black and blue (as 6d.)	1·25	1·25
50	7½c. black and rose-carmine (as 9d.)	1·25	1·25
51	10c. black and light brown (as 1s.)	2·00	1·25
52	25c. black and ultramarine (as 2s. 6d.)	7·00	7·50
53	50c. black and light emerald (as 5s.)	24·00	20·00
54	1r. black and violet (as 10s.)	50·00	38·00
42/54 *Set of* 13		80·00	70·00

Following a volcanic eruption the island was evacuated on 10 October 1961, but resettled in 1963.

TRISTAN DA CUNHA RESETTLEMENT 1963
(30)

1963 (12 Apr). Tristan Resettlement. As Nos. 176/188 of St Helena, but Wmk Mult Script CA (sideways on 1d., 2d., 7d., 10d., 2s. 6d., 10s), optd with T **30**.

No.	Description	Unused	Used
55	1d. bright blue, dull violet, yellow and carmine	15	1·00
56	1½d. yellow, green, black and light drab	2·00	70
57	2d. scarlet and grey	25	1·00
58	3d. light blue, black, pink and deep blue	30	1·00
	a. Black printed double*	£300	
	w. Wmk inverted	£750	£850
59	4½d. yellow-green, green, brown and grey	50	60
60	6d. red, sepia and light yellow-olive	3·00	30
61	7d. red-brown, black and violet	50	30
62	10d. brown-purple and light blue	50	30
63	1s. greenish yellow, bluish green and brown	50	30
64	1s.6d. grey, black and slate-blue	6·50	1·00
65	2s.6d. red, pale yellow and turquoise	1·00	45
66	5s. yellow, brown and green	5·00	1·00
	w. Wmk inverted	90·00	80·00
67	10s. orange-red, black and blue	6·00	1·00
55/67 *Set of* 13		23·00	8·00

* No. 58a shows the outline round the Queen's head printed double.

1963 (2 Oct). Freedom from Hunger. As No. 146 of Antigua.

No.	Description	Unused	Used
68	1s.6d. carmine	50	30

1964 (1 Feb). Red Cross Centenary. As Nos. 147/148 of Antigua.

No.	Description	Unused	Used
69	3d. red and black	20	15
70	1s.6d. red and blue	30	20

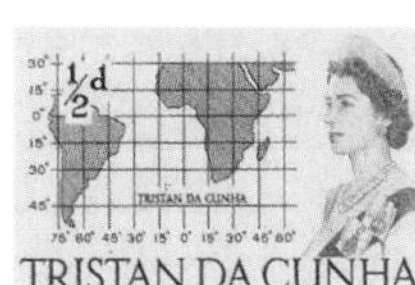

31 South Atlantic Map

32 Flagship of Tristao da Cunha, 1506

33 *Heemstede* (Dutch East Indiaman), 1643

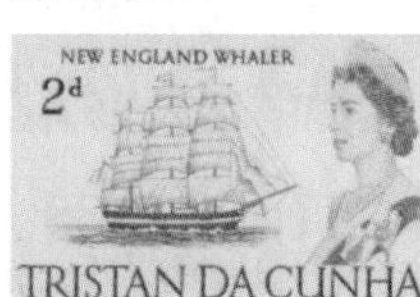

34 *Edward* (American Whaling ship), 1864

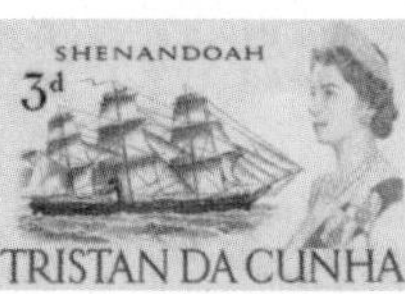

35 *Shenandoah* (Confederate warship), 1873

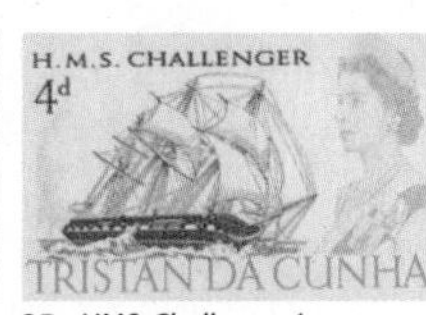

35a HMS *Challenger* (survey ship), 1873

36 HMS *Galatea* (screw frigate), 1867

H.M.S. CILICIA
TRISTAN DA CUNHA

37 HMS *Cilicia* (transport), 1942

38 Royal Yacht *Britannia*

39 HMS *Leopard* (frigate)

40 *Tjisadane* (liner)

41 *Tristania* (crayfish trawler)

42 *Boissevain* (cargo liner)

43 *Bornholm* (liner)

44 Queen Elizabeth II

44a *RSA* (research vessel)

(Queen's portrait by Anthony Buckley. Des, eng and recess B.W.)

1965 (17 Feb)–**67**. Designs as Types **31/44a**. W w **12** (sideways on £1). P 11½×11 (vert) or 11×11½ (horiz).

71	**31**	½d. black and ultramarine	15	30
72	**32**	1d. black and emerald-green	1·00	15
73	**33**	1½d. black and blue	1·00	15
74	**34**	2d. black and purple	1·00	15
75	**35**	3d. black and turquoise-blue	1·00	15
75*a*	**35a**	4d. black and orange (1.9.67)	3·00	4·00
76	**36**	4½d. black and brown	1·00	15
77	**37**	6d. black and green	1·25	15
78	**38**	7d. black and rose-red	2·25	30
79	**39**	10d. black and chocolate	1·25	55
80	**40**	1s. black and carmine	1·25	30
81	**41**	1s.6d. black and yellow-olive	7·50	2·50
82	**42**	2s.6d. black and orange-brown	3·50	4·00
83	**43**	5s. black and violet	9·50	3·50
84	**44**	10s. deep blue and carmine	1·75	1·25
84*a*	**44a**	10s. black and deep turquoise-blue (1.9.67)	14·00	11·00
84*b*	**44**	£1 deep blue and orange-brown (1.9.67)	8·00	11·00
71/84*b* *Set of 17*			50·00	35·00

1965 (11 May*). ITU Centenary. As Nos. 166/167 of Antigua.

85	3d. orange-red and grey	20	15
86	6d. reddish violet and yellow-orange	30	15

* This is the local date of issue; the stamps were not released in London until 17 May.

1965 (25 Oct). International Co-operation Year. As Nos. 168/169 of Antigua.

87	1d. reddish purple and turquoise-green	20	15
88	6d. deep bluish green and lavender	50	25

1966 (24 Jan). Churchill Commemoration. As Nos. 170/173 of Antigua.

89	1d. new blue	35	40
	a. Value omitted	£1400	
90	3d. deep green	1·00	50
91	6d. brown	1·25	65
92	1s.6d. bluish violet	1·40	70
89/92 *Set of 4*		3·50	2·00

No. 89a was caused by misplacement of the gold and also shows the country inscription moved to the right.

45 HMS *Falmouth* (frigate) at Tristan and Soldier of 1816

(Des V. Whiteley. Litho Harrison)

1966 (15 Aug). 150th Anniversary of Tristan Garrison. W w **12** (sideways*). P 14½.

93	**45**	3d. multicoloured	15	10
		w. Wmk Crown to right of CA	7·00	
94		6d. multicoloured	15	15
95		1s.6d. multicoloured	20	25
96		2s.6d. multicoloured	25	25
93/96 *Set of 4*			65	65

* The normal sideways watermark shows Crown to left of CA, *as seen from the back of the stamp.*

1966 (1 Oct*). World Cup Football Championship. As Nos. 176/177 of Antigua.

97	3d. violet, yellow-green, lake and yellow-brown	30	10
98	2s.6d. chocolate, blue-green, lake and yellow-brown	70	20

* Released in St Helena on 1 July in error.

1966 (1 Oct). Inauguration of WHO Headquarters, Geneva. As Nos. 178/179 of Antigua.

99	6d. black, yellow-green and light blue	65	30
100	5s. black, light purple and yellow-brown	1·10	70

1966 (1 Dec). 20th Anniversary of UNESCO. As Nos. 196/198 of Antigua.

101	10d. slate-violet, red, yellow and orange	25	15
	w. Wmk Crown to right of CA	45·00	
102	1s.6d. orange-yellow, violet and deep olive	40	20
103	2s.6d. black, bright purple and orange	45	25
101/103 *Set of 3*		1·00	55

* The normal sideways watermark shows Crown to left of CA, *as seen from the back of the stamp.*

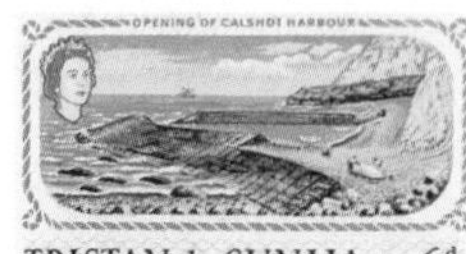

46 Calshot Harbour

(Des V. Whiteley. Litho D.L.R.)

1967 (2 Jan). Opening of Calshot Harbour. P 14×14½.

104	**46**	6d. multicoloured	10	10
105		10d. multicoloured	10	10
106		1s.6d. multicoloured	10	15
107		2s.6d. multicoloured	15	20
104/107 *Set of 4*			30	45

(**47**)

48 Prince Alfred, First Duke of Edinburgh

1967 (10 May). No. 76 surch with T **47**.

108	4d. on 4½d. black and brown	10	10

(Des M. Goaman. Litho Harrison)

1967 (10 July). Centenary of First Duke of Edinburgh's Visit to Tristan. W w **12**. P 14½.

109	**48**	3d. multicoloured	10	10
110		6d. multicoloured	10	10
111		1s.6d. multicoloured	10	10
112		2s.6d. multicoloured	15	15
109/112 *Set of 4*			30	30

49 Wandering Albatross

(Des V. Whiteley. Photo Harrison)

1968 (15 May). Birds. T **49** and similar horiz designs. Multicoloured. W w **12**. P 14×14½.

113	4d. Type **49**	30	30
114	1s. Wilkins's Finch	35	30
115	1s.6d. Tristan Thrush	40	55
116	2s.6d. Greater Shearwater	60	65
113/116 *Set of 4*		1·50	1·60

53 Union Jack and Dependency Flag

(Des Jennifer Toombs. Litho D.L.R.)

1968 (1 Nov). 30th Anniversary of Tristan da Cunha as a Dependency of St Helena. T **53** and similar horiz design. W w **12** (sideways). P 14.

117	**53**	6d. multicoloured	20	30
118	–	9d. sepia, blue and turquoise-blue	20	35
119	**53**	1s.6d. multicoloured	30	40
120	–	2s.6d. carmine, blue and turquoise-blue	40	40
117/120 *Set of 4*			1·00	1·25

Design: 9d., 2s.6d. St Helena and Tristan on chart.

55 Frigate

(Des and recess B.W.)

1969 (1 June). Clipper Ships. T **55** and similar horiz designs. W w **12**. P 11×11½.

121	4d. new blue	60	50
122	1s. carmine (full-rigged ship)	60	60
123	1s.6d. blue-green (barque)	65	95
124	2s.6d. chocolate (full-rigged clipper)	70	1·10
121/124 *Set of 4*		2·25	2·75

59 Sailing Ship off Tristan da Cunha

(Des Jennifer Toombs. Litho Format)

1969 (1 Nov). United Society for the Propagation of the Gospel. T **59** and similar horiz designs. Multicoloured. W w **12** (sideways). P 14½×14.

125	4d. Type **59**	60	30
126	9d. Islanders going to first Gospel service	15	30
127	1s.6d. Landing of the first minister	15	40
128	2s.6d. Procession outside St Mary's Church	20	40
125/128 *Set of 4*		1·00	1·25

63 Globe and Red Cross Emblem

(Des and litho B.W.)

1970 (1 June). Centenary of British Red Cross. T **63** and similar designs. W w **12** (sideways on vert designs). P 13.

129	**63**	4d. light emerald, scarlet and deep bluish green	10	25
130		9d. bistre, scarlet and deep bluish green	15	30
131	–	1s.9d. light drab, scarlet and ultramarine	40	45
132	–	2s.6d. reddish purple, scarlet and ultramarine	45	55
129/132 *Set of 4*			1·00	1·40

Design: Vert—1s.9d., 2s.6d., Union Jack and Red Cross Flag.

64 Crawfish and Longboat

(Des Harrison. Litho Enschedé)

1970 (1 Nov). Crawfish Industry. T **64** and similar horiz design. Multicoloured. W w **12**. P 12½×13.

133	4d. Type **64**	30	30
134	10d. Packing and storing Crawfish	35	35
135	1s.6d. Type **64**	45	60
136	2s.6d. As 10d.	45	70
133/136 *Set of 4*		1·40	1·75

STAMP BOOKLETS

1957 (30 May)–**58**. Black on blue cover. Postmarked 'MY 30 57' on back cover. Stapled.

SB1	3s.6d. booklet containing 8×½d. and 4×1d., 4×1½d., 4×3d. and 4×4d. (Nos. 14/16, 19/20) in blocks of 4	£350
	a. Postmarked 'JA 24 58' on back cover (24.1.58)	£300
	b. Without postmark	£325

1958 (Jan). Black on red cover. Without postmark. Stapled.

SB2	3s.6d. Contents as No. SB1	55·00

1960 (Feb). Black on green cover. Stitched.

SB3	3s.6d. booklet containing 8×½d. and 4×1d., 4×1½d., 4×3d. and 4×4d. (Nos. 28/30, 33/34) in blocks of 4	30·00

1965 (17 Feb). Black on green cover. Stapled.

SB4	4s.2d. booklet containing 8×½d. and 4×1d., 4×1½d., 4×3d. and 4×6d. (Nos. 71/73, 75, 77) in blocks of 4	6·00

The booklet covers were reprinted with amended postage rates and released by the Crown Agents on 21 September 1970.

POSTAGE DUE STAMPS

D 1

3d	3d	d
Normal	Lower serif at left of '3' missing (R. 9/1)	**4d.** Ball of 'd' broken and serif at top damaged (R. 9/5). Other stamps in the fifth vertical row show slight breaks to the ball of the 'd'.

(Typo D.L.R.)

1957 (1 Feb). Chalk-surfaced paper. Wmk Mult Script CA. P 14.

D1	D **1**	1d. scarlet	1·75	16·00
D2		2d. orange-yellow	2·50	4·75
		a. Large 'd'	30·00	
D3		3d. green	2·50	5·50
		a. Missing serif	50·00	
D4		4d. ultramarine	4·50	7·00
		a. Broken 'd'	60·00	
D5		5d. lake	2·50	27·00
D1/D5 *Set of 5*			12·00	55·00

For illustration of No. D2a see above No. D1 of Basutoland.

POSTAL FISCAL STAMPS

NATIONAL
SAVINGS
(F **1**)

1970 (15 May). No. 77 optd with T F **1** in red.

F1	6d. black and green	20	30

No. F1 was originally intended as a National Savings Stamp, but also retained postal validity.

Trucial States

The Trucial States consisted of Abu Dhabi, Ajman (with Manama), Dubai, Fujeira, Ras al Khaima. Sharjah and Umm al Qiwain. However the following issue of stamps was only put into use in Dubai, despite the inscription 'TRUCIAL STATES'.

The first organised postal service in Dubai commenced on 19 August 1909 when an Indian Branch Office, administered from Karachi, was opened, using the unoverprinted stamps of India, principally the ½a. and 1a. values.

The initial cancellation was a single-ring type inscribed 'DUBAI B.O. PERSIAN GULF', which remained in use until 1933.

1909 Cancellation

Its replacement was of the Indian double-circle type showing a similar inscription.

Dubai was upgraded to Sub-Post Office status on 1 April 1942 and this change was reflected in a new double-ring mark inscribed 'DUBAI' only. At the same time the office was provided with a single-ring handstamp which also incorporated a cancelling device of seven wavy lines.

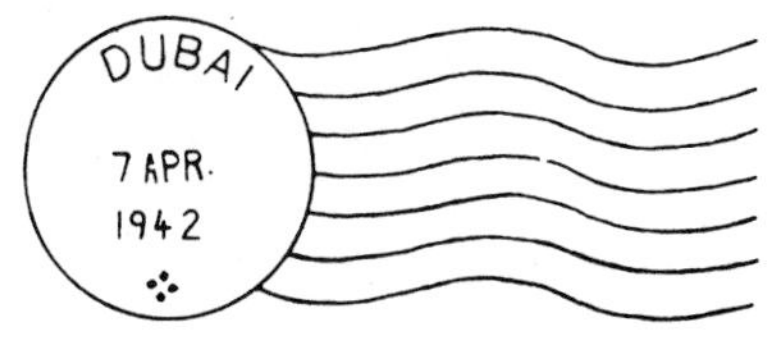

1942 Handstamp (*illustration reduced: actual size 65×27 mm*)

A further version of the double-ring type appeared in 1946, showing the 'PERSIAN GULF' inscription restored to the lower segment of the postmark.

In October 1947 control of the Dubai Post Office passed to Pakistan whose stamps were used there until the end of March 1948.

On 1 April 1948 the post office was transferred, yet again, to British control and Great Britain stamps surcharged for use in the British Postal Agencies in Eastern Arabia were then sold in Dubai until 6 January 1961, being cancelled with British style single and double-ring postmarks.

Stamps of the British Postal Agencies in Eastern Arabia (Nos. 81, 83 and 85/86) overprinted 'AJMAN', 'FUJAIRAH' or 'UMM AL QAIWAIN' are bogus.

(Currency. 100 naye paise = 1 rupee)

1 Palms

2 Dhow

(Des M. Goaman. Photo Harrison (T **1**). Des M. Farrar-Bell. Recess D.L.R. (T **2**))

1961 (7 Jan). P 15×14 (T **1**) or 13×12½ (T **2**).

1	**1**	5n.p. green	1·75	1·75
2		15n.p. red-brown	60	1·50
3		20n.p. bright blue	1·75	2·00
4		30n.p. orange-red	60	50
5		40n.p. reddish violet	60	50
6		50n.p. bistre	60	75
7		75n.p. grey	60	1·50
8	**2**	1r. green	9·50	4·50
9		2r. black	8·50	22·00
10		5r. carmine-red	12·00	28·00
11		10r. deep ultramarine	15·00	30·00
1/11 *Set of 11*			45·00	80·00

The Dubai Post Department took over the postal services on 14 June 1963. Later issues for Dubai will be found in the Stanley Gibbons *Arabia catalogue*.

Turks and Caicos Islands

TURKS ISLANDS

DEPENDENCY OF JAMAICA

A branch of the British Post Office opened at Grand Turk on 11 December 1854 replacing an earlier arrangement under which mail for the islands was sorted by local R.M.S.P. agents.

No. CC 1 is known used between 22 October 1857 and 20 April 1862.

GRAND TURK

CROWNED-CIRCLE HANDSTAMPS

CC **1**

CC1	CC **1** TURKS-ISLANDS (Oct 1857)	*Price on cover*	£5500

PRICES FOR STAMPS ON COVER TO 1945

Nos. 1/5	*from* × 30
No. 6	—
Nos. 7/20	*from* × 50
Nos. 20*a*/48	—
Nos. 49/52	*from* × 12
Nos. 53/57	*from* × 10
Nos. 58/65	*from* × 20
Nos. 66/69	*from* × 5
Nos. 70/72	*from* × 10
Nos. 101/109	*from* × 8
Nos. 110/126	*from* × 6
Nos. 129/139	*from* × 4
Nos. 140/153	*from* × 12
Nos. 154/190	*from* × 3
Nos. 191/193	*from* × 10
Nos. 194/205	*from* × 2

1

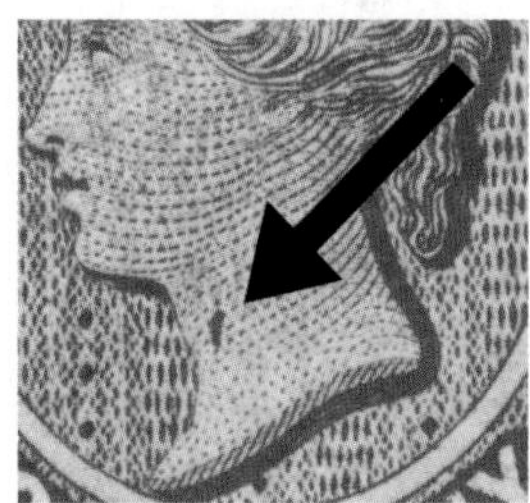

Throat flaw (R. 3/4)

(Recess P.B.)

1867 (4 Apr). No wmk. P 11–12½.

1	**1**	1d. dull rose	65·00	60·00
		a. Throat flaw	£250	£250
2		6d. black	£120	£140
3		1s. dull blue	£100	60·00

1873–79. Wmk Small Star. W w **2** (sideways on Nos. 5 and 6). P 11–12½×14½–15½.

4	**1**	1d. dull rose-lake (7.73)	55·00	50·00
		a. Throat flaw	£225	£225
		b. Wmk sideways	90·00	90·00
		ba. Throat flaw	£325	£350
5		1d. dull red (1.79)	60·00	60·00
		a. Imperf between (horiz pair)	£30000	
		b. Throat flaw	£250	£250
		c. Wmk upright		
6		1s. lilac (1.79)	£5000	£2000

1881 (1 Jan). Stamps of the preceding issues surcharged locally, in black. Sheets of 30 (10×3).

There are 12 different settings of the ½d., nine settings of the 2½d., and six settings of the 4d.

$\frac{1}{2}$	$\frac{1}{2}$
(**2**)	(**3**)

Setting 1. T **2**. Long fraction bar. Two varieties in a horizontal pair repeated 15 times in the sheet.

7	½ on 6d black	£100	£170

Setting 2. T **3**. Short fraction bar. Three varieties in a vertical strip repeated ten times in sheet.

Setting 3. Similar to setting 2, but the middle stamp of the three varieties has a longer bar.

8 ½ on 6d. black (*setting 2 only*) £100 £150
9 ½ on 1s. dull blue £140 £200
a. Surch double £8000

(4) (5) (6)

Three varieties in a vertical strip repeated ten times in sheet.
Setting 4. Types **4**, **5**, **6**.
Setting 5. Types **4** (without bar), **5**, **6**.
Setting 6. Types **4**, **5**, **6** (without bar).
Setting 7. Types **4** (shorter thick bar), **6**, **6**.

10 ½ on 1d. dull red (*setting 7 only*) (Type **6**)
a. Type **4** (shorter thick bar) £16000
11 ½ on 1s. dull blue (*setting 6 and 7*) (Type **4**) £2000
a. Type **4** (shorter thick bar) £3000
b. Type **5** £1500
c. Type **6** £1200
d. Type **6** (without bar) £2500
e. Surch double (Type **4**) £14000
f. Surch double (Type **5**) £14000
g. Surch double (Type **6** without bar)..
12 ½ on 1s. lilac (Type **4**) £275 £425
a. Without bar £600
b. With short thick bar £550 £750
c. Surch double £4000
cb. Surch double and short thick bar £14000
13 ½ on 1s. lilac (Type **5**) £160 £300
a. Surch double £3750
14 ½ on 1s. lilac (Type **6**) £150 £275
a. Without bar £700
b. Surch double £8000
ba. Surch double and without bar £14000

Care should be taken in the identification of Types **6** and **7** which are very similar. For the 1s. value some varieties of No. 9 are often confused with Nos. 11b/c.

(7) (8) (9) (10)

Setting 8. T **7**. Three varieties in a vertical strip. All have a very short bar.

15 ½. on 1d dull red 85·00 £160
a. Throat flaw £350
b. Surch double £7500

Setting 9. T **8**. Single unit surcharge. Bar long and thick and '1' leaning a little to left.

16 ½ on 1d. dull red £200 £350
a. Surch double £6000
b. Throat flaw £700

Setting 10. Types **9** and **10**. 15 varieties repeated twice in a sheet. Ten are of T **9** (Rows 1 and 2), five of T **10** (Row 3).

17 ½ on 1d. dull red (Type **9**) 60·00 £150
a. Surch double £6500
18 ½ on 1d. dull red (Type **10**) 95·00 £200
a. Surch double £11000
b. Throat flaw £350
19 ½ on 1s. lilac (Type **9**) £100 £225
20 ½ on 1s. lilac (Type **10**) £180 £400
20*a* ½. on 1s dull blue (Type **9**) £12000
20*b* ½ on 1s. dull blue (Type **10**) £22000

Types **9** and **11**. The difference is in the position of the '2' in relation to the '1'. In setting 10 the '2' is to the left of the '1' except on No. 10 (where it is directly below the '1') and in setting 11 it is to the right except on No. 2 (where it is to the left, as in setting 10).

(11) (12) (13) (14)

Setting 11. Types **9** and **11** to **14**. 15 varieties repeated twice in a sheet. Nine of T **11**, three of T **12**, and one each of Types **9**, **13** and **14**.

Setting 12. Similar to last, but T **13** replaced by another T **12**.

21 ½ on 1d. dull red (Type **11**) £120 £225
22 ½ on 1d. dull red (Type **12**) £325
a. Throat flaw £1300
23 ½ on 1d. dull red (Type **13**) £1100
a. Throat flaw £1100
24 ½ on 1d. dull red (Type **14**) £700
24*a* ½ on 1s. dull blue (Type **11**) £22000

T **9** from these settings, where it occurs on position 2, can only be distinguished from similar stamps from setting 10 when *se-tenant* with T **11**.

In setting 11 T **13** occupied R. 3/4 in the setting (5×3), corresponding to the position of the 'Throat flaw' on the left half of each sheet of 30 (10×3). Nos. 23 and 23a therefore exist in equal quantities.

(15) (16)

Setting 1. T **15**. Single unit surcharge. Fraction in very small type.

25 2½ on 6d. black £16000

Setting 2. T **16**. Two varieties repeated 15 times in a sheet. Large '2' on level with top of the '1', long thin bar.

26 2½ on 6d. black £400 £600
a. Imperf between (horiz pair) £42000
b. Surch double £18000

(17) (18) (19)

Setting 3. T **17**. Single unit surcharge. As T **16**, but large '2' not so high up.

27 2½ on 1s. lilac £4000

Setting 4. T **18**. Three varieties in a vertical strip repeated ten times in sheet. Large '2' placed lower and small bar.

28 2½ on 6d. black £250 £450
a. Surch double £17000

Setting 5. T **19**. Three varieties in a vertical strip repeated ten times in sheet. '2' further from '½', small fraction bar.

29 2½ on 1s. lilac £550 £1000

(20) (21)

Setting 6. Types **20** and **21**. 15 varieties. Ten of T **20** and five of T **21**, repeated twice in a sheet.

30 2½ on 1s. lilac (Type **20**) £14000
31 2½ on 1s. lilac (Type **21**) £25000

(22) (23) (24)

Setting 7. T **22**. Three varieties in a vertical strip, repeated ten times in a sheet.

32 2½ on 6d. black £9500
33 2½ on 1s. dull blue £28000

Setting 8. Types **23** and **24**. 15 varieties. Ten of T **23** and five of T **24** repeated twice in a sheet.

34 2½ on 1d. dull red (Type **23**) £800
35 2½ on 1d. dull red (Type **24**) £1600
a. Throat flaw £4750
36 2½ on 1s. lilac (Type **23**) £600 £900
a. Surch '½' double £4750
37 2½ on 1s. lilac (Type **24**) £1200
a. Surch '½' double £9000

(25) (26) (27)

Setting 9. Types **25**, **26**, and **27**. 15 varieties. Ten of T **25**, three of T **26**, one of T **26** without bar, and one of T **27**, repeated twice in a sheet.

38 2½ on 1s. dull blue (Type **25**) £1100
39 2½ on 1s. dull blue (Type **26**) £3750
40 2½ on 1s. dull blue (Type **26**) (without bar) £15000
41 2½ on 1s. dull blue (Type **27**) £15000

(28) (29) (30)

Setting 1. T **28**. '4' 8 mm high, pointed top.

42 4 on 6d. black £750 £350

Settings 2-6. Types **29** and **30**.

43 4 on 6d. black (Type **29**) £110 £160
44 4 on 6d. black (Type **30**) £400 £550
45 4 on 1s. lilac (Type **29**) £475 £750
a. Surch double
46 4 on 1s. lilac (Type **30**) £2500
a. Surch double
47 4 on 1d. dull red (Type **29**) £750 £475
48 4 on 1d. dull red (Type **28**) £850 £550

The components of these settings can only be distinguished when in blocks. Details are given in the handbook by John J. Challis.

31 (32)

(Typo (No. 50) or recess D.L.R.)

1881. Wmk Crown CC (sideways* on T **1**). P 14.

49 **1** 1d. brown-red (10.81) 85·00 £100
a. Throat flaw £300 £375
50 **31** 4d. ultramarine (Die I) (8.81) £170 60·00
w. Wmk inverted — £400
51 **1** 6d. olive-black (10.81) £160 £200
52 1s. slate-green (10.81) £200 £150

* The normal sideways watermark shows Crown to right of CC, *as seen from the back of the stamp*.

Nos. 49 and 51/52 also exist showing Crown to left of CC, but due to the position of the watermark such varieties are difficult to detect on single stamps. Reversed watermarks are also known.

1882–85. Wmk Crown CA (reversed on 1d.). P 14.

53 **31** ½d. blue-green (Die I) (2.82) 27·00 32·00
a. Pale green (12.85) 7·50 6·50
b. Top left triangle detached £400
w. Wmk inverted £250
55 **1** 1d. orange-brown (10.83) £100 38·00
a. Bisected (½d.) (*on cover*) † £5000
b. Throat flaw £375 £150
x. Wmk normal (not reversed) £190 £110
56 **31** 2½d. red-brown (Die I) (2.82) 45·00 17·00
57 4d. grey (Die I) (10.84) 40·00 4·25
a. Bisected (2d.) (*on cover*) † £5000

For illustration of 'top left triangle detached' variety see above No. 21 of Antigua.

1887 (July)–**89.** Wmk Crown CA.

(a) P 12

58 **1** 1d. crimson-lake 42·00 9·00
a. Imperf between (horiz pair) £28000
b. Throat flaw 90·00 23·00
x. Wmk reversed 24·00 6·00

(b) P 14

59 **1** 6d. yellow-brown (2.89) 5·00 7·00
s. Optd 'SPECIMEN' 50·00
60 1s. sepia 7·00 5·00

During a shortage of 1d. stamps a supply of JAMAICA No. 27 was sent to the Turks and Caicos Islands in April 1889 and used until replaced by No. 61. *Price from £250 used.*

1889 (May). Surch at Grand Turk with T **32**.

61 **31** 1d. on 2½d. red-brown 24·00 21·00
a. 'One' omitted £1600
b. Bisected (½d.) (*on cover*) † £5000

No. 61a was caused by misplacement of the surcharge. Stamps from the same sheet can be found with the surcharge reading 'Penny One'.

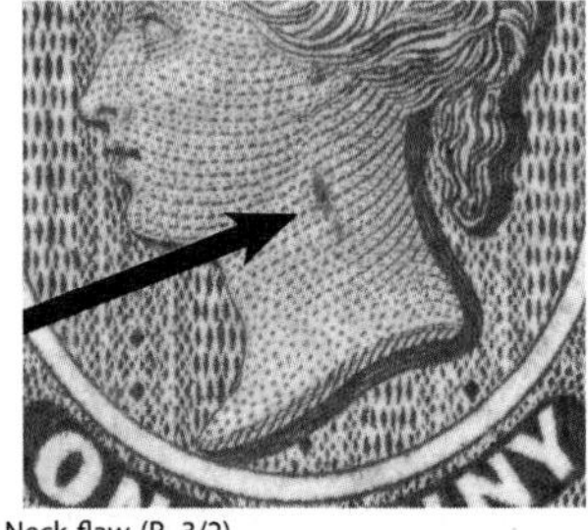

Neck flaw (R. 3/2)

1889–93. Wmk Crown CA. P 14.

62 **1** 1d. crimson-lake (7.89) 8·50 6·50
a. Bisected (½d.) (*on cover*) † £4750
b. Throat flaw 28·00 28·00
c. Neck flaw 48·00 48·00
x. Wmk reversed 75·00
63 1d. lake 7·00 4·50
a. Bisected (½d.) (*on cover*) † £4750
b. Throat flaw 22·00 22·00
c. Neck flaw 40·00 40·00
64 1d. pale rosy lake 7·00 8·50
b. Throat flaw 22·00 35·00
c. Neck flaw 40·00 50·00
65 **31** 2½d. ultramarine (Die II) (4.93) 7·00 4·75
s. Optd 'SPECIMEN' 50·00

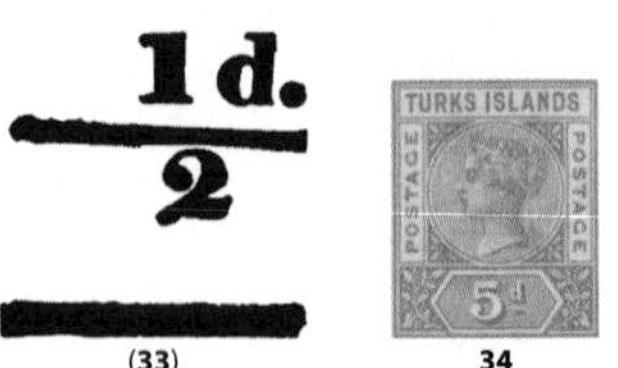

(33) **34**

1893 (10 June). No. 57 surch at Grand Turk with T **33**.

Setting 1. Bars between '1d.' and '2' separate, instead of continuous across the rows of stamps.

66 ½d. on 4d. grey £3500 £1500

Setting 2. Continuous bars. Thin and thick bar 10¾ mm apart. '2' under the '1'.

67 ½d. on 4d. grey £200 £140

Setting 3. As last, but bars 11¾ mm apart.

68 ½d. on 4d. grey £180 £190

Setting 4. Bars 11 mm apart. Five out of the six varieties in the strip have the '2' below the space between the '1' and 'd'.

69 ½d. on 4d. grey £225 £180

There is a fifth setting, but the variation is slight.

(Typo D.L.R.)

1893–95. Wmk Crown CA. P 14.

70 **31** ½d. dull green (Die II) (12.93) 7·00 4·25
71 4d. dull purple and ultramarine (Die II) (5.95) 25·00 27·00
72 **34** 5d. olive-green and carmine (6.94) 12·00 27·00
a. Bisected (2½d.) (*on cover*) † £4750
70/72 *Set of 3* 40·00 50·00
71s/72s Optd 'SPECIMEN' *Set of 2* £100

TURKS AND CAICOS ISLANDS

35 Badge of the Islands　**36** Badge of the Islands

The dates on the stamps have reference to the political separation from Bahamas.

(Recess D.L.R.)

1900 (10 Nov)–**04**. Wmk Crown CA (½d. to 1s.) or Wmk Crown CC (2s., 3s.). P 14.

No.	Type	Description	Unused	Used
101	**35**	½d. green	2·75	4·00
		x. Wmk reversed	£170	
		xs. Ditto. Optd 'SPECIMEN'	£190	
102		1d. red	3·50	75
		w. Wmk inverted	£120	
		x. Wmk reversed	£170	
103		2d. sepia	1·00	1·25
		w. Wmk inverted		
		x. Wmk reversed	£130	
104		2½d. blue	11·00	16·00
		a. *Greyish blue* (1904)	1·75	1·00
		aw. Wmk inverted	£120	
		ay. Wmk inverted and reversed	—	£225
105		4d. orange	3·75	7·00
106		6d. dull mauve	2·50	6·50
107		1s. purple-brown	3·25	23·00
108	**36**	2s. purple	50·00	80·00
109		3s. lake	80·00	£110
101/109 *Set of 9*			£130	£200
101s/109s Optd 'SPECIMEN' *Set of 9*			£250	

Nos. 101/107 exist without watermark or with double-lined lettering from the marginal watermark due to the way in which full sheets were cut for printing.

1905–08. Wmk Mult Crown CA. P 14.

No.	Type	Description	Unused	Used
110	**35**	½d. green	7·00	15
		x. Wmk reversed	—	£200
111		1d. red	20·00	50
		w. Wmk inverted	£200	
		x. Wmk reversed	£200	
112		3d. purple/*yellow* (1908)	2·25	6·00
		s. Optd 'SPECIMEN'	50·00	
		w. Wmk inverted		
110/112 *Set of 3*			26·00	6·00

37 Turk's-head Cactus　**38**

(Recess D.L.R.)

1909 (2 Sept)–**11**. Wmk Mult Crown CA. P 14.

No.	Type	Description	Unused	Used
115	**37**	¼d. rosy mauve (1910)	1·75	1·00
		w. Wmk inverted	£200	
116		¼d. red (1911)	60	40
		w. Wmk inverted		
117	**38**	½d. yellow-green	75	40
		w. Wmk inverted		
		x. Wmk reversed	65·00	
		y. Wmk inverted and reversed	£170	
118		1d. red	1·25	40
119		2d. greyish slate	6·00	1·40
120		2½d. blue	8·50	2·25
		w. Wmk inverted		
		x. Wmk reversed	80·00	90·00
		xs. Ditto opt 'SPECIMEN'	£110	
121		3d. purple/*yellow*	2·50	2·00
122		4d. red/*yellow*	3·25	5·00
123		6d. purple	7·00	3·00
124		1s. black/*green*	8·00	4·50
		w. Wmk inverted	£275	
125		2s. red/*green*	45·00	75·00
126		3s. black/*red*	48·00	40·00
115/126 *Set of 12*			£110	£120
115s/126s Optd 'SPECIMEN' *Set of 12*			£275	

See also Nos. 154 and 162.

39

WAR TAX
(40)

1913 (1 Apr)–**21**. Wmk Mult Crown CA. P 14.

No.	Type	Description	Unused	Used
129	**39**	½d. green	50	1·75
		w. Wmk inverted		
130		1d. red	1·00	2·25
		a. *Bright rose-scarlet*	1·10	2·00
		ax. Wmk reversed	85·00	
		b. *Rose-carmine* (1918)	3·75	7·00
131		2d. greyish slate	2·25	3·50
132		2½d. ultramarine	2·25	3·00
		aw. Wmk inverted		
		b. *Bright blue* (1918)	4·25	3·00
133		3d. purple/*yellow*	2·25	11·00
		a. *On lemon*	16·00	
		b. *On yellow-buff*	4·00	12·00
		c. *On orange-buff*	1·75	
		cx. Wmk reversed	£110	
		d. *On pale yellow*	2·75	12·00
134		4d. red/*yellow*	1·00	9·50
		a. *On orange-buff*	1·75	7·50
		ab. 'A' of 'CA' missing from wmk		
		as. Optd 'SPECIMEN'	48·00	
		b. *Carmine on pale yellow*	7·50	16·00
135		5d. pale olive-green (18.5.16)	6·50	22·00
136		6d. dull purple	2·50	3·50
		w. Wmk inverted		
		x. Wmk reversed		
137		1s. brown-orange	1·50	5·00
		w. Wmk inverted		
138		2s. red/*blue-green*	29·00	60·00
		a. *On greenish white* (1919)	32·00	70·00
		b. *On emerald* (3.21)	48·00	75·00
		bs. Optd 'SPECIMEN'	55·00	
		bx. Wmk reversed	£275	
139		3s. black/*red*	15·00	26·00
129/139 *Set of 11*			55·00	£120
129s/139s Optd 'SPECIMEN' *Set of 11*			£200	

1917 (3 Jan). Optd locally with T **40** at bottom of stamp.

No.	Type	Description	Unused	Used
140	**39**	1d. red	10	1·75
		a. Opt double	£180	£250
		ab. Opt double (in horiz pair with normal)	£400	
		b. 'TAX' omitted		
		c. 'WAR TAX' omitted in vert pair with normal	£700	
		d. Opt inverted at top	65·00	85·00
		e. Opt double, one inverted	£110	
		f. Opt inverted only, in pair with No. 140e	£600	
141		3d. purple/*yellow-buff*	1·25	9·50
		a. Opt double	£100	
		b. *On lemon*	4·25	15·00
		ba. Opt double	£100	£130
		bb. Opt double, one inverted	£325	

The overprint was in a setting of 60, using a plate supplied by De La Rue, applied twice to the sheets of 120. One sheet of the 1d. exists with the right-hand impression of the setting misplaced one row to the left so that stamps in vertical row 6 show a double overprint (No. 140ab). It appears that the right-hand vertical row on this sheet had the overprint applied at a third operation.

In Nos. 140e/140f the inverted overprint is at foot and reads 'TAX WAR' owing to displacement. No. 140e also exists with 'WAR' omitted from the inverted overprint.

In both values of the first printings the stamp in the bottom left-hand corner of the sheet has a long 'T' in 'TAX', and on the first stamp of the sixth row the 'X' is damaged and looks like a reversed 'K'. The long 'T' was subsequently converted.

1917 (Oct). Second printing with overprint at top or in middle of stamp.

No.	Type	Description	Unused	Used
143	**39**	1d. red	10	1·25
		a. Inverted opt at bottom or centre	50·00	
		c. Opt omitted (in pair with normal)	£650	
		d. Opt double, one at top, one at bottom	65·00	
		e. As d., but additional opt in top margin	£120	
		f. Pair, one as d., the other normal	£325	
		g. Pair, one opt inverted, one normal	£650	
		h. Double opt at top (in pair with normal)	£275	
		i. Opt double	48·00	60·00
144		3d. purple/*yellow*	60	2·50
		a. Opt double	50·00	
		b. Opt double, one inverted	£350	
		c. *On lemon*	4·50	

1918 (18 Dec). Overprinted with T **40**.

No.	Type	Description	Unused	Used
145	**39**	3d. purple/*yellow* (R.)	22·00	60·00
		a. Opt double	£325	

WAR TAX **(41)**　WAR TAX **(42)**　WAR TAX **(43)**

1918 (26 June). Optd with T **41** in London by D.L.R.

No.	Type	Description	Unused	Used
146	**39**	1d. rose-carmine	20	3·00
		a. *Bright rose-scarlet*	15	2·50
		aw. Wmk inverted	75·00	
147		3d. purple/*yellow*	6·50	9·00
146s/147s Optd 'SPECIMEN' *Set of 2*			85·00	

1919 (14 Apr). Optd with T **41** in London by D.L.R.

No.	Type	Description	Unused	Used
148	**39**	3d. purple/*orange-buff* (R.)	20	6·00
		s. Optd 'SPECIMEN'	45·00	

1919 (17 Apr). Local overprint. T **40**, in violet.

No.	Type	Description	Unused	Used
149	**39**	1d. bright rose-scarlet	2·00	7·50
		a. 'WAR' omitted (in pair with normal)	£200	
		b. Opt double	21·00	
		c. Opt double in pair with normal	£120	
		d. Opt double, one inverted		
		e. Opt triple		
		f. *Rose-carmine*	9·00	19·00
		fa. Opt double		
		w. Wmk inverted	35·00	

1919 (20 Aug). Optd locally with T **42**.

No.	Type	Description	Unused	Used
150	**39**	1d. scarlet	10	2·50
		a. Opt double	£150	£180
151		3d. purple/*orange-buff*	45	2·75
		w. Wmk inverted	40·00	
		x. Wmk reversed	40·00	

1919 (17 Dec). Optd locally with T **43**.

No.	Type	Description	Unused	Used
152	**39**	1d. scarlet	20	4·00
		a. Opt inverted		
153		3d. purple/*orange-buff*	2·00	4·25
		w. Wmk inverted	40·00	
		x. Wmk reversed	25·00	
		y. Wmk inverted and reversed	12·00	35·00

The two bottom rows of this setting have the words 'WAR' and 'TAX' about 1 mm further apart.

1921 (23 Apr). Wmk Mult Script CA. P 14.

No.	Type	Description	Unused	Used
154	**37**	¼d. rose-red	4·75	27·00
155	**39**	½d. green	3·50	7·50
156		1d. carmine-red	1·00	5·50
157		2d. slate-grey	1·00	20·00
		y. Wmk inverted and reversed	95·00	
158		2½d. bright blue	1·75	7·50
		x. Wmk reversed	£130	
159		5d. sage-green	12·00	70·00
160		6d. purple	7·00	70·00
		w. Wmk inverted		
		x. Wmk reversed	£100	
161		1s. brown-orange	13·00	48·00
154/161 *Set of 8*			38·00	£225
154s/161s Optd 'SPECIMEN' *Set of 8*			£160	

44　**45**

(Recess D.L.R.)

1922 (20 Nov)–**26**. P 14.

No.	Type	Description	Unused	Used
		(a) Wmk Mult Script CA		
162	**37**	¼d. black (11.10.26)	1·50	1·00
163	**44**	½d. yellow-green	5·50	5·00
		a. *Bright green*	5·50	5·00
		b. *Apple-green*	8·00	12·00
164		1d. brown	50	3·25
165		1½d. scarlet (24.11.25)	9·00	17·00
166		2d. slate	50	5·00
167		2½d. purple/*pale yellow*	50	1·75
168		3d. bright blue	50	5·00
169		4d. red/*pale yellow*	1·25	19·00
		ax. Wmk reversed	£100	
		b. *Carmine/pale yellow*	4·50	18·00
170		5d. sage-green	85	22·00
		y. Wmk inverted and reversed	£110	
171		6d. purple	70	13·00
		x. Wmk reversed	£120	
172		1s. brown-orange	80	23·00
173		2s. red/*emerald* (24.11.25)	2·00	13·00
		(b) Wmk Mult Crown CA		
174	**44**	2s. red/*emerald*	21·00	£110
175		3s. black/*red*	5·00	42·00
162/175 *Set of 14*			45·00	£250
162s/175s Optd 'SPECIMEN' *Set of 14*			£250	

1928 (1 Mar). Inscr 'POSTAGE & REVENUE'. Wmk Mult Script CA. P 14.

No.	Type	Description	Unused	Used
176	**45**	½d. green	75	50
177		1d. brown	75	70
178		1½d. scarlet	75	4·50
179		2d. grey	75	50
180		2½d. purple/*yellow*	75	5·00
181		3d. bright blue	75	11·00
182		6d. purple	75	7·50
183		1s. brown-orange	3·75	7·50
184		2s. red/*emerald*	8·50	38·00
185		5s. green/*yellow*	13·00	35·00
186		10s. purple/*blue*	60·00	£120
176/186 *Set of 11*			80·00	£200
176s/186s Optd 'SPECIMEN' *Set of 11*			£200	

1935 (6 May). Silver Jubilee. As Nos. 91/94 of Antigua, but ptd by Waterlow. P 11×12.

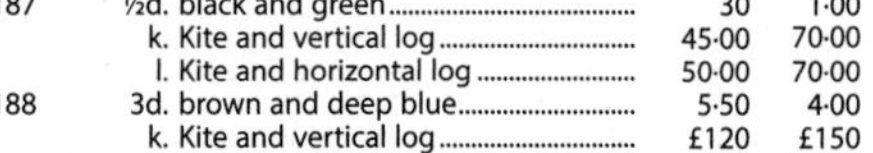

No.	Type	Description	Unused	Used
187		½d. black and green	30	1·00
		k. Kite and vertical log	45·00	70·00
		l. Kite and horizontal log	50·00	70·00
188		3d. brown and deep blue	5·50	4·00
		k. Kite and vertical log	£120	£150
189		6d. light blue and olive-green	1·75	5·50
		k. Kite and vertical log	£100	£160
190		1s. slate and purple	1·75	4·00
		k. Kite and vertical log	£100	£150
187/190 *Set of 4*			8·50	14·00
187s/190s Perf 'SPECIMEN' *Set of 4*			£100	

For illustrations of plate varieties see Omnibus section following Zanzibar.

1937 (12 May). Coronation. As Nos. 95/97 of Antigua, but ptd by D.L.R. P 14.

No.	Type	Description	Unused	Used
191		½d. myrtle-green	10	10
		a. *Deep green*	40·00	40·00
192		2d. grey-black	1·00	65
193		3d. bright blue	1·00	65
191/193 *Set of 3*			1·75	1·25
191s/193s Perf 'SPECIMEN' *Set of 3*			90·00	

46 Raking Salt　**47** Salt Industry

(Recess Waterlow)

1938 (18 June)–**45**. Wmk Mult Script CA. P 12½.

No.	Type	Description	Unused	Used
194	**46**	¼d. black	20	10
195		½d. yellowish green	9·00	15
		a. *Deep green* (6.11.44)	2·75	70
196		1d. red-brown	75	10
197		1½d. scarlet	75	15
198		2d. grey	1·00	30
199		2½d. yellow-orange	13·00	1·25
		a. *Orange* (6.11.44)	6·00	3·50

200 3d. bright blue 70 30
201 6d. mauve 22·00 3·75
201*a* 6d. sepia (9.2.45) 50 20
202 1s. yellow-bistre 5·00 14·00
202*a* 1s. grey-olive (9.2.45) 50 20
203 **47** 2s. deep rose-carmine 48·00 19·00
a. Bright rose-carmine (6.11.44) 23·00 23·00
204 5s. yellowish green 60·00 27·00
a. Deep green (6.11.44) 55·00 30·00
205 10s. bright violet 32·00 7·50
194/205 *Set of* 14 £130 60·00
194s/205s Perf 'SPECIMEN' *Set of* 14 £375

1946 (4 Nov). Victory. As Nos. 110/111 of Antigua.
206 2d. black 10 15
207 3d. blue 15 20
206s/207s Perf 'SPECIMEN' *Set of* 2 80·00

1948 (13 Sept). Royal Silver Wedding. As Nos. 112/113 of Antigua.
208 1d. red-brown 15 10
209 10s. mauve 14·00 20·00

50 Badge of the Islands

51 Flag of Turks and Caicos Islands

52 Map of islands

53 Queen Victoria and King George VI

(Recess Waterlow)

1948 (14 Dec). Centenary of Separation from Bahamas. Types **50/53**. Wmk Mult Script CA. P 12½.
210 **50** ½d. blue-green 2·25 15
211 2d. carmine 2·25 15
212 **51** 3d. blue 1·75 15
213 **52** 6d. violet 1·75 30
214 **53** 2s. black and bright blue 1·25 2·25
215 5s. black and green 2·00 8·00
216 10s. black and brown 4·25 8·00
210/216 *Set of* 7 14·00 17·00

1949 (10 Oct). 75th Anniversary of UPU. As Nos. 114/117 of Antigua.
217 2½d. red-orange 20 2·50
218 3d. deep blue 2·25 2·25
219 6d. brown 30 3·00
220 1s. olive 20 50
217/220 *Set of* 4 2·75 7·50

54 Bulk Salt Loading

55 Salt Cay

56 Caicos mail

57 Grand Turk

58 Sponge diving

59 South Creek

60 Map

61 Grand Turk Light

62 Government House

63 Cockburn Harbour

64 Government offices

65 Loading salt

66 Dependency's Badge

(Recess Waterlow)

1950 (1 Aug). Types **54/66**. Wmk Mult Script CA. P 12½.
221 **54** ½d. green 85 40
222 **55** 1d. red-brown 1·25 75
223 **56** 1½d. deep carmine 1·25 55
224 **57** 2d. red-orange 1·50 40
225 **58** 2½d. grey-olive 1·25 50
226 **59** 3d. bright blue 1·25 40
227 **60** 4d. black and rose 4·00 70
228 **61** 6d. black and blue 3·50 50
229 **62** 1s. black and blue-green 3·00 40
230 **63** 1s.6d. black and scarlet 16·00 3·25
231 **64** 2s. emerald and ultramarine 7·00 4·50
232 **65** 5s. blue and black 27·00 8·50
233 **66** 10s. black and violet 28·00 28·00
221/233 *Set of* 13 85·00 42·00

1953 (2 June). Coronation. As No. 120 of Antigua, but ptd by B.W. & Co.
234 2d. black and orange-red 60 1·25

67 MV *Kirksons*

68 Greater Flamingoes in flight

(Recess Waterlow)

1955 (1 Feb). Types **67/68**. Wmk Mult Script CA. P 12½.
235 **67** 5d. black and bright green 1·75 1·00
236 **68** 8d. black and brown 3·00 70

69 Queen Elizabeth II (after Annigoni)

70 Bonefish

71 Red Grouper

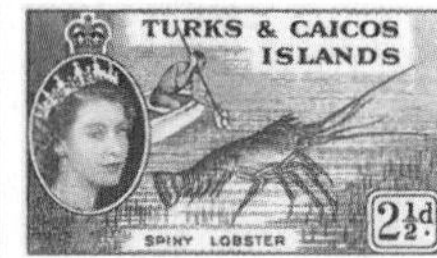
72 Spiny Lobster

73 Albacore

74 Mutton Snapper

75 Permit

76 Queen or Pink Conch

77 Greater Flamingoes

78 Spanish Mackerel

79 Salt Cay

80 *Uakon* (Caicos sloop)

81 Cable Office

82 Dependency's Badge

(Recess B.W.)

1957 (25 Nov). Types **69/82**. W w **12**. P 13½×14 (1d.), 14 (10s.) or 13½ (others).
237 **69** 1d. deep blue and carmine 60 20
238 **70** 1½d. grey-green and orange 30 30
239 **71** 2d. red-brown and olive 30 15
240 **72** 2½d. carmine and green 30 15
241 **73** 3d. turquoise-blue and purple 30 15
242 **74** 4d. lake and black 1·25 15
243 **75** 5d. slate-green and brown 1·50 40
244 **76** 6d. carmine-rose and blue 2·00 55
245 **77** 8d. vermilion and black 3·25 20
246 **78** 1s. deep blue and black 1·25 10
247 **79** 1s.6d. sepia and deep ultramarine 20·00 2·50
248 **80** 2s. deep ultramarine and brown 16·00 3·00
249 **81** 5s. black and carmine 11·00 2·75
250 **82** 10s. black and purple 26·00 8·00
237/250 *and* 253 *Set of* 15 £120 30·00

83 Map of the Turks and Caicos Islands

(Photo D.L.R.)

1959 (4 July). New Constitution. Wmk Mult Script CA. P 13½×14.
251 **83** 6d. deep olive and light orange 80 70
252 8d. violet and light orange 80 40

84 Brown Pelican

(Des Mrs. S. Hurd. Photo Harrison)

1960 (1 Nov). W w **12**. P 14×14½.
253 **84** £1 sepia and deep red 48·00 16·00

CROWN COLONY

1963 (4 June). Freedom from Hunger. As No. 146 of Antigua.
254 8d. carmine 30 15

1963 (2 Sept). Red Cross Centenary. As Nos. 147/148 of Antigua.
255 2d. red and black 15 50
256 8d. red and blue 30 50

1964 (23 Apr). 400th Birth Anniversary of William Shakespeare. As No. 164 of Antigua.
257 8d. green 30 10

1965 (17 May). ITU Centenary. As Nos. 166/167 of Antigua.
258 1d. vermilion and brown 10 10
259 2s. light emerald and turquoise-blue 20 20

1965 (25 Oct). International Co-operation Year. As Nos. 168/169 of Antigua.
260 1d. reddish purple and turquoise-green 10 15
261 8d. deep bluish green and lavender 20 15

1966 (24 Jan). Churchill Commemoration. As Nos. 170/173 of Antigua.
262 1d. new blue 10 10
263 2d. deep green 20 10
264 8d. brown 35 10
a. Gold ptg double £160
265 1s.6d. bluish violet 50 1·10
262/265 Set of 4 1·00 1·25

The price quoted for No. 264a is for examples with the two impressions clearly separated. Examples with the two impressions nearly co-incident are worth considerably less.

1966 (4 Feb). Royal Visit. As Nos. 271/272 of Bahamas.
266 8d. black and ultramarine 40 10
267 1s. 6d. black and magenta 60 20

85 Andrew Symmer going ashore

(Des V. Whiteley. Photo D.L.R.)

1966 (1 Oct). Bicentenary of Ties with Britain T **85** and similar horiz designs. P 13½.
268 1d. deep blue and orange 10 10
269 8d. red, blue and orange-yellow 20 15
270 1s.6d. multicoloured 25 20
268/270 *Set of* 3 50 40
Designs: 1d. T **85**; 8d. Andrew Symmer and Royal Warrant; 1s.6d. Arms and Royal Cypher.

1966 (1 Dec). 20th Anniversary of UNESCO. As Nos. 196/198 of Antigua.
271 1d. slate-violet, red, yellow and orange. 10 10
272 8d. orange-yellow, violet and deep olive 40 10
273 1s.6d. black, bright purple and orange 65 40
271/273 *Set of* 3 1·00 50

88 Turk's-head Cactus

89 Boat-building

90 Arms of Turks and Caicos Islands

91 Queen Elizabeth II

(Des V. Whiteley. Photo Harrison)

1967 (1 Feb). Designs as Types **88/91**. W w **12**. P 14½×14 (vert) or 14×14½ (horiz).

274	1d. olive-yellow, vermilion and bright bluish violet	10	10
275	1½d. brown and orange-yellow	1·50	10
276	2d. deep slate and deep orange-yellow	20	10
277	3d. agate and dull green	20	10
278	4d. bright mauve, black and turquoise	2·75	10
279	6d. sepia and new blue	2·25	10
280	8d. yellow, turquoise-blue and deep blue	55	10
281	1s. maroon and turquoise	20	10
282	1s.6d. orange-yellow, lake-brown and deep turquoise-blue	50	20
283	2s. multicoloured	1·25	2·00
284	3s. maroon and turquoise-blue	3·50	40
285	5s. ochre, blue and new blue	2·00	2·75
286	10s. multicoloured	5·00	3·00
287	£1 Prussian blue, silver and crimson	5·00	13·00
274/287 *Set of* 14		22·00	19·00

Designs: Vert 1d. T **88**. As T **88**—2d. Donkey; 3d. Sisal industry 6d. Salt industry; 8d. Skin-diving; 1s.6d. Water-skiing. Horiz 1½d. T **89**. As T **89**—4d. Conch industry; 1s. Fishing; 2s. Crawfish industry; 3s. Maps of Turks and Caicos Islands and West Indies; 5s. Fishing industry. 10s. T **90**. £1 T **91**.

102 Turks Islands 1d. Stamp of 1867

(Des R. Granger Barrett. Photo Harrison)

1967 (1 May). Stamp Centenary. T **102** and similar horiz designs. W w **12**. P 14½.

288	1d. black and light magenta	15	10
	w. Wmk inverted	50·00	
289	6d. black and bluish grey	25	15
290	1s. black and turquoise-blue	25	15
288/290 *Set of* 3		60	30

Designs: 1d. T **102**; 6d. Queen Elizabeth 'stamp' and Turks Islands 6d. stamp of 1867; 1s. Turks Islands 1s. stamp of 1867.

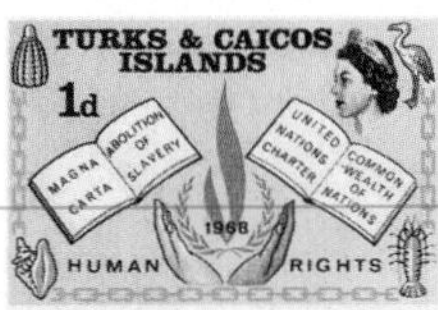

104 Human Rights Emblem and Charter

(Des R. Granger Barrett. Photo Harrison)

1968 (1 Apr). Human Rights Year. W w **12**. P 14×14½.

291	**104**	1d. multicoloured	10	10
292		8d. multicoloured	15	15
293		1s.6d. multicoloured	15	15
291/293 *Set of* 3			30	30

105 Dr Martin Luther King and 'Freedom March'

(Des V. Whiteley. Photo Harrison)

1968 (1 Oct). Martin Luther King Commemoration. W w **12**. P 14×14½.

294	**105**	2d. yellow-brown, blackish brown and deep blue	10	10
295		8d. yellow-brown, blackish brown and lake	15	15
296		1s.6d. yellow-brown, blackish brown and violet	15	15
294/296 *Set of* 3			30	30

(New Currency. 100 cents = 1 dollar)

(**106**)

107 The Nativity with John the Baptist

1969 (8 Sept)–**71**. Decimal currency. Nos. 274/287 surch as T **106** by Harrison & Sons, and new value (¼c.) as T **90**.

297	¼c. pale greenish grey and multicoloured	10	10
	a. Bronze-green and multicoloured (2.2.71)	1·75	30
298	1c. on 1d. olive-yellow, vermilion and bright bluish violet	10	10
	a. Wmk sideways	10	10
299	2c. on 2d. deep slate and deep orange-yellow	10	10
	a. Wmk sideways	10	10
300	3c. on 3d. agate and dull green	10	10
	a. Wmk sideways	10	10
301	4c. on 4d. bright mauve, black and turquoise	3·50	10
302	5c. on 6d. sepia and new blue	10	10
	a. Wmk sideways	10	60
303	7c. on 8d. yellow, turquoise-blue and deep blue	10	10
	a. Wmk sideways	10	40
304	8c. on 1½d. brown and orange-yellow	10	10
	w. Wmk inverted	38·00	
305	10c. on 1s. maroon and turquoise	20	10
306	15c. on 1s.6d. orange-yellow, lake-brown and deep turquoise-blue	25	10
	a. Wmk sideways	20	25
307	20c. on 2s. multicoloured	30	25
308	30c. on 3s. maroon and turquoise-blue	55	35
309	50c. on 5s. ochre, blue and new blue	1·25	45
310	$1 on 10s. mulicoloured	2·50	3·00
311	$2 on £1 Prussian blue, silver and crimson	2·75	15·00
	a. Wmk sideways	2·75	8·00
297/311 *Set of* 15		10·50	18·00
298a/311a *Set of* 7		3·00	8·50

The 4, 8, 10, 20, 30, 50c., and $1 exist with PVA gum as well as gum arabic.

No. 311 was only on sale through the Crown Agents.

(Des adapted by V. Whiteley. Litho D.L.R.)

1969 (20 Oct). Christmas. Scenes from 16th-century *Book of Hours*. T **107** and similar vert design. Multicoloured. W w **12**. P 13×12½.

312	1c. Type **107**	10	10
313	3c. The Flight into Egypt	10	10
314	15c. Type **107**	15	10
315	30c. As 3c.	25	20
312/315 *Set of* 4		40	40

109 Coat of Arms

110 *Christ bearing the Cross*

(Des L. Curtis. Litho B.W.)

1970 (2 Feb). New Constitution. Multicoloured; background colours given. W w **12** (sideways). P 13×12½.

316	**109**	7c. brown	40	25
317		35c. deep violet-blue	60	25

(Des, recess and litho Enschedé)

1970 (17 Mar). Easter. Details from the *Small Engraved Passion* by Dürer. T **110** and similar vert designs. W w **12** (sideways). P 13×13½.

318	5c. olive-grey and blue	10	10
319	7c. olive-grey and vermilion	10	10
320	50c. olive-grey and red-brown	60	1·00
318/320 *Set of* 3		70	1·10

Designs: 5c. T **110**; 7c. *Christ on the Cross*; 50c. *The Lamentation of Christ*

113 Dickens and Scene from *Oliver Twist*

(Des Sylvia Goaman. Recess and litho D.L.R.)

1970 (17 June). Death Centenary of Charles Dickens. T **113** and similar horiz designs. W w **12** (sideways). P 13.

321	1c. black and yellow-brown/*yellow*	10	50
322	3c. black and Prussian blue/*flesh*	20	40
323	15c. black and grey blue/*flesh*	60	20
324	30c. black and drab/*blue*	80	40
321/324 *Set of* 4		1·50	1·40

Designs (each incorporating portrait of Dickens as in T **113**, and a scene from one of his novels): 1c. T **113**; 3c. *A Christmas Carol*; 15c. *Pickwick Papers*; 30c. *The Old Curiosity Shop*.

114 Ambulance–1870

(Des Harrison. Litho B.W.)

1970 (4 Aug). Centenary of British Red Cross. T **114** and similar horiz design. Multicoloured. W w **12**. P 13½×14.

325	1c. Type **114**	10	70
326	5c. Ambulance–1970	20	10
	a. Wmk sideways	30	10
	ab. Grey omitted	£350	
327	15c. Type **114**	40	15
	a. Wmk sideways	50	10
328	30c. As 5c.	50	20
	a. Wmk sideways	60	40
325/328 *Set of* 4		1·00	1·00

115 Duke of Albemarle and Coat of Arms

(Des V. Whiteley. Litho Enschedé)

1970 (1 Dec). Tercentenary of Issue of Letters Patent. T **115** and similar horiz design. Multicoloured. W w **12**. P 12½×13½.

329	1c. Type **115**	10	30
330	8c. Arms of Charles II and Elizabeth II	25	40
331	10c. Type **115**	25	15
332	35c. As 8c.	55	75
329/332 *Set of* 4		1·00	1·40

Uganda

PRICES FOR STAMPS ON COVER TO 1945

The type-written stamps of Uganda, Nos. 1/53, are very rare used on cover.

Nos. 54/60	*from* × 20
No. 61	—
Nos. 70/75	*from* × 12
No. 76	—
Nos. 84/90	*from* × 20
No. 91	—
Nos. 92/93	*from* × 40

PROTECTORATE

Following a period of conflict between Islamic, Protestant and Roman Catholic factions, Uganda was declared to be in the British sphere of influence by the Anglo-German Agreement of July 1890. The British East Africa Company exercised a variable degree of control until 27 August 1894 when the country was declared a British Protectorate.

Before the introduction of Nos. 84/91 the stamps of Uganda were only valid for internal postage. Letters for overseas were franked with British East Africa issues on arrival at Mombasa.

(Currency. 200 cowries = 1 rupee)

'U G' 50 — 1

'U G' 20 — 2

TYPE-WRITTEN STAMPS. Nos. 1/53 were type-written by the Revd. E. Millar at Mengo for the Uganda administration. For all 'printings' a thin laid paper was used, and all issues were imperforate and ungummed. The laid lines are invariably horizontal, with the exception of Nos. 19a, 20a and 38b.

The original typewriter used had wide letters, but in late April, 1895 Millar obtained a new machine on which the type face was in a narrower fount.

Each sheet was made up of whatever values were required at the time, so that different values can be found *se-tenant* or *tête-bêche*. These last were caused by the paper being inverted in the machine so that space at the foot could be utilised.

For the first issue the sheets were of 117 (9×13), but with the introduction of the narrower width (Nos. 17 onwards) a larger number of stamps per sheet, 143 (11×13), was adopted.

PRICES. The prices of Nos. 1/53 vary greatly according to condition. The thin paper used is subject to creasing, staining and thinning. Catalogue quality is for fine examples, with borders visible on at least three sides. Used stamps are usually found with manuscript crosses in pencil, crayon or ink; examples with initials, dates or place names may command a premium, but note that stamps cancelled to order with circular datestamps (usually at Kampala in 1898) tend to be worth less.

1895 (20 Mar). Wide letters. Wide stamps, 20 to 26 mm wide.

No.	Type		Unused	Used
1	1	10 (c.) black	£4250	£2250
2		20 (c.) black	£7500	£1800
		a. 'U A' for 'U G'	†	£6500
3		30 (c.) black	£2000	£1600
4		40 (c.) black	£6000	£2250
5		50 (c.) black	£1400	£1100
		a. 'U A' for 'U G'	†	£8500
6		60 (c.) black	£2500	£2250

It is now believed that the 5, 15 and 25 cowries values in this width, formerly listed, do not exist.

1895 (May). Wide stamps with pen-written surcharges, in black.

No.	Type		Unused	Used
8	1	5 on 10 (c.) black	†	£70000
9		10 on 30 (c.) black	†	£70000
10		10 on 50 (c.) black	†	£70000
11		15 on 10 (c.) black	†	£50000
12		15 on 20 (c.) black	†	£70000
13		15 on 40 (c.) black	†	£60000
14		15 on 50 (c.) black	†	£70000
15		25 on 50 (c.) black	†	£70000
16		50 on 60 (c.) black	†	£70000

The manuscript provisionals, Nos. 9/16 come from the Mission at Ngogwe, most of the manuscript surcharges including the initials of the Revd. G. R. Blackledge stationed there. But No. 8, known only in *se-tenant* form with an unsurcharged pair of No. 1 *on cover*, was initialled 'E.M.' by Revd. E. Millar, presumably at Mengo.

1895 (Apr). Wide letters. Narrow stamps, 16 to 18 mm wide.

No.	Type		Unused	Used
17	1	5 (c.) black	£3250	£1300
18		10 (c.) black	£3250	£1600
19		15 (c.) black	£2000	£1500
		a. Vertically laid paper	†	£5000
20		20 (c.) black	£3250	£1500
		a. Vertically laid paper	†	£6500
21		25 (c.) black	£1800	£1600
22		30 (c.) black	£8500	£8500
23		40 (c.) black	£8000	£8000
24		50 (c.) black	£3750	£4250
25		60 (c.) black	£8000	£8500

A used pair of No. 19a and two used examples of No. 20a have been seen. With the exception of No. 38b, Nos. 1/53 otherwise show the laid lines horizontal.

To qualify as Nos. 22/25, which are very rare stamps, examples must show borders on both vertical sides and not exceed 18 mm in width. Examples not fulfilling both criteria can only be classified as belonging to the 'Wide stamps' group, Nos. 3/6.

1895 (May). Narrow letters. Narrow stamps 16 to 18 mm wide.

No.	Type		Unused	Used
26	2	5 (c.) black	£1900	
27		10 (c.) black	£2000	
28		15 (c.) black	£2000	
29		20 (c.) black	£1700	
30		25 (c.) black	£1900	
31		30 (c.) black	£2250	
32		40 (c.) black	£1900	
33		50 (c.) black	£2000	
34		60 (c.) black	£2750	

1895 (Nov). Narrow letters. Narrow stamps, 16–18 mm wide. Change of colour.

No.	Type		Unused	Used
35	2	5 (c.) violet	£700	£650
36		10 (c.) violet	£650	£650
37		15 (c.) violet	£1100	£600
38		20 (c.) violet	£475	£300
		a. 'G U' for 'U G'		
		b. Vertically laid paper	£3000	
39		25 (c.) violet	£1800	£1600
40		30 (c.) violet	£2250	£1100
41		40 (c.) violet	£2250	£1500
42		50 (c.) violet	£2000	£1500
43		100 (c.) violet	£2500	£3000

Stamps of 35 (c.) and 45 (c.) have been recorded in violet, on vertically laid paper. They were never prepared for postal use, and did not represent a postal rate, but were type-written to oblige a local official. (*Price £2750 each, unused*)

'V.96.R' 25 'Uganda'

3

1896 (June).

No.	Type		Unused	Used
44	3	5 (c.) violet	£750	£1000
45		10 (c.) violet	£850	£650
46		15 (c.) violet	£750	£750
47		20 (c.) violet	£400	£225
48		25 (c.) violet	£700	£900
49		30 (c.) violet	£800	£850
50		40 (c.) violet	£900	£900
51		50 (c.) violet	£750	£800
52		60 (c.) violet	£1600	£2000
53		100 (c.) violet	£1500	£2000

(New Currency. 16 annas = 1 rupee)

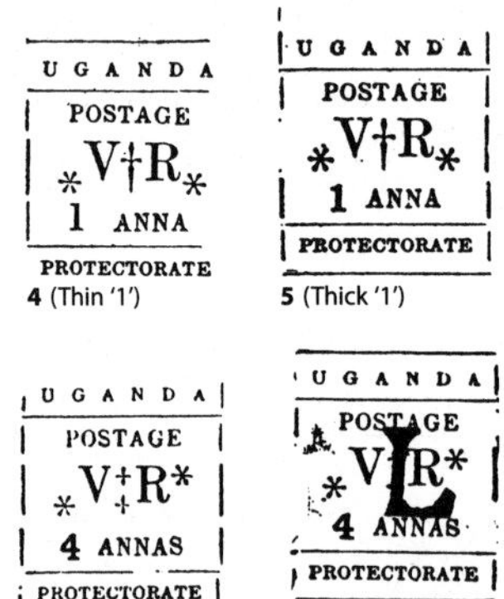

4 (Thin '1') 5 (Thick '1') 6 7

In the 2a. and 3a. the dagger points upwards; the stars in the 2a. are level with the top of 'VR'. The 8a. is as T **6** but with left star at top and right star at foot. The 1r. has three stars at foot. The 5r. has central star raised and the others at foot.

(Type-set by the Revd. F. Rowling at Lubwa's, in Usoga)

1896 (7 Nov). Thick white wove paper (Nos. 54/58) or thin yellowish paper ruled with vertical lines 9 mm apart (Nos. 59/61).

*(a) Types **4/6***

No.	Type		Unused	Used
54	4	1a. black	£110	£100
		a. Small 'o' in 'POSTAGE'	£600	£600
55	5	1a. black	23·00	26·00
		a. Small 'o' in 'POSTAGE'	85·00	£100
56	6	2a. black	29·00	35·00
		a. Small 'o' in 'POSTAGE'	£100	£120
57		3a. black	29·00	45·00
		a. Small 'o' in 'POSTAGE'	£120	£180
58		4a. black	32·00	38·00
		a. Small 'o' in 'POSTAGE'	£120	£130
59		8a. black	40·00	48·00
		a. Small 'o' in 'POSTAGE'	£140	£180
60		1r. black	85·00	£100
		a. Small 'o' in 'POSTAGE'	£350	£425
61		5r. black	£275	£350
		a. Small 'o' in 'POSTAGE'	£900	£1100

*(b) Optd 'L', in black as in T **7** for local use, by a postal official, R. R. Racey, at Kampala*

No.	Type		Unused	Used
70	4	1a. black	£190	£170
		a. Small 'o' in 'POSTAGE'	£1400	£1200
71	6	2a. black	£120	£120
		a. Small 'o' in 'POSTAGE'	£550	£600
72		3a. black	£275	£325
		a. Small 'o' in 'POSTAGE'	£1700	£2000
73		4a. black	£120	£160
		a. Small 'o' in 'POSTAGE'	£550	
74		8a. black	£200	£300
		a. Small 'o' in 'POSTAGE'	£1500	£1900
75		1r. black	£375	£450
		a. Small 'o' in 'POSTAGE'	£2000	
76		5r. black	£22000	£22000

Tête-bêche pairs of all values may be found owing to the settings of 16 (4×4) being printed side by side or above one another. They are worth a premium. The variety with small 'O' occurs on R. 3/1.

8

9

UGANDA
(10)

(Recess D.L.R.)

1898 (Nov)–**1902**. P 14.

(a) Wmk Crown CA

No.	Type		Unused	Used
84	8	1a. scarlet	7·00	4·50
		a. Carmine-rose (1902)	2·25	1·75
86		2a. red-brown	11·00	11·00
87		3a. pale grey	22·00	45·00
		a. Bluish grey	21·00	20·00
		x. Wmk reversed	£325	
88		4a. deep green	17·00	10·00
89		8a. pale olive	15·00	30·00
		a. Grey-green	38·00	50·00

(b) Wmk Crown CC

No.	Type		Unused	Used
90	9	1r. dull blue	60·00	65·00
		a. Bright blue	70·00	80·00
91		5r. brown	£110	£130
84/91 *Set of 7*			£200	£225
84s/91s Optd 'SPECIMEN' *Set of 7*			£200	

Examples of No. 86 are known bisected to pay the 1 anna rate during a shortage of 1a. stamps at the post office in Masindi in late 1899 and early 1900.

Nos. 84/89 exist without watermark or with double-lined lettering from the marginal watermark due to the way in which sheets were cut for printing.

On 1 April 1901 the postal administrations of British East Africa and Uganda were merged. Subsequent issues to 1962 are listed under KENYA, UGANDA and TANGANYIKA.

1902 (Feb). T **11** of British East Africa (Kenya, Uganda, and Tanganyika) optd with T **10**.

No.		Unused	Used
92	½a. yellow-green	3·00	2·25
	a. Opt omitted (in pair with normal)	£5500	
	b. Opt inverted (at foot)	£2250	
	c. Opt double	£2750	
	w. Wmk inverted	£400	
	x. Wmk reversed	—	£325
93	2½a. deep blue (R.)	5·00	3·25
	a. Opt double	£600	
	b. Inverted 'S' (R. 1/1)	£120	£100
	x. Wmk reversed	£375	
	y. Wmk inverted and reversed	£375	

The Eastern Province of Uganda was transferred to British East Africa on 1 April 1902.

SELF-GOVERNMENT

(New Currency. 100 cents = 1 East African, later Uganda shilling)

11 Ripon Falls and Speke Memorial

(Des S. Scott. Recess B.W.)

1962 (28 July). Centenary of Speke's Discovery of Source of the Nile. W w **12**. P 14.

No.	Type		Unused	Used
95	11	30c. black and red	20	25
96		50c. black and slate-violet	20	10
97		1s.30 black and green	1·25	25
98		2s.50 black and blue	2·50	2·25
95/98 *Set of 4*			3·75	2·50

INDEPENDENT

12 Murchison Falls

13 Tobacco-growing

14 Mulago Hospital

1s.30 Dome flaw–a large white flaw to left of dome of Namirembe Cathedral (Pl. 1A-1A, R. 9/10)

(Des V. Whiteley. Photo Harrison)

1962 (9 Oct)–**64**. Independence. Various designs as Types **12/14**. P 15×14 (5c. to 50c.) or 14½ (others).

No.	Description	Unused	Used
99	5c. deep bluish green	10	10
100	10c. reddish brown	10	10
	a. Brown (coil)	10	1·00
	b. Deep yellow-brown (17.10.64)	10	10
101	15c. black, red and green	10	10
102	20c. plum and buff	10	10
103	30c. blue	10	10
104	50c. black and turquoise-green	10	10
105	1s. sepia, red and turquoise-green	1·25	20
106	1s.30 yellow-orange and violet	25	10
	a. Dome flaw	35·00	
107	2s. black, carmine and light blue	50	70
108	5s. vermilion and deep green	8·00	2·25
109	10s. slate and chestnut	4·25	4·75
110	20s. brown and blue	4·50	21·00
99/110 *Set of* 12		17·00	26·00

Designs: As Types **12/13**—5c. T **12**; 10c. T **13**; 15c. Coffee growing; 20c. Ankole cattle; 30c. Cotton; 50c. Mountains of the Moon. As T **14**—1s. T **14**; 1s.30, Cathedrals and Mosque; 2s. Makerere College; 5s. Copper mining; 10s. Cement industry; 20s. Parliament Buildings.

15 South African Crowned Crane

(Photo Harrison)

1965 (20 Feb). International Trade Fair, Kampala. P 14½×14.

No.	Type	Description	Unused	Used
111	**15**	30c. multicoloured	15	10
112		1s.30 multicoloured	25	10

16 Black Bee-eater

17 African Jacana

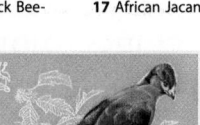

18 Ruwenzori Turaco

(Des Mrs. R. Fennessy. Photo Harrison)

1965 (9 Oct). Birds. Various designs as Types **16/18**. P 15×14 (5c., 15c., 20c., 40c., 50c.), 14×15 (10c., 30c., 65c.) or 14½ (others).

No.	Description	Unused	Used
113	5c. multicoloured	10	10
114	10c. chestnut, black and light blue	10	10
115	15c. yellow and sepia	20	10
116	20c. multicoloured	20	10
117	30c. black and brown-red	1·50	10
118	40c. multicoloured	1·00	1·75
119	50c. grey-blue and reddish violet	25	10
	a. White bird (grey-blue omitted)	£1700	
120	65c. orange-red, black and light grey	2·00	2·75
121	1s. multicoloured	50	10
122	1s.30 chestnut, black and yellow	4·50	30
123	2s.50 multicoloured	3·50	65
124	5s. multicoloured	6·00	4·00
125	10s. multicoloured	9·00	11·00
126	20s. multicoloured	20·00	38·00
113/126 *Set of* 14		42·00	48·00

Designs: Vert as T **16**—5c. T **16**; 15c. Orange Weaver; 20c. Narina Trogon; 40c. Blue-breasted Kingfisher; 50c. Whale-headed Stork. Horiz as T **17**—10c. T **17**; 30c. Sacred Ibis; 65c. Red-crowned Bishop. As T **18**. Vert—1s.30, African Fish Eagle; 5s. Lilac-breasted Roller. Horiz—1s. T **18**; 2s.50, Great Blue Turaco; 10s. Black-collared Lovebird; 20s. South African Crowned Crane.

The 15c., 40c., 65c., and 1s. exist with PVA gum as well as gum arabic.

19 Carved Screen

(Des Mrs. R. Fennessy. Photo Harrison)

1967 (26 Oct). 13th Commonwealth Parliamentary Association Conference. T **19** and similar horiz designs. Multicoloured. P 14.

No.	Description	Unused	Used
127	30c. Type **19**	10	10
128	50c. Arms of Uganda	10	10
129	1s.30 Parliamentary Building	10	10
130	2s.50 Conference Chamber	15	1·75
127/130 *Set of* 4		30	1·75

20 *Cordia abyssinica*

21 *Acacia drepanolobium*

(Des Mrs. R. Fennessy. Photo Harrison)

1969 (9 Oct)–**74**. Flowers. Various designs as Types **20/21**. Chalk-surfaced paper. P 14½×14 (5c. to 70c.) or 14 (others).

No.	Description	Unused	Used
131	5c. brown, green and light olive-yellow	10	1·00
	a. Glazed, ordinary paper (11.4.73)	40	10
132	10c. multicoloured	10	10
	a. Glazed, ordinary paper (27.9.72)	40	10
133	15c. multicoloured	40	10
134	20c. bluish violet, yellow-olive and pale sage-green	15	10
	a. Glazed, ordinary paper (27.9.72)	40	10
135	30c. multicoloured	20	10
136	40c. reddish violet, yellow-green and pale olive-grey	20	10
137	50c. multicoloured	20	10
138	60c. multicoloured	45	2·75
	a. Glazed, ordinary paper (9.5.73)	17·00	40
139	70c. multicoloured	25	30
	a. Glazed, ordinary paper (27.9.72)	1·00	45
140	1s. multicoloured	20	10
	a. Glazed, ordinary paper (22.1.71)	1·00	10
141	1s.50 multicoloured (cobalt background)	25	10
	a. Glazed, ordinary paper (3.2.71)	50	10
	b. Azure background (chalk-surfaced paper) (21.1.74)	55	30
142	2s.50 multicoloured	30	1·25
	a. Glazed, ordinary paper (3.2.71)	1·25	10
143	5s. multicoloured	40	1·60
	a. Glazed, ordinary paper (3.2.71)	1·75	10
144	10s. multicoloured	50	4·50
	a. Glazed, ordinary paper (3.2.71)	3·75	10
145	20s. multicoloured	1·00	6·00
	a. Glazed, ordinary paper (22.1.71)	12·00	15
131/145 *Set of* 15		3·50	15·00
131a/145a *Set of* 11		35·00	1·40

Designs: As T **20**—5c. T **20**; 10c. *Grewia similis*; 15c. *Cassia. didymobotrya*; 20c. *Coleus barbatus*; 30c. *Ockna ovata*; 40c. *Ipomoea spathulata*; 50c. *Spathodea nilotica*; 60c. *Oncoba spinosa*; 70c. *Carissa edulis*. As T **21**—1s. T **21**; 1s.50, *Clerodendrum myricoides*; 2s.50, *Acanthus arboreus*; 5s. *Kigelia aethiopium*; 10s. *Erythrina abyssinica*; 20s. *Monodora myristica*.

Some of the glazed ordinary paper printings were available in Uganda some time before the London release dates which are quoted in the listings.

STAMP BOOKLETS

1962 (9 Oct). Black on buff cover. Stitched.

No.	Description	Price
SB1	5s. booklet containing 10c., 15c., 20c., 30c. and 50c. (Nos. 100/104), each in block of 4	6·50

1965. Black on blue (No. SB2) or buff (No. SB3) covers. Stitched.

No.	Description	Price
SB2	3s. booklet containing 4×15c. and 8×30c. (Nos. 115, 117) in blocks of 4	10·00
SB3	5s. booklet containing 4×15c. and 4×50c., and 8×30c. Nos. 115, 117, 119) in blocks of 4	11·00

1970. Black on blue (No. SB4) or buff (No. SB5) covers. Stitched.

No.	Description	Price
SB4	3s. booklet containing 4×5c. and 4×10c., and 8×30c. (Nos. 131/132, 135) in blocks of 4	15·00
SB5	5s. booklet containing 4×5c., 4×10c. and 4×50c., and 8×30c. (Nos. 131/132, 135, 137) in blocks of 4	15·00

POSTAGE DUE STAMPS

The Postage Due stamps of Kenya, Uganda and Tanganyika were used in Uganda until 2 January 1967.

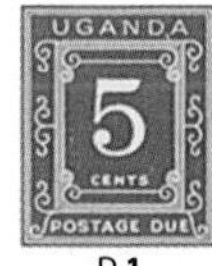

D **1**

(Litho D.L.R.)

1967 (3 Jan). Chalk-surfaced paper. P 14×13½.

No.	Type	Description	Unused	Used
D1	D **1**	5c. scarlet	20	4·50
D2		10c. green	20	5·00
D3		20c. deep blue	35	5·00
D4		30c. red-brown	40	6·50
D5		40c. bright purple	60	15·00
D6		1s. orange	1·50	13·00
D1/D6 *Set of* 6			3·00	45·00

1970 (31 Mar). As Nos. D1/D6, but on glazed ordinary paper. P 14×15.

No.	Type	Description	Unused	Used
D7	D **1**	5c. scarlet	15	3·25
D8		10c. green	15	2·50
D9		20c. deep blue	25	3·00
D10		30c. red-brown	35	4·25
D11		40c. bright purple	55	5·50
D7/D11 *Set of* 5			1·25	17·00

TELEGRAPH STAMPS

T **1** T **2**

1902 (1 June). Black on coloured paper. Pin perf 12.

No.	Type	Description	Unused	Used
T1	T **1**	2a. on *blue-green*	£120	75·00
		a. Seriffed 'G' in lower 'TELEGRAPHS'	£200	£130
T2		4a. on *yellow*	£130	90·00
		a. Seriffed 'G' in lower 'TELEGRAPHS'	£225	£150
T3		6a. on *magenta*	£140	£110
		a. 'SIK' for 'SIX' in upper half	£250	£160
		b. Seriffed 'G' in lower 'TELEGRAPHS'	£250	£180
T4		8a. on *rose*	£180	£120
		a. Seriffed 'G' in lower 'TELEGRAPHS'	£275	£200
T5		12a. on *green*	£250	£190
		a. On greyish blue	£300	£250
		b. Seriffed 'G' in lower 'TELEGRAPHS'	£375	£275
T6	T **2**	1r. on white laid paper	£325	£110
		a. Stop for comma after lower 'TELEGRAPHS'	£375	£150
		b. No stop after lower 'RUPEE'	£375	£150
		c. on white wove paper	—	£120
T7		2r. on *yellow*	£325	£140
		a. Stop for comma after lower 'TELEGRAPHS'	£375	£180
T8		3r. on *blue-green*	£550	£325
		a. Stop for comma after lower 'TELEGRAPHS'	£650	£375
T9		4r. on *magenta*	£750	£375
		a. Stop for comma after lower 'TELEGRAPHS'	£850	£425
		b. No stop after lower 'RUPEES'	£850	£425
T10		5r. on *rose*	£850	£400
		a. Stop for comma after lower 'TELEGRAPHS'	£950	£450
T11		10r. on *greyish blue*	£1400	£700
		a. Stop for comma after lower 'TELEGRAPHS'	£1600	£850
T12		20r. on white laid paper	£2250	£1100
		a. Stop for comma after lower 'TELEGRAPHS'	£2750	£1300
		b. No stop after lower 'RUPEES'	£2750	£1300

Nos. T1/T5 were printed in sheets of 56 (14×4), from stereotyped plates formed from an original typeset row of seven.

Nos. T6/T12 were in sheets of 48 (12×4), similarly formed from an original typeset row of six.

No. T3a occurs on the seventh and 14th stamp of each row.

The variety with seriffed 'G' occurs on the first and eighth stamp of each row.

Nos. T7/T9 are known with the 'S' of 'RUPEES' omitted but these are of proof status.

Unused prices are for whole stamps. Used prices are for half stamps, as the stamps were bisected in use, following the practice of the Ceylon and India telegraph departments. The upper halves remained on the receipts handed back to senders, while the lower halves were originally retained for official record purposes.

Victoria *see* Australia

Virgin Islands *see* British Virgin Islands

Western Australia *see* Australia

Western Samoa *see* Samoa

Zambia

INDEPENDENT

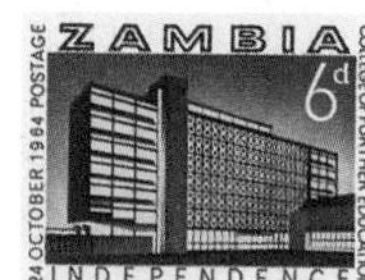

11 President Kaunda and Victoria Falls   **12** College of Further Education, Lusaka

(Des M. Goaman (3d., 6d.), Gabriel Ellison (1s.3d.). Photo Harrison)

1964 (24 Oct). Independence. Types **11/12** and similar vert design. P 13½×11½ (6d.) or 14½×13½ (others).

91	**11**	3d. sepia, yellow-green and blue	10	10
92	**12**	6d. deep violet and yellow	15	20
93	–	1s.3d. red, black, sepia and orange	20	25
91/93 *Set of 3*			40	50

Design: 1s.3d. Barotse dancer.

14 Maize-Farmer and Silo   **15** Health–Radiographer

21 Fishing at Mpulungu   **22** Tobacco Worker

(Des Gabriel Ellison. Photo Harrison)

1964 (24 Oct). Types **14/15**, **21/22** and similar designs. P 14½ (½d. to 4d.), 14½×13½ (1s.3d., 2s. and £1) or 13½×14½ (others).

94		½d. red, black and yellow-green	10	1·50
95		1d. brown, black and bright blue	10	10
96		2d. red, deep brown and orange	10	10
97		3d. black and red	10	10
98		4d. black, brown and orange	15	10
99		6d. orange, deep brown and deep bluish green	30	10
100		9d. carmine, black and bright blue	15	10
101		1s. black, yellow-bistre and blue	15	10
102		1s.3d. light red, yellow, black and blue	20	10
103		2s. bright blue, black, deep brown and orange	25	30
		a. Black (detail of heads) omitted	£300	
104		2s.6d. black and orange-yellow	1·00	35
105		5s. black, yellow and green	1·00	1·00
106		10s. black and orange	4·50	4·75
107		£1 black, brown, yellow and red	2·00	7·50
94/107 *Set of 14*			9·00	14·00

Designs: Vert (as T **15**)— 1d. T **15**; 2d. Chinyau dancer; 3d. Cotton-picking. (As T **22**)—1s. 3d. T **22**; 2s. Tonga basket-making; £1 Makishi dancer. Horiz (as T **14**)—½d. T **14**; 4d. Angoni bull. (As T **21**)— 6d. Communications, old and new; 9d. Zambezi sawmills and Redwood flower; 1s. T **21**, 2s.6d. Luangwa Game Reserve; 5s. Education—student; 10s. Copper mining.

Nos. 94/95 and 97 exist in coils, constructed from normal sheets.

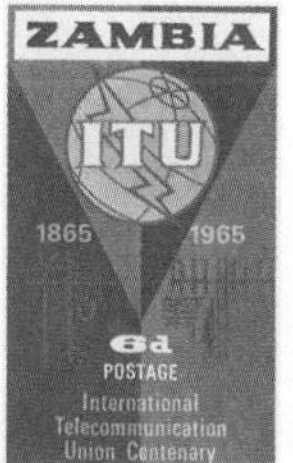

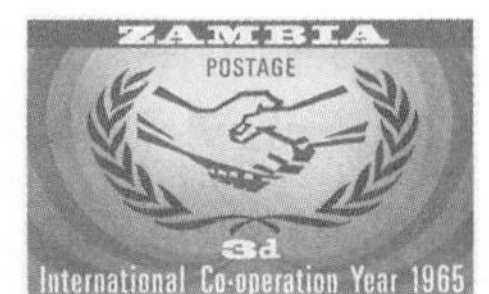

28 ITU Emblem and Symbols   **29** ICY Emblem

(Photo Harrison)

1965 (26 July). ITU Centenary. P 14×14½.

108	**28**	6d. light reddish violet and gold	15	10
109		2s.6d. brownish grey and gold	85	1·50

(Photo Harrison)

1965 (26 July). International Co-operation Year. P 14½.

110	**29**	3d. turquoise and gold	15	10
111		1s.3d. ultramarine and gold	45	45

30 State House, Lusaka   **34** WHO Building and UN Flag

(Des Gabriel Ellison. Photo Harrison)

1965 (18 Oct). First Anniversary of Independence. T **30** and similar multicoloured designs. No wmk. P 13½×14½ (3d.), 14×13½ (6d.) or 13½×14 (others).

112		3d. Type **30**	10	10
113		6d. Fireworks, Independence Stadium	10	10
		a. Bright purple (fireworks) omitted	£160	
114		1s.3d. *Clematopsis (vert)*	15	10
115		2s.6d. *Tithonia diversifolia (vert)*	30	1·25
112/115 *Set of 4*			50	1·25

(Des M. Goaman. Photo Harrison)

1966 (18 May). Inauguration of WHO Headquarters, Geneva. P 14½.

116	**34**	3d. lake-brown, gold and new blue	40	10
		a. Gold omitted	£120	
117		1s.3d. gold, new blue and deep bluish violet	1·40	95

35 Proposed University Building   **36** National Assembly Building

(Des Gabriel Ellison. Photo Harrison)

1966 (12 July). Opening of Zambia University. P 14½.

118	**35**	3d. blue-green and copper-bronze	10	10
119		1s.3d. reddish violet and copper-bronze	20	10

The building shown on T **35** was never built.

(Des Gabriel Ellison. Photo Harrison)

1967 (2 May). Inauguration of National Assembly Building. P 14½.

120	**36**	3d. black and copper-bronze	10	10
121		6d. olive-green and copper-bronze	10	10

37 Airport Scene

(Des Gabriel Ellison. Photo Harrison)

1967 (2 Oct). Opening of Lusaka International Airport. P 13½×14½.

122	**37**	6d. violet-blue and copper-bronze	15	10
123		2s.6d. brown and copper-bronze	60	1·00

38 Youth Service Badge   **39** 'Co-operative Farming'

(Des Gabriel Ellison. Photo Harrison)

1967 (23 Oct). National Development. Types **38/39** and similar designs. P 13½×14½ (6d., 1s.6d.) or 14½×13½ (others).

124		4d. black, red and gold	10	10
125		6d. black, gold and violet-blue	10	10
126		9d. black, grey-blue and silver	15	50
127		1s. multicoloured	50	10
128		1s.6d. multicoloured	70	2·25
124/128 *Set of 5*			1·40	2·75

Designs: Vert—4d. T **38**; 9d. 'Communications'; 1s. Coalfields. Horiz—6d. T **39**; 1s.6d. Road link with Tanzania.

(New Currency. 100 ngwee = 1 kwacha)

43 Lusaka Cathedral   **44** Baobab Tree

52 Chokwe Dancer   **53** Kafue Railway Bridge

(Des Gabriel Ellison. Photo Harrison)

1968 (16 Jan). Decimal Currency. Types **43/44**, **52/53** and similar designs. P 13½×14½ (1, 3, 15, 50n.) or 14½×13½ (others).

129		1n. multicoloured	10	10
		a. Copper-bronze (including value) omitted	£180	
		b. Ultramarine (windows) omitted	£225	
130		2n. multicoloured	10	10
131		3n. multicoloured	10	10
132		5n. bistre-brown and copper-bronze	10	10
		a. Coil stamp. P 14½	1·00	1·50
133		8n. multicoloured	15	10
		a. Copper-bronze (background) omitted		
		b. Blue (of costumes) omitted	£160	
134		10n. multicoloured	35	10
135		15n. multicoloured	2·75	10
136		20n. multicoloured	4·75	10
137		25n. multicoloured	25	10
138		50n. chocolate, red-orange and copper-bronze	30	15
139		1k. royal blue and copper-bronze	7·50	20
140		2k. black and copper-bronze	1·25	1·25
129/140 *Set of 12*			15·00	1·75

Designs: Horiz (as T **43**)—1n. T **43**; 3n. Zambia Airways Vickers VC-10 jetliner. (As T **53**)—15n. *Imbrasia zambesina* (moth); 1k. T **53**; 2k. Eland. Vert (as T **44**)—2n. T **44**; 5n. National Museum, Livingstone; 8n. Vimbuza dancer; 10n. Tobacco picking. (As T **52**)—20n. South African Crowned Cranes; 25n. Angoni warrior; 50n. T **52**.

All values exist with PVA gum as well as gum arabic.

Nos. 129/130 and 132 exist in coils, constructed from normal sheets it is believed that the 5n. perf 14½ came from a late release.

55 Ndola on Outline of Zambia   **56** Human Rights Emblem and Heads

(Des Gabriel Ellison. Photo Harrison)

1968 (29 June). Trade Fair, Ndola. P 14.

141	**55**	15n. green and gold	10	10

(Des Gabriel Ellison. Photo and die-stamped (gold emblem) Harrison)

1968 (23 Oct). Human Rights Year. P 14.

142	**56**	3n. deep blue, pale violet and gold	10	10

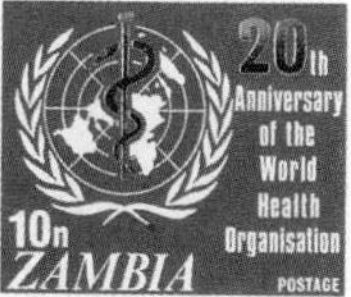

57 WHO Emblem   **58** Group of Children

(Des Gabriel Ellison. Photo and die-stamped (gold staff and '20') Harrison)

1968 (23 Oct). 20th Anniversary of World Health Organisation. P 14.

143	**57**	10n. gold and bluish violet	10	10

(Des Gabriel Ellison. Photo and die-stamped (gold children) Harrison)

1968 (23 Oct). 22nd Anniversary of UNICEF. P 14.

144	**58**	25n. black, gold and ultramarine	15	70

59 Copper Miner   **61** Zambia outlined on Map of Africa

(Des Gabriel Ellison. Photo Harrison)

1969 (18 June). 50th Anniversary of International Labour Organisation. T **59** and similar design. P 14½×13½ (3n.) or 13½×14½ (25n.).

145	**59**	3n. copper-bronze and deep violet	25	10
146	–	25n. pale yellow copper-bronze and blackish brown	1·00	1·00

Design: Horiz—25n. Poling a furnace.

A used example of No. 145 exists with the copper-bronze omitted.

(Des Gabriel Ellison. Photo Harrison)

1969 (23 Oct). International African Tourist Year. T **61** and similar multicoloured designs. P 14×14½ (5n., 25n.) or 14½×14 (others).

147	5n. Type **61**	10	10
148	10n. Waterbuck (*horiz*)	15	10
149	15n. Kasaba Bay Golden Perch (*horiz*)	35	40
150	25n. Carmine Bee-eater	1·00	1·75
147/150 *Set of* 4		1·40	2·00

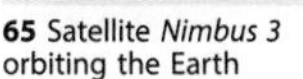

65 Satellite *Nimbus 3* orbiting the Earth — **66** Woman collecting Water from Well

(Des Gabriel Ellison. Litho Enschedé)

1970 (23 Mar). World Meteorological Day. P 13×10½.

151	**65**	15n. multicoloured	20	50

(Des V. Whiteley (from local designs). Litho B.W.)

1970 (4 July). Preventive Medicine. T **66** and similar vert designs. P 13½×12.

152	3n. multicoloured	15	10
153	15n. multicoloured	30	30
154	25n. greenish blue, rosine and sepia	65	70
152/154 *Set of* 3		1·00	1·00

Designs: 3n. T **66**; 15n. Child on scales; 25n. Child being immunized.

67 *Masks* (mural by Gabriel Ellison) — **68** Ceremonial Axe

(Des Gabriel Ellison. Litho Harrison)

1970 (8 Sept). Conference of Non-Aligned Nations. P 14×14½.

155	**67**	15n. multicoloured	30	30

(Des Gabriel Ellison. Litho D.L.R.)

1970 (30 Nov). Traditional Crafts. T **68** and similar multicoloured designs. P 13½ (15n.), 12½ (25n.) or 14 (others).

156	3n. Type **68**	10	10
157	5n. Clay Smoking-Pipe Bowl	10	10
158	15n. Makishi Mask (30×47 *mm*)	35	30
159	25n. Kuomboka Ceremony (72×19 *mm*)	55	1·00
156/159 *Set of* 4		1·00	1·40
MS160 133×83 mm. Nos. 156/159. Imperf		5·00	13·00

STAMP BOOKLETS

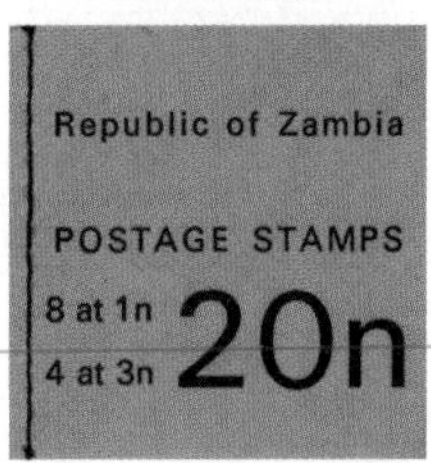

B **2**

1968. Black on buff covers as T B **2** (No. SB2), or size 82×58 mm (No. SB3). Stitched.

SB2	20n. booklet containing 8×1n. and 4×3n. (Nos. 129, 131) in blocks of 4	4·25
SB3	30n. booklet containing 12×1n. and 6×3n. (Nos. 129, 131) in blocks of 6	4·25

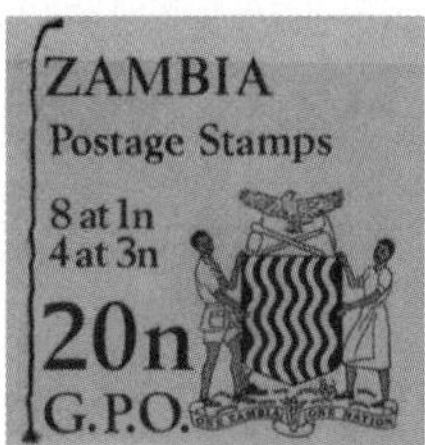

B **3**

1970 (26 Aug). Black on green cover as T B **3** (No. SB4) or black on rose cover, size 82×58 mm (No. SB5). Stitched.

SB4	20n. booklet containing 8×1n. and 4×3n. (Nos. 129, 131) in blocks of 4	6·50
SB5	30n. booklet containing 12×1n. and 6×3n. (Nos. 129, 131) in blocks of 6	6·50

POSTAGE DUE STAMPS

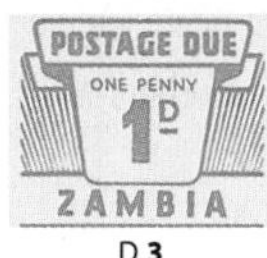

D **3**

(Des D. Smith. Litho Govt Printer, Lusaka)

1964 (24 Oct). P 12½.

D11	D **3**	1d. orange	35	2·50
D12		2d. deep blue	35	2·50
D13		3d. lake	45	1·75
D14		4d. ultramarine	45	2·25
D15		6d. purple	45	2·25
D16		1s. light emerald	55	4·25
D11/D16 *Set of* 6			2·25	14·00

In all values the left-hand vertical row of the sheet is imperf at left and the bottom horizontal row is imperf at foot. The above were crudely perforated, resulting in variations in the sizes of the stamps.

The above were withdrawn on 15 January 1968 and thereafter decimal currency postage stamps were used for postage due purposes with appropriate cancellations.

Zanzibar

An Indian post office opened in Zanzibar in November 1868, but was closed for political reasons on 1 April of the following year. Little has survived from this period. Subsequently mail was forwarded via Seychelles or, later, Aden.

Stamps of INDIA were used in Zanzibar from 1 October 1875 until 10 November 1895, when the administration of the postal service was transferred from India to British East Africa. Separate cancellations for Zanzibar are known from 1 June 1878.

Z **1** — Z **1a**

Stamps of INDIA cancelled with T Z **1** (1878–1879)

1865. (Nos. 54/65).

Z1	1a. deep brown	£650
Z2	2a. orange	£650

1866–78. (Nos. 69/72).

Z2*a*	4a. green (Die I)	£650
Z3	4a. blue-green (Die II)	£650

1865. (Nos. 54/65).

Z4	½a. blue (Die II)	£600

Surviving covers show that T Z **1** was normally used as a datestamp, struck clear of the stamps which were obliterated by a rhomboid of bars, but examples of the c.d.s. used as a cancel are known.

Stamps of INDIA cancelled with T Z **1a**.

1865. (Nos. 54/65).

Z7	2a. orange	£800

In T Z **1a** the word 'ZANZIBAR' is shorter than in Types Z **1** and Z **3**. It was generally used as an arrival mark but cancellations on adhesives are known.

Z **2**

Stamps of INDIA cancelled with T Z **2** (1879–1882).

1865. (Nos. 54/65).

Z10	8p. mauve	£500
Z11	1a. deep brown	19·00
Z12	2a. orange	35·00
	a. Brown-orange	18·00

1866–78. (Nos. 69/72).

Z13	4a. green (Die I)	£120
Z14	4a. blue-green (Die II)	32·00

1868. (Nos. 73/74).

Z15	8a. rose (Die II)	£120

1873. (Nos. 75/76).

Z16	½a. blue (Die II)	19·00

1874. (Nos. 77/79).

Z17	1r. slate	£425

1876. (Nos. 80/82).

Z18	6a. pale brown	£150
Z19	12a. Venetian red	£350

1882. (No. 90).

Z19*a*	1a.6p. sepia	£275

OFFICIAL STAMPS

1874–82. (Nos. O31/O37).

Z19*b*	1a. brown	£425
Z20	2a. orange	£375
Z21	4a. green (Die I)	£475
Z22	8a. rose (Die II)	£650

Z **3**

Stamps of INDIA cancelled with T Z **3** (1882–1884)

1865. (Nos. 54/65).

Z25	1a. deep brown	75·00
Z26	2a. brown-orange	45·00
	aa. Orange	80·00

1866–78. (Nos. 69/72).
Z26*a* 4a. green (Die I) £110
Z27 4a. blue-green (Die II) 50·00

1868. (Nos. 73/74).
Z28 8a. rose (Die II) 90·00

1873. (Nos. 75/76).
Z29 ½a. blue (Die II) 40·00

1874. (Nos. 77/79).
Z29*a* 1r. slate £325

1876. (Nos. 80/82).
Z30 6a. pale brown 85·00
Z31 12a. Venetian red £325

1882–83. (Nos. 84/101).
Z32 1a. brown-purple 55·00
Z33 1a.6p. sepia 60·00
Z34 3a. orange 55·00

OFFICIAL STAMPS

1867–73. (Nos. O20/O30*a*).
Z35 2a. orange £425
Z36 8a. rose £550

Z 4 Z 5

Stamps of INDIA cancelled with T Z **4** (June 1884–May 1887) (between January and September 1885 the postmark was used without year numerals).

1865. (Nos. 54/65).
Z38 8p. purple £550
Z39 1a. deep brown £225
Z40 2a. brown-orange 40·00

1866–78. (Nos. 69/72).
Z41 4a. green (Die I) £250
Z41*a* 4a. blue-green (Die II) 40·00

1868. (Nos. 73/74).
Z42 8a. rose (Die II) 50·00

1873. (Nos. 75/76).
Z43 ½a. blue (Die II) 30·00

1874. (Nos. 77/79).
Z44 1r. slate £350

1876. (Nos. 80/82).
Z45 6a. pale brown £100
Z45*a* 12a. Venetian red £275

1882–86. (Nos. 84/101).
Z46 ½a. blue-green 25·00
Z47 1a. brown-purple 27·00
Z48 1a.6p. sepia 21·00
Z49 2a. blue 60·00
Z50 3a. orange 15·00
Z51 4a. olive-green 45·00
Z52 4a.6p. yellow-green 25·00
Z53 8a. dull mauve 60·00
Z54 1r. slate 48·00

OFFICIAL STAMPS

1867–73. (Nos. O20/O30*a*).
Z55 2a. orange £375

1874–82. (Nos. O31/O37).
Z55*a* ½a. blue £140
Z56 1a. brown £140
Z56*a* 2a. orange £350

1883–95. (Nos. O37*a*/O48).
Z57 1a. brown-purple £250

Stamps of INDIA cancelled with T Z **5** (1887–1894).

1865. (Nos. 54/65).
Z58 8p. purple £475
Z59 2a. brown-orange £225

1868. (Nos. 73/74).
Z59*a* 8a. rose (Die II) £350

1873. (Nos. 75/76).
Z59*b* ½a. blue (Die II) £170

1876. (Nos. 80/82).
Z60 6a. pale brown 25·00
Z61 12a. Venetian red £100

1882–90. (Nos. 84/101).
Z62 ½a. blue-green 8·00
Z63 9p. aniline carmine 90·00
Z64 1a. brown-purple 6·00
Z65 1a.6p. sepia 10·00
Z66 2a. blue 8·00
Z67 3a. orange 10·00
Z68 3a. brown-orange 7·50
Z69 4a. olive-green 40·00
Z70 4a.6p. yellow-green 12·00
Z71 8a. dull mauve 25·00
Z72 12a. purple/*red* 90·00
Z73 1r. slate 18·00

1891. (No. 102).
Z74 2½a. on 4a.6p. yellow-green 9·00

1892–95. (Nos. 103/106).
Z75 2a.6p. yellow-green 6·00

OFFICIAL STAMPS

1867–73. (Nos. O20/O30*a*).
Z75*a* 4a. green £550

1874–82. (Nos. O31/O71.
Z76 ½a. blue £100
Z77 1a. brown £160
Z78 2a. yellow £350

Z 6

Z 7

Stamps of INDIA cancelled with T Z **6**, inscribed 'REG' (registration) or 'PAR' (parcel) (1888–1895).

1876. (Nos. 80/82).
Z80 6a. pale brown 32·00
Z80*a* 12a. Venetian red £250

1882–90. (Nos. 84/101).
Z81 ½a. blue-green 45·00
Z82 9p. aniline carmine £100
Z83 1a. brown-purple 10·00
Z84 1a.6p. sepia 15·00
Z85 2a. blue 17·00
Z86 3a. orange 30·00
Z87 3a. brown-orange 25·00
Z88 4a. olive-green 17·00
Z89 4a.6p. yellow-green 35·00
Z90 8a. dull mauve 28·00
Z91 12a. purple/*red* 95·00
Z92 1r. slate 24·00

1891. (No. 102).
Z93 2½a. on 4a.6p. yellow-green 38·00

1892–95. (Nos. 103/106).
Z94 2a.6p. yellow-green 20·00

Stamps of INDIA cancelled with T Z **7** (1894–1895).

1876. (Nos. 80/82).
Z95 6a. pale brown £120

1882–90. (Nos. 84/101).
Z100 ½a. blue-green 35·00
Z101 9p. aniline carmine £150
Z102 1a. brown-purple 42·00
Z103 1a.6p. sepia 95·00
Z104 2a. blue 35·00
Z105 3a. brown-orange 95·00
Z106 4a. olive-green 95·00
Z107 8a. dull mauve £120
Z108 12a. purple/*red* £150
Z109 1r. slate £130

1892–95. (Nos. 103/106).
Z110 2a.6p. yellow-green 19·00

1895. (Nos. 107/109).
Z111 2r. carmine and yellow-brown £850

A French post office was opened on the island on 1 February 1889 and this service used the stamps of FRANCE until 1894 when specific stamps for this office were provided. The French postal service on the island closed on 31 July 1904 and it is known that French stamps were again utilised during the final month.

A German postal agency operated in Zanzibar between 27 August 1890 and 31 July 1891, using stamps of GERMANY.

PRICES FOR STAMPS ON COVER TO 1945

Nos. 1/2	—
Nos. 3/16	*from* × 30
No. 17	*from* × 8
No. 18	*from* × 25
Nos. 19/21	—
No. 22	*from* × 40
Nos. 23/25	*from* × 25
No. 26	*from* × 40
Nos. 27/40	—
Nos. 41/46	*from* × 25
Nos. 156/168	*from* × 15
Nos. 169/177	—
Nos. 178/187	*from* × 20
Nos. 188/204	*from* × 15
Nos. 205/209	*from* × 20
Nos. 210/238	*from* × 15
Nos. 239/245	—
Nos. 246/259	*from* × 8
Nos. 260/260f	—
Nos. 261/330	*from* × 4
Nos. D1/D3	*from* × 8
No. D4	*from* × 1
No. D5	*from* × 15
No. D6	—
No. D7	*from* × 1
Nos. D8/D12	*from* × 15
No. D13	*from* × 1
No. D14	—
Nos. D15/D16	*from* × 6
No. D17	*from* × 4
Nos. D18/D24	*from* × 15
Nos. D25/D30	*from* × 30

PROTECTORATE

(Currency. 12 pies = 1 anna. 16 annas = 1 rupee)

Zanzibar
(1)

1895 (14 Nov)–**96.** Nos. 81, 85, 90/96, 98/101, 103 and 106/109 of India (Queen Victoria) optd with T **1** by *Zanzibar Gazette*.

(a) In blue
1 ½a. blue-green £25000 £5500
2 1a. plum £3000 £500
j. 'Zanzidar' (R. 4/6, 8/5) † £25000

(b) In black
3 ½a. blue-green 4·50 5·00
j. 'Zanzidar' (R. 4/6, 8/5) £1300 £700
k. 'Zanibar' (R. 7/2) £1300 £1700
l. Diaeresis over last 'a' (R. 10/5) £2000 £2000
m. Opt double, one albino £225
4 1a. plum 4·75 3·75
j. 'Zanzidar' (R. 4/6, 8/5) — £4000
k. 'Zanibar' (R. 7/2) £1700 £2000
l. Diaeresis over last 'a' (R. 10/5) £4750
p. Opt in blue-black £130 £100
pj. 'Zanzidar' (R. 4/6, 8/5) † £6000
5 1a.6p. sepia 5·00 4·75
j. 'Zanzidar' (R. 4/6, 8/5) £4000 £1200
k. 'Zanibar' (R. 7/2) £1600 £1700
m. Diaeresis over last 'a' (R. 10/5) £1600
6 2a. pale blue 9·50 8·50
7 2a. blue 10·00 9·00
j. 'Zanzidar' (R. 4/6, 8/5) £7500 £3000
k. 'Zanibar' (R. 7/2) £6000 £2750
l. Diaeresis over last 'a' (R. 10/5) £3000
m. Opt double £275
n. Opt double, one albino £275
8 2½a. yellow-green 9·00 5·00
j. 'Zanzidar' (R. 4/6, 8/5) £7500 £1800
k. 'Zanibar' (R. 7/2) £700 £1400
l. 'Zapzibar'
n. Diaeresis over last 'a' (R.10/5) £2500 £1900
o. Second 'z' italic (R. 10/1) £450 £650
p. Opt double, one albino £275
10 3a. brown-orange 12·00 17·00
j. 'Zanzidar' (R. 4/6, 8/5) £1000 £1900
k. 'Zanizbar' (R. 1/9) £6500 £7000
11 4a. olive-green 20·00 18·00
j. 'Zanzidar' (R. 4/6, 8/5) £10000 £4250
12 4a. slate-green 21·00 24·00
l. Diaeresis over last 'a' (R. 10/5) £5000
m. Opt double, one albino
13 6a. pale brown 20·00 11·00
j. 'Zanzidar' (R. 4/6, 8/5) £10000 £4250
k. 'Zanibar' (R. 7/2) £800 £1400
l. 'Zanzibarr' £7500 £6000
m. Opt double £300
n. Opt double, one albino £170
o. Opt triple, two albino £225
14 8a. dull mauve 48·00 28·00
j. 'Zanzidar' (R 4/6, 8/5) £10000 £8000
15 8a. magenta (2.96) 25·00 30·00
l. Diaeresis over last 'a' (R. 10/5) £8000
16 12a. purple/*red* 18·00 11·00
j. 'Zanzidar' (R.4/6, 8/5) £10000 £4500
17 1r. slate £130 90·00
j. 'Zanzidar' (R 4/6, 8/5) £9500 £6000
18 1r. green and aniline carmine (7.96) 21·00 40·00
j. Opt vert downwards £425
19 2r. carmine and yellow-brown £110 £120
j. 'r' omitted £28000
k. 'r' inverted £4000 £5000
20 3r. brown and green 95·00 £100
j. 'r' omitted £28000
k. 'r' inverted £6000 £6000
l. Opt double, one albino £1600
21 5r. ultramarine and violet £100 £130
j. 'r' omitted £28000
k. 'r' inverted £4750 £7500
l. Opt double, one inverted £850
m. Opt double, one albino £1600
3/21 *Set of* 15 £500 £500

Forged examples of the blue overprints, Nos. 1/2, can be found on piece with genuine cancellations as T Z **7**, dated '13 FE 97'.

There were a number of different settings for this overprint.

Values to 1r. were initially overprinted from settings of 120 (12×10) including one which showed 'Zanzidar' on R. 4/6 and R. 8/5 (soon corrected) and 'Zanizbar' on R. 1/9 (also soon corrected). Later supplies of these values were overprinted from settings of 80 (8×10) for the 6a. only or 60 (6×10) for the others. One of these settings included 'Zanibar' on R. 7/2. Another late setting, showed a diaeresis over last 'a' on R. 10/5.

Many forgeries of this overprint exist and also bogus errors.

MINOR VARIETIES. The following minor varieties of type exist on Nos. 1/21:

A. First 'Z' antique (sloping serifs) (all values)
B. Broken 'p' for 'n' (all values to 1r.)
C. Tall second 'z' (all values)
D. Small second 'z' (all values)
E. Small second 'z' and inverted 'q' for 'b' (all values)
F. Second 'z' Gothic (lower limb bent upwards) (½a. to 12a. and 1r.) (No. 18) (black opts only)
G. No dot over 'i' (all values to 1r.)
H. Inverted 'q' for 'b' (all values to 1r.)
I. Arabic '2' for 'r' (all values to 1r.) (black opts only)

Varieties D and E are worth the same as normal examples, A (2, 3, 5r.) and C normal plus 50%, G and I from 3 times normal, A (values to 1r.), F and H from 4 times normal and B from 5 times normal.

2½ (2) 2½ (3) 2½ (4) 2½ (5)

1895–98. Provisionals.

I. Stamps used for postal purposes

(a) No. 5 surch in red (30.11.95)
22 **2** 2½ on 1a.6p. sepia 75·00 55·00
j. 'Zanzidar' £1600 £1300
k. 'Zanizbar' £4750 £1900
l. Inverted '1' in '½' £1100 £900

(b) No. 4 surch in black (11.5.96)

23 **3** 2½ on 1a. plum £180 £100
24 **4** 2½ on 1a. plum £475 £275
j. Inverted '1' in '½' £2750
25 **5** 2½ on 1a. plum £200 £110

2½ **(6)** 2½ **(7)** 2½ **(8)**

(c) No. 6 surch in red (15.8.96)

26 **6** 2½ on 2a. pale blue 70·00 42·00
j. Inverted '1' in '½' £450 £275
k. Roman 'I' in '½' £250 £160
l. 'Zanzibar' double, one albino £160
m. 'Zanzibar' triple, two albino £300
27 **7** 2½ on 2a. pale blue £190 £110
j. '2' of '½' omitted £16000
k. '2²' for '2½' £24000
l. '1' of '½' omitted £16000 £6500
m. Inverted '1' in '½' £3500 £1700
n. 'Zanzibar' double, one albino £500
28 **8** 2½ on 2a. pale blue £5000 £2500

No. 28 only exists with small 'z' and occurs on R. 2/2 in the setting of 60.

(d) No. 5 surch in red (15.11.96)

29 **6** 2½ on 1a.6p. sepia £180 £180
j. Inverted '1 in '½' £1500 £1200
k. Roman 'I' in '½' £900 £900
l. Surch double, one albino £350
30 **7** 2½ on 1a.6p. sepia £425 £400
l. Surch double, one albino £800
31 **8** 2½ on 1a.6p. sepia £24000 £17000

No. 31 only exists with small 'z' and occurs on R. 2/2 in the setting of 60.

II. Stamps prepared for official purposes. Nos. 4, 5 and 7 surch as before in red (1.98)

32 **3** 2½ on 1a. plum £250 £700
33 **4** 2½ on 1a. plum £450 £1000
34 **5** 2½ on 1a. plum £275 £700
35 **3** 2½ on 1a.6p. sepia 90·00 £250
j. Diaeresis over last 'a' £8000
36 **4** 2½ on 1a.6p. sepia £225 £600
37 **5** 2½ on 1a.6p. sepia £130 £350
j. 'b' and 'r' of 'Zanzibar' inserted by hand £2250
38 **3** 2½ on 2a. dull blue £140 £350
39 **4** 2½ on 2a. dull blue £325 £650
40 **5** 2½ on 2a. dull blue £160 £425

It is doubtful whether Nos. 32/40 were issued to the public.

1896. Nos. 65/66, 68 and 71/73 of British East Africa (Queen Victoria), optd with T **1**.

41 ½a. yellow-green (23.5) 45·00 24·00
42 1a. carmine-rose (1.6) 45·00 17·00
j. Opt double £750 £900
k. Opt double, one albino £325
43 2½a. deep blue (R.) (24.5) 90·00 48·00
j. Inverted 'S' in 'ANNAS' (R. 1/1) £1200 £750
44 4½a. orange-yellow (12.8) 50·00 60·00
45 5a. yellow-bistre (12.8) 65·00 40·00
j. 'r' omitted — £4000
46 7½a. mauve (12.8) 55·00 65·00
41/46 *Set of* 6 £300 £225

MINOR VARIETIES. The various minor varieties of type detailed in the note below No. 21 also occur on Nos. 22 to 46 as indicated below:

A. Nos. 23, 25, 27, 30, 35, 38, 41/46
B. Nos. 22/23, 26, 29/30, 32/33, 36, 39, 44/46
C. Nos. 22, 25/26, 32, 36, 38, 40/46
D. Nos. 22/46
E. Nos. 22/46
F. Nos. 22, 25/26, 29, 41/46
G. Nos. 25/26, 29, 35, 37/38, 40/46
H. Nos. 22, 41/46 (on the British East Africa stamps this variety occurs in the same position as variety C)
I. Nos. 26, 29, 35, 38, 41/46

The scarcity of these varieties on the surcharges (Nos. 22/40) is similar to those on the basic stamps, but examples on the British East Africa values (Nos. 41/46) are more common.

PRINTERS. All Zanzibar stamps up to T **37** were printed by De La Rue & Co.

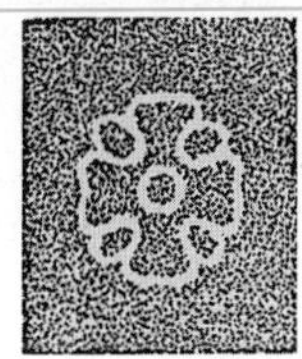
12

13

14 Sultan Seyyid Hamad-bin-Thwain

No right serif to left-hand '4' (R. 1/1)

No fraction bar at right (R. 2/1)

1896 (Dec). Recess. Flags in red on all values. W **12**. P 14.

156 **13** ½a. yellow-green 4·00 2·50
157 1a. indigo 4·25 1·75
158 1a. violet-blue 7·00 4·50
159 2a. red-brown 4·75 75
160 2½a. bright blue 16·00 1·50
161 2½a. pale blue 18·00 1·50
162 3a. grey 19·00 10·00
163 3a. bluish grey 22·00 12·00
164 4a. myrtle-green 13·00 6·00
165 4½a. orange 8·00 8·00
a. No right serif to left-hand '4' £275 £275
b. No fraction bar at right (R. 2/1) £275 £275
166 5a. bistre 9·50 6·00
a. Bisected (2½a.) (*on cover*) † £4500
167 7½a. mauve 8·50 8·50
168 8a. grey-olive 11·00 8·50
169 **14** 1r. blue 26·00 9·00
170 1r. deep blue 38·00 14·00
171 2r. green 30·00 9·50
172 3r. dull purple 32·00 9·50
173 4r. lake 27·00 13·00
174 5r. sepia 32·00 13·00
156/174 *Set of* 15 £200 95·00
156s/174s Optd 'SPECIMEN' *Set of* 15 £275

The ½, 1, 2, 2½, 3 and 8a. are known without wmk, these being from edges of the sheets.

1897 (5 Jan). No. 164 surch as before, in red by the *Zanzibar Gazette.*

175 **3** 2½ on 4a. myrtle-green 95·00 55·00
176 **4** 2½ on 4a. myrtle-green £325 £275
177 **5** 2½ on 4a. myrtle-green £120 80·00
175/177 *Set of* 3 £475 £375

There were two settings of the surcharge, the first comprised 26 of T **3**, 10 of T **4** and 24 of T **5**. The composition of the second setting is unknown.

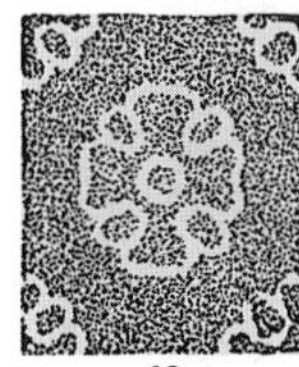
18

1898 (Apr). Recess. W **18**. P 14.

178 **13** ½a. yellow-green 1·50 35
179 1a. indigo 5·50 1·25
a. Greenish black 7·00 1·50
180 2a. red-brown 11·00 2·25
a. Deep brown 13·00 2·25
181 2½a. bright blue 5·00 30
182 3a. grey 9·50 1·25
183 4a. myrtle-green 3·75 2·00
184 4½a. orange 17·00 1·25
a. No right serif to left-hand '4' £400 £110
b. No fraction bar at right (R. 2/1) £400 £110
185 5a. bistre 21·00 2·25
a. Pale bistre 23·00 3·00
186 7½a. mauve 21·00 2·75
187 8a. grey-olive 22·00 3·25
178/187 *Set of* 10 £100 15·00

19

20 Sultan Seyyid Hamoud-bin-Mohammed bin Said

1899 (June)–**1901**. Recess. Flags in red. W **18** (Nos. 188/199) or W **12** (others). P 14.

188 **19** ½a. yellow-green 2·75 60
a. Wmk sideways 27·00 9·00
189 1a. indigo 4·50 20
a. Wmk sideways 50·00 2·75
190 1a. carmine (1901) 4·75 20
191 2a. red-brown 6·00 1·75
192 2½a. bright blue 5·50 1·00
193 3a. grey 8·00 3·25
194 4a. myrtle-green 8·00 4·00
195 4½a. orange 18·00 11·00
196 4½a. blue-black (1901) 21·00 15·00
197 5a. bistre 8·50 3·25
198 7½a. mauve 8·50 10·00
199 8a. grey-olive 8·50 7·50
200 **20** 1r. blue 26·00 15·00
201 2r. green 29·00 25·00
202 3r. dull purple 50·00 55·00
203 4r. lake 60·00 75·00
204 5r. sepia 80·00 £100
188/204 *Set of* 17 £300 £275
188s/204s Optd 'SPECIMEN' *Set of* 17 £325

One **(21)** Two & Half **(22)** Two & Half **(22a)** Thin open 'w' (R. 2/2, 3/4) Two & Half **(22b)** Serif to foot of 'f' (R. 3/1)

1904 (June). Nos. 194/196 and 198/199 surch as Types **21** and **22**, in black or lake (L.) by *Zanzibar Gazette* in setting of 30 (6×5).

205 **19** 1 on 4½a. orange 4·00 7·00
206 1 on 4½a. blue-black (L.) 7·00 18·00
207 2 on 4a. myrtle-green (L.) 14·00 18·00
208 2½ on 7½a. mauve 17·00 24·00
a. Opt Type **22a** 90·00 £110
b. Opt Type **22b** £150 £190
c. 'Hlaf' for 'Half' £16000
209 2½ on 8a. grey-olive 30·00 40·00
a. Opt Type **22a** £150 £180
b. Opt Type **22b** £250 £300
c. 'Hlaf' for 'Half' £15000 £10000
205/209 *Set of* 5 65·00 95·00

23

24

Monogram of Sultan Seyyid Ali bin Hamoud bin Naherud

1904 (8 June). Typo. Background of centre in second colour. W **18**. P 14.

210 **23** ½a. green 3·00 50
211 1a. rose-red 3·00 10
212 2a. brown 5·50 45
213 2½a. blue 5·00 35
214 3a. grey 6·50 2·25
215 4a. deep green 5·00 1·60
216 4½a. black 6·00 2·50
217 5a. yellow-brown 7·50 3·25
218 7½a. purple 9·00 8·50
219 8a. olive-green 7·00 7·00
220 **24** 1r. blue and red 38·00 29·00
a. Wmk sideways £100 35·00
221 2r. green and red 48·00 55·00
a. Wmk sideways £275 £375
222 3r. violet and red 65·00 95·00
223 4r. claret and red 70·00 £110
224 5r. olive-brown and red 70·00 £110
210/224 *Set of* 15 £300 £375
210s/224s Optd 'SPECIMEN' *Set of* 15 £200

25

26

27 Sultan Ali bin Hamoud

28 View of Port

1908 (May)–**09**. Recess. W **18** (sideways on 10r. to 30r.). P 14.

225 **25** 1c. pearl-grey (10.09) 2·25 30
226 3c. yellow-green 16·00 10
a. Wmk sideways 9·00 1·25
227 6c. rose-carmine 11·00 10
a. Wmk sideways 13·00 3·00
228 10c. brown (10.09) 7·50 3·00
229 12c. violet 19·00 4·00
a. Wmk sideways 16·00 1·25
230 **26** 15c. ultramarine 21·00 40
a. Wmk sideways 20·00 6·50
231 25c. sepia 8·50 1·00
232 50c. blue-green 13·00 9·00
233 75c. grey-black (10.09) 16·00 20·00
234 **27** 1r. yellow-green 50·00 12·00
a. Wmk sideways £120 16·00
235 2r. violet 25·00 21·00
a. Wmk sideways £300 80·00
236 3r. orange-bistre 42·00 60·00
237 4r. vermilion 70·00 £110
238 5r. steel-blue 75·00 75·00
239 **28** 10r. blue-green and brown £225 £375
s. Optd 'SPECIMEN' 70·00
240 20r. black and yellow-green £650 £850
s. Optd 'SPECIMEN' £100
241 30r. black and sepia £750 £1100
a. Wmk upright
s. Optd 'SPECIMEN' £120
242 40r. black and orange-brown £950
s. Optd 'SPECIMEN' £150
243 50r. black and mauve £900
s. Optd 'SPECIMEN' £150
244 100r. black and steel-blue £1300
s. Optd 'SPECIMEN' £200
245 200r. brown and greenish black £1800
s. Optd 'SPECIMEN' £275
225/238 *Set of* 14 £325 £275
225s/238s Optd 'SPECIMEN' *Set of* 14 £325

The 3, 6, 12, 15c. 'SPECIMEN' always show wmk sideways.

29 Sultan Khalifa bin Harub

30 Sailing Canoe

31 Dhow

1913. Recess. W **18** (sideways on 75c. and 10r. to 200r.). P 14.

No.	Type	Description	Unused	Used
246	**29**	1c. grey	50	1·00
247		3c. yellow-green	1·50	75
248		6c. rose-carmine	1·75	20
249		10c. brown	1·25	3·75
250		12c. violet	1·50	75
251		15c. blue	4·00	1·00
252		25c. sepia	1·50	3·00
253		50c. blue-green	4·75	8·00
254		75c. grey-black	3·00	7·00
		a. Wmk upright	£150	
		as. Optd 'SPECIMEN'	95·00	
255	**30**	1r. yellow-green	28·00	20·00
256		2r. violet	22·00	40·00
257		3r. orange-bistre	27·00	65·00
258		4r. scarlet	42·00	90·00
259		5r. steel-blue	55·00	55·00
260	**31**	10r. green and brown	£225	£425
260*b*		20r. black and green	£375	£700
		bs. Optd 'SPECIMEN'	90·00	
260*c*		30r. black and brown	£400	£850
		cs. Optd 'SPECIMEN'	90·00	
260*d*		40r. black and vermilion	£700	£1100
		ds. Optd 'SPECIMEN'	£160	
260*e*		50r. black and purple	£700	£1200
		es. Optd 'SPECIMEN'	£150	
260*f*		100r. black and blue	£950	
		fs. Optd 'SPECIMEN'	£180	
260*g*		200r. brown and black	£1400	
		gs. Optd 'SPECIMEN'	£225	
246/260 *Set of* 15			£350	£650
246s/260as Optd 'SPECIMEN' *Set of* 15			£375	

1914–22. Wmk Mult Crown CA (sideways on 10r.). P 14.

No.	Type	Description	Unused	Used
261	**29**	1c. grey	80	25
		w. Wmk inverted	†	£450
262		3c. yellow-green	1·25	10
		a. Dull green	9·50	20
		w. Wmk inverted	†	£300
263		6c. deep carmine	1·25	20
		a. Bright rose-carmine	1·00	10
		aw. Wmk inverted	†	£300
		ay. Wmk inverted and reversed	†	£350
264		8c. purple/*pale yellow* (1922)	1·50	7·50
265		10c. myrtle/*pale yellow* (1922)	1·00	30
266		15c. deep ultramarine	1·75	8·50
268		50c. blue-green	5·00	8·00
269		75c. grey-black	3·00	38·00
270	**30**	1r. yellow-green	5·50	3·75
271		2r. violet	19·00	20·00
272		3r. orange-bistre	27·00	50·00
273		4r. scarlet	32·00	85·00
		y. Wmk inverted and reversed	£275	
274		5r. steel-blue	17·00	65·00
		w. Wmk inverted	£275	
275	**31**	10r. green and brown	£225	£750
261/275 *Set of* 14			£300	£950
261s/275s Optd 'SPECIMEN' *Set of* 14			£375	

1921–29. Wmk Mult Script CA (sideways on 10r. to 30r.). P 14.

No.	Type	Description	Unused	Used
276	**29**	1c. slate-grey	30	13·00
		x. Wmk reversed	£300	
277		3c. yellow-green	4·50	8·00
278		3c. orange-yellow (1922)	40	10
		w. Wmk inverted		
279		4c. green (1922)	60	3·25
280		6c. carmine-red	40	50
		w. Wmk inverted	£325	
		x. Wmk reversed	†	£425
281		6c. purple/*blue* (1922)	45	10
		w. Wmk inverted	†	£425
282		10c. brown	80	16·00
283		12c. violet	50	30
		w. Wmk inverted	£475	
284		12c. carmine-red (1922)	50	40
285		15c. blue	65	15·00
286		20c. indigo (1922)	1·00	30
287		25c. sepia	1·00	32·00
288		50c. myrtle-green	4·25	9·00
		y. Wmk inverted and reversed	£200	£300
289		75c. slate	2·50	65·00
290	**30**	1r. yellow-green	7·00	3·50
291		2r. deep violet	3·50	17·00
292		3r. orange-bistre	7·00	7·50
293		4r. scarlet	12·00	48·00
294		5r. Prussian blue	27·00	75·00
		w. Wmk inverted	£350	
295	**31**	10r. green and brown	£225	£500
296		20r. black and green	£425	£800
		s. Optd 'SPECIMEN'	£150	
297		30r. black and brown (1929)	£350	£750
		s. Perf 'SPECIMEN'	£150	
276/295 *Set of* 20			£275	£750
276s/295s Optd 'SPECIMEN' *Set of* 20			£425	

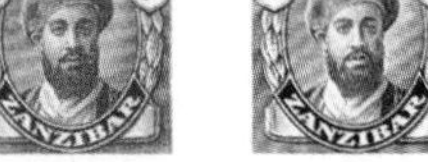
32 Sultan Khalifa bin Harub   33

1926–27. T **32** ('CENTS' in serifed capitals). Recess. Wmk Mult Script CA. P 14.

No.	Type	Description	Unused	Used
299	**32**	1c. brown	1·00	10
300		3c. yellow-orange	30	15
301		4c. deep dull green	30	1·25
302		6c. violet	30	10
303		8c. slate	1·00	4·50
304		10c. olive-green	1·00	40
305		12c. carmine-red	3·00	10
306		20c. bright blue	60	30
307		25c. purple/*yellow* (1927)	17·00	2·50
308		50c. claret	4·75	35
309		75c. sepia (1927)	40·00	42·00
299/309 *Set of* 11			60·00	45·00
299s/309s Optd 'SPECIMEN' *Set of* 11			£200	

(New Currency. 100 cents = 1 shilling)

1936 (1 Jan). T **33** ('CENTS' in sans-serif capitals), and Types **30/31**, but values in shillings. Recess. Wmk Mult Script CA. P 14×13½–14.

No.	Type	Description	Unused	Used
310	**33**	5c. green	10	10
311		10c. black	15	10
312		15c. carmine-red	20	1·25
313		20c. orange	20	10
314		25c. purple/*yellow*	20	10
315		30c. ultramarine	20	10
316		40c. sepia	20	20
317		50c. claret	30	10
318	**30**	1s. yellow-green	75	10
319		2s. slate-violet	4·50	1·75
320		5s. scarlet	27·00	7·00
321		7s.50 light blue	45·00	42·00
322	**31**	10s. green and brown	45·00	32·00
310/322 *Set of* 13			£110	75·00
310s/322s Perf 'SPECIMEN' *Set of* 13			£250	

Nos. 310/322 remained current until 1952 and the unused prices are therefore for unmounted examples.

36 Sultan Khalifa bin Harub

1936 (9 Dec). Silver Jubilee of Sultan. Recess. Wmk Mult Script CA. P 14.

No.	Type	Description	Unused	Used
323	**36**	10c. black and olive-green	3·25	30
324		20c. black and bright purple	4·50	2·75
325		30c. black and deep ultramarine	15·00	1·50
326		50c. black and orange-vermilion	15·00	7·00
323/326 *Set of* 4			35·00	10·50
323s/326s Perf 'SPECIMEN' *Set of* 4			£120	

37 *Sham Alam* (Sultan's dhow)

VICTORY ISSUE 8TH JUNE 1946
(38)

1944 (20 Nov). Bicentenary of Al Busaid Dynasty. Recess. Wmk Mult Script CA. P 14.

No.	Type	Description	Unused	Used
327	**37**	10c. ultramarine	1·00	5·50
		a. 'C' of 'CA' missing from wmk	£800	
328		20c. red	1·50	3·75
		a. 'C' of 'CA' missing from wmk	£800	
329		50c. blue-green	1·50	60
		a. 'A' of 'CA' missing from wmk	—	£850
330		1s. dull purple	1·50	1·75
		a. 'A' of 'CA' missing from wmk	£950	
327/330 *Set of* 4			5·00	10·50
327s/330s Perf 'SPECIMEN' *Set of* 4			£120	

1946 (11 Nov). Victory. Nos. 311 and 315 optd with T **38**.

No.	Type	Description	Unused	Used
331	**33**	10c. black (R.)	20	50
332		30c. ultramarine (R.)	30	50
331s/332s Perf 'SPECIMEN' *Set of* 2			90·00	

1949 (10 Jan). Royal Silver Wedding. As Nos. 112/113 of Antigua.

No.	Type	Description	Unused	Used
333		20c. orange	30	1·50
334		10s. brown	25·00	40·00

1949 (10–13 Oct). 75th Anniversary of UPU. As Nos. 114/117 of Antigua.

No.	Type	Description	Unused	Used
335		20c. red-orange (13.10)	30	4·00
336		30c. deep blue	1·75	3·00
		a. 'C' of 'CA' missing from wmk	£900	
337		50c. magenta	1·00	3·50
		a. 'A' of 'CA' missing from wmk	£900	
338		1s. blue-green (13.10)	1·00	4·50
335/338 *Set of* 4			3·50	13·50

39 Sultan Khalifa bin Harub

40 Seyyid Khalifa Schools, Beit-el-Ras

1952 (26 Aug)–**55.** Wmk Mult Script CA. P 12½ (cent values) or 13 (shilling values).

No.	Type	Description	Unused	Used
339	**39**	5c. black	10	10
340		10c. red-orange	10	10
341		15c. green	3·00	3·75
		a. Yellow-green (12.11.53)	6·50	3·75
342		20c. carmine-red	75	70
343		25c. reddish purple	1·00	10
344		30c. deep bluish green	1·25	10
		a. Deep green (29.3.55)	16·00	4·75
345		35c. bright blue	1·25	4·50
346		40c. deep brown	1·25	1·25
		a. Sepia (12.11.53)	6·50	2·00
347		50c. violet	3·50	10
		a. Deep violet (29.3.55)	8·50	1·00
348	**40**	1s. deep green and deep brown	60	10
349		2s. bright blue and deep purple	3·00	2·50
350		5s. black and carmine-red	3·50	9·00
351		7s.50 grey-black and emerald	28·00	28·00
352		10s. carmine-red and black	10·00	18·00
339/352 *Set of* 14			50·00	60·00

41 Sultan Khalifa bin Harub

(Photo Harrison)

1954 (26 Aug). Sultan's 75th Birthday. Wmk Mult Script CA. Chalk-surfaced paper. P 13×12.

No.	Type	Description	Unused	Used
353	**41**	15c. deep green	15	10
354		20c. rose-red	15	10
355		30c. bright blue	20	10
356		50c. purple	50	10
357		1s.25 orange-red	40	75
353/357 *Set of* 5			1·25	1·00

42 Cloves

43 *Urnmoja Wema* (dhow)

44 Sultan's Barge

45 Map of East African Coast

46 Minaret Mosque

47 Dimbani Mosque

48 Kibweni Palace

(Des W. J. Jennings (T **42**), A. Farhan (T **43**), Mrs. M. Broadbent (T **44**, T **46**), R. A. Sweet (T **45**), A. S. B. New (T **47**), B. J. Woolley (T **48**). Recess B.W.)

1957 (26 Aug). W w **12**. P 11½ (5c., 10c.), 11×11½ (15c., 30c., 1s.25), 14×13½ (20c., 25c., 35c., 50c.,), 13½×14 (40c., 1s., 2s.) or 13×13½ (5s., 7s.50, 10s.).

No.	Type	Description	Unused	Used
358	**42**	5c. orange and deep green	10	40
359		10c. emerald and carmine-red	10	10
360	**43**	15c. green and sepia	30	2·75
361	**44**	20c. ultramarine	15	10
362	**45**	25c. orange-brown and black	45	1·25
363	**43**	30c. carmine-red and black	20	1·25
364	**45**	35c. slate and emerald	45	20
365	**46**	40c. brown and black	15	10
366	**45**	50c. blue and grey-green	60	30
367	**47**	1s. carmine and black	20	30
368	**43**	1s.25 slate and carmine	3·50	20
369	**47**	2s. orange and deep green	4·50	2·25
370	**48**	5s. deep bright blue	5·00	2·00
371		7s.50 green	17·00	4·00
372		10s. carmine	17·00	7·00
358/372 *Set of* 15			45·00	19·00

The 10c. exists from coils made up from normal sheets.

49 Sultan Seyyid Sir Abdullah bin Khalifa

50 Protein Foods

(Recess B.W.)

1961 (17 Oct). As Types **42/48**, but with portrait of Sultan Sir Abdullah as in T **49**. W w **12**. P 13×13½ (20s.), others as before.

No.	Type	Description	Unused	Used
373	**49**	5c. orange and deep green	50	1·25
374		10c. emerald and carmine-red	40	10
375	**43**	15c. green and sepia	75	3·75
376	**44**	20c. ultramarine	40	30
377	**45**	25c. orange-brown and black	2·75	1·75
378	**43**	30c. carmine-red and black	3·25	3·50

379	**45**	35c. slate and emerald	4·00	5·50
380	**46**	40c. brown and black	40	20
381	**45**	50c. blue and grey-green	4·25	10
382	**47**	1s. carmine and black	50	1·50
383	**43**	1s.25 slate and carmine	4·25	8·50
384	**47**	2s. orange and deep green	1·00	4·75
385	**48**	5s. deep bright blue	3·50	13·00
386		7s.50 green	3·50	22·00
387		10s. carmine	4·50	13·00
388		20s. sepia	17·00	28·00
373/388 *Set of 16*			42·00	95·00

The 10c. exists from coils made up from normal sheets.

(Des M. Goaman. Photo Harrison)

1963 (4 June). Freedom from Hunger. W w **12**. P 14×14½.

389	**50**	1s.30 sepia	1·25	75

INDEPENDENT

51 Zanzibar Clove

53 'Religious Tolerance' (mosques and churches)

(Photo Harrison)

1963 (10 Dec). Independence. Portrait of Sultan Seyyid Jamshid bin Abdullah. Types **51**, **53** and similar vert designs. P 12½.

390	30c. multicoloured	25	1·25
391	50c. multicoloured	25	1·00
392	1s.30, multicoloured	25	4·00
393	2s.50, multicoloured	35	4·75
	a. Green omitted	†	£700
390/3 *Set of 4*		1·00	10·00

Designs: 30c. T **51**; 50c. 'To Prosperity' (Zanzibar doorway); 1s.30, T **53**; 2s.50, 'Towards the Light' (Mangapwani Cave).

REPUBLIC

When the Post Office opened on 14 January 1964, after the revolution deposing the Sultan, the stamps on sale had the portrait cancelled by a manuscript cross. Stamps thus cancelled *on cover* or *piece* used between January 14 and 17 are therefore of interest.

JAMHURI 1964

(**55**= 'Republic')

1964 (17 Jan). Locally handstamped as T **55** in black.

(i) Nos. 373/388

394	**49**	5c. orange and deep green	1·25	1·00
395		10c. emerald and carmine-red	1·25	20
396	**43**	15c. green and sepia	2·50	2·75
397	**44**	20c. ultramarine	1·75	1·50
398	**45**	25c. orange-brown and black	2·75	20
399	**43**	30c. carmine-red and black	1·50	1·00
400	**45**	35c. slate and emerald	2·75	1·50
401	**46**	40c. brown and black	1·75	1·75
402	**45**	50c. blue and grey-green	2·75	10
403	**47**	1s. carmine and black	1·50	1·00
404	**43**	1s.25 slate and carmine	1·25	3·00
405	**47**	2s. orange and deep green	2·00	2·25
406	**48**	5s. deep bright blue	1·75	1·75
407		7s.50 green	2·00	1·75
408		10s. carmine	2·00	1·75
409		20s. sepia	2·50	7·50

(ii) Nos. 390/393 (Independence)

410	30c. multicoloured	1·00	3·50
411	50c. multicoloured	60	2·00
412	1s.30 multicoloured	1·25	2·50
413	2s.50 multicoloured	1·40	4·00
	a. Green omitted	£425	
394/413 *Set of 20*		32·00	35·00

T **55** occurs in various positions—diagonally, horizontally or vertically.

NOTE. Nos. 394 to 413 are the only stamps officially authorised to receive the handstamp but it has also been seen on Nos. 353/357, 389 and the D25/D30 Postage Dues. There are numerous errors such as inverted and double opts, and pairs, one without handstamp, but it is impossible to distinguish between cases of genuine oversight and those made deliberately at the request of purchasers.

JAMHURI 1964 (**56**)

JAMHURI 1964 (**57**)

1964 (28 Feb). Optd by Bradbury Wilkinson.

*(i) As T **56** on Nos. 373/388*

414	**49**	5c. orange and deep green	10	10
415		10c. emerald and carmine-red	10	10
416	**43**	15c. green and sepia	20	10
417	**44**	20c. ultramarine	10	10
418	**45**	25c. orange-brown and black	30	10
419	**43**	30c. carmine-red and black	20	10
420	**45**	35c. slate and emerald	30	10
421	**46**	40c. brown and black	10	10
422	**45**	50c. blue and grey-green	30	10
423	**47**	1s. carmine and black	10	10
424	**43**	1s.25 slate and carmine	2·00	3·00
425	**47**	2s. orange and deep green	50	40
426	**48**	5s. deep bright blue	50	35
427		7s.50 green	65	7·00
428		10s. carmine	1·25	8·00
429		20s. sepia	2·25	8·00

The opt T **56** is set in two lines on Types **46/48**.

The 10c. exists from coils made up from normal sheets.

*(ii) As T **57** on Nos. 390/393 (Independence)*

430	30c. multicoloured	10	10
431	50c. multicoloured	10	10
432	1s.30, multicoloured	10	10
433	2s.50, multicoloured	15	65
	a. Green omitted	£160	
414/433 *Set of 20*		8·00	25·00

The opt T **57** is set in one line on No. 432.

For the set inscribed 'UNITED REPUBLIC OF TANGANYIKA AND ZANZIBAR' see Nos. 124/127 of Tanganyika.

58 Axe, Spear and Dagger

59 Zanzibari with Rifle

(Litho German Bank Note Ptg Co, Leipzig)

1964 (21 June). Types **58/59** and similar designs inscr. 'JAMHURI ZANZIBAR 1964'. Multicoloured. P 13×13½ (vert) or 13½×13 (horiz).

434	5c. Type **58**	20	10
435	10c. Bow and arrow breaking chains	30	10
436	15c. Type **58**	30	10
437	20c. As 10c	50	10
438	25c. Type **59**	50	10
439	30c. Zanzibari breaking manacles	30	10
440	40c. Type **59**	50	10
441	50c. As 30c	30	10
442	1s. Zanzibari, flag and Sun	30	10
443	1s.30 Hands breaking chains (*horiz*)	30	1·75
444	2s. Hand waving flag (*horiz*)	30	30
445	5s. Map of Zanzibar and Pemba on flag (*horiz*)	1·00	5·50
446	10s. Flag on Map	4·75	7·50
447	20s. National Fag (*horiz*)	4·50	26·00
434/447 *Set of 14*		12·50	38·00

68 Soldier and Maps

69 Building Construction

(Litho German Bank Note Ptg Co, Leipzig)

1965 (12 Jan). First Anniversary of Revolution. P 13×13½ (vert) or 13½×13 (horiz).

448	**68**	20c. apple-green and deep green	10	10
449	**69**	30c. chocolate and yellow-orange	10	10
450	**68**	1s.30 light blue and ultramarine	15	15
451	**69**	2s.50 reddish violet and rose	20	75
448/451 *Set of 4*			50	1·00

T **68** is inscribed 'PEMPA' in error for 'PEMBA'.

70 Planting Rice

(Litho German Bank Note Ptg Co, Leipzig)

1965 (17 Oct). Agricultural Development. T **70** and similar horiz design. P 13×12½.

452	**70**	20c. sepia and blue	10	1·00
453	–	30c. sepia and magenta	10	1·00
454	–	1s.30 sepia and yellow-orange	25	2·00
455	**70**	2s.50 sepia and emerald	35	7·00
452/455 *Set of 4*			70	10·00

Design: 30c., 1s.30, Hands holding rice.

72 Freighter, Tractor, Factory, and Open Book and Torch

73 Soldier

(Litho German Bank Note Ptg Co, Leipzig)

1966 (12 Jan). Second Anniversary of Revolution. P 12½×13.

456	**72**	20c. multicoloured	25	20
457	**73**	50c. multicoloured	25	50
458	**72**	1s.30 multicoloured	25	30
459	**73**	2s.50 multicoloured	30	2·25
456/459 *Set of 4*			1·00	3·00

For stamps with similar inscription or inscribed 'TANZANIA' only, and with commemorative date 26th April 1966, see Nos. Z142/Z145 of TANZANIA.

74 Tree-felling

75 Zanzibar Street

(Litho German Bank Note Ptg Co, Leipzig)

1966 (5 June). Horiz designs as Types **74**, and **75**. P 12½×13 (50c., 10s.) or 13×12½ (others).

460	5c. maroon and yellow-olive	70	80
461	10c. brown-purple and bright emerald	70	80
462	15c. brown-purple and light blue	70	80
463	20c. ultramarine and light orange	40	20
464	25c. maroon and orange-yellow	40	30
465	30c. maroon and ochre-yellow	70	20
466	40c. purple-brown and rose-pink	80	20
467	50c. green and pale greenish yellow	80	20
468	1s. maroon and bright blue	80	20
469	1s. 30 maroon and turquoise	80	3·00
470	2s. brown-purple and light blue-green	80	40
471	5s. rose-red and pale blue	1·25	7·00
472	10s. crimson and pale yellow	2·25	18·00
473	20s. deep purple-brown and magenta	7·00	42·00
460/473 *Set of 14*		16·00	65·00

Designs: 5c., 20s. T **74**; 10c., 1s. Clove cultivation; 15, 40c. Chair-making; 20c., 5s. Lumumba College; 25c., 4s. 30, Agriculture; 30c., 2s. Agricultural workers; 50c.,10s. T **75**.

81 Education

(Litho D.L.R.)

1966 (25 Sept). Introduction of Free Education. P 13½×13.

474	**81**	50c. black, light blue and orange	10	1·00
475		1s.30 black, light blue and yellow-green	25	1·75
476		2s.50 black, light blue and pink	80	4·50
474/476 *Set of 3*			1·00	6·50

82 ASP Flag

(Litho D.L.R.)

1967 (5 Feb). Tenth Anniversary of Afro-Shirazi Party (ASP). T **82** and similar multicoloured design. P 14.

477	30c. Type **82**	35	1·75
478	50c. Vice-President M. A. Karume of Tanzania, flag and crowd (*vert*)	20	1·00
479	1s.30 As 50c	35	2·25
480	2s.50 Type **82**	50	3·75
477/480 *Set of 4*		1·25	8·00

84 Voluntary Workers

(Photo Delrieu)

1967 (20 Aug). Voluntary Workers Brigade. P 12½×12.

481	**84**	1s.30 multicoloured	25	2·25
482		2s.50 multicoloured	75	5·50

POSTAGE DUE STAMPS

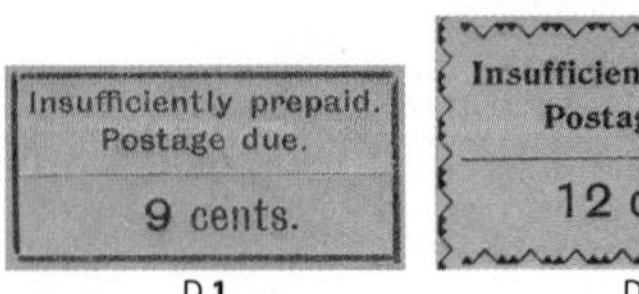

D **1**

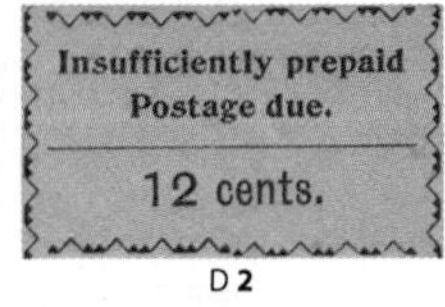

D **2**

(Types D **1** and D **2** typo by the Government Printing Office)

1926–30. Rouletted 10, with imperf sheet edges. No gum.

D1	D **1**	1c. black/*orange* (1930)	11·00	£160
D2		2c. black/*orange* (1930)	4·50	85·00
D3		3c. black/*orange* (1929)	5·00	70·00
		a. 'cent.s' for 'cents'	£160	£550
D4		6c. black/*orange*	—	£7000
		a. 'cent.s' for 'cents'	†	£24000
D5		9c. black/*orange* (1929)	2·75	45·00
		a. 'cent.s' for 'cents'	27·00	£200
D6		12c. black/*orange* (1929)	£15000	£12000
		a. 'cent.s' for 'cents'	†	£21000
		b. 'I' of 'Insufficiently' omitted (R. 3/2)	†	£21000

No.	Type	Description	Unused	Used
D7		12c. black/*green*	£1500	£600
		a. 'cent.s' for 'cents'	£4000	£1700
D8		15c. black/*orange* (1929)	2·75	45·00
		a. 'cent.s' for 'cents'	27·00	£200
D9		18c. black/*salmon*	5·50	60·00
		a. 'cent.s' for 'cents'	55·00	£300
D10		18c. black/*orange* (1929)	29·00	90·00
		a. 'cent.s' for 'cents'	85·00	£400
D11		20c. black/*orange* (1929)	4·50	80·00
		a. 'cent.s' for 'cents'	55·00	£375
D12		21c. black/*orange* (1929)	3·50	55·00
		a. 'cent.s' for 'cents'	48·00	£275
D13		25c. black/*magenta*	£2750	£1300
		a. 'cent.s' for 'cents'	£7000	£4000
D14		25c. black/*orange* (1929)	£20000	£18000
D15		31c. black/*orange* (1929)	9·50	£130
		a. 'cent.s' for 'cents'	70·00	£1200
D16		50c. black/*orange* (1929)	21·00	£275
		a. 'cent.s' for 'cents'	£130	£1700
D17		75c. black/*orange* (1929)	80·00	£750
		a. 'cent.s' for 'cents'	£300	

Initial printings, except the 1c. and 2c., contained the error 'cent.s' for 'cents' on R. 4/1 in the sheets of ten (2×5). The error was corrected on subsequent supplies of the 3c., 9c. and 15c.

It is known that examples of these stamps used before early 1929 were left uncancelled on the covers. Uncancelled examples of Nos. D4, D6/D7 and D13/D14 which are not in very fine condition, must be assumed to have been used.

1930–33. Rouletted 5. No gum.

No.	Type	Description	Unused	Used
D18	D **2**	2c. black/*salmon* (1932)	28·00	42·00
		a. Wide space between '2' and 'cents' (R. 1/2)	—	£325
D19		3c. black/*rose* (1933)	3·50	70·00
D21		6c. black/*yellow*	3·25	38·00
D22		12c. black/*blue* (1931)	4·50	32·00
D23		25c. black/*rose*	10·00	£150
D24		25c. black/*lilac* (1933)	30·00	90·00
D18/D24 *Set of 6*			70·00	£375

The wide space variety No. D18a occurred only on one of the four printings of the 2c. value.

D **3**

(Typo D.L.R.)

1936 (1 Jan)–**62**. Wmk Mult Script CA. P 14.

No.	Type	Description	Unused	Used
D25	D **3**	5c. violet	8·50	14·00
		a. Chalk-surfaced paper (18.7.56)	35	20·00
D26		10c. scarlet	7·50	2·75
		a. Chalk-surfaced paper (6.3.62)	35	13·00
D27		20c. green	2·50	7·00
		a. Chalk-surfaced paper (6.3.62)	35	32·00
D28		30c. brown	20·00	24·00
		a. Chalk-surfaced paper (18.7.56)	35	15·00
D29		40c. ultramarine	10·00	29·00
		a. Chalk-surfaced paper (18.7.56)	75	50·00
D30		1s. grey	17·00	38·00
		a. Chalk-surfaced paper (18.7.56)	1·00	26·00
D25/D30 *Set of 6*			60·00	£100
D25a/D30a *Set of 6*			2·75	£140
D25s/D30s Perf 'SPECIMEN' *Set of 6*			£140	

Unused prices for D25/D30 are for unmounted examples.

For postage due stamps handstamped 'JAMHURI 1964', see note below No. 413.

All Zanzibar issues were withdrawn on 1 January 1968 and replaced by Tanzania issues. Zanzibar stamps remained valid for postage in Zanzibar for a limited period.

Zululand *see* South Africa

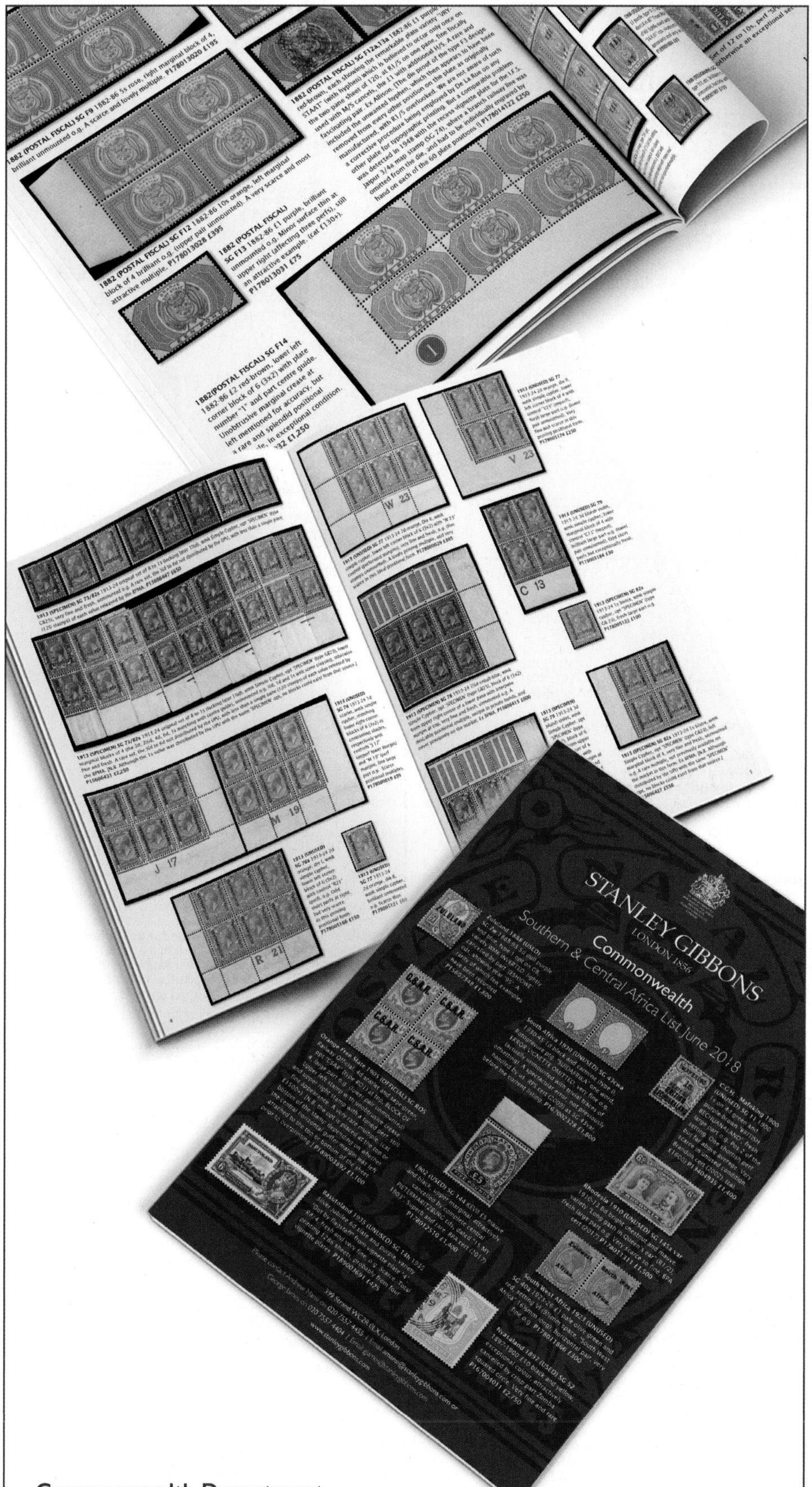

Set Prices for British Empire Omnibus Issues

The composition of these sets is in accordance with the tables on the following pages. Only such items considered basic stamps are included; varieties such as shades, perforation changes and watermark changes are excluded.

Stamps issued in connection with any of the events by countries which are no longer in the British Commonwealth and which are not listed in the *Part 1 Catalogue* are omitted.

1935 SILVER JUBILEE

	PRICE *Un*	*Used*
1935. Silver Jubilee.		
Complete set of 250 stamps	£1600	£2000

Country	*Catalogue Nos.*	*Stamps*
Great Britain	453/456	4
Antigua	91/94	4
Ascension	31/34	4
Australia	156/158	3
Nauru	40/43	4
New Guinea	206/207	2
Papua	150/153	4
Bahamas	141/144	4
Barbados	241/244	4
Basutoland	11/14	4
Bechuanaland	111/114	4
Bermuda	94/97	4
British Guiana	301/304	4
British Honduras	143/146	4
British Solomon Islands	53/56	4
Canada	335/340	6
Newfoundland	250/253	4
Cayman Islands	108/111	4
Ceylon	379/382	4
Cyprus	144/147	4
Dominica	92/95	4
Egypt-British Forces	A10	1
Falkland Islands	139/142	4
Fiji	242/245	4
Gambia	143/146	4
Gibraltar	114/117	4
Gilbert and Ellice Islands	36/39	4
Gold Coast	113/116	4
Grenada	145/8	4
Hong Kong	133/136	4
India	240/246	7
Jamaica	114/117	4
Kenya, Uganda and Tanganyika	124/127	4
Leeward Islands	88/91	4
Malaya-Straits Settlements	256/259	4
Malta	210/13	4
Mauritius	245/248	4
Montserrat	94/97	4
Morocco Agencies		
British Currency	62/65	4
Spanish Currency	149/152	4
French Currency	212/215	4
Tangier	238/240	3
New Zealand	573/575	3
Cook Islands	113/115	3
Niue	69/71	3
Western Samoa	177/9	3
Nigeria	30/33	4
Northern Rhodesia	18/21	4
Nyasaland	123/126	4
St. Helena	124/127	4
St. Kitts-Nevis	61/64	4
St. Lucia	109/112	4
St. Vincent	142/145	4
Seychelles	128/131	4
Sierra Leone	181/184	4
Somaliland Protectorate	86/89	4
South Africa	65/68	4×2
Southern Rhodesia	31/34	4
South West Africa	88/91	4
Swaziland	21/24	4
Trinidad and Tobago	239/242	4
Turks and Caicos Islands	187/189	4
Virgin Islands	103/106	4
Total		250

The concept initiated by the 1935 Silver Jubilee omnibus issue has provided a pattern for a series of Royal commemoratives over the past 50 years which have introduced countless collectors to the hobby.

The Crown Colony Windsor Castle design by Hugo Fleury is, surely, one of the most impressive produced to the 20th-century and its reproduction in the recess process by three of the leading stamp-printing firms of the era has provided a subject for philatelic research which has yet to be exhausted.

Each of the three, Bradbury Wilkinson & Co. and Waterlow and Sons, who both produced 15 issues, together with De La Rue & Co. who printed 14, used a series of vignette (centre) plates coupled with individual frame plates for each value. All were taken from dies made by Waterlow. Several worthwhile varieties exist on the frame plates but most interest has been concentrated on the centre plates, each of which was used to print a considerable number of different stamps.

Sheets printed by Bradbury Wilkinson were without printed plate numbers, but research has now identified 12 centre plates which were probably used in permanent pairings. Stamps from some of these centre plates have revealed a number of prominent plate flaws, the most famous of which, the extra flagstaff, has been eagerly sought by collectors for many years.

Extra flagstaff (Plate '1' R. 9/1)

Short extra flagstaff (Plate '2' R. 2/1)

Lightning conductor (Plate '3' R. 2/5)

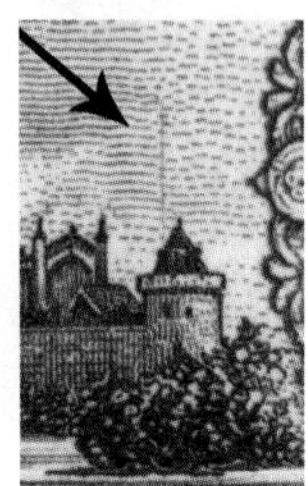

Flagstaff on right-hand turret (Plate '5' R. 7/1)

Double flagstaff (Plate '6' R. 5/2)

De La Rue sheets were initially printed with plate numbers, but in many instances these were subsequently trimmed off. Surviving examples do, however, enable a positive identification of six centre plates, 2A, 2B, (2A), (2B), 4 and 4/ to be made. The evidence of sheet markings and plate flaws clearly demonstrates that there were two different pairs of plates numbered 2A 2B. The second pair is designated (2A) (2B) by specialist collectors to avoid further confusion. The number of major plate flaws is not so great as on the Bradbury, Wilkinson sheets, but four examples are included in the catalogue.

Diagonal line by turret (Plate 2A R. 10/1 and 10/2)

Dot to left of chapel (Plate 2B R. 8/3)

Dot by flagstaff (Plate 4 R. 8/4)

Dash by turret (Plate 4/ R. 3/6)

Much less is known concerning the Waterlow centre plate system as the sheets did not show plate numbers. Ten individual plates have, so far, been identified and it is believed that these were used in pairs. The two versions of the kite and log flaw from plate '2' show that this plate exists in two states.

Damaged turret (Plate '1' R. 5/6)

Kite and vertical log (Plate '2A' R. 10/6)

Kite and horizontal log (Plate '2B' R. 10/6)

Bird by turret (Plate '7' R. 1/5)

1937 CORONATION

1937. Coronation.		
Complete set of 202 stamps	£200	£270

Country	*Catalogue Nos*	*Stamps*
Great Britain	461	1
Aden	13/15	3
Antigua	95/97	3
Ascension	35/37	3
Australia		
Nauru	44/47	4
New Guinea	208/211	4
Papua	154/157	4
Bahamas	146/148	3
Barbados	245/247	3
Basutoland	15/17	3
Bechuanaland	115/117	3
Bermuda	107/109	3
British Guiana	305/307	3
British Honduras	147/149	3
British Solomon Islands	57/59	3
Canada	356	1
Newfoundland	254/6, 257/67	14
Cayman Islands	112/14	3
Ceylon	383/5	3
Cyprus	148/50	3
Dominica	96/8	3
Falkland Islands	143/5	3
Fiji	246/8	3
Gambia	147/9	3
Gibraltar	118/20	3
Gilbert and Ellice Islands	40/2	3
Gold Coast	117/19	3
Grenada	149/51	3
Hong Kong	137/9	3
Jamaica	118/20	3
Kenya, Uganda and Tanganyika	128/30	3
Leeward Islands	92/4	3
Malaya-Straits Settlements	275/7	3
Malta	214/16	3
Mauritius	249/51	3
Montserrat	98/100	3
Morocco Agencies		
Spanish Currency	164	1
French Currency	229	1
Tangier	244	1
New Zealand	599/601	3
Cook Islands	124/6	3
Niue	72/4	3
Nigeria	46/8	3
Northern Rhodesia	22/4	3
Nyasaland	127/9	3
St. Helena	128/30	3
St. Kitts-Nevis	65/7	3
St. Lucia	125/7	3
St. Vincent	146/8	3
Seychelles	132/4	3
Sierra Leone	185/7	3
Somaliland Protectorate	911/2	3
South Africa	71/5	5×2
Southern Rhodesia	36/9	4
South West Africa	97/104	8×2
Swaziland	25/7	3
Trinidad and Tobago	243/5	3
Turks and Caicos Islands	191/3	3
Virgin Islands	107/9	3
Total		202

1945–1946 VICTORY

1945–46. Victory.
Complete set of 164 stamps .... 65·00 95·00

Country	Catalogue Nos.	Stamps
Great Britain	491/492	2
Aden	28/29	2
Seiyun	12/13	2
Shihr and Mukalla	12/13	2
Antigua	110/111	2
Ascension	48/49	2
Australia	213/215	3
Bahamas	176/177	2
Barbados	262/263	2
Basutoland	29/31	3×2
Bechuanaland	129/131	3×2
Bermuda	123/124	2
British Guiana	320/321	2
British Honduras	162/163	2
British Solomon Islands	73/74	2
Burma	64/67	4
Cayman Islands	127/128	2
Ceylon	400/401	2
Cyprus	164/165	2
Dominica	110/111	2
Falkland Islands	164/165	2
Falkland Islands Dependencies	G17/18	2
Fiji	268/269	2
Gambia	162/163	2
Gibraltar	132/133	2
Gilbert and Ellice Islands	55/56	2
Gold Coast	133/134	2
Grenada	164/165	2
Hong Kong	169/170	2
India	278/281	4
Hyderabad	53	1
Jamaica	141/142	2
Kenya, Uganda and Tanganyika	155/156	2
Leeward Islands	115/116	2
Malta	232/233	2
Mauritius	264/265	2
Montserrat	113/114	2
Morocco Agencies		
Tangier	253/254	2
New Zealand	667/677	11
Cook Islands	146/149	4
Niue	98/101	4
Western Samoa	215/218	4
Nigeria	60/61	2
Northern Rhodesia	46/47	2
Nyasaland	158/159	2
Pakistan		
Bahawalpur	O19	1
Pitcairn Islands	9/10	2
St Helena	141/142	2
St Kitts-Nevis	78/79	2
St Lucia	142/143	2
St Vincent	160/161	2
Seychelles	150/151	2
Sierra Leone	201/202	2
Somaliland Protectorate	117/118	2
South Africa	108/110	3×2
Southern Rhodesia	64/67	4
South West Africa	131/133	3×2
Swaziland	39/41	3×2
Trinidad and Tobago	257/258	2
Turks and Caicos Islands	206/207	2
Virgin Islands	122/123	2
Zanzibar	331/332	2
Total		164

1948 ROYAL SILVER WEDDING

1948–49. Royal Silver Wedding.
Complete set of 138 stamps £2250 £2500

Country	Catalogue Nos.	Stamps
Great Britain	493/4	2
Aden	30/1	2
Seiyun	14/15	2
Shihr and Mukalla	14/15	2
Antigua	112/13	2
Ascension	50/1	2
Bahamas	194/5	2
Bahrain	61/2	2
Barbados	265/62	2
Basutoland	36/7	2
Bechuanaland	136/7	2
Bermuda	125/6	2
British Guiana	322/3	2
British Honduras	164/5	2
British Postal Agencies in Eastern Arabia	25/26	2
British Solomon Islands	75/76	2
Cayman Islands	129/130	2
Cyprus	166/167	2
Dominica	112/113	2
Falkland Islands	166/167	2
Falkland Islands Dependencies	G19/20	2
Fiji	270/271	2
Gambia	164/165	2
Gibraltar	134/135	2
Gilbert and Ellice Islands	57/58	2
Gold Coast	147/148	2
Grenada	166/167	2
Hong Kong	171/172	2
Jamaica	143/144	2
Kenya, Uganda and Tanganyika	157/158	2
Kuwait	74/75	2
Leeward Islands	117/118	2
Malaya		
Johore	131/132	2
Kedah	70/71	2
Kelantan	55/56	2
Malacca	1/2	2
Negri Sembilan	40/41	2
Pahang	47/48	2
Penang	1/2	2
Perak	122/123	2
Perlis	1/2	2
Selangor	88/89	2
Trengganu	61/62	2
Malta	249/250	2
Mauritius	270/271	2
Montserrat	115/116	2
Morocco Agencies		
Spanish Currency	176/177	2
Tangier	255/256	2
Nigeria	62/63	2
North Borneo	350/351	2
Northern Rhodesia	48/49	2
Nyasaland	161/162	2
Pitcairn Islands	11/12	2
St Helena	143/144	2
St Kitts-Nevis	80/81	2
St Lucia	144/145	2
St Vincent	162/163	2
Sarawak	165/166	2
Seychelles	152/153	2
Sierra Leone	203/204	2
Singapore	31/32	2
Somaliland Protectorate	119/120	2
South Africa	125	1×2
South West Africa	137	1×2
Swaziland	46/47	2
Trinidad and Tobago	259/260	2
Turks and Caicos Islands	208/209	2
Virgin Islands	124/125	2
Zanzibar	333/334	2
Total		138

1949 75th ANNIVERSARY OF UPU

1949. UPU 75th Anniversary.
Complete set of 310 stamps £325 £700

Country	Catalogue Nos.	Stamps
Great Britain	449/502	4
Aden	32/35	4
Seiyun	16/19	4
Shihr and Mukalla	16/19	4
Antigua	114/117	4
Ascension	52/55	4
Australia	232	1
Bahamas	196/199	4
Bahrain	67/70	4
Barbados	267/270	4
Basutoland	38/41	4
Bechuanaland	138/141	4
Bermuda	130/133	4
British Guiana	324/327	4
British Honduras	172/175	4
British Postal Agencies in Eastern Arabia	31/34	4
British Solomon Islands	77/80	4
Brunei	96/99	4
Cayman Islands	131/134	4
Ceylon	410/412	3
Cyprus	168/171	4
Dominica	114/117	4
Falkland Islands	168/171	4
Falkland Islands Dependencies	G31/34	4
Fiji	272/275	4
Gambia	166/169	4
Gibraltar	136/139	4
Gilbert and Ellice Islands	59/62	4
Gold Coast	149/152	4
Grenada	168/171	4
Hong Kong	173/176	4
India	325/328	4
Jamaica	145/148	4
Kenya, Uganda and Tanganyika	159/162	4
Kuwait	80/83	4
Leeward Islands	119/122	4
Malaya		
Johore	148/51	4
Kedah	72/75	4
Kelantan	57/60	4
Malacca	18/21	4
Negri Sembilan	63/66	4
Pahang	49/52	4
Penang	23/26	4
Perak	124/127	4
Perlis	3/6	4
Selangor	111/114	4
Trengganu	63/66	4
Malta	251/254	4
Mauritius	272/275	4
Montserrat	117/120	4
Morocco Agencies		
Tangier	276/279	4
New Hebrides	64/67, F77/80	4+4
Nigeria	64/67	4
North Borneo	352/355	4
Northern Rhodesia	50/5	4
Nyasaland	163/166	4
Pakistan		
Bahawalpur	43/46, O28/31	4+4
Pitcairn Islands	13/16	4
St Helena	145/148	4
St Kitts-Nevis	82/85	4
St Lucia	160/163	4
St Vincent	178/181	4
Sarawak	167/170	4
Seychelles	154/157	4
Sierra Leone	205/208	4
Singapore	33/36	4
Somaliland Protectorate	121/124	4
South Africa	128/130	3×2
Southern Rhodesia	68/69	2
South West Africa	138/140	3×2
Swaziland	48/51	4
Tonga	88/91	4
Trinidad and Tobago	261/264	4
Turks and Caicos Islands	217/220	4
Virgin Islands	126/129	4
Zanzibar	335/338	4
Total		310

1951 INAUGURATION OF BWI UNIVERSITY COLLEGE

1951. BWI University College.
Complete set of 28 stamps .... 12·00 30·00

Country	Catalogue Nos.	Stamps
Antigua	118/119	2
Barbados	283/284	2
British Guiana	328/329	2
British Honduras	176/177	2
Dominica	118/119	2
Grenada	185/186	2
Jamaica	149/150	2
Leeward Islands	123/124	2
Montserrat	121/122	2
St. Kitts-Nevis	92/93	2
St. Lucia	164/165	2
St. Vincent	182/183	2
Trinidad and Tobago	265/266	2
Virgin Islands	130/131	2
Total		28

1953 CORONATION

1953. Coronation.
Complete set of 106 stamps £150 £100

1953–1954 ROYAL VISIT

1953–54. Royal Visit.
Complete set of 13 stamps .... 7·50 4·50

1958 CARIBBEAN FEDERATION

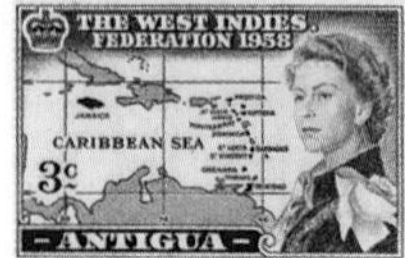

1958. Caribbean Federation.
Complete set of 30 stamps .... 26·00 21·00

1963 FREEDOM FROM HUNGER

1963. Freedom from Hunger.
Complete set of 77 stamps £160 £110

1963 RED CROSS

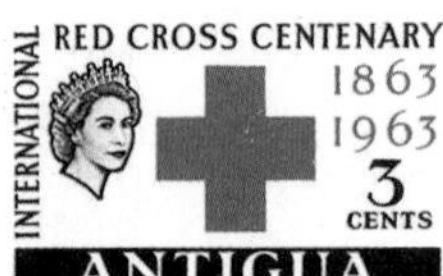

1963. Red Cross Centenary.
Complete set of 108 stamps and 2 miniature sheets. £190 £225

1964 SHAKESPEARE

1964. Shakespeare. 400th Birth Anniversary.
Complete set of 25 stamps .... 14·00 10·00

1965 ITU CENTENARY

1965. ITU Centenary.
Complete set of 112 stamps and 1 miniature sheet... £140 £110

1965 ICY

1965. ICY
Complete set of 107 stamps and 2 miniature sheets. £110 90·00

1965–1967 CHURCHILL

1965–67. Churchill.
Complete set of 182 stamps £260 £225

1966 ROYAL VISIT

1966. Royal Visit to the Caribbean.
Complete set of 34 stamps .... 32·00 18·00

1966 FOOTBALL WORLD CUP

1966. World Cup Football Championship.
Complete set of 68 stamps and 2 miniature sheets... £140 90·00

1966 WHO HEADQUARTERS

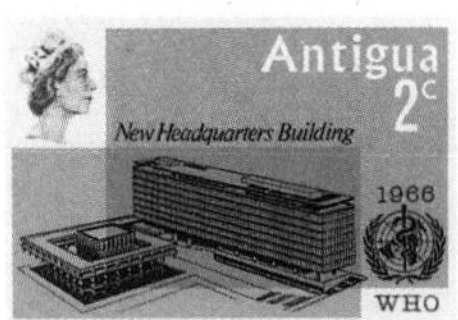

1966. WHO New Headquarters.
Complete set of 58 stamps and 1 miniature sheet... 90·00 75·00

1966-67 UNESCO ANNIVERSARY

1966–67. UNESCO 20th Anniversary.
Complete set of 110 stamps and 1 miniature sheet... £180 £170

1935 SILVER JUBILEE TO 1966 UNESCO

Issuing countries	1935 Silver Jubilee	1937 Coronation	1945–47 Victory	1948 Silver Wedding	1949 UPU.	1951 BWI Univ	1953 Coronation	1953–54 Royal Visit	1958 Caribbean Federation	1963 FFH.	1963 Red Cross	1964 Shakespeare	1965 ITU.	1965–66 ICY.	1965–66 Churchill	1966 Royal Visit	1966 Football Cup	1966 WHO.	1966 UNESCO.
Great Britain	4	1	2	2	4	—	4	—	—	2+2	3+3	5+4	2+2	2+2	2+2	—	3+3	—	—
Aden / South Arabian Federation	—	3	2	2	4	—	1	1	—	1	2	—	—	2	4	—	2	2	3
Seiyun	—	—	2	2	4	—	1	—	—	—	—	—	7	—	1	—	7	—	—
Shihr and Mukalla	—	—	2	2	4	—	1	—	—	—	—	—	—	8	3	—	8+**MS**	—	—
Antigua	4	3	2	2	4	2	1	—	3	1	2	1	2	2	4	2	2	2	3
Ascension	4	3	2	2	4	—	1	—	—	1	2	—	2	2	4	—	2	2	3
Australia	3	—	3	—	1	—	3	3	—	—	1	—	1	1	1	—	—	—	—
Bahamas	4	3	2	2	4	—	1	—	—	1	2	1	2	2	4	2	2	2	3
Bahrain	—	—	—	2	4	—	4	—	—	—	—	—	—	—	—	—	—	—	—
Barbados	4	3	2	2	4	2	1	—	3	—	—	—	2	—	4	2	—	—	3
Basutoland / Lesotho	4	3	3×2	2	4	—	1	—	—	1	2	—	2	2	4	—	—	—	4
Bechuanaland / Botswana	4	3	3×2	2	4	—	1	—	—	1	2	1	2	2	4	—	—	—	—
Bermuda	4	3	2	2	4	—	1	1	—	1	2	—	2	2	4	—	2	—	3
British Antarctic Territory	—	—	—	—	—	—	—	—	—	—	—	—	—	—	4	—	—	—	—
British Guiana / Guyana	4	3	2	2	4	2	1	—	—	1	2	—	2	2	2	2	—	—	—
British Honduras	4	3	2	2	4	2	1	—	—	1	2	—	2	2	4	—	—	—	—
British P.A's in Eastern Arabia	—	—	—	2	4	—	4	—	—	—	—	—	—	—	—	—	—	—	—
British Solomon Islands	4	3	2	2	4	—	1	—	—	1	2	—	2	2	4	—	2	2	3
British Virgin Islands	4	3	2	2	4	2	1	—	—	1	2	1	2	2	4	2	—	—	3
Brunei	—	—	—	—	4	—	—	—	—	1	—	—	2	2	4	—	2	2	3
Burma	—	—	4	—	—	—	—	—	—	—	—	—	—	—	—	—	—	—	—
Canada	6	1	—	—	—	—	1	—	—	—	—	—	—	1	1	—	—	—	—
Newfoundland	4	14	—	—	—	—	—	—	—	—	—	—	—	—	—	—	—	—	—
Cayman Islands	4	3	2	2	4	—	1	—	—	1	2	1	2	2	4	2	2	2	3
Ceylon	4	3	2	—	3	—	1	1	—	2	—	—	2	2	—	—	—	2	2
Cook Islands	3	3	4	—	—	—	2	—	—	—	—	—	—	—	6	—	—	—	—
Cyprus	4	3	2	2	4	—	1	—	—	2	2	4	3	2	—	—	—	—	1
Dominica	4	3	2	2	4	2	1	—	3	1	2	1	2	2	4	2	2	2	3
Egypt/ British Forces in Egypt	1	—	—	—	—	—	—	—	—	—	—	—	—	—	—	—	—	—	—
Falkland Islands	4	3	2	2	4	—	1	—	—	1	2	1	2	2	4	—	—	—	—
Falkland Island Dependencies	—	—	2	2	4	—	1	—	—	—	—	—	—	—	—	—	—	—	—
Fiji	4	3	2	2	4	—	1	1	—	1	2	—	2	2	4	—	2	2	—
Gambia	4	3	2	2	4	—	1	—	—	1	2	1	2	—	3	—	—	—	—
Gibraltar	4	3	2	2	4	—	1	1	—	1	2	1	2	2	4	—	2	2	3
Gilbert and Ellice Islands	4	3	2	2	4	—	1	—	—	1	2	—	2	2	4	—	2	2	3
Gold Coast / Ghana	4	3	2	2	4	—	1	—	—	3	4+**MS**	—	4+**MS**	4+**MS**	—	—	5+**MS**	4+**MS**	5+**MS**
Grenada	4	3	2	2	4	2	1	—	3	1	2	—	2	2	4	2	2	2	3
Hong Kong	4	3	2	2	4	—	1	—	—	1	2	—	2	2	4	—	—	2	3
India	7	—	4	—	4	—	—	—	—	1	1	—	1	1	—	—	—	—	—
Hyderabad	—	—	1	—	—	—	—	—	—	—	—	—	—	—	—	—	—	—	—
Ireland	—	—	—	—	—	—	—	—	—	2	2	—	2	2	—	—	—	—	—
Jamaica	4	3	2	2	4	2	1	1	3	2	2	—	1	—	2	4	—	—	—
K.U.T. / East Africa	4	3	2	2	4	—	1	1	—	4	2	—	4	4	—	—	—	—	4
Kuwait	—	—	—	2	4	—	4		—		—	—	—	—	—	—	—	—	—
Leeward Islands	4	3	2	2	4	2	1	—	—	—	—	—	—	—	—	—	—	—	—
Malayan States, etc.	4	3	—	22	44	—	11	—	—	3	—	—	3	—	—	—	—	—	—
North Borneo	—	—	—	2	4	—	1	—	—	1	—	—	—	—	—	—	—	—	—
Sarawak	—	—	—	2	4	—	1	—	—	1	—	—	—	—	—	—	—	—	—
Maldive Islands	—	—	—	—	—	—	—	—	—	7	5	—	—	5+**MS**	6	—	—	—	6
Malta	4	3	2	2	4	—	1	1	—	1	2	—	—	—	4	—	—	—	—
Mauritius	4	3	2	2	4	—	1	—	—	1	2	—	2	2	4	—	—	—	3
Montserrat	4	3	2	2	4	2	1	—	3	1	2	1	2	2	4	2	—	2	3
Morocco Agencies / Tangier	15	3	2	4	4	—	4	—	—	—	—	—	—	—	—	—	—	—	—
Nauru	4	4	—	—	—	—	—	—	—	—	—	—	—	—	—	—	—	—	—
New Hebrides / Vanuatu (English and French inscr)	—	—	—	—	4+4	—	1	—	—	1+1	2+2	—	2+2	2+2	4+4	—	2+2	2+2	3+3
New Zealand	3	3	11	—	—	—	5	2	—	—	—	—	1	1	1	—	—	—	—
Tokelau Islands	—	—	—	—	—	—	1	—	—	—	—	—	—	—	—	—	—	—	—
Nigeria	4	3	2	2	4	—	1	—	—	2	3+**MS**	—	3	3	—	—	—	—	3
Niue	3	3	4	—	—	—	2	—	—	—	—	—	—	—	—	—	—	—	—
Northern Rhodesia / Zambia	4	3	2	2	4	—	1	—	—	—	—	—	2	2	—	—	—	2	—
Nyasaland / Malawi	4	3	2	2	4	—	1	—	—	—	—	—	—	—	—	—	—	—	—
Pakistan	—	—	—	—	—	—	—	—	—	2	1	—	1	2	—	—	—	—	1
Bahawalpur	—	—	1	—	4+4	—	—	—	—	—	—	—	—	—	—	—	—	—	—
Papua New Guinea / Papua	4	4	—	—	—	—	—	—	—	—	1	—	—	—	—	—	—	—	—
New Guinea	2	4	—	—	—	—	—	—	—	—	—	—	—	—	—	—	—	—	—
Pitcairn Islands	—	—	2	2	4	—	1	—	—	1	2	—	2	2	4	—	2	2	3
Rhodesia and Nyasaland	—	—	—	—	—	—	—	—	—	—	1	—	—	—	—	—	—	—	—
St Helena	4	3	2	2	4	—	1	—	—	1	2	—	2	2	4	—	2	2	3
St Kitts-Nevis	4	3	2	2	4	2	1	—	3	—	2	—	2	2	4	2	2	2	3
St Lucia	4	3	2	2	4	2	1	—	3	1	2	1	2	2	4	2	2	2	3
St Vincent	4	3	2	2	4	2	1	—	3	1	2	—	2	—	4	2	—	2	3
Samoa	3	—	4	—	—	—	2	—	—	—	—	—	—	—	—	—	—	4	—
Seychelles	4	3	2	2	4	—	1	—	—	1	2	—	2	2	4	—	2	2	3
Sierra Leone	4	3	2	2	4	—	1	—	—	2	3	—	—	—	11	—	—	—	—
Singapore	—	—	—	2	4	—	1	—	—	—	—	—	—	—	—	—	—	—	—
Somaliland Protectorate	4	3	2	2	4	—	1	—	—	—	—	—	—	—	—	—	—	—	—
South Africa	4×2	5×2	3×2	1×2	3×2	—	1	—	—	—	2	—	2	—	—	—	—	—	—
Southern Rhodesia	4	4	4	—	2	—	1	—	—	—	—	—	3	—	1	—	—	—	—
South West Africa	4	8×2	3×2	1×2	3×2	—	5	—	—	—	2	—	—	—	—	—	—	—	—
Swaziland	4	3	3×2	2	4	—	1	—	—	1	2	—	2	2	4	—	—	—	3
Tonga	—	—	—	—	4	—	—	—	—	1	2	—	—	—	—	—	—	—	—
Trinidad and Tobago	4	3	2	2	4	2	1	—	3	3	—	—	—	1	—	4	—	—	—
Tristan da Cunha	—	—	—	—	—	—	1	—	—	1	2	—	2	2	4	—	2	2	3
Turks and Caicos islands	4	3	2	2	4	—	1	—	—	1	2	1	2	2	4	2	—	—	3
Zanzibar	—	—	2	2	4	—	—	—	—	1	—	—	—	—	—	—	—	—	—
Total number of stamps	250	202	164	138	310	28	106	13	30	77	108 +2**MS**	25	112 +**MS**	107 +2**MS**	182	34	68 +2**MS**	58 +**MS**	110 +**MS**

Index

Dear Catalogue User,

As a collector and Stanley Gibbons catalogue user for many years myself, I am only too aware of the need to provide you with the information you seek in an accurate, timely and easily accessible manner. Naturally, I have my own views on where changes could be made, but one thing I learned long ago is that we all have different opinions and requirements.

I would therefore be most grateful if you would complete the form overleaf and return it to me. Please contact Lorraine Holcombe (lholcombe@stanleygibbons.com) if you would like to be emailed the questionnaire.

Very many thanks for your help.

Yours sincerely,

Hugh Jefferies,
Editor.

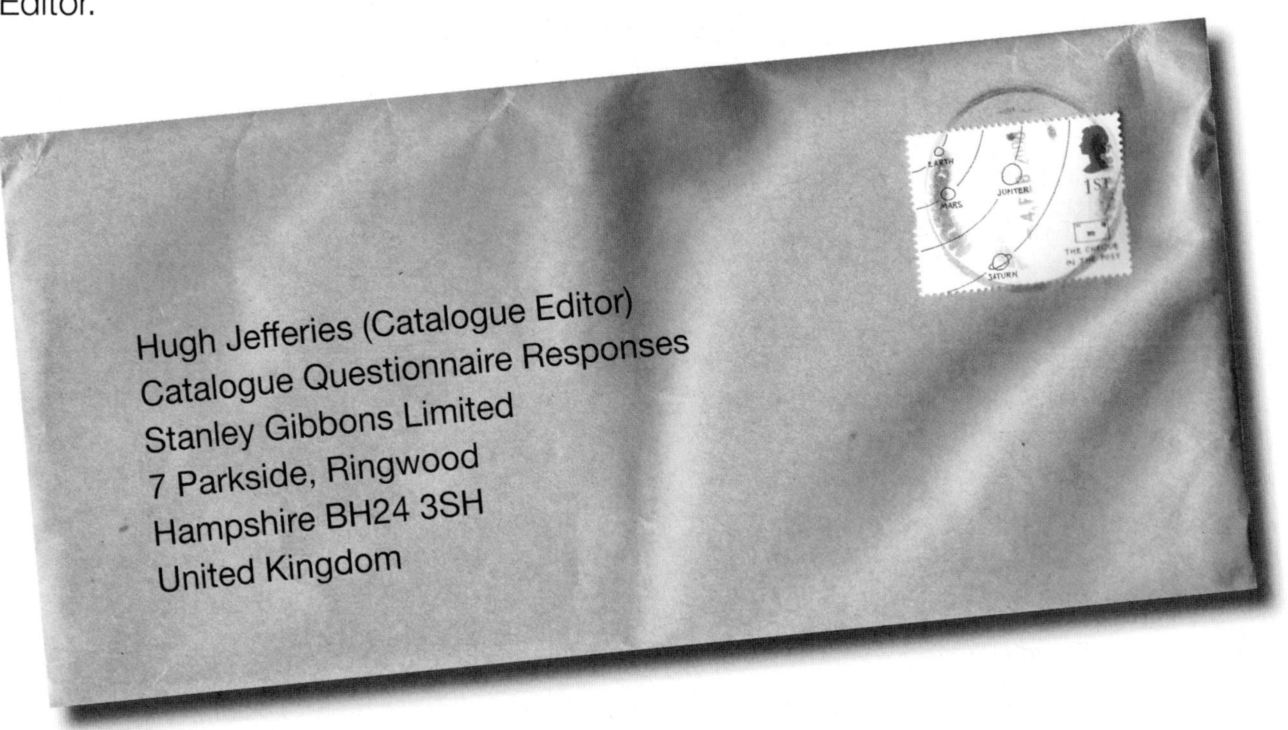

Questionnaire

2019 Commonwealth & British Empire Stamps 1840-1970

1. Level of detail
   Do you feel that the level of detail in this catalogue is:
   a. too specialised O
   b. about right O
   c. inadequate O

2. Frequency of issue
   How often would you purchase a new edition of this catalogue?
   a. Annually O
   b. Every two years O
   c. Every three to five years O
   d. Less frequently O

3. Design and Quality
   How would you describe the layout and appearance of this catalogue?
   a. Excellent O
   b. Good O
   c. Adequate O
   d. Poor O

4. How important to you are the prices given in the catalogue:
   a. Important O
   b. Quite important O
   c. Of little interest O
   d. Of no interest O

5. Would you be interested in an online version of this catalogue?
   a. Yes O
   b. No O

6. Do you like the format?
   a. Yes O
   b. No O

7. What changes would you suggest to improve the catalogue? E.g. Which other features would you like to see included?
   ....
   ....
   ....
   ....

8. What Countries are you interested in?
   ....
   ....
   ....
   ....

9. Would you be interested in receiving information, brochures and auction catalogues on these countries?
   a. Yes O
   b. No O

   If so please give your contact details below.

   Name: ....
   Address: ....
   ....
   ....
   ....
   Email: ....
   Telephone: ....

10. Which other Stanley Gibbons catalogues do you buy?
    a. ....
    b. ....
    c. ....

Many thanks for your comments.

Please complete and return it to: Hugh Jefferies (Catalogue Editor)
Stanley Gibbons Limited, 7 Parkside, Ringwood, Hampshire BH24 3SH, United Kingdom
or email: lholcombe@stanleygibbons.com to request a soft copy